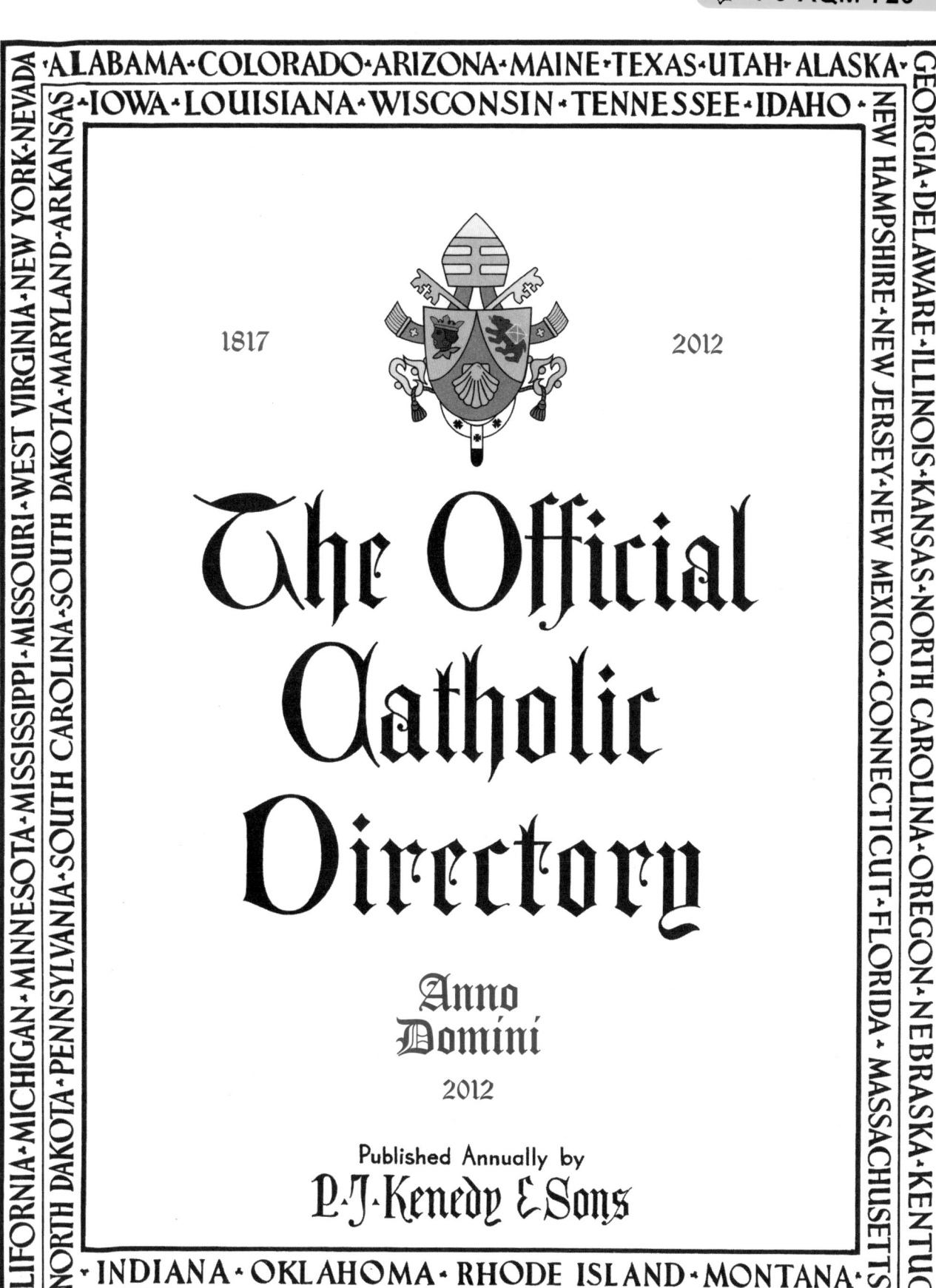

ALABAMA · COLORADO · ARIZONA · MAINE · TEXAS · UTAH · ALASKA · GEORGIA · DELAWARE · ILLINOIS · KANSAS · NORTH CAROLINA · OREGON · NEBRASKA · KENTUCKY

IOWA · LOUISIANA · WISCONSIN · TENNESSEE · IDAHO · NEW HAMPSHIRE · NEW JERSEY · NEW MEXICO · CONNECTICUT · FLORIDA · MASSACHUSETTS

1817 2012

The Official Catholic Directory

Anno Domini

2012

Published Annually by

P. J. Kenedy & Sons

INDIANA · OKLAHOMA · RHODE ISLAND · MONTANA

HAWAII · WASHINGTON · VIRGINIA · VERMONT · WYOMING · OHIO

NORTH DAKOTA · PENNSYLVANIA · SOUTH CAROLINA · SOUTH DAKOTA · MARYLAND · ARKANSAS

CALIFORNIA · MICHIGAN · MINNESOTA · MISSISSIPPI · MISSOURI · WEST VIRGINIA · NEW YORK · NEVADA

The Official Catholic Directory

P.J. Kenedy & Sons, Publishers

Robert Docherty
Publisher

Jeanne LoGiurato Hanline
Publisher Emeritus

FOREWORD

Throughout our long history of publishing the primary goal of *The Official Catholic Directory*® P.J. Kenedy & Sons has always been to provide a detailed and thorough portrait of the holy Roman Catholic Church in the United States. Nothing would be accomplished without the help and cooperation of the many ecclesiastical authorities, diocesan officials, religious and laity. These individuals were instrumental in organizing the vast and substantial amount of information needed to publish this successful directory. We wish to thank them for all of their tireless work and invaluable assistance.

In the 2012 edition of *The Official Catholic Directory*® we have added our special features including a first hand account of this year's awe-inspiring consistory where Cardinals Dolan and O'Brien received their birettas. Also included is an exclusive piece on using social media tools, such as Twitter, to catechize and minister to the church's population, an informative research study conducted by the Center for Applied Research in the Apostolate which tracks the evolution of the priesthood since Vatican II, and even more thought provoking articles.

Along with Volume One, we have included *The Official Catholic Directory, Part II* in your subscription. Produced in the fall, the supplement contains updates and new listings not present in the main volume, along with the archdioceses and dioceses of the world reprinted with permission from the Vatican.

We are proud to produce a directory which offers an accurate and thorough portrait of the Catholic Church in the United States. Our goal is to continue to serve the Catholic community by continually improving this unique and valuable reference tool.

Sincerely,

Robert Docherty
Publisher

Jeanne LoGiurato Hanline
Publisher Emeritus

300 Connell Drive, Suite 2000, Berkeley Heights, New Jersey 07922 (908) 673-1000 (800) 473-7020

Cross Catholic Outreach Upholds the Church's Commitment to Charity And Evangelization

James Cavnar, president of Cross Catholic Outreach, in recent meetings with Cardinal Sarah, President of the Pontifical Council Cor Unum. CCO has collaborated with the Holy Father's relief outreach for many years.

By **Msgr. Ted Bertagni**

Strong leadership is critical to the success of any difficult endeavor. Fortunately, **Cross Catholic Outreach** *(fomerly known as Cross International Catholic Outreach)* has been blessed by the guidance of an outstanding group of Catholic leaders — men who understand the plight of the poor and are committed to the Catholic Church's role in alleviating hardships by ministering to the poorest of the poor through charity and evangelization.

In addition to having Edwin Cardinal O'Brien as its Patron, Cross Catholic Outreach has six prominent U.S. Catholic leaders serving on its board of directors: Most Rev. Sam Jacobs (Chairman); Most Rev. Thomas Rodi; Most Rev. Dennis Schnurr; Most Rev. Kevin W. Vann; Most Rev. Edward J. Slattery; and Most Rev. Richard Garcia. Each of these men brings unique strengths to the work of Cross Catholic Outreach.

Relying on this leadership has benefited Cross Catholic Outreach in several ways. It has kept the organization at the center of Catholic Church strategies, it has helped Cross forge stronger relationships with bishops serving in developing countries, and it has helped our outreach achieve more powerful partnerships with Catholic parishes in the U.S.

To date, more than 60 bishops and archbishops in the U.S. and abroad have endorsed Cross Catholic Outreach, and many of these Catholic leaders have encouraged priests in their dioceses to involve Cross in their parish life and mission activities. They credit Cross Catholic Outreach for providing life-saving services to the poor worldwide and with giving American parishes effective ways of supporting special service projects overseas.

"The goal of our Outreach Priest program is to highlight the important mission work being accomplished by Catholic parishes and missions overseas. Our Outreach Priests visit U.S. parishes to share inspiring stories about the priests, nuns and lay leaders serving in the trenches, among the poor," Jim Cavnar explained. Cavnar, the president of Cross Catholic Outreach, is also proud of the ministry's unique relationship with the Pontifical Council ***Cor Unum***. and its president, Cardinal Robert Sarah.

Commending Cross Catholic Outreach, the Cardinal recently wrote:

"In the face of such pressing needs, many look to the Holy Father for help, both spiritual and material. As President of the Vatican Dicastery responsible for His charitable solicitude, I wish to encourage the possibilities for aid that come from our collaboration with Cross Catholic Outreach. Such help is a most commendable expression of the Catholic Church's care for the poor and needy, making manifest the charity of Christ. Through the outreach made possible by our collaboration, we achieve this object of service in ways that impact directly the lives of the suffering in many parts of the world — for example, feeding the hungry, providing medicines to the sick, responding to the needs of refugees, being a support in times of natural disaster.

"We hope that even more can be accomplished in the years ahead, and so encourage Cross Catholic Outreach to remain a resolute advocate for the poor through parish visits, educational programs, and other activities. This is an effective way for American Catholics to know about serious needs worldwide, and be given a reliable channel to become personally involved through prayer and financial support."

Although collaborations with Cor Unum represent only one part of Cross Catholic Outreach's extensive mission, the Cardinal's comments underscore the importance of our Universal Church and demonstrate how important Catholic programs are to blessing the poor for the glory of God.

For more information about Cross Catholic Outreach, its Outreach Priests programs or opportunities for project support, contact the ministry at 561-392-9212. Online information is available at www.CrossCatholic.org.

2011 Year in Review

The introduction of the English translation of the Roman Missal topped the religious news stories of 2011, and Pope Benedict XVI was again the top newsmaker, according to the annual poll conducted by Catholic News Service.

The continued effect of the global economic downturn was second among the 30 news stories on the ballot, the democracy movement in the Middle East, dubbed the Arab Spring, took third place.

When the editors' poll was first conducted in 1962, the overwhelming choice for top story was the opening of the Second Vatican Council. Last year, editors chose the recovery and rebuilding effort that followed the devastating January earthquake in Haiti as the top religious story of the year and Pope Benedict as the top newsmaker.

Rounding out the top five for religious news stories were the Irish church's sex abuse scandal and the issue of religious freedom. Pope Benedict who has been the top religious

©TOMAS HAJEK DREAMSTIME

newsmaker in the CNS poll every year since 2006, took first place this year for his travels to Croatia, Benin, Germany and Spain; his declaration of the upcoming Year of Faith; and his meetings with U.S. bishops, which were to continue into 2012.

Roman Missal an evangelization tool

Cardinal Donald Wuerl didn't have a problem with the fact that there would be some missteps and some wrong words spoken during the first weeks of using the new English translation of the Roman Missal at Mass. "We are going to have to live with the fact that not every celebration is going to be perfect," the archbishop of Washington said during a December 6th teleconference. "But that can be inviting to some people who are afraid that they are going to do the wrong thing. They might say, 'That's the same struggle I'm having'". Cardinal Wuerl, who co-wrote "The Mass: The Glory, the Mystery, the Tradition" with Mike Aquilina, joined in a panel discussion about the impact of the new translation, which went into use in the United States on the first Sunday of Advent, November 27th.

As 2011 drew to a close, American Catholics were greeting the new missal translation with a mostly positive response and finding some unexpected spiritual benefits in the need to pay closer attention to the words spoken at Mass, at least for a while.

Economic hardship hits nearly all

It's not new, but it's still news: The economy remains in a funk and it has spread to many nations around the world. Although the "Great Recession," which officially started December 2007, was declared over in June 2009, U.S. unemployment numbers were staying stubbornly around 9 percent. In December, the figure dipped to 8.6 percent, the lowest it's been since the second full month of Barrack Obama's presidency, but that was because nearly three times as many people quit looking for work as found jobs. The number of poor Americans has grown to roughly 49 million, or close to one in six overall.

©DIRK ERCKEN DREAMSTIME

New Jersey's Catholic bishops, in a November 21st statement, called on Americans to "address the critical needs of the poor who live among us.... We cannot ignore children who go to bed hungry, parents who are jobless, families who are homeless, the sick who suffer without medical care or the elderly who live in infested or unsafe housing". Most leading economic indicators show little change. And working Americans, in terms of "consumer confidence", still seem wary over the prospect of losing their job or the possibility of a second recession.

"We cannot ignore children who go to bed hungry, parents who are jobless, families who are homeless, the sick who suffer without medical care or the elderly who live in infested or unsafe housing".

Arab spring uprising roils Middle East

What turned out to be a year-long Arab spring of grass-roots uprisings in 2011 left several countries with new leadership and a death toll in the tens of thousands, most from a full-scale civil war in Libya. Meanwhile, protests in Israel and efforts by Palestinians to obtain full recognition in the

United Nations ramped up pressure for achieving a two-state solution to peace.

The wave of protests began December 18, 2010, in Tunisia after Mohamed Bouazizi set himself on fire to protest police corruption and to publicize his problems with trying to run a small business. By the time Bouazizi died of his injuries in early January, public protests had taken root in Tunis and other cities. Longtime President Zine el Abidine Ben Ali stepped down under pressure January 14 and fled to Saudi Arabia. Since then, Tunisia has dissolved its political police force and other institutions associated with the Ben Ali regime and moved toward creating a new government.

The spirit that overtook Tunisia in January spread, leading to the resignation of Yemen's prime minister and to the overthrow of the governments of Egypt and Libya, following protests that turned violent, and then to outright war in Libya. In a dozen other countries, unprecedented protests ranged from peaceful and fairly restrained, as in Jordan and Lebanon, to brutally violent in Syria. By May, border clashes in Israel were connected to the uprising spirit.

Focus shifts to Irish abuse scandal

In 2011, the epicenter of the Catholic Church's clergy sex abuse scandal moved from the United States to Europe prompting a church-state crisis in Ireland and a heightened response from the Vatican. But problems persisted in the United States, where Bishop Robert Finn of Kansas City – St. Joseph, Missouri, tried to avoid a criminal misdemeanor indictment for failing to report a priest suspected of child abuse and, following a devastating grand jury report in Philadelphia, a former archdiocesan secretary of the clergy was facing criminal charges of failing to protect children from alleged abusers.

Nationwide reports released during 2011, as mandated by the U.S. bishops' "Charter for the Protection of Children and Young People," showed that reported cases of child sexual abuse in U.S. dioceses and religious institutes declined between 2008 and 2009, as did the costs to dioceses and religious orders for lawsuits and other allegation-related expenses. The long-awaited report on "The Causes and Context of Sexual Abuse of Minors by Catholic Priests in the United States, 1950-2010," conducted by the John Jay College of Criminal Justice of the City University of New York and commissioned by the independent National Review Board was released in May. It said there is "no single identifiable 'cause' of sexually abusive behavior toward minors" and encouraged steps to deny abusers "the opportunity to abuse".

But much of the abuse-related attention during the year was focused on Ireland. Where fallout continued from two government reports issued in 2009 – the first detailing decades of neglect and abuse of children in church-run residential institutions, the second faulting the Archdiocese of Dublin for the way it handled 325 sex abuse claims in the years 1975-2004.

A new report on similar problems in the Diocese of Cloyne and charges by Irish Prime Minister Enda Kenny that the Vatican attempted to "frustrate an inquiry in a sovereign, democratic republic as little as three years ago" led the Vatican to withdraw its diplomatic representative to the country, Archbishop Giuseppe Leanza. Ireland then decided to close its embassy to the Vatican, citing economic factors, but continued diplomatic relations with the Holy See. An apostolic visitation ordered by Pope Benedict XVI to assess the

Irish sex abuse problem was completed in 2011 and its results were expected to be released early in 2012.

Bishops' concerns on religious liberty rise

Concerns that religious liberty is being eroded by government action and policy-making prompted the U.S. Conference of Catholic Bishops to open a campaign in 2011 to head off what they consider dangers to the rights of people of faith and conscience. The bishops' concerns deepened as the year progressed, leading to the formation of an Ad Hoc Committee for Religious Liberty in September. The 10 bishops on the committee are working to shape public policy and coordinate the church's response on the issue.

Bishop William Lori of Bridgeport, Connecticut, (now archbishop of Baltimore) was named to chair the committee, and he wasted no time in taking the bishops' concerns to various public forums. Addressing the bishops November 14th at their fall meeting in Baltimore, Bishop Lori said there seems to be a pattern of culture and law to treat religion "as merely a private matter between an individual and one's own God. Instead of promoting toleration of differing religious views, some laws, some decisions and some administrative regulations treat religion not as a contributor to our nations' common morality but as a divisive and disruptive force better kept out of public life," he said.

The issue posed such deep concerns that Archbishop (now Cardinal) Timothy M. Dolan of New York, president of the bishops' conference, pursued a private meeting with President Barack Obama at the White House. Archbishop Dolan said

he came away from the November 8th meeting "a bit more at peace than when I entered" the Oval Office.

Immigration action in the states and courts

With a politically divided Congress putting immigration on the don't-even-bother list of stagnate legislation, action on the subject in 2011 fell to state legislatures and federal courts where challenges focused on whether states have the right to act on immigration. Between court cases and election-year rhetoric, however, 2012 promises to give the issue a much higher profile. The Supreme Court agreed December 12th to consider the constitutionality of Arizona's S.B. 1070, a package of restrictions on immigrants and requirements for law enforcement officers to determine people's immigration status, which was to have taken effect in summer of 2010.

Injunctions have blocked some of the most-criticized parts of the law, including mandatory requirements for police to check on immigration status and criminalizing various forms of assistance to undocumented immigrants. That includes the response to a lawsuit by the Department of Justice challenging the state's right

"The prayers and support from around the world," he said "are a great source of strength and reinforce the image of us all sharing a common humanity under God our Father".

to step into immigration law, normally the purview of the federal government. The 9th U.S. Circuit Court of Appeals in April upheld the federal District Court's prohibition on parts of the law from taking effect. That set up the state's appeal to the Supreme Court. The court will likely hear the case in April 2012, with a ruling expected by the time the court adjourns for the summer.

Natural disasters prompt charity outpour

Natural disasters around the world and all across the United States this year prompted prayers, charitable giving and outreach amid unthinkable destruction. The devastation across the globe included an earthquake and tsunami in Japan, flooding in Australia and a drought in Africa. The United States also was particularly hard hit with a string of natural disasters: unprecedented summer heat and drought in the Southwest, deadly tornadoes, a massive blizzard in the Northeast, major river floods in the Midwest, and an earthquake on the East Coast followed by a hurricane that caused massive flooding.

In early March, a tsunami and magnitude 9 earthquake struck Japan, devastating parts of its coast and leaving nearly 20,000 people dead and hundreds of thousands homeless. It also triggered a meltdown at a nuclear power plant, releasing radiation and forcing tens of thousands of Japanese to evacuate their homes. Maryknoll Father, Jim Mylet, who lives in Japan, noted that in the midst of the devastation Catholics and others there were buoyed by the support they had received. "The prayers and support from around the world," he said "are a great source of strength and reinforce the image of us all sharing a common humanity under God our Father".

For pope, year of evangelization, travel

An interfaith meeting in Assisi, a new book on Jesus of Nazareth and a website-launching tap on an iPad were among the highlights of 2011 for Pope Benedict XVI. Although the year saw a further cutback in individual papal audiences, the 84-year old pope still enjoyed a productive and busy 12 months, meeting privately with nearly 400 church or civil leaders, addressing more than 180 groups and presiding over 40 public liturgies.

The pope traveled to Croatia, Spain for World Youth Day, Germany and Benin, delivering 60 speeches on the road. In weekly talks at the Vatican, attended by nearly half a million people, he gave a series of reflections on the great teachers of the church and on prayer, a continuation of the "back to basics" approach that has marked his pontificate.

The reduction of papal meetings and the introduction of a rolling platform for his entrance into St. Peter's Basilica fueled speculation about the pope's health. Close observers say that, like most octogenarians, the pontiff tires more easily today but that he suffers no serious health problems. The year 2011 saw two of Pope Benedict's favorite themes come into clearer focus: new evangelization and religious liberty. Increasingly, he has linked the two topics telling bishops that both tasks require courageous truth telling in sometimes hostile environments.

Honor, Humility and Humor

Featured as Cardinals Timothy Dolan and Edwin O'Brien Receive Their Birettas

BY CINDY WOODEN, CATHOLIC NEWS SERVICE

Cardinals Timothy M. Dolan of New York and Edwin F. O'Brien, grand master of the Equestrian Order of the Holy Sepulcher of Jerusalem, joined the College of Cardinals Feb. 18, 2012, with much prayer, a conference and several humorous quips. After the consistory in St. Peter's Square, where they knelt before the pope and received their birettas, a three-cornered red hat, the two new U.S. cardinals were asked separately what went through their minds as they ascended the steps toward the altar. Both said they were hoping they wouldn't trip and fall in front of all those people.

Cardinals Dolan and O'Brien were among 22 new cardinals from 13 countries created in Pope Benedict XVI's fourth consistory. The pope brought the total number of cardinals up to a record-breaking 213. On the day of the consistory there were 125 cardinals under the age of 80 and therefore eligible to vote in a conclave to elect a new pope. Just over half, 63, of the so-called "cardinal-electors" were named to the College

U.S. Cardinal Dolan embraces fellow cardinal during consistory
©PAUL HARING/CNS

of Cardinals by Pope Benedict. The other 62 were made cardinals by Blessed John Paul II.

The consistory took place in the context of a prayer service. After the Gospel reading, the pope told the cardinals that love and service, not an air of importance, are to mark their lives as cardinals. "Dominion and service, egoism and altruism, possession and gift, self-interest and gratuitousness: These profoundly contrasting approaches confront each other in every age and place," Pope Benedict said, but the cardinals must model their lives on that of Jesus, who loved others to the point of giving up his life for them. On the eve of the consistory, Cardinal Dolan had said he and his brothers are called to be "scarlet audiovisual aids" for all Catholics, who also are called "to be ready to suffer and die for Jesus".

In his homily at the consistory, Pope Benedict prayed that "Christ's total gift of self on the cross" would be "the foundation, stimulus and strength" of the new cardinals' faith and that it would be reflected in their love and charity toward others. Cardinal O'Brien, who was still serving as administrator of the Archdiocese of Baltimore when he became a cardinal, told reporters afterward that the whole ceremony underlined how becoming a cardinal "is not a reward, it brings on greater responsibilities, something the pope experiences every day". He said that when he knelt before the pope, "I thanked him; I said I'd serve him completely with my whole heart". Cardinal Dolan said, "The Gospel and the homily were very sobering," because they recalled the words of Jesus that "we're not in it for the prestige, we're not in it for the honor, we're not in it for the glory. We're in it to serve".

St. Peter's Basilica was filled to overflowing for the ceremony, and several thousand people, disappointed to have traveled so far and gotten up so early in the morning to no avail, sat in a sunny St. Peter's Square watching on large video screens. During the ceremony, Pope Benedict placed rings on the fingers of the 22 new cardinals and assigned them a "titular church" in Rome; the assignment of the title to a church makes them full members of the Rome clergy, which is what the earliest cardinals in the church were. For several centuries, the clergy of Rome elected the pope, who is the bishop of Rome.

Cardinal O'Brien's titular church is the historic Church of St. Sebastian on the Palatine Hill. With foundations dating back at least to the 10th century, it stands amid the ruins of imperial Roman residences. It was built on the site of ancient Rome's Temple of the Unconquered Sun and is believed to be the place where St. Sebastian was martyred in the third century. Cardinal Dolan's titular church, Our Lady of Guadalupe, is much more modern -- it was consecrated in 1932, and is home to a bustling parish community in Rome's Monte Mario neighborhood.

The College of Cardinals sometimes is referred to as "the pope's senate," and as Pope Benedict explained, the new members of the college would "be called to consider and evaluate the events, the problems and the pastoral criteria which concern the mission of the entire church". In fact, they started their new work 24 hours before they actually became cardinals. Pope Benedict called the new and old members of the college together for a daylong discussion of the "new evangelization," a global effort to strengthen the

Pope Benedict said, but the cardinals must model their lives on that of Jesus, who loved others to the point of giving up his life for them.

faith of all Catholics, revive the faith of those who have strayed and reach out to people who never have believed in Jesus.

Pope Benedict had chosen Cardinal Dolan to lead the day's discussion and by all accounts, including Pope Benedict's, the cardinal did a brilliant job clearly outlining the challenges, offering suggestions and doing so in a way filled with good humor. Cardinal Dolan told the gathering that secularism has had an easy time spreading through many traditionally Christian cultures because so many Christians do not know their faith and do not grasp the truth it teaches. While the New York prelate did not downplay the challenges the church faces in reviving the faith of its members and bringing the Gospel to those who have never heard it, he delivered his assessment with his characteristic smile and broad gestures, telling Pope Benedict and the cardinals that evangelization requires joy and love. The pope spoke at the end of the evening session, after 27 cardinals and cardinals-designate had taken the floor to comment on Cardinal Dolan's presentation or offer reflections based on their own experience.

Pope Benedict told the assembly that the teachings of the Second Vatican Council, which opened in 1962, were important for "rediscovering the relevance of Jesus and of faith" today, and he echoed Cardinal Dolan's call for a true renewal of catechesis to combat what has been defined as "religious illiteracy," a lack of knowledge and understanding about church teaching that makes Catholics easy prey for a culture that tries to lead them from belief. Cardinal Dolan had told his fellow cardinals that while secularism "is invading every aspect of daily life," it also is true that most people, on some level, still ques-

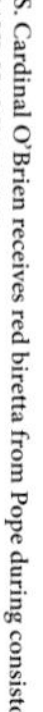

U.S. Cardinal O'Brien receives red biretta from Pope during consistory.
©PAUL HARING/CNS

tion the ultimate meaning of life and still ponder the idea of God. "Even a person who brags about being secular and is dismissive of religion has within an undeniable spark of interest in the beyond, and recognizes that humanity and creation is a dismal riddle without the concept of some kind of creator," he said. Every Christian has an obligation to help seekers find answers that make sense.

After the conference on new evangelization, it was time for the tradition and innovation, solemnity and festivity, high honor and a call to sacrifice that are key parts of the creation of new cardinals. The hushed moment when each churchman knelt before the pope and received his red hat as a cardinal contrasted sharply with the mood in the Apostolic Palace and the Vatican's Paul VI Audience Hall that same evening when the public -- literally anyone who wanted to come -- was invited in to congratulate the new cardinals.

A consistory is a gathering of cardinals with the pope. According to the Code of Canon Law, an ordinary consistory is called for consultation or for the celebration "of especially solemn acts," such as the creation of new cardinals or a vote approving the canonization of candidates for sainthood. And the Feb. 18 consistory brought both elements together. Just moments after the new cardinals were created, in their first official act in their new role, the new cardinals were asked to join their peers in voicing their assent to the canonization of seven new saints, including Blessed Kateri Tekakwitha, an American Indian, and Blessed Marianne Cope of Molokai, Hawaii. The pope announced at the consistory that the canonization ceremony would be celebrated Oct. 21 at the Vatican.

The morning after the consistory, the new cardinals concelebrated Mass with Pope Benedict to mark the feast of the Chair of St. Peter, a solemnity focused on the teaching authority of St. Peter and his successors, the popes. That authority, Pope Benedict said, comes not from power, but from fidelity to the faith handed down through the centuries. "The church is not self-regulating, she does not determine her own structure, but receives it from the word of God, to which she listens in faith as she seeks to understand it and to live it," the pope said in his homily Feb. 19. To illustrate his homily, the pope used the towering sculpture in the apse of St. Peter's Basilica: Gian Lorenzo Bernini's "The Chair of St. Peter," which features a throne supported by statues of four early Christian theologians and topped by a stained-glass window of a dove, representing the Holy Spirit. "The Catholic Church is like a window into which the light of truth shines and through which a response of love should radiate", the pope said. "Bernini set his throne on the statues of two doctors of the church from the East and two from the West, representing the unity and diversity within the universal church," he said. The support of the theologians "teaches us that love rests upon faith. Love collapses if man no longer trusts in God and disobeys him".

The two U.S. cardinals, who were surrounded by television cameras, photographers and reporters every time they stepped out in public while in Rome and at the Vatican, met the press at the Pontifical North American College and shared both humorous quips and serious reflections. Cardinal O'Brien said the consistory's universal flavor was a reminder that every Catholic, whether lay or ordained, has a responsibility for the whole church and not just for one parish or diocese. While "one hopes it doesn't happen too soon," the most important task of a Catholic

"Dolan, you've got temptations galore. I've always had them and now I've got one more, to let this go to my head literally. And you can't because it's all about humility, and it's all about service and love and being close to God and his people".

cardinal is to elect a new pope, Cardinal O'Brien said. "It's a weighty responsibility and always in the back of one's mind".

Cardinal Dolan told reporters that a bit earlier he had been reading the Gospel story of the devil tempting Christ and said to himself, "Dolan, you've got temptations galore. I've always had them and now I've got one more, to let this go to my head literally. And you can't because it's all about humility, and it's all about service and love and being close to God and his people".

Lighter moments were provided by Italian newspapers touting Cardinal Dolan as one of the front-runners to become pope someday, even before he officially became a cardinal. A reporter asked Cardinal O'Brien if he thought Cardinal Dolan had a chance, and Cardinal O'Brien responded, "His mother thinks so". When Cardinal Dolan was asked directly, he told reporters he didn't understand the question and moved on, but later he did tell reporters he had a big ambition. "As grateful as I am for being a cardinal, I really want to be a saint," he said. "I mean that, and I've got a long way to go, but it's all about holiness, it's all about friendship with Jesus and it's all about being a saint. That's what I want to be".

CINDY WOODEN *a Vatican correspondant for Catholic News Service, has lived in Rome since 1989. This was her ninth consistory.*

Social Media and the Church

BY LISA M. HENDEY

With the Catholic Church ministering to an increasingly wired global congregation, it is apparent that dioceses and parishes will need to harness the power and efficacy of technology tools to communicate with, catechize and minister to the population we serve. A look at recent statistics from the Pew Internet and American Life Project shows that 78% of all adults use the Internet. Of these, nearly 70% are active on social networking sites and that number continues to grow in younger demographic groups. With the meteoric rise in both social networking and adoption of mobile technologies, the Catholic Church finds herself poised to embrace digital solutions to embark upon the New Evangelization.

©ANDRES RODRIGUEZ DREAMSTIME

Vatican Takes the Lead

To observe the increasing role technology is playing in the Church today, one can look to the Vatican -- and indeed to Pope Benedict XVI himself -- for a taste of the changing tides. While photo opportunities such as the first "Papal Tweet" on the popular site Twitter and Pope Benedict XVI's remote lighting of the Vatican Christmas tree from an iPad may be largely symbolic, evidence of the Vatican's commitment to emerging technologies is increasingly evident. The launch of a new Vatican News portal (www.News.va), its active presence on a YouTube channel with nearly seven million views, and daily papal postings on Twitter during the season of Lent show the Vatican's commitment to employing all available tools in the New Evangelization.

On the heels of the Beatification of Blessed John Paul II, the Pontifical Councils for Social Communications and Culture jointly sponsored the first ever Vatican Bloggers Meeting. This gathering of 150 independent bloggers from around the world exemplified the capacity of social media to not only begin a dialogue, but to see the exchange of ideas continue to flourish long after a single day's event. Conversations begun under the shadow of St. Peter's Basilica, simulcast to the attending bloggers in five different languages and via streaming video to a worldwide audience, continue now over a year later on Facebook.

Fr. Antonio Spadaro, S. J., editor of the influential Jesuit journal Civilta Cattolica and a recent nominee to the Pontifical Council for Culture, calls this era one which demands a "cyber theology", saying that, "The net and the culture of cyberspace today pose new challenges to our ability to formulate and to listen to a symbolic language that speaks of possibility and of signs of transcendence in our lives".

USCCB Provides Direction

Since use of new media in the daily communications, catechesis and socialization of dioceses around the country is on the rise, the United States Conference of Catholic Bishops recognized the need to offer guidelines for those involved with social media. According to Helen Osment, Secretary of Communications for the USCCB, the recently released USCCB Social Media Guidelines (http://www.usccb.org/about/communications/social-media-guidelines.cfm) were promulgated as a compliment to the last several World Communications Day messages as a tool for those employed by the Church and her associated entities. The USCCB itself actively maintains numerous blogs in both English and Spanish and holds a daily dialogue with over 35,000 members at its robust Facebook community. Osment notes that the active Facebook page is open and closely monitored, but that the conversation is typically one of mutual respect. The USCCB is also active on Twitter and offers daily steaming video of homilies and online coverage of news related events. In all of their efforts online, Osment notes that the USCCB's emphasis centers on engagement rather than numbers. She recommends that parishes view their use of social media primarily as a tool for creating and fostering community with an eye towards gathering together in spirit as a compliment to Sunday Mass and traditional parish activities. She is heartened at the growing number of parishes around the country who are using technology to pray with and for one another and to build lasting community and fellowship.

Dioceses Around the Country Embrace and Create

Around the United States, at the diocesan and parish level, exciting advances are being made in the deployment and creative usage of emerging technologies. "With the same budget concerns in tough economic times as every other large organization, the Archdiocese of Boston is turning to social media and new technologies to turn them into resource multipliers," states Domenico Bettinelli, Jr., Creative Director for the Archdiocese of Boston's Pilot New Media Group. "We're looking at tools such as live video streaming for meetings, workshops, and classes; distance learning tools through a partnership with MyCatholicFaithDelivered.com; and even the new iBooks Author program for the iPad to create catechetical books and resources for archdiocesan initiatives. These relatively low-cost tools give us the ability to do more with so much less".

In the Diocese of Fort Wayne-South Bend, an atmosphere of innovation is fostered by Bishop Kevin C. Rhoades. Megan Oberhausen, Associated Director for the Office of Youth Ministry at the Secretariat for Evangelization and Special Ministries explains, "This year at our annual high school youth rally, we offered 'Text the Bishop' utilizing mobile technology to in-

With the meteoric rise in both social networking and adoption of mobile technologies, the Catholic Church finds herself poised to embrace digital solutions to embark upon the New Evangelization.

vite teens at the event to send text messages to our Bishop who read and responded to their questions. We also plan on using video technology to offer virtual campus ministry meetings, where campus groups can watch a teaching video posted to YouTube and then participate in discussions using online forums. Using social media and new technology is especially important in our work with young people; it is the most effective way of reaching out to teens and young adults. It communicates a quality and credibility to the work of evangelization, and sets an example of how new media and technology can be used in the work of the Gospel".

Getting Started with New Media

For parishes and organizations looking to get started with or to better employ social media technologies, radio host, author and national speaker Greg Willits of the non-profit apostolate New Evangelizers offers sage advice. "Start Small and think locally," counsels Willits. "Add a blog or start a podcast. Grow your community virtually as well as in-person".

Social media consultant and author Meredith Gould recommends that pastors seek support, training and assistance from parishioners who have been trained in the latest tools. Consider forming a technology committee made up of knowledgeable parishioners from a variety of ages and situations, including parish young adult and youth leaders.

Jeff Geerling is the Chief Technical Officer for flockNote, a communications system for Catholic parishes, dioceses, schools and organizations. Geerling advises, "The mainstream brands that are connecting with their audiences well today are realizing that people want to share and reply to things that relate to them personally. Catholic leaders need to adapt to this reality by making their communications initiatives more reliable, more personal and simpler".

As a starting point in building your communications strategy, consider starting with the following initiatives:

❶ **Website** – Strongly consider using Content Management System (CMS) software system that provides website authoring, collaboration, and administration tools such as WordPress, Drupal, Joomla. As a compliment to the website and using the software listed above or the simple Blogger platform, Pastors and key staff should work together to create dialogue on the site with short but regularly scheduled blog posts which are open to commenting by readers. Team member collaboration, effective editing and close moderation of online discussions are key to the success of any website or blog.

❷ **Social Networking Presence** – Start with a parish or organization Facebook page that serves as both a means for conveying information and a tool for building community. Compliment a well-established Facebook presence with a Twitter feed and a Google+ presence.

❸ **Email Communications** – Invest in a robust system such as flockNote or Constant Contact that will enable you to send regular, well-written and effective messages that include the parish bulletin or organizational newsletter, special announcements and appeals, and important reminders and prayer requests.

❹ **Podcasting** – Employ simple and inexpensive software or CMS plugins and a smartphone or inexpensive digital recorder to audio podcast weekly homilies and special speakers.

❺ **Video** – Create an online repository for simple video features on a platform such as YouTube. Use Ustream.tv or Justin.tv to live stream parish activities or to host virtual events and gatherings. Try the "hangout" feature on Google+ or Skype group calling for small group video conferencing, prayer groups and informal conversations online.

To learn more about the use of emerging technologies in your parish or organization, follow the CatholicTechTalk.com blog, take part in weekly Church and Social Media Twitter chats at http://churchsocmed.blogspot.com/, visit the website for The Church and New Media by Brandon Vogt at http://www.churchandnewmedia.com/ and consider attending the annual Catholic New Media Convention sponsored by SQPN.com.

Going Mobile

The recent Pew Internet study reporting that 46% of Americans now own "smartphones" continues to point to use of mobile devices as an ever increasing trend. For parishes and organizations, this should provoke an interest in providing mobile versions of parish websites, engaging in group text communications strategies, and realizing that younger generations are increasingly likely to ignore the paper parish bulletin in favor of its online Facebook or Twitter presence.

The great news for Catholics is that applications developers are creating new faith oriented apps at a fast pace. Patrick

Leinen, one of the key players in the mobile development startup Little iApps, calls the worldwide media frenzy that surrounded the launch of their highly publicized Confession app "humbling". Little iApps' team of developers continues to be on the forefront of creating apps that enable Catholics to respond to Pope Benedict XVI's recent exhortations to use technology to "witness consistently" in our proclamation of gospel truths.

Supporting the Families We Serve

Today's parishes and non-profit organizations have the great responsibility of serving families who are often pulled in multiple directions. Media watchdog groups refer to the current group of young adults ages 18 to 34 as "Generation C", citing their digitally connected behavior as a major trait in not only their consumption of media, but also their decision making processes.

Barbara K. Baker, Division Director of Marketing, Sales and Internet for Franciscan Media explains the need for the Church to be responsive to her increasingly wired congregation. "The Church needs to remain relevant to families within their daily lives," offers Baker. "We must not become a 'Sunday Mass only' place of

"The mainstream brands that are connecting with their audiences well today are realizing that people want to share and reply to things that relate to them personally. Catholic leaders need to adapt to this reality by making their communications initiatives more reliable, more personal and simpler".

The following mobile apps are recommended to smartphone owners who desire to use their mobile devices for faith formation and personal spirituality:

- **Divine Office** – Pray with an audio and text version of the official set of daily prayers from the Liturgy of the Hours of the Roman Catholic Church (Breviary)
- **Confession:** A Roman Catholic App -- With a personalized examination of conscience for each user, password protected profiles, and a step-by-step guide to the sacrament, this app invites Catholics to prayerfully prepare for and participate in the Rite of Penance.
- **Catholic News Live** – Aggregate news from hundreds of different Catholic websites on mobile devices, and enable the sharing of news and blog posts directly from the source.
- **iPieta** – Gain access to a vast library of Catholic documents, teachings, writings, prayers, and calendars for personal devotion, apologetics, and evangelization.
- **Saint of the Day** – Text and audio features include a brief saint biography, commentary on the saint's relevance to daily life, and a reflective quote from Scripture, the saint, or another spiritual writer.

ministry and access". Author, speaker and media consultant Meredith Gould concurs, saying, "If we want families to live in sync with a Catholic ethos, we must be able to use tools to convey that ethos and sacramental imagination". Gould suggests following the example of Protestant and non-denominational churches who have embraced technology effectively to preach the Gospel and to fulfill the Great Commission.

Steve Nelson, Executive Director of the Star Quest Production Network (SQPN), works in conjunction wtih SQPN Founder and CEO Fr. Roderick Vonhögen and a worldwide team of Catholic new media enthusiasts to create engaging media that serves the Church, evangelizes the world, and forms authentic community. From that vantage point, Nelson observes, "I don't think it's any secret that the family unit is suffering because of the insidious prevalence of the online world in our lives. Young people often say, 'It's not real until it's on Facebook.' What a commentary that is! The Church cannot cede the online world to the evil forces, or just the secular forces, that are answering our young people's quest for knowledge, understanding, and community. The Church has to go toe-to-toe with them".

In a practical sense, this means parishes must not only use social media tools to communicate with their congregations, but that they must also actively educate families on the safe and moral use of technology.

What's Next

Around the globe the laity are joining ordained clery and religious in embracing the call to the New Evangelization in new and creative ways. American seminarians studying in Rome produce viral videos. A California congregation encourages parishioners to "check in" on mobile devices before entering church to share their parish with friends on Facebook. A group of women from six different states gather weekly on Google+ to study the writings of St. Louis de Montford and pray together for their families. And these are simply a few of the creative ways everyday Catholics are mixing technology and faith.

With new media tools, ingenuity and a sincere commitment to the Truth, the potential for sharing the good news of the gospel is limitless.

LISA M. HENDEY *is the founder and editor of* www.CatholicMom.com *and the author of* A Book of Saints for Catholic Moms. *An active speaker, radio guest and podcaster, Lisa lives with her family in Fresno, California and worships at St. Anthony of Padua, where Lisa serves as Parish Webmaster.*

Conversation Starters

Dialogue and Deliberation During Vatican II

BY RICHARD GAILLARDETZ

Many Catholics over 50 are struggling with the realization that many younger Catholics, particularly seminarians and younger priests, do not share their sense of indebtedness to the Second Vatican Council. As one of those "over-50" Catholics, I am convinced that we overlook the influence of the council at our peril. The council's enduring significance is not limited to the 16 documents it promulgated, however. There is much the church today can learn from a consideration of the actual conduct of the council.

Yves Congar, the great 20th-century Dominican ecclesiologist and a key theological consultant at Vatican II, believed that councils manifest a deeper reality fundamental to the church itself—conciliarity. In an essay that has been influential in postconciliar ecclesiology ("The Council as an Assembly and the Church as Essentially Conciliar"), Father Congar complained of the tendency to treat councils as mere juridical events. He insisted that councils were, in some sense, a representation of the entire church. They effected "a totalization of the memory of the church". If he is correct, then the key

ecclesial dynamics that were at work at the council ought also to be present in the life of our church today.

Every ecumenical council manifests or puts on display, to some extent, what the church really is. What happens at ecumenical councils is more than the writing, debate, revision and approval of documents. At an ecumenical council, saints and sinners, the learned and the ignorant gather together. They share their faith, voice their concerns, pray, argue, gossip, forge alliances and compromises, enter into political intrigue, rise above that intrigue to discern the movements of the Spirit, worry about preserving the great tradition in which their identity is rooted, seek to understand the demands of the present moment and hope for a better future.

That those who gather at a council carry lofty titles (pope, patriarch, cardinal, archbishop, bishop, religious superior, theologian) and wear somewhat unusual garb should not distract us from the fact that, at heart, they are brothers and sisters (women did play their part, however circumscribed it may have been) in the faith to all other Catholic Christians. Their deliberations represent, in a dramatic form, what the church is called to be.

Father Congar argued against the idea, floated by some during the preparations for Vatican II, that it might be possible to have "a council by writing". In such a view, it would have been sufficient for the bishops to have drafts of documents mailed to them. They would then submit written comments and suggestions, after which an amended version would be returned to them for a final vote. Congar rejected such a proposal as an ecclesial sham. He insisted instead that it was necessary for the bishops to actually gather together to deliberate as an episcopal body on the needs and concerns of the church. He knew that there were crucial ecclesial dynamics that could come into play only if the bishops were allowed the opportunity for genuine deliberation and discernment. Consider three of those dynamics.

Catholicity of Dialogue

The first dynamic pertains to the catholicity of dialogue. Here I am using the term catholic in line with its etymological roots. The Greek word katholikos is derived from the root, kat'holou, "pertaining to or oriented toward the whole". Catholicity affirms the fundamental unity-in-diversity of the church. Ecclesial dialogue is catholic to the extent that it freely engages different perspectives and insights. During the four sessions of the council, bishops were introduced to other prelates from diverse countries and continents, who looked at key pastoral and theological issues from strikingly different perspectives. One of the more felicitous decisions of the council concerned the seating of bishops in the aula (the nave of St. Peter's Basilica where the main meetings of the council were conducted). The bishops were seated in order according to episcopal seniority rather than by region. This created the circumstances in which an Italian bishop, for example, might sit next to a bishop from Africa.

This arrangement made possible a fruitful exchange of diverse perspectives and insights. Indeed, some of the most important work of the council was accomplished at the coffee bars (nicknamed after two Gospel characters, Bar-Jonah and Bar-Abbas) kept open behind the bleachers in the aula. Bishops, after struggling to stay awake during one mind-numbing Latin speech after another, found respite at these coffee bars and often engaged in frank conversation about a variety of topics. It was the sustained, face-to-face conversation and sharing of diverse experiences that opened episcopal eyes to new

What happens at ecumenical councils is more than the writing, debate, revision and approval of documents. At an ecumenical council, saints and sinners, the learned and the ignorant gather together.

©BOGGY DREAMSTIME

We discover the guidance of the Spirit and penetrate the power and significance of God's word through ecclesial conversation and the opportunity to interact with believers who offer us different insights, experiences and questions.

possibilities. These conversations were further facilitated by informal gatherings of bishops like the 22 bishops who met regularly at the Domus Mariae hotel and were committed to encouraging a more wide-ranging deliberation than was possible within the aula. These bishops met weekly to discuss topics being considered by the council. They included among their number key representatives from the various episcopal conferences and served as a sort of clearing house for ideas and proposals, facilitating workable compromises on disputed topics. Council bishops also had opportunities to interact with theologians (periti) and non-Catholic observers, who offered their own remarks regarding the issues being considered by the council.

It was the many opportunities for discussion and debate, both formal and informal, that allowed the bishops to discern the impulse of the Spirit. Even the common prayer of the council deepened this catholicity of dialogue. Daily liturgies were celebrated on a rotating basis among the diverse liturgical traditions, East and West. Many council participants recorded in their journals and diaries the transformative impact of these celebrations as experiences of a church immeasurably richer in diversity than they had previously imagined.

The catholicity of dialogue evident at the council shines a harsh light on the situation of our church today. We seek to live our faith in a culture that has become increasingly uncivil. We too often encounter demonizing rhetoric on cable television, talk radio and in the blogosphere. Yet the council reminds us of the Christian obligation to respectful conversation with people whose views may differ markedly from our own. The conduct of the council teaches us that a precondition for genuine ecclesial discernment is the conviction that none of us individually has all the answers. We discover the guidance of the Spirit and penetrate the power and significance of God's word through ecclesial conversation and the opportunity to interact with believers who offer us different insights, experiences and questions.

Humble Learning

A second dynamic evident at the council was the bishops' commitment to humble learning. In the century before the council it had become common to divide the church into two parts: a teaching church (ecclesia docens) made up of the clergy and a learning church (ecclesia discens) consisting of the laity. This way of imagining the church dangerously overlooked the fact that bishops do not have a monopoly on divine truth. They do not receive supernaturally infused knowledge at their episcopal ordination. It is not the case that a priest with a shaky understanding of the doctrine of the Trinity on the day before his episcopal ordination would suddenly be able to give learned lectures on the topic on the day after ordination! As St. Cyprian of Carthage sagely pointed out in the third century, bishops must themselves be learners before they can be teachers (Epistle 74, 10).

Historians of Vatican II will point out the remarkable willingness of so many of the council bishops to become students once again. It is easy to forget that a good number of bishops, then as now, found that their pastoral responsibilities made it difficult for them to keep up with current historical, biblical and theological scholarship. As the council proceeded, many bishops sought the expert input of some of the many distinguished theologians and ecumenical observers who were in Rome at the time. Many regularly attended evening lectures offered by leading theologians. Bishop Albino Luciani (the future Pope John Paul I) admitted, according to an article in The National Catholic Reporter (Oct. 4, 2002), that during the council he tried to spend each afternoon in his room studying. He explained, referring to the Pontifical Gregorian University in Rome, conducted by the Jesuits:

[E]verything I learned at the Gregorian is useless now. I have to become a student again. Fortunately I have an African bishop as a neighbor in the bleachers in the council hall, who gives me the texts of the experts of the German bishops. That way I can better prepare myself.

Vatican II reminds us that we are all disciples of Jesus and, therefore, lifelong learners. This is as true for the pope as it is for children preparing for first Communion. Our pilgrim church does not so much possess the truth as it humbly lives into it, as it were, knowing full well that, this side of Jesus' Second Coming, we shall not have the fullness of truth ("Dogmatic Constitution on Divine Revelation," No. 8). We are all baptized into a great school of discipleship from which none of us ever graduates. Christ, our teacher, showed impatience only toward those who were arrogant in their certitude.

Openness to the World

The final dynamic evident in the council's deliberations was its openness to the world. Pope John XXIII himself set the tone for this openness. Many have wrongly accused Pope John of being a naïve optimist, a remarkable accusation on the face of it, when one considers that during World War I he had served as a medical stretcher bearer, tending to the injured and maimed victims of that bloody conflict. Later, as a church diplomat, he held ecclesiastical posts in such global hotspots as Bulgaria, Turkey and France.

Pope John knew well the evils present in the world, but he was convinced that we must not exaggerate those evils and succumb to a dark apocalypticism. In his many addresses and homilies he evinced an attitude of respectful yet critical engagement with the world. In "Humanae Salutis," the apostolic constitution with which he formally convoked the council, the pope warned of "distrustful souls" who "see only darkness burdening the face of the earth". And in his opening address at the council, he noted the advice he sometimes received from "prophets of gloom" who see "nothing but prevarication and ruin" in the world today.

Pope John XXIII was convinced that Christians must be willing to read "the signs of the times" and enter into a more constructive engagement with the world. Indeed the history of the council can be read as a long struggle among the council bishops to acquire a form of balanced engagement in which the church could preach the Gospel of Jesus Christ with a humble confidence, challenging the forces of hate and greed even as it affirmed the signs of God's reign already present in the world. Over the course of the council the bishops became convinced that the times demanded a church that lived in vulnerable and open mission to the world, effecting a transformation from within as leaven. The council thereby turned its back on that preconciliar tendency to stand in severe judgment of the world from some privileged Olympian heights.

Here again the council's conduct and attitude offer insight for our modern church, for we still hear far too many apocalyptic pronouncements regarding "a culture of death" and a "toxic secularism". The council reminds us that we must not yield in the face of evil, but neither can we close our eyes to the signals of grace always present where humans seek justice and truth and ask the great questions about life's meaning and ultimate significance.

Over the next three years we will have ample opportunity to celebrate the teaching of Vatican II as a breathtaking achievement and summons for today's church. Yet we should never forget that the council, in its conduct and deliberations, was a manifestation of the church in a dramatic and intense form. As an event of the church, the council reminds us that our church today must 1) continue to practice the catholicity of dialogue, 2) maintain a commitment to humble learning and inquiry and 3) sustain an openness to the world in which we have been sent. If we are faithful to these tasks, perhaps we can fulfill the hope of Pope John XXIII for an ecclesial renewal that will restore "the simple and pure lines that the face of the church of Jesus had at its birth".

RICHARD GAILLARDETZ *is the Joseph McCarthy Professor of Catholic Systematic Theology at Boston College, Chestnut Hill, Mass. He is the co-author, with Catherine Clifford, of* Keys to the Council: Unlocking the Teaching of Vatican II *(Liturgical Press).*

U.S. Priesthood

Since Vatican II

BY DR. MARY L. GAUTIER, PH.D.
Center for Applied Research in the Apostolate (CARA) at Georgetown University

A lot has changed in the half-century since Vatican II, for lay Catholics and clergy alike. A recently released book, *Same Call, Different Men: The Evolution of the Priesthood since Vatican II*, explores the history and direction of the Catholic priesthood in this country over the past 40 years. This study was the fifth in a series of periodic surveys of priests that began in 1970, most sponsored by the National Federation of Priests' Councils (NFPC), which examine trends in the composition, ministry, attitudes, and behaviors of priests.

© JEFFREY WILLIAMS DREAMSTIME

For this most recent study, researchers from the Center for Applied Research in the Apostolate (CARA) at Georgetown University, Dr. Mary L. Gautier, Dr. Paul M. Perl, and Fr. Stephen J. Fichter, surveyed a national random sample of 2,400 diocesan and 800 religious priests in 2009. This survey replicated important questions from previous studies to track trends in the composition, ministry, attitudes, and behaviors of priests. A few new questions were added to address issues that were unheard of in 1970, such as sharing ministry with laity, multicultural ministry, working with international priests, and ministry after the clergy sexual abuse crisis. In addition to the survey, selected priests from the study participated in focus groups and individual interviews in early 2010.

Same Call, Different Men describes the demographics of today's priests, sources of priestly satisfaction, challenges in priestly life and ministry, collaboration in ministry, and the multicultural reality of priestly ministry today. It also deals with the sexual abuse crisis and its effect on priests. It looks toward the future, examining characteristics and attitudes of the priests who are encouraging new candidates for the diocesan and religious priest-

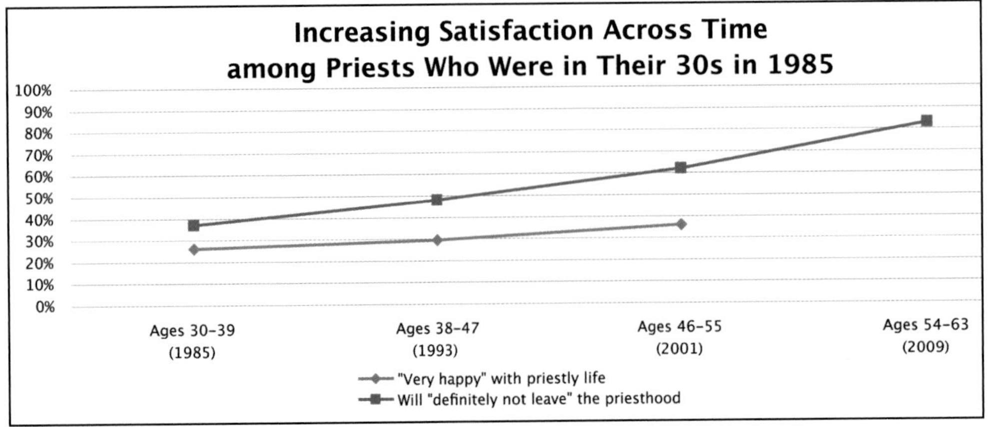

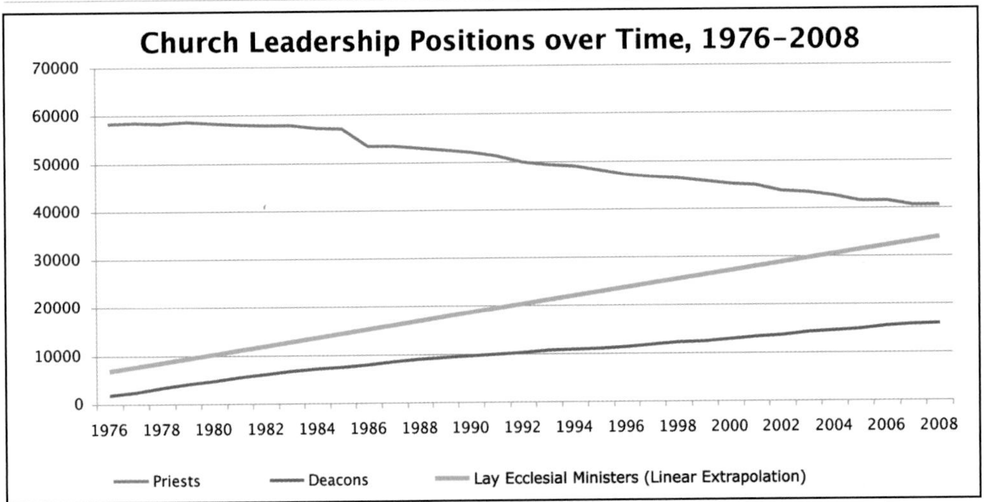

hood. Some of the important results and trends identified in the study include the following:

Four Decades of Change in U.S. Catholic Population

▪ Catholics have been increasing at about 1 to 2 percent a year, approximately keeping pace with the growth in the U.S. population overall. Growth is increasing in the suburbs and cities of the South and Southwest, in areas that lack the Catholic infrastructure (parishes, schools, seminaries, and colleges and universities) and personnel (priests and religious) of the Northeast and Upper Midwest. The effect of this trend is that dioceses in the Northeast and Upper Midwest have been closing parishes and schools that no longer have enough parishioners to sustain them, while dioceses in the South and Southwest are under increasing pressure to build more and larger parishes and schools to accommodate the demand.

▪ In addition, the Catholic population is becoming increasingly diverse as a result of immigration to the United States from Catholic population centers around the world. Hispanics, in particular, are underrepresented in the priest population relative to their presence in the Catholic Church in the United States. For priests, this means that they are sometimes challenged to accommodate a variety of cultures and language groups within a single parish.

▪ In 1970, there were fewer than 800 Catholics for every priest and about 2,500

Selected Problems, by Year

(Percentage saying each is a "Great Problem for me Personally")

	1970	1985	1993	2001	2009
The way authority is exercised in the Church	26%	21%	26%	24%	30%
Difficulty really reaching people today	16	7	10	7	18
Too much work	8	11	15	16	17
Unrealistic demands and expectations of lay people	7	15	18	13	15
Being expected to represent Church teachings I have difficulty with	—[1]	—[1]	14	13	15
Relationship with the bishop of the diocese in which you work	—[1]	8	11	7	14
Uncertainty about the future of the Church	9	5	11	10	12
Celibacy or lifelong commitment to chastity	11	15	14	10	11
Loneliness of priestly life	15	14	15	13	11
Relationships with superiors or pastor	12	9	8	7	10

[1]Not asked

In fact, the trend data show that priests ordained in the years following Vatican II (who were in their 30s in 1985) are more satisfied now, in their mid-50s to mid-60s, than they were in 1985. And younger priests in 2009 are more satisfied than younger priests were in years past.

Catholics per parish. By 2009, there were more than 1,600 Catholics for every priest and more than 3,600 Catholics per parish.

Changes in Priestly Demographics

▪ In 1970 there were about 58,000 total priests in the United States, their average age was 35, and less than 10 percent of them were over the age of 65. In 2009 there were about 41,000 priests overall, with an average age of 63 and more than 40 percent over the age of 65. In 1970, only 3 percent of priests were retired and 97 percent were in active ministry. In 2009, 78 percent of priests were in active ministry, 7 percent were semi-retired and 15 percent fully retired. In fact, the graying of the priesthood is the one trend that is perhaps having the most immediate impact on priestly life in the United States.

▪ The number of seminarians, in decline in the 1970s and 1980s, has stabilized over the last twenty-five years to about 3,500 seminarians enrolled in theology each year. However, ordinations are still only about a third of the number that is needed to compensate for those priests who are retiring, dying, or leaving active ministry. Bishops in many dioceses are struggling to find ways to stretch fewer priests to assume responsibility for more than one parish and are bringing in priests from outside the United States to help out as well. In 2009, more than a quarter of theologate-level seminarians in U.S. seminaries were foreign born and three in ten newly ordained priests were foreign born.

▪ With so many fewer priests available in 2009, 75 percent of active diocesan priests and 38 percent of active religious priests are assigned to full-time parish work. Another 18 percent of active diocesan and 29 percent of religious priests do part-time parish ministry. So only 7 percent of diocesan and 33 percent of active religious priests have entirely non-parish duties.

Priestly Satisfaction and Challenges

▪ Despite the dwindling number of priests available for active ministry, the addi-

Selected Sources of Satisfaction, by Year

(Percentage saying each is a "Great" importance as a source of satisfaction)

	1970	1985	1993	2001	2009
Joy of administering the sacraments and presiding over the liturgy	80%	87%	92%	90%	94%
Satisfaction of preaching the Word	—[1]	—[1]	82	80	83
Being part of a community of Christians who are working together to share the Good News of the Gospel	63	65	69	62	73
Opportunity to work with many people and be a part of their lives	72	72	74	67	71
Opportunity to exercise intellectual and creative abilities	52	46	53	55	58
Challenge of being the leader of a Catholic Christian community	38	39	46	47	42
Organizing and administering the work of the Church	31	32	33	34	30
Engaging in efforts at social reform	22	20	23	23	25
Respect that comes to the priestly office	23	21	23	25	22

[1]Not asked

tional workload for those remaining, and the effects of the clergy sex abuse scandal, morale and satisfaction among priests has actually improved over time. In fact, the trend data show that priests ordained in the years following Vatican II (who were in their 30s in 1985) are more satisfied now, in their mid-50s to mid-60s, than they were in 1985. And younger priests in 2009 are more satisfied than younger priests were in years past.

▪ The problems in life and ministry cited by priests have remained relatively stable over the past 40 years, except for a dramatic increase in the percentage who mention "too much work" and "unrealistic demands and expectations of laypeople". A listing of selected problems, and how they have changed over time, is in the accompanying table.

The Contemporary Context

▪ Priests today appreciate the necessity for the Charter for the Protection of Children and Young People adopted in 2002 by the U.S. Conference of Catholic Bishops, but many consider the application of its zero-tolerance aspects to be unnecessarily harsh and inflexible. They fear this has the potential of undermining the relationship between a bishop or religious superior and his priests.

▪ The present shortage of priests, combined with the expanded role of the laity as defined in the documents of Vatican II, have resulted in a situation whereby there are more lay ecclesial ministers than priests serving in full-time parish ministry. As the numbers of priests decline and the number of Catholics continues to increase, collaborative ministry is becoming the norm.

▪ In response to the increased diversity in the church today, at least two-thirds of the priests surveyed in 2009 felt it was important to have open discussions about ministry in ethnic or multicultural parishes, multiculturalism and diversity, and collaboration with international priests.

It is encouraging that members of the youngest ordination cohort—priests of the Millennial generation ordained since 1992—are much more likely than others to have encouraged someone to become a priest during the previous 6 months.

▪ Past research shows that the principal factor in encouraging priestly vocations is the example of happy and productive priests. It is encouraging that members of the youngest ordination cohort—priests of the Millennial generation ordained since 1992—are much more likely than others to have encouraged someone to become a priest during the previous 6 months.

The first study in the series was commissioned by what is now the U.S. Conference of Catholic Bishops (then called the National Conference of Catholic Bishops or NCCB) and completed in 1970 by Fr. Andrew Greeley of the National Opinion Research Center (NORC) at the University of Chicago. The next three studies in the series (in 1985, 1993, and 2001) were conducted by Dr. Dean Hoge and colleagues at The Catholic University of America. The most recent study was taken up by CARA at the request of NFPC after Dr. Hoge's death in 2009.

Same Call, Different Men: The Evolution of the Priesthood since Vatican II, by Mary L. Gautier, Paul M. Perl, and Stephen J. Fichter, published in April 2012, is available from Liturgical Press, PO Box 7500, Collegeville, MN 56321-7500 (www.litpress.org).

MARY L. GAUTIER, PH.D. *is a senior research associate at the Center for Applied Research in the Apostolate (CARA) at Georgetown University, where she edits* The CARA Report, *a research quarterly, and other CARA publications. She is co-author of five books on Catholics in the United States.*

Profile - Deacon Paul Sullivan

Designing Deacon

Paul J. Sullivan Masters the Art of Heraldry

BY RICK SNIZEK

Bathed in the natural light streaming through four oblong skylights in the ceiling overhead, the artist sets out to practice his craft. Although Deacon Paul J. Sullivan has a modest office downstairs in the comfortable, airy home he shares with Kathleen, his wife of 23 years, and son Ryan, 20, his preferred workspace is at the head of the long dining room table on the main floor.

The setting for the family's home, which is located across from a nature preserve a short distance inland from the tranquil waters of Rhode Island's Narragansett Bay, is a constant reminder to Sullivan of the beauty of God's creation and provides him with the inspiration he needs to create painstakingly the coats of arms that represent some of the highest officials in the worldwide Catholic Church.

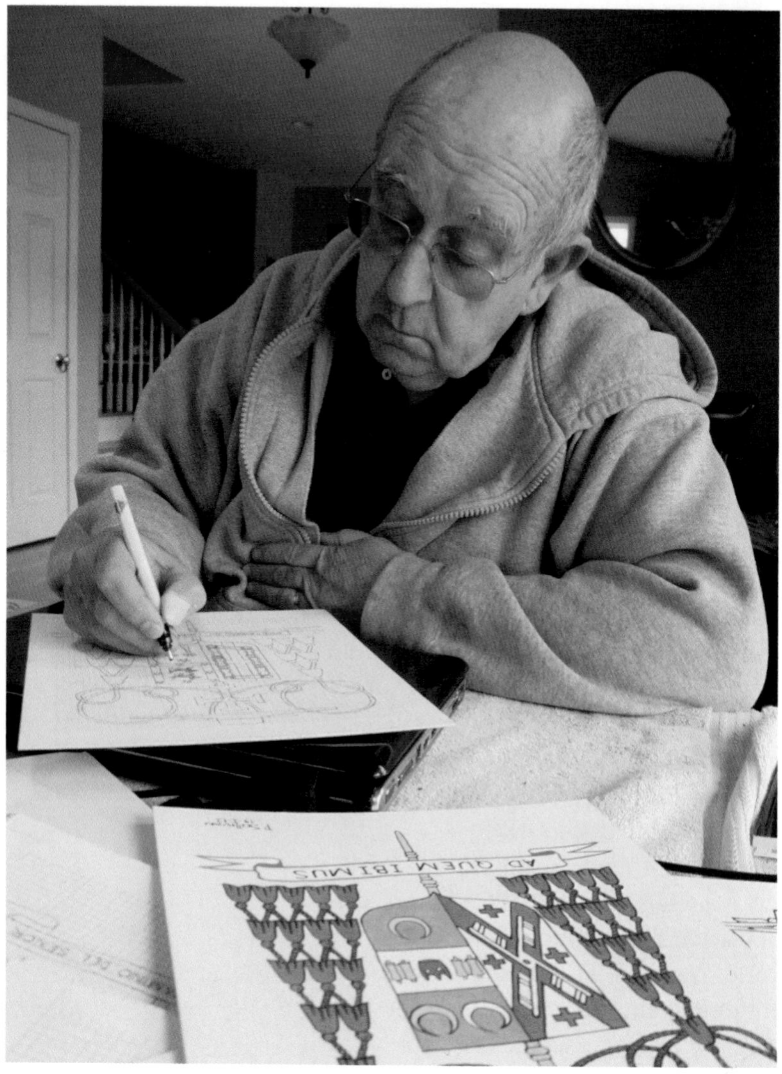

Being chosen to redesign the coat of arms for Bishop Thomas J. Tobin, who was installed in 2005 as the eighth Bishop of Providence, represents for him a significant moment in his professional artistic career. "I'm honored to have been able to serve our bishop," he says.

For more than 35 years Sullivan has produced such works as an artist in the genre of heraldry — the art and science of creating or emblazoning a coat of arms — a subject that has fascinated him since the age of 10. According to Sullivan, the art form is one that dates back to the time of the Old Testament. "The representation of people with a graphic design goes back to the pharaohs," says Sullivan, 64, noting how royal names were encapsulated within a cartouche, or oval, in Egyptian hieroglyphics, to highlight their import in society.

Unlike the dress shirt, tie and sweater vest he usually sports when at work 30 miles to the north, where he serves as director of deacons for the Diocese of Providence, Sullivan at home prefers the comfort and mobility afforded by a zippered soft cotton sweatshirt when creating in his home studio.

Arrayed before him on the long, chocolate brown dining room table are several of his current projects. Some are finished or are nearing completion, while others are just beginning to take shape. At the center is the coat of arms and its blazon — or visual description of a coat of arms' design — for newly appointed Cardinal Timothy M. Dolan, the archbishop of New York, and president of the United States Conference of Catholic Bishops.

The design incorporates the important change in color from green to red of the cardinal's galero at the top, and the addition of another row of red tassels below to signify Cardinal Dolan's new responsibilities in the church. Sullivan said it was especially rewarding to have been chosen to produce Cardinal Dolan's coat of arms. He is also very appreciative of the cardinal's thoughtfulness and compassion in assuring him of special remembrance at his Masses and in his prayers after learning in January that Sullivan had suffered a stroke.

On Martin Luther King Day, Sullivan and his wife were at their local YMCA exercising in a water aerobics class. The first signs began to appear soon after the 45-minute class ended, and he was getting dressed to leave for home. "I noticed I was having trouble putting on my left sock and shoe," Sullivan said. He also developed a backache and had a restless night. The next morning, the symptoms persisted and worsened. "The whole left side of my face became dropped," he said. At that point, his wife Kathleen, a hospice nurse, recognized that he was in need of immediate medical attention and rushed him to the hospital, where he was given the sacrament of the anointing of the sick.

Two months later, the only outward sign to those who know Sullivan that he had recently experienced a life-threatening medical condition is the cane he still uses in ambulating between the chancery and cathedral, where he assists in celebrating the noontime Mass on weekdays. Although he still has some difficulty at this stage with his balance, he reports that most of his strength has returned. He credits the professional physical therapy sessions he faithfully participates in several times each week with speeding him along on his road to wellness. "I am ahead of the curve for what is expected of me in recovery," he says.

The stroke he experienced in January was not the first time that Sullivan has experienced a life-threatening health issue. About 20 years ago he was hospitalized with an acute lung infection that claimed the life of the creator of the Muppets. "I had the same type of pneumonia that had killed Jim Henson," he said. "I almost died three times in a three-week period". Doctors peeled off a portion of the outside surface of one of his lungs, but he survived the illness with no lasting effects.

Sullivan's fascination with creating what is also known in the artistic field as a "heraldic achievement" or "armorial achievement" began when he was a child growing up in the Edgewood section of Cranston, R.I. The son of Allyn, a dentist, and Isabel, a stay at home mom, Sullivan and his family moved to Cranston when he was about five years old.

A family friend, Msgr. Thomas Maloney, was chosen in the 1960s to serve as auxiliary bishop of Providence. Following World War II, then-Father Maloney was sent to Belgium to re-open the American seminary where he served as rector of the

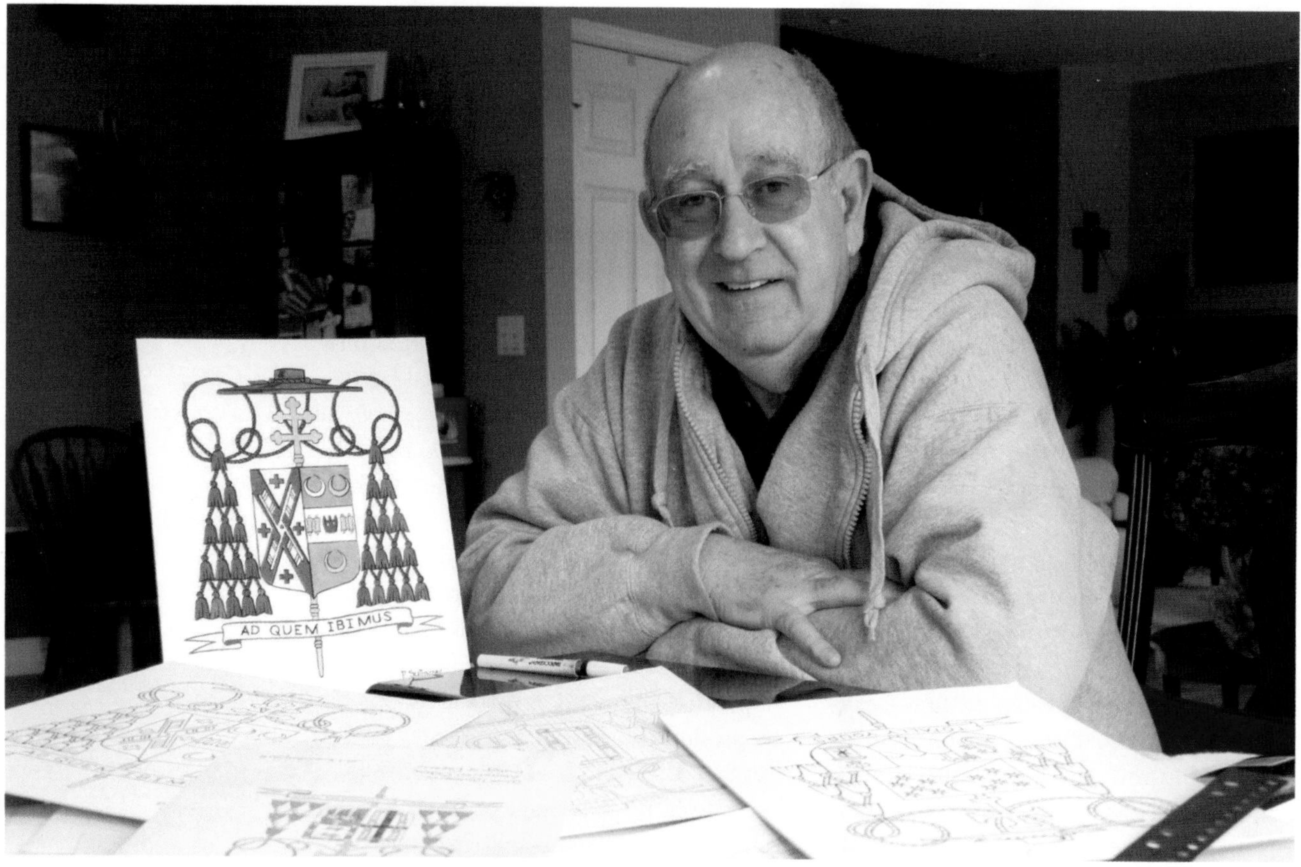

©RICK SNIZEK

American College of Louvain. During his time there, Father Maloney was promoted to a monsignor. He would later be chosen by then-Providence Bishop Russell J. McVinney to serve his diocese as an auxiliary bishop. Returning to the diocese and preparing for his installation, Msgr. Maloney paid a visit to the Sullivan family home. "All the stuff he brought home with him just fascinated me as a 10-year-old. I must have drawn his coat of arms a hundred times," Sullivan said.

Although Bishop Maloney passed away from cancer only two years after his ordination, the heraldic spirit never flickered for the young Sullivan, who would attend Bishop Hendricken High School, which was then-run by the Holy Cross Brothers, and go on to earn a bachelor's degree in business management from Providence-College, run by the Dominican friars.

His interest in art remained only that at that point in his life; he embarked instead on a more concrete professional path, designing and writing code for computer systems for several different companies in Connecticut and Rhode Island, including five years as a systems analyst at Brown University. "This was a hobby on the side," Sullivan said of his artwork. Over the years to come, he would learn much more about the craft of creating heraldic achievements and even amass a personal library on the subject. It was during his study of the art form, he came to realize that he too could make his mark in this uncommon field.

In studying the work of one heraldic achievement artist, Sullivan noted a discrepancy between the artwork and the technical description of the creation. In order to match the artwork produced, the blazon called for a description of a five-petaled flower. Instead the narrative should have described a maline cross, with arms terminating in anchors. In heraldry, the detailed description that accompanies each coat of arms – known as a blazon – is intended to create the same visual image for the reader, as one would appreciate by viewing the finished artwork directly. In noticing the error, he realized that he possessed the skills necessary to be a successful artist in this form.

Sullivan soon formed his own small business, P. Sullivan & Company, and began to advertise his services as an artist in this specialty medium that today he says employs less than a dozen people. In 1976, when Sullivan was in his early 30s, he was commissioned to create his first heraldic achievement. Bishop Eugene Gerber of the Diocese of Dodge City, Kansas sought Sullivan's artistic services to mark his installation to the episcopacy. "I had a bishop take a chance on my work, and I'm grateful for that," Sullivan says.

In a field where one's talents become known to prospective clients primarily through reputation and word of mouth referrals, he was commissioned to create two additional coats-of-arms that year, and four the following year. He has expanded his business to the point where he has created as many as 31 heraldic achievements over the course of a year, for bishops and cardinals from all over the world. His creations span the globe, from Albania – the farthest east – to Wellington, New Zealand in the west. In the Southern Hemisphere, Sullivan has created artwork for prelates in Kenya and Liberia, and in Georgetown, Guyana.

When he returned to Rhode Island to care for his ailing parents, his life would change in more ways than one. "I was the bachelor son who helped out at home," he says. With both parents confined to hospital beds set up in the living room of the family home, Sullivan arranged for nursing care in the home.

"That's how I met my wife. It was her first call as a visiting nurse. God sent her right to my front door," he recalls fondly. "She's a bona fide angel," Sullivan says with a smile. Although he would lose his parents to health complications in close proximity to each other, he and Kathleen would eventually marry and later have a son.

Ryan, 20, followed in his father's footsteps graduating from Bishop Hendricken High School, and is now in his sophomore year at Stonehill College, a small, Catholic college outside of Boston, where he majors in physics and mathematics. He is proud of his father's dedication to his faith as a deacon, and of the many artistic creations he has produced for so many prelates of the church. "The church is very much like a family to him," Ryan said of his father. In addition to his responsibilities at the diocese, Sullivan is also active in his parish, St. Thomas More, where he is a member of the RCIA team, among other church committees and groups. Ryan described his father as a "really good guy" who has always been very respectful of him. "He gave me the tools to start thinking for myself," he added.

About two years before Ryan was born, Sullivan began his formation as a deacon. He had learned after Mass one day that the diocese would reopen its diaconate program. After discussing it with his wife, who encouraged him to apply, he joined the program. He was ordained a deacon on Oct. 15, 1994 — on the feast of St. Theresa of Avila — and was appointed director of deacons in 2006. Sullivan is proud of the work of all those involved in the program, and is looking forward to seeing the 21 men currently in formation be ordained in February, 2013. "The needs in our communities are absolutely so desperate," he says, point-

"There's still a tremendous hunger out there and that's why the ministry of the diaconate is so necessary," Sullivan said.

"I have an ability that God has given me to do something for the church, and I am thankful that I have that ability," Sullivan says.

ing to the more than 90 nursing homes and 60 assisted living facilities across the diocese where residents are hungry for spiritual enrichment. While priests visit as often as they can, the visits by deacons can truly have an impact for the homebound that cannot make it to church. "There's still a tremendous hunger out there and that's why the ministry of the diaconate is so necessary," Sullivan said.

Father Timothy D. Reilly, chancellor of the Diocese of Providence, feels the church is blessed to have Sullivan's talents as an artist and his administrative capabilities as director of deacons at work in its mission. "He puts his unique gifts to good use. He's very dedicated and has taken great pride in the next class of deacons, almost a paternal pride," Father Reilly says. "I see Deacon Paul's excitement in serving God that way".

Through the years, Sullivan has continued to expand his artistic offerings, but didn't have to look too far in late 2009 for his next client. When Msgr. Robert C. Evans was chosen to serve as the auxiliary bishop of Providence, he commissioned Sullivan to produce his coat of arms. "I chose a more traditional design as well as two symbols: an anchor capped with a 'chi rho,' the first two letters of Christ as they appear in Greek, an ancient Christian symbol, and a star representing the Blessed Virgin Mary, 'Stella Maris' ('Star of the Sea')," said Bishop Evans, as he recalled the process he employed to create his Episcopal coat of arms.

The anchor Bishop Evans chose appears on the state flag of Rhode Island and is a symbol of hope, which is also the state motto. "Being the 'Ocean State', I thought it appropriate that the Blessed Mother be represented by a nautical image as the one guiding us into a safe port," Bishop Evans continued. "Finally, I chose as a motto 'spe salvi' ('saved by hope') which includes the word 'hope' as a number of Providence bishops in the past have chosen to do, and also as a way to honor Pope Benedict XVI who chose as the title for his encyclical on hope the phrase 'spe salvi' from Saint Paul's letter to the Romans. Having made these decisions, I then engaged Deacon Paul Sullivan to translate the above into approved heraldic language and imagery. I am very pleased with the result". Sullivan said it was an honor for him to be asked by Bishop Evans to create his first coat of arms. "I have an ability that God has given me to do something for the church, and I am thankful that I have that ability," Sullivan says.

He reflects on the lasting impact of what he creates as a legacy he will one day leave behind. "There will be people around the country and around the world who, 50 years from now when I'm dead, will look at my artwork". ■

RICK SNIZEK *is an award-winning writer and photojournalist. He currently serves as editor of the* Rhode Island Catholic.

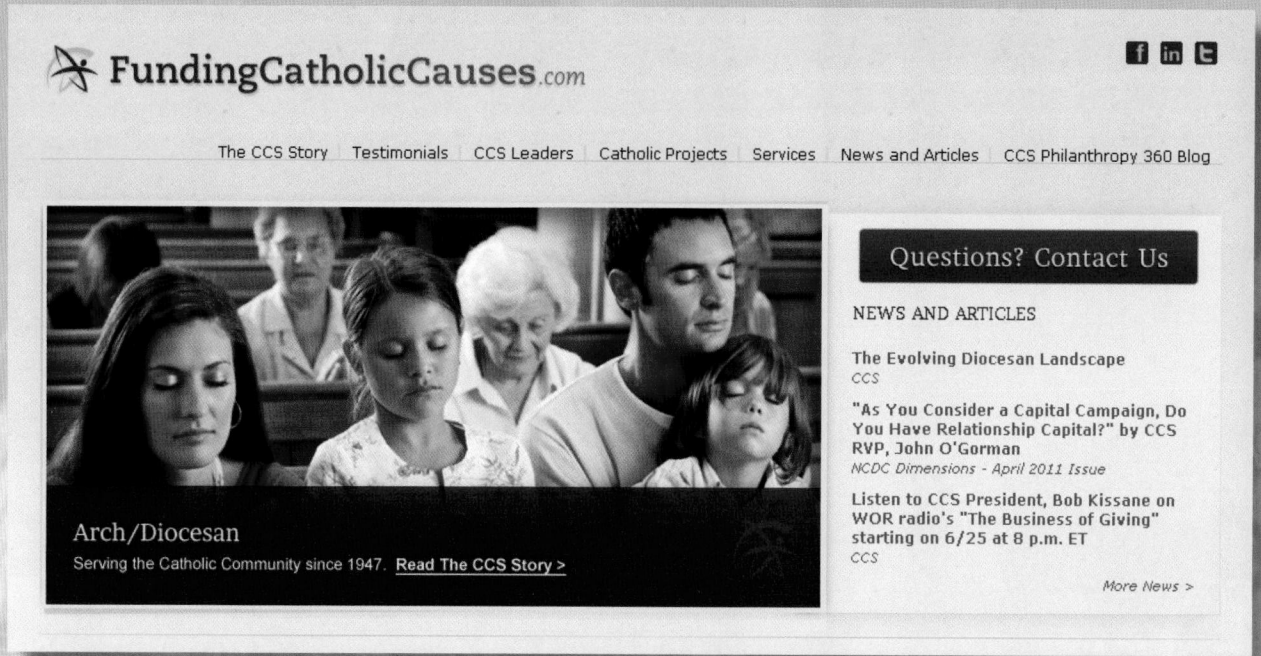

CM ALMY
Three American Lane
PO Box 2644
Greenwich, CT 06836
800.225.2569 www.almy.com
Timeless design, devoted craftsmanship, fine materials and friendly, trustworthy service. These are the hallmarks of CM Almy, outfitters to the church & clergy since 1892.

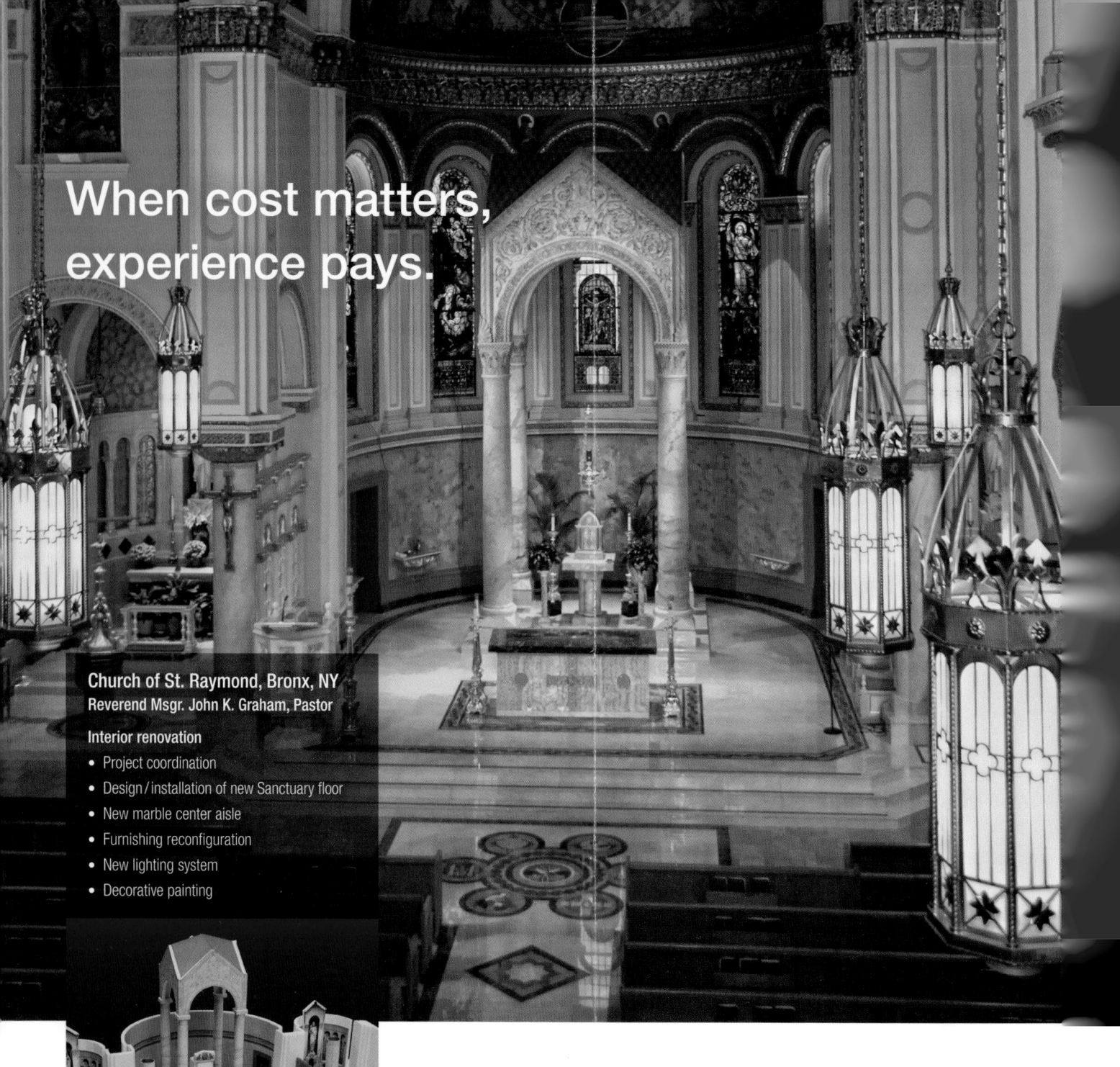

The Official Catholic Directory

for the Year of Our Lord

2012

GIVING STATUS OF THE CATHOLIC CHURCH AS OF JANUARY 1, 2012

Containing Ecclesiastical Statistics of

THE UNITED STATES, PUERTO RICO,
THE VIRGIN ISLANDS, AGANA, CAROLINE AND MARSHALL ISLANDS,
AND FOREIGN MISSIONARY ACTIVITIES.

The information contained in this Directory is derived from reports submitted to the publishers by the ecclesiastical authorities of the countries concerned, and neither the publishers nor the ecclesiastical authorities assume responsibility for any errors or omissions.

P.J. KENEDY & SONS

Publishers of the Holy Apostolic See

For inquiries call: 908-673-1000, or write:
300 Connell Drive, Suite 2000, Berkeley Heights, NJ 07922
To place an order call: 1-800-473-7020

The Official Catholic Directory®

Published by P.J. Kenedy & Sons in association with National Register Publishing

Printed and bound in the United States of America
International Standard Book Number: 978-0-87217-014-8
International Standard Serial Number: 0078-3854
Library of Congress Catalog Card Number: 81-30961

CONTENTS

ARCHDIOCESES AND DIOCESES

APOSTOLATE

PRELATURE OF THE HOLY CROSS AND OPUS DEI

EASTERN CHURCHES

TERRITORIAL SEES

MISSION SECTION

RELIGIOUS INSTITUTION SECTION

GENERAL SUMMARY

THE ARCHDIOCESES AND DIOCESES OF THE UNITED STATES—BY STATES

A—Indicates Archdiocese. The Archdiocese of Washington includes the District of Columbia and five counties of Maryland. Dioceses traverse state license in the following instances only: Cheyenne includes all of Yellowstone National Park; South Norwich includes Fisher's Island; Wilmington includes the eastern shores of Maryland; and Gallup includes parts of Arizona and New Mexico.

A USER'S GUIDE TO *THE OFFICIAL CATHOLIC DIRECTORY*®

Each year the editors of ***The Official Catholic Directory***® seek added ways of serving their subscribers. Although the book may never answer every question, this is th conscientious goal; its format, arrangement and editorial features are directed toward the convenience and needs of the public. Comments and suggestions are welcome. Fo the benefit of the subscriber and a more efficient use of ***The Official Catholic Directory***® and its cross references, a summary of the contents and their meaning follows

***The Official Catholic Directory*® Glossary**
A listing of some of the ecclesiastical terms and organizations found in the *Directory.*

The Governing Bodies in Vatican City
A chronological table of the **Supreme Roman Pontiffs**; the **Pope**, and an alphabetical list of the **College of Cardinals**; the duties of each of the agencies of the **Roman Curia**, and other commissions and institutions associated with the Holy See, along with their officers; a list of the **Seminaries** and **National Colleges** in Rome; the **Apostolic Nunciature** and the **Permanent Observer Mission to the United Nations**, with their staff. As foreign organizations, these entities are not included in the USCCB group tax exemption ruling ("Group Ruling").

The Catholic Church in the United States (Provinces)
The archdioceses and dioceses of the United States arranged under the provinces to which they belong, listed with their active archbishops and bishops.

Ecclesiastical forms of address recognized in the United States. Formal forms of address for correspondence with the clergy in the United States.

U.S. Cardinals, Archbishops, Bishops, Archabbots and Abbots
An alphabetical list of Cardinals, Archbishops, Bishops, Archabbots and Abbots, arranged within their specific title. Also listed is their address and status, followed by a hierarchical/chronological list by year.

United States Conference of Catholic Bishops
The United States Conference of Catholic Bishops is a permanent institute composed of Catholic bishops of the United States of America in and through which the bishops exercise in a communal or collegial manner the pastoral mission entrusted to them by the Lord Jesus of sanctification, teaching, and leadership, especially by devising forms and methods of the apostolate suitably adapted to the circumstances of the times. Such exercise is intended to offer appropriate assistance to each bishop in fulfilling his particular ministry in the local Church, to effect a commonality of ministry addressed to the people of the United States of America, and to foster and express communion with the Church in other nations within the Church universal, under the leadership of its chief pastor, the Pope.

Victims Assistance Coordinators pages.

Alphabetical Places List
The cities, towns, and villages where there is a church with a resident priest, or a Catholic institution, or both, together with the abbreviations of the archdiocese or diocese to which it belongs.

Dioceses and Archdioceses (in alphabetical sequence)
The most detailed information on the Catholic Church in the United States, including the Military Services, Eastern Churches, Personal Prelatures, and Apostolates to the Hungarians and Lithuanians. Listings are in alphabetical order according to the name of the diocese/archdiocese and include the diocesan curia and administrative offices; a parish-by-parish listing of clergy, churches, missions, and parochial schools; information on institutions, and the religious institutes of men and women located in the diocese/archdiocese; and a statistical profile for each diocese/archdiocese.

United States Territorial Sees
This section contains information on U.S. territories similar to that found in the preceding section.

American Foreign Missions
This section highlights the Religious working specifically in foreign countries. Each Province lists their U.S. members and the countries they serve in. For specific address requests, contact the mission office listed.

Missionary Activities
Organizations involved in missionary work in the U.S. and foreign countries.

United States Conference of Secular Institutes
An alphabetical list of secular organizations and their purposes.

U.S. Catholic Mission Association
An alphabetical list of countries served by the U.S. Catholic Mission Association, detailing the number and religious order or laity personnel working there.

Mission Churches
A list, by city, of mission churches in the U.S. and the parishes to which they are attached.

Religious Institutes of Men and Women
An alphabetical list of religious institutes of men and of women, using a P.J. Kenedy identification number. Each listing contains the general headquarters, provinces, provincialates, a summary of legal titles and holdings taken from the individual archdioceses and dioceses within the *Directory*, various forms of ministry and works statistical data of personnel, and representation in the U.S. dioceses and archdioceses Foreign religious institutes are not included in the USCCB Group Ruling.

Special Care Facilities
An alphabetical list of special care facilities by state and diocese.

Religious Order Initials for Men and **Religious Order Initials for Women**
Indexes of abbreviations relevant to the religious institute name and the applicabl identification number.

Diocesan and Religious Priests
An alphabetical list of diocesan and religious priests denoting their year of ordinatior the archdiocese or diocese they are assigned to or work in, and the church or institutio with which they are affiliated.

Necrology of U.S. Cardinals, Archbishops, Bishops, Archabbots, Abbots, an Priests
An alphabetical list of the U.S. hierarchy and priests who have died since the last issu of the *Directory*, along with their date of death and last assignment.

The General Summary
A 40+ page general summary of statistics arranged alphabetically by state, listing th archdiocese first within each state, followed by the dioceses. This information, extracte from the Statistical Overview of each diocese/archdiocese, pertains to personne parishes, health and welfare, education, and specific sacramental figures, as well a Catholic and total population figures for each diocese/archdiocese. U.S. territorie and Eastern Church statistics are also included.

Map of Catholic Diocesan and Province Boundaries in the United States
Map defining the diocesan, archdiocesan, provincial, and state boundaries.

Products & Services Guide
Includes a diverse array of products and services offered to the Catholic communit

***The Official Catholic Directory*®**
Provides a comprehensive listing of archdioceses and dioceses of the world. Als contains mid-year updates to the U.S. (arch)dioceses. More information on *Th OfficialCatholic Directory Part II* can be obtained from the publisher.

SPECIAL NOTATIONS USED IN THE DIRECTORY

An asterisk (*) denotes a tax-exempt organization that has its own IRS exemptio status and is not covered by the USCCB Group Ruling. The Group Ruling allows for th exemption from federal income tax of all Catholic institutions listed in *The Offici Catholic Directory*® for that year. The exemption was established in 1946 and has bee extended every year since then.

[CEM] in a parish listing indicates that a cemetery is connected to the parish.

[JC] indicates a joint cemetery, which is a cemetery being utilized by more than or parish. A number following [CEM] or [JC] indicates the number of cemeteries owne by the parish or joint cemeteries shared with other parishes.

A dagger † next to a name in the Necrology denotes a deceased priest. A Maltese cros ✠ denotes a deceased member of the hierarchy.

THE GENERAL SUMMARY

Certain terms used in the General Summary may need additional explanation.

Extern Priests are priests who have not been incardinated into the diocese in whic they are currently working and residing.

Health Care Centers include ancillary care systems, medical centers, sanitorium and hospices.

Specialized Homes refers to institutions which provide aid to abused children adults, halfway homes, AIDS patients, ARC patients, ex-offenders, pregnant wome adjudicated delinquents, or runaway youths.

Special Centers for Social Services are institutions or services that provi assistance, such as hotline centers, food banks, homeless centers, legal aid service or counseling services.

Residential Care of Children refers to orphanages, as opposed to day care center

Non-residential Schools for Handicapped are day schools which provide regul and religious education for physically and/or mentally handicapped students.

Received into Full Communion is used to describe people who have been baptiz earlier in life and have now been received into full communion in the Catholic Churc

THE OFFICIAL CATHOLIC DIRECTORY® GLOSSARY

Abbot

The superior of an autonomous community of men religious. He has general and sacramental jurisdiction over his community. The head of a prominent monastery or a congregation consisting of several monasteries is an *archabbot*.

Advocate

An ecclesiastical advocate is someone approved by Church authority to safeguard the rights of a party in a canonical process by arguments regarding the law and the facts of the case. [Cf. c. 1481 and CLSA Comm., p. 967]

Apostolate

Apostolate is the mission of Christ and participation in it. Its object is to bring Christ to others, its goal is the greater glory of God, its scope is universal. The work is carried out by every human agency by which the life of grace may be given or increased in the soul. A mandate from the Church is essential to the Catholic apostolate.

Archbishop

A bishop of a main or metropolitan diocese in an ecclesiastical province. The term is equivalent to *metropolitan* in the Western Church. It may also be granted to other ordinaries and non-residential bishops, and to the ordinary of a diocese outside a province.

Auditor

An official of a diocesan court, who gathers evidence and testimony and draws up a record of an ecclesiastical case.

Bishop

A bishop, by divine institution, carries on the work of the apostles. By reason of episcopal consecration, he shares in the triple apostolic function of teacher of doctrine, priest of sacred worship, and minister of church government. Bishops are responsible for the pastoral care of their dioceses. In addition, bishops have a responsibility to act in council to guide the Church. The term *eparch* is used in Eastern-rite churches.

The bishop to whom a particular or local church is entrusted is called a *diocesan bishop* or a *residential bishop*. Some other bishops receive *Titular Sees* over which they exercise no pastoral authority.

When the pastoral needs of a diocese or archdiocese warrant, an *auxiliary bishop* may be assigned to aid the residential bishop in governing his diocese. An auxiliary bishop is assigned when the residential bishop needs assistance in carrying out his duties because of ill health, advanced age, or amount of work. An auxiliary bishop does not have the right of succession within his diocese.

In special circumstances, such as the advanced age or ill health of a diocesan bishop, a *coadjutator bishop* may be appointed to assist the principal bishop of a diocese. Coadjutator bishops have the *right of succession* in the diocese of their appointment from the time the See becomes vacant upon the death or retirement of its bishop.

Brother

A man who is a member of a religious order, but is not ordained or studying for the priesthood.

Cana Conference

A Catholic family movement, originally designed to aid married couples and families in their spiritual and interpersonal relationships. The program is now divided into *Pre-Cana,* for couples engaged to be married, and *Cana Conferences,* programs for married people.

Catholic Fraternal Organizations

National Catholic fraternal organizations operating in the United States include the Knights of Columbus and the Knights of Peter Claver. These organizations are not included in the USCCB group tax exemption ruling.

Censor Librorum

A theologian empowered by a bishop to judge a book's soundness in regard to Church teaching before publication.

Chancellor

The office of the chancellor (or the *chancery*) evolved from the practice in the early Church of appointing an official to sign and preserve the letters of the bishop. The first function of the chancellor in the present day is gathering, arranging, and safeguarding the acts of the diocesan curia. Dispensations and other official documents also originate from the chancery. In many dioceses, the chancellor continues to exercise ordinary jurisdiction as delegated by the diocesan bishop. He or she may be assisted by a separate official, the *vice-chancellor.*

Chapter

The *general chapter* of a religious order is an assembly of elected or appointed members and provincials. General chapters are convened for the election of officers, amendments to the constitution, and discussion and legislation of matters of concern to members and the order as a whole.

A *provincial chapter* conducts elections and handles legislation on a provincial level. The assembly is comprised of superiors and representatives of the religious.

A *chapter of canons* is a group of diocesan priests, appointed by the bishop of a diocese, with assigned authority or responsibilities.

College of Cardinals

The College of Cardinals is made up of the cardinals of the Church, who advise the Pope, assist in the central administration of the Church, head the various curial offices and congregations, administer the Holy See during a vacancy, and elect a new Pope. There are three ranks in the College of Cardinals, corresponding to the historical origins of cardinals in the Roman Catholic Church. All cardinals are bishops, but their rank within the College of Cardinals is characterized by one of the hierarchical ranks of bishop, priest, or deacon. Cardinals are given honorary title to churches in the city of Rome. [CF. c. 350; CLSA Comm., pp. 288-289]

1. Cardinal Bishops

There are two types of Cardinal Bishops: 1) those appointed by the Pope as titular bishops to one of the six suburban dioceses of Rome, and 2) Eastern-rite Patriarchs who are heads of Sees with apostolic origins that have been assigned to the College of Cardinals.

2. Cardinal Priests

Heads of Sees outside the city of Rome are assigned a "titular church," one of the churches in Rome. They have no pastoral authority over their titular church.

3. Cardinal Deacons

Cardinals of diaconal rank are bishops without Sees who head the various departments, offices, congregations, committees, and the Secretariat of State of the Roman Curia.

Confraternity of Christian Doctrine [CCD]

A lay organization established for religious education throughout a person's entire life. The term is currently used to describe Catholic parish-based religious education of children from kindergarten through high school. At the diocesan level, the offices are now more commonly known as offices of *religious education* or *Christian formation.* Nationally, the confraternity's religious education component has been taken over by the USCCB's Department of Education. It still exists as a separate entity under the USCCB Administrative Board, with responsibility for licensing religious and spiritual literature.

Consolidated School

The term, as used in the *Directory,* may refer to a school that takes students from more than one parish, or a school that was formed by the consolidation of two or three other schools. In both cases, it is a means of keeping a Catholic school in a given area open by taking students from the surrounding areas, regardless of parish boundaries.

Convent

In common usage, the term refers to a house of women religious. Originally, it referred to a building where members of religious institutes lived, and was not restricted to communities of women.

Cursillo

The *cursillo de cristianidad*, or "little course in Christianity," is a three-day program for achieving spiritual renewal or spiritual awakening. It seeks to convey a new sense of individual and organized apostolic action. The program, conducted by priests and laypeople, consists of a three-day weekend focused on prayer, study, and Christian action, and a follow-up program known as the *post-cursillo.*

Deacons

The diaconate is the first order or grade in ordained ministry. Its origins are in early apostolic times, when deacons preached and baptized under the direction of the presbyters or bishops. Any man who is to be ordained to the priesthood must first be ordained as a *transitional deacon.* Deacons serve in the ministry of liturgy, of the word, and of charity.

In 1967, Pope Paul VI reinstituted the *Permanent Diaconate* for men who do not plan to become ordained priests. Although men ordained as permanent deacons are sometimes referred to as "married deacons," the permanent diaconate is open to both married and unmarried men, with the understanding that after ordination, they may not marry even after the death of a spouse. Under the authority of the diocesan bishop, they perform the same functions as the transitional deacons while, at the same time, retaining their roles in society as family and business men.

Dean/Vicar Forane

The title of a priest appointed by the bishop to aid him in administering the parishes in a certain vicinity, called a "deanery," or "vicariates forane." The function of a dean, or vicar forane, involves promotion, coordination, and supervision of the common pastoral activity within the deanery or vicariate.

Defender of the Bond

A member of a diocesan tribunal, either a cleric or a lay person, holding a graduate degree in canon law, who is appointed by the diocesan bishop for cases concerning the nullity of sacred ordination or the nullity or dissolution of the marriage bond. The defender of the bond is responsible for a review of the evidence, scrutiny of the briefs, examination of witnesses, and maintenance of proper procedures during the trial. The defender also deals with some situations concerning the content of the litigation rather than the legal procedures.

Diocesan Consultors

An advisory council of diocesan priests, as appointed by a diocesan bishop, that assists in the administrative affairs of the diocese.

Diocesan Curia

The personnel and offices assisting the diocesan bishop in directing the pastoral activity, administration, and the exercise of judicial power of his diocese. The curia includes among its officers laity and religious as well as clergy. Principal officers of a diocesan curia are the vicar general of the diocese, the chancellor, officials of the diocesan tribunal, examiners, consultors, auditors, the promoter of justice and the defender of the bond.

Diocese

The standard term for a territorial division of the Church, entrusted to a bishop who rules in his own name as local ordinary, and not as a delegate of another. The chief diocese of a province is an *archdiocese.* It is headed by an archbishop. A diocese is usually limited to a definite territory so that it comprises all the faithful who inhabit that territory. [Cf. cc. 369 and 372, #1] In Eastern-rite churches, the term eparchy is used.

Eastern-rite [Oriental] Church

The term used to describe the Catholic churches which developed in Eastern Europe, Asia, and Africa. The Eastern-rite churches have their own distinctive liturgical and organizational systems. Each is considered equal to the Latin rite within the Church.

Eastern Catholic Association

The eastern catholic association is the association of all Eastern Catholic Bishops in the United States. All Eastern Catholic Bishops, diocesan bishops (and their equivalent in law) and auxiliaries are members. The Association represents the Armenian, Chaldean, Maronite Melikite, Romanian, Ruthenian and Ukrainian Churches. The Syriac, Syro-Malabar and Russian churches are also represented but without a bishop member since they are presently have no established hierarchy in the United States.

Ecumenism/Ecumenical Movement

A movement for spiritual understanding and unity among Christians and their churches. The term is also extended to apply to efforts toward greater understanding and cooperation between Christians and members of other faiths.

Exarch/Exarchy

A church jurisdiction, similar to a diocese, established for Eastern-rite Catholics living outside their native land. The head of an exarchy, usually a bishop, is an *exarch.*

Hierarchy

In general, the term refers to the ordered body of clergy, divided into bishops, priests, and deacons. In Catholic practice, the term refers to the bishops of the world or of a particular region.

Holy Name Society

A lay organization which seeks to aid its members in living a genuinely Christian life. The society organizes retreats and other spiritual and devotional exercises.

Holy See

The term refers to the diocese of Rome. Used in reference to the governance of the Church, it refers to the Pontiff, the Roman Curia, and the Sacred College.

Legion of Mary

A lay organization established to assist the clergy in the sanctification of its members' souls, and the spread of the Christian faith and spiritual service to others. Members participate in almost every form of social service and Catholic action, including evangelization. The organization was founded in 1921.

Metropolitan

The archbishop of an archdiocese in a province. He has limited supervisory powers and influence over the other dioceses and bishops in the province.

Military Ordinariate [Archdiocese for the Military Services, U.S.A.]

A nonterritorial diocese for American Catholics and their dependents who are in the military or affiliated with the armed forces. Personnel employed by or engaged in diplomatic missions for the U.S. government in countries where U.S. military forces are stationed also belong to the Military Ordinariate.

Mission

A mission, or *quasi-parish,* is a parish which has not been established because it lacks one or more of the following qualifications: a resident pastor; necessary financial resources; territorial boundaries; or a natural grouping by way of rite, nationality, or language. Missions are attached to some parishes under the care of their pastors.

Moderator of the Curia

A bishop or priest, appointed by the diocesan bishop, who is concerned primarily with administrative matters and with supervising those working in the curia.

Monastery

An autonomous community house of a religious order, which may or may not be a monastic order. The term is used more specifically to refer to a community house of men religious or women religious in which they lead a contemplative life separate from the world.

Monsignor

An honorary ecclesiastical title granted by the Pope to some diocesan priests. In the United States, the title is given to the vicar general of a diocese. In Europe, the title is also given to bishops.

Newman Apostolate

An apostolate to the Catholic college and university community, now commonly known as "campus ministry."

Notary

An elected or appointed ecclesiastical official who acts as a secretary in formal church proceedings. The notary records the minutes, testimony, etc., of the proceedings.

Opus Dei

A personal prelature dedicated to spreading through society an awareness of the call to Christian virtue, awareness, and witness in one's life and work. The organization was founded in 1928 and in 1950, it received Vatican approval as a secular institution. In 1982, it was designated a personal prelature, the *Prelature of the Holy Cross and Opus Dei.* Members are not members of a religious order, do not take vows, and do not live in community.

Ordinary

Diocesan bishops, religious superiors, and certain other diocesan authorities with jurisdiction over the clergy in a specific geographical area, or the members of a religious order.

Ordination/Ordain

The sacramental rite by which a "sacred order" is conferred (diaconate, priesthood, episcopacy).

Papal Audience

Request for attendance at papal audiences and similar functions may be addressed to: Bishops' Office for United States Visitors to the Vatican. Postal address: North American College, Via dell 'Umilta 30, 00187 Rome, Italy. Tel.: 011-39-06-6900-1821; Fax: 011-39-06-679-1448.

Papal Representatives

There are three types of representatives of the Roman Pontiff:

1) those who represent him to particular churches and civil government;

2) those who represent him to particular churches;

3) those who represent him in international organizations or at various conferences and meetings. [Cf. c. 363; CLSA Comm., p. 302]

1. Apostolic Nuncio

In the United States, the papal representative is sent by the Pope to both the local church and to the government. His title is Apostolic Nuncio.

2. Legate

An individual appointed by the Pope to be his personal representative to a nation, international conference, or local church. The legate may be chosen from the local clergy of a country.

3. Permanent Observer to the United Nations

The Apostolic See maintains permanent legates below the ambassadorial level to several world organizations. Since the papal representative does not enjoy the right to vote within the organization, his title at the United Nations is that of *Observer*.

Parish

A specific community of the Christian faithful within a diocese, which has its own church building, under the authority of a *pastor* who is responsible for providing them with ministerial service. Most parishes are formed on a geographic basis, but they may be formed along national or ethnic lines.

Parish Coordinator

A deacon, religious, or lay person who is responsible for the pastoral care of parish. The parish coordinator is in charge of the day-to-day life of the parish in the areas of worship, education, pastoral service and administration.

Pastor

A priest in charge of a parish or congregation. He is responsible for administering the sacraments, instructing the congregation in the doctrine of the Church, and other services to the people of the parish.

Pastoral Associate

A member of the laity who is part of a parish ministry team.

Pastoral Council

A consultative body which the pastor or bishop consults concerning the pastoral activity within the diocese. Its members include laity, religious, and clergy. The pastoral council's purpose is to study practical situations, difficulties and problems, and make concrete recommendations and proposals to the diocesan bishop. The pastoral council is always subject to the final authority of the pastor or bishop.

Patriarch

The Pope is the traditional "Patriarch of the West." All other bishops in the Latin Rite, even those with the honorary title of "Patriarch," are subject to him. Similarly, patriarchs within nations have only an honorary title unless special provisions are made otherwise. Eastern-rite Patriarchs are subject to the Pope while serving as heads of the faithful belonging to their rites throughout the world.

Personal Prelature

In addition to the territorial arrangement of the Church into particular or local churches or dioceses, canon law also provides for non-territorial areas of religious jurisdiction, incorporating secular clergy and deacons. Membership is also open to lay persons. These *prelatures* are established to meet specific pastoral or missionary needs at the regional, national, or international level without infringing on the rights of the local bishops. A prelature is presided over by a *personal prelate,* who is an ordinary with the right to establish seminaries and ordain priests as members of the prelature.

Canon law also allows for laity to be associated in the works of prelatures without being withdrawn from the jurisdiction of their own diocesan bishop.

Personal prelatures are jurisdictional structures of a secular type which are established by the Holy See as an instrument within the hierarchical pastoral work of the Church to carry out special pastoral or missionary tasks. Personal prelatures are based on the principle of insertion into the local Church. In this they differ essentially from the personal dioceses, such as those constituted for the faithful of a particular rite, which are based on the principle of independence or autonomy in regard to local Churches.

Vatican II provided for setting up personal prelatures (see Decree, Presbyterorum ordinis, no. 10). Additional norms were established in subsequent pontifical legislation (see Motu proprio Ecclesiae Sanctae no. 1, no. 4, August 6, 1966 and the Apostolic Constitution Regimini Ecclesiae Universae, no. 49, no. 1, Aug. 15, 1967). General legislation concerning personal prelatures is contained in canons 294 to 297 of the 1983 Code of Canon Law.

Personal prelatures are to be established by the Holy See after hearing the views of the respective Episcopal Conferences (can. 294). They are governed by a Prelate according to statutes given by the Holy See. The Prelate is their proper Ordinary, who may incardinate priests and must look after their spiritual and temporal welfare (can. 295). Lay people can dedicate themselves by means of a contractual agreement, to the apostolic activities of the prelature; the statutes are to specify the manner of this organic cooperation (can. 296). And the statutes are also to determine the relations of the prelature with the Ordinaries of the places in which the prelature works, with the prior consent of the Ordinaries (can. 297).

Presbyteral Council

Also known as the *priests' council,* the presbyteral council is the principal consultative body mandated by the Code of Canon Law to advise the diocesan bishop in matters of pastoral governance. It consists of bishops and priests serving the diocese.

Propagation of the Faith

An organization, headquartered in Rome, which distributes aid to Catholic missions and organizes the work of missionaries all over the world. The organization has responsibility for fostering missionary vocations, assigning missionaries to field work, defining ecclesiastical boundaries and assigning clergy to them, and encouraging training and installation of native-born clergy.

Promoter of Justice

A cleric or lay person, holding a graduate degree in canon law, who is appointed by the diocesan bishop to serve in the role of a "prosecuting attorney" in trials of crimes against church law and of other judicial litigations in the diocese. A promoter of justice may be appointed for a specific case by the bishop.

Province

A defined geographic area containing an archdiocese, or *Metropolitan See,* and at least one diocese, or *Suffragen See.* The archbishop of the archdiocese has no direct powers over the Suffragen Sees, but does have limited advisory and appellate authority and obligations. The term also refers to a territorial grouping of particular churches or communities, or a territory of a religious order.

Provincial

The superior of the communities of a religious order that constitute a province.

Provincial Council

An assembly of the bishops of an ecclesiastical province, called by the metropolitan archbishop. The term is also used in reference to the provincial superior of a province, along with his or her chief advisors.

Receptions into the Church

Can take two forms: baptism of those not previously validly baptized, or "reception into full communion" with the Church for those who have already been baptized, in which case a profession of faith affects the reception.

Religious Education Department

The ECA has established the ECDD-The Eastern Conference of Diocesan Directors of Religious Education which oversees, through God With Us Publications, all publications of catechtical materials published by it and used in Eastern Catholic Churches, mainly of Byzantine tradition.

Religious Priest/Diocesan Priest

Religious, or regular, priests are those who are professed members of a religious order or institute. Religious clergy live according to the rule of their respective orders. In pastoral ministry, they are under the jurisdiction of their local bishop, as well as the superiors of their order. Diocesan, or secular, priests are under the direction of their local bishop. They commit to serving their congregations and other institutions.

Retreat

A period of time spent in meditation and religious exercise. Retreats may take various forms, from traditional closed forms, to open retreats, which do not disengage the participants from day-to-day life. Both clergy and lay people of all ages participate in retreats. Houses and centers providing facilities for retreats are *retreat houses.*

Rite of Christian Initiation of Adults [RCIA]

The liturgical book containing the norms and rituals of the Catholic Church for people who wish to join the Church. Part of the book is intended for baptized Christians who wish to become Catholics. The term is used in a general sense to refer to the process of entering the Catholic Church.

Roman Curia

The official collective name for the administrative agencies and courts, and their officials, who assist the Pope in governing the Church. Members are appointed and granted authority by the Pope.

St. Vincent DePaul Society

Originally known as the *Conference of Charity,* this is an organization of lay people who serve the poor through spiritual and material works of mercy. The society operates stores, rehabilitation workshops, food centers, shelters, criminal justice and other programs.

Scholastic

A member of a religious order who has completed his novitiate, but has not yet been ordained.

Scholastic Teaching

Usually refers to Scholastic Philosophy, which is the basis for much Catholic Theology. It comes from the canonical "schools" of the 12th-13th centuries, St. Thomas Aquinas, St. Bonaventure, St. Albert the Great, etc., who developed "scholasticism" based mainly on Aristotle. It is the semi-official philosophy of the Church.

Secular Institute

Canonically erected institute of consecrated life for single laity and clerics who strive for the perfection of charity and work for the sanctification of the world while remaining in a lifestyle within the world.

See

The word is taken from the Latin word "sedes" ("seat"), and is used to denote a diocese or ecclesiastical district. The term *Holy See* is reserved to the diocese of Rome whose bishop is the Pope. U.S. Territorial Sees are dioceses located on territory of the United States of America, but are members of episcopal confereences other than the United States Conference of Catholic Bishops.

Seminary

An educational institution for men preparing for *Holy Orders.* The term originates from the time of St. Augustine, when those preparing for the priesthood were educated in the "cathedral school." During the Middle Ages, the clergy were educated in a university setting where faculties of philosophy, theology, and canon law existed. Eventually individual dioceses or provinces came to establish their own schools for educating their clerical students. Traditional seminaries date from the Council of Trent in the 16th century.

A school for the spiritual, academic, and pastoral education and formation of priesthood candidates is known as a *major seminary* in which the focus is on philosophical and theological education. To prepare for entrance into a major seminary, a period of study is set aside for the required courses in the humanities and the sciences in institutions called *minor seminaries.*

Serra Club

Local units of *Serra International,* an organization which promotes vocations to the priesthood and religious life, and offers instruction to lay leaders.

Sister

The term, in the strictest sense, refers to women religious who belong to institutes which have professed simple vows. However, in everyday usage, the term is used for any woman religious.

Sodality

A group of laity established for the promotion of Christian life and worship, or some other religious purpose.

Special Centers for Social Services

This would seem to overlap with Specialized Homes. Some of the categorization is fairly arbitrary. Catholic Charities might have its own proper distinctions for government or private funding purposes.

Specialized Homes

Includes such institutions as homes for handicapped (e.g., Misericordia Homes), youth homes (e.g., Maryville, Mercy Boys and Girls, Homes), homes for battered women, drug rehab centers, homes for unwed mothers, etc.

Superior

The head of a religious order or congregation. He or she may be the head of a province, or an individual house.

Synod

A gathering of designated officials and representatives of a church, that has legislative and policy-making powers.

1. Synod of Bishops

The Synod of Bishops is a consultative body, unless explicitly stated otherwise by His Holiness, expressing the communion of the hierarchy. A synod of bishops meets in general assembly, either in "Ordinary" or "Extraordinary" session, when the matter for treatment concerns the whole Church and in "Special Assembly" when the matter deals directly with a definite region or regions.

2. Synod of Oriental Churches

The synods of the Oriental Churches enjoy various prerogatives including the right to elect bishops, regulate discipline and exercise pastoral authority in their respective churches.

3. Diocesan Synod

A diocesan synod is an expression of the communion of the particular church. A diocesan synod enjoys the participation of priests, women and men religious and laypersons; the bishop is the sole legislator.

Territorial Sees

Dioceses located on territory of the United States, but are members of episcopal conferences other than the United States Conference of Catholic Bishops.

Theologate

An institution which provides the last four years of study for candidates for the priesthood.

Titular See

A former diocese which no longer physically or geographically exists. Titular Sees are given as an honorary title to certain bishop not serving as a chief pastor of a diocese, i.e., auxiliary bishops, papal representatives, and bishops of the Roman Curia.

Tribunal

A tribunal (court) is the name given to the person or persons who exercise the Church's judicial powers. By its very nature, this procedure involves the determination of a legal controversy. A major concern of tribunals is conducting the process leading to the dissolution or annulment of marriages. In ecclesiastical matters, definite procedural norms for conducting a trial are found in the Code of Canon Law to settle disputes. There are various grades of tribunals, including diocesan tribunals, the first court of trial for most cases; regional and metropolitan tribunals, located in an archdiocese, the appellate court for all cases tried within the province; and the tribunals of the Holy See, which act as the Church's central appellate court, try cases reserved to the Holy See, deal with questions of procedure and jurisdiction of the other courts, and act as the Church's supreme court.

United States Conference of Catholic Bishops

The United States Conference of Catholic Bishops is a permanent institute composed of Catholic bishops of the United States of America in and through which the bishops exercise in a communal or collegial manner the pastoral mission entrusted to them by the Lord Jesus of sanctification, teaching, and leadership, especially by devising forms and methods of the apostolate suitably adapted to the circumstances of the times. Such exercise is intended to offer appropriate assistance to each bishop in fulfilling his particular ministry in the local Church, to effect a commonality of ministry addressed to the people of the United States of America, and to foster and express communion with the Church in other nations within the Church universal, under the leadership of its chief pastor, The Pope.

Vicar

The appointment of a priest or a bishop as an *episcopal vicar* is an option given to a diocesan bishop when he needs a deputy for governing a specific territory within the diocese, a group of persons or a specific rite, or a type of apostolic work within the diocese.

By Church law, the diocesan bishop is the judge of all cases in the diocesan tribunal of first trial. He must appoint a priest with ordinary power to judge cases not reserved to the bishop himself. This priest must have a graduate degree in canon law. He is called the *judicial vicar,* and is sometimes referred to as the chief judge or officialis. He may be given another priest as an assistant with the title of *adjutant judicial vicar*.

A bishop or priest appointed to participate in the executive (administrative) governance of the diocese with executive jurisdiction as a deputy of the diocesan bishop is a *vicar general.* The appointment of a vicar general is mandatory for every diocese. This office is designed to facilitate and unify diocesan administration.

Vicar for Religious

A priest appointed by a bishop to act as his representative in dealing with the religious communities in his diocese.

Information for this glossary was taken from the *Catholic News Service's Stylebook on Religion,* the *Modern Catholic Dictionary,* published by Doubleday and Company, Inc., the *Concise Oxford Dictionary of the Christian Church,* published by Oxford University Press, and the *Encyclopedic Dictionary of Religion,* published by the Sisters of St. Joseph of Philadelphia. The publishers of the *Official Catholic Directory* also wish to thank the Vice Chancellors of the Archdiocese of Chicago for their work in the preparation of this glossary.

THE SUPREME ROMAN PONTIFFS

St. Peter of Bethsaida in Galilee, Prince of the Apostles, who received from Jesus Christ the Supreme Pontifical Power to be transmitted to his Successors, resided first at Antioch, then at Rome for twenty-five years where he was martyred in the year 64, or 67 of the common reckoning.

Pontiff	END OF PONTIFICATE, A.D.
St. Linus	76
St. Anacletus or Cletus	88
St. Clement I	97
St. Evaristus	105
St. Alexander I	115
St. Sixtus I	125
St. Telesphorus	136
St. Hyginus	140
St. Pius I	155
St. Anicetus	166
St. Soterus	175
St. Eleuterius	189
St. Victor I	199
St. Zephyrinus	217
St. Callistus I	222
St. Urban I	230
St. Pontian	235
St. Anterus	236
St. Fabian	250
St. Cornelius	253
St. Lucius I	254
St. Stephen I	257
St. Sixtus II	258
St. Dionysius	268
St. Felix I	274
St. Eutychian	283
St. Caius	296
St. Marcellinus	304
St. Marcellus I	309
St. Eusebius	309
St. Melchiades	314
St. Sylvester I	335
St. Mark	336
St. Julius I	352
Liberius	366
St. Damasus I	384
St. Siricius	399
St. Anastasius I	401
St. Innocent I	417
St. Zozimus	418
St. Boniface I	422
St. Celestine I	432
St. Sixtus III	440
St. Leo I (the Great)	461
St. Hilary	468
St. Simplicius	483
St. Fclix III or II	492
St. Gelasius I	496
Anastasius II	498
St. Symmacus	514
St. Hormisdas	523
St. John I	526
St. Felix IV or III	530
Boniface II	532
John II	535
St. Agapitus	536
St. Silverius	537
Vigilius	555
Pelagius I	561
John III	574
Benedict I	579
Pelagius II	590
St. Gregory I (the Great)	604
Sabinianus	606
Boniface III	607
St. Boniface IV	615
St. Deusdeditus or Adeodatus I	618
Boniface V	625
Honorius I	638
Severinus	640
John IV	642
Theodore I	649
St. Martin I	655
St. Eugene I	657
St. Vitalian	672
Adeodatus II	676
Donus I	678
St. Agathonus	681
St. Leo II	683
St. Benedict II	685
John V	686
Conon	687
St. Sergius I	701
John VI	705
John VII	707
Sisinnius	708
Constantine	715
St. Gregory II	731
St. Gregory III	741
St. Zachary	752
Stephen III	757
St. Paul I	767
Stephen IV	772
Adrian I	795
St. Leo III	816
Stephen V	817
St. Paschal I	824
Eugene II	827
Valentine	827
Gregory IV	844
Sergius II	847
St. Leo IV	855
Benedict III	858
St. Nicholas I (the Great)	867
Adrian II	872
John VIII	882
Marinus I	884
St. Adrian III	885
Stephen VI	891
Formosus	896
Boniface VI	896
Stephen VII	897
Romanus	897
Theodore II	897
John IX	900
Benedict IV	903
Leo V	903
Sergius III	911
Anastasius III	913
Landus	914
John X	928
Leo VI	928
Stephen VIII	931
John XI	935
Leo VII	939
Stephen IX	942
Marinus II	946
Agapitus II	955
John XII	964
Leo VIII	965
Benedict V	966
John XIII	972
Benedict VI	974
Benedict VII	983
John XIV	984
John XV	996
Gregory V	999
Sylvester II	1003
John XVII	1003
John XVIII	1009
Sergius IV	1012
Benedict VIII	1024
John XIX	1032
Benedict IX	1044
Benedict IX	1045
Sylvester III	1045
Gregory VI	1046
Clement II	1047
Benedict IX	1048
Damasus II	1048
St. Leo IX	1054
Victor II	1057
Stephen X	1058
Nicholas II	1061
Alexander II	1073
St. Gregory VII	1085
B. Victor III	1087
B. Urban II	1099
Paschal II	1118
Gelasius II	1119
Callistus II	1124
Honorius II	1130
Innocent II	1143
Celestine II	1144
Lucius II	1145
B. Eugene III	1153
Anastasius IV	1154
Adrian IV	1159
Alexander III	1181
Lucius III	1185
Urban III	1187
Gregory VIII	1187
Clement III	1191
Celestine III	1198
Innocent III	1216
Honorius III	1227
Gregory IX	1241
Celestine IV	1241
Innocent IV	1254
Alexander IV	1261
Urban IV	1264
Clement IV	1268
B. Gregory X	1276
B. Innocent V	1276
Adrian V	1276
John XXI	1277
Nicholas III	1280
Martin IV	1285
Honorius IV	1287
Nicholas IV	1292
St. Celestine V	1296
Boniface VIII	1303
B. Benedict XI	1304
Clement V	1314
John XXII	1334
Benedict XII	1342
Clement VI	1352
Innocent VI	1362
B. Urban V	1370
Gregory XI	1378
Urban VI	1389
Boniface IX	1404
Innocent VII	1406
Gregory XII	1415
Martin V	1431
Eugene IV	1447
Nicholas V	1455
Callistus III	1458
Pius II	1464
Paul II	1471
Sixtus IV	1484
Innocent VIII	1492
Alexander VI	1503
Pius III	1503
Julius II	1513
Leo X	1521
Adrian VI	1523
Clement VII	1534
Paul III	1549
Julius III	1555
Marcellus II	1555
Paul IV	1559
Pius IV	1565
St. Pius V	1572
Gregory XIII	1585
Sixtus V	1590
Urban VII	1590
Gregory XIV	1591
Innocent IX	1591
Clement VIII	1605
Leo XI	1605
Paul V	162
Gregory XV	162
Urban VIII	164
Innocent X	165
Alexander VII	166
Clement IX	166
Clement X	167
B. Innocent XI	168
Alexander VIII	169
Innocent XII	170
Clement XI	172
Innocent XIII	172
Benedict XIII	173
Clement XII	174
Benedict XIV	175
Clement XIII	176
Clement XIV	177
Pius VI	179
Pius VII	182
Leo XII	182
Pius VIII	183
Gregory XVI	184
Pius IX	187
Leo XIII	190
St. Pius X	191
Benedict XV	192
Pius XI	193
Pius XII	195
John XXIII	196
Paul VI	197
John Paul I	197
John Paul II	200
Benedict XVI	now reignin

PART I
Hierarchy of the Catholic Church

The Hierarchy, as the supreme governing body of the Catholic Church, consists of the Roman Pontiff, the successor of Peter, and the Bishops joined together with him and never without him (canons 330,331,336) in one apostolic college to provide for the common good of the Church. The Roman Pontiff in the exercise of his office is assisted by the College of Cardinals, and further by the departments also called "dicasteries" of the Roman Curia. The Bishops, of whom some bear the titles of Patriarch and Archbishop, are united with the Roman Pontiff in the governance of the whole Church; the Bishops, when assigned to particular Sees, are individually responsible for the teaching, sanctification and governance of their particular Church. Apostolic Vicars and Prefects together with certain Abbots and other Prelates are also joined in this work.

HIS HOLINESS THE POPE

Bishop of Rome and Vicar of Jesus Christ,
Successor of St. Peter, Prince of the Apostles,
Supreme Pontiff of the Universal Church.
Primate of Italy.
Archbishop and Metropolitan of the Roman Province,
Sovereign of Vatican City State.
Servant of the Servants of God

Benedict XVI

JOSEPH RATZINGER

The present successor of St. Peter was born in Marktl am Inn, Diocese of Passau, April 16, 1927; ordained Priest, June 29, 1951; appointed Archbishop of Munchen und Freising March 25, 1977 and consecrated May 28, 1977; Proclaimed and created Cardinal June 27, 1977. Elected Pope, April 19, 2005; installed April 24, 2005.

VATICAN CITY

Vatican City is the smallest state in the world, occupying 108.7 acres, of which about one third is covered with buildings and is situated on the right side of the Tiber River. Vatican City has territory, population, and sovereignity. This territory, limited as it is, suffices to guarantee the spiritual and temporal independence needed for the exercise of the Holy See's spiritual mission. In 1870 the Kingdom of Italy seized all Vatican possessions which for several centuries had constituted the papal temporal domain. But even after 1870 the Holy See continued to regard itself as a separate entity in international law, and was recognized as such by numerous states with which it retained normal diplomatic relations. After long discussions the Holy See and the then Kingdom of Italy signed the Lateran Pacts on February 11, 1929, so that the complete and independent authority of the Vatican State was and is recognized by the Italian state.

The Sovereign of this small state is His Holiness, the Pope.

The government presently is administered by a Pontifical Commission of which His Eminence Giovanni Cardinal Lajolo is President.

THE COLLEGE OF CARDINALS

The Cardinals constitute a special college and they assist the Roman Pontiff collegially when they are called together to deal with questions of major importance; they do so individually when they assist the Pope especially in the daily care of the universal Church by means of the different offices which they perform (canons 349-350). The Cardinals who are under eighty years of age elect his successor.

The College of Cardinals is divided into three ranks: Cardinal-Bishops, Cardinal-Priests, and Cardinal-Deacons. The College of Cardinals, when complete formerly consisted of 70 members: 6 Cardinal Bishops, 50 Cardinal Priests and 14 Cardinal Deacons, but the late Pontiffs, Pope John XXIII and Pope Paul VI enlarged the College of Cardinals. At the moment the maximum number of Cardinal electors (those under 80 years of age) must not exceed 120.

The Cardinal Bishops (except the Patriarch-Cardinals of the Oriental Rites), have as Titular Sees the Suburban Sees of Rome, which are: Porto Santa Rufina, Albano, Palestrina, Sabina, Frascati, Velletri, Segni. The Cardinal Dean has united to his See the See of Ostia. The Cardinal Priests take their title from the Titular Churches to which they are appointed: the Cardinal Deacons are appointed to other Churches called Deaconries. The first Cardinal Bishop is Dean; the first Cardinal Priest is First Priest; and the first Cardinal Deacon is First Deacon of the Sacred College. The Dean has the right of ordaining the new Pope if he is not already a bishop; the First Deacon has the right of proclaiming him and investing him with the sacred Pallium. On the death of the Pontiff, the Cardinal Camerlengo has the Administration of the affairs of the Holy See.

Sometimes the Roman Pontiff promotes a person to the dignity of Cardinal but does not make public his name and keeps it in pectore. Upon the publication of his name, this Cardinal enjoys his right of precedence from the day on which his name was reserved in pectore by the Pope (cfr. Can. 351¶ 3).

The Cardinals of the Holy Roman Church

(Listed in Alphabetical Order)

Abril y Castello, Santos (Cardinal Deacon), Diaconate of San Ponziano, Archpriest of the papal basilica of St. Mary Major; Born in Alfambra, Diocese of Teruel, September 21, 1935. Created and proclaimed February 18, 2012. Address: Via dell'Erba 1, 00193 Rome, Italy.

Agnelo, Geraldo Majella (Cardinal Priest), Titular of San Gregorio Magno alla Magliana Nuova, Archbishop Emeritus of Sao Salvador da Bahia;

born in Juiz de Fora, October 19, 1933. Created and proclaimed February 21, 2001. Address: Rua Ten. Fernando Tuy, 318, Edf Mansao Central Park, apt. 102, Pituba, 41830-498, Salvador, B.A. Brasile.

Agré, Bernard (Cardinal Priest), Titular of San Giovanni Crisostomo a Monte Sacro Alto, Archbishop Emeritus of Abidjan; born in Monga, Archdiocese of Abidjan, March 2, 1926. Created and proclaimed February 21, 2001. Address: 06 B.P. 2806, Abidjan 06, Cote D'Ivoire.

Agustoni, Gilberto (Cardinal Priest) Titular of Ss. Urbano e Lorenzo a Primaporta, Prefect Emeritus of the Supreme Tribunal of the Apostolic Signatura; born in Schaffhausen, Switzerland, Diocese of Basel, July 26, 1922. Created and proclaimed November 26, 1994. Address: Piazza della Citta Leonina 9, 00193 Rome, Italy.

Alencherry, George (Cardinal Priest), Titular of San Bernardo alle Terme, Major Archbishop of Ernakulam-Angamaly of the Syro-Malabars, India; Born in Thuruthy, Archdiocese of Changanacherry of the Syro-Malabars, April 19, 1945. Created and proclaimed February 18, 2012. Address: Major Archbishop's Home, P.O. Box 2580 Kochi-682031, Ernakulam, Kerala, India.

Álvarez Martinez, Francisco (Cardinal Priest), Titular of Santa Maria Regina Pacis a Monte Verde, Archbishop Emeritus of Toledo; born in Santa Eulalia de Ferrones Llanera, Archdiocese of Oviedo, July 14, 1925. Created and proclaimed February 21, 2001. Address: Calle Doctor Gómez Ulla 10, 3° drcha., 28028 Madrid, Spain.

Amato, Angelo, S.D.B. (Cardinal Deacon), Diaconate of St. Mary in Aquiro, Prefect of the Congregation for the Causes of Saints; born in Molfetta (Bari, Italy) June 8, 1938. Created and proclaimed November 20, 2010. Address: 00120 Vatican City State.

Amigo Vallejo, Carlos, O.F.M. (Cardinal Priest), Titular of Santa Maria di Monserrato degli Spagnoli, Archbishop Emeritus of Seville; born in Medina de Rioseco, Diocese of Valladolid, August 23, 1934. Created and proclaimed October 21, 2003. Address: Calle Burgo de Osma 57, 28033 Madrid, Spain.

Angelini, Fiorenzo (Cardinal Priest), Titular of S. Spirito in Sassia; President Emeritus of the Pontifical Council for Pastoral Assistance to Health Care Workers; born in Rome, Italy, August 1, 1916. Created and proclaimed June 28, 1991. Address: Via della Conciliazione 15, 00193 Rome, Italy.

Antonelli, Ennio (Cardinal Priest), Titular of Sant'Andrea delle Fratte, President of the Pontifical Council for the Family, Archbishop Emeritus of Florence; born in Todi, Diocese of Orvieto-Todi, November 18, 1936. Created and proclaimed October 21, 2003. Address: Piazza S. Calisto 16, 00153 Rome, Italy.

Antonetti, Lorenzo (Cardinal Priest), Titular of Saint Agnes in Agone; President Emeritus of the Administration of the Patrimony of the Apostolic See; born in Romagnano Sesia, diocese of Novara, July 31, 1922. Created and proclaimed February 21, 1998. Address: Casa del Clero, Via Sartoretti 5, 28010 Miasino (Novara) Italy.

Aponte Martinez, Luis (Cardinal Priest), Titular of S. Maria Madre della Provvidenza a Monte Verde, Archbishop Emeritus of San Juan de Puerto Rico; born in Lajas, diocese of Mayaguez, August 4, 1922. Created and proclaimed March 5, 1973. Address: Urbanizacion San Ignacio, Calle San Alejandro 1763, San Juan, PR 00927, Puerto Rico.

Araujo, Serafim Fernandes de (Cardinal Priest), Titular of S. Luigi Maria Grignion de Montfort, Archbishop Emeritus of Belo Horizonte, Brazil; born in Minas Novas, Diocese of Aracuai, August 13, 1924. Created and proclaimed February 21, 1998. Address: Av. Brasil 1666 5 andar, Bairro dos Funcionários, 30140-003 Belo Horizonte, MG, Brazil.

Arinze, Francis (Cardinal Bishop), Titular of the suburbicarian Church of Velletri-Segni; Prefect Emeritus of the Congregation for Divine Worship and the Discipline of the Sacraments; born in Eziowelle, Archdiocese of Onitsha, November 1, 1932. Created and proclaimed May 25, 1985. Address: Largo del Colonnato 3, 00193 Rome, Italy.

Arns, Paul Evaristo, O.F.M. (Cardinal Priest), Titular of S. Antonio da Padova in Via Tuscolana, Archbishop Emeritus of Sao Paulo; born in Forquilhinha, Diocese of Criciuma, September 14, 1921. Created and proclaimed March 5, 1973. Address: C.P. 916, Rua Antonietta Altenfelder 1000, 02717-170, Sao Paulo, SP, Brazil.

Assis, Raymundo Damasceno (Cardinal Priest), Titular of Our Lady Immaculate al Tiburtino, Archbishop of Aparecida, Brazil; born in Capela Nova, February 15, 1937. Created and proclaimed November 20, 2010. Address: Curia Metropolitana, Rua Barao do Rio Branco 412, 12570-000 Aparecida, SP, Brazil.

Aviz, Joao Braz de (Cardinal Deacon), Diaconate of Sant'Elena fuori Porta Prenestina, prefect of the Congregation for Institutes of Consecrated Life and Societies of Apostolic Life; Born in Mafra, Diocese of Joinville, April 24, 1947. Created and proclaimed February 18, 2012. Address: 00120 Vatican City State, Europe.

Backis, Audrys Juozas (Cardinal Priest), Titular of Nativita di Nostro Signore Gesu Cristo a Via Gallia, Archbishop of Vilnius; born in Kaunas, February 1, 1937. Created and proclaimed February 21, 2001. Address: Sventaragio 4, LT-01122 Vilnius, Lithuania.

Bagnasco, Angelo (Cardinal Priest), title of the Gran Madre di Dio, Archbishop of Genoa (Italy), born in Pontevico, Diocese of Brescia, January 14, 1943. Created and proclaimed November 24, 2007. Address: Arcivescovado, Piazza Matteotti 4, 16123 Genova, Italy.

Baldelli, Fortunato (Cardinal Deacon), Diaconate of St. Anselm on the Aventine, Major Penitentiary Emeritus; born in Valfabbrica, Diocese of Assisi-Nocera Umbra-Gualdo Tadino, Italy, August 6, 1935. Created and proclaimed November 20, 2010.

Barbarin, Philippe Xavier Ignace (Cardinal Priest), Titular of Santissima Trinita al Monte Pincio, Archbishop of Lyon; born in Rabat, Morocco, October 17, 1950. Created and proclaimed October 21, 2003. Address: Archeveche, 1 Place de Fourviere, 69321 Lyon, Cedex 05, France.

Bartolucci, Domenico (Cardinal Deacon), Diaconate of the Most Holy Names of Jesus and Mary in Via Latia; Former Director of the Sistine Chapel; born in Borgo San Lorenzo, Firenze, May 7, 1919. Created and proclaimed November 20, 2010. Address: Via Monte della Farina 64, 00186 Rome, Italy.

Baum, William Wakefield (Cardinal Priest), Titular of Santa Croce in Via Flaminia; Major Penitentiary Emeritus; born in Dallas, Texas, November 21, 1926. Created and proclaimed, May 24, 1976. Address: Little Sisters of the Poor, 4200 Harewood Road, NE Washington, DC, U.S.A.

Becker, Karl Josef, S.J. (Cardinal Deacon), Diaconate of San Giuliano Martire, Professor emeritus of the Pontifical Gregorian University and for many years consultor of the Congregation for the Doctrine of the Faith: Born in Koln, April 18, 1928. Created and proclaimed February 18, 2012. Address: Piazza della Pilotta 4, 00186 Rome, Italy.

Bergoglio, Jorge Mario, S.J. (Cardinal Priest), Titular of San Roberto Bellarmino, Archbishop of Buenos Aires; born in Buenos Aires, December 17, 1936. Created and proclaimed February 21, 2001. Address: Avda. Rivadavia 415, C1002AAC Buenos Aires, Argentina.

Bertello, Giuseppe (Cardinal Deacon), Diaconate of Santi Vito, Modesto e Crescenzia, President of the Pontifical Commission for Vatican City State and of the Governorate of Vatican City State; Born in Foglizzo, Diocese of Ivrea, October 1, 1942. Created and proclaimed February 18, 2012. Address: Palazzo del Governatorato, 00120 Vatican City State, Europe.

Bertone, Tarcisio, S.D.B. (Cardinal Bishop), Titular of the Suburbicarian Church of Frascati, Secretary of State, Camerlengo of the Holy Roman Church; Archbishop Emeritus of Genova; born in Romano Canavese, Diocese of Ivrea, Italy, December 2, 1934. Created and proclaimed October 21, 2003. Address: 00120 Vatican City State.

Betori, Giuseppe (Cardinal Priest), Titular of San Marcello, Archbishop of Florence, Italy; Born in Foligno February 25, 1947. Created and proclaimed February 18, 2012. Address: Arcivescovado, Piazza S. Giovanni 3, 50123 Firenze, Italy.

Biffi, Giacomo (Cardinal Priest), Titular of Ss. Giovanni Evangelista e Petronio, Archbishop Emeritus of Bologna; born in Milan, June 13, 1928. Created and proclaimed May 25, 1985. Address: Villa Edera, Via S. Ruffillo 5/A, 40068 S. Lazzaro Di Savena (Bologna), Italy.

Bozanic, Josip (Cardinal Priest), Titular of San Girolamo dei Croati, Archbishop of Zagreb; born in Rijeka, Croatia, March 20, 1949. Created and proclaimed October 21, 2003. Address: Nadbiskupski Duhovni Stol, Kaptol 21, p.p. 553, 10000 Zagreb, Croatia.

Brady, Sean Baptist (Cardinal Priest), Titular of Sts. Quiricus and Julitta, Archbishop of Armagh, Ireland, born in Laragh (Drumcalpin), Diocese of Kilmore, August 16, 1939. Created and proclaimed November 24, 2007. Address: Ara Coeli, Cathedral Road, Armagh BT61 7QY, Ireland.

Brandmuller, Walter (Cardinal Deacon), Diaconate of St. Julian of the Flemish, Presidente Emeritus of the Pontifical Commission for Historical Sciences; born in Ansbach, Archdiocese of Bamberg, January 5, 1929. Created and proclaimed November 20, 2010. Address: 00120 Vatican City State.

Burke, Raymond Leo (Cardinal Deacon), Diaconate of St. Agatha of the Goths, Prefect of the Supreme Tribunal of the Apostolic Signatura; born in Richland Center, Diocese of La Crosse, June 30, 1948. Created and proclaimed November 20, 2010. Address: Via Rusticucci 13, 00193 Rome, Italy.

Cacciavillan, Agostino (Cardinal Priest), Titular of the Holy Guardian Angels at Citta Giardino, President Emeritus of Administration of the Patrimony of the Apostolic See; born in Novale, Diocese of Vincenza, August 14, 1926. Created and proclaimed February 21, 2001. Address: 00120 Vatican City State, Europe.

Caffarra, Carlo (Cardinal Priest), Titular of Saint John the Baptist of the Florentines, Archbishop of Bologna; born in Samboseto di Busseto, Diocese of Fidenza, June 1, 1938. Created and proclaimed March 24, 2006. Address: Via Altabella 6, 40126 Bologna, Italy.

Calcagno, Domenico (Cardinal Deacon), Diaconate of Annunciazione della Beata Vergine Maria a Via Ardeatina, President of the Administration of the Patrimony of the Apostolic See; Born in Tramontana di Parodi Ligure, Archdiocese of Genova, February 3, 1943. Created and proclaimed February 18, 2012. Address: 00120 Vatican City State, Europe.

Canestri, Giovanni (Cardinal Priest), Titular of S. Andrea della Valle, Archbishop Emeritus of Genoa; born in Castelspina, Diocese of Alessandria, September 30, 1918. Created and proclaimed June 28, 1988. Address: Via Cernaia 9, 00185 Rome, Italy.

Canizares Llovera, Antonio (Cardinal Priest), Titular of Saint Pancras, Prefect of the Congregation for Divine Worship and the Discipline of the Sacraments, Archbishop Emeritus of Toledo; born in Utiel, Archdiocese of Valencia, October 10, 1945. Created and proclaimed March 24, 2006. Address: 00120 Vatican City State, Europe.

Carles Gordo, Ricardo Maria (Cardinal Priest), Titular of S. Maria Consolatrice al Tiburtino, Archbishop Emeritus of Barcelona, Spain; born in Valencia, September 24, 1926. Created and proclaimed November 26, 1994, Address: General Vives 29, 08017 Barcelona, Spain.

Cassidy, Edward Idris (Cardinal Priest), Titular of S. Maria in Via Lata, President Emeritus of the Pontifical Council for Promoting Christian Unity; born in Sydney, Australia, July 5, 1924. Created and proclaimed June 28, 1991. Address: 16 Coachwood Dr., Warabrook, NSW 2304, Australia.

Castrillón Hoyos, Dario (Cardinal Priest), Titular of the Most Holy Name of Mary at Trajan's Forum, President Emeritus of the Pontifical Commission Ecclesia Dei, Prefect Emeritus of the Congregation for Clergy; born in Medellin July 4, 1929. Created and proclaimed February 21, 1998. Address: Piazza della Citta Leonina 1, 00193 Rome, Italy.

Ce', Marco (Cardinal Priest), Titular of S. Marco, Patriarch Emeritus of Venice; born in Izano, Diocese of Crema, July 8, 1925. Created and proclaimed June 30, 1979. Address: Dorsoduro 2807, 30123 Venezia, Italy.

Cheli, Giovanni (Cardinal Priest), Titular of Ss. Cosmos and Damian at Via Sacra, President Emeritus of the Pontifical Council for the Pastoral Care of Migrants and Itinerant People; born in Torino, October 4, 1918. Created and proclaimed February 21, 1998. Address: Piazza S. Calisto 16, 00153 Rome, Italy.

Cheong Jinsuk, Nicholas (Cardinal Priest), Titular of Mary Immaculate of Lourdes at Boccea, Archbishop of Seoul; born in Seoul, December 7, 1931. Created and proclaimed March 24, 2006. Address: Archbishop's House, Chung-gu Myong-dong 2-ka, Seoul 100-809, Korea.

Cipriani Thorne, Juan Luis (Cardinal Priest), Titular of San Camillo di Lellis, Archbishop of Lima; born in Lima, December 28, 1943. Created and proclaimed February 21, 2001. Address: Calle Los Nogales 249, San Isidro, Lima 27, Peru.

Clancy, Edward Bede (Cardinal Priest), Titular of S. Maria in Vallicella, Archbishop Emeritus of Sydney; born in Lithgow, Diocese of Bathurst, December 13, 1923. Created and proclaimed June 28, 1988. Address: 70 Market St., P.O. Box 246, Randwick NSW 2031, Australia.

Coccopalmerio, Francesco (Cardinal Deacon), Diaconate of San Giuseppe dei Falegnami, President of the Pontifical Council for Legislative Texts;

Born in San Giuliano Milanese, Archdiocese of Milan, March 6, 1938. Created and proclaimed February 18, 2012. Address: 00120 Vatican City State, Europe.

Collins, Thomas Christopher (Cardinal Priest), Titular of San Patrizio, Archbishop of Toronto, Canada; Born in Guelph, Diocese of Hamilton, January 16, 1947. Created and proclaimed February 18, 2012. Address: 1155 Yonge Street, Toronto, ON M4T 1W2, Canada.

Comastri, Angelo (Cardinal Deacon), Deacon of St. Salvatore in Lauro, Vicar General of His Holiness for the Vatican City, Archpriest of the Saint Peter's Basilica and President of the Fabric of Saint Peter's, born in Sorano, Diocese of Pitigliano-Sovano-Orbetello, Italy, September 17, 1943. Created and Proclaimed November 24, 2007. Address: 00120 Vatican City State, Europe.

Connell, Desmond (Cardinal Priest), Titular of San Silvestro in Capite, Archbishop Emeritus of Dublin; born in Dublin, March 24, 1926. Created and proclaimed February 21, 2001. Address: 29 Iona Road, Dublin 9, Ireland.

Coppa, Giovanni (Cardinal Deacon), Deacon of St. Linus, Apostolic Nuncio Emeritus; born in Alba, Italy, November 9, 1925. Created and proclaimed November 24, 2007. Address: 00120 Vatican City State, Europe.

Cordero Lanza di Montezemolo, Andrea (Cardinal Deacon), Deacon of Saint Mary in Portico, Archpriest Emeritus of the Basilica of St. Paul Outside-the-Walls; born in Turin, August 27, 1925. Created and proclaimed March 24, 2006. Address: Piazza della Citta Leonina, 9, 00193 Rome, Italy.

Cordes, Paul Josef (Cardinal Deacon), Diaconate of St. Lawrence in Piscibus. President Emeritus of the Pontifical Council "Cor Unum"; born in Kirchhundem, Archdiocese of Paderborn, Germany, September 5, 1934. Created and proclaimed November 24, 2007. Address: 00120 Vatican City State, Europe.

Cottier, Georges Marie Martin, O.P. (Cardinal Deacon), Deacon of Santi Domenico e Sisto, Theologian Emeritus of the Pontifical Household; born in Geneve, April 25, 1922. Created and proclaimed October 21, 2003. Address: 00120 Vatican City State, Europe.

Danneels, Godfried (Cardinal Priest), Titular of S. Anastasia, Archbishop Emeritus of Malines-Brussels; born in Kanegem, Diocese of Brugge, June 4, 1933. Created and proclaimed February 2, 1983. Address: Aartsbisdom, Wollemarkt 15, B-2800 Mechelen, Belgium.

Daoud, Ignace Moussa I (Cardinal Bishop), Patriarch Emeritus of Antioch of the Maronites; born in Meskane, Archeparchy of Homs of the Syrians, September 18, 1930. Created and proclaimed February 21, 2001. Address: Piazza della Citta Leonina 9, 00193 Rome, Italy.

Darmaatmadja, Julius Riyadi, S.J. (Cardinal Priest), Titular of S. Cuore di Maria, Archbishop Emeritus of Jakarta, Indonesia; born in Muntilan, Archdiocese of Semarang, December 20, 1934. Created and proclaimed November 26, 1994. Address: Keuskupan Agung, Jl. Katedral 7, Jakarta 10710, Indonesia.

De Giorgi, Salvatore (Cardinal Priest), Titular of S. Maria in Ara Coeli, Archbishop Emeritus of Palermo; born in Vernole, Archdiocese of Lecce, September 6, 1930. Created and proclaimed February 21, 1998. Address: Via di Porta Angelica 31, 00193 Roma, Italy.

Delly, Emmanuel III (Cardinal Bishop), Patriarch of Babylon of the Chaldeans, Iraq; born in Telkaif, October 6, 1927; elected Patriarch December 3, 2003. Address: Patriarcat Chaldeen Catholique, P.O. Box 6112, Al-Mansour, Baghdad, Iraq.

De Paolis, Velasio, C.S. (Cardinal Deacon), Diaconate of Jesus the Good Shepherd alla Montagnola, Presidente Emeritus of the Prefecture for the Economic Affairs of the Holy See; born in Sonnino, Diocese of Latina-Terracina-Sezze-Priverno, Italy, September 19, 1935. Created and proclaimed November 20, 2010. Address: Piazza del S. Uffizio 11, 00193 Rome, Italy.

Dias, Ivan (Cardinal Priest), Titular of Spirito Santo alla Ferratella, Archbishop of Bombay; Prefect Emeritus of the Congregation for the Evangelization of Peoples; born in Mumbai, April 14, 1936. Created and proclaimed February 21, 2001. Address: Residenza Cardinale J.H. Newman, Via Giosue Carducci 2, Scala D, Piano 2, 00187 Rome, Italy.

DiNardo, Daniel N. (Cardinal Priest), Titular of St. Eusebius, Archbishop of Galveston-Houston, born in Steubenville (Ohio), U.S.A., May 23, 1949. Created and proclaimed November 24, 2007. Address: 1700 San Jacinto St., P.O. Box 907, Houston, TX 77001-0907.

Dolan, Timothy Michael (Cardinal Priest), Titular of Nostra Signora di Guadalupe a Monte Mario, Archbishop of New York, U.S.A.; Born in Saint Louis February 6, 1950. Created and proclaimed February 18, 2012. Address: 1011 First Avenue, New York, NY 10022, U.S.A.

do Nascimento, Alexandre (Cardinal Priest), Titular of San Marco in Agro Laurentino, Archbishop Emeritus of Luanda; born in Malanje, Angola, March 1, 1925. Created and proclaimed February 2, 1983. Address: Rua Américo Júlio de Carvalho 97-99, Luanda, Angola.

Duka, Dominik Jaroslav, O.P. (Cardinal Priest), Titular of Santi Marcellino e Pietro, Archbishop of Prague, Czech Republic; Born in Hradec Kralove April 26, 1943. Created and proclaimed February 18, 2012. Address: Arcibiskupsky Ordinariat, Hradcanske nam. 56/16, 119 02 Praha 1, Czech Republic.

Dziwisz, Stanislaw (Cardinal Priest), Titular of Saint Mary del Popolo, Archbishop of Krakow; born in Raba Wyzna, Archdiocese of Krakow, April 27, 1939. Created and proclaimed March 24, 2006. Address: ul. Franciszkanska 3, 31-004 Krakow, Poland.

Egan, Edward M. (Cardinal Priest), Titular of Santi Giovanni e Paolo, Archbishop Emeritus of New York; born in Oak Park, Chicago, February 4, 1932. Created and proclaimed February 21, 2001. Address: Chapel of the Sacred Hearts of Jesus & Mary, 325 East 33rd Street, New York, NY 10016.

Eijk, Willem Jacobus (Cardinal Priest), Titular of San Callisto, Archbishop of Utrecht, Netherland; Born in Duivendrecht, Diocese of Haarlem-Amsterdam, June 22, 1953. Created and proclaimed February 18, 2012. Address: Maliebaan 38-40, 3581 CR Utrecht, Netherland.

Erdõ, Péter (Cardinal Priest), Titular of Santa Balbina, Archbishop of Esztergom-Budapest; born in Budapest, June 25, 1952. Created and proclaimed October 21, 2003. Address: Primasi es Erseki Hivatal, Uri u 62, H-1014 Budapest, Hungary.

Errázuriz Ossa, Francisco Javier (Cardinal Priest), Titular of Santa Maria della Pace, Archbishop Emeritus of Santiago de Chile; born in Santiago de Chile, September 5, 1933. Created and proclaimed February 21, 2001. Address: Simon Bolivar 2845, Santiago, Chile.

Estepa Llaurens, Jose Manuel (Cardinal Priest), Titular of St. Gabriel the Archangel all'Acqua Traversa, Archbishop Emeritus for Military Services; born in Andujar, Diocese of Jaen, Spain, January 1, 1929. Created and proclaimed November 20, 2010. Address: Gustavo Fernandez Balbuena 40, 28002 Madrid, Spain.

Etchegaray, Roger (Cardinal Bishop), Titular of the suburbicarian church of Porto-Santa Rufina, President Emeritus of the Pontifical Council for Justice and Peace, Vice Dean of the College of Cardinals born in Espelette, Diocese of Bayonne, September 25, 1922. Created and proclaimed June 30, 1979. Address: Piazza San Calisto 16, 00153 Rome, Italy.

Falcao, Jose Freire (Cardinal Priest), Titular of S. Luca a Via Prenestina, Archbishop Emeritus of Brasilia; born in Erere, Diocese of Limoeiro do Norte, October 23, 1925. Created and proclaimed June 28, 1988. Address: SHIGS 707, Bl.HL casa 74, Asa Sul, 70351-708 Brazilia, D.F., Brazil.

Farina, Raffaele, S.D.B. (Cardinal Deacon), Deacon of St. John della Pigna, Archivist and Librarian of the Holy Roman Church, born in Buonalbergo, Diocese of Ariano Irpino-Lacedonia, Italy, September 24, 1933. Created and proclaimed November 24, 2007. Address: 00120 Vatican City State, Europe.

Filoni, Fernando (Cardinal Deacon), Diaconate of Nostra Signora di Coromoto in San Giovanni di Dio, Prefect of the Congregation for the Evangelization of Peoples; Born in Manduria, Diocese of Oria, April 15, 1946. Created and proclaimed February 18, 2012. Address: Via Urbano VIII 16, 00165 Rome, Italy.

Furno, Carlo (Cardinal Priest), Titular St. Humphrey, Grand Master Emeritus of the Equestrian Order of the Holy Sepulchre of Jerusalem; born in Bairo Canavese, Diocese of Ivrea, December 2, 1921. Created and proclaimed November 26, 1994. Address: Piazza della Citta Leonina 1, 00193 Rome, Italy.

George, Francis E., O.M.I. (Cardinal Priest) Titular of S. Bartolomeo all'Isola, Archbishop of Chicago; born in Chicago, Illinois, U.S.A., January 16, 1937. Created and proclaimed February 21, 1998. Address: 835 N. Rush St., Chicago, IL 60611-2030.

Glemp, Jozef (Cardinal Priest), Titular of S. Maria in Trastevere, Archbishop Emeritus of Warsaw; born in Inowroclaw, Archdiocese of Gniezno, December 18, 1929. Created and proclaimed February 2, 1983. Address: ul. Miodowa 17-19, 00-246 Warsaw, Poland.

Gracias, Oswald (Cardinal Priest), Titular of St. Paul of the Cross in Corviale. Archbishop of Bombay (India), born in Bombay, December 24, 1944. Created and proclaimed November 24, 2007. Address: Archbishop's House, 21 Nathalal Parekh Marg, Mumbai-400001, India.

Grech, Prosper, O.S.A. (Cardinal Deacon), Diaconate of Santa Maria Goretti, Professor emeritus of several Roman universities and consultor of the Congregation for the Doctrine of the Faith; Born in Birgu, Archdiocese of Malta, December 24, 1925. Created and proclaimed February 18, 2012. Address: Via Paolo VI 25, 00193 Rome, Italy.

Grocholewski, Zenon (Cardinal Priest), Titular of St. Nicholas in Carcere, Prefect of the Congregation for Catholic Education; born in Brodki, Archdiocese of Poznan, October 11, 1939. Created and proclaimed February 21, 2001. Address: Piazza della Cancelleria 1, 00186 Rome, Italy.

Gulbinowicz, Henryk Roman (Cardinal Priest), Titular dell'Immacolata Concezione di Maria a Grottarossa, Archbishop Emeritus of Wroclaw; born in Sukiskes, Archdiocese of Vilnius, October 17, 1923. Created and proclaimed May 25, 1985. Address: ul. Katedralna 15, 50-328 Wroclaw, Poland.

Herranz Casado, Julian (Cardinal Deacon), Deacon of Saint Eugenius, President Emeritus of the Pontifical Council for the Interpretation of Legislative Texts; born in Baena, Diocese of Cordoba, March 31, 1930. Created and proclaimed October 21, 2003. Address: Borgo Santo Spirito 16, 00193 Rome, Italy.

Honoré, Jean (Cardinal Priest), Titular of Santa Maria della Salute a Primavalle, Archbishop Emeritus of Tours; born in Saint-Brice-en-Cogles, Archdiocese of Rennes, August 13, 1920. Created and proclaimed February 21, 2001. Address: 1 Allee de la Rocaille, 37390 La Membrolle-sur-Choisille, France.

Hummes, Claudio, O.F.M. (Cardinal Priest), Titular of Sant' Antonio da Padova in Via Merulana, Prefect Emeritus of the Congregation for the Clergy; born in Montenegro, Archdiocese of Porto Alegre, August 8, 1934. Created and proclaimed February 21, 2001. Address: Rua Oscar Bressane, 383 (Bosque da Saude), 04151-040 Sao Paulo, SP, Brazil.

Husar, Lubomyr, M.S.U. (Cardinal Priest), Titular of Santa Sofia a Via Boccea, Major Archbishop Emeritus of Kyiv-Halye of the Ukrainians; born in Lviv, February 26, 1933. Created and proclaimed February 21, 2001. Address: vul. Riznytcka II -B/28-29, P.O. Box B-125, 01011 Kyiv, Ukraine.

Jaworski, Marian (Cardinal Priest), Titular of St. Sisto, Archbishop Emeritus of Lviv of the Latins; born in Lviv August 21, 1926. Created and reserved in pectore February 21, 1998; proclaimed February 21, 2001. Address: ul. Samczuka 14/a, 79011 Lviv, Ukraine.

Karlic, Estanislao Esteban (Cardinal Priest), Titular of the Our Lady of Sorrows in Piazza Buenos Aires, Archbishop Emeritus of Paraná. Created and proclaimed November 24, 2007. Address: Av. Don Bosco 2553, 3100 Parana, Argentina.

Kasper, Walter (Cardinal Priest), Titular of All Saints on the New Appian Way, President Emeritus of the Pontifical Council for Promoting Christian Unity; born in Heidenheim/Brenz, Diocese of Rottenburg-Stuttgart, March 5, 1933. Created and proclaimed February 21, 2001. Address: Piazza della Citta Leonina 1, 00193 Rome, Italy.

Keeler, William Henry (Cardinal Priest), Titular of S. Maria degli Angeli, Archbishop Emeritus of Baltimore; born in San Antonio, Texas, March 4, 1931. Created and proclaimed November 26, 1994. Address: 2525 Pot Spring Rd. S-726, Timonium, Maryland 21093. U.S.A.

Kitbunchu, Michael Michai (Cardinal Priest), Titular of S. Lorenzo in Panisperna, Archbishop of Bangkok; born in Samphran, Archdiocese Emeritus of Bangkok, January 25, 1929. Created and proclaimed February 2, 1983. Address:Baan Phu Waann Center, 2/4 Moo 6, Phetkasem Road, Thakham, Sampran, Nakon Pathom 73110, Thailand.

Koch, Kurt (Cardinal Deacon), Diaconate of Our Lady of the Sacred Heart, President of the Pontifical Council for Promoting Christian Unity; born in Emmenbrucke, Diocese of Basel, March 15, 1950. Created and proclaimed November 20, 2010. Address: 00120 Vatican City State, Europe.

Korec, Jan Chryzostom, S.J. (Cardinal Priest), Titular of Ss. Fabiano e Venanzio a Villa Fiorelli, Bishop Emeritus of Nitra; born in Bosany,

Diocese of Nitra, January 22, 1924. Created and proclaimed June 28, 1991. Address: Hradna 2, SK-949 01 Nitra, Slovakia.

Lajolo, Giovanni (Cardinal Deacon), Deacon of St. Mary Liberatrice in Monte Testaccio, President Emeritus of the Pontifical Commission for the Vatican City State and of the Governorate of Vatican City State; born in Novara, Italy, January 3, 1935. Created and proclaimed November 24, 2007. Address: 00120 Vatican City State, Europe.

Law, Bernard Francis (Cardinal Priest), Titular of S. Susanna, Archpriest Emeritus of the Patriarchal Basilica of Saint Mary Major; born in Torreon, November 4, 1931. Created and proclaimed May 25, 1985. Address: 00120 Vatican City State, Europe.

Lehmann, Karl (Cardinal Priest), Titular of San Leone I, Bishop of Mainz; born in Sigmaringen, Archdiocese of Freiburg im Breisgau, May 16, 1936. Created and proclaimed February 21, 2001. Address: Bischofsplatz 2A, D-55116 Mainz, Germany.

Levada, William Joseph (Cardinal Deacon), Deacon of Saint Mary in Domnica, Prefect of the Congregation for the Doctrine of the Faith; born in Long Beach, Archdiocese of Los Angeles, June 15, 1936. Created and proclaimed March 24, 2006. Address: 00120 Vatican City State, Europe.

Lopez Rodriguez, Nicolas de Jesus (Cardinal Priest), Titular of S. Pio X alla Balduina, Archbishop of Santo Domingo; born in Barranca, Diocese of La Vega, October 31, 1936. Created and proclaimed June 28, 1991. Address: Calle Pellerano Alfau 1, Ciudad Colonial, Santo Domingo, Dominican Republic.

Lourdusamy, D. Simon (Cardinal Priest), Titular of S. Maria delle Grazie alle Fornaci fuori Porta Cavalleggeri, Prefect Emeritus of the Congregation for the Oriental Churches; born in Kalleri, Archdiocese of Pondicherry and Cuddalore, February 5, 1924. Created and proclaimed May 25, 1985. Address: Via dei Corridori 64, 00193 Rome, Italy.

Lozano Barragan, Javier (Cardinal Deacon), Deacon of St. Michael the Archangel, President Emeritus of the Pontifical Council for Pastoral Assistance to Health Care; born in Toluca, Mexico, January 26, 1933. Created and proclaimed October 21, 2003. Address: Piazza S. Calisto 16, 00153 Rome, Italy.

Macharski, Franciszek (Cardinal Priest), Titular of S. Giovanni a Porta Latina, Archbishop Emeritus of Krakow; born in Krakow, May 20, 1927. Created and proclaimed June 30, 1979. Address: ul. Franciszkanska 3, 31-004 Krakow, Poland.

Mahony, Roger M. (Cardinal Priest), Titular of Ss. Quattro Coronati, Archbishop Emeritus of Los Angeles; born in Hollywood, California, Archdiocese of Los Angeles, February 27, 1936. Created and proclaimed June 28, 1991. Address: 10834 Moorpark Street, North Hollywood, CA 91602-2206, U.S.A.

Maida, Adam Joseph (Cardinal Priest), Titular of Ss. Vitale, Valeria, Gervasio e Protasio, Archbishop Emeritus of Detroit; born in East Vandergrift, Pennsylvania, Diocese of Greensburg, March 18, 1930. Created and proclaimed November 26, 1994. Address: 44045 Five Mile Road, Plymouth MI 48170, U.S.A.

Marchisano, Francesco Cardinal (Cardinal Deacon), Deacon of Santa Lucia del Gonfalone, President Emeritus of the Labor Office of the Apostolic See; born in Racconigi, Italy, June 25, 1929. Created and proclaimed October 21, 2003. Address: Piazza San Calisto 16, 00153 Rome, Italy.

Martinez Sistach, Lluis (Cardinal Priest), Titular of St. Sebastian at the Catacombs, Archbishop of Barcelona; Created and proclaimed November 24, 2007. Address: Arzobispado, Carrer del Bisbe 5, 08002 Barcelona, Spain.

Martinez Somalo, Eduardo (Cardinal Priest), Titular of SS. Nome di Gesu', Chamberlain Emeritus of the Holy Roman Church; born at Banos de Rio Tobia, Diocese of Calahorra y La Calzada-Logrono, March 31, 1927. Created and proclaimed June 28, 1988. Address: 00120 Vatican City State, Europe.

Martini, Carlo Maria, S.J. (Cardinal Priest), Titular of S. Cecilia, Archbishop Emeritus of Milan; born in Turin, February 15, 1927. Created and proclaimed February 2, 1983. Address: "Aloisianum", Via San Luigi Gonzaga 8, 21013 Gallarate (Varese), Italy.

Martino, Renato Raffaele (Cardinal Deacon), Deacon of St. Francis of Paola ai Monti, President Emeritus of the Pontifical Council for Justice and Peace, President of the Pontifical Council for the Pastoral Care of Migrants; born in Salerno, Italy, November 23, 1932. Created and proclaimed October 21, 2003. Address: Via Pancrazio Pfeiffer 10, 00193 Rome, Italy.

Marx, Reinhard (Cardinal Priest), Titular of St. Corbinian, Archbishop of Munchen and Freising, Germany; born in Geseke, Archdiocese of Paderborn, September 21, 1953. Created and proclaimed November 20, 2010. Address: Werneckstr, 24, D-80802 Munchen, Germany.

Mazombwe, Medardo Joseph (Cardinal Priest), Titular of St. Emerentiana at Tor Fiorenza, Archbishop Emeritus of Lusaka, Zambia; born in Chundamira, Diocese of Chipata, September 24, 1931. Created and proclaimed November 20, 2010. Address: P.O. Box 31179, 10101 Lusaka, Zambia.

McCarrick, Theodore E. (Cardinal Priest), Titular of Santi Nereo e Achilleo, Archbishop Emeritus of Washington; born in New York, July 7, 1930. Created and proclaimed February 21, 2001. Address: P.O. Box 29260, Washington, DC 20017, U.S.A.

Medina Estévez, Jorge Arturo (Cardinal Priest), Titular of St. Saba, Prefect Emeritus of the Congregation for Divine Worship and the Discipline of the Sacraments; born in Santiago de Chile, December 23, 1926. Created and proclaimed February 21, 1998. Address: Av. Pehuén 7240, Dpto. 100 Las Condes, Santiago 6782144 Chile.

Meisner, Joachim (Cardinal Priest), Titular of S. Pudenziana, Archbishop of Cologne; born in Breslau, December 25, 1933. Created and proclaimed February 2, 1983. Address: Kardinal-Frings-Strasse 10, D-50668 Koln 1, Germany.

Mejía, Jorge María (Cardinal Priest), Titular of St. Jerome of Charity, Librarian Emeritus and Archivist Emeritus of the Holy Roman Church; born in Buenos Aires, January 31, 1923. Created and proclaimed February 21, 2001. Address: Piazza S. Calisto 16, 00153 Rome, Italy.

Monsengwo Pasinya, Laurent (Cardinal Priest), Titular of St. Mary "Regina Pacis" at Ostia Mare, Archbishop of Kinshasa, Democratic Republic of Congo; born in Mongobele, Diocese of Inongo, October 7, 1939. Created and proclaimed November 20, 2010. Address: Archeveche, Avenue del'Universite, B.P. 8431, Kinshasa 1, Republic Democratic of Congo.

Monteiro de Castro, Manuel (Cardinal Deacon), Diaconate of San Domenico di Guzman, Penitentiary Major; Born in Santa Eufemia de Prazins-Guimaraes, Archdiocese of Braga, March 29, 1938. Created and proclaimed February 18, 2012. Address: 00120 Vatican City State, Europe.

Monterisi, Francesco (Cardinal Deacon), Diaconate of St. Paul alla Regola, Archpriest of the Papal Basilica of St. Paul's Outside-the-Walls; born in Barletta, Italy, May 28, 1934. Created and proclaimed November 20, 2010. Address: 00120 Vatican City State, Europe.

Muresan, Lucian (Cardinal Priest), Titular of Sant'Atanasio, Major Archbishop of Fagaras and Alba Julia of the Romanians, Romania; Born in Ferneziu, May 23, 1931. Created and proclaimed February 18, 2012. Address: Str. Petru Pavel Aron 2, RO-515400 Blaj, AB, Romania.

Murphy-O'Connor, Cormac (Cardinal Priest), Titular of Santa Maria sopra Minerva, Archbishop Emeritus of Westminster; born in Reading, Diocese of Portsmouth, August 24, 1932. Created and proclaimed February 21, 2001. Address: St. Edward's, 7 Duke's Avenue, Chiswick, London W4 2AA, England.

Naguib, Antonios (Cardinal Bishop), Patriarch of Alexandria of the Copts; born in Minya, Egypt, March 7, 1935; ordained October 30, 1960; elected Bishop of Minya of the Copts July 26, 1977; consecrated September 9, 1977; resigned September 29, 2002; elected Patriarch of Alexandria of the Copts March 30, 2006. Address: Patriarcat Copte Catholique, B.P. 69, 34 Rue Ibn Sandar, Saray El Koubbeh, 11712 Le Caire, Egypte.

Nagy, Stanislaw, S.C.I. (Cardinal Deacon), Deacon of Santa Maria della Scala; born in Bieru Stary, Archdiocese of Katowice, September 30, 1921. Created and proclaimed October 21, 2003. Address: c/o University of Lublin, UL. Saska 2, 30-715 Krakow, Poland.

Napier, Wilfrid Fox, O.F.M. (Cardinal Priest), Titular of San Francesco d'Assisi ad Acilia, Archbishop of Durban; born in Swartberg, Diocese of Kokstad, March 8, 1941. Created and proclaimed February 21, 2001. Address: 154 Gordon Rd., Durban 4001, Kwazulu-Natal, South Africa.

Nicora, Attilio (Cardinal Deacon), Deacon of St. Filippo Neri in Eurosia, President Emeritus of the Administration of the Patrimony of the Apostolic See; Pontifical Legate for the Basilicas of St. Francis and St. Mary of the Angels in Assisi; born in Varese, Italy, March 16, 1937. Created and proclaimed October 21, 2003. Address: 00120 Vatican City State, Europe.

Njue, John (Cardinal Priest), Titular of the Most Precious Blood of Our Lord Jesus Christ. Archbishop of Nairobi (Kenya), born in Ngandori, 1944. Created and proclaimed November 24, 2007. Address: Archbishop's House, P.O. Box 14231, Nairobi, Kenya.

Nycz, Kazimierz (Cardinal Priest), Titular of Sts. Sylvester and Mariano ai Monti, Archbishop of Warszawa, Poland; born in Stara Wies, February 1, 1950. Created and proclaimed November 20, 2010. Address: Kuria Metropolitalna, ul. Miodowa 17-19, 00-246 Warszawa, Poland.

Obando Bravo, Miguel, S.D.B. (Cardinal Priest), Titular of S. Giovanni Evangelista a Spinaceto, Archbishop Emeritus of Managua; born in La Libertad, Diocese of Juigalpa, February 2, 1926. Created and proclaimed May 25, 1985. Address: Arzobispado, Apartado 2008, Managua, Nicaragua.

O'Brien, Edwin Frederick (Cardinal Deacon), Diaconate of San Sebastiano al Palatino, Grand master of the Equestrian Order of the Knights of the Holy Sepulchre of Jerusalem. Born in New York April 8, 1939. Created and proclaimed February 18, 2012. Address: 00120 Vatican City State, Europe.

O'Brien, Keith Michael Patrick (Cardinal Priest), Titular of Santi Gioacchino e Anna al Tuscolano, Archbishop of Saint Andrews and Edinburgh; born in Ballycastle, County Antrim, Northern Ireland, March 17, 1938. Created and proclaimed October 21, 2003. Address: Archbishop's House, 42 Greenhill Gardens, Edinburgh EH10 4BJ, Scotland, Great Britain.

Okogie, Anthony Olubunmi (Cardinal Priest), Titular of Beata Vergine Maria del Monte Carmelo a Mostacciano, Archbishop of Lagos; born in Lagos, June 16, 1936. Created and proclaimed October 21, 2003. Address: P.O. Box 8, 19 Catholic Mission Street, Lagos, Nigeria.

O'Malley, Sean Patrick, O.F.M.Cap. (Cardinal Priest), Titular of Saint Mary of Victory, Archbishop of Boston; born in Lakewood, Diocese of Cleveland, June 29, 1944. Created and proclaimed March 24, 2006. Address: 66 Brooks Drive, Braintree, MA 02184, U.S.A.

Ortega y Alamino, Jaime Lucas (Cardinal Priest), Titular of Ss. Aquila e Priscilla, Archbishop of San Cristobal de La Habana, Cuba; born in Jaguey Grande, Diocese of Matanzas, October 18, 1936. Created and proclaimed November 26, 1994. Address: Calle Habana 152, La Habana, 10100 Cuba.

Ouellet, Marc, P.S.S. (Cardinal Priest), Titular of Santa Maria in Traspontina, Prefect of the Congregation for Bishops; Archbishop Emeritus of Quebec; born in Lamotte, Diocese of Amos, June 8, 1944. Created and proclaimed October 21, 2003. Address: 00120 Vatican City State, Europe.

Panafieu, Bernard Louis Auguste Paul (Cardinal Priest), Titular of San Gregorio Barbarigo alle Tre Fontane, Archbishop Emeritus of Marseille; born in Chatellerault, Archdiocese of Poitiers, January 26, 1931. Created and proclaimed October 21, 2003. Address: Residence du Quinsan, 84210 Venasque, France.

Paskai, Laszlo, O.F.M. (Cardinal Priest), Titular of S. Teresa al Corso d'Italia, Archbishop Emeritus of Esztergom-Budapest; born at Szeged, May 8, 1927. Created and proclaimed June 28, 1988. Address: Dobozy Mihaly u. 12, H-2500 Esztergom, Hungary.

Patabendige Don, Albert Malcolm Ranjith (Cardinal Priest), Titular of St. Lawrence in Lucina, Archbishop of Colombo, Sri Lanka; born in Polgahawela, Diocese of Kurunegala, November 15, 1947. Created and proclaimed November 20, 2010. Address: Archbishop's Home, 976 Gnanartha Pradeepaya Mawatha, Colombo 08. Sri Lanka.

Pell, Georges Marie Martin (Cardinal Priest), Titular of Santa Maria Domenica Mazzarello, Archbishop of Sydney; born in Ballarat, Australia, June 8, 1941. Created and proclaimed October 21, 2003. Address: St. Mary's Cathedral, St. Mary's Road, Sydney NSW 2000, Australia.

Pengo, Polycarp (Cardinal Priest), Titular of Nostra Signora de La Salette, Archbishop of Dar-es-Salaam, Tanzania; born in Mwazye, Diocese of Sumbawanga, August 5, 1944. Created and proclaimed February 21, 1998. Address: Archbishop's House, P.O. Box 167, Dar-es-Salaam, Tanzania.

Pham Minh Man, Jean-Baptiste (Cardinal Priest), Titular of San Giustino, Archbishop of Ho Chi Minh; born in Than-Pho, Ca Mau, Diocese of Can Tho, in the year 1934. Created and proclaimed October 21, 2003. Address: Toa Tong Giam Muc,

189 Nguyen Dinh Chieu, Q-3 Thanh-Pho Ho Chi Minh, Vietnam.

Piacenza, Mauro (Cardinal Deacon), Diaconate of St. Paul at the Three Fountains, Prefect of the Congregation for the Clergy; born in Genoa, Italy, September 15, 1944. Created and proclaimed Novemeber 20, 2010. Address: 00120 Vatican City State, Europe.

Pimenta, Simon Ignatius (Cardinal Priest), Titular of S. Maria Regina Mundi a Torre Spaccata, Archbishop Emeritus of Bombay; born in Marol, Archdiocese of Bombay, March 1, 1920. Created and proclaimed June 28, 1988. Address: Archbishop's House, 21 Nathalal Parekh Marg, Mumbai-400001, India.

Piovanelli, Silvano (Cardinal Priest), Titular of S. Maria delle Grazie a Via Trionfale, Archbishop Emeritus of Florence; born in Ronta di Mugello, Archdiocese of Florence, February 21, 1924. Created and proclaimed May 25, 1985. Address: Via Dante da Castiglione 32, 50010 Trespiano, Italy.

Poletto, Severino (Cardinal Priest), Titular of San Giuseppe in Via Trionfale, Archbishop Emeritus of Turin; born in Salgareda, Diocese of Treviso, March 18, 1933. Created and proclaimed February 21, 2001. Address: Strada della Rovere, Fraz. Testona, 10024 Moncalieri (Torino), Italy.

Policarpo, Jose da Cruz (Cardinal Priest), Titular of St. Anthony in Campo Marzio, Patriarch of Lisbon; born in Alvorninha, Patriarchate of Lisbon, February 26, 1936, created and proclaimed February 21, 2001. Address: Casa Patriarcal, Quinta deo Cabeco, Rua do Seminario, 1885-076 Moscavide, Portugal.

Poupard, Paul (Cardinal Priest), Titular of S. Prassede, President Emeritus of the Pontifical Council of Culture, President Emeritus of the Pontifical Council for Interreligious Dialogue; born in Bouzille, Diocese of Angers, August 30, 1930. Created and proclaimed May 25, 1985. Address: Piazza San Calisto 16, 00153 Rome, Italy.

Pujats, Janis (Cardinal Priest), Titular of Santa Silvia, Archbishop Emeritus of Riga; born in Nautrani, Diocese of Rezekne-Aglona, November 14, 1930. Created and proclaimed February 21, 2001. Address: Maza Pils iela 2/a, 1050 Riga, Latvia.

Puljic, Vinko (Cardinal Priest), Titular of S. Chiara a Vigna Clara, Archbishop of Sarajevo, Bosnia-Herzegovina; born in Prijecani, Diocese of Banja Luka, September 8, 1945. Created and proclaimed November 26, 1994. Address: Kaptol 7, BiH-71000 Sarajevo, Bosnia Herzegovina.

Quezada Toruño, Rodolfo (Cardinal Priest), Titular of San Saturnino, Archbishop Emeritus of Guatemala; born in Guatemala City, March 8, 1932. Created and proclaimed October 21, 2003. Address: Casa Arzobispal, Km. 15 Carretera Roosevelt 4-54, Zona 3 de Mixco, 01057 Ciudad de Guatemala, Guatemala.

Ravasi, Gianfranco (Cardinal Deacon), Diaconate of St. George in Velabro, President of the Pontifical Council for Culture & President of the Pontifical Commission for the Cultural Heritage of the Church and for Sacred Archaeology; born in Merate, Archdiocese of Milan, Italy, October 18, 1942. Created and proclaimed November 20, 2010. Address: Piazza della Citta Leonina 9, 00193 Rome, Italy.

Re, Giovanni Battista (Cardinal Bishop), Titular of the suburbicanan Church of Sabina Poggio-Mirteto, Prefect Emeritus of the Congregation for Bishops; born in Borno, Diocese of Brescia, January 30, 1934. Created and proclaimed February 21, 2001. Address: 00120 Vatican City State, Europe.

Ricard, Jean-Pierre (Cardinal Priest), Titular of Saint Augustine, Archbishop of Bordeaux; born in Marseille, September 26, 1944. Created and proclaimed March 24, 2006. Address: 183 cours de la Somme, CS 21368, 33034 Bordeaux CEDEX, France.

Ries, Julien (Cardinal Deacon), Diaconate of Sant'Antonio di Padova a Circonvallazione Appia, Priest of the diocese of Namur and professor emeritus of religious history at the Catholic University of Leuven, Belgium; Born in Fouches, Diocese of Namur, April 19, 1920. Created and proclaimed February 18, 2012. Address: Famille Spirituelle L'Oeuvre, Maison Damas, Place de Villers-St-Amand 2, 7812 Villers-Notre-Dame, Belgium.

Rigali, Justin Cardinal (Cardinal Priest), Titular of Santa Prisca, Archbishop Emeritus of Philadelphia; born in Los Angeles, California, April 19, 1935. Created and proclaimed October 21, 2003. Address: P.O. Box 11886, Knoxville TN 37939, U.S.A.

Rivera Carrera, Norberto (Cardinal Priest), Titular of S. Francesco d' Assisi a Ripa Grande, Archbishop of Mexico City; born in Tepehuanes, Archdiocese of Durango, June 6, 1942. Created and proclaimed February 21, 1998. Address: Camelia 110, Col. Florida, Deleg. Alvaro Obregon, 01030 Mexico D.F., Mexico.

Robles Ortega, Francisco (Cardinal Priest), Titular of St. Mary of the Presentation, Archbishop of Guadalajara, born in Mascota, Jalisco, Diocese of Tepic, March 2, 1949. Created and proclaimed November 24, 2007. Address: Alfredo R. Plascencia 995, Col. Chapultepec Country, Apartado 61-33, 44620 Guadalajara, Jal., Mexico.

Rode, Franc, C.M. (Cardinal Deacon), Deacon of Saint Francis Xavier at Garbatella, Prefect Emeritus of the Congregation for the Institutes of Consecrated Life and Societies of Apostolic Life; born in Ljubljana, September 23, 1934. Created and proclaimed March 24, 2006. Address: Piazza del S. Uffizio 11, 00193 Rome, Italy.

Rodríguez Maradiaga, Oscar Andrés, S.D.B. (Cardinal Priest), Titular of Santa Maria della Speranza, Archbishop of Tegucigalpa; born in Tegucigalpa, December 29, 1942. Created and proclaimed February 21, 2001. Address: 3 Calle N. 11-13, Tegucigalpa, Honduras.

Romeo, Paolo (Cardinal Priest), Titular of St. Mary Hodegetria of the Sicilians, Archbishop of Palermo, Italy; born in Acireale, Diocese of Catania, February 20, 1938. Created and proclaimed November 20, 2010. Address: Via Matteo Bonello 2, 90134 Palermo, Italy.

Rosales, Gaudencio B. (Cardinal Priest), Titular of the Most Holy Name of Mary in Via Latina, Archbishop Emeritus of Manila; born in Batangas City, Archdiocese of Lipa, August 10, 1932. Created and proclaimed March 24, 2006. Address: 121 Arzobispo St., Intramuros, P.O. Box 132, 1099 Manila, Philippines.

Rouco Varela, Antonio Maria (Cardinal Priest), Titular of S. Lorenzo in Damaso, Archbishop of Madrid, Spain; born in Villalba, Diocese of Mondonedo-Ferrol, August 24, 1936. Created and proclaimed February 21, 1998. Address: Calle San Justo 2, 28005 Madrid, Spain.

Rubiano Sáenz, Pedro (Cardinal Priest), Titular of Trasfigurazione di Nostro Signore Gesu Cristo, Archbishop Emeritus of Bogotá; born in Cartago, September 13, 1932. Created and proclaimed February 21, 2001. Address: Calle 94 N. 9-51, Apdo 305, Bogota, Colombia.

Ruini, Camillo (Cardinal Priest), Titular of S. Agnese Fuori le Mura, Vicar General Emeritus of His Holiness for the Diocese of Rome; born in Sassuolo, Diocese of Reggio Emilia-Guastalla, February 19, 1931. Created and proclaimed June 28, 1991. Address: Viale Vaticano 42, 00120 Vatican City State.

Rylko, Stanislaw (Cardinal Deacon), Deacon of the Sacred Heart of Christ the King, President of the Pontifical Council for the Laity; born in Andrychow, Diocese of Bielsko-zywiec, Poland, July 4, 1945. Created and proclaimed November 24, 2007. Address: 00120 Vatican City State, Europe.

Sales, Eugenio de Araujo (Cardinal Priest), Titular of S. Gregorio VII, Archbishop Emeritus of Sao Sebastiao do Rio de Janeiro; born in Acari, Diocese of Caico, November 8, 1920. Created and proclaimed April 28, 1969. Address: Rua Visconde de Piraja 339, 8. andar, 22410-003 Rio de Janeiro, RJ, Brazil.

Sandoval Iniguez, Juan (Cardinal Priest), Titular of Nostra Signora di Guadalupe e S. Filippo Martire in Via Aurelia, Archbishop Emeritus of Guadalajara, Mexico; born in Yahualica, Diocese of San Juan de los Lagos, March 28, 1933. Created and proclaimed November 26, 1994. Address: Morelos 244, 45500 San Pedro Tlaquepaque, Jal., Mexico.

Sandri, Leonardo (Cardinal Deacon), Deacon of Sts. Blaise and Charles ai Catinari, Prefect of the Congregation for the Oriental Churches; born in Buenos Aires, November 18, 1943. Created and proclaimed November 24, 2007. Address: 00120 Vatican City State, Europe.

Santos, Alexandre Jose Maria dos, O.F.M. (Cardinal Priest), Titular of S. Frumenzio ai Prati Fiscali, Archbishop Emeritus of Maputo; born in Zavala, Diocese of Inhambane, March 18, 1924. Created and proclaimed June 28, 1988. Address: Av. Julius Nyerere 882, Maputo, Mozambique.

Sarah, Robert (Cardinal Deacon), Diaconate of St. John Bosco in Via Tuscolana, President of the Pontifical Council "Cor Unum", Archbishop Emeritus of Conakry, Guinea; born in Ourous, Archdiocese of Conakry, June 15, 1945. Created and proclaimed November 20, 2010. Address: 00120 Vatican City State, Europe.

Saraiva Martins, José, C.M.F. (Cardinal Bishop), Titular of the Suburbicaria Church of Palestrina, Prefect Emeritus of the Congregation for the Causes of Saints; born in Gagos, Diocese of Guarda, January 6, 1932. Created and proclaimed February 21, 2001. Address: Via Pancrazio Pfeiffer 10, 00193 Rome, Italy.

Sardi, Paolo (Cardinal Deacon), Diaconate of Our Lady of Help in Via Tuscolana, Patron of the Sovereign Military Order; born in Ricaldone, Diocese of Acqui, September 1, 1934. Created and proclaimed November 20, 2010. Address: 00120 Vatican City State.

Sarr, Theodore-Adrien (Cardinal Priest) Titular of St. Lucy a Piazza d'Armi, Archbishop of Dakar (Senegal); born in Fadiouth, Archdiocese of Dakar, November 28, 1936. Created and proclaimed November 24, 2007. Address: Archeveche, Avenue Jean XXIII, Dakar, Senegal.

Scheid, Eusebio Oscar, S.C.I. (Cardinal Priest), Titular of Santi Bonifacio e Alessio, Archbishop Emeritus of Sao Sebastiao de Rio de Janeiro; born in Bom Retiro, Diocese of Joacaba, December 8, 1932. Created and proclaimed October 21, 2003. Address: Rua Erminio Neves da Silva 113, 12246-008 Sao Jose dos Campos, SP, Brazil.

Scherer, Odilo Pedro (Cardinal Priest) Titular of St. Andrew al Quirinale, Archbishop of Sao Paulo, born in Sao Francisco, Diocese of Santo Angelo, Brazil, September 21, 1949. Created and proclaimed November 24, 2007. Address: Rua Alfredo Maia 195, Bairro da Luz, 01106-010 Sao Paulo, SP, Brazil.

Schönborn, Christoph, O.P. (Cardinal Priest), Titular of Gesu' Divin Lavoratore, Archbishop of Vienna, Austria; born in Skalsko, Diocese of Litomerice, January 22, 1945. Created and proclaimed February 21, 1998. Address: Rotenturmstrasse 2, A-1010 Vienna, Austria.

Schwery, Henri (Cardinal Priest), Titular of Ss. Protomartiri a Via Aurelia Antica, Bishop Emeritus of Sion; born in Saint Leonard, Diocese of Sion, June 14, 1932. Created and proclaimed June 28, 1991. Address: Rue des Ecoles 16, CH-1958 Saint-Leonard, Switzerland.

Scola, Angelo Cardinal (Cardinal Priest), Titular of Santi XII Apostoli, Patriarch of Venice; born in Malgrate, Archdiocese of Milan, November 7, 1941. Created and proclaimed October 21, 2003. Address: Palazzo Arcivescovile, Piazza Fontana 2, 20122 Milan, Italy.

Sebastiani, Sergio (Cardinal Priest), Titular of St. Eustace, President Emeritus of the Prefecture for the Economic Affairs of the Holy See; born in Montemonaco, Diocese of San Benedetto del Tronto-Ripatransone-Montalto, April 11, 1931. Created and proclaimed February 21, 2001. Address: Via Rusticucci 13, 00193 Rome, Italy.

Sepe, Crescenzio (Cardinal Priest), Titular of the Most Merciful Father, Archbishop of Naples; born in Carinaro, Diocese of Aversa, June 2, 1943. Created and proclaimed February 21, 2001. Address: Largo Donnaregina 23, 80138 Napoli, Italy.

Sfeir, Nasrallah Pierre (Cardinal Bishop), Patriarch Emeritus of Antioch of the Maronites, Lebanon; born in Reyfoun, Lebanon, Eparchy of Sarba of the Maronites, May 15, 1920. Created and proclaimed November 26, 1994. Address: Patriarcat Maronite, Bkerke, Lebanon.

Sgreccia, Elio (Cardinal Deacon), Diaconate of St. Angelo in Pescheria, President Emeritus of the Pontifical Academy for Life; born in Nidastore di Arcevia, Ancona, Italy, June 6, 1982. Created and proclaimed November 20, 2010. Address: Piazza Uffizio 11, 00193 Rome, Italy.

Shan Kuo-hsi, Paul, S.J. (Cardinal Priest), Titular of S. Crisogono, Bishop Emeritus of Kaohsiung, Taiwan; born in Puyang, Diocese of Taming, December 3, 1923. Created and proclaimed February 21, 1998. Address: Bishop's House, 125 Szu-Wei 3rd Rd., Kaohsiung 80250, Taiwan.

Silvestrini, Achille (Cardinal Priest), Titular of S. Benedetto fuori Porta S. Paolo, Prefect Emeritus of the Congregation for Oriental Churches; born in Brisighella, Diocese of Faenza-Modigliana, October 25, 1923. Created and proclaimed June 28, 1988. Address: Palazzina della Zecca, 00120 Vatican City State, Europe.

Simonis, Adrianus Johannes (Cardinal Priest), Titular of S. Clemente, Archbishop Emeritus of Utrecht; born in Lisse, Diocese of Rotterdam, November 26, 1931. Created and proclaimed May 25, 1985. Address: Mariapolis Mariënkroon, Abjlaan 8, NL-5253 VP Nienwkuijk NB, Netherlands.

Sodano, Angelo (Cardinal Bishop), Titular of the suburbicarian church of Ostia, Secretary Emeritus of State; Dean of the College of Cardinals; born in Isola d'Asti, Diocese of Asti, November 23, 1927. Created and proclaimed June 28, 1991. Address: 00120 Vatican City State, Europe.

Stafford, James Francis (Cardinal Priest), Titular of St. Peter in Montorio, Major Apostolic Penitentiary Emeritus. Born in Baltimore, Maryland, U.S.A., July 26, 1932. Created and proclaimed February 21, 1998. Address: Piazza S. Calisto 16, 00153 Rome, Italy.

Szoka, Edmund Casimir (Cardinal Priest), Titular of Ss. Andrea e Gregorio al Monte Celio, President Emeritus of the Pontifical Commission for Vatican City State; President Emeritus of the Governatorate of Vatican City State. Born in Grand Rapids, Michigan, September 14, 1927. Created and proclaimed June 28, 1988. Address: 891 McDonald Drive, Northville, MI 48167, U.S.A.

Tauran, Jean-Louis Pierre (Cardinal Deacon), Deacon of St. Apollonaris at the Neronian-Alexandrian Bath; President of the Pontifical Council for Interreligious Dialogue; born in Bordeaux, April 5, 1943. Created and proclaimed October 21, 2003. Address: 00120 Vatican City State, Europe.

Terrazas Sandoval, Julio, C.Ss.R. (Cardinal Priest), Titular of San Giovanni Battista de' Rossi, Archbishop of Santa Cruz de la Sierra; born in Valle Grande, Archdiocese of Santa Cruz de la Sierra, March 7, 1936. Created and proclaimed February 21, 2001. Address: Calle Paquio Esquina Achachairu S/N, Santa Cruz, Bolivia.

Tettamanzi, Dionigi (Cardinal Priest), Titular of Ss. Ambrogio e Carlo, Archbishop Emeritus of Milan, Italy; born in Renate, Archdiocese of Milan, March 14, 1934. Created and proclaimed February 21, 1998. Address: Villa S. Cuore, Via S. Cuore 7, 20844 Tregasio di Triuggio (Monza Brianza), Italy.

Tomko, Jozef (Cardinal Priest), Titular of S. Sabina, Prefect Emeritus of the Congregation for the Evangelization of Peoples; President Emeritus for the Pontifical Committee for International Eucharistic Congresses; born in Udavske, Archdiocese of Kosice, March 11, 1924. Created and proclaimed May 25, 1985. Address: Via della Conciliazione 44, 00193 Rome, Italy.

Tong Hon, John (Cardinal Priest), Titular of Regina Apostolorum, Bishop of Hong Kong, China; Born in Hong Kong, July 31, 1939. Created and proclaimed February 18, 2012. Address: Catholic Diocese Centre 12F, 16 Caine Road, Hong Kong, China.

Tonini, Ersilio (Cardinal Priest), Titular of Ss. Redentore a Val Melaina, Archbishop Emeritus of Ravenna-Cervia, Italy; born in Centovera di San Giorgio Piacentino, Diocese of Piacenza-Bobbio, July 20, 1914. Created and proclaimed November 26, 1994. Address: Via Santa Teresa 8, 48100 Ravenna, Italy.

Toppo, Telesphore Placidus (Cardinal Priest), Titular of Sacro Cuore di Gesu agonizzante a Vitinia, Archbishop of Ranchi; born in Chainpur, India, October 15, 1939. Created and proclaimed October 21, 2003. Address: P.O. Box 5, Dr. Camil Bulcke Path, Ranchi-834001 Jharkhand, India.

Tucci, Roberto, S.J. (Cardinal Priest), Titular of St. Ignatius of Loyola at Campo Marzio; born in Naples, Italy, April 19, 1921. Created and proclaimed February 21, 2001. Address: Via Di Porta Pinciana 1, 00187 Rome, Italy.

Tumi, Christian Wiyghan (Cardinal Priest), Titular of Ss. Martiri dell' Uganda a Poggio Ameno, Archbishop Emeritus of Douala; born in Kikaikelaki, Diocese of Kumbo, October 15, 1930. Created and proclaimed June 28, 1988. Address: Archeveche, B.P. 179, Douala, Cameroon.

Turcotte, Jean-Claude (Cardinal Priest), Titular of Nostra Signora del Ss. Sacramento e Santi Martiri Canadesi, Archbishop of Montreal, Canada; born in Montreal, June 26, 1936. Created and proclaimed November 26, 1994. Address: 1071 rue de la Cathedrale, Montreal, Q.C. H3B 2V4, Canada.

Turkson, Peter Kodwo Appiah (Cardinal Priest), Titular of San Liborio, President of the Pontifical Council for Justice and Peace; born in Wassaw Nsuta, Archdiocese of Cape Coast, October 11, 1948. Created and proclaimed October 21, 2003. Address: 00120 Vatican City State, Europe.

Urosa Savino, Jorge Liberato (Cardinal Priest), Titular of Saint Mary ai Monti, Archbishop of Caracas, Santiago de Venezuela; born in Caracas, August 28, 1942. Created and proclaimed March 24, 2006. Address: Arzobispado, Apartado 954, Monajas a Gradillas, Plaza Bolivar, Caracas 1010-A, Venezuela.

Vallini, Agostino (Cardinal Priest), Titular of Saint Peter Damian ai Monti di San Paolo, Vicar General of His Holiness for the Diocese of Rome, Archpriest of the Patriarchal Lateran Basilica; born in Poli, Diocese of Tivoli, April 17, 1940. Created and proclaimed March 24, 2006. Address: Piazza S. Giovanni in Laterano 4, 00184 Rome, Italy.

Vanhoye, Albert, S.J. (Cardinal Deacon), Deacon of Saint Mary of Mercy and Saint Adrian at Villa Albani, Former Rector of the Pontifical Biblical Institute and Former Secretary of the Pontifical Biblical Commission; born in Hazebrouck, Diocesi of Lille, July 24, 1923. Created and proclaimed March 24, 2006. Address: Pontificio Istituto Biblico, Via della Pilotta 25, 00187 Rome, Italy.

Veglio, Antonio Maria (Cardinal Deacon), Diaconate of San Cesareo in Palatio, President of the Pontifical Council for the Pastoral Care of Migrants and Itinerant Peoples; Born in Macerata Feltria, Diocese of San Marino-Montefeltro, February 3, 1938. Created and proclaimed February 18, 2012. Address: Piazza S. Calisto 16, 00153 Rome, Italy.

Vela Chiriboga, Raul Eduardo (Cardinal Priest),Titular of St. Mary in Via, Archbishop Emeritus of Quito, Ecuador; born in Riobamba, Diocese of Omonima, January 1, 1934. Created and proclaimed November 20, 2010. Address: Calle Juan Manuel Acuna E5-60 y Jose de Ascazubi, Apartado 17-41-0004, Conocoto, Quito, Ecuador.

Versaldi, Giuseppe (Cardinal Deacon), Diaconate of Sacro Cuore di Gesu a Castro Pretorio, President of the Prefecture for the Economic Affairs of the Holy See; Born in Villarboit, Archdiocese of Vercelli, July 30, 1943. Created and proclaimed February 18, 2012. Address: 00120 Vatican City State, Europe.

Vidal, Ricardo J. (Cardinal Priest), Titular of Ss. Pietro e Paolo a Via Stiense, Archbishop Emeritus of Cebu; born in Mogpoc, Diocese of Boac, February 6, 1931. Created and proclaimed May 25, 1985. Address: 234 D. Jakosalem Str., P.O. Box 52, 6000 Cebu City, Philippines.

Vingt-Trois, Andre (Cardinal Priest) Titular of San Luigi dei Francesi, Archbishop of Paris; born in Paris, November 7, 1942. Created and proclaimed November 24, 2007. Address: 32 rue de Barbet de Jouy, 75007 Paris, France.

Vlk, Miloslav (Cardinal Priest), Titular of S. Croce in Gerusalemme, Archbishop Emeritus of Prague, Czech Republic; born in Lisnice-Sepekov, Diocese of Ceske Budejovice, May 17, 1932. Created and proclaimed November 26, 1994. Address: Arcibiskupsky Ordinariat, Hradcanske nam. 56/16, 119 02 Praha 1, Czech Republic.

Wamala, Emmanuel (Cardinal Priest), Titular of S. Ugo, Archbishop Emeritus of Kampala, Uganda; born in Kamaggwa, Diocese of Masaka, December 15, 1926. Created and proclaimed November 26, 1994. Address: Archbishop's House, P.O. Box 14125, Mengo- Kampala, Uganda.

Wetter, Friedrich (Cardinal Priest), Titular of S. Stefano al Monte Celio, Archbishop Emeritus of Munich und Freising; born in Landau, Diocese of Speyer, February 20, 1928. Created and proclaimed May 25, 1985. Address: Vinzenz-von-Paul-Strasse 1, D-81671 Munchen, Germany.

Williams, Thomas Stafford (Cardinal Priest), Titular of Gesu' Divin Maestro alla Pineta Sacchetti, Archbishop Emeritus of Wellington; born in Wellington, March 20, 1930. Created and proclaimed February 2, 1983. Address: 40 Walton Ave., Waikanae Park, Kapiti 5036, New Zealand.

Woelki, Rainer Maria (Cardinal Priest), Titular of San Giovanni Maria Vianney, Archbishop of Berlin, Germany; Born in Koln, August 18, 1956. Created and proclaimed February 18, 2012. Address: Niederwallstr. 8-9, D-10117 Berlin, Germany.

Wuerl, Donald William (Cardinal Priest), Titular of St. Peter in Chains, Archbishop of Washington, U.S.A.; born in Pittsburgh, November 12, 1940. Created and proclaimed November 20, 2010. Address: P.O. Box 29260, Washington DC 20017, U.S.A.

Zen Ze-kiun, Joseph (Cardinal Priest), Titular of Saint Mary Mother of the Redeemer at Tor Bella Monaca, Archbishop Emeritus of Hong Kong; born in Shanghai, January 13, 1932. Created and proclaimed March 24, 2006. Address: Salesian House of Studies, 18 Chai Wan Road, Shaukiwan, Hong Kong, China.

Zubeir Wako, Gabriel (Cardinal Priest), Titular of Sant' Atanasio a Via Tiburtina, Archbishop of Khartoum; born in Mboro, Diocese of Wau, February 27, 1941. Created and proclaimed October 21, 2003. Address: P.O. Box 49, Khartoum, Sudan.

Patriarchs

Alexandria (Egypt), Coptic Rite— His Beatitude Antonios Cardinal Naguib, born in Minya, Egypt, March 7, 1935; ordained October 30, 1960; elected Bishop of Minya of the Copts, July 26, 1977; consecrated September 9, 1977; resigned September 29, 2002; elected Patriarch of Alexandria of the Copts, March 30, 2006. Address: Patriarcat Copte Catholique, B.P. 69, 34 Rue Ibn Sandar, Saray El Koubbeh, 11712 Le Caire, Egypte.

Antioch (Syria), Syriac Rite— His Beatitude Ignace Joseph III Younan, born in Hassaké November 15, 1944; elected Patriarch February 15, 2009. Address: Rue Damas, B.P. 116-5087, 1106-2010 Beyrouth, Lebanon.

Maronite Rite— His Beatitude Bechara Boutros Rai, OMM, born in Himlaya, February 25, 1940; elected Patriarch March 15, 2011. Address: Patriarcat Maronite, Bkerke, Lebanon.

Melkite Greek Catholic— His Beatitude Gregoire III Laham, born December 15, 1932 in Daraya; elected Patriarch November 29, 2000. Address: B.P. 22249, Avenue Az-Zeitoon 12, Bab Charki, Damascus, Syria.

Jerusalem (Israel)— His Beatitude Fouad Twal, born in Madaba, Israel, October 23, 1940; succeeded Patriarch of Jerusalem of the Latins June 21, 2008. Address: Patriarcat Latin, P.O. Box 14152, 91141 Jerusalem (Old City).

Babylon of the Chaldeans— His Beatitude Emmanuel III Cardinal Delly, born in Telkaif, October 6, 1927; elected Patriarch December 3, 2003. Address: Patriarcat Chaldeen Catholique, P.O. Box 6112, Al-Mansour, Baghdad, Iraq.

Cilicia of the Armenians— His Beatitude Nerses Bedros XIX Tarmouni, born in LeCaire January 17, 1940; elected Patriarch October 7, 1999. Address: Patriarcat Armenien Catholique, Rue de L'Hopital Orthodoxe, Jeitaoui, 2078 5605 Beyrouth, Lebanon.

East Indies— Most Rev. Filipe Neri António Sebastiaó Do Rosario Ferrao, Archbishop of Goa and Damao; born in Aldona, Archdiocese of Goa, January 20, 1953; promoted Archbishop January 16, 2004. Address: Paco Patriarcal P.O. Box 216, Panaji, Goa-403001, India.

Lisbon, (Portugal)— His Eminence Jose da Cruz Policarpo, born in Alvorninha, Patriarchate of Lisbon, February 26, 1936; consecrated June 29, 1978; appointed Coadjutor Archbishop of the Patriarchate of Lisbon March 5, 1997; promoted Patriarch March 24, 1998; elevated to the College of Cardinals February 21, 2001. Address: Mosteiro de Sao Vicente De Fora, Campo de Santa Clara 1100-472 Lisbon, Portugal.

Venice, (Italy)— His Excellency Archbishop Francesco Moraglia, Archbishop of Venezia; born in May 25, 1953; appointed Archbishop of Venezia January 31, 2012. Address: Curia Patriarcale, S. Marco 320/a, 30124 Venice, Italy.

Synod of Bishops

Synodus Episcoporum: Secretary General: Most Rev. Archbishop Nikola Eterovic, General Secretariat: Palazzo del Bramante, Via della Conciliazione, 34, 00193 Rome, Italy. Tel: 06.69.88.48.21 or 06.69.88.43.24; Fax: 06.69.88.33.92; Email: synodus@synod.va

Office of Labor of the Apostolic See

Officium Laboris Apostolicae Sedia President: His Excellency Bishop Giorgio Corbellini, Assessor of the Presidency: Prof. Angelo Pandolfo, Assessor of the Presidency: Prof. Giovanni Giustiniani, Office: Via della Conciliazione, 1, 00193 Rome, Italy. Tel: 69.88.44.49. Fax: 69.88.38.00. Email: ulsa1@ulsa.va.

The Roman Curia

The present norms regarding the Roman Curia were publicly announced June 28, 1988, in the Pastor Bonus - Constitutio Apostolica de Romana Curia, and published in A.A.S. LXXX/1988, Commentarium Officiale; pp. 841-934. The Supreme Pontiff usually conducts business of the universal Church by means of the Roman Curia, which fulfills its duty in his name and by his authority for the good and the service of the Churches; it consists of the Secretariat of State or the Papal Secretariat, congregations, tribunals and other institutions, whose structure and competency are defined in special law (can. 360). The Roman curia is the complex of departments and institutes which assist the Roman Pontiff in the exercise of his supreme pastoral function for the good and service of the universal Church and of the particular churches, by which the unity of faith and communion of the people of God is strengthened and the mission is promoted which is proper to the Church in the world.

I. THE SECRETARIAT OF STATE TO HIS HOLINESS

The Secretariat of State

The Secretariat of State is the dicastery of the Roman Curia which works most closely with the Supreme Pontiff in the exercise of his universal mission (*Pastor Bonus*, Art. 39). The Secretariat of State is presided over by a Cardinal who assumes the title of Secretary of State. As the Pope's first Collaborator in the governance of the universal Church, the Cardinal Secretary of State is the one primarily responsible for the diplomatic and political activity of the Holy See, in some circumstances representing the person of the Supreme Pontiff himself.

The Secretariat of State includes two sections, namely: the First Section that is headed by an Archbishop, the *Substitute for General Affairs*, assisted by a Prelate, the *Assessor for General Affairs*; and the Second Section of the Secretariat of State headed by an Archbishop, the *Secretary for Relations with States*, aided by a Prelate, the *Under-Secretary for Relations with States*, and assisted by Cardinals and Bishops.

Secretary of State: His Eminence Tarcisio Cardinal Bertone.
Office: Apostolic Palace, 00120 Vatican City State, Europe. Tel: 06-69.88.39.13; Fax: 06-69.88.52.55.

First Section: For General Affairs

In conformity with Arts. 41-44 of *Pastor Bonus*, the Section for General Affairs or the First Section is responsible for handling matters regarding the everyday service of the Supreme Pontiff, both in caring for the universal Church and in dealing with the dicasteries of the Roman Curia. It attends to the preparation of whatever documents the Holy Father entrusts to it. It enacts the provisions for appointments within the Roman Curia and keeps custody of the Lead Seal and the Fisherman's Ring. It regulates the duties and activity of the Holy See's Representatives, especially in relation to the local Churches. It attends to all that concerns the Embassies accredited to the Holy See. It supervises the Holy See's official communication agencies and is responsible for publishing the "Acta Apostolicae Sedis" and the "Annuario Pontificio".

Substitute: Most Rev. Archbishop Giovanni Angelo Becciu.
Assessor: Rev. Msgr. Peter Bryan Wells.
Office: Apostolic Palace, 00120 Vatican City State, Europe. Tel: 06.69.88.34.38; Fax: 06.69.88.50.88; E-mail: sostituto@sds.va.

Second Section: For Relations with States

On the basis of Arts. 45-47 of Pastor Bonus, the Section for Relations with States or Second Section has the specific duty of attending to matters which involve civil governments. It has responsibility for the Holy See's diplomatic relations with States, including the establishing of Concordats or similar agreements; for the Holy See's presence in international organizations and conferences; in special circumstances, by order of the Supreme Pontiff and in consultation with the competent dicasteries of the Curia, provides for appointments to particular Churches, and for their establishment or modification; in close collaboration with the Congregation for Bishops, it attends to the appointment of Bishops in countries which have entered into treaties or agreements with the Holy See in accordance with the norms of international law.

Secretary: Most Rev. Archbishop Dominique Mamberti.
Undersecretary: Rev. Msgr. Ettore Balestrero.
Office: Apostolic Palace, 00120 Vatican City State, Europe. Tel: 06.69.88.30.14; Fax: 06.69.88.53.64; E-mail: rapportistati@sds.va.

II. THE CONGREGATIONS

By the name of department (dicasteria) is understood: the congregations, tribunals, councils and offices, namely the Apostolic Camera, the Administration of the Patrimony of the Apostolic See, and the Prefecture of Economic Affairs of the Holy See. The departments are juridically equal among themselves. Attached to the institutes of the Roman Curia are the Prefecture of the Papal Household and the Office of Liturgical Celebrations of the Supreme Pontiff.

The Congregation for the Doctrine of the Faith

The proper function of the Congregation on the Doctrine of the Faith is to promote and safeguard the doctrine of faith and morals in the whole Catholic world; therefore, those things belong to it which touch this matter in any way. Fulfilling the function of promoting doctrine, it fosters studies in order that the understanding of the faith might grow and that a response can be prepared under the light of faith for new questions arising from developments in science and human culture. It is a help to bishops, whether individually or gathered in assemblies, in the exercise of the function by which they are constituted authentic teachers and doctors of the faith as well as the office by which they are held to safeguard and promote the integrity of that faith. This Sacred Congregation reproves doctrines opposed to the principles of the faith after the interested Bishops of a region have been heard. It studies the books referred to it and, if necessary, reproves them after the author has been heard and has had an opportunity to defend himself and after the Ordinary has been forewarned. It also examines whatever concerns "the privilege of the faith" whether in law and in fact. It is competent to pass judgment on errors about the faith according to the norms of an ordinary process. It safeguards the dignity of the sacrament of Penance. The Congregation proceeds administratively or judicially according to the nature of the question to be treated.

Prefect: His Eminence William Joseph Cardinal Levada.
Secretary: Most Rev. Luis Francisco Ladaria Ferrer, S.J.
Undersecretary: Rev. Msgr. Damiano Marzotto Caotorta.
Office: Piazza del S. Uffizio 11, 00193 Rome, Italy. Tel: 06.69.89.59.11; Fax: 06.69.88.34.09.

The Congregation for the Oriental Churches

This Congregation considers those matters, whether regarding persons or things, which touch on the Eastern Catholic Churches. It treats all questions which pertain either to persons, or to discipline, or to the rites of the Oriental Churches, even if they are mixed in that by the nature of the thing or of persons they involve Latins. Territories in which a major part of the Christians belong to Oriental rites are subject only to this Congregation. Even in Latin territories it carefully supervises the faithful of Oriental rites and provides as much as possible for their spiritual needs even by the establishment of their own hierarchy if the number of faithful and circumstances require this.

Prefect: His Eminence Leonardo Cardinal Sandri.
Secretary: Most Rev. Archbishop Cyril Vasil, S.J.
Undersecretary: Rev. Msgr. Maurizio Malvestiti.
Office: Via della Conciliazione 34, 00193 Rome, Italy. Tel: 06.69.88.42.81; E-mail: cco@orientchurch.va.

The Congregation for Divine Worship and the Discipline of the Sacraments

This congregation does those things which pertain to the Apostolic See as to the moderation and promotion of the sacred liturgy, especially the sacraments, with due regard for the competence of the Congregation on Doctrine of the Faith. It fosters and safeguards the discipline of the sacraments, especially what pertains to their valid and licit celebration; moreover, it concedes favors and dispensations for matters which are not contained in the facilities of diocesan bishops in this line. It alone examines the non-consummation of a marriage and the presence of causes for the granting of a dispensation and everything connected with them. It has competence with regard to the obligations connected with major orders and it examines questions about the validity of sacred ordination.

Prefect: His Eminence Antonio Cardinal Canizares Llovera.
Secretary: Most Rev. Archbishop Joseph Augustine Di Noia, O.P.
Undersecretaries: Rev. Anthony Ward, S.M.; Rev. Msgr. Juan Miguel Ferrer Grenesche.
Office: Piazza Pio XII 10, 00193 Rome, Italy. Tel: 06.69.88.40.05; Fax: 06.69.88.34.99; E-mail: cultdiv@ccdds.va.

The Congregation for the Causes of Saints

The Congregation for the Causes of Saints is competent in all matters which in any way pertain to the Beatification of Servants of God or to the Canonization of the Blessed or to the Preservation of Relics.

This Congregation is divided into three offices.

Prefect: His Eminence Angelo Cardinal Amato, S.D.B.
Secretary: Most Rev. Archbishop Marcello Bartolucci.
Undersecretary: Rev. Boguslaw Turek, C.S.M.A.
Office: Piazza Pio XII 10, 00193 Rome, Italy. Tel: 06.69.88.42.47; Fax: 06.69.88.19.35.

The Congregation for Bishops

This congregation examines what pertains to the constitution and provision of particular churches as well as the exercise of the episcopal function in the Latin Church, except for the competence of the Congregation for the Evangelization of Peoples. It belongs to the Congregation for Bishops to propose to the Roman Pontiff, for approval, the constitution of new dioceses, provinces and regions; to divide, unite and realign them after consulting the interested Episcopal Conferences; it deals also with the erection of the military ordinariates and, after consulting the Episcopal Conference, prelacies for special pastoral ministries for various regions or social groups. This Congregation provides also for the naming of bishops, apostolic administrators, coadjutors and auxiliaries of bishops, military and other vicars and prelates enjoying personal jurisdiction. It is competent for all things that have to do with bishops and publishes norms which, through the Episcopal Conference, provide for the more urgent needs of the faithful.

Prefect: His Eminence Marc Cardinal Ouellet
Secretary: Most Rev. Archbishop Manuel Monteiro de Castro.
Undersecretary: Rev. Msgr. Giovanni Maria Rossi.
Adjunct Undersecretary: Rev. Msgr. Serge Poitras.
Office: Piazza Pio XII 10, 00193 Rome, Italy. Tel: 06.69.88.42.17; Fax: 06.69.88.53.03.

Pontifical Commission for Latin America

(Directly responsible to Congregation for Bishops)
President: His Eminence Marc Cardinal Ouellet.
Secretary: Prof. Guzman Carriquiry

The Congregation for the Evangelization of Peoples or for the Propagation of the Faith

It belongs to this congregation to direct and coordinate throughout the world the work of the evangelization of peoples itself and missionary cooperation, while respecting the competence of the Congregation for Eastern Churches. It is competent for those things which pertain to all the missions established for the spread of the Kingdom of Christ throughout the world and therefore for whatever is connected with the assignment and transferal of the necessary ministers, for describing ecclesiastical boundaries and proposing those who will govern them. It encourages also the development of an indigenous clergy. The congregation sponsors missionary initiatives and promotes missionary vocations and spirituality. In the territories subject to it, the Congregation has charge of all that pertains to the holding of synods and councils, to the establishing of episcopal conferences and to the review of their statutes and decrees. The Congregation has a Supreme Council for the direction of Pontifical Missionary Works, on which depend the general Councils of the Missionary Union of the Clergy, the Society for the Propagation of the Faith, the Society of St. Peter the Apostle, and the Society of the Holy Childhood.

Prefect: His Eminence Fernando Cardinal Filoni.

Secretary: Most Rev. Archbishop Savio Hon Tai-Fai, S.D.B.

Adjunct Secretary: Most Rev. Archbishop Piergiuseppe Vacchelli.

Undersecretary: Rev. Massimo Cenci, P.I.M.E.

Office: Palazzo di Propaganda Fide, Piazza di Spagna 48, 00187 Rome, Italy. Tel: 06.69.87.92.99; Fax: 06.69.88.01.18; E-mail: Segreteria@propagandafide.va.

The Congregation for the Clergy

With due regard for the rights of bishops and their conferences, this congregation examines those things which concern priests and deacons of the secular clergy with regard to their persons, pastoral ministry, matters which are in support of the exercise of these things, and in all this provides opportune assistance to the bishops. The Congregation has many functions: studies, proposes and urges the means and aids by which priests strive for sanctity. This office also has charge of everything which concerns the work and discipline of the diocesan clergy. Particularly it promotes the preaching of the Word of God and the works of the apostolate and organization of catechesis, evaluates and approves pastoral and catechetical directories, fosters national and international Catechetical Congresses and indicates the opportune norms for religious instruction of children, young people and adults. The Congregation looks also to the preservation and administration of the temporal goods of the Church without prejudice to the other Congregations which have temporal goods committed to their vigilance.

Prefect: His Eminence Mauro Cardinal Piacenza.

Secretary: Most Rev. Archbishop Celso Morga Iruzubieta.

Undersecretary: Rev. Msgr. Antonio Neri.

Office: Piazza Pio XII 3, 00193 Rome, Italy. Tel: 06.69.88.41.51; Fax: 06.69.88.48.45; E-mail: clero@cclergy.va.

The Congregation for Institutes of Consecrated Life and for Societies of Apostolic Life

The principal function of this congregation is to promote and supervise, in the whole Latin Church, the practices of the evangelical counsels as they are exercised in approved forms of consecrated life and at the same time the activities of societies of apostolic life. The Congregation takes care of Religious Institutes of Consecrated Life and Secular Institutes.

Religious Institutes: the Congregation is entrusted with the affairs of all religious institutes of the Latin Rite and their members. It is also competent in matters which pertain to societies of common life, whose members live like religious, or to Third Orders as such.

Secular Institutes: the Congregation is competent in the same way, all else being equal, for Apostolic Societies which, although not religious, make a true and complete profession of the evangelical counsels in the world.

Prefect: His Eminence João Cardinal Braz de Aviz.

Secretary: Most Rev. Archbishop Joseph William Tobin, C.SS.R.

Undersecretaries: Sister Enrica Rosanna, F.M.A.; Rev. Sebastiano Paciolla, O.Cist.

Office: Piazza Pio XII 3, 00193 Rome, Italy. Tel: 06.69.89.25.11; Fax: 06.69.88.45.26.

The Congregation for Catholic Education (of Seminaries and Institutes of Studies)

This Congregation expresses and exercises the Apostolic See's solicitude for the formation of those who are called to holy orders as well as for the promotion and organization of Catholic education. It is competent for all that pertains to the formation of clerics and the Catholic education both of clerics and of the laity.

The Congregation has many functions and is charged with the direction, discipline and temporal administration of seminaries and whatever touches the education of the diocesan clergy and the scientific formation of religious and secular institutes.

The Congregation oversees universities, faculties, athenaea and any institute of higher learning which has the name "Catholic" in so far as they depend on the authority of the Church, not excluding those directed by religious or the laity.

The Congregation cares for the establishment of parochial and diocesan schools; watches over all Catholic schools below the level of a university and faculty, as well as all institutes of instruction or education dependent on the authority of the Church.

Also within the Congregation is located the Pontifical Work for Vocations, which is charged with coordinating and promoting the work of fostering all ecclesiastical vocations.

Prefect: His Eminence Zenon Cardinal Grocholewski.

Secretary: Most Rev. Archbishop Jean-Louis Bruguès, O.P.

Undersecretary: Rev. Msgr. Angelo Vincenzo Zani.

Office: Piazza Pio XII 3, 00193 Rome, Italy. Tel: 06.69.88.41.67; Fax: 06.69.88.41.72.

III. TRIBUNALS

Apostolic Penitentiary

The competence of this Tribunal is concerned with those matters which pertain to the internal forum, for both the sacramental and non-sacramental internal forum. It is competent in matters pertaining to the granting and use of indulgences.

Major Penitentiary: His Eminence Manuel Cardinal Monteiro de Castro.

Office: Piazza della Cancelleria 1, 00186 Rome, Italy. Tel: 06.69.88.75.26; Fax: 06.69.8875.57.

Supreme Tribunal of the Apostolic Signatura

This department, in addition to the function which it exercises as Supreme Tribunal, consults that justice may be correctly administered in the Church.

With the many functions, the Apostolic Signatura judges the matters assigned to it in the Code of Canon Law; it prorogues the competence of tribunals; it extends the forum for strangers in Rome to cases of matrimonial nullity in extraordinary circumstances and for grave reasons; it supervises the proper administration of justice; it provides for the establishment of regional and interregional tribunals; it enjoys the rights assigned to it in concordats between the Holy See and the various nations.

The Tribunal settles questions about the exercise of administrative ecclesiastical power which are referred to it. It also passes on conflicts of competence among the departments of the Holy See; it examines administrative matters referred to it by the Congregations of the Roman Curia as well as questions committed to it by the Holy Father.

Prefect: His EminenceRaymond Leo Cardinal Burke.

Secretary: Most Rev. Bishop Frans Daneels, O.Praem.

Office: Piazza della Cancelleria 1, 00186 Rome, Italy. Tel: 06.69.88.75.20; Fax: 06.69.88.75.53.

Tribunal of the Roman Rota

This tribunal acts as a higher instance at the Apostolic See, usually in the grade of appeal, for safeguarding rights in the Church; it fosters the unity of jurisprudence and, through its own sentences, is a help to lower tribunals. It is also a court of first instance for cases specified in the law and for others committed to the Rota by the Roman Pontiff. The greater part of its decisions concern the nullity of marriage. In such cases its competence includes marriages between two Catholics, between a Catholic and non-Catholic, and between two non-Catholic parties whether one or both of the baptized parties belongs to a Latin or Oriental Rite.

Dean: Most Rev. Bishop Antoni Stankiewicz.

Office: Piazza della Cancelleria 1, 00186 Rome, Italy. Tel: 06.69.88.75.02; Fax: 06.69.88.75.54.

IV. PONTIFICAL COUNCILS

Pontifical Council for the Laity

This council is competent in those matters which pertain to the Apostolic See in promoting and coordinating the apostolate of the lay persons and, generally, in those things which look to the Christian life of lay persons as such. The norms were published in the apostolic letter, Catholicam Christi Ecclesiam of January 6, 1967 (A.A.S., LIX, pp. 25-28).

President: His Eminence Stanislaw Cardinal Rylko.

Secretary: Most Rev. Bishop Josef Clemens.

Undersecretary: Rev. Msgr. Miguel Delgado Galindo.

Office: Piazza S. Calisto 16, 00153 Rome, Italy. Tel: 06.69.86.93.00; Fax: 06.69.88.72.14; E-mail: pcpl@laity.va; youth@laity.va; gmg@laity.va

Pontifical Council for Promoting Christian Unity

The function of this Council is to concentrate in an appropriate way on initiatives and ecumenical activities for the restoration of unity among Christians. It has charge of relations with those of other communities; considers the correct interpretation and observance of the principles of ecumenism; promotes Catholic groups and coordinates the efforts at unity, both on the national and international levels; institutes colloquies on ecumenical questions and activities with Churches and ecclesial communities separated from the Holy See; deputes Catholic observers for Christian congresses; invites to Catholic gatherings observers of the separated brethren; orders into practice conciliar decrees on ecumenical matters. Furthermore, it is competent for all questions concerning religious relations with Judaism.

President: His Eminence Kurt Cardinal Koch.

Secretary: Most Rev. Bishop Brian Farrell, L.C.

Office: Via della Conciliazione 5, 00193 Rome, Italy. Tel: 06.69.88.30.72; Fax: 06.69.88.53.65; E-mail: office@christianunity.va.

Commission for Religious Relations with Jews

Secretary: Rev. Norbert Hoffman, S.D.B.

Pontifical Council for the Family

This Council promotes the pastoral care of families and fosters their rights and dignity in the Church and in civil society, in order that they might ever more suitably fulfill their own functions.

President: His Eminence Ennio Cardinal Antonelli.

Secretary: Most Rev. Bishop Jean Laffitte.

Undersecretary: Rev. Carlos Simón Vázquez.

Office: Piazza S. Calisto 16, 00153 Rome, Italy. Tel: 06.69.88.72.43; Fax: 06.69.88.72.72; E-mail: pcf@family.va

Pontifical Council for Justice and Peace

This Council looks to those things which will promote justice and peace in the world according to the Gospel and the social teaching of the Church.

President: His Eminence Peter Kodwo Appiah Cardinal Turkson.

Secretary: Most Rev. Bishop Mario Toso, S.D.B.

Undersecretary: Dr. Flaminia Giovanelli.

Office: Piazza S. Calisto 16, 00153 Rome, Italy. Tel 06.69.87.99.11; Fax: 06.69.88.72.05; E-mail pcjustpax@justpeace.va.

Pontifical Council Cor Unum

This Council shows the solicitude of the Catholic Church toward the needy, in order that human fraternity might be fostered and the charity of Christ be made manifest.

President: His Eminence Robert Cardinal Sarah.

Secretary: Rev. Msgr. Giovanni Pietro Dal Toso.

Undersecretary: Rev. Msgr. Segundo Tejado Muñoz.

Office: Palazzo San Pio X, Via della Conciliazione 5, 00193 Rome, Italy. Tel: 06.69.88.94.11; Fax: 06.69.88.73.01; E-mail: corundum@corunum.va.

Pastoral Council for the Pastoral Care of Migrants and Itinerant People

This Council directs the pastoral concern of the Church toward the special needs of those who are forced to leave their own native land or who perhaps lack one; it also sees that there is appropriate study of the questions which touch on this matter.

President: His Eminence Antonio Maria Cardinal Vegliò.
Secretary: Most Rev. Archbishop Joseph Kalathiparambil.
Undersecretary: Rev. Gabriele Ferdinando Bentoglio, C.S.
Office: Piazza S. Calisto 16, 00153 Rome, Italy. Tel: 06.69.88.71.93; Fax: 06.69.88.71.11; E-mail: office@migrants.va.

Pontifical Council for the Pastoral Assistance to Health Care

This Council shows the solicitude of the Church for the sick by aiding those who carry out a ministry toward the sick and suffering, in order that the apostolate of mercy, which they carry out, may ever more suitably respond to new needs.

President: Most Rev. Archbishop Zygmunt Zimowski.
Secretary: Rev. Msgr. Jean-Marie Mpendawatu.
Undersecretary: Very Rev. Augusto Chendi, M.I.
Office: Via della Conciliazione 3, 00193 Rome, Italy. Tel: 06.69.88.31.38; Fax: 06.69.88.31.39; E-mail: opersanit@hlthwork.va.

Pontifical Council for the Intepretation of Legislative Texts

The function of this Council consists especially in interpreting the Church's laws.

President: His Eminence Francesco Cardinal Coccopalmerio.
Vice President: Most Rev. Archbishop Bruno Bertagna.
Secretary: Most Rev. Bishop Juan Ignacio Arrieta Ochoa De Chinchetru.
Undersecretary: Rev. Msgr. José Aparecido Gonçalves de Almeida.
Office: Palazzo delle Congregazioni Piazza Pio XII 10, 00193 Rome, Italy. Tel: 06.69.88.40.08; Fax: 06.69.88.47.10.

Pontifical Council for Inter-Religious Dialogue

This Council fosters and moderates relations with members and bodies of religions which do not carry the name of Christian, as well as with those who in any way possess a religious spirit. It fosters studies and promotes relations with non-Christians to bring about an increase in mutual respect and seeks ways to establish a dialogue with them; it receives and carefully weighs the wishes of the Ordinaries; it provides for the formation of those who participate in dialogue.

President: His Eminence Jean-Louis Cardinal Tauran.
Secretary: Most Rev. Archbishop Pier Luigi Celata
Undersecretary: Rev. Msgr. Andrew Thanya-anan Vissanu.
Office: Via della Conciliazione 5, 00193 Rome, Italy. Tel: 06.69.88.43.21; Fax: 06.69.88.44.94; E-mail: dialogo@interrel.va.

Commission for Religious Relations with Muslims

Secretary: Rev. Msgr. Khaled Akasheh.

Pontifical Council for Culture

The Council embodies the Church's pastoral concern over the relationship between faith and cultures. Its tasks include: studying unbelief and religious indifference, as present in different cultures; supporting the Church's inculturation of the Gospel; promoting initiatives of dialogue between faith and culture, as well as dialogue with those who do not believe in God. Its activities include seminars, intercultural exchanges, and coordinating the activities of Pontifical Academies and the Pontifical Commission for the Cultural Patrimony of the Church. An important hope of the Council is to show faith as the inspiration of science, literature and the arts.

President: His Eminence Gianfranco Cardinal Ravasi.
Secretary: Most Rev. Bishop Bathelemy Adoukonou.
Undersecretary: Rev. Msgr. Melchor José Sánchez de Toca y alameda.
Office: Via della Conciliazione 5, 00193 Rome, Italy. Tel: 06.69.89.38.11; Fax: 06.69.88.73.68; E-mail: cultura@cultura.va.

Pontifical Council for Social Communications

This Council is involved in questions touching on the instruments of social communication so that the proclamation of salvation and human progress might be promoted even through them in order to foster civil culture.

President: Most Rev. Archbishop Claudio Maria Celli.
Secretary: Rev. Msgr. Paul Tighe.
Adjunct Secretary: Rev. Msgr. Giuseppe Antonio Scotti.
Undersecretary: Dr. Angelo Scelzo.
Office: Via della Conciliazione 5, 00193 Rome, Italy. Tel: 06.69.89.18.00; Fax: 06.69.89.18.40; E-mail: pccs@vatican.va.

Pontifical Council for Promoting New Evangelization

The Council pursues its own ends both by encouraging reflection on topics of the new evangelization, and by identifying and promoting suitable ways and means to accomplish it.

President: Most Rev. Archbishop Salvatore Fisichella.
Secretary: Most Rev. Archbishop Jose Octavio Ruiz Arenas.
Undersecretary: Rev. Msgr. Graham Bell.
Office: Via della Conciliazione 5, 00193 Rome, Italy. Tel: 06.69.86.95.00; Fax: 06.69.86.95.21.

V. OFFICES

Apostolic Camera

The Apostolic Camera is presided over by the cardinal chamberlain of the Holy Roman Church, assisted by the vice-chamberlain together with certain prelates chamberlain. It chiefly exercises the function which is given to it in the special law on the vacancy of the Apostolic See.

Camerlengo: His Eminence Tarcisio Cardinal Bertone, Secretary of State.

Administration of the Patrimony of the Apostolic See

This Office is competent to administer the goods proper to the Holy See, the income from which is destined to support the expenditures necessary for the functions of the Roman Curia.

Extraordinary Section: Handles the duties committed to it by the Sovereign Pontiff.
President: His Eminence Domenico Cardinal Calcagno.
Secretary: Rev. Msgr. Luigi Misto.
Office: Apostolic Palace, 00120 Vatican City State, Europe. Tel: 06.69.89.34.03; Fax: 06.69.88.31.41; E-mail: apsa-ss@apsa.va.

Prefecture of the Economic Affairs of the Holy See

The Prefecture has the function of supervising and governing the administration of goods which belong to the Holy See or which it is in charge of, no matter what kind of autonomy they may perhaps enjoy. This is directed by a Commission of three Cardinals and coordinates and watches over the administration of the possessions of the Holy See. It receives the reports on the receipts and disbursements of the Church's goods and the various budgets.

President: His Eminence Giuseppe Cardinal Versaldi.
Secretary: Rev. Lucio Angel Vallejo Valda.
Office: Largo del Colonnato 3, 00193 Rome, Italy. Tel: 06.69.88.42.63; Fax: 06.69.88.50.11.

Prefecture of the Papal Household

The Prefecture looks after the internal order of the pontifical household and supervises everything which pertains to discipline and service either by clergy or laity who constitute the pontifical chapel and family. It is in charge of the Apostolic Palace and is at the service of the Holy Father, both there and wherever he goes. It arranges audiences with His Holiness and supervises papal ceremonies other than the strictly liturgical.

Prefect: Most Reverend Archbishop James M. Harvey.

Office of the Liturgical Celebrations of the Supreme Pontiff

This Office prepares whatever is necessary for liturgical and other sacred celebrations which are carried out by the Supreme Pontiff or in his name and, in keeping with existing prescription of liturgical law, to supervise them.

Master of Ceremonies: Rev. Msgr. Guido Marini.

Central Office of Statistics of the Church

This Office gathers and organizes the data which seems necessary or useful for a better understanding of the state of the Church and for assistance to its Bishops.

Director: Rev. Msgr. Vittorio Formenti.
Tel: 06.69.88.34.93; 06.69.88.36.55; Fax: 06.69.88.38.16.

VI. COMMISSIONS AND COMMITTEES

Pontifical Commission for the Cultural Heritage of the Church

President: His Eminence Gianfranco Cardinal Ravasi.
Secretary: Dr. Francesco Buranelli.

Pontifical Commission for Sacred Archeology

President: His Eminence Gianfranco Cardinal Ravasi.
Secretary: Rev. Msgr. Giovanni Carrù.

Pontifical Biblical Commission

President: His Eminence William Cardinal Levada
Secretary: Rev. Klemens Stock, S.J.

Pontifical Commission "Ecclesia Dei"

President: His Eminence William Cardinal Levada
Secretary: Rev. Msgr. Guido Pozzo

International Theological Commission

President: His Eminence William Cardinal Levada
Secretary General: Rev. Serge Thomas Bonino, O.P.

Pontifical Commission for the Vatican City State

President: His Eminence Giuseppe Cardinal Bertello.

Pontifical Committee for the International Eucharistic Congresses

President: Most Rev. Archbishop Pietro Marini.

Pontifical Committee for Historical Sciences

President: Rev. Bernard Ardura, O.Praem.
Secretary: Rev. Cosimo Semeraro, S.D.B.

VII. INSTITUTIONS CONNECTED WITH THE HOLY SEE

Press Office of the Holy See

Director: Rev. Federico Lombardi, S.J.

Vatican Secret Archives

Archivist: His Eminence Raffaele Cardinal Farina, S.D.B.
Prefect: Most Rev. Bishop Sergio B. Pagano.

Vatican Apostolic Library

Librarian: His Eminence Raffaele Cardinal Farina, S.D.B.
Prefect: Rev. Cesare Pasini.

Sr. Jacinta Coscia, F.S.E.

Vatican Polyglot Press

Director General: Rev. Pietro Migliasso, S.D.B.

L'Osservatore Romano

Editor-in-Chief: Prof. Giovanni Maria Vian.

Secretary: Dr. Gaetano Vallini.
English Language Weekly - Contact Person: (Vacant)
Translations of English, French, Spanish, German, Portuguese, and Polish editions available.

Vatican Publishing House
President: Rev. Msgr. Giuseppe Antonio Scotti.
Director: Rev. Giuseppe Costa, S.D.B.

Vatican Radio
Director General: Rev. Frederico Lombardi, S.J.

Vatican Television Centre
President of the Administrative Council: Most Rev. Archbishop Claudio Maria Celli.
Director General: Rev. Federico Lombardi, S.J.

St. Peter's Basilica
Archpriest: His Eminence Angelo Cardinal Comastri.

Fabric of St. Peter's
President: His Eminence Angelo Cardinal Comastri.

Office of Papal Charities
Almoner: Most Rev. Archbishop Felix Del Blanco Prieto.

Pontifical Academy of Sciences
President: Prof. Werner Arber.

Pontifical Academy of Social Sciences
President: Prof. Mary Ann Glendon.

Pontifical Academy for Life
President: Most Rev. Bishop Ignacio Carrasco de Paula.

Pontifical Academy of Theology
President: Rev. Manlio Sodi, S.D.B.

Institute for Works of Religion
Director General: Mr. Paolo Cipriani

VIII. AMERICANS WORKING IN THE ROMAN CURIA

Secretariat of State I. Section for General Affairs: Rev. Msgr. Peter Wells; Rev. Msgr. William Millea; Rev. Reginald Foster, O.C.D.; Rev. Daniel Gallagher.

Congregation for the Doctrine of the Faith: His Eminence William J. Cardinal Levada, Prefect; Most Rev. Archbishop Joseph DiNoia, O.P.; Rev. Msgr. Charles Brown; Rev. Msgr. Robert P. Deeley; Rev. Steven Lopes.

Congregation for Divine Worship and the Discipline of the Sacraments: Rev. Msgr. Thomas Fucinaro.

Congregation for Causes of Saints: Rev. Msgr. Robert Sarno.

Congregation for Bishops: Rev. Andrew Baker; Rev. Thomas W. Powers.

Congregation for Evangelization of People: Most Rev. Charles A. Schleck, C.S.C. (Retired); Sr. Raffaella Petrini, F.S.E.

Congregation for the Clergy: Rev. Msgr. J. Anthony McDaid.

Congregation for The Institutes of Consecrated Life and for Societies of Apostolic Life: Sr. Sharon Holland, I.H.M.

Apostolic Penitentiary: His Eminence Fortunato Cardinal Baldelli

Supreme Tribunal of the Apostolic Signatura: Most Rev. Archbishop Raymond L. Burke, Prefect; Rev. Msgr. Joseph Punderson.

Tribunal of the Roman Rota: Rev. Msgr. Kenneth Boccafola; Rev. Msgr. Robert Sable.

Pontifical Council For Promoting Christian Unity: Rev. Msgr. John Radano; Rev. Gregory J. Fairbanks.

Pontifical Council for Justice and Peace: Rev. Msgr. James Reinert; Rev. Msgr. Anthony R. Frontiero.

Pontifical Council for Interreligious Dialogue: Sr. Judith Zoebelein, F.S.E.

Pontifical Council "Cor Unum": Rev. Anthony J. Figueiredo.

Administration for the Patrimony of the Apostolic See: Sr. Judith Zoebelein, F.S.E.

Prefecture of the Papal Household: Most Rev. James M. Harvey, Prefect.

Pontifical Commission Ecclesia Dei: Rev. Msgr. Arthur Calkins.

International Theological Commission: Rev. Peter D Akpunonu.

Apostolic Vatican Library: Rev. Laurence Spiteri.

Equestrian Order of the Knights of the Holy Sepulchre of Jerusalem: His Eminence Edwin F. Cardinal O'Brien, Grand Master.

L'Osservatore Romano: For subscription information for North America please contact: The Cathedral Foundation, Inc. 320 Cathedral St., Baltimore, MD 21201. Tel: 410-547-5380; Fax: 410-385-0113.

Synod of Bishops: Rev. Msgr. John Abruzzese.

Papal Basilica of Saint Mary Major: His Eminence Bernard F. Law, Archpriest; Rev. Msgr. Paul Brendan McInerny.

Residence for American Diocesan Priests working in the Roman Curia: Villa Stritch, Via della Nocetta 63, 00164 Rome, Italy. Tel: 011 39 06 6616 2662; or 6616 2676; Fax 011 39 06 6616 2700. Rev. Msgr. Robert J. Sarno, Dir. Rev. Msgr. John Abruzzese, Vice Dir.

INSTITUTES OF GRADUATE STUDIES IN ROME

Pontifical Gregorian University (Associated with the Pontifical Biblical Institute and the Pontifical Oriental Institute. Constituted in 1552. *Address*: Piazza della Pilotta 4, 00187 Rome, Italy. His Eminence Zenon Cardinal Grocholewski, Grand Chancellor; Very Rev. Pachó Adolfo Nicolás, S.J. Vice Chancellor; Very Rev. François-Xavier Dumortier, S.J., Rector; Very Rev. José Abrego de Lacy, S.J., Rector of the Biblical Institute; Very Rev. James M. McCann, S.J., Rector of the Oriental Institute.

Pontifical Lateran University Founded in 1824. *Address*: Piazza S. Giovanni in Laterano 4, 00184 Rome, Italy. His Eminence Agostino Cardinal Vallini, Grand Chancellor; Most Rev. Bishop Enrico dal Covolo Rector.

Pontifical Urban University Founded in 1627. *Address*: Via Urbano VIII 16, 00165 Rome, Italy. His Eminence Ivan Cardinal Dias, Grand Chancellor; Rev. Cataldo Zuccaro, Rector.

Pontifical University of St. Thomas Aquinas Founded in 1580. *Address*: Largo Angelicum 1, 00184 Rome, Italy. Very Rev. Bruno Cadore, O.P., Master General of the Order of Preachers and Grand Chancellor; Very Rev. Charles Morerod, O.P., Rector.

Pontifical Salesian University Founded in 1940. *Address*: Piazza Ateneo Salesiano 1, 00139 Rome, Italy. Very Rev. Pascual Chávez Villanueva, Grand Chancellor; Very Rev. Carlo Nanni, Rector.

Faculty of Christian and Classical Humanities Very Rev. Pascual Chávez Villanueva, Rector; Very Rev. Mario Maritano, S.D.B., Dean.

Pontifical University of the Holy Cross Founded in 1984. *Address:* Piazza di S. Apollinare, 49, 00186 Rome, Italy. Most Rev. Bishop Javier Echevarría, Prelate of Opus Dei and Grand Chancellor; Rev. Prof. Luis Romero, Rector.

Pontifical Antonianum University Founded in 1933. *Address*: Via Merulana 124, 00185 Rome, Italy. Very Rev. José Rodriguez Carballo, O.F.M., Minister General of the Order of Friars Minor and Grand Chancellor; Very Rev. Johannes Baptist Freyer, O.F.M., Rector.

Pontifical Atheneum of St. Anselm Founded in 1687. *Address*: Piazza Cavalieri di Malta 5, 00153 Rome, Italy. Very Rev. Wolf D. Notker, O.S.B., Abbot Primate of the Benedictine Confederation and Grand Chancellor; Very Rev. Juan Javier Flores Arcas, O.S.B., Rector.

Pontifical Athenaeum Regina Apostolorum Founded in 1993. *Address*: Via Degli Aldobrandeschi, 190, 00163 Rome, Italy. Very Rev. Alvaro Corcuera, L.C., Grand Chancellor; Very Rev. Pedro Barrajon, L.C., Rector.

Pontifical Institute of Sacred Music Founded in 1911. *Address*: Via di Torre Rossa 21, 00165, Rome, Italy. His Eminence Zenon Cardinal Grocholewski, Grand Chancellor; Rev. Msgr. Valentin Miserachs Grau, President.

Pontifical Institute of Christian Archeology Founded in 1925. *Address*: Via Napoleone III 1, 00185 Rome, Italy. His Eminence Zenon Cardinal Grocholewski, Grand Chancellor; Prof. Nicolai Fiocchi, Rector.

Pontifical Theological Faculty St. Bonaventure Erected in 1935. *Address:* Via del Serafico 1, 0014[illegible] Rome, Italy. Very Rev. Marco Tasca, O.F.M.Conv. Grand Chancellor and Minister General of the Orde[r] of Friars Minor Conventual; Rev. Domenico Paoletti O.F.M.Conv., President.

Pontifical Theological Faculty Teresianum Founde[d] in 1935. *Address*: Piazza S. Pancrazio 5-A, 00152 Rome Italy. Very Rev. Saverio Cannistra del Sacro Cuore O.C.D., Grand Chancellor; Very Rev. Aniano Alvarez Suarez, President.

Pontifical Theological Faculty Marianum Founde[d] in 1666. *Address:* Viale Trenta Aprile 6, 00153 Rome Italy. Very Rev. Angel M. Ruiz Garnica, Prior Genera[l] of the Order of Servants of Mary and Grand Chancel[-]lor; Very Rev. Silvano M. Maggiani, O.S.M., Presi[-]dent.

Pontifical Institute for Arabic and Islamic Stud[-]ies Founded in 1926. *Address:* Viale di Trastevere 9[illegible] 00153 Rome, Italy. His Eminence Zenon Cardina[l] Grocholewski, Grand Chancellor; Rev. Prof. Richar[d] Baawobr, Superior General of the Missionaries [of] Africa and Vice Grand-Chancellor; Rev. Prof. Migue[l] Angel Ayuso Gvixot, M.C.C.J., President.

Pontifical Faculty of Educational Science[s] Auxilium Founded in 1970. *Address:* Via Cremolin[o] 141, 00166 Rome, Italy. Very Rev. Pascual Cháve[z] Villanueva, Grand Chancellor; Mother Yvonn[e] Reungoat, Superior General of the Daughters of Mar[y] Help of Christians and Vice-Grand Chancellor; Siste[r] Giuseppina Del Core, President.

SEMINARIES AND NATIONAL COLLEGES IN ROME

Pontifical Roman Major Seminary Founded in 1565 by Pius IV. Address: Piazza S. Giovanni in Laterano 4, 00184 Rome, Italy. Rev. Msgr. Giovanni Tani, Rector.

Pontifical Roman Minor Seminary Address: Viale Vaticano 42, 00165 Rome, Italy. Rev. Msgr. Paolo Selvadagi, Rector.

North American College (Pontifical) Corporate Title: The American College of the Roman Catholic Church of the United States. A Maryland Corporation. Founded in 1859 by Pope Pius IX. Postal Address: 00120 Vatican City State, Europe. Rev. Msgr. James F. Checchio, Rector. (See AMERICAN CO[L]LEGES ABROAD for further details.)

Armenian College (Pontifical) Founded on March 1883. Address: Salita S. Nicola da Tolentino 17, 001[8] Rome, Italy. Rev. Joseph Antoine Kélékian, Recto[r].

Beda College (Pontifical) Founded in 1852. Address: Viale San Paolo 18, 00146 Rome, Italy. Rev. Charles R. Strange, Rector.

Belgian College (Pontifical) Founded in 1844. Rev. Address: Via G.B. Pagano 35, 00167 Rome, Italy.

Canadian College (Pontifical) Founded in 1888. Address: Via Crescenzio 75, 00193 Rome, Italy. Rev. Charles Langlois, P.S.S., Rector.

Capranica College (Almo) Founded in 1457 by Cardinal Capranica. Address: Piazza Capranica 98, 00186 Rome, Italy. Rev. Msgr. Ermenegildo Manicardi, Rector.

Ethiopian College (Pontifical) Founded on October 1, 1919 and February 12, 1930. Address: 00120 Citta del Vaticano, Europe. Rev. P. Keflemariam Bernhanemeskel, C.M., Rector.

French Seminary (Pontifical) Founded on October 10, 1853. Address: Via di S. Chiara 42, 00186 Rome, Italy. Rev. Yves-Marie Fradet, C.S.Sp., Rector.

German-Hungarian College (Pontifical) Founded on August 31, 1552. Address: Via S. Nicola da Tolentino 13, 00187 Rome, Italy. Rev. P. Franz Meures, S.J., Rector.

Greek College (Pontifical) Founded on January 13, 1577. Address: Via del Babuino 149, 00187 Rome, Italy. Very Rev. Manuel Nin, O.S.B., Rector.

English College (Venerabile) Founded on May 1, 1579. Address: Via Monserrato 45, 00186 Rome, Italy. Rev. Msgr. Nicholas Hudson, Rector.

Irish College (Pontifical) Founded in 1628. Address: Via dei Ss. Quattro 1, 00184 Rome, Italy. Rev. Msgr. Liam Bergin, Rector.

Lithuanian College (Pontifical) Founded on May 1, 1948. Address: Via Casalmonferrato 20, 00182 Rome, Italy. Rev. Msgr. Petras Siurys, Rector.

Maronite College Founded on June 17, 1584. Address: Via Porta Pinciana 18, 00187 Rome, Italy. Rev. Hanna G. Alwan, O.M.M., Rector.

Nepomucene College (Pontifical) Address: Via Concordia 1, 00183 Rome, Italy. Rev. Msgr. Jan Mráz, Rector.

Philippine College (Pontifical) Founded on June 29, 1961. Address: Via Aurelia 490, 00165 Rome, Italy. Rev. Msgr. Ruperto C. Santos, Rector.

Dutch College (Pontifical) Founded on October 26, 1930. Address: Via Ercole Rosa 1, 00153 Rome, Italy.

Brazilian College (Pio Brasiliano) (Pontifical) Founded in 1934 by Pius XI. Address: Via Aurelia 527, 00165 Rome, Italy. Very Rev. Joao Roque Rohr. S.J., Rector.

Latin American College (Pio Latino Americano) (Pontifical) Founded November 21, 1858. Address: Via Aurelia Antica 408, 00165 Rome, Italy. Rev. José A. González Prado, S.J., Rector.

Polish College (Pontifical) Founded in 1582-84. Address: Piazza Remuria 2-A, 00153 Rome, Italy. Rev. Msgr. Tadeusz Karkosz, Rector.

Portuguese College (Pontifical) Founded on October 28, 1900. Address: Via Nicolo V 3, 00165 Rome, Italy. Rev. José Manuel Garcia Cordeiro, Rector.

Russian College of S. Theresa of the Child Jesus (Pontifical) Founded on August 15, 1929. Address: Via Carlo Cattaneo 2/A, 00185 Rome, Italy. Rev. Alojz Cvikl, S.J., Rector.

Ukrainian College of Saint Josephat (Pontifical) Founded on December 18, 1897. Address: Passeggiata del Gianicolo 7, 00165 Rome, Italy. Rev. Genésio Viomar, O.S.B.M., Rector.

College of St. Jerome of the Croatians (Pontifical) Founded on August 1, 1901. Address: Via Tomacelli 132, 00186 Rome, Italy. Rev. Msgr. Jure Bogdan.

St. Thomas Aquinas Founded in 1948. Address: Via degli Ibernesi 20, 00184 Rome, Italy. Very Rev. Luke Douglas Buckles, O.P., Rector.

Scots College (Pontifical) Founded on December 5, 1600. Address: Via Cassia 481, 00189 Rome, Italy. Rev. Paul G. Milarvie, Rector.

Spanish College of St. Joseph (Pontifical) Founded on April 1, 1892. Address: Via Di Torre Rossa 2, 00165 Rome, Italy. Very Rev. Mariano Herrera Fraile, Rector.

Teutonic College of St. Mary of the Soul (Pontifical Institute) Founded in 1406. Address: Via della Pace 20, 00186 Rome, Italy. Rev. Msgr. Franz Xaver Brandmayr, Rector.

Teutonic College (S. Maria in Camposanto), for the study of Sacred Archaeology and Ecclesiastical History Founded on November 21, 1876. Address: Via della Sagrestia 17, 00120 Citta del Vaticano, Europe. Rev. Msgr. Erwin Gatz, Rector.

Polish Ecclesiastical Institute (Pontifical) Founded in 1910. Address: Via Pietro Cavallini, 38, 00193 Rome, Italy. Rev. Msgr. Boguslaw Kosmider, Rector.

American Church Santa Susanna Address: Via Venti Settembre 15, Postal Address: Via Antonio Salandra 6, 00187 Rome, Italy. Tel: 011 39 6 488.2748; Fax: 011 39 6 474.0236. Very Rev. Paul G. Robichaud, C.S.P., Rector; Rev. Gregory Apparcel, C.S.P., Vice Rector; Rev. Dennis W. Hickey, C.S.P., Vice Rector.

AMERICAN COLLEGES ABROAD

North American College, Rome, Italy *(Pontifical)* Corporate Title: The American College of the Roman Catholic Church of the United States. A Maryland Corporation. Operates under the auspices of a special committee of the United States Conference of Catholic Bishops. President: His Eminence Cardinal Francis George. Founded in 1859 by Pope Pius IX, to bring American seminarians and student priests into close association with the Holy See. Seminarians live and take their priestly formation at the College, while studying at the theological universities in Rome. Three major departments: Seminary, Graduate and Institute for Continuing Theological Education.

Postal Address: North American College, 00120 Vatican City State, Europe. Tel: (011 39 06) 68 49 31; Administration Fax: (011 39 06) 686 7561; Business office Fax: (011 39 06) 686 4095; Email: pnac@pnac.org; Website: www.pnac.org.

Administration: Rev. Msgr. James F. Checchio, Rector; Lory Mondaini, Secretary, Office of the Rector; Rev. Msgr. Daniel H. Mueggenborg, Vice Rector for Administration and Director of Admissions; Raffaella Granellini, Secretary, Office of the Vice Rector for Administration; Sr. Susan Hooks, O.S.B., Asst. to Vice Rector for Admin. and Comptroller; Ms. Mary DiDonato, Executive Director, Institutional Advancement, Washington, D.C.

Seminary: Rev. Msgr. Robert D. Gruss, Vice Rector for Seminary Life, Director of Human Formation; Elena Panti, Secretary, Office of the Vice Rector and Office of Admissions; Maria Soggiu, Secretary, Office of the Vice Rector; Laura Panarese, Visa Coordinator; Rev. Joseph V. Betschart, Academic Dean; Rev. Jeffrey Burrill, Director of Apostolic Formation; Rev. James Quigley, O.P., Director of Homiletics; Rev. David G. Songy, O.F.M.Cap., Director of Counseling Services; Rev. Kurt Belsole, O.S.B., Director of Liturgical Formation; Rev. John J. Costello, Director of Pastoral Formation; Dr. Gianfranco De Luca, Director of Liturgical Music, Seminary Choir Director; Rev. Joseph G. Hanefeldt, Director of Spiritual Formation, Spiritual Director; Rev. Brendan G. Lally, S.J., Spiritual Director; Rev. Brendan Hurley, S.J., Spiritual Director; Rev. Msgr. William J. Lyons, Spiritual Director; Rev. Michael Hickin, Spiritual Director; Rev. Gregory J. Fairbanks, Adjunct Spiritual Director; Rev. Thomas W. Powers, Adjunct Spiritual Director; Rev. Msgr. Anthony Frontiero, Adjunct Spiritual Director; Rev. Msgr. Anthony Figueiredo, Adjunct Spiritual Director; Sr. Rebecca Abel, O.S.B., Librarian.

Institute for Continuing Theological Education, Fall & Spring 12-week sabbatical sessions for priests. Rev. Michael Wensing, Director of ICTE, Adjunct Formation Director, romeshabat@pnac.org; Carol Salfa, Secretary, Institute for Continuing Theological Education.

Graduate Department: Casa Santa Maria, Residence of North American College for post-graduate priests.Graduate priests 72 from 42 US Dioceses and from several other English speaking countries. *Postal Address*: Via dell'Umiltà 30, 00187 Rome, Italy. Fax: (011 39 06) 6900 1823. Rev. Msgr. Francis Kelly, Superior, fkelly@pnac.org.

Bishops' Office for United States Visitors to the Vatican, *Postal Address*: Via dell'Umiltà 30, 00187 Rome, Italy. Tel: (011 39 06) 6900 1821; Fax: (011 39 06) 679 1448; Email: visitorsoffice@pnac.org; Website: www.pnac.org/general/visiting_vatican.htm. Request for attendance at Papal audiences and similar functions may be addressed to this office. Rev. Msgr. Roger C. Roensch, Dir.

Office for Development of the North American College, *Postal Address*: 3211 Fourth St., N.E., Washington, DC 20017-1194. Tel: 202-541-5403; Fax: 202-722-8804. E-mail: mdodinato@usccb.org. Ms. Mary DiDonato, Executive Director.

The Apostolic Nunciature

Established As Apostolic Delegation January 24, 1893; Established as Apostolic Nunciature January 10, 1984.
Address: 3339 Massachusetts Ave., N.W., Washington, DC 20008. Tel: 202-333-7121. Fax: 202-337-4036.

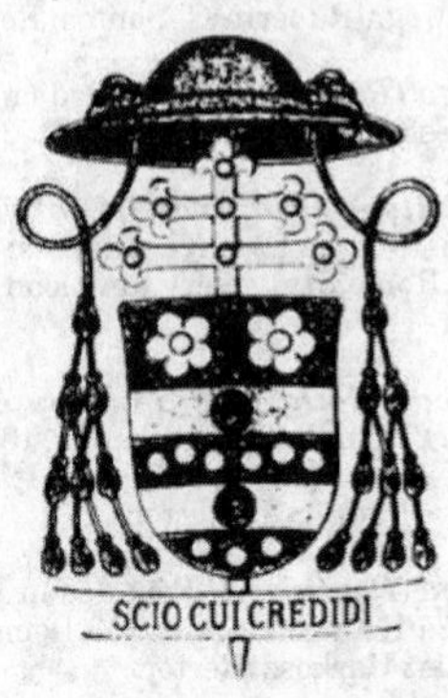

APOSTOLIC NUNCIO TO THE UNITED STATES

His Excellency
Archbishop Carlo Maria Vigano
Titular Archbishop of Ulpiana

Archbishop Carlo Maria Viganò was born on January 16, 1941 in Varese, Italy. He was ordained a priest on March 24, 1968 and incardinated in the Diocese of Pavia (Italy). He has a Doctorate in both Canon and Civil Law *(Utroque Iure).*His Excellency started his service in the Diplomatic Corps of the Holy See as *Attaché* in 1973 in Iraq and Kuwait. In 1976 he was transferred to the Apostolic Nunciature in Great Britain. From 1978 until 1989 he worked at the Secretariat of State of Vatican City. On April 4, 1989 he was nominated *Special Envoy* with the functions of *Permanent Observer* to the European Council in Strasbourg. He was elected Archbishop on April 3, 1992. On April 26, 1992 he was consecrated and made Titular Archbishop of Ulpiana. He was nominated Pro-Apostolic Nuncio in Nigeria, on April 3, 1992. On April 4, 1998 he was nominated Delegate for the Pontifical Representations. Archbishop Viganò served as Secretary General of the Governorate of the Vatican City State from July 16, 2009 until September 3, 2011. On October 19, 2011 Pope Benedict XVI appointed him Apostolic Nuncio to the United States.

Rev. Msgr. Jean-Francois Lantheaume, J.C.D., *First Counselor*; Rev. Msgr. Angelo Accattino, J.C.D., *Second Counselor*; Rev. Msgr. Fermín Emilio Sosa Rodríguez, J.C.D., *Second Counselor*.

Rev. Msgr. John H. Maksymowicz, S.T.L., *Secretary*; Rev. Msgr. Joseph W. Pokusa, M.A., J.C.D., *Secretary*; Rev. Msgr. Richard E. Marchese, S.T.L., Ph.D., *Secretary*; Rev. Msgr. Gregory W. Gordon, S.T.L., *Secretary*; Rev. Michael McCormack, O.P., S.T.L., *Secretary;* Brother Joseph J. Britt, C.F.X., *Archivist*.

Former Apostolic Delegates:

His Eminence Francesco Cardinal Satolli	1893-1896
His Eminence Sebastiano Cardinal Martinelli	1896-1902
His Eminence Diomede Cardinal Falconio	1902-1911
His Eminence Giovanni Cardinal Bonzano	1911-1922
His Eminence Pietro Cardinal Fumasoni-Biondi	1922-1933
His Eminence Amleto G. Cardinal Cicognani	1933-1958
His Eminence Egidio Cardinal Vagnozzi	1958-1967
His Eminence Luigi Cardinal Raimondi	1967-1973
His Excellency Most Reverend Jean Jadot	1973-1980
His Eminence Pio Cardinal Laghi	1980-1984

Apostolic Pro-Nuncios:

His Eminence Pio Cardinal Laghi	1984-1990
His Eminence Agostino Cardinal Cacciavillan	1990-1998

Apostolic Nuncios:

His Excellency Most Reverend Gabriel Montalvo	1998-2006
His Excellency Most Reverend Pietro Sambi	2006-2011
His Excellency Most Reverend Carlo Maria Vigano	2011-

The Permanent Observer Mission of the Holy See to the United Nations

Established January 26, 1964

Office Address: 25 E. 39th St., New York, NY 10016. Tel.: 212-370-7885; Fax: 212-370-9622.
E-mail: office@holyseemission.org. Website: www.holyseemission.org.

PERMANENT OBSERVER OF THE HOLY SEE TO THE UNITED NATIONS

His Excellency
The Most Reverend

FRANCIS A. CHULLIKATT
Titular Archbishop of Ostra
Apostolic Nuncio

Born in Bolghatty, India, on 20 March 1953. Ordained a priest for the Diocese of Verapoly in 3 June 1978.
Completed a doctorate in Canon Law and entered the diplomatic service of the Holy See in 1988.
Served at the Apostolic Nunciatures in Honduras, various countries of southern Africa, and the Philippines, at the Mission to the United Nations in New York and at the Secretariat of State in the Vatican.
Appointed Apostolic Nuncio to Iraq and Jordan on 29 April 2006. Ordained Titular Archbishop of Ostra on 25 June 2006.
Appointed Permanent Observer of the Holy See to the United Nations in New York on 17 July 2010.
Office Address: 25 E. 39th St., New York, NY 10016. Tel: 212-370-7885; Fax: 212-370-9622.

Rev. Mauro Cionini, *Second Secretary*; Rev. Christopher Pollard, *Attaché*; Rev. Philip J. Bené, *Attaché;* Rev. Justin Wylie, *Attaché*.

Former Permanent Observers:

Rev. Msgr. Alberto Giovannetti	1964-1973
His Eminence Giovanni Cardinal Cheli	1973-1986
His Eminence Renato Cardinal Martino	1986-2002
His Excellency Archbishop Celestino Migliore	2002-2010

The United States Embassy to the Holy See

Established United States Embassy to the Holy See January 10, 1984.

Address: Via Delle Terme Deciane, 26 00153 Rome, Italy. Tel: 011-39-06-4674-3428; Fax: 011-39-06-575-8346.
APO Address: U.S. Embassy to the Holy See, PSC 59, Box 66, APO AE 09624.

UNITED STATES AMBASSADOR TO THE HOLY SEE

Your Excellency The Honorable

DR. MIGUEL HUMBERTO DÍAZ

Ambassador Díaz, the first Hispanic to represent the United States at the Vatican earned his bachelor's degree from Saint Thomas University in Miami Gardens, FL and his master's and doctorate from the University of Notre Dame in Indiana. Prior to his appointment, Ambassador Díaz was a professor of theology at the College of Saint Benedict in St. Joseph, MN and St. John's University in Collegeville, MN. He has also taught at Barry University in Miami Shores, FL, Saint Vincent de Paul Regional Seminary in Boyton Beach, FL, the University of Dayton in Ohio and at Notre Dame. Ambassador Díaz is a board member of the Catholic Theological Society of America and former president of the Academy of Catholic Theologians of the United States. He is the author of the book "On Being Human: U.S. Hispanic and Rahnerian Perspectives" which earned him the Hispanic Theological Initiative's 2002 Book of the Year award from Princeton Theological Seminary. He is also co-editor of the book, "From the Heart of Our People" Latino Explorations in Catholic Systematic Theology."

Former Ambassadors to the Holy See:

The Honorable William A. Wilson 1984-1986
The Honorable Frank Shakespeare 1986-1989
The Honorable Thomas Patrick Melady 1989-1993
The Honorable Raymond Flynn 1993-1997
The Honorable Corinne Claiborne Boggs 1997-2001
The Honorable James Nicholson 2001-2005
The Honorable Francis Rooney 2005-2008
The Honorable Mary Ann Glendon 2008-2009

The Catholic Church in the United States

The organizational structure of the Catholic Church in the United States consists of 33 Provinces with as many Archdioceses (Metropolitan Sees); 149 Suffragan Sees (Dioceses); The Military Archdiocese; four Eastern-Rite jurisdictions immediately subject to the Holy See in Rome. The Eparchies of St. Maron (Maronites), Newton (Melkites), St. Thomas the Apostle of Detroit (Chaldeans) and St. George Martyr of Canton, Ohio (Romanians), St. Thomas of Chicago of the Syro-Malabarians. Each of these jurisdictions is under the direction of an Archbishop and Bishop called an Ordinary, who has apostolic responsibility and authority for the pastoral service of the people in his care.

The structure includes the territorial episcopal conference known as the United States Conference of Catholic Bishops. In and through this body, which is strictly ecclesiastical and has defined juridical authority, the Bishops exercise their collegiate pastorate over the Church in the entire country.

Related to the USCCB is the civil corporation and operational secretariat through which the Bishops, in cooperation with other members of the Church, act on a wider-than-ecclesiastical scale for the good of the Church and society in the United States.

The following is a list of the thirteen regions in the United States and provinces within those regions.

Region I: Includes the states of Maine, Vermont, New Hampshire, Massachusetts, Rhode Island, and Connecticut. Provinces of Boston and Hartford; Eparchy of Stamford and Eparchy for Melkites.

Region II: Includes the state of New York. Province of New York and Eparchy of St. Maron; Syro-Malankara Catholic Exarchate in USA.

Region III: Includes the states of New Jersey and Pennsylvania. Provinces of Newark and Philadelphia; Archeparchy of Philadelphia, Ukrainian Archeparchy of Pittsburgh, Byzantine Eparchy of Passaic, and Eparchy of Our Lady of Nareg for Armenian Catholics.

Region IV: Includes the states of Delaware, District of Columbia, Maryland, Virgin Islands, Virginia and West Virginia. Provinces of Baltimore, Washington, and the Military Archdiocese.

Region V: Includes the states of Alabama, Kentucky, Louisiana, Mississippi and Tennessee. Provinces of Louisville, Mobile and New Orleans.

Region VI: Includes the states of Michigan and Ohio. Provinces of Cincinnati, Detroit; Eparchy of Parma, Apostolic Exarchate for Chaldeans, and Apostolic Exarchate for Romanians.

Region VII: Includes the states of Illinois, Indiana and Wisconsin. Provinces of Chicago, Indianapolis, Milwaukee; Eparchy of St. Nicholas in Chicago-Ukrainian.

Region VIII: Includes the states of Minnesota, North Dakota and South Dakota. Provinces of St. Paul and Minneapolis.

Region IX: Includes the states of Kansas, Missouri and Nebraska. Provinces of Dubuque, Kansas City in Kansas, Omaha and St. Louis.

Region X: Includes the states of Arkansas, Oklahoma and Texas (excluding El Paso). Provinces of Galveston-Houston, Oklahoma City and San Antonio.

Region XI: Includes the states of California, Hawaii and Nevada. Provinces of Los Angeles and San Francisco (excluding Salt Lake City); Holy Protection of Mary Byzantine Catholic Eparchy of Phoenix.

Region XII: Includes the states of Alaska, Idaho, Montana, Oregon and Washington. Provinces of Anchorage, Portland and Seattle.

Region XIII: Includes the states of Utah, Arizona, New Mexico, Colorado and Wyoming. Provinces of Denver, Santa Fe, part of San Francisco, Salt Lake City, and El Paso.

Region XIV: Includes the states of Georgia, North and South Carolina and Florida. Provinces of Atlanta and Miami.

Please refer to individual Diocesan and Archdiocesan listing for complete and detailed information. The following list does not include the retired Archbishops or retired Bishops.

PROVINCE OF ANCHORAGE

Includes the State of Alaska.

Archdiocese of Anchorage, AK—Most. Rev. Roger L. Schwietz, O.M.I., Archbishop of Anchorage.

Diocese of Fairbanks, AK—Most Rev. Donald J. Kettler, Bishop of Fairbanks.

Diocese of Juneau, AK—Most Rev. Edward J. Burns, Bishop of Juneau.

PROVINCE OF ATLANTA

Includes the States of Georgia, North Carolina and South Carolina.

Archdiocese of Atlanta, GA—Most Rev. Wilton D. Gregory, Archbishop of Atlanta. Most Rev. Luis R. Zarama, Auxiliary Bishop.

Diocese of Charleston, SC—Most Rev. Robert E. Guglielmone, Bishop of Charleston.

Diocese of Charlotte, NC—Most Rev. Peter J. Jugis, Bishop of Charlotte.

Diocese of Raleigh, NC—Most Rev. Michael F. Burbidge, Bishop of Raleigh.

Diocese of Savannah, GA—Most Rev. Gregory J. Hartmayer, O.F.M.Conv., Bishop of Savannah.

PROVINCE OF BALTIMORE

Includes the States of Maryland (except Montgomery, Prince Charles, St. Mary's, Calvert and Charles Counties), Delaware, Virginia and West Virginia.

Archdiocese of Baltimore, MD—Most Rev. William E. Lori, Archbishop of Baltimore. Most Rev. Mitchell T. Rozanski, Auxiliary Bishop. Most Rev. Denis J. Madden, Auxiliary Bishop.

Diocese of Arlington, VA—Most Rev. Paul S. Loverde, Bishop of Arlington.

Diocese of Richmond, VA—Most Rev. Francis X. DiLorenzo, Bishop of Richmond.

Diocese of Wheeling-Charleston, WV—Most Rev. Michael J. Bransfield, Bishop of Wheeling-Charleston.

Diocese of Wilmington, DE—Most Rev. W. Francis Malooly, Bishop of Wilmington.

PROVINCE OF BOSTON

Includes the States of Maine, New Hampshire, Vermont and Massachusetts.

Archdiocese of Boston, MA—His Eminence Sean Patrick Cardinal O'Malley, O.F.M.Cap., Archbishop of Boston. Most Rev. Walter J. Edyvean, Auxiliary Bishop. Most Rev. Arthur L. Kennedy, Auxiliary Bishop. Most Rev. John A. Dooher, Auxiliary Bishop. Most Rev. Robert F. Hennessey, Auxiliary Bishop. Most Rev. Peter J. Uglietto, Auxiliary Bishop.

Diocese of Burlington, VT—Most Rev. Salvatore R. Matano, Bishop of Burlington.

Diocese of Fall River, MA—Most Rev. George W. Coleman, Bishop of Fall River.

Diocese of Manchester, NH—Most Rev. Peter A. Libasci, Bishop of Manchester. Most Rev. Francis J. Christian, Auxiliary Bishop.

Diocese of Portland, ME—Most Rev. Richard J. Malone, Bishop of Portland.

Diocese of Springfield, MA—Most Rev. Timothy A. McDonnell, Bishop of Springfield in Massachusetts.

Diocese of Worcester, MA—Most Rev. Robert J. McManus, Bishop of Worcester.

PROVINCE OF CHICAGO

Includes the State of Illinois.

Archdiocese of Chicago, IL—His Eminence Francis Cardinal George, O.M.I., Archbishop of Chicago. Most Rev. John R. Manz, Auxiliary Bishop. Most Rev. Joseph N. Perry, Auxiliary Bishop. Most Rev. Francis J. Kane, Auxiliary Bishop. Most Rev. George J. Rassas, Auxiliary Bishop. Most Rev. Alberto Rojas, Auxiliary Bishop. Most Rev. Andrew P. Wypych, Auxiliary Bishop.

Diocese of Belleville, IL—Most Rev. Edward K. Braxton, Bishop of Belleville.

Diocese of Joliet, IL—Most Rev. R. Daniel Conlon, Bishop of Joliet. Most Rev. Joseph M. Siegel Auxiliary Bishop.

Diocese of Peoria, IL— Most Rev. Daniel R. Jenky, C.S.C., Bishop of Peoria.

Diocese of Rockford, IL—Most Rev. David J. Malloy, Bishop of Rockford.

Diocese of Springfield, IL—Most Rev. Thomas J. Paprocki, Bishop of Springfield.

PROVINCE OF CINCINNATI

Includes the State of Ohio.

Archdiocese of Cincinnati, OH—Most Rev. Dennis M. Schnurr, Archbishop of Cincinnati. Most Rev. Joseph R. Binzer, Auxiliary Bishop.

Diocese of Cleveland, OH—Most Rev. Richard Gerard Lennon, Bishop of Cleveland. Most Rev. Roger W. Gries, O.S.B., Auxiliary Bishop.

Diocese of Columbus, OH—Most Rev. Frederick F. Campbell, Bishop of Columbus.

Diocese of Steubenville, OH—Vacant See.

Diocese of Toledo, OH—Most Rev. Leonard P. Blair, Bishop of Toledo.

Diocese of Youngstown, OH—Most Rev. George V. Murry, S.J., Bishop of Youngstown.

PROVINCE OF DENVER

Includes the States of Colorado and Wyoming.

Archdiocese of Denver, CO—Vacant See. Most Rev. James D. Conley, Apostolic Administrator.

Diocese of Cheyenne, WY—Most Rev. Paul D. Etienne, Bishop of Cheyenne.

Diocese of Colorado Springs, CO—Most Rev. Michael J. Sheridan, Bishop of Colorado Springs.

Diocese of Pueblo, CO—Most Rev. Fernando Isern, Bishop of Pueblo.

PROVINCE OF DETROIT

Includes the State of Michigan.

Archdiocese of Detroit, MI—Most Rev. Allen H. Vigneron, Archbishop of Detroit. Most Rev. Francis R. Reiss, Auxiliary Bishop. Most Rev. Donald F. Hanchon, Auxiliary Bishop. Most Rev. Michael Byrnes, Auxiliary Bishop. Most Rev. Jose Arturo Cepeda Escobedo, Auxiliary Bishop.

Diocese of Gaylord, MI—Most Rev. Bernard A. Hebda, Bishop of Gaylord.

Diocese of Grand Rapids, MI—Most Rev. Walter A. Hurley, Bishop of Grand Rapids.

Diocese of Kalamazoo, MI—Most Rev. Paul J. Bradley, Bishop of Kalamazoo.

Diocese of Lansing, MI—Most Rev. Earl A. Boyea, Bishop of Lansing.

Diocese of Marquette, MI—Most Rev. Alexander K. Sample, Bishop of Marquette.

Diocese of Saginaw, MI—Most Rev. Joseph R. Cistone, Bishop of Saginaw.

PROVINCE OF DUBUQUE

Includes the State of Iowa.

Archdiocese of Dubuque, IA—Most Rev. Jerome Hanus, O.S.B., Archbishop of Dubuque.

Diocese of Davenport, IA—Most Rev. Martin J. Amos, Bishop of Davenport.

Diocese of Des Moines, IA—Most Rev. Richard E. Pates, Bishop of Des Moines.

Diocese of Sioux City, IA—Most Rev. R. Walker Nickless, Bishop of Sioux City.

PROVINCE OF GALVESTON-HOUSTON

Includes the State of Texas except Atascosa, Bandera, Bexar, Comal, Edwards, Frio, Gillespie, Gonzales, Guadalupe, Karnes, Kendall, Kerr, Kinney, McMullen, Medina, Real, Uvalde, Val Verde and Wilson Counties.

Archdiocese of Galveston-Houston, TX—His Eminence Daniel Cardinal DiNardo, Archbishop of Galveston-Houston. Most Rev. George A. Sheltz, Auxiliary Bishop.

Diocese of Austin, TX— Most Rev. Joe S. Vasquez, Bishop of Austin.

Diocese of Beaumont, TX—Most Rev. Curtis John Guillory, S.V.D., Bishop of Beaumont.

Diocese of Brownsville, TX—Most Rev. Daniel E. Flores, Bishop of Brownsville.

Diocese of Corpus Christi, TX—Most Rev. William M. Mulvey, Bishop of Corpus Christi.

Diocese of Tyler, TX—Vacant See.

Diocese of Victoria, TX—Most Rev. David E. Fellhauer, Bishop of Victoria in Texas.

PROVINCE OF HARTFORD

Includes the States of Connecticut and Rhode Island.

Archdiocese of Hartford, CT—Most Rev. Henry J. Mansell, Archbishop of Hartford. Most Rev. Christie A. Macaluso, Auxiliary Bishop.

Diocese of Bridgeport, CT—Vacant See.

Diocese of Norwich, CT—Most Rev. Michael R. Cote, Bishop of Norwich.

Diocese of Providence, RI—Most Rev. Thomas J. Tobin, Bishop of Providence. Most Rev. Robert C. Evans, Auxiliary Bishop.

PROVINCE OF INDIANAPOLIS

Includes the State of Indiana.

Archdiocese of Indianapolis, IN—Vacant See. Most Rev. Christopher J. Coyne, Apostolic Administrator.

Diocese of Evansville, IN—Most Rev. Charles C. Thompson, Bishop of Evansville.

Diocese of Fort Wayne-South Bend, IN—Most Rev. Kevin C. Rhoades, Bishop of Fort Wayne-South Bend.

Diocese of Gary, IN—Most Rev. Dale J. Melczek, Bishop of Gary.

Diocese of Lafayette in Indiana, IN—Most Rev. Timothy Doherty, Bishop of Lafayette in Indiana.

PROVINCE OF KANSAS CITY, KANSAS

Includes the State of Kansas.

Archdiocese of Kansas City, KS—Most Rev. Joseph F. Naumann, Archbishop of Kansas City.

Diocese of Dodge City, KS—Most Rev. John B. Brungardt, Bishop of Dodge City.

Diocese of Salina, KS—Most Rev. Edward J. Weisenburger, Bishop of Salina.

Diocese of Wichita, KS—Most Rev. Michael Owen Jackels, Bishop of Wichita.

PROVINCE OF LOS ANGELES

Includes Southern California and Central California.

Archdiocese of Los Angeles, CA—Most Rev. Jose H. Gomez, Archbishop of Los Angeles. Most Rev. Thomas J. Curry, Auxiliary Bishop. Most Rev. Gerald E. Wilkerson, Auxiliary Bishop. Most Rev. Edward W. Clark, Auxiliary Bishop. Most Rev. Oscar Azarcon Solis, Auxiliary Bishop. Most Rev. Alexander Salazar, Auxiliary Bishop.

Diocese of Fresno, CA—Most Rev. Armando Xavier Ochoa, Bishop of Fresno.

Diocese of Monterey, CA—Most Rev. Richard J. Garcia, Bishop of Monterey.

Diocese of Orange, CA—Most Rev. Tod David Brown, Bishop of Orange in California. Most Rev. Dominic Mai Luong, Auxiliary Bishop.

Diocese of San Bernardino, CA—Most Rev. Gerald R. Barnes, Bishop of San Bernardino. Most Rev. Rutilio del Riego, Auxiliary Bishop.

Diocese of San Diego, CA—Most Rev. Robert H. Brom, Bishop of San Diego. Most Rev. Cirilo Flores, Coadjutor Bishop.

PROVINCE OF LOUISVILLE

Includes the States of Kentucky and Tennessee.

Archdiocese of Louisville, KY—Most Rev. Joseph E. Kurtz, Archbishop of Louisville.

Diocese of Covington, KY—Most Rev. Roger J. Foys, Bishop of Covington.

Diocese of Knoxville, TN—Most Rev. Richard F. Stika, Bishop of Knoxville.

Diocese of Lexington, KY—Most Rev. Ronald W. Gainer, Bishop of Lexington.

Diocese of Memphis, TN—Most Rev. J. Terry Steib, S.V.D., Bishop of Memphis.

Diocese of Nashville, TN—Most Rev. David R. Choby, Bishop of Nashville.

Diocese of Owensboro, KY—William F. Medley, Bishop of Owensboro.

PROVINCE OF MIAMI

Includes the State of Florida.

Archdiocese of Miami, FL—Most Rev. Thomas G. Wenski, Archbishop of Miami.

Diocese of Orlando, FL—Most Rev. John G. Noonan, Bishop of Orlando.

Diocese of Palm Beach, FL—Most Rev. Gerald M. Barbarito, Bishop of Palm Beach.

Diocese of Pensacola-Tallahassee, FL—Most. Rev. Gregory L. Parkes, Bishop of Pensacola-Tallahassee.

Diocese of St. Augustine, FL—Most Rev. Felipe de Jesus Estevez, Bishop of St. Augustine.

Diocese of St. Petersburg, FL—Most Rev. Robert N. Lynch, Bishop of St. Petersburg.

Diocese of Venice, FL—Most Rev. Frank J. Dewane, Bishop of Venice.

PROVINCE OF MILWAUKEE

Includes the State of Wisconsin.

Archdiocese of Milwaukee, WI—Most Rev. Jerome E. Listecki, Archbishop of Milwaukee. Most Rev. Donald J. Hying, Auxiliary Bishop.

Diocese of Green Bay, WI—Most Rev. David L. Ricken, Bishop of Green Bay. Most Rev. Robert F. Morneau, Auxiliary Bishop.

Diocese of La Crosse, WI—Most Rev. William P. Callahan, Bishop of La Crosse.

Diocese of Madison, WI—Most Rev. Robert C. Morlino, Bishop of Madison.

Diocese of Superior, WI—Most Rev. Peter F. Christensen, Bishop of Superior.

PROVINCE OF MOBILE

Includes the states of Alabama and Mississippi.

Archdiocese of Mobile, AL—Most Rev. Thomas J. Rodi, Archbishop of Mobile.

Diocese of Biloxi, MS—Most Rev. Roger P. Morin, Bishop of Biloxi.

Diocese of Birmingham, AL—Most Rev. Robert J. Baker, Bishop of Birmingham.

Diocese of Jackson, MS—Most Rev. Joseph N. Latino, Bishop of Jackson.

PROVINCE OF NEWARK

Includes the State of New Jersey.

Archdiocese of Newark, NJ—Most Rev. John J. Myers, Archbishop of Newark. Most Rev. Edgar M. da Cunha, S.D.V., Auxiliary Bishop. Most Rev. Thomas A. Donato, Auxiliary Bishop. Most Rev. John W. Flesey, Auxiliary Bishop. Most Rev. Manuel A. Cruz, Auxiliary Bishop.

Diocese of Camden, NJ—Most Rev. Joseph A. Galante, Bishop of Camden.

Diocese of Metuchen, NJ—Most Rev. Paul G. Bootkoski, Bishop of Metuchen.

Diocese of Paterson, NJ—Most Rev. Arthur J. Serratelli, Bishop of Paterson.

Diocese of Trenton, NJ—Most Rev. David M. O'Connell, Bishop of Trenton.

PROVINCE OF NEW ORLEANS

Includes the State of Louisiana.

Archdiocese of New Orleans, LA—Most Rev. Gregory M. Aymond, Archbishop of New Orleans. Most Rev. Shelton J. Fabre, Auxiliary Bishop.

Diocese of Alexandria, LA—Most Rev. Ronald P. Herzog, Bishop of Alexandria.

Diocese of Baton Rouge, LA—Most Rev. Robert William Muench, Bishop of Baton Rouge.

Diocese of Houma-Thibodaux, LA—Most Rev. Sam G. Jacobs, Bishop of Houma-Thibodaux.

Diocese of Lafayette, LA—Most Rev. Michael C. Jarrell, Bishop of Lafayette.

Diocese of Lake Charles, LA—Most Rev. Glen J. Provost, Bishop of Lake Charles.

Diocese of Shreveport, LA —Most Rev. Michael G. Duca, Bishop of Shreveport.

PROVINCE OF NEW YORK

Includes the State of New York.

Archdiocese of New York, NY—His Eminence Timothy Cardinal Dolan, Archbishop of New York. Most Rev. Josu Iriondo, Auxiliary Bishop. Most Rev. Dominick J. Lagonegro, Auxiliary Bishop. Most Rev. Dennis J. Sullivan, Auxiliary Bishop. Most Rev. Gerald T. Walsh, Auxiliary Bishop.

Diocese of Albany, NY—Most Rev. Howard J. Hubbard, Bishop of Albany.

Diocese of Brooklyn, NY—Most Rev. Nicholas A. DiMarzio, Bishop of Brooklyn. Most Rev. Frank J. Caggiano, Auxiliary Bishop. Most Rev. Octavio Cisneros, Auxiliary Bishop.

Diocese of Buffalo, NY—Most Rev. Edward U. Kmiec, Bishop of Buffalo. Most Rev. Edward M. Grosz, Auxiliary Bishop.

Diocese of Ogdensburg, NY—Most Rev. Terry R. LaValley, Bishop of Ogdensburg.

Diocese of Rochester, NY—Most Rev. Matthew H. Clark, Bishop of Rochester.

Diocese of Rockville Centre, NY—Most Rev. William Francis Murphy, Bishop of Rockville Centre. Most Rev. John C. Dunne, Auxiliary Bishop. Most Rev. Paul H. Walsh, Auxiliary Bishop.

Diocese of Syracuse, NY—Most Rev. Robert J. Cunningham, Bishop of Syracuse.

PROVINCE OF OKLAHOMA CITY

Includes States of Arkansas and Oklahoma.

Archdiocese of Oklahoma City, OK—Most Rev. Paul S. Coakley, Archbishop of Oklahoma City.

Diocese of Little Rock, AR—Most Rev. Anthony Basil Taylor, Bishop of Little Rock.

Diocese of Tulsa, OK—Most Rev. Edward J. Slattery, Bishop of Tulsa.

PROVINCE OF OMAHA

Includes the State of Nebraska.

Archdiocese of Omaha, NE—Most Rev. George J. Lucas, Archbishop of Omaha.

Diocese of Grand Island, NE—Most Rev. William J. Dendinger, Bishop of Grand Island.

Diocese of Lincoln, NE—Most Rev. Fabian W. Bruskewitz, Bishop of Lincoln.

PROVINCE OF PHILADELPHIA

Includes the State of Pennsylvania.

Archdiocese of Philadelphia, PA—Most Rev. Charles J. Chaput, Archbishop of Philadelphia. Most Rev. John J. McIntyre, Auxiliary Bishop. Most Rev. Michael J. Fitzgerald, Auxiliary Bishop. Most Rev. Daniel E. Thomas, Auxiliary Bishop. Most Rev. Timothy Senior, Auxiliary Bishop.

Diocese of Allentown, PA—Most Rev. John O. Barres, Bishop of Allentown.

Diocese of Altoona-Johnstown, PA—Most Rev. Mark L. Bartchak, Bishop of Altoona-Johnstown.

Diocese of Erie, PA—Most Rev. Donald W. Trautman, Bishop of Erie.

Diocese of Greensburg, PA—Most Rev. Lawrence E. Brandt, Bishop of Greensburg.

Diocese of Harrisburg, PA—Most Rev. Joseph P. McFadden, Bishop of Harrisburg.

Diocese of Pittsburgh, PA—Most Rev. David A. Zubik, Bishop of Pittsburgh. Most Rev. William J. Waltersheid, Auxiliary Bishop.

Diocese of Scranton, PA—Most Rev. Joseph C. Bambera, Bishop of Scranton.

PROVINCE OF PORTLAND IN OREGON

Includes the States of Oregon, Idaho and Montana.

Archdiocese of Portland, OR—Most Rev. John G.

Vlazny, Archbishop of Portland in Oregon.
Diocese of Baker, OR—Most Rev. Liam S. Cary, Bishop of Baker.
Diocese of Boise, ID—Most Rev. Michael P. Driscoll, Bishop of Boise.
Diocese of Great Falls-Billings, MT—Most Rev. Michael W. Warfel, Bishop of Great Falls-Billings.
Diocese of Helena, MT— Most Rev. George Leo Thomas, Bishop of Helena.

PROVINCE OF ST. LOUIS

Includes the State of Missouri.
Archdiocese of St. Louis, MO—Most Rev. Robert J. Carlson, Archbishop of St. Louis. Most Rev. Edward M. Rice, Auxiliary Bishop.
Diocese of Jefferson City, MO—Most Rev. John Raymond Gaydos, Bishop of Jefferson City.
Diocese of Kansas City-St. Joseph, MO—Most Rev. Robert W. Finn, Bishop of Kansas City-St. Joseph.
Diocese of Springfield-Cape Girardeau, MO—Most Rev. James V. Johnston, Jr., Bishop of Springfield-Cape Girardeau.

PROVINCE OF ST. PAUL AND MINNEAPOLIS

Includes the States of Minnesota, South Dakota and North Dakota.
Archdiocese of St. Paul and Minneapolis, MN—Most Rev. John C. Nienstedt, Archbishop of St. Paul and Minneapolis. Most Rev. Lee A. Piche, Auxiliary Bishop.
Diocese of Bismarck, ND—Most Rev. David D. Kagan, Bishop of Bismarck.
Diocese of Crookston, MN—Most Rev. Michael J. Hoeppner, Bishop of Crookston.
Diocese of Duluth, MN—Most Rev. Paul D. Sirba, Bishop of Duluth.
Diocese of Fargo, ND—Most Rev. Samuel J. Aquila, Bishop of Fargo.
Diocese of New Ulm, MN—Most Rev. John M. LeVoir, Bishop of New Ulm.
Diocese of Rapid City, SD—Most Rev. Robert D. Gruss, Bishop of Rapid City.
Diocese of St. Cloud, MN—Most Rev. John F. Kinney, Bishop of St. Cloud.
Diocese of Sioux Falls, SD—Most Rev. Paul J. Swain, Bishop of Sioux Falls.
Diocese of Winona, MN—Most Rev. John M. Quinn, Bishop of Winona.

PROVINCE OF SAN ANTONIO

Includes the State of Texas except Walker, San Jacinto, Galveston, Grimes, Montgomery, Waller, Harris, Fort Bend, Brazoria and Austin Counties.
Archdiocese of San Antonio, TX—Most Rev. Gustavo Garcia-Siller, M.SP.S., Archbishop of San Antonio. Most Rev. Oscar Cantu, Auxiliary Bishop.
Diocese of Amarillo, TX—Most Rev. Patrick J. Zurek, Bishop of Amarillo.
Diocese of Dallas, TX—Most Rev. Kevin J. Farrell, Bishop of Dallas. Most Rev. John D. Deshotel, Auxiliary Bishop. Most Rev. Mark J. Seitz, Auxiliary Bishop.
Diocese of El Paso, TX—Vacant See.
Diocese of Fort Worth, TX—Most Rev. Kevin W. Vann, Bishop of Fort Worth.
Diocese of Laredo, TX—Most Rev. James A. Tamayo, Bishop of Laredo.
Diocese of Lubbock, TX—Most Rev. Placido Rodriguez, C.M.F., Bishop of Lubbock.
Diocese of San Angelo, TX—Most Rev. Michael D. Pfeifer, O.M.I., Bishop of San Angelo.

PROVINCE OF SAN FRANCISCO

Includes Northern California and the States of Nevada, Utah and Hawaii.
Archdiocese of San Francisco, CA—Most Rev. George H. Niederauer, Archbishop of San Francisco. Most Rev. William J. Justice, Auxiliary Bishop. Most Rev. Robert W. McElroy, Auxiliary Bishop.
Diocese of Honolulu, HI—Most Rev. Clarence R. Silva, Bishop of Honolulu.
Diocese of Las Vegas, NV—Most Rev. Joseph A. Pepe, Bishop of Las Vegas.
Diocese of Oakland, CA—Most Rev. Salvatore J. Cordileone, Bishop of Oakland.
Diocese of Reno, NV—Most Rev. Randolph R. Calvo, Bishop of Reno.
Diocese of Sacramento, CA—Most Rev. Jaime Soto, Bishop of Sacramento.
Diocese of Salt Lake City, UT—Most Rev. John C. Wester, Bishop of Salt Lake City.
Diocese of San Jose, CA—Most Rev. Patrick J. McGrath, Bishop of San Jose in California. Most Rev. Thomas A. Daly, Auxiliary Bishop.
Diocese of Santa Rosa, CA— Most Rev. Robert F. Vasa, Bishop of Santa Rosa in California.
Diocese of Stockton, CA—Most Rev. Stephen E. Blaire, Bishop of Stockton.

PROVINCE OF SANTA FE

Includes the States of New Mexico and Arizona.
Archdiocese of Santa Fe, NM—Most Rev. Michael J. Sheehan, Archbishop of Santa Fe.
Diocese of Gallup, NM—Most Rev. James S. Wall, Bishop of Gallup.
Diocese of Las Cruces, NM—Most Rev. Ricardo Ramirez, C.S.B., Bishop of Las Cruces.
Diocese of Phoenix, AZ—Most Rev. Thomas J. Olmsted, Bishop of Phoenix. Most Rev. Eduardo A. Nevares, Auxiliary Bishop.
Diocese of Tucson, AZ—Most Rev. Gerald F. Kicanas, Bishop of Tucson.

PROVINCE OF SEATTLE

Includes the State of Washington.
Archdiocese of Seattle, WA—Most Rev. James P. Sartain, Archbishop of Seattle. Most Rev. Eusebio L. Elizondo, M.Sp.S., Auxiliary Bishop.
Diocese of Spokane, WA—Most Rev. Blasé J. Cupich, Bishop of Spokane.
Diocese of Yakima, WA—Most Rev. Joseph J. Tyson, Bishop of Yakima.

PROVINCE OF WASHINGTON

Includes the District of Columbia, and Montgomery, Prince Georges, Charles, Calvert and St. Mary's Counties in Maryland, also Virgin Islands.
Archdiocese of Washington, DC—His Eminence Donald Cardinal Wuerl, Archbishop of Washington. Most Rev. Martin D. Holley, Auxiliary Bishop. Most Rev. Francisco Gonzalez, S.F., Auxiliary Bishop. Most Rev. Barry C. Knestout, Auxiliary Bishop.
Diocese of St. Thomas, V.I.—Most Rev. Herbert A. Bevard, Bishop of St. Thomas in the Virgin Islands.

MILITARY

Archdiocese for the Military Services—Most Rev. Timothy P. Broglio, Archbishop for the Military Services. Most Rev. Richard B. Higgins, Auxiliary Bishop. Most Rev. F. Richard Spencer, Auxiliary Bishop. Most Rev. Neal J. Buckon, Auxiliary Bishop.

EASTERN CATHOLIC JURISDICTIONS

ANTIOCHENE TRADITION

Maronite Rite—
Eparchy of St. Maron of Brooklyn—Most Rev. Gregory J. Mansour, Bishop of St. Maron.
Eparchy of Our Lady of Lebanon of Los Angeles—Most Rev. Robert J. Shaheen, Bishop of Our Lady of Lebanon of Los Angeles.

Syrian Rite—
Diocese of Our Lady of Deliverance—Most Rev. Yousif Habash, Bishop of Our Lady of Deliverance.

ARMENIAN TRADITION

Armenian Catholic Eparchy of Our Lady of Nareg in the United States of America and Canada—Most Rev. Mikael A. Mouradian, Armenian Catholic Eparch of Our Lady of Nareg.

CHALDEAN TRADITION

Eparchy of St. Thomas the Apostle—Most Rev. Ibrahim N. Ibrahim, Eparch of St. Thomas the Apostle.
Eparchy of St. Peter the Apostle—Most Rev. Sarhad Y. Jammo, Eparch of St. Peter the Apostle.

CONSTANTINOPOLITAN TRADITION

Melkite - Greek Rite—
Eparchy of Newton—Most Rev. Nicholas J. Samra, Eparch of Newton.

Romanian Rite—
Romanian Catholic Diocese of St. George's in Canton—Most Rev. John Michael Botean, Bishop for the Romanian Catholic Diocese of Canton.

Ruthenian Rite—
Metropolitan Archbishop for Pittsburgh Byzantine—Most Rev. William C. Skurla, Archbishop for Pittsburgh, Byzantine.
Byzantine Eparchy of Parma—Most Rev. John M. Kudrick, Bishop of Parma.
Byzantine Catholic Eparchy of Passaic—Vacant See.
Holy Protection of Mary Byzantine Catholic Eparchy of Phoenix—Most Rev. Gerald N. Dino, Bishop of Holy Protection of Mary Byzantine.
Russian Rite—
Two parishes—

Ukrainian Rite—
Metropolitan Archdiocese of Philadelphia Ukrainian—Most Rev. Stefan Soroka, Archbishop of Philadelphia Ukrainian. Most Rev. John Bura, Auxiliary Bishop.
Ukrainian Catholic Diocese of St. Josaphat in Parma—Vacant See. Most Rev. John Bura, Apostolic Administrator.
Diocese of St. Nicholas in Chicago for Ukrainians—Most Rev. Richard S. Seminack, Bishop of St. Nicholas of Chicago.
Ukrainian Catholic Diocese of Stamford—Most Rev. Paul Patrick Chomnycky, O.S.B.M., Bishop of Stamford.

Syro-Malabar—
St. Thomas Syro-Malabar Catholic Diocese of Chicago—Most Rev. Jacob Angadiath, Bishop of St. Thomas Syro-Malabar.

Syro-Malankara—
Syro-Malankara Catholic Exarchate in USA—Most Rev. Thomas Mar Eusebius Naickamparambil, Bishop of Syro-Malankara.

ECCLESIASTICAL FORMS OF ADDRESS RECOGNIZED IN THE UNITED STATES

These are the formal forms of address used in correspondence:

CARDINALS:

Address on envelope: His Eminence (Christian name) Cardinal (Surname)

Salutation: Your Eminence:

Concluding a letter: I have the honor to be, Your Eminence, *etc.*

ARCHBISHOPS:

Address on envelope: Most Reverend N_______ N_______

Salutation: Your Excellency:

Concluding a letter: I have the honor to be, Your Excellency, *etc.*

BISHOPS:

Address on envelope: Most Reverend N_______ N_______

Salutation: Your Excellency:

Concluding a letter: I have the honor to be, Your Excellency, *etc.*

ABBOTS:

Address on envelope: Right Reverend N_______ N_______ *(add religious order initials)*

Salutation: Right Reverend Abbot:

Concluding a letter: I have the honor to be, Right Reverend Abbot, *etc.*

PROTONOTARIES APOSTOLIC:

Address on envelope: Rev. Msgr. N_______ N_______

Salutation: Rev. Msgr.:

Concluding a letter: I am, Rev. Msgr., *etc.*

PRELATE OF HONOR OF HIS HOLINESS:

Address on envelope: Rev. Msgr. N_______ N_______

Salutation: Rev. Msgr.:

Concluding a letter: I am, Rev. Msgr., *etc.*

CHAPLAIN TO HIS HOLINESS:

Address on envelope: Rev. Msgr. N_______ N_______

Salutation: Rev. Msgr.:

Concluding a letter: I am, Rev. Msgr., *etc.*

SECULAR PRIESTS:

Address on envelope: Rev. N_______ N_______

Salutation: Dear Reverend Father:

Concluding a letter: I am, Reverend Father, *etc.*

RELIGIOUS ORDER PRIESTS:

Address on envelope: Rev. N_______ N_______ *(add religious order initials)*

Salutation: Dear Reverend Father:

Concluding a letter: I am, Reverend Father, *etc.*

DEACONS:

Address on envelope: Deacon N_______

Salutation: Dear Deacon N_______

Concluding a letter: I am, Respectfully yours, *etc.*

BROTHERS:

Address on envelope: Brother N_______

Salutation: Dear Brother N_______

Concluding a letter: I am, Respectfully yours, *etc.*

SISTERS:

Address on envelope: Sister N_______

Salutation: Dear Sister N_______

Concluding a letter: I am, Respectfully yours, *etc.*

AN ALPHABETICAL LIST OF THE

Cardinals, Archbishops, Bishops, Archabbots & Abbots of the United States

CARDINALS

His Eminence William W. Baum, Major Penitentiary emeritus, Via Rusticucci 13, 00193 Rome, Italy.
His Eminence Daniel N. DiNardo, Archbishop of Galveston-Houston, 1700 San Jacinto St., Houston, TX 77002.
His Eminence Timothy M. Dolan, Archbishop of New York, 1011 First Ave., New York, NY 10022.
His Eminence Edward M. Egan, Archbishop emeritus of New York, 1011 First Ave., New York, NY 10022.
His Eminence Francis E. George, o.m.i., Archbishop of Chicago, 835 N. Rush St., Chicago, IL 60611-2030.
His Eminence William H. Keeler, Archbishop emeritus of Baltimore, 320 Cathedral St., Baltimore, MD 21201.
His Eminence Bernard F. Law, Archbishop emeritus of Boston, Archpriest of the Patriarchal Liberian Basilica of St. Mary Major, Patriarcale Basilica Liberiana di Santa Maria Maggiore, 00120 Vatican City.
His Eminence, William J. Levada, Prefect, Congregation for the Doctrine of the Faith, Palazzo del S. Uffizio, 00120 Vatican City State.
His Eminence Roger M. Mahony, Archbishop emeritus of Los Angeles, 10834 Moorpark St., North Hollywood, CA 91602-2206.
His Eminence Adam J. Maida, Archbishop emeritus of Detroit, 1234 Washington Blvd., Detroit, MI 48226.
His Eminence Theodore E. McCarrick, Archbishop emeritus of Washington, DC, P.O. Box 29260, Washington, DC 20017.
His Eminence Edwin F. O'Brien, Grand Master of Equestrian Order of the Holy Sepulchre of Jerusalem, 00120 Vatican City.
His Eminence Sean P. O'Malley, o.f.m.cap., Archbishop of Boston, 66 Brooks Dr., Braintree, MA 02184-3839.
His Eminence Justin F. Rigali, Archbishop emeritus of Philadelphia, P.O. Box 11886, Knoxville, TN 37939.
His Eminence J. Francis Stafford, Major Penitentiary emeritus, Piazza S. Calisto 16, Vatican City State, Europe 00120.
His Eminence Edmund C. Szoka, President emeritus Pontifical Commission, Vatican City State, Europe. 00120.
His Eminence Donald W. Wuerl, Archbishop of Washington, 5001 Eastern Ave., Hyattsville, MD 20782-3447.

ARCHBISHOPS

His Excellency,
The Most Reverend

Apuron, Anthony Sablan, o.f.m.cap., Archbishop of Agana, 196-B Cuesta San Ramon, Agana, Guam 96910.
Aymond, Gregory M., Archbishop of New Orleans, 7887 Walmsley Ave., New Orleans, LA 70125.
Beltran, Eusebius J., Archbishop emeritus of Oklahoma City, P.O. Box 32180, Oklahoma City, OK 73123.
Broglio, Timothy P., Archbishop for the Military Services, 1025 Michigan Ave., N.E., P.O. Box 4469, Washington, DC 20017-0469.
Brunett, Alexander J., Archbishop emeritus of Seattle, 710 9th Ave., Seattle, WA 98104.
Buechlein, Daniel M., o.s.b., Archbishop emeritus of Indianapolis, 1400 N. Meridian St. Indianapolis, IN 46206.
Carlson, Robert J., Archbishop of St. Louis, 20 Archbishop May Dr., St. Louis, MO 63119-5738.
Chaput, Charles J., o.f.m. cap., Archbishop of Philadelphia, 222 N. 17th St., Philadelphia, PA 19103-1299.
Coakley, Paul S., Archbishop of Oklahoma City, 7501 Northwest Expwy., Oklahoma City, OK 73132.
Cronin, Daniel A., Archbishop emeritus of Hartford, 469 Bloomfield Ave., Bloomfield, CT 06002.
Curtiss, Elden F., Archbishop emeritus of Omaha, 100 N. 62nd St., Omaha, NE 68132-2795.
Dimino, Joseph T., Archbishop emeritus for the Military Services, P.O. Box 4469, Washington, DC 20017.
Favalora, John C., Archbishop emeritus of Miami, 9401 Biscayne Blvd., Miami Shores, FL 33138.
Fiorenza, Joseph A., Archbishop emeritus of Galveston-Houston, 1700 San Jacinto, Houston, TX 77002.
Flores, Patrick F., Archbishop emeritus of San Antonio, P.O. Box 28410, San Antonio, TX 78228.
Flynn, Harry J., Archbishop emeritus of St. Paul and Minneapolis, 226 Summit Ave., St. Paul, MN 55102.
Garcia-Siller, Gustavo, m.sp.s., Archbishop of San Antonio, P.O. Box 28410, San Antonio, TX 78228-0410.
Gerety, Peter Leo, Archbishop emeritus of Newark, 60 Home Ave., Rutherford, NJ 07070.
Gomez, Jose H., Archbishop of Los Angeles, 3424 Wilshire Blvd., Los Angeles, CA 90010.
Gonzalez, Roberto O., o.f.m., Archbishop of San Juan, P.O. Box 9021967, San Juan, PR 00902-1967.
Gregory, Wilton D., Archbishop of Atlanta, 2401 Lake Park Dr,. Smyrna, GA 30080-8862.
Hanus, Jerome G., o.s.b., Archbishop of Dubuque, 1229 Mt. Loretto Ave., P.O. Box 479, Dubuque, IA 52004-0479.
Hughes, Alfred C., Archbishop emeritus of New Orleans, 7887 Walmsley Ave., New Orleans, LA 70125.
Hunthausen, Raymond G., Archbishop emeritus of Seattle, 710 9th Ave., Seattle, WA 98104.

His Excellency,
The Most Reverend

Hurley, Francis T., Archbishop emeritus of Anchorage, 225 Cordova St., Anchorage, AK 99501.
Keleher, James P., Archbishop emeritus of Kansas City in Kansas, 12615 Parallel Pkwy., Kansas City, KS 66109.
Kucera, Daniel W., o.s.b., Archbishop emeritus of Dubuque, Villa Raphael, 1155 Mt. Loretta Ave., Dubuque, IA 52003.
Kurtz, Joseph E., Archbishop of Louisville, 212 E. College St., P.O. Box 1073, Louisville, KY 40201.
Lipscomb, Oscar H., Archbishop emeritus of Mobile, 400 Government St., Mobile, AL 36602.
Listecki, Jerome E., Archbishop of Milwaukee, 3501 S. Lake Dr., P.O. Box 070912, Milwaukee, WI 53207-0912.
Lori, William E., Archbishop of Baltimore, 320 Cathedral St., Baltimore, MD 21201.
Lucas, George J., Archbishop of Omaha, 100 N. 62nd St., Omaha, NE 68132-2795.
Mansell, Henry J., Archbishop of Hartford, 134 Farmington Ave., Hartford, CT 06105-3784.
Myers, John Joseph, Archbishop of Newark, 171 Clifton Ave., Newark, NJ 07104-9500.
Naumann, Joseph F., Archbishop of Kansas City in Kansas, 12615 Parallel Pkwy., Kansas City, Kansas 66109.
Niederauer, George H., Archbishop of San Francisco, One Peter Yorke Way, San Francisco, CA 94109-6602.
Nienstedt, John C., Archbishop of St. Paul and Minneapolis, 226 Summit Ave., St. Paul, MN 55102.
Pilarczyk, Daniel E., Archbishop emeritus of Cincinnati, 100 E. Eighth St., Cincinnati, OH 45202.
Quinn, John R., Archbishop emeritus of San Francisco, 1100 Woodside Rd., Redwood City, CA 94061.
Rodi, Thomas J., Archbishop of Mobile, 400 Government St., Mobile, AL 36602.
Sartain, James Peter, Archbishop of Seattle, 710 9th Ave., Seattle, WA 98104.
Schnurr, Dennis M., Archbishop of Cincinnati, 100 E. Eighth St., Cincinnati, OH 45202-2129.
Schulte, Francis B., Archbishop emeritus of New Orleans, 320 S. Roberts Rd., Rosemont, PA 19010.
Schwietz, Roger L., o.m.i., Archbishop of Anchorage, 225 Cordova St., Anchorage, AK 99501.
Sheehan, Michael J., Archbishop of Santa Fe, Catholic Center, 4000 St. Joseph's Pl., N.W., Albuquerque, NM 87120.
Skurla, William C., Metropolitan Archbishop of Pittsburgh, Byzantine, 66 Riverview Ave., Pittsburgh, PA 15214.
Soroka, Stefan, Archbishop of the Ukrainian Catholic Archeparchy of Philadelphia, 827 N. Franklin St., Philadelphia, PA 19123.

His Excellency,
The Most Reverend

Sulyk, Stephen, Archbishop emeritus of the Ukrainian Catholic Archeparchy of Philadelphia, 827 N. Franklin St., Philadelphia, PA 19123.
Vigneron, Allen H., Archbishop of Detroit, 1234 Washington Blvd., Detroit, MI 48226.
Vlazny, John G., Archbishop of Portland in Oregon, 2838 E. Burnside St., Portland, OR 97214-1895.
Weakland, Rembert G., o.s.b. Archbishop emeritus of Milwaukee, Wilson Commons, 1400 W. Sonata Dr., #218, Milwaukee, WI 53221.
Wenski, Thomas G., Archbishop of Miami, 9401 Biscayne Blvd., Miami Shores, FL 33138.

BISHOPS

Adamec, Joseph V., Bishop emeritus of Altoona-Johnstown, 504 Holliday Hills Dr., Hollidaysburg, PA 16648.
Allue, Emilio, s.d.b., Retired Auxiliary Bishop of Boston, St. Theresa of Avila Rectory, 10 Saint Theresa Ave., Boston, MA 02132.
Amos, Martin John, Bishop of Davenport, 780 W. Central Park Ave., Davenport, IA 52804-1901.
Anderson, Moses B., s.s.e., Retired Auxiliary Bishop of Detroit, 1234 Washington Blvd., Detroit, MI 48226.
Angadiath, Jacob, Bishop of St. Thomas Syro-Malabar Catholic Diocese of Chicago, 372 S. Prairie Ave., Elmhurst, IL 60126-4020.
Angell, Kenneth A., Bishop emeritus of Burlington, 55 Joy Dr., South Burlington, VT 05403.
Aquila, Samuel J., Bishop of Fargo, 5201 Bishops Blvd., Ste. A, Fargo, ND 58104-7605.
Arias, David, o.a.r., Retired Auxiliary Bishop of Newark, St. Joseph of the Palisades Rectory, 6401 Palisade Ave., West New York, NJ 07093.
Baker, Robert J., Bishop of Birmingham, P.O. Box 12047, Birmingham, AL 35202.
Balke, Victor, Bishop emeritus of Crookston, 1200 Memorial Dr., Crookston, MN 56716.
Baltakis, Paul A., o.f.m., Bishop emeritus for Lithuanian Catholics Outside Lithuania, St. Anthony's Friary, P.O. Box 980, 28 Beach Ave., Kennebunkport, ME 04046.
Bambera, Joseph C., Bishop of Scranton, 300 Wyoming Ave., Scranton, PA 18503.
Banks, Robert J., Bishop emeritus of Green Bay, P.O. Box 23825, Green Bay, WI 54305-3825.
Barbarito, Gerald, Bishop of Palm Beach, 9995 N. Military Tr., Palm Beach Gardens, FL 33410.
Barnes, Gerald R., Bishop of San Bernardino, 1201 E. Highland Ave., San Bernardino, CA 92404.

His Excellency,
The Most Reverend

Barres, John O., Bishop of Allentown, 4029 W. Tilghman St., Allentown, PA 18104.

Bartchak, Mark L., Bishop of Altoona-Johnstown, 927 S. Logan Blvd., Hollidaysburg, PA 16648.

Batakian, Manuel, Eparch emeritus of Our Lady of Nareg, 21 Nassau Ave., Brooklyn NY 11222.

Bevard, Herbert A., Bishop of St. Thomas in the Virgin Islands, P.O. Box 301825, Charlotte Amalie, VI 00803.

Binzer, Joseph R., Auxiliary Bishop of Cincinnati, 100 E. Eighth St., Cincinnati, OH 45202-2129.

Blair, Leonard P., Bishop of Toledo, 1933 Spielbusch Ave., Toledo, OH 43604-5360.

Blaire, Stephen E., Bishop of Stockton, 212 N. San Joaquin St., Stockton, CA 95202.

Boland, J. Kevin, Bishop emeritus of Savannah, 601 E. Liberty St., Savannah, GA 31401.

Boland, Raymond J., Bishop emeritus of Kansas City-St. Joseph, 2552 Gillham Rd., Kansas City, MO 64108.

Boles, John P., Retired Auxiliary Bishop of Boston, 841 E. Broadway, Boston, MA 02127.

Bootkoski, Paul G., Bishop of Metuchen, 10 Library Pl., Metuchen, NJ 08840.

Bosco, Anthony G., Bishop emeritus of Greensburg, 723 E. Pittsburgh St., Greensburg, PA 15601.

Botean, John M., Bishop of the Romanian Catholic Eparchy of St. George's in Canton, 1325 Skyway St., N.E., Canton, OH 44721.

Boyea, Earl A., Bishop of Lansing, 228 N. Walnut St., Lansing, MI 48933.

Bradley, Paul J., Bishop of Kalamazoo, 215 N. Westnedge Ave., Kalamazoo, MI 49007-3760.

Brandt, Lawrence E., Bishop of Greensburg, 723 E. Pittsburgh St., Greensburg, PA 15601.

Bransfield, Michael J., Bishop of Wheeling-Charleston, 1300 Byron St., P.O. Box 230, Wheeling, WV 26003.

Braxton, Edward K., Bishop of Belleville, 222 S. Third St., Belleville, IL 62220-1985.

Brom, Robert H., Bishop of San Diego, P.O. Box 85728, San Diego, CA 92186-5728.

Brown, Tod D., Bishop of Orange, Marywood Center, 2811 E. Villa Real Dr., Orange, CA 92867.

Brucato, Robert A., Retired Auxiliary Bishop of New York, John Cardinal O'Connor Clergy Residence, 5655 Arlington Ave., Bronx, NY 10471.

Brungardt, John B., Bishop of Dodge City, 910 Central Ave., Dodge City, KS 67801.

Bruskewitz, Fabian W., Bishop of Lincoln, P.O. Box 80328, Lincoln, NE 68510-0328.

Buckon, Neal, Auxiliary Bishop for the Military Services, 1025 Michigan Ave., P.O. Box 4469, Washington, DC 20017-0469.

Bura, John, Auxiliary Bishop of Philadelphia for Ukrainians & Apostolic Admin. of St. Josaphat in Parma, 5720 State Rd., P.O. Box 347180, Parma, OH 44134-7180.

Burbidge, Michael F., Bishop of Raleigh, 715 Nazareth St., Raleigh, NC 27606.

Burns, Edward J., Bishop of Juneau, 415 Sixth St., #300, Juneau, AK 99801.

Byrnes, Michael J., Auxiliary Bishop of Detroit, 1234 Washington Blvd., Detroit, MI 48226.

Caggiano, Frank J., Auxiliary Bishop of Brooklyn, 310 Prospect Park W., Brooklyn, NY 11215.

Callahan, William P., o.f.m.conv., Bishop of La Crosse, 3710 East Ave., P.O. Box 4004, La Crosse, WI 54602-4004.

Calvo, Randolph R., Bishop of Reno, 290 S. Arlington Ave., Reno, NV 89501-1713.

Camacho, Tomas A., Bishop emeritus of Chalan Kanoa, Our Lady of Mt. Carmel, P.O. Box 500745 CK, Saipan, MP 96950.

Campbell, Frederick F., Bishop of Columbus, 198 E. Broad St., Columbus, OH 43215.

Cantu, Oscar, Auxiliary Bishop of San Antonio, 2718 W. Woodlawn Ave., P.O. Box 28410, San Antonio, TX 78228-0410.

Carmody, Edmond, Bishop emeritus of Corpus Christi, 620 Lipan St., P.O. Box 2620, Corpus Christi, TX 78403.

Carmon, Dominic, s.v.d., Retired Auxiliary Bishop of New Orleans, 3270 Continental Dr., Kenner LA 70065-2663.

His Excellency,
The Most Reverend

Cary, Liam S., Bishop of Baker, P.O. Box 5999, Bend, OR 97708

Casiano-Vargas, Ulises, Bishop emeritus of Mayaguez, P.O. Box 2272, Mayaguez, PR 00709.

Catanello, Ignatius, Retired Auxiliary Bishop of Brooklyn, 175-20 74th Ave., Flushing, NY 11366.

Cepeda Escobedo, Jose A, Auxiliary Bishop of Detroit, 1234 Washington Blvd., Detroit, MI 48226

Charron, Joseph L., c.pp.s., Bishop emeritus of Des Moines, 601 Grand Ave., Des Moines, IA 50309.

Chavez, Gilbert E., Retired Auxiliary Bishop of San Diego, P.O. Box 85728, San Diego, CA 92186.

Choby, David R., Bishop of Nashville, 2400 - 21st Ave., S., Nashville, TN 37212.

Chomnycky, Paul P., o.s.b.m., Eparch of Stamford Ukrainians, 14 Peveril Rd., Stamford, CT 06902-3019.

Christensen, Peter F., Bishop of Superior, 1201 Hughitt Ave., Box 969, Superior, WI 54880.

Christian, Francis J., Auxiliary Bishop of Manchester, St. Joseph Cathedral, 145 Lowell St., Manchester, NH 03104.

Cisneros, Octavio, Auxiliary Bishop of Brooklyn, Holy Child Jesus, 111-11 86th Ave., Richmond Hill, NY 11418-1613.

Cistone, Joseph R., Bishop of Saginaw, 5800 Weiss St. Saginaw, MI 48603-2762.

Clark, Edward W., Auxiliary Bishop of Los Angeles, Our Lady of the Angels Pastoral Region, 5835 W. Slauson, Culver City, CA, 90230.

Clark, Matthew H., Bishop of Rochester, 1150 Buffalo Rd., Rochester, NY 14624.

Coleman, George W., Bishop of Fall River, 47 Underwood St., Fall River, MA 02720.

Conley, James D., Auxiliary Bishop of Denver, 1300 S. Steele St., Denver, CO 80210.

Conlon, R. Daniel, Bishop of Joliet, 425 Summit St., Joliet, IL 60435.

Connolly, Thomas J., Bishop emeritus of Baker, P.O. Box 5999, Bend, OR 97708.

Cooney, Patrick R., Bishop emeritus of Gaylord, 611 W. North St., Gaylord, MI 49735-8349.

Cordileone, Salvatore J., Bishop of Oakland, 2121 Harrison St., Ste. 100, Oakland, CA 94612.

Corrada del Rio, Alvaro, s.j., Bishop of Mayaguez, P.O. Box 2272, Mayaguez, PR 00681.

Costello, Thomas J., Retired Auxiliary Bishop of Syracuse, 1515 Midland Ave, P.O. Box 511, Syracuse, NY 13205.

Cote, Michael R., Bishop of Norwich, 201 Broadway, Norwich, CT 06360.

Coyne, Christopher J., Apostolic Admin. of Indianapolis, 1400 N. Meridian St., Indianapolis, IN 46206.

Cruz, Manuel A., Auxiliary Bishop of Newark, 171 Clifton Ave., Newark, NJ 07104.

Cserhati, Ferenc, Bishop to Hungarians, Ung.Kath.Delegatur, Landwehrstr.66, D-80336, Munchen, Germany.

Cullen, Edward P., Bishop emeritus of Allentown, P.O. Box F, 4029 W. Tilghman St., Allentown, PA 18105.

Cummins, John S., Bishop emeritus of Oakland, 617 Prospect Ave., Oakland, CA 94610.

Cunningham, Robert Joseph, Bishop of Syracuse, 240 E. Onondaga St., Syracuse, NY 13202.

Cupich, Blasé J., Bishop of Spokane, 1023 Riverside Ave., P.O. Box 1453, Spokane, WA 99210-1453.

Curlin, William G., Bishop emeritus of Charlotte, 3005 Markworth Ave., Charlotte, NC 28210-6432.

Curry, Thomas J., Auxiliary Bishop of Los Angeles, Santa Barbara Pastoral Region, 3240 Calle Pinon, Santa Barbara, CA 93105.

da Cunha, Edgar M., s.d.v., Auxiliary Bishop of Newark, 171 Clifton Ave., Newark, NJ 07104-0500.

Daily, Thomas V., Bishop emeritus of Brooklyn, 7200 Douglaston Pkwy., Douglaston, NY 11362.

Daly, James J., Retired Auxiliary Bishop of Rockville Centre, P.O. Box 9023, Rockville Centre, NY 11571-9023.

Daly, Thomas A., Auxiliary Bishop of San Jose, 1150 N. First St., Ste. 100, San Jose, CA 95112.

D'Arcy, John M., Bishop emeritus of Fort Wayne-South Bend, P.O. Box 390, Fort Wayne, IN 46801.

His Excellency,
The Most Reverend

del Riego, Rutilio J., Auxiliary Bishop of San Bernardino, 1201 E. Highland Ave., San Bernardino, CA 92404.

Dendinger, William J., Bishop of Grand Island, 2708 Old Fair Rd., Grand Island, NE, 68803.

Deshotel, J. Douglas, Auxiliary Bishop of Dallas, 3725 Blackburn, P.O. Box 190507, Dallas, TX 75219.

DeSimone, Louis A., Retired Auxiliary Bishop of Philadelphia, St. Justin Martyr Rectory, 1222 Hagysford Rd., Narberth, PA 19072.

Dewane, Frank J., Bishop of Venice, P.O. Box 2006, Venice, FL 34284-2006.

DiLorenzo, Francis X., Bishop of Richmond, 7800 Carousel Lane, Richmond, VA 23294.

DiMarzio, Nicholas A., Bishop of Brooklyn, 310 Prospect Park W., Brooklyn, NY 11215.

Dino, Gerald N., Bishop of Holy Protection of Mary Byzantine Catholic Eparchy of Phoenix, 8105 N. 16th St., Phoenix, AZ 85020.

Doherty, Timothy L., Bishop of Lafayette in Indiana, P.O. Box 260, Lafayette, IN 47902-0260.

Donato, Thomas A., Auxiliary Bishop of Newark, St. Henry's Parish, 82 W. 29th St., Bayonne, NJ 07002.

Donnelly, Robert W., Retired Auxiliary Bishop of Toledo, 1933 Spielbusch Ave., Toledo, OH 43604-5360.

Dooher, John, Auxiliary Bishop of Boston, 236 Pleasant St., Weymouth, MA 02190.

Doran, Thomas G., Bishop emeritus of Rockford, P.O. Box 7044, Rockford, IL 61125.

Dorsey, Norbert L., c.p., Bishop emeritus of Orlando, 50 E. Robinson St., Orlando, FL 32801.

Doueihi, Stephen Hector, Bishop emeritus of the Maronite Eparchy of St. Maron of Brooklyn, 113 Remsen St., Brooklyn, NY 11201-4212.

Dougherty, John M., Retired Auxiliary Bishop of Scranton, 300 Wyoming Ave., Scranton, PA 18503.

Driscoll, Michael P., Bishop of Boise, 1501 Federal Way, Boise, ID 83705.

Duca, Michael G., Bishop of Shreveport, 3500 Fairfield Ave., Shreveport, LA 71104.

DuMaine, R. Pierre, Bishop emeritus of San Jose, 20 Willow Rd., Unit 43, Menlo Park, CA 94025.

Dunne, John C., Auxiliary Bishop of Rockville Centre, P.O. Box 39, Farmingdale, NY 11735-0039.

Dupre, Thomas L., Bishop emeritus of Springfield in Massachusetts, P.O. Box 1730, Springfield, MA 01101-1730.

Edyvean, Walter J., Auxiliary Bishop of Boston, St. Patrick, 44 E. Central St., Natick, MA 01760.

Elizondo, Eusebio L., Auxiliary Bishop of Seattle, 710 9th Ave., Seattle, WA 98104.

Elya, John A., b.s.o., Eparch emeritus of Newton, 30 East St., Methuen, MA 01844.

Escobedo, Jose Arturo Cepeda, Auxiliary Bishop of Detroit, 1234 Washington Blvd., Detroit, MI 48226.

Estevez, Felipe J., Bishop of St. Augustine, 11625 Old St. Augustine Rd., Jacksonville, FL 32258.

Etienne, Paul D., Bishop of Cheyenne, P.O. Box 1468, Cheyenne, WY 82003-1468.

Evans, Robert C., Auxiliary Bishop of Providence, One Cathedral Sq., Providence, RI 02903-3695.

Fabre, Shelton J., Auxiliary Bishop of New Orleans, 7887 Walmsley Ave., New Orleans, LA 70125-3496.

Farrell, Kevin J., Bishop of Dallas, 3725 Blackburn, P.O. Box 190507, Dallas, TX 75219.

Fellhauer, David E., Bishop of Victoria, P.O. Box 4070, Victoria, TX 77903.

Fernandez Torres, Daniel, Bishop of Arecibo, 206 Dr. Salas St., P.O. Box 616, Arecibo, PR 00613.

Finn, Robert W., Bishop of Kansas City-St. Joseph, P.O. Box 419037, Kansas City, MO 64141.

Fitzgerald, Michael J., Auxiliary Bishop of Philadelphia, 222 N. 17th St.,, Rm. 530, Philadelphia, PA 19103-1299.

Fitzsimons, George K., Bishop emeritus of Salina, P.O. Box 980, Salina, KS 67402-0980.

Flanagan, Thomas J., Retired Auxiliary Bishop of San Antonio, P.O. Box 28410, San Antonio, TX 78228-0410.

Flesey, John W., Auxiliary Bishop of Newark, Most Blessed Sacrament, 787 Franklin Lake Rd., Franklin Lakes, NJ 07417.

Fliss, Raphael M., Bishop emeritus of Superior, 7218 Ogden Ave., P.O. Box 3067, Superior, WI 54880.

His Excellency,
The Most Reverend

Flores, Cirilo, Coadjutor Bishop of San Diego, P.O. Box 85728, San Diego, CA 92186-5728.

Flores, Daniel E., Bishop of Brownsville, 1910 University Blvd., P.O. Box 2279, Brownsville, TX 78522-2279.

Foley, David E., Bishop emeritus of Birmingham, 2121 Third Ave., N., Birmingham, AL 35203.

Foys, Roger J., Bishop of Covington, P.O. Box 15550, Covington, KY 41015-0550.

Franklin, William E., Bishop emeritus of Davenport, 780 W. Central Park Ave., Davenport, IA 52804-1901.

Friend, William B., Bishop emeritus of Shreveport, 3575 Broken Woods Dr. #301, Coral Springs, FL 33065

Gainer, Ronald W., Bishop of Lexington, 1310 W. Main St., Lexington, KY 40508-2048.

Galante, Joseph A., Bishop of Camden, 631 Market St., P.O. Box 708, Camden, NJ 08101.

Galeone, Victor B., Bishop emeritus of St. Augustine, 11625 Old St. Augustine Rd., Jacksonville, FL 32258.

Garcia, Richard J., Bishop of Monterey, 425 Church St., Monterey, CA 93940.

Garland, James H., Bishop emeritus of Marquette, 300 Rock St., Marquette, MI 49855.

Gaydos, John R., Bishop of Jefferson City, P.O. Box 104900, Jefferson City, MO 65110-4900.

Gelineau, Louis E., Bishop emeritus of Providence, St. Antoine Residence, 10 Rhodes Ave., North Smithfield, RI 02896.

Gendron, Odore, Bishop emeritus of Manchester, P.O. Box 310, Manchester, NH 03105-0310.

Gerber, Eugene J., Bishop emeritus of Wichita, 424 N. Broadway, Wichita, KS 67202.

Gerry, Joseph J., o.s.b., Bishop emeritus of Portland in Maine, St. Anselm Abbey, 100 St. Anselm Dr., Manchester, NH 03102-1310.

Gettelfinger, Gerald A., Bishop emeritus of Evansville, 12222 St. Wendel Rd., Evansville, IN 47720.

Gilmore, Ronald M., Bishop emeritus of Dodge City, 910 Central Ave., Box 137, Dodge City, KS 67801.

Goedert, Raymond E., Retired Auxiliary Bishop of Chicago, P.O. Box 1979, Chicago, IL 60690.

Gonzalez, Francisco, s.f., Auxiliary Bishop of Washington, P.O. Box 29260, Washington, DC 20017.

Gonzalez Medina, Ruben Antonio, c.m.f., Bishop of Caguas, P.O. Box 8698, Caguas, PR 00726.

Gorman, John R., Retired Auxiliary Bishop of Chicago, 10731 W. 131st. St., Orland Park, IL 60462.

Gossman, F. Joseph, Bishop emeritus of Raleigh, 2401 Crusader Dr., Raleigh, NC 27606.

Gracida, Rene H., Bishop emeritus of Corpus Christi, 620 Lipan St., P.O. Box 2620, Corpus Christi, TX 78403.

Grahmann, Charles V., Bishop emeritus of Dallas, 3725 Blackburn, P.O. Box 190507, Dallas, TX 75219.

Gries, Roger W., o.s.b., Auxiliary Bishop of Cleveland, 1230 Ansel Rd., Cleveland, OH 44109.

Griffin, James A., Bishop emeritus of Columbus, 198 E. Broad St., Columbus, OH 43215.

Grosz, Edward M., Auxiliary Bishop of Buffalo, Blessed Sacrament Parish, 1035 Delaware Ave., Buffalo, NY 14209-1605.

Gruss, Robert D., Bishop of Rapid City, 606 Cathedral Dr., Rapid City, SD 57701.

Guglielmone, Robert E., Bishop of Charleston, 119 Broad St., P.O. Box 818, Charleston, SC 29402.

Guillory, Curtis J., Bishop of Beaumont, 710 Archie St., P.O. Box 3948, Beaumont, TX 77704-3948.

Gumbleton, Thomas J., Retired Auxiliary Bishop of Detroit, 1234 Washington Blvd., Detroit, MI 48226.

Habash, Yousif, Bishop of Our Lady of Deliverance, 317 Ave. E. Bayonne, NJ 07002-4678.

Hanchon, Donald F., Auxiliary Bishop of Detroit, 1234 Washington Blvd., Detroit, MI 48226.

Hanifen, Richard C., Bishop emeritus of Colorado Springs, 228 N. Cascade Ave., Colorado Springs, CO 80903.

Harrington, Bernard J., Bishop emeritus of Winona, 55 W. Sanborn St., P.O. Box 588, Winona, MN 55987.

Hart, Joseph H., Bishop emeritus of Cheyenne, Box 1468, Cheyenne, WY 82003-1468.

Hartmayer, Gregory J., Bishop of Savannah, 601 E. Liberty St., Savannah, GA 31401-5196.

His Excellency,
The Most Reverend

Hebda, Bernard A., Bishop of Gaylord, 611 W. North St., Gaylord, MI 49735-8349.

Hennessey, Robert F., Auxiliary Bishop of Boston, 841 E. Broadway, Boston, MA 02127-2302.

Hermann, Robert J., Retired Auxiliary Bishop of St. Louis, 20 Archbishop May Dr., St. Louis, MO 63119.

Hernandez Rivera, Enrique M., Bishop emeritus of Caguas, HC 04 Box 44015, Caguas, PR 00727.

Herzog, Ronald P., Bishop of Alexandria, P.O. Box 7417, Alexandria, LA 71306-0417.

Higgins, Richard B., Auxiliary Bishop for the Military Services, P.O. Box 4469, Washington, DC 20017-0469.

Higi, William L., Bishop emeritus of Lafayette in Indiana, 610 Lingle Ave., Lafayette, IN 47902.

Hoeppner, Michael J., Bishop of Crookston, 1200 Memorial Dr., Crookston, MN 56716.

Holley, Martin D., Auxiliary Bishop of Washington, P.O. Box 29260, Washington, DC 20017.

Houck, William R., Bishop emeritus of Jackson, P.O. Box 2248, Jackson, MS 39225-2248.

Howze, Joseph L., Bishop emeritus of Biloxi, P.O. Box 6067, Mobile, AL 36660-0067.

Hubbard, Howard J., Bishop of Albany, 125 Eagle St., Albany, NY 12202.

Hughes, Edward T., Bishop emeritus of Metuchen, 914 Milford-Warren Glen Rd., Milford NJ 08848-1619.

Hughes, William A., Bishop emeritus of Covington, Carmel Manor, 100 Carmel Manor Rd., Ft. Thomas, KY 41075-2395.

Hurley, Walter A., Bishop of Grand Rapids, Cathedral Square Center, 360 Division Ave., S., Grand Rapids, MI 49503-4539.

Hying, Donald J., Auxiliary Bishop of Milwaukee, 3501 S. Lake Dr., Milwaukee, WI 53207.

Ibrahim, Ibrahim, Bishop-Eparch to St. Thomas the Apostle (Chaldean), 25603 Berg Rd., Southfield, MI 48033.

Imesch, Joseph L., Bishop emeritus of Joliet, 425 Summit St., Joliet, IL 60435.

Iriondo, Josu, Auxiliary Bishop of New York, St. Anthony Padua Parish, 832 W. 166th St., Bronx, NY 10459.

Irwin, Francis X., Retired Auxiliary Bishop of Boston, Saint Raphael Parish, 38 Boston Ave., Medford, MA 02155.

Isern, Fernando, Bishop of Pueblo, 101 N. Greenwood, Pueblo, CO 81003.

Jackels, Michael O., Bishop of Wichita, 424 N. Broadway, Wichita, KS 67202.

Jacobs, Sam, Bishop of Houma-Thibodaux, P.O. Box 505, Schriever, LA 70395.

Jakubowski, Thad J., Retired Auxiliary Bishop of Chicago, 6002 W. Berteau Ave., Chicago, IL 60634-1630.

Jammo, Sarhad Y., Bishop of St. Peter the Apostle (Chaldean), 1627 Jamacha Way, El Cajon, CA 92019.

Jarrell, Michael, Bishop of Lafayette, 1408 Carmel Dr., Lafayette, LA 70501.

Jenky, Daniel R., c.s.c., Bishop of Peoria, 419 N.E. Madison Ave., Peoria, IL 61603-3720.

Johnston, Jr., James V., Bishop of Springfield-Cape Girardeau, The Catholic Center, 601 S. Jefferson Ave., Springfield, MO 65806.

Jugis, Peter J., Bishop of Charlotte, 1123 S. Church St., Charlotte, NC 28203.

Justice, William J., Auxiliary Bishop of San Francisco, One Peter Yorke Way, San Francisco, CA 94109-6602.

Kagan, David D., Bishop of Bismarck, 420 Raymond St., P.O. Box 1575, Bismarck, ND 58502-1575.

Kane, Francis, Auxiliary Bishop of Chicago, 1641 W. Diversey, Chicago, IL 60614.

Kennedy, Arthur L., Auxiliary Bishop of Boston, 66 Brooks Dr., Braintree, MA 02184-3839.

Kettler, Donald J., Bishop of Fairbanks, 1316 Peger Rd., Fairbanks, AK 99709.

Kicanas, Gerald F., Bishop of Tucson, P.O. Box 31, Tucson AZ 85702.

Kinney, John F., Bishop of St. Cloud, 214 Third Ave., S., Box 1248, St. Cloud, MN 56302-1248.

Kmiec, Edward U., Bishop of Buffalo, 77 Oakland Pl., Buffalo, NY 14222-1241.

His Excellency,
The Most Reverend

Knestout, Barry C., Auxiliary Bishop of Washington, P.O. Box 29260, Washington, DC 20017.

Kudrick, John M., Bishop of Parma, 1900 Carlton Rd., Parma, OH 44134.

Lagonegro, Dominick J., Auxiliary Bishop of New York, Sacred Heart, 301 Ann St., Newburgh, NY 12550-5467.

Latino, Joseph N., Bishop of Jackson, P.O. 2248, Jackson, MS 39225-2248.

LaValley, Terry R., Bishop of Ogdensburg, P.O. Box 369, Ogdensburg, NY 13669.

Lazaro Martinez, Felix, sch.p., Bishop of Ponce, P.O. Box 32205, Estancion 6, Ponce, PR 00732-2205.

Leibrecht, John J., Bishop emeritus of Springfield-Cape Girardeau, 1152 W. Camino Alto St., Springfield, MO 65810.

Lennon, Richard G., Bishop of Cleveland, 1404 E. Ninth St., Cleveland, OH 44114.

Lessard, Raymond W., Bishop emeritus of Savannah, St. Vincent de Paul Seminary, 10701 S. Military Tr., Boynton Beach, FL 33436-4899.

LeVoir, John M., Bishop of New Ulm, 1400 6th St. N., New Ulm, MN 56073.

Libasci, Peter A., Bishop of Manchester, 153 Ash St., P.O. Box 310, Manchester, NH 03105.

Lohmuller, Martin N., Retired Auxiliary Bishop of Philadelphia, Villa Maria House of Studies, 1410 Almshouse Rd., Jamison, PA 18929.

Losten, Basil, Eparch emeritus of Stamford of the Ukrainians, 122 Clovelly Rd., Stamford, CT 06902-3019.

Lotocky, Innocent, o.s.b.m., Bishop emeritus of St. Nicholas in Chicago, 2245 W. Rice St., Chicago, IL 60622.

Loverde, Paul S., Bishop of Arlington, 200 N. Glebe Rd., Arlington, VA 22203.

Lynch, Robert N., Bishop of St. Petersburg, P.O. Box 40200, St. Petersburg, FL 33743-0200.

Lyne, Timothy J., Retired Auxiliary Bishop of Chicago, Holy Name Cathedral, 730 N. Wabash, Chicago, IL 60611.

Macaluso, Christie A., Auxiliary Bishop of Hartford, 134 Farmington Ave., Hartford, CT 06105-3784.

Madden, Denis J., Auxiliary Bishop of Baltimore, 320 Cathedral St., Baltimore, MD 21201.

Madera, Joseph J., m.sp.s., Retired Auxiliary Bishop for the Military Services, P.O. Box 4469, Washington, DC 20017.

Maginnis, Robert P., Retired Auxiliary Bishop of Philadelphia, St. Edmond Home for Children, 320 S. Roberts Rd., Rosemont, PA 19010.

Maguire, Joseph F., Bishop emeritus of Springfield in Massachusetts, 76 Elliot St., P.O. Box 1730, Springfield, MA 01102-1730.

Mai Luong, Dominic, Auxiliary Bishop of Orange, 2811 E. Villa Real Dr., Orange, CA 92867.

Mallona Txertudi, Inaki, c.p. Bishop emeritus of Arecibo, Hogar Irma Fe Pol, #52 Calle Comercio, Lares, PR 00669.

Malloy, David J., Bishop of Rockford, 555 Colman Ctr. Dr., P.O. Box 7044, Rockford, IL 61125.

Malone, Richard Joseph, Bishop of Portland in Maine, 510 Ocean Ave., Portland, ME 04104-7559.

Malooly, William Francis, Bishop of Wilmington, P.O. Box 2030, Wilmington, DE 19899.

Mansour, Gregory J., Bishop of the Eparchy of St. Maron of Brooklyn, 109 Remsen St., Brooklyn, NY 11201.

Manz, John R., Auxiliary Bishop of Chicago, 1400 S. Austin Blvd., Cicero, IL 60804.

Marconi, Dominic A., Retired Auxiliary Bishop of Newark, 71 Washington Ave., Chatham, NJ 07928.

Martino, Joseph F., Bishop emeritus of Scranton, Regina Coeli Residence for Priests, 685 York Rd., Warminster, PA 18974.

Matano, Salvatore R., Bishop of Burlington, 55 Joy Dr., South Burlington, VT 05403.

McCarthy, James F., Retired Auxiliary Bishop of New York, St. Elizabeth Ann Seton, 1377 N. Main St., Shrub Oak, NY 10588.

McCarthy, John E., Bishop emeritus of Austin, 6225 E. Hwy. 290 E., Austin, TX 78723.

His Excellency,
The Most Reverend

McCormack, John B., Bishop emeritus of Manchester, 153 Ash St., P.O. Box 310, Manchester, NH 03105.
McCormack, William J., Retired Auxiliary Bishop of New York, 142 E. 29th St., New York, NY 10016.
McDonald, Andrew J., Bishop emeritus of Little Rock, St. Joseph's Home, 80 W. Northwest Hwy., Palatine, IL 60067.
McDonnell, Charles J., Retired Auxiliary Bishop of Newark, 34 Maple Ave., Hackensack, NJ 07601.
McDonnell, Timothy A., Bishop of Springfield in Massachusetts, P.O. Box 1730, Springfield, MA 01102-1730.
McElroy, Robert W., Auxiliary Bishop of San Francisco, One Peter Yorke Way, San Francisco, CA 94109-6602.
McFadden, Joseph P., Bishop of Harrisburg, 4800 Union Deposit Rd., Harrisburg, PA 17111-3710.
McGrath, Patrick J., Bishop of San Jose, 1150 N. First St., Ste. 100, San Jose, CA 95112.
McIntyre, John J., Auxiliary Bishop of Philadelphia, 222 N. 17th St., Rm. 830, Philadelphia, PA 19103-1299.
McLaughlin, Bernard J., Retired Auxiliary Bishop of Buffalo, 204 Knoche Rd., Tonawanda, NY 14150.
McManus, Robert J., Bishop of Worcester, 49 Elm St., Worcester, MA 01609.
McRaith, John J., Bishop emeritus of Owensboro, 529 Cedar St., Owensboro, KY 42301.
Medley, William F., Bishop of Owensboro, 600 Locust St., Owensboro, KY 42301.
Melczek, Dale J., Bishop of Gary, 9292 Broadway, Merrillville, IN 46410.
Mengeling, Carl F., Retired Bishop of Lansing, 228 N. Walnut St., Lansing, MI 48933.
Mikloshazy, Attila, s.j., Retired Bishop for Hungarians, St. Augustine's Seminary, 2661 Kingston Rd., Scarborough, Ontario, Canada, M1M 1M3.
Milone, Anthony M., Bishop emeritus of Great Falls-Billings, 7600 S. 42nd St., Bellevue, NE 68147-1702.
Morin, Roger P., Bishop of Biloxi, 1790 Popps Ferry Rd., Biloxi, MS 39532-2118.
Morlino, Robert C., Bishop of Madison, 702 S. High Point Rd., Madison, WI 53744-4983.
Morneau, Robert F., Auxiliary Bishop of Green Bay, 333 Hilltop Dr., Green Bay, WI 54301-2713.
Moskal, Robert M., Bishop emeritus of St. Josaphat in Parma, 5720 State Rd., Parma, OH 44134.
Mouradian, Mikael Antoine, Eparch of Our Lady of Nareg, 21 Nassau Ave., Brooklyn, NY 11222.
Moynihan, James M., Bishop emeritus of Syracuse, 240 E. Onondaga St., Syracuse, NY 13202.
Muench, Robert W., Bishop of Baton Rouge, 1800 S. Acadian Thruway, P.O. Box 2028, Baton Rouge, LA 70821-2028.
Mulvee, Robert E., Bishop emeritus of Providence, 30 Fenner St., Providence, RI 02903.
Mulvey, Wm. Michael., Bishop of Corpus Christi, 620 Lipan St., P.O. Box 2620, Corpus Christi, TX, 78403-2620.
Murphy, William F., Bishop of Rockville Centre, P.O. Box 9023, Rockville Centre, NY 11571-9023.
Murray, James A., Bishop emeritus of Kalamazoo, 215 N. Westnedge Ave., Kalamazoo, MI 49007-3760.
Murry, George V., s.j., Bishop of Youngstown, 144 W. Wood St., Youngstown, OH 44503.
Naickamparambil, Thomas Mar Eusebius, Bishop of Syro-Malankara Catholic Exarchate, 950 Hillside Ave., New Hyde Park, NY 11040.
Nevares, Eduardo A., Auxiliary Bishop of Phoenix, 400 E. Monroe St., Phoenix, AZ 85004-2336.
Nevins, John J., Bishop emeritus of Venice, P.O. Box 2006, Venice, FL 34284-2006.
Newman, William C., Retired Auxiliary Bishop of Baltimore, 5300 N. Charles St., Baltimore, MD 21201.
Nickless, R. Walker, Bishop of Sioux City, 1821 Jackson St., P.O. Box 3379, Sioux City, IA 51102-3379.
Noonan, John G., Bishop of Orlando, 50 E. Robinson St., Orlando, FL 32801.
O'Brien, Thomas J., Bishop emeritus of Phoenix, 400 E. Monroe St., Phoenix, AZ 85004-2336.
O'Connell, Anthony J., Bishop emeritus of Palm Beach, 1098 Mepkin Abbey Rd., Moncks Corner, SC 29461-4796.

His Excellency,
The Most Reverend

O'Connell, David M., c.m., Bishop of Trenton, 701 Lawrenceville Rd., Trenton, NJ 08648.
O'Neill, Arthur J., Bishop emeritus of Rockford, 3330 Maria Linden Dr., Rockford, IL 61114.
Ochoa, Armando, Bishop of Fresno, 1550 N. Fresno St,. Fresno, CA 93703-3788.
Olivier, Leonard J., s.v.d., Retired Auxiliary Bishop of Washington, 619 Tenth St., N.W., Washington, DC 20001-4587.
Olmsted, Thomas J., Bishop of Phoenix, 400 E. Monroe St., Phoenix, AZ 85004-2336.
Ottenweller, Albert H., Bishop emeritus of Steubenville, 2544 Parkwood Ave., Toledo, OH 43610-1317.
Paprocki, Thomas J., Bishop of Springfield in Illinois, 1615 W. Washington St., P.O. Box 3187, Springfield, IL 62708-3187.
Parkes, Gregory L., Bishop of Pensacola-Tallahassee, P.O. Drawer 13284, Pensacola, FL 32591.
Pates, Richard E., Bishop of Des Moines, 601 Grand Ave., Des Moines, IA 50309.
Pena, Raymundo J., Bishop emeritus of Brownsville, 300 N. Nebraska Ave., San Juan, TX 78589.
Pepe, Joseph A., Bishop of Las Vegas, 336 Cathedral Way, Las Vegas, NV 89109.
Perry, Joseph N., Auxiliary Bishop of Chicago, P.O. Box 733, South Holland, IL 60473-0733.
Pevec, A. Edward, Retired Auxiliary Bishop of Cleveland, 28700 Euclid Ave., Wickliffe, OH 44092.
Pfeifer, Michael D., o.m.i., Bishop of San Angelo, P.O. Box 1829, San Angelo, TX 76902.
Piche, Lee A., Auxiliary Bishop of St. Paul and Minneapolis, 226 Summit Ave., St. Paul, MN 55102.
Pilla, Anthony M., Bishop emeritus of Cleveland, 28700 Euclid Ave., Wickliffe, OH 44092.
Popp, Bernard F., Retired Auxiliary Bishop of San Antonio, Padua Place, 80 Peter Baque Rd., San Antonio, TX 78209.
Provost, Glen J., Bishop of Lake Charles, 414 Iris St., P.O. Box 3223, Lake Charles, LA 70602.
Quinn, A. James, Retired Auxiliary Bishop of Cleveland, 2345 Bassett Rd., Westlake, OH 44145.
Quinn, Francis A., Bishop emeritus of Sacramento, 8840 E. 22nd St., Tucson, AZ 85710.
Quinn, John M., Bishop of Winona, 55 W. Sanborn St., P.O. Box 588, Winona, MN 55987.
Ramirez, Ricardo, c.s.b., Bishop of Las Cruces, 1280 Med Park Dr., Las Cruces, NM 88005.
Ramos Morales, Eusebio, Bishop of Fajardo-Humacao, Apartado 888, Fajardo, PR 00738.
Rassas, George J., Auxiliary Bishop of Chicago, 200 N. Milwaukee Ave., Ste. 200, Libertyville, IL 60048-2250.
Reilly, Daniel P., Bishop emeritus of Worcester, St. Paul Cathedral, 38 High St., Worcester, MA 01609.
Reiss, Francis R., Auxiliary Bishop of Detroit, 36800 Schoolcraft Rd., Livonia, MI 48154.
Rhoades, Kevin C., Bishop of Fort Wayne-South Bend, P.O. Box 390, Fort Wayne, IN 46801.
Ricard, John H., s.s.j., Bishop emeritus of Pensacola-Tallahassee, 11 N. B St., Pensacola, FL 32501.
Rice, Edward M., Auxiliary Bishop of St. Louis, 20 Archbishop May Dr., St. Louis, MO 63119-5738.
Ricken, David L., Bishop of Green Bay, 1825 Riverside Dr., Green Bay, WI 54301.
Rivera Perez, Hector M., Retired Auxiliary Bishop of San Juan, P.O. Box 31155, San Juan, PR 00929-2155.
Rizzotto, Vincent M., Retired Auxiliary Bishop of Galveston-Houston, P.O. Box 907, Houston, TX 77001-0907.
Rodimer, Frank J., Bishop emeritus of Paterson, 1082 Greenpond Rd., Newfoundland, NJ 07435.
Rodriguez, Placido, c.m.f., Bishop of Lubbock, P.O. Box 98700, Lubbock, TX 79499-8700.
Rojas, Alberto, Auxiliary Bishop of Chicago, 1850 S. Throop St., Chicago, IL 60608.
Roque, Francis X., Retired Auxiliary Bishop for the Military Services, P.O. Box 4469, Washington, DC 20017.
Rosazza, Peter A., Retired Auxiliary Bishop of Hartford, 467 Bloomfield Ave., Bloomfield, CT 06002-2999.

His Excellency,
The Most Reverend

Rose, Robert J., Bishop emeritus of Grand Rapids, 1200 104th, Apt. 4, Byron Center, MI 49315.
Rozanski, Mitchell T., Auxiliary Bishop of Baltimore, 320 Cathedral St., Baltimore, MD 21201.
Rueger, George E., Retired Auxiliary Bishop of Worcester, St. Stephen's Rectory, 16 Hamilton St., Worcester, MA 01604.
Ryan, Daniel L., Bishop emeritus of Springfield in Illinois, St. John Vianney Villa, 1464 Green Trail Dr., Naperville, IL 60540-8359.
Ryan, Sylvester D., Bishop emeritus of Monterey, 425 Church St., Monterey, CA 93940.
Salazar, Alexander, Auxiliary Bishop of Los Angeles, 3424 Wilshire Blvd., Los Angeles, CA 90010-2241.
Samo, Amando, Bishop of the Caroline Islands, P.O. Box 939, Chuuk, Caroline Islands, FM 96942.
Sample, Alexander K., Bishop of Marquette, 1004 Harbor Hills Dr., Marquette, MI 49855.
Samra, Nicholas J., Eparch of Newton, 3 VFW Pkwy., West Roxbury, MA 02132.
Sansaricq, Guy A., Retired Auxiliary Bishop of Brooklyn, St. Matthew, 1123 Eastern Pkwy., Brooklyn, NY 11213-4801.
Sartoris, Joseph M., Retired Auxiliary Bishop of Los Angeles, San Pedro Pastoral Region, 1988 Rolling Vista Dr., #21, Lomita, CA 90717-3761.
Schlarman, Stanley G., Bishop emeritus of Dodge City, 2620 Lebanon Ave., Belleville, IL 62221.
Seitz, Mark J., Auxiliary Bishop of Dallas, 3725 Blackburn, P.O. Box 190507, Dallas, TX 75219.
Seminack, Richard S., Bishop of St. Nicholas in Chicago for Ukrainians, 2245 W. Rice St., Chicago, IL 60622.
Senior, Timothy C., Auxiliary Bishop of Philadelphia, 222 N. 17th St., Rm. 1200, Philadelphia, PA 19103-1299.
Serratelli, Arthur J., Bishop of Paterson, 777 Valley Rd., Clifton, NJ 07013.
Sevilla, Carlos, s.j., Bishop emeritus of Yakima, 5301-A Tieton Dr., Yakima, WA 98908.
Shaheen, Robert J., Bishop of Our Lady of Lebanon, 1021 S. 10th St., St. Louis, MO 63104.
Sheldon, Gilbert I., Bishop emeritus of Steubenville, 609 N. Seventh St., Steubenville, OH 43952.
Sheltz, George A., Auxiliary Bishop of Galveston-Houston, P.O. Box 907, Houston, TX 77001-0907.
Sheridan, Michael J., Bishop of Colorado Springs, 228 N. Cascade Ave., Colorado Springs, CO 80903.
Siegel, Joseph M., Auxiliary Bishop of Joliet, 425 Summit St., Joliet, IL 60435.
Silva, Clarence, Bishop of Honolulu, 1184 Bishop St., Honolulu, HI 96813.
Sirba, Paul D., Bishop of Duluth, 2830 E. Fourth St., Duluth, MN 55812.
Sklba, Richard J., Retired Auxiliary Bishop of Milwaukee, 836 N. Broadway, Milwaukee, WI 53202-3608.
Skylstad, William S., Bishop emeritus of Spokane, W. 1023 Riverside Ave., Spokane, WA 99201.
Slattery, Edward J., Bishop of Tulsa, P.O. Box 690240, Tulsa, OK 74169.
Smith, John M., Bishop emeritus of Trenton, Villa Vianney, 2301 Lawrenceville Rd., Trenton, NJ 08648.
Snyder, John J., Bishop emeritus of St. Augustine, 5 Casa San Pedro, 1714
Soens, Lawrence D., Bishop emeritus of Sioux City, 1703 - W. 25th, Apt. 208, Sioux City, IA 51103-1700. State Rd. 13, Ste. 6, Jacksonville, FL 32259.
Solis, Oscar A., Auxiliary Bishop of Los Angeles, 3555 St. Pancratius Pl., Lakewood, CA 90712-1416.
Soto, Jaime, Bishop of Sacramento, 2110 Broadway, Sacramento, CA 95818-2541.
Spencer, F. Richard, Auxiliary Bishop for the Military Services, 1025 Michigan Ave., N.E., P.O. Box 4469, Washington, DC 20017-0469.

His Excellency,
The Most Reverend

Speyrer, Jude, Bishop emeritus of Lake Charles, 118 Marcus Dr., Carenco, LA 70502.

Steib, J. Terry, s.v.d., Bishop of Memphis, The Catholic Center, P.O. Box 341669, Memphis, TN 38184-1669.

Steiner, Kenneth D., Retired Auxiliary Bishop of Portland in Oregon, 2838 E. Burnside St., Portland, OR 97214.

Stika, Richard F., Bishop of Knoxville, 805 Northshore Dr., S.W., Knoxville, TN 37919.

Straling, Phillip F., Bishop emeritus of Reno, 290 S. Arlington Ave., Reno, NV 89501-1713.

Sullivan, Dennis J., Auxiliary Bishop of New York, 452 Madison Ave., New York, NY 10022.

Sullivan, Joseph M., Retired Auxiliary Bishop of Brooklyn, Queen of All Saints, 300 Vanderbilt Ave., Brooklyn, NY 11205-3696.

Sullivan, Walter F., Bishop emeritus of Richmond, 3203 Hawthorne Ave., Richmond, VA 23227.

Swain, Paul J., Bishop of Sioux Falls, 523 N. Duluth Ave., Sioux Falls, SD 57104.

Symons, J. Keith, Bishop emeritus of Palm Beach, P.O. Box 7, Alma, MI 48801-0007.

Tafoya, Arthur N., Bishop emeritus of Pueblo, 101 N. Greenwood., Pueblo, CO 81003.

Tamayo, James A., Bishop of Laredo, Chancery, 1901 Corpus Christi St., Laredo, TX 78043.

Taylor, Anthony B., Bishop of Little Rock, 2500 N. Tyler St., P.O. Box 7565, Little Rock, AR 72217.

Thomas, Daniel E., Auxiliary Bishop of Philadelphia, 222 N. 17th St., Rm. 930, Philadelphia, PA 19103.

Thomas, Elliott G., Bishop emeritus of St. Thomas, in the Virgin Islands, Natl. Shrine of Divine Mercy, 2 Prospect Hill Rd., Stockbridge, MA 01262.

Thomas, George, Bishop of Helena, 515 N. Ewing, P.O. Box 1729, Helena, MT 59624-1729.

Thompson, Charles C., Bishop of Evansville, 4200 N. Kentucky Ave., P.O. Box 4169, Evansville, IN 47724-0169.

Thompson, David B., Bishop emeritus of Charleston, 4479 Downing Pl., Mount Pleasant, SC 29466.

Timlin, James C., Bishop emeritus of Scranton, Villa St. Joseph, 1600 Green Ridge St., Dunmore, PA 18509.

Tobin, Thomas J., Bishop of Providence, One Cathedral Sq., Providence, RI 02903-3695.

Trautman, Donald W., Bishop of Erie, 205 W. 9th St., P.O. Box 10397, Erie, PA 16514.

Tyson, Joseph J., Bishop of Yakima, 5301-A Tieton Dr., Yakima, WA 98908.

Uglietto, Peter J., Auxiliary Bishop of Boston, 66 Brooks Dr., Braintree, MA 02184-3839.

Valero, Rene, Retired Auxiliary Bishop of Brooklyn, 7200 Douglaston Pkwy., Douglaston NY 11362.

Vann, Kevin W., Bishop of Fort Worth, 800 W. Loop 820 S., Fort Worth, TX 76108.

Vasa, Robert F., Bishop of Santa Rosa, 985 Airway Ct., Santa Rosa, CA 95403.

Vasquez, Joe S., Bishop of Austin, 6225 E. Hwy. 290 E., Austin, TX 78723.

Wall, James S., Bishop of Gallup, 711 S. Puerco Dr., P.O. Box 1338, Gallup, NM 87305.

Walsh, Daniel F., Bishop emeritus of Santa Rosa, 985 Airway Ct., Ste. B, Santa Rosa, CA 95403.

Walsh, Gerald T., Auxiliary Bishop of New York, St. Joseph's Seminary, 201 Seminary Ave., Yonkers, NY 10704.

Walsh, Paul H., Auxiliary Bishop of Rockville Centre, Western Vicariate, Diocese of Rockville Centre, P.O. Box 933, Roosevelt, NY 11575-0933.

Waltersheid, William J., Auxiliary Bishop of Pittsburgh, 111 Blvd. of the Allies, Pittsburgh, PA 15222-1618.

Wang, Ignatius, Retired Auxiliary Bishop of San Francisco, Holy Name of Jesus Church, 1555 39th Ave., San Francisco, CA 94122.

Warfel, Michael, Bishop of Great Falls-Billings, 121 23rd St. S., Great Falls, MT 59401-3939.

Wcela, Emil A., Retired Auxiliary Bishop of Rockville Centre, Church of St. John the Evangelist, 546 St. John's Place, Riverhead, NY 11901.

Weigand, William K., Bishop emeritus of Sacramento, Pastoral Center, 2110 Broadway, Sacramento CA 95818.

Weisenburger, Edward J., Bishop of Salina, 103 N. Ninth, P.O. Box 980, Salina, KS 67402-0980.

Weitzel, John Quinn, m.m., Bishop of Samoa-Pago Pago, Fatuoaiga, P.O. Box 596, Pago Pago, American Samoa 96799.

Wester, John Charles, Bishop of Salt Lake City, 27 C St., Salt Lake City, UT 84103-2397.

Wilkerson, Gerald E., Auxiliary Bishop of Los Angeles, 15101 San Fernando Mission Blvd., Mission Hills, CA 91345-1109.

Williams, James K., Bishop emeritus of Lexington, 1310 W. Main St., Lexington, KY 40508.

Winter, William J., Retired Auxiliary Bishop of Pittsburgh, St. John Vianney Manor, 2600 Morange Rd., Pittsburgh, PA 15205.

Wypych, Andrew P., Auxiliary Bishop of Chicago, 2330 W. 118th St., Chicago, IL 60643.

Yanta, John W., Bishop emeritus of Amarillo, 1800 N. Spring St., P.O. Box 5644, Amarillo, TX 79117-5644.

Zarama, Luis R., Auxiliary Bishop of Atlanta, 2401 Lake Park Dr., Smyrna, GA 30080-8862.

Zipfel, Paul A., Bishop emeritus of Bismarck, University of Mary, 7500 University Dr., Bismarck, ND 58502-1575.

Zubik, David A., Bishop of Pittsburgh, 111 Blvd. of the Allies, Pittsburgh, PA 15222-1618.

Zurek, Patrick J., Bishop of Amarillo, 1800 N. Spring St., Amarillo, TX 79117.

U.S. HIERARCHY SERVING IN OTHER COUNTRIES

His Excellency,
The Most Reverend

Adams, Edward J., Titular Archbishop of Scala, Archbishop Apostolic Nuncio to Greece, Athenai, 154 52 Paleo Psychico, Odos Mavili, 2.

Balvo, Charles D., Titular Archbishop of Castello, Apostolic Nuncio to New Zealand, Wellington 6041, P.O. Box 14-044, 112 Queen's Dr.

Blume, Michael August, s.v.d., Titular Archbishop of Alexanum, Apostolic Nuncio in Benin and Togo, B.P. 20790, Lome, Togo.

Burke, Raymond L., Prefect of the Apostolic Signatura in Rome, Palazzo della Cancelleria, 00186 Roma, Piazza della Cancelleria, 1.

Bustros, Cyril Salim, s.m.s.p., Archbishop of Beirut and Jbeil, 655 rue de Damas, B.P. 11-901 Beyrouth, Liban.

Cardone, Christopher, o.p., Bishop of Auki, Solomon Islands, P. O. Box A 13, Auki, Malaita, Solomon Islands.

Echevarria, Javier, Prelate of the Prelature of the Holy Cross and Opus Dei, Viale Bruno Buozzi 73, 00197, Rome, Italy.

Gilbert, Edward J., c.ss.r., Archbishop of Port of Spain, 27 Maraval Rd., St. Clair Port of Spain, Trinidad & Tobago.

Gullickson, Thomas E., Apostolic Nuncio to Ukraine, 252054 Kyiv, vul Turhenivska 40.

Harvey, James M., Titular Archbishop of Memfi, Prefect of the Papal Household, 00120 Vatican City State, Europe.

Heim, Capistrano F., o.f.m., Prelate emeritus of Itaituba, Brazil, C.P. 171, 68181-970 Itaituba, PA, Brazil.

Hermes, Heriberto, o.s.b., Bishop Prelate emeritus of Cristalandia, Brazil, C.P. 05, Praca da Catedral s/n, 77490-00, Cristalandia, TO, Brazil.

Howaniec, Henry Theophilus, o.f.m., Bishop emeritus of Holy Trinity in Almaty, Kazakhstan, Kabanbai Batyra St., 77/16, 050000 Almaty, Kazakhstan.

Kurtz, Robert, c.r., Bishop of Hamilton-in-Bermuda, P.O. Box SN629, Southhampton SNBX Bermuda.

La Fay, Michael, o.carm., Bishop Prelate of Sicuani, Peru, Apartado 46, Jiron Hipolio Unanue 236, Plaza de Armas, Sicuani, via Cuzco, Peru.

Lonchyna, Hlib, m.s.u., Titular Bishop of Bareta, Apostolic Administrator of Great Britain (Ukrainian), 22 Binney St., London, W1Y 1YN, England, Great Britain.

Manning, Elias James, o.f.m.conv., Bishop of Valenca, Brazil, C.P. 87332, 27600-000 Valenca, RJ, Brazil.

Meeking, Basil, Bishop emeritus of Christchurch, New Zealand, St. John Fisher House, 190 Brougham St., Sydenham Christchurch 8023 New Zealand.

Muldoon, Thomas A., o.f.m., Bishop of Juticalpa, Honduras, Apartado 2, Juticalpa, Olancho 16101, Honduras.

Novak, Alfred E., c.ss.r., Bishop emeritus of Paranagua, Brazil, C.P. 531, 83203-970 Paranagua, PR, Brazil

Pelletier, Donald L., m.s., Bishop emeritus of Morondava Madagascar, Bishop's House, P.O. Box 132, Morondava 619, Madagascar.

Potocnak, Joseph J., s.c.j., Bishop emeritus of De Aar, South Africa, P.O. Box 73, 1 Van Riebeeck Str., De Aar 7000, South Africa.

Reichert, Stephen J., o.f.m.cap., Archbishop of Madang, Papua New Guinea, P. O. Box 750, Madang, Papua New Guinea.

Scarpone, Gerald, o.f.m., Bishop emeritus of Comayagua, Honduras, Obispado, Calle de la Catedral, Apartado 41, 12101 Comayagua, Honduras.

Schmitz, Paul Ervin, o.f.m.cap., Vicariate Apostolic of Bluefields, Apartado Postal 8, Bluefields, R.A.A.S., Nicaragua, C.A.

Tiedemann, Neil, c.p., Bishop of Mandeville, Jamaica, P.O. Box 8, 20 Perth Rd., Mandeville, Manchester, Jamaica.

Turley, Daniel Thomas, o.s.a., Bishop of Chulucanas, Peru, Obispado, Calle Cuzco 381, Chulucanas, Depto. de Piura, Peru.

Zywiec, David Albin, o.f.m.cap., Auxiliary Bishop, Vicariate Apostolic of Bluefields, Apartado Postal 8, Bluefields, R.A.A.S., Nicaragua, C.A.

OTHER HIERARCHY RESIDING IN THE UNITED STATES

His Excellency,
The Most Reverend

Bennett, Gordon D., s.j., Bishop emeritus of Mandeville, P.O. Box 45041, Los Angeles, CA 90045.

Boland, Ernest B., o.p., Bishop emeritus of Multan, St. Thomas Aquinas Priory, Providence College, 333 Eaton St., Providence, RI 02918-0001.

McNabb, John Conway, o.s.a., Bishop emeritus of Chulucanas, Peru, St. Clare of Montefalco Parish, 1401 Whittier Rd., Grosse Point Park, MI 48230.

McNaughton, William J., m.m., Bishop emeritus of Inchon, P.O. Box 304, Maryknoll, NY 10545.

Pearce, George H., s.m., Archbishop emeritus of Suva, 10 Rhodes Ave., N. North Smithfield, RI 02896.

Sabatini, Lawrence, c.s., Bishop emeritus of Kamloops, Canada, Holy Rosary Church, 612 N. Western Ave., Chicago, IL 60612.

Sowada, Alphonse, o.s.c., Bishop emeritus of Agats, Indonesia, 308 3rd St., S., Sauk Rapids, MN 56379.

ARCHABBOTS

The Right Reverend

DuVall, Justin, o.s.b., St. Meinrad Archabbey, N. 100 Hill Dr., St. Meinrad IN 47577.

Knaebel, Bonaventure, o.s.b., (Resigned), St. Meinrad Archabbey, N. 100 Hill Dr., St. Meinrad, IN 47577.

Maher, Paul R., o.s.b., (Resigned) St. Vincent Archabbey, 300 Fraser Purchase Rd., Latrobe, PA 15650-2686.

Nowicki, Douglas R., o.s.b., St. Vincent Archabbey, 300 Fraser Purchase Rd., Latrobe, PA 15650-2686.

Reilly, Lambert, o.s.b., (Resigned) St. Meinrad Archabbey, N. 100 Hill Dr., St. Meinrad, IN 47577.

ABBOTS

The Right Reverend

Anderson, Hugh R., o.s.b., St. Procopius Abbey, 5601 College Rd., Lisle, IL 60532.

Anderson, Philip, o.s.b., Our Lady of the Annunciation of Clear Creek Monestery, 5804 W. Monastery Rd., Hulbert, OK 74441.

Antonucci, Richard, o.praem., Daylesford Abbey, 220 S. Valley Rd., Paoli, PA 19301.

Balsavich, Marion E., o.s.b., Retired. St. Bede Abbey, Peru, IL 61354.

Bamberger, John E., o.c.s.o., Retired. Abbey of Genesee, Piffard, NY 14533.

Barnes, Robert, o.c.s.o., Cistercian Abbey of Our Lady of the Holy Cross, 901 Cool Spring Ln., Berryville, VA 22611- 2700.

Bataille, Vincent, o.s.b., Resigned. Marmion Abbey, 850 Butterfield Rd., Aurora, IL 60502.

Benedict, Francis, o.s.b., Resigned. St. Andrew's Abbey, 31001 N. Valyermo Rd., Valyermo, CA 93563.

Benkert, Gerald, o.s.b., Resigned. Marmion Abbey, 850 Butterfield Rd., Aurora, IL 60502.

Berndt, Alan, o.s.b., Retired. Blue Cloud Abbey, P.O. Box 98, Marvin, SD 57251.

Bock, David R., o.c.s.o., Retired. New Melleray Abbey, Order of Cistercians of the Strict Observance, 6632 Melleray Circle, Peosta, IA 52068.

Boyce, Edmund J., o.s.b., St. Benedict's Abbey, 12605 224th Ave., Benet Lake, WI 53102.

Boyle, Joseph, o.c.s.o., St. Benedict's Monastery, 1012 Monastery Rd., Snowmass, CO 81654.

Brahill, John, o.s.b., Marmion Abbey, 850 Butterfield Rd., Aurora, IL 60502.

Brown, Justin, o.s.b., St. Joseph Abbey, 75376 River Rd., St. Benedict, LA 70457.

Burnett, Oscar, o.s.b., Retired. Belmont Abbey, 100 Belmont-Mount Holly Rd., Belmont, NC 28012-1802.

Camacho, Isaac, o.s.b., St. Leo Abbey, Box 2350, Saint Leo, FL 33574.

Carr, Christian Aidan, o.c.s.o., Retired. Mepkin Abbey, 1098 Mepkin Abbey Rd., Moncks Corner, SC 29461-4796.

Clark, Victor J., o.s.b., Retired. St. Bernard Abbey, 1600 St. Bernard Dr., S.E., Cullman, AL 35055.

Clarke, Brian H., o.s.b., Retired. St. Mary Abbey, Delbarton, Mendham Rd., Morristown, NJ 07960.

Cole, Edwin J., o.s.b., St. Anselm Church, 530 S. Mason Rd., St. Louis, MO 63141.

Connor, James, o.c.s.o., Retired. Assumption Abbey, Rte. 5, P.O. Box 1056, Ava, MO 65608.

Corpus, Roger, o.s.b., Retired. St. Bede Abbey, Peru, IL 61354.

Cyr, David J., o.s.b., Retired. Marmion Abbey, 850 Butterfield Rd., Aurora, IL 60502.

Dagher, George, b.s.o., Retired. Basilian Salvatorian Order American Headquarters, 30 East St., Methuen, MA 01844.

Davis, Thomas X., o.c.s.o., Retired. Abbey of New Clairvaux, Trappist, P.O. Box 80, Vina, CA 96092.

De Wane, Thomas E., o.praem., Retired. St. Norbert Abbey, 1016 N. Broadway, De Pere, WI 54115-2697.

Denburger, John J., o.c.s.o., Abbey of the Genesee, Piffard, NY 14533.

Dimitrijevich, Nicholas, Our Lady of the Valley, P.O. Box 419, Gloverville, SC 29828.

Dosch, Leander, o.c.s.o., Abbey of the Holy Trinity, 1250 S. 9500 E., Huntsville, UT 84317.

Driscoll, William J., o.mar., Monastery of the Most Holy Trinity, 67 Dugway Rd., Petersham, MA 01366-9725.

Duerr, Gregory, o.s.b. Mt. Angel Abbey, St. Benedict, OR 97373.

Dzikowicz, Justin E., o.s.b., Retired. St. Paul's Abbey, Newton, NJ 07860.

Eberle, Peter, o.s.b., Retired. Mt. Angel Abbey, St. Benedict, OR 97373.

Farkasfalvy, Denis, o.cist., Cistercian Abbey of Our Lady of Dallas, 3550 Cistercian Rd., Irving, TX 75039.

Flaherty, Malachy, o.c.s.o., Abbey of Our Lady of the Holy Trinity, 1250 S. 9500 E., Huntsville, UT 84317.

Freeman, Brendan J., o.c.s.o., New Melleray Abbey, Order of Cistercians of the Strict Observance, 6632 Melleray Circle, Peosta, IA 52068-9736.

Frerking, Thomas, o.s.b., Abbey of St. Mary and St. Louis, 500 S. Mason Rd., St. Louis, MO 63141.

Garber, Andrew V., o.s.b., Resigned. St. Benedict Abbey, Benet Lake, WI 53102.

Geraets, David, o.s.b., Monastery of the Risen Christ, P.O. Box 3931, San Luis Obispo, CA 93405.

Gumula, Stanislaus, o.c.s.o., Mepkin Abbey, 1098 Mepkin Abbey Rd., Moncks Corner, SC 29461-4796.

Hacker, Louis, o.s.b., Corpus Christi Abbey, HCR 2, Box 6300, Sandia, TX 78383.

Harrison, Cyprian, o.c.s.o., Retired. Assumption Abbey, Rte. 5, Box 1056, Ava, MO 65608.

Hayes, Eugene, o.praem., St. Michael Abbey, 19292 El Toro Rd., Silverado, CA 92676-9710.

Hayes, Giles, o.s.b. St. Mary's Abbey, Delbarton, 230 Mendham Rd., Morristown, NJ 07960.

Heidgen, Warren J., o.s.b., Retired. Holy Cross Abbey, 2951 Hwy. 50, Canon City, CO 81212.

Hein, Kenneth, o.s.b., Retired Abbot, Holy Cross Abbey, 2951 E. Hwy. 50, Canon City, CO 81212.

Hillenbrand, Thomas, o.s.b., Retired. Blue Cloud Abbey, P.O. Box 98, Marvin, SD 57251.

Hinches, Augustine J., o.s.b., Resigned. St. Paul Abbey, Newton, NJ 07860.

Holmes, W. Caedmon, o.s.b., Abbey of St. Gregory the Great, 285 Cory's Ln., Portsmouth, RI 02871.

Homick, Joseph, Holy Transfiguration Monastery, 17001 Tomki Rd., Redwood Valley, CA 95470.

Johnson, Bernard, o.c.s.o., Retired. Abbey of New Clairvaux Trappist, P. O. Box 80, Vina, CA 96092.

Kalcic, Dismas B., o.s.b., Retired. St. Procopius Abbey, 5601 College Rd., Lisle, IL 60532.

Keating, Thomas, o.c.s.o., Contemplative Outreach, Ltd., 10 Landmark Dr., Ste. 117, P.O. Box 208, Cornwall, NY 12518.

Klassen, John, o.s.b., St. John's Abbey of the Order of St. Benedict, 31802 County Rd. 159, Collegeville, MN 56321.

Kodell, Jerome, o.s.b., Subiaco Abbey, Subiaco, AR 72865.

Koehler, Ralph, o.s.b., Retired. St. Benedict's, Abbey, Atchison, KS 66002.

Lawrence, Philip, o.s.b., Monastery of Christ in the Desert, Abiquiu, NM 87510.

Leavy, Matthew K., o.s.b., St. Anselm Abbey, Manchester, NH 03102.

Liebl, Michael, o.s.b., Mount Michael Benedictine Abbey, 22520 Mount Michael Rd., Elkhorn, NE 68022.

Liprie, James, o.s.b., Abbot of Our Lady of Guadalupe Abbey, Pecos, NM 87552.

Logan, John M., o.praem., Daylesford Abbey, 220 S. Valley Rd., Paoli, PA 19301.

Lugo, Martin, o.s.b., Retired. St. Gregory's Abbey, Shawnee, OK 74804.

Macul, Joel P., o.s.b., St. Paul's Abbey, Newton, NJ 07860.

Massoth, Charles, o.s.b., Retired. St. Gregory Abbey, Shawnee, OK 74801.

Matter, Robert, o.c.s.o., Retired. Assumption Abbey, Rte. 5, Box 1056, Ava, MO 65608.

McCaffrey, Edmund F., Former Abbot-Ordinary Belmont Abbey, P.O. Box 70548, Myrtle Beach, SC 29572-0028.

McCarthy, Peter, o.c.s.o., The Cistercian (Trappist) Abbey of Our Lady of Guadalupe, Lafayette, OR 97127.

McCorkell, Edward, o.c.s.o., Retired. Cistercian Abbey of Our Lady of the Holy Cross, 901 Cool Spring Ln., Berryville, VA 22611-2700.

McDermott, Benedict, o.s.b., Mary Mother of Church Abbey, 12829 River Rd., Richmond, VA 23238-7206.

McGonigle, Kevin, o.s.b., Retired. Conception Abbey, Conception, MO 64433.

Meagher, Cletus D., o.s.b., St. Bernard Abbey, 1600 St. Bernard Dr., S.E., Cullman, AL 35055.

Moore, Patrick, o.s.b., Resigned. Assumption Abbey, P.O. Box A, Richardton, ND 58652.

Morcone, Nicholas J., o.s.b., Glastonbury Abbey, 16 Hull St., Hingham, MA 02043.

Murphy, Austin, o.s.b., St. Procopius Abbey, 5601 College Rd., Lisle, IL 60532.

Neville, Gary, o.praem., Abbot St. Norbert Abbey, 1016 N. Broadway, DePere, WI 54115-2697.

O'Connor, Philip J., o.c.s.o., Retired. New Melleray Abbey, 6500 Melleray Circle, Peosta, IA 52068.

Odenbrett, Stephen, o.s.b., Our Lady of Guadalupe Abbey, Pecos, NM 87552.

Parcher, Adrian, o.s.b., Resigned. St. Martin's Abbey, 5000 Abbey Way, S.E., Lacey, WA 98503.

Polan, Gregory, o.s.b., Abbot of Conception Abbey, Conception, MO 64433.

Purcell, Owen, o.s.b., Retired. St. Benedict's Abbey, Atchison, KS 66002.

Quinkert, Denis, o.s.b., Blue Cloud Abbey, P.O. Box 98, Marvin, SD 57251.

Regan, Patrick, o.s.b., Retired. St. Joseph Abbey, St. Benedict, LA 70457.

Rigby, Luke, o.s.b., Abbey of St. Mary and St. Louis, 500 S. Mason Rd., St. Louis, MO 63141.

Rivera, Oscar, o.s.b., San Antonio Abad Abbey of the Order of St. Benedict, P.O. Box 729, Humacao, PR 00792.

Roberts, Augustine, o.c.s.o., St. Joseph Abbey, Spencer, MA 01562.

Rooney, Marcel, o.s.b., Conception Abbey, Conception, MO 64433.

Rossi, Ronald, o.praem., Retired. Daylesford Abbey, 220 S. Valley Rd., Paoli, PA 19301.

Roth, Neal G., o.s.b., St. Martin's Abbey, 5000 Abbey Way, S.E., Lacey, WA 98503-7500.

Ryska, Leo M., o.s.b., Retired. St. Benedict's Abbey and Retreat Center, Benet Lake, WI 53102.

Schoofs, Robert, o.s.b., Retired. St. Benedict's Abbey, Benet Lake, WI 53102.

Scott, Mark A., o.c.s.o., Retired. Assumption Abbey, Rte. 5, Box 1056, Ava, MO 65608.

Senecal, Barnabas, o.s.b., St. Benedict's Abbey, Atchison, KS 66002.

Serna, F. Mark, o.s.b., Retired. Abbey of St. Gregory the Great, 785 Cory's Ln., Portsmouth, RI 02871.

Shea, Aidan, o.s.b., St. Anselm's Abbey, 4501 South Dakota Ave., N.E., Washington, DC 20017.

Solari, Placid D., o.s.b., Belmont Abbey, 100 Belmont-Mount Holly Rd., Belmont, NC 28012-1802.

Stark, Matthew, o.s.b., Retired. Abbey of St. Gregory the Great, 285 Cory's Ln., Portsmouth, RI 02871.

Stasyszen, Lawrence, o.s.b., St. Gregory's Abbey, Shawnee, OK 74804.

Thompson, Damien, o.c.s.o., Retired. Abbey of Our Lady of Gethsemani of the Order of Cistercians of the Strict Observance, Trappist, KY 40051.

Tremel, Jerome G., o.praem., Retired. Daylesford Abbey Norbertine Canonry, 220 S. Valley Rd., Paoli, PA 19301-1900.

Valvano, Melvin J., o.s.b., Retired. Newark Abbey, 528 Dr. Martin Luther King Jr. Blvd., Newark, NJ 07102.

Veilleux, Armand J., o.s.c.o., Monastery of the Holy Spirit, 2625 Hwy. 212 S.W., Conyers, GA 30094-4044.

Vollmer, Edward J., o.s.b., Retired. Holy Cross Abbey, P.O. Box 1510, Canon City, CO 81215-1510.

Vorderlandwehr, Adrian R., o.s.b., Retired. St. Gregory Abbey, Shawnee, OK 74801.

Vuong, M. John Lam Dinh, o.cist., Retired. St. Joseph Monastery, 21010 Lucerne Valley Cutoff, P.O. Box 960, Lucerne Valley, CA 92356.

Wagner, Lawrence, o.s.b., Retired. Assumption Abbey, P.O. Box A, Richardton, ND 58652.

Walsh, Raphael, o.s.b., Resigned. Mount Michael Benedictine Abbey, Elkhorn, NE 68022.

Wangler, Brian, o.s.b., Assumption Abbey, P.O. Box A, Richardton, ND 58652.

Wechter, David L., o.c.s.o., Retired. New Melleray Abbey, 6500 Melleray Circle, Peosta, IA 52068.

Wiseman, James, o.s.b., Retired. St. Anselm's Abbey, 4501 South Dakota Ave., N.E., Washington, DC 20017.

Wolff, Theodore, o.s.b., Resigned. Mount Michael Benedictine Abbey, 22520 Mount Michael Rd., Elkhorn, NE 68022.

Wood, Joseph, o.s.b., Retired. Mt. Angel Abbey, St. Benedict, OR 97373.

Wright, Charles, o.s.b., Prince of Peace Abbey, 650 Benet Hill Rd., Oceanside, CA 92058-1253.

A LIST OF CARDINALS IN THE UNITED STATES IN THE ORDER OF THEIR SENIORITY

CARDINALS

His Eminence William Cardinal Baum, Vatican City State
His Eminence Bernard Cardinal Law, Vatican City State
His Eminence Edmund Cardinal Szoka, Vatican City State
His Eminence Roger Cardinal Mahony, Los Angeles
His Eminence William Cardinal Keeler, Baltimore
His Eminence Adam Cardinal Maida, Detroit
His Eminence Francis Cardinal Stafford, Vatican City State
His Eminence Francis Cardinal George, o.m.i., Chicago
His Eminence Edward Cardinal Egan, New York
His Eminence Theodore Cardinal McCarrick, Washington
His Eminence Justin Cardinal Rigali, Philadelphia
His Eminence William Cardinal Levada, Vatican City State
His Eminence Sean Patrick Cardinal O'Malley, o.f.m.cap., Boston
His Eminence Daniel Cardinal DiNardo, Galveston-Houston
His Eminence Donald Cardinal Wuerl, Washington
His Eminence Timothy Cardinal Dolan, New York
His Eminence Edwin Cardinal O'Brien, Vatican City State

A CHRONOLOGICAL LIST OF CARDINAL, ARCHBISHOP & BISHOP ACTIVITY BY YEAR

1962

Bishop

Hunthausen, Raymond G., Appointed July 8. Ordained June 1, 1946. Bishop of Helena.

1966

Bishop

Gerety, Peter Leo, Appointed March 4. Ordained June 29, 1939. Coadjutor Bishop of Portland (in Maine).

1967

Bishops

Broderick, Edwin B., Appointed March 4. Ordained May 30, 1942. Auxiliary Bishop of New York.

Gerety, Peter Leo, Appointed Feb. 18. Ordained June 29, 1939. Apostolic Administrator of Portland (in Maine).

Quinn, John R., Appointed Oct. 21. Ordained July 19, 1953. Auxiliary Bishop of San Diego.

1968

Bishops

Cronin, Daniel A., Appointed June 10. Ordained Dec. 20, 1952. Auxiliary Bishop of Boston.

Gossman, F. Joseph, Appointed July 15. Ordained Dec. 17, 1955. Auxiliary Bishop of Baltimore.

Gumbleton, Thomas J., Appointed March 8. Ordained June 2, 1956. Auxiliary Bishop of Detroit.

McLaughlin, Bernard J., Appointed Dec. 28. Ordained Dec. 21, 1935. Retired Auxiliary Bishop of Buffalo.

O'Neill, Arthur J., Appointed Aug. 19. Ordained March 27, 1943. Bishop of Rockford.

1969

Bishops

Broderick, Edwin B., Appointed March 19. Ordained May 30, 1942. Bishop of Albany.

Gerety, Peter Leo, Succeeded to See Sept. 15. Bishop of Portland (in Maine).

1970

Bishops

Baum, William, Appointed Feb. 18. Ordained May 12, 1951. Bishop of Springfield-Cape Girardeau.

Bosco, Anthony G., Appointed May 14. Ordained June 7, 1952. Auxiliary Bishop of Pittsburgh.

Cronin, Daniel A., Appointed Oct. 30. Ordained Dec. 20, 1952. Bishop of Fall River.

Flores, Patrick F., Appointed March 18. Ordained May 26, 1956. Auxiliary Bishop of San Antonio.

Hurley, Francis T., Appointed Feb. 4. Ordained June 16, 1951. Auxiliary Bishop of Juneau.

Lohmuller, Martin N., Appointed Feb. 11. Ordained June 3, 1944. Auxiliary Bishop of Philadelphia.

Sullivan, Walter F., Appointed Oct. 20. Ordained May 9, 1953. Auxiliary Bishop of Richmond.

1971

Bishops

Connolly, Thomas J., Appointed May 4. Ordained April 8, 1947. Bishop of Baker.

Gelineau, Louis E., Appointed Dec. 6. Ordained June 5, 1954. Bishop of Providence.

Gracida, Rene H., Appointed Dec. 6. Ordained May 23, 1959. Auxiliary Bishop of Miami.

Hurley, Francis T., Appointed July 20. Ordained June 16, 1951. Bishop of Juneau.

Losten, Basil, Appointed March 15. Ordained June 10, 1957. Auxiliary Bishop of Philadelphia Ukrainian.

Maguire, Joseph F., Appointed Dec. 1. Ordained June 29, 1945. Auxiliary Bishop of Boston.

Szoka, Edmund, Appointed June 15. Ordained June 5, 1954. Bishop of Gaylord.

1972

Archbishop

Quinn, John R., Appointed Dec. 13. Ordained July 19, 1953. Archbishop of Oklahoma City.

Bishops

Howze, Joseph L., Appointed Nov. 8. Ordained May 7, 1959. Auxiliary Bishop of Jackson.

McDonald, Andrew J., Appointed July 4. Ordained May 8, 1948. Bishop of Little Rock.

Snyder, John J., Appointed Dec. 19. Ordained June 9, 1951. Auxiliary Bishop of Brooklyn.

1973

Archbishop

Baum, William, Appointed May 9. Ordained May 12, 1951. Archbishop of Washington.

Bishops

Imesch, Joseph L., Appointed Feb. 8. Ordained Dec. 16, 1956. Auxiliary Bishop of Detroit.

Law, Bernard, Appointed Oct. 22. Ordained May 21, 1961. Bishop of Springfield-Cape Girardeau.

Lessard, Raymond W., Appointed March 5. Ordained Dec. 16, 1956. Bishop of Savannah.

Sullivan, Walter F., Appointed April 30. Ordained May 9, 1953. Apostolic Administrator of Richmond.

1974

Archbishop

Gerety, Peter Leo, Appointed April 2. Ordained June 29, 1939. Archbishop of Newark.

Bishops

Angell, Kenneth A., Appointed Aug. 9. Ordained May 26, 1956. Auxiliary Bishop of Providence.

Chavez, Gilbert E., Appointed April 19. Ordained March 19, 1960. Auxiliary Bishop of San Diego.

Cummins, John S., Appointed Feb. 26. Ordained Jan. 24, 1953. Auxiliary Bishop of Sacramento.

Daily, Thomas V., Appointed Dec. 31. Ordained Jan. 10, 1952. Auxiliary Bishop of Boston.

D'Arcy, John M., Appointed Dec. 31. Ordained Feb. 2, 1957. Auxiliary Bishop of Boston.

Gendron, Odore J., Appointed Dec. 12. Ordained May 31, 1947. Retired Bishop of Manchester.

Hanifen, Richard C., Appointed July 6. Ordained June 6, 1959. Auxiliary Bishop of Denver.

Hughes, William A., Appointed July 23. Ordained April 6, 1946. Auxiliary Bishop of Youngstown.

Ottenweller, Albert H., Appointed April 17. Ordained June 19, 1943. Auxiliary Bishop of Toledo.

Pilarczyk, Daniel E., Appointed Nov. 12. Ordained Dec. 20, 1959. Auxiliary Bishop of Cincinnati.

Sullivan, Walter F., Succeeded to See June 6. Bishop of Richmond.

1975

Archbishop

Hunthausen, Raymond G., Appointed Feb. 25. Ordained June 1, 1946. Archbishop of Seattle.

Bishops

Fitzsimons, George K., Appointed May 27. Ordained March 18, 1961. Auxiliary Bishop of Kansas City-St. Joseph.

Gossman, F. Joseph, Appointed April 8. Ordained Dec. 17, 1955. Bishop of Raleigh.

Gracida, Rene H., Appointed Oct. 1. Ordained May 23, 1959. Bishop of Pensacola-Tallahassee.

Mahony, Roger M., Appointed Jan. 7. Ordained May 1, 1962. Auxiliary Bishop of Fresno.

Reilly, Daniel P., Appointed June 17. Ordained May 30, 1953. Bishop of Norwich.

1976

Cardinal

Baum, William Cardinal, Created May 24. Prefect of Sacred Congregation for Catholic Education, Vatican.

Archbishop

Hurley, Francis T., Appointed May 4. Ordained June 16, 1951. Archbishop of Anchorage.

Bishops

Balke, Victor, Appointed July 7. Ordained May 24, 1958. Bishop of Crookston.

Broderick, Edwin B., Appointed June 3. Exec. Dir. Catholic Relief Services; resigned Bishop of Albany.
Casiano-Vargas, Ulises, Appointed March 4. Ordained May 30, 1967. Bishop of Mayaguez.
Curtiss, Elden F., Appointed March 4. Ordained May 24, 1958. Bishop of Helena.
Gerber, Eugene J., Appointed Oct. 16. Ordained May 19, 1959. Bishop of Dodge City.
Hart, Joseph H., Appointed July 1. Ordained May 1, 1956. Bishop of Cheyenne.
Hughes, Edward T., Appointed June 14. Ordained May 31, 1947. Auxiliary Bishop of Philadelphia.
Kinney, John F., Appointed Nov. 16. Ordained Feb. 2, 1963. Auxiliary Bishop of St. Paul-Minneapolis.
Losten, Basil H., Appointed June 8. Ordained June 10, 1957. Apostolic Administrator Philadelphia Ukrainian.
Maguire, Joseph F., Appointed April 3. Ordained June 29, 1945. Coadjutor Bishop of Springfield.
Marconi, Dominic A., Appointed May 3. Ordained May 30, 1953. Auxiliary Bishop of Newark.
Pena, Raymundo, J., Appointed Oct. 16. Ordained May 25, 1957. Auxiliary Bishop of San Antonio.
Sheldon, Gilbert I., Appointed April 20. Ordained Feb. 28, 1953. Auxiliary Bishop of Cleveland.
Stafford, J. Francis, Appointed Jan. 27. Ordained Dec. 15, 1957. Auxiliary Bishop of Baltimore.
Timlin, James C., Appointed Aug. 3. Ordained July 16, 1951. Auxiliary Bishop of Scranton.

1977

Archbishops

Quinn, John R., Appointed Feb. 22. Ordained July 19, 1953. Archbishop of San Francisco.
Weakland, Rembert, G., o.s.b., Appointed Sept. 20. Ordained June 24, 1951. Archbishop of Milwaukee.

Bishops

Cummins, John S., Appointed May 3. Ordained Jan. 24, 1953. Bishop of Oakland.
Daly, James J., Appointed Feb. 28. Ordained May 22, 1948. Auxiliary Bishop of Rockville Centre.
Howze, Joseph L., Appointed March 1. Ordained May 7, 1959. Bishop of Biloxi from Auxiliary Bishop of Jackson.
Hubbard, Howard J., Appointed Feb. 1. Ordained Dec. 18, 1963. Bishop of Albany.
Kucera, Daniel W., o.s.b., Appointed June 6. Ordained May 26, 1949. Auxiliary Bishop of Joliet.
Losten, Basil H., Appointed Sept. 20. Ordained June 10, 1957. Bishop of Stamford.
Maguire, Joseph F., Succeeded to See Nov. 4. Bishop of Springfield.
McCarrick, Theodore E., Appointed May 24. Ordained May 31, 1958. Auxiliary Bishop of New York.
Mulvee, Robert E., Appointed Feb. 15. Ordained June 30, 1957. Auxiliary Bishop of Manchester.
Ottenweller, Albert H., Appointed Oct. 11. Ordained June 19, 1943. Bishop of Steubenville.
Rodimer, Frank J., Appointed Dec. 13. Ordained May 19, 1951. Bishop of Paterson.
Skylstad, William, Appointed Feb. 22. Ordained May 21, 1960. Bishop of Yakima.
Steiner, Kenneth, Appointed Dec. 6. Ordained May 19, 1962. Auxiliary Bishop of Portland in Oregon.

1978

Bishops

Beltran, Eusebius J., Appointed Feb. 28. Ordained May 14, 1960. Bishop of Tulsa.
Costello, Thomas J., Appointed Jan. 10. Ordained June 5, 1954. Auxiliary Bishop of Syracuse.
DuMaine, R. Pierre, Appointed April 28. Ordained June 5, 1957. Auxiliary Bishop of San Francisco.
Flores, Patrick F., Appointed April 4. Ordained May 26, 1956. Bishop of El Paso.
Morneau, Robert F., Appointed Dec. 19. Ordained May 28, 1966. Auxiliary Bishop of Green Bay.
Quinn, Francis A., Appointed April 28. Ordained June 15, 1946. Auxiliary Bishop of San Francisco.
Rosazza, Peter A., Appointed Feb. 28. Ordained June 29, 1961. Auxiliary Bishop of Hartford.
Straling, Phillip F., Appointed July 18. Ordained March 19, 1959. Bishop of San Bernardino.

1979

Archbishop

Flores, Patrick F., Appointed Aug. 28. Ordained May 26, 1956. Archbishop of San Antonio.

Bishops

Clark, Matthew H., Appointed May 2. Ordained Dec. 19, 1962. Bishop of Rochester.
Fiorenza, Joseph A., Appointed Sept. 4. Ordained May 29, 1954. Bishop of San Angelo.
Fliss, Raphael M., Appointed Nov. 6. Ordained May 26, 1956. Coadjutor Bishop of Superior.
Friend, William B., Appointed Aug. 31. Ordained May 7, 1959. Auxiliary Bishop of Alexandria-Shreveport.
Griffin, James A., Appointed June 30. Ordained May 28, 1960. Auxiliary Bishop of Cleveland.
Houck, William R., Appointed March 28. Ordained May 19, 1951. Auxiliary Bishop of Jackson.
Hughes, William A., Appointed April 13. Ordained April 6, 1946. Bishop of Covington.
Imesch, Joseph L., Appointed June 30. Ordained Dec. 16, 1956. Bishop of Joliet.
Keeler, William H., Appointed July 24. Ordained July 17, 1955. Auxiliary Bishop of Harrisburg.
Madera, Joseph J., m.sp.s., Appointed Dec. 18. Ordained June 15, 1957. Coadjutor Bishop of Fresno.
McCarthy, John E., Appointed Jan. 23. Ordained May 26, 1956. Auxiliary Bishop of Galveston-Houston.
Nevins, John J., Appointed Feb. 6. Ordained June 6, 1959. Auxiliary Bishop of Miami.
Pilla, Anthony M., Appointed June 30. Ordained May 23, 1959. Auxiliary Bishop of Cleveland.
Quinn, Francis A., Appointed Dec. 18. Ordained June 15, 1946. Bishop of Sacramento.
Rivera, Hector M., Appointed June 11. Ordained June 12, 1966. Auxiliary Bishop of San Juan.
Rivera, Enrique Hernandez, Appointed June 11. Ordained June 8, 1968. Auxiliary Bishop of San Juan.
Schlarman, Stanley G., Appointed March 13. Ordained July 13, 1958. Auxiliary Bishop of Belleville.
Sklba, Richard J., Appointed Nov. 6. Ordained Dec. 20, 1959. Auxiliary Bishop of Milwaukee.
Snyder, John J., Appointed Oct. 2. Ordained June 9, 1951. Bishop of St. Augustine.

1980

Archbishops

Lipscomb, Oscar H., Appointed July 29. Ordained July 15, 1956. Archbishop of Mobile.
Sulyk, Stephen, Appointed Dec. 29. Archbishop of Philadelphia Ukrainian.

Bishops

Kucera, Daniel W., o.s.b., Appointed March 11. Ordained May 26, 1949. Bishop of Salina.
Madera, Joseph J., m.sp.s., Succeeded to See July 1. Bishop of Fresno.
Mahony, Roger M., Appointed Feb. 26. Ordained May 1, 1962. Bishop of Stockton.
Pena, Raymundo J., Appointed April 29. Ordained May 25, 1957. Bishop of El Paso.
Pilla, Anthony M., Appointed Nov. 18. Ordained May 23, 1959. Bishop of Cleveland.
Speyrer, Jude, Appointed Jan. 29. Ordained July 25, 1953. Bishop of Lake Charles.
Sullivan, Joseph M., Appointed Oct. 7. Ordained June 2, 1956. Auxiliary Bishop of Brooklyn.
Tafoya, Arthur N., Appointed July 1. Ordained May 12, 1962. Bishop of Pueblo.
Valero, Rene, Appointed Oct. 7. Ordained June 2, 1956. Auxiliary Bishop of Brooklyn.
Weigand, William K., Appointed Sept. 3. Ordained May 25, 1963. Bishop of Salt Lake City.

1981

Archbishops

Marcinkus, Paul C., Appointed Sept. 26. Ordained May 3, 1947. Titular Archbishop of Orta, Vatican City State.
Szoka, Edmund C., Appointed March 28. Ordained June 5, 1954. Archbishop of Detroit.

Bishops

DeSimone, Louis A., Appointed June 27. Ordained May 10, 1952. Auxiliary Bishop of Philadelphia.
Dumaine, R., Pierre, Appointed Jan. 27. Ordained June 5, 1957. Bishop of San Jose.
Grahmann, Charles V., Appointed June 30. Ordained March 17, 1956. Auxiliary Bishop of San Antonio.
Hughes, Alfred C., Appointed July 21. Ordained Dec. 15, 1957. Auxiliary Bishop of Boston.
Lotocky, Innocent, o.s.b.m., Appointed Jan. 29. Ordained Nov. 24, 1940. Bishop of St. Nicholas Chicago.
McCarrick, Theodore E., Appointed Nov. 24. Bishop of Metuchen.
Milone, Anthony M., Appointed Nov. 10. Ordained Dec. 15, 1957. Auxiliary Bishop of Omaha.
Moskal, Robert M., Appointed Aug. 3. Ordained March 25, 1963. Auxiliary Bishop of the Archeparchy of Philadelphia.
O'Brien, Thomas J., Appointed Nov. 24. Ordained May 7, 1961. Bishop of Phoenix.
Ramirez, Ricardo, c.s.b., Appointed Oct. 27. Ordained Dec. 10, 1966. Auxiliary Bishop of San Antonio.
Rivera, Enrique Hernandez, Appointed Feb. 13. Ordained June 8, 1968. Bishop of Caguas.
Rose, Robert J., Appointed Oct. 13. Ordained Dec. 21, 1955. Bishop of Gaylord.
Ryan, Daniel L., Appointed Aug. 14. Ordained May 3, 1956. Auxiliary Bishop of Joliet.
Schulte, Francis B., Appointed June 27. Ordained May 10, 1952. Auxiliary Bishop of Philadelphia.
Symons, J. Keith, Appointed Jan. 16. Ordained May 18, 1958. Auxiliary Bishop of St. Petersburg.
Walsh, Daniel F., Appointed June 30. Ordained March 30, 1963. Auxiliary Bishop of San Francisco.

1982

Archbishop

Pilarczyk, Daniel E., Appointed Nov. 2. Ordained Dec. 20, 1959. Archbishop of Cincinnati.

Bishops

Anderson, Moses B., s.s.e., Appointed Dec. 3. Ordained May 30, 1958. Auxiliary Bishop of Detroit.
Cooney, Patrick, R., Appointed Dec. 7. Ordained Dec. 20, 1959. Auxiliary Bishop of Detroit.
Friend, William B., Appointed Nov. 23. Bishop of Alexandria-Shreveport.
Gerber, Eugene J., Appointed Nov. 23. Ordained May 19, 1959. Bishop of Wichita.
Grahmann, Charles V., Appointed April 14. Ordained March 17, 1956. Bishop of Victoria.
Kinney, John F., Appointed June 28. Ordained Feb. 2, 1963. Bishop of Bismarck.
Kmiec, Edward V., Appointed Aug. 26. Ordained Dec. 20, 1961. Auxiliary Bishop of Trenton.
McRaith, John J., Appointed Oct. 23. Ordained Feb. 21, 1960. Bishop of Owensboro.
Melczek, Dale J., Appointed Dec. 3. Ordained June 6, 1964. Auxiliary Bishop of Detroit.
Pevec, Edward A., Appointed April 13. Ordained April 29, 1950. Auxiliary Bishop of Cleveland.
Ramirez, Ricardo, c.s.b., Appointed Aug. 31. Ordained Dec. 10, 1966. Bishop of Las Cruces.
Stafford, J. Francis, Appointed Nov. 16. Ordained Dec. 15, 1957. Bishop of Memphis.

1983

Archbishop

Kucera, Daniel, W., Appointed Dec. 20. Archbishop of Dubuque.

Bishops

Apuron, Anthony S., o.f.m.cap., Appointed Dec. 8. Auxiliary Bishop of Agana.
Arias, David, o.a.r., Appointed Jan. 25. Auxiliary Bishop of Newark.
Brom, Robert, Appointed March 25. Bishop of Duluth.
Carlson, Robert, J., Appointed Nov. 22. Auxiliary Bishop of St. Paul-Minneapolis.
Dimino, Joseph, Appointed March 29. Auxiliary Bishop of Military Services.
Gracida, Rene, Appointed May 19. Bishop of Corpus Christi.
Gregory, Wilton, Appointed Oct. 31. Auxiliary Bishop of Chicago.
Griffin, James, Appointed Feb. 7. Bishop of Columbus.
Hanifen, Richard, Appointed Nov. 10. Bishop of Colorado Springs.
Keeler, William, Appointed Nov. 10. Bishop of Harrisburg.
Levada, William, J., Appointed March 29. Auxiliary Bishop of Los Angeles.
Lyne, Timothy, Appointed Oct. 31. Auxiliary Bishop of Chicago.
Maida, Adam, Appointed Nov. 8. Bishop of Green Bay.
Moskal, Robert, Appointed Dec. 5. Bishop of St. Josaphat in Parma.
Popp, Bernard, Appointed June 7. Auxiliary Bishop of San Antonio.
Quinn, A. James, Appointed Oct. 14. Auxiliary Bishop of Cleveland.
Rodriquez, Placido, Appointed Oct. Auxiliary Bishop of Chicago.
Roque, Francis, Appointed March 29. Auxiliary Bishop of Military Services.

Ryan, Daniel, Appointed Nov. 22. Bishop of Springfield in Illinois.
Schlarmann, Stanley, Appointed March 1. Bishop of Dodge City.
Sheehan, Michael, J., Appointed March 29. Bishop of Lubbock.
Soens, Lawrence, Appointed June 15. Bishop of Sioux City.
Steib, James Terry, s.v.d., Appointed Dec. 6. Auxiliary Bishop of St. Louis.
Symons, J. Keith, Appointed Sept. 29. Bishop of Pensacola-Tallahassee.
Vlazny, John G., Appointed Oct. 31. Auxiliary Bishop of Chicago.

1984

Archbishop
Law, Bernard, Appointed Jan. 24. Archbishop of Boston.

Bishops
Baltakis, Paul, Appointed June 1. Bishop for the Lithuanian Apostolate.
Camacho, Tomas A., Appointed Nov. 8. Bishop of Chalan Kanoa.
Daily, Thomas, Appointed July 17. Bishop of Palm Beach.
Donnelly, Robert, Appointed March 20. Auxiliary Bishop of Toledo.
Fiorenza, Joseph, A., Appointed Dec. 18. Bishop of Galveston-Houston.
Fitzsimons, George, Appointed March 22. Bishop of Salina.
Garland, James, H., Appointed June 25. Auxiliary Bishop of Cincinnati.
Higi, William, Appointed April 7. Bishop of Lafayette in Indiana.
Houck, William, Appointed April 24. Bishop of Jackson.
Keleher, James, Appointed Oct. 23. Bishop of Belleville.
Leibrecht, John, Appointed Oct. 23. Bishop of Springfield-Cape Girardeau.
Nevins, John, J., Appointed July 17. Bishop of Venice.
Newman, William, Appointed July 2. Auxiliary Bishop of Baltimore.
O'Malley, Sean, P., o.f.m.cap., Appointed May 30. Coadjutor Bishop of St. Thomas Virgin Islands.
Ricard, John, s.s.j., Appointed May 29. Auxiliary Bishop of Baltimore.
Timlin, James, Appointed April 24. Bishop of Scranton.
Williams, J. Kendrick, Appointed April 15. Auxiliary Bishop of Covington.

1985

Cardinal
Law, Bernard Cardinal, Created May 25. Archbishop of Boston.

Archbishop
Mahony, Roger, Appointed July 16. Archbishop of Los Angeles.

Bishops
Apuron, Anthony S., o.f.m.cap., Appointed Oct. 27. Apostolic Administrator of Agana.
Banks, Robert J., Appointed June 26. Auxiliary Bishop of Boston.
Corrada del Rio, Alvaro, s.j., Appointed Aug. 4. Auxiliary Bishop of Washington.
D'Arcy, John M., Appointed Feb. 26. Bishop of Fort Wayne-South Bend.
Egan, Edward M., Appointed April 1. Auxiliary Bishop of New York.
Fliss, Raphael M., Succeeded to See June 27. Bishop of Superior.
Ibrahim, Ibrahim, Appointed Sept. 14. Eparch of St. Thomas the Apostle.
McCarthy, John E., Appointed Dec. 24. Bishop of Austin.
Mulvee, Robert E., Appointed Feb. 16. Bishop of Wilmington.
O'Malley, Sean, P., o.f.m.cap., Succeeded to See Oct. 16. Bishop of St. Thomas Virgin Islands.
Pfeifer, Michael, o.m.i., Appointed July 26. Bishop of San Angelo.
Schulte, Francis B., Appointed June 4. Bishop of Wheeling-Charleston.
Trautman, Donald W., Appointed Feb. 27. Auxiliary Bishop of Buffalo.
Wuerl, Donald, Appointed Dec. 3. Auxiliary Bishop of Seattle.

1986

Archbishops
Apuron, Anthony S., o.f.m.cap., Succeeded to See May 11. Archbishop of Agana.
Gerety, Peter, Leo, Retired June. Archbishop of Newark.
Levada, William J., Appointed July 1. Archbishop of Portland in Oregon.
McCarrick, Theodore E., Appointed June 1. Archbishop of Newark.
Stafford, J. Francis, Appointed June 3. Archbishop of Denver.

Bishops
Dorsey, Norbert, c.p., Appointed Jan. 10. Auxiliary Bishop of Miami.
Elya, John A., b.s.o., Appointed April 2. Auxiliary Bishop of Newton.
Favalora, John C., Appointed June 16. Bishop of Alexandria.
Flynn, Harry, Appointed April 19. Coadjutor Bishop of Lafayette.
Foley, David, Appointed May 3. Auxiliary Bishop of Richmond.
Friend, William B., Appointed June 1. Bishop of Shreveport.
Gerry, Joseph J., o.s.b., Appointed April 21. Auxiliary Bishop of Manchester.
Hughes, Edward, Appointed Dec. 11. Bishop of Metuchen.
McCormack, William J., Appointed Dec. 23. Auxiliary Bishop of New York.
Ochoa, Armando, Appointed Dec. 29. Auxiliary Bishop of Los Angeles.
Weitzel, John Q., m.m., Appointed Oct. 29. Bishop of Samoa-Pago Pago.

1987

Bishops
Adamec, Joseph V., Appointed March 12. Bishop of Altoona-Johnstown.
Bosco, Anthony G., Appointed April 14. Bishop of Greensburg.
Buechlein, Daniel, M., o.s.b., Appointed Jan. 20. Bishop of Memphis.
Franklin, William, E., Appointed Jan. 29. Auxiliary Bishop of Dubuque.
Guillory, Curtis, Appointed Dec. 29. Auxiliary Bishop of Galveston-Houston.
Hanus, Jerome, G., o.s.b., Appointed July 6. Bishop of St. Cloud.
Milone, Anthony M., Appointed Dec. 14. Bishop of Great Falls-Billings.
Myers, John J., Appointed July 14. Coadjutor Bishop of Peoria.
Rueger, George, Appointed Jan. 19. Auxiliary Bishop of Worcester.
Samo, Amando, Appointed May 10. Auxiliary Bishop of The Carolines-Marshalls.
Smith, John M., Appointed Dec. 1. Auxiliary Bishop of Newark.
Vlazny, John G., Appointed May 19. Bishop of Winona.
Walsh, Daniel F., Appointed June 9. Bishop of Reno-Las Vegas.

1988

Cardinal
Szoka, Edmund Cardinal, Created June 29. Pres. Prefecture for Economic Affairs of the Holy See, Vatican.

Archbishop
Schulte, Francis B., Appointed Dec. 13. Archbishop of New Orleans.

Bishops
Boland, Raymond J., Appointed Feb. 2. Bishop of Birmingham.
Brown, Tod D., Appointed Dec. 27. Bishop of Boise.
Carmody, Edmond, Appointed Nov. 8. Auxiliary Bishop of San Antonio.
Chaput, Charles, o.f.m.cap., Appointed April 11. Bishop of Rapid City.
Curlin, William G., Appointed Dec. 20. Auxiliary Bishop of Washington.
DiLorenzo, Francis, Appointed Jan. 26. Auxiliary Bishop of Scranton.
Dunne, John C., Appointed Oct. 21. Auxiliary Bishop of Rockville Centre.
Egan, Edward, M., Appointed Nov. 8. Bishop of Bridgeport.
Gerry, Joseph, J., o.s.b., Appointed Dec. 27. Bishop of Portland (in Maine).
Gonzalez, Roberto O., o.f.m., Appointed July 19. Auxiliary Bishop of Boston.
Gorman, John R., Appointed Feb. 16. Auxiliary Bishop of Chicago.
Jakubowski, Thaddeus J., Appointed Feb. 16. Auxiliary Bishop of Chicago.
Loverde, Paul S., Appointed Feb. 3. Auxiliary Bishop of Hartford.
McGrath, Patrick, J., Appointed Dec. 6. Auxiliary Bishop of San Francisco.
McLaughlin, Bernard J., Retired Jan. 15. Auxiliary Bishop of Buffalo.
O'Connell, Anthony J., Appointed June 7. Bishop of Knoxville.
Olivier, Leonard J., s.v.d., Appointed Dec. 20. Auxiliary Bishop of Washington.
Sevilla, Carlos A., s.j., Appointed Dec. 6. Auxiliary Bishop of San Francisco.
Wcela, Emil A., Appointed Oct. 21. Auxiliary Bishop of Rockville Centre.
Williams, J. Kendrick, Appointed March 2. Bishop of Lexington.
Winter, William J., Appointed Dec. 27. Auxiliary Bishop of Pittsburgh.
Wuerl, Donald, Appointed Feb. 11. Bishop of Pittsburgh.

1989

Archbishop
Keeler, William, Appointed April 6. Archbishop of Baltimore.

Bishops
Brom, Robert, Appointed April 22. Coadjutor Bishop of San Diego.
Charron, Joseph L., c.pp.s., Appointed Nov. 6. Auxiliary Bishop of St. Paul-Minneapolis.
Cooney, Patrick, R., Appointed Nov. 21. Bishop of Gaylord.
Driscoll, Michael P., Appointed Dec. 19. Auxiliary Bishop of Orange.
Favalora, John, C., Appointed March 7. Bishop of St. Petersburg.
Flynn, Harry J., Succeeded to the See May 13. Bishop of Lafayette.
Gettelfinger, Gerald A., Appointed March 11. Bishop of Evansville.
Grahmann, Charles V., Appointed Dec. 18. Coadjutor Bishop of Dallas.
Grosz, Edward, Appointed Nov. 22. Auxiliary Bishop of Buffalo.
Jacobs, Sam, Appointed July 1. Bishop of Alexandria.
Mikloshazy, Attila, s.j., Appointed Aug. 12. Bishop for the Apostolate to the Hungarians.
Rose, Robert J., Appointed July 11. Bishop of Grand Rapids.
Samra, Nicholas J., Appointed June 29. Auxiliary Bishop of Newton.
Schwietz, Roger L., o.m.i., Appointed Dec. 12. Bishop of Duluth.
Thompson, David B., Appointed May 9. Coadjutor Bishop of Charleston.
Zipfel, Paul A., Appointed May 16. Auxiliary Bishop of St. Louis.

1990

Archbishop
Maida, Adam J., Appointed June 11. Archbishop of Detroit.

Bishops
Banks, Robert J., Appointed Oct. 16. Bishop of Green Bay.
Blaire, Stephen E., Appointed Feb. 17. Auxiliary Bishop of Los Angeles.
Brom, Robert H., Succeeded to the See July 10. Bishop of San Diego.
Daily, Thomas V., Appointed Feb. 20. Bishop of Brooklyn.
Dorsey, Norbert M., c.p., Appointed March 20. Bishop of Orlando.
Dupre, Thomas L., Appointed April 19. Auxiliary Bishop of Springfield in Massachusetts.
Fellhauer, David E., Appointed April 19. Bishop of Victoria.
George, Francis E., o.m.i., Appointed July 10. Bishop of Yakima.
Grahmann, Charles V., Succeeded to See July 14. Bishop of Dallas.

Muench, Robert W., Appointed May 8. Auxiliary Bishop of New Orleans.
Myers, John J., Succeeded to See Jan. 23. Bishop of Peoria.
Ryan, Sylvester D., Appointed Feb. 17. Auxiliary Bishop of Los Angeles.
Skylstad, William S., Appointed April 17. Bishop of Spokane.
Symons, J. Keith, Appointed June 2. Bishop of Palm Beach.
Thompson, David B., Succeeded to See Feb. 22. Bishop of Charleston.
Trautman, Donald W., Appointed July 16. Bishop of Erie.

1991

Cardinal
Mahony, Roger Cardinal, Created June 28. Archbishop of Los Angeles.

Archbishops
Cronin, Daniel A., Appointed Dec. 9. Archbishop of Hartford.
Dimino, Joseph T., Succeeded to the See June 21. Archbishop of the Military Services.
Hunthausen, Raymond G., Retired Aug. Archbishop of Seattle.

Bishops
Goedert, Raymond E., Appointed July 8. Auxiliary Bishop of Chicago.
Madera, Joseph J., m.sp.s., Appointed May 28. Auxiliary Bishop of the Military Services.
Maguire, Joseph F., Retired Dec. Bishop of Springfield.
Smith, John M., Appointed June 24. Bishop of Pensacola-Tallahassee.
Txertudi, Inaki Mallona, c.p., Appointed Dec. 14. Bishop of Arecibo.

1992

Archbishops
Beltran, Eusebius J., Appointed Nov. 24. Archbishop of Oklahoma City, from Bishop of Tulsa.
Buechlein, Daniel M., o.s.b., Appointed July 14. Archbishop of Indianapolis, from Bishop of Memphis.

Bishops
Angell, Kenneth A., Appointed Oct. 10. Bishop of Burlington, from Auxiliary Bishop of Providence.
Barnes, Gerald R., Appointed Jan. 28. Auxiliary Bishop of San Bernardino.
Boles, John P., Appointed April 14. Auxiliary Bishop of Boston.
Bruskewitz, Fabian W., Appointed March 24. Bishop of Lincoln.
Carmody, Edmond, Appointed March 24. Bishop of Tyler, from Auxiliary Bishop of San Antonio.
Carmon, Dominic, s.v.d., Appointed Dec. 16. Auxiliary Bishop of New Orleans.
Galante, Joseph A., Appointed Oct. 13. Auxiliary Bishop of San Antonio.
Garland, James H., Appointed Oct. 10. Bishop of Marquette, from Auxiliary Bishop of Cincinnati.
Jarrell, Michael Charles, Appointed Dec. 29. Bishop of Houma-Thibodaux.
Kmiec, Edward Urban, Appointed Oct. 13. Bishop of Nashville, from Auxiliary Bishop of Trenton.
Mansell, Henry J., Appointed Nov. 24. Auxiliary Bishop of New York.
O'Malley, Sean P., o.f.m.cap., Appointed June 16. Bishop of Fall River from Bishop of St. Thomas, Virgin Islands.
Ottenweller, Albert H., Retired April. Bishop of Steubenville.
Ryan, Sylvester D., Appointed Jan. 21. Bishop of Monterey, from Auxiliary Bishop of Los Angeles.
Sheldon, Gilbert I., Appointed Jan. 28. Bishop of Steubenville, from Auxiliary Bishop of Cleveland.
Tobin, Thomas J., Appointed Nov. 3. Auxiliary Bishop of Pittsburgh.

1993

Archbishops
Curtiss, Elden F., Appointed May 4. Archbishop of Omaha, from Bishop of Helena.
Keleher, James P., Transferred Sept. 8. Archbishop of Kansas City in Kansas, from Bishop of Belleville.
Sheehan, Michael J., Appointed April 6. Archbishop of Santa Fe.

Bishops
Boland, Raymond J., Appointed June 22. Bishop of Kansas City-St. Joseph, from Bishop of Birmingham, June.
Charron, Joseph L., c.pp.s. Appointed Nov. 12. Bishop of Des Moines, from Auxiliary Bishop of St. Paul and Minneapolis.
Elya, John A., b.s.o. Appointed Dec. 7. Bishop of Newton from Auxiliary Bishop of Newton.
Franklin, William E., Appointed Nov. 12. Bishop of Davenport, from Auxiliary Bishop of Dubuque.
Gregory, Wilton, Appointed Dec. 29. Bishop of Belleville from Auxiliary Bishop of Chicago.
Harrington, Bernard J., Appointed Nov. 23. Auxiliary Bishop of Detroit.
Hughes, Alfred C., Appointed Sept. 7. Bishop of Baton Rouge, from Auxiliary Bishop of Boston.
Lotocky, Innocent, Resigned July. Bishop of St. Nicholas of Chicago.
Loverde, Paul S., Appointed Nov. 11. Bishop of Ogdensburg, from Auxiliary Bishop of Hartford.
Popp, Bernard F., Retired March. Auxiliary Bishop of San Antonio.
Quinn, Francis A., Retired Nov. Bishop of Sacramento.
Slattery, Edward J., Appointed Nov. 11. Bishop of Tulsa.
Steib, James Terry, s.v.d. Appointed March 23. Bishop of Memphis, from Auxiliary Bishop of St. Louis.
Tamayo, James A., Appointed Jan. 26. Auxiliary Bishop of Galveston-Houston.
Thomas, Elliot G., Appointed Oct. 10. Bishop of St. Thomas, Virgin Islands.
Weigand, William K., Appointed Nov. 3. Bishop of Sacramento from Bishop of Salt Lake City.
Wiwchar, Michael, c.ss.r. Appointed July 15. Bishop of St. Nicholas in Chicago for Ukrainians.

1994

Cardinals
Keeler, William Cardinal, Created Nov. 26. Archbishop of Baltimore.
Maida, Adam Cardinal, Created Nov. 26. Archbishop of Detroit.

Archbishops
Favalora, John C., Appointed Nov. 3. Archbishop of Miami.
Flynn, Harry J., Appointed Feb. 2. Coadjutor Archbishop of St. Paul-Minneapolis.
Hanus, Jerome, G., o.s.b. Appointed Aug. 23. Coadjutor Archbishop of Dubuque.
Rigali, Justin F., Appointed Jan. 25. Archbishop of St. Louis.

Bishops
Barbarito, Gerald, Appointed June 28. Auxiliary Bishop of Brooklyn.
Brunett, Alexander J., Appointed April 19. Bishop of Helena.
Burke, Raymond L., Appointed Dec. 10. Bishop of La Crosse.
Carlson, Robert J., Appointed Jan. 13. Coadjutor Bishop of Sioux Falls, from Auxiliary Bishop of St. Paul-Minneapolis.
Catanello, Ignatius, Appointed June 28. Auxiliary Bishop of Brooklyn.
Cullen, Edward P., Appointed Feb. 8. Auxiliary Bishop of Philadelphia.
Curlin, William G., Appointed Feb. 22. Bishop of Charlotte, from Auxiliary Bishop of Washington.
Curry, Thomas J., Appointed Feb. 8. Auxiliary Bishop of Los Angeles.
DiLorenzo, Francis X., Appointed Oct. 4. Bishop of Honolulu.
Doran, Thomas G., Appointed April 19. Bishop of Rockford.
Foley, David E., Appointed March 22. Bishop of Birmingham, from Auxiliary Bishop of Richmond.
Galante, Joseph A., Appointed April 5. Bishop of Beaumont from Auxiliary Bishop of San Antonio.
Lohmuller, Martin N., Retired Oct. Auxiliary Bishop of Philadelphia.
McDonnell, Charles J., Appointed March 15. Auxiliary Bishop of Newark.
Niederauer, George H., Appointed Nov. 3. Bishop of Salt Lake City.
O'Neill, Arthur J., Retired April. Bishop of Rockford.
Reilly, Daniel P., Appointed Oct. 27. Bishop of Worcester.
Rodriguez, Placido, c.m.f., Appointed April 5. Bishop of Lubbock, from Auxiliary Bishop of Chicago.
Samo, Amando, Appointed Feb. Coadjutor Bishop of the Caroline Islands.
Sartoris, Joseph M., Appointed Feb. 8. Auxiliary Bishop of Los Angeles.
Yanta, John W., Appointed Oct. 27. Auxiliary Bishop of San Antonio.

1995

Archbishops
Flynn, Harry J., Appointed Sept. 8. From Coadjutor to Archbishop of St. Paul-Minneapolis.
Hanus, Jerome G., o.s.b., Succeeding as Archbishop of Dubuque from status of Coadjutor.
Kucera, Daniel W., Retired Oct. Archbishop of Dubuque.
Quinn, John R., Retired Dec. Archbishop of San Francisco.
Levada, William J., Succeeding as Archbishop of San Francisco Dec.

Bishops
Barnes, Gerald R., Appointed Dec. 28. Bishop of San Bernardino, from Auxiliary of same Diocese.
Boland, J. Kevin, Appointed Feb. 7. Bishop of Savannah.
Braxton, Edward K., Appointed March 28. Auxiliary Bishop of St. Louis.
Carlson, Robert J., Succeeding as Bishop of Sioux Falls in March, from status of Coadjutor.
Cote, Michael R., Appointed May 9. Auxiliary Bishop of Portland in Maine.
Dougherty, John M., Appointed Feb. 7. Auxiliary Bishop of Scranton.
Dupre, Thomas L., Appointed March 14. Bishop of Springfield, from Auxiliary Bishop of Springfield.
Gonzalez, Roberto O., o.f.m., Appointed May 16. Coadjutor Bishop of Corpus Christi, from Auxiliary Bishop of Boston.
Hughes, William A., Retired July. Bishop of Covington.
Kicanas, Gerald F., Appointed Jan. 24. Auxiliary Bishop of Chicago.
Kinney, John F., Appointed May 8. Bishop of St. Cloud from Bishop of Bismarck.
Lessard, Raymond W., Retired Feb. Bishop of Savannah.
Lori, William E., Appointed Feb. 27. Auxiliary Bishop of Washington.
Lynch, Robert N., Appointed Dec. 4. Bishop of St. Petersburg.
Lyne, Timothy J., Retired Jan. 24. Auxiliary Bishop of Chicago.
Mansell, Henry J., Appointed April 18. Bishop of Buffalo, from Auxiliary Bishop of New York.
McCormack, John B., Appointed Nov. Auxiliary Bishop of Boston.
Melczek, Dale J., Appointed Nov. 9. Coadjutor Bishop of Gary.
Mengeling, Carl F., Appointed Nov. Bishop of Lansing.
Moynihan, James M., Appointed April 29. Bishop of Syracuse.
Mulvee, Robert Edward, Appointed Feb. 7. Coadjutor Bishop of Providence from Bishop of Wilmington.
Murphy, William F., Appointed Nov. Auxiliary Bishop of Boston.
Murry, George V., s.j. Appointed Jan. 24. Auxiliary Bishop of Chicago.
Pena, Raymundo J., Appointed May 23. Bishop of Brownsville, from Bishop of El Paso.
Samo, Amando, Appointed March. Bishop of the Caroline Islands.
Smith, John M., Named Coadjutor of Trenton from Bishop of Pensacola-Tallahassee.
Straling, Phillip F., Appointed March 21. Bishop of Reno, from Bishop of San Bernadino.
Tobin, Thomas J., Appointed Bishop of Youngstown, from Auxiliary of Pittsburgh.
Walsh, Daniel F., Appointed Bishop of Las Vegas March 21.

1996

Archbishop
George, Francis, E. o.m.i., Appointed Archbishop of Portland in Oregon from Bishop of Yakima, April.

Bishops
Allue, Emilio, s.d.b., Appointed Auxiliary Bishop of Boston, July 24.
Aymond, Gregory M., Appointed Auxiliary Bishop of New Orleans, Nov. 19.
Botean, John Michael, Appointed Bishop of Romanian Catholic Diocese of St. George in Canton.
Christian, Francis J., Appointed Auxiliary Bishop of Manchester, April 2.
Daly, James J., Retired Auxiliary Bishop of Rockville Centre, July.

DiMarzio, Nicholas A., Appointed Auxiliary Bishop of Newark, Sept.
Doueihi, Hector, Appointed Bishop of St. Maron of Brooklyn.
Irwin, Francis X., Appointed Auxiliary Bishop of Boston, July 24.
Maginnis, Robert P., Appointed Auxiliary Bishop of Philadelphia, Jan. 23.
Manz, John R., Appointed Auxiliary Bishop of Chicago, Jan. 23.
Martino, Joseph F., Appointed Auxiliary Bishop of Philadelphia, Jan. 23.
Melczek, Dale J., Succeeded to Bishop of Gary, June 1.
Muench, Robert W., Appointed Bishop of Covington from Auxiliary Bishop of New Orleans, Jan. 5.
Nienstedt, John C., Appointed Auxiliary Bishop of Detroit, June 11.
O'Brien, Edwin F., Appointed Auxiliary Bishop of New York.
Ochoa, Armando, Appointed Bishop of El Paso from Auxiliary Bishop of Los Angeles, April.
Sevilla, Carlos A., s.j. Appointed Bishop of Yakima from Auxiliary Bishop of San Francisco Dec. 31.
Vigneron, Allen H., Appointed Auxiliary Bishop of Detroit June 11.
Warfel, Michael, Appointed Bishop of Juneau Nov. 19.
Younan, Joseph, Appointed Bishop of Our Lady of Deliverance of Newark.
Zipfel, Paul A., Appointed Bishop of Bismarck from Auxiliary Bishop of St. Louis Dec. 31.

1997

Archbishops

Brunett, Alexander J., Appointed Archbishop of Seattle, Oct.
Chaput, Charles J., o.f.m.cap., Appointed Archbishop of Denver Feb. 18, 1997, from Bishop of Rapid City.
Dimino, Joseph T., Retired Archbishop for the Military Services, Aug.
George, Francis, E. o.m.i., Appointed Archbishop of Chicago from Archbishop of Portland in Oregon from Bishop of Yakima, April.
O'Brien, Edwin F., Appointed Archbishop for the Military Services from Auxiliary Bishop of New York.
Vlazny, John G., Appointed Archbishop of Portland in Oregon, Oct.

Bishops

Bennett, Gordon D., Appointed Auxiliary Bishop of Baltimore, Dec. 23.
Bootkoski, Paul G., Appointed Auxiliary Bishop for the Archdiocese of Newark, July.
Brucato, Robert A., Appointed Auxiliary Bishop for the Archdiocese of New York, July.
Cullen, Edward P., Appointed Bishop of Allentown from Auxiliary Bishop of Philadelphia, Dec 16.
DeSimone, Louis A., Retired Auxiliary Bishop of Philadelphia, April.
DiNardo, Daniel N., Appointed Coadjutor Bishop of Sioux City, Aug. 19.
Garcia, Richard J., Appointed Auxiliary Bishop of Sacramento, Nov.
Gaydos, John R., Appointed June 24. Bishop of Jefferson City.
Gelineau, Louis E., Retired Bishop of Providence, June.
Gonzalez, Roberto O., Appointed Bishop of Corpus Christi, March 31.
Gracida, Rene H., Retired Bishop of Corpus Christi, April.
Hughes, Edward T., Retired Bishop of Metuchen, Sept.
Jenky, Daniel R., c.s.c., Appointed Auxiliary Bishop of Fort Wayne-South Bend.
Macaluso, Christie A., Appointed Auxiliary Bishop of Hartford, March 18.
Mulvee, Robert E., Succeeds as Bishop of Providence from Coadjutor Bishop of Providence, June.
Murray, James A., Appointed Bishop of Kalamazoo, Nov.
Naumann, Joseph F., Appointed Bishop of St. Louis, July.
Ricard, John H., s.s.j., Appointed Bishop of Pensacola-Tallahassee, Jan.
Sheridan, Michael J., Appointed Auxiliary Bishop of St. Louis, July.
Smith, John M., Succeeds as Bishop of Trenton from Coadjutor Bishop of Trenton, July.
Wenski, Thomas G., Appointed Auxiliary Bishop for the Archdiocese of Miami, June 23.
Wilkerson, Gerald E., Appointed Auxiliary Bishop of Los Angeles, Nov. 5.
Yanta, John W., Appointed Bishop of Amarillo, from Auxiliary of San Antonio in Jan.
Zubik, David A., Appointed Auxiliary Bishop of Pittsburgh Feb. 18.

1998

Cardinals

George, Francis Cardinal, o.m.i., Created Feb. 21. Archbishop of Chicago.
Stafford, Francis Cardinal, Pres.-Pontifical Council for the Laity, Vatican.

Bishops

Brown, Tod D., Appointed Bishop of Orange from Bishop of Boise, June.
Cupich, Blase J., Appointed Bishop of Rapid City, July 6.
DiNardo, Daniel N., Appointed Bishop of Sioux City, Dec.
Flanagan, Thomas Joseph, Appointed Auxiliary Bishop of San Antonio, Jan. 5.
Gilmore, Ronald M., Appointed Bishop of Dodge City, May.
Harrington, Bernard J., Appointed Bishop of Winona, from Auxiliary Bishop of Detroit, Nov.
Harvey, James M., Bishop and Prefect of the Papal Household, March.
McCormack, John B., Appointed Bishop of Manchester from Auxiliary Bishop of Boston, July.
McManus, Robert Joseph, Appointed Auxiliary Bishop of Providence, Dec. 1.
Murry, George V., s.j., Appointed Coadjutor to St. Thomas Virgin Islands, May.
Perry, Joseph N., Appointed Auxiliary Bishop of Chicago, May.
Rivera, Enrique Hernandez, Retired Bishop of Caguas, July.
Schlarman, Stanley G., Retired Bishop of Dodge City, May 12.
Soens, Lawrence D., Retired Bishop of Sioux City, Nov.
Symons, Joseph K., Retired Bishop of Palm Beach, June.
Wester, John Charles, Appointed Auxiliary Bishop of San Francisco, June 30.
Zurek, Patrick J., Appointed Auxiliary Bishop of San Antonio, Jan. 5.

1999

Bishops

Baker, Robert J. Appointed Bishop of Charleston July 12.
Barbarito, Gerald M., Appointed Bishop of Ogdensburg, from Auxiliary Bishop of Brooklyn.
Blair, Leonard P., Appointed Auxiliary Bishop of Detroit.
Blaire, Stephen E., Appointed Bishop of Stockton, from Auxiliary Bishop of Los Angeles, Sept.
Campbell, Frederick F., Appointed Auxiliary Bishop of St. Paul and Minneapolis, March.
DiMarzio, Nicholas A., Appointed Bishop of Camden.
Driscoll, Michael P., Appointed Bishop of Boise, from Auxiliary Bishop of Orange, Jan.
Dumaine, Pierre, Retired Bishop of San Jose, Nov.
Galante, Joseph A., Appointed Coadjutor Bishop of Dallas, from Bishop of Beaumont, Nov. 23.
Kurtz, Joseph E., Appointed Bishop of Knoxville, Dec.
Loverde, Paul S., Appointed Bishop of Arlington, from Bishop of Ogdensburg, Jan.
Lucas, George J., Appointed Bishop of Springfield, Illinois, Oct. 19.
McCarthy, James F., Auxiliary Bishop of New York, May.
McGrath Patrick J., Succeeded to Bishop of San Jose, from Coadjutor, Nov. 27.
Morlino, Robert C. Appointed Bishop of Helena July 6.
Murry, George V., s.j., Appointed Bishop to St. Thomas Virgin Islands, June 30.
O'Connell, Anthony J., Resigned Bishop of Palm Beach, from Bishop of Knoxville.
Olmsted, Thomas J., Appointed Coadjutor Bishop of Wichita, Feb.
Ricken, David L., Appointed Coadjutor Bishop of Cheyenne, Dec.
Ryan, Daniel L., Retired Bishop of Springfield in Illinois, Oct.
Sartain, J. Peter, Appointed Bishop of Little Rock, Dec.
Thomas, Elliot G., Retired Bishop of St. Thomas Virgin Islands, June 30.
Thomas, George, Appointed Auxiliary Bishop of Seattle, Nov. 19.
Thompson, David B., Retired Bishop of Charleston, July.
Vasa, Robert F., Appointed Bishop of Baker, Nov. 19.

2000

Archbishops

Egan, Edward M., Appointed Archbishop of New York, from Bishop of Bridgeport, June.
Gonzalez, Roberto O., o.f.m., Archbishop of San Juan.
McCarrick, Theodore E., Appointed Archbishop of Washington from Archbishop of Newark, Dec.
Schwietz, Roger L., o.m.i., Appointed Coadjutor Archbishop of Anchorage from Bishop of Duluth, Jan.
Soroka, Stephen, Appointed Archbishop of the Ukrainian Archeparchy of Philadelphia.
Sulyk, Stephen, Retired Archbishop of Philadelphia Ukrainian, Nov.

Bishops

Aymond, Gregory M., Appointed Coadjutor Bishop of Austin, June.
Batakian, Manuel, Appointed Exarch for Armenian Catholics in U.S.A. and Canada, Nov. 30.
Braxton, Edward K., Appointed Bishop of Lake Charles, Dec. 11.
Carmody, Edmond, Appointed Bishop of Corpus Christi, from Bishop of Tyler, Feb. 2.
Connolly, Thomas J., Retired Bishop of Baker, Jan.
Corrada del Rio, Alvaro, s.j. from Auxiliary Bishop of Washington; Administrator of Caguas to Bishop of Tyler.
Guillory, Curtis J., Appointed Bishop of Beaumont from Auxiliary Bishop of Galveston-Houston, June.
Listecki, Jerome E., Appointed Auxiliary Bishop of Chicago, Nov. 7.
Malone, Richard J., Appointed as Auxiliary Bishop of Boston, Feb.
Malooly, William Frances, Appointed Auxiliary Bishop of Baltimore, Dec. 11.
McDonald, Andrew J., Retired Bishop of Little Rock, Jan.
Serratelli, Arthur J., Appointed Auxiliary Bishop of Newark, July 3.
Shaheen, Robert J., Eparch of Our Lady of Lebanon, Dec. 4.
Snyder, John J., Retired Bishop of St. Augustine, Dec.
Soto, Jaime, Appointed Auxiliary Bishop of Orange, March 23.
Speyrer, Jude, Resigned Bishop of Lake Charles, Dec.
Tamayo, James A., Appointed Bishop of Laredo, July 3.
Walsh, Daniel F., Appointed Bishop of Santa Rosa, April 4.

2001

Cardinals

Egan, Edward Cardinal, M., Created Feb. 21, Archbishop of New York.
McCarrick, Theodore Cardinal, E., Created Feb., Archbishop of Washington.

Archbishops

Hughes, Alfred C., Coadjutor Archbishop of New Orleans from Bishop of Baton Rouge, Feb.
Hurley, Francis T., Retired Archbishop of Anchorage, March 3.
Myers, John J., Appointed Archbishop of Newark, July.
Schwietz, Roger L., o.m.i., Succeeded March 3, as Archbishop of Anchorage from Coadjutor Archbishop of Anchorage.

Bishops

Amos, Martin John, Appointed Auxiliary Bishop of Cleveland, April 3.
Aquila, Samuel J., Appointed Coadjutor Bishop of Fargo June 12.
Angadiath, Jacob, Appointed Bishop of St. Thomas Syro-Malabar Catholic Diocese of Chicago, March 12.
Aymond, Gregory M., Appointed Bishop of Austin from Coadjutor Bishop of Austin, Jan. 2.
Clark, Edward W., Appointed Auxiliary Bishop of Los Angeles, Jan. 16.
Dolan, Timothy, M., Appointed Auxiliary Bishop of St. Louis, June 19.

Edyvean, Walter, Appointed Auxiliary Bishop of Boston, June 29.
Farrell, Kevin, Appointed Auxiliary Bishop of Washington, D.C., Dec. 28.
Galeone, Victor, Appointed Bishop of St. Augustine, June 26.
Gerber, Eugene J., Retired Bishop of Wichita, Oct.
Gomez, Jose H., Appointed Auxiliary Bishop of Denver, Jan. 22.
Gonzalez, Francisco, Appointed Auxiliary Bishop of Washington, Dec.
Gries, Roger W., o.s.b., Appointed Auxiliary Bishop of Cleveland, April 3.
Hart, Joseph H., Retired Bishop of Cheyenne, Sept. 26.
Howze, Joseph L., Retired Bishop of Biloxi, May 15.
Iriondo, Josu, Appointed Auxiliary Bishop of New York, Oct. 29.
Kicanas, Gerald F., Appointed Coadjutor Bishop of Tucson, from Auxiliary Bishop of Chicago, Oct. 30.
Lagonegro, Dominick J., Appointed Auxiliary Bishop of New York, Oct. 29.
Lennon, Richard, Appointed Auxiliary Bishop of Boston, June 29.
Lori, William E., Bishop of Bridgeport from Auxiliary Bishop of Washington, Jan. 16.
McCarthy, John E., Retired Bishop of Austin, Jan. 2.
McCormack, William J., Retired Auxiliary Bishop of New York, Oct.
McDonnell, Timothy A., Appointed Auxiliary Bishop of New York, Oct. 29.
Medina, Ruben Antonio Gonzalez, c.m.f., Bishop of Caguas.
Muench, Robert W., Appointed Bishop of Baton Rouge, from Bishop of Covington, Dec. 14.
Murphy, William, Appointed Bishop of Rockville Centre from Auxiliary Bishop of Boston June 26.
Myers, John, J., Appointed Archbishop of Newark from Bishop of Peoria, July 24.
Nienstedt, John C., Appointed Bishop of New Ulm, from Auxiliary Bishop of Detroit.
Olmsted, Thomas J., Succeeds as Bishop of Wichita, from Coadjutor Bishop, Oct. 4.
Pates, Richard E., Appointed Auxiliary Bishop of St. Paul and Minneapolis.
Pepe, Joseph A., Appointed Bishop of Las Vegas, April 6.
Pevec, Edward A., Retired Auxiliary Bishop of Cleveland, April.
Ricken, David, Appointed Bishop of Cheyenne, Sept. 26.
Rizzotto, Vincent, Appointed Auxiliary Bishop of Galveston-Houston, June 22.
Rodi, Thomas, Appointed Bishop of Biloxi, May 15.
Schnurr, Dennis M., Appointed Bishop of Duluth, Jan.18.
Sheridan, Michael, Appointed Coadjutor Bishop of Colorado Springs from Auxiliary Bishop of St. Louis Dec. 3.
Vasquez, Jose S., Appointed Auxiliary Bishop of Galveston-Houston, Nov. 29.

2002

Cardinal

Law, Bernard, Retired Archbishop of Boston, Dec.

Archbishops

Dolan, Timothy, M., Appointed Archbishop of Milwaukee, June 25.
Hughes, Alfred C., Succeeds as Archbishop of New Orleans from Coadjutor, Jan. 3.
Schulte, Francis B., Retired Archbishop of New Orleans, Jan.
Weakland, Rembert G., o.s.b., Retired Archbishop of Milwaukee, May 24.

Bishops

Aquila, Samuel J., Succeeds as Bishop of Fargo, March18.
Bootkoski, Paul G., Appointed Bishop of Metuchen from Auxiliary Bishop of Newark, Jan. 4.
Boyea Earl A., Appointed Auxiliary Bishop of Detroit, July 22.
Burbidge, Michael F., Installed as Auxiliary Bishop of Philadelphia, Sept. 5.
Conlon, R. Daniel, Appointed Bishop of Steubenville, June.
Cordileone, Salvatore J., Appointed Auxiliary Bishop of San Diego, July.
Curlin, William G., Retired Bishop of Charlotte, Sept. 10.
Foys, Roger J., Appointed Bishop of Covington, May 30.
Gainer, Ronald W., Appointed Bishop of Lexington, Dec. 12.
Hermann, Robert J., Appointed Auxiliary Bishop of St. Louis, Oct. 16.
Jammo, Sarhad Y., Appointed Bishop of Eparchy of St. Peter the Apostle (Chaldean), May 4.
Jarrell, Michael C., Appointed Bishop of Lafayette in Louisiana, Nov. 8.
Jenky, Daniel R., c.s.c., Appointed Bishop of Peoria, from Auxiliary Bishop of Fort Wayne-South Bend, Feb. 11.
Kettler, Donald J., Appointed Bishop of Fairbanks, June 6.
Kudrick, John M., Installed as Bishop of Parma, July 10.
Lazaro, Felix, Appointed Coadjutor Bishop of Ponce, March.
Marconi, Dominic A., Retired Auxiliary Bishop of Newark, July.
McCarthy, James F., Retired Auxiliary Bishop of New York, June.
O'Connell, Anthony J., Resigned Bishop of Palm Beach, March.
O'Malley, Sean P., o.f.m.cap., Appointed as Bishop of Palm Beach, Sept. 3.
Pevec, Edward A., Retired Auxiliary Bishop of Cleveland, Sept. 1.
Sartoris, Joseph M., Retired Auxiliary Bishop of Los Angeles, Dec. 31.
Sheldon, Gilbert I., Retired as Bishop of Steubenville, Aug. 6.
Skurla, William, Appointed Bishop of the Eparchy of Van Nuys, Feb. 19.
Wang, Ignatius, Appointed Auxiliary Bishop of San Francisco, Dec. 12.
Williams, J. Kendrick, Retired Bishop of Lexington, June 11.

2003

Cardinal

Rigali, Justin Cardinal, Created Oct. 21, Archbishop of Philadelphia.

Archbishops

Burke, Raymond L., Appointed Archbishop of St. Louis, Dec. 2.
Cronin, Daniel A., Retired as Archbishop of Hartford, Oct. 20.
Mansell, Henry J., Appointed as Archbishop of Hartford, Oct. 20.
O'Malley, Sean P., o.f.m.cap., Appointed as Archbishop of Boston, July 1.
Rigali, Justin F., Appointed as Archbishop of Philadelphia, July 21.

Bishops

Anderson, Moses B., s.s.e., Retired Auxiliary Bishop of Detroit, Oct. 24.
Baltakis, Paul A., Retired Bishop for the Lithuanian Apostolate, July.
Banks, Robert J., Retired Bishop of Green Bay, Oct. 10.
Barbarito, Gerald M., Appointed Bishop of Palm Beach, July 1.
Blair, Leonard P., Appointed Bishop of Toledo, Dec. 4.
Coleman, George W., Appointed Bishop of Fall River, April 30.
Cote, Michael R., Appointed Bishop of Norwich, March 10.
Cummins, John S., Retired Bishop of Oakland, Oct. 1.
da Cunha, Edgar M., s.d.v., Appointed Auxiliary Bishop of Newark, June 27.
Daily, Thomas V., Retired Bishop of Brooklyn, Aug. 1.
DiMarzio, Nicholas A., Appointed Bishop of Brooklyn, Aug. 1.
Dinh Mai Luong, Dominic Appointed Auxiliary Bishop of Orange, April 25.
Estevez, Felipe J., Appointed Auxiliary Bishop of Miami, Nov. 21.
Garcia-Siller, Gustavo, m.sp.s., Appointed Auxiliary Bishop of Chicago, Jan. 23.
Goedert, Raymond E., Retired Auxiliary Bishop of Chicago, Jan. 23.
Gorman, John R., Retired Auxiliary Bishop of Chicago, Jan. 23.
Hanifen, Richard C., Retired Bishop of Colorado Springs, Jan.
Houck, William R., Retired Bishop of Jackson, Jan. 3.
Hurley, Walter A., Appointed Auxiliary Bishop of Detroit, July 7.
Jacobs, Sam G., Appointed Bishop of Houma-Thibodaux, Aug. 1.
Jakubowski, Thaddeus J., Retired Auxiliary Bishop of Chicago, Jan. 23.
Jugis Peter J., Appointed Bishop of Charlotte, Aug. 1.
Kane, Francis Appointed Auxiliary Bishop of Chicago, Jan. 23.
Kicanas, Gerald F., Succeeded as Bishop of Tucson, March 7.
Latino, Joseph N., Appointed Bishop of Jackson, Jan. 3.
Lazaro, Felix, Succeeded as Bishop of Ponce, June.
Luong, Dominic Mai, Appointed Auxiliary Bishop of Orange in California, April.
Martino, Joseph F., Appointed Bishop of Scranton, July 25.
Morin, Roger P., Appointed Auxiliary Bishop of New Orleans, Feb. 11.
Morlino, Robert C., Appointed Bishop of Madison, May 22.
Newman, William C., Retired Auxiliary Bishop of Baltimore, Aug. 28.
O'Brien, Thomas J., Resigned Bishop of Phoenix, June 18.
Olmsted, Thomas J., Appointed Bishop of Phoenix, Nov. 25.
Paprocki, Thomas J., Appointed Auxiliary Bishop of Chicago, Jan. 23.
Quinn, John M., Appointed Auxiliary Bishop of Detroit, July 7.
Reiss, Francis R., Appointed Auxiliary Bishop of Detroit, July 7.
Rose, Robert J., Retired as Bishop of Grand Rapids, Oct. 13.
Seminack, Richard S. Appointed Bishop of St. Nicholas in Chicago Ukrainian, March 24.
Sheridan, Michael, J., Succeeded as Bishop of Colorado Springs, Jan. 30.
Solis, Oscar A., Appointed Auxiliary Bishop of Los Angeles, Dec. 11.
Sullivan, Walter F., Retired as Bishop of Richmond, Sept. 16.
Timlin, James, C., Retired Bishop of Scranton, July 25.
Vigneron, Allen H., Appointed Coadjutor Bishop of Oakland Jan. 9; succeeded as Bishop of Oakland, Oct. 1.
Walsh, Paul H., Appointed Auxiliary Bishop of Rockville Centre, April 2.
Wenski, Thomas G., Named Coadjutor Bishop of Orlando, June 30.
Zubik, David A., Appointed Bishop of Green Bay, Oct. 10.

2004

Archbishops

DiNardo, Daniel N., Appointed Coadjutor Archbishop of Galveston-Houston from Coadjutor Bishop of Galveston-Houston, Dec. 29.
Fiorenza, Joseph A., Appointed Archbishop of Galveston-Houston, Dec. 29.
Flores, Patrick F., Retired Archbishop of San Antonio, Dec. 29.
Gomez, Jose H., Appointed Archbishop of San Antonio, Dec. 29.
Gregory, Wilton D., Appointed Archbishop of Atlanta, Dec. 9.
Naumann, Joseph F., Named Coadjutor Archbishop of Kansas City in Kansas, Jan. 7.

Bishops

Arias, David, Retired Auxiliary Bishop of Newark, May 21.
Bosco, Anthony G., Retired Bishop of Greensburg, Jan. 2.
Bradley, Paul J., Appointed Auxiliary Bishop of Pittsburgh, Dec. 16.
Brandt, Lawrence E., Appointed Bishop of Greensburg, Jan. 2.
Bransfeld, Michael D., Appointed Bishop of Wheeling-Charleston, Dec. 9.
Bustros, Cyrille S., Appointed Eparch of Newton, June 22.
Campbell, Frederick F., Appointed Bishop of Columbus, Oct. 14.
Carlson, Robert J., Appointed Bishop of Saginaw, Dec. 29.
Cistone, Joseph R., Appointed Auxiliary Bishop of Philadelphia, June 8.
Coakley, Paul S., Appointed Bishop of Salina, Oct. 21.
Costello, Thomas J., Retired Auxiliary Bishop of Syracuse, March 23.

Cunningham, Robert Joseph, Appointed Bishop of Ogdensburg, March 9.
Dendinger, William J., Appointed Bishop of Grand Island, Oct. 14.
DiLorenzo, Francis X., Appointed Bishop of Richmond, March 31.
Donato, Thomas A., Appointed Auxiliary Bishop of Newark, May 21.
Dorsey, Norbert L., Retired Bishop of Orlando, Nov. 13.
Doueihi, Hector, Retired Bishop of St. Maron of Brooklyn, Jan. 12.
Dupre, Thomas L., Retired Bishop of Springfield, Feb. 11.
Elya, John A., Retired Eparch of Newton, June 22.
Finn, Robert W., Named Coadjutor Bishop of Kansas City-St. Joseph, March.
Fitzsimons, George K., Retired Bishop of Salina, Oct. 21.
Flesey, John W., Appointed Auxiliary Bishop of Newark, May 21.
Galante, Joseph A., Appointed Bishop of Camden from Coadjutor Bishop of Dallas, March 23.
Gerry, Joseph, J., o.s.b., Retired Bishop of Portland, Feb. 10.
Griffin, James A., Retired Bishop of Columbus, Oct. 14.
Herzog, Ronald P., Appointed Bishop of Alexandria, Nov. 4.
Higgins, Richard B., Appointed Auxiliary Bishop for the Military Services, May 7.
Holley, Martin D., Appointed Auxiliary Bishop of Washington, May 18.
Kmiec, Edward U., Appointed Bishop of Buffalo, Aug. 12.
Listecki, Jerome E., Appointed Bishop of La Crosse, Dec. 29.
Madera, Joseph J., Retired Auxiliary Bishop for the Military Services, Sept. 15.
Malone, Richard J., Appointed Bishop of Portland in Maine, Feb.
Mansour, Gregory J., Appointed Bishop of the Eparchy of St. Maron, Brooklyn, Jan.
McDonnell, Charles J., Retired Auxiliary Bishop of Newark, May 21.
McDonnell, Timothy A., Appointed Bishop of Springfield in Massachusetts, March.
McFadden, Joseph P., Appointed Auxiliary Bishop of Philadelphia, June 8.
McManus, Robert J., Appointed Bishop of Worcester, March.
Olivier, Leonard J., Retired Auxiliary Bishop of Washington, May 18.
Reilly, Daniel P., Retired Bishop of Worcester, March.
Rhoades, Kevin C., Appointed Bishop of Harrisburg, Oct. 14.
Rodimer, Frank J., Retired Bishop of Paterson, June 1.
Roque, Francis X., Retired Auxiliary Bishop for the Military Services, Sept. 15.
Rozanski, Mitchell T., Appointed Auxiliary Bishop of Baltimore, July 3.
Salazar, Alexander, Appointed Auxiliary Bishop of Los Angeles, Sept. 7.
Serratelli, Arthur J., Appointed Bishop of Paterson, June 1.
Sullivan, Dennis J., Appointed Auxiliary Bishop of New York June, 28.
Thomas, George, Appointed Bishop of Helena from Auxiliary Bishop of Seattle, March 23.
Walsh, Gerald T., Appointed Auxiliary Bishop of New York, June 28.
Wenski, Thomas G., Succeeded as Bishop of Orlando, Nov. 13.

2005

Archbishops

Keleher, James P., Retired Archbishop of Kansas City in Kansas, Jan. 15.
Levada, William J., Appointed Prefect of the Congregation for the Doctrine of the Faith, May 13.
Naumann, Joseph F., Succeeded as Archbishop of Kansas City in Kansas, Jan. 15.
Niederauer, George H., Appointed Archbishop of San Francisco, Dec. 15.

Bishops

Angell, Kenneth A., Retired Bishop of Burlington, Nov. 9.
Boland, Raymond, Retired Bishop of Kansas City-St. Joseph, May 24.
Braxton, Edward K., Appointed Bishop of Belleville, March 15.
Calvo, Randolph R., Appointed Bishop of Reno, Dec. 23.
Choby, David R., Appointed Bishop of Nashville, Dec. 20.
del Riego, Rutilio, Appointed Auxiliary Bishop of San Bernardino, July 26.
Elizondo, Eusebio L., Appointed Auxiliary Bishop of Seattle, May 12.
Flanagan, Thomas J., Retired Auxiliary Bishop of San Antonio, Dec. 15.
Finn, Robert W., Succeeded as Bishop of Kansas City-St. Joseph, May 24.
Foley, David E., Retired Bishop of Birmingham, May 10.
Garland, James H., Retired Bishop of Marquette, Dec. 13.
Hurley, Walter A., Appointed Bishop of Grand Rapids, June 21.
Jackels, Michael O., Appointed Bishop of Wichita, Jan. 28.
Madden, Denis J., Appointed Auxiliary Bishop of Baltimore, May 10.
Matano, Salvatore R., Succeeded as Bishop of Burlington from Coadjutor, Nov. 9.
Mulvee, Robert E., Retired Bishop of Providence, March 31.
Nickless, R. Walker, Appointed Bishop of Sioux City, Nov. 10.
Noonan, John, Appointed Auxiliary Bishop of Miami, June 21.
Rueger, George E., Retired Auxiliary Bishop of Worcester, Jan. 25.
Sample, Alexander K., Appointed Bishop of Marquette, Dec. 13.
Samra, Nicholas J., Retired Auxiliary Bishop of Newton, Jan. 11.
Silva, Clarence, Appointed Bishop of Honolulu, May 17.
Straling, Phillip F., Retired Bishop of Reno, June 21.
Sullivan, Joseph, Retired Auxiliary Bishop of Brooklyn, May 12.
Tobin, Thomas J., Appointed Bishop of Providence, March 31.
Tyson, Joseph J., Appointed Auxiliary Bishop of Seattle, May 12.
Valero, Rene A., Retired Auxiliary Bishop of Brooklyn, Oct. 27.
Vann, Kevin W., Succeeded as Bishop of Fort Worth from Coadjutor, July 12.
Winter, William J., Retired Auxiliary Bishop of Pittsburgh, May 20.

2006

Cardinals

Levada, William Cardinal, Created March 24, Prefect of the Congregation for the Doctrine of the Faith.
McCarrick, Theodore Cardinal, Retired Archbishop of Washington DC, May 16.
O'Malley, Sean Patrick Cardinal, Created March 24, Archbishop of Boston.

Archbishops

DiNardo, Daniel N., Succeeded as Archbishop of Galveston-Houston, Feb. 28.
Fiorenza, Joseph A., Retired Archbishop of Galveston-Houston, Feb. 28.
Wuerl, Donald W., Appointed Archbishop of Washington DC, May 16.

Bishops

Amos, Martin, Appointed Bishop of Davenport, Oct. 12.
Boles, John Patrick, Retired Auxiliary Bishop of Boston, Oct. 12.
Brucato, Robert A., Retired Auxiliary Bishop of New York, Oct. 31.
Bura, John, Appointed Auxiliary Bishop of Philadelphia Ukrainian, Jan. 3.
Burbidge, Michael F., Appointed Bishop of Raleigh, June 8.
Caggiano, Frank, Appointed Auxiliary Bishop of Brooklyn, June 6.
Carmon, Dominic, s.v.d., Retired Auxiliary Bishop of New Orleans, Dec. 13.
Chomnycky, Paul, o.s.b.m., Appointed Bishop of Stamford, Jan. 3.
Cisneros, Octavio, Appointed Auxiliary Bishop of Brooklyn, June 6.
Dewane, Frank J., Appointed Coadjutor Bishop of Venice, April 25.
Donnelly, Robert W., Retired Auxiliary Bishop of Toledo, May 30.
Dooher, John, Appointed Auxiliary Bishop of Boston, Oct. 12.
Fabre, Shelton J., Appointed Auxiliary Bishop of New Orleans, Dec. 13.
Flores, Daniel E., Appointed Auxiliary Bishop of Detroit, Oct. 28.
Franklin, William E., Retired Bishop of Davenport, Oct. 12.
Friend, William B., Retired Bishop of Shreveport, Dec. 20.
Garcia, Richard J., Appointed Bishop of Monterey in California, Dec. 19.
Gossman, F. Joseph, Retired Bishop of Raleigh, June 8.
Gumbleton, Thomas J., Retired Auxiliary Bishop of Detroit, Feb. 2.
Hennessey, Robert, Appointed Auxiliary Bishop of Boston, Oct. 12.
Imesch, Joseph J., Retired Bishop of Joliet in Illinois, May 16.
Lennon, Richard G., Appointed Bishop of Cleveland, April 4.
Losten, Basil H., Retired Bishop of Stamford, Jan. 3.
Mikloshazy, Attila, s.j., Retired Bishop of Apostolate to Hungarians, April.
Milone, Anthony M., Retired Bishop of Great Falls, July 12.
Pilla, Anthony M., Retired Bishop of Cleveland, April 4.
Rassas, George J., Appointed Auxiliary Bishop of Chicago, Feb. 2.
Rizzotto, Vincent, Retired Auxiliary Bishop of Galveston-Houston, Nov. 6.
Ryan, Sylvester D., Retired Bishop of Monterey in California, Dec. 19.
Sansaricq, Guy, Appointed Auxiliary Bishop of Brooklyn, June 6.
Sartain, James, Appointed Bishop of Joliet in Illinois, May 16.
Swain, Paul J., Appointed Bishop of Sioux Falls, Aug. 31.
Thomas, Daniel E., Appointed Auxiliary Bishop of Philadelphia, June 8.

2007

Cardinals

DiNardo, Daniel Cardinal, Created Nov. 24, Archbishop of Galveston-Houston.
Keeler, William Cardinal, Retired Archbishop of Baltimore, July 12.

Archbishops

Broglio, Timothy P., Appointed Archbishop for the Military Services Nov. 19.
Kurtz, Joseph E., Appointed Archbishop of Louisville, June 12.
Nienstedt, John C., Appointed Coadjutor Archbishop of St. Paul and Minneapolis, April 24.
O'Brien, Edwin F., Appointed Archbishop of Baltimore, July 12.

Bishops

Baker, Robert J., Appointed Bishop of Birmingham, Aug. 14.
Balke, Victor H. Retired Bishop of Crookston, Sept. 28.
Callahan, William P., Appointed Auxiliary Bishop of Milwaukee, Oct. 30.
Charron, Joseph L., c.pp.s., Retired Bishop of Des Moines, April 10.
Chavez, Gilbert, Retired Auxiliary Bishop of San Diego, June 1.
Christensen, Peter F., Appointed Bishop of Superior, June 28.
Cserhati, Ferenc, Appointed Bishop for the Apostolate to Hungarians, June 15.
Dewane, Frank J., Succeeded as Bishop of Venice, Jan. 19.
Dino, Gerald N., Appointed Bishop of Van Nuys, Dec. 6.
Farrell, Kevin J., Appointed Bishop of Dallas, March 6.
Fernandez Torres, Daniel, Appointed Auxiliary Bishop of San Juan, Feb. 14.
Fliss, Raphael M., Retired Bishop of Superior, June 28.
Grahmann, Charles V., Retired Bishop of Dallas, March 6.

Hoeppner, Michael J., Appointed Bishop of Crookston, Sept. 28.
Libasci, Peter A., Appointed Auxiliary Bishop of Rockville Centre, April 3.
Murry, George V., s.j., Appointed Bishop of Youngstown, Jan. 30.
Nevins, John J., Retired Bishop of Venice, Jan. 19.
Provost, Glen J., Appointed Bishop of Lake Charles, March 6.
Skurla, William C., Appointed Bishop of Passaic, Dec. 6.
Soto, Jaime, Appointed Coadjutor Bishop of Sacramento, Oct. 11.
Warfel, Michael W., Appointed Bishop of Great Falls-Billings, Nov. 20.
Wcela, Emil A., Retired Auxiliary Bishop of Rockville Centre, April 3.
Wester, John C., Appointed Bishop of Salt Lake City, Jan. 8.
Zubik, David A., Appointed Bishop of Pittsburgh, July 18.

2008

Archbishops

Burke, Raymond L., Resigned Archbishop of St. Louis, June 27.
Flynn, Harry J., Retired Archbishop of St. Paul and Minneapolis, May 2.
Lipscomb, Oscar H., Retired Archbishop of Mobile, April 2.
Nienstedt, John C., Succeeded to Archbishop of St. Paul and Minneapolis, May 2.
Rodi, Thomas J., Appointed Archbishop of Mobile, April 2.
Schnurr, Dennis M., Appointed Coadjutor Archbishop of Cincinnati, Oct. 17.

Bishops

Bevard, Herbert A., Appointed Bishop of St. Thomas in the Virgin Islands, July 7.
Boyea, Earl A., Appointed Bishop of Lansing, Feb. 27.
Cantu, Oscar, Appointed Auxiliary Bishop of San Antonio, April 10.
Conley, James D., Appointed Auxiliary Bishop of Denver, April 10.
Cruz, Manuel A., Appointed Auxiliary Bishop of Newark, June 9.
Duca, Michael G., Appointed Bishop of Shreveport, April 1.
Johnston, Jr., J. Vann, Appointed Bishop of Springfield-Cape Girardeau, Jan. 24.
Justice, William J., Appointed Auxiliary Bishop of San Francisco, April 10.
Knestout, Barry C., Appointed Auxiliary Bishop of Washington, Nov. 18.
Leibrecht, John J., Retired Bishop of Springfield-Cape Girardeau, Jan. 24.
LeVoir, John M., Appointed Bishop of New Ulm, July 14.
Malooly, W. Francis, Appointed Bishop of Wilmington, July 7.
Mengeling, Carl F., Retired Bishop of Lansing, Feb. 27.
Pates, Richard E., Appointed Bishop of Des Moines, April 10.
Quinn, A. James, Retired Auxiliary Bishop of Cleveland, June 14.
Quinn, John M., Appointed Coadjutor Bishop of Winona, Oct. 15.
Ramos Morales, Eusebio, Appointed Bishop of Fajardo-Humacao, March 11.
Ricken, David L., Appointed Bishop of Green Bay, July 9.
Soto, Jaime, Succeeded as Bishop of Sacramento, Nov. 29.
Taylor, Anthony B., Appointed Bishop of Little Rock, April 10.
Weigand, William K., Retired Bishop of Sacramento, Nov. 29.
Yanta, John W., Retired Bishop of Amarillo, Jan. 3.
Zurek, Patrick J., Appointed Bishop of Amarillo, Jan. 3.

2009

Cardinals

Egan, Edward Cardinal, Retired Archbishop of New York, Feb. 23.
Maida, Adam Cardinal, Retired Archbishop of Detroit, Jan. 5.

Archbishops

Aymond, Gregory M., Appointed Archbishop of New Orleans, June 12.
Carlson, Robert J., Appointed Archbishop of St. Louis, April 21.
Curtiss, Elden Francis, Retired Archbishop of Omaha, June 3.
Dolan, Timothy M., Appointed Archbishop of New York, Feb. 23.
Hughes, Alfred C., Retired Archbishop of New Orleans, June 12.
Listecki, Jerome E., Appointed Archbishop of Milwaukee, Nov. 14.
Lucas, George J., Appointed Archbishop of Omaha, June 3.
Pilarczyk, Daniel E., Retired Archbishop of Cincinnati, Dec. 21.
Schnurr, Dennis M., Appointed Archbishop of Cincinnati, Dec. 21.
Vigneron, Allen H., Appointed Archbishop of Detroit, Jan. 5.

Bishops

Barres, John O., Appointed Bishop of Allentown, May 27.
Bradley, Paul J., Appointed Bishop of Kalamazoo, April 6.
Burns, Edward J., Appointed Bishop of Juneau, Jan. 19.
Cistone, Joseph R., Appointed Bishop of Saginaw, May 20.
Cooney, Patrick R., Retired Bishop of Gaylord, Oct. 7.
Cordileone, Salvatore J., Appointed Bishop of Oakland, March 23.
Cullen, Edward P., Retired Bishop of Allentown, May 27.
Cunningham, Robert J., Appointed Bishop of Syracuse, April 21.
D'Arcy, John M., Retired Bishop of Fort Wayne-South Bend, Nov. 14.
Dougherty, John M., Retired Auxiliary Bishop of Scranton, Aug. 31.
Etienne, Paul D., Appointed Bishop of Cheyenne, Oct. 19.
Evans, Robert C., Appointed Auxiliary Bishop of Providence, Oct. 15.
Flores, Cirilo, Appointed Auxiliary Bishop of Orange, Jan. 5.
Flores, Daniel E., Appointed Bishop of Brownsville, Dec. 9.
Guglielmone, Robert E., Appointed Bishop of Charleston, Jan. 24.
Harrington, Bernard J., Retired Bishop of Winona, May 7.
Hebda, Bernard A., Appointed Bishop of Gaylord, Oct. 7.
Irwin, Francis Xavier, Retired Auxiliary Bishop of Boston, Oct. 12.
Isern, Fernando, Appointed Bishop of Pueblo, Oct. 15.
Martino, Joseph F., Retired Bishop of Scranton, Aug. 31.
McRaith, John J., Retired Bishop of Owensboro, Jan. 5.
Medley, William F., Appointed Bishop of Owensboro, Dec. 15.
Morin, Roger P., Appointed Bishop of Biloxi, March 2.
Moskal, Robert M., Retired Bishop of St. Josaphat in Parma, July 29.
Moynihan, James M., Retired Bishop of Syracuse, April 21.
Murray, James A., Retired Bishop of Kalamazoo, April 6.
Pena, Raymundo J., Retired Bishop of Brownsville, Dec. 9.
Piche, Lee A., Appointed Auxiliary Bishop of St. Paul and Minneapolis, May 27.
Quinn, John M., Appointed Bishop of Winona, May 7.
Rhoades, Kevin C., Appointed Bishop of Fort Wayne-South Bend, Nov. 14.
Rivera, Hector M., Retired Auxiliary Bishop of San Juan, PR, Oct. 31.
Senior, Timothy, Appointed Auxiliary Bishop of Philadelphia, June 8.
Siegel, Joseph M., Appointed Auxiliary Bishop of Joliet, Oct. 28.
Sirba, Paul D., Appointed Bishop of Duluth, Oct. 15.
Stika, Richard F., Appointed Bishop of Knoxville, Jan. 12.
Tafoya, Arthur N., Retired Bishop of Pueblo, Oct. 15.
Wall, James S., Appointed Bishop of Gallup, Feb. 5.
Wang, Ignatius, Retired Auxiliary Bishop of San Francisco, May 16.
Zarama, Luis R., Appointed Auxiliary Bishop of Atlanta, July 27.

2010

Cardinal

Wuerl, Donald Cardinal, Created Nov. 20, Archbishop of Washington.

Archbishops

Beltran, Eusebius J., Retired Archbishop of Oklahoma City, Dec. 16.
Brunett, Alexander J., Retired Archbishop of Seattle, Sept. 16.
Coakley, Paul S., Appointed Archbishop of Oklahoma City, Dec. 16.
Favalora, John C., Retired Archbishop of Miami, April 20.
Garcia-Siller, Gustavo, m.sp.s., Appointed Archbishop of San Antonio, Oct. 14.
Gomez, Jose Horacio, Appointed Coadjutor Archbishop of Los Angeles, April 6.
Sartain, James Peter, Appointed Archbishop of Seattle, Sept. 16.
Wenski, Thomas G., Appointed Archbishop of Miami, April 20.

Bishops

Allue, Emilio Simeon, Retired Auxiliary Bishop of Boston, June 30.
Bambera, Joseph C., Appointed Bishop of Scranton, Feb. 23.
Brungardt, John B., Appointed Bishop of Dodge City, Dec. 15.
Callahan, William P., o.f.m.conv., Appointed Bishop of La Crosse, June 11.
Camacho, Tomas A., Retired Bishop of Chalan Kanoa, April 6.
Carmody, Edmond, Retired Bishop of Corpus Christi, Jan. 18.
Catanello, Ignatius A., Retired Auxiliary Bishop of Brooklyn, Sept. 20.
Cupich, Blasé J., Appointed Bishop of Spokane, June 30.
Deshotel, John D., Appointed Auxiliary Bishop of Dallas, March 11.
Doherty, Timothy, Appointed Bishop of Lafayette in Indiana, May 12.
Fernandez Torres, Daniel, Appointed Bishop of Arecibo, Sept. 24.
Fitzgerald, Michael J., Appointed Auxiliary Bishop of Philadelphia, June 22.
Gilmore, Ronald M., Retired Bishop of Dodge City, Dec. 15.
Habash, Yousif, Appointed Bishop of Our Lady of Deliverance, April 12.
Hermann, Robert J., Retired Auxiliary Bishop of St. Louis, Dec. 1.
Higi, William L., Retired Bishop of Lafayette in Indiana, May 12.
Kennedy, Arthur L., Appointed Auxiliary Bishop of Boston, June 30.
LaValley, Terry R., Appointed Bishop of Ogdensburg, Feb. 23.
Maginnis, Robert P., Retired Auxiliary Bishop of Philadelphia, June 8.
McElroy, Robert W., Appointed Auxiliary Bishop San Francisco, July 6.
McFadden, Joseph P., Appointed Bishop of Harrisburg, June 22.
McIntyre, John J., Appointed Auxiliary Bishop of Philadelphia, June 8.
Mulvey, William M., Appointed Bishop of Corpus Christi, Jan. 18.
Naickamparambil, Thomas Mar Eusebius, Appointed Bishop of Syro-Malankara Catholic Exarchate, July 14.
Nevares, Eduardo A., Appointed Auxiliary Bishop of Phoenix, May 11.
Noonan, John G., Appointed Bishop of Orlando, Oct. 23.
O'Connell, David M., Succeeded as Bishop of Trenton, Dec. 1.
Paprocki, Thomas J., Appointed Bishop of Springfield in Illinois, April 20.
Rice, Edward M., Appointed Auxiliary Bishop of St. Louis, Dec. 1.
Rosazza, Peter A., Retired Auxiliary Bishop of Hartford, June 30.
Sansaricq, Guy, Retired Auxiliary Bishop of Brooklyn, Oct. 6.
Seitz, Mark J., Appointed Auxiliary Bishop of Dallas, March 11.
Sklba, Richard J., Retired Auxiliary Bishop of Milwaukee, Oct. 18.
Skylstad, William S., Retired Bishop of Spokane, June 30.
Smith, John M., Retired Bishop of Trenton, Dec. 1.

Spencer, F. Richard, Appointed Auxiliary Bishop for the Military Services, May 22.
Txertudi, Inaki Mallona, c.p., Retired Bishop of Arecibo, Sept. 24.
Uglietto, Peter J., Appointed Auxiliary Bishop of Boston, June 30.
Vasquez, Joe S., Appointed Bishop of Austin, Jan. 26.

2011

Cardinals
Mahony, Roger Cardinal, Retired Archbishop of Los Angeles, March 1.
Rigali, Justin Cardinal, Retired Archbishop of Philadelphia, July 19.

Archbishops
Buechlein, Daniel Mark, o.s.b., Retired Archbishop of Indianapolis, Sept. 21.
Chaput, Charles J., o.f.m.cap., Appointed Archbishop of Philadelphia, July 19.
Gomez, Jose H., Succeeded as Archbishop of Los Angeles, March 1.

Bishops
Adamec, Joseph V., Retired Bishop of Altoona-Johnstown, Jan. 14.
Bartchak, Mark L., Appointed Bishop of Altoona-Johnstown, Jan. 14.
Batakian, Manuel, Retired Eparch of Our Lady of Nareg, May 21.
Binzer, Joseph R., Appointed Auxiliary Bishop of Cincinnati, April 6.
Boland, J. Kevin, Retired Bishop of Savannah, July 19, 2011.
Buckon, Neal J., Appointed Auxiliary Bishop for the Military Services, Jan. 3.
Byrnes, Michael, Appointed Auxiliary Bishop of Detroit, March 22.
Casiano Vargas, Ulises Aurelio, Retired Bishop of Mayaguez, July 6.
Conley, James D., Appointed Apostolic Administrator of Denver, Sept. 8.
Conlon, R. Daniel, Appointed Bishop of Joliet in Illinois, May 17.
Corrada del Rio, Alvaro, s.j., Appointed Bishop of Mayaguez, July 6.
Coyne, Christopher J., Appointed Auxiliary Bishop of Indianapolis, Jan.14 and Appointed Apostolic Administrator of Indianapolis Sept. 21.
Daly, Thomas A., Appointed Auxiliary Bishop of San Jose, March 16.
Escobedo, Jose Arturo Cepeda, Appointed Auxiliary Bishop of Detroit, April 18.
Estevez, Felipe de Jesus, Appointed Bishop of St. Augustine April 27.
Galeone, Victor Benito, Retired Bishop of St. Augustine, April 27.
Gettelfinger, Gerald A., Retired Bishop of Evansville, April 26.
Gruss, Robert D., Appointed Bishop of Rapid City, May 26.
Hanchon, Donald F., Appointed Auxiliary Bishop of Detroit, March 22.
Hartmayer, Gregory J., Appointed Bishop of Savannah, July 19.
Hying, Donald J., Appointed Auxiliary Bishop of Milwaukee, May 26.
Kagan, David D., Appointed Bishop of Bismarck, Oct. 19.
Libasci, Peter A., Appointed Bishop of Manchester, Sept. 19.
McCormack, John B., Retired Bishop of Manchester, Sept. 19.
Mouradian, Mikael A., Appointed Eparch of Our Lady of Nareg, May 21.
Ochoa, Armando X., Appointed Bishop of Fresno, Dec. 1.
Ricard, John H., Retired Bishop of Pensacola-Tallahassee, March 11.
Rojas, Alberto, Appointed Auxiliary Bishop of Chicago, June 13.
Samra, Nicholas J., Appointed Eparch of Newton, June 15.
Sevilla, Carlos A., Retired Bishop of Yakima, April 12.
Steiner, Kenneth D., retired Auxiliary Bishop of Portland in Oregon, Nov. 25.
Thompson, Charles C., Appointed Bishop of Evansville, April 26.
Tyson, Joseph J., Appointed Bishop of Yakima, April 12.
Vasa, Robert Francis, Appointed Coadjutor Bishop of Santa Rosa, Jan. 24.
Walsh, Daniel F., Retired Bishop of Santa Rosa, June 30.
Waltersheid, William J., Appointed Auxiliary Bishop of Pittsburgh, Feb. 25.
Wypych, Andrew P., Appointed Auxiliary Bishop of Chicago, June 13.
Zipfel, Paul A., Retired Bishop of Bismarck, Oct. 19.

2012

Cardinal
Dolan, Timothy Cardinal, Created Feb. 18, Archbishop of New York.

Archbishops
Lori, William E., Appointed Archbishop of Baltimore, March 20.
Skurla, William C., Appointed Archbishop of Pittsburgh, Byzantine, Jan. 19.

Bishops
Cary, Liam S., Appointed Bishop of Baker, March 8.
Doran, Thomas G., Retired Bishop of Rockford, March 20.
Flores, Cirilo, Appointed Coadjutor Bishop of San Diego, Jan. 4.
Malloy, David J., Appointed Bishop of Rockford, March 20.
Parkes, Gregory L., Appointed Bishop of Pensacola-Tallahassee, March 20.
Sheltz, George A., Appointed Auxiliary Bishop of Galveston-Houston, Feb. 21.
Weisenburger, Edward J., Appointed Bishop of Salina, Feb. 6.

United States Conference of Catholic Bishops

Address—3211 Fourth St., N.E., Washington, DC 20017-1194. Tel: 202-541-3000; Web Site: www.usccb.org.

The United States Conference of Catholic Bishops is a permanent institute composed of Catholic bishops of the United States of America in and through which the bishops exercise in a communal or collegial manner the pastoral mission entrusted to them by the Lord Jesus of sanctification, teaching, and leadership, especially by devising forms and methods of the apostolate suitably adapted to the circumstances of the times. Such exercise is intended to offer appropriate assistance to each bishop in fulfilling his particular ministry in the local Church, to effect a commonality of ministry addressed to the people of the United States of America, and to foster and express communion with the Church in other nations within the Church universal, under the leadership of its chief pastor, the Pope.

OFFICES

President—Cardinal Timothy M. Dolan
Vice President—Archbishop Joseph E. Kurtz
Treasurer—Bishop Michael J. Bransfield
Secretary—Bishop George Vance Murry, S.J.

USCCB GENERAL SECRETARIAT

General Secretary—Rev. Msgr. David J. Malloy
General Secretary - Elect—Rev. Msgr. Ronny Jenkins
Rev. J. Brian Bransfield, M.Div., M.A., S.T.L.
Associate General Secretary—Mr. Bruce E. Egnew
Ms. Nancy Wisdo

STAFF OFFICES

Finance & Accounting—Mrs. Joyce Jones
General Counsel—Mr. Anthony R. Picarello, Esq.
General Services—Mr. Keith Manley
Government Relations—Ms. Nancy Wisdo
Human Resources—Ms. Linda Hunt
Information Technology—Mr. John A. Galotta
Child & Youth Protection—Ms. Teresa M. Kettelkamp

USCCB COMMITTEES
I. EXECUTIVE LEVEL
ADMINISTRATIVE COMMITTEE

President—Cardinal Timothy M. Dolan
Members—Cardinal Daniel N. DiNardo
Cardinal Donald W. Wuerl
Archbishop Wilton D. Gregory, S.L.D.
Bishop Earl Boyea (Region VI)
Bishop Edward K. Braxton (Region VII)
Bishop Michael F. Burbidge, D.D., Ed.D., V.G. (Region XIV)
Auxiliary Bishop Oscar Cantu (Region X)
Bishop Francis J. Christian, Ph.D. (Region I)
Bishop Robert J. Cunningham, D.D., J.C.L. (Region II)
Bishop Blase J. Cupich
Bishop Thomas J. Curry, D.D., Ph.D., V.G.
Bishop Kevin Joseph Farrell, D.D.
Bishop Roger J. Foys (Region V)
Bishop Howard J. Hubbard
Bishop William J. Justice (Region XI)
Bishop Richard J. Malone
Bishop R. Walker Nickless (Region IX)
Bishop Thomas J. Paprocki, S.T.L., J.D., J.C.D.
Bishop Mitchell T. Rozanski, D.D., V.G. (Region IV)
Bishop Michael J. Sheridan, S.Th.D. (Region XIII)
Bishop Paul D. Sirba (Region VIII)
Bishop William C. Skurla (Region XV)
Bishop Jaime Soto, M.S.W.
Bishop Joseph J. Tyson (Region XII)
Bishop Gabino Zavala
Bishop David A. Zubik (Region III)
Vice President—Archbishop Joseph E. Kurtz
Treasurer—Bishop Michael J. Bransfield
Secretary—Bishop George V. Murry, S.J.

ADMINISTRATIVE COMMITTEE-REGIONAL ALTERNATES

Alternate (Region I)—Bishop Robert Hennessey
Alternate (Region II)—Bishop Ignatius Catanello, D.D., Ph.D., V.E.
Alternate (Region III)—Bishop Edgar M. da Cunha, S.D.V., D.D.
Alternate (Region IV)—Archbishop Timothy P. Broglio
Alternate (Region V)—Bishop Ronald William Gainer
Alternate (Region VI)—Bishop R. Daniel Conlon
Alternate (Region VII)—Bishop William P. Callahan, O.F.M.Conv.
Alternate (Region VIII)—Bishop John LeVoir
Alternate (Region IX)—Archbishop Paul S. Coakley, D.D., S.T.L.
Alternate (Region X)—Bishop Michael D. Pfeifer, O.M.I.
Alternate (Region XI)—Bishop Rutilio J. del Riego
Alternate (Region XII)—Bishop Donald J. Kettler
Alternate (Region XIII)—Bishop James S. Wall
Alternate (Region XIV)—Bishop Robert Guglielmone
Alternate (Region XV)—Bishop Jacob Angadiath

EXECUTIVE COMMITTEE

Chairman—Cardinal Timothy M. Dolan
Members—Bishop Arthur J. Serratelli, S.T.D., S.S.L., D.D.
Vice President—Archbishop Joseph E. Kurtz
Treasurer—Bishop Michael J. Bransfield
Secretary—Bishop George Vance Murry, S.J.
Staff—Rev. Msgr. David J. Malloy

BUDGET AND FINANCE

Chairman—Bishop Michael J. Bransfield
Members—Cardinal Edmund Szoka
Bishop Kevin Joseph Farrell, D.D.
Bishop Gerald Frederick Kicanas, D.D.
Bishop Timothy Senior
Staff—Mr. Bruce E. Egnew
Rev. Msgr. Ronny E. Jenkins, S.T.L., J.C.D.
Peter Canine
Mrs. Joyce Jones
Ms. Nancy Wisdo

Audit Subcommittee

Chairman—Bishop Kevin J. Farrell, D.D.
Members—Bishop Michael F. Burbidge, D.D., Ed.D., V.G.
Bishop Mitchell T. Rozanski, D.D., V.G.

PRIORITIES AND PLANS

Chairman—Bishop George Vance Murry, S.J.
Vice Chairman—Bishop Michael J. Bransfield
Members—Bishop Earl Boyea (Region VI)
Bishop Edward K. Braxton (Region VII)
Bishop Michael F. Burbidge, D.D., Ed.D., V.G. (Region XIV)
Bishop Oscar Cantu (Region X)
Bishop Francis J. Christian, Ph.D. (Region I)
Bishop Robert J. Cunningham, D.D., J.C.L. (Region II)
Bishop Roger J. Foys (Region V)
Bishop William J. Justice (Region XI)
Bishop R. Walker Nickless (Region IX)
Bishop Mitchell T. Rozanski, D.D., V.G. (Region IV)
Bishop Michael J. Sheridan, S.Th.D. (Region XIII)
Bishop Paul D. Sirba (Region VIII)
Bishop William C. Skurla (Region XV)
Bishop Joseph J. Tyson (Region XII)
Bishop David A. Zubik (Region III)
Consultants—Rev. Msgr. David J. Malloy
Staff Coordinator—Rev. J. Brian Bransfield, M.Div., M.A., S.T.L.
Staff—Mr. Bruce E. Egnew
Rev. Msgr. Ronny E. Jenkins, S.T.L., J.C.D.
Paul Henderson
Mrs. Joyce Jones
Ms. Helen Osman
Ms. Nancy Wisdo

II. GENERAL MEMBERSHIP LEVEL
STANDING COMMITTEES
COMMITTEE ON CANONICAL AFFAIRS AND CHURCH GOVERNANCE

Chairman—Bishop Thomas J. Paprocki, S.T.L., J.D., J.C.D.
Chairman - Elect—Archbishop Timothy P. Broglio
Members—Archbishop John J. Myers, D.D., J.C.D.
Bishop R. Daniel Conlon
Bishop Salvatore J. Cordileone, J.C.D.
Bishop Thomas George Doran, D.D., J.C.D.
Bishop David Eugene Fellhauer
Bishop Peter J. Jugis
Bishop David L. Ricken, D.D., J.C.L.
Bishop Kevin W. Vann, J.C.D., D.D.
Consultants—Bishop Mark Bartchak
Rev. John J. Coughlin, O.F.M.
Sr. Sharon A. Euart, R.S.M., J.C.D.
Dr. Kurt Martens
Staff—Rev. Msgr. Ronny E. Jenkins, S.T.L., J.C.D.
Ms. Siobhan M. Verbeek, J.C.L.

COMMITTEE ON CATHOLIC EDUCATION

Chairman—Bishop Thomas J. Curry, D.D., Ph.D., V.G.
Chairman - Elect—Bishop Joseph P. McFadden, D.D.
Members—Bishop Oscar Cantu, S.T.D.
Bishop John C. Dunne
Bishop Walter J. Edyvean, S.T.D.
Bishop Ronald William Gainer
Bishop Francis J. Kane
Bishop Joseph P. McFadden, D.D.
Bishop Richard E. Pates
Bishop John C. Wester, V.G.
Consultants—Bishop Michael J. Sheridan, S.Th.D.
Dr. John Convey
Dr. Michael Galligan-Stierle
Sr. Mary Elizabeth Galt, B.V.M.
Ms. Jennifer Kraska
Dr. Mary McDonald
Rev. Martin Moran
Dr. Karen Ristau
Ms. Mary Ellen Russell
Staff—Sr. Suzanne Bellenoit, S.S.J.
Ms. Barbara Humphrey McCrabb
Mrs. Marie A. Powell
Ms. Terry Thames

COMMITTEE ON CLERGY, CONSECRATED LIFE, AND VOCATIONS

Chairman—Archbishop Robert J. Carlson
Members—Cardinal Sean P. O'Malley, O.F.M.Cap., Ph.D.
Bishop Samuel J. Aquila
Bishop Earl Boyea
Bishop Edward K. Braxton
Bishop Michael F. Burbidge, D.D., Ed.D., V.G.
Bishop Octavio Cisneros
Bishop Daniel E. Thomas
Rev. Msgr. Steven Callahan
Consultants—Archbishop Paul S. Coakley
Bishop Robert J. Shaheen
Rev. Robert Barron
Deacon Gerald Dupont
Sr. Rose McDermott, S.S.J.
Mrs. Rose Sullivan
Staff—Rev. W. Shawn McKnight, S.T.D.
Sr. Mary Joanna Ruhland, R.S.M.

COMMITTEE ON COMMUNICATIONS

Chairman—Bishop Gabino Zavala, D.D., J.C.L., V.G.
Members—Archbishop Gregory M. Aymond
Archbishop Dennis M. Schnurr
Bishop Michael J. Bransfield
Bishop Ronald P. Herzog
Bishop John B. McCormack, D.D.
Bishop Joseph A. Pepe
Consultants—Mr. Patrick Brannigan
Ms. Carolina Guevara
Deacon Gregory Kandra
Mr. Frank Morock
Dr. Owen Phelps, Ph.D.
Mr. Jeff Smith
Mrs. Annette Gonzales Taylor
Mrs. Penny Wiegert
Staff—Mr. Enrico Donzelli
Mr. David Felber
Paul Henderson
Ms. Helen Osman
Mr. Anthony J. Spence
Sr. Mary Ann Walsh

Subcommittee on the Catholic Communications Campaign

Chairman—Archbishop Dennis M. Schnurr
Members—Bishop Michael J. Bransfield
Bishop Thomas J. Costello, D.D., V.G.
Bishop Richard J. Garcia, D.D.
Bishop Martin D. Holley, D.D., V.G.
Consultants—Ms. Carolina Guevara
Deacon Gregory Kandra
Mr. Frank Morock
Dr. Owen Phelps, Ph.D.
Mr. Jeff Smith
Mrs. Annette Gonzales Taylor
Mrs. Penny Wiegert
Staff—Mr. Enrico Donzelli
Mr. David Felber
Paul Henderson
Ms. Helen Osman
Mr. Anthony J. Spence
Sr. Mary Ann Walsh

COMMITTEE ON CULTURAL DIVERSITY IN THE CHURCH

Chairman—Bishop Jaime Soto, M.S.W.
Members—Archbishop Charles J. Chaput, O.F.M.Cap., D.D.
Bishop Gerald R. Barnes
Bishop Randolph R. Calvo
Bishop Rutilio J. del Riego
Bishop Martin D. Holley, D.D., V.G.
Staff—Rev. Allan F. Deck, S.J.

Subcommittee on African American Affairs

Chairman—Bishop Martin D. Holley, D.D., V.G.
Members—Bishop Herbert A. Bevard
Bishop Oscar Cantu, S.T.D.
Bishop Manuel A. Cruz
Bishop Shelton J. Fabre
Bishop Curtis J. Guillory, S.V.D.
Bishop Joseph N. Perry
Bishop Glen J. Provost
Bishop John H. Ricard, S.S.J.
Consultants—Deacon Arthur Miller
Mrs. Geralyn Shelvin
Staff—Ms. Beverly A. Carroll

Subcommittee on Asian and Pacific Islanders
Chairman—Bishop Randolph R. Calvo
Members—Bishop Jacob Angadiath
Bishop William Justice
Bishop Dominic M. Luong, D.D., V.G.
Bishop Clarence Silva
Bishop Oscar Azarcon Solis
Bishop Dennis J. Sullivan
Bishop Joseph J. Tyson
Bishop Joe Steve Vasquez
Consultants—Rev. Paul Lee
Ms. Teresita Nuval
Staff—Ms. Cecile Motus

Subcommittee on Hispanic Affairs
Chairman—Bishop Gerald R. Barnes
Members—Bishop Octavio Cisneros, (Region II)
Bishop Daniel E. Flores, S.T.D., (Region VI)
Archbishop J. Peter Sartain, D.D., S.T.L., (Region VII)
Bishop Joe Steve Vasquez, (Region X)
Bishop Cirilo B. Flores, (Region XI)
Bishop Joseph A. Pepe
Bishop Eusebio Elizondo, M.Sp.S., J.C.D., (Region XII)
Bishop Felipe de Jesus Estevez, (Region XIV)
Consultants—Rev. Msgr. Eberto Diaz
Ms. Maria Johnson
Staff—Mr. Alejandro Aguilera-Titus

Subcommittee on Native American Catholics
Chairman—Archbishop Charles J. Chaput, O.F.M.Cap., D.D.
Members—Archbishop Alexander J. Brunett, D.D., Ph.D.
Bishop Peter F. Christensen, M.A.S.
Bishop Robert J. Cunningham, D.D., J.C.L.
Bishop Ronald P. Herzog, D.D.
Bishop Donald J. Kettler
Bishop Alexander K. Sample
Bishop George L. Thomas
Consultants—Sr. Kateri Mitchell, S.S.A.
Rev. Wayne C. Paysse
Staff—Rev. Maurice Henry Sands

Subcommittee on Pastoral Care of Migrants, Refugees, and Travelers
Chairman—Bishop Rutilio J. del Riego
Members—Bishop J. Kevin Boland
Bishop Edgar M. da Cunha, S.D.V., D.D.
Bishop Frank J. Dewane
Bishop John F. Kinney, D.D., J.C.D.
Bishop John R. Manz
Bishop John H. Ricard, S.S.J.
Bishop Guy Sansaricq
Consultants—Archbishop Jerome E. Listecki
Staff—Sr. Myrna Tordillo, M.S.C.S.

COMMITTEE ON DIVINE WORSHIP

Chairman—Archbishop Gregory M. Aymond, D.D.
Members—Cardinal Francis E. George, O.M.I.
Cardinal Justin F. Rigali
Bishop Edward K. Braxton
Bishop Octavio Cisneros
Bishop Daniel E. Flores, S.T.D.
Bishop Ronald P. Herzog, D.D.
Bishop Arthur Joseph Serratelli, S.S.L., S.T.D., D.D.
Bishop Daniel E. Thomas
Consultants—Rev. Donald Senior, C.P., S.T.D.
Bishop David A. Zubik
Rev. Msgr. John H. Burton
Rev. Msgr. Kevin W. Irwin, S.T.D., M.A.
Rev. Juan J. Sosa
Ms. Lisa A. Tarker
Staff—Rev. Richard B. Hilgartner
Sr. Doris M. Turek, S.S.N.D.

Subcommittee on Hispanics and the Liturgy
Chairman—Bishop Octavio Cisneros
Members—Archbishop Gustavo Garcia-Siller, M.Sp.S.
Archbishop Jose H. Gomez, S.T.D.
Bishop Carlos Arthur Sevilla, S.J., D.D.
Bishop Luis R. Zarama
Consultants—Rev. Heliodero Lucatero
Rev. Jorge I. Perales
Mr. Rogelio Zelada
Staff—Sr. Doris M. Turek, S.S.N.D.

COMMITTEE ON DOCTRINE

Chairman—Cardinal Donald W. Wuerl
Members—Archbishop Daniel M. Buechlein, O.S.B., D.D.
Archbishop Jose H. Gomez, S.T.D., D.D.
Archbishop Allen H. Vigneron, D.D.
Bishop Leonard P. Blair
Bishop William E. Lori, S.T.D.
Bishop Robert J. McManus, D.D., S.T.D.
Bishop Kevin C. Rhoades, D.D., S.T.L., J.C.L.
Bishop Arthur J. Serratelli, S.T.D., S.S.L., D.D.
Consultants—Cardinal Francis E. George, O.M.I.
Archbishop John C. Nienstedt
Rev. Steven C. Boguslawski, O.P., M.A., M.Div., S.T.M., S.T.L., Ph.D.
Sr. Sara Butler, M.S.B.T., Ph.D.
Dr. Peter Casarella
Dr. John C. Cavadini, Ph.D.
Rev. John McDermott
Staff—Dr. James Legrys
Ms. Siobhan M. Verbeek, J.C.L.
Rev. Thomas G. Weinandy, O.F.M.Cap.

Subcommittee on the Translation of Scripture Text
Chairman—Bishop Arthur J. Serratelli, S.T.D., S.S.L., D.D.
Members—Cardinal Justin F. Rigali
Bishop Blase J. Cupich
Bishop Anthony B. Taylor
Staff—Ms. Siobhan M. Verbeek, J.C.L.
Rev. Thomas G. Weinandy, O.F.M.Cap.

COMMITTEE ON DOMESTIC JUSTICE AND HUMAN DEVELOPMENT

Chairman—Bishop Stephen E. Blaire, D.D.
Chairman-Elect—Bishop Howard J. Hubbard
Members—Archbishop Gregory M. Aymond
Archbishop Gustavo Garcia-Siller, M.Sp.S.
Bishop Martin D. Holley, D.D., V.G.
Bishop Robert W. McElroy
Bishop Ricardo Ramirez, C.S.B.
Bishop Jaime Soto
Bishop David A. Zubik
Consultants—Mr. Ray Boshara
Ms. Meghan Clark, Ph.D.
Mr. John Garvey
Mr. Morgan McGrath
Mr. John Sweeney
Mr. Anthony Williams
Staff—Ms. Cecilia Calvo
Mr. John Carr
Mr. Anthony Granado
Mr. Thomas Mulloy
Ms. Kathy Saile

Subcommittee on the Catholic Campaign for Human Development
Chairman—Bishop Jaime Soto
Members—Bishop Michael Patrick Driscoll
Bishop Howard J. Hubbard
Bishop Francis J. Kane
Bishop J. Terry Steib, S.V.D.
Bishop David A. Zubik
Consultants—Rev. Edward B. Branch
Ms. Christine (Cris) Doby
Mr. Richard Fowler
Mr. Robert Gorman, A.C.S.W., B.C.S.W.
Rev. Michael P. Jacques, S.S.E., V.F.
Ms. Martina O'Sullivan, M.S.W.
Ms. Kerry A. Robinson
Dr. Richard Wood
Staff—Ms. Bonita Anderson
Mr. John Carr
Mr. W. Randy Kessler
Ms. Gloria Luna Moorman
Ms. Sandy Mattingly-Paulen
Mr. Ralph McCloud
Ms. Kathy Saile

COMMITTEE ON ECUMENICAL AND INTERRELIGIOUS AFFAIRS

Chairman—Archbishop Wilton D. Gregory, S.L.D.
Chairman-Elect—Bishop Denis J. Madden
Members—Bishop Stephen E. Blaire, D.D.
Bishop Daniel E. Flores, S.T.D.
Bishop John R. Gaydos
Bishop Denis J. Madden
Bishop William F. Murphy, J.C.L., LL.D., S.T.D.
Bishop Thomas J. Olmsted, J.C.L.
Representatives—Rev. Dennis McManus
Dr. Christopher Ruddy
Rev. Frank Ruff
Consultants—Cardinal William Keeler
Archbishop Oscar H. Lipscomb, D.D., Ph.D.
Archbishop John C. Nienstedt
Bishop Tod D. Brown, D.D.
Bishop Ronald P. Herzog, D.D.
Bishop Howard J. Hubbard
Bishop Edward U. Kmiec, D.D., S.T.L.
Bishop John C. Reiss, D.D., J.C.D.
Bishop Placido Rodriguez, C.M.F.
Bishop Carlos Arthur Sevilla, S.J., D.D.
Bishop Richard J. Sklba
Bishop John C. Wester
Bishop William S. Skylstad, D.D.
Staff—Rev. James Massa, Exec. Dir.
Rev. Ronald G. Roberson, C.S.P.
Rev. Leo Walsh, S.T.D.

COMMITTEE ON EVANGELIZATION AND CATECHESIS

Chairman—Bishop Richard J. Malone
Chairman-Elect—Bishop David L. Ricken
Members—Cardinal Donald W. Wuerl
Archbishop Paul S. Coakley
Bishop Robert Joseph Baker
Bishop Leonard P. Blair
Bishop Sam G. Jacobs
Bishop Gregory John Mansour
Bishop Jaime Soto, M.S.W.
Bishop Daniel F. Walsh, D.D.
Consultants—Archbishop Alfred C. Hughes, S.T.D.
Mr. Robert McCarty, N.F.C.Y.M.
Rev. John E. Hurley, C.S.P.
Rev. Msgr. John E. Kozar
Ms. Leland Nagel
Ms. Carol Obrokta
Ms. Diana Dudoit Raiche
Ms. Maruja Sedano
Staff—Rev. J. Brian Bransfield, M.Div., M.A., S.T.L.
Ms. Jeannine Marino
Dr. Michael Steier
Dr. Jem Sullivan

Subcommittee on the Catechism
Chairman—Bishop Leonard P. Blair, D.D., S.T.D.
Members—Cardinal Daniel N. DiNardo
Archbishop George J. Lucas
Archbishop Allen H. Vigneron, D.D.
Bishop Kevin C. Rhoades
Bishop Arthur J. Serratelli, S.T.D., S.S.L., D.D.
Consultants—Archbishop Alfred C. Hughes, S.T.D.
Rev. John Pollard
Staff—Rev. J. Brian Bransfield, M.Div., M.A., S.T.L.
Ms. Jeannine Marino
Dr. Jem Sullivan

COMMITTEE ON INTERNATIONAL JUSTICE AND PEACE

Chairman—Bishop Howard J. Hubbard
Chairman-Elect—Archbishop Edwin F. O'Brien, S.T.D., D.D.
Ex-Officio—Bishop William F. Murphy
Members—Cardinal Theodore E. McCarrick
Archbishop Edwin F. O'Brien, S.T.D., D.D.
Archbishop Thomas G. Wenski
Bishop Frank J. Dewane
Bishop Gerald Kicanas
Bishop Richard E. Pates
Bishop Ricardo Ramírez, C.S.B., D.D.
Bishop John H. Ricard, S.S.J.
Bishop William S. Skylstad, D.D.
Consultants—Cardinal Justin F. Rigali
Archbishop Timothy P. Broglio
Archbishop Jose H. Gomez
Bishop Stephen E. Blaire
Bishop John C. Wester
Major Gen. William F. Burns, (Ret.)
Ambassador Mary Ann Glendon
Dr. Maryann Cusimano Love
Dr. John Steinbruner
Staff—Mr. John Carr
Dr. Stephen M. Colecchi
Mrs. Virginia L. Farris
Mr. Gerry Flood
Mr. Stephen R. Hilbert
Rev. Juan Jose Molina, O.SS.T.

COMMITTEE ON LAITY, MARRIAGE, FAMILY LIFE, AND YOUTH

Chairman—Bishop Kevin C. Rhoades
Members—Archbishop Paul S. Coakley
Bishop John O. Barres, S.T.D., J.C.L., D.D.
Bishop Paul J. Bradley
Bishop Daniel E. Flores, S.T.D.
Bishop Martin D. Holley, D.D., V.G.
Bishop George J. Rassas
Advisors—Mr. Christopher Anderson
Mrs. Christine Codden
Ms. Donna Dausman
Ms. Theresa H. Farnan, Ph.D.
Ms. Marilyn Santos
Consultants—Bishop Jaime Soto, D.D., M.S.W.
Bishop John C. Wester, V.G.
Staff—Ms. Sheila Garcia
Sr. Eileen McCann, C.S.J.
Dr. H. Richard McCord
Ms. Theresa Notare

COMMITTEE ON MIGRATION

Chairman—Archbishop Jose H. Gomez, S.T.D.
Members—Archbishop Gustavo Garcia-Siller, M.Sp.S.
Archbishop Thomas G. Wenski
Bishop Nicholas A. DiMarzio
Bishop John R. Manz
Auxiliary Bishop Eduardo A. Nevares, V.G.
Bishop Anthony B. Taylor
Bishop Kevin W. Vann, J.C.D., D.D.
Bishop Luis R. Zarama
Consultants—Cardinal Roger M. Mahony
Cardinal Theodore E. McCarrick
Cardinal Justin F. Rigali
Bishop Daniel E. Flores, S.T.D.
Bishop Martin D. Holley, D.D., V.G.
Bishop Ricardo Ramirez, C.S.B.
Bishop James Anthony Tamayo, D.D.
Bishop John C. Wester
Sr. RayMonda DuVall, C.H.S.
Rev. Daniel G. Groody, C.S.C.
Mr. Kenneth Hackett
Sr. Gaye L. Moorhead, R.S.M.
Mr. Loc Nguyen
Ms. Maria Odom
Mr. Allen Sanchez
Staff—Mr. Kevin Appleby
Ms. Anastasia Brown
Mr. Johnny Young

COMMITTEE ON NATIONAL COLLECTIONS

Chairman—Bishop Kevin Joseph Farrell, D.D.
Members—Cardinal Theodore E. McCarrick
Cardinal Justin F. Rigali
Archbishop Jose H. Gomez
Archbishop Dennis M. Schnurr

Bishop Michael J. Bransfield
Bishop John H. Ricard, S.S.J.
Bishop Jaime Soto, D.D., M.S.W.
Bishop Michael W. Warfel
Consultants—Sr. Janice Bader, C.P.P.S.
Mr. Jim Caldarola
Rev. John Cusick
Staff—Ms. Mary Mencarini Campbell
Ms. Gina Laurent
Mr. Patrick Markey
Dr. Declan Murphy
Rev. Andrew Small, O.M.I.
Dr. David J. Suley

Subcommittee on Catholic Home Missions
Chairman—Bishop Michael W. Warfel
Members—Archbishop Paul S. Coakley
Archbishop Stefan Soroka
Bishop Peter F. Christensen, M.A.S.
Bishop Curtis J. Guillory, S.V.D.
Bishop Thomas J. Olmsted
Bishop Joseph S. Vasquez
Coadjutor Bishop Robert F. Vasa
Staff—Mr. Patrick Markey
Mr. Kenneth Ong
Dr. David J. Suley

Subcommittee on the Church in Africa
Chairman—Bishop John H. Ricard, S.S.J.
Members—Cardinal Theodore E. McCarrick
Cardinal Sean P. O'Malley, O.F.M.Cap., Ph.D.
Archbishop Wilton D. Gregory, S.L.D.
Bishop Martin D. Holley, D.D., V.G.
Bishop Howard J. Hubbard
Bishop Gerald Kicanas
Bishop John C. Wester
Consultants—Mr. Brian Gleeson
Rev. Msgr. John E. Kozar
Mr. Fritz Zuger
Staff—Mr. Patrick Markey
Dr. David J. Suley

Subcommittee on the Church in Central and Eastern Europe
Chairman—Cardinal Justin F. Rigali
Members—Cardinal Adam Maida
Cardinal Theodore E. McCarrick
Archbishop John J. Myers, J.C.D., D.D.
Archbishop Stefan Soroka
Bishop John R. Gaydos
Bishop Richard F. Stika
Bishop Blase J. Cupich, S.T.D.
Staff—Mr. Vincent L. Bus
Mr. Patrick Markey
Dr. Declan Murphy

Subcommittee on the Church in Latin America
Chairman—Archbishop Jose H. Gomez
Members—Cardinal Sean P. O'Malley, O.F.M.Cap., Ph.D.
Archbishop Robert J. Carlson
Archbishop Thomas G. Wenski
Bishop Octavio Cisneros
Bishop Eusebio Elizondo, M.Sp.S., J.C.D.
Bishop Cirilo B. Flores
Bishop John R. Manz
Bishop Joe Steve Vasquez
Consultant—Rev. Kevin M. McDonough
Staff—Mr. Kevin Day
Mr. Patrick Markey
Rev. Andrew Small, O.M.I.

COMMITTEE ON PRO-LIFE ACTIVITIES
Chairman—Cardinal Daniel N. DiNardo
Members—Cardinal Justin F. Rigali
Archbishop Joseph F. Naumann, V.G., D.D.
Bishop Daniel E. Flores, S.T.D.
Bishop Martin D. Holley, D.D., V.G.
Bishop William E. Lori, S.T.D.
Bishop Gregory John Mansour
Bishop Robert J. McManus
Bishop J. Terry Steib, S.V.D.
Consultants—Cardinal Francis E. George, O.M.I.
Cardinal Roger M. Mahony
Cardinal Sean P. O'Malley, O.F.M.Cap.
Cardinal Donald W. Wuerl
Archbishop Charles J. Chaput, O.F.M.Cap., D.D.
Archbishop Joseph E. Kurtz
Bishop Robert W. Finn
Bishop William F. Murphy
Ms. Helen Alvare, Esq.
Mr. Carl Anderson
Dr. John M. Haas, Ph.D., S.T.L., K.M.
Rev. J. Daniel Mindling, O.F.M.Cap.
Ms. Gail Quinn
Mr. Moe Wosepka
Dr. John Brehany, Ph.D.
Staff—Mr. Richard M. Doerflinger, M.A.
Mr. Thomas Grenchik
Mary McClusky
Ms. Deirdre McQuade
Ms. Susan Wills

COMMITTEE ON THE PROTECTION OF CHILDREN AND YOUNG PEOPLE
Chairman—Bishop Blase J. Cupich
Chairman-Elect—Bishop R. Daniel Conlon
Members—Bishop Richard J. Malone (Region I)
Bishop Dennis J. Sullivan (Region II)
Bishop Timothy Senior (Region III)
Bishop Mitchell T. Rozanski, D.D., V.G. (Region IV)
Bishop Richard F. Stika (Region V)
Bishop Bernard A. Hebda (Region VI)
Bishop Edward K. Braxton (Region VII)
Bishop John LeVoir (Region VIII)
Bishop Michael O. Jackels, S.T.D. (Region IX)
Bishop Patrick J. Zurek, D.D. (Region X)
Bishop Clarence Silva (Region XI)
Bishop Michael W. Warfel (Region XII)
Bishop Paul D. Etienne (Region XIII)
Bishop John G. Noonan (Region XIV)
Bishop Gerald N. Dino (Region XV)
Consultants—Very Rev. Thomas P. Cassidy, S.C.J.
Rev. Paul Lininger, O.F.M.Conv.
Staff—Rev. Msgr. Ronny E. Jenkins, S.T.L., J.C.D.
Ms. Teresa M. Kettelkamp
Ms. Mary Jane Doerr
Rev. W. Shawn McKnight, S.T.D.
Ms. Helen Osman
Mr. Anthony R. Picarello, Esq.
Sr. Mary Ann Walsh

AD HOC COMMITTEE FOR THE DEFENSE OF MARRIAGE
Chairman—Bishop Salvatore J. Cordileone
Members—Cardinal Donald W. Wuerl
Bishop William E. Lori, S.T.D.
Bishop Gabino Zavala, D.D., J.C.L., V.G.
Consultants—Mr. Carl Anderson
Mr. Hosffman Ospino
Staff—Rev. J. Brian Bransfield, M.Div., M.A., S.T.L.
Mr. Andrew Lichtenwalner
Dr. H. Richard McCord
Ms. Deirdre McQuade
Mr. Anthony R. Picarello, Esq.
Ms. Nancy Wisdo

TASK FORCE ON HEALTH CARE
Chairman—Bishop Kevin C. Rhoades
Members—Cardinal Daniel N. DiNardo
Archbishop Charles J. Chaput, O.F.M.Cap., D.D.
Archbishop Henry J. Mansell
Bishop Timothy L. Doherty
Bishop Felipe de Jesus Estevez
Bishop Robert Joseph McManus
Bishop Thomas J. Paprocki, S.T.L., J.D., J.C.D.
Bishop Kevin W. Vann, J.C.D., D.D.
Coadjutor Bishop Robert F. Vasa
Consultants—Dr. John M. Haas, Ph.D., S.T.L., K.M.
Rev. J. Daniel Mindling, O.F.M.Cap., S.T.D.
Ms. Janice L. Benton
Dr. John Brehany, Ph.D.
Sr. Carol Keehan, D.C.
Staff—Mr. John Carr
Mr. Richard M. Doerflinger, M.A.
Mr. Tom Grenchik
Ms. Kathy Saile
Rev. Thomas G. Weinandy, O.F.M.Cap.
Ms. Nancy Wisdo
Mrs. Christina Zvir

TASK FORCE ON THE SPANISH LANGUAGE BIBLE
Chairman—Archbishop Jose H. Gomez, D.D., S.T.D., V.G.
Members—Bishop Arthur J. Serratelli, S.T.D., S.S.L., D.D.
Bishop Jaime Soto, D.D., M.S.W.
Bishop Gabino Zavala
Bishop Patrick J. Zurek, D.D., V.G.
Staff—Mr. Alejandro Aguilera-Titus
Sr. Doris M. Turek, S.S.N.D.

AMERICAN COLLEGE OF LOUVAIN
Chairman—Bishop David L. Ricken, D.D., J.C.L.
Members
Region I—Bishop Robert C. Evans, D.D., J.C.L.
Region II—Bishop Octavio Cisneros
Region III—Bishop Arthur Joseph Serratelli, S.S.L., S.T.D., D.D.
Region IV—Bishop Richard B. Higgins, S.T.L., D.D.
Region V—Bishop Shelton J. Fabre
Region VI—Bishop Roger W. Gries, O.S.B., D.D., M.Ed.
Region VII—Bishop David L. Ricken, D.D., J.C.L.
Region VIII—Bishop Lee Piche
Region IX—Bishop Michael Owen Jackels
Region X—Bishop James Anthony Tamayo, D.D.
Region XI—Deacon John Luong
Region XII—Bishop George L. Thomas, D.D., Ph.D., V.G.
Region XIII—Bishop Fernando Isern, D.D.
Region XIV—Bishop John G. Noonan
Region XV—Bishop John Michael Botean, D.D.
Consultant—Rev. Msgr. Ross A. Shecterle, Rector
Staff—Rev. Msgr. Ronny E. Jenkins, S.T.L., J.C.D.

NORTH AMERICAN COLLEGE, ROME
Chairman—Archbishop John J. Myers, J.C.D., D.D.
Vice-Chairman—Archbishop John C. Nienstedt
Treasurer—Bishop Frank J. Dewane
Secretary—Bishop Patrick J. Zurek, D.D.
Members
Region I—Bishop Walter J. Edyvean, S.T.D.
Region II—Bishop William F. Murphy, J.C.L., LL.D., S.T.D.
Region III—Archbishop John J. Myers, D.D., J.C.D.
Region IV—Cardinal Donald W. Wuerl
Region V—Bishop Glen John Provost
Region VI—Bishop Bernard A. Hebda, J.C.L., J.D.
Region VII—Bishop Thomas George Doran, D.D., J.C.D.
Region VIII—Archbishop John C. Nienstedt
Region IX—Bishop Richard E. Pates
Region X—Bishop Patrick J. Zurek, D.D., V.G.
Region XI—Bishop Robert H. Brom, D.D.
Region XII—Bishop Michael W. Warfel
Region XIII—Archbishop Daniel E. Sheehan, D.D., J.C.D.
Region XIV—Bishop Frank J. Dewane
Region XV—Bishop John M. Kudrick
Consultant—Mr. James Crowley
Staff—Rev. Msgr. Daniel H. Mueggenborg
Mrs. Mary DiDonato
Rev. Msgr. James Checchio, J.C.D., M.B.A.

BOARD OF DIRECTORS: CATHOLIC LEGAL IMMIGRATION NETWORK, INC.
Chairman—Bishop Jaime Soto, D.D., M.S.W.
Members—Archbishop Jose H. Gomez, D.D., S.T.D., V.G.
Archbishop Thomas G. Wenski
Bishop Frank J. Dewane
Bishop Nicholas DiMarzio
Bishop Richard J. Garcia, D.D.
Bishop Joseph A. Pepe, D.D., J.C.D.
Bishop James Anthony Tamayo, D.D.
Bishop John C. Wester
Sr. Anne Curtis, R.S.M.
Sr. Sally Duffy, S.C.
Sr. RayMonda DuVall, C.H.S.
Sr. Maureen Joyce, R.S.M.
Mr. Vincent Pitta
Ms. Nancy Wisdo
Mr. Johnny Young
Secretary—Mr. Mark Franken, Exec. Dir.

BOARD OF DIRECTORS: CATHOLIC RELIEF SERVICES (CRS)
Chairman—Cardinal Timothy M. Dolan
Members—Cardinal Theodore E. McCarrick
Archbishop Timothy P. Broglio
Archbishop Michael Jarboe Sheehan, S.T.L., J.C.D.
Bishop J. Kevin Boland
Bishop Joseph R. Cistone
Bishop Frank J. Dewane
Bishop Daniel E. Flores, S.T.D.
Bishop Martin D. Holley, D.D., V.G.
Bishop Denis J. Madden
Bishop Richard J. Malone
Bishop John C. Wester
Dr. Viva Bartkus
Mrs. Constance L. Proctor
Judge Geraldine Rivera
Bishop William P. Callahan, O.F.M.Conv.
Sr. Carol Keehan, D.C.
Staff—Rev. Msgr. David J. Malloy

BOARD OF TRUSTEES: CONFRATERNITY OF CHRISTIAN DOCTRINE, INC.
President—Cardinal Timothy M. Dolan
Members—Cardinal Donald W. Wuerl
Archbishop Joseph E. Kurtz
Staff—Ms. Mary Elizabeth Sperry
Bishop Michael J. Bransfield
Bishop George Vance Murry, S.J.

NATIONAL REVIEW BOARD
Chair—Ms. Diane M. Knight, A.C.S.W., C.I.S.W.
Members—Dr. Emmet M. Kenney, Jr., M.D.
Justice Robert Charles Kohm
Dr. Susan Steibe-Pasalich, Ph.D.
Mr. Stephen A. Zappala, Jr.
Dr. Ana Marie Catanzaro, Ph.D.
Mr. Michael J. Clark
Dr. Antoine M. Garibaldi, Ph.D.
Dr. Charles H. Handel, Ed.D.
Judge Anna Moran, J.D.
Mr. Al Notzon, III
Dr. Thomas Plante, Ph.D.
Judge Geraldine Rivera
Dr. Ruben Gallegos, Ph.D.
Staff—Ms. Mary Jane Doerr
Ms. Teresa M. Kettelkamp

NATIONAL ADVISORY COUNCIL
Chairman—Dr. Robert J. McCann Spokane, WA
Chairman-Elect—Rev. Miguel A. Gonzalez Orlando, FL
Members—Bishop William Justice
Bishop William C. Skurla
Very Rev. John G. Basarab, M.A. Annandale, VA (Region XV)
Rev. William Neuhaus, V.F. Covington, KY (Region V)
Rev. Msgr. Lawrence J. Carroll Fairfield, CT (Region I)
Rev. Mark A. Eckman, M.Div. Pittsburgh, PA (Region III)
Rev. Msgr. John F. Canary Chicago, IL (Region VII)
Rev. Msgr. Heberto M. Diaz, Jr. Brownsville, TX (Region X)
Very Rev. Gary Zender Renton, WA (Region XII)
Rev. Daniel Aubin Ocala, FL
Rev. Daniel Dorsey Cincinnati, OH

Sr. Catherine Marie Hopkins, O.P. Nashville, TN
Sr. Lynn Jarrell, O.S.U., M.A., J.C.D. Louisville, KY
Sr. Yolanda Tarango, C.C.V.I. San Antonio, TX
Members At Large—Ms. Charlene Harris Sacramento, CA
Ms. Barbara Jean Harty-Golder Lookout Mountain, TN
Regional Representatives
Region I—Mrs. Patricia Collins Caribou, ME
Mr. Angel Fernandez-Chavero New Haven, CT
Region II—Vacant, Member
Region III—Ms. Kelly Caddy Pittsburgh, PA
Mr. Raymond D. Sellman Moon Township, PA
Region IV—Ms. Virginia Berg Fairfax, VA
Deacon Thomas E. McFeely Chesapeake, VA
Region V—Vacant, Member
Region VI—Dr. Benjamin Brown Ypsilanti, MI
Ms. Rosita Kintz Lansing, MI
Region VII—Dr. Cheryl Zuccaro, M.D.
Vacant, Member
Region VIII—Mr. Hoa Her Circle Pines, MN
Vacant, Member
Region IX—Mrs. Renee Miller Grand Island, NE
Dr. John Purk, D.D.S. Roeland Park, KS
Region X—Mrs. Lori Hines San Angelo, TX
Mr. Fernando Montemayor Laredo, TX
Region XI—Mr. Tac Pham Tustin, CA
Mrs. Laura Lopez San Bernardino, CA
Region XII—Ms. Barbara Aston Moscow, ID
Mr. Todd Cooper Portland, OR
Region XIII—Ms. Jeanette De Melo Denver, CO
Mr. Michael Valdo Albuquerque, NM
Region XIV—Mrs. Mary Jo Anderson Orlando, FL
Dr. Paul Thigpen Savannah, GA
Region XV—Mr. James DuBois Fenton, MD
Ms. Helen M. Kennedy Blairsville, PA
Staff—Mrs. Melissa Boyle
Mr. Bruce E. Egnew

RELATED ORGANIZATIONS

***Catholic Legal Immigration Network, Inc. (CLINIC) Theological College**
National Office, 415 Michigan Ave., N.E. Ste. 200 Washington, DC 20017. Tel: 202-635-2556 Fax: 202-635-2649 Email: national@cliniclegal.org Web: www.cliniclegal.org
Corporate Officers:—Bishop Richard J. Garcia, D.D., Chm. & Pres., Bishop Anthony B. Taylor, Vice Pres., Sr. Sally Duffy, S.C., Treas., Ms. Maria Odom, Exec. Dir. & Sec.
Members:—Bishop Jaime Soto, D.D., M.S.W., Bishop Nicholas A. DiMarzio, Bishop Thomas G. Wenski, D.D., Bishop Joseph Anthony Pepe, D.D., J.C.D., Bishop Eusebio Elizondo, M.Sp.S., J.C.D., Bishop Richard J. Garcia, D.D., Archbishop Jose H. Gomez, Bishop Anthony B. Taylor, Bishop Kevin W. Vann, J.C.D., D.D., Auxiliary Bishop Luis R. Zarama, J.C.L., V.G., Auxiliary Bishop Eduardo A. Nevares, V.G., Sr. RayMonda DuVall, C.H.S., Sr. Sally Duffy, S.C., Ms. Marguerite (Peg) Harmon, Mr. James T. McGibbon, Mr. Vincent Pitta, Ambassador Johnny Young, Mr. John Wilhelm, Ms. Nancy Wisdo
The Catholic Legal Immigration Network, Inc. (CLINIC), a subsidiary of the United States Catholic Conference of Bishops (USCCB), operates a legal support agency for a rapidly growing national network of Catholic immigration programs. CLINIC advocates for transparent, fair and generous immigration policies, and expresses the Church's commitment to the full membership of migrants in U.S. society.

Catholic Relief Services

Catholic Relief Services-USSCB
CRS World Headquarters, 228 W. Lexington St. Baltimore, MD 21201-3413. Tel: 866-608-5978 Web: www.crs.org Dr. Carolyn Y. Woo, Pres.
Catholic Relief Services Board of Directors
Chairman—Bishop Gerald Kicanas
Members—Bishop J. Kevin Boland, Dr. Viva Bartkus, Bishop William P. Callahan, O.F.M.Conv., Bishop Joseph R. Cistone, D.D., V.G., Archbishop Paul Coakley, Mr. Glenn Creamer, Bishop Frank J. Dewane, Bishop Daniel E. Flores, S.T.D., Dr. Patrick T. Harker, Bishop Martin D. Holley, D.D., V.G., Rev. Msgr. Ronny E. Jenkins, S.T.L., J.C.D., Sr. Carol Keehan, D.C., Archbishop George J. Lucas, Bishop Denis J. Madden, Bishop Richard J. Malone, Cardinal Theodore E. McCarrick, Mrs. Constance L. Proctor, Geraldine E. Rivera, Archbishop Michael J. Sheehan, Bishop John C. Wester
Staff—Ms. Christine Tucker, Chief of Staff, Mr. Sean Callahan, Exec. Vice Pres., Overseas Operations, Mr. Mark Palmer, Exec. Vice Pres., & Chief Financial Officer, Mr. David Piraino, Exec. Vice Pres., Human Resources, Mr. Michael Wiest, Exec. Vice Pres., Charitable Giving and Awareness, Dr. Carolyn Y. Woo, Pres.
Catholic Relief Services is the official international humanitarian agency of the Catholic community in the United States. CRS alleviates suffering and provides assistance to people in need in nearly 100 countries, without regard to race, religion or nationality.
CRS was founded in 1943 by the bishops of the United States to assist the poor and disadvantaged outside this country — helping people in need for more than 65 years.
CRS is efficient and effective directing more than 95 percent of the agency's expenditures directly to programs that benefit the poor overseas. Our agency touches more than 100 million lives, by addressing the root causes and effects of poverty, promoting human dignity, and helping to build more just and peaceful societies.
Our relief and development work is accomplished through programs of emergency response, HIV, health, agriculture, education, microfinance and peacebuilding.
We serve Catholics in the United States by inviting them to live out their faith as part of one human family.
For more information, please visit www.crs.org.

RELATED ORGANIZATIONS

National Religious Retirement Office
3211 Fourth St. Washington, DC 20017-1194. Tel: 202-541-3215 Sr. Janice Bader, C.P.P.S., Exec. Dir.
The Mission of the National Religious Retirement Office is to coordinate the National Collection for the Retirement Fund for Religious and to distribute these monies to eligible religious institutes for their retirement needs. The office also provides retirement planning and educational assistance to religious institutes. The National Religious Retirement Office is sponsored by the Conference of Major Superiors of Men, the Conference of Major Superiors of Women Religious, the Leadership Conference of Women Religious and the United States Conference of Catholic Bishops.

The USCCB Commission on Certification and Accreditation
3211 South Lake Dr., Ste. 317 St. Francis, WI 53235-3702. Tel: 414-486-0139 Fax: 414-489-0006 Dr. C. Vanessa White, Board Chair, Dr. Kay Sheskaitis, I.H.M., Exec. Dir.
Established in 1982 by the Administrative Board of the United States Conference of Catholic Bishops, the USCCB Commission serves as an accrediting commission of the Catholic Bishops of the United States, establishes accreditation standards, policies, and procedures, and accredits quality ministry formation programs that prepare persons for ministry. The USCCB/CCA also approves certification standards and procedures for the certification of specialized ecclesial ministers by (Arch)Dioceses and organizations.

NATIONAL ORGANIZATIONS

Listing in this category is not related to classification under Canon Law as a public juridic person.

American Catholic Correctional Chaplains Association
c/o Catholic Social Services, 100 E. Eighth St. Cincinnati, OH 45202-2193. Tel: 920-324-6298 Fax: 920-324-6254 Email: info@catholiccorrectionalchaplains.org Web: catholiccorrectionalchaplains.org Auxiliary Bishop Barry C. Knestout, D.D., V.G., Episcopal Advisor, Paul E. Rogers, Pres., Rev. Michael Koncik, C.Ss.R., Vice Pres., Mr. Teodoro Rael, Treas., Christine M. Shimrock, Sec., Rev. Mark C. Schmieder, Past Pres., Sr. Peggy Devaney, I.H.M., Certification Chair
The Board of Directors include the Episcopal Advisor and Elected Officers. Address all Communications to the Executive Secretary.
A nonprofit organization for the purposes of unifying and implementing the Church's corrective and restorative efforts for the spiritual welfare of persons committed to the Catholic Chaplains' care, and to foster a Catholic approach to issues of criminal justice in accord with the principles of Sacred Scripture and Catholic social justice teaching. Affiliated with the Social Development and World Peace Department, USCCB, the International Commission of Catholic Prison Pastoral Care, American Correctional Association, American Correctional Chaplains Association, National Council on Crime and Delinquency and The Catholic University of America, it was established with approval of the American Bishops in 1952. Grants USCCB-recognized certification to qualified members.
Publication: tri-annually, ACCCA Newsletter.

American Catholic Historical Association (1919)
Fordham University, Dealy Hall, Rm. 637, 441 E. Fordham Bronx, NY 10458. Tel: 718-817-3830 Fax: 718-817-5690 Email: acha@fordham.edu Dr. Thomas F.X. Noble, Pres., Rev. R. Bentley Anderson, S.J., Sec. & Treas.
A membership organization, founded to promote the study of church history understood in the broad sense and to assist American Catholics and other members in all fields of history.

The American College of the Roman Catholic Church of the United States-North American College (1859)
3211 Fourth St., N.E. Washington, DC 20017-1194. Tel: 202-541-5411 Fax: 202-722-8804 Email: nac@usccb.org Archbishop John J. Myers, J.C.D., D.D., Chm., Rev. Msgr. James Checchio, J.C.D., M.B.A., Rector
The College is owned and operated by the Bishops of the United States and incorporated under the laws of the State of Maryland.

Apostleship of the Sea of the United States of America (AOSUSA)
1500 Jefferson Dr. Port Arthur, TX 77642-0646. Tel: 409-985-4545 Fax: 409-985-5945 Email: aosusa@sbcglobal.net Very Rev. Sinclair Oubre, J.C.L., E.V., Pres., Ms. Doreen M. Badeaux, Sec. Gen.
AOSUSA is an association of the faithful of Catholic maritime chaplains, cruise ship priests, seafarers, deacons, religious, lay ecclesial ministers, and affiliates serving the people of the sea in ports throughout the USA.
Publication: AOS USA Maritime E-News.

Association of Catholic Diocesan Archivists
Archdiocese of Chicago Archives & Record Ctr., 711 W. Monroe Chicago, IL 60661. Tel: 312-534-4400 Bishop Thomas J. Paprocki, D.D., J.C.D., S.T.D., Episcopal Moderator, William Bissenden, Pres., , Peggy Lavelle, Vice Pres. & Pres. Elect, Brian Fahey, Treas., Michele Levandoski, Sec.
The Association of Catholic diocesan archivists first met in 1979 and formally organized the Association of Catholic Diocesan Archivists in 1982. The organization promotes professionalism in the management of diocesan archives in the United States and Canada, and fosters cooperation between diocesan archivists and others on regional, national and international levels. Membership information is available through the above address and telephone number.

Catholic Academy for Communication Arts Professionals
National Office, 1645 Brook Lynn Dr., Ste. 2 Dayton, OH 45432-1944. Tel: 937-458-0265 Fax: 937-458-0263 Email: admin@catholicacademy.org Web: www.catholicacademy.org Mr. Frank Morock, Pres., Ms. Sally A. Oberski, 1st. Vice Pres.
The Catholic Academy for Communication Arts Professionals is the U.S. affiliate of SIGNIS, the international Vatican-approved organization for communication. The Catholic Academy grew out of the international merger of two other associations founded in the 1920's in Europe: UNDA for radio and television and OCIC the International Catholic Organization for Cinema. These groups joined to form the Catholic Academy in October 2002. The Catholic Academy is a national network of broadcasters, communications directors, public relations personnel, independent producers, syndicators, internet and other media professionals. This national network provides professional support and access to a broad base of experience and resources. Principal activities of the Catholic Academy: annual General Assembly for all members, annual Gabriel Awards for excellence in commercial and religious communications.
Publication: electronic newsletter, White Papers.

Catholic Association of Diocesan Ecumenical and Interreligious Officers (CADEIO)
1009 Stafford Ave. Fredericksburg, VA 22401. Fax: 540-371-0251 Email: frrooney@stmaryfred.org Cell: 703-309-8719 Rev. Donald J. Rooney, M.A., M.Div., Pres., Rt. Rev. (non-Abbot) Alexei Smith, M.A., M.Div., Vice Pres., Rev. Erich Rutten, M.A., M.Div., Treas., Rev. Msgr. George Appleyard, V.G., Sec.
CADEIO (formerly NADEO) is the Catholic Association of Ecumenical and Interreligious Officers who serve as delegates of dialogue on behalf of their bishops of (Arch)Dioceses and Eparchies in the United States: to promote collaboration which advances the work of Christian unity and

interreligious understanding; to arrange programs for continuing formation and education of the membership; and to cooperate with the Bishops' Committee for Ecumenical and Interreligious Affairs of the United States Conference of Catholic Bishops, and with other ecumenical and interreligious networks and agencies.

Publication: quarterly Newsletter; annual booklets on various ecumenical and interreligious topics, Handbook for Catholic Ecumenical Officers.

Catholic Association of Teachers of Homiletics (CATH)

St. Meinrad School of Theology, 200 Hill Dr. St. Meinrad, IN 47577.

Officers—Rev. Guerric DeBona, O.S.B., Pres., Dr. Deborah A. Organ, D.Min., Vice Pres., Very Rev. Donald J. Heet, O.S.F.S., Sec. & Treas.

Catholic Campus Ministry Association

National Office, 1118 Pendleton St., Ste. 300 Cincinnati, OH 45202-8805. Tel: 513-842-0167 Fax: 513-842-0171

Founded in 1969 by campus ministers, the association promotes the mission of the Church in higher education and implements the 1985 Pastoral Letter on Campus Ministry through educational programs and services, leadership, the development of cooperative relationships with other organizations and development activities. Membership is open to individuals interested in campus ministry.

Publications: Crossroads, bimonthly publication; The Catholic Campus Ministry Directory.

Catholic Cemetery Conference

National Office, 1400 S. Wolf Rd., Bldg. 3 Hillside, IL 60162. Tel: 888-850-8131 Web: www.catholiccemeteryconference.org Dennis Fairbank, Exec. Dir., Bishop John M. Quinn, Episcopal Moderator

The Conference is an organization of Diocesan Directors of Cemeteries and parish cemetery administrators from throughout the United States, Canada, Australia, Italy and Guam. Guided by the principle: "That burial of the dead is one of the Corporal Works of Mercy," the Conference promotes high standards of Catholic cemetery management, development, operation and maintenance consistent with Christian service to the Catholic community; and fosters and promotes the religious, charitable and educational interests of Catholic cemeteries and the people they serve.

Founded in 1949, the Catholic Cemetery Conference (CCC) helps cemetery staff enhance their skills in caring for the deceased and comforting their loved ones through ministry, education, networking and service opportunities.

Publications: monthly magazine, Catholic Cemetery; various booklets on cemetery management & evaluation services; funeral liturgy at the cemetery. Annual Convention; John Carroll University-Summer Seminar on Leadership; smaller cemeteries seminar.

Catholic Charities USA

Sixty-six Canal Center Plaza, Ste. 600 Alexandria, VA 22314. Tel: 703-549-1390 Fax: 703-549-1656 Rev. Larry Snyder, Pres., Bishop Michael P. Driscoll, D.D., M.S.W., Episcopal Liaison

Catholic Charities USA is a national network of more than 1,700 local Catholic Charities agencies and institutions that provide help and create hope for more than 10.2 million people a year regardless of their religious, social, or economic backgrounds.

For more than 280 years, local Catholic Charities agencies have been providing a wide range of vital services in their communities ranging from day care, adoption, and refugee resettlement to advocacy, counseling, and emergency food and housing. Today, the Catholic Charities network is made up of more than 62,000 staff and 243,000 volunteers. In addition, more than 6,100 individuals serve as volunteer members of local boards.

The National Office-Catholic Charities USA-was founded in 1910 as the National Conference of Catholic Charities by the Most Rev. Thomas J. Shahan and Rt. Rev. Msgr. William J. Kerby in cooperation with lay leaders of the Society of St. Vincent De Paul.

Catholic Charities USA provides its members a national voice, networking opportunities, training and technical assistance, program development, and financial support.

Catholic Charities USA has been commissioned by the U.S. Catholic bishops to represent the Catholic community in times of domestic disaster. Catholic Charities USA also provides disaster preparedness training to dioceses and agencies to mitigate the disruption of business and services consequent to natural disasters.

Pope Benedict XVI has named Fr. Larry Synder, President of Catholic Charities USA, to the Dicastery of Cor Unum, which oversees the church's charitable activities.

Publications: Charities USA, a quarterly membership magazine; an annual report; an annual survey of Catholic Charities services nationwide; and various publications on issues of concern to Catholic Charities agencies.

The Catholic Communications Foundation (CCF)

c/o 6363 St. Charles Ave. New Orleans, LA 70118. Dr. William H. Hummell, Board Member & Contact Person

The Catholic Communications Foundation was established and is supported by Catholic Fraternal Benefit Societies. Its mission is to assist the communications apostolates of the Catholic Church in the United States, with particular emphasis at the diocesan level. The Foundation awards religious communications training scholarships.

The Catholic Health Association of the United States (1919)

Headquarters, 4455 Woodson Rd. Saint Louis, MO 63134. Tel: 314-427-2500 Fax: 314-427-0029 Web: www.chausa.org Sr. Carol Keehan, D.C., Pres. & CEO, Sr. Patricia A. Talone, R.S.M., Ph.D., Vice Pres. Mission Svcs., Michael F. Rodgers, Sr. Vice Pres. Public Policy and Advocacy, Rhonda Mueller, Senior Vice Pres. Finance & Opers., J. Fred Caesar, Sr., Special Asst. to the Pres., Lisa J. Gilden, Vice Pres. Gen. Counsel, Ed Giganti, Vice Pres. Communications & Mktg., Elaine Bauer, Vice Pres. Strategic Initiatives

CHA represents the combined strength of its members, more than 2,000 Catholic healthcare sponsors, systems, facilities, and related organizations. Founded in 1915, CHA unites members to advance selected strategic directions. Presents annual awards recognizing contribution to the health ministry by organizations and individuals. Sponsors continuing education for healthcare personnel.

Service Areas: Planning and Policy Development, Public Policy and Advocacy, Communications, Sponsorship, Ethics and Mission Services. Annual Assembly: Annual assembly and membership meeting for Catholic healthcare leaders.

Publications: 6 times-year, Health Progress; bimonthly Catholic Health World; booklets, books & audiovisual on healthcare, Church-related subjects.

Catholic Kolping Society of America (1849)

(Please direct all correspondence to the National Administrator).

1223 Van Houten Clifton, NJ 07013. Patricia Farkas, Natl. Admin.

The Society was founded by Rev. Adolph Kolping in Cologne, Germany, and established in the United States in 1856. The Catholic Kolping Society of America is a part of the world-wide Kolping movement and belongs to the International Kolping Society. There are 12 branches in principal cities of the United States with a combined membership of approximately 2,500. The membership is open to men and women of all ages. The Society's mission statement reads: We, the members of the Catholic Kolping Society of America, extend the vision of our founder, Blessed Adolph Kolping, by promoting the development of the individual and family; we foster a sense of belonging and friendship through our program of spiritual, educational, charitable and social activities.

Catholic Medical Association

National Headquarters, 29 Bala Ave. Ste. 205 Bala Cynwyd, PA 19004. Tel: 484-270-8002 Fax: 866-666-2319 Email: info@cathmed.org Web: www.cathmed.org

Officers (2011-2012)—John F. Brehany, Ph.D., S.T.L., Exec. Dir., Maricela P. Moffitt, M.D., Pres,. John I. Lane, M.D., Pres. Elect, Paul J. Braaton, M.D., Vice Pres., Peter Morrow, M.D., Treas., Lester A. Ruppersberger, D.O., Sec.

Upholding the principles of the Catholic faith in the science and practice of medicine.

Catholic Volunteer Network

6930 Carroll Ave., Ste. 820 Takoma Park, MD 20912-4423. Tel: 301-270-0900 Tel: 800-543-5046 Email: info@catholicvolunteernetwork.org Web: www.catholicvolunteernetwork.org Bishop Oscar Solis, Episcopal Advisor

Catholic Volunteer Network promotes, recruits and refers volunteers to missions in the United States and overseas. We represent nearly 200 faith-based volunteer programs worldwide and work with the U.S. dioceses, religious communities and the private sector to determine their needs for help. Catholic Volunteer Network (CVN) is committed to the goal that every Catholic man and woman be invited to consider a period of service in the missions, as a vital and important manifestation of the baptismal call of all Catholic people. Currently over 14,000 men and women are serving in CVN member mission programs offering their gifts and abilities in full-time service to people in need and living their Catholic faith more fully. These volunteers are serving domestically for a summer, six months, a year or more, and they are serving internationally for two or more years at a time. They are single and married, recent college graduates and early retirees, doctors and teachers, parish ministers and social workers, community organizers, computer programmers, legal aides and more. Gatherings: Annual Conference; Formation Workshop, Training Seminars.

Publications: annual, Response: Directory of Volunteer Opportunities; monthly, How Can I Help?; quarterly, FaithWorks.

Awards: The Father George Mader Award, given annually to honor organizations and individuals who promote the value of lay mission service. The Bishop Joseph A. Francis Award to honor organizations and individuals who promote community service.

The Catholic Press Association of the United States and Canada, Inc.

205 W. Monroe St., Ste. 470 Chicago, IL 60606. Tel: 312-380-6789 Fax: 312-361-0256 Web: www.catholicpress.org Bishop Gabino Zavala

Board of Directors—Greg Erlandson, Pres., Mrs. Penny Wiegert, Past Pres., Robert DeFrancesco, Vice Pres., Matthew Schiller, Treas., Malea Hargett, Sec., Timothy M. Walter, Exec. Dir., Mark Zimmerman, William Howard, Peter P. Finney, Jr., Rev. Pat McCloskey, Paul Henderson, Robert Lockwood, Brian Gray, Lynn Monahan, Michael Krokos

The Catholic Press Association of the United States and Canada, Inc., is the trade and professional association of Catholic newspapers, magazines, and general publishers in the U.S. and Canada and their staff personnel. The CPA was established in 1911. It serves a professional Catholic press market of nearly 2,000 persons working in more than 600 publications with a wide promotion and representation of Catholic press interests in social media, education, and professional development.

The Catholic Theological Society of America

c/o John Carroll University, 20700 N. Park Blvd. University Hts, OH 44118. Tel: 216-397-4980 Fax: 216-397-1804

Board Members—John E. Thiel, Pres., Fairfield, CT, Susan A. Ross, Pres. Elect, Chicago IL, Richard R. Gaillardetz, Vice Pres., Chestnut Hill, MA, M. Theresa Moser, RSCJ, Sec., San Francisco, CA, Jozef D. Zalot, Treas., Cincinnati, OH, Mary Ann Hinsdale, Past Pres., Chestnut Hill, MA, Michael E. Lee, Bronx, NY, Sr. Kathleen McManus, O.P., Portland, OR, Sr. Judith A. Merkle, S.N.D.deN., Niagara University, NY, Elena Procario-Foley, New Rochelle, NY, Mary Jane Ponyik, Dir., University Hts., OH

An association of professional theologians. Its purpose is to promote studies and research in theology within the Roman Catholic tradition, to relate theological science to current problems, and to foster a more effective theological education by providing a forum for an exchange of views among theologians and with scholars in other disciplines.

Catholic Youth Foundation USA

415 Michigan Ave., Ste. 40 Washington, DC 20017-4503. Tel: 202-636-3825 Fax: 202-526-7544 Email: info@cyfusa.org Web: cyfusa.org Donald R. McCrabb, D.Min., Exec. Dir.

Catholic Youth Foundation USA (CYFUSA) is assuring a faithful future by promoting effective and innovative youth ministry. CYFUSA also provides full financial support to the national youth ministry office of the Catholic Church. CYFUSA makes all of the following possible: scholarships for youth and youth leaders to attend the National Catholic Youth Conference and the National Conference for Catholic Youth Ministry; awards annual grants to local, diocesan, regional, and national youth ministry projects; development of youth ministry programs for culturally diverse communities; outreach to youth in crisis; training of youth ministers; and full support of the work of the National Federation for Catholic Youth Ministry.

Conference for Catholic Facility Management

P.O. Box 016 Kensington, MD 20895-0016. Tel: 301-946-3704 Fax: 301-946-3705 Email: destwolr@adw.org Web: www.ccfm.net Jim Zielinski, Pres., Richard deStwolinski, Acting Exec. Dir., William Krammer, Vice Pres., Janis Balentine, Sec., Andre Villere, Jr., Treas.

Mindful of their special ministry in the Roman Catholic Church in facility and real estate matters, the members of the CCFM united to be of service to the Church in ministry of facility and real estate concerns. In particular, this organization promotes the spiritual growth of its membership; promotes facility and real estate knowledge and expertise in service to the local and national Church, facilitates the exchange of ideas and information through personal contacts, quarterly newsletters and annual meetings.

The Conference of Major Superiors of Men of the United States, Inc.

8808 Cameron St. Silver Spring, MD 20910. Tel: 301-588-4030 Fax: 301-587-4575 Abbot Giles P. Hayes, O.S.B., Pres., Very Rev. Thomas H. Smolich, S.J., Vice Pres., Bro. Ronald Talbot, S.C., Sec. & Treas., Rev. John A. Pavlik, O.F.M.Cap., Exec. Dir.

A canonical conference of the major superiors of religious communities and institutes of men for the purpose of promoting the spiritual and apostolic welfare of priests and brothers.

The Confraternity of Christian Doctrine, Inc.

3211 Fourth St., N.E. Washington, DC 20017. Tel: 202-541-3098 Fax: 202-541-3089 Mary Elizabeth Sperry, Assoc Dir.

Members—Bishop George V. Murry, S.J., Cardinal Timothy M. Dolan, Cardinal Donald W. Wuerl, Archbishop Joseph E. Kurtz, D.D., Bishop Michael J. Bransfield

The Confraternity is a distinct entity, separately incorporated and directed by a Board of Trustees from the United States Conference of Catholic Bishops. The purpose of the Corporation is to foster and promote the teachings of Christ as understood and handed down by the Roman Catholic Church. To this end it licenses use of the Lectionary for Mass and the New American Bible, translations made from the original languages.

Council of Major Superiors of Women Religious in the United States of America

1211 Lawrence St., N.E. P.O. Box 4467 Washington, DC 20017-0467. Tel: 202-832-2575 Fax: 202-832-6325 Mother Regina Marie Gorman, O.C.D., Chairperson

A canonically erected conference of Major Superiors of women's religious communities established in 1992 to promote mutual support among them and to foster coordination and cooperation with the Bishops' conference and individual Bishops.

Diocesan Fiscal Management Conference

National Office, P.O. Box 60210 San Angelo, TX 76906. Bishop Kevin J. Farrell, D.D., Episcopal Moderator, Leslie Maiman, M.B.A., M.T.S., Exec. Dir.

Mindful of their special ministry in the Roman Catholic Church as the extension of the Diocesan Bishop in fiscal matters, the members of the DFMC unite to be of service to the Church in the ministry of fiscal management.

In particular, this organization promotes the spiritual growth of its members; promotes financial and administrative knowledge and expertise in service to the local and national Church; facilitates the free exchange of ideas and information, and serves as a liaison among the fiscal managers of the Dioceses and Archdioceses of the Church.

Diocesan Information Systems Conference

National Office, 226 Summit Ave. Saint Paul, MN 55102-2197. Tel: 651-291-4439 Fax: 651-290-1627 Email: info@discinfo.org Archbishop Richard E. Pates, D.D., Episcopal Moderator, Mary Jo Jungwirth, Pres., Lee Jones, Vice Pres., Dale Jonasson, M.S., Sec. & Treas.

The members of DISC unite to be of service to the Roman Catholic Church in information systems matters. The DISC organization serves as a liaison among technology managers for Archdioceses, Dioceses and related entities.

In particular, this organization promotes the spiritual growth of its members, provides technical expertise in Information Technology, promotes professional technical services to the local and national church communities, encourages the development of professional relationships among its members and facilitates the free exchange of technical information and ideas.

Federation of Diocesan Liturgical Commissions

National Office, 415 Michigan Ave., N.E., Ste. 70 Washington, DC 20017. Tel: 202-635-6990 Fax: 202-529-2452 Web: www.FDLC.org Ms. Lisa A. Tarker, Exec. Dir., Rev. Msgr. John H. Burton, Chm., Dr. Judy Bullock, Vice Chm., Rev. Michael D. Balash, Treas., Rev. Tom Ranzino, B.A., M.A., Delegate-at-Large, Ms. Lesa Truxaw, Delegate-at-Large

The FDLC is a voluntary association of all diocesan liturgical commissions/offices from the United States. Two members of each diocesan liturgical commission/office serve as diocesan representatives to the FDLC. From this membership are elected 24 representatives (two from each of the 12 Episcopal regions) to serve as the National Board of Directors. The day-to-day activities of the FDLC are directed by the Executive Director. The FDLC relates closely to the Bishops because its membership consists of their appointees. The Federation serves the Bishops and local commissions in matters of ongoing liturgical renewal. It also serves through education and other coordinated services requested by individual commissions or through consultation and voting at national meetings. The FDLC is organized and operated exclusively for religious and educational purposes.

Instituto Nacional Hispano de Liturgia, Inc.

620 Michigan Ave., N.E. Washington, DC 20064. Tel: 202-319-6450 Fax: 202-319-6449 Rev. Juan J. Sosa, Pres., Sr. Paulina Hurtado, O.P., Vice Pres., Mrs. Mary Frances Reza, Sec.

The Instituto is a national organization committed to assisting the bishops of the country in promoting the liturgical reforms mandated by the Second Vatican Council, while it studies, reflects and celebrates more authentically the Catholic faith from the various religious traditions of Hispanics who reside in the United States. Instituto members assist the Church at the national, diocesan and parish levels by providing lectures, translations, and other Spanish and bilingual resources that may meet the liturgical needs of Hispanics whenever they surface. Membership to the organization is open to all persons and institutions interested in liturgy. Board members meet twice a year, members meet annually. National Conference every 2 years and/or symposium on liturgical topics.

International Catholic Migration Commission (ICMC) & ICMC, Inc.

c/o USCCB 3211 Fourth St., N.E. Washington, DC 20017-1194. John Klink, Pres., Johan Ketelers, Sec. Gen., Jane Bloom, U.S. Liaison Officer

Provides technical assistance and coordination in area of service to migrants and refugees. Nonprofit New York Corporation.

International Catholic Stewardship Council, Inc. (ICSC)

National Office, 1275 K St., N.W., Ste. 880 Washington, DC 20005. Tel: 800-352-3452 Tel: 202-289-1093 Fax: 202-682-9018 Email: icsc@catholicstewardship.org Web: www.catholicstewardship.org Bishop Paul G. Bootkoski, D.D., Bishop of Metuchen, NJ, Episcopal Moderator, Michael Murphy, Exec. Dir.

Through its annual conference, Stewardship and Development Institutes, publications and audio materials, ICSC allows people committed to Christian stewardship to gather, share ideas, and learn from each other. At one with the universal church, ICSC fosters solidarity of stewardship as a way of life in parishes and dioceses all over the world. Membership in ICSC is extended to several categories of Christian stewards: (Arch)dioceses, parishes, Catholic associations and professional firms from the United States and around the world. Members receive a number of essential benefits to enable them to live stewardship and bring this way of life to others in their communities and organizations.

ICSC encourages the growing professionalism of diocesan stewardship and development procedures and programs, as well as the development of parish-centered stewardship renewal aimed at increasing the time, talent and treasure contributed by parishioners. These principles of stewardship outlined in the 1992 USCCB Pastoral Letter: Stewardship: A Disciple's Response.

For a complete list of services and publications contact the ICSC office or visit the ICSC Website at www.catholicstewardship.org. Membership information is available upon request.

Jesuit Conference, Inc.

1016 16th St., N.W., Ste. 400 Washington, DC 20036. Tel: 202-462-0400 Fax: 202-328-9212 Rev. Thomas H. Smolich, S.J., Pres., Rev. Gerard L. Stockhausen, S.J., Ph.D., Exec. Sec.

Ladies of Charity of the United States of America (LCUSA)

National Center, P.O. Box 31697 Saint Louis, MO 63131-0697. Tel: 314-344-1184 ext 102 Fax: 314-344-2989 Web: www.famvin.org/LCUSA MaryAnn Morovitz, Pres. 2007-2008, Bishop Howard James Hubbard, D.D., Episcopal Chm. , Rev. Richard Gielow, C.M., Spiritual Advisor

Ladies of Charity in the United States of America (LCUSA) is a national organization with local associations of Ladies of Charity as its members. The local Associations are dedicated to the service of the poor in their communities in the spirit of St. Vincent de Paul, St. Louise de Marillac and St. Elizabeth Ann Seton. Nationally about 10,000 members contribute volunteer hours and financial support to services that may include the operation of a thrift shop, food pantry, meal and transportation services. LCUSA participates in social co-responsibility as a member of the International Association of Charities. They are advocates for the disadvantaged and the poor and help to empower the poor to help themselves. National Assembly annually.

Publications; quarterly, Servicette.

Leadership Conference of Women Religious in the United States of America

Office, 8808 Cameron St. Silver Spring, MD 20910. Tel: 301-588-4955 Fax: 301-587-4575 Sr. Mary Hughes, O.P., Ed.D., Past Pres., Sr. Pat Farrell, O.S.F., Pres., Sr. Florence Deacon, O.S.F., Ph.D., Pres. Elect, Sr. Sheila Megley, R.S.M., Treas., Sr. Barbara Blesse, O.P., M.A., M.Div., Sec., Sr. Janet Mock, C.S.J., B.A., Acting Exec. Dir.

A conference of leaders of U.S. women religious congregations, founded in 1956, canonically approved in 1959 with a name change in 1972 and canonical approval of revised by-laws in 1972 and 1989, to promote a developing understanding and living of religious life, to assist members to carry out more collaboratively their service of leadership, to provide a vehicle for dialogue with the Bishops' Conference and other ecclesiastical authority, and to collaborate with other groups concerned with the needs of society in continuing the mission of Christ in the world today.

Lithuanian Roman Catholic Federation of America

4545 W. 63rd St. Chicago, IL 60629. Tel: 312-585-9500 Bishop Paul Baltakis, O.F.M., Episcopal Advisor, Saulius V. Kuprys, Pres.

A not-for-profit corporation founded in 1906 in Wilkes-Barre, PA, to promote and coordinate religious, educational and charitable activities among Lithuanian American Catholics, their organizations, institutions, religious communities, and parishes (for detailed information regarding religious institutions please refer to the Apostolate for Lithuanians).

Mariological Society of America (1949)

Secretariat: Marian Library, University of Dayton Dayton, OH 45469-1390. Tel: 937-229-4294 Fax: 937-229-4258 Rev. Thomas A. Thompson, S.M., Exec. Sec.

The objects and purposes of this organization are to promote interest and research in the theology of the Virgin Mary. Professional and associate membership. Proceedings of annual meeting published in Marian Studies. Annual convention in late May or early June.

National Apostolate for Inclusion Ministry NAFIM (1967)

Mailing Address, P.O. Box 218 Riverdale, MD 20738-0218. Tel: 800-736-1280 Tel: 301-699-9500 Fax: 240-220-8374 Email: qnafim@aol.com Web: www.nafim.org Bishop Mitchell T. Rozanski, D.D., V.G., Episcopal Moderator, Deacon Lawrence R. Sutton, Ph.D., Pres., Barbara J. Lampe, Exec. Dir., Dennis McNulty, E-Journal

Established in 1967 to promote the full participation of persons with intellectual disabilities in the life of the Catholic Church. Formerly known as National Apostolate with Persons with Mental Retardation (NAPMR) 1992-1997, National Apostolate with Mentally Retarded Persons (NAMRP) 1974-1992 and National Apostolate for the Mentally Retarded (NAMR) 1967-1974.

Publications: internet journal; newsletter; pamphlets; training materials.

National Association for Treasurers of Religious Institutes, Inc. (NATRI) (1981)

8824 Cameron St. Silver Spring, MD 20910. Tel: 301-587-7776 Fax: 301-589-2897 Web: www.trcri.org

Serving finance officers and staffs of religious institutes by assisting them in fulfilling their stewardship responsibilities. An annual national conference, seminar for new personnel in financial offices, and a consulting service are key program components. All Roman Catholic religious institutes are eligible for membership in NATRI and currently approximately 585 belong.

Publication: annual membership and service directories and other miscellaneous publications 5 times a year; Accounting and Financial Management.

National Association of African American Catholic Deacons, Inc.

Office of the President, 1418 Glen View Rd. Yellow Springs, OH 45387. Tel: 937-974-1588 Tel: 937-767-5381 Fax: 937-767-7465 Deacon Paul E. Richardson, Pres. Yellow Springs, OH, Deacon Joseph Connor, Vice Pres., Seattle, WA, Deacon Alfred Mitchell, Sec., Atlanta, GA, Deacon Jerry Lett, Treas., Lithonia, GA, Deacon Marvin Threatt, Immediate Past-Pres., Spring Valley, CA

Members At Large:—Deacon Arthur L. Miller, Windsor, CT, Deacon Jimmie L. Boyd, Sr., Buffalo, NY, Deacon Keith McKnight, Jersey City, NJ, Deacon Ralph Cyrus, Ft. Washington, MD, Deacon Emith Fludd, St. Croix, VI, Deacon Dexter Watson, Chicago, IL, Deacon Oliver Washington, Cincinnati, OH, Deacon Dunn Cumby, Oklahoma City, OK, Deacon A. Stephen Pickett, Lenoir, SC

Wives Representatives:—Magnolia Cumby, Oklahoma City, OK, Barbara Connor, Seattle, WA

To establish an organization of Permanent deacons of African heritage ordained in the Roman Catholic Church. To promote unity among deacons of African descent by facilitating effective communication network on a national, regional, and diocesan level. To be a pro-active organization in promoting and contributing to the future of the African American family with emphasis on African American men. To promote justice, peace, equality, an end to racism, and the sharing of resources among all peoples in light of the social teachings of the Roman Catholic Church.

National Association of Catholic Chaplains

National Office, 4915 S. Howell Ave., Ste. 501 Milwaukee, WI 53207-6159. Tel: 414-483-4898 Fax: 414-483-6712 Email: info@nacc.org Web: www.nacc.org Archbishop Paul S. Coakley, D.D., S.T.L., Alan E. Bowman, M.Div., M.B.A., B.C.C., Pres. & Chm. Bd., Mr. David A. Lichter, Exec. Dir.

The National Association of Catholic Chaplains advocates for the profession of spiritual care and educates, certifies, and supports chaplains, clinical pastoral educators, and all members who continue the healing ministry of Jesus in the name of the Church.

Publication: 6 times-year, journal-newsletter, Vision; 26 times-year (every other Monday), email newsletter, NACC Now.

The National Association of Catholic Family Life Ministers

300 College Park Dayton, OH 45469-2512. Tel: 937-431-5443 Fax: 937-431-5443 Email: nacflm@udayton.edu David Abele, CFO, Lorrie Gramer, Pres., Deacon Thomas Fogle, Pres. Elect

The National Association of Church Personnel Administrators (NACPA)

Headquarters, 100 E. Eighth St. Cincinnati, OH 45202. Tel: 513-421-3134 Fax: 513-421-3085 Web: www.nacpa.org Rev. Msgr. Patrick J. Pollard, Bd. Pres., Mary Jo Moran, Ph.D., S.P.H.R., Exec. Dir.

The National Association of Church Personnel Administrators (NACPA) is a membership association of lay, religious and clergy serving dioceses, parishes, religious congregations and other church-related institutions. The purpose of the Association is to promote justice in the workplace where the Church is the employer through ethical and just standards and to provide programs and resources that assist members in developing competencies in human resource management grounded in gospel values.

National Association of Diaconate Directors (1977)

National Office, 7625 N. High St. Columbus, OH 43235-1499. Tel: 614-985-2276 Email: naddinfo@nadd.org Web: www.nadd.org Deacon Gerald W. DuPont, Chm., Deacon Steve Rangel, Vice Chm., Deacon Michael F. Jelley, Sec. & Treas., Deacon Thomas R. Dubois, Exec. Dir.

NADD serves formation directors, deacon directors, vicars for deacons, and other diocesan personnel who are responsible to their bishops for the formation of deacon candidates and the continued professional development and education of deacons following ordination. The Association takes a leadership role relating to national and regional issues of the diaconate and serves as a consultant to the USCCB Committee for Clergy, Consecrated Life and Vocations. The Association leadership is comprised of an Executive Director, Executive Committee and a Board of Directors representing each of the 14 USCCB regions. NADD promotes expertise through the National Directory Institute, annual conventions, regional meetings, research, newsletters, and by providing consultation teams which evaluate formation programs upon request of the ordinary.

National Association of Diocesan Directors of Campus Ministry

305 Michigan Ave. Detroit, MI 48226. Tel: 313-237-5962 Mrs. Rakhi McCormick, Contact Person

National Association of Pastoral Musicians

National Office, 962 Wayne Ave., Ste. 210 Silver Spring, MD 20910-4461. Tel: 240-247-3000 Fax: 240-247-3001 Email: npmsing@npm.org Web: www.npm.org Dr. J. Michael McMahon, Pres. & CEO, Ms. Joanne Werner, Chm. Bd. of Directors , Cardinal Daniel Cardinal DiNardo, Episcopal Moderator

The National Association of Pastoral Musicians fosters the art of musical liturgy. The members of NPM serve the Catholic Church in the United States as musicians, clergy, liturgists, and other leaders of prayer. Regular parish membership includes both parish musicians and parish clergy. Individual membership is also available.

NPM programs include an annual national convention for musicians, clergy, and other leaders, as well as institutes for cantors, choir directors, guitarists, and ensemble musicians in addition to programs in pastoral liturgy, chant, music with children, and handbells. Several webinars are held each year on topics of interest and concern to musicians and other liturgical leaders. NPM provides a Job Hotline to assist musicians seeking employment and parishes searching for musicians. The Association also sponsors certification programs for organists, cantors, and professional directors of music ministries.

The Association is directed by a 5-member Board of Directors, advised by a 40-member NPM Council and served by a 9-person staff. There is a division for professional directors of music ministries as well as special interest sections for cantors, choir directors, organists, clergy, ensemble musicians, pianists, composers, diocesan directors of music, music educators, military musicians, campus ministers, youth, pastoral liturgy, chant, and musicians serving African American parishes, Hispanic communities, Asian Pacific Rim communities, and religious congregations.

Publications include Pastoral Music (five times annually); Pastoral Music Notebook (twice monthly by e-mail); Sunday Word for Pastoral Musicians (weekly by e-mail); The Liturgical Singer (four times annually); as well as e-newsletters for clergy and professional directors of music ministries. The NPM website provides a wealth of free resources, including music planning suggestions, access to official church documents, and downloadable recordings of chants for the Mass.

National Black Catholic Clergy Caucus

Resurrection Catholic Missions, Office, 2815 Forbes Dr. Montgomery, AL 36110.

Board of Directors:—Rev. Anthony Bozeman, S.S.J., Pres., Rev. Kenneth Taylor, V.F., Vice Pres., New Orleans, LA, Rev. Roy Lee, Sec., Atlanta, GA, Deacon Jerry Lett, Treas., Lithonia, GA, Deacon Dunn Cumby, Immediate Past Pres., Oklahoma, OK, Bro. Herman D. Johnson, O.P., Men Religious Representative, New Orleans, LA, Mr. Anthony Onyango, Seminarian Representative, Rev. Jeffery Ott, O.P., New Orleans, LA, Deacon Paul E. Richardson, Pres. NAAACD, Yellow Springs, OH

Members At Large:—Rev. Christopher L. Coleman, Ph.D., Brooklyn, NY, Rev. Victor H. Cohea, New Orleans, LA

The National Black Catholic Clergy Caucus serves as a fraternity for Black Catholic Clergy and Religious to support the spiritual, theological, educational and ministerial growth of its members. It is a vehicle to bring the contributions of the Black Community to fruition within the Catholic Church.

National Catholic Committee on Scouting Executive Committee (1934)

1325 W. Walnut Hill Ln. P.O. Box 152079 Irving, TX 75015-2079. Fax: 972-580-2535 Bishop Robert Guglielmone, Bishop of Charleston, SC, Episcopal Liaison, William Davies, Past Chm. (Minneapolis, MN), Gerard Scanlon, Vice Chm. (New York, NY), Edward Martin, Vice Chm. (Medina, OH), Susan Barriball, Vice Chm. (Chesterton, IN), Rev. Stephen B. Salvador, Natl. Chap. (Fall River, MA), John Halloran, Natl. Chm. (Lake Charles, LA), Rev. Raymond L. Fecteau, Past Natl. Chap. (Darnestown, MD) , Mr. Austin Cannon, Vice Chm. (Bellmore, NY), Rev. Michael P. Hanifin, Assoc. Natl. Chap. (Yorba Linda, CA), Mr. Michael F. Gannon, Vice Chm. (Silver Spring, MD)

A voluntary organization of clergy and laymen, members include a chaplain and lay chairman from all of the dioceses in the United States Conferences. It serves as an advisory committee to the Boy Scouts of America. It has the responsibility of promoting and guiding cooperative contracts between the proper authorities of the Catholic Church in the United States and the Boy Scouts of America.

National Catholic Conference for Total Stewardship (NCCTS)

National Office, 300 Liguori Dr. Liguori, MO 63057-9998. Tel: 636-464-3666 Fax: 636-464-4717 Email: fanov@aol.com Robert Winkler, Chm., Rev. Francis A. Novak, C.Ss.R., Pres., Adelaide Herrell, Sec.

The mission of the National Catholic Conference for Total Stewardship (NCCTS) is to initiate in dioceses and parishes the concept of total stewardship through a pastoral process called Celebrating Life as a Catholic Christian (CLCC). The concept joins the three basic elements of the bible: Evangelization, Discipleship and Service, and through the CLCC process presents them as a single unit not as separate apostolates. The CLCC manual defines the 3 elements, choosing key paragraphs and explanatory excerpts from 20 modern day papal documents. The process first updates active church-going Catholics in sound catechetics and eucharistic spirituality. At the same time the process prepares and motivates them to reach out to lapsed, non-regular church-going Catholics making person-to-person contact with them and with RCIA graduates. They join a Small Ecclesial Faith Community (SEFC) connected to the parish. Active parishoners in SEFC's constitute a welcoming environment for those in need of returning to the faith and those in need of retaining it. In them they experience Catholic fellowship, inter-personal sharing, communal and personal prayer and study official church teachings. Through the CLCC process returnees and recent converts are further formed in doctrine and spirituality for full membership in the Church, for encountering Christ in the sacraments, for enjoying "communion" with all Catholics and for Celebrating Life as Catholic Christians both in vocation and mission.

National Catholic Council on Alcoholism and Related Drug Problems, Inc.

Headquarters, 1601 Joslyn Rd. Lake Orion, MI 48360. Tel: 800-626-6910 ext 1200 Fax: 248-391-0210 Email: ncca@guesthouse.org Web: www.ncatoday.org Richard Thibodeau, Exec. Dir., Rev. Msgr. Thomas M. Haggerty, Pres.

NCCA is an agency of the Church, affiliated with the U.S. Conference of Catholic Bishops, and under the auspices of Guest House, Inc., is dedicated to the promotion of adequate treatment for all clergy, men and women religious, and laity who are suffering from alcoholism and other drug dependencies. NCCA also provides educational programs including workshops for dioceses, an Annual Conference, also educational and "Spirituality Support" resources, including free booklet: "Prayers For Addicted Persons and Their Loved Ones", also "Serenity Prayer Bookmarks", "Spirituality and Recovery From Addictions", also: "When They Won't (or Can't) Quit Alcohol or Drugs", also the Blue Book of Conference Proceedings. The NCCA seeks to help those struggling to overcome an addiction and those engaged in pastoral ministry, including outreach to the nation's jail and prison ministries.

National Catholic Development Conference, Inc. (1968)

86 Front St. Hempstead, NY 11550. Tel: 516-481-6000 Web: www.ncdc.org Sr. Georgette Lehmuth, O.S.F., Pres. & CEO, Mark Melia, Chm., Curtis Yarlott, Vice Chm., Mrs. Paulette Karas, Sec., Keith Zekind, Treas.

NCDC leads the Catholic development community toward excellence in the ministry of ethical fundraising through education, resources, networking and advocacy. As the United States' largest association of religious philanthropies, NCDC affirms the mission of each of its members by working for and with them as fundraisers. The hallmark of NCDC is the promotion of the integrity of its member organizations to donors, the media and the general public. To this end, all members are required to fully adhere to the NCDC Code of Stewardship and Ethics and support the Donor Bill of Rights. Central to NCDC's existence are the many services provided to its membership: advocacy, regional seminars, the annual Conference and Exposition, informative publications, educational resources and other specialized services geared to meet member needs.

Publications: Dimensions (10 times a year); E-Newsletters: Newswire, Essentials, Breaking News, Jobs eBulletin, Workshop and Programming; Stewardship for Mission, Toward a Theology of Fundraising; A Call to Accountability: Where Donors and Mission Meet.

National Catholic Educational Association (1904)

National Headquarters, 1005 N. Glebe Ave., Ste. 525 Arlington, VA 22201. Tel: 800-711-6232 Fax: 703-243-0025 Archbishop Wilton D. Gregory, S.L.D., Bd. Chair, Karen M. Ristau, Ed.D., Pres.

The National Catholic Educational Association (NCEA) has been providing leadership and service to American Catholic educators since 1904. NCEA's institutional and individual memberships represent Catholic education at all levels and in a variety of settings: preschools, elementary and secondary schools, parish catechetical/religious education programs, diocesan offices, colleges, universities and seminaries. The Association advances the educational and catechetical mission of the Church; provides leadership and service to its members; articulates the contribution of Catholic education to the Church and society; proclaims the uniqueness of Catholic schools; advocates recognition of and support for Catholic education in parish, school, college and university communities; enhances and supports leadership among the members; and fosters local, national and international collaboration.

National Catholic Office for the Deaf (1971)

NCOD Office, 7202 Buchanan St. Landover Hills, MD 20784-2236. Tel: 301-577-1684 Fax: 301-577-1684 Email: info@ncod.org Web: www.ncod.org Teletype: 301-577-4184 Eileen Colarusso, NCOD Bd. Pres.

The NCOD, established by the Catholic pastoral workers of the deaf in 1971 at Trinity College, Washington, DC is devoted to coordinating the Church's pastoral ministry to deaf and hard-of-hearing persons at the national level; developing special liturgies, catechetical texts and materials; organizing workshops, leadership programs, and national and regional pastoral workers meetings; coordinating a training program for ministers with the deaf; and serving as an information and referral center for all those involved in this special ministry as well as members of the deaf community and their families. Policy is established by a board of directors elected by the members.

Publication: pastoral journal, Vision.

National Catholic Partnership on Disability

415 Michigan Ave., N.E., Ste. 95 Washington, DC 20017-4501. Tel: 202-529-2933 Fax: 202-529-4678 Web: www.ncpd.org Teletype: 202-529-2934 Ms. Janice L. Benton, Exec. Dir., Ms. Susanna Herro, Chm.

Established to foster and facilitate the challenges of "Pastoral Statement of U.S. Catholic Bishops on People with Disabilities." Provides resources and enhances visibility of diocesan offices addressing access and inclusion; works with USCCB staff and other national Catholic organizations in advocating for disability involvement and concerns; collaborates with other ministries of the church to enhance meaningful participation; affirms the culture of life through promoting the giftedness of all people with assorted disabilities at all stages of the life cycle. Mission is promoted through appropriate media, consultation, lectures, workshops, and regional gatherings.

National Catholic Rural Life Conference

National Headquarters, 4625 Beaver Ave. Des Moines, IA 50310-2145. Tel: 515-270-2634 Fax: 515-270-9447 Email: info@ncrlc.com Web: www.ncrlc.com Bishop Frank J. Dewane, Pres. Bd. , James F. Ennis, Exec. Dir.

The National Catholic Rural Life Conference is a membership organization grounded in a spiritual tradition which brings together the Church, care for creation and care for community. The NCRLC fosters programs of direct service and systemic change. As an educator in the faith, the NCRLC seeks to relate religion to the rural world; develops support services for rural pastoral ministers; serves as a prophetic voice and as a catalyst and convener for social justice.

National Catholic Student Coalition (1988)

45 Lovett Ave. Newark, DE 19711. Tel: 302-463-5538 Fax: 302-368-2548 Email: ncsc@catholicstudent.org Web: www.catholicstudent.org Joe Ewing, Natl. Chm., Jessi Steenbergen, External Affairs Liaison

The National Catholic Student Coalition (NCSC) is a national coalition of Catholic student communities in institutes of higher education. The coalition provides a platform for Catholic students to reflect, speak, and act on issues within the university, the Church and society. The NCSC promotes the development of campus ministry and Catholic lay and religious leaders for the Church and society. The NCSC is a member of the International Movement of Catholic Students. Membership is open to groups or individuals associated with Catholic student groups in higher education. The NCSC holds an annual leadership conference.

Publication: The Catholic Collegian.

The National Center for Urban Ethnic Affairs (1971)

National Office, P.O. Box 20, Cardinal Station Washington, DC 20064. Tel: 202-232-3600 Tel: 202-319-5128 Tel: 202-319-6188 Dr. John A. Kromkowski, Pres., Rev. Msgr. Salvatore E. Polizzi, Chm., Rev. George F. McLean, O.M.I., Sec. Treas.

"The great task incumbent on all men of good will is to restore the relations of the human family in truth, in justice, in love, and in freedom." (Pope John XXIII, Peace on Earth.) The independent program of this nonprofit organization has evolved from the efforts initiated by the former Task Force on Urban Problems of the United States Catholic Conference. Its aims and purposes are to continue the expression of the Catholic Church's concern for the problems facing our urban society. NCUEA promotes the celebration of cultural pluralism in America and bridges the gaps between groups of various ethnic and cultural traditions. The Center disseminates information, conducts research, develops and supports programs concerned with ethnic Americans and urban society. The Center in association with various community and church groups develops workshops, conferences, and programs related to the quality of human life, national priorities and the development of an urban mission strategy. The Center is also associated with public and private agencies in developing urban economic, social, and intercultural programs, etc.

The National Conference for Catechetical Leadership (NCCL)

125 Michigan Ave., N.E. Washington, DC 20017. Tel: 202-884-9753 Fax: 202-884-9756 Web: www.nccl.org Dr. Anne D. Roat, Pres., Mr. Leland Nagel, Exec. Dir.

A voluntary organization composed of diocesan and parish catechetical personnel, academics specializing in religious education, and various associate and affiliated members, including publishers of catechetical materials. The Conference operates on three levels: national, regional and provincial. The purpose of the Conference is to promote and develop professional competence within catechetical leadership and to assist its members in their roles as leaders in the Church's catechetical ministry through networking, resource development, research, training, consultation and advocacy. The Conference is committed to collaboration with other national groups concerned with catechesis/religious education as a means of expanding and coordinating a service to catechetical ministry.

National Conference of Catholic Airport Chaplains (NCCAC)

Chicago O'Hare International Airport, P.O. Box 66353 Chicago, IL 60666-0353. Tel: 773-686-2636 Fax: 773-686-0130 Email: office@nccac.us Web: www.nccac.us Rev. Michael G. Zaniolo, S.T.L., C.A.C., Pres. (Chicago O'Hare International Airport), Rev. Philip S. Majka, Vice Pres. (Dulles International Airport), Deacon Philip Disparte, Sec. (Chicago O'Hare International Airport), Deacon Dennis E. Jordan, C.A.C., Treas. (Miami International Airport), Archbishop Jerome E. Listecki, Archbishop of Milwaukee, Episcopal Liaison

This Conference provides support and communication for all Catholics performing pastoral ministry to airport & airline workers, and travelers; in affiliation with USCCB Secretariat of Cultural Diversity in the Church, Subcommittee on Pastoral Care of Migrants, Refugees and Travelers.

National Council of Catholic Women

200 N. Glebe Rd., Ste. 725 Arlington, VA 22203. Tel: 703-224-0990 Fax: 703-224-0991 Email: nccw01@nccw.org Web: www.nccw.org Judy Powers, Pres., Joanne E. Dunne, Interim Exec. Dir.

The NCCW consists of Catholic women's organizations in the United States, numbering 3,000+ local, diocesan, national organizations and individual members. It delivers programs through 3,200+ Spirituality, Leadership and Service Commissions and the Annual Convention.

Publications: bimonthly, Catholic Woman; monthly, NCCW Connect.

National Federation for Catholic Youth Ministry, Inc. (NFCYM) (1981)

415 Michigan Ave., N.E., Ste. 40 Washington, DC 20017-4502. Tel: 202-636-3825 Bishop Martin D. Holley, D.D., V.G., Episcopal Advisor, Robert J. McCarty, D.Min., Exec. Dir., Michal Horace, Chm.

A membership association of diocesan youth offices and collaborating organizations, founded after a reorganization of the USCC Department of Education and the National CYO Federation. The NFCYM fosters the development of youth ministry in the "United States to, with, by, and for youth." The NFYCM mission is "to serve those who serve the young church". Members of the Federation work through diocesan, regional and national structures to provide national leadership, resources and vision for adults and youth in youth ministry. Key services include the biennial National Conference on Catholic Youth Ministry (for adults working with youth); the biennial National Catholic Youth Conference (for teenagers and their adult chaperones); the development of resources for parish workers; religious recognitions for Catholic Girl Scouts/Camp Fire; position papers on current topics and issues in youth ministry; regional and diocesan consultations and programs for diocesan youth ministry leaders.

National Organization for Continuing Education of Roman Catholic Clergy, Inc. (NOCERCC)

333 N. Michigan Ave., Ste. 1205 Chicago, IL 60601. Tel: 312-781-9450 Fax: 312-442-9709 Email: nocercc@nocercc.org Web: www.nocercc.org Rev. Richard L. Chiola, Ph.D., Pres., Dr. Mary Ann Boyarski, Ed.D., Vice Pres., Rev. Patrick M. Carrion, Sec. & Treas., Mr. James H. Alphen, M.B.A., Exec. Dir., Bishop Gregory J. Hartmayer, O.F.M.Conv., Member-at-Large, Rev. John S. Sledziona, C.M., Member-at-Large

The National Organization for Continuing Education of Roman Catholic Clergy (NOCERCC) is a membership association of dioceses and religious communities and other interested organizations and individuals committed to the Church's mission to promote and support ongoing formation for priests and presbyterates. Founded in 1973, the National Organizaiton for Continuing Education of Roman Catholic Clergy (NOCERCC) is a membership association of dioceses, religious communities and other interested organizations and individuals committed to the Church's mission to promote and support ongoing formation for priests and presbyterates. Professional and formational services offered include an annual convention; an annual orientation workshop; regional meetings; programs that dioceses and religious communities can host for clergy and other pastoral ministers; a quarterly newsletter; and other practical resouorces in diverse media.

Publications: newsletter, Handbook for Directors of Ongoing Formation of Priests, Sabbatical Opportunities, Priestly Relationships: Freedom through Boundaries.

National Pastoral Center for the Chinese Apostolate, Inc.
Sacred Heart of Jesus, 14277 Preston Rd., Apt. 1027 Dallas, TX 75240. Tel: 972-716-0077 Rev. Paul P. Pang, O.F.M., Dir.

National Pastoral Life Center
Headquarters, 18 Bleecker St. New York, NY 10012-2404. Tel: 212-431-7825 Fax: 212-274-9786 Email: nplc@nplc.org Web: www.nplc.org Rev. John E. Hurley, C.S.P., Exec. Dir., Hope Villella, Dir. Social Action & Pastoral Planning, Ms. Elizabeth O'Connor, Editor Church Magazine, Mr. Peter Denio, Dir. Catholic Common Ground Initiative and Pastoral Svcs., Mr. Carl Barnes, Devel. Dir.

The Center is an information, training, and consulting resource for diocesan and parish leaders. The Center conducts and staffs educational and training programs for pastors and others in ministry. It also sponsors pastoral ministry conventions, social justice conferences, the Common Ground Initiative colloquia, conducts pastoral research, and serves as a resource and referral center for parish and diocesan staffs. The Center is home to the roundtable association for Diocesan social action directors and the conference for the pastoral planning and council development.

Publications: Church Magazine; Center Papers, books, pastoral pamphlets and other publications.

North American Pastoral Center for Czech Catholics
344 Koch Ave. Placentia, CA 92870-1928. Tel: 714-524-0092 Fax: 714-637-6789 Bishop Peter Esterka, Pres.

The Papal Foundation
Office, 150 Monument Rd., Ste. 609 Bala Cynwyd, PA 19004. Tel: 610-535-6340 Tel: 610-535-6341 Fax: 610-535-6343 Email: jcoffey@thepapalfoundation.com Mr. James V. Coffey, M.A., Vice Pres. Devel.

Cardinal Members—Cardinal William Keeler, Cardinal Daniel N. DiNardo, Cardinal Edward M. Egan, Cardinal Francis E. George, O.M.I., Cardinal Roger M. Mahony, Cardinal Adam Maida, Cardinal Theodore E. McCarrick, Cardinal Sean P. O'Malley, O.F.M.Cap., Cardinal Justin F. Rigali

Trustees—Cardinal Timothy M. Dolan, Archbishop Jose H. Gomez, S.T.D., Archbishop John J. Myers, D.D., J.C.D., Cardinal Donald Cardinal Wuerl, Chm., Bishop Michael J. Bransfield, Pres., Bishop Michael F. Burbidge, Sec., Bishop Kevin J. Farrell, D.D., Bishop Richard F. Stika, Bishop Joseph A. Pepe, D.D., J.C.D., Timothy R. Busch, Lisa Goodmaster, Frank J. Hanna, III, Elmer F. Hansen, Jr., Treas., Ken Kenworthy, Patricia Lynch, Judy Rauenhorst Mahoney, Timothy Maguire, Eustace Mita, James Nolen, III, Carol Saeman, J. Eustace Wolfington

The Parish Evaluation Project
3195 S. Superior St. Milwaukee, WI 53207. Tel: 414-483-7370 Fax: 414-483-7380 Email: pep@pitnet.net Web: www.pepparish.org Rev. Thomas P. Sweetser, S.J., Co-Dir., Wendy Rappe, Co-Dir.

The Parish Evaluation Project is a nonprofit organization under the laws of Wisconsin, whose purpose is to provide religious and educational services to Catholic parishes in the United States in the areas of surveying, needs assessment, leadership skills, goal setting, evaluation techniques, staff development, pastoral council formation and other resources helpful in parish planning and renewal.

Pax Christi U.S.A., National Catholic Peace Movement
1225 Otis St., N.E. Washington, DC 20017-2516. Tel: 202-635-2741 Fax: 202-832-9494 Sr. Josie Chrosniak, H.M., Chair, Mary Pat O'Gorman, Vice Chm., Bishop Gabino Zavala, Pres., Greet Vanaerschot, Intl. Sec., Jack McHale, Treas.

Pax Christi USA is the national Catholic peace movement, reaching more than half a million Catholics in the United States each year. Our membership includes more than 100 U.S. bishops, 800 parishes, 650 religious communities and 250 local groups. Pax Christi USA is a section of Pax Christi International, the international Catholic peace movement with consultative status at the United Nations.

Publications: bimonthly newspaper and peace education materials.

Religious Brothers Conference
National Office, 5401 S. Cornell Ave. Chicago, IL 60615. Tel: 773-595-4023 Fax: 773-595-4087 Email: rbc@ctu.edu Web: brothersonline.org Bro. Thomas Osorio, O.H., Pres., Bro. Herman D. Johnson, O.P., Vice Pres., Bro. Michael Moran, C.P., Treas., Bro. John Byrd, F.M.S., Sec., Bro. Stephen Synan, F.M.S., Exec. Dir.

Publication: Brothers' Voice; Reflections.

Religious Formation Conference
National Office, 8820 Cameron St. Silver Spring, MD 20910-4152. Tel: 301-588-4938 Fax: 301-585-7649 Sr. Violet Grennan, M.F.I.C., Exec. Dir., Sr. Jeanine Tisot, R.S.M., Chm.

A national organization which assists Women and Men Religious who are engaged in the ministry of initial and on-going formation in their congregations.

The Resource Center for Religious Institutes
8824 Cameron St. Silver Spring, MD 20910. Tel: 301-589-8143 Fax: 301-589-2897 Email: trcri@trcri.org Web: www.trcri.org Rev. Daniel Ward, O.S.B., Exec. Dir.

The Slovak Catholic Federation (1911)
315 Wyoming Ave. Scranton, PA 18503-1237. Tel: 570-344-7231 Fax: 570-344-4749 Email: frfrosty@gmail.com Web: www.slovakcatholicfederation.org Rev. Philip A. Altavilla, V.G., Pres., Bishop Joseph Victor Adamec, D.D., S.T.L., Episcopal Advisor, Rev. Msgr. Thomas A. Derzack, M.Div., Spiritual Dir., Dolores M. Evanko, Sec. & Treas.

Founded by Father Joseph Murgas at Wilkes-Barre, Pennsylvania as a nonprofit corporation to promote and coordinate religious and social activities among Slovak Catholic fraternal benefit societies, religious communities, Slovak parishes and individuals in order to address the pastoral needs of Slovak Catholics at home and abroad.

United States Catholic Mission Association
Hecker Center, 3025 Fourth St., N.E., Ste. 100 Washington, DC 20017. Tel: 202-832-3112 Fax: 202-832-3688 Email: uscma@uscatholicmission.org Web: www.uscatholicmission.org Teresita Gonzalez de la Maza, Pres., Rev. Michael Montoya, M.J., Exec Dir.

The USCMA was juridically established September 1, 1981. Its members include U.S. missioners, mission organizations, diocesan mission offices, and others concerned about the mission of the Church and global solidarity. The Association seeks to help missioners to stay up-to-date on mission and world trends, to promote greater global awareness, sensibility, and solidarity in the U.S., and periodically to be a voice for U.S. missioners speaking out in defense of the poor and oppressed throughout the world. USCMA activities include a national conference that highlights specific mission themes and issues, liaison and cooperation with missionary bodies of other Christian churches. The USCMA is responsible for gathering statistical data on the U.S. missionary personnel, which is published biannually.

Publications: quarterly newsletter, Mission Update; reports, U.S. Catholic Missionary Statistics, and education programs on mission and global awareness.

NATIONAL ORGANIZATIONS WITH INDIVIDUAL I.R.S. RULINGS

Beginning Experience
International Ministry Center, 1657 Commerce Dr. South Bend, IN 46628. Tel: 574-283-0279 Tel: 866-610-8877 Fax: 574-283-0287 Email: imc@beginningexperience.org Web: www.beginningexperience.org Bishop Patrick J. Zurek, D.D., Episcopal Moderator, Kathleen Murphy, Exec. Dir., Steven Oldham, Pres., Beverly Howell, Vice Pres., Susan Ackerman, Sec., Carolyn Rhode, Treas.

Beginning Experience is a copyrighted weekend program to help divorced, separated and widowed persons, as well as their families, work through the trauma of the loss of their spouse and make a new beginning in life. The program was designed by and for Catholics and has its roots in sound Catholic tradition and the sacramental life of the Church. True to the ecumenical spirit in the Church since Vatican II, it has been open to persons of all faiths from the beginning. The Beginning Experience weekend was originated in 1974 by Sr. Josephine Stewart in Fort Worth, TX. It has spread throughout the United States as well as other countries. Trained teams make the Beginning Experience weekend available on a regular basis. It also serves as an informational and materials resource for the establishment of support groups to minister to the needs of the divorced, separated and widowed and their families at various points in their growth process.

Canon Law Society of America
The Hecker Center, 3025 4th St., N.E., Ste. 111 Washington, DC 20017-1102. Tel: 202-832-2350 Fax: 202-832-2331 Email: info@clsa.org Sr. Sharon A. Euart, R.S.M., J.C.D., Exec. Coord., Mrs. Rita F. Joyce, J.D., J.C.L., Pres., Rev. John R. Vaughan, J.C.D., Vice Pres., Ms. Zabrina R. Decker, J.C.L., Sec., Rev. Gregory T. Bittner, J.D., J.C.L., Treas.

A membership association of Bishops, Clergy, Religious and Laity for the purpose of promoting research and professional collaboration in the area of Canon Law.

Catholic Engaged Encounter, Inc.
4239 Shirley Rd. Richmond, VA 23225. Tel: 800-339-9790 Jim Dyk, Sandy Dyk, Rev. Jay Biber

Catholic Library Association
205 W. Monroe St., Ste. 314 Chicago, IL 60606-5061. Tel: 312-739-1776 Fax: 312-739-1778 Email: cla@cathla.org Web: www.cathla.org Malachy R. McCarthy, Pres.

The Catholic Mutual Relief Society of America
10843 Old Mill Rd. Omaha, NE 68154-2600. Tel: 402-551-8765 Mr. Joseph Beveridge, Pres. & CEO, Mr. Michael Intrieri, Exec. Vice Pres. & COO

The Catholic Relief Insurance Company of America
76 St. Paul St., Ste. 500 Burlington, VT 05401. Tel: 402-551-8765 Mr. Joseph Beveridge, Pres., Mr. Michael Intrieri, Vice Pres.

Conference for Pastoral Planning and Council Development
P.O. Box 45625 Philadelphia, PA 19149. Tel: 215-333-0993 Email: cppcd@cppcd.org Web: www.cppcd.org Mr. Robert Choiniere, Chair, Fran Stratton, Acting Admin. Dir.

National Association for Lay Ministry (NALM)
National Office, 6896 Laurel St., N.W. Washington, DC 20012. Tel: 202-541-5300 Email: nalm@nalm.org Web: www.nalm.org Mr. Christopher Anderson, Exec. Dir.

The National Association for Lay Ministry is a professional organization which supports, educates and advocates for lay ministers and promotes the development of lay ministry in the Catholic Church. Rejoicing in our baptismal call to be disciples of Jesus Christ and claiming our vocation to minister in the Roman Catholic Church, we value: 1) the universal call to holiness; 2) sharing in the mission and ministry of Jesus; 3) faith that works for justice; 4) the dignity of each person and the richness that results from diversity; 5) the ongoing conversion of persons and structures; 6) collaboration in ministry and participative Church leadership, and; 7) the life experiences lay ministers bring to ministry from their unique relationships and responsibilities as family members, workers, and citizens.

Publications: National Certification Standards for Lay Ecclesial Ministers; Moving Ministry Forward; Study Guide: CoWorkers in the Vineyard of the Lord; National Certification Standards for Pastoral Ministers.

National Catholic Conference for Interracial Justice (NCCIJ) (1959)
Office, 1200 Varnum St., N.E. Washington, DC 20017-2796. Tel: 202-529-6480 Fax: 202-526-1262 Archbishop Charles J. Chaput, O.F.M.Cap., D.D., Co. Chm., Hon. Lindy Boggs, Co. Chm., Deacon Joseph M. Conrad, Exec. Dir.

Established to implement the teaching of the Catholic Church on cultural and racial justice and to promote the church's vision of multicultural, multiracial understanding, mutual respect and collaboration.

The National Catholic Risk Retention Group, Inc.

National Office, 801 Warrenville Rd., Ste. 175 Lisle, IL 60532-4334. Tel: 630-725-0986 Tel: 877-486-2774 Fax: 630-725-1374 Michael J. Bemi, Pres. & CEO, Rev. Jay C. Haskin, M.Ch.A., Chm. Bd., Mr. John M. Scholl, C.P.C.U., A.I.M., Vice Pres., Mr. John J. Maxwell, CPA, Treas.

The Company is wholly owned by 66 Catholic (Arch)Dioceses and one Catholic Risk Pooling Trust. It underwrites excess liability insurance for Dioceses and other Church organizations listed in the Official Catholic Directory. Coverage is always subject to a minimum self-insured retention or underlying coverage of $250,000. Maximum limits of coverage available are $14,750,000. The company has the capability to underwrite insurance in all states, Territories and Possessions of the U.S.

National Catholic Young Adult Ministry Association

c/o Diocese of Joliet Young Adult Ministry, Chicago Office, 101 W. Airport Rd. Romeoville, IL 60446. Tel: 815-834-4047 Fax: 202-526-7544 Email: info@ncyama.org Web: www.ncyama.org Rakhi Roy McCormick, Pres., Paul Jarzembowski, Exec. Dir., Lauren Gaffey, Treas.

Founded in 1982, NCYAMA is an organization supporting those who minister to and with single and married people in their late teens, twenties or thirties. We develop and promote programs and resources while providing opportunities for networking and communication. We advocate for the full integration of young adults in the life of the Catholic faith community in order to connect them with Jesus, the Church, the mission of the Church and their peers.

Publication: electronic newsletter.

National Conference of Diocesan Vocation Directors (1962)

National Office, 440 W. Neck Rd. Huntington, NY 11743. Tel: 631-645-8210 Fax: 631-812-0249 Email: office@ncdvd.org Rev. Msgr. Robert Panke, Pres., Mrs. Rosemary C. Sullivan, Exec. Dir.

NCDVD is a professional organization that supports, educates and provides resources for diocesan vocation directors as they promote all Church vocations, but particularly diocesan priesthood. This organization serves all dioceses associated with the United States Conference of Catholic Bishops.

Publications: four times a year, Newsletter; documents of interest & training institutes; Meetings annually for Regional Conferences and a National Convention.

The National Federation of Priests' Councils (1968)

National Office, 333 N. Michigan Ave., Ste. 1205 Chicago, IL 60601-4002. Tel: 312-442-9700 Tel: 888-271-6372 Fax: 312-442-9709 Email: nfpc@nfpc.org Web: www.nfpc.org Rev. Richard Vega, Pres., Mr. Victor J. Doucette, Dir. Events Coord., Mr. Terry Oldes, Business Mgr., Mr. David Philippart, Dir. Devel., Mr. Alan Szafsaniec, Research Asst.

The NFPC promotes priestly fraternity by facilitating communication among priests' councils, provides a forum for priests to discuss pastoral matters, enables priests' councils to speak with a common voice, promotes and collaborates on programs of pastoral research, furthers the spiritual renewal of priestly life, collaborates with national lay and religious groups in ways that promote renewal in the Church, collaborates with the USCCB in addressing the needs of the Church in the U.S.A., encourages priests' councils to promote justice in light of the social teachings of the Church, and participates in developing a national and universal perspective of church and ministry.

The NFPC represents over 116 priests' councils, priests' associations and affiliates. Elected delegates of member councils meet annually to set policy, and a national executive board meets regularly to carry out the work of the NFPC, assisted by standing committees. Member councils represent approximately 26,000 priests.

Publications: quarterly newsletter, Touchstone; weekly; NFPC This Week; books, Income Tax for Priests Only, The Laborer Is Worthy of His Hire, International Priests in America, The First Five Years of Priesthood, Evolving Visions of the Priesthood, Stewards of God's Mysteries.

National Institute for the Word of God

Headquarters, 487 Michigan Ave., N.E. Washington, DC 20017. Tel: 203-562-6193 ext 147 Email: wjburke@dhs.edu Web: www.wordofgodinstitute.org

Episcopal Advisory Board—Archbishop John R. Quinn, Bishop David E. Foley, D.D., Bishop Patrick R. Cooney, S.T.B., S.T.L., D.D., Bishop William G. Curlin, D.D.

Staff—Rev. John W. Burke, O.P., Exec. Dir., William H. Graham, Assoc. Dir., Mary Graham, Sec., Very Rev. Joseph P. Allen, O.P., B.A., Admin. & Treas.

Board of Advisors—Rev. Msgr. Raymond East, Rev. James Patrick Moroney, Rev. Rutilio J. del Riego, Rev. James Walsh, Martha Fernandez, Carol Graham Lehan, Mary Ann McGuire, Michael M. McGuire

The Institute is an unaffiliated nonprofit organization incorporated under the laws of the District of Columbia, whose purpose is to promote, support, conduct and assist in any way whatsoever educational, liturgical, and remedial programs and activities, public and private, through the use of any and all media, to further effective communication of the revealed word of God, as the primary pastoral work of the Church. Ongoing efforts include the dissemination of scriptural, theological and pastoral aids such as books, films and tape albums, and the conducting of parish missions, conferences and retreats for clergy and laity.

National Service Committee of the Catholic Charismatic Renewal of the United States, Inc.

P.O. Box 628 Locust Grove, VA 22508-0628. Rev. Robert E. Hogan, B.B.D., Chm., Walter Matthews, Exec. Dir.

Our focus is to foster baptism in the Holy Spirit in the life of the Church in the United States and throughout the world, to broaden and deepen the understanding that baptism in the Holy Spirit is the Christian inheritance of all, and to strengthen the Catholic Charismatic Renewal. The National Service Committee has established and supported numerous programs to help further our mission. Some of the activities and programs include the establishment of Chariscenter USA, which serves as the national headquarters for our committee and a national office for the Catholic Charismatic Renewal.

Publications: Magazine, "Pentecost Today"; Leaders' training materials as well as an annual national conference, outreach to youth ministers, and evangelization training. The NSC has supported the International Catholic Charismatic Renewal Office in Rome.

The North American Forum on the Catechumenate

125 Michigan Ave., N.E. Washington, DC 20017-1102. Tel: 202-884-9758 Fax: 202-884-9747 James Schellman, Exec. Dir.

The North American Forum on the Catechumenate is an international network committed to the implementation of the Rite of Christian Initiation of Adults. The work of FORUM is overseen by a Board of Directors of seven elected representatives. A variety of institutes are offered in co-sponsorship with a hosting diocese to serve the local Church. FORUM networks with other U.S., Canadian and international groups, promotes research into issues raised by Christian Initiation (including outreach to the inactive through a process of Re-Membering Church), and provides a newsletter which focuses on the impact of Christian Initiation on the Church as well as key issues related to its implementation.

Worldwide Marriage Encounter

National Office, 2210 E. Highland Ave., Ste. 106 San Bernardino, CA 92404. Tel: 909-863-9963 Fax: 909-863-9986

Secretariat Team—Rev. Emile Frische, M.H.M., Anthony Witczak, Catherine Witczak

Organized to foster a program of Christian information to instruct married couples in the means to find God's plan and matrimony in their lives, for their own spiritual development and the betterment of all humankind; and to develop, foster and disseminate an adult catechesis supporting, furthering and building upon such instruction. Worldwide Marriage Encounter offers the marriage encounter weekend experience in 150 dioceses in the United States as well as in 88 foreign countries. In the United States over 1,500,000 couples and over 5,000 priests and bishops have experienced the Worldwide weekend.

Publication: EMatrimony online at ematrimony.org.

MISCELLANEOUS

Catholic Committee for Refugees & Children

3211 Fourth St., N.E. Washington, DC 20017-1194. Fax: 202-722-8755 Ambassador Johnny Young, Pres.

Incorporated since 1954, the Catholic Committee for Refugees and Children was founded to counsel and cooperate with European refugees during and after World War II. Since that time its mission has been expanded to include service to refugees worldwide. It has a special mandate from the bishops concerning its work with children through international child welfare, child care or placement, and international adoption. The USCCB Committee on Migration serves as the Board of Directors for CCRC.

National Association of State Catholic Conference Directors

An Association of the Directors of the State Catholic Conferences, organized in 1968 to facilitate and encourage the exchange of information among its members pertaining to the activities, programs and organization of the Conferences. A State Catholic Conference is a Church agency composed of the dioceses within a state to provide for the coordination of the public policy concerns of the Church. Thus a Conference of the Church communicates with state government, other Church Agencies, non-Catholic churches and secular agencies. Bishops, priests, religious and lay persons are involved in the work of the State Conferences. National Association: USCCB, 3211 4th St., N.E., Washington, DC 20017-1194.

ALASKA

Alaska Conference of Catholic Bishops, 225 Cordova St., Anchorage, AK 99501. Tel: 907-297-7744; Fax: 907-279-3885
Executive Director: Ms. Mary Gore

ARIZONA

Arizona Catholic Conference, 400 E. Monroe St., Phoenix, AZ 85004-2336. Tel: 602-354-2391; Fax: 602-354-2466
Chairman: Bishop Thomas J. Olmsted, J.C.D.
Executive Director: Ron Johnson

CALIFORNIA

California Conference of Catholic Bishops, 1119 K St., 2nd Fl., Sacramento, CA 95814. Tel: 916-313-4000; Fax: 916-313-4066; Email: conference@cacatholic.org; Web: www.cacatholic.org
President: Bishop Gerald E. Wilkerson, D.D., V.G.
Vice President: Bishop Jaime Soto, D.D., M.S.W.
Secretary-Treasurer: Bishop Richard J. Garcia, D.D.
Executive Director: Mr. Edward Dolejsi

COLORADO

Colorado Catholic Conference, 1535 Logan St., Denver, CO 80203. Tel: 303-894-8808; Fax: 303-894-7939; Email: ccc@cocatholicconference.org; Web: www.cocatholicconference.org
Executive Director: Jennifer Kraska

CONNECTICUT

Connecticut Catholic Conference, 134 Farmington Ave., Hartford, CT 06105. Tel: 860-524-7882; Fax: 860-525-0750; Email: ccc@ctcatholic.org
President and Chairman of the Board: Archbishop Henry J. Mansell
Secretary: Bishop Michael Richard Cote, D.D.
Executive Director: Michael Culhane, B.A., M.A., J.D.

FLORIDA

Florida Catholic Conference, 201 W. Park Ave., Tallahassee, FL 32301-7760. Tel: 850-222-3803; Fax: 850-681-9548
President: Bishop Thomas G. Wenski, D.D.
Executive Director: Dr. D. Michael McCarron, Ph.D.

GEORGIA

Georgia Catholic Conference, 3600 Mansell Rd., Ste. 300, Alpharetta, GA 30022. Tel: 770-521-8799; Email: fmulcahy@tbtlaw.com
Executive Director: Francis J. Mulcahy, Esq.

HAWAII

Hawaii Catholic Conference, 6301 Pali Hwy., Kaneohe, HI 96744. Tel: 808-203-6704; Fax: 808-261-7022; Email: hcc@rcchawaii.org
Director: Deacon Walter H. Yoshimitsu

ILLINOIS

Catholic Conference of Illinois, 65 E. Wacker Pl., Ste. 1620, Chicago, IL 60601. Tel: 312-368-1066 108 E. Cook St., Springfield, IL 62704. Tel: 217-528-9200
Chairman: His Eminence Francis Cardinal George, O.M.I., Ph.D., S.T.D.
Executive Director: Robert F. Gilligan
Director of Government Relations: Zachary Wichmann
Director of Social Services/Social Justice: Marilou Gervacio
Director of Communications: Mary Massingale

INDIANA

Indiana Catholic Conference, 1400 N. Meridian St., Indianapolis, IN 46202. Tel: 317-236-1455; Fax: 317-236-1456; Email: icc@archindy.org
General Chairman: Vacant
Executive Director: Glenn Tebbe

IOWA

Iowa Catholic Conference, 530-42nd St., Des Moines, IA 50312-2707. Tel: 515-243-6256; Fax: 515-243-6257; Email: info@iowacatholicconference.org; Web: www.iowacatholicconference.org
President: Archbishop Jerome Hanus, O.S.B.
Directors: Bishop Martin J. Amos, D.D.
Bishop Richard E. Pates
Secretary-Treasurer-Director: Bishop R. Walker Nickless
Executive Director: Thomas Chapman

KANSAS

Kansas Catholic Conference, 204 SW 8th Ave., Topeka, KS 66603. Tel: 785-227-9247; Web: www.kscathconf.org
Chairman: Archbishop Joseph F. Naumann, V.G., D.D.
Executive Director: Michael M. Schuttloffel
Associate Director: Ms. Beatrice E. Swoopes

KENTUCKY

Catholic Conference of Kentucky, 1042 Burlington Ln., Frankfort, KY 40601. Tel: 502-875-4345; Fax: 502-875-2841
Chairman: Archbishop Joseph E. Kurtz, D.D.
Executive Director: Rev. Patrick D. Delahanty

LOUISIANA

Louisiana Conference of Catholic Bishops, 2431 S. Acadian Thruway, Ste. 250, Baton Rouge, LA 70808. Tel: 225-344-7120; Fax: 225-383-9591
Chairman: Archbishop Gregory M. Aymond, D.D.
Executive Director: Mr. Daniel J. Loar
Associate Director: Mr. Robert M. Tasman
Business Manager: Mrs. Barbara Bovard

MARYLAND

Maryland Catholic Conference, 10 Francis St., Annapolis, MD 21401-1714. Tel: 410-269-1155; Fax: 410-269-1790
Chairman: His Eminence Edwin F. O'Brien, S.T.D., D.D.
Executive Director: Mary Ellen Russell

MASSACHUSETTS

Massachusetts Catholic Conference, 150 Staniford St. W. End Pl., Ste. 5, Boston, MA 02114. Tel: 617-367-6060
Executive Director: James F. Driscoll

MICHIGAN

Michigan Catholic Conference, 510 S. Capitol Ave., Lansing, MI 48933. Tel: 517-372-9310; Fax: 517-372-3940
Chairman: Archbishop Allen Vigneron
Vice Chairman: Bishop Walter Allison Hurley
Secretary-Treasurer: Mr. Robert Asmussen
President & CEO: Mr. Paul A. Long

MINNESOTA

Minnesota Catholic Conference, 475 University Ave. W., Ste. B, Saint Paul, MN 55103-1959. Tel: 651-227-8777; Fax: 651-227-2675
President: Archbishop John C. Nienstedt
Secretary-Treasurer: Bishop John LeVoir
Executive Director: Jason Adkins
Education Director: Dr. Peter Noll

MISSOURI

Missouri Catholic Conference, 600 Clark Ave., P.O. Box 1022, Jefferson City, MO 65102. Tel: 573-635-7239; Fax: 573-635-7431
General Chairman: Archbishop Robert J. Carlson
Executive Chairman: Bishop John R. Gaydos
Executive Director: J. Michael Hoey
General Counsel: Tyler McClay
Staff Associate: Rita Linhardt
Communications Director: Melissa Varner

MONTANA

Montana Catholic Conference, P.O. Box 1708, Helena, MT 59624. Tel: 406-442-5761; Fax: 406-442-9047; Email: mccadmin@bresnan.net; Web: www.montanacc.org
President: Mr. James Ziegler
Vice President: Mr. Craig Eddy
Secretary-Treasurer: Sr. Judy Lund, O.P.
Executive Director: Mr. Moe Wosepka

NEBRASKA

Nebraska Catholic Conference, 215 Centennial Mall South, Ste. 310, Lincoln, NE 68508-1890. Tel: 402-477-7517
President: Archbishop George J. Lucas
Directors: Bishop Fabian Wendelin Bruskewitz, D.D., S.T.D.
Bishop William J. Dendinger, D.D., M.A.
Executive Director: James R. Cunningham

NEVADA

Nevada Catholic Conference, 290 S. Arlington Ave., Ste. 200, Reno, NV 89501-1713. Tel: 775-684-9028; Fax: 775-348-8619
Executive Director: John Cracchiolo

NEW JERSEY

New Jersey Catholic Conference, 149 N. Warren St., Trenton, NJ 08608. Tel: 609-989-1120; Fax: 609-989-1152; Email: info@njcathconf.com; Web: www.njcathconf.com
President: Archbishop John J. Myers, D.D., J.C.D.
Executive Director: Deacon Patrick R. Brannigan

NEW YORK

New York State Catholic Conference, 465 State St., Albany, NY 12203. Tel: 518-434-6195
President: His Eminence Timothy M. Dolan
Vice President: Bishop Nicholas A. DiMarzio, D.D., Ph.D.
Secretary-Treasurer: Bishop William Francis Murphy, S.T.D., L.H.D.
Chairman-Public Policy Committee: Bishop Howard James Hubbard, D.D.
Executive Director: Richard E. Barnes

NORTH DAKOTA

North Dakota Catholic Conference, 103 S. 3rd St., Ste. 10, Bismarck, ND 58501. Tel: 701-223-2519; Fax: 701-223-6075
President: Bishop Samuel J. Aquila, D.D.
Vice President: Bishop Paul Albert Zipfel
Executive Director: Christopher Dodson

OHIO

Catholic Conference of Ohio, 9 E. Long St., Ste. 201, Columbus, OH 43215. Tel: 614-224-7147; Email: cco@ohiocathconf.org
President: Archbishop Dennis M. Schnurr, J.C.D., D.D.
Vice President: Bishop Richard G. Lennon
Secretary-Treasurer: Bishop Frederick F. Campbell, Ph.D., D.D.
Executive Director: Carolyn M. Jurkowitz

OREGON

Oregon Catholic Conference, 2838 E. Burnside St., Portland, OR 97214. Tel: 503-234-5334; Fax: 503-234-2545
President: Archbishop John G. Vlazny
Secretary-Treasurer: Rev. Msgr. Dennis O'Donovan

PENNSYLVANIA

Pennsylvania Catholic Conference, 223 North St., P.O. Box 2835, Harrisburg, PA 17105. Tel: 717-238-9613; Fax: 717-238-1473
Chairman: His Eminence Justin Cardinal Rigali
President: Bishop Joseph P. McFadden, D.D., V.G.
Vice President: Rev. Msgr. Lawrence T. Persico, J.C.L., V.G.
Secretary: Rev. Msgr. Peter Waslo, J.C.L.
Executive Director: Dr. Robert J. O'Hara
Treasurer: Rev. Msgr. Michael E. Servinsky, V.G., S.T.L., J.C.L., D.Min.

TEXAS

Texas Catholic Conference, 1625 Rutherford Ln., Bldg. D, Austin, TX 78754-5105. Tel: 512-339-9882
Co-Chairmen: Archbishop Jose H. Gomez, S.T.D., D.D.
His Eminence Daniel Cardinal DiNardo
Executive Director: Mr. Andrew Rivas
Associate Director: Jennifer Carr
Director of Education: Margaret McGettrick
Director, Catholic Archives of Texas: Susan Eason
Director of Accreditation: Marsha Solana

WASHINGTON

Washington State Catholic Conference, 710 Ninth Ave., Seattle, WA 98104. Tel: 206-301-0556; Fax: 206-301-0558; Web: www.thewscc.org
President: Archbishop J. Peter Sartain, D.D., S.T.L.
Executive Director: Sr. Sharon Park, O.P.
Office Manager: Theresa Ferguson

WEST VIRGINIA

Catholic Conference of West Virginia, 1114 Virginia St. E., Charleston, WV 25301. Tel: 304-342-8175; Fax: 304-344-3907
Director: Rev. Msgr. P. Edward Sadie, S.T.L., V.F.
Executive Secretary: Very Rev. Brian P. O'Donnell, S.J., Ph.D.

WISCONSIN

Wisconsin Catholic Conference, 131 W. Wilson St., Rm. 1105, Madison, WI 53703. Tel: 608-257-0004; Fax: 608-257-0376
President: Archbishop Jerome E. Listecki
Vice President: Bishop Robert C. Morlino
Executive Director: John Huebscher
Associate Director Respect Life & Social Concerns: Barbara A. Sella
Associate Director Education & Health Care: Kim Wadas

Alphabetical List of Places in the United States

This comprehensive list includes all cities and towns in the United States in which a Catholic Institution is located.

The abbreviations identify each city or town to the corresponding Diocese or Archdiocese.

Abbeville, LA LAF
SC CHR
Abbott, TX FWT
Abbottstown, PA HBG
Aberdeen, MD BAL
MS JKS
SD SFS
WA SEA
Abilene, KS SAL
TX SAN
Abingdon, IL PEO
MD BAL
VA RIC
Abington, MA BO
PA PH
Abiquiu, NM SFE
Abita Springs, LA NO
Absecon, NJ CAM
Acme, MI GLD
Acton, MA BO
ME PRT
Acushnet, MA FR
Ada, MI GR
MN CR
OH COL
OK OKL
Adams, MA SPR
MN WIN
NY OG
WI LC
Adamsville, AL BIR
Addison, IL JOL
NY ROC
Adel, GA SAV
IA DM
Adelanto, CA SB
Adelphi, MD WDC
Adena, OH STU
Adkins, TX SAT
Adrian, MI LAN
MN WIN
Advance, MO SPC
Affton, MO STL
Agawam, MA SPR
Agua Dulce, TX CC
Aguilar, CO PBL
Ahoskie, NC R
Aiea, HI HON
Aiken, SC CHR
Ainsworth, NE GI
Aitkin, MN DUL
Ajo, AZ TUC
Akron, CO DEN
IA SC
NY BUF
OH CLV
OH NTN
OH SJP
OH PRM
Alakanuk, AK FBK
Alameda, CA OAK
Alamo, TX BWN
Alamogordo, NM LSC
Alamosa, CO PBL
Albany, CA OAK
GA SAV
IL RCK
KY L
LA BR
MN SCL
NY ALB
OR P
TX FWT
Albemarle, NC CHL
Albers, IL BEL
Albert Lea, MN WIN
Albertville, MN STP
Albia, IA DAV
Albion, IN FTW
MI KAL
NE OM
NY BUF
PA E
RI PRO
Albuquerque, NM HPM
NM SFE
Alburgh, VT BUR
Alcoa, TN KNX
Alden, NY BUF
Aledo, IL PEO
TX FWT
Alexander City, AL BIR
Alexandria, IN LFT
KY COV
LA ALX
MN SCL
SD SFS
VA ARL
VA WDC
Alexandria Bay, NY OG
Alexis, IL PEO
Alfred, ME PRT
NY BUF
Algoma, WI GB
Algona, IA SC
Algonquin, IL RCK
Alhambra, CA LA
Alice, TX CC
Alief, TX GAL
Aliquippa, PA PBR
PA PIT
PA SJP
Aliso Viejo, CA ORG
Allegan, MI KAL
Allegany, NY BUF
Allen, TX DAL
Allen Park, MI DET
MI PRM
Allendale, MI GR
NJ NEW
Allenspark, CO DEN
Allenton, MI DET
WI MIL
Allentown, NJ TR
PA ALN
PA OLD
PA PSC
Alleyton, TX VIC
Alliance, NE GI
OH Y
Allison Park, PA PIT
Allston, MA BO
Alma, MI SAG
Alma Center, WI LC
Almond, NY BUF
WI LC
Aloha, OR P
Alpena, MI GLD
Alpha, NJ MET
Alpharetta, GA ATL
Alpine, CA SD
MI GR
TX ELP
Alsip, IL CHI
Alta Loma, CA SB
Altadena, CA LA
Altamont, IL SFD
NY ALB
Altamonte Springs, FL ORL
Alton, IA SC
IL SFD
TX BWN
Altona, NY OG
Altoona, IA DM
PA ALT
PA SJP
WI LC
Alturas, CA SAC
Altus, AR LR
OK OKL
Alva, OK OKL
Alvin, TX GAL
Alviso, CA SJ
Ama, LA NO
Amargosa Valley, NV LAV
Amarillo, TX AMA
Ambia, IN LFT
Ambler, PA PH
Amboy, IL RCK
Ambridge, PA PBR
PA SJP
PA PIT
Amelia, LA HT
OH CIN
VA RIC
Amenia, NY NY
American Canyon, CA SR
American Falls, ID B
American Fork, UT SLC
Americus, GA SAV
Amery, WI SUP
Ames, IA DUB
Amesbury, MA BO
Amherst, MA SPR
NY BUF
OH CLV
VA RIC
WI LC
Amite, LA BR
Amity, OR P
Amityville, NY RVC
Amory, MS JKS
Amsterdam, NY ALB
NY STF
OH STU
Anaconda, MT HEL
Anacortes, WA SEA
Anacostia, Washington, DC WDC
Anadarko, OK OKL
Anaheim, CA HPM
CA ORG
Anaheim Hills, CA LA
Anahuac, TX BEA
Anamoose, ND FAR
Anamosa, IA DUB
Anchorage, AK ANC
AK HPM
Andale, KS WCH
Andalusia, AL MOB
IL PEO
Anderson, CA SAC
IN LFT
SC CHR
TX GAL
Andice, TX AUS
Andover, KS WCH
MA BO
NJ PAT
OH Y
Andrews, NC CHL
TX SAN
Angels Camp, CA STO
Angleton, TX GAL
Angola, IN FTW
NY BUF
Angus, MN CR
Aniak, AK FBK
Ankeny, IA DM
Ann Arbor, MI LAN
MI OLL
Anna, IL BEL
OH CIN
Annandale, MN STP
VA ARL
VA PSC
Annapolis, MD BAL
Annawan, IL PEO
Anniston, AL BIR
Annville, PA HBG
Anoka, MN STP
Anson, TX LUB
Ansonia, CT HRT
CT STF
Anthem, AZ PHX
Anthon, IA SC
Anthony, NM LSC
Antigo, WI GB
Antioch, CA OAK
IL CHI
TN NSH
Anton Chico, NM SFE
Antonito, CO PBL
Anza, CA SB
Apache Junction, AZ TUC
Apalachicola, FL PT
Apex, NC R
NC SYM
Apollo, PA GBG
Apopka, FL ORL
FL SJP
Apple Creek, MO STL
Apple Valley, CA SB
Applegate, CA SAC
Appleton, MN NU
WI GB
Appomattox, VA RIC
Aptos, CA MRY
Arabi, LA NO
Aransas Pass, TX CC
Arbor Vitae, WI SUP
Arcade, NY BUF
Arcadia, CA LA
FL VEN
WI LC
Arcata, CA SR
Archbald, PA SCR
Archbold, OH TOL
Arcola, IL SFD
Arden, NC CHL
Ardmore, OK OKL
PA PH
Ardsley, NY NY
PA PH
Argo, IL CHI
Argyle, MI SAG
MN CR
MO JC
WI MAD
Arkadelphia, AR LR
Arkansas City, KS WCH
Arkansaw, WI LC
Arlington, MA BO
MN NU
SD SFS
TX FWT
VA ARL
VA WDC
VT BUR
WA SEA
Arlington Heights, IL CHI
Arma, KS WCH
Armada, MI DET
Armonk, NY NY
Armour, SD SFS
Armstrong, IA SC
Armstrong Creek, WI GB
Arnaudville, LA LAF
Arnold, MD BAL
MO STL
PA SJP
Arroyo Grande, CA MRY
Arroyo Seco, NM SFE
Artesia, CA LA
NM LSC
Arvada, CO DEN
Arvin, CA FRS
Asbury Park, NJ TR
Ash Fork, AZ PHX
Ashaway, RI PRO
Ashburn, VA ARL
Ashburnham, MA WOR
Ashdown, AR LR
Asheboro, NC CHL
Asherton, TX LAR
Asheville, NC CHL
Ashford, CT NOR
Ashfork, AZ PHX
Ashkum, IL JOL
Ashland, IL SFD
KS DOD
KY LEX
MA BO

MT	GF
NE	LIN
OH	CLV
OR	P
PA	ALN
VA	RIC
WI	SUP
Ashland City, TN	NSH
Ashley, PA	SCR
Ashtabula, OH	Y
Ashton, IA	SC
Aspen, CO	DEN
Aspinwall, PA	PIT
Assonet, MA	FR
Assumption, IL	SFD
Aston, PA	PH
Astoria, NY	BRK
OR	P
Atascadero, CA	MRY
Atchison, KS	KCK
Atco, NJ	CAM
Athens, AL	BIR
GA	ATL
NY	ALB
OH	STU
TN	KNX
TX	TYL
WI	LC
WV	WH
Atherton, CA	SFR
Athol, MA	WOR
Athol Springs, NY	BUF
Atkins, AR	LR
Atkinson, IL	PEO
NE	OM
Atlanta, GA	ATL
GA	SAM
GA	NTN
TX	TYL
Atlantic, IA	DM
Atlantic Beach, FL	STA
Atlantic City, NJ	CAM
Atlantic Highlands, NJ	TR
Atmore, AL	MOB
Attica, IN	LFT
NY	BUF
OH	TOL
Attleboro, MA	FR
Attleboro Falls, MA	FR
Atwater, CA	FRS
Atwood, KS	SAL
Au Sable Forks, NY	OG
AuGres, MI	SAG
Auburn, AL	MOB
CA	SAC
IA	SC
IL	SFD
IN	FTW
KY	OWN
MA	WOR
ME	PRT
MI	SAG
NE	LIN
NH	MAN
NY	ROC
NY	STF
WA	SEA
Auburn Hills, MI	DET
Auburndale, WI	LC
Audubon, IA	DM
PA	PH
Augusta, GA	NTN
GA	SAV
KS	WCH
KY	COV
ME	PRT
MI	KAL
MO	STL
Ault, CO	DEN
Aumsville, OR	P
Auriesville, NY	ALB
Aurora, CO	DEN
IL	JOL
IL	RCK
IL	ROM
IN	IND
KS	SAL
MN	DUL
MO	SPC
NE	LIN
NY	ROC
OH	Y
Austin, MN	WIN
TX	AUS
TX	OLL
Austintown, OH	Y
OH	SJP
Ava, IL	BEL
MO	SPC
Avalon, CA	LA
NJ	CAM
Ave Maria, FL	VEN
Avella, PA	PBR
PA	PIT
Avenal, CA	FRS
Avenel, NJ	MET
Avenue, MD	WDC
Averill Park, NY	ALB
Avilla, IN	FTW
Aviston, IL	BEL
Avoca, IA	DM
PA	SCR
Avon, CT	HRT
MA	BO
MN	SCL
NY	ROC
OH	CLV
Avon By The Sea, NJ	TR
Avon Lake, OH	CLV
Avon Park, FL	VEN
Avondale, AZ	PHX
CO	PBL
LA	NO
PA	PH
Avonmore, PA	GBG
Axtell, KS	KCK
Ayer, MA	BO
Aztec, NM	GLP
Azusa, CA	LA
Babbitt, MN	DUL
Babylon, NY	RVC
Bad Axe, MI	SAG
Baden, PA	PIT
Badger, MN	CR
Bagdad, AZ	PHX
Bagley, MN	CR
Bailey, CO	COS
Baileyville, KS	KCK
ME	PRT
Bainbridge, GA	SAV
NY	SY
Bainbridge Island, WA	SEA
Bairdford, PA	PIT
Baker, MT	GF
OR	BAK
Baker City, OR	BAK
Bakersfield, CA	FRS
Bala Cynwyd, PA	PH
Baldwin, KS	KCK
LA	LAF
MI	GR
NY	RVC
Baldwin Park, CA	LA
Baldwinsville, NY	SY
Baldwinville, MA	WOR
Ballinger, TX	SAN
Ballston Lake, NY	ALB
Ballston Spa, NY	ALB
Ballwin, MO	STL
Bally, PA	ALN
Balmorhea, TX	ELP
Balsam Lake, WI	SUP
Baltic, CT	NOR
Baltimore, MD	BAL
MD	PSC
MD	PHU
Bancroft, IA	SC
Bandera, TX	SAT
Bandon, OR	P
Bangall, NY	NY
Bangor, ME	PRT
MI	KAL
PA	ALN
WI	LC
Banks, OR	P
Bannister, MI	SAG
Banquete, TX	CC
Bantam, CT	HRT
Baptistown, NJ	MET
Bar Harbor, ME	PRT
Baraboo, WI	MAD
Baraga, MI	MAR
Barberton, OH	CLV
OH	PRM
Barbourville, KY	LEX
Bardonia, NY	NY
Bardstown, KY	L
Bardwell, KY	OWN
Barefoot Bay, FL	ORL
Barhamsville, VA	RIC
Bark River, MI	MAR
Barker, NY	BUF
Barling, AR	LR
Barnegat, NJ	TR
Barnesville, MD	WDC
MN	CR
OH	STU
PA	ALN
Barre, MA	WOR
VT	BUR
Barrett Station, TX	GAL
Barrington, IL	CHI
RI	PRO
Barron, WI	SUP
Barrow, AK	FBK
Barryville, NY	NY
Barstow, CA	SB
Bartelso, IL	BEL
Bartlesville, OK	TLS
Bartlett, IL	CHI
TN	MEM
Barton, VT	BUR
Bartonville, IL	PEO
Bartow, FL	ORL
Bascom, OH	TOL
Basehor, KS	KCK
Basile, LA	LAF
Basking Ridge, NJ	MET
Bassfield, MS	BLX
Bastrop, LA	SHP
TX	AUS
Batavia, IL	RCK
NY	BUF
OH	CIN
Batesburg–Leesville, SC	CHR
Batesville, AR	LR
IN	IND
MS	JKS
Bath, NY	ROC
OH	CLV
PA	ALN
Bathgate, ND	FAR
Baton Rouge, LA	BR
Battle Creek, MI	KAL
NE	OM
Battle Ground, WA	SEA
Battle Lake, MN	SCL
Battle Mountain, NV	RNO
Baudette, MN	CR
Baxley, GA	SAV
Bay City, MI	PRM
MI	SAG
TX	VIC
Bay Head, NJ	TR
Bay Minette, AL	MOB
Bay Point, CA	OAK
Bay Shore, NY	RVC
Bay St. Louis, MS	BLX
Bay Village, OH	CLV
Bayard, NM	LSC
Bayfield, WI	SUP
Bayonne, NJ	NEW
NJ	OLD
NJ	PSC
Bayou LaBatre, AL	MOB
Bayport, MN	STP
Bayside, NY	BRK
Baytown, TX	GAL
Bayville, NJ	TR
NY	RVC
Beach, ND	BIS
Beacon, NY	NY
Beacon Falls, CT	HRT
Bear, DE	WIL
Bear Creek, PA	SCR
Beardsley, MN	NU
Beardstown, IL	SFD
Beatrice, NE	LIN
Beattie, KS	KCK
Beattyville, KY	LEX
Beaufort, SC	CHR
Beaumont, CA	SB
TX	BEA
Beaver, PA	PBR
PA	PIT
Beaver Crossing, NE	LIN
Beaver Dam, AZ	PHX
KY	OWN
WI	MIL
Beaver Falls, PA	PIT
Beaver Island, MI	GLD
Beaver Meadows, PA	PSC
Beavercreek, OH	CIN
Beaverdale, PA	PBR
Beaverton, OR	P
Beaverville, IL	JOL
Beckemeyer, IL	BEL
Becker, MN	SCL
Beckley, WV	WH
Bedford, IN	IND
MA	BO
NH	MAN
NY	NY
OH	CLV
OH	PRM
PA	ALT
TX	FWT
VA	RIC
Beebe, AR	LR
Beech Grove, IN	IND
Beemer, NE	OM
Beeville, TX	CC
Bel Air, MD	BAL
Belchertown, MA	SPR
Belcourt, ND	FAR
Belding, MI	GR
Belen, NM	SFE
Belfield, ND	BIS
ND	STN
Belgium, WI	MIL
Belgrade, MN	SCL
Bell City, LA	LKC
Bell Gardens, CA	LA
Bella Vista, AR	LR
Bellaire, MI	GLD
OH	STU
Belle, MO	JC
WV	WH
Belle Chasse, LA	NO
Belle Fontaine, AL	MOB
Belle Fourche, SD	RC
Belle Glade, FL	PMB
Belle Harbor, NY	BRK
Belle Plaine, IA	DUB
MN	STP
Belle Rose, LA	BR
Belle Vernon, PA	GBG
Belleair, FL	SP
Bellechester, MN	STP
Bellefontaine, OH	CIN
Bellefonte, PA	ALT
Bellerose, NY	BRK
Belleview, FL	ORL
Belleville, IL	BEL
KS	SAL
MI	DET
NJ	NEW
WI	MAD
Bellevue, IA	DUB
KY	COV
MI	LAN
NE	OM
OH	TOL
PA	PIT
WA	SEA
Bellflower, CA	LA
Bellingham, MA	BO
WA	SEA
Bellmawr, NJ	CAM
Bellmore, NY	RVC
Bellows Falls, VT	BUR
Bellport, NY	RVC
Bellville, TX	GAL
Bellwood, IL	CHI
IL	SYM
NE	LIN
PA	ALT
Belmar, NJ	TR
Belmond, IA	DUB
Belmont, CA	SFR
MA	BO
MA	OLN
MI	GR
NC	CHL
NH	MAN
NY	BUF
WI	MAD
Beloit, KS	SAL
WI	MAD
WI	MIL
Belpre, KS	DOD
Belt, MT	GF
Belton, MO	KC
TX	AUS
Beltsville, MD	PSC
MD	WDC
Belvidere, IL	RCK
NJ	MET
Belzoni, MS	JKS
Bemidji, MN	CR
Bemus Point, NY	BUF
Ben Bolt, TX	CC
Benavides, TX	CC
Bend, OR	BAK
Bendena, KS	KCK
Benedict, MD	WDC
Benedicta, ME	PRT
Benet Lake, WI	MIL
Benicia, CA	SAC
Benkelman, NE	LIN
Bennington, VT	BUR
Bensalem, PA	PH
Bensenville, IL	JOL
Benson, AZ	TUC
MN	NU
Bentleyville, PA	PIT
Benton, AR	LR
IL	BEL
MO	SPC
WI	MAD
Benton City, WA	YAK
Benton Harbor, MI	KAL
Bentonville, AR	LR
Benwood, WV	WH

Berea, KY	LEX
OH	CLV
Beresford, SD	SFS
Bergen, NY	BUF
Bergenfield, NJ	NEW
Berkeley, CA	OAK
Berkeley Heights, NJ	NEW
Berkeley Springs, WV	WH
Berkley, MI	DET
MI	SYM
Berlin, MA	WOR
MD	WDC
MD	WIL
NH	MAN
NJ	CAM
WI	MAD
Bernalillo, NM	SFE
Bernardsville, NJ	MET
Berryville, AR	LR
VA	ARL
Bertha, MN	SCL
Bertram, TX	AUS
Berwick, LA	LAF
PA	HBG
PA	PHU
Berwyn, IL	CHI
PA	PH
Bessemer, AL	BIR
MI	MAR
Bethalto, IL	SFD
Bethany, MO	KC
WV	WH
Bethany Beach, DE	WIL
Bethel, AK	FBK
CT	BGP
OH	CIN
VT	BUR
Bethel Park, PA	PIT
Bethesda, MD	WDC
Bethlehem, CT	HRT
PA	ALN
PA	PHU
PA	PSC
Bethpage, NY	RVC
Bettendorf, IA	DAV
Beulah, ND	BIS
Beverly, MA	BO
OH	STU
Beverly Hills, CA	LA
FL	SP
MI	DET
Beverly Shores, IN	GRY
Bicknell, IN	EVN
Biddeford, ME	PRT
Big Bear Lake, CA	SB
Big Bend, WI	MIL
Big Lake, AK	ANC
MN	SCL
TX	SAN
Big Pine Key, FL	MIA
Big Rapids, MI	GR
Big Spring, TX	SAN
Big Stone City, SD	SFS
Big Stone Gap, VA	RIC
Big Sur, CA	MRY
Big Timber, MT	GF
Bigelow, AR	LR
Bigfork, MN	DUL
MT	HEL
Billerica, MA	BO
Billings, MO	SPC
MT	GF
Biloxi, MS	BLX
Binghamton, NY	SY
NY	PSC
Birch Run, MI	SAG
Bird Island, MN	NU
Birmingham, AL	BIR
AL	NTN
AL	OLL
MI	DET
Birmingham (Hoover), AL	BIR
Birnamwood, WI	GB
Bisbee, AZ	TUC
ND	FAR
Biscoe, NC	CHL
Bishop, CA	FRS
TX	CC
Bismarck, ND	BIS
Biwabik, MN	DUL
Bixby, OK	TLS
Black Canyon City, AZ	PHX
Black Creek, WI	GB
Black Diamond, WA	SEA
Black Mountain, NC	CHL
Black River, NY	OG
Black River Falls, WI	LC
Blackfoot, ID	B
Blacksburg, VA	RIC
Blackstone, MA	WOR
VA	RIC
Blackwell, OK	OKL
Blackwood, NJ	CAM
Bladensburg, MD	WDC
Blaine, MN	STP
Blair, NE	OM
Blairstown, NJ	MET
Blairsville, GA	ATL
PA	GBG
Blakely, GA	SAV
Blanchardville, WI	MAD
Blanco, NM	GLP
TX	AUS
Blasdell, NY	BUF
Blauvelt, NY	NY
NY	CAM
Blessing, TX	VIC
Block Island, RI	PRO
Bloomer, WI	LC
Bloomfield, CT	HRT
IN	EVN
NJ	NEW
NJ	PAT
NM	GLP
Bloomfield Hills, MI	DET
Blooming Prairie, MN	WIN
Bloomingdale, IL	JOL
OH	STU
Bloomington, CA	SB
IL	PEO
IN	IND
MN	STP
TX	VIC
WI	MAD
Bloomsburg, PA	HBG
Bloomsbury, NJ	MET
Bloomsdale, MO	STL
Blountstown, FL	PT
Blue Bell, PA	PH
Blue Earth, MN	WIN
Blue Grass, IA	DAV
Blue Island, IL	CHI
Blue Point, NY	RVC
Blue Ridge, GA	ATL
Blue Springs, MO	KC
Bluefield, WV	WH
Bluffton, IN	FTW
MN	SCL
OH	TOL
SC	CHR
Blythe, CA	SB
Blytheville, AR	LR
Blythewood, SC	CHR
Boalsburg, PA	ALT
Boardman, OH	Y
OH	PBR
OH	ROM
OR	BAK
Bobtown, PA	PIT
Boca Grande, FL	VEN
Boca Raton, FL	PMB
Boerne, TX	SAT
Bogalusa, LA	NO
Bogota, NJ	NEW
Bohemia, NY	RVC
Boise, ID	B
Bokeelia, FL	VEN
Bolingbrook, IL	JOL
Bolivar, MO	SPC
NY	BUF
OH	COL
PA	GBG
TN	MEM
Bolton, CT	NOR
Bolton Landing, NY	ALB
Bonduel, WI	GB
Bonesteel, SD	RC
Bonfield, IL	JOL
Bonham, TX	DAL
Bonifay, FL	PT
Bonita, CA	LA
CA	SD
Bonita Springs, FL	VEN
Bonne Terre, MO	STL
Bonner, MT	HEL
Bonners Ferry, ID	B
Bonnots Mill, MO	JC
Boone, IA	SC
NC	CHL
Booneville, AR	LR
MS	JKS
Boonsboro, MD	BAL
Boonton, NJ	PAT
Boonville, IN	EVN
MO	JC
NC	CHL
NY	SY
Boothwyn, PA	PH
Bordelonville, LA	ALX
Bordentown, NJ	TR
Borger, TX	AMA
Borrego Springs, CA	SD
Boscobel, WI	MAD
Bossier City, LA	SHP
Boston, MA	BO
NY	BUF
Boswell, PA	ALT
Bothell, WA	SEA
Botkins, OH	CIN
Bottineau, ND	FAR
Boulder, CO	DEN
MT	HEL
Boulder City, NV	LAV
Boulder Creek, CA	MRY
Boulder Junction, WI	SUP
Bound Brook, NJ	MET
Bountiful, UT	SLC
Bourbonnais, IL	JOL
Bourg, LA	HT
Bovina, TX	AMA
Bowdle, SD	SFS
Bowie, MD	WDC
Bowling Green, KY	OWN
MO	JC
OH	TOL
Bowlus, MN	SCL
Bowman, ND	BIS
Bowmansville, NY	BUF
Box Elder, MT	GF
Boyce, LA	ALX
Boyceville, WI	LC
Boyd, WI	LC
Boyertown, PA	ALN
Boylston, MA	WOR
Boyne City, MI	GLD
Boynton Beach, FL	PMB
Boys Town, NE	OM
Bozeman, MT	HEL
Brackettville, TX	SAT
Braddock, PA	PBR
PA	PIT
Bradenton, FL	VEN
Bradenton Beach, FL	VEN
Bradenville, PA	PBR
Bradford, IN	IND
OH	CIN
PA	E
RI	PRO
VT	BUR
Bradley, IL	JOL
Bradley Beach, NJ	TR
Bradshaw, MD	BAL
Brady, TX	SAN
Brady's Bend, PA	GBG
Braham, MN	SCL
Braidwood, IL	JOL
Brainard, NE	LIN
Brainerd, MN	DUL
Braintree, MA	BO
Braithwaite, LA	NO
Branchville, NJ	PAT
Brandenburg, KY	L
Brandon, FL	SP
FL	SYM
MN	SCL
SD	SFS
VT	BUR
Brandywine, MD	WDC
Branford, CT	HRT
FL	STA
Branson, MO	SPC
Brant Beach, NJ	TR
Brasher Falls, NY	OG
Brattleboro, VT	BUR
Brawley, CA	SD
Brazil, IN	IND
Brazoria, TX	GAL
Brea, CA	ORG
Breaux Bridge, LA	LAF
Breckenridge, MN	SCL
TX	FWT
Brecksville, OH	CLV
OH	PRM
Breda, IA	SC
Breese, IL	BEL
Bremen, IN	FTW
OH	COL
Bremerton, WA	SEA
Bremond, TX	AUS
Brenham, TX	AUS
Brentwood, CA	OAK
MO	STL
NY	RVC
TN	NSH
Brevard, NC	CHL
Brewerton, NY	SY
Brewster, MA	FR
MN	WIN
NY	NY
WA	SPK
Brewton, AL	MOB
Briarcliff Manor, NY	NY
Briarwood, NY	BRK
Brick, NJ	TR
Brick Town, NJ	TR
Bridal Veil, OR	P
Bridge City, TX	BEA
Bridgehampton, NY	RVC
Bridgeport, CT	BGP
CT	STF
MI	SAG
NE	GI
NY	SY
OH	STU
PA	PH
PA	PHU
TX	FWT
WV	WH
Bridger, MT	GF
Bridgeton, MO	STL
NJ	CAM
Bridgeview, IL	CHI
Bridgeville, PA	PIT
Bridgewater, MA	BO
NJ	MET
SD	SFS
Bridgman, MI	KAL
Bridgton, ME	PRT
Brigantine, NJ	CAM
Briggsville, WI	MAD
Brigham City, UT	SLC
Brighton, CO	DEN
IL	SFD
MA	BO
MI	DET
MI	LAN
Brillion, WI	GB
Brimfield, IL	PEO
MA	SPR
Brimley, MI	MAR
Brinkley, AR	LR
Bristol, CT	HRT
IN	FTW
PA	PH
PA	PHU
RI	PRO
VA	RIC
VT	BUR
WI	MIL
Bristow, IN	IND
VA	ARL
Britt, IA	DUB
Britton, SD	SFS
Broad Brook, CT	HRT
Broadalbin, NY	ALB
Broadus, MT	GF
Broadview, IL	CHI
Broadview Heights, OH	CLV
Brockport, NY	ROC
Brockton, MA	BO
MA	SAM
MA	NY
Brockway, PA	E
Brodheadsville, PA	SCR
Broken Arrow, OK	TLS
Broken Bow, NE	GI
Bronson, MI	KAL
Bronx, NY	NY
NY	CHI
NY	MCE
NY	SYM
NY	STF
Bronxville, NY	NY
Brookeville, MD	WDC
Brookfield, CT	BGP
IL	CHI
MO	JC
WI	MIL
Brookhaven, MS	JKS
PA	PH
Brookings, OR	P
SD	SFS
Brooklandville, MD	BAL
Brookline, MA	BO
MA	ROM
Brooklyn, CT	NOR
IA	DAV
MI	LAN
NY	BRK
NY	OLN
NY	SAM
NY	NTN
NY	STF
OH	CLV
OH	SJP
OH	NTN
Brooklyn Center, MN	STP
Brooklyn Park, MN	STP
Brookpark, OH	CLV
Brooksville, FL	SP
FL	SJP
KY	COV
MS	JKS
Brookville, IN	IND

NY	RVC
PA	E
Broomall, PA	PH
Broomfield, CO	DEN
Brooten, MN	SCL
Broussard, LA	LAF
Browerville, MN	SCL
Brown Deer, WI	MIL
Brownfield, TX	LUB
Browning, MT	HEL
Browns Mills, NJ	TR
Browns Valley, MN	SCL
Brownsburg, IN	IND
Brownstown, IN	IND
Brownsville, PA	GBG
PA	PBR
TN	MEM
TX	BWN
Brownville, NY	OG
Brownwood, TX	SAN
Bruce, MS	JKS
Bruno, NE	LIN
Brunswick, GA	SAV
MD	BAL
ME	PRT
MO	JC
OH	CLV
OH	PRM
Brush, CO	DEN
Brushton, NY	OG
Brusly, LA	BR
Brussels, IL	SFD
WI	GB
Bryan, OH	TOL
TX	AUS
Bryant, IN	LFT
Bryantown, MD	WDC
Bryn Mawr, PA	PH
Bryson City, NC	CHL
Buchanan, MI	KAL
NY	NY
Buckeye, AZ	PHX
Buckeye Lake, OH	COL
Buckeystown, MD	BAL
Buckhannon, WV	WH
Buckley, WA	SEA
Buckner, MO	KC
Bucksport, ME	PRT
Bucyrus, KS	KCK
OH	TOL
Buda, TX	AUS
Budd Lake, NJ	PAT
Buena Park, CA	ORG
Buena Vista, CO	COS
Buffalo, IA	DAV
MN	STP
MO	SPC
NY	BUF
NY	STF
SD	RC
TX	TYL
WY	CHY
Buffalo Grove, IL	CHI
Buford, GA	ATL
Buhl, ID	B
MN	DUL
Bulger, PA	PIT
Bullhead City, AZ	PHX
Buna, TX	BEA
Bunkie, LA	ALX
Bunnell, FL	STA
Burbank, CA	LA
IL	CHI
Burgaw, NC	R
Burgettstown, PA	PIT
Burien, WA	SEA
Burkburnett, TX	FWT
Burke, SD	RC
VA	ARL
Burleson, TX	FWT
Burley, ID	B
Burlingame, CA	SFR
Burlington, CO	COS
IA	DAV
KS	KCK
KY	COV
MA	BO
NC	R
NJ	TR
TX	AUS
VT	BUR
WA	SEA
WI	MIL
Burnet, TX	AUS
Burney, CA	SAC
Burnham, IL	CHI
Burns, OR	BAK
Burnsville, MN	STP
Burr Ridge, IL	JOL
Burton, MI	LAN
OH	PRM
Burtonsville, MD	WDC
Bushnell, FL	ORL
IL	PEO
Bushton, KS	WCH
Bushwood, MD	WDC
Butler, AL	MOB
MO	KC
NJ	PAT
PA	PBR
PA	PIT
WI	MIL
Butner, NC	R
Butte, MT	HEL
NE	OM
Butternut, WI	SUP
Buttonwillow, CA	FRS
Buxton, NC	R
Buzzards Bay, MA	FR
Byers, CO	DEN
Byron, CA	OAK
IL	RCK
MN	WIN
Byron Center, MI	GR
MI	KAL
Cabery, IL	JOL
Cable, WI	SUP
Cabot, PA	PIT
Cadet, MO	STL
Cadillac, MI	GLD
Cadiz, KY	OWN
OH	STU
Cadogan, PA	GBG
Cadott, WI	LC
Cadyville, NY	OG
Cahokia, IL	BEL
Cairo, IL	BEL
NY	ALB
Calais, ME	PRT
Caldwell, ID	B
KS	WCH
NJ	NEW
OH	STU
TX	AUS
Caledonia, MI	GR
MN	WIN
NY	ROC
WI	MIL
Calexico, CA	SD
Calhan, CO	COS
Calhoun, GA	ATL
KY	OWN
Caliente, NV	LAV
Califon, NJ	MET
California, KY	COV
MO	JC
PA	PIT
California City, CA	FRS
Calimesa, CA	SB
CA	HPM
Calipatria, CA	SD
Calistoga, CA	SR
Callahan, FL	STA
Callaway, MN	CR
Callicoon, NY	NY
Calmar, IA	DUB
Calumet, MI	MAR
Calumet City, IL	CHI
Calumet Park, IL	CHI
Calvert City, KY	OWN
Camanche, IA	DAV
Camarillo, CA	LA
Camas, WA	SEA
Cambria, CA	MRY
Cambria Heights, NY	BRK
Cambridge, MA	BO
MD	WIL
MN	SCL
NE	LIN
NY	ALB
OH	STU
VT	BUR
WI	MAD
Cambridge City, IN	IND
Cambridge Springs, PA	E
Camden, AL	MOB
AR	LR
ME	PRT
MS	JKS
NJ	CAM
NY	SY
SC	CHR
TN	MEM
WV	WH
Camdenton, MO	JC
Cameron, LA	LKC
MO	KC
TX	AUS
Camillus, NY	SY
Camp Douglas, WI	LC
Camp Hill, PA	HBG
Camp Springs, KY	COV
MD	WDC
Camp Verde, AZ	PHX
Campbell, CA	SJ
CA	SPA
MO	SPC
NE	LIN
OH	Y
OH	PBR
Campbell Hall, NY	STF
Campbellsport, WI	MIL
Campbellsville, KY	L
Campo, CA	SD
Campti, LA	ALX
Campus, IL	PEO
Canaan, CT	HRT
Canadaigua, NY	ROC
Canadian, TX	AMA
Canal Fulton, OH	Y
Canal Winchester, OH	COL
Canandaigua, NY	ROC
Canaseraga, NY	BUF
Canastota, NY	SY
Canby, MN	NU
OR	P
Candler, FL	ORL
NC	CHL
Cando, ND	FAR
Candor, NC	CHL
Caney, KS	WCH
Canfield, OH	Y
Cankton, LA	LAF
Cannon Falls, MN	STP
Canoga Park, CA	LA
Canon City, CO	PBL
Canonsburg, PA	PBR
PA	PIT
Canterbury, CT	NOR
Canton, GA	ATL
IL	PEO
MA	BO
MI	DET
MO	JC
MS	JKS
NY	OG
OH	Y
OH	ROM
PA	SCR
SD	SFS
TX	TYL
Cantonment, FL	PT
Canutillo, TX	ELP
Canyon, TX	AMA
Canyon Lake, TX	SAT
Capac, MI	DET
Cape Charles, VA	RIC
Cape Coral, FL	VEN
Cape Elizabeth, ME	PRT
Cape Girardeau, MO	SPC
Cape May, NJ	CAM
Cape May Court House, NJ	CAM
Cape May Point, NJ	CAM
Cape Vincent, NY	OG
Capitola, CA	MRY
Captain Cook, HI	HON
Capulin, CO	PBL
Carbondale, CO	DEN
IL	BEL
PA	SCR
Cardington, OH	COL
Carefree, AZ	PHX
Carencro, LA	LAF
Carey, OH	TOL
Caribou, ME	PRT
Carle Place, NY	RVC
Carleton, MI	DET
Carlin, NV	RNO
Carlinville, IL	SFD
Carlisle, AR	LR
IA	DM
KY	LEX
MA	BO
PA	HBG
Carlos, MN	SCL
Carlsbad, CA	SD
NM	LSC
TX	SAN
Carlton, MN	DUL
Carlyle, IL	BEL
Carmel, CA	MRY
IN	LFT
NY	NY
Carmel Valley, CA	MRY
Carmi, IL	BEL
Carmichael, CA	SAC
Carmichaels, PA	PIT
Carnegie, PA	PIT
PA	SJP
PA	SAM
Carney's Point, NJ	CAM
Caro, MI	SAG
Carol Stream, IL	JOL
Carolina, RI	PRO
Carpentersville, IL	RCK
Carpinteria, CA	LA
Carrington, ND	FAR
Carrizo Springs, TX	LAR
Carrizozo, NM	LSC
Carroll, IA	SC
Carrollton, GA	ATL
IL	SFD
KY	COV
MO	KC
OH	STU
TX	DAL
TX	FWT
Carrolltown, PA	ALT
Carson, CA	LA
ND	BIS
Carson City, MI	GR
NV	RNO
Carteret, NJ	MET
NJ	PSC
NJ	PHU
Cartersville, GA	ATL
Carterville, IL	BEL
Carthage, MO	SPC
MS	JKS
NY	OG
TX	TYL
Carthagena, OH	CIN
Caruthersville, MO	SPC
Carver, MA	BO
MN	STP
Cary, IL	RCK
NC	R
NC	PSC
NC	SAM
Casa Grande, AZ	TUC
Cascade, CO	COS
IA	DUB
Casco, ME	PRT
WI	GB
Caseville, MI	SAG
Caseyville, IL	BEL
Cashion, AZ	PHX
Cashmere, WA	YAK
Cashton, WI	LC
Casper, WY	CHY
Caspian, MI	MAR
Cass City, MI	SAG
Cass Lake, MN	DUL
Casselberry, FL	ORL
Casselton, ND	FAR
Cassopolis, MI	KAL
Cassville, MO	SPC
WI	MAD
Castine, ME	PRT
Castle Hayne, NC	R
Castle Rock, CO	COS
WA	SEA
Castleton, NY	ALB
VT	BUR
Castleton On Hudson, NY	ALB
Castro Valley, CA	OAK
Castroville, CA	MRY
TX	SAT
Catasauqua, PA	ALN
Catawissa, MO	STL
PA	HBG
Catharine, KS	SAL
Cathedral City, CA	SB
Cato, WI	GB
Catonsville, MD	BAL
Catskill, NY	ALB
Cattaraugus, NY	BUF
Cavalier, ND	FAR
Cave Creek, AZ	PHX
Cayucos, CA	MRY
Cazenovia, NY	SY
WI	LC
Cecil, PA	PIT
WI	GB
Cecilia, LA	LAF
Cedar, MI	GLD
Cedar City, UT	SLC
Cedar Falls, IA	DUB
Cedar Grove, NJ	NEW
WI	MIL
Cedar Knolls, NJ	PAT
Cedar Lake, IN	GRY
Cedar Park, TX	AUS
Cedar Rapids, IA	DUB
NE	OM
Cedarburg, WI	MIL
Cedarhurst, NY	RVC
Cedartown, GA	ATL
Celebration, FL	ORL
Celestine, IN	EVN
Celina, OH	CIN
Centennial, CO	DEN
Center, CO	PBL
ND	BIS

TX TYL
Center Harbor, NH MAN
Center Line, MI DET
MI MCE
Center Moriches, NY RVC
Center Ossipee, NH MAN
Center Ridge, AR LR
Center Valley, PA ALN
Centereach, NY RVC
Centerport, NY RVC
Centerville, IA DAV
LA LAF
MA FR
MN STP
OH CIN
SD SFS
TN NSH
Central City, IA DUB
KY OWN
NE OM
PA ALT
Central Falls, RI PRO
Central Islip, NY RVC
Central Point, OR P
Central Square, NY SY
Central Valley, UT SLC
Centralia, IL BEL
MO JC
WA SEA
Centreville, MD WIL
Ceres, CA SPA
CA STO
Cerrillos, NM SFE
Chadds Ford, PA PH
Chadron, NE GI
Chadwicks, NY SY
Chaffee, MO SPC
Chagrin Falls, OH CLV
Chalfont, PA PH
Chalmette, LA NO
Chama, NM SFE
Chamberino, NM LSC
Chamberlain, SD SFS
Chambersburg, PA HBG
Chamblee, GA ATL
Chamois, MO JC
Champaign, IL PEO
Champion, MI MAR
Champlain, NY OG
Chandler, AZ PHX
OK OKL
Chanhassen, MN STP
Channahon, IL JOL
Channelview, TX GAL
Channing, MI MAR
Chantilly, VA ARL
Chanute, KS WCH
Chaparral, NM LSC
Chapel Hill, NC R
Chapin, SC CHR
Chapman, KS SAL
Chappaqua, NY NY
Chappell, NE GI
Chappell Hill, TX AUS
Chaptico, MD WDC
Chardon, OH CLV
Charenton, LA LAF
Chariton, IA DM
Charleroi, PA PBR
PA PIT
Charles City, IA DUB
Charles Town, WV WH
Charleston, AR LR
IL SFD
MO SPC
MS JKS
SC CHR
WV WH
Charlestown, IN IND
MA BO
NH MAN
Charlevoix, MI GLD
Charlotte, IA DAV
MI LAN
NC CHL
TX SAT
VT BUR
Charlotte Hall, MD WDC
Charlottesville, VA RIC
Charlton, MA WOR
Charlton City, MA WOR
Chaska, MN STP
Chassell, MI MAR
Chataignier, LA LAF
Chatawa, MS JKS
Chateaugay, NY OG
Chatfield, MN WIN
Chatham, IL SFD
MA FR
NJ PAT
NY ALB

Chatsworth, CA LA
IL PEO
Chattahoochee, FL PT
Chattanooga, TN KNX
Chauvin, LA HT
Chazy, NY OG
Chebanse, IL JOL
Cheboygan, MI GLD
Cheektowaga, NY BUF
Chefornak, AK FBK
Chehalis, WA SEA
Chelan, WA YAK
Chelmsford, MA BO
Chelsea, MA BO
MI LAN
Cheltenham, PA PH
Cheney, WA SPK
Cheneyville, LA ALX
Chenoa, IL PEO
Chepachet, RI PRO
Cheraw, SC CHR
Cherokee, IA SC
Cherokee Village, AR LR
Cherry, IL PEO
Cherry Hill, NJ CAM
NJ PHU
Cherry Valley, NY ALB
Cherryvale, KS WCH
Chesaning, MI SAG
Chesapeake, OH STU
VA RIC
Cheshire, CT HRT
MA SPR
Chest Springs, PA ALT
Chester, CT NOR
IL BEL
MD WIL
MT GF
NJ PAT
NY NY
PA PH
PA PHU
SC CHR
VT BUR
WV WH
Chesterfield, MO STL
NJ TR
VA RIC
Chesterland, OH CLV
OH ROM
Chesterton, IN GRY
Chestertown, MD WIL
NY ALB
Chestnut Hill, MA BO
Chetek, WI SUP
Chevak, AK FBK
Cheverly, MD WDC
Chewelah, WA SPK
Cheyenne, WY CHY
Cheyenne Wells, CO COS
Chicago, IL CHI
IL EST
IL STN
IL SYM
IL LIT
IL DET
Chicago Heights, IL CHI
Chicago Ridge, IL CHI
Chickasaw, AL MOB
Chickasha, OK OKL
Chico, CA SAC
Chicopee, MA SPR
Chicora, PA PIT
Chiefland, FL STA
Childress, TX AMA
Childs, MD WIL
Chillicothe, IL PEO
MO KC
OH COL
Chillum, MD WDC
Chiloquin, OR BAK
Chilton, WI GB
Chimayo, NM SFE
China, TX BEA
China Spring, TX AUS
Chincoteague Island, VA RIC
Chinle, AZ GLP
Chino, CA SB
Chino Hills, CA SB
Chino Valley, AZ PHX
Chinook, MT GF
Chipley, FL PT
Chippewa Falls, WI LC
Chippewa Lake, OH CLV
Chisholm, MN DUL
Chittenango, NY SY
Chokio, MN SCL
Choteau, MT HEL
Chowchilla, CA FRS
Chrisney, IN EVN
Christiansburg, VA RIC

Christopher, IL BEL
Christoval, TX SAN
Chula Vista, CA SD
Church Point, LA LAF
Churchville, NY ROC
Churdan, IA SC
Churubusco, IN FTW
Cibecue, AZ GLP
Cicero, IL CHI
IN LFT
NY SY
Cimarron, NM SFE
Cincinnati, OH CIN
OH OLL
Cinnaminson, NJ TR
Circle, MT GF
Circleville, OH COL
Citronelle, AL MOB
Citrus Heights, CA SAC
Citrus Springs, FL SP
Claflin, KS DOD
Clairton, PA PBR
PA PIT
Clanton, AL BIR
Clara City, MN NU
Clare, MI SAG
Claremont, CA LA
NH MAN
Claremore, OK TLS
Clarence, NY BUF
PA ALT
Clarendon, TX AMA
Clarendon Hills, IL JOL
Clarinda, IA DM
Clarion, IA DUB
PA E
Clarissa, MN SCL
Clark, NJ NEW
SD SFS
Clarkesville, GA ATL
Clarklake, MI LAN
Clarks Green, PA SCR
Clarks Summit, PA SCR
Clarksburg, CA SAC
WV WH
Clarksdale, MS JKS
Clarkson, KY OWN
NE OM
Clarkston, MI DET
WA SPK
Clarksville, AR LR
IN IND
MD BAL
PA PIT
TN NSH
TX TYL
VA RIC
Clawson, MI DET
Claxton, GA SAV
Clay Center, KS SAL
Claymont, DE WIL
Clayton, MO STL
NC R
NJ CAM
NM SFE
NY OG
Cle Elum, WA YAK
Clear Lake, IA DUB
MN SCL
SD SFS
WI SUP
Clearfield, PA E
Clearlake, CA SR
Clearville, PA ALT
Clearwater, FL SP
MN STP
Clearwater Beach, FL SP
Cleburne, TX FWT
Clemmons, NC CHL
Clemson, SC CHR
Clermont, FL ORL
IA DUB
Cleveland, GA ATL
MN STP
MS JKS
NY SY
OH CLV
OH OLL
OH ROM
OH SJP
OH PRM
TN KNX
TX BEA
Cleveland Heights, OH CLV
Clewiston, FL VEN
Clifford, PA SCR
Cliffside Park, NJ NEW
NJ NTN
Clifton, AZ TUC
IL JOL
NJ PAT

TX FWT
VA ARL
Clifton Forge, VA RIC
Clifton Heights, PA PH
PA PHU
Clifton Park, NY ALB
Clifton Springs, NY ROC
Clint, TX ELP
Clinton, AR LR
CT NOR
IA DAV
IL PEO
IN IND
KY OWN
MA WOR
MD WDC
MO KC
MS JKS
NC R
NJ MET
NY SY
OH CLV
OK OKL
TN KNX
WI MAD
Clinton Township, MI DET
MI PRM
Clintonville, WI GB
Clintwood, VA RIC
Clio, MI LAN
Cloquet, MN DUL
Closter, NJ NEW
Cloudcroft, NM LSC
Cloutierville, LA ALX
Cloverdale, CA SR
OH TOL
Cloverport, KY OWN
Clovis, CA FRS
NM SFE
Clute, TX GAL
Clyde, KS SAL
MO KC
NY ROC
OH TOL
Clymer, NY BUF
PA GBG
PA PBR
Coachella, CA SB
Coal City, IL JOL
Coal Township, PA HBG
Coal Valley, IL PEO
Coalinga, CA FRS
Coalport, PA E
Coalton, WV WH
Coates, MN STP
Coatesville, PA PH
PA PSC
Cobden, IL BEL
Cobleskill, NY ALB
Cockeysville, MD BAL
Cocoa, FL ORL
Cocoa Beach, FL ORL
Coconut Creek, FL PSC
Coconut Grove, FL MIA
Coden, AL MOB
Cody, WY CHY
Coeur d'Alene, ID B
Coffeyville, KS WCH
Coggon, IA DUB
Cohasset, MA BO
Cohoes, NY ALB
NY STF
Colbert, WA SPK
Colby, KS SAL
WI LC
Colchester, CT NOR
CT STF
VT BUR
Cold Spring, KY COV
MN SCL
NY NY
Coldwater, MI KAL
OH CIN
Colebrook, NH MAN
Coleman, MI SAG
TX SAN
WI GB
Colerain, OH STU
Coleraine, MN DUL
Colfax, CA SAC
IA DAV
IL PEO
LA ALX
NC CHL
WA SPK
College Park, MD WDC
College Point, NY BRK
College Station, TX AUS
Collegeville, MN SCL
PA PH
Colleyville, TX FWT

Place	Code
Collierville, TN	MEM
Collingdale, PA	PH
Collings Lakes, NJ	CAM
Collingswood, NJ	CAM
Collinsville, CT	HRT
IL	SFD
OK	TLS
Collyer, KS	SAL
Colma, CA	SFR
Colo, IA	DUB
Cologne, MN	STP
Colon, NE	LIN
Colona, IL	PEO
Colonia, NJ	MET
Colonial Beach, VA	ARL
Colonial Heights, VA	RIC
Colonie, NY	ALB
Colorado City, TX	SAN
Colorado Springs, CO	COS
Colstrip, MT	GF
Colton, CA	SB
NY	OG
WA	SPK
Colts Neck, NJ	TR
Columbia, CT	NOR
IL	BEL
MD	BAL
MO	JC
MS	BLX
PA	HBG
SC	CHR
TN	NSH
VA	RIC
Columbia City, IN	FTW
Columbia Falls, MT	HEL
Columbia Heights, MN	STP
Columbia Station, OH	CLV
Columbiana, OH	Y
Columbus, GA	SAV
IN	IND
KS	WCH
MS	JKS
MT	GF
NE	OM
OH	COL
OH	SYM
OH	PRM
TX	VIC
WI	MAD
Columbus Grove, OH	TOL
Columbus Junction, IA	DAV
Colusa, CA	SAC
Colver, PA	ALT
Colville, WA	SPK
Colwich, KS	WCH
Combined Locks, WI	GB
Comfort, TX	SAT
Comfrey, MN	NU
Commack, NY	RVC
Commerce, CA	LA
TX	DAL
Commerce City, CO	DEN
Compton, CA	LA
Conception, MO	KC
Conception Junction, MO	KC
Concord, CA	SJ
CA	OAK
MA	BO
MI	LAN
NC	CHL
NH	MAN
Concord Twp., OH	CLV
Concordia, KS	SAL
Condon, OR	BAK
Conejos, CO	PBL
Conemaugh, PA	ALT
PA	PBR
Congers, NY	NY
Congress, AZ	PHX
Conifer, CO	DEN
Conklin, MI	GR
Conneaut, OH	Y
Conneaut Lake, PA	E
Conneautville, PA	E
Connell, WA	SPK
Connellsville, PA	GBG
Connersville, IN	IND
Conrad, MT	HEL
Conroe, TX	GAL
Conshohocken, PA	PH
Constable, NY	OG
Constableville, NY	OG
Continental, OH	TOL
Convent, LA	BR
Convent Station, NJ	PAT
Converse, TX	SAT
Conway, AR	LR
MI	GLD
MO	SPC
PA	PIT
SC	CHR
Conway Springs, KS	WCH
Conyers, GA	ATL
GA	SJP
Conyngham, PA	SCR
Cook, MN	DUL
Cookeville, TN	NSH
Coolidge, AZ	TUC
Coon Rapids, IA	SC
MN	STP
Coon Valley, WI	LC
Coopersburg, PA	ALN
Cooperstown, ND	FAR
NY	ALB
Coopersville, MI	GR
Coos Bay, OR	P
Copake Falls, NY	ALB
Copemish, MI	GLD
Copenhagen, NY	OG
Copiague, NY	RVC
Coplay, PA	ALN
Copley, OH	CLV
Coppell, TX	DAL
TX	SYM
Copperas Cove, TX	AUS
Copperhill, TN	KNX
Copperopolis, CA	STO
Copperton, UT	SLC
Coquille, OR	P
Coral, PA	GBG
Coral Gables, FL	MIA
Coral Springs, FL	MIA
FL	SYM
Coralville, IA	DAV
Coram, NY	RVC
Coraopolis, PA	PIT
Corbin, KY	LEX
Corcoran, CA	FRS
MN	STP
Cordele, GA	SAV
Cordova, AK	ANC
TN	MEM
Corfu, NY	BUF
Corinth, MS	JKS
NY	ALB
Cornelius, OR	P
Cornell, WI	LC
Corning, AR	LR
CA	SAC
IA	DM
KS	KCK
NY	ROC
OH	COL
Cornucopia, WI	SUP
Cornville, AZ	PHX
Cornwall, NY	NY
PA	HBG
Cornwall–on–Hudson, NY	NY
Corona, CA	SB
NY	BRK
Coronado, CA	SD
Corpus Christi, TX	CC
Corrales, NM	SFE
Corralitos, CA	MRY
Corry, PA	E
Corsicana, TX	DAL
Cortaro, AZ	TUC
Cortez, CO	PBL
Cortland, NE	LIN
NY	SY
OH	Y
Cortlandt Manor, NY	NY
NY	SYM
Corvallis, OR	P
Corydon, IN	IND
Coshocton, OH	COL
Costa Mesa, CA	ORG
Cotati, CA	SR
Cottage City, MD	WDC
Cottage Grove, MN	STP
OR	P
WI	MAD
Cottonport, LA	ALX
Cottonwood, AZ	PHX
ID	B
MN	NU
Cotulla, TX	LAR
Coudersport, PA	E
Coulee City, WA	YAK
Council Bluffs, IA	DM
Council Grove, KS	WCH
Country Club Hills, IL	CHI
Countryside, IL	CHI
Coushatta, LA	SHP
Coventry, CT	NOR
RI	PRO
Covina, CA	LA
Covington, GA	ATL
IN	LFT
KY	COV
LA	NO
OH	CIN
TN	MEM
VA	RIC
WA	SEA
Coweta, OK	TLS
Cowiche, WA	YAK
Cox's Creek, KY	L
Coxsackie, NY	ALB
Cozad, NE	GI
Crabtree, PA	GBG
Craig, AK	JUN
CO	DEN
Cranberry Township, PA	PIT
Crandon, WI	GB
WI	SUP
Crane, TX	SAN
Cranford, NJ	NEW
Cranston, RI	PRO
Crawford, NE	GI
Crawfordsville, IN	LFT
Crawfordville, FL	PT
Creighton, NE	OM
PA	PIT
Crescent, PA	PIT
Crescent City, CA	SR
FL	STA
Crescent Springs, KY	COV
Cresco, IA	DUB
PA	PSC
PA	SCR
Cresskill, NJ	NEW
Cresson, PA	ALT
Crest Hill, IL	JOL
Crestline, CA	SB
OH	TOL
Creston, IA	DM
Crestone, CO	PBL
Crestview, FL	PT
Crestview Hills, KY	COV
Crestwood, KY	L
MO	STL
NY	NY
Crete, NE	LIN
Creve Coeur, IL	PEO
MO	STL
Crivitz, WI	GB
Crockett, CA	OAK
TX	TYL
Crofton, MD	BAL
NE	OM
Croghan, NY	OG
Cromwell, CT	NOR
Crookston, MN	CR
Crooksville, OH	COL
Cropwell, AL	BIR
Crosby, MN	DUL
ND	BIS
TX	GAL
Cross Plains, WI	MAD
Cross Village, MI	GLD
Crossett, AR	LR
Crosslake, MN	DUL
Crossville, TN	KNX
Croswell, MI	SAG
Croton Falls, NY	NY
Croton–on–Hudson, NY	NY
Crow Agency, MT	GF
Crowley, LA	LAF
TX	FWT
Crown, PA	E
Crown Point, IN	GRY
Crownpoint, NM	GLP
Crownsville, MD	BAL
Croydon, PA	PH
Crozet, VA	RIC
Crystal, MN	STP
Crystal City, MO	STL
TX	LAR
Crystal Falls, MI	MAR
Crystal Lake, IL	RCK
Crystal River, FL	SP
Crystal Springs, MS	JKS
Cuba, MO	JC
NM	GLP
NY	BUF
Cuba City, WI	MAD
Cudahy, CA	LA
WI	MIL
Cuero, TX	VIC
Cullman, AL	BIR
Cullom, IL	PEO
Culpeper, VA	ARL
Culver, IN	FTW
Culver City, CA	LA
Cumberland, KY	LEX
MD	BAL
RI	PRO
WI	SUP
Cumming, GA	ATL
Cunningham, KS	WCH
Cupertino, CA	SJ
Curdsville, KY	OWN
Curtis, NE	LIN
Curwensville, PA	E
Cushing, OK	TLS
Custar, OH	TOL
Custer, MI	GR
SD	RC
WI	LC
Cut Bank, MT	HEL
Cut–Off, LA	HT
Cutchogue, NY	RVC
Cutler, CA	FRS
Cuyahoga Falls, OH	CLV
Cynthiana, KY	COV
Cypress, CA	ORG
D'Hanis, TX	SAT
D'Iberville, MS	BLX
Dade City, FL	SP
Dahlgren, IL	BEL
Dahlonega, GA	ATL
Daingerfield, TX	TYL
Dakota Dunes, SD	SFS
Dale, IN	EVN
Dale City, VA	ARL
Dalhart, TX	AMA
Dallas, GA	ATL
OR	P
PA	SCR
TX	DAL
Dallastown, PA	HBG
Dalton, GA	ATL
MA	SPR
PA	SCR
Daly City, CA	SFR
Dalzell, IL	PEO
Damar, KS	SAL
Damascus, MD	WDC
Damiansville, IL	BEL
Damon, TX	GAL
Dana Point, CA	ORG
Danbury, CT	BGP
CT	NTN
CT	SAM
CT	PSC
IA	SC
TX	GAL
Dane, WI	MAD
Dania Beach, FL	MIA
Danielson, CT	NOR
Dannemora, NY	OG
Danvers, MA	BO
Danville, AR	LR
CA	OAK
IL	PEO
IN	IND
KY	LEX
OH	COL
PA	HBG
VA	RIC
Daphne, AL	MOB
Darby, PA	PH
Dardanelle, AR	LR
Dardenne Prairie, MO	STL
Darien, CT	BGP
IL	JOL
Darien Center, NY	BUF
Darlington, PA	PIT
WI	MAD
Darnestown, MD	SYM
MD	WDC
Dartmouth, MA	SAM
Darwin, MN	NU
Dauphin, PA	HBG
Dauphin Island, AL	MOB
Davenport, CA	MRY
IA	DAV
WA	SPK
Davey, NE	LIN
David, KY	LEX
David City, NE	LIN
Davidson, NC	CHL
Davidsonville, MD	BAL
Davidsville, PA	ALT
Davie, FL	MIA
Davis, CA	SAC
Davisburg, MI	DET
Davison, MI	LAN
Dawson, MN	NU
NE	LIN
Dawson Springs, KY	OWN
Dawsonville, GA	ATL
Dayton, KY	COV
KY	SYM
MN	STP
NV	RNO
OH	CIN
OH	OLL
OH	PRM
TN	KNX
TX	BEA
WA	SPK
WY	CHY

Daytona Beach, FL ORL
Dayville, CT NOR
De Forest, WI MAD
De Funiak Springs, FL PT
De Motte, IN LFT
De Pere, WI GB
De Queen, AR LR
De Ridder, LA LKC
De Smet, SD SFS
De Soto, MO STL
De Witt, MI LAN
DeBary, FL ORL
DeKalb, IL RCK
DeLand, FL ORL
DePue, IL PEO
DeQuincy, LA LKC
DeSmet, ID B
DeWitt, IA DAV
NY SY
Deal, NJ TR
Dearborn, MI DET
MI STN
MI ROM
Dearborn Heights, MI DET
MI STN
Deatsville, AL MOB
Decatur, AL BIR
GA ATL
IL SFD
IN FTW
MI KAL
TX FWT
Decherd, TN NSH
Decorah, IA DUB
Dedham, IA SC
MA BO
Deep River, CT NOR
Deephaven, MN STP
Deer Lodge, MT HEL
Deer Park, NY RVC
TX GAL
WA SPK
Deer River, MN DUL
Deerbrook, WI GB
Deerfield, IL CHI
KS DOD
MI LAN
Deerfield Beach, FL MIA
Defiance, IA DM
MO STL
OH TOL
Deford, MI SAG
Del City, OK OKL
Del Norte, CO PBL
Del Rio, TX SAT
Deland, FL ORL
Delano, CA FRS
MN STP
Delanson, NY ALB
Delavan, IL PEO
WI MIL
Delaware, OH COL
Delaware City, DE WIL
Delcambre, LA LAF
Delhi, IA DUB
NY ALB
Dell Rapids, SD SFS
Delmar, IA DAV
NY ALB
Delmont, PA GBG
Delphi, IN LFT
Delphos, OH TOL
Delran, NJ TR
Delray Beach, FL NTN
FL PMB
Delta, CO PBL
Delta Junction, AK FBK
Delton, MI KAL
Deltona, FL ORL
Demarest, NJ NEW
Deming, NM LSC
Demopolis, AL BIR
Demotte, IN LFT
Denham Springs, LA BR
Denison, IA SC
TX DAL
Denmark, WI GB
Dennison, OH COL
Dent, MN SCL
Denton, NE LIN
TX FWT
Denver, CO DEN
CO HPM
CO STN
NC CHL
Denver City, TX LUB
Denville, NJ PAT
Depauw, IN IND
Depew, NY BUF
Dequincy, LA LKC
Derby, CT HRT
KS WCH
NY BUF
Derby Line, VT BUR
Derry, NH MAN
PA GBG
Derwood, MD WDC
Des Allemands, LA NO
Des Moines, IA DM
WA SEA
Des Plaines, IL CHI
Descanso, CA SD
Desert Hot Springs, CA SB
Deshler, OH TOL
Destin, FL PT
Destrehan, LA NO
Detroit, MI DET
MI EST
MI ROM
MI STN
MI OLL
Detroit Lakes, MN CR
Deville, LA ALX
Devils Lake, ND FAR
Devine, TX SAT
Devon, PA PH
Dewey, OK TLS
Dexter, ME PRT
MI LAN
MO SPC
NM LSC
Diamond Bar, CA LA
Diamondhead, MS BLX
Diberville, MS BLX
Diboll, TX TYL
Dickeyville, WI MAD
Dickinson, ND BIS
TX GAL
Dickson, TN NSH
Dickson City, PA SCR
Dieterich, IL SFD
Dighton, KS DOD
MA FR
Dilley, TX SAT
Dillingham, AK ANC
Dillon, MT HEL
SC CHR
Dilworth, MN CR
Dime Box, TX AUS
Dimmitt, TX AMA
Dimock, SD SFS
Dinuba, CA FRS
Dittmer, MO STL
Dix Hills, NY RVC
Dixon, CA SAC
IL RCK
MO JC
NM SFE
Dobbs Ferry, NY NY
Dodge, NE OM
WI LC
Dodge Center, MN WIN
Dodge City, KS DOD
Dodgeville, WI MAD
Dolan Springs, AZ PHX
Dolgeville, NY ALB
Dona Ana, NM LSC
Donaldson, IN FTW
Donaldsonville, LA BR
Donegal, PA GBG
Doniphan, MO SPC
NE LIN
Donna, TX BWN
Donora, PA PBR
PA PIT
Doral, FL ARL
FL MIA
Doraville, GA ATL
Dorchester, MA BO
Dorr, MI KAL
Dos Palos, CA FRS
Dothan, AL MOB
Douglas, AZ TUC
GA SAV
MA WOR
MI KAL
WY CHY
Douglassville, PA ALN
Douglaston, NY BRK
NY MCE
Douglasville, GA ATL
Dousman, WI MIL
Dover, DE WIL
MA BO
NH MAN
NH SAM
NJ PAT
OH COL
TN NSH
Dover Plains, NY NY
Dowagiac, MI KAL
Downers Grove, IL JOL
Downey, CA LA
Downieville, CA SAC
Downingtown, PA PH
Downs, IL PEO
Doylesburg, PA HBG
Doylestown, OH CLV
PA PH
WI MAD
Dracut, MA BO
Drake, ND FAR
Draper, UT SLC
Drayton, ND FAR
Dresden, OH COL
Drexel Hill, PA PH
Dripping Springs, TX AUS
Drummond, MT HEL
Drums, PA SCR
Dryden, MI DET
Du Bois, PA E
PA PBR
Du Quoin, IL BEL
Duarte, CA LA
Dublin, CA OAK
GA SAV
OH COL
Dubois, IL BEL
IN EVN
Dubuque, IA DUB
Dudley, MA WOR
PA ALT
Dufur, OR BAK
Dulac, LA HT
Dulce, NM GLP
Duluth, GA ATL
MN DUL
MN SUP
Dumas, AR LR
TX AMA
Dumfries, VA ARL
Dumont, NJ NEW
Dunbar, PA GBG
Duncan, OK OKL
Duncansville, PA ALT
Duncanville, TX DAL
Dundas, IL BEL
Dundee, IL RCK
MI DET
Dunedin, FL SP
Dunellen, NJ MET
NJ PSC
Dunkerton, IA DUB
Dunkirk, IN LFT
NY BUF
Dunlap, IA DM
TN KNX
Dunmore, PA PSC
PA SCR
Dunn, NC R
Dunnellon, FL ORL
Dunseith, ND FAR
Dunsmuir, CA SAC
Dunwoody, GA ATL
Dupo, IL BEL
Dupont, LA ALX
PA SCR
Duquesne, PA PBR
PA PIT
Durand, IL RCK
MI LAN
WI LC
Durango, CO PBL
Durant, OK TLS
Durham, CT NOR
NC R
NH MAN
Durhamville, NY SY
Duryea, PA SCR
Dushore, PA SCR
Duson, LA LAF
Dutton, MT HEL
Duvall, WA SEA
Duxbury, MA BO
Dwight, IL PEO
NE LIN
Dyer, IN GRY
Dyersburg, TN MEM
Dyersville, IA DUB
Dysart, PA ALT
Eagan, MN STP
Eagle, ID B
WI MIL
Eagle Butte, SD RC
Eagle Grove, IA DUB
Eagle Harbor, MI STN
Eagle Lake, TX VIC
Eagle Pass, TX LAR
Eagle River, AK ANC
WI SUP
Earlimart, CA FRS
Earling, IA DM
Earlington, KY OWN
Earlville, IA DUB
IL PEO
Earth City, MO STL
East Aurora, NY BUF
East Berlin, CT HRT
East Bernard, TX VIC
East Bloomfield, NY ROC
East Boston, MA BO
East Brady, PA E
PA GBG
East Bridgewater, MA BO
East Brookfield, MA WOR
East Brunswick, NJ MET
NJ PSC
East Carbon, UT SLC
East Chicago, IN GRY
IN ROM
East China, MI DET
East Dubuque, IL RCK
East Elmhurst, NY BRK
East Falmouth, MA FR
East Freetown, MA FR
East Glendale, NY BRK
East Grand Forks, MN CR
East Grand Rapids, MI GR
East Greenbush, NY ALB
East Greenwich, RI PRO
East Hampton, CT NOR
NY RVC
East Hanover, NJ PAT
East Hartford, CT HRT
CT SYM
East Haven, CT HRT
East Helena, MT HEL
East Islip, NY RVC
East Jordan, MI GLD
East Lansdowne, PA PH
East Lansing, MI LAN
East Liverpool, OH Y
East Longmeadow, MA SPR
East Lyme, CT NOR
East McKeesport, PA PIT
East Meadow, NY RVC
East Millinocket, ME PRT
East Moline, IL PEO
East Newark, NJ NEW
East Norriton, PA PH
East Northport, NY RVC
East Orange, NJ NEW
East Palestine, OH Y
East Palo Alto, CA SJ
CA SFR
East Patchogue, NY RVC
East Peoria, IL PEO
IL RCK
East Pittsburgh, PA PBR
PA PIT
East Providence, RI PRO
East Rochester, NY ROC
East Rockaway, NY RVC
East Rutherford, NJ NEW
East Saint Louis, IL BEL
East Sandwich, MA FR
East Stroudsburg, PA SCR
East Syracuse, NY SY
East Taunton, MA FR
East Tawas, MI GLD
East Templeton, MA WOR
East Troy, WI MIL
East Vandergrift, PA GBG
East Wenatchee, WA YAK
East Windsor, CT HRT
Easthampton, MA SPR
Eastlake, OH CLV
Eastman, GA SAV
WI LC
Easton, CA FRS
CT BGP
KS KCK
MD WIL
MO KC
PA ALN
PA SAM
Eastpointe, MI DET
Eaton, OH CIN
Eaton Rapids, MI LAN
Eatontown, NJ TR
NJ CAM
Eau Claire, WI LC
Eau Galle, WI LC
Ebensburg, PA ALT
Ebony, VA RIC
Echo, LA ALX
Ecorse, MI DET
Edcouch, TX BWN
Eddystone, PA PH
Eddyville, KY OWN
Eden, NC CHL
NY BUF
SD SFS
TX SAN

Place	Code
WI	MIL
Eden Prairie, MN	STP
Eden Valley, MN	SCL
Edenton, NC	R
Edgar, WI	LC
Edgard, LA	NO
Edgefield, SC	CHR
Edgeley, ND	FAR
Edgemere, MD	BAL
Edgerton, OH	TOL
WI	MAD
Edgewater, MD	BAL
NJ	NEW
Edgewood, IA	DUB
KY	COV
MD	BAL
Edina, MN	STP
MO	JC
Edinboro, PA	E
Edinburg, TX	BWN
TX	SYM
Edinburgh, IN	IND
Edison, NJ	MET
Edisto Island, SC	CHR
Edmond, OK	OKL
Edmonds, WA	SEA
Edmonton, KY	L
Edmore, MI	GR
Edna, TX	VIC
Edroy, TX	CC
Edwards, CO	DEN
Edwardsburg, MI	KAL
Edwardsville, IL	SFD
PA	PHU
Effingham, IL	SFD
KS	KCK
Egg Harbor, WI	GB
Egg Harbor City, NJ	CAM
Egg Harbor Township, NJ	CAM
Eggertsville, NY	BUF
Egypt, OH	CIN
El Cajon, CA	SD
CA	OLD
CA	OLL
CA	SPA
El Campo, TX	VIC
El Centro, CA	SD
El Cerrito, CA	OAK
El Dorado, AR	LR
KS	WCH
El Dorado Hills, CA	SAC
CA	SPA
El Dorado Springs, MO	SPC
El Mirage, AZ	PHX
El Monte, CA	LA
El Paso, IL	PEO
TX	ELP
El Reno, OK	OKL
El Rito, NM	SFE
El Segundo, CA	LA
CA	NTN
El Sobrante, CA	OAK
Elberon, NJ	TR
Elberta, AL	MOB
Elbow Lake, MN	SCL
Elburn, IL	RCK
Elcho, WI	GB
Eldersburg, MD	BAL
Eldon, MO	JC
Eldora, IA	DUB
Eldorado, IL	BEL
TX	SAN
WI	MIL
Eldred, PA	E
Eldridge, IA	DAV
Elgin, IL	RCK
NE	OM
OK	OKL
TX	AUS
Elizabeth, CO	COS
IL	RCK
MN	SCL
NJ	NEW
NJ	PHU
NJ	PSC
PA	PIT
Elizabeth City, NC	R
Elizabethton, TN	KNX
Elizabethtown, IL	BEL
KY	L
NY	OG
PA	HBG
Elk City, OK	OKL
Elk Grove, CA	SAC
Elk Grove Village, IL	CHI
Elk Mound, WI	LC
Elk Point, SD	SFS
Elk Rapids, MI	GLD
Elk River, MN	SCL
Elkader, IA	DUB
Elkhart, IA	DM
IN	FTW
KS	DOD
Elkhart Lake, WI	MIL
Elkhorn, NE	OM
WI	MIL
Elkins, WV	WH
Elkins Park, PA	PH
Elkland, PA	SCR
Elko, NV	RNO
Elkridge, MD	BAL
Elkton, FL	STA
KY	OWN
MD	WIL
VA	RIC
Elkview, WV	WH
Ellenburg, NY	OG
Ellenburg Center, NY	OG
Ellendale, ND	FAR
Ellensburg, WA	YAK
Ellenville, NY	NY
Ellicott City, MD	BAL
Ellicottville, NY	BUF
Ellijay, GA	ATL
Ellington, CT	NOR
Ellinwood, KS	DOD
Ellis, KS	SAL
Ellis Grove, IL	BEL
Ellisville, MO	STL
Ellsworth, KS	SAL
ME	PRT
WI	LC
Ellwood City, PA	PIT
Elm Creek, NE	GI
Elm Grove, WI	MIL
Elma, IA	DUB
NY	BUF
WA	SEA
Elmendorf, TX	SAT
Elmer, NJ	CAM
Elmhurst, IL	JOL
IL	SYM
NY	BRK
Elmhurst Twp., PA	SCR
Elmira, MI	GLD
NY	ROC
Elmira Heights, NY	STF
Elmont, NY	MCE
Elmore, AL	MOB
OH	DET
Elmsford, NY	NY
Elmwood, IL	PEO
WI	LC
Elmwood Park, IL	CHI
NJ	NEW
Elon, NC	R
Eloy, AZ	TUC
Elrama, PA	PIT
Elrosa, MN	SCL
Elsa, TX	BWN
Elsberry, MO	STL
Elsmere, KY	COV
Elton, LA	LKC
Eltopia, WA	SPK
Elverson, PA	PH
Elwood, IN	LFT
Ely, MN	DUL
NV	LAV
Elyria, OH	CLV
Elyria Township, OH	CLV
Elysburg, PA	HBG
Elysian, MN	STP
Emerson, NE	OM
NJ	NEW
Emery, SD	SFS
Emeryville, CA	OAK
Emily, MN	DUL
Emlenton, PA	E
Emmaus, PA	ALN
Emmetsburg, IA	SC
Emmett, ID	B
MI	DET
Emmitsburg, MD	BAL
Emmonak, AK	FBK
Empire, MI	GLD
Emporia, KS	KCK
Emporium, PA	E
Encinal, TX	LAR
Encinitas, CA	SD
Encino, CA	LA
Enderlin, ND	FAR
Endicott, NY	SY
Endwell, NY	SY
Enfield, CT	HRT
NH	MAN
England, AR	LR
Englewood, CO	DEN
FL	VEN
NJ	NEW
OH	CIN
Englewood Cliffs, NJ	NEW
Enid, OK	OKL
Ennis, TX	DAL
Enola, PA	HBG
Enosburg Falls, VT	BUR
Enterprise, AL	MOB
OR	BAK
Enumclaw, WA	SEA
Ephraim, UT	SLC
Ephrata, PA	HBG
WA	YAK
Epping, NH	MAN
Epworth, IA	DUB
Equality, IL	BEL
Erath, LA	LAF
Erdenheim, PA	PH
Erie, KS	WCH
MI	DET
PA	E
PA	PBR
Erlanger, KY	COV
Ernest, PA	PBR
Escanaba, MI	MAR
Escondido, CA	SD
Esmond, ND	FAR
Esopus, NY	NY
Espanola, NM	SFE
Essex, CT	NOR
MD	BAL
Essex Junction, VT	BUR
Essexville, MI	SAG
Essington, PA	PH
Estacada, OR	P
Estes Park, CO	DEN
Estherville, IA	SC
Ettrick, WI	LC
Euclid, MN	CR
OH	CLV
OH	PRM
Eudora, KS	KCK
Eufaula, AL	MOB
Eugene, MO	JC
OR	P
Eunice, LA	LAF
Eupora, MS	JKS
Eureka, CA	SR
IL	PEO
KS	WCH
MO	STL
MT	HEL
NV	RNO
SD	SFS
Eureka Springs, AR	LR
Eustis, FL	ORL
Eutaw, AL	BIR
Evangeline, LA	LAF
Evans City, PA	PIT
Evans Mills, NY	OG
Evanston, IL	CHI
IL	MCE
WY	CHY
Evansville, IL	BEL
IN	EVN
WI	MAD
Evart, MI	GR
Eveleth, MN	DUL
Everett, MA	BO
PA	ALT
WA	SEA
Evergreen, CO	DEN
LA	ALX
Evergreen Park, IL	CHI
Everson, PA	GBG
Ewa, HI	HON
Ewa Beach, HI	HON
Ewen, MI	MAR
Ewing, MO	JC
NE	OM
Excelsior, MN	STP
Excelsior Springs, MO	KC
Exeter, CA	FRS
NE	LIN
NH	MAN
PA	SCR
RI	PRO
Exton, PA	PH
Fabens, TX	ELP
Fair Haven, NJ	TR
VT	BUR
Fair Lawn, NJ	NEW
Fair Oaks, CA	SAC
Fairbank, IA	DUB
Fairbanks, AK	FBK
Fairborn, OH	CIN
Fairbury, IL	PEO
NE	LIN
Fairchance, PA	GBG
Fairchild, WI	LC
Fairdale, KY	L
Fairfax, CA	SFR
MN	NU
OK	TLS
SD	RC
VA	ARL
VT	BUR
Fairfield, CA	SAC
CT	BGP
IA	DAV
IL	BEL
KY	L
MT	HEL
NJ	NEW
OH	CIN
PA	HBG
TX	TYL
VT	BUR
Fairfield Bay, AR	LR
Fairfield Glade, TN	KNX
Fairhaven, MA	FR
Fairhope, AL	MOB
Fairlawn, OH	CLV
OH	OLL
Fairless Hills, PA	PH
Fairmont, MN	WIN
WV	WH
Fairmont City, IL	BEL
Fairmount, ND	FAR
Fairport, NY	ROC
Fairport Harbor, OH	CLV
Fairview, NJ	NEW
PA	E
Fairview Heights, IL	BEL
Fairview Park, OH	CLV
OH	PRM
Faith, SD	RC
Falcon, CO	COS
Falconer, NY	BUF
Falfurrias, TX	CC
Fall Creek, WI	LC
Fall River, MA	FR
MA	SAM
MA	STF
Fallbrook, CA	SD
Fallentimber, PA	ALT
Fallon, NV	RNO
Falls, PA	SCR
Falls Church, VA	ARL
VA	SYM
Falls City, NE	LIN
TX	SAT
Falls Creek, PA	E
Fallsington, PA	PH
Fallston, MD	BAL
Falmouth, KY	COV
MA	FR
Fancy Farm, KY	OWN
Far Rockaway, NY	BRK
Fargo, ND	FAR
Faribault, MN	STP
Farley, IA	DUB
Farmer City, IL	PEO
Farmers Branch, TX	SYM
Farmersville, IL	SFD
Farmingdale, NJ	TR
NY	RVC
Farmington, CT	HRT
IA	DAV
IL	PEO
ME	PRT
MI	DET
MI	OLN
MN	STP
MO	STL
NH	MAN
NM	GLP
PA	GBG
Farmington Hills, MI	DET
MI	OLD
Farmingville, NY	RVC
Farmville, NC	R
VA	RIC
Farnham, NY	BUF
Farrell, PA	E
Faulkner, MD	WDC
Faulkton, SD	SFS
Fayette, IA	DUB
MO	JC
MS	JKS
OH	TOL
Fayetteville, AR	LR
GA	ATL
IL	BEL
NC	R
NC	SAM
NY	SY
OH	CIN
TN	NSH
TX	AUS
Feasterville, PA	PH
Federal Way, WA	SEA
Feeding Hills, MA	SPR
Fellsmere, FL	PMB
Felton, CA	MRY

Place	Code
Fenelton, PA	PIT
Fennimore, WI	MAD
Fennville, MI	KAL
Fenton, LA	LKC
MI	LAN
MO	STL
Ferdinand, IN	EVN
Fergus Falls, MN	SCL
Ferguson, MO	STL
Fernandina Beach, FL	STA
Ferndale, CA	SR
MI	DET
WA	SEA
Fernley, NV	RNO
Ferriday, LA	ALX
Ferris, TX	DAL
Fertile, MN	CR
Fessenden, ND	FAR
Festus, MO	STL
Fife, WA	SEA
Fillmore, CA	LA
NY	BUF
Fincastle, VA	RIC
Findlay, OH	TOL
Finleyville, PA	PIT
Firebaugh, CA	FRS
Fisher, MN	CR
Fishers, IN	LFT
Fishers Island, NY	NOR
Fishkill, NY	NY
Fiskdale, MA	WOR
Fitchburg, MA	WOR
Flagler Beach, FL	STA
Flagstaff, AZ	PHX
Flanders, NJ	PAT
NJ	PSC
Flandreau, SD	SFS
Flasher, ND	BIS
Flat Rock, MI	DET
Flatonia, TX	AUS
TX	VIC
Fleming Island, FL	STA
Flemingsburg, KY	COV
Flemington, NJ	MET
Flint, MI	LAN
MI	OLL
TX	TYL
Flint Hill, MO	STL
Floodwood, MN	DUL
Flora, IL	BEL
Floral City, FL	SP
Floral Park, NY	BRK
NY	RVC
Florence, AL	BIR
AZ	TUC
CO	PBL
KY	COV
OR	P
SC	CHR
SD	SFS
TX	AUS
WI	GB
Floresville, TX	SAT
Florham Park, NJ	PAT
Florida, NY	NY
Florida City, FL	MIA
Florissant, MO	STL
Flossmoor, IL	CHI
Flourtown, PA	PH
Flower Mound, TX	FWT
Flowery Branch, GA	ATL
Flowood, MS	JKS
Floydada, TX	LUB
Floyds Knobs, IN	IND
Flushing, MI	LAN
MI	PRM
NY	BRK
OH	STU
Foley, AL	MOB
MN	SCL
Follansbee, WV	WH
Folly Beach, SC	CHR
Folsom, CA	SAC
LA	NO
Fond Du Lac, WI	MIL
Fond du Lac, WI	MIL
Fonda, IA	SC
NY	ALB
Fontana, CA	SB
CA	HPM
WI	MIL
Footville, WI	MAD
Force, PA	E
Ford City, PA	GBG
PA	SJP
Fordsville, KY	OWN
Fordyce, NE	OM
Foreman, AR	LR
Forest, MS	JKS
Forest City, IA	DUB
NC	CHL
PA	SCR
Forest Grove, OR	P
Forest Hill, MD	BAL
Forest Hills, NY	BRK
Forest Lake, MN	STP
Forest Park, IL	CHI
Forestburgh, NY	NY
Foreston, MN	SCL
Forestport, NY	SY
Forestville, CT	HRT
MD	WDC
Forked River, NJ	TR
Forks, WA	SEA
Forman, ND	FAR
Forney, TX	DAL
Forrest City, AR	LR
Forsyth, MO	SPC
MT	GF
Fort Ann, NY	ALB
Fort Ashby, WV	WH
Fort Atkinson, WI	MAD
Fort Benton, MT	GF
Fort Bragg, CA	SR
Fort Branch, IN	EVN
Fort Calhoun, NE	OM
Fort Collins, CO	DEN
Fort Covington, NY	OG
Fort Davis, TX	ELP
Fort Defiance, AZ	GLP
Fort Dodge, IA	SC
Fort Edward, NY	ALB
Fort Gratiot, MI	DET
Fort Hancock, TX	ELP
Fort Jennings, OH	TOL
Fort Jones, CA	SAC
Fort Kent, ME	PRT
Fort Lauderdale, FL	MIA
FL	SYM
FL	SAM
Fort Leavenworth, KS	KCK
Fort Lee, NJ	NEW
Fort Loramie, OH	CIN
Fort Lupton, CO	DEN
Fort Madison, IA	DAV
Fort Mc Clellan, AL	BIR
Fort Mill, SC	CHR
Fort Mitchell, AL	MOB
KY	COV
Fort Monroe, VA	RIC
Fort Morgan, CO	DEN
Fort Myers, FL	VEN
Fort Myers Beach, FL	VEN
Fort Oglethorpe, GA	ATL
Fort Payne, AL	BIR
Fort Pierce, FL	PMB
FL	PSC
Fort Pierre, SD	RC
Fort Plain, NY	ALB
Fort Recovery, OH	CIN
Fort Riley, KS	SAL
Fort Scott, KS	WCH
Fort Shaw, MT	GF
Fort Smith, AR	LR
Fort Stockton, TX	SAN
Fort Sumner, NM	SFE
Fort Thomas, KY	COV
Fort Thompson, SD	SFS
Fort Totten, ND	FAR
Fort Walton Beach, FL	PT
Fort Washington, MD	WDC
Fort Wayne, IN	FTW
Fort Worth, TX	FWT
Fort Wright, KY	COV
Fort Yates, ND	BIS
Fortuna, CA	SR
Fortville, IN	IND
Fosston, MN	CR
Foster, RI	PRO
Foster City, CA	SFR
Fostoria, OH	TOL
Fountain City, WI	LC
Fountain Hill, PA	ALN
Fountain Hills, AZ	PHX
Fountain Valley, CA	ORG
Fowler, CA	FRS
IN	LFT
KS	DOD
MI	LAN
Fowlerville, MI	LAN
Fox Chase Manor, PA	PH
PA	PHU
Fox Lake, WI	MIL
Fox Point, WI	MIL
Foxborough, MA	BO
Foxfield, CO	DEN
Foxholm, ND	BIS
Frackville, PA	ALN
PA	PHU
Framingham, MA	BO
MA	SYM
Francis Creek, WI	GB
Franconia, MN	STP
Frankenmuth, MI	SAG
Frankfort, IL	JOL
IN	LFT
KS	KCK
KY	LEX
MI	GLD
NY	ALB
Franklin, IN	IND
KY	OWN
LA	LAF
MA	BO
MN	NU
NC	CHL
NH	MAN
NJ	PAT
OH	CIN
PA	E
TN	NSH
TX	AUS
VA	RIC
WI	MIL
WV	WH
Franklin Furnace, OH	STU
Franklin Lakes, NJ	NEW
Franklin Park, IL	CHI
Franklin Square, NY	RVC
Franklinton, LA	NO
Franklinville, NY	BUF
Fraser, MI	DET
Frazee, MN	CR
Frazier Park, CA	FRS
Frederic, WI	SUP
Frederick, CO	DEN
MD	BAL
Fredericksburg, TX	SAT
VA	ARL
Fredericktown, MO	SPC
PA	PIT
Fredonia, KS	WCH
NY	BUF
WI	MIL
Free Soil, MI	GR
Freeburg, IL	BEL
MO	JC
Freedom, PA	PIT
WI	GB
Freehold, NJ	TR
Freeland, MI	SAG
PA	PSC
PA	SCR
Freeport, IL	RCK
MN	SCL
NY	RVC
PA	GBG
TX	GAL
Freer, TX	CC
Freeville, NY	ROC
Fremont, CA	SJ
CA	SYM
CA	OAK
MI	GR
NE	OM
OH	TOL
French Lick, IN	IND
French Settlement, LA	BR
Frenchburg, KY	LEX
Frenchtown, MT	HEL
Frenchville, ME	PRT
PA	E
Fresh Meadows, NY	BRK
NY	STF
Fresno, CA	FRS
Friday Harbor, WA	SEA
Fridley, MN	STP
Friend, NE	LIN
Friendsville, PA	SCR
Friendswood, TX	GAL
Friona, TX	AMA
Frisco, CO	DEN
TX	DAL
TX	FWT
Front Royal, VA	ARL
Frontenac, KS	WCH
MN	STP
MO	STL
Frostburg, MD	BAL
Fruita, CO	PBL
Fruitland, ID	B
Fryburg, PA	E
Fulda, MN	WIN
Fullerton, CA	ORG
NE	OM
Fulton, IL	RCK
KY	OWN
MD	BAL
MO	JC
NY	SY
TX	CC
Fultonville, NY	ALB
Fuquay–Varina, NC	R
Gadsden, AL	BIR
Gaffney, SC	CHR
Gagetown, MI	SAG
Gahanna, OH	COL
Gaines, MI	LAN
Gainesville, FL	STA
GA	ATL
TX	FWT
VA	ARL
Gaithersburg, MD	WDC
Galena, AK	FBK
IL	RCK
MD	WIL
Galena Park, TX	GAL
Gales Ferry, CT	NOR
Galesburg, IL	PEO
Galeton, PA	E
Galion, OH	TOL
Gallatin, MO	KC
TN	NSH
Galliano, LA	HT
Gallipolis, OH	STU
Gallitzin, PA	ALT
Galloway, NJ	CAM
Gallup, NM	GLP
Galt, CA	SAC
Galva, IL	PEO
Galveston, TX	GAL
Gambrills, MD	BAL
Ganado, AZ	GLP
TX	VIC
Garberville, CA	SR
Garciasville, TX	BWN
Garden, MI	MAR
Garden City, KS	DOD
MI	DET
NY	RVC
SC	CHR
TX	SAN
Garden Grove, CA	ORG
Garden Plain, KS	WCH
Gardena, CA	LA
Gardendale, AL	BIR
Gardiner, NY	NY
Gardner, KS	KCK
MA	WOR
Gardnerville, NV	RNO
Garfield, NJ	NEW
NJ	SYM
NM	LSC
Garfield Heights, OH	CLV
Garland, TX	DAL
TX	MCE
TX	SYM
Garner, IA	DUB
NC	R
NC	SJP
Garnerville, NY	NY
Garnett, KS	KCK
Garretson, SD	SFS
Garrett, IN	FTW
Garrett Park, MD	WDC
Garrettsville, OH	Y
Garrison, MN	DUL
ND	BIS
NY	NY
Garwood, NJ	NEW
Gary, IN	GRY
WV	WH
Garyville, LA	NO
Gas City, IN	LFT
Gassaway, WV	WH
Gastonia, NC	CHL
Gate City, VA	RIC
Gates Mills, OH	CLV
Gatesville, TX	AUS
Gatlinburg, TN	KNX
Gautier, MS	BLX
Gaylord, MI	GLD
MN	NU
Gays Mills, WI	LC
Geddes, SD	SFS
Genesee, ID	B
Genesee Depot, WI	MIL
Geneseo, IL	PEO
ND	FAR
NY	ROC
Geneva, IL	RCK
IN	FTW
NE	LIN
NY	ROC
OH	Y
Genoa, IL	RCK
NE	OM
OH	TOL
WI	LC
George West, TX	CC
Georgetown, CA	SAC
CT	BGP
DE	WIL
IL	PEO

Place	Code
IN	IND
KY	LEX
MA	BO
MN	CR
OH	CIN
SC	CHR
TX	AUS
Georgiaville, RI	PRO
Gering, NE	GI
Germantown, IL	BEL
MD	WDC
NY	ALB
OH	CIN
TN	MEM
WI	MIL
Gervais, OR	P
Gettysburg, PA	HBG
SD	SFS
Getzville, NY	BUF
Ghent, MN	NU
Gibbon, MN	NU
Gibbsboro, NJ	CAM
Gibbstown, NJ	CAM
Gibraltar, MI	DET
Gibson, LA	HT
Gibson City, IL	JOL
Gibsonburg, OH	TOL
Gibsonia, PA	PBR
PA	PIT
Giddings, TX	AUS
Gig Harbor, WA	SEA
Gilbert, AZ	HPM
AZ	PHX
IA	DUB
MN	DUL
Gilberts, IL	RCK
Gilbertville, IA	DUB
MA	WOR
Gilford, NH	MAN
Gillespie, IL	SFD
Gillett, WI	GB
Gillette, WY	CHY
Gilman, IL	JOL
MN	SCL
WI	SUP
Gilmer, TX	TYL
Gilroy, CA	SJ
Girard, KS	WCH
OH	Y
PA	E
PA	PBR
Girardville, PA	ALN
Gladewater, TX	TYL
Gladstone, MI	MAR
MO	KC
NJ	PAT
Gladwin, MI	SAG
Gladwyne, PA	PH
Glandorf, OH	TOL
Glasco, NY	NY
Glasgow, KY	L
MO	JC
MT	GF
Glassboro, NJ	CAM
Glassport, PA	PIT
Glastonbury, CT	HRT
CT	STF
Glen Allen, VA	RIC
VA	SAM
Glen Burnie, MD	BAL
Glen Carbon, IL	SFD
Glen Cove, NY	RVC
NY	STF
Glen Dale, WV	WH
Glen Echo, MD	WDC
Glen Ellyn, IL	JOL
Glen Head, NY	RVC
Glen Lyon, PA	SCR
Glen Mills, PA	PH
Glen Rock, NJ	NEW
Glen Rose, TX	FWT
Glen Ullin, ND	BIS
Glenburn, ND	BIS
Glencoe, MN	NU
Glendale, AZ	PHX
AZ	SPA
CA	LA
CA	OLN
NY	BRK
WI	MIL
Glendale Heights, IL	JOL
Glendive, MT	GF
Glendora, CA	LA
Glenmora, LA	ALX
Glennallen, AK	ANC
Glenns Ferry, ID	B
Glenolden, PA	PH
Glenrock, WY	CHY
Glens Falls, NY	ALB
Glenshaw, PA	PIT
Glenside, PA	PH
Glenview, IL	CHI
IL	SYM
Glenville, NY	ALB
WV	WH
Glenwood, AR	LR
IA	DM
IL	CHI
MN	SCL
Glenwood City, WI	SUP
Glenwood Springs, CO	DEN
Globe, AZ	TUC
Gloucester, MA	BO
NJ	CAM
VA	RIC
Gloversville, NY	ALB
Gloverville, SC	CHR
Gluckstadt, MS	JKS
Glyndon, MD	BAL
Gobernador, NM	GLP
Gobles, MI	KAL
Goddard, KS	WCH
Godfrey, IL	SFD
Goetzville, MI	MAR
Goffstown, NH	MAN
Gold Hill, OR	P
Golden, CO	DEN
Golden Meadow, LA	HT
Golden Valley, MN	STP
Goldendale, WA	YAK
Goldsboro, NC	R
Goldthwaite, TX	AUS
Goleta, CA	LA
Goliad, TX	VIC
Gonic, NH	MAN
Gonzales, CA	MRY
LA	BR
TX	SAT
Goodhue, MN	STP
Gooding, ID	B
Goodland, KS	SAL
Goodman, WI	GB
Goodrich, MI	LAN
Goodyear, AZ	PHX
AZ	TUC
Goose Creek, SC	CHR
Gordon, NE	GI
Gorham, KS	SAL
ME	PRT
NH	MAN
Goshen, CT	HRT
IN	FTW
NY	NY
Gould, AR	LR
Gouldsboro, PA	SCR
Gouverneur, NY	OG
Gowanda, NY	BUF
Gower, MO	KC
Graceville, MN	NU
Graford, TX	FWT
Grafton, IL	SFD
MA	WOR
ND	FAR
NY	ALB
OH	CLV
WI	MIL
WV	WH
Graham, TX	FWT
Grambling, LA	SHP
Grampian, PA	E
Granada Hills, CA	LA
Granbury, TX	FWT
Granby, CO	DEN
CT	HRT
MA	SPR
Grand Bay, AL	MOB
Grand Blanc, MI	LAN
Grand Canyon, AZ	PHX
Grand Chenier, LA	LKC
Grand Coteau, LA	LAF
Grand Coulee, WA	YAK
Grand Forks, ND	FAR
Grand Haven, MI	GR
Grand Island, NE	GI
NY	BUF
Grand Isle, LA	HT
Grand Junction, CO	PBL
IA	SC
Grand Ledge, MI	LAN
Grand Marais, MI	MAR
MN	DUL
Grand Meadow, MN	WIN
Grand Mound, IA	DAV
Grand Prairie, TX	DAL
TX	FWT
Grand Rapids, MI	GR
MI	STN
MN	DUL
OH	TOL
Grand Rivers, KY	OWN
Grand Ronde, OR	P
Grand Terrace, CA	SB
Grandview, MO	KC
WA	YAK
Grandville, MI	GR
Granger, IA	DM
IN	FTW
TX	AUS
WA	YAK
Grangeville, ID	B
Granite Bay, CA	SAC
Granite City, IL	SFD
Granite Falls, MN	NU
Graniteville, VT	BUR
Grant, NE	LIN
Grants, NM	GLP
Grants Pass, OR	P
Granville, IA	SC
IL	PEO
NY	ALB
OH	COL
Grapevine, TX	FWT
Grass Lake, MI	LAN
Grass Valley, CA	SAC
Gray, LA	NO
LA	PBR
Grayling, MI	GLD
Grayslake, IL	CHI
Grayson, KY	LEX
Great Barrington, MA	SPR
Great Bend, KS	DOD
PA	SCR
Great Falls, MT	GF
VA	ARL
Great Meadows, NJ	MET
Great Mills, MD	WDC
Great Neck, NY	RVC
Greeley, CO	DEN
KS	KCK
Green Bay, WI	GB
Green Isle, MN	NU
Green Lake, WI	MAD
Green Pond, NJ	PAT
Green River, WY	CHY
Green Valley, AZ	TUC
Greenacres, FL	PMB
FL	SAM
Greenbelt, MD	WDC
Greenbrae, CA	SFR
Greenbush, MN	CR
Greencastle, IN	IND
PA	HBG
Greendale, WI	MIL
Greene, IA	DUB
NY	SY
Greeneville, TN	KNX
Greenfield, CA	MRY
IA	DM
IL	SFD
IN	IND
MA	SPR
OH	CIN
WI	MIL
Greenfield Center, NY	ALB
Greenlawn, NY	RVC
Greenleaf, WI	GB
Greenport, NY	RVC
Greensboro, GA	ATL
NC	CHL
Greensburg, IN	IND
KS	DOD
PA	GBG
PA	PBR
PA	PIT
Greenup, IL	SFD
Greenville, AL	MOB
IL	SFD
ME	PRT
MI	GR
MS	JKS
NC	R
NH	MAN
NY	ALB
OH	CIN
PA	E
RI	PRO
SC	CHR
TX	DAL
WI	GB
Greenwald, MN	SCL
Greenwell Springs, LA	BR
Greenwich, CT	BGP
NY	ALB
Greenwood, IN	IND
MS	JKS
SC	CHR
WI	LC
Greenwood Lake, NY	NY
Greer, SC	CHR
SC	SAM
Gregory, SD	RC
TX	CC
Grenada, MS	JKS
Grenora, ND	BIS
Grenville, SD	SFS
Gresham, OR	P
WI	GB
Gretna, LA	NO
NE	OM
Grey Eagle, MN	SCL
Greybull, WY	CHY
Gridley, CA	SAC
Griffin, GA	ATL
Griffith, IN	GRY
Grinnell, IA	DAV
KS	SAL
Griswold, CT	NOR
IA	DM
Groom, TX	AMA
Grosse Ile, MI	DET
Grosse Pointe, MI	DET
Grosse Pointe Farms, MI	DET
Grosse Pointe Park, MI	DET
Grosse Tete, LA	BR
Groton, CT	NOR
NY	ROC
SD	SFS
Grove, OK	TLS
Grove City, MN	NU
OH	COL
PA	E
Grove Hill, AL	MOB
Groveport, OH	COL
Groves, TX	BEA
Groveton, NH	MAN
Grovetown, GA	SAV
Grulla, TX	BWN
Gruver, TX	AMA
Guadalupe, AZ	PHX
CA	LA
Guasti, CA	SB
Guerneville, CA	SR
Guernsey, WY	CHY
Gueydan, LA	LAF
Guilderland, NY	ALB
Guilderland Center, NY	ALB
Guilford, CT	HRT
IN	IND
Gulf Breeze, FL	PT
Gulf Shores, AL	MOB
Gulfport, FL	SP
MS	BLX
Gun Barrel City, TX	TYL
Gunnison, CO	PBL
Guntersville, AL	BIR
Gurnee, IL	CHI
Gustine, CA	FRS
Guthrie, KY	OWN
OK	OKL
Guthrie Center, IA	DM
Guttenberg, IA	DUB
Guymon, OK	OKL
Guys Mills, PA	E
Gwinn, MI	MAR
Gwynedd Valley, PA	PH
Hacienda Heights, CA	LA
Hackberry, LA	LKC
Hackensack, MN	DUL
NJ	NEW
Hackettstown, NJ	MET
Haddon Heights, NJ	CAM
Haddonfield, NJ	CAM
Hadley, MA	SPR
Hagaman, NY	ALB
Hagerstown, MD	BAL
MD	SYM
Hague, ND	BIS
Hahnville, LA	NO
Haiku, HI	HON
Hailey, ID	B
Haines, AK	JUN
Haines City, FL	ORL
Haines Falls, NY	ALB
Hainesport, NJ	TR
NJ	CAM
Halbur, IA	SC
Hale, MI	GLD
Haledon, NJ	PAT
Hales Corners, WI	MIL
Halethorpe, MD	BAL
Half Moon Bay, CA	SFR
Hallandale Beach, FL	MIA
Hallettsville, TX	VIC
Hallock, MN	CR
Hallowell, ME	PRT
Halstead, KS	WCH
Haltom City, TX	FWT
Ham Lake, MN	STP
Hamburg, IA	DM
NJ	PAT
NY	BUF
PA	ALN
Hamden, CT	HRT
Hamel, MN	STP

Hamilton, AL	BIR
MA	BO
MO	KC
MT	HEL
NJ	TR
NY	SY
OH	CIN
TX	AUS
VA	ARL
Hamilton Square, NJ	TR
Hamlet, IN	GRY
NC	CHL
Hamlin, NY	ROC
Hammond, IN	GRY
IN	NTN
LA	BR
WI	SUP
Hammondsport, NY	ROC
Hammonton, NJ	CAM
Hampden, MA	SPR
Hampshire, IL	RCK
Hampstead, NC	R
NH	MAN
Hampton, IA	DUB
MN	STP
NH	MAN
NJ	MET
VA	RIC
Hampton Bays, NY	RVC
Hamptonville, NC	CHL
Hamtramck, MI	DET
MI	STN
Hana, HI	HON
Hanahan, SC	CHR
Hanceville, AL	BIR
Hancock, MD	BAL
MI	MAR
NY	ALB
Hanford, CA	FRS
Hankinson, ND	FAR
Hannibal, MO	JC
NY	SY
Hanover, IL	RCK
KS	SAL
MA	BO
MD	BAL
NH	MAN
PA	HBG
Hanover Park, IL	CHI
Hanover Township, PA	SCR
Hanoverton, OH	Y
Hanson, MA	BO
Hapeville, GA	ATL
Happy, TX	AMA
Harahan, LA	NO
Harbor Beach, MI	SAG
Harbor Springs, MI	GLD
Harborcreek, PA	E
Hardin, IL	SFD
KY	OWN
MT	GF
Hardinsburg, KY	OWN
Hardwick, VT	BUR
Harker Heights, TX	AUS
Harlan, IA	DM
KY	LEX
Harlingen, TX	BWN
Harlowton, MT	HEL
Harmony, MN	WIN
Harper, KS	WCH
TX	SAT
Harper Woods, MI	DET
Harrah, OK	OKL
Harriman, NY	NY
TN	KNX
Harrington, WA	SPK
Harrington Park, NJ	NEW
Harrisburg, IL	BEL
PA	HBG
PA	PSC
Harrison, AR	LR
MI	SAG
NJ	NEW
NY	NY
OH	CIN
Harrison City, PA	GBG
Harrison Township, MI	DET
Harrisonburg, VA	RIC
Harrisonville, MO	KC
Harrisville, MI	DET
MI	GLD
NY	OG
RI	PRO
WV	WH
Harrodsburg, KY	LEX
Hart, MI	GR
Hartford, CT	HRT
CT	STF
MI	KAL
SD	SFS
WI	MIL

Hartford City, IN	LFT
Hartington, NE	OM
Hartland, WI	MIL
Hartman, AR	LR
Hartsdale, NY	NY
Hartshorne, OK	TLS
Hartsville, SC	CHR
Hartwell, GA	ATL
Harvard, IL	RCK
MA	WOR
NE	LIN
Harvey, IL	CHI
LA	NO
ND	FAR
Harvey Cedars, NJ	TR
Harveys Lake, PA	SCR
Harwichport, MA	FR
Harwick, PA	PIT
Harwinton, CT	HRT
Harwood, ND	FAR
Harwood Heights–Norridge, IL	CHI
Hasbrouck Heights, NJ	NEW
Haskell, NJ	PAT
Hastings, MI	KAL
MN	STP
NE	LIN
PA	ALT
Hastings–on–Hudson, NY	NY
Hatboro, PA	PH
Hatch, NM	LSC
Hatfield, MA	SPR
PA	PH
Hatley, WI	LC
Hattiesburg, MS	BLX
Hattieville, AR	LR
Haubstadt, IN	EVN
Hauppauge, NY	RVC
Havana, IL	PEO
Havelock, NC	R
Haverford, PA	PH
Haverhill, MA	BO
Haverstraw, NY	NY
Havertown, PA	PH
Havre, MT	GF
Havre de Grace, MD	BAL
Hawaiian Gardens, CA	LA
Hawarden, IA	SC
Hawesville, KY	OWN
Hawi, HI	HON
Hawk Point, MO	STL
Hawk Run, PA	PBR
Hawley, MN	CR
PA	SCR
Haworth, NJ	NEW
Hawthorne, CA	LA
NJ	PAT
NV	RNO
NY	NY
Hayden, AZ	TUC
Haydenville, MA	SPR
Hayfield, MN	WIN
Hays, KS	SAL
MT	GF
Haysville, KS	WCH
Hayward, CA	OAK
WI	SUP
Hazard, KY	LEX
Hazel Crest, IL	CHI
Hazel Green, WI	MAD
Hazel Park, MI	DET
Hazelton, ND	BIS
Hazelwood, MO	STL
Hazen, ND	BIS
Hazleton, PA	PSC
PA	SCR
Healdsburg, CA	SR
Healdton, OK	OKL
Healy, AK	FBK
Hearne, TX	AUS
Heart Butte, MT	HEL
Heath, OH	COL
Hebbronville, TX	CC
TX	LAR
Heber Springs, AR	LR
Hebron, CT	NOR
IN	GRY
ND	BIS
NE	LIN
Hector, MN	NU
Hedgesville, WV	WH
Helena, AR	LR
MT	HEL
OH	TOL
Helenwood, TN	KNX
Hellertown, PA	ALN
Helmetta, NJ	MET
Helmville, MT	HEL
Helotes, TX	SAT
TX	SYM
Helper, UT	SLC
Hemet, CA	SB

Hemlock, MI	SAG
Hemphill, TX	TYL
Hempstead, NY	RVC
NY	STF
TX	GAL
Henderson, KY	OWN
MN	NU
NC	R
NV	LAV
TX	TYL
Hendersonville, NC	CHL
TN	NSH
Hennessey, OK	OKL
Henniker, NH	MAN
Henning, MN	SCL
Henrico, VA	RIC
Henrietta, NY	ROC
TX	FWT
Henry, IL	PEO
SD	SFS
Henryetta, OK	TLS
Heppner, OR	BAK
Herculaneum, MO	STL
Hercules, CA	OAK
Hereford, AZ	TUC
TX	AMA
Herington, KS	SAL
Herkimer, NY	ALB
Hermann, MO	JC
Herminie, PA	GBG
PA	PBR
Hermiston, OR	BAK
Hermitage, MO	JC
PA	E
PA	PBR
Hermosa Beach, CA	LA
Hernando, MS	JKS
Herndon, VA	ARL
Heron Lake, MN	WIN
Herreid, SD	SFS
Herrin, IL	BEL
Herron, MI	GLD
Herscher, IL	JOL
Hershey, PA	HBG
Hesperia, CA	SB
Hessmer, LA	ALX
Hettinger, ND	BIS
Heuvelton, NY	OG
Hewitt, NJ	PAT
WI	LC
Hewlett, NY	RVC
Hialeah, FL	MIA
Hiawatha, IA	DUB
KS	KCK
Hibbing, MN	DUL
Hickman, KY	OWN
Hickory, NC	CHL
Hickory Hills, IL	CHI
Hicksville, NY	RVC
OH	TOL
Hidalgo, TX	BWN
Higganum, CT	NOR
Higgins Lake, MI	GLD
Higginsville, MO	KC
High Bridge, NJ	MET
High Point, NC	CHL
High Ridge, MO	STL
High Springs, FL	STA
Highland, CA	SB
IL	SFD
IN	GRY
MI	DET
NY	NY
WI	MAD
Highland Beach, FL	PMB
Highland Falls, NY	NY
Highland Heights, KY	COV
OH	CLV
Highland Lakes, NJ	PAT
Highland Mills, NY	NY
Highland Park, IL	CHI
MI	DET
NJ	MET
Highland Springs, VA	RIC
Highlands, NJ	TR
TX	GAL
Highlands Ranch, CO	COS
Highmore, SD	SFS
Hightstown, NJ	TR
Highwood, IL	CHI
Hilbert, WI	GB
Hill City, KS	SAL
MN	DUL
Hillcrest Heights, MD	WDC
Hilliard, OH	COL
Hillman, MI	GLD
MN	SCL
Hills, IA	DAV
Hillsboro, IL	SFD
MO	STL
ND	FAR

OH	CIN
OR	P
TX	FWT
WI	LC
Hillsborough, NC	R
NH	MAN
NJ	MET
NJ	PHU
Hillsborough Township, NJ	PSC
Hillsdale, MI	LAN
NJ	NEW
Hillside, IL	CHI
NJ	NEW
NJ	PHU
Hillsville, PA	PIT
Hilltown, PA	PH
Hilmar, CA	FRS
Hilo, HI	HON
Hilton, NY	ROC
Hilton Head Island, SC	CHR
Hinckley, MN	DUL
NY	SY
OH	CLV
Hinesburg, VT	BUR
Hinesville, GA	SAV
Hingham, MA	BO
Hinsdale, IL	JOL
Hinton, WV	WH
Hitchcock, TX	GAL
Ho Ho Kus, NJ	NEW
Hobart, IN	GRY
Hobbs, NM	LSC
Hobe Sound, FL	PMB
Hoboken, NJ	NEW
Hobson, TX	SAT
Hockessin, DE	WIL
Hodge, LA	SHP
Hodgenville, KY	L
Hoffman Estates, IL	CHI
Hogansburg, NY	OG
Hohenwald, TN	NSH
Hoisington, KS	DOD
Holbrook, AZ	GLP
MA	BO
NY	RVC
Holden, MO	KC
Holdingford, MN	SCL
Holdrege, NE	LIN
Holgate, OH	TOL
Holiday, FL	SP
Holland, MI	GR
NY	BUF
PA	PH
Holland Patent, NY	SY
Hollandale, WI	MAD
Holley, NY	BUF
Hollidaysburg, PA	ALT
Hollis, NY	BRK
NY	SYM
Hollis Hills, NY	BRK
Hollister, CA	MRY
Holliston, MA	BO
Holly, CO	PBL
MI	DET
Holly Springs, MS	JKS
Hollywood, CA	STN
FL	MIA
MD	WDC
Holmdel, NJ	TR
Holmen, WI	LC
Holstein, IA	SC
Holton, KS	KCK
Holts Summit, MO	JC
Holtville, CA	SD
Holy Cross, AK	FBK
IA	DUB
Holyoke, CO	DEN
MA	SPR
Homer, AK	ANC
NY	SY
Homer City, PA	PBR
Homer Glen, IL	JOL
IL	PRM
Homestead, FL	MIA
PA	PIT
Hometown, IL	CHI
Homewood, IL	CHI
IL	JOL
Homosassa, FL	SP
Hondo, TX	SAT
Honeoye, NY	ROC
Honeoye Falls, NY	ROC
Honesdale, PA	SCR
Honey Brook, PA	PH
Honokaa, HI	HON
Honolulu, HI	HON
HI	STN
Hood River, OR	BAK
Hooksett, NH	MAN
Hoopa, CA	SR
Hooper, NE	OM

Place	Code
Hooper Bay, AK	FBK
Hoopeston, IL	PEO
Hoosick Falls, NY	ALB
Hooversville, PA	ALT
Hopatcong, NJ	PAT
Hope, AR	LR
Hope Mills, NC	R
Hope Valley, RI	PRO
Hopedale, MA	WOR
OH	STU
Hopelawn, NJ	MET
Hopewell, NJ	TR
VA	RIC
Hopewell Junction, NY	NY
Hopkins, MN	STP
Hopkinsville, KY	OWN
Hopkinton, IA	DUB
MA	BO
Hoquiam, WA	SEA
Horace, ND	FAR
Horicon, WI	MIL
Horizon City, TX	ELP
Hornell, NY	ROC
Horse Branch, KY	OWN
Horseheads, NY	ROC
Horseshoe Bay, TX	AUS
Horseshoe Bend, AR	LR
Horsham, PA	PH
Horton, KS	KCK
Hortonville, WI	GB
Hoschton, GA	ATL
Hospers, IA	SC
Hot Springs, SD	RC
VA	RIC
Hot Springs National Park, AR	LR
Hot Springs Village, AR	LR
Houck, AZ	GLP
Houghton, IA	DAV
MI	MAR
Houlton, ME	PRT
Houma, LA	HT
Housatonic, MA	SPR
House Springs, MO	STL
Houston, MN	WIN
MO	SPC
TX	GAL
TX	OLL
TX	PBR
TX	STN
TX	MCE
Houtzdale, PA	E
Hoven, SD	SFS
Howard, SD	SFS
Howard Beach, NY	BRK
Howard City, MI	GR
Howardstown, KY	L
Howell, MI	LAN
NJ	TR
Howells, NE	OM
Howes, SD	RC
Howland, ME	PRT
Hoxie, KS	SAL
Hoyt Lakes, MN	DUL
Hubbard, OH	Y
Hubertus, WI	MIL
Hudson, FL	SP
MA	BO
MI	LAN
NH	MAN
NY	ALB
NY	STF
OH	CLV
WI	SUP
Hudson Falls, NY	ALB
Huffman, TX	GAL
Hughson, CA	STO
Hugo, MN	STP
OK	TLS
Hugoton, KS	DOD
Hulbert, OK	TLS
Hull, MA	BO
Humble, TX	GAL
Humboldt, IA	SC
SD	SFS
TN	MEM
Humphrey, NE	OM
Hungerford, TX	VIC
Hunlock Creek, PA	SCR
Hunt Valley, MD	BAL
Hunter, NY	STF
Huntersville, NC	CHL
Huntingburg, IN	EVN
Huntingdon, PA	ALT
Huntingdon Valley, PA	PH
PA	SYM
Huntington, IN	FTW
NY	RVC
WV	WH
Huntington Beach, CA	ORG
Huntington Park, CA	LA
Huntington Station, NY	RVC
Huntingtown, MD	WDC
Huntley, IL	RCK
Huntsville, AL	BIR
AR	LR
OH	CIN
TX	GAL
UT	SLC
Hurley, NM	LSC
NY	NY
WI	SUP
Huron, CA	FRS
OH	TOL
SD	SFS
Hurricane, WV	WH
Hurst, TX	FWT
Hurt, VA	RIC
Hurtsboro, AL	MOB
Huslia, AK	FBK
Hutchinson, KS	WCH
MN	NU
Hutto, TX	AUS
Huttonsville, WV	WH
Hyannis, MA	FR
Hyattsville, MD	WDC
Hyde Park, MA	BO
NY	NY
UT	SLC
Hydes, MD	BAL
Iberia, MO	JC
Ida, MI	DET
Ida Grove, IA	SC
Idabel, OK	TLS
Idaho Falls, ID	B
Idaho Springs, CO	DEN
Idalou, TX	LUB
Idyllwild, CA	SB
Ignacio, CO	PBL
Ijamsville, MD	BAL
Ilion, NY	ALB
Illiopolis, IL	SFD
Imlay City, MI	DET
Immaculata, PA	PH
Immokalee, FL	VEN
Imogene, IA	DM
Imperial, CA	SD
MO	STL
NE	LIN
PA	PIT
Inchelium, WA	SPK
Incline Village, NV	RNO
Independence, IA	DUB
KS	WCH
KY	COV
LA	BR
MO	KC
OH	CLV
OR	P
WI	LC
Indialantic, FL	ORL
Indian Creek, IL	CHI
Indian Head, MD	WDC
Indian Lake, NY	OG
Indian River, MI	GLD
Indian Rocks Beach, FL	SP
Indiana, PA	GBG
Indianapolis, IN	IND
IN	PRM
Indianola, IA	DM
MS	JKS
NE	LIN
Indiantown, FL	PMB
Indio, CA	SB
Inez, TX	VIC
Ingalls, KS	DOD
Ingleside, IL	CHI
TX	CC
Inglewood, CA	LA
Ingram, TX	SAT
Inkster, MI	DET
Interlachen, FL	STA
Interlaken, NY	ROC
International Falls, MN	DUL
Intervale, NH	MAN
Inver Grove Heights, MN	STP
Inverness, FL	SP
IL	CHI
Inwood, NY	RVC
WV	WH
Iola, KS	WCH
Ione, CA	SAC
WA	SPK
Ionia, MI	GR
Iota, LA	LAF
Iowa, LA	LKC
Iowa City, IA	DAV
Iowa Falls, IA	DUB
Iowa Park, TX	FWT
Ipswich, MA	BO
SD	SFS
Ira Township, MI	DET
Ireland, IN	EVN
Irene, SD	SFS
Iron Mountain, MI	MAR
Iron River, MI	MAR
WI	SUP
Irons, MI	GR
Ironton, MO	SPC
OH	STU
Ironwood, MI	MAR
Iroquois, SD	SFS
Irvine, CA	ORG
KY	LEX
Irving, TX	DAL
TX	PBR
Irvington, KY	OWN
NJ	NEW
NY	NY
Irvington–on–the–Hudson, NY	NY
Irwin, IL	JOL
PA	GBG
Irwindale, CA	LA
Isanti, MN	SCL
Iselin, NJ	MET
Ishpeming, MI	MAR
Island Park, NY	RVC
Island Pond, VT	BUR
Isle La Motte, VT	BUR
Isleta, NM	SFE
Isleton, CA	SAC
Islip, NY	RVC
Islip Terrace, NY	RVC
Issaquah, WA	SEA
Italy, TX	DAL
Itasca, IL	CHI
IL	JOL
Ithaca, MI	SAG
NY	ROC
Ivanhoe, MN	NU
Ivesdale, IL	PEO
Jabor, Jaluit, MI	MI
Jackman, ME	PRT
Jackson, CA	SAC
GA	ATL
KY	LEX
MI	LAN
MN	WIN
MO	SPC
MS	JKS
NE	OM
NJ	TR
OH	COL
TN	MEM
WY	CHY
Jackson Heights, NY	BRK
Jacksonville, AL	BIR
AR	LR
FL	OLD
FL	SAM
FL	STA
IL	SFD
NC	R
TX	TYL
Jacksonville Beach, FL	STA
Jaffrey, NH	MAN
Jal, NM	LSC
Jamaica, NY	NY
NY	BRK
Jamaica Estates, NY	BRK
Jamaica Plain, MA	BO
MA	OLD
MA	SAM
MA	STF
Jamesburg, NJ	MET
Jamestown, KY	L
ND	FAR
NY	BUF
OH	CIN
RI	PRO
TN	KNX
Jamison, PA	PH
Jamul, CA	SD
Janesville, MN	WIN
WI	MAD
Jarrell, TX	AUS
Jasper, AL	BIR
GA	ATL
IN	EVN
TX	BEA
Jay, ME	PRT
Jeanerette, LA	LAF
Jeannette, PA	GBG
PA	SJP
Jefferson, IA	SC
LA	NO
MA	WOR
NC	CHL
OH	Y
SD	SFS
TX	TYL
WI	MAD
Jefferson City, MO	JC
TN	KNX
Jefferson Hills, PA	PIT
Jeffersonville, IN	IND
NY	NY
Jemez Pueblo, NM	SFE
Jemez Springs, NM	SFE
Jena, LA	ALX
Jenison, MI	GR
Jenkins, KY	LEX
Jenkintown, PA	PH
PA	PHU
Jennings, LA	LKC
Jensen Beach, FL	PMB
Jermyn, PA	SCR
Jerome, ID	B
Jersey City, NJ	NEW
NJ	PSC
NJ	PHU
Jersey Shore, PA	SCR
Jerseyville, IL	SFD
Jessup, PA	PSC
PA	SCR
Jesup, GA	SAV
IA	DUB
Jetmore, KS	DOD
Jewett City, CT	NOR
Jim Falls, WI	LC
Jim Thorpe, PA	ALN
Joanna, SC	CHR
Jobstown, NJ	TR
Joelton, TN	NSH
Johannesburg, MI	GLD
John Day, OR	BAK
Johns Creek, GA	ATL
Johns Island, SC	CHR
Johnsburg, IL	RCK
Johnson City, NY	SY
NY	STF
TN	KNX
Johnson Creek, WI	MAD
Johnsonburg, PA	E
Johnston, IA	DM
RI	PRO
Johnston City, IL	BEL
Johnstown, CO	DEN
NY	ALB
OH	COL
PA	ALT
PA	SJP
PA	PBR
Joliet, IL	JOL
Jolon, CA	MRY
Jonesboro, AR	LR
GA	ATL
Jonesburg, MO	JC
Jonestown, MS	JKS
Jonesville, VA	RIC
Joplin, MO	SPC
Joppa, MD	BAL
Jordan, MN	STP
NY	SY
Jordan Valley, OR	BAK
Jourdanton, TX	SAT
Julesburg, CO	DEN
Julian, CA	SD
Junction, TX	SAN
Junction City, KS	SAL
OH	COL
OR	P
WI	LC
Juneau, AK	JUN
Jupiter, FL	PMB
Justice, IL	CHI
Kahoka, MO	JC
Kahuku, HI	HON
Kahului, HI	HON
Kailua, HI	HON
Kailua–Kona, HI	HON
Kalaheo, HI	HON
Kalamazoo, MI	KAL
Kalaupapa, HI	HON
Kalida, OH	TOL
Kalispell, MT	HEL
Kalkaska, MI	GLD
Kalona, IA	DAV
Kalskag, AK	FBK
Kaltag, AK	FBK
Kamiah, ID	B
Kamuela, HI	HON
Kanab, UT	SLC
Kandiyohi, MN	NU
Kane, PA	E
Kaneohe, HI	HON
Kankakee, IL	JOL
Kannapolis, NC	CHL
Kansas City, KS	KCK
MO	KC
Kansasville, WI	MIL
Kapaa, HI	HON
Kaplan, LA	LAF
Kapolei, HI	HON
Karnes City, TX	SAT

Place	Code
Kathleen, GA	SAV
Katonah, NY	NY
Katy, TX	GAL
Kaufman, TX	DAL
Kaukauna, WI	GB
Kaunakakai, HI	HON
Kawkawlin, MI	SAG
Kayenta, AZ	GLP
Keams Canyon, AZ	GLP
Keansburg, NJ	TR
Kearney, MO	KC
NE	GI
Kearneysville, WV	WH
Kearns, UT	SLC
Kearny, AZ	TUC
NJ	NEW
Keene, NH	MAN
NY	OG
Keeseville, NY	OG
Keizer, OR	P
Kekaha, HI	HON
Keller, TX	FWT
WA	SPK
Kelley's Island, OH	TOL
Kelliher, MN	CR
Kellnersville, WI	GB
Kellogg, ID	B
Kelly, KS	KCK
Kelso, MO	SPC
WA	SEA
Kemmerer, WY	CHY
Kenai, AK	ANC
Kenansville, NC	R
Kendall, WI	LC
Kendall Park, NJ	MET
Kendallville, IN	FTW
Kenedy, TX	SAT
Kenilworth, NJ	NEW
Kenmare, ND	BIS
Kenmore, NY	BUF
NY	STF
Kennebunk, ME	PRT
Kenner, LA	NO
Kennesaw, GA	ATL
Kennett, MO	SPC
Kennett Square, PA	PH
Kennewick, WA	YAK
Kenosha, WI	MIL
Kensington, CA	OAK
CT	HRT
MD	WDC
Kent, CT	HRT
MN	SCL
OH	Y
PA	GBG
WA	SEA
Kentfield, CA	SFR
Kentland, IN	LFT
Kenton, OH	COL
Kenyon, MN	STP
Keokuk, IA	DAV
Keota, IA	DAV
Kerens, TX	DAL
Kerhonkson, NY	STF
Kerman, CA	FRS
Kermit, TX	ELP
WV	WH
Kernersville, NC	CHL
Kerrville, TX	SAT
Kersey, PA	E
Keshena, WI	GB
Ketchikan, AK	JUN
Kettering, OH	CIN
Kewanee, IL	PEO
Kewaskum, WI	MIL
Kewaunee, WI	GB
Key Biscayne, FL	MIA
Key Largo, FL	MIA
Key West, FL	MIA
Keyport, NJ	TR
Keyser, WV	WH
Keystone Heights, FL	STA
Kickapoo (Edwards), IL	PEO
Kiel, WI	GB
Kieler, WI	MAD
Kihei, HI	HON
Kilgore, TX	TYL
Kilkenny, MN	STP
Killdeer, ND	BIS
Killeen, TX	AUS
Killingworth, CT	NOR
Kilmarnock, VA	ARL
Kiln, MS	BLX
Kimball, MN	SCL
NE	GI
SD	SFS
Kimberling City, MO	SPC
Kimberly, WI	GB
Kimberton, PA	PH
Kincaid, IL	SFD
Kinde, MI	SAG

Place	Code
Kinder, LA	LKC
Kindred, ND	FAR
King City, CA	MRY
King of Prussia, PA	PH
Kingfisher, OK	OKL
Kingman, AZ	PHX
KS	WCH
Kings Park, NY	RVC
Kingsburg, CA	FRS
Kingsford, MI	MAR
Kingsland, TX	AUS
Kingsley, MI	GLD
Kingsport, TN	KNX
Kingston, MA	BO
NY	NY
PA	PSC
PA	SCR
RI	PRO
Kingstree, SC	CHR
Kingsville, MD	BAL
OH	Y
TX	CC
Kingwood, TX	GAL
WV	WH
Kinnelon, NJ	PAT
Kinsley, KS	DOD
Kinston, NC	R
Kiowa, KS	DOD
Kirkland, WA	SEA
Kirksville, MO	JC
Kirkwood, MO	STL
NY	SY
Kirtland, OH	CLV
Kissimmee, FL	ORL
Kittanning, PA	GBG
Kittery, ME	PRT
Kitty Hawk, NC	R
Klamath Falls, OR	BAK
Klawock, AK	JUN
Knights Landing, CA	SAC
Knightstown, IN	IND
Knottsville, KY	OWN
Knox, IN	GRY
Knox City, TX	FWT
Knoxville, IA	DAV
TN	KNX
TN	PBR
Kodiak, AK	ANC
Kohler, WI	MIL
Kokomo, IN	LFT
Koloa, HI	HON
Konawa, OK	OKL
Kosciusko, MS	JKS
Kotlik, AK	FBK
Kotzebue, AK	FBK
Kountze, TX	BEA
Kouts, IN	GRY
Koyukuk, AK	FBK
Krakow, WI	GB
Kranzburg, SD	SFS
Krebs, OK	TLS
Kremmling, CO	DEN
Krotz Springs, LA	LAF
Kula, HI	HON
Kulpmont, PA	HBG
Kutztown, PA	ALN
Kyle, TX	AUS
L'Anse, MI	MAR
La Canada Flintridge, CA	LA
La Conner, WA	SEA
La Crescent, MN	WIN
La Crescenta, CA	LA
La Crosse, WI	LC
La Feria, TX	BWN
La Follette, TN	KNX
La Grande, OR	BAK
La Grange, IL	CHI
TX	AUS
TX	VIC
La Grange Park, IL	CHI
La Grulla, TX	BWN
La Habra, CA	ORG
La Jolla, CA	SD
La Joya, NM	SFE
TX	BWN
La Junta, CO	PBL
La Luz, NM	LSC
La Marque, TX	GAL
La Mesa, CA	SD
CA	STN
NM	LSC
La Mirada, CA	LA
La Moure, ND	FAR
La Pine, OR	BAK
La Place, LA	NO
La Plata, MD	WDC
La Porte, IN	GRY
TX	GAL
La Porte City, IA	DUB
La Pryor, TX	LAR
La Puente, CA	LA

Place	Code
La Quinta, CA	SB
La Salle, IL	PEO
La Valle, WI	MAD
La Verne, CA	LA
La Vernia, TX	SAT
La Vista, NE	OM
LaBelle, FL	VEN
LaCenter, KY	OWN
LaCoste, TX	SAT
LaCrosse, KS	DOD
LaGrange, GA	ATL
IN	FTW
KY	L
LaGrangeville, NY	NY
Labadieville, LA	BR
Lac du Flambeau, WI	SUP
Lacey, WA	SEA
Laceyville, PA	SCR
Lackawanna, NY	BUF
NY	STF
Lacombe, LA	NO
Lacon, IL	PEO
Lacona, IA	DM
Laconia, NH	MAN
Ladd, IL	PEO
Ladera Ranch, CA	ORG
Ladue, MO	STL
Lady Lake, FL	ORL
Ladysmith, VA	RIC
WI	SUP
Lafayette, CA	OAK
CO	DEN
IN	LFT
LA	LAF
MN	NU
NY	SY
OR	P
TN	NSH
Lafayette Hill, PA	PH
Lafferty, OH	STU
Lafitte, LA	NO
Laflin, PA	SCR
Lago Vista, TX	AUS
Lagrange, OH	CLV
Laguna, NM	GLP
Laguna Beach, CA	ORG
Laguna Heights, TX	BWN
Laguna Hills, CA	ROM
Laguna Niguel, CA	ORG
Laguna Woods, CA	ORG
Lagunitas, CA	SFR
Lahaina, HI	HON
Laingsburg, MI	LAN
Lake Andes, SD	SFS
Lake Ariel, PA	SCR
Lake Arrowhead, CA	SB
Lake Arthur, LA	LKC
Lake Benton, MN	SFS
Lake Charles, LA	LKC
Lake City, FL	STA
IA	SC
MI	GLD
MN	WIN
SC	CHR
Lake Clear, NY	OG
Lake Dallas, TX	FWT
Lake Elmo, MN	STP
Lake Forest, CA	ORG
IL	CHI
Lake Geneva, WI	MIL
Lake George, NY	ALB
Lake Harmony, PA	ALN
Lake Havasu City, AZ	PHX
Lake Hopatcong, NJ	PAT
Lake Jackson, TX	GAL
Lake Katrine, NY	NY
Lake Leelanau, MI	GLD
Lake Linden, MI	MAR
Lake Mills, WI	MAD
Lake Nebagamon, WI	SUP
Lake Odessa, MI	GR
Lake Orion, MI	DET
Lake Oswego, OR	P
Lake Ozark, MO	JC
Lake Park, MN	CR
Lake Placid, FL	VEN
NY	OG
Lake Providence, LA	SHP
Lake Ridge, VA	ARL
Lake Ronkonkoma, NY	RVC
Lake Saint Louis, MO	STL
Lake Station, IN	GRY
Lake Stevens, WA	SEA
Lake View, NY	BUF
Lake Villa, IL	CHI
Lake Village, AR	LR
IN	LFT
Lake Wales, FL	ORL
Lake Worth, FL	PMB
Lake Zurich, IL	CHI
Lakehurst, NJ	TR

Place	Code
Lakeland, FL	ORL
LA	BR
MN	STP
Lakemont, Altoona, PA	ALT
Lakeport, CA	SR
MI	DET
Lakeside, CA	SD
Lakeview, OR	BAK
Lakeville, CT	HRT
MA	BO
MN	STP
Lakeway, TX	AUS
Lakewood, CA	LA
CO	DEN
CO	OLL
NJ	TR
NY	BUF
OH	CLV
OH	PRM
WA	SEA
WI	GB
Lakewood Ranch, FL	VEN
Lakin, KS	DOD
Lakota, ND	FAR
Lamar, CO	PBL
MO	SPC
Lamberton, MN	NU
Lambertville, NJ	MET
Lame Deer, MT	GF
Lamesa, TX	LUB
Lamont, CA	FRS
Lamoure, ND	FAR
Lampasas, TX	AUS
Lanai City, HI	HON
Lanark Village, FL	PT
Lancaster, CA	LA
KY	LEX
MA	WOR
NH	MAN
NY	BUF
NY	STF
OH	COL
PA	HBG
SC	CHR
TX	DAL
WI	MAD
Lancing, TN	KNX
Land O'Lakes, FL	SP
WI	SUP
Lander, WY	CHY
Landisville, NJ	CAM
Landover Hills, MD	MCE
MD	WDC
Lanesville, IN	IND
Lanett, AL	BIR
Langdon, ND	FAR
Langhorne, PA	PH
Langley, OK	TLS
WA	SEA
Lanham, MD	WDC
Lansdale, PA	PH
Lansdowne, MD	BAL
PA	PH
Lanse, MI	MAR
Lansford, ND	FAR
PA	ALN
PA	PSC
Lansing, IA	DUB
IL	CHI
KS	KCK
MI	LAN
MI	NTN
NY	ROC
Lantana, FL	PMB
Laona, WI	GB
Lapeer, MI	DET
Laramie, WY	CHY
Larchmont, NY	NY
Larchwood, IA	SC
Laredo, TX	LAR
Largo, FL	SP
MD	WDC
Larimore, ND	FAR
Larkspur, CA	SFR
Larned, KS	DOD
Larose, LA	HT
Las Animas, CO	PBL
Las Cruces, NM	LSC
Las Vegas, NM	SFE
NV	HPM
NV	SYM
NV	LAV
NV	OLL
NV	SPA
Lastrup, MN	SCL
Latham, NY	ALB
Lathrop, CA	STO
Laton, CA	FRS
Latrobe, PA	GBG
PA	PBR
PA	SJP

Lauderdale–by–the–Sea, FL MIA
Laughlin, NV LAV
Laupahoehoe, HI HON
Laurel, MD BAL
MD WDC
MS BLX
MT GF
NE OM
Laurence Harbor, NJ MET
Laurie, MO JC
Laurinburg, NC R
Lavallette, NJ TR
Laveen, AZ PHX
Laverock, PA PH
Lawler, IA DUB
Lawrence, KS KCK
MA BO
MA NTN
MA SAM
NE LIN
Lawrenceburg, IN IND
KY LEX
TN NSH
Lawrenceville, GA ATL
IL BEL
NJ TR
Lawtell, LA LAF
Lawton, OK OKL
Layton, UT SLC
Le Center, MN STP
Le Mars, IA SC
Le Roy, NY BUF
Le Sueur, MN STP
LeClaire, IA DAV
Lead, SD RC
Leadville, CO COS
League City, TX GAL
Leavenworth, KS KCK
WA YAK
Leawood, KS KCK
Lebanon, CT NOR
IL BEL
IN LFT
KY L
MO SPC
NH MAN
OH CIN
OR P
PA HBG
TN NSH
VA RIC
Lebanon Junction, KY L
Lebeau, LA LAF
Lecanto, FL SP
Leckrone, PA GBG
Lecompte, LA ALX
Ledyard, IA SC
Lee, IL RCK
MA SPR
Lee Center, NY SY
Leechburg, PA GBG
Leeds, AL BIR
Lees Summit, MO KC
Leesburg, FL ORL
VA ARL
Leesville, LA ALX
Leetonia, OH Y
Lefor, ND BIS
Lehigh Acres, FL VEN
Lehighton, PA ALN
Leicester, MA WOR
Leigh, NE OM
Leipsic, OH TOL
Leisenring, PA PBR
Leisure City, FL MIA
Leitchfield, KY OWN
Leland, MS JKS
Lemay, MO STL
Lemhi, ID B
Lemmon, SD RC
Lemon Grove, CA SD
Lemont, IL CHI
Lemoore, CA FRS
Lena, IL RCK
Lenexa, KS KCK
Lenni, PA PH
Lennox, SD SFS
Lenoir, NC CHL
Lenoir City, TN KNX
Lenox, IA DM
MA SPR
Lenox Dale, MA SPR
Leominster, MA WOR
Leon, IA DM
Leonardtown, MD WDC
Leonia, NJ NEW
Leonville, LA LAF
Leopold, IN IND
MO SPC
Leslie, MI LAN
Levelland, TX LUB
Levittown, NY RVC
PA PH
PA PSC
Lewes, DE WIL
Lewis Run, PA E
Lewisburg, PA HBG
TN NSH
Lewisport, KY OWN
Lewiston, ID B
ME PRT
MI GLD
MN WIN
NY BUF
Lewistown, IL PEO
MT GF
PA HBG
Lewisville, TX FWT
TX OLL
Lexington, KY LEX
MA BO
MA OLN
MI SAG
MO KC
MS JKS
NC CHL
NE GI
OH TOL
SC CHR
TN MEM
VA RIC
Lexington Park, MD WDC
Libby, MT HEL
Liberal, KS DOD
Liberty, IL SFD
IN IND
KY L
MO KC
NY NY
TN NSH
TX BEA
Liberty Township, OH CIN
Libertytown, MD BAL
Libertyville, IL CHI
Lidderdale, IA SC
Lidgerwood, ND FAR
Liebenthal, KS DOD
Lighthouse Point, FL MIA
Ligonier, IN FTW
PA GBG
Liguori, MO STL
Lihue, HI HON
Lilburn, GA ATL
Lillian, AL MOB
Lilly, PA ALT
Lima, NY ROC
OH TOL
Lime Ridge, WI MAD
Limerick, ME PRT
PA PH
Limestone, NY BUF
Limon, CO COS
Lincoln, CA SAC
IL PEO
KS SAL
ME PRT
NE LIN
NH MAN
RI NTN
RI SAM
RI PRO
Lincoln City, OR P
Lincoln Park, MI DET
NJ PAT
Lincolnton, NC CHL
Lincroft, NJ TR
Lindale, TX TYL
Linden, CA STO
NJ NEW
NJ PSC
VA ARL
Lindenhurst, NY RVC
NY STF
Lindenwold, NJ CAM
Lindsay, CA FRS
NE OM
TX FWT
Lindsborg, KS WCH
Lindstrom, MN STP
Linesville, PA E
Linn, MO JC
Lino Lakes, MN STP
Linthicum Heights, MD BAL
Linton, IN EVN
ND BIS
Linwood, MA WOR
MI SAG
NJ CAM
PA PH
Lisbon, ND FAR
NY OG
OH Y
Lisbon Falls, ME PRT
Lisle, IL JOL
Lismore, MN WIN
Litchfield, CT HRT
IL SFD
MN NU
NH MAN
OH CLV
Lithia Springs, GA ATL
Lithonia, GA ATL
Lititz, PA HBG
Little Canada, MN STP
Little Chute, WI GB
Little Compton, RI PRO
Little Egg Harbor Twp, NJ TR
Little Falls, MN SCL
NJ OLN
NJ PAT
NY ALB
Little Ferry, NJ NEW
Little Hocking, OH STU
Little River, KS WCH
Little Rock, AR LR
Littlefield, TX LUB
Littlestown, PA HBG
Littleton, CO COS
CO DEN
MA BO
NH MAN
Live Oak, FL STA
Livermore, CA OAK
Liverpool, NY SY
Livingston, AL BIR
CA FRS
IL SFD
MT GF
NJ NEW
TX BEA
Livingston Manor, NY NY
Livonia, LA BR
MI DET
MI MCE
MI PRM
MI OLL
NY ROC
Llano, TX AUS
Lock Haven, PA ALT
Lockeford, CA STO
Lockhart, TX AUS
Lockport, IL JOL
LA HT
NY BUF
Locust Valley, NY STF
Lodge Grass, MT GF
Lodi, CA STO
NJ NEW
WI MAD
Logan, IA DM
KS SAL
OH COL
WV WH
Logansport, IN LFT
Loganville, GA SYM
Loma Linda, CA SB
Lombard, IL JOL
IL OLL
Lomira, WI MIL
Lomita, CA LA
Lompoc, CA LA
London, KY LEX
OH COL
Londonderry, NH MAN
Lone Pine, CA FRS
Lone Tree, IA DAV
Long Beach, CA LA
MS BLX
NY RVC
Long Branch, NJ TR
Long Grove, IA DAV
Long Island City, NY BRK
NY STF
NY ROM
Long Lake, MN STP
Long Prairie, MN SCL
Long Valley, NJ PAT
Longboat Key, FL VEN
Longbranch, WA SEA
Longmeadow, MA SPR
Longmont, CO DEN
Longview, TX TYL
WA SEA
Longville, MN DUL
Longwood, FL ORL
FL SYM
Lonsdale, MN STP
Loogootee, IN EVN
Lookout Mountain, GA ATL
Loomis, CA SAC
Loose Creek, MO JC
Lorain, OH CLV
OH SJP
OH PRM
Lords Valley, PA SCR
Lordsburg, NM LSC
Loreauville, LA LAF
Loretto, KY L
MN STP
PA ALT
TN NSH
Los Alamitos, CA ORG
Los Alamos, NM SFE
Los Altos, CA SJ
Los Altos Hills, CA SJ
Los Angeles, CA LA
CA OLL
CA OLN
Los Banos, CA FRS
Los Fresnos, TX BWN
Los Gatos, CA SJ
CA HPM
CA MRY
Los Lunas, NM SFE
Los Nietos, CA LA
Los Ojos, NM SFE
Los Osos, CA MRY
Lost Nation, IA DAV
Lott, TX AUS
Loudonville, NY ALB
OH CLV
Louisa, KY LEX
Louisburg, KS KCK
NC R
Louisiana, MO JC
Louisville, CO DEN
KY L
KY SYM
MS JKS
OH Y
Loup City, NE GI
Loveland, CO DEN
OH CIN
Lovell, WY CHY
Lovelock, NV RNO
Loves Park, IL RCK
Lovilia, IA DAV
Loving, NM LSC
Lovingston, VA RIC
Lovington, NM LSC
Lowell, IN GRY
MA BO
MI GR
OH STU
VT BUR
Lowellville, OH Y
Lower Brule, SD RC
SD SFS
Lower Burrell, PA GBG
Lowry, MN SCL
Lowville, NY OG
Loyal, WI LC
Lubbock, TX LUB
Lucan, MN NU
Lucerne Valley, CA SB
Lucinda, PA E
Ludington, MI GR
Ludlow, KY COV
MA SPR
MA STF
VT BUR
Luebbering, MO STL
Lufkin, TX TYL
Lukachukai, AZ GLP
Luling, LA NO
TX AUS
Lumberton, MS BLX
NC R
NM GLP
TX BEA
Lunenburg, MA WOR
Luray, VA ARL
Lusk, WY CHY
Lutherville, MD BAL
Lutz, FL SP
Luverne, MN WIN
Luxemburg, IA DUB
WI GB
Luzerne, PA SCR
Lydia, LA LAF
Lyford, TX BWN
Lykens, PA HBG
Lynbrook, NY RVC
Lynch, NE OM
Lynchburg, VA RIC
Lynden, WA SEA
Lyndhurst, NJ NEW
OH CLV
Lyndon Station, WI LC
Lyndora, PA PBR
PA SJP
Lynn, MA BO
Lynnfield, MA BO
Lynnwood, WA SEA

Place	Code
Lynwood, CA	LA
Lyon Mountain, NY	OG
Lyons, IL	CHI
KS	WCH
NE	OM
NY	ROC
WI	MIL
Lytle, TX	SAT
Mableton, GA	ATL
Mabton, WA	YAK
Macclenny, FL	STA
Macdona, TX	SAT
Machias, ME	PRT
Mackinac Island, MI	MAR
Mackinaw City, MI	GLD
Macomb, IL	PEO
MI	DET
Macon, GA	SAV
MO	JC
Madawaska, ME	PRT
Madeira Beach, FL	SP
Madelia, MN	WIN
Madera, CA	FRS
Madill, OK	OKL
Madison, AL	BIR
CT	HRT
FL	PT
IL	SFD
IL	STN
IN	IND
MN	NU
MS	JKS
NE	OM
NJ	PAT
OH	CLV
SD	SFS
TN	NSH
TN	SYM
VA	ARL
WI	MAD
WV	WH
Madison Heights, MI	DET
Madison Lake, MN	STP
MN	WIN
Madisonville, KY	OWN
LA	NO
TN	KNX
TX	TYL
Madras, OR	BAK
Madrid, IA	SC
NY	OG
Magee, MS	JKS
Maggie Valley, NC	CHL
Magna, UT	SLC
Magnolia, AR	LR
DE	WIL
TX	GAL
Magnolia Springs, AL	MOB
Mahanoy City, PA	ALN
PA	PSC
Mahnomen, MN	CR
Mahomet, IL	PEO
Mahopac, NY	NY
Mahtomedi, MN	STP
Mahwah, NJ	NEW
Maine, NY	SY
Makawao, HI	HON
Makoti, ND	BIS
Malakoff, TX	TYL
Malden, MA	BO
Malibu, CA	LA
Malone, NY	OG
Malta, MT	GF
Malvern, AR	LR
PA	PH
Malverne, NY	RVC
Mamaroneck, NY	NY
Mammoth, AZ	TUC
Mammoth Lakes, CA	STO
Mamou, LA	LAF
Man, WV	WH
Manahawkin, NJ	TR
Manalapan, NJ	TR
NJ	MCE
Manasquan, NJ	TR
Manassas, VA	ARL
VA	PHU
Manawa, WI	GB
Mancelona, MI	GLD
Manchaug, MA	WOR
Manchester, CT	HRT
IA	DUB
MD	BAL
MI	LAN
MO	STL
NH	MAN
NH	PRT
NH	STF
NH	NTN
TN	NSH
Manchester Center, VT	BUR
Manchester Township, NJ	TR
Manchester by the Sea, MA	BO
Mandan, ND	BIS
Mandaree, ND	BIS
Manderson, SD	RC
Mandeville, LA	NO
Mangum, OK	OKL
Manhasset, NY	RVC
Manhattan, IL	JOL
KS	SAL
Manhattan Beach, CA	LA
Manheim, PA	HBG
Manistee, MI	GLD
Manistique, MI	MAR
Manitou Beach, MI	LAN
Manitowish Waters, WI	SUP
Manitowoc, WI	GB
WI	MIL
Mankato, KS	SAL
MN	WIN
Manley, NE	LIN
Manlius, NY	SY
Manly, IA	DUB
Manning, IA	SC
Mannington, WV	WH
Manomet, MA	BO
Manor, TX	AUS
Manorville, NY	RVC
Mansfield, LA	SHP
MA	FR
OH	TOL
PA	SCR
TX	FWT
Manson, IA	SC
Mansura, LA	ALX
Mantador, ND	FAR
Manteca, CA	STO
Manteno, IL	JOL
Mantua, NJ	CAM
OH	Y
Manvel, ND	FAR
TX	GAL
Manville, NJ	MET
RI	PRO
Many, LA	SHP
Maple City, MI	GLD
Maple Glen, PA	PH
Maple Grove, MN	STP
Maple Heights, OH	CLV
Maple Hill, KS	KCK
Maple Lake, MN	STP
Maple Mount, KY	OWN
Maple Park, IL	RCK
Maple Shade, NJ	TR
Mapleton, IA	SC
MN	WIN
Mapleville, RI	PRO
Maplewood, MN	STP
MO	STL
NJ	NEW
WI	GB
Maquoketa, IA	DUB
Marana, AZ	TUC
Marathon, FL	MIA
NY	SY
WI	LC
Marathon City, WI	LC
Marble, MN	DUL
Marble Falls, TX	AUS
Marblehead, MA	BO
OH	PRM
OH	TOL
Marbury, AL	MOB
Marceline, MO	JC
Marcellus, NY	SY
Marco Island, FL	VEN
Marcus Hook, PA	PH
Marengo, IA	DAV
IL	RCK
Marfa, TX	ELP
Margaretville, NY	ALB
Margate, FL	MCE
FL	MIA
FL	SYM
NJ	CAM
Margate City, NJ	CAM
Maria Stein, OH	CIN
Mariah Hill, IN	EVN
Marianna, AR	LR
FL	PT
Maricopa, AZ	TUC
Marienthal, KS	DOD
Marietta, GA	ATL
NY	SY
OH	STU
Marina, CA	MRY
Marine, IL	SFD
Marine City, MI	DET
Marine on St. Croix, MN	STP
Marinette, WI	GB
Marion, IA	DUB
IL	BEL
IN	LFT
KS	WCH
KY	OWN
MA	FR
OH	COL
SD	SFS
VA	RIC
Marionville, MO	SPC
Mariposa, CA	FRS
Marked Tree, AR	LR
Markham, IL	CHI
Marksville, LA	ALX
Marlboro, NJ	TR
NY	NY
Marlborough, CT	HRT
MA	BO
Marlette, MI	SAG
Marlin, TX	AUS
Marlinton, WV	WH
Marlton, NJ	TR
Marmora, NJ	CAM
Marne, MI	GR
Marquette, MI	MAR
Marrero, LA	NO
Marriottsville, MD	BAL
Mars Hill, NC	CHL
Marseilles, IL	PEO
Marshall, AK	FBK
IL	SFD
MI	KAL
MN	NU
MO	JC
TX	TYL
Marshalltown, IA	DUB
Marshfield, MA	BO
MO	SPC
WI	LC
Marthasville, MO	STL
Martin, KY	LEX
OH	TOL
SD	RC
TN	MEM
Martindale, TX	AUS
Martinez, CA	OAK
Martins Creek, PA	ALN
Martins Ferry, OH	STU
Martinsburg, MO	JC
WV	WH
Martinsville, IN	IND
NJ	MET
VA	RIC
Marty, SD	SFS
Marvin, SD	SFS
Mary Esther, FL	PT
Marydel, MD	WIL
Maryknoll, NY	NY
Maryland Heights, MO	STL
Marylhurst, OR	P
Marysville, CA	SAC
KS	KCK
MI	DET
OH	COL
PA	HBG
WA	SEA
Maryville, IL	SFD
MO	KC
Masaryktown, FL	SP
Mascoutah, IL	BEL
Mashpee, MA	FR
Mason, MI	LAN
OH	CIN
Mason City, IA	DUB
Masontown, PA	GBG
Maspeth, NY	BRK
Massapequa, NY	RVC
Massapequa Park, NY	RVC
Massena, IA	DM
NY	OG
Massillon, OH	Y
OH	PBR
Mastic Beach, NY	RVC
Masury, OH	Y
Matamoras, PA	SCR
Matawan, NJ	TR
NJ	MET
NJ	PSC
Mathews, VA	RIC
Mathis, TX	CC
Mattapan, MA	BO
Mattapoisett, MA	FR
Mattawa, WA	YAK
Mattawan, MI	KAL
Matteson, IL	CHI
Matthews, NC	CHL
Mattoon, IL	SFD
Mauldin, SC	CHR
Maumee, OH	TOL
Maurepas, LA	BR
Maurice, LA	LAF
Mauriceville, TX	BEA
Mauston, WI	LC
Maximo, OH	Y
May's Lick, KY	COV
Maybee, MI	DET
Maybrook, NY	NY
Mayer, AZ	PHX
Mayetta, KS	KCK
Mayfield, KY	OWN
Maynard, MA	BO
OH	STU
Maynardville, TN	KNX
Mays Landing, NJ	CAM
Maysel, WV	WH
Maysville, KY	COV
Mayville, MI	SAG
ND	FAR
WI	MIL
Maywood, CA	LA
IL	CHI
IL	SYM
NJ	NEW
Mazomanie, WI	MAD
Mc Kean, PA	E
Mc Leansboro, IL	BEL
McAdoo, PA	ALN
PA	PSC
PA	PHU
McAfee, NJ	PAT
McAlester, OK	TLS
McAllen, TX	BWN
McCall, ID	B
McCamey, TX	SAN
McCloud, CA	SAC
McComb, MS	JKS
McConnellsburg, PA	ALT
McConnelsville, OH	STU
McCook, NE	LIN
McCormick, SC	CHR
McDonald, OH	Y
PA	PIT
McDonough, GA	ATL
McEwen, TN	NSH
McFarland, CA	FRS
WI	MAD
McGehee, AR	LR
McGrath, AK	FBK
McGregor, MN	DUL
TX	AUS
McHenry, IL	RCK
McKees Rocks, PA	PBR
PA	PIT
PA	SJP
McKeesport, PA	PBR
PA	PIT
PA	ROM
PA	SJP
McKenzie Bridge, OR	P
McKinleyville, CA	SR
McKinney, TX	DAL
McLaughlin, SD	RC
McLean, VA	ARL
VA	WDC
VA	NTN
McMechen, WV	WH
McMinnville, OR	P
TN	NSH
McMurray, PA	PIT
McNary, AZ	GLP
McPherson, KS	WCH
McRae, GA	SAV
McSherrystown, PA	HBG
Mead, CO	DEN
NE	LIN
Meade, KS	DOD
Meadow Lands, PA	PIT
Meadowbrook, PA	PH
Meadville, PA	E
Mecca, CA	SB
Mechanicsburg, OH	CIN
PA	HBG
Mechanicsville, IA	DAV
MD	WDC
VA	RIC
Mechanicville, NY	ALB
Medfield, MA	BO
Medford, MA	BO
MN	WIN
NJ	TR
NY	RVC
OK	OKL
OR	P
WI	SUP
Media, PA	PH
Medical Lake, WA	SPK
Medicine Lodge, KS	DOD
Medina, MN	STP
NY	BUF
OH	CLV
Medway, MA	BO
Meeker, CO	DEN
Megargel, TX	FWT

Place	Code
Meherrin, VA	RIC
Melbourne, FL	ORL
KY	COV
Melbourne Beach, FL	ORL
Melcher, IA	DAV
Mellen, WI	SUP
Mellette, SD	SFS
Melrose, IA	DAV
MA	BO
MN	SCL
WI	LC
Melrose Park, IL	CHI
PA	PHU
Melville, LA	LAF
NY	RVC
Melvindale, MI	DET
Memphis, MI	DET
MO	JC
TN	MEM
TX	AMA
Mena, AR	LR
Menahga, MN	SCL
Menands, NY	ALB
Menard, TX	SAN
Menasha, WI	GB
Mendham, NJ	PAT
Mendocino, CA	SR
Mendon, MI	KAL
NY	ROC
Mendota, CA	FRS
IL	PEO
MN	STP
Mendota Heights, MN	OLL
MN	STP
Menlo Park, CA	SJ
CA	SFR
Menoken, ND	BIS
Menominee, MI	MAR
Menomonee Falls, WI	MIL
Menomonie, WI	LC
Mentor, MN	CR
OH	CLV
Mentor–on–the–Lake, OH	PRM
Mequon, WI	MIL
Merced, CA	FRS
Mercedes, TX	BWN
Mercer, PA	E
WI	SUP
Mercer Island, WA	SEA
Merchantville, NJ	CAM
Meredith, NH	MAN
Meriden, CT	HRT
KS	KCK
Meridian, ID	B
MS	JKS
Merion Station, PA	PH
Mermentau, LA	LAF
Merrick, NY	RVC
Merrill, IA	SC
MI	SAG
OR	BAK
WI	SUP
Merrillville, IN	GRY
IN	PRM
Merrimac, MA	BO
Merrimack, NH	MAN
Merritt Island, FL	ORL
Mesa, AZ	PHX
ID	B
Mescalero, NM	LSC
Mesilla, NM	LSC
Mesilla Park, NM	LSC
Mesquite, NV	LAV
TX	DAL
Metairie, LA	NO
Metaline Falls, WA	SPK
Metamora, IL	PEO
Methuen, MA	BO
MA	NTN
Metropolis, IL	BEL
Metuchen, NJ	MET
Mexia, TX	AUS
Mexico, MO	JC
NY	SY
Meyersdale, PA	ALT
Meyersville, TX	VIC
Miami, AZ	TUC
FL	ARL
FL	SJP
FL	SAM
FL	MIA
FL	NTN
FL	PSC
OK	TLS
Miami Beach, FL	MIA
Miami Gardens, FL	MIA
Miami Lakes, FL	MIA
Miami Shores, FL	MIA
Miami Springs, FL	MIA
Miamisburg, OH	CIN
Michigan Center, MI	LAN

Place	Code
Michigan City, IN	GRY
Middle Village, NY	BRK
Middleborough, MA	BO
Middlebourne, WV	WH
Middleburg, FL	STA
VA	ARL
Middleburg Heights, OH	CLV
Middleburgh, NY	ALB
Middlebury, CT	HRT
VT	BUR
Middlefield, CT	NOR
Middlesboro, KY	LEX
Middlesex, NJ	MET
Middleton, MA	BO
WI	MAD
Middletown, CA	SR
CT	NOR
DE	WIL
MD	BAL
NJ	TR
NY	NY
NY	STF
OH	CIN
PA	HBG
RI	PRO
Middletown Springs, VT	BUR
Midland, MD	BAL
MI	SAG
PA	PIT
TX	SAN
Midland City, AL	MOB
Midland Park, NJ	NEW
Midlothian, IL	CHI
VA	RIC
Midvale, UT	SLC
Midway City, CA	ORG
Midwest City, OK	OKL
Miesville, MN	STP
Mifflintown, PA	HBG
Milaca, MN	SCL
Milan, IL	PEO
MI	LAN
MO	JC
NM	GLP
OH	TOL
Milbank, SD	SFS
Miles, TX	SAN
Miles City, MT	GF
Milford, CT	HRT
DE	WIL
IA	SC
MA	WOR
MI	DET
NH	MAN
NJ	MET
OH	CIN
PA	SCR
UT	SLC
Mililani, HI	HON
Mililani Town, HI	HON
Mill Creek, WA	SEA
Mill Valley, CA	SFR
Milladore, WI	LC
Millbrae, CA	OLL
CA	SFR
Millbrook, NY	NY
Millbury, MA	WOR
Milledgeville, GA	ATL
Millen, GA	SAV
Miller, SD	SFS
Miller City, OH	TOL
Millersburg, OH	COL
PA	HBG
Millersville, MD	BAL
Millington, TN	MEM
Millis, MA	BO
Millstadt, IL	BEL
Millstone Township, NJ	TR
Milltown, NJ	MET
Millville, MA	WOR
NJ	CAM
NJ	PHU
Milmont Park, PA	PH
Milnor, ND	FAR
Milpitas, CA	SJ
CA	SYM
Milroy, MN	NU
Milton, FL	PT
LA	LAF
MA	BO
NY	NY
PA	HBG
VT	BUR
WI	MAD
Milton Freewater, OR	BAK
Milwaukee, WI	MIL
WI	NTN
WI	STN
Milwaukie, OR	P
Mims, FL	ORL
Minden, LA	SHP

Place	Code
NE	LIN
Mineola, NY	RVC
TX	TYL
Mineral, VA	RIC
Mineral Point, WI	MAD
Mineral Ridge, OH	Y
Mineral Wells, TX	FWT
Minersville, PA	ALN
PA	PSC
PA	PHU
Minerva, OH	STU
Minetto, NY	SY
Mingo Junction, OH	PBR
OH	STU
Minneapolis, KS	SAL
MN	OLL
MN	STP
MN	STN
MN	PRM
Minneota, MN	NU
Minnetonka, MN	STP
Minong, WI	SUP
Minonk, IL	PEO
Minooka, IL	JOL
Minot, ND	BIS
Minster, OH	CIN
Minto, ND	FAR
Minturn, CO	DEN
Mio, MI	GLD
Miramar, FL	MIA
Miramar Beach, FL	PT
Mishawaka, IN	FTW
IN	STN
Mishicot, WI	GB
Misquamicut, RI	PRO
Mission, KS	KCK
SD	RC
TX	BWN
Mission Hill, SD	SFS
Mission Hills, CA	LA
Mission Viejo, CA	ORG
Missoula, MT	HEL
Missouri City, TX	GAL
TX	SYM
Missouri Valley, IA	DM
Mitchell, IN	IND
NE	GI
SD	SFS
Mitchellville, MD	WDC
Moab, UT	SLC
Moberly, MO	JC
Mobile, AL	MOB
Mobridge, SD	SFS
Mocanaqua, PA	SCR
Mocksville, NC	CHL
Modesto, CA	STO
Modoc, IL	BEL
Mogadore, OH	Y
Mohall, ND	BIS
Mohawk, NY	ALB
Mohnton, PA	ALN
Mokane, MO	JC
Mokena, IL	JOL
Molalla, OR	P
Moline, IL	PEO
KS	WCH
Momence, IL	JOL
Monaca, PA	PIT
Monahans, TX	ELP
Moncks Corner, SC	CHR
Mondovi, WI	LC
Monee, IL	JOL
Monessen, PA	GBG
PA	PBR
Moneta, VA	RIC
Monett, MO	SPC
Monkton, MD	BAL
Monmouth, IL	PEO
OR	P
Monmouth Beach, NJ	TR
Monmouth Junction, NJ	MET
Monona, IA	DUB
WI	MAD
Monongah, WV	WH
Monongahela, PA	PIT
Monponsett, MA	BO
Monroe, CT	BGP
GA	ATL
LA	SHP
MI	DET
NC	CHL
NY	NY
OH	CIN
WA	SEA
WI	MAD
Monroe City, MO	JC
Monroe Township, NJ	MET
Monroeville, AL	MOB
IN	FTW
OH	TOL
PA	PBR

Place	Code
PA	PIT
Monrovia, CA	LA
Monsey, NY	NY
Monson, MA	SPR
Mont Belvieu, TX	BEA
Mont Clare, PA	PSC
Montague, MI	GR
NJ	PAT
Montauk, NY	RVC
Montclair, CA	SB
NJ	NEW
Monte Vista, CO	PBL
Montebello, CA	LA
Montegut, LA	HT
Montello, WI	MAD
Monterey, CA	MRY
IN	LFT
Monterey Park, CA	LA
Montevallo, AL	BIR
Montevideo, MN	NU
Montezuma, OH	CIN
Montfort, WI	MAD
Montgomery, AL	MOB
IN	EVN
MN	STP
NY	NY
WV	WH
Montgomery City, MO	JC
Monticello, AR	LR
IA	DUB
IL	PEO
IN	LFT
KY	LEX
MN	STP
NY	NY
UT	SLC
Montoursville, PA	SCR
Montpelier, OH	TOL
VA	RIC
VT	BUR
Montrose, CA	LA
CA	OLN
CO	PBL
IL	SFD
MI	LAN
MO	KC
NY	NY
PA	SCR
SD	SFS
Montvale, NJ	NEW
Montville, NJ	PAT
Monument, CO	COS
Moodus, CT	NOR
Mooers, NY	OG
Mooers Forks, NY	OG
Moon Township, PA	PIT
Moore, OK	OKL
Moore Haven, FL	VEN
Moorefield, WV	WH
Moorestown, NJ	TR
Mooresville, IN	IND
NC	CHL
Mooreton, ND	FAR
Moorhead, MN	CR
Moorpark, CA	LA
Moose Lake, MN	DUL
Moosup, CT	NOR
Mora, MN	SCL
NM	SFE
Moraga, CA	OAK
Moreauville, LA	ALX
Morehead, KY	LEX
Morehead City, NC	R
Morenci, AZ	TUC
Moreno Valley, CA	SB
Morgan, MN	NU
Morgan City, LA	HT
LA	LAF
Morgan Hill, CA	SJ
Morganfield, KY	OWN
Morganton, NC	CHL
Morgantown, KY	OWN
WV	WH
WV	PBR
WV	SYM
Morganza, LA	BR
MD	WDC
Moriarty, NM	SFE
Morning View, KY	COV
Morrice, MI	LAN
Morrilton, AR	LR
Morris, IL	JOL
IN	IND
MN	SCL
NY	ALB
Morris Plains, NJ	PAT
Morrisdale, PA	E
Morrison, IL	RCK
Morrisonville, IL	SFD
NY	OG
Morristown, NJ	PAT

Place	Code
NY	OG
TN	KNX
Morrisville, NY	SY
PA	PH
VT	BUR
Morro Bay, CA	MRY
Morrow, LA	LAF
OH	CIN
Morse, LA	LAF
Morse Bluff, NE	LIN
Morton, IL	PEO
MN	NU
PA	PH
TX	LUB
WA	SEA
Morton Grove, IL	CHI
IL	SYM
IL	MCE
Moscow, ID	B
PA	SCR
TN	MEM
Moses Lake, WA	YAK
Mosinee, WI	LC
Moss Beach, CA	SFR
Moss Bluff, LA	LKC
Moss Point, MS	BLX
Mott, ND	BIS
Moulton, AL	BIR
TX	VIC
Moultrie, GA	SAV
Mound, MN	STP
Mound Bayou, MS	JKS
Mound City, IL	BEL
Moundsville, WV	WH
Mount Airy, MD	BAL
Mount Angel, OR	P
Mount Arlington, NJ	PAT
Mount Calvary, WI	MIL
Mount Carmel, IL	BEL
PA	HBG
PA	PHU
Mount Carroll, IL	RCK
Mount Clemens, MI	DET
Mount Dora, FL	ORL
Mount Ephraim, NJ	CAM
Mount Holly, NJ	TR
Mount Hope, KS	WCH
Mount Horeb, WI	MAD
Mount Ida, AR	LR
Mount Jewett, PA	E
Mount Joy, PA	HBG
Mount Laurel, NJ	TR
Mount Morris, MI	LAN
Mount Olive, IL	SFD
NC	R
Mount Pleasant, IA	DAV
MI	SAG
PA	GBG
SC	CHR
TX	TYL
Mount Pocono, PA	SCR
Mount Rainier, MD	WDC
Mount Shasta, CA	SAC
Mount St. Francis, IN	IND
Mount St. Joseph, OH	CIN
Mount Sterling, IL	SFD
KY	LEX
Mount Union, PA	ALT
Mount Vernon, AL	MOB
IA	DUB
IL	BEL
IN	EVN
KY	LEX
MO	SPC
NY	NY
TX	TYL
WA	SEA
Mount Victoria, MD	WDC
Mount Washington, KY	L
Mountain City, TN	KNX
Mountain Grove, MO	SPC
Mountain Home, AR	LR
ID	B
TX	SAT
Mountain Home A F B, ID	B
Mountain Lakes, NJ	PAT
Mountain Top, PA	SCR
Mountain View, AR	LR
CA	SJ
HI	HON
MO	SPC
Mountain Village, AK	FBK
Mountainair, NM	SFE
Mountainside, NJ	NEW
Mountlake Terrace, WA	SEA
Moville, IA	SC
Moweaqua, IL	SFD
Moxee, WA	YAK
Mt Zion, IL	SFD
Mt. Airy, NC	CHL
Mt. Kisco, NY	NY
Mt. Lebanon, PA	PIT
Mt. Prospect, IL	CHI
Mt. Vernon, OH	COL
Mt. Zion, IL	SFD
Muenster, TX	FWT
Mukwonago, WI	MIL
Muleshoe, TX	LUB
Mullen, NE	GI
Mullens, WV	WH
Mullica Hill, NJ	CAM
Mulvane, KS	WCH
Muncie, IN	LFT
Muncy, PA	SCR
Munday, TX	FWT
Mundelein, IL	CHI
Munger, MI	SAG
Munhall, PA	PBR
PA	PIT
Munich, ND	FAR
Munising, MI	MAR
Munjor, KS	SAL
Munnsville, NY	SY
Munster, IN	GRY
IN	STN
IN	PRM
Murdock, MN	NU
Murfreesboro, TN	NSH
Murphy, NC	CHL
Murphysboro, IL	BEL
Murray, KY	OWN
UT	OLL
UT	SLC
Murrieta, CA	SB
Murrysville, PA	GBG
Muscatine, IA	DAV
Muscoda, WI	MAD
Muse, PA	PIT
Muskego, WI	MIL
Muskegon, MI	GR
Muskegon Heights, MI	GR
Muskogee, OK	TLS
Mustang, OK	OKL
Myerstown, PA	HBG
Myrtle Beach, SC	CHR
Myrtle Creek, OR	P
Mystic, CT	NOR
Naalehu, HI	HON
Naches, WA	YAK
Nacogdoches, TX	TYL
Nada, TX	VIC
Nadeau, MI	MAR
Nahant, MA	BO
Nampa, ID	B
Nanakuli, HI	HON
Nanticoke, PA	PHU
PA	SCR
Nantucket, MA	FR
Nanty–Glo, PA	ALT
PA	PBR
Nanuet, NY	NY
Napa, CA	SR
Naperville, IL	JOL
Naples, FL	VEN
Napoleon, IN	IND
ND	FAR
OH	TOL
Napoleonville, LA	BR
Naranja, FL	MIA
Narberth, PA	PH
Narragansett, RI	PRO
Narrowsburg, NY	NY
Nashotah, WI	MIL
Nashua, IA	DUB
NH	MAN
Nashville, AR	LR
IL	BEL
IN	IND
KS	WCH
TN	NSH
Nashwauk, MN	DUL
Nassau, NY	ALB
Nassau Bay, TX	GAL
Natchez, LA	ALX
MS	JKS
Natchitoches, LA	ALX
Natick, MA	BO
National City, CA	SD
Natrona Heights, PA	PIT
Naugatuck, CT	HRT
Nauvoo, IL	PEO
Navajo, NM	GLP
Navarre, FL	PT
OH	Y
Navasota, TX	GAL
Nazareth, KY	L
MI	KAL
PA	ALN
TX	AMA
Nebraska City, NE	LIN
Necedah, WI	LC
Nederland, TX	BEA
Needham, MA	BO
Needles, CA	SB
Needville, TX	GAL
Neenah, WI	GB
Neffs, OH	STU
Negaunee, MI	MAR
Neillsville, WI	LC
Nekoosa, WI	LC
Neligh, NE	OM
Nelsonville, OH	STU
Nenana, AK	FBK
Neodesha, KS	WCH
Neola, IA	DM
Neopit, WI	GB
Neosho, MO	SPC
WI	MIL
Neptune, NJ	TR
Nerinx, KY	L
Nesbit, MS	JKS
Nesconset, NY	RVC
Nespelem, WA	SPK
Nesquehoning, PA	ALN
PA	PSC
Ness City, KS	DOD
Netcong, NJ	PAT
Nevada, MO	KC
Nevada City, CA	SAC
Nevis, MN	CR
New Albany, IN	IND
MS	JKS
OH	COL
New Alexandria, PA	GBG
New Almelo, KS	SAL
New Athens, IL	BEL
New Baden, IL	BEL
New Baltimore, MI	DET
MI	MCE
PA	ALT
New Bavaria, OH	TOL
New Bedford, MA	FR
MA	SAM
New Berlin, IL	SFD
NY	SY
WI	MIL
New Bern, NC	R
New Bethlehem, PA	E
New Blaine, AR	LR
New Bloomfield, PA	HBG
New Boston, MI	DET
OH	COL
TX	TYL
New Braunfels, TX	SAT
New Bremen, OH	CIN
New Brighton, MN	STP
PA	PIT
New Britain, CT	HRT
CT	PSC
CT	STF
New Brunswick, NJ	MET
NJ	PSC
NJ	PHU
New Buffalo, MI	KAL
New Cambria, MO	JC
New Canaan, CT	BGP
New Caney, TX	GAL
New Carlisle, IN	FTW
OH	CIN
New Castle, DE	WIL
IN	IND
PA	PIT
PA	SAM
VA	RIC
New City, NY	NY
New Cumberland, PA	HBG
WV	WH
New Cuyama, CA	LA
New Derry, PA	GBG
New Egypt, NJ	TR
New England, ND	BIS
New Fairfield, CT	BGP
New Franken, WI	GB
New Freedom, PA	HBG
New Hampton, IA	DUB
New Harmony, IN	EVN
New Hartford, CT	HRT
NY	SY
New Haven, CT	HRT
CT	STF
IN	FTW
KY	L
MO	STL
New Hill, NC	R
New Holland, PA	HBG
New Holstein, WI	GB
WI	MIL
New Hope, KY	L
MN	STP
PA	PH
New Hyde Park, NY	MCE
NY	RVC
New Iberia, LA	LAF
New Ipswich, NH	MAN
New Kensington, PA	GBG
New Lebanon, NY	ALB
New Lenox, IL	JOL
New Lexington, OH	COL
New Lisbon, WI	LC
New London, CT	NOR
MN	NU
NH	MAN
OH	TOL
WI	GB
New Lothrop, MI	SAG
New Madrid, MO	SPC
New Market, MN	STP
New Martinsville, WV	WH
New Melle, MO	STL
New Middletown, OH	Y
New Milford, CT	HRT
NJ	NEW
New Monmouth, NJ	TR
New Munich, MN	SCL
New Munster, WI	MIL
New Orleans, LA	NO
LA	PBR
New Oxford, PA	HBG
New Paltz, NY	NY
New Philadelphia, OH	COL
PA	ALN
New Port Richey, FL	SP
FL	PSC
New Prague, MN	STP
New Providence, NJ	NEW
New Richland, MN	WIN
New Richmond, OH	CIN
WI	SUP
New Riegel, OH	TOL
New Ringgold, PA	ALN
New River, AZ	PHX
New Roads, LA	BR
New Rochelle, NY	NY
NY	MCE
New Rockford, ND	FAR
New Salem, ND	BIS
PA	GBG
PA	PBR
New Smyrna Beach, FL	ORL
New Trier, MN	STP
New Ulm, MN	NU
TX	VIC
New Vernon, NJ	PAT
New Vienna, IA	DUB
New Washington, OH	TOL
New Waverly, TX	GAL
New Windsor, NY	NY
New York, NY	NY
NY	PSC
NY	STF
New York Mills, NY	SY
Newark, CA	OAK
DE	WIL
NJ	NEW
NJ	PHU
NJ	PSC
NY	ROC
OH	COL
Newaygo, MI	GR
Newberg, OR	P
Newberry, MI	MAR
SC	CHR
Newburg, MD	WDC
WI	MIL
Newburgh, IN	EVN
NY	NY
Newbury, OH	CLV
Newbury Park, CA	LA
Newburyport, MA	BO
Newcastle, WY	CHY
Newcomb, NY	OG
Newcomerstown, OH	COL
Newfane, NY	BUF
Newfield, NJ	CAM
Newington, CT	HRT
Newman, CA	STO
Newmarket, NH	MAN
Newnan, GA	ATL
Newport, KY	COV
MI	DET
NH	MAN
NY	ALB
OR	P
RI	PRO
TN	KNX
VT	BUR
WA	SPK
Newport Beach, CA	ORG
Newport News, VA	RIC
Newry, PA	ALT
Newtok, AK	FBK
Newton, IA	DAV
IL	BEL
IL	SFD

Place	Code
KS	WCH
MA	BO
NC	CHL
NJ	PAT
WI	GB
Newton Falls, OH	Y
OH	PBR
Newton Grove, NC	R
Newtown, CT	BGP
PA	PH
Newtown Square, PA	PH
PA	SAM
Nez Perce, ID	B
Niagara, WI	GB
Niagara Falls, NY	BUF
NY	STF
Niagara University, NY	BUF
Niantic, CT	NOR
Niceville, FL	PT
Nicholasville, KY	LEX
Nichols, IA	DAV
Nicholson, PA	SCR
Nicktown, PA	ALT
Nicollet, MN	NU
Nightmute, AK	FBK
Niles, IL	CHI
MI	KAL
OH	Y
Nine Mile Falls, WA	SPK
Nipomo, CA	MRY
Nisswa, MN	DUL
Nitro, WV	WH
Nixa, MO	SPC
Nixon, TX	SAT
Noblesville, IN	LFT
Nogales, AZ	TUC
Nokomis, FL	VEN
IL	SFD
Nome, AK	FBK
Norco, CA	SB
LA	NO
Norcross, GA	ATL
GA	SYM
Norfolk, MA	BO
NE	OM
NY	OG
VA	RIC
Norge, VA	RIC
Normal, IL	PEO
Norman, OK	OKL
Normandy, MO	STL
Norridge, IL	CHI
Norris, TN	KNX
Norristown, PA	PH
North Adams, MA	SPR
North Andover, MA	BO
North Arlington, NJ	NEW
North Attleboro, MA	FR
North Augusta, SC	CHR
North Aurora, IL	RCK
North Baltimore, OH	TOL
North Bay, NY	SY
North Beach, MD	WDC
North Bend, NE	OM
OH	CIN
OR	P
North Bennington, VT	BUR
North Bergen, NJ	NEW
North Bethesda, MD	WDC
North Branch, MI	DET
MN	STP
North Branford, CT	HRT
North Brookfield, MA	WOR
North Brunswick, NJ	MET
North Caldwell, NJ	NEW
North Canton, OH	Y
North Cape May, NJ	CAM
North Charleston, SC	CHR
North Chili, NY	ROC
North Collins, NY	BUF
North Conway, NH	MAN
North Creek, NY	ALB
North Dartmouth, MA	FR
North Dighton, MA	FR
North East, PA	E
North Easton, MA	FR
North English, IA	DAV
North Falmouth, MA	FR
North Fond du Lac, WI	MIL
North Fort Myers, FL	VEN
North Grafton, MA	WOR
North Grosvenordale, CT	NOR
North Guilford, CT	HRT
North Haledon, NJ	PAT
North Haven, CT	HRT
North Highlands, CA	SAC
North Hills, CA	LA
North Hollywood, CA	LA
CA	OLD
CA	SPA
CA	NTN

Place	Code
North Huntingdon, PA	GBG
PA	PBR
North Jackson, OH	Y
OH	OLL
North Judson, IN	GRY
North Kingstown, RI	PRO
North Lake, WI	MIL
North Las Vegas, NV	LAV
North Lauderdale, FL	MIA
North Lima, OH	Y
North Little Rock, AR	LR
North Manchester, IN	FTW
North Mankato, MN	NU
North Merrick, NY	RVC
North Miami, FL	MIA
North Miami Beach, FL	MIA
North Muskegon, MI	GR
North Myrtle Beach, SC	CHR
North Olmsted, OH	CLV
North Oxford, MA	WOR
North Palm Beach, FL	PMB
North Plainfield, NJ	MET
North Plains, OR	P
North Platte, NE	GI
NE	LIN
North Pole, AK	FBK
North Port, FL	SJP
FL	VEN
North Providence, RI	PRO
North Reading, MA	BO
North Ridgeville, OH	CLV
North Riverside, IL	CHI
North Royalton, OH	CLV
OH	PRM
North Saint Paul, MN	STP
North Scituate, RI	PRO
North Smithfield, RI	PRO
North Stonington, CT	NOR
North Syracuse, NY	SY
North Tonawanda, NY	BUF
North Vernon, IN	IND
North Wales, PA	PH
North Wildwood, NJ	CAM
North Wilkesboro, NC	CHL
Northampton, MA	SPR
PA	ALN
PA	PHU
Northboro, MA	WOR
Northbridge, MA	WOR
Northbrook, IL	CHI
IL	OLD
Northern Cambria, PA	ALT
PA	PBR
PA	SJP
Northfield, IL	CHI
MA	SPR
MN	STP
NJ	CAM
OH	CLV
VT	BUR
Northford, CT	HRT
Northglenn, CO	DEN
Northlake, IL	CHI
IL	NTN
Northport, NY	RVC
WA	SPK
Northridge, CA	LA
Northvale, NJ	NEW
Northville, MI	DET
NY	ALB
Northwood, OH	PRM
Norton, KS	SAL
MA	FR
OH	CLV
VA	RIC
Nortonville, KS	KCK
Norwalk, CA	LA
CT	BGP
IA	DM
OH	TOL
Norway, ME	PRT
MI	MAR
Norwell, MA	BO
Norwich, CT	NOR
NY	SY
Norwichtown, CT	NOR
Norwood, MA	BO
MN	STP
NJ	NEW
NY	OG
PA	PH
Notre Dame, IN	FTW
Novato, CA	SFR
Novi, MI	DET
Nulato, AK	FBK
Nutley, NJ	NEW
Nyack, NY	NY
Nyssa, OR	BAK
O Fallon, IL	BEL
O'Donnell, TX	LUB
O'Fallon, MO	STL

Place	Code
O'Neill, NE	OM
Oak Brook, IL	JOL
Oak Creek, WI	MIL
Oak Forest, IL	CHI
Oak Grove, KY	OWN
LA	SHP
MN	STP
Oak Harbor, OH	TOL
WA	SEA
Oak Hill, WV	WH
Oak Lawn, IL	CHI
Oak Park, IL	CHI
MI	DET
MI	EST
Oak Park Heights, MN	STP
Oak Ridge, NJ	PAT
TN	KNX
Oak Ridge–Milton, NJ	PAT
Oakbrook Terrace, IL	JOL
IL	OLL
Oakdale, CA	STO
CT	NOR
IL	BEL
LA	LKC
MN	STP
NE	OM
NY	RVC
PA	PIT
Oakes, ND	FAR
Oakfield, NY	BUF
Oakhurst, CA	FRS
Oakland, CA	OAK
MD	BAL
NJ	NEW
Oakland City, IN	EVN
Oakland Gardens, NY	BRK
Oakland Park, FL	MIA
Oakley, CA	OAK
KS	SAL
MI	SAG
Oaklyn, NJ	CAM
Oakmont, PA	PIT
Oakville, CA	SR
CT	HRT
MO	STL
Oberlin, KS	SAL
LA	LKC
OH	CLV
Obernburg, NY	NY
Ocala, FL	ORL
Occidental, CA	SR
Ocean Beach, NY	RVC
Ocean City, MD	WIL
NJ	CAM
Ocean Grove, NJ	TR
Ocean Springs, MS	BLX
Oceanside, CA	SD
NY	RVC
Oconee, IL	SFD
Oconomowoc, WI	MIL
Oconto, WI	GB
Oconto Falls, WI	GB
Odebolt, IA	SC
Odell, IL	PEO
Odem, TX	CC
Odenton, MD	BAL
Odessa, MO	KC
TX	SAN
Oelwein, IA	DUB
Ogallala, NE	GI
Ogden, IA	SC
UT	SLC
Ogdensburg, NJ	PAT
NY	OG
Ogema, MN	CR
Oglala, SD	RC
Oglesby, IL	PEO
Ohio, IL	PEO
Ohkay Owingeh, NM	SFE
Oil City, PA	E
Ojai, CA	LA
Okanogan, WA	SPK
Okarche, OK	OKL
Okawville, IL	BEL
Okeechobee, FL	PMB
Okeene, OK	OKL
Okemos, MI	LAN
Oklahoma City, OK	OKL
OK	SYM
Oklee, MN	CR
Okmulgee, OK	TLS
Olathe, KS	KCK
Old Bridge, NJ	MET
Old Fields, WV	WH
Old Forge, NY	OG
PA	PSC
PA	SCR
Old Hickory, TN	NSH
Old Lyme, CT	NOR
Old Mill Creek, IL	CHI
Old Monroe, MO	STL

Place	Code
Old Orchard Beach, ME	PRT
Old Saybrook, CT	NOR
Old Tappan, NJ	NEW
Old Town, ME	PRT
Old Westbury, NY	RVC
Oldenburg, IN	IND
Oldsmar, FL	SP
Olean, NY	BUF
NY	PSC
NY	SAM
Olema, CA	SFR
Olive Branch, MS	JKS
Olive Hill, KY	LEX
Olivia, MN	NU
Olmito, TX	BWN
Olmitz, KS	DOD
Olmsted Falls, OH	CLV
Olney, IL	BEL
MD	WDC
Olpe, KS	KCK
Olton, TX	LUB
Olympia, WA	HPM
WA	ROM
WA	SEA
Olympia Fields, IL	CHI
Olyphant, PA	PHU
PA	SCR
Omaha, NE	OM
NE	STN
Omak, WA	SPK
Omer, MI	PRM
Omro, WI	GB
Ona, WV	WH
Onaga, KS	KCK
Onalaska, WI	LC
Onamia, MN	SCL
Onawa, IA	SC
Onaway, MI	GLD
Oneida, NY	SY
WI	GB
Onekama, MI	GLD
Oneonta, AL	BIR
NY	ALB
Onida, SD	SFS
Onley, VA	RIC
Onset, MA	FR
Onsted, MI	DET
Ontario, CA	SB
NY	ROC
OR	BAK
Ontonagon, MI	MAR
Opelika, AL	MOB
Opelousas, LA	LAF
Oquossoc, ME	PRT
Oracle, AZ	TUC
Oradell, NJ	NEW
Oran, MO	SPC
Orange, CA	OLL
CA	ORG
CT	HRT
MA	SPR
NJ	NEW
TX	BEA
VA	ARL
Orange Beach, AL	MOB
Orange Cove, CA	FRS
Orange Grove, TX	CC
TX	SYM
Orange Park, FL	STA
Orangeburg, NY	NY
SC	CHR
Orangevale, CA	SAC
Orbisonia, PA	ALT
Orchard Lake, MI	DET
Orchard Park, NY	BUF
Ord, NE	GI
Orefield, PA	ALN
Oregon, IL	RCK
OH	TOL
WI	MAD
Oregon City, OR	P
Oreland, PA	PH
Orem, UT	SLC
Orient, SD	SFS
Oriental, NC	R
Orinda, CA	OAK
Orion, IL	PEO
Oriska, ND	FAR
Oriskany Falls, NY	SY
Orland, CA	SAC
Orland Hills, IL	CHI
Orland Park, IL	CHI
Orlando, FL	ORL
FL	PSC
FL	SAM
Orleans, MA	FR
NE	LIN
Ormond Beach, FL	ORL
Orofino, ID	B
Orono, ME	PRT
Oroville, CA	SAC

Place	Code
WA	SPK
Orr, MN	DUL
Orrtanna, PA	HBG
Orrville, AL	MOB
OH	CLV
Ortonville, MI	DET
MN	NU
Orwell, OH	Y
VT	BUR
Orwigsburg, PA	ALN
Osage, IA	DUB
Osage City, KS	KCK
Osakis, MN	SCL
Osawatomie, KS	KCK
Osborne, KS	SAL
Osceola, AR	LR
IA	DM
NE	LIN
WI	SUP
Oscoda, MI	GLD
Osgood, IN	IND
OH	CIN
Oshkosh, WI	GB
Oskaloosa, IA	DAV
Oslo, MN	CR
Osmond, NE	OM
Osprey, FL	VEN
Osseo, MN	STP
Ossian, IA	DUB
Ossineke, MI	GLD
Ossining, NY	NY
Osterville, MA	FR
Oswego, IL	JOL
KS	WCH
NY	SY
Othello, WA	SPK
Otis Orchards, WA	SPK
Otisville, MI	LAN
NY	NY
Otsego, MI	KAL
Ottawa, IL	PEO
KS	KCK
OH	TOL
Ottawa (Naplate), IL	PEO
Otter River, MA	WOR
Ottoville, OH	TOL
Ottsville, PA	PH
Ottumwa, IA	DAV
Ouray, CO	PBL
Overgaard, AZ	GLP
Overland, MO	STL
Overland Park, KS	KCK
Overton, NV	LAV
Ovid, MI	LAN
NY	ROC
Oviedo, FL	ORL
Owasso, OK	TLS
Owatonna, MN	WIN
Owego, NY	ROC
Owen, WI	LC
Owensboro, KY	OWN
Owensville, MO	JC
OH	CIN
Owings, MD	WDC
Owings Mills, MD	BAL
Owingsville, KY	LEX
Owosso, MI	LAN
Oxford, CT	HRT
IA	DAV
IN	LFT
MA	WOR
MI	DET
MS	JKS
NJ	MET
OH	CIN
PA	PH
Oxford Junction, IA	DUB
Oxnard, CA	LA
CA	ROM
Oxon Hill, MD	WDC
Oyster Bay, NY	RVC
Ozark, AL	MOB
AR	LR
MO	SPC
Ozona, TX	SAN
Ozone Park, NY	BRK
NY	STF
Pacific, MO	STL
Pacific Grove, CA	MRY
Pacific Palisades, CA	LA
Pacifica, CA	SFR
Pacoima, CA	LA
Paden City, WV	WH
Paducah, KY	OWN
Page, AZ	GLP
Pagosa Springs, CO	PBL
Pahala, HI	HON
Pahoa, HI	HON
Pahokee, FL	PMB
Pahrump, NV	LAV
Paia, HI	HON
Paincourtville, LA	BR
Painesville, OH	CLV
Paintsville, KY	LEX
Pajaro, CA	MRY
Pala, CA	SD
Palacios, TX	VIC
Palatine, IL	CHI
IL	STN
Palatka, FL	STA
Palestine, TX	TYL
Palisades Park, NJ	NEW
Palm Bay, FL	ORL
Palm Beach, FL	PMB
Palm Beach Gardens, FL	PMB
Palm City, FL	PMB
Palm Coast, FL	STA
Palm Desert, CA	SB
Palm Harbor, FL	SP
Palm Springs, CA	SB
FL	PMB
Palmdale, CA	LA
Palmer, AK	ANC
MA	SPR
Palmerton, PA	ALN
PA	PHU
Palmetto, FL	VEN
Palms, MI	SAG
Palmview, TX	BWN
Palmyra, MO	JC
NE	LIN
NY	ROC
PA	HBG
VA	RIC
WI	MAD
Palo Alto, CA	SJ
Palos Heights, IL	CHI
Palos Hills, IL	CHI
Palos Park, IL	CHI
IL	STN
Pampa, TX	AMA
Pana, IL	SFD
Panama, IA	DM
Panama City, FL	PT
Panama City Beach, FL	PT
Panhandle, TX	AMA
Panna Maria, TX	SAT
Panora, IA	DM
Panorama City, CA	LA
Paola, KS	KCK
Paoli, IN	IND
PA	PH
Paonia, CO	PBL
Papaikou, HI	HON
Papillion, NE	OM
Paradis, LA	NO
Paradise, CA	SAC
MI	MAR
Paradox, NY	ALB
Paragould, AR	LR
Paramount, CA	LA
Paramus, NJ	NEW
Parchment, MI	KAL
Pardeeville, WI	MAD
Paris, AR	LR
IL	SFD
KY	LEX
TN	MEM
TX	TYL
Park, KS	SAL
Park City, UT	SLC
Park Falls, WI	SUP
Park Forest, IL	CHI
IL	JOL
Park Hills, KY	COV
MO	STL
Park Rapids, MN	CR
Park Ridge, IL	CHI
NJ	NEW
Park River, ND	FAR
Parker, AZ	TUC
CO	COS
SD	SFS
Parkers Prairie, MN	SCL
Parkersburg, WV	WH
Parkesburg, PA	PH
Parkland, FL	MIA
Parkman, OH	CLV
Parks, LA	LAF
Parkston, SD	SFS
Parkton, MD	BAL
Parkville, MD	BAL
Parlier, CA	FRS
Parlin, NJ	MET
Parma, OH	CLV
OH	PRM
OH	SJP
Parma Heights, OH	CLV
Parnell, MO	KC
Parrish, FL	VEN
Parshall, ND	BIS
Parsippany, NJ	PAT
Parsons, KS	WCH
Pasadena, CA	LA
MD	BAL
TX	GAL
Pascagoula, MS	BLX
Pasco, WA	SPK
Pascoag, RI	PRO
Paso Robles, CA	MRY
Pass Christian, MS	BLX
Passaic, NJ	PAT
NJ	PHU
NJ	PSC
Patagonia, AZ	TUC
Patchogue, NY	RVC
Paterson, NJ	PAT
Patterson, CA	STO
LA	LAF
NY	NY
Pattison, TX	GAL
Patton, PA	ALT
PA	PBR
Paulding, OH	TOL
Paulina, LA	BR
Pavilion, NY	BUF
Paw Paw, MI	KAL
Pawcatuck, CT	NOR
Pawhuska, OK	TLS
Pawleys Island, SC	CHR
Pawling, NY	NY
Pawnee Rock, KS	DOD
Pawtucket, RI	PRO
Paxico, KS	KCK
Paxton, IL	JOL
MA	WOR
Paynesville, MN	SCL
Payneville, KY	L
Payson, AZ	PHX
AZ	TUC
UT	SLC
Pe Ell, WA	SEA
Peabody, MA	BO
Peachtree City, GA	ATL
Peapack, NJ	MET
Pearce, AZ	TUC
Pearisburg, VA	RIC
Pearl, MS	JKS
Pearl City, HI	HON
Pearl River, LA	NO
NY	NY
Pearland, TX	GAL
Pearsall, TX	SAT
Pecatonica, IL	RCK
Peckville, PA	SCR
Pecos, NM	SFE
TX	ELP
Peebles, OH	CIN
Peekskill, NY	NY
NY	PSC
Pekin, IL	PEO
Pelham, AL	BIR
NH	MAN
NY	NY
Pelham Manor, NY	NY
Pelican Rapids, MN	SCL
Pella, IA	DAV
Pellston, MI	GLD
Pembina, ND	FAR
Pembine, WI	GB
Pembroke, MA	BO
Pembroke Pines, FL	MIA
Pen Argyl, PA	ALN
Pena Blanca, NM	SFE
Penacook, NH	MAN
Penasco, NM	SFE
Pender, NE	OM
Pendleton, OR	BAK
Penelope, TX	FWT
Penfield, IL	PEO
NY	ROC
Peninsula, OH	CLV
Penitas, TX	BWN
Penn Hills, PA	PIT
Penn Yan, NY	ROC
Penndel, PA	PH
Penngrove, CA	SR
Pennington, NJ	TR
Pennsauken, NJ	CAM
Pennsburg, PA	PH
Pensacola, FL	PT
Peoria, AZ	PHX
IL	OLL
IL	PEO
Peoria Heights, IL	PEO
Peosta, IA	DUB
Peotone, IL	JOL
Pepper Pike, OH	CLV
Pepperell, MA	BO
Pequannock, NJ	PAT
Pequot Lakes, MN	DUL
Peralta, NM	SFE
Perham, MN	SCL
Perkins, MI	MAR
Perris, CA	SB
CA	SPA
Perry, FL	PT
IA	DM
KS	KCK
ME	PRT
MO	JC
NY	BUF
OH	CLV
OK	OKL
Perryopolis, PA	GBG
PA	PBR
Perrysburg, OH	TOL
Perryton, TX	AMA
Perryville, MD	WIL
MO	STL
Perth Amboy, NJ	MET
NJ	PHU
NJ	PSC
Peru, IL	PEO
IN	LFT
NY	OG
Peshtigo, WI	GB
Pesotum, IL	PEO
Petal, MS	BLX
Petaluma, CA	SR
Peterborough, NH	MAN
Petersburg, AK	JUN
IL	SFD
IN	EVN
NE	OM
TX	LUB
VA	RIC
WV	WH
Petersham, MA	SAM
MA	WOR
Petoskey, MI	GLD
Pettus, TX	CC
Pevely, MO	STL
Pewamo, MI	GR
Pewaukee, WI	MIL
Pewee Valley, KY	L
Pflugerville, TX	AUS
Pharr, TX	BWN
Phelan, CA	SB
Phenix City, AL	MOB
Philadelphia, MS	JKS
PA	PH
PA	SYM
PA	SAM
PA	PSC
PA	MCE
PA	PHU
Philip, SD	RC
Philippi, WV	WH
WV	OLL
Philipsburg, PA	ALT
Phillips, WI	SUP
Phillipsburg, KS	SAL
NJ	MET
NJ	PSC
Philo, IL	PEO
Philpot, KY	OWN
Phlox, WI	GB
Phoenicia, NY	NY
Phoenix, AZ	HPM
AZ	PHX
AZ	OLL
AZ	OLD
AZ	NTN
AZ	STN
AZ	SYM
NY	SY
Phoenixville, PA	PH
Picayune, MS	BLX
Pickens, SC	CHR
Pickerel, WI	GB
Pickerington, OH	COL
Pico Rivera, CA	LA
Piedmont, CA	OAK
MO	SPC
OK	OKL
SD	RC
Pierce, NE	OM
Pierce City, MO	SPC
Pierceton, IN	FTW
Piermont, NY	NY
Pierre, SD	SFS
Pierre Part, LA	BR
Pierron, IL	SFD
Pierz, MN	SCL
Piffard, NY	ROC
Pigeon, MI	SAG
Pigeon Forge, TN	KNX
Pikeville, KY	LEX
Pilot Grove, MO	JC
Pilot Knob, MO	SPC
Pilot Point, TX	FWT
Pilot Station, AK	FBK
Pinckney, MI	LAN

Place	Code
Pinckneyville, IL	BEL
Pinconning, MI	SAG
Pine Apple, AL	MOB
Pine Bluff, AR	LR
Pine Bluffs, WY	CHY
Pine Bush, NY	NY
Pine City, MN	DUL
NY	ROC
Pine Island, MN	STP
NY	NY
Pine Knoll Shores, NC	R
Pine Mountain, GA	SAV
Pine Plains, NY	NY
Pine Prairie, LA	LAF
Pine Ridge, SD	RC
Pine River, MN	DUL
Pinecrest, FL	MIA
Pinedale, WY	CHY
Pinehurst, NC	R
Pinellas Park, FL	SP
Pinetop, AZ	GLP
Pineville, LA	ALX
WV	WH
Pinole, CA	OAK
Pinon, AZ	GLP
Pipestone, MN	WIN
Piqua, OH	CIN
Pirtleville, AZ	TUC
Piscataway, NJ	MET
Pisek, ND	FAR
Pismo Beach, CA	MRY
Pittsboro, NC	R
Pittsburg, CA	OAK
KS	WCH
TX	TYL
Pittsburgh, PA	PBR
PA	SJP
PA	PIT
Pittsfield, IL	SFD
MA	SPR
MA	STF
NH	MAN
Pittsford, NY	ROC
VT	BUR
Pittston, PA	PSC
PA	SCR
Pittstown, NJ	MET
Pittsville, WI	LC
Placentia, CA	NTN
CA	ORG
Placerville, CA	SAC
Plain, WI	MAD
Plain City, OH	COL
Plainfield, CT	NOR
IL	JOL
IN	IND
NJ	NEW
WI	GB
Plains, KS	DOD
MT	HEL
PA	SCR
Plainsboro, NJ	MET
Plainview, MN	WIN
NE	OM
NY	RVC
TX	LUB
Plainville, CT	HRT
KS	SAL
MA	BO
Plaistow, NH	MAN
Planada, CA	FRS
Plankinton, SD	SFS
Plano, IL	JOL
TX	DAL
Plant City, FL	SP
Plantation, FL	MIA
Plantation Key, FL	MIA
Plantersville, TX	GAL
Plantsville, CT	HRT
Plaquemine, LA	BR
Platte, SD	SFS
Platte Center, NE	OM
Platte City, MO	KC
Plattekill, NY	NY
Platteville, CO	DEN
WI	MAD
Plattsburg, MO	KC
Plattsburgh, NY	OG
Plattsmouth, NE	LIN
Plaucheville, LA	ALX
Playa del Rey, CA	LA
Plaza, ND	BIS
Pleasant City, OH	PBR
Pleasant Grove, AL	BIR
Pleasant Hill, CA	OAK
MO	KC
Pleasant Mount, PA	SCR
Pleasant Prairie, WI	MIL
Pleasant Valley, NY	NY
Pleasanton, CA	OAK
TX	SAT

Place	Code
Pleasantville, NJ	CAM
NJ	SAM
NY	NY
Plentywood, MT	GF
Plover, WI	LC
WI	SUP
Plum, PA	PIT
Plum City, WI	LC
Plymouth, IN	FTW
MA	BO
MI	DET
MI	NTN
MI	LAN
MN	STP
NC	R
NH	MAN
OH	TOL
PA	PHU
PA	SCR
WI	MIL
Plymouth Meeting, PA	PH
Pocahontas, AR	LR
IA	SC
Pocasset, MA	FR
Pocatello, ID	B
Pocomoke City, MD	WIL
Pocono Pines, PA	SCR
Pocono Summit, PA	PSC
Point Arena, CA	SR
Point Lookout, NY	RVC
Point Pleasant, NJ	TR
WV	WH
Point Pleasant Beach, NJ	TR
Point Richmond, CA	OAK
Pointe A La Hache, LA	NO
Poland, OH	Y
Polo, IL	RCK
Polonia, WI	LC
Polson, MT	HEL
Pomeroy, OH	STU
WA	SPK
Pomfret, CT	NOR
MD	WDC
Pomona, CA	LA
NJ	CAM
Pompano Beach, FL	MIA
Pompey, NY	SY
Pompton Lakes, NJ	NY
NJ	PAT
Pompton Plains, NJ	PAT
Ponca, NE	OM
Ponca City, OK	OKL
Ponchatoula, LA	BR
LA	NO
Ponte Vedra Beach, FL	STA
Pontiac, IL	PEO
MI	DET
Pontotoc, MS	JKS
Poolesville, MD	WDC
Poplar, MT	GF
Poplar Bluff, MO	SPC
Poquonock, CT	HRT
Porcupine, SD	RC
Port Allegany, PA	E
Port Allen, LA	BR
Port Angeles, WA	SEA
Port Aransas, TX	CC
Port Arthur, TX	BEA
Port Austin, MI	SAG
Port Barre, LA	LAF
Port Carbon, PA	ALN
Port Charlotte, FL	VEN
Port Chester, NY	NY
Port Clinton, OH	TOL
Port Edwards, WI	LC
Port Ewen, NY	NY
Port Gibson, MS	JKS
Port Henry, NY	OG
Port Huron, MI	DET
Port Isabel, TX	BWN
Port Jefferson, NY	RVC
Port Jefferson Station, NY	RVC
Port Jervis, NY	NY
Port Lavaca, TX	VIC
Port Leyden, NY	OG
Port Murray, NJ	MET
Port Neches, TX	BEA
Port Orange, FL	ORL
Port Orchard, WA	SEA
Port Reading, NJ	MET
Port Richey, FL	SP
Port Sanilac, MI	SAG
Port St. Joe, FL	PT
Port St. Lucie, FL	PMB
Port Sulphur, LA	NO
Port Tobacco, MD	WDC
Port Townsend, WA	SEA
Port Vue, PA	PIT
Port Washington, NY	RVC
WI	MIL
Port Wentworth, GA	SAV

Place	Code
Portage, IN	GRY
MI	KAL
PA	ALT
PA	PBR
WI	MAD
Portage Des Sioux, MO	STL
Portageville, MO	SPC
Portales, NM	SFE
Porter, TX	GAL
Porterfield, WI	GB
Porterville, CA	FRS
Portland, CT	NOR
IN	LFT
ME	PRT
MI	GR
OR	P
OR	OLL
OR	HPM
TX	CC
Portola, CA	SAC
Portola Valley, CA	SFR
Portsmouth, IA	DM
NH	MAN
OH	COL
RI	PRO
VA	RIC
Posen, IL	CHI
MI	GLD
Poseyville, IN	EVN
Post, TX	LUB
Post Falls, ID	B
Poteau, OK	TLS
Poteet, TX	SAT
Poth, TX	SAT
Potomac, MD	WDC
Potomac Falls, VA	ARL
Potosi, MO	STL
WI	MAD
Potsdam, NY	OG
Pottstown, PA	PH
PA	PHU
PA	PSC
Pottsville, PA	ALN
Poughkeepsie, NY	NY
Poulsbo, WA	SEA
Poultney, VT	BUR
Poway, CA	SD
Powell, OH	COL
WY	CHY
Powhatan, LA	ALX
VA	RIC
WV	WH
Poynette, WI	MAD
Prague, NE	LIN
OK	OKL
Prairie View, TX	GAL
Prairie Village, KS	KCK
Prairie du Chien, WI	LC
Prairie du Rocher, IL	BEL
Prairie du Sac, WI	MAD
Prairieburg, IA	DUB
Prairieville, LA	BR
Pratt, KS	DOD
Prattville, AL	MOB
Prayer Town, TX	AMA
Premont, TX	CC
Prescott, AZ	PHX
MI	GLD
WI	LC
Prescott Valley, AZ	PHX
Presho, SD	RC
Presidio, TX	ELP
Preston, CT	NOR
IA	DUB
Prestonsburg, KY	LEX
Price, UT	SLC
Prichard, AL	MOB
Priest River, ID	B
Primos, PA	PH
Prince Frederick, MD	WDC
Princess Anne, MD	WIL
Princeton, FL	MIA
IL	PEO
IN	EVN
KY	OWN
MA	WOR
MN	SCL
NJ	TR
WI	MAD
WV	WH
Princeton Jct., NJ	TR
Princeville, IL	PEO
Prineville, OR	BAK
Prior Lake, MN	STP
Proctor, MN	DUL
VT	BUR
WV	WH
Progreso, TX	BWN
Prophetstown, IL	RCK
Prospect, CT	HRT
KY	L

Place	Code
PA	PIT
Prospect Heights, IL	CHI
Prospect Park, NJ	PAT
Prosser, WA	YAK
Protivin, IA	DUB
Providence, RI	PRO
Provincetown, MA	FR
Prudenville, MI	GLD
Pryor, MT	GF
OK	TLS
Pueblo, CO	PBL
Pueblo of Acoma, NM	GLP
Pulaski, NY	SY
PA	PIT
TN	NSH
WI	GB
Pullman, WA	SPK
Punta Gorda, FL	VEN
Punxsutawney, PA	E
PA	PBR
Purcell, OK	OKL
Purcellville, VA	ARL
Put–In–Bay, OH	TOL
Putnam, CT	BUR
CT	NOR
Putney, VT	BUR
Puyallup, WA	SEA
Pylesville, MD	BAL
Quaker Hill, CT	NOR
Quakertown, PA	PH
Quarryville, PA	HBG
Queen Creek, AZ	PHX
Queens, NY	BRK
Queens Village, NY	BRK
Queensbury, NY	ALB
Quemado, NM	GLP
Questa, NM	SFE
Quicksburg, VA	ARL
Quincy, CA	SAC
FL	PT
IL	SFD
MA	BO
WA	YAK
Quinlan, TX	DAL
Quinque, VA	RIC
Quinton, VA	RIC
Raceland, LA	HT
Racine, WI	MIL
Radcliff, KY	L
Radnor, PA	PH
PA	OLN
Radom, IL	BEL
Raeford, NC	R
Raeville, NE	OM
Rahway, NJ	MCE
NJ	PSC
NJ	NEW
Rainelle, WV	WH
Rainier, OR	P
Raleigh, NC	R
NC	SJP
Ralls, TX	LUB
Ralston, NE	OM
Ramah, NM	GLP
Ramey, PA	E
PA	SJP
Ramona, CA	SD
Ramsey, IL	SFD
MN	STP
NJ	NEW
Rancho Cordova, CA	SAC
Rancho Cucamonga, CA	SB
Rancho Dominguez, CA	LA
Rancho Palos Verdes, CA	LA
Rancho Santa Fe, CA	SD
Rancho Santa Margarita, CA	ORG
Ranchos De Taos, NM	SFE
Rancocas, NJ	TR
Randall, MN	SCL
Randallstown, MD	BAL
Randolph, MA	BO
NE	OM
NJ	PAT
VT	BUR
Random Lake, WI	MIL
Ranger, TX	FWT
Ransomville, NY	BUF
Rantoul, IL	PEO
Rapid City, SD	RC
Rapid River, MI	MAR
Rapids City, IL	PEO
Rapson, MI	SAG
Raritan, IL	PEO
NJ	MET
Ratcliff, AR	LR
Raton, NM	SFE
Ravena, NY	ALB
Ravenna, KY	LEX
MI	GR
NE	GI
OH	Y

Place	Code
Ravenswood, WV	WH
Rawlins, WY	CHY
Ray Township, MI	DET
Raymond, IL	SFD
MS	JKS
WA	SEA
Raymondville, NY	OG
TX	BWN
Raymore, MO	KC
Rayne, LA	LAF
Raynham Center, MA	FR
Raytown, MO	KC
Rayville, LA	SHP
Raywick, KY	L
Raywood, TX	BEA
Reading, MA	BO
OH	CIN
PA	ALN
PA	PHU
Readsboro, VT	BUR
Readville, MA	BO
Red Bank, NJ	TR
Red Bluff, CA	SAC
Red Bud, IL	BEL
Red Cloud, NE	LIN
Red Hook, NY	NY
Red Lake, MN	CR
Red Lake Falls, MN	CR
Red Lodge, MT	GF
Red Oak, IA	DM
Red Springs, NC	R
Red Wing, MN	STP
Redding, CA	SAC
Redding Ridge, CT	BGP
Redfield, SD	SFS
Redford, MI	DET
NY	OG
Redford Township, MI	DET
Redgranite, WI	GB
Redlands, CA	SB
Redmond, OR	BAK
WA	SEA
Redondo Beach, CA	LA
Redwood City, CA	SJ
CA	SFR
Redwood Falls, MN	NU
Redwood Valley, CA	STN
Reed, KY	OWN
Reed City, MI	GR
Reedley, CA	FRS
Reedsburg, WI	MAD
Reedsport, OR	P
Reese, MI	SAG
Reeseville, WI	MIL
Refugio, TX	CC
Regent, ND	BIS
Rego Park, NY	BRK
Rehoboth Beach, DE	WIL
Reidsville, NC	CHL
Reinbeck, IA	DUB
Remington, IN	LFT
Remsen, IA	SC
Remus, MI	GR
Renault, IL	BEL
Reno, NV	RNO
Renovo, PA	ALT
Rensselaer, IN	LFT
NY	ALB
Renton, WA	SEA
Renville, MN	NU
Republic, MI	MAR
MO	SPC
PA	GBG
WA	SPK
Reseda, CA	LA
Reserve, LA	NO
NM	GLP
Reston, VA	ARL
Revere, MA	BO
Revillo, SD	SFS
Reynolds, IN	LFT
ND	FAR
Reynoldsburg, OH	COL
Reynoldsville, PA	E
Rhinebeck, NY	NY
Rhineland, MO	JC
Rhinelander, WI	SUP
Rhodell, WV	WH
Rialto, CA	SB
Rib Lake, WI	SUP
Ribera, NM	SFE
Rice, MN	SCL
Rice Lake, WI	SUP
Riceville, IA	DUB
Rich Fountain, MO	JC
Richardson, TX	DAL
Richardton, ND	BIS
Richboro, PA	PH
Richeyville, PA	PIT
Richfield, MN	STP
OH	CLV
Richfield Springs, NY	ALB
Richford, VT	BUR
Richland, IA	DAV
NJ	CAM
NY	SY
WA	YAK
Richland Center, WI	LC
Richmond, CA	OAK
IL	RCK
IN	IND
KY	LEX
MI	DET
MN	SCL
MO	KC
OH	STU
TX	GAL
VA	RIC
VT	BUR
Richmond Heights, MO	STL
Richmond Hill, GA	SAV
NY	BRK
Richwood, TX	GAL
WV	WH
Richwoods, MO	STL
Ridge, MD	WDC
Ridge Manor, FL	SP
Ridgecrest, CA	FRS
Ridgefield, CT	BGP
NJ	NEW
Ridgefield Park, NJ	NEW
Ridgeland, SC	CHR
Ridgely, MD	WIL
Ridgeway, WI	MAD
Ridgewood, NJ	NEW
NY	BRK
Ridgway, IL	BEL
PA	E
Ridley Park, PA	PH
Riegelsville, PA	PH
Rifle, CO	DEN
Ringtown, PA	ALN
Ringwood, NJ	PAT
Rio Bravo, TX	LAR
Rio Grande, OH	STU
Rio Grande City, TX	BWN
Rio Hondo, TX	BWN
Rio Rancho, NM	SFE
Rio Rico, AZ	TUC
Rio Vista, CA	SAC
Ripley, MS	JKS
OH	CIN
Ripon, CA	STO
WI	MIL
Rittman, OH	CLV
Ritzville, WA	SPK
River Edge, NJ	NEW
River Falls, WI	LC
WI	SUP
River Forest, IL	CHI
River Grove, IL	CHI
River Ridge, LA	NO
River Rouge, MI	DET
Riverbank, CA	STO
Riverdale, CA	FRS
GA	ATL
IL	CHI
MD	WDC
NY	NY
Riverdale Park, MD	WDC
Riverhead, NY	RVC
NY	STF
Riverside, CA	SB
CT	BGP
IA	DAV
IL	CHI
NJ	TR
RI	PRO
Riverton, IL	SFD
NJ	TR
UT	SLC
WY	CHY
Riverview, FL	SP
MI	DET
Riviera, TX	CC
Riviera Beach, FL	PMB
Roanoke, IL	PEO
IN	FTW
VA	RIC
VA	SAM
Roanoke Rapids, NC	R
Roaring Brook Twp., PA	SCR
Roaring Spring, PA	ALT
Robbinsdale, MN	STP
Robertsdale, AL	MOB
Robesonia, PA	ALN
Robinson, IL	SFD
Robinsonville, MS	JKS
Robstown, TX	CC
Rochelle, IL	RCK
Rochelle Park, NJ	NEW
Rochester, IL	SFD
IN	LFT
MI	DET
MN	WIN
NH	MAN
NY	NTN
NY	STF
NY	ROC
PA	PIT
Rochester Hills, MI	DET
Rock Creek, OH	Y
Rock Falls, IL	RCK
Rock Hill, SC	CHR
Rock Island, IL	PEO
Rock Rapids, IA	SC
Rock Springs, WY	CHY
Rock Valley, IA	SC
Rockaway, NJ	PAT
OR	P
Rockaway Beach, NY	BRK
Rockaway Park, NY	BRK
Rockaway Point, NY	BRK
Rockdale, IL	JOL
TX	AUS
Rockford, IA	DUB
IL	RCK
MI	GR
OH	CIN
Rockland, MA	BO
WI	LC
Rockledge, FL	ORL
Rocklin, CA	SAC
Rockport, IN	EVN
TX	CC
Rocksprings, TX	SAT
Rockville, CT	NOR
IN	IND
MD	WDC
MN	SCL
VA	RIC
Rockville Centre, NY	RVC
Rockwall, TX	DAL
Rockwell, IA	DUB
Rockwell City, IA	SC
Rockwood, MI	DET
Rocky Ford, CO	PBL
Rocky Hill, CT	HRT
Rocky Mount, MO	STL
NC	R
VA	RIC
Rocky Point, NY	RVC
Rocky River, OH	CLV
Rodeo, CA	OAK
Roebling, NJ	TR
NJ	PSC
NJ	ROM
Roeland Park, KS	KCK
Rogers, AR	LR
MN	STP
TX	AUS
Rogers City, MI	GLD
Rogersville, TN	KNX
Roggen, CO	DEN
Rohnert Park, CA	SR
Rolette, ND	FAR
Rolla, MO	JC
ND	FAR
Rolling Meadows, IL	CHI
Rolling Prairie, IN	GRY
Rollingstone, MN	WIN
Roma, TX	BWN
Rome, GA	ATL
NY	SY
Rome City, IN	FTW
Romeo, MI	DET
Romeoville, IL	JOL
Romney, WV	WH
Romulus, MI	DET
Ronan, MT	HEL
Ronceverte, WV	WH
Ronkonkoma, NY	RVC
Roosevelt, NY	RVC
UT	SLC
Roosevelt Island, NY	NY
Rootstown, OH	Y
Rosalia, WA	SPK
Rosamond, CA	FRS
Roscoe, PA	PIT
SD	SFS
Roscommon, MI	GLD
Roseau, MN	CR
Rosebud, SD	RC
Roseburg, OR	P
Rosebush, MI	SAG
Rosedale, MS	JKS
NY	BRK
Roseland, NE	LIN
NJ	NEW
Roselle, IL	JOL
NJ	NEW
Roselle Park, NJ	NEW
Rosemead, CA	LA
Rosemont, IL	CHI
PA	PH
Rosemount, MN	STP
Rosenberg, TX	GAL
Rosendale, NY	NY
Roseto, PA	ALN
Roseville, CA	SAC
MI	DET
MN	STP
Rosharon, TX	MCE
Rosholt, SD	SFS
WI	LC
Roslindale, MA	BO
Roslyn, NY	RVC
PA	PH
Rosman, NC	CHL
Ross, CA	SFR
Rossford, OH	SJP
OH	TOL
Rossville, KS	KCK
Roswell, GA	ATL
GA	PSC
NM	LSC
Rotan, TX	LUB
Rothschild, WI	LC
Round Lake, IL	CHI
NY	ALB
Round Rock, TX	AUS
Roundup, MT	GF
Rouses Point, NY	OG
Rouseville, PA	E
Rowena, TX	SAN
Rowland Heights, CA	LA
Rowlett, TX	DAL
Roxboro, NC	R
Roxbury, MA	BO
Roy, NM	SFE
Royal, IA	SC
Royal City, WA	YAK
Royal Oak, MI	DET
Royal Palm Beach, FL	PMB
Royalton, IL	BEL
MN	SCL
Royersford, PA	PH
Rubicon, WI	MIL
Ruby, AK	FBK
Rudolph, WI	LC
Rudyard, MI	MAR
Rugby, ND	FAR
Ruidoso, NM	LSC
Rulo, NE	LIN
Rumford, ME	PRT
RI	PRO
Rumson, NJ	TR
Runge, TX	SAT
Runnemede, NJ	CAM
Running Springs, CA	SB
Rupert, ID	B
Rush, NY	ROC
Rush City, MN	STP
Rushford, MN	WIN
NY	BUF
Rushville, IL	PEO
IN	IND
Ruskin, FL	SP
Russell, KS	SAL
MA	SPR
Russells Point, OH	CIN
Russellton, PA	PIT
Russellville, AL	BIR
AR	LR
KY	OWN
MO	JC
Russia, OH	CIN
Ruston, LA	SHP
Ruth, MI	SAG
Rutherford, NJ	NEW
Ruthven, IA	SC
Rutland, MA	WOR
VT	BUR
Rutledge, TN	KNX
Ryan, IA	DUB
Rydal, PA	PH
Rye, NY	NY
Rye Beach, NH	MAN
Sabattus, ME	PRT
Sabetha, KS	KCK
Sabinal, TX	SAT
Sac City, IA	SC
Sacaton, AZ	PHX
Saco, ME	PRT
Sacramento, CA	HPM
CA	NTN
CA	STN
CA	SYM
CA	SAC
Saddle Brook, NJ	NEW
Saddle River Borough, NJ	NEW
Safety Harbor, FL	SP
Safford, AZ	TUC
Sag Harbor, NY	RVC

Saginaw, MI	SAG
Sahuarita, AZ	TUC
St. Agatha, ME	PRT
St. Albans, ME	PRT
NY	BRK
VT	BUR
WV	WH
St. Amant, LA	BR
St. Ann, MO	STL
St. Anne, IL	JOL
St. Anthony, ID	B
IN	EVN
MN	STP
ND	FAR
St. Augustine, FL	STA
St. Benedict, KS	KCK
LA	NO
OR	P
Saint Benedict, OR	P
Saint Bernard, LA	NO
St. Bonaventure, NY	BUF
Saint Bonaventure, NY	BUF
St. Bonifacius, MN	STP
St. Catharine, KY	L
Saint Charles, IL	RCK
St. Charles, MI	SAG
MN	WIN
MO	STL
St. Clair, MI	DET
MO	STL
PA	ALN
Saint Clair, PA	ALN
St. Clair Shores, MI	DET
St. Clairsville, OH	STU
Saint Cloud, FL	ORL
St. Cloud, MN	SCL
MN	SYM
Saint Cloud, MN	SCL
St. Columbans, NE	OM
St. Croix, IN	IND
St. David, AZ	TUC
St. Edward, NE	OM
St. Elizabeth, MO	JC
St. Francis, KS	SAL
KY	L
MN	SCL
SD	RC
WI	MIL
St. Francisville, LA	BR
St. Gabriel, LA	BR
St. George, UT	SLC
St. Hedwig, TX	SAT
Saint Helen, MI	GLD
Saint Helena, CA	SR
St. Helena Island, SC	CHR
St. Helens, OR	P
Saint Henry, OH	CIN
St. Ignace, MI	MAR
St. Ignatius, MT	HEL
St. Inigoes, MD	WDC
St. James, LA	BR
MN	WIN
Saint James, MO	JC
NY	RVC
St. John, FL	STA
IN	GRY
KS	DOD
ND	FAR
Saint John, WA	SPK
St. Johns, AZ	GLP
FL	STA
MI	LAN
Saint Johnsbury, VT	BUR
St. Joseph, LA	ALX
MI	KAL
Saint Joseph, MN	SCL
St. Joseph, MO	KC
MO	STN
Saint Leo, FL	SP
St. Leo, MN	NU
St. Libory, IL	BEL
NE	GI
St. Louis, MI	SAG
MO	PRM
Saint Louis, MO	STL
St. Louis, MO	STL
Saint Louis, MO	OLL
St. Louis, MO	STN
St. Louis County, MO	STL
St. Louis Park, MN	STP
St. Lucas, IA	DUB
St. Maries, ID	B
St. Martin, MN	SCL
OH	CIN
St. Martinville, LA	LAF
Saint Mary, MO	STL
Saint Mary Of The Woods, IN	IND
St. Mary's, MO	BEL
St. Mary's City, MD	WDC
St. Marys, AK	FBK
GA	SAV

IA	DM
Saint Marys, IA	DM
St. Marys, KS	KCK
OH	CIN
PA	E
Saint Marys, PA	E
St. Marys, WV	WH
Saint Meinrad, IN	IND
St. Michael, AK	FBK
MN	STP
ND	FAR
PA	ALT
St. Michaels, AZ	GLP
St. Nazianz, WI	GB
WI	ROM
St. Paul, KS	WCH
MN	STP
Saint Paul, MN	STP
St. Paul, MN	SYM
MO	STL
NE	GI
OR	P
VA	RIC
St. Paul Park, MN	STP
St. Pete Beach, FL	SP
Saint Peter, MN	NU
St. Peters, MO	STL
St. Petersburg, FL	SP
Saint Petersburg, FL	SP
FL	PSC
St. Petersburg, FL	SJP
St. Regis Falls, NY	OG
St. Robert, MO	JC
St. Rose, IL	BEL
St. Simons Island, GA	SAV
St. Stephen, MN	SCL
Saint Stephens, WY	CHY
St. Theresa, WI	MIL
St. Thomas, MO	JC
St. Xavier, MT	GF
Salado, TX	AUS
Salamanca, NY	BUF
Salem, IL	BEL
IN	IND
MA	BO
MA	STF
MO	SPC
NH	MAN
NY	ALB
OH	Y
OR	P
SD	SFS
VA	RIC
WV	WH
Salida, CO	COS
Salina, KS	SAL
Salinas, CA	MRY
Saline, MI	LAN
Salisbury, MD	WIL
MO	JC
NC	CHL
PA	ALT
Sallisaw, OK	TLS
Salmon, ID	B
Salt Lake City, UT	SLC
Salt Point, NY	NY
Saltaire, NY	RVC
Salyersville, KY	LEX
Sammamish, WA	SEA
San Andreas, CA	STO
San Angelo, TX	SAN
San Anselmo, CA	SFR
San Antonio, FL	SP
TX	OAK
TX	SAT
TX	SYM
TX	OLL
San Benito, TX	BWN
San Bernardino, CA	SB
CA	NTN
San Bruno, CA	SFR
San Carlos, AZ	TUC
CA	SFR
San Clemente, CA	ORG
San Diego, CA	SD
CA	NTN
CA	SPA
CA	HPM
CA	STN
TX	CC
San Dimas, CA	LA
San Elizario, TX	ELP
San Fernando, CA	LA
CA	SYM
San Fidel, NM	GLP
San Francisco, CA	SFR
CA	STN
San Gabriel, CA	LA
San Isidro, TX	BWN
San Jacinto, CA	SB
San Jose, CA	SJ
CA	NTN

San Juan, TX	BWN
San Juan Bautista, CA	MRY
San Juan Capistrano, CA	ORG
San Leandro, CA	OAK
San Lorenzo, CA	OAK
San Luis, AZ	TUC
CO	PBL
San Luis Obispo, CA	HPM
CA	MRY
San Manuel, AZ	TUC
San Marcos, CA	SD
TX	AUS
San Marino, CA	LA
San Mateo, CA	SFR
San Miguel, CA	MRY
NM	LSC
San Pablo, CA	OAK
San Patricio, NM	LSC
San Pedro, CA	LA
San Rafael, CA	SFR
San Ramon, CA	OAK
San Saba, TX	AUS
San Ysidro, CA	SD
Sanborn, IA	SC
MN	NU
Sanbornville, NH	MAN
Sand Lake, MI	GR
Sand Springs, OK	TLS
Sanderson, TX	SAN
Sandoval, IL	BEL
Sandpoint, ID	B
Sandstone, MN	DUL
Sandusky, MI	SAG
OH	TOL
Sandwich, IL	RCK
Sandy, OR	P
UT	SLC
Sandy Hook, KY	LEX
Sandyston, NJ	PAT
Sanford, FL	ORL
ME	PRT
MI	SAG
NC	R
Sanger, CA	FRS
Sanibel, FL	VEN
Santa Ana, CA	ORG
CA	SYM
CA	SPA
Santa Barbara, CA	LA
Santa Clara, CA	SJ
CA	STN
NM	LSC
Santa Clarita, CA	LA
Santa Claus, IN	EVN
Santa Cruz, CA	MRY
NM	SFE
Santa Fe, NM	SFE
Santa Fe Springs, CA	LA
Santa Margarita, CA	MRY
Santa Maria, CA	LA
Santa Monica, CA	LA
Santa Paula, CA	LA
Santa Rosa, CA	SR
NM	SFE
TX	BWN
Santa Rosa Beach, FL	PT
Santa Susana Knolls, CA	LA
Santa Ynez, CA	LA
Santa Ysabel, CA	SD
Santee, CA	SD
SC	CHR
Sapulpa, OK	TLS
Saranac, MI	GR
Saranac Lake, NY	OG
Sarasota, FL	VEN
Saratoga, CA	SJ
NY	ALB
WY	CHY
Saratoga Springs, NY	ALB
Sardinia, NY	BUF
Sarita, TX	CC
Sartell, MN	SCL
Satanta, KS	DOD
Saugerties, NY	NY
Saugus, MA	BO
Sauk Centre, MN	SCL
Sauk City, WI	MAD
Sauk Rapids, MN	SCL
Sauk Village, IL	CHI
Saukville, WI	MIL
Sault Sainte Marie, MI	MAR
Sausalito, CA	SFR
Savage, MN	STP
Savanna, IL	RCK
Savannah, GA	SAV
MO	KC
TN	MEM
Saxon, WI	SUP
Sayre, PA	PHU
PA	SCR
Sayreville, NJ	MET

Sayville, NY	RVC
Scales Mound, IL	RCK
Scammon Bay, AK	FBK
Scappoose, OR	P
Scarborough, ME	PRT
Scarsdale, NY	NY
Scenic, AZ	PHX
Schaller, IA	SC
Schaumburg, IL	CHI
Scheller, IL	BEL
Schenectady, NY	ALB
Schererville, IN	GRY
Schertz, TX	SAT
Schiller Park, IL	CHI
Schnellville, IN	EVN
Schofield, WI	LC
Schriever, LA	HT
Schroon Lake, NY	OG
Schulenburg, TX	VIC
Schuyler, NE	OM
Schuylerville, NY	ALB
Schuylkill Haven, PA	ALN
Schwenksville, PA	PH
Scio, OR	P
Scituate, MA	BO
Scobey, MT	GF
Scotch Plains, NJ	NEW
Scotia, CA	SR
NY	ALB
Scotland, SD	SFS
Scott, LA	LAF
Scott AFB, IL	BEL
Scott City, KS	DOD
MO	SPC
Scott Twp., PA	SCR
Scottdale, PA	GBG
PA	PBR
Scotts Valley, CA	MRY
Scottsbluff, NE	GI
Scottsboro, AL	BIR
Scottsburg, IN	IND
Scottsdale, AZ	PHX
AZ	SPA
Scottsville, KY	OWN
NY	ROC
VA	RIC
Scottville, MI	GR
Scranton, AR	LR
IA	SC
PA	NTN
PA	PHU
PA	PSC
PA	SCR
PA	SAM
Sea Cliff, NY	RVC
Sea Girt, NJ	TR
Sea Isle City, NJ	CAM
Seaford, DE	WIL
NY	RVC
Seal Beach, CA	ORG
Sealy, TX	GAL
Searcy, AR	LR
Seaside, CA	MRY
OR	P
Seaside Heights, NJ	TR
Seaside Park, NJ	TR
Seat Pleasant, MD	WDC
Seattle, WA	HPM
WA	NTN
WA	SEA
WA	STN
Seaview, WA	SEA
Sebastian, FL	PMB
Sebastopol, CA	SR
Sebewaing, MI	SAG
Seboyeta, NM	GLP
Sebree, KY	OWN
Sebring, FL	VEN
OH	Y
Secane, PA	PH
Secaucus, NJ	NEW
Secretary, MD	WIL
Security, CO	COS
Sedalia, CO	COS
MO	JC
Sedona, AZ	PHX
Sedro Woolley, WA	SEA
Seekonk, MA	FR
Seelyville, IN	IND
Seffner, FL	SP
FL	SYM
Seguin, TX	SAT
Selah, WA	YAK
Selby, SD	SFS
Selden, KS	SAL
NY	RVC
Seligman, AZ	PHX
Selinsgrove, PA	HBG
Sellersburg, IN	IND
Sellersville, PA	PH
Selma, AL	MOB

Place	Code
CA	FRS
TX	SAT
Selmer, TN	MEM
Selz, ND	FAR
Seminole, FL	SP
OK	OKL
TX	LUB
Semmes, AL	MOB
Senatobia, MS	JKS
Seneca, IL	PEO
KS	KCK
MO	SPC
WI	LC
Sentinel Butte, ND	BIS
Sequim, WA	SEA
Sesser, IL	BEL
Setauket, NY	RVC
Severn, MD	BAL
Severna Park, MD	BAL
Seward, AK	ANC
KS	DOD
NE	LIN
PA	GBG
Sewell, NJ	CAM
Sewickley, PA	PIT
Seymour, CT	HRT
IL	PEO
IN	IND
TN	KNX
TX	FWT
WI	GB
Shady Cove, OR	P
Shadyside, OH	STU
Shafter, CA	FRS
Shaker Heights, OH	CLV
Shakopee, MN	STP
Shallotte, NC	R
Shallowater, TX	LUB
Shamokin, PA	HBG
PA	PHU
Shamrock, TX	AMA
Shandon, OH	CIN
Shannon, IL	RCK
Sharon, CT	HRT
KS	DOD
MA	BO
PA	E
WI	MIL
Sharon Hill, PA	PH
Sharon Township, MN	STP
Sharpsburg, PA	PIT
Sharpsville, PA	E
Shavertown, PA	SCR
Shaw, MS	JKS
Shaw Island, WA	SEA
Shawano, WI	GB
Shawnee, KS	KCK
OK	OKL
Shawnee Mission, KS	KCK
Shawneetown, IL	BEL
Sheboygan, WI	MIL
Sheboygan Falls, WI	MIL
Sheffield, MA	SPR
OH	CLV
PA	E
PA	PBR
Sheffield Lake, OH	CLV
Shelbina, MO	JC
Shelburne, VT	BUR
VT	SAM
Shelburne Falls, MA	SPR
Shelby, MI	GR
MS	JKS
MT	HEL
NC	CHL
NE	LIN
OH	TOL
Shelby Twp., MI	DET
MI	EST
Shelbyville, IL	SFD
IN	IND
KY	L
TN	NSH
Sheldon, IA	SC
Sheldon Springs, VT	BUR
Shell Knob, MO	SPC
Shell Lake, WI	SUP
Shelter Island Heights, NY	RVC
Shelton, CT	BGP
WA	SEA
Shenandoah, IA	DM
PA	ALN
PA	PHU
Shepherd, MI	SAG
Shepherdstown, WV	WH
Shepherdsville, KY	L
Sheppton, PA	ALN
Sherborn, MA	BO
Sherburne, NY	SY
Sheridan, MT	HEL
OR	P
WY	CHY
Sherman, CT	BGP
IL	SFD
TX	DAL
Sherman Oaks, CA	LA
CA	HPM
CA	ROM
Sherrill, NY	SY
Sherwood, AR	LR
OR	P
WI	GB
Shieldsville, MN	STP
Shillington, PA	ALN
Shiloh, IL	BEL
Shiner, TX	VIC
Shinglehouse, PA	E
Shinnston, WV	WH
Shippensburg, PA	HBG
Shiprock, NM	GLP
Shirley, MA	BO
Shoemakersville, PA	ALN
Shohola, PA	SCR
Shoreham, NY	RVC
Shoreline, WA	SEA
Shoreview, MN	STP
Shorewood, IL	JOL
WI	MIL
Short Hills, NJ	NEW
Shoshone, ID	B
Show Low, AZ	GLP
Shreveport, LA	SHP
Shrewsbury, MA	WOR
MO	STL
Shrub Oak, NY	NY
Shullsburg, WI	MAD
Shumway, IL	SFD
Sibley, IA	SC
Sicklerville, NJ	CAM
Sidney, MT	GF
NE	GI
NY	ALB
OH	CIN
Sierra Madre, CA	LA
Sierra Vista, AZ	TUC
Sigel, IL	SFD
Signal Mountain, TN	KNX
Sigourney, IA	DAV
Sikeston, MO	SPC
Siler City, NC	R
Silex, MO	STL
Siloam Springs, AR	LR
Silsbee, TX	BEA
Silver Bay, MN	DUL
Silver City, NM	LSC
Silver Creek, NE	OM
NY	BUF
Silver Lake, MN	NU
Silver Spring, MD	PHU
MD	WDC
Silverado, CA	ORG
Silverton, OR	P
TX	AMA
Silvis, IL	PEO
Simi Valley, CA	LA
Simmesport, LA	ALX
Simpsonville, SC	CHR
Simsbury, CT	HRT
Sinking Spring, PA	ALN
Sinsinawa, WI	MAD
Sinton, TX	CC
Sioux Center, IA	SC
Sioux City, IA	SC
Sioux Falls, SD	SFS
Sioux Rapids, IA	SC
Siren, WI	SUP
Sisseton, SD	SFS
Sisters, OR	BAK
Sistersville, WV	WH
Sitka, AK	JUN
Skaneateles, NY	SY
Skiatook, OK	TLS
Skidmore, TX	CC
Skillman, NJ	MET
Skokie, IL	CHI
Skowhegan, ME	PRT
Slater, MO	JC
Slatersville, RI	PRO
Slatington, PA	ALN
Slaton, TX	LUB
Slayton, MN	WIN
Sleepy Eye, MN	NU
Sleepy Hollow, NY	NY
Slickville, PA	GBG
Slidell, LA	NO
Slinger, WI	MIL
Slingerlands, NY	ALB
Slippery Rock, PA	PIT
Sloan, NY	BUF
Sloatsburg, NY	NY
NY	STF
Smethport, PA	E
Smiley, TX	SAT
Smith Center, KS	SAL
Smithfield, NC	R
RI	PRO
VA	RIC
Smithton, IL	BEL
Smithtown, NY	RVC
Smithville, MO	KC
TN	NSH
TX	AUS
Smock, PA	GBG
Smyrna, DE	WIL
GA	ATL
TN	NSH
Sneedville, TN	KNX
Snellville, GA	ATL
Snohomish, WA	SEA
Snoqualmie, WA	SEA
Snowflake, AZ	GLP
Snowmass, CO	DEN
Snyder, NE	OM
NY	BUF
TX	LUB
Sobieski, WI	GB
Socorro, NM	SFE
TX	ELP
Soda Springs, ID	B
Soddy Daisy, TN	KNX
Solana Beach, CA	SD
Soldotna, AK	ANC
Soledad, CA	MRY
Solomon, AZ	TUC
KS	SAL
Solomons, MD	WDC
Solon, IA	DAV
OH	CLV
OH	PRM
OH	SJP
Solon Springs, WI	SUP
Solvang, CA	LA
Solvay, NY	SY
Somers, NY	NY
Somers Point, NJ	CAM
Somerset, KY	LEX
MA	FR
NJ	MET
NJ	SAM
NJ	SYM
NJ	PSC
OH	COL
PA	ALT
TX	SAT
WI	SUP
Somersville, CT	NOR
Somersworth, NH	MAN
Somerton, AZ	TUC
Somerville, MA	BO
NJ	MET
TN	MEM
TX	AUS
Somonauk, IL	RCK
Sonoita, AZ	TUC
Sonoma, CA	SR
Sonora, CA	STO
TX	SAN
Soquel, CA	MRY
Sorrento, LA	BR
Sound Beach, NY	RVC
Sour Lake, TX	BEA
South Abington Township, PA	SCR
South Amboy, NJ	MET
South Amherst, OH	CLV
South Barre, MA	WOR
South Beloit, IL	RCK
South Bend, IN	FTW
IN	NTN
South Boston, MA	BO
VA	RIC
South Bound Brook, NJ	MET
South Burlington, VT	BUR
South Charleston, OH	CIN
WV	WH
South Dartmouth, MA	FR
South Deerfield, MA	SPR
MA	STF
South Easton, MA	FR
South El Monte, CA	LA
South Euclid, OH	CLV
South Fork, PA	ALT
South Gate, CA	LA
CA	SYM
South Glastonbury, CT	HRT
South Glens Falls, NY	ALB
South Grafton, MA	WOR
South Hadley, MA	SPR
South Haven, MI	KAL
South Heart, ND	BIS
South Hero, VT	BUR
South Hill, VA	RIC
South Holland, IL	CHI
South Houston, TX	GAL
South Huntington, NY	RVC
South Hutchinson, KS	WCH
South Kingstown, RI	PRO
South Lake Tahoe, CA	SAC
South Lyon, MI	DET
South Mantoloking, NJ	TR
South Milwaukee, WI	MIL
South Orange, NJ	NEW
South Ozone Park, NY	BRK
South Park, PA	PIT
South Pasadena, CA	LA
South Pittsburg, TN	KNX
South Plainfield, NJ	MET
South Portland, ME	PRT
South Richmond Hill, NY	BRK
South River, NJ	MET
South San Francisco, CA	SFR
South Sioux City, NE	OM
South St. Paul, MN	STP
South Tucson, AZ	TUC
South Wilmington, IL	JOL
South Windsor, CT	HRT
South Yarmouth, MA	FR
Southampton, NY	RVC
PA	PH
Southaven, MS	JKS
Southborough, MA	WOR
Southbridge, MA	WOR
Southbury, CT	HRT
Southern Pines, NC	R
Southfield, MI	DET
MI	EST
MI	SYM
Southgate, KY	COV
MI	DET
Southington, CT	HRT
Southold, NY	RVC
Southport, NC	R
Southwest Ranches, FL	MIA
Southwick, MA	SPR
Spalding, MI	MAR
NE	GI
Sparkill, NY	NY
Sparks, MD	BAL
NV	RNO
Sparta, IL	BEL
MI	GR
NJ	PAT
TN	NSH
WI	LC
Spartanburg, SC	CHR
Spearfish, SD	RC
Spearman, TX	AMA
Spearville, KS	DOD
Speculator, NY	OG
Spencer, IA	SC
IN	IND
MA	WOR
WV	WH
Spencerport, NY	ROC
Spencerville, OH	TOL
Spicer, MN	NU
Spillville, IA	DUB
Spirit Lake, IA	SC
Splendora, TX	GAL
Spokane, WA	SPK
Spokane Valley, WA	HPM
WA	SPK
Spooner, WI	SUP
Spotswood, NJ	MET
Spotsylvania, VA	ARL
Spreckels, CA	MRY
Spring, TX	GAL
Spring Branch, TX	SAT
Spring City, PA	PH
Spring Green, WI	MAD
Spring Grove, IL	RCK
PA	HBG
Spring Hill, FL	SP
TN	NSH
Spring House, PA	PH
Spring Lake, MI	GR
NJ	TR
Spring Mills, PA	ALT
Spring Valley, CA	SD
IL	PEO
MN	WIN
NY	NY
NY	MCE
NY	STF
WI	LC
Springbrook, IA	DUB
NY	BUF
Springdale, AR	LR
PA	PIT
Springer, NM	SFE
Springerville, AZ	GLP
Springfield, CO	PBL
GA	SAV
IL	SFD
KY	L

Place	Code
MA	SAM
MA	SPR
MN	NU
MO	SPC
NE	OM
NJ	NEW
OH	CIN
OR	P
OR	STN
PA	PH
SD	SFS
TN	NSH
VA	ARL
VA	WDC
VT	BUR
Springfield Gardens, NY	BRK
Springville, IA	DUB
NY	BUF
Spruce Pine, NC	CHL
Spur, TX	LUB
Stafford, TX	GAL
TX	SYM
VA	ARL
Stafford Springs, CT	NOR
Stamford, CT	BGP
CT	STF
NY	ALB
TX	LUB
Stanberry, MO	KC
Standish, ME	PRT
MI	SAG
Stanford, CA	SJ
MT	GF
Stanley, ND	BIS
WI	LC
Stanton, CA	ORG
KY	LEX
NE	OM
TN	MEM
TX	SAN
Stanwood, WA	SEA
Staples, MN	SCL
Stapleton, NE	GI
Star City, AR	LR
IN	LFT
Star Lake, NY	OG
Starke, FL	STA
Starkville, MS	JKS
State College, PA	ALT
PA	PBR
Staten Island, NY	NY
NY	STF
Statesboro, GA	SAV
Statesville, NC	CHL
Staunton, IL	SFD
VA	RIC
Stayton, OR	P
Ste. Genevieve, MO	STL
Ste. Marie, IL	SFD
Steamboat Springs, CO	DEN
Stebbins, AK	FBK
Steele, ND	FAR
Steelton, PA	HBG
Steger, IL	JOL
Steinauer, NE	LIN
Stella Niagara, NY	BUF
Stephen, MN	CR
Stephenson, MI	MAR
Stephenville, TX	FWT
Sterling, CO	DEN
IL	RCK
MA	WOR
VA	ARL
Sterling Heights, MI	DET
MI	EST
MI	PRM
MI	OLD
Stetsonville, WI	SUP
Steubenville, OH	STU
Stevens Point, WI	LC
Stevenson, MD	BAL
Stevensville, MT	HEL
Stewart, MN	NU
Stewartsville, NJ	MET
Stewartville, MN	WIN
Stickney, IL	CHI
Still River, MA	WOR
Stillwater, MN	STP
NY	ALB
OK	TLS
Stirling, NJ	PAT
Stockbridge, MA	SPR
WI	GB
Stockdale, TX	SAT
Stockholm, NJ	PAT
Stockton, CA	STO
IL	RCK
Stone Harbor, NJ	CAM
Stone Lake, WI	SUP
Stone Mountain, GA	ATL
Stoneboro, PA	E
Stoneham, MA	BO
Stoneville, NC	CHL
Stonewall, TX	SAT
Stonewood, WV	WH
Stonington, CT	NOR
IL	SFD
Stony Point, NY	NY
Storm Lake, IA	SC
Storrs, CT	NOR
Stoughton, MA	BO
WI	MAD
Stow, MA	BO
OH	CLV
Stowe, PA	PH
VT	BUR
Strafford, PA	PH
Strandquist, MN	CR
Strasburg, ND	BIS
Stratford, CT	BGP
TX	AMA
WI	LC
Stratton, CO	COS
Strawberry Point, IA	DUB
Streamwood, IL	CHI
Streator, IL	PEO
Streetsboro, OH	Y
Strongsville, OH	CLV
Stroudsburg, PA	SCR
Struthers, OH	Y
Strykersville, NY	BUF
Stuart, FL	PMB
IA	DM
NE	OM
Studio City, CA	LA
Sturgeon Bay, WI	GB
Sturgis, KY	OWN
MI	KAL
SD	RC
Sturtevant, WI	MIL
Stuttgart, AR	LR
Stuyvesant, NY	ALB
Suamico, WI	GB
Subiaco, AR	LR
Sublette, IL	RCK
Sublimity, OR	P
Succasunna, NJ	PAT
Sudbury, MA	BO
Suffern, NY	NY
Suffield, CT	HRT
Suffolk, VA	RIC
Sugar Creek, MO	KC
MO	PRM
Sugar Grove, IL	RCK
OH	COL
Sugar Land, TX	GAL
Sugar Notch, PA	SCR
Sugarloaf, PA	PSC
Suitland, MD	WDC
Sulligent, AL	BIR
Sullivan, IL	SFD
IN	EVN
MO	STL
WI	MAD
Sullivan's Island, SC	CHR
Sulphur, LA	LKC
Sulphur Springs, TX	TYL
Summerfield, FL	ORL
KS	KCK
MI	DET
Summerhill, PA	ALT
Summersville, WV	WH
Summerton, SC	CHR
Summerville, SC	CHR
Summit, IL	CHI
NJ	NEW
Summit Hill, PA	ALN
Sumner, IA	DUB
WA	SEA
Sumter, SC	CHR
Sun City, AZ	PHX
CA	SB
Sun City Center, FL	SP
Sun City West, AZ	PHX
Sun Lakes, AZ	PHX
Sun Prairie, WI	MAD
Sun Valley, CA	LA
ID	B
NV	RNO
Sunapee, NH	MAN
Sunbury, OH	COL
PA	HBG
Suncook, NH	MAN
Sunland Park, NM	LSC
Sunman, IN	IND
Sunny Hills, FL	PT
Sunny Isles Beach, FL	MIA
Sunnyside, WA	YAK
Sunnyvale, CA	SJ
Sunrise, FL	MIA
Sunriver, OR	BAK
Sunset Hills, MO	STL
Superior, AZ	TUC
NE	LIN
WI	SUP
Suring, WI	GB
Surprise, AZ	PHX
Susanville, CA	SAC
Susquehanna, PA	SCR
Sussex, NJ	PAT
Sutherlin, OR	P
Sutter Creek, CA	SAC
Sutton, MA	WOR
NE	LIN
Suttons Bay, MI	GLD
Swainsboro, GA	SAV
Swampscott, MA	BO
Swan Lake, MT	HEL
Swansboro, NC	R
Swansea, MA	FR
Swanton, OH	TOL
VT	BUR
Swarthmore, PA	PH
Swartswood, NJ	PAT
Swartz Creek, MI	LAN
Swedesboro, NJ	CAM
Swedesburg, PA	PH
Sweeny, TX	GAL
Sweet Home, OR	P
TX	VIC
Sweetwater, TX	SAN
Swinomish, WA	SEA
Switzerland, FL	STA
Swormville, NY	BUF
Swoyersville, PA	SCR
Sybertsville, PA	PSC
Sycamore, IL	RCK
OH	TOL
Sykeston, ND	FAR
Sykesville, PA	E
PA	PBR
Sylacauga, AL	BIR
Sylmar, CA	LA
Sylva, NC	CHL
Sylvania, GA	SAV
OH	TOL
Syosset, NY	RVC
Syracuse, IN	FTW
KS	DOD
NE	LIN
NY	SY
NY	STF
Tabb, VA	RIC
Taberg, NY	SY
Tabernacle, NJ	TR
Tabor, SD	SFS
Tacoma, WA	SEA
Taft, CA	FRS
TX	CC
Taftville, CT	NOR
Tahlequah, OK	TLS
Tahoe City, CA	SAC
Takoma Park, MD	WDC
Talcott, WV	WH
Talkeetna, AK	ANC
Talladega, AL	BIR
Tallahassee, FL	PT
Tallassee, AL	MOB
Tallmadge, OH	CLV
Tallulah, LA	ALX
Tama, IA	DUB
Tamaqua, PA	ALN
Tamarac, FL	MIA
Tamaroa, IL	BEL
Tampa, FL	SP
FL	SAM
Tampico, IL	RCK
Tanana, AK	FBK
Taneytown, MD	BAL
Tannersville, PA	SCR
Taos, NM	SFE
Tappahannock, VA	RIC
Tappan, NY	NY
Tarboro, NC	R
Tarentum, PA	PBR
PA	PIT
Tariffville, CT	HRT
Tarkio, MO	KC
Tarpon Springs, FL	SP
Tarrytown, NY	NY
Tarzana, CA	LA
Taunton, MA	FR
Tavernier, FL	MIA
Tawas City, MI	GLD
Taylor, MI	DET
TX	AUS
Taylor Mill, KY	COV
Taylors, SC	CHR
Taylors Falls, MN	STP
Taylorsville, UT	SLC
Taylorville, IL	SFD
Tazewell, VA	RIC
Tea, SD	SFS
Teaneck, NJ	NEW
Techny, IL	CHI
Tecumseh, MI	LAN
NE	LIN
Tehachapi, CA	FRS
Tekamah, NE	OM
Tekoa, WA	SPK
Tell City, IN	IND
Teller, AK	FBK
Telluride, CO	PBL
Temecula, CA	SB
Tempe, AZ	PHX
Temperance, MI	DET
Temple, TX	AUS
Temple City, CA	LA
Temple Terrace, FL	SP
Tenafly, NJ	NEW
Tennessee Ridge, TN	NSH
Tequesta, FL	PMB
Terre Haute, IN	IND
Terrell, TX	DAL
Terrytown, LA	NO
Terryville, CT	HRT
CT	STF
Teutopolis, IL	SFD
Tewksbury, MA	BO
Texarkana, AR	LR
TX	TYL
Texas City, TX	GAL
The Colony, TX	STN
The Dalles, OR	BAK
The Rock, GA	ATL
The Woodlands, TX	GAL
Theriot, LA	HT
Thermopolis, WY	CHY
Thibodaux, LA	HT
Thief River Falls, MN	CR
Thomas, WV	WH
Thomasboro, IL	PEO
Thomaston, CT	HRT
Thomasville, GA	SAV
NC	CHL
Thompson, CT	NOR
ND	FAR
OH	CLV
Thompson Falls, MT	HEL
Thomson, GA	ATL
Thoreau, NM	GLP
Thornton, CO	DEN
Thornwood, NY	NY
Thorp, WI	LC
Thousand Oaks, CA	LA
CA	OLL
Three Bridges, NJ	MET
Three Forks, MT	HEL
Three Lakes, WI	SUP
Three Oaks, MI	KAL
Three Rivers, CA	FRS
MA	SPR
MI	KAL
TX	CC
Throop, PA	SCR
Tiburon, CA	SFR
Tickfaw, LA	BR
Ticonderoga, NY	OG
Tidioute, PA	E
Tierra Amarilla, NM	SFE
Tiffin, OH	TOL
Tifton, GA	SAV
Tigard, OR	P
Tigerton, WI	GB
Tijeras, NM	SFE
Tilden, NE	OM
Tillamook, OR	P
Tilton, NH	MAN
Tiltonsville, OH	STU
Timber Lake, SD	RC
Timonium, MD	BAL
Tinley Park, IL	CHI
Tintah, MN	SCL
Tioga, LA	ALX
ND	BIS
Tipp City, OH	CIN
Tipton, CA	FRS
IA	DAV
IN	LFT
KS	SAL
MO	JC
Tishomingo, OK	OKL
Titusville, FL	ORL
NJ	TR
PA	E
Tiverton, RI	PRO
Tivoli, NY	NY
TX	CC
Toccoa, GA	ATL
Tohatchi, NM	GLP
Tok, AK	FBK
Toksook Bay, AK	FBK
Toledo, OH	TOL
WA	SEA

Place	Code
Tolland, CT	NOR
Tolleson, AZ	PHX
Tolono, IL	PEO
Toluca, IL	PEO
Tomah, WI	LC
Tomahawk, WI	SUP
Tomales, CA	SFR
Tomball, TX	GAL
Tombstone, AZ	TUC
Tome, NM	SFE
Toms River, NJ	TR
NJ	PHU
NJ	PSC
Tonawanda, NY	BUF
Tonganoxie, KS	KCK
Tonica, IL	PEO
Tonkawa, OK	OKL
Tonopah, AZ	PHX
NV	LAV
Tontitown, AR	LR
Tooele, UT	SLC
Topawa, AZ	TUC
Topeka, KS	KCK
Toppenish, WA	YAK
Topping, VA	RIC
Topsfield, MA	BO
Toronto, OH	PBR
OH	STU
Torrance, CA	LA
Torrington, CT	HRT
CT	SAM
WY	CHY
Totowa, NJ	PAT
Towanda, PA	SCR
Tower, MN	DUL
Town and Country, MO	STL
Towner, ND	FAR
Townsend, MA	BO
MT	HEL
TN	KNX
Towson, MD	BAL
Tracy, CA	STO
MN	NU
Tracyton, WA	SEA
Traer, IA	DUB
Trafford, PA	GBG
Tranquillity, CA	FRS
Trappist, KY	L
Travelers Rest, SC	CHR
Traverse City, MI	GLD
Tremont, PA	ALN
Trempealeau, WI	LC
Trenary, MI	MAR
Trenton, IL	BEL
MI	DET
NE	LIN
NJ	TR
NJ	PHU
NJ	PSC
NJ	ROM
OH	CIN
Tres Pinos, CA	MRY
Trevorton, PA	HBG
Triangle, VA	ARL
Tribes Hill, NY	ALB
Tribune, KS	DOD
Trinidad, CO	PBL
Trinity, FL	SP
TX	TYL
Tripp, SD	SFS
Troy, AL	MOB
IL	SFD
KS	KCK
MI	DET
MI	EST
MO	STL
NY	ALB
NY	STF
NY	SAM
OH	CIN
VT	BUR
Truckee, CA	SAC
Trumansburg, NY	ROC
Trumbull, CT	BGP
CT	PSC
Trussville, AL	BIR
Truth or Consequences, NM	LSC
Truxton, NY	SY
Tryon, NC	CHL
Tualatin, OR	P
Tuba City, AZ	GLP
Tubac, AZ	TUC
Tuckahoe, NY	NY
Tucker, GA	ATL
Tuckerton, NJ	TR
Tucson, AZ	HPM
AZ	TUC
AZ	STN
Tucumcari, NM	SFE
Tujunga, CA	LA
CA	OLN
Tukwila, WA	SEA
Tulare, CA	FRS
Tularosa, NM	LSC
Tulelake, CA	SAC
Tulia, TX	AMA
Tullahoma, TN	NSH
Tully, NY	SY
Tulsa, OK	OLL
OK	TLS
Tunkhannock, PA	SCR
Tununak, AK	FBK
Tupelo, MS	JKS
Tupper Lake, NY	OG
Turlock, CA	SPA
CA	STO
Turners Falls, MA	SPR
Turnersville, NJ	CAM
Turtle Creek, PA	PIT
Turton, SD	SFS
Tuscaloosa, AL	BIR
Tuscola, IL	SFD
Tuscumbia, AL	BIR
Tuskegee Institute, AL	MOB
Tustin, CA	ORG
CA	ROM
Tutwiler, MS	JKS
Tuxedo, NY	NY
Twain Harte, CA	STO
Twentynine Palms, CA	SB
Twin Falls, ID	B
Twin Lake, MI	GR
Twin Lakes, WI	MIL
Twinsburg, OH	CLV
Twisp, WA	SPK
Two Harbors, MN	DUL
Two Rivers, WI	GB
Tybee Island, GA	SAV
Tyler, MN	NU
TX	TYL
Tyndall, SD	SFS
Tyngsborough, MA	BO
Tyringham, MA	SPR
Tyrone, GA	ATL
PA	ALT
Ubly, MI	SAG
Uhland, TX	AUS
Ukiah, CA	SR
CA	STN
Ulysses, KS	DOD
NE	LIN
Umbarger, TX	AMA
Unadilla, NY	ALB
Unalakleet, AK	FBK
Unalaska, AK	ANC
Uncasville, CT	NOR
Underhill Center, VT	BUR
Underwood, MN	SCL
ND	BIS
Union, KY	COV
MO	STL
NJ	NEW
SC	CHR
Union City, CA	OAK
CT	HRT
IN	LFT
NJ	NEW
OK	OKL
PA	E
TN	MEM
Union Gap, WA	YAK
Union Grove, WI	MIL
Uniondale, NY	RVC
Uniontown, KY	OWN
OH	Y
OH	CLV
PA	GBG
PA	PBR
PA	SAM
Unionville, CT	HRT
United, PA	GBG
Universal, IN	IND
University City, MO	STL
University Heights, OH	CLV
University Park, PA	ALT
Upland, CA	SB
Upper Darby, PA	PH
Upper Marlboro, MD	WDC
Upper Montclair, NJ	NEW
Upper Saddle River, NJ	NEW
Upper Sandusky, OH	TOL
Upper St. Clair, PA	PBR
Upsala, MN	SCL
Upton, MA	WOR
Urbana, IL	PEO
OH	CIN
Urbandale, IA	DM
Utica, IL	PEO
KY	OWN
MI	DET
NY	SY
NY	NTN
NY	SAM
NY	STF
OH	COL
Uvalde, TX	SAT
Uwchlan, PA	PH
Uxbridge, MA	WOR
Vacaville, CA	SAC
Vacherie, LA	BR
Vail, AZ	TUC
Valatie, NY	ALB
Valdez, AK	ANC
Valdosta, GA	SAV
Vale, NC	CHL
OR	BAK
Valentine, NE	GI
Valhalla, NY	NY
Valier, MT	HEL
Valinda, CA	LA
Vallejo, CA	SAC
Valley, NE	OM
WA	SPK
Valley Center, CA	SD
KS	WCH
Valley City, ND	FAR
OH	CLV
Valley Lee, MD	WDC
Valley Park, MO	STL
Valley Stream, NY	MCE
NY	RVC
Valmeyer, IL	BEL
Valparaiso, IN	GRY
NE	LIN
Valrico, FL	SP
Valyermo, CA	LA
Van Alstyne, TX	DAL
Van Buren, AR	LR
ME	PRT
Van Horn, TX	ELP
Van Horne, IA	DUB
Van Nuys, CA	LA
Van Wert, OH	TOL
Vanceburg, KY	COV
Vancleave, MS	BLX
Vancouver, WA	SEA
Vandalia, IL	SFD
MO	JC
OH	CIN
Vanderbilt, TX	VIC
Vandergrift, PA	GBG
Vanderwagen, NM	GLP
Vashon, WA	SEA
Vassar, MI	SAG
Vaughn, NM	SFE
Vega, TX	AMA
Velva, ND	FAR
Veneta, OR	P
Venice, CA	LA
FL	VEN
Ventnor, NJ	CAM
PA	PH
Ventura, CA	LA
CA	ROM
Verdigre, NE	OM
Vergennes, VT	BUR
Vermilion, OH	TOL
Vermillion, MN	STP
SD	SFS
Vernal, UT	SLC
Verndale, MN	SCL
Vernon, CA	LA
CT	NOR
NY	SY
TX	FWT
Vernon Hills, IL	CHI
Vernonia, OR	P
Vero Beach, FL	PMB
Verona, NJ	NEW
NY	SY
PA	PIT
WI	MAD
Verplanck, NY	NY
Versailles, CT	NOR
KY	LEX
OH	CIN
Veseli, MN	STP
Vesper, WI	LC
Vestaburg, MI	GR
Vestal, NY	SY
Vicksburg, MI	KAL
MS	JKS
Victor, IA	DAV
NY	ROC
Victoria, KS	SAL
MN	STP
TX	VIC
Victorville, CA	SB
Vidalia, GA	SAV
LA	ALX
Vidor, TX	BEA
Vienna, IL	BEL
MO	JC
OH	Y
VA	ARL
WV	WH
Viera, FL	ORL
Villa Grove, IL	SFD
Villa Hills, KY	COV
Villa Maria, PA	PIT
Villa Park, IL	JOL
Villa Ridge, MO	STL
Villanova, PA	PH
Villanueva, NM	SFE
Ville Platte, LA	LAF
Vina, CA	SAC
Vincennes, IN	EVN
Vine Grove, KY	L
Vineland, NJ	CAM
Vineyard Haven, MA	FR
Vinita, OK	TLS
Vinton, IA	DUB
LA	LKC
Viola, KS	WCH
Violet, LA	NO
Virden, IL	SFD
Virgil, IL	RCK
Virginia, MN	DUL
Virginia Beach, VA	RIC
Virginia City, NV	RNO
Virginia Dale, CO	DEN
Viroqua, WI	LC
Visalia, CA	FRS
Vista, CA	SD
Vivian, LA	SHP
Volga, IA	DUB
Volo, IL	CHI
Voluntown, CT	NOR
Von Ormy, TX	SAT
Voorheesville, NY	ALB
Vulcan, MI	MAR
WaKeeney, KS	SAL
Wabash, IN	FTW
Wabasha, MN	WIN
Wabasso, MN	NU
Wabeno, WI	GB
Waco, TX	AUS
Waconia, MN	STP
Waddington, NY	OG
Wadena, MN	SCL
Wading River, NY	RVC
Wadsworth, IL	CHI
OH	CLV
Waggaman, LA	NO
Wagner, SD	SFS
Wagon Mound, NM	SFE
Wagoner, OK	TLS
Wahiawa, HI	HON
Wahkon, MN	SCL
Wahoo, NE	LIN
Wahpeton, ND	FAR
Waialua, HI	HON
Waianae, HI	HON
Waihee, HI	HON
Wailuku, HI	HON
Waimanalo, HI	HON
Waipahu, HI	HON
Waite Park, MN	SCL
Wake Forest, NC	R
Wakefield, MA	BO
MI	MAR
RI	PRO
Wakeman, OH	TOL
Walbridge, OH	TOL
Walden, NY	NY
Waldorf, MD	WDC
Waldport, OR	P
Waldron, AR	LR
Walhalla, ND	FAR
Walker, IA	DUB
MN	DUL
Walkersville, MD	BAL
Walkerton, IN	FTW
IN	GRY
Wall, PA	PBR
SD	RC
TX	SAN
Walla Walla, WA	SPK
Wallace, ID	B
NE	LIN
Walled Lake, MI	DET
Wallingford, CT	HRT
PA	PH
VT	BUR
Wallington, NJ	NEW
Wallis, TX	GAL
Walls, MS	JKS
Walnut, CA	LA
IL	PEO
Walnut Creek, CA	OAK
Walnut Grove, CA	SAC
MN	NU
Walnut Ridge, AR	LR
Walnutport, PA	ALN

Place	Code
Walpole, MA	BO
Walsenburg, CO	PBL
Walsh, IL	BEL
Walterboro, SC	CHR
Waltham, MA	BO
Walton, KY	COV
NY	ALB
Wamego, KS	KCK
Wanatah, IN	GRY
Wantagh, NY	RVC
Wapakoneta, OH	CIN
Wapato, WA	YAK
Wapella, IL	PEO
Wappingers Falls, NY	NY
Wapwallopen, PA	SCR
War, WV	WH
Warba, MN	DUL
Ward, SC	CHR
Ware, MA	SPR
Wareham, MA	FR
Warminster, PA	PH
Warner, NH	MAN
Warner Robins, GA	SAV
Warren, AR	LR
IL	RCK
MA	WOR
MI	DET
MI	STN
MI	EST
MI	OLL
MI	NTN
MN	CR
NJ	MET
OH	Y
OH	PBR
PA	E
RI	PRO
Warrens, WI	LC
Warrensburg, MO	KC
NY	ALB
Warrenton, MO	STL
VA	ARL
Warrenville, IL	JOL
Warrington, PA	PH
PA	PHU
Warroad, MN	CR
Warsaw, IL	PEO
IN	FTW
KY	COV
MO	JC
NY	BUF
Warson Woods, MO	STL
Warwick, NY	NY
RI	PRO
Wasco, CA	FRS
OR	BAK
Waseca, MN	WIN
Washburn, WI	SUP
Washington, DC	PHU
DC	SAM
DC	WDC
GA	ATL
IA	DAV
IL	PEO
IN	EVN
KS	SAL
LA	LAF
MI	DET
MO	STL
NC	R
NJ	MET
NJ	SYM
PA	PIT
TX	AUS
VA	ARL
Washington Court House, OH	COL
Washington Depot, CT	HRT
Washington Township, NJ	NEW
Washingtonville, NY	NY
Wasilla, AK	ANC
Watchung, NJ	MET
Waterbury, CT	HRT
CT	SAM
VT	BUR
Waterflow, NM	GLP
Waterford, CT	NOR
CT	NTN
MI	DET
NY	ALB
PA	E
WI	MIL
Waterloo, IA	DUB
IL	BEL
IN	FTW
NY	ROC
WI	MAD
Watersmeet, MI	MAR
Watertown, CT	HRT
MA	BO
MN	STP
NY	OG
SD	SFS
WI	MAD
Waterville, ME	PRT
ME	SAM
MN	STP
NY	SY
WA	YAK
Watervliet, MI	KAL
NY	ALB
NY	STF
Watford City, ND	BIS
Wathena, KS	KCK
Watkins, MN	NU
MN	SCL
Watkins Glen, NY	ROC
Watseka, IL	JOL
Watsonville, CA	MRY
Waubun, MN	CR
Wauchula, FL	VEN
Waucoma, IA	DUB
Wauconda, IL	CHI
Waukee, IA	DM
Waukegan, IL	CHI
Waukesha, WI	MIL
Waukon, IA	DUB
Waumandee, WI	LC
Waunakee, WI	MAD
Waupaca, WI	GB
Waupun, WI	MIL
Wauregan, CT	NOR
Wausau, WI	LC
Wausaukee, WI	GB
Wauseon, OH	TOL
Wautoma, WI	GB
Wauwatosa, WI	MIL
Wauzeka, WI	LC
Waveland, MS	BLX
Waverly, IA	DUB
KY	OWN
MN	STP
NE	LIN
OH	COL
Waxahachie, TX	CHL
TX	DAL
Waycross, GA	SAV
Wayland, MA	BO
MI	KAL
NY	ROC
Waymart, PA	SCR
Wayne, IL	JOL
MI	DET
NE	OM
NJ	PAT
PA	PH
WV	WH
Waynesboro, GA	SAV
MS	BLX
PA	HBG
VA	RIC
Waynesburg, OH	Y
OH	STU
PA	PIT
Waynesville, NC	CHL
OH	CIN
Wayside, NJ	TR
Wayzata, MN	STP
Weatherford, OK	OKL
TX	FWT
Weatherly, PA	ALN
Weaverville, CA	SAC
Webb City, MO	SPC
Webster, MA	WOR
MN	STP
NY	ROC
SD	SFS
WI	SUP
Webster City, IA	DUB
Webster Groves, MO	STL
Webster Springs, WV	WH
Wedron, IL	PEO
Weed, CA	SAC
Weedsport, NY	ROC
Weimar, TX	VIC
Weiner, AR	LR
Weirton, WV	WH
WV	PBR
Weiser, ID	B
Welch, WV	WH
Wellesley, MA	BO
Wellesley Hills, MA	BO
Wellfleet, MA	FR
Wellington, FL	PMB
KS	WCH
OH	CLV
Wellpinit, WA	SPK
Wells, ME	PRT
MN	WIN
NV	RNO
Wellsboro, PA	SCR
Wellsburg, WV	WH
Wellston, OH	COL
Wellsville, NY	BUF
Wellton, AZ	TUC
Welsh, LA	LKC
Wenatchee, WA	YAK
Wendell, NC	R
Wendover, UT	SLC
Wenona, IL	PEO
Wentzville, MO	STL
Wernersville, PA	ALN
Weslaco, TX	BWN
Wesley, IA	SC
Wesley Hills, NY	NY
Wessington Springs, SD	SFS
West, TX	AUS
West Allis, WI	MIL
WI	SYM
West Babylon, NY	RVC
West Bend, IA	SC
WI	MIL
West Bloomfield, MI	DET
MI	EST
West Boylston, MA	WOR
West Branch, IA	DAV
MI	GLD
West Brandywine, PA	PH
West Bridgewater, MA	BO
West Brookfield, MA	WOR
West Brooklyn, IL	RCK
West Burlington, IA	DAV
West Chazy, NY	OG
West Chester, OH	CIN
PA	PH
West Chicago, IL	JOL
West Clarksville, NY	BUF
West Conshohocken, PA	PH
West Covina, CA	LA
CA	OLL
West Deptford, NJ	CAM
West Des Moines, IA	DM
West Easton, PA	PHU
West End, NJ	TR
West Falls, NY	BUF
West Fargo, ND	FAR
West Frankfort, IL	BEL
West Greenwich, RI	PRO
West Grove, PA	PH
West Harrison, IN	IND
NY	NY
West Hartford, CT	HRT
West Harwich, MA	FR
West Haven, CT	HRT
CT	MCE
UT	SLC
West Hazleton, PA	SCR
West Hempstead, NY	RVC
NY	SYM
West Hollywood, CA	LA
FL	MIA
West Hyattsville, MD	WDC
West Islip, NY	RVC
West Jefferson, OH	COL
West Jordan, UT	SLC
West Lafayette, IN	LFT
West Liberty, IA	DAV
KY	LEX
WV	WH
West Linn, OR	P
West Long Branch, NJ	TR
West Memphis, AR	LR
West Middlesex, PA	E
West Mifflin, PA	PIT
West Milford, NJ	PAT
West Milton, OH	CIN
West Monroe, LA	SHP
West New York, NJ	NEW
West Newton, PA	GBG
West Nyack, NY	NY
NY	SYM
West Orange, NJ	NEW
West Palm Beach, FL	PMB
West Park, NY	NY
West Paterson, NJ	NTN
NJ	PAT
West Peoria, IL	PEO
West Pittston, PA	SCR
West Plains, MO	SPC
West Point, IA	DAV
MS	JKS
NE	OM
NY	NY
VA	RIC
West Portsmouth, OH	COL
West Redding, CT	BGP
West River, MD	BAL
West Roxbury, MA	BO
MA	NTN
West Rutland, VT	BUR
West Sacramento, CA	SAC
West Salem, OH	CLV
WI	LC
West Sedona, AZ	PHX
West Seneca, NY	BUF
West Simsbury, CT	HRT
West Springfield, MA	SPR
West St. Paul, MN	STP
West Stockbridge, MA	SPR
West Sunbury, PA	PIT
West Trenton, NJ	TR
West Union, IA	DUB
OH	CIN
West Valley, NY	BUF
West Valley City, UT	SLC
West Warren, MA	WOR
West Warwick, RI	PRO
West Wyoming, PA	SCR
West Yellowstone, MT	HEL
Westampton, NJ	TR
Westborough, MA	WOR
Westbrook, CT	NOR
ME	PRT
Westbury, NY	PSC
NY	RVC
Westchester, IL	CHI
Westcliffe, CO	PBL
Westerly, RI	PRO
Western Springs, IL	CHI
Westernport, MD	BAL
Westerville, OH	COL
OH	NTN
Westfield, IN	LFT
MA	SPR
NJ	NEW
NY	BUF
VT	BUR
Westford, MA	BO
Westhampton Beach, NY	RVC
Westlake, LA	LKC
OH	CLV
Westlake Village, CA	LA
Westland, MI	DET
Westminster, CA	ORG
CO	DEN
MA	WOR
MD	BAL
Westmont, IL	JOL
Westmorland, CA	SD
Weston, CT	BGP
FL	MIA
MA	BO
MO	KC
NE	LIN
PA	SCR
VT	BUR
WI	LC
WV	WH
Westphalia, IA	DM
MI	LAN
MO	JC
Westport, CT	BGP
MA	FR
SD	SFS
Westville, IL	PEO
Westville Grove, NJ	CAM
Westwego, LA	NO
Westwood, CA	SAC
MA	BO
NJ	NEW
Wethersfield, CT	HRT
Wever, IA	DAV
Wewahitchka, FL	PT
Wexford, PA	PIT
Weyauwega, WI	GB
Weymouth, MA	BO
Wharton, NJ	PAT
TX	VIC
Wheat Ridge, CO	DEN
Wheatfield, IN	LFT
Wheatland, IA	DAV
WY	CHY
Wheaton, IL	GB
IL	PEO
IL	JOL
MD	WDC
MN	SCL
Wheelersburg, OH	COL
Wheeling, IL	CHI
WV	WH
WV	SJP
WV	OLL
Whippany, NJ	PAT
NJ	PHU
Whistler, AL	MOB
White, SD	SFS
White Bear Lake, MN	STP
White Castle, LA	BR
White Cloud, MI	GR
White Deer, TX	AMA
White Haven, PA	SCR
White Lake, MI	DET
SD	SFS
WI	GB
White Mills, KY	L

White Oak, PA PIT
White Pigeon, MI KAL
White Pine, MI MAR
White Plains, NY NY
NY PSC
NY SAM
White River, SD RC
White River Junction, VT BUR
White Salmon, WA YAK
White Sulphur Springs, MT HEL
WV WH
White Swan, WA YAK
Whitefield, ME PRT
Whitefish, MT HEL
Whitefish Bay, WI MIL
Whitehall, MT HEL
NY ALB
PA ALN
WI LC
Whitehouse, OH TOL
TX TYL
Whitehouse Station, NJ MET
Whitelaw, WI GB
Whiteriver, AZ GLP
Whitesboro, NY SY
Whitestone, NY BRK
Whitesville, KY OWN
Whitethorn, CA SR
Whiteville, NC R
Whitewater, CO PBL
WI MIL
Whiting, IN GRY
IN PRM
NJ TR
Whitinsville, MA WOR
Whitman, MA BO
Whitney, PA GBG
Whitney Point, NY SY
Whittemore, IA SC
MI GLD
Whittier, CA LA
Wichita, KS STN
KS WCH
Wichita Falls, TX FWT
Wickatunk, NJ TR
Wickenburg, AZ PHX
Wickford, RI PRO
Wickliffe, OH CLV
Wiggins, MS BLX
Wilber, NE LIN
Wilbraham, MA SPR
Wilbur, WA SPK
Wilburton, OK TLS
Wilcox, PA E
Wilder, KY COV
Wildomar, CA SB
CA NTN
Wildwood, FL ORL
MO STL
NJ CAM
PA PIT
Wilkes–Barre, PA PHU
PA SCR
PA SAM
PA PSC
Willard, OH TOL
WI LC
Willcox, AZ TUC
Williams, AZ PHX
CA SAC
IA DUB
Williams Bay, WI MIL
Williamsburg, IA DAV
KY LEX
PA ALT
VA PSC
VA RIC
Williamson, WV WH
Williamsport, IN LFT
MD BAL
PA SCR
Williamston, MI LAN
NC R
Williamstown, KY COV
MA SPR
NJ CAM
PA HBG
Williamsville, NY BUF
NY SAM
Willimantic, CT NOR
CT STF
Willingboro, NJ TR
Willington, CT NOR
Williston, FL STA
ND BIS
VT BUR
Williston Park, NY RVC
Willits, CA SR
Willmar, MN NU
Willoughby, OH CLV
Willoughby Hills, OH CLV
Willow City, ND FAR
Willow Grove, PA PH
Willow River, MN DUL
Willow Springs, IL CHI
MO SPC
Willowick, OH CLV
Willows, CA SAC
Willsboro, NY OG
Wilmerding, PA PIT
Wilmette, IL CHI
Wilmington, CA LA
DE PHU
DE WIL
IL JOL
MA BO
NC R
OH CIN
VT BUR
Wilmore, PA ALT
Wilmot, SD SFS
Wilson, KS SAL
NC R
Wilsonville, OR P
Wilton, CT BGP
IA DAV
ND BIS
ND STN
Wimberley, TX AUS
Wimbledon, ND FAR
Winamac, IN LFT
Winchendon, MA WOR
Winchester, CA SB
KY LEX
MA BO
VA ARL
Winchester Center, CT HRT
Wind Lake, WI MIL
Windber, PA ALT
PA PBR
Winder, GA ATL
Windham, CT NOR
ME PRT
NH MAN
NY ALB
OH Y
Windom, MN WIN
Windsor, CA SR
CO DEN
CT HRT
ME PRT
NC R
NY SY
VT BUR
Windsor Locks, CT HRT
Windthorst, TX FWT
Winfield, AL BIR
IL JOL
KS WCH
Winlock, WA SEA
Winnebago, NE OM
Winneconne, WI GB
Winnemucca, NV RNO
Winner, SD RC
Winnetka, CA LA
IL CHI
Winnfield, LA ALX
Winnie, TX BEA
Winnsboro, LA ALX
SC CHR
Winona, MN WIN
Winooski, VT BUR
Winslow, AR LR
AZ GLP
ME PRT
Winsted, CT HRT
MN NU
Winston–Salem, NC CHL
Winter, WI SUP
Winter Garden, FL ORL
Winter Haven, FL ORL
Winter Park, FL ORL
Winter Springs, FL ORL
Winterhaven, CA SD
Winters, CA SAC
TX SAN
Winterset, IA DM
Wintersville, OH STU
Winthrop, MA BO
MN NU
Wisconsin Dells, WI MAD
Wisconsin Rapids, WI LC
WI SUP
Wishek, ND FAR
Wisner, NE OM
Wittenberg, WI LC
Wixom, MI DET
Woburn, MA BO
Wofford Heights, CA FRS
Wolcott, CT HRT
NY ROC
Wolf Point, MT GF
Wolfeboro, NH MAN
Wolfforth, TX LUB
Wonder Lake, IL RCK
Wonewoc, WI LC
Wood Dale, IL JOL
Wood Ridge, NJ NEW
Wood River, IL SFD
NE GI
Woodbourne, NY NY
Woodbridge, CT HRT
NJ MET
VA ARL
Woodburn, OR P
Woodbury, CT HRT
MN STP
NJ CAM
NY RVC
Woodbury Heights, NJ CAM
Woodcliff Lake, NJ NEW
Woodhaven, MI DET
NY BRK
Woodhull, IL PEO
Woodinville, WA SEA
Woodlake, CA FRS
Woodland, CA SAC
WA SEA
Woodland Hills, CA LA
Woodland Park, CO COS
NJ PAT
NJ PSC
Woodlawn, VA RIC
Woodridge, IL JOL
Woodruff, WI SUP
Woods Hole, MA FR
Woodsboro, TX CC
Woodsfield, OH STU
Woodside, NY BRK
Woodstock, GA ATL
IL RCK
MD BAL
NY NY
VA ARL
VT BUR
Woodsville, NH MAN
Woodville, FL PT
MS JKS
TX BEA
Woodward, OK OKL
Woodworth, LA ALX
Woonsocket, RI NTN
RI STF
RI PRO
SD SFS
Wooster, OH CLV
Worcester, MA NTN
MA SAM
MA WOR
NY ALB
Worland, WY CHY
Worthington, IA DUB
MN WIN
OH COL
Wrangell, AK JUN
Wray, CO DEN
Wrentham, MA BO
Wright, KS DOD
Wrightsville Beach, NC R
Wrightwood, CA SB
Wurtsboro, NY NY
Wyalusing, PA SCR
Wyandanch, NY RVC
Wyandotte, MI DET
Wyckoff, NJ NEW
Wylie, TX DAL
Wymore, NE LIN
Wynantskill, NY ALB
Wyncote, PA PH
Wyndmere, ND FAR
Wyndmoor, PA PH
Wynne, AR LR
Wynnewood, PA PH
PA OLN
Wynot, NE OM
Wyoming, IL PEO
MI GR
OH CIN
PA SCR
Wytheville, VA RIC
Xenia, OH CIN
Yakima, WA YAK
Yakutat, AK JUN
Yale, MI DET
Yalesville, CT HRT
Yamhill, OR P
Yankton, SD SFS
Yardley, PA PH
Yardville, NJ TR
Yarmouth, ME PRT
Yarnell, AZ PHX
Yatesboro, PA GBG
Yazoo City, MS JKS
Yeadon, PA PH
Yellow Springs, OH CIN
Yellville, AR LR
Yelm, WA SEA
Yerington, NV RNO
Yoakum, TX VIC
Yoder, IN FTW
Yonges Island, SC CHR
Yonkers, NY NY
NY STF
NY NTN
NY MCE
Yorba Linda, CA ORG
York, NE LIN
PA HBG
SC CHR
York Haven, PA HBG
Yorktown, TX VIC
VA RIC
Yorktown Heights, NY NY
Yorkville, IL JOL
Youngstown, NY BUF
OH Y
OH PBR
OH SJP
OH OLL
Youngsville, LA LAF
PA E
Youngtown, AZ PHX
Youngwood, PA GBG
Yountville, CA SR
Ypsilanti, MI LAN
Yreka, CA SAC
Yuba City, CA SAC
Yucaipa, CA SB
Yucca Valley, CA SB
Yukon, OK OKL
PA GBG
Yulan, NY NY
Yuma, AZ TUC
CO DEN
Zachary, LA BR
Zaleski, OH COL
Zanesville, OH COL
OH NTN
Zapata, TX LAR
Zelienople, PA PIT
Zenda, KS WCH
Zephyr Cove, NV RNO
Zephyrhills, FL SP
Zillah, WA YAK
Zion–Beach Park, IL CHI
Zionsville, IN LFT
Zumbrota, MN STP
Zuni, NM GLP
Zwolle, LA SHP

Diocesan Abbreviations

ARCHDIOCESES AND DIOCESES

(ALB) Albany (New York)
(ALN) Allentown (Pennsylvania)
(ALT) Altoona-Johnstown (Pennsylvania)
(ALX) Alexandria (Louisiana)
(AGN) Agana (Guam)
(AMA) Amarillo (Texas)
(ANC) Anchorage (Alaska)
(ARE) Arecibo (Puerto Rico)
(ARL) Arlington (Virginia)
(ATH) Apostolate To Hungarians (Washington, DC)
(ATL) Atlanta (Georgia)
(AUS) Austin (Texas)
(B) Boise (Idaho)
(BAK) Baker (Oregon)
(BAL) Baltimore (Maryland)
(BEA) Beaumont (Texas)
(BEL) Belleville (Illinois)
(BGP) Bridgeport (Connecticut)
(BIR) Birmingham (Alabama)
(BIS) Bismarck (North Dakota)
(BLX) Biloxi (Mississippi)
(BO) Boston (Massachusetts)
(BR) Baton Rouge (Louisiana)
(BRK) Brooklyn (New York)
(BUF) Buffalo (New York)
(BUR) Burlington (Vermont)
(BWN) Brownsville (Texas)
(CAM) Camden (New Jersey)
(CC) Corpus Christi (Texas)
(CGS) Caguas (Puerto Rico)
(CHI) Chicago (Illinois)
(CHK) Chalan Kanoa
(CHL) Charlotte (North Carolina)
(CHR) Charleston (South Carolina)
(CHY) Cheyenne (Wyoming)
(CI) Caroline Islands
(CIN) Cincinnati (Ohio)
(CLV) Cleveland (Ohio)
(COL) Columbus (Ohio)
(COS) Colorado Springs (Colorado)
(COV) Covington (Kentucky)
(CR) Crookston (Minnesota)
(DAL) Dallas (Texas)
(DAV) Davenport (Iowa)
(DEN) Denver (Colorado)
(DET) Detroit (Michigan)
(DM) Des Moines (Iowa)
(DOD) Dodge City (Kansas)
(DUB) Dubuque (Iowa)
(DUL) Duluth (Minnesota)
(E) Erie (Pennsylvania)
(ELP) El Paso (Texas)
(EST) Eparchy of Saint Thomas the Apostle
(EVN) Evansville (Indiana)
(FAJ) Fajardo-Humacao (Puerto Rico)
(FAR) Fargo (North Dakota)
(FBK) Fairbanks (Alaska)
(FgM) Foreign Mission Section
(FR) Fall River (Massachusetts)
(FRS) Fresno (California)
(FTW) Fort Wayne-South Bend (Indiana)
(FWT) Fort Worth (Texas)
(GAL) Galveston-Houston (Texas)
(GLD) Gaylord (Michigan)
(GB) Green Bay (Wisconsin)
(GBG) Greensburg (Pennsylvania)
(GF) Great Falls-Billings (Montana)
(GI) Grand Island (Nebraska)
(GLP) Gallup (New Mexico)
(GR) Grand Rapids (Michigan)
(GRY) Gary (Indiana)
(HBG) Harrisburg (Pennsylvania)
(HEL) Helena (Montana)
(HON) Honolulu (Hawaii)
(HPM) Holy Protection of Mary (Arizona)
(HRT) Hartford (Connecticut)
(HT) Houma-Thibodaux (Louisiana)
(IND) Indianapolis (Indiana)
(JC) Jefferson City (Missouri)
(JKS) Jackson (Mississippi)
(JOL) Joliet in Illinois
(JUN) Juneau (Alaska)
(KAL) Kalamazoo (Michigan)
(KC) Kansas City-St. Joseph (Missouri)
(KCK) Kansas City in Kansas
(KNX) Knoxville (Tennessee)
(L) Louisville (Kentucky)
(LA) Los Angeles (California)
(LAF) Lafayette (Louisiana)
(LAN) Lansing (Michigan)
(LAR) Laredo (Texas)
(LC) La Crosse (Wisconsin)
(LEX) Lexington (Kentucky)
(LFT) Lafayette in Indiana
(LIN) Lincoln (Nebraska)
(LIT) Lithuanian Apostolate for Lithuanian Catholics
(LKC) Lake Charles (Louisiana)
(LR) Little Rock (Arkansas)
(LSC) Las Cruces (New Mexico)
(LUB) Lubbock (Texas)
(LAV) Las Vegas (Nevada)
(MAD) Madison (Wisconsin)
(MAN) Manchester (New Hampshire)
(MAR) Marquette (Michigan)
(MCE) Syro-Malankara Exarchate (New York)
(MEM) Memphis (Tennessee)
(MET) Metuchen (New Jersey)
(MGZ) Mayaguez (Puerto Rico)
(MI) Marshall Islands
(MIA) Miami (Florida)
(MIL) Milwaukee (Wisconsin)
(MO) Military Services (Maryland)
(MOB) Mobile (Alabama)
(MRY) Monterey in California
(NEW) Newark (New Jersey)
(NO) New Orleans (Louisiana)
(NOR) Norwich (Connecticut)
(NSH) Nashville (Tennessee)
(NTN) Newton (Melkite, United States)
(NU) New Ulm (Minnesota)
(NY) New York (New York)
(OAK) Oakland (California)
(OG) Ogdensburg (New York)
(OKL) Oklahoma City (Oklahoma)
(OLD) Our Lady of Deliverance Syriac (Union City, New Jersey)
(OLL) Our Lady of Lebanon of Los Angeles (California)
(OLN) Our Lady of Nareg for Armenian Catholics (New York)
(OM) Omaha (Nebraska)
(ORG) Orange in California
(ORL) Orlando (Florida)
(OWN) Owensboro (Kentucky)
(P) Portland in Oregon
(PAT) Paterson (New Jersey)
(PBL) Pueblo (Colorado)
(PBR) Pittsburgh Byzantine (Pennsylvania)
(PCE) Ponce (Puerto Rico)
(PEO) Peoria (Illinois)
(PH) Philadelphia (Pennsylvania)
(PHU) Philadelphia Ukrainian (Pennsylvania)
(PHX) Phoenix (Arizona)
(PIT) Pittsburgh (Pennsylvania)
(PMB) Palm Beach (Florida)
(POC) Personal Ordinariate of the Chair of St. Peter
(POD) Prelature of the Holy Cross and Opus Dei
(PRM) Parma Byzantine (Ohio)
(PRO) Providence (Rhode Island)
(PRT) Portland (Maine)
(PSC) Passaic Byzantine (New Jersey)
(PT) Pensacola-Tallahassee (Florida)
(R) Raleigh (North Carolina)
(RC) Rapid City (South Dakota)
(RCK) Rockford (Illinois)
(RIC) Richmond (Virginia)
(RNO) Reno (Nevada)
(ROC) Rochester (New York)
(ROM) Romanian (Byzantine) (Ohio)
(RVC) Rockville Centre (New York)
(SAC) Sacramento (California)
(SAG) Saginaw (Michigan)
(SAL) Salina (Kansas)
(SAM) St. Maron of Brooklyn (U.S.A.)
(SAN) San Angelo (Texas)
(SAT) San Antonio (Texas)
(SAV) Savannah (Georgia)
(SB) San Bernadino (California)
(SC) Sioux City (Iowa)
(SCL) St. Cloud (Minnesota)
(SCR) Scranton (Pennsylvania)
(SD) San Diego (California)
(SEA) Seattle (Washington)
(SFD) Springfield in Illinois
(SFE) Santa Fe (New Mexico)
(SFR) San Francisco (California)
(SFS) Sioux Falls (South Dakota)
(SHP) Shreveport (Louisiana)
(SJ) San Jose in California
(SJN) San Juan (Puerto Rico)
(SJP) St. Josaphat in Parma (Ohio)
(SLC) Salt Lake City (Utah)
(SP) St. Petersburg (Florida)
(SPA) Eparchy of St. Peter the Apostle (Chaldean)
(SPC) Springfield-Cape Girardeau (Missouri)
(SPK) Spokane (Washington)
(SPP) Samoa-Pago Pago
(SPR) Springfield in Massachusetts
(SR) Santa Rosa in California
(STA) St. Augustine (Florida)
(STF) Stamford Ukrainian (Connecticut)
(STL) St. Louis (Missouri)
(STN) St. Nicholas in Chicago Ukrainian
(STO) Stockton (California)
(STP) St. Paul and Minneapolis (Minnesota)
(STU) Steubenville (Ohio)
(STV) St. Thomas, Virgin Islands
(SUP) Superior (Wisconsin)
(SY) Syracuse (New York)
(SYM) St. Thomas Syro-Malabar (Illinois)
(TLS) Tulsa (Oklahoma)
(TOL) Toledo (Ohio)
(TR) Trenton (New Jersey)
(TUC) Tucson (Arizona)
(TYL) Tyler (Texas)
(VEN) Venice (Florida)
(VIC) Victoria in Texas
(WCH) Wichita (Kansas)
(WDC) Washington (District of Columbia)
(WH) Wheeling-Charleston (West Virginia)
(WIL) Wilmington (Delaware)
(WIN) Winona (Minnesota)
(WOR) Worcester (Massachusetts)
(Y) Youngstown (Ohio)
(YAK) Yakima (Washington)

Diocese of Albany

(Dioecesis Albanensis)

Most Reverend

HOWARD J. HUBBARD, D.D.

Bishop of Albany; ordained December 18, 1963; appointed February 1, 1977; ordained and installed March 27, 1977. *Res.: 125 Eagle St., Albany, NY 12202.* Tel: 518-462-3804.

REJOICE WE ARE HIS PEOPLE

Chancery Office: Pastoral Center, 40 N. Main Ave., Albany, NY 12203. Tel: 518-453-6600; Fax: 518-453-6795.

Web: www.rcda.org

Email: chancery@rcda.org

ESTABLISHED APRIL 23, 1847.

Square Miles 10,419.

(Incorporated by a special act of the Legislature of the State of New York, April 12, 1941, with the title "The Roman Catholic Diocese of Albany, New York").

Comprises the entire Counties of Albany, Columbia, Delaware, Fulton, Green, Montgomery, Otsego, Rensselaer, Saratoga, Schenectady, Schoharie, Warren and Washington and that part of Herkimer and Hamilton Counties, south of the northern line of the townships of Ohio and Russia, as existing in 1872 in the State of New York.

For legal titles of parishes and diocesan institutions, consult the Chancery Office.

STATISTICAL OVERVIEW

Personnel	
Bishop	1
Priests: Diocesan Active in Diocese	121
Priests: Diocesan Active Outside Diocese	4
Priests: Retired, Sick or Absent	88
Number of Diocesan Priests	213
Religious Priests in Diocese	63
Total Priests in Diocese	276
Ordinations:	
Diocesan Priests	1
Transitional Deacons	1
Permanent Deacons	2
Permanent Deacons in Diocese	108
Total Brothers	68
Total Sisters	656
Parishes	
Parishes	128
With Resident Pastor:	
Resident Diocesan Priests	95
Resident Religious Priests	8
Without Resident Pastor:	
Administered by Deacons	5
Administered by Religious Women	8
Administered by Lay People	11
Missions	13
Pastoral Centers	7
New Parishes Created	1
Closed Parishes	2
Professional Ministry Personnel:	
Brothers	6
Sisters	31
Lay Ministers	220
Welfare	
Catholic Hospitals	3
Total Assisted	1,260,500
Health Care Centers	17
Total Assisted	73,150
Homes for the Aged	7
Total Assisted	1,200
Residential Care of Children	4
Total Assisted	117
Day Care Centers	3
Total Assisted	216
Specialized Homes	18
Total Assisted	559
Special Centers for Social Services	75
Total Assisted	90,000
Residential Care of Disabled	17
Total Assisted	84
Other Institutions	18
Total Assisted	861
Educational	
Diocesan Students in Other Seminaries	7
Total Seminarians	7
Colleges and Universities	4
Total Students	10,000
High Schools, Diocesan and Parish	4
Total Students	1,109
High Schools, Private	3
Total Students	968
Elementary Schools, Diocesan and Parish	20
Total Students	4,570
Elementary Schools, Private	2
Total Students	286
Catechesis/Religious Education:	
High School Students	8,267
Elementary Students	18,662
Total Students under Catholic Instruction	43,869
Teachers in the Diocese:	
Brothers	2
Sisters	12
Lay Teachers	724
Vital Statistics	
Receptions into the Church:	
Infant Baptism Totals	3,297
Minor Baptism Totals	101
Adult Baptism Totals	74
Received into Full Communion	139
First Communions	3,752
Confirmations	3,275
Marriages:	
Catholic	680
Interfaith	295
Total Marriages	975
Deaths	4,146
Total Catholic Population	330,000
Total Population	1,392,464

Former Bishops—His Eminence JOHN CARDINAL MCCLOSKEY, D.D., ord. Jan. 12, 1834; appt. Bishop of Axiere and Coadjutor to the Bishop of New York, Nov. 21, 1843; cons. March 10, 1844; transferred to Albany, May 21, 1847; promoted to New York, May 6, 1864; created Cardinal Priest of the Holy Roman Church, March 15, 1875, under the title Sanctae Mariae supra Minervam; died Oct. 10, 1885; Rt. Rev. JOHN J. CONROY, ord. May 21, 1842; appt. Bishop July 7, 1865; cons. Oct. 15, 1865; resigned Oct. 16, 1877; transferred to the See of Curium, March 22, 1878; died Nov. 20, 1895; Rt. Rev. Msgrs. FRANCIS MCNEIRNY, D.D., ord. Aug. 17, 1854; appt. Bishop of Rhesina and Coadjutor to the Bishop of Albany, Dec. 22, 1871; cons. April 21, 1872; appt. Administrator of the Diocese of Albany, Jan. 18, 1874; Bishop of Albany, by right of succession, Oct. 16, 1877; died Jan. 2, 1894; THOMAS M. A. BURKE, D.D., ord. June 30, 1864; preconized May 18, 1894; cons. July 1, 1894; died Jan 20, 1915; THOMAS F. CUSACK, D.D., ord. May 30, 1885; cons. Titular Bishop of Themiscyra and Auxiliary to the Archbishop of New York, April 25, 1904; transferred to Albany, July 5, 1915; died July 12, 1918; Most Revs. EDMUND F. GIBBONS, D.D., ord. May 27, 1893; appt. Bishop, Feb. 1, 1919; cons. March 25, 1919; resigned Nov. 10, 1954; transferred to See of Verbe; died June 19, 1964; WILLIAM A. SCULLY, D.D., ord. Sept. 20, 1919; appt. Coadjutor Bishop "cum jure successionis," Aug. 21, 1945; cons. Oct. 24, 1945; succeeded to See, Nov. 10, 1954; died Jan. 5, 1969; EDWARD J. MAGINN, D.D., ord. June 10, 1922; appt. Titular Bishop of Curium & Auxiliary Bishop of Albany June 27, 1957; appt. Apostolic Admin. for the Diocese of Albany Jan. 10, 1966; appt. ended March 18, 1969; died Aug. 21, 1984.; EDWIN B. BRODERICK, D.D., ord. May 30, 1942; appt. Titular Bishop of Tizica and Auxiliary of New York, March 8, 1967; cons. April 21, 1967; transferred to Albany, March 19, 1969; resigned June 2, 1976; appt. Exec. Dir. Catholic Relief Services, June 3, 1976; retired Sept. 1985; died July 2, 2006.

Pastoral Center—Pastoral Center, 40 N. Main Ave., Albany, 12203. Tel: 518-453-6600; Fax: 518-453-6793. Office Hours: Mon.-Fri. 8:30-4:30.

Vicar General and Moderator of the Curia—Rev. MICHAEL A. FARANO, Pastoral Center, 40 N. Main Ave., Albany, 12203-1422. Tel: 518-453-6612.

Chancellors—Pastoral Center, 40 N. Main Ave., Albany, 12203. Tel: 518-453-6612. Rev. KENNETH DOYLE, Chancellor Pub. Information; ELIZABETH SIMCOE, Chancellor Pastoral Svcs.

Chief Financial Officer—Mr RICHARD FARRELL, 40 N. Main Ave., Albany, 12203. Tel: 518-453-6640.

Insurance Office—Catholic Mutual Group, 33 Elk St., Albany, 12207. Tel: 518-445-6250; Fax: 518-445-6253. JON ROCCO, Claims & Risk Mgr. Email: jrocco@catholicmutual.org; KATHLEEN WILLIAMS, Asst. Claims & Risk Mgr. Email: kwilliams@catholicmutual.org; CHERYL DYKSTRA, Sec. Email: cdykstra@catholicmutual.org.

Office of Human Resources—JOYCE C. TARANTINO, Esq., Dir. Email: joyce.tarantino@rcda.org; PAMELA BENNETT, Administrative Asst., 40 N. Main Ave., Albany, 12203. Tel: 518-453-6635; Fax: 518-453-8446. Email: diocesan.hr@rcda.org.

Pastoral Planning—Deacon FRANK C. BERNING, Dir. Email: frank.berning@rcda.org. Assistants: MARY REILLY. Tel: 518-453-6661; SARA LAFOUNTAIN. Tel: 518-453-6611.

Archivist—Sr. NOLA BRUNNER, C.S.J., 40 N. Main Ave., Albany, 12203. Tel: 518-453-6669. Email: nola.brunner@rcda.org.

Office of Canonical Services—40 N. Main Ave., Albany, 12203. Tel: 518-453-6620; Fax: 518-453-6778. Office Hours: 8:30-4:30 (By appointment only)

Vicar Judicial—Rev. JAMES I. DONLON, J.C.D.

Adjutant Vicar Judicial—Rev. PETER J. SULLIVAN III, J.C.L.

Judges—Revs. DAVID V. BERBERIAN, J.C.L.; ANTHONY M. BARRATT; JAMES I. DONLON, J.C.D.; PETER J. SULLIVAN III, J.C.L.

Defender of the Marriage Bond in First Instance—Rev. DAVID V. BERBERIAN, J.C.L.

Promoter of Justice—Rev. DAVID V. BERBERIAN, J.C.L.

Advocates—Revs. THOMAS KRUPA; JAMES LEFEBVRE (Retired); JOSEPH O'BRIEN; Very Rev. JOHN L.

MOYNA, V.F.; MEG BERGH.

Bishop's Delegate for Marriage Dispensations—Revs. JAMES I. DONLON, J.C.D.; PETER J. SULLIVAN III, J.C.L.

Notaries—MARTHA MCEWAN; MARY FIORILLO.

Interdiocesan Tribunal for the Province of NY Archdiocese— (Second Instance Appeal Court), Rev. MICHAEL T. MARTINE, Vicar Judicial, 201 Seminary Ave., Yonkers, 10704-1852. Tel: 914-968-4301; 800-293-6598; Fax: 914-968-4466.

Presbyteral Council—Most Rev. HOWARD JAMES HUBBARD, D.D., Pres.; Revs. JOHN O'KANE; PAUL G. CATENA; JAMES A. EBERT; PAUL BURKOWSKI, C.SS.R.; THOMAS BERARDI; ANTHONY F. LIGATO; JAMES FITZMAURICE; PETER PAGONES, Chm.; JOSEPH FALLETTA; THOMAS MORETTE; MARTIN J. FISHER; KENNETH DOYLE, Chancellor; JAMES I. DONLON, J.C.D.; Mr RICHARD FARRELL, CFO; Rev. MICHAEL A. FARANO, Vicar Gen. & Moderator of the Curia.

Diocesan Board of Consultors—Revs. PAUL G. CATENA; JOSEPH FALLETTA; JOHN O'KANE; MARTIN J. FISHER; PAUL BURKOWSKI, C.SS.R.; THOMAS BERARDI; ANTHONY F. LIGATO; JAMES A. EBERT; THOMAS MORRETTE; JAMES FITZMAURICE; PETER PAGONES, Chm.; JAMES I. DONLON, J.C.D., Canonical Consultant to the Bd.

Deans—Revs. JOHN BRADLEY, Albany City; GEOFFREY D. BURKE, Albany County Suburban Deanery; GORDON POLENZ, Delaware County & Otsego County; JOHN A. MOLYN, Colombia County; DONALD CZELUSNIAK, Fulton County and Montgomery County; Very Rev. JOHN L. MOYNA, V.F., Greene County; Revs. ANTHONY M. BARRATT, Herkimer County; RANDALL P. PATTERSON, Northern Albany County and Northern Rensselaer County; THOMAS KRUPA, Southern Rensselaer County; Very Rev. DOMINIC INGEMIE, Saratoga; Revs. PETER PAGONES, Schenectady County; THOMAS HOLMES, Schoharie County; THOMAS BERARDI, Warren County & Washington County.

Diocesan Offices and Directors

Unless otherwise indicated all Diocesan Offices and Directors are located at: *The Pastoral Center, 40 N. Main Ave., Albany, 12203*. Tel: 518-453-6600; Fax: 518-453-6793.

Office of Real Property—NOEL A. OLSEN, Dir. Tel: 518-453-6623.

Administrative Review Board (Due Process)—Rev. DAVID V. BERBERIAN, J.C.L., Chm., St. Mary's Rectory, 10 Lodge St., Albany, 12207. Tel: 518-462-4254. Email: dvberberian@msn.com.

Apostleship of Prayer—Rev. ROBERT MCGUIRE, S.J., Fultonville, 12072. Tel: 518-853-3033, Ext. 233.

Bishop's Appeal—THOMAS PRINDLE, Exec. Dir. Tel: 518-453-6680.

Black Catholic Apostolate of the Diocese of Albany—Rev. KOFI NTSIFUL-AMISSAH, Admin., Office: St. Joan of Arc Parish, 76 Menand Rd., Menands, 12204. Tel: 518-462-9604.

Korean Catholic Apostolate of Albany—Rev. JEOUNG KEUN KANG, 80 Slingerland St., Albany, 12202. Tel: 518-275-0350. Email: jkkangtt@hanmail.net; Mr. JONGWOO CHOI, Contact, 28 Dublin Ct., Latham, 12110. Tel: 518-817-6852. Email: jongwoochoi66@yahoo.com.

Vietnamese Apostolate—Rev. LOUIS VAN THANH, c/o St. Patrick's Rectory, 55 Grand St., Newburgh, 12550. Tel: 845-561-0888.

Campus Ministry—CATHERINE REED, Diocesan Dir., Albany Collegiate Interfaith Center, Chapel House/UAlbany, 1400 Washington Ave., Albany, 12222. Tel: 518-489-8573; Fax: 518-489-8975.

Catholic Deaf Ministry—Rev. JAMES E. CLARK, Chap. Tel: 518-877-8506, Ext. 303 (Office); Cell: 518-423-1883. Email: deaf@rcda.org. Web: www.deafalbany.catholicweb.com.

Cemeteries—RICHARD TOUCHETTE, Exec. Dir., Catholic Cemeteries of the Roman Catholic Diocese of Albany, 48 Cemetery Ave., Menands, Albany, 12204. Tel: 518-432-4953. Web: www.rcdacemeteries.org. Email: rick.touchette@rcda.org.

Censor Librorum—Rev. JOHN R. ROOS, J.C.D. (Retired).

Architecture and Building Commission—Rev. RANDALL P. PATTERSON, Chm.; LORI CHERA, Coord. Tel: 518-453-6622; Fax: 518-453-6792. Email: abc@rcda.org.

Public Information—Rev. KENNETH DOYLE, Chancellor. Tel: 518-453-6612; KENNETH GOLDFARB, Dir. Communications. Tel: 518-453-6618.

Cursillo in Christian Living—Co Spiritual Directors: Deacon MARTIN BECKMAN; Mrs. SALLY BECKMAN, 746 Western Ave., Albany, 12203. Tel: 518-489-0873; ALLAN JOHNSON, Lay Dir., 207 Glen Ave., Scotia, 12302. Tel: 518-377-1425.

Diocesan Service Committee for Charismatic Renewal—Liaisons: Deacon JERRY GRIGAITIS; MARIE GRIGAITIS, 25 Par Del Rio, Clifton Park, 12065. Tel: 518-371-7911. Email: dcnjmgrigaitis@aol.com.

Diocesan Stewardship Office—THOMAS PRINDLE, Exec. Dir. Tel: 518-453-6680.

Office of Information Technology—GERALYN A. FOX, Dir. Tel: 518-453-6685; Fax: 518-453-6779.

Catholic Charities of Diocese of Albany, Inc.; St. Vincent's Child Care Society, Inc.—Mr. VINCENT W. COLONNO, CEO & Sec. to Bishop for Health & Social Svcs. & Sec. St. Vincent's Child Care Society, Inc. Tel: 518-453-6650; Fax: 518-453-6792; MICHELE KELLY, CFO.

Catholic Charities Agencies and Commissions—THERESA LUX, Dir., Catholic Charities of Columbia & Greene Counties, 431 E. Allen St., Hudson, 12534. Tel: 518-828-8660; JOHN NASSO, Dir., Catholic Charities of Fulton & Montgomery Counties, 4 Nicholas St., Johnstown, 12095. Tel: 518-762-8313; TERRY LEONARD, Dir., Catholic Charities of Herkimer County, 61 West St., Ilion, 13357. Tel: 315-894-9917; Mr. VINCENT W. COLONNO, Dir., Catholic Charities of Delaware & Otsego Counties, 176 Main St., Oneonta, 13820. Tel: 607-432-0061; Sr. CHARLA COMMINS, C.S.J., Dir., Catholic Charities of Saratoga, Warren & Washington Counties, 142 Regent St., Saratoga, 12866. Tel: 518-587-5000; DEBORAH DAMM O'BRIEN, Dir., Catholic Charities Sr. Svcs. in Schenectady County. Tel: 518-372-5667; Mr. VINCENT W. COLONNO, Dir. Roarke Center - Troy, NY. Tel: 518-453-6650; Mr. VINCENT W. COLONNO, Dir., Catholic Charities of Schoharie County, 489 W. Main St., Cobleskill, 12043. Tel: 518-234-3581; JOSEPH POFIT, Dir., Commission on Aging. Tel: 518-453-6650; DAVID KACZYNSKI, Dir. Commission on Restorative Justice. Tel: 518-453-6650; BARBARA DITOMMASO, Dir., Commission on Peace & Justice. Tel: 518-453-6650; RENEE BENSON, Dir., Catholic Charities Caregivers Support Svcs., 100 Slingerland St., Albany, 12202. Tel: 518-449-2001; Sr. MARY ANN LOGIUDICE, R.S.M., Dir., Community Maternity Svcs., 27 N. Main Ave., Albany, 12203. Tel: 518-482-8836; ANN OGDEN, Dir., Catholic Charities Disabilities Svcs., 1 Park Pl., Ste. 200, Albany, 12205. Tel: 518-783-1111; DEBORAH DAMM O'BRIEN, Dir., Catholic Charities Housing Office, 40 N. Main Ave., Albany, 12203. Tel: 518-459-0183; DEBORAH DAMM O'BRIEN, Dir., Diocesan Housing, Svcs. & Property, 41 N. Main Ave., Albany, 12203. Tel: 518-459-0183; Mr. VINCENT W. COLONNO, Dir., Catholic Charities of Rensselaer County. Tel: 518-453-6650; Mr. VINCENT W. COLONNO, Dir. Sunnyside Child Development Center, 9th St. at Ingalls Ave., Troy, 12180. Tel: 518-214-5986; DEBORAH DAMM O'BRIEN, Dir., Hispanic Outreach Svcs., 40 N. Main Ave., Albany, 12203. Tel: 518-453-6655; ANGELA KELLER, Dir., Catholic Charities AIDS Svcs., 100 Slingerland St., Albany, 12202. Tel: 518-449-3581; JOSEPH POFIT, Dir. Diocesan Community Health Alliance, 40 N. Main Ave., Albany, 12203. Tel: 518-453-6650; SHANNON KELLY, Dir. Diocesan Jail Ministry, 40 N. Main Ave., Albany, 12203. Tel: 518-453-6650.

United Tenants of Albany—Co Directors: ROGER MARKOVICS; MARIA MARKOVICS, 33 Clinton Ave., Albany, 12207. Tel: 518-436-8997.

Catholic Campaign for Human Development—MARY OLSEN, Dir., Catholic Campaign for Human Devel., 40 N. Main Ave., Albany, 12203. Tel: 518-453-6650.

Catholic Relief Services—MARY OLSEN, Dir., Catholic Relief Svcs.; DAVID MEYERS, Dir., Immigration Svcs., Catholic Charities of the Diocese of Albany, 40 N. Main Ave., Albany, 12203. Tel: 518-453-6650.

Health and Hospitals Office—Mr. VINCENT W. COLONNO, Bishop's Rep. Tel: 518-453-6650.

Catholic Women's Service League—Co Presidents: KATHERINE UNDERWOOD; VERONICA BLENDELL. Moderators: Bros. JAMES MCMANUS, F.S.C.; RICHARD LEO MCALICE, F.S.C.; Rev. ROBERT J. HOHENSTEIN, Spiritual Advisor, c/o LaSalle School, 391 Western Ave., Albany, 12203. Tel: 518-242-4731.

Ladies of Charity—CANDICE STELLATO, Pres., 36 Carolanne Dr., Delmar, 12054. Tel: 518-439-7767. Email: candice.stellato@yahoo.com.

Spiritual Director—Rev. PATRICK J. BUTLER, St. Edward the Confessor, 569 Clifton Park Rd., Clifton Park, 12065. Tel: 518-371-7372.

Society of St. Vincent de Paul—EDWARD KILMER, Pres., 1880 Watt St., Schenectady, 12304. Tel: 518-374-0572; Cell: 518-312-0339; EDWARD NARE, Diocesan Central Council Pres., 202 S. Ballston Ave., Scotia, 12302. Tel: 518-374-2548.

St. Luke's Guild of Catholic Physicians—c/o Chancery, 40 N. Main Ave., Albany, 12203. Tel: 518-453-6612. Email: stlukes.guild@rcda.org. Deacon FRANK THOMAS, M.D., Contact.

Consultation Center of the Diocese of Albany— A nonprofit Mental Health Center which provides quality professional psychological counseling services and educational programs in the area of mental health to individuals and groups.

Office—Rev. THOMAS E. KONOPKA, L.C.S.W., Dir.; Sr. MARY FRANCES BECK, S.N.J.M., Admin. Dir.; Revs. JOHN J. MALECKI, Ph.D., Psychologist (Retired); ANTHONY J. CHIARAMONTE, Ph.D., Counselor; KATHLEEN STIFFEN, Sec., 790 Lancaster St., Albany, 12203. Tel: 518-489-4431; Fax: 518-489-5189. Email: consultation.center@rcda.org. Web: consultationcenteralbany.org.

Psychological Counseling— Provides individual therapy, marriage and couples counseling, psychological testing and consultative services to individuals and groups in matters calling for psychological expertise.

Group Therapy— Provides a variety of different kinds of therapy groups.

Educational Programs— Offers lectures and workshops in the area of mental health and personal growth. The Center also offers specialized workshops and training programs to meet the needs of various groups.

Spiritual Direction— Provides a program of individual spiritual direction for any person interested in developing a deeper relationship with God.

Counseling for Laity—Sr. ANNE BRYAN SMOLLIN, C.S.J., Ph.D., Exec. Dir. Tel: 518-453-6625; Fax: 518-453-6793. Email: anne.smollin@rcda.org. Provides individual, family, marital and group psychological counseling-therapy by certified trained therapists. The staff provides services for the Young Married program and assessments for second marriages. Consultation and training programs are offered upon request. Workshops and lectures offered on select topics.

Diocesan Coordinator of Pastoral Care—Ms. HARLEY MCDEVITT, Pastoral Center: 40 N. Main Ave., Albany, 12203-1422. Tel: 518-641-6823. Email: harley.mcdevitt@rcda.org.

Diocesan Pastoral Council—Mr. DAVID AMICO, Admin., Pastoral Center, 40 N. Main Ave., Albany, 12203-1422. Tel: 518-453-6670. Email: david.amico@rcda.org.

Prevention Services - Catholic Schools Office—VACANT, Prog. Dir. Tel: 518-453-6771; Fax: 518-453-6667 Services students, faculty and parents of Catholic schools in the diocese.

Ecumenical and Interreligious Affairs of the Roman Catholic Diocese of Albany, Commission for—Mrs. AUDREY HUGHES; Deacon RAYMOND SULLIVAN, Ph.D., Assoc. Dir.; JOAN HOLMAN; JOAN LIPSCOMB; KATHLEEN DUFF; Mr. FRANK M. PELL; Revs. ROBERT LOESCH, Protestant Min.; JAMES KANE, Dir.; DAVID MICKIEWICZ; GEORGE BRENNAN; Mr. KASHIF THOMAS GILL; Bro. ROBERT GILROY, C.S.C.; Mr. EDWARD FALTERMAN; Ms. ANNE SNYDER; MARYANN POSTAVA-DAVIGNON, Sec.

"The Evangelist"— Diocesan Newspaper, Albany Catholic Press Assoc., Inc. KATE BLAIN, Editor. Tel: 518-453-6688; Fax: 518-453-8448.

Holy Name Societies—Pastoral Center, 40 N. Main Ave., Albany, 12203-1422. Tel: 518-453-6612.

Office of Lay Ministry Formation—Tel: 518-453-6670. DAVID G. AMICO, Dir. Tel: 518-453-6670.

Formation for Priesthood/Vocation Awareness—Sr. ROSEMARY ANN CUNEO, C.R.; Rev. JAMES J. WALSH. Tel: 518-453-6690.

Legion of Mary—Holy Mother and Child Parish, 405 Palmer Ave., Corinth, 12822. Email: angel409@frontiernet.net. Contacts: MAMIE DERSTYNE, North Hudson Valley Curia. Tel: 518-677-3363; ANNA DESCHARMARS, Corinth. Tel: 518-654-6437; MARY BETHEL, Glens Falls. Tel: 518-792-2526.

Office of Evangelization, Catechesis and Family Life—JEANNE SCHREMPF, Diocesan Dir.; STEPHEN MAWN, Assoc. Dir., Catechist Formation & Respect Life; TRACY COFFEY, Administrative Asst. & Media Resource Center/Marriage Preparation; DAVID STAGLIANO, Assoc. Dir., Youth & Young Adult Ministry; JOYCE SOLIMINI, Assoc. Dir., Adult, Family and Intergenerational Catechesis; Rev. ROBERT LONGOBUCCO, Clergy Assoc.; MARY FAY, Assoc. Dir. Marriage Preparation & Enrichment; ROSEMARIE TOBIN, Consultant: Catechesis of Persons with Developmental Disabilities/Special Needs.

Permanent Deacons Office—Deacons MICHAEL MCDONALD, Administrative Advocate for Deacons & Dir. Office of Diaconate. Tel: 518-453-6678; FRANK C. BERNING, Dir. Diaconate Formation. Tel: 518-453-6670; RAYMOND SULLIVAN, Ph.D., Dir. Ongoing Formation & Continuing Education of Deacons. Tel: 518-453-6678.

Catholic Foundation—Most Rev. HOWARD JAMES HUBBARD, D.D., Pres.; THOMAS PRINDLE, Exec. Dir.

Office of Prayer & Worship—ELIZABETH SIMCOE, Dir. & Chancellor for Pastoral Svcs.; MARYANN POSTAVA-DAVIGNON, Sec., 40 N. Main Ave., Albany, 12203. Tel: 518-453-6645; Fax: 518-453-6793. Email: prayer&worship@rcda.org.

Administrative Advocate for Priests—Rev. DAVID V. BERBERIAN, J.C.L. Tel: 518-453-6643.

Priests Placement Committee—Revs. RONALD MENTY, Chm. Tel: 518-453-6643; L. EDWARD DEIMEKE; JOHN J. BRADLEY; ROBERT J. HOHENSTEIN; DAVID V. BERBERIAN, J.C.L.

Priestly Life and Ministry Council—Tel: 518-664-3354. Revs. CHRISTOPHER DEGIOVINE, Chm.; JAMES BELOGI; MICHAEL CAMBI; THOMAS J. HAYES, D.Min.; DOMINIC ISOPO; JOHN T. PROVOST; DANIEL P. RYAN; ERWIN SCHWEIGARDT (Retired); PATRICK BUTLER; RONALD MENTY; ANTHONY F. LIGATO; THOMAS KRUPA.

Minister to Active Priests and Priests in Special Circumstances—Rev. THOMAS BERARDI.

Ministers to Retired Priests—Revs. PAUL COX (Retired); GEORGE G. ST. JOHN (Retired); JOHN D. KIRWIN (Retired); RICHARD J. LESKOVAR (Retired).

Ongoing Formation and Continuing Education for Priests—Members: Revs. THOMAS LAWLESS, Advisory; DAVID MICKIEWICZ; THOMAS MORRETTE; PETER J. MURRAY, S.J.; THOMAS J. HAYES, D.Min., Chm.; RONALD MENTY, Administrative Advocate for Priests - Advisory; ANTHONY J. CHIARAMONTE, Ph.D.

Priests Retirement Board/Priests Retirement Plan Board—Revs. JOHN T. PROVOST, Chm. Tel: 518-674-3818; JOSEPH ANSELMENT (Retired); JOSEPH A. BARKER (Retired); WINSTON L. BATH; RICHARD J. LESKOVAR (Retired); J. THOMAS CONNERY (Retired); JOSEPH DWORAK (Retired); JAMES LEFEBVRE (Retired); RONALD MENTY, Administrative Advocate for Priests & Ex Officio; ERWIN H. SCHWEIGARDT (Retired); Mr RICHARD FARRELL, CFO & Ex Officio.

Administrative Advocate for Deacons—Deacon MICHAEL MCDONALD, Administrative Advocate for Deacons & the Office of Diaconate. Tel: 518-453-6678.

Propagation of the Faith-Pontifical Society—Tel: 518-453-6675. Rev. MICHAEL A. FARANO, Dir.

Schools: Diocesan School Board—

Chair—Ms. LYNN MCGUIRE. Tel: 518-783-8695.

Diocesan School Office—Sr. MARY JANE HERB, I.H.M., Ph.D., Supt. Schools. Tel: 518-453-6602; Mr. JOHN SOJA, Asst. Supt., Admin. Svcs. Tel: 518-453-6666; Ms. TERRI MCGRAW, Asst. Supt. for Instructional Svcs. Tel: 518-453-6666; VACANT, Prevention Svcs. Prog. Tel: 518-453-6771; JOANN GAMELLO, Business Mgr. Tel: 518-453-6604; SAL CARBONE, Safety Coord. Tel: 518-853-4001; VACANT, Dir. Educational Technology. Tel: 518-453-6666; Ms. TRISH LA TORRE, Dir. Educational Advancement & External Affairs. Tel: 518-453-6676.

Scouting—Deacons PETER R. QUINN, Chap., 2305 County Rte. 5, New Lebanon, 12125-0448. Tel: 518-794-0544; WILLIAM H. GAUL JR., Assoc. Dir., 12 Woodlake Dr., Gansevoort, 12831-1817. Tel: 518-587-4631.

St. Bernard's School of Theology and Ministry—Sr. KATHERINE HANLEY, C.S.J., Dir. & Assoc. Dean. Tel: 518-453-6760; Fax: 518-453-6793. Email: stbernards@rcda.org.

Vicar for Religious—Sr. NOLA BRUNNER, C.S.J. Tel: 518-453-6669.

Women's Commission—c/o Chancery, 40 N. Main Ave., Albany, 12203. Tel: 518-453-6612. Email: womens.commission@rcda.org. RUTH JOJO, Contact. Tel: 518-272-6914.

Assistance Coordinator—THERESA F. RODRIGUES. Tel: 518-453-6646. Email: assistance.coordinator@rcda.org.

Vocations and Vocation Awareness Program—Sr. ROSEMARY ANN CUNEO, C.R. Tel: 518-674-3818. Email: rosemary.cuneo@rcda.org. Web: www.albanyvocations.org; Rev. JAMES J. WALSH. Tel: 518-453-6690.

CLERGY, PARISHES, MISSIONS AND PAROCHIAL SCHOOLS

CITY OF ALBANY

(ALBANY COUNTY)

1—CATHEDRAL OF THE IMMACULATE CONCEPTION (1848) Rev. William H. Pape, Rector. In Res., Most Rev. Howard James Hubbard.
Rectory Office—125 Eagle St., 12202. Tel: 518-463-4447; Fax: 518-436-5177. Email: ecathedr@nycap.com. Web: www.cathedralic.com.
Religious Education Office—Tel: 518-436-7918.
Cathedral Social Services—Tel: 518-463-2279.
Catechesis/Religious Program—(Combined with St. Francis of Assisi) Thomas Fowler, D.R.E. Students 29.
Convent—93 Park Ave., 12202. Tel: 518-436-7697. Sisters 6.

2—ALL SAINTS CATHOLIC CHURCH Rev. Ronald Menty; Deacons Gary O'Connor; Timothy J. McAuliffe.
Parish Office: 1168 Western Ave., 12203. Tel: 518-482-4497; Fax: 518-482-4719. Email: office@allsaintsalbany.org.
School—All Saints Catholic Academy, (Grades PreK-8), 10 Rosement St., 12203. Tel: 518-438-0066; Fax: 518-438-0066. Sr. Mary Ellen Owens, Prin. Sisters 1; Lay Teachers 16; Students 150.
Catechesis/Religious Program—(Combined with Holy Cross) Students 138.

3—BLESSED SACRAMENT Revs. John Bradley; Quy Vo; Sr. Judith Kapp, R.S.M., Pastoral Assoc. In Res., Revs. George G. St. John (Retired); Anthony D. Gulley (Retired).
Res.: 607 Central Ave., 12206. Tel: 518-482-3375; Fax: 518-482-3376.
School—(Grades PreK-8), 605 Central Ave., 12206. Tel: 518-438-5854; Fax: 518-438-1532. Sr. Patricia Lynch, R.S.M., Prin. Sisters of Mercy 2; Lay Teachers 16; Students 250.
Catechesis/Religious Program—Tel: 516-446-0997. Rosemarie Reed, D.R.E.; Cathy Fredette, D.R.E. Clustered with St. Mary. Students 202.
Shrine—Shrine of Our Lady of the America's 279 Central Ave., 12206. Tel: 518-465-3685; Fax: 518-462-5487. Rev. Francis O'Connor, Chap.
Sister Maureen Joyce Center—369 Livingston Ave., 12208. Tel: 518-462-9885.

4—ST. CASIMIR, For inquiries for parish records, please contact Blessed Sacrament.

5—ST. CATHERINE OF SIENA, Merged with St. Theresa of Avila, Albany to form Parish of Mater Christi, Albany. Worship Site.

6—CHURCH OF THE HOLY CROSS, Merged with St. Margaret Mary, Albany to form All Saints Catholic Church, Albany.

7—ST. FRANCIS OF ASSISI PARISH (2010), (Formed from merger of St. James and St. John-St. Ann.) Revs. John Lanese, Sacramental Min.; Cabell B. Marbury, Sacramental Min. (Retired); Paul Smith, Sacramental Min. (Retired); Leo P. O'Brien, Sacramental Min. (Retired); Deacons James E. O'Rourke; Raymond Sullivan, Parish Life Dir.; Sr. Patricia Houlihan, C.S.J., Pastoral Assoc. Prayer & Worship; Jo-Ann Garrison, Pastoral Assoc. for Admin. & Business Mgr.; Sr. Phyllis Mauger, C.S.J., Pastoral Care.
391 Delaware Ave., 12209. Tel: 518-434-4028; Fax: 518-434-1097. Email: stfrancesofassisi;parish@gmail.com.
Catechesis/Religious Program—Roberta Grieco, Faith Formation. Students 36.
Worship Sites—
St. John-St. Ann—88 Fourth St., 12202. Tel: 518-472-9091.

8—ST. GEORGE, Closed. For inquiries for Sacramental records, please contact St. Joan of Arc/The Black Apostolate, Menands.

9—HOLY FAMILY PARISH (2005) [JC] Closed. For inquiries for parish records, contact Blessed Sacrament, Albany.

10—ST. JAMES, Merged with St. John-St. Ann to form St. Francis of Assisi Parish.

11—ST. JOHN-ST. ANN, Merged with St. James to form St. Francis of Assisi Parish.

12—ST. JOSEPH, Records are kept at Sacred Heart of Jesus, Albany.
Parish Office—33 Walter St., 12204. Tel: 518-463-3286; Fax: 518-462-0506.

13—ST. MARGARET MARY, Merged with Church of the Holy Cross, Albany to form All Saints Catholic Church, Albany. Worship Site.

14—ST. MARY Rev. James Lefebvre (Retired); Deacons George Witko; Walter Ayres.
Res.: 10 Lodge St., 12207-2196. Tel: 518-462-4254; Fax: 518-462-4255.
Catechesis/Religious Program— Clustered with Blessed Sacrament.

15—OUR LADY HELP OF CHRISTIANS, (German), Closed. For inquiries for parish records please see Cathedral of the Immaculate Conception.

16—OUR LADY OF ANGELS, [CEM], Suppressed. For inquiries for parish records please contact Blessed Sacrament, Albany.

17—PARISH OF MATER CHRISTI Rev. Kenneth Doyle; Deacons Gerald Ladouceur; James E. O'Rourke; Sr. Margery Halpin, R.S.M., Pastoral Assoc. In Res., Rev. John Tallman.
40 Hopewell St., 12208. Email: materchristi@nycap.rr.com.
Res.: 40 Collins Pl., 12208. Tel: 518-489-3204; Fax: 518-482-3721.
School—Mater Christi School, (Grades PreK-8), 35 Hurst Ave., 12208. Tel: 518-489-3111; Fax: 518-489-5863. Theresa L. Ewell, Prin. Lay Teachers 20; Students 200; Pre-K 8.
Catechesis/Religious Program—Bernadette McSparron, D.R.E. Students 452.

18—ST. PATRICK, Suppressed. For inquiries for parish records please contact Blessed Sacrament, Albany.

19—SACRED HEART OF JESUS Rev. Kofi Ntsiful Amissah.
31 Walter St., 12204. Tel: 518-434-0680.
Catechesis/Religious Program—Dawn Hewitt, D.R.E.

20—ST. TERESA OF AVILA, Merged with St. Catherine of Siena, Albany to form Parish of Mater Christi, Albany.

21—ST. VINCENT DE PAUL C. Elizabeth Rowe-Manning, Parish Life Dir.; Deacon Martin Beckman.
Parish Office: 900 Madison Ave., 12208. Tel: 518-489-5408; Fax: 518-489-5474.
Catechesis/Religious Program—Susan Sweeney, D.R.E. Students 159.

OUTSIDE THE CITY OF ALBANY

ALTAMONT, ALBANY CO., ST. LUCY/ST. BERNADETTE Sr. Mary Lou Liptak, R.S.M., Parish Life Dir.; Rev. Paul Smith, Sacramental Min. (Retired).
Parish House—P.O. Box 678, 12009. Tel: 518-861-8770; Fax: 518-861-8770. 1757 Helderberg Tr., Berne, 12023. Tel: 518-872-1131. Email: slucys@nycap.rr.com.
Catechesis/Religious Program—Tel: 518-861-5810. Leah Kedik, D.R.E. Students 187.

AMSTERDAM, MONTGOMERY CO.

1—ST. CASIMIR, (Lithuanian), [CEM] Closed. For inquiries for parish records, contact St. Mary's, Amsterdam.

2—ST. JOHN THE BAPTIST, (Polish), [CEM] Closed. For inquiries for parish records, contact St. Stanislaus, Amsterdam

3—ST. JOSEPH, See separate listing. Canonically merged in 1980 into St. Joseph-St. Michael-Our Lady of Mount Carmel. All inquiries should be directed to the listed address, 39 St. John St. & 58 Grove St., Amsterdam, NY 12010.

4—ST. JOSEPH-ST. MICHAEL-OUR LADY OF MOUNT CARMEL, [CEM 3], Canonically merged parishes in 1980. Rev. Lawrence J. Decker.
Mailing Address: 39 John St., P.O. Box 699, 12010.
Office & Res.: 39 St. John St., 12010. Tel: 518-843-3250; Fax: 518-843-4070. Email: mt.carmel699@albany.twcbc.com.
Catechesis/Religious Program— Cynthia Kuzia, D.R.E. Students 55.

5—ST. MARY, [CEM] Rev. John M. Medwid.
Res.: 156 E. Main St., 12010. Tel: 518-842-4500; Fax: 518-843-1068. Email: smcpadre@nycap.rr.com.
School—St. Mary Institute, (Grades PreK-8), 10 Kopernik Dr., 12010. Tel: 518-842-4100; Fax: 518-842-0217. Email: virgigliog@smik8.org. Giovanni Virgilio, Prin. Lay Teachers 19; Students 212.
Catechesis/Religious Program—Sr. Agnes Clare, S.A., D.R.E. Students 302.

6—ST. MICHAEL THE ARCHANGEL, See separate listing. Canonically merged in 1980 into St. Joseph-St. Michael-Our Lady of Mount Carmel. All inquiries should be directed to the listed address, 39 St. John St. & 58 Grove St., Amsterdam, NY 12010.

7—OUR LADY OF MT. CARMEL, (Italian), See separate listing. Canonically merged in 1980 into St. Joseph-St. Michael-Our Lady of Mount Carmel. All inquiries should be directed to the listed address, 39 St. John St. & 58 Grove St., Amsterdam, NY 12010.

8—ST. STANISLAUS, (Polish), [CEM] Rev. Robert De Martinis.
Res.: 46 Cornell St., 12010. Tel: 518-842-2771; Fax: 518-842-2621. Email: ssoffice@verizon.net.
Catechesis/Religious Program—Dolores Dybas, D.R.E. Students 30.
Convent—46 Cornell St., 12010. Tel: 518-842-2621.

ATHENS, GREENE CO, ST. PATRICK Rev. Richard D. Shaw, Sacramental Min.; Sr. Mary L. Mazza, C.N.D., Parish Life Dir.
Res.: 19 N. Franklin St., 12015. Tel: 518-945-1656; Fax: 518-945-3042. Email: patrickofathens@aol.com. Web: www.stpatrickathenscatskill.org.
Catechesis/Religious Program—Email: stpatsff@yahoo.com. Linda S. Bruno, D.R.E. Tel: 518-947-9444. Students 107.

AVERILL PARK, RENSSELAER CO., ST. HENRY (1868) [CEM 2] Rev. John T. Provost; Deacons Frank S. Lukovits; John W. Novak; Robert Pasquarelli.
Res.: Crystal Lake Rd., P.O. Box 550, 12018. Tel: 518-674-3818; Fax: 518-674-1043.
Catechesis/Religious Program—Mary Lee Kopache, Coord. Faith Formation (High School); Marie Frost, Coord. Faith Formation (Elem. School). Students 380.

BALLSTON LAKE, SARATOGA CO., OUR LADY OF GRACE

(1922) Dorothy A. Sokol, Parish Life Dir. In Res., Rev. John Varno, Sacramental Min. (Retired).
Res.: 73 Midline Rd., 12019. Tel: 518-399-5713; Fax: 518-399-5761. Web: www.ourladyofgracechurchny.com.
Catechesis/Religious Program—Tel: 518-384-0109. Mary Salm, D.R.E. Students 646.

BALLSTON SPA, SARATOGA CO., ST. MARY, [CEM] Revs. Thomas J. Kelly; Jay John Benedict Atherton; Deacon Ronald T. Hogan.
Res.: 167 Milton Ave., 12020. Tel: 518-885-7411; Fax: 518-885-6863.
School—(Grades PreK-5), 40 Thompson St., 12020. Tel: 518-885-7300; Fax: 518-855-7378. Michelle Lezon, Prin. Sisters 1; Lay Teachers 23; Students 212.
Catechesis/Religious Program—Jake Stomieroski, D.R.E. Students 791.

BERLIN, RENSSELAER CO., SACRED HEART, Merged with St. John Francis Regis, Grafton to form Parish of Our Lady of the Snow, Grafton.

BOLTON LANDING, WARREN CO., BLESSED SACRAMENT, [CEM] Kathleen L. Sousa, Parish Life Dir.; Rev. Thomas Berardi, Sacramental Min.
Res.: 12 Goodman Ave., P.O. Box 266, 12814.
Church: Goodman Ave., P.O. Box 266, 12814. Tel: 518-644-3861.
Catechesis/Religious Program—Eileen Scott, D.R.E. Students 29.

BROADALBIN, FULTON CO., ST. JOSEPH Rev. Neil Draves-Arpaia; Deacon Joseph S. Pagano.
Res.: 7 North St., P.O. Box 538, 12025-0538. Tel: 518-863-4736; Fax: 518-883-6381. Email: stjosephschurch@yahoo.com.
Catechesis/Religious Program—Patricia Cardone, D.R.E. Students 152.

CAIRO, GREENE CO., SACRED HEART Rev. Jeremiah Nunan.
Res.: 35 Church St., 12413. Tel: 518-622-3319; Fax: 518-622-0131.
Catechesis/Religious Program—Mrs. Camille Thiesen, D.R.E. Students 153.
Shrine—Our Lady of Knock Shrine P.O. Box 223, East Durham, Greene Co. 12423. Tel: 518-634-7448. Email: sacredheartofficecairony@verizon.net.
Mission—St. Mary 2052 Rte. 145, East Durham, Greene Co. 12423.

CAMBRIDGE, WASHINGTON CO., ST. PATRICK, [CEM] Jeffrey C. Peck, Parish Life Dir.; Rev. Liam Condon, Sacramental Min.; Michele Ruland, Parish Life Assoc.
Res.: 17 S. Park St., 12816-1248. Tel: 518-677-2757; Fax: 518-677-2810. Email: stpatrick18@verizon.net.
Catechesis/Religious Program—Students 85.

CANAJOHARIE, MONTGOMERY CO., ST. PETER'S AND PAUL'S, [CEM] Merged with St. James, Fort Plain & St. Patrick, St. Johnsville to form Parish of Our Lady of Hope, Fort Plain. Worship Site.

CASTLETON ON HUDSON, RENSSELAER CO., SACRED HEART, [CEM 2] Rev. Thomas Krupa.
Res.: 3 Catholic Way, 12033-1543. Tel: 518-732-2155; Fax: 518-732-4906.
Catechesis/Religious Program—Tel: 518-732-1106; Fax: 518-732-4960. Lisa McGarvey, Pastoral Assoc. for Faith Formation K-6; Katherine Monty, Pastoral Assoc. for Faith Formation (7-12) & Youth Min. Students 295.

CATSKILL, GREENE CO., ST. PATRICK Sr. Mary L. Mazza, C.N.D., Parish Life Dir.; Rev. Richard D. Shaw, Sacramental Min.; Mrs. Theresa E. St. Germain, Pastoral Assoc. for Faith Formation.
Res.: 157 Bridge St., 12414. Tel: 518-943-3150; Fax: 518-943-5257. Email: patrickcatskill@gmail.com. Web: www.stpatrickathenscatskill.org.
School—(Grades PreK-8), 80 Woodland Ave., 12414. (School closed June 6, 2007.)
Catechesis/Religious Program—Linda S. Bruno, D.R.E. Students 74.

CHATHAM, COLUMBIA CO., ST. JAMES Rev. Gary Paul Gelfenbien; Deacon Peter Trawinski.
Res.: 129 Hudson Ave., 12037. Tel: 518-392-4991; Fax: 518-392-9205.
Catechesis/Religious Program—Sharon Koomler, C.R.E. Students 248.

CHERRY VALLEY, OTSEGO CO., ST. THOMAS THE APOSTLE Mrs. Karen J. Walker, Parish Life Coord.; Rev. John R. Roos, Sacramental Min. (Retired); Deacon Richard Brown.
Mailing Address: P.O. Box 246, 13320.
Res.: 24 Maple Ave., 13320. Tel: 607-264-3779; Fax: 607-264-3779. Email: stthomascv@nycap.rr.com. Web: turnpikecatholics.com.
Catechesis/Religious Program—Mrs. Karen J. Walker, Faith Formation Coord. Students 14.

CHESTERTOWN, WARREN CO.

1—ST. JOHN THE BAPTIST, Merged with Blessed Sacrament, Hague to form Parish of St. Isaac Jogues, Chestertown. Worship Site.

2—PARISH OF ST. ISAAC JOGUES Rev. John O'Kane.
Res.: 86 Riverside Dr., P.O. Box 471, 12817. Tel: 518-494-5229. Email: northernpointscluster@frontiernet.net. Web: northernpointscluster.org.
Catechesis/Religious Program—Barbara Carlozzi, D.R.E. Students 64.

CLAVERACK, COLUMBIA CO., ST. JOHN VIANNEY, Merged with St. Bridget, Copake Falls to form Parish of Our Lady of Hope, Copake Falls. Worship Site.

CLIFTON PARK, SARATOGA CO., ST. EDWARD THE CONFESSOR Rev. Patrick J. Butler; Deacons Walter MacKinnon; Eugene Kelenski.
Office: Tel: 518-371-7372; Fax: 518-371-1206. Email: stedwards@stedwardsny.org. Web: stedwardsny.org.
Church: 569 Clifton Park Center Rd., 12065-4838.
Catechesis/Religious Program—Students 1,301.

CLINTON HEIGHTS, RENSSELAER CO., ST. MARY Rev. David R. LeFort.
Res.: 163 Columbia Tpke., East Greenbush, 12144-3521. Tel: 518-449-2232; Fax: 518-449-2234.
School— Closed. For further information, contact St. Mary's Parish.
Catechesis/Religious Program—Austin J. Byrnes, D.R.E. Students 227.

COBLESKILL, SCHOHARIE CO., ST. VINCENT DE PAUL, [CEM] Rev. Thomas Holmes, Sacramental Min.; Deacon Gary Surman; Sr. Connie James, S.N.D., Parish Life Dir.; Greg Rys, Campus Min.
Res.: 138 Washington Ave., 12043. Tel: 518-234-2892; Fax: 518-234-3699. Email: vincentdepaul@verizon.net.
Catechesis/Religious Program—Students 175.

COHOES, ALBANY CO.

1—ST. AGNES-ST. PATRICK, Closed. For inquiries for parish records contact Holy Trinity, Cohoes.

2—ST. BERNARD, Closed. For inquiries for parish records contact Holy Trinity, Cohoes.

3—HOLY TRINITY, [CEM] Rev. James A. Ebert; Deacons Albert Schrempf; Gerard Matthews; Kathleen Curtin, Youth Min.
Res.: 122 Vliet Blvd., 12047-1842. Tel: 518-237-2373; Fax: 518-238-9427. Email: holytrinity@nycap.rr.com. Web: www.holytrinity.cohoesonline.com.
See Cohoes Catholic School, Cohoes under Consolidated Elementary Schools located in the Institution section.
Catechesis/Religious Program—Email: htpfaithformation@nycap.rr.com. Karen T. Beattie, C.R.E. Students 146.

4—ST. JOSEPH, (French), [CEM] Closed. For inquiries for parish records contact Holy Trinity, Cohoes.

5—ST. MARIE, Closed. For inquiries for parish records contact Holy Trinity, Cohoes.

6—ST. MICHAEL, [CEM] Rev. Peter Tkocz.
Res.: 36 Page Ave., 12047. Tel: 518-237-5151.
Office: 20 Page Ave., 12047. Fax: 518-237-5151 (Call First). Email: parishinfo@stmichaelsofcohoes.org. Web: www.stmichaelsofcohoes.org.
Catechesis/Religious Program—Karen T. Beattie, D.R.E. Students 54.

7—ST. RITA-SACRED HEART, Closed. For inquiries for parish records, contact Holy Trinity, Cohoes.

COLONIE, ALBANY CO.

1—ST. CLARE Rev. Thomas E. Konopka, Sacramental Min.; Nancy A. Volks, Parish Life Dir.; Deacon Gary Riggi.
Res.: 1947 Central Ave., 12205-4299. Tel: 518-456-3112; Fax: 518-456-1072. Email: rstclare@nycaprr.com. Web: www.stclares.nycap.rr.com.
Catechesis/Religious Program—Tel: 518-456-3113. Email: stclarefaithformsec@nycap.rr.com. Mary Nicholson, Coord. Faith Formation & Youth Ministry. Students 436.

2—OUR LADY OF MERCY, Merged with St. Francis de Sales, Loudonville to form Christ Our Light Roman Catholic Church, Loudonville.

COOPERSTOWN, OTSEGO CO., ST. MARY, [CEM 2] Rev. John P. Rosson.
Res.: 31 Elm St., 13326. Tel: 607-547-2213; Fax: 607-547-5742.
Catechesis/Religious Program—Dr. Theresa Russo, D.R.E.

COPAKE FALLS, COLUMBIA CO.

1—ST. BRIDGET, [CEM] Merged with St. John Vianney, Claverack to form Parish of Our Lady of Hope, Copake Falls. Worship Site.

2—PARISH OF OUR LADY OF HOPE Rev. George Brennan; Mary Burntitius, Faith Formation Coord.; Steven M. Gubler, Parish Office Mgr.
Res.: 8074 State Rte. 22, 12517. Tel: 518-329-4711; Fax: 518-329-4240. Email: ourladyofhope2009@yahoo.com.
Catechesis/Religious Program—Students 51.

CORINTH, COLUMBIA CO.

1—HOLY MOTHER AND CHILD PARISH Rev. Kenneth J. Swain.
Office: 405 Palmer Ave., 12822. Tel: 518-654-2113; Fax: 518-654-9119. Email: angel409@frontiernet.net.
Res.: 323 Lake Ave., P.O. Box 470, Lake Luzerne, 12846. Tel: 518-696-2625.
Catechesis/Religious Program—Margaret Watkins, D.R.E.; Pat Melillo, D.R.E. Students 106.

2—IMMACULATE CONCEPTION, [CEM] Merged with Holy Infancy, Lake Luzerne to form Holy Mother and Child Parish, Corinth. Worship Site.

COXSACKIE, GREENE CO., ST. MARY, [CEM] Very Rev. John L. Moyna; Deacon Michael McDonald.
Res.: 80 Mansion St., 12051. Tel: 518-731-8800; Fax: 518-731-8505.
Catechesis/Religious Program— Mr. Robert DesRosiers, D.R.E. Students 221.

CRESCENT, SARATOGA CO., ST. MARY'S CHURCH Rev. Joseph Cebula.
Parish Center—86 Church Hill Rd., Waterford, 12188. Tel: 518-371-9632; Fax: 518-371-7235. Email: fr.cebula@nycap.rr.com. Web: rcda.org/churches/StMarysCrescent.
Catechesis/Religious Program—Tel: 518-371-9521. Email: smcff@nycap.rr.com. Mary Anne Cureau, C.R.E. Students 395.

DELANSON, SCHENECTADY CO., OUR LADY OF FATIMA Lynn O'Rourke, Parish Life Dir.; Rev. Paul Engel, Sacramental Min. (Retired); Angela Caraher, Pastoral Assoc.
Res.: 1735 Alexander Rd., P.O. Box 219, 12053-0219. Tel: 518-895-2788; Fax: 518-895-2788. Email: pldatolf@nycap.rr.com. Web: rcda.org/churches/ourladyoffatima.
Catechesis/Religious Program—Students 120.

DELHI, DELAWARE CO., ST. PETER Rev. Edward Golding.
Res.: 8 Franklin St., 13753. Tel: 607-746-2503; Fax: 607-746-7651.
Catechesis/Religious Program—Ann Burgin, Faith Formation Moderator. Students 35.

DELMAR, ALBANY CO., ST. THOMAS THE APOSTLE Revs. Thomas J. Hayes; James D. Daley, Pastor Emeritus (Retired); Richard J. Leskovar, Weekend Asst. (Retired); Deacon Alfred Manzella.
Res.: 35 Adams Pl., 12054. Tel: 518-439-4951; Fax: 518-439-0108. Email: office@stthomasdelmar.org. Web: www.stthomasdelmar.org.
School—(Grades PreK-8), 42 Adams Pl., 12054. Tel: 518-439-5573; Fax: 518-478-9773. Web: www.stthomas-school.org. Mr. Thomas Kane, Prin. Lay Teachers 25; Students 214.
Catechesis/Religious Program—Tel: 518-439-3945. Students 910.

DOLGEVILLE, HERKIMER CO., ST. JOSEPH, [CEM 2] Rev. William A. Gorman.
Res.: 31 N. Helmer Ave., 13329. Tel: 315-429-8338. Email: sjdolgeville@verizon.net.
Catechesis/Religious Program—Students 39.

EAST GREENBUSH, RENSSELAER CO., HOLY SPIRIT Rev. Joseph O'Brien; Deacon William Dringus; Kathleen M. Rosenbaum, Parish Assoc.
Res.: 667 Columbia Tpke., 12061. Tel: 518-477-7925; Fax: 518-477-8108. Email: holyspiriteg@nycap.rr.com. Web: www.rcda.org/churches/holyspiritchurch.
School—(Grades PreK-8), 54 Highland Dr., 12061. Tel: 518-477-5739; Fax: 518-477-5743. Email: hssoffice@nycap.rr.com. Web: http://holyspiritschooleg.com. Anne Cowling, Prin.; Monica Parmenter, Librarian. Lay Teachers 21; Students 221.
Catechesis/Religious Program—Tel: 518-477-8108. Tracy Penk-Masucci, Coord. Youth Ministry; Maria Collins, Coord. Childrens Faith Formation. Students 426.

EDMESTON , OSWEGO CO., NATVITY OF B.V.M., Closed. For inquiries for parish records, contact Holy Cross, Morris.

FONDA, MONTGOMERY CO., ST. CECILIA, [CEM] Rev. Patrick Gallagher, O.F.M.Conv.
Mailing Address: P.O. Box 837, 12068.
Res.: 26 Broadway, 12068. Tel: 518-853-4195.
Catechesis/Religious Program—Lenora Fiorenza, D.R.E. Students 60.

FORT ANN, WASHINGTON CO., ST. ANN Rev. Michael Flannery.
Res.: 85 George St., P.O. Box 226, 12827. Tel: 518-639-5218; Fax: 518-639-4073. Email: frpastor@nycap.rr.com.
Catechesis/Religious Program—(Combined with Our Lady of Hope, Whitehall) Students 67.

FORT EDWARD, WASHINGTON CO., ST. JOSEPH, [CEM] Revs. Thomas Babiuch; Harold Wessell, Assoc. for Faith Formation.
Res.: 166 Broadway, 12828. Tel: 518-747-5117; Fax: 518-747-3444.
Catechesis/Religious Program—Tel: 518-747-5117, Ext. 816. Students 119.

FORT PLAIN, MONTGOMERY CO.

1—ST. JAMES, Merged with St. Peter's and Paul's, Canajoharie & St. Patrick, St. Johnsville to form Parish of Our Lady of Hope, Fort Plain. Worship Site.

2—PARISH OF OUR LADY OF HOPE Rev. Dennis Murphy.

Mailing Address: 115 Reid St., P.O. Box 287, 13339-0287.
Office: 119 Reid St., P.O. Box 287, 13339-0287. Tel: 518-993-3822; Fax: 518-993-3823. Email: ourladyofhope@frontier.com.
Catechesis/Religious Program—Debra DiVisconti, D.R.E. Students 115.

FRANKFORT, HERKIMER CO.
1—ST. MARY, Merged with SS. Peter & Paul, Frankfort, to form Our Lady Queen of Apostles, Frankfort, Jan. 8, 1995.
2—OUR LADY QUEEN OF APOSTLES (1995) [CEM] Rev. Anthony M. Barratt.
414 Frankfort St., 13340.
Res.: 109 West St., Ilion, 13357. Tel: 518-894-2025; 315-894-3766; Fax: 315-894-2025.
Catechesis/Religious Program—Michelle Deutschman, C.R.E. Students 205.
3—SS. PETER & PAUL, Merged with St. Mary, Frankfort, to form Our Lady Queen of Apostles, Frankfort, Jan. 8, 1995.

GERMANTOWN, COLUMBIA CO., RESURRECTION, [CEM] Merged with Church of St. Mary, Hudson to form Parish of the Holy Trinity, Hudson. Worship Site.

GLENS FALLS, WARREN CO.
1—ST. ALPHONSUS, [CEM] Closed. For inquiries for parish records contact St. Mary, Glens Falls.
2—ST. MARY Rev. Joseph Manerowski; Deacons F. David Powers. Tel: 518-792-0989, Ext. 35; Joseph Tyrrell. Tel: 518-792-0989, Ext. 35.
Res.: 62 Warren St., 12801-4530. Tel: 518-792-0989; Fax: 518-792-0251. Email: dwoodward@nycap.rr.com; rmattes@nycap.rr.com. Web: www.stmaryglensfalls.parishesonline.com.
School—St. Mary's/St. Alphonsus Regional School, (Grades PreK-8), 10-12 Church St., 12801. Tel: 518-792-3178; Fax: 518-792-6056. Mrs. Kathryn Mahoney Fowler, Prin.
Catechesis/Religious Program—Tel: 518-792-0989, Ext. 15. Jo Kaczmarek, Pastoral Assoc. for Faith Formation. Tel: 518-792-0798; Fax: 518-792-0798; Maria Polidore, Pastoral Assoc. Youth Min. Email: molidire@nycap.rr.com. Students 350.

GLENVILLE, SCHENECTADY CO., IMMACULATE CONCEPTION Rev. Jerome R. Gingras; Deacon Michael Melanson. In Res., Rev. Thomas Connery.
Res.: 400 Saratoga Rd., 12302. Tel: 518-399-9168; Fax: 518-384-3278. Email: icchurch4w@gmail.com. Web: www.ic-glenville.com.
Catechesis/Religious Program—Tel: 518-399-9210. Email: cic4kids@nycap.rr.com. Christine Goss, Pastoral Assoc. for Youth Ministries; Madeline Fretto, Pastoral Assoc. Faith Formation. Students 684.

GLOVERSVILLE, FULTON CO.
1—CHURCH OF THE HOLY SPIRIT Revs. Donald Czelusniak; Rendell Torres.
Res.: 149 S. Main St., 12078. Tel: 518-725-3143; Fax: 518-725-7245. Email: holyspirit@nycap.rr.com.
Catechesis/Religious Program—Tel: 518-725-1213; 518-773-8590; Fax: 518-725-7245. Karen Hoose, D.R.E. Students 130.
2—ST. MARY, See separate listing. Canonically merged with Our Lady of Mount Carmel in 1990. See St. Mary of Mount Carmel.
3—ST. MARY OF MT. CARMEL, [CEM] Merged Consolidated from Our Lady of Mount Carmel and St. Mary in 1990.; Merged with Sacred Heart, Gloversville to form Church of the Holy Spirit, Gloversville.; Worship Site.
4—SACRED HEART, Merged with St. Mary of Mt. Carmel, Gloversville to form Church of the Holy Spirit, Gloversville.

GRAFTON, RENSSELAER CO.
1—ST. JOHN FRANCIS REGIS, Merged with Sacred Heart, Berlin to form Parish of Our Lady of the Snow, Grafton. Worship Site.
2—PARISH OF OUR LADY OF THE SNOW Eva Swiontkowski de Nardis, Parish Life Dir. Fax: 518-279-3055. Email: ourladyofthesnow@verizon.net; Rev. Kenneth Gregory, Sacramental Min.
13 Owen Rd., P.O. Box 234, 12082. Tel: 518-279-4943. Email: ourladyofthesnow@verizon.com.
Catechesis/Religious Program—Vici Armsby, Pastoral Assoc. Faith Formation. Students 32.

GRAND GORGE, DELAWARE CO., ST. PHILIP NERI, Merged with Sacred Heart, Stamford to form Sacred Heart/St. Philip Neri, Stockton

GRANVILLE, WASHINGTON CO.
1—ST. MARY, Closed. For inquiries for parish records contact the chancery.
2—ST. MARY'S ROMAN CATHOLIC CHURCH ROMAN CATHOLIC COMMUNITY OF GRANVILLE, Consolidated St. Mary's, All Saints, and Our Lady of Mount Carmel. Rev. Joseph Arockiasamy; Deacon Jon Ramey.
Res.: 23 Bulkley Ave., 12832. Tel: 518-642-1262. Email: rcathcom@roadrunner.com.
Parish Center—All Saints House, Morrison Ave., 12832.
Catechesis/Religious Program—Mary King, D.R.E. Students 207.

GREEN ISLAND, ALBANY CO., ST. JOSEPH, Merged with St. Brigid's, Immaculate Conception, Our Lady of Mt. Carmel, St. Patrick's & Sacred Heart of Mary, Watervliet to form Immaculate Heart of Mary, Watervliet. Church not closed.

GREENFIELD CENTER, SARATOGA CO., ST. JOSEPH Rev. Simon Udemgia, Sacramental Min.; Deacon Gary Pilcher, Parish Life Dir.
Res.: 3159 Rte. 9N, 12833-0568. Tel: 518-893-7680; Fax: 518-893-0472.
Mission—St. Paul 771 Rte. 29, P.O. Box 136, Rock City Falls, Saratoga Co. 12863. Tel: 518-885-4877.

GREENVILLE, GREENE CO., ST. JOHN THE BAPTIST Rev. James Schiffer, C.P.; Deacon Peter Sedlmeir; Connie Parente, Pastoral Assoc.
Office: 4987 Rte. 81, P.O. Box 340, 12083. Tel: 518-966-8317; Fax: 518-966-4652.
Catechesis/Religious Program—Students 173.

GREENWICH, WASHINGTON CO., ST. JOSEPH Rev. Martin J. Fisher; Deacon Herbert Howley.
Res.: 36 Bleecker St., 12834. Tel: 518-692-2159; Fax: 518-692-8706. Email: parish@nycap.rr.com.

GUILDERLAND, ALBANY CO.
1—CHRIST THE KING Revs. James Fitzmaurice, Admin.; Paul G. Catena; Deacon Joseph Markham.
Res.: 20 Sumpter Ave., 12203. Tel: 518-456-1644; Fax: 518-456-4070. Email: CTKathy@nycap.rr.com. Web: CTKparishny.org.
Catechesis/Religious Program—Nancy Paino, D.R.E. Students 439.
2—ST. MADELEINE SOPHIE Revs. James Belogi; Robert Powhida; Deacons Earle Flatt; Mark Leonard.
Res.: 3500 Carman Rd., Schenectady, 12303. Tel: 518-355-0421; Fax: 518-355-0412. Email: pstmadel@nycap.rr.com. Web: www.smsparish.org.
School—(Grades PreK-5), 3510 Carman Rd., Schenectady, 12303. Tel: 518-355-3080; Fax: 518-355-3106. Email: stmadeleinesophie@yahoo.com. Miss Teresa Kovarovic, Prin.; Cathy Aloisi, Librarian. Lay Teachers 21; Students 152.
Catechesis/Religious Program—3514 Carman Rd., Schenectady, 12303. Tel: 518-355-3115. Donna Simone, Pastoral Assoc. for Faith Formation; Terri Bouchard, Pastoral Assoc. for Faith Formation. Students 1,025.

HAGAMAN, MONTGOMERY CO., ST. STEPHEN, [CEM] Rev. Martin DeRose.
Res.: 51 Pawling St., P.O. Box 81, 12086. Tel: 518-843-2951.
Mission—St. Mary's Galway, Saratoga Co.
Catechesis/Religious Program—Therese DeBiere Craig, D.R.E. Students 121.

HAGUE, WARREN CO., BLESSED SACRAMENT, Merged with St. John the Baptist, Chestertown to form Parish of St. Isaac Jogues, Chestertown. Worship Site-Summer only.

HAINES FALLS, GREENE CO.
1—IMMACULATE CONCEPTION, [CEM] Merged with Sacred Heart, Palenville to form Immaculate Conception, Haines Falls. Worship Site.
2—SACRED HEART-IMMACULATE CONCEPTION CHURCH Rev. Anthony Motta.
67 N. Lake Rd., P.O. Box 379, 12436. Tel: 518-589-5577.
Res.: Mountain House Rd., 12436.
Mission—St. Mary's Church Rte. 23A, Hunter, 12442.
Shrine—Wayside Shrine of the Immaculate Conception, Greene Co.

HANCOCK, DELAWARE CO., ST. PAUL THE APOSTLE, [CEM 2] Rev. Christopher J. Welch.
Res.: 330 W. Main St., 13783. Tel: 607-637-2571; Fax: 607-637-3203. Email: stpauls@hancock.net. Web: www.stpaulshancock.org.
Catechesis/Religious Program—Patricia Brown, D.R.E. Students 58.

HERKIMER, HERKIMER CO.
1—ST. ANTHONY-ST. JOSEPH Rev. Thomas Lawless.
Res.: 228 S. Main St., 13350. Tel: 315-866-2892; 315-866-6373 (Parish Office); Fax: 315-867-6186. Email: stsanthonyandjoseph@verizon.net.
Catechesis/Religious Program—344 S. Washington St., 13350. Kevin Foss, D.R.E., (Grades K-10). Tel: 315-866-6821. Students 72.
2—ST. FRANCIS DE SALES, [CEM] Rev. Mark Cunningham; Deacon William Henkel.
Parish Center—219 N. Bellinger St., 13350. Tel: 315-866-4282; Fax: 315-866-9043.
Res.: 25 Park Pl. S., 13350. Tel: 315-866-7103.
School—(Grades PreK-6), 220 Henry St., 13350. Tel: 315-866-4831. Sr. Rosalie Kelly, C.S.J., Prin. Sisters of St. Joseph of Carondolet 3; Lay Teachers 8; Students 150.
Catechesis/Religious Program—Students 265.
Convent—One Park Pl., 13350. Tel: 315-866-4492.

HOOSICK FALLS, RENSSELAER CO., IMMACULATE CONCEPTION, [CEM] Rev. Thomas Zelker.
Res.: 67 Main St., 12090. Tel: 518-686-5064; Fax: 518-686-1625. Email: immconcept@roadrunner.com. Web: immaculateconcephf.org.
School—St. Mary Academy, (Grades PreK-8), 4 Parsons Ave., 12090. Tel: 518-686-4314; Fax: 518-686-5957. Email: rebeccamartin15@gmail.com. Web: stmaryshf.com. Mrs. Rebecca Martin, Prin. Lay Teachers 13; Students 157.

HUDSON FALLS, WASHINGTON CO.
1—IMMACULATE HEART OF MARY (Sandy Hill), (French), See separate listing. Canonically merged with St. Paul, Hudson Falls. Now called Church of St. Mary's/St. Paul's, Roman Catholic Community of Hudson Falls/Kingsbury.
2—ST. PAUL (Sandy Hill), (French), See separate listing. Canonically merged with Immaculate Heart of Mary parish, Hudson Falls. Now called Church of St. Mary's/St. Paul's, Roman Catholic Community of Hudson Falls/Kingsbury.
3—ROMAN CATHOLIC COMMUNITY OF HUDSON FALLS/KINGSBURY (Sandy Hill) [CEM 2] Rev. Thomas Babiuch; Mrs. Patty Fitzgerald, Sec. & Office Mgr.
Res.: 11 Wall St., 12839. Tel: 518-747-4823; Fax: 518-747-2265.
Catechesis/Religious Program—Peter Derway, D.R.E. Students 187.

HUDSON, COLUMBIA CO.
1—CHURCH OF ST. MARY, Merged Canonically merged with Our Lady of Mount Carmel and Our Lady of Perpetual Help-Sacred Heart in 1991. ; Merged with Resurrection, Germantown to form Parish of the Holy Trinity, Hudson.; Worship Site.
2—OUR LADY OF MT. CARMEL, See separate listing. Canonically merged with Church of St. Mary in 1991. All inquiries should be directed to P.O. Box 323, Hudson, NY 12534. Tel: 518-828-1334.
3—OUR LADY OF PERPETUAL HELP-SACRED HEART, (Polish), See separate listing. Canonically merged with Church of St. Mary in 1991. All inquiries should be directed to P.O. Box 323, Hudson, NY 12534. Tel: 518-828-1334.
4—PARISH OF THE HOLY TRINITY Rev. Winston L. Bath; Deacon Charles O'Neill. In Res., Rev. Theodore J. Gerken (Retired).
Res.: 429 E. Allen St., P.O. Box 323, 12534. Tel: 518-828-1334 (Hudson Office); 518-537-6136 (Germantown Office). Email: rcgtown@valstar.net; stmaryhudson@mhcable.com.
Catechesis/Religious Program—Students 210.
Mission—Nativity Linlithgo, Columbia Co.

ILION, HERKIMER CO., ANNUNCIATION, [CEM] Rev. Anthony M. Barratt; Deacon James Bower.
Res.: 109 West St., 13357. Tel: 315-894-3766; Fax: 315-894-1550. Email: achurch@twcny.rr.com. Web: www.annunciationilion.org.
Catechesis/Religious Program—Students 203.

JOHNSONVILLE, RENSSELAER CO., ST. MONICA'S CHURCH, Merged with St. John the Baptist, Schaghticoke to form Church of the Holy Trinity, Schaghticoke.

JOHNSTOWN, FULTON CO.
1—ST. ANTHONY, (Slovak), [CEM] Consolidated with Immaculate Conception, Johnstown and St. Patrick, Johnstown to form Holy Trinity, Johnstown.
2—HOLY TRINITY PARISH Rev. Thomas Morrette.
Parish Offices: 207 Glebe St., 12095. Tel: 518-762-2636; 518-762-2011; Fax: 518-762-6920. Email: rcchurch@holytrinityjohnstown.com. Web: www.holytrinityjohnstown.com. In Res., Rev. Ronald G. Matulewicz (Retired).
Catechesis/Religious Program—Cynthia Kollar, D.R.E. Students 205.
3—IMMACULATE CONCEPTION, (Italian), [CEM 3] Consolidated with St. Anthony, Johnstown and St. Patrick, Johnstown to form Holy Trinity, Johnstown.
4—ST. PATRICK, [CEM] Consolidated with Immaculate Conception, Johnstown and St Anthony, Johnstown to form Holy Trinity Parish, Johnstown.

LAKE GEORGE, WARREN CO., SACRED HEART Rev. Thomas Berardi.
Res.: 50 Mohican St., 12845. Tel: 518-668-2046; Fax: 518-668-4377. Email: kathy@sacredheartcatholiccommunity.com. Web: www.sacredheartcatholiccommunity.com.
Catechesis/Religious Program—Irene Filippelli, D.R.E.; Torie Wattendorf, D.R.E. Students 270.

LAKE LUZERNE, WARREN CO., HOLY INFANCY, [JC] Merged with Immaculate Conception, Corinth to form Holy Mother and Child Parish, Corinth. Worship Site.

LATHAM, ALBANY CO.
1—ST. AMBROSE Rev. Francis J. DuBois; Deacon Helmut Neurohr.
Res.: 347 Old Loudon Rd., 12110. Tel: 518-785-1351; Fax: 518-785-1951. Email: office@churchofstambrose.org. Web: www.churchofstambrose.org.
School—(Grades PreK-8) Tel: 518-785-6453; Fax: 518-785-8370. James Leveskas, Prin. Email: albstamb@rcdaschools.org. Sisters 1; Lay Teachers 17; Students 196.
Catechesis/Religious Program—Mary Kay Frederick, D.R.E.; Mark Trudeau, Life Teen Youth Min. Students 515.
2—OUR LADY OF THE ASSUMPTION Rev. Geoffrey D.

Burke.
Res.: 498 Watervliet-Shaker Rd., 12110. Tel: 518-785-0234; Fax: 518-785-0420. Web: www.rcda.org/churches/ourladyoftheassumption.
Catechesis/Religious Program—Tel: 518-785-1605. Linda Berkery, D.R.E.; Rosemary Gavin, Youth Min. Students 582.

LITTLE FALLS, HERKIMER CO.

1—HOLY FAMILY, [CEM] Rev. Thomas Lawless; Sr. Marilyn Hayes, C.S.J., Pastoral Assoc.; Deacons Michael Carbone; Joseph DeLorenzo; Mary Puznowski, Music Dir. (1992 Merger of St. Mary's, St. Joseph's & Sacred Heart)
Office: 763 E. Main St., 13365. Tel: 315-823-3410; Fax: 315-823-2701. Email: hfplf@ntcnet.com. Web: www.rcda.org/churches/holy_family_parish_sts_anthony_joseph.
Catechesis/Religious Program—Lisa LaCoppola, D.R.E. & Youth Min. Students 157.

2—ST. JOSEPH, Consolidated with St. Mary and Sacred Heart to form Holy Family Parish, Little Falls.

3—ST. MARY, Consolidated with St. Joseph and Sacred Heart to form Holy Family Parish, Little Falls.

4—SACRED HEART, (Polish), Consolidated with St. Joseph and St. Mary to form Holy Family Parish, Little Falls.

LOUDONVILLE, ALBANY CO.

1—CHRIST OUR LIGHT ROMAN CATHOLIC CHURCH Rev. David E. Noone.
Church & Offices: 1 Maria Dr., 12211. Tel: 518-489-8386; Fax: 518-489-6910. Email: christourlight1@gmail.com.
Res.: 15 Exchange St., 12205. Tel: 518-489-8386.
Old Church—15 Exchange St., 12205.

2—ST. FRANCIS DE SALES (1972) Merged with Our Lady of Mercy, Colonie to form St. Francis de Sales, Loudonville. Worship Site.

3—ST. PIUS X Revs. Michael A. Farano; Paul Butler.
Mailing Address: 23 Crumitie Rd., 12211. In Res., Rev. James J. Walsh.
School—(Grades PreK-8), 79 Upper Loudon Rd., 12211. Tel: 518-465-4539; Fax: 518-465-4895. Dennis Mullahy, Prin. Students 700.
Catechesis/Religious Program—Judy Rinalli, D.R.E.; Brian Evers, D.R.E. Students 635.

MARGARETVILLE, DELAWARE CO., SACRED HEART Rev. Paul G. Catena.
Res.: Academy St., 12455. Tel: 845-586-2665. Email: shparish@live.com.
Catechesis/Religious Program—Students 122.
Mission—St. Ann Andes, Delaware Co.

MECHANICVILLE, SARATOGA CO., ASSUMPTION-ST. PAUL, Consolidated with St. Peter the Apostle, Stillwater to form Roman Catholic Community of All Saints on the Hudson, Stillwater.

MENANDS, ALBANY CO., ST. JOAN OF ARC Rev. Kofi Ntsiful Amissah.
Parish Office & Res.: 76 Menand Rd., 12204. Tel: 518-463-0378; Fax: 518-463-0489. Email: sjoa@nycap.rr.com.
Catechesis/Religious Program—Students 32.

MIDDLEBURGH, SCHOHARIE CO.

1—ST. CATHERINE, Merged with St. Joseph, Schoharie to form Parish of Our Lady of the Valley, Middleburgh. Worship Site.

2—PARISH OF OUR LADY OF THE VALLEY Rev. Thomas Holmes.
Res.: 111 Wells Ave., 12122. Tel: 518-827-5132. Email: stcath56@midtel.net.
Catechesis/Religious Program—Tel: 518-239-6587. Martha Conroy, D.R.E. Students 72.

MOHAWK, HERKIMER CO., BLESSED SACRAMENT Sr. Mary Jo Tallman, C.S.J., Parish Life Dir.; Rev. Mark Cunningham, Sacramental Min.
Res.: 54 E. Main St., 13407. Tel: 315-866-1752.
Catechesis/Religious Program—Students 241.

MORRIS, OTSEGO CO., HOLY CROSS, Unassigned.
Res.: 96 Main St., P.O. Box 118, 13808-0118. Tel: 607-263-5143. Email: hcchurch@frontiernet.net.
Catechesis/Religious Program—Maureen E. Joy, Parish Life Coord. Students 24.

NASSAU, RENSSELAER CO., ST. MARY, [CEM] Revs. John T. Provost; Antone Kandrac, O.F.M.Conv., Pastor Emeritus.
Res.: 26 Church St., P.O. Box 435, 12123. Tel: 518-766-2701; Fax: 518-766-7535.
Catechesis/Religious Program—Linda Ridzi, D.R.E. Students 101.

NEW LEBANON, COLUMBIA CO., IMMACULATE CONCEPTION, [CEM] Rev. John Close; Deacon Peter R. Quinn.
Church and Shrine of Our Lady of Lourdes: 732 U.S. Rte. 20, P.O. Box 218, 12125. Tel: 518-794-7651; 518-766-5651; Fax: 518-766-5651.
Mission—St. Joseph's Stephentown, Rensselaer Co.

NEWPORT, HERKIMER CO., ST. JOHN THE BAPTIST Rev. William A. Gorman.
Res.: Main St., Box 475, 13416. Tel: 315-845-8017. Email: stjohnthebaptist@ntcnet.com.
Catechesis/Religious Program—Mrs. Barbara Sigona, D.R.E. Students 104.

NORTH CREEK, WARREN CO., ST. JAMES, [CEM] Rev. John O'Kane; Sr. M. Francesca Husselbeck, R.S.M., Parish Life Dir.
Parish Center: 223 Main St., P.O. Box 23, 12853. Tel: 518-251-2518; Fax: 518-251-2518.
Catechesis/Religious Program— Karen Smith, D.R.E.; Joyce Parker, D.R.E. Students 45.

NORTHVILLE, FULTON CO., ST. FRANCIS OF ASSISI Rev. Neil Draves-Arpaia, Admin.; Deacon Joseph S. Pagano.
Mailing Address: P.O. Box 126, 12134.
Res.: 501 Bridge St., 12134. Tel: 518-863-4736; Fax: 518-863-4128.

ONEONTA, OTSEGO CO., ST. MARY, [CEM] Revs. Joseph Benintende; Bernard Osei Ampong; Lawrence Curran, Campus Ministry, Neuman House, 77 Spruce St., 13820. Tel: 607-432-4400; Fax: 607-432-6437.
Res.: 39 Walnut St., 13820. Tel: 607-432-3920; Fax: 607-432-6437. Web: stmarysoneonta.org/church.
School—(Grades N-6), 5588 State Hwy. 7, 13820. Tel: 607-432-1450; Fax: 607-433-1656. Web: stmarysoneonta.org/school. Patricia Bliss, Prin.; Nancy Jankura, Librarian. Religious 1; Lay Teachers 16; Students 122.
Catechesis/Religious Program—Tel: 607-431-9320. Carmel Ann Sperti DeArmas, D.R.E. Students 275.

PALENVILLE, GREENE CO., SACRED HEART, Merged with Immaculate Conception, Haines Falls to form Sacred Heart-Immaculate Conception, Haines Falls. Worship Site.

PHILMONT, COLUMBIA CO., SACRED HEART, [CEM] Merged with Holy Cross, West Taghkanic to form St. John Vianney, Philmont.

PITTSTOWN, RENSSELAER CO., ST. GEORGE, Closed. For inquiries for parish records, contact Immaculate Conception, Hoosick Falls.

QUEENSBURY, WARREN CO., OUR LADY OF THE ANNUNCIATION Rev. Joseph Busch.
Res.: 448 Aviation Rd., 12804. Tel: 518-793-9677; Fax: 518-793-9678.
Catechesis/Religious Program— Catherine Vesterby, C.R.E.; David W. Oakes, Youth Min. Students 721.

RAVENA, ALBANY CO., ST. PATRICK, [CEM] Rev. James J. Kane; Deacon James E. O'Rourke.
Res.: 21 Main St., 12143. Tel: 518-756-3145; Fax: 518-756-8411. Web: www.tcosp.com.
Catechesis/Religious Program—Frank Julian, Faith Formation Min. Students 183.

RENSSELAER, RENSSELAER CO.

1—ST. JOHN THE EVANGELIST, [CEM] Consolidated with St. Joseph, Rensselaer to form Parish of St. John the Evangelist and St. Joseph's, Rensselaer.

2—ST. JOSEPH (1915) Consolidated with St. John the Evangelist, Rensselaer to form Parish of St. John the Evangelist and St. Joseph's, Rensselaer.

3—PARISH OF ST. JOHN THE EVANGELIST AND ST. JOSEPH'S Rev. R. Adam Forno.
Res.: 50 Herrick St., 12144.
Parish Office—P.O. Box 256, 12144. Tel: 518-465-0482; 518-463-4401; Fax: 518-449-7088. Email: sjesjparish@aol.com. Web: www.churchofstjohnstjoseph.org.
Catechesis/Religious Program—Combined program with St. Joseph. Linda Remington, D.R.E. Students 142.

RICHFIELD SPRINGS, OTSEGO CO.

1—ST. JOSEPH, [CEM] Merged with St. Joseph, West Winfield to form St. Joseph the Worker, Richfield Springs. Worship Site.

2—ST. JOSEPH THE WORKER Rev. Terence P. Healy, Sacramental Min.; Nancy Brown, Pastoral Assoc.
Mailing Address: 35 Canadarago St., 13439.
Business Office: P.O. Box 791, 13439.
Res.: 305 W. Main St., West Winfield, 13491-2904. Tel: 315-858-1682; Fax: 315-858-1682. Email: stjosephsrichfield@verizon.net.
Catechesis/Religious Program—Tel: 315-822-3191 (West Winfield site). Email: sntjos9@aol.com. Students 40.

ROTTERDAM, SCHENECTADY CO., ST. GABRIEL THE ARCHANGEL Ms. Annette Brooks, Parish Life Dir.; Revs. James Belogi, Sacramental Min.; Robert Powhida, Sacramental Min. In Res., Rev. Kenneth Tunney (Retired).
Res.: 3040 Hamburg St., Schenectady, 12303. Tel: 518-355-6600; Fax: 518-355-6604. Email: stgaberectory@aol.com. Web: www.stgabrielschurch.com.
Catechesis/Religious Program—Tel: 518-355-4193. Email: chs3040@msn.com. Donna Simone, Pastoral Assoc. for Faith Formation; Alexandra Saucedo, Pastoral Assoc. for Faith Formation. Students 291.

ST. JOHNSVILLE, MONTGOMERY CO., ST. PATRICK, Merged with St. James, Fort Plain & St. Peter's & Paul's, Canajoharie to form Parish of Our Lady of Hope, Fort Plain. Worship Site.

SALEM, WASHINGTON CO., HOLY CROSS, [CEM] Jeffrey C. Peck, Parish Life Dir.
Res.: 247 Main St., P.O. Box 357, 12865. Tel: 518-854-7626.

SARATOGA SPRINGS, SARATOGA CO.

1—ST. CLEMENT Revs. Paul Borowski, C.Ss.R.; Timothy Keating, C.Ss.R.; Arthur Tuttle, C.Ss.R.; Deacons Larry Willette, Pastoral Assoc.; Arthur Turcotte, Pastoral Assoc.; Lee Hanson, Pastoral Assoc.; William H. Gaul Jr.
Res.: 231 Lake Ave., 12866. Tel: 518-584-6122; Fax: 518-584-2644. Web: stclementschurch.com.
School—231 Lake Ave., 12866. Tel: 518-584-7350; Fax: 518-587-2623. Mrs. Jane E. Kromm, Prin. Lay Teachers 23; Students 291.
Catechesis/Religious Program—Tel: 518-587-3611. Rev. Cornelius Draves-Arpaia (PHX), Dir. Whole Community Catechesis; Kurt Lawrence, Youth Ministry; Denise Salage, Coord. - Sacramental Prep for Children. Students 576.
Chapel—Gansevoort, St. Therese, Tel: 518-587-3180. Deacon Danny Boyd.

2—ST. PETER, [CEM] Very Rev. Dominic Ingemie; Revs. Robert J. LeFevre, Pastor Emeritus (Retired); Matthew Wetsel.
Rectory—241 Broadway, 12866. Tel: 518-584-2375; Fax: 518-584-5471. Email: stpetersar@nycap.rr.com. Web: www.stpeteronline.org.
Priest Res.: 88 Regent St., 12866. Tel: 518-584-8127.
Catechesis/Religious Program— Rita Usher. Tel: 518-587-4487. Students 534.

SCHAGHTICOKE, RENSSELAER CO.

1—CHURCH OF THE HOLY TRINITY, [CEM] Merged with Church of St. Bonaventure, Speigletown to form Transfiguration Parish, Troy. For parish records contact Transfiguration Parish, Troy.

2—ST. JOHN THE BAPTIST, Merged with St. Monica, Johnsonville to form Church of the Holy Trinity, Schaghticoke.

SCHENECTADY, SCHENECTADY CO.

1—ST. ANTHONY, (Italian), Revs. Richard A. Carlino; Anthony De Franco, Pastor Emeritus (Retired); Sr. Maria Rose Querini, M.P.V., Pastoral Assoc.
Parish Office—331 Seward Pl., 12305. Tel: 518-374-4591; Fax: 518-377-5245. Email: info@stanthonyschurch.net. Web: stanthonyschurch.net.
Catechesis/Religious Program—1840 Van Vranken Ave., 12308. Tel: 518-393-0748; 518-847-3044. Sr. Dolores Puglis, M.P.V., D.R.E. Students 88.
Convent—1834 Van Vranken Ave., 12308. Tel: 518-346-2060.

2—CHURCH OF ST. ADALBERT, (Polish), [CEM] Deacon Joseph M. Cechnicki, Parish Life Coord.; Sr. Bernadette Filter, C.R., Pastoral Assoc. for Elderly.
Rectory—Res.: 550 Lansing St., 12303-1195. Tel: 518-346-4204; Fax: 518-346-0348.
Catechesis/Religious Program—Tel: 518-372-8372. Daniel Pepe, D.R.E.; Arlene Parisi, Coord. Faith Formation. Students 89.

3—SS. CYRIL AND METHODIUS, Closed. For inquiries for parish records contact Our Lady of Mount Carmel, Schenectady.

4—ST. HELEN Rev. Robert Longobucco.
Res.: 1803 Union St., 12309. Tel: 518-346-6137; Fax: 518-346-5390. Email: helen1803@aol.com.
School—(Grades PreK-5), 1801 Union St., 12309. Tel: 518-382-8225; Fax: 518-382-2226. Jennifer Chatain, Prin. Lay Teachers 22; Students 250.
Catechesis/Religious Program—Tel: 518-377-3119. Students 502.

5—HOLY CROSS, Closed. For inquiries for parish records, contact St. John the Evangelist, Schenectady.

6—IMMACULATE CONCEPTION, Merged with Our Lady of the Assumption to form Our Lady Queen of Peace.

7—ST. JOHN THE BAPTIST, [CEM] Closed. For inquiries for parish records, contact St. John the Evangelist, Schenectady.

8—ST. JOHN THE EVANGELIST Revs. Richard A. Carlino; Anthony Curran; Deacon Frank Schickel. In Res., Rev. Leopold Kamundo.
Res.: 802 Union St., 12308. Fax: 518-372-0992.
Office: 816 Union St., 12308. Tel: 518-372-3381; Fax: 518-372-0992.
School—(Grades PreK-6), 806 Union St., 12308. Tel: 518-393-5331; Fax: 518-374-4663. Marie Keenan, Prin. Lay Teachers 171; Students 231.
Catechesis/Religious Program—Tel: 518-372-3381, Ext. 110; Fax: 518-372-0962. Jeanne Marie Hawkey, D.R.E. Combined with St. Mary and Holy Cross Students 650.

9—ST. JOSEPH, (German), [CEM 2] Rev. Michael Hogan.
Res.: 225 Lafayette St., 12305. Tel: 518-374-4466; Fax: 518-382-7711.
Church: 600 State St., 12305.
Catechesis/Religious Program—Daniel Pepe, D.R.E.; Kay Skelly, D.R.E. Students 40.
Mission—St. Margaret of Cortona 2 Putnam St., Rotterdam Junction, 12150.

10—ST. LUKE Rev. Dominic Isopo.

Res.: 1241 State St., 12304. Tel: 518-346-3405; Fax: 518-346-3406. Email: slrcc7@aol.com. Web: stlukesofschenectady.org.
Catechesis/Religious Program—Doreen Wright, D.R.E. Students 151.
11—St. Mary, (Polish), [CEM] Closed. For inquiries for parish records, contact St. John the Evangelist, Schenectady.
12—Our Lady of Fatima Deacon Richard J. Thiesen, Parish Life Dir.
Res.: 2216 Rosa Rd., 12309. Tel: 518-370-3136; Fax: 518-370-3137. Email: admin@olfatima.cc. Web: www.olfatima.cc.
Catechesis/Religious Program—Tel: 518-370-0027. Patricia Policastro, C.R.E. Students 205.
13—Our Lady of Mt. Carmel, (Italian), Revs. Robert J. Hohenstein; Anastacio Segura, Diocesan Ministry to Spanish Apostolate.
Res.: 1255 Pleasant St., 12303. Tel: 518-393-4109; Fax: 518-393-4100. Email: olmc1255@aol.com. Web: olmc-schenectady.com.
Our Lady of Mt. Carmel Center—1274 Pleasant St., 12303. Tel: 518-372-0336.
Catechesis/Religious Program—Tel: 518-372-8372. Jacquline Burgoyne, D.R.E. Students 36.
14—Our Lady of the Assumption, Closed. For inquiries for parish records contact Our Lady Queen of Peace, Schenectady.
15—Our Lady Queen of Peace (2010) Revs. Vincent J. Ciotoli; David Hammond; Deacon Joseph Brennan.
210 Princetown Rd., 12303. Tel: 518-346-4926.
Catechesis/Religious Program—Debbie Ploetz, D.R.E. Students 493.
Worship Site—
Former Our Lady of the Assumption, Rotterdam—
16—St. Paul the Apostle Revs. Peter Pagones; Daniel P. Ryan; Deacon Gregory Zoltowski.
Res.: 2777 Albany St., 12304. Tel: 518-377-8886; Fax: 518-377-4371. Email: stpaulsmail1@yahoo.com.
School—Closed., 16 Van Zandt St., 12304. Tel: 518-377-0506.
Catechesis/Religious Program—Daniel Pepe, Faith Formation Dir. (7-11); Arlene Parisi, Faith Formation Coord. (K-6). Students 215.
17—Sacred Heart-St. Columba, Merged with St. Joseph, Schenectady. For inquiries for parish records contact St. Joseph.
18—St. Thomas the Apostle, Closed. For inquiries for parish records please see Our Lady of Mt. Carmel, Schenectady.
Schoharie, Schoharie Co., St. Joseph, Closed. For inquiries for parish records please contact Our Lady of the Valley, Middleburgh.
Schuylerville, Saratoga Co.
1—Notre Dame-Visitation, [CEM 2] Rev. Martin J. Fisher.
Parish House—18 Pearl St., 12871. Tel: 518-695-3391; Fax: 518-695-3391.
Catechesis/Religious Program—Tel: 518-695-3318; Fax: 518-695-4854. Marie Ehlinger, D.R.E. Students 130.
Convent—
2—Visitation of the Blessed Virgin Mary, Closed. For inquiries for parish records contact Notre Dame de Lourdes Parish, Schuylerville.
Scotia, Schenectady Co., St. Joseph Church Rev. Peter Russo; Deacons John P. Crane; Stephen M. Lape.
Res.: 231 Second St., 12302. Tel: 518-346-4960.
Parish Center—Office: 45 MacArthur Dr., 12302. Tel: 518-346-2316; Fax: 518-374-3383. Email: stjosephs1@verizon.net. Web: mysite.verizon.net/stjosephs1.
Catechesis/Religious Program—Tel: 518-374-3382. Donna Simone, D.R.E.; Ruth Moon, Youth Min. Students 250.
Sidney, Delaware Co., Sacred Heart Rev. Gordon Polenz; Deacons Thomas E. Luby; Michael R. Donnell.
Res.: 15 Liberty St., 13838. Tel: 607-563-1591; Fax: 607-563-7066. Email: revgordon@frontiernet.net.
Catechesis/Religious Program—Fax: 607-563-7066. Email: formingfaith@gmail.com. Paula Ciborowski, D.R.E.; Kimberly Ayres, Youth Min. Students 145.
Mission—St. Ambrose Unadilla, Otsego Co. (Closed)
Mission—St. Paul Franklin, Delaware Co. (Closed)
South Glens Falls, Saratoga Co., St. Michael the Archangel Rev. Guy A. Childs, Admin.
Res.: 80 Saratoga Ave., 12803. Tel: 518-792-5859; Fax: 518-792-5850. Email: smichael@nycap.rr.com.
Catechesis/Religious Program—James M. Gorman, D.R.E. Students 271.
South Kortright, Delaware Co., Church of the Most Precious Blood of Jesus, Merged with Sacred Heart, Stamford.
Speigletown, Rensselaer Co., St. Bonaventure, Closed. As of 7/1/2010 Sacramental records are at Transfiguration Parish, Troy.
Stamford, Delaware Co.
1—Sacred Heart, [CEM] Rev. Michael Cambi; Marlies Kneis, Pastoral Assoc. for Faith Formation.
Res.: 27 Harper St., 12167. Tel: 607-652-7170; Fax: 607-652-9250. Email: sheartchurch@stny.rr.com; pastorshc2@stny.rr.com.
Catechesis/Religious Program—Combined with St. Philip Neri Mission. Louise Evans, D.R.E. Students 100.
Mission—St. Philip Neri Grand Gorge, 12434.
2—Sacred Heart, Merged with St. Philip Neri, Grand Gorge to form Sacred Heart/St. Philip Neri, Stamford
Stillwater, Saratoga Co.
1—St. Peter the Apostle, [CEM] Consolidated with Assumption/St. Paul, Mechanicville to form Roman Catholic Community of All Saints on the Hudson, Stillwater.
2—Roman Catholic Community of All Saints on the Hudson, Formed from consolidation of St. Peter the Apostle Stillwater, NY and Assumption-St. Paul, Mechanicville, NY. Deacon Mark Leonard, Admin.
Res.: 881 Hudson Ave., P.O. Box 519, 12170. Tel: 518-664-3354; Fax: 518-664-9971.
Catechesis/Religious Program—Students 312.
Mission—St. Isaac Jogues Saratoga Lake, Saratoga Co. (Summer)
Stottville, Columbia Co., Holy Family, Merged with St. Mary/Nativity, Stuyvesant Falls to form Church of St. Joseph, Stuyvesant. Worship Site.
Stuyvesant, Columbia Co.
1—Church of St. Joseph Rev. Joseph Falletta.
Church & Res.: 1820 U.S. Rte. 9, 12173. Tel: 518-799-5411; 518-779-3050 (Res.); Fax: 518-799-3144.
Catechesis/Religious Program—Students 23.
2—Nativity/St. Mary's, Merged with Holy Family, Stottville to form Church of St. Joseph, Stuyvesant. Worship Site.
Stuyvesant Falls, Columbia Co., St. Mary/Nativity, [CEM] Merged with Holy Family, Stottville to form Church of St. Joseph, Stuyvesant.
Summit, Schoharie Co., St. Anna, Closed. For inquiries for parish records, contact St. Vincent de Paul, Cobleskill.
Tribes Hill, Montgomery Co., Sacred Heart Revs. Patrick Gallagher, O.F.M.Conv.; Mark Steed, O.F.M.Conv.
Res.: 111 Third Ave., P.O. Box 264, 12177. Tel: 518-829-7301. Email: usacredh@nycap.rr.com.
Catechesis/Religious Program—Tel: 518-762-7732. Lenora Fiorenza, D.R.E. Students 53.
Troy, Rensselaer Co.
1—St. Anthony of Padua (Shrine Church), (Italian), Rev. Mario F. Julian, O.F.M.; Bro. Philip Hira, O.F.M., Parish Asst.; Deacon Moises Gutierrez.
Friary: 28 State St., 12180-3916. Tel: 518-273-8622; Fax: 518-273-2731.
Catechesis/Religious Program—(Combined with St. Joseph, Troy), Tel: 518-283-5760. Students 6.
2—St. Augustine Revs. James Spenard, O.S.A.; Alfred J. Ellis, O.S.A.
Res.: 25 115th St., 12182. Tel: 518-235-3861; Fax: 518-233-0284. Email: jass@nycap.rr.com.
School—(Grades N-6), 525 Fourth Ave., 12182. Tel: 518-235-7287; Fax: 518-237-7943. Email: staug@nycap.rr.com. James R. Clement, Prin. Lay Teachers 12; Students 195.
Catechesis/Religious Program—Cindy Brisson, D.R.E. Students 198.
3—St. Francis de Sales, Closed. For inquiries for parish records, contact Our Lady of Victory, Troy.
4—Holy Trinity, (Polish), Rev. Romaeus Cooney, O.Carm., Admin.
Mailing Address: *St. Joseph's Priory*, 416 Third St., 12180. Tel: 518-274-6720; Fax: 518-272-6503.
5—St. Joseph, [CEM] Rev. Timothy Ennis, O.Carm.; Deacon Charles Wojton. In Res., Rev. Romaeus Cooney, O.Carm.
Res.: 416 Third St., 12180. Tel: 518-274-6720; Fax: 518-272-6503. Email: stjoes-carm@nycap.rr.com.
Catechesis/Religious Program—Joanne Barnes, D.R.E. Students 56.
6—St. Lawrence, Closed. For inquiries for parish records contact St. Joseph Parish, Troy.
7—St. Mary, Closed. For inquiries for parish records, contact St. Joseph, Troy.
8—St. Michael the Archangel Sr. Katherine Arseneau, C.S.J., Parish Life Dir.; Revs. Arthur A. Toole, Sacramental Min. (Retired); James Mackey, Sacramental Min. (Retired); Barbara Berger, Pastoral Assoc. Tel: 518-283-6110, Ext. 13.
Church: 175 Williams Rd., 12180. Tel: 518-283-6110; Fax: 518-283-3938.
Catechesis/Religious Program—Students 330.
Mission—Van Rensselaer Manor, County Nursing Home North Greenbush, Rensselaer Co.
Mission—The Springs Nursing Home, Rensselaer Co.
9—Our Lady of Victory Rev. Randall P. Patterson; Deacons Gerald Christiano; Brian Lewis. In Res., Rev. Joseph A. Barker (Retired).
Res.: 55 N. Lake Ave., 12180. Tel: 518-273-7609; 518-273-7602 (Office); Fax: 518-273-0310. Email: olvbusoffice@nycap.rr.com. Web: olv-troy.4lpi.com.
School—Our Lady of Victory Education Center, (Grades PreK), 451 Marshland Ct., 12180. Tel: 518-274-6202; Fax: 518-271-8680. Rev. Randall P. Patterson, Dir.
Catechesis/Religious Program—Email: mtuiteolv@nycap.rr.com. Maryanne Tuite, D.R.E. Students 376.
10—St. Patrick, Closed. For inquiries for parish records, contact St. Anthony of Padua, Troy.
11—St. Paul the Apostle, Closed. For inquiries for parish records, contact Our Lady of Victory, Troy.
12—St. Peter, [CEM] Closed. For inquiries for parish records, contact St. Anthony of Padua, Troy.
13—Sacred Heart Deacon Neil Hook, Interim Admin.; Revs. John Yanas; James Vaughan, Pastor Emeritus (Retired); Augustine Tufail; Suzanne Turner, Associate Pastoral Admin.
Res.: 310 Spring Ave., 12180. Tel: 518-274-1363; Fax: 518-274-8720.
School—(Grades PreK-6), 308 Spring Ave., 12180. Tel: 518-274-3655; Fax: 518-274-8270. Susan Holland, Prin.; Mona Zimmerman, Librarian. Lay Teachers 17; Students 172.
Catechesis/Religious Program—Marie Venaglia, D.R.E. Students 195.
14—Transfiguration Parish (2010), Formed from merger of Holy Trinity, Schaghticoke and Church of St. Bonaventure, Speigletown. Rev. George Fleming.
50 Hillview Dr., 12182. Tel: 518-235-0337. Email: general-office@transfigurationparish40.org.
Worship Sites—
St. Bonaventure—
Holy Trinity—
15—St. Williams, Closed. For inquiries for parish records, contact Sacred Heart, Troy.
Ushers, Saratoga Co., Corpus Christi Rev. James E. Clark; Deacon John Tierney.
Mailing Address: P.O. Box 628, Round Lake, 12151-0628. Email: ccorpus@nycap.rr.com.
Res.: 23 Pepperbush Pl., Ballston Spa, 12020. Tel: 518-877-8506 (Office); Fax: 518-877-5620 (Office).
Catechesis/Religious Program—Tel: 518-877-8506, Ext. 302. Sr. Sue Wieczynski, R.S.M., Dir. Whole Community Catechesis. (Generations of Faith Program) 900.
Valatie, Columbia Co., St. John the Baptist, [CEM] Rev. John A. Molyn.
Res.: 1025 Kinderhook St., 12184. Tel: 518-758-9401; Fax: 518-758-9409. Email: stjohnthebapistch@nycap.rr.com. Web: home.nycap.rr.com/stjohn.
Catechesis/Religious Program—Tel: 518-758-1828. Email: faithformation@fairpoint.net. Connie Smith, D.R.E. Students 436.
Voorheesville, Albany Co., St. Matthew Rev. Thomas H. Chevalier; Deacon Paul M. Davignon; Ms. Ellie Dorn, Youth Min.
Res.: 25 Mountainview St., 12186-9551. Tel: 518-765-2805; Fax: 518-765-3701. Email: stmatthewsvoorheesville@verizon.net. Web: www.stmatthewsvoorheesville.org.
Catechesis/Religious Program—Ms. Suzanne Schultz, D.R.E. Students 318.
Walton, Delaware Co., St. John the Baptist Rev. Edward Golding.
Mailing Address: 25 Benton Ave., 13856-0315.
Res.: 15 Benton Ave., 13856-0315. Tel: 607-865-4720.
Catechesis/Religious Program—Ann Burgin, Faith Formation Moderator. Students 78.
Mission—Holy Family 14918 State Hwy. 30, Downsville, Delaware Co. 13755.
Warrensburg, Warren Co., St. Cecilia, [CEM] Rev. Paul Cox, Sacramental Min. (Retired); Sr. Linda Hogan, C.S.J., Parish Life Dir.
Res.: 3802 Main St., 12885-1629. Tel: 518-623-3021. Web: www.stceciliaschurch.com.
Catechesis/Religious Program—Tel: 518-361-3765. Students 70.
Waterford, Saratoga Co.
1—St. Anne, Closed. For inquiries for parish records, contact St. Mary of the Assumption, Waterford.
2—St. Mary of the Assumption, [CEM] Rev. David Kelley, O.S.A. In Res., Rev. Michael Stanley, O.S.A.
Res.: 119 Broad St., 12188-2397. Tel: 518-237-3131; Fax: 518-237-9625.
School—St. Mary's Catholic School, 12 Sixth St., 12188. Tel: 518-237-0652; Fax: 518-233-0898. Mary Rushkoski, Prin. Lay Teachers 20; Students 245.
Catechesis/Religious Program—Cathleen Olmstead, D.R.E. Faith Formation Program is located at St. Mary of the Assumption. Students 152.
Watervliet, Albany Co.
1—St. Brigid, Merged with Immaculate Conception, Our Lady of Mt. Carmel, St. Patrick's and Sacred Heart of Mary, Watervliet & St. Joseph,

Green Island, to form Immaculate Heart of Mary, Watervliet. Church not closed.

2—IMMACULATE CONCEPTION, (Polish), [CEM] Merged with St. Brigid's, Our Lady of Mt. Carmel, St. Patrick's, Sacred Heart of Mary, Watervliet & St. Joseph's, Green Island to form Immaculate Heart of Mary, Watervliet. Church not closed.

3—IMMACULATE HEART OF MARY Leadership Team:, Rev. L. Edward Deimeke; Deacon Thomas Nash.
Parish Office: 2416 7th Ave., 12189. Tel: 518-273-6020; Fax: 518-273-3978. Email: ihm@rcpw.org. Web: www.rcpw.org.
Rectory—695 Fifth Ave., 12189. Tel: 518-687-2107.
School—St. Brigid's Regional School, (Grades PreK-8), 700 Fifth Ave., 12189.
Catechesis/Religious Program—Sharon C. Kowalski, D.R.E. Students 139.

4—OUR LADY OF MT. CARMEL, (Italian), Merged with St. Brigid's, Immaculate Conception, St. Patrick's, Sacred Heart of Mary, Watervliet & St. Joseph, Green Island to form Immaculate Heart of Mary, Watervliet. Church not closed.

5—ST. PATRICK, Merged with St. Brigid's, Immaculate Conception, Our Lady of Mt. Carmel, Sacred Heart of Mary, Watervliet & St. Joseph's Green Island, to form Immaculate Heart of Mary, Watervliet. Church not closed.

6—SACRED HEART OF MARY, Closed. Consolidated with St. Brigid's, Immaculate Conception, Our Lady of Mt. Carmel, St. Patrick's, Watervliet & St. Joseph's, Green Island to form Immaculate Heart of Mary, Watervliet.

WEST TAGHKANIC, COLUMBIA CO., HOLY CROSS, Merged with Sacred Heart, Philmont, to form St. John Vianney, Claverack, NY 12153-0477. Tel: 518-851-1333.

WEST WINFIELD, HERKIMER CO., ST. JOSEPH, [CEM] Merged with St. Joseph, Richfield Springs to form St. Joseph the Worker, Richfield Springs. Worship Site.

WHITEHALL, WASHINGTON CO.

1—NOTRE DAME DES VICTOIRES, Merged with Our Lady of Angels, Whitehall to form Our Lady of Hope, Whitehall.

2—OUR LADY OF ANGELS, Merged with Notre Dame des Victoires, Whitehall to form Our Lady of Hope, Whitehall.

3—OUR LADY OF HOPE Rev. Michael Flannery.
Res.: 9 Wheeler Ave., 12887. Tel: 518-499-1656; Fax: 518-499-2489.
Catechesis/Religious Program—Combined with Chapel of the Assumption. Patti Abbott, A.R.E. & Youth Min. Students 55.
Chapel—Assumption, Huletts Landing

WINDHAM, GREENE CO., ST. THERESA OF CHILD JESUS Rev. James Schiffer, C.P.
Res.: Main St., 12496. Tel: 518-734-3352.
Catechesis/Religious Program—Tel: 518-734-9685; Fax: 518-734-3352. Margaret Reinold Gulino, D.R.E. Students 128.
Mission—St. Joseph's Chapel Ashland, Greene Co.

WORCESTER, OTSEGO CO., ST. JOSEPH Rev. Ronald Lee Green, M.M., Admin.
Res.: 181 Main St., P.O. Box 156, 12197. Tel: 607-397-9373; Fax: 607-397-7732.
Mission—St. Mary [CEM] Schenevus, Otsego Co.

WYNANTSKILL, RENSSELAER CO., ST. JUDE THE APOSTLE Rev. Anthony F. Ligato, Admin.; Deacon Warren A. Safford.
43 Brookside Ave., P.O. Box 347, 12198-0347.
Res.: 6 Schuyler Ct., P.O. Box 347, 12198-0347. Tel: 518-283-1162; Fax: 518-286-2808. Email: stjude@nycap.rr.com. Web: stjude-church.com.
Parish Office: 42 Dana Ave., 12198-0347.
School—(Grades PreK-6), 35 Dana Ave., 12198. Tel: 518-283-0333; Fax: 518-283-0475. Email: albsjs@rcdaschools.org. Web: www.rcdaschools.org/stjude/. Cathleen Carney, Admin. Lay Teachers 18; Students 203.

Chaplains of Public Institutions

ALBANY. *Albany County Jail*. (Assigned to Deanery Priests).
Albany County Nursing Home. Rev. Anthony Curran, Rev. Anthony C. Nicklas, (Orthodox).
Albany Medical Center Hospital. Revs. Kenneth Gregory, Robert E. DeLeon, C.S.C.
Capital District Psychiatric Center. Deacon Charles Hall.
Columbia County Jail. Rev. Theodore J. Gerken (Retired).
Memorial Hospital. Rev. John T. Kelly.
New York State Department of Corrections. Deacon Donald Thomas Sharrow, Ministerial Prog. Coord. Tel: 518-457-8106.
St. Peter's Hospital. Rev. John Tallman, Chap., Rev. Terrence O'Neil, Chap., Deacon Martin Beckman, Chap., David Dietsche, Chap., Mr. Younas Azad, Chap., Ms. Sally Conklin, Chap., Mr. J. Erik Swift, Chap.
University Heights Nursing Home. Sr. Jane Carr, R.S.M., Chap.
Veterans' Administration Hospital. Deacon Gerald Ladouceur, Revs. Joseph Grasso, C.PP.S., Paul Tartaglia (Retired).

COMSTOCK. *Great Meadows Correctional Institution*. Deacon Miguel Fabian, Chap., Rev. Michael Flannery, Sacramental Min.

COXSACKIE. *Coxsackie Correctional Facility*. Rev. Richard D. Shaw, Sacramental Min., Deacon Lawrence Groesbeck, Chap., Very Rev. John L. Moyna, V.F., Chap., Regional Medical Unit.
Greene Correctional Facility. Deacon Steven Young, Chap., Rev. Richard D. Shaw, Sacramental Min.

GLENS FALLS. *Glens Falls Hospital*. Sr. Donna Irvine, S.S.N.D., Chap.
Hudson Correctional Facility. Gerald Van Alstine, Chap.

SCHENECTADY. *Ellis Hospital*. Ms. Angela Marczewski, Deacon Gary Riggi.
Hallmark Nursing Home. Deacon Earle Flatt, Chap.
Schenectady County Nursing Home. Madelyn Thorne, Chap.

TROY. *Samaritan Hospital*. Deacons Frank S. Lukovits, Moses Guitterrez.
Seton Health. Deacon Albert Schrempf.
Van Rensselaer Manor. Vacant.

WILTON. *Mount McGregor Correctional Facility*. Rev. Dennis Tamburello, O.F.M., Sacramental Min., Lois Lippincott-Pino, Chap.

Special Assignment:
Most Rev.—
Hubbard, Howard James, D.D., Bishop, Roman Catholic Diocese of Albany
Revs.—
Berberian, David V., J.C.L., 40 N. Main Ave., 12203-1422.
Broderick, Richard, Pueblo to Pueblo Program, 330 Brownell Rd., Cambridge, 12816.
Chepaitis, Peter, O.F.M., 26C Mill Ln., P.O. Box 42, Middleburgh, 12122.
Chiaramonte, Anthony J., Ph.D., 790 Lancaster St., 12203. Consultation Center
Cullinane, Briant, O.F.M.Conv., P.O. Box 629, Rensselaer, 12144.
Curran, Anthony, St. Paul the Apostle Rectory, 277 Albany St., Schenectady, 12304.
DeGiovine, Christopher, 432 Western Ave., 12203. College of St. Rose
DeLeon, Robert E., C.S.C., 495 Maple Ln., Valatie, 12184.
Donlon, James I., J.C.D., 40 N. Main Ave., 12203. Judicial Vicar, Tribunal, Pastoral Center
Farano, Michael A., Vicar Gen. & Dir. Society of the Propagation of Faith, 2 Fairview Rd., Loudonville, 12211.
Finn, Firmin, O.F.M.Conv., 1 Jeanne Jugan Ln., Latham, 12110.
Fragomeni, Richard, 5401 S. Cornell Ave., Chicago, IL 60615.
Frisoni, Matthew H., Oblates of St. Francis de Sales, 721 Lawrence St., N.E., Washington, DC 20017.
Gregory, Kenneth, Chap., Albany Medical Center, 12208.
Kelly, John T., Chap., Memorial Hospital, 600 N. Blvd., 12010.
Konopka, Thomas E., L.M.S.W., Dir. Consultation Center, 465 State St., 12203.
L'Arche, Jeffrey, M.S., B.S., S.T.B., Our Lady of LaSalette Shrine, Lessome Ln., Altamont, 12009.
Murray, Peter J., S.J., 136 Shrine Rd., Fultonville, 12072.
Shaw, Richard D., Chap., Coxsackie Correctional Facility, P.O. Box 232, New Baltimore, 12124. Sacramental Min., Greene County Correctional Facility
Sullivan, Peter J., III, J.C.L., 40 N. Main Ave., 12203. Adjutant Vicar Judicial Tribunal, Pastoral Center
Tallman, John, Chap., St. Peter's Hospital, Mater Christi, 40 Collins Pl., 12208.
Van Thanh, Louis, Vietnamese Apostolate, 55 Grand St., Newburgh, 12550.
Vosko, Richard, Liturgical Design Consultant, 4611 Foxwood Dr., P.O. Box 2217, Clifton Park, 12605.
You, Simon (Kwanggun), Korean Apostolate, 80 Slingerlands St., 12202.

On Duty Outside the Diocese:
Revs.—
Fragomeni, Richard, Chicago Theological Institute, 5401 S. Cornell Ave., Chicago, IL 60615-5698.
Hurst, Thomas R., S.S., Theological College, 5400 Roland Ave., Baltimore, MD 21210.
O'Keeffe, Joseph, P.O. Box 793, Enfield, NH 03748.

Military Chaplains:
Revs.—
O'Keeffe, Joseph, P.O. Box 793, Enfield, NH 03748.
Rutherford, Donald I., CH (MG), HQDA (DACH-2B), 2700 Pentagon, Rm. 2A514A, Washington, DC 20310-2700.

Leave of Absence:
Revs.—
Celeste, Charles R.
Cournoyer, Michael R.
Raiche, Brian
Rossi, Desmond
Tressic, David L.

Retired:
Revs.—
Ahern, Bernard, 4418 Poppy Tree Ln., Jacksonville, FL 32258.
Allie, Stanley J., 1201 Bogard Rd., Wasilla, AK 99643.
Amato, Joseph, 1056 Nantucke Rd., Venice, FL 34293.
Anselment, Joseph, 23 Tiffany Dr., Glens Falls, 12801.
Antos, Paul J., 1149 Highland Park Rd., Niskayuna, 12309.
Baniak, Walter, St. Peter's Nursing & Rehab., 301 Hackett Blvd., 12208.
Barker, Joseph, Our Lady of Victory, 55 N. Lake Ave., Troy, 12180.
Brucker, George W., 25 St. Anthony Ln., Rensselaer, 12144.
Cairns, John L., 23 Oak Brook Commons, Clifton Park, 12065.
Cantwell, Edward F., 429 E. Allen St., Hudson, 12534.
Clemente, Michael, The Eddy, 15 E. Ascot Ln., Niskayuna, 12309.
Cox, Paul, P.O. Box 134, Kattskill Bay, 12844.
Cyvas, Matthew, 555 68th Ave., St. Petersburg Beach, FL 33706.
D'Agostino, Joseph, Teresian House, 200 Washington Ave. Ext., 12203.
Daley, James D., 69 Murray Ave., Delmar, 12054.
De Franco, Anthony, Teresian House, 200 Washington Ave. Ext., 12203.
De Pascale, Daniel, CDR, 2750 Biarritz Ct., Ponte Vedra Beach, FL 32802.
Donnelly, Robert, 100 White Pine Dr., 12203.
Doyle, Donald, 178 E. Sanford St., Glens Falls, 12801.
Dunbar, Francis, 20 1/2 Williams St., Whitehall, 12887.
Dworak, Joseph J., 4 Wood Lake Rd., Apt. #1, 12203.
Dybas, Richard W., 1786 Union St., Rm. 336, Schenectady, 12309.
Engel, Paul, 3 Raymond Dr., Altamont, 12009.
Esmond, William, Ledgewood Village, Rte. 149, 17 Ledgewood Dr., Lake George, 12845.
Facci, John, S.A.C., 802 Union St., Schenectady, 12308.
French, John F., 15 Priorslee Ln., Williamsburg, VA 23185.
Gaffigan, Charles A., 66 James St., Schenectady, 12304.
Gaffigan, William J., 111 Stewart St., Amsterdam, 12010.
Gerken, Theodore J., 207 S. Main St., P.O. Box 335, Germantown, 12526.
Girzone, Joseph, 107 Joshua Ln., Altamont, 12209.
Gulley, Anthony D., Blessed Sacrament, 607 Central Ave., 12206.
Gulley, James, Teresian House, 200 Washington Ave. Ext., 12203.
Halloran, Joseph, Teresian House, 200 Washington Ave. Ext., 12203.
Ianotti, Pascal, 204 Linden Ct., Amsterdam, 12010.
Jupin, Alan D., Rosegarden Apts., Bldg. 7, Apt. 6, Latham, 12110.
Kelly, Donald F., 38 Paine St., Green Island, 12183.
Kirwin, John D., 94 Lincoln Ave., Saratoga Springs, 12866.
Lamanna, Alfred, The Prospect Inn, 20 N. Prospect St., Apt. J, Herkimer, 13350.
Lefebvre, James, St. Mary's Rectory, 10 Lodge St., 12207.
LeFevre, Robert J., 2 Jaipur Ln., Saratoga Springs, 12866.
Leskovar, Richard J., 4 Woodlake Rd., Apt. 7, 12203.
Lonergan, J. Barry, 187 E. Sanford St., Glens Falls, 12801.
Mackey, James, 38 Oak Brook Commons, Clifton Park, 12065.
Maher, Daniel J., 2305 Florence Dr., Latham, 12110.
Malecki, John J., Ph.D., Teresian House, 200 Washington Ave. Ext., 12203.
Marbury, Cabell B., 99 Slingerland St., 12202.
Markert, Leo, 133 Saratoga Rd., Bldg. S, Apt. #5, Glenville, 12302.
Matulewicz, Ronald G., St. Joseph Rectory, 7 North

St., P.O. Box 538, Broadalbin, 12025.
McCloskey, Francis G., 1094 Mountain Ave., #4, Purling, 12470.
McTavey, Lawrence, V.F., 89B Church Hill Rd., Waterford, 12188.
Nabozny, Peter, 27 St. Anthony Ln., Rensselaer, 12144.
Nusbaum, Daniel C., Ph.D., 2701 Chicago Blvd., Detroit, MI 48206.
O'Brien, Leo P., Avila, 100 White Pine Dr., 12203.
O'Connor, Frank, 465 State St., 12203.
O'Grady, John F., S.S.D., S.T.D., 1000 Quayside Ter., #2104, Miami, FL 33138.
O'Neill, James, 38 Middletown Rd., P.O. Box 421, Waterford, 12188.
Ophals, Donald J., St. Ambrose Rectory, 347 Old Loudon Rd., Latham, 12110.
Pereira, Cyril F., 2256 Burdett Ave., #2017, Troy, 12180.
Piechocki, Raymond S., 100 Charles Ln., Apt. M-7, Amsterdam, 12010.
Potvin, Leo F., 73 1st St., Ilion, 13357.
Powers, Thomas M., Teresian House, 200 Washington Ave. Ext., 12203.
Purcell, Robert, P.O. Box 169, Margaretville, 12455.
Rebeyro, Lloyd, 4 Proctor Ct., Loudonville, 12211. Tel: 518-265-9974
Redmond, Paul V., P.O. Box 458, Emmitsburg, MD 21727.
Rooney, John J., St. Joseph Apts., #4115, 2 Jeanne Jugan Ln., Latham, 12110.
Roos, John R., J.C.D., 203 Elm St., Apt. 7, Cobleskill, 12043.
Ryan, Edward J., Teresian House, 200 Washington Ave., 12203.
Schmitt, Michael T., 133 Saratoga Rd. Bldg. H, Apt. 12, Glenville, 12302.
Schweigardt, Erwin H., 1570 Kingston Ave., Schenectady, 12303.
Shanley, Owen F., P.O. Box 914, Broadalbin, 12025.
Sipperly, Edward, P.O. Box 317, Clifton Park, 12065.
Smith, Paul, 37 Parkwood St. E., 12203.
St. John, George G., 607 Central Ave., 12206.
Swierzowski, Stanislaus J., 48 Van Derveer St., Amsterdam, 12010.
Tartaglia, Paul, 465 State St., 12203. (June-Nov.)
Testa, Richard, St. Joseph Apts., 2 Jeanne Jugan Ln., Latham, 12110.
Titta, Santino, 19 Juniper Pl., Grant City, 10306.
Toole, Arthur A., 38 Oak Brook Commons, Clifton Park, 12065.
Touchette, Marc L., Eddy Village Green, 16 Posinello Way, Cohoes, 12047.
Tremblay, Nellis, P.O. Box 134, Kattskill Bay, 12844.
Tunny, Kenneth J., St. Gabriel's Rectory, 3040 Hamburg St., Schenectady, 12303.
Turnbull, William, 89A Church Hill Rd., Waterford, 12188.
Urban, Carl, 48 Annabelle Pl., Schenectady, 12306-5789.
Vail, Thomas, 76 Moreland St., Little Falls, 13365.
Varno, John, 73 Midline Rd., Ballston Lake, 12019.
Vaughan, James, 310 Spring Ave., Troy, 12180.
Waldron, John F., 418 Shaker Run, Apt 419, 12205.
Weider, Gregory, 7 Eastmount Dr., Apt. 216, Slingerlands, 12159.
Young, Peter G., 40 Eagle St., 12207.

Permanent Deacons:
Ayers, Walter, St. Mary's, Albany
Baechel, Kenneth, Saint Augustine, FL 32080. (Relocated)
Bandel, Arthur, Blessed Sacrament, Bolton Landing
Bazinet, William, St. Joseph's, Fort Edward; St. Mary's/St. Paul's, Hudson Falls
Beckman, Martin L., St. Vincent de Paul, Albany; Pastoral Services- St. Peter's Hospital, Albany
Berning, Frank C., St. Joseph's, Scotia; Dir. Initial Formation for the Diaconate; Diocesan Director of Pastoral Planning
Bower, James W., Annunciation, Ilion
Boyd, Danny S., St. Therese Mission, Gansevoort, Admin.
Brady, Robert, (Retired), 100 White Pine Dr., Apt. 325, 12203. Deacon Life and Ministry Council (Retired)
Brennan, Joseph, Our Lady of the Assumption, Rotterdam
Brett, William, Chap., Our Lady of Mercy Life Center, Guilderland; Legion of Mary
Brown, Richard Dr., St. Thomas the Apostle, Cherry Valley
Carbone, Michael S., Holy Family, Little Falls
Cechnicki, Joseph M., St. Adalbert's, Schenectady; Deacon Life and Ministry Council; Diaconate Formation Faculty
Christiano, Gerald, (Retired), 14 Woods Path, Troy, 12182-1636.
Cohen, Andrew, St. Francis of Assisi, Albany
Colton, Thomas, (On Leave)
Crane, John, St. Joseph's, Scotia
Davignon, Paul M., St. Matthews, Voorheesville
DeLorenzo, Joseph, Holy Family, Little Falls
Devine, Patrick, (On Duty Outside Diocese) (Relocated)
Donnell, Michael, Sacred Heart, Sidney
Dorsch, Warren, Parish of Our Lady of Hope, Copake Falls; Chaplain, Hudson Correctional Facility; Columbia County Sheriff & Jail; Albany Medical Center
Dringus, William, Holy Spirit Church, East Greenbush
Fabian, Miguel, Hispanic Community, Albany
Flatt, Earle, St. Madeleine Sophie, Guiderland
Garcia-Lopez, Angel, Holy Family Parish, Hispanic Community, Albany; Coxsackie & Greene Correctional
Gaul, William H., Jr., St. Clement's, Saratoga Springs
Gorman, William, D.Min., Ph.D., (On Duty Outside Diocese) (Relocated)
Grigaitis, Jerry, (Retired), Co-liaison for Catholic Charismatic Renewal; St. Edward the Confessor, Clifton Park
Groesbeck, Lawrence, Hale Creek Correctional Facility
Gutierrez, Moises, St. Anthony of Padua, Troy; Samaritan Hospital, Troy
Hall, Charles H., III, Capitol District Psychiatric Center, Albany
Hanson, Lee, St. Clement, Saratoga Springs
Henkel, William, St. Francis de Sales, Herkimer; Office of Evangelization, Catechesis, & Family Life
Herlihy, Frank, Sacred Heart, Lake George
Hewitt, William, (Retired)
Hogan, Ronald T., St. Mary's, Ballston Spa
Hook, J. Neil, (Retired), Diocesan Liturgy Committee, Interim Admin.; Sacred Heart, Troy
Jones, Dennis, (On Leave)
Kelenski, Eugene, St. Edward's, Clifton Park
Kisselback, Paul, St. Mary's, Crescent
Ladouceur, Gerald J., Mater Christi, Albany; Stratton VA Hospital, Albany
Lape, Stephen M., St. Joseph's, Scotia
Leonard, Mark J., St. Madeleine Sophie, Schenectady
Levine, Brian, St. Peter's, Saratoga Springs
Lewis, Brian, Our Lady of Victory, Troy
Luby, Thomas T., Rural Ministry, Sacred Heart, Sidney
Lukovits, Frank S., St. Henry, Averill Park; Samaritan Hospital, Troy
MacKinnon, Walter, St. Edward, Clifton Park
Manno, Peter, (Retired), St. Joseph's, Dolgeville
Mansfield, E. Gregory, Assumption-St. Paul's, Mechanicville
Manzella, Alfred R., St. Thomas, Delmar
Markham, Joseph, Christ the King, Albany; Pre-Cana Coord.
Matthews, Gerard, Holy Trinity, Cohoes
McAuliffe, Timothy J., All Saints, Albany; Diaconate Board
McDonald, Michael, Administrative Advocate for Deacons; St. Mary's, Coxsackie
Melanson, Michael, Immaculate Conception, Glenville; Master of Ceremonies; Deacon Life and Ministry Council
Nahm, George H., (Retired)
Nash, Thomas, Immaculate Heart of Mary, Watervliet; Green Island
Neurohr, Helmut N., St. Ambrose, Latham
Novak, John W., (Retired)
O'Connell, Thomas, (Retired)
O'Connor, Gary, All Saints Catholic Church, Albany
O'Connor, Gerard, (Retired)
O'Neill, Charles, Parish of the Holy Trinity, Hudson
O'Rourke, James E., St. Patrick's, Ravena
Pagano, Joseph S., St. Francis of Assisi, Northville; St. Joseph, Broadalbin
Pasquarelli, Robert, St. Henry's, Averill Park
Picher, Gary, St. Joseph, Greenfield Center, Parish Life Director
Powers, David F., St. Mary's, Glen Falls
Quinn, Peter R., Immaculate Conception, New Lebanon, Assoc. Dir. Catholic Scouting
Riggi, Gary, Ellis Hospital, Schenectady
Roemer, Paul W., (Retired)
Rucinski, Robert T., (Retired)
Ryba, Michael, Parish Administrator, St. Stanislaus, Amsterdam; Montgomery County Convalescent Home, Montgomery County Prison
Safford, Warren A., St. Jude the Apostle, Wynantskill
Sakowicz, Albert, (Retired), Parish of Our Lady of Hope, Fort Plain, Canajoharie
Salamone, Sam, (Retired)
Schickel, Frank, St. Mary & St. John the Evangelist, Schenectady
Schrempf, Albert G., Holy Trinity, Cohoes; Seton Health, Troy
Sedlmeir, Peter, St. John the Baptist, Greenville
Sharrow, Thomas, St. Helen's, Schenectady
Sheppeck, Michael, (Retired)
Skelly, John, St. Mary's, Nassau
Solar, Richard, (Retired)
Solomon, Edward R., St. Joseph's, Greenfield Center; St. Paul's Mission, Rock City Falls
South, Owen D., (Retired)
Stosiek, Martin, (Retired)
Sullivan, Raymond, Ph.D., St. Francis of Assisi, Albany, Parish Life Dir.; Ongoing Formation of Ordained Deacons; Master of Ceremonies
Surman, Dr. Gary, St. Vincent, Cobleskill; Office of Evangelization, Catechesis, & Family Life
Tapia, Raymon, St. John the Evangelist, Schenectady
Thiesen, Richard J., Our Lady of Fatima, Schenectady, Parish Life Director
Thomas, Frank, M.D., Our Lady of Grace, Ballston Spa; St. Luke's Guild
Tierney, John, Corpus Christi, Round Lake (Ushers)
Trawinski, Peter, St. James, Chatham; Master of Ceremonies; Liturgy sub-committee; Deacon Life and Ministry Council
Turcotte, Arthur W., (Retired)
Tyrell, Joseph, St. Mary's, Glens Falls
Valenti, Charles, St. Michael's, Cohoes
Velez, Randy, St. Mary's, Cooperstown
Washburn, Richard, Holy Trinity, Hudson
Willette, Lawrence, St. Clement, Saratoga Springs
Wilson, Gerald, Our Lady of Annunciation, Queensbury
Witko, George, St. Mary, Albany
Wojton, Charles, St. Joseph, Troy
Wubbenhorst, Robert H., (Retired), Parish of St. Isaac Jogues, Chestertown
Yankowski, Frank, St. Michael the Archangel, Troy
Zoltowski, Gregory, (Retired)

INSTITUTIONS LOCATED IN THE DIOCESE

[A] SEMINARIES, RELIGIOUS OR SCHOLASTICATES

CATSKILL. *St. Anthony Friary*, 24 Harrison St., P.O. Box 487, 12414-0487. Tel: 518-943-3451; Fax: 518-943-1573. Revs. Michael Dominic W. Ledoux, O.F.M.; Regis Gallo, O.F.M.; Valerian Faugno, O.F.M.; Albin Fusco, O.F.M.; Albert McMahon, O.F.M.; Paul Guido, O.F.M.; Bros. Lawrence Stumpo, O.F.M.; Vincent de Paul Ciaravino, O.F.M., Dir., Health Care & Local Min. Order of Friars Minor. Priests 6; Brothers 2.

RENSSELAER. *Conventual Franciscan Friars Immaculate Conception Province, Provincialate/ Office of the Treasurer*, P.O. Box 629, 12144. Tel: 518-472-1000; 518-472-1016; Fax: 518-472-1013. Email: brorayl@juno.com. Web: www.franciscanseast.org. 77 St. Francis Pl., 12144. Very Rev. Justin Biase, O.F.M.Conv., Min. Prov.; Friar Raymond Sobocinski, O.F.M. Conv., Province Treas. Order Friars Minor Conventual. Priests 1; Brothers 1.

[B] COLLEGES AND UNIVERSITIES

ALBANY. *St. Bernard's School of Theology and Ministry at Albany*, 40 N. Main Ave., 12203. Tel: 518-453-6760; Fax: 518-453-6793. Email: stbernards@rcda.org. Web: stbernards.edu. Sr. Katherine Hanley, C.S.J., Assoc. Dean. Extension Program of St. Bernard's School of Theology and Ministry, Rochester, NY. Graduate School of Theology & Ministry Studies.

The College of Saint Rose (Corporate Name), 432 Western Ave., 12203. Tel: 518-454-5111; 800-657-8556; Fax: 518-458-5447. Web: www.strose.edu. Dr. Mark Sullivan, Pres.; Dr. David Szczerbacki, Provost & Vice Pres. Academic Affairs; Marcus Buckley, Vice Pres. Fin. & Admin.; Karin Carr, Vice Pres. Inst. Advancement; Judith A. Kelly, Registrar; Dennis McDonald, Vice Pres. Student Affairs; Mary Grondahl, Vice Pres. Enrollment Management; Rev. Christopher DeGiovine, Chap. & Dean Spiritual Life; Peter Koonz, Dir. Library Svcs. Founded by the Sisters of St. Joseph of Carondelet in 1920. Priests 1; Sisters 3; Lay Teachers 207; Students 4,863.

Maria College, 700 New Scotland Ave., 12208. Tel: 518-438-3111; Fax: 518-438-7170. Web: MariaCollege.edu. Sr. Laureen Fitzgerald, Pres.; Dr. Margie Byrd, Dean for Academic Affairs; Ms. Laurie Gilmore, Dir. Admissions; Ms. Deborah Corrigan, Dean Students; Mrs. Frances Bernard, Dir. Business Affairs; Sr. Rose Hobbs, R.S.M.,

Librarian. Two-Year College with a Bachelors Completion Program (RN-BS) for registered nurses. Sisters of Mercy 9; Sisters of St. Joseph 1; Lay Teachers 32; Students 800.

LOUDONVILLE. *Siena College* 12211. Tel: 518-783-2300; Fax: 518-783-4293. Web: www.siena.edu. Revs. Kevin Mullen, O.F.M., Ph.D., Pres.; Kenneth Paulli, O.F.M., Chief of Staff, President's Cabinet; Linda Richardson, Ph.D., Vice Pres. Academic Affairs; Paul Stec, Vice Pres. Fin. & Admin.; David Smith, Vice Pres. Develop. & External Affairs; Ned Jones, Vice Pres. Enrollment Mgmt.; Dr. Maryellen Gilroy, Vice Pres. Student Affairs; Rev. Greg Jakubowicz, O.F.M., Chap.; Mary Lawyer, Asst. Vice Pres., Financial Aid; Mark Frost, Asst. Vice Pres. Facilities; James A. Serbalik, Registrar; Gary B. Thompson, Dir. of Library.

Siena College, Founded in 1937 by the Franciscan Friars, Order of Friars Minor, Province of the Most Holy Name of Jesus. Students 3,292; Full Time 182; Part Time 304.

The Friary: Most Rev. Capistrano Heim, O.F.M.; Revs. Greg Jakubowicz, O.F.M., Chap.; Richard Biasiotto, O.F.M.; William L. Beaudin, O.F.M., Chap., Guardian-Siena Friary; Julian A. Davies, O.F.M.; Ambrose Donehue, O.F.M.; Matthias Doyle, O.F.M.; Daniel P. Dwyer, O.F.M.; Peter A. Fiore, O.F.M.; Capistran Hanlon, O.F.M.; Linh Hoang, O.F.M.; Gerard Lee, O.F.M., Dir., St. Francis Chapel; Kevin Mullen, O.F.M., Ph.D., Pres.; Russell T. Murray, Dir. Franciscon Center for Svc. & Advocacy; Gerald R. Mudd, O.F.M.; Daniel C. Nelson, O.F.M.; Kenneth Paulli, O.F.M.; Reginald J. Reddy, O.F.M.; Blaise R. Reinhart, O.F.M.; Dennis Tamburello, O.F.M.; John E. Van Hook, O.F.M.; Bros. Brian C. Belanger, O.F.M.; Romuald Chinetsky, O.F.M.; Walter Liss, O.F.M., Vicar; Edgardo Zoa, O.F.M.

[C] HIGH SCHOOLS, DIOCESAN

ALBANY. *Bishop Maginn High School*, 99 Slingerland St., 12202. Tel: 518-463-2247; Fax: 518-463-9880. Email: principal@bishopmaginn.org. Web: www.bishopmaginn.org. Mr. Joseph Grasso, Assoc. Head of School; Joseph Salamack, Head of School. Priests 1; Sisters 1; Lay Teachers 16; Students 150.

AMSTERDAM. *Bishop Scully High School*, Upper Church St., 12010. Tel: 518-842-4100. Closed.

SARATOGA SPRINGS. *Saratoga Central Catholic High School*, (Grades 6-12), 247 Broadway, 12866. Tel: 518-587-7070; Fax: 518-587-0678. Email: scc@saratogacentralcatholic.org. Web: www.saratogacatholic.org. Mr. L. Stephen Lombard, Prin. Lay Teachers 22; Students 222.

SCHENECTADY. *Notre Dame-Bishop Gibbons School*, (Grades 6-12), (Coed) (grades 6-12), 2600 Albany St., 12304. Tel: 518-393-3131; Fax: 518-370-3817. Email: info@ndbg.org. Ninette Kondratowicz, Co-Prin. (High School); Mr. Richard Harrigan, Co-Prin. (Middle School). Lay Teachers 29; Students 302.

TROY. *Catholic Central High School*, (Grades 7-12), 625 Seventh Ave., 12182. Tel: 518-235-7100; Fax: 518-237-1796. Email: cchsprincipal@yahoo.com. Web: www.cchstroy.org. Mr. Christopher Bott, Prin.; Howard Lustig, Asst. Prin.; Frederick Talarico, Middle School Dean. Sisters 2; Lay Teachers 37; Students 500.

[D] HIGH SCHOOLS, PRIVATE

ALBANY. *Academy of the Holy Names Upper, Middle and Lower Schools*, (Grades PreK-12), 1073 New Scotland Rd., 12208. Tel: 518-438-7895; Fax: 518-438-7368. Web: www.ahns.org. Dr. Eva C. Joseph, Pres. (PreK-12); Ms. Mary Anne Vigliante, Prin. (Grades 9-12); Ms. Susan Bulmer, Prin. (Grades PreK-8). Sisters 6; Lay Teachers 71; Students 294.

The Christian Brothers' Academy of Albany, (Grades 6-12), 12 Airline Dr., 12205. Tel: 518-452-9809; Fax: 518-452-9804. Web: www.cbaalbany.org. Mr. James Schlegel, Prin.; Ms. Diane Babbie, Librarian. Brothers of the Christian Schools., JROTC College Prep. Program. Brothers 6; Lay Teachers 36; Students 402.

Mercy High, Private School for Girls Closed., c/o 40 N. Main Ave., 12203.

TROY. *LaSalle Institute*, (Grades 6-12), 174 Williams Rd., 12180. Tel: 518-283-2500; Fax: 518-283-6265. Email: info@lasalleinstitute.org. Web: www.lasalleinstitute.org. Bro. Carl Malacalza, F.S.C., Prin.; Mrs. Frances Lengua, Librarian. Brothers of the Christian Schools. Brothers 8; Sisters 1; Lay Teachers 35; Students 410.

[E] ELEMENTARY SCHOOLS, PRIVATE

LOUDONVILLE. *Saint Gregory's School*, (Grades N-8), 121 Old Niskayuna Rd., 12211-1399. Tel: 518-785-6621; Fax: 518-782-1364. Email: marrao@saintgregoryschool.org. Web: www.saintgregorysschool.org. Jeffry P. Loomis, Head of School. An independent Catholic day school for boys staffed by laity (Nursery-8). Girls admitted in Nursery through Kindergarten classes. Lay Teachers 22; Students 139.

[F] CONSOLIDATED ELEMENTARY SCHOOLS

ALBANY. *Cathedral Academy*, 75 Park Ave., 12202. Tel: 518-449-5232. Closed.

COHOES. *Cohoes Catholic School* Closed., One St. Marie's Ln., 12047. Tel: 518-235-5202; Fax: 518-453-6666.

GLEN FALLS. *St. Mary's/St. Alphonsus Regional Catholic School*, (Grades PreK-8), 10-12 Church St., Glens Falls, 12801. Tel: 518-792-3178; Fax: 518-792-6056. Web: www.smsaschool.org. Mrs. Kathryn Mahoney-Fowler, Prin.

WATERFORD. *St. Mary's School*, (Grades PreK-8), 12 Sixth St., 12188. Tel: 518-237-0652; Fax: 518-233-0898. Email: stmarys1@nycap.rr.com. Web: www.smswaterford.org. Mary Rushkoski, Prin. Part Time 1; Lay Teachers 22; Students 260.

[G] RESIDENTIAL INSTITUTIONS FOR CHILDREN & ADOLESCENTS

ALBANY. *Saint Anne Institute*, 160 N. Main Ave., 12206. Tel: 518-437-6500; Fax: 518-437-6555. Email: rriccio@s-a-i.org. Web: www.stanneinstitute.org. Richard C. Riccio, Exec. Dir. Email: rriccio@s-a-i.org. Residential and Community-based Preventive Service Center. Regents accredited and certified junior and senior H.S. for the emotionally handicapped and Preschool program for 3-4 year olds who are speech-impaired and emotionally disturbed. Residential care, critical care, and Day Treatment for young women ages 12-18. Family Services, Vocational Training, Sex Abuse Prevention and Juvenile Sex Offender Programs for male and female adolescents in crisis and their families. Residential 129; Day Treatment 40; Juvenile Sex Offender & Sex Abuse Prevention Families 90.

St. Catherine's Center for Children, 40 N. Main Ave., 12203. Tel: 518-453-6700; Fax: 518-453-8443. Web: www.st-cath.org. Ms. Helen Hayes, Exec. Dir. Residential and day treatment, group homes and foster family programs for children with special needs. Community based prevention programs; Parent aides; Parent Training; Transitional Program for Homeless Families. Total Assisted Annually 1,250.

LaSalle School, Inc., 391 Western Ave., 12203. Tel: 518-242-4731; Fax: 518-242-4747. Email: information@lasalle-school.org. Web: www.lasalle-school.org. Mr. William Wolff, Exec. Dir. Residential and day programs, independent living program, sexual victim/offender program, licensed substance abuse treatment program, and preventative services for boys (ages 12-18) and their families in New York State. Registered New York State Junior and Senior High School and certified School of Special Education. Brothers of the Christian Schools 8; Prevention Families 64; Resident Students 83; Day Students 44; Community Connections 21.

The La Salle School Foundation of Albany Tel: 518-242-4731; Fax: 518-242-4744.

WATERVLIET. *St. Colman's Home* 12189. Tel: 518-273-4911; Fax: 518-273-3312. Sr. Mary Regina, Dir.; Rev. Kenneth Gregory, Chap. Sisters of the Presentation of the B.V.M. Children 45.

[H] GENERAL HOSPITALS

ALBANY. *St. Clare's Corporation*, 40 N. Main Ave., 12203-1422. Tel: 518-453-6650; Fax: 518-453-6792. Joseph Profiti, Pres.

St. Clare's Holding Company, Inc., 40 N. Main Ave., 12203-1422. Tel: 518-453-6650. Web: www.stclares.org.

St. Peter's Health Care Services, 315 S. Manning Blvd., 12208. Tel: 518-525-1550; Fax: 518-525-1520. Email: sboyle@stpetershealthcare.org. Web: www.stpetershealthcare.org. Mr. Steven P. Boyle, Pres. & CEO.

Affiliated Management Service Corp., 1300 Massachusetts Ave., Troy, 12180. Tel: 518-268-5520; Fax: 518-268-5257. Email: sstgeorge@setonhealth.org. Mr. Scott St. George, Vice Pres. Opers. Troy Acute Care.

The Eddy Licensed Home, 433 River St., Troy, 12180. Tel: 518-274-6200; Fax: 518-274-2908. Email: mazzaccom@nehealth.com. Web: www.nehealth-.com. Michelle Mazzacco, Vice Pres. & Dir.

Family Life Information Center, 315 S. Manning Blvd., 12208. Tel: 518-525-1388; Fax: 518-525-1728. Web: www.sphcs.org. Margaret Murabito, Community Nurse Educator.

St. Peter's Addiction Recovery Center, 8 Mercycare Ln., Guilderland, 12084. Tel: 518-452-6700.

St. Peter's Hospital of the City of Albany, 315 S. Manning Blvd., 12208. Tel: 518-525-1550; 518-525-1388 (Education Sites for Natural Family Planning); Fax: 518-525-1520. Email: sboyle@sphcs.org. Web: www.sphcs.org. Mr. Steven P. Boyle, Pres. & CEO; Rev. John Tallman, Chap. Bed Capacity 442; Patients Assisted Annually 500,000.

AMSTERDAM. *St. Mary's Healthcare*, 427 Guy Park Ave., 12010. Tel: 518-842-1900; Fax: 518-842-0107. Web: smha.org. Mr. Victor Giulianelli, FACHE, Pres. & CEO. Sisters of St. Joseph of Carondelet 7; Sisters of the Resurrection 1; Bed Capacity 313; Patients Assisted Annually 360,048; Daughters of Charity 2.

The Auxiliary of St. Mary's Healthcare, 427 Guy Park Ave., 12010.

St. Mary's Healthcare Foundation, 427 Guy Park Ave., 12010.

RENSSELAER. *The Community Hospice*, 295 Valley View Blvd., 12144. Tel: 518-285-8150; Fax: 518-285-8151. Web: www.communityhospice.org. Ronald F. Watson, Pres. & CEO.

TROY. *Seton Health System, Inc.*, 1300 Massachusetts Ave., 12180. Tel: 518-268-5000; Fax: 518-268-5257. Email: info@setonhealth.org. Web: www.setonhealth.org. Mr. Scott St. George, Interim Pres. & CEO; Shafi Thomas, Dir. Spiritual Care; Sr. Clarisse Correia, Chm. Bd. of Directors.

Seton Health System, Inc. Daughters of Charity of St. Vincent de Paul. Sisters 8; Bed Capacity 196; Patients Assisted Annually 315,000.

Seton Health at Schuyler Ridge aka Leonard Nursing Home One Abele Dr., Clifton Park, 12065. Tel: 518-371-1400. Email: ssmith@setonhealth.org. Web: schuylerridge.org. Sandy Smith, Exec. Dir.

[I] SERVICES FOR ELDERLY

ALBANY. *St. Peter's Licensed Home Care Agency*, 159 Wolf Rd., 12205. Tel: 518-525-6099; Fax: 518-525-6002. Email: bsmith@stpetershealthcareservices.org. Sr. Jean McGinty, R.S.M.

GERMANTOWN. *The Carmelite System, Inc.*, 646 Woods Rd., 12526-5617. Tel: 518-537-7500; Fax: 518-537-7501. Email: xsusansan@carmelitesystem.org. Web: Carmelitesystem.org. Sr. M. Mark Louis Anne Randall, O.Carm., Chair.

[J] NURSING AND AGED HOMES

ALBANY. *McAuley Living Services*, 310 S. Manning Blvd., 12208. Tel: 518-437-8400; Fax: 518-437-8418. Email: mhulihan@stpetershealthcare.org. Sisters Amy Kennedy, Exec. Dir.; Stella Dillon, R.S.M., Diocesan Contact Person for Pastoral Care. Tel: 518-437-8400. Sisters of Mercy of the Americas - Northeast Community.

Teresian House (1974) 200 Washington Ave. Ext., 12203. Tel: 518-456-2000; Fax: 518-456-1142. Email: info@teresianhouse.com. Web: www.teresianhouse.com. Sisters Pauline Brecanier, O.Carm., Admin.; Joan Lewis, O.Carm., Coord. Pastoral Care; Rev. Jeffrey L'Arche, M.S., B.S., S.T.B., Chap. Carmelite Sisters for the Aged and Infirm.Roman Catholic Diocese of Albany., Corporate Title: Teresian House Nursing Home Co., Inc. Bed Capacity 300; Respite Beds 2.

Teresian House Foundation

Villa Mary Immaculate dba St. Peter's Nursing & Rehabilitation Center 301 Hackett Blvd., 12208. Tel: 518-525-7600; Fax: 518-525-7673. Email: gcooper@stpetershealthcare.org. Web: www.sphcs.org. Glen Cooper, Exec. Dir.

AMSTERDAM. *Mt. Loretto Nursing Home*, 302 Swart Hill Rd., 12010. Tel: 518-842-6790; Fax: 518-843-5993. Email: mtloretto@superior.net. Web: www.MountLoretto.com. Mr. Brian Chamberlin, Admin.; Sr. Joan Thomas, C.S.J., Dir. Pastoral Care. Health Care Facility, 24 Hour Skilled Nursing Care, Hospice, IV Therapy & Rehab.; Conducted by the Sisters of the Holy Family of Nazareth and the Sisters of the Resurrection. Capacity 180.

CASTLETON. *Resurrection Nursing Home* 12033. Tel: 518-732-7617; Fax: 518-732-4211. Email: rnh@resnursinghome.org. Web: www.resnursinghome.org. Conducted by the Sisters of the Holy Family of Nazareth and the Sisters of Resurrection., Nursing Home (Established 1962); Corporate Name: Resurrection Nursing Home, Inc. Bed Capacity 80.

CATSKILL. *St. Joseph's Villa Senior Living Services*, 38 Prospect Ave., 12414. Tel: 518-453-6650; Fax: 518-453-6650. *Pastoral Center, Diocese of Albany*, 40 N. Main Ave., 12203-1422.

CLIFTON PARK. *Seton Health at Schuyler Ridge aka Leonard Nursing Home* One Abele Dr., 12065. Tel: 518-371-1400; Fax: 518-371-1240. Email: ssmith@

setonhealth.org. Web: schuylerridge.org. Sandy Smith, Exec. Dir.

GERMANTOWN. *Avila Institute of Gerontology, Inc.*, 600 Woods Rd., 12526. Tel: 518-537-5000; Fax: 518-537-4725. Email: srpeter@avilainstitute.org. Web: www.avilainstitute.org. Sisters Michelle Anne Reho, O.Carm., Pres.; Peter Lillian, O.Carm., Dir. Carmelite Sisters for the Aged and Infirm., (Educational Institute)

GUILDERLAND. *Our Lady of Mercy Life Center*, 2 Mercycare Ln., 12084. Tel: 518-464-8100; Fax: 518-464-8111. Web: www.stpetershealthcare.org. Wesley I. Hale, Exec. Dir.

LATHAM. *Our Lady of Hope Residence, Little Sisters of the Poor*, 1 Jeanne Jugan Ln., 12110-3098. Tel: 518-785-4551; Fax: 518-213-4499. Email: lmmothersuperior@littlesistersofthepoor.org. Mary Bernard Nettle, Pres.; Rev. Firmin Finn, O.F.M.Conv. Nursing Facility 36; Apartments for the Elderly 48.

[K] APARTMENTS FOR ELDERLY

ALBANY. *Bishop Broderick Apartments Housing Development Fund Co., Inc. dba Bishop Broderick Apts.* 50 Prescott St., 12205. Tel: 518-869-7441; Fax: 518-869-0443. Email: bbacommunitymanager@yahoo.com. Web: www.depaulhousing.com. Pamela Rost, Community Mgr. Affordable housing for seniors and people with physical disabilities.

C.S.C. Housing Development Fund Co., Inc. dba Sanderson Court Senior Apts. 6 Carondelet Dr., Watervliet, 12189. Tel: 518-782-1123; Fax: 518-782-1125. Email: scfm6@yahoo.com. Web: www.depaulhousing.com. Caitlin Beck, Community Mgr. Affordable housing for seniors.

Cusack Community Service Corporation, 40 N. Main Ave., 12203. Tel: 518-459-0183; Fax: 518-459-0202. Email: Deborah.DammOBrien@rcda.org.

DePaul Housing Management Corp., 41 N. Main Ave., 12203. Tel: 518-459-0183; Fax: 518-459-0202. Email: diocesan.housing@rcda.org. Web: www.depaulhousing.com. Deborah Damm O'Brien, Exec. Dir.; Jill McLellan Phelps, Dir. Affordable Housing Admin.; Rhonda Finehout, Dir. Housing Mgmt. Managing diocesan sponsored housing for persons who are elderly or mobility impaired.

Teresian House Housing Corporation dba Avila Retirement Community 100 White Pine Dr., 12203. Tel: 518-452-4250; Fax: 518-452-4251. Email: cpolacko@avilaretirement.com. Web: www.avilaretirement.com. Christy Polacko Durant, Dir. Senior Retirement Community. Apartments and cottages.

St. Vincent Apartments Housing Development Fund Co., Inc. dba St. Vincent's Apts. 475 Yates St., 12208. Tel: 518-482-8915; Fax: 518-489-1220. Email: mrmsva@nycap.rr.com. Web: www.depaulhousing.com. Lorraine Caroccia, Community Mgr. Affordable housing for seniors and people with physical disabilities. Total Apartments 59.

CLIFTON PARK. *Halfmoon Housing Development Fund Co., Inc. dba Bishop Hubbard Senior Apartments* 54 Katherine Dr., 12065. Tel: 518-383-2705; Fax: 518-383-6350. Email: lrosamino5@yahoo.com. Web: www.depaulhousing.com. Affordable housing for seniors and people with physical disabilities. Total Apartments 49.

DELHI. *Delhi Housing Development Fund Co., Inc. I and II dba Delhi Senior Community* 7 Main St., 13753. Tel: 607-746-8142; Fax: 607-746-6546. Email: dsc7@delhitel.net. Web: www.depaulhousing.com. Rick Ackerly, Community Mgr. Total Apartments 45.

LATHAM. *LSOP Housing, Inc.*, 2 Jeanne Jugan Ln., 12110. Tel: 518-785-4551; Fax: 518-213-4499. Email: lmmothersuperior@littlesistersofthepoor.org. Mary Bernard Nettle, Pres.

NORTH GREENBUSH. *S.J. Housing Development Fund Company, Inc. dba St. Jude's Apartments* 50 Dana Ave., Wynantskill, 12198. Tel: 518-283-5690; Fax: 518-283-5893. Email: bwsjabmsa@yahoo.com. Web: www.depaulhousing.com. Barbara Weatherwax, Community Mgr. Affordable housing for seniors and people with physical disabilities. Apartments 49.

RENSSELAER. *East Greenbush Housing Development Fund Co., Inc. dba Branson Manor Senior Apartments* 3 Grandview Dr., 12144. Tel: 518-283-8280; Fax: 518-283-8292. Email: bwsjabmsa@yahoo.com. Web: www.depaulhousing.com. Barbara Weatherwax, Community Mgr. Affordable housing for seniors and people with physical disabilities. Total Apartments 49.

Franciscan Heights Community Service Corp. dba Franciscan Heights Senior Community 1 St. Anthony Ln., 12144. Tel: 518-432-3555; Fax: 518-432-3553. Web: www.depaulhousing.com. Cheryl Walton, Community Mgr. Apartments and Cottages 85.

ROTTERDAM. *Rotterdam Housing Development Fund Co., Inc. dba Father Leo O'Brien Senior Community* 3151 Marra Ln., Schenectady, 12303. Tel: 518-357-4424; Fax: 518-357-9377. Email: flobtlc@nycap.rr.com. Web: www.depaulhousing.com. Karen Sorensen, Community Mgr. Affordable housing for seniors. Total Apartments 49.

SCHENECTADY. *LCS Housing Development Fund Company, Inc. dba The Lawrence Commons* 2660 Albany St., 12304. Tel: 518-393-2412; Fax: 518-346-2686. Email: flobtlc@nycap.rr.com. Web: www.depaulhousing.com. Karen Sorensen, Community Mgr. Affordable housing for people with physical disabilities. Apartments 12.

SLINGERLANDS. *Marie-Rose Manor HDFCI dba Marie Rose Manor* 100 Marquis Dr., 12159. Tel: 518-459-0204; Fax: 518-459-0527. Email: mrmsva@nycap.rr.com. Web: www.depaulhousing.com. Lorraine Caroccia, Community Mgr. Affordable housing for seniors. Total Apartments 49.

WATERVLIET. *Delatour Housing Development Fund Company, Inc. dba Carondelet Commons Senior Apartments* 2 Carondelet Dr., 12189. Tel: 518-783-0444; Fax: 518-783-0456. Email: cccahousing@yahoo.com. Web: www.depaulhousing.com. Brenda Rosekrans, Community Mgr. Affordable housing for seniors and people with physical disabilities. Total Apartments 49.

Fontbonne Manor Housing Development Fund Company, Inc. dba Fontbonne Manor Senior Apts. 10 Carondelet Dr., 12189. Tel: 518-782-2780; Fax: 518-782-2778. Email: scfm6@yahoo.com. Web: www.depaulhousing.com. Caitlin Beck, Community Mgr. Affordable housing for seniors. Total Apartments 49.

Italian-American Housing Development Fund Co., Inc. dba Cabrini Acers Senior Apts. 4 Carondelet Dr., 12189. Tel: 518-785-0050; Fax: 518-785-0110. Email: cccahousing@yahoo.com. Web: www.depaulhousing.com. Brenda Rosekrans, Community Mgr. Affordable housing for seniors and people with physical disabilities. Total Apartments 49.

[L] MONASTERIES AND RESIDENCES OF PRIESTS AND BROTHERS

ALBANY. *Vincentian Fathers Residence*, 96 Menands Rd., 12204-1499. Tel: 518-462-1881. Email: revlasma@yahoo.com. Rev. Lawrence F. Asma, C.M. Priests 1.

LAKE GEORGE. *St. Mary of the Lake*, P.O. Box 31, 12845. Tel: 518-668-5594. c/o 40 N. Main Ave., 12203. Rev. Ken McGuire, C.S.P., Dir. Summer retreat of the Paulist Fathers.

RENSSELAER. *Franciscan Mission House*, 517 Washington Ave., 12144. Tel: 518-465-0062; Fax: 518-472-1013. Web: www.thefma.org. Rev. Antone Kandrac, O.F.M.Conv.; Bro. Leo Merriman, O.F.M.Conv. Promotion Center for Order's Missions.

Provincialate, Immaculate Conception Friary - Order of Friars Minor Conventual (1872) (Immaculate Conception Province), 77 St. Francis Pl., P.O. Box 629, 12144. Tel: 518-472-1000; Fax: 518-472-1013. Email: Biasej@aol.com. Web: www.franciscanseast.org. Very Rev. Justin Biase, O.F.M.Conv., Min. Prov.; Bro. Raymond Sobocinski, O.F.M.Conv., Province Treas. & Guardian; Revs. Henry Madigan, O.F.M.Conv.; Rufino Maloney, O.F.M.Conv.; Firmin Finn, O.F.M.Conv., Chap.; Antone Kandrac, O.F.M.Conv.; Giles Van Wormer, O.F.M.Conv.; Bro. Andre Picotte, O.F.M.Conv. (Corporate Name: Order Minor Conventuals, Inc.)

SARATOGA SPRINGS. *St. John Neumann Residence*, 233 Lake Ave., 12866-2729. Tel: 518-584-7500; Fax: 518-581-8421. Redemptorist Priests and Brothers of the Baltimore Province.

VALATIE. *St. Joseph Center* Residence for retired Holy Cross Brothers and Priests., 495 Maple Ln., 12184. Tel: 518-784-9481; Fax: 518-784-9494. Email: BEBCSC@hotmail.com. Rev. Robert E. DeLeon, C.S.C., Pastoral Care Albany Medical Center & Chap., St. Joseph Center In Res. Rev. James P. Madden, C.S.C.; Bro. Edward Boyer, C.S.C., B.A., M.M.Ed., Dir.

[M] CONVENTS AND RESIDENCES FOR SISTERS

ALBANY. *Daughters of Charity of St. Vincent de Paul - St. Louise House* Home for the Senior Sisters of the Daughters of Charity of St. Vincent de Paul, 96 Menand Rd., 12204-1499. Tel: 518-462-5593; Fax: 518-462-5025.

Daughters of Charity of St. Vincent de Paul House, 96 Menand Rd., 12204-1499. Tel: 518-462-5593; Fax: 518-462-5025. Web: www.daughtersofcharity.org.

Religious of the Sacred Heart, 128 W. Lawrence St., 12203. Tel: 518-489-8280; Fax: 518-489-8280. Sr. Marie Buonato, R.S.C.J., Area Dir.

Sisters of Mercy of the Americas - Northeast Community, 310 S. Manning Blvd., 12208. Tel: 518-437-3000; Fax: 518-437-3030. Sr. Jane Somerville, R.S.M., Life & Ministry Admin. Sisters 110.

Sisters of the Holy Names of Jesus and Mary, U.S. - Ontario Province, Regional Center, 258 Partridge St., 12208. Tel: 503-675-7125; Fax: 503-675-7138. Email: meholohan@snjmuson.org. Web: www.snjmusontario.org. (Corporate Name: Sisters of the Holy Names of Jesus and Mary of the New York Province, Inc.)

CASTLETON ON HUDSON. *Provincial House, The Congregation of the Sisters of the Resurrection of Our Lord* Jesus Christ, Juniorate and Novitiate of the Sisters of the Resurrection Province of St. Joseph Senior Religious Trust, 35 Boltwood Ave., 12033-1097. Tel: 518-732-2226; Fax: 518-732-2898. Email: crsister@resurrectionsisters.org. Web: www.resurrectionsisters.org. Sisters Dolores Stepien, C.R., Prov. Supr.; Christine Bykowski, C.R., Local Supr.; Dolores Palermo, C.R., Dir. Novices.

Jesus Christ, Province of St. Joseph Senior Religious Trust, Juniorate and Novitiate of the Sisters of the Resurrection. Sisters 24. *Chaplain's Residence*, 34 Boltwood Ave., 12033.

Retreat and Vacation Home, 325 Madonna Lake Rd., Cropseyville, 12052-1819. Tel: 518-279-1673.

DELMAR. *Franciscan House, Mill Hill Sisters* Regional House, 703 Derzee Ct., 12054. Tel: 518-512-4362; Fax: 518-512-4362. Sr. Judith Dever, F.M.S.J., Admin. Sisters 2.

GERMANTOWN. *St. Teresa's Motherhouse*, Avila on the Hudson, 600 Woods Rd., 12526-5639. Tel: 518-537-5000; Fax: 518-537-5226. Email: smrc@stmhcs.org. Web: www.carmelitesisters.com. Sr. M. Mark Louis Anne Randall, O.Carm., Supr. Gen.; Rev. Joseph E. Finch, Chap. Carmelite Sisters for the Aged and Infirm., Motherhouse and Novitiate. Sisters 31.

Postulation Office Tel: 518-537-5000; Fax: 518-537-5226. Sr. M. Angeline Teresa, O.Carm., Servant of God; Rev. Mario Esposito, O.Carm., Vice Postulator; Andrea Ambrosi, Postulator.

LATHAM. *Provincial House of the Sisters of St. Joseph of Carondelet (Albany Province)* 12110-4799. Tel: 518-783-3500; Fax: 518-783-3672. Email: sszczerbacki@csjalbany.org. Web: www.csjalbany.org. Rev. Geoffrey D. Burke, Chap.; Sisters Mary Anne Rodgers, C.S.J., Province Leadership Team; Nancy Gregg, C.S.J., Province Leadership Team; Ann Christi Brink, C.S.J., Province Leadership Team; Charla Commins, C.S.J., Province Leadership Team; Mary Jo Tallman, C.S.J., Province Leadership Team; Eileen McCann, C.S.J., Province Leadership Team. Sisters 387.

WATERVLIET. *St. Colman's Convent* 12189. Tel: 518-273-4911; Fax: 518-273-3312. Sr. M. Carmel, P.B.V.M., Supr. Motherhouse and Novitiate of Sisters of the Presentation of the B.V.M.

[N] HOUSES OF PRAYER AND RETREAT HOUSES

AURIESVILLE. *Jesuit Retreat House (Auriesville) - Inactive, Shrine of Our Lady of Martyrs*, 136 Shrine Rd., Fultonville, 12072. Tel: 518-853-3033; Fax: 518-853-3051. Web: www.martyrshrine.org.

Shrine of Our Lady of Martyrs, Fultonville, 12072. Tel: 518-853-3033; Fax: 518-853-3051. Email: office@martyrshrine.org. Web: www.martyrshrine.org. Revs. Peter J. Murray, S.J., Supr. & Dir.; Robert McGuire, S.J., Vice Postulator Cause of Kateri Tekakwitha; Bro. Ted Bender, S.J. National Shrine of the Jesuit Martyrs of North America. Priests 2; Brothers 1.

CHESTERTOWN. *The Priory of St. Benedict, Inc.*, 135 Priory Rd., P.O. Box 336, 12817-0336. Tel: 518-494-3733; Fax: 518-494-3733. Email: prioryretreat@yahoo.com. Web: www.prioryretreathouse.org. Sr. Constance M. Messitt, C.S.J., Dir.

MIDDLEBURGH. *Bethany Ministries*, 176 Mill Ln., P.O. Box 432, 12212. Tel: 518-827-4699. Email: bethmin@midtel.net. Web: www.midtel.net/~bethmin. Rev. Peter Chepaitis, O.F.M., Dir.

PARADOX. *Pyramid Life Center* Corporation Name: Albany Catholic Youth Association, Inc., 12858. Tel: 518-585-7545; Fax: 518-585-7545. Email: monicaplc@aol.com. Web: www.pyramidlife.org. Sr. Monica Murphy, C.S.J., Dir. Summer, fall and winter retreat house, located at Pyramid Lake.

QUEENSBURY. *Wellsprings Outreach*, 230 Robert Gardens N., #5, 12804. Tel: 518-745-1617. Email: info@wsprings.org. Web: www.wsprings.org. Bro. Michael Laratonda, F.M.S., Dir. Programs in

Spirituality (Holistic Retreats & Workshops Chapter Facilitation for Religious Congregations, Spiritual Direction)

SCHENECTADY. *Dominican Retreat and Conference Center*, 1945 Union St., 12309. Tel: 518-393-4169; Fax: 518-393-4525. Email: dslcny@nycap.rr.com. Web: www.dslcny.org. Sr. Susan M. Zemgulis, O.P., Admin. Residence Facilities for 50; Non-resident Facilities for 90 to 100.

STILLWATER. *Still Point Interfaith Retreat House*, 20 Still Point Rd., Mechanicville, 12118. Tel: 518-587-4967; Fax: 518-587-4967. Email: stillpt423@aol.com. Web: www.stillpointretreatcenter.com. Sisters Rowena Fay, Dir.; Anne Leger, Dir.; Nicole St. John, Dir.

UNADILLA. *Gilead, Inc.*, 1011 State Hwy. 7, 13849. Tel: 607-369-2845. Email: tngilead@aol.com. Eucharistic Community

VALATIE. *St. Joseph Center*, 495 Maple Ln., 12184. Tel: 518-784-9481; Fax: 518-784-9494. Email: bebcsc@hotmail.com. Bro. Edward Boyer, C.S.C., B.A., M.M.Ed., Dir.

[O] YOUTH TREATMENT FACILITIES

ALBANY. *Hospitality House Therapeutic Community Inc.*, 271 Central Ave., 12206. Tel: 518-434-6468; Fax: 518-434-6302. Email: lbecker@hospitalityhouse.info. A private, not-for-profit, intensive residential treatment program for males, 18 years or older, with a history of drug and/or substance abuse.

ALTAMONT. *Bernard and Caroline Cobb Memorial School*, 100-300 Mt. Presentation Way, P.O. Box 503, 12009. Tel: 518-861-6446; Fax: 518-861-5228. Email: cobbmemorialschool@verizon.net. Web: www.cobbmemorialschool.org. Sr. Mary Thomas, P.B.V.M., Prin. 12-month special education program for students 5-21 years. Lay Teachers 7.

[P] SHRINES

ALTAMONT. *La Salette Shrine* 1109 Berne-Altamont Rd., 12009-3440. Tel: 518-861-8159; Fax: 518-861-7052. Email: fr.jeff@verizon.net. Rev. Jeffrey L'Arche, M.S., B.S., S.T.B., Dir.; Bros. Anthony Casso, M.S., B.A., Assoc.; Donald Wininski, M.S., B.A., Assoc. Corporate Titles: Missionaries of Our Lady of La Salette Inc., Altamont, NY; La Salette Seminary, Altamont, NY.

FONDA. *The National Shrine of Blessed Kateri Tekakwitha and Friary* P.O. Box 627, 12068. Tel: 518-853-3646. Email: office@katerishrine.com. Web: www.katerishrine.com. Friar Mark Steed, O.F.M.Conv., Shrine Dir. & Guardian; Bro. James Amrhein, O.F.M.Conv., Assoc. Dir.; Friar Patrick Gallagher, O.F.M.Conv., Local Pastor.

[Q] CAMPUS MINISTRY

ALBANY. *New York State University at Albany* , (Albany Collegiate Interfaith Center, Inc.) with offices at Albany-Chapel House., 1400 Washington Ave., 12222. Tel: 518-489-8573; Fax: 518-489-8573. Email: pbutler@uamail.albany.edu. Catherine Reid, Campus Min.

COBLESKILL. *State University of New York College of Agricultural & Technology at Cobleskill* Main St., P.O. Box 124, 12175. Tel: 518-234-2892. Rev. Thomas Berardi.

DELHI. *State University of New York College of Agricultural & Technology at Delhi* St. Peter Rectory, 8 Franklin St., 13753. Tel: 607-746-2503.

GLENS FALLS. *Adirondack Community College* c/o 40 N. Main Ave., 12203. Tel: 518-793-9677.

HUDSON. *Columbia-Greene Community College* P.O. Box 1000, 12534. Tel: 518-828-4181.

LOUDONVILLE. *Siena College* 12211. Tel: 518-783-2332; Fax: 518-783-2549. Email: chaplainsoffice@siena.edu. Web: www.siena.edu. Kate Kaufman-Burns, Dir. of Liturgical Arts; Rev. Greg Jakubowicz, O.F.M., Chap.; Colleen Sheedy, Asst. College Chap.; Michele Stefanik, Assoc. Campus Min.

ONEONTA. *Newman Clubs - SUNY Oneonta and Hartwick College* Newman House, 77 Spruce St., 13820. Tel: 607-432-4400. Email: newmanhouse@stny.rr.com. Carol A. Blazina, Pres. of Foundation & Bd. of Dir. Corporate Title: Oneonta Newman Foundation.

SARATOGA. *Skidmore College* 815 N. Broadway, 12866. Tel: 518-580-5682; Fax: 518-580-5555. Email: cminnery@skidmore.edu. Catherine W. Minnery, Coord. Catholic Student Life.

SCHENECTADY. *Catholic Chaplain, Union College Reamer Hall*, 807 Union St., 12308-3152. Tel: 518-388-6087. Email: bolandt@union.edu. Web: www.union.edu/studentlife/religious_programs/catholic. Deacon Frank Thomas, M.D., Chap.

TROY. *Hudson Valley Community College* 80 Vandenburgh Ave., 12180. Tel: 518-629-7168. Email: langhnan@hvcc.edu. Web: www.hvcc.edu. Sr. Nancy Langhart, O.S.F., Campus Min.

The Rensselaer Newman Foundation RPI Chaplains Office-RU # 3514, 110 Eighth St., 12180. Tel: 518-276-6518; Fax: 518-274-5945. Email: fred@rpi.edu. Web: www.christsunofjustice.org. Richard M. Hartt, Pres.; Rev. Edward Kacerguis, Chap.

University Parish of Christ Sun of Justice 12180. Tel: 518-274-7793; Fax: 518-274-5945. Rev. Edward Kacerguis.

Chapel + Cultural Center 10 Tom Phelan Pl., 12180. Tel: 518-274-7793; Fax: 518-274-5945. 10 Phelan Pl., 12180.

Russell Sage College Campus Ministry Office, Rm. #304 Student Center, 12180. Tel: 518-244-4507. Email: cuneor@sage.edu. Sr. Rosemary Ann Cuneo, C.R.

[R] MISCELLANEOUS LISTINGS

ALBANY. *Birthright of Albany*, 586 Central Ave., 12206. Tel: 518-438-2978; Fax: 518-438-2978.

Broderick Community Service Organization, 40 N. Main Ave., 12203-1422. Mr Richard Farrell, Contact Person.

Burke Community Service Corp., Inc., 40 N. Main Ave., 12203. Tel: 518-453-6623; Fax: 518-453-6792. Email: noel.olsen@rcda.org.

Care for Life Foundation, 40 N. Main Ave., 12203-1422. Tel: 518-453-6650. Email: joseph.profit@rcda.org. Joseph Profit, Contact Person.

The Cathedral Restoration Corp., 40 N. Main Ave., 12203. Tel: 518-463-4447; Fax: 518-436-5177. Email: ecathedra@nycap.rr.com. Rev. William H. Pape, Sec. & Treas.

Diocesan AIDS Services, 100 Slingerlands St., 12202. Tel: 518-449-3581; Fax: 518-426-3662.

Diocesan Investment and Loan Trust, 40 N. Main Ave., 12203-1422. Tel: 518-641-6948.

Emmaus House, 45 Trinity Pl., 12202. Tel: 518-482-4966. Fred Boehrer, Co-Dir.; Diana Conroy, Co-Dir. Albany Catholic Worker Community. Bed Capacity 8; Total Assisted Annually 200; Total Staff 12.

Family Rosary Albany Office, 16 Cornell Ave., 12203. Tel: 518-452-3082; Fax: 518-452-3956. Email: lrhatigan@hcfm.org. Web: www.hcfm.org. Laetitia Rhatigan, Albany Mission Dir. Sponsored by Congregation of Holy Cross (Eastern Prov.)

Crusade for Family Prayer, Inc., North Easton, MA. Tel: 508-238-4095; Fax: 508-238-3953. Rev. John P. Phalen, C.S.C., Pres. Sponsored by Congregation of Holy Cross (Eastern Prov.)

Family Theater Ministries, 16 Cornel Ave., 12207. Tel: 518-452-3082.

The Foundation of the Roman Catholic Diocese of Albany, New York, Inc., 40 N. Main Ave., 12203. Tel: 518-453-6680; Fax: 518-453-8440.

St. Francis Chapel Wolf Road Shoppers Park, 145A Wolf Rd., 12205. Tel: 518-459-2854; Fax: 518-783-4195. Web: www.TimesUnion/communities/StFrancischapel. Revs. Gerard Lee, O.F.M., Dir. Email: catglee@aol.com; Richard Biasiotto, O.F.M.; Ambrose Donehue, O.F.M.; Reginald J. Reddy, O.F.M.; Gerald R. Mudd, O.F.M. Order of Friars Minor Province of the Most Holy Name of Jesus.

Kenwood Braille Association, Inc., Kenwood Convent of the Sacred Heart, 799 S. Pearl St., 12202. Tel: 518-465-3341; Fax: 518-465-3663. Sr. Priscilla Meier, R.S.C.J., Dir.

Korean Apostolate of the Roman Catholic Diocese of Albany, 17 Exchange St., 12202. Tel: 518-429-5566.

LaSalle Albany, Inc., Christian Brothers Academy, 12 Airline Rd., 12205. Tel: 518-452-9809; Fax: 518-452-9804. Email: schlegel@cbaalbany.org. Web: www.cbaalbany.org. Mr. James Schlegel, Prin.

McCloskey Community Service Corporation, 41 N. Main Ave., 12203. Tel: 518-459-0183; Fax: 518-459-0202. Email: Diocesan.Housing@rcda.org. Deborah Damm O'Brien, Exec. Dir.

Mercy Cares for Kids, 310 S. Manning Blvd., 12208. Tel: 518-525-5437; Fax: 518-525-6514. Web: www.stpetershealthcare.org. Mr. Steven P. Boyle, Pres. & CEO.

Mill Hill Sisters Charitable Trust, 703 Derzee Ct., Delmar, 12054. Tel: 518-512-4362. Email: jdever001@nycap.rr.com.

New York State Catholic Conference, 465 State St., 12203. Tel: 518-434-6195; Fax: 518-434-9796. Email: info@nyscatholic.org. Web: www.nyscatholic.org. Richard E. Barnes, Exec. Dir.

Noonan Community Service Corporation, 40 N. Main Ave., 12203-1422. Tel: 518-453-6641; Fax: 518-453-8454. Rev. Joseph Benintende, Contact Person.

St. Peter's Auxiliary, 315 S. Manning Blvd., 12208. Tel: 518-525-1550; Fax: 518-525-1003. Mr. Steven P. Boyle, Pres. & CEO.

St. Peter's Licensed Home Care Agency, 159 Wolf Rd., 12205. Tel: 518-525-6000; Fax: 518-525-6002. Web: www.stpetershealthcare.org. Mr. Steven P. Boyle, Pres. & CEO.

Sisters of the Holy Names of Jesus & Mary of the New York Province, Inc., 1061 New Scotland Ave., 12208-1198. Tel: 503-675-7125; Fax: 503-675-7138. Email: meholohan@snjmuson.org. Continuing Support Charitable Trust to provide for the needs of the Tutwiler Clinic, Tutwiler, Mississippi.

St. Peter's Hospital Foundation, Inc., 319 S. Manning Blvd., Ste. 114, 12208. Tel: 518-482-4433; Fax: 518-482-4593. Web: www.stpetershealthcare.org. Peter D. Semenza, Exec. Dir.

Support Fund Trust of the Province of St. Thomas of Villanova, c/o 40 N. Main Ave., 12203.

Warde Services Corporation, Inc., 159 Wolf Rd., 12205. Tel: 518-525-1550; Fax: 518-525-1520. Mr. Steven P. Boyle, Pres. & CEO.

CASTLETON ON HUDSON. *Cooperative Christian Ministries of Schodack, Inc. aka CCMS The Anchor* 92 S. Main St., 12033-0092. Tel: 518-732-4120. Formal Name: C.C.M. of Schodack

GERMANTOWN. *Oneness in Peace Center, Inc.*, 49 Main St., 12526. Tel: 518-537-5678. Email: information@onenessinpeace.org. Web: www.onenessinpeace.org. Sr. Vergilia Jim, O.S.F., Co-Dir, Prog. Presenter & Peace Educator; Claire Langie, Co-Dir, Prog. Presenter & Peace Educator.

GUILDERLAND CENTER. *Christ Child Society of Albany*, P.O. Box 423, 12085. Tel: 518-355-0739. Annette Guido, Pres.

LATHAM. *The Sister M. Athanasia Gurry Trust Fund of the Sisters of St. Joseph*, 385 Watervliet-Shaker Rd., 12110-4799. Tel: 518-783-3538; Fax: 518-783-1123.

MECHANICVILLE. *Albany, New York Chapter of Magnificat, Inc.*, 178 George Thompson Rd., 12118. Tel: 518-664-4374. Email: albanymagnificat@gmail.com. Web: www.albanymagnificat.com.

MENANDS. *Catholic Cemeteries of the Roman Catholic Diocese of Albany, New York*, 48 Cemetery Ave., 12204. Tel: 518-432-4953; Fax: 518-427-8035. Richard Touchette, Contact Person.

Medicus Christi, LTD, 16 MacAffer Dr., 12204-1208. Tel: 518-852-0130. Joseph Marotta, M.D., Contact Person.

NISKAYUNA. *Villa Fusco Child Day Care (Pre-K)*, 955 Balltown Rd., 12309. Tel: 518-377-1613; Fax: 518-377-1613. Email: fcppschaloux@yahoo.com; ebere66@yahoo.com. Sr. Caroline Anochirim, Supr. Daughters of Charity of the Most Precious Blood. Capacity 14.

NORTH CREEK. *North Country Ministry, Inc., Leaven House*, 32 Circle Ave., P.O. Box 111, 12853. Tel: 518-251-4460; Fax: 518-251-5483. Email: ncm32@frontiernet.net. Bro. James Posluszny, C.S.C., Dir.

RENSSELAER. *Assisi in Albany, Inc.*, 77 St. Francis Pl., 12144. Tel: 518-265-0747; Fax: 518-472-1013. Rev. Anthony Kall, O.F.M.Conv.

Circles of Mercy, Inc., 11 Washington St., Ste. A, 12144. Tel: 518-462-0899; Fax: 518-462-2892. Email: circlesofmercy@nycap.rr.com. Web: www.circlesofmercy.org. Richard S. Zazycki, Exec. Dir.

Franciscans in Collaborative Ministry, Inc., 77 St. Francis Pl., 12144. Tel: 518-472-1000; Fax: 518-472-1013. Very Rev. Justin Biase, O.F.M.Conv., Minister Prov.

Franciscorps, Inc., 77 St. Francis Pl., 12144. Tel: 518-472-1000; Fax: 518-472-1013. Email: francorps@gmail.com. Web: www.Franciscanseast.org.

Order of Friars Minor Conventual Immaculate Conception Province Charitable Trust (Established 1990), P.O. Box 629, 12144. Tel: 518-472-1000; Fax: 518-472-1013. Email: brorayl@juno.com. Web: www.Franciscanseast.org. Bro. Raymond Sobosinski, Trustee & Treas.

The Community Hospice Foundation, Inc., 295 Valley View Blvd., 12144. Tel: 518-285-8150; Fax: 518-285-8192. Web: www.communityhospice.org. Stephen J. Manny, Dir. Devel.

SCHENECTADY. *Secular Order of Discalced Carmelites*, P.O. Box 408, 12301. Tel: 518-393-5027. Email: carmel1352@localnet.com. Pamela Taranto, Pres.

TROY. *Catholic School Administrators' Association of New York State*, 525 Fourth Ave., 12182. Tel: 518-273-1205; Fax: 518-273-1206. Email: nysadm@nycap.rr.com; csaanys@nycap.rr.com. Web: www.csaanys.org. Carol Geddis, Exec. Dir.

Seton Auxiliary, Inc., 1300 Massachusetts Ave., 12180. Tel: 518-268-5505. Email: eproche@setonhealth.org. Web: setonhealth.org. Colleen P. Roche, Community Educ. & Volunteers.

Seton Health Foundation, Inc., 1300 Massachusetts Ave., P.O. Box 985, 12180. Tel: 518-268-5503; Fax: 518-268-5799. Email: msteiner@setonhealth.org.

Web: setonhealth.org. Marica M. Steiner, Exec. Dir.

VALATIE. *Holy Cross International, Inc., St. Joseph Spiritual Life Center*, 495 Maple Ln., 12184. Tel: 518-784-9481. Email: sjcval@berk.com.

[S] SUMMER CAMPS

ALBANY. *Camp Scully*, 40 N. Main Ave., 12203. Tel: 518-453-6613; 518-283-1617 (Synders Lake); Fax: 518-453-6792. Web: campscully.squarespace.com. *Summer Address*, 24 Camp Scully Way, Wynantskill, 12198. Tel: 518-283-1617. A program of Catholic Charities of the Diocese of Albany; Day & resident camp for children 5-17. Under direction of Catholic Charities of the Diocese of Albany. Financed by local Youth Bureaus, the Albany Catholic Diocese, USDA Summer Program and by contributions. Capacity 80.

TROY. *Troy CYO Day Camp*, 237 Fourth St., Box 867, 12180. Tel: 518-274-2630; Fax: 518-274-2734. Raymond R. Piscitelli, Exec. Dir. Sponsored by Troy Youth Organization, Inc. for Boys and Girls, ages 5-12 yrs.

RELIGIOUS INSTITUTES OF MEN REPRESENTED IN THE DIOCESE

For further details refer to the corresponding bracketed number in the Religious Institutes of Men or Women section.

[0140]—*The Augustinians*—O.S.A.

[0330]—*Brothers of the Christian Schools* (New York Prov.)—F.S.C.

[0600]—*Brothers of the Congregation of Holy Cross* (Eastern Prov.)—C.S.C.

[]—*Carmelite Fathers*—O.Carm.

[0310]—*Congregation of Christian Brothers* (Eastern US)—C.F.C.

[1330]—*Congregation of the Mission* (Eastern Prov.)—C.M.

[]—*Franciscan Friars* (Immaculate Conception Prov.)—O.F.M.

[0480]—*Friars Minor Conventual* (Prov. of Immaculate Conception)—O.F.M.Conv.

[0690]—*Jesuit Fathers and Brothers* (New York Prov.)—S.J.

[]—*Marist Brothers*—F.M.S.

[0720]—*The Missionaries of Our Lady of La Salette* (Prov. of Our Lady of Seven Dolors)—M.S.

[0520]—*Order of Friars Minor* (Most Holy Name Prov.)—O.F.M.

[1070]—*Redemptorist Fathers* (Baltimore Prov.)—C.Ss.R.

RELIGIOUS INSTITUTES OF WOMEN REPRESENTED IN THE DIOCESE

[0330]—*Carmelite Sisters for the Aged and Infirm*—O.Carm.

[2980]—*Congregation of Notre Dame*—C.N.D.

[0760]—*Daughters of Charity of St. Vincent de Paul*—D.C.

[0740]—*Daughters of Charity of the Most Precious Blood*—D.C.P.B.

[1070-17]—*Dominican Sisters - Congregation of St. Catherine de Ricci*—O.P.

[]—*Dominican Sisters of Amityville*—O.P.

[1170]—*Felician Sisters*—C.S.S.F.

[1190]—*Franciscan Sisters of the Atonement*—S.A.

[2340]—*Little Sisters of the Poor*—L.S.P.

[2070]—*Religious of the Holy Union of the Sacred Hearts*—S.U.S.C.

[4180]—*Religious Venerini Sisters*—M.P.V.

[2970]—*School Sisters of Notre Dame*—S.S.N.D.

[2150]—*Sister Servants of the Immaculate Heart of Mary* (Michigan)—I.H.M.

[2160]—*Sister Servants of the Immaculate Heart of Mary* (Pennsylvania)—I.H.M.

[2575]—*Sisters of Mercy of the Americas* (Albany)—R.S.M.

[2990]—*Sisters of Notre Dame de Namur*—S.N.D.deN.

[]—*Sisters of St. Francis of the Neumann Communities*—O.S.F.

[1660]—*Sisters of St. Francis of the Providence of God*—O.S.F.

[3840]—*Sisters of St. Joseph of Carondelet*—C.S.J.

[1830]—*Sisters of the Good Shepherd of Mary*—R.G.S.

[1990]—*Sisters of the Holy Names of Jesus and Mary*—S.N.J.M.

[3320]—*Sisters of the Presentation of the B.V.M.*—P.B.V.M.

[3480]—*Sisters of the Resurrection*—C.R.

[4070]—*Society of the Sacred Heart*—R.S.C.J.

DIOCESAN CEMETERIES

ALBANY. *Our Lady of Angels Cemetery*, 1389 Central Ave., 12205. Tel: 518-463-0134; Fax: 518-427-8035. Email: info@rcdacemeteries.org. Web: www.rcdacemeteries.org. Mailing Address: 48 Cemetery Ave., Menands, 12204.

COHOES. *St. Agnes Cemetery*, 79 St. Agnes Hwy., 12047. Tel: 518-463-0134; Fax: 518-427-8035. Email: info@rcdacemeteries.org. Web: www.rcdacemeteries.org. Mailing Address: 48 Cemetery Ave., Menands, 12204.

COLONIE. *St. Patrick Cemetery*, 150 Troy Rd., Watervliet, 12189. Tel: 518-463-0134; Fax: 518-427-8035. Email: info@rcdacemeteries.org. Web: www.rcdacemeteries.org. Mailing Address: 48 Cemetery Ave., Menands, 12204.

GLENMONT. *Our Lady Help of Christians Cemetery*, Mailing Address: 48 Cemetery Ave., Menands, 12204. 41 Jolley Rd., 12077. Tel: 518-463-0134; Fax: 518-427-8035. Email: info@rcdacemeteries.org. Web: www.rcdacemeteries.org.

GLENVILLE. *St. Anthony Cemetery*, 27 Glenridge Rd., 12302. Tel: 518-463-0134; Fax: 518-427-8035. Email: info@rcdacemeteries.org. Web: www.rcdacemeteries.org. Mailing Address: 48 Cemetery Ave., Menands, 12204.

MENANDS. *St. Agnes Cemetery*, 48 Cemetery Ave., 12204. Tel: 518-463-0134; Fax: 518-427-8035. Email: info@rcdacemeteries.org. Web: www.rcdacemeteries.org.

Calvary Cemetery, Mailing Address: 48 Cemetery Ave., 12204. 481 Rte. 9 W., Glenmont, 12077. Tel: 518-463-0134. Email: info@rcdacemeteries.org.

ROTTERDAM. *Holy Cross Cemetery*, Mailing Address: 48 Cemetery Ave., Menands, 12204. 1456 Dunnsville Rd., 12306. Tel: 518-463-0134. Email: info@rcdacemeteries.org. Web: www.rcdacemeteries.org.

SCHENECTADY. *St. Cyril & St. Method Cemetery*, Mailing Address: 48 Cemetery Ave., Menands, 12204. 611 Duanesburg Rd., Rotterdam, 12306. Tel: 518-463-0134; Fax: 518-427-8035. Email: info@rcdacemeteries.org. Web: www.rcdacemeteries.org.

St. Mary's Cemetery, Mailing Address: 48 Cemetery Ave., Menands, 12204. 738 McClellan St., 12304. Tel: 518-463-0134; Fax: 518-427-8035. Email: info@rcdacemeteries.org. Web: www.rcdacemeteries.org.

Most Holy Redeemer Cemetery, 2501 Troy Rd., Niskayuna, 12309. Tel: 518-463-0134; Fax: 518-427-8035. Email: info@rcdacemeteries.org. Web: www.rcdacemeteries.org. Mailing Address: 48 Cemetery Ave., Menands, 12204.

TROY. *St. Jean Baptiste Cemetery*, Mailing Address: 48 Cemetery Ave., Menands, 12204. 968 Spring Ave. Ext., 12180. Tel: 518-463-0134; Fax: 518-427-8035. Email: info@rcdacemeteries.org. Web: rcdacemeteries.org.

St. John Cemetery, 250 Cemetery Ave., 12180. Tel: 518-463-0134; Fax: 518-427-8035. Email: info@rcdacemeteries.org. Web: www.rcdacemeteries.org. Mailing Address: 48 Cemetery Ave., Menands, 12204.

St. Mary's Cemetery of Troy, Inc., 79 Brunswick Rd., 12180. Tel: 518-463-0134; Fax: 518-427-8035. Email: info@rcdacemeteries.org. Web: rcdacemeteries.org. Mailing Address: 48 Cemetery Ave., Menands, 12204.

WATERVLIET. *Immaculate Conception Cemetery*, 29 Delatour Rd., 12189. Tel: 518-463-0134; Fax: 518-427-8035. Email: info@rcdacemeteries.org. Web: www.rcdacemeteries.org. Mailing Address: 48 Cemetery Ave., Menands, 12204.

NECROLOGY

† Campagnone, Nicholas, (Retired)—Died Jan. 14, 2011

† Cronin, Brian, (Retired)—Died Aug. 27, 2011

† Douglas, Louis, (Retired)—Died May 11, 2011

† Lynch, Patrick J., (Retired)—Died May 25, 2011

Diocese of Alexandria

(Dioecesis Alexandrina in Louisiana)

Most Reverend

RONALD P. HERZOG

Bishop of Alexandria; ordained June 1, 1968; appointed Bishop of Alexandria October 27, 2004; ordained and installed January 5, 2005. *Mailing Address: P.O. Box 7417, Alexandria, LA 71306-0417.* Tel: 318-445-6424, Ext. 201; Fax: 318-767-1230. Email: rherzog@diocesealex.org.

Chancery Office: 4400 Coliseum Blvd., P.O. Box 7417, Alexandria, LA 71306. Tel: 318-445-2401 (Receptionist); 318-445-6424 (Auto Attendant); Fax: 318-448-6121.

Web: www.diocesealex.org

ERECTED AS DIOCESE OF NATCHITOCHES JULY 29, 1853.

Square Miles 11,108.

Transferred to Alexandria August 6, 1910 and became Diocese of Alexandria.

Redesignated Diocese of Alexandria-Shreveport on January 12, 1977; split, forming two Dioceses, the Diocese of Alexandria and the Diocese of Shreveport as of June 16, 1986.

Comprises the Counties (parishes) of Rapides, Avoyelles, Concordia, Catahoula, LaSalle, Grant, Natchitoches, Vernon, Tensas, Caldwell, Winn, Franklin and Madison.

For legal titles of parishes and diocesan institutions, consult the Chancery Office.

STATISTICAL OVERVIEW

Personnel	
Bishop	1
Priests: Diocesan Active in Diocese	30
Priests: Diocesan Active Outside Diocese	6
Priests: Retired, Sick or Absent	18
Number of Diocesan Priests	54
Religious Priests in Diocese	11
Total Priests in Diocese	65
Extern Priests in Diocese	13
Ordinations:	
Transitional Deacons	1
Permanent Deacons in Diocese	6
Total Brothers	3
Total Sisters	29
Parishes	
Parishes	44
With Resident Pastor:	
Resident Diocesan Priests	29
Resident Religious Priests	15
Missions	21
Professional Ministry Personnel:	
Brothers	3
Sisters	29
Lay Ministers	15
Welfare	
Catholic Hospitals	1
Total Assisted	205,250
Health Care Centers	1
Total Assisted	350
Homes for the Aged	1
Total Assisted	104
Special Centers for Social Services	8
Total Assisted	925
Residential Care of Disabled	1
Total Assisted	202
Other Institutions	1
Total Assisted	58,900
Educational	
Diocesan Students in Other Seminaries	7
Total Seminarians	7
High Schools, Diocesan and Parish	3
Total Students	691
Elementary Schools, Diocesan and Parish	7
Total Students	1,771
Catechesis/Religious Education:	
High School Students	825
Elementary Students	1,836
Total Students under Catholic Instruction	5,130
Teachers in the Diocese:	
Brothers	3
Sisters	6
Lay Teachers	21
Vital Statistics	
Receptions into the Church:	
Infant Baptism Totals	552
Minor Baptism Totals	71
Adult Baptism Totals	41
Received into Full Communion	154
First Communions	593
Confirmations	423
Marriages:	
Catholic	124
Interfaith	63
Total Marriages	187
Deaths	599
Total Catholic Population	43,484
Total Population	383,421

Former Bishops—Rt. Revs. AUGUSTUS M. MARTIN, ord. Sept. 25, 1825; cons. Nov. 30, 1853; died Sept. 29, 1875; FRANCIS XAVIER LERAY, ord. March 19, 1852; cons. Bishop of Natchitoches, April 22, 1877; named Bishop of Janopolis, Coadjutor of New Orleans, and Administrator of Natchitoches, Oct. 23, 1879; promoted to the See of New Orleans, Dec. 1883; died Sept. 23, 1887; ANTHONY DURIER, D.D., ord. Oct. 27, 1856; cons. March 19, 1885; died Feb. 28, 1904; Most Revs. CORNELIUS VAN DE VEN, ord. May 31, 1890; cons. Nov. 30, 1904; made assistant at the Pontifical Throne, Nov. 12, 1929; died May 8, 1932; DANIEL FRANCIS DESMOND, D.D., ord. June 9, 1911; cons. Bishop of Alexandria Jan. 5, 1933; died Sept. 11, 1945; CHARLES P. GRECO, D.D., ord. July 25, 1918; cons. Feb. 25, 1946; retired May 22, 1973; died Jan. 20, 1987; LAWRENCE P. GRAVES, D.D., J.C.L., ord. June 11, 1942; cons. April 25, 1969; installed Bishop of Alexandria, Sept. 18, 1973; retired July 14, 1982; died Jan. 15, 1994; WILLIAM B. FRIEND, ord. Oct. 30, 1979; installed Bishop of Alexandria-Shreveport Jan. 11, 1983; then after Diocese of Alexandria-Shreveport was divided into two dioceses June 16, 1986; installed Bishop of Shreveport July 30, 1986; JOHN C. FAVALORA, ord. Dec. 20, 1961; appt. Bishop of Alexandria June 16, 1986; ord. and installed July 29, 1986; installed Bishop of St. Petersburg May 16, 1989; installed Archbishop of Miami Dec. 20, 1994; SAM G. JACOBS, ord. June 6, 1964; appt. Bishop of Alexandria July 1, 1989; ord. and installed Aug. 24, 1989; appt. Bishop of Houma-Thibodaux Aug. 1, 2003; installed Oct. 10, 2003.

St. Joseph Catholic Center—Diocese of Alexandria, 4400 Coliseum Blvd., Alexandria, 71303-3597. Mailing Address: P.O. Box 7417, Alexandria, 71306-0417. Tel: 318-445-2401 Receptionist; 318-445-6424 Auto-Attendant; Fax: 318-448-6121. Web: www.diocesealex.org. Office Hours: Mon.-Thurs. 8-5, Fri. 8-12:30.

All offices as above unless listed otherwise. Send requests for matrimonial dispensations to the Diocesan Tribunal.

COORDINATING STAFF

Vicar General—Rev. SCOTT CHEMINO, V.G., J.C.L. Tel: 318-445-6424, Ext. 204. Email: frschemino@diocesealex.org.

Episcopal Vicar for Administration—Rev. BRUCE MILLER, J.C.L., E.V., J.V. Tel: 318-445-6424, Ext. 261; Fax: 318-767-0872. Email: frbmiller@diocesealex.org.

Chancellor—Rev. CHAD A. PARTAIN, Chancellor & Archivist. Tel: 318-445-6424, Ext. 228. Email: frcpartain@diocesealex.org.

Director of Catholic Charities and Special Ministries—(family life and worship) Rev. RICK GREMILLION. Tel: 318-445-6424, Ext. 226. Email: frgrem@diocesealex.org.

Superintendent of Catholic Schools—Mr. THOMAS ROQUE. Tel: 318-445-6424, Ext. 224. Email: troque@diocesealex.org.

Director of Development and Public Affairs—ANN MASDEN. Tel: 318-445-6424, Ext. 210. Email: amasden@diocesealex.org.

Chief Financial Officer—DAVID BROOK. Tel: 318-445-6424, Ext. 214. Email: dbrook@diocesealex.org.

Director of Religious Formation and Training—(Steubenville Conference) CHRISTINA THERIOT. Tel: 318-445-6424, Ext. 231. Email: ctheriot@diocesealex.org.

Secretary to the Bishop—DEBORAH DEOROSAN. Tel: 318-445-6424, Ext. 201; Fax: 318-767-1230. Email: ddeorosan@diocesealex.org.

Other Diocesan Services

Archivist—Rev. CHAD A. PARTAIN. Tel: 318-445-6424, Ext. 228. Email: frcpartain@diocesealex.org.

Vicar for Clergy—Rev. CRAIG SCOTT, V.C., Mailing Address: P.O. Box 7056, Alexandria, 71306-0056. Tel: 318-445-7141, Ext. 12. Email: frcscott@strita.org.

Communications—ANN MASDEN, Communications Dir. Tel: 318-445-6424, Ext. 210. Email: amasden@diocesealex.org; JEANNIE PETRUS, Editor of The Church Today & Coord. Evangelization. Tel: 318-445-6424, Ext. 255. Email: jpetrus@diocesealex.org.

Continuing Education of the Clergy—Rev. ADAM FREDERICK TRAVIS, Mailing Address: P.O. Box 7056, Alexandria, 71306-0056. Email: fathertravis@gmail.com.

Diaconate Program—Rev. DANIEL P. O'CONNOR, V.F., Dir., 401 21st St., Alexandria, 71301-6500. Tel: 318-445-9748, Ext. 16. Email: frdan@bellsouth.net.

Diocesan Tribunal— (canonical services) PATRICIA THOMAS, Moderator of the Tribunal Chancery. Tel: 318-445-6424, Ext. 263; Fax: 318-767-0872. Email: pthomas@diocesealex.org.

Judges—Revs. BRUCE MILLER, J.C.L., E.V., J.V. Tel: 318-445-6424, Ext. 261. Email: frbmiller@diocesealex.org; SCOTT CHEMINO, V.G., J.C.L. Tel: 318-445-6424, Ext. 204. Email: frschemino@diocesealex.org.

Defender of the Bond and Promoter of Justice—Rev. JAMES A. FERGUSON, J.C.L. Tel: 318-445-6424, Ext. 265. Email: frjferguson@diocesealex.org.

Notary—MARY ANN MANUEL. Tel: 318-445-6424, Ext. 262. Email: mmanuel@diocesealex.org.

Hispanic Ministry—LAURA GASPAR DE ALBA, Mailing Address: P.O. Box 7417, Alexandria, 71306-0417.

Tel: 318-445-6424, Ext. 258; Rev. MARTIN L. LAIRD, P.O. Box 130, Mansura, 71350. Tel: 318-964-2921.

Liturgy Commission—Rev. JOSE A. ROBLES-SANCHEZ, Chm., 2211 E. Texas Ave., Alexandria, 71301-4207. Tel: 318-445-4588. Email: frjose@cabrinichurch.com.

Maryhill Renewal Center—Mr. PAUL ANDRIES, Property Mgr., 600 Maryhill Rd., Pineville, 71360-4196. Tel: 318-640-1378; 318-792-1570. Email: cnorris@diocesealex.org.

Protection of Children—

Program Director—PAM DELRIE. Tel: 318-445-6424, Ext. 213. Email: pdelrie@diocesealex.org.

Victim Assistance Minister—MARY GIRARD, L.M.F.T., L.P.C., 5501 C John Eskew Blvd., Alexandria, 71303-3725. Tel: 318-449-8571, Ext. 13.

Administrator and Assessor, Code of Pastoral Conduct—Rev. SCOTT CHEMINO, V.G., J.C.L. Tel: 318-445-6424, Ext. 223. Email: frschemino@diocesealex.org.

Coordinator for Religious—VACANT.

Vocations and Seminarians—Revs. KENNETH J. MICHIELS, Dir., Mailing Address: 105 South St., Leesville, 71446. Tel: 337-239-2656. Email: stmichaelschurch@bellsouth.net; BLAKE PAUL DESHAUTELLE, Assoc. Dir.

College of Consultors—Rev. SCOTT CHEMINO, V.G., J.C.L.; Rev. Msgr. STEVE J. TESTA, V.F.; Revs. ANTONY AELAVANTHARA, V.F.; FERREOLUS D'CRUZ, V.F.; DANIEL P. O'CONNOR, V.F.; CRAIG SCOTT, V.C.; JAMES A. FERGUSON, J.C.L.; RYAN P. HUMPHRIES, V.F.; KENNETH J. MICHIELS; CHAD A. PARTAIN, Chancellor.

Presbyteral Council—Elected Members: Revs. JAMES A. FERGUSON, J.C.L.; RYAN P. HUMPHRIES, V.F.; ADAM FREDERICK TRAVIS; CHAD A. PARTAIN; DANIEL P. O'CONNOR, V.F., Chm.; LOUIS E. SKLAR. Appointed Members: Revs. PETER KULIGOWSKI, V.F.; KENNETH J. MICHIELS; BRUCE MILLER, J.C.L., E.V., J.V.; CRAIG SCOTT, V.C., Vicar for Clergy; Rev. Msgr. STEVE J. TESTA, V.F. Ex Officio: Rev. SCOTT CHEMINO, V.G., J.C.L., Ex Officio.

Deans—Revs. RYAN P. HUMPHRIES, V.F., Natchitoches Deanery; PETER KULIGOWSKI, V.F., Eastern Deanery; DANIEL P. O'CONNOR, V.F., Central Deanery; Rev. Msgr. STEVE J. TESTA, V.F., Avoyelles Deanery.

Diocesan Representatives

Boy Scouts of America—

Region 5 Chaplain—VACANT.

Diocesan, Region 5 & Louisiana Purchase Council Chaplain—Rev. STEPHEN J. BRANDOW, Mailing Address: P.O. Box 39, Tioga, 71477-0039. Tel: 318-473-0010, Ext. 2539.

Catholic Relief Services—Rev. RICK GREMILLION. Tel: 318-445-6424, Ext. 226. Email: frgrem@diocesealex.org.

Louisiana Interchurch Council—Rev. SCOTT CHEMINO, V.G., J.C.L., Ecumenical Liaison. Tel: 318-445-6424, Ext. 204. Email: frschemino@diocesealex.org.

Holy Childhood Association—Rev. Msgr. STEVE J. TESTA, V.F., Dir. Tel: 318-445-6424, Ext. 225.

Propagation of the Faith and Foreign Mission Education—Rev. Msgr. STEVE J. TESTA, V.F., Dir. Tel: 318-445-6424, Ext. 225.

CLERGY, PARISHES, MISSIONS AND PAROCHIAL SCHOOLS

CITY OF ALEXANDRIA

(RAPIDES PARISH)

1—ST. FRANCIS XAVIER CATHEDRAL (1834) Revs. James A. Ferguson, Rector; Peter A. Faulk; Robert Garrione.
Res.: 626 Fourth St., 71301-8424. Tel: 318-445-1451; Fax: 318-445-1433. Email: vannatta@sfxcathedral.org. Web: www.sfxcathedral.org.
Catechesis/Religious Program—Students 19.

2—ST. FRANCES XAVIER CABRINI (1947) Revs. Jose A. Robles-Sanchez (Puerto Rico); Jorge Antonio Velez Lopez.
Office: 2211 E. Texas Ave., 71301-4207. Tel: 318-445-4588; Fax: 318-443-7156.
Res.: 2012 Wedgewood Ave., 71301. Tel: 318-445-4588; Fax: 318-443-7156. Web: www.cabrinichurch.com.
School—(Grades PreK-8), 2215 E. Texas Ave., 71301. Tel: 318-448-3333; Fax: 318-448-3343. Web: www.cabrinischool.com. Joseph Wiederholt, Prin.; Jackie Pousson, Librarian. Lay Teachers 10; Students 89.
Catechesis/Religious Program—Students 99.

3—ST. JAMES MEMORIAL (1911) Rev. Remigius Owuamanam, S.M.M.M. (Nigeria).
Res.: 900 Daspit St., 71302.
Church: 714 Winn St., 71301. Tel: 318-487-9512; Fax: 318-445-9826.
Catechesis/Religious Program—Students 17.

4—ST. JULIANA (1959) Rev. Remigius Owuamanam, S.M.M.M. (Nigeria).
Res.: 900 Daspit St., 71302-5343. Tel: 318-445-6700; Fax: 318-445-9826.
Catechesis/Religious Program—Students 18.

5—OUR LADY OF PROMPT SUCCOR (1947) Revs. Daniel P. O'Connor; Emmanuel Chinaka. In Res., Rev. Christudas Nayak (India).
Res.: 401 21st St., 71301-7022. Tel: 318-445-3693; Fax: 318-445-8471. Email: olpsc@bellsouth.net. Web: www.olpschurch.org.
School—(Grades PreK-6), 420 21st St., 71301. Tel: 318-487-1862; Fax: 318-473-9321. Email: olpsoffice@promptsuccor.org. Jo Tassin, Prin.; Jackie Whitcher, Librarian. Lay Teachers 45; Students 509.
Catechesis/Religious Program—Paul Hood, D.R.E. Students 250.

6—ST. RITA (1940) Revs. Michael Craig Scott, V.C.; Adam Frederick Travis.
Mailing Address: P.O. Box 7056, 71306.
Office: 3822 Bayou Rapides Rd., 71303. Tel: 318-445-7120; Fax: 318-448-0704. Email: strita@strita.org. Web: www.strita.org.
Res.: 214 N. 17th St., 71301. Tel: 318-445-7120.
Church: 4401 Bayou Rapides Rd., 71303. Tel: 318-448-9599.
Child Development Center—1005 Seip Dr., 71303. Tel: 318-448-9999; Fax: 318-445-3003. Email: cdc@strita.org.
Catechesis/Religious Program—Tel: 318-445-7141, Ext. 15. Sr. Nell Murray, M.S.C., D.R.E. Students 154.

OUTSIDE THE CITY OF ALEXANDRIA

BELLEDEAU, AVOYELLES PARISH, ST. MARTIN OF TOURS (1950) [CEM] Rev. Silverino Kwebuza, A.J. (Uganda). In Res., Rev. Daniel Corkery (Ireland) (Retired).
Res.: P.O. Box 98, Hessmer, 71341-4234.
Catechesis/Religious Program—Tel: 318-563-8772. Roxanna Moreau, D.R.E.

BORDELONVILLE, AVOYELLES PARISH, ST. PETER (1903) [CEM] Rev. Msgr. Steve J. Testa.
Mailing Address: P.O. Box 31, 71320-0031.
Res.: 4702 Hwy. 451, 71320-0031. Tel: 318-997-2151; Fax: 318-997-2159. Email: stpeter@centurytel.net.
Catechesis/Religious Program—Tel: 318-997-2502. Pattie Moyeaux, D.R.E. Students 26.

BOYCE, RAPIDES PARISH, ST. MARGARET (1936) Rev. Kurian Zachariah (India).
Res.: 402 Ryan St., 71409. Tel: 318-793-8811; Fax: 318-793-8815.
Catechesis/Religious Program—Cloteal Powell, D.R.E. Students 14.
Mission—St. Cyril Flatwoods, Rapides Parish.
Mission—St. Margaret Mary Gorum, Natchitoches Parish.

BROUILLETTE, AVOYELLES PARISH, ST. GENEVIEVE (1953) [CEM] Rev. Jose Pallipurath, O.S.B.Silv. (India).
Res.: 4052 Hwy. 452, Marksville, 71351-3530. Tel: 318-253-9237; Fax: 318-253-0703.
Catechesis/Religious Program—Cindy Dupuy, D.R.E. Students 39.

BUNKIE, AVOYELLES PARISH, ST. ANTHONY OF PADUA (1904) [CEM] Rev. Jack H. Michalchuk (Canada).
Res.: 409 St. John St., P.O. Box 719, 71322-0719. Tel: 318-346-7274; Fax: 318-346-7475. Email: stanthonyscathol@bellsouth.net. Web: stanthony_bunkie.org.
School—(Grades PreK-8), 116 S. Knoll St., 71322. Tel: 318-346-2739; Fax: 318-346-9191. Martha Coulon, Prin.; Kim Juneau, Librarian. Sisters 2; Lay Teachers 13; Students 225.
Catechesis/Religious Program—Karen McCoy, D.R.E. Students 44.

CAMPTI, NATCHITOCHES PARISH, NATIVITY OF THE BLESSED VIRGIN MARY (1831) [CEM 3] Rev. Ryan P. Humphries.
Res.: 119 Tally St., 71411. Tel: 318-476-2116. Email: peggy@nativityofbvm.com.
Mission—St. Joseph Trichel, Natchitoches Parish.
Mission—Our Lady of the Holy Rosary Black Lake, Natchitoches Parish.
Catechesis/Religious Program—Students 16.

CHENEYVILLE, RAPIDES PARISH, ST. JOSEPH (1966) [CEM] Rev. Scott Chemino.
Res.: P.O. Box 446, 71325-0446. Tel: 318-279-2394; Fax: 318-279-2394.

CLOUTIERVILLE, NATCHITOCHES PARISH, ST. JOHN THE BAPTIST (1816) [CEM] Rev. Kenneth Obiekwe (Nigeria).
Mailing Address: P.O. Box 40, 71416-0040.
Res.: 423 Hwy. 495, 71416-0040. Tel: 318-379-2231; Fax: 318-379-2236.
Catechesis/Religious Program—Students 30.
Mission—Holy Rosary Emmanuel, Natchitoches Parish.
Mission—Holy Family Monet Ferry, Natchitoches Parish.

COLFAX, GRANT PARISH, ST. JOSEPH (1897) Rev. Harold Imamshah (Trinidad and Tobago).
Res.: 139 Second St., P.O. Box 243, 71417-0243. Tel: 318-627-3952.
Mission—St. Patrick P.O. Box 158, Montgomery, Grant Parish 71454.
Catechesis/Religious Program—Students 16.

COTTONPORT, AVOYELLES PARISH, ST. MARY ASSUMPTION (1889) [CEM 4] Rev. Jamie Medina-Cruz (Puerto Rico).
Mailing Address: P.O. Box 1123, 71327-1123.
Res.: 820 Front St., 71327-1123. Tel: 318-876-3681; Fax: 318-876-3686. Email: stmarychurch@kricket.net.
School—(Grades PreK-8) Tel: 318-876-3651; Fax: 318-876-2955. Email: smsangels@kricket.net. Amanda Hemphill, Prin. Lay Teachers 12; Students 210.
Catechesis/Religious Program—Students 125.

DEVILLE, RAPIDES PARISH

1—STS. FRANCIS AND ANNE CATHOLIC CHURCH (2010) Rev. Joy Antony Retnazihamoni (India).
Mailing Address: P.O. Box 3147, Pineville, 71361.
Church: 143 Boone Miller Rd., 71328-9445. Tel: 318-443-5118; Fax: 318-443-7344. Email: joyr_antony@yahoo.com.
Catechesis/Religious Program—Rudy Mitchel, D.R.E. Students 115.

2—ST. JOHN THE BAPTIST (1942) [CEM 2] Rev. Paul Kunnumpuram, M.S.F.S. (India).
Res.: 1024 Hwy. 1207, P.O. Box 7, 71328-0007. Tel: 318-466-5587; Fax: 318-466-5265.
Catechesis/Religious Program—Students 110.
Mission—St. Winifred Effie, Avoyelles Parish.
Mission—St. John the Baptist Moncla, Avoyelles Parish.

DUPONT, AVOYELLES PARISH, IMMACULATE CONCEPTION (1945) [CEM] Rev. George Krosfield (India).
Res.: P.O. Box 385, 71329-0385. Tel: 318-922-3243; Fax: 318-922-3976.
Catechesis/Religious Program—Tel: 318-922-3707. Angie Dixon, D.R.E. Students 55.

ECHO, RAPIDES PARISH, ST. FRANCIS DE SALES (1894) [CEM] Rev. Scott Chemino.
Res.: P.O. Box 37, 71330-0037. Tel: 318-563-4530; Fax: 318-563-4530.
Catechesis/Religious Program—Tel: 318-564-4340. Students 77.

EVERGREEN, AVOYELLES PARISH, LITTLE FLOWER (1928) [CEM 2] Rev. Bartholomew Ibe (Nigeria).
Mailing Address: P.O. Box 20, 71333-0020.
Res.: 2912 Main St., 71333-0020. Tel: 318-346-2840; Fax: 318-346-4989. Email: litflowr@bellsouth.net.
Catechesis/Religious Program—Students 9.
Mission—St. Charles Goudeau, Avoyelles Parish.

FERRIDAY, CONCORDIA PARISH, ST. PATRICK (1952) [JC] Rev. Louis E. Sklar.
Res.: P.O. Box 369, 71334. Tel: 318-757-3834.
Catechesis/Religious Program—Students 4.
Mission—St. Gerard P.O. Box 863, Jonesville, Catahoula Parish 71343. Tel: 318-339-6143.

GLENMORA, RAPIDES PARISH, ST. LOUIS (1941) Rev. Binochan Pallipparambil, O.S.B.Silv. (India).
Res.: 826 8th St., P.O. Box 636, 71433-0636. Tel: 318-748-8324.
Catechesis/Religious Program—Students 37.
Mission—St. Peter [CEM] Elmer, Rapides Parish.
Mission—St. Jude Sieper, Rapides Parish.

HESSMER, AVOYELLES PARISH, ST. ALPHONSUS (1898) [CEM] Rev. Edwin Rodriguez-Hernandez (Puerto Rico).
Mailing Address: P.O. Box 66, 71341-0066.
Res.: 3659 Main St., 71341-0066. Tel: 318-563-4550; Fax: 318-563-8395.
Catechesis/Religious Program—Tel: 318-542-6098. Tina Laborde, D.R.E. Students 150.

ISLE BREVELLE, NATCHITOCHES PARISH, ST. AUGUSTINE'S (1856) [CEM] Rev. Jacob Thomas (India).
Res.: 2262 Hwy. 484, Natchez, 71456-3622. Tel: 318-379-2521; Fax: 318-379-6085.
Catechesis/Religious Program—Mr. Thomas Roque, D.R.E. Students 46.
Mission—St. Charles Bermuda, Natchitoches Parish.
Mission—St. Anne Old River, Natchitoches Parish.

JENA, LASALLE PARISH, ST. MARY (1949) Rev. Keith E. Ishmael.
Mailing Address: P.O. Box 2240, 71342. Tel: 318-992-1019.
Catechesis/Religious Program—Students 43.
Mission—St. Edward Fishville, Grant Parish 71467. P.O. Box 669, Pollock, 71467.

LECOMPTE, RAPIDES PARISH, ST. MARTIN (1993) Rev. Pedro J. Sierra-Posada (Colombia).

Res.: 1904 Union St., P.O. Box 459, 71346-0459. Tel: 318-776-7820; Fax: 318-776-9921. Email: stmartinscatholi@bellsouth.net. Web: www.diocesealex.org/stmartin.
Catechesis / Religious Program—Tel: 318-748-7389; Fax: 318-748-7389. Cathy Andries, D.R.E. Students 44.
Mission—Our Lady of Guadalupe, Tel: 318-308-9021.
Catechesis / Religious Program—Tel: 318-448-1068. Students 97.

LEESVILLE, VERNON PARISH, ST. MICHAEL (1946) Revs. Kenneth J. Michiels; Anthony Catella.
Res.: 202 W. Harriet, 71446. Tel: 337-239-2656; Fax: 337-239-2657.
Catechesis / Religious Program—Tel: 337-238-4941. Tammy Cecil, D.R.E. Students 150.

MANSURA, AVOYELLES PARISH

1—OUR LADY OF PROMPT SUCCOR (1937) Rev. Jose Palathara, C.M.I. (India).
Res.: 1910 Escude St., P.O. Box 67, 71350-0067. Tel: 318-964-2654; Fax: 318-964-2654.
Catechesis / Religious Program—Students 7.

2—ST. PAUL THE APOSTLE (1796) [CEM] Revs. Chad A. Partain; Martin L. Laird.
Mailing Address: P.O. Box 130, 71350-0130.
Res.: 1879 Leglise St., 71350-0130. Tel: 318-964-2921; Fax: 318-964-2921.
Catechesis / Religious Program—Students 76.

MARKSVILLE, AVOYELLES PARISH

1—HOLY GHOST (1919) [CEM 2] Rev. Ignatius A. Ibe, S.M.M.M. (Nigeria).
Res.: 121 S. Preston St., 71351-3034. Tel: 318-253-7131; Fax: 318-253-7136. Email: holyghostchur783@bellsouth.net.
Catechesis / Religious Program—Students 79.
Mission—St. Richard, Avoyelles Parish 71351.

2—ST. JOSEPH'S (1869) [CEM 2] Revs. Rusty P. Rabalais; Abraham Varghese (India).
Res.: 141 S. Washington, 71351-3025. Tel: 318-253-7561 (Office); Fax: 318-253-8871. Email: stjosephofc@kricket.net.
Catechesis / Religious Program—Students 225.

3—OUR LADY OF LOURDES (1948) [CEM 4] Rev. Silverino Kwebuza, A.J. (Uganda).
Res.: 1315 Eggbend Rd., 71351-4223. Tel: 318-253-9936; Fax: 318-253-6300. Email: lourdeschurch@bellsouth.net.
Catechesis / Religious Program—Students 60.

MOREAUVILLE, AVOYELLES PARISH

1—OUR LADY OF SORROWS (1944) [CEM] Rev. Jose Palanthara.
Mailing Address: P.O. Box 247, 71355-0247.
Res.: 524 Main St., 71355-0247. Tel: 318-985-2968. Email: ols_moreauville@yahoo.com.
Catechesis / Religious Program—

2—SACRED HEART (1860) [CEM] Rev. Marc A. Noel (Canada).
Res.: 9986 Bayou Des Glaises St., 71355-9702. Tel: 318-985-2774; Fax: 318-985-2397. Email: shc_moreauville@yahoo.com. Web: www.shcmoreauville.org.
School—(Grades PreK-8), 9968 Bayou Des Glaises, P.O. Box 179, 71355. Tel: 318-985-2772; Fax: 318-985-2164. Email: shs@kricket.net. Sr. Sandra Norsworthy, O.L.S., Prin.; Rhonia Smith, Librarian. Sisters of Our Lady of Sorrows 3; Lay Teachers 22; Students 322.
Catechesis / Religious Program—Students 118.

NATCHITOCHES, NATCHITOCHES PARISH

1—ST. ANTHONY OF PADUA (1935) [JC] Revs. John O'Brien (Canada); Thomas Elmus Paul.
Res.: 911 Fifth St., P.O. Box 432, 71458-0432. Tel: 318-352-2559; Fax: 318-352-2528. Email: spadua@bellsouth.net.
Catechesis / Religious Program—Students 176.

2—HOLY CROSS (1968) Rev. Jason E. Gootee.
Res.: 129 Second St., P.O. Box 211, 71458-0211. Tel: 318-352-2615; Fax: 318-352-8989.
Catechesis / Religious Program—Students 41.

3—IMMACULATE CONCEPTION (1728) [CEM] Revs. James A. Foster; Irion St. Romain.
Res.: 145 Church St., P.O. Box 13, 71458-0013. Tel: 318-352-3422; Fax: 318-352-3822.
School—St. Mary, (Grades PreK-12), 1101 E. Fifth St., P.O. Box 2070, 71458-2070. Tel: 318-352-8394; Fax: 318-352-5798. Alan Powers, Prin. & High School Prin. Lay Teachers 24; Students 269.
High School—Lay Teachers 18; Students 91.
Catechesis / Religious Program—Students 91.

PINEVILLE, RAPIDES PARISH, SACRED HEART (1933) Revs. Bruce Miller; Stephen Soares.
Res.: 600 Lakeview, P.O. Drawer 3009, 71360-7519. Tel: 318-445-2496; Fax: 318-443-0808.
Catechesis / Religious Program—Students 219.

PLAUCHEVILLE, AVOYELLES PARISH, MATER DOLOROSA (1879) [CEM] Rev. Charles J. Morgan.
Res.: P.O. Box 9, 71362-0009. Tel: 318-922-3131; Fax: 318-922-3664.
School—(Grades PreK-8) Tel: 318-922-3401; Fax: 318-922-3776. Bro. Anthony Dugas, F.S.E., Prin. Brothers of the Holy Eucharist 3; Lay Teachers 5; Students 147.
High School—Bro. Anthony Dugas, F.S.E., Prin. Brothers of the Holy Eucharist 3; Sisters 2; Lay Teachers 5; Students 91.
Catechesis / Religious Program—Bro. Paul Casey, F.S.E., D.R.E. Students 67.

POWHATAN, NATCHITOCHES PARISH, ST. FRANCIS OF ASSISI (1952) Rev. Antony Aelavanthara.
Res.: P.O. Box 82, 71066-0082. Tel: 318-352-8819; Fax: 318-352-8008.
Catechesis / Religious Program—Students 7.
Mission—St. Anne [CEM] Spanish Lake, Natchitoches Parish.

REXMERE, AVOYELLES PARISH, ST. MICHAEL (1964) [CEM] Rev. Msgr. Steve J. Testa.
Res.: 4702 Hwy. 451, P.O. Box 31, Bordelonville, 71320-0031. Tel: 318-997-2151; Fax: 318-997-2159. Email: stpeter@centurytel.net.
Catechesis / Religious Program—

ST. JOSEPH, TENSAS PARISH, ST. JOSEPH (1940) [JC] Rev. Peter Kuligowski (Poland).
Mailing Address: P.O. Box 198, 71366-0198.
Res.: 919 Plank Rd., 71366-0198. Tel: 318-766-3565; Fax: 318-766-4564.
Catechesis / Religious Program—Students 15.
Mission—St. Francis of Assisi Waterproof, Tensas Parish.

SIMMESPORT, AVOYELLES PARISH, CHRIST THE KING (1935) [CEM] Rev. Dwight De Jesus (Philippines).
Res.: 657 Main St., P.O. Box 186, 71369-0186. Tel: 318-941-2381; Fax: 318-941-2381. Email: cthe@centurytel.net.
Catechesis / Religious Program—Tel: 318-941-5159. Gwen Barr, D.R.E. Students 47.

TALLULAH, MADISON PARISH, ST. EDWARD (1936) Rev. Ferreolus D'Cruz (India).
Res.: 204 Hwy. 80 E., P.O. Box 1308, 71282-1308. Tel: 318-574-1677; Fax: 318-574-1636. Email: stedward@bellsouth.net.
Catechesis / Religious Program—Students 32.

TIOGA, RAPIDES PARISH, IMMACULATE HEART OF MARY (1971) Rev. Rick Gremillion.
P.O. Box 687, 71477-0687. Tel: 318-640-5314 (Res.); 318-640-9446 (Office); Fax: 318-640-3864. Email: ihmarychurch@suddenlink.net.
Res.: 1220 Tioga Rd., Ball, 71405.
Catechesis / Religious Program—Helen Craig, D.R.E. Students 131.

VIDALIA, CONCORDIA PARISH, OUR LADY OF LOURDES (1887) [JC] Rev. George Pookkattu, C.M.I. (India).
Res.: 503 Texas St., P.O. Box 460, 71373. Tel: 318-336-5450; Fax: 318-336-9770. Email: ollourdes@bellsouth.net.
Catechesis / Religious Program—Tel: 601-446-5757. Brigid Martin, D.R.E. Students 19.

WINNFIELD, WINN PARISH, OUR LADY OF LOURDES (1988) Rev. Christian Iheanyichukwu Ogbonna (Nigeria).
Res.: 772 Country Club Rd., P.O. Box 1412, 71483-1412. Tel: 318-628-2561; Fax: 318-628-4653.
Mission—St. William 4580 Main St., P.O. Box 1232, Olla, La Salle Parish 71465. Tel: 318-495-5356; Fax: 318-495-3579.
Catechesis / Religious Program—Students 30.

WINNSBORO, FRANKLIN PARISH, ST. MARY (1945) Rev. James Nellikunnell, C.M.I. (India).
Res.: 1712 West St., 71295-3240. Tel: 318-435-8580; Fax: 318-435-2002. Email: stmarysc c@bellsouth.net.
Catechesis / Religious Program—Cindy Futch, D.R.E. Students 34.
Mission—St. John 7900 Hwy. 165, Columbia, Caldwell Parish 71295.

WOODWORTH, RAPIDES PARISH, CONGREGATION OF MARY, MOTHER OF JESUS ROMAN CATHOLIC CHURCH, WOODWORTH, LOUISIANA (2008) Rev. John Pardue.
9323 Hwy. 165 S., P.O. Box 408, 71485. Tel: 318-487-9894. Email: mmjwoodworth@att.net. In Res., Rev. Blake Paul Deshautelle.
Catechesis / Religious Program—Linda Kelly, D.R.E. Students 8.

Chaplains of Public Institutions

ALEXANDRIA. *Christus St. Frances Cabrini Hospital*, 3330 Masonic Dr., 71301. Tel: 318-487-1122. Revs. Christudas Nayak (India), Robert Garrione.
Rapides Regional Medical Center, 211 4th St., 71301. Tel: 318-769-3000. Rev. Peter A. Faulk.

PINEVILLE. *Central Louisiana State Hospital*, W. Shamrock Ave., P.O. Box 5031, 71361. Tel: 318-484-6357; 318-484-6352. Rev. Stephen J. Brandow.
Veterans Administration Medical Center, Shreveport Hwy., 71360. Tel: 318-473-0010. Rev. Stephen J. Brandow, Staff Chap.

On Duty Outside the Diocese:
Revs.—
Braquet, David J., Archdiocese of New Orleans
DeCoste, Wade (Canada)
Mathews, Ronald J., Disciples of the Lord Jesus Christ, Channing, TX
Vead, Victor P., Federal Correctional Complex, Beaumont, TX

Military Chaplains:
Rev.—
Brocato, John K.

Absent on Leave:
Rev.—
Deevy, Edward

Retired:
Rev. Msgrs.—
Bordelon, Roland
Hoppe, Ronald C.
Lyons, Frederick J.
Timmermans, John (The Netherlands)
Revs.—
Allen, Terry
Corkery, Daniel (Ireland)
Cunningham, John H.
Fey, Thomas J.
Hasieber, Joseph S.
Lemoine, Russell J.
Messina, Angelo
Montalbano, Joseph E.
Roy, James
Ryan, John (Ireland)
Thompson, August L.
Viviano, Nino
Zagst, Bernard L.

Permanent Deacons:
Daigrepont, William, Avoyelles Prison Ministry
Foster, John, (Retired)
Giaco, Vincent, Chap., Christus St. Frances Cabrini Hospital
Gremillion, Norman, Immaculate Conception, Dupont
Peltier, Joseph, (Retired), St. Augustine, Isle Brevelle
Plaisance, Paul J., (Retired)

INSTITUTIONS LOCATED IN THE DIOCESE

[A] HIGH SCHOOLS, DIOCESAN

ALEXANDRIA. *Holy Savior Menard Central*, (Grades 7-12), 4603 Coliseum Blvd., 71303. Tel: 318-445-8233; Fax: 318-448-8170. Email: hsmenard@centuryinter.net. Mr. Joel Desselle, Prin.; Rev. Michael Craig Scott, V.C., Pres.; Clint Guillory, Librarian. Junior & High School. Lay Teachers 35; Students 482.

[B] GENERAL HOSPITALS

ALEXANDRIA. *Christus Health Central Louisiana dba Christus St. Frances Cabrini Hospital* 3330 Masonic Dr., 71301. Tel: 318-487-1122; Fax: 318-448-6754. Web: www.cabrini.org. Mr. Stephen Wright, Regl. Pres. & CEO; Rev. Christudas Nayak (India), Dir. Pastoral Care. Sisters of Charity of the Incarnate Word 2; Bed Capacity 283; Total Staff 1,785; Patients Assisted Annually 204,900.
Christus St. Frances Cabrini Hospital Foundation of Alexandria, Inc., 3330 Masonic Dr., 71301. Tel: 318-448-6580; Fax: 318-443-3072. Email: michael.davis@christushealth.org. Web: www.christuscabrinifoundation.org.
Dubuis Hospital of Alexandria, 3330 Masonic Dr., 71301. Tel: 318-448-4938; Fax: 318-483-4033. Web: www.dubuis.org. Mr. Stephen Peters, Admin. Bed Capacity 33; Total Staff 100; Patients Assisted Annually 350.

[C] PROTECTIVE INSTITUTIONS

ALEXANDRIA. *St. Mary's Residential Training School, Inc.*, P.O. Drawer 7768, 71306. Tel: 318-445-6443; Fax: 318-449-8520. Email: sistercarla@stmarys-rts.org. Web: www.stmarys-rts.org. Sr. Carla Bertani, O.L.S., Admin. Congregation of the Sisters of Our Lady of Sorrows of the U.S.A., Inc. Sisters 2; Lay Staff 350; Bed Capacity 202; Students 202.
Our Lady of Sorrows Community Homes, 347 Browns Bend Rd., 71303. Tel: 318-487-8897; Fax: 318-487-9987. Email: carlabols@aol.com. Congregation of the Sisters of Our Lady of Sorrows of the U.S.A., Inc. Sisters 3; Lay Staff 18; Bed Capacity 20; Residents 20.

[D] HOMES FOR AGED

ALEXANDRIA. *Our Lady's Manor, Inc.*, 402 Monroe St., 71301. Tel: 318-473-2560; Fax: 318-443-2449. Ms. Christina Brumley, Admin. Apartments 104.

[E] RESIDENCES OF PRIESTS AND BROTHERS

PLAUCHEVILLE. *Brothers of the Holy Eucharist*, P.O. Box 25, 71362. Tel: 318-922-3630. Bro. Andre M. Lucia, F.S.E., Supr. Brothers 4.

[F] CONVENTS AND RESIDENCES FOR SISTERS

ALEXANDRIA. *Congregation of the Marianites of Holy Cross, St. Rita Convent*, 1717 Ashley Ave., 71301. Tel: 318-448-8001. Sisters 3.

Congregation of the Sisters of Charity of the Incarnate Word, Nazareth Community, 340 Park Pl., 71301-3942. Tel: 318-473-9329; Fax: 318-473-9377. Sisters 2.

Sisters of Our Lady of Sorrows, St. Joseph Convent, 440 Browns Bend Rd., 71303. Tel: 318-443-1553; Fax: 318-443-0994. Email: stjoe97@aol.com. Sisters 5.

Sisters of the Holy Family, 3110 Georges Ln., 71301. Tel: 318-619-8573. Sr. Patricia Ann Williams, S.S.F., Local Leader. Sisters 3.

MOREAUVILLE. *Sisters of Our Lady of Sorrows, Sacred Heart Convent*, P.O. Box 179, 71355. Tel: 318-985-2994. Sisters 3.

[G] RETREAT HOUSES

PINEVILLE. *Maryhill Renewal Center*, 600 Maryhill Rd., 71360. Tel: 318-640-1378; 318-792-1570; Fax: 318-640-8604. Email: cnorris@diocesealex.org. Web: www.diocesealex.org. David Brook, CFO.

[H] CATHOLIC CHARITIES AND SPECIAL MINISTRIES

ALEXANDRIA. *Catholic Charities and Special Ministries*, 4400 Coliseum Blvd., P.O. Box 7417, 71306. Tel: 318-445-2401; Fax: 318-448-6121. Email: frgrem@diocesealex.org. Web: www.diocesealex.org. Rev. Rick Gremillion, Dir.

[I] NEWMAN CENTERS

ALEXANDRIA. *Louisiana State University at Alexandria Catholic Student Center*, 8100 Hwy. 71-S, 71302-9633. Tel: 318-473-6494. Mrs. Lynn Ray, Dir.; Rev. Blake Paul Deshautelle, Chap.

NATCHITOCHES. *Northwestern State University Holy Cross Catholic Student Center*, 129 Second St., P.O. Box 211, 71458. Tel: 318-352-2615; Fax: 318-352-8989. Email: holycrosscm@gmail.com. Rev. Jason E. Gootee, Chap.

[J] MISCELLANEOUS

ALEXANDRIA. *Catholic Charitable Endowment of Alexandria*, 4400 Coliseum Blvd., 71303. Tel: 318-445-2401; Fax: 318-448-6121.

The Catholic Foundation of North-Central Louisiana, Inc., P.O. Box 12833, 71315. Tel: 318-487-9222. Joseph L. Hebert, Pres.; Mrs. Betty Chop, Sec.

Manna House, 2655 Lee St., P.O. Box 6011, 71307. Tel: 318-445-9053. Mr. Chuck Westerchil, Pres. Board of Directors.

RELIGIOUS INSTITUTES OF MEN REPRESENTED IN THE DIOCESE

For further details refer to the corresponding bracketed number in the Religious Institutes of Men or Women section.

[]—*Apostles of Jesus (Uganda)*—A.J.
[]—*Benedictine Monks* (India)—O.S.B.Silv.
[0620]—*Brothers of the Holy Eucharist*—F.S.E.
[0275]—*Carmelites of Mary Immaculate*—C.M.I.
[0520]—*Franciscan Friars*—O.F.M.
[]—*Missionaries of St. Francis de Sales* (France)—M.S.F.S.
[]—*Sons of Mary Mother of Mercy (Nigeria)*—S.M.M.M.

RELIGIOUS INSTITUTES OF WOMEN REPRESENTED IN THE DIOCESE

[2410]—*Congregation of the Marianites of Holy Cross*—M.S.C.
[0470]—*Congregation of the Sisters of Charity of the Incarnate Word*—C.C.V.I.
[1950]—*Congregation of the Sisters of the Holy Family*—S.S.F.
[1010]—*Sisters of Divine Providence of San Antonio, Texas*—C.D.P.
[3120]—*Sisters of Our Lady of Sorrows*—O.L.S.
[]—*Sisters of the Living Word*—S.L.W.

DIOCESAN CEMETERIES

LECOMPTE. *Lecompte Cemetery*
PINEVILLE. *Maryhill Cemetery for Clergy*

NECROLOGY

† Susi, Rev. Msgr. Joseph M., (Retired)—Died Oct. 21, 2011

An asterisk (*) denotes an organization that has established tax-exempt status directly with the IRS and is not covered by the USCCB Group Ruling.

Diocese of Allentown

(Dioecesis Alanopolitana)

Most Reverend

JOHN O. BARRES, S.T.D., J.C.L., D.D.

Bishop of Allentown; ordained October 21, 1989; appointed Bishop of Allentown May 27, 2009; installed July 30, 2009. *Office: 4029 W. Tilghman St., Allentown, PA 18104.*

Most Reverend

EDWARD P. CULLEN, D.D.

Retired Bishop of Allentown; appointed Auxiliary Bishop of Philadelphia and Titular Bishop of Paria in Preconsilare February 8, 1994; consecrated April 14, 1994; appointed Bishop of Allentown December 16, 1997; installed Third Bishop of Allentown February 9, 1998; retired May 27, 2009. *Office: 4029 W. Tilghman St., Allentown, PA 18104. Mailing Address: Bishop's Office, P.O. Box F, Allentown, PA 18105.*

ESTABLISHED JANUARY 28, 1961.

Square Miles 2,773.

Comprises the Counties of Berks, Carbon, Lehigh, Northampton and Schuylkill in the State of Pennsylvania.

Chancery Office: 4029 W. Tilghman St., Allentown, PA 18104. Mailing Address: P.O. Box F, Allentown, PA 18105-1538. Tel: 610-437-0755; Fax: 610-433-7822.

STATISTICAL OVERVIEW

Personnel	
Bishop	1
Retired Bishops	1
Priests: Diocesan Active in Diocese	127
Priests: Diocesan Active Outside Diocese	10
Priests: Retired, Sick or Absent	67
Number of Diocesan Priests	204
Religious Priests in Diocese	67
Total Priests in Diocese	271
Extern Priests in Diocese	2
Ordinations:	
Diocesan Priests	1
Transitional Deacons	1
Permanent Deacons in Diocese	107
Total Brothers	11
Total Sisters	320
Parishes	
Parishes	104
With Resident Pastor:	
Resident Diocesan Priests	100
Resident Religious Priests	4
Without Resident Pastor:	
Administered by Priests	13
Missions	2
Pastoral Centers	26
Welfare	
Catholic Hospitals	2
Total Assisted	510,945
Health Care Centers	2
Total Assisted	4,760
Homes for the Aged	11
Total Assisted	474
Day Care Centers	1
Total Assisted	152
Specialized Homes	2
Total Assisted	565
Special Centers for Social Services	6
Total Assisted	30,537
Residential Care of Disabled	1
Total Assisted	59
Educational	
Diocesan Students in Other Seminaries	17
Total Seminarians	17
Colleges and Universities	2
Total Students	5,809
High Schools, Diocesan and Parish	7
Total Students	3,513
Elementary Schools, Diocesan and Parish	38
Total Students	8,926
Non-residential Schools for the Disabled	3
Total Students	186
Catechesis/Religious Education:	
High School Students	229
Elementary Students	16,226
Total Students under Catholic Instruction	34,906
Teachers in the Diocese:	
Priests	2
Sisters	28
Lay Teachers	807
Vital Statistics	
Receptions into the Church:	
Infant Baptism Totals	2,780
Adult Baptism Totals	135
Received into Full Communion	2,915
First Communions	3,513
Confirmations	3,694
Marriages:	
Catholic	525
Interfaith	282
Total Marriages	807
Deaths	2,854
Total Catholic Population	271,482
Total Population	1,272,222

Former Bishops—Most Revs. JOSEPH MCSHEA, D.D., appt. Titular Bishop of Mina and Auxiliary Bishop of Philadelphia Feb. 8, 1952; cons. March 19, 1952; appt. Bishop of Allentown Feb. 15, 1961; installed April 11, 1961; retired Feb. 8, 1983; died Nov. 28, 1991; THOMAS J. WELSH, D.D., J.C.D., appt. Titular Bishop of Scattery Island and Auxiliary Bishop of Philadelphia, Feb. 18, 1970; cons. April 2, 1970; appt. First Bishop of Arlington, June 4, 1974; installed Aug. 13, 1974; appt. Bishop of Allentown, Feb. 8, 1983; installed Second Bishop of Allentown, March 21, 1983; retired Dec. 16, 1997; died Feb. 19, 2009; EDWARD PETER CULLEN, D.D., ord. May 19, 1962; appt. Auxiliary Bishop of Philadelphia and Titular Bishop of Paria in Preconsilare Feb. 8, 1994; cons. April 14, 1994; appt. Bishop of Allentown Dec. 16, 1997; installed Third Bishop of Allentown Feb. 9, 1998; retired May 27, 2009.

Vicar General—Rev. Msgr. ALFRED A. SCHLERT, J.C.L., V.G., 4029 W. Tilghman St., Allentown, 18105-1538. Mailing Address: P.O. Box F, Allentown, 18105-1538. Tel: 610-437-0755; Fax: 610-433-7822.

Chancellor—Rev. Msgr. GERALD E. GOBITAS, Th.M., 4029 W. Tilghman St., Allentown, 18105-1538. Mailing Address: P.O. Box F, Allentown, 18105-1538. Tel: 610-437-0755; Fax: 610-433-7822.

Vice Chancellor—Rev. Msgr. DAVID L. JAMES, V.E., M.Div., J.C.L., 4029 W. Tilghman St., Allentown, 18105-1538. Tel: 610-437-0755; Fax: 610-433-7822. Mailing Address: P.O. Box F, Allentown, 18105-1538.

Secretary to the Bishop—Rev. Msgr. GERALD E. GOBITAS, Th.M., 4029 W. Tilghman St., Allentown, 18105. Mailing Address: P.O. Box F, Allentown, 18105-1538. Tel: 610-437-0755; Fax: 610-433-7822.

Council of Priests/Diocesan Consultors—4029 W. Tilghman St., P.O. Box F, Allentown, 18105. Tel: 610-437-0755; Fax: 610-433-7822.

College of Consultors—Rev. Msgrs. ALFRED A. SCHLERT, J.C.L., V.G.; THOMAS D. BADDICK, Th.M.; THOMAS A. DERZACK, M.Div.; Rev. ROBERT T. FINLAN, M.Div., M.A., M.Ed.; Rev. Msgrs. JOHN P. MURPHY; GERALD E. GOBITAS, Th.M.; DAVID L. JAMES, V.E., M.Div., J.C.L.; STEPHEN J. RADOCHA, V.F., M.Div.; JAMES J. REICHERT.

Ex Officio Members—Rev. Msgrs. ALFRED A. SCHLERT, J.C.L., V.G.; GERALD E. GOBITAS, Th.M.

Elected Members—Rev. Msgr. JOHN P. MURPHY; Revs. KENNETH A. MEDVE; JOSEPH T. WHALEN, M.Div.; Rev. Msgr. EDWARD R. SACKS, M.Ed.; Revs. THOMAS P. BORTZ, M.Div., S.T.B.; RONALD P. BOWMAN, M.Div., M.A.; ANDREW N. GEHRINGER, M.Div., M.A., S.T.B.; ROBERT T. FINLAN, M.Div., M.A., M.Ed.; DAVID J. KOZAK, J.C.L.; JOSEPH F. TOBIAS, M.S.C.; DEOGRATIAS RWEGASIRA, A.J.; Rev. Msgr. ROBERT M. FORST (Retired).

Appointed Members—Revs. SCOTT R. ARDINGER, M.Div., M.A., S.T.B.; ERIC R. ARNOUT, M.Div.; ADAM C. SEDAR, M.Div., M.A.; Rev. Msgrs. JOSEPH A. DESANTIS, M.Div.; WILLIAM T. BAKER, S.T.L.; DAVID L. JAMES, V.E., M.Div., J.C.L.; Rev. JEROME A. TAUBER, M.Div., S.T.B.

Finance Council—Most Rev. JOHN O. BARRES, S.T.D., J.C.L., D.D.; Rev. Msgr. ALFRED A. SCHLERT, J.C.L., V.G., 4029 W. Tilghman St., P.O. Box F, Allentown, 18105-1538. Tel: 610-437-0755; Fax: 610-433-7822; Mr. DENNIS DOMCHEK; Mr. P. MICHAEL EHLERMAN; Ms. AUDRA J. HOFFMAN; Mr. JOHN F. HORRIGAN JR.; Mr. HERMAN L. RIJ; Mr. PAUL E. HUCK; Mr. ROBERT J. SNYDER; Mr. JAMES A. TIEFENBRUNN; THOMAS F. TRAUD, Esq.; Mr. KERRY A. WROBEL.

Victim Assistance Coordinator—Mrs. HELEN P. KELLEHER, L.S.W. Tel: 800-791-9209; Fax: 610-791-1878. Email: hkelleher@allentowndiocese.org.

Censor of Books—Rev. Msgr. JAMES J. MULLIGAN, S.T.L.

Diocesan Tribunal—Very Rev. JOHN J. PAUL, M.S.C., V.J., S.T.L., J.C.D., Judicial Vicar, 202 N. 17th St., Allentown, 18104. Tel: 610-434-3200; Fax: 610-433-3104.

Judges—Rev. Msgrs. DAVID J. MORRISON (Retired); THOMAS P. KOONS, V.R., J.C.L., M.A., M.Div.; VICTOR F. FINELLI, J.C.L., Th.M., M.Div.

Promoter of Justice—Rev. Msgr. DAVID L. JAMES, V.E., M.Div., J.C.L.

Defenders of the Bond—Rev. Msgr. DAVID L. JAMES,

V.E., M.Div., J.C.L.; Rev. DAVID J. KOZAK, J.C.L.; Rev. Msgr. ALFRED A. SCHLERT, J.C.L., V.G.

Secretary—VACANT.

Advocates—Rev. Msgr. DAVID L. JAMES, V.E., M.Div., J.C.L.; Revs. ANDREW N. GEHRINGER, M.Div., M.A., S.T.B.; KEITH R. LASKOWSKI, M.Div., M.A., S.T.B.; BRIAN M. MILLER; STANLEY M. MOCZYDLOWSKI, M.B.A., M.Div.; MICHAEL E. MULLINS, M.Div., M.A., S.T.B.; ERIC N. TOLENTINO, M.Div.; Deacons THOMAS H. MILLER; WILLIAM R. HASSLER; THOMAS B. REIMER; CU T. THAN; MICHAEL V. WOODALL.

Notaries—Mrs. PATRICIA ECHTERNACH; Mrs. KATHLEEN SNYDER.

Vicar for Religious—Rev. Msgr. THOMAS P. KOONS, V.R., J.C.L., M.A., M.Div., Diocesan Tribunal, 202 N. 17th St., Allentown, 18104-5605. Tel: 610-434-3200; Fax: 610-433-3104. Email: tkoons@allentowndiocese.org.

Vicars Forane—Rev. Msgrs. JOHN G. CHIZMAR, V.F., M.Div., Carbon Deanery; DANIEL J. YENUSHOSKY, V.F., Th.M., Lehigh Deanery; DENNIS T. HARTGEN, V.F., Berks Deanery; STEPHEN J. RADOCHA, V.F., M.Div., Northampton Deanery; EDWARD J. O'CONNOR, M.Th., M.S.W., V.F., Schuylkill Deanery.

Human Resources—Mr. RONALD J. JACOBS, SPHR Dir., Mailing Address: P.O. Box F, Allentown, 18105-1538. Tel: 610-871-5200, Ext. 204; Fax: 610-871-5211. Email: rjacobs@allentowndiocese.org.

Secretariat for Clergy—Rev. Msgr. GERALD E. GOBITAS, Th.M., Sec., Mailing Address: P.O. Box F, Allentown, 18105-1538. Tel: 610-437-0755; Fax: 610-433-7822. Email: ggobitas@allentowndiocese.org.

Priest Personnel Office—Rev. Msgr. GERALD E. GOBITAS, Th.M., Dir., Mailing Address: P.O. Box F, Allentown, 18105-1538. Tel: 610-437-0755; Fax: 610-433-7822.

Holy Family Villa for Priests—Rev. Msgr. GERALD E. GOBITAS, Th.M., Rector, 1325 Prospect Ave., Bethlehem, 18018-4916. Tel: 610-694-0395; Fax: 610-694-9990.

Permanent Diaconate Office—Rev. Msgr. MICHAEL J. CHABACK, S.T.D., Dir., 2145 Madison Ave., Bethlehem, 18018-4642. Tel: 610-866-0581; Fax: 610-867-8702. Email: diaconate@allentowndiocese.org.

Vocations Office—Rev. Msgr. DAVID L. JAMES, V.E., V.R., M.Div., J.C.L., Dir., 4029 W. Tilghman St., Allentown, 18105-1538. Tel: 610-437-0755; Fax: 610-433-7822. Email: djames@allentowndiocese.org. Web: beapriest.com.

Priestly Life and Ministry Office—Rev. Msgr. JAMES J. MULLIGAN, S.T.L., Dir., Queenship of Mary Rectory, 1324 Newport Ave., Northampton, 18067-1442. Tel: 610-262-1885; Fax: 610-262-4192.

Secretariat for Catholic Life and Evangelization—MARY FRAN HARTIGAN, M.A., Sec., 900 S. Woodward St., Allentown, 18103-4179. Tel: 610-289-8900; Fax: 610-289-7917. Email: mhartigan@allentowndiocese.org.

Office of Faith Formation—MARY FRAN HARTIGAN, M.A., Dir., 900 S. Woodward St., Allentown, 18103-4179. Tel: 610-289-8900; Fax: 610-289-7917. Email: mhartigan@allentowndiocese.org.

Office of Marriage and Family Life Formation—Dr. CARMINA CHAPP, Coord. Email: cchapp@allentowndiocese.org; Mrs. CARLA NEUPAUER, Asst. Coord. Tel: 610-289-8900; Fax: 610-289-7917. Email: cneupauer@allentowndiocese.org.

Office of Youth and Young Adult Ministry—Rev. ALLEN J. HOFFA, M.Div., Coord. Email: ahoffa@allentowndiocese.org; Mrs. MARY ELLEN JOHNS, B.A., Asst. Coord. Tel: 610-289-8900; Fax: 610-289-7917. Email: mjohns@allentowndiocese.org.

Office of Adult Formation—Dr. CARMINA CHAPP, Coord. Tel: 610-289-8900; Fax: 610-289-7917. Email: cchapp@allentowndiocese.org.

Office of Rite of Christian Initiation of Adults (RCIA)—Rev. SCOTT R. ARDINGER, M.Div., M.A., S.T.B., Coord. Tel: 610-289-8900; Fax: 610-289-7917. Email: sardinger@allentowndiocese.org.

Office of Pro-Life and Social Concerns—Mr. MATTHEW HUMMEL, Coord., 900 S. Woodward St., Allentown, 18103-4179. Tel: 610-289-8900; Fax: 610-289-7917. Email: mhummel@allentowndiocese.org.

Office of Pro-Life Activities and Social Concerns—Mr. MATTHEW HUMMEL, Coord. Email: mhummel@allentowndiocese.org; Mrs. MARY ANN GENNA, Asst. Coord. Tel: 610-289-8900; Fax: 610-289-7917. Email: mgenna@allentowndiocese.org.

Office of Multi-Cultural Affairs—Mrs. MARY ANN GENNA, Coord. Tel: 610-289-8900; Fax: 610-289-7917. Email: mgenna@allentowndiocese.org.

Office of Hispanic Affairs—Rev. ANDREW N. GEHRINGER, M.Div., M.A., S.T.B., Dir. Tel: 610-289-8900; Fax: 610-289-7917. Email: agehringer@allentowndiocese.org.

Office of Prison Ministry—Rev. WILLIAM N. SEIFERT, M.Div., Coord. Tel: 610-289-8900; Fax: 610-289-7917. Email: wseifert@allentowndiocese.org.

Office of Ministry with Persons with Disabilities—Sr. JANICE MARIE JOHNSON, R.S.M., Coord. Tel: 610-289-8900; Fax: 610-289-7917. Email: jjohnson@allentowndiocese.org.

Office of Ecumenical and Interreligious Dialogue—Rev. Msgr. JOHN S. MRAZ, M.A., M.Ed., M.Div., Dir., 2174 Lincoln Ave., Northampton, 18067-1257. Tel: 610-965-2426; Fax: 610-967-1099. Email: churchofstann@rcn.com.

Office of Worship—Rev. SCOTT R. ARDINGER, M.Div., M.A., S.T.B., Dir., 900 S. Woodward St., Allentown, 18103-4179. Tel: 610-289-8900; Fax: 610-289-7917. Email: sardinger@allentowndiocese.org.

Secretariat for Temporal Affairs—Mr. MARK E. SMITH, CPA, CFO & Sec., P.O. Box F, Allentown, 18105-1538. Tel: 610-871-5200, Ext. 205; Fax: 610-871-5211. Email: msmith@allentowndiocese.org.

Banking and Investments—Mr. MARK D. HULLINGER, Dir., P.O. Box F, Allentown, 18105-1538. Tel: 610-871-5200, Ext. 288; Fax: 610-871-5211. Email: mhullinger@allentowndiocese.org.

Accounting Services—JEFFREY K. BUCK, Controller. Tel: 610-871-5200, Ext. 102; Fax: 610-871-5211. Email: jbuck@allentowndiocese.org; Mr. THOMAS O. KERN, C.E.B.S., Benefits & Payroll Mgr. Tel: 610-871-5200, Ext. 109; Fax: 610-871-5211. Email: tkern@allentowndiocese.org.

Parish and School Support Services—Mrs. LESLIE SHIROCK. Tel: 610-871-5200, Ext. 228; Fax: 610-871-5211. Email: lshirock@allentowndiocese.org.

Information Systems—VACANT. Tel: 610-871-5200, Ext. 239; Fax: 610-871-5211.

Cemeteries—Rev. Msgr. WILLIAM F. BAVER, M.Div., Th.M., C.C.C.E., K.C.H.S., Dir., P.O. Box F, Allentown, 18105-1538. Tel: 610-871-5200, Ext. 234; Fax: 610-871-5211. Email: wbaver@allentowndiocese.org.

Insurance and Real Estate—Ms. KELLY C. BRUCE, A.R.M., Dir. Tel: 610-871-5200, Ext. 203. Email: kbruce@allentowndiocese.org.

Secretariat for Stewardship and Development—Mr. JAMES S. FRIEND JR., P.O. Box F, Allentown, 18105-1538. Tel: 610-871-5200, Ext. 210; Fax: 610-871-5211. Email: jfriend@allentowndiocese.org.

Secretariat for Catholic Education—Mr. PHILIP J. FROMUTH, M.Ed., Sec., 2145 Madison Ave., Bethlehem, 18017-4642. Tel: 610-866-0581; Fax: 610-867-8702. Email: pfromuth@allentowndiocese.org.

Elementary School Religious Education—Ms. BARBARA AMABILE, Asst. Supt. Email: bamabile@allentowndiocese.org.

Religious Education—Ms. BARBARA AMABILE, Asst. Supt. Email: bamabile@allentowndiocese.org.

Curriculum, Supervision and Professional Development (Elementary/Secondary Schools)—Sr. ANITA PATRICK GALLAGHER, I.H.M., Asst. Supt. Email: agallagher@allentowndiocese.org.

Personnel (Elementary and Secondary)—Sr. ROBERTA PETERS, I.H.M., Asst. Supt. Email: rpeters@allentowndiocese.org.

Early Childhood Education—Sr. ANITA PATRICK GALLAGHER, I.H.M., Asst. Supt. Email: agallagher@allentowndiocese.org.

Secondary Schools—VACANT, Asst. Supt.

Special Education Programs—Mr. LOUIS RUSNOCK, Dir. Tel: 610-866-0581, Ext. 25; Fax: 610-867-8702. Email: lrusnock@allentowndiocese.org.

Government Programs—Ms. KATHLEEN BONDI, Dir. Tel: 610-866-0581; Fax: 610-867-8702. Email: kbondi@allentowndiocese.org.

Instructional Technology—Ms. KATHLEEN BONDI, Dir. Tel: 610-866-0581; Fax: 610-867-8702. Email: kbondi@allentowndiocese.org.

Board of Education—Mr. EUGENE M. LENNON, Pres.

Secretariat for Catholic Human Services—Mrs. HELEN P. KELLEHER, L.S.W., Sec., 2141 Downyflake Ln., Allentown, 18103-4774. Tel: 610-791-3888; Fax: 610-791-1878. Email: hkelleher@allentowndiocese.org.

Catholic Charities—Mrs. HELEN P. KELLEHER, L.S.W., Exec. Dir., 2141 Downyflake Ln., Allentown, 18103-4774. Tel: 610-791-3888; Fax: 610-791-1878. Web: catholiccharityad.org.

Catholic Senior Housing and Health Care Services, Inc.—

Holy Family Manor—Mrs. HEATHER KESSLER, N.H.A., Admin., 1200 Spring St., Bethlehem, 18018. Tel: 610-865-5595; Fax: 610-997-5442. Web: www.hfmanor.org.

Holy Family Residential Services—Mrs. KAREN ABRUZZESE, Coord., 1200 Spring St., Bethlehem, 18018. Tel: 610-865-5595; Fax: 610-997-8454. Web: www.hfmanor.org.

Collaborative Residential and Home Care Services—SANDRA LEE LEVENGOOD, M.B.A., R.N., Exec. Dir., 1223 Pottsville Pike, Shoemakersville, 19555-1719. Tel: 570-385-5522; Fax: 570-385-5287. Email: slevengood@covenanthc.org.

Diocesan Medical Ethicist—Rev. Msgr. JAMES J. MULLIGAN, S.T.L., Dir., Queenship of Mary Rectory, 1324 Newport Ave., Northampton, 18067-1442. Tel: 610-262-1885; Fax: 610-262-4192.

Saint Vincent De Paul Society—Rev. FRANCIS P. STRAKA, Spiritual Advisor; Ms. ELIZABETH HARRISON, Pres. Diocesan Council, 969 Port Carbon St., Pottsville, 17901. Tel: 570-622-6289.

Secretariat for External Affairs—Mr. MATTHEW T. KERR, Dir., Mailing Address: P.O. Box F, Allentown, 18105-1538. Tel: 610-871-5200, Ext. 265; Fax: 610-439-7694. Email: mkerr@allentowndiocese.org.

Office of Communications—Mr. MATTHEW T. KERR, Dir. Tel: 610-871-5200, Ext. 265; Fax: 610-439-7694. Email: mkerr@allentowndiocese.org.

Office of Government Affairs—Mr. MATTHEW T. KERR, Dir. Tel: 610-871-5200, Ext. 265; Fax: 610-439-7694. Email: mkerr@allentowndiocese.org.

The A.D. Times—Mrs. JILL M. CARAVAN, Editor & Dir. Tel: 610-871-5200, Ext. 264; Fax: 610-439-7694. Email: adtimes@allentowndiocese.org.

Allentown Catholic Communications, Inc.—Most Rev. JOHN O. BARRES, S.T.D., J.C.L., D.D., Pres.; Rev. Msgr. ALFRED A. SCHLERT, J.C.L., V.G., Sec. Tel: 610-871-5200, Ext. 264; Fax: 610-439-7694.

Affiliated Organizations

American Catholic Overseas Aid Fund—Mailing Address: P.O. Box F, Allentown, 18105-1538. Tel: 610-437-0755; Fax: 610-433-7822.

Blue Army of Our Lady of Fatima—2483 Community Dr., Bath, 18014. Tel: 610-614-1218. Email: thesixfamily@enter.net. Mr. MICHAEL A. SIX, Pres.; Rev. DOMINIC THAO PHAM, M.Div., Spiritual Dir.

Catholic Daughters of the Americas—Rev. FLOYD CAESAR JR., Diocese Committee Chap.

Ashland - Court St. Joan of Arc #225—Rev. JOHN W. BAMBRICK, Chap.

Easton - Court Easton #358—Rev. DEOGRATIAS RWEGASIRA, A.J., Chap.

Frackville - Court St. James #1029—Rev. ROBERT T. FINLAN, M.Div., M.A., M.Ed., Chap.

Girardville - Court St. Cecilia #1529—Rev. EDWARD B. CONNOLLY, M.Div., M.Ed., Chap.

Jim Thorpe - Court Ryan #911—Rev. JAMES J. WARD, M.Div., Chap.

Shenandoah - Court Annunciation #175—VACANT, Chap.

Catholic Men of Good News (CMOGN)—Rev. LARRY J. HESS, M.A., Our Lady of Good Counsel, 436 S. 2nd St., Bangor, 18013-2514. Tel: 610-588-5445; Fax: 610-599-6997.

Charismatic Renewal—Rev. LARRY J. HESS, M.A., Bishop's Liaison. Assistants: Rev. CLIFTON E. BISHOP; Deacon ANTHONY T. CAMPANELL, Our Lady of Good Counsel Rectory, 436 S. 2nd St., Bangor, 18013-2514. Tel: 610-588-5445; Fax: 610-599-6997. Email: olgc2002@epix.net.

Courage—Mailing Address: P.O. Box F, Allentown, 18105-1538. Tel: 610-217-5557.

Cursillo Movement—Rev. MARTIN F. KERN, Spiritual Dir., St. Columbkill Rectory, 200 Indian Spring Rd., Boyertown, 19512-2008. Tel: 610-367-2371; Fax: 610-369-0242.

Father Walter Ciszek Prayer League, Inc. (The)—Rev. Msgr. RONALD C. BOCIAN, M.Ed., Bd. Pres., The Ciszek Center, 231 N. Jardin St., Shenandoah, 17976-1642. Tel: 570-462-2270; Fax: 570-462-2274. Email: fwccenter@verizon.net. Web: www.ciszek.org.

Holy Name Societies—Rev. PAUL L. ROTHERMEL, M.Div., Th.M., M.A., Most Blessed Trinity Rectory, P.O. Box 35, Tremont, 17981-0035. Tel: 570-695-3648; Fax: 570-695-2275.

Knights of Columbus—

St. Peter the Fisherman Council #10772, Lake Harmony, District #41—ANTHONY VASSALLO, Grand Knight, Mailing Address: P.O. Box 892, Blakeslee, 18610. Tel: 570-430-3522. Email: webmaster@kofc10772.com.

St. Joseph the Worker Council #10921, Orefield, District #33—JAMES MUELLER, Grand Knight, Mailing Address: 5211 Wagonwheel Dr., Schnecksville, 18078. Tel: 610-769-0555. Email: jim@jnsc.org.

St. Paul Council #10922, Allentown, District #33—VACANT, Grand Knight.

Calvary Council #528, Allentown, District #32—RONALD WALBERT, Grand Knight, Mailing Address: 843 W. Greenleaf St., Allentown, 18102. Tel: 610-349-5942.

Sarto Council #1322, Ashland District #54—FRANK BIRSTER, Grand Knight, Mailing Address: 1109

Centre St., Ashland, 17921. Tel: 570-875-2929. Email: mgm@ptd.net.

Father DeNisco Council #3862, Bangor, District #34—GREGORY KENNEDY, Grand Knight, Mailing Address: 1759 Mountain Rd., Saylorsburg, 18353. Tel: 570-922-5366. Email: erjon@ptd.net.

Trinity Council #313, Bethlehem, District #32—JOHN F. SPIRK JR., Grand Knight, Mailing Address: 404 Apollo Dr., Bethlehem, 18017. Tel: 610-954-0347. Email: jspirk@northampton.com.

Union Council #345, Easton, District #34—WILLIAM EISMONT, Grand Knight, Mailing Address: 2680 Upper Way, Easton, 18040. Tel: 610-258-4810. Email: wteismont@ptd.net.

St. Ann Council #12886, Emmaus, District #33—RONALD SCHOCK, Grand Knight, Mailing Address: 1541 Par Causeway, Wescosville, 18106. Tel: 610-391-0255. Email: larkschock@enter.net.

Rev. James A. Hogan Council #2580, Frackville, District #39—THOMAS MALLOY, Grand Knight, Mailing Address: 13 N. 6th St., Frackville, 17931. Tel: 570-874-1843. Email: tjmalloy@verizon.net.

Father Sheridan Council #748, Girardville, District #40—VACANT, Grand Knight.

Damien Council #598, Jim Thorpe, District #41—(Serving Jim Thorpe, Lehighton, Nesquehoning and the surrounding areas). CHRISTOPHER A. HEERY, Grand Knight, 154 Semmels Hill Rd., Lehighton, 18235. Tel: 570-386-9210. Email: cahi@desales.edu.

Archbishop Ryan Council #1552, Lansford, District #41—FRANK SERINA, Grand Knight, Mailing Address: 107 W. Bertsch St., Lansford, 18232. Tel: 570-645-5221.

Mahanoy City Council #549, Mahanoy City, District #40—GEORGE KRALL, Grand Knight, Mailing Address: 214 W. Spruce St., Mahanoy City, 17948.

St. Benedict Council #14654, Mohnton, District #28—JOHN COCCO, Grand Knight, Mailing Address: 247 Gebhart School Rd., Mohnton, 19540. Tel: 610-856-5176. Email: grandknight@knightsofsaintbenedict.org.

Our Lady of the Sacred Heart Council #4282, Nazareth, District #34—WILLIAM J. TANZOSH, Grand Knight, Mailing Address: 615 Hill Ave., Nazareth, 18064. Tel: 610-759-3161. Email: billsjustplain@verizon.net.

Queenship of Mary Council #4050, Northampton, District #34—JOHN HABIAK, Grand Knight, Mailing Address: 1128 Sherwood Dr., Laurys Station, 18059. Tel: 610-262-4569.

Lafayette Council #2522, Palmerton, District #41—VACANT, Grand Knight.

Schuylkill Council #431, Pottsville, District #39—GEORGE F. HALCOVAGE JR., Grand Knight, Mailing Address: 1282 Oak Terr., Pottsville, 17901. Tel: 570-640-2013. Email: georgejr@ptd.net.

Reading Council #793, Reading, District #28—LEONARD WECKEL, Grand Knight, Mailing Address: 570 Guldin Rd., Blandon, 19510. Tel: 610-223-0800.

Holy Eucharist Council #4198, Reading, District #28—JOHN KUZMINSKI, Grand Knight, Mailing Address: 527 Park Ave., Reading, 19611. Tel: 610-372-5561.

Father John Newman Council #14009, Saint Clair, District #39—ANTHONY KLAZAS, Grand Knight, Mailing Address: 545 E. Lawton St., Saint Clair, 17970. Tel: 570-617-9403. Email: heidi318@verizon.net.

Francis Cardinal Brennan Council #618, Shenandoah, District #40—WILLIAM APPLEGATE, Grand Knight, Mailing Address: 108 N. White St., Shenandoah, 17976. Tel: 570-985-7476.

Holy Name Council #7179, Shillington, District #28—RONALD SZURGOT, Grand Knight, Mailing Address: 410 March St., Shillington, 19607. Tel: 610-796-8092.

Light of Christ Council #8726, Sinking Spring, District #28—ANTHONY CALDERONI, Grand Knight, Mailing Address: 2314 Gring Dr., Reading, 19607. Tel: 610-927-3208. Email: calderoni@verizon.net.

Father Henry Baker Council #2711, Tamaqua, District #43—JOSEPH HNAT, Grand Knight, Mailing Address: 24 W. High St., Coaldale, 18218. Tel: 570-645-3930.

St. Nicholas Council #12105, Weatherly, District #42—VACANT, Grand Knight.

District #28—JOSEPH PASCUZZI, District Deputy, Mailing Address: 3337 Harrison Ave., Reading, 19605. Tel: 610-921-2481. Email: jlpascuzzi@enter.net.

District #32—JOSEPH DADAY, District Deputy, Mailing Address: 960 Yorkshire Rd., Bethlehem, 18017. Tel: 610-428-3617. Email: jdaday@shh.org.

District #33—ROBERT GOWELL, District Deputy, Mailing Address: 1794 Applewood Dr., Orefield, 18069. Tel: 610-391-9855. Email: marshalbob@verizon.net.

District #34—BRUCE WERMANN, District Deputy, Mailing Address: 5621 Heather Lane, Laurys Station, 18059. Tel: 610-262-0191. Email: spundt2@verizon.net.

District #39—JOHN MATULEVICH, District Deputy, Mailing Address: 17 Cinder Alley, Saint Clair, 17970. Tel: 570-429-1596. Email: jmat@ptd.net.

District #40—JOSEPH RUTH, District Deputy, Mailing Address: 1428 Long Lane Rd., Lenhartsville, 19534. Tel: 610-756-6970. Email: joruth@state.pa.us.

District #41—DAVID MICHAEL, District Deputy, Mailing Address: P.O. Box 612, Albrightsville, 18210. Tel: 570-722-1234.

District #43—WILLIAM ZAMMER, District Deputy, Mailing Address: 32 Rymin Rd., Tamaqua, 18252. Tel: 570-668-5300. Email: zammerw@ptd.net.

District #54—DAVID SHINSKIE, District Deputy, Mailing Address: 307 Chestnut St., Kulpmont, 17834. Tel: 570-373-1355. Email: david.shinskie@erieinsurance.com.

Legatus—Mr. LEN MARRELLA, 25 Pinewood Rd., Wyomissing, 19610-1972. Tel: 610-478-1148; Fax: 610-288-5801; Mrs. DEE MARRELLA; Rev. Msgr. JOHN P. MURPHY, Chap.

Legion of Mary—Mr. JOE AKKARA, Pres., 29 Mulligan Dr., Reading, 19606. Tel: 610-301-5139.

National Shut-In Visitation Society—VACANT, Natl. Dir., Holy Rosary, 237 Franklin St., Reading, 19602-1034. Tel: 610-373-5579.

Operation Rice Bowl—Rev. Msgr. JOHN P. MURPHY, Dir., St. Thomas More, 1040 Flexer Ave., Allentown, 18103-5520. Tel: 610-433-7413; Fax: 610-433-2308.

Our Lady's Missionaries of the Eucharist—VACANT A Public Association of Christ's Faithful. Magnificat House, 640 E. Main St., Birdsboro, 19508. Tel: 610-582-3333; Fax: 610-582-2456. Email: olme@olme.org. Web: www.olme.org.

Secular Franciscan Order - St. Francis Fraternity—St. Francis Retreat House, 3918 Chipman Rd., Easton, 18045-3014. Tel: 610-258-3053; Fax: 610-258-2412. NANCY SNYDER, S.F.O., Min., 1296 Hedgerow Dr., Easton, 18040. Tel: 610-252-5230. Email: lmpnurpara@msn.com.

Serra Clubs—

Serra Club of Allentown—Rev. Msgr. DANIEL J. YENUSHOSKY, V.F., Th.M., Chap.; Mrs. MARIE MAZZINI, Pres., 3282 Golden Key Rd., New Tripoli, 18066. Tel: 610-285-2002. Email: m.mazzini@att.net.

Forks of the Delaware Serra—Rev. ERIC N. TOLENTINO, M.Div., Chap.; Mr. VINCENT PRESTO, Vice Pres. Vocations, 59 Central Dr., Easton, 18045. Tel: 610-253-0223. Email: vpresto@stokeselectric.com.

Serra Club of Bethlehem—Rev. ANTHONY P. MONGIELLO, Chap.; JOHN M. TOBIN, Pres., 872 Media St., Bethlehem, 18017. Tel: 610-868-0250. Email: jmt872@msn.com.

Serra Club of Reading—Rev. PAUL L. ROTHERMEL, M.Div., Th.M., M.A., Chap.; Mr. STEPHEN C. HAHN, Pres., 31 Sycamore Dr., Reading, 19606. Tel: 610-779-8477.

Carbon/Schuylkill Serra Club—Rev. JAMES C. BECHTEL, M.Div., Chap.; DIANE SURAVICZ, Vice Pres. Programs, 1877 Quakake Rd., Weatherly, 18255. Tel: 570-427-8724.

Catholic Business Owners Alliance—Mailing Address: P.O. Box F, Allentown, 18105-1538. Tel: 610-871-5200, Ext. 210. RAY BISHOP, Pres.; Mr. JAMES S. FRIEND JR., Diocesan Representative.

St. Thomas More Society—Cathedral of St. Catharine of Siena, 1825 W. Turner St., Allentown, 18104. Tel: 610-433-6461; Fax: 610-433-5452. Email: info@stmsallentown.org. Web: www.stmsallentown.org. Mr. JOHN L. KRAJSA JR., Pres.

Third Order Dominican Expectation of Blessed Virgin Mother Chapter—Dr. FELICIDAD QUILO, Moderator, Notre Dame of Bethlehem Church, 1861 Catasauqua Rd., Bethlehem, 18018-1298. Tel: 610-691-6761.

Third Order Secular Carmelites—Holy Rosary Parish, 237 Franklin St., Reading, 19602-1034. Tel: 610-373-5579.

Miscellaneous Affiliated Organizations

Dayspring Homes, Inc.—Mr. DWAYNE ALBRIGHT, CEO; CATHY BEWLEY, Dir. Mission; Sr. FRANCIS BISLAND, C.P.S., Mailing Address: P.O. Box 158, Reading, 19607-0172. Tel: 610-374-9036; Fax: 610-374-9086. Email: dayspringhomes@dayspringhomes.org.

Mary's Shelter—BRENDA GEHRING, M.S.W., Prog. Dir.; DANIELLE MONAHAN, M.S.W., Asst. Exec. Dir., 325 S. 12th St., Reading, 19602-2021. Tel: 610-376-1973; Fax: 610-376-5391. Email: maryshelterrdg@verizon.net. Web: www.marysshelter.org.

Mary's Home—CHRISTINE FOLK, Exec. Dir., 736 Upland Ave., Reading, 19607. Tel: 610-603-8010; Fax: 610-603-8012. Email: chris@marysshelter.org; marysshelterrdg@verizon.net. Web: www.marysshelter.org.

Stephen's Place, Inc.—Sr. VIRGINIA LONGCOPE, M.S.C., M.S.W., Dir., 729 Ridge Ave., Bethlehem, 18015-3621. Tel: 610-861-7677; Fax: 610-861-7677. Email: vlongcope@msn.com. Web: www.stephens-place.com.

CLERGY, PARISHES, MISSIONS AND PAROCHIAL SCHOOLS

CITY OF ALLENTOWN

(LEHIGH COUNTY)

1—CATHEDRAL OF ST. CATHARINE OF SIENA (1919), (Indian), Rev. Msgr. Andrew R. Baker; Revs. Eric N. Tolentino; Brian M. Miller; Deacon William Hassler. Students 350.
Res.: 1825 W. Turner St., 18104. Tel: 610-433-6461; Fax: 610-433-5452. Email: cathsec@ptd.net.
See John Vianney Regional School under Regional Catholic Elementary Schools, Diocesan located in the Institution section.
Catechesis/Religious Program—Tel: 610-432-7655. Sr. Laura Berryman, S.C.C., D.R.E. Students 485.

2—ST. FRANCIS OF ASSISI (1928) Rev. Msgr. Victor F. Finelli; Deacon Robert P. Young. In Res., Rev. Msgr. Thomas P. Koons.
Res.: 801 N. 11th St., 18102-1304. Tel: 610-433-6102; Fax: 610-434-6972.
Business Office—1046 W. Cedar St., 18102-1304. Tel: 610-433-6102; Fax: 610-434-6972. Email: stephe@ptd.net.
Parish Center—1046 W. Cedar St., 18102-1304.
See St. John Vianney Regional School under Regional Catholic Elementary Schools, Diocesan located in the Institution section.
Catechesis/Religious Program—Tel: 610-435-0364. Email: stfrancisprep@yahoo.com. Marianne Schubert, D.R.E. Students 100.

3—IMMACULATE CONCEPTION (1857) [CEM], (Declared National Shrine of Our Lady of Guadalupe, Mother of the Americas 1974). Rev. Msgr. Albert J. Byrne; Deacon Richard L. Benkovic. In Res., Rev. Edwin V. Schwartz (Retired).
Res.: 501 Ridge Ave., 18102. Tel: 610-433-4404; Fax: 610-433-8401.
Schools-See St. Elizabeth Regional School under Regional Catholic Elementary Schools, Diocesan located in the Institution section.
Catechesis/Religious Program—Students 20.

4—ST. JOHN THE BAPTIST, (Slovak), [CEM] Rev. Dominik P. Kalata.
Res.: 924 N. Front St., 18102-1912. Tel: 610-432-0034; Fax: 610-432-2776. Email: stjohn924@aol.com. Web: www.saintjohnthebaptist.net.
See St. Elizabeth Regional School under Regional Catholic Elementary Schools, Diocesan located in the Institution section.
Convent—920 N. Front St., 18102-1998. Tel: 610-434-1471.

5—OUR LADY HELP OF CHRISTIANS (1927) Rev. John S. Pendzick. In Res., Rev. Clifton E. Bishop; Rev. Msgr. Robert M. Forst (Retired).
Res.: 444 N. Jasper St., 18109-2666. Tel: 610-432-9384; Fax: 610-782-9297.
School—934 Hanover Ave., 18109-2011. Tel: 610-433-1592; Fax: 610-434-7123. Ms. Mary K. Vanya, Prin.
Catechesis/Religious Program—Students 185.
Convent—922 Hanover Ave., 18109-2011. Tel: 610-433-4915.

6—ST. PAUL (1928) Rev. Andrew N. Gehringer, Admin.; Deacons Gary Granato; Cu T. Than; Saul Hernandez. In Res., Rev. Gregory R. Karpyn, Pastoral Ministry, Allentown Hospitals & Nursing Homes.
Res.: 920 S. Second St., 18103. Tel: 610-797-9733; Fax: 610-797-9537. Email: sprcc1@rcn.com.
Church: Second St. & Susquehanna St., 18103.
See John Vianney Regional School under Regional Catholic Elementary Schools, Diocesan located in the Institution section.
Catechesis/Religious Program—Students 100.

7—SS. PETER AND PAUL (1912), (Polish), Rev. Dominik P. Kalata.

Parish Office: 924 N. Front St., 18102. Tel: 610-432-0034; Fax: 610-432-2776.
Res.: 1065 Fullerton Ave., 18102.
See St. Elizabeth Regional School under Regional Catholic Elementary Schools, Diocesan located in the Institution section.
Catechesis/Religious Program—Students 4.

8—SACRED HEART OF JESUS (1869) [CEM] Rev. Msgr. John J. Grabish; Rev. Angel L. Garcia Almodovar; Deacons Roberto Reyes; Julian Corchado; Jose M. Santos Gonzalez.
Res.: 336 N. Fourth St., 18102-3008. Tel: 610-434-5171; Fax: 610-434-2441.
School—(Grades PreK-8), 325 N. Fourth St., 18102-3007. Tel: 610-437-3031; Fax: 610-437-2724. Email: altlsh@ptd.net. James Krupka, Prin. Lay Teachers 13; Students 325.
Catechesis/Religious Program—317 N. 4th St., 18102. Tel: 610-434-5171, Ext. 21; Fax: 610-434-2441. Ms. Katharine Watt, D.R.E. Students 286.

9—ST. STEPHEN OF HUNGARY (1915), (Hungarian), Rev. William N. Seifert.
Res.: 510 W. Union St., 18101-2307. Tel: 610-439-0111; Fax: 610-439-6048. Email: ststephenofhun@aol.com.
See Sacred Heart School, Allentown under Regional Catholic Elementary Schools, Diocesan located in the Institution section.

10—ST. THOMAS MORE (1966) Rev. Msgr. John P. Murphy; Rev. Keith A. Mathur; Deacons James R. Duncan; James Toolan; Ralph J. Jaccodine; Fredic W. Lash Jr.; Thomas F. Schubella. In Res., Rev. Allen J. Hoffa.
Res.: 1040 Flexer Ave., 18103-5520. Tel: 610-433-7413; Fax: 610-433-2308. Email: rectory@stmchurchallentown.org. Web: www.stmchurchallentown.org.
School—Tel: 610-432-0396; Fax: 610-432-1395. Email: altlstm@ptd.com. Web: www.stmschoolpa-.com. Dr. Carl P. Weber, Prin. Bernardine Sisters 2; Lay Teachers 47; Students 620.
Catechesis/Religious Program—Tel: 610-437-3491; Fax: 610-437-4935. Kevin Damitz, D.R.E. Students 601.
Convent—992 Flexer Ave., 18103-3664. Tel: 610-437-9520; Fax: 610-432-9359.

OUTSIDE CITY OF ALLENTOWN

ASHLAND, SCHUYLKILL CO.

1—ST. JOSEPH (1856) [CEM] Rev. John W. Bambrick. 1115 Walnut St., 17921-1845.
Res.: 802 Pine St., 17921-1845. Tel: 570-875-1521; Fax: 570-875-2635.
See Trinity Academy at the Father Walter J. Ciszek Education Center, Shenandoah under Regional Catholic Elementary Schools, Diocesan located in the Institution section.
Catechesis/Religious Program—Students 53.

2—ST. MAURITIUS (1856), (German), [CEM] Rev. John W. Bambrick.
Office: 1115 Walnut St., 17921. Tel: 570-875-1521; Fax: 570-875-2635.
Res.: 802 Pine St., 17921. Fax: 570-875-2635.
See Trinity Academy at the Father Walter J. Ciszek Education Center, Shenandoah under Regional Catholic Elementary Schools, Diocesan located in the Institution section.
Catechesis/Religious Program—Tel: 570-875-1521. Students 27.

BALLY, BERKS CO., MOST BLESSED SACRAMENT (1741) [CEM] Rev. Msgr. Edward J. Coyle; Rev. Michael J. Briggman, Pastor Emeritus (Retired); Deacons Thomas J. Murphy; Michael J. Boyle.
Res.: 610 Pine St., Box C, 19503-1003. Tel: 610-845-2460; Fax: 610-845-2660.
See St. Francis Academy, Bally under Regional Catholic Elementary Schools, Diocesan located in the Institution section.
Catechesis/Religious Program—Students 625.

BANGOR, NORTHAMPTON CO., OUR LADY OF GOOD COUNSEL (1915) [CEM] Rev. Stephen L. Maco.
Res.: 436 S. Second St., 18013-2514. Tel: 610-588-5445; Fax: 610-599-6997. Email: olgc2002@epix.net.
See Our Lady of Mt. Carmel School, Roseto under Regional Catholic Elementary Schools, Diocesan located in the Institution section.
Catechesis/Religious Program—Tel: 570-897-6941; 610-588-2602. Elizabeth Thompson, D.R.E.; Pricilla Pecca, D.R.E. Students 136.
Mission—St. Vincent de Paul 720 Delaware Ave., Portland, Northampton Co. 18351.

BARNESVILLE, SCHUYLKILL CO., ST. RICHARD (1950) Rev. Joseph T. Whalen.
Res.: 799 Barnesville Dr., 18214-9747. Tel: 570-467-2315; Fax: 570-467-2462.
Catechesis/Religious Program—

BATH, NORTHAMPTON CO., SACRED HEART OF JESUS (1920) [CEM] Rev. Msgr. Francis A. Nave; Deacon Lewis T. Ferris.
Res.: 210 E. Northampton St., 18014-1625. Tel: 610-837-7874; Fax: 610-837-4570. Email: office@sacredheartchurch.com. Web: www.sacredheartchurch.com.
School—(Grades PreK-8), 115 Washington St., 18014-1524. Tel: 610-837-6391; Fax: 610-837-2469. Email: office@shschool.us. Web: www.sacred-heart-school.com. Mrs. Donna M. Blaszka, Prin.; Mary Kay Duckworth, Librarian. Students 113.
Catechesis/Religious Program—Mrs. Rose Prentice, D.R.E. Tel: 610-837-7874, Ext. 26. Students 599.

BETHLEHEM, LEHIGH CO.

1—ASSUMPTION B.V.M. (1927) Rev. Msgrs. John J. Martin; Robert J. Coll, Pastor Emeritus (Retired); Deacons Richard Thoden; Donald W. Elliott; William F. Urbine.
Res.: 4101 Old Bethlehem Pike, 18015-9097. Tel: 610-867-7424; Fax: 610-867-8301. Email: abvmrect@ptd.net. Web: www.assumptionbethlehem.com.
See St. Michael the Archangel School, Coopersburg under Regional Catholic Elementary Schools, Diocesan located in the Institution section.
Catechesis/Religious Program—Tel: 610-814-0712. Christina Bigatel Durback, D.R.E. Students 595.

2—NOTRE DAME OF BETHLEHEM (1954) Rev. Msgr. Thomas D. Baddick; Rev. Patrick H. Lamb; Deacon Michael W. Doncsecz. In Res., Revs. Achilles Ayaton; Bernard J. Ezaki.
Res.: 1861 Catasauqua Rd., 18018-1298. Tel: 610-866-4371; Fax: 610-866-9065. Web: www.churchofndbeth.org.
School—(Grades K-8), 1835 Catasauqua Rd., 18018-1211. Tel: 610-866-2231; Fax: 610-866-4374. Email: altlndb@ptd.net. Web: www.ndbeth.org. Mrs. Kathy Maziarz, Prin.; Mrs. Rosalie Wertman, Librarian. Lay Teachers 27; Students 404.
Catechesis/Religious Program—Tel: 610-866-1418. Mrs. Stephanie Kalavoda, D.R.E. Students 274.

3—SS. SIMON AND JUDE (1917) Rev. Msgr. William F. Baver; Deacons Reuben H. Hartzell Jr.; Jeffrey R. Trexler.
Res.: 730 W. Broad St., 18018. Tel: 610-866-5582; Fax: 610-866-2992.
See Seton Academy, Bethlehem under Regional Catholic Elementary Schools.
Catechesis/Religious Program—Tel: 610-866-5582, Ext. 7. Students 58.

BETHLEHEM, NORTHAMPTON CO.

1—ST. ANNE (1929) Revs. Anthony P. Mongiello; A. Braham; Deacons Francis J. Cosgrove; Richard L. Gergar.
Res.: 450 E. Washington Ave., 18017-5944. Tel: 610-867-5039; Fax: 610-882-4094. Email: st.annes.rectory@verizon.net. Web: www.stannebethlehem.catholicweb.com.
School—(Grades PreK-8), 375 Hickory St., 18017-5944. Tel: 610-868-4182; 610-868-7513 (pre-school); Fax: 610-868-8709. Email: altnsa@ptd.net. Web: www.stannebethlehem.org. Mrs. Annette M. Filler, Prin. Students 390.
Catechesis/Religious Program—Students 180.

2—HOLY GHOST (1871), (German), [CEM] Rev. Wayne E. Killian; Rev. Msgr. Richard J. Loeper, Pastor Emeritus (Retired); Deacon Franklin J. Chiles.
See Seton Academy, Bethlehem under Regional Catholic Elementary Schools, Diocesan located in the Institution section.
Holy Ghost Pre-School—Tel: 610-867-5939. Mrs. Jane Zakovitch, Dir.
Catechesis/Religious Program—Tel: 610-867-9382. Mrs. Mary C. Elliott, D.R.E.

3—HOLY INFANCY (1861) [CEM] Rev. Msgr. Robert J. Biszek; Rev. Robson Luis Weber; Rev. Msgr. Joseph R. Sobiesiak; Deacons Nicasio Rodriguez; Manuel Ramirez; Rodoberto Matos.
Res.: 312 E. Fourth St., 18015-1706. Tel: 610-866-1121; Fax: 610-866-7094. Email: holyinfancy@aol.com.
School—(Grades PreK-8), 127 E. 4th St., 18015-1707. Tel: 610-868-2621; Fax: 610-868-5402. Email: altnhi@ptd.net. Sr. Joyce Valese, S.S.J., Prin. Students 170.
Catechesis/Religious Program— Sr. Moira Frawley, O.S.F., D.R.E. Tel: 610-866-1121, Ext. 12. Students 377.
Convent—Sisters of St. Joseph, 202 E. 4th St., 18015-1704. Tel: 610-867-7384. Email: sjoyce@onecommail.com.
Convent—Poor Sisters of St. Joseph, Casa Belen, 305 E. Fourth St., 18015. Tel: 610-867-4030. Email: hnasbelen@att.net. Sr. Rosa B. But, P.S.S.J., Supr.

4—INCARNATION OF OUR LORD PARISH (2008) [CEM], Formed by the merger of Our Lady of Pompeii, St. John Capistrano, St. Joseph, St. Stanislaus and SS. Cyril and Methodius, Bethlehem. Rev. Stanley M. Moczydlowski.
Thomas and Buchanan Sts., 18015.
Rectory—617 Pierce St., 18015-3498. Tel: 610-866-3391; Fax: 610-866-6490.
See Seton Academy, Bethlehem under Regional Catholic Elementary Schools, Diocesan located in the Institution section.
Convent—520 Buchanan St., 18015-3499. Tel: 610-866-0275.
Catechesis/Religious Program—Students 18.

5—OUR LADY OF PERPETUAL HELP (1963) Rev. Msgr. Edward R. Sacks; Rev. Eric R. Arnout; Deacons Joseph G. Buragino; George C. Kelly Jr. In Res., Rev. Msgr. David J. Morrison (Retired).
Res.: 3219 Santee Rd., 18020. Tel: 610-867-8409; Fax: 610-867-4870.
School—3221 Santee Rd., 18020. Tel: 610-868-6570; Fax: 610-868-7941. Lay Teachers 14; Students 295.
Catechesis/Religious Program—Students 484.

6—SACRED HEART OF JESUS (1936) Rev. Robert J. George; Deacon Hugh Carlin.
Res.: 1817 First St., 18020. Tel: 610-865-5042; Fax: 610-865-1912. Email: shchbeth@etd.net.
Catechesis/Religious Program—Tel: 610-867-0221. Students 100.

BOYERTOWN, BERKS CO., ST. COLUMBKILL (1921) Rev. Martin F. Kern; Deacons Michael Woodall; Joseph L. Paschall Jr.
Res.: 200 Indian Spring Rd., 19512-2008. Tel: 610-367-2371; Fax: 610-369-0242. Email: pastor@stcolumbkill.com. Web: stcolumbkill.com.
See St. Francis Academy, Bally under Regional Catholic Elementary Schools, Diocesan located in the Institution section.
Catechesis/Religious Program—Sr. Nancy Kramer, S.S.J., D.R.E.; Constance Boyer, D.R.E. Students 645.

CATASAUQUA, LEHIGH CO., ANNUNCIATION B.V.M.-ST. MARY'S (1857), (German), [CEM] Rev. Anthony M. Drouncheck; Deacon Joseph H. Bogusky.
Res.: 122 Union St., 18032-1923. Tel: 610-264-0332; Fax: 610-264-5271.
Catechesis/Religious Program—Tel: 610-264-9383. Christina Moriarty, D.R.E. Students 64.

CATASAUQUA, NORTHAMPTON CO.

1—ST. ANDREW (1902), (Slovak), [CEM] Rev. Eric J. Gruber, Admin.
Mailing Address: 1001 2nd St., 18032-2764. Tel: 610-264-1972; Fax: 610-264-2105.
Church: 1229 3rd St., North Catasauqua, 18032.
Schools-See Our Lady of Hungary Regional School, Northampton under Regional Catholic Elementary Schools, Diocesan located in the Institution section.
Catechesis/Religious Program—Tel: 610-264-1972. Regina Marhefka, D.R.E. Located at St Lawrence, Catasauqua Students 14.

2—ST. LAWRENCE THE MARTYR (Lehigh Co.) (1858) [CEM 2] Rev. Eric J. Gruber, Admin.; Deacon Thomas B. Reimer.
Res.: 1001 Second St., 18032. Tel: 610-264-1972; Fax: 610-264-2105.
School— Please see separate listing under Regional Catholic Elementary Schools, Diocesan in the Institutions section.
Catechesis/Religious Program—Students 70.

COOPERSBURG, LEHIGH CO., ST. JOSEPH (1926) [CEM] Rev. Thomas R. Buckley; Deacon Dennis P. Meyer.
Res.: 5050 St. Joseph's Rd., 18036-8920. Tel: 610-965-2877; Fax: 610-965-8317. Email: stjoes@ptd.net. Web: www.st-mikes.com.
See St. Michael the Archangel School, Limeport & Colesville under Regional Catholic Elementary Schools, Diocesan located in the Institution section.
Catechesis/Religious Program—Tel: 610-965-0590. Students 225.

COPLAY, LEHIGH CO., ST. PETER (1927), (Austrian—Hungarian), [CEM] Rev. Msgr. William E. Handges.
Res.: 4 S. Fifth St., 18037. Tel: 610-262-2417; Fax: 610-262-2652.
See Christ the King School, Whitehall under Regional Catholic Elementary Schools, Diocesan located in the Institution section.
Catechesis/Religious Program—Students 90.

DOUGLASSVILLE, BERKS CO., IMMACULATE CONCEPTION (1916) [CEM 2] Rev. Msgr. John B. McCann; Deacon Paul J. Hiryak Jr. In Res., Rev. Msgrs. Richard J. Loeper (Retired); Thomas J. Birch (Retired).
Res.: 905 Chestnut St., 19518-9006. Tel: 610-582-2411; Fax: 610-404-2609. Email: secretary@icbvm.org. Web: www.icbvm.org.
School—Immaculate Conception Academy, (Grades K-8), 903 Chestnut St., 19518. Tel: 610-404-8645; Fax: 610-404-4890. Mrs. Christine Foley, Prin. Students 220.
Catechesis/Religious Program—Tel: 610-582-3880; Fax: 610-404-2609. Patricia Tarquinio, D.R.E. Students 494.

EASTON, NORTHAMPTON CO.

1—ST. ANTHONY OF PADUA (1909), (Italian), [CEM] Rev. Msgr. Edward S. Zemanik; Deacon Charles A. DeBellis.
Res.: 900 Washington St., 18042-4342. Tel: 610-253-7188; Fax: 610-253-6184.
See Easton Catholic School, Easton under Regional Catholic Elementary Schools, Diocesan, located in the Institution section.

Catechesis/Religious Program—Mrs. Karen Donato, D.R.E. Students 191.
Convent—910 Washington St., 18042. Tel: 610-258-7792; Fax: 610-258-7792.

2—ST. JANE FRANCES DE CHANTAL (1920) [JC] Rev. Msgr. Stephen J. Radocha; Rev. Keith R. Laskowski; Deacons Robert W. Rodgers; Ranulfo Raymundo; Joseph H. Pufko; John A. Hanni; Noreen McDonough, Business Mgr.
4049 Hartley Ave., 18045.
Res.: 123 S. Nulton Ave., 18045-3791. Tel: 610-253-3553; Fax: 610-253-5711. Web: www.stjanesofeastonpa.com.
School—(Grades PreK-8), 1900 Washington Blvd., 18042-4619. Tel: 610-253-8442; Fax: 610-253-2427. Email: altnsjf@ptd.net. Mrs. Isabel Conlin, Prin.; Wendy Reidinger, Librarian. Lay Teachers 23; Students 476.
Catechesis/Religious Program—Tel: 610-253-7794, Ext. 13. Kevin Kimmel, D.R.E. (Children); Mrs. Teresa Rodgers, Dir. Adult Rel. Formation. Students 592.

3—OUR LADY OF MERCY PARISH (2008), Formed by the merger of St. Bernard, St. Joseph and St. Michael, Easton. Public oratory for weekday masses: St. Bernard, 134 S. 5th St. Revs. Deogratias Rwegasira, A.J. (Tanzania); Venantius K. Twinomuhwezi, A.J.; Deacons Jose F. DeCastro; Henry J. Fleck Jr.
St. Joseph and Davis Sts., 18042. In Res., Rev. Elias Munyaneza, A.J.
Office: 132 S. Fifth St., 18042-4418. Tel: 610-252-7381; Fax: 610-252-6757. Email: info@olomercy.com. Web: www.olomercy.com.
Rectory—129 Davis St., 18042-6295.
Catechesis/Religious Program—Mrs. Johanna Florez, D.R.E. (Coord.). Students 160.

EMMAUS, LEHIGH CO., ST. ANN (1931) [CEM] Rev. Msgr. John S. Mraz; Rev. Dominic Thao Pham; Deacon Dominic F. Amedeo Jr.
Res.: 415 S. Sixth St., 18049-3703. Tel: 610-965-2426; Fax: 610-967-1099.
School—(Grades PreK-8), 435 S. 6th St., 18049. Tel: 610-965-9220; Fax: 610-967-4521. Diana Kile, Prin.; Holly Haydorn, Librarian. Sisters 1; Lay Teachers 23; Students 303.
Catechesis/Religious Program—Tel: 610-965-6888. Cris Kimock, D.R.E. Students 425.
Convent—526 Fairview St., 18049. Tel: 610-965-6818.

FOUNTAIN HILL, LEHIGH CO., ST. URSULA (Bethlehem P.O.) (1919) Rev. Robert J. Potts; Deacon David K. Rohner. In Res., Rev. Avitus Kazi Siriwa, A.J.
Res.: 1300 Broadway, 18015-4099. Tel: 610-867-5122; Fax: 610-867-6569.
See Bethlehem under Regional Catholic Elementary Schools, Diocesan located in the Institution section.
Catechesis/Religious Program—Tel: 610-861-2897. Students 47.

FRACKVILLE, SCHUYLKILL CO.

1—ST. ANN (1924), (Polish), Rev. Robert T. Finlan.
Mailing Address: 7 S. Broad Mountain Ave., 17931-1800.
Res.: 99 N. Line St., 17931-1310. Tel: 570-874-0610; Fax: 570-874-0969.
Schools-See Trinity Academy at the Father Walter J. Ciszek Education Center, Shenandoah under Regional Catholic Elementary Schools, Diocesan located in the Institution section.
Catechesis/Religious Program—Kimberly Mikulski, D.R.E. Students 30.

2—ANNUNCIATION B.V.M. (1917), (Lithuanian), [CEM] Rev. Robert T. Finlan.
Mailing Address: 7 S. Broad Mountain Ave., 17931-1800.
Res.: 99 N. Line St., 17931-1310. Tel: 570-874-0610; Fax: 570-874-0969.
Schools-See Trinity Academy at the Father Walter J. Ciszek Education Center, Shenandoah under Regional Catholic Elementary Schools, Diocesan located in the Institution section.
Catechesis/Religious Program—Kimberly Mikulski, D.R.E. Students 35.

3—ST. JOSEPH (1909) [CEM] Rev. Robert T. Finlan.
Mailing Address: 14 N. Nice St., 17931-1310.
Res.: 99 N. Line St., 17931-1310. Tel: 570-874-0610; Fax: 570-874-0969.
See Trinity Academy at the Father Walter J. Ciszek Education Center, Shenandoah under Regional Catholic Elementary Schools, Diocesan located in the Institution section.
Catechesis/Religious Program—Kimberly Mikulski, D.R.E.

GIRARDVILLE, SCHUYLKILL CO.

1—ST. JOSEPH (1870) [CEM] Rev. Edward B. Connolly.
Mailing Address & Parish Center: 260 N. 2nd, 17935-1338. Tel: 570-276-6033; Fax: 570-276-6032. Email: stjospar@verizon.net.
See Trinity Academy at the Father Walter J. Ciszek Education Center, Shenandoah under Regional Catholic Elementary Schools, Diocesan located in the Institution section.
Catechesis/Religious Program—Edward M. Wascavage, D.R.E. Students 27.

2—ST. VINCENT DE PAUL (1907), (Lithuanian), [CEM] Revs. Edward B. Connolly; David M. Liebner, Pastor Emeritus (Retired).
Res.: 260 N. Second St., 17935. Tel: 570-276-6033; 570-276-6239; Fax: 570-276-6032. Email: stvdppar@verizon.net.
See Trinity Academy at the Father Walter Ciszek Education Center, Shenandoah under Regional Catholic Elementary Schools, Diocesan located in the Institution section.
Catechesis/Religious Program—Students 9.

GORDON, SCHUYLKILL CO., OUR LADY OF GOOD COUNSEL (1922) Revs. John W. Bambrick; Thomas A. Horan, Pastor Emeritus (Retired), 802 Pine St., Ashland, 17921.
Mailing Address: 1115 Walnut St., Ashland, 17921.
Res.: 802 Pine St., Ashland, 17921-1845. Tel: 570-875-1521; Fax: 570-875-2635.
See Trinity Academy at the Father Walter J. Ciszek Education Center, Shenandoah under Regional Catholic Elementary Schools, Diocesan located in the Institution section.
Catechesis/Religious Program—Sr. Elizabeth Kealy, I.H.M., D.R.E. Students 10.

HAMBURG, BERKS CO., ST. MARY (1854) [CEM] Rev. Donald W. Cieniewicz; Deacon Henry G. Gordon.
Res.: 94 Walnut Rd., P.O. Box 189, 19526. Tel: 610-562-7657; Fax: 610-562-0379. Email: stmaryhamburg@aol.com. Web: www.rc.net/allentown/stmaryhamb.
Catechesis/Religious Program—Email: stmaryprep@stmaryhamburg.org. Mrs. Brenda Cordier, D.R.E. Students 185.
Station—Hamburg State School and Hospital, Tel: 610-562-6063.

HELLERTOWN, NORTHAMPTON CO., ST. THERESA OF THE CHILD JESUS (1925) Rev. Jerome A. Tauber; Deacon Gerald R. Schmidt. In Res., Rev. Msgr. Alfred A. Schlert.
Res.: 1408 Easton Rd., 18055-1127. Tel: 610-838-7045; Fax: 610-838-0932. Email: sttheresacj@enter.net.
School—(Grades PreK-8), 300 Leonard St., 18055-1199. Tel: 610-838-8161; Fax: 610-838-1915. Email: altnst@ptd.net. Mrs. Louise Glass, Prin.; Kenneth Westgate, Librarian. Lay Teachers 14; Students 130.
Catechesis/Religious Program—Tel: 610-838-7645. Students 131.
Convent—255 Wilson Ave., 18055-1454.

JIM THORPE, CARBON CO.

1—IMMACULATE CONCEPTION (1848) [CEM] Rev. James J. Ward.
Res.: 180 W. Broadway, 18229. Tel: 570-325-2791; Fax: 570-325-2427.
See St. Joseph Regional Academy, Jim Thorpe under Regional Catholic Elementary Schools, Diocesan located in the Institution section.
Catechesis/Religious Program—Mrs. Kathleen D. Merkel, C.R.E. Students 65.

2—ST. JOSEPH (1871) [CEM] Rev. Francis J. Baransky.
Res.: 526 North St., 18229. Tel: 570-325-3731; Fax: 570-325-2523.
Schools-See St. Joseph Regional Academy, Jim Thorpe under Regional Catholic Elementary Schools, Diocesan located in the Institution section.
Catechesis/Religious Program—Mrs. Kathleen D. Merkel, D.R.E. Students 82.

KUTZTOWN, BERKS CO., ST. MARY (1919) Rev. Msgr. Walter T. Scheaffer.
Res.: 14833 Kutztown Rd., 19530. Tel: 610-683-7443; 610-683-7466 (Church); Fax: 610-683-7625. Email: stmarysktown@verizon.net. Web: www.stmaryskutztown.com.
Catechesis/Religious Program—Tel: 610-683-6454. Students 232.

LAKE HARMONY, CARBON CO., ST. PETER THE FISHERMAN (1982) Rev. Msgr. John G. Chizmar; Deacon John F. Thompson.
Res.: Lake Dr., P.O. Box 237, 18624-0237. Tel: 570-722-2034; Fax: 570-722-1348. Email: stpeter@ptd.net.
Catechesis/Religious Program—Students 118.

LANSFORD, CARBON CO.

1—ST. KATHARINE DREXEL PARISH (2008) [CEM 3], Formed by the merger of St. John the Baptist, St. Mary & SS. Cyril and Methodius Parishes, Coaldale and St. Ann, St. Michael & SS. Peter and Paul Parishes, Lansford. Rev. Kenneth A. Medve; Deacon James P. Henninger.
Mailing Address: 124 E. Abbott St., 18232-0177. Tel: 570-645-2282; Fax: 570-645-2754.
Rectory—41 E. Ruddle St., Coaldale, 18218-1206.
See Our Lady of the Angels Academy, Lansford under Regional Catholic Elementary Schools, Diocesan located in the Institution section.
Catechesis/Religious Program—Students 50.

LEHIGHTON, CARBON CO., SS. PETER AND PAUL (1885), (German), [CEM] Rev. Michael E. Ahrensfield.
Res.: 260 N. Third St., 18235-1595. Tel: 610-377-3690; Fax: 610-377-0721. Email: sspp@ptd.net. Web: www.ssppchurch.com.
School—307 Coal St., 18235-1458. Tel: 610-377-4466; Fax: 610-377-8881. Email: altcspp@ptd.net. Web: www.sppschool.org. Mrs. Sherry Ambrose, Prin. Students (Early childhood to 8) 100.
Catechesis/Religious Program—Students 105.

LOST CREEK, SCHUYLKILL CO., ST. MARY MAGDALEN (1879) [JC] Rev. Msgr. Ronald C. Bocian.
Res. & Parish Office: 129 S. Jardin St., Shenandoah, 17976-2226. Tel: 570-462-1916; Fax: 570-462-1980. Email: rccos@shenhgts.net. Web: saintmarymagdalen.catholicweb.com.
See Trinity Academy at the Father Walter J. Ciszek Education Center, Shenandoah under Regional Catholic Elementary Schools, Diocesan located in the Institution section.

MAHANOY CITY, SCHUYLKILL CO.

1—BLESSED TERESA OF CALCUTTA PARISH (2000), Formed by the merger of Assumption B.V.M., St. Canicus, St. Casimir, St. Fidelis, St. Joseph & Sacred Heart, Mahanoy City; Our Lady of Siluva, Maizeville. Rev. Kevin P. Gallagher; Deacon Joseph J. Costa.
600 W. Mahanoy Ave., 17948.
Office: 614 W. Mahanoy Ave., 17948-2416. Tel: 570-773-2771; Fax: 570-773-1937. Email: btoc@ptd.net.
See Trinity Academy, Shenandoah under Regional Catholic Elementary Schools, Diocesan located in the Institution section.
Catechesis/Religious Program—Students 142.

MARTINS CREEK, NORTHAMPTON CO., ST. ROCCO (1929) Rev. Msgr. James J. Reichert.
Res.: 6658 School St., Box 421, 18063-0010. Tel: 610-258-9059; Fax: 610-258-4780. Email: strocco@enter.net. Web: strocco.org.
See Immaculate Conception School, Pen Argyl under Regional Catholic Elementary Schools, Diocesan located in the Institution section.
Catechesis/Religious Program—Students 101.

MCADOO, SCHUYLKILL CO.

1—ALL SAINTS PARISH (2008), Formed by the merger of Immaculate Conception, Kelayres; St. Kunegunda, St. Mary & St. Patrick, McAdoo; St. Michael & St. Bartholomew, Tresckow. Rev. Ronald J. Minner.
36 E. Washington Ave., 18237-1842. Tel: 570-929-1073; Fax: 570-929-1073. Email: churchofallsaints@earthlink.net.
Catechesis/Religious Program—Sr. Eleanore Joseph, I.H.M., D.R.E. Students 149.

MINERSVILLE, SCHUYLKILL CO.

1—ST. MATTHEW THE EVANGELIST (2008), Formed by the merger of St. Stanislaus Kostka, St. Francis of Assisi & St. Barbara, Minersville; St. Mary, Star of the Sea, Branchdale. Rev. Leo J. Maletz.
135 Spruce St., 17954.
Parish Center: 120 Oak St., 17954. Tel: 570-544-5485.
Rectory—139 Spruce St., 17954-1642. Tel: 570-544-2211; Fax: 570-544-2317. Email: ssk1905@verizon.net. Web: www.stmatthewtheevangelistparish.org.
See All Saints Regional School, Pottsville, under Regional Catholic Elementary Schools, Diocesan located in the Institution section.
Catechesis/Religious Program—301 Heffner St., 17954. Tel: 570-544-3766. Ms. Rosalie Novack, C.R.E. Students 74.

2—ST. MICHAEL THE ARCHANGEL PARISH (2008), Formed by the merger of Our Lady of Mount Carmel & St. Vincent de Paul, Minersville; St. Kieran, Heckscherville. Rev. Adam C. Sedar.
541 Sunbury St., 17954.
Rectory—538 Sunbury St., 17954-1015. Tel: 570-544-4741; Fax: 570-544-4742. Email: st.michaelthearchangelminers@hotmail.com.
See All Saints Regional School, Pottsville, under Regional Catholic Elementary Schools, Diocesan located in the Institution section.
Catechesis/Religious Program—Sr. Catherine T. Brennan, S.S.J., D.R.E.
Convent—Tel: 570-544-2016. Email: ssjmin@comcast.net.

MOHNTON, BERKS CO., ST. BENEDICT'S (1955) Rev. Philip F. Rodgers. In Res., Rev. Robert C. Quinn (Retired).
Res.: 2020 Chesnut Hill Rd., 19540-8243. Tel: 610-856-1006; Fax: 610-856-1035. Email: stbenedict2020@dejazzd.com.
See La Salle Academy and Early Childhood Center, Shillington under Regional Catholic Elementary Schools, Diocesan located in the Institution section.
Catechesis/Religious Program—Tel: 610-370-0199; 610-856-5146. Ms. Valerie Christo-Pinheiro, D.R.E. Students 274.

NAZARETH, NORTHAMPTON CO., HOLY FAMILY (1908) [CEM 2] Revs. Joseph F. Tobias, M.S.C.; Walter Downs, M.S.C., Senior Priest; Jonas Tandayu, M.S.C.; Deacon Donald J. Dupont, Gracedale Ministry.
Res.: 23 Forest Dr., 18064-1300. Tel: 610-759-0870; Fax: 610-746-2026. Email: hfp23@rcn.com. Web: holyfamilyparish.myownparish.com.
School—(Grades PreK-8), 17 Convent Ave., 18064-1324. Tel: 610-759-5642; Fax: 610-759-0386. Web: holyfamilynazareth.com. Mrs. Colette Fisher, Prin. Lay Teachers 22; Students 309.
Catechesis/Religious Program—Tel: 610-759-2623 (Grades K-8). Email: elyd@holyfamily-edu.org. Donna Ely, D.R.E. Students 676.

NESQUEHONING, CARBON CO.
1—ST. FRANCIS OF ASSISI PARISH (2008), Formed by the merger of Immaculate Conception, Sacred Heart and Our Lady of Mount Carmel Parishes, Nesquehoning. Rev. Francis P. Schoenauer.
Mill and Radcliff Sts., 18240.
Rectory—15 E. Garibaldi Ave., 18240-1109. Tel: 570-669-6321; Fax: 570-669-9440. Email: iccnesq@ptd.net.
See Our Lady of the Angels Academy, Lansford under Regional Catholic Elementary Schools, Diocesan located in the Institution section.
Catechesis/Religious Program—Students 26.

NEW PHILADELPHIA, SCHUYLKILL CO.
1—HOLY CROSS PARISH (2008) [CEM 3], Formed by the merger of Holy Family & Sacred Heart, New Philadelphia; St. Anthony of Padua, Cumbola. Rev. Edward J. Essig.
101 Valley St., 17959.
Office & Rectory: 99 Valley St., 17959-1103. Tel: 570-277-6800; Fax: 570-277-0528. Email: hfchurch@f-tech.net.
See Assumption BVM Elementary School, Pottsville under Regional Catholic Elementary Schools, Diocesan located in the Institution section.
Catechesis/Religious Program—Students 80.

NORTHAMPTON, NORTHAMPTON CO.
1—ASSUMPTION OF THE BLESSED VIRGIN MARY (1922), (Slovak), [CEM] Rev. Francis P. Straka; Deacon Anthony L. Brasten.
Res.: 2174 Lincoln Ave., 18067-1257. Tel: 610-262-2559; Fax: 610-262-1613. Email: bvm1922@rcn.com.
See Good Shepherd School, Northampton under Regional Catholic Elementary Schools, Diocesan located in the Institution section.
Catechesis/Religious Program—Tel: 610-262-7343. Mrs. Linda Santucci, C.R.E. Students 189.
2—QUEENSHIP OF MARY PARISH (2008), Formed by the merger of Our Lady of Hungary & St. Michael, Northampton. Rev. Msgr. John S. Campbell; Deacon Joseph F. Godiska.
1308 Newport Ave., 18067. In Res., Rev. Msgrs. Michael J. Chaback, Dir. Office of Permanent Diaconate; James J. Mulligan, Dir. Office of Priestly Life and Ministry.
Rectory—1324 Newport Ave., 18067-1442. Tel: 610-262-2227; Fax: 610-262-4192. Email: queenshipofmary@rcn.com.
See Good Shepherd School, Northampton under Regional Catholic Elementary Schools, Diocesan located in the Institution section.

OREFIELD, LEHIGH CO., ST. JOSEPH THE WORKER (1948) Rev. Msgr. Robert J. Wargo; Rev. Kevin M. Gualano; Deacons Anthony T. Campanell; Bruno Schettini; Charles A. Coyle. In Res., Rev. Scott R. Ardinger; Rev. Msgr. Joseph P.T. Smith.
Res.: 1879 Applewood Dr., 18069-9507. Tel: 610-395-2876; Fax: 610-395-2616. Email: stjc@ptd.net. Web: stjoseph-theworker.org.
School—(Grades K-8), 1858 Applewood Dr., 18069-9535. Tel: 610-395-7221; Fax: 610-395-7904. Email: altlsj@ptd.net. Mrs. Jody Myers, Prin. Students 400.
Catechesis/Religious Program—Tel: 610-395-4920. Students 938.

PALMERTON, CARBON CO., SACRED HEART (1908) [CEM] Rev. William T. Campion; Deacon William P. Pitts.
Res.: 243 Lafayette Ave., 18071-1511. Tel: 610-826-2335; Fax: 610-826-5360. Email: shpmtn@ptd.net. Web: www.shcpalmerton.org.
See St. John Neumann Regional School, Palmerton-Slatington under Regional Catholic Elementary Schools, Diocesan located in the Institution section.
Catechesis/Religious Program—Tel: 610-826-2849. Dr. Edward Girard, C.R.E.

PEN ARGYL, NORTHAMPTON CO., ST. ELIZABETH OF HUNGARY (1929) [CEM] Rev. Msgr. Vincent P. York.
Res.: 300 W. Babbitt Ave., 18072-0126. Tel: 610-863-4777; Fax: 610-863-7449.
See Immaculate Conception School, Pen Argyl under Regional Catholic Elementary Schools, Diocesan located in the Institution section.
Catechesis/Religious Program—Tel: 610-614-0268. Suzanne Engler, C.R.E. Students 145.
Convent—111-115 Lobb Ave., 18072. Tel: 610-863-9214.

PORT CARBON, SCHUYLKILL CO., ST. STEPHEN (1847) [CEM] Rev. David W. Karns.
Res.: 218 Valley St., 17965-1636. Tel: 570-622-6600; Fax: 570-622-9817. Email: saintstephen2@verizon.net. Cemetery office 570-622-6600
Catechesis/Religious Program—Students 40.

POTTSVILLE, SCHUYLKILL CO.
1—ST. JOHN THE BAPTIST (1841), (German), [CEM 3] Rev. David J. Loeper; Deacon Luis R. Visot.
Res.: 913 Mahantongo St., 17901-3024. Tel: 570-622-5470; Fax: 570-622-4589. Email: stjohnthebaptist@verizon.net.
See All Saints Elementary School, Pottsville under Regional Catholic Elementary Schools, Diocesan located in the Institution section.
Catechesis/Religious Program—Students 126.
2—ST. PATRICK (1827) [CEM 3] Rev. Msgr. Edward J. O'Connor; Rev. Jason F. Stokes; Deacon John E. Quirk. In Res., Rev. John Little.
Res.: 319 Mahantongo St., 17901-3012. Tel: 570-622-1802; Fax: 570-622-2593.
See All Saints Elementary School, Pottsville under Regional Catholic Elementary Schools, Diocesan located in the Institution section.
Catechesis/Religious Program—Mrs. Peterine Wojcik, D.R.E. Students 179.

READING, BERKS CO.
1—ST. ANTHONY OF PADUA (1914), (Polish), Rev. Larry J. Hess.
Res.: 501 Summit Ave., 19611-1964. Tel: 610-685-5505; Fax: 610-685-1101. Email: stanthony2009@stanthonyreading.org. Web: www.stanthonyreading.org.
Catechesis/Religious Program—Students 25.
Convent—234 Grace St., 19611-1946. Tel: 610-372-8578.
2—ST. CATHARINE OF SIENA (1925) Rev. Msgr. Edward R. Domin; Rev. Eugene P. Ritz, Parochial Vicar; Deacons Richard A. Horst; Craig A. Fry.
Res.: 2427 Perkiomen Ave., 19606. Tel: 610-779-4005; Fax: 610-779-0859.
Church: 4975 Boyertown Pike, 19606. Tel: 610-779-4090.
School—(1925) 2330 Perkiomen Ave., 19606-2048. Tel: 610-779-5810; Fax: 610-779-6888. Email: altbscs@ptd.net. Sr. M. Teresa Ballisty, I.H.M., Prin. Sisters 4; Lay Teachers 20; Students 265.
Catechesis/Religious Program—Tel: 610-779-8535. Constance Fry, D.R.E., (K-5); Lorraine Gajewski, D.R.E., (6-8). Students 505.
Convent—2328 Perkiomen Ave., 19606. Tel: 610-779-5583.
Chapel—
3—SS. CYRIL AND METHODIUS (1895), (Slovak), Rev. Charles S. Sperlak; Deacon John J. Allison.
Res.: 449 S. Sixth St., 19602-2410. Tel: 610-373-0627; Fax: 610-371-9532.
Catechesis/Religious Program—Kathleen Shaulis, D.R.E. Students 34.
Convent—502 S. Sixth St., 19602-2706. Tel: 610-375-8001.
4—HOLY GUARDIAN ANGELS (1929) Rev. Msgrs. Dennis T. Hartgen; Francis X. Barrett, Pastor Emeritus (Retired); Rev. Christopher M. Zelonis; Deacon John B. Gallagher.
Res.: 3121 Kutztown Rd., 19605-2659. Tel: 610-921-2729; Fax: 610-921-8886. Web: www.hgaparish-.com.
Schools-see Holy Guardian Angels Regional School, Reading under Regional Catholic Elementary Schools, Diocesan located in the Institution section.
Catechesis/Religious Program—3125 Kutztown Rd., 19605. Tel: 610-929-1416; Fax: 610-929-1623. Mrs. Rose Quaglia, D.R.E. Students 369.
5—HOLY ROSARY (1904), (Italian), Unassigned.
Res.: 237 Franklin St., 19602-1034. Tel: 610-373-5579; Fax: 610-372-0130. Email: holyrosarychurch01@comcast.net. Web: www.holyrosaryreading.com.
Catechesis/Religious Program—Sr. Marita Olango, F.D.Z., D.R.E. Students 22.
Convent—234 Franklin St., 19602-1035. Tel: 610-375-9072; Fax: 610-375-4895. Email: srdivinezeal@hotmail.com. Sr. Angelie Marie Inoferio, F.D.Z., Supr.
Mission—Holy Rosary Chapel Schuylkill Ave., Berks Co. 19601. Tel: 610-376-4383.
6—ST. JOSEPH (1891) Rev. George R. Winne; Sr. Mary Ellen Broderick, I.H.M., Pastoral Assoc.; Deacon Francisco De La Gracia Colon.
Res.: 1018 N. Eighth St., 19604-2210. Tel: 610-376-2976; Fax: 610-376-2825. Email: stjosephchurchreading@yahoo.com.
See Holy Guardian Angels Regional School, Reading under Regional Catholic Elementary Schools, Diocesan located in the Institution section.
Catechesis/Religious Program—Students 200.
7—ST. MARGARET (1920) Rev. John M. Gibbons; Deacons John P. Konopelski; Ramon L. Rolon; Gregory G. Schneider.
Res.: 925 Centre Ave., 19601-2105. Tel: 610-376-2919; Fax: 610-376-2462. Email: stmrgrt@verizon.net.
School—Tel: 610-375-1882; Fax: 610-376-2291. Email: stmargaretoffice@comcast.net. Web: www.sm-sreading.com. Sr. Marian Michele Smith, I.H.M., Prin. Students 186.
Catechesis/Religious Program—Tel: 610-376-2919. Sr. Honoria Smith, D.R.E.
Convent—233 Spring St., 19601-2121. Tel: 610-372-1302. Email: stmgrtconvent@holmail.com.
8—ST. MARY (1888), (Polish), [CEM] Rev. Leo S. Stajkowski.
250 S. 12th St., 19602-2046. Tel: 610-376-6321; Fax: 610-376-1378. In Res., Rev. Robert Tobolski, M.S.C.
Catechesis/Religious Program—Students 9.
9—ST. PAUL (1860), (German), [CEM] Rev. Msgr. William T. Baker; Rev. Quyet A. Pham.
Res.: 151 N. 9th St., 19601. Tel: 610-372-1531; Fax: 610-372-7478. Email: stpaulsrcchurch@comcast.net.
Catechesis/Religious Program—Students 461.
10—ST. PETER THE APOSTLE (1752) [CEM] Rev. Msgr. Thomas J. Orsulak; Rev. David J. Kozak; Deacons Jesus Centeno; Mariano Torres; Julio Colon; Fernando L. Torres; Leopoldo Alvarado.
Res.: 326 S. Fifth St., 19602-2311. Tel: 610-372-9652; Fax: 610-374-3351. Email: stpeterchurch@comcast.net.
School—225 S. Fifth St., 19602-1816. Tel: 610-374-2447; Fax: 610-374-3415. Email: altbsp@ptd.com. Sr. Anna Musi, I.H.M., Prin. Students 325.
Catechesis/Religious Program—Sr. Margaret Pavluchuk, I.H.M., D.R.E. Students 344.
Convent—218 S. Fifth St., 19602-1841. Tel: 610-373-6185. Email: speter7@aol.com. Sr. Mary Ellen Broderick, I.H.M., Supr.

RINGTOWN, SCHUYLKILL CO., ST. MARY (1923) [CEM] Rev. James M. Torpey.
Mailing Address: P.O. Box F, 17967-9731.
Res.: 84 N. Center, P.O. Box F, 17967-9731. Tel: 570-889-3850; Fax: 570-889-5005.
See Trinity Academy at the Father Walter J. Ciszek Education Center, Shenandoah under Regional Catholic Elementary Schools, Diocesan located in the Institution section.
Catechesis/Religious Program—

ROBESONIA, BERKS CO., ST. FRANCIS DE SALES (1982) Rev. Mark J. Wrightson, O.S.F.S.; Sr. Mary Heffron, I.H.M., Pastoral Assoc.
Res.: 320 N. Church St., 19551. Tel: 610-693-5851; Fax: 610-693-5852. Email: stfrancisrob82@verizon.net. Web: www.stfrancisroby.org.
Catechesis/Religious Program—Email: marijoccd@verizon.net. Students 153.

ROSETO, NORTHAMPTON CO., OUR LADY OF MT. CARMEL (1897), (Italian), [CEM 2] Revs. James G. Prior, C.M.; Thomas W. Prior, C.M.
P.O. Box 422, 18013.
Rectory—560 N. Sixth St., Bangor, 18013. Tel: 610-588-2183; Fax: 610-588-6973.
See Our Lady of Mt. Carmel School, Roseto under Regional Catholic Elementary Schools, Diocesan located in the Institution section.
Catechesis/Religious Program—Students 72.

SAINT CLAIR, SCHUYLKILL CO.
1—ST. CLARE OF ASSISI PARISH (2008), Formed by the merger of St. Mary, Immaculate Conception, St. Casimir, SS. Peter and Paul & St. Boniface. Rev. Msgr. William F. Glosser.
Mill and Hancock Sts., 17970.
Rectory—250 E. Hancock St., St. Clair, 17970-1049. Tel: 570-429-0701; 570-429-0370 (Office); Fax: 570-429-0630. Email: scassisi@ptd.net.
See Assumption BVM School, Pottsville under Regional Catholic Elementary Schools, Diocesan located in the Institution section.
Catechesis/Religious Program—Mrs. Kazimiera Hornberger, D.R.E. Students 101.

SCHUYLKILL HAVEN, SCHUYLKILL CO., ST. AMBROSE (1851) [CEM] Rev. Msgr. Edward S. Zemanik; Rev. Kevin J. Bobbin; Deacon Edward E. Freed.
Res.: 201 Randel St., 17972-1495. Tel: 570-385-1031; Fax: 570-385-1035. Email: sambrosel@comcast.net.
School—(Grades PreK-8), 302 Randel St., 17972-1421. Tel: 570-385-2377; Fax: 570-385-2387. Email: altssa@ptd.net. Web: www.pottsville.com/stambrose. Anne B. Curry, Prin. Students 158.
Catechesis/Religious Program—Tel: 570-385-2472. Sr. Dolorita Nachajska, C.S.F.N., D.R.E. Students 294.

SHENANDOAH, SCHUYLKILL CO.
1—ANNUNCIATION (1870) [CEM] Rev. Msgr. Ronald C. Bocian. In Res., Rev. Charles J. Dene.
Res. & Office Center: 129 S. Jardin St., 17976-2209. Tel: 570-462-1916; Fax: 570-462-1980.

See Trinity Academy at the Father Walter J. Ciszek Education Center, Shenandoah under Regional Catholic Elementary Schools, Diocesan located in the Institution section.
Convent—229 W. Cherry St., 17976. Tel: 570-462-1024.
Catechesis/Religious Program—Students 54.

2—ST. CASIMIR (1872), (Polish), [CEM] Rev. Msgr. Ronald C. Bocian; Teofil Galezniak, Music Min.; Stanley Pietkiewicz, Business Mgr.
Res.: 108 W. Cherry St., 17976-2207. Tel: 570-462-1968; Fax: 570-462-1388.
See Trinity Academy at the Father Walter J. Ciszek Education Center, Shenandoah under Regional Catholic Elementary Schools, Diocesan located in the Institution section.
Catechesis/Religious Program—Tel: 570-773-1142. Kay Hornberger, D.R.E. Students 19.
Convent—233 N. Jardin St., 17976. Tel: 570-462-0877; Fax: 570-462-9318.

3—ST. GEORGE (1891), (Lithuanian), [CEM 5] Rev. Msgr. Ronald C. Bocian.
Res.: 129 S. Jardin St., 17976. Tel: 570-462-1989; Fax: 570-462-1980.
See Trinity Academy at the Father Walter J. Ciszek Education Center, Shenandoah under Regional Catholic Elementary Schools, Diocesan located in the Institution section.
Catechesis/Religious Program—Kay Hornberger, D.R.E. Students 23.

4—OUR LADY OF MT. CARMEL (1914), (Italian), [CEM] Rev. Msgr. Ronald C. Bocian.
Res.: 129 S. Jardin St., 17976. Tel: 570-462-1989; Fax: 570-462-1980.
See Trinity Academy at the Father Walter J. Ciszek Education Center, Shenandoah under Regional Catholic Elementary Schools, Diocesan located in the Institution section.
Catechesis/Religious Program—Students 14.

5—ST. STANISLAUS (1898), (Polish), [CEM] Rev. Msgr. Ronald C. Bocian; Maria Rittle, Music Min.; Stanley Pietkiewicz, Business Mgr.
Res.: 108 W. Cherry St., 17976. Tel: 570-462-1968; Fax: 570-462-1388.
See Trinity Academy at the Father Walter J. Ciszek Education Center, Shenandoah under Regional Catholic Elementary Schools, Diocesan located in the Institution section.
Catechesis/Religious Program—Tel: 570-773-1142. Kay Hornberger, D.R.E. Students 6.

6—ST. STEPHEN (1899), (Slovak), [CEM] Rev. Msgr. Ronald C. Bocian.
Church: 14-16 E. Oak St., 17976.
Res.: 108 W. Cherry St., 17976-2207. Tel: 570-462-1968; Fax: 570-462-1388.
See Trinity Academy at the Father Walter J. Ciszek Education Center, Shenandoah under Regional Catholic Elementary Schools, Diocesan located in the Institution section.
Catechesis/Religious Program—Students 7.

SHEPPTON, SCHUYLKILL CO., ST. JOSEPH (1894) [CEM] [JC] Rev. James M. Torpey.
Res.: 14 E. Oak St., P.O. Box 118, 18248-0118. Tel: 570-384-0517. Email: smrc@epix.net.
Catechesis/Religious Program—Students 11.
Mission—St. John the Baptist P.O. Box 118, Oneida, Schuylkill Co. 18248.

SHILLINGTON, BERKS CO., ST. JOHN BAPTIST DE LA SALLE (1948) Rev. Richard H. Clement; Rev. Msgr. Thomas J. Birch, Pastor Emeritus (Retired).
Mailing Address: 420 Holland St., 19607. Tel: 610-777-1697; Fax: 610-777-4468. Email: stjohnbaptist.delasalle@verizon.net. Web: www.catholic-church.org/baptist-delasalle. In Res., Rev. Thomas P. Bortz.
Res.: 400 Holland St., 19607. Tel: 610-777-1365.
See La Salle Academy and Early Childhood Center, Shillington under Regional Catholic Elementary Schools, Diocesan located in the Institution section.
Catechesis/Religious Program—Bernadette H. Yohn, D.R.E. Students 221.

SINKING SPRING, BERKS CO., ST. IGNATIUS LOYOLA (1965) Rev. Msgr. James A. Treston; Rev. Cletus S. Onyegbule; Deacon William L. Autrey.
Res.: 2810 St. Alban's Dr., 19608-1028. Tel: 610-678-3767; Fax: 610-678-4483. Email: ignatiusrect@aol.com. Web: www.stignatiusreading.org.
School—(Grades PreK-8), 2700 St. Albans Dr., Reading, 19609. Tel: 610-678-0111; Fax: 610-670-5795. Mr. Robert Birmingham, Prin.; Mrs. Ann Rutkoski, Librarian. Sisters of the Third Order of St. Francis 1; Lay Teachers 37; Students 518.
Catechesis/Religious Program—2710 St. Alban's Dr., Reading, 19609. Tel: 610-678-0676; Fax: 610-678-4274. Students 658.
Convent—2601 St. Alban's Dr., West Lawn, 19609. Tel: 610-678-2769.

SLATINGTON, LEHIGH CO., ASSUMPTION B.V.M. (1883) [CEM] Rev. Joseph L. Grembocki; Deacon Fredic Bloom.
Res.: 633 W. Washington St., 18080-1618. Tel: 610-767-2214; Fax: 610-767-2702.
See St. John Neumann Regional School, Palmerton-Slatington under Regional Catholic Elementary Schools, Diocesan located in the Institution section.
Catechesis/Religious Program—Students 97.

SUMMIT HILL, CARBON CO.

1—ST. JOSEPH (1850) [CEM 3] Rev. James J. Burdess.
Mailing Address & Res.: 118 N. Market St., 18250-1108. Tel: 570-645-2664; Fax: 570-645-3037. Email: stjs@ptd.net. Web: www.stjscatholicchurch.org.
Church: 462 W. Ludlow St., 18250-1108.
See Our Lady of the Angels Academy, Lansford under Regional Catholic Elementary Schools, Diocesan located in the Institution section.
Catechesis/Religious Program— Twinned with Coaldale/Lansford. Students 30.

TAMAQUA, SCHUYLKILL CO.

1—ST. JEROME (1833) Rev. James C. Bechtel.
Res.: 266 W. Broad St., 18252-1819. Tel: 570-668-2301; Fax: 570-668-4406. Email: stjeromes@verizon.net. Web: www.parishesonline.com/stjerometamaqua.
School—250 W. Broad St., 18252-1819. Tel: 570-668-2757; Fax: 570-668-6101. Email: altssj@ptd.net. Mary Ann Mansell, Prin.; Mrs. Michelle Mansell, Pre-School Dir. Tel: 570-668-2651. Lay Teachers 9; Students 152.
Catechesis/Religious Program—Tel: 570-668-4416. Jane Habel, D.R.E.; Kristin Osenbach, Dir. Adult Formation. Students 157.

2—SS. PETER AND PAUL (1911), (Lithuanian), [CEM] [JC] Rev. William J. Linkchorst.
Res.: 307 Pine St., 18252. Tel: 570-668-1150; Fax: 570-668-6933.
See St. Jerome Regional School, Tamaqua under Regional Catholic Schools Diocesan located in the Institution Section.
Catechesis/Religious Program—Tel: 570-668-4416. Students 75.

TREMONT, SCHUYLKILL CO.

1—MOST BLESSED TRINITY PARISH (2008), Formed by the merger of Immaculate Conception, Tremont, Sacred Heart, Newtown & SS. Peter and Paul, Tower City. Rev. Paul L. Rothermel.
Mailing Address: P.O. Box 35, 17981-0035. Tel: 570-695-3648; Fax: 570-695-2275. Email: mostbt@wtvaccess.com.
Rectory—113 Cherry St., 17981.
See Assumption BVM, Pottsville, under Regional Catholic Elementary Schools, Diocesan located in the Institution section.
Catechesis/Religious Program—Students 60.

WALNUTPORT, NORTHAMPTON CO., ST. NICHOLAS (1974) [CEM] Rev. Msgr. Thomas A. Derzack; Deacon Michael W. Kudla.
4412 Mountain View Dr., 18088-9728.
Res.: 1152 Oak Rd., 18088-9728. Tel: 610-767-3107; Fax: 610-760-6241. Email: stnickll@ptd.net. Web: stnicholaswalnutport.parishesonline.com.
See St. John Neumann Regional School, Palmerton-Slatington under Regional Catholic Elementary Schools, Diocesan located in the Institution section.
Catechesis/Religious Program—Students 127.

WEATHERLY, CARBON CO.

1—OUR LADY OF LOURDES PARISH (2008), Formed by the merger of St. Nicholas, Weatherly and St. Mary, Beaver Meadows. Rev. Floyd Caesar Jr.
Rectory—318 Plane St., 18255-1012. Tel: 570-427-4123; Fax: 570-427-4615. Email: oll318@metrocast.net.
See McAdoo Catholic Elementary School, McAdoo under Regional Catholic Elementary Schools, Diocesan located in the Institution section.
Catechesis/Religious Program—Barbara Braun, D.R.E. Students 144.

WEST READING, BERKS CO., SACRED HEART (1917), (German), Rev. Msgr. Joseph A. DeSantis; Deacon William R. Kase.
Lakeview Dr. at Cherry St., P.O. Box 6217, Reading, 19610-0217. Tel: 610-372-4010; Fax: 610-372-4926. Email: shc6217@aol.com. Web: www.shrcparish.org. In Res., Rev. Gregory R. Karpyn.
Res.: 740 Cherry St., 19611.
School—701 Franklin St., 19611-1029. Tel: 610-373-3316; Fax: 610-375-7299. Email: altbsh@ptd.net. Mrs. Katherine Napolitano, Prin. Lay Teachers 12; Students 161.
Catechesis/Religious Program—Tel: 610-374-5430. Ms. Valerie Christo-Pinheiro, D.R.E. Students 112.

WHITEHALL, LEHIGH CO.

1—ST. ELIZABETH (1941) Rev. Msgr. Anthony D. Muntone, S.T.L.; Rev. Michael E. Mullins.
Res.: 618 Fullerton Ave., 18052-6726. Tel: 610-266-0695; Fax: 610-266-1548. Email: adm1936@sercc.org. Web: www.sercc.org.
See St. Elizabeth Regional School, Whitehall under Regional Catholic Elementary Schools, Diocesan located in the Institution section.

2—HOLY TRINITY (1928) Rev. Msgr. Daniel J. Yenushosky; Deacons Eugene J. Wyrwa; Michael J. Laroche. In Res., Rev. Msgr. David L. James.
Res.: 4102 S. Church St., 18052-2415. Tel: 610-262-9315; Fax: 610-261-3576.
See Good Shepherd Catholic School, Northampton under Regional Catholic Elementary Schools, Diocesan located in the Institution section.
Catechesis/Religious Program—Mrs. Barbara Majkowski, C.R.E. Students 243.

3—ST. JOHN THE BAPTIST (1927) [CEM] Rev. Joseph J. Campion.
Res.: 3024 S. Ruch St., 18052. Tel: 610-262-2260; Fax: 610-262-1935. Email: stjohnsstiles@verizon.net.
See Good Shepherd Catholic School, Northampton under Regional Catholic Elementary Schools, Diocesan located in the Institution section.
Catechesis/Religious Program—Irene M. Quigley, D.R.E. Students 75.

Chaplains of Public Institutions

ALLENTOWN. *Country Meadows.* (St. Catharine of Siena)
Devon House Personal Care Home (1930). (St. Thomas More)
Good Shepherd Home and Rehabilitation Hospital. Deacon Cu T. Than. (St. Paul)
Lehigh County Prison. (Sacred Heart)
Lehigh Valley Hospital, Allentown Campus, 17th and Chew Sts., 18103. (St. Catharine of Siena)
Lehigh Valley Hospital at Cedar Crest, Tel: 610-402-8465 Pastoral Care. Rev. Joseph P. Becker, O.S.F.S., M.A., Deacon Anthony L. Brasten. (St. Thomas More)
Liberty Nursing Center. (St. Catharine of Siena)
St. Luke's Hospital, Allentown Campus. (St. Catharine of Siena)
Luthercrest. (St. Joseph, Orefield)
Manor Care Nursing Home, 1265 S. Cedar Crest Blvd., 18103. Rev. Gregory R. Karpyn, B.A., M.A., M.Div., (St. Paul).
New Seasons Personal Care Home. (St. Thomas More)
Phoebe Devitt Home. (St. Catharine of Siena)
Westminster Village. (Our Lady Help of Christians)

ASHLAND. *Ashland Regional Medical Center.* Administered by St. Mauritius, Ashland; St. Joseph, Ashland; St. Joseph, Girardville; St. Vincent de Paul, Girardville; Our Lady of Good Counsel, Gordon.

BETHLEHEM. *Atria.* (Notre Dame of Bethlehem)
Lehigh Valley Muhlenberg Medical Center. (Notre Dame of Bethlehem)
Lehigh Valley Muhlenberg Rehab Center. (Notre Dame of Bethlehem)
Lutheran Manor of the Lehigh Valley, Inc. (Notre Dame of Bethlehem)
Manor Care Nursing and Rehabilitation Centers I and II. (Notre Dame of Bethlehem)

COALDALE. *Edgemont Lodge Assisted Living Personal Care Home.* St. Katharine Drexel, Lansford
St. Luke's Miners Memorial Medical Center. St. Katharine Drexel, Lansford

EASTON. *Easton Home.* (Our Lady of Mercy)
Easton Hospital. (Priests of Easton Area)
Easton Nursing Center. (Our Lady of Mercy)
Northampton County Prison. (Our Lady of Mercy)
Praxis. (Our Lady of Mercy)

FOUNTAIN HILL. *Cedarbrook.* (Lehigh County Home) St. Ursula.
St. Luke's Hospital. (St. Ursula)

FRACKVILLE. *SCI-Mahoney.* Vacant. (State Correctional Institution)

HAMBURG. *Hamburg Center.* (St. Mary)
Laurel Nursing Center. (St. Mary)

LEHIGHTON. *Gnaden Huetten Memorial Hospital.* (SS. Peter and Paul)
Gnaden Huetten Nursing Home. (SS. Peter & Paul)
Mahoning Valley Nursing Home. (SS. Peter & Paul)

MACUNGIE. *Lehigh Center Nursing Home*, 1718 Spring Creek Rd., 18062. Rev. Gregory R. Karpyn, B.A., M.A., M.Div. St. Paul, Allentown
Lehigh Commons Personal Care Home, 1680 Spring Creek Rd., 18062. Rev. Gregory R. Karpyn, B.A., M.A., M.Div. St. Paul, Allentown

MINERSVILLE. *Federal Correctional Institution Schuylkill*, P.O. Box 700, 17954-0700. Tel: 570-544-7191; Fax: 570-544-7196. Sr. Patricia Weldman, Chap. Email: pweldman@bop.gov.

NAZARETH. *Gracedale.* Deacon Donald J. Dupont. (Northampton County Home) Holy Family.

NEW TRIPOLI. *Jenny's Country Manor.* (St. Joseph the Worker, Orefield)

ORWIGSBURG. *Orwigsburg Center.* (St. Ambrose, Schuylkill Haven)

Pinebrook Personal Care Center. (St. Ambrose, Schuylkill Haven)
PALMERTON. *Palmerton Hospital*. Rev. William T. Campion, M.Div., Th. M, Chap. (Sacred Heart)
POTTSVILLE. *Luther Ridge*. (St. Patrick)
Manor Care. (St. Patrick)
Providence Place. (St. Patrick)
Schuylkill County Prison. St. Patrick, Pottsville
Schuylkill Manor. (St. Patrick)
York Terrace Nursing Home. (St. John)
READING. *Berks County Prison*. (St. Ignatius Loyola, Sinking Spring; St. Peter, Reading - Spanish Speaking Inmates)
Berks-Heim. (Berks County Home; St. Ignatius Loyola, Sinking Spring)
Villa St. Elizabeth, 1201 Museum Rd., 19611. (Sacred Heart, West Reading)
Wyomissing Nursing and Rehabilitation Center, 1000 E. Wyomissing Blvd., 19611. (Sacred Heart)
SCHUYLKILL HAVEN. *Rest Haven County Home*. (St. Ambrose)
SINKING SPRING. *Columbia Cottage*. (St. Ignatius Loyola)
TREXLERTOWN. *Mosser Nursing Home*. (St. Joseph the Worker, Orefield)
WEATHERWOOD. *Carbon County District Home*. (Our Lady of Lourdes, Weatherly)
Heritage Hill (Personal Care). (Our Lady of Lourdes, Weatherly)
WERNERSVILLE. *Phobe Berks Village*. (St. Ignatius Loyola)
State Hospital. Deacon Richard A. Horst.
WESCOSVILLE. *Lehigh County Home*. (Cedarbrook) (St. Catharine of Siena, Allentown.)
WEST READING. *Manorcare Health Services*, 425 Buttonwood St., 19611. (Sacred Heart)
Reading Hospital and Medical Center. Rev. Gregory R. Karpyn, B.A., M.A., M.Div., Chap., Deacon William R. Kase. (Sacred Heart)
Spruce Manor Nursing and Rehabilitation Center, 220 S. Fourth Ave., 19611. (Sacred Heart)
WYOMISSING. *County Meadows*. (St. Ignatius Loyola, Sinking Spring)
Highlands at Wyomissing, 2000 Cambridge Ave., 19610. (Sacred Heart, West Reading)

On Duty Outside the Diocese:
Rev. Msgrs.—
Bartkus, Algimantas A. (BRK), 85-22 150th St., Jamaica, NY 11435-2826.
Callaghan, Aloysius R., Rector & Vice Pres., The Saint Paul Seminary School of Divinity, 2260 Summit Ave., St. Paul, MN 55105-5050. Tel: 651-962-5050
Revs.—
Czartoryński, David F., 437 Arch Ridge Loop, Seffner, FL 33584-3703.
Gillis, David C., St. Ann Church, P.O. Box 530218, Debary, FL 32753-0218. Tel: 386-668-8270
Thomas, James J., 905 N. Allerton Rd., Belleville, IL 62221.

Military Chaplains:
Revs.—
Butera, Christopher S., M.Div., M.A., Chap., 14 Crain St., Fort Rucker, AL 36362-2209.
Connolly, James M.T., Lt., CHC, 313 Riverwood Ct., Virginia Beach, VA 23454-3232.
Dermott, William R., Chap., 100 E. Ocean View Ave., Apt. 511, Norfolk, VA 23503-1632. Tel: 757-227-3490

Unassigned:
Revs.—
Brennan, Edmund J.
Margarito, Luis A. Bonilla, M.Div.
Onushco, William J.

Retired:
Rev. Msgrs.—
Barrett, Francis X., 3021 Countryside Blvd., Apt. A30, Clearwater, FL 33761.
Benestad, Thomas J., M.Div., 1299 Ocean Blvd. K-2, Boca Raton, FL 33432-7729.
Birch, Thomas J., Immaculate Conception BVM Rectory, 905 Chestnut St., Douglassville, 19518-9006.
Coll, Robert J., 2956 Gilford Way, Naples, FL 34119-7523.
Dooley, Joseph P., Carver House, 337 Carver Dr., Bethlehem, 18017.
Forst, Robert M., Our Lady Help of Christians Rectory, 444 N. Jasper St., 18109-2699.
Hoban, Thomas E., St. John the Baptist, 3024 Ruch Ave., Whitehall, 18052.
Loeper, Richard J., M.A., Immaculate Conception Rectory, 905 Chestnut St., Douglassville, 19518-9006.
Merman, Raymond F., Holy Family Villa, 1325 Prospect Ave., Bethlehem, 18018.
Morrison, David J., Our Lady of Perpetual Help Parish Center, 3219 Santee Rd., Bethlehem, 18020-2833.
Ott, Alfred R., V.F., M.Div., Holy Family Villa, 1325 Prospect Ave., Bethlehem, 18018.
Rigney, Dennis A., 580 Yellow Pine Dr., Auburn, 17922.
Wassel, Anthony F., 36 Clay St., New Philadelphia, 17959.
Revs.—
Bolez, Edward C., 1340 W. Linden St., 18102.
Brady, James J., Holy Family Villa, 1325 Prospect Ave., Bethlehem, 18018-4916.
Braudis, Joseph M., Holy Family Villa, 1325 Prospect Ave., Bethlehem, 18018-4916.
Briggman, Michael J., Holy Family Villa, 1325 Prospect Ave., Bethlehem, 18018-4916.
Conte, John P., Holy Family Villa, 1325 Prospect Ave., Bethlehem, 18018-4916.
Dagle, Harold F., M.A., St. Mary, 2N. 8th St., Lebanon, 17046.
Fromholzer, Francis J., P.O. Box F, 18105.
Gillespie, Francis T., Holy Family Villa, 1325 Prospect Ave., Bethlehem, 18018-4916.
Grundowski, Francis M., P.O. Box 13553, Reading, 19612-3553.
Halabura, Stephen J., Holy Family Villa, 1325 Prospect St., Bethlehem, 18018-4916.
Hulko, Joseph D., Holy Family Villa, 1325 Prospect Ave., Bethlehem, 18018-4916.
Jones, William P., Holy Family Manor Nursing Home, 1200 Spring St., Bethlehem, 18018-4915.
Kerestus, Thomas J., P.O. Box F, 18105.
Lawrence, Michael S., P.O. Box F, 18105-1538.
Lofton, James J., 1759 Tanglewood Rd., Orwigsburg, 17961.
McElduff, Edward W., 2586 Mountain Rd., Slatington, 18080.
McKenna, F. Charles, Holy Family Villa, 1325 Prospect Ave., Bethlehem, 18018-4916.
Mihalak, James J., P.O. Box F, 18105-1538.
O'Donnell, William J., Holy Family Manor, 1200 Spring St., Bethlehem, 18018-4940.
Paskowicz, Marian, 469 Ridge Line Ct., Dayton, OH 45458.
Quinn, Robert C., St. Benedict Rectory, 2020 Chestnut Hill Rd., Mohnton, 19540.
Sattler, Frederick F., Holy Family Villa, 1325 Prospect Ave., Bethlehem, 18018.
Schwartz, Edwin V., Immaculate Conception, 501 Ridge Ave., 18102.

Permanent Deacons:
Allison, John J., (Retired)
Alvarado, Leopoldo, St. Peter, Reading
Amedeo, Dominick F., Jr., St. Ann, Emmaus
Autrey, William L., St. Ignatius Loyola, Sinking Spring
Benkovic, Richard L., Immaculate Conception, Allentown
Bloom, Fredic, Assumption B.V.M., Slatington
Bogusky, Joseph H., Annunciation B.V.M., Catasauqua
Boyle, Michael J., Most Blessed Sacrament, Bally
Brasten, Anthony L., Assumption B.V.M., Northampton; Lehigh Valley Hospital Center, Allentown
Buragino, Joseph G., (Retired)
Campanell, Anthony T., St. Joseph the Worker, Orefield
Carlin, Hugh, Sacred Heart, Bethlehem (Miller Heights)
Centeno, Jesus, (Retired)
Chiles, Franklin J., (Retired)
Close, Richard B., (Serving outside diocese)
Colon, Francisco De La Gracia, St. Joseph, Reading
Colon, Julio, St. Peter, Reading
Corchado, Julian, Sacred Heart of Jesus, Allentown
Cosgrove, Francis J., (Retired)
Costa, Joseph J., Blessed Teresa of Calcutta, Mahanoy City
Coyle, Charles A., (Retired)
Cummings, John D., (Retired)
Danyi, Frank J., Jr., (Retired)
De Bellis, Charles A., (Retired)
De Jesus, Roberto, (On Duty Outside the Diocese)
DeCastro, Jose F., Our Lady of Mercy, Easton
Doncsecz, Michael W., Notre Dame of Bethlehem, Bethlehem
Duncan, James R., St. Thomas More, Allentown
Dupont, Donald J., Holy Family, Nazareth; Northampton County Home, Gracedale
Elliott, Donald W., Assumption B.V.M., Bethlehem
Ferris, Lewis T., Sacred Heart, Bath
Flanley, Eugene M., Jr.
Fleck, Henry J., Jr., (Retired)
Freed, Edward E., St. Ambrose, Schuylkill Haven
Fry, Craig A., St. Catharine of Siena, Reading
Gallagher, John B., Holy Guardian Angels, Reading
Gergar, Richard L., St. Anne, Bethlehem
Godiska, Joseph F., (Retired)
Gonzalez, Jose M., (Retired)
Gordon, Henry G., Office of the Permanent Diaconate and St. Mary, Hamburg
Granato, Gary J., St. Paul, Allentown
Hanni, John A., St. Jane Frances de Chantal, Easton
Hartzell, Reuben H., Jr., SS. Simon and Jude, Bethlehem
Hassler, William R., Cathedral of St. Catharine of Siena, Allentown
Henninger, James P., St. Katharine Drexel, Lansford
Hernandez, Saul, St. Paul, Allentown
Hiryak, Paul J., Jr., Immaculate Conception Blessed Virgin Mary, Douglassville
Horst, Richard A., Wernersville State Hospital, Wernersville; St. Catharine of Siena, Reading
Hunkele, Thomas H., (Retired)
Jaccodine, Ralph J., (Retired)
Kase, William R., Sacred Heart, West Reading
Kelly, George C., Jr., Our Lady of Perpetual Help, Bethlehem
Konopelski, John P., (Retired)
Koval, Edward P., (On Duty Outside the Diocese)
Kudla, Michael W., St. Nicholas, Walnutport
LaPolice, George D., (Retired)
Laroche, Michael J., Holy Trinity, Whitehall
Lash, Fredic W., Jr., St. Thomas More, Allentown
Maggitti, Alexander L., Sr., (Retired)
Matos, Rodoberto, Holy Infancy, Bethlehem
Meyer, Dennis P., St. Joseph, Coopersburg
Miller, Thomas H., Incarnation, Bethlehem
Monahan, Brian J., (Retired)
Morales, Edison, (On Duty Outside the Diocese)
Mroz, John J., St. Joseph, Jim Thorpe
Murphy, John W., Jr., (Retired)
Murphy, Thomas J., St. Francis Academy and Most Blessed Sacrament, Bally
Najera-Ramirez, Francisco, St. Paul, Reading
Paschall, Joseph L., Jr., (Retired)
Pitts, William P., Sacred Heart, Palmerton
Pogash, John F., (Retired)
Pufko, Joseph H., St. Jane Frances de Chantel, Easton
Quirk, John E., St. Patrick, Pottsville
Ramirez, Manuel L., Holy Infancy, Bethlehem
Raymundo, Ranulfo, St. Jane Frances de Chantal, Easton
Reimer, Thomas B., St. Lawrence the Martyr, Catasauqua
Reyes, Roberto, Sacred Heart of Jesus, Allentown
Rodgers, Robert W., Chap., Eastern Hospital; St. Jane Frances de Chantal, Easton
Rodriguez, Nicasio, (Retired)
Rodriguez-Trejo, Jose N., (On Duty Outside the Diocese)
Rohner, David K., St. Ursula, Fountain Hill
Rolon, Ramon L., St. Margaret, Reading
Sablone, Stephen F., St. Francis de Sales, Robesonia; St. Scholastica, Lecanto, FL
Santos-Gonzalez, Jose M., Sacred Heart of Jesus, Allentown
Schettini, Bruno, St. Joseph the Worker, Orefield
Schmidt, Gerald R., Office of the Permanent Diaconate; St. Theresa of the Child Jesus, Hellertown
Schneider, Gregory G., St. Margaret, Reading
Setlock, John A., St. Richard, Barnesville
Sheridan, John, (Retired)
Shubella, Thomas F., St. Thomas More, Allentown
Solis, Alfonso D., (Retired)
Than, Cu T., Good Shepherd Home and Rehabilitation Hospital; St. Paul, Allentown
Thoden, Richard M., Jr., Assumption B.V.M., Bethlehem
Thompson, John F., (Retired)
Toolan, James, St. Thomas More, Allentown
Torres, Fernando L., (Retired)
Torres, Mariano, St. Peter, Reading
Trexler, Jeffrey R., Ph.D., SS. Simon & Jude, Bethlehem
Tyson, Robert J., (Retired)
Visot, Luis R., (Retired)
Wagner, William J., (Retired)
Wilkinson, Raymond, (Retired)
Wisser, Bernard M.
Woodall, Michael V., St. Columbkill, Boyertown
Wyrwa, Eugene J., Holy Trinity, Whitehall
Young, Robert P., St. Francis of Assisi, Allentown
Urbine, William F., Assumption B.V.M, Bethlehem; Office of the Permanent Diaconate

INSTITUTIONS LOCATED IN THE DIOCESE

[A] SEMINARIES, RELIGIOUS OR SCHOLASTICATES

CENTER VALLEY. *Sacred Heart Villa, Missionaries of the Sacred Heart*, 3300 Station Ave., 18034-9563. Tel: 610-282-1415, Ext. 21; Fax: 610-282-0610. Email: mscvilla@aol.com. Web: www.misacor-usa.org. Very Revs. E. Michael Camilli, M.S.C., S.T.L., M.S.L.S., H.E.L., Supr./Rector; John J. Paul, M.S.C., V.J., S.T.L., J.C.D.; Revs. Thomas Carney, M.S.C.; Thomas Keller, M.S.C.; Ronald Leinen, M.S.C., Ph.D.; Joseph T. Muller, M.S.C.; Leo Petit, M.S.C., M.A.; Robert Tobolski, M.S.C.; Bros. Nicholas Lanese, M.S.C.; John Peralta, M.S.C.; Robert Murphy, M.S.C.; Alois Schirmers, M.S.C.; Anton Freitas, M.S.C.; George Farkas, M.S.C.; John Rose, M.S.C.; Warren Perreto. Priests 10; Brothers 8; Total Staff 6.

WERNERSVILLE. *Jesuit Center-Jesuit Community* (1930) P.O. Box 223, 19565-0223. 501 N. Church Rd., 19565-0223. Tel: 610-678-8085; Fax: 610-678-8747. Email: jescntbus@jesuitcenter.org. Web: www.jesuitcenter.org. Rev. Joseph A. Currie, S.J., Rector. Priests 19; Brothers 3; Sisters 1; Lay Staff 12; Total Staff 16. In Res. Revs. Bert Akers, S.J.; John P. Barron, S.J.; James A. Borbely, S.J.; Henry G. Coster, S.J.; James J. Ditillo, S.J.; Robert J. Dullahan, S.J.; Francis P. Gillespie, S.J.; Lucien F. Longtin, S.J.; William D. Lynn, S.J.; John J. Martinez, S.J.; John T. McCaslin, S.J.; Edwin J. Sanders, S.J.; Joseph P. Sanders; William J. Sneck, S.J.; D. Gilbert Sweeney, S.J.; Robert D. Wiesenbaugh, S.J.; Justin Whittington, S.J.; Bros. Thomas S. Kretz, S.J.; James C. Lemon, S.J.; Thomas R. Williams, S.J.

[B] COLLEGES AND UNIVERSITIES

CENTER VALLEY. *DeSales University*, 2755 Station Ave., 18034-9568. Tel: 610-282-1100; Fax: 610-282-1480. Email: admiss@desales.edu. Web: www.DeSales.edu. Very Rev. Bernard F. O'Connor, O.S.F.S., Ph.D., Pres.; Rev. Alexander T. Pocetto, O.S.F.S., Ph.D., Senior Vice Pres.; Mrs. Linda Zerbe, Dean Students; Mrs. Mary Birkhead, Dean Enrollment Mgmt.; Mr. Thomas Mantoni, Registrar; Mr. Robert J. Snyder, Vice Pres. Admin., Fin. & Environment; Mr. Thomas Campbell, Vice Pres. Devel.; Dr. Karen Doyle Walton, Vice Pres. Academic Affairs & Provost; Rev. John A. Hanley, O.S.F.S., M.Div., M.R.E., Dir. Campus Min.; Mr. Michael Sweetana, Dir. Fin. & Treas.; Dr. Gerard Joyce, Vice Pres. for Student Life; Revs. Joseph P. Becker, O.S.F.S., M.A.; Douglas C. Burns, O.S.F.S., M.Div.; Very Rev. Thomas F. Dailey, O.S.F.S., S.T.D., Dir. Salesian Ctr. for Faith & Culture; Revs. Daniel G. Gambet, O.S.F.S., Ph.D., Pres. Emeritus; Peter J. Leonard, O.S.F.S., Ph.D., Dean of Graduate Educ.; Deacon George Kelly, M.A., Dir. Inst. Research; Revs. Gerard J. Schubert, O.S.F.S., Ph.D.; Mark Plaushin, O.S.F.S., M.Div., Exec. Dir., Public Safety; Mrs. Debbie Malone, Dir., Library; Bros. Daniel P. Wisniewski, O.S.F.S., Ph.D.; Joseph G. Schodowski, O.S.F.S., A.A.; Sr. John Marie Schauber, O.S.F.S.; Revs. Robert Rutledge, O.S.F.S., Ph.D., Asst. Prof., Biology; John O'Neill, O.S.F.S., M.Div., Asst., Pres.; John Fisher, O.S.F.S., Ed.D., Dir., Educational Initiatives & Salesian Ctr. Asst.; Mr. Timothy McIntire, O.S.F.S., Instructor, Theology. Coeducational liberal arts college conducted by the Oblates of St. Francis de Sales (1965); Accredited. Priests 6; Brothers 1; Sisters 1; Lay Teachers 285; Students 3,170.

READING. *Alvernia University* (1958) 19607. Tel: 610-796-8200; Fax: 610-796-8324. Email: tom.flynn@alvernia.edu. Web: www.alvernia.edu. Thomas F. Flynn, Ph.D., Pres.; Ms. Sharon Neal, Dir. Library & Educ. Svcs.; Dr. Shirley Williams, Provost; Dr. Joseph Cicula, Vice Pres. Univ. Life & Student Learning Experience; Sr. Roberta McKelve, O.S.F, Special Asst., Pres., Mission; Mr. Douglas Smith, Vice Pres., Fin. & Admin.; Mr. Michael Pressimone, Vice Pres., Inst. Advancement; Mr. John McCloskey Jr., Vice Pres., Enrollment Mgmt; Ms. Beki Stein, Registrar; Dr. Evelina Panayotova, Dir., Inst. Research; Mr. Jay Worrell, Exec. Dir., Center for Community Engagement. Bernardine Sisters of the Third Order of St. Francis., Catholic Franciscan University, coeducational, accredited, offering undergraduate & graduate education in Liberal Arts & Professional Programs & Doctoral Program in Leadership. Sisters 2; Lay Teachers 97; Students 4,052.

[C] HIGH SCHOOLS, DIOCESAN

ALLENTOWN. *Allentown Central Catholic High School*, 301 N. Fourth St., 18102-3098. Tel: 610-437-4601; Fax: 610-437-6760. Email: altlcchs@ptd.net. Web: www.acchs.info. Mrs. Yvonne G. McCarthy, Prin.; Mr. William F. Tielman Jr., Vice Prin. Priests 1; Lay Teachers 47; Students 790.

BANGOR. *Pius X High School*, 580 Third Ave., 18013-1399. Tel: 610-588-3291; Fax: 610-599-3048. Email: altnpxhs@ptd.net. Web: www.piusxhs.com. Mr. James Angeline, Prin. Sisters 1; Lay Teachers 23; Students 299.

BETHLEHEM. *Bethlehem Catholic High School*, 2133 Madison Ave., 18017-4699. Tel: 610-866-0791; Fax: 610-866-9892. Email: altnbchs@ptd.net. Web: www.BethlehemCatholichs.org. Mr. John P. Petruzzelli, Prin.; Mrs. Diane Young, Vice Prin.; Mr. Michael Grasso, Dean of Student Life; Mr. Richard F. Mazza, Dir. Admissions; Rev. Bernard J. Ezaki, Dir. Spiritual Activities; Very Rev. Peter J. Hosak, M.S., Guidance Counselor; Ms. Christine M. Chew, Dir. Institutional Advancement; Mrs. Mary Ann Harmanos, Librarian. Founded as two-year commercial high school, 1897.; Founded as four-year comprehensive high school, 1925. Sisters of St. Joseph 1; Priests 2; Lay Teachers 39; Students 759.

EASTON. *Notre Dame High School*, 3417 Church Rd., 18045-2999. Tel: 610-868-1431; Fax: 610-868-6710. Email: altnndhs@ptd.net. Web: www.ndcrusaders.org. Mr. Joseph R. Kramer Jr., Prin.; Mr. James E. Steiner, Vice Prin.; Rev. Robert J. George, M.Div., Chap.; Michelle Bonner, Librarian. Priests 1; Lay Teachers 39; Students 520.

POTTSVILLE. *Nativity B.V.M. High School*, One Lawtons Hill, 17901-2795. Tel: 570-622-8110; Fax: 570-622-0454. Email: altsnhs@ptd.net. Web: www.nativitybvm.net. Mrs. Lynn Sabol, Prin.; Mrs. Jennifer Daubert, Dir. Devel. Lay Teachers 18; Students 189.

READING. *Berks Catholic* (Formed by the merger of Holy Name & Central Catholic.), 955 E. Wyomissing Blvd., 19611-1799. Tel: 610-374-8361; Fax: 610-374-4309. Tony Balistrere, Prin.; Rev. Thomas P. Bortz, M.Div., S.T.B., Chap. Lay Teachers 42; Enrollment 710.

TAMAQUA. *Marian Catholic High School*, 166 Marian Ave., 18252. Tel: 570-467-3335; Fax: 570-467-0186. Email: altsmhs@ptd.net. Web: www.mariancatholicshs.org. Sr. Bernard Agnes, I.H.M., Prin.; Justen Hackenberg, Dir. Student Svcs; Rev. Kenneth A. Medve, Chap. Priests 1; Sisters (Servants of the Immaculate Heart of Mary) 3; Lay Teachers 27; Students 311.

[D] REGIONAL CATHOLIC ELEMENTARY SCHOOLS, DIOCESAN

ALLENTOWN. *St. John Vianney Regional School* (Formed by the merger of Cathedral School, St. Francis of Assisi School & St. Paul School, Allentown), 210 N. 18th St., 18104. Tel: 610-435-8981; Fax: 610-437-7951. Mrs. Robin Fredericks, Prin. Lay Teachers 25; Students 395.

Sacred Heart School, (Grades PreK-8), 325 N. Fourth St., 18102-3007. Tel: 610-437-3031; Fax: 610-437-2724. Email: altlsh@ptd.net. James Krupka, Prin. Serving Sacred Heart & St. Stephen, Allentown. Lay Teachers 11; Students 321.

BALLY. *St. Francis Academy*, 668 Pine St., 19503. Tel: 610-845-7364; Fax: 610-845-2223. Email: sfacademy@aol.com. Web: www.sfabally.org. Deacon Thomas J. Murphy, Prin. Serving Most Blessed Sacrament, Bally, St. Columbkill, Boyertown, and St. Mary, Kutztown. Lay Teachers 10; Students 187.

BETHLEHEM. *St. Michael the Archangel School* Serving Assumption B.V.M., Bethlehem; St. Joseph, Coopersburg (Limeport)

Primary Bldg. (Grades K-4), 5040 St. Joseph's Rd., Coopersburg, 18036. Tel: 610-965-4441; Fax: 610-965-1030; Tel: 610-965-9383 (PreSchool).

Middle School (Grades 5-8), Main Office., 4121 Old Bethlehem Pike, 18015. Tel: 610-867-8422; 610-867-7892 (Pre-school); Fax: 610-865-2098. Lori L. Rutkiewicz, M.Ed., Prin. Priests 2; Lay Teachers 26; Students (K-8) 320.

Seton Academy, (Grades K-8), 623 6th Ave., 18018-5224. Tel: 610-867-9530; Fax: 610-868-6784. Email: altlset@ptd.net. Web: www.setonacademypa.org. Dr. Patricia A. Coughlin, Prin. Serving SS. Simon and Jude, Holy Ghost, St. Ursula & Incarnation of Our Lord. Lay Teachers 12; Students 118.

The Aquinas Program (Elementary Level), 623 6th Ave., 18018-5224. Tel: 610-867-5930; Fax: 610-868-6784. Mr. Louis Rusnock, Supvr.; Dr. Patricia A. Coughlin, Prin.; Tracy Prostko, Librarian.

JIM THORPE. *St. Joseph Regional Academy*, (Grades K-8), 25 W. 6th St., 18229-2120. Tel: 570-325-3186; Fax: 570-325-9451. Email: altcsjra@ptd.net. Ms. Melissa Cuzzola-Novatnack, Prin. Serving St. Joseph, Immaculate Conception, Jim Thorpe, St. Peter the Fisherman, and Lake Harmony. Lay Teachers 8; Students 118.

LANSFORD. *Our Lady of the Angels Academy* (1999) (Grades PreK-8), 123 E. Water St., 18232-2001. Tel: 570-645-7170; Fax: 570-645-5278. Email: altcola@ptd.net. Web: www.oloa.net. Sr. Regina Elinich, I.H.M., Prin. Serving St. Katharine Drexel, Lansford; St. Francis of Assisi, Nesquehoning & St. Joseph, Summit Hill. Sisters 2; Lay Teachers 8; Students 109.

MCADOO. *McAdoo Catholic Elementary School*, (Grades PreK-8), 35 N. Cleveland St., 18237-1915. Tel: 570-929-1442; Fax: 570-929-3016. Email: altsmacc@ptd.net. Sr. Amy Summers, I.H.M., Prin.; Mrs. Rita Prekopa, Librarian. Serving St. Patrick, St. Kunegunda, St. Mary, McAdoo; St. Bartholomew, St. Michael, Tresckow; Immaculate Conception, Kelayres; St. Nicholas, Weatherly; St. Mary, Beaver Meadows; Church of All Saints, McAdoo; Our Lady of Lourdes, Weatherly. Sisters 2; Lay Teachers 10; Students 123.

NORTHAMPTON. *Good Shepherd Catholic School*, 1300 Newport Ave., 18067. Tel: 610-262-9171; Fax: 610-262-2202. Email: altngs@ptd.net. Web: www.gscatholic.com. Irene M. Quigley, M.Ed., Prin.; Christine Siebler, Librarian. Serving Our Lady of Hungary, Assumption B.V.M., Northampton; St. Lawrence and St. Andrew, Catasauqua; St. Peter, Coplay; St. John the Baptist & Holy Trinity, Whitehall. Lay Teachers 18; (K-8) 280; (Pre-K) 32.

PALMERTON-SLATINGTON. *St. John Neumann Regional School*, (Grades K-3), Serving St. Nicholas, Berlinsville; Sacred Heart, Palmerton; Assumption B.V.M., Slatington.

(Grades 4-8), 259 Lafayette Ave., 18071. Tel: 610-826-2354; Fax: 610-826-6444. Email: altcsjn@ptd.net. Sr. Virginia Stephanie, S.S.J., M.S., Prin. Sisters 1; Lay Teachers 8; Students 80.

(Grades K-3), 641-645 W. Washington St., Slatington, 18080. Tel: 610-767-2935; Fax: 610-767-2948. Email: altcsjn@ptd.net.

PEN ARGYL. *Immaculate Conception School*, (Grades K-6), Babbitt Ave. & Heller Ave., 18072. Tel: 610-863-4816; Fax: 610-863-8158. Email: altnics@ptd.net. Web: www.immaculateconceptionschool.net. Sr. Maria Luz, O.P., Prin.; Mrs. Bernie Tucker, Librarian. Serving St. Elizabeth, Pen Argyl; St. Rocco, Martins Creek. Sisters 5; Lay Teachers 4; Students 154.

POTTSVILLE. *Assumption BVM School*, (Grades K-8), 112 S. Seventh St., 17901-3079. Tel: 570-622-0106; 570-622-1765; Fax: 570-622-4737. Email: altsabvm@ptd.net. Web: www.assumptionbvmschool.net. Miss Kimberly A. Fetter, Prin. Serving St. Patrick, St. John the Baptist, Pottsville, St. Matthew the Evangelist, St. Michael the Archangel, Minersville & Most Blessed Trinity, Tremont; St. Clare of Assisi; St. Clair; Holy Cross, New Philadelphia; St. Stephen, Millersville. Lay Teachers 10; Students 121.

READING. *Holy Guardian Angels Regional School, Reading*, (Grades PreK-8), 3125 Kutztown Rd., 19605-2659. Tel: 610-929-4124; Fax: 610-929-1623. Email: altbhga@ptd.net. Web: www.hgaparish.com. Mrs. Maureen Wallin, Prin.; Carolyn Santoro, Librarian. Serving Holy Guardian Angels and St. Joseph, Reading. Lay Teachers 24; Students 425.

St. Ignatius Loyola School, (Grades PreK-8), 2700 St. Alban's Dr., 19609-1134. Tel: 610-678-0111; Fax: 610-670-5795. Email: altbsil@ptd.net. Web: www.stignatiusvikings.org. Mr. Robert Birmingham, Prin.; Mrs. Ann Rutkoski, Librarian. Serving St. Ignatius Loyola, Sinking Spring; St. Francis de Sales, Robesonia. Sisters 1; Lay Teachers 26; Students 404.

ROSETO. *Our Lady of Mt. Carmel School* (1953) 80 Ridge St., 18013-1398. Tel: 610-588-2629; Fax: 610-588-3423. Email: altnolmc@ptd.net. Web: www.olmc-roseto.org. Mr. Joseph Yannuzzi, Prin. Serving Our Lady of Mt. Carmel, Roseto and Our Lady of Good Counsel, Bangor. Lay Teachers 11; Students 150.

SHENANDOAH. *Trinity Academy at the Father Walter J. Ciszek Education Center*, (Grades PreK-8), 233 W. Cherry St., 17976. Tel: 570-462-3927; Fax: 570-462-4603. Email: altsta@ptd.net. Sr. Mary Ann Spaetti, I.H.M., Prin.; Barbara Eiche, Librarian. Serving Annunciation, St. Casimir, St. George, Our Lady of Mt. Carmel, St. Stanislaus, St. Stephen, Shenandoah; St. Mary Magdalen, Lost Creek; St. Mary, Ringtown; St. Joseph, Annunciation, St. Ann, Frackville; Our Lady of Good Counsel, Gordon; St. Joseph, St. Vincent de Paul, Girardville; St. Joseph, St. Mauritius,

Ashland; Blessed Theresa of Calcutta, Mahanoy City; St. Joseph, Sheppton. Religious 4; Lay Teachers 10; Students 170.

SHILLINGTON. *La Salle Academy*, (Grades PreK-8), 440 Holland St., 19607-3260. Tel: 610-777-7392; Fax: 610-777-1280. Email: altblsa@ptd.net. Web: www.lsabear.org. Dr. Patti Fisher, Psy.D., M.Ed., Prin.; Diana McNamara, Librarian. Serving St. John Baptist de La Salle, Shillington; St. Benedict, Mohnton; St. Anthony, Millmont. Lay Teachers 18; Students 214.

TAMAQUA. *St. Jerome Regional School* (1919) 250 W. Broad St., 18252-1819. Tel: 570-668-2757; Fax: 570-668-6101. Email: altssj@ptd.net. Web: www.sjrschool.com. Mary Ann Mansell, Prin. Serving St. Jerome, SS. Peter and Paul, Tamaqua. Lay Teachers 9; Students 157.

WHITEHALL. *St. Elizabeth Regional School* (1953) 433 Pershing Blvd., 18052. Tel: 610-264-0143; Fax: 610-264-1563. Email: altlse@ptd.net. Web: www.sercc.org/school. Sr. Bonita Smith, R.S.M., Prin.; Mrs. Lisa Capece, Librarian. Serving St. Elizabeth, Whitehall; Annunciation, Catasauqua. Religious 1; Lay Teachers 9; Students 178.

[E] SPECIAL SCHOOLS

ALLENTOWN. *Mercy Special Learning Center* (1954) 830 S. Woodward St., 18103-3440. Tel: 610-797-8242; Fax: 610-797-9092. Email: altlmslc@pdt.net. Web: www.mercyspeciallearning.org. Bridget L. Muehlencamp, Prin.; Mr. Louis Rusnock, Supvr. Ages: 18 months to post 21. Lay Teachers 8; Students 85.

EASTON. *The Aquinas Program - Secondary Level Notre Dame High School*, 3417 Church St., 18045-2999. Tel: 610-868-1431; Fax: 610-868-8710. Email: altnndhs@ptd.net. Mr. Joseph R. Kramer Jr., Prin.; Mr. Louis Rusnock, Supvr. Students 62.

POTTSVILLE. *St. Joseph Center for Special Learning*, 2075 W. Norwegian St., 17901-1907. Tel: 570-622-4638; Fax: 570-622-3420. Email: altssjc@ptd.net. Web: www.stjosephctr.com. Julia Leibensperger, Prin. Lay Teachers 3; Students 30.

READING. *The Aquinas Program St. Margaret School*, 233 Spring St., 19601-2121. Tel: 610-375-1882; Fax: 610-376-2291. Email: altbsmg@ptd.net. Sr. Marian Michele Smith, I.H.M., Prin.; Mr. Louis Rusnock, Dir. Tel: 610-866-0581, Ext. 25; ,Fax: 610-867-8702. Students 18.

SHILLINGTON. *John Paul II Center for Special Learning* (1982) 1092 Welsh Rd., 19607-0097. Tel: 610-777-0605; Fax: 610-777-0682. Email: info@johnpauliicenter.org. Web: www.johnpaulIIcenter.org. Mrs. Mary A. Adams, Prin.; Mrs. Becky Burton, Dir. Devel. Lay Teachers 4; Students 42.

WEST READING. *Alvernia Montessori School at Sacred Heart School* (1969) (Grades N-K), 211 Grace St., 19611. Tel: 610-396-0882. Sr. Ann Marie Coll, Prin. Bernardine Sisters, O.S.F. 4; Lay Teachers 1; Students 65.

[F] CATHOLIC CHARITIES AND SOCIAL AGENCIES

ALLENTOWN. *Catholic Charities*, 2141 Downyflake Ln., 18103-4774. Tel: 610-791-3888; Fax: 610-791-1878. Web: www.catholiccharityad.org. Mrs. Helen P. Kelleher, L.S.W., Exec. Dir. of Catholic Charities. Parish-based Counseling Centers: St. Columbkill, Boyertown; St. Joseph, Jim Thorpe; St. Mary's, Kutztown; St. Jerome, Tamaqua, Sacred Heart, Bath; St. Katharine Drexel, Lansford; St. Anthony of Padua, Easton; Annunciation B.V.M., Shenandoah.

Branch Offices: (For Lehigh and Northampton Cos.); (For Schuylkill and Carbon Cos.); (For Berks Co.)

Branch Office, 530 Union Blvd., 18109-3230. Tel: 610-435-1541; Fax: 610-435-4367.

13 Westwood Rd., Pottsville, 17901-1800. Tel: 570-628-0466; Fax: 570-628-3343.

Berks County Branch Office, The Madison Building, 400 Washington St., Ste. 100, Reading, 19601-3966. Tel: 610-376-7144; Fax: 610-376-7145.

[G] GENERAL HOSPITALS

ALLENTOWN. *Sacred Heart Hospital* (1912) 421 Chew St., 18102-3490. Tel: 610-776-4500; Fax: 610-776-4559. Web: shh.org. Mr. John Nespoli, Pres. & CEO; Rev. John G. Hilferty, Chap. & Dir. Pastoral Care. Priests 1; Deacons 1; Sisters 1; Bed Capacity 215; Skilled Nursing Beds 22; Patients Assisted Annually 179,456; Total Staff 1,275.

READING. *Bornemann Health Corporation* (1990) *c/o Saint Regional Health Network*, 2500 Bernville Rd., P.O. Box 316, 19603-0316. Tel: 610-378-2300; Fax: 610-378-2798. Web: www.sjmcberks.org. Mr. John Morahan, Pres. & CEO. Total Assisted (Physician Visits) 720; Total Staff 22.

Saint Joseph Medical Center, 2500 Bernville Rd., P.O. Box 316, 19603-0316. Tel: 610-378-2000; Fax: 610-378-2798. John R. Morahan, Pres. & CEO; Sr. Janet Henry, Vice Pres., Mission & Ministry. Opened Aug. 26, 1873. Sisters 5; Total Staff 1,323; Bed Capacity 212; Bassinets 22; Patients Assisted Annually 319,793.

[H] SKILLED NURSING FACILITIES

BETHLEHEM. *Holy Family Manor of Catholic Senior Housing and Health Care Services, Inc.* (1963) Holy Family Manor: a division of Catholic Senior Housing and Health Care Services, Inc., 1200 Spring St., 18018. Tel: 610-865-5595; Fax: 610-997-8454. Email: hkessler@hfmanor.org. Web: www.hfmanor.org. Judee Bavaria, Pres.; Mrs. Heather Kessler, N.H.A., Admin.; Mr. Robert Rakow, Interim Exec. Dir.; Rev. Clifton E. Bishop, Chap. Skilled and intermediate nursing care facility for the aged, chronically ill, or invalid. Capacity 208; Total Assisted 421; Total Staff 323.

SHOEMAKERSVILLE. *Covenant Home Care*, 1223 Pottsville Pike, 19555-1719. Tel: 800-726-8761; Fax: 570-385-5287. Email: slevengood@covenanthc.org. Web: www.covenanthc.org. Sandra Lee Levengood, M.B.A., R.N., Exec. Dir.

[I] HOMES AND SERVICES FOR THE ELDERLY AND CONVALESCENT

BETHLEHEM. *Grace Mansion Personal Care Home of Catholic Senior Housing and Health Care Services, Inc.*, 1200 Spring St., 18018. Tel: 610-865-6748; Fax: 610-997-8444. Email: kabruzzese@HFManor.org. Web: www.hfmanor.org. Mrs. Karen Abruzzese, Admin. Personal care home for 25 elderly. Total in Residence 23; Total Staff 13; Total Assisted 23.

Holy Family Apartments of Catholic Housing Corporation of Bethlehem, 330-338 13th Ave., 18018. Tel: 610-866-4603; Fax: 610-866-1622. Email: hfabeth@epix.net. Josephine Dries, Mgr.; Mark Mason, Dir. Catholic housing for the elderly. Total Staff 2; Apartments 50; Residents 50.

Trexler Pavilion, Assisted Living Residence of Catholic Senior Housing and Health Care Services, Inc., 1220 Prospect Ave., 18018. Tel: 610-868-7776; Fax: 610-865-7775. Email: kabruzzese@HFManor.org. Web: www.hfmpc.org. Mary Jo Kuebler, Admin. Personal care/assisted living facility for 23 elderly. Total in Residence 23; Total Staff 10; Total Assisted 27.

EASTON. *Antonian Towers*, 2405 Hillside Ave., 18042. Tel: 610-258-2033; Fax: 610-258-6541. Email: antoniantowers@verizon.net. Mark Mason, Dir.; Mrs. Judith Kern, Mgr. Catholic housing for the elderly. Apartments 50; Total in Residence 50; Total Staff 2.

NEW PHILADELPHIA. *Holy Family Apartments of Catholic Housing Corporation of New Philadelphia, c/o Neumann Apartments*, 25 N. Nichols St., St. Clair, 17970. Tel: 570-429-0699; Fax: 570-429-2368. Email: neumann@ptd.com. Apartments 11; Total Staff 2.

ORWIGSBURG. *Holy Family Adult Day Care at St. Francis Center of Catholic Charities of the Diocese of Allentown, Inc.*, 900 W. Market St., 17961. Tel: 570-366-2924; Fax: 570-366-2301. Email: lherb@allentowndiocese.org. Mrs. Linda Herb, Dir. Day care for the elderly. Total Staff 7; Clients 34.

Holy Family Assisted Living Residence of Catholic Senior Housing and Health Care Services, Inc., 900 W. Market St., 17961. Tel: 570-366-2912; Fax: 570-366-7781. Web: www.hfmanor.org. Deborah Bayliff, L.P.N., Admin.; Mrs. Karen Abruzzese, Dir. Residential Svcs. Personal care/assisted living facility for 59 elderly of Holy Family Manor. Total in Residence 55; Total Staff 21; Total Assisted 73.

POTTSVILLE. *Queen of Peace Apartments of Catholic Housing Corporation of Schuylkill County*, 777 Water St., 17901. Tel: 570-628-4504; Fax: 570-628-4712. Email: qpeace@comcast.net. Mark Mason, Dir.; Mrs. Diana Hess, Mgr. Catholic housing for the elderly. Apartments 48; Total in Residence 48; Total Staff 2.

READING. *Queen of Angels Apartments of Catholic Housing Corporation of Northern Berks County*, 22 Rothermel St., Hyde Park, 19605. Tel: 610-921-3115; Fax: 610-921-8576. Email: qangels@comcast.net. Mark Mason, Dir. Email: mmason@cshhcs.org; Hazel C. Black, Mgr. Catholic housing for the elderly. Apartments 45; Total in Residence 47; Total Staff 3.

Sacred Heart Villa - Personal Care Community of the Missionary Sisters of the Most Sacred Heart of Jesus (2003) 51 Seminary Ave., 19605. Tel: 610-929-5751; Fax: 610-929-0762. Email: sacredheartvilla@comcast.com. Web: sacredheartvilla-readingpa.org. Sr. Mary Anne Bigos, M.S.C., Admin. Bed Capacity 100; Total Assisted 78; Total Staff 56.

SAINT CLAIR. *Neumann Apartments of Catholic Housing Corporation of St. Clair*, 25 N. Nichols St., St. Clair, 17970. Tel: 570-429-0699; Fax: 570-429-2368. Email: neumann@ptd.com. Mark Mason, Dir.; Ms. Patricia Harris. Catholic housing for the elderly. Apartments 24; Total in Residence 24; Total Staff 2; Total in Residence 24; Total Staff 2.

[J] HOMES FOR PRIESTS

BETHLEHEM. *Holy Family Villa*, 1325 Prospect Ave., 18018-4916. Tel: 610-694-0395; Fax: 610-694-9990. In Res. Rev. Msgrs. Raymond F. Merman (Retired); Alfred R. Ott, V.F., M.Div. (Retired); Revs. James J. Brady (Retired); Joseph M. Braudis (Retired); Michael J. Briggman (Retired); Robert R. Fagan (Retired); Francis T. Gillespie (Retired); Stephen J. Halabura (Retired); Thomas Horan (Retired); Joseph D. Hulko (Retired); F. Charles McKenna (Retired); Luigi Palmieri (Retired); John J. Duminiak (Retired); John P. Conte (Retired); Joseph A. Sheehan (Retired); Frederick F. Sattler (Retired).

ORWIGSBURG. *St. Francis Villa for Priests*, 900 W. Market St., 17961-1008. Rev. Thomas Shanfelt, Rector.

[K] MONASTERIES AND RESIDENCES OF PRIESTS AND BROTHERS

BETHLEHEM. *The Barnabite Fathers Barnabite Spiritual Center*, 4301 Hecktown Rd., 18020-9704. Tel: 610-691-8648. Email: BarnabiteSpiritualCenter@gmail.com. Web: www.barnabites.com. Revs. Anthony M. Bianco, C.R.S.P., M.A.; Robert B. Kosek, C.R.S.P., Ph.D., Supr., Mod. of Spiritual Center; Paul M. Marconi, C.R.S.P., Vicar.

CENTER VALLEY. *Oblates of St. Francis de Sales*, Wills Hall, 2755 Station Ave., 18034-9568. Tel: 610-282-3300; Fax: 610-282-3962. Email: thomas.dailey@desales.edu. Web: www.desales.edu. Total in Residence 17. In Res. Very Rev. Thomas F. Dailey, O.S.F.S., S.T.D., Supr.; Rev. John Fisher, O.S.F.S., Ed.D.; Very Rev. Bernard F. O'Connor, O.S.F.S., Ph.D., Pres.; Revs. Joseph P. Becker, O.S.F.S., M.A.; Douglas C. Burns, O.S.F.S., M.Div.; Daniel G. Gambet, O.S.F.S., Ph.D.; J. Charles Goliath, O.S.F.S.; John A. Hanley, O.S.F.S., M.Div., M.R.E.; Peter J. Leonard, O.S.F.S., Ph.D.; John O'Neill, O.S.F.S., M.Div.; Mark Plaushin, O.S.F.S., M.Div.; Alexander T. Pocetto, O.S.F.S., Ph.D.; Robert Rutledge, O.S.F.S., Ph.D.; Bro. Joseph G. Schodowski, O.S.F.S., A.A.; Rev. Gerard J. Schubert, O.S.F.S., Ph.D.; Bro. Daniel P. Wisniewski, O.S.F.S., Ph.D.

EASTON. *St. Francis Friary*, 3908 Chipman Rd., 18045-3014. Tel: 610-515-0867; Fax: 610-515-0902. Web: www.catholic-church.org/stfran-retreat. Revs. William Reisteter, O.F.M.; Miles Pfalzer, O.F.M., Guardian; Daniel Havron, O.F.M.; Bros. Mark Ligett, O.F.M., Vicar; Edward Skutka, O.F.M.; Edward Demyanovich, O.F.M. Franciscan Province of St. John the Baptist. Brothers 3; Total in Residence 6.

NEW RINGGOLD. *Cistercian Monastery, St. Mary's Priory*, 70 Schuylkill Rd., 17960-9703. Tel: 570-943-2645; Fax: 570-943-3035. Very Rev. Luke Anderson, S.O.Cist., Th.M., Ph.D., Prior; Rev. Hugh Montague, S.O.Cist., M.A., Th.M. Fathers 3.

[L] CONVENTS AND RESIDENCES OF SISTERS

BETHLEHEM. *St. Joseph Convent*, 2133 Madison Ave., 18017-4642. Tel: 610-865-4691; Fax: 610-866-9892. Email: ssj2133@aol.com. Sisters 10.

Monocacy Manor (1947) 395 Bridle Path Rd., 18017. Tel: 610-866-2597; Fax: 610-861-7478. Web: www.schoolsistersosf.org. Sr. Bernadine Marie Stemnock, O.S.F., Prov. Min. School Sisters of the Third Order Regular United States Prov. Professed Sisters 21.

COOPERSBURG. *Carmelite Monastery* (1931) St. Therese of the Child Jesus and St. Mary Magdalen de Pazzi, St. Therese's Valley., 3551 Lanark Rd., 18036-9324. Tel: 610-797-3721; Fax: 610-797-8510. Sr. Mary Gertrude, O.Carm., Mother Prioress; Rev. Msgr. Thomas P. Koons, V.R., J.C.L., M.A., M.Div., Chap. Carmelite Nuns of the Ancient Observance (Calced) O.Carm. Professed Nuns 7.

EMMAUS. *Transfiguration Priory* (1998) 526 Fairview St., 18049-3837. Tel: 610-965-6818. Email: monasteryosb@enter.net. Sr. Martina Revak, O.S.B., Coord. Corporate Title: Benedictine Sisters of Baltimore, Ministries in the fields of education, pastoral ministry, hospitality and spirituality; A mission house of the Benedictine Sisters of Baltimore, Emmanuel Monastery. Members 3.

MAHANOY CITY. *St. Joseph Convent*, 536 W. South St., 17948-2422. Tel: 570-773-1420. Sr. M. Regine, M.C., Supr. Missionaries of Charity. Sisters 5.

NESQUEHONING. *Our Lady of Perpetual Help House of*

Prayer, 140 W. Mill St., 18240-1225. Tel: 570-669-9858. Email: hopnesq@ptd.net. Sr. Anne Elise Darreff, I.H.M., Supr. Email: ihmsae@aol.com. Sister Servants of the Immaculate Heart of Mary. Sisters 3.

PEN ARGYL. *Dominican Daughters of the Immaculate Mother*, 115 Lobb Ave., 18072. Tel: 610-863-9214; Fax: 610-863-9214. Email: ddimpa@epix.net. Sr. Maria Angelita, O.P., Supr. Sisters 6.

READING. *The Bernardine Sisters of the Third Order of Saint Francis*, 450 St. Bernardine St., 19607-1737. Tel: 484-334-6976; Fax: 484-334-6977. Email: RobertaAnn@bfranciscan.org. Web: www.bfranciscan.org. Sr. Marilisa H. da Silva, O.S.F., Congregational Min.

The Bernardine Sisters of the Third Order of Saint Francis, Generalate, (aka Bernardine Franciscan Sisters).

Bethany Convent, 1214 N. 14th St., 19604. Tel: 610-372-1753. Web: www.mscreading.org. Sisters Theresa Molchanow, M.S.C., Dir. Lay MSC; Barbara Daniels, M.S.C., Prov. Leadership Team & Treas. Sisters 3.

Chevalier House, 43 Seminary Ave., 19605. Tel: 610-929-8348; Fax: 610-929-0762. Web: www.mscreading.org. Sr. Virginia Marie Chnapko, M.S.C., Coord. Sisters 3.

St. Clare Convent, 465 St. Bernardine St., 19607-1736. Tel: 610-777-4590; Fax: 610-777-3973. Web: www.bfranciscan.org. Sr. Paula Nowak, O.S.F., Contact Person. Bernardine Franciscan Sisters. Sisters 2.

Hannibal House - Spiritual Center (1887) *Daughters of Divine Zeal, F.D.Z.*, 1526 Hill Rd., 19602-1410. Tel: 610-375-1738; 610-375-9072; Fax: 610-375-2188. Email: srdivinezeal@hotmail.com. Sisters 3.

House of Nazareth (Casa Nazaret), 532 Spruce St., 19602. Tel: 610-378-1947; Fax: 610-374-3351. Email: nazarethouse@comcast.net. Sr. Rosa But, Supr. Residence of the Poor Sisters of St. Joseph who work in Spanish Apostolate of Berks County. Sisters 3.

Saint Ignatius Convent, 2601 St. Alban Dr., 19609-1132. Tel: 610-678-2769. Sr. M. Patricia Brennan, O.S.F., Local Min. Sisters 2.

St. Joseph Villa (1967) 464 Bernardine St., 19607. Tel: 610-777-5556; Fax: 610-777-5545. Email: jeananthony@saintjosephvilla.com. Web: www.bfrancisan.org. Sisters Jean Anthony Rodgers, O.S.F., Admin.; La Verne Grippe, O.S.F.; Rev. Msgr. Edward W. Sarzynski, Chap. Home of the Retired Bernardine Sisters of the Third Order of St. Francis. Sisters 91.

MSC Province Center, 2811 Moyers Ln., 19605. Tel: 610-929-5944; Fax: 610-929-3634. Email: mscsisters@aol.com. Web: www.mscreading.org. Sr. Lorraine Molchanow, M.S.C., Province Leader. Provincial offices of Missionary Sisters of the Sacred Heart of Jesus. Sisters 2. *Our Lady of the Sacred Heart Convent*, 2811 Moyers Ln., 19605. Tel: 601-929-5944; Fax: 610-929-3634. Email: mscsisters@aol.com. Sisters 3.

Precious Blood Convent (1885) 1094 Welsh Rd., P.O. Box 97, 19607-0097. Tel: 610-777-1624; Fax: 610-777-3359. Email: cps.shillington@comcast.net. Web: www.cpsnap.com. Sisters Mary William Verhoeven, C.P.S, Prov. Supr.; Ethelyn Tucker, C.P.S., Local Supr. Residence for Missionary Sisters of the Precious Blood. Sisters 23.

Sacred Heart Convent, 460 St. Bernardine St., 19607-1737. Tel: 484-334-7000; Fax: 484-334-6808. Email: skateri@bfranciscan.org. Web: www.bfranciscan.org. Sr. Kateri Peake, O.S.F., Admin. Tel: 610-777-7221; Rev. Msgr. Edward W. Sarzynski, Chap. Motherhouse; Residence for Bernardine Sisters of Third Order of St. Francis. Professed Sisters 46; Total Staff 3.

Sacred Heart Villa, 51 Seminary Ave, 19605-2621. Tel: 610-929-5751; Fax: 610-929-0762. Email: mscsisters_shv@comcast.net. Sisters Marie Raymond Gazo, M.S.C., Local Supr.; Lorraine Molchanow, M.S.C., Prov. Supr. Motherhouse, Retirement Home of Missionary Sisters of the Most Sacred Heart of Jesus., Attended by Chaplain. Professed Sisters 30.

WEATHERLY. *Sisters of Peace Pentecost*, 484 Pump House Rd., 18255. Tel: 570-427-2467; Fax: 570-427-2545. Email: pentecosty@hanmail.net.

[M] RETREAT HOUSES

BETHLEHEM. *St. Francis Center for Renewal (Monocacy Manor)* (1948) 395 Bridle Path Rd., 18017. Tel: 610-867-8890; Fax: 610-861-7478. Email: stfranciscenter@gmail.com. Web: www.catholic-church.org/stfrancis-cfn. Sr. M. Barbara DeStefano, O.S.F., Dir. Weekend retreats (68) and days of recollection (70); retreats for men and women, marriage encounter; engaged encounters; parish retreats; workshops; youth groups; weekends; privately directed retreats; private retreats, spiritual direction. Professed Sisters 6; Lay Staff 4; Total Staff 10.

EASTON. *St. Francis Retreat House*, 3918 Chipman Rd., 18045-3014. Tel: 610-258-3053; Fax: 610-258-2412. Email: stfranrh@localnet.com. Web: www.stfrancisretreathouse.org. Rev. Daniel Havron, O.F.M., Dir. of Retreat & Prog.; Mr. Michael Markle, Exec. Dir. Retreatants 129.

ORWIGSBURG. *St. Francis Center*, 900 W. Market St., 17961-1006. Tel: 570-366-1016; Fax: 570-366-1017. Diocesan Agencies with Facilities in the St. Francis Center:

Holy Family Adult Day Care Tel: 570-366-2924; Fax: 570-366-2301. Email: lherb@allentowndiocese.org. Mrs. Linda Herb, Dir.

Holy Family Assisted Living Tel: 570-366-2912; Fax: 570-366-7781. Email: dbayliff@hfmanor.com. Deborah Bayliff, L.P.N., Admin.

READING. *Mariawald Renewal Center*, 1094 Welsh Rd., P.O. Box 97, 19607-0097. Tel: 610-777-0135; Fax: 610-777-3359. Email: mariawald@aol.com. Web: www.mariawaldrenewal.com. Diane Ross, Admin. Single, double, and triple occupancy. Units 16.

[N] CENTERS FOR SPIRITUAL GROWTH

READING. *Bernardine Franciscan Sisters Spirituality and Conference Center*, 460 St. Bernardine St., 19607-1737. Tel: 484-334-6807; Fax: 484-334-6808. Email: bfcc@bfranciscan.org. Sr. Barbara Ann Winnals, S.S.J., Dir. The Center shares space at the Bernardine Franciscan Motherhouse. Able to provide space for days of reflection and workshops for groups up to 125 persons. Spiritual direction and directed/private retreats available. Total Staff 2.

WERNERSVILLE. *Jesuit Center* (1971) 19565. Tel: 610-670-3640; Fax: 610-670-3650. Email: jescntsec@jesuitcenter.org. Web: www.jesuitcenter.org. Rev. Joseph A. Currie, S.J., Rector; Susan Bowers, Dir. of Spiritual Growth Programs; Revs. John P. Barron, S.J.; William J. Sneck, S.J.; Lucien F. Longtin, S.J.; Kathryn M. Fitzgerald, D.Min.; Sisters Maria McCoy, S.S.J.; Sarah Lamb, I.H.M. Directed retreats, programs in prayer, discernment, psychology and spirituality. Priests 3; Total Assisted (9710 overnight & 822 day only) 10,532; Total Staff 7.

[O] NEWMAN CENTERS

ALLENTOWN. *The Newman Center* 2339 Liberty St., 18104. Tel: 484-664-3122; Fax: 484-664-3123. Rev. John A. Krivak, M.Div., Th.M., M.Ed., Ed.D., Diocesan Dir., Campus Ministry.

Albright College (Reading) Christopher House, 15207 Kutztown Rd., Kutztown, 19530-9281. Tel: 610-223-6206; Fax: 610-683-8467. Email: christopherhouse@kutztown.edu. Web: www.kutztown.edu/activities/clubs/newmancenter/home.htm/. Rev. Richard C. Brensinger, M.Div., Campus Ministry.

DeSales University (Center Valley) 2755 Station Ave., Center Valley, 18034-9568. Tel: 610-282-1100, Ext. 1898; Fax: 610-282-1772. Email: johnhanley@desales.edu. Rev. John A. Hanley, O.S.F.S., M.Div., M.R.E.

Alvernia College Office of Campus Ministry, 400 St. Bernardine St., Reading, 19607. Tel: 610-796-8300; Fax: 610-796-8324.

Cedar Crest College (Allentown) Rev. John A. Krivak, M.Div., Th.M., M.Ed., Ed.D. See Muhlenberg College

Kutztown University (Kutztown) Christopher House, 15207 Kutztown Rd., Kutztown, 19530-9218. Tel: 610-683-8380; Fax: 610-683-8467. Email: christopherhouse@kutztown.edu. Web: www.kutztown.edu/activities/clubs/newmancenter/home.htm/. Rev. Richard C. Brensinger, M.Div.

Lafayette College (Easton) Newman House, 119 McCartney St., Easton, 18042-7647. Tel: 610-253-5044; Fax: 610-253-1391. Email: buterbaughi@lafayette.edu; nhcenter@rcn.com. Mr. Ian Buterbaugh.

Lehigh University (Bethlehem) Newman Center at Lehigh University, 417 Carlton Ave., Bethlehem, 18015-1583. Tel: 610-758-4148; Fax: 610-758-6392. Email: wek4@lehigh.edu. Rev. Wayne E. Killian, M.A., M.S.

Moravian College (Bethlehem) Newman Center at Moravian College, 1309 Main St., Bethlehem, 18018-6650. Tel: 610-625-7922; Fax: 610-625-7885. Email: killian@moravian.edu. Rev. Wayne E. Killian, M.A., M.S.

Muhlenberg College (Allentown) Newman Center, 2339 Liberty St., 18104-5586. Tel: 484-664-3122; Fax: 464-664-3123. Rev. John A. Krivak, M.Div., Th.M., M.Ed., Ed.D.

Penn State University Campus Ministry Coordinator Office: Penn State Schuylkill Campus. Tel: 570-385-6262.

[P] MISCELLANEOUS

ALLENTOWN. *Eastern Pennsylvania Scholarship Foundation*, P.O. Box F, 18105-1538. Tel: 610-871-5200, Ext. 216; Fax: 610-871-5211. Email: svargas@allentowndiocese.org. Web: www.allentowndiocese.org/giving. Mr. James S. Friend Jr., Sec.; Mrs. Silvia Vargas, Dir., Catholic School Devel. & Admin., Eastern, PA Scholarship Foundation.

BATH. *Blue Army of Our Lady of Fatima*, 2483 Community Dr., 18014. Tel: 484-284-0639. Email: thesixfamily@gmail.com. Rev. Dominic Thao Pham, M.Div., Spiritual Dir.

BETHLEHEM. *Stephen's Place*, 729 Ridge Ave., 18015-3621. Tel: 610-861-7677. Email: vlongcope@msn.com. Sr. Virginia Longcope, M.S.C., Dir. A nonprofit residential community designed to meet the needs of the adult non-violent offender with a history of substance abuse.

Third Order Dominican Expectation of the Blessed Mother Chapter, Notre Dame of Bethlehem Church, 1861 Catasququa Rd., 18018-1298. Tel: 610-691-6761. Dr. Felicidad Quilo, Mod.

CENTER VALLEY. *Mission Vehicle Association, Inc.*, 3300 Station Ave., 18034-9563.

EASTON. *Secular Franciscan Fraternity, Secular Franciscan Order, St. Francis Retreat House*, 3918 Chipman Rd., 18045-3014. Tel: 610-258-3053; Fax: 610-258-2412.

NORTHAMPTON. *Apostles of Jesus* (1968) 829 Main St., 18067-1838. Tel: 610-502-1732; Fax: 610-502-1733. Email: worldaj@email.com. Web: www.apostlesofjesus.org. Rev. Paul O. Gaggawala, A.J., Supr.

ORWIGSBURG. *Seton Manor, Inc.*, 1000 Seton Dr., 17961. Tel: 570-366-0400; Fax: 570-366-1970. Web: www.setonmanor.org. Mrs. Jackie Robinson. Total Staff 200; Bed Capacity 120.

READING. *Association of Franciscan Colleges and Universities, Inc., Alvernia University*, 400 St. Bernardine St., Francis Hall, Rm. #307, 19607. Tel: 610-796-8200; Fax: 610-796-8324. Email: kevin.godfrey@alvernia.edu. Dr. Kevin Godfrey, Exec. Dir.

Bernardine Franciscan Sisters Congregational Leadership Offices, 450 St. Bernardine St., 19607-1737. Tel: 484-334-6976; Fax: 484-334-6977.

Bernardine Franciscan Sisters Mission and Ministries Charitable Trust, 450 St. Bernardine St., 19607-1737. Tel: 484-334-6976; Fax: 484-334-6977. Email: RobertaAnn@bfranciscan.org. Web: www.bfranciscan.org. Sr. Marilisa H. da Silva, O.S.F., Congregational Min.

Bernardine Franciscans, Delaware County, 450 St. Bernardine St., 19607-1737. Tel: 484-334-6976; Fax: 484-334-6977. Email: RobertaAnn@bfranciscan.org. Web: www.bfranciscan.org. Sr. Marilisa H. da Silva, O.S.F., Congregational Min.

Mary's Home (2001) 736 Upland Ave., 19607. Tel: 610-603-8010; Fax: 610-603-8012. Email: dani@marysshelter.org. Web: www.marysshelter.org. Christine Folk, Exec. Dir. Transitional home for mothers and babies. Bed Capacity 10; Total Assisted Annually 35; Total Staff 10.

Mary's Shelter, 736 Upland Ave., 19607. Tel: 610-376-1973; Fax: 610-376-5391. Email: dani@marysshelter.org. Web: www.marysshelter.org. Christine Folk, Exec. Dir.; Danielle Monahan, M.S.W., Asst. Exec. Dir. A residence for pregnant, homeless young women and teens.

SHENANDOAH. *Apostles of Jesus*, P.O. Box 215, 17976-0215. Tel: 570-233-1864; Fax: 570-462-1235. Email: worldaj@email.com. Web: www.apostlesofjesus.org. Revs. Paul O. Gaggawala, A.J., Regl. Supr. & Dir.; Peter C. Mainza, A.J., Sec.

WERNERSVILLE. **ISECP, Inc.*, P.O. Box 223, 19565-0223. Tel: 410-868-0582. Email: jim.borbely@yahoo.com. Web: www.isecp.org. Rev. James A. Borbely, S.J., Admin.

RELIGIOUS INSTITUTES OF MEN REPRESENTED IN THE DIOCESE

For further details refer to the corresponding bracketed number in the Religious Institutes of Men or Women section.

[]—*Apostles of Jesus*—A.J.

[]—*Cistercian Monks of the Strict Observance*—O.Cist.

[0160]—*Clerics Regular of St. Paul* (Bernabite Fathers)—C.R.S.P.

[1330]—*Congregation of the Mission (Vincentian Fathers)* (Eastern Prov.)—C.M.

[0520]—*Franciscan Fathers* (St. John the Baptist Province)—O.F.M.

[0690]—*Jesuit Fathers* (Maryland Prov.)—S.J.

[1110]—*Missionaries of the Sacred Heart* (American Prov.)—M.S.C.

[0920]—*Oblates of St. Francis de Sales*—O.S.F.S.

RELIGIOUS INSTITUTES OF WOMEN REPRESENTED IN THE DIOCESE

[0120]—*Angelic Sisters of St. Paul*—A.S.S.P.

[1810]—*Bernardine Sisters of the Third Order of St.*

Francis (Bernardine Franciscan Sisters)—O.S.F.

[0320]—*Carmelite Nuns of the Ancient Observance*—O.Carm.

[]—*Congregation of Sisters of Holy Family of Nazareth*—C.S.F.N.

[0795]—*Daughters of Divine Zeal*—F.D.Z.

[1065]—*Dominican Daughters of the Immaculate Mother*—O.P.

[2710]—*Missionaries of Charity*—M.C.

[]—*Missionary Sisters of the Most Sacred Heart of Jesus*—M.S.C.

[2850]—*Missionary Sisters of the Precious Blood*—C.P.S.

[3250]—*Poor Sisters of St. Joseph*—P.S.S.J.

[1700]—*School Sisters of the Third Order of St. Francis* (United States Prov.)—O.S.F.

[0660]—*Sisters of Christian Charity*—S.C.C.

[]—*Sisters of Mercy* (Mid-Atlantic Community)—R.S.M.

[3700]—*Sisters of St. Benedict*—O.S.B.

[]—*Sisters of St. Francis of Philadelphia* (Glen Riddle)—O.S.F.

[3830]—*Sisters of St. Joseph*—S.S.J.

[2170]—*Sisters, Servants of the Immaculate Heart of Mary*—I.H.M.

[]—*Sisters, Servants of the Immaculate Heart of Mary* (Scranton Province)—I.H.M.

DIOCESAN CEMETERIES

ALLENTOWN. *Resurrection*, 547 N. Krocks Rd., 18106-9732. Tel: 610-395-3819; Fax: 610-366-3713. Mr. Larry Hillanbrand, Supt.

BETHLEHEM. *Holy Saviour*, 2575 Linden St., 18017-3842. Tel: 610-866-2372; Fax: 610-866-9277. Mr. Larry Hillanbrand, Supt.; Mr. James D. Reich, Sales Mgr.

NECROLOGY

† della Picca, Rev. Msgr. Paul B., (Retired)—Died Sept. 22, 2011

† Losito, Rev. Msgr. Felix A., Reading, PA Holy Rosary.—Died Nov. 3, 2011

† Masiar, Paul E., (Retired)—Died July 3, 2011

An asterisk (*) denotes an organization that has established tax-exempt status directly with the IRS and is not covered by the USCCB Group Ruling.

Diocese of Altoona-Johnstown

(Dioecesis Altunensis-Johnstoniensis)

Most Reverend

MARK L. BARTCHAK

Bishop of Altoona-Johnstown; ordained May 15, 1981; appointed Bishop of Altoona-Johnstown January 14, 2011; installed April 19, 2011. *Chancery Office: 927 S. Logan Blvd., Hollidaysburg, PA 16648.*

Most Reverend

JOSEPH V. ADAMEC, D.D., S.T.L.

Bishop Emeritus of Altoona-Johnstown; ordained July 3, 1960; appointed Bishop of Altoona-Johnstown March 17, 1987; ordained and installed May 20, 1987; retired January 14, 2011. *Res.: 504 Holliday Hills Dr., Hollidaysburg, PA 16648.*

ESTABLISHED DIOCESE OF ALTOONA, MAY 27, 1901.

Square Miles 6,674.

Redesignated Diocese of Altoona-Johnstown, October 9, 1957.

Comprises the Counties of Bedford, Blair, Cambria, Centre, Clinton, Fulton, Huntingdon and Somerset in the State of Pennsylvania.

For legal titles of parishes and diocesan institutions, consult the Chancery Office.

The Chancery: 927 S. Logan Blvd., Hollidaysburg, PA 16648. Tel: 814-695-5579; Fax: 814-695-8894.

Web: www.ajdiocese.org

Email: tdegol@dioceseaj.org

STATISTICAL OVERVIEW

Personnel	
Bishop	1
Retired Bishops	1
Priests: Diocesan Active in Diocese	76
Priests: Diocesan Active Outside Diocese	3
Priests: Retired, Sick or Absent	41
Number of Diocesan Priests	120
Religious Priests in Diocese	56
Total Priests in Diocese	176
Extern Priests in Diocese	1
Ordinations:	
Diocesan Priests	1
Religious Priests	2
Transitional Deacons	1
Permanent Deacons	1
Permanent Deacons in Diocese	36
Total Brothers	8
Total Sisters	70
Parishes	
Parishes	88
With Resident Pastor:	
Resident Diocesan Priests	71
Resident Religious Priests	13
Without Resident Pastor:	
Administered by Deacons	3
Administered by Religious Women	1
Missions	5
Welfare	
Health Care Centers	1
Total Assisted	253
Homes for the Aged	3
Total Assisted	288
Special Centers for Social Services	2
Total Assisted	26,678
Educational	
Diocesan Students in Other Seminaries	3
Total Seminarians	3
Colleges and Universities	2
Total Students	4,379
High Schools, Private	4
Total Students	1,005
Elementary Schools, Diocesan and Parish	20
Total Students	4,482
Catechesis/Religious Education:	
High School Students	2,589
Elementary Students	6,080
Total Students under Catholic Instruction	18,538
Teachers in the Diocese:	
Priests	5
Scholastics	331
Brothers	1
Sisters	7
Lay Teachers	327
Vital Statistics	
Receptions into the Church:	
Infant Baptism Totals	925
Minor Baptism Totals	51
Adult Baptism Totals	75
Received into Full Communion	134
First Communions	1,154
Confirmations	1,427
Marriages:	
Catholic	286
Interfaith	166
Total Marriages	452
Deaths	1,538
Total Catholic Population	90,507
Total Population	652,258

Former Bishops—Rt. Rev. EUGENE A. GARVEY, D.D., ord. Sept. 22, 1869; cons. Sept. 8, 1901; died Oct. 22, 1920; Most Revs. JOHN JOSEPH MCCORT, D.D., ord. Oct. 14, 1883; cons. Titular Bishop of Azotus and Auxiliary to the Archbishop of Philadelphia, Sept. 17, 1912; appt. Coadjutor cum jure successionis to the Bishop of Altoona, Jan. 27, 1920; appt. Bishop of Altoona, Oct. 22, 1920; appt. Assistant at the Pontifical Throne, Oct. 5, 1933; died April 21, 1936; RICHARD T. GUILFOYLE, D.D., ord. June 2, 1917; appt. Aug. 8, 1936; cons. Nov. 30, 1936; died June 10, 1957; HOWARD J. CARROLL, D.D., ord. April 2, 1927; appt. Dec. 5, 1957; cons. Jan. 2, 1958; died March 21, 1960; J. CARROLL MCCORMICK, D.D., ord. July 10, 1932; cons. April 20, 1947; appt. June 25, 1960; transferred to See of Scranton March 4, 1966; retired Feb. 15, 1983; died Nov. 2, 1996; JAMES J. HOGAN, D.D., ord. Dec. 8, 1937; appt. Titular Bishop of Philomelium and Auxiliary of Trenton, Nov. 27, 1959; cons. Feb. 25, 1960; appt. to the See of Altoona-Johnstown May 23, 1966; retired Oct. 17, 1986; died June 14, 2005; JOSEPH V. ADAMEC, D.D., S.T.L., ord. July 3, 1960; appt. Bishop of Altoona-Johnstown March 17, 1987; ord. and installed May 20, 1987; retired Jan. 14, 2011.

Diocesan Officials

Bishop—Most Rev. MARK LEONARD BARTCHAK, J.C.D., 927 S. Logan Blvd., Hollidaysburg, 16648. Tel: 814-695-5579; Fax: 814-695-8894.

Secretary to the Bishop—Deacon ROBERT D. BAILEY, Episcopal Master of Ceremonies, 927 S. Logan Blvd., Hollidaysburg, 16648. Tel: 814-695-5579; Fax: 814-695-8894. Email: rbailey@dioceseaj.org.

Retired Bishop—Most Rev. JOSEPH V. ADAMEC, D.D., S.T.L., 504 Holliday Hills Dr., Hollidaysburg, 16648. Tel: 814-317-7714.

Secretary for Communications—Mr. TONY DEGOL, 925 S. Logan Blvd., Hollidaysburg, 16648. Tel: 814-695-5579; Fax: 814-695-8894. Email: tdegol@dioceseaj.org.

Vicar General—Rev. Msgr. MICHAEL E. SERVINSKY, V.G., S.T.L., J.C.L., D.Min. Tel: 814-944-6676 (Res.). 927 S. Logan Blvd., Hollidaysburg, 16648. Tel: 814-695-5579; Fax: 814-695-8894.

Judicial Vicar—Very Rev. JOHN D. BYRNES, J.V., J.C.L., 933 S. Logan Blvd., Hollidaysburg, 16648. Tel: 814-693-9485; 814-886-2235 (Res.); Fax: 814-695-8894.

Bishop's Vicar for Religious—Very Rev. ANTHONY FRANCIS SPILKA, O.F.M.Conv., St. Francis of Assisi, 120 Barron Ave., Johnstown, 15906. Tel: 814-539-1632; Fax: 814-536-7024.

Chancellor—Mrs. TERESA M. STAYER, 927 S. Logan Blvd., Hollidaysburg, 16648. Tel: 814-695-5579; Fax: 814-695-8894. Email: tstayer@dioceseaj.org.

Episcopal Master of Ceremonies—Deacon ROBERT D. BAILEY, 927 S. Logan Blvd., Hollidaysburg, 16648. Tel: 814-695-5579; Fax: 814-695-8894. Email: rbailey@dioceseaj.org.

Vicars Forane

Allegheny Deanery—Very Rev. ANDREW C. STANKO, V.F., St. John Vianney Rectory, 3513 William Penn Ave., Johnstown, 15909. Tel: 814-322-4789.

Altoona Deanery—Rev. Msgr. STANLEY B. CARSON, V.F., Sacred Heart Rectory, 511-20 St., Altoona, 16602. Tel: 814-943-8553; Fax: 814-943-1556.

Cambria Deanery—Very Rev. LEONARD E. VOYTEK, V.F., St. Elizabeth Ann Seton Rectory, 605 Graham Ave., Windber, 15963. Tel: 814-467-7191.

Northern Deanery—Very Rev. NEIL R. DADEY, V.F., St. John the Evangelist Rectory, 134 E. Bishop St., Bellefonte, 16823. Tel: 814-355-3134.

Juniata Deanery—Very Rev. CLEMENT G. GARDNER, V.F., St. Michael Rectory, 301 Spruce St., Hollidaysburg, 16648. Tel: 814-695-0912.

Johnstown Deanery—Very Rev. MARK S. BEGLY, V.F., Our Mother of Sorrows Rectory, 407 Tioga St., Johnstown, 15905. Tel: 814-535-7646; Fax: 814-536-7850.

Prince Gallitzin Deanery—Rev. Msgr. TIMOTHY J. SWOPE, V.F., Basilica of St. Michael the Archangel Rectory, 321 St. Mary's St., P.O. Box 10, Loretto, 15940-0010. Tel: 814-472-8551 Minor Basilica.

Southern Deanery—Very Rev. DANIEL J. O'NEILL, V.F., St. Peter Rectory, 433 W. Church St., Somerset, 15501. Tel: 814-443-6574; Fax: 814-445-7766.

Diocesan Offices

Building Commission—Mr. GERALD MCMULLEN, Chm., 728 Ben Franklin Hwy., Ebensburg, 15931. Tel: 814-472-0603. Email: jmcmullen@dioceseaj.org.

Campus Ministry—Rev. Msgr. MICHAEL A. BECKER, Coord., Mailing Address: St. John the Evangelist Rectory, 309 Lotz Ave., Lakemont, Altoona, 16602. Tel: 814-942-5503; Fax: 814-943-8832.

Catholic Charities—Mrs. JEAN JOHNSTONE, Exec. Dir., 1300 12th Ave., P.O. Box 1349, Altoona, 16603. Tel: 814-944-9388; Fax: 814-941-2677. Email: jjohnstone@dioceseaj.org.

Altoona Offices—1300 12th Ave., P.O. Box 1349, Altoona, 16603. Tel: 814-944-9388; Fax: 814-941-2677.

Johnstown Offices—321 Main St., Ste. 5 G, Johnstown, 15901. Tel: 814-535-6538; Fax: 814-535-2235. Email: jjohnstone@dioceseaj.org.

Bellefonte Offices—213 E. Bishop St., Bellefonte, 16823. Tel: 814-353-0502; Fax: 814-353-0515. Email: jjohnstone@dioceseaj.org.

"The Catholic Register"—Rev. Msgr. TIMOTHY P. STEIN, Editor, Mailing Address: P.O. Box 413, Hollidaysburg, 16648. Tel: 814-695-7563; Fax: 814-695-7517. Email: tstein@dioceseaj.org.

Catholic Relief Services & Foreign Mission Outreach—Rev. ROBERT J. KELLY, Ph.D., Dir. Email: rkelly@dioceseaj.org; Sr. PATTI ROSSI, C.S.J., Assoc. Dir., 933 S. Logan Blvd., Hollidaysburg, 16648. Tel: 814-695-5579; Fax: 814-696-6725. Email: prossi@dioceseaj.org.

Cemetery Commission—Rev. SEAN K. CODE, St. Joan of Arc, 692 Glendale Valley Blvd., Frugality, 16639-6505. Tel: 814-943-5437. Email: SSJoanAndThomasPA53@dishmail.net.

Chancery—Mrs. TERESA M. STAYER, Chancellor, 927 S. Logan Blvd., Hollidaysburg, 16648. Tel: 814-695-5579; Fax: 814-695-8894. Email: tstayer@dioceseaj.org.

Children and Youth Protection/Safe Environment Office—Sr. DONNA MARIE LEIDEN, S.C., Dir., 933 S. Logan Blvd., Hollidaysburg, 16648. Tel: 814-693-9333; Fax: 814-696-6725. Email: dleiden@dioceseaj.org.

Communications—Mr. TONY DEGOL, 925 S. Logan Blvd., Hollidaysburg, 16648. Tel: 814-695-5579; Fax: 814-695-8894. Email: tdegol@dioceseaj.org.

Commission for Life and Justice—Mrs. SUSAN STITH, Diocesan Liaison, 5379 Portage St., Lilly, 15938. Tel: 814-886-5551. Email: sstith@dioceseaj.org.

Development—Mr. CHRISTOPHER F. RINGKAMP, Dir., 925 S. Logan Blvd., P.O. Box 409, Hollidaysburg, 16648. Tel: 814-695-5577; Fax: 814-696-9516. Email: cringkamp@dioceseaj.org.

Diaconal Formation—Deacons GENE P. NERAL, Dir., 925 S. Logan Blvd., Hollidaysburg, 16648. Tel: 814-693-9870; Fax: 814-695-8894. Email: gneral@dioceseaj.org; MICHAEL L. RUSSO, Assoc. Dir. Email: michael.russo@atlanticbb.net.

Diocesan Liturgy Committee—Mr. GEORGE PISULA, Chm., 925 S. Logan Blvd., Hollidaysburg, 16648. Tel: 814-693-9870. Email: ggpisula@atlanticbb.net; jnoonan@dioceseaj.org.

Dmitri Manor - Priests' Residence - St. Mary's Lane—Rev. Msgr. ROBERT J. SALY, 927 S. Logan Blvd., Hollidaysburg, 16648. Tel: 814-696-4698; 814-696-4126 (Res.).

Ecumenical Minister—Rev. DANIEL SINISI, T.O.R., St. Francis University, P.O. Box 600, Loretto, 15940-0600. Tel: 814-472-3001; Fax: 814-472-3003.

Education—Sr. DONNA MARIE LEIDEN, S.C., Dir. Email: dleiden@dioceseaj.org; Mrs. COLLEEN KRUG, Administrative Asst. Email: ckrug@dioceseaj.org; 933 S. Logan Blvd., Hollidaysburg, 16648. Tel: 814-693-1401; Fax: 814-696-6725.

Elementary Education—Sr. MARK PLESCHER, C.S.A., Asst. Dir., 933 S. Logan Blvd., Hollidaysburg, 16648. Tel: 814-693-1401; Fax: 814-696-6725. Email: mplescher@dioceseaj.org.

Director of Facilities—Mr. GERALD MCMULLEN, 728 Ben Franklin Hwy., Ebensburg, 15931. Tel: 814-472-7500, Ext. 109; Fax: 814-472-8020. Email: jmcmullen@dioceseaj.org.

Family Life Office—Mrs. SUSAN STITH, Dir. Email: sstith@dioceseaj.org; 5379 Portage St., Lilly, 15938-1091. Tel: 814-886-5551; Fax: 814-886-7697. Email: familylife@dioceseaj.org.

Finance—Mr. LARRY R. SUTTON, CFO. Email: lsutton@dioceseaj.org; Mr. MATTHEW REILLY, CPA, Comptroller. Email: mreilly@dioceseaj.org; Mrs. JEANNE BRYAN, Accounting Asst. Email: jbryan@dioceseaj.org; 927 S. Logan Blvd., Hollidaysburg, 16648. Tel: 814-695-5579; Fax: 814-695-8894.

Fulton County Catholic Mission—Sr. MARGIE MONAHAN, C.C.W. Email: sistermargie@comcast.net; 110 S. Third St., Mc Connellsburg, 17233. Tel: 717-485-5917; 717-485-0661; Fax: 717-485-3855.

Holy Childhood—Rev. ROBERT J. KELLY, Ph.D., Dir. Email: rkelly@dioceseaj.org; Sr. PATTI ROSSI, C.S.J., Assoc. Dir., 933 S. Logan Blvd., Hollidaysburg, 16648. Tel: 814-695-5579; Fax: 814-696-6725. Email: prossi@dioceseaj.org.

Information Technology—Mr. DON LAYO, Dir., 927 S. Logan Blvd., Hollidaysburg, 16648. Tel: 814-695-5579; Fax: 814-695-8894. Email: dlayo@dioceseaj.org.

Network Support Specialist—Mr. DAVID EGER, 927 S. Logan Blvd., Hollidaysburg, 16648. Tel: 814-695-5579; Fax: 814-695-8894. Email: deger@dioceseaj.org.

Network Support Technicians—Mr. GREGORY CLAPPER. Email: gclapper@dioceseaj.org; Mr. JAMES ECKENRODE, 927 S. Logan Blvd., Hollidaysburg, 16648. Tel: 814-695-5579; Fax: 814-695-8894. Email: jeckenrode@dioceseaj.org.

Technology/Implementation Coordinator—Mrs. ALISON LINK. Email: alink@dioceseaj.org.

Inter-Faith Minister—Very Rev. MARK S. BEGLY, V.F., Our Mother of Sorrows Rectory, 415 Tioga St., Johnstown, 15905. Tel: 814-535-7646; Fax: 814-536-7850.

Liturgy—Rev. Msgr. ROBERT C. MAZUR, 925 S. Logan Blvd., Hollidaysburg, 16648. Tel: 814-693-9870; Fax: 814-695-8894.

Ongoing Formation of the Clergy—Rev. Msgr. TIMOTHY J. SWOPE, V.F., Mailing Address: P.O. Box 99, Loretto, 15940-0099. Tel: 814-472-5441; Fax: 814-472-5446.

Parish Life Office—925 S. Logan Blvd., Hollidaysburg, 16648. Tel: 814-693-9605; Fax: 814-696-9516. Rev. Msgr. ROBERT C. MAZUR, Dir.

Adult Enrichment—Deacon MICHAEL L. RUSSO, Ministerial Coord., St. Patrick School, 925 Park Ave., Johnstown, 15902. Tel: 814-361-2000. Email: michael.russo@atlanticbb.net.

Christian Initiation of Adults—Mrs. JEANNE THOMPSON, Ministerial Coord. Tel: 814-693-9605; Fax: 814-696-9516. Email: jthompson@dioceseaj.org.

Lay Ecclesial Ministry—Deacon MICHAEL L. RUSSO, Ministerial Coord., St. Patrick School, 925 Park Ave., Johnstown, 15902. Tel: 814-361-2000. Email: michael.russo@atlanticbb.net.

Diocesan Contact for Parish Pastoral Councils—Rev. Msgr. ROBERT C. MAZUR, Ministerial Coord. Tel: 814-693-9605; Fax: 814-696-9516.

Sacramental Preparation/Confirmation Process/Religious Education—Mrs. FRANCINE M. SWOPE, Ministerial Coord., 933 S. Logan Blvd., Hollidaysburg, 16648. Tel: 814-693-1401; Fax: 814-696-6725. Email: fswope@dioceseaj.org.

Stewardship—Rev. Msgr. ROBERT C. MAZUR, Ministerial Coord. Tel: 814-693-9605; Fax: 814-696-9516.

Ministerial Coordinator of Evangelization/Catholics Returning—Sr. LINDA LAMAGNA, C.C.W., Ministerial Coord., St. Monica/St. Augustine Parishes, P.O. Box 231, Chest Springs, 16624. Tel: 814-674-3712. Email: sllamagna@verizon.net.

Youth Ministry—Mrs. FRANCINE M. SWOPE, Ministerial Coord., 933 S. Logan Blvd., Hollidaysburg, 16648. Tel: 814-693-1401; Fax: 814-696-6725. Email: fswope@dioceseaj.org.

Permanent Deacons Formation Ministry and Life—Deacon GENE P. NERAL, 925 S. Logan Blvd., Hollidaysburg, 16648. Tel: 814-693-9870; 814-695-8894; Fax: 814-695-8894. Email: gneral@dioceseaj.org.

Presbyteral Council—Rev. ANGELO J. PATTI, Chm., St. Andrew Rectory, 1621 Ferndale Ave., Johnstown, 15905. Tel: 814-288-4324; Fax: 814-288-6750. Email: pastor@standrewchurch.com.

Priests' Personnel Board—Rev. Msgr. MICHAEL E. SERVINSKY, V.G., S.T.L., J.C.L., D.Min., 927 S. Logan Blvd., Hollidaysburg, 16648. Tel: 814-695-5579; Fax: 814-695-8894.

Priests' Retirement Plan—Rev. WALTER J. MOLL JR., 927 S. Logan Blvd., Hollidaysburg, 16648. Tel: 814-695-5579; Fax: 814-696-8894.

Propagation of the Faith—Rev. ROBERT J. KELLY, Ph.D., Dir. Email: rkelly@dioceseaj.org; Sr. PATTI ROSSI, C.S.J., Assoc. Dir., 933 S. Logan Blvd., Hollidaysburg, 16648. Tel: 814-695-5579; Fax: 814-696-6725. Email: prossi@dioceseaj.org.

Retreat & Conference Center—Mailing Address: St. John the Baptist Retreat Center, P.O. Box 10, New Baltimore, 15553. Tel: 814-733-2210; Fax: 814-733-2966.

St. Vincent de Paul Society—Mr. ANTHONY CONSIGLIO, Exec. Dir., 927 Franklin St., Johnstown, 15905. Tel: 814-539-4627; Fax: 814-536-1272. Email: avcdepaul@verizon.net. Web: www.svdpcares.org.

Scouting—Rev. JOSEPH T. ORR, St. Agnes, 310 W. Water St., Lock Haven, 17745. Tel: 570-748-4594; Fax: 570-893-8229.

Self Insurance Program—Mr. DAVE ROSS, Gallagher Bassett Insurance Service, 540 Pellis Rd., Ste. 3000, Greensburg, 15601. Tel: 800-831-3247; Fax: 724-836-8684.

Temporalities—Mr. LARRY R. SUTTON, CFO, 927 S. Logan Blvd., Hollidaysburg, 16648. Tel: 814-695-5579; Fax: 814-695-8894. Email: lsutton@dioceseaj.org.

Tribunal—Very Rev. JOHN D. BYRNES, J.V., J.C.L. Email: jbyrnes@dioceseaj.org; Rev. DAVID R. RIZZO, J.C.L., 927 S. Logan Blvd., Hollidaysburg, 16648. Tel: 814-693-9485; 814-943-6185 (Res.); Fax: 814-695-8894.

Victims' Advocate—Sr. MARILYN WELCH, C.C.W., 927 S. Logan Blvd., Hollidaysburg, 16648. Tel: 814-695-5579; Fax: 814-695-8894.

Vocation—Rev. ALLEN P. ZETH, Dir., Prince Gallitzin Chapel House, 357 St. Mary's St., P.O. Box 99, Loretto, 15940-0099. Tel: 814-472-5441; Fax: 814-472-5446. Email: azeth@dioceseaj.org.

CLERGY, PARISHES, MISSIONS AND PAROCHIAL SCHOOLS

CITY OF ALTOONA

(BLAIR COUNTY)

1—CATHEDRAL OF THE BLESSED SACRAMENT (1851) Rev. Msgrs. Robert C. Mazur, Rector; Roy F. Kline (Retired); Rev. John Michael Gibbons; Deacons John J. Szwarc; James F. Leap, (Retired); John R. Rys.
Church: One Cathedral Square, Altoona, 16601-3315. Tel: 814-944-4603; Fax: 814-942-4337. Email: altcathedral@dioceseaj.org. Web: www.altoonacathedral.org.
Catechesis/Religious Program—Andrew R. Motyke, Dir. Music. Students 117.

2—HOLY ROSARY (1901) Rev. Msgr. Michael E. Servinsky.
Res.: 900 N. Fourth St., Altoona, 16601. Tel: 814-944-6676; Fax: 814-946-9207.
Catechesis/Religious Program—Tel: 814-942-8641. Mrs. Jeanette L. Fabbri, D.R.E. Students 63.

3—IMMACULATE CONCEPTION (1860) [CEM], (St. Mary's) Rev. Msgr. Timothy P. Stein.
Res.: 1405 Fifth Ave., Altoona, 16602. Tel: 814-942-2416.
See Altoona Central Catholic School, Altoona under Elementary Diocesan Schools located in the Institution section.
Catechesis/Religious Program—Mr. James Mock, D.R.E. Students 86.

4—ST. JOHN THE EVANGELIST (1921) Rev. Msgr. Michael A. Becker; Deacon Gene P. Neral.
Res.: 309 Lotz Ave., Lakemont, Altoona, 16602. Tel: 814-942-5503. Email: stjohnchurch@atlanticbb.net.
School—311 Lotz Ave., Altoona, 16602. Tel: 814-943-4966; Fax: 814-943-8832. Tabatha Griffin, Prin. Lay Teachers 9; Students 111.
Catechesis/Religious Program—Tel: 814-943-4966. Mrs. Jane Adams, D.R.E. Students 133.

5—ST. LEO THE GREAT (1911) Merged with SS. Peter & Paul to form Our Lady of Fatima, Altoona.

6—ST. MARK'S (1889) Very Rev. Ronald V. Osinski.
Catechesis/Religious Program—Tel: 814-942-2488. Students 78.
Chapel—Valley View Home for the Aged, Tel: 814-944-0845.
Chapel—Bellemeade Manor, Tel: 814-942-2423.

7—OUR LADY OF FATIMA (1995) [CEM] Rev. James D. Zatalava.
Res.: 2010 12th Ave., Altoona, 16601. Tel: 814-942-0371; Fax: 814-942-0372. Email: olfoffio@hotmail.com. Web: www.ourladyoffatimaaltoona.org.
See Altoona Central Catholic School, Altoona under Elementary Diocesan Schools located in the Institution section.
Catechesis/Religious Program—1304 13th Ave., Altoona, 16603. Tel: 814-943-7423. Students 8.

8—OUR LADY OF LOURDES (1923) Rev. David R. Rizzo.
Res.: 2716 Broad Ave., Altoona, 16601. Tel: 814-943-6185; Fax: 814-943-1968.
Catechesis/Religious Program—Tel: 814-943-1685. Colleen Sheehan, D.R.E. Students 65.

9—OUR LADY OF MT. CARMEL (1905), (Italian), Revs. Frank Scornaienchi, T.O.R.; Terrence T. Smith, T.O.R. In Res., Rev. William Santre, T.O.R. (Retired).
Res.: 806 11th St., Altoona, 16602. Tel: 814-942-8501; Fax: 814-944-2208. Email: olmc806@aol.com.

Web: www.mountcarmelaltoona.com.
See Altoona Central Catholic School, Altoona under Elementary Diocesan Schools located in the Institution section.
Catechesis/Religious Program—Tel: 814-931-3995. Mrs. Dona Baughman, C.R.E. Students 141.
Convent—
Mission—Our Lady of the Assumption (1925) 15 1/2 Hileman St., Altoona, Blair Co. 16602.

10—SS. PETER AND PAUL (1911), (Polish), Merged with St. Leo the Great to form Our Lady of Fatima, Altoona.

11—ST. ROSE OF LIMA (1924) Rev. Brian R. Saylor. In Res., Rev. Carl A. Spishak (Retired).
Res.: 5514 Roselawn Ave., Altoona, 16602. Tel: 814-944-8509; Fax: 814-942-8345. Web: www.stroselima.com.
School—5519 Sixth Ave., Altoona, 16602. Tel: 814-942-7835; Fax: 814-942-1095. Patricia Ronan, Prin. Lay Teachers 13; Students 201.
Catechesis/Religious Program—Students 133.

12—SACRED HEART (1890) Rev. Msgr. Stanley B. Carson.
Res.: 511 20th St., Altoona, 16602. Tel: 814-943-8553; Fax: 814-943-1556. Email: sacredheart511@verizon.net. Web: www.sacredheartaltoona.org.
Formation Center—2009 Sixth Ave., Altoona, 16602. Tel: 814-944-3922.
Catechesis/Religious Program—Students 142.

13—ST. THERESE OF THE CHILD JESUS (1927) Rev. D. Timothy Grimme; Deacon Thomas J. McFee.
Res.: 2301 5th St., Altoona, 16601-3863. Tel: 814-942-4479; Fax: 814-942-1873. Email: sttheresealtoona@catholicweb.com. Web: http://home.catholicweb.com/sttheresealtoona.
See Altoona Central Catholic School, Altoona under Elementary Diocesan Schools located in the Institution section.
Catechesis/Religious Program—Mary Beth Schmidhamer, D.R.E. Students 131.

CITY OF JOHNSTOWN

(CAMBRIA COUNTY)

1—ST. JOHN GUALBERT CATHEDRAL (1835) [CEM 2] Revs. James F. Crookston, Rector; John F. Brezovec; Clarence S. Bridges; Deacons John J. Concannon, (Retired); Bruce L. Becker.
Res.: 117 Clinton St., P.O. Box 807, Johnstown, 15907. Tel: 814-536-0117; Fax: 814-535-6771. Email: cathedral@floodcity.net.
Catechesis/Religious Program—124 Maple Ave., Johnstown, 15901. Tel: 814-535-4228. Students 62.

2—ST. ANDREW (1956) Rev. Angelo J. Patti.
Res.: 1621 Ferndale Ave., Johnstown, 15905. Tel: 814-288-4324; Fax: 814-288-6750. Email: pastor@standrewschurch.com. Web: www.standrewschurch.com.
School—(Grades PreK-8), 1621 Ferndale Ave., Johnstown, 15905. Tel: 814-288-2811; Fax: 814-288-6750. Email: gguaetta@standrewschurch.com. Lay Teachers 11; Students 179.
Catechesis/Religious Program—Email: mclark@standrewschurch.com. Students 68.

3—ST. ANTHONY'S (1905), (Italian), Merged with SS. Peter & Paul, Johnstown to form St. Clare of Assisi, Johnstown.

4—ST. BARNABAS (1954), (Slovenian), Merged with St. Gregory, Johnstown to form SS. Gregory & Barnabas, Johnstown.

5—ST. BENEDICT'S (1911) Revs. David S. Peles; Derek Fairman; Michael Wolfe.
Res.: 2310 Bedford St., Johnstown, 15904. Tel: 814-266-9718, Ext. 101; Fax: 814-269-4220. Email: SBpastor@atlanticbb.net. Web: www.stbenedictchurch.org.
School—2306 Bedford St., Johnstown, 15904. Tel: 814-266-3837; Fax: 814-266-7718. Web: www.sbpanthers.org. Mr. George Nace, Prin. Lay Teachers 22; Students 259.
Catechesis/Religious Program—Sr. Cindy Burns, D.R.E. (High School). Tel: 814-266-9718, Ext. 301; Mrs. Michelle Robatin, D.R.E. (Elem). Tel: 814-266-9718, Ext. 302. Students 290.

6—SS. CASIMIR & EMERICH (1997), (Polish—Hungarian), [CEM 2] Closed. For inquiries for parish records please see Resurrection Roman Catholic Church (814-539-5788).

7—ST. CLARE OF ASSISI (2000), (Italian—Slovak), [CEM 2] Rev. Leo Arnone; Deacon Samuel M. Cammarata.
Office: 110 Maple Ave., Johnstown, 15901. Tel: 814-535-1133; Fax: 814-535-1664. Email: stclareofassisi@atlanticbb.net.
Res.: 124 Maple Ave., Johnstown, 15901.
See Central Catholic Academy, Johnstown under Elementary Diocesan Schools located in the Institution section.
Catechesis/Religious Program—Tel: 814-535-2360. Students 27.

8—ST. CLEMENT'S (1956) Rev. William E. Rosenbaum.
Res. & Church: 114 Lindberg Ave., Johnstown, 15905. Tel: 814-255-4422; Fax: 814-255-2623. Email: stclementchurch@atlanticbb.net. Web: www.stclementaj.org.
See Cathedral Catholic Academy under Education Consolidated Elementary Schools located in the Institution section.
Catechesis/Religious Program—Sr. Dolores Partsch, C.S.J., D.R.E. Students 135.

9—ST. COLUMBA'S (1888) [CEM] Closed. For inquiries for parish records please see Resurrection Roman Catholic Church (814-539-5788).

10—ST. EMERICH'S (1905), (Hungarian), Merged with St. Casimir's, Johnstown to form SS. Casimir & Emerich, Johnstown.

11—ST. FRANCIS OF ASSISI (1922), (Slovak), [CEM] Very Rev. Anthony Francis Spilka, O.F.M.Conv.
Res.: 120 Barron Ave., Johnstown, 15906. Tel: 814-539-1632; Fax: 814-539-5888. Email: sfassisich@atlanticbbn.net.
Catechesis/Religious Program—Students 62.

12—SS. GREGORY & BARNABAS (2001) Rev. Robert L. Ruston; Deacon Thomas M. Papinchak.
Res.: 120 Boltz St., Johnstown, 15902. Tel: 814-536-6818; Fax: 814-534-0651. Email: sgsb925@hotmail.com. Web: www.gregbar.org.
Catechesis/Religious Program—Students 134.

13—ST. GREGORY'S (1919) Merged with St. Barnabas, Johnstown to form SS. Gregory & Barnabas, Johnstown.

14—IMMACULATE CONCEPTION (1859), (German), [CEM] Closed. For inquiries for parish records please see Resurrection Roman Catholic Church (814-539-5788).

15—ST. JOSEPH'S (1852), (German), Merged with Our Lady of Mercy to form St. John Gualbert Cathedral, Johnstown.
See Central Catholic Elementary School, Johnstown under Elementary Diocesan Schools located in the Institution section.

16—ST. MICHAEL'S (1910), (German), Very Rev. Anthony Francis Spilka, O.F.M.Conv.
Mailing Address: 180 Gilbert St., Johnstown, 15906.
Res.: 120 Barron Ave., Johnstown, 15906. Tel: 814-539-1632; Fax: 814-539-5888.
Catechesis/Religious Program— (Clustered with St. Francis of Assisi) Students 63.

17—OUR LADY OF MERCY (1921) Merged with St. Joseph to form St. John Gualbert Cathedral, Johnstown.

18—OUR MOTHER OF SORROWS (1920) Very Rev. Mark S. Begly.
Res.: 407 Tioga St., Johnstown, 15905. Tel: 814-535-7646; Fax: 814-536-7850. Email: office@omostoday.com. Web: www.omostoday.com.
School—430 Tioga St., Johnstown, 15905. Tel: 814-539-5315; Fax: 814-539-5315. Mrs. Pamela Seidel, Prin. Lay Teachers 20; Students 252.
Catechesis/Religious Program—Tel: 814-255-1264. Mrs. Karen Fink, D.R.E. Students 179.

19—ST. PATRICK'S (1904) Rev. Matthew A. Reese.
Res.: 609 Park Ave., Johnstown, 15902. Tel: 814-539-2186; Fax: 814-539-2410.
Catechesis/Religious Program—Students 36.

20—SS. PETER AND PAUL'S (1918) Merged with St. Anthony, Johnstown to form St. Clare of Assisi, Johnstown.

21—RESURRECTION ROMAN CATHOLIC CHURCH (2009) [CEM] [JC] Rev. Alan E. Thomas.
Parish Office: 408 Eighth Ave., Johnstown, 15906. Tel: 814-539-5788; Fax: 814-539-8845.
Worship Site: 324 Chestnut St., Johnstown, 15906.
Catechesis/Religious Program—Tel: 814-535-5409. Students 62.

22—ST. ROCHUS (1900), (Croatian), [CEM] Closed. For inquiries for parish records please see Resurrection Roman Catholic Church (814-539-5788).

23—ST. STEPHEN, FIRST KING OF HUNGARY (1891), (Slovak), [CEM] Closed. For inquiries for parish records please see Resurrection Roman Catholic Church (814-539-5788).

24—ST. THERESE OF THE CHILD JESUS (1929), (Slovenian), [CEM] Rev. Bernard Karmanocky, O.F.M.
Res.: 536 Decker Ave., Johnstown, 15906. Tel: 814-539-7633; Fax: 814-539-7633.
See West End Catholic School, Johnstown under Elementary Diocesan Schools located in the Institution section.
Convent—702 Saybrook Pl., Johnstown, 15906.
Mission—St. Anne's (1935) 533 Woodland Ave., Moxham, Cambria Co. 15902. Tel: 814-539-7633.
Catechesis/Religious Program—Tel: 814-536-2287. Students 45.

25—VISITATION OF THE B.V.M. (1927) Rev. Barry J. Baroni; Deacon John E. Sroka.
Res.: 1127 McKinley Ave., Johnstown, 15905. Tel: 814-536-6110; Fax: 814-536-3709. Email: visitation@floodcity.net. Web: www.visitationchurch.net.
Catechesis/Religious Program—Tel: 814-535-2341. Students 47.

OUTSIDE THE CITIES OF ALTOONA AND JOHNSTOWN

ACOSTA, SOMERSET CO., ST. JOHN THE BAPTIST'S (1912) Merged with St. Joseph, Boswell, and St. Stanislaus, Boswell, to form All Saints Church, Boswell.

ASHVILLE, CAMBRIA CO., ST. THOMAS AQUINAS (1889) [CEM] Rev. Sean K. Code.
Mailing Address: 692 Glendale Valley Blvd., Fallentimber, 16639. Tel: 814-943-5437. Email: ssjoanandthomasonpa53@dishmail.net.
Catechesis/Religious Program—Students 56.

BAKERTON, CAMBRIA CO., SACRED HEART (1904) Merged with St. Patrick, Spangler, to form St. Jude, Elmora.

BARNESBORO, CAMBRIA CO.

1—CHRIST THE KING (1993) Merged with St. Stanislaus Kostka, Barnesboro; St. John the Baptist, Northern Cambria; Our Lady of Mt. Carmel, Northern Cambria; Holy Cross, Northern Cambria to form Prince of Peace, Northern Cambria.

2—ST. STANISLAUS KOSTKA (1906), (Polish), Merged with Christ the King, Barnesboro; St. John the Baptist, Northern Cambria; Our Lady of Mt. Carmel, Northern Cambria; Holy Cross, Northern Cambria to form Prince of Peace, Northern Cambria.

BEANS COVE, BEDFORD CO., SEVEN DOLORS B.V.M. (1878) [CEM] Rev. Richard B. Tomkosky.
Mailing Address: 2174 Beans Cove Rd., Clearville, 15535-7901. Tel: 814-767-9522; Fax: 814-767-8158.
Res.: 161 E. First Ave., Everett, 15537. Tel: 814-652-5854.
Catechesis/Religious Program—Students 10.

BEAVERDALE, CAMBRIA CO.

1—ST. AGNES (1909) Merged with St. Joseph, Beaverdale, and Corpus Christi, Dunlo, to form Holy Spirit Church, Beaverdale.

2—HOLY SPIRIT (1995) [CEM 2] Closed. For inquiries for parish records please see Saint Michael, St. Michael, PA (814-495-9640).

3—ST. JOSEPH'S (1904), (Slovak), Merged with St. Agnes, Beaverdale, and Corpus Christi, Dunlo, to form Holy Spirit Church, Beaverdale.

BEDFORD, BEDFORD CO., ST. THOMAS (1816) [CEM 2] Rev. Donald W. Dusza.
Res.: 215 E. Penn St., 15522. Tel: 814-623-5526; Fax: 814-623-1741. Web: www.stthomasbedford.com.
School—129 W. Penn St., 15522. Tel: 814-623-8873; Fax: 814-623-1208. Sarah Bordi, Prin. Lay Teachers 7; Students 56.
Catechesis/Religious Program—Tel: 814-623-6023. Mrs. Amelie Regester, D.R.E. Students 108.

BELLEFONTE, CENTRE CO., ST. JOHN THE EVANGELIST'S (1828) [CEM 2] Very Rev. Neil R. Dadey; Rev. Brian Lee Warchola; Deacon Thomas E. Boldin.
Res.: 134 E. Bishop St., 16823. Tel: 814-355-3134; Fax: 814-355-4820. Email: stjcatholic@comcast.net. Web: www.catholicchurchbellefonte.catholicweb.com.
School—(Grades PreK-5), 116 E. Bishop St., 16823. Tel: 814-355-7859; Fax: 814-355-2939. Email: twendt@saintjohnsch.com. Web: www.stjohnsch.com. Kristina Tice, Prin.; Mrs. Karen Moore, Librarian. Lay Teachers 8; Students 124.
Catechesis/Religious Program—Tel: 814-355-3134. Students 237.

BELLWOOD, BLAIR CO., ST. JOSEPH'S (1890) Rev. David H. Roesch.
Res.: 623 E. Third St., 16617. Tel: 814-742-7075. Email: sanjoe3@aol.com. Web: stjosephbellwood.org.
Catechesis/Religious Program—Tel: 814-742-7894. Students 103.

BOSWELL, SOMERSET CO.

1—ALL SAINTS (1995) [CEM 3] Rev. Justin A. Ratajczak, O.F.M.Conv.
Res.: 325 Quemahoning St., 15531. Tel: 814-629-5551; Fax: 814-629-5677. Email: allsaints.parish@verizon.net.
Catechesis/Religious Program—Students 49.

2—ST. STANISLAUS (1901), (Polish), Merged with St. John the Baptist, Acosta to form All Saints Church, Boswell.

CARROLLTOWN, CAMBRIA CO., ST. BENEDICT'S (1846) [CEM 3] Rev. Jude W. Brady, O.S.B.; Bro. Francis Ehnat, O.S.B.
Res.: 100 Main St., P.O. Box 447, 15722. Tel: 814-344-6548; Fax: 814-344-8656. Email: sbcjwb@comcast.net. Web: saintbenedictchurch.com.
School—119 S. Church St., 15722. Tel: 814-344-6512; Fax: 814-344-8530. Email: sbsct@dioceseaj.org. Sisters 2; Brothers 1; Lay Teachers 10; Students 110.
Catechesis/Religious Program—Suzanne Bills, D.R.E. Students 221.

CASSANDRA, CAMBRIA CO., ST. AGNES (1909) Closed. For inquiries for parish records contact the chancery.

CENTRAL CITY, SOMERSET CO.

1—ST. JOHN THE BAPTIST (1917), (Slovak), Merged with Sacred Heart of Jesus, Central City to form Our Lady Queen of Angels, Central City.

2—OUR LADY QUEEN OF ANGELS (1999) [CEM 2] Rev. Joseph D. Maurizio Jr.
Res.: 738 Sunshine Ave., 15926-1233. Tel: 814-754-5224; Fax: 814-754-4447 (24 hrs a day). Email: queenofangels@wpia.net. Web: www.ladyqueenofangels.org.
Catechesis/Religious Program—Students 41.

3—SACRED HEART OF JESUS (1914), (Polish), Merged with St. John the Baptist, Central City to form Our Lady Queen of Angels, Central City.

CHEST SPRINGS, CAMBRIA CO., ST. MONICA'S (1859) [CEM] Rev. Joseph W. Fleming.
Res.: 803 St. Augustine Rd., Dysart, 16636. Tel: 814-674-8550.
Church: 3037 Colonel Drake Hwy., 16624. Tel: 814-674-3712.
Catechesis/Religious Program—Students 64.

CLARENCE, CENTRE CO.

1—ST. MICHAEL'S (1900), (Slovak), [CEM] Merged with St. Mary's, Snow Shoe to form Queen of Archangels, Clarence.

2—QUEEN OF ARCHANGELS (2005) [CEM 2] Rev. Lubomir J. Strecok.
102 Church St., 16829. Tel: 814-387-6762. Email: queenofarchangelspa@verizon.net.
Catechesis/Religious Program—Tel: 814-387-6762. Students 94.
Mission— 204 S. 4th St., Snow Shoe, Centre Co. 16874.

COLVER, CAMBRIA CO., HOLY FAMILY (1912), (Polish), [CEM] Rev. Bernard F. Grega.
Res.: 562 Fifth St., P.O. Box 543, 15927. Tel: 814-748-7054; Fax: 814-748-7254.
Catechesis/Religious Program—Sr. Anna Marie, S.A., D.R.E. Students 47.

CONEMAUGH, CAMBRIA CO.

1—ASSUMPTION OF B.V.M. (1910) [CEM] Merged with Sacred Heart, Conemaugh to form Church of the Transfiguration, Conemaugh.

2—CHURCH OF THE TRANSFIGURATION (2008) [CEM 2] Rev. Robert C. Hall.
Res.: 340 Second St., 15909. Tel: 814-535-2250; Fax: 814-536-9770. Email: shasec@comcast.net.
Catechesis/Religious Program—Mrs. Louise Brezovic, D.R.E. Students 61.

3—SACRED HEART (1902) [CEM] Merged with Assumption of B.V.M., Conemaugh to form Church of the Transfiguration, Conemaugh.

COUPON, CAMBRIA CO., ST. JOSEPH'S (1855) [CEM 2] Closed. For inquiries for parish records please see St. Demetrius, Gallitzin (814-886-7941).

CRESSON, CAMBRIA CO.

1—ST. ALOYSIUS (1838) [CEM] Very Rev. John D. Byrnes.
Res.: 7911 Admiral Peary Hwy., 16630. Tel: 814-886-2235. Email: stals16630@yahoo.com. Web: www.saintaloysiuscresson.org.
See All Saints Catholic School under Elementary Diocesan Schools located in the Institution section.
Catechesis/Religious Program—Tel: 814-886-2669. Marcia E. Hammond, D.R.E. Students 124.

2—ST. FRANCIS XAVIER (1908) [CEM] Rev. Valentine J. Bradley.
Res.: 211 Powell Ave., 16630. Tel: 814-886-2374; Fax: 814-886-2498.
See All Saints Catholic School under Elementary Diocesan Schools located in the Institution section.
Catechesis/Religious Program—Tel: 814-886-2374. Mrs. Tracey Ingold, Dir. Faith Formation. Students 122.

DAVIDSVILLE, SOMERSET CO., ST. ANNE (1911) [CEM 2] Rev. Michael Lewandowski, O.F.M.Conv.
Mailing Address: 205 Woodstown Hwy., P.O. Box 500, 15928. Tel: 814-479-2664; Fax: 814-479-7702. Email: sannep@atlanticbb.net.
Catechesis/Religious Program—Students 48.

DUDLEY, HUNTINGDON CO., IMMACULATE CONCEPTION (1856) [CEM] Rev. Bernard L. White.
Res.: 1416 Dudley Rd., P.O. Box 188, 16634. Tel: 814-635-2919.
Catechesis/Religious Program—Students 45.

DUNCANSVILLE, BLAIR CO., ST. CATHERINE OF SIENA (1963) Rev. Msgr. Robert J. Saly.
Mailing Address: Old Rte. 22, P.O. Box 88, 16635. Tel: 814-696-4126; Fax: 814-693-7518. Email: sienaelm@verizon.net.
Res.: 417 Elm Ln., 16635.
Catechesis/Religious Program—P.O. Box 88, 16635. Debra Terchanik, D.R.E. Students 73.

DUNLO, CAMBRIA CO., CORPUS CHRISTI (1903) Merged with St. Agnes and St. Joseph, Beaverdale to form Holy Spirit Church, Beaverdale.

EBENSBURG, CAMBRIA CO., HOLY NAME (1816) [CEM] Rev. Msgr. Arnold L. Gaus.
Mailing Address: 500 N. Julian St., 15931. Tel: 814-472-7244; Fax: 814-472-7249. Email: holynameebg@verizon.net. Web: www.holynameebg.org.
School—Tel: 814-472-8817; Fax: 814-471-0500. Email: holynameelementary@comcast.net. Mrs. Robin McMullen, Prin. Lay Teachers 16; Students 220.
Catechesis/Religious Program—Students 344.

EHRENFELD, CAMBRIA CO., OUR LADY OF MT. CARMEL (1892) Merged with St. James and St. Anthony's, South Fork to form Most Holy Trinity, South Fork.

ELMORA, CAMBRIA CO., ST. JUDE (1995) Closed. For inquiries for parish records contact the chancery.

EMEIGH, CAMBRIA CO., MOST PRECIOUS BLOOD, See separate listing. See Christ the King, Barnesboro.

EVERETT, BEDFORD CO., ST. JOHN THE EVANGELIST (1971) Rev. Richard B. Tomkosky.
Res.: 161 E. First Ave., 15537. Tel: 814-652-5854; Fax: 814-652-5854.
Church: 163 E. First Ave., 15537.
Catechesis/Religious Program—Students 15.

FALLENTIMBER, CAMBRIA CO.

1—ST. JOAN OF ARC (1995) Rev. Sean K. Code.
Res.: 692 Glendale Valley Blvd., 16639. Tel: 814-943-5437. Email: ssjoanandthomasonpa53@dishmail.net.
Catechesis/Religious Program—Tel: 814-672-5123. Mrs. Nancy Francisco, D.R.E. Students 17.

2—ST. MARY MAGDALEN'S (1889) Closed. Merged with St. Richard's Mission, Blandburg to form St. Joan of Arc Church, Fallentimber.

GALLITZIN, CAMBRIA CO.

1—ST. DEMETRIUS (2000) [CEM 2] Rev. Albert H. Ledoux.
Res.: 811 Church St., 16641. Tel: 814-886-7941; Fax: 814-886-5673.
Catechesis/Religious Program—Students 107.

2—OUR LADY OF CZESTOCHOWA (1903), (Polish), Merged with St. Patrick, Gallitzin to form St. Demetrius, Gallitzin.

3—ST. PATRICK'S (1850) Merged with Our Lady of Czestochowa, Gallitzin to form St. Demetrius, Gallitzin.

HASTINGS, CAMBRIA CO., ST. BERNARD (1890) [CEM 2] Rev. Thaddeus E. Rettger, O.S.B.
Res.: 148-Apt. 2 Seventh Ave., P.O. Box 497, 16646. Tel: 814-247-6558; Fax: 814-247-8522.
Catechesis/Religious Program—Tel: 814-247-6415. Mrs. Mary Patterson, D.R.E. Students 117.
Mission—*St. Boniface Chapel* 1278 Main St., St. Boniface, Cambria Co. 16675.

HOLLIDAYSBURG, BLAIR CO.

1—ST. MARY'S (1841) [CEM 2] Rev. Anthony J. Legarski; Deacons Charles R. Ahearn; Charles R. Ahearn.
Res.: 312 Clark St., 16648. Tel: 814-695-0622; Fax: 814-696-9609. Email: smcforyou@hotmail.com. Web: www.webparish.com/aj/saintmarys.
See Hollidaysburg Consolidated Catholic Elementary, Hollidaysburg under Elementary Diocesan Schools located in the Institution section.
Catechesis/Religious Program—Tel: 814-695-5678. Mrs. Connie Curfman, D.R.E. Students 143.

2—ST. MICHAEL'S (1862), (German), [CEM] Very Rev. Clement G. Gardner.
Res.: 301 Spruce St., 16648. Tel: 814-695-0912; Fax: 814-693-9820. Web: www.stmichael-hldg-pa.org.
See Hollidaysburg Consolidated Catholic Elementary, Hollidaysburg under Elementary Diocesan Schools located in the Institution section.
Catechesis/Religious Program—Tel: 814-695-9735. Email: susu1949@aol.com. Susan M. Teske, D.R.E. Students 286.

HOOVERSVILLE, SOMERSET CO., HOLY FAMILY (1911) [CEM] Rev. Karl Kolodziejski, O.F.M.Conv.
Res.: 321 Sugar St., P.O. Box 187, 15936. Tel: 814-798-2933; Fax: 814-798-8601.
Catechesis/Religious Program—Students 31.

HUNTINGDON, HUNTINGDON CO., MOST HOLY TRINITY (1826) [CEM] Rev. David J. Arseneault.
Res.: 524 Mifflin St., 16652. Tel: 814-643-0160; Fax: 814-643-0160. Email: mhtcc@comcast.net. Web: www.mhtcc.org.
Catechesis/Religious Program—Students 185.

LILLY, CAMBRIA CO.

1—ST. BRIGID'S (1883) Merged with Our Lady of Mount Carmel, Lilly to form Our Lady of the Alleghenies, Lilly.

2—OUR LADY OF MT. CARMEL (1910), (Polish), Merged with St. Brigid, Lilly to form Our Lady of the Alleghenies, Lilly.

3—OUR LADY OF THE ALLEGHENIES (1995) [CEM 2] Rev. Msgr. John R. Sasway.
Res.: 608 Main St., 15938. Tel: 814-886-2504; Fax: 814-884-4952. Email: olallegh@comcast.net.
Catechesis/Religious Program—Tel: 814-886-2161. Sr. Theresa M. Kukla, S.S.C.J., D.R.E. Students 101.

LOCK HAVEN, CLINTON CO.

1—ST. AGNES (1873) [CEM] Rev. Joseph T. Orr; Deacons Philip Gibson; Calvin J. Young.
Res.: 3 E. Walnut St., 17745. Tel: 570-748-4594; Fax: 570-893-8229. Email: stagnespa@comcast.net. Web: www.stagneslh.org.
See Lock Haven Catholic School under Immaculate Conception, Lock Haven.
Catechesis/Religious Program—Email: stagnespa.pat@comcast.net. Students 92.

2—IMMACULATE CONCEPTION (1852) [CEM] Sr. Nancy E. Spence, C.C.W., Parochial Admin.
Res.: 310 W. Water St., 17745. Tel: 570-748-4535; Fax: 570-748-1674. Email: ic1852@comcast.net.
School—*Lock Haven Catholic School*, Tel: 570-748-7252. Michele Alexander, Prin. Students 27.
Catechesis/Religious Program—Fax: 570-893-8229. Students 50.

LORETTO, CAMBRIA CO., BASILICA OF ST. MICHAEL THE ARCHANGEL (1799) [CEM] Rev. Msgr. Timothy J. Swope; Deacon Michael Condor Jr. Tel: 814-886-4948. In Res., Rev. Allen P. Zeth.
Res.: 321 St. Mary, P.O. Box 10, 15940. Tel: 814-472-8551; Fax: 814-471-4959. Web: www.basilica-loretto.org.
School—301 St. Elizabeth St., 15940. Tel: 814-472-9117; Fax: 814-472-9117. Judy M. Noel, Prin. Lay Teachers 9; Students 157.
Catechesis/Religious Program—Tel: 814-505-8817. Robert Sutton, D.R.E. (Elementary & High School). Students 139.

MCCONNELLSBURG, FULTON CO., ST. STEPHEN'S (1962) Rev. Joseph C. Nale.
Res.: 303 Lincoln Way E., 17233. Tel: 717-485-3723; Fax: 717-485-3855.
Catechesis/Religious Program—Tel: 717-485-0661. Students 30.

MEYERSDALE, SOMERSET CO., SS. PHILIP AND JAMES (1850) [CEM 2] Rev. James M. Dugan.
Res.: 247 High St., 15552. Tel: 814-634-8150; Fax: 814-634-0983.
Catechesis/Religious Program—Students 66.
Mission—*St. Gregory* (1907) Church St., Berlin, Somerset Co. 15530.

MOUNT UNION, HUNTINGDON CO., ST. CATHERINE OF SIENA (1912) [CEM] Rev. George D. Koharchik.
Mailing Address: 205 W. Market St., 17066.
Res.: 203 W. Market St., 17066. Tel: 814-542-4582. Email: stcatherine@comcast.net.
Catechesis/Religious Program—Students 44.

MUNDYS CORNER, CAMBRIA CO., ST. JOHN VIANNEY'S (1950) Very Rev. Andrew C. Stanko.
Res.: 3513 William Penn Ave., Johnstown, 15909. Tel: 814-322-4789; Fax: 814-322-3799. Email: stjohnvianney@atlanticbb.net. Web: www.sjvcc.com.
Catechesis/Religious Program—Tel: 814-322-1149. Yvonne Allbaugh. Students 87.

NANTY-GLO, CAMBRIA CO., ST. MARY'S (1902) [CEM] Merged with SS. Timothy & Mark, Twin Rocks Rev. Martin A. Cingle; Deacon James J. Janosik.
Res.: 1020 Caroline St., 15943. Tel: 814-749-9103; Fax: 814-749-5463. Email: mirrorsmcl@aol.com.
Catechesis/Religious Program—Mrs. Rosemary Conzo, D.R.E. Students 105.

NEW BALTIMORE, ST. JOHN THE BAPTIST (1829) [CEM] Rev. George I. Jakopac.
Res.: 101 Findley St., P.O. Box 10, 15553. Tel: 814-733-2210; Fax: 814-733-2966.
Catechesis/Religious Program—Students 76.

NEWRY, BLAIR CO., ST. PATRICK'S (1816) [CEM 2] Rev. Msgr. Anthony B. Little.
P.O. Box 398, 16665.
Res.: 704 Patrick Ln., 16665. Tel: 814-695-3413; Fax: 814-695-1733. Email: stpatricksnewry@yahoo.com. Web: www.saintpatricknewry.org.
School—Tel: 814-695-3819; Fax: 814-695-5274. Sisters 2; Lay Teachers 8; Students 60.
Catechesis/Religious Program—Mrs. Linda Guiffre, D.R.E. Students 90.

NICKTOWN, CAMBRIA CO., ST. NICHOLAS (1861) [CEM] Rev. Chad R. Ficorilli, O.S.B.
Res.: 1169 Alverda Rd., P.O. Box 37, 15762. Tel: 814-948-9614; Fax: 814-948-5232. Email: info@saintnicholasparish.org. Web: www.saintnicholasparish.org.
See Northern Cambria Catholic School, Nicktown under Elementary Schools Diocesan located in the Institution section.
Catechesis/Religious Program—Students 139.

NORTHERN CAMBRIA, CAMBRIA CO.

1—HOLY CROSS (1893) Merged with St. Stanislaus Kostka, Barnesboro; Christ the King, Barnesboro; St. John the Baptist, Northern Cambria; Our Lady of Mt. Carmel, Northern Cambria to form Prince of Peace, Northern Cambria.

2—ST. JOHN THE BAPTIST (1896), (Slovak), Merged with St. Stanislaus Kostka, Barnesboro; Christ the King, Barnesboro; Holy Cross, Northern Cambria; Our Lady of Mt. Carmel, Northern Cambria to form Prince of Peace, Northern Cambria.

3—OUR LADY OF MT. CARMEL (1908), (Italian), Merged with St. Stanislaus Kostka, Barnesboro; Christ the King, Barnesboro; Holy Cross, Northern Cambria; St. John the Baptist, Northern Cambria to form Prince of Peace, Northern Cambria.

4—PRINCE OF PEACE (2000) [CEM 5] Rev. Lawrence L. Lacovic.
Res.: 811 Chestnut Ave., 15714. Tel: 814-948-6842; Fax: 814-948-6585.

School—Tel: 814-948-8900. See Elementary Diocesan Schools under Institutions Located in the Diocese.
Catechesis/Religious Program—Deacon Bernard J. Zernick, D.R.E. Students 160.

ORBISONIA, HUNTINGDON CO., ST. MARY'S (1840) [CEM 2] Rev. Joseph C. Nale.
Mailing Address: 20896 Croghan Pike, 17243-9000. Tel: 814-447-3172; Fax: 814-447-9030. Email: valumbra@embarqmail.com.
Res.: 303 Lincoln Way E., McConnellsburg, 17233. Tel: 717-485-3723.
Catechesis/Religious Program—Students 21.

PATTON, CAMBRIA CO.
1—ST. GEORGE (1907), (Slovak), Merged with Our Lady of Perpetual Help, Patton and St. Lawrence to form Queen of Peace, Patton.
2—OUR LADY OF PERPETUAL HELP (1892) Merged with St. George, Patton, and St. Lawrence to form Queen of Peace, Patton.
3—QUEEN OF PEACE (1995) [CEM 2] Rev. Ananias Buccicone, O.S.B.
Res.: 907 Sixth Ave., 16668. Tel: 814-674-8983; Fax: 814-674-8805. Email: qpchurch@verizon.net.
Catechesis/Religious Program—Tel: 814-674-3645. Thomas Price, D.R.E. Students 137.

PENNS VALLEY, CENTRE CO., BLESSED KATERI TEKAKWITHA (1986) [JC] Very Rev. Neil R. Dadey; Rev. Brian Lee Warchola.
Res.: 3503 Penns Valley Rd., Spring Mills, 16875. Tel: 814-422-8983.
Catechesis/Religious Program—Students 75.

PHILIPSBURG, CENTRE CO., SS. PETER AND PAUL (1868) [CEM] [JC] Rev. Robert J. Kelly.
Res.: 400 S. Fourth St., 16866. Tel: 814-342-1700; Fax: 814-342-5480. Email: rjkll@psu.edu.
Catechesis/Religious Program—Jerry Craven, D.R.E. Students 100.

PORTAGE, CAMBRIA CO.
1—ASSUMPTION B.V.M. (1907), (Slovak), Merged with Sacred Heart of Jesus to form Our Lady of the Sacred Heart, Portage
2—ST. JOHN THE BAPTIST (1923), (Hungarian), [CEM] Merged with Our Lady of the Sacred Heart, Portage.
3—ST. JOSEPH'S (1898) Rev. Walter J. Moll Jr.
Res.: 509 Caldwell Ave., 15946. Tel: 814-736-4279; Fax: 814-736-4764.
Catechesis/Religious Program—Tel: 814-736-9214. Mary E. Heinrich, D.R.E. Students 134.
4—OUR LADY OF THE SACRED HEART (1999), (Polish—Hungarian), [CEM 3] Rev. Matthew Misurda.
601 Mountain Ave., 15946. Tel: 814-736-4239. Email: OLSHparish@hotmail.com.
Res.: 806 Hammers St., 15946-1737. Tel: 814-736-9770.
Catechesis/Religious Program—Students 89.
5—SACRED HEART OF JESUS (1909), (Polish), Merged with Assumption of the Blessed Virgin Mary, Portage to form Our Lady of the Sacred Heart, Portage.

RENOVO, CLINTON CO., ST. JOSEPH'S (1869) [CEM 3] Rev. Charles Chidindu Ugo.
Res.: 925 Huron Ave., 17764. Tel: 570-923-0172; Fax: 570-923-0172.
Catechesis/Religious Program—Judy M. Kurutz, D.R.E. Students 43.

REVLOC, CAMBRIA CO., MOST HOLY REDEEMER (1920) Closed. For inquiries for parish records contact the chancery.

ROARING SPRING, BLAIR CO., ST. THOMAS MORE (1969) Rev. Leo A. Lynch, Admin.
Res.: 825 Williams St., 16673. Tel: 814-224-4522; Fax: 814-224-4522.
Catechesis/Religious Program—Students 74.

ST. AUGUSTINE, CAMBRIA CO., ST. AUGUSTINE (1847) [CEM] Rev. Joseph W. Fleming.
Res.: 803 St. Augustine Rd., Dysart, 16636. Tel: 814-674-8550.
Catechesis/Religious Program—Students 91.

ST. BONIFACE, CAMBRIA CO., ST. BONIFACE CHAPEL (1859) Merged to form St. Bernard, Hastings.

ST. LAWRENCE, CAMBRIA CO., ST. LAWRENCE'S (1853) Merged with Our Lady of Perpetual Help and St. George, Patton to form Queen of Peace, Patton.

ST. MICHAEL, CAMBRIA CO., ST. MICHAEL'S (1913) [CEM] Rev. Charles F. Bodziak.
Res.: 751 Locust St., Box 103, 15951. Tel: 814-495-9640; Fax: 814-495-9424. Email: saintmichaelsecretaries@yahoo.com. Web: www.saintmichaelchurch.weebly.com.
Catechesis/Religious Program—Students 172.

SNOW SHOE, CENTRE CO., ST. MARY'S (1865), (Irish), [CEM] Merged with St. Michael, Clarence to form Queen of Archangels, Clarence.

SOMERSET, SOMERSET CO.
1—ST. PETER IN CHAINS (1995) Mailing Address: *S.C.I.-Somerset*, 1590 Walters Mill Rd., 15501-0001. Tel: 814-443-8100.
2—ST. PETER'S (1920) [CEM] Very Rev. Daniel J. O'Neill.
Res.: 433 W. Church St., 15501. Tel: 814-443-6574; Fax: 814-445-7766.
School—Tel: 814-445-6662. Email: principal@stpetersparish.com. Mrs. Jill Harris, Prin. Lay Teachers 7; Students 105.
Catechesis/Religious Program—Students 177.

SOUTH FORK, CAMBRIA CO.
1—ST. ANTHONY'S (1905), (Polish), Merged with St. James, South Fork and Our Lady of Mt. Carmel, Ehrenfeld to form Most Holy Trinity, South Fork.
2—ST. JAMES (1906) Merged with St. Anthony, South Fork and Our Lady of Mt. Carmel, Ehrenfeld to form Most Holy Trinity, South Fork.
3—MOST HOLY TRINITY (1995) [CEM 2] Rev. Robert P. Reese.
Res.: 550 Main St., 15956. Tel: 814-495-4419; Fax: 814-495-9104. Email: rectory@mostholytrinitychurch.com. Web: www.mostholytrinitychurch.com.
Catechesis/Religious Program—Tel: 814-495-4028. Mrs. Betty Rosmus, D.R.E. Students 51.

SPANGLER, CAMBRIA CO., ST. PATRICK'S (1902) Merged with Sacred Heart, Bakerton to form St. Jude, Elmora.

STATE COLLEGE, CENTRE CO.
1—GOOD SHEPHERD (1989) Rev. Charles M. Amershek Jr.; Deacons Michael A. Ondik Jr. Tel: 814-237-1857; Jack E. Orlandi. Tel: 814-692-7472.
Mailing Address: 867 Gray's Woods Blvd., P.O. Box 8186, 16805.
Res.: 835 Gray's Woods Blvd., P.O. Box 8186, 16805. Tel: 814-238-7463. Email: gsoffice@goodshepherd-sc.org. Web: www.goodshepherd-sc.org.
Church: Tel: 814-238-2110; Fax: 814-238-3484.
Catechesis/Religious Program—Tel: 814-238-0649. Email: dirred@goodshepherd-sc.org. Margaret M. Meyers, Dir. Faith Formation. Students 380.
2—OUR LADY OF VICTORY (1908) Rev. Msgr. David A. Lockard; Revs. Matthew Baum; Chinemere Onyeocha; Deacon David C. Lapinski.
Res.: 820 Westerly Pkwy., 16801. Tel: 814-237-7832; Fax: 814-237-6709. Email: office@ourladyofvictory.com. Web: ourladyofvictory.com.
Preschool—Tel: 814-238-6616. Lay Teachers 10; Students 90.
School—800 Westerly Pkwy., 16801. Tel: 814-238-1592; Fax: 814-238-4553. Web: olvcatholicschool.org. Kathleen Bechdel, Prin. Lay Teachers 26; Students 286.
Catechesis/Religious Program—Tel: 814-237-7832, Ext. 221. Email: ecorsaro@ourladyofvictory.com. Students 418.

SUMMERHILL, CAMBRIA CO., ST. JOHN (1903) [CEM] Rev. Alfred Patterson, O.S.B.
Res.: 538 Main St., P.O. Box 248, 15958. Tel: 814-495-5241; Fax: 814-495-9522. Email: stjic@verizon.net.
Mission—Immaculate Conception (1854) 1640 New Germany Rd., P.O. Box 248, New Germany, Cambria Co. 15958.
Catechesis/Religious Program—Kimberly Gates, C.R.E. Students 163.

TWIN ROCKS, CAMBRIA CO.
1—ST. CHARLES (1917) Merged with Immaculate Conception Mission, Vintondale to form SS. Timothy & Mark Church, Twin Rocks & SS. Timothy & Mark Chapel, Vintondale.
2—SS. TIMOTHY & MARK (1995) [CEM] Merged with St. Mary, Nanty Glo (Tel: 814-749-9103; Fax: 814-749-5463).

TYRONE, BLAIR CO., ST. MATTHEW (1853) [CEM 2] Rev. Jozef Kovacik.
Res.: 1205 Cameron Ave., 16686. Tel: 814-684-1480; Fax: 814-684-7969. Email: stmatthewtyrone@gmail.com. Cemeteries: Oak Grove & St Luke's.
School—1105 Cameron Ave., 16686. Tel: 814-684-3510; Fax: 814-684-7833. Melissa McMullen, Prin. Lay Teachers 6; Students 69.
Catechesis/Religious Program—Students 100.

WEST SALISBURY, SOMERSET CO., ST. MICHAEL'S (1887) [CEM 2] Deacon William R. Underhill, Parochial Admin.; Rev. Nathan Munsch, O.S.B., Sacramental Min.
Res.: 1316 St. Paul Rd., Salisbury, 15558-0036. Tel: 814-662-2958.
Mission—St. Mary's (1906) 215 Warrens Mill Rd., Meyersdale, Somerset Co. 15552. Tel: 814-662-2958. P.O. Box 36, Salisbury, 15558-0036.
Catechesis/Religious Program—Tel: 301-689-9189. Students 29.

WILLIAMSBURG, BLAIR CO., ST. JOSEPH (1861) [CEM 2] Rev. Aron M. Maghsoudi.
Res.: 628 W. First St., 16693. Tel: 814-832-2137; Fax: 814-832-1025. Email: frleo52@comcast.net.
Catechesis/Religious Program—Students 30.

WILMORE, CAMBRIA CO., ST. BARTHOLOMEW'S (1840) [CEM] Rev. Robert P. Reese.
185 Church Hill Rd., P.O. Box 96, 15962.
Res.: 550 Main St., South Fork, 15956. Tel: 814-495-4419; Fax: 814-495-9104.
Catechesis/Religious Program—Students 37.

WINDBER, SOMERSET CO.
1—ST. ANTHONY OF PADUA (1908), (Italian), [CEM] Revs. Roderick N. Soha, T.O.R.; Adrian Tirpak, T.O.R.; Mark Reifel, T.O.R.
Res.: 2201 Graham Ave., 15963. Tel: 814-467-7292; Fax: 814-467-9182.
School—St. Benedict School, Tel: 814-266-3837; Fax: 814-266-7718. Students 2.
School—St. Andrew School, Tel: 814-288-2811; Fax: 814-288-6750.
School—St. Clement School, Tel: 814-255-1964; Fax: 814-255-2623.
School—St. Thomas, (Bedford), Tel: 814-623-5526; Fax: 814-623-1741.
Catechesis/Religious Program—Tel: 814-467-9670. Violet Bunk, D.R.E.; Roxann Newcomer, D.R.E. Students 92.
2—SS. CYRIL AND METHODIUS (1906), (Slovak), [CEM 2] Rev. George M. Gulash.
Res.: 604 Graham Ave., 15963. Tel: 814-467-7042.
Catechesis/Religious Program—600 Graham Ave., 15963. Tel: 814-467-9670. Students 22.
3—ST. ELIZABETH ANN SETON (2000) [CEM 2] Very Rev. Leonard E. Voytek; Deacon Thaddeus J. Janisko.
Res.: 605 Graham Ave., 15963. Tel: 814-467-7191; Fax: 814-467-1621.
Catechesis/Religious Program—Windber Catechetical Center, P.O. Box 36, 15963. Tel: 814-467-9670; Fax: 814-467-9670. Violet Bunk, D.R.E. Students 122.
4—HOLY CHILD JESUS (1921), (Irish), Closed. For inquiries for sacramental records, please contact SS. Cyril & Methodius.
5—ST. JOHN CANTIUS (1898), (Polish), Merged with St. Mary's, Windber to form St. Elizabeth Ann Seton, Windber.
6—ST. MARY'S (1914), (Hungarian), Merged with St. John Cantius, Windber to form St. Elizabeth Ann Seton, Windber.

Chaplains of Public Institutions

ALTOONA. *Altoona Regional Health System, Altoona Hospital Campus*, Howard Ave. & Seventh St., 16601. Tel: 814-946-2011.
Altoona Hospital Campus, 620 Howard Ave., 16601. Tel: 841-946-2011. Rev. Christopher Panagoplos, T.O.R., Chap.
Veterans Medical Center, 2907 Pleasant Valley Blvd., 16602. Tel: 814-943-8164. Revs. David H. Roesch, Chap., Anthony J. Legarski, Assoc. Chap.

JOHNSTOWN. *Conemaugh Health System*.
Memorial Medical Center, 1086 Franklin St., 15905. Tel: 814-534-9000. Revs. John F. Brezovec, Chap. Tel: 814-534-9250; Fax: 814-534-3507, James Smyka, O.F.M.Conv., Chap.
Good Samaritan Medical Center, 1020 Franklin St., 15905. Tel: 814-534-9000. Revs. John F. Brezovec, Chap. Tel: 814-534-9250; Fax: 814-534-3507, James Smyka, O.F.M.Conv., Chap.
Memorial Medical Center Lee Campus, 320 Main St., 15901. Tel: 814-534-6000. Revs. John F. Brezovec, Chap. Tel: 814-534-9250; Fax: 814-534-3507, James Smyka, O.F.M.Conv., Chap.

BELLEFONTE. *State Correctional Institution - Rockview Our Lady of the Mount*, Box A, 16823. Tel: 814-355-4874, Ext. 232. Deacon Thomas E. Boldin, Catholic Chap. & Admin., 2139 Zion Rd., 16823. Tel: 814-355-4234, Rev. Brian Lee Warchola, Sacramental Min. Tel: 814-355-3134 (Res.).

CRESSON. *State Correctional Institution*, P.O. Box A, 16630. Tel: 814-886-8181. Rev. Aron M. Maghsoudi, Chap. Tel: 814-832-2137 (Res.).

EBENSBURG. *Laurel Crest Rehabilitation & Special Care Center*, 429 Manor Dr., 15931. Tel: 814-472-8100, Ext. 3119. Vacant.

HUNTINGDON. *State Correctional Institution*, St. Dismas, 1100 Pike St., 16652. Tel: 814-643-6520, Ext. 213. Rev. Aron M. Maghsoudi, Sac. Min. Tel: 814-832-2137 (Res.), Deacon Thomas J. McFee, Chap. & Admin.

LORETTO. *Federal Correctional Institution*, P.O. Box 1000, 15940. Tel: 814-472-4140, Ext. 155. Vacant.

SMITHFIELD. *State Correctional Institution*, 1120 Pike St., Huntingdon, 16652. Tel: 814-643-6520. Rev. David J. Arseneault, Sacramental Min. Tel: 814-643-0160 (Res.), Deacon Thomas J. McFee, Chap.

SOMERSET. *State Correctional Institution*, St. Peter in Chains, 1590 Walters Mill Rd., 15510. Tel: 814-443-8100. Rev. James M. Dugan, Chap. & Pastor.
State Correctional Institution, Laurel Highlands, 5706 Glades Pike Rd., P.O. Box 631, 15501. Tel: 814-445-6501. Rev. James M. Dugan, Sacramental Min., Deacon Joseph W. Visinsky, Chap.

On Duty Outside the Diocese:
Rev.—
Slovikovski, John J., Theological College, 401 Michigan Ave., N.E., Washington, DC 20017.

Military Chaplains:
Rev.—
Halka, Frantisek A., 1 Scottsdale Ct., Columbia, SC 29229. U.S. Army

Priests on Medical Leave:
Rev.—
Kurdziel, Dennis M.

Absent on Leave:
Revs.—
Kuligowski, Peter J.
Leahey, Patrick R.
Norcavage, Albert R.

Retired:
Rev. Msgrs.—
Biller, Harold N., 201 W. High St., Apt. 202, Ebensburg, 15931.
Kline, Roy F., Blessed Sacrament Cathedral, One Cathedral Sq., P.O. Box 33, Altoona, 16601. Tel: 814-944-1909
Lenz, Paul A., The Catholic University, Curley Hall #113, Washington, DC 20064.
Mabon, Thomas K., 703 Lincoln-Lee Manor, 231 Walnut St., Johnstown, 15904. Tel: 814-535-2991
Panza, Paul D., P.A., Our Lady of Alleghenies Personal Care Res., 1037 S. Logan Blvd., 16648.
Przybocki, Bernard A., 7923 Admiral Peary Hwy., Cresson, 16630.
Saylor, Philip, Mid Town Square, 310 S. Allen St., State College, 16801.
Tomaselli, Samuel J., 855 W. Sanner St., 15501.
Valko, George J., 5922 Willow Bridge Loop, Ellenton, FL 34222.
Wadas, Ignatius C., John Paul Manor II, 856 Cambria St., Cresson, 16630.

Revs.—
Balestino, Francis P., P.O. Box 817, Johnstown, 15907.
Becker, David R., 505 McIntosh Ln., 16648. Tel: 814-935-3588
Bendzella, Sylvester J., 150 Saint Marys Ln., Apt./Ste. 3, 16648.
Boslett, Donald E., 3037 Colonel Drake Hwy., Box 132, Chest Springs, 16624. Tel: 814-674-8327
Coveney, James B., M.A., M.Div., Dmitri Manor, 150 St. Mary's Ln., Ste. 4, 16648.
Crosser, Raymond G., 100 Beckman Dr., 6F, Altoona, 16602.
Dykas, Benjamin, Town House Towers, 420 Vine St., Apt. 2402, Johnstown, 15906. Tel: 814-539-4776
Ellias, John J., 118 Mechanic St., Everett, 15537.
George, J. Clark, 150 Saint Marys Ln., Apt./Ste. 2, 16648.
Gergel, Stephen J., Lt. USN, 116 Lake Manor Dr., Kingsland, GA 31548.
Imgrund, Norman P., 2257 Sulpher Run Rd., Jersey Shore, 17740.
Joly, Henry L., 228 Piedmont Dr., Duncansville, 16635.
Knapik, Andrew G., P.O. Box 111, Bellefonte, 16823.
Mulvehill, Louis J., John Paul II Manor, 856 Cambria St., Cresson, 16630.
Robine, Paul M., 21 Country Club Rd., Cresson, 16630. Tel: 814-866-2573
Spishak, Carl A., St. Rose of Lima, 5514 Roselawn Ave., Altoona, 16602. Tel: 814-944-8509

Permanent Deacons:
Ahearn, Charles R., St. Mary, Hollidaysburg
Bailey, Robert D., Secretary to the Bishop and Episcopal Master of Ceremonies
Beavers, Thomas T., St. John the Baptist, New Baltimore
Becker, Bruce L., St. John Gualbert Cathedral, Johnstown
Boldin, Thomas E., Chap., St. John the Evangelist, Bellefonte, Catholic Chap. & Admin.; Our Lady of the Mount-SCI, Rockview
Buige, Thomas M., St. John Vianney, Mundy's Corner
Cammarata, Samuel M., St. Clare of Assisi, Johnstown
Concannon, John J., St. John Gualbert Cathedral, Johnstown
Condor, Michael, Jr., Basilica of St. Michael, Loretto
Dalla Valle, Joseph R., St. Patrick, Johnstown
Gibson, Philip, St. Agnes, Lock Haven
Golden, Richard T., Most Holy Trinity, S. Fork & St. Bartholomew, Wilmore
Hornick, David G., St. Michael, St. Michael
Ivanits, Laszlo P., Penn State Catholic Campus Ministry
Janisko, Thaddeus J., St. Elizabeth Ann Seton, Windber
Janosik, James J., St. Mary, Nanty Glo
Kolonich, Ronald A., St. Peter, Somerset
Lapinski, David C., Our Lady of Victory, State College
Leap, James F., Cathedral of the Blessed Sacrament, Altoona
Little, Scott Q., Our Mother of Sorrows, Johnstown
Luke, Steve A., St. Augustine, St. Augustine; St. Monica, Chest Springs
McFee, Thomas J., St. Therese of the Child Jesus, Altoona; Chap., Smithfield, SCI; Chap. & Admin., St. Dismas, SCI Huntingdon
Neral, Gene P., St. John the Evangelist, Lakemont
Ondik, Michael A., Jr., (Retired), Good Shepherd, State College
Orlandi, Jack E., Good Shepherd, State College
Papinchak, Thomas M., SS. Gregory & Barnabas, Johnstown
Pyle, Jay A., All Saints, Boswell
Russo, Michael L., St. Benedict, Johnstown
Rys, John R., Cathedral of the Blessed Sacrament, Altoona
Sroka, John E., Visitation of the BVM, Johnstown
Szwarc, John J., Cathedral of the Blessed Sacrament, Altoona
Underhill, William R., SS. Philip & James, Meyersdale; St. Gregory, MacDonaldton; Admin. St. Michael, West Salisbury; St. Mary, Pocahontas
Visinsky, Joseph W., Holy Family, Hooversville & Chap. at SCI Laurel
Woomer, James L., Sr., St. Rose of Lima, Altoona
Young, Calvin J., Immaculate Conception, Lock Haven; Lock Haven Univ., Lock Haven; St. Agnes, Lock Haven
Zernick, Bernard J., Prince of Peace, Northern Cambria

INSTITUTIONS LOCATED IN THE DIOCESE

[A] COLLEGES AND UNIVERSITIES (NON-DIOCESAN)

CRESSON
Mount Aloysius College (1853) 7373 Admiral Peary Hwy., 16630. Tel: 814-886-4131; Fax: 814-886-2978. Email: cmiller@mtaloy.edu. Web: www.mtaloy.edu. Dr. Thomas P. Foley, Pres.; Mr. Frank Crouse, Vice Pres. Enrollment Management; Dr. Timothy Fulop, Senior Vice Pres. Academic Affairs; Dr. Jane Grassadonia, Vice Pres. Student Affairs. Sisters of Mercy. Sisters 6; Lay Teachers 65; Total Staff 225; Students 2,000.

LORETTO
St. Francis University, P.O. Box 600, 15940-0600. Tel: 814-472-3001; Fax: 814-472-3003. Email: vsoyka@francis.edu. Web: www.francis.edu. Rev. Gabriel Zeis, T.O.R., Pres.; Dr. Patricia Serotkin, Vice Pres. Strategic Initiatives; Dr. Wayne Powel, Provost; Erin McCloskey, Vice Pres. Enrollment Mgmt.; Robert Datsko, Vice Pres. Finance; Mr. Robert Crusciel, Vice Pres. Advancement; Mr. Randy Frye, Dean Business; T. J. Brecciaroli, Dir. Residence Life; Ms. Sandra Balough, Dean Library Svcs.; Ms. Julie Barris, Dir. Career Devel. & Continuing Educ.; Mr. George Pyo, Dir. Computer Svcs.; Mr. Dominick Peruso, Assoc. Dir. Student Activities; Ms. Renee Bernard, Dir. Advising & Retention, Ctr. Acad. Success; Robert Krimmel, Dir. Athletics; Mr. David Wilson, Dir. Counseling; Rev. Daniel Sinisi, T.O.R., Vice Pres. Mission Effectiveness & Ministry; Bro. Gabriel Mary Amato, T.O.R., Coord. Dorothy Day Center; Revs. Nathan Malavolti, T.O.R., Asst. Professor Chemistry; Malachi VanTassell, T.O.R., Adjunct Asst. Professor Accounting; Joseph Chancler, T.O.R., Adjunct Instructor Math; Christopher Dobson, T.O.R., Dir. Campus Ministry; Bro. Shamus McGrenra, T.O.R., Dir. Intl. Admissions; Revs. Shawn Roberson, T.O.R., Campus Min.; Patrick Donahoe, T.O.R., Campus Min. & Mission Effectiveness; Matthew Russick, T.O.R., Campus Min. Priests 10; Lay Professors 112; Students 2,379.

[B] HIGH SCHOOLS, PRIVATE

ALTOONA. **Bishop Guilfoyle Catholic High School*, 2400 Pleasant Valley Blvd., 16602. Tel: 814-944-4014; Fax: 814-944-8695. Email: bkubitza@bguilfoyle.org. Web: www.bishopguilfoyle.org. Bernard G. Kubitza, Pres. & Prin.; Sr. Beverly Hmel, I.H.M., Curriculum Dir.; Joan Donnelly, Vice Prin.; Linda Alianiello, Librarian. Sisters 1; Lay Teachers 24; Total Staff 43; Students 330.

JOHNSTOWN. **Bishop McCort Catholic High School*, 25 Osborne St., 15905. Tel: 814-536-8991; Fax: 814-535-4118. Email: ksalem@mccort.org. Web: www.mccort.org. Mr. Kenneth S. Salem, Prin. & Contact Person; Mrs. Janet Skelly, Librarian; Sr. Donna Marie Leiden, S.C., Dir. Educ. Priests 1; Deacons 1; Sisters 1; Lay Teachers 33; Students 410.

EBENSBURG. **Bishop Carroll Catholic High School*, 728 Ben Franklin Hwy., 15931. Tel: 814-472-7500; Fax: 814-472-8020. Web: bishopcarroll.com. Lorie Ratchford, Prin.; Nicole Petrunak, Librarian. Priests 2; Brothers 1; Lay Teachers 23; Students 227.

[C] ELEMENTARY DIOCESAN SCHOOLS

ALTOONA. *Altoona Central Catholic School*, (Grades PreK-8), 1400 4th Ave., 16602. Tel: 814-944-1250; Fax: 814-944-1452. Email: altoonaccs1@aol.com. Web: altoonacentralcatholic.com. Jeffery F. Maucieri, Prin. Lay Teachers 23; Students 303.
424 Wopsononock Ave., 16601. Tel: 814-381-7011; Fax: 814-381-7015.
1400 4th Ave., 16602. Tel: 814-944-1250; Fax: 814-944-1452. Email: altoonaccs1@aol.com.

BOALSBURG. *St. Joseph's Catholic Academy*, 901 Boalsburg Pike, 16827.

CRESSON. *All Saints Catholic School*, (Grades PreK-8), 220 Powell Ave., 16630. Tel: 814-886-7942; Fax: 814-886-7942. Email: allsaints@ascsknights.org. Mrs. Susan Glass, Prin. Consolidation of the following parishes: St. Francis Xavier; St. Aloysius; Our Lady of the Allegheneies; St. Thomas Aquinas; Our Lady of the Sacred Heart; St. Demetrius; St. Bartholomew; St. Joseph. Sisters 2; Lay Teachers 10; Preschool 55; Students 118.

HOLLIDAYSBURG. *Hollidaysburg Consolidated Catholic Elementary School*, (Grades PreK-8), Spruce & Wayne Sts., P.O. Box 599, 16648. Tel: 814-695-6112; Fax: 814-696-8960. Email: espencer@hcssaints.org. Web: www.daj.k12.pa.us/hcs/. Mrs. Elaine Spencer, Prin. Consolidation of the following parishes: St. Michael's; St. Mary's. Lay Teachers 10; Students 148.

NICKTOWN. *Northern Cambria Catholic School*, 3278 Blue Goose Rd., P.O. Box 252, 15762. Tel: 814-948-8900; Fax: 814-948-8720. Email: nccs@northerncambriacatholic.org. Sr. Mary Lee Przybylski, C.S.S.F., Prin.; Ellen Hoover, Librarian. Consolidation of the following parishes: St. Nicholas & Prince of Peace. Sisters 1; Lay Teachers 12; Students 108.

[D] EDUCATION CONSOLIDATED ELEMENTARY SCHOOLS

JOHNSTOWN. *Cathedral Catholic Academy*, (Grades PreK-8), Consolidated schools of St. John Gualbert Cathedral, St. Clement & St. Clare of Assisi., 110 Lindberg Ave., 15905. Tel: 814-255-1964; Fax: 814-255-1964. Email: rbatzel@ccacademy.org. Mrs. Rosemary Batzel, Prin. Lay Teachers 13; Students 165.

[E] GENERAL HOSPITALS (NON-DIOCESAN)

JOHNSTOWN
Good Samaritan Medical Center, 1020 Franklin St., 15905. Tel: 814-534-9000; Fax: 814-539-0264. Email: stucker@conemaugh.org. Rev. John F. Brezovec, Chap.; Mr. Steven E. Tucker, Pres. Skilled Nursing Care Center Beds 74; Patients Assisted Annually 253; Total Staff 58.

[F] HOMES FOR AGED (NON-DIOCESAN)

HOLLIDAYSBURG
Garvey Manor (1965) 1037 S. Logan Blvd., 16648. Tel: 814-695-5571; Fax: 814-695-8516. Web: www.garveymanor.org. Sr. M. Joachim Anne Ferenchak, O.Carm., Admin. Senior Care Complex: Nursing, Personal Care, Independent Living. Carmelite Sisters for the Aged and Infirm 7; Aged Residents 180; Total Assisted Annually 250; Patients Assisted Annually 300; Total Staff 310; Bed Capacity 180.
St. Leonard's Home, Inc., 601 N. Montgomery St., 16648. Tel: 814-695-9581; Fax: 814-695-2606. Email: srcindy@juno.com. Sr. Cynthia Meyer, C.S.F.N., Exec. Dir.

St. Leonard's Home, Inc. Sisters of the Holy Family of Nazareth 1; Bed Capacity 28; Total Staff 15; Total Assisted Annually 35.

(DIOCESAN)

HOLLIDAYSBURG

Dmitri Manor Priests' Residence, St. Mary's Ln., 16648. Tel: 814-696-4698. Rev. Msgr. Robert J. Saly. Aged Residents 3; Staff 1; Bed Capacity 12.

[G] MONASTERIES AND RESIDENCES OF PRIESTS AND BROTHERS

(NON-DIOCESAN)

HOLLIDAYSBURG

St. Joseph Friary, 501-503 Walnut St., 16648. Tel: 814-695-5802. Revs. Leonard Blostic, T.O.R. (Retired); Gerard M. Connolly, T.O.R.; Christopher Panagoplos, T.O.R., Priest Chap. Altoona Regl. Health System, Local Min.

LORETTO

St. Bonaventure Friary, P.O. Box 155, 15940-0155. Tel: 814-693-2824; Fax: 814-693-2831. Revs. Bernard Tickerhoof, T.O.R., Dir. Novices; Shawn Roberson, T.O.R., Dir. Postulants. Priests 2; Novices 2; Postulants 3.

St. Francis Friary at Mount Assisi, 141 St. Francis Dr., P.O. Box 40, 15940-0040. Tel: 814-693-2827; Fax: 814-693-2882. Web: www.franciscanstor.org. Revs. Patrick George, T.O.R. Tel: 814-472-5324, Ext. 302; Augustine Belinda, T.O.R.; Alex Bombera, T.O.R.; David Bonarrigo, T.O.R., Faculty Bishop Carroll H.S.; Gervase Cain, T.O.R.; Marion Deck, T.O.R.; Simon Mary Engler, T.O.R.; Jack Grinnen, T.O.R.; Colman J. McGarril, T.O.R.; James V. Morman, T.O.R., Local Minister; Francis Moyher, T.O.R.; Daniel J. Mulkern, T.O.R.; Aidan Mullaney; Christian R. Oravec, T.O.R., Prov. Tel: 814-472-3001; Arnold Petrosky, T.O.R.; Emil Resconich, T.O.R.; Shawn Roberson, T.O.R., Postulants Dir., Dir. Retreats; Bernard Tickerhoof, T.O.R., Novices Dir.; Andre Strittmatter, T.O.R.; Benjamin Medeiros, T.O.R., Archivist; Malachi VanTassell, T.O.R., Faculty-St. Francis Univ./Prov. Econome/Vicar; Jude Ventiquattro, Dir. Healthcare; Matthew Russick, Faculty-Bishop Carrol H.S.; Sean Sullivan, T.O.R.; Bros. Gabriel Mary Amato, T.O.R., Dir., Dorothy Day Center; Edward Bennett, T.O.R.; Callistus Gerardi, T.O.R.; Damien Koehler, T.O.R.; Stephen Liebal, T.O.R.; Bernard Nicolosi, T.O.R.; Norman MeNelis, T.O.R. Priests 24; Brothers 7; Novices 6; Postulants 2.

NEWRY

St. Bernardine Monastery (1925) 768 Monastery Rd., P.O. Box 117, 16648. Tel: 814-695-3992; 814-693-0166; Fax: 814-695-1611. Web: www.franciscanfriars.org. Most Rev. Bonaventure Midili, T.O.R. (Retired); Very Revs. J. Patrick Quinn, T.O.R., Min. Provincial & Local Min.; Adalbert Wolski, T.O.R. (Retired); Revs. Kenneth La Pan, T.O.R. (Retired); Carl Vacek, T.O.R.; Fabian Sheganoski, T.O.R. (Retired); Very Rev. Eugene Kubina, T.O.R. (Retired); Rev. Cyprian J. Mercieca, T.O.R. (Retired); Bro. Stephen P. Baker, T.O.R. (Retired). Priests 8; Brothers 1. *Franciscan Friars, T.O.R. Development Office and Mass Association*, P.O. Box 139, 16648. Tel: 814-695-3802; Fax: 814-695-1611. Email: info@thefranciscanfriars.org. Web: www.thefranciscanfriars.org. Tim Beresnyek, Dir. Devel. & Mass Association. *Province Econome's Office* (1925) P.O. Box 117, 16648. Tel: 814-696-3321; Fax: 814-695-1611. Email: wlinhares@gmail.com. Web: www.franciscanfriarstor.com. Rev. William P. Linhares, T.O.R., Provincial Econome.

[H] CONVENTS AND RESIDENCES FOR SISTERS

(NON-DIOCESAN)

ALTOONA

Our Lady of Perpetual Help Convent, 445 Baynton Ave., #A, 16602. Tel: 814-942-3819. Sisters, Servants of the Immaculate Heart of Mary. Total in Residence 1; Total Staff 1.

St. John of the Cross Convent, 35 Seneca Ave., 16602. Tel: 814-942-5747; Fax: 814-942-8052. Email: sllamagna@verizon.net. Carmelite Community of the Word. Total in Residence 2.

CRESSON

Sister Servants of the Most Sacred Heart of Jesus (1894) Provincial House, 866 Cambria St., 16630-1713. Tel: 814-886-4223; Fax: 814-886-4735. Email: sacredheartsistersusa@catholic.org. Sr. Jacinta Miryam Hanley, S.S.C.J., Prov. Supr. Sisters 25; Personnel 25; Novices 1; Aspirants 2. *John Paul II Manor Personal Care Home* Tel: 814-886-7961; Fax: 814-886-7987. Email: johnpaul2manor@juno.com. Total in Residence 45; Total Staff 18.

EBENSBURG

Carmelite Community of the Word (1971) St. Therese Convent, 218 W. Lloyd St., 15931. Tel: 814-472-9457; Fax: 814-472-5105. Email: ebensburgccw@aol.com. Total in Residence 3.

Sisters of St. Ann Mother House, 1120 N. Center St., P.O. Box 328, 15931. Tel: 814-472-9354; Fax: 814-472-9354. Email: sistersann@verizon.net. Sr. Diana L. Polanco, Supr. Sisters of St. Ann. Total in Residence 4.

GALLITZIN

Carmelite Community of the Word-Incarnation Center, 394 Bem Rd., 16641. Tel: 814-886-4098; Fax: 814-886-7115. Web: ccwsisters.org. Sr. Marilyn Welch, C.C.W., Admin. Gen. Total in Residence 3.

Little Sisters of Jesus, 347 Tunnel Hill St., 16641. Tel: 814-886-4679. Sr. Laura Lee Seubert, Supr. Total in Residence 3.

LORETTO

Carmel of St. Therese of Lisieux (1927) 2101 Manor Dr., P.O. Box 57, 15940-0057. Tel: 814-472-8620; Fax: 814-472-6231. Web: www.lorettocarmel.com. Sr. John of the Cross, O.C.D., Prioress. Discalced Carmelite Nuns. Nuns with Solemn Vows 10.

MCCONNELLSBURG

Carmelite Community of the Word, Fulton County Mission, 110 S. Third St., 17223. Tel: 717-485-5917; 717-485-0661; Fax: 717-485-3855. Email: sistermargie@comcast.net. Total in Residence 2.

PORTAGE

Sister Servants of the Most Sacred Heart of Jesus, Sacred Heart Novitiate, 1872 Munster Rd., 15946. Tel: 814-886-4459. Sisters Maria Kotch, S.S.C.J., Local Supr.; Ryszarda Wittbrodt, S.S.C.J., Dir., Formation. Sisters 3; Novices 1; Aspirants 2.

[I] CAMPUS MINISTRY

ALTOONA. *Office of Campus Ministry Saint John the Evangelist Rectory*, 309 Lotz Ave., 16602. Tel: 814-942-5503; Fax: 814-943-8832. Rev. Msgr. Michael A. Becker, Coord.

Juniata College 1905 More St., Huntington, 16652. Tel: 814-641-3362 (Office); Fax: 814-641-3317. Ms. Lisa Baer, Campus Min.; Rev. David J. Arseneault, Chap.

Lock Haven University (Lock Haven) Newman Center, 445 W. Main St., Lock Haven, 17745. Tel: 570-748-8592; Fax: 570-748-8592 (Call ahead). Sr. Karen Grusek, C.C.W., Campus Min.; Rev. Joseph T. Orr, Sacramental Min.

Mount Aloysius College (Cresson) 7373 Admiral Peary Hwy., Cresson, 16630. Tel: 814-886-6476; Fax: 814-886-2978. Sr. Nancy Donovan, R.S.M., Dir. Campus Ministry; Ann Schwartz, Campus Min.

Penn State University, Altoona Edith Davis Eve Chapel Room 113, 3000 Ivyside Park, 16601. Tel: 814-949-5137. Andre McCarville, Campus Min.

Penn State University, University Park 205C Pasquerilla Spiritual Center, University Park, 16802. Tel: 814-865-4281; Fax: 814-865-2972. Revs. Matthew T. Laffey, O.S.B., Dir. Campus Ministry; David R. Griffin, O.S.B., Campus Min.; Deacon Laszlo P. Ivanits, Campus Min.; Mr. Phillip Torbert, Dir. Music & Liturgy.

St. Francis University (Loretto) P.O. Box 600, Loretto, 15940. Tel: 814-472-3391; Fax: 814-472-2776. Rev. Christopher Dobson, T.O.R., Dir. Campus Ministry. Tel: 814-472-3391; Mr. Paul Girardi, Campus Min. Tel: 814-472-3367; Revs. Shawn Roberson, T.O.R., Campus Min.; Patrick Donoughe, T.O.R., Campus Min.; Matthew Russick, T.O.R., Campus Min.

University of Pittsburgh at Johnstown 450 Schoolhouse Rd., Johnstown, 15904. Tel: 814-269-2007; Fax: 814-269-7128. Jonathan Jerome, Campus Min.; Rev. Matthew A. Reese, Chap. & Sacramental Min.

[J] NEWMAN CENTERS

(NON-DIOCESAN)

UNIVERSITY PARK

Penn State Catholic Community 205 Pasquerilla Spiritual Center, 16802. Tel: 814-865-4281; Fax: 814-865-2972. Email: catholic@psu.edu. Web: www.psu.edu/catholic. Revs. Matthew T. Laffey, O.S.B., Dir.; David R. Griffin, O.S.B., Campus Min.; Deacon Laszlo P. Ivanits, Campus Min. Catholic Students attending Penn State University 9,500; Total in Residence 2; Total Staff 6.

[K] MISCELLANEOUS LISTINGS

(NON-DIOCESAN)

BEDFORD

St. Mary's House of Solitude, Passionist Community, 2970 Imlertown Rd., 15522-8101. Tel: 814-623-1796; Fax: 814-623-2457. Rev. Silvan Rouse, C.P., Supr.

HOLLIDAYSBURG

Second Century Scholarship Fund (2001) *Diocese of Altoona-Johnstown*, 925 S. Logan Blvd., 16648. Tel: 814-695-5577; Fax: 814-696-9516. Email: ringkamp@dioceseaj.org. Web: www.secondcenturyfund.org. Mr. Christopher F. Ringkamp, Devel. Dir.; Mr. Larry R. Sutton, Corporate Sec. Student Scholarships 788.

LORETTO

American Parish Youth Center, Inc., P.O. Box 40, 15940. Tel: 814-693-2885; Fax: 814-693-2881. Email: framarco@aol.com.

Prince Gallitzin Chapel House (Diocesan), P.O. Box 99, 15940. Tel: 814-472-5441; Fax: 814-472-5446. Email: azeth@dioceseaj.org.

Office of Vocations, Prince Gallitzin Chapel House, 357 St. Mary's St., P.O. Box 99, 15940-0099. Tel: 814-472-5441; Fax: 814-472-5446. Email: azeth@dioceseaj.org. Rev. Allen P. Zeth, Dir.

Office of Ongoing Formation of Clergy, P.O. Box 99, 15940-0099. Tel: 814-472-5441; Fax: 814-472-5446. Rev. Msgr. Timothy J. Swope, V.F.

NEW BALTIMORE

St. John The Baptist Retreat Center, P.O. Box 10, 15553. Tel: 814-733-2210; Fax: 814-733-2966. Total in Residence 1; Total Staff 6.

RELIGIOUS INSTITUTES OF MEN REPRESENTED IN THE DIOCESE

For further details refer to the corresponding bracketed number in the Religious Institutes of Men or Women section.

[0200]—*Benedictine Monks*—O.S.B.

[0470]—*The Capuchin Friars*—O.F.M.Cap.

[1000]—*Congregation of the Passion*—C.P.

[0480]—*Conventual Franciscans* (St. Anthony of Padua Prov.)—O.F.M.Conv.

[0520]—*Franciscan Friars*—O.F.M.

[0560]—*Third Order Regular of Saint Francis* (Provs. of Sacred Heart, Immaculate Conception)—T.O.R.

RELIGIOUS INSTITUTES OF WOMEN REPRESENTED IN THE DIOCESE

[0100]—*Adorers of the Blood of Christ*—A.S.C.

[0315]—*Carmelite Community of the Word*—C.C.W.

[0330]—*Carmelite Sisters for the Aged and Infirm*—O.Carm.

[3710]—*Congregation of the Sisters of Saint Agnes*—C.S.A.

[0420]—*Discalced Carmelite Nuns*—O.C.D.

[1070-03]—*Dominican Sisters*—O.P.

[1170]—*Felician Sisters*—C.S.S.F.

[2330]—*Little Sisters of Jesus*—L.S.J.

[3630]—*Servants of the Most Sacred Heart of Jesus*—S.S.C.J.

[0570]—*Sisters of Charity of Seton Hill, Greensburg, Pennsylvania*—S.C.

[2575]—*Sisters of Mercy of the Americas* (Dallas Regional Community)—R.S.M.

[1620]—*Sisters of Saint Francis of Millvale, Pennsylvania*—O.S.F.

[3780]—*Sisters of Ss. Cyril and Methodius*—SS.C.M.

[3718]—*Sisters of St. Ann* (Italy)—S.S.A.

[3830]—*Sisters of St. Joseph*—C.S.J.

[1970]—*Sisters of the Holy Family of Nazareth*—C.S.F.N.

[3260]—*Sisters of the Precious Blood (Ohio)*—C.PP.S.

[2160]—*Sisters, Servants of the Immaculate Heart of Mary* (Scranton, PA)—I.H.M.

[4160]—*Vincentian Sisters of Charity*—V.S.C.

NECROLOGY

† Bender, Philip M., (Retired)—Died May 23, 2011

† Conrad, James H., (Retired)—Died Oct. 28, 2010

† Myers, Regis F., (Retired)—Died Jan. 13, 2011

Diocese of Amarillo

(Dioecesis Amarillensis)

Most Reverend

PATRICK J. ZUREK, D.D.

Bishop of Amarillo; ordained June 29, 1975; appointed Auxiliary Bishop of San Antonio and Titular Bishop of Tamugadi January 5, 1998; consecrated February 16, 1998; appointed Bishop of Amarillo January 3, 2008; installed Feb. 22, 2008.

Most Reverend

JOHN W. YANTA, D.D.

Retired Bishop of Amarillo; ordained March 17, 1956; appointed Titular Bishop of Naratcata and Auxiliary Bishop of San Antonio October 27, 1994; consecrated December 30, 1994; appointed Bishop of Amarillo January 21, 1997; installed March 17, 1997; retired January 3, 2008.

Diocesan Pastoral Center: 1800 N. Spring St., P.O. Box 5644, Amarillo, TX 79117-5644. Tel: 806-383-2243; Fax: 806-383-8452.

Web: www.amarillodiocese.org

ERECTED A DIOCESE BY POPE PIUS XI, AUGUST 25, 1926.

Square Miles 25,800.

Comprises that part of the State of Texas known as the Panhandle, and extending thence southward; bounded on the east by Oklahoma, and by the eastern county line of Childress and by the southern lines Childress, Hall, Briscoe, Swisher, Castro and Parmer Counties; the western boundary is the New Mexico state line from the southern line of Parmer County, Texas, northward to the northwestern corner of the Panhandle of Texas. There are 26 counties.

For legal titles of parishes and diocesan institutions, consult the Chancery Office.

STATISTICAL OVERVIEW

Personnel	
Bishop	1
Retired Bishops	1
Priests: Diocesan Active in Diocese	26
Priests: Diocesan Active Outside Diocese	2
Priests: Retired, Sick or Absent	12
Number of Diocesan Priests	40
Religious Priests in Diocese	4
Total Priests in Diocese	44
Extern Priests in Diocese	10
Ordinations:	
Diocesan Priests	1
Permanent Deacons	16
Permanent Deacons in Diocese	60
Total Sisters	87
Parishes	
Parishes	38
With Resident Pastor:	
Resident Diocesan Priests	21
Resident Religious Priests	3
Without Resident Pastor:	
Administered by Priests	14
Missions	11
Professional Ministry Personnel:	
Brothers	1
Sisters	2
Lay Ministers	10
Welfare	
Homes for the Aged	1
Total Assisted	74
Day Care Centers	1
Total Assisted	89
Specialized Homes	5
Total Assisted	657
Special Centers for Social Services	1
Total Assisted	300
Other Institutions	1
Total Assisted	4
Educational	
Diocesan Students in Other Seminaries	7
Total Seminarians	7
High Schools, Diocesan and Parish	1
Total Students	136
Elementary Schools, Diocesan and Parish	4
Total Students	568
Catechesis/Religious Education:	
High School Students	2,149
Elementary Students	3,532
Total Students under Catholic Instruction	6,392
Teachers in the Diocese:	
Priests	2
Sisters	6
Lay Teachers	62
Vital Statistics	
Receptions into the Church:	
Infant Baptism Totals	1,052
Minor Baptism Totals	156
Adult Baptism Totals	59
Received into Full Communion	116
First Communions	1,086
Confirmations	686
Marriages:	
Catholic	176
Interfaith	30
Total Marriages	206
Deaths	307
Total Catholic Population	50,237
Total Population	427,927

Former Bishops—Most Revs. RUDOLPH ALOYSIUS GERKEN, D.D., ord. June 10, 1917; cons. April 26, 1927; installed Bishop of Amarillo, April 28, 1927; elevated to the Metropolitan See of Santa Fe, NM, June 2, 1933; died March 2, 1943; ROBERT E. LUCEY, ord. May 14, 1916; cons. May 1, 1934; installed May 16, 1934; elevated to the Metropolitan See of San Antonio, Jan. 22, 1941; LAURENCE J. FITZSIMON, D.D., ord. May 17, 1921; cons. Oct. 22, 1941; installed Nov. 5, 1941; died July 2, 1958; JOHN L. MORKOVSKY, appt. Auxiliary of Amarillo, Dec. 22, 1955; named Bishop of Amarillo, Aug. 18, 1958; transferred to as Coadjutor Bishop of Galveston-Houston "cum jure successionis," April 16, 1963; LAWRENCE M. DEFALCO, D.D., ord. June 11, 1942; appt. April 16, 1963; cons. May 30, 1963; installed June 13, 1963; retired Aug. 28, 1979; died Sept. 22, 1979; LEROY T. MATTHIESEN, D.D., M.A., LITT.D, ord. March 10, 1946; appt. March 25, 1980; ord. Bishop, May 30, 1980; retired Jan. 21, 1997; died March 22, 2010.; JOHN W. YANTA, D.D., ord. March 17, 1956; appt. Titular Bishop of Naratcata and Auxiliary Bishop of San Antonio Oct. 27, 1994; cons. Dec. 30, 1994; appt. Bishop of Amarillo Jan. 21, 1997; installed March 17, 1997; retired Jan. 3, 2008.

Diocesan Officials

Diocesan Pastoral Center—1800 N. Spring St., Amarillo, 79107. Tel: 806-383-2243; Fax: 806-383-8452. Web: www.amarilodiocese.org. *Mailing Address: P.O. Box 5644, Amarillo, 79117-5644.*

Vicar General—Very Rev. PHU T. PHAN, J.C.L., Bel.

Moderator of the Curia—Rev. Msgr. HAROLD L. WALDOW.

Vicar of Clergy—Rev. Msgr. HAROLD L. WALDOW.

Vicars Forane—Revs. JOHN VALDEZ, South Deanery; HECTOR MADRIGAL, Central Deanery; FRANCISCO PENEZ, East Deanery; SCOTT RAEF, North Deanery.

Diocesan Tribunal—

Judicial Vicar—Very Rev. PHU T. PHAN, J.C.L., Bel.

Defenders of the Bond—Rev. Msgr. JAMES C. GURZYNSKI (Retired); Rev. MIECZYSLAW "MITCHELL" PRZEPIORA.

Advocates—Revs. JOSE GOMEZ; DAVID CONTRERAS; HECTOR MADRIGAL; FRANCISCO PEREZ; DANIEL A. DREHER; TONY NEUSCH.

Notaries—Ms. CAROL SANFORD; Ms. SUSAN GARNER; Deacon FLOYD ASHLEY.

Chancellor—Rev. FRANCISCO PEREZ.

Archivist—Ms. SUSAN GARNER.

Executive Assistant to the Bishop—Deacon FLOYD ASHLEY.

Diocesan Advisory Councils

Presbyteral Council—Rev. Msgrs. JOSEPH T. TASH; JOSEPH BIXENMAN; Rev. LUPE MAYORGA. Bishop's Appointee: Ex Officio: Very Rev. PHU T. PHAN, J.C.L., Bel, Vicar Gen.; Rev. Msgr. HAROLD L. WALDOW, Vicar of Clergy; Revs. JOHN VALDEZ, Dean; HECTOR MADRIGAL, Dean; FRANCISCO PEREZ, Dean; SCOTT RAEF, Dean.

College of Consultors—Rev. Msgrs. HAROLD L. WALDOW; REX NICHOLL; Rev. JOHN VALDEZ; Rev. Msgrs. MICHAEL P. COLWELL; JOSEPH T. TASH; Very Rev. PHU T. PHAN, J.C.L., Bel, Vicar Gen.; Rev. Msgr. JOSEPH BIXENMAN; Rev. FRANCISCO PEREZ.

Diocesan Pastoral Council—Rev. Msgr. HAROLD L. WALDOW, Liaison.

Priests' Pension Plan Retirement Committee—Rev. Msgrs. JOSEPH T. TASH; RAYMOND CROSIER; Revs. FRANCISCO PEREZ; DAVID CONTRERAS.

Vocation Development Team—Revs. SCOTT RAEF, Dir.; JOHN VALDEZ; FRANCISCO PEREZ; TONY NEUSCH.

Deacon Director—Deacon BLAINE WESTLAKE.

Diocesan Departments

Director of Youth—OSCAR GUZMAN.

Office for the Catholic Schools—Rev. ROBERT BUSCH, Ph.D., Supt.

Christian Formation Commission—Sr. JANET ABBACHI, S.S.N.D.

Department of Communications—CHRIST ALBRACHT, Editor "The West Texas Catholic".

Department of Finances and Ecclesiastical Properties—

Fiscal Manager—PHIL WHITSON, CFO.
Director of Administrative Services—PATSY GRAHAM.
Office of Development and Stewardship—KIM RICHARD, Dir.
United Catholic Appeal—KIM RICHARD, Dir.
Webmaster/IT Manager—JOE GARCIA.

General Auxiliary Pastoral Services

Diocesan Attorney—FREDERICK J. GRIFFIN, 504 S. Polk, Amarillo, 79101.
Promoter of Justice—Rev. Msgr. MICHAEL P. COLWELL. Email: mcolwell@amarillodiocese.org.
Victim Assistance Coordinator—BELINDA TAYLOR GONZALEZ, Mailing Address: P.O. Box 5644, Amarillo, 79117-5644. Tel: 806-372-7960.
Charter Review Board—LOUISE ROSS, Chm.; BELINDA TAYLOR GONZALEZ; FRANK JONES; DOROTHY GUGGEMOS; ZEKE CASTRO; CHARLES MESTAS.
Ex Officio—Very Rev. PHU T. PHAN, J.C.L., Bel; Rev. Msgr. HAROLD L. WALDOW; Deacon BLAINE WESTLAKE; FREDERICK J. GRIFFIN.
Coalition for Catholic Social Services - CCSS—VACANT.
Catholic Historical Society—Ms. SUSAN GARNER, Pres.; ANN WELD, Museum Cur.
Rural Life Director—VACANT.
Holy Childhood Association—VACANT.
Propagation of the Faith—Rev. MIECZYSLAW "MITCHELL" PRZEPIORA.
Rite of Christian Initiation of Adults Commission—Sr. JANET ABBACHI, S.S.N.D.; Rev. Msgr. HAROLD L. WALDOW.

Auxiliary Pastoral Services for Laity

Diocesan Council of Catholic Women—Rev. Msgr. REX NICHOLL, Mod.; EMILY SANCHEZ, Pres., 1200 S. Washington, Amarillo, 79102.
Director of Prison Ministry—Deacons BLAINE WESTLAKE; MARK SEIDLITZ, Coord.
Marriage Encounter—Rev. Msgr. MICHAEL P. COLWELL.
Engaged Encounter—Directors: Deacon BLAINE WESTLAKE; LOUISE WESTLAKE.
Diaconate Office Secretary—MOLLY VILLEGAS.
Catholic Student Center at West Texas A & M University—Rev. DANIEL A. DREHER, Dir. Campus Min. & Chap.; BETTY ARAGON, Asst. Dir., 2614 Fourth Ave., Canyon, 79015. Tel: 806-655-4345.
Scouting—Deacon ROBERT SMITH.
Serra Club—DAVID HUDSON, Pres.
Natural Family Planning—Dr. FAYE USALA, Coord. Tel: 806-379-9224.
Cursillo Movement—Rev. Msgr. REX NICHOLL, Spiritual Dir. Lay Directors: LUPE GOMEZ, Amarillo; MARISOL CASTANON, Amarillo.
A.C.T.S. Movement—Rev. Msgr. HAROLD L. WALDOW, Spiritual Dir. Retrouvallie: ROB GRIFFITH; MARY GRIFFITH. Tel: 806-477-6262.
Family Life Commission—STEPHANIE FRAUSTO.
Vicar for Religious— (Pending)
Office for the Permanent Diaconate—Deacon BLAINE WESTLAKE, Coord.
Continuing Education of Clergy—Rev. Msgr. HAROLD L. WALDOW.
Priests' Retirement—PATSY GRAHAM.
Neocatechumenite—Rev. Msgr. ARTURO MEZA, Contact, Our Lady of Loreto, Silverton, 79257. Tel: 806-823-2548.

CLERGY, PARISHES, MISSIONS AND PAROCHIAL SCHOOLS

CITY OF AMARILLO

(POTTER COUNTY)

1—SACRED HEART CATHEDRAL, Closed. This parish ceased to exist 1/19/75. For inquiries contact the Diocese of Amarillo: P.O. Box 5644, Amarillo, TX 79117-5644. Tel: 806-383-2243.

2—BLESSED SACRAMENT Rev. Ignacio Candelas, O.F.M.; Deacons Mark Seidlitz; Rene Perea.
Res.: 4112 S.E. 25th St., 79103. Tel: 806-374-1132; Fax: 806-372-3631.
Catechesis/Religious Program—Ms. Bernice Noggler, D.R.E. Students 136.

3—ST. FRANCIS Rev. Bellamkonda Chinnaiah, Parochial Admin.
Res.: 5005 Klinke Rd., 79108-9628. Tel: 806-335-1872.
Catechesis/Religious Program—Verlyn Walunas, C.R.E. Students 29.

4—ST. HYACINTH'S Rev. James Schmitmeyer; Deacon Arnold Schwertner.
Res.: 4500 W. Hills Tr., 79106. Tel: 806-358-1351; Fax: 806-467-1708. Email: sth4500@juno.com. Web: sthyacinthamarillo.org.
Catechesis/Religious Program—Lori Greer, C.R.E. Students 49.

5—ST. JOSEPH'S Rev. Hector Madrigal; Deacons Leo Ramos; Willy Montao. In Res., Rev. John Ohlig (LUB).
Res.: 4122 Bonham St., 79110. Tel: 806-355-5621; Fax: 806-355-5622.
See St. Joseph's School, Amarillo under Elementary Schools, City-Wide located in the Institution section.
St. Joseph Day Care Center—4108 S. Bonham, 79110. Tel: 806-359-1604; Fax: 806-353-3340. Gail Saiz, Dir. Students 89.
Catechesis/Religious Program—Students 54.

6—ST. LAURENCE CHURCH Revs. Juan Rubio, O.F.M.; Gabriel Garcia, O.F.M.; Ignacio Candelas, O.F.M.; Diego Rivera, O.F.M.; Jaime Hernandez, O.F.M.; Bro. Alberto Alvarado, O.F.M.; Deacons Alfredo Alarcon; David Duenes; Pablo Morales; Miguel Tovar; Andy Gonzalez.
Res.: 2300 N. Spring St., 79107. Tel: 806-383-2261; Fax: 806-383-2266.
Catechesis/Religious Program—Sr. Benicia Ramirez, D.R.E. Students 294.

7—ST. MARTIN DE PORRES MISSION Rev. Msgr. Rex Nicholl.
Res.: 1507 N. Adams St., 79107. Tel: 806-376-8871.
Catechesis/Religious Program—

8—ST. MARY'S CATHEDRAL Rev. Msgr. Harold L. Waldow; Deacons Floyd Ashley; Robert Smith; John Peters; Bill Allein.
Res.: 1200 Washington St., 79102. Tel: 806-376-7204; Fax: 806-376-7972.
See St. Mary's School and St. Mary's Montessori Preschool, Amarillo under Elementary Schools, City-Wide located in the Institution section.
Catechesis/Religious Program—Ms. Bernice Noggler, D.R.E. Students 314.

9—OUR LADY OF GUADALUPE Rev. Jose Gomez; Deacon Armando Esparza.
Res.: 1210 E. 11th Ave., 79102. Tel: 806-372-1128; Fax: 806-372-2225. Web: www.ourladyofguadalupeamarillo.com.
Catechesis/Religious Program—Rosa Mores, D.R.E. Students 175.

10—OUR LADY OF VIETNAM Rev. John Tran Tinh, C.M.C.
Res.: 3334 N.E. 20th Ave., 79107. Tel: 806-383-0467; Fax: 806-383-0467.
Catechesis/Religious Program—Students 110.

11—ST. THOMAS THE APOSTLE Rev. Msgr. Joseph T. Tash; Deacons Terry Pevehouse; Blaine Westlake; Phillip Eugene Whitson; Stanley Martin Drozell. In Res., Rev. Daniel A. Dreher.
Res.: 4100 Coulter Dr., 79109. Tel: 806-358-1016; Fax: 806-358-2529.
Catechesis/Religious Program—Eileen Dolan, D.R.E. Students 431.

OUTSIDE THE CITY OF AMARILLO

BORGER, HUTCHINSON CO., ST. JOHN THE EVANGELIST Rev. Msgr. Michael P. Colwell; Deacon Zeferino Jimenez.
Res.: 201 St. John's Rd., 79007. Tel: 806-274-7064; Fax: 806-274-3941.
Catechesis/Religious Program—Jennifer Crittenden, D.R.E. Students 235.
Mission—*St. Ann's* Stinnett, Hutchinson Co.

BOVINA, PARMER CO., ST. ANN'S Rev. Anthony Swamy Aakula, Parochial Admin.; Deacon Teodoro Chavez.
Res.: Box 660, 79009. Tel: 806-251-1511.
Catechesis/Religious Program—Ginger Trimble, C.R.E. Students 172.

CANADIAN, HEMPHILL CO., SACRED HEART Rev. Salibindla Balashowreddy; Deacon Jose Jesus Gutierrez.
Rectory—721 Main St., 79014. Tel: 806-323-9705; Fax: 806-323-9705.
Church: 804 Kingman Ave., 79014. Tel: 806-323-6608.
Catechesis/Religious Program—Students 80.

CANYON, RANDALL CO., ST. ANN'S Very Rev. Phu T. Phan; Deacons Gabriel Rivas; August Hesse III; John David Rausch.
Mailing Address: P.O. Box 59, 79015.
Res.: 605 38th St., 79015. Tel: 806-655-3302; Fax: 806-655-3384.
Catechesis/Religious Program—Ms. Carol Sanford, D.R.E. Students 230.

CHILDRESS, CHILDRESS CO., HOLY ANGELS Rev. David Contreras.
Res.: 308 Ave. B, S.W., P.O. Box 608, 79201. Tel: 940-937-3946; Fax: 940-937-0668.
Catechesis/Religious Program—Students 80.

CLARENDON, DONLEY CO., ST. MARY'S Rev. Arokia Raj Samala; Deacon Pedro Juarez.
Res.: 815 McClelland St., P.O. Drawer C, 79226. Tel: 806-874-3910.
Catechesis/Religious Program—Debra Kuhl, C.R.E. Students 7.

DALHART, HARTLEY CO., ST. ANTHONY OF PADUA Rev. Scott Raef; Deacons Ronald Hein; Louis Paul Artho.
Res.: 411 Texas Blvd., Box 1029, 79022. Tel: 806-244-4128; Fax: 806-244-7128.
School—(Grades K-6), 1302 Oak St., 79022. Tel: 806-244-4811; Fax: 806-244-4811. Karen Graff, Interim Prin.; Dorothy Kuster, Librarian. School Sisters of the Third Order of St. Francis 3; Lay Teachers 6; Students 105.
Catechesis/Religious Program—Javita Anzaldua, C.R.E.; Suzanne Foley, C.R.E. Students 210.
Convent—1301 Oak Ave., 79022. Tel: 806-244-2390. Email: stanthon@xit.net. School Sisters of St. Francis 2.
Mission—*St. Mary's* Texline, Dallum Co.

DIMMITT, CASTRO CO., IMMACULATE CONCEPTION Rev. Arthur Rodriguez; Deacons Jose Garcia; John Nino.
Res.: 710 W. Halsell St., 79027. Tel: 806-647-4219 (Church); 806-647-0105 (Office).
Catechesis/Religious Program—Mary Helen Flores, C.R.E. Students 185.
Mission—*St. John's* Hart, Castro Co.

DUMAS, MOORE CO., SS. PETER AND PAUL Rev. Juan Carlos Barragan; Deacons Joseph A. Schwertner; Jim Clements; Joe Beauchamp.
Res.: 815 S. Maddox, Box 503, 79029. Tel: 806-935-5002; Fax: 806-934-3382.
Catechesis/Religious Program—Maria Guttierrez, D.R.E. Students 357.
Mission—*Christ the King* P.O. Box 681, Sunray, Moore Co. 79086. Rev. Joseph Papaiah; Deacon Wayne Norrell.

FRIONA, PARMER CO., ST. TERESA OF JESUS Rev. Anthony Swamy Aakula; Deacon Jose Correa.
Res.: 401 W. 17th, 79035-9601. Tel: 806-250-2871; Fax: 806-250-3549.
Catechesis/Religious Program—Olga De Lao, C.R.E. Students 172.

GROOM, CARSON CO., IMMACULATE HEART OF MARY, [CEM] Rev. Arokia Raj Samala.
Res.: 411 Ware Ave., P.O. Box 130, 79039. Tel: 806-248-7584.
Catechesis/Religious Program—Renee Weinheimer, C.R.E. Students 31.

GRUVER, HANSFORD CO., CRISTO REDENTOR Rev. Gregory Bunyan.
Res. & Mailing Address: P.O. Box 28, 79040. Tel: 806-733-5236.
Catechesis/Religious Program—Esperanza Vega, C.R.E. Students 60.

HAPPY, SWISHER CO., HOLY NAME OF JESUS, [CEM] Rev. George Kalampatt; Rev. Msgr. Mario Stortz (Retired).
Res.: 317 W. Main, P.O. Box 128, 79042. Tel: 806-558-2871.
Catechesis/Religious Program—Students 24.

HEREFORD, DEAF SMITH CO.

1—ST. ANTHONY'S Revs. John Valdez; Haider Quintero, Parochial Vicar.
Business Office—114 Sunset Dr., 79045. Tel: 806-364-6150; Fax: 806-364-0969.
Res.: 115 N. 25 Mile Ave., 79045. Tel: 806-364-2793; Fax: 806-364-0969.
School—(Grades PreK-5), 120 W. Park Ave., 79045. Tel: 806-364-1952. Linda Aranda, Prin.; Susan Hicks, Librarian. Lay Teachers 10; Students 99.
Catechesis/Religious Program—Students 358.

2—SAN JOSE Very Rev. Joseph E. Bixenman; Deacons Emilio Fuentes; Richard Mendez; Paul Herrera.
Res.: 735 Brevard, 79045. Tel: 806-364-5053; Fax: 806-364-2880.
Catechesis/Religious Program—Tel: 806-364-5053. Students 394.

MEMPHIS, HALL CO., SACRED HEART Rev. David Contreras.
Mailing Address: 213 N. Third St., P.O. Box 239, 79245. Tel: 806-259-2178.
Catechesis/Religious Program—Mrs. Juanita Garza, D.R.E. Students 40.

NAZARETH, CASTRO CO., HOLY FAMILY Rev. Ken Keller; Deacons Jerome Brockman; Bob Birkenfeld; Henry Wilhelm.
Res.: 210 St. Joseph, P.O. Box 100, 79063. Tel: 806-945-2616; Fax: 806-945-2564.
Catechesis/Religious Program—Gladys Fortenberry, D.R.E. Students 131.

PAMPA, GRAY CO., ST. VINCENT DE PAUL Revs. Francisco Perez; Joseph Ravi.
Res.: 810 W. 23rd St., 79065. Tel: 806-665-5665; Fax: 806-665-2840.
Catechesis/Religious Program—Students 314.

PANHANDLE, CARSON CO., ST. THERESA Rev. Mieczyslaw "Mitchell" Przepiora.
Res.: P.O. Box 366, 79068. Tel: 806-537-3677.
Catechesis/Religious Program—Judy Neusch, D.R.E. Students 28.

PERRYTON, OCHILTREE CO., IMMACULATE CONCEPTION Rev. J. Guadalupe Mayorga; Deacons Jose Cano; Serigo Estrada; Manuel Moreno Jr.
Res.: 1000 S.W. 15th Ave., 79070. Tel: 806-435-3802; Fax: 806-648-1490.
Catechesis/Religious Program—Maria Gallardo,

D.R.E. (Elementary). Students 375.
Mission—St. Peter Booker, Lipscomb Co. Deacon Felix Tudon.

SILVERTON, BRISCOE CO., OUR LADY OF LORETTO Rev. Cesar Salazar.
303 Pulitzer St., 79257. Tel: 806-823-2548.
Mission—Elizabeth Ann Seton P.O. Box 28, Turkey, Hall Co. 79261. Tel: 806-396-5687.
Mission—St. Juan Diego P.O. Box 62, Quitaque, 79255.

SPEARMAN, HANSFORD CO., SACRED HEART Rev. Gregory Bunyan.
Res.: 901 S. Roland, P.O. Box 127, 79081. Tel: 806-659-2166; Fax: 806-659-2166.
Catechesis/Religious Program—Oliva Salgado, D.R.E. Students 157.
Mission—Cristo Redentor P.O. Box 238, Gruver, Hansford Co. 79040.

STRATFORD, SHERMAN CO., ST. JOSEPH'S Rev. Carlos Eduardo Castro; Deacon Willie F. Artho.
Mailing Address: Box 28, 79084. Tel: 806-366-5687.
Catechesis/Religious Program—Annie Duran, D.R.E. Students 117.
Mission—Our Lady of Guadalupe Box 28, Cactus, Sherman Co. 79084. Tel: 806-396-5687.

TULIA, SWISHER CO., CHURCH OF THE HOLY SPIRIT Rev. Marco A. Gonzalez; Deacon Jackie Gunnels.
Res.: 513 S. Austin, P.O. Box 25, 79088. Tel: 806-995-3191; Fax: 806-995-3286.
Catechesis/Religious Program—Leslie Briones, D.R.E. Students 170.
Mission—St. Paul the Apostle P.O. Box 231, Kress, Swisher Co. 79052. Tel: 806-823-2548.

UMBARGER, RANDALL CO., ST. MARY'S, [CEM] Rev. George Kalampatt; Deacon Bill Dorsey.
22830 Pondaseta St., 79091.
Res.: P.O. Box 105, 79091. Tel: 806-499-3531.
Catechesis/Religious Program—Judy Neusch, D.R.E. Students 40.

VEGA, OLDHAM CO., IMMACULATE CONCEPTION Rev. Barnabas Radke, Parochial Admin.; Deacon Raymond Artho.
Res.: P.O. Box 250, 79092. Tel: 806-267-0154.
Catechesis/Religious Program—Michelle Baca, D.R.E. Students 50.

WELLINGTON, COLLINGSWORTH CO., OUR MOTHER OF MERCY Rev. Tony Neusch; Deacon Jose Velasco.
P.O. Box 49, Shamrock, 79079.
Church: 1108 Floydada, 79095. Tel: 806-256-5358; Fax: 806-256-2829.
Catechesis/Religious Program—Students 14.
Mission—St. Patrick Shamrock, Wheeler Co.

WHITE DEER, CARSON CO., SACRED HEART Rev. Mieczyslaw "Mitchell" Przepiora, Admin.
Box 427, 79097. Tel: 806-883-4781.
Catechesis/Religious Program—Natalie Davis, D.R.E. Students 17.

On Duty Outside the Diocese:
Revs.—
Afunugo, Emmanuel, D.D.
Rosolen, Emil

Unassigned:
Rev.—
Lindley, Philip

Retired:
Rev. Msgrs.—
Greka, David, Allpena, MI
Gurzynski, James C., 2229 Loucust, 79109.
Hickey, John, Corpus Christi, TX
Kuehler, Norbert, 4210 N.E. 18th, 79107. Chaplain Franciscan Sisters
Malnar, Matthew, Independence, WI
Stalter, Cal, 1300 S. Harrison, #809, 79102.
Stortz, Mario, Rt. 1, Box 174, Tulia, 79088.
Revs.—
Choong, Norbert, 5906 Aspen Ave., N.E., Albuquerque, NM 87110.
McGhee, Jim, Keller, TX
Sweeney, Edward, 2400 E. Willow Creek, 79108.
Wood, Michael, Baltic, CT

Permanent Deacons:
Alarcon, Alfredo, St. Laurence Cathedral, Amarillo
Allein, Bill, St. Mary's, Amarillo
Artho, Louis Paul, St. Anthony's Church, Dalhart
Artho, Raymond, Immaculate Conception, Vega
Artho, Willie F., (Retired), St. Joseph's Church, Stratford
Ashley, Floyd, St. Mary's Church, Amarillo; Admin. Asst. to Bishop Zurek
Beauchamp, Joe, Sts. Peter and Paul, Dumas
Birkenfeld, Bob, Holy Family Church, Nazareth
Blunt, Orvel Ray, (Retired)
Brockman, Jerome, Holy Family, Nazareth
Brown, Jim, (Retired)
Cano, Jose, Immaculate Conception, Perryton
Chaves, Teodoro, St. Ann's Church, Bovina
Clements, Jim, Sts. Peter & Paul, Dumas
Cloud, Jonny E., (Retired)
Correa, Jose, St. Teresa's Church, Friona
Dollins, Belvin G., (Retired)
Dorsey, Bill, St. Mary's, Umbarger
Drozell, Stanley Martin, St. Thomas the Apostle Church, Amarillo
Duenes, David, St. Laurence Cathedral, Amarillo
Esparza, Armando, Our Lady of Guadalupe, Amarillo
Estrada, Sergio, Immaculate Conception, Perryton
Frausto, Joseph, (Unassigned)
Fuentes, Emilio, Sr., (Retired), San Jose Church, Hereford
Gallegos, Hector, (Retired), Our Lady of Guadalupe, Amarillo
Garcia, Vicente H., (Retired)
Gonzales, Roberto, (Retired), St. John's, Hart
Gonzalez, Andy, St. Laurence Church, Amarillo
Grossman, Jerry, (On Leave of Absence)
Guerrero, Jesse, (Prison Ministry)
Gunnells, Jackie, Church of the Holy Spirit, Tulia
Gutierrez, Jose Jesus, Sacred Heart Church, Canadian
Gutierrez, Robert, (Retired)
Hein, Ronald, St. Anthony's Church, Dalhart
Hernandez, Mauro, (Retired)
Hesse, August, III, (Retired)
Jimenez, Zeferino, St. John's Church, Borger
Juarez, Pedro, St. Mary's, Clarendon
Keller, Robert C., (Outside the Diocese)
Mason, Wilbur, (Retired)
Mendez, Ricardo, San Jose Church, Hereford
Montano, Willie, St. Joseph's, Amarillo
Morales, Pablo, St. Laurence Church, Amarillo
Moreno, Manuel, Jr., Immaculate Conception Church, Perryton
Nino, John, Immaculate Conception, Dimmitt
Norrell, Wayne, Christ the King Church, Sunray
Perez, Jesus Rene, Blessed Sacrament Church, Amarillo
Peters, John, St. Mary's, Amarillo
Pevehouse, Terry, St. Thomas the Apostle Church, Amarillo
Ramos, Leo, St. Joseph, Amarillo
Rausch, John David, St. Ann's Church, Amarillo
Reid, Timothy, (Outside the Diocese)
Rivas, Gabriel, St. Ann's Church, Canyon
Ruiz, Jesse P., (On Duty Outside the Diocese)
Schwertner, Arnold, St. Hyacinth's
Schwertner, Joseph A.
Seidlitz, Mark, Blessed Sacrament Church, Amarillo and Prison Ministry
Smith, Robert, St. Mary's Church, Amarillo
Tovar, Miguel, St. Laurence Church, Amarillo
Tudon, Felix, St. Peter's, Booker
Valdez, Pete, (Leave of Absence)
Velasco, Jose, Our Lady of Mercy, Wellington; Shamroci
Velo, Jose, (On Leave)
Westlake, Blaine, St. Thomas Church, Amarillo; Coord. Deacons/Safe Environment
Whitson, Phillip Eugene, St. Thomas the Apostle, Amarillo
Wilhelm, Josepl, Holy Family Church, Nazareth

INSTITUTIONS LOCATED IN THE DIOCESE

[A] HIGH SCHOOLS, CITY-WIDE

AMARILLO. *Holy Cross Catholic Academy*, (Grades 6-12), (Coed), 4114 S. Bonham, 79110-1113. Tel: 806-355-9637; Fax: 806-353-9520. Email: hcca124@swbell.net. Web: www.holycrosscatholicacademy.org. Rev. Robert Busch, Ph.D., Prin.; Laveta Peters, Librarian. Priests 2; Sisters 3; Lay Teachers 10; Students 121.

[B] ELEMENTARY SCHOOLS, CITY-WIDE

AMARILLO. *St. Joseph's School*, (Grades PreK-5), 4118 Bonham St., 79110. Tel: 806-359-1604; Fax: 806-359-1605. Email: stjosephelem@catholicexchange.com. Web: http://stjosephcatholicschoolamarillo.weebly.com/index.html. Angie Seidenbenger, Prin.; Evelyn Mula, Librarian. Priests 1; Sisters 3; Lay Teachers 4; Students 109.

St. Mary School and St. Mary's Montessori Preschool, (Grades K-6), 1200 S. Washington St., 79102. Tel: 806-376-9112; Fax: 806-376-9112. Email: lreynolds@stmarysamarillo.com. Kathi Lewis, Prin.; Julie Scrimpsher, Montessori Asst.; Amanda McDonald, Librarian. Sisters 2; Lay Teachers 115; Students 232.

[C] HOMES FOR THE AGED

PANHANDLE. *St. Ann's Nursing Home*, P.O. Box 1444, 79068. Tel: 806-537-3194; Fax: 806-537-3003. Email: stannsnh@amaonline.com. Jimmie Sue Chisum, Admin.

St. Joseph's Home for Retired Priests, P.O. Box 1179, 79068. Rev. James Hutzler (Retired).

[D] COALITION OF CATHOLIC SOCIAL SERVICES

AMARILLO. **Catholic Family Service, Inc.*, 200 S. Tyler St., 79101. Tel: 806-376-4571; Fax: 806-345-7911. Email: gbcree@catholicfamily.net. Web: www.catholicfamilyservice.org. Box 15127, 79105-5127. Nancy Koons, Exec. Dir.

Downtown Women's Center, Inc., 409 S. Monroe, 79101. Tel: 806-372-3625; Fax: 806-372-9026. Email: diann@dwcenter.org. Diann Gilmore, Exec. Dir.

[E] CATHOLIC CHILDREN'S DEVELOPMENT CENTERS

AMARILLO. *Amarillo Catholic Children's Development Centers*

St. Joseph Campus, 4108 Bonham St., P.O. Box 19726, 79114. Tel: 806-353-7043. Gail Saiz, Dir. Teachers 5; Caregivers 11; Students 89.

[F] RETREAT HOUSES

AMARILLO. *Bishop DeFalco Retreat Center*, 2100 N. Spring St., 79107. Tel: 806-383-1811; Fax: 806-383-6919. Email: bdrc@1s.net. Web: www.bdrc.org. Deacon Robert Smith, Exec. Dir.

Bishop DeFalco Retreat Center Foundation

CANYON. *St. Benedict Monastery Retreat/Spirituality Center*, 17825 S. Western St., 79015. Tel: 806-655-9317; Fax: 806-655-9736. Email: nuns@osbcanyontx.org. Web: www.osbcanyontx.org. Sr. Hildegard Varga, O.S.B., Admin.

CHANNING. *Prayer Town Emmanuel Retreat House*, 404 Holy Way, P.O. Box 64, Prayer Town, 79010. Tel: 806-534-2312; Fax: 806-534-2223. Email: sisters@dljc.org. Web: www.dljc.org. Sr. Magdalena Casas-Nava, Coord. The Disciples of the Lord Jesus Christ.

[G] CONVENTS AND RESIDENCES FOR SISTERS

AMARILLO. *St. Francis Convent, Novitiate and U.S. Provincial House*, 4301 N.E. 18th St., 79107. Tel: 806-383-5769; Fax: 806-383-6545. Email: franpro@worldnet.att.net. Sisters Sol Diaz, Prov. Supr.; Conchita Carillo, Prov. Supr. Franciscan Sisters of Mary Immaculate of the Third Order of St. Francis. Sisters 13.

St. Francis Mission Community, O.S.F., LaVerna Convent, 203 S. Avondale, 79106. Tel: 806-352-2981. Email: franciscan@erfwireless.net. Sr. Charlotte Lyjan, O.S.F., Prov., Lubbock House. Sisters 4.

Madres Clarisas Capuchinas, Capuchin Nuns of St. Clare, 4201 N.E. 18th Ave., 79107. Tel: 806-383-9877. Sr. Theresa Cortes, O.S.C., Abbess. Sisters 17.

CANYON. *St. Benedict's Monastery*, 17825 S. Western, 79015. Tel: 806-655-9317; Fax: 806-655-9736. Email: nuns@osbcanyontx.org. Web: www.osbcanyontx.org. Sr. Mary Hawkins, O.S.B., Prioress. Sisters 4.

CHANNING. *Disciples of the Lord Jesus Christ*, 404 Holy Way, P.O. Box 64, Prayer Town, 79010. Tel: 806-534-2312; Fax: 806-534-2223. Email: sisters@dljc.org. Web: www.dljc.org. Sr. Lucy Lukasiewicz, Supr. Gen.; Revs. Ron Mathews, Chap.; Frank Pavone.

PANHANDLE. *Sancta Maria Convent (North American Region and Novitiate)*, 119 Franciscan Way, P.O. Box 906, 79068-0906. Tel: 806-537-3182; Fax: 806-537-5498. Email: schsrs@gmail.com. Web: www.panhandlefranciscans.org. Sr. Jean Marie Lara, Regl. Supr. School Sisters of the Third Order of St. Francis. Sisters 21.

[H] CAMPUS MINISTRY

CANYON. *Catholic Student Center at West Texas A & M University* 2610 Fourth Ave., 79015. Tel: 806-655-4345; Fax: 806-655-0534. Email: cscwtamu@arn.net. Web: www.wtcsc.org. Rev. Daniel A. Dreher, Chap. & Dir.; Betty Aragon, Asst. Dir.

[I] MISCELLANEOUS LISTINGS

AMARILLO. *Amarillo Catholic School System*, 1800 N. Spring St., 79107. Tel: 806-383-2243, Ext. 110; Fax: 806-383-8452. Rev. Robert Busch, Ph.D., Supt. of Catholic Schools.

Amarillo Scholarship Endowment and Assistance

Fund, 1800 N. Spring St., 79107. Tel: 806-383-2243; Fax: 806-383-8452. Rev. Robert Busch, Ph.D., Supt. of Catholic Schools.

**Catholic Radio of the Texas High Plains*, 701 S. Pierce, Ste. 101, 79101. Tel: 806-350-1360; Fax: 806-350-1361.

Engaged Encounter, 1800 N. Spring St., 79107. Tel: 806-383-2243; Fax: 806-383-8452. Email: bwestlake@amarillodiocese.org. Deacon Blaine Westlake, Dir.

Holy Family Parish of Nazareth, Texas Endowment Foundation, Diocese of Amarillo, 1800 N. Spring St., 79107. Tel: 806-383-2243; Fax: 806-383-8452. Email: pwhitson@amarillodiocese.org. Phil Whitson, CFO; Most Rev. Patrick J. Zurek, D.D., Bd.; Rev. Ken Keller.

Marriage Encounter, 1800 N. Spring, 79107. Tel: 806-376-6498. Email: pvkrat@msn.com. Rev. Msgr. Michael P. Colwell; Patrick Kratochvil, Ecclesiastical Team; Virginia Kratochvil, Ecclesiastical Team.

Monsignor B.A. Erpen Trust Fund (1985) Diocese of Amarillo, 1800 N. Spring, 79107. Tel: 806-383-2243; Fax: 806-383-8452. Email: joelo2046@dellnet.com. Phil Whitson, CFO; Most Rev. Patrick J. Zurek, D.D., Trustee; Rev. Msgr. Harold L. Waldow, Trustee.

Pope John Paul II House of Discernment (2005) 1501 N. Adams, 79107. Tel: 806-373-5400. Email: mcolwell@amarillodiocese.org. Rev. Msgr. Michael P. Colwell, Vocation Dir.

Project Solidarity (1999) Diocese of Amarillo, 1800 N. Spring, 79107. Tel: 806-383-2243; Fax: 806-383-8452. Email: mcolwell@amarillodiocese.org. Rev. Msgr. Michael P. Colwell, Chancellor & Vicar Gen.

Roman Catholic Diocese of Amarillo Deposit and Loan Fund, 1800 N. Spring St., 79107. Tel: 806-383-2243; Fax: 806-383-8452. Email: pwhitson@amarillodiocese.org. Phil Whitson, CFO; Most Rev. Patrick J. Zurek, D.D.; Very Rev. Joseph E. Bixenman.

Texas Panhandle Catholic Endowment Foundation (1985) 1800 N. Spring, 79107. Tel: 806-383-2243; Fax: 806-383-8452. Email: pwhitson@amarillodiocese.org. Most Rev. Patrick J. Zurek, D.D., Trustee; Robert Neslage, Trustee; Ed Wieck, Trustee; Frank Walsh, Trustee; Daniel Martinez, Trustee; Dr. Anh My Do, Trustee.

RELIGIOUS INSTITUTES OF MEN REPRESENTED IN THE DIOCESE

For further details refer to the corresponding bracketed number in the Religious Institutes of Men or Women section.

[0275]—*Carmelite of Mary Immaculate*—C.M.I.

[]—*Congregation of Mother Coredemptrix*—C.M.C.

[]—*Provincia de los SS. Francisco and Santiago* (Mexico)—A.R.

RELIGIOUS INSTITUTES OF WOMEN REPRESENTED IN THE DIOCESE

[0230]—*Benedictine Sisters of Pontifical Jurisdiction* (Little Rock, AR)—O.S.B.

[]—*Congregation of the School Sisters of Notre Dame*—S.S.N.D.

[0965]—*Disciples of the Lord Jesus Christ*—D.L.J.C.

[1500]—*Franciscan Sisters of Mary Immaculate of the Third Order of St. Francis of Assisi*—F.M.I.

[]—*Missionary Catechist Sisters of St. Joseph* (Mexico)—O.F.M.

[1695]—*School Sisters of the Third Order of St. Francis, (Panhandle, Texas)*—O.S.F.

[1705]—*Sisters of the Third Order of St. Francis of Assisi*—O.S.F.

[]—*St. Clare Capuchin Sisters*—C.P.C.

NECROLOGY

† Chen, Raphael, (Retired)—Died May 4, 2011

† Sherry, Brendan, (Retired)—Died March 30, 2011

An asterisk (*) denotes an organization that has established tax-exempt status directly with the IRS and is not covered by the USCCB Group Ruling.

Archdiocese of Anchorage

(Archidioecesis Ancoragiensis)

Most Reverend

ROGER L. SCHWIETZ, O.M.I., D.D.

Archbishop of Anchorage; ordained December 20, 1967; appointed Bishop of Duluth December 12, 1989; consecrated and installed Bishop of Duluth February 2, 1990; appointed Coadjutor Archbishop of Anchorage January 18, 2000; succeeded to the See March 3, 2001.

Most Reverend

FRANCIS T. HURLEY

Archbishop Emeritus of Anchorage; ordained June 16, 1951; appointed Titular Bishop of Daimlaig and Auxiliary of Juneau February 4, 1970; consecrated March 19, 1970; appointed Bishop of Juneau July 20, 1971; installed September 8, 1971; appointed Archbishop of Anchorage May 4, 1976; installed July 8, 1976; retired March 3, 2001.

ESTABLISHED FEBRUARY 9, 1966.

Square Miles 138,985.

Comprises the Third Judicial Division of Alaska.

For legal titles of parishes and archdiocesan institutions, consult the Chancery Office.

Chancery Office: 225 Cordova St., Anchorage, AK 99501. Tel: 907-297-7700; Fax: 907-279-3885.

Web: www.archdioceseofanchorage.org

Email: mail@caa-ak.org

STATISTICAL OVERVIEW

Personnel	
Archbishops	1
Retired Archbishops	1
Priests: Diocesan Active in Diocese	22
Priests: Diocesan in Foreign Missions	1
Priests: Retired, Sick or Absent	2
Number of Diocesan Priests	25
Religious Priests in Diocese	11
Total Priests in Diocese	36
Extern Priests in Diocese	11
Permanent Deacons in Diocese	18
Total Brothers	1
Total Sisters	20
Parishes	
Parishes	23
With Resident Pastor:	
Resident Diocesan Priests	15
Resident Religious Priests	8
Without Resident Pastor:	
Administered by Lay People	1
Missions	6
Professional Ministry Personnel:	
Brothers	1
Sisters	20
Lay Ministers	76
Welfare	
Catholic Hospitals	1
Total Assisted	78,251
Health Care Centers	5
Total Assisted	10,685
Homes for the Aged	1
Total Assisted	641
Residential Care of Children	2
Total Assisted	18
Special Centers for Social Services	3
Total Assisted	17,382
Educational	
Diocesan Students in Other Seminaries	4
Total Seminarians	4
High Schools, Diocesan and Parish	1
Total Students	78
High Schools, Private	1
Total Students	42
Elementary Schools, Diocesan and Parish	3
Total Students	315
Elementary Schools, Private	1
Total Students	49
Catechesis/Religious Education:	
High School Students	724
Elementary Students	1,714
Total Students under Catholic Instruction	2,926
Teachers in the Diocese:	
Lay Teachers	75
Vital Statistics	
Receptions into the Church:	
Infant Baptism Totals	454
Minor Baptism Totals	35
Adult Baptism Totals	50
Received into Full Communion	54
First Communions	429
Confirmations	297
Marriages:	
Catholic	47
Interfaith	41
Total Marriages	88
Deaths	144
Total Catholic Population	37,089
Total Population	400,000

Former Archbishops—Most Revs. JOSEPH T. RYAN, D.D., Archbishop of Anchorage; ord. June 3, 1939; cons. March 25, 1966; installed April 14, 1966; transferred to as Coadjutor Military Vicar of U.S. Armed Forces Dec. 13, 1975; appt. First Archbishop of the Archdiocese for the Military Services, U.S.A., March 16, 1985; died Oct. 9, 2000; FRANCIS T. HURLEY, D.D. (Retired), Archbishop of Anchorage; ord. June 16, 1951; appt. Titular Bishop of Daimlaig and Auxiliary of Juneau, Feb. 4, 1970; cons. March 19, 1970; appt. Bishop of Juneau, July 20, 1971; installed Sept. 8, 1971; appt. Archbishop of Anchorage, May 4, 1976; installed July 8, 1976; retired March 3, 2001.

Chief Operating Officer and Chief Finance Officer—Rev. STEVEN C. MOORE.

Vicar General—Very Rev. THOMAS C. LILLY, V.G.

Pastoral Center—

Chancellor—VACANT.

Vice Chancellor—Mrs. EILEEN T. KRAMER, 225 Cordova St., Anchorage, 99501. Tel: 907-297-7712; Fax: 907-279-3885.

Secretary to Archbishop Emeritus—Ms. JOANN WHITE.

Secretary to Archbishop Roger L. Schwietz, O.M.I.—KIMBERLY BAKIC.

Office of Stewardship/Development—Ms. JULIE VAREE. Tel: 907-297-7718.

Tribunal—225 Cordova St., Anchorage, 99501-2409. Tel: 907-297-7724.

Judicial Vicar—Rev. THOMAS T. BRUNDAGE, J.C.L.

Judge—Deacon WILLIAM FINNEGAN, J.C.L.

Defenders of the Bond—Rev. SCOTT GARRETT, J.C.L.; Mrs. MIRIAM DONOHUE.

Notaries—Sr. JOAN OBERLE, C.PP.S.; Mrs. EILEEN T. KRAMER; KIMBERLY BAKIC; Revs. VINCENT BLANCO; WILLIAM HANRAHAN.

Diocesan Consultors—Very Rev. THOMAS C. LILLY, V.G.; Revs. SCOTT MEDLOCK; RICHARD D. TERO; ANTHONY PATALINO, O.P.; STEVEN C. MOORE; FRED BUGARIN; WILLIAM HANRAHAN; THOMAS T. BRUNDAGE, J.C.L.

Archdiocesan Offices and Directors

Apostleship of the Sea— Port Chaplain: SALLY BOSTWICK, Anchorage.

Archdiocesan Newspaper— "Catholic Anchor" JOEL DAVIDSON, Editor, Pastoral Center, 225 Cordova St., Anchorage, 99501. Tel: 907-297-7730.

Magadan Mission—Rev. MICHAEL SHIELDS.

Campaign for Human Development—Deacon JAMES "MICK" FORNELLI.

Catholic Relief Services—Ms. BONNIE CLER.

Catholic Social Services—SUSAN BOMALASKI, Exec. Dir.; ELLEN KRSNAK, Dir. Community Rels.; MARY BETH BRAGIEL, Deputy Dir., 3710 E. 24th St., Anchorage, 99508. Tel: 907-276-5590; Fax: 907-258-1091.

Board Members—ROGER CHAN; ROSE CARROLL SUWANNEE; Rabbi MICHAEL OBLATH, Ex Officio; MICHAEL FREDERICKS; BILLIE R. KORSUNSKIY; MAURICE COYLE, M.D.; Ms. MONICA ANDERSON; KARA MORIARTLY; PATRICK GILMORE; PATRICIA PETRIVELLI; Ms. ERNESTINE FLEECE; WALTER WILLIAMS IV; MICHELLE EGAN; WILLIAM GRANGER; LOTTIE MICHAEL; MARIA TAGLIAVENTO.

Hispanic Ministry—Rev. DOMINIC DEMAIO, O.P.; Sisters LORRAINE REAUME, O.P.; MARIE ANGELA DIAZ, D.C.

Korean Ministry—Rev. AN KWANG-SUNG, 7206 Lake Otis Pkwy., Anchorage, 99507. Tel: 907-333-5307; Fax: 907-333-2888; Sisters JOANNA CHOE; CECILIA PARK.

Native Ministry—Sr. FRANCES VISTA, D.C., Dir.

Office of Finance—Rev. STEVEN C. MOORE, CFO. Tel: 907-297-7726; Ms. MONIKA SCOTT, Comptroller. Tel: 907-297-7723.

Faith Formation & Ministry Development—DOUGLAS STEWART, Dir. Tel: 907-297-7732.

Permanent Diaconate—Deacon JAMES "MICK" FORNELLI.

Propagation of the Faith—Ms. JULIE VAREE, Dir.

Retreats—ALAN MUISE, Dir., Holy Spirit Center, 10980

Hillside Dr., Anchorage, 99507. Tel: 907-346-2343, Ext. 205.

Superintendent of Schools—BENJAMIN EVELAND. Tel: 907-297-7790.

Victim Assistance Coordinator—VIVIAN FINLAY, M.Ed., L.M.F.T.; VERA HURSH. Tel: 907-297-7786.

Vocations—Rev. LEO WALSH, S.T.D.

Director of Seminarians—Very Rev. THOMAS C. LILLY, V.G.

CLERGY, PARISHES, MISSIONS AND PAROCHIAL SCHOOLS

CITY OF ANCHORAGE

1—HOLY FAMILY CATHEDRAL (1915) [JC] Revs. Anthony Patalano, O.P.; Augustine Hilander, O.P.; Lukasz Misko, O.P.
Mailing Address: 811 W. 6th Ave., 99501-2093. Tel: 907-276-3455; Fax: 907-258-9785. Email: holyfamilycathedral@alaska.com. In Res., Rev. Dominic DeMaio, O.P.
Catechesis/Religious Program—Bro. Justin Gable, O.P., D.R.E. Students 110.

2—ST. ANTHONY Rev. Fred Bugarin; H. William Goehring, Business Mgr.
Res.: 825 S. Klevin St., 99508-2698. Tel: 907-333-5544; Fax: 907-338-3864.
Catechesis/Religious Program—Students 65.

3—ST. BENEDICT Rev. Leo Walsh; Deacons Ted Greene; Desiderio L. Martinez.
Res.: 8110 Jewel Lake Rd., 99502. Tel: 907-243-2195; Fax: 907-243-0088. Email: info@stbenedictsak.com. Web: www.stbenedictsak.com.
Catechesis/Religious Program—Students 177.

4—CORP. OF ST. CHRISTOPHER BY THE SEA CHURCH Very Rev. Thomas C. Lilly, Canonical Pastor.
P.O. Box 405, Unalaska, 99685. Tel: 907-581-4022; Fax: 907-581-2979.
Catechesis/Religious Program—Students 39.

5—CORP. OF OUR LADY OF THE LAKE CHURCH (2007) Revs. Scott Garrett, Canonical Pastor; Luzvimindo Flores, Parochial Vicar; Katherine Bishop, Parish Dir.
P.O. Box 520769, Big Lake, 99652. Tel: 907-892-6492; Fax: 907-892-6497.
Catechesis/Religious Program—Students 24.
Mission—St. Christopher P.O. Box 412, Willow, 99688.

6—CORP. OF ST. ANDREW KIM PARISH OF THE KOREAN COMMUNITY Rev. An Kwang-Sung.
7206 Lake Otis Pkwy., 99507. Tel: 907-333-5307; Fax: 907-333-2888.
Catechesis/Religious Program—Sisters Joanna Choe, D.R.E.; Cecilia Park, D.R.E.; Phillip W. Lee, D.R.E. Students 53.

7—ST. ELIZABETH ANN SETON (1975) Very Rev. Thomas C. Lilly.
2901 E. Huffman Rd., 99516. Tel: 907-345-4466; Fax: 907-345-6361.
Catechesis/Religious Program—Students 386.
Mission—Our Lady of the Snows Girdwood, 99587. Tel: 907-783-1171. Email: reservations@chapelourladyofthesnows.org. Web: www.chapelourladyofthesnows.org.

8—HOLY CROSS (1984) Revs. Rafail A. Saiz; Leo Walsh, Canonical Pastor; Sr. Loretta Luecke, C.PP.S., Parish Life Dir.
Res.: 2627 Lore Rd., 99507. Tel: 907-349-8388; Fax: 907-344-3388. Email: loretta@alaska.net. Web: www.holycrossalaska.net.
Catechesis/Religious Program—Mrs. Janine Redding, Dir., Faith Formation & R.C.I.A.; Theresa Austin, Dir., Youth & Young Adult Ministry. Students 140.

9—OUR LADY OF GUADALUPE (1970) Rev. Vincent Blanco.
Res.: 3900 Wisconsin St., 99517. Tel: 907-248-2000; Fax: 907-245-1600. Email: olg@olgalaska.org.
Catechesis/Religious Program—LeAndra Childs, D.R.E. Students 216.

10—ST. PATRICK (1971) Revs. Scott Medlock; Daniel J. Hebert; Deacons Felix Maguire; James Fornelli; Jon Hermon.
Res.: 2111 Muldoon Rd., 99504-3699. Tel: 907-337-1538; Fax: 907-337-5460. Email: stpatricks@st.patsak.org. Web: www.st.patsak.org.
Catechesis/Religious Program—Julia Thomas, Dir. Faith Formation. Students 395.

11—ST. PAUL MIKI, Closed. For inquiries for parish records contact St. Elizabeth Ann Seton Parish, Anchorage.

OUTSIDE THE CITY OF ANCHORAGE

CORDOVA, VALDEZ-CORDOVA CO., ST. JOSEPH Rev. Thomas Killeen, O.M.I.
Res.: 220 Adams Ave., P.O. Box 79, 99574. Tel: 907-424-3637. Email: stjoecor@gci.net.
Catechesis/Religious Program—Students 30.

DILLINGHAM, DILLINGHAM CO., HOLY ROSARY Revs. Nelson Marilag (Philippines); Scott Garrett, Canonical Pastor.
Res.: P.O. Box 810, 99576. Tel: 907-842-5581. Email: holyrosaryalaska@hotmail.com. Web: www.holyrosaryalaska.org.
Catechesis/Religious Program—Students 10.
Mission—St. Theresa P.O. Box 269, Naknek, Bristol Bay Borough 99633. Tel: 907-246-6652.

EAGLE RIVER, ANCHORAGE BOROUGH, ST. ANDREW (1968) Rev. Thomas T. Brundage; Deacon Jim Lee.
Res.: 16300 Domain Ln., 99577. Tel: 907-694-2170; Fax: 907-694-1385. Email: parishsecretary@aksaintandrews.org. Web: www.aksaintandrews.org.
Catechesis/Religious Program—Email: deb@aksaintandrews.org. Mrs. Deb Marino, Dir. Faith Formation. Students 260.

GLENNALLEN, VALDEZ-CORDOVA CO., HOLY FAMILY (1955) Rev. Frank Reitter.
Mailing Address: P.O. Box 126, 99588. Fax: 907-822-4208.
Catechesis/Religious Program—Students 7.

HOMER, KENAI PENINSULA BOROUGH, ST. JOHN THE BAPTIST, 255 Ohlson Ln., 99603. Tel: 907-235-8436; Fax: 907-235-5251. Email: st.john@gcl.net. Pastoral Team:, Revs. Roger Bergkamp, O.M.I.; Andrew Sensenig, O.M.I., Priest Mod.; Joseph Dowling, O.M.I.
Res.: 222 W. Redoubt Ave., Soldotna, 99669.
Mission—St. Peter the Apostle Box 39290, Ninilchik, 99639. Tel: 907-567-3490.
Mission—St. James the Apostle Seldovia, 99663.
Catechesis/Religious Program—Students 33.

KENAI, KENAI PENINSULA BOROUGH, OUR LADY OF THE ANGELS, 225 S. Spruce Rd., 99611. Pastoral Team:, Revs. Roger Bergkamp, O.M.I.; Andrew Sensenig, O.M.I., Priest Mod.; Joseph Dowling, O.M.I.; Pako Whannell, Parish Life Coord.
Res.: 222 W. Redoubt Ave., Soldotna, 99669. Tel: 907-283-4555.
Catechesis/Religious Program—Students 61.

KODIAK, KODIAK ISLAND BOROUGH, ST. MARY'S Rev. Joseph Classen.
Res.: 2934 Mill Bay Rd., 99615. Tel: 907-486-5411; Fax: 907-486-2719.
Catechesis/Religious Program—Students 47.

PALMER, MATANUSKA-SUSITNA BOROUGH, ST. MICHAEL (1935) Most Rev. Roger L. Schwietz, O.M.I., Canonical Pastor; Matthew Beck, Parish Life Dir.; Rev. Jaime Mencias, Parochial Vicar.
Res.: 432 E. Fireweed Ave., 99645. Tel: 907-745-3229; Fax: 907-746-7040. Email: frontdesk@st-mikesparish.org. Web: www.st-mikesparish.org.
Catechesis/Religious Program—Mrs. Joanne Rousculp, D.R.E. Students 101.

SEWARD, KENAI PENINSULA BOROUGH, SACRED HEART Rev. Richard Tero; Deacon Walter Corrigan.
Res.: 409 Fifth Ave., P.O. Box 207, 99664. Tel: 907-224-5414. Email: walcor@arctic.net.
Catechesis/Religious Program—Ms. Joanne Frey, D.R.E. Students 24.
Mission—St. John Neumann Church P.O. Box 737, Cooper Landing, 99572. Tel: 907-595-1300.

SOLDOTNA, KENAI PENINSULA BOROUGH, OUR LADY OF PERPETUAL HELP (1961) Pastoral Team:, Revs. Roger Bergkamp, O.M.I.; Andrew Sensenig, O.M.I., Priest Mod.; Joseph Dowling, O.M.I.; Marlys Verba, Parish Life Coord.
Res.: 222 W. Redoubt Ave., 99669. Tel: 907-262-4749; Fax: 907-262-5542 (Call 907-262-4725 before sending fax).
Catechesis/Religious Program—Students 77.

TALKEETNA, MATANUSKA-SUSITNA BOROUGH, ST. BERNARD (1970) Renamary Rauchenstein, Dir.; Rev. Scott Garrett, Canonical Pastor.
Res.: P.O. Box 510, 99676. Tel: 907-733-2424 (msg. phone); Fax: 907-733-2425. Email: rstein@matnet.com.
Mission—St. Philip Benizi P.O. Box 13475, Trapper Creek, 99683.

VALDEZ, VALDEZ-CORDOVA CO., ST. FRANCIS XAVIER (1908) Rev. Frank Reitter; Deacon Daniel Stowe.
Res.: 341 Pioneer Dr., P.O. Box 908, 99686. Tel: 907-835-4556; Fax: 907-835-3583. Email: stfrnxav@cvalaska.net.
Catechesis/Religious Program—Kena Lull, D.R.E.; Jamie Schnider, D.R.E. Students 45.

WASILLA, MATANUSKA-SUSITNA BOROUGH, SACRED HEART, [CEM] Rev. Scott Garrett.
Res.: 1201 Bogard Rd., 99654-6523. Tel: 907-376-5087; Fax: 907-373-1156. Email: shparish@mtaonline.net. Web: www.sacredheartwasilla.org.
Catechesis/Religious Program—Students 141.

On Duty Outside Archdiocese:
Rev.—
Shields, Michael, Magadan, Russia

Retired:
Revs.—
Abele, Alan Carl, 340 N. Worthy, Marblehead, OH 43440.
Desso, Leo C., 1925 Gaylord St., Butte, MT 59701.

Permanent Deacons:
Allor, Raymond W., (Retired), Albany, OR
Cable, Jay, Wasilla
Corrigan, Walter, Seward
Ernst, Richard, Kenai
Foreman, Dennis, (Retired), Anchorage
Fornelli, James, Anchorage
Frost, William, Wasilla
Greene, Theodore, Anchorage
Hermon, Jon, Anchorage
Hoffman, Louis, (Retired)
Hostman, James, (Retired), Eagle River
Larroque, Robert, (Retired), Portland, OR
Lee, Jim, St. Andrew, Eagle River
Leuenberger, Curt, Palmer
Maguire, Felix M., Anchorage
Martinez, Dez, Anchorage
Moore, Harry, Palmer
Pearson, Bill, Loxley, AL
Schutt, David E., Wasilla
Stowe, Daniel, Valdez

INSTITUTIONS LOCATED IN THE ARCHDIOCESE

[A] GRADE SCHOOLS, HIGH SCHOOLS PAROCHIAL

ANCHORAGE. *St. Elizabeth Ann Seton School*, (Grades K-6), 2901 E. Huffman Rd., 99516. Tel: 907-345-3712; Fax: 907-345-2910. Email: jimbailey@akseas.com. Web: www.akseas.com. James Bailey, Prin.; Beth Lottridge, Librarian. Lay Teachers 12; Students 162.

Holy Rosary Academy, (Grades K-12), 1010 W. Fireweed Ln., 99503. Tel: 907-276-5822; Fax: 907-258-1055. Web: www.holyrosaryacademy.net. John Fleming, Acting Exec. Dir.; Tim Main, Teacher. Lay Teachers 15; Students 91.

Lumen Christi High School, (Grades 7-12), 8110 Jewel Lake Rd., Bldg. D., 99502. Tel: 907-245-9231; Fax: 907-245-9232. Email: info@lumenchristiak.com. Web: www.lumenchristiak.com. Thomas Sorci, Prin. Students 75; Total Staff 6.

KODIAK. *St. Mary's*, (Grades PreK-8), 2932 Mill Bay Rd., 99615. Tel: 907-486-3513; Fax: 907-486-3117. Catherine Nuno, Prin. Lay Teachers 8; Students 94.

WASILLA. *Corp. of Our Lady of the Valley Catholic School, Inc.*, (Grades K-8), 260 Nelson Ave., 99654. Tel: 907-376-0883; Fax: 907-376-0853. Theresa Sand, Prin. Staff 6; Students 59.

[B] GENERAL HOSPITALS

ANCHORAGE. *Providence Alaska Medical Center*, 3200 Providence Dr., P.O. Box 196604, 99519. Tel: 907-212-2211; Fax: 907-212-3041. Mr. E. Al Parrish, CEO; Ms. Monica Anderson, Chief Mission Integration Officer. Properties, entities, and divisions owned or operated: Providence Health System--Washington; Providence Alaska Medical Center, Anchorage, AK, Providence Extended Care Center, Anchorage, AK, Providence Health System Housing* dba- Providence Horizon House, Anchorage, AK. Bed Capacity 326; Patients Assisted Annually 78,251; Staff 2,400.

KODIAK. *Providence Kodiak Island Medical Center*, 717 E. Rezanof Dr., 99615. Tel: 907-481-2400; Fax: 907-481-2419. Skilled Nursing 19; Total Assisted Annually 1,720; Total Staff 18.

SEWARD. *Providence Seward Medical Center*, 417 First Ave., 99664. Tel: 907-224-5205; Fax: 907-224-7248. Bed Capacity 6; Total Assisted Annually 3,225; Total Staff 114.

VALDEZ. *Providence Valdez Medical Center*, 911 Meals Ave., P.O. Box 550, 99686-0550. Tel: 907-835-2249; Fax: 907-835-1980. Bed Capacity 11; Skilled Nursing 12; Total Assisted 2,695; Total Staff 84.

[C] NURSING HOMES

ANCHORAGE. *Providence Extended Care Center*, 4900 Eagle St., 99503. Tel: 907-562-2281; Fax: 907-762-0280. Jody Howorth, Admin.

Sisters of Providence in Washington. Bed Capacity 140; Patients Assisted Annually 519; Staff 303.

[D] CATHOLIC SOCIAL SERVICES

ANCHORAGE. *Brother Francis Shelter*, 1021 E. Third Ave., 99501. Tel: 907-277-1731. Mr. Dewayne Harris, Dir. Overnight shelter for homeless men and women.

Catholic Social Services Center, 3710 E. 20th St., 99508. Tel: 907-276-5590; Fax: 907-258-1091. Email: sbomalaski@cssalaska.org. Web: www.cssalaska.org.

Catholic Social Services Center, 3710 E. 20th Ave., 99508. Tel: 907-276-5590; Fax: 907-258-1091. Email: sbomalaski@cssalaska.org. Karen Ferguson, Dir., Immigration & Refugee Svcs.; Sharon Lilja, Pregnancy Support & Adoption Dir.; Linda Bond, Prog. Mgr., St. Francis House.

Charlie Elder House, 1513 Wintergreen, 99508. Tel: 907-277-8622; Fax: 907-277-2326. Benita Stepp, Deputy Dir.

Clare House, 420 W. 54th Ave., 99518. Tel: 907-563-4545. Temporary shelter for homeless women and women with children.

McAuley Manor, 3015 Yale Dr., 99508. Tel: 907-279-5772; Fax: 907-279-5774. Residence for homeless teenage girls.

KODIAK. *Marian Center, Inc.*, P.O. Box 8756, 99615. Tel: 907-486-3820; Fax: 907-486-2605. Email: mariancenter@alaska.com.

[E] CONVENTS AND RESIDENCES FOR SISTERS

ANCHORAGE. *Daughters of Charity*, 3424 E. 15th Ave., 99508. Tel: 907-258-3424; Fax: 907-258-3424. Email: docanchorage@aol.com. Sisters 3.

Sisters of Perpetual Adoration, 2645 E. 72nd Ave., 99507. Tel: 907-344-3330; Fax: 907-522-2945. Sisters 3.

Sisters of St. Paul de Chartres, 7206 Lake Otis Pkwy., 99507. Tel: 907-258-3273; Fax: 907-333-2888. Sisters 2.

[F] RETREAT HOUSES

ANCHORAGE. *Holy Spirit Center*, 10980 Hillside Dr., 99507. Tel: 907-346-2343; Fax: 907-346-2140. Email: hsc@holyspiritcenterak.org. Web: www.holyspiritcenterak.org. Alan Muise, Admin.

[G] MISCELLANEOUS

ANCHORAGE. *Archdiocese of Anchorage Priests Pension Trust*, 225 Cordova St., 99501. Tel: 907-297-7700; Fax: 907-279-3885.

**St. Catherine of Siena CUF Chapter, Inc.*, P. O. Box 220106, 99522-0106. 2928 McCollie Ave., 99517.

Catholic Foundation of Alaska, 225 Cordova St., 99501. Tel: 907-297-7700; Fax: 907-279-3885.

Catholic Retreat House Ministries, Inc., 225 Cordova St., 99501. Tel: 907-297-7700; Fax: 907-279-3885.

Covenant House Alaska, 609 F St., 99501. Tel: 907-272-1255; Fax: 907-272-1466. Ms. Deirdre Cronin, Exec. Dir. Program for homeless and runaway youth.

Providence Alaska Foundation, Anchorage, Alaska, 3200 Providence Dr., P.O. Box 196694, 99519-6604. Tel: 907-261-3600; Fax: 907-212-3048. Email: janice.six@providence.org. Web: www.providence.org/alaska. Janice Six, Devel. Officer; Susan Ruddy, Pres.

Providence Health System Housing dba Providence Horizon House 4140 Folker Ave., 99508. Tel: 907-261-4140; Fax: 907-562-4160. Email: ssamet@provak.org. Jamie Benard, Prog. Dir. Staff 53; Patients Assisted Annually 80; Guests 80.

Providence Home Health Care, Anchorage, Alaska, 3546 Latouche St., Ste. 101, 99508. Tel: 907-563-0130; Fax: 907-563-0135. Email: klum@provak.org. Deborah Seidl, Prog. Dir.

PALMER. *Bishop's Attic II, Inc.*, 840 S. Bailey St., 99645. Tel: 907-745-1316; Fax: 907-745-4209. Email: batwo@mtaonline.net.

RELIGIOUS INSTITUTES OF MEN REPRESENTED IN THE ARCHDIOCESE

For further details refer to the corresponding bracketed number in the Religious Institutes of Men or Women section.

[0780]—*Marist Fathers*—S.M.

[0854]—*Missionary Society of St. Paul of Nigeria*—M.S.P.

[0910]—*Oblates of Mary Immaculate*—O.M.I.

[0430]—*Order of Preachers-Dominicans* (Oakland Prov.)—O.P.

RELIGIOUS INSTITUTES OF WOMEN REPRESENTED IN THE ARCHDIOCESE

[1070]—*Adrian Dominican Sisters, Congregation of the Most Holy Rosary*—O.P.

[0760]—*Daughters of Charity of St. Vincent DePaul*—D.C.

[2330]—*Little Sisters of Jesus*—L.S.J.

[3190]—*Nuns of Perpetual Adoration of the Blessed Sacrament* (Mexico)—A.P.

[2575]—*Sisters of Mercy of the Americas* (Merion, PA)—R.S.M.

[]—*Sisters of Mercy of the Americas* (Albany, NY)

[3980]—*Sisters of St. Paul de Chartres*—S.P.C.

[1960]—*Sisters of the Holy Family*—S.H.F.

[2183]—*Sisters of the Immaculate Heart of Mary, Mother of Christ* (Nigeria)

[3270]—*Sisters of the Most Precious Blood* (O'Fallon, MO)—C.PP.S.

NECROLOGY

† Houck, Peter, (Retired)—Died Jan. 19, 2011

An asterisk (*) denotes an organization that has established tax-exempt status directly with the IRS and is not covered by the USCCB Group Ruling.

Diocese of Arlington

(Dioecesis Arlingtonensis)

Most Reverend

PAUL S. LOVERDE, D.D., S.T.L., J.C.L.

Bishop of Arlington; ordained December 18, 1965; appointed Titular Bishop of Ottabia and Auxiliary Bishop of Hartford February 3, 1988; consecrated April 12, 1988; appointed Bishop of Ogdensburg November 11, 1993; installed as Eleventh Bishop of Ogdensburg January 17, 1994; appointed Bishop of Arlington January 25, 1999; installed as Third Bishop of Arlington March 25, 1999.

The Chancery: 200 N. Glebe Rd., Ste. 914, Arlington, VA 22203. Tel: 703-841-2500; Fax: 703-524-5028.

ESTABLISHED AUGUST 13, 1974.

Square Miles 6,541.

Comprises the following 21 Counties in Northern Virginia: Arlington, Clarke, Culpeper, Fairfax, Fauquier, Frederick, King George, Lancaster, Loudoun, Madison, Northumberland, Orange, Page, Prince William, Rappahannock, Richmond, Shenandoah, Spotsylvania, Stafford, Warren and Westmoreland and the 7 independent cities of Alexandria, Fairfax City, Falls Church, Fredericksburg, Manassas, Manassas Park and Winchester.

For legal titles of parishes and diocesan institutions, consult the Chancery Office.

STATISTICAL OVERVIEW

Personnel	
Bishop	1
Abbots	1
Priests: Diocesan Active in Diocese	130
Priests: Diocesan Active Outside Diocese	16
Priests: Diocesan in Foreign Missions	1
Priests: Retired, Sick or Absent	14
Number of Diocesan Priests	160
Religious Priests in Diocese	61
Total Priests in Diocese	221
Extern Priests in Diocese	27
Ordinations:	
Diocesan Priests	3
Transitional Deacons	3
Permanent Deacons	16
Permanent Deacons in Diocese	61
Total Brothers	11
Total Sisters	132
Parishes	
Parishes	68
With Resident Pastor:	
Resident Diocesan Priests	58
Resident Religious Priests	10
Missions	6
Pastoral Centers	1
Professional Ministry Personnel:	
Sisters	48
Lay Ministers	191
Welfare	
Health Care Centers	1
Total Assisted	239
Day Care Centers	31
Total Assisted	2,253
Specialized Homes	2
Total Assisted	600
Special Centers for Social Services	11
Total Assisted	43,998
Other Institutions	1
Total Assisted	291
Educational	
Diocesan Students in Other Seminaries	32
Total Seminarians	32
Colleges and Universities	3
Total Students	4,961
High Schools, Diocesan and Parish	4
Total Students	3,775
High Schools, Private	2
Total Students	539
Elementary Schools, Diocesan and Parish	38
Total Students	11,904
Elementary Schools, Private	1
Total Students	214
Catechesis/Religious Education:	
High School Students	2,885
Elementary Students	31,572
Total Students under Catholic Instruction	55,882
Teachers in the Diocese:	
Priests	6
Sisters	34
Lay Teachers	1,275
Vital Statistics	
Receptions into the Church:	
Infant Baptism Totals	5,035
Minor Baptism Totals	2,193
Adult Baptism Totals	1,274
Received into Full Communion	695
First Communions	8,161
Confirmations	6,852
Marriages:	
Catholic	726
Interfaith	825
Total Marriages	1,551
Deaths	1,569
Total Catholic Population	453,916
Total Population	2,968,486

Former Bishops—Most Revs. THOMAS J. WELSH, D.D., J.C.D., appt. Titular Bishop of Scattery Island and Auxiliary Bishop of Philadelphia on Feb. 18, 1970; cons. April 2, 1970; appt. as 1st Bishop of Arlington on June 4, 1974; installed on Aug. 13, 1974; transferred to the See of Allentown, Feb. 8, 1983; resigned Dec. 16, 1997; appt. Diocesan Administrator; retired Feb. 9, 1998; died Feb. 19, 2009.; JOHN R. KEATING, D.D., J.C.D., ord. Dec. 20, 1958; appt. Second Bishop of Arlington on June 7, 1983; cons. and installed on Aug. 4, 1983; died March 22, 1998.

The Chancery

The Chancery—200 N. Glebe Rd., Ste. 914, Arlington, 22203. Tel: 703-841-2500; Fax: 703-524-5028. Office Hours: Mon.-Fri. 8:30-4:30; Address all official business to this office.

Bishop—Most Rev. PAUL S. LOVERDE, D.D., S.T.L., J.C.L., 200 N. Glebe Rd., Ste. 914, Arlington, 22203. Tel: 703-841-2511.

Secretary to the Bishop—Rev. DANIEL F. HANLEY, 200 N. Glebe Rd., Ste. 914, Arlington, 22203. Tel: 703-841-2511; Fax: 703-524-5028.

Vicar General for Administration and Moderator of the Curia—Very Rev. MARK S. MEALEY, O.S.F.S., J.C.D., Ph.D., V.G., J.V., 200 N. Glebe Rd., Ste. 914, Arlington, 22203. Tel: 703-841-2587; Fax: 703-524-5028.

Vicar General for Pastoral Services—Rev. FRANK J. READY, V.G., 200 N. Glebe Rd., Ste. 901, Arlington, 22203. Tel: 703-841-3857; Fax: 703-841-8472.

Chancellor and General Counsel—MARK E. HERRMANN, Esq., 200 N. Glebe Rd., Ste. 914, Arlington, 22203. Tel: 703-841-2524; Fax: 703-524-5028.

Episcopal Vicar for Faith Formation and Director of the Diaconate Formation Program—Rev. THOMAS P. FERGUSON, J.C.L., 200 N. Glebe Rd., Ste. 914, Arlington, 22203. Tel: 703-841-2563; Fax: 703-524-5028.

Bishop's Delegate for Priests—Rev. PAUL D. SCALIA, 200 N. Glebe Rd., Ste. 901, Arlington, 22203. Tel: 703-841-3809; Fax: 703-841-8472.

Bishop's Delegate for Retired Priests and Permanent Diaconate—Rev. JOHN C. CREGAN, V.F., 200 N. Glebe Rd., Ste. 901, Arlington, 22203. Tel: 703-841-3809; Fax: 703-841-8472.

Diocesan Finance Officer—TIMOTHY R. COTNOIR, CPA, 200 N. Glebe Rd., Ste. 914, Arlington, 22203. Tel: 703-841-2543; Fax: 703-524-5028.

Finance & Accounting Office—ANN DEPUE, CPA, Controller. Tel: 703-841-3813; Fax: 703-524-5028; JOEL GORZA, Asst. Controller, 200 N. Glebe Rd., Ste. 914, Arlington, 22203. Tel: 703-841-3842; Fax: 703-524-5028.

Director of Diocesan Charities—ART BENNETT, 200 N. Glebe Rd., Ste. 506, Arlington, 22203. Tel: 703-841-3835; Fax: 703-841-3840.

Deans—Revs. ROBERT J. RIPPY, J.C.L., V.F.; JOHN C. CREGAN, V.F.; WILLIAM P. SAUNDERS, Ed.D., V.F.; LEO J. ZONNEVELD, C.I.C.M., V.F., Ph.D.; ROBERT C. CILINSKI, V.F.; JOHN D. KELLY, V.F.

Vicar for Religious—Rev. FRANK J. READY, V.G. Tel: 703-841-3857; Fax: 703-841-8472.

The Tribunal

The Tribunal—200 N. Glebe Rd., Ste. 524, Arlington, 22203. Tel: 703-841-2555; Fax: 703-841-0693.

Judicial Vicar—Very Rev. MARK S. MEALEY, O.S.F.S., J.C.D., Ph.D., V.G., J.V. Tel: 703-841-2587; Fax: 703-841-0693.

Adjutant Judicial Vicar—Rev. LEE R. ROOS, J.C.L. Tel: 703-841-2563; Fax: 703-841-0693.

Diocesan Judges—Revs. PAUL F. DELADURANTAYE, S.T.D.; THOMAS P. FERGUSON, J.C.L.; Mrs. TARA A. MCINTOSH, J.C.L.; Very Rev. MARK S. MEALEY, O.S.F.S., J.C.D., Ph.D., V.G., J.V.; Revs. LEE R. ROOS, J.C.L.; WILLIAM J. RUHL, O.S.F.S., S.T.D. (Retired); DAVID A. WHITESTONE, J.C.L.

Defenders of the Bond—Rev. PAUL A. BERGHOUT; Deacons CHARLES A. COUTU; WILLIAM J. DONOVAN, J.C.L.; Revs. JOHN P. MOSIMANN; DONALD J. PLANTY, J.C.D.; GREGORY S. THOMPSON; MATTHEW H. ZUBERBUELER.

Promoter of Justice—VACANT.

Auditor—Mrs. JOYCE M. KIDD MACDONALD, J.C.L.

Advocates—Revs. BRIAN G. BASHISTA; RONALD J. GRIPSHOVER JR.; EDWARD R. HORKAN; ANTHONY J. KILLIAN; JAMIE R. WORKMAN.

Advocate & Procurator—VACANT.

Notaries—Revs. RAMON A. BAEZ; EDWARD J. BRESNAHAN; KEVIN J. FIMIAN; ANDREW J. HEINTZ; MICHAEL J. R. KELLY; WILSON I. KORPI; BJORN C. LUNDBERG; MARK MULLANEY; CHARLES C. SMITH; DIEM JOSEPH QUANG VU; CHRISTOPHER T. VACCARO; ROBERT J. WAGNER; JASON WEBER.

Diocesan Offices

Diocesan Offices— Unless otherwise noted, all offices are located at: *200 N. Glebe Rd., Arlington, 22203.*

Accounting Office—MONICA GRIFFIN, Accounting Dir., Ste. 600. Tel: 703-841-2756.

Archives—MARK E. HERRMANN, Esq., Ste. 914. Tel: 703-841-2524.

Arlington Catholic Herald, Inc.—MICHAEL F. FLACH, Editor & Gen. Mgr.; ANN AUGHERTON, Mng. Editor, Ste. 600. Tel: 703-841-2590; Fax: 703-524-2782. Web: www.catholicherald.com.

Bishop's Lenten Appeal—ROBERT P. MUELLER, Prog. Dir., Ste. 811. Tel: 703-841-2545; Fax: 703-528-3057; JUANITA PADGETT, Pledge Coord., Ste. 811. Tel: 703-841-2570; Fax: 703-528-3057.

Campus Ministry—Rev. PETER W. NASSETTA, Y.A., Bishop's Liaison, 4515 Roberts Rd., Fairfax, 22032. Tel: 703-425-0022.

*Catholic Charities of the Diocese of Arlington—Ste. 506*Web: www.ccda.net. ART BENNETT, Pres. Tel: 703-841-3835; Fax: 703-841-3840.

Catholic Charities Fredericksburg Office—305 Hanson Ave., Ste. 180, Fredericksburg, 22401. Tel: 540-371-1124.

Western Regional Office—100 Dry Mill Rd., Unit 102, Leesburg, 20175. Tel: 703-443-2481.

Parish Based Catholic Charities Loudoun Office—At Christ the Redeemer Parish, 46833 Harry Byrd Hwy., Sterling, 20164. Tel: 703-421-2317.

Parish Based Catholic Charities Prince William Office—All Saints Church, 9300 Stonewall Rd., Manassas, 20110. Tel: 703-368-4500.

*Center for Adoption and Pregnancy Services—*TERESA MCDONOUGH, M.S.W., L.C.S.W., Prog. Dir., 5294 Lyngate Ct., Burke, 22015. Tel: 703-425-0100.

Christ House Emergency Shelter—131 S. West St., Alexandria, 22314. Tel: 703-549-8644.

*Catholic Charities Communications—*KATIE WALKER, Dir. Tel: 703-841-3833.

*Elderly Services—*THOMAS GRODEK, Prog. Dir., St. Martin de Porres Senior Center, 4650 Taney Ave., Alexandria, 22304. Tel: 703-751-2766.

Emergency Assistance—131 S. West St., Alexandria, 22314. Tel: 703-548-4227.

*Family Services—*DAVID CAVANAUGH, M.S.W., L.C.S.W., Prog. Dir., 200 N. Glebe Rd., Ste. 250, Arlington, 22203. Tel: 703-841-2531.

*Hogar Hispano-Legal Assistance to Immigrants—*JOHN ODENWELDER, M.B.A., Prog. Dir., 6201 Leesburg Pike, Ste. 307, Falls Church, 22044. Tel: 703-534-9805.

*Parish Liaison Network—*SALLY O'DWYER, Prog. Dir. Tel: 703-841-3831.

*Prison Ministry—*Sr. CONSTANCIA V. PARCASIO, S.N.D.S., Prog. Dir. Tel: 703-841-3832.

*Saint Margaret of Cortona Transitional Residences—*AMY WHITE, Prog. Dir., 1423 G St., Apt. K, Woodbridge, 22191. Tel: 703-910-4845.

*Services for Disabled Persons/Car Ministry—*HARRY BURKE, Prog. Dir., 3838 Cathedral Ln., Arlington, 22203. Tel: 703-841-2531.

*Catholic Education, Office of Catechetics—*Rev. PAUL F. DELADURANTAYE, S.T.D., Sec. Relg. Educ. & The Liturgy, Ste. 503. Tel: 703-841-2554; Fax: 703-524-8670; Mrs. PROVIE RYDSTROM, Coord. Pastoral Ministry for the Hearing Impaired. Tel: 703-978-7997 (V-TTD); Mrs. NADINE HALLUMS, Dir., Spec. Rel. Educ. (SPRED). Tel: 703-569-2428.

*Office of Catholic Schools—*Sisters BERNADETTE MCMANIGAL, B.V.M., Supt. of Schools, Ste. 503. Tel: 703-841-2519; Fax: 703-524-8670; KARL ANN HOMBERG, S.S.J., Asst. Supt. for Elementary Educ.; ELIZABETH ROACH, Asst. Supt. for Instruction and Personnel; RENEE WHITE, Dir. Mktg., Enrollment & Special Projects; DIANE ELLIOTT, M.Ed., Special Svcs. Coord.; ROBERT QUARTUCCIO, CPA, School Finance Officer.

*Child Protection and Safety—*Deacon MARQUES R. SILVA, Dir., Ste. 914. Tel: 703-841-3847.

*Communications Office—*CAITLIN BOOTSMA, Interim Dir., Ste. 914. Tel: 703-841-2517; Fax: 703-524-5028. Email: communications@arlingtondiocese.org.

*Development Office—*ROBERT P. MUELLER, Dir., Ste. 811. Tel: 703-841-2545; Fax: 703-528-3057.

*Information Services—*KIMBERLY T. MURPHY, Dir. Tel: 703-841-3825; Fax: 703-841-4786.

Office of Planning, Construction and Facilities—Ste. 704. Tel: 703-841-2572; Fax: 703-276-9486. J. REID HERLIHY, Dir.; MARK ANTHONY, Dir. Planning; PETER B. FISHER, Construction Mgr.; FRANCIS PAREK, Construction Mgr.; JOHN AMARANTIDES, Facilities Mgr.

*Ecumenical and Interreligious Affairs Commission—*Rev. DONALD J. ROONEY, M.A., M.Div., Chm. Tel: 540-373-6491.

*Human Resources—*EUGENE F. RITZENTHALER, Dir., Ste. 600. Tel: 703-841-3854.

*Family Life Office—*THERESE BERMPOHL, Dir., Ste. 523. Tel: 703-841-2550; Fax: 703-807-2032. Email: familylife@arlingtondiocese.org.

*Gabriel Project-Pregnancy Assistance Program—*SARAH LAPIERRE, Prog. Dir., Ste. 814. Tel: 703-841-3812.

Marriage Preparation & Enrichment— Conferences for the Engaged TOM O'NEILL. Tel: 703-841-3807.

*Natural Family Planning—*Tel: 703-841-2550.

*Project Rachel Post-Abortion Outreach—*SARAH LAPIERRE, Prog. Dir. Tel: 703-841-2504; 888-456-4673 (24 hrs.). Email: projectrachel@arlingtondiocese.org.

*Respect Life/Pro-Life Activities—*Sr. CLARE HUNTER, F.S.E., Prog. Dir. Tel: 703-841-2550. Email: respectlife@arlingtondiocese.org.

*Young Adult Ministry—*ERIN KISLEY, Prog. Dir. Tel: 703-841-2549. Email: yam@arlingtondiocese.org.

*Liturgy, Office of Sacred—*Rev. PAUL F. DELADURANTAYE, S.T.D., Sec. for the Liturgy, Ste. 503. Tel: 703-841-2554; RICHARD GIBALA, Diocesan Music Coord. Tel: 703-524-2815.

*Permanent Diaconate—*Rev. JOHN C. CREGAN, V.F., Ste. 901. Tel: 703-841-3809; Fax: 703-841-8472.

*Diaconal Formation Program—*Revs. THOMAS P. FERGUSON, J.C.L., Dir. Tel: 703-841-2563; FRANK J. READY, V.G., Coord. Spiritual Formation. Tel: 703-841-3857.

*Pontifical Mission Societies and Propagation of the Faith—*Rev. PATRICK L. POSEY, Dir. Tel: 703-532-8815.

*Spanish Apostolate—*Rev. JOSE EUGENIO HOYOS, Dir.; IVONNE GRANADOS, Prog. Coord., Ste. 820. Tel: 703-841-3882.

*Office of Migration and Refugee Services—*SEYOUM BERHE, Dir., 80 N. Glebe Rd., Arlington, 22203. Tel: 703-524-2154; Fax: 703-524-2741.

*Risk Management, Office of—*MARY STEWART, Dir., Ste. 600. Tel: 703-841-2503; Fax: 703-841-4786.

*Victim Assistance Coordinator—*PATRICIA MUDD, M.S.W., A.C.S.W. Tel: 703-841-2530; ADLIN DE CARDI, M.A. Tel: 703-841-2730.

*Vocations, Office of—*Revs. BRIAN G. BASHISTA, Dir.; DANIEL F. HANLEY, Promoter Vocations; ANDREW J. FISHER, Coord. Hispanic Men Vocations.

*Youth Ministry, Office of—*KEVIN BOHLI, Dir., Ste. 519. Tel: 703-841-2559; Fax: 703-807-2032.

*Catholic Scouting Information—*Rev. EDWARD R. HORKAN, Chap., Ste. 519. Tel: 703-841-2559; Fax: 703-807-2032.

*Scouting & Camp Fire, Diocesan Committee on—*PATRICK BERNEY, Chm., 1701 Gelding Ln., Vienna, 22182. Tel: 730-255-2445. Email: pmberney@hotmail.com.

Consultative Bodies

*Clergy Personnel Board—*Rev. JOHN C. CREGAN, V.F., 200 N. Glebe Rd., Ste. 901, Arlington, 22203. Tel: 703-841-3809; Fax: 703-841-8472.

*Diaconal Council—*Deacons THOMAS M. BELLO, Chm. Tel: 703-448-9677; NICHOLAS LADUCA, Vice Chm. Tel: 703-323-4608.

*Diocesan Consultors—*Rev. ROBERT C. CILINSKI, V.F.; Very Rev. MARK S. MEALEY, O.S.F.S., J.C.D., Ph.D., V.G., J.V.; Revs. FRANK J. READY, V.G.; ROBERT J. RIPPY, J.C.L., V.F.; WILLIAM P. SAUNDERS, Ed.D., V.F.; DAVID P. MENG; TERRY W. SPECHT; DAVID A. WHITESTONE, J.C.L.

*Diocesan Finance Council—*Most Rev. PAUL S. LOVERDE, D.D., S.T.L., J.C.L., Chm. Tel: 703-841-2511; TIMOTHY R. COTNOIR, CPA, Diocesan Finance Officer. Tel: 703-841-2543.

*Diocesan School Board—*MAUREEN BLAKE, Chm. Tel: 703-494-3879.

*Presbyteral Council—*Most Rev. PAUL S. LOVERDE, D.D., S.T.L., J.C.L., Pres.; Rev. PHILLIP M. COZZI, Recording Sec.

*Sisters' Council—*Sr. CECILIA DWYER, O.S.B., Pres. Tel: 703-361-0106.

CLERGY, PARISHES, MISSIONS AND PAROCHIAL SCHOOLS

COUNTY OF ARLINGTON

1—CATHEDRAL OF ST. THOMAS MORE (1938) Revs. Robert J. Rippy; Jason Weber; Deacon Samuel M. Taub, (Retired). In Res., Rev. Paul F. deLadurantaye.
Res.: 3901 Cathedral Ln., 22203. Tel: 703-525-1300; 703-525-0450; Fax: 703-528-5760. Web: www.cathedralstm.org.
School—(Grades PreK-8), 105 N. Thomas St., 22203. Tel: 703-528-6781; Fax: 703-528-5048. Email: stmoffice@stmschool.org. Web: www.stmschool.org. Ms. Eleanor S. McCormack, Prin. Lay Teachers 27; Students 334.
*Catechesis/Religious Program—*Tel: 703-528-6781, Ext. 26. Kristin Grasson, D.R.E. Students 131.

2—ST. AGNES (1936) Revs. Lee R. Roos; Carroll L. Oubre, Parochial Vicar. In Res., Revs. Frank J. Ready; Cedric M. Wilson, O.S.A.
Res. & Office: 1910 N. Randolph St., 22207-3046. Tel: 703-525-1166; Fax: 703-243-2840. Email: parishoffice.stagnes@verizon.net. Web: www.saintagnes.org.
School—(Grades PreK-8), 2024 N. Randolph St., 22207. Tel: 703-527-5423; Fax: 703-527-6325. Kristine Carr, Prin. Lay Teachers 38; Students 406.
*Catechesis/Religious Program—*Tel: 703-527-1129. Email: re.stagnes@verizon.net. Bernadette Michael, D.R.E. Students 330.

3—ST. ANN (1947) Revs. Donald C. Greenhalgh; Lino Rico Rostro; Deacon William J. Donovan.
Res.: 5300 10th St. N., 22205. Tel: 703-528-6276; Fax: 703-522-4758.
School—(Grades PreK-8), 980 N. Frederick St., 22205. Tel: 703-525-7599; Fax: 703-525-2687. Ms. Mary E. Therrell, Prin.; Mary Herrington, Librarian. Lay Teachers 23; Students 151.
*Catechesis/Religious Program—*Tel: 703-528-6199. Students 480.

4—ST. CHARLES BORROMEO (1909) Rev. Horace H. Grinnell. In Res., Rev. Clement Aapengnuo.
Res.: 3304 N. Washington Blvd., 22201. Tel: 703-527-5500; Fax: 703-527-5505. Email: parishoffice@stcharleschurch.org. Web: www.stcharleschurch.org.
School—(Grades PreK-8), 3299 N. Fairfax Dr., 22201. Tel: 703-527-0608; Fax: 703-526-0262. Email: office@stcharles.k12.va.us. Web: www.stcharles.k12.va.us. Mrs. Linda Lacot, Prin. Lay Teachers 14; Students 200.
*Catechesis/Religious Program—*Tel: 703-527-5500, Ext. 17. Mrs. Anne Marie Kaufman, D.R.E. Students 768.
Convent—Benedictine Sisters of Virginia, 3299 N. Fairfax Dr., 22201. Tel: 703-527-1026; Fax: 703-526-0262.

5—HOLY MARTYRS OF VIETNAM (1979), (Vietnamese), Revs. John Baptist Vuong Duc Nguyen, O.P.; Thich Ngo, O.P.; Luan Pho, O.P.; Deacon Michael Kien Minh Pham, D.R.E.
Res.: 915 S. Wakefield St., 22204. Tel: 703-553-0370; Fax: 703-553-0371. Email: cttdarlington@yahoo.com. Web: www.cttdva.net.
*Catechesis/Religious Program—*Tel: 703-471-0137. Students 555.

6—OUR LADY OF LOURDES (1946) Revs. Robert E. Avella; Robert A. Lange, Parochial Vicar (Retired). In Res., Revs. Brian G. Bashista; Paul A. Berghout.
Res.: 830 S. 23rd St., 22202. Tel: 703-684-9261; 703-684-9211; Fax: 703-684-6342. Email: olol@comcast.net. Web: www.ololcc.net.
*Catechesis/Religious Program—*Marian Hartzell, D.R.E. Students 131.

7—OUR LADY, QUEEN OF PEACE (1945) Revs. Timothy J. Hickey, C.S.Sp.; Thomas P. Tunney, C.S.Sp., Parochial Vicar. In Res., Rev. Robert J. Richter.
Res.: 2700 S. 19th St., 22204. Tel: 703-979-5580; Fax: 703-979-5590. Email: office@olqpva.org. Web: olqpva.org.
*Catechesis/Religious Program—*Email: kremedios@olqpva.org. Kathleen Remedios, D.R.E. Students 297.

OUTSIDE THE COUNTY OF ARLINGTON

ALEXANDRIA, ALEXANDRIA CO.

1—BLESSED SACRAMENT (1946) Revs. John C. Cregan; Anthony J. Killian; Terry A. Cramer.
1427 W. Braddock Rd., 22302.
Res.: 1407 W. Braddock Rd., 22302. Tel: 703-998-6100. Web: www.blessedsacramentcc.org.
School—(Grades PreK-8), 1417 W. Braddock Rd., 22302. Tel: 703-998-4170; Fax: 703-998-5033. Mrs. Valerie Garcia, Prin.; Sue Knight, Librarian. Lay Teachers 40; Students 327.
Catechesis/Religious Program— Susan Doyle, D.R.E. Students 451.

2—ST. JOSEPH'S (1915) Rev. Francis M. Hull, S.S.J.; Deacon Albert Anderson.
Res.: 711 N. Columbus St., 22314. Tel: 703-836-3725; Fax: 703-837-9066. Web: stjosephva.org.
*Catechesis/Religious Program—*Tel: 703-924-5448. Mrs. Beverly Anderson, D.R.E. Students 36.

3—ST. MARY'S (1795) [CEM] Revs. Dennis W. Kleinmann; Robert L. Ruskamp; Michael J. R. Kelly. In Res., Rev. Jean-Claude Atusameso.
Res.: 310 Duke St., 22314. Tel: 703-836-4100; Fax: 703-549-3605. Web: www.saintmaryparish.net.
School—(Grades PreK-8), 400 Green St., 22314. Tel: 703-549-1646; Fax: 703-519-0840. Web: www.smsva.org. Mrs. Janet Cantwell, Prin.; Karen Kelly, Librarian. Lay Teachers 46; Students 709.
*Catechesis/Religious Program—*Tel: 703-836-5450. Jeanne Guerin, D.R.E. Students 278.

4—ST. RITA (1914) Rev. Daniel N. Gee. In Res., Rev. Edwin E. Perez; Rev. Msgr. Jeremiah H. McCarthy.
Res.: 3815 Russell Rd., 22305. Tel: 703-836-1640; Fax: 703-836-7825. Email: saintritarectory@speakeasy.net. Web: www.stritaparish.org.
School—(Grades K-8), 3801 Russell Rd., 22305. Tel: 703-548-1888; Fax: 703-519-9389. Email: saintritaalexandria@worldnet.att.net. Web: www.saintrita-school.org. Mrs. Mary Pat Schlickenmaier, Prin. Sisters of St. Joseph 2; Lay Teachers 13; Students 230.
*Catechesis/Religious Program—*Tel: 703-836-1356. Betsy Nunn, D.R.E. Students 189.
Convent—Sisters of St. Joseph, 231 W. Glebe Rd., 22305. Tel: 703-683-1929.

ALEXANDRIA, FAIRFAX CO.

1—GOOD SHEPHERD (1965) Rev. Thomas P. Ferguson; Deacon Thomas G. White Jr. In Res., Revs. Luis Quinones; Ricardo Martin Pinillos.
Church & Mailing Address: 8710 Mount Vernon Hwy., 22309. Tel: 703-780-4055; Fax: 703-842-8232.

Email: office@gs-cc.org. Web: www.gs-cc.org.
Res.: 3510 Surry Dr., 22309.
Catechesis/Religious Program—Joan Sheppard, D.R.E. Students 1,163.

2—ST. LAWRENCE (Franconia) (1967) Rev. Christopher J. Mould. In Res., Revs. Tomasz Medrek; Andrew Szymakowski.
Res.: 6222 Franconia Rd., 22310. Tel: 703-971-4378; Fax: 703-971-0331. Email: st.lawrence@cox.net. Web: saintlawrenceparish.com.
Catechesis/Religious Program—Tel: 703-971-8541. Anna Krestyn, D.R.E. Students 213.

3—ST. LOUIS (1949) Revs. Richard A. Mullins; Mark F. Carrier. In Res., Revs. Paul L. Dudzinski; Joseph Tatro.
Res.: 2907 Popkins Ln., 22306. Tel: 703-765-4421; Fax: 703-765-1750.
School—(Grades K-8), 2901 Popkins Ln., 22306. Tel: 703-768-7732; Fax: 703-768-3836. Daniel Baillargeon, Prin. Lay Teachers 24; Students 410.
Catechesis/Religious Program— Mr. Patrick Krisak, D.R.E. Students 224.

4—QUEEN OF APOSTLES (1963) Revs. Marcus A. Pollard; Andrew J. Heintz. In Res., Rev. Andrew Luong; Deacon Richard C. Caporiccio.
Res.: 4329 Sano St., 22312. Tel: 703-354-8711; Fax: 703-354-0766. Web: www.queenofapostles.org.
School—(Grades K-8), 4409 Sano St., 22312. Tel: 703-354-0714; Fax: 703-354-1820. Mark S. Moran, Prin. Lay Teachers 16; Students 185.
Catechesis/Religious Program—Jennifer Guarnizo, D.R.E. Students 243.

ANNANDALE, FAIRFAX CO.

1—ST. AMBROSE (1966) Revs. Andrew J. Fisher; Stephen Holmes. In Res., Rev. Charles W. Merkle III.
Church & Office Mailing Address: 3901 Woodburn Rd., 22003. Tel: 703-280-4400; Fax: 703-280-1123. Email: information@stambroseva.org. Web: www.stambroseannandale.org.
Res.: 3825 Woodburn Rd., 22003. Tel: 703-280-4400; Fax: 703-280-1123.
School—(Grades K-8), 3827 Woodburn Rd., 22003. Tel: 703-698-7171; Fax: 703-698-7170. Web: stambroseschool.org. Barbara Dalmut, Prin.; Marcia Healy, Librarian. Lay Teachers 15; Students 189.
Catechesis/Religious Program—Tel: 703-280-1122; Fax: 703-280-1123. Email: dre@stambroseannandale.org. Ms. Simone Rizkallah, D.R.E. & Dir. Youth Activities. Students 218.

2—HOLY SPIRIT (1964) Revs. Terry W. Specht; Joseph R. Kenna, Parochial Vicar.
Mailing Address: 5121 Woodland Way, 22003. Email: holyspiritparish@cox.net. Web: www.holyspiritchurch.us.
School—(Grades PreK-8), 8800 Braddock Rd., 22003. Tel: 703-978-7117; Fax: 703-978-7438. Mrs. Sarah O'Fallon, Prin. (Extended Day Care available) Lay Teachers 30; Students 377.
Catechesis/Religious Program—Tel: 703-978-8925. Email: religious.ed@holyspiritchurch.us. Ms. Ana Lisa Pinon, D.R.E. Students 617.

3—ST. MICHAEL (1953) Revs. Jerry Pokorsky; Kevin J. Beres; Kevin J. Fimian; Deacons David S. McCaffrey; Roger T. Ostrom. In Res., Rev. Joseph J. Clark.
Res.: 7401 St. Michael's Ln., 22003. Tel: 703-256-7822; Fax: 703-256-7122.
School—(Grades K-8) Tel: 703-256-1222; Fax: 703-941-9474. Web: www.stmikes22003.org. Sr. Therese Elizabeth Bauer, Prin. Sisters (Servants of the Immaculate Heart of Mary) 5; Lay Teachers 19; Students 206.
Catechesis/Religious Program—Tel: 703-941-9403. Email: dre@stmikes22003.org. Deacon David S. McCaffrey, D.R.E. Students 210.
Convent—Sisters, Servants of the Immaculate Heart of Mary, 7421 St. Michael's Ln., 22003. Tel: 703-256-2130.

ASHBURN, LOUDOUN CO., ST. THERESA (1991) Revs. Richard M. Guest; Daniel S. Spychala.
Rectory—43367 Icepond Dr., 20147. Tel: 703-729-9036; Fax: 703-729-9036.
Church: 21371 St. Theresa Ln., 20147.
School—(Grades K-8), 21370 St. Theresa Ln., 20147. Tel: 703-729-3577; Fax: 703-729-8068. Web: sttheresa-ashburn.com. Carol Krichbaum, Prin.; Mrs. Kit McKeon, Librarian. Lay Teachers 36; Students 477.
Catechesis/Religious Program—Tel: 703-729-3714; Fax: 703-729-9036. Email: reoffice@sttheresa-ashburn.org. Students 1,531.

BURKE, FAIRFAX CO., CHURCH OF THE NATIVITY (W. Springfield) (1973) Revs. Richard B. Martin; Wilson I. Korpi.
Mailing Address: 6400 Nativity Ln., 22015. Tel: 703-455-2400; Fax: 703-455-6832.
Res.: 9523 Lyra Ct., 22015. Tel: 703-913-2306. Web: www.nativityburke.org.
School—(Grades PreK-8), 6398 Nativity Ln., 22015. Tel: 703-455-2300; Fax: 703-569-8109. Web: www.nativityschool.org. Ms. Maria E. Kelly, Prin. Lay Teachers 18; Students 312.
Catechesis/Religious Program—Tel: 703-455-0372. Sisters Donatella Merulla, A.R., D.R.E.; Mary Attilia Todaro, A.R., D.R.E. Students 1,432.
Convent—Handmaids of Reparation of the Sacred Heart of Jesus, 6300 Capella Ave., 22015. Tel: 703-455-4180.

CHANTILLY, FAIRFAX CO.

1—ST. TIMOTHY (1969) Revs. Gerald Weymes; William M. Aitcheson; Stephen J. Schultz, Parochial Vicar; Deacon David E. Conroy Sr. In Res., Rev. Anthony J. Pinizzotto, O.S.F.S.
Res.: 13807 Poplar Tree Rd., 20151. Tel: 703-378-7461; Tel: 703-378-7646; Fax: 703-378-7552. Email: mbuonocore@sttimothyparish.org. Web: www.sttimothyparish.org.
School—(Grades K-8), 13809 Poplar Tree Rd., 20151. Tel: 703-378-6932; Fax: 703-378-1273. Patricia Kobyra, Prin.; Ms. Karen Tierny, Librarian. Sisters 1; Lay Teachers 40; Students 585.
Catechesis/Religious Program—Tel: 703-378-9143; Fax: 703-378-7552. Maria Ho, D.R.E. Students 1,163.

2—ST. VERONICA (1999) Revs. Edward C. Hathaway; Charles C. Smith; Deacon J. Paul Ochenkowski.
3460 Centreville Rd., 20151. Tel: 703-773-2000; Fax: 703-773-2001. Email: info@stveronica.net. Web: www.stveronica.net.
School—(Grades K-8), 3460B Centreville Rd., 20151. Tel: 703-773-2020; Fax: 703-773-2021. Web: www.stveronicaschool.org. Mary Baldwin, Prin.; Julie Kopping, Librarian. Students 361; Lay Staff 33.
Catechesis/Religious Program—Students 403.

CLIFTON, FAIRFAX CO.

1—ST. ANDREW THE APOSTLE (1989) Revs. John D. Kelly; Mark Mullaney, Parochial Vicar. In Res., Rev. Russell Raj Yesudhas, O.C.D.
Res.: 6720 Union Mill Rd., 20124. Tel: 703-817-1770; Fax: 703-817-0928.
School—(Grades PreK-8) Tel: 703-817-1774; Fax: 703-817-1721. Glenda Sigg, Prin. Lay Teachers 21; Students 278.
Catechesis/Religious Program—Tel: 703-817-1773. Mrs. Delores Nelson, D.R.E. Students 756.

2—ST. CLARE OF ASSISI (1981) Rev. Thomas J. Lehning.
Church & Rectory: 12409 Henderson Rd., 20124. Tel: 703-266-1310; 703-266-7293; Fax: 703-266-7011. Email: office@stclareclifton.org. Web: www.stclareclifton.org.
Catechesis/Religious Program—Peggy Mattei, D.R.E. Students 82.

COLONIAL BEACH, WESTMORELAND CO., ST. ELIZABETH OF HUNGARY (1906) [JC] Revs. Francis M. De Rosa; Vincent D. Bork.
Res.: 21 Irving Ave., 22443. Tel: 804-224-7221; Fax: 804-224-3137. Email: office@elizant.com. Web: www.elizant.com.
Catechesis/Religious Program—Sally Cullin, D.R.E. Students 81.
Mission—St. Anthony's [CEM] 11 Irving Ave., Westmoreland Co. 22443.

CULPEPER, CULPEPER CO., PRECIOUS BLOOD (1880) [CEM] Rev. Leo J. Zonneveld, C.I.C.M.; Deacon Ramon Tirado.
Res.: 114 E. Edmondson St., 22701. Tel: 540-825-8945; Fax: 540-825-8987.
Catechesis/Religious Program—Tel: 540-825-1339. Ms. Patricia Reed, D.R.E. Students 351.

DALE CITY, PRINCE WILLIAM CO., HOLY FAMILY (1970) Revs. Gerard Creedon; Stephen F. McGraw; John T. O'Hara; Deacons Vincent Einsmann; Richard L. Demers; Joseph L. Santiago. In Res., Rev. Matthew H. Zuberbueler.
Res.: 14190 Ferndale Rd., 22193. Tel: 703-670-8161; Fax: 703-670-8323. Email: parishoffice@holyfamilydalecity.org. Web: www.holyfamilycatholicchurchdalecity.org.
School—(Grades PreK-8) Tel: 703-670-3138. Web: www.holyfamilyinfolink.com. Joseph M. McLaughlin, Prin. Email: principal@hfccdc.com; Judi Peacott, Dir. (PreK); Ashley Brunacci, Librarian. Lay Teachers 19; Students 255.
Catechesis/Religious Program—Tel: 703-670-8161, Ext. 308. Reyes Ruiz, D.R.E. Students 711.

FAIRFAX, FAIRFAX CO.

1—ST. MARY OF SORROWS (1858) [CEM] Revs. James S. Barkett; Stefan P. Starzynski.
Mailing & Parish Center Address: 5222 Sideburn Rd., 22032-2640. Tel: 703-978-4141; Fax: 703-978-2568. Email: kathyc@stmaryofsorrows.org. Web: stmaryofsorrows.org.
Historic Church—5612 Ox Rd., Fairfax Station, 22039.
Res.: 11112 Fairfax Station Rd., Fairfax Station, 22039.
Catechesis/Religious Program— Esther Silva, D.R.E., (PreK-8); Brian Kissinger, Youth Min. Students 1,015.

2—ST. PAUL CHUNG (1986), (Korean), Revs. Peter Hoin Kwak; Jungha Kim; Deacon Paul Lee.
Res.: 4708 Rippling Pond Dr., 22033-5077. Tel: 703-818-9707; Fax: 703-968-3013. Email: sthasang@gmail.com. Web: www.stpaulchung.org.
Church & Mailing Address: 4712 Rippling Pond Dr., 22033-5077. Tel: 703-968-3010.
Catechesis/Religious Program—

FAIRFAX CITY, FAIRFAX CO., ST. LEO'S (1957) Revs. David A. Whitestone; Ramon A. Baez; Robert J. Wagner; Deacons Jose J. Lopez; Noel Vivaldi.
Res.: 3700 Old Lee Hwy., 22030. Tel: 703-273-5369; Fax: 703-273-2371.
School—(Grades PreK-8), 3704 Old Lee Hwy., 22030. Tel: 703-273-1211; Fax: 703-273-6913. Mr. David DiPippa, Prin.; Cynthia Washington, Asst. Prin. Lay Teachers 28; Students 449.
Catechesis/Religious Program—Tel: 703-273-4868; Fax: 703-273-0994. Lee Cena, D.R.E.; Erik Teter, Asst. Youth Min. Tel: 703-591-6089; Nina Deboeck, Youth Min. Students 658.
Station—Fairfax Nursing Home, Tel: 703-273-7705.
Station—Commonwealth Care Center 22030. Tel: 703-934-5060.
Station—The Gardens at Fair Oaks 22030. Tel: 703-278-1001.
Station—Sunrise Assisted Living at George Mason 22030. Tel: 703-934-5069.

FALLS CHURCH, FAIRFAX CO.

1—ST. ANTHONY'S (1952) Revs. Kevin B. Walsh; Matthew J. DeForest; Deacons Mario Mendoza; Thomas M. Bello. In Res., Revs. Alex Diaz-Amaya; Jose Eugenio Hoyos.
Res.: 3305 Glen Carlyn Rd., 22041. Tel: 703-820-7111; Fax: 703-379-9195.
Catechesis/Religious Program—Lia Salinas, D.R.E. Students 782.

2—ST. JAMES (1892) [CEM] Revs. Patrick L. Posey; Edward R. Horkan; Philip S. Majka; Deacon James A. Fishenden. In Res., Revs. Joseph Elamparayil, O.C.D.; Edmund C. Ani.
Res.: 905 Park Ave., 22046. Tel: 703-532-8815; Fax: 703-533-7644. Email: rectory@stjamescatholic.org; sjcc@stjamescatholic.org. Web: www.stjamescatholic.org.
School—(Grades K-8), 830 W. Broad St., 22046. Tel: 703-533-1182, Ext. 100; Fax: 703-532-8316. Email: mainoffice@saintjamesschool.org. Sr. Nancy J. Kindelan, I.H.M., Prin. Sisters (Servants of the Immaculate Heart of Mary) 4; Lay Teachers 40; Students 575.
Catechesis/Religious Program—Sr. Joyce Carolyn Bell, I.H.M., D.R.E. Students 392.
Convent—Sisters, Servants of the Immaculate Heart of Mary, 101 N. Spring St., 22046. Tel: 703-532-2388.

3—ST. PHILIP (1963) Revs. Denis M. Donahue; Luke R. Dundon; Tarsicio Buitrago.
Res.: 7500 St. Philip's Ct., 22042. Tel: 703-573-3808; Fax: 703-560-2832. Email: stphilipsparish@gmail.com. Web: www.stphilipsparish.com.
Convent—7504 St. Philip's Ct., 22042. Tel: 703-204-0837. Sisters 5.
Catechesis/Religious Program—Students 345.

FREDERICKSBURG, FREDERICKSBURG CO.

1—ST. JUDE (2003) Rev. James C. Hudgins; Deacons Robert F. Borchert; Robert A. Lyons.
Church: 10725 Courthouse Rd., 22407. Tel: 540-891-7350; Fax: 540-891-1810. Email: parishoffice@stjudechurch.us. Web: www.stjudespotsy.org.
Res.: 10101 Chatham Ct., 22408. Tel: 540-710-1060.
Catechesis/Religious Program—Tel: 540-891-1262. Joyce Franklin, D.R.E. Students 246.

2—ST. MARY OF THE IMMACULATE CONCEPTION (1858) Revs. Donald J. Rooney; Bjorn C. Lundberg, Parochial Vicar; Edward J. Bresnahan. In Res., Rev. Frederick H. Edlefsen.
Res.: 1009 Stafford Ave., 22401-5418. Tel: 540-373-6491; Fax: 540-371-0251. Email: stmary@stmaryfred.org. Web: www.stmaryfred.org.
Catechesis/Religious Program— Aristides Lucas, D.R.E. Students 1,038.
Convent—Oblate Sisters of St. Francis de Sales, St. Mary Convent, 1316 Royston St., 22401. Tel: 540-371-1652; Fax: 540-371-1652.

3—ST. PATRICK (1983) Revs. John A. Ziegler; Ronald J. Gripshover Jr.; Deacons David Conroy; John J. McClay; William D. Pivarnik.
Tel: 540-785-5299; Fax: 540-785-5692. Email: office@saintpatrickparish.org. Web: www.saintpatrickparish.org.
School—(Grades PreK-8), 9151 Ely's Ford Rd., 22407. Tel: 540-786-2277; Fax: 540-785-2213. Email: saintpatrick123@yahoo.com. Web: saintpatrick-school.com. Mr. George Elliott, Prin. Lay Teachers 16; Students 231.

Catechesis/Religious Program—Tel: 540-785-7857; Fax: 540-785-5758. Email: stpatsreligioused@comcast.net. Philip Camill, D.R.E. Students 553.

FRONT ROYAL, WARREN CO., ST. JOHN THE BAPTIST (1884) Revs. Jerome W. Fasano; Richard T. Carr.
Res.: 123 W. Main St., 22630. Tel: 540-635-3780; Fax: 540-635-2683. Email: stjohns@shentel.net. Web: www.sjtb.org.
Catechesis/Religious Program—Julie Luckey, D.R.E. Students 433.

GAINESVILLE, PRINCE WILLIAM CO., HOLY TRINITY (2001) Revs. Thomas P. Vander Woude; Jerry A. Wooton, Parochial Vicar; Deacon Lawrence B. Henry.
Church: 8213 Linton Hall Rd., 20155. Web: www.holytrinityparish.net.
Res.: 13260 McCartney Ct., Bristow, 20136. Tel: 703-753-6700; Fax: 703-753-6286. Web: www.holytrinityparish.net.
Catechesis/Religious Program—Email: ReligiousEd@holytrinityparish.net. Michele Leary, D.R.E. Students 1,800.

GORDONSVILLE, ORANGE CO., ST. MARK'S (1972) Merged with St. John's, Orange to form St. Isidore the Farmer, Orange.

GREAT FALLS, FAIRFAX CO., ST. CATHERINE OF SIENA (1979) Rev. Alexander R. Drummond.
Mailing Address: 1020 Springvale Rd., 22066. Tel: 703-759-4350; Fax: 703-759-3753. Email: office@saintcatherineschurch.org.
School—Siena Academy, Tel: 703-759-4129. Email: sienaacademy@saintcatherineschurch.org. Sr. Janet Siepker, F.S.E., Head of School. Students 125.
Catechesis/Religious Program—Tel: 703-759-3530; Fax: 703-759-7941. Anson Groves, D.R.E. Students 188.

HERNDON, FAIRFAX CO., ST. JOSEPH (1950) Revs. James Angert, T.O.R.; Patrick Donahoe, T.O.R., Parochial Vicar; Timothy Harris, T.O.R., Parochial Vicar; Alberto Bueno, T.O.R.; Zygmunt Mazanowksi, T.O.R.
Res.: 750 Peachtree St., 20170. Tel: 703-880-4300; Fax: 703-880-4320. Email: mkirby@sjcherndon.org. Web: www.sjcherndon.org.
School—(Grades K-8) Tel: 703-880-4350. Mrs. Joan Cargill, Prin.; Mrs. Cindi Conroy, Asst. Prin.; Mrs. Heather Brown, Librarian. Lay Teachers 30; Students 585.
Catechesis/Religious Program—Students 621.

KILMARNOCK, LANCASTER CO., ST. FRANCIS DE SALES (1966) [CEM 2] Revs. James C. Bruse; John M. O'Donohue.
Res.: 154 E. Church St., P.O. Box 759, 22482-0759. Tel: 804-435-1511; Fax: 804-436-9614. Email: stfrancis@va.metrocast.net.
Catechesis/Religious Program—Fax: 804-436-9614. Students 66.
Mission—St. Paul 811 Long Point Rd., P.O. Box 65, Hague, Westmoreland Co. 22469. Tel: 804-472-3090; Fax: 804-423-3092. Email: saintpaul@hughes.net.

LAKE RIDGE, PRINCE WILLIAM CO., ST. ELIZABETH ANN SETON (1976) Revs. David P. Meng; James R. Searby, Parochial Vicar; Deacon Robert Warner.
Mailing Address: 12805 Valleywood Dr., 22192. Tel: 703-494-4008; Fax: 703-494-1995.
Catechesis/Religious Program—Tel: 703-494-3966; Fax: 703-494-8005. Jackie Ezersky, D.R.E. (Grades K-5); Kathy Lord, D.R.E. (Middle School); Kevin Heider, Youth Min.; Jessica Watjen, Youth Min. Students 522.

LEESBURG, LOUDOUN CO., ST. JOHN THE APOSTLE (1926) [CEM] Revs. John P. Mosimann; Francis J. Peffley.
Mailing Address: 101 Oakcrest Manor Dr., N.E., 20176-2221. Tel: 703-777-1317; Fax: 703-771-9016. Email: church@stjohnleesburg.com. Web: stjohnleesburg.com.
Res.: 302 N. King St., N.E., 20176. Tel: 703-777-6477.
Catechesis/Religious Program—Tel: 703-777-3891. Email: dre@stjohnleesburg.com. Edward V. Spinelli, D.R.E. Students 1,147.

LURAY, PAGE CO., OUR LADY OF THE VALLEY (1954) Rev. Christopher Lemme, T.O.R.
Mailing Address: 200 Collins Ave., 22835. Tel: 540-743-4919; Fax: 540-743-2490.
Catechesis/Religious Program—Mrs. Elizabeth Hutchins, D.R.E.; Mary Nestor, Youth Min.; Michael Nestor, Youth Min. Students 35.

MADISON, MADISON CO., OUR LADY OF THE BLUE RIDGE (1977) Rev. Michael T. Orlowsky.
Res.: 692 Lonnie Burke Rd., 22727. Tel: 540-948-4144; Fax: 540-948-3325.
Catechesis/Religious Program—Students 48.

MANASSAS, PRINCE WILLIAM CO.

1—ALL SAINTS (1879) Revs. Robert C. Cilinski; John H. Melmer, Parochial Vicar; Juan Puigbo, Parochial Vicar; Jeb S. Donelan, Parochial Vicar; Deacons John W. Eberlein; Richard O'Connell.
Res.: 9300 Stonewall Rd., 20110. Tel: 703-368-4500; Fax: 703-257-9299. Web: www.allsaintsvachurch.org.
School—(Grades PreK-8), 9294 Stonewall Rd., 20110. Tel: 703-368-4400; Fax: 703-393-2157. Web: www.allsaintsschool.org. Mr. David E. Conroy Jr., Prin.; Mrs. Elba Campagna, Asst. Prin. Lay Teachers 24; Students 552.
Catechesis/Religious Program—Tel: 703-393-2142. Samantha Welsh, D.R.E., (Elementary-English); Clarissa Maciel, D.R.E. (Elementary-Spanish); Rob Tessier, Youth Min. (Junior-Senior High School & College). Students 1,086.

2—SACRED HEART (1984) [CEM] Rev. Michael J. Bazan; Deacon Gerald J. Moore.
Mailing Address: 12975 Purcell Rd., 20112-3217. Tel: 703-590-0030; Fax: 703-590-0141. In Res., Rev. Devaraju Arockiasamy.
Res.: 6258 Terrapin Dr., 20112. Tel: 703-791-5131.
Catechesis/Religious Program—Tel: 703-590-0256. Kathleen Burr, D.R.E. Students 369.

MCLEAN, FAIRFAX CO.

1—ST. JOHN THE BELOVED (1913) Revs. Paul D. Scalia; James M. Poumade; Deacon Joseph G. Benin. In Res., Rev. Franklyn M. McAfee.
Res.: 6420 Linway Ter., 22101. Tel: 703-356-7916; Fax: 703-356-4517.
School—(Grades PreK-8), 6422 Linway Ter., 22101. Tel: 703-356-7554; Fax: 703-448-3811. Web: www-.stjohnacademy.org. Peter Schultz, Headmaster; Barbara Gray, Librarian. Lay Teachers 26; Students 273.
Catechesis/Religious Program—Tel: 703-356-5275. Ms. Laura Pennefather, D.R.E. Students 282.

2—ST. LUKE (1961) Rev. David L. Martin. In Res., Rev. Jamie R. Workman.
Res.: 7001 Georgetown Pike, 22101. Tel: 703-356-1255; Fax: 703-442-0848. Email: parishoffice@saintlukemclean.org. Web: www.saintlukemclean.org.
School—(Grades K-8), 7005 Georgetown Pike, 22101. Tel: 703-356-1508; Fax: 703-356-1141. Web: www.saintlukeschool.com. Mark A. Cosenza, Prin. Lay Teachers 18; Students 230.
Catechesis/Religious Program—Tel: 703-356-8419; Fax: 703-356-5988. Joyce Franklin, D.R.E. Students 750.

MIDDLEBURG, LOUDOUN CO., ST. STEPHEN THE MARTYR (1975) Rev. William B. Schardt; Deacon Jack M. Ligon.
Mailing Address: 23331 Sam Fred Rd., 20117-3221. Tel: 540-687-6433; Fax: 540-687-5170. Web: www.saint-stephen.org.
Res.: 23309 Sam Fred Rd., 20117.
Church: Intersection of Rtes. 50 & Sam Fred Rd., 20117.
Catechesis/Religious Program—Students 882.
Mission—St. Katharine Drexel Mission 14535 John Marshall Hwy., Ste. 210, Gainesville, Prince William Co. 20155. Tel: 703-754-8444; Fax: 703-754-7334.
Mission—Corpus Christi Mission 15100 Enterprise St., Ste. 300, Chantilly, 20151. Tel: 703-378-1037; Fax: 703-378-4442. Rev. Michael G. Taylor, Admin.

ORANGE, ORANGE CO.

1—ST. ISIDORE THE FARMER (2002) Rev. Terrence R. Staples; Deacon Thomas M. Fursman.
Res.: 14405 St. Isidore Way, 22960. Tel: 540-672-4933; Fax: 540-661-4204. Email: stisidore@nexet.net.
Church: 14414 St. Isidore Way, 22960-2573.
Catechesis/Religious Program—Students 62.

2—ST. JOHN'S (1946) Merged with St. Mark's, Gordonsville to form St. Isidore the Farmer, Orange.

POTOMAC FALLS, LOUDOUN CO., OUR LADY OF HOPE (2000) Revs. William P. Saunders; William Schierer.
Res.: 20648 Belwood Ct., 20165. Email: info@ourladyofhope.net. Web: www.ourladyofhope.net.
School—(Grades K-8), 46633 Algonkian Pkwy., 20165. Tel: 703-433-6760; Fax: 703-433-6761. Email: school@ourladyofhope.net. Web: www.school.ourladyofhope.net. Mary Beth Pittman, Prin. Lay Teachers 15; Students 218.
Catechesis/Religious Program—Cathy Plummer, D.R.E. Students 561.

PURCELLVILLE, LOUDOUN CO., ST. FRANCIS DE SALES (1967) Revs. Ronald S. Escalante; Edwin T. Tewes; Deacon Lawrence V. Hammel.
Res.: 37730 St. Francis Ct., 20132. Tel: 540-338-6381; Fax: 540-338-6431. Email: secretary@saintfrancisparish.org. Web: stfrancisdesalescatholicchurch.org.
Catechesis/Religious Program—Tel: 540-338-4497. Melissa Gobs, D.R.E.; Janice Rees, C.R.E. Students 888.

RESTON, FAIRFAX CO.

1—ST. JOHN NEUMANN (1979) Revs. Thomas E. Murphy, O.S.F.S.; Robert Mancini, O.S.F.S. In Res., Revs. William M. Rutledge, O.S.F.S.; William N. Dougherty, O.S.F.S.; Joseph T. Brennan, O.S.F.S.
Res.: 11900 Lawyers Rd., 20191-4299. Tel: 703-860-8510; Fax: 703-860-2136. Web: www.saintjn.org.
Catechesis/Religious Program—Tel: 703-860-2815. Mrs. Mary Lyons, D.R.E. Students 1,393.

2—ST. THOMAS A BECKET (1970) Rev. Paul M. Grankauskas.
1418 Greenmont Ct., 20190. Web: www.stbchurch.com.
Catechesis/Religious Program—Tel: 703-689-3816. Betsy Coffey, Dir., Middle & High School Faith Formation (6-12); Susan Reilly, Dir., Pre-K-Grade 5 Faith Formation. Students 672.

SPOTSYLVANIA, SPOTSYLVANIA CO., ST. MATTHEW (1999) Revs. Paul M. Eversole; Augustine Tran; Deacons Edward F. Whelan Jr.; John A. Hubbarth; Paul A. Gregory; Linda Long, Music Min.
Mailing Address: 8200 Robert E. Lee Dr., 22553. Tel: 540-582-5575; Fax: 540-582-8639.
Catechesis/Religious Program—Tel: 540-582-8469. Joanne Warren, D.R.E. Students 252.

SPRINGFIELD, FAIRFAX CO.

1—ST. BERNADETTE (1959) Revs. Kevin J. Larsen; Joseph Q. Vu; Deacon William D. Powers. In Res., Rev. Luis Fernando Franco Henao.
Res.: 7600 Old Keene Mill Rd., 22152-2022. Tel: 703-451-8576; Fax: 703-269-1121. Email: office@stbernpar.org. Web: www.stbernpar.org.
School—(Grades PreSchool-8), 7602 Old Keene Mill Rd., 22152-2099. Tel: 703-451-8696. Email: school@stbernschool.org. Web: www.stbernpar.org. Mrs. Patricia Beeks, Prin. Lay Teachers 30; Students 492.
Catechesis/Religious Program—Tel: 703-451-8576, Ext. 36. Email: religioused@stbernpar.org. David Wallace, D.R.E. Students 483.

2—ST. RAYMOND OF PENAFORT (1997) Revs. John C. De Celles, Admin.; Mark A. Pilon; John Lovell. In Res., Rev. Joby Thomas, M.C.B.S.
Parish Office & Res.: 8750 Pohick Rd., 22153. Tel: 703-440-0535; Fax: 703-440-0538.
Catechesis/Religious Program—Email: strayccd@aol.comTel: 703-440-0537. Maria Ammirati, D.R.E.; Kristin Smith, Youth Min. Students 665.

STAFFORD, STAFFORD CO., ST. WILLIAM OF YORK (1971) Revs. Robert J. DeMartino; Geronimo A. Magat, Parochial Vicar; Bryan W. Belli, Parochial Vicar.
Res. & Mailing Address: 3130 Jefferson Davis Hwy., 22554. Tel: 540-659-1102; Fax: 540-659-5637. Web: www.swoycc.org.
School—(Grades PreK-8) Tel: 540-659-5207; Fax: 540-659-9863. Web: www.stwillschool.org. Mr. Frank P. Nicely, Prin.; Mrs. Katie Moloko, Librarian. Lay Teachers 18; Students 203.
Catechesis/Religious Program—Tel: 540-659-5705. Mr. Timothy J. Nacey, D.R.E. Students 587.

STERLING, LOUDOUN CO., CHRIST THE REDEEMER (1972) Revs. C. Donald Howard, S.A.; Arthur M. Johnson, S.A. In Res., Revs. Bernard R. Palka, S.A.; William F. Schmidt, S.A.
Res.: 12494 Cliff Edge Dr., Herndon, 20170. Tel: 703-430-1686.
Church: 46833 Harry Byrd Hwy., 20164. Tel: 703-430-0811; Fax: 703-430-1590.
Catechesis/Religious Program—Tel: 703-430-0813; Fax: 703-430-1590. Ms. Harvesta Greene Williams, D.R.E.; Mr. Jay Cuasay, D.R.E.; Mrs. M. Amelia Silva, D.R.E. Hispanic. Students 647.

TRIANGLE, PRINCE WILLIAM CO., ST. FRANCIS OF ASSISI (1957) Revs. Charles J. Miller, O.F.M.; Kevin J. Downey, O.F.M.; John J. Heffernan, O.F.M.; Deacons James B. Doyle; Francisco Flores.
Res.: 18414 Cabin Rd., 22172. Tel: 703-221-4575. Web: www.stfrncis.org.
Church: 18825 Fuller Heights Rd., 22172. Tel: 703-221-4044; Fax: 703-221-3246.
School—(Grades PreK-8) Tel: 703-221-3868; Fax: 703-221-0700. Dr. Tricia Barber, Prin.; Geri Weindelmayer, Librarian. Lay Teachers 16; Students 337.
Catechesis/Religious Program—Tel: 703-221-4978. Sr. Janice Urbanec, D.R.E. Students 988.

VIENNA, FAIRFAX CO.

1—ST. MARK (1965) [CEM] Rev. Patrick Holroyd.
Res.: 9970 Vale Rd., 22181. Tel: 703-281-9100; Fax: 703-281-0675. Web: www.stmark.org.
School—(Grades PreK-8), 9972 Vale Rd., 22181. Tel: 703-281-9103. Roberta Etzel, Prin.; Elizabeth Posey, Librarian. Lay Teachers 28; Students 400.
Catechesis/Religious Program—Tel: 703-938-1948. Mickey Edwards, D.R.E.; Isaac Garcia, D.R.E. Students 726.

2—OUR LADY OF GOOD COUNSEL (1956) Revs. William J. Metzger, O.S.F.S.; Lewis S. Fiorelli, O.S.F.S., Parochial Vicar; William J. Ruhl, O.S.F.S. (Retired); Stephen E. Shott, O.S.F.S. In Res., Very Rev. Mark S. Mealey, O.S.F.S.
Office & Mailing Address: P.O. Box 97, 22183-0097. Tel: 703-938-2828; Fax: 703-938-2829. Email: administration_receptionist@olgcva.org. Web: www.olgcva.org.
Res.: 8601 Wolftrap Rd., 22182.
School—(Grades K-8) Tel: 703-938-3600; Fax: 703-938-2933. Web: olgcschool.org. Mr. Austin Poole,

Prin.; Susan McFaden, Librarian. Lay Teachers 30; Students 453.
Catechesis/Religious Program—Tel: 703-896-7414. Jessica Dennis, D.R.E. Students 625.

WARRENTON, FAUQUIER CO., ST. JOHN THE EVANGELIST (1874) Revs. James R. Gould; Mark E. Moretti, Parochial Vicar.
Res.: 271 Winchester St., 20186. Tel: 540-347-2922; Fax: 540-347-1274. Email: info@stjohntheevangelist.org. Web: www.stjohntheevangelist.org.
School—(Grades PreK-8), 111 King St., 20186. Tel: 540-347-2458; Fax: 540-349-8007. Arthur Fairweather, Prin. Lay Teachers 21; Students 250.
Catechesis/Religious Program—Sherin Murphy, D.R.E. Students 620.

WASHINGTON, RAPPAHANNOCK CO., ST. PETER (2005) Rev. Christopher D. Murphy; Deacon Charles A. Coutu.
12762 Lee Hwy., 22747. Tel: 540-675-3432; Fax: 540-675-1053.
Catechesis/Religious Program—Email: our4chickadees@aol.comTel: 540-547-9970. Students 60.

WINCHESTER, FREDERICK CO., SACRED HEART OF JESUS (1870) [CEM] Revs. Stanley J. Krempa; Michael J. Dobbins, Parochial Vicar; Deacon Edward L. Christianson.
Res.: 130 Keating Dr., 22601-2806. Tel: 540-662-5858; Fax: 540-667-6156.
School—(Grades PreK-8), 110 Keating Dr., 22601-2806. Tel: 540-662-7177. Mrs. Rebecca McTavish, Prin.; Mrs. Dolores Sirbaugh, Librarian. Lay Teachers 18; Students 190.
Catechesis/Religious Program—Tel: 540-662-2651. Julia Carty, D.R.E. Students 855.
Mission—St. Bridget of Ireland Berryville, Clarke Co.

WOODBRIDGE, PRINCE WILLIAM CO., OUR LADY OF ANGELS (1959) Revs. J. Kevin O'Keefe, Parochial Admin.; Michael R. Duesterhaus, Parochial Vicar; Christopher T. Vaccaro; Deacons Danny E. Johnson; Emil P. Myskowski. In Res., Rev. Milton Acevedo.
Res.: 13752 Mary's Way, 22191. Tel: 703-494-2444; 703-494-5015; Fax: 703-494-0005. Web: www.olacc.org.
Catechesis/Religious Program—Tel: 703-494-3696; Fax: 703-494-3117. Email: religioused@olacc.org. Students 698.

WOODSTOCK, SHENANDOAH CO., ST. JOHN BOSCO (1888) Revs. Wilhelm J. Ettner; Richard J. Ley, Parochial Vicar. In Res., Rev. Zacharis Martinez.
Res.: 315 N. Main St., 22664. Tel: 540-459-4448; Fax: 540-459-4406. Email: office@sjbwoodstock.org. Web: www.sjbwoodstock.org.
Catechesis/Religious Program—Tel: 540-436-9342. Linda Spiker, D.R.E. Students 154.
Mission—Our Lady of the Shenandoah 240 Fretzel Way, P.O. Box 654, Basye, Shenandoah Co. 22810. Tel: 540-856-2411; Fax: 540-856-3043.

DIOCESAN MISSION PARISH

DOMINICAN REPUBLIC

1—SAN FRANCISCO DE ASIS, BANICA Revs. Keith M. O'Hare; Christopher D. Murphy.
Mailing Address: BM #7038, 3508 NW114 Ave., Doral, FL 33178.

2—SAN JOSE, PEDRO SANTANA Revs. Keith M. O'Hare; Christopher D. Murphy.
Mailing Address: BM #7038, 3508 NW 114 Ave., Doral, FL 33178.

On Duty Outside the Diocese:
Revs.—
Albertson, Eric J., Chap. Lt.Col., Fort Belvoir, VA
Gross, Lee W., S.T.L., Mount St. Mary Seminary, Emmitsburg, MD
Heisler, John F., Pontifical College Josephinum, Columbus, OH
Mode, Daniel L., Chap., LCDR, Groton, CT
Murphy, Christopher D., St. Joseph, Pedro Santana & Banica, Domincan Republic
Pollard, Christopher J., Permanent Observer, Mission of the Holy See to the United Nations, New York, NY
Riley, John J., Augustine Institute, Denver, CO
Terrien, Lawrence B., S.S., Dir. Spiritual Life Progs., Systematic Theology, St. Mary's Seminary & University, 5400 Roland Ave., Baltimore, MD 21210-1994
Weston, Michael D., Basilica of the National Shrine of the Immaculate Conception, Washington D.C.

Military Chaplains:
Revs.—
Albertson, Eric J., Chap., Lt.Col., Fort Belvoir, VA
Mode, Daniel L., Chap., CRMD, Virgina Beach, VA

On Leave of Absence:
Revs.—
Buckner, Christopher M.
Erbacher, William J.
Hamilton, Daniel E.
Tran, Nhi Dinh
Tucker, James A.

Retired:
Rev. Msgrs.—
Cosby, R. Roy, M.A., V.G., Rockville, VA
Hendrick, Frank J., Pinehurst, NC
Mahler, Frank E., Annandale, VA
Revs.—
Biniek, Joseph P., New Orleans, LA
Brooks, Robert C., Arlington, VA
Dair, Richard J., Annandale, VA
Daly, Jerome R., Fort Belvoir, VA
Irace, Dominic P., Lake Worth, FL
McGuill, Martin, J.C.D., Ft. Myer, VA
Mendez, Francisco, Annandale, VA
O'Brien, Cornelius, County Cork, Ireland
Richardson, M. Paul, Richmond, VA
Trinkle, Clarence M., Linden, VA
Trong, John T.B., Annandale, VA
Watkins, Clarence N., Falls Church, VA

Permanent Deacons:
Allen, Charles C., St. Francis of Assisi, Triangle
Anderson, Albert, St. Joseph, Alexandria
Arquette, Lester K., (Retired)
Avery, Dale R., Nativity, Burke
Bayne, James L., (Leave of Absence)
Bello, Thomas M., St. Anthony, Falls Church
Benin, Joseph G., St. John the Beloved, McLean
Bernaola, Alberto G., St. Mary Fredericksburg
Betit, Eugene D., (Leave of Absence)
Borchert, Robert F., St. Jude, Fredericksburg
Braun, Richard L., (Leave of Absence)
Burrell, Richard L., (Leave of Absence)
Caporiccio, Richard C., Queen of Apostles, Alexandria
Christianson, Edward L., Sacred Heart of Jesus, Winchester
Conroy, David E., Sr., St. Timothy, Chantilly; St. Patrick, Fredericksburg
Coutu, Charles A., St. Peter, Washington
deLadurantaye, Robert E., (Retired)
Demers, Richard L., Holy Family, Dale City
Dixon, Stephen J., St. Rita, Alexandria
Donovan, William J., J.C.L., St. Ann, Arlington
Eberlein, John W., All Saints, Manassas
Einsmann, W. Vincent, Holy Family, Dale City
Emley, William P., (Leave of Absence)
Fishenden, James A., St. James, Falls Church
Flores, Francisco, St. Francis of Assisi, Triangle
Fursman, Thomas M., St. Isidore The Farmer, Orange
Galvez, Rene A., Annunciation, West Hollywood, FL
George, Paul J., (Leave of Absence)
Gregory, Paul A., St. Matthew, Spotsylvania
Hammel, Lawrence V., St. Francis de Sales, Purcellville
Henry, Lawrence B., (Retired)
Hubbarth, John A., St. Matthew, Spotsylvania
Johnson, Danny E., Our Lady of Angels, Woodbridge
Kenski, Frank G., (Retired)
LaDuca, Nicholas J., Corpus Chrisit, South Riding
Lee, Paul, St. Paul Chung, Fairfax
Ligon, Jack M., St. Stephen the Martyr, Middleburg
Lopez, Jose J., St. Leo the Great, Fairfax
Lyons, Robert A., St. Jude, Fredericksburg
Malinowski, Leonard P., (Retired)
Mallon, John B., (Leave of Absence)
McCaffrey, David S., St. Michael, Annandale
McClay, John J., St. Patrick, Fredericksburg
Mendoza, Mario L., St. Anthony, Falls Church
Meyers, Jeffrey M., St. Mary, Fairfax
Moore, Gerald J., Sacred Heart, Manassas
Myskowski, Emil P., Our Lady of Angels, Woodbridge
Nguyen, Vincent Cong, St. Philip, Falls Church
Nickle, Dennis E., (Leave of Absence)
O'Connell, Richard T., All Saints, Manassas
Ochenkowski, J. Paul, St. Veronica, Chantilly
Ostrom, Roger T., St. Michael, Annandale
Pardo, Jose I., St. Charles Borromeo, Arlington
Pham, Kien Minh, Holy Martyrs of Vietnam, Arlington
Pivarnik, William D., (Retired)
Powers, William D., St. Bernadette, Springfield
Pyrek, William J., St. Jude the Apostle, Lewes, DE
Ramirez, Eduardo A., (Leave of Absence)
Resendes, Daniel F., (Retired)
Santiago, Joseph L., Holy Family, Dale City
Silva, Marques R., St. Mary, Fairfax
Singer, Joseph R., (Retired)
Smith, Richard P., St. William of York, Stafford
Soutuyo, Francisco R., (Leave of Absence)
Taub, Samuel M., (Retired)
Tirado, Ramon, Precious Blood, Culpeper
Vivaldi, Noel, St. Leo the Great, Fairfax
Wagner, John A., St. John Neumann, Reston
Wagner, Robert W., St. Elizabeth Ana, Seton, Lake Ridge
Whelan, Edward F., Jr., St. Matthew, Spotsylvania
White, Thomas G., Jr., Good Shepherd, Alexandria
Wolter, Thomas W.

INSTITUTIONS LOCATED IN THE DIOCESE

[A] COLLEGES AND UNIVERSITIES

ARLINGTON. *Marymount University*, 2807 N. Glebe Rd., 22207. Tel: 703-522-5600; Fax: 703-284-1595. Email: admissions@marymount.edu. Web: www.marymount.edu. Dr. Matthew D. Shank, Pres.; Rev. David M. Sharland, Y.A., Campus Min.; Zary Mostashari, Librarian; Rev. John P. Peterson, Y.A., Asst. Chap. Religious of the Sacred Heart of Mary., Resident and Non-resident coed students. Sisters 6; Lay Faculty & Staff 593; Students 3,600.

FRONT ROYAL. *Christendom College*, 134 Christendom Dr., 22630. Tel: 540-636-2900; Fax: 540-636-1655. Web: www.christendom.edu. Timothy T. O'Donnell, S.T.D., Pres.; Andrew Armstrong, Library Dir. Resident and Non-resident students. Priests 2; Lay Teachers 45; Students 425. In Res. Rev. Donald J. Planty, J.C.D.

[B] GRADUATE SCHOOLS

ARLINGTON. **The Institute for the Psychological Sciences, Inc.*, 2001 Jefferson Davis Hwy., Ste. 511, 22202. Tel: 703-416-1441; Fax: 703-416-8588. Email: info@ipsciences.edu. Web: www.ipsciences.edu. Gladys Sweeney, Ph.D., Dean; Rev. Charles Sikorsky, L.C. Dedicated to the development and promotion of approaches to psychology founded in the Catholic vision of the human person. Master of Science (M.S.) and Doctor of Psychology (Psy.D.) degrees in Clinical Psychology. Priests 2; Lay Facility 12; Lay Adjunct Faculty 5; Total Staff 11; Total Enrollment 82.

ALEXANDRIA. *Notre Dame Graduate School of Christendom College*, 4407 Sano St., 22312. Tel: 703-658-4304; Fax: 703-658-2318. Email: ndgs@christendom.edu. Web: www.christendom.edu/grad. Kristin P. Burns, Ph.D., Dean; Heidi Kalian, Registrar & Business Officer; Joseph Arias, Librarian. Priests 9; Sisters 1; Lay Teachers 12; Total Staff 4; Total Enrollment 200.

[C] DISTANCE UNIVERSITY

HAMILTON. *The Catholic Distance University*, 120 E. Colonial Hwy., 20158-9012. Tel: 888-254-4238; Fax: 540-338-4788. Email: cdu@cdu.edu. Web: www.cdu.edu. Most Rev. Paul S. Loverde, D.D., S.T.L., J.C.L., Bd. Chm.; Marianne Evans Mount, Ph.D., Pres.; Dr. Robert Royal, Ph.D., Dean Graduate Progs.; Sr. Mary Margaret Ann Schlather, S.N.D., Dean Catechetical Progs.; Rev. Bevil Bramwell, O.M.I., Ph.D., Dean Undergraduate Progs. Accredited University and Catechetical Institute offering M.A. in theology, B.A. degree completion in theology, A.A degree in catholic studies, catechetical diploma, advanced catechist certificates, continuing education, online seminars. All programs through distance and online education. No residency required. Adjunct Faculty 41; Staff 14; Total Staff 45; Students 1,800.

[D] HIGH SCHOOLS, DIOCESAN

ARLINGTON. *Bishop Denis J. O'Connell High School*, 6600 Little Falls Rd., 22213. Tel: 703-237-1400; Fax: 703-237-1465. Email: mrohrbach@bishopoconnell.org. Web: www.bishopoconnell.org. Kathleen Prebble, Pres.; Dr. Joseph E. Vorbach III, Ph.D., Prin.; Mr. John J. Gutter, Asst. Prin.; Sr. Catherine Hill, I.H.M., Asst. Prin.; Rev. James C. Hudgins, Chap. & Asst. Prin.; Mrs. Sue Baxter, Librarian. Priests 1; Sisters 5; Teachers 104; Total Staff 46; Students 1,218.

ALEXANDRIA. *Bishop Ireton High School*, 201 Cambridge Rd., 22314. Tel: 703-751-7606; Fax: 703-212-8173. Email: info@bishopireton.org. Web: www.bishopireton.org. Mr. Tim Hamer, Prin.; Rev. Edwin E. Perez, Chap.; Lindagale Dube, Librarian. Priests 1; Brothers 1; Sisters 2; Lay Teachers 60; Students 821.

DUMFRIES. *Pope John Paul the Great Catholic High School*, 17700 Dominican Dr., 22026. Tel: 703-445-0300; Fax: 703-445-0301. Web: www.jpthegreat.org. Sr. Mary Jordan Hoover, O.P., Prin.; Shawn McNulty, Asst. Prin. Student Life; Carl Patton, Asst. Prin. Academics; Rev. Matthew H. Zuberbueler, Chap.; Mrs. Cynthia Trax, Librarian; Donald Turner, Dir. Facilities; Dr. Patricia Smith, Dir. Guidance; Jennifer Cole, Dir. Admissions; Lori Strickland, Registrar; Dianna Tillgtson, Dir. Devel.; Joseph Redding, Business Mgr. Priests 1; Sisters 3; Lay Staff 36; Students 484.

FAIRFAX. *Paul VI Catholic High School*, 10675 Fairfax Blvd., 22030. Tel: 703-352-0925; Fax: 703-273-9845. Email: website@paulvi.net. Web: www.paulvi.net. Mrs. Virginia Colwell, Prin.; Thomas G. Opfer, Asst. Prin. & Dean of Academics; Eileen Hanley, Dir. of Admissions & Asst. Prin.; Rev. Joel D. Jaffe, Chap. & Asst. Prin.; Mary Jane Cochrane, Librarian. Priests 1; Deacons 1; Lay Teachers 81; Students 965.

[E] ELEMENTARY SCHOOLS, PRIVATE

BRISTOW. *Linton Hall*, (Grades PreK-8), 9535 Linton Hall Rd., 20136. Tel: 703-368-3157; Fax: 703-368-3036. Email: lintonhall@aol.com. Web: www.lintonhall.edu. Mrs. Elizabeth Poole, Prin.; Sr. Mary Patricia Herrity, O.S.B., Librarian. Benedictine Sisters of Virginia 4; Lay Teachers 22; Students 205.

[F] INTERPAROCHIAL SCHOOLS

CULPEPER. *Epiphany School*, (Grades PreK-8), Precious Blood, 114 E. Edmondson St., 22701. Tel: 540-825-9017; Fax: 540-825-8987. Email: office@epiphanycatholicschool.org. Web: www.epiphanycatholicschool.org. Wendy Murphy, Prin. Sponsoring parishes: Precious Blood, Culpeper; Our Lady of the Blue Ridge, Madison; St. Isidore, Orange and St. Peter Mission, Washington, VA. Lay Teachers 12; Students 135.

FALLS CHURCH. *Corpus Christi School*, (Grades PreK-8), And Early Childhood Center, 3301 Glen Carlyn Rd., 22041. Tel: 703-820-7450; Fax: 703-820-9635. Email: info@corpuschristischool.org. Web: www.corpuschristischool.org. J. A. Garcia, Prin.; Ann Stich, Dir. Early Childhood Center; D. Krafchek, Librarian. Sponsoring parishes: St. Anthony and St. Philip. Lay Teachers 25; Students 450.

FREDERICKSBURG. *Holy Cross Academy*, (Grades PreK-8), 250 Stafford Lakes Pkwy., 22406. Tel: 540-286-1600; Fax: 540-286-1625. Email: holycrossacademy@verizon.net. Web: www.holycrossweb.com. Sr. Susan Louise Eder, O.S.F.S., Prin.; Jennifer Buer, Librarian. Sponsoring parish: St. Mary, Fredericksburg. Oblate Sisters of St. Francis de Sales 4; Lay Teachers 28; Total Staff 42; Students 533.

WOODBRIDGE. *St. Thomas Aquinas Regional School*, (Grades PreK-8), 13750 Mary's Way, 22191. Tel: 703-491-4447; Fax: 703-492-8828. Email: office@aquinastars.org. Web: www.aquinastars.org. Sr. Maria Goretti Baker, O.P., Prin.; Mrs. Judy Beda, Librarian. Sponsoring parishes: Our Lady of Angels, Woodbridge; St. Elizabeth Ann Seton, Lake Ridge; and Sacred Heart, Manassas. Dominican Sisters, Congregation of St. Cecilia 4; Lay Teachers 34; Total Staff 64; Students 520.

[G] DAY CARE AND CHILD LEARNING CENTERS

ARLINGTON. *Holy Martyrs of Vietnam Child Enrichment Day Care Center* (Children 2 1/2-5 years), 915 S. Wakefield St., 22204. Tel: 703-920-1049; Fax: 703-553-0371. Email: tamila915@cs.com. Dr. Tamila Mostamandy, Dir. Lay Teachers 3; Students 38.

ALEXANDRIA. *Blessed Sacrament Grade School and Early Childhood Center*, (Grades PreK-8), 1417 W. Braddock Rd., 22302. Tel: 703-998-4170; Fax: 703-998-5033. Email: schoolinfo@blessedsacramentcc.org. Web: www.BlessedSacramentcc.org. Mrs. Valerie Garcia, Prin. Lay Teachers 45; Students 338.

St. Gabriel's (Children 2-5 years), 4319 Sano St., 22312. Tel: 703-354-0395; Fax: 703-354-0395. Sr. Maria D. Gonzalez, P.S.S.J., Local Supr. Poor Sisters of St. Joseph (Buenos Aires). Sisters 6; Lay Teachers 6; Students 50.

FALLS CHURCH. *Corpus Christi Early Childhood Center* (Children 3-5 years), 7506 St. Philip's Ct., 22042. Tel: 703-573-4570; Fax: 703-573-6832. Laura Zybrick, Prin.; Amy Fry, Dir.; Ann Stich, Dir. Sponsoring Parishes: St. Anthony and St. Philip. Lay Teachers 7; Students 174.

St. Joseph's Preschool (Children 2-5 years), 203 N. Spring St., 22046. Tel: 703-533-8441; Fax: 703-462-8621. Rodney Torp, Dir. Lay Teachers 22; Students 100.

[H] MONASTERIES AND RESIDENCES OF PRIESTS AND BROTHERS

ARLINGTON. *Missionhurst, C.I.C.M.-Central House and Provincialate*, 4651 N. 25th St., 22207. Tel: 703-528-3800; Fax: 703-528-5355. Email: provincial@missionhurst.org. Web: www.missionhurst.org. Revs. Anselme Malonda Nkuanga, C.I.C.M., Prov. Supr.; Joseph Giordano, C.I.C.M., Provincial Treas. & Dir. Promotion; Michael Hann, C.I.C.M., Rector; William Wyndaele, C.I.C.M.; John B. Peters, C.I.C.M.; Joseph Dewaele, C.I.C.M.; Randy Gonzales, C.I.C.M., Dir., Promotion; John Morel, C.I.C.M.

American I.H.M. Province, Inc.

Immaculate Heart Missions, Inc.

Missionhurst, Inc., Congregation of the Immaculate Heart of Mary foreign and home missions.

BERRYVILLE. *Cistercian Abbey of Our Lady of the Holy Cross*, 901 Cool Spring Ln., 22611-2700. Tel: 540-955-1425; Fax: 540-955-1356. Email: holycross@hcava.org. Web: www.hcava.org. Rt. Revs. Robert T. Barnes, O.C.S.O., Abbot; Edward McCorkell, O.C.S.O. (Retired); Revs. Edmund Flynn, O.C.S.O., Treas.; Paschal Balkan, O.C.S.O.; Andrew Gries, O.C.S.O.; Vincent Collins, O.C.S.O.; Maurice Flood, O.C.S.O.; Joseph Wittstock, O.C.S.O.; James Orthmann, O.C.S.O., Novice Master & Vocation Dir.; Malachy Marrion, O.C.S.O.; Bros. Stephen Maguire, O.C.S.O.; Barnabas Brownsey, O.C.S.O.; Christopher Harmon, O.C.S.O.; Edward McLean, O.C.S.O.; Luke Scheuerell, O.C.S.O.; Benedict Simmonds, O.C.S.O.; James Sommers, O.C.S.O.; Martin Statz, O.C.S.O.; Joseph Vantu, O.C.S.O., Prior; Efrain Sosa, O.C.S.O. Order of Cistercians of the Strict Observance (Trappist). Community 20; Residents 18; Priests 10; Solemnly Professed Non-priest Monks 10.

[I] CONVENTS AND RESIDENCES FOR SISTERS

ARLINGTON. *Religious of the Sacred Heart of Mary, Marymount Convent*, 2807 N. Glebe Rd., 22207-4299. Tel: 703-284-1495; Fax: 703-284-5992. Email: francisca.grace@marymount.edu. Web: www.rshm.org. Sisters Irene Cody; Francisca Grace; Jacqueline Murphy. Sisters 3.

Sisters Servants of the Immaculate Heart of Mary, 6600 Little Falls Rd., 22213. Tel: 703-237-1424; Fax: 703-237-1465. Email: ihmdjo@yahoo.com. Web: www.ihmimmaculata.org. Sr. Rose Marie DeCarlo, I.H.M., Supr. Sisters 8.

ALEXANDRIA. *Congregation of the Sisters of the Holy Cross*, 5582 First Statesman Ln., 22312. Tel: 703-658-9519.

Sisters of the Holy Cross, Inc. Sisters 2.

Daughters of St. Paul, 1025 King St., 22314. Tel: 703-549-3806; 703-549-1323 (Convent); Fax: 703-683-2568. Email: alexandria@pauline.org. Web: www.pauline.org. Sr. Christine Virginia, F.S.P., Local Supr.

St. Gabriel Convent, 4319 Sano St., 22312. Tel: 703-354-0395; Fax: 703-354-0395. Email: mgonzalezruiz@verizon.net. Sr. Maria D. Gonzalez, P.S.S.J., Local Supr. Poor Sisters of St. Joseph's Buenos Aires Regional House and Novitiate 5.

Poor Clare Monastery of Mary, Mother of the Church, 2505 Stonehedge Dr., 22306. Tel: 703-768-4918; Fax: 703-765-2985. Observing the Primitive Rule of St. Clare. Solemnly Professed 13; Simply (Temporary) Professed 1; Novices 1.

BRISTOW. *St. Benedict Monastery*, Benedictine Sisters of Virginia, 9535 Linton Hall Rd., 20136-1217. Tel: 703-361-0106; Fax: 703-361-0254. Email: cdwyerosb@comcast.net. Web: www.osbva.org. Sr. Cecilia Dwyer, O.S.B., Prioress. Tel: 703-368-4848. B.E.A.C.O.N.: Benedictine Educational Assistance Community Outreach to Neighbors, Benedictine Pastoral Center, Linton Hall School, Benedictine Counseling Center. Professed Sisters 29; Sisters Resident at Motherhouse 26.

FAIRFAX. *Adorers of the Holy Cross*, 10917 Marilta Ct., 22030. Tel: 703-591-0862; Fax: 703-591-0862. Email: mtgdlva@yahoo.com. Sr. Elizabeth Lien Nguyen, M.T.G., Supr. Sisters 8.

Sisters of Our Lady of La Salette (Grenoble, France), 10600 Cedar Ave., 22030-3112. Tel: 703-691-4294; Fax: 703-691-1767. Email: marijosnds@verizon.net; lasalette.sisters@yahoo.com. Web: www.geocities.com/lasalettesisters. Sr. Maria Josephine S. Valenton, S.N.D.S., Asst. Gen. & Mission Supr., U.S.A.

FRONT ROYAL. *Pax Christi Institute*, 1769 Quicksburg Rd., Quicksburg, 22847. Tel: 540-740-9108; Fax: 540-740-4236. Email: paxchristisister@yahoo.com. Sr. Mercedes Martinez, P.C.I., Supr. Sisters 2.

LINDEN. *Saint Dominic's Monastery, Dominican Nuns (Contemplative)*, 2636 Monastery Rd., 22642-5371. Tel: 540-635-3259; Fax: 540-635-5086. Email: lindenopnuns@aol.com. Sr. Mary Fidelis Stoll, O.P., Prioress. Solemnly Professed 6; Simply Professed 1; Novices 3; Postulants 3.

WOODBRIDGE. *Dominican Sisters Convent* (Congregation of St. Cecilia), 5009 Bobcat Ct., 22193. Tel: 703-878-7823; Fax: 703-878-7824. Email: smj.hoover@jpthegreat.org. Sr. Mary Jordan Hoover, O.P., Supr. Dominican Sisters. Sisters 7.

[J] RETREAT HOUSES

BERRYVILLE. *Retreat House, Holy Cross Abbey*, 901 Cool Spring Ln., 22611-2700. Tel: 540-955-4383; Fax: 540-955-1356. Email: information@hcava.org. Web: www.hcava.org.

MCLEAN. *Dominican Retreat House*, 7103 Old Dominion Dr., 22101-2799. Tel: 703-356-4243; Fax: 703-893-4502. Email: sragnes@dominicanretreat.org. Web: www.dominicanretreat.org. Dominican Sisters of St. Catherine De Ricci., Accommodations for 41 persons. Sisters 5.

[K] CAMPUS MINISTRY

ARLINGTON. *Marymount University* 2807 N. Glebe Rd., 22207. Tel: 703-284-1607; Fax: 703-284-3850. Email: father.david@marymount.edu. Web: www.marymount.edu. Revs. John P. Peterson, Y.A., Asst. Chap.; David M. Sharland, Y.A., Chap. & Dir. Campus Ministry

FAIRFAX. *George Mason University, Catholic Campus Ministry* 4515 Roberts Rd., 22032. Tel: 703-425-0022; Fax: 703-425-0753. Email: pnassett@gmu.edu. Web: gmuccm.org. Rev. Peter W. Nassetta, Y.A., Chap. & Dir. Campus Ministry; John More, Asst. Campus Min.

St. Robert Bellarmine Chapel George Mason University, 4515 Roberts Rd., 22032. Tel: 703-425-0022; Fax: 703-425-0753. Rev. Peter W. Nassetta, Y.A.; John More, Campus Min.; Catherine Horan, Asst. Campus Min. Catholic Campus Ministry.

FREDERICKSBURG. *University of Mary Washington* Catholic Campus Ministry, 1614 College Ave., 22401. Tel: 540-373-6746; Fax: 540-518-9086. Email: father@umwccm.org. Web: umwccm.org. Rev. Frederick H. Edlefsen, Chap.; Molly Milroy, Asst. to the Chap.; Veronica Knickerbocker, Admin. Asst.

[L] MISCELLANEOUS

ARLINGTON. *Arlington Diocesan Investment and Loan Corp.*, 200 N. Glebe Rd., Ste. 914, 22203. Tel: 703-841-2500; Fax: 703-524-5028. Very Rev. Mark S. Mealey, O.S.F.S., J.C.D., Ph.D., V.G., J.V., Pres.

The Foundation for the Catholic Diocese of Arlington, Inc., 200 N. Glebe Rd., Ste. 914, 22203. Tel: 703-841-2500; Fax: 703-524-5028. Very Rev. Mark S. Mealey, O.S.F.S., J.C.D., Ph.D., V.G., J.V., Pres.

Rooted in Faith-Forward in Hope, Inc., 200 N. Glebe Rd., Ste. 914, 22203. Tel: 703-841-2500; Fax: 703-524-5028. Very Rev. Mark S. Mealey, O.S.F.S., J.C.D., Ph.D., V.G., J.V., Pres.

The Women's Apostolate to Youth, 5600 N. 16th St., 22205. Tel: 703-534-5821. Email: robinmaas@verizon.net. Web: womensapostolatetoyouth.blogspot.com. Dr. Robin Maas, Dir.

Youth Apostles Institute, An Association of Christian Faithful, 1600 Carlin Ln., McLean, 22101-4100. Tel: 703-556-0914; Fax: 703-556-9455. Email: administrator@youthapostles.org. Web: www.youthapostles.org. Revs. John P. Peterson, Y.A., Dir.; Ramon Dominguez, Y.A.; Michael F. Kuhn, Y.A.; Peter W. Nassetta, Y.A.; David M. Sharland, Y.A.; Mr. Thomas Duesterhaus; Mr. Thomas Yehl.

FAIRFAX. *Alpha Omega Clinic and Consultation Services*, 3607A Chain Bridge Rd., Ste. 105, 22030. Tel: 301-767-1733; Fax: 301-767-1743. Email: alphaomegaclinic@verizon.net. Web: www.aoccs.org.

**Divine Mercy Care*, 11096A Lee Hwy. Ste. 101, 22030. Tel: 703-934-5552, Ext. 304; Fax: 703-766-5500. Email: info@divinemercycare.org. Web: www.divinemercycare.org. John Bruchalski, M.D., F.A.C.O.G., Board Chm.

FRONT ROYAL. **Human Life International*, 4 Family Life Ln., 22630. Tel: 540-635-7884; Fax: 540-622-6247. Email: hli@hli.org. Web: www.hli.org. Rev. Shenan J. Boquet, Pres.

**Seton Home Study School*, 1350 Progress Dr., 22630. Tel: 540-636-9990; Fax: 540-636-1602. Email: info@setonhome.org. Web: www.setonhome.org. Dr. Mary K. Clark, Dir.

MCLEAN. *Crusaders of St. Mary*, 2001 Great Falls St., 22101. Tel: 703-536-3546. Email: aperezalca@cox.net. Antonio Perez-Alcala, Local Dir.

SPOTSYLVANIA. *St. Francis Catholic Worker West*, 9631 Peppertree Rd., 22553. Tel: 540-972-3218. Web:

www.catholicworker.org. Mr. John Mahoney, Vice Pres. Total in Residence 2.

VIENNA. *Mount Tabor Society, Inc.*, 2363 Hunter Mill Rd., 22181. Tel: 703-938-2564. Rev. Paul G. Wynants, C.I.C.M., Dir. A House of Prayer and Christian Community.

RELIGIOUS INSTITUTES OF MEN REPRESENTED IN THE DIOCESE

For further details refer to the corresponding bracketed number in the Religious Institutes of Men or Women section.

[]—*Apostles of Jesus*—A.J.

[0350]—*Cistercians Order of the Strict Observance* (Trappists)—O.C.S.O.

[0650]—*Congregation of the Holy Spirit*—C.S.Sp.

[]—*Diocesan Laborer Priests*

[0260]—*Discalced Carmelite Friars*—O.C.D.

[0520]—*Franciscan Friars* (Holy Name Prov.)—O.F.M.

[0530]—*Franciscan Friars of the Atonement*—S.A.

[0860]—*Missionhurst Congregation of the Immaculate Heart of Mary*—C.I.C.M.

[0920]—*Oblates of St. Francis de Sales* (Wilmington-Philadelphia Prov.)—O.S.F.S.

[]—*Order of St. Augustine (Augustinians)*—O.S.A.

[0975]—*Society of Our Lady of the Most Holy Trinity*—S.O.L.T.

[0700]—*St. Joseph Society of the Sacred Heart* (Baltimore, MD)—S.S.J.

[0560]—*Third Order Regular of Saint Francis* (Sacred Heart Prov.)—T.O.R.

[]—*Vietnamese Dominican Fathers* (Calgary, Alberta, Canada)—O.P.

[]—*Youth Apostles*—Y.A.

RELIGIOUS INSTITUTES OF WOMEN REPRESENTED IN THE DIOCESE

[4155]—*Adorers of the Holy Cross*—M.T.G.

[0230]—*Benedictine Sisters of Virginia*—O.S.B.

[1920]—*Congregation of the Sisters of the Holy Cross*—C.S.C.

[0960]—*Daughters of Wisdom*—D.W.

[1070-17]—*Dominican Sisters Congregation of St. Catherine deRicci*—O.P.

[1070-07]—*Dominican Sisters Congregation of St. Cecilia*—O.P.

[1365]—*Franciscan Missionary Sisters of the Infant Jesus*—F.M.I.J.

[1250]—*Franciscan Sisters of the Eucharist*—F.S.E.

[]—*Franciscan Sisters of the Immaculate Conception of Glasgow, Scotland*—O.S.F.

[1880]—*Handmaidens of Reparation of the Sacred Heart of Jesus*—A.R.

[3060]—*Oblate Sisters of St. Francis de Sales*—O.S.F.S.

[3760]—*Order of St. Clare (Cloistered)*—P.C.C.

[]—*Pax Christi Institute* (Corpus Christi, TX)—P.C.I.

[0950]—*Pious Society of Daughters of St. Paul*—F.S.P.

[3250]—*Poor Sisters of St. Joseph*—P.S.S.J.

[3465]—*Religious of the Sacred Heart of Mary* (Eastern North Amer. Prov.)—R.S.H.M.

[]—*Sisters of Charity of the Blessed Virgin Mary*—B.V.M.

[2575]—*Sisters of Mercy of the Americas*—R.S.M.

[2990]—*Sisters of Notre Dame*—S.N.D.

[3000]—*Sisters of Notre Dame de Namur*—S.N.D.deN.

[]—*Sisters of Our Lady of La Salette* (Grenoble, France)—S.N.D.S.

[3893]—*Sisters of St. Joseph of Chestnut Hill* (Philadelphia)—S.S.J.

[]—*Sisters of St. Paul of Chartres*—S.P.C.

[]—*Sisters of the Holy Cross*—C.S.C.

[]—*Sisters of the Humility of Mary*—H.M.

[2170]—*Sisters, Servants of the Immaculate Heart of Mary*—I.H.M.

NECROLOGY

✠ Estabrook, Most Rev. Joseph W., Auxiliary Bishop for the Military Services, U.S.A.—Died Feb. 4, 2012

† Cassidy, Rev. Msgr. Thomas J., (Retired)—Died Oct. 1, 2011

† Loftus, Joseph J., (Retired)—Died April 2, 2011

An asterisk (*) denotes an organization that has established tax-exempt status directly with the IRS and is not covered by the USCCB Group Ruling.

Archdiocese of Atlanta

(Archidioecesis Atlantensis)

Most Reverend

WILTON D. GREGORY, S.L.D.

Archbishop of Atlanta; ordained May 9, 1973; appointed Auxiliary Bishop of Chicago and Titular Bishop of Oliva October 31, 1983; consecrated December 13, 1983; appointed Bishop of Belleville December 29, 1993; installed February 10, 1994; appointed Archbishop of Atlanta December 9, 2004; installed January 17, 2005.

Most Reverend

LUIS R. ZARAMA

Auxiliary Bishop of Atlanta; ordained November 27, 1993; appointed Auxiliary Bishop of Atlanta and Titular Bishop of Bararus July 27, 2009; consecrated September 29, 2009.

Catholic Center Archdiocese of Atlanta: 2401 Lake Park Dr., Smyrna, GA 30080-8862. Tel: 404-920-7300; Fax: 404-920-7301.

Web: www.archatl.com

ESTABLISHED JULY 2, 1956.

Square Miles 21,445.

Canonically Erected November 8, 1956; created an Archdiocese February 21, 1962.

Comprises the 69 Counties in the northern part of the State of Georgia, north of and including the following counties: Lincoln, McDuffie, Warren, Hancock, Baldwin, Putnam, Jasper, Monroe, Upson, Meriwether and Troup

Patrons of the Archdiocese: I. Our Blessed Lady under the title of the Immaculate Heart of Mary; II. Saint Pius X.

For legal titles of parishes and archdiocesan institutions, consult the Archbishop's office.

STATISTICAL OVERVIEW

Personnel	
Archbishops	1
Auxiliary Bishops	1
Abbots	1
Priests: Diocesan Active in Diocese	150
Priests: Diocesan Active Outside Diocese	2
Priests: Retired, Sick or Absent	30
Number of Diocesan Priests	182
Religious Priests in Diocese	69
Total Priests in Diocese	251
Extern Priests in Diocese	23
Ordinations:	
Diocesan Priests	7
Transitional Deacons	3
Permanent Deacons	16
Permanent Deacons in Diocese	235
Total Brothers	33
Total Sisters	86
Parishes	
Parishes	88
With Resident Pastor:	
Resident Diocesan Priests	69
Resident Religious Priests	19
Missions	9
Professional Ministry Personnel:	
Brothers	10
Sisters	11
Lay Ministers	163
Welfare	
Catholic Hospitals	5
Total Assisted	348,989
Homes for the Aged	3
Total Assisted	95
Special Centers for Social Services	5
Total Assisted	22,000
Educational	
Diocesan Students in Other Seminaries	38
Total Seminarians	38
High Schools, Diocesan and Parish	3
Total Students	2,444
High Schools, Private	4
Total Students	1,363
Elementary Schools, Diocesan and Parish	15
Total Students	6,191
Elementary Schools, Private	4
Total Students	1,883
Catechesis/Religious Education:	
High School Students	8,816
Elementary Students	30,050
Total Students under Catholic Instruction	50,785
Teachers in the Diocese:	
Priests	17
Brothers	3
Sisters	15
Lay Teachers	1,143
Vital Statistics	
Receptions into the Church:	
Infant Baptism Totals	7,741
Minor Baptism Totals	707
Adult Baptism Totals	546
Received into Full Communion	1,166
First Communions	8,514
Confirmations	4,806
Marriages:	
Catholic	956
Interfaith	348
Total Marriages	1,304
Deaths	1,315
Total Catholic Population	119,235
Total Population	332,598

Former Bishops—Most Revs. FRANCIS E. HYLAND, D.D., J.C.D., appt. Titular Bishop of Gomphi and Auxiliary Bishop of Savannah-Atlanta, Oct. 15, 1949; cons. Dec. 21, 1949; First Bishop of Atlanta, July 17, 1956; installed on Nov. 8, 1956; resigned and appointed Titular Bishop of Bisica, Oct. 11, 1961; died Jan. 31, 1968; PAUL J. HALLINAN, D.D., appt. Bishop of Charleston, Sept. 9, 1958; cons. Oct. 28, 1958; elevated to the Archiepiscopal dignity, Feb. 21, 1962; installed First Archbishop of Atlanta, March 29, 1962; died March 27, 1968; JOSEPH L. BERNARDIN, D.D., appt. Auxiliary of Atlanta, March 9, 1966; cons. April 26, 1966; appt. Gen. Sec. U.S.C.C., April 5, 1968; died Nov. 14, 1996.; THOMAS A. DONNELLAN, appt. Bishop of Ogdensburg, March 4, 1964; cons. April 9, 1964; appt. to Atlanta, May 29, 1968; installed July 16, 1968; died Oct. 15, 1987; EUGENE A. MARINO, S.S.J., D.D., appt. Auxiliary of Washington, July 15, 1974; appt. Archbishop of Atlanta, March 14, 1988; installed May 5, 1988; resigned July 10, 1990; died Nov. 12, 2000; JAMES P. LYKE, O.F.M., Ph.D., appt. Auxiliary Bishop of Cleveland and Titular Bishop of Fornos Maggiore, June 30, 1979; cons. Aug. 1, 1979; appt. Apostolic Administrator Archdiocese of Atlanta, July 10, 1990; appt. Archbishop of Archdiocese of Atlanta, April 30, 1991; installed June 24, 1991; Palium conferred June 29, 1991; died Dec. 27, 1992; JOHN FRANCIS DONOGHUE, D.D., ord. June 4, 1955; appt. Bishop of Charlotte Nov. 6, 1984; installed second Bishop Dec. 18, 1984; appt. Archbishop of Atlanta June 22, 1993; installed Aug. 18, 1993; retired Dec. 9, 2004; died Nov. 11, 2011.

Vicars General—Most Rev. LUIS R. ZARAMA, J.C.L., V.G.. Email: lzarama@archatl.com; Rev. Msgr. W. JOSEPH CORBETT, V.G., Moderator of the Curia. Tel: 404-920-7315; Fax: 404-920-7316. Email: jcorbett@archatl.com. Senior Executive Assistants: KIRIAL DEROZAS-MILES. Tel: 404-920-7319; Fax: 404-920-7316. Email: kderozas-miles@archatl.com; LISA JONES. Tel: 404-920-7321; Fax: 404-920-7316. Email: ljones@archatl.com.

Chancellor—Tel: 404-920-7325; Fax: 404-920-7326. Deacon DENNIS J. DORNER. Tel: 404-920-7325; Fax: 404-920-7326. Email: ddorner@archatl.com; MARDESSA SMITH, Exec. Asst. Tel: 404-920-7328; Fax: 404-920-7326. Email: mwsmith@archatl.com; KELLY KNIGHT, Administrative Asst. Tel: 404-920-7307; Fax: 404-920-7326. Email: kknigh@archatl.com.

Judicial Vicar—Very Rev. PEDRO POLOCHE, J.C.L., J.V., 2401 Lake Park Dr., Smyrna, 30080-8862. Tel: 404-920-7500; Fax: 404-920-7501. Email: ppoloche@archatl.com.

Secretary for Finance—BRADLEY WILSON, CFO, 2401 Lake Park Dr., Smyrna, 30080-8862. Tel: 404-920-7404; Fax: 404-920-7401. Email: bwilson@archatl.com.

Secretary for Catholic Charities—JOSEPH J. KRYGIEL, 2401 Lake Park Dr., Smyrna, 30080-8862. Tel: 404-885-7476; Fax: 404-885-7477. Email: jkrygiel@catholiccharitiesatlanta.org.

Secretary for Communications—PATRICIA CHIVERS, 2401 Lake Park Dr., Smyrna, 30080-8862. Tel: 404-920-7344; Fax: 404-920-7341. Email: pchivers@archatl.com.

Secretary for Schools—DIANE STARKOVICH, Ph.D., 2401 Lake Park Dr., Smyrna, 30080-8862. Tel: 404-920-7700; Fax: 404-920-7701. Email: dstarkovich@archatl.com.

Secretary for Office of Formation and Discipleship—AMY S. DANIELS, 2401 Lake Park Dr., Smyrna, 30080-8862. Tel: 404-920-7624; Fax: 404-920-7621. Email: adaniels@archatl.com.

Secretary for Human Resources—CHARLES THIBAUDEAU, 2401 Lake Park Dr., Smyrna, 30080-8862. Tel: 404-920-7482; Fax: 404-920-7481. Email: cthibaudeau@archatl.com.

Archbishop's Office—Most Rev. WILTON D. GREGORY,

S.L.D., Office of the Archbishop, 2401 Lake Park Dr., Smyrna, 30080-8862. Tel: 404-920-7300; Fax: 404-920-7301. Email: archbishop@archatl.com. Web: www.archatl.com; KENYA GRAHAM, Senior Exec. Asst. Tel: 404-920-7303; Fax: 404-920-7301. Email: kgraham@archatl.com; GERALDINE DEW, Administrative Asst. Tel: 404-920-7304; Fax: 404-920-7301. Email: gdew@archatl.com.

College of Consultors—Most Rev. LUIS R. ZARAMA, J.C.L., V.G.; Rev. Msgr. W. JOSEPH CORBETT, V.G.; Rev. FRANCIS G. MCNAMEE; Very Revs. PEDRO POLOCHE, J.C.L., J.V.; PETER J. RAU, V.F.; Revs. JAMES A. SCHILLINGER, S.T.L., V.F.; PAUL W. BERNY, M.Div.; Very Revs. ALBERT W. JOWDY, V.F., M.Div.; JOHN WALSH, V.F.

Deans—Very Rev. PETER J. RAU, V.F., North Metro Deanery; Rev. G. PHILIP RYAN, V.F., Southeast Deanery; Very Revs. TERENCE CRONE, V.F., Northeast Deanery; ALBERT W. JOWDY, V.F., M.Div., Northeast Metro Deanery; DAVID MCGUINNESS, V.F., East Deanery; Revs. JOHN KOZIOL, O.F.M.Conv., V.F., South Deanery; DANIEL J. FLEMING, V.F., Southwest Deanery; Very Revs. JAMES D. DUFFY, S.M., M.Div., V.F., Central Deanery; RANDALL T. MATTOX, V.F., M.Div., Northwest Deanery; JOHN WALSH, V.F., Northwest Metro Deanery; Rev. JOHN KOZIOL, O.F.M.Conv., V.F., South Deanery; Very Revs. JAMES D. DUFFY, S.M., M.Div., V.F., Central Deanery; TERENCE CRONE, V.F., Northeast Deanery.

Priest Personnel—2401 Lake Park Dr., Smyrna, 30080-8862. Rev. FRANCIS G. MCNAMEE, Dir. Email: frfrank@ctking.com; JUNE OWENS, Exec. Asst. Tel: 404-920-7333; Fax: 404-920-7331. Email: jowens@archatl.com.

Vicars for Clergy—Rev. Msgr. FRANCIS PHUONG; Rev. FRANCIS G. MCNAMEE; Very Revs. KEVIN J. HARGADEN, M.Div.; RICHARD B. MORROW (Retired); PEDRO POLOCHE, J.C.L., J.V.; Rev. Msgr. HENRY C. GRACZ.

Vicar for Consecrated Life—Sr. MARGARET MCANOY, I.H.M., 2401 Lake Park Dr., Smyrna, 30080-8862. Tel: 404-920-7652.

Archdiocesan Offices

Archives and Records—2401 Lake Park Dr., Smyrna, 30080-8862. Tel: 404-920-7694. Deacon DENNIS J. DORNER, Chancellor. Email: ddorner@archatl.com; CAROLYN DENTON, Dir. Archives & Records. Tel: 404-920-7692. Email: cdenton@archatl.com; BRIDGET T. LERETTE, C.A., Archivist. Tel: 404-920-7693. Email: blerette@archatl.com; Research Room: Tel: 404-920-7694.

Black Catholic Ministry—2401 Lake Park Dr., Smyrna, 30080-8862. Tel: 404-920-7530; Fax: 404-920-7531. Web: www.obcm.org. CHARLES PREJEAN, Dir. Tel: 404-920-7534; Fax: 404-920-7531. Email: cprejean@archatl.com.

Campus Ministry—2401 Lake Park Dr., Smyrna, 30080-8862. Tel: 404-920-7620; Fax: 404-920-7621. Web: www.archatl.com. VACANT.

Catholic Charities of the Archdiocese of Atlanta, Inc.—2401 Lake Park Dr., Smyrna, 30080-8862. Tel: 404-888-7816; Fax: 404-885-7477 (Confidential Fax). Web: www.catholiccharitiesatlanta.org. JOSEPH J. KRYGIEL, Sec. Catholic Charities, CEO & Member of the Secretariat. Tel: 404-885-7476; Fax: 404-885-7477. Email: jkrygiel@catholiccharitiesatlanta.org. Village of St. Joseph Counseling Services, Pregnancy, Parenting & Adoption Program, Immigration Legal Services Program, Refugee Resettlement Services, Disaster Preparedness & Response, Family Enrichment Program, Parish Social Justice Ministries; ROCCO TESTANI, Catholic Charities Bd. Chm. Tel: 404-853-8390. Email: rocco.testani@sutherland.com; JOSEPH GALVIN, COO. Tel: 404-885-7258; Fax: 404-888-7816. Email: jgalvin@catholiccharitiesatlanta.org; KELLEY KENER, Sr. Dir. Devel. & Mktg. Tel: 404-885-7474; Fax: 404-885-7477. Email: kkener@catholiccharitiesatlanta.org.

Catholic Housing Initiatives, Inc.—JOSEPH J. KRYGIEL, 2401 Lake Park Dr., Smyrna, 30080-8862. Tel: 404-885-7476; Fax: 404-885-7477.

Saint Joseph Place—2973 Butner Rd., S.W., Atlanta, 30331. Tel: 404-346-0745; Fax: 404-346-0747. LARGINE JOHNSON, Mgr.

Catholic Construction Services, Inc.—2401 Lake Park Dr., Smyrna, 30080-8862. Tel: 404-920-7860; Fax: 404-920-7861. GEORGE BARRIE, Pres., CEO & Member of the Secretariat. Tel: 404-920-7862; Fax: 404-920-7861. Email: gbarrie@archatl.com; DONNA L. WORLEY, Office Mgr. & Land Acquisitions. Tel: 404-920-7863; Fax: 404-920-7861. Email: dworley@archatl.com; RACHEL WHITE, Administrative Asst. Tel: 404-920-7865; Fax: 404-920-7861. Email: rwhite@archatl.com.

Field Representatives/Quality Control—RANDY HOOD. Tel: 404-920-7867; Fax: 404-920-7861. Email: rhood@archatl.com; DICK JANSEN. Tel: 404-920-7864; Fax: 404-920-7861. Email: djansen@archatl.com.

Project Managers—DENNIS W. KELLY. Tel: 404-920-7868; Fax: 404-920-7861. Email: dkelly@archatl.com; CARL TREVATHAN. Tel: 404-920-7866; Fax: 404-920-7861. Email: ctrevathan@archatl.com.

Catholic Foundation of North Georgia—780 Johnson Ferry Rd., Ste. 750, Atlanta, 30342. Tel: 404-497-9440; Fax: 404-497-9442. Web: www.cfnga.org. NANCY DINKA COVENY, Exec. Dir. Email: ncoveny@cfnga.org; DIANE DUQUETTE, Dir. Gift Planning. Email: dduquette@cfnga.org; AUBREY WHITTIER, Exec. Asst. Email: awhittier@cfnga.org.

Catholic Schools—2401 Lake Park Dr., Smyrna, 30080-8862. Tel: 404-920-7700; Fax: 404-920-7701. Web: www.archatl.com. DIANE STARKOVICH, Ph.D., Supt. & Member of the Secretariat. Tel: 404-920-7700; Fax: 404-920-7701. Email: dstarkovich@archatl.com; THOMAS R. CAMPBELL, Assoc. Supt. Tel: 404-920-7706; Fax: 404-920-7701. Email: tcampbell@archatl.com; MEGAN HUME, Asst. to Supt. Tel: 404-920-7708; Fax: 404-920-7701. Email: mhume@archatl.com; NANCY DILLY, School Psychologist. Tel: 404-920-7713; Fax: 404-920-7701. Email: ndilly@archatl.com; TERRY GRAHAM, Dir. Parish Pre-Schools. Tel: 404-920-7704; Fax: 404-920-7701. Email: tgraham@archatl.com; CECI MCAULIFFE, Dir. Special Svcs. Tel: 404-920-7705; Fax: 404-920-7701. Email: cmcauliffe@archatl.com; DONNA TOMLINSON, Administrative Asst. to School Psychologist. Tel: 404-920-7709; Fax: 404-920-7701. Email: dtomlinson@archatl.com; TAMARA CROCKETT, Receptionist & Administrative Asst. Tel: 404-920-7702; Fax: 404-920-7701. Email: tcrockett@archatl.com.

Chancery Facility Management (CFM)—2401 Lake Park Dr., Smyrna, 30080. Tel: 404-920-7876; Fax: 404-920-7875. ROB MCKINNON, Dir. Email: rmckinnon@archatl.com; PORTIA RILEY, Office Mgr. Email: priley@archatl.com. Facililties Supervisors: ARTHUR GLOVER. Email: aglover@archatl.com; JOE TRUITT. Email: jtruitt@archatl.com; CHRISTOPHER WYNNE. Email: cwynne@archatl.com.

Child and Youth Protection—2401 Lake Park Dr., Smyrna, 30080-8862. Tel: 404-920-7550; 888-437-0764 (24 Hour Reporting Hotline); Fax: 404-920-7551. Email: ocyp@archatl.com. MARY SUSAN STUBBS, Dir. & Victim Asst. Coord. Tel: 404-920-7550; Cell: 404-456-4043; Tel: 888-437-0764 24 Hour Reporting Hotline; Fax: 404-920-7551. Email: sstubbs@archatl.com; JENNIFER BROEL, Dir. Safe Environment. Tel: 404-920-7550; 888-437-0764 (24 Hour Reporting Hotline); Fax: 404-920-7551; MARIANNE "MAC" FRONEK, Sec. Tel: 404-920-7550; Fax: 404-920-7551. Email: mfronek@archatl.com.

Communications—2401 Lake Park Dr., Smyrna, 30080-8862. Tel: 404-920-7340; Fax: 404-920-7341. Web: www.archatl.com. PATRICIA CHIVERS, Dir. & Member of the Secretariat. Tel: 404-920-7344; Fax: 404-920-7341. Email: pchivers@archatl.com; MEAGHAN SCHROEDER, Asst. Dir. Communications. Tel: 404-920-7345; Fax: 404-920-7341. Email: mschroeder@archatl.com; JONATHON HANTEN, Web Devel. Tel: 404-920-7343; Fax: 404-920-7341. Email: jhanten@archatl.com; DAVID PACE, Creative Dir. Tel: 404-920-7342; Fax: 404-920-7341. Email: dpace@archatl.com; JOY PLACE, Administrative Asst. Tel: 404-920-7346; Fax: 404-920-7341. Email: jplace@archatl.com; MARIA BRASWELL, Translator. Tel: 404-920-7349; Fax: 404-920-7341. Email: mbraswell@archatl.com.

"The Georgia Bulletin"—MARY ANNE CASTRANIO, Exec. Editor. Tel: 404-920-7440; Fax: 404-920-7431. Email: mcastranio@archatl.com.

Respect Life—MARY BOYERT, Dir. Tel: 404-920-7362; Fax: 404-920-7361. Email: mboyert@archatl.com.

Jail and Prison Ministry—Deacon RICHARD P. TOLCHER, Dir. Tel: 404-920-7357; Fax: 404-920-7356. Email: rtolcher@archatl.com.

Social Justice Ministries—KAT DOYLE, Dir. Tel: 404-920-7897. Email: kdoyle@archatl.com; LESLYE COLVIN. Tel: 404-920-7898; Fax: 404-920-7896. Email: lcolvin@archatl.com.

Georgia Catholic Conference—FRANK MULCAHY, Dir. Tel: 404-920-7367. Email: fmulcahy@archatl.com.

Disabilities Ministry—Mr. ED MCCOY, Dir. Tel: 404-920-7682; Fax: 404-920-7681. Email: emccoy@archatl.com.

Court of Appeals - Province of Atlanta—2401 Lake Park Dr., Smyrna, 30080-8862. Tel: 404-920-7560; Fax: 404-920-7561.

Judicial Vicar—Very Rev. PAUL J. HACHEY, S.M., J.C.L., M.C.L., M.Div. Email: phachey@archatl.com; MARGUERITE V. FORTINO, B.M., Sec. Email: mfortino@archatl.com.

Defenders of the Bond—Rev. Msgr. PETER A. DORA, M.Div.; Rev. DANIEL J. MCCORMICK, B.A.; Ms. ROBERTA I. SIEGWALD.

Judges—Rev. GREGORY D. GOOLSBY, M.Div., J.D.; Very Rev. ALBERT W. JOWDY, V.F., M.Div.; Rev. VICTOR A. GALIER, M.Div.; Rev. Msgr. R. DONALD KIERNAN, P.A., D.P.A., Ph.D., LL.D.; Very Rev. RICHARD B. MORROW (Retired); Rev. JAMES A. SCHILLINGER, S.T.L., V.F.

Advocates—Rev. Msgr. HENRY C. GRACZ; Rev. PAUL W. BERNY, M.Div.; Very Rev. RANDALL T. MATTOX, V.F., M.Div.; Revs. VICTOR J. REYES, M.Div.; ERIC HILL, M.Div.; Very Rev. KEVIN J. HARGADEN, M.Div.; Deacons DENNIS J. DORNER; PAUL S. SWOPE JR.

Notaries—MARGUERITE V. FORTINO, B.M.; MARIANNE "MAC" FRONEK.

Promoter of Justice—Rev. DANIEL J. MCCORMICK, B.A.

Office For Divine Worship—2401 Lake Park Dr., SE, Smyrna, 30080. Rev. THEODORE R. BOOK, S.L.L., Dir. Tel: 404-920-7228; Fax: 404-920-7336. Email: tbook@archatl.com; PATRICIA DEJARNETT, Ph.D., Asst. to Dir. Tel: 404-920-7339; Fax: 404-920-7336; CLAIRE GILLIGAN, Assoc. Dir. Tel: 404-920-7337; Fax: 404-920-7336. Email: cgilligan@archatl.com.

Office of Formation and Discipleship—2401 Lake Park Dr., Smyrna, 30080-8862. Tel: 404-920-7620; Fax: 404-920-7621. Web: www.archatl.com. AMY S. DANIELS, Dir. & Member of the Secretariat. Tel: 404-920-7624; Fax: 404-920-7621. Email: adaniels@archatl.com; IVONNE S. VREELAND, Office Mgr. Tel: 404-920-7623; Fax: 404-920-7621. Email: ivreeland@archatl.com; AN D. TRAN, Communications Coord. Tel: 404-920-7634; Fax: 404-920-7621. Email: atran@archatl.com.

Associate Director of Religious Education—Tel: 404-920-7620; Fax: 404-920-7621. Email: ofd@archatl.com.

Assistant Director of Family Life/Pastoral Care—Tel: 404-920-7620; Fax: 404-920-7621. Email: ofd@archatl.com.

Assistant Director of Youth/Young Adult—Tel: 404-920-7620; Fax: 404-920-7621. Email: ofd@archatl.com.

Religious Education Administrative Assistant—Tel: 404-920-7620; Fax: 404-920-7621. Email: ofd@archatl.com.

Associate Director Professional Development—Tel: 404-920-7620; Fax: 404-920-7621. Email: ofd@archatl.com.

Professional Development Administrative Assistant—Tel: 404-920-7620; Fax: 404-920-7621. Email: ofd@archatl.com.

Associate Director of Evangelization—Tel: 404-920-7620; Fax: 404-920-7621. Email: ofd@archatl.com.

Retrouvaille—Coordinators: SCOTT HALL; DENISE HALL, 2401 Lake Park Dr., S.E., Smyrna, 30080. Tel: 770-495-8592. Web: www.retrouvailleofatlanta.org.

Engaged Encounter—Coordinators: YVONNE GREEN; JIM GREEN, 2401 Lake Park Dr., S.E., Smyrna, 30080. Tel: 404-216-9502. Web: www.atlcee.org.

LLASU-Llamados a Ser Uno— (Marriage preparation in Spanish). Co Directors: MIGUEL ZUMARAN; VANGIE ZUMARAN, 2401 Lake Park Dr., S.E., Smyrna, 30080. Tel: 678-327-6388. Web: www.archatl.com.

Family Ministry/Pastoral Care Ministry—IVONNE S. VREELAND, Office Mgr. Tel: 404-885-7484; Fax: 404-885-7473. Email: ivreeland@archatl.com.

Family Ministry—

*Retrouvaille—2401 Lake Park Dr., S.E., Smyrna, 30080*Web: www.retrouvailleofatlanta.org.

Finance Office—2401 Lake Park Dr., Smyrna, 30080-8862. Tel: 404-920-7400; Fax: 404-920-7401. BRADLEY WILSON, CFO & Member of the Secretariat. Tel: 404-920-7404; Fax: 404-920-7401. Email: bwilson@archatl.com; MICHAEL WARREN, Controller. Tel: 404-920-7411; Fax: 404-920-7401. Email: mwarren@archatl.com; ELSA RULLAN, Planning Mgr. Tel: 404-920-7403; Fax: 404-920-7401. Email: erullan@archatl.com; PATRICK WARNER, Parish Systems Mgr. Tel: 404-920-7410; Fax: 404-920-7401. Email: pwarner@archatl.com; ANN PITRA, Office Mgr. Tel: 404-920-7426; Fax: 404-920-7401. Email: apitra@archatl.com; MELISSA CHAPMAN, Accounting Mgr. Tel: 404-920-7405; Fax: 404-920-7401. Email: mchapman@archatl.com; MARY ANN BROWN, Accounting Asst. Tel: 404-920-7407; Fax: 404-920-7401. Email: mabrown@archatl.com; JEFFREY DEAN, Payroll Mgr. Tel: 404-920-7418. Email: jdean@archatl.com; ANDY HOECKELE, Cash Receipts Clerk. Tel: 404-920-7419. Email: ahoeckele@archatl.com; LINDA HARDEN, Accounting Asst. Tel: 404-920-7425. Email: lharden@archatl.com; NEEMA MOLLEL, Staff Accountant. Tel: 404-920-7406. Email: nmollel@archatl.com; SHANNON WIGGINS, Training Coord. Tel: 404-920-7408. Email: swiggins@archatl.com; EDWARD ROSSER, Parish Systems Support. Tel: 404-920-7409. Email: erosser@archatl.com; PATRICIA BISHOP, Accounting Clerk. Tel: 404-920-7610. Email: pbishop@archatl.com;

JON BOKINA, Internal Auditor. Tel: 404-920-7421. Email: jbokina@archatl.com; RICHARD SHEEDWITH, Internal Auditor. Tel: 404-920-7422. Email: rsheedwith@archatl.com; PERLA FREED, Support Svcs. Accountant. Tel: 404-920-7416. Email: pfreed@archatl.com.

Hispanic Ministry—2401 Lake Park Dr., Smyrna, 30080-8862. Tel: 404-920-7540; Fax: 404-920-7541. Web: www.archatl.com. JAIRO MARTINEZ, Dir. Email: jemartinez@archatl.com; ROCIO ZAMARRON, Office Mgr. Email: rzamarron@archatl.com.

Human Resources—2401 Lake Park Dr., Smyrna, 30080-8862. Tel: 404-920-7480; Fax: 404-920-7481. Web: www.archatl.com. CHARLES THIBAUDEAU, Dir. & Member of the Secretariat. Tel: 404-920-7482; Fax: 404-920-7481. Email: cthibaudeau@archatl.com; MARQUITA RICHBURG, Human Resources Mgr. Tel: 404-920-7483; Fax: 404-920-7481. Email: mrichburg@archatl.com; JENNIFER BROEL, Dir. Safe Environment. Tel: 404-920-7553; Fax: 404-920-7551; MARIANNE "MAC" FRONEK, Exec. Asst. Tel: 404-920-7552; Fax: 404-920-7551. Email: mfronek@archatl.com; LILY GALLAGHER, Benefits Mgr. Tel: 404-920-7485; Fax: 404-920-7481. Email: lgallagher@archatl.com; ROSA MONTANO-PARKER, Senior Benefits Specialist. Tel: 404-920-7486; Fax: 404-920-7481. Email: rmontano-parker@archatl.com; STEPHANIE LANDRUM, Volunteer Coord. Tel: 404-920-7489; Fax: 404-920-7481; CHAUNDRA LOUARD, Human Resources Specialist. Tel: 404-920-7488; Fax: 404-920-7481. Email: clouard@archatl.com; ERIN HAWTHORNE, HR Staff Specialist. Tel: 404-920-7495; Fax: 404-920-7481. Email: ehawthorne@archatl.com. Receptionists: DESTINY MARQUEZ; GISELLA COTTER. Tel: 404-920-7800; Fax: 404-920-7481. Email: chanceryreceptionist@archatl.com. Human Resources Assistants: BRENDA POLLOCK. Tel: 404-920-7484; Fax: 404-920-7481. Email: bpollock@archatl.com; DALIA KINSEY. Tel: 404-920-7490; Fax: 404-920-7481. Email: dkinsey@archatl.com.

Information Technology—2401 Lake Park Dr., Smyrna, 30080-8862. Tel: 404-920-7450; Fax: 404-920-7451. TOM POPE, Dir. Tel: 404-920-7452; Fax: 404-920-7451. Email: tpope@archatl.com; TOMASZ KASPRZYK, Information Technology Mgr. Tel: 404-920-7455; Fax: 404-920-7451. Email: tkasprzyk@archatl.com; CHAD SIGLER, Sr. Systems Analyst. Tel: 404-920-7456; Fax: 404-920-7451. Email: csiglar@archatl.com; SANDRA LONG, Sr. Software Analyst. Tel: 404-920-7453; Fax: 404-920-7451. Email: slong@archatl.com; GINA BENNETT, Sr. Systems Analyst. Tel: 404-920-7458; Fax: 404-920-7451. Email: gbennett@archatl.com; STEPHANIE COOPER, Systems Support Specialist I. Tel: 404-920-7457; Fax: 404-920-7451. Email: scooper@archatl.com; ANGEL ROSA, Support Specialist II. Tel: 404-920-7454; Fax: 404-920-7451. Email: arosa@archatl.com.

Metropolitan Tribunal—2401 Lake Park Dr., Smyrna, 30080-8862. Tel: 404-920-7500; Fax: 404-920-7501. Web: www.archatl.com/offices/tribunal. Email: tribunal@archatl.com.

Judicial Vicar—Very Rev. PEDRO POLOCHE, J.C.L., J.V., 2401 Lake Park Dr., Smyrna, 30080-8862. Tel: 404-920-7500; Fax: 404-920-7501. Email: ppoloche@archatl.com.

Executive Secretary to the Judicial Vicar—DIANE GILSDORF. Tel: 404-920-7507; Fax: 404-920-7501. Email: dgilsdorf@archatl.com.

Adjutant Judicial Vicars—Rev. Msgr. STEPHEN T. CHURCHWELL, J.C.D. Email: schurchwell@archatl.com; Rev. MICHAEL U. ONYEKURU, J.C.D. Email: monyekuru@archatl.com.

Court Administrator—Dr. DAVID CASTRONOVO, J.D., J.C.D., Court Admin. Tel: 404-920-7510. Email: dcastronovo@archatl.com.

Archdiocesan Judges—Rev. Msgr. EDWARD J. DILLON, J.C.D.; Rev. MICHAEL U. ONYEKURU, J.C.D.; Dr. DAVID CASTRONOVO, J.D., J.C.D., Court Admin.

Court Expert—Dr. ED YAROSZ, Ed.D., Consulting Psychologist. Tel: 404-920-7526.

Defenders of the Bond—Deacon ALFRED T. SAMORANSKI. Tel: 404-920-7515. Email: asamoranski@archatl.com; Dr. ELYN MACEK, J.D., J.C.L. (Cand.). Tel: 404-920-7516. Email: emacek@archatl.com.

Auditors—Very Rev. PEDRO POLOCHE, J.C.L., J.V., (English & Spanish). Tel: 404-920-7500. Email: ppoloche@archatl.com; Bro. NICHOLAS WOLFLA, O.F.M.Conv., J.C.L., Chief Auditor. Tel: 404-920-7511. Email: nwolfla@archatl.com; CATHERINE MCCARTY. Tel: 404-920-7519. Email: cmccarty@archatl.com; Dr. ROBERT BROOKS, J.D. Tel: 404-920-7517. Email: rbrooks@archatl.com.

Advocates—Rev. BALAPPA SELVARAJ, J.C.L., Chief Advocate. Tel: 404-920-7524. Email: bselvaraj@archatl.com; JEAN GUETTLER. Tel: 404-920-7502. Email: jsmith@archatl.com; DOROTHY WESSELMAN. Tel: 404-920-7525. Email: dwesselman@archatl.com; JOSEPH TOVAR, (English & Spanish). Tel: 404-920-7503. Email: jtovar@archatl.com.

Notaries—WENDY A. ABRAHAM, Case Mgr. & Chief Notary. Tel: 404-920-7509. Email: wabraham@archatl.com; KARREN DEBOW, Instructor for Informal Cases. Tel: 404-920-7505. Email: kdebow@archatl.com; PAM ROQUE, (English & Spanish) (Transcriptionist). Tel: 404-920-7508. Email: proque@archatl.com.

Case Sponsor Coordinator—Deacon WHITNEY ROBICHAUX.

Permanent Diaconate—2401 Lake Park Dr., Smyrna, 30080-8862. Tel: 404-920-7325; Fax: 404-920-7326. Deacon DENNIS J. DORNER, Dir. Office of Permanent Diaconate. Tel: 404-920-7325; Fax: 404-920-7326. Email: ddorner@archatl.com; Rev. TIMOTHY M. HEPBURN, Office of Permanent Diaconate & Spiritual Dir., Catholic Center at Georgia Tech, 172 Fourth St., NW, Atlanta, 30313. Tel: 404-920-7462; Fax: 404-920-7461. Email: frhepburn@gmail.com; Deacon PAUL S. SWOPE JR., Assoc. Dir. Formation, Office of Permanent Diaconate. Tel: 404-920-7382; Fax: 404-920-7326. Email: sswope@archatl.com; MARDESSA SMITH, Exec. Asst. Tel: 404-920-7328; Fax: 404-920-7326. Email: mwsmith@archatl.com; Most Rev. LUIS R. ZARAMA, J.C.L., V.G., Episcopal Delegate. Tel: 404-920-7315; Fax: 404-920-7316. Email: lzarama@archatl.com; KIRIAL DEROZAS-MILES. Tel: 404-920-7319; Fax: 404-920-7316. Email: kderozas-miles@archatl.com.

Stewardship—2401 Lake Park Dr., Smyrna, 30080-8862. Tel: 404-920-7600; Fax: 404-920-7601. Web: www.archatl.com. STEVE SILER, Exec. Dir. Stewardship. Tel: 404-920-7603; Fax: 404-920-7601. Email: ssiler@archatl.com; CHRISTINE HEUSINGER, Assoc. Dir. Stewardship. Tel: 404-920-7605; Fax: 404-920-7601. Email: cheusinger@archatl.com; ESTELA MORALES, Administrative Asst. Tel: 404-920-7604; Fax: 404-920-7601. Email: emorales@archatl.com; MARY ELLEN CENZALLI, Assoc. Dir. Devel. Tel: 404-920-7602; Fax: 404-920-7601. Email: mcenzalli@archatl.com; TRACY ZELCZAK, Database Admin. Tel: 404-920-7606; Fax: 404-920-7601. Email: tzelczak@archatl.com; SARAH VANDEUSEN, Data Entry Supvr. Tel: 404-920-7607. Email: svandeusen@archatl.com.

Office of Formation and Discipleship—2401 Lake Park Dr., Smyrna, 30080-8862. Tel: 404-920-7620; Fax: 404-920-7621. Web: www.archatl.com. IVONNE S. VREELAND, Office Mgr. Tel: 404-920-7623; Fax: 404-920-7621. Email: ivreeland@archatl.com.

Catechetical Ministry—

Office for Youth Ministry—

Inculturation Ministry—

Office for Young Adult Ministry—

Office for Adult Ministry—

Office of Planning and Facilities—2401 Lake Park Dr., Smyrna, 30080. Tel: 404-920-7850; Fax: 404-920-7851. PETER F. FALETTI, Dir. Tel: 404-920-7855; Fax: 404-920-7851. Email: pfaletti@archatl.com; JENNIFER MILES, Planning Analyst. Tel: 404-920-7852. Email: jmiles@archatl.com.

Vocations—2401 Lake Park Dr., Smyrna, 30080-8862. Tel: 404-920-7460; Fax: 404-920-7461. Web: www.calledbychrist.com. Rev. TIMOTHY M. HEPBURN, Dir. Tel: 404-920-7460; Fax: 404-920-7461. Email: thepburn@archatl.com; SALLY SCARDASIS, Exec. Asst. Tel: 404-920-7463; Fax: 404-920-7461. Email: sscardasis@archatl.com; LIVIA DOMINGUES, Intl. Liaison & Finance Analyst. Tel: 404-920-7464; Fax: 404-920-7461. Email: ldomingues@archatl.com; MICHAEL FERRIN, Assoc. Dir. Vocations. Tel: 404-920-7465; Fax: 404-920-7461. Email: mferrin@archatl.com.

Other Archdiocesan Offices

AACCW—DANA WILLIS, Pres., 2771 Bracken Wood Dr., Snellville, 30039. Tel: 770-365-4396. Email: willisdanalee@yahoo.com; Rev. WILLIAM M. WILLIAMS, Spiritual Moderator, Queen of Angels Catholic Church, 1326 Washington Rd., Thomson, 30824. Tel: 706-595-2913; Fax: 706-595-9636. Email: ourladyqofa@comcast.net.

Cursillo—Sr. MARGARET MCANOY, I.H.M., Dir., 2401 Lake Park Dr., Smyrna, 30080-8862. Tel: 404-920-7652. Email: mmcanoy@archatl.com.

Georgia Catholic Conference—FRANK MULCAHY, 2401 Lake Park Dr., Smyrna, 30080-8862. Tel: 404-920-7367. Email: fmulcahy@georgiacc.org.

Boy Scouts—Deacon THOMAS E. GOTSCHALL, Chap., 525 Indian Mill Ct., Alpharetta, 30022. Tel: 770-490-9436. Email: gotschall@mindspring.com.

Archdiocesan Councils, Boards, Commissions, and Committees

Atlanta Conference of Sisters—Sr. MARGARET MCANOY, I.H.M., 2401 Lake Park Dr., Smyrna, 30080-8862. Tel: 404-920-7652; Fax: 404-920-7611. Email: mmcanoy@archatl.com.

Audit Committee—KIERAN QUINN, Chm.

Benefits Committee—ROCHESTER ANDERSON, Chm.

Budget and Operations Committee—VALERIE LANDAU, Chm.

Catholic Charities of the Archdiocese of Atlanta, Inc.—ROCCO TESTANI, Chm.; SCOTT GARRETT, Co Chm.; JENNY KEOUGH, Sec.

Council of Priests—Rev. JEFFERY OTT, O.P., Chm., Our Lady of Lourdes Catholic Church, 25 Boulevard, N.E., Atlanta, 30312. Tel: 404-522-6776; Fax: 404-222-0202. Email: jefferyott@gmail.com.

Eucharistic Congress Committee—Deacon DENNIS J. DORNER, Chancellor & Dir. Office of Permanent Diaconate. Tel: 404-920-7325; Fax: 404-920-7326. Email: ddorner@archatl.com; MARDESSA SMITH, Exec. Asst. Tel: 404-920-7328; Fax: 404-920-7326. Email: mwsmith@archatl.com.

Finance Council—KIERAN QUINN, Chm.

Investment Committee—MICHAEL MOHR, Chm.

Advisory Board on Sexual Abuse of Minors—Rev. Msgr. EDWARD J. DILLON, J.C.D., Promoter of Justice.

Liturgical Commission—Rev. THEODORE R. BOOK, S.L.L., 2401 Lake Park Dr., Smyrna, 30080-8862. Tel: 404-920-7338; Fax: 404-920-7336. Email: tbook@archatl.com.

Project Review Committee—HAL BARRY, Chm.

St. George Village—Catholic Community Retirement Center, 11350 Woodstock Rd., Roswell, 30075. Mr. MARK A. LOWELL, Exec. Dir. Tel: 678-987-0404; ZANDRA ANDERSON, Concierge Supvr.

Board of Directors—Most Revs. WILTON D. GREGORY, S.L.D.; LUIS R. ZARAMA, J.C.L., V.G.; GEORGE AULBACH; Rev. Msgr. W. JOSEPH CORBETT, V.G., Moderator of the Curia; BRADLEY WILSON, CFO, Archdiocese of Atlanta; Rev. Msgr. STEPHEN T. CHURCHWELL, J.C.D.; GARY MEADER; ROBERT FINK; KENNETH R. WEBER.

Council of Deacons—Deacon KEVIN F. TRACY, Chm.

Diaconate Advisory Board—Deacon DENNIS J. DORNER, Facilitator.

Archdiocese of Atlanta Pastoral Council—Most Rev. WILTON D. GREGORY, S.L.D., Chm.

Archdiocesan School Advisory Council—BRIAN NEWHALL, Chm.

CLERGY, PARISHES, MISSIONS AND PAROCHIAL SCHOOLS

CITY OF ATLANTA

(FULTON COUNTY)

1—CATHEDRAL OF CHRIST THE KING (1936) [CEM] Most Rev. Wilton D. Gregory, Archbishop of Atlanta; Rev. Francis G. McNamee; Very Rev. Richard B. Morrow (Retired); Revs. Jorge Arevalo, Parochial Vicar; Jaime Rivera, Parochial Vicar; Michael Silloway, Parochial Vicar; Deacons Whitney Robichaux; Scott J.N. McNabb; John J. McManus; Gerald Zukauckas; Ronald Comeaudad.

Church: 2699 Peachtree Rd., N.E., Atlanta, 30305. Tel: 404-233-2145; Fax: 404-233-9711. Web: www.cathedralofchristtheking.org.

See Cathedral of Christ the King Catholic School, Atlanta under Archdiocesan Schools, located in the Institution section.

Catechesis/Religious Program—Tel: 404-267-3694; Fax: 404-233-4984. Web: www.religiousled.com. Students 676.

2—ST. ANTHONY OF PADUA (1903) Rev. Victor A. Galier; Deacons Joseph Barker; Leviticus Jelks; William H. Simmons III.

Church: 928 Ralph David Abernathy Blvd., S.W., Atlanta, 30310. Tel: 404-758-8861; Fax: 404-755-6755. Web: parishesonline.com/scripts/hostedsites/org.asp?ID= 12639.

Catechesis/Religious Program—Fax: 404-755-6755. Students 27.

3—HOLY CROSS (1964) Revs. Richard K. Tibbetts; Fausto Marquez, Parochial Vicar; Deacons Cece Reimer; Tom Silvestri; James Weiss; Dayle H. Geroski. In Res., Rev. Edward A.J. Danneker (Retired).

Church & Res.: 3175 Hathaway Ct., Atlanta, 30341. Tel: 770-939-3501; Fax: 770-723-7013. Email: office@holycrossatlanta.org. Web: www.holycrossatlanta.org.

Catechesis/Religious Program—Tel: 770-939-3501, Ext. 233; 770-939-3501, Ext. 235. Barbara Garvin,

D.R.E.; Aida Buseta, C.R.E. (K-5). Students 700.
Mission—Holy Vietnamese Martyrs (2003) Revs. Tuan Quoc Tran, Admin.; Tran Duy Hung, Parochial Vicar; Tan Pham, S.J., Parochial Vicar.

4—HOLY SPIRIT (1964) Rev. Msgr. Edward J. Dillon; Revs. Nicholas G. Azar, Parochial Vicar; Paul A. Burke, Parochial Vicar; Deacons William F. McCarthy; Allen Underwood; Stephen G. Demko. In Res., Rev. John C. Fallon.
Church: 4465 Northside Dr., N.W., Atlanta, 30327. Tel: 404-252-4513; Fax: 404-252-1162. Web: hscatl-.com.
See Holy Spirit Preparatory School, Atlanta, under Independent Schools located in the Institution Section
Catechesis/Religious Program—Students 621.
Mission—Centro Catolico del Espiritu Santo 120 Northwood Dr., Ste. B5-8, Atlanta, Fulton Co. 30342. Tel: 404-303-9927; Fax: 404-303-0620.

5—IMMACULATE HEART OF MARY (1958) Revs. James A. Schillinger; Juan Anzora, Parochial Vicar; Deacon Robert J. Hauert.
Church: 2855 Briarcliff Rd., N.E., Atlanta, 30329. Tel: 404-636-1418; Fax: 404-636-4394. Web: www.i-hmatlanta.org.
See Immaculate Heart of Mary Catholic School, Atlanta under Archdiocesan Schools, located in the Institution section.
Catechesis/Religious Program—Students 504.

6—ST. JUDE (1960) [CEM] Rev. Msgr. James J. Fennessy; Revs. Rosenilton Do Carmo Araujo, Parochial Vicar; Daniel Ketter, Parochial Vicar; Armando Herrejon-Lopez, Parochial Vicar; Adam Z. Ozimek, Parochial Vicar; Deacons Robert Riddett; James A. Tramonte.
Church: 7171 Glenridge Dr. N.E., Atlanta, 30328. Tel: 770-394-3896; Fax: 770-399-7866. Web: www-.stjudeatlanta.net.
See St. Jude the Apostle Catholic School, Atlanta under Archdiocesan Schools, located in the Institution section.
Catechesis/Religious Program—Students 322.

7—MOST BLESSED SACRAMENT (1960) Rev. Bruce W. Wilkinson; Deacon Fred Tocca.
Church: 2971 Butner Rd., S.W., Atlanta, 30331. Tel: 404-349-0176; Fax: 404-349-0178. Web: www.mbschurch.com.
Rectory—1926 Austin Rd., Atlanta, 30331. Tel: 404-349-1406.
Catechesis/Religious Program—Tel: 404-629-1287. Students 69.

8—OUR LADY OF LOURDES (1912) Revs. Jeffery Ott, O.P.; Bruce Schultz, O.P.; Deacon Chester H. Griffin.
Church: 25 Boulevard, N.E., Atlanta, 30312. Tel: 404-522-6776; Fax: 404-222-0202. Web: www.lourdesatlanta.org.
Catechesis/Religious Program—Students 89.

9—OUR LADY OF THE ASSUMPTION (1951) Very Rev. James D. Duffy, S.M.; Rev. John J. Sullivan, S.M., Parochial Vicar; Bro. Ernest Morasci, S.M.; Deacons Bill Bevacqua; Chris Thompson; Terry Biglow; Antonius Anugerah; Edward Patterson; William H. O'Donoghue.
Church: 1350 Hearst Dr., N.E., Atlanta, 30319. Tel: 404-261-7181; Fax: 404-364-1913. Web: www.ola-church.org.
See Our Lady of the Assumption Catholic School, Atlanta under Archdiocesan Schools, located in the Institution section.
Catechesis/Religious Program—Students 285.
Chapel—Marist School 3790 Ashford Dunwoody Rd., Atlanta, 30319. Tel: 770-457-7201; Fax: 770-457-8402. Web: www.marist.com.
Chapel—St. Joseph Hospital 5665 Peachtree Dunwoody Rd., NE, Atlanta, 30319. Tel: 404-851-7001; Fax: 404-851-5901. Web: www.stjosephsatlanta.org.
Chapel—Sisters of Mercy Convent at St. Joseph's Hospital, Tel: 404-255-6427.

10—ST. PAUL OF THE CROSS (1954) Revs. Jerome McKenna, C.P.; Glenn Maga, C.P., Parochial Vicar; Deacons George Smith; Hilliard M. Lee Jr.; Joseph Goolsby.
Church: 551 Harwell Rd., N.W., Atlanta, 30318. Tel: 404-696-6704; Fax: 404-696-4735. Email: info@spcatl.catholicweb.com. Web: www.spcatl.catholicweb.com.
Catechesis/Religious Program—Students 131.

11—SHRINE OF THE IMMACULATE CONCEPTION (1848) Rev. Msgr. Henry C. Gracz; Deacons William Payne; Bart DeSandre.
Church: 48 Martin Luther King, Jr. Dr., S.W., Atlanta, 30303-3599. Tel: 404-521-1866; Fax: 404-524-2297. Email: theshrine@mindspring.com. Web: www.catholicshrineatlanta.org.
Catechesis/Religious Program—Students 50.

12—THE BASILICA OF THE SACRED HEART OF JESUS (1880) Revs. T. J. Meehan; Mario Lopez Castro, Parochial Vicar; Deacons Wayne D. Smith; Michael K. Balfour; Marino Gonzalez.
Church: 353 Peachtree St., N.E., Atlanta, 30308. Tel: 404-522-6800; Fax: 404-524-5440. Web: www.sacredheartatlanta.org.
Catechesis/Religious Program—Students 310.
Mission—San Felipe de Jesus 925 Conley Rd., Forest Park, Clayton Co. 30297. Tel: 404-675-0540. Revs. Jacques E. Fabre, C.S., Admin. & Spiritual Dir.; Rubens Sylvain, C.S., Parochial Vicar.

OUTSIDE CITY OF ATLANTA

ALPHARETTA, FULTON CO., ST. THOMAS AQUINAS (1972) [CEM] Revs. Gregory D. Goolsby; Roberto Herrera, Parochial Vicar; Deacons William W. Keeling; Edmund LaHouse; John Strachan; Kevin F. Tracy; Arthur Lerma; Jose I. Pupo; Robert Brunton; Steven W. Shawcross.
Church: 535 Rucker Rd., 30004. Tel: 770-475-4501; Fax: 770-772-0355. Web: www.sta.org.
Catechesis/Religious Program—Tel: 770-475-4508. Students 1,816.

ATHENS, CLARKE CO., ST. JOSEPH (1873) Very Rev. David McGuinness; Rev. Omar Loggiodice, Parochial Vicar; Deacons Jim Gaudin; Robert J. Kepshire; Scott E. Medine.
Church: 134 Prince Ave., 30601. Tel: 706-548-6332; Fax: 706-354-1783.
See St. Joseph's Catholic School, Athens under Archdiocesan Schools, located in the Institution section.
Catechesis/Religious Program—Students 493.
Chapel—St. Mary's Hospital, Tel: 706-389-3000; Fax: 706-389-3931. Email: ploome@stmarysathens.org. Web: www.stmarysathens.org. Nurses 342; Total Staff 1,421.
Chapel—Catholic Student Center at The University of Georgia 1344 S. Lumpkin St., 30605-1345. Tel: 706-543-2293; Fax: 706-543-2541. Web: www.uga.edu/cc. Revs. Thomas F. Vigliotta, O.F.M., Dir. Campus Ministry; David L. Hyman, O.F.M., Assoc. Campus Min.

BLAIRSVILLE, UNION CO., ST. FRANCIS OF ASSISI (1966) [CEM] [JC] Revs. Joseph Liem Nguyen; Arturo Haro-Palos, Parochial Vicar; Deacons Lawrence Casey; Paul Dietz; John P. McGuire.
Church: 3717 Hwy. 515 E., 30512-3288. Tel: 706-745-6400; Fax: 706-745-1468. Email: saintfrancis@windstream.net.
Catechesis/Religious Program—Students 100.

BLUE RIDGE, FANNIN CO., ST. ANTHONY (1976) [CEM] Rev. John T. Conway; Deacons Loris Sinanian; John Mason.
E. Main St., P.O. Box 1448, 30513. Tel: 706-632-5970; Fax: 706-632-2120. Email: stanthony@tds.net. Web: www.stanthonyblueridge.parishesonline.com.
Catechesis/Religious Program—Students 14.

CALHOUN, GORDON CO., ST. CLEMENT (1958) Rev. Joseph Shaute; Deacon Bradford Krupa.
Mailing Address: 875 Hwy. 53, S.W., 30701. Tel: 706-629-2345; Fax: 706-625-5219. Email: stclementcalhoun@yahoo.com. Web: www.stclementsga.org.
Catechesis/Religious Program—Students 355.

CANTON, CHEROKEE CO., OUR LADY OF LASALETTE (1984) Rev. Victor J. Reyes; Deacons Charles E. Carignan; John Stanley.
2941 Sam Nelson Rd., 30114. Tel: 770-479-8923 (Office); Fax: 770-479-6025 (Office).
Catechesis/Religious Program—Students 87.

CARROLLTON, CARROLL CO., CHURCH OF OUR LADY OF PERPETUAL HELP (1962) [CEM] Rev. Rafael Carballo; Deacon Jon Gary Atkinson.
Church: 210 Old Center Point Rd., 30117. Tel: 770-832-8977; Fax: 770-832-1666.
Newman Center West Georgia College—
Catechesis/Religious Program—Students 354.

CARTERSVILLE, BARTOW CO., ST. FRANCIS OF ASSISI (1969) [JC] Very Rev. Daniel Stack; Deacon James H. Williams.
Church: 850 Douthit Ferry Rd., 30120. Tel: 770-382-4549; Fax: 770-382-4506. Web: www.st-francis-cartersville.org.
Catechesis/Religious Program—Wendy Sosa, Dir. Faith Formation; Cindy Caughman, Youth Min. Students 370.

CEDARTOWN, POLK CO., ST. BERNADETTE (1941) [JC] Very Rev. Jose Duvan Gonzalez.
Church: 101 S. College St., 30125. Tel: 770-748-1517.
Catechesis/Religious Program—Fax: 770-748-1517. Students 294.

CLARKESVILLE, HABERSHAM CO., ST. MARK (1964), (Hispanic), Rev. Jose Luis Hernandez-Ayala; Deacon Richard Marinchak.
Mailing Address: 5410 Hwy. 197 S., 30523. Tel: 706-754-4518; Fax: 706-754-9751.
Res.: 488 Windridge Rd., 30523. Tel: 706-839-6576.
Catechesis/Religious Program—Students 273.
Mission—St. Helena P.O. Box 534, Clayton, Rabun Co. 30525. Tel: 706-782-5152; Fax: 706-782-5152. Email: sthelenachurchclayton@windstream.net.

CLEVELAND, WHITE CO., ST. PAUL THE APOSTLE (1964) Revs. Vincent Sullivan; Arturo Haro-Palos, Parochial Vicar.
1243 Hulsey Rd., 30528. Tel: 706-865-4474; Fax: 706-219-3009. Web: stpaulcleveland.com.
Catechesis/Religious Program—Laurie Vitek, D.R.E. Students 175.

CONYERS, ROCKDALE CO., ST. PIUS X (1974) Revs. John C. Kieran; Timothy Gallagher, Parochial Vicar; Deacons Brian Kilkelly; Fred Johns; Joseph Rhodes; Stuart A. Mead; Fernando Barrueta.
Church: 2621 Hwy. 20, S.E., 30013-2424. Tel: 770-483-3660; Fax: 770-483-7006.
Catechesis/Religious Program—Tel: 770-929-1017. Students 484.

COVINGTON, NEWTON CO., ST. AUGUSTINE OF HIPPO (1977) Rev. Roberto Orellana.
Church: 11524 Hwy. 278 E., 30014. Tel: 770-787-1064; Fax: 770-787-0871. Email: office@staugcc.org. Web: home.catholicweb.com/StAugustineCovington/.
Catechesis/Religious Program—Tel: 770-787-9052. Students 148.
Mission—St. James 562 Vine St., Madison, Morgan Co. 30650. Tel: 706-342-9661; Fax: 706-342-2860. Deacon Herbert C. Berding, Admin.

CUMMING, FORSYTH CO.

1—ST. BRENDAN THE NAVIGATOR (2000) Revs. Robert A. Frederick; Fabio A. Alvarez, Parochial Vicar; Deacons Roger A. Fraser; William J. Monahan; Eduardo J. Rubio; Robert H. Grimaldi.
4633 Shiloh Rd., 30040. Tel: 770-205-7969; Fax: 770-205-5040. Web: www.stbrendansatl.com.
Catechesis/Religious Program—Students 1,075.

2—GOOD SHEPHERD (1975) Revs. Francis X. Richardson; Ignacio Morales; Deacons Donald N. Nadeau; Ralph LaMachia.
Church: 3740 Holtzclaw Rd., 30041. Tel: 770-887-9861; Fax: 770-887-2241. Web: www.goodshepherdcumming.com.
Catechesis/Religious Program—Tel: 770-887-9861, Ext. 16. Students 601.

DAHLONEGA, LUMPKIN CO., ST. LUKE (1960) Revs. Neil Dhabliwala; Ignacio Morales, Parochial Vicar; Deacon Dennis J. Dorner.
Church: 91 N. Park St., 30533. Tel: 706-864-4779; Fax: 706-864-2568. Email: deacon@stlukercc.org. Web: www.stlukercc.org.
Catechesis/Religious Program—Isaac Hathaway Jr., Youth Min. & Campus Min.; Kelly Peffer, D.R.E.
Station—North Georgia College and State University (Newman Club) 91 N. Park St., 30597. Email: college@stlukercc.org. Web: www.ngcsucatholic.org.

DALLAS, PAULDING CO., ST. VINCENT DE PAUL (2003) Rev. Adrian C.H. Pleus; Deacons Jose Perez; James McDermott; Stephen J. Bek.
680 W. Memorial Dr., 30132. Tel: 770-443-0566 (Office); Fax: 770-443-1612 (Office). Email: svdpchurch@bellsouth.net. Web: saintvincentdepaulchurch.org.
Catechesis/Religious Program—Tel: 770-443-0566; Fax: 770-443-1612. Students 300.

DALTON, WHITFIELD CO., ST. JOSEPH (1941) [JC] Revs. Paul D. Williams Jr.; Juan de Dios Oliveros, Parochial Vicar.
Church & Res.: 968 Haig Mill Lake Rd., 30720. Tel: 706-278-3107; Fax: 706-278-6902. Web: www.sjccdalton.com.
Catechesis/Religious Program—Cathy Blevins, D.R.E. Students 1,259.
Mission—Capella Santo Toribio Romo Crandall, 30711.

DAWSONVILLE, DAWSON CO., CHRIST THE REDEEMER CATHOLIC CHURCH (1982) Rev. Brian J. Higgins; Deacons Kenneth Williams; Ray Richardson.
Church: 991 Kilough Church Rd., 30534. Tel: 706-265-1361; Fax: 706-265-1363.
Catechesis/Religious Program—Students 91.

DECATUR, DEKALB CO.

1—STS. PETER AND PAUL (1959) [JC] Rev. Bryan D. Small; Deacons Jerry Lett; Alfred Mitchell; Augustin Pierre-Louis.
Res: 2372 Collier Dr., 30032. Tel: 404-241-5862 (Office); Fax: 404-241-5839 (Office). Web: www.stspandp.com.
Church: 2560 Tilson Rd., 30032.
See St. Peter Claver Regional Catholic School, Decatur under Archdiocesan Schools, located in the Institution section.
Catechesis/Religious Program—Gloria George-Patrick, D.R.E. Students 118.

2—ST. THOMAS MORE (1941) Rev. Msgr. Paul Fogarty; Rev. Brian Lorei, Parochial Vicar.
Church: 636 W. Ponce de Leon Ave., 30030. Tel: 404-378-4588; Fax: 404-378-0506. Web: www.stmgaparish.org.
See St. Thomas More Catholic School, Decatur under Archdiocesan Schools, located in the Institution section.
Catechesis/Religious Program—Students 324.

DORAVILLE, DEKALB CO., KOREAN MARTYRS CATHOLIC CHURCH (1977) Revs. Tae-su Michael Ha, S.J.; Hyong-Nyol Ryu, S.J., Parochial Vicar; Stefano Young-hoon Kim, S.J., Parochial Vicar.
6003 Buford Hwy., N.E., 30340. Tel: 770-455-1380; Fax: 770-455-4262. Web: www.kmccga.org.

Catechesis/Religious Program—Students 30.

DOUGLASVILLE, DOUGLAS CO., ST. THERESA OF THE CHILD JESUS (1985) Revs. Fernando Molina-Restrepo; Kizito Okeke, Parochial Vicar; Deacons Ronald A. St. Michel; Terry M. Holmer; Charles Patrick; Israel D. Melara.
Church: 4401 Prestley Mill Rd., 30135. Tel: 770-489-7115; Fax: 770-489-4873. Web: www.sainttheresacatholicchurch.org.
Catechesis/Religious Program—Tel: 770-942-9765. Students 660.

DULUTH, GWINNETT CO., ST. MONICA (1994) Revs. John F. Durkin Jr.; Thomas Zahuta, Parochial Vicar; Deacons Bob Tipton; John Koppenaal; Edward Rademacher; Joseph R. Carter; William L. Bohn.
1700 Buford Hwy., 30097. Tel: 678-584-9947; Fax: 678-584-9760. Web: www.saintmonicas.com.
Rectory—3393 Forrestwood Dr., Suwanee, 30024.
Catechesis/Religious Program—Tel: 678-584-9947. Students 760.

DUNWOODY, DEKALB CO., ALL SAINTS (1977) Rev. Msgr. Hugh M. Marren; Revs. Daniel J. McCormick, Parochial Vicar; William T. Hao, Parochial Vicar; Deacons William Garrett; Edward Krise; Paul Lee Doppel.
Church: 2443 Mount Vernon Rd., 30338-3099. Tel: 770-393-3255; Fax: 770-913-0140. Web: www.allsaints.us.
Catechesis/Religious Program—Students 625.

ELLIJAY, GILMER CO., GOOD SAMARITAN CATHOLIC CHURCH (1986) Very Rev. Randall T. Mattox.
55 Church St., 30540. Tel: 706-636-2772; Fax: 706-636-2776.
Catechesis/Religious Program—Students 95.

FAYETTEVILLE, FAYETTE CO., ST. GABRIEL (1993) Rev. Michael L. McWhorter; Deacons I. Carl McBride; Donald S. Parker.
Church: 152 Antioch Rd., 30215-5702. Tel: 770-461-0492; Fax: 770-461-0374. Email: stgabrielchurch@comcast.net. Web: www.stgabrielaga.com.
Catechesis/Religious Program—Tel: 770-461-0493. Students 397.

FLOWERY BRANCH, HALL CO., PRINCE OF PEACE (1978) Revs. Eric J. Hill; Patrick S. Scully, S.M., Parochial Vicar; Deacons Michael R. Jones; William Speed; Al Samoranski; Michael Woods; Nicholas Johnson.
Church: 6439 Spout Springs Rd., 30542. Tel: 770-945-2244; Fax: 770-945-4599. Email: princeofpeace@popcatholicchurch.org. Web: www.popcatholicchurch.org.
Catechesis/Religious Program—Students 1,356.

FORT OGLETHORPE, CATOOSA CO., ST. GERARD MAJELLA (1952) Rev. Liam Coyne.
3049 LaFayette Rd., 30742. Tel: 706-861-9410; Fax: 706-866-0574. Email: stgeradmin@bellsouth.net.
Catechesis/Religious Program—Tel: 706-861-0563. Students 56.

GAINESVILLE, HALL CO., ST. MICHAEL (1933) Revs. Jaime Barona; William Canales, Parochial Vicar; Dominic Tran, Parochial Vicar; Deacons Michael Kennedy; Gary Roche; Gilberto Perez; Luis Londono; Kenneth W. Lampert.
Church: 1440 Pearce Cir., N.E., 30501-2457. Tel: 770-534-3338; Fax: 770-535-2440. Web: www.saintmichael.cc.
Catechesis/Religious Program—Students 1,514.

GREENSBORO, GREENE CO., CHRIST OUR KING AND SAVIOR (1992), Consolidation of Christ Our Savior, Eatonton, and Christ Our King, Greensboro. Rev. G. Philip Ryan.
Church: 6341 Lake Oconee Pkwy., 30642. Tel: 706-453-7292; Fax: 706-453-7095. Email: admin@cokas.org. Web: www.cokas.org.
Catechesis/Religious Program—Students 72.

GRIFFIN, SPALDING CO., SACRED HEART (1941) Rev. Dennis R. Juan; Deacons Felix Marrero; Kenneth P. Bishop.
Church: 1323 MacArthur Dr., 30224. Tel: 770-227-2378; Fax: 770-227-6440. Email: shpriest@comcast.net.
Catechesis/Religious Program—Tel: 770-227-2898. Students 67.

HAPEVILLE, DEKALB CO., ST. JOHN THE EVANGELIST (1954) Revs. Edward Thein; Hernan Quevedo Rodriguez, Parochial Vicar; Deacon Tom Stonecipher.
Res.: 3370 Sunset Ave., 30354.
Church: 230 Arnold St., Atlanta, 30354-1530. Tel: 404-768-5647; Fax: 404-767-6416.
See St. John the Evangelist School, Hapeville under Archdiocesan Schools, located in the Institution section.
Catechesis/Religious Program—Fax: 404-767-6416. Mrs. Daphny Keel, C.R.E. Students 280.

HARTWELL, HART CO., SACRED HEART OF JESUS (1977) [CEM] [JC] Rev. Rafael Castano Fernandez; Deacons Jerry Korte; Barry Phillips.
Church: 1009 Benson St., 30643. Tel: 706-376-4112; Fax: 706-376-4112. Email: shj.parish@gmail.com. Web: www.sacredheartofhartwell.com.
Catechesis/Religious Program—Tel: 864-958-0601. Email: stgus8@bellsouth.net. Students 123.

JACKSON, BUTTS CO., SAINT MARY, MOTHER OF GOD CATHOLIC CHURCH (1960) Rev. Mark F. Fischer.
359 Old Griffin Rd., P.O. Box 901, 30233. Tel: 770-775-4162; Fax: 770-775-4174. Email: stmarysinjackson@bellsouth.net.
Catechesis/Religious Program—Students 54.

JASPER, PICKENS CO., OUR LADY OF THE MOUNTAINS (2004) Rev. Charles A. Byrd Jr.
Church: 1908 Waleska Hwy. 108, 30143. Tel: 706-253-3078; Fax: 706-253-3077. Email: ladyofthemts@ellijay.com.
Catechesis/Religious Program—Students 170.

JOHNS CREEK, FULTON CO.

1—ST. BENEDICT (1987) Revs. Paul Flood; Carlos Quintero, Parochial Vicar; Joseph Mullakkara, M.S.F.S., Parochial Vicar; Charles Okeke, Parochial Vicar; Deacons Gerard G. Kazin; John D. Puetz; Ronald Carr.
Res.: 11085 Parson's Rd., Duluth, 30097.
Church: 11045 Parson's Rd., 30097. Tel: 770-442-5903; Fax: 770-442-0744. Web: www.stbenedict.net.
Catechesis/Religious Program—Tel: 678-992-2511; Fax: 770-442-0744. Students 1,372.
Mission—Mision del Divino Nino Jesus 4400 Abbotts Bridge Rd., Duluth, Gwinnett Co. 30097. Tel: 678-417-7912.

2—ST. BRIGID (1998) [CEM] Rev. Msgr. David P. Talley; Rev. Gilbert Exume, Parochial Vicar; Deacons Dennis J. Dorner; James A. LaFreniere; Leo Gahafer; Tom Huff.
3400 Old Alabama Rd., 30022. Tel: 678-393-0060; Fax: 678-393-0071. Email: office@saintbrigid.org. Web: www.saintbrigid.org.
See Holy Redeemer Catholic School, Alpharetta under Archdiocesan Schools located in the Institution section
Catechesis/Religious Program—Students 1,178.

JONESBORO, CLAYTON CO., ST. PHILIP BENIZI (1965) Revs. John Koziol, O.F.M.Conv.; Abelardo Huanca Martinez, O.F.M.Conv., Parochial Vicar; Michael Kolodziej, O.F.M.Conv., Parochial Vicar; Deacons Joseph C. Anzalone; Peter B. Swan Sr.; Richard P. Tolcher; Etienne Francisco Rodriguez; Gregory L. Pecore; Matias A. Casal; Julio V. Martinez; Leonard P. Chambliss Jr.
Church: 591 Flint River Rd., 30238-3452. Tel: 770-478-0178; Fax: 770-471-2079. Web: www.stphilipbenizi.org.
Catechesis/Religious Program—Students 284.

KENNESAW, COBB CO., ST. CATHERINE OF SIENA (1981) Revs. John M. Matejek, Admin.; Manuel de Jesus Rivas, Parochial Vicar; Deacons Richard Conti; Burgess "David" Grubbs; Stephen Ponichtera; Thomas J. Ryan; Miguel A. Echevarria; Ronald Manning.
Res.: 1644 Ben King Rd., 30144. Web: stcatherinercc.org.
Church: 1618 Ben King Rd., N.W., 30144. Tel: 770-428-7139; Fax: 770-428-0131.
See St. Catherine of Siena Catholic School, Kennesaw under Archdiocesan Schools, located in the Institution section.
Catechesis/Religious Program— Joan Hennes, D.R.E. Students 1,300.

LAGRANGE, TROUP CO., ST. PETER (1936) Rev. Theodore Book; Deacon Wayne Nacey.
Church: 200 LaFayette Pkwy., 30241. Tel: 706-884-4224; Fax: 706-884-1624. Web: www.stpeterslagrange.com.
Catechesis/Religious Program—Lyss Feria, D.R.E. Students 158.
Mission—St. Elizabeth Seton P.O. Box 638, Warm Springs, Meriwether Co. 31830. Tel: 706-846-5223.

LAWRENCEVILLE, GWINNETT CO.

1—ST. LAWRENCE (1974) [CEM] Very Rev. Albert W. Jowdy; Rev. Juan F. Areiza, Parochial Vicar; Deacons A.B. King III; Patrick Fagan; Terry D. Millinger; Richard Downey.
Church: 319 Grayson Hwy., 30046. Tel: 770-963-8992; Fax: 770-963-1710. Web: www.saintlaw.org.
Catechesis/Religious Program—Tel: 770-962-2765. Students 775.

2—ST. MARGUERITE D'YOUVILLE (1994) Revs. James Harrison; Joseph Mendes, M.S.F.S.; Piotr Nowacki, S.Chr., Parochial Vicar; Deacons George D. Angelich; Albert L. Feliu.
Church: 85 Gloster Rd., 30044. Tel: 770-381-7337; Fax: 770-381-6568.
Catechesis/Religious Program—Students 187.

LILBURN, GWINNETT CO.

1—ST. JOHN NEUMANN (1977) Rev. John T. Howren; Deacons Michael T. Byrne; Greg Ollick; William H. Marten.
Church: 801 Tom Smith Rd., 30047-2299. Tel: 770-923-6633; Fax: 770-381-7856. Web: www.sjnlilburn.com.
See St. John Neumann Catholic School, Lilburn under Archdiocesan Schools located in the Institution section.
Catechesis/Religious Program—Becky Wakim, D.R.E. Students 841.

2—ST. STEPHEN THE MARTYR (1999) Revs. Patrick H.M. Donaghey; John Paul Ezeonyido, Parochial Vicar; Deacons Evelio Garcia-Carreras; Michael K. Mobley Sr.; Richard C. Kaszycki.
Church & Res.: 5373 Wydella Rd., 30047. Tel: 770-381-7488; Fax: 770-923-8061. Web: www.ststephenthemartyr.info.
Catechesis/Religious Program—Students 167.

LITHIA SPRINGS, DOUGLAS CO., ST. JOHN VIANNEY (1958) Revs. Jude Michael Krill, O.F.M.Conv.; Paulino Matus Castillo, O.F.M.Conv., Parochial Vicar; Timothy Lyons, O.F.M., Parochial Vicar; Deacons Francis Przybylek; Felix Rentas; Miguel Class.
Church: 1920 Skyview Dr., 30122. Tel: 770-941-2807; 770-745-5445 (Res.); Fax: 770-941-5821. Web: www.sjvpar.com.
Catechesis/Religious Program—Students 482.

LITHONIA, DEKALB CO., CHRIST OUR HOPE (1984) Rev. Guyma Noel; Deacon Gerald A. Collins.
1786 Wellborn Rd., 30058. Tel: 770-482-5017; Fax: 770-482-9476. Web: www.christourhopeatl.org.
Catechesis/Religious Program—Students 25.

LOOKOUT MOUNTAIN, WALKER CO., OUR LADY OF THE MOUNT (1947) [JC] Very Rev. Richard P. Wise.
Church: 1227 Scenic Hwy., 30750. Tel: 706-820-0680; 706-820-2691 (Res.); Fax: 706-820-2797. Web: www.olmga.org. (Memorial Garden For Ashes)
Catechesis/Religious Program—Students 75.
Mission—St. Katharine Drexel 109 New England Rd., P.O. Box 1032, Trenton, Dade Co. 30753-1032.

MABLETON, COBB CO., ST. FRANCIS DE SALES (1999) Revs. Howard Venette, F.S.S.P.; Matthew McCarthy, F.S.SP., Parochial Vicar; Deacon Douglas J. Anderson.
Church: 587 Landers Dr., 30126. Tel: 770-948-6888; 770-745-3464 (Res.); Fax: 770-948-6888. Web: www.francisdesales.com.
Catechesis/Religious Program—Randall Mandock, D.R.E. Students 72.

MARIETTA, COBB CO.

1—ST. ANN (1978) Revs. Thomas A. Reilly, M.S.; Raymond G. Cadran, M.S., Parochial Vicar; John Gabriel, M.S., Parochial Vicar; Joseph LaMartine Eliscar, M.S., Parochial Vicar; Deacons Edmund M. Grabowy; J. Nicholas Morning; Bobby Allen Jennings; Robert Klein.
Church: 4905 Roswell Rd., N.E., 30062. Tel: 770-552-6400; 770-552-6400 (Res.); Fax: 770-552-6420. Web: www.st-ann.org.
Catechesis/Religious Program—Tel: 770-552-6400, Ext. 6044; Fax: 770-552-6421. Students 1,700.

2—CHURCH OF THE TRANSFIGURATION (1977) Rev. Msgr. Patrick A. Bishop; Rev. Juan Jose Sanchez Teran, Parochial Vicar; Deacons Tom Coffey; Jim Easterwood; Jose G. Espinosa; Paul A. Gorski; Philip Miles.
Church: 1815 Blackwell Rd., N.E., 30066-2911. Tel: 770-977-1442; 770-977-2756 (Res.); Fax: 770-578-1415. Email: staff@transfiguration.com. Web: www.transfiguration.com.
Catechesis/Religious Program—Joyce Guris, D.R.E. Students 1,852.

3—HOLY FAMILY (1973) Revs. Darragh Griffith; Armando Herrejon-Lopez, Parochial Vicar; Stewart Wilber, Parochial Vicar; Deacons Al Gallagher; John P. Duffield.
Church: 3401 Lower Roswell Rd., 30068-3974. Tel: 770-973-0038; Fax: 770-578-0475. Web: www.holyfamilycc.org.
Catechesis/Religious Program—Students 326.

4—ST. JOSEPH (1952) Revs. John P. Walsh; Michael S. Sherliza, Parochial Vicar; Javier Munoz, Parochial Vicar; Deacons Thomas Shaver; Joseph C. Eustace; Bruce Reed; Francis Devereux; Norman K. Keller; Jose T. Merlo-Quintero.
Church: 87 Lacy St., N.W., 30060. Tel: 770-422-5633; Fax: 770-422-1148. Web: www.saintjosephcc.org.
See St. Joseph Catholic School, Marietta under Archdiocesan Schools, located in the Institution section.
Catechesis/Religious Program—Tel: 770-422-5633, Ext. 51; Fax: 770-422-1472. Students 1,382.

MCDONOUGH, HENRY CO., ST. JAMES THE APOSTLE (1979) Revs. James Flanagan; Mansueto P. Palang, Parochial Vicar; Deacon Patrick (Pat) J. Gillespie.
1000 Decatur Rd., Hwy. 155, 30252. Web: www.stjamesapostle.com. In Res., Rev. Msgr. Terry W. Young (Retired).
Church: 1000 Decatur Rd., 30252. Tel: 770-957-5441; Fax: 770-957-0383.
Catechesis/Religious Program—Email: mmartin@stjamesapostle.com. Students 541.

MILLEDGEVILLE, BALDWIN CO., SACRED HEART OF JESUS (1874) Rev. Dung Nguyen; Deacon Cesar Basilio.
Church: 110 N. Jefferson St., P.O. Box 754, 31061. Tel: 478-452-2421 (Res.); Fax: 478-454-1110.

Catechesis/Religious Program—Students 97.

MONROE, WALTON CO., ST. ANNA (1951) [JC] Rev. Daniel R. Toof; Deacon Thomas J. Metzger.
Church: 836 E. Spring St., 30655. Tel: 770-267-7637; Fax: 770-267-0465. Web: www.st-annas.com.
Catechesis/Religious Program—Tel: 770-267-0420; Fax: 770-267-4134. Students 192.

NEWNAN, COWETA CO.

1—ST. GEORGE (1952) [JC] Rev. Austin Fogarty; Deacons James R. Bishop; Steve Beers; Paul S. Swope Jr.
Church: 771 Roscoe Rd., 30263. Tel: 770-251-5353; Fax: 770-251-2053. Email: lbrunelle@numail.org. Web: www.stgeorgecatholicchurch.org.
Catechesis/Religious Program—Tel: 770-254-9933. Students 212.

2—ST. MARY MAGDALENE (1999) Rev. Daniel J. Fleming; Deacon David C. Sandlin.
3 Village Rd., 30265-6162. Tel: 770-253-1888; Fax: 770-253-1290. Email: smmcc@smmcatholic.org. Web: www.smmcatholic.org.
Catechesis/Religious Program—Tel: 770-253-1888. Students 427.

NORCROSS, GWINNETT CO.

1—MARY OUR QUEEN CATHOLIC CHURCH (1994) Revs. David M. Dye, Admin.; Stephen J. Lyness, Parochial Vicar; Yuen Caballejo, Prison Ministry Chap.; Deacons James E. Stone; Joseph Ruberte.
Church: 6260 The Corners Pkwy., 30092. Tel: 770-416-0002; Fax: 770-416-1846. Email: office@maryourqueen.com. Web: www.maryourqueen.com.
Catechesis/Religious Program—Tel: 770-416-9799. Email: reled@maryourqueen.com. Students 182.

2—SAINT PATRICK (1968) Revs. Refugio Onate-Melendez; Cyril Soo-Gil Chae, Parochial Vicar; Henry Atem, Parochial Vicar; Deacon Jose Narvaez.
Church & Res.: 2140 Beaver Ruin Rd., 30071. Tel: 770-448-2028; 770-446-2041 (Res.); Fax: 770-448-7046. Web: www.stpatricksga.org.
Catechesis/Religious Program—Tel: 770-448-6386. Students 622.
Mission—Our Lady of the Americas 4603 Lawrenceville Hwy., Lilburn, Gwinnet Co. 30047. Tel: 770-717-1517; Fax: 770-717-1312. Revs. Luis Guillermo-Cordoba, Admin.; Carlos Bustamante, Parochial Vicar.

PEACHTREE CITY, FAYETTE CO., HOLY TRINITY (1973), (Hispanic), Revs. John Murphy; Pavol Brenkus, Parochial Vicar; Dairo Antonio Rico, Parochial Vicar; Deacons Anthony F. Cuomo; Nemour Michel Landaiche; Terry S. Blind; Hector M. Vargas; Mark A. Sholander.
Church: 101 Walt Banks Rd., 30269. Tel: 770-487-7672; Fax: 770-486-9152. Web: www.holytrinitypt-c.org.
See Our Lady of Mercy Catholic High School, Fairburn under Archdiocesan Schools located in the Institution section.
See St. Pius X Catholic High School, Atlanta under Archdiocesan Schools located in the Institution section
Catechesis/Religious Program—Tel: 770-487-0175. Students 834.

RIVERDALE, CLAYTON CO., OUR LADY OF VIETNAM (1989), (Vietnamese), [JC] Rev. Msgr. Francis Pham Van Phuong; Rev. Peter Duc Vu, Parochial Vicar; Deacons Peter Hung Viet Huynh; Joseph Phu Nguyen.
Church: 91 Valley Hill Rd., 30274. Tel: 770-472-9963; 770-471-8453 (Res.); Fax: 770-473-5211.
Catechesis/Religious Program—Students 475.

THE ROCK, UPSON CO., ST. PETER THE ROCK (2005) Rev. Neil Herlihy; Deacon Tilton (T.C.) Meuninck.
3594 Barnesville Hwy., P.O. Box 280, 30285. Tel: 706-648-2599; Fax: 706-648-4040. Web: www.stpetertherock.com.
Catechesis/Religious Program—Sherre Rohling, C.R.E. Students 77.

ROME, FLOYD CO., ST. MARY (1930) Rev. Patrick J. Kingery; Deacons Stuart L. Neslin; Jose M. Orellana.
Res.: 911 N. Broad St., 30161. Tel: 706-290-9100; Fax: 706-295-1717. Web: www.smcrome.org.
See St. Mary Catholic School, Rome under Archdiocesan Schools, located in the Institution section.
Catechesis/Religious Program—Ballard Betz, D.R.E. & Youth Dir.; LouAnn Ellsworth, C.R.E. Students 508.

ROSWELL, FULTON CO.

1—ST. ANDREW (1981) Very Rev. Michael G. Kingery; Rev. Carlos Vargas, Parochial Vicar; Deacons William Keen; Thomas E. Gotschall; Jose G. Campos; Gary E. Schantz.
Res.: 115 River Lake Ct., 30075. Tel: 770-552-0485.
Church: 675 Riverside Rd., 30075. Tel: 770-641-9720; Fax: 770-641-8584. Email: admin@standrewcatholic.com. Web: www.standrewcatholic.com.
Catechesis/Religious Program—Tel: 770-641-9720, Ext. 253; Fax: 770-641-8584. Email: religiousedu@standrewcatholic.com. Students 340.

2—ST. PETER CHANEL (1998) Very Rev. Peter J. Rau; Revs. Llane Briese, Parochial Vicar; Thang M. Pham, Parochial Vicar; Deacons Keith M. Kolodziej; Martin J. Lampe; Jesus Nerio; Michael Bickerstaff; Scott A. Sparks; John Wojcik; David J. Thomasberger; Tom Blond, Business Mgr.; Jane Jackson, Music Min.; Megan Busch, Youth Min.
11330 Woodstock Rd., 30075. Tel: 678-277-9424; Fax: 678-277-9423. Web: www.stpeterchanel.org.
See Queen of Angels Catholic School, Roswell under Archdiocesan Schools located in the Institution section
See Blessed Trinity Catholic High School, Roswell under Archdiocesan Schools located in the Institution section
Catechesis/Religious Program—Tel: 678-832-1230. Cathy Marbury, D.R.E. Students 1,110.

SMYRNA, COBB CO., ST. THOMAS THE APOSTLE (1966) Revs. James H. Kuczynski, M.S.; Jaime Molina-Juarez, M.N.M., Parochial Vicar; Jose Luis Manjaly, M.S., Parochial Vicar; Pedro Chingandu, M.S., Parochial Vicar; Deacons Michael Garrett; Earl D. Jackson.
Church: 4300 King Springs Rd., 30082. Tel: 770-432-8579; Fax: 770-432-8570. Email: stthomasga@stthomastheapostle.org. Web: stthomastheapostle.org.
Catechesis/Religious Program—Tel: 770-432-5296. Email: ssenecal@stthomastheapostle.org. Students 1,213.

SNELLVILLE, GWINNETT CO., ST. OLIVER PLUNKETT (1978) Revs. James A. Henault, M.S.; Neil G. Jones, M.S., Parochial Vicar; Juan de la Cruz, Parochial Vicar; Deacons William Jindrich; Rafael Cintron.
Church & Res.: 3200 Brooks Dr., 30078. Tel: 770-979-3827 (Res.); Fax: 770-985-6590. Email: oplunkett@stolivers.com. Web: www.stolivers.com.
Catechesis/Religious Program—Tel: 770-978-6751. Students 957.

STONE MOUNTAIN, DEKALB CO., CORPUS CHRISTI (1971) [JC] Revs. John Molyneux, C.M.F.; Richard DeTore, C.M.F., Parochial Vicar; Peter Pedroza, C.M.F.; Deacons John J. McManus; Ken W. Melvin. In Res., Rev. Gregory D. Kenny, C.M.F.
Church: 600 Mountain View Dr., 30083. Tel: 770-469-0395; Fax: 770-469-0568. Web: www.corpuschristicc.org.
Catechesis/Religious Program—Tel: 770-469-0597; Fax: 770-469-0568. Richard Dick, D.R.E. Students 331.

THOMSON, MCDUFFIE CO., QUEEN OF ANGELS (1955) Rev. William M. Williams.
Church: 1326 Washington Rd., 30824. Tel: 706-595-2913; Fax: 706-595-9636.
Catechesis/Religious Program—Email: ourladyqofa@comcast.net. Students 47.

TOCCOA, STEPHENS CO., ST. MARY (1956) [JC] Very Rev. Terence Crone; Deacon John Burke.
Res.: 231 Rothell Rd. Ext., 30577. Tel: 706-886-2819; Fax: 706-886-8770. Email: stmary@windstream.net. Web: www.stmarystoccoaga.com.
Catechesis/Religious Program—Students 25.

TYRONE, FULTON CO., ST. MATTHEW (1979) Very Rev. Kevin J. Hargaden; Deacons William Hampton; Jim G. Weeks; Gayle P. Peters; King E. Cooper.
Church: 215 Kirkley Rd., 30290-9549. Tel: 770-964-5804; Fax: 770-964-1228. Web: www.saintmatthew.us.
See Our Lady of Victory Catholic School, Tyrone under Archdiocesan Schools located in the Institution section
Catechesis/Religious Program—Students 296.

WASHINGTON, WILKES CO., ST. JOSEPH (1840) [CEM] [JC 2] Rev. Christopher Williamson.
Church: 1015 N. By Pass Hwy. 78 W., P.O. Box 632, 30673. Tel: 706-678-2110; Fax: 706-678-3353. Email: stjosephs@nu-z.net.
Catechesis/Religious Program—Students 18.
Mission—St. Mary P.O. Box 632, Elbert Co. 30678.
Station—Purification Hwy. 47, Sharon, Talifero Co. 30631.

WINDER, BARROW CO., ST. MATTHEW (1999) Revs. Leo C. Holleran, M.S.; Salomon Garcia, Parochial Vicar; Deacons Tim Kirksey; Richard A. Mickle; Lawrence J. Welsh.
25 Wilkins Rd., S.W., 30680-1009. Tel: 770-867-4876; Fax: 770-867-6034. Email: busmgr@saintmatthewcc.org. Web: www.saintmatthewcc.org.
Rectory—450 Winston Manor Dr., 30680.
Catechesis/Religious Program—Students 323.

WOODSTOCK, CHEROKEE CO., ST. MICHAEL THE ARCHANGEL (1995) Revs. Larry Niese; Paul Moreau, L.C., Parochial Vicar; Deacons William H. Heinsch; Bernard J. Casey; Victor L. Taylor.
Church & Res.: 490 Arnold Mill Rd., 30188. Tel: 770-516-0009.
Catechesis/Religious Program—Tel: 770-516-9699; Fax: 770-516-4664. Students 1,012.

Chaplains of Public Institutions

ATLANTA. *Atlanta Veterans Administration Hospital*, 1670 Clairmont Rd., Decatur, 30033. Tel: 404-321-6111. Rev. Daniel J. McCormick, B.A.
Cobb County Jail, 1825 County Services Pkwy., Marietta, 30060. Tel: 770-499-4200. Rev. Yuen Caballejo.
Dobbins Air Force Base. Vacant.
94 AW/HC, 1311 Patrol Rd., Dobbins Air Force Base, 30069-5003. Tel: 404-919-4955; 404-919-4956.
Fort McPherson.
Office of the Garrison Chaplain, Bldg. 51, Fort McPherson, 30330-5000. Tel: 404-752-2616. Rev. Fred W. Wendel, Chap.
Office of the FORSCOM Chap., 1777 Hardee Ave., S.W., Fort McPherson, 30330. Tel: 404-464-6030. Vacant.
Hartsfield Jackson International Airport, Interfaith Airport Chaplaincy, P.O. Box 20801, 30320. Tel: 404-762-1051. Web: www.airportchapel.org. Deacons Donald A. Kelsey, Ray Egan, Alfred Mitchell, Mark A. Sholander, Terry S. Blind, Dayle H. Geroski, Whitney Robichaux.
Prison Apostolate. Rev. John C. Fallon, Chap.
U.S. Penitentiary, 601 McDonough Blvd., 30315. Tel: 404-635-5100. Vacant.

JACKSON. *Georgia Diagnostic & Classification Center, Diagnostic & Classification*, 2978 Hwy. 36 W., 30233. Tel: 770-504-2000. Deacon Thomas O. Silvestri, Chap.

Special or Other Archdiocesan Assignment:
Rev. Msgrs.—
Churchwell, Stephen T., J.C.D., Vicar for Senior Priests & Adjutant Judicial Vicar of the Metropolitan Tribunal
Corbett, W. Joseph, V.G., Vicar Gen. & Moderator of the Curia
Giusta, Frank J., Chap. (Retired), Emory Crawford Long Hospital, Emory University Hospital, The Emory Clinic, Winship Cancer Institute & Wesley Woods Center Complex, Emory University Orthopaedics and Spine Hospital
Lopez, Richard J., Chap., St. Pius X High School
Very Revs.—
Hachey, Paul J., S.M., J.C.L., M.C.L., M.Div., Judicial Vicar, Court of Appeals
Poloche, Pedro, J.C.L., J.V., Metro. Tribunal
Revs.—
Adams, James P., Chap., Our Lady of Mercy High School
Ballman, Luke R., S.T.L., Dir. Vocations & Rector, St. Charles Borromeo House of Formation
Berny, Paul W., M.Div., Chap., Blessed Trinity Catholic School
Branch, Edward B., Chap., Atlanta University
Caballejo, Yuen, Chap., Prison Ministry Catholic Charities of the Archdiocese of Atlanta
Dhabliwala, Neil
Grave, Miguel de Peralta, St. Joseph Hosp.
Hennessy, Thomas J., Chap., Our Lady of Perpetual Help Home, Atlanta
Hepburn, Timothy M., Chap., Georgia Institute of Technology
Hyman, David L., O.F.M., Chap., University of Georgia
Lyness, Stephen J., Chap., Georgia State University
Morris, Joseph E., Chap., Kennesaw State University
Natad, Diosmar, Master of Ceremonies for the Most Reverend Wilton D. Gregory
Peek, Kevin T., B.A., M.Div., Campus Min., GA. Tech
Selvaraj, Balappa, J.C.L., Cf. Adv. Metro. Tribunal
Small, Bryan D., Chap., Emory University & Agnes State College
Vigliotta, Thomas F., O.F.M., Chap., University of Georgia
Wilber, Stewart, Counselor, Catholic Charities of the Archdiocese of Atlanta

---

Without Archdiocesan Assignment or Faculties:
Revs.—
Anderson, John
Bailey, Ricardo, (Leave of Absence)
Doyle, N. Brendan
Jean, Thony Roody, (Leave of Absence)
Kieran, Richard A., (Medical Leave)
Kinast, Robert L., (On Sabbatical)
Mateus, Norberto, (Medical Leave)
Schoenfield, Andres H., (Leave of Absence)
Sotelo, Fabio A., (Leave of Absence)
St. Fleur, Maxis, (Leave of Absence)
Zivic, Richard A.

On Duty Outside the Archdiocese:
Revs.—
Craig, David, Holy Spirit Catholic Church, 1420 7th St. N., Fargo, ND 58102.
Gadziala, Timothy, J.C.L., Diocese of Mandeville,

P.O. Box 8, Mandeville, Jamaica.
Kinast, Robert L., Center for Theological Reflection, 102 Gulf Blvd. #301, Indian Rocks Beach, FL 33785.
Silloway, Michael, Pontifical North American 00120 Vatican City State.

Graduate Studies:
Rev.—
Allen, Joshua, Pontifical North American College 00120 Vatican City State.

Military Chaplains:
Revs.—
Ha, Hieu Minh, United States Regular Army
McCormick, Patrick J., 3308 E. 15th St., Panama City, FL 32405.
Wendel, Fred W., United States Regular Army, 1270 Polo Rd., Apt. 1431, Columbia, SC 29223.

On Leave of Absence:
Revs.—
Anderson, John R.
Bailey, Ricardo
Doyle, N. Brendan
Jean, Thony Roody
Kieran, Richard A.
Kinast, Robert L., (On Sabbatical)
Mateus, Norberto
Schoenfield, Andres H.
Sotelo, Fabio A.
St. Fleur, Maxis
Zivic, Richard A.

Retired:
Rev. Msgrs.—
Donovan, Walter J., St. George Village, 11350 Woodstock Rd., Apt. 2122, Roswell, 30075. Sacred Heart Church, 353 Peachtree St., Atlanta, 30308.
Giusta, Frank J., P.O. Box 160019, Atlanta, 30316.
Herbert, Leo P., 3131 N. Druid Hills Rd., Apt 2206, Decatur, 30033-2646.
Hoffman, William G., St. George Village, 11350 Woodstock Rd., Apt. 2124, Roswell, 30075. Tel: 770-645-2340. Email: msgrbill@yahoo.com
Young, Terry W., V.F., 1000 Decatur Rd. (GA Hwy. 155), Mcdonough, 30253-1779.
Very Rev.—
Morrow, Richard B., 2699 Peachtree Rd., Atlanta, 30305. Cathedral of Christ the King
Revs.—
Adamski, John S., 41 Finch Tr., Atlanta, 30308.
Curran, Anthony T., 915 N. Rock St., Shamokin, PA 17872.
Danneker, Edward A.J., Holy Cross Catholic Church, 3175 Hathaway Ct., NE, Atlanta, 30341.
Dullea, Denis, 11350 Woodstock Rd., Roswell, 30075.
Foley, Walter W., 561 Raindrop Circle, Hartwell, 30643.
Horan, Ray, 318 Memory Ln., Martin, 30557.
Kane, Terence, 294 John Austin Way, Hartwell, 30643.
Medlin, Douglas S., P.O. Box 224, Sautee Nacoochee, 30571.
O'Connor, Edward, St. George Village, 11350 Woodstock Rd., Roswell, 30075.
Redden, Michael J., 1413 Oak Knoll Dr., Conyers, 30012.
Rudd, Thad B., 540 Ascension Trail, Cleveland, 30528.
Ryan, Tim, 1310 Primrose Dr., Roswell, 30076.
Sexstone, James H., Saint Thomas Aquinas Catholic Church, 535 Rucker Rd., Alpharetta, 30004.

Permanent Deacons:
Anderson, Douglas J., St. Francis De Sales, Mableton
Angelich, George D., St. Marguerite D'Youville, Lawrenceville
Anugerah, Antonius, Our Lady of the Assumption, Atlanta
Anzalone, Joseph C., St. Philip Benizi, Jonesboro
Anzalone, Joseph S., (On Duty Outside the Archdiocese)
Atkinson, Jon G., Our Lady of Perpetual Help, Carrollton
Balfour, Michael K., Sacred Heart, Atlanta
Barker, Joseph J., St. Anthony, Atlanta
Barone, John J., St. Mark, Clarkesville; On Duty Outside of Diocese
Barrueta, Fernando, Saint Pius X, Conyers
Basilio, Cesar, Sacred Heart, Milledgeville
Bathea, Val, (On Duty Outside the Archdiocese)
Beckman, Richard F., (Retired)
Bedard, Walter T., Sr., (Retired)
Beers, Steven (Steve), St. George's, Newnan
Bek, Stephen J., St. Vincent de Paul, Dallas
Berding, Herbert C., (Retired), St. James, Madison
Bevacqua, Bill J., Our Lady of the Assumption, Atlanta
Bickerstaff, Michael, St. Peter Chanel, Roswell
Biglow, Ernest, Our Lady of the Assumption, Atlanta
Bishop, James R., St. George's, Newnan
Bishop, Kenneth P., Sacred Heart, Griffin
Blind, Terry S., Holy Trinity, Peachtree City
Bobb, William, St. George Village, Roswell
Bohn, William L., Saint Monica, Duluth
Borsavage, Charles T., (Inactive)
Brown, Raymond E., (On Duty Outside the Archdiocese)
Brunton, Robert, St. Thomas Aquinas, Alpharetta
Burke, John, St. Mary's, Toccoa
Byrne, Michael T., St. John Neumann, Lilburn
Campos, Jose G., St. Andrew, Roswell
Carignan, Charles E., Our Lady of LaSalette, Canton
Carr, Ronald, St. Benedict, Johns Creek
Carter, Joseph R., St. Monica, Duluth
Casal, Matias A., St. Philip Benizi, Jonesboro
Casey, Bernard J., St. Michael the Archangel, Woodstock
Casey, Lawrence B., St. Francis of Assisi, Blairsville
Chambliss, Leonard P., Jr., St. Philip Benizi, Jonesboro
Cintron, Rafael, St. Oliver Plunkett, Snellville
Coffey, Thomas, Church of the Transfiguration, Marietta
Collins, Gerald A., Christ Our Hope, Lithonia
Comeau, Ronald A., (Retired), Cathedral of Christ the King, Atlanta
Connell, Jerry F., (Retired)
Conti, Richard J., St. Catherine of Siena, Kennesaw
Cooper, King E., St. Matthew, Tyrone
Coughlin, Frank F., (Retired)
Cuomo, Anthony F., Holy Trinity, Peachtree City
Demko, Stephen G., Holy Spirit, Atlanta
DeSandre, Bart R., (Retired/Active), Shrine of the Immaculate Conception, Atlanta
Devereux, Francis, St. Joseph, Marietta
Dietz, Paul E., St. Francis of Assisi, Blairsville
Doppel, Paul Lee, All Saints, Dunwoody
Dorner, Dennis J., Chancellor, Dir. Permanent Diaconate, St. Brigid, Johns Creek; St. Luke the Evangelist, Dahlonega
Duffield, John P., Holy Family, Marietta
Easterwood, James M., (Retired)
Echevarria, Miguel A., St. Catherine of Siena, Kennesaw
Egan, Raymond F., Chancery, Atlanta; Interfaith Airport Chaplaincy
Espinosa, Jose G., Transfiguration, Mariett; Holy Spirit Mission, Sandy Springs
Eustace, Joseph C., St. Joseph, Marietta
Fagan, Patrick, St. Lawrence, Lawrenceville
Feliu, Albert L., St. Marguerite D'Youville, Lawrenceville
Figueredo, Alberto, (Inactive)
Ford, Stanley B., (On Leave of Absence)
Fraser, Roger A., St. Brendan, Cumming
Gahafer, Leo, St. Brigid, Johns Creek
Gallagher, Alexander S., Holy Family, Marietta
Galvis, Enrique L., (Retired)
Garcia-Carreras, Evelio, St. Stephen the Martyr, Lilburn
Garrett, Michael, St. Thomas the Apostle, Smyrna
Garrett, William, All Saints, Dunwoody
Gaudin, James M., Jr., St. Joseph's, Athens
Geroski, Dayle H., The Interfaith Airport Chaplaincy, Inc., Atlanta
Gillespie, Patrick (Pat) J., St. James the Apostle, McDonough
Gonzalez, Marino, Sacred Heart, Atlanta
Goolsby, Joseph B., (Retired)
Gorski, Paul A., Transfiguration, Marietta
Gotschall, Thomas E., St. Andrew, Roswell
Grabowy, Edmund M., St. Ann's, Marietta
Gregerson, Robert J., (On Duty Outside of Archdiocese)
Griffin, Chester H., Our Lady of Lourdes, Atlanta
Grimaldi, Robert H., St. Brendan, Cumming
Gross, Benedict, (Retired)
Grubbs, Burgess "David", St. Catherine of Siena, Kennesaw
Hampton, William (Bill) L., St. Matthew's, Tyrone
Hanson, David, St. Helena Catholic Mission, Clayton; On Duty Outside of Archdiocese
Hauert, Robert J., St. Stephen the Martyr, Lilburn
Heinsch, William H., St. Michael the Archangel, Woodstock
Henrich, Robert A., (On Duty Outside the Archdiocese)
Hettel, Louis A., (Retired)
Holmer, Terry M., St. Theresa, Douglasville
Huff, Tom, St. Brigid, Johns Creek
Hunkele, Thomas H., (Retired)
Huynh, Hung Viet (Vic), Our Lady of Vietnam, Riverdale
Jackson, Earl D., St. Thomas the Apostle, Smyrna
Jelks, Leviticus, St. Anthony's, Atlanta
Jennings, Bobby Allen, St. Ann, Marietta
Jimenez, Arturo P., (Retired)
Jindrich, William L., St. Oliver Plunkett, Snellville
Johns, Fred, St. Pius X, Conyers
Johnson, Nicholas, Prince of Peace, Flowery Branch
Jones, Frederick T., (Retired)
Jones, Michael R., Prince of Peace, Flowery Branch
Kaszycki, Richard C., St. Steven the Martyr, Lilburn
Kazin, Gerard G., St. Benedict, Duluth
Keeling, William W., St. Thomas Aquinas, Alpharetta
Keen, William, St. Andrew's, Roswell
Keller, Norman K., St. Joseph, Marietta
Kelsey, Donald A., (Retired)
Kennedy, Michael L., St. Michael's, Gainesville
Kepshire, Robert J., St. Joseph, Athens
Kilkelly, Brian, St. Pius X, Conyers
King, A.B., III, St. Lawrence, Lawrenceville
Kirksey, Timothy K., St. Matthew's Church, Winder
Klein, Robert, St. Ann, Marietta
Kolodziej, Keith M., St. Peter Chanel Church, Roswell
Korte, Jerry R., Sacred Heart of Jesus, Hartwell
Krise, Edward, All Saints, Dunwoody
Krupa, Bradford, St. Clement, Calhoun
LaFreniere, James A., St. Brigid, Alpharetta
LaHouse, Edmund J., St. Thomas Aquinas, Alpharetta
LaMachia, Ralph, Good Shepherd, Cumming
Lampe, Martin J., St. Peter Chanel Church, Roswell
Lampert, Kenneth W., St. Michael, Gainesville
Landaiche, Nemour Michel, Holy Trinity, Peachtree City
Lange, William G., (Retired)
Lee, Hilliard M., Jr., St. Paul of the Cross, Atlanta
Lerma, Arthur, St. Thomas Aquinas, Alpharetta
Lett, Jerry M., Sts. Peter & Paul, Decatur
Londono, Luis, St. Michael, Gainesville
Mac Donald, Will, (Retired)
Mackin, Thomas F., (Retired)
Manning, Ronald, St. Catherine of Siena, Kennesaw
Marchildon, Donald W., (Retired)
Marinchak, Richard J., St. Mark's, Clarkesville
Marrero, Felix, Sacred Heart, Griffin
Marsh, Curtis D., St. Catherine Laboure, Jefferson
Marten, William H., St. John Neumann, Lilburn
Martinez, Julio V., St. Philip Benizi, Jonesboro
Martorell, Gerardo G., (Retired)
Mason, John, St. Anthony's, Blue Ridge
Mc Carthy, Kevin J., (On Duty Outside the Archdiocese)
McBride, Carl I., St. Gabriel's, Fayetteville
McCarthy, William F., Holy Spirit, Atlanta
McDermott, James, St. Vincent de Paul, Dallas
McGrane, Thomas J., (On Duty Outside the Archdiocese)
McGuire, John P., St. Anthony, Blue Ridge
McHugh, Al C., (Retired)
McKenzie, William, St. Patrick, Norcross
McManus, John J., J.D., J.C.L. , Cathedral of Christ the King, Atlanta; Corpus Christi, Stone Mountain
McNabb, Scott J.N., Cathedral of Christ the King, Atlanta
Mead, Stuart A., St. Pius X, Conyers
Medine, Scott E., St. Joseph, Athens
Melara, Israel D., St. Theresa, Douglasville
Melvin, Ken W., Corpus Christi, Stone Mountain
Merlo-Quintero, Jose T., St. Joseph, Marietta
Metzger, Thomas J., St. Anna, Monroe
Meuninck, Tilton (T.C.), St. Peter the Rock, The Rock, GA
Mickle, Richard (Rich) A., St. Matthew, Winder
Miles, Philip, Church of the Transfiguration, Marietta
Millinger, Terry D., St. Lawrence, Lawrenceville
Mitchell, Alfred, Sts. Peter & Paul, Decatur; Interfaith Chaplaincy Airport
Mobley, Michael K., Sr., St. Stephen the Martyr, Lilburn
Monahan, William J., St. Brendan Church, Cumming
Moncrief, Wayland, (On Duty Outside the Archdiocese)
Moore, Dennis, (Retired)
Morning, J. Nicholas, St. Ann, Marietta
Mure, Samuel M., (Retired)
Nacey, Wayne, St. Peter, LaGrange
Nadeau, Donald N., Good Shepherd, Cumming
Narvaez, Jose A., St. Patrick's, Norcross
Nerio, Jesus, St. Peter Chanel Church, Roswell
Neslin, Stuart L., St. Mary, Rome
Nguyen, Joseph Phu, Our Lady of Vietnam, Riverdale

O'Brien, Michael J., Our Lady of the Assumption, Atlanta
O'Donoghue, William H., Our Lady of the Assumption, Atlanta
O'Neill, Robert A., (Retired)
Ollick, Gregory, St. John Neumann, Lilbur; St. Mary, Toccoa
Orellana, Jose M., St. Mary, Rome
Parker, Donald S., St. Gabriel, Fayetteville
Patrick, Charles, St. Theresa, Douglasville
Patterson, Edward, Our Lady of the Assumption, Atlanta
Payne, William E., Jr., Shrine of the Immaculate Conception, Atlanta
Pecore, Gregory L., St. Philip Benizi, Jonesboro
Perez, Gilberto, Saint Michael, Gainesville
Perez, Jose, St. Vincent de Paul, Dallas
Peters, Gayle P., St. Matthew, Tyrone
Peterson, John R., Prince of Peace, Flowery Branch
Ponichtera, Stephen, St. Catherine of Siena, Kennesaw
Przybylek, Francis, St. John Vianney, Lithia Springs
Publicover, Bruce C., (Retired)
Puetz, John D., St. Benedict, Duluth
Pupo, Jose I., St. Thomas Aquinas, Alpharetta
Rademacher, Edward, St. Monica, Duluth
Readdy, Robert G., (Retired)
Reed, William Bruce, Jr., St. Joseph, Marietta
Reimer, Cecil R., Holy Cross, Atlanta
Rentas, Felix, St. John Vianney, Lithia Springs
Rhodes, Joseph, St. Pius X, Conyers
Rich, Robert M., (Retired)
Richardson, Raymond L., (Retired w/Faculties)
Riddett, Robert, St. Jude the Apostle, Atlanta
Rivera, Prudencio I., (Retired)
Robichaux, Whitney F., Jr., Cathedral of Christ the King, Atlanta; Interfaith Chaplaincy Airport
Roche, Gary J., St. Mark, Clarkesville
Rodriguez, Etienne Francisco, St. Philip Benizi, Jonesboro
Ruberte, Joseph, Mary Our Queen, Norcross
Rubio, Eduardo J., St. Brendan the Navigator, Cumming
Ryan, Thomas J., St. Catherine of Siena, Kennesaw
Sambrone, Fred J., Jr., (Retired)
Samoranski, Alfred T., Prince of Peace, Buford
Sandlin, David C., St. Mary Magdalene, Newnan
Schantz, Gary E., St. Andrew, Roswell
Shaver, Thomas R., St. Joseph's, Marietta
Shawcross, Steven W., St. Thomas Aquinas, Alpharetta
Shoemaker, John W., (Retired)
Sholander, Mark A., The Interfaith Airport Chaplaincy, Inc., Atlanta; Holy Spirit, Peachtree City
Shuler, Thomas B., John XXIII Seminary
Silvestri, Thomas D., Holy Cross, Atlanta; Chap., Georgia Diagnostic and Correctional Center, Jackson
Simmons, William H., III, St. Anthony of Padua, Atlanta
Sinanian, Loris R., St. Anthony's, Blue Ridge
Smith, George, St. Paul of the Cross, Atlanta
Smith, Robert B., (Retired)
Smith, Wayne D., Sacred Heart, Atlanta
Sparks, Scott A., St. Peter Chanel, Roswell
Speed, William (Bill) E., Prince of Peace, Flowery Branch
St. Michel, Ronald A., St. Theresa, Douglasville
Stagg, James A., (On Duty Outside the Archdiocese)
Stewart, James M., (Retired)
Stone, James E., Mary Our Queen, Norcross
Stonecipher, Thomas L., St. John the Evangelist, Hapeville
Strachan, John S., St. Thomas Aquinas, Alpharetta
Suever, Richard M., (Retired)
Sutter, Edward L., Our Lady of the Mountain, Jasper
Swan, Peter B., Sr., St. Philip Benizi, Jonesboro
Swope, Paul S., Jr., Assoc. Dir. Formation, St. George, Newnan
Thibodeau, Richard, St. Paul the Apostle, Cleveland
Thomasberger, David J., St. Peter Chanel, Roswell
Thompson, Chris, Our Lady of Assumption, Atlanta
Tipton, Robert F., St. Monica, Duluth
Tocca, Fred, Most Blessed Sacrament, Atlanta
Tolcher, Richard P., St. Philip Benizi, Jonesboro
Tracy, Kevin F., St. Thomas Aquinas, Alpharetta
Tramonte, James A., St. Jude the Apostle, Sandy Springs
Underwood, Froilan (Allen) V., Holy Spirit, Atlanta
Vargas, Hector M., Holy Trinity, Peachtree City
Weeks, Jim G., St. Matthew's, Tyrone
Weiss, Dr. James (Jim), Holy Cross, Atlanta
Welsh, Lawrence J., St. Matthew, Winder
Whitmeyer, Eugene, (Retired)
Williams, James H., St. Francis of Assisi, Cartersville
Williams, Kenneth, Christ Redeemer Mission, Dawsonville
Wojcik, John, St. Peter Chanel, Roswell
Woods, Michael, Prince of Peace, Flowery Branch
Zaworski, Thomas E., (Retired)
Zukauckas, Gerald, Cathedral of Christ the King, Atlanta

INSTITUTIONS LOCATED IN THE ARCHDIOCESE

[A] SEMINARIES, RELIGIOUS OR SCHOLASTICATES

ATLANTA. *Aquinas Center of Theology at Emory University*, 1256 Briarcliff Rd, Bldg. A, Rm. 221, 30306. Tel: 404-727-8860; Fax: 404-727-8862. Email: baoster@emory.edu. Web: www.aquinas.emory.edu. Joseph Foltz Esq., Chair; Dr. Phillip Thompson, Dir. Total Staff 2.

[B] ARCHDIOCESAN SCHOOLS, PARISH

ATLANTA. *Cathedral of Christ the King Catholic School* (1937) (Grades K-8), (Co-ed), 46 Peachtree Way N.E., 30305. Tel: 404-233-0383; Fax: 404-266-0704. Email: pmwarner@christking.org. Web: www.christking.org. Mrs. Peggy Warner, Prin.; Tricia Ward, Asst. Prin.; Melanie Brent, Librarian. Lay Teachers 39; Students 565.

Immaculate Heart of Mary Catholic School (1958) (Grades K-8), 2855 Briarcliff Rd., N.E., 30329. Tel: 404-636-4488; Fax: 404-636-1853. Web: www.ihmschool.org. James Lee, Prin.; Bob Baldonado, Asst. Prin.; Sandy Wilson, Librarian. Lay Teachers 36; Students 504.

St. Jude the Apostle Catholic School (1962) (Grades K-8), 7171 Glenridge Dr., N.E., 30328. Tel: 770-394-2880; Fax: 770-804-9248. Web: saintjude.net. Patty Childs, Prin.; Eleneora Straub, Librarian. Lay Teachers 30; Students 517.

Our Lady of the Assumption Catholic School (1952) (Grades PreK-8), 1320 Hearst Dr., N.E., 30319. Tel: 404-364-1902; Fax: 404-364-1914. Email: office@olaschool.org. Web: olaschool.org. Anita Nagel, Prin.; Diane Miller-Deasy, Librarian. Lay Teachers 39; Students 521.

St. Pius X Catholic High School (1958) (Coed), 2674 Johnson Rd., N.E., 30345. Tel: 404-636-3023; Fax: 404-633-8387. Email: spellman@spx.org. Web: spx.org. Mr. Stephen Spellman, Prin.; Ruth McCullough, Dean Academics; Rachel Braham, Dean Students; Edye Simpson, Dean Students; Mark Kelly, Athletic Dir.; Chuck Byrd, Admissions; Rev. Msgr. Richard J. Lopez; Rev. Dan Rogaczewski; Robin Tanis, Librarian. Priests 2; Teachers 94; Students 1,116; Total Staff 40.

ATHENS. *St. Joseph Catholic School* (1949) (Grades PreK-8), 134 Prince Ave., 30601. Tel: 706-543-1621; Fax: 706-543-0149. Email: tbortle@sjsathens.org. Web: sjsathens.org. Charles J. Martin, Prin.; Karen Roberts, Librarian. Lay Teachers 20; Students 255.

DECATUR. *St. Peter Claver Regional Catholic School* (2001) (Grades PreK-8), 2560 Tilson Rd., 30032. Tel: 404-241-3063; Fax: 404-241-4382. Email: pmoors@spc-school.org. Web: www.spc-school.org. Pamela Moors, M.Ed., Prin.; Oree Williams III, Admission & Devel. Dir.; Eileen Rice, Librarian. Lay Teachers 15; Students 150.

St. Thomas More Catholic School (1950) (Grades K-8), 630 W. Ponce De Leon Ave., 30030. Tel: 404-373-8456; Fax: 404-377-8554. Email: stm@stmga.org. Web: www.stmga.org. Mrs. Terry Collis, Prin.; Eileen Maron, Admissions; Ansley Murphey, Devel.; Laura Ayala, Librarian. Lay Teachers 31; Students 473.

FAYETTEVILLE. *Our Lady of Mercy Catholic High School*, 861 Evander Holyfield Hwy., 30214. Tel: 770-461-2202; Fax: 770-461-9353. Email: ddorsel@mercycatholic.org. Web: www.mercycatholic.org. Daniel Dorsel, Prin.; Sandra Livsey-Martin, Admissions; William Schmitz, Athletic Dir.; Timothy Wojcik, Librarian; Rev. James P. Adams, Chap. Priests 1; Lay Teachers 33; Total Staff 34; Total Enrollment 358.

HAPEVILLE. *St. John the Evangelist Catholic School* (1954) (Grades PreK-8), 240 Arnold St., 30354. Tel: 404-767-4312; Fax: 404-767-0359. Web: sjccs.org. Karen Vogtner, B.S., M.Ed., Prin.; Kathy Van Meter, Librarian. Lay Teachers 22; Students 323; Sisters 1.

JOHN'S CREEK. *Holy Redeemer Catholic School* (1999) (Grades K-8), 3380 Old Alabama Rd., Johns Creek, 30022. Tel: 770-410-4056; Fax: 770-410-1454. Web: www.hrcatholicschool.org. Lauren Schell, Prin.; Sue Kalinauskas, Asst. Prin.; Emily Davis, Librarian. Lay Teachers 32; Students 504.

KENNESAW. *St. Catherine of Siena Catholic School* (2002) (Grades K-8), 1618 Ben King Rd., 30144. Tel: 770-419-8601; Fax: 678-626-0000. Web: www.scsiena.org. Sr. Mary Jacinta, O.P., Prin.; Vinita John, Librarian. Sisters 4; Lay Teachers 43; Total Staff 47; Total Enrollment 430.

LILBURN. *St. John Neumann Regional* (1986) (Grades K-8), (Regional), 791 Tom Smith Rd., S.W., 30047. Tel: 770-381-0557; Fax: 770-381-0276. Email: crusader@sjnrcs.org. Web: www.sjnrcs.org. Alex Porto, Prin.; Janet Kent. Lay Teachers 38; Students 481.

MARIETTA. *St. Joseph Catholic School* (1953) (Grades K-8), 81 Lacy St., 30060. Tel: 770-428-3328; Fax: 770-424-2960. Email: jbrodell@stjosephschool.org. Web: stjosephschool.org. Patricia Allen, Ed.S., Prin.; Jill Ramsey, Vice Prin. Lay Teachers 30; Students 484.

ROME. *St. Mary's Catholic School* (1945) (Grades PreK-8), 401 E. Seventh St., 30161. Tel: 706-234-4953; Fax: 706-234-3030. Web: www.smsrome.org. John H. Tarpley, Prin.; Theresa Cox, Librarian. Lay Teachers 25; Students 280.

ROSWELL. *Blessed Trinity Catholic High School* (2000) 11320 Woodstock Rd., 30075. Tel: 678-277-9083; Fax: 678-277-9756. Email: fmoore@btcatholic.org. Web: www.btcatholic.org. Frank Moore, Prin.; Mr. Richard Martin, Asst. Prin.; Brian Marks, Asst. Prin.; Susan Dorner, Asst. Prin.; Alan Keel, Librarian; Revs. Paul W. Berny, M.Div., Chap.; Augustine Tran, J.C.L. . Priests 2; Lay Teachers 70; Total Staff 108; Total Enrollment 970.

Queen of Angels Catholic School (1999) (Grades K-8), 11340 Woodstock Rd., 30075. Tel: 770-518-1804; Fax: 770-518-0945. Email: kwood@qaschool.org. Web: www.qaschool.org. Dr. Kathy Wood, Ph.D., Prin.; Mrs. Molly Carlin, Asst. Prin.; Mrs. Sue VanRooyen, Librarian. Lay Teachers 35; Students 504; Total Staff 60.

TYRONE. *Our Lady of Victory Catholic School* (1999) (Grades PreK-8), 211 Kirkley Rd., 30290. Tel: 770-306-9026; Fax: 770-306-0323. Web: www.olvpatriots.org. Linda Grace, Prin.; Angela Williams, Librarian. Lay Teachers 19; Admin/Facilities Staff 5; Total Staff 29; Total Enrollment 214.

[C] INDEPENDENT SCHOOLS

ATLANTA. **Donnellan School Inc. dba Holy Spirit Preparatory School* 4449 Northside Dr., 30327. Tel: 678-904-2811 (Office); Fax: 678-904-2811. Web: www.holyspiritprep.org. Gareth N. Genner, Pres.; Bob Pelletier, High School Prin.; Rev. Paul Moreau, L.C., B.A., Head Chap.; Kelly Corsetti, Librarian. Priests 1; Lay Teachers 114.

(Grades 7-12), Upper School Campus: 4449 Northside Dr., 30327. Tel: 678-904-2811. Bob Pelletier, High School Prin.

(Grades K-6), Lower School Campus: 4820 Long Island Dr., 30342. Tel: 404-255-0900. Linda Anthony, Prin.; Linda Ehlers, Librarian.

(Grades PreK), Preschool: 4465 Northside Dr., 30327. Tel: 404-252-8008. Dara Liberatore, Early Childhood Prin.; Linda Ehlers, Librarian.

Marist School, (Grades 7-12), 3790 Ashford Dunwoody, N.E., 30319-1899. Tel: 770-457-7201; 770-451-1316 (Res.); Fax: 770-457-8402. Email: marist@marist.com. Web: www.marist.com. Revs. Joel M. Konzen, S.M., Prin.; Francis J. Kissel, S.M.; Ralph F. Olek, S.M., Supr.; David D. Musso, S.M., Chap.; John H. Harhager, S.M., Pres.; John Walls, S.M., Dir. Campus Ministry; William F. Rowland, S.M., Spec. Asst. to Pres. A Private Catholic School.; College Preparatory Day School conducted by The Marist Fathers and Brothers. Corporate Title: Marist School, Inc. Priests 7; Lay Faculty 112; Total Staff 194; Students 1,080. In Res. Revs. Lawrence R. Schmuhl, S.M. (Retired); Charles A. Girard, S.M., Prov. Archivist; Very Rev. Paul J. Hachey, S.M., J.C.L., M.C.L., M.Div., Court of Appeals.

ATHENS. **Monsignor Donovan Catholic High School* (2003) 590 Lavender Rd., 30606. Tel: 706-433-0223; Fax: 706-433-0229. Email: jnasworthy@mdchs.org. Web: www.mdchs.org. Patrick J. Yuran, Prin.; Virginia Stutsman, Asst. Prin.; Liz Edwards, Librarian. Teachers 17; Total Staff 9; Students 101.

CUMMING. **Pinecrest Academy, Inc.* (1993) (Grades PreK-12), 955 Peachtree Pkwy., 30041. Tel: 770-888-4477; Fax: 770-888-0404. Email: pinecrestacademy@pinecrestacademy.org. Web: www.pinecrestacademy.org. Rick Swygman, Exec. Dir.; John H. Tarpley, Prin. High School; Fernada Paez, Formation Dir. Girls & Lower School; Robert Bruckner, Admissions; Rev. Dominic Pham, L.C., Chap.; Bro. Gabriel Lewis, L.C.; Rev. Todd Belardi, L.C.; Emily Smolynsky, Librarian.

Priests 3; Brothers 2; Female Consecrated 4; Lay Teachers 90; Students 870.

DULUTH. *Notre Dame Academy* (2005) (Grades PreK-8), 4635 River Green Pkwy., 30096. Tel: 678-387-9385 (Office); Fax: 678-990-9353. Email: dorr@ndacademy.org. Web: www.ndacademy.org. Debra Orr, Head of School; Julia Derucki, Prin. Upper Elementary & Middle School; Stacy Stanford, Advancement Dir.; Gary Hegarty, Dir., Fin. & Opers. Independent, Marist Sponsored School, Preschool program for children ages 3 & 4

Early Years School, Notre Dame Academy, 3345 Peachtree Industrial Blvd., 30096. Tel: 678-387-9385 (Office); Fax: 678-990-9353. Email: mhole@ndacademy.org. Web: www.ndacademy.org. Molly Hole, Prin. Primary Years & Admissions Dir. Independent, Marist Sponsored School Lay Teachers 50.

[D] GENERAL HOSPITALS

ATHENS. *St. Mary's Health Care System*, 1230 Baxter St., 30606-3791. Tel: 706-389-3930; Fax: 706-389-3931. Email: dmckenna@stmarysathens.org. Web: www.stmarysathens.org. Mr. Don McKenna, Pres. & CEO; Sr. Patricia Loom, S.N.D.deN., Vice Pres. Mission Svcs. Sisters of Mercy, South Central Region. Other Sister Personnel 3; Nurses 465; Bed Capacity 196; Patients Assisted Annually 13,000; Total Staff 1,348.

[E] SPECIAL HOSPITALS

ATLANTA. *Saint Joseph's Mercy Care Services* (1985) 424 Decatur St., 30312-1848. Tel: 678-843-8500; Fax: 678-843-8501. Email: aebberwein@sjha.org. Division of Saint Joseph's Health System. Operates Saint Joseph's Mercy Care Services (Atlanta, Georgia). Operates Mercy Senior Care (Rome, Georgia). Total Staff 140; Sisters 1; Total Assisted 22,000.

Our Lady of Perpetual Help Home, 760 Pollard Blvd., S.W., 30315. Tel: 404-688-9515; Fax: 404-588-9568. Web: olphhome.org. Sr. Miriam Smith, O.P., Supr.; Rev. Joseph Mullakkara, M.S.F.S., Chap.

Servants of Relief for Incurable Cancer Dominican Sisters of Hawthorne, Nursing Home for Free Care of Cancer Patients. Priests 1; Sisters 11; Total Staff 32; Patients Assisted Annually 150; Bed Capacity 35.

ROME. *Mercy Senior Care, Inc.*, P.O. Box 866, 30162-0866. Tel: 706-291-8496; Fax: 706-295-5953. Email: rlawler@sjha.org. Sr. Angela Marie Ebberwein, R.S.M., Vice Pres.; Rita Lawler, Dir. Total Staff 18; Total Assisted 500.

[F] MONASTERIES AND RESIDENCES OF PRIESTS

ATLANTA. *Augustine House, Dominicans Friars of Atlanta*, 220 Renaissance Pkwy. N.E., Unit 1313, 30308. Tel: 404-549-3223. Revs. Bruce Schultz, O.P., Supr.; Jeffery Ott, O.P.

Marist Provincial Office, Society of Mary - Atlanta Province, P.O. Box 81144, 30366-1144. Tel: 770-458-1435; Fax: 770-458-1044. Email: provincialoffice@marist.com; tgkeating@msn.com. Web: www.societyofmaryusa.org. P.O. Box 81144, 30366-1144. Very Rev. Timothy G. Keating, S.M., Prov.

ALPHARETTA. *Legionaries of Christ, Incorporated*, 55 Club Ct., 30005. Tel: 770-671-8778; Fax: 678-916-7543. Web: www.legionariesofchrist.org. Revs. Guillermo Serra, L.C., Asst., Territorial Dir.; Dominic Pham, L.C., Chap.; Robert Presutti, L.C., Exec. Dir., Pinecrest Academy; Peter Devereux, L.C.; Bros. Gabriel Lewis, L.C., Formation Instructor; Christopher Gronotte, L.C., Formation Instructor; Michael Baggot, L.C., Teacher, Pinecrest Academy. Total in Residence 5.

Norcross Pastoral Center, Inc., 55 Club Ct., 30005. Tel: 770-671-8778; Fax: 678-916-7543. Web: www.legionariesofchrist.org. Revs. Jose Felix Ortega, L.C., Contact Person; Timothy Moran, Retreats & Promotion Work; David Daly, L.C., Supr. & Retreat Work. Email: ddaly@legionaries.org; Juan Gabriel Guerra, L.C., Retreat Work; Martin Connor, L.C. *Legionaries of Christ*, 2595 Spalding Dr., Atlanta, 30350. Tel: 770-394-2158; Fax: 770-393-0934. Web: www.legionariesofchrist.org. Rev. Richard Sutter, L.C., Formation Dir., Pinecrest Academy.

CONYERS. *The Monastery of the Holy Spirit*, 2625 Hwy. 212 S.W., 30094-4044. Tel: 770-483-8705; Fax: 770-760-0989. Email: monastery@trappist.net. Web: www.trappist.net. Rev. Anthony Delisi, O.C.S.O.; Bro. Elias Marechal, O.C.S.O., Master of Novices; Revs. Francis Michael Stiteler, O.C.S.O., Abbot; Richard Donarski, O.C.S.O.; Methodius Telnack, O.C.S.O., Prior; Malachy Corley, O.C.S.O.; Gerard Gross, O.C.S.O., Office Sub Prior; Jerome J. Hickey, O.C.S.O. (Retired); Luke C. Kot, O.C.S.O. (Retired); Ed Morley, O.C.S.O.; John M. O'Brien, O.C.S.O.; Eduardo Rodriguez, O.C.S.O.; Thomas F. Smith, O.C.S.O.; Matt G. Torpey, O.C.S.O., Master of Juniors. Priests 15; Professed Brothers 20; Postulants 2; Novices 2. Located Elsewhere: Rev. James Stephen Behrens, O.C.S.O.

SNELLVILLE. *The Missionaries of St. Francis De Sales* (1838) 3474 Pate Dr., 30039. Tel: 770-972-0202; Fax: 770-963-3774. Web: www.basilluyethop.org. Revs. Joseph Mullakkara, M.S.F.S., Local Supr.; John C. DeVore, M.S.F.S.; Martin Kopchik, M.S.F.S., Dir. Vocations & Spirituality Center; Jose Maliekal, M.S.F.S.; Joseph Mendes, M.S.F.S.; Abraham Puthiaparampil, M.S.F.S.

[G] CONVENTS AND RESIDENCES OF SISTERS

ATLANTA. *Missionaries of Charity* (1993) 995 St. Charles Ave., N.E., 30306-4211. Tel: 404-892-5111. Sisters 4; Total Assisted 300.

Sisters of Good Shepherd, 3244 Wanda Woods Dr., 30340-4510. Tel: 770-491-6292; Fax: 770-908-8777. Email: srmak77@bellsouth.net. Sr. M. Anita Kristofco, Contact Person. Sisters 4.

BUFORD. *Missionary Sisters of the Sacred Heart "Ad Gentes"* (1949) 6401 New Bethany Rd., 30518. Tel: 678-482-1530; Fax: 678-482-1530. Email: xeniagonzalez@bellsouth.net. Sisters Inés G. Ramos Tapia, M.A.G., B.A., M.A., Gen. Coord. of M.A.G. Sisters in U.S.A.; Beatriz Taneco Bieira, M.A.G., B.A., L.P., Pastoral Assoc.; Xenia Gonzalez, M.A.G., B.A., M.A., Treas. & Pastoral Assoc.; Veronica F. Ramos, M.A.G., B.A., M.A., Pastoral Assoc.; Esther Ordonez, M.A.G., B.A., Pastoral Assoc.; Maria L. Ramos, M.A.G., Pastoral Assoc.; Pilar Hinojosa, M.A.G., B.A., Pastoral Assoc. To serve the Hispanic Community. Sisters 7.

SNELLVILLE. *Monastery of the Visitation* (Maryfield), 2055 Ridgedale Dr., 30078. Tel: 770-972-1060. Sr. Mary Jane Frances Williams, V.H.M., Supr. Strictly cloistered contemplative Office of First Federation. Private retreats for women interested in a religious vocation. U.S. Professed Sisters 11; Novices 1.

[H] RETREAT HOUSES

ATLANTA. *Ignatius House*, 6700 Riverside Dr., N.W., 30328-2710. Tel: 404-255-0503; Fax: 404-256-0776. Email: smachek@ignatiushouse.org. Web: www.ignatiushouse.org. Revs. Albert C. Louapre, S.J., Retreat Dir.; Niel Jarreau, S.J., Retreat Dir.; Edward P. Buvens, S.J., Retreat Dir.; Maria Greta Cressler, Lay Exec. Dir.; Rev. Edward Salazar, Retreat Dir. Total in Residence 4; Total Staff 9.

CONYERS. *Monastery of the Holy Spirit*, 2625 Hwy. 212, S.W., 30094. Tel: 770-760-0959; Fax: 770-760-0989. Email: rhouse@trappist.net. Web: www.trappist.net. Private retreats for men and women.

HOSCHTON. *Sisters of the Cenacle*, 5913 Jackson Trail Rd., 30548. Tel: 706-654-3460; Fax: 706-654-1459. Sisters Susan Arcaro, R.C.; Barbara Young, R.C. Congregation of Our Lady of the Retreat in the Cenacle., Retreat Ministry, Spiritual Development Programs, Spiritual Direction, and Other Forms of Spiritual Ministry. Sisters 2.

[I] CAMPUS MINISTRY CENTERS

ATLANTA. *Campus Ministry Archdiocese of Atlanta*, 2401 Lake Park Dr., 30080-8862. Tel: 404-885-7413; Fax: 404-885-7473.

Atlanta University Complex-The Catholic Center 809 Beckwith St., S.W., 30314-3720. Tel: 404-755-9394; Fax: 404-755-3460. Rev. Edward B. Branch, Campus Min.

Kennesaw State University 3487 Campus Loop Rd., Kennesaw, 30144. Tel: 770-423-9909; Fax: 770-423-9605. Web: www.kennesaw.edu. Rev. Joseph E. Morris, Chap.

Emory University, Agnes Scott College 1753 N. Decatur Rd., N.E., 30307. Tel: 404-636-7237; Fax: 404-636-6099. Web: www.emory.edu. Rev. Diosmar Natad, Chap.

Georgia Institute of Technology 172 4th St., N.W., 30313. Tel: 404-892-6759; Fax: 404-829-6759. Web: www.gatech.edu. Rev. Kevin T. Peek, B.A., M.Div., Chap.

Oglethorpe University 4484 Peachtree Rd., N.E., 30319. Tel: 404-261-1441. Web: www.oglethorpe.edu.

University of Georgia - Catholic Student Center 1344 S. Lumpkin St., Athens, 30605. Tel: 706-543-2293; Fax: 706-543-2541. Web: www.uga.edu/cc. Revs. Thomas F. Vigliotta, O.F.M., Dir. Campus Ministry; David L. Hyman, O.F.M., Assoc. Campus Min. (Athens)

North Georgia College , (Dahlonega), *St. Luke the Evangelist Church*, 91 N. Park St., Dahlonega, 30533. Tel: 706-864-4779; Fax: 706-864-2568. Web: www.northgeorgia.edu. Rev. Neil Dhabliwala.

Dalton Junior College , (Dalton), *Church of St. Joseph*, 1775 Old Haigmill Rd., Dalton, 30720. Tel: 706-278-3107; Fax: 706-278-6902. Web: www.daltonstate.edu.

Brenau College St. Michael's Catholic Church - 1440 Pearce Cir., N.E., Gainesville, 30501-2457. Tel: 706-534-3338; Fax: 706-535-2440. Web: www.onlinebrenau.edu. (Gainesville)

LaGrange Jr. College 200 LaFayette Pkwy., LaGrange, 30240. Tel: 706-884-4224; Fax: 706-884-1624. Web: www.lagrange.edu. Rev. Theodore Book, S.L.L., Chap. (LaGrange)

Georgia College & State University , (Milledgeville), *Sacred Heart Church*, 1730 Columbine Rd., Milledgeville, 31061. Tel: 478-453-7758. Email: cesar.basilio@thielekanolin.com.

Shorter College , (Rome), *St. Mary's Church*, 911 N. Broad St., Rome, 30161. Tel: 706-295-7014; Fax: 706-295-1717. Web: www.shorter.edu.

Dekalb Community College , (Stone Mountain), *Corpus Christi Church*, 600 Mountain View Dr., Stone Mountain, 30083. Tel: 770-469-0395; Fax: 770-469-6822. Web: www.dekalbtech.org. Rev. Leonard Brown, C.M.F.

Catholic Center Georgia State University Student Center, Ste. 330, P.O. Box 3965, 30302. Rev. Theodore Book, S.L.L., Chap.

[J] CATHOLIC CONTINUING CARE RETIREMENT CENTER

ROSWELL. *St. George Village-Catholic Community Retirement Center*, 11350 Woodstock Rd., 30075. Tel: 770-645-2340. Web: www.stgeorgevillage.com. Mr. Mark A. Lowell, Exec. Dir.

[K] MISCELLANEOUS LISTINGS

ATLANTA. *Allegre Point Senior Residences, Inc.*, 621 North Ave., Ste. A150, 30308. Tel: 404-549-5349; Fax: 877-693-2333. Web: www.mercyhousing.org.

Bon Secours Charity Health System Inc., 191 Peachtree St., Ste. 1500, 30303.

Bon Secours New York Health System Inc., 191 Peachtree St., Ste. 1500, 30303.

The Catholic Charismatic Renewal for the Archdiocese of Atlanta, 1786 Wellborn Rd., Lithonia, 30058. Tel: 770-482-5017; Fax: 770-482-9476. Email: contact@atlccr.org. Web: www.atlccr.org.

Christ Child Society of Atlanta, P.O. Box 88705, 30356. Tel: 404-520-9900. Email: treasurer@christchildatlanta.org.

Good Shepherd Services of Atlanta, Inc. (1993) (Incorporated as Good Shepherd Corporation)

Main Office, 2426 Shallowford Terr., 30341. Tel: 770-455-9379; Fax: 770-451-0156. Email: shepherdatlanta@yahoo.com. Sr. Christine Truong, M.S.W., M.A., Exec. Dir.

Good Shepherd Outreach Center, 2426 Shallowford Ter., 30341. Tel: 770-455-9379; Fax: 770-451-0156. Sr. M. Catherine Massei, Pres. Sisters 2.

St. Joseph's 125th Anniversary Capital Campaign, Inc., 5673 Peachtree Dunwoody Rd., N.E., 30342.

Saint Joseph's at East Georgia, Inc., 5665 Peachtree Dunwoody Rd., N.E., 30342. Tel: 706-453-5031; Fax: 706-453-2812. Paul G. Justice Esq., Asst. Sec.

Saint Joseph's Health System (1985) 5665 Peachtree Dunwoody Rd., N.E., Ste. 650, 30342. Tel: 678-843-7120; Fax: 678-843-7339. Web: www.stjosephsatlanta.org. Howard Watts, CEO; Bill Garrett, Chief Mission Officer. Sponsorship. Holding Company Sponsored by Sisters of Mercy of Americas, South Central Community Inc., which operates: Saint Joseph's Hospital of Atlanta, Inc.; Saint Joseph's Mercy Foundation, Inc.; Saint Joseph's Mercy Care Services, Inc.; Saint Joseph's Research Institute Inc. and Saint Joseph's East Georgia.

Saint Joseph's Mercy Foundation (1981) 5665 Peachtree Dunwoody Rd., Ste. 650, 30342-1746. Tel: 678-843-5715; Fax: 678-843-7339. Email: bgarrett@sjha.org. Web: www.stjosephsatlanta.org. William Garrett, Pres. Priests 1; Total Staff 8; Total Assisted 10,000.

Mercy Housing Pembroke, Inc., 621 North Ave., N.E. Ste. A-150, 30308. Tel: 404-873-3887; Fax: 877-693-2333. Web: www.mercyhousing.org.

Mercy Services Downtown, Inc., 424 Decatur St., 30312. Tel: 678-843-8500; Fax: 678-843-8501. Paul G. Justice Esq., Vice Pres. & Gen Counsel Sec.

National Consultants for Education, Inc., 5 Concourse Pkwy., Ste. 750, 30328. Tel: 770-828-4950; Fax: 770-828-4955. Email: businessoffice@nceducation.org; egrandio@nceducation.org. Web: www.nceducation.org. Rev. Jose Felix Ortega, L.C., Dir.

Patrons of the Arts in the Vatican Museums, Inc., 4449 Northside Dr., 30328. Tel: 678-904-2811, Ext. 235; Fax: 404-221-1006. Gareth N. Genner, Dir. & Sec.

Renovacion Carismatica Catolica Hispana De Atlanta, 490 Arnold Mill Rd., Woodstock, 30188. Tel: 678-213-0685; Fax: 770-516-4664. Email: rcchatlanta@yahoo.com.

The Solidarity Association, Five Concourse Pkwy., Ste. 200, 30328. Frank J. Hanna III, Moderator & Trustee; Gareth N. Genner, Trustee, Sec. & Treas.; Rev. Msgr. Edward J. Dillon, J.C.D., Spiritual Advisor; Elizabeth Hanna, Trustee; David Hanna, Trustee; Sally Hanna, Trustee.

ALPHARETTA. *Home and Family, Inc.* (1996) 6445 Shiloh Rd., Ste. B, 30005. Tel: 678-679-2480; Fax: 678-679-2481. Email: office@missionnetworkatlanta.org. Revs. Dominic Pham, L.C., Supr.; Peter Devereux, L.C.

**Mission Network USA, Inc.*, 6445 Shiloh Rd., Ste. B, 30005. Tel: 628-679-2480; Fax: 678-679-2481. Web: www.cywn.net.

Youth for the Third Millennium, Inc., 6445 Shiloh Rd., Ste. B, 30005. Tel: 914-773-1368. Email: jfortega@legionaries.org. Rev. Jose F. Ortega, L.C., Sec. & Treas.

BLAIRSVILLE. *Faith Enrichment Institute, Inc.* (1989) 173 Dills Rd. Ext., 30512. Tel: 404-402-4022; Fax: 706-781-3673. Email: peglor@windstream.net. Deacon Loris Sinanian.

CONYERS. *Magnificat - Joyful Visitation Chapter, Inc.* (1922) 3295 Creekside Dr., 30094. Tel: 770-929-0405. Email: gowa@bellsouth.net. Beth Gowasack, Coord.

**Rosary Army Corp.*, 1805 Overlake Dr. Ste. C, 30013. Tel: 770-918-1101. Email: greg@rosaryarmy.com. Web: rosaryarmy.com. P.O. Box 82721, 30013. Greg Willits, Pres.; Jennifer Willits, Sec. & Treas.

COVINGTON. *Society of Our Lady of the Most Holy Trinity, SOLT Lay Community*, 110 Aspen Dr., 30016-5824. Tel: 706-819-9215. Email: frpauldamian@netzero.net. Rev. John S. Zachary, Lay Formation Dir.

CUMMING. *Vocation Action Circle, Inc.*, 2820 Bordeaux Blvd., 30041. Tel: 678-648-2620. Email: jmgonzales@vocation.com.

HAPEVILLE. **Mother and Unborn Baby Care, Inc. dba Advice and Aid Pregnancy Problem Center* 411 King Arnold St., 30354.

ROSWELL. **Catholics Come Home*, 560 W. Crossville Rd., Ste. 101, 30075. Tel: 678-585-7886; Fax: 678-585-7854.

**Virtue Media, Inc.*, 560 W. Crossville Rd., Ste. 101, 30075. Tel: 770-559-5533; Fax: 678-585-7854.

SANDY SPRINGS. *LCNA Atlanta, Incorporated*, 55 Club Ct., Alpharetta, 30005. Tel: 914-773-1368. Email: jfortega@legionaries.org. Rev. Jose F. Ortega, L.C., Asst. Sec.

Legion of Christ, Atlanta, Inc., 55 Club Ct., Alpharetta, 30005. Tel: 770-671-8778. Bro. Viet Tran, L.C., Vice Pres.

SMYRNA. *AOA Properties Holding, Inc.*, 2401 Lake Park Dr. S.E., 30080. Tel: 400-920-7800; Fax: 404-920-7801. Bradley Wilson, CFO & Sec.

Archdiocese of Atlanta Priests Payroll Services, 2401 Lake Park Dr., S.E., 30080-8862.

Catholic Education of North Georgia, Inc., 2401 Lake Park Dr. S.E., 30080. Tel: 404-920-7800; Fax: 404-920-7801. Bradley Wilson, CFO.

G.R.A.C.E. Scholars, Inc., 2401 Lake Park Dr. S.E., 30080. Tel: 404-920-7900; Fax: 404-920-7901. Email: gracescholars@archatl.com. Web: www.gracescholars.org. David Brown, Dir.; Christopher Vaughan, Coord.

TUCKER. *Catholic Metro League of Atlanta, Inc.*, 3799 Gleneagles Ct., 30084.

RELIGIOUS INSTITUTES OF MEN REPRESENTED IN THE ARCHDIOCESE

For further details refer to the corresponding bracketed number in the Religious Institutes of Men or Women section.

[0350]—*Cistercians Order of the Strict Observance-Trappists*—O.C.S.O.

[0360]—*Claretian Missionaries* (Eastern Province)—C.M.F.

[]—*Congregation of the Missionaries of Saint Charles Scalabranians*—C.S.

[1000]—*Congregation of the Passion* (Prov. of St. Paul of the Cross)—C.P.

[0480]—*Conventual Franciscans* (Prov. of St. Anthony of Padua, Baltimore)—O.F.M.Conv

[0520]—*Franciscan Friars* (Prov. of the Most Holy Name of Jesus)—O.F.M.

[0690]—*Jesuit Fathers and Brothers* (New Orleans Prov.)—S.J.

[0730]—*Legionaries of Christ*—L.C.

[0780]—*Marist Fathers* (San Francisco-Washington Prov.)—S.M.

[0720]—*The Missionaries of Our Lady of La Salette*—M.S.

[]—*Missionaries of St. Francis de Sales* (Annecy, France)—M.S.F.S.

[]—*Missionaries of the Nativity of Mary*—M.N.M.

[]—*Order of Friars Preachers Dominicans*—O.P.

[1065]—*The Priestly Fraternity of St. Peter*—F.S.S.P.

[]—*Salesians of St. John Bosco*—S.D.B.

[]—*Society of Christ*—S.Chr.

[]—*Society of Our Lady of the Most Holy Trinity*—S.O.L.T.

[]—*Society of St. Paul*—S.S.P.

RELIGIOUS INSTITUTES OF WOMEN REPRESENTED IN THE ARCHDIOCESE

[3110]—*Congregation of Our Lady of the Retreat in the Cenacle*—R.C.

[1070-13]—*Dominican Sisters (Adrian, MI)*—O.P.

[]—*Dominican Sisters of St. Cecilia* (Nashville, TN)

[1070-23]—*Dominican Sisters of St. Rose of Lima (Hawthorne, NY)*—O.P.

[]—*Dominican Sisters of Vietnam*

[1070-03]—*Dominican Sisters (Sinsinawa, WI)*—O.P.

[]—*Franciscan Sisters of Our Lady of Refuge* (Mexico)—R.F.R.

[1840]—*Grey Nuns of the Sacred Heart (Yardley, PA)*—G.N.S.H.

[1870]—*Handmaids of the Sacred Heart of Jesus (Philadelphia, PA)*—A.C.J.

[]—*Holy Family Sisters of the Needy* (Nigeria)—H.F.S.N.

[2575]—*Institute of the Sisters of Mercy of the Americas* (Merion, PA; Rochester, NY; Baltimore, MD)—R.S.M.

[2710]—*Missionaries of Charity*—M.C.

[]—*Missionary Sisters of the Most Sacred Heart* (Reading, PA)

[2800]—*Missionary Sisters of the Most Sacred Heart of Jesus of Hiltrup* (Reading, PA)—M.S.C.

[]—*Missionary Sisters of the Sacred Heart "Ad Gentes"* (Mexico)—M.A.G.

[]—*Sisters of Jesus of Kkottongnae* (Korea)

[3840]—*Sisters of St. Joseph of Carondelet (St. Louis, MO)*—C.S.J.

[3830-15]—*Sisters of St. Joseph of Concordia (Concordia, KS)*—C.S.J.

[]—*Sisters of the Blessed Sacrament* (Nigeria)

[1830]—*The Sisters of the Good Shepherd (Silver Spring, MD)*—R.G.S.

[4190]—*Sisters of the Visitation*—V.H.M.

[]—*Sisters of the Visitation of Holy Mary*

[2150]—*Sisters, Servants of the Immaculate Heart of Mary (Monroe, MI)*—I.H.M.

ARCHDIOCESAN CEMETERIES

CARROLLTON. *Our Lady of Perpetual Help, Our Lady of Help Church*, 210 Old Center Point Rd., 30117. Tel: 770-832-8977; Fax: 770-832-1666. Email: olphcc@gmail.com.

SHARON. *Locust Grove, Archdiocese of Atlanta*, 2401 Lake Park Dr., 30080. Tel: 404-920-7800.

Purification, St. Joseph's Catholic Church, U.S. Hwy. 78, P.O. Box 632, Washington, 30673.

SPARTA. *Sparta, Archdiocese of Atlanta*, 2401 Lake Park Dr., 30080. Tel: 404-920-7800.

WASHINGTON. *Saint Patrick's, St. Joseph's*, US Hwy. 78, P.O. Box 632, 30673. Email: frtom4nfp@stpatricks-norcross.org.

NECROLOGY

✠ Donoghue, Most Rev. John F., Retired Archbishop of Atlanta.—Died Nov. 11, 2011

† Dillman, Alan M., (Retired)—Died Jan. 7, 2011

† Druding, John C., (Retired)—Died Feb. 12, 2011

An asterisk (*) denotes an organization that has established tax-exempt status directly with the IRS and is not covered by the USCCB Group Ruling.

Diocese of Austin

(Dioecesis Austiniensis)

Most Reverend

JOE S. VÁSQUEZ

Bishop of Austin; ordained June 30, 1984; appointed Titular Bishop of Cova and Auxiliary Bishop of Galveston-Houston November 30, 2001; ordained January 23, 2002; appointed Bishop of Austin January 26, 2010; installed March 8, 2010. *Office: 6225 Hwy. 290 E., Austin, TX 78723.*

Most Reverend

JOHN E. MCCARTHY, D.D.

Retired Bishop of Austin; ordained May 26, 1956; appointed Titular Bishop of Pasadena and Auxiliary Bishop of Galveston-Houston January 15, 1979; appointed Bishop of Austin December 19, 1985; retired January 2, 2001.

Pastoral Center: 6225 Hwy. 290 E., Austin, TX 78723. Tel: 512-949-2400; Fax: 512-949-2520.

Web: www.austindiocese.org

Email: info@austindiocese.org

ERECTED 1947.

Square Miles 21,000.

Comprises the Counties of Mills, Hamilton, San Saba, Lampasas, Coryell, McLennan, Limestone, Bell, Falls, Robertson, Mason, Llano, Burnet, Williamson, Milam, Brazos, Blanco, Travis, Bastrop, Lee, Burleson, Washington, Hays, Caldwell and the part of Fayette County north of the Colorado River in the State of Texas.

For legal titles of parishes and diocesan institutions, consult the Chancery Office.

STATISTICAL OVERVIEW

Personnel	
Bishop	1
Retired Bishops	1
Priests: Diocesan Active in Diocese	93
Priests: Diocesan Active Outside Diocese	10
Priests: Retired, Sick or Absent	39
Number of Diocesan Priests	142
Religious Priests in Diocese	54
Total Priests in Diocese	196
Extern Priests in Diocese	30
Ordinations:	
Diocesan Priests	2
Transitional Deacons	4
Permanent Deacons in Diocese	168
Total Brothers	43
Total Sisters	96
Parishes	
Parishes	101
With Resident Pastor:	
Resident Diocesan Priests	80
Resident Religious Priests	18
Without Resident Pastor:	
Administered by Priests	3
Missions	22
Pastoral Centers	4
Professional Ministry Personnel:	
Brothers	3
Sisters	23
Lay Ministers	176
Welfare	
Catholic Hospitals	5
Total Assisted	1,836,646
Homes for the Aged	2
Total Assisted	189
Day Care Centers	2
Total Assisted	300
Specialized Homes	2
Total Assisted	155
Special Centers for Social Services	4
Total Assisted	27,000
Educational	
Diocesan Students in Other Seminaries	44
Total Seminarians	44
Colleges and Universities	1
Total Students	5,285
High Schools, Diocesan and Parish	4
Total Students	1,054
High Schools, Private	2
Total Students	475
Elementary Schools, Diocesan and Parish	16
Total Students	3,348
Elementary Schools, Private	1
Total Students	863
Catechesis/Religious Education:	
High School Students	9,149
Elementary Students	27,621
Total Students under Catholic Instruction	47,839
Teachers in the Diocese:	
Priests	3
Sisters	4
Lay Teachers	507
Vital Statistics	
Receptions into the Church:	
Infant Baptism Totals	7,984
Minor Baptism Totals	660
Adult Baptism Totals	394
Received into Full Communion	722
First Communions	7,707
Confirmations	4,291
Marriages:	
Catholic	1,137
Interfaith	284
Total Marriages	1,421
Deaths	1,600
Total Catholic Population	518,940
Total Population	2,809,636

Former Bishops—Most Revs. LOUIS J. REICHER, D.D., ord. Dec. 6, 1918; appt. first Bishop of Austin Nov. 29, 1947; cons. April 14, 1948; died Feb. 23, 1984; VINCENT M. HARRIS, D.D., ord. March 19, 1938; appt. Bishop of Beaumont July 4, 1966; cons. Sept. 28, 1966; transferred to Austin April 21, 1971; succeeded to the See Nov. 16, 1971; retired Feb. 25, 1986; died March 31, 1988; JOHN E. MCCARTHY, D.D. (Retired), Bishop of Austin; ord. May 26, 1956; appt. Titular Bishop of Pasadena and Auxiliary Bishop of Galveston-Houston, Jan. 23, 1979; cons. March 14, 1979; appt. Bishop of Austin, Dec. 24, 1985; installed Feb. 25, 1986; retired Jan. 2, 2001; GREGORY M. AYMOND, ord. May 10, 1975; appt. Titular Bishop of Acolla and Auxiliary Bishop of New Orleans Nov. 19, 1996; ord. Jan. 10, 1997; appt. Coadjutor Bishop of Austin June 1, 2000; installed Aug. 3, 2000; succeeded to the See of Austin Jan. 2, 2001; appt. Archbishop of New Orleans, June 12, 2009; installed Aug. 20, 2009.

Vicar General—Rev. Msgr. MICHAEL J. SIS.

Moderator of the Curia—Rev. Msgr. MICHAEL J. SIS.

Diocesan Administrator—VACANT.

Pastoral Center—Mailing Address: 6225 Hwy. 290 E., Austin, 78723. Tel: 512-949-2400; Fax: 512-949-2524. Office Hours: Mon.-Fri. 8:30-5.

Notary—Deacon RON WALKER.

Deans—

Austin North—Very Rev. DANIEL E. GARCIA.

Austin Central—Rev. Msgr. THOMAS FRANK.

Austin South—Very Rev. GLYNN (BUD) ROLAND JR.

Bastrop / Lockhart—Very Rev. GEORGE JOSEPH.

Brenham / La Grange—Very Rev. JAMES OLNHAUSEN.

Bryan / College Station—Rev. Msgr. JOHN MALINOWSKI (Retired).

Georgetown / Round Rock—Very Rev. MICHAEL O'CONNOR.

Killeen / Temple—Very Rev. RICHARD O'ROURKE, M.S.C.

Lampasas / Marble Falls—Very Rev. JAIRO LOPEZ.

San Marcos—Very Rev. BRIAN EILERS.

Waco—Very Rev. EDWARD KARASEK.

Presbyteral Council—Most Rev. JOE S. VASQUEZ; Rev. Msgrs. LOUIS PAVLICEK (Retired); ELMER HOLTMAN (Retired); JOHN A. MCCAFFREY; Very Rev. DANIEL E. GARCIA; Rev. SAMUEL HOSE; Very Rev. GEORGE JOSEPH; Revs. PAUL F. MCCALLUM (Retired); JAMES MISKO; EDWARD KOHARCHIK, C.S.P., M.A., M.S.; EDWARD C. NOWAK, C.S.P., B.S., M.Div.; ANTHONY ODIONG; DAVID KONDERLA; Very Rev. JAMES OLNHAUSEN; Revs. TIMOTHY V. VAVEREK; WILLIAM A. WACK, C.S.C.; FRANK ZLOTKOWSKI, C.S.C.; JUAN CARLOS LOPEZ; Very Rev. ALBERT LAFORET JR.; Rev. DANIEL LIU. Ex Officio: Rev. Msgr. MICHAEL J. SIS; Rev. HARRY DEAN; Very Rev. CHRISTOPHER FERRER, J.C.L., Consulting Member.

Secretariats and Secretariat Directors—

Business and Finance—MARY BETH KOENIG, Dir.

Administration—Deacon RON WALKER, Dir.

Formation and Spirituality—CHERYL MAXWELL, Dir.

Stewardship, Development and Communication—SCOTT WHITAKER, Dir.

Justice and Charity—BARBARA BUDDE, M.A., Dir.

Clergy and Religious—Rev. Msgr. MICHAEL J. SIS, Dir.

Family Life—

Office of Black Catholics—

Religious Education and Formation—

Youth, Young Adult and Campus Ministry—

Office of Worship—

Cedarbrake Retreat Center—

College of Consultors—Very Rev. DANIEL E. GARCIA; Rev. SAMUEL HOSE; Very Revs. GEORGE JOSEPH; JAMES OLNHAUSEN; Rev. Msgr. JOHN A.

McCaffrey; Rev. James Misko; Rev. Msgr. Elmer Holtman (Retired); Revs. Juan Carlos Lopez; David Konderla; Rev. Msgr. Michael J. Sis.

Canonical and Tribunal Services—6225 E. Hwy. 290, Austin, 78723-1025. Tel: 512-949-2479; Fax: 512-949-2522. Direct all inquiries concerning marriage nullity, dispensation and permissions to this address.

Judicial Vicar—Very Rev. Christopher Ferrer, J.C.L.

Adjutant Judicial Vicar—Rev. Jozef Musiol, S.D.S., J.C.D.

Diocesan Tribunal Judges—Rev. Robert L. Kincl, M.A., S.T.L., J.C.L.; Very Rev. Christopher Ferrer, J.C.L.; Rev. Anthony Nwudah, J.C.L.

Defenders of the Bond—Rev. Kirby Garner, M.Div.; Robert Pine, M.Sc.

Notaries—Deacons Raymond Sanders Jr., M.S., M.A., Ed.D.; Ralph Arevalo Jr.; Donald Gessler, M.D., M.B.A.; Kevin Nissen; Mr. Harvey Bollich, Ph.D.; Joanne Sanders, M.R.E.; Deborah R. Patin; Janie Cuellar; W. Blake Dominguez, M.A.; Thomas Howard, J.D.; Deacon John Pickwell; Robert Pine, M.Sc.; DeAnn Walker, J.D.; Patricia Thompson, M.A., M.R.E., M.A.A.C.C.D. Office Manager: Deborah R. Patin. Administrative Assistants: Janie Cuellar; Robert Pine, M.Sc.

Advocates— Priests, Deacons, Religious, and Parish Associates exercising ministry in the Diocese of Austin. Advocates for the Respondent in English: W. Blake Dominguez, M.A.; Deacon Donald Gessler, M.D., M.B.A.; Thomas Howard, J.D.

Advocate for the Respondent in Spanish—Deacon Ralph Arevalo Jr.

Auditor—Mr. Harvey Bollich, Ph.D.

Assessors—DeAnn Walker, J.D.; Deacons John Pickwell; Kevin Nissen; Raymond Sanders Jr., M.S., M.A., Ed.D.; Joanne Sanders, M.R.E.

Assistant Auditor—Patricia Thompson, M.A., M.R.E., M.A.A.C.C.D.

Finance Council—Most Rev. Joe S. Vasquez, Bishop of Austin; Campbell McGinnis; Karl Kuykendall; Jim Smolik; Mary Beth Koenig; Jose Montemayor; Patricia Ohlendorf; John McGovern; Rev. Msgrs. Michael J. Sis; John A. McCaffrey; Deacon Deason L. Switzer; Mr. Don E. Cox.

Diocesan Archives and Records—Deacon Ron Walker, Chancellor, Mailing Address: 6225 Hwy. 290 E., Austin, 78723. Tel: 512-949-2400.

Office of Black Catholics—Mr. Johnnie Dorsey, Dir., Mailing Address: 6225 Hwy. 290 E., Austin, 78723. Tel: 512-949-2449. Email: johnnie-dorsey@austindiocese.org.

Facility Planning—Patrick Baker, Dir., Mailing Address: 6225 Hwy. 290 E., Austin, 78723. Tel: 512-949-2433; Fax: 512-949-2525.

Catholic Campaign for Human Development—Barbara Budde, M.A., Mailing Address: 6225 Hwy. 290 E., Austin, 78723. Tel: 512-949-2471.

Catholic Charities of Central Texas—Melinda Rodriquez, 1817 E. 6th St., Austin, 78702. Tel: 512-651-6102.

Immigration Legal Services—Mark Kinzler, Dir., Catholic Charities of Central Texas, 1817 E. 6th St., Austin, 78702. Tel: 512-651-6110.

Marywood Children & Family Services—Mailing Address: 6225 Hwy. 290 E., Austin, 78723. Tel: 512-472-9251; 800-251-5433; Fax: 512-472-4829. Carolyn Chamberlain, Dir. Tel: 512-949-2806.

Catholic Schools Office—Dr. Ned F. Vanders, Ph.D., Supt., Mailing Address: 6225 Hwy. 290 E., Austin, 78723. Tel: 512-949-2498; Fax: 512-949-2520.

Stewardship and Development—Scott Whitaker, Dir., Mailing Address: 6225 Hwy. 290 E., Austin, 78723. Tel: 512-949-2441; Fax: 512-949-2520.

"Catholic Spirit" Newspaper—Shelley Metcalf, Editor, Mailing Address: 6225 Hwy. 290 E., Austin, 78723. Tel: 512-949-2443; Fax: 512-949-2523. Email: catholic.spirit@austindiocese.org.

Office of Youth, Young Adult and Campus Ministry—Alison Koederitz, Dir., Mailing Address: 6225 Hwy. 290 E., Austin, 78723. Tel: 512-949-2465; Fax: 512-949-2520; Rev. Jesus Ferras, I.S.P., Coord. Hispanic Young Adult Ministry. Tel: 512-949-2466; Angie Harmon, Prog. Coord. Young Adult Ministry. Tel: 512-949-2467.

Cemeteries—Patrick Baker, Mailing Address: 6225 Hwy. 290 E., Austin, 78723. Tel: 512-949-2418.

Hispanic Ministry—Edgar Ramirez, 6225 Hwy. 290 E., Austin, 78723. Tel: 512-949-2468.

Communications—Christian Gonzalez, Dir., Mailing Address: 6225 Hwy. 290 E., Austin, 78723. Tel: 512-949-2456.

Human Resources—Carmen Cortes-Harms, HR Coord., Mailing Address: 6225 Hwy. 290 E., Austin, 78723. Tel: 512-949-2451; Fax: 512-949-2524.

Priestly Life and Formation Committee—Rev. Harry Dean, Chm., Mailing Address: 6225 Hwy. 290 E., Austin, 78723. Tel: 512-949-2431; Fax: 512-949-2524.

Council of Catholic Women—Judy Edwards, Pres., 1315 Barak Ln., Bryan, 77802. Tel: 979-846-0617. Email: judithl@suddenlink.net. Web: www.adccw.com.

Cursillo—Mailing Address: Our Lady of Guadalupe Cursillo Center, 200 W. FM 487, P.O. Box 65, Jarrell, 76537. Tel: 512-746-2041. Silvia Villarreal, Center Dir., 200 W. FM 487, Jarrell, 76537. Tel: 512-746-2041; 254-541-4567. Spanish: Silvia Villarreal, 200 W. FM 487, Jarrell, 76537. Tel: 512-746-2041 (Office); 254-541-4567. English: Adolfo Alvarez, Pres., Mailing Address: P.O. Box 142486, Austin, 78714-2486. Tel: 512-784-7964. Email: wu_doc1@hotmail.com.

Deaf Ministry—Deacon Patrick Murray, Dir., St. Ignatius Church, 2309 Euclid St., Austin, 78704. Email: mpatrick@austin.rr.com.

Diaconate—Deacon Ron Walker, Dir., Mailing Address: 6225 Hwy. 290 E., Austin, 78723. Tel: 512-949-2452.

Diaconate Formation—Associate Directors: Deacons Tom Johnson; Sidney (Butch) Prewitt, 6225 Hwy. 290 E., Austin, 78723. Tel: 512-949-2400; Fax: 512-949-2520.

Ecumenism—Rev. Charles L. Covington, Dir., St. Louis Church, 7601 Burnet Rd., Austin, 78757. Tel: 512-454-0384.

Catholic Family Counseling and Family Life Office—Guadalupe Garcia, Dir., Mailing Address: 6225 Hwy. 290 E., Austin, 78723. Tel: 512-949-2493; Fax: 512-949-2527.

Holy Childhood—Charlene O'Connell, M.A., 6225 Hwy. 290 E., Austin, 78723. Tel: 512-949-2470.

Criminal Justice Ministry—Deacon E. Generes (Doots) Dufour, Dir., 6225 Hwy. 290 E., Austin, 78723. Tel: 512-949-2400.

Mission Council—Barbara Budde, M.A., Contact, Mailing Address: 6225 Hwy. 290 E., Austin, 78723. Tel: 512-949-2471.

Office of Hispanic Ministry—Edgar Ramirez, Dir., Mailing Address: 6225 Hwy. 290 E., Austin, 78723. Tel: 512-949-2468.

Social Concerns and Parish Social Ministries—Barbara Budde, M.A., Dir., Mailing Address: 6225 Hwy. 290 E., Austin, 78723. Tel: 512-949-2471.

Propagation of the Faith—Deacon Bill Hobby, Dir. Tel: 512-949-2427.

Department of Religious Education & Formation—Dr. Geri Telepak, D.Min., Ed.D., Dir. Tel: 512-949-2469; Fax: 512-949-2520; Charlene O'Connell, M.A., Assoc. Dir. Rel. Educ. Tel: 512-949-2470; Vacant, Coord. Hispanic Catechesis, Mailing Address: 6225 Hwy. 290 E., Austin, 78723. Tel: 512-949-2400; Fax: 512-949-2520.

Office of Pro-Life Activities & Chaste Living—Marie Seale, Dir., Mailing Address: 6225 Hwy. 290 E., Austin, 78723. Tel: 512-949-2487; Fax: 512-949-2520.

Rural Life—Rev. Msgr. Emilian Foltyn, Dir., 8626 FM 1105, Jarrell, 76537-1522. Tel: 512-863-3020.

Serra Club - Austin—Rita Vagilica, 11405 Taterwood Dr., Austin, 78750. Tel: 512-219-5825.

Serra Club - Central Texas—C. David Broecker, Pres., 1417 Elizabeth Circle, Salado, 76571. Tel: 254-247-1776. Email: cbroecker@vvm.com.

Special Collections—Scott Whitaker, Dir., Mailing Address: 6225 Hwy. 290 E., Austin, 78723. Tel: 512-949-2441; Fax: 512-949-2520.

Vicar for Clergy—Rev. Harry Dean, Mailing Address: 6225 Hwy. 290 E., Austin, 78723. Tel: 512-949-2431; Fax: 512-949-2524. Email: fr-harry-dean@austindiocese.org.

Office for Religious—Sr. Helen Brewer, D.C., Dir., Mailing Address: 6225 Hwy. 290 E., Austin, 78723. Tel: 512-949-2401; Fax: 512-949-2524.

Ethics and Integrity in Ministry—Emily Hurlimann, Coord., Mailing Address: 6225 Hwy. 290 E., Austin, 78723. Tel: 512-949-2447.

Victim Assistance Coordinator—Patricia Stankus. Tel: 512-949-2400. Email: pat-stankus@austindiocese.org.

Vocations—Rev. Brian McMaster, Dir., Mailing Address: 6225 Hwy. 290 E., Austin, 78723. Tel: 512-949-2405. Email: fr-brian-mcmaster@austindiocese.org. Associate Directors: Rev. Jonathan D. Raia, St. William, 620 Round Rock W. Dr., Round Rock, 78681. Tel: 512-600-8154; Very Rev. Glynn (Bud) Roland Jr., St. John Neumann, 5455 Bee Cave Rd., Austin, 78746. Tel: 512-328-3220; Rev. Msgr. Louis Pavlicek (Retired), St. William, 1105 Deer Run, Round Rock, 78681. Tel: 512-763-6495; Revs. Daniel Liu, St. Dominic Savio Catholic High School, 905 Duncan Lane, Austin, 78705. Tel: 512-388-8846; James M. Ekeocha, St. Luke, 2807 Oakdale, Temple, 76502. Tel: 254-773-1561; Rafael Padilla, Ascension, 804 Pine St., Bastrop, 78602. Tel: 512-321-3552; Rev. Msgr. Michael J. Sis, Pastoral Center: 6225 Hwy. 290 E., Austin, 78723. Tel: 512-949-2402; Julie Gray, Admin. Asst., Pastoral Center: 6225 Hwy. 290 E., Austin, 78723. Tel: 512-949-2430.

Diocesan Institute for Ecclesial Ministry—6225 Hwy. 290 E., Austin, 78723. Tel: 512-949-2400. Dr. Geri Telepak, D.Min., Ed.D., Dir., 6225 Hwy. 290 E., Austin, 78723. Tel: 512-949-2469.

Legal Services—6225 Hwy. 290 E., Austin, 78723. Tel: 512-949-2400. Deacon Ron Walker, Gen. Counsel. Tel: 512-949-2452.

Worship Office—Mailing Address: 6225 Hwy. 290 E., Austin, 78723. Tel: 512-949-2400. Cheryl Maxwell, Dir. Tel: 512-949-2453.

CLERGY, PARISHES, MISSIONS AND PAROCHIAL SCHOOLS

CITY OF AUSTIN

(Travis County)

1—St. Mary Cathedral (1852) Very Rev. Albert Laforet Jr., Rector; Revs. Germanus Rayen, O.F.M.Cap., Parochial Vicar; Juntack (John) Kim, Parochial Vicar; Deacons Willie Cortez; Ron Walker; Vincent A. Boyle; Guadalupe Rodriguez Jr.
Res.: 203 E. 10th St., 78701. Tel: 512-476-6182; Fax: 512-476-8799. Email: office@smcaustin.org. Web: www.smcaustin.org.
School—Cathedral School of St. Mary, (Grades PreK-8), 910 San Jacinto, 78701. Tel: 512-476-1480; Fax: 512-476-9922. Mary Margaret Hitt, Prin.; Janet O'Dwyer, Librarian. Lay Teachers 16; Students 136.
Catechesis/Religious Program—Tel: 512-476-4801; Fax: 512-476-8799. Students 250.

2—St. Albert The Great (1987) [CEM] Rev. Isidore Ndagizimana (Uganda); Deacon Al Cuevas; Storm Knien, Music Min.
Res.: 12041 Bittern Hollow, 78758. Tel: 512-837-7825; Fax: 512-834-2377.
Catechesis/Religious Program— Annemarie Weis, D.R.E. Students 493.

3—St. Andrew Kim Taegon Korean Catholic Church (1984), (Korean), Rev. Francis Chung.
Church: 6523 Emerald Forest, 78745. Tel: 512-326-3225; Fax: 512-326-2554.
Catechesis/Religious Program—Students 55.

4—St. Austin (1908) Revs. Charles Kullmann, C.S.P.; Steven Bell, C.S.P. In Res., Revs. Edward C. Nowak, C.S.P.; Robert P. Michele, C.S.P.
Res.: 2026 Guadalupe St., 78705. Tel: 512-477-9471; Fax: 512-477-9430.
School—(Grades PreK-8), 1911 San Antonio St., 78705. Tel: 512-477-3751; Fax: 512-477-3079. Web: www.staustinschool.org. Barbara Kennedy, Prin.; Kathy Hymel, Librarian. Lay Teachers 20; Students 224.
Catechesis/Religious Program—Tel: 512-477-9471, Ext. 302. Students 258.

5—St. Catherine of Siena (1979) Revs. Patrick Coakley, M.S.C.; Masilamani Rajamanickam; Deacons Larry Terrell, (Retired); Christopher Schroeder; Jesse Casarez; Arthur Cavazos.
Church: 4800 Convict Hill Rd., 78749. Tel: 512-892-2420; Fax: 512-892-0488.
Catechesis/Religious Program—Tel: 512-892-2426; Fax: 512-892-0488. Pamela Neuman, D.R.E. Students 1,130.

6—Church of the Resurrection, Emmaus (1963) [CEM] [JC] Revs. Samuel Hose; Luis Alberto Caceres, Parochial Vicar; Deacons Terry Guilbert; John Hill; Jesse Martinez.
Mailing Address & Res.: 1718 Lohman's Crossing, Lakeway, 78734. Tel: 512-261-8500; Fax: 512-261-8200.
Catechesis/Religious Program—Students 868.
Chapel—Queen of Angels 20600 Siesta Shores Rd., Spicewood, Travis Co. 78669. Tel: 512-264-3355. P.O. Box 448, Spicewood, 78669-0448.

7—Cristo Rey (1950), (Hispanic), Revs. Mario Castro Martinez, O.F.M.Conv.; Guillermo Aguilar Alamilla, O.F.M.Conv., Parochial Vicar; Deacon Agapito Lopez.
2208 E. 2nd St., 78702. Fax: 512-477-1099 (Office). Res.: 2107 E. 2nd St., 78702. Tel: 512-474-6376.
Catechesis/Religious Program—2215 E. 2nd St., 78702. Tel: 512-477-1099. Sr. Irene Tapia, F.M.A., D.R.E. Students 1,100.

8—Holy Cross (1936), (African American), Rev. Basil Aguzie, M.S.P.

1610 E. 11th St., 78702. Tel: 512-472-3741; Fax: 512-472-3783. Email: holycrossaustin@grandecom.net. Web: www.holycrossaustin.org.
Res.: 1607 E. 11th St., 78702. Tel: 512-322-0603.
Catechesis/Religious Program—Tel: 512-276-7924. Jessica Cortez, D.R.E. Students 65.

9—HOLY VIETNAMESE MARTYRS CATHOLIC CHURCH - AUSTIN, TEXAS (1990), (Vietnamese), Rev. Msgr. Joe Van Anh Nguyen; Deacon Hoa Mai.
Res.: 1107 E. Yager Ln., 78753. Tel: 512-834-8483; Fax: 512-821-1155.
Catechesis/Religious Program—Students 602.

10—ST. IGNATIUS MARTYR (1937) Revs. William A. Wack, C.S.C.; Michael Couhig, C.S.C.; James Martin, C.S.C.; Deacon Patrick Murray; Tony Ross, Parish Admin.
Res.: 2308 Euclid Ave., 78704. Tel: 512-442-3602; Fax: 512-916-4440.
School—(Grades PreK-8), 120 W. Oltorf St., 78704. Tel: 512-442-8547; Fax: 512-442-8685. Todd Blahnik, Prin.; Deborah Stavely, Librarian. Lay Teachers 20; Aides 3; Students 269.
Catechesis/Religious Program—Tel: 512-442-8656. Sirene Brunell, D.R.E. Students 460.

11—ST. JOHN NEUMANN (1984) Very Rev. Glynn (Bud) Roland Jr.; Rev. Adrian Chishimba, Parochial Vicar; Deacons Mike Gesch; David Sekel; Manuel Torres.
Res.: 5455 Bee Cave Rd., 78746. Tel: 512-328-3220; Fax: 512-328-3226.
Rectory—Tel: 512-494-6335.
Catechesis/Religious Program—Students 955.

12—ST. JULIA (1957), (Hispanic), Rev. Bradford Hernandez; Deacons Ralph Arevalo Jr.; Kevin Nissen.
Mailing Address: 3010 Lyons Rd., 78702. Tel: 512-926-4186; Fax: 512-926-7414.
Res.: 900 Tillery Rd., 78702.
Catechesis/Religious Program—Students 400.

13—ST. LOUIS (1952) Revs. Larry Covington; Manuel Montenegro-Calero; Oliver Weerakkody; Deacons Rob Embry; Donald Turner; Richard Bigelow; Tony Pynes; Luis Villa.
Res.: 7601 Burnet Rd., 78757. Tel: 512-454-0384; Fax: 512-454-2010.
School—(Grades PreK-8) Tel: 512-454-0384, Ext. 242; Fax: 512-454-7252. Mrs. Patricia Romanies, Prin.; Brian Kemp, Librarian. Lay Teachers 24; Students 245.
Catechesis/Religious Program—Tel: 512-454-0384, Ext. 225. Tommy Sustaita, D.R.E. Youth Ministries; Amy Allert, D.R.E., Adult Ministries; Dr. Tina Juarez Bailey, D.R.E., Childhood Ministries; Sumayah Abullarade, D.R.E., Hispanic Adult & Family Ministries. Students 885.

14—ST. MARGARET OF SCOTLAND (1984) Closed. For inquiries for parish records contact the chancery.

15—NUESTRA SENORA DE DOLORES (1952), (Hispanic), Rev. Albert Capello Ruiz; Deacon Hector Rosales.
Res.: 1111 Montopolis Dr., 78741. Tel: 512-385-4333; Fax: 512-385-6116.
Catechesis/Religious Program—Tel: 512-385-4333. Sr. Rose Moreno, F.H.M., D.R.E. Students 656.
Convent—Hijas De La Misericordia, Tel: 512-385-5090; Fax: 512-389-0692. Sisters 2.

16—OUR LADY OF GUADALUPE (1907), (Hispanic), Rev. Florencio Rodriguez, T.O.R.; Deacons Mario Renteria; William "Billy" Atkins; Natalie Rodriguez, Business Mgr.
1206 E. 9th St., 78702.
Rectory—912 Lydia, 78702. Tel: 512-478-7955 (Parish Office); 512-478-4132 (Rectory); Fax: 512-478-8377.
Catechesis/Religious Program—Sr. Anita Franz, O.S.F., D.R.E. Students 260.

17—ST. PAUL (1989) Revs. Hector Vega, I.S.P.; Christian Christenson, I.S.P.; Deacons John Pickwell; Solomon Villegas.
Res.: 10000 David Moore Dr., 78748. Tel: 512-280-7230.
Catechesis/Religious Program—Tel: 512-280-4460, Ext. 122; Fax: 512-280-7219. Ana Jackoskie, D.R.E. Students 352.

18—ST. PETER THE APOSTLE (1962) Rev. Richard Tijerina.
Mailing Address: P.O. Box 17575, 78760-7575.
Res.: 4600 E. Ben White Blvd., 78741. Tel: 512-442-0655.
Catechesis/Religious Program—Tel: 512-444-7477. Students 143.

19—SACRED HEART (1958) Revs. Matthew C. Iwuji; John Paul Hudson; Deacons Jesse M. Garza, (Retired); Robert Martinez; Jose Chavez. In Res., Rev. Anthony Nwudah.
Res.: 5909 Reicher Dr., 78723. Tel: 512-926-2552; Fax: 512-926-5138.
Catechesis/Religious Program—Tel: 512-926-2116; Fax: 512-926-2983. Students 1,100.

20—SAN FRANCISCO (1941), (Hispanic), Rev. Cesar Jaime Guzman Diaz.
Res.: 9110 Hwy. 183 S., 78747. Tel: 512-243-1404; Fax: 512-243-2995.
Catechesis/Religious Program—Fax: 512-243-2995. Students 528.
Mission—San Juan Diego 216 Stony Point Dr., Del Valle, Travis Co. 78617. Tel: 512-247-2476. Web: www.sanjuandiego.org.

21—SAN JOSE (1939) Revs. Tom Frank; Kevin Rai, Parochial Vicar; Charlie Garza, Parochial Vicar; Deacons Joe Gutierrez; Romeo Sanchez; Alfred Benavides; Jose Mendez.
Res.: 2435 Oak Crest Ave., 78704. Tel: 512-444-7587; Fax: 512-443-1212.
Catechesis/Religious Program—Tel: 512-444-4664. Students 1,300.

22—SANTA BARBARA CATHOLIC CHURCH -AUSTIN, TEXAS (1991), (Hispanic), Rev. John Boiko.
Mailing Address: 13713 FM 969, 78724. Tel: 512-276-7718.
Catechesis/Religious Program—Students 318.

23—ST. THERESA (1968) Rev. Msgr. William C. Brooks; Rev. Emmanuel Okwaraocha, Parochial Vicar; Deacons Ray James; Donald Gessler; George Zacek.
Res.: 4311 Small Dr., 78731. Tel: 512-451-5121; Fax: 512-453-6824.
Rectory—4405 Enclove Cove, 78731. Tel: 512-323-6160.
School—(Grades PreK-8) Tel: 512-451-7105; Fax: 512-451-8808. Gracie Burback, Prin.; Jayne Uglum, Librarian. Lay Teachers 40; Students 433.
Catechesis/Religious Program—Tel: 512-451-2940; Fax: 512-453-6824. Sandy Nevills, D.R.E. Students 920.

24—ST. THOMAS MORE (1978) Revs. Larry Stehling; Wade Russell; Deacons Peter Schwab; Thomas Mallinger; Thomas Johnson; Daniel Wright.
Office: 10205 Ranch Rd., 620 N., 78726. Tel: 512-258-1161; Fax: 512-258-8812.
Catechesis/Religious Program—Tel: 512-258-1944; Fax: 512-331-9248. Cynthia Klaer-Jordan, D.R.E. Students 1,078.

25—ST. THOMAS MORE CHAPEL (1958) Closed. For inquiries for sacramental records please see St Mary's Cathedral, (512-476-6182). Res: 1600 N. Congress, Austin, TX 78701.

26—ST. VINCENT DE PAUL (1995) Very Rev. Daniel E. Garcia; Rev. Ronald Joseph Feather; Deacon David Boren.
Mailing Address: 9500 Neenah Ave., 78717. Tel: 512-255-1389; Fax: 512-246-2373.
Rectory—13007 Partridge Bend, 78729. Tel: 512-249-1549.
Catechesis/Religious Program—Fax: 512-246-2373. Mhel Galaviz, C.R.E.; Debbie Hess, C.R.E.; Chris Ochoa, Youth Min. Students 598.

OUTSIDE CITY OF AUSTIN

ANDICE, WILLIAMSON CO., SANTA ROSA (1937) [CEM] Rev. Eliseus Ibeh, M.S.P.; Deacon Marc Washburne.
Mailing Address: 6571 FM 970, Florence, 76527. Tel: 254-793-2047; Fax: 254-793-3247. 6571 FM 970, 78628.
Catechesis/Religious Program—Tel: 254-793-2056; 254-793-2047 (Church); Fax: 254-793-3247. Denise Mackew, D.R.E. Students 123.

BASTROP, BASTROP CO., ASCENSION CATHOLIC CHURCH (1864) Rev. Rafael Padilla Valdez; Deacon Bill Hobby.
905 Water St., 78602. Tel: 512-321-3552; Fax: 512-332-0404.
Res.: 905 Pecan St., 78602.
Catechesis/Religious Program—Sr. Cal Leopold, O.S.F., D.R.E. Students 304.

BELTON, BELL CO., CHRIST THE KING (1969) Rev. James Misko; Deacons Armando Aguirre; Steve Pina; William Shoemake.
Res.: 210 E. 24th Ave., 76513. Tel: 254-939-0806; 254-939-6109 (Rectory); Fax: 425-962-6914.
Catechesis/Religious Program—Krissie Lastovica, D.R.E. Students 363.

BERTRAM, BURNET CO., HOLY CROSS (1941) Attended by Our Mother of Sorrows, Burnet. Rev. Vincent Chacko, I.M.S. (India).
Mailing Address: P.O. Box 94, 78605. Tel: 512-355-2972.
Catechesis/Religious Program—Tel: 512-699-0376; Fax: 512-355-2972. Liz Barta, D.R.E. Students 65.

BLANCO, BLANCO CO., ST. FERDINAND (1940) [CEM] Rev. Justin Udomah.
Res.: 25 Main St., 78606. Tel: 830-833-4447; Fax: 830-833-9978.
Catechesis/Religious Program—Tel: 830-833-0444. Students 86.
Mission—Good Shepherd P.O. Box 1608, Johnson City, Blanco Co. 78636. Tel: 830-833-5227.
Mission—St. Mary's Help of Christians CR 473, Twin Sisters, Blanco Co. 78606.

BREMOND, ROBERTSON CO., ST. MARY (1879) [CEM] Rev. Celso A. Yu, M.F. (Philippines).
Res.: 715 N. Main St., 76629. Tel: 254-746-7789; Fax: 254-746-7789.
Catechesis/Religious Program—Tel: 254-746-7789. Students 105.

BRENHAM, WASHINGTON CO., ST. MARY OF THE IMMACULATE CONCEPTION (1870) [CEM] Rev. David J. Ivey (LA); Deacons Bill Januszewski; Steve Medina.
Office: 701 Church St., 77833.
Rectory—608 S. Baylor, 77833. Tel: 979-836-4441; Fax: 979-836-9383.
Catechesis/Religious Program—Tel: 979-830-8331. Sr. Kathleen Skog, O.S.F., D.R.E. Students 552.
Mission—Sacred Heart Latium, 77833.

BRYAN, BRAZOS CO.

1—ST. ANTHONY (1896), (Italian), [JC] Rev. Patrick Ebner; Deacons Ellis Abraham; Glen Milton; Andy Perrone; Bill Scarmardo.
Res.: 401 S. Parker, 77803. Tel: 979-823-8145; Fax: 979-823-6001.
Catechesis/Religious Program—Tel: 979-822-3700. Students 262.
Mission—San Salvador, Brazos Co. 77803.

2—ST. JOSEPH (1873) [CEM 2] Rev. Msgr. John A. McCaffrey; Deacons Gary Nelson; Patrick Gallagher.
Res.: 600 E. 26th St., 77803. Tel: 979-822-2721; Fax: 979-779-3120.
School—(Grades PreK-12), 600 S. Coulter Dr., 77803. Tel: 979-822-6641; Fax: 979-779-2810. Mrs. Beatrice Janssen, Pres. & Prin.; Melissa Slater, Librarian. Lay Teachers 46; Students 463.
Catechesis/Religious Program—Tel: 979-823-5568; Fax: 979-779-3120. John Valentino, Youth Min.; Lisa Storemski, D.R.E. Students 592.

3—SAN SALVADOR, Attended by Mission of St. Anthony, Bryan Rev. Patrick Ebner.
Mailing Address: 401 S. Parker, 77803. Tel: 979-823-8145.

4—SANTA TERESA (1940), (Hispanic), Rev. Raymundo Chavez Vazquez; Deacon Fred Molina.
Res.: 1212 Lucky, 77803. Tel: 979-822-2932; Fax: 979-822-6957. Email: st.teresa@verizon.net.
Catechesis/Religious Program—Tel: 979-822-5557. Laura Cisneros, English & Spanish D.R.E. Students 665.

BUDA, HAYS CO., SANTA CRUZ (1941) Revs. Kirby Garner; Rito Davila, Parochial Vicar; Deacons Rodolfo Gonzalez; Rey Garza; John Riojas; Benjamin Garcia; Robert Johnson, Business Mgr.; Juanita Rodriguez, Parish Sec.
1100 Main St., 78610. P.O. Box 187, 78610-0187.
Res.: 1100 Main St., 78610. Tel: 512-312-2520; Fax: 512-295-2034.
School—(Grades PreK-6), 1100 Main St., P.O. Box 160, 78610. Tel: 512-312-2137; Fax: 512-312-2143. Susan Flanagan, Prin. Students 163.
Catechesis/Religious Program—Tel: 512-312-2520, Ext. 137; 512-312-2520, Ext. 129. Joanna Rubio, D.R.E.; Lupita Bodony, High School D.R.E. & Youth Ministry. Students 1,406.

BURLINGTON, MILAM CO., ST. MICHAEL (1879) Attended by St. Ann, Rosebud. Rev. Michael Ajewole, M.S.P.
85 Church Ave., 76519. Tel: 254-869-2169.
Catechesis/Religious Program—See St. Ann, Rosebud. Patsy Moeller, D.R.E. Students 2.

BURNET, BURNET CO., OUR MOTHER OF SORROWS (1941) Rev. Vincent Chacko, I.M.S. (India).
Res.: 507 Buchanan Dr., 78611-2304. Tel: 512-756-4410; Fax: 512-756-1573.
Catechesis/Religious Program—Maria Kyle, D.R.E. Students 199.
Mission—Holy Cross P.O. Box 94, Bertram, Burnet Co. 78605. Tel: 512-699-0376. Email: lbarta@austinrr.com.

CALDWELL, BURLESON CO., ST. MARY (1895), (Hispanic), [CEM] Rev. Brion Zarsky; Deacons John Young; Samuel Reyes.
Res.: 509 N. Thomas, 77836. Tel: 979-567-3667; Fax: 979-567-0749.
Catechesis/Religious Program—Students 300.
Mission—Holy Rosary [CEM] 8610 FM 2774, Burleson Co. 77836. Tel: 979-535-7704.

CALVERT, ROBERTSON CO., ST. MARY (1876), (Hispanic), [CEM] Closed. See St. Mary's Church, Hearne.

CAMERON, MILAM CO., ST. MONICA (1883) [CEM] Rev. Dimitrij Colankin; Michael Schoppe, Business Mgr.
Mailing Address: P.O. Box 673, 76520. Tel: 254-697-2107; Fax: 254-697-3334.
Church: 306 S. Nolan Ave., 76520.
Catechesis/Religious Program—Derek Brazeal, D.R.E.; Jim Lloyd, Youth Min.; Kerry Lloyd, Youth Min. Students 98.

CEDAR PARK, WILLIAMSON CO., ST. MARGARET MARY (1942) Revs. Le-Minh Pham; Javier Toscano; Deacons Phillip Roberge; Paul Rodriguez; John Murphy.
Res.: 12451 R.R. 2243, Leander, 78641. Tel: 512-259-3126.
Catechesis/Religious Program—Tel: 512-260-0162; Fax: 512-259-9658. Robin Hambright, D.R.E. Students 1,235.

CHAPPELL HILL, WASHINGTON CO., ST. STANISLAUS (1889), (Polish), [CEM] [JC 2] Rev. Jozef Musiol, S.D.S.

Res.: 9175 FM 1371, 77426. Tel: 979-836-3030; Fax: 979-836-7170.
Catechesis/Religious Program—Students 30.

CHINA SPRING, MCLENNAN CO., ST. PHILIP CATHOLIC CHURCH - CHINA SPRING, TEXAS (1996) Attended by Mission of St. Eugene, McGregor. Rev. Jose Luis Azcona, Pastoral Admin.
Mailing Address: P.O. Box 430, 76633. Tel: 254-836-4425; Fax: 254-751-8428. Email: barbaraanncallaway@hot.rr.com. 13095 Old China Spring Church Rd., 76633.
Catechesis/Religious Program—Tel: 254-836-1969; Fax: 254-836-0600. Students 66.

COLLEGE STATION, BRAZOS CO.
1—ST. MARY (1926) Revs. David Konderla; William R. Straten; Deacons Bill Scott Jr.; David Reed; Switzer Deason.
603 Church Ave., 77840.
Res.: 600 Church Ave., 77840. Tel: 979-846-5717; Fax: 979-846-4493. Email: info@aggiecatholic.org. Web: www.aggiecatholic.org.
Catechesis/Religious Program—Students 75.
2—ST. THOMAS AQUINAS (1982) Revs. Edwin Kagoo; Uche Obikwelu, Parochial Vicar; Deacons Theodore Baker; Frank Ashley; Dave Mayes; Ronald Fernandes.
Res.: 2541 Earl Rudder Fwy. S., 77845. Tel: 979-680-1412; 979-693-6994 (Office); Fax: 979-260-4502.
Catechesis/Religious Program—Nancy Blanco, D.R.E. Students 652.

COPPERAS COVE, CORYELL CO., HOLY FAMILY (1963) Rev. Christopher J. Downey; Deacons Tim Dorsey; James Hayden.
Res.: 1001 Georgetown Rd., 76522. Tel: 254-547-3735; Fax: 254-547-3735.
Catechesis/Religious Program—Tel: 254-547-0090. Natalie Czajka, D.R.E. Students 337.

CYCLONE, BELL CO., ST. JOSEPH (1902), (Czech—German), [CEM] Rev. Walter J. Matus.
Mailing Address: 20120 FM 485, Burlington, 76519.
Catechesis/Religious Program—Students 58.
Mission—Ss. Cyril & Methodius Burlington. FM 485, Marak, Milam Co. 76519. Tel: 254-985-2280.
Res.: 6633 FM 2269, Buckholts, 76518.

DIME BOX, LEE CO., ST. JOSEPH (1909) [CEM] Rev. Anthony Alphonse.
Mailing Address: 8282 FM 141, 77853.
Church: Farm-Market Rd. 141, 77853.
Catechesis/Religious Program—Students 17.
Mission—Holy Family (1990) P.O. Box 541, Lexington, Lee Co. 78947. Tel: 979-773-2500.

DRIPPING SPRINGS, HAYS CO., ST. MARTIN DE PORRES (1974) Rev. Edward Koharchik, C.S.P.; Deacons Edward Rositas; Daniel Pearson.
Mailing Address: P.O. Box 1062, 78620. Tel: 512-858-5667; Fax: 512-858-1467. Email: stmartindp@austin.rr.com. Web: stmartindp.org.
Church: 26160 Ranch Rd. 12, P.O. Box 1062, 78620.
Catechesis/Religious Program— Mary Armatta, D.R.E. Students 360.

ELGIN, BASTROP CO., SACRED HEART (1908), (Hispanic), [JC] Very Rev. George Joseph; Deacons Larry Dunne; Channing Fell; Richard Botello.
206 W. 12th St., 78621.
Res.: 400 W. 11th St., 78621. Tel: 512-281-4478; Fax: 512-281-2527.
Catechesis/Religious Program—Tel: 512-281-3536, Ext. 205. Students 459.

ELK, MCLENNON CO., ST. JOSEPH (1925) [CEM] Attended by St. Martin, Tours. Rev. Msgr. Isidore Rozycki.
Mailing Address: 301 St. Martins Church Rd., West, 76691. Tel: 254-822-1145; Fax: 254-822-0171.
Res.: 9656 Elk Rd., West, 76691.
Catechesis/Religious Program—Tel: 254-863-5919. Julie Arersman, D.R.E. Students 66.

ELLINGER, FAYETTE CO., ST. MARY CATHOLIC CHURCH (1855), (Czech), [CEM] Attended by St. John Catholic Church, Fayetteville. Rev. Steven Nesrsta.
Mailing Address: P.O. Box 57, Fayetteville, 78940. Tel: 979-378-2277; Fax: 979-378-4407.
Catechesis/Religious Program—209 E. Bell St., Fayetteville, 78940. Students 23.

FAYETTEVILLE, FAYETTE CO., ST. JOHN THE BAPTIST (1870), (Czech), [CEM] Rev. Steven Nesrsta; Deacon Robert Jasek.
Mailing Address: P.O. Box 57, 78940. Tel: 979-378-2277; Fax: 979-378-4407.
Res.: 205 E. Bell St., 78940. Tel: 979-378-2003.
Catechesis/Religious Program— Janice Kasmiersky, D.R.E. Students 90.
Mission—St. Mary Ellinger/Hostyn Hill, Fayette Co. 78940.
Mission—St. Martin Warrenton, Fayette Co. 78940.

FRANKLIN, ROBERTSON CO., ST. FRANCIS OF ASSISI (1997) Revs. David Leibham; Joseph Kim; Deacon Luis Doriocourt.
Mailing Address: P.O. Box 543, 77856. Tel: 979-828-9025 (Rectory); 979-828-1269 (Office).
Res.: 1371 W. FM 1644, 77856.
Catechesis/Religious Program—Students 60.

FRENSTAT, BURLESON CO., HOLY ROSARY (1888), (Czech), [CEM 2] Attended by St. Mary's, Caldwell Rev. Brion Zarsky.
Mailing Address: 6978 SH 36 S., Caldwell, 77836-5462. Tel: 979-567-4994.
Church: 8610 FM 2774, Caldwell, 77836. Fax: 979-535-7704.
Rectory—509 N. Thomas, Caldwell, 77836. Tel: 979-567-3667.
Catechesis/Religious Program—Tel: 979-596-2606. Students 26.

GATESVILLE, CORYELL CO., OUR LADY OF LOURDES CATHOLIC CHURCH - GATESVILLE, TEXAS (1946) Rev. Timothy V. Vaverek.
Res.: 1108 W. Main St., 76528-1123. Tel: 254-865-6710; Fax: 254-865-9065.
Catechesis/Religious Program— Velma Lewis, D.R.E. Students 61.

GEORGETOWN, WILLIAMSON CO., ST. HELEN (1932) Revs. Robert Becker; Jairo Sandoval Pliego, Parochial Vicar; Deacons Frank Monroe; Joe Ruiz; Vern Dawson.
Res.: 2700 E. University Ave., 78626-7300. Tel: 512-943-0259; Fax: 512-863-8558.
School—(Grades PreK-8) Tel: 512-868-0744; Fax: 512-869-3244. Sr. Mary Jean Olsovsky, Prin.; Laura Zarate, Librarian. Teachers 22; Students 189.
Catechesis/Religious Program—Tel: 512-863-0799. Dr. Santiago Ramirez, D.R.E. Students 663.

GIDDINGS, LEE CO., ST. MARGARET (1944), (German—Hispanic), [JC] Very Rev. James Robert Olnhausen.
Res.: 526 S. Grimes St., 78942. Tel: 979-542-0217; Fax: 979-542-4186.
Catechesis/Religious Program— Suzanne Peschke, D.R.E. (Upper Grades); Roxanna Madero, D.R.E. (Lower Grades). Students 300.
Mission—St. Mary's in Pin Oak Smithville. 732 FM 2104, Pin Oak, Bastrop Co. 78957.

GOLDTHWAITE, MILLS CO., ST. PETER (1885) [JC] Attended by St. Mary, San Saba. Very Rev. Jairo Lopez; Deacon Richard Menchaca, Pastoral Admin.
Res.: 1212 Reynolds St., P.O. Box 352, 76844. Tel: 325-648-3732; Fax: 325-648-3732.
Catechesis/Religious Program—Tel: 325-648-2903; Fax: 325-648-2903. Tani Menchaca, D.R.E. Students 50.

GRANGER, WILLIAMSON CO., SS. CYRIL AND METHODIUS (1891), (Czech), [CEM 2] [JC] Very Rev. Joseph Nisari (Pakistan).
Mailing Address: P.O. Box 608, 76530.
Res.: 300 W. Davilla, 76530. Tel: 512-859-2223; Fax: 512-859-2223. Email: sscmchurch@gmail.com. Web: www.sscmchurch.org.
School—(Grades PreK-6), P.O. Box 248, 76530. Tel: 512-859-2927; Fax: 512-859-2649. Mrs. Angela Warner, Prin.; Monica Schwertner, Librarian. Lay Teachers 8; Students 55.
Catechesis/Religious Program—104 N. Brazas, P.O. Box 956, 76530. Tel: 512-859-2634. Cara Finn, D.R.E. Students 120.

HAMILTON, HAMILTON CO., ST. THOMAS CATHOLIC CHURCH - HAMILTON, TEXAS (1965) [JC] Attended by Our Lady of Lourdes, Gatesville Rev. Timothy V. Vaverek.
Res.: 843 Nicholson Ave., 76531. Tel: 254-386-5513.
Catechesis/Religious Program—Students 41.

HARKER HEIGHTS, BELL CO., ST. PAUL CHONG HASANG (1986) Very Rev. Richard O'Rourke, M.S.C.; Rev. Gyo Jeong Joseph Lee, C.P.; Deacons Peter Kim; Klaus Adam; Ms. Margaret Hunt, Pastoral Assoc.
Mailing Address: P.O. Box 2414, 76548.
Res.: 1000 E. FM 2410, 76548. Tel: 254-698-4110; 254-698-4338; Fax: 254-698-4608.
Catechesis/Religious Program—Mrs. Victoria Biehle, D.R.E. Students 436.

HEARNE, ROBERTSON CO., ST. MARY (1872), (Italian—Mexican-American), [CEM] Rev. David Leibham.
Res.: 402 W. First St., 77859. Tel: 979-279-2233; Fax: 979-279-9606.
Catechesis/Religious Program— Madeline Zeig, D.R.E. Students 215.

HORSESHOE BAY, BURNET CO., ST. PAUL THE APOSTLE (1982) Rev. Ruben M. Patino, C.S.P.
Mailing Address: P.O. Box 8019, 78657. Tel: 830-598-8342; Fax: 830-598-1274.
Res.: 201 Dalton Cir., 78657.
Catechesis/Religious Program—Students 28.

HUTTO, WILLIAMSON CO., ST. PATRICK (2000) Very Rev. Christopher Ferrer; Deacons Kenneth Ryan; Gumisindo Gonzales.
Mailing Address: 2500 Limmer Loop, 78634. Tel: 512-759-3712; Fax: 512-759-3728.
Res.: 536 Will Smith Cir., 78634. Tel: 512-846-2118.
Catechesis/Religious Program—Students 241.

JARRELL, WILLIAMSON CO., HOLY TRINITY CATHOLIC CHURCH - CORN HILL, TEXAS (1889), (Czech—German), [CEM] Rev. Msgr. Emilian Foltyn; Deacon Gene (Roy) Davis.
Res.: 8626 FM 1105, 76537. Tel: 512-863-0401; Fax: 512-868-9505. Email: trinity@thegateway.net.
Catechesis/Religious Program—Tel: 512-863-3020. Debie Klaus, D.R.E. Students 59.

KILLEEN, BELL CO., ST. JOSEPH (1954) Revs. Adam Martinez; Vincent Romuals, S.R.C.; Deacons Michael Aaronson; James Rodgers.
Res.: 2903 E. Rancier Ave., 76543. Tel: 254-634-7878; Fax: 254-634-1508.
School—(Grades PreK-5), 2901 E. Rancier Ave., 76543. Tel: 254-634-7272; Fax: 254-634-1224. Becky Kirkland, Prin.; Mrs. Debbie Istas, Librarian. Lay Teachers 13; Students 119.
Catechesis/Religious Program—Tel: 254-634-7878, Ext. 213; Fax: 254-634-1508. Students 422.

KINGSLAND, LLANO CO., ST. CHARLES BORROMEO CATHOLIC CHURCH - KINGSLAND, TEXAS (1965) Rev. Bernard Nguyen Hung; Deacons Larry Crochet; Ronald Woods.
Mailing Address: P.O. Box 1748, 78639. 205 Trinity Dr., 78639.
Church: 1927 Hwy. 1431, 78639.
Rectory—1927 Hwy. 1431, 78639. Tel: 325-388-3742.
Catechesis/Religious Program—Tel: 830-598-7327. Students 25.
Mission—Our Lady of the Lake (Sunrise Beach) 304 Hillview Dr., Horseshoe Bay, Burnet Co. 78657-6043.

KOVAR, BASTROP CO., STS. PETER AND PAUL (1906), (Czech), Now a mission of St. Paul, Smithville. Mailing Address: 204 Mills St., Smithville, TX 78957. Tel: 512-237-2179., 309 Stolle Ln., Flatonia, 78941.

KYLE, HAYS CO., ST. ANTHONY MARIE DE CLARET (1909), (Hispanic), Revs. Juan Carlos Lopez; Matthew Kinney, Parochial Vicar; Deacons John Peca; Joe Flores; Richard Duecker; Aurelio Medina, (Retired).
Res.: 801 N. Burleson St., P.O. Box 268, 78640. Tel: 512-268-5311 (Church); Fax: 512-268-0144.
Rectory—279 Greene, 78640. Tel: 512-523-9122.
Catechesis/Religious Program—Maryrae Stein, D.R.E. Students 1,000.

LA GRANGE, FAYETTE CO., SACRED HEART OF JESUS (1886) [JC] Rev. Joseph Varickamackal (India); Deacons Mike Meismer; Frank J. (Jay) Vocelka.
Mailing Address: Box 548, 78945. Tel: 979-968-3430; Fax: 979-968-5740.
Res.: 539 E. Pearl, 78945. Tel: 979-968-6030.
School—(Grades PreK-6) Tel: 979-968-3223; Fax: 979-968-6382. Elmer Faykus, Prin. Lay Teachers 15; Students 152.
Catechesis/Religious Program—Tel: 979-968-3430, Ext. 6. Debbie Greene, C.R.E. Students 218.

LAGO VISTA, TRAVIS CO., OUR LADY OF THE LAKE CATHOLIC CHURCH - LAGO VISTA, TEXAS (1970) [CEM] Rev. Don Loftin; Deacons Terry Martin; Ed Faulk.
Mailing Address: 6100 Lohman Ford Rd., 78645. Tel: 512-267-2644; Fax: 512-267-2649.
Rectory—20400 Dawn Dr., 78645. Tel: 512-267-1524.
Catechesis/Religious Program—Students 81.

LAMPASAS, TRAVIS CO., ST. MARY OF THE IMMACULATE CONCEPTION (1885) Rev. Pedro Castillo (Colombia); Deacon Carlos Jasso.
Church & Mailing Address: 701 N. Key Ave., 76550-0866. Tel: 512-556-5544; Fax: 512-556-6967.
Catechesis/Religious Program—Students 163.
Mission—Good Shepherd Catholic Church (1927) 411 W. Main St., Lometa, Lampasas Co. 76853.

LATIUM, WASHINGTON CO., SACRED HEART CATHOLIC CHURCH - LATIUM, TEXAS (1872) [CEM] Attended by St. Mary, Brenham., 701 Church St., Brenham, 77833. Tel: 979-836-4441.

LEXINGTON, LEE CO., HOLY FAMILY CATHOLIC CHURCH - LEXINGTON, TEXAS (1990) [JC], Mission of St. Joseph, Dime Box. Rev. Anthony Alphonse.
Mailing Address: 8282 FM 141, Dime Box, 77853. Tel: 979-884-3100.
Res.: 1027 FM 696 East of Hwy. 77, 78947. Tel: 979-773-2500.
Catechesis/Religious Program—Students 46.

LLANO, LLANO CO., HOLY TRINITY CATHOLIC CHURCH - LLANO, TEXAS (1890) Rev. Melvin Dornak; Deacon George Lillard.
Mailing Address: P.O. Box 698, 78643. Tel: 325-247-4481; Fax: 325-248-0691. 708 Bessemer, 78643.
Catechesis/Religious Program—Students 41.
Mission—St. Joseph 216 Ave. B, Mason, Mason Co. 76856. Tel: 325-347-6932.

LOCKHART, CALDWELL CO., ST. MARY (1887) [CEM 2] Rev. Alberto J. Borruel; Deacons Guadalupe Aguilar; William Long; William Haywood; Patrick Venglar.
Res.: 205 W. Pecan, 78644. Tel: 512-398-4649; Fax: 512-398-2285. Web: stmaryslockhart.org.
Catechesis/Religious Program—Tel: 512-398-3506. Eva Mendez, D.R.E. Students 560.

LOMETA, LAMPASAS CO., GOOD SHEPHERD (1927) Attended by St. Mary, Lampasas. Rev. Pedro Castillo (Colombia); Deacon Carlos Jasso.

Mailing Address: 701 N. Key Ave., Lampasas, 76550-0866. Tel: 512-556-5544; Fax: 512-556-6967.
Church: 500 W. Main St., 76853.
Catechesis/Religious Program—Students 29.

LOTT, FALLS CO., SACRED HEART (1905), (Italian—German), [CEM] Attended by St. Joseph, Marlin. Rev. John Kelley.
Mailing Address: P.O. Box 371, Marlin, 76661. Tel: 254-803-8888; Fax: 254-803-8888.
Res.: 213 N. 6th St., 76656.
Catechesis/Religious Program— Clustered with St. Joseph, Marlin. Students 170.

LULING, CALDWELL CO., ST. JOHN THE EVANGELIST (1879) [CEM] Rev. Howard Goertz; Deacons Wilfred Dub Hargraves; Paul Easterling.
500 E. Travis St., 78648.
Res.: 400 S. Pecan Ave., 78648. Tel: 830-351-5043; Fax: 830-875-3533.
Catechesis/Religious Program—Students 145.

MANOR, TRAVIS CO., ST. JOSEPH (1876), (Hispanic), [JC] Rev. Ernesto Elizondo; Deacon William Vela.
Mailing Address: P.O. Box 389, 78653. Tel: 512-272-4004 (Rectory); Fax: 512-272-8939.
Catechesis/Religious Program—Students 283.

MARAK, MILAM CO., SS. CYRIL AND METHODIUS CATHOLIC CHURCH - MARAK, TEXAS (1903), (Czech), [CEM] [JC 2], Attended from St. Joseph's, Cyclone. Rev. Walter J. Matus.
Mailing Address: 20120 FM 485, Burlington, 76519. Tel: 254-985-2280.
Res.: 6633 FM 2266, Buckholts, 76518.
Catechesis/Religious Program—Tel: 254-697-4861. Students 40.

MARBLE FALLS, BURNET CO., ST. JOHN THE EVANGELIST (1961) Very Rev. Jairo Lopez; Deacons Eraclio Solorzano; Paul Lavallee; Edward Holicky.
Church: 105 Hwy. 1431 E., 78654. Tel: 830-693-5134; Fax: 830-798-9574.
Catechesis/Religious Program—Tel: 830-693-3279. Students 311.

MARLIN, FALLS CO., ST. JOSEPH (1872), (Italian—Polish), Rev. John Kelley.
Mailing Address: Box 371, 76661. Tel: 254-803-8888; Fax: 254-803-8888.
Church: 311 Oakes St., Box 371, 76661.
Catechesis/Religious Program— Mr. Charles Yesak, D.R.E. Students 113.
Mission—Sacred Heart [CEM] 6th & Hackberry, Lott, Falls Co. 76656.

MARTINDALE, CALDWELL CO., IMMACULATE HEART OF MARY (1908) Rev. Antonio Perez, Admin.; Deacon Johnny Ojeda.
Mailing Address: P.O. Box 117, 78655. Tel: 512-357-6573; Fax: 512-357-2667.
Church: 312 Lockhart St., 78655.
Catechesis/Religious Program—Tel: 512-357-9076. Georgina Cruz, D.R.E. Students 60.

MASON, MASON CO., ST. JOSEPH (1873) Attended by Holy Trinity, Llano. Rev. Melvin Dornak.
Mailing Address: P.O. Box 698, Llano, 78643.
Church: 216 Ave. B, 76856. Tel: 325-347-6932; Fax: 325-248-0691.
Catechesis/Religious Program—Tel: 325-347-5327. Gladys Garner, D.R.E. Students 44.

MCGREGOR, MCLENNAN CO., ST. EUGENE CATHOLIC CHURCH - MCGREGOR, TEXAS (1958), (Hispanic), [JC] Rev. Jose Luis Azcona.
Res.: 207 N. Johnson Dr., 76657. Tel: 254-840-3174; Fax: 254-840-0174.
Catechesis/Religious Program—Students 200.
Mission—Our Lady of San Juan 207 N. Johnson Dr., Moody, McLennan Co. 76657. Tel: 254-853-9011.
Mission—St. Philip 13095 Old China Spring Rd., P.O. Box 430, China Spring, McLennan Co. 76633. Tel: 254-836-4425.

MEXIA, LIMESTONE CO., ST. MARY (1886) [JC] Rev. Carlo Benjamin Magnaye, M.F.; Deacons Daniel Ramirez; Dwight Mahoney; Richard Johnson.
Res. & Mailing Address: 606 N. Bonham St., 76667. Tel: 254-562-3619; Fax: 254-562-6377.
Catechesis/Religious Program—Filomena Contrekas, D.R.E.; Gladys Mendoza, D.R.E. Students 289.

MOODY, MCLENNAN CO., OUR LADY OF SAN JUAN CATHOLIC MISSION CHURCH - MOODY, TEXAS (1991), (Hispanic), Mission of St. Eugene, McGregor. Rev. Jose Luis Azcona.
Church: 207 N. Johnson Dr., Mc Gregor, 76657. Tel: 254-840-3174; Fax: 254-840-0174.
Catechesis/Religious Program—Tel: 254-853-9011. Students 35.

OLD WASHINGTON-ON-THE-BRAZOS, WASHINGTON CO., BLESSED VIRGIN MARY (1849), (African American), Attended by St. Ann, Somerville. Rev. Nock W. Russell; Deacon Limas Sweed Sr.
Mailing Address: P.O. Box 485, Washington, 77880.
Catechesis/Religious Program—Students 10.

PFLUGERVILLE, TRAVIS CO., ST. ELIZABETH (1932) Revs. Pedro Garcia-Ramirez; Steve Sauser; Deacons Alejandro Lara; Barry Ryan; Emmanuel Nwokocha.
Mailing Address: 1520 N. Railroad Ave., 78660. Tel: 512-251-9838; Fax: 512-251-9868.
Res.: 1104 Lincoln Sparrow Cove, 78660.
Catechesis/Religious Program—Tel: 512-251-9842; Fax: 572-251-9868. Students 1,305.

PIN OAK, BASTROP CO., ST. MARY (1866), (German), [CEM] Attended by St. Margaret, Giddings. Very Rev. James Robert Olnhausen.
Mailing Address: *c/o St. Margaret Catholic Church*, 526 S. Grimes St., Giddings, 78942. Tel: 979-542-0217; Fax: 979-542-4186.
Church: 732 FM 2104, Smithville, 78957.
Catechesis/Religious Program—Roxanna Madero, D.R.E.; Suzanne Peschke, D.R.E. Students 7.

ROCKDALE, MILAM CO., ST. JOSEPH (1880) Rev. Ramon Frayna; Deacons Gus Coelho; Donald Sims.
Mailing Address: P.O. Box 548, 76567. Tel: 512-446-2049; Fax: 512-446-0411.
Rectory—521 E. Davilla St., 76567. Tel: 512-446-2196.
Church: 234 San Gabriel St., 76567.
Catechesis/Religious Program—Theresa Alvarez, D.R.E. Students 180.

ROCKNE, BASTROP CO., SACRED HEART (1876), (German), [CEM] Rev. Dariusz Ziebowicz, S.D.S.; Deacons Roger Muehr; Alvin Frerich.
Mailing Address: 4045 FM 535, Bastrop, 78602. Tel: 512-321-7991; Fax: 512-303-2723.
Church: Farm-Market Rd., 78602.
Catechesis/Religious Program—Tel: 512-303-3311. Students 210.
Mission—Assumption of the Blessed Virgin Mary [CEM] String Prairie, Bastrop Co. Tel: 830-839-4580.

ROGERS, BELL CO., ST. MATTHEW (1991) Revs. Tom Chamberlain; Ramiro Tarazona, Parochial Vicar.
Mailing Address: 707 S. 6th St., Temple, 76504.
Church: 10451 E. Hwy. 1290, 76569. Tel: 254-773-6779.
Catechesis/Religious Program—Students 69.

ROSEBUD, FALLS CO., ST. ANN (1915) [CEM] Rev. Michael Ajewole, M.S.P.
Mailing Address: 85 Church Ave., Burlington, 76519. Tel: 254-869-2525.
Church: 511 S. Stalworth St., 76570. Tel: 254-869-2169; Fax: 254-869-2169. Web: www.stannandstmichaelchurches.org.
Catechesis/Religious Program—Tel: 254-583-0309. Students 88.
Mission—St. Michael (1879) Burlington.

ROUND ROCK, WILLIAMSON CO.

1—ST. JOHN VIANNEY (1997) Very Rev. Michael J. O'Connor; Deacons Gene Saienga; Frank McCormick.
Catechesis/Religious Program—Fax: 512-218-8272. Students 395.

2—ST. WILLIAM (1956) Revs. Dean E. Wilhelm; Jonathan D. Raia, Parochial Vicar; Deacons Concho Castillo, (Retired); Richard Kotrola; Dennis Egan; Rudy Rios.
Mailing Address & Office: 620 Round Rock W. Dr., 78681. Tel: 512-255-4473; Fax: 512-255-8126. Email: office@saintwilliams.org. Web: www.saintwilliams.org.
Rectory—1105 Deer Run, 78681. Tel: 512-358-6063.
Catechesis/Religious Program—Tel: 512-600-8172. Students 1,748.

SALADO, BELL CO., ST. STEPHEN (1989) Rev. Gregory McLaughlin; Deacon Jose Jimenez.
Mailing Address: P.O. Box 662, 76571. Tel: 254-947-8037; Fax: 254-947-8091.
Rectory—601 FM 2268, 76751. Tel: 254-947-5582.
Church: 601 FM 2268 (Holland Rd.), P.O. Box 662, 76751. Tel: 254-947-8037; Fax: 254-947-8091.
Catechesis/Religious Program—Laura Snyder, D.R.E. Students 147.

SAN MARCOS, HAYS CO., ST. JOHN THE EVANGELIST (1883) Revs. Victor Mayorga (Colombia); Mark Hamlet; Deacons Domingo Vargas; Jesse Mojica; Luis F. Silguero.
Res.: 624 E. Hopkins, 78666. Tel: 512-353-8969; Fax: 512-396-7522.
Catechesis/Religious Program—Tel: 512-353-5065. Students 810.
Mission—Guadalupe Chapel 218 Roosevelt, Hays Co. 78666.

SAN SABA, SAN SABA CO., ST. MARY (1967), (Hispanic), Very Rev. Jairo Lopez, Admin.
Mailing Address: P.O. Box 415, 76877. Tel: 325-372-3679; Fax: 325-372-6569. Email: stmarys@centex.net.
Church: 504 W. Wallace, 76877.
Catechesis/Religious Program—Tani Menchaca, D.R.E., (Goldthwaite); Michael Bohensky, D.R.E. (San Saba). Students 90.

SATIN, SATIN FALLS CO., SANTA RITA SHRINE (1917), (Hispanic), Attended by St. Francis, Waco., Mailing Address: 301 Jefferson Ave., Waco, 76701. Tel: 254-752-8434; Fax: 254-752-2415.

SMITHVILLE, BASTROP CO., ST. PAUL CATHOLIC CHURCH (1896) Rev. Pius T. Mathew, Admin.; Deacon Bernard Meuth.
Res.: 204 Mills St., 78957. Tel: 512-237-3299; Fax: 512-237-3299 (call first). Email: stpaul_business@austin.rr.com.
Catechesis/Religious Program—Tel: 512-237-3299. Mitchell Herring, D.R.E. Students 118.
Mission—Sts. Peter and Paul Kovar, Bastrop Co.

SOMERVILLE, BURLESON CO., ST. ANN (1913) Rev. Nock W. Russell.
Mailing Address: P.O. Box 99, 77879. Tel: 979-596-1966; Fax: 979-596-2857.
Church: 333 Thornberry Rd., 77879.
Catechesis/Religious Program—Sr. Mary John Della Morte, D.R.E. Students 5.
Mission—Blessed Virgin Mary Chapel (1849) [JC] Washington. 17370 Sweed Rd., Old Washington, Washington Co. 77880. Tel: 936-878-2659.

STONY POINT, TRAVIS CO., SAN JUAN DIEGO MISSION OF DOLORES - STONY POINT (1987), (Mexican), Attended by San Francisco Javier, Austin. Rev. Cesar Jaime Guzman Diaz.
Mailing Address: 9110 U.S. Hwy. 183 S., 78747.
Church: 216 Stony Point Dr., Del Valle, 78617. Tel: 512-247-2476; Fax: 512-243-2995.
Catechesis/Religious Program—Students 59.

STRING PRAIRIE, BASTROP CO., ST. MARY OF THE ASSUMPTION (1876), (German), [CEM] Attended by Sacred Heart, Rockne. Rev. Dariusz Ziebowicz, S.D.S.
Mailing Address: 4045 FM 535, Bastrop, 78602. Tel: 830-839-4580; Fax: 512-303-2723.
Catechesis/Religious Program—Tel: 830-540-4089. Mrs. Deanna Seidel, D.R.E. Students 55.

SUNRISE BEACH, LLANO CO., OUR LADY OF THE LAKE, Attended by St. Charles Borromeo, Kingsland Rev. Bernard Nguyen Hung.
304 Hillview Dr., Horseshoe Bay, 78657. Tel: 830-598-7327.

TAYLOR, WILLIAMSON CO.

1—ST. MARY OF THE ASSUMPTION (1877) [CEM] Rev. Msgr. Lonnie A. Urban; Deacon David Pustka.
Res.: 408 Washburn St., 76574. Tel: 512-352-2175; 512-365-2175; Fax: 512-365-5313.
School—(Grades PreK-8) Tel: 512-352-2313. Dr. Barbara Gibson, Prin.; Dolores Hernandez, Librarian. Sisters 2; Lay Teachers 18; Students 179.
Catechesis/Religious Program—Tel: 512-352-2133. Frances Albert, D.R.E. Students 206.
Convent—317 E. 4th St., 76574. Tel: 512-352-2144.

2—OUR LADY OF GUADALUPE (1914), (Hispanic), [CEM] Rev. Efrain Villanueva; Deacon Alfredo Torres.
Res.: 113 Dickey St., 76574. Tel: 512-365-2380; Fax: 512-365-1733.
Catechesis/Religious Program—Students 323.

TEMPLE, BELL CO.

1—ST. LUKE (1969) [CEM] [JC] Rev. James M. Ekeocha; Deacons Jerome J. Klement; James Madsen; Robert George.
Res.: 2807 Oakdale, 76502. Tel: 254-773-1561; Fax: 254-773-4623.
Catechesis/Religious Program—Tel: 254-773-2330. Students 425.

2—ST. MARY (1883) [JC] Rev. Sales T. (Ranjan) Cletus; Deacons Bonifacio (Barney) Rodriguez; Robert J. Snigger.
Res.: 1018 S. 7th St., 76504. Tel: 254-773-4541; Fax: 254-774-7044.
Rectory—1004 S. 7th St., 76504. Tel: 254-773-3238.
School—(Grades PreK-8), 1019 S. 7th St., 76504. Tel: 254-778-8141; Fax: 254-778-1396. James Melone, Prin.; Bernadette Hickman, Librarian. Lay Teachers 20; Students 230.
Catechesis/Religious Program—Tel: 254-773-1980. Loris Edwards, D.R.E. Students 184.

3—OUR LADY OF GUADALUPE CATHOLIC CHURCH - TEMPLE, TEXAS (1952), (Hispanic), Revs. Tom Chamberlain; Ramiro Tarazona; Deacons J. Margarito Alvarado; Joe Vela; Rafael Ozuna.
Res.: 707 S. 6th St., 76504. Tel: 254-778-1304; Fax: 254-773-5469.
Catechesis/Religious Program—Students 405.
Mission—St. Mathew

TOURS, MCLENNAN CO., ST. MARTIN (1870), (German—Czech), [CEM] Rev. Msgr. Isidore Rozycki.
Res.: 301 St. Martin's Church Rd., West, 76691-2135. Tel: 254-822-1145; Fax: 254-822-0171.
Catechesis/Religious Program—Tel: 254-822-1026. Jennifer Varga, D.R.E.; Kayla Sinkule, D.R.E. Students 141.
Mission—St. Joseph Elk, McLennon Co. 76691.

UHLAND, HAYS CO., ST. MICHAEL (1924), (Hispanic), [CEM] [JC] Rev. Antonio Perez; Deacon W. J. Ham.
Church and Mailing: 80 S. Old Spanish Tr., 78640. Tel: 512-398-7475; Fax: 512-398-7156.
Catechesis/Religious Program—Carolyn Martinez, D.R.E. Students 75.

WACO, MCLENNAN CO.

1—ST. FRANCIS ON THE BRAZOS (1924), (Hispanic), [JC] Very Rev. Roman Burgos, T.O.R.; Deacon Jessie C. Garza.

Mailing Address: 315 Jefferson Ave., 76701.
Res.: 301 Jefferson Ave., 76701. Tel: 254-752-8434; Fax: 254-752-2415.
Nursery & Kindergarten—612 N. 3rd St., 76701. Tel: 254-753-5565; Fax: 254-757-0537. Sr. Maria Izquierdo, F.H.M., Prin. Sisters 4; Lay Teachers 6; Students 131.
Catechesis/Religious Program—Tel: 254-752-1159. Students 410.
Convent—612 N. 3rd St., 76701. Tel: 254-753-5565.

2—ST. JEROME (1982) Rev. Rakshaganathan Selvaraj; Deacons Joseph Potter; Rae Carter; Greg George; Raymond Jones.
9820 Chapel Rd., 76712.
Res.: 9200 Yellowstone, 76712. Tel: 254-666-7722; Fax: 254-666-4848.
Catechesis/Religious Program—Lisa Sanders, D.R.E. Students 400.

3—ST. JOHN THE BAPTIST (1953), (African American), Rev. Cyril Ngbede Ejaidu; Sylvia Glynn, Business Admin. & Finance Sec.
Mailing Address: P.O. Box 585, 76704-0585.
Res.: 1312 Dallas St., 76704-0585. Tel: 254-753-6742.
Catechesis/Religious Program—Students 4.

4—ST. JOSEPH (1950) Rev. Robert Herald.
Res.: 1011 Boston St., 76705.
Catechesis/Religious Program—Tel: 254-799-6646. Rosemary Berrios, D.R.E. Students 70.

5—ST. LOUIS (1964) Rev. John Michael Guzaldo.
Res.: 2001 N. 25th St., P.O. Box 5040, 76708. Tel: 254-754-1221; Fax: 254-754-4019.
School—(Grades PreK-8) Tel: 254-754-2041; Fax: 254-754-2091. Louis Gonzales, Prin.; Linda Adkins, Librarian. Lay Teachers 42; Students 311.
Catechesis/Religious Program—Antonia Duran, D.R.E. Students 200.

6—ST. MARY OF THE ASSUMPTION (1870) Rev. Joseph F. Geleney Jr.; Deacons James Fitzpatrick; James Poole; Jerry Opperman.
Church & Mailing Address: 1401 Washington Ave., 76701. Tel: 254-753-0146; Fax: 254-753-5100.
Catechesis/Religious Program—Terri Bukowski, D.R.E. Students 74.

7—SACRED HEART CATHOLIC CHURCH - WACO, TEXAS (1957), (Spanish), Rev. Lawrence Soler, T.O.R.; Deacons Tony Arocha; Lorenzo Garcia; George Shields; Robert Wehrer.
Res.: 2621 Bagby Ave., 76711. Tel: 254-756-0449; Fax: 254-756-6302.
Catechesis/Religious Program—Tel: 254-756-2390. Students 495.

WARRENTON, FAYETTE CO., ST. MARTIN CATHOLIC CHURCH - WARRENTON, TEXAS (1888) [CEM], Historic chapel, mission of St John, Fayetteville., Mailing Address: P.O. Box 57, Fayetteville, 78940.

WEST, MCLENNAN CO., ST. MARY, CHURCH OF THE ASSUMPTION (1892), (Czech), [CEM] Very Rev. Edward Karasek; Rev. Anthony Odiong (Nigeria).
Mailing Address: P.O. Box 276, 76691. Tel: 254-826-3705; Fax: 254-826-5497.
Church: 303 S. Harrison, 76691. Tel: 254-826-3705; Fax: 254-826-5497.
School—(Grades PreK-8) Tel: 254-826-5991; Fax: 254-826-7047. Ericka Sammons, Prin. Lay Teachers 11; Students 145.
Catechesis/Religious Program—Dianne Mendiola, D.R.E.; Nancy Polasek, D.R.E. Students 425.

WESTPHALIA, FALLS CO., CHURCH OF THE VISITATION (1883), (German), [CEM] Rev. Walter Dhanwar, I.M.S.; Deacons Bill Smetana; Charlie Wright.
Res.: 144 County Rd. 3000, Lott, 76656-3827. Tel: 254-584-4983; 254-275-4488; Fax: 254-584-4983.
Catechesis/Religious Program—Tel: 254-584-4407. Marilyn Rudloff, D.R.E. Students 129.

WIMBERLEY, HAYS CO., ST. MARY (1956) [CEM] Revs. Gregory Hanks, Admin. Pro Tem; Everett Trebtoske, Pastor Emeritus (Retired).
Res.: 6 Palos Verdes, 14711 Ranch Rd. 12, 78676. Tel: 512-847-9181 (Church); Fax: 512-847-5573.
Catechesis/Religious Program—Tel: 512-847-1662. Minerva Martinez, D.R.E. Students 176.

Chaplains of Public Institutions

AUSTIN. *St. David's Hospital*. Attended by St. Austin Catholic Church., 2010 Guadalupe, 78705. Tel: 512-477-9471. Vacant.
School for the Blind. Attended by St. Louis Church., 7601 Burnet Rd., 78757. Tel: 512-454-0384. Vacant.
School for the Deaf, 2309 Euclid St., 78704. Tel: 512-442-3602. Attended by St. Ignatius Catholic Church.
Seton/Brackenridge Hospital, Tel: 512-324-7480; 512-324-7106. Revs. Paulinus Iwuji, S.M.M.M., Chap., Seton Healthcare Facilities, Jude Ndugbu, Dell Children's Hospital, Anthony Nwudah, J.C.L., Seton Healthcare Facilities, Frank Zlotkowski, C.S.C., Chap., Brackenridge Hospital.
State Hospital, 4110 Guadalupe, 78751. Tel: 512-836-1213. Attended by St. Austin Church, Tel: 512-477-9471.

GATESVILLE. *Texas Department of Criminal Justice*, P.O. Box 665, 76528. Rev. Timothy V. Vaverek.

GIDDINGS. *State School*, Tel: 979-542-0217. Very Rev. James Robert Olnhausen. Attended by St. Margaret, Giddings. Tel: 409-542-3380.

MEXIA. *State School*, 606 N. Bonham, 76667. Tel: 254-562-3619. Rev. Carlo Benjamin Magnaye, M.F.

TEMPLE. *V.A. Hospital*, 1901 S. First St., 76501. Tel: 254-778-4811, Ext. 4879. Vacant.

WACO. *V.A. Hospital*, 4800 Memorial Dr., 76711. Tel: 254-752-6581. Vacant.

Chaplains of the Military:
Revs.—
George, George C., Chap., 15519 Luna Ridge, Helotes, 78023.
Johnson, Charles W., (LT), C.H.C., U.S.N., CRMD USS Theodore Roosevelt, CVN 71, Apo, AE 09599-2871.
Nielson, Kenneth (Karl), U.S. Army

On Duty Outside the Diocese:
Rev. Msgr.—
Jenkins, Ron, USCCB, 3211 4th St. N.E., Washington, DC 20017. Tel: 202-541-3100, Ext. 11
Revs.—
Koehl, Keith, P.O. Box 140309, Irving, 75014.
McNeil, Joel
Strieder, Leon, St. Mary Seminary, University of St. Thomas, Houston, Texas, 9845 Memorial Dr., Houston, 77024.

Retired:
Rev. Msgrs.—
Brennan, Ralph, 921 St. Edward's Dr., 78704. Tel: 512-493-0130
Deane, Joseph, John Paul Residence for Priests, 2610 E. University Ave., # 701, Georgetown, 78626.
Deering, Mark, 4700 Westchester, 76710. Tel: 254-772-5263
Goertz, Victor, 2610 E. University Ave., #202, Georgetown, 78626.
Holtman, Elmer, 2805 Ranch Rd., 2341, Burnet, 78611.
Johnson, Oliver F., 7709 Beckett Rd., #2134, 78749.
Malinowski, John C., P.O. Box 3931, Bryan, 77805.
Mazurkiewicz, Harry, 2848 Ehlinger-Becker, Fayetteville, 78940.
Miller, Frank, 501 Meadow Dr., #12, West, 76691.
Pavlicek, Louis, 620 Round Rock W. Dr., Round Rock, 78681.
Reyes, Lonnie C.
Schmitt, Joseph J., 6100 Lohman Ford Rd., Lago Vista, 78645.
Wozniak, Louis, 2212 Rifle Bend Dr., Georgetown, 78626. Tel: 512-864-1907
Zientek, Benedict, P.O. Box 2447, Brenham, 77834.
Revs.—
Benish, William, 450 Discovery Blvd., Room 210, Cedar Park, 78613. Tel: 254-741-1412
Carr, Walter, 1006 Salem Ln., 78753.
Chalupa, Fred, J.C.L., John Paul II Residence for Priests, 2610 E. University Ave., #201, Georgetown, 78626.
Clancy, "Ray", 13836 W. Sola Dr., Sun City West, AZ 85375.
Dowling, Ray, 11300 W. Parmer Ln., Cedar Park, 78613.
Evans, James L., 6704 Cypress Pt. N., 78746. Tel: 512-306-8698
Ferrer, Gonzalo, 160 Biels Loop, Killeen, 76542.
Frazer, Joseph, P.O. Box 1083, Penney Farms, FL 32079.
Geniesse, Joseph F., C.S.C., 2111 Brackenridge St., 78704.
Goertz, Bernard C., 585 Shiloh Rd., Bastrop, 78602.
Hanus, Thomas J., P.O. Box 141, Lyons, 77863.
Higgens, Peter, 105 Island Dr., #D, Horseshoe Bay, 78657.
Leddy, Leonard, Western Hill Village, 3000 W. Adams Ave., #301, Temple, 76504.
Lee, Sang Yil, 867 Riverside Dr., Killeen, 76542. Tel: 254-285-1501
Mahoney, Bernard, 1722 Chippendale, Houston, 77018.
McCabe, Peter
McCallum, Paul F., John Paul II Residence for Priests, 2610 E. University Ave., #101, Georgetown, 78626.
Mikkelson, Scott, John Paul II Residence for Priests, 2610 E. University, #702, Georgetown, 78626.
Niemira, Thomas, Lorena, 76655.
Romanski, Gregory A., 8017 Raintree Pl., 78759.
Shepard, Eugene, 308 Mechanic, Weimar, 78962.
Smith, Gerald, 4800 Convict Hill, 78749.
Trebtoske, Everett, 14711 Ranch Rd. 12, Wimberley, 78676.
Tzanakas, George M., John Paul II Residence for Priests, 2610 E. University Ave., #102, Georgetown, 78626.
Van Winkle, Charles, C.S.C., 2111 Brackenridge St., 78704.

Permanent Deacons:
Aaronson, Michael, St. Joseph, Killeen
Abraham, Ellis, St. Anthony, Bryan
Adam, Klaus, St. Paul Chong Hasang, Harker Heights
Aguilar, Guadalupe, St. Mary, Lockhart
Aguirre, Armando, Christ the King, Belton
Alvarado, J. Margarito, Our Lady of Guadalupe, Temple
Arellano, Joe, St. Peter the Apostle, Austin
Arevalo, Ralph, St. Julia, Austin
Arocha, Antonio, Sacred Heart, Waco
Ashley, Frank, St. Thomas Aquinas, College Station
Atkins, William "Billy", Our Lady of Guadalupe, Austin
Baker, Ted, St. Thomas Aquinas, College Station
Banda, Cruz, Jr., St. Albert the Great, Austin
Barkley, Roy, St. Joseph, Manor
Beltran, Victor, St. Eugene, McGregor
Benavides, Alfred, San Jose, Austin
Bigelow, Richard, St. Louis, Austin
Boren, David, St. Vincent de Paul, Austin
Botello, Richard, Sacred Heart, Elgin
Boyle, Vincent A., St. Mary Cathedral, Austin
Cardona, David, Serving in Diocese of St. Petersburg, FL
Carter, Rae, St. Jerome, Waco
Casarez, Jesse, St. Catherine of Siena, Austin
Castillo, Concepcion, (Retired)
Cavazos, Arthur, Catherine of Siena, Austin
Chavez, Jose, Sacred Heart, Austin
Clapp, Ron, (Inactive)
Coelho, Gus, St. Joseph, Rockdale
Colley, Earl, St. Monica, Cameron
Collins, Roger, (Retired)
Colon, Willie, (Retired)
Consentino, John, (Retired)
Cortez, Willie, St. Mary Cathedral, Austin
Crochet, Larry, (Retired)
Cuevas, Alfonso, St. Albert the Great, Austin
Davis, Gene (Roy), Holy Trinity, Corn Hill
Dawson, Vern, St. Helen, Georgetown
De La Garza, John, University Catholic Center, Austin
Deason, Switzer, St. Mary, College Station
Desorcie, Allen, St. Vincent de Paul, Austin
Doriocourt, Luis, St. Francis of Assisi, Franklin
Dorsey, Timothy, Holy Family, Copperas Cove
Duecker, Richard, St. Anthony, Kyle
Dufour, Generes "Doots", Diocesan Criminal Justice Ministry
Dunne, Larry, Sacred Heart, Elgin
Duran, Everardo "Lalo", (Retired)
Easterling, Paul, St. John the Evangelist, Luling
Egan, Dennis, St. William, Round Rock
Embry, Rob, St. Louis, Austin
Endris, Lou, (Retired)
Esquivel, Benito, St. Ferdinand, Blanco; Good Shepard, Johnson City
Fahlund, Nelson, (Inactive)
Fell, Channing, Scared Heart, Elgin
Fernandes, Ronald, St. Thomas Aquinas, College Station
Fitzpatrick, Jim, St. Mary, Church of the Assumption, Waco
Flores, Joe, St. Anthony, Kyle
Franklin, John, (Retired)
Frerich, Alvin, Sacred Heart, Rockne
Gallagher, Pat, St. Joseph, Bryan
Garcia, Ben, Santa Cruz, Buda
Garcia, Lorenzo, Sacred Heart, Waco
Garza, Jesse M., (Retired)
Garza, Jessie C., (Retired)
Garza, Juan, (Retired)
Garza, Rey, Santa Cruz, Buda
George, Gregory, St. Jerome, Waco
George, Robert, St. Luke, Temple
Gesch, Michael, St. John Neumann, Austin
Gessler, Donald, M.D., M.B.A., St. Theresa, Austin
Gonzales, Gumisindo, St. Patrick, Hutto
Gonzalez, Rodolfo, Santa Cruz, Buda
Guerrero, Jorge, St. Mary, Wimberly
Guilbert, Terry, Emmaus Parish, Lakeway
Gutierrez, Joe, San Jose, Austin
Ham, W. J., St. Michael, Uhland
Hansen, Clarence, (Inactive)
Hargraves, Wilfred (Dub), St. John, Luling
Hayden, Tim, Holy Family, Copperas Cove
Haywood, Daryl, St. Mary, Lockhart
Hill, John, Jr., Emmaus, Lakeway
Hipskind, Gregory, (Inactive)

Hobby, Bill, Ascension, Bastrop; Diocesan Vice Chancellor
Holicky, Edward, Jr., St. John the Evangelist, Marble Falls
James, Ray, (Retired)
Januszewski, Bill, (Retired)
Jasek, Frank, St. Peter Catholic Student Center, Waco
Jasek, Robert, St. John, Fayetteville
Jasso, Carlos, St. Mary, Lampasas
Jimenez, Jose, St. Stephen, Salado
Johnson, Richard, St. Mary, Mexia
Johnson, Tom, St. Thomas More, Austin; Assoc. Dir. Diaconate Formation
Jones, Fred, Catholic Community, Fort Hood
Jones, Ray, St. Jerome, Waco
Kennedy, Pat, (Retired)
Kim, Peter, St. Paul Chong Hasang, Harker Heights
Klement, Jerry, St. Luke, Temple
Kotrola, Richard, St. William, Round Rock
Krotzer, Philip, (Inactive)
Lara, Alejandro, St. Elizabeth, Pflugerville
Lastovica, Ronnie, Christ the King, Belton
Lavallee, Paul, St. John the Evangelist, Marble Falls
Lawrence, John, (Retired)
Ledesma, Robert, (Inactive)
Lilliard, George, Holy Trinity, Llano
Long, Bill, St. Mary, Lockhart
Lopez, Agapito, Cristo Rey, Austin
Luna, Conception, St. Mary, Hearne
Luna, Willie, (Inactive)
Lupo, Daniel, St. Thomas More, Austin
Madsen, James, St. Luke, Temple
Mahoney, Dwight, St. Mary, Mexia
Mai, Hoa, Holy Vietnamese Martyrs, Austin
Mallinger, Thomas, St. Thomas More, Austin
Martin, Terry, St. Mary, Lago Vista
Martinez, Jesse, Emmaus, Lakeway
Martinez, Roberto, Sacred Heart, Austin
Mayes, Dave, St. Thomas Aquinas, College Station
McCormick, Frank, St. John Vianney, Round Rock
Medina, Aurelio, (Retired)
Meismer, Mike, Sacred Heart, La Grange
Menchaca, Richard, St. Peter, Goldthwaite
Mendez, Jose, San Jose, Austin
Meuth, Bernard, St. Paul, Smithville
Milton, Glen, (Inactive)
Mojica, Jessie, St. John, San Marcos
Molina, Fred, Santa Teresa, Bryan
Monroe, Frank, J.D., St. Helen, Georgetown
Montag, Eugene J., (Retired)
Moore, Ray, (Inactive)
Morales, David, (Retired)
Moran, Elias, (Inactive)
Morse, Eugene, (Retired)
Muehr, Roger, Sacred Heart, Rockne
Murphy, John, St. Margaret Mary, Cedar Park
Murray, Patrick, St. Ignatius, Austin
Nelson, Gary, St. Joseph, Bryan
Nissen, Kevin, St. Julia, Austin
Nwokocha, Emmanuel, St. Elizabeth, Pflugerville
O'Neill, John, (Retired)
Ojeda, Johnny, Immaculate Heart of Mary, Martindale
Opperman, Jerry, St. Mary of the Assumption, Waco
Orton, Dick, (Retired)
Ozuna, Rafael, (Inactive)
Pearson, Daniel, St. Martin de Porres, Dripping Springs
Peca, John M., St. Anthony, Kyle
Perrone, Andy, St. Anthony, Bryan
Pfuntner, Jordan, (Retired)
Pickwell, John, St. Paul, Austin; Canonical & Tribunal Services
Pina, Steve, Christ the King, Belton
Poole, James, St. Mary, Church of the Assumption, Waco
Potter, Joseph, (Retired)
Prewitt, Sidney (Butch), Assoc. Dir. Diaconate Formation
Pustka, David, St. Mary of the Assumption, Taylor
Pynes, Tony, Serving on the Diocese of Charleston
Ramirez, Daniel, St. Mary, Mexia
Reed, David, St. Mary, College Station
Renteria, Mario, Our Lady of Guadalupe, Austin
Reyes, Samuel, St. Mary, Caldwell
Riojas, John, Santa Cruz, Buda
Rios, Rudy, (Inactive)
Roberge, Philip R., St. Margaret Mary, Cedar Park
Rodgers, James, St. Joseph, Killeen
Rodriguez, Bonifacio, St. Mary, Temple
Rodriguez, Guadalupe, Jr., St. Mary Cathedral, Austin
Rodriguez, J. Paul, St. Margaret Mary, Cedar Park
Romero, Toby, (Inactive)
Rosales, Hector, Dolores, Austin
Rositas, Edward, St. Martin de Porres, Dripping Springs
Ruiz, Joe, St. Helen, Georgetown
Ryan, Barry, St. Elizabeth, Pflugerville
Ryan, Kenneth, St. Patrick, Hutto
Saienga, Gene, St. John Vianney, Round Rock
Sanchez, Romeo, San Jose, Austin
Sanders, Raymond, Jr., M.S., M.A., Ed.D., (Retired)
Scarmardo, Bill, St. Anthony, Bryan
Schroeder, Christopher, St. Catherine, Austin
Schwab, Peter, Ph.D., St. Thomas More, Austin
Scott, Bill, (Retired)
Sekel, David, St. John Neumann, Austin
Shieldes, George, (Retired)
Shoemake, William, Christ the King, Belton
Silguero, Luis F., St. John, San Marcos
Sims, Donald, St. Joseph, Rockdale
Sis, Ray, (Retired)
Smetana, Bill, Visitation, Westphalia
Snigger, Robert J., St. Mary, Temple
Solorzano, Eraclio, St. John the Evangelist, Marble Falls
Sweed, Limas, Blessed Virgin Mary, Washington
Terrell, John Larry, (Inactive)
Thornton, Johnnie, Sts. Cyril & Methodius, Granger
Torres, Alfredo, Our Lady of Guadalupe, Taylor
Torres, Manuel, St. John Neumann, Austin
Turner, Donald, St. Louis, Austin
Tyboroski, Julian, (Retired)
Vargas, Domingo, (Inactive)
Vela, Joe, Our Lady of Guadalupe, Temple
Vela, William, St. Joseph, Manor
Venglar, Patrick, St. Mary, Lockhart; H.L. Grant Student Center, Texas State, San Marcos
Villa, Luis, St. Louis, Austin
Villegas, Solomon, St. Paul, Austin
Vocelka, Frank J. (Jay), Sacred Heart, La Grange
Vochoska, Kenneth, (Inactive)
Vogler, Fred, (Inactive)
Walker, Ron, St. Mary Cathedral, Austin; Dir. of Diaconal Ministry; Chancellor
Washburne, Marc, Santa Rosa, Andice
Wearden, Glen, (Retired)
Wehrer, Robert, Sacred Heart, Waco
Weilert, Otto, (Retired)
Weynand, Joe, (Retired)
Woods, Ronald, St. Charles Borromeo, Kingsland
Wright, Charlie, Visitation, Westphalia
Wright, Dan, St. Thomas More, Austin
Young, John, St. Mary, Caldwell
Zacek, George, St. Theresa, Austin

INSTITUTIONS LOCATED IN THE DIOCESE

[A] COLLEGES AND UNIVERSITIES

AUSTIN. *St. Edward's University*, 3001 S. Congress Ave., 78704-6489. Tel: 512-448-8400; Fax: 512-448-8492. Email: seu.admit@stedwards.edu. Web: www.stedwards.edu. Dr. George E. Martin, Pres. Established in 1878 by the Congregation of Holy Cross and chartered by the state in 1885. Priests 2; Holy Cross Brothers 14; Sisters 4; Lay Professors 522; Total Staff 960; Students 5,285. Officers: Revs. Louis Brusatti, C.M., Dean School of Humanities; Rick Wilkinson, C.S.C., Dir. Campus Ministry; Sr. Donna M. Jurick, S.N.D., Exec. Vice Pres.; Bros. Richard Daly, C.S.C.; Joseph Harris, C.S.C.; George Klawitter, C.S.C.; Gerald Muller, C.S.C.; John Perron, C.S.C.; Edwin Reggio, C.S.C.; Paige Booth, Vice Pres. Mktg. & Enrollment; David Waldron, Vice Pres. Information Technology; Rhonda Cartwright, Vice Pres. Financial Affairs; Helene Caudill, Interim Dean of New College; Dr. Lance Hayes, Registrar; Dr. Marianne F. Hopper, Dean Univ. Programs; Michael Larkin, Vice Pres. for Univ. Advancement; Marsha C. Kelliher, Dean School of Mgmt. & Business; Dr. George E. Martin, Pres.; Dr. Sandra L. Pacheco, Vice Pres. Student Affairs; Thomas Mitzel, Dean, School Natural Sciences; Dr. Thomas Evans, Assoc. Vice Pres., Professional Educ. & Global Initiatives; Dr. Grant W. Simpson, Dean, School Educ.; Dr. Brenda Vallance, Dean, School Behavioral & Social Sciences; Cristina Bordin, Pres. Asst.; Josie Barrett, Pres. Asst.; Bhuban Pandey, Assoc. Vice Pres., Inst. Effectiveness & Research.

[B] HIGH SCHOOL, DIOCESAN

AUSTIN. *St. Dominic Savio Catholic High School*, 9300 Neenah Ave., 78717. Tel: 512-388-8846; Fax: 512-388-1335. Mr. Kevin J. Calkins, Prin. Priests 1; Sisters 1; Lay Teachers 23; Students 282.

San Juan Diego Catholic High School (2002) 800 Herndon Ln., 78704. Tel: 512-804-1935; Fax: 512-804-1937. Email: info@sjdchs.org. Web: sjdchs.org. Pamela S. Jupe, Prin.; Lori Jasper, Librarian; Laura MacLean, Dean of Academics. Priests 1; Sisters 1; Lay Teachers 17; Total Staff 28; Total Enrollment 165.

BRYAN. *St. Joseph High School*, 600 S. Coulter, 77803. Tel: 979-822-6641; Fax: 979-779-2810. Mrs. Beatrice Janssen, Prin. & Pres.; Melissa Slater, Librarian. Lay Teachers 46; Students 392.

WACO. *Reicher Catholic High School* (1954) 2102 N. 23rd St., 76708. Tel: 254-752-8349; Fax: 254-752-8408. Email: ajones@reicher.org. Web: www.reicher.org. Mrs. Arlene Anderson Jones, Prin.; Michele Lacina, Librarian. Deacons 1; Lay Teachers 30; Students 215.

[C] HIGH SCHOOL, PRIVATE

AUSTIN. *St. Michael's Catholic Academy* (1984) 3000 Barton Creek Blvd., 78735. Tel: 512-328-2323; Fax: 512-328-2327. Email: sscamardo@smca.com. Web: www.smca.com. Sharon S. Scarmardo, Prin.; Ayne Ray, Librarian. Priests 1; Lay Teachers 39; Students 388.

TEMPLE. *Holy Trinity Catholic High School* (1997) 6608 W. Adams Ave., 76502. Tel: 254-771-0787; Fax: 254-771-2285. Email: info@holytrinitychs.org. Web: www. holytrinitychs.org. Christopher Mosmeyer, Prin.; Mary Ann Clark, Librarian. Lay Teachers 16; Total Staff 14; Total Enrollment 87.

[D] ELEMENTARY SCHOOL, DIOCESAN

AUSTIN. *Holy Family Catholic School* (2000) (Grades PreK-8), 9400 Neenah Ave., 78717. Tel: 512-246-4455; Fax: 512-246-4454. Email: hfcs@holyfamilycs.org. Web: www.holyfamilycs.org. Joan Wagner, Ph.D., Prin.; Donald Kenner, Librarian. Lay Teachers 26; Total Staff 42; Students 482.

[E] ELEMENTARY SCHOOL, PRIVATE

AUSTIN. *St. Gabriel's Catholic School*, (Grades PreK-8), (Legal name: Southwest Austin Catholic School Inc.), 2500 Wimberly Ln., 78735. Tel: 512-327-7755; Fax: 512-327-4334. Web: sgs-austin.org. Steve Balak, Head, School; Misty Poe, Head, Middle School; Rebecca Hammel, Head, Lower School. Lay Teachers 42; Total Enrollment 381.

[F] GENERAL HOSPITALS

AUSTIN. **Seton Healthcare*, 1345 Philomena St., 78723. Tel: 512-324-1923. Web: www.seton.net. Charles J. Barnett, Pres. & CEO. d/b/a's: Dell Children's Medical Center, Austin; Seton Bertram Healthcare Center, Bertram; Seton Burnet Healthcare Center, Burnet; Seton Edgar B. Davis Hospital, Luling; Seton Highland Lakes Hospital, Burnet; Seton Kozmetsky Community Health Center, Austin; Seton Lampasas Healthcare Center, Lampasas; Seton Lockhart Family Health Center, Lockhart; Seton Marble Falls Healthcare Center, Marble Falls; Seton McCarthy Community Health Center, Austin; Seton Medical Center Austin, Austin; Seton Medical Center Hays, Kyle; Seton Medical Center Williamson, Round Rock; Seton Northwest Hospital, Austin; Seton Pflugerville Healthcare Center, Pflugerville; Seton Shoal Creek Hospital, Austin; Seton Smithville Regional Hospital, Smithville; Seton Southwest Hospital, Austin; Seton Topfer Community Health Center, Austin. Bed Capacity 1,668; Total Assisted Annually 883,314; Staff 11,826.

BRYAN. *Burleson St. Joseph Health Center of Caldwell, Texas*, 2801 Franciscan Dr., 77802. Tel: 979-776-2599; Fax: 409-774-4590. Email: info@mail.st-joseph.org. Web: www.st-joseph.org. Anthony D. Pfitzer, Pres. & CEO, St. Joseph Health System; John Hughson, BSJHC Admin. Total Staff 70; Patients Assisted Annually 17,669; Bed Capacity 25.

St. Joseph Regional Health Center, 2801 Franciscan Dr., 77802. Tel: 979-776-3777; Fax: 979-774-4590. Email: tpfitzer@st-joseph.org. Web: www.st-joseph.org. Anthony D. Pfitzer, Pres. & CEO, St. Joseph Health System; Rev. Msgr. John C. Malinowski, Chap. (Retired); Robert Upchurch, Bd. Chm. Sisters of St. Francis of Sylvania, OH 4; Bed Capacity 254; Patients Assisted Annually 384,000; Total Staff 1,659.

St. Joseph Services Corp., 2801 Franciscan Dr., 77802. Tel: 979-776-3777; Fax: 979-774-4590. Email: info@mail.st-joseph.org. Web: www.st-joseph.org. Anthony D. Pfitzer, Pres. & CEO, St. Joseph Health System; George Nelson, Bd. Chm. Sisters of St. Francis of Sylvania, OH 4; Bed Capacity 329; LTC Beds 237; Patients Assisted Annually 407,971; LTC Staff 167; Total Staff 2,500.

WACO. *Providence Healthcare Network* (1904) 6901 Medical Pkwy., P.O. Box 2589, 76702-2589. Tel: 254-751-4000; Fax: 254-751-4769. Email: kkeahey@phn-waco.org. Web: www.providence.net. Kent A. Keahey, M.B.A., B.B.A., Pres. & CEO; Sr. Cecile Matushek, D.C., Vice Pres. Mission. Providence Health Center-Medical/Surgical/OB/

Pediatrics Acute Care; DePaul Center - Psychiatric Care; Providence Park - Independent Living, Assisted Living & Long Term Care Facilities; Providence Home Care. Daughters of Charity of St. Vincent de Paul 5; Bed Capacity 607; Patients Assisted Annually 210,686; Total Staff 2,482.

[G] MONASTERIES AND RESIDENCES OF PRIESTS AND BROTHERS

AUSTIN. *Brother Andre Residence* (1985) 2111 Brackenridge St., 78704. Tel: 512-351-9780. Web: www.southerncsc.org. Revs. Harold W. Essling, C.S.C.; Joseph F. Geniesse, C.S.C. (Retired); Charles Van Winkle, C.S.C. (Retired); Barry E. Cabell, C.S.C.; L. Peter Logsdon, C.S.C.

Congregation of Holy Cross, Moreau Province (1837) Tel: 512-442-7856; Fax: 512-444-3133. Web: www.brothersofholycross.org. Corporate Title: Congregation of Holy Cross, Moreau Province, Inc.

Brother John Baptist Province Center (1956) 1101 St. Edward's Dr., 78704-6512. Tel: 512-442-7856; Fax: 512-444-3133. Web: www.holycross-sw.org. Bros. William Zaydak, C.S.C., Prov. Supr.; Donald Blauvelth, C.S.C, Vicar Prov.; William Nick, C.S.C., M.Ed., Councilor & Steward; Richard Daly, C.S.C., Councilor; Joel Giallanza, C.S.C.; Lawrence Backus, C.S.C. Total in Province 85. *Brother Vincent Pieau Residence* (1997) 921 St. Edward Dr., 78704. Tel: 512-493-0121; Fax: 512-493-0158. Bro. Harold Ehlinger, C.S.C., Dir. Priests 3; Brothers 24. *St. Joseph Hall Residence, St. Edward's University*, 3001 S. Congress Ave., 78704. Tel: 512-448-8628; Fax: 512-448-8638. Email: nick1040@gmail.com. Bros. William Nick, C.S.C., M.Ed., Dir.; Howard Metz, Asst. Dir. Brothers 16. *Moreau House, St. Edward's University*, 3001 S. Congress Ave., 78704. Tel: 512-448-8595; Fax: 512-448-8638. Email: larrya@stedwards.edu. Web: holycrossbrothers.org. Bros. Larry Atkinson, C.S.C., M.Ed., Dir.; John Perron, C.S.C.

Dominican Friars of Austin (1960) 2502 Comburg Castle Way, 78748-5258. Tel: 512-282-3908; Fax: 512-280-9011. Email: chiefop@att.net. Revs. James A. McDonough, O.P., Supr.; Henry Groover, O.P.; Gerardo Guerra-Mayaudon, O.P. Tel: 512-292-3381; Gerald Mendoza, O.P.; Ralph Rogawski, O.P., 6008 Club Terrace, 78741. Tel: 512-385-1719; Bro. Angel Mendez, O.P.

Moreau House, Congregation of Holy Cross Moreau Province, Inc., #1069, 3001 S. Congress, 78704. Tel: 512-448-8595; Fax: 512-448-8638. Email: larrya@stedwards.edu. Web: holycrossbrothers.org. Bros. Larry Atkinson, C.S.C., M.Ed.; John Perron, C.S.C.

Schoenstatt Fathers, 7839 Wheel Rim Cir., 78749. Tel: 512-301-8762; Fax: 512-301-8564. Revs. Christian Christensen, I.S.P.; Jesus Ferras, I.S.P.; Marcelo Aravena, I.S.P.

St. Joseph's Hall, 3001 S. Congress Ave., 78704. Tel: 512-448-8628; Fax: 512-448-8638. Email: nick1040@gmail.com. Web: www.holycrossbrothers.org. Bro. William Nick, C.S.C., M.Ed., Dir. Priests 2; Brothers 16.

BREMOND. *Clerical Congregation Missionaries of Faith* (1972) 715 N. Main St., 76629-5173. Tel: 254-746-7789; Fax: 254-746-7789. Email: jyucmf@hotmail.com. Web: www.mftexas.catholicweb.com. Rev. Celso A. Yu, M.F. (Philippines), Supr.

BURLINGTON. *Missionary Society of St. Paul, MSP*, P.O. Box 85, 76519. Tel: 254-869-2169. Rev. Michael Ajewole, M.S.P.

GEORGETOWN. *Pope John Paul II, Residence for Priests*, 2610 E. University Ave., #1001, 78626. Tel: 512-868-3454; Fax: 512-949-2520.

[H] CONVENTS AND RESIDENCES FOR SISTERS

AUSTIN. *Congregation of Marianites of Holy Cross, M.S.C.*, 2809 Onslow Dr., 78748. Tel: 512-904-9070; Fax: 512-804-1937. Sr. Stephanie Brignac, M.S.C., Contact Person.

Congregation of the Sisters of the Holy Cross, La Casa Convent, 2213 Euclid Ave., 78704. Tel: 512-441-6693.

Sisters of the Holy Cross, Inc.

Congregation of the Sisters of the Holy Cross (1975) Loretto Convent, 2301 E. Side Dr., 78704-5214. Tel: 512-441-3850; Fax: 512-441-3850. Email: alicecondon@aol.com. Sisters 4.

Congregation of the Sisters of the Holy Cross, Our Lady of Victory Convent, 2215 Euclid Ave., 78704-5214. Tel: 512-441-2927.

Sisters of the Holy Cross, Inc. Sisters 6.

Daughters of Charity of St. Vincent De Paul, 8013 Greenslope Dr., 78759. Tel: 512-453-9656. Email: dc31st@yahoo.com. Sisters 4.

Other Addresses: *Daughters of Charity of St. Vincent De Paul*, 5803 Fairlane Dr., 78757-4414. Tel: 512-452-8980. Email: dcfairlane@sbcglobal.net. Sisters 3. *Daughters of Charity of St. Vincent De Paul*, 8013 Greenslope Dr., 78759. Tel: 512-340-0081. Email: austindc1633@sbcglobal.net. Sisters 3.

Daughters of Mary Help of Christians (Salesian Sisters of St. John Bosco), St. Mary Mazzarello Convent, 2109 E. Second St., 78702. Tel: 512-474-2312; Fax: 512-474-2314. Email: itapia@craustin.com. Sisters 4.

Franciscan Sisters Daughters of Mercy (Hermanas Franciscanas Hijas de la Misericordia) (1856) *House of Formation*, 1207 Montopolis Dr., 78741. Tel: 512-389-3411; 512-385-5090. Sr. Rose Moreno, F.H.M., M.A., Regl. Supr. Sisters 2.

St. Francis Convent, 612 N. 3rd St., Waco, 76701. Tel: 254-753-6816; Fax: 254-757-0537. Sisters 4.

Missionary Catechists of Divine Providence (1946) 921 St. Edward's Dr., 78704. Tel: 512-793-0123; 512-949-2468; Fax: 512-949-2520. Email: sr_celia_ann_cavazos@austindiocese.org.

Missionary Sisters of the Immaculate Conception of the Mother of God, 4211-B Shoalwood, 78756. Tel: 512-451-2890. Email: jreisch@prodigy.net.

Sinsinawa Dominican Sisters (1848) 6008 Club Terr., 78741. Tel: 512-385-1719. Sisters 2.

Sisters of Charity of the Incarnate Word, 8233 Summer Side Dr., 78759. Tel: 512-451-0272; 512-231-9512 (Home); Fax: 512-451-0284.

Sisters of Divine Providence, 4604 Molera Dr., 78749. Tel: 512-324-1000.

Sisters, Servants of the Immaculate Heart of Mary, 2606 East Side Dr., 78704. Tel: 512-442-5295.

BRENHAM. *Monastery of St. Clare* (1985) 900 Geney St., 77833. Tel: 979-836-2444. Email: srangela@franciscanpoorclares.org. Web: www.franciscanpoorclares.org. Sr. Angela Chandler, O.S.C., Abbess. Sisters 3.

Pax Christi Sisters, 9300 Hwy. 105, 77833.

Sisters of St. Francis of Our Lady of Lourdes (O.S.F.) (1916) 605A Church St., 77833. Tel: 979-836-9481; Fax: 979-830-2277. Sisters 2.

BRYAN. *Sisters of St. Francis of Our Lady of Lourdes*, 2514 Clare Ct. Apt. C, 77802. Tel: 979-777-0578; Fax: 409-774-4590. Email: info@mail.st-joseph.org. Web: www.st-joseph.org. Sisters 5.

BURNET. *Sisters of the Holy Cross, Inc.*, 1910 Sunset Cliff, 78611.

SOMERVILLE. *Missionary Ecumenical*, P.O. Box 367, 77879. Tel: 979-595-1494; Fax: 979-596-1494. Sisters 2.

WACO. *Daughters of Charity of St. Vincent De Paul*, 2416 Colcord, 76707. Tel: 254-753-3817. Email: cmatushek@grandecom.net. Sisters 2. 6901 Old McGregor Rd., 76712. Tel: 254-399-7575. Email: hewittdc@aol.com. Sisters 5.

Franciscan Sisters Daughters of Mercy (Franciscanas Hijas de la Misericordia), 612 N. Third St., 76701. Tel: 254-753-5565. Sisters 4. 1207 Montopolis Dr., 78741. Sisters 2.

[I] HOMES FOR THE AGED & HANDICAPPED

BRYAN. *St. Joseph Manor* (1999) 2333 Manor Dr., 77802. Tel: 979-821-7330; Fax: 979-821-7301. Email: hcottrell@st-joseph.org. Anthony D. Pfitzer, Pres. & CEO, St. Joseph Health System; Harold O. Cottrell, BBA, Exec. Dir. Bed Capacity 121; Total Staff 98; Total Assisted Annually 107.

CALDWELL. *Burleson St. Joseph Manor*, 1022 Presidential Corridor, Hwy. 21E, 77836. Tel: 979-567-0920; Fax: 979-567-4811. Email: pbeathard@st-joseph.org. Anthony D. Pfitzer, Pres. & CEO, St. Joseph Health System. Bed Capacity 112; Staff 69; Total Assisted Annually 82.

[J] MISSION CENTERS

SOMERVILLE. *St. Ann Mission Center*, P.O. Box 367, 77879. Tel: 979-596-1696; Fax: 979-596-1496. Sr. M. John DellaMorte, M.E., Supr. Missionary Ecumenical. Day Care Students 20; Total Staff 2.

WACO. *St. Francis Mission Center*, 612 N. Third St., 76701. Tel: 254-753-5565; Fax: 254-757-0537. Email: barbarajhtexas@hotmail.com. Sisters Jacinta Amengual, F.H.M., Supr.; Maria Izquierdo, F.H.M., Catechetical, Kindergarten & Nursery; Catherine Vallespir, F.H.M., Catechetical, Kindergarten & Nursery. Franciscan Sisters Daughters of Mercy. Sisters 4; Total Staff 12.

[K] RENEWAL CENTERS

BELTON. *Cedarbrake Renewal Center* (1979) 5602 S. Hwy. 317 N., P.O. Box 58, 76513-0058. Tel: 254-780-2436; Fax: 254-780-2684. Email: cedarbrake@austindiocese.org. Total in Residence 2; Total Staff 12.

[L] NEWMAN APOSTOLATE

AUSTIN. *University Catholic Center* 2010 University Ave., 78705. Tel: 512-476-7351; Fax: 512-476-7377. Email: catholic@utcatholic.org. Web: www.utcatholic.org. Revs. Edward C. Nowak, C.S.P., B.S., M.Div., Dir.; Jamie Baca, C.S.P., M.Div., Assoc. Dir.; Deacon John De La Garza. Serving the Catholic community at the University of Texas. Total Staff 11.

BRYAN. *Blinn College Catholic Student Union Blinn College*, 2423 Blinn Blvd., 77802. Tel: 979-209-7430; Fax: 979-209-7430. P.O. Box 6030, 77805-6030. For Catholic students attending Blinn Jr. College. Staff 1.

COLLEGE STATION. *St. Mary's Catholic Center* 603 Church Ave., 77840. Tel: 979-846-5717; Fax: 979-846-4493. Email: info@aggiecatholic.org. Web: www.aggiecatholic.org. Revs. David Konderla; Christopher J. Downey; Deacons Bill Scott Jr.; David Reed; Switzer Deason. Campus ministry at Texas A&M University and Blinn College. Total in Residence 2; Total Staff 45.

SAN MARCOS. *Texas State University, H.L. Grant Catholic Student Center* 100 Concho St., 78666. Tel: 512-392-5925; Fax: 512-392-5922. Email: office@txstatecatholic.org. Web: www.txstatecatholic.org. Very Rev. Brian Joseph Eilers, Dir.; Deacon Patrick Venglar, Business Admin. Catholic Students attending Texas State University.

WACO. *St. Peter Catholic Student Center at Baylor University* 1415 S. 9th St., P.O. Box 6060, 76706-0060. Tel: 254-757-0636; Fax: 254-714-0639. Email: office@baylorcatholic.org. Web: www.baylorcatholic.org. Rev. Anthony Odiong (Nigeria), Dir.; Deacon Frank Jasek, Spiritual Dir.; Debbie Shannon, Admin. Asst. & Center Coord. For Catholic students attending Baylor University, Texas State Technical College, and McLennan Community College.

[M] FOUNDATIONS, ENDOWMENTS & TRUSTS

AUSTIN. *Blue Ladies Minerals, Inc.*, 1201 W. 38th St., 78705-1056. Tel: 512-324-1990; Fax: 512-324-1989. Ken Gladish, Pres.

Catholic Foundation - Diocese of Austin, Mailing Address: 6225 Hwy. 290 E., 78723. Tel: 512-949-2400; Fax: 512-949-2520.

Clergy Medical and Retirement Trust of the Diocese of Austin The Diocese of Austin Pension Plan Committee

Clerical Endowment Fund, P.O. Box 276, West, 76691. Tel: 254-826-3705. Very Rev. Edward Karasek.

CMC Foundation of Central Texas aka Children's Medical Center Foundation of Central Texas 4900 Mueller Blvd., 78723. Tel: 512-324-0170; Fax: 512-324-0798. Web: www.childrensaustin.org. Ms. Missy Wood, Vice Pres. & Exec. Dir.

Father Bernard C. Goertz Scholarship Trust Fund, Sacred Heart Church, 4045 FM 535, Bastrop, 78602.

Fickett Health Legacy, Inc., 12011 W. 38th St., 78705. Tel: 512-324-1990; Fax: 512-324-7989. Charles Scarborough, Sec.

Holy Family Catholic School Foundation (2000) 9400 Neenah Ave., 78717. Tel: 512-246-4455; Fax: 512-246-4454. Email: hfcs@holyfamilycs.org. Web: www.holyfamilycs.org. Joan Wagner, Ph.D., Contact Person.

John J. Kearns Memorial Charitable Trust Fund, Mailing Address: P.O. Box 5040, Waco, 78708.

Seton Fund of the Daughters of Charity of St. Vincent de Paul, Inc., 1201 W. 38th St., 78705. Tel: 512-324-1990. Web: www.setonfund.org. Ken Gladish, Pres.

Seton Hays Foundation, 6001 Kyle Pkwy., Kyle, 78640. Tel: 512-504-5061; Fax: 512-268-8710. Web: www.setonhaysfoundation.org. Gerald Hill, Exec. Dir. & Vice Pres. Develop.

St. Joseph's Foundation of Bryan, 2801 Franciscan Dr., Bryan, 77802. Tel: 979-774-4087. Thomas J. Pool, Exec.

St. Joseph's School Memorial Endowment Fund, 600 E. 26th St., Bryan, 77803. Tel: 979-822-2721; Fax: 979-779-3120. Rev. Msgr. John A. McCaffrey.

St. Jude Foundation, Inc., 1306 N. Park, Brenham, 77833.

St. Michael's Foundation, 3000 Barton Creek Blvd., 78735.

Sts. Cyril & Methodius School Endowment, P.O. Box 201, Granger, 76530. Very Rev. Joseph Nisari (Pakistan).

Twenty-Six Doors, Inc., 1201W. 38th St., 78705. Tel: 512-324-1990; Fax: 512-324-1989. Charles Scarborough, Sec.

Vincare Services of Austin Foundation aka Saint Louise House (2000) 2026 Guadalupe St., 78705. Tel: 512-302-0027; Fax: 512-326-2290. Web: saintlouisehouse.org. Sharon Bieser, Exec. Dir.

BRYAN. *St. Joseph Memorial Endowment Fund*, St. Joseph's, 600 E. 26th, 77803. Tel: 979-822-2721;

Fax: 979-779-3120. Email: frjohn@stjosephbcs.org. Web: www.stjosephbcs.org. Rev. Msgr. John A. McCaffrey.

ROUND ROCK. *Seton Williamson Foundation*, 201 Seton Pkwy., WI 78665. Tel: 512-324-4118; Fax: 512-246-1442. Web: www.setonwilliamsonfdn.org. Donna Budak, Pres.

[N] MISCELLANEOUS

AUSTIN. *Catholic Archives of Texas*, P.O. Box 13124, 78711-3124. Tel: 512-476-6296; Fax: 512-476-3715. Email: archives@txcatholic.org. Web: www.catholicarchivesoftx.org. Susan Eason, Archive Dir.; Eric J. Hartmann, Asst. Archivist. Historical collection of the Church in the Southwest and Texas from 1519.

Catholic Family Fraternal of Texas. KJZT, P.O. Box 18896, 78760-8896. Tel: 512-444-9586; Fax: 512-444-6887. Loretta Stahl, Pres.

Catholic Southwest, 1600 Congress Ave., Ste. B, 78701. Tel: 817-251-5451; Fax: 512-339-8670. P.O. Box 13285, 78711. Dr. Richard Fossey, Editor.

Juan Diego Missionary Society, 4606 E. St. Elmo, 78744. Tel: 512-731-8434; Fax: 512-441-0928. Email: jdms1981@gmail.com. Elias and Christina Limon, Dir.

Juan Diego Work/Study Program, Inc., 800 Herndon Ln., 78704. Tel: 512-804-1935; Fax: 512-804-1937. Web: www.sjdchs.org. Pamela S. Jupe, Prin.

Ladies of Charity of Austin, TX (1890) P.O. Box 9566, 78766. Tel: 512-507-0068; Fax: 512-267-5578. Email: mmoya@aol.com. Web: www.ladiesofcharityaustin.com. Monique Urtado, Pres.

North Central Catholic School Corporation (1996) 9400 Neenah Ave., 78717. Tel: 512-246-4455; Fax: 512-246-4454. Email: hfcs@holyfamilycs.org. Web: www.holyfamilycs.org.

Seton Cove - A Spirituality Center, 3708 Crawford St., 78731. Tel: 512-451-0272; Fax: 512-451-0284. Email: setoncove@seton.org. Web: setoncove.net. Staff 8.

Society of St. Katharine Drexel, 1800 Brookhaven Dr., 78704. Tel: 512-329-5052. Carole Buckman, Pres.

**Society of St. Vincent de Paul, Diocesan Council of Austin*, P.O. Box 9070, 78766.

Texas Catholic Conference, P.O. Box 13285, 78711. 1600 N. Congress Ave., Suite B, 78701. Tel: 512-339-9882; Fax: 512-339-8670. Web: www.txcatholic.org. Jeffery Patterson, Exec. Dir.; Jennifer Carr-Allmon, Assoc. Dir.; Margaret McGettrick, Dir. Educ.; Marsha Solana, Dir. Accreditation; Susan Eason, Dir. Catholic Archives of Texas.

Texas Catholic Historical Society, c/o Texas Catholic Conference, P.O. Box 13285, 78711. 1600 N. Congress Ave., Ste. B, 78701. Tel: 512-339-9882; Fax: 512-339-8670. Rev. Robert Wright, O.M.I., Pres.

VIDES Volunteers International Development Education and Solidarity, 2109 E. 2nd St., 78702. Tel: 512-320-1913. Email: director@vides.us. Web: www.vides.us. Sr. Mary Gloria Mar, F.M.A., Prog. Dir. VIDES USA (Central Office) and VIDES East USA (Satellite Office)

BASTROP. *Ladies of Charity of Bastrop, TX*, P.O. Box 1060, 78602. Tel: 512-321-9819; Fax: 512-321-1647. Email: locbastrop@aol.com. Putzie Martin, Pres.

BUDA. *St. Mary's Academy Alumnae Association*, 16005 Scenic Oak Tr., 78610. Tel: 512-312-0836. Email: cattal@austin.rr.com. Catherine Attal, Contact Person.

LAGRANGE. *Catholic Union of Texas, The K.J.T.* (1889) P.O. Box 297, La Grange, 78945-0297. Tel: 979-968-5877; Fax: 979-968-5823. Email: president@kjtnet.org. Web: www.kjtnet.org. Christopher L. Urban, Pres. KJT NEWS (official publication).

ROUND ROCK. *Christ the Child Society of Texas, Capital Area, Inc.* (2004) P.O. Box 5953, 78683. Tel: 512-246-8934. Email: amrschultz@yahoo.com; ofelia_melendez@yahoo.com. Julie Schultz, Pres.; Ofelia Melendez, Pres.-Elect.

WACO. *Ladies of Charity of Waco, TX* (1895) 622 N. 36th St., 76710. Tel: 254-752-2009; Fax: 254-753-5059. Email: Lbb622@aol.com. Lorraine Brooks, Financial Sec.

RELIGIOUS INSTITUTES OF MEN REPRESENTED IN THE DIOCESE

For further details refer to the corresponding bracketed number in the Religious Institutes of Men or Women section.

[0600]—*Congregation of Holy Cross-Brothers* (Moreau Prov.)—C.S.C.

[0610]—*Congregation of Holy Cross-Priests* (Indiana Prov., Notre Dame, IN)—C.S.C.

[]—*Congregation of the Passionists*—C.P.

[0480]—*Conventual Franciscans* (Mt. Francis, IN)—O.F.M.Conv.

[]—*Indian Missionary Society* (Varanasi, UP, India)—I.M.S.

[0690]—*Jesuit Fathers and Brothers* (New Orleans Province, LA)—S.J.

[]—*Missionaries of Faith* (U.S. Region, Bremond, TX)—M.F.

[]—*Missionaries of St. Paul* (Houston, TX)—M.S.P.

[1110]—*Missionaries of the Sacred Heart* (San Antonio, TX)—M.S.C.

[0430]—*Order of Preachers-Dominicans* (New Orleans, LA)—O.P.

[1030]—*Paulist Fathers* (Jamaica Estates, NY)—C.S.P.

[]—*Redemptorist Fathers*—C.Ss.R.

[]—*Secular Order of Schoenstatt Priests*—I.S.P.

[1200]—*Society of the Divine Savior* (Polish Province, US, Porth, TX)—S.D.S.

[]—*Sons of Mary Mother of Mercy*—S.M.M.M.

[0470]—*The Capuchin Friars*—O.F.M.Cap.

[0560]—*Third Order Regular of Saint Francis* (Vice-Province of Santa Maria de Guadalupe, Mexico)—T.O.R.

RELIGIOUS INSTITUTES OF WOMEN REPRESENTED IN THE DIOCESE

[]—*Apostles of the Interior Life*—A.V.I.

[]—*Benedictines of Perpetual Adoration*—O.S.B.

[0470]—*Congregation of Sisters of Charity of the Incarnate Word* (Houston, Texas)—C.C.V.I.

[1010]—*Congregation of Divine Providence* (San Antonio, TX)—C.D.P.

[0760]—*Daughters of Charity of St. Vincent de Paul* (St. Louis, MO)—D.C.

[0850]—*Daughters of Mary Help of Christians* (San Antonio, TX)—F.M.A.

[]—*Daughters of St. Theresa* (Uganda)—D.S.T.

[1070-19]—*Dominican Sisters* (Houston, TX)—O.P.

[1070-03]—*Dominican Sisters* (Sinsinawa, WI)—O.P.

[]—*Dominican Sisters of Mary, Mother of the Eucharist*—O.P.

[]—*Ecumenica Missioneries* (Rome, Italy)—M.E.

[]—*Eudist Servants of the Eleventh Hour* (Tijuana, Mexico)—E.S.E.H.

[]—*Franciscan Poor Clares* Corpus Christi, TX—O.S.C.

[1235]—*Franciscan Sisters Daughters of Mercy (Franciscanas Hijas de la Misericordia)* (U.S. delegation: Waco, TX)—F.H.M.

[1430]—*Franciscan Sisters of Our Lady of Perpetual Help* (St. Louis, MO)—O.S.F.

[1855]—*Handmaids of the Holy Child Jesus*—H.H.C.J.

[]—*Hermanas Dominicas "Siervas del Senor"*—O.P.

[2410]—*Marianites of Holy Cross* (New Orleans, LA)—M.S.C.

[2690]—*Missionary Catechists of Divine Providence* (San Antonio, TX)—M.C.D.P.

[2760]—*Missionary Sisters of the Immaculate Conception* (Paterson, NJ)—S.M.I.C.

[3760]—*Order of St. Clare* (Brenham, TX)—O.S.C.

[2970]—*School Sisters of Notre Dame* (St. Louis, MO; Dallas, TX)—S.S.N.D.

[]—*Sisters for Christian Community*—S.F.C.C.

[1530]—*Sisters of St. Francis of Our Lady of Lourdes* (Sylvania, OH)—O.S.F.

[1920]—*Sisters of the Holy Cross* (Notre Dame, IN)—C.S.C.

[]—*Sisters of Jesus the Savior*—S.J.S.

[3000]—*Sisters of Notre Dame de Namur* (Cincinnati, OH)—S.N.D.deN.

[]—*Sisters of Sacred Sciences* (India)—S.S.S.

[]—*Sisters of St. Francis of Assisi*—O.S.F.

[]—*Sisters of St. John Bosco* (Taylor, TX)—S.J.B.

[2150]—*Sisters, Servants of the Immaculate Heart of Mary* (Monroe, MI)—I.H.M.

[]—*U.S. Association of Consecrated Virgins*

NECROLOGY

† Elmer, Rev. Msgr. Charles, (Retired)—Died Sept. 4, 2011

† Anukam, Anselm A., Temple, TX St. Mary.—Died May 22, 2011

An asterisk (*) denotes an organization that has established tax-exempt status directly with the IRS and is not covered by the USCCB Group Ruling.

Diocese of Baker

(Dioecesis Bakeriensis)

Most Reverend

LIAM S. CARY

Bishop of Baker; ordained September 5, 1992; appointed Bishop of Baker March 8, 2012.

Most Reverend

THOMAS J. CONNOLLY, D.D., J.C.D.

Retired Bishop of Baker; ordained April 8, 1947; appointed May 4, 1971; consecrated June 30, 1971; retired January 2000. *Res.: P.O. Box 5999, Bend, OR 97708.*

Diocesan Pastoral Office: P.O. Box 5999, Bend, OR 97708. Tel: 541-388-4004; Fax: 541-388-2566.

Email: chancellor@dioceseofbaker.org

ESTABLISHED JUNE 19, 1903.

Square Miles 66,826.

Comprises the Counties of Baker, Crook, Deschutes, Gilliam, Grant, Harney, Hood River, Jefferson, Klamath, Lake, Malheur, Morrow, Sherman, Umatilla, Union, Wallowa, Wasco and Wheeler in the State of Oregon.

For legal titles of parishes and diocesan institutions, consult the Chancery Office.

STATISTICAL OVERVIEW

Personnel	
Bishop	1
Retired Bishops	1
Priests: Diocesan Active in Diocese	17
Priests: Diocesan Active Outside Diocese	4
Priests: Retired, Sick or Absent	15
Number of Diocesan Priests	36
Religious Priests in Diocese	9
Total Priests in Diocese	45
Extern Priests in Diocese	10
Permanent Deacons in Diocese	12
Total Sisters	9
Parishes	
Parishes	31
With Resident Pastor:	
Resident Diocesan Priests	24
Resident Religious Priests	7
Missions	28
Professional Ministry Personnel:	
Sisters	9
Lay Ministers	20
Welfare	
Catholic Hospitals	4
Total Assisted	161,261
Homes for the Aged	4
Total Assisted	189
Day Care Centers	1
Total Assisted	20
Special Centers for Social Services	6
Total Assisted	69,514
Educational	
Diocesan Students in Other Seminaries	2
Total Seminarians	2
Elementary Schools, Diocesan and Parish	5
Total Students	512
Catechesis/Religious Education:	
High School Students	726
Elementary Students	2,068
Total Students under Catholic Instruction	3,308
Teachers in the Diocese:	
Priests	1
Sisters	2
Lay Teachers	37
Vital Statistics	
Receptions into the Church:	
Infant Baptism Totals	907
Minor Baptism Totals	65
Adult Baptism Totals	41
Received into Full Communion	122
First Communions	929
Confirmations	618
Marriages:	
Catholic	141
Interfaith	28
Total Marriages	169
Deaths	260
Total Catholic Population	34,142
Total Population	509,474

Former Bishops—Most Revs. CHARLES J. O'REILLY, D.D., ord. June 29, 1890; appt. June 24, 1903; cons. Bishop of Baker City, Aug. 25, 1903; transferred to the See of Lincoln March 20, 1918; died Feb. 4, 1923; LEO F. FAHEY, D.D., ord. May 29, 1926; appt. Titular Bishop of Ipsus and Coadjutor "cum jure successionis" March 13, 1948; cons. May 26, 1948; died March 31, 1950; JOSEPH F. MCGRATH, D.D., appt. assistant at the Pontifical Throne, Bishop of Baker City; ord. Dec. 21, 1895; appt. Dec. 21, 1918; cons. March 25, 1919; died April 12, 1950; FRANCIS P. LEIPZIG, D.D., ord. April 14, 1920; appt. Bishop of Baker July 18, 1950; cons. Sept. 12, 1950; retired May 4, 1971; died Jan. 17, 1981; THOMAS J. CONNOLLY, D.D., J.C.D. (Retired), ord. April 8, 1947; appt. May 4, 1971; cons. June 30, 1971; retired Nov. 19, 1999; ROBERT FRANCIS VASA, ord. May 22, 1976; appt. Bishop of Baker Nov. 19, 1999; cons. and installed Jan. 26, 2000; appt. Coadjutor Bishop of Santa Rosa in California Jan. 24, 2011; installed March 6, 2011.

Vicar General—Very Rev. JOSEPH N. REINIG.

Judicial Vicar—VACANT.

Chancellor—VACANT.

Diocesan Pastoral Office—Mailing Address: P.O. Box 5999, Bend, 97708. Tel: 541-388-4004; Fax: 541-388-2566. *911 S.E. Armour, Bend, 97702.*

Receptionists and Secretaries—PATTI RAUSCH; VIRGINIA MOHR.

Diocesan Tribunal—Tel: 541-388-4010.

Judicial Vicar and Chief Judge—Rev. JUDE E. ONOGBOSELE, Judge Pro Tem.

Judge—VACANT.

Defenders of the Bond and Promoters of Justice—Revs. LEO F. WECKERLE (Retired); CHRISTOPHER AGOHA, S.M.M.M.

Tribunal Assistant—MARILYN RANSOM.

Coordinator and Notary—VIRGINIA MOHR.

Council of Priests and Diocesan Consultors—Very Rev. JOSEPH N. REINIG; Revs. JAMES A. RADLOFF; CHARLES CHIKA NNABUIFE; ROBERT GREINER; BAILEY CLEMENS; CHRISTOPHER AGOHA, S.M.M.M.; Very Revs. STANISLAUS STRZYZ; FRANCIS X. EKWUGHA; Rev. FRANCIS AKANO.

Deans—Central: Very Rev. JOSEPH N. REINIG. Eastern: Very Rev. STANISLAUS STRZYZ. Northern: Very Rev. GERALD W. CONDON. Southern: Very Rev. RICHARD O. FISCHER. Western: Very Rev. RONALD E. MAAG.

Diocesan Offices and Directors

Board of Education—ROGER RICHMOND, Supt.; Very Revs. TODD UNGER; FRANCIS X. EKWUGHA; Revs. CHRISTOPHER AGOHA, S.M.M.M.; CHARLES CHIKA NNABUIFE; JUDE NWACHUKWU, S.M.M.M., Principals of Schools and Representatives from each Parish School Board.

Building Committee—HOPE BURKE; JOHN G. SCHIEMER; Very Rev. JOSEPH N. REINIG.

Campus Ministry Apostolate—VACANT, 829 S.W. Second Ave., Ontario, 97914. Tel: 541-889-8469.

Catholic Services—GLORIA SHEEHY, 60185 High Valley Rd., Union, 97883.

Church Property, Administration of—JOSEPH LA CASSE, Realtor.

Diocesan Attorney—Mr. GREGORY LYNCH.

Diocesan Development Office—JOHN G. SCHIEMER, Mailing Address: P.O. Box 5999, Bend, 97708. Tel: 541-388-4004.

Diocesan Finance Minister—HOPE BURKE.

Diocesan Financial Board—HOPE BURKE; JOHN G. SCHIEMER; RICHARD GRALL; JOSEPH LA CASSE; CRAIG MINNIS.

Diocesan Superintendent of Schools—ROGER RICHMOND, Mailing Address: P.O. Box 5999, Bend, 97708. Tel: 541-388-4004; Fax: 541-388-2566.

Director of Campaign for Human Development—Very Rev. RONALD E. MAAG, Mailing Address: St. Mary Church, P.O. Box 693, Hood River, 97031. Tel: 541-386-3373.

Director of Catholic Hospitals—Very Rev. JOSEPH N. REINIG, Mailing Address: P.O. Box 5999, Bend, 97708.

Friends of the Catholic University of America—VACANT.

Health and Retirement Board—Very Revs. RONALD E. MAAG; RICHARD O. FISCHER; TODD UNGER, Sec. & Treas.; STANISLAUS STRZYZ, Chm.

Office of Worship and Spirituality—VACANT.

Natural Family Planning—Deacon GUSTAVO RUIZ, Mailing Address: P.O. Box 5999, Bend, 97708. Tel: 541-388-4004.

Director of Youth Ministry—Rev. JAMES A. RADLOFF, Mailing Address: P.O. Box 5999, Bend, 97708. Tel: 541-388-4004.

Director of Religious Education—JILL SCHWARTZ, P.O. Box 5999, Bend, 97708. Tel: 541-388-4004.

Director of Hispanic Ministry and Adult Faith Development—Deacon GUSTAVO RUIZ, Mailing Address: P.O. Box 5999, Bend, 97708. Tel: 541-388-4004.

Priests' Continuing Education Committee—Very Rev. RONALD E. MAAG.

R.C.I.A. Office—VACANT.

Diocesan Scout Director—JANET SCHWARZ, 20980 Via Bonita, Bend, 97702. Tel: 541-388-4004.

Victim Assistance Coordinator—ANGELINA MONTOYA. Tel: 541-388-9271.

Vocation Promoter—Rev. JAMES A. RADLOFF, Mailing Address: P.O. Box 5999, Bend, 97708. Tel: 541-388-4004.

CLERGY, PARISHES, MISSIONS AND PAROCHIAL SCHOOLS

BAKER CITY

(COUNTY OF BAKER), CATHEDRAL OF ST. FRANCIS DE SALES (1871) [CEM] Rev. Julian Cassar (Malta), Rector.
Res.: 2235 First St., Baker, 97814. Tel: 541-523-4521; Fax: 541-523-8362. Email: julianmlt@uci.net. Web: www.saintfranciscathedral.com.
Catechesis/Religious Program—Tamara Skidmore, D.R.E. Students 135.
Mission—St. Therese Halfway, Baker Co.

OUTSIDE BAKER CITY

ARLINGTON, GILLIAM CO., ST. FRANCIS, See separate listing. Now a mission of St. John, Condon.

BEND, DESCHUTES CO., ST. FRANCIS OF ASSISI (1904) Very Rev. Francis X. Ekwugha (Nigeria); Rev. Joseph Levine; Deacon Bob Walling.
Office: 2450 N.E. 27th St., 97701. Tel: 541-382-3631; Fax: 541-385-8879. Web: www.stfrancisbend.org.
Day Care—Tel: 541-389-3906. Students 20.
School—(Grades PreK-8) Tel: 541-382-4701; Fax: 541-312-9111. Web: www.saintfrancisschool.net. Julie Roberts, Head Teacher. Lay Teachers 18; Students 217.
Catechesis/Religious Program—Duke Johnson, D.R.E. Students 220.
Diocese of Baker - Latino Community Association—Tel: 541-312-2084.

BOARDMAN, MORROW CO., OUR LADY OF GUADALUPE Rev. Edwardo Nebelung.
Mailing Address: P.O. Box 1277, 97818. Tel: 541-481-2024.
Catechesis/Religious Program—Students 124.

BURNS, HARNEY CO., HOLY FAMILY (1899) Very Rev. Stanislaus Strzyz.
Res.: 685 N. Fairview Ave., 97720. Tel: 541-573-2613.
Catechesis/Religious Program—620 N. Egan St., 97720. Andrea Nichols, D.R.E. Students 80.
Mission—Our Lady of Loretto Drewsey, Harney Co.
Mission—St. Thomas Crane, Harney Co.
Mission—St. Charles Juntura, Malheur Co.

CHILOQUIN, KLAMATH CO., OUR LADY OF MT. CARMEL (1927) Rev. Innocent Onwukwe Diala (Nigeria).
Res.: 503 W. Chocktoot, P.O. Box 396, 97624. Tel: 541-783-2411; Fax: 541-783-2411.
Catechesis/Religious Program—
Mission—St. James the Apostle Bly, Klamath Co.

CONDON, GILLIAM CO., ST. JOHN (1925) Rev. Peter Obinna Umekwe (Nigeria).
Mailing Address: P.O. Box 485, 97823.
Res.: 412 W. Walnut St., 97823. Tel: 541-384-5271; Fax: 541-384-5271.
Catechesis/Religious Program—Students 13.
Mission—St. Catherine Fossil, Wheeler Co.
Mission—St. Francis (1931)

DUFUR, WASCO CO., ST. ALPHONSUS (1911) Rev. Fabian Nwokorie (Nigeria).
Res.: P.O. Box 395, 97021. Tel: 541-467-2580.
Catechesis/Religious Program—Students 1.
Mission—St. Mary Maupin, Wasco Co. 97037.

ELGIN, UNION CO., ST. MARY (1966) See separate listing. Now a mission of Our Lady of the Valley, La Grande.

ENTERPRISE, WALLOWA CO., ST. KATHERINE'S (1923) Rev. Francis Obijekwu, S.M.M.M. (Nigeria).
Res.: 301 E. Garfield St., P.O. Box 370, 97828. Tel: 541-426-3043.
Parish Office—Tel: 541-426-4008.
Catechesis/Religious Program—Students 22.
Mission—St. Pius X S. Pine St., Wallowa, Wallowa Co. 97885.

HEPPNER, MORROW CO., ST. PATRICK'S (1887) Very Rev. Gerald W. Condon.
Res.: 525 Gale St., P.O. Box 633, 97836. Tel: 541-676-9462.
Catechesis/Religious Program—Mary Ann Elguezabal, D.R.E. Students 45.
Mission—St. William Mailing Address: P.O. Box 633, 97836. 10 Main St., Ione, 97843.
Catechesis/Religious Program—Jeri Mc Elligott, D.R.E. Students 29.

HERMISTON, UMATILLA CO., OUR LADY OF ANGELS (1910) Revs. Daniel J. Maxwell; Theodore Nnabugo (Nigeria); Deacon Jesus Esparaza; Kay Edwards, Administrative Asst.
Res.: 565 Hermiston Ave., 97838. Tel: 541-567-5812; Fax: 541-564-0933.
Catechesis/Religious Program—Tel: 541-567-3825. Michelle Edwards, D.R.E. Students 383.

HOOD RIVER, HOOD RIVER CO., IMMACULATE CONCEPTION (1906) [CEM] Very Rev. Ronald E. Maag; Deacons Lou DeSitter, Pastoral Assoc.; David Raj, Pastoral Assoc.
Res.: 1501 Belmont Ave., P.O. Box 693, 97031. Tel: 541-386-3373; Fax: 541-386-1451.
Catechesis/Religious Program—Tel: 541-387-6797. Maria Ramirez, D.R.E., (Spanish); Sharon Foss, D.R.E., (English); Patricia Romero, Youth Min. Students 310.

IONE, MORROW CO., ST. WILLIAM, See separate listing. Now a mission of St. Patrick's, Heppner.

JOHN DAY, GRANT CO., ST. ELIZABETH (1939) Rev. Bartholomew Ifionu, S.M.M.M. (Nigeria).
Res.: 111 S.W. 2nd St., P.O. Box 189, 97845. Tel: 541-575-1459; Fax: 541-575-1459.
Catechesis/Religious Program—Tel: 541-575-0415.
Mission—St. Anne Monument, Grant Co.
Mission—St. Charles Seneca, Grant Co.
Mission—St. Katherine Long Creek, Grant Co.

JORDAN VALLEY, MALHEUR CO., ST. BERNARD (1915) Rev. Joseph Levine.
Res.: P.O. Box 186, 97910. Tel: 541-586-2266; Fax: 541-586-2448.
Catechesis/Religious Program—Lily Garrard, D.R.E. Students 12.
Mission—Holy Family Arock Rd., Arock, Malheur Co. 97902.

KLAMATH FALLS, KLAMATH CO.

1—ST. PIUS X (1957) [CEM] Very Rev. Richard O. Fischer. In Res., Rev. Ildefonce Mapara, O.S.B. (Tanzania).
Res.: 4880 Bristol Ave., 97603. Tel: 541-884-4242; Fax: 541-885-8724.
Catechesis/Religious Program—Tel: 541-882-7593; Fax: 541-882-7593. Mary Holder, D.R.E. Students 177.

2—SACRED HEART (1904) Rev. Rogatian Urassa.
Res.: 815 High St., 97601. Tel: 541-884-4566; Fax: 541-882-0472.
Catechesis/Religious Program—Tel: 541-882-4864. Michele Laughlin, D.R.E. Students 60.

LA GRANDE, UNION CO., OUR LADY OF THE VALLEY (1914), (Under the title of the Immaculate Conception) Revs. Christopher Agoha, S.M.M.M. (Nigeria); Gabriel U. Ezeh, S.M.M.M. (Nigeria).
Parish Office: 1002 L Ave., 97850. Tel: 541-963-7341; Fax: 541-963-7341.
Res.: 1101 4th St., 97850. Tel: 541-963-0006.
School—Marian Academy, (Grades PreSchool-K) Lay Teachers 3; Students 20.
Catechesis/Religious Program—Tel: 541-963-0861. Charlene Storoe, D.R.E. Students 44.
Mission—St. Anthony North Powder, Union Co.
Mission—St. Mary P.O. Box 97, Elgin, Union Co. 97827. Tel: 541-437-8101. Deacon Joseph Garlitz.
Catechesis/Religious Program—Nancy Wheeling, D.R.E. Students 28.
Mission—Sacred Heart (1905) 340 S. 10th St., P.O. Box 473, Union, Union Co. 97883.
Catechesis/Religious Program—Tel: 541-562-5486. Kathy Goodman, D.R.E.; Sherry Mendoza, D.R.E. Students 6.

LA PINE, DESCHUTES CO., HOLY REDEEMER (1983) Rev. Jose Thomas Mudakodiyil (India).
Res.: 16137 Burgess Rd., P.O. Box 299, 97739. Tel: 541-536-3571; 541-536-1177 (Rectory); Fax: 541-536-5647.
Catechesis/Religious Program—Tel: 541-536-1992. Debbie Garrett, D.R.E. Students 34.
Mission—Our Lady of the Snows Gilchrist, Klamath Co.
Mission—Holy Family Christmas Valley, Lake Co.
Mission—Holy Trinity 18143 Cottonwood Rd., Sunriver, Deschutes Co. 97707.

LAKEVIEW, LAKE CO., ST. PATRICK (1912) Rev. Anthony Mbaegbu (Nigeria).
Res.: 163 S. G St., P.O. Box 29, 97630. Tel: 541-947-2741; Fax: 541-947-2756. Email: saintpatrick@tnet.biz.
Catechesis/Religious Program—185 S. G St., 97630. Tel: 541-947-3875. Students 66.
Mission—St. Richard Adel, Lake Co.
Mission—St. Thomas Plush, Lake Co.
Mission—St. John the Apostle Paisley, Lake Co.

MADRAS, JEFFERSON CO., ST. PATRICK (1955) Rev. Luis M. Flores-Alva.
Res.: 341 S.W. J St., P.O. Box 786, 97741. Tel: 541-475-2936; Fax: 541-475-0539. Email: stpat@bkateri.org.
Catechesis/Religious Program—Tel: 541-475-2444. Elouise Kirsch, D.R.E. Students 214.
Mission—Blessed Kateri Tekakwitha P.O. Box 764, Warm Springs, Jefferson Co. 97761. Tel: 541-553-1235. (Indian Reservation)

MERRILL, KLAMATH CO., ST. AUGUSTINE (1939) Rev. Francis Akano (Nigeria).
Res.: 905 E. Front St., P.O. Box 340, 97633. Tel: 541-798-5823.
Catechesis/Religious Program—Tel: 541-891-6907. Debbie Wallace, D.R.E. Students 35.
Mission—St. Frances Cabrini Bonanza, Klamath Co. Tel: 541-545-6002.

MILTON FREEWATER, UMATILLA CO., ST. FRANCIS OF ASSISI (1940) Rev. Juan Carlos Chiarinoti (Argentina).
Res.: 925 Vining, 97862. Tel: 541-938-5436; Fax: 541-938-3536.
Catechesis/Religious Program—Students 100.

NYSSA, MALHEUR CO., ST. BRIDGET OF KILDARE (1951) Rev. Andrew Szymakowski, F.S.S.P.
Res.: 504 Locust, 97913-3235. Tel: 541-372-3133; Fax: 541-372-5620.
Catechesis/Religious Program—Students 92.

ONTARIO, MALHEUR CO., BLESSED SACRAMENT (1911) Revs. Jude Nwachukwu, S.M.M.M. (Nigeria); Joseph Levine; Mrs. Frances A. Schaffer, Pastoral Assoc.
Office: 829 S.W. Second Ave., 97914-2695. Tel: 541-889-8469; Fax: 541-889-8483.
School—Saint Peter, (Grades K-5), 98 S.W. Ninth St., 97914. Tel: 541-889-7363; Fax: 541-889-2852. Lay Teachers 5; Students 60.
Catechesis/Religious Program—Tel: 541-889-8404. Angelica Corona, D.R.E.; Tim Cables, Youth Min. Students 233.

PENDLETON, UMATILLA CO.

1—ST. ANDREW'S INDIAN MISSION (1847) [CEM] Rev. Michael J. Fitzpatrick, S.J.
Res.: 48022 St. Andrews Rd., 97801. Tel: 541-276-6155; Fax: 541-276-0767.
Catechesis/Religious Program—Tel: 541-276-0767. Fern Oliver, D.R.E. Students 51.
Mission—Sacred Heart 5th St. & College St., Athena, Umatilla Co. 97813.

2—ST. MARY (1902) [CEM] Rev. Bailey Clemens; Deacon Martin Omar Tores. In Res., Rev. Albert Lakra.
Res.: 800 S.E. Court Ave., 97801. Tel: 541-276-3615; Fax: 541-276-7484.
Catechesis/Religious Program—Tel: 541-276-6163. Shirley Baker, C.R.E. Students 70.
Mission—St. Helen (1930) 740 S.W. Birch, P.O. Box V, Pilot Rock, 97868.
Catechesis/Religious Program—Students 4.

PILOT ROCK, UMATILLA CO., ST. HELEN (1930) See separate listing. Now a mission of St. Mary, Pendleton.

PRINEVILLE, CROOK CO., ST. JOSEPH (1943) Rev. Robert Greiner.
Res.: 150 E. First, P.O. Box 1315, 97754. Tel: 541-447-6475; Fax: 541-416-9141.
Catechesis/Religious Program—200 E. First St., P.O. Box 721, 97754. Tel: 541-447-1227; Fax: 541-389-0888. Dolores Wettstein, D.R.E. Students 100.

REDMOND, DESCHUTES CO., ST. THOMAS (1941) Very Rev. Todd Unger.
Res.: 1720 N.W. 19th, 97756. Tel: 541-923-3390; Fax: 541-548-6630.
School—St. Thomas Academy, (Grades PreSchool-4), 1740 N.W. 9th St., 97756. Lay Teachers 4; Students 62.
Catechesis/Religious Program—Tel: 541-923-0597. Mary Lehnertz, D.R.E. Students 125.

SISTERS, DESCHUTES CO., ST. EDWARD THE MARTYR (1984) Rev. Jude E. Onogbosele. In Res., Rev. James A. Radloff.
Res.: 123 Trinity Way, P.O. Box 489, 97759-0489. Tel: 541-549-0751 (Rectory); 541-549-9391 (Office); Fax: 541-549-1057.
Catechesis/Religious Program—Marcia Rietmann, C.R.E. Students 51.

THE DALLES, WASCO CO., ST. PETER (1848) [CEM] Rev. Charles Chika Nnabuife.
Res.: 1222 W. 10th St., P.O. Box 41, 97058. Tel: 541-296-2026; Fax: 541-296-5835.
School—St. Mary, (Grades PreK-8), 1112 Cherry Heights Rd., 97058. Tel: 541-296-6004; Fax: 541-296-7858. Kim Koch, Admin. Lay Teachers 13; Students 221.
Catechesis/Religious Program—1111 W. 10th, P.O. Box 41, 97058. Students 30.

UNION, UNION CO., SACRED HEART (1905) See separate listing. Now a mission of Our Lady of the Valley, La Grande.

VALE, MALHEUR CO., ST. PATRICK (1946) Rev. Camillus Fernando (Sri Lanka).
Res.: 690 A St. W., P.O. Box J, 97918. Tel: 541-473-3906; Fax: 541-473-3906.
Catechesis/Religious Program—Tel: 541-473-3848. Kelly Hartman, D.R.E. Students 38.
Mission—St. Joseph Unity, Baker Co.

WASCO, MALHEUR CO., ST. MARY (1954) Rev. Fabian Nwokorie (Nigeria).
Res.: 807 Barnett St., P.O. Box 14, 97065. Tel: 541-442-8560; Fax: 541-442-8569. Email: finwoko@yahoo.com.
Catechesis/Religious Program—Bob O'Dell, D.R.E.; Cindy Brown, Youth Min.
Mission—St. John the Baptist Grass Valley, Sherman Co.

Military Services:
Rev.—
Colvin, Andrew, CHC, USN, 5527 N.W. Lause Way, Silverdale, WA 98383.

On Duty Outside the Diocese:
Rev.—
Hickie, J. Noel, Sacred Heart General Hospital, 1305 Willagillespie Rd., Eugene, 97401.

Retired:
Revs.—
Albrecht, Louis Henry, 802A Rice St., Honolulu, HI 96819. Tel: 541-963-7341
Bower, Lawrence C., 215 Woodward Blvd., Summerville, SC 29483. Tel: 843-815-1285
Cribbin, Austin J., 220 Newcastle Rd., Klamath Falls, 97601.
Dreisbach, Charles V., 2308 Newcastle, Klamath Falls, 97601. Tel: 541-882-6016
Fisher, A. J., 1200 W. Dimond #14105, Anchorage, AK 99515.
Homes, Dennis, 1501 9th St. S., #528, Great Falls, MT 59401. Tel: 406-452-1994
Hopp, Raymond, 1800 N. 4th St. #28, Lakeview, 97630.
Jasper, John, 4300 Albany Dr., Apt. L132, San Jose, CA 95129.
Kiely, Cornelius, Casilla 09-15825, Guayaquil, Ecuador.
Reeves, Joseph, P.O. Box 1380, Redmond, 97756. Tel: 503-690-3643
Scanlan, Thomas R., 1188 N.E. 27th St., Lot 101, 97701.
Weckerle, Leo F., 10979 S.W. Shad Rd., Terrebonne, 97760. Tel: 541-923-6828

INSTITUTIONS LOCATED IN THE DIOCESE

[A] GENERAL HOSPITALS

BAKER CITY. *Saint Alphonsus - Baker City, Inc.*, 3325 Pocahontas Rd., 97814. Tel: 541-523-6461 (Hospital); Fax: 541-523-8151. Email: leanneirsik@chiwest.com. Leanne Irsik, CEO; Steve Brocato, Chm. Bed Capacity 25; Nursing Home Beds 90; Patients Assisted Annually 20,114; Nursing Home 91; Staff 223.

HOOD RIVER. *Providence Hood River Memorial Hospital*, 811 13th St., 97031. Tel: 541-386-3911; Fax: 541-387-6462. Email: mark.thomas@providence.org. Web: www.providence.org. Edward Frysinger, CEO. Total Staff 500; Bed Capacity 25; Patients Assisted Annually 160,000.

ONTARIO. *Saint Alphonsus - Ontario, Inc.*, 351 S.W. Ninth St., 97914. Tel: 541-881-7000; Fax: 541-881-7184. Web: holyrosary-ontario.org. Wes Colvin, Pres.; Mr. Kenneth Hart, Bd. Chm.; Mr. Mark Bekkedahl, Vice Pres. Mission Integration. Bed Capacity 49; Total Staff 463; Patients Assisted Annually 73,189.

PENDLETON. *St. Anthony Hospital*, 1601 S.E. Court Ave., 97801. Tel: 541-276-5121; Fax: 541-278-3227. Email: vonnismonton@chiwest.com. Web: www.sahpendleton.org. Randall L. Mee, Pres. & CEO. Sisters of St. Francis of Philadelphia 2; Bed Capacity 49; Patients Assisted Annually 87,370; Staff 335.

[B] MONASTERIES AND RESIDENCES FOR PRIESTS AND BROTHERS

GILCHRIST. *Monastery of Annunciation Hermitage*, 146640 Hwy. 97, La Pine, 97739-9127. Tel: 541-433-2903; Fax: 215-995-7911. Email: w146640@hotmail.com. Rev. Arsenius.

[C] MISCELLANEOUS

BEND. *Baker Diocese Investment and Loan Corporation*, P.O. Box 5999, 97708.
Bend Volunteer Corps, P.O. Box 682, 97709. Tel: 541-318-4636. Email: mary@bendvolunteercorps.org. Web: www.bendvolunteercorps.org. Kristin Meagher, Exec. Dir.; Mary Dean, Dir. Recruiting.
The Health and Retirement Association of the Diocese of Baker, Oregon, 911 S.E. Armour St., P.O. Box 5999, 97708. Tel: 541-296-7979; Fax: 541-296-5835. Email: tunger@netcnct.net. Very Rev. Todd Unger, Plan Admin.
The Legacy of Faith Catholic Community Foundation of Oregon, P.O. Box 5999, 97708. Tel: 541-388-4004; Fax: 541-388-2566. John G. Schiemer, Exec. Dir.

HOOD RIVER. *Dethman Manor*, 1205 Montello St., 97031. Tel: 541-386-5111; Fax: 541-387-6356.
Providence Brookside Manor, 1550 Brookside Dr., 97031. Tel: 541-387-6370; Fax: 541-387-8272.
Providence Down Manor, 1950 Sterling Pl., 97031. Tel: 541-386-5115; Fax: 541-386-2456.
Providence Hood River Memorial Hospital Foundation, 810 12th St., P.O. Box 149, 97031. Tel: 541-387-6474; Fax: 541-387-6462.

KLAMATH FALLS. *St. Maurus Hanga Abbey*, 4880 Bristol Ave., 97603.

SUNRIVER. *Holy Trinity Community Outreach Care and Share*, 18160 Cottonwood Rd., PMB 763, 97707. Tel: 541-593-5990; Fax: 541-593-5991.

RELIGIOUS INSTITUTES OF MEN REPRESENTED IN THE DIOCESE

For further details refer to the corresponding bracketed number in the Religious Institutes of Men or Women section.

[]—*The Institute of the Incarnate Word*

[0690]—*Jesuit Fathers and Brothers* (Oregon Prov.)—S.J.

[]—*St. Maurus Hanga Abbey*

[]—*Sons of Mary Mother of Mercy*—S.M.M.M.

RELIGIOUS INSTITUTES OF WOMEN REPRESENTED IN THE DIOCESE

[2470]—*Maryknoll Sisters of St. Dominic*—M.M.

[]—*Sisters of Mary of Kakamega*

[]—*Sisters of Providence, Mother Joseph Providence*

[1650]—*Sisters of St. Francis of Philadelphia*—O.S.F.

[1990]—*Sisters of the Holy Names of Jesus and Mary*—S.N.J.M.

NECROLOGY

† Jarboe, Raymond, (Retired)—Died May 4, 2011
† Van Sickler, Robert, (Retired)—Died Feb. 18, 2011

An asterisk (*) denotes an organization that has established tax-exempt status directly with the IRS and is not covered by the USCCB Group Ruling.

Archdiocese of Baltimore

(Archidioecesis Baltimorensis)

His Eminence

WILLIAM CARDINAL KEELER, D.D., J.C.D.

Retired Archbishop of Baltimore; ordained July 17, 1955; appointed Titular Bishop of Ulcinium and Auxiliary Bishop of Harrisburg July 24, 1979; ordained Bishop September 21, 1979; appointed Bishop of Harrisburg November 10, 1983; installed January 4, 1984; appointed Archbishop of Baltimore April 6, 1989; installed as Fourteenth Archbishop of Baltimore May 23, 1989; created Cardinal Priest November 26, 1994; retired July 12, 2007. *Office: 320 Cathedral St., Baltimore, MD 21201.* Tel: 410-547-5437.

Most Reverend

WILLIAM C. NEWMAN, D.D., V.G.

Retired Auxiliary Bishop of Baltimore; ordained May 29, 1954; appointed Auxiliary Bishop of Baltimore and Titular Bishop of Numluli May 25, 1984; installed Bishop July 2, 1984; retired August 28, 2003. *Office: 320 Cathedral St., Baltimore, MD 21201.* Tel: 410-547-5438. *Res.: 5300 N. Charles St., Baltimore, MD 21201.*

Most Reverend

WILLIAM E. LORI, S.T.D.

Archbishop of Baltimore; ordained May 14, 1977; appointed Titular Bishop of Bulla and Auxiliary Bishop of Washington April 20, 1995; appointed Bishop of Bridgeport January 23, 2001; installed March 19, 2001; appointed Archbishop of Baltimore March 20, 2012. *Office: 320 Cathedral St., Baltimore, MD 21201.* Tel: 410-547-5446.

Chancery Office: 320 Cathedral St., Baltimore, MD 21201. Tel: 410-547-5446; Fax: 410-727-8234.

Web: www.archbalt.org

Email: chancery@archbalt.org

Most Reverend

MITCHELL T. ROZANSKI

Auxiliary Bishop of Baltimore; ordained November 24, 1984; appointed Auxiliary Bishop of Baltimore and Titular Bishop of Walla Walla July 3, 2004; installed August 24, 2004. *Office: 320 Cathedral St., Baltimore, MD 21201.* Tel: 410-547-5438.

Most Reverend

DENIS J. MADDEN

Auxiliary Bishop of Baltimore; ordained April 1, 1967; appointed Auxiliary Bishop of Baltimore and Titular Bishop of Baia May 10, 2005; ordained August 24, 2005. *Office: 320 Cathedral St., Baltimore, MD 21201.* Tel: 410-547-5452.

Square Miles 4,801.

Established a Diocese November 6, 1789; Established an Archdiocese April 8, 1808.

Comprises the City of Baltimore and Allegany, Anne Arundel, Baltimore, Carroll, Frederick, Garrett, Harford, Howard and Washington Counties.

By a Decree of the Sacred Congregation of the Propaganda, July 19, 1858, approved by His Holiness, Pius IX, July 25, 1858, "Prerogative of Place" was conferred on the Archdiocese of Baltimore. By the explicit words of said decree of the Holy See, the Archbishop of Baltimore takes precedence over all Archbishops of the United States (not Cardinals) in Councils, gatherings and meetings of whatever kind of the Hierarchy (in concillis, coetibus et comitiis quibuscumque) regardless of the seniority of other Archbishops in promotion or ordination. Decree signed by Cardinal Barnabo, August 15, 1858.

For legal titles of parishes and archdiocesan institutions, consult the Chancery Office.

STATISTICAL OVERVIEW

Personnel	
Retired Cardinals	1
Auxiliary Bishops	2
Retired Bishops	1
Priests: Diocesan Active in Diocese	187
Priests: Diocesan Active Outside Diocese	17
Priests: Retired, Sick or Absent	45
Number of Diocesan Priests	249
Religious Priests in Diocese	227
Total Priests in Diocese	476
Extern Priests in Diocese	52
Ordinations:	
Diocesan Priests	1
Transitional Deacons	4
Permanent Deacons	14
Permanent Deacons in Diocese	168
Total Brothers	69
Total Sisters	860
Parishes	
Parishes	146
With Resident Pastor:	
Resident Diocesan Priests	91
Resident Religious Priests	28
Without Resident Pastor:	
Administered by Priests	20
Administered by Deacons	3
Administered by Lay People	4
Missions	7
Closed Parishes	7
Professional Ministry Personnel:	
Brothers	1
Sisters	25
Lay Ministers	175
Welfare	
Catholic Hospitals	5
Total Assisted	1,864,800
Health Care Centers	4
Total Assisted	2,772
Homes for the Aged	27
Total Assisted	4,225
Residential Care of Children	9
Total Assisted	1,429
Day Care Centers	6
Total Assisted	5,025
Specialized Homes	5
Total Assisted	756
Special Centers for Social Services	40
Total Assisted	359,747
Residential Care of Disabled	1
Total Assisted	255
Other Institutions	1
Total Assisted	7,219
Educational	
Seminaries, Diocesan	2
Students from This Diocese	18
Students from Other Diocese	229
Diocesan Students in Other Seminaries	11
Total Seminarians	29
Colleges and Universities	4
Total Students	11,315
High Schools, Diocesan and Parish	7
Total Students	3,384
High Schools, Private	13
Total Students	7,363
Elementary Schools, Diocesan and Parish	42
Total Students	16,104
Elementary Schools, Private	7
Total Students	1,111
Non-residential Schools for the Disabled	1
Total Students	116
Catechesis/Religious Education:	
High School Students	2,430
Elementary Students	22,589
Total Students under Catholic Instruction	64,441
Teachers in the Diocese:	
Priests	40
Brothers	8
Sisters	64
Lay Teachers	2,587
Vital Statistics	
Receptions into the Church:	
Infant Baptism Totals	5,860
Adult Baptism Totals	481
Received into Full Communion	793
First Communions	5,828
Confirmations	5,299
Marriages:	
Catholic	877
Interfaith	430
Total Marriages	1,307
Deaths	4,167
Total Catholic Population	510,328
Total Population	3,148,690

Former Archbishops—Most Revs. JOHN CARROLL, D.D., cons. Aug. 15, 1790; Archbishop, April 8, 1808; died Dec. 3, 1815; LEONARD NEALE, D.D., cons. Coadjutor, Dec. 7, 1800; acceded to the Dec. 3, 1815; died June 18, 1817; AMBROSE MARECHAL, S.S., D.D., cons. Dec. 14, 1817; died Jan. 29, 1828; JAMES WHITFIELD, D.D., cons. May 25, 1828; died Oct. 19, 1834; SAMUEL ECCLESTON, S.S., D.D., cons. Sept. 14, 1834; died April 22, 1851; FRANCIS PATRICK KENRICK, D.D., cons. June 6, 1830; Coadjutor Bishop of Philadelphia; promoted to Aug. 19, 1851; died July 8, 1863; MARTIN JOHN SPALDING, D.D., cons. Sept. 10, 1848; Coadjutor Bishop of Louisville; promoted to May 6, 1864; died Feb. 7, 1872; JAMES ROOSEVELT BAYLEY, D.D., cons. Oct. 30, 1853; Bishop of Newark; promoted to July 30, 1872; died Oct. 3, 1877; His Eminence JAMES CARDINAL GIBBONS, D.D., cons. Vicar Apostolic of North Carolina, Aug. 16, 1868; transferred to See of Richmond, July 30, 1872; promoted to See of Baltimore, Oct. 3, 1877; created Cardinal Priest of S. Maria in Trastevere, June 7, 1886; died March 24, 1921; Most Revs. MICHAEL J. CURLEY, D.D., cons. Bishop of St. Augustine, June 30, 1914; promoted to Aug. 10, 1921; died May 16, 1947; FRANCIS P. KEOUGH, D.D., cons. Bishop of Providence, May 22, 1934; promoted to Nov. 29, 1947; died Dec. 8, 1961; LAWRENCE CARDINAL SHEHAN, cons. Auxiliary Bishop of Baltimore, Dec. 12, 1945; transferred to Diocese of Bridgeport, Aug. 25, 1953; appt. Coadjutor Archbishop of Baltimore, July 10, 1961; acceded to the Dec. 8, 1961; created Cardinal Priest of S. Clemente, Feb. 22, 1965; retired March 25, 1974; died Aug. 26, 1984; WILLIAM DONALD BORDERS, D.D. (Retired), appt. Bishop of Orlando, May 2, 1968; cons. June 14, 1968; promoted to March 25, 1974; installed June 26, 1974; retired April 6, 1989; died April 19, 2010.; His Eminence WILLIAM CARDINAL KEELER, ord. July 17, 1955; appt. Titular Bishop of Ulcinium and Auxiliary Bishop of Harrisburg July 24, 1979;

ord. Bishop Sept. 21, 1979; appt. Bishop of Harrisburg Nov. 10, 1983; installed Jan. 4, 1984; appt. Archbishop of Baltimore April 6, 1989; installed as Fourteenth Archbishop of Baltimore May 23, 1989; created Cardinal Priest Nov. 26, 1994; retired July 12, 2007.; EDWIN F. O'BRIEN, ord. May 29, 1965; appt. Titular Bishop of Tizica and Auxiliary Bishop of New York Feb. 6, 1996; cons. March 25, 1996; appt. Coadjutor April 8, 1997; succeeded as Ordinary to the Military Services Aug. 12, 1997; appt. Archbishop of Baltimore July 12, 2007; installed as 15th Archbishop of Baltimore Oct. 1, 2007; appt. Grand Master of the Equestrian Order of the Holy Sepulchre of Jerusalem Aug. 29, 2011; elevated to Cardinal Feb. 18, 2012.

Vicars General—Most Revs. WILLIAM C. NEWMAN, D.D., V.G. (Retired); MITCHELL T. ROZANSKI, D.D., V.G.; DENIS J. MADDEN, D.D., V.G.; Rev. Msgr. RICHARD W. WOY, V.G., Moderator of the Curia.

Office of the Cardinal Archbishop Emeritus—St. Stephen's Green at Mercy Ridge, 2525 Pot Spring Rd., Timonium, 21093.

Chancery Office—320 Cathedral St., Baltimore, 21201. Tel: 410-547-5446; Fax: 410-727-8234. Office Hours: Mon.-Fri. 9-5; Closed holidays.

Chancellor—Dr. DIANE L. BARR, J.C., J.C.D. Tel: 410-547-5446.

Canonical Adviser, Office of—Canonical & Theological Consultants to the Archbishop: Rev. Msgr. RONNY JENKINS, J.C.D.; Rev. JAMES J. CONN, S.J. Tel: 410-547-5435.

Consultors— (vacant)

Office of the St. Elizabeth Ann Seton Vicariate—Most Rev. MITCHELL T. ROZANSKI, D.D., V.G., Eastern Vicar. Tel: 410-547-5438. Email: svicar@archbalt.org; Dr. THOMAS E. LITTLE, Pastoral Assoc. Tel: 410-547-5376. Email: thomas.little@archbalt.org; Deacon CHARLES H. HIEBLER JR., Asst. Pastoral Planner, 320 Cathedral St., Baltimore, 21201. Tel: 410-547-5456; Fax: 410-727-5432. Email: chiebler@archbalt.org.

Interdiocesan Tribunal of Appeals of the Province of Baltimore—320 Cathedral St., Baltimore, 21201. Tel: 410-547-5512; Fax: 410-576-6932. Email: interdiocesan.tribunal@archbalt.org.

Judicial Vicar—Rev. WILLIAM GRAHAM, O.F.M.Cap., J.C.L.; Rev. Msgr. THOMAS SHREVE, Adjutant Judicial Vicar & Judge; Mrs. M. TERESA EWEN, Sec. Interdiocesan Tribunal & Notary.

Metropolitan Tribunal—320 Cathedral St., Baltimore, 21201. Tel: 410-547-5533; Fax: 410-576-6932. Email: metropolitan.tribunal@archbalt.org.

Judicial Vicar—Rev. GILBERT J. SEITZ, J.C.L.

Adjutant Judicial Vicar—Rev. JOHN B. WARD, J.C.L., J.D. Email: jward@archbalt.org.

Judge—Rev. MICHAEL J. CARRION.

Defender of the Bond—Rev. Msgr. ROBERT A. ARMSTRONG, P.A. (Retired).

Advocates—Mr. STEPHEN R. BEARD; Sisters KATHERINE BELL, R.S.M.; JUDITH CIANFROGNA, S.S.J.; SUSAN ENGEL, M.H.S.H.; Deacon NICHOLAS FEURER; Ms. MARGARET GAUGHAN; Deacon JOHN L. MANLEY; Mrs. TERESA MARTH; Deacon LAWRENCE G. MATHENY; Rev. Msgr. EDWARD M. MILLER; Deacon HUGH H. MILLS JR.; Mr. JOE MULICK; Deacon WILLIAM NAIRN; Ms. CAROLYN NOLAN; Mr. GERARD NOVAK; Rev. DONALD J. PARSON; Ms. CAMILLA RAWE; Deacon EDWARD SULLIVAN.

Notaries—Deacon NEIL A. CRISPO; Mrs. PATRICIA WALLS.

Office of the St. John Neumann Vicariate—Most Rev. DENIS J. MADDEN, D.D., V.G.; Mr. ALBERT SCHARBACH, Pastoral Assoc. to the Neumann Vicar. Tel: 410-547-5488; Fax: 410-727-5432.

Archdiocesan Offices and Directors

African American Catholic Ministries, Archdiocesan Office of—THERESE WILSON FAVORS, Dir., 320 Cathedral St., Baltimore, 21201. Tel: 410-625-8472; Fax: 410-625-8485. Email: aacm@archbalt.org.

Archdiocesan Directory—Mr. CHRISTOPHER GUNTY, Mailing Address: P.O. Box 777, Baltimore, 21203. Tel: 443-524-3150 Official directory of the Archdiocese of Baltimore. Published annually by The Catholic Review. $45 per copy.

Archdiocesan Pastoral Council— (See Pastoral Council Archdiocesan).

Archives-Archivist—TRICIA PYNE, Ph.D., 5400 Roland Ave., Baltimore, 21210. Tel: 410-864-4074 (By appointment); Fax: 410-864-3690. Email: archives@stmarys.edu. Web: stmarys.edu/archives.

Boy Scouts— (See Catholic Youth Activities).

Building Commission—NOLAN MCCOY, Contact Person. Tel: 410-547-5335.

Catholic Campaign For Human Development, Archdiocese of Baltimore, Inc.—GLYNDON L. BAILEY, Chair, 320 Cathedral St., Baltimore, 21201. Tel: 410-235-5136; 410-547-5446.

Catholic Review Media—Most Rev. EDWIN F. O'BRIEN, S.T.D., D.D., Publisher & Chm.; Mr. CHRISTOPHER GUNTY, Assoc. Publisher & Editor, Mailing Address: P.O. Box 777, Baltimore, 21203. Tel: 443-524-3150; Fax: 443-524-3155. Web: catholicreview.org. Publishers of The Catholic Review, Official Archdiocesan Directory, Catholic International and Cathedral Foundation Press.

Catholic Charities, Inc.—Mr. WILLIAM J. MCCARTHY JR., Exec. Dir., 320 Cathedral St., Baltimore, 21201. Tel: 410-547-5490. Web: www.cc-md.org.

Department of Catholic Schools—Dr. BARBARA MCGRAW EDMONDSON, Exec. Dir. & Supt. Catholic Schools, 320 Cathedral St., Baltimore, 21201-4419. Tel: 410-547-5515. Email: barbara.edmondson@archbalt.org.

Department of Evangelization—Rev. JOHN E. HURLEY, C.S.P., Exec. Dir., 320 Cathedral St., Baltimore, 21201-4419. Tel: 410-547-5321. Email: john.hurley@archbalt.org.

"The Catholic Review"—Most Rev. EDWIN F. O'BRIEN, S.T.D., D.D., Publisher; Mr. CHRISTOPHER GUNTY, Assoc. Publisher & Editor; PAUL MCMULLEN, Mng. Editor, Mailing Address: 880 Park Ave., Baltimore, 21203. Tel: 443-263-0259; Fax: 443-524-3160. Web: www.catholicreview.org. Newspaper of the Archdiocese of Baltimore. Established 1913. Published every Thursday by the Cathedral Foundation, Inc.

Clergy Personnel, Division of—Rev. Msgr. JAMES W. HANNON, Div. Dir. Tel: 410-547-5302. Email: jhannon@archbalt.org. Administrative Assistants: Mrs. CINDY ORR. Tel: 410-547-5550. Email: corr@archbalt.org; Mrs. CAROL PURWIN. Tel: 410-547-5427. Email: cpurwin@archbalt.org; 320 Cathedral St., Rm. 620, Baltimore, 21201.

Commission for Ecumenical and Interreligious Affairs—VACANT.

Communications Office—SEAN CAIN, Vice Chancellor & Dir. Communications, 320 Cathedral St., Baltimore, 21201. Tel: 410-547-5379; Fax: 410-625-8480. Email: scain@archbalt.org.

Deacon Personnel Board—Deacons RON THOMPSON, Liaison. Email: rthompson@archbalt.org; MICHAEL A. DODGE; DAVID A. PAGE; JOHN COMEGNA; Mrs. CAROL MATHENY; Deacons GEORGE SISSON; MARTIN E. WOLF; KEVIN F. REID; Mrs. MICHELLE SHELDON-RUBIO.

Development, Department of—PATRICK MADDEN, Exec. Dir.; GREGORY LEITNER, Regl. Devel. Dir. & Dir Institutional Advancement of the Basilica; BRENT DAILEY, Dir. Devel.; SHEILA CANELOS, Dir. Fiscal Devel.; CESSY TORSELLA, Exec. Asst.; JENNIFER SMITH, Dir. Advancement Svcs.; MELANIE TORSELLA, Research Mgr.; JENNIFER HAMMOND, Grants Admin.; MATTHEW ANTHONY, Asst. Dir.

Employee Benefits, Division of—PETRA PHELPS, Dir., 320 Cathedral St., Baltimore, 21201. Tel: 410-547-5317; Fax: 410-783-5993. Email: pphelps@archbalt.org.

Financial Administration, Board of—Most Rev. EDWIN F. O'BRIEN, S.T.D., D.D., Chm.; WILLIAM J. BAIRD III, Exec. Dir. Mgmt. Svcs. & CFO, 320 Cathedral St., Baltimore, 21201. Tel: 410-547-5322.

Fiscal Services, Division of—JOHN M. MATERA, CPA, Controller, 320 Cathedral St., Baltimore, 21201. Tel: 410-547-5313; Fax: 410-332-8233. Email: fiscal@archbalt.org.

Courage— A ministry for same sex attracted persons. Rev. Msgr. JAMES P. FARMER, Dir.

Hispanic Ministries, Office of—MARIA T.P. JOHNSON, Dir., 320 Cathedral St., Baltimore, 21201. Tel: 410-547-5363; Fax: 410-625-8485. Email: mtpjohnson@archbalt.org.

Holy Childhood Association—Deacon RODRIGUE MORTEL, M.D., 320 Cathedral St., Baltimore, 21201. Tel: 410-625-8450. Email: rmortel@archbalt.org.

Human Resource Services, Division of—MICHELLY B. MERRICK, SPHR, Dir., 320 Cathedral St., Baltimore, 21201. Tel: 410-547-5448; Fax: 410-234-2953. Email: mmerrick@archbalt.org.

Human Resources Committee—LEONARD STROM, Exec. Dir. Tel: 410-547-5556.

Information Technology, Division of—WILLIAM A. GLOVER, Dir. & C.I.O., 320 Cathedral St., Baltimore, 21201. Tel: 410-547-5539; Fax: 410-332-8233. Email: it@archbalt.org.

Insurance Committee—WILLIAM FRANEY, Chm.; PETRA PHELPS, Sec., 320 Cathedral St., Baltimore, 21201. Tel: 410-547-5317; Fax: 410-783-5993. Email: pphelps@archbalt.org.

Lay Employees Retirement Board—RAYMOND BRUSCA, Chm.; PETRA PHELPS, Sec., 320 Cathedral St., Baltimore, 21201. Tel: 410-547-5317; Fax: 410-783-5993. Email: pphelps@archbalt.org.

League of the Little Flower—RUTH A. PULS, Dir., 320 Cathedral St., Baltimore, 21201. Tel: 410-547-5470. Email: llf@archbalt.org.

Management Services, Department of—WILLIAM J. BAIRD III, Exec. Dir. & CFO, 320 Cathedral St., Baltimore, 21201. Tel: 410-547-5322; Fax: 410-332-8233. Email: mgmtserv@archbalt.org.

Maryland Catholic Conference—Mrs. MARY ELLEN RUSSELL, Exec. Dir., 10 Francis St., Annapolis, 21401. Tel: 410-269-1155 (Bal.); 301-261-1979 (Wash.); Fax: 410-269-1790. Email: info@mdcathcon.org. Web: www.mdcathcon.org.

Catechetical and Pastoral Formation, Division of—RUTH A. PULS, Dir. Tel: 410-547-5470. Email: rpuls@archbalt.org; ARMANDO GARCIA, Coord. Hispanic Pastoral Formation. Email: agarcia@archbalt.org; LAURI PRZYBYSZ, Coord. Marriage & Family Life. Tel: 410-547-5420. Email: lprzybysz@archbalt.org; Ms. MAE RICHARDSON, Coord. Pastoral Leadership Formation. Tel: 410-547-5415. Email: mae.richardson@archbalt.org; Sr. SALLY RUSSELL, S.S.J., Coord. Curriculum & Catechist Formation. Tel: 410-547-5414. Email: sally.russell@archbalt.org; MICHAEL RUZICKI, Coord. Adult & Sacramental Formation. Tel: 410-547-5417. Email: michael.ruzicki@archbalt.org.

Missions Office—Most Rev. EDWIN F. O'BRIEN, S.T.D., D.D., Gen. Dir.; Deacon RODRIGUE MORTEL, M.D., Dir., 320 Cathedral St., Baltimore, 21201. Tel: 410-547-5498; Fax: 410-625-8486. Email: rmortel@archbalt.org.

Moderator of the Curia—Rev. Msgr. RICHARD W. WOY, V.G., 320 Cathedral St., Baltimore, 21201. Tel: 410-547-5447; Fax: 410-727-5432. Email: rwoy@archbalt.org.

New Cathedral Cemetery—4300 Old Frederick Rd., Baltimore, 21229. Tel: 410-566-7770; Fax: 410-566-0709.

Office of Diaconate—Rev. Msgr. JAY F. O'CONNOR, Dir. Tel: 410-547-5427; Deacon RON THOMAS, Asst. Dir. Tel: 410-547-5558. Email: rthomas@archbalt.org. Administrative Assistants: Mrs. CINDY ORR; Mrs. CAROL PURWIN, 320 Cathedral St., Rm. 620, Baltimore, 21201. Tel: 410-547-5427. Email: deacons@archbalt.org.

Office of Pastoral Service for Senior and Retired Clergy—Rev. SALVATORE LIVIGNI, Dir., 320 Cathedral St., Baltimore, 21201. Tel: 410-547-5382. Email: slivigni@archbalt.org.

Permanent Deacon Formation Program—Rev. PATRICK CARRION, B.A., S.T.D., S.T.M., M.A.S. Email: pcarrion@archbalt.org.

Presbyteral Council— (vacant)

Priest Personnel Board—Rev. Msgr. LLOYD AIKEN; Rev. JOHN A. WILLIAMSON; Rev. Msgrs. KEVIN T. SCHENNING; EDWARD M. MILLER; Revs. JERRY FRANCIK; CHRISTOPHER P. MOORE; STEPHEN E. HOOK; JAMES P. KIESEL; EUGENE NICKOL; Rev. Msgrs. MARTIN E. FEILD; JAMES O. MCGOVERN, V.F. (Retired).

Prison Ministry for the Archdiocese of Baltimore—Deacon SEIGFRIED PRESBERRY, Dir. Prison Ministry. Tel: 410-547-5575.

Real Estate and Facilities Management, Division of—NOLAN MCCOY, Dir. Facilities & Real Estate; HUGH ANDES, Catholic Center Bldg. Mgr.; MATTHEW REGAN, Capital Project Mgr.; DOUG JOHNSON, Capital Project Mgr.; MYRTLE BUCHANAN, Office Mgr.; DAVE OWENS, Capital Projects Mgr.; ROBERT CLANCY, Project Mgr., 320 Cathedral St., Baltimore, 21201. Tel: 410-547-5367; Fax: 410-837-2932.

St. Vincent de Paul Society— Baltimore Council: Most Rev. EDWIN F. O'BRIEN, S.T.D., D.D., Honorary Pres.; Rev. JOHN J. LOMBARDI, Spiritual Advisor; KEVIN G. MEYD, Pres.; JOHN J. SCHIAVONE, Pres. & CEO, 2305 N. Charles St., Ste. 300, Baltimore, 21218. Tel: 410-662-0500; Fax: 410-662-0508. Web: www.vincentbaltimore.org.

Senior Priests' Retirement Board—Rev. JAMES PROFFITT; PETRA PHELPS, Sec.

Office of Research and Planning—320 Cathedral St., Baltimore, 21201. Fax: 410-727-5432.

Executive Director—Rev. Msgr. ROBERT L. HARTNETT, Exec. Dir. Tel: 443-540-6630. Email: bob.hartnett@archbalt.org.

Associate Directors—Mrs. MARY ELLEN FISE. Tel: 410-547-5454. Email: mfise@archbalt.org; MARK PACIONE. Tel: 410-547-5373. Email: mpacione@archbalt.org.

Technology Advisory Committee—WILLIAM GRESKOVICH, Chm.

Vicar for African-American Catholic Ministries—Most Rev. DENIS J. MADDEN, D.D., V.G.

Vicar for Hispanic Ministry—Most Rev. MITCHELL T. ROZANSKI, D.D., V.G.

Office of Consecrated Life—Sr. MARIA LUZ ORTIZ, M.H.S.H., Archbishop's Delegate for Relg. Tel: 410-547-5584. Email: marialuz@archbalt.org.

Office of Child and Youth Protection—ALISON J. D'ALESSANDRO, Dir. Tel: 410-547-5348. Email: adalessandro@archbalt.org.

Vocation Office—Rev. T. AUSTIN MURPHY JR., Dir. Tel: 410-547-5426; Fax: 410-234-2953. Email: vocations@archbalt.org.

Youth and Young Adult Ministry, Division of—D. SCOTT MILLER, Dir., 320 Cathedral St., Baltimore, 21201. Tel: 410-547-5372; Fax: 410-625-8481. Email: smiller@archbalt.org.

Associated Catholic Charities, Inc.

Catholic Charities— Associated Catholic Charities, Inc. (Catholic Charities) is Maryland's leading private provider of human services. The agency welcomes and serves people in need, regardless of faith, race or other circumstances. Through more than 80 programs, Catholic Charities improves the lives of children and families, seniors, the disadvantaged, and people with developmental disabilities. Headquartered in Baltimore, the agency operates in the city and nine Maryland counties under the auspices of the Roman Catholic Archdiocese of Baltimore. *Catholic Charities, 320 Cathedral St., Baltimore, 21201.* Tel: 410-547-5490. Email: info@cc-md.org. Web: www.cc-md.org. For detailed information on specific Catholic Charities and its programs, please refer to the Institution Section.

Executive Director—Mr. WILLIAM J. MCCARTHY JR., Catholic Charities, 320 Cathedral St., 3rd Fl., Baltimore, 21201-4493. Tel: 410-547-5490.

CLERGY, PARISHES, MISSIONS AND PAROCHIAL SCHOOLS

METROPOLITAN BALTIMORE

(BALTIMORE CITY AND BALTIMORE COUNTY)

1—CATHEDRAL OF MARY OUR QUEEN (1954) [CEM] Rev. Msgrs. J. Bruce Jarboe, Rector; Robert A. Armstrong, Rector Emeritus (Retired); Rev. Peter Literal; Deacons Charles Hiebler; Ray Moreau; William W. Senft. In Res., Rev. Msgrs. James W. Hannon; Richard W. Woy; Revs. Joseph F. Breighner; John E. Hurley, C.S.P.
Res.: 5200 N. Charles St., 21210-2098. Tel: 410-464-4000; Fax: 410-464-4060. Web: www.cathedralofmary.org.
School—(Grades K-8), 111 Amberly Way, 21210-2098. Tel: 410-464-4100; Fax: 410-464-4137. Sr. Josephann Wagoner, S.S.N.D., Prin. Lay Teachers 30; Students 450.
Catechesis/Religious Program—5200 N. Charles St., 21210. Tel: 410-464-4004. Mrs. Sherri Rachuba, D.R.E. Students 210.
Youth & Family Life—Tel: 410-464-4012. Ms. Meghan Cosgrove, Dir.
Office of Music Ministry—Tel: 410-464-4020. Daniel Sansone.

2—ST. AGNES (Catonsville) (1852) [CEM] Rev. Michael DeAscanis; Deacon John Ames; Marianne Gregory, Music Min.
Res.: 5422 Old Frederick Rd., 21229. Tel: 410-744-2900; Fax: 410-744-8304. Email: stagnes@archbalt.org. Web: www.stagnescatholicchurch.org.
Catechesis/Religious Program—Amanda Barrick, D.R.E. & Youth Min. Students 185.

3—ST. ALPHONSUS, SHRINE OF (1845), (Lithuanian), Rev. Msgr. Arthur Bastress. In Res., Rev. William F. Spacek, Univ. of Maryland Hospital Chap.; Deacon Hugh H. Mills Jr., Business Mgr.
Res.: 114 W. Saratoga St., 21201. Tel: 410-685-6090; Fax: 410-244-1670. Email: alphonsus@verizon.net. Web: www.stalphonsusbalt.org.

4—ST. AMBROSE (1907), (African American), Rev. Paul Zaborowski, O.F.M.Cap.; Deacons Seigfried Presberry; Steven Rubio; Betty Butler, Music Min.; Derrick A. Hewlett, Music Min. In Res., Revs. Roman Kozacheson, O.F.M.Cap; William Graham, O.F.M.Cap.
Res.: 4502 Park Heights Ave., 21215. Tel: 410-367-9918; Fax: 410-542-6056. Email: pastor@saintambrose.com. Web: www.saintambrose.com.
School—(Grades K-8), 4506 Park Heights Ave., 21215. Tel: 410-664-2373; Fax: 410-664-0857. Email: principal@stambrose.org. Pamela Sanders, Prin. Lay Teachers 24; Students 187.
Catechesis/Religious Program—Sr. Mary Stephen Beauford, O.S.P., D.R.E. Students 50.
Outreach Center—, (St. Vincent de Paul Society), 3445 Park Heights Ave., 21215. Tel: 410-225-0870. Ms. Laura Spada, Dir.

5—ST. ANDREW, Closed. 1974. Parish records available at the Chancery. Tel: 410-547-5446.

6—ST. ANN (1873), (African American), Twinned with St. Wenceslaus, Baltimore. Rev. Peter A. Lyons, T.O.R.; Deacon James E. Bee; Sr. Edna Maier, S.N.D., Pastoral Admin. In Res., Rev. Jordan Hite, T.O.R.
Res.: 528 E. 22nd St., 21218. Tel: 410-235-8169; Fax: 410-235-8253.
Catechesis/Religious Program—Students 35.

7—ANNUNCIATION (1968) Rev. Thomas E. Walsh, O.F.M.Conv.; Sr. Susan Engel, M.H.S.H., Pastoral Assoc.; John Holland, Music Min.
Res.: 5212 McCormick Ave., 21206. Tel: 410-866-4020; Fax: 410-866-2754. Email: cota.parish@verizon.net. Web: www.sites.google.com/site/church of the annunciation.
Catechesis/Religious Program—Tel: 410-866-4706. Mrs. Kathy Brotzman, C.R.E. Students 63.

8—ST. ANTHONY OF PADUA (1884), Twinned with Most Precious Blood. Revs. Ty S. Hullinger; Anthony Abiamiri. Email: akabiamiri@comcast.net; Deacons Joseph C. Krysiak; Joseph Schultz; Christian Lafferty, Dir. Kingdom Ministries.
Res.: 4414 Frankford Ave., 21206. Tel: 410-488-0400; Fax: 410-488-0032. Email: sapmpb@comcast.net. Web: www.stampb.org.
Catechesis/Religious Program—Tel: 410-488-0400; Fax: 410-488-0032. Students 22.

9—ASCENSION (Halethorpe) (1913) Rev. John A. Williamson; Deacon Thomas J. Yannuzzi; Bonnie Kabara, Music Min.
Res.: 4603 Poplar Ave., 21227. Tel: 410-242-2292; Fax: 410-242-6807. Email: ascebalt@archbalt.org. Web: www.ascensionbaltimore.org.
Catechesis/Religious Program—Mrs. Marie Murphy, D.R.E.; Cathy Carlin, D.R.E. Students 105.

10—ST. ATHANASIUS (1891) Rev. Robert A. DiMattei Jr.; Deacon Michael A. Dodge; Teresa Stevens, Coord. Family Ministry.
Res.: 4708 Prudence St., 21226. Tel: 410-355-5740; Fax: 410-355-8122. Web: www.athanasius.org.
Catechesis/Religious Program—Tel: 410-355-2540. Mary Beth Barnes, D.R.E.; Leo Quinn, Youth Min. Students 70.

11—ST. AUGUSTINE (Elkridge) (1844) [CEM] Rev. John A. Williamson.
Res.: 5976 Old Washington Rd., Elkridge, 21075. Tel: 410-796-1520; Fax: 410-796-8172. Web: www.staugustinechurch.org.
School—(Grades PreK-8), 5990 Old Washington Rd., Elkridge, 21075. Tel: 410-796-3040; Fax: 410-579-1165. Web: www.staug-md.org. Mrs. Patricia Schratz, Prin. School Sisters of Notre Dame 2; Lay Teachers 9; Students 262.
Catechesis/Religious Program—Tel: 410-796-8150. Cathy Carlin, C.R.E.; Mary Jane Thomas, Dir. Adult Faith Formation; Marty Link, Coord. Youth Min. Students 455.

12—ST. BARNABAS, Closed. 1931. Parish records available at St. Pius V Church. Tel: 410-523-1930.

13—BASILICA OF THE NATIONAL SHRINE OF THE ASSUMPTION OF THE BLESSED VIRGIN MARY (1806), (Co-Cathedral). Corporate Title: The Trustees of the Catholic Cathedral Church of Baltimore (The Basilica); Basilica of the Assumption Historic Trust, Inc. Established for the Preservation of the Basilica as a National Landmark of American Architecture. Rev. Msgr. Arthur F. Valenzano, Rector. In Res., Rev. Adam Parker.
The Archbishop's Residence—408 N. Charles St., 21201. Tel: 410-727-3564; Fax: 410-539-0407. Web: www.baltimorebasilica.org. Most Rev. Edwin F. O'Brien.
Parish Office—

14—ST. BENEDICT (1893) Rt. Rev. Paschal A. Morlino, O.S.B.; Deacon Edward Whitesell; Mrs. Maggie Barrick, Pastoral Coord.
Res.: 2612 Wilkens Ave., 21223. Tel: 410-947-4988; Fax: 410-947-6009. Email: pamorlino@aol.com. Web: www.saintbenedict.org.
Catechesis/Religious Program—Theresa Lingenfelter, D.R.E.; Mr. Kenneth Podowski, Youth Min. Students 38.

15—ST. BERNARD, (Korean), Closed. For parish records prior to 1989 contact the chancery office. For parish records past 1989 contact Holy Korean Martyrs, Baltimore.

16—ST. BERNARDINE (1928), (African American), Rev. Msgr. Edward M. Miller; Deacons Wardell Barksdale; Philip W. Harcum, (Retired).
Res.: 3812 Edmondson Ave., 21229. Tel: 410-362-8664; Fax: 410-945-0459. Email: stbernardine@archbalt.org. Web: www.stbernardinechurch.org.
Catechesis/Religious Program—618 Mt. Holly St., 21229. Tel: 410-362-8978. Beverly White, D.R.E. Students 122.

17—BLESSED SACRAMENT CHURCH (1911) Rev. Joseph L. Muth Jr.; Deacon Paul D. Shelton; Sr. Marie Mack, S.S.N.D., Pastoral Admin.
Res.: 4103 Old York Rd., 21218-1237. Tel: 410-323-0424; Fax: 410-323-4478. Email: blesssac@aol.com.
Catechesis/Religious Program—Students 7.

18—ST. BRIGID (1854) Rev. Joseph G. Bochenek; Bette Brocato, Pastoral Assoc.
Res.: 911 S. Ellwood Ave., 21224. Tel: 410-563-1717; Fax: 410-563-1776. Email: sbrigid@archbalt.org. Web: www.saintbrigid-canton.com.
Catechesis/Religious Program—Jo Ellen Shorb, C.R.E., Youth Min. Students 50.

19—ST. CASIMIR (1902) Rev. Dennis Grumsey, O.F.M.Conv.; Bernadette Vece, Pastoral Assoc. & Music Dir. In Res., Revs. Timothy Kulbicki, O.F.M.Conv.; Romuald Meogrossi, O.F.M.Conv.
Res.: 2736 O'Donnell St., 21224. Tel: 410-276-1981; Fax: 410-732-7436. Email: st.casimir@verizon.net. Web: www.stcasimir.org.
School—*St. Casimir Catholic School*, (Grades PreK-8), 1035 S. Kenwood Ave., 21224. Tel: 410-342-2681; Fax: 410-342-5715. Email: school@stcasimirschool.us. Web: www.stcasimirschool.us. Noreen Heffner, Prin. See separate listing.
Catholic Community at Relay— (1972) 5025 Cedar Ave., 21227. Tel: 410-247-4033; Fax: 410-247-2557. Email: admin@ccr.comcastbiz.net. Peg Mooney, Admin.; Geralyn Magan, Coord. Total Staff 2.

20—ST. CECILIA (1902), Twinned with Immaculate Conception, Baltimore. Rev. Sylvester Peterka, C.M.; Bro. William Stover, C.M., Pastoral Assoc.
Res.: 3300 Clifton Ave., 21216. Tel: 410-624-3600; Fax: 410-945-0157. Email: ourchurches@comcast.net.
Catechesis/Religious Program—Joseph Parham Sr., D.R.E. Students 39.

21—ST. CHARLES BORROMEO (Pikesville) (1848) [CEM] Rev. Msgr. Lloyd Aiken; Rev. Raymond C. Chase; Deacon Stephen R. Roscher; Christopher Welsh, Pastoral Assoc.
Res.: 101 Church Ln., 21208. Tel: 410-486-5400; Fax: 410-486-5421. Email: charlesst@comcast.net. Web: www.ourstcharles.org.
Catechesis/Religious Program—Betty Schmedes, Youth Min.; Donna Cooper, C.R.E. Students 92.

22—CHRIST THE KING (Dundalk) (1957) Closed. For inquiries for parish records please see St. Rita, Baltimore.

23—CHURCH OF THE IMMACULATE CONCEPTION (Towson) (1883) [CEM] Rev. Joseph F. Barr; Rev. Msgr. Edward J. Lynch, Pastor Emeritus (Retired); Rev. Stewart Bullock; Deacon Kevin F. Reid. In Res., Rev. T. Austin Murphy Jr.
Res.: 200 Ware Ave., Towson, 21204. Tel: 410-427-4700; Fax: 410-427-4795. Email: info@theimmaculate.org. Web: www.theimmaculate.org.
School—(Grades PreK-8), 112 Ware Ave., Towson, 21204. Mrs. Madeline Meaney, Prin.
Catechesis/Religious Program—*School of Religion* Students 140.

24—ST. CLARE (Essex) (1956) Revs. C. Lou Martin; Juan Vazquez-Rubio, O.SS.T.; Rev. Msgr. Thomas J. Tewes (Retired); Deacons Paul Mann, Pastoral Assoc.; Edison Morales, Hispanic Min.
Res.: 714 Myrth Ave., 21221-4898. Tel: 410-687-6011; Fax: 410-687-3054. Web: www.saintclare.org.
Catechesis/Religious Program—Tel: 410-686-7693; Fax: 410-687-2518. Mrs. Susan Bangert, C.R.E. Students 140.

25—ST. CLEMENT (Lansdowne) (1891) Deacon Paul A. Gifford, Pastoral Life Dir.; Revs. Thomas R. Malia; Jesus Aguirre. Serving the Spanish and English speaking communities of Lansdowne, Baltimore Highlands, Riverview, Lakeland, Westport, and Morrel Park.
Res.: 2700 Washington Ave., 21227. Tel: 410-242-1025; Fax: 410-242-1227. Web: www.stclement1.org.
Catechesis/Religious Program—Dan Miller, Youth Min. Students 80.

26—ST. CLEMENT MARY HOFBAUER (Rosedale) (1925) Rev. Donald Grzymski, O.F.M.Conv.; Deacons Nicholas Feurer; Francis Zeiler. In Res., Revs. Bernard Dudek, O.F.M. Conv.; Thomas E. Walsh, O.F.M.Conv.
Res. & Parish Office: 1212 Chesaco Ave., 21237. Tel: 410-686-6188; Fax: 410-686-6198. Email: parishoffice@stclementmh.org. Web: www.stclementmh.org.
School—(Grades PreK-8), 1216 Chesaco Ave., 21237. Tel: 410-686-3316. Email: inquiry@stclemmh.org. Web: www.stclemmh.org. Mrs. Pamela Walters, Prin. Lay Teachers 20; Students 308.
Catechesis/Religious Program—Tel: 410-391-5028. Mrs. Patricia Wagner, C.R.E. Email: pwagner@archbalt.org. Students 90.

27—CORPUS CHRISTI (1881) Rev. Martin H. Demek; Deacons Frank Hodges; Fritz Bauerschmidt; Ms. Betty W. Lafferty, Pastoral Assoc.; Daniel Meyer, Music Min.
Res.: 110 W. Lafayette Ave., 21217. Tel: 410-523-4161; Fax: 410-669-0349. Email: cchristi@archbalt.org. Web: www.corpuschristibaltimore.org.
Catechesis/Religious Program—Stephanie Roberts, D.R.E. Students 70.

28—ST. DOMINIC (1906) Rev. Ty S. Hullinger; Sr. Catherine Manning, S.S.N.D., Pastoral Assoc.; Deacon James L. Mann Jr.
Res.: 5302 Harford Rd., 21214. Tel: 410-426-0360; Fax: 410-444-6963. Email: stdominic@archbalt.org.
Catechesis/Religious Program—Tel: 410-426-0360. Susan Donnelly, D.R.E. Students 30.

29—ST. EDWARD (1880) Rev. Evod E. Shao, C.S.Sp.; Sr. Anita B. Smith, O.S.F., Pastoral Assoc.; Deacon Carl A. Anderson.
Res.: 901 Poplar Grove St., 21216-4350. Tel: 410-362-2000; Fax: 410-945-7113. Email: stedwardsparish@verizon.net. Web: www.stedwardschurchmd.org.
Catechesis/Religious Program—Dr. Cre Saundra Sills, D.R.E. Students 70.

30—ST. ELIZABETH OF HUNGARY (1895) Rev. Robert Sisk, T.O.R.
Mailing & Office Address: 2638 E. Baltimore St., 21224. Tel: 410-675-8260; Fax: 410-675-2530. Email: stliz1@comcast.net. Web: www.stelizabethofhungarychurchmd.org.
Res.: 2638 E. Baltimore St., 21224.
Catechesis/Religious Program—Students 20.

31—FOURTEEN HOLY MARTYRS, Closed. 1964. Parish records available at St. Martin Church. Tel: 410-947-1242.

32—ST. FRANCIS OF ASSISI (1927) Rev. Msgr. William F. Burke; Sr. Katherine Bell, R.S.M., Pastoral Assoc.
Res.: 3615 Harford Rd., 21218. Tel: 410-235-5136; Fax: 410-467-9503. Email: sfabalt@archbalt.org.
School—(Grades PreK-8), 3617 Harford Rd., 21218. Tel: 410-467-1683; Fax: 410-467-9449. Rebecca Malone, Prin. Lay Teachers 19; Students 233.
Catechesis/Religious Program—Sr. Katherine M. Bell, R.S.M., D.R.E.; Frederick Buettner, Dir. Youth Min. Students 50.

33—ST. FRANCIS XAVIER (1793) Revs. James E. McLinden, S.S.J.; Stanley K. Ihuoma, S.S.J.; Kenyatta Haridison, Music Min.
Res.: 1501 E. Oliver St., 21213. Tel: 410-727-3103; 410-727-3104; Fax: 410-625-9587. Email: j1mclinden@aol.com. Web: www.josephite.com/parish/md/sfx.
Catechesis/Religious Program—Tel: 410-837-0556. Sr. Magdala Marie Gillbert, O.S.P., D.R.E. Students 117.

34—ST. GABRIEL (1997), Formerly St. Lawrence and Our Lady of Perpetual Help, Woodlawn. Rev. Msgr. Thomas L. Phillips; Rev. Juan Vazquez-Rubio, O.SS.T., Hispanic Ministry.
Parish Office: 6950 Dogwood Rd., 21244-2658. Tel: 410-298-8888; Fax: 410-944-7409. Email: stgabriel@archbalt.org. Web: www.stgabrielch.org.
See John Paul Regional Catholic School, Inc., Baltimore under Elementary/Middle Schools, Private located in the Institution section.
Catechesis/Religious Program—Sr. Sonia Marie Fernandez, Dir. Christian Formation.

35—ST. GREGORY THE GREAT (1884), (African American), Rev. Msgr. Damien G. Nalepa; Sisters Anthonia Ugwu, O.S.P., Pastoral Assoc.; Mary Charlotte Marshall, O.S.P., Dir. Evangelization; Louise G. Tildon, Senior Pastoral Advisor; Gloria Williams, Social Outreach Dir.
Res. & Church: 1542 N. Gilmor St., 21217-2304. Tel: 410-523-0061; 410-523-0063; Fax: 410-669-1385. Email: sggreat@archbalt.org.
Catechesis/Religious Program—Shirley Hampton, C.R.E. Students 52.

36—HOLY CROSS (1858), (German), [CEM] Rev. Patrick Carrion; Deacon Richard Clemens; Sr. Vicki Staub, S.S.J., Dir. Ministry & Volunteers.
Res.: 110 E. West St., 21230. Tel: 410-752-8498; Fax: 410-752-2703. Web: www.southbaltcatholic.org.
Church: 108 E. West St., 21230.
Catechesis/Religious Program— Dorris van Gaal, Dir. Faith Formation. Students 35.

37—HOLY KOREAN MARTYRS (1989), (Korean), [CEM] Rev. Joseph Y. Kim.
Res.: 5801 Security Blvd., 21207. Tel: 410-265-8885; Fax: 410-265-1655. Email: kmartyrs@archbalt.org.
Catechesis/Religious Program—Students 165.

38—HOLY ROSARY (1887), (Polish), [CEM] Revs. Zdzislaw Nawrocki, S.Ch.; Richard Philiposki, S.Ch., Curator.
Res.: 408 S. Chester St., 21231. Tel: 410-732-3960; Fax: 410-675-4917. Web: www.holyrosarypl.org.
Catechesis/Religious Program—Students 35.

39—ST. IGNATIUS CHURCH (1856) Revs. William Watters, S.J.; Edward M. Ifkovits, S.J.; Deacon Paul Webber, Business & Plant Mgr.
Church: 740 N. Calvert St., 21202. Tel: 410-727-3848; Fax: 410-837-8883. Email: parish@st-ignatius.net. Web: www.st-ignatius.net.
Jesuit Community of St. Ignatius Parish: 102 E. Madison St., 21202. Tel: 410-727-8729.
School—St. Ignatius Loyola Academy, (Grades 6-8) Tel: 410-539-8268; Fax: 410-539-4821. John Ciccone, Pres.
Catechesis/Religious Program—Students 30.

40—IMMACULATE CONCEPTION (1850), (African American), Twinned with St. Cecilia, Baltimore. Rev. Sylvester Peterka, C.M.; Bro. William Stover, C.M., Pastoral Assoc. & Dir. Outreach.
Res.: 3300 Clifton Ave., 21216. Tel: 410-624-3600; Fax: 410-945-0157.
Catechesis/Religious Program—Debra Curry, D.R.E. Students 26.

41—IMMACULATE HEART OF MARY (Baynesville) (1948) Revs. Michael W. Carrion; James Risacher, Weekend Asst.; Emmanuel Fale, Weekend Asst.; Deacons John R. Martin; Kenneth Pivec; Garrett Brown, Dir. Outreach Min.
Res.: 8501 Loch Raven Blvd., 21286. Tel: 410-668-7935; Fax: 410-661-6560. Web: www.immaculateheartofmary.com.
School—(Grades PreK-8) Tel: 410-668-8466; Fax: 410-668-6171. Amy Belz, Prin. Lay Teachers 33; Students 505.
Catechesis/Religious Program—Tel: 410-661-3820; Fax: 410-661-3838. Amie Post, Dir. Faith Formation. Students 138.

42—ST. ISAAC JOGUES (1968) Rev. H. Martin Hammond; Sr. Patricia Tryon, S.N.D.deN., Pastoral Assoc.; Deacons Al Rose, (Retired); James Westwater; Frank O'Keefe.
Church Office: 9215 Old Harford Rd., 21234. Tel: 410-661-4888; Fax: 410-882-1484. Email: sij@archbalt.org. Web: www.sij.org.
Res.: 9400 Old Harford Rd., 21234.
Catechesis/Religious Program—Tel: 410-665-2561; 410-668-3686 Youth Ministry Office. Sr. John Francis Kearney, S.S.N.D., Dir. Faith Formation; Barbara Ward, Dir. Evangelization; Kenneth Goedeke Jr., Coord. Youth Ministry. Students 452.

43—ST. JAMES AND ST. JOHN, Closed. 1986. Parish records available at the Chancery. Tel: 410-547-5446.
See Queen of Peace Elementary Cluster, St. James and St. John School, Baltimore under Elementary Schools, Regional and Community located in the Institution section.

44—ST. JEROME (1887) Merged with St. Martin and St. Peter the Apostle, Baltimore to form Transfiguration Roman Catholic Church, Baltimore.

45—ST. JOHN GERMAN CATHOLIC CHURCH, Closed. in 1841. Original records, stored at The Catholic Center, are available to researchers on microfilm at the Maryland State Archives in Annapolis.

46—ST. JOHN THE EVANGELIST, Closed. in 1966. Parish records available at the Chancery. Tel: 410-547-5446.

47—ST. JOSEPH, Closed. in 1962. Parish records available at Holy Cross Rectory. Tel: 410-752-8498.

48—ST. JOSEPH (Fullerton) (1850), (German), [CEM] Rev. Msgr. Kevin T. Schenning; Rev. Roque G. Lim; Deacons William J. DeAngelis; Charles A. Baynes; William S. Albaugh. In Res., Rev. Msgr. A. Thomas Baumgartner (Retired).
Res.: 8420 Belair Rd., 21236. Tel: 410-256-1630; Fax: 410-529-2990. Web: www.stjoefullerton.org.
School—(Grades PreK-8), 8416 Belair Rd., 21236. Tel: 410-256-8026; Fax: 410-529-7234. Email: office@stjoefullerton.org. Web: www.stjoeschool.org. Mrs. Phyllis Karko, Prin. Lay Teachers 25; Students 490.
Catechesis/Religious Program—Lauren Arroyo, Youth Min. Students 421.

49—ST. JOSEPH PASSIONIST MONASTERY PARISH (1868) Rev. William Murphy, C.P.; Frank J. McGloin, Pastoral Assoc. In Res., Revs. Robert Carbonneau, C.P.; Alban Harmon, C.P.; Thomas McCann, C.P.; Bro. Edward Hall, C.P.
Res.: 251 S. Morley St., 21229. Tel: 410-566-0877; Fax: 410-233-4974. Email: info@sjmp.org. Web: www.sjmp.org.
Catechesis/Religious Program—Students 80.

50—ST. JUDE SHRINE (1917), (Italian), Revs. Louis F. Micca, S.A.C., Pastoral Dir.; Joseph Kuchar, S.A.C., Assoc. Pastoral Dir. In Res., Rev. John G. Biermann, S.A.C.
Res.: 308 N. Paca St., P.O. Box 1455, 21203. Tel: 410-685-6026; Fax: 410-244-5728.
St. Jude Shrine Corp.—512 W. Saratoga St., 21203. Tel: 410-685-6026. Web: www.stjudeshrine.org.

51—ST. KATHARINE OF SIENNA, Closed. in 1986. Parish records available at St. Wenceslaus Church. Tel: 410-675-7304.

52—ST. LAWRENCE (1962) Merged with The Shrine of Our Lady of Perpetual Help, Baltimore, to form St. Gabriel Parish, Baltimore. Records available at St. Gabriel Parish.

53—ST. LEO (1881), (Italian), Rev. Salvatore C. Furnari, S.A.C.; Sr. Mary Catherine Duerr, S.U.S.C., Pastoral Care.
Res.: 227 S. Exeter St., 21202-4451. Tel: 410-675-7275; Fax: 410-675-8292.
School—St. Casimir Catholic School, (Grades PreK-8), See separate listing., Tel: 410-685-8505. Noreen Heffner, Prin.
Catechesis/Religious Program—Mary Ann Blattermann, D.R.E.

54—LITTLE FLOWER, SHRINE OF (1926) Rev. Michael J. Orchik; Deacon Henry L. Siarkowski; Tony Magliano, Pastoral Assoc. In Res., Rev. James Miles.
Res.: 2854 Brendan Ave., 21213. Tel: 410-483-1700; Fax: 410-488-6482. Email: slflower@netzero.net.
Catechesis/Religious Program—Barbara G. Talley, C.R.E. Students 17.

55—ST. LUKE (Edgemere) (1888) Rev. Msgr. Joseph S. Lizor Jr.
Res.: 7517 North Point Rd., Edgemere, 21219-1499. Tel: 410-477-5200; Fax: 410-477-5996. Email: stlukromcathchur@yahoo.com. Web: www.stlukeedgemere.org.
School—Our Lady of Hope/St. Luke's School, (Grades PreK-8) Tel: 410-288-2793. Sr. Irene Mary Pryle, S.S.N.D., Prin.
Catechesis/Religious Program—Tel: 410-477-5201; Fax: 410-477-2022. Doris Lundin, C.R.E. Students 91.

56—ST. MARK (Catonsville) (1888) Rev. Christopher Whatley; Deacon Seigfried Presberry; Beth O'Connell, Health Care Min. In Res., Revs. Peter Tianzhi Chen; John L. Kelly (Retired).
Res.: 30 Melvin Ave., Catonsville, 21228. Tel: 410-744-6560; Fax: 410-747-3182. Email: smcatons@archbalt.org. Web: www.stmarkchurch-catonsville.org.
School—(Grades PreK-8), 26 Melvin Ave., 21228. Tel: 410-744-6560, Ext. 250; Fax: 410-747-3188. Email: mwarthen@stmark-school.org. Web: www.stmark-school.org. Mary Jo Warthen, Prin.
Catechesis/Religious Program—Anne Kidwell, D.R.E.; Rae Ellen Clegg, C.R.E. (Confirmation). Students 869.

57—ST. MARTIN (1865), (African American), Merged with St. Jerome and St. Peter the Apostle, Baltimore to form Transfiguration Roman Catholic Church, Baltimore.

58—ST. MARY OF THE ASSUMPTION (1849) [CEM] Rev. Patrick Besel; Deacon Miguel Sainz.
Res.: 5502 York Rd., 21212. Tel: 410-435-5900; Fax: 410-435-1287.
Catechesis/Religious Program—Miss Lisa O'Reily, D.R.E., Coord. Youth Min. Students 13.

59—ST. MARY, STAR OF THE SEA (1868) Rev. Patrick Carrion; Deacons Richard Clemens; George Russell.
Res.: 110 E. West St., 21230. Tel: 410-685-2255; Fax: 410-752-2703. Web: www.southbaltcatholic.org.
Catechesis/Religious Program—1528 E. Fort Ave., 21230. Tel: 410-752-8498. Dorris van Gaal, Dir. Faith Formation. Twinned with Holy Cross & Good Counsel Students 35.
Convent—Sisters of St. Joseph, 1410 Riverside Ave., 21230. Tel: 410-752-4344; Fax: 410-685-0692.

60—ST. MATTHEW (1949) Rev. Joseph L. Muth Jr.
Res.: 5401 Loch Raven Blvd., 21239. Tel: 410-433-2300; Fax: 410-433-5263. Email: stmattrc@verizon.net. Web: www.stmattrc.org.
See Cardinal Shehan School, Baltimore under Elementary Schools, Regional and Community located in the Institution section.
Catechesis/Religious Program—Tel: 410-444-4563; Fax: 410-444-6502. Email: reledym1@tripod.com. Students 90.
Convent—Comboni Missionary Sisters, 5405 Loch Raven Blvd., 21239. Tel: 410-323-1469; Fax: 410-323-9632. Email: sisters@comboniesrs.com. Web: www.combonisrs.com.
Immigration Outreach Services Center, Inc.—Tel: 410-323-8564; Fax: 410-323-8598. Email: jmkholloway@msn.com. Web: www.ioscbaltimore-.org.

61—ST. MICHAEL (Broadway) (1852), (Hispanic), Closed. For inquiries for parish records contact the chancery.

62—ST. MICHAEL (Overlea) (1914) Rev. James L. Sorra, Admin.; Deacon Henry C. Davis, Pastoral Assoc. Tel: 410-665-1054, Ext. 109. In Res., Rev. Msgr. Jay F. O'Connor. Tel: 410-665-1054, Ext. 152; Rev. Salvatore Livigni (Retired). Tel: 410-665-1054, Ext. 108.
Res.: 2 Willow Ave., 21206. Tel: 410-665-1054; Fax: 410-665-4024. Email: parish@smoverlea.org.
School—(Grades K-8), 10 Willow Ave., 21206. Tel: 410-668-8797; Fax: 410-663-9277. Mrs. Patricia Rohde Kelly, Prin. Tel: 410-668-8797, Ext. 122; Robert Wuenschel, Asst. Prin. Tel: 410-668-8797, Ext. 123. Lay Teachers 16; Students 395.
Catechesis/Religious Program—Nikki Lux, D.R.E. Tel: 410-668-8797, Ext. 106. Students 125.

63—ST. MILDRED CHURCH, Closed. in 1967. Parish records available at Our Lady of Hope Rectory. Tel: 410-284-6600.

64—ST. MONICA, Closed. 1959. Parish records available at the Chancery. Tel: 410-547-5446.

65—MOST PRECIOUS BLOOD (1948), Twinned with St.

Anthony of Padua, Baltimore. Revs. Ty S. Hullinger; Anthony Abiamiri; Deacons Joseph C. Krysiak; Joseph Schultz; Lisa O'Reilly, Pastoral Assoc. Office: 4414 Frankford Ave., 21206. Tel: 410-488-0400; Fax: 410-488-0032. Email: sapmpb@comcast.net. Web: www.stampb.org.
Church: 5010 Bowleys Ln., 21206.
Catechesis / Religious Program—Rev. Anthony Abiamiri, D.R.E. Twinned with St. Anthony of Padua, Baltimore.

66—New All Saints (1912), (African American), Rev. Donald A. Sterling.
Res.: 4408 Liberty Heights Ave., 21207. Tel: 410-542-0445; Fax: 410-542-8852. Email: office@newallsaintschurch.org. Web: www.naschurch.org.
Catechesis / Religious Program—Laura Thomas, D.R.E. Tel: 410-542-0445, Ext. 148; Kirk Johnson, Dir. Youth Ministry. Tel: 410-542-0445, Ext. 139. Students 35.

67—Our Lady of Fatima (1951) Revs. Arthur Gildea, C.Ss.R.; Richard K. Poetzel, C.Ss.R.; Bro. DeSales Zimpfer, C.Ss.R.; Sr. Julianne Hau, M.H.S.H., Pastoral Assoc.; Deacon Alphonse Bankard III. In Res., Revs. Edwin Foley, C.Ss.R.; Jack Fiske, C.Ss.R.
Res.: 6420 E. Pratt St., 21224. Tel: 410-633-9393; Fax: 410-631-7239; 410-633-8699.
Catechesis / Religious Program—Tel: 410-633-6526. Sr. Rita Dorn, S.S.N.D., D.R.E. Students 47.

68—Our Lady of Good Counsel (1859) Rev. Patrick Carrion; Deacons Richard Clemens; George Russell. Office: 1532 E. Fort Ave., 21230. Tel: 410-752-0205; Fax: 410-576-0929. Web: www.southbaltcatholic.org.
Catechesis / Religious Program—Fax: 410-752-2703. Dorris van Gaal, Dir. Faith Formation. Students 35.

69—Our Lady of Hope (1967) Rev. William F. Franken; Deacon Herman S. Wilkins.
Res.: 1727 Lynch Rd., 21222. Tel: 410-284-6600; Fax: 410-282-9361. Email: lhope@archbalt.org. Web: www.ourladyofhopedundalk.com.
School—(Grades PreK-8), 8003 N. Boundary Rd., 21222. Tel: 410-288-2793; Fax: 410-288-2850. Email: olhsls@aol.com. Web: www.olhsls.com. Sr. Irene Mary Pryle, S.S.N.D., Prin. School Sisters of Notre Dame 2; Lay Teachers 24; Students 311.
Catechesis / Religious Program—8003 N. Boundary Rd. Tel: 410-282-3120; Fax: 410-282-9361. Mrs. Bonnie Nagel, Youth Min. Students 155.
Convent—8001 N. Boundary Rd., 21222. Tel: 410-282-3800; Fax: 410-288-2850. School Sisters of Notre Dame

70—Our Lady of La Vang (2000) Rev. Joseph Chuc Tran.
335 Sollers Point Rd., 21222. Tel: 410-282-1497; Fax: 410-282-1497. Email: olol_baltimore@yahoo.com. Web: www.olol-baltimore.net.
Catechesis / Religious Program—Duong Nguyen, D.R.E.

71—Our Lady of Lourdes, Closed. 1995. Parish records available at The New All Saints Church. Tel: 410-542-0445.

72—Our Lady of Mount Carmel (Middle River) (1887) Rev. Msgr. Robert L. Hartnett; Rev. John Rapisarda; Deacon Charles A. Baynes, Pastoral Assoc.
Res.: 1704 Old Eastern Ave., 21221. Tel: 410-686-4972; Fax: 410-574-8785. Web: www.parish.olmcmd.org.
Catechesis / Religious Program—Tel: 410-238-1167; Fax: 410-574-8785. Caroline Hemling, D.R.E.; Missy Lawrence, Youth Min. Students 187.

73—Our Lady of Perpetual Help (1936) Merged with St. Lawrence, Baltimore, to form St. Gabriel Parish, Baltimore. Records available at St. Gabriel.

74—Our Lady of Pompei (1924) Rev. Luigi Esposito. Res.: 3600 Claremont St., 21224. Tel: 410-675-7790; Fax: 410-563-9067. Email: lpompei@archbalt.org. Web: www.olpmd.org.
School—Archbishop Borders School, (Grades PreK-8), 201 S. Conkling St., 21224. Tel: 410-276-6534; Fax: 410-276-6915. Ms. Mary Catherine Marshal, Prin. Lay Teachers 10; Students 160.
Catechesis / Religious Program—Mrs. Dorothy Locco, D.R.E.

75—Our Lady of Sorrows, Closed. 1935. Parish records available at Holy Cross Rectory. Tel: 410-752-8498.

76—Our Lady of the Angels Catholic Community (Catonsville) (1993), Service senior citizens w/in community. Rev. Leo J. Larrivee, S.S.; Sisters Eileen McKeever, S.S.N.D., Pastoral Assoc.; Patricia Huesman, S.S.N.D., Pastoral Assoc.; Deacon Jack Coster.
Mailing Address: 711 Maiden Choice Ln., Catonsville, 21228. Tel: 410-247-4779; Fax: 410-737-8826. Email: llarrive@archbalt.org.

77—Our Lady of Victory (Arbutus) (1952) Rev. Timothy Klunk; Deacon William Jauquet.
Res.: 4414 Wilkens Ave., 21229. Tel: 410-242-0131; 410-242-0180; Fax: 410-242-6963. Email: ol.victory@verizon.net. Web: www.olvictory.org.
School—(Grades PreK-8), 4416 Wilkens Ave., 21229. Tel: 410-242-3688; Fax: 410-242-8867. Thomas E. Riddle, Prin. Lay Teachers 24; Students 475.
Catechesis / Religious Program—Tel: 410-242-9533. Email: smithgl@mail.olvschool.com. Gloria Smith, D.R.E. Students 57.

78—Our Lady, Queen of Peace (1953), (Middle River) Rev. Kevin A. Mueller; Deacon Gerald Anthony Roberts. In Res., Rev. Paul C. Sparklin.
Res.: 10003 Bird River Rd., 21220. Tel: 410-686-3085; Fax: 410-687-1916. Email: qpeace@archbalt.org. Web: www.olqpmd.org.
Catechesis / Religious Program—Tel: 410-686-3085, Ext. 120; Fax: 410-687-1916. Kathy Shadrach, C.R.E.; Debbie Boblitz, C.R.E. Students 98.

79—St. Patrick, Closed. Now a Mission of Sacred Heart of Jesus, Baltimore.

80—St. Paul's (1888) Closed. Parish records available at St. Francis Xavier. Tel: 410-727-3103.

81—St. Peter Claver (1888), (African American), Rev. Ray P. Bomberger, S.S.J.
Res.: 1546 N. Fremont Ave., 21217. Tel: 410-669-0512; Fax: 410-383-8227. Email: spclaver@verizon.net.
Catechesis / Religious Program—Dorothy Kutcherman, D.R.E.; Ernestine Watkins, Youth Min. Students 54.

82—St. Peter the Apostle (1842) Merged with St. Jerome and St. Martin, Baltimore to form Transfiguration Roman Catholic Church, Baltimore.

83—SS. Philip and James (1897) Rev. Carleton Parker Jones, O.P.; Ron Meyers, Pastoral Assoc.
Res.: 2801 N. Charles St., 21218. Tel: 410-235-2294; Fax: 410-243-5262. Email: info@philipandjames.org. Web: www.philipandjames.org.
Catechesis / Religious Program—

84—St. Pius V (1878), (African American), [JC] Rev. Ray P. Bomberger, S.S.J.
Res.: 907 Edmondson Ave., P.O. Box 16550, 21217-0550. Tel: 410-669-0512; Fax: 410-383-8227. Email: stpiusv@archbalt.org.
Catechesis / Religious Program—Mrs. Jean Brent, D.R.E.; Sonja Smith, Youth Min.; Michael Smith, Youth Min. Students 11.

85—St. Pius X (1957) Carol J. Pacione, Pastoral Life Dir. Tel: 410-427-7515; Rev. Samuel Lupico (Retired). Tel: 410-427-7508.
Parish Office—6428 York Rd., 21212. Tel: 410-427-7500; Fax: 410-377-2651.
School—(Grades PreK-8), 6432 York Rd., 21212. Tel: 410-427-7400; Fax: 410-377-9738. Email: principal@stpius10.org. Mrs. Massie Dates, Prin. Lay Teachers 29; Students 402; School Sisters of Notre Dame 3.
Catechesis / Religious Program—Tel: 410-427-7500. Mrs. Pinky Howard, Dir. Adult & Family Min.; Amy Buttarazzi, Dir. Children's Ministry. Tel: 410-427-7511; Mark Parchment, Dir. Youth Ministry. Tel: 410-427-7517. Students 240.

86—St. Rita (1922) Deacons John Langmead, Pastoral Life Dir. Tel: 410-284-0388, Ext. 18; George T. Evans.
Res.: 2907 Dunleer Rd., 21222. Tel: 410-284-0388; Fax: 410-284-3998.
Catechesis / Religious Program—Tel: 410-284-7355. Sr. Michael Marie Hartman, I.H.M., Adult Faith Formation. Tel: 410-284-0388, Ext. 15. Students 85.

87—St. Rose of Lima (1914) Rev. Robert A. DiMattei Jr. In Res., Rev. Charles F. Klein.
Res.: 3803 4th St., 21225. Tel: 410-355-8515; Fax: 410-354-3392. Email: strose@archbalt.org. Web: www.stroseparish.org.
Catechesis / Religious Program—Mary Beth Barnes, D.R.E.; Lee Quinn, Youth Min. Students 43.

88—Sacred Heart of Jesus (1873) Revs. Robert Wojtek, C.Ss.R.; Gerard J. Knapp, C.Ss.R.; Andrew Carr, C.Ss.R.; Uriel Useda, C.Ss.R.; Deacons James S. Clack; Edison Morales; Richard D. Novak. In Res., Rev. John Bauer, C.Ss.R.; Bro. Raphael Rock, C.Ss.R.
Res.: 600 S. Conkling St., 21224-4203. Tel: 410-342-4336; Fax: 410-522-2022. Email: shjesus@archbalt.org.
Catechesis / Religious Program—Olga E. Diaz, D.R.E. & RCIA Coord. Students 45.
Mission—St. Patrick (Broadway) (1792) Bank St. & Broadway, 21231. Email: smikepat95@hotmail.com.

89—Sacred Heart of Mary (1925) [CEM] Rev. George J. Gannon, Admin.; Rev. Msgr. Richard E. Parks, Pastor Emeritus (Retired); Bro. William Ciganek, C.F.X.; Deacon Douglas P. Kendzierski.
Res.: 6736 Youngstown Ave., 21222-1097. Tel: 410-633-2828; Fax: 410-633-0349. Email: stmary@archbalt.org. Web: www.shmparish.org.
Catechesis / Religious Program—Michael Demski, D.R.E.; Noel Fell, Youth Coord. Students 123.

90—Shrine of the Sacred Heart (Mt. Washington) (1867) Rev. William A. Au. Tel: 410-466-6884, Ext. 12; Sr. Carol Czyzewski, F.S.S.J., Pastoral Assoc. Tel: 410-466-6884, Ext. 15; Deacon Mark Soloski. Tel: 410-466-6884, Ext. 13.
Res.: 1701 Regent Rd., 21209. Tel: 410-466-6884; Fax: 410-664-0523. Email: shshrine@archbalt.org. Web: www.theshrine.org.
Catechesis / Religious Program—Tel: 410-466-6884, Ext. 14. Bernetta Palaslk, Dir. Faith Formation. Tel: 410-466-6884, Ext. 16. Students 168.

91—St. Stanislaus Kostka (1880), (Polish), Closed. For inquiries for parish records please contact St. Casimir, Baltimore. Tel: 410-276-1981; 732-7436 (fax).

92—St. Thomas Aquinas (1867) Rev. Silvester Kim, Admin.; Deacon Richard W. Montalto.
Res.: 1008 W. 37th St., 21211. Tel: 410-366-4488; Fax: 410-366-8352. Email: staquinas@archbalt.org. Web: www.stthomasaquinasbaltimore.parishesonline.com.
Catechesis / Religious Program— Susan Sousa, C.R.E.; Annemarie Vallonga, Youth Min. Students 40.

93—St. Thomas More (1961) Rev. Brian A. Zielinski, O.Praem.; Deacon Michael P. McCoy; Sr. Kathleen Haughey, S.N.D., Pastoral Assoc.
Parish Center & Mailing Address: 6806 McClean Blvd., 21234. Tel: 410-444-6500; Fax: 410-444-6502.
See Cardinal Shehan School, Baltimore under Elementary Schools, Regional and Community located in the Institution section.
Catechesis / Religious Program—Tel: 410-444-4563. Suzannah M. Keating, D.R.E. & Youth Ministry. Students 39.

94—Transfiguration Catholic Community (2004) Rev. Augustine Etemma Inwang, M.S.P. (Nigeria). Office: 775 W. Hamburg St., 21230. Tel: 410-685-5044 (Office); Fax: 410-625-2406. Email: spabalt@archbalt.org.
Res.: *St. Ambrose Friary*, 4502 Park Heights Ave., 21215. Tel: 410-685-5044.
Catechesis / Religious Program—Mary O'Shiro, C.R.E. Students 84.

95—St. Ursula (Parkville) (1937) Rev. Stephen E. Hook; Rev. Msgr. A. Thomas Baumgartner, Pastor Emeritus (Retired); Revs. Lawrence P. Adamczyk; Emmanuel T. Mensah; Deacons Richard F. Morris; Frank Rongione Sr.; Robert G. Keenan; Michael R. Baxter. In Res., Rev. Gerald Hynes, C.P. (Retired).
Res.: 8801 Harford Rd., 21234. Tel: 410-665-2111; Fax: 410-665-0758. Email: stursula@comcast.net. Web: www.stursulaparish.org.
Catechesis / Religious Program—Tel: 410-655-4106. Laura Wetherington, D.R.E. Tel: 410-377-5323; Betty Schmedes, Dir. Youth Ministry. Tel: 410-882-3910. Students 716.

96—St. Veronica (1945), (African American), Very Rev. Donald M. Fest, S.S.J.; Deacon Jhan Harris.
Res.: 806 Cherry Hill Rd., 21225. Tel: 410-355-7466; Fax: 410-355-7741.
Catechesis / Religious Program—Jackie Wise, Youth Min.; Reyward Pinckney, Youth Min. Students 108.

97—St. Vincent de Paul (1841) [CEM] Rev. Richard T. Lawrence.
Res.: 120 N. Front St., 21202-4804. Tel: 410-962-5078; Fax: 410-962-8427. Web: stvchurch.org.
St. Vincent de Paul Church Historic Trust, Inc.—Tel: 410-962-5078.
Jonestown Planning Council, Inc.—Tel: 410-962-5078.
Jonestown Day Care Center, Inc.—
Catechesis / Religious Program—Students 55.

98—St. Wenceslaus (1872) Rev. Peter A. Lyons, T.O.R. In Res., Rev. Jordan Hite, T.O.R.
Res.: 2111 Ashland Ave., 21205. Tel: 410-675-7304; Fax: 410-675-5746. Web: www.stwen.org.
See Queen of Peace Elementary Cluster, St. James and St. John School, Baltimore under Elementary Schools, Regional and Community located in the Institution section.
Catechesis / Religious Program—Students 43.

99—St. William of York (1914) Rev. Michael DeAscanis.
Res.: 600 Cooks Ln., 21229. Tel: 410-566-2140; Fax: 410-362-5475. Email: swybalt@archbalt.org. Web: www.stwilliamofyorkchurch.org.
Catechesis / Religious Program—Tel: 410-566-6152. Peggy Mrozek, D.R.E. (Children); Wayne Hipley, Youth Min. Students 45.

OUTSIDE METROPOLITAN BALTIMORE

Aberdeen, Harford Co., St. Joan of Arc (1920) Rev. William Foley; Deacon Daniel Kopczyk.
Office: 222 S. Law St., 21001. Tel: 410-272-4535; 410-575-6909; Fax: 410-272-9025. Email: parish@stjoanarc.org.
Res.: 223 S. Law St., 21001.
School—(Grades K-8), 230 S. Law St., 21001. Tel: 410-272-1387; Fax: 410-272-1959. Email: school@stjoanarc.org. Dr. Jane Towery, Prin. Lay

Teachers 16; Students 199.
Catechesis/Religious Program—Tel: 410-272-6944. Students 152.

ABINGDON, HARFORD CO., ST. FRANCIS DE SALES (1866) [CEM] Rev. Charles M. Wible; Deacons Richard Stine; James C. Sullivan; Alex Rodriguez; Beth Marchiano, Parish Mgr.
Res.: 1450 Abingdon Rd., 21009. Tel: 410-676-5119; 410-679-4555; Fax: 410-676-7520. Email: sfabing@archbalt.org. Web: www.stfrancisabingdon.org.
Catechesis/Religious Program—Tel: 410-676-3354. Doris McKibbon, Dir. Preschool; Elizabeth Taneyhill, Dir. Evangelization & Adult Catechesis; Betty Burlin, Coord. High School Catechesis & Sacramental Prep (9-12); Patrick Perkins, Coord. Middle School Catechesis; Diane Lewis, C.R.E. Elementary Catechesis & Youth Minister. Students 700.

ANNAPOLIS, ANNE ARUNDEL CO.

1—ST. ANDREW BY THE BAY (Annapolis) (1981) Rev. Jeffrey S. Dauses; Deacons James C. Monaghan Jr., Pastoral Assoc.; David Tengwell; Mr. Zachary Stachowski, Music Min. & Liturgy.
Parish Center—701 College Pkwy., 21409. Tel: 410-974-4366; Fax: 410-974-4339. Email: sabbanna@archbalt.org. Web: www.standrewbythebay.org.
Catechesis/Religious Program—Erin Tate, C.R.E.; Mrs. Stephany Crane, A.R.E.; Lisa Franceschini, Youth Min. Students 609.

2—ST. MARY (1853) [CEM] Revs. John G. Tizio, C.Ss.R.; Blas Caceres, C.Ss.R.; Andrew Costello, C.Ss.R.; Patrick Flynn, C.Ss.R.; Daniel Francis, C.Ss.R.; Eric Hoog, C.Ss.R.; Fabio Mavin Morales, C.Ss.R.; John Harrison, C.Ss.R.; Joseph Krastel, C.Ss.R.; Kevin Milton, C.Ss.R.; Deacons Leroy S. Moore; Anthony F. Norcio. In Res., Rev. Alphonsus Olive, C.Ss.R.
Res.: 109 Duke of Gloucester St., 21401. Tel: 410-263-2396; 410-269-6092; Fax: 410-263-3027.
School—(Grades K-8), 111 Duke of Gloucester St., 21401. Tel: 410-263-2869; Fax: 410-269-6513. Rebecca McNealey, Prin. Sisters 1; Lay Teachers 47; Students 814.
High School—113 Duke of Gloucester St., 21401. Tel: 410-263-3294; Fax: 410-269-7843. Richard Bayhan, Prin. School Sisters of Notre Dame 1; Lay Teachers 37; Students 486.
Catechesis/Religious Program—Tel: 410-990-4779; Fax: 410-263-7381. Stephen Beard, D.R.E. Students 1,498.
Convent—4 Shipwright St., 21401. Tel: 410-269-0568. School Sisters of Notre Dame 2.
Mission—St. John Neuman 620 N. Bestgate Rd., Anne Arundel Co. 21401. Tel: 410-266-2498; Fax: 410-266-2497.

BEL AIR, HARFORD CO., ST. MARGARET (1905) Rev. Msgr. G. Michael Schleupner; Revs. Francis X. Callahan, Pastor Emeritus (Retired); John Cunningham; C. Douglas Kenney; Mrs. Mary Ellen Bates, Business Mgr.; Michael Britt, Music Mgr.; Jane O'Hara, Outreach Coord.; Deacons Patrick J. Goles; Victor Petrosino; Martin E. Wolf; John Chott; James DeCapite; Steven Roth.
Res.: 141 Hickory Ave., 21014. Tel: 410-838-6969; Fax: 410-879-2518. Web: www.stmargaret.org.
School—(Grades PreK-8), 205 Hickory Ave., 21014. Tel: 410-879-1113. Email: smsch@archbalt.org. Madeleine Hobik, Prin. Lay Teachers 30; Students 863.
Catechesis/Religious Program—Tel: 410-838-4224. Mrs. Marge Troilo, C.R.E. Preschool; Kristin Rupprecht, Youth & Young Adult Ministry Coord.; Marie DeKowski, C.R.E. Students 1,600.
Mission—St. Mary Magdalen 1716 Churchville Rd., Harford Co. 21015.

BOONSBORO, WASHINGTON CO., ST. JAMES BOONSBORO ROMAN CATHOLIC CONGREGATION, INC. (2008) Rev. John J. Jicha; Paul Schmitt, Liturgical Ministry.
121 N. Main St., 21713. Tel: 301-432-2887. Email: johnjjicha@gmail.com. Web: www.stjamesmd.org.
Catechesis/Religious Program—Brigitte Schmidt, C.R.E.

BRADSHAW, BALTIMORE CO., ST. STEPHEN (1863) [CEM] Revs. Lawrence F. Kolson; Paul Breczinski; Deacons Frank R. Laws; Timothy D. Maloney.
Res.: 8030 Bradshaw Rd., 21087. Tel: 410-592-7071; Fax: 410-592-6803. Email: ststephen@archbalt.org. Web: www.ststephenbradshaw.org.
School—(Grades PreK-8), 8028 Bradshaw Rd., 21087. Tel: 410-592-7617; Fax: 410-592-7330. Email: sssch@archbalt.org. Mrs. Mary M. Patrick, Prin. Lay Teachers 25.
Catechesis/Religious Program—Tel: 410-592-8666. Sr. Angela DeFontes, O.S.F., D.R.E.; Kellie Reynolds, Coord. Youth & Young Adult Min. Students 402.

BRUNSWICK, FREDERICK CO., ST. FRANCIS OF ASSISI (1893) [CEM] Deacons Lawrence P. Teixeira, Pastoral Life Dir.; Chuck McCandless; Faye Williams, Business Mgr.
Res.: 113 First Ave., 21716. Tel: 301-834-9185; Fax: 301-834-4162. Email: office@stfrancis-stmary.org. Web: www.stfrancis-stmary.org.
Catechesis/Religious Program—Patricia Martz, Faith Formation Admin. Students 90.
Mission—St. Mary's Petersville, Frederick Co. 21758.

BUCKEYSTOWN, FREDERICK CO., ST. JOSEPH-ON-CARROLLTON MANOR (1811) [CEM] Rev. Lawrence K. Frazier; Deacon Gregory Rausch.
Mailing Address: P.O. Box 33, 21717. Tel: 301-663-0907; Fax: 301-874-0247. Email: office@stjoesbuckeystown.org. Web: www.stjoesbuckeystown.org.
Res.: 5843 Manor Woods Rd., Frederick, 21703.
Catechesis/Religious Program—Tel: 301-663-0907, Ext. 12; Fax: 301-874-0247. Therese Ivanisin, D.R.E.; Ashley Arominski, Coord. Youth Ministry; Jeanne Geisinger, Faith Formation Asst. Students 354.

CLARKSVILLE, HOWARD CO., ST. LOUIS (1855) [CEM] Rev. Msgr. Joseph L. Luca; Rev. P. Gregory Rapisarda; Deacons Fred L. Mauser; Matthew A. Podniesinski; Marianne M. Faulstich, Pastoral Assoc.; Mary S. Helfrich, Dir. Devel.
Res.: 12500 Clarksville Pike, 21029. Tel: 410-531-6040; Fax: 410-531-6191. Email: parishoffice@stlouisparish.org. Web: www.stlouisparish.org.
School—(Grades PreK-8) Tel: 410-531-6664; Fax: 410-531-6690. Web: www.stlouisparish.org/school. Mrs. Mary Theresa Weiss, Prin. Sisters 1; Lay Teachers 27; Students 475.
Catechesis/Religious Program—Tel: 410-531-6688; Fax: 410-531-6689. Web: www.stlouisparish.org/reled. Victoria Yozwiak, D.R.E.; Patrick Sprankle, Dir. Youth Ministry. Students 1,330.

COCKEYSVILLE, BALTIMORE CO., ST. JOSEPH (1852) [CEM] Rev. Msgr. Paul G. Cook; Rev. Gonzalo Cadavid-Rivera; Sr. Rose Lindner, S.S.N.D., Pastoral Assoc.; Deacon Edward Sulivan; Ann Marie Labin, Pastoral Assoc. & Parish Nurse.
Res.: 101 Church Ln., 21030. Tel: 410-683-0600; Fax: 410-628-2956.
School—(Grades K-8), 105 Church Ln., 21030. Fax: 410-628-6814. Terrance Golden, Prin. Sisters 2; Lay Teachers 25; Students 406.
Catechesis/Religious Program—Fax: 410-628-6814. Marie Lybolt, D.R.E.; Kathleen Paul, Youth & Young Adult Ministry. Students 442.

COLUMBIA, HOWARD CO., ST. JOHN THE EVANGELIST (1967) Revs. Gerard J. Bowen. Tel: 410-964-1425, Ext. 315; Ferdinand Ezenwachi. Tel: 410-964-1425, Ext. 313; Leandro Fazolini, Hispanic Ministry. Tel: 410-964-1425, Ext. 320; Deacon James J. Benjamin. Tel: 410-730-1543.
5885 Robert Oliver Pl., 21045. Tel: 410-964-1434.
Interfaith Centers—10431 Twin Rivers Rd., 21044. Tel: 410-964-1425; Fax: 410-730-9253. Web: www.sjerc.org. (Wilde Lake)
Catechesis/Religious Program—Tel: 410-964-1440. Wyman A. Scott IV, D.R.E., Youth & Young Adults. Tel: 410-964-1425, Ext. 316; Kathleen Armstrong, D.R.E.; Mr. Peter Barbernitz, Evangelization. Tel: 410-964-1430. Students 490.

CRESAPTOWN, ALLEGANY CO., ST. AMBROSE (1886) [CEM] Closed. For inquiries for parish records contact the chancery.

CROFTON, ANNE ARUNDEL CO., ST. ELIZABETH ANN SETON (1976) Rev. Edward C. Connelly. Tel: 410-721-5770, Ext. 234; Sr. Katherine O'Donnell, R.S.M., Pastoral Assoc. Tel: 410-721-5770, Ext. 233; Deacon Frederick Seibold; Mr. Jack O'Malley, Administrative Assoc. Tel: 410-721-5770, Ext. 227.
Office: 1800 Seton Dr., 21114. Tel: 410-721-5770; Fax: 410-721-5508. Email: setonparish@seaton.org. Web: www.seaseton.org.
See School of the Incarnation, Inc., Gambrills under Elementary Schools, Regional and Community located in the Institution section.
Catechesis/Religious Program—Tel: 410-721-5774. Michael MacDonald, Coord. Youth Ministry. Tel: 410-721-5774, Ext. 229; Nancy Connell, Admin. Faith Formation. Tel: 410-721-5774, Ext. 222. Students 280.

CUMBERLAND, ALLEGANY CO.

1—ST. MARY (1900), (Italian), [CEM] Closed. For inquiries for parish records contact the chancery.

2—OUR LADY OF THE MOUNTAINS, ROMAN CATHOLIC CONGREGATION, INC. 2011, (Irish), [CEM] Revs. Gregory Chervenak, O.F.M.Cap.; Stephen Fernandes, O.F.M.Cap.; Bernard Finerty, O.F.M-.Cap. Tel: 301-777-3131, Ext. 6; Eric Gauchat, O.F.M.Cap., Catholic Health Care Ministry. Tel: 301-777-3131, Ext. 7; Deacons Fred Passauser, Parish Mgr.; David A. Conley, (Retired); Loren Mooney; Francis L. Werner Jr.; Teresa Files, Exec. Asst. to Pastor & Parish Mgr.
Res.: 201 N. Centre St., 21502. Tel: 301-777-1750; Fax: 301-777-2669. Email: spcumber@archbalt.org.
School—Bishop Walsh School, (Grades PreK-12), 700 Bishop Walsh Rd., 21502. Tel: 301-724-5360. Shelby Webb, Prin.
Catechesis/Religious Program—Tel: 301-724-0288. Monica Beck, C.R.E.; Mary Ann Daley, Coord. Youth Ministry. Tel: 301-777-3131, Ext. 2. Students 74.
Convent—School Sisters of Notre Dame, 209 N. Centre St., 21502.

3—ST. PATRICK, Merged For inquiries for parish records contact Our Lady of the Mountains, Cumberland.

4—SS. PETER AND PAUL (1848), (German), [CEM] Closed. For inquiries for parish records contact the chancery.

DAVIDSONVILLE, ANNE ARUNDEL CO., HOLY FAMILY (1929) Rev. Andrew Aaron; Deacon Thomas W. Beales.
Res.: 826 W. Central Ave., P.O. Box 130, 21035-0130. Tel: 410-269-0586; 301-261-7399; Fax: 410-798-5315. Email: office@hfccmail.org. Web: www.holy-familychurch.com.
See School of the Incarnation under Elementary Schools, Regional and Community located in the Institution section.
Catechesis/Religious Program—Tel: 410-798-5680. Sharon Graham, A.R.E. Tel: 410-798-5680, Ext. 30; Meg O'Neill, Adult Enrichment Coord. Tel: 410-798-5680, Ext. 34; Jonathan Benitez, Youth Min. Tel: 410-798-5680, Ext. 33. Students 576.

EDGEWATER, ANNE ARUNDEL CO., OUR LADY OF PERPETUAL HELP (1976) Rev. Joseph J. Cosgrove. Tel: 443-203-1002, Ext. 16; Deacon Stephen H. Cooley.
Res.: 515 Loch Haven Rd., 21037. Tel: 443-203-1002; Fax: 410-798-0076. Web: www.olph.net.
See School of the Incarnation, Gambrills under Elementary Schools, Regional and Community in the Institution Section.
Catechesis/Religious Program—Patricia Dixon, A.R.E. Tel: 443-203-1002, Ext. 14. Students 125.

EDGEWOOD, HARFORD CO., PRINCE OF PEACE (1977) Rev. Jack Ward.
Office Address—2600 Willoughby Beach Rd., 21040-3412. Tel: 410-679-5912; Fax: 410-676-0326. Email: ppedgewd@archbalt.org.
Catechesis/Religious Program—Sr. Susanne Bunn, M.H.S.H., Dir. Faith Formation. Students 84.

ELLICOTT CITY, HOWARD CO.

1—OUR LADY OF PERPETUAL HELP (1893) [CEM] Revs. Erik J. Arnold; McLean Cummings; Sr. Lorraine McGraw, O.S.F., Pastoral Assoc. Tel: 410-747-4334, Ext. 314; Lisa Sliker, Parish Admin.
Res.: 4795 Ilchester Rd., 21043-6898. Tel: 410-747-4334; Fax: 410-747-4399. Email: olphparish@archbalt.org. Web: www.olphparish.org.
School—(Grades K-8), 4801 Ilchester Rd., Elliott City, 21043. Tel: 410-744-4251; Fax: 410-788-5210. Rose Goeres, Prin. Lay Teachers 22; Students 230.
Catechesis/Religious Program—Tel: 410-747-0131; Fax: 410-788-8905. Mrs. Judy Gruel, D.R.E.; Mrs. Kristen Fisher, Youth Min. (Middle School); Erin White, Dir. Youth Ministry (High School). Students 561.

2—ST. PAUL (1838) [CEM] Revs. Matthew T. Buening; Thomas J. Donaghy (Retired); Deacon Joseph E. Knepper; Patricia Frederick, Pastoral Assoc.
Res.: 3755 St. Paul St., 21043. Tel: 410-465-1670; Fax: 410-313-8551. Email: parish_office@stpaulec.org. Web: www.stpaulec.org.
Catechesis/Religious Program—Tel: 410-465-0622. Becky Clark, Youth Min. Students 237.

3—RESURRECTION (1974) Rev. Msgr. John A. Dietzenbach. Tel: 410-461-9111, Ext. 202; Rev. Warren V. Tanghe; Deacons Ray H. Britt, (Retired); John Comegna. In Res., Rev. Edward S. Szymanski, Chap. Howard Co. General Hospital.
Office: 3175 Paulskirk Dr., 21042-2698. Tel: 410-461-9111, Ext. 201; Fax: 410-203-9419.
School—Resurrection/St. Paul, (Grades K-8), 3155 Paulskirk Dr., 21042-2698. Tel: 410-461-9111, Ext. 242; Fax: 410-461-8621. Karen Murphy, Prin. Lay Teachers 32; Students 452.
Catechesis/Religious Program—Tel: 410-461-9111, Ext. 221. Kate Kleintank, D.R.E. Tel: 410-461-9111, Ext. 222; Laura Nisonger, A.R.E. Tel: 410-461-9111, Ext. 223; Martha Bode, Dir. Adult Education. Tel: 410-461-9111, Ext. 204; Fernando Cartagena, Youth Min. Tel: 410-461-9111, Ext. 206. Students 820.

EMMITSBURG, FREDERICK CO.

1—ST. ANTHONY SHRINE (1805) [CEM] Ms. Barbara Anderson, Pastoral Life Dir.; Deacon John A. Hawkins.
Res. & Office Address: 16150 St. Anthony Rd., 21727. Tel: 301-447-2367; Fax: 301-447-3618. Email: sasolmc@archbalt.org. Web: www.emmitsburg.net/sasolmc.
Catechesis/Religious Program—Tel: 301-271-4099; Fax: 301-271-7127. Sr. M. Valent Rusin, F.S.S.J., D.R.E. & Pastoral Min. Students 36.

2—ST. JOSEPH (1793) [CEM 2] Revs. John J. Holliday, C.M.; Charles F. Krieg, C.M.; Stephen P. Trzecieski, C.M., Chap.; Deacon Robert L. Baker. In Res., Rev.

Robert J. Prior, C.M., Chap. St. Elizabeth Ann Seton Shrine.
Res.: 47 DePaul St., 21727. Tel: 301-447-2326; Fax: 301-447-3579. Email: stjosephemmitsburg@comcast.net. Web: www.stjosephemmitsburg.org.
Catechesis/Religious Program—Rina Roca, Dir. Faith Formation; Roberta Alvarez, Coord. Youth Ministry. Students 110.

FALLSTON, HARFORD CO., ST. MARK (1887) Rev. Gerard C. Francik; Deacons Charles W. Hicks, (Retired); Marty Perry; Mrs. Charlotte Henderson, Pastoral Assoc.
Mailing Address: 2407 Laurel Brook Rd., 21047.
Res.: 812 Reckord Rd., 21047. Tel: 410-879-9110; Fax: 410-877-0576.
Catechesis/Religious Program—Tel: 410-879-1706; Fax: 410-877-3502. Mrs. Bridgit Goedekl, Catechetical Leader. Students 554.

FREDERICK, FREDERICK CO.

1—ST. JOHN THE EVANGELIST (1763) [CEM] Rev. Msgr. Richard J. Murphy; Rev. Miguel Mateo, S.F.; Deacons John L. Manley; Daniel C. Roff; Michael J. Currens.
Res.: 112 E. Second St., 21701. Tel: 301-662-8288; Fax: 301-698-1832. Email: parish@stjohn-frederick.org. Web: www.stjohn-frederick.org.
See St. John Regional Catholic School, Frederick under Elementary Schools, Regional and Community located in the Institution section.
Catechesis/Religious Program—Tel: 301-662-6722; Fax: 301-695-7024. Julie St. Croix, D.R.E., Elementary and Family Catechesis; Irene Wunderlich, Dir. Youth Min.; Ms. Amy Spessard, Dir. Evangelization. Students 387.

2—ST. KATHARINE DREXEL ROMAN CATHOLIC CONGREGATION, INC. (2000) Rev. Keith W. Boisvert; Deacons Jeff Sutterman; Doug Nathan; Leah Huber, Pastoral Assoc.; Brian McCrohan, Pastoral Assoc.; Barbara Miller, Pastoral Assoc.; Kathy Moore, Pastoral Assoc.
8428 Opossumtown Pike, 21702. Tel: 301-360-9581; Fax: 301-360-9582. Email: stkatharinedrexel@saintdrexel.org. Web: www.saintdrexel.org.
Catechesis/Religious Program—Laura Weber, D.R.E. Students 175.

FROSTBURG, ALLEGANY CO., ST. MICHAEL (1852) [CEM] Revs. Richard Gray, Temp. Admin.; Eric Gauchat, O.F.M.Cap., Sacramental Min.; Deacons W. Frederick Passquer, Pastoral Assoc.; Harold C. Bradley.
Res.: 44 E. Main St., 21532. Tel: 301-689-6767; Fax: 301-689-6411. Email: smfrostb@archbalt.org.
Catechesis/Religious Program—Tel: 301-689-2898. Camilla Rawe, C.R.E.; Kathleen Broadwater, Coord. Youth Ministry. Students 95.

FULTON, HOWARD CO., ST. FRANCIS OF ASSISI (1988) Rev. Dennis P. Diehl; Deacon Joseph McKenna; Berta Sabrio, Dir. Liturgy & Music; Tracey Eberhardt, Dir. Health Ministry.
Office: 8300 Old Columbia Rd., 20759. Tel: 410-792-0470; Fax: 410-792-0472. Email: office@instrumentofpeace.org. Web: www.instrumentofpeace.org.
Catechesis/Religious Program—Becki Kaman, Youth Min. Students 491.

GAMBRILLS, ANNE ARUNDEL CO., CHURCH OF THE HOLY APOSTLES (2004) Rev. James P. Kiesel; Sr. Angela Case, S.S.J., Asst. for Community Life & Adult Prog.; Deacon Keith D. Chase; Katie Jenkins, Asst. Music Min.
Res.: 1755 Urby Dr., Crofton, 21114. Web: www.holyapostlesmd.org.
See School of the Incarnation, Inc., Gambrills under Elementary Schools, Regional and Community located in the Institution section.
Church of the Holy Apostles Roman Catholic Congregation, Inc.—Tel: 410-519-2291; Fax: 410-519-2299.
Catechesis/Religious Program—Michele Dougherty, Faith Formation, Sacramental Prep & Youth Ministry. Students 200.

GLEN BURNIE, ANNE ARUNDEL CO.

1—CHURCH OF THE GOOD SHEPHERD (1972) Rev. Msgr. Richard J. Bozzelli; Revs. John L. Kelly, Pastor Emeritus (Retired); Jesse L. Bolger.
Res.: 1451 Furnace Ave., 21060. Tel: 410-761-4607; Fax: 410-761-6019. Email: goodshepherd9@comcast.net. Web: www.goodshepherdgb.org.
See Arthur Slade Regional Catholic School, Glen Burnie under Elementary Schools, Regional and Community located in the Institution section.
Catechesis/Religious Program—Students 48.

2—CRUCIFIXION, CHURCH OF THE (1972) Rev. Msgr. Richard J. Bozzelli; Rev. Jesse L. Bolger.
Rectory—100 Scott Ave., 21060. Tel: 410-768-4880; Fax: 410-768-5025.
Catechesis/Religious Program—Tel: 410-766-5070 (Holy Trinity).

3—HOLY TRINITY (1919) Rev. Msgr. Richard J. Bozzelli; Revs. Jesse L. Bolger; J. Kevin Farmer; Anthony Adawu (Ghana); Goddswill Agbagwa; Brandon Carr (Retired); Sydney Griffith; Joseph McDonough; Deacon Kevin T. Brown; Lou Costanzo, Business Mgr. In Res., Rev. Jesus Aguirre Guzman, (Diocese of Oruro).
Res.: 7436 Baltimore-Annapolis Blvd., 21061. Tel: 410-766-1214. Email: office@holytrinitycc.org. Web: www.holytrinitycc.org.
Parish Center—126 Dorsey Rd., 21061. Tel: 410-766-5070; Fax: 410-760-6738.
See Monsignor Slade Catholic School, Glen Burnie under Elementary Schools, Regional and Community located in the Institution section.
Catechesis/Religious Program—Tel: 410-768-3890; Fax: 410-760-6738. Pat Stanley, D.R.E. (PreK-5); Joyce Pagan, Youth Min. Students 500.

GLYNDON, BALTIMORE CO., SACRED HEART (1873) Rev. Msgr. Lloyd Aiken; Rev. Marc L. Lanoue; Sr. Judith Cianfrogna, S.S.J., Pastoral Assoc.; Deacons James A. Ryan; Stephen D. Cotter; Sr. Helen Wiegmann, S.S.J., Health Care Ministry.
65 Sacred Heart Ln., P.O. Box 3672, 21071-3672. Tel: 410-833-1696; Fax: 410-833-2676. Email: parish@shgparish.org. Web: www.shgparish.org.
School—(Grades PreK-8), 63 Sacred Heart Ln., P.O. Box 3672, 21071-3672. Tel: 410-833-0857; Fax: 410-833-0914. Email: school@shgschool.org. Web: www.shgsc.org. Mrs. Sherri Wright, Prin. Sisters 1; Lay Teachers 39; Students 775.
Catechesis/Religious Program—Tel: 410-833-8515. Sisters Karen Washabaugh, S.S.J., D.R.E.; Cecilia Cyford, S.S.J., D.R.E. Students 574.
Convent—Sacred Heart, 81 Sacred Heart Ln., P.O. Box 3672, 21071-3677. Tel: 410-526-1327.

GRANTSVILLE, NORTHERN GARRETT CO., ST. ANN (1976) Rev. Richard Gray, Temp. Admin.; Deacon W. Frederick Passauer, Pastoral Assoc.
c/o St. Michael, 44 E. Main St., Frostburg, 21532.
Res.: 12814 New Germany Rd., 21536. Tel: 301-689-6767; Fax: 301-689-6411. Email: sagrants@archbalt.org.
Catechesis/Religious Program—Camilla Rawe, C.R.E.; Kathleen Broadwater, Youth Min. Students 37.

HAGERSTOWN, WASHINGTON CO.

1—ST. ANN (1966) Revs. Martin S. Nocchi; Christopher P. Moore, Admin.; Deacons William Nairn; Richard M. Kunkel, (Retired); Gary Fulmer.
Res.: 12817 Cathedral Ave., 21742. Tel: 301-791-2727. Email: church@stannchurch.com. Web: www.stannhagerstown.parishesonline.com.
Church: 1525 Oak Hill Ave., 21742. Tel: 301-733-0410; Fax: 301-733-6218.
Catechesis/Religious Program—Tel: 301-733-0410, Ext. 20. Rita Mahoney, Adult Faith Formation Coord.; Theresa Prymuszewski, Faith Formation. Students 284.

2—ST. JOSEPH (1951) Rev. Christopher P. Moore.
Res.: 17630 Virginia Ave., 21740-7829. Tel: 301-797-9445; Fax: 301-797-2490. Email: stjoe319@verizon.net. Web: www.parishesonline.com/stjosephhagerstown.
Catechesis/Religious Program—Tel: 301-790-1610. Denise Kuhna, D.R.E.; Neil Becker, Youth Min.; Angie Viar, Office Mgr. Students 160.

3—ST. MARY (1790) Revs. J. Collin Poston; James Nirappel.
Res.: 224 W. Washington St., 21740. Tel: 301-739-0390; Fax: 301-739-7082. Email: church@saintmarysonline.org. Web: www.saintmarysonline.org.
School—(Grades K-8), 218 Washington St., Hagertown, 21740. Tel: 301-733-1184; Fax: 301-745-4997. Web: www.stmarycatholicschool.org. Mrs. Patricia McDermott, Prin. School Sisters of Notre Dame 2; Lay Teachers 24; Students 260.
Catechesis/Religious Program—Tel: 301-790-2444. Jan McCarter, D.R.E. Students 166.
Mission—St. Michael 31 S. Martin St., Clear Spring, Washington Co. 21722.

HANCOCK, WASHINGTON CO., ST. PETER'S (1834) [CEM] Rev. John J. Lombardi, Admin.
Res. & Mailing Address: 16 E. High St., 21750. Tel: 301-678-6339; Fax: 301-678-6608. Email: officestpeter@verizon.net.
Mission—St. Patrick's (1860) [CEM] 12517 St. Patrick Rd., S.E., Little Orleans, Allegany Co. 21766.
Catechesis/Religious Program—Miss Susan Taylor, A.R.E. Students 85.

HAVRE DE GRACE, HARFORD CO., ST. PATRICK'S (1847) [CEM] Rev. William J. O'Brien III; Sr. Frances Schiminsky, O.S.F., Pastoral Assoc.; Mary Wancowicz, Admin.; Richard Allen, Dir. Music; Paschal J. Venanzi, Business Mgr.
Res.: 615 Congress Ave., 21078. Tel: 410-939-2525; 410-575-6741; Fax: 410-575-6490. Email: sphgrace@archbalt.org.
Catechesis/Religious Program—Tel: 410-939-2544. Nancy Elder, A.R.E. Students 145.

HICKORY, HARFORD CO., ST. IGNATIUS (1792) [CEM] Rev. Msgr. James Barker; Revs. Stephen Sutton; Hector Mateus-Ariza; Deacons Ralph Trautwein, Pastoral Assoc.; Peter J. Calabrese; Lee A. Benson; Deborah Czawlytko, Pastoral Assoc. & Parish NurseWeb: www.stignatiushickory.org; James Foxwell, Dir. Music Min. In Res., Rev. Kennard Muller (Retired).
Res.: 533 E. Jarrettsville Rd., Forest Hill, 21050-1603. Tel: 410-879-1926; 410-838-2106; Fax: 410-879-1352.
Catechesis/Religious Program—Tel: 410-879-9390. Robert Kovacs, Dir. Adult Faith Formation; Doris Wheeler, A.R.E.; Cetta York, Coord. Family Ministry; Susan Strickroth, C.R.E.; Susanna Bredehoeft, Dir. Youth Min. Students 1,280.

HUNT VALLEY, BALTIMORE CO., CATHOLIC COMMUNITY OF ST. FRANCIS XAVIER (1988) Rev. Frank J. Brauer; Rev. Msgr. Thomas J. Donellan, Pastor Emeritus; Deacon Donald Murray.
13717 Cuba Rd., P.O. Box 407, 21030. Tel: 410-785-0356; Fax: 410-785-1628. Email: info@ccsfx.net. Web: www.ccsfx.org.
Catechesis/Religious Program—Patricia Allshouse, C.R.E.; Ms. Joanie Carlson, Coord. Middle School; Mr. John Mojzisek, Youth Min. Students 445.

HYDES, BALTIMORE CO., ST. JOHN THE EVANGELIST (1822) [CEM] Rev. Msgrs. Richard E. Cramblitt; Richard W. Woy; Deacon Frederick X. Schoennagel Jr.
13305 Long Green Pike, 21082. In Res., Most Rev. William C. Newman (Retired).
Res.: 6536 Cherry Hill Rd., Baldwin, 21013. Tel: 410-817-9693. Email: sjehydes@sjehydes.org. Web: www.stjohnhydes.org.
Catechesis/Religious Program—M. Theresa Konitzer, D.R.E.; Mrs. M. Colleen Sisolak, Youth & Young Adult Ministry; Christopher Deaver, Dir. Adult Faith Formation. Students 427.

IJAMSVILLE, FREDERICK CO., ST. IGNATIUS OF LOYOLA (1983) Rev. Michael J. Jendrek. Tel: 301-695-8845, Ext. 206; Deacons Larry Matheny; David J. Ebner; Paul Szczerowski, Music Min.
Office: 4103 Prices Distillery Rd., 21754. Tel: 301-695-8845; Fax: 301-695-0259. Email: pastor@e-stignatius.org. Web: www.e-stignatius.org.
Res.: 4914 Bush Creek Dr., Monrovia, 21770. Tel: 301-865-5783.
See St. John Regional Catholic School, Frederick under Elementary Schools, Regional and Community located in the Institution section.
Catechesis/Religious Program—Carol Smith, Coord. Faith Formation & Youth Ministry. Tel: 301-695-8845, Ext. 210. Students 764.

JESSUP, ANNE ARUNDEL CO., ST. LAWRENCE MARTYR (1866) [CEM] Revs. Victor Scocco, O.SS.T.; Binoy Akkalayil, O.SS.T.; Deacon John Sedlevicius. In Res., Rev. Alfonso Serna, O.SS.T.
Res.: 7669 Clark Rd., Hanover, 21076. Tel: 410-799-1970; Fax: 410-799-1143. Email: office@stlawrencemartyr.org. Web: www.saint-lawrencemartyr.org.
See Arthur Slade Regional Catholic School, Glen Burnie under Elementary Schools, Regional and Community located in the Institution section.
Catechesis/Religious Program—St. Lawrence School of Religion, P.O. Box 1188, 2821 Jessup Rd., 20794. Tel: 410-799-7790; Fax: 410-799-7291. Mrs. Valerie Magnuson, D.R.E. Students 76.

JOPPA, HARFORD CO., CHURCH OF THE HOLY SPIRIT (1963) Rev. Joseph C. Simmons.
Res.: 540 Joppa Farm Rd., 21085. Tel: 410-679-2191; Fax: 410-679-2874. Email: hspiritchurch@aol.com. Web: www.hspiritchurch.org.
Catechesis/Religious Program—Tel: 410-679-5912. Sr. Susanne Bunn, M.H.S.H., Dir. Faith Formation. Students 99.

LAUREL, ANNE ARUNDEL CO., RESURRECTION OF OUR LORD (1968) Rev. Mark Bialek, Admin.; Daniel Pereira, Dir. Music; Kathleen Leddy, Office Mgr.
Res.: 407 Forest Bridge Ct., 20724. Tel: 301-498-7107; Fax: 410-792-8337. Email: rollaure@archbalt.org. Web: www.resurrectionofourlord.com.
Office Address: 8402 Brock Bridge Rd., 20724. Tel: 410-792-7982; Fax: 410-792-8337. Email: office@resurrectionofourlord.com. Web: www.resurrectionofolurlord.com.
Catechesis/Religious Program—Tel: 301-498-9803. Students 174.

LIBERTYTOWN, FREDERICK CO., ST. PETER (1821) [CEM] Rev. Jason Worley; Deacons Michael Misulia; John R. Martin; Gerald B. Jennings.
P.O. Box 278, 21762.
Res.: 9201 Green Valley Rd., 21762. Tel: 301-898-5111 (Office); 301-898-9069 (Rectory); Fax: 301-898-0465. Web: www.stpeters-libertytown.org.
9190 Church St., 21762.
Catechesis/Religious Program—Anne Mason, C.R.E. (Children); Ms. Caroline Nolan, C.R.E. (Adults); Kenn DeMoll, C.R.E. (Youth). Students 713.

LINTHICUM HEIGHTS, ANNE ARUNDEL CO., ST. PHILIP NERI (1964) Rev. Dale Picarella; Deacon Robert Keeley.
Parish Center—6405 S. Orchard Rd., 21090-2628. Tel: 410-859-0571; Fax: 410-859-5047. Email: info@stphilip-neri.org. Web: www.saintphilipchurch.org.
School—(Grades K-8), 6401 Orchard Rd., 21090. Tel: 410-859-1212; Fax: 410-859-5480. Email: spnschool@archbalt.org. Kate Daley, Prin. Lay Teachers 24; Students 389.
Catechesis/Religious Program—Tel: 410-859-4950, Ext. 224; 410-859-0571, Ext. 224 (Rel. Ed. Office). Hilary Bateman, Dir. Youth Ministry. Students 310.

LONACONING, ALLEGANY CO., ST. MARY OF THE ANNUNCIATION (1865) [CEM] Closed. For inquiries for parish records contact the chancery.

MANCHESTER, CARROLL CO., ST. BARTHOLOMEW (1864) Rev. Michael J. Roach.
Mailing Address & Parish Center: 3071 Park Ave., 21102. Tel: 410-239-8881.
Res.: 2940 Park Ave., P.O. Box 448, 21102-0448. Tel: 410-239-8207; Fax: 410-239-3216.
Catechesis/Religious Program—Thomas Abbott, C.R.E. (Adult); Lynn Szymanski, C.R.E.; Linda Sterner, Youth Coord. Students 466.

MIDDLETOWN, FREDERICK CO., HOLY FAMILY CATHOLIC COMMUNITY (1986) Rev. Msgr. Robert J. Jaskot; Rev. John Charles Moore, Pastor Emeritus (Retired); Deacon George Sisson.
Res.: 3240 Old National Pike, 21769. Tel: 301-371-3239.
Church & Mailing Address: 7321 Burkittsville Rd., 21769. Tel: 301-473-4800; Fax: 301-371-6810. Email: info@hfccmd.org. Web: www.hfccmd.org.
Catechesis/Religious Program—Mr. Ricardo Valdez, Dir. Faith Formation; Carolyn Kilonsky, Coord. Youth Ministry. Email: ckilonsky@hfccmd.org. Students 522.

MIDLAND, ALLEGANY CO., ST. JOSEPH (1891), (Irish), [CEM] Revs. Richard Gray, Temp. Admin.; Eric Gauchat, O.F.M.Cap., Sacramental Min.; Deacons W. Frederick Passauer, Pastoral Assoc.; Harold C. Bradley.
Mailing Address: 19925 Church St., P.O. Box 1, 21542. Tel: 301-463-6770; Fax: 301-463-6729. Email: stjoemid@archbalt.org.
Catechesis/Religious Program—Kathleen Broadwater, C.R.E. & Youth Ministry. Students 23.

MILLERSVILLE, ANNE ARUNDEL CO., OUR LADY OF THE FIELDS (1902) [CEM] Rev. G. Eugene Nickol. Tel: 410-923-7016; Deacons Anthony Grillo; Edward J. Stoops; Nancy Manstof, Parish Mgr. Tel: 410-923-7002.
1070 Cecil Ave. S., 21108. Tel: 410-923-6070; Fax: 410-923-6978. In Res., Rev. Jose Opalda.
Res.: 1069 S. Cecil Ave., 21108. Tel: 410-987-1551; Fax: 410-987-9723. Email: lfields@archbalt.org. Web: www.ourladyofthefields.org.
See School of the Incarnation, Inc., Gambrills under Elementary Schools, Regional and Community located in the Institution section.
Catechesis/Religious Program—Tel: 410-923-2195. Donna Fischer, D.R.E. Tel: 410-923-6953; Scott Link, Coord.Youth Min. Tel: 410-923-6955; Sue Dobrzykowski, Coord. Adult Faith Formation. Tel: 410-923-6954. Students 1,052.

MOUNT SAVAGE, ALLEGANY CO., ST. PATRICK (1863) [CEM] Closed. For inquiries for parish records contact the chancery.

OAKLAND, GARRETT CO., ST. PETER THE APOSTLE (1852) [CEM] Rev. Donald J. Parson; Deacon Donald P. Battista.
Res.: 208 S. Fourth St., 21550. Tel: 301-334-2202; Fax: 301-334-9006. Web: www.catholicchurchofsoutherngarrettcounty.org.
Catechesis/Religious Program—Betty Eaton, D.R.E. Students 67.
Mission—St. Peter at the Lake Deep Creek Lake, Garrett Co. Dolores Gloeckl, Lake Center Coord.

ODENTON, ANNE ARUNDEL CO., ST. JOSEPH (1924) Rev. William L. Viola; Deacons C. Richard Swann, (Retired); David A. Page.
Mailing Address & Church: 1283 Odenton Rd., 21113. Tel: 410-551-9238; Fax: 410-674-4761. Email: parish@sjodenton.org. Web: www.stjosephodenton.org.
See School of the Incarnation, Inc., Gambrills under Elementary Schools, Regional and Community located in the Institution section.
Catechesis/Religious Program—Patricia Dieterich, A.R.E. Students 236.

PARKTON, BALTIMORE CO., OUR LADY OF GRACE (1974) Rev. Samuel V. Young; Sr. Mary Therese White, O.S.F., Pastoral Assoc.
Res.: 425 Everett Rd., Monkton, 21111. Fax: 410-329-6830. Web: www.olgrace.com.
Parish Center—18310 Middletown Rd., 21120. Tel: 410-329-6826; Fax: 410-329-6830. Email: ehagner@ourladygrace.org.
Catechesis/Religious Program—Dr. Jack Buchner, Faith Formation Pastoral Assoc.; Deborah Webber, Coord. Youth Ministries. Students 472.

PASADENA, ANNE ARUNDEL CO.

1—ST. JANE FRANCES DE CHANTAL (Riviera Beach) (1946) Rev. Msgr. Carl F. Cummings; Deacon Robert Vlcej.
Res.: 8499 Virginia Ave., 21122-3097. Tel: 410-255-4646; Fax: 410-437-5191. Web: www.stjane.org.
School—(Grades PreK-8), 8513 Saint Jane Dr., 21122. Tel: 410-255-4750; Fax: 410-360-6720. Mrs. Michelle Jones, Prin.; Renee Hammond, Vice Prin. Lay Teachers 23; Students 574.
Catechesis/Religious Program—Tel: 410-437-4727. Katie Torrey, C.R.E.; Claire Horvath, Youth Ministry Coord.; Betsey Green, Music Min. Students 361.

2—OUR LADY OF THE CHESAPEAKE (1980) Rev. Brian M. Rafferty; Jack Streb, Coord. Liturgical Ministries; Mary Laber, Community Outreach; Judy Glinka, Admin. Asst.; Patricia Hild, Sec.
Church: 8325 Ventnor Rd., 21122. Tel: 410-255-3677; Fax: 410-437-7527. Email: info@olchesapeake.org. Web: www.olchesapeake-.org.
See Arthur Slade Regional Catholic School, Glen Burnie under Elementary Schools, Regional and Community in the Institution Section.
Catechesis/Religious Program—Fax: 410-437-7527. Carole Dowell, Faith Formation; Mr. Brian Harrison, Rel. Formation; Tim Janiszewski, Youth Ministry. Students 456.

POPLAR SPRINGS, HOWARD CO., ST. MICHAEL (1879) [CEM] Revs. Michael J. Ruane; Kurt J. Klismet, O.SS.T., Weekend Asst.; Deacons Harbey Santiago; Clifford L. Britton; Judy Turner, Liturgy Coord.
Res.: 1200 St. Michaels Rd., Mount Airy, 21771-3202. Tel: 410-489-4211; 410-442-2845. Email: smpoplar@archbolt.org. Web: www.stmichaelspoplarsprings.org.
Parish Center—Tel: 410-489-7667; 410-442-1717; Fax: 410-442-1486. Email: smpoplar@archbalt.org. Web: www.stmichaelspoplarsprings.org.
Catechesis/Religious Program—Tel: 410-489-7667; Fax: 410-442-1486. Stacey Ford, D.R.E.; Theodore P. Burkhardt, Youth & Young Adult Ministry; Joann Wozniak, A.R.E. Students 820.

PYLESVILLE, HARFORD CO., ST. MARY (1855) [CEM] Rev. A. Henry Kunkel III; Deacons Simon M. Driesen; Gary Dumer Jr.; Phillip Seneschal; Barbara Sadler, Business Mgr.; Diana Weidner, Admin. Asst.
Res.: 1021 St. Mary's Rd., 21132. Tel: 410-838-7471; 410-452-5166; 410-879-4015; Fax: 410-452-8493. Web: www.stmaryspylesville.org.
Catechesis/Religious Program— Janet Young, Coord. Faith Formation; Rachel Bittner, Youth Min. Students 353.

RANDALLSTOWN, BALTIMORE CO., HOLY FAMILY (1876) [CEM] Revs. Andrew S. Mohl; Walter J. McGovern (Retired); Dennis W. Kast, Business Mgr. Tel: 410-922-3800. In Res., Rev. Msgr. William A. Collins (Retired).
Res., Church & Office: 9531 Liberty Rd., 21133. Tel: 410-922-3800; Fax: 410-922-3804.
Catechesis/Religious Program—9531 Liberty Rd., 21133. Tel: 410-922-2805. Students 107.

SEVERN, ANNE ARUNDEL CO., ST. BERNADETTE (1972) Rev. Michael A. Murphy; Ann McDonald, Pastoral Life Dir. Tel: 410-969-2785; Andrea Montrose, Pastoral Assoc. Tel: 410-969-2872.
Res.: 801 Stevenson Rd., 21144. Tel: 410-969-2783; Fax: 410-969-2789. Web: www.stbernadette.org.
See Arthur Slade Regional Catholic School, Glen Burnie under Elementary Schools, Regional and Community located in the Institution section.
Catechesis/Religious Program—Tel: 410-969-2786. Pat Radford, C.R.E. Email: pradford@stbernadette.org; Carolyn Matthews, D.R.E.; Marge Sholl, Coord. Youth Ministry. Students 225.

SEVERNA PARK, ANNE ARUNDEL CO., ST. JOHN THE EVANGELIST (1927) Revs. James Proffitt; Michael Foppiano; Deacons Ronald Thompson; Dean Lopata; Joanne Ibex, Music Min. Email: jibex@stjohnsp.org. In Res., Rev. Msgr. John J. Auer (Retired).
Res.: 689 Ritchie Hwy., S.E., 21146. Tel: 410-647-4884; Fax: 410-544-3047. Web: www.stjohnsp.org.
School—(Grades K-8), 669 Ritchie Hwy., 21146. Tel: 410-647-2283; Fax: 410-431-5438. Sr. Linda Larsen, S.S.J., Prin. Sisters of St. Joseph, Chestnut Hill 5; Lay Teachers 30; Students 460.
Catechesis/Religious Program—Tel: 410-647-4892; Fax: 410-431-8912. John Poland, D.R.E.; Jen Mayer, Adult Faith Formation. Tel: 410-647-4892, Ext. 2155. Email: jmayer@stjohnsp.org; Cassandra Anderson, Youth Min. Tel: 410-647-3346, Ext. 2153. Email: canderson@stjohnsp.org. Students 770.
Convent—679 Ritchie Hwy., 21146. Tel: 410-647-2041. Sisters of St. Joseph 6.

SYKESVILLE, CARROLL CO., ST. JOSEPH (1868) [CEM] Revs. Terence P. Weik, S.M.; Paul A. Reich, S.M.; George Onida, S.M.; Neville O'Donohue, S.M.; Deacons Michael Dvorak; Karl Bayhi; Robert LeBlanc, Liturgy & Music Min.
Office: 915 Liberty Rd., 21784. Tel: 443-920-9191; Fax: 443-920-9192. Email: parishoffice@saintjoseph.cc. Web: www.stjosepheldersburg.org.
Res.: 6049 Kennard Ct., Eldersburg, 21784. Tel: 410-795-2722.
Catechesis/Religious Program—Tel: 410-552-5402; Fax: 410-795-7516. Nora Rozelle, D.R.E. (First Sacraments); Jackie Antkowiak, Adult Formation. Students 1,295.

TANEYTOWN, CARROLL CO., ST. JOSEPH (1797) [CEM] Rev. Msgr. Martin E. Feild; Deacons Darrell W. Smith; Stanley Wise, (Retired).
Res.: 44 Frederick St., 21787. Tel: 410-756-2500; Fax: 410-756-1260. Email: sjtaney@archbalt.org.
Catechesis/Religious Program—Tel: 410-876-8108. Terry A. Smith, C.R.E. Students 182.

THURMONT, FREDERICK CO., OUR LADY OF MOUNT CARMEL (1856) [CEM] Rev. John F. Lesnick; Ms. Barbara Anderson, Parish Life Dir.; Sr. M. Valenta Rusin, F.S.S.J., Pastoral Min. & Dir. Rel. Educ.; Deacon John A. Hawkins.
Office: 16150 St. Anthony Rd., Emmitsburg, 21727. Tel: 301-447-2367; Fax: 301-447-3618. Email: sasolmc@archbalt.org. Web: www.emmitsburg.net/sasolmc.
Church: 103 N. Church St., 21788.
Catechesis/Religious Program—18 N., Altamont Ave., 21788. Tel: 301-271-4099; Fax: 301-271-7127. Sr. M. Valent Rusin, F.S.S.J., Pastoral Min./DRE. Tel: 301-271-4099. Students 94.

TIMONIUM, BALTIMORE CO., CHURCH OF THE NATIVITY (1968) Rev. Michael White; Tom Corcoran, Pastoral Assoc.
20 E. Ridgely Rd., 21093. Tel: 410-252-6080; Fax: 410-252-2657. Web: www.churchnativity.tv.
Catechesis/Religious Program—Students 562.

WALKERSVILLE, FREDERICK CO., ST. TIMOTHY (1980) Deacon Jim Barth; Linda Lebo, Music & Liturgy Coord. Tel: 301-845-8041.
200 Glade Blvd., 21793.
Church: 8651 Biggs Ford Rd., 21793. Tel: 301-845-8043; Fax: 301-845-4902.
Catechesis/Religious Program—Tel: 301-845-8025. Yvette Leith, D.R.E.; Jim Schrader, A.R.E. Coord.; Marissa Alspaugh, Dir. Youth Faith Formation. Students 275.

WEST RIVER, ANNE ARUNDEL CO., OUR LADY OF SORROWS (1866) [CEM] Rev. Mark Logue.
Res.: 101 Owensville Rd., 20778. Tel: 410-867-2059; Fax: 410-867-8276. Email: frmark@olos.us. Web: www.olos.us.
Catechesis/Religious Program—Tel: 410-867-1941. Mary Catherine Haines, D.R.E. Students 309.

WESTERNPORT, ALLEGANY CO., ST. PETER (1857) [CEM] Revs. Richard Gray, M.S.S.A., Temp. Admin.; Eric Gauchat, O.F.M.Cap., Sacramental Min.; Deacons W. Frederick Passauer, Pastoral Assoc.; Harold C. Bradley.
Res.: 127 Church St., 21562. Tel: 301-359-3055; Fax: 301-359-0657. Email: stpeter127@verizon.net.
Catechesis/Religious Program—Tel: 301-359-9832. Kathleen Broadwater, C.R.E. & Youth Ministry; Doug Baker, D.R.E. Students 71.
Mission—St. Gabriel Barton, 21521.

WESTMINSTER, CARROLL CO., ST. JOHN (1853) [CEM] Rev. Msgr. James P. Farmer; Revs. Louis A. Bianco; Lawrence P. Adamczyk; Deacons Donald W. Miller; Joseph M. Cinquino; Mark Ripper; Paul G. Cooke; William Fallon.
Res.: 43 Monroe St., 21157. Tel: 410-848-4744; 410-876-2248; Fax: 410-857-1519. Email: sjwestmi@archbalt.org. Web: www.sjwest.org.
Catechesis/Religious Program—Tel: 410-848-8443. Paul D. Gallagher, D.R.E.; Jordan Tippett, C.R.E (5-8); Bethany Fischer, D.R.E. (Confirmation). Students 968.

WILLIAMSPORT, WASHINGTON CO., ST. AUGUSTINE (1854) Revs. John J. Jicha; John T. Carter, Pastor Emeritus (Retired); Rev. Msgr. Alfred E. Smith, Pastor Emeritus (Retired).
Res.: 32 E. Potomac St., 21795. Tel: 301-223-7959; Fax: 301-223-9506. Web: www.staugustinemd.org.
Catechesis/Religious Program—Sherry Brodnan, C.R.E.; David Gentile, Youth Ministry High School. Students 35.

WOODSTOCK, BALTIMORE CO., ST. ALPHONSUS RODRIGUEZ (1869) [CEM] Rev. Joseph P. Lacey, S.J.; Dee Papania, Pastoral Assoc.; Beth Sembly, Music Min.
Res.: 10800 Old Court Rd., 21163-1107. Tel: 410-461-5267; Fax: 410-750-7286. Email: stalphonsus@comcast.net.
Catechesis/Religious Program—De Papania, D.R.E.; Valerie Herrington, Youth Min. Students 246.

SHRINES, NATIONAL SHRINE OF ST. ELIZABETH ANN SETON Mrs. Karen Harding, Dir.
333 S. Seton Ave., Emmitsburg, 21727. Tel: 301-447-6606; Fax: 301-447-6061. Email: office@setonshrine.org. Web: www.setonshrine.org.

Chaplains of Public Institutions

BALTIMORE. *Baltimore City Detention Center - Men*, 401 Eager St., 21202. Tel: 410-523-0061. Rev. Msgr. Damien G. Nalepa, V.F., Chap.
Baltimore City Jail Detention Center - Women, 401 Eager St., 21202. Tel: 410-209-4216. Sr. Kathy Dougherty, O.F.M., Chap.
Carroll County Detention Center. Debbie Loveland, Volunteer Coord. Tel: 410-857-1201.
Franklin Square Hospital Center. Covered on rotating basis by Our Lady of Mt. Carmel; St. Clare; St. Anthony; Most Precious Blood; Our Lady Queen of Peace; Our Lady of La Vang; St. Elizabeth of Hungry; Church of the Annuciation; St. Rita; St. Stephen Bradshaw
Greater Baltimore Medical Center, Tel: 410-427-4700. Immaculate Conception, Towson; St. Leo, Baltimore
Harbor Hospital (1959)Tel: 410-685-2255. St. Veronica
James Lawrence Kernan Hospital, Tel: 410-298-8888. St. Gabriel, Woodlawn
Johns Hopkins Bayview Medical Center, Tel: 410-633-9393. Our Lady of Fatima; St. Leo; Sacred Heart of Mary
Johns Hopkins Hospital. St. Brigid; Our Lady of La Vang; St. Leo
Maryland Correctional Adjustment Center, 401 E. Madison St., 21201. Tel: 410-539-5445. Rev. Charles J. Canterna.
Maryland General Hospital. St. Ignatius; Church of Immaculate Conception
Maryland Penitentiary Complex, 954 Forest St., 21202. Rev. Charles J. Canterna, Chap. Tel: 410-539-5445.
Mt. Washington Pediatric Hospital, Tel: 410-466-6884. Shrine of the Sacred Heart
Northwest Hospital Center, Tel: 410-922-3800. Holy Family, Randallstown; New All Saints, Baltimore
Sheppard Pratt Hospital, Tel: 410-427-4700. Immaculate Conception, Towson
Sinai Hospital of Baltimore. Covered on rotating basis by St. Ambrose; Shrine of the Sacred Heart
Union Memorial Hospital. SS. Philip & James, Blessed Sacrament & St. Thomas Aquinas
University of Maryland Medical System. St. Leo; St. Mary, Star of the Sea; Holy Cross
University of Maryland- R. Adams Crowley Shock Trauma. Rev. Lawrence Schulmeister, O.S.F.

ANNAPOLIS. *Anne Arundel Medical Center*, Tel: 410-263-2397. St. Andrew by the Bay (Cape St. Clare); St. Mary, Annapolis

COLUMBIA. *Howard County General Hospital*, Tel: 410-964-1425. St. John the Evangelist, Columbia; St. Francis of Assisi, Fulton; St. Louis, Clarksville; Church of the Resurrection, Ellicott City

CUMBERLAND. *Federal & State Correctional Facilities* 21505. Rev. Ty S. Hullinger, S.T.B. Tel: 301-264-3521. St. Mary's, Cumberland
Western Maryland Regional Medical Center, Tel: 301-777-2990. St. Mary, Cumberland

FREDERICK. *Frederick Memorial Hospital*. Tel: 301-662-8288. St. John the Evangelist, Frederick

HAGERSTOWN. *Brook Lane Psychiatric Hospital*, Tel: 301-733-0410. St. Ann, Hagerstown
Maryland Correction Training Center 21740.
Roxbury Correctional Institution 21740. Tel: 240-420-1601. Mr. Bob Lashinsky, Volunteer Coord. Tel: 240-420-1601.

HAVRE DE GRACE. *Harford Memorial Hospital*, Tel: 410-939-2525. St. Patrick, Havre de Grace

GLEN BURNIE. *Baltimore Washington Medical Center*. Covered on rotating basis by Holy Trinity; Good Shepherd; St. Bernadette (Severn), Our Lady of the Chesapeake; Church of the Crucifixion; St. Jane Frances de Chantal; St. Joseph, Odenton

JESSUP. *Brockbridge Correction Facility*, 7931 Brockbridge Rd., 20794. Tel: 410-792-0470. Tracey Eberhardt, Volunteer Coord.
Clifton T. Perkins Hospital 20794. Tel: 410-547-5475. Rev. Msgr. John J. Auer (Retired).
Maryland Correctional Institution for Women 20794. Tel: 410-547-5475. Kathy Reid, Volunteer Coord. Tel: 410-795-7838, Ext. 113.
Maryland Correctional Institution-Jessup 20794. Jim Sanders, Chap. Tel: 410-799-0100, Ext. 2836.
Patuxent Institution 20794. Tel: 410-518-9977. Bill Cornolius, Volunteer Coord.
Toulson Boot Camp 20794. John Reinhard, Volunteer Coord. Tel: 410-730-6289.

OAKLAND. *Garrett County Memorial Hospital*, Tel: 301-334-2204. St. Peter the Apostle, Oakland

WESTMINSTER. *Carroll County General Hospital*, Tel: 410-848-4744. St. John, Westminster

---

Special Assignment:
Rev. Msgrs.—
FitzGerald, John L., Apostleship of the Sea
Hannon, James W.
O'Connor, Jay F., Dir., Div. Clergy Personnel
Woy, Richard W., V.G., Vicar Gen., Catholic Ctr.
Revs.—
Bonadio, Joseph J., S.S., M. Rel.Ed., D.Min., S.T.L. (Retired), Oak Crest
Breighner, Joseph F., Retreats & Missions
Canterna, Charles J., Spiritual Dir., Lay Missionaries Charity, Prison Min.
Chase, Raymond C., St. Charles Borromeo & Catholic Charities
Cote, E. Joseph J., SSND Motherhouse
Ferri, Gregory J., Hospital Chap., Hartford County Hospitals
Gosnell, Stephen D., Hospital Chap., Mercy Medical Ctr.
Henry, Paul J., Jr., Retreats and Missions
Johnson, Lawrence M., Stella Maris
Lesnick, John F., Chap., Frederick Memorial Hospital; St. Anthony Shrine
Maillet, Paul A., S.S., B.Mus., M.M., M.Div., S.T.L., S.T.D.
Malia, Thomas R., Hospital Chap., Mercy Medical; St. Clements
Murphy, Michael A., Mt. St. Joseph High School
Murphy, T. Austin, Jr., Vocation Dir., Vocations Office
Nolan, Brian P., Mt. St. Mary's Univ.
Parker, Adam J., Sec., Archbishop
Patalinghug, Leo E., S.T.L., Mt. St. Mary's Seminary
Ryan, Thomas, Newman Ctr., Towson Univ.
Seitz, Gilbert J., J.C.L., Tribunal, Interim Judicial Vicar, Metropolitan Tribunal
Spacek, William F., Hospital Chap., Univ. MD Hospital
Sparklin, Paul C., Hospital Chap., John Hopkins Hospital
Szymanski, Edward S., Chap., St. John Columbia; St. Louis; St. Paul; OLPH; Resurrection; St. Francis, Fulton

---

On Duty Outside the Archdiocese:
Revs.—
Burnham, Martin J., S.T.B., M.Div., Theological College; The Catholic Univ. of America
Byrne, Glenn F., St. Camillus Church
Cadavid-Rivera, Gonzalo, Studying Canon Law at Pontificia Universidad Javeriana
Callaghan, Michael, St. Philip Oratory
Cummings, McLean A., The Vatican, Congregation for Oriental Churches
Farmer, J. Kevin, Holy Trinity; Crucifixion & Good Shepherd
Hendricks, Edward S., Frostburg State, Dir., High Educ. & Campus Min.
Hilgartner, Richard B., USCCB
Jakopac, George I., St. John the Baptist
Lobert, Richard C., Chap. & Head, Theology Dept.
Morey, Robert E., St. Anthony Catholic Church
Warman, William C., VA Hospital

Military Chaplains:
Revs.—
Gills, Thomas, Air Force
Goulet, Daniel R., Battalion Chap.
Kruse, David B., Air Force; Kadena Air Base, Okinawa, Japan
Ochalek, Arkadiusz, Chap., Basic Officer Leader Course
Wood, Tyson J., US Army

Priests Sick or Absent:
Revs.—
Bonderenko, Thomas
DoBranski, John V.
Fell, Timothy J.
Golueke, Thomas J.
Harris, Raymond L.
Kightlinger, Jon T.
Mahon, M. Shawn
Martin, Raymond D.
McFadden, Frank
Messina, John
O'Brien, John E., Jr.
Peach, Peter of Jesus, O.Carm.
Richardson, Stephen S.
Robbins, John W.
Rock, Larry G.
Schenk, Charles
Thornsberry, Michael J.
Zeller, Leonard H.

Retired:
His Eminence—
Keeler, William Cardinal, 14th Archbishop of Baltimore, Mercy Ridge, S726, 2525 Pot Spring Rd., Timonium, 21093.
Most Rev.—
Newman, William C., D.D., V.G., Auxiliary Bishop of Baltimore, Mercy Ridge S201, 2525 Pot Spring Rd., Timonium, 21093.
Rev. Msgrs.—
Amato, Nicholas P., P.O. Box 40, Whiteford, 21160.
Armstrong, Robert A., P.A., Mercy Ridge, S718, 2525 Pot Spring Rd., Timonium, 21093.
Auer, John J., St. John the Evangelist, 689 Ritchie Hwy., Severna Park, 21146.
Baumgartner, A. Thomas, St. Joseph, Fullerton, 8420 Bel Air Rd., 21236-3098.
Bozel, Robert A., Stella Maris, 2300 Dulaney Valley Rd., Rm. 308, Timonium, 21093.
Byrnes, Paul A., 210 Hazelhurst Ln., Swanton, 21561.
Collins, William A., 9533 Liberty Rd., Randallstown, 21133.
Collopy, John C., Mercy Ridge S733, 2525 Pot Spring Rd., Timonium, 21093.
Donellen, Thomas J., Hampton House, 204 E. Joppa Rd., #507, Towson, 21204.
Hobbs, James V., 206 E. Main St., Thurmont, 21788.
Kenney, Jeremiah F., Mercy Ridge S633, 2525 Pot Spring Rd., Timonium, 21093.
Lynch, Edward J., Mercy Ridge S735, 2525 Pot Spring Rd., Timonium, 21093.
McGovern, James O., V.F., 1815 Vincenza Dr., Unit A, Eldersburg, 21784.
Meisel, Charles F., Mercy Ridge S614, 2525 Pot Spring Rd., Timonium, 21093.
Mieczkowski, Chester J., 7305 German Hill Rd., 21222.
Moeller, George B., Mercy Ridge S728, 2525 Pot Spring Rd., Timonium, 21093.
Parks, Richard E., 205 Robwood Rd., 21222.
Smith, Alfred E., 224 Sunbrook Ln., Hagerstown, 21742.
Tewes, Thomas J., 3905 Darleigh Rd., #E3, Nottingham, 21236.
Tillman, Richard H.
Revs.—
Abrahams, John J., 46 Abrahams Rd., Port Deposit, 21904.
Albright, Robert E., 7415 Chesapeake Rd., 21220.
Bonadio, Joseph J., S.S., M. Rel.Ed., D.Min., S.T.L., Oak Crest, 8800 Walther Blvd., 21234.
Bowen, John W., S.S., M.A., S.T.L., St. Charles Villa, 603 Maiden Choice Ln., 21228.
Buttner, Michael T., 304 Willrich Cir., J, Forest Hill, 21050.
Callahan, Francis X., Mercy Ridge S628, 2525 Pot Spring Rd., Timonium, 21093.
Carey, David M., 6 Ecoway Ct., Apt. 3D, Towson, 21286.
Carney, John J.
Carr, Brendan, Mercy Ridge S734, 2525 Pot Spring Rd., Timonium, 21093.
Carter, John T., Mercy Ridge, S618, 2525 Pot Spring Rd., Timonium, 21093.
Donaghy, Thomas J., Ph.D., 1104 Main St., 2nd Fl., Darby, PA 19023.
Dukehart, Claude H., S.S., M.A., S.T.D., St. Charles Villa, 603 Maiden Choice Ln., 21228.
Gallagher, John J.
Gesy, Lawrence J., 7121 Queen St., Kearneysville, WV 25430.
Hartgen, William E., Jr., S.S., M.A.
Hill, Edward T.
Hipsley, Milton A., Dublin Ct., DEM1, 2525 Pot Spring Rd., Timonium, 21093.
Holthaus, Paul G., Mercy Ridge X617, 2525 Pot Spring Rd., Timonium, 21093.
Hughes, Joseph B., 2034 Park Ave., 21217.
Karoor, Isaac M., 1111 King Arthur Ct., Sykesville, 21784.
Kelly, John L., St. Mark's Catonsville, 30 Melvin Rd., Catonsville, 21228.
Klein, Charles R., Church of the Good Shepherd, 1451 Furnace Ave., Glen Burnie, 21060.
Krach, Joseph W., St. Stephens Green AL315, 2525 Pot Spring Rd., Timonium, 21093.
LaPorta, Ross Anthony
Lardner, Gerald V., S.S., S.T.B., M.A., Ph.D., 3601 Greenway, Apt. 102, 21218.
Limmer, George A., 716 Naples Dr., Hagerstown, 21740.
Lippold, John L., St. Stephen's Green, 2525 Pot Spring Rd., Timonium, 21093.
Livigni, Salvatore, St. Michael's, 10 Willow Ave., 21206.
Loskarn, George
Lupico, Samuel, St. Elizabeth Hall, #C210, 2300 Dulaney Valley Rd., Timonium, 21093.
Mattingly, John F., S.S., M.A., M.S.L.S., S.S.L., St. Charles Villa, 603 Maiden Choice Ln., 21228.
McGovern, Walter J., Holy Family Rectory, 9533 Liberty Rd., Randallstown, 21133.
Messer, Joseph V., St. Stephen's Green AL309, 2525 Pot Spring Rd., Timonium, 21093.

Moody, William J., 86 Mt. Pleasant St., Frostburg, 21532.
Moore, John Charles, 868 Waterford Dr., Frederick, 21702-4088.
Muller, Kennard, St. Ignatius Church, 533 E. Jarrettsville Rd., Forest Hill, 21050-1603.
Muller, Myles, Mercy Ridge S727, 2525 Pot Spring Rd., Timonium, 21093.
O'Meara, Joseph, 5422 Old Frederick Rd., 21229.
Peterson, Casimir M., S.T.L., J.C.D., Reparation Society of the Immaculate Heart of Mary, 7920 Beverly Ave., 21234-5308.
Purvey, John J., Mercy Ridge, S635, 2525 Pot Spring Rd., Timonium, 21093.
Reitz, Louis M., S.S., S.T.L., M.S.L.S., M.Ed., St. Pius X, 6428 York Rd., 21212.
Roman, Manuel R., Heartlands, 3004 N. Ridge Rd., H102, Ellicott City, 21043.
Rose, Alphonse G., 5510 Woodlawn Rd., 21210.
Snouffer, Philip T., 8820 Walther Blvd., Apt. 1401, 21234.
Spillane, Michael Joseph
Thomas, Paul K., 637 Dover St., 21230.
Tittler, Leo R., St. Michael, 10 Willow Ave., 21206.
Vu Dinh Hoat, Rochus
Wenderoth, Joseph R., 16745 Wesley Chapel Rd., Monkton, 21111.
Wilson, Stuart T., 5269 N. Spring Pointe, Tucson, AZ 85749.
Witthauer, Paul G., Briarwood Estates, 719 Gregwood Ct., 21222.
Wojciechowski, Richard P., St. Stephens Green AL306, 2525 Pot Spring Rd., Timonium, 21093.
Zoubek, Ronald, 1 Greenwood Ave., 21206.

Permanent Deacons:
Albaugh, William S., St. Joseph, Fullerton
Ames, John, St. Agnes; St. William of York
Anderson, Carl A., St. Edward, Baltimore
Antczak, George W., Holy Rosary
Awalt, R. Donald, St. Joseph, Cockeysville
Bagley, Kevin, St. Leo the Great
Bankard, Alphonse C., III, Our Lady of Fatima, Baltimore
Barksdale, Wardell, St. Bernardine
Barth, Jim, St. Timothy Parish, Walkersville
Battista, Donald P., St. Peter the Apostle, Oakland
Bauerschmidt, Frederick C., Corpus Christi
Baxter, Michael R., St. Ursula
Baynes, Charles A., Our Lady of Mount Carmel & St. Joseph's Belair Rd.
Beales, Thomas W., Holy Family, Davidsonville
Bee, James E., St. Ann, Baltimore
Beimel, Leroy W., (Retired)
Benjamin, James, St. John the Evangelist, Columbia
Benson, Lee A., St. Ignatius, Hickory
Bolgiano, Richard, (On Duty Outside the Diocese)
Boscoe, John J., (Retired)
Bradley, Harold C., St. Michael, Frostburg; St. Peter, Westernport; St. Gabriel, Barton; St. Joseph, Midland; St. Mary, Lonaconing; St. Ann, Grantsville
Britt, Ray H., Resurrection, Ellicott City
Britton, Clifford L., St. Gabriel Parish
Brown, Kevin T., Holy Trinity, Glen Burnie
Chase, Keith D., Church of the Holy Apostles
Chesnavage, Albert W., (Retired)
Ciesla, Paul R., (Retired)
Cinquino, Joseph M., St. John, Westminster
Clemens, Richard W., Catholic Community of S. Baltimore
Comegna, John, Church of the Resurrection, Ellicott City
Concordia, Louis R., North Carolina
Conley, David A., St. Mary, Cumberland
Cook, Charles E., (Retired)
Cook, Thomas P., Our Lady of Sorrows, Owensville
Cooke, Paul G., St. John, Westminster
Coster, John E., Our Lady of the Angels Parish
Currens, Michael J., St. John the Evangelist, Frederick
Davis, Henry C., St. Michael the Archangel, Overlea
DeAngelis, William J., St. Joseph, Fullerton
DeCapite, James, St. Margaret, Bel Air
Derouaux, Bert, (Retired)
Dodge, Michael A., St. Athanasius; St. Rose of Lima Parish
Driesen, Simon M., St. Mary's, Pylesville
Dumer, Gary, Jr., St. Mary's, Pylesville
Dvorak, Michael A., St. Joseph, Eldersburg
Ebner, David J., St. Ignatius of Loyola, Ijamsville
Evans, George T., St. Rita
Fallon, William L., St. John, Westminster
Feurer, Nicholas E., St. Clement Mary Hofbauer
Fitzpatrick, T. Kelly, (On Duty Outside the Diocese)
Fulmer, Gary Lee, St. Ann, Hagerstown
Gardner, Edward L., Sr., (On Duty Outside the Diocese) St. Mary; Star of the Sea, Ocean City
Gifford, Paul A., PLD at St. Clement I, Lansdowne
Goles, Patrick J., St. Margaret, Bel Air
Graham, Robert L., (On Duty Outside the Diocese)
Gramling, John C., Immaculate Conception, Towson
Grillo, Anthony, Our Lady of the Fields
Gross, Theodore C., (Retired)
Hacker, Robert J., (Retired)
Harcum, Philip W., (Retired)
Harris, Jhan M., St. Veronica, Baltimore
Hawkins, John A., (Unassigned)
Heathcott, Brent L., Our Lady of the Fields, Millersville
Herzog, Robert, (On Duty Outside the Diocese)
Hicks, Charles W., St. Mark, Fallston
Hiebler, Charles H., Jr., Cathedral of Mary Our Queen
Hodges, Frank P., Corpus Christi
Jauquet, William, Our Lady of Victory
Jennings, Gerald B., St. Peter the Apostle, Libertytown
Keeley, Robert L., St. Philip Neri
Keenan, Robert G., St. Ursula
Kendzierski, Douglas P., Sacred Heart of Mary Parish
Knepper, Joseph E., St. Paul, Ellicott City
Kopczyk, Daniel R., St. Joan of Arc
Kosla, Albert F., (Retired)
Krysiak, Joseph C., (Retired)
Kunkel, Richard M., St. Ann, Hagerstown
Lancaster, Scott R., St. Louis, Clarksville
Langmead, John T., PLD, St. Rita Parish
Laws, Francis R., St. Stephen, Bradshaw
Lopata, Dean M., St. John, Severna Park
Lynne, Robert O., (Retired)
MacKnew, J. Donald, (Retired)
Malinowski, Bob A., (Retired)
Maloney, Timothy D., St. Stephen Parish
Manley, John L., St. John the Evangelist, Frederick
Mann, James L., Jr., St. Dominic
Mann, Paul T., St. Clare
Martin, John M., Immaculate Heart of Mary; Genesis Cromwell & Loch Raven Nursing Homes
Martin, John R., St. Peter Parish, Libertytown
Matheny, Lawrence G., St. Ignatius of Loyola, Ijamsville
Matthews, Russell, Charles Hickey School & St. Francis Xavier, Baltimore
Mauser, Fred L., St. Louis, Clarksville
McAndrews, George F., (Retired)
McCoy, Michael P., St. Thomas More
McKenna, John I., St. Clement, Lansdown
McKenna, Joseph, St. Francis of Assisi, Fulton
Miller, Donald W., St. John, Westminster
Miller, Eugene J., Jr., (Unassigned)
Mills, Hugh H., Jr., St. Alphonsus, Baltimore
Misulia, Michael, St. Peter the Apostle, Libertytown
Monaghan, James C., St. Andrew by the Bay
Montalto, Richard W., St. Thomas Aquinas
Mooney, Loren, St. Patrick, Cumberland
Moore, LeRoy S., St. Mary, Annapolis
Moore, Timothy J., St. Timothy, Walkersville
Morales, Edison, Sacred Heart of Jesus (Sagrado Corazon de Jesus)
Moreau, Ray, (On Duty Outside the Diocese)
Morris, Richard F., St. Ursula
Murray, J. Donald, St. Francis Xavier, Hunt Valley
Nairn, William P., St. Ann, Hagerstown
Nathan, Douglas J., St. Katherine Drexel
Norcio, Anthony F., Ph.D., St. Mary, Annapolis; Asst. Dir., Deacon Formation
Novak, Richard D., Sacred Heart of Jesus (Sagrado Corazon de Jesus)
O'Keefe, Francis, St. Issac Jogues
O'Neill, Harry St. A., Oak Crest
Oliver, Robert W., (On Duty Outside the Diocese)
Page, David A., St. Joseph, Odenton
Parrish, John N.
Passauer, W. Fred, St. Joseph, Midland; St. Michael, Frostburg; St. Mary of the Annunciation, Lonaconing; St. Patrick, Mt. Savage; St. Ann, Grantsville; St. Peter, Westernport and St. Gabriel, Barton
Perry, Martin, St. Mark, Fallston
Perry, Samuel R., (On Duty Outside the Diocese)
Petrosino, Victor R., St. Margaret, Bel Air
Piet, Stanley G., (Retired)
Pinkney, Willard A., Jr., (Retired)
Pitocco, Nickolas, (On Duty Outside the Diocese)
Pivec, J. Kenneth, Immaculate Heart of Mary and Loch Raven Nursing Home
Presberry, Seigfried, Dir., Prison Ministry, St. Mark, Catonsville
Prosser, James J., Our Lady of Grace Parish, Parkton
Rafter, John J., Jr., St. Jane Frances de Chantal
Rausch, P. Gregory, M.D., St. Joseph-on-Carrollton Manor
Reid, Kevin F., Immaculate Conception, Towson
Reinsfelder, Edward J., (On Duty Outside the Diocese)
Ripper, Mark, St. John, Westminster
Roberts, Gerald A., Our Lady Queen of Peace
Rodriguez, Alex, St. Francis de Sales
Roff, Daniel C., St. John, Frederick
Rongione, Frank, St. Ursula
Roscher, Stephen R., St. Charles Borromeo, Pikesville
Rose, Alan, St. Isaac Jogues
Rubio, Steven, St. Matthew
Russell, George A., Catholic Community of S. Baltimore
Ryan, James A., Sacred Heart, Glyndon
Sainz, Miguel E., St. Mary of the Assumption, Govans/Hispanic
Santiago, Harbey, St. Michael, Poplar Springs
Schoennagel, Frederick, St. John the Evangelist, Hydes
Schott, Robert G., Immaculate Conception, Connellsville, PA
Schultz, Joseph L., St. Anthony of Padua/Most Precious Blood
Sedlevicius, John, St. Lawrence the Martyr, Jessup
Seibold, Frederick, St. Elizabeth Ann Seton, Crofton
Seneschal, Phillip, St. Mary of the Assumption, Pylesville
Senft, William W., Cathedral of Mary Our Queen
Shelton, Paul D., St. Mary's and Blessed Sacrament
Shepard, Robert M., Basilica and MD State Prison System
Siarkowski, Henry L., Shrine of the Little Flower
Sisson, George, Holy Family CC, Middletown
Smith, Darrell, St. Joseph, Taneytown
Smith, H. Todd, St. Joseph, Sykesville
Soloski, Mark, Shrine of the Sacred Heart, Mt. Washington
Stine, Richard J., St. Francis de Sales, Abingdon
Stoops, Edward J., Our Lady of the Fields
Stretmater, Daniel J., (On Duty Outside the Diocese)
Sullivan, Edward R., St. Joseph, Cockeysville
Sullivan, James C., St. Francis de Sales, Abingdon
Sutterman, Jeffrey M., St. Katharine Drexel
Swann, C. Richard, (Retired)
Teixeira, Lawrence P., St. Francis of Assisi, Brunswick; St. Mary, Petersville
Tengwall, David L., St. Andrew by the Bay
Thomas, Charles, (On Duty Outside the Diocese)
Thompson, Ronald, St. John, Severna Park
Trautwein, Ralph, St. Ignatius, Hickory
Vassie, Frederick S., (On Duty Outside the Diocese)
Wachter, George G., Springfield Hospital Center
Walker, George W., Jr., Diocese of Wilmington, DE; St. John the Apostle, Milford, DE
Weber, Paul A., St. Ignatius, Baltimore
Werner, Francis L., Jr., St. Patrick, Cumberland
Westwater, James, St. Isaac Jogues; Asst. Dir., Deacon Formation
Whitesell, Edward, St. Benedict
Wilkins, Herman S., Our Lady of Hope
Wise, Stanley, St. Joseph, Taneytown
Witherspoon, Willard, Jr., St. Peter Claver/St. Pius V
Wolf, Martin E., Maryland Correctional Institutions; St. Margaret's, Bel Air
Yannuzzi, Thomas J., Ascension Parish
Zeiler, Francis, St. Clement Mary Hofbauer; Clergy Liaison, Project Rachel

INSTITUTIONS LOCATED IN THE ARCHDIOCESE

[A] SEMINARIES, ARCHDIOCESAN

BALTIMORE. *St. Mary's Seminary and University,* 5400 Roland Ave., 21210-1994. Tel: 410-864-4000; Fax: 410-864-4278. Web: www.stmarys.edu. Most Rev. Edwin F. O'Brien, S.T.D., D.D., Archbishop of Baltimore, Chancellor, Chm. Board of Trustees.

St. Mary's Seminary and University Priests 17; Diocesan Seminarians 74; Diocesan Seminarians on Pastoral Leave 8; Lay Teachers 7.

Officers of the Administration: Revs. Thomas R. Hurst, S.S., S.T.L., Ph.D., Pres. Rector; Timothy Kulbicki, O.F.M.Conv., B.A., S.T.B., H.E.D., Assoc. Prof. Church History & Academic Dean, School Theology; Richard G. Childs, M.B.A., Vice Pres., Finance; Michael J. Gorman, Ph.D., Dean, Ecumenical Institute of Theology; Ms. Paula Thigpen, M.A., M.Div., Univ. Registrar; Mrs. Elizabeth L. Visconage, B.S., Vice Pres., Advancement & Human Resources; Thomas Raszewski, Dir. Library Svcs.; Rev. Edward Griswold, D.Min., Ph.D., S.T.L., Vice Rector & Dir. Pastoral Formation; Rev. Msgr. David

I. Fulton, J.C.D., S.T.D., Dir., Continuing Formation Programs, Priests; Arryn Milne, B.S., Dir., Information Svcs.; Revs. Renato Lopez, S.S., S.S.L., Dir., Liturgy; Lawrence B. Terrien, S.S., Ph.D., S.T.D., Dir., Spiritual Life Progs.

Academic Faculty: Revs. Michael L. Barre, S.S., S.T.L., Ph.D., Prof., Sacred Scripture; Daniel J. Doherty, S.S., B.A., M.A., M.Div., S.T.L., Asst. Prof. Pastoral Theology; Patricia Fosarelli, M.D., D.Min., Lecturer Pastoral Theology; Rev. Msgr. David I. Fulton, J.C.D., S.T.D., Asst. Prof. Canon Law; Michael J. Gorman, Ph.D., Dean, Ecumenical Institute of Theology & Prof. Sacred Scripture; Revs. Thomas R. Hurst, S.S., S.T.L., Ph.D., Assoc. Prof. Sacred Scripture; Robert F. Leavitt, S.S., S.T.D., Prof. Systematic Theology; Renato Lopez, S.S., S.S.L., Asst. Prof. Sacred Scripture & Dir. Liturgy; William Miller, S.J., M.Div., Ph.D., Assoc. Prof. Sacred Scripture; Hy K. Nguyen, S.S., M.Div., M.A., S.T.D., Asst. Prof. Systematic Theology; Peter Paul Seaton, Ph.L., Ph.D., Asst. Prof. Philosophy; Revs. Lawrence B. Terrien, S.S., Ph.D., S.T.D.; Leonardo J. Gajardo, S.S., B.A., J.C.L., S.T.B., Asst. Prof., Canon Law; Timothy A. Kulbicki, O.F.M.Conv., S.T.B., H.E.D., B.A., Assoc. Prof., Church History; Rafael M. Ramirez, S.S., B.A., M.Div., M.A., S.T.L., S.T.D., S.T.B., Asst. Prof., Sacred Scripture.

Adjunct Academic Faculty: Myrelle D'Abreu, ESL Coord.; Revs. Edward Griswold, D.Min., Ph.D., S.T.L., Instructor Homiletics; Austin Murphy, Instructor Pastoral Year; Bill Scalia, Lecturer English; Leo White, Instructor Philosophy; Deacon George Russell, B.A., M.A., Ph.D., Ph.L., Adjunct Prof., Philosophy; Revs. John J. Slovikovski, M.Div., M.A., Ph.D. (Cand.), B.A., Adjunct Instructor, Moral Theology; Thomas J. Burke, O.SS.T., S.T.M., S.T.D., B.A., Adjunct Assoc. Prof., Systematic Theology; Patrick Carrion, B.A., S.T.D., S.T.M., M.A.S., Adjunct Instructor, Pastoral Theology; Rev. Msgr. Robert J. Jaskot, B.S., S.T.L., S.T.B., Adjunct Instructor, Sacremental Theology.

Ecumenical Institute of Theology, 5400 Roland Ave., 21210. Tel: 410-864-4200; Fax: 410-864-4205. Michael J. Gorman, M.Div., Ph.D., Dean. Students 258.

EMMITSBURG. *Mount St. Mary's Seminary* (1808) 21727-7797. Tel: 301-447-5295; Fax: 301-447-5895. Email: seminaryinfo@msmary.edu. Web: www.msmary.edu/seminary.

An integral part of the corporation known as Mount St. Mary's University and Seminary. Priests 14; Lay Teachers 8; Lay Administrators 3; Support Staff 4; Diocesan Seminarians 158; Religious Seminarians 8; Total Enrollment 166.

Administration: Dr. Thomas H. Powell, Pres.; Rev. Msgr. Steven P. Rohlfs, S.T.L., S.T.D., Vice Pres. & Rector; Revs. Brian M. Doerr, Vice Rector, Human Formation; Lee W. Gross, S.T.L., Dean of Students & Asst. Prof., Liturgy & Systematic Theology; J. Daniel Mindling, O.F.M.Cap., S.T.D., Academic Dean & Prof., Moral Theology; John J. Dietrich, M.A., M.Div., Dir. Spiritual Formation; Rev. Msgr. Stuart W. Swetland, S.T.D., M.Div., S.T.L., Flynn Chair, Christian Ethics; Rev. Kenneth D. Brighenti, Ph.D., Vice Rector, Pastoral Formation; Dir. Pastoral Field Educ.; Mr. Charles L. Kuhn, Dir. Library; Mr. Phil McGlade, Dir. Seminary Devel. & Alumni Rels.; Mrs. Amelia Y. Rodriguez, Seminary Registrar; Mrs. Rosemary S. Mick, Seminary Records & Canonicals; Mrs. Susan L. Nield, Admin. Asst., Rector & Coord., Admissions.

Full Time Faculty: Revs. Frederick L. Miller, S.T.D., S.T.L., Assoc. Prof., Systematic Theology; Thomas J. Lane, S.S.L., S.T.D., Asst. Prof., Sacred Scripture; Lawrence J. Donohoo, S.T.D., Ph.D., Assoc. Prof. Systematic Theology, Formation Advising, Spiritual Direction; Leo E. Patalinghug, S.T.L., Prof. Homiletics, Pastoral Theology; Charles P. Connor, S.T.L., Asst. Prof., Church History, Systematic Theology; Dr. Christopher J. Anadale, Ph.D., Dir., Masters Arts, Philosophical Studies; William A. Bales, Ph.D., Assoc. Prof., Sacred Scripture; Paige E. Hochschild, Ph.D., Asst. Dir., Pre-Theology & Asst. Prof. Philosophy Adjunct Faculty; John D. Love, S.T.D., Asst. Prof., Systematic Theology; Owen M. Phelan, Ph.D., Asst. Prof., Church History; Steven C. Smith, Ph.D., Asst. Prof., Sacred Scripture; Deborah Wentling, M.A., ESL Coord.; Ms. Julia Panker, Organist/Dir. Liturgical Music; Mr. John Williams, Coord., Pastoral Activities; Mrs. Caroline Purcell, M.A., ESL Instructor.

Part Time Faculty: Revs. Ronald S. Gillis, S.T.L., J.C.D., Ph.D., Spiritual Dir.; Michael J. Roach; Lawrence J. McNeil, D.Min.; Dr. Carol L. Houghton, S.T.D., J.C.D.; Cynthia Fraga-Canadas, Ph.D., Adjunct Prof. Pastoral Spanish.

[B] COLLEGES AND UNIVERSITIES

BALTIMORE. **Loyola University in Maryland*, 4501 N. Charles St., 21210. Tel: 410-617-2000; Fax: 410-617-2176. Web: www.loyola.edu. Rev. Brian F. Linnane, S.J., Pres. Priests 14; Lay Teachers 501; Total Staff 1,295; Total Enrollment 6,067.

Loyola Graduate Center-Columbia Campus, 8890 McGaw Rd., Columbia, 21045-5245. Tel: 410-617-7600; Fax: 410-617-7643.

Loyola Graduate Center-Timonium Campus, 2034 Greenspring Dr., Timonium, 21093. Tel: 410-617-1500; Fax: 410-617-1518. Revs. Brian F. Linnane, S.J., Pres.; James J. Miracky, S.J., Dean Loyola College; Dr. Timothy Law Snyder, Vice Pres. Academic Affairs; Dr. Karyl Leggio, Dean Sellinger School of Business & Mgmt.; Dr. Susan Donovan, Exec. Vice Pres. Student Devel. & Dean Students; Randall Gentzler, Vice Pres. Finance & Treas.; Terrence Sawyer, Vice Pres. Admin.; Marc Camille, Vice Pres. Enrollment Mgmt. & Communications; Megan Gillick, Vice Pres. Advancement; Shelia Horton, Vice Pres., Student Devel. & Dean, Students; Ilona McGuiness, Ph.D., Dean of First Year Students & Academic Svcs.; Revs. Charles Borges, S.J.; Hank Hilton, S.J.; Joseph S. Rossi, S.J.; James F. Salmon, S.J.

Jesuit Community of Loyola University, Inc. Tel: 410-617-2318; Fax: 410-617-2125. Revs. Ronald J. Amiot, S.J.; Charles Borges, S.J.; Timothy B. Brown, S.J.; John Conley, S.J.; John M. Dennis, S.J., M.Ed.; Frank R. Haig, S.J.; Francis G. Hilton, S.J.; James Kelly, S.J.; Brian F. Linnane, S.J.; Brian O. McDermott, S.J.; Francis J. Nash, S.J.; John W. Peck, S.J.; Joseph S. Rossi, S.J.; James F. Salmon, S.J.; Mr. Samuel J. Sawyer, S.J.; Rev. Luis A. Tampe, S.J., Affiliate Instructor.

Mount St. Agnes College Tel: 410-617-2271; Fax: 410-617-5413. Sisters of Mercy of the Americas., (Merged with Loyola College.)

Notre Dame of Maryland University, 4701 N. Charles St., 21210. Tel: 410-435-0100; Fax: 410-532-5791. Web: www.ndm.edu. Patricia J. Mitchell, Chm. Bd. of Trustees; Dr. Mary Pat Seurkamp, Ph.D., Pres.; Sr. Christine DeVinne, Vice Pres. Academic Affairs; Heidi Fletcher Roller, Vice Pres. Enrollment Mgmt.; Thomas Maher, Vice Pres. Fin. & Admin.; Sharon Bogdan, Registrar; Patricia Bosse, Vice Pres. Institutional Advancement; Sr. Eileen O'Dea, Vice Pres. Mission. School Sisters of Notre Dame. Sisters 23; Lay Professors 83; Students 2,929; Residents 260; Total Staff 189.

EMMITSBURG. *Mount Saint Mary's University* (1808) 21727. Tel: 301-447-6122; Fax: 301-447-5634. Email: communications@msmary.edu. Web: www.msmary.edu. Dr. Thomas Powell, Pres.; Mr. Charles L. Kuhn, Librarian; Mr. David C. Reeder, Dir. Fin. Aid; Dr. David Rehm, Provost; Ms. Leona Sevick, Assoc. Provost; Mr. Michael Post, Vice Pres., Enrollment Mgmt.; Ms. Margot Rhoades, Registrar; Mr. Dan Soller, Exec. Vice Pres.; Michael Malewicki, Vice Pres., Business & Finance; Rev. Msgrs. Steven P. Rohlfs, S.T.L., S.T.D., Vice Pres. & Rector; Stuart W. Swetland, S.T.D., M.Div., S.T.L., Vice Pres., Catholic Identity; Revs. Brian P. Nolan, Chap.; Paul V. Redmond (Retired); James Donohue, C.R.; Thomas Smith, Chap. of the Grotto; Mr. Bob Brennan, Vice Pres., Inst. Advancement. Priests 8; Sisters 2; Lay Teachers 171; Total Enrollment 2,305.

[C] HIGH SCHOOLS, ARCHDIOCESAN

BALTIMORE. *Archbishop Curley High School* (1961) 3701 Sinclair Ln., 21213. Tel: 410-485-5000; Fax: 410-483-2545. Email: jbenicewicz@archbishopcurley.org. Web: www.archbishopcurley.org. Revs. Joseph Benicewicz, O.F.M.Conv., Pres.; Vincent Gluc, O.F.M.Conv., Vocation Dir. & Guardian; Matthew Foley, O.F.M.Conv., Campus Min.; Bros. Daniel Lutolf, O.F.M.Conv., Teacher; Douglas McMillan, O.F.M.Conv., Teacher; Phil Piercy, Prin.; Ms. Ann Kennedy, Librarian. Administered by Order of Friars Minor Conventual, St. Anthony of Padua Province (USA). Priests 2; Brothers 2; Lay Teachers 41; Students 530; Total Staff 63.

The Seton Keough High School (1988) 1201 Caton Ave., 21227-1092. Tel: 410-646-4444; Fax: 443-573-0107. Web: setonkeough.com. Ms. Karen Hanrahan, Pres.; Ms. Angela Calamari, Prin.; Josiah LaTona, Vice Prin.; Ms. Laurie Manuel, Librarian. Sisters 1; Lay Teachers 35; Students 374.

CUMBERLAND. *Bishop Walsh School* (1966) (Grades PreK-12), 700 Bishop Walsh Rd., 21502. Tel: 301-724-5360; Fax: 301-722-0555. Email: swebb@bishopwalsh.org. Web: www.bishopwalsh.org. Sisters Phyllis McNally, S.S.N.D., M.Ed., Pres.; Kathleen Jancuk, S.S.N.D., M.Ed., Reading Specialist; Shelby Webb, Prin.; Mrs. Ann Workmeister, Asst. Prin.; Wendy Walker, Librarian. School Sisters of Notre Dame. Sisters 3; Lay Teachers 37; Students 465.

ESSEX. *Our Lady of Mount Carmel Catholic School*, 1706 Old Eastern Ave., 21221. Tel: 410-686-1023.

SEVERN. *Archbishop Spalding High School* (1966) 8080 New Cut Rd., 21144. Tel: 410-969-9105; Fax: 410-969-1026. Email: info@archbishopspalding.org. Web: www.archbishopspalding.org. Kathleen K. Mahar, Pres.; Lewis VanWambeke, Prin. Lay Teachers 92; Students 1,200.

[D] HIGH SCHOOLS, PRIVATE

BALTIMORE. *Calvert Hall* (1845) 8102 La Salle Rd., 21286. Tel: 410-825-4266; Fax: 410-825-6826. Email: chc@calverthall.com. Web: www.calverthall.com. Bro. Thomas Zoppo, F.S.C., Pres.; Mr. Joseph Baker, Asst. Prin. Academic Affairs; Mr. Charles Stembler, Asst. Prin. Student Affairs; Mr. Louis Heidrick, Prin.; Ms. Elsie Paliath, Librarian. Conducted by the Brothers of the Christian Schools (F.S.C.). Brothers 12; Lay Teachers 90; Students 1,225.

The Catholic High School of Baltimore (1939) 2800 Edison Hwy., 21213. Tel: 410-732-6200; Fax: 410-732-7639. Email: chsb@thecatholichighschool.org. Web: www.thecatholichighschool.org. Dr. Barbara Nazelrod, Pres.; Mrs. Marti Meyd, Prin.; Jan Bandzwolck, Vice Prin.; Mary Sunday, Librarian. The Sisters of St. Francis of Philadelphia. Sisters 9; Lay Teachers 31; Students 314; Total Staff 60.

Cristo Rey Jesuit High School, 420 Chester St., 21231. Tel: 410-727-3255; Fax: 443-573-9898. Rev. John W. Swope, S.J., Pres.; Thomas A. Malone, Prin.; Katherine Sorci, Librarian. Priests 1; Scholastics 1; Lay Teachers 30; Staff 37; Students 311.

St. Frances Academy (1828) (Coed), 501 E. Chase St., 21202. Tel: 410-539-5794; Fax: 410-685-2650. Email: sfa@sfacademy.org. Web: www.sfacademy.org. Sr. John Francis Schilling, O.S.P., Pres.; Deacon Curtis Turner, Prin.; Ms. Mary Missouri, Asst. Prin.; Mr. Doral Palley, Asst. Prin.; Ms. Linda Wilson, Guidance. Oblate Sisters of Providence. Sisters 3; Lay Teachers 17; Students 180.

Institute of Notre Dame (1847) 901 Aisquith St., 21202. Tel: 410-522-7800; Fax: 410-522-7810. Email: info@indofmd.org. Web: indofmd.org. Dr. Mary L. Funke, Pres.; Ann Seeley, Prin.; Mrs. Diana Franz, Asst. Prin.

Institute of Notre Dame, Inc. Sisters 3; Lay Teachers 29; Lay Employees 27; Counselors 2; Students 347.

Loyola Blakefield (1952) (Grades 6-12), P.O. Box 6819, 21285-6819. Tel: 410-823-0601; Fax: 410-823-5277. Email: admin@loyolablakefield.org. Web: www.loyolablakefield.org. Revs. Thomas A. Pesci, S.J., Pres.; F. Joseph Michini, S.J., Chap.; Lloyd George, S.J.; Mr. Anthony I. Day, Prin.; Mrs. Theresa K. Darr, Librarian. Priests 3; Lay Teachers 89; Students 1,004.

Mercy High School (1960) 1300 E. Northern Pkwy., 21239-1998. Tel: 410-433-8880; Fax: 410-323-8816. Email: mercy@mercyhighschool.com. Web: www.mercyhighschool.com. Sr. Carol E. Wheeler, R.S.M., Pres.; Jo Ann Lazzeri, Vice Pres. Academic Affairs; Pegeen D'Agostino, Prin.; Claire Hruban, Librarian. Sisters of Mercy of the Americas. Sisters 6; Lay Teachers 48; Students 355; Total Staff 72.

Mount de Sales Academy (1952) 700 Academy Rd., 21228. Tel: 410-744-8498; Fax: 410-744-8314. Email: mdsa@mountdesales.org. Web: www.mountdesales.org. Sr. Anne Catherine, Prin.; Judi Lanciotti, Vice Prin.; Sr. Peter Marie, O.P., Vice Prin.; Mrs. Alice Carpenter, Librarian. Sisters 6; Lay Teachers 50; Students 502.

Mt. St. Joseph College High School (1876) 4403 Frederick Ave., 21229. Tel: 410-644-3300; Fax: 410-646-6220. Email: barry@admin.msjnet.edu. Web: www.msjnet.edu. Bro. James M. Kelly, C.F.X., Pres.; Mr. Barry J. Fitzpatrick, Prin. Xaverian Brothers. Priests 1; Brothers 2; Lay Teachers 93; Students 1,044; Total Staff 148.

BEL AIR. *The John Carroll School* (1964) 703 E. Churchville Rd., 21014. Tel: 410-879-2480; Fax: 410-836-8514. Email: jcs@johncarroll.org. Web: www.johncarroll.org. Ms. Madelyn A. Ball, Prin.; Mrs. Patti Murphy Dohn, Campus Min.; Theresa Burlas, Librarian. Priests 1; Sisters 1; Lay Teachers 60; Students 690; Total Staff 101.

FREDERICK. *Saint John's Catholic Prep* (1829) (Coed), 889 Butterfly Ln., 21703. Tel: 301-662-4210; Fax: 301-662-5166. Email: mschultz@saintjohnsprep.org. Web: www.saintjohnsprep.org. Mr. Gordon Oliver, Pres.; Mr. Christopher Cosentino, Prin.; Ms. Melissa Minsker, Librarian. Lay Teachers 30; Total Staff 55; Students 275.

HAGERSTOWN. *St. Maria Goretti High School* (1955) (Coed), 1535 Oak Hill Ave., 21742. Tel: 301-739-4266; Fax: 301-739-4261. Email: goretti@goretti.org. Web: www.goretti.org. Mr. Richard E. Fairley, Prin. Lay Teachers 23; Students 211;

Total Staff 39; Support Staff 7; Administrators 9.

[E] MIDDLE/HIGH SCHOOLS, PRIVATE

BROOKLANDVILLE. *Maryvale Preparatory School* (1945) (Grades 6-12), (Girls), 11300 Falls Rd., 21022-1490. Tel: 410-252-3366; Fax: 410-308-1497. Email: grahamm@maryvale.com. Web: www.maryvale.com. Sr. Shawn Marie Maguire, S.N.D.deN., Headmistress & Pres.; Donna Bridickas, Prin.; Barbara Lipsky, Librarian. Sisters of Notre Dame de Namur 1; Lay Teachers 38; Students 362; Total Staff 30.

TOWSON. *Notre Dame Preparatory School* (1873) (Grades 6-12), 815 Hampton Ln., 21286. Tel: 410-825-6202; Fax: 410-832-5355. Web: www.notredameprep.com. Sr. Patricia McCarron, S.S.N.D., Headmistress; Ms. Laurie Jones, Prin.; Mrs. Ellen Cullen, Librarian.
Notre Dame Preparatory School, Inc. Sisters 4; Lay Teachers 91; Students 772; Total Staff 140.

[F] ELEMENTARY/MIDDLE SCHOOLS, REGIONAL AND COMMUNITY

BALTIMORE. *John Paul Regional Catholic School, Inc.*, (Grades PreK-8), 6946 Dogwood Rd., 21244. Tel: 410-944-0367; Fax: 410-265-5316. Email: office@jprcs.org. Web: www.jprcs.org. Mrs. Theresa Brooks, Prin.; Mrs. Patricia Little, Librarian. Early Childhood Program. Lay Teachers 17; Students 198.

[G] ELEMENTARY SCHOOLS, PRIVATE

BALTIMORE. *Mother Seton Academy*, (Grades 6-8), 2215 Greenmont Ave., 21218-5421. Tel: 410-563-2833; Fax: 410-563-7353. Web: www.mothersetonacademy.org. Laura Minakowski, Prin.; Sisters Charmaine Krohe, S.S.N.D., Pres.; Patricia Maxa, S.S.N.D., Admin. Asst. Innovative Middle School for Inner City Youth. Brothers 2; Sisters 7; Lay Teachers 4; Lay Volunteers 2; Students 72.
Sisters Academy of Baltimore, Inc. (2004) (Grades 5-8), 139 First Ave., 21227. Tel: 410-242-1212; Fax: 410-242-5104. Web: www.sistersacademy.org. Sisters Delia Dowling, S.S.N.D., Pres.; Debra Liesen, S.S.N.D., Prin.; Dorothy Daiger, S.S.N.D., Librarian; Kathleen Donnelly, Admin. Asst.; Sr. Virginia Maria Brune, S.S.N.D., Teacher. Religious 3; Lay Teachers 11; Students 65.

ELLICOTT CITY. *Trinity School* (1941) (Grades PreK-8), 4985 Ilchester Rd., 21043. Tel: 410-744-1524; Fax: 410-744-3617. Email: admintrin@trinityschoolmd.org. Web: trinityschoolmd.org. Sr. Catherine Phelps, S.N.D.deN., Prin.; Anne Howard, Librarian. Sisters of Notre Dame de Namur 2; Lay Teachers 30; Students 360.

EMMITSBURG. *Mother Seton School*, (Grades PreK-8), 100 Creamery Rd., 21727. Tel: 301-447-3161; Fax: 301-447-3914. Email: office@mothersetonschool.org. Web: www.mothersetonschool.org. Sr. JoAnne Goecke, D.C., Prin.; Ms. Teri Monacelli, Librarian. Daughters of Charity of St. Vincent de Paul 3; Lay Teachers 20; Students 310.

FREDERICK. *The Visitation Academy* (1846) (Grades PreK-8), 200 E. 2nd St., 21701. Tel: 301-662-2814; Fax: 301-695-8549. Email: contact@thevisitationacademy.org. Web: www.thevisitationacademy.org. Lynne Kirby, Prin.; Ms. Danielle Adams, Librarian. Lay Teachers 21; Students 108.

HYDES. *St. John Long Green Valley Roman Catholic Elementary School*, 13311 Long Green Pike, 21082.

[H] ELEMENTARY SCHOOLS, REGIONAL AND COMMUNITY

BALTIMORE. *St. Agnes Roman Catholic Elementary School*, (Grades PreK-8), 603 St. Agnes Ln., 21229. Tel: 410-747-4070; Fax: 410-747-0138. Email: information@stagnesschool.net. Web: www.stagnesschool.net. Ms. Susan Banks, Prin.
Archbishop Borders School, (Grades PreK-8), Language Immersion School Partner Language Spanish, 201 S. Conkling St., 21224. Tel: 410-276-6534; Fax: 410-276-6915. Email: principal@abbschool.com. Mary C. Marshall, Prin. Students 130; Lay Staff 17.
Cardinal Shehan School, (Grades PreK-8), 5407 Loch Raven Blvd., 21239-2996. Tel: 410-433-2775; Fax: 410-323-6131. Web: cardinalshehanschool.org. Sr. Rita Michelle, O.S.P., Prin.; Mrs. Corinne Davidson, Asst. Prin.; Mrs. Lisa Taylor, Librarian. Serving St. Matthew and St. Thomas More Parishes. Sisters 4; Lay Teachers 23; Students 334.
St. Ignatius Loyola Academy (1993) (Grades 6-8), 740 N. Calvert St., 21202. Tel: 410-539-8268; Fax: 410-539-4821. Email: teresascott@saintignatius.org. John Ciccone, Pres.; Mrs. Teresa Scott, Prin. Middle School for boys from low income families. Lay Teachers 16; Students 69.
Queen of Peace Elementary Cluster, St. James and St. John School (1847) (Grades PreK-8), 1012 Somerset St., 21202. Tel: 410-342-3222; Fax: 410-675-8262. Mrs. LaUanah King-Cassell, Prin. Lay Teachers 19; Students 291.
St. Thomas Aquinas School, (Grades PreK-8), 3710 Roland Ave., 21211. Tel: 410-889-4618; Fax: 410-889-1956. Email: stasch@archbalt.org. Web: www.stthomasaquinasschool.us. Sr. Marie Rose Gustatus, S.S.N.D., Prin. Lay Teachers 24.
St. Ursula Roman Catholic Elementary School, 8900 Harford Rd., 21234-4193. Tel: 410-335-3533; Fax: 410-661-1620. Email: jkelly2@archbalt.org. Sr. Joan Kelly, S.N.D.deN., Prin.

ESSEX. *Our Lady of Mount Carmel Catholic School*, 1702 Old Eastern Ave., 21221. Tel: 410-686-1023 (6-12); 410-686-0859 (Lower School); 410-687-8513 (Infant Care/Pre-School); Fax: 410-686-2361 (6-12); 410-686-4916 (Lower School). Email: olmchsch@archbalt.org. Web: www.olmcmd.org. Mrs. Kathleen Sipes, Pres.; Christopher Ashby, Prin., Upper School; Christine Olszewsk, Prin., Lower School.

FREDERICK. *St. John Regional Catholic School*, (Grades PreK-8), 8414 Opossumtown Pike, 21702. Tel: 301-662-6722; Fax: 301-695-7024. Email: ksmith@SJRCS.org. Web: www.sjrcs.org. Mrs. Karen Smith, Prin.; Mr. Paul Fer, Asst. Prin.; Karen Gawinske, Librarian. Lay Teachers 35; Students 575.

GAMBRILLS, ANNE ARUNDEL. *School of the Incarnation, Inc.* (1999) (Grades K-8), 2601 Symphony Ln., 21054. Tel: 410-519-2285; Fax: 410-519-2286. Email: lshipley@schooloftheincarnation.org. Web: www.schooloftheincarnation.org. Mrs. Lisa Shipley, Prin.; Anne Umerlik, Librarian. An interparish school of the Archdiocese of Baltimore established 1999. Parishes: Church of the Holy Apostles, Gambrills; Our Lady of the Fields, Millersville; St. Joseph, Odenton; Our Lady of Perpetual Help, Edgewater; Holy Family, Davidsonville and St. Elizabeth Ann Seton, Crofton. Lay Staff 31; Lay Teachers 41; Students 756.

GLEN BURNIE. *Monsignor Slade Catholic School* (1954) (Grades K-8), 120 Dorsey Rd., 21061. Tel: 410-766-7130; Fax: 410-787-0594. Email: mscs@msladeschool.com. Web: www.msladeschool.com. Gregory E. Jones, Prin.; Laura Lodowski, Librarian. Serving Glen Burnie, Pasadena, Hanover and Severn Parishes. Lay Teachers 40; Students 770.

HYDES. *St. John the Evangelist School (Hydes)*, 13311 Long Green Pike, 21082. Tel: 410-592-9585, Ext. 120; Fax: 410-817-4548. Email: school@stjohnhydes.org. Mrs. Genevieve Delcher, Prin.

KINGSVILLE. *St. Stephen School* (1863) (Grades PreK-8), 8028 Bradshaw Rd., 21087-1807. Tel: 410-592-7617; Fax: 410-592-7330. Email: sssch@archbalt.org. Web: www.ststephenbradshaw.org. Mrs. Mary M. Patrick, Prin.; Mrs. Linda Boschert, Librarian & Music. Lay Teachers 20; Instructional Aides 4.

PARKTON. *Our Lady of Grace Roman Catholic Elementary School*, 18310 Middletown Rd., 21120. Tel: 410-329-6956, Ext. 130. Mrs. Byrdie Ricketts, Prin.

WESTMINSTER. *St. John School (Westminster) Roman Catholic Elementary School*, 45 Monroe St., 21157. Tel: 410-848-7455; Fax: 410-848-2822. Email: hwalker@sjwest.org. Mrs. Harriann Walker, Prin.

[I] SPECIAL EDUCATION

BALTIMORE. *St. Elizabeth School, Inc.*, 801 Argonne Dr., 21218-1998. Tel: 410-889-5054; Fax: 410-889-2356. Email: info@stelizabeth-school.org. Web: www.stelizabeth-school.org. Christine Manlove, Ed.D., Exec. Dir.; Mr. Andy Parsley, Prin.; Ed McAnnulla, Librarian. Sisters of St. Francis of Assisi 3; Lay Teachers 23; Other Lay Staff 52; Aides 57; Children 116.

TIMONIUM. *Villa Maria School* (Timonium Campus), 2300 Dulaney Valley Rd., 21093. Tel: 410-252-6343; Fax: 410-560-1347. Jack Pumphrey, Admin. & Dir. Education. Non-public (Level V and VI) special education for children with emotional/multiple disabilities, ages 11-15. Lay Teachers 22; Teacher Aides 20; Children 120.
Villa Maria School at St. Vincent's Center, 2600 Pot Spring Rd., 21093. Tel: 410-252-3725; Fax: 410-561-8109. Non-public level V & VI special education for children with emotional/multiple disabilities ages 4-11. Lay Teachers 7; Teacher Aides 9; Children 54.
Villa Maria School of Harford County, 1370 Brass Mill Rd., Belcamp, 21017. Tel: 410-297-4100; Fax: 410-273-9555. Non-public level 5 special education for children with emotional/multiple disabilities ages 5-15. Lay Teachers 9; Teacher Aides 6; Children 40.

[J] CHILD CARE CENTERS

BALTIMORE. *Bon Secours Family Support Center*, 26 N. Fulton Ave., 21223. Tel: 410-362-3629; Fax: 410-362-3649. Web: www.bonsecours.org/bshsi. Brenda K. Jones, Svc. Coord.; Lori H. Fagan, Exec. Dir.
Bon Secour of Maryland Foundation, Inc. Total Staff 16; Total Assisted Annually 220.
St. Frances Outreach Center, 1026 Brentwood Ave., 21202-4203. Tel: 410-685-1975; Fax: 410-332-1299. Sr. Brenda Motte, O.S.P., Dir. Total Assisted 20; Total Staff 1.
Good Shepherd Center, 4100 Maple Ave., 21227. Tel: 410-247-2770; Fax: 410-247-3242. Email: info@goodshepherdcenter.org. Web: www.goodshepherdcenter.org. Derrick Boone, Psy.D., Pres. & CEO; Laurie Zimmerli, Prin.; Sr. Mary Carol McClenon, Mission Integration Coord.; Susan Hirschman, Librarian.
House of the Good Shepherd of the City of Baltimore, Residential psychiatric treatment for adolescent girls with emotional and behavioral problems. Sisters 10; Lay Teachers 15; Capacity 105; Students 103; Total Assisted 168; Total Staff 295.
Mount Providence Child Development Center, 701 Gun Rd., 21227. Tel: 410-247-0449; Fax: 410-247-1150. Web: www.oblatesisters.com. Sr. Brenda Cherry, O.S.P., Dir. Oblate Sisters of Providence. Sisters 3; Lay Teachers 12; Students 80; Total Staff 16.

TIMONIUM. *Francis X. Gallagher Services*, 2520 Pot Spring Rd., 21093. Tel: 410-252-4005; Fax: 410-560-3495. Email: jhillman@cc-md.org. Web: www.catholiccharities-md.org/programs/gallagher. Mark J. Schulz, Admin. Residential, day habilitation and medical day programs for the people with developmental disabilities. Residential Capacity 262; Day Capacity 240; Total Assisted 360; Total Staff 410.
St. Vincent's Villa, 2300 Dulaney Valley Rd., 21093. Tel: 410-252-4700; Fax: 410-252-3040. Email: jhackbar@catholiccharities-md.org. Web: www.catholiccharities-md.org. Mark Greenberg, Dir., Child & Family Svcs.; Rev. Raymond C. Chase, Chap.; Katie Cashin, Spiritual Devel. Coord. St. Vincent's Villa is a part of Catholic Charities Child and Family Services, providing residential care as part of a continuum of mental health, educational and family services. Clients 6,000; Total Staff 825.

[K] GENERAL HOSPITALS

BALTIMORE. *St. Agnes HealthCare, Inc.*, 900 Caton Ave., 21229-5299. Tel: 410-368-6000; Fax: 410-368-2109. Email: info@stagnes.org. Web: www.stagnes.org. Dr. Ann Hazelwood, Dir. Pastoral Care; Bonnie Phipps, Pres. & CEO; Revs. Inniah Christy Arockiaraj, M.A., M.S., Ph.L., Chap.; Simonraj Savarimathu. Ascension Health. Priests 2; Sisters 11; Bed Capacity 307; Patients Assisted Annually 478,365; Total Staff 2,824.
St. Agnes Foundation, Inc. Tel: 410-368-3155; Fax: 410-368-3533. (Subsidiary of St. Agnes Health-Care, Inc.)
Bon Secours Baltimore Health Corporation, Inc. (1919) 2000 W. Baltimore St., 21223. Tel: 410-362-3000; Fax: 410-362-3126. Email: inforequest@bshsi.org. Web: www.bonsecoursbaltimore.org. Samuel L. Ross, M.D., M.S., CEO; Bro. Arthur Caliman, C.F.X., Bd. Pres.; Glendora Hughes, Bd. Chair; Sr. Mary Skopal, S.S.J., Dir. of Pastoral Care. Bon Secours Ministry. Sisters of Bon Secours 5; Bed Capacity 141; Patients Assisted Annually 204,907; Total Staff 935.
The following are tax exempt subsidiaries of the Bon Secours Baltimore Health Corporation, Inc.
Bon Secours Hospital Baltimore, Inc. (1920)
Bon Secours Community Health Works, Inc. (1994) Email: ghughes@mail.mchr.state.md.us.
Bon Secours of Maryland Foundation, Inc. (1991)
Good Samaritan Hospital, 5601 Loch Raven Blvd., 21239. Tel: 443-444-8000; Fax: 443-444-4599. Web: www.goodsam-md.org. Jeffrey A. Matton, Pres.; Shirley Roth, Vice Pres. Nursing; Rev. Guy Kagere, Dir. Pastoral Care; Deborah Bena, R.N., Health Min. Coord.; Anthony Read, Board Chm. Adult acute care teaching hospital with a strong tradition of community care and home to more than 200 hospital based physicians. Bed Capacity 317.
Mercy Health Services Inc., 301 St. Paul Pl., 21202. Tel: 410-332-9000; Fax: 410-962-1303. Email: rrice@mdmercy.com. Web: www.mdmercy.com. Thomas Mullen, Pres. & CEO; Revs. Stephen D. Gosnell; Thomas R. Malia, Chap. & Asst. to

Mission Pres.; Sr. Mary Harper, R.S.M., Chap.; Rev. Augustine Etemma Inwang, M.S.P. (Nigeria); Kathy Ault, Dir. Pastoral Care. Institute of the Sisters of Mercy of the Americas., Subsidiaries: Mercy Medical Center Inc.; St. Paul Place Specialists, Inc.; Healthcare for the Homeless; Maryland Family Care; Mercy Transitional Care; Stella Maris, Inc.; Cardinal Shehan Center, Inc.; Mercy Health Foundation, Inc.; Mercy Ridge. Sisters 14; Employees 3,738; Patients Assisted Annually 732,853; Bed Capacity 226; Total Staff 3,913.

TOWSON. *St. Joseph Medical Center, Inc.* (1864) 7601 Osler Dr., 21204. Tel: 410-337-1000; Fax: 410-337-1024. Email: susannedecrane@catholichealth.net. Web: www.stjosephtowson.com. Charles Neumann, Pres. & CEO; Susanne DeCrane, Ph.D., Vice Pres., Mission & Dir. Spiritual Care. Sisters of St. Francis of Philadelphia. Sisters 4; Nurses 670; Beds 263; Patients Assisted Annually 309,812; Total Staff 2,210.

Chaplains: Affiliate of Catholic Health Initiatives. Revs. Alfonso Serna, O.SS.T.; Robert Phillips, S.J.; Sr. Anna M. Keenaghan, O.S.F., Chap.; Jane Mayrer; Maureen O'Brien; Kathy Edelmann.

[L] NURSING HOMES (SKILLED) AND REHABILITATION CENTERS

BALTIMORE. *Belvedere Green at Good Samaritan*, 1651 E. Belvedere Ave., 21239. Tel: 410-433-7255. Jeffrey A. Malton, Pres.; Shirley Roth, Vice Pres. Nursing; Rev. Guy Kagere, Dir. of Pastoral Care; Deborah Bena, R.N., Health Min. Coord.; Anthony Read, Board Chm.

Dismas House West, 105 S. Mount St., 21223-0435. Tel: 410-566-9400; Fax: 410-233-1622. P.O. Box 4435, 21223-0435. Joseph J. Kruse Jr., Exec Dir.; Barbara Fleming, Admin. Svcs. Facilitator. Non-Sectarian-Use Diocesan Property Rehabilitation center under contract to the Maryland Division of Corrections to provide inmate services. Total Staff 26; Total Assisted Annually 200.

Good Samaritan Nursing Center, 1601 E. Belvedere Ave., 21239. Tel: 443-451-5700. Jeffrey A. Malton, Pres.; Cesare A. Tapino, Admin.

The Neighborhoods at St. Elizabeth Rehabilitation and Nursing Center, 3320 Benson Ave., 21227-1035. Tel: 410-644-7100; Fax: 410-646-6589. Email: info@catholiccharities-md.org. Web: www.catholiccharities-md.org. Ms. Christine Mour, N.H.A., Admin.; Rev. Godswill Agbagwa, Chap.

St. Elizabeth Rehabilitation and Nursing Center., Sponsored by Associated Catholic Charities. Sisters 1; Bed Capacity 162; Total Assisted 285; Total Staff 220.

EMMITSBURG. *St. Joseph's Ministries, Inc.*, 331 S. Seton Ave., 21727. Tel: 301-447-7000; Fax: 301-447-7015. Email: info@stcatherinesnursingcenter.com. Web: stcatherinesnursingcenter.com. Annie Isaac, Admin. & CEO. Sponsored by Ascension Health. Bed Capacity 99; Total Assisted 150; Total Staff 215.

[M] HOMES FOR AGED

BALTIMORE. *St. Charles Villa*, 603 Maiden Choice Ln., 21228-3697. Tel: 410-747-1211; Fax: 410-747-2460. Revs. John L. Bitterman, S.S., S.T.B., M.A., Dir.; Joseph J. Bonadio, S.S., M. Rel.Ed., D.Min., S.T.L. (Retired); John W. Bowen, S.S., M.A., S.T.L. (Retired); Albert C. Giaquinto, S.S., M.A., S.T.L. (Retired); Claude H. Dukehart, S.S., M.A., S.T.D. (Retired); Edward J. Frazer, S.S., M.A., S.T.L. (Retired); John F. Mattingly, S.S., M.A., M.S.L.S., S.S.L. (Retired); John E. McMurry, S.S., S.T.L., Ph.D. (Retired); Vincent deP. McMurry, S.S., M.A., S.T.L. (Retired); John H. Olivier, S.S., M.A., S.T.B. (Retired). Priests 10; Total in Residence 10; Total Staff 5.

St. Joseph's Nursing Home (1934) 1222 Tugwell Dr., 21228. Tel: 410-747-0026; Fax: 410-747-0386. Email: st.josephs@stjosephs.net. Rev. Joseph Dorniak, O.F.M.Conv.; Sr. Krystyna Mroczek, Admin.

Sisters Servants of Mary Immaculate, Inc. Sisters 11; Residents 44; Total Assisted 80; Total Staff 63.

St. Martin's Home for Aged, Little Sisters of the Poor, Baltimore Inc., 601 Maiden Choice Ln., 21228. Tel: 410-744-9367; Fax: 410-747-6380. Email: msbaltimore@littlesistersofthepoor.org. Web: www.littlesistersofthepoorbaltimore.org. Sisters 16; Intermediate Care Beds 42; Assisted Living 22; Apartments 16; Aged Residents 80; Total Staff 120; Total Assisted 84.

TIMONIUM. *Stella Maris* (1953) 2300 Dulaney Valley Rd., 21093. Tel: 410-252-4500 (office); Fax: 410-560-9675. Email: ljohnson@stellamaris.com. Web: www.stellamarisinc.com. Sr. Karen McNally, R.S.M., Chief Admin. Officer; Rev. Lawrence M. Johnson, Dir. of Pastoral Care. The management corporation for all programs of Stella Maris. Long-term care; sub-acute care; home health; rehabilitative services; in-patient and home hospice; skilled home care; personal care; independent living; counseling/bereavement services for adults and children; and Senior day care. All applications for the facilities of the Center are processed directly through the Admissions Office at Stella Maris. Lay Personnel 724; Sisters 7; Staff 730; Residents 383; Bed Capacity 412; Total Assisted 139,930.

[N] SOCIAL SERVICES

BALTIMORE. *Franciscan Center* (1968) 101 W. 23rd St., 21218. Tel: 410-467-5340; Fax: 410-467-4569. Email: emcnally@franciscancenterbaltimore.org. Web: www.franciscancenterbaltimore.org. Edward McNally, M.B.A., M.Div., J.D., Pres. & CEO. Sisters of St. Francis of Assisi. Total Assisted 180,000; Total Staff 21.

Mount Providence Reading Center, 701 Gun Rd., 21227. Tel: 410-247-0448; Fax: 410-242-4963. Email: sisterconstance@oblatesisters.com. Web: www.oblatesisters.com. Sr. M. Constance Fenwick, O.S.P., Dir. Oblate Sisters of Providence. Students 56; Total Assisted 56; Total Staff 4.

Trinitarian Counseling Services, Inc., 8400 Park Heights Ave., P.O. Box 5719, 21282. Tel: 410-486-5764; Fax: 410-486-0614. Email: treasurer@trinitarians.org. Rev. William J. Moorman, O.SS.T., Ph.D., Dir. Total Assisted 12; Total Staff 1.

EMMITSBURG. *Seton Center, Inc.*, 16840 S. Seton Ave., 21727. Tel: 301-447-6102; Fax: 301-447-1748. Email: setoncenterinc@doc.org. Web: www.setoncenterinc.org. Sr. Salvatrice Murphy, D.C., Admin. Daughters of Charity., Social Service; Outreach; Thrift Shop. Total Assisted 8,000.

PASADENA. *Mary's Center, Inc.* (1990) P.O. Box 1804, 21123-1804. Tel: 410-761-8082; 301-739-1234 (Hagerstown); Fax: 410-761-0330. 7567 Ritchie Hwy., Glen Burnie, 21061. Pregnancy Support Svcs. Free pregnancy tests; material assistance to women & babies in need. Additional offices in Hagerstown, MD (1200 Dual Hwy.) & Baltimore, MD (805 N. Calvert St.) Total Assisted 721; Total Staff 28.

[O] ASSOCIATED CATHOLIC CHARITIES

BALTIMORE. *Associated Catholic Charities, Inc. (Catholic Charities)*

For more information on Catholic Charities and its programs please contact:

Catholic Charities, 320 Cathedral St., 3rd Floor, 21201-4421. Tel: 410-547-5490. Email: info@catholiccharities-md.org. Web: www.catholiccharities-md.org.

Management Team:

Associated Catholic Charities Inc., 320 Cathedral St., 3rd Floor, 21201-4421. Tel: 410-547-5333; Fax: 410-752-2873. Mr. William J. McCarthy Jr., Exec. Dir.

Associated Catholic Charities Inc., 228 W. Lexington St., 21201-3432. Tel: 410-261-6775; Fax: 410-889-0203. Mary Anne O'Donnell, Dir. Community Svcs. Div.

Associated Catholic Charities Inc., 320 Cathedral St., 3rd Floor, 21201-4421. Tel: 410-547-5459; Fax: 410-752-2873. Scott Becker, CFO.

Associated Catholic Charities Inc., 320 Cathedral St., 21201-4421. Tel: 410-547-5481; Fax: 410-576-2179. Angelo Boer, Dir., Devel. and Communications Div.

Associated Catholic Charities Inc., 2520 Pot Spring Rd., Timonium, 21093-2795. Tel: 410-252-4005, Ext. 104; Fax: 410-560-3495. Mark J. Schulz, Dir., Lifetime Svcs. Division.

Associated Catholic Charities Inc., 1966 Greenspring Dr., Ste. 200, Timonium, 21093. Tel: 443-798-3416; Fax: 410-561-3056. Dale R. McArdle, Dir., Housing Svcs. Div.

Associated Catholic Charities Inc., 1966 Greenspring Dr., Ste. 200, Timonium, 21093. Tel: 443-798-3390; Fax: 410-561-7728. Kathleen H. Mills, Dir., Human Resources Div.

Associated Catholic Charities Inc., 2300 Dulaney Valley Rd., Timonium, 21093-2739. Tel: 410-252-4700, Ext. 101; Fax: 410-252-3040. Mark Greenberg, Dir., Children & Family Svcs. Division Management Team: Jim Tucker, Dir. Information Technology, 1966 Greenspring Dr., Ste. 200, Timonium, 21093. Tel: 410-561-6469; Fax: 410-561-7755; Mr. William J. McCarthy Jr.; Angelo Boer; Mark Greenburg; Dale R. McArdle; Kathy Mills; Mary Anne O'Donnell; Mark J. Schulz; Scott Becker.

Associated Catholic Charities Inc., 2300 Dulaney Valley Rd., Timonium, 21093. Tel: 410-252-4700, Ext. 103; Fax: 410-252-3040. Mary Rode, Admin. Villa Maria Continuum.

Services For Children and Families:

Harford County, Early Head Start, 34 N. Philadelphia Blvd., Aberdeen, 21001. Tel: 410-273-5650; Fax: 410-272-6082.

Carroll County, Head Start and Early Head Start and PreK School, 255 Clifton Blvd., Ste. 101, Westminster, 21157. Tel: 410-871-2450; 410-876-8503; Fax: 410-876-8630.

Center for Family Services - International Adoptions, 2601 N. Howard St., 21218. Tel: 410-685-2363; Fax: 410-685-2365.

Center for Family Services - Family to Family Respite, 2601 N. Howard St., 21218. Tel: 410-685-2363; Fax: 410-685-2365.

Center for Family Services - Pregnancy, Parenting and Domestic Adoption Svcs., 2601 N. Howard St., 21218. Tel: 410-685-2363; Fax: 410-685-2365.

Center for Family Services - Therapeutic Alternative Shelter Care (TASC), 1301 Continental Dr., Ste. 101, Abingdon, 21009. Tel: 410-538-3388; Fax: 410-538-3376.

Center for Family Services - Resource Services, 2601 N. Howard St., 21218. Tel: 410-685-2363; Fax: 410-685-2365.

Center for Family Services - Treatment Foster Care, 2601 N. Howard St., 21218. Tel: 410-685-2363; Fax: 410-685-2365.

1301 Continental Dr., Suite 101, Abingdon, 21009. Tel: 410-676-4002; Fax: 410-676-7365.

St. Jerome's Head Start, 915 Sterrett St., 21230-2502. Tel: 410-685-1700; Fax: 410-685-2546.

Treatment Foster Care HOPE Program, 2601 N. Howard St., 21218. Tel: 410-685-2363; Fax: 410-685-2365.

Baltimore City Child and Adolescent Response (Foster/Kinship Care Stabilization Program), 1118 S. Light St., 21230. Tel: 410-727-4800; Fax: 410-727-5853.

St. Vincent's Villa Diagnostic Evaluation and Treatment Program, 2600 Pot Spring Rd., Timonium, 21093. Tel: 410-252-4000; Fax: 410-561-8109.

Villa Maria - Behavioral Health Clinics: (9 locations)

Anne Arundel County Out-Patient Mental Health Clinic, 1438 Defense Hwy., Ste. 202, Gambrills, 21054. Tel: 410-451-0682; Fax: 410-451-0701.

Lansdowne Out-Patient Mental Health Clinic, 2700 Washington Ave., 21227. Tel: 410-368-3984; Fax: 410-536-1290.

Harford County Out-Patient Mental Health Clinic, 1301 Continental Dr., Ste. 101, Abingdon, 21009. Tel: 410-676-4002; Fax: 410-676-7365.

Carroll County Out-Patient Mental Health Clinic, 255 Clifton Blvd., Ste. 302, Westminster, 21157. Tel: 410-848-2037; Fax: 410-848-5273.

Frederick County Out-Patient Mental Health Clinic, 116 E. 2nd St., Frederick, 21701. Tel: 301-694-6654; 301-898-7900 (Voicemail); Fax: 301-694-8221.

Hagerstown Out-Patient Mental Health Clinic, 229 N. Potomac St., Hagerstown, 21740-3812. Tel: 301-733-5858; Fax: 301-733-5626.

Mountain Maryland Out-Patient Mental Health Clinic and Allegany County School Mental Health Services, 517 Oldtown Rd., Front, Cumberland, 21502. Tel: 301-777-8685; Fax: 301-777-8687.

Fallstaff Out-Patient Mental Health Clinic, 6999 Reisterstown Rd., 21215. Tel: 410-585-0598; Fax: 410-585-0589.

Home-Based Respite Program (Cecil, Harford, Baltimore County & Baltimore City), 2601 N. Howard St., 21218. Tel: 410-685-2363; Fax: 410-685-2364.

In-Home Intervention Services, 2601 N. Howard St., 21218. Tel: 410-685-2363; Fax: 410-685-2364.

St. Vincent's Villa Residential Treatment Center, 2600 Pot Spring Rd., Timonium, 21093-2739. Tel: 410-252-4000; Fax: 410-561-8109. 2300 Dulaney Valley Rd., Timonium, 21093. Tel: 410-252-4700; Fax: 410-252-3040.

Safe Start, 1301 Continental Dr., Ste. 101, Abingdon, 21009-2338. Tel: 410-676-4002; Fax: 410-676-7365.

Villa Maria School, 2300 Dulaney Valley Rd., Timonium, 21093-2739. Tel: 410-252-6343; Fax: 410-560-1347.

Villa Maria School of Harford County, 1370 Brass Mill Rd., Belcamp, 21017. Tel: 410-297-4101; Fax: 410-273-9555. Rick Frank, Prin.

Villa Maria School at St. Vincent's Center, 2600 Pot Spring Rd., Timonium, 21093-2732. Tel: 410-252-3725; Fax: 410-453-9712.

Villa Maria School at St. Vincent's Center Type III Diagnostic Program, 2600 Pot Spring Rd., Timonium, 21093. Tel: 410-252-4000; Fax: 410-453-9712.

Villa Maria School-Based Mental Health Programs Baltimore County, Harford County, Baltimore City, 2300 Dulaney Valley Rd., Timonium, 21093. Tel: 410-252-4700; Fax: 410-252-3040. Carl Fornoff, Contact Person (Balt. Co.); Diane Shannon, Contact Person (Balt. City & Hartford Co.).

Parochial School Consultation Program, 2300 Dulaney Valley Rd., Timonium, 21093. Tel: 410-252-4700; Fax: 410-252-3040.
St. Vincent's Therapeutic Group Home, 1422 Gibsonwood Rd., Catonsville, 21228-2523. Tel: 410-788-9440; Fax: 410-788-4668.
Lansdowne Therapeutic After School Program, 2700 Washington Ave., 21227. Tel: 410-368-3984; Fax: 410-536-1290.
Timonium Therapeutic After School Program, 2300 Dulaney Valley Rd., Timonium, 21093-2739. Tel: 410-252-4700; Fax: 410-252-3040.
Residential Respite Program, 2300 Dulaney Valley Rd., Timonium, 21093. Tel: 410-252-4700; Fax: 410-252-3040.
Family Support Group Resource Center, 2300 Dulaney Valley Rd., Timonium, 21093. Tel: 410-252-4700; Fax: 410-252-3040.
Family Systems Navigator, 2300 Dulaney Valley Rd., Timonium, 21093. Tel: 410-252-4700; Fax: 410-252-3040.
Villa Maria at Edgewood Middle School, 2311 Willoughby Beach Rd., Edgewood, 21040. Tel: 410-612-1523; Fax: 410-612-1518.
Head Start Mental Health Consultation (Baltimore City, Baltimore, Harford and Carroll Counties), 1301 Continental Dr., Abingdon, 21009. Tel: 410-676-4002; Fax: 410-676-7365.
Timonium Out-Patient Mental Health Clinic, 2300 Dulaney Valley Rd., Timonium, 21093. Tel: 410-252-4700; Fax: 410-561-9073.
White Oak Counseling (White Oak School), 2300 Dulaney Valley Rd., Timonium, 21093. Tel: 410-252-4700, Ext. 126; Fax: 410-561-9073.
Baltimore City Regional Expanded School Mental Health/Early Childhood Mental Health Services, 6999 Reisterstown Rd., 21215. Tel: 410-545-0598; Fax: 410-585-0589.
Brief Strategic Family Therapy, 2300 Dulaney Valley Rd., Timonium, 21093. Tel: 410-252-4700, Ext. 262 (Timonium & Dundalk Office); 410-368-3984 (Lansdown Office).
Carroll County Head Start-Parents as Teachers, 255 Clifton Blvd., Ste. 101, Westminster, 21157. Tel: 410-848-2037.
Dundalk Outpatient Mental Health Clinic, 2901 Dunleer Rd., Dundalk, 21222. Tel: 410-252-4700, Ext. 262.
Early Childhood Mental Health Screening in seven Maryland Counties., 2300 Dulaney Valley Rd., Timonium, 21093. Tel: 410-252-7664.
Kinship Care Systems Navigations, 2901 Dunleer Rd., Dundalk, 21222. Tel: 443-652-2296.
Making All the Children Healthy (M.A.T.C.H.) Mental Health Assessment, 2601 N. Howard St., 21218. Tel: 410-659-4050; Fax: 410-685-2364.
Mental Health Counseling for Deaf Clients (Fallstaff Outpatient Mental Health Clinic), 6999 Resiterstown Rd., 21215. Tel: 410-585-0598.
Mountain Maryland/Garrett County Lighthouse Collaboration, 20 Oak Rd., Oakland, 21550. Tel: 301-334-9126.
School Based Mental Health Services (Allegany, Anne Arundel, Baltimore, Baltimore City, Washington, Frederick and Harford County), 2300 Dulaney Valley Rd., Timonium, 21093. Tel: 410-252-4700; Fax: 410-252-3040.
Therapeutic Mentoring Program, 2600 Pot Spring Rd., Timonium, 21093. Tel: 410-252-4000; Fax: 410-561-8109.
Community Services:
Anna's House, P.O. Box 88, Bel Air, 21014-0088. Tel: 410-803-2130; Fax: 410-638-1753.
Esperanza Center/Immigration Legal Services, 430 S. Broadway, 21231-2410. Tel: 410-522-2668; 410-534-8015; Fax: 410-675-1451.
**Cherry Hill Town Center (Cherry Hill Town Center, Inc.)* Program now part of Lifetime Services Division.
Christopher Place Employment Academy, 725 Fallsway, 21202. Tel: 443-983-9045; Fax: 410-962-8933.
Families That Work, 17 W. Franklin St., 21201. Tel: 410-659-3750; Fax: 410-244-6069.
Holden Hall, 761 W. Hamburg St., 21230. Tel: 410-347-9830; Fax: 410-347-9831.
Legislative Education Group Advocacy Networks (LEG), 228 W. Lexington St., Ste. 220, 21201-3432. Tel: 410-261-6783; Fax: 410-889-0203.
My Sister's Place Women's Center, 17 W. Franklin St., 21201. Tel: 410-727-3523; Fax: 410-727-1611.
My Sister's Place Lodge, 111 W. Mulberry St., 21201-3619. Tel: 410-528-9002; Fax: 410-528-9004.
Our Daily Bread, 725 Fallsway, 21202. Tel: 443-986-9045; Fax: 410-962-8932.
Parish Social Ministry, 228 W. Lexington St., Ste. 220, 21201-3432. Tel: 410-261-6782; Fax: 410-889-0203.
Project FRESH Start (Family Relocation, Empowerment, and Self-Help), 228 W. Lexington St., Ste. 220, 21201-3432. Tel: 410-261-6777; Fax: 410-889-0203.
Project SERVE (Service and Education through Residential Volunteer Experience), 228 W. Lexington St., Ste. 220, 21201-3432. Tel: 410-261-6774; Fax: 410-889-0203.
Alternative Spring Break, 228 W. Lexington St., Ste. 220, 21201-3432. Tel: 410-261-6774; Fax: 410-889-0203.
Employment Services, 725 Fallsway, 21202. Tel: 443-986-9043; Fax: 410-962-8930.
Samaritan Center, 17 W. Franklin St., 21201. Tel: 410-659-4020; Fax: 410-659-0642.
Sarah's House, 2015 20th St., Fort Meade, 20755-1301. Tel: 410-551-7722; Fax: 410-551-7279.
Social Concerns, 228 W. Lexington St., Ste. 220, 21201-3432. Tel: 410-261-6783; Fax: 410-889-0203.
Senior Community Service Employment Program (SCSEP), 228 W. Lexington St., Ste. 220, 21201-3432. Tel: 410-261-6765; Fax: 410-235-5781.
Services for Seniors:
Catholic Charities Senior Housing at Abingdon, 3001 St. Clair Dr., Abingdon, 21009. Tel: 410-273-0915; Fax: 410-273-0916. Debbie Seigle, Contact Person.
ACC Green House Residences, Inc., 320 Cathedral St., 21201. Tel: 410-547-5459; Fax: 410-752-2873. Web: www.cc-md.org. Scott Becker, Contact Person.
Answers for the Aging, 3310 Benson Ave., 21227-1035. Tel: 410-646-0100; 888-502-7587; Fax: 410-646-0500.
Caritas House Assisted Living, 3308 Benson Ave., 21227. Tel: 410-646-6600; Fax: 410-646-6565.
Catholic Charities Housing Application/Information Requests, 1966 Greenspring Dr., Ste. 200, Timonium, 21093. Tel: 443-798-3424.
**Catholic Charities Senior Housing at Arundel Woods (Glen Burnie Senior Housing, Inc.)*, 403 W. Ordnance Rd., Glen Burnie, 21061. Tel: 410-424-3535; Fax: 410-424-4484.
Catholic Charities Senior Housing at Basilica Place (The Catholic Charities Housing, Inc.), 124 W. Franklin Street, 21201-4576. Tel: 410-539-0418; Fax: 410-752-6207.
**Catholic Charities Senior Housing at Coursey Station (Coursey Station Apartments, Inc.)*, 200 First Ave., Lansdowne, 21227. Tel: 410-242-6167; Fax: 410-242-3459.
Catholic Charities Senior Housing at DePaul House (DePaul House, Inc.), 3300 Benson Ave., 21227-1030. Tel: 410-644-8484; Fax: 410-644-1334.
**Catholic Charities Senior Housing at Friendship Station (Odenton Senior Housing, Inc.)*, 1212 Odenton Rd., Odenton, 21113-1629. Tel: 410-519-6085; Fax: 410-519-6092.
Catholic Charities Senior Housing at Our Lady of Fatima II, 6420 E. Pratt St., 21224. Tel: 410-631-3555; Fax: 410-631-3556. Web: www.cc-md.org. Dale R. McArdle, Vice Pres.
**Catholic Charities Senior Housing at Owings Mills New Town (Owings Mills Senior Housing, Inc.)*, 9733 Groffs Mill Dr., Owings Mills, 21117. Tel: 410-902-8222; Fax: 410-902-0250.
**Catholic Charities Senior Housing at Reister's Clearing (Reisterstown Gardens Senior Housing, Inc.)*, 304 Cantata Ct., Reisterstown, 21136-6471. Tel: 410-517-4994; Fax: 410-517-0095.
**Catholic Charities Senior Housing at Reister's View (Reisterstown Village Senior Housing, Inc.)*, 306 Cantata Ct., Reisterstown, 21136-6472. Tel: 410-517-4994; Fax: 410-517-4995.
Catholic Charities Senior Housing at St. Charles House (St. Charles House, Inc.), 11 Church Ln., Pikesville, 21208-6607. Tel: 410-484-6125.
**Catholic Charities Senior Housing at Aberdeen*, 901 Barnett La., Aberdeen, 21001. Tel: 410-273-0435; Fax: 410-273-0439.
**Catholic Charities Senior Housing at St. Joachim House (St. Joachim House, Inc.)*, 3310 Benson Ave., 21227-1075. Tel: 410-644-8269; Fax: 410-525-9227.
**Catholic Charities Senior Housing at St. Luke's Place (St. Luke's Apartments, Inc.)*, 2825 Lodge Farm Rd., Edgemere, 21219-1347. Tel: 410-477-3661; Fax: 410-477-0199.
**Catholic Charities Senior Housing at Starner Hill Apartments (Backbone Housing, Inc.)*, 25 N. Pennsylvania Ave., Grantsville, 21536-0489. Tel: 301-895-5842; Fax: 301-895-3762.
**Catholic Charities Senior Housing at Trinity House Apartments (Trinity House Apartments, Inc.)*, 409 Virginia Ave., Towson, 21286-5372. Tel: 410-825-5288; Fax: 410-825-5592.
**Catholic Charities Senior Housing at Holy Korean Martyrs (Woodlawn Senior Housing, Inc.)*, 5500 Lexington Rd., Woodlawn, 21207. Tel: 410-944-5959; Fax: 410-944-0555.
Cherry Hill SeniorLife Center, 606 Cherry Hill Rd., Ste. 201, 21225-1229. Tel: 410-354-5101; Fax: 410-354-5103.
Congregate Housing Services Program, 1966 Greenspring Dr., Timonium, 21093. Tel: 443-798-3417; Fax: 410-561-3056.
Everall Gardens, 6100 Everall Ave., Overlea, 21206. Tel: 410-444-5850; Fax: 410-444-0190.
Catholic Charities Senior Housing at Friendship Village, 1208 Odenton Rd., Odenton, 21113. Tel: 410-305-0480; Fax: 410-305-0481.
Kessler Park, 4230 Hollins Ferry Rd., Lansdowne, 21227. Tel: 410-247-9244; Fax: 410-247-9245.
Pastoral Care at the Jenkins Senior Living Community, 3320 Benson Ave., 21227. Tel: 410-646-6513; Fax: 410-646-6541.
Catholic Charities Senior Housing at Our Lady of Fatima I, 6410 E. Pratt St., 21224. Tel: 410-631-6191; Fax: 410-631-6192.
St. Ann Adult Day Services, 3320 Benson Ave., 21227-1001. Tel: 410-646-6533; Fax: 410-644-0840.
The Neighborhoods at St. Elizabeth Rehabilitation and Nursing Center (Jenkins Memorial Nursing Home, Inc.), 3320 Benson Ave., 21227-1035. Tel: 410-644-7100; Fax: 410-646-6589.
Catholic Charities Senior Housing at St. Mark's, 19 Winters Ln., Catonsville, 21228. Tel: 410-788-0972.
Services for People with Developmental Disabilities:
Francis X. Gallagher Services, 2520 Pot Spring Rd., Timonium, 21093-2795. Tel: 410-252-4005; Fax: 410-560-3495. Programs include vocational, adult medical day & residential services.
The Bethany Community, Inc. Tel: 410-252-4005; Fax: 410-560-3495.
Group homes constructed and operated under the U.S. Dept. of Housing and Urban Development's Section 202-8 Program:
3731 Ellerslie Ave., 21218.
2421 Pot Spring Rd., Timonium, 21093.
2292 Dulaney Valley Rd., Timonium, 21093.
18314 Middletown Rd., Parkton, 21120.
3400 Benson Ave., 21227.
8240 Jumpers Hole Rd., Millersville, 21108.
4607 Mountain Rd., Pasadena, 21122.
2560 Pot Spring Rd., Timonium, 21093.
625 Belfast Rd., Sparks, 21152.
4605 Mountain Rd., Pasadena, 21122.
751 Argonne Dr., 21218.
47 Church Rd., Arnold, 21012.
1925 Rockhaven Ave., 21228.
Other Associated Catholic Charities, Inc. Corporations:
661 Corporation, 320 Cathedral St., 21201. Tel: 410-547-5469.
The Children's Fund, Inc., 320 Cathedral St., 21201. Tel: 410-547-5469; Fax: 410-752-2873.

[P] RETREAT HOUSES FOR MEN, WOMEN AND YOUTH

SPARKS. *Msgr. Clare J. O'Dwyer Retreat House*, 15523 York Rd., P.O. Box 310, 21152. Tel: 410-666-2400; Fax: 410-472-3281. Email: odwyer@archbalt.org. Web: www.msgrodwyer.org. Total Staff 9.

[Q] MONASTERIES AND RESIDENCES OF PRIESTS AND BROTHERS

BALTIMORE. *St. Ambrose Friary*, 4502 Park Heights Ave., 21215. Tel: 410-367-0334; Fax: 410-542-6056. Revs. William Graham, O.F.M.Cap., J.C.L., Tribunal Office, Archdiocese of Baltimore; Paul Zaborowski, O.F.M.Cap., Pastor St. Ambrose Parish; Roman Kozacheson, O.F.M.Cap, Pastoral Min. Good Shepherd Hospital. *Colombiere Jesuit Community* St. Claude La Colombiere Jesuit Community., 5704 Roland Ave., 21210-1399. Tel: 410-532-1334; Fax: 410-532-1419. Revs. William C. Rickle, S.J., Supr., Asst. for Latino Ministries. Tel: 443-451-1659; 443-921-1335 (Office); Theodore E.A. Brady, S.J.; James A. Casciotti, S.J., Socius, Admonitor to Prov. & Prov. Consultor. Tel: 410-532-1423; 443-921-1317; William A. Dawson, S.J.; Edward Glynn, S.J., Min. Tel: 410-532-1431; Robert K. Judge, S.J.; Joseph Kennedy, S.J.; Liborio J. LaMartina, S.J., Resident Archivist & Sacristan. Tel: 410-532-1420; Thomas P. Martin, S.J., Subminister, Asst. Community Treas. & House Confessor; William H. Millerd, S.J.; Francis X. Metzbower, S.J.; Francis X. Moan, S.J., House Consultor; Bro. Claude L. Ory, S.J.; Revs. Joseph A. Panuska, S.J.; Thomas E. Peacock, S.J. Tel: 410-532-1438; Joseph M. Ritzman, S.J.; William P. Ryan, S.J., Prov. Treas. & Revisor for Houses & Apostolic Works. Tel: 410-532-1433; 443-921-1321 (Office); William J. Walsh; Joseph J. Hayden, S.J., Min.; Vincent deP. Alagia, S.J., Pastoral Ministry; Walter A. Buckius, S.J.; Bro. Paul Cawthorne, S.J., Fleet Maintenance; Revs. John J. Coll, S.J.; G. Richard Dimler, S.J., Pastoral Ministry; Bernard G. Filmyer, S.J., Pastoral Ministry.
Congregation of the Holy Spirit, 2846 W. Lafayette Ave., 21216.
Ferdinand Wheeler Jesuit Community, 3048 Guilford Ave., 21218. Tel: 410-338-1296; Fax: 443-921-1347. Email: tkuller@hotmail.com. Revs.

Michael Simone, S.J.; Thomas J. Kuller, S.J.; Dinesh Braganza, S.J.; Roberto A.R. Carampatan, S.J., Graduate Student; John S. Dear, S.J.; Mr. Luis Infante, S.J., Graduate Student. Priests 6; Brothers 1; Scholastics 1.

Holy Trinity Monastery, 8400 Park Heights Ave., P.O. Box 5719, 21282-0719. Tel: 410-486-5171; Fax: 410-486-0614. Web: trinitarians.org. Priests 62. In Residence - Holy Trinity Monastery Baltimore Very Rev. J. Edward Owens, O.SS.T., Min. Provincial; Revs. Kurt J. Klismet, O.SS.T., Prov. Treas. & Dir. Devel.; David Colella, O.SS.T; Joseph J. Gross, O.SS.T; Juan Vasquez-Rubio, O.SS.T.; Alberto Rodriguez, O.SS.T.; Alfonso Serna, O.SS.T.; John Dorn, O.SS.T.; Aaron M. Dowdell, O.SS.T., M.A., S.T.B.; Jojo George Padinjare Pariyathu Parampil, O.SS.T.; Joshy Abraham Mappilaparambil, O.SS.T. Assigned Elsewhere Rome, Italy Very Rev. Albert M. Anuszewski, O.SS.T., Gen Councilor & Economer Gen.; Most Rev. Jose T. Narlaly, O.SS.T., Min. Gen. Archdiocese of Baltimore, MD - Assigned Elsewhere Revs. Thomas J. Burke, O.SS.T., S.T.M., S.T.D., B.A.; William J. Moorman, O.SS.T., Ph.D.; Victor Scocco, O.SS.T., Pastor; Binoy Akkalayil, O.SS.T. Diocese of Belleville, IL Bro. Eric Beardsley, O.SS.T. Diocese of Las Vegas, NV Revs. Edward Wagner, O.SS.T.; Michael Conway, O.SS.T. Archdiocese of Los Angeles, CA Very Rev. William J. Axe, O.SS.T., Prov. Councilor; Rev. Frank Whatley, O.SS.T. Archdiocese of Miami, FL Rev. William Sullivan, O.SS.T. Archdiocese of Philadelphia, PA Rev. Vincent Bechamps, O.SS.T.; Very Rev. James R. Day, O.SS.T., Prov. Councilor; Rev. Thomas A. Morris, O.SS.T. Archdiocese of San Antonio, TX Rev. Tom Dymowski, O.SS.T. Diocese of Trenton, NJ Revs. Ken Borgesen, O.SS.T.; Philip Cordisco, O.SS.T.; Daniel Houde, O.SS.T.; Ireneusz Ekiert, O.SS.T.; Charles J. Flood, O.SS.T.; Boby Kurian Kumbakeel, O.SS.T.; Gerard Lynch, O.SS.T.; Santhosh George Kozhippandan, O.SS.T. Diocese of Victoria, TX Rev. Raphael Baidoo, O.SS.T.; Very Rev. Stanley W. DeBoe, O.SS.T., Prov. Councilor; Rev. Adelson S. Moreira, O.SS.T.; Bro. Patrick G. Wildgen, O.SS.T.; Rev. Juan Antonio Perez-Ojeda, O.SS.T. Archdiocese of Washington, DC Very Rev. Damian Anuzewski, O.SS.T., Prov. Sec./Acting Rector DeMatha Catholic High School; Rev. Lawrence C. Hernandez, O.SS.T.; Very Rev. Juan Molina, O.SS.T., Prov. Councilor Assigned in India Revs. Anthony Pullukattu, O.SS.T.; Baiju Parakkal, O.SS.T.; Bitaju Puthenpurakal, O.SS.T.; Francis Kulathingal, O.SS.T.; Janil Joseph Chakkiath, O.SS.T.; Joseph Muthuplackal, O.SS.T.; Mathew Maniamkerry, O.SS.T.; Poulose Chalackal, O.SS.T.; Pradeep Puthenveettil, O.SS.T.; Simine G. Fernandez, O.SS.T.; Xavier Kachappilly, O.SS.T.; Roy Kurian Kalachalil, O.SS.T.; Sajeev Joseph, O.SS.T.; Augustine Varghese Vadakathalakal, O.SS.T.; Binoj Mathew Puthenpurackal, O.SS.T.; Jolly Pappachan Thekkinen, O.SS.T.; Jins Valiyakulathil, O.SS.T.; Joshi Antony Kombarakkaran, O.SS.T.; Shinu Mathew Malekunnel, O.SS.T.; Sibi Antony Palatty, O.SS.T.; Sibi Rocky Puthussery, O.SS.T.

Immaculate Heart of Mary Friary, 4220 Erdman Ave., 21213. Tel: 410-485-5511; Fax: 410-483-2545. Email: jbenicewicz@archbishopcurley.org. Revs. Vincent Gluc, O.F.M.Conv.; Joseph Benicewicz, O.F.M.Conv.; Matthew Foley, O.F.M.Conv.; Bros. Douglas McMillan, O.F.M.Conv., Vicar; Daniel Lutolf, O.F.M.Conv. Residence of Franciscan Friars, O.F.M.Conv., conducting Archbishop Curley High School. Priests 3; Brothers 2; Total Staff 5.

Jesuit Community of Loyola University, Inc., Loyola University, 4603 Millbrook Rd., 21212-4721. Tel: 410-617-2318; Fax: 410-617-2125. Email: bomcdermott@loyola.edu. Revs. David G. Allen, S.J.; Ronald J. Amiot, S.J.; Charles Borges, S.J.; Timothy B. Brown, S.J.; James L. Connor, S.J.; John M. Dennis, S.J., M.Ed.; John R. Donahue, S.J.; Lloyd George, S.J.; Frank R. Haig, S.J.; Francis G. Hilton, S.J.; James Kelly, S.J.; Brian F. Linnane, S.J., Pres. Loyola College; Brian O. McDermott, S.J., Rector; F. Joseph Michini, S.J.; William T. Miller, S.J.; James J. Miracky, S.J.; Francis J. Nash, S.J.; Konrad Noronha, S.J.; Thomas A. Pesci, S.J.; Robert L. Phillips, S.J.; Joseph S. Rossi, S.J.; Peter F. Ryan, S.J., S.T.L., S.T.D.; James F. Salmon, S.J.; James M. Shea, S.J.; Luis A. Tampe, S.J.; John W. Peck, S.J.; George Joseph Sebastian, S.J. Total in Residence 29.

Jesuit Mission Bureau, Maryland Province Inc., 8600 LaSalle Rd., Ste. 620, Towson, 21286-2014. Tel: 443-921-1310; Fax: 443-921-1313. Email: advancement@mdsj.org. Web: www.mdsj.org.

Jesuit Seminary Guild, Maryland Province, Inc., 8600 La Salle Rd., Ste. 620, Towson, 21286-2014. Tel: 443-921-1310; Fax: 443-921-1313. Email: advancement@mdsj.org. Web: www.mdsj.org.

St. Joseph Society of the Sacred Heart House of Central Administration, 1130 N. Calvert St., 21202. Tel: 410-727-3386; Fax: 410-727-1006. Email: josephite1@aol.com. Web: www.josephite.com. Very Rev. Edward J. Chiffriller, S.S.J., Supr. Gen.; Revs. Michael L. Thompson, S.S.J., Vicar Gen.; Thomas R. Frank, S.S.J., Consultor Gen.; Very Rev. Nelson A. Moreira, S.S.J., Treas. & Rector; Mrs. Carla Canady, Asst. Archivist; Revs. John F. Byrne, S.S.J. (Retired); N. Wilfrid DesRosiers, S.S.J. (Retired); James A. Hayes, S.S.J. (Retired); Joseph J. Rimshaw, S.S.J. (Retired). Priests 12.

St. Joseph's Manor, 911 W. Lake Ave., 21210-1022. Tel: 410-323-3829; Fax: 410-435-1853. Very Revs. Stephen F. Brett, S.S.J., Rector; Matthew J. O'Rourke, S.S.J., Vice Rector; Revs. Daniel Bastianelli, S.S.J.; Joseph M. Calamari, S.S.J.; Michael J. Farrell, S.S.J.; James A. Hayes, S.S.J. (Retired); Vincent P. Keenan, S.S.J.; Peter J. Kenney, S.S.J.; Edward J. Lawlor, S.S.J. (Retired); Edward J. Mullowney, S.S.J.; Bro. Charles Douglas, S.S.J. Home for retired priest & brothers of St. Joseph's Society of the Sacred Heart. Priests 10; Brothers 1.

St. Joseph's Passionist Community, 251 S. Morley St., 21229. Tel: 410-566-0877; Fax: 410-233-4974. Email: info@sjmp.org. Web: www.sjmp.org. Rev. Robert Carbonneau, C.P.; Bro. Edward Hall, C.P.; Revs. Alban Harmon, C.P., J.C.L.; Thomas McCann, C.P.; William Murphy, C.P. Congregation of the Most Holy Cross and Passion of Our Lord Jesus Christ. Priests 4; Brothers 1.

Pallottine Center for Apostolic Causes, 512 W. Saratoga St., 21201. Tel: 410-685-3063; Fax: 410-234-1459. Rev. Peter T. Sticco, S.A.C., Dir.

St. Jude Shrine-Pallottine Missions; Pallottine Center for Apostolic Causes, Inc., Promotional Center for St. Jude Shrine.

Society of St. Sulpice, Province of the United States (Associated Sulpicians of the United States), 5408 Roland Ave., 21210-1988. Tel: 410-323-5070; Fax: 410-433-6524. Email: provincial@sulpicians.org. Web: sulpicians.org. Very Revs. Ronald D. Witherup, S.S., S.T.L., S.T.M., Ph.D., Supr. General, 6 rue du Regard, Paris 75006 France; Thomas R. Ulshafer, S.S., S.T.L., Ph.D., Prov. Supr., Dubourg House, 4210 N. Charles St., Apt. 6, 21218-1041; Rev. Gerald D. McBrearity, S.S., M.A., S.T.B., D.Min., Dir. Formation, Coord. Human & Spiritual Formation, Dir. Basselins Advisor & Spiritual Dir. Theological College of The Catholic University of America, 401 Michigan Ave., NE, Washington, DC 20017-1578. Represented in the Archdioceses and Dioceses of: Baltimore, Bridgeport, Dallas, Lansing, Los Angeles, Monterey, Oakland, Scranton, San Antonio, San Francisco, San Jose, Springfield-Cape Girardeau, and Washington, DC. Also in France & Italy.; Missions: Kabwe & Lusaka in Zambia, Central Africa Priests in Society of St. Sulpice 73; Priests at Provincial House 4; Priest Candidates 9.

Members and Candidates on Individual Assignments: Revs. Cornelius Hankomoone, S.S., S.T.L., S.T.D., Rector & Faculty, Emmaus Regl. Supr. Spirituality Center, Emmaus Spirituality Centre, P.O. Box 320084-Woodlands, Lusaka, Zambia; Timothy C. Chikweto, S.S., S.T.L., Scripture, Emmaus Spiritually Ctr., Lusaka, Zambia; Lewis B. Chilufya, S.S., S.T.L., S.T.D., Human Devel., Emmaus Spiritually Ctr., Lusaka, Zambia; Smart H. Chinyanwa, S.S., B.D., Ph.L., Philosophy & Metaphysics, St. Augustine's Major Seminary, Kabwe, Zambia; Thomas R. Hurst, S.S., S.T.L., Ph.D., Pres.-Rector, Vice Chancellor, St. Mary's Seminary & University, 5400 Roland Ave., 21210-1994; Melvin C. Blanchette, S.S., M.A., Ph.D., Advisor & Spiritual Dir., Theological College of The Catholic University of America, 401 Michigan Ave, N.E., Washington, DC 20017-1578. Tel: 202-756-4915; Fax: 202-756-4909; Daniel J. Doherty, S.S., B.A., M.A., M.Div., S.T.L., Pastoral Theology & Asst. Dir. Pastoral Formation, St. Mary's Seminary & University, 5400 Roland Ave., 21210-1994; Paul A. Maillet, S.S., B.Mus., M.M., M.Div., S.T.L., S.T.D., Sacred Scripture, St. Patrick Seminary & Univ. Tel: 202-756-5400; Fax: 202-756-4909; Daniel F. Moore, S.S., M.A., S.T.L., S.T.D., Dir. Discernment & Admissions, Provincial Sec., Theological College of The Catholic University of America, 401 Michigan Ave., NE, Washington, DC 20017-1578. Tel: 202-756-4914; Fax: 202-756-4909; Anthony J. Pogorelc, S.S., M.Div., M.S., Ph.D., Dir. Pastoral Formation Prog., Advisor & Spiritual Dir., Theological College of The Catholic University of America, 401 Michigan Ave, N.E., Washington, DC 20017-1578. Tel: 202-756-4912; Fax: 202-756-4909; David D. Thayer, S.S., S.T.L., Ph.D., Advisor/Spirit. Dir. & Dir. of Intellectual Formation, Catholic University of America, c/o Theological College, 401 Michigan Ave, N.E., Washington, DC 20017-1578. Tel: 202-756-4911; Fax: 202-756-4909; Victor S. Shikaputo, S.S., S.T.L., S.T.D., St. Dominic Seminary Academic Dean, Moral Theology & Regl. Coord. Discernment, St. Dominic's Major Seminary, P.O. Box 320191, Woodlands, Lusaka, Zambia; Joseph T. Ky, S.S., M.A. (Retired), The Congregation of the Mother Co-Redemptrix, 1900 Grand Ave., Carthage, MO 64836-3500. Tel: 417-358-7137; William E. Hartgen Jr., S.S., M.A. (Retired), 634 E St., N.E., Washington, DC 20002-5230. Tel: 202-236-7745; John S. Kselman, S.S., S.T.L., Ph.D., Sacred Scripture, St. Patrick's Seminary & University, 320 Middlefield Rd., Menlo Park, CA 94025-3596; Addison G. Wright, S.S., M.A., S.S.L., S.T.D. (Retired), 24 Killian Ave., Trumbull, CT 06611-4118. Tel: 203-268-3610; James W. Lothamer, S.S., S.T.B., M.A., Ph.D., Parochial Vicar, Diocese Lansing. Tel: 517-223-8684; Fax: 517-223-0813; James P. Oberle, S.S., S.T.B., S.T.L., Ph.D., Dir. Spiritual & Liturgical Formation, Holy Trinity Seminary, 3131 Vince Hagen Dr., Irving, TX 75062; James S. Tucker, S.S., M.A., M.S., Ph.D., Spiritual Advisor, Assumption Seminary, 2600 W. Woodlawn Ave., San Antonio, TX 78228-5196. Tel: 210-734-5137, Ext. 36; Cale J. Crowley, S.S., M.Div., Ph.D.; Patrick Simutowe, S.S., S.T.L., Graduate Studies, Accademia Alfonsiana, College Pontifical Canadien, 75 Crescenzio, Rome 00193 Italy. Tel: 011-260-95-915273; Fax: 001-260-1-263-404; Gerald V. Lardner, S.S., S.T.B., M.A., Ph.D. (Retired), 3601 Greenway, Apt. 102, 21218-2450. Tel: 443-983-5992; Fax: 410-747-2460; Joseph J. Bonadio, S.S., M. Rel.Ed., D.Min., S.T.L., Chap. Oak Crest Retirement Center (Retired), St. Charles Villa, 603 Maiden Choice Ln., 21228-3697. Tel: 410-747-2055; Fax: 410-747-2460; John W. Bowen, S.S., M.A., S.T.L., St. Mary Seminary & Univ. Alumni News Ed. (Retired), St. Charles Villa, 603 Maiden Choice Ln., 21228-3697. Tel: 410-719-2842; Fax: 410-747-2460; C. Henry Dukehart, S.S., M.A., S.T.D. (Retired), St. Charles Villa, 603 Maiden Choice Ln., 21228-3697. Tel: 410-455-5382; Fax: 410-747-2460; Edward J. Frazer, S.S., M.A., S.T.L. (Retired), St. Charles Villa, 603 Maiden Choice Ln., 21228-3697. Tel: 410-719-7191; Fax: 410-747-2460; Albert C. Giaquinto, S.S., M.A., S.T.L. (Retired), St. Charles Villa, 603 Maiden Choice Ln., 21228-3697. Tel: 410-744-2049; Fax: 410-747-2460; John F. Mattingly, S.S., M.A., M.S.L.S., S.S.L. (Retired), St. Charles Villa, 603 Maiden Choice Ln., 21228-3697. Fax: 410-747-2460; Vincent deP. McMurry, S.S., M.A., S.T.L. (Retired), St. Charles Villa, 603 Maiden Choice Ln., 21228-3697. Fax: 410-747-2460. Email: vdpmcmss@aol.com; John H. Olivier, S.S., M.A., S.T.B (Retired), St. Charles Villa, 603 Maiden Choice Ln., 21228-3697. Tel: 410-747-3587; Fax: 410-747-2460; Hy K. Nguyen, S.S., M.Div., M.A., S.T.D., Systematic Theology, St. Mary's Seminary and University, 5400 Roland Ave., 21210-1994. Tel: 410-864-4258; Fax: 410-864-4278; William J. Flynn, S.S., S.T.L., M.S., D.Min. (Retired), Villa St. Joseph, 1600 Green Ridge St., Dunmore, PA 18509. Tel: 570-254-6233; Fax: 570-254-6233; Peter F. Chirico, S.S., S.T.D., B.B.A. (Retired), St. Martin's Home for the Aged, 601 Maiden Choice Ln., 21228-3698. Tel: 410-744-1528; William J. Lee, S.S., M.A., Ph.D. (Retired), St. Martin's Home for the Aged, 601 Maiden Choice Ln., 21228-3698. Tel: 410-788-0455; Peter W. Gray, S.S., M.A., Ph.D., Special Assignment, 113 Maple Ridge Rd., Reisterstown, 21136-6518; John E. McMurry, S.S., S.T.L., Ph.D., Asst. Dir., Sulpician Retirement Community (Retired); John C. Kemper, S.S., M.Div., M.A., D.Min., Vice Pres. Advancement & Dir. St. Mary's Spiritual Center & Historic Site, St. Mary's Spiritual Center & Historic Site, 600 N. Paca St., 21201-1920; Leo J. Larrivee, S.S., M.A. (Theol.), M.A. (Hist.), Dubourg House, 4210 N. Charles St., Apt. 3, 21218-1041. Fax: 410-737-8826; John L. Bitterman, S.S., S.T.B., M.A., Dir./Supr Sulpician Retirement Community, St. Charles Villa, 603 Maiden Choice Ln., 21228-3697. Tel: 410-323-5070; Fax: 410-433-6524; Gerald L. Brown, S.S., M.Div., Ph.D., Co-Dir., Pastoral Year Prog. (Retired), St. Patrick's Seminary & University, 320 Middlefield Rd., Menlo Park, CA 94025-3596. Tel: 650-289-3357; Fax: 650-322-0997; Phillip J. Brown, J.D., S.T.B., J.C.D., Rector, Theological College, Theological College of The Catholic University of America, 401 Michigan Ave., N.E., Washington, DC 20017-1578. Tel: 202-756-4910; Fax: 202-756-4909; Vincent D. Bui, S.S., M.A., S.T.B., J.C.L., Dean, Students, St. Patrick's Seminary & University, 320 Middlefield Rd., Menlo Park, CA 94025; Frederick J. Cwiekowski, S.S., M.A., S.T.D., Systematic Theology (Retired), St. Patrick's Seminary & University, 320 Middlefield Rd., Menlo Park, CA 94025-3596. Tel: 650-328-2544; Fax: 650-322-0997;

Philip S. Keane, S.S., S.T.D., Special Asst., Provincial (Retired), St. Mary's Seminary & University, 5400 Roland Ave., 21210-1994; Nam J. Kim, S.S., M.A., S.T.L., S.T.D., Sabbatical, St. Patrick's Seminary & University, 320 Middlefield Rd., Menlo Park, CA 94025-3563. Tel: 408-533-5073; Fax: 650-322-0997; Eugene J. Konkel, S.S., M.A., S.T.L., Spiritual Direction (Retired), St. Patrick's Seminary & University, 320 Middlefield Rd., Menlo Park, CA 94025-3596. Tel: 650-326-3825; Fax: 650-322-0997; Gerald D. Coleman, S.S., M.A., S.T.L., Ph.D., Vice Pres. Corp. Ethics Daughters of Charity Health System, St. Pius Rectory, 1100 Woodside Rd., Redwood City, CA 94061-3627. Tel: 650-298-9953; 650-298-9953; Louis M. Reitz, S.S., S.T.L., M.S.L.S., M.Ed. (Retired), St. Pius X Rectory, 6428 York Rd., 21212-2111. Tel: 410-377-5417; Lawrence B. Terrien, S.S., Ph.D., S.T.D., Dir. Spiritual Life Programs, Systematic Theology, St. Mary's Seminary & University, 5400 Roland Ave., 21210-1994; James E. Myers, S.S., M.Div., Dir. of Vatican II Institute, Vatican II Institute, St. Patrick's Seminary & University, 320 Middlefield Rd., Menlo Park, CA 94025-3596. Tel: 650-328-1731; Fax: 650-325-6765; James L. McKearney, S.S., M.Div., S.T.L., S.T.D., Pres., Rector & Vice Chancellor, St. Patrick's Seminary and University, 320 Middlefield Rd., Menlo Park, CA 94025-3563. Tel: 650-839-1290; Fax: 650-322-0997; J. Michael Strange, S.S., M.A., M.T.S., St. Vincent de Paul Parish, 2320 Green St., San Francisco, CA 94123-4625. Tel: 415-922-7203; Howard P. Bleichner, S.S., M.A., Dr. Theol., Prof. Systematic Theol. (Retired), 2-1151 E. Cliff Dr., Santa Cruz, CA 95062-4835. Tel: 831-475-5724; Richard M. Gula, S.S., S.T.L., S.T.M., Ph.D., Dir. Personnel & Supvr., Province Properties, 1514 Oxford St., Apt. 303, Berkeley, CA 94709-1502. Tel: 510-649-8259; Fax: 510-549-9466; Richard B. MacDonough, S.S., S.T.L., Ph.D., Adjunct Spiritual Direction, St. John's Seminary (Retired), 647 Bluewater Way, Port Hueneme, CA 93041-3559. Tel: 805-482-3470. *St. Mary's Seminary & University*, 5400 Roland Ave., 21210-1994. Tel: 410-864-4000; Fax: 410-864-4278. Revs. Michael L. Barre, S.S., S.T.L., Ph.D., Sacred Scripture, St. Mary's Seminary & University, 5400 Roland Ave., 21210-1994. Tel: 410-435-1973; Robert F. Leavitt, S.S., S.T.D., Systematic Theology, 16131 Old York Rd., Monkton, 21111. Tel: 410-864-3611; Luis R. Corneli Esq., S.S., J.D., J.C.L., Graduate Studies, Pontifical Gregorian Univ., St. Mary's Seminary & University, 5400 Roland Ave., 21210-1994; Gladstone H. Stevens, S.S., M.A., S.T.L., Ph.D., Vice Rector, Academic Dean, Systematic Theology, St. Patrick's Seminary & University, 320 Middlefield Rd., Menlo Park, CA 94025-3563; Shoba Nyambe, B.D., Graduate Studies, Pontifical Univ., St. Patrick's College, Dublin, Emmaus Spirituality Centre, P.O. Box 320084, Woodlands, Lusaka, Zambia; Renato Lopez, S.S., S.S.L., New Testament, Introduction to Theology, Dir. Liturgy, St. Mary's Seminary & University, 5400 Roland Ave., 21210-1994; Jeffrey A. Hubbard, B.A., S.T.B., M.Div., Graduate Studies, The Catholic Univ., St. Patrick's Seminary & University, 320 Middlefield Rd., Menlo Park, CA 94025-3563; Noel R. de Lira, A.B., S.T.B., S.T.L., Catholic Doctrine, Spiritual Dir. & Advisor, St. Patrick's Seminary & University, 320 Middlefield Rd., Menlo Park, CA 94025-3563; Victor Mwanamwambwa, S.S., B.D., Graduate Studies, Loyola Univ., MD, Emmaus Spirituality Centre, P.O. Box 320084, Woodlands, Lusaka, Zambia. St. Mary's Seminary & Univ., Baltimore, MD; John J. Slovikovski, M.Div., M.A., Ph.D. (Cand.), B.A., Advisor & Spiritual Dir., Theological College of The Catholic University of America, 401 Michigan Ave., NE, Washington, DC 20017-1578; Inniah Christy Arockiaraj, M.A., M.S., Ph.L., Philosophy; Martin J. Burnham, S.T.B., M.Div., Formation Faculty; Eugene H. Mwanza, B.D., Emmaus Spirituality Ctr., Lusaka, Zambia. (Sulpician Cand.) African Heritage; Rafael M. Ramirez, S.S., B.A., M.Div., M.A., S.T.L., S.T.D., S.T.B., Sacred Scripture, Latin; Jaime E. Robledo, M.Div., S.T.L., Ph.D. (Cand.), Philosophical & Medical Ethics, Advisor & Spiritual Dir.; Leonardo J. Gajardo, S.S., B.A., J.C.L., S.T.B., Canon Law.

Xaverian Brothers Generalate, 4409 Frederick Ave., 21229. Tel: 410-644-0034; Fax: 410-644-2762. Email: brother@xaverianbrothers.org. Web: xaverianbrothers.org. Bros. Lawrence Harvey, C.F.X., Gen. Supr.; Daniel Skala, C.F.X., Vicar Gen.; Ms. Alice Hession, Dir. Xaverian Sponsored Schools; Bros. Paul J. Murray, C.F.X., Gen. Councillor U.S. Personnel; Thomas Klar, C.F.X., Properties Mgr.; John Hamilton, C.F.X., Gen. Councillor Formation; Cornelius Hubbuch, C.F.X., Pastoral Care; Mr. Shawn Lynch, Business Mgr.; Bros. Jeremiah O'Leary, C.F.X., Peace & Justice; James Connolly, C.F.X., Dir. Memberships: Vocations/Volunteers; Peter Campbell, C.F.X., J.D., Treas. & Finance Officer. Legal Titles and Schools Sponsored: Xaverian Brothers USA, Inc. (f/k/a The American Central Province of the Xaverian Brothers Inc., The American Northeast Province of the Xaverian Brother, Inc., and the Working Boys Home, Inc.); St. Mary's-Ryken High School, Inc.; Our Lady of Good Counsel High School, Inc.; St. Xavier High School, Inc.; Xaverian High School, Inc.; Mt. St. Joseph High School, Inc.; Xaverian Brothers Auxiliary; St. Michael's High School Alumni Association; Nazareth Regional High School, Inc.; St. John's Preparatory School, Inc.; St. John's High School, Inc.; Xaverian Brothers High School, Inc.; Malden Catholic High School, Inc.; Xavier High School, Inc.; Isidore Charitable Trust. Brothers 235.

CUMBERLAND. *The Friary*, 300 1/2 E. Oldtown Rd., 21502. Tel: 301-777-7946; Fax: 301-759-3568. Email: ppaul@archbalt.org. Revs. Bernard Finerty, O.F.M.Cap., Vicar & Assoc. Pastor SS. Peter & Paul (Cumberland) & St. Ambrose (Cresaptown).; Eric Gauchat, O.F.M.Cap., Assoc. Pastor SS. Peter & Paul (Cumberland) & St. Ambrose (Cresaptown).; Stephen Fernandes, O.F.M.Cap., Vicar & Assoc. Pastor, Our Lady of the Mountains; Gregory Chervanek, O.F.M.Cap., Guardian & Mountain Maryland Health Care Priest.

Province of St. Augustine of the Capuchin Order Priests 4.

ELDERSBURG. *Society of Mary (Marianists), Marianist Community*, 6049 Kennard Ct., 21784. Tel: 410-795-2722; Fax: 410-795-7516. Rev. Richard Kuhn, S.M.; Bros. Frank O'Donnell, S.M.; Gerard Sullivan, S.M. Priests 1; Brothers 2.

ELLICOTT CITY. *Friary of St. Joseph Cupertino*, 12290 Folly Quarter Rd., 21042-1425. Tel: 410-531-2800; Fax: 410-531-2801. Rev. Joseph Dorniak, O.F.M.Conv.; Bro. Gerry Seipp, O.F.M.Conv., Dir. Hospitality. Conventual Franciscan Friars., Corporate Title: Franciscan Friars Minor Conventuals of MD, Inc. *Friars Minor Conventual Shrine of St. Anthony* Tel: 410-531-2800; Fax: 410-531-2801. *Companions of St. Anthony*, 12290 Folly Quarter Rd., 21042. Tel: 410-531-2800; Fax: 410-531-2801. *Companions Evangelization & Mail Order Office* Tel: 410-988-9833; Fax: 410-988-9705. Rev. Michael Heine, O.F.M.Conv., Guardian & Co-Dir., Postulancy; Bro. Daniel Geary, O.F.M.Conv., Co-Dir., Postulancy; Rev. Steven Frenier, O.F.M.Conv., Exec. Dir., Shrine.

Order of Friars Minor Conventual, 12300 Folly Quarter Rd., 21042-1419. Tel: 410-531-1400; Fax: 410-531-4881. Email: provse@saprov.org. Web: www.stanthonyprovince.org. Revs. Joachin Giermek, O.F.M.Conv.; Robert Twele Esq., O.F.M.Conv., Counselor Catholic Re4lief Svs.

Order of Friars Minor Conventual, St. Anthony of Padua Province, U.S.A., Inc.; Franciscan Minor Conventuals of Maryland, Inc. of Ellicott City, MD.; The Franciscan Fathers, Minor Conventuals, of St. Stanislaus Church of Baltimore City, Inc.; Franciscan Friars, St. Anthony of Padua Province, Education Fund, Inc.; Franciscan Friars, St. Anthony of Padua Province, Fund for the Aged and Infirm Friars, Inc.; St. Francis of Assisi Community, Inc., Companions of St. Anthony. St. Stanislaus Cemetery Inc; AnthonyCorps, Inc. Fr. Justin Ministry Fund, Inc. Total in Residence 138.

On Assignment Outside the U.S.A.: Revs. Matteo Luo, O.F.M.Conv., Curia Generale dei Frati Minori Conventualli, Piazza Ss. Apostoli 51, Rome 00187 Italy. Tel: 011-39-06-699-571; Fax: 011-39-06-699-57321; Donald Kos, O.F.M.Conv., Convento S. Antonio, 56, Viale Guido Baccelli, 56, Rome 00153 Italy. Tel: 011-39-06-572-993-11; Fax: 011-39-06-572-993-42; David Blowey, O.F.M.Conv., Mag-9sawang 11at, 4120, P.O. Box 080, Tagaytay, Cavite, Philippines. Tel: 046-431-12-74-; Fax: 011-254-2-88420; Vincent Lachendro, O.F.M.Conv., Asato Catholic Church, 3-7-2 Asato, Naha, Okinawa 902-0067 Japan. Tel: 011-81-98-863-2020; Fax: 011-81-98-863-8474 Metro Manila; Very Rev. James McCurry, O.F.M.Conv., Min. Prov.; Revs. Thomas Reist, O.F.M.Conv.; Richard-Jacob Forcier, O.F.M.Conv., Province Sec.; Martin Breski, O.F.M.Conv., Dir. Franciscan Mission Assoc.; Mitchell Sawicki, O.F.M.Conv., Province Treas.; Jude Winkler, O.F.M.Conv., Asst. Gen., Rome; Stephen King, O.F.M.Conv.; Paul Miskvewicz, O.F.M.Conv., Delegate United Kingdom & Ireland.

Individual Assignment Within the U.S.A.: *Sisters of Providence Infirmary*, 1233 Main St., Holyoke, MA 01040-5399.

EMMITSBURG. *Vincentian House*, P.O. Box 376, 21727. Tel: 301-447-2326; Fax: 301-447-3579. Email: stjosephemmitsburg@comcast.net. Web: www.emmitsburg.net/stjosephparish. Revs. John J. Holliday, C.M., Pastor, Supr.; Charles F. Krieg, C.M., Parochial Vicar/Asst. Supr.; Robert J. Prior, C.M., Chap.; Stephen P. Trzecieski, C.M., Chap. Priests 4.

TOWSON. *Jesuit Jamshedpur Mission Society, Inc.*, 8600 La Salle Rd., Ste. 620, 21286-2014. Tel: 443-921-1310; Fax: 443-921-1313. Email: advancement@mdsj.org. Web: www.mdsj.org.

Maryland Province of the Society of Jesus, 8600 LaSalle Rd., Ste. 620, 21286-2014. Tel: 443-921-1310; Fax: 443-921-1313. Web: www.mdsj.org. Revs. James M. Shea, S.J., Provincial; James A. Casciotti, S.J., Socius; Timothy J. Stephens, S.J., Treas.; William C. Rickle, S.J., Asst. Latino Ministries; Liborio J. LaMartina, S.J., Resident Archivist; Ronald J. Amiot, S.J., Asst. Healthcare Planning; Richard S. McCouch, S.J., Asst. Secondary Educ.

Corporation of the Roman Catholic Clergymen, Maryland

Military Chaplains: Revs. Paul J. Shaughnessy, S.J., Naval War College, 686 Cushing Rd., Newport, RI 02841-1207. Tel: 760-763-3510; Christopher S. Fronk, S.J.

Priests of the Province Serving Abroad: Rev. Eugene J. Barber, S.J., Resid. S. Pedro Claver, Casilla 452, Africa, Chile. Tel: 011-56-58-22-9402; Fax: 011-56-58-22-9402; Bro. Guy J. Consolmagno, S.J.; Revs. Edgar J. Debany, S.J., P.O. Box 223, Surulere, Lagos State, Nigeria. Tel: 011-234-1-7733535; James M. Desjardins, S.J., UL. Levitana 38, P.O. Box "Inigo", 630051 Novosibirsk, Russia. Tel: 011-7-3832-77-2013; Fax: 011-7-3832-77-1413; Eugene M. Geinzer, S.J.; Brendan Hurley, S.J.; Michael J. Kuchera, S.J., Pont. Ist Orientale, Piazza S. Maria Maggiore 7, Rome 00187 Italy. Tel: 011-39-06-44741-7154; Fax: 011-39-06-446-5576; Michael J. Lynch, S.J.; Paul K. Rourke, S.J., Collegium Internationale del gesu, Piazza del Gesu 45, Rome 00186 Italy; Michael J. Woods, S.J.

Priests of the Province Serving Elsewhere: Revs. David E. Barry, S.J.; Raymond T. Gawronski, S.J., St. John Vianney Theological Seminary, 1300 S. Steele St., Denver, CO 80210-2599. Tel: 303-282-3404; 303-282-3449 (Office); James N. Gelson, S.J., 3510 S. Ocean Blvd., Highland Beach, FL 33487-3326. Tel: 561-272-4409; Fax: 561-278-8509; Robert J. McTeigue, S.J.; A. Richard Sotelo, S.J., P.O. Box 972141, El Paso, TX 79997-2141. Tel: 915-845-3899; Fax: 915-298-5325.

[R] CONVENTS AND RESIDENCES FOR SISTERS

BALTIMORE. *Carmelite Communities Assoc.*, 1318 Dulaney Valley Rd., 21286-1399. Tel: 410-823-7415. Email: info@baltimorecarmel.org. Web: www.ccacarmels.org.

Carmelite Sisters of Baltimore (1790) 1318 Dulaney Valley Rd., 21286-1399. Tel: 410-823-7415; Fax: 410-823-7418. Email: info@baltimorecarmel.org. Web: www.baltimorecarmel.org. Sr. Colette Ackerman, O.C.D., Prioress. Discalced Carmelite Nuns. Professed Sisters 17.

Chesapeake Province of the Sisters of Notre Dame de Namur, Provincial Offices, 305 Cable St., 21210-2511. Tel: 410-243-1993; Fax: 410-243-2279. Email: ches.prov@sndden.org. Web: www.sndden.org.

Chesapeake Province of the Sisters of Notre Dame de Namur, Inc. Sisters in Province 66; Sisters in Baltimore Diocese 45.

Administrative Team: Sisters Barbara Ann English, S.N.D.; Agnes Rose McNally, S.N.D.; Kathleen O'Brien, S.N.D.; Mary Margaret Pignone, S.N.D.; Margaret Shawn Scanlan, S.N.D.

Comboni Missionary Sisters, 5405 Loch Raven Blvd., 21239-2902. Tel: 410-323-1469; Fax: 410-323-9632. Email: sisters@combonisrs.com. Web: www.combonisrs.com. Sisters Andre T. Rothschild, C.M.S., Supr.; Joan Ramus, C.M.S.; Ilaria Buonriposi, C.M.S.; Emma W. Wachira, C.M.S. Sisters 4.

Contemplative Sisters of the Good Shepherd (CGS), 4140 Maple Ave., Halethorpe, 21227-4099. Tel: 410-247-1485; Fax: 410-247-1513. Web: goodshepherdsisters.org. Sr. Clare Szlachetka, Local Supr. Sisters 8.

Daughters of Charity, 900 S. Caton Ave., 21229. Tel: 410-368-2885; Fax: 410-368-3509. Email: stagneshouse@stagnes.org. Sr. Vincentia Goeb, D.C., Local Supr. Total in Residence 11.

Little Sisters of Jesus-Regional Residence, 400 N. Streeper St., 21224-1230. Tel: 410-327-7863. Web: www.rc.net/org/littlesisters. Sr. Lynn Flear, Regl. Supr. Sisters 5.

Little Sisters of the Poor-Provincial Residence (1869) 601 Maiden Choice Ln., 21228-3698. Tel: 410-744-9367; Fax: 410-747-0601. Email: mpbaltimore@littlesistersofthepoor.org. Web: www.littlesistersofthepoor.org. Sisters Alice Marie Jones, L.S.P., Supr.; Loraine Maguire, L.S.P., Provincial. Sisters 16; Total Assisted 67; Total Staff 130.

Maria Health Care Center, Inc., 6401 N. Charles St., 21212. Tel: 410-377-3011; Fax: 410-377-6042. Email: gsciamanna@ssndba.org. Sr. Grace Sciamanna, S.S.N.D., Admin. Health Center for School Sisters of Notre Dame and other Religious Congregations.

Mercy Villa Convent, Inc., 6806 Bellona Ave., 21212. Tel: 410-377-2450. Diane T. Bair, CFO.

Mission Helper Center, 1001 W. Joppa Rd., 21204-3787. Tel: 410-823-8585; Fax: 410-825-6355. Email: lcornell@missionhelpers.org. Web: www.missionhelpers.org. Sisters Loretta Cornell, M.H.S.H., Pres.; Dolores Glick, Vice Pres.; Elizabeth Langmead, M.H.S.H., Treas.; Claire Cartier, Office Mgr. Sisters 23; Sisters in Diocese 45; Total Staff 10.

Missionaries of Charity (1950) Gift of Hope Convent, 818 N. Collington Ave., 21205. Tel: 410-732-6056. Sr. Vineeth, M.C., Supr. Sisters 5; Total Assisted Annually 800; Total in Residence 10.

Our Lady of Mt. Providence Convent-Motherhouse, 701 Gun Rd., 21227. Tel: 410-242-8500; Fax: 410-242-4963. Email: srcrescentia@oblatesisters.com. Sisters Mary Alexis Fisher, O.S.P., Supr. Gen.; Mary Clarice Proctor, O.S.P., Asst. Gen.; Mary Crescentia, Proctor, Sec.; Sharon Young, Treas. Oblate Sisters of Providence., Attended by Sulpician Fathers and Josephite Fathers. Sisters in the Motherhouse 54; Oblate Sisters 72; Sisters in the Diocese 59; Total Staff 30.

The School Sisters of Notre Dame Atlantic-Midwest Province (1876) 6401 N. Charles St., 21212. Tel: 410-377-7774; Fax: 410-377-5363. Email: kcornell@amssnd.org. Web: www.atlanticmidwest.org. Sr. Kathleen Cornell, S.S.N.D., Prov. Leader; Rev. E. Joseph Cote, Chap. Sisters in Province 552; Sisters in Diocese 225.

Atlantic-Midwest Province of the School Sisters of Notre Dame, Inc.

SSND Service Corporation

SSND Care, Inc.

SSND Real Estate Holding Corporation

SSND Real Estate Trust

SSND Continuing Care Trust

SSND Charitable Annuity Trust

Atlantic-Midwest Province Endowment Trust

School Sisters of Notre Dame in the City of Baltimore, Inc., 6401 N. Charles St., 21212. Tel: 410-337-7774; Fax: 410-377-5363.

Sisters of the Good Shepherd (1864) 4100 Maple Ave., 21227-4099. Tel: 410-247-2770; Fax: 410-242-5890. Email: mregina@goodshepherdcenter.org. Sr. M. Regina Long, R.G.S., Supr. Sisters 10; Total Staff 2.

Sisters of the Good Shepherd-St. Joseph Residence (1864) 4130 Maple Ave., 21227-4007. Tel: 410-247-3898; Fax: 410-242-5890. Sr. Nora Pat O'Flannigan, Local Leader. Infirmary for the Mid-North America Province. Sisters 16; Total Staff 36.

Sisters Servants of Mary Immaculate, Inc., 1220 Tugwell Dr., 21228. Tel: 410-747-1353; Fax: 410-747-0386. Sr. Krystyna Mroczek, Prov. Supr. Convent and Novitiate. Sisters 19.

St. Anthony, 4500 Frankford Ave., 21206. Tel: 410-488-0054. Sisters 6.

St. Clare of Assisi, Inc. (2003) 3725 Ellerslie Ave., 21218. Tel: 410-235-9277; Fax: 410-243-2569. Email: etcarr@msn.com. Web: www.lakeosfs.org. Sisters Ellen Carr, O.S.F., Admin. Dir.; Jodene Wydeven, O.S.F., Local Coord. Clare of Assisi, Inc. operates Clare Court Convent, a retirement residence for members of The Sisters of St. Francis of Assisi, Inc. These sisters were Franciscan Sisters of Baltimore prior to the merger of the two congregations in 2001. Sisters 8; Staff 13.

The Villa (1971) 6806 Bellona Ave., 21212-1299. Tel: 410-377-2450; Fax: 410-377-2501. Mrs. Carol Zaicko, Admin.

Mercy Villa Convent, Inc., Convent for Retired Sisters of Mercy, Mission Helpers of the Sacred Heart, and other religious. Sisters 70; Total Staff 70.

CATONSVILLE. *All Saints Sisters of the Poor*, 1501 Hilton Ave., P.O. Box 3127, 21228-0127. Tel: 410-747-4104; Fax: 410-747-3321. Sisters Christina Christie, Prioress; Emily Ann Lindsey, Sub-Prioress. All Saints is a traditional Community desiring to uphold orthodox Christian faith and morality and to support the Apostolic tradition in ministry and practice. We are united by our common commitment to the One Lord Jesus Christ and by the desire to live for Him.

EMMITSBURG. *Daughters of Charity of St. Vincent de Paul, Province of St. Louise-Holy Family House* 21727. Tel: 301-447-3121; Fax: 301-447-6038. Web: www.daughtersofcharity.org.

Villa St. Michael, LLC, 333 S. Seton Ave., 21727-9299. Tel: 301-447-3121; Fax: 301-447-7082. Retirement Home of Daughters of Charity of St. Vincent de Paul., Home for the Senior Sisters of the Daughters of Charity of St. Vincent de Paul

St. Vincent Care Center LLC, 333 S. Seton Ave., 21727-9299. Tel: 301-447-3121; Fax: 301-447-7082. Home for the Senior Sisters of the Daughters of Charity of St. Vincent de Paul

LUTHERVILLE. *Emmanuel Monastery* (1971) 2229 W. Joppa Rd., 21093-4601. Tel: 410-821-5792; Fax: 410-296-9560. Email: bensrs@emmanuelosb.org. Web: www.emmanuelosb.org. Benedictine Sisters of Baltimore., Ministering in Education, Pastoral Ministry, Retreats and Spiritual Direction, Social Services, Justice Ministry, Hospital Ministry, and Business Admin. Sisters 16.

MARRIOTTSVILLE. *Sisters of Bon Secours, C.B.S., Leadership Office* (1824) 21104. Tel: 410-442-1333; Fax: 410-442-1394. Web: www.bonsecours.org. Sr. Rose Marie Jasinski, C.B.S., Pres. Retired Sisters (in Baltimore) 8; Retired Sisters (in USA) 12; Total in Residence (Baltimore) 18; Total in Residence (In USA) 28; Total Staff 60.

STEVENSON. *Maryland Province Center* (1934) 1531 Greenspring Valley Rd., 21153. Tel: 410-486-5599; Fax: 410-486-5466. Email: sndmd@aol.com. Web: www.sndden.org. Sisters Carol Lichtenberg, S.N.D.deN., Prov. Moderator; Colette Didier, S.N.D.deN., Prov. Leadership; Judith Clemens, S.N.D.deN., Prov. Leadership.

Baltimore Province of the Sisters of Notre Dame de Namur, Inc.

Sisters of Notre Dame de Namur, Maryland Province, Charitable Trust

Cemetery Perpetual Trust, Additional Projects Sponsored: Maryland Province Center, Stevenson, MD; Villa Julie Residence, Stevenson, MD; Notre Dame Academy, Villanova, PA; Trinity School, Ellicott City, MD; Maryvale Preparatory School, Brooklandville, MD.; Additional Projects Co-Sponsored: The Development Office, a joint project of the Maryland, Chesapeake & Notre Dame Base Communities Provinces; Director: Ms. Marion Connolly; Sisters Academy of Baltimore, co-sponsored by the School Sisters of Notre Dame, The Sisters of Bon Secours, The Sisters of Notre Dame de Namur and The Sisters of Mercy. Sisters in Province 85; Sisters in Diocese 46; Total Staff 3.

Villa Julie Residence, 1531 Greenspring Valley Rd., 21153. Tel: 410-486-6946; Fax: 410-484-6930. Email: sndvilla@aol.com. Web: www.sndden.org. Residence for retired Sisters of Notre Dame de Namur Sisters 25.

Maria Health Care, 6401 N. Charles St., 21212-1016. Tel: 410-377-7774. Sisters of Notre Dame de Namur 4.

The Villa, 6806 Bellona Ave., 21212. Tel: 410-377-2450. Sisters of Notre Dame de Namur 2.

[S] NEWMAN CENTERS

BALTIMORE. *Division Of Campus Ministry For Universities And Colleges Archdiocese of Baltimore, Dept. of Evangalization*, 320 Cathedral St., 21201. Tel: 410-547-5321; Fax: 410-625-8481. 43 Monroe St., Westminster, 21157. Tel: 410-848-8443. Email: pgallagher@sjwest.org. Purpose: To bring the presence of the Church to college and university campuses by offering spiritual, liturgical, social, service and educational experiences to the campus communities of non-Catholic academic institutions within the Archdiocese.

Coppin State University St. Cecilia Church, 3300 Clifton Ave., 21216. Tel: 410-624-3600. Email: frsy7@hotmail.com.

Frostburg State University Osborne Newman Center, 130 S. Broadway, Frostburg, 21532. Tel: 301-689-5041. Email: kbroadwater@archbalt.org.

Johns Hopkins University SS. Philip & James, 2801 N. Charles St., 21218. Tel: 410-235-2294.

McDaniel College St. John Church, 43 Monroe St., Westminster, 21157. Tel: 410-848-8443. Email: pgallagher@sjwest.org.

Morgan State University St. Matthew Church, 5401 Loch Raven Blvd., 21239. Tel: 410-433-2300. Email: joemuth@verizon.net.

Stevenson University Sacred Heart Church, 65 Sacred Heart Ln., P.O. Box 3672, Glyndon, 21071-3672. Tel: 410-833-1696. Email: srjude@shgparish.org.

Towson University Newman Center, 7909 York Rd., Towson, 21204. Tel: 410-828-0622. Email: tryan@archbalt.org.

University of Maryland, Baltimore County (UMBC) Our Lady of Perpetual Help, Ellicott City, 4795 Ilchester Rd., Ellicott City, 21043. Tel: 410-747-4334. Email: frjohn@umbc.edu.

Goucher College/Hood College/UMAB Email: kbroadwater@archbalt.org.

Catholic Universities in the Archdiocese:

Loyola University 4501 N. Charles St., 21210. Tel: 410-617-2444; Fax: 410-617-2052. Email: jdennis@loyola.edu. Rev. Jack Dennis, S.J., Dir. Campus Ministry.

Mount St. Mary's University Emmitsburg, 21727. Tel: 301-447-5223; Fax: 301-447-5868. Email: nolan@msmary.edu. Rev. Brian P. Nolan, Chap. & Dir. Campus Ministry.

Notre Dame of Maryland University 4701 N. Charles St., 21210. Tel: 410-532-5565; Fax: 410-532-5796. Email: mlees@ndm.edu. Melissa Lees, Dir. Campus Ministry.

[T] FOUNDATIONS, FUNDS AND TRUSTS

BALTIMORE. *Archbishop Curley High School Endowment Trust*, 3701 Sinclair Ln., 21213. Tel: 410-485-5000; Fax: 410-483-2545. Rev. Joseph Benicewicz, O.F.M.Conv.

Bon Secours of Maryland Foundation, Inc. aka Bon Secours Community Works (1919) 26 N. Fulton Ave., 21223. Tel: 410-362-3199; Fax: 410-362-3443. Email: george_kleb@bshsi.org. Total Staff 27; Total Assisted 9,657.

The following are tax exempt subsidiaries of the Bon Secours of Maryland Foundation, Inc.

Bon Secours Housing, Inc. aka Hollins Terrace (1983)

Bon Secours Housing II, Inc. aka Benet House (1987)

Unity Properties, Inc. (1993)

Bon Secours Baltimore Development, Inc. (2005)

The Catholic Community Foundation of the Archdiocese of Baltimore, Inc., 320 Cathedral St., 21201. Tel: 443-263-1925; Fax: 410-625-8485. Email: pmadden@archbalt.org. Web: www.ccfmd.org. Patrick Madden, Exec. Dir.

Chancery Office, 320 Cathedral St., 21201. Tel: 410-547-5444; Fax: 410-727-8234. Email: chancery@archbalt.org. Web: www.archbalt.org. Dr. Diane L. Barr, J.C., J.C.D., Chancellor. Tel: 410-547-5446.

Archbishop of Baltimore Annual Appeal Trust/Cardinal's Lenten Appeal Tel: 410-547-5439; Fax: 410-727-8234.

Archdiocesan Health Plan Trust Fund Agreement Tel: 410-547-5317; Fax: 410-783-5993.

Archdiocesan General Insurance Program Trust Tel: 410-547-5317; Fax: 410-783-5993.

Archdiocesan Priests Post-Retirement Benefits Plan Trust Fund, 320 Cathedral St., 21201. Tel: 410-547-5317; Fax: 410-783-5993. Email: pphelps@archbalt.org. Petra R. Phelps, Contact Person.

Cemetery Continuing Care Trust St. Patrick's Havre de Grace, Cemetery Continuing Care Trust; Holy Cross Cemetery Continuing Care Trust; St. Joseph, Fullerton, Cemetery-Continuing Care Trust Agreement; St. Mary of the Assumption, Govans, Cemetery Continuing Care Trust; St. Mary's, Pylesville Cemetery, Continuing Care Trust

Christian Brothers Community Support Charitable Trust Tel: 732-380-7926.

Corpus Christi Jenkins Memorial Trust, Inc. Tel: 410-523-4161; Fax: 410-523-5745.

Dart, Inc.

The Dr. Charles J. Foley Sr. and Mildred H. Foley Memorial Endowment Trust Tel: 410-547-5322; Fax: 410-332-8233. Provides annual support for over 300 programs and agencies of the Archdiocese.

Franciscan Sisters of Baltimore, Inc., Trust Tel: 410-235-2496; Fax: 410-243-2569.

The Gallagher Family Fund, 320 Cathedral St., 21201. Tel: 410-547-5322; Fax: 410-332-8233.

**G S Housing, Inc.*

John Paul II Regional School, Inc. (Grades PreK-8) Tel: 410-944-0367; Fax: 410-265-5316.

The Marion Burk Knott Scholarship Fund, Educational Trust Tel: 301-603-9501.

Marianist Charitable Trust Tel: 410-366-1300; Fax: 410-889-5743.

Maryvale Educational Fund, Inc. Tel: 410-252-3366; Fax: 410-561-1826.

Mercy Primary Care Group, Inc. Tel: 410-332-9000; Fax: 410-962-1303.

The National Black Catholic Congress, Inc. Tel: 410-547-8496; Fax: 410-752-3958. Email: nbcc@nbccongress.org. Web: www.nbccongress.org.

Neumann Early Childhood Center, Inc. Tel: 410-547-5495.

Our Lady of Good Counsel Historic Trust, Inc. Tel: 410-752-0205; Fax: 410-576-0929.

Plan of Self-Insurance Trust Tel: 410-547-5317; Fax: 410-783-5993.

The Priests Continuing Education and Formation Endowment Trust Tel: 410-547-5317; Fax: 410-783-5993.

St. Gregory the Great Housing Committee, Inc. Tel: 410-523-0061; Fax: 410-669-1385.

St. Jane Frances Educational Endowment Trust Tel: 410-255-4750; Fax: 410-350-6720.

St. John Neumann Regional School, Inc. Tel: 301-724-4055; Fax: 301-724-4827.

St. John the Evangelist School Endowment Trust,

689 Ritchie Hwy., Severna Park, 21146. Tel: 410-647-2283.

St. Jude Shrine Corporation Tel: 410-685-6026; Fax: 410-244-5728.

St. Mark's Parish School Endowment Trust Tel: 410-747-6613; Fax: 410-747-3188.

St. Peter's Cemetery Restoration Fund, Inc. Tel: 410-547-5300; Fax: 410-332-8233.

St. Pius V Housing Committee, Inc. Tel: 410-523-1930; Fax: 410-523-8164.

St. Vincent De Paul Historic Trust, Inc. Tel: 410-547-5377; Fax: 410-625-8483.

Sacred Heart Community Health Services, Inc. Tel: 301-723-5222.

Sacred Heart Foundation, Inc. Tel: 301-723-5222.

Sacred Heart Hospital of the Sisters of Charity, Inc. Tel: 410-723-5222.

School Sisters of Notre Dame in the City of Baltimore Charitable Trust, Inc. Tel: 410-377-7774; Fax: 410-377-5363.

Sisters of Notre Dame de Namur Charitable Trusts Tel: 410-255-1577.

Sisters of Notre Dame de Namur, Maryland Province, Charitable Trust Tel: 410-486-5382; Fax: 410-486-5466.

Women's Auxiliary Board Tel: 410-547-5356. Funds provide partial tuition for thousands of low income students in designated Baltimore City Catholic Schools.

**St. Elizabeth School Foundation, Inc.*, 801 Argonne Dr., 21218-1998. Tel: 410-889-5054; Fax: 410-889-2356. Diane Darrah, Pres.

The Immaculate Heart of Mary School Endowment Trust, 8501 Loch Raven Blvd., 21286. Tel: 410-668-7935; Fax: 410-668-6171. Rev. Michael W. Carrion.

St. Joseph Manor Foundation, Inc., 1130 N. Calvert St., 21202. Tel: 410-727-3386; Fax: 410-727-1006. Email: superiorgeneral@josephite.com. Web: www.josephite.com. Very Rev. William L. Norvel, S.S.J., Contact Person.

The Josephite Retirement and Disability Benefits Trusts (2003) 1130 N. Calvert St., 21202. Tel: 410-727-3386; Fax: 410-727-1006. Email: superiorgeneral@josephite.com. Web: www.josephite.com. Very Rev. William L. Norvel, S.S.J., Supr. Gen.

The Josephite Seminarian Education Trust (2003) 1130 N. Calvert St., 21202. Tel: 410-727-3386; Fax: 410-727-1006. Email: superiorgeneral@josephite.com. Web: www.josephite.com. Very Rev. William L. Norvel, S.S.J., Supr. Gen.

St. Luke Parish Education Endowment Trust, 7517 N. Point Rd., 21219. Tel: 410-477-5200; Fax: 410-477-5996. Email: stlukegemere@yahoo.com. Purpose: to support the youth of the parish who attend catholic schools. Total Assisted 43; Total Staff 1.

St. Matthew's Parish Endowment Trust, 5401 Loch Raven Blvd., 21239. Tel: 410-433-2300. Email: stmattrc@verizon.net. Rev. Joseph L. Muth Jr., Contact Person.

Mercy Health Foundation, Inc., 301 St. Paul Pl., 21202. Tel: 410-332-9874; Fax: 410-685-7464. Email: nkoas@mdmercy.com. Web: mdmercy.com. Thomas R. Mullen, Pres.

Partners in Excellence - Scholarship Fund, 320 Cathedral St., 21201. Tel: 410-547-5356. The fund provides partial tuition assistance to low income families wishing to send their children to a Catholic School in the Baltimore Metropolitan Area.

The Paul Van Gerwin Religious & Charitable Trust, 4409 Frederick Ave., 21229. Tel: 941-484-9641. Email: pcampbell@xaverianbrothers.org. Bro. Peter Campbell, C.F.X., J.D., Contact Person.

The Sacred Heart of Mary Cemetery Continuing Care Trust, 6736 Youngstown Ave., 21222. Tel: 410-633-2828; Fax: 410-633-0349. Rev. George J. Gannon.

The Seton Keough High School Endowment Trust, 1201 Caton Ave., 21227. Tel: 410-646-4444; Fax: 443-573-0107. Web: setonkeough.com.

St. Thomas Aquinas School Foundation Trust, 3710 Roland Ave., 21211. Tel: 410-889-4618; Fax: 410-889-1956. Email: starch@archbalt.org. Larry Glose, Contact Person.

BEL AIR. *John Carroll Foundation of the Roman Catholic Archdiocese of Baltimore, The John Carroll School*, 703 E. Churchville Rd., 21014. Tel: 410-879-2480; Fax: 410-836-8514.

ANNAPOLIS. *St. Andrew by the Bay Endowment Trust*, 701 College Pkwy., 21409. Tel: 410-974-4366; Fax: 410-974-4339. Email: sabbanna@archbalt.org. Web: standrewbythebay.org. Rev. Jeffrey S. Dauses.

COCKEYSVILLE. *St. Joseph, Texas Endowment Trust*, 101 Church Ln., 21030. Tel: 410-683-0600; Fax: 410-628-2956. Email: pcook@sjpmd.org. Rev. Msgr. Paul G. Cook, Contact Person; Rev. Ernest W. Cibelli.

CUMBERLAND. *The SS. Peter & Paul Parish Endowment Trust*, 109 N. Smallwood St., 21502-2992. Tel: 301-777-3131, Ext. 5; Fax: 301-759-3568. Email: ppaul@archbalt.org.

ELKRIDGE. *St. Augustine School Education Endowment Trust*, 5990 Old Washington Rd., 21075. Tel: 410-796-3040; Fax: 410-579-1165. Web: www.staug-md.org. Mrs. Patricia Schratz, Prin.

ELLICOTT CITY. *The St. Paul's Parish Endowment Trust*, 3755 St. Paul St., 21043. Tel: 410-465-1670; Fax: 410-313-8551. Email: stpaulsrc@aol.com. Rev. Matthew T. Buening.

FROSTBURG. *St. Michael School Endowment Trust*, 44 E. Main St., 21532. Tel: 301-689-6767; Fax: 301-689-6411. Email: smfrostb@archbalt.org. Rev. Richard Gray, Admin.

St. Joseph Midland Parish Endowment Trust, 44 E. Main St., 21532. Tel: 301-463-6770. Deacon W. Fred Passauer.

St. Joseph, Midland Cemetery Continuing Care Trust, 44 E. Main St., 21532. Tel: 301-463-6770. Deacon W. Fred Passauer.

GLEN BURNIE. *The Church of the Good Shepherd Parish Endowment Trust*, 1451 Furnace Ave., 21060. Tel: 410-761-4607; Fax: 410-761-6019. Rev. Msgr. Richard J. Bozzelli; Rev. Jesse L. Bolger.

KINGSVILLE. *St. Stephen School Endowment Trust*, 8028 Bradshaw Rd., 21087-1807. Tel: 410-592-7617; Fax: 410-592-7330.

MARRIOTTSVILLE. *Bon Secours Health System, Inc.*, 1505 Marriottsville Rd., 21104. Tel: 410-442-3505; Fax: 410-442-3256. Web: www.bshsi.org. Donald G. Seitz, M.D., Chair & Bd. of Directors; Richard J. Statuto, CEO & Pres.

Bon Secours, Inc., 1505 Marriottsville Rd., 21104. Tel: 410-442-3505; Fax: 410-442-3256. Web: www.bshsi.org.

PASADENA. *St. Jane Frances Educational Endowment Trust*, 8499 Virginia Ave., 21122. Tel: 410-255-4646; Fax: 410-437-5191. Email: postmaster@stjane.org. Web: stjane.org.

SYKESVILLE. *St. Joseph Catholic Community Endowment Trust*, 915 Liberty Rd., 21784. Tel: 443-920-9191; Fax: 443-920-9192. Email: parishoffice@saintjoseph.cc. Web: www.stjosepheldersburg.org. Revs. Terence P. Weik, S.M.; Paul A. Reich, S.M.; Neville O'Donohue, S.M.; George Onida, S.M.; Deacons Karl Bayhi; Michael Dvorak.

TOWSON. *The Immaculate Conception Elementary School Endowment Trust*, 200 Ware Ave., 21204. Tel: 410-427-4700; Fax: 410-427-4795. Email: info@theimmaculate.org. Web: www.theimmaculate.org. Rev. Joseph F. Barr.

WESTERNPORT. *St. Peter's, Westernport, School Endowment Trust*, 127 Church St., 21562. Tel: 301-359-3055; Fax: 301-359-0657.

[U] MISCELLANEOUS

BALTIMORE. *African Conference of Catholic Clergy & Religious in the United States, Inc.*, 309 Cathedral St., 3rd Fl., 21201. Tel: 443-982-5230. Web: www.accrus.org. Rev. Martin C. Emeh, Pres.

Saint Agnes Hospital Foundation, Inc., 900 Caton Ave., SAHC Box 123, 21229. Tel: 410-368-3155; Fax: 410-368-3533. Web: www.stagnes.org/foundation-main.htm. Ms. Malinda B. Small, Pres.

Alhambra, International Order of (1904) Supreme Headquarters, 4200 Leeds Ave., 21229. Tel: 410-242-0660; Fax: 410-536-5729. Email: salaam@orderofalhambra.org. Web: www.OrderAlhambra.org. Roger J. Reid, Exec. Dir. Nonprofit organization dedicated to assisting the developmentally disabled.

The Baltimore Catholic League, Inc., 2850 N. Ridge Rd., #207, Ellicott City, 21043. Tel: 410-461-4612; Fax: 410-480-3764.

Basilica of the Assumption Historic Trust, Inc., 409 N. Charles St., 21201. Tel: 410-727-3565; Fax: 410-539-0407. Web: www.baltimorebasilica.org. Gregory Leitner, Devel. Dir.; Kathy Wandishin, Devel. Exec.Asst.

Bon Secours Baltimore Development, Inc., 26 N. Fulton Ave., 21223. Tel: 410-362-3199; Fax: 410-362-3443. Email: george_kleb@bshsi.org.

Bon Secours Baltimore Health System Foundation, 2000 W Baltimore St, 21223. Tel: 410-362-3513; Fax: 410-362-3126. Christiane Walker, Chief Devel. Officer.

**Cardijn Associates, Inc* (1994) 4513 Bayonne Ave., 21206. Tel: 410-488-7936. Ms. Nancy Lee Conrad, Sec.

Caroline Center (1996) 900 Somerset St., 21202. Tel: 410-563-1303; Fax: 410-563-1302. Email: carolinecenter@caroline-center.org. Web: Caroline-Center.org. Sr. Patricia McLaughlin, S.S.N.D., Exec. Dir.

The Caroline Freiss Center, Inc., Employment training education for low income women. Total Assisted Annually 180; Total Staff 20.

Cathedral Library, 5200 N. Charles St., 21210. Tel: 410-464-4041. Laura M. Perry, Dir. Staffed by the Catholic Evidence League.; Maintain a lending library open to anyone in the archdiocese on Sunday & Monday, from 10:00 AM-2:00 PM. Total Staff 11.

Catholic Alumni Club of Baltimore (1961) P.O. Box 22305, 21203-2305. Tel: 410-580-1250; Fax: 410-771-7191. Email: info@cacbaltimore.org. Web: www.cacbaltimore.org.

Catholic Evidence League, c/o Cathedral of Mary Our Queen, 5200 N. Charles St., 21210. Tel: 410-296-5170; Fax: 410-296-5152.

Catholic Relief Services Foundation, Inc., 228 W. Lexington St., 21201. Tel: 410-951-7546; Fax: 443-825-3886. Rev. Robert Twele Esq., O.F.M.Conv., Sec.

Catholic Relief Services, United States Conference of Catholic Bishops, 228 W. Lexington St., 21201. Tel: 410-625-2220; Fax: 410-234-2986. Web: www.crs.org. Dr. Carolyn Y. Woo, Pres. For a more detailed explanation of this organization, please consult the A-pages located in the front of the Directory.

Catholic Single Again Council of Baltimore, The Villa, 6806 Belona Ave., 21212-1219. Tel: 410-485-8313. Email: singleagaincouncil@yahoo.com. Web: www.singleagain.itgo.com. Mary Ann Leard, Pres.

Catholic War Veterans USA, Inc., 5256 Milfield Rd., 21237. Tel: 410-933-0766. James Barlow, Dept. Commander; Rev. Coman Timoney, Post Chap.

Christian Life Community Regional Information Center (1967) 615 Rest Ave., Catonsville, 21228. Tel: 410-465-1312; Fax: 410-646-0500. Email: cazieba@yahoo.com. Web: www.clc-usa.org. Carol A. Zieba, Regional Chm.; Carol Montagnese, Treas. CLC is a lay organization that forms and sustains men and women, adults and youth, who commit themselves to the church and its mission in the world and feel the urgent need to unite their human life in all its dimensions with the fullness of their Christian faith and to work for social justice. Members come together in community to share their experience of Ignatian spirituality and mission.

Cristo Rey Corporate Internship Program, Inc., 420 S. Chester St., 21231. Tel: 410-727-3255; Fax: 443-573-9898. Janet Shock, Dir.

Esperanza Center Health Services Inc., 320 Cathedral St., 21201. Tel: 443-825-3450; Fax: 443-573-6100. Mr. William J. McCarthy Jr., Dir.

Food for Thought, Inc., 1625 E. Baltimore, 21231. Tel: 410-563-0081; Fax: 410-327-1345. Email: srmaryannh@aol.com. Sr. Mary Ann Hartnett, S.S.N.D., Dir. Tutorial program for children & adult literacy.

**Franciscan Youth Center, Inc.* (1985) Stone House, Clare Court, 3725 Ellersile Ave., 21218. Tel: 410-235-3577; Fax: 410-243-8191. Email: info@fycbaltimore.org. Web: www.fycbaltimore.org. Derryck D. Fletcher, Exec. Dir.; Ruth Maria Allen, Office Mgr. Staff 26; Total Assisted 110.

Friends of Ijebu-Ode Diocese, Inc., 1130 N. Calvert St., 21202. Tel: 410-727-3386; Fax: 410-727-1006. Very Rev. Nelson A. Moreira, S.S.J., Sec.-Treas.

**G S Properties, Inc.*, 5601 Loch Raven Blvd., 21239. Tel: 410-772-6719; Fax: 410-772-6998. Web: www.medstarhealth.org.

Ignatian Volunteer Corps, 801 St. Paul St., 21202. Tel: 410-752-4686; Fax: 410-752-8480. Email: info@ivcusa.org. Web: www.ivcusa.org. Ms. Mary C. McGinnity, Exec. Dir.; Rev. James R. Conroy, S.J., Founder; Jennifer Anthony, Dir. Finance & Admin.

Johns Hopkins Hospital, Dept. of Pastoral Care, 600 N. Wolfe St., Halsted 144, 21287-4170. Tel: 410-955-5842; Fax: 410-502-6765. Email: psparkl1@jhmi.edu. Rev. Paul C. Sparklin. Total Staff 20.

Legion of Mary, 502 Old Stone Pl., Bel Air, 21015-1812. Tel: 410-893-3607. Elissa Passalacqua, Pres. Baltimore Comitium, governing body for the Legion of Mary in the Baltimore Archdiocese.

Marian House, Inc., 949 Gorsuch Ave., 21218. Tel: 410-467-4121; Fax: 410-467-6709. Web: www.marianhouse.org. Katie Allston, LCSW-C, Exec. Dir.

Maryland Family Care, Inc., 301 St. Paul Pl., 21202. Tel: 410-332-1902; Fax: 410-332-9134. Email: hleek@mercymed.com. Helen Leek, Vice Pres.

Mission Helper Productions, Inc., 1001 W. Joppa Rd., 21204-3787. Tel: 410-823-8585, Ext. 241; Fax: 410-296-4050. Email: aguinan@missionhelpers.org; ckennedy@missionhelpers.org. Web: missionhelperproductions.org. Sisters Anne Guinan, M.H.S.H., Dir.; Caritas Kennedy, R.S.M., Assoc. Dir. A nonprofit video production house which provides full service professional, relatively low-cost, video production for independent producers and nonprofit socially concerned groups or individuals.

Mother Seton House on Paca Street, Inc., 600 N. Paca St., 21201. Tel: 410-728-6464; Fax: 410-669-8140. Web: www.stmarysspiritualcenter.org. Rev. John C. Kemper, S.S., M.Div., M.A., D.Min., Dir. The Mother Seton House on Paca Street is part of the St. Mary's Spiritual Center and Historic Site. The federal style house served as home (1808) and school for St. Elizabeth Ann Seton, America's first native-born canonized saint. Also on the site is the Historic Seminary Chapel that served the needs of our nation's first Roman Catholic Seminary (1791). The Historic Site is owned and operated by the Society of St. Sulpice, Province of the US. The site is open Monday-Friday from 12 noon to 3:30 pm and Saturday-Sunday from 1-3 pm. Entrance to the site is free, with off street parking.

The Mount Saint Agnes Theological Center for Women, Inc., 909 Poplar Hill Rd., 21210. Tel: 410-435-7500; Fax: 410-435-9522. Email: wisdom@mountsaintagnes.org. Web: www.mountsaintagnes.org. Sr. Mary Aquin O'Neill, R.S.M., Ph.D., Founding Dir.; Sacha M. Ludwig, Assoc. Dir. Total Staff 4.

**Murphy Initiative for Justice and Peace*, 1001 W. Joppa Rd., 21204. Tel: 410-823-8585, Ext. 244. Rosemary Thompson, Exec. Dir.

My Sister's Place Women's Center Fund, Inc., 320 Cathedral St., 21201. Tel: 410-547-5469. Email: bmccarth@cc-md.org. Mr. William J. McCarthy Jr., Contact Person.

Nigeria-Igbo Catholic Community, P.O. Box 66027, 21239. Tel: 443-850-6673. Email: office@niccchurch.org. Web: www.niccchurch.org. Raymond Anuforo, Chm. Tel: 443-850-6673; Clement Anyadike, Sec. Tel: 443-910-3647; Simon Nwaigwe, Vice Chm. Tel: 202-250-0889; Rev. Anthony Abiamm. Purpose: to provide an environment for all Igbos in the Baltimore Metropolitan area to worship in their native language.

Our Daily Bread Employment Center Fund, Inc., 320 Cathedral St., 21201. Tel: 410-547-5469. Email: bmccarth@cc-md.org. Mr. William J. McCarthy Jr., Contact Person.

Pallottine Charitable, Educational and Apostolic Ministry Trust, 512 W. Saratoga St., 21201. Tel: 410-685-3064.

Radio Mass of Baltimore, Inc., St. Ignatius Church, 740 N. Calvert St., 21202. Tel: 410-539-7812; Fax: 410-837-8883. Rev. James A. Casciotti, S.J., Dir.; Mrs. Carolyn Dunne, Admin. Mass is broadcast every Sunday morning from St. Ignatius Church at 9:30 A.M., WBAL, 1090 AM Radio Dial.

Reparation Society of the Immaculate Heart of Mary, Inc. (1946) Fatima House, 7920 Beverly Ave., 21234. Tel: 410-665-1199. Rev. Casimir M. Peterson, S.T.L., J.C.D., Pres. & Spiritual Dir. (Retired). Purpose: To promote prayer and penance in reparation to the Immaculate Heart of Mary in accordance with the message of Fatima. Volunteers 4; Total in Residence 1.

Sarah's House Fund, Inc., 320 Cathedral St., 21201. Tel: 410-547-5469. Email: bmccarth@cc-md.org. Mr. William J. McCarthy Jr., Contact Person.

Serra Club, 320 Cathedral St., 21201. Tel: 410-547-5426; Fax: 410-234-2953. Web: www.becomeapriest.org. Rev. Austin Murphy, Vocations Dir.

Society of St. Sulpice Foundation US, Inc., 5408 Roland Ave., 21210. Tel: 410-323-5074; Fax: 410-433-6524. Very Rev. Thomas R. Ulshafer, S.S., S.T.L., Ph.D., Contact Person.

Stella Maris Seafarers' Center, 320 Cathedral St., 21201. Tel: 443-845-7227; Fax: 410-288-5504. Email: aosbalt@gmail.com. Web: www.aosbalt.org. Rev. Msgr. John L. FitzGerald, Dir. Member of Apostleship of the Sea (USA).; Christian hospitality services in the Catholic tradition with spiritual, temporal, and emotional support for seafarers and their families. Also, transportation to and from ships for their crew members to the local Stella Maris Maritime Center and the city.

St. Thomas More Society of Maryland Inc., 36 S. Charles St., Ste. 1700, 21201-3101. Tel: 410-244-7005; Fax: 410-332-0269. Bruce Powell, Pres. The local branch of the St. Thomas More Society.

**The Thomas O'Neill Catholic Health Care Fund, Inc.*, 5601 Lock Raven Blvd., 21239. Tel: 410-772-6719; Fax: 410-772-6998.

Union of Catholic Apostolate USA, Inc., 512 W. Saratoga St., 21201. Tel: 410-685-6026, Ext. 1355; Fax: 410-244-5728. Email: usncc@sacapostles.org. Robert H. Gay, Pres.

ANNAPOLIS. *Christ Child Society of Annapolis*, P.O. Box 1801, 21401. Tel: 410-991-3895. Mary Morris, Pres.

Mid-Atlantic Catholic Schools Consortium, 10 Francis St., 21401. Tel: 301-908-7812; Fax: 410-269-1790. Email: mehrutka@gmail.com. Mary Ellen Hrutka, Exec. Dir.

Redemptorist Office for Mission Advancement, 107 Duke of Gloucester St., 21401. Tel: 410-288-8755; Fax: 410-990-1083. Web: redemptorists.net. Rev. Daniel Francis, C.Ss.R., Dir.

ARNOLD. **Walking With Purpose, Inc.*, P.O. Box 97, 21012. Tel: 410-703-9132. Email: walkingwithpurpose@yahoo.com. Web: www.walkingwithpurpose.com. Lisa Brenninkmeyer, Chm.

CROWNSVILLE. *Holy Name Society (Union)* (1911) 1649 Severn Chapel Rd., 21032. Tel: 410-923-2596. Rev. Michael W. Carrion, Archdiocesan Dir.; Bill Schummer, Pres. Purpose: Support Right to Life, Anti-Pornography, High School Scholarship Grants, Canonization of Blessed John of Vercelli, Support the Archbishop's discernment supper fund and works of charity.

**Springhill Center for Family Development*, 1134 Bacon Ridge Rd., 21032. Tel: 410-923-8900. Rev. John Hopkins, L.C., Exec. Dir.; Carrie Osborn, Contact Person. A Catholic organization enriching and strengthening family life in the community; addresses the needs of the modern family through quality programs and counseling services.

DUNKIRK. *Family of the Americas Foundation, Inc.* (1977) P.O. Box 1170, 20754-1170. Tel: 301-627-3346; 800-443-3395; Fax: 301-627-0847. Email: familyplanning@yahoo.com. Web: familyplanning.net.

ELLICOTT CITY. *AnthonyCorps, Inc.* (2003) 12300 Folly Quarter Rd., 21042. Tel: 410-531-1400; Fax: 410-531-4881. Email: treasurer1@saprov.org. Rev. Mitchell Sawicki, O.F.M.Conv., Treas.

The Baltimore Catholic League, 4725 Dorsey Hall Dr., Ste. A-610, 21042. Tel: 410-461-4612; Fax: 410-461-4613. John E. Degele Jr.

Christlife, Inc. (1995) 12280 Folly Quarter Rd., 21042. Tel: 410-531-7701; Fax: 410-531-7702. Email: info@christlife.org. Web: www.christlife.org. Mr. Dave Nodar, Dir.

**Faith Journeys Foundation, Inc.*, P.O. Box 1222, 21041. Tel: 410-744-0305. Email: fjourneys@aol.com. Web: www.faithjourneys.org. Ms. Lynn A. Cassella-Kapusinski, B.A., M.F.A., M.S., N.C.C., Pres. & Founder.

Fr. Justin Ministry Fund, Inc., 12300 Folly Quarter Rd., 21042. Tel: 410-531-1400; Fax: 410-531-4881. Email: treasurer1@saprov.org. Revs. Mitchell Sawicki, O.F.M.Conv.; Richard-Jacob Forcier, O.F.M.Conv.

OWINGS MILLS. *Knights of Columbus, Maryland State Council*, 10815 Stang Rd., 21117-4607. Tel: 410-521-6200; Fax: 410-521-0203. Email: kc-md@comcast.net. Rev. Donald Grzymski, O.F.M.Conv., State Chap.; Richard V. Siejack, State Deputy; Romeo Gauthier, Exec. Sec.

SEVERN. *Catholic Daughters of the Americas*, 124 Lillian Ave., 21144. Tel: 410-551-4241. Nina Lindsey, State Regent. Religious, charitable and educational to serve the needs of the Church and community through apostolate, renewal, community and youth. Catholic women 18 years or older in good standing with the Church are eligible for membership.

TIMONIUM. *Odenton Senior Housing II, Inc.*, 1966 Greenspring Dr., Ste. 200, 21093. Tel: 443-798-3416; Fax: 410-561-3056. Web: www.cc-md.org. Dale R. McArdle, Contact Person.

TOWSON. *Jesuit Educational Association of Maryland, Inc.*, 8600 LaSalle Rd., Ste. 620, 21286-2014. Tel: 443-921-1310; 443-921-1315; Fax: 443-921-1313. Email: rmccouch@mdsj.org. Web: www.mdsj.org.

RELIGIOUS INSTITUTES OF MEN REPRESENTED IN THE ARCHDIOCESE

For further details refer to the corresponding bracketed number in the Religious Institutes of Men or Women section.

[0200]—*Benedictine Monks (Latrobe, PA)*—O.S.B.
[0330]—*Brothers of the Christian Schools* (Baltimore Prov.)—F.S.C.
[0470]—*The Capuchin Friars* (Prov. of St. Augustine)—O.F.M.Cap.
[0400]—*Crosier Fathers*—O.S.C.
[]—*Franciscan Friars Conventual*—O.F.M.Conv.
[0520]—*Franciscan Friars (Most Holy Name)*—O.F.M.
[]—*Franciscan Third Order Regular*—T.O.R.
[]—*St. Joseph's Society of the Sacred Heart*—S.S.J.
[]—*Josephite Fathers & Brothers*—S.S.J.
[0730]—*Legionaries of Christ*—L.C.
[]—*The Marianists*—S.M.
[0854]—*Missionary Society of St. Paul of Nigeria*—M.S.P.
[]—*Norbertine Fathers* (Immaculate Conception Priory, DE)—O.Praem.
[]—*Pallottines*—S.A.C.
[]—*Passionists*—C.P.
[1070]—*Redemptorist Fathers* (Baltimore Prov.)—C.SS.R.
[1260]—*Society of Christ*—S.Ch.
[]—*Society of Jesus*—S.J.
[]—*Sulpicians*—S.S.
[]—*Trinitarians*—O.SS.T.
[]—*Vincentians*—C.M.
[]—*Xaverian Brothers*—C.F.X.

RELIGIOUS INSTITUTES OF WOMEN REPRESENTED IN THE ARCHDIOCESE

[]—*All Saints Sisters of the Poor*—A.S.S.P.
[0230]—*Benedictine Sisters of Pontifical Jurisdiction* (Baltimore)—O.S.B.
[]—*Carmelites*—O.C.D.
[0690]—*Comboni Missionary Sisters*—C.M.S.
[]—*Congregation of the Sister of Merciful Jesus*—C.S.M.J.
[0760]—*Daughters of Charity of St. Vincent de Paul*—D.C.
[1070-03]—*Dominican Sisters*—O.P.
[1070-13]—*Dominican Sisters*—O.P.
[1115]—*Dominican Sisters of Peace*—O.P.
[1470]—*Franciscan Sisters of St. Joseph*—F.S.S.J.
[1840]—*Grey Nuns of the Sacred Heart* (Pennsylvania)—G.N.S.H.
[]—*Holy Union Sisters*—S.U.S.C.
[2330]—*Little Sisters of Jesus*—L.S.J.
[2340]—*Little Sisters of the Poor*—L.S.P.
[2470]—*Maryknoll Sisters* (New York)—M.M.
[2720]—*Mission Helpers of the Sacred Heart*—M.H.S.H.
[2710]—*Missionaries of Charity* (New York)—M.C.
[]—*Missionary Servants of the Most Blessed Trinity*—M.S.B.T.
[3040]—*Oblate Sisters of Providence*—O.S.P.
[]—*Oblates of St. Martha*
[3465]—*Religious of the Sacred Heart of Mary* (New York)—R.S.H.M.
[]—*Religious Sisters of Mercy Sisters of Mercy of the Americas*—R.S.M.
[2970]—*School Sisters of Notre Dame*—S.S.N.D.
[]—*Sisters for Christian Community*—C.F.C.C.
[]—*Sisters of Bon Secours*—C.B.S.
[0640]—*Sisters of Charity* (Halifax)—S.C.
[]—*Sisters of Mercy of the Americas*—R.S.M.
[3000]—*Sisters of Notre Dame de Namur*—S.N.D.deN.
[]—*Sisters of Notre Dame de Namur*—S.N.D.deN.
[]—*Sisters of Notre Dame de Namur* (Ohio Prov.)—S.N.D.deN.
[1705]—*Sisters of St. Francis of Assisi*—O.S.F.
[1650]—*Sisters of St. Francis of Philadelphia*—O.S.F.
[3893]—*Sisters of St. Joseph*—S.S.J.
[]—*Sisters of the Good Shepherd*—R.G.S.
[]—*Sisters of the Good Shepherd - Contemplative*
[1990]—*Sisters of the Holy Names of Jesus and Mary*—S.N.J.M.
[]—*Sisters of the Humility of Mary* (Villa Maria, PA)—H.M.
[3610]—*Sisters Servants of Mary Immaculate*—S.S.M.I.
[2160]—*Sisters, Servants of the Immaculate Heart of Mary*—I.H.M.
[4120]—*Ursuline Nuns, of the Congregation of Kentucky*—O.S.U.

ARCHDIOCESAN CEMETERIES

BALTIMORE. *New Cathedral Cemetery*, 4300 Old Frederick Rd., 21229. Tel: 410-566-7770; Fax: 410-566-0709.

NECROLOGY

† Strempeck, Rev. Msgr. Martin R., (Retired)—Died Feb. 8, 2011
† Hemler, Edward B., (Retired)—Died July 27, 2011
† Lafferty, Charles L., (Retired)—Died Aug. 17, 2011
† Paulits, Walter J., (Retired)—Died June 4, 2011
† Shaum, David W., (Retired)—Died Oct. 6, 2011

Diocese of Baton Rouge

(Dioecesis Rubribaculensis)

Most Reverend

ROBERT WILLIAM MUENCH, D.D.

Bishop of Baton Rouge; ordained May 18, 1968; appointed Titular Bishop of Mactaris and Auxiliary Bishop of New Orleans May 8, 1990; consecrated June 29, 1990; appointed Bishop of Covington January 5, 1996; installed March 19, 1996; appointed Fifth Bishop of Baton Rouge December 15, 2001; installed March 14, 2002. *Office: Bishop's Office, P.O. Box 2028, Baton Rouge, LA 70821-2028.* Tel: 225-242-0247; Fax: 225-336-8768. Email: Bishop@diobr.org.

Chancery Office: Catholic Life Center, 1800 S. Acadian Thruway, P.O. Box 2028, Baton Rouge, LA 70821-2028. Tel: 225-387-0561; Fax: 225-336-8789.

Web: www.diobr.org

Email: chancery@diobr.org

ESTABLISHED JULY 20, 1961.

Square Miles 5,513.

Comprises the civil parishes (counties) of Ascension, Assumption, East Baton Rouge, West Baton Rouge, Iberville, Pointe Coupee, East Feliciana, West Feliciana, St. Helena, Tangipahoa, Livingston and St. James in the State of Louisiana.

For legal titles of parishes and diocesan institutions, consult the Chancery Office.

STATISTICAL OVERVIEW

Personnel	
Bishop	1
Priests: Diocesan Active in Diocese	50
Priests: Retired, Sick or Absent	23
Number of Diocesan Priests	73
Religious Priests in Diocese	35
Total Priests in Diocese	108
Extern Priests in Diocese	6
Ordinations:	
Diocesan Priests	2
Religious Priests	1
Transitional Deacons	3
Permanent Deacons in Diocese	66
Total Brothers	15
Total Sisters	95
Parishes	
Parishes	68
With Resident Pastor:	
Resident Diocesan Priests	34
Resident Religious Priests	8
Without Resident Pastor:	
Administered by Priests	25
Administered by Lay People	1
Professional Ministry Personnel:	
Sisters	5
Lay Ministers	92
Welfare	
Catholic Hospitals	3
Total Assisted	625,003
Homes for the Aged	7
Total Assisted	735
Specialized Homes	5
Total Assisted	357
Special Centers for Social Services	8
Total Assisted	227,093
Educational	
Diocesan Students in Other Seminaries	15
Total Seminarians	15
Colleges and Universities	1
Total Students	1,860
High Schools, Diocesan and Parish	6
Total Students	2,197
High Schools, Private	2
Total Students	2,003
Elementary Schools, Diocesan and Parish	23
Total Students	10,927
Catechesis/Religious Education:	
High School Students	3,561
Elementary Students	8,338
Total Students under Catholic Instruction	28,901
Teachers in the Diocese:	
Priests	2
Brothers	2
Sisters	10
Lay Teachers	945
Vital Statistics	
Receptions into the Church:	
Infant Baptism Totals	2,474
Minor Baptism Totals	137
Adult Baptism Totals	153
Received into Full Communion	285
First Communions	2,487
Confirmations	2,040
Marriages:	
Catholic	512
Interfaith	185
Total Marriages	697
Deaths	1,702
Total Catholic Population	225,979
Total Population	969,104

Former Bishops—Most Revs. ROBERT E. TRACY, D.D., LL.D., appt. Titular Bishop of Sergentza and Auxiliary of Lafayette March 18, 1959; cons. May 19, 1959; appt. First Bishop of Baton Rouge Aug. 10, 1961; retired March 21, 1974; died April 4, 1980; JOSEPH V. SULLIVAN, S.T.D., appt. Titular Bishop of Tagamuta and Auxiliary of Kansas City-St. Joseph March 3, 1967; cons. April 3, 1967; appt. Second Bishop of Baton Rouge Aug. 5, 1974; died Sept. 4, 1982; STANLEY JOSEPH OTT, S.T.D., appt. Titular Bishop of Nicives and Auxiliary of New Orleans May 24, 1976; cons. June 29, 1976; appt. Third Bishop of Baton Rouge Jan. 18, 1983; died Nov. 28, 1992; ALFRED C. HUGHES, S.T.D., ord. Dec. 15, 1957; appt. Auxiliary of Boston and Titular Bishop of Massimiana in Bizacena, July 21, 1981; cons. Sept. 14, 1981; appt. to Baton Rouge Sept. 7, 1993; installed Fourth Bishop of Baton Rouge, Nov. 4, 1993; appt. Coadjutor Archbishop of New Orleans, Feb. 16, 2001; installed May 2, 2001.

Vicar General/Moderator of the Curia—Very Rev. THAN N. VU, S.T.L., V.G.

Chancery Office—Catholic Life Center, 1800 S. Acadian Thruway, P.O. Box 2028, Baton Rouge, 70821-2028. Tel: 225-387-0561; Fax: 225-336-8789. Email: chancery@diobr.org. Office Hours: Mon.-Fri. 8:30-4:30.

Chancellor—Very Rev. THOMAS C. RANZINO.

Diocesan Tribunal—Catholic Life Center, 1800 S. Acadian Thruway, P.O. Box 1087, Baton Rouge, 70821-1087. Tel: 225-336-8755; Fax: 225-242-0229. Email: tribunal@diobr.org.

Judicial Vicar—Very Rev. PAUL D. COUNCE, J.C.L., M.C.L.

Promoter of Justice—Very Rev. VINCENT J. DUFRESNE, S.T.L., J.C.L., V.F.

Judges—Rev. Msgrs. WILLIAM L. GREENE (Retired); GERALD M. LEFEBVRE (Retired); Very Rev. FRANK M. UTER, V.F.; Revs. JAMIN S. DAVID, J.C.L.; MICHAEL J. MORONEY; Mrs. JACLYN O'BRIEN MCEACHERN, J.C.D.

Defenders of the Bond—Very Rev. VINCENT J. DUFRESNE, S.T.L., J.C.L., V.F.; Rev. GARLAND T. BELSOME; Very Rev. THAN N. VU, S.T.L., V.G.; Revs. MATTHEW P. LORRAIN; GERARD R. MARTIN; PAUL A. MCDUFFIE.

Notaries—Mrs. V. EILEEN BOURGEOIS; Mrs. PATRICIA F. SONIAT; Mrs. ANN T. BOLTIN.

College of Consultors—Very Revs. PAUL D. COUNCE, J.C.L., M.C.L.; THAN N. VU, S.T.L., V.G.; MILES D. WALSH, S.T.D., V.F.; Revs. MICHAEL J. SCHATZLE; MATTHEW C. DUPRE; THOMAS P. DUHE, M.Ed.

Diocesan Pro-Vicar—

Pro-Vicar for Religious Men and Women—Sr. LUCY SILVIO, C.S.J.

Diocesan Corporation (The Roman Catholic Church of the Diocese of Baton Rouge)—Most Rev. ROBERT WILLIAM MUENCH, D.D., Pres.; Very Revs. THAN N. VU, S.T.L., V.G., Vice Pres.; THOMAS C. RANZINO, Sec.; Mr. JOSEPH E. INGRAHAM, Treas.

Diocesan Offices and Directors

Apostolate to the Deaf—Mrs. CAROLE B. MONTGOMERY, Dir., 2585 Brightside Lane, Baton Rouge, 70820-3504. Tel: 225-766-9320; 225-769-0223; Fax: 225-766-6615. Email: hearingimpaired@diobr.org.

Archives and Records Management—Mrs. ANN T. BOLTIN, Mailing Address: P.O. Box 2028, Baton Rouge, 70821-2028. Tel: 225-242-0224; Fax: 225-242-0299. Email: archives@diobr.org.

Black Catholics—Deacon ALFRED P. ADAMS SR., Mailing Address: P.O. Box 30, Convent, 70723-0030. Tel: 225-562-3255. Email: bcatholics@diobr.org.

Campus Ministry—Rev. ROBERT F. STINE, Mailing Address: LSU Box 25131, Baton Rouge, 70803-0106. Tel: 225-344-8595; Fax: 225-344-1920. Email: rstine@diobr.org.

Catholic Charismatic Renewal—Rev. HENRY W. GAUTREAU, Ph.D. (Retired), 421 D Longwood Ct., Baton Rouge, 70806-4048. Tel: 225-346-8873. Email: hgautreau@diobr.org.

Catholic Charities of the Diocese of Baton Rouge, Inc.—Mr. DAVID C. AGUILLARD, M.P.A., M.H.A., Exec. Dir., Office, 1900 S. Acadian Thruway, P.O. Box 1668, Baton Rouge, 70821-1668. Tel: 225-336-8770; Fax: 225-336-8745. Email: ccsgen@ccdiobr.org. Web: www.ccdiobr.org.

Catholic Social Services— Maternity & Adoption Dept. Mrs. JANICE ALLEN, 1900 S. Acadian Thruway, P.O. Box 1668, Baton Rouge, 70821-1668. Tel: 225-336-8708; Fax: 225-336-8745. Email: adopt@ccdiobr.org. Web: www.adoptbatonrouge.com.

Social and Community Responsibility Department—Ms. JENNIFER HILL. Email: jhill@ccdiobr.org.

Cemeteries—Very Rev. FRANK M. UTER, V.F., P.O. Box 1609, Denham Springs, 70727-1609. Tel: 225-665-5359; Fax: 225-665-4422. Email: futer@diobr.org.

Child and Youth Protection Office—Mrs. AMY J. CORDON, Dir., Mailing Address: P.O. Box 2028, Baton Rouge, 70821-2028. Tel: 225-242-0202; Fax:

225-242-0233. Email: childprotection@diobr.org.

Clergy Personnel—Rev. ROBERT F. STINE, Dir., Christ the King and Catholic Center, LSU Box 25131, Baton Rouge, 70803-0106. Tel: 225-344-8595; Fax: 225-344-1920. Email: rstine@diobr.org.

Board Members—Revs. GERALD R. MARTIN; MICHAEL J. ALELLO; ROBERT F. STINE; GREGORY J. DAIGLE; Very Rev. RANDY M. CUEVAS, S.T.L., V.F.; Deacon DONALD J. MUSSO.

Ecumenical Affairs—Rev. MICHAEL J. MORONEY, 14040 Greenwell Springs Rd., Greenwell Springs, 70739-3302. Tel: 225-261-4650; Fax: 225-261-5650. Email: ecumenism@diobr.org.

Evangelization and Catechesis Office—Mrs. RHONDA PARENTON, Dir., Mailing Address: P.O. Box 2028, Baton Rouge, 70821-2028. Tel: 225-242-0137; Fax: 225-242-0245. Email: evangelization@diobr.org.

Communications—Mrs. MARY BETH CHEVALIER, Media Liaison. Tel: 225-242-0256. Email: mchevalier@diobr.org; Mr. STEVE LEE, Mailing Address: Catholic Life Channel 15, P.O. Box 2028, Baton Rouge, 70821-2028. Tel: 225-242-0215; Fax: 225-242-0134. Email: television@diobr.org.

Continuing Formation for the Clergy—Very Rev. RANDY M. CUEVAS, S.T.L., V.F., Dir., St. Albert the Great Student Center, 409 W. Dakota St., Hammond, 70401-2517. Tel: 985-345-7206; Fax: 985-345-7223. Email: clergyformation@diobr.org.

Stewardship Office—Mr. MARK J. BLANCHARD, Dir., Mailing Address: P.O. Box 2028, Baton Rouge, 70821-2028. Tel: 225-336-8790; Fax: 225-336-8710. Email: stewardship@diobr.org.

Finance—Mr. JOSEPH E. INGRAHAM, Fiscal Officer, Mailing Address: P.O. Box 2028, Baton Rouge, 70821-2028. Tel: 225-387-0561; Fax: 225-336-8789. Email: jingraham@diobr.org.

Human Resources—ANITA L. KRAIL, S.P.H.R., Dir., Mailing Address: P.O. Box 2028, Baton Rouge, 70821-2028. Tel: 225-387-0561; Fax: 225-336-8789. Email: akrail@diobr.org.

Hispanic Apostolate—Mrs. MARIA ROSA EADS, Dir.; Rev. ELIECER MONTANEZ, M.C.M., Chap., 7520 Florida Blvd., Baton Rouge, 70806-4702. Tel: 225-927-8700; Fax: 225-927-8787. Email: hapostol@bellsouth.net.

Newspaper "The Catholic Commentator"—Mrs. LAURA G. DEAVERS, Exec. Editor & Gen. Mgr., Office, 1800 S. Acadian Thruway, Baton Rouge, 70821-1668. Email: tcc@diobr.org; Mailing Address: P.O. Drawer 14746, Baton Rouge, 70898-4746. Tel: 225-387-0983; Fax: 225-336-8710.

Marriage and Family Life Department—Deacon MICHAEL T. CHIAPPETTA, Dir., Office: 1800 S. Acadian Thruway, P.O. Box 2028, Baton Rouge, 70821-2028. Tel: 225-336-8770; Fax: 225-336-8745. Email: mflgen@diobr.org.

Permanent Diaconate Office—Deacon DONALD J. MUSSO, Dir., 15615 Old Jefferson Hwy., Baton Rouge, 70817-6311. Tel: 225-752-6230; Fax: 225-756-5014. Email: diaconate@diobr.org.

Presbyteral Council—Rev. THOMAS P. DUHE, M.Ed.; Very Rev. PAUL D. COUNCE, J.C.L., M.C.L.; Revs. MATTHEW C. DUPRE; CHARLES R. LANDRY; JASON P. PALERMO; PAUL A. GROS; CHRISTOPHER J. DECKER; NICHOLAS JOHN NUTTER III; AYO E. EFODIGBUE, M.S.P.; MICHAEL J. MORONEY; Very Rev. MILES D. WALSH, S.T.D., V.F.; Rev. MICHAEL J. ALELLO; Very Rev. THAN N. VU, S.T.L., V.G.; Rev. MICHAEL J. SCHATZLE.

Propagation of the Faith and Association of Holy Childhood—Rev. NICHOLAS JOHN NUTTER III, Dir., P.O. Box 2028, Baton Rouge, 70821-2028. Tel: 225-242-0115; Fax: 225-242-0343. Email: missions@diobr.org.

Catholic Schools—Dr. MELANIE B. VERGES, Ed.D., Supt.; Deacon JOSEPH M. SCIMECA, Asst. Supt., Mailing Address: P.O. Box 2028, Baton Rouge, 70821-2028. Tel: 225-336-8735; Fax: 225-336-8711. Email: secretary@csobr.org.

Separated and Divorced—VACANT.

Serra Clubs—Rev. MATTHEW P. LORRAIN, Spiritual Advisor, Mailing Address: P.O. Box 2028, Baton Rouge, 70821-2028. Tel: 225-336-8778; Fax: 225-336-8710. Email: vocations@diobr.org.

Society of St. Vincent De Paul—Mr. MICHAEL J. ACALDO, CEO. Email: macaldo@svdpbr.com; Deacon ESNARD F. GREMILLION, Spiritual Advisor, Mailing Address: P.O. Box 127, Baton Rouge, 70821-0127. Tel: 225-383-7837.

Victim Assistance Coordinator—Mrs. AMY J. CORDON, Mailing Address: P.O. Box 2028, Baton Rouge, 70821-2028. Tel: 225-242-0202; Fax: 225-242-0233. Email: childprotection@diobr.org.

Vietnamese Apostolate—Rev. TAN VIET NGUYEN, I.C.M., Dir., 2580 Tecumseh St., Baton Rouge, 70805-7999. Tel: 225-357-4787; Fax: 225-355-9794.

Vocations—Rev. MATTHEW P. LORRAIN, Dir.; Sr. LUCY SILVIO, C.S.J., Assoc. Dir., Mailing Address: P.O. Box 2028, Baton Rouge, 70821-2028. Tel: 225-336-8778; Fax: 225-336-8710. Email: vocations@diobr.org.

Worship, Office of—Very Rev. THOMAS C. RANZINO, Dir., Mailing Address: P.O. Box 2028, Baton Rouge, 70821-2028. Tel: 225-387-0561; Fax: 225-336-8789. Email: worship@diobr.org.

Youth and Young Adult Ministry—Mrs. BRIGITTE BURKE, Assoc. Dir., Mailing Address: P.O. Box 2028, Baton Rouge, 70821-2028. Tel: 225-336-8751; Fax: 225-336-8765. Email: youth@diobr.org.

CLERGY, PARISHES, MISSIONS AND PAROCHIAL SCHOOLS

CITY OF BATON ROUGE

(EAST BATON ROUGE PARISH)

1—ST. JOSEPH CATHEDRAL (1792) [CEM 3] Very Rev. Paul D. Counce. In Res., Deacon Jodi A. Moscona.
Res.: 412 North St., 70802-5496. Tel: 225-387-5928; Fax: 225-387-5929. Email: office@cathedralofstjoseph.org. Web: www.cathedralofstjoseph.org.
Catechesis/Religious Program—Students 16.

2—ST. AGNES (1917) Rev. Joseph M. Camilleri; Deacon Thomas Traylor. In Res., Revs. Clifton Hill, C.Ss.Sp.; Michael Jung, O.S.B.
Res.: 749 East Blvd., 70802-6398. Tel: 225-383-4127; Fax: 225-383-4154. Email: saintagnes@bellsouth.net.
Catechesis/Religious Program—Tel: 225-338-1511. Ms. Margaret Granger, C.R.E. Students 136.

3—ST. ALOYSIUS (1955) Very Rev. Than N. Vu; Rev. Jamin S. David; Deacons John A. Jung Jr.; John W. Veron.
Mailing Address: 2025 Stuart Ave., 70808-3998. Tel: 225-343-6657; Fax: 225-344-6847. Email: saghb@cox.net. Web: www.aloysius.org.
School—(Grades PreK-8) Tel: 225-383-3871; Fax: 225-383-4500. Mr. John L. Bennett, Prin.; Anne Blanchard, Librarian. Lay Teachers 75; Students 1,170.
Catechesis/Religious Program—Mrs. Patricia Greely, D.R.E. Students 154.

4—STS. ANTHONY OF PADUA AND LE VAN PHUNG (1920) Rev. Tan Viet Nguyen, I.C.M.
Res.: 2305 Choctaw Dr., 70805-7910. Tel: 225-357-4800; Fax: 225-354-0611. Web: www.gxvnbatonrouge.org.
Catechesis/Religious Program—Students 364.

5—ST. CHARLES BORROMEO (1964) Closed. For inquiries for parish records contact St. Gerard Majella, Baton Rouge.

6—CHRIST THE KING (1980) Revs. Robert F. Stine; C. Todd Lloyd.
Mailing Address: LSU Box 25131, 70803-0106. In Res., Rev. Eliecer Montanez, M.C.M.
Office: 11 Fraternity Ln., 70803. Tel: 225-344-8595; Fax: 225-344-1920. Email: rstine@ctk-lsu.org. Web: www.ctk-lsu.org.
Catechesis/Religious Program—Mrs. Rebecca East, D.R.E. Students 55.

7—ST. FRANCIS DE SALES PARISH (1979), (Catholic Deaf Center) Mrs. Carole B. Montgomery, Exec. Dir.
Res.: 2585 Brightside Dr., 70820-3504. Tel: 225-766-9320; 866-311-5292 (Video Phone); Fax: 225-766-6615. Email: hearingimpaired@diobr.org.
Catechesis/Religious Program—Fax: 225-766-6615. Mrs. Carole B. Montgomery, D.R.E. Students 13.

8—ST. FRANCIS XAVIER (1918) Rev. Edward Chiffriller, S.S.J.
Res.: 1143 S. 11th St., 70802-4997. Tel: 225-246-2727; Fax: 225-343-4259. Email: stfrancisxavier@bellsouth.net. Web: www.stfrancisxavierchurch.net.
School—(Grades K-8) Tel: 225-387-6639; Fax: 225-383-1215. Sr. Joseph Charles, S.S.F., Prin.; Geraldine Devernay, Librarian. Lay Teachers 9; Students 87.
Catechesis/Religious Program—Students 80.

9—ST. GEORGE (1908) [CEM] Revs. Michael J. Schatzle; P. Brent Maher; Deacons Albert R. Ellis; Jeff Rufus Easley.
Office: 7808 St. George Dr., 70809-4699. Tel: 225-293-2212; Fax: 225-291-8063. Web: www.st-george.org.
School—(Grades PreK-8), 7880 St. George Dr., 70809-4699. Tel: 225-293-1298. Mrs. Lizette Leader, Prin. Lay Teachers 65; Students 1,076.
Catechesis/Religious Program—Mrs. Cherry Riggs, D.R.E.; Mrs. Karen Fawley, D.R.E. Students 90.

10—ST. GERARD MAJELLA (1944) Revs. Marcel E. Okwara, C.Ss.R.; Matthew Bonk, C.Ss.R. In Res., Rev. Samuel C. Maranto, C.Ss.R.
Res.: 3808 Gerard St., 70805-2834. Tel: 225-355-2553; Fax: 225-356-7472. Email: stgmc@earthlink.net.
School—(Grades PreK-6), 3655 St. Gerard Ave., 70805-2898. Tel: 225-355-1437; Fax: 225-355-1879. Ms. Joanie Hudson, Prin. Lay Teachers 18; Students 238.
Catechesis/Religious Program—

11—IMMACULATE CONCEPTION (1953) Very Rev. Thomas F. Clark, S.J.; Rev. Derrick J. Weingartner, S.J.
Res.: 1565 Curtis St., 70807-4906. Tel: 225-775-7067; Fax: 225-775-0775. Email: clarktf@hotmail.com.
Catechesis/Religious Program—Students 84.

12—ST. JEAN VIANNEY (1975) Very Rev. Thomas C. Ranzino; Deacons Brent Duplessis; Daniel S. Borne.
Res.: 16166 S. Harrell's Ferry Rd., 70816-3199. Tel: 225-753-7950; Fax: 225-753-7965. Email: churchinfo@stjeanvianney.org. Web: www.stjeanvianney.org.
School—(Grades K-8), 16266 S. Harrell's Ferry Rd., 70816-3103. Tel: 225-751-1831; Fax: 225-752-8774. Mrs. Wendy Gilmore, Prin.; Kerry Ferrara, Librarian. Lay Teachers 49; Students 501.
Preschool—Tel: 225-752-5356. Mrs. Amie Williams, Dir. Lay Teachers 13; Students 89.
Catechesis/Religious Program—Students 102.

13—ST. JUDE THE APOSTLE (1966) Rev. Caye A. Nelson III; Deacons Frank E. Bains; James J. Morrissey; Curt P. Reeson. In Res., Rev. Michael J. Collins (Retired).
Res.: 9150 Highland Rd., 70810-4096. Tel: 225-766-2431; Fax: 225-766-0722. Email: stjude@stjudecatholic.org. Web: stjudecatholic.org.
School—(Grades PreK-8) Tel: 225-769-2344; Fax: 225-769-0671. Web: stjudebr.org. Mrs. Karen Jakuback, Prin.; Mrs. Terri Legendre, Librarian. Lay Teachers 34; Students 577.
Catechesis/Religious Program—Students 102.

14—ST. LOUIS, KING OF FRANCE (1966) Rev. Nicholas John Nutter III. In Res., Rev. Msgr. Leo Guillot (Retired).
Res.: 2121 N. Sherwood Forest Dr., 70815-1962. Tel: 225-275-7280; Fax: 225-275-5845. Email: slkfadm@bellsouth.net. Web: www.slkfbr.org.
School—(Grades PreK-8), 2311 N. Sherwood Forest Dr., 70815-1997. Tel: 225-273-3932; Fax: 225-273-3978. Mrs. Mary Clare Polito, Prin.; Carol Speyrer, Librarian. Lay Teachers 19; Students 200.
Catechesis/Religious Program—Students 76.

15—MOST BLESSED SACRAMENT (1979) Rev. Philip F. Spano; Deacon Donald J. Musso.
Res. & Mailing Address: 15165 Old Jefferson Hwy., 70817-6311. Tel: 225-752-6230; Fax: 225-756-5014. Web: www.mbsparish.org.
School—(Grades K-8), 8033 Barringer Rd., 70817-6000. Tel: 225-751-0273; Fax: 225-753-7259. Mrs. Maria I. Cloessner, Prin.; Ellen Manint, Librarian. Lay Teachers 28; Students 553.
Catechesis/Religious Program—Tel: 225-751-5867; Fax: 225-751-6738. Mr. David P. Planche, D.R.E. Students 329.

16—OUR LADY OF MERCY (1947) Very Rev. Miles D. Walsh; Rev. Arun John, I.M.S. (India); Deacon Richard H. Grant.
Office: 445 Marquette Ave., 70806-4497. Tel: 225-926-1883; Fax: 225-923-0448.
Res.: 450 Marquette Ave., 70806-4497. Email: admin@olomchurch.com.
School—(Grades PreK-8), 400 Marquette Ave., 70806-4498. Tel: 225-924-1054; Fax: 225-923-2201. Email: tvilla@olomschool.org. Web: www.olomschool.org. Mrs. Tina Villa, Prin.; Kirsten Steintrager, Librarian. Lay Teachers 52; Students 810.
Catechesis/Religious Program—Students 144.

17—ST. PATRICK (1974) Rev. Gerard R. Martin; Deacon J. Peter Walsh.
Res.: 12424 Brogdon Ln., 70816-4801. Tel: 225-753-5750; Fax: 225-756-9636. Email: stpatrickbr@aol.com. Web: www.stpatrickbr.org.
Catechesis/Religious Program—Ms. Lisa Trahan, D.R.E. Students 149.

18—ST. PAUL THE APOSTLE (1960) Rev. Vincent Alexius, S.V.D.; Deacon Benjamin J. Dunbar.
Res.: 3912 Gus Young Ave., 70802-1727. Tel: 225-383-2537; Fax: 225-383-3702. Email: stpaulbr@aol.com. Web: www.stpaulbr.webs.com.
Catechesis/Religious Program—Mrs. Vera Dunbar, D.R.E. Students 85.

19—ST. PIUS X (1963) Rev. Frank B. Bass; Deacon Esnard F. Gremillion.
Office: 6380 Hooper Rd., 70811-2499. Tel: 225-357-5935; Fax: 225-357-6005.
Catechesis/Religious Program—Students 44.

20—SACRED HEART OF JESUS (1928) Rev. Paul A. McDuffie; Deacon Joseph M. Scimeca.
Res.: 2250 Main St., 70802-3198. Tel: 225-387-6671; Fax: 225-387-6674. Email: info@sacredheartbtr.com. Web: www.sacredheartbtr.com.

School—(Grades PreK-8) Tel: 225-383-7481; Fax: 225-383-1810. Mrs. Joan R. Hutson, Prin.; Catherine Fontenot, Librarian. Sisters of St. Joseph 2; Lay Teachers 29; Students 496.
Catechesis/Religious Program—Ms. Vicki Nacol, D.R.E. Students 51.

21—ST. THOMAS MORE (1959) Rev. Thomas P. Duhe; Deacon Clayton Hollier.
Office: 11441 Goodwood Blvd., 70815-6299. Tel: 225-275-3940; Fax: 225-275-1407. Email: info@stmchurch.org. Web: stmchurch.org.
School—(Grades PreK-8), 11400 Sherbrook Dr., 70815. Tel: 225-275-2820; Fax: 225-275-0376. Dr. Judy Armstrong, Prin.; Mrs. Felice Bourg, Librarian. Lay Teachers 59; Students 862.
Preschool—11500 Sherbrook Dr., 70815. Tel: 225-272-3477; Fax: 225-272-0468. Ms. Angie Ducote, Dir. Lay Teachers 12; Students 120.
Catechesis/Religious Program—Students 47.

OUTSIDE THE CITY OF BATON ROUGE

ALBANY, LIVINGSTON PARISH, ST. MARGARET QUEEN OF SCOTLAND (1910) [CEM] Rev. Joseph Arogyasami, I.M.S. (India).
Res.: P.O. Box 100, 70711-0100. Tel: 225-567-3573; Fax: 225-567-2031.
Catechesis/Religious Program—Ms. Mary Herbert, D.R.E. Tel: 225-567-3573. Students 119.
Chapel—Springfield, St. Thomas

AMITE, TANGIPAHOA PARISH, ST. HELENA (1868) Rev. Mark B. Beard; Deacon Michael A. Agnello.
Mailing Address: 122 S. First St., 70422-2701.
Res.: 121 S. First St., 70422-2701. Tel: 985-748-9057; Fax: 985-748-9094. Email: sthelenacatholic@bellsouth.net.
Catechesis/Religious Program—Students 117.
Chapel—Greensburg, St. Jude; Kentwood, St. Elizabeth

BAKER, EAST BATON ROUGE PARISH, ST. ISIDORE THE FARMER (1958) Rev. Frank B. Bass; Deacons Willie Berthelot; Micheal J. Joseph; Donald L. Ard.
Res.: 5657 Thomas Rd., 70811-7356. Tel: 225-775-8850 (Office); Fax: 225-775-7072. Email: parishoffice@stisidorecommunity.org. Web: www.stisidorecommunity.org.
Catechesis/Religious Program—Ms. Monice Oliphant, D.R.E. Students 45.

BAYOU PIGEON, IBERVILLE PARISH, ST. JOAN OF ARC (1965) Rev. Joey F. Angeles.
Res.: 39315 Hwy. 75, Plaquemine, 70764-9629. Tel: 225-545-8213; Fax: 225-545-8213.
Catechesis/Religious Program—Students 11.
Chapel—Bayou Sorrell, St. Catherine Laboure

BELLE ROSE, ASSUMPTION PARISH, ST. JULES (1912) [CEM 2] Rev. Andrew Merrick.
Res.: P.O. Box 38, 70341-0038. Tel: 225-473-8569; Fax: 225-473-2950. Email: stjuleschurch@charterinternet.com.
Catechesis/Religious Program—Students 7.
Chapel—Brusly/St. Martin, St. Martin

BRUSLY, WEST BATON ROUGE PARISH, ST. JOHN THE BAPTIST (1835) Rev. Matthew C. Dupre; Deacon Samuel C. Collura.
Res.: P.O. Box 248, 70719-0248. Tel: 225-749-2189; 225-749-3387; Fax: 225-749-1921. Email: sjbcc@sjbcc.brcoxmail.com.
Catechesis/Religious Program—Mrs. Peggy LeBlanc, D.R.E. Students 400.

CONVENT, ST. JAMES PARISH, ST. MICHAEL THE ARCHANGEL (1812) [CEM 2] Very Rev. Vincent J. Dufresne; Rev. Paul A. Gros; Deacon Alfred P. Adams Sr.
Mailing Address: P.O. Box 129, Paulina, 70763. Tel: 225-869-5751; Fax: 225-869-4166. Email: riverroadcatholic@att.net. Web: www.riverroadcatholic.com.
Church: 6490 LA Highway 44, 70763.
Catechesis/Religious Program—Students 74.

DARROW, ASCENSION PARISH, ST. ANTHONY OF PADUA (1962) Rev. Michael A. Galea.
Mailing Address: P.O. Box 9, Sorrento, 70778. Tel: 225-675-8126; Fax: 225-675-6150.
Church: 37311 LA Highway 22, 70725.
Catechesis/Religious Program—Tel: 225-675-6528. Combined with St. Anne, Sorrento

DENHAM SPRINGS, LIVINGSTON PARISH, IMMACULATE CONCEPTION (1960) Very Rev. Frank M. Uter; Rev. Amal Raj Savarimuthu, I.M.S.; Deacons Peter Schlette; Michael T. Chiappetta; Rudolph W. Stahl.
Mailing Address: P.O. Box 1609, 70727-1609.
Res.: 865 Hatchell Ln., 70726. Tel: 225-665-5359; Fax: 225-665-4422. Web: www.icc-msh.org.
Catechesis/Religious Program—Tel: 225-665-5926. Students 1,090.
Chapel—Livingston, Sacred Heart of Jesus, Tel: 225-686-7322.

DONALDSONVILLE, ASCENSION PARISH

1—ASCENSION OF OUR LORD JESUS CHRIST (1772) [CEM] Rev. Ju Hyung Paul Yi.
Res.: P.O. Box 508, 70346-0508. Tel: 225-473-3176; Fax: 225-473-3256.
Catechesis/Religious Program—Students 15.

2—ST. CATHERINE OF SIENA (1924) Rev. Ayo E. Efodigbue, M.S.P.
Res.: P.O. Box 428, 70346-0428. Tel: 225-473-8350; Fax: 225-473-9978.
Catechesis/Religious Program—Mrs. Ivory Joseph, D.R.E. Students 99.

3—ST. FRANCIS OF ASSISI (1884) [CEM] Rev. Ju Hyung Paul Yi.
Res.: 818 W. Tenth St., 70346-9501. Tel: 225-473-8302; Fax: 225-474-0348.
Catechesis/Religious Program—Students 7.

FRENCH SETTLEMENT, LIVINGSTON PARISH, ST. JOSEPH (1849) [CEM] Rev. Jason P. Palermo; Deacon James A. Little.
Res.: 15710 Louisiana Hwy. 16, 70733-9802. Tel: 225-698-3110; Fax: 225-698-1512. Email: stjosephfs@eatel.net.
Catechesis/Religious Program—Tel: 225-698-6318. Mrs. Barbara Bethelot, D.R.E. Students 192.

GONZALES, ASCENSION PARISH

1—ST. MARK (1973) Rev. Rubin R. Reynolds; Deacon Mario P. (Sam) Sammartino.
Res.: 42021 Hwy. 621, 70737-9354. Tel: 225-647-8461; Fax: 225-647-5125. Email: mail@stmarkgonzales.org. Web: www.stmarkgonzales.org.
Catechesis/Religious Program—Peggy Villavaso, D.R.E. Students 705.

2—ST. THERESA OF AVILA (1918) [CEM] Rev. Gary T. Belsome; Deacon William Blair.
Res.: 1022 N. Burnside Ave., 70737-2551. Tel: 225-647-6588; Fax: 225-647-2223. Email: sttheresa@eatel.net. Web: www.sttheresaofavila.org.
School—212 E. New River St., 70737-2499. Tel: 225-647-2803; Fax: 225-647-7814. Ms. Chris Musso, Prin. Lay Teachers 26; Students 411.
Catechesis/Religious Program—Mrs. Alice Blair, D.R.E. Students 230.

GRAMERCY, ST. JAMES PARISH, MOST SACRED HEART OF JESUS (1961) Very Rev. Vincent J. Dufresne; Rev. Paul A. Gros.
Mailing Address: P.O. Box 129, Paulina, 70763-0129. Tel: 225-869-5751; Fax: 225-869-4166. Email: sacredheart3@cox.net. Web: www.riverroadcatholic.com.
Church: 616 E. Main St., 70052.
Catechesis/Religious Program—Mrs. Diana Cantillo, D.R.E. (Elementary); Mrs. Melissa Laurent, D.R.E. (High School). Students 200.

GREENWELL SPRINGS, EAST BATON ROUGE PARISH, ST. ALPHONSUS LIGUORI (1962) Rev. Michael J. Moroney; Deacons J. Phillip BeJeaux; Robert J. Kusch; Ronald James Hebert.
Res.: 14040 Greenwell Springs Rd., 70739-3302. Tel: 225-261-4650; Fax: 225-261-5650. Web: www.st-alphonsus.net.
School—(Grades PreK-8), 13940 Greenwell Springs Rd., 70739. Tel: 225-261-5299; Fax: 225-261-2795. Web: www.stalphonsusbr.org. Mrs. Cynthia Ryals, Prin.; Melissa Bordelon, Librarian. Lay Teachers 26; Students 428.
Catechesis/Religious Program—Olga Johnson, D.R.E. Students 451.

GROSSE TETE, IBERVILLE PARISH, ST. JOSEPH (1904) [CEM] Revs. John Joseph Kunnaseril, I.M.S.; Sylvester Minj, I.M.S.
Res.: P.O. Box 8, 70740-0008. Tel: 225-625-2438; Fax: 225-625-3513. Email: frsanjayims@yahoo.com.
Catechesis/Religious Program—Tel: 225-625-2485; Fax: 225-625-3513. Students 25.

HAMMOND, TANGIPAHOA PARISH, HOLY GHOST (1902) Revs. Roberto Merced, O.P.; John Boll, O.P.; Cayet N. Mangiaracina, O.P.; Deacons Wallace L. Gainey Jr.; Mauricio Salazar, O.P.
Res.: 601 N. Oak St., 70401-2529. Tel: 985-345-3360; Fax: 985-542-4191. Email: holyghostchurch@I-55.com. Web: www.i-55.com/holyghost.
School—(Grades PreK-8), 507 Oak St., 70401-2598. Tel: 985-345-0977; Fax: 985-542-6545. Ms. Tangee Daugereaux, Prin. Lay Teachers 44; Students 775.
Catechesis/Religious Program—Tel: 985-345-3360, Ext. 28; Fax: 985-542-4191. Mrs. Trisha Labbe, D.R.E. Students 190.

INDEPENDENCE, TANGIPAHOA PARISH, MATER DOLOROSA (1908) Rev. Howard R. Adkins; Deacons Alfred P. Zeringue; Roger A. Navarra; Natale J. Garofalo.
620 3rd St., 70443.
Res.: P.O. Box 349, 70443-0349. Tel: 985-878-9639; Fax: 985-878-6260.
School—(Grades PreK-8), P.O. Box 380, 70443-0380. Tel: 985-878-4295; Fax: 985-878-4888. Mrs. Linda P. Wisinger, Prin. Lay Teachers 12; Students 173.
Catechesis/Religious Program—Tel: 985-878-2852. Ms. Carol A. Young, D.R.E. Students 107.
Chapel—Husser, St. Dominic

LABADIEVILLE, ASSUMPTION PARISH, ST. PHILOMENA (1847) [CEM] Rev. Michael J. Alello.
Res.: P.O. Box 99, 70372-0099. Tel: 985-526-4247; Fax: 985-526-4128. Email: stphilomena@charterinternet.com. Web: www.stphilomenachurch.org.
Catechesis/Religious Program—Students 132.

LAKELAND, POINTE COUPEE PARISH, IMMACULATE CONCEPTION (1859) [CEM 2] Rev. Gregory J. Daigle.
Res.: P.O. Box 158, 70752-0158. Tel: 225-627-5124; Fax: 225-627-5125.
Catechesis/Religious Program—Students 193.

LIVONIA, POINTE COUPEE PARISH, ST. FRANCES XAVIER CABRINI (1955) [CEM] Revs. John Joseph Kunnaseril, I.M.S.; Sylvester Minj, I.M.S.
Res.: 3523 Hwy. 78, P.O. Box 128, 70755-0128. Tel: 225-637-2396; Fax: 225-637-2390. Email: stfrances@spillwaycable.com.
Catechesis/Religious Program—Students 221.
Chapel—Fordoche, St. Catherine of Siena

MARINGOUIN, IBERVILLE PARISH, IMMACULATE HEART OF MARY (1964) [CEM] Revs. John Joseph Kunnaseril, I.M.S.; Sylvester Minj, I.M.S.
Mailing Address: P.O. Box 8, Grosse Tete, 70740-0008.
Res.: 11140 Hwy. 77, 70757-9703. Tel: 225-625-2438; Fax: 225-625-3513.
Catechesis/Religious Program—Students 32.

MAUREPAS, LIVINGSTON PARISH, ST. STEPHEN THE MARTYR (1964) Rev. Jason P. Palermo.
Res.: 22494 Hwy. 22, 70449-3404. Tel: 225-695-6310; Fax: 225-695-6039. Email: saintstephen@eatel.net.
Catechesis/Religious Program—Tel: 225-695-6310; Fax: 225-695-6039. Students 71.

MORGANZA, POINTE COUPEE PARISH, ST. ANN (1872) [CEM 3] Rev. Keun-Soo Lee.
Res.: 182 Church St., P.O. Box 128, 70759-0128. Tel: 225-694-3781; Fax: 225-694-3711. Email: stanns@bellsouth.net.
Catechesis/Religious Program—Tel: 225-694-2132. Mrs. Sharon LeCoq, D.R.E. Students 66.
Chapel—Innis, St. Vincent De Paul

NAPOLEONVILLE, ASSUMPTION PARISH

1—ST. ANNE (1874) [CEM 2] Rev. J. Joel LaBauve.
Res.: P.O. Box 99, 70390-0090. Tel: 985-369-6656; Fax: 985-369-9718. Email: stanne02@att.net. Web: www.renewthebcc.com.
Catechesis/Religious Program—Tel: 985-369-2130. Kathy Landry, D.R.E. Students 208.

2—ST. BENEDICT THE MOOR (1911) [CEM 2] Rev. John Osom, M.S.P.
Res.: 5479 Hwy. 1, 70390-2410. Tel: 985-369-7225; Fax: 985-369-2772. Email: stbenedictchurch@charter.net.
Catechesis/Religious Program—twinned with St. Augustine. Mrs. Jerilyn S. Williams, D.R.E.; Mrs. Pamela Alcorn, D.R.E. Tel: 985-369-7727. Students 90.
Chapel—Klotzville, St. Augustine, Tel: 225-473-9670.

NEW ROADS, POINTE COUPEE PARISH

1—ST. AUGUSTINE (1923) Rev. Lowell D. Case, S.S.J.; Deacon Thomas Robinson.
Res.: 809 New Roads St., P.O. Box 548, 70760-0548. Tel: 225-638-7553; Fax: 225-638-2947. Email: staug812@bellsouth.net.
Catechesis/Religious Program—Students 144.

2—ST. MARY OF FALSE RIVER (1865) [CEM 2] Rev. Msgr. Robert H. Berggreen; Deacon Thomas M. Robinson.
Res.: 348 W. Main St., 70760-3587. Tel: 225-638-9665; Fax: 225-638-6346. Email: stmaryfr@bellsouth.net. Web: www.stmarysfr.org.
Catechesis/Religious Program—Tel: 225-638-6508. Mrs. Emily Froeba, D.R.E. Students 85.
Chapel—Pointe Coupee, St. Francis

PAINCOURTVILLE, ASSUMPTION PARISH, ST. ELIZABETH (1840) [CEM] Rev. Andrew Merrick.
Mailing Address: P.O. Box 1, 70391-0001.
Res.: 6057 St. Elizabeth St., 70391. Tel: 985-369-7398; Fax: 985-369-9892. Email: stelizabeth@charter.net.
Catechesis/Religious Program—Students 33.

PAULINA, ST. JAMES PARISH, ST. JOSEPH (1900) [CEM] Very Rev. Vincent J. Dufresne; Rev. Paul A. Gros.
Mailing Address: P.O. Box 129, 70763-0129.
Church: 2130 Rectory St., 70763-0129. Tel: 225-869-5751; Fax: 225-869-4166. Email: riverroadcatholic@att.net. Web: www.riverroadcatholic.com.
Catechesis/Religious Program—Mrs. Melissa Laurent, D.R.E. (High School); Mrs. Donna Waguespack, D.R.E. (Elementary). Students 458.
Chapel—Lutcher, Our Lady of Prompt Succor

PIERRE PART, ASSUMPTION PARISH, ST. JOSEPH THE WORKER (1858) [CEM 2] Rev. Clarence J. Waguespack.
Res.: 1022 Bayou Dr., P.O. Box 190, 70339-0190. Tel: 985-252-6008; Fax: 985-252-8011. Email: office@sjworker.org.
Catechesis/Religious Program—Tel: 985-252-6633. Mrs. Georgiana C. Cox, D.R.E. Students 370.

PLAQUEMINE, IBERVILLE PARISH

1—ST. CLEMENT OF ROME (1964) Closed. For inquiries for parish records contact St. John the Evangelist, Plaquemine.

2—ST. JOHN THE EVANGELIST (1850) [CEM] Very Rev. Cleo J. Milano.
Office:—57805 Main St., 70764-2531.
Res.: 57810 Plaquemine St., 70764-2538. Tel: 225-687-2402; Fax: 225-687-1587.
Catechesis/Religious Program—Students 189.

PLATTENVILLE, ASSUMPTION PARISH, ASSUMPTION OF THE BLESSED VIRGIN MARY (1793) [CEM] Rev. J. Joel LaBauve.
Mailing Address: P.O. Box 99, Napoleonville, 70390-0099. Tel: 985-369-6656; Fax: 985-369-9718. Email: stanne02@att.net.
Church: Hwy. 308, 70393.
Catechesis/Religious Program—Kathy Landry, D.R.E. Students 204.

PONCHATOULA, TANGIPAHOA PARISH, ST. JOSEPH (1875) [CEM] Revs. John D. Sims, O.P.; Cayet N. Mangiaracina, O.P.; Deacon Larry Melancon.
Mailing Address: P.O. Box 368, 70454-0368. Tel: 985-386-3749; Fax: 985-386-4188. Email: kauchak@i-55.com.
Church: 255 N. 8th St., 70454.
School—(Grades PreK-8), 175 N. Eighth St., 70454-3306. Tel: 985-386-6421; Fax: 985-386-0560. Dr. Gerard Toups, Prin. Lay Teachers 25; Students 411.
Catechesis/Religious Program—Ms. Denise Arnondin, D.R.E. Students 263.

PORT ALLEN, WEST BATON ROUGE PARISH, HOLY FAMILY (1920) Rev. David E. Allen.
Res.: P.O. Box 290, 70767-0290. Tel: 225-383-1838; Fax: 225-383-1839. Email: holyfamilycathol@bellsouth.net.
School—(Grades K-8), 335 N. Jefferson Ave., 70767-2798. Tel: 225-344-4100; Fax: 225-344-1928. Mrs. Brenda Fremin, Prin.; Glenda Manuel, Librarian. Lay Teachers 38; Students 390.
Preschool—415 N. Jefferson Ave., 70767-2727. Tel: 225-343-6541; Fax: 225-344-4100. Jennifer Malbrough, Dir. Lay Teachers 5; Students 30.
Catechesis/Religious Program—Tel: 225-336-4463. Students 55.

PRAIRIEVILLE, ASCENSION PARISH, ST. JOHN THE EVANGELIST (1919) Rev. Eric V. Gyan; Deacons Randy Clement; Claude H. Bourgeois Jr.; Edwin J. Martin.
Res.: 15208 Hwy. 73, 70769-3507. Tel: 225-673-8307; Fax: 225-673-8680. Email: stjohnchurch@eatel.net.
School—St. John Primary School, (Grades PreK-K), 37407 Duplessis Rd., 70769-4321. Tel: 225-677-8238 (Office). Mrs. Tina Schexnaydre, Prin. Lay Teachers 14; Students 367.
Catechesis/Religious Program—Tel: 225-673-8680. Mr. Horace Shows, D.R.E. Students 1,239.

ST. AMANT, ASCENSION PARISH, HOLY ROSARY (1905) [CEM 2] Revs. Jon C. Koehler; Boby Alex (India); Deacon Eliazar Salinas Jr.
Res.: 44450 Hwy. 429, 70774-4597. Tel: 225-647-5321; Fax: 225-647-5322. Email: holyrosary@eatel.net. Web: www.holyrcc.org.
Catechesis/Religious Program—Students 619.
Chapel—Lake, Sacred Heart

ST. FRANCISVILLE, WEST FELICIANA PARISH, OUR LADY OF MOUNT CARMEL (1874) Rev. J. Cary Bani.
Res.: P.O. Box 1249, 70775-1249. Tel: 225-635-3630; Fax: 225-635-2344. Email: olmcchurch@bellsouth.net.
Catechesis/Religious Program—Students 167.
Chapel—Jackson, Our Lady of Perpetual Help, Tel: 225-635-3630.
Chapel—Angola, St. Augustine, Louisiana State Penitentiary [CEM]Tel: 225-655-4411, Ext. 2028.

ST. GABRIEL, IBERVILLE PARISH, ST. GABRIEL THE ARCHANGEL (1769) [CEM] Rev. Charles R. Landry; Deacon Thomas E. Labat Sr.
Res.: 3625 Hwy. 75, 70776-9411. Tel: 225-642-8441; Fax: 225-642-8491. Email: stgabrielcatholi@bellsouth.net.
Catechesis/Religious Program—Students 39.

ST. JAMES, ST. JAMES PARISH, ST. JAMES (1767) [CEM] Rev. Christopher J. Decker; Deacon Henry Zeringue.
Res.: 6613 Hwy. 18, 70086-9054. Tel: 225-265-4210; Fax: 225-265-4225.
Catechesis/Religious Program—Tel: 225-265-9549. Mrs. Janel W. Gordon, D.R.E. Students 125.

SORRENTO, ASCENSION PARISH, ST. ANNE (1963) Rev. Michael A. Galea; Deacon Jerry Braud.
Res.: P.O. Box 9, 70778-0009. Tel: 225-675-8126; Fax: 225-675-6150.
Catechesis/Religious Program—Tel: 225-675-6528. Mrs. Lisa Westerfield, C.R.E. Attended by St. Anthony of Padua, Darrow Students 98.

TICKFAW, TANGIPAHOA PARISH, OUR LADY OF POMPEII (1973) Rev. Roberto Merced, O.P.; Deacon Albert Levy.
14450 Hwy. 442, 70466.
Res.: P.O. Box 276, 70466-0276. Tel: 985-345-8957; Fax: 985-542-8490.

VACHERIE, ST. JAMES PARISH
1—OUR LADY OF PEACE (1864) [CEM] Very Rev. Michael A. Miceli.
Res.: 13281 Hwy. 644, 70090-3102. Tel: 225-265-3953; Fax: 225-265-2507. Email: olopeace@bellsouth.net.
Catechesis/Religious Program—Students 211.
2—ST. PHILIP (1873) [CEM] Rev. Christopher J. Decker.
Res.: 1175 Hwy. 18, 70090-9527. Tel: 225-265-4085; Fax: 225-265-9348. Email: stphilip@bellsouth.net.
Catechesis/Religious Program—Mrs. Janel W. Gordon, D.R.E. Students 123.

WHITE CASTLE, IBERVILLE PARISH, OUR LADY OF PROMPT SUCCOR (1899) [CEM 2] Rev. Joey F. Angeles.
Mailing Address: P.O. Box 249, 70788-0249. Tel: 225-545-3635; Fax: 225-545-8615. Email: olpschurch@cox.net. 32615 Bowie St., 70788.
Catechesis/Religious Program—Students 62.

ZACHARY, EAST BATON ROUGE PARISH, ST. JOHN THE BAPTIST (1964) Rev. M. Jeffery Bayhi; Deacon Ronald D. LeGrange.
Res.: 4727 McHugh Dr., 70791-3935. Tel: 225-654-5778; Fax: 225-654-5796.
Catechesis/Religious Program—Tel: 225-654-5885; Fax: 225-654-5294. Mrs. Dorothy Kuhlman, D.R.E. Students 422.
Chapel—Clinton, Our Lady of the Assumption

Chaplains of Public Institutions

BATON ROUGE. *Baton Rouge General Medical Center*, P.O. Box 3611, 70821-3611. Tel: 225-387-7000. Rev. Michael Jung, O.S.B., Chap.

ANGOLA. *Louisiana State Penitentiary*, P.O. Box 428, 70712-0428. Tel: 225-655-4411, Ext. 2028; 225-655-3243. Rev. J. Cary Bani. St. Augustine Chapel.

ST. GABRIEL. *Hunt Correctional Institute*. Jules Tolivar, Chap.
Mailing Address: P.O. Box 174, 70776-0174. Tel: 225-642-3306. Deacon Claude H. Bourgeois Jr.
LA Correctional Institute For Women, Mailing Address: P.O. Box 26, 70726-0026. Tel: 225-642-5529, Ext. 240. Sr. Linda Songy, S.C.S.C., Chap.

Special Assignment:
Rev.—
Ferrier, Francis V., S.J., 4101 Plaza Tower Dr. #233, 70816-4381. Tel: 225-291-2444 Nursing homes not under Catholic auspices.

Medical Leave:
Rev.—
Sheldon, Alexander J.

Leave:
Rev.—
Labbe, Jason M., S.T.L.

Retired:
Rev. Msgrs.—
Frey, Andrew F., 274 Marquette Ave., 70806-4417. Tel: 225-929-8917
Greene, William L., 3111 Kleinert Ave., 70806-6833. Tel: 225-336-0903
Guillot, Leo, St. Louis King of France, 2121 N. Sherwood Forest Dr., 70815-1962. Tel: 225-275-7280
Lefebvre, Gerald M., P.O. Box 84126, 70884-4126. Tel: 225-925-8241
Revs.—
Blanchard, Donald V., 9124 Old Hammond Hwy., #46, 70809-1380. Tel: 225-361-0818
Brunet, Jules A., 604 Country Club Blvd., Thibodaux, 70301. Tel: 985-209-5701
Burns, Gerald H., 7915 Menlo Ave., 70808. Tel: 225-388-5374
Carville, John, S.T.D., 3553 Hyacinth St., 70808-2849. Tel: 225-383-8320
Collins, Michael J., 9150 Highland Dr., 70810-4096. Tel: 225-766-2431
Dugas, Jerome A., 24520 Ferdinand St., Plaquemine, 70764. Tel: 225-687-1291
Gautreau, Henry W., Ph.D., 421-D Longwood Ct., 70806. Tel: 225-346-8873
Hall, Howard B., P.O. Box 457, 70821-0457. Tel: 225-245-1862
Laird, Kenneth W., 3331 Myrtle Grove, 70810-1232. Tel: 225-262-1517
Marcell, Robert G., P.O. Box 80783, 70898-0783. Tel: 225-346-8258
Mascarella, Patrick J., 144 Highland Park Dr., 70808-5631. Tel: 225-252-2806
McDonald, A. John, 333 Lee Dr., #323, 70808-4974. Tel: 225-767-8237
Messina, Victor G., 438 Alello Dr., 70806-4531. Tel: 225-927-7633
Palang, Mansueto P., 535 Rucker Rd., Alpharetta, GA 30004. Tel: 770-475-4501
Russo, Anthony J., 4145 Pine Park Dr., 70809-2385. Tel: 225-226-8569
Sheehy, Sean O., Ed.D., Listowel, Meen, County Kerry Ireland.
Vavasseur, Henry C., St. Mary of False River Parish, 348 Main St., New Roads, 70760-3587. Tel: 225-939-1924
Young, Gerard F., P.O. Box 345, Darrow, 70725-0345. Tel: 225-278-2466

Permanent Deacons:
Adams, Alfred P., Sr., St. Michael the Archangel, Convent
Agnello, Michael A., St. Helena, Amite
Ard, Donald L., St. Isidore Parish; Baker & Dixon Correctional Institute
Bains, Frank E., St. Jude the Apostle, Baton Rouge
BeJeaux, J. Phillip, St. Alphonsus Liguori, Greenwell Springs
Berthelot, Willie M., St. Isidore the Farmer, Baker
Blair, William B., St. Theresa of Avila, Gonzales
Borne, Daniel S., St. Jean Vianney, Baton Rouge
Bourgeois, Claude H., Jr., St. John the Evangelist, Prairieville
Brady, Eugene F., Nursing Homes Coord., Baton Rouge
Braud, Jerry W., St. Anne Church, Sorrento
Broussard, Patrick James, Jr., Holy Family, Port Allen
Campeaux, Barry G., (Retired), (Diocese of New Orleans)
Chiappetta, Michael T., Dir. Marriage & Family Life, Immaculate Conception, Denham Springs
Christophe, Norman, (Retired), (Oklahoma City)
Clement, Randall A., St. John the Evangelist, Prairieville
Collura, Samuel C., St. John the Baptist, Brusly
Decker, Guy E., (Retired)
Dunbar, Benjamin J., St. Paul the Apostle, Baton Rouge
Duplessis, W. Brent, St. Jean Vianney, Baton Rouge
Easley, Jeff Rufus, St. George, Baton Rouge
Ellis, Albert R., St. George, Baton Rouge
Ferguson, H. John, III, (On Leave)
Furlow, Robert E., Jr., (Leave of Absence)
Garofalo, Natale J., Mater Dolorosa, Tangipahoa Prison
Gauthreaux, Edward Joseph, St. Catherine of Siena, Donaldsonville
Gonzales, Steven Carl, Holy Rosary, St. Amant
Grant, Richard H., Our Lady of Mercy, Baton Rouge
Gremillion, Esnard F., St. Pius X, Baton Rouge
Hebert, Ronald James, St. Alphonsus Church, Greenwell Springs
Hollier, Clayton A., St. Thomas More Church, Baton Rouge
Holtman, Williams H., Most Blessed Sacrament, Baton Rouge
Joseph, Micheal J., St. Isidore the Farmer, Baker
Jung, John A., Jr., St. Aloysius & Nursing Home Ministry, Baton Rouge
Kusch, Robert J., St. Alphonsus Liguori, Greenwell Springs
Labat, Thomas E., Sr., St. Gabriel Church, St. Gabriel
LeGrange, Ronald D., St. John the Baptist, Zachary
Levy, Albert, Our Lady of Pompeii, Tickfaw
Little, James A., St. Joseph Church, French Settlement
Malinoski, Thomas J., (Retired)
Martin, Edwin J., St. John Evangelist, Prairieville
Melancon, Larry, St. Joseph, Ponchatoula
Morrissey, James J.
Moscona, Jodi A., St. Joseph Cathedral, Baton Rouge
Musso, Donald J., Most Blessed Sacrament, Baton Rouge
Navarra, Roger A., Mater Dolorosa, Independence
Nola, Angelo S., Our Lady of Mt. Carmel, St. Francisville
Oubre, Ricky P., Our Lady of Peace, Vacherie
Patterson, Ricky Anthony, St. Louis King of France, Baton Rouge
Reeson, Curles P., St. Jude The Apostle, Baton Rouge
Rhodes, Frank W., (Retired), Denham Springs
Ricard, Alfred J., II, St. John the Evangelist, Plaquemine
Robinson, Thomas H., St. Mary & St. Augustine, New Roads
Salinas, Eliazar, Jr., Holy Rosary, St. Amant
Sammartino, Mario P. (Sam), St. Mark, Gonzales
Schanzbach, Dr. Milton, (Retired)
Schlette, Peter, Immaculate Conception, Denham Springs
Scimeca, Joseph M., Sacred Heart of Jesus, Baton Rouge
St. Pierre, Thomas J.
Stahl, Rudolph W., Immaculate Conception, Denham Springs; Jetson Correctional Institute

Traylor, John T., St. Agnes, Baton Rouge
Veron, John W., St. Aloysius, Baton Rouge
Walsh, J. Peter, St. Patrick, Baton Rouge
Wax, James E., (Retired)
Zeringue, Alfred P., Mater Dolorosa, Independence
Zeringue, Henry J., St. James, St. James

INSTITUTIONS LOCATED IN THE DIOCESE

[A] COLLEGES AND UNIVERSITIES

BATON ROUGE. *Our Lady of the Lake College*, 7434 Perkins Rd., 70808-4380. Tel: 225-768-1710; Fax: 225-768-0811. Email: sandra.harper@ ololcollege.edu. Web: www.ololcollege.edu. Dr. Sandra Harper, Pres. Lay Teachers 110; Students 1,860.

[B] DIOCESAN HIGH SCHOOLS, INTERPAROCHIAL

BATON ROUGE. *Redemptorist Diocesan Regional High School*, (Grades 7-12), 4000 St. Gerard Ave., 70805-2999. Tel: 225-357-0936; Fax: 225-357-4555. Email: redemptortist@rhsbr.org. Web: www.rhsbr.org. John W. Sanders, Prin.; Brian R. Menard, Admin.; Kathy Mendoza, Librarian. Serving parishes in Baton Rouge, Baker, Brusly, Denham Springs, Greenwell Springs, Lakeland, New Roads, Gonzales, Port Allen, St. Gabriel, Zachary, Plaquemine, Maringouin, Prairieville and Clinton. Lay Teachers 27; Students 342.

St. Michael the Archangel Diocesan Regional High School, 17521 Monitor Ave., 70817-2640. Tel: 225-753-9782; Fax: 225-753-0605. Email: stmichaelhigh@csobr.org. Web: www.smhsbr.org. P.O. Box 86110, 70879-6110. Ellen B. Lee, Prin.; Ms. Amy Donaldson, Librarian. Sisters 1; Lay Teachers 54; Students 720.

DONALDSONVILLE. *Ascension Catholic Diocesan Regional School*, (Grades PreK-12), 311 St. Vincent St., 70346-2697. Tel: 225-473-9227; Fax: 225-473-9235. Email: darlenel@ ascensioncatholic.org. Sandy Pizzolato, Prin. Serving parishes in Donaldsonville, St. James, Belle Rose, Vacherie, White Castle, Darrow, Gonzales, Convent, Paincourtville and Plattenville. Lay Teachers 32; Students 475.

HAMMOND. *St. Thomas Aquinas Regional Catholic High School*, 14520 Voss Dr., 70401-9801. Tel: 985-542-7662; Fax: 985-542-4010. Email: stthomasaquinas@csobr.org. Web: www.stafalcons.org. Mr. Jose Becerra, Prin.; Ms. Virginia Bravata, Librarian. Dominican Sisters, Springfield, IL. Lay Teachers 32; Students 397.

NEW ROADS. *Catholic High School of Pointe Coupée*, (Grades 7-12), 504 Fourth St., 70760-3499. Tel: 225-638-9313; Fax: 225-638-6471. Email: highschooloffice@catholicpc.com. Web: www.catholicpc.com. Mrs. Colleen Caillet, Prin. Serving parishes in Lakeland, Livonia, Morganza, New Roads and Maringouin. Lay Teachers 25; Students 321.

PLAQUEMINE. *St. John Interparochial High School*, (Grades 7-12), 24250 Regina St., 70764-3598. Tel: 225-687-3056; Fax: 225-687-3530. Email: info@ stjohnschool.org. Web: www.stjohnschool.org. Mr. David W. Dean, Admin.; Mrs. Cherie Schlatre, Prin.; Mrs. Tonya Orcino, Librarian. Serving parishes in Plaquemine, Brusly, Port Allen, Grosse Tete, St. Gabriel and White Castle. Lay Teachers 16; Students 120.

[C] HIGH SCHOOLS, PRIVATE

BATON ROUGE. *Catholic High School*, (Grades 8-12), 855 Hearthstone Dr., 70806-5599. Tel: 225-383-0397; Fax: 225-383-0381. Email: info@ catholichigh.org. Web: www.catholichigh.org. Mr. Gerald E. Tullier, Pres.; Mrs. Lisa Harvey, Prin.; Mrs. Amanda Graves, Librarian. Brothers of the Sacred Heart 3; Lay Teachers 82; Boys 1,033.

**St. Joseph's Academy*, 3015 Broussard St., 70808-1198. Tel: 225-383-7207; Fax: 225-344-5714. Email: harvisol@sjabr.org. Web: www.sjabr.org. Mrs. Jan Rhorer Breen, Pres.; Mrs. Linda Harvison, Prin.; Mrs. Rebecca V. Stagg, Librarian. Sisters of St. Joseph 4; Lay Teachers 74; Girls 918.

[D] DIOCESAN ELEMENTARY SCHOOLS, INTERPAROCHIAL

DONALDSONVILLE. *Ascension Catholic Interparochial School*, (Grades PreK-12), 311 St. Vincent St., 70346-3499. Tel: 225-473-9227; Fax: 225-473-8559. Email: darlene@ascensioncatholic.org; ascensionelem@csobr.org. Sandy Pizzolato, Prin. Serving parishes in Donaldsonville, St. James, Belle Rose, Vacherie, White Castle, Darrow, Gonzales, Convent, Paulina, Paincourtville, and Plattenville. Lay Teachers 22; Students 402.

Redemptorist Elementary School and Guardian Angels Center, (Grades PreK-8), 3655 St. Gerard Ave., 70805-2898. Tel: 225-355-1437 (office); Fax: 225-355-1879. Email: redemptoristelem@csobr.org. Brian R. Menard, Admin.; Mrs. Joan R. Hutson, Prin.; Ms. Erica Walker, Prin.

NEW ROADS. *Catholic Elementary School of Pointe Coupee*, (Grades PreK-6), 304 Napoleon St., 70760-3527. Tel: 225-638-9313; Fax: 225-638-9953. Email: elementaryoffice@catholicpc.com. Web: www.catholicpc.com. Mrs. Melissa Cline, Prin.; Ms. Kathy Holloway, Librarian. Serving parishes in Lakeland, Livonia, Morganza, New Roads and Maringouin. Lay Teachers 23; Students 396.

PAINCOURTVILLE. *St. Elizabeth Interparochial*, (Grades PreK-8), P.O. Drawer M, 70391-0420. Tel: 985-369-7402; Fax: 985-369-1527. Email: St.Elizabeth@csobr.org. Ms. Paula Simoneaux, Prin.; Ms. Celeste Comeaux, Librarian. Serving parishes in Belle Rose, Bertrandville, Napoleonville, Paincourtville, Pierre Part, Plattenville and Labadieville. Religious Sisters 2; Lay Teachers 14; Students 221.

PAULINA. *St. Peter Chanel Interparochial School*, (Grades PreK-8), 2590 LA Hwy 44, 70763. Tel: 225-869-5778; Fax: 225-869-8131. Email: chanel.school@stpchanel.org. Web: www.stpchanel.org. Mrs. Joanna Foltz, Prin.; Mrs. Sharon Poche, Librarian. Serving parishes in Paulina, Gramercy, Convent, Vacherie, St. James and Grand Point. Lay Teachers 16; Students 241.

PLAQUEMINE. *St. John Interparochial Elementary/ Middle School*, (Grades PreK-8), 58645 St. Clement Ave., 70764-3599. Tel: 225-687-6616; Fax: 225-687-6280. Email: info@stjohnschool.org. Web: www.stjohnschool.org. Mr. David W. Dean, Admin.; Mrs. Bernardine Legendre, Prin.; Ms. Amy John, Librarian. Serving parishes in Plaquemine, Brusly, Grosse Tete, White Castle, Baton Rouge, St. Gabriel, Maringouin, Bayou Pigeon, and Donaldsonville. Lay Teachers 23; Students 372.

[E] SCHOOL, EXCEPTIONAL CHILDREN

BATON ROUGE. *Redemptorist Special Education Program*, 3655 St. Gerard Ave, 70805. Tel: 225-356-4239; Fax: 225-356-4239. Email: sbourgere@ rhsbr.org. Web: www.csobr.org. Mrs. Shirley Bourgere, Dir. Special Educ. Guardian Angels Center (6-13 yrs.) and Career Ed. Center (14-21 yrs.); Redemptorist Elementary Teachers 5; Speech Therapist 1; Students 60.

[F] GENERAL HOSPITALS

BATON ROUGE. *Our Lady of the Lake Regional Medical Center*, 5000 Hennessy Blvd., 70808-4398. Tel: 225-765-6565; Fax: 225-766-5645. Web: www.olorlmc.com. Sr. Kathleen Cain, O.S.F., Supr.; Mr. K. Scott Wester, CEO; Revs. Thomas Danso (Ghana); Donatus O. Ajoko (Nigeria). Franciscan Missionaries of Our Lady (North American Province). Bed Capacity 736; Sisters 19; Patients Assisted Annually 332,597.

Tau Center, 8080 Margaret Ann Dr., 70809-3444. Tel: 225-767-1320; Fax: 225-767-1327.

GONZALES. *St. Elizabeth Hospital*, 1125 W. Hwy. 30, 70737-5000. Tel: 225-647-5071; Fax: 225-647-6066. Web: www.steh.com. Mrs. Dolores LeJeune, R.N., Pres. & CEO. Bed Capacity 78; Total Staff 740; Patients Assisted Annually 90,379.

NAPOLEONVILLE. *Our Lady of the Lake Assumption Community Hospital, Inc.*, 135 Highway 402, 70390-2217. Tel: 985-369-3600; Fax: 985-369-4271. Mr. Wayne M. Arboneaux, CEO. Bed Capacity 60; Total Staff 72.

[G] HOMES AND SPECIAL CARE FACILITIES

BATON ROUGE. *Elderly Housing of Our Lady of the Lake Medical Center*, 5000 Hennessy Blvd., 70808-4398. Tel: 225-765-6565. Ms. Patricia Hima, Dir.

Chateau Louise, 7565 Bishop Ott Dr., 70806. Tel: 225-926-5918. Ms. Patricia Hima, Exec. Dir. Housing for elderly and handicapped persons.

Assisi Village, Inc., of Our Lady of the Lake Medical Center, 7585 Bishop Ott Dr., 70806-8922. Tel: 225-926-5918; Fax: 225-927-1742. Housing facilities for elderly persons.

Calais House, Inc., of Our Lady of the Lake Medical Center, 7545 Bishop Ott Dr., 70806-8900. Tel: 225-927-1889; Fax: 225-927-1742. Housing facilities for elderly persons.

Villa St. Francis, Inc., of Our Lady of the Lake Medical Center, 7575 Bishop Ott Dr., 70806-8906. Tel: 225-927-0070; Fax: 225-927-1742. Housing facilities for elderly and handicapped persons.

Ollie Steele Burden Manor, 4250 Essen Ln., 70809-2196. Tel: 225-926-0091; Fax: 225-926-4937. Ms. Susan Folse, M.S., N.F.A., Admin. Our Lady of the Lake Regional Medical Center, Our Lady of the Lake Pastoral Care. Total Staff 172; Bed Capacity 164.

[H] MONASTERIES AND RESIDENCES OF PRIESTS OR BROTHERS

BATON ROUGE. *Brothers of the Sacred Heart*, 4345 Woodside Dr., 70808. Tel: 225-223-6920. Bro. Xavier Werneth, S.C., Supr. Brothers 4; Ordained 1.

St. Gerard Residence, P.O. Box 53900, 70892-3900. Tel: 225-355-3377; Fax: 225-355-6200. Web: www.novp.org. Priests 2; Brothers 2. In Res. Revs. Gerald Siebold, C.Ss.R.; Samuel C. Maranto, C.Ss.R.; Bro. Clement J. Furno, C.Ss.R.

Incarnatio Consecratio Missio (Vietnamese Institute), 2580 Choctaw Dr., 70805-7999. Tel: 225-357-1204; Fax: 225-354-0611. Email: nvhung@ bellsouth.net. Very Rev. Hung Viet Nguyen, I.C.M. (Vietnam), Supr. General; Revs. Martin Thanh Nguyen, I.C.M.; Peter Neuman, I.C.M.

[I] CONVENTS AND RESIDENCES FOR SISTERS

BATON ROUGE. *Congregation of St. Joseph*, 3134 Hundred Oaks Ave., 70808. Tel: 225-332-2999; Fax: 225-379-7930. Email: ameridier@ csjoseph.org. Web: sistersofstjoseph.org. Sr. Patricia Sullivan, C.S.J., Admin. Sisters of St. Joseph 17.

St. Joseph Spirituality Center, 2980 Kleinert Ave., 70806-6800. Tel: 225-383-3349; Fax: 225-336-4874.

Maryville Novitiate and Provincial House, 4200 Essen Ln., 70809-2196. Tel: 225-926-1627; Fax: 225-925-5268. Email: kathleencain@fmolhs.org. Web: www.fmolsisters.com. *North American Province*, 4200 Essen Ln., 70809-2196. Tel: 225-927-7481; 225-926-1627; Fax: 225-925-5268. Sr. Kathleen Cain, O.S.F., Prov. Supr. Final Vows 23.

[J] RETREAT HOUSES

BATON ROUGE. *Bishop Robert E. Tracy Center*, P.O. Box 2028, 70821-2028. Tel: 225-336-8750; Fax: 225-336-8725. Email: tracycenter@diobr.org. 1800 S. Acadian Thruway, P.O. Box 2028, 70821-2028. Mr. Samuel N. Scimeca, Admin.

CONVENT. *Manresa House of Retreats*, Office: P.O. Box 89, 70723-0089. Tel: 225-562-3596; 800-782-9431; Fax: 225-562-3147. Email: manresahr@ bellsouth.net. Mr. Tim Murphy, Dir.; Revs. Peter J. Callery, S.J., Assoc. Dir.; John J. Callahan, S.J., Assoc. Dir.; Clyde Le Blanc, S.J., Assoc. Dir.; Anthony G. Rausehuber, S.J.

PONCHATOULA. *Rosaryville/Spirit Life Center*, 39003 Rosaryville Rd., 70454-7001. Tel: 225-294-5039; 800-627-9183; Fax: 225-294-3510. Email: rosaryville@charter.net. Web: www.rosaryvillela.com. Susan Satter, Acting Dir.

[K] CAMPUS MINISTRY

BATON ROUGE. *Christ the King Parish and Catholic Center Louisiana State University*, LSU Box 25131, 70803-0106. Tel: 225-344-8595; Fax: 225-344-1920. Email: rstine@ctk-lsu.org. Web: www.ctk-lsu.org. Revs. Robert F. Stine; C. Todd Lloyd.

11 Fraternity Ln., 70803. Total Catholic Students 15,000.

Martin Luther King, Jr. Catholic Student Center St. Joseph Chapel, Southern University, 586 Harding Blvd., 70807-5301. Tel: 225-775-8691; Fax: 225-775-2702. Email: glundysj@aol.com. Rev. Derrick J. Weingartner, S.J., Chap. & Dir. Total Catholic Students 3,000.

HAMMOND. *St. Albert the Great Catholic Student Center* 409 W. Dakota St., 70401-2517. Tel: 985-345-7206; Fax: 985-345-7223. Email: saintal@ bellsouth.net. Very Rev. Randy M. Cuevas, S.T.L., V.F., Dir. Serving Southeastern Louisiana University. Catholic Students 4,500.

[L] MISCELLANEOUS

BATON ROUGE. *Bishop Stanley J. Ott Shelter Program*, P.O. Box 127, 70821-0127. Tel: 225-383-7343; Fax: 225-383-6623. Email: macaldo@svdpbr.com. Mr. Michael J. Acaldo, CEO. Guest Nights of Shelter 25,000.

Catholic Charities of the Diocese of Baton Rouge, Inc., 1900 S. Acadian Thruway, 70808-1688. Tel: 225-336-8770; Fax: 225-336-8745. Email: daguillard@ccdiobr.org. Web: www.ccdiobr.org. Mailing Address: P.O. Box 1668, 70821-1668. Mr. David C. Aguillard, M.P.A., M.H.A., Exec. Dir.

Joseph Homes, Inc.

Child Nutrition Program, P.O. Box 66578, 70896-6578. Lynda Carville, Supvr.

Closer Walk Ministries, Inc., P.O. Box 87279, 70879-8279. Tel: 225-615-7085; Fax: 225-615-7086. Rev. M. Jeffery Bayhi, Pres.; Damien Calato, Exec. Dir.

FMOL Health Systems, Inc., 4200 Essen Ln., 70809-2196. Tel: 225-923-2701; Fax: 225-926-4846. Email: jfinan@fmolhs.com. Web: www.fmolhs.org. Mr. John J. Finan Jr., Pres. & CEO.

Franciscan Ministry Fund, Inc., 4200 Essen Ln., 70809. Sr. Kathleen Cain, O.S.F., Contact Person.

Haiti Mission, Inc., 4200 Essen Ln., 70809-2196. Tel: 225-926-1627; Fax: 225-925-5268. Email: barcenea@ololrmc.com. Sr. Kathleen Cain, O.S.F., Pres. Organized and under the supervision of the Franciscan Missionaries of Our Lady, North American Province.

MAGNIFICAT-Baton Rouge Chapter, 16047 Hickory Knoll, 70810-9515. Tel: 225-752-5678. Mrs. Mary Kestler, Coord. A Ministry to Catholic Women.

Maternity & Adoption, 1900 S. Acadian Thruway, 70808. Tel: 225-336-8708; Fax: 225-336-8703. Email: adopt@ccdiobr.org. Web: www.adoptbatonrouge.com. Mailing Address: P.O. Box 4785, 70821-4785. Mrs. Janice Allen, Dir.

St. Michael's Home (Vietnamese), 2305 Choctaw Dr., 70805-7999. Tel: 225-357-1204; Fax: 225-354-0611. Email: nvhung@bellsouth.net. 2580 Tecumseh St., 70805-7999. Very Rev. Hung Viet Nguyen, I.C.M. (Vietnam), Supr. Gen. Tel: 225-355-9794.

Missionaries of Charity Queen of Peace Home and Soup Kitchen, 737 East Blvd., 70802-6399. Tel: 225-383-8367. Missionaries of Charity.

PACE, Inc., Franciscan Missionaries of Our Lady, 4200 Essen Ln., 70809. Tel: 225-923-2701; Fax: 225-926-4846. Sr. Brendan Mary Ronayne, O.S.F., Contact Person.

Redemptorist Fathers of Baton Rouge, Inc., Redemptorist Residence, P.O. Box 53900, 70892. 5354 Plank Rd., 70805. Tel: 225-355-3377; Fax: 225-355-6200. Revs. Samuel C. Maranto, C.Ss.R.; Gerald Siebold, C.Ss.R.; Bro. Clement J. Furno, C.Ss.R.

**Sisters of St. Joseph - St. Paul Center, Mr. David Jones*, 3920 Gus Young Ave., 70802-1727. Tel: 225-344-8590; Fax: 225-387-5169. Email: spalc@juno.com. Mr. David Jones, Dir.

**SJA Foundation*, 3015 Broussard St., 70808.

**St. Vincent DePaul Community Pharmacy, Inc.*, Mailing Address: P.O. Box 127, 70821-0127. Tel: 225-383-7450; Fax: 225-383-4774. Email: macaldo@svdpbr.com. Mr. Michael J. Acaldo, CEO. Prescriptions Filled 32,400.

St. Vincent DePaul Dining Room, Mailing Address: P.O. Box 127, 70821-0127. Tel: 225-383-7837; 225-383-7439; Fax: 225-383-6623. Email: macaldo@svdpbr.com. Mr. Michael J. Acaldo, CEO. Meals Served 218,644.

St. Vincent DePaul Stores, Mailing Address: P.O. Box 127, 70821-0127. Tel: 225-267-5447; Fax: 225-267-5157. Email: macaldo@svdpbr.com. Mr. Michael J. Acaldo, CEO. Tel: 225-383-7837.

[M] FOUNDATIONS, FUNDS AND TRUSTS

BATON ROUGE. *Baton Rouge Chancery Office*, Mailing Address: P.O. Box 2028, 70821-2028. 1800 S. Acadian Thruway, 70808-1698. Tel: 225-387-0561; Fax: 225-336-8789. Email: chancery@diobr.org.

Ascension Catholic Interparochial School Endowment Fund, Donaldsonville. Tel: 225-473-9227; Fax: 225-473-9235.

Bishop Stanley J. Ott Works of Mercy Trust Tel: 225-387-0561; Fax: 225-336-8789.

Diocese of Baton Rouge Clergy Retirement Plan Tel: 225-387-0561; Fax: 225-336-8789.

Diocese of Baton Rouge Lay Retirement Plan Tel: 225-387-0561; Fax: 225-336-8715.

Catholic Foundation of the Diocese of Baton Rouge Tel: 225-387-0561; Fax: 225-336-8715.

Nim Pecquet Holy Family School Foundation, Port Allen. Tel: 225-344-4100; Fax: 225-344-1928.

Our Lady of Perpetual Help Trust Tel: 225-635-3630; Fax: 225-635-2344.

Pamphile and Mabyn Donaldson Trust for St. Louis King of France Church Tel: 225-275-7280; Fax: 225-275-5845.

Pointe Coupee Catholic Interparochial School Endowment Fund, New Roads. Tel: 225-638-9313; Fax: 225-638-6471.

The Roman Catholic Church of The Diocese of Baton Rouge, Deposit and Loan Fund, Inc., 1800 S. Acadian Thruway, 70808-1698. Tel: 225-387-0561; Fax: 225-336-8789. Mr. Joseph E. Ingraham, CFO.

Sacred Heart School Endowment Fund Tel: 225-383-7481; Fax: 225-383-1810.

St. Aloysius School Endowment Fund Tel: 225-383-3871; Fax: 225-383-4500.

St. Joseph Cathedral Cemetery Fund Tel: 225-387-5928; Fax: 225-387-5929.

St. Joseph Cathedral Trust Tel: 225-387-5928; Fax: 225-387-5929.

St. Theresa of Avila Catholic School Educational Foundation, Gonzales. Tel: 225-647-2803; Fax: 225-647-7814.

St. Thomas More School Endowment Trust Tel: 225-275-2820; Fax: 225-275-0376.

Veritas Foundation, Hammond. Tel: 985-542-7662; Fax: 985-542-4010.

CHS Foundation, 855 Hearthstone Dr., 70806. Tel: 225-389-0978; Fax: 225-389-0983. Mr. Gerald E. Tullier, Pres.

Our Lady of the Lake Foundation, 5000 Hennessy Blvd., 70808-9907. Tel: 225-765-5000; Fax: 225-765-6480.

CONVENT. *Hynes Fund*, Tel: 800-782-9431; Fax: 225-562-3147. Mailing Address: P.O. Box 89, 70723-0089. Mr. Tim Murphy, Dir.

The Administrators of the Rev. John W. Hynes, S.J., Manresa Memorial Endowment Fund, Inc.

RELIGIOUS INSTITUTES OF MEN REPRESENTED IN THE DIOCESE

For further details refer to the corresponding bracketed number in the Religious Institutes of Men or Women section.

[0200]—*Benedictine Monks* (St. Joseph Abbey, St. Benedict, LA)—O.S.B.

[0620]—*Brothers of the Holy Eucharist*—F.S.E.

[1100]—*Brothers of the Sacred Heart* (New Orleans Prov.)—S.C.

[]—*Congregation of the Holy Spirit*—C.S.Sp.

[1070]—*Congregation of the Most Holy Redeemer-Redemptorists*—C.Ss.R.

[]—*Incarnatio Consecratio Missio*—I.C.M.

[]—*Indian Missionary Society*—I.M.S.

[]—*Misioneros de Cristo Maestro*—M.C.M.

[0854]—*Missionaries of St. Paul*—M.S.P.

[0430]—*Order of Preachers-Dominicans* (Prov. of St. Martin de Porres)—O.P.

[0690]—*Society of Jesus* (New Orleans Prov.)—S.J.

[0420]—*Society of the Divine Word* (Southern Prov.)—S.V.D.

[0700]—*St. Joseph's Society of the Sacred Heart-Josephites*—S.S.J.

RELIGIOUS INSTITUTES OF WOMEN REPRESENTED IN THE DIOCESE

[]—*Congregation of the Mother of Carmel*—C.M.C.

[3832]—*Congregation of the Sisters of St. Joseph*—C.S.J.

[]—*Congregation of the Sisters of the Holy Family*—S.S.F.

[]—*Daughters of Mary Mother of the Church*—D.M.

[]—*Dominican Sisters of St. Mary*—O.P.

[1380]—*Franciscan Missionaries of Our Lady*—O.S.F.

[2187]—*Incarnatio Consecratio Missio*—I.C.M.

[2410]—*Marianites of Holy Cross*—M.S.C.

[2590]—*Mercedarian Sisters of the Blessed Sacrament*—H.M.S.S.

[2710]—*Missionaries of Charity*—M.C.

[2970]—*School Sisters of Notre Dame*—S.S.N.D.

[]—*Sisters of Mercy of Holy Cross*—S.C.S.C.

[]—*Sisters of St. Joseph of Carondelet* (Albany Province)—C.S.J.

[3830-16]—*Sisters of St. Joseph of Springfield, Mont Marie*—S.S.J.

[2940]—*Sisters of the Most Holy Sacrament*—M.H.S.

[4070]—*Society of the Sacred Heart*—R.S.C.J.

NECROLOGY

† Youngs, Fred A., (Retired)—Died March 7, 2011

An asterisk (*) denotes an organization that has established tax-exempt status directly with the IRS and is not covered by the USCCB Group Ruling.

Diocese of Beaumont

(Dioecesis Bellomontensis)

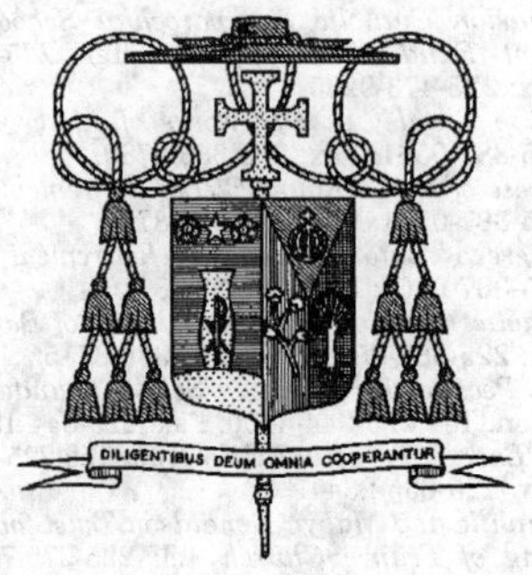

Most Reverend

CURTIS JOHN GUILLORY, S.V.D., D.D.

Bishop of Beaumont; ordained December 16, 1972; appointed Titular Bishop of Stagno and Auxiliary Bishop of Galveston-Houston December 29, 1987; consecrated February 19, 1988; appointed Bishop of Beaumont June 2, 2000; installed July 28, 2000. *Mailing Address: P.O. Box 3948, Beaumont, TX 77704-3948. Office: 710 Archie St., Beaumont, TX 77701-2802.* Tel: 409-924-4310; Fax: 409-838-4511.

Catholic Pastoral Center: 710 Archie St., Beaumont, TX 77701-2802. Mailing Address: P.O. Box 3948, Beaumont, TX 77704-3948. Tel: 409-924-4300; Fax: 409-838-4511.

Web: www.dioceseofbmt.org

Email: chancery@dioceseofbmt.org

ESTABLISHED SEPTEMBER 29, 1966.

Square Miles 7,878.

Comprises the counties of Chambers, Hardin, Jasper, Jefferson, Liberty, Newton, Orange, Polk and Tyler.

For legal titles of parishes and diocesan institutions, consult the Catholic Pastoral Center.

STATISTICAL OVERVIEW

Personnel	
Bishop	1
Priests: Diocesan Active in Diocese	28
Priests: Diocesan Active Outside Diocese	3
Priests: Retired, Sick or Absent	15
Number of Diocesan Priests	46
Religious Priests in Diocese	23
Total Priests in Diocese	69
Extern Priests in Diocese	4
Permanent Deacons in Diocese	32
Total Brothers	3
Total Sisters	22
Parishes	
Parishes	44
With Resident Pastor:	
Resident Diocesan Priests	26
Resident Religious Priests	18
Missions	4
Professional Ministry Personnel:	
Lay Ministers	44
Welfare	
Catholic Hospitals	3
Total Assisted	406,107
Special Centers for Social Services	7
Total Assisted	4,723
Educational	
Diocesan Students in Other Seminaries	6
Seminaries, Religious	1
Students Religious	7
Total Seminarians	13
High Schools, Diocesan and Parish	1
Total Students	431
Elementary Schools, Diocesan and Parish	5
Total Students	1,167
Catechesis/Religious Education:	
High School Students	1,622
Elementary Students	6,221
Total Students under Catholic Instruction	9,454
Teachers in the Diocese:	
Sisters	1
Lay Teachers	135
Vital Statistics	
Receptions into the Church:	
Infant Baptism Totals	1,381
Adult Baptism Totals	178
Received into Full Communion	249
First Communions	1,289
Confirmations	1,004
Marriages:	
Catholic	150
Interfaith	94
Total Marriages	244
Deaths	710
Total Catholic Population	72,117
Total Population	616,838

Former Bishops—Most Revs. VINCENT M. HARRIS, D.D., ord. March 19, 1938; appt. Bishop of Beaumont, July 4, 1966; cons. Sept. 28, 1966; installed as First Bishop of Beaumont, Sept. 29, 1966; appt. Titular Bishop of Rotaria and Coadjutor with right of succession to the Bishop of Austin, TX, April 21, 1971; succeeded to See as Second Bishop of Austin, Nov. 16, 1971; died March 31, 1988; WARREN L. BOUDREAUX, J.C.D., D.D., ord. May 30, 1942; appt. Titular Bishop of Calynda and Auxiliary Bishop of Lafayette, LA, May 19, 1962; cons. July 25, 1962; appt. second Bishop of Beaumont, June 4, 1971; installed Aug. 25, 1971; appt. first Bishop of Houma-Thibodaux, March 2, 1977; installed as first Bishop of Houma-Thibodaux, June 5, 1977; died Oct. 6, 1997; BERNARD J. GANTER, D.D., ord. May 22, 1952; appt. first Bishop of Tulsa, Dec. 19, 1972; cons. and installed, Feb. 7, 1973; appt. third Bishop of Beaumont, Oct. 3, 1977; installed Dec. 13, 1977; died Oct. 9, 1993; JOSEPH A. GALANTE, D.D., J.C.D., ord. May 16, 1964; appt. Titular Bishop of Equilum & Auxiliary Bishop of San Antonio Oct. 13, 1992; cons. Dec. 11, 1992; appt. Bishop of Beaumont, April 5, 1994; installed May 9, 1994; appt. Coadjutor Bishop of Dallas, Nov. 23, 1999; installed Jan. 14, 2000; appt. Bishop of Camden, March 23, 2004; installed April 30, 2004.

Catholic Pastoral Center—710 Archie St., Beaumont, 77701-2802. Tel: 409-924-4300; Fax: 409-838-4511 Office Hours: 8-5. *Mailing Address: P.O. Box 3948, Beaumont, 77704-3948.*

Vicar General and Moderator of the Curia—Rev. Msgr. MICHAEL A. JAMAIL, J.C.D., Ed.D., Mailing Address: P.O. Box 3948, Beaumont, 77704-3948. Tel: 409-924-4303; Fax: 409-838-4511.

Episcopal Vicars—Central Vicariate: Rev. Msgr. WILLIAM MANGER, M.Ed., E.V., Mailing Address: St. Anne, P.O. Box 3429, Beaumont, 77704-3429. Eastern Vicariate: Very Rev. JOSEPH P. DALEO, Mailing Address: St. Mary Church, 912 W. Cherry Ave., Orange, 77630-5017. Northern Vicariate: Very Rev. RONALD B. FOSHAGE, M.S., St. Michael, P.O. Box 239, Jasper, 75951. Southern Vicariate: Very Rev. SINCLAIR OUBRE, J.C.L., E.V., Mailing Address: St. John the Evangelist, P.O. Box 123, Port Arthur, 77641-0123. Western Vicariate: Very Rev. JOSEPH KHANH HO, S.T.L., J.C.L., Holy Trinity, P.O. Box 290, Mont Belvieu, 77580-0290.

Diocesan College of Consultors—Very Rev. JOSEPH KHANH HO, S.T.L., J.C.L.; Rev. Msgr. MICHAEL A. JAMAIL, J.C.D., Ed.D.; Rev. CLIFTON LABBE, S.V.D.; Rev. Msgr. KENNETH R. GREIG; Rev. JOHN CLANCY COON, MA.P.S.; Rev. Msgr. BENNIE J. PATILLO, M.Ed.; Revs. THOMAS E. PHELAN, M.S.W.; D. STEPHEN MCCRATE, S.T.L.; CHARLES ATUAH, M.S.P.; DAVID A. EDWARDS, M.Div.; Very Rev. LUONG QUANG TRAN, J.C.L.

Presbyteral Council—Very Rev. JOSEPH KHANH HO, S.T.L., J.C.L.; Rev. Msgr. MICHAEL A. JAMAIL, J.C.D., Ed.D.; Revs. HENRY DAVIS, S.S.J.; STEVEN L. LEGER, S.T.L., J.C.L.; MARTIN LESTER NELSON, J.C.L.; Rev. Msgrs. BENNIE J. PATILLO, M.Ed.; DAN MALAIN, D.Min.; Revs. M. SHANE BAXTER, S.T.L.; CHARLES ATUAH, M.S.P.; MICHAEL A. STROTHER, M.Div.; Very Rev. LUONG QUANG TRAN, J.C.L.

Clergy Personnel Board—Rev. Msgr. BENNIE J. PATILLO, M.Ed., Chm., Mailing Address: P.O. Box 3948, Beaumont, 77704-3948.

Chancellor—Sr. ESTHER DUNEGAN, I.W.B.S., J.C.L., Mailing Address: Catholic Pastoral Center, P.O. Box 3948, Beaumont, 77704-3948. Tel: 409-924-4304; Fax: 409-838-4511.

Chief Financial Officer—LAURA J. WILLIAMS, CPA, Mailing Address: Catholic Pastoral Center, P.O. Box 3948, Beaumont, 77704-3948. Tel: 409-924-4313; Fax: 409-838-4511.

Diocesan Finance Council—LAURA J. WILLIAMS, CPA, Mailing Address: P.O. Box 3948, Beaumont, 77704-3948.

Human Resources Director—BEVERLY ESCAMILLA, P.H.R., Mailing Address: Catholic Pastoral Center, P.O. Box 3948, Beaumont, 77704-3948. Tel: 409-924-4314; Fax: 409-924-4396; 409-838-4511.

Diocese of Beaumont Retirement Committee—Mr. ROBERT M. CORE, Chm., Mailing Address: P.O. Box 3948, Beaumont, 77704-3948. Tel: 409-924-4314.

Tribunal—Mailing Address: Catholic Pastoral Center, 710 Archie St., P.O. Box 3948, Beaumont, 77704-3948. Tel: 409-924-4319; Fax: 409-838-4511.

Judicial Vicar—Very Rev. LUONG QUANG TRAN, J.C.L.

Diocesan Judges—Very Rev. LUONG QUANG TRAN, J.C.L., Judicial Vicar; Rev. Msgr. KENNETH R. GREIG; Rev. STEVEN L. LEGER, S.T.L., J.C.L.; Very Rev. JOSEPH KHANH HO, S.T.L., J.C.L.; Rev. MARTIN LESTER NELSON, J.C.L.; Very Rev. SINCLAIR OUBRE, J.C.L., E.V.; Rev. Msgr. BENNIE J. PATILLO, M.Ed.; Sr. ESTHER DUNEGAN, I.W.B.S., J.C.L.

Promoter of Justice—Rev. Msgr. MICHAEL A. JAMAIL, J.C.D., Ed.D.

Defender of Bond—Rev. Msgr. MICHAEL A. JAMAIL, J.C.D., Ed.D.

Psychologists for the Tribunal—RAY COXE, Ph.D.; Rev. Msgr. MICHAEL A. JAMAIL, J.C.D., Ed.D.

Secretary-Notary—MARILYN PRICE; Sr. BARBARA ANNE OSTERHAUS, C.V.I., Sec.

Victim Assistance Coordinator—Mrs. BECKY RICHARD, M.S., L.P.C., Mailing Address: 2780 Eastex Freeway, Beaumont, 77703. Tel: 409-924-4400, Ext. 4433; Fax: 409-832-0145. Email: brichard@catholiccharitiesbmt.org.

Diocesan Departments

Apostleship of the Sea—Very Rev. SINCLAIR OUBRE, J.C.L., E.V., Diocesan Dir., 1500 Jefferson Dr.,

Port Arthur, 77642. Tel: 409-982-5111; Fax: 409-985-5945. Email: aos-beaumont@dioceseofbmt.org.

Lifelong Catholic Formation / Education—LORRAINE S. DELUCA, Ed.D., Dir., Mailing Address: P.O. Box 3948, Beaumont, 77704-3948. Tel: 409-924-4323; Fax: 409-838-4511.

Catholic Schools—MARCIA STEVENS, Supt., Mailing Address: P.O. Box 3948, Beaumont, 77704-3948. Tel: 409-924-4322; Fax: 409-838-4511.

Office of Stewardship & Communications—LETTY LANZA, Dir., Mailing Address: P.O. Box 3948, Beaumont, 77704-3948. Tel: 409-924-4302; Fax: 409-838-4511.

East Texas Catholic Newspaper—710 Archie St., Beaumont, 77701-2802. Tel: 409-924-4350; Fax: 409-838-4511. Ms. KAREN GILMAN, Editor.

Diaconate, Permanent Diaconate—Rev. Msgr. JEREMIAH J. MCGRATH, D.Min., Vicar, Mailing Address: St. Anthony Cathedral Basilica, P.O. Box 3309, Beaumont, 77704-3309. Tel: 409-833-6433; Fax: 409-833-6688; Deacon STEVEN OBERNUEFEMANN, Dir., 210 Thornridge, Bridge City, 77611-2355. Tel: 409-735-6005; Fax: 409-838-4511.

Diaconate Formation—Very Rev. SINCLAIR OUBRE, J.C.L., E.V., Dir. Tel: 409-924-4303; Fax: 409-838-4511; Sr. ESTHER DUNEGAN, I.W.B.S., J.C.L., Assoc. Dir., Diocese of Beaumont, P.O. Box 3948, Beaumont, 77704-3948. Tel: 409-924-4304; Fax: 409-838-4511.

Holy Childhood—LETTY LANZA, Mailing Address: P.O. Box 3948, Beaumont, 77704-3948. Tel: 409-924-4316; Fax: 409-838-4511.

Propagation of the Faith: Mission Coop—LETTY LANZA, Mailing Address: P.O. Box 3948, Beaumont, 77704-3948. Tel: 409-924-4316; Fax: 409-838-4511.

Hispanic Ministry, Diocesan—Mr. JESUS ABREGO, Dir., Mailing Address: P.O. Box 3948, Beaumont, 77704-3948. Tel: 409-924-4331; Fax: 409-838-4511.

African American Ministry—LINDA DUHON-LACOUR, Dir., Mailing Address: P.O. Box 3948, Beaumont, 77704-3948. Tel: 409-924-4325; Fax: 409-838-4511.

Worship; Liturgical Commission; Diocesan Choir—Mrs. ROSALIND SANCHEZ, M.A., Dir., Mailing Address: P.O. Box 3948, Beaumont, 77704-3948. Tel: 409-924-4321; Fax: 409-838-4511.

Principal Master of Episcopal Ceremonies—Deacon DAVID LUTHER, Mailing Address: Rte. 7, Box 46-1, Jasper, 75951-9294. Tel: 409-384-1521.

Family Life Ministry & Respect Life Liaison—JEROME CABEEN, Dir., Mailing Address: P.O. Box 3948, Beaumont, 77704-3948. Tel: 409-924-4390; Fax: 409-838-4511.

Criminal Justice Ministry—Deacon HARRY DAVIS, Dir., Mailing Address: P.O. Box 3948, Beaumont, 77704-3948. Tel: 409-924-4329; Fax: 409-838-4511.

Director of Seminarians—Rev. ANDREW MOORE, M.Div., Mailing Address: Infant Jesus Church, P.O. Box 8180, Lumberton, 77657. Tel: 409-755-1734; Fax: 409-755-2833.

Vocations—Rev. M. SHANE BAXTER, S.T.L., Mailing Address: P.O. Box 3948, Beaumont, 77704-3948. Tel: 409-924-4361; Fax: 409-832-4129.

Office of Youth Ministry—TEX PHELPS, Dir., Mailing Address: P.O. Box 3948, Beaumont, 77704-3948. Tel: 409-924-4362; Fax: 409-838-4511.

Ecumenical Interreligious Affairs Officer—Rev. Msgr. JEREMIAH J. MCGRATH, D.Min., Mailing Address: St. Anthony Cathedral Basilica, P.O. Box 3309, Beaumont, 77704-3309. Tel: 409-833-6433; Fax: 409-833-6688.

Committees, Boards, Commissions

Diocesan Review Board—Mailing Address: P.O. Box 3948, Beaumont, 77704-3948.

Diocesan African American Commission—Mr. WILLIAM JAMES CARTER, Chm., Mailing Address: P.O. Box 3948, Beaumont, 77704-3948. Tel: 409-924-4325; Fax: 409-838-4511.

Diocesan Building Commission—HAMIL CUPERO JR., Chm., Mailing Address: P.O. Box 3948, Beaumont, 77704. Tel: 409-924-4313.

Catholic Committee on Scouting—Mr. DAVID PECORA, Chm., 1152 Sunmeadow, Beaumont, 77706. Tel: 409-338-3008.

Catholic Daughters of America—JANE BONNIN, District Deputy, Mailing Address: P.O. Box 7851, Beaumont, 77726. Tel: 409-883-5234.

Catholic Women, Council of—Rev. MARTIN LESTER NELSON, J.C.L., Moderator, Mailing Address: Our Lady of Victory, P.O. Box 1359, Sour Lake, 77659-1359.

Charismatic Prayer Renewal—Rev. Msgr. WILLIAM MANGER, M.Ed., E.V., Group Liaison, Mailing Address: St. Anne Church, P.O. Box 3429, Beaumont, 77704-3429.

Southeast Texas ACTS Mission Chapter—Rev. Msgr. WILLIAM MANGER, M.Ed., E.V., Liaison, Mailing Address: St. Anne Church, P.O. Box 3429, Beaumont, 77704-3429. Tel: 409-832-9963; Fax: 409-832-9964.

Commission for Continuing Education of Clergy & Religious—Rev. PETER C. FUNK, Chm., Holy Family Retreat Center, 9920 N. Major Dr., Beaumont, 77713-7618. Tel: 409-899-5617; Fax: 409-899-3161.

R.C.I.A. Commission—LORRAINE S. DELUCA, Ed.D., Chm., Mailing Address: P.O. Box 3948, Beaumont, 77704-3948. Tel: 409-924-4323; Fax: 409-838-4511.

Diocesan School Board—MICHAEL FULJENZ, Pres., 8255 White Rd., Beaumont, 77706. Tel: 409-860-1620 (Office); Cell: 409-658-4533. Email: stacey@universalcoin.com; BILL SCOTT, Vice Pres., 140 Grandchase, Nederland, 77627. Tel: 409-727-4801 (Office). Email: kdaleo@tgsgroup.com.

Vocation Board—Rev. M. SHANE BAXTER, S.T.L., Vocations Dir.

CLERGY, PARISHES, MISSIONS AND PAROCHIAL SCHOOLS

CITY OF BEAUMONT

(JEFFERSON COUNTY)

1—ST. ANTHONY CATHEDRAL BASILICA (1879) Rev. Msgr. Jeremiah J. McGrath; Deacons Laurence David; Keith Fontenot. In Res., Revs. George Kalappura, C.M.I.; Joseph Kattakkara, C.M.I.
Res.: 700 Jefferson St., P.O. Box 3309, 77704-3309. Tel: 409-833-6433; Fax: 409-833-8996. Email: support@stanthonycathedral.org. Web: stanthonycathedral.org.
School—(Grades PreK-8), 850 Forsythe, 77701-2890. Tel: 409-832-3486; Fax: 409-838-9051. Email: pwalters@stanthonycathedralschool.org. Phyllis Walters, Prin.; Sherridan Shakour, Librarian. Lay Teachers 18; Students 203.
Catechesis / Religious Program—Students 174.

2—ST. ANNE (1937) Rev. Msgr. William Manger; Rev. Rodel Faller, Parochial Vicar. In Res., Rev. Msgr. Michael A. Jamail.
Res.: Calder Ave. & 11th, P.O. Box 3429, 77704-3429. Tel: 409-832-9963; Fax: 409-832-9964. Email: stannechurch@gtbizclass.com. Web: www.stannebmt.org.
School—(Grades PreK-8), 375 N. 11th St., 77702-1834. Web: www.stannecatholic.org. Amy Delgado, Prin.; Ana Wallace, Librarian. (Formerly St. Anne Tri-Parish School) Lay Teachers 40; Students 561.
Catechesis / Religious Program—Tel: 409-832-8107; Fax: 409-832-5099. Email: drestanne@gtbizclass.com. Students 117.

3—BLESSED SACRAMENT (1915), (African American), [CEM] Revs. Henry Davis, S.S.J.; Jerome Ugochukwu Cletus, S.S.J., Parochial Vicar.
Res.: 780 Porter St., 77701-7198. Tel: 409-833-6089; Fax: 409-833-6091. Email: blessed780@hotmail.com.
Catechesis / Religious Program—Tel: 409-833-1909. Students 30.

4—CRISTO REY (1951), (Hispanic), Rev. Luis Urriza, O.S.A.
Res.: 767 Ave. A, 77701. Tel: 409-835-7788; Fax: 409-835-7788.
Catechesis / Religious Program—Tel: 409-835-7240. Students 536.

5—ST. JOSEPH (1905), (Italian—Vietnamese), Rev. Khue Si Bui.
Res.: 1115 Orange St., 77701-4392. Tel: 409-835-5662; Fax: 409-832-7717. Email: josephcbmt@aol.com.
Catechesis / Religious Program—Students 60.

6—ST. JUDE THADDEUS (1978) Revs. John Hughes; Constantino Barrera, Parochial Vicar; David A. Edwards, Parochial Vicar; Deacon Gordon Cabra.
Res.: 6825 Gladys, 77706-3239. Tel: 409-866-5088; Fax: 409-866-1866. Email: stjude@stjudebmt.org. Web: www.stjudebmt.org.
Catechesis / Religious Program—Tel: 409-866-9595. Students 474.

7—OUR LADY OF THE ASSUMPTION (1951) Rev. Antony Paulose, C.M.I., Parochial Admin.; Deacon Harry Davis.
Res.: 4445 Ave. A, 77705-4998. Tel: 409-835-5343; Fax: 409-835-5344. Email: oloa4445@gt.rr.com.
Catechesis / Religious Program—Students 40.

8—OUR MOTHER OF MERCY (1937), (African American), Revs. Henry Davis, S.S.J.; Jerome Ugochukwu Cletus, S.S.J., Parochial Vicar.
Res.: 3390 Sarah St., 77705-3098. Tel: 409-842-5533; Fax: 409-842-4710. Email: omomchurch@sbcglobal.net. Web: josephite.com/parish/tx/omom.
School—(Grades PreK-6) Dorothy Wheaton, Prin.; Gwen Williams, Librarian. Lay Teachers 8; Students 64.
Catechesis / Religious Program—Tel: 409-842-0112. Students 221.

9—ST. PIUS X (1954) Rev. Joseph Dang, S.V.D., Parochial Admin.
Res.: 5075 Bigner Rd. at East Lucas, 77708-5299. Tel: 409-892-3316; Fax: 409-892-8916. Email: joeoanhdangsvd@yahoo.com. Web: catholic.web.com/stpiusxbmt.
Catechesis / Religious Program—Tel: 409-892-6052. Students 58.

OUTSIDE THE CITY OF BEAUMONT

AMES, LIBERTY CO., OUR MOTHER OF MERCY (1903), (African American), [CEM] Rev. George Okeahialam, M.S.P.
Res.: P.O. Box 264, Liberty, 77575-0264. Tel: 936-336-3004; Fax: 936-336-5955. Email: ourmotherofmercyames@yahoo.com.
Catechesis / Religious Program—Students 35.

ANAHUAC, CHAMBERS CO., OUR LADY OF LIGHT (1938) Rev. Neil A. Arce.
Res.: Rte. 2, Box 1-F, 77514-9001. Tel: 409-267-3158; Fax: 409-267-4047. Email: neilofjesus@hotmail.com.
Catechesis / Religious Program—Students 115.

BRIDGE CITY, ORANGE CO., ST. HENRY (1948) Rev. Steven L. Leger; Deacon Hazen Kenney.
Mailing Address: P.O. Box 427, 77611-0427.
Res.: 475 W. Round Bunch Rd., 77611-2448. Tel: 409-735-2422; Fax: 409-738-2158. Email: office@sthenrybctx.org. Web: www.sthenrybctx.org.
Catechesis / Religious Program—Tel: 409-735-8642; Fax: 409-697-1013. Students 281.

BUNA, JASPER CO., ST. FRANCIS OF ASSISI MISSION (1968) Rev. Delphyn J. Meeks.
Mailing Address: P.O. Box 1688, 77612-1688. Tel: 409-994-3456. Email: stfrancism@att.net.
Catechesis / Religious Program—Tel: 409-994-3456. Students 14.

CHEEK, JEFFERSON CO., ST. MARTIN DE PORRES MISSION (1972), (African American), Rev. James McClintock; Deacon Allan Santos.
Mailing Address: 9894 Gilbert, 77705. Tel: 409-794-2548; Fax: 409-794-3411. Email: stmarycc@hotmail.com.
Catechesis / Religious Program—(with St. Mary, Fannett), Tel: 409-794-1725. Students 17.

CHINA, JEFFERSON CO., OUR LADY OF SORROWS (1918) Very Rev. Luong Quang Tran.
Res.: P.O. Box 38, 77613-0038. Tel: 409-752-3571; Fax: 409-752-5134. Email: olos1@sbcglobal.net.
Catechesis / Religious Program—Students 126.

CLEVELAND, LIBERTY CO., ST. MARY (1950) Rev. Eric Groner, S.V.D.; Deacons David Mueller; Larry Terrell.
Res.: P.O. Box 816, 77328-0816. Tel: 281-592-2985; Fax: 281-592-7247. Email: stmarycleveland01@sbcglobal.net. Web: www.stmarycleveland-tx.org.
Catechesis / Religious Program—Students 525.

CORRIGAN, POLK CO., ST. MARTIN DE PORRES MISSION (1971), (Hispanic), Rev. Clifton Labbe, S.V.D.; Deacon Jose A. Vitela.
Mailing Address: P.O. Box 930, Livingston, 77351-0930. Tel: 936-967-8385; Fax: 936-967-4657. 104 Gossett Rd., 75939. Tel: 936-398-2807. Email: stjoe@eastex.net. Web: stjoseph-livingston-tx.org.
Catechesis / Religious Program—Students 58.

DAYTON, LIBERTY CO., ST. JOSEPH THE WORKER (1945) [CEM] Rev. Michael Long Vu, S.V.D., Parochial Admin.
Res.: P.O. Box 640, 77535-0640. Tel: 936-258-5735; Fax: 936-258-7220. Email: stjosephdayton@yahoo.com.
Catechesis / Religious Program—Students 141.

EASTGATE, LIBERTY CO., ST. ANNE MISSION (1918) Rev. Michael Long Vu, S.V.D., Parochial Admin.
Mailing Address: P.O. Box 640, Dayton, 77535-0640. Tel: 936-258-5735; Fax: 936-258-7220. Email: stjosephdayton@yahoo.com.

FANNETT, JEFFERSON CO., ST. MARY (1964), Formerly St. Mary, Hamshire (1899). Rev. James McClintock, Parochial Admin.; Deacon Allan Santos.
Res.: 9894 Gilbert Rd., 77705-8878. Tel: 409-794-2548; Fax: 409-794-3411. Email: stmarycc@hotmail.com.
Catechesis / Religious Program—Tel: 409-794-1725; Fax: 409-794-3411. Students 283.

GROVES, JEFFERSON CO.

1—IMMACULATE CONCEPTION (1928) Rev. Msgr. Kenneth R. Greig; Deacon Steven Obernuefemann. In Res., Rev. M. Shane Baxter.
Res.: 6250 Washington, P.O. Box 967, 77619-0967. Tel: 409-962-0255; Fax: 409-963-3464. Email: icc-groves@gtbizclass.com.
Catechesis / Religious Program—Students 77.

2—St. Peter the Apostle (1972) Rev. Msgr. Kenneth R. Greig; Deacon Thomas Ewing Jr.
Res.: 2049 Taft Ave., 77619-4953. Tel: 409-962-8365; Fax: 409-962-8366. Email: stpeters4072@sbcglobal.net.
Catechesis/Religious Program—Tel: 409-962-3661. Students 208.

Jasper, Jasper Co., St. Michael (1952) Very Rev. Ronald B. Foshage, M.S.; Deacons David Luther; William (Bill) Lawrence.
Res.: P.O. Box 239, 75951-0239. Tel: 409-384-2447; Fax: 409-384-2447.
Catechesis/Religious Program—Students 108.
Station—Toledo Village

Kirbyville, Jasper Co., Our Lady of La Salette Mission (1948) Very Rev. Ronald B. Foshage, M.S.; Deacons David Luther; William (Bill) Lawrence.
Mailing Address: P.O. Box 239, Jasper, 75951-0239. Tel: 409-384-2447; Fax: 409-384-2447.
Catechesis/Religious Program—Students 50.

Kountze, Hardin Co., Holy Spirit Mission (1986) Rev. Andrew Moore.
470 Monroe, 77625-5414. Tel: 409-246-4457 (Office); Fax: 409-246-4623. Email: virginiamonk16@yahoo.com.
Catechesis/Religious Program—Students 38.

Liberty, Liberty Co., Immaculate Conception (1756) [CEM] Rev. Sebastian Myladiyil, S.V.D.
Res.: 411 Milam, 77575-4730. Tel: 936-336-7267; Fax: 936-336-9740. Email: iccliberty@comcast.net.
Catechesis/Religious Program—Students 290.

Livingston, Polk Co., St. Joseph (1970) Rev. Clifton Labbe, S.V.D.; Deacon Mike Marion.
Res.: P.O. Box 930, 77351-0930. Tel: 936-967-8385; Fax: 936-967-4657. Email: stjoe@eastex.net. Web: www.stjoseph-livingston-tx.org.
Catechesis/Religious Program—Tel: 936-646-4685. Students 184.

Lumberton, Hardin Co., Infant Jesus (1948) Rev. Andrew Moore.
Res.: P.O. Box 8180, 77657-0180. Tel: 409-755-1734; Fax: 409-755-2833. Email: cslegros@gt.rr.com.
Catechesis/Religious Program—Students 210.

Mauriceville, Orange Co., St. Maurice (1966) Rev. Delphyn J. Meeks.
Res.: P.O. Box 940, 77626-0940. Tel: 409-745-4060; Fax: 409-745-4272. Email: stmaurice2@aol.com.
Catechesis/Religious Program—Students 51.

Mont Belvieu, Chambers Co., Holy Trinity (2003) Very Rev. Joseph Khanh Ho; Deacon Eugene R. LeBlanc.
Mailing Address: P.O. Box 290, 77580-0290.
Church: 3515 Trinity, 77580. Email: office@htcc-mb.org. Web: www.holytrinitymb.org.
Catechesis/Religious Program—Students 200.

Nederland, Jefferson Co., St. Charles Borromeo (1923) Rev. Msgr. Dan Malain; Rev. David D. Placette, Parochial Vicar; Deacons Dallas Broussard; Chris Penning, D.O.
Res.: 130 Hardy Ave., 77627-7326. Tel: 409-722-3413; Fax: 409-722-2020. Email: stcharles@gt.bizclass.com. Web: stcharlesnederland.com.
Catechesis/Religious Program—Tel: 409-722-0421; Fax: 409-722-5848. Students 662.

Orange, Orange Co.

1—St. Francis of Assisi (1978) Rev. Thomas E. Phelan; Deacon Hector Maldonado.
Church: 4300 Meeks Dr., 77632-4508. Tel: 409-883-9153; Fax: 409-883-9154. Email: stfrancisorangetx@gt.twcbc.com. Web: www.stfrancisorange.org.
Catechesis/Religious Program—Tel: 409-883-8232. Email: jbroussard@gt.twcbc.com. Students 215.

2—St. Mary (1880) [CEM] Very Rev. Joseph P. Daleo; Deacon Melvin Payne.
Res.: 912 W. Cherry St., 77630-5017. Tel: 409-883-2883; Fax: 409-883-3547. Email: stmary@gtbizclass.com.
School—(Grades PreK-8), 2600 Bob Hall Rd., 77630-2418. Tel: 409-883-8913; Fax: 409-883-0827. Denise Willingham, Prin.; Kristi Braquet, Librarian. Lay Teachers 20; Students 192.
Catechesis/Religious Program—Tel: 409-886-0841; Fax: 409-886-0841. Students 88.

3—St. Therese (1924), (African American), Rev. Anselm Eke, M.S.P.; Deacon Julian Richard.
Res.: 1409 N. Sixth St., 77630-3927. Tel: 409-883-3783; Fax: 409-883-4918. Email: sttherese2770@att.net.
Catechesis/Religious Program—Students 22.

Orangefield, Orange Co., St. Helen (1938) Rev. George Kindangen, C.M.I., Parochial Admin.; Deacon Timothy Istre.
Res.: 8105 FM 1442, 77630-8197. Tel: 409-735-2200 (Office); Fax: 409-735-7786. Email: sthelen2009@yahoo.com.
Catechesis/Religious Program—Tel: 409-735-7028. Students 112.

Port Arthur, Jefferson Co.

1—St. Catherine of Siena (1954) Rev. Duc Duong; Deacon Jim Gard.
Res.: 3706 Woodrow Dr., 77642-2320. Tel: 409-962-5715; Fax: 409-962-4775. Email: jonig@stcatherinechurch.net.
School—(Grades PreK-8) Haidee Todora, Prin.; Mary Anne Sigur, Librarian. Lay Teachers 17; Students 170.
Catechesis/Religious Program—Students 99.

2—St. James (1929) Rev. John Clancy Coon. In Res., Rev. R. Eathan Oakes.
Res.: 3617 Gulfway Dr., 77642-3675. Tel: 409-985-8865; Fax: 409-985-3847. Email: jefferyhlewis@sbcglobal.net. Web: www.patx.us/stjames.
Catechesis/Religious Program—Students 16.

3—St. John (1951), (African American), Very Rev. Sinclair Oubre; Deacon Willie Posey.
Res.: P.O. Box 123, 77641-0123. Tel: 409-985-8010; Fax: 409-982-8691. Email: aos-beaumont@dioceseofbmt.org.
Catechesis/Religious Program—Tel: 409-985-8010; Fax: 409-982-8691. Students 27.

4—St. Joseph (1951) Rev. D. Stephen McCrate; Deacon Luis Javier Magana.
Res.: 4600 Procter St., 77642-1365. Tel: 409-982-6409; Fax: 409-983-5383. Email: stjochurch@att.net. Web: www.patx.us/stjoseph.
Catechesis/Religious Program—Tel: 409-982-0667. Students 333.

5—St. Mary (1903), (African American), Merged with Sacred Heart, Port Arthur in 2006 to form Sacred Heart-St. Mary Parish, Port Arthur.

6—Our Lady of Guadalupe (1927), (Hispanic), Revs. Telesforo R. Blanco, O.S.A.; Urbano Saenz, O.S.A., Parochial Vicar.
Res.: 3648 S. Sgt. Lucian Adams Dr., 77642-6100. Tel: 409-962-6777; Fax: 409-963-0669. Email: trb@gtbizclass.com. Web: www.patx.us/olgchurch.
Catechesis/Religious Program—Tel: 409-962-2247. Students 333.

7—Queen of Vietnam (1977), (Vietnamese), Revs. Francis Vinh Vu, C.M.C.; Martin Vanban Tran, C.M.C., Parochial Vicar.
Res.: 801 Ninth Ave., 77642-3329. Tel: 409-983-7676; Fax: 409-982-1212. Email: queenofvnchurch@hotmail.com.
Catechesis/Religious Program—Students 190.
Convent—1148 Ninth Ave., 77642. Tel: 409-985-5102; Fax: 409-985-5102. Dominican Sisters 3.

8—Sacred Heart (1915), (African American), Merged with St. Mary, Port Arthur in 2006 to form Sacred Heart-St. Mary Parish, Port Arthur.

9—Sacred Heart-St. Mary Parish (2006) Rev. Charles Atuah, M.S.P.
920 Booker T. Washington Ave., 77640-4923. Tel: 409-985-5104; Fax: 409-982-0106. Email: sacredheart@gt.rr.com.
Catechesis/Religious Program—Students 50.

10—St. Therese the Little Flower of Jesus (1928) Rev. Rejimon George, C.M.I., Parochial Admin.
Res.: 6412 Garnet Ave., 77640-1308. Tel: 409-736-1536; Fax: 409-736-2113. Email: officelittleflower@gtbizclass.com. Web: www.patx.us/sttherese.
Catechesis/Religious Program—Students 81.

Port Neches, Jefferson Co., St. Elizabeth (1922) Rev. Msgr. Bennie J. Patillo.
Res.: 2006 Nall St., 77651-3714. Tel: 409-727-8874; Fax: 409-727-8875. Email: stebeth@stelizabethchurch.net. Web: stelizabethchurch.net.
Catechesis/Religious Program—Tel: 409-722-5941. Students 384.

Raywood, Liberty Co., Sacred Heart (1952), (African American), [CEM] Rev. George Okeahialam, M.S.P.
Res.: P.O. Box 429, 77582. Tel: 936-587-4631; Fax: 936-587-1012. Email: sacredheartchurchraywood@yahoo.com.
Catechesis/Religious Program—Students 11.

Sabine Pass, Jefferson Co., St. Paul Mission (1955) Closed. in 2009. For inquiries for parish records contact St. John, Port Arthur.

Sam Rayburn, Jasper Co., St. Raymond Mission (1970) Very Rev. Ronald B. Foshage, M.S.
Mailing Address: P.O. Box 239, Jasper, 75951-0239. Tel: 409-384-2447.

Silsbee, Hardin Co., St. Mark the Evangelist (1940) Rev. Msgr. James Vanderholt (Retired); Deacon Glen Hebert.
Res.: 905 N. Ninth St., 77656. Tel: 409-287-3287; Fax: 409-385-0806. Email: mevangelist@sbcglobal.net.
Catechesis/Religious Program—Students 80.

Sour Lake, Hardin Co., Our Lady of Victory (1906) 225 Barkley, P.O. Box 1359, 77659. In Res., Rev. Martin Lester Nelson.
Res.: 210 W. Barkley, P.O. Box 1359, 77659. Tel: 409-287-3287; Fax: 409-287-3271. Email: olov1@att.net. Web: olovsourlake.org.
Catechesis/Religious Program—Students 106.

Vidor, Orange Co., Our Lady of Lourdes (1938) Rev. Paul Sumler.
Res.: 1600 N. Main, 77662-3014. Tel: 409-769-2865; Fax: 409-769-2865. Email: ourladyoflourdes@sbcglobal.net. Web: ololvidor.c-paluch.com.
Catechesis/Religious Program—Tel: 409-769-6758. Students 137.

Winnie, Chambers Co., St. Louis (1947) Rev. Neil A. Arce.
Res.: 315 W. Buccaneer Dr., 77665-9711. Tel: 409-296-4200; Fax: 409-296-9715. Email: slccoffice@windstream.net. Web: www.slcc-winnie.org.
Catechesis/Religious Program—Tel: 409-296-4925. Students 275.

Woodville, Tyler Co., Our Lady of the Pines (1950) Rev. Michael A. Strother, Parochial Admin.
Res.: P.O. Box 2029, 75979-2029. Tel: 409-283-5367; Fax: 409-283-2219. Email: olopcc@sbcglobal.net.
Catechesis/Religious Program—Students 37.

Chaplains of Public Institutions

Beaumont. *Memorial Hermann Baptist Hospital.* Rev. Charles Atuah, M.S.P.

Jefferson County. *Convalescent Home Ministry.* Revs. George Kalappura, C.M.I., Joseph Kattakkara, C.M.I.

Prisons

Livingston. *Beaumont - Federal Correctional Complex.* Deacon Thomas Ewing Jr.
Livingston: Polunsky Unit - Death Row. Deacon Jose A. Vitela, Chap.

On Duty Outside the Diocese:
Rev.—
DeFrancisco, Joseph, S.T.D., St. Ambrose University, Davenport, IA 52803.

On Leave:
Revs.—
Badeaux, Kevin, J.C.L.
Baluyot, Michael

Military Chaplains:
Rev.—
Beck, R. Patrick, Lackland Air Force Base, 9914 W. Military Dr., Apt. 1407, San Antonio, 78251.

Retired:
Rev. Msgrs.—
Culotta, Salvador J.
Dempsey, James
Montondon, Walter, Chap. Col.
Revs.—
Delarue, Louis
Iglesias, Clement
Mudd, Earl
Pucar, August, M.Div.
Romero, Joseph J.
Stratman, Joseph, M.Th.
Sumler, Kevin

Permanent Deacons:
Arceneaux, Jude, St. Anne, Beaumont
Blankenstein, Eddie, (Retired)
Broussard, Dallas, St. Charles Borromeo, Nederland
Cabra, Gordon, St. Jude Thaddeus, Beaumont
Cockburn, Rudy, (Retired)
David, Laurence, St. Anthony Cathedral Basilica, Beaumont
Davis, Harry, Dir., Office of Criminal Justice Ministry, Our Lady of the Assumption, Beaumont; Assoc. Dir., Permanent Diaconate
Dubois, Harvey, (Retired)
Ewing, Thomas, Jr., St. Peter the Apostle, Groves; Beaumont Federal Correctional Complex
Fontenot, Keith, Dir., Permanent Diaconate, St. Anthony Cathedral Basilica, Beaumont
Gard, Jim, St. Catherine of Siena, Port Arthur
Gros, Robert, (Retired)
Hebert, Glen, St. Mark the Evangelist Church, Silsbee
Istre, Timothy, St. Helen, Orangefield
Kenny, Hazen, St. Henry, Bridge City
Lawrence, William (Bill), St. Michael, Jasper; Our Lady of LaSalette, Kirbyville and St. Raymond, Rayburn
LeBlanc, E. R., Holy Trinity, Mont Belvieu
Luther, David, Principal Master of Episcopal Ceremonies, St. Michael, Jasper; Our Lady of LaSalette, Kirbyville; St. Raymond, Rayburn
Magana, Luis Javier, St. Joseph, Port Arthur
Maldonado, Hector, St. Francis of Assisi, Orange
Marion, Mike, St. Joseph, Livingston
Mueller, David, St. Mary, Cleveland
Obernuefemann, Steven, Immaculate Conception, Groves

Payne, Melvin, St. Mary, Orange
Penning, Chris, D.O., St. Charles, Nederland
Posey, Willie, St. John, Port Arthur; Apostleship of the Sea
Richard, Julian, St. Therese, Orange
Santos, Allan, St. Mary, Fannett
Scheurich, Joseph, (Retired)
Stanley, John G., (Retired)
Terrell, Larry, St. Mary, Cleveland
Vitela, Joe, St. Joseph, Livingston; St. Martin de Porres, Corrigan; Criminal Justice Ministry
Wycliff, Wilbert, (Retired)

INSTITUTIONS LOCATED IN THE DIOCESE

[A] HIGH SCHOOLS, DIOCESAN

BEAUMONT. *Monsignor Kelly Catholic High School*, 5950 Kelly Dr., 77707. Tel: 409-866-2351; Fax: 409-866-0917. Email: rbemis@kelly.beaumont.tx.us. Web: www.kelly.beaumont.tx.us. Mr. Roger Bemis, Prin.; Rev. Constantino Barrera, Chap.; Nina Felix, Librarian. Sisters 1; Lay Teachers 33; Students 431.

[B] GENERAL HOSPITALS

BEAUMONT. *CHRISTUS Health Southeast Texas - CHRISTUS Hospital - St. Elizabeth* (1962) 2830 Calder Ave., P.O. Box 5405, 77726-5405. Tel: 409-892-7171; Fax: 409-899-8191. Web: www.christusste.org. Paul Trevino, Admin.; Revs. Emmanuel Chikezie (Nigeria), Chap.; Leonard Ogbonna (Nigeria), Chap. Operated by CHRISTUS Health Southeast Texas. Bed Capacity 431; Patients Assisted Annually 239,998.

JASPER. *CHRISTUS Health Southeast Texas dba Jasper Memorial Hospital* 1275 Marvin Hancock Dr., 75951. Tel: 409-384-5461; Fax: 409-383-0622. Email: deborah.wiegand@christushealth.org. Deborah Wiegand, R.N., CEO Admin. Operated by CHRISTUS Health Southeast Texas. Bed Capacity 59; Patients Assisted Annually 38,251.

PORT ARTHUR. *CHRISTUS Health Southeast Texas - CHRISTUS Hospital - St. Mary* (1930) 3600 Gates Blvd., P.O. Box 3696, 77643. Tel: 409-985-7431; Fax: 409-989-1033. Web: www.christushospital.org. Ms. Ellen Jones, CEO & Pres.; Mr. Wayne Moore, Admin.; Rev. Joe Mundadan, Chap. Operated by CHRISTUS Health Southeast Texas. Bed Capacity 227; Patients Assisted Annually 127,858.

[C] MONASTERIES AND RESIDENCES OF PRIESTS AND BROTHERS

BEAUMONT. *Holy Cross Monastery*, 9920 N. Major Dr., 77713-7618. Tel: 409-899-3554; Fax: 409-899-3558. Email: porter@holycrossmonks.org. Web: www.holycrossmonks.org. Benedictine Monks

[D] NEWMAN CENTERS

BEAUMONT. *Lamar University-Catholic Student Center* 1010 E. Virginia, P.O. Box 3948, 77704-3948. Tel: 409-924-4360; Fax: 409-832-4129. Email: vocationsandcampus@dioceseofbmt.org. Rev. M. Shane Baxter, S.T.L., Dir.

[E] RETREAT CENTERS

BEAUMONT. *Holy Family Retreat Center*, 9920 N. Major Dr., 77713-7618. Tel: 409-899-5617; Fax: 409-899-3161. Email: retreatcenter@dioceseofbmt.org. Web: www.dioceseofbmt.org/holyfamily/index.html. Rev. Peter C. Funk, Dir.; Bro. Michael Gallagher, Asst. Dir.

[F] SOCIAL AGENCIES - Catholic Charities of Southeast Texas

BEAUMONT. *Catholic Charities of Southeast Texas*, 2780 Eastex Fwy., 77703-4617.

Physical Address, 2780 Eastex Fwy., 77703-4617. Tel: 409-924-4400; Fax: 409-832-0145. Email: catholiccharities@catholiccharitiesbmt.org. Web: www.catholiccharitiesbmt.org. Carol R. Fernandez, Pres. & CEO.

Counseling Services, 2780 Eastex Fwy., 77703-4617. Tel: 409-924-4418; Fax: 409-832-0145. Ms. Christie Byrne, M.S., L.P.C., Dir.

Elijah's Place (2003) Tel: 409-924-4419; Fax: 409-832-0145. Randi Fertitta, M.S., L.P.C., L.P.A., Dir.

Hospitality Center, 3959 Gulfway Dr., Port Arthur, 77642. Tel: 409-982-4842; Fax: 409-983-7145. 2780 Eastex Fwy., 77703. Christina Green, Dir.

Immigration Services, 2780 Eastex Fwy., 77703-4617. Tel: 409-924-4413; Fax: 409-832-0145. Alma Garza-Cruz, Dir.

Parish Social Ministry, 2780 Eastex Fwy., 77703-4617. Tel: 409-924-4415; Fax: 409-832-0145.

Disaster Trauma & Loss, 2780 Eastex Fwy., 77703-4617. Randi Fertitta, M.S., L.P.C., L.P.A., Dir. Tel: 409-924-4426; Fax: 409-832-0145.

[G] FOUNDATIONS, ENDOWMENTS AND TRUSTS

BEAUMONT. *St. Anthony School Foundation, Inc.*, 850 Forsythe, 77701. Tel: 409-832-3486; Fax: 409-813-3337. Web: stanthonycathedralschool.org. Tom Flanagan, Pres.

Catholic Clerical Student Fund, P.O. Box 3948, 77704-3948. Ms. Renella Primeaux, Diocesan Representative.

The Catholic Foundation of the Diocese of Beaumont, Inc., P.O. Box 3948, 77704-3948. Tel: 409-924-4313; Fax: 409-838-4511. Laura J. Williams, CPA, Sec. & Treas.

CHRISTUS Health Foundation of Southeast Texas, 2830 Calder Ave., 77702. Tel: 409-899-7555; Fax: 409-899-7346. Web: www.christushealthfoundationsetx.org.

Monsignor Kelly Catholic High School Foundation, Inc., 5950 Kelly Dr., 77707. Tel: 409-866-2351; Fax: 409-866-0917. Hubert Oxford III, Pres.

ORANGE. *St. Mary School Foundation, Inc.*, 912 Cherry St., 77630. Tel: 409-883-2883; Fax: 409-883-3547. Email: stmary@gtbizclass.com.

[H] MISCELLANEOUS

BEAUMONT. *Abiding Place Catholic Charismatic Renewal Center*, 4440 Chaison, 77705. Email: ncl890@aol.com. Ms. Nita Chavis, Dir.

PORT ARTHUR. *Apostleship of the Sea of the United States of America (AOSUSA)* (1976) 1500 Jefferson Dr., 77642-0646. Tel: 409-985-4545; Fax: 409-985-5945. Email: aosusa@sbcglobal.net. Web: www.aos-usa.org. Very Rev. Sinclair Oubre, J.C.L., E.V., Pres. Email: aos-beaumont@dioceseofbmt.org; Sr. Myrna Tordillo, AOS National Dir.; Ms. Doreen M. Badeaux, Sec. General.

RELIGIOUS INSTITUTES OF MEN REPRESENTED IN THE DIOCESE

For further details refer to the corresponding bracketed number in the Religious Institutes of Men or Women section.

[0140]—*The Augustinians* (Prov. of Castile, Spain)—O.S.A.

[]—*Benedictine Monks*—O.S.B.

[0275]—*Carmelites of Mary Immaculate* (Chanda, India)—C.M.I.

[]—*Carmelites of Mary Immaculate* (Andhra Pradesh, India)—C.M.I.

[]—*Congregation of the Mother Coredemptrix* (Missouri)—C.M.C.

[0720]—*The Missionaries of Our Lady of La Salette* (Prov. of Mary Queen)—M.S.

[]—*Missionary Society of St. Paul*—M.S.P.

[0420]—*Society of the Divine Word* (Southern Province of St. Augustine)—S.V.D.

[0700]—*St. Joseph's Society of the Sacred Heart* (Baltimore)—S.S.J.

RELIGIOUS INSTITUTES OF WOMEN REPRESENTED IN THE DIOCESE

[2190]—*Congregation of the Incarnate Word and Blessed Sacrament* (Houston, TX)—C.V.I.

[]—*Daughters of Mary Mother of Mercy*—D.M.M.M.

[1070-19]—*Dominican Sisters*—O.P.

[]—*Missionary Carmelites of St. Teresa* (Houston)—C.M.S.T.

[]—*Sisters of the Destitute* (India)—S.D.

[2205]—*Sisters of the Incarnate Word and Blessed Sacrament* (Corpus Christi)—I.W.B.S.

[]—*Vietnamese Dominican Sisters* (Houston)—O.P.

DIOCESAN CEMETERIES

BEAUMONT. *Blessed Sacrament Cemetery*, c/o Blessed Sacrament Church, 780 Porter St., 77701. Tel: 409-833-6089; Fax: 409-833-6091.

Hebert Catholic Cemetery-Stivers Lane, c/o Diocese of Beaumont, P.O. Box 3948, 77704-3948. Tel: 409-924-4313. Laura J. Williams, CPA, CFO.

AMES. *Our Mother of Mercy Cemetery*, c/o Our Mother of Mercy Church, P.O. Box 264, Liberty, 77575-0264. Tel: 936-336-3004; Fax: 936-336-5955.

EASTGATE. *St. Anne Cemetery*, c/o St. Joseph, the Worker Church, P.O. Box 640, Dayton, 77535-0640. Tel: 936-258-5735; Fax: 936-258-7220.

LIBERTY. *Immaculate Conception Cemetery*, c/o Immaculate Conception Church, 411 Milam, 77575-4730. Tel: 936-336-7267; Fax: 936-336-9740.

ORANGE. *St. Mary Cemetery, c/o St. Mary Church*, 912 W. Cherry St., 77630-5017. Tel: 409-883-7390; Fax: 409-883-7390.

PORT ARTHUR. *Calvary Cemetery, Diocese of Beaumont*, P.O. Box 3948, 77704-3948. Tel: 409-924-4313; Fax: 409-722-8312; 409-838-4511.

NECROLOGY

(No Deaths)

An asterisk (*) denotes an organization that has established tax-exempt status directly with the IRS and is not covered by the USCCB Group Ruling.

Diocese of Belleville

(Dioecesis Bellevillensis)

Most Reverend

EDWARD K. BRAXTON, Ph.D., S.T.D.

Bishop of Belleville; ordained May 13, 1970; appointed Auxiliary Bishop of St. Louis and Titular Bishop of Macomades Rusticiana March 28, 1995; ordained May 17, 1995; appointed Bishop of Lake Charles December 12, 2000; installed February 22, 2001; appointed Bishop of Belleville March 15, 2005; installed June 22, 2005. *Mailing Address: The Chancery, 222 S. Third St., Belleville, IL 62220.* Tel: 618-277-8181.

The Chancery: 222 S. Third St., Belleville, IL 62220-1985. Tel: 618-277-8181; Fax: 618-277-0387.

Web: www.diobelle.org

Email: info@diobelle.org

Erected January 7, 1887.

Square Miles 11,678.

Comprises Illinois south of the northern limits of the Counties of St. Clair, Clinton, Marion, Clay, Richland and Lawrence.

For legal titles of parishes and diocesan institutions, consult the Chancery Office.

STATISTICAL OVERVIEW

Personnel	
Bishop	1
Retired Bishops	1
Priests: Diocesan Active in Diocese	61
Priests: Diocesan Active Outside Diocese	1
Priests: Retired, Sick or Absent	45
Number of Diocesan Priests	107
Religious Priests in Diocese	34
Total Priests in Diocese	141
Extern Priests in Diocese	17
Ordinations:	
Diocesan Priests	1
Permanent Deacons in Diocese	27
Total Brothers	11
Total Sisters	309
Parishes	
Parishes	117
With Resident Pastor:	
Resident Diocesan Priests	67
Resident Religious Priests	10
Without Resident Pastor:	
Administered by Priests	35
Administered by Deacons	1
Administered by Religious Women	3
Administered by Lay People	1
Professional Ministry Personnel:	
Sisters	16
Lay Ministers	78
Welfare	
Catholic Hospitals	5
Total Assisted	524,344
Homes for the Aged	2
Total Assisted	237
Day Care Centers	3
Total Assisted	201
Specialized Homes	1
Total Assisted	14
Special Centers for Social Services	3
Total Assisted	275,000
Educational	
Diocesan Students in Other Seminaries	5
Total Seminarians	5
High Schools, Diocesan and Parish	3
Total Students	1,129
Elementary Schools, Diocesan and Parish	29
Total Students	4,971
Catechesis/Religious Education:	
High School Students	419
Elementary Students	4,250
Total Students under Catholic Instruction	10,774
Teachers in the Diocese:	
Priests	6
Sisters	8
Lay Teachers	400
Vital Statistics	
Receptions into the Church:	
Infant Baptism Totals	1,138
Minor Baptism Totals	75
Adult Baptism Totals	126
Received into Full Communion	187
First Communions	1,353
Confirmations	1,475
Marriages:	
Catholic	294
Interfaith	188
Total Marriages	482
Deaths	1,194
Total Catholic Population	91,550
Total Population	860,658

Former Bishops—Most Revs. JOHN JANSSEN, D.D., ord. Nov. 19, 1858; cons. April 25, 1888; died July 2, 1913; HENRY J. ALTHOFF, D.D., ord. July 26, 1902; appt. Dec. 4, 1913; cons. Feb. 24, 1914; died July 3, 1947; ALBERT R. ZUROWESTE, D.D., ord. June 8, 1924; appt. Nov. 29, 1947; cons. Jan. 29, 1948; retired Sept. 3, 1976; died March 28, 1987; WILLIAM M. COSGROVE, D.D., ord. Dec. 18, 1943; Auxiliary Bishop of Cleveland June 19, 1968; cons. Sept. 3, 1968; appt. Bishop of Belleville Sept. 3, 1976; installed Oct. 28, 1976; retired May 19, 1981; died Dec. 11, 1992; JOHN N. WURM, S.T.D., Ph.D., ord. April 3, 1954; Auxiliary Bishop of St. Louis June 25, 1976; cons. Aug. 17, 1976; appt. Bishop of Belleville Sept. 19, 1981; installed Nov. 4, 1981; died April 27, 1984; JAMES P. KELEHER, S.T.D., M.Ed., ord. April 12, 1958; appt. Bishop of Belleville Oct. 23, 1984; cons. Dec. 11, 1984; transferred to Kansas City, KS Sept. 8, 1993; WILTON D. GREGORY, S.L.D., ord. May 9, 1973; appt. Auxiliary Bishop of Chicago and Titular Bishop of Oliva Oct. 31, 1983; cons. Dec. 13, 1983; appt. Bishop of Belleville Dec. 29, 1993; installed Feb. 10, 1994; appt. Archbishop of Atlanta Dec. 9, 2004; installed Jan. 17, 2005.

Diocese of Belleville Chancery Office—222 S. Third St., Belleville, 62220-1985. Tel: 618-277-8181; Fax: 618-277-0387.

Diocesan Pastoral Center—2620 Lebanon Ave., Belleville, 62221. Tel: 618-235-9601; Fax: 618-235-7416.

Vicar General—Very Rev. JOHN W. MCEVILLY, V.G.

Moderator of the Curia—Very Rev. JOHN W. MCEVILLY, V.G.

Chancellor for Canonical Affairs—Rev. KENNETH J. YORK, J.C.L.

Chancellor of Administration & Pastoral Services—Mr. DAVID R. SPOTANSKI.

Vicar for Priests—Most Rev. STANLEY G. SCHLARMAN, D.D. (Retired).

Administrative Assistant to the Bishop—Mrs. ANGELA BARBER.

Administrative Assistant to the Vicar General & Chancellor—Mrs. LINDA KREHER.

Archivist—Sr. MARY KENAN WOLFF, S.S.N.D., Diocesan Pastoral Center, 2620 Lebanon Ave., Bldg. 6, Belleville, 62221-3299. Tel: 618-235-9601, Ext. 1562; Fax: 618-235-7115.

Diocesan Tribunal—Diocesan Pastoral Center, 2620 Lebanon Ave., Belleville, 62221. Tel: 618-212-0050; Fax: 618-212-0055. Address all rogatory commissions to the Judicial Vicar at the Tribunal.

Judicial Vicar—Very Rev. JAMES M. NALL, J.C.L.

Judges—Very Rev. JAMES M. NALL, J.C.L.; Rev. Msgr. JAMES E. MARGASON, M.Div., J.C.L.

Promoter Justitiae—Rev. PAUL R. WIENHOFF, J.C.L.

Defensores Vinculi—Rev. Msgrs. DONALD W. EICHENSEER (Retired); THOMAS D. FLACH, V.F.; Rev. PAUL R. WIENHOFF, J.C.L.

Advocate—Very Rev. JOHN T. MYLER, S.T.D., V.F.

Notaries—Mrs. RENEE QUIRIN; Mrs. JACQUELINE MATT.

Diocesan Consultors—Very Revs. JOHN W. MCEVILLY, V.G.; C. RAYMOND SCHULTZ, V.F.; Rev. Msgr. WILLIAM P. MCGHEE; Revs. URBAN OSUJI, C.M.; KENNETH J. YORK, J.C.L., Chancellor; JAMES E. DEITERS; Very Rev. DANIEL J. JUREK, V.F.; Rev. PAUL R. WIENHOFF, J.C.L.; Most Rev. STANLEY G. SCHLARMAN, D.D. (Retired); Very Rev. JOHN T. MYLER, S.T.D., V.F.; Revs. TREVOR K. MURRY; DAVID M. WILKE.

Diocesan Deans—Very Revs. JOHN T. MYLER, S.T.D., V.F., Belleville Deanery; C. RAYMOND SCHULTZ, V.F., East St. Louis Deanery; JOHN C. IFFERT, V.F., East Deanery; Rev. Msgr. JAMES A. BUERSTER, V.F., North Central Deanery; Very Revs. DANIEL J. JUREK, V.F., West Deanery; ROBERT B. FLANNERY, V.F., South Deanery.

Diocesan Finance Office—Mr. JAMES MROCZKOWSKI, CFO; Mr. DAVID WAELTZ, Comptroller, Chancery Office. Tel: 618-277-8181; Fax: 618-277-0819.

Diocesan Finance Council—Most Rev. EDWARD K. BRAXTON, Bishop of Belleville; Mrs. JEANETTE BAX-KURTZ; Very Rev. JOHN W. MCEVILLY, V.G.; Mr. JAMES MROCZKOWSKI, CFO; Deacon LINUS KLOSTERMANN; Mr. DAVID FIELDS; Sr. THERESA MARKUS, S.S.N.D.; Mr. RAYMOND HEINEN; Mr. JAMES L. BURKE; Mr. MICHAEL HOPKINS; Mr. GREGORY HOWELL; Rev. KENNETH J. YORK, J.C.L.; Very Rev. JOHN C. IFFERT, V.F.; Mr. JOHN SMITH, Chm.; Mr. JOHN REED.

Diocesan Pastoral Council—Most Rev. EDWARD K. BRAXTON, Bishop of Belleville; Mr. JERRY DESOTO; Mr. DAVID R. SPOTANSKI, Chancellor of Admin. & Pastoral Svcs.; Mr. DENNIS LAAKE; Ms. PHYLLIS MENSING; Mr. FRANCIS MYER; Mr. BRIAN NIERMAN; Deacon DONALD DEITZ; Sr. DIANE M. TURNER, S.S.N.D.; Rev. VON C. DEEKE; Ms. KATHY MULVIN. Tel: 618-277-8181; Fax: 618-277-0387.

Building Commission, Chancery Office—Rev. Msgr. JEROME D. HARTLEIN, Chm.; Deacon DONALD DEITZ; Mr. HERB FOPPE.

Catholic Campaign for Human Development—2620 Lebanon Ave., Belleville, 62221. Tel: 618-235-9601.

Catholic Charities of Southern Illinois— Formerly Catholic Charities *8601 W. Main St., Belleville, 62223.* Tel: 618-394-5900.

Catholic Social Service of Southern Illinois—Mr. GARY HUELSMANN, Dir. Email: ghuelsmann@cssil.org.
Main Office—
Belleville—8601 W. Main St., Ste. 201, Belleville, 62223. Tel: 618-394-5900; Fax: 618-394-5909. Mr. BRAD BECK, Regl. Dir. Tel: 618-688-1161.
Carbondale—214 S. University, Carbondale, 62901. Tel: 618-351-0743. Ms. MARY LOU LOOS, Regl. Dir.
Mount Vernon—219 Withers Dr., Mount Vernon, 62864. Tel: 618-244-0344; Fax: 618-244-1445. Ms. PAM FLOTA, Regl. Dir.
Mount Carmel—120 W. Fifth St., P.O. Box 23, Mount Carmel, 62863. Tel: 618-263-3863; Fax: 618-263-4559. Mr. DON GOFF, Regl. Dir.
Belleville—Don Bosco Children's Center, 900 Royal Heights Rd., Ste. 200, Belleville, 62226. Tel: 618-688-1150; Fax: 618-277-7084. Mr. GEORGE FERGUSON, M.S.W., Dir. Email: georgef@cssil.org.
Olney—Fox River Senior Assisted Living, 1016 Parker St., Olney, 62450. Tel: 618-392-6168; Fax: 618-392-6170. Ms. JESSICA SLATER, Dir. Email: jessicas@cssil.org.
Catholic Urban Programs—Coordinators: Mr. JOSEPH P. HUBBARD; Mr. GERARD F. HASENSTAB; CHRISTINE YORK, Case Mgr., #7 Vieux Carre Dr., East Saint Louis, 62203. Tel: 618-398-5616. Mailing Address: P.O. Box 3310, East Saint Louis, 62203.
Holy Angels Shelter—Ms. PATRICIA LEWIS, Co Dir.; Ms. PAULYN SNYDER, Co Dir., 1410 N. 37th St., East St. Louis, 62204. Tel: 618-874-4079.
Griffin Center—Sr. JULIA HUISKAMP, D.C., Dir., 2630 Lincoln Ave., East St. Louis, 62204. Tel: 618-874-2500. De Shields-Robinson Center, 1235 McCasland, East St. Louis, 62201. Tel: 618-874-0637. Roosevelt Center, 1328 N. 44th St., East St. Louis, 62204. Tel: 618-271-9859. Weather-Owens Center, 1400 Missouri Ave., East St. Louis, 62201. Tel: 618-271-1250; Ms. DIANE SONNEMAN, Dir. Educational Programs; ALEXANDRA GRAHAM, Site Dir.
Family Center—705 Summit, East Saint Louis, 62201. Tel: 618-875-7295. Sisters CAROL LEHMKUHL, O.P., Site Dir.; MARY ANN BUHR, O.P., Asst. Site Dir.; ANN GREGORY BISCHOF, O.P., Prog. Dir., 705 Summit, East St. Louis, 62201. Tel: 618-875-7295.
Neighborhood Law Office—7 Vieux Carre, East Saint Louis, 62203. Mailing Address: P.O. Box 3310, East Saint Louis, 62203. Tel: 618-398-1100; Fax: 618-398-1101. Ms. KATHLEEN O'KEEFE, Advocate.
Catholic Diocese of Belleville Cemetery Association, Chancery Office—DEE DEE MURRAY, Contact, Mt. Carmel. Tel: 618-397-0181. Covers: Immaculate Conception, Centreville; Holy Cross, Fairview Heights; St. Phillips, East St. Louis, IL
Child Protection Office and Victim Assistance Coordinator—Mrs. LYNN MUSCARELLO, Dir., Diocesan Pastoral Center, 2620 Lebanon Ave., Bldg. 5, Belleville, 62221. Tel: 618-212-0050, Ext. 1212; Fax: 618-212-0055.
Clergymen's Aid Society—Rev. Msgr. MARVIN C. VOLK, St. James, 405 W. Madison, Millstadt, 62260. Tel: 618-476-3513; Fax: 618-476-7357.
Communications—Mr. DAVID R. SPOTANSKI, Dir. Tel: 618-277-8181, Ext. 1071.
Diocesan Development Office—222 S. Third St., Belleville, 62220. Tel: 618-277-8181. Mr. DAVID R. SPOTANSKI, Chancellor of Admin. & Pastoral Svcs. Tel: 618-277-8181, Ext. 1071; Mr. RANDY FLACHSBART, Dir. Planned Giving. Tel: 618-277-8181, Ext. 1321; Ms. JUDY PHILLIPS, Dir. Foundations & Corporations, Chancery Office. Tel: 618-277-8181, Ext. 1141; Fax: 618-277-0387.
Diocesan Liturgical Commission—Rev. DAVID M. DARIN, Chm. Tel: 618-235-9601, Ext. 1442.
Diocesan Outreach Apostolate— Serving Alexander and Pulaski Counties. Daystar Community Program, *909 Washington Ave., Cairo, 62914.* Tel: 618-734-0178. Ms. SHERRY MILLER, Dir. Email: sherrym47@yahoo.com.
Diaconate, Office of Permanent—VACANT, Vicar for Deacons; Deacons ROBERT LANTER, Coord. of Deacon, Diocesan Pastoral Center, 2620 Lebanon Ave., Belleville, 62221. Tel: 618-235-9601, Ext. 1482; DONALD DEITZ, Pres. Deaconate Community; Rev. EUGENE H. WOJCIK, Dir. Deacon Formation.
Office of Vocation and Deacon Formation—Mrs. PATTI WARNER, Administrative Asst., Diocesan Pastoral Center. Tel: 618-235-9601, Ext. 1452.
Diocesan Council of Catholic Women—Rev. DENNIS F. VOSS, Diocesan Moderator (Retired); Mrs. JANET MOLINAROLO, Pres., Diocesan Pastoral Center, 2408 W. North, Harrisburg, 62946.
Ecumenical and Interreligious Affairs—Very Rev. ROBERT B. FLANNERY, V.F., 303 S. Poplar St., Carbondale, 62901. Tel: 618-457-4556.
Formation of Priests—Very Rev. JOHN T. MYLER, S.T.D., V.F., Chm., Cathedral of St. Peter, 200 W. Harrison St., Belleville, 62220. Tel: 618-234-1166; Rev. JAMES R. DEITERS, 1411 Cross, Shiloh, 62269. Tel: 618-632-3562.
Office of Education—2620 Lebanon Ave., Bldg. 6, Belleville, 62221. Tel: 618-235-9601. Mr. THOMAS H. POSNANSKI, Dir., Diocesan Pastoral Center. Tel: 618-235-9601, Ext. 1152.
Religious Education and Catechesis—Mr. RUSSELL PETERSON, Assoc. Dir. Tel: 618-235-9601, Ext. 1042.
Diocesan Board of Education—Mr. BEN FUEHNE, Pres.
Hispanic Ministry—Sr. CECILIA MARIE HELLMANN, A.S.C., Dir., 2620 Lebanon Ave., Belleville, 62221. Tel: 618-235-9601, Ext. 1292.
Holy Childhood Association—Very Rev. JOHN T. MYLER, S.T.D., V.F., Cathedral of St. Peter, 200 W. Harrison St., Belleville, 62220. Tel: 618-234-1166.
Hospitals—Rev. EUGENE J. NEFF, Delegate, Ministry to Sick and Aged, 2620 Lebanon Ave., Belleville, 62221. Tel: 618-235-9991.
Insurance Commission—Mr. JAMES MROCZKOWSKI, Dir., Chancery Office.
Catholic Mutual Group—Mr. WILLIAM P. JOHNSON, Claims & Risk Mgr., Diocesan Pastoral Center. Tel: 618-233-1090.
Office of Worship—Diocesan Pastoral Center, 2620 Lebanon Ave., Belleville, 62221. Tel: 618-235-9601. Mrs. SUE HUETT, Dir. Worship, Diocesan Pastoral Center. Tel: 618-235-9601, Ext. 1442.
Newman Catholic Student Center—Mr. TIM TAYLOR, Dir., 715 S. Washington St., Carbondale, 62901. Tel: 618-529-3311; Rev. PATTINIKUTTIGE KINGSLEY NONIS, Campus Min.
Newman Auxiliary—Ms. MARGE MANGAN, Pres., 9741 Stilley's Mill Dr., Marion, 62959. Tel: 618-982-2218.
Newspaper, "The Messenger"—Diocesan Pastoral Center, 2620 Lebanon Ave., Belleville, 62221. Tel: 618-233-8670. Ms. LIZ QUIRIN, Editor, Diocesan Pastoral Center.
Ondessonk, Camp— Diocese of Belleville, Department of Outdoor Education: Mr. DAN KING, Exec. Dir., 3760 Ondessonk Rd., Ozark, 62972. Tel: 618-695-2489; Fax: 618-695-3593.
Respect Life/Project Rachel Pastoral Center—Pastoral Center. Mrs. LAURIE EDWARDS, Diocesan Pastoral Center, 2620 Lebanon Ave., Belleville, 62221. Tel: 618-235-9601, Ext. 1332.
Propagation of the Faith—Very Rev. JOHN T. MYLER, S.T.D., V.F., Cathedral of St. Peter, 200 W. Harrison St., Belleville, 62220. Tel: 618-234-1166.
Office of Review Board—Ms. JOANN PISEL, Chancery - Diocese of Belleville: 222 S. Third St., Belleville, 62220. Tel: 800-640-3044 (Hotline).
Office of Youth Ministry—Diocesan Pastoral Center, 2620 Lebanon Ave., Belleville, 62221. Tel: 618-235-9601. Mr. GARY LANDOLL, Dir. Tel: 618-235-9601, Ext. 1302; Rev. BERNARD C. GOEDDE JR., Spiritual Moderator.
Rural Life Conference—Deacon DOUG SPARLING, Dir., 1945 Etherton Rd., Murphysboro, 62966. Tel: 618-687-9618. Email: dsparling@siu.edu.
St. Vincent de Paul Society—Mr. MICHAEL JOHNSON, Store Mgr.; Mr. JOSEPH P. HUBBARD, Pres.; Ms. PATRICIA HOGREBE, Dir. Devel., 13 Vieux Carre Dr., Ste. 2, East St. Louis, 62205. Tel: 618-271-6230. Mailing Address: P.O. Box 3310, East Saint Louis, 62205.
Sick and Aged (Ministry)—Rev. EUGENE J. NEFF, Dir., Diocesan Pastoral Center. Tel: 618-235-9991.
Vocation Office—Pastoral Center, 2620 Lebanon Ave., Belleville, 62221. Tel: 618-235-9601, Ext. 1482. Co Directors: Rev. Msgr. WILLIAM P. MCGHEE, Diocesan Pastoral Center; Revs. TREVOR K. MURRY; DAVID M. WILKE.

CLERGY, PARISHES, MISSIONS AND PAROCHIAL SCHOOLS

CITY OF BELLEVILLE

(ST. CLAIR COUNTY)

1—CATHEDRAL OF ST. PETER (1842) [CEM] Very Rev. John T. Myler, Rector; Rev. Joseph Oganda; Deacons Robert Becker; Donald Deitz.
Res.: 200 W. Harrison St., 62220-2090. Tel: 618-234-1166; Fax: 618-234-2957. Web: www.stpeterscathedral.info.
School—Cathedral School, 200 S. Second St., 62220. Tel: 618-233-6414; Fax: 618-233-3587. Web: cgs-belleville.com. Catherine (Kay) Bennett, Prin. School Sisters of Notre Dame 1; Lay Teachers 14; Students 163.
Cathedral Grade School Early Learning Center—200 S. 2nd St., 62220. Tel: 618-233-6414. Ms. Patty Birkner, Dir.
Catechesis/Religious Program—Sr. Theresa Markus, S.S.N.D., D.R.E.; Miss Jane Stock, D.R.E.; Mr. Charles York, Business Mgr. Students 175.

2—ST. AUGUSTINE OF CANTERBURY (1955) Rev. Patrick Okwumuo (Nigeria).
Res.: 1910 W. Belle St., 62226. Tel: 618-233-3813; Fax: 618-233-3946.
School—St. Mary - St. Augustine School, 1900 W. Belle, 62226. Tel: 618-234-4958; Fax: 618-234-3360. Sandra Baechle, Prin. Merged school with St. Mary. Lay Teachers 14; Students 122.
Catechesis/Religious Program—(Combined with St. Mary, Belleville) Students 26.

3—BLESSED SACRAMENT (1927) Rev. Matthew Elie, Admin.
Res.: 8707 W. Main St., 62223. Tel: 618-397-2287; Fax: 618-397-2269.
School—8809 W. Main St., 62223. Tel: 618-397-1111; Fax: 618-397-8431. Ms. Claire Hatch, Prin. Lay Teachers 13; Students 194.
Catechesis/Religious Program—Students 31.
Convent—

4—CHAPEL OF ST. JOHN CHILDREN'S HOME, [CEM] Very Rev. John W. McEvilly.
Mailing Address: *Chancery Office*, 222 S. Third St., 62220. Tel: 618-277-8181; Fax: 618-277-0387.

5—ST. HENRY (1925) Rev. Kenneth J. York.
Res.: 5315 W. Main St., 62226. Tel: 618-233-2423; Fax: 618-233-9879.
Catechesis/Religious Program—Students 70.

6—ST. LUKE (1883) Revs. David M. Darin, Canonical Pastor; Sean Palas, Parochial Vicar; Deacon Robert Lanter; Sr. Grace Marie Mueller, S.S.N.D., Parish Life Coord.
Res.: 301 N. Church St., 62220. Tel: 618-236-1124; Fax: 618-236-1125. Email: stluke301@aol.com. Web: www.stlukebelleville.org.
Catechesis/Religious Program—Tel: 618-236-1839. Students 37.

7—ST. MARY (1893) Rev. Msgr. William P. McGhee.
Res.: 1706 W. Main St., 62226. Tel: 618-233-2391; Fax: 618-233-9201. Email: stmarychurch1893@sbcglobal.net. Web: www.st-marybelleville.org.
See St. Mary - St. Augustine School under St. Augustine of Canterbury, Belleville for details.
Catechesis/Religious Program— Ms. Ann Bach, D.R.E. Tel: 618-277-1652. Twinned with St. Augustine, Belleville. Students 90.

8—OUR LADY QUEEN OF PEACE (1955) Very Rev. John W. McEvilly; Ms. Karen Ferrara, Business Mgr.
Res.: 5923 N. Belt W., 62223. Tel: 618-234-6196; Fax: 618-234-6217. Email: qpparish@qofp.com.
School—5915 N. Belt W., 62223. Tel: 618-234-1206; Fax: 618-234-6123. Email: qpschool@qofp.com. Web: www.qofp.com. Ms. Sharon Needham, Prin. Lay Teachers 15; Students 205.
Catechesis/Religious Program—Students 29.

9—ST. TERESA OF THE CHILD JESUS (1926), (Little Flower) Revs. David M. Darin; Sean Palas, Parochial Vicar.
Res.: 1201 Lebanon Ave., 62221. Tel: 618-233-3500; Fax: 618-233-9703. Email: stteresa@charter.net. Web: www.stteresa.pvt.k.12.il.us.
School—1108 Lebanon Ave., 62221. Tel: 618-235-4066; Fax: 618-235-7930. Mr. Dennis Grimmer, Prin. Lay Teachers 20; Students 289.
Catechesis/Religious Program—Students 80.

OUTSIDE THE CITY OF BELLEVILLE

ALBERS, CLINTON CO., ST. BERNARD (1908) [CEM] Rev. John J. Joyce.
Res.: 202 N. Broadway, P.O. Box 10, 62215. Tel: 618-248-5112; Fax: 618-248-5595. Email: stbernard@charter.net.
Catechesis/Religious Program—Tel: 618-248-5134; Fax: 618-248-5134 (Call First). Sr. Joan Stoverink, A.S.C., D.R.E. Students 102.

ANNA, UNION CO., ST. MARY (1857) Rev. Federico Higuera; Sr. Joan Backes, S.S.N.D., Pastoral Assoc. & D.R.E.
Res.: 402 Freeman, 62906. Tel: 618-833-5835; Fax: 618-833-8220. Email: st_marys@frontier.com.
Catechesis/Religious Program—Tel: 618-833-3131. Students 62.

AVA, JACKSON CO., ST. ELIZABETH (1890) Rev. Leo J. Hayes.
Res.: 606 W. George St., 62907. Tel: 618-426-3321; Fax: 608-426-3321.
Catechesis/Religious Program—Tel: 618-497-8724. Students 4.

AVISTON, CLINTON CO., ST. FRANCIS OF ASSISI (1865), (German), [CEM] Rev. Daniel L. Friedman; Deacon Charles Litteken, Ministry Dir.
Res.: 251 S. Clinton, Box 93, 62216-0093. Tel: 618-228-7219; Fax: 618-228-7320. Email: parish@stfrancisav.org. Web: www.stfrancisav.org.
Catechesis/Religious Program—Students 365.

BARTELSO, CLINTON CO., ST. CECILIA (1885), (German), Rev. Henry J. Fischer.
Res.: 304 S. Washington St., P.O. Box 176, 62218.

Tel: 618-765-2162; Fax: 618-765-2264. Email: cechbart@frontier.com.
Catechesis/Religious Program— Ms. Betty Budde, C.R.E.; Ms. Ellen Huegen, C.R.E. Students 172.

BEAVER PRAIRIE, CLINTON CO., ST. FELICITAS (1883) [CEM] Revs. Edward F. Schaefer; Lawrence M. Nickels, O.F.M., Sacramental Min.; Sr. Diane M. Turner, S.S.N.D., Pastoral Life Coord.
Mailing Address: 13322 Church Rd., Carlyle, 62231. Tel: 618-594-3040; Fax: 618-594-3040.
Catechesis/Religious Program—Students 22.

BECKEMEYER, CLINTON CO., ST. ANTHONY (1905) [CEM] Rev. Charles W. Tuttle; Deacon Robert Lippert, Parish Life Coord.
Res.: 451 W. 3rd St., P.O. Box 305, 62219. Tel: 618-227-8236; Fax: 618-227-8630. Email: stanthny@papadocs.com.
Catechesis/Religious Program— Combined with All Saints, Breese. Students 42.

BENTON, FRANKLIN CO., ST. JOSEPH (1872) [CEM] Rev. Joseph L. Trapp.
Res.: 506 W. Main, 62812. Tel: 618-438-9941; Fax: 618-438-9941. Email: stjoecc@frontier.com.
Catechesis/Religious Program—Students 58.

BREESE, CLINTON CO.
1—ST. AUGUSTINE (1912) [CEM] Rev. Charles W. Tuttle; Deacon Robert Lippert, Parish Life Coord.
Res.: 525 S. Third St., 62230. Tel: 618-526-4362; Fax: 618-526-4362. Email: augustine306@att.net.
Catechesis/Religious Program—Students 121.
2—ST. DOMINIC (1858) [JC] Rev. Patrick N. Peter.
Res.: 493 N. Second St., 62230. Tel: 618-526-7746; Fax: 618-526-7755. Email: saintdominic@papadocs.com.
Catechesis/Religious Program— Ms. Phyllis Mensing, D.R.E. Students 82.

BRIDGEPORT, LAWRENCE CO., IMMACULATE CONCEPTION (1856) [CEM] Rev. Bernardine Nganzi (Uganda).
Mailing Address: 1006 Collins, Lawrenceville, 62439. Tel: 618-943-5255. Email: stlawrence@avenuebb.com.
Catechesis/Religious Program—Students 19.

CAHOKIA, ST. CLAIR CO.
1—ST. CATHERINE LABOURE (1959) Closed. For inquiries for parish records contact the chancery.
2—HOLY FAMILY (1699) [CEM 3] Rev. Paul R. Wienhoff.
Res.: 116 Church St., 62206. Tel: 618-337-4548; Fax: 618-332-1699. Email: holyfamily1699@yahoo.com.
Catechesis/Religious Program—Joint with Sacred Heart, Dupo Students 40.

CAIRO, ALEXANDER CO., ST. PATRICK (1838) [CEM] Rev. John Agbasiere, S.M.M.M. (Nigeria).
Res.: 517 Walnut, Mound City, 62963. Tel: 618-734-2061; Fax: 618-734-9823.
Church: 312 Ninth St., 62914.
Catechesis/Religious Program—Ms. Mary Helen Wissinger, D.R.E.

CARBONDALE, JACKSON CO., ST. FRANCIS XAVIER (1900) Very Rev. Robert B. Flannery.
Res.: 303 S. Poplar St., 62901-2709. Tel: 618-457-4556; Fax: 618-457-7368. Email: sfrancis@globaleyes.net. Web: wwwstfx.org.
Catechesis/Religious Program—Ms. Toni Intravaia, D.R.E. Students 129.

CARLYLE, CLINTON CO., ST. MARY (1853) [CEM], (Immaculate Conception) Rev. George A. Mauck.
Res.: 1171 Jefferson St., Box 179, 62231. Tel: 618-594-2225; Fax: 618-594-4638. Email: stmary@sbcglobal.net. Web: www.carlylecatholicchurch.com.
Catechesis/Religious Program—Tel: 618-594-2284. Ms. Ellen Knolhoff, D.R.E. Students 242.

CARMI, WHITE CO., ST. POLYCARP (GERMAN) (1847) [CEM] Rev. Stephen A. Rudolphi.
Res.: 209 Fourth St., 62821. Tel: 618-382-7732. Email: wccath@frontier.com.
Catechesis/Religious Program—Students 30.

CARTERVILLE, WILLIAMSON CO., CHURCH OF THE HOLY SPIRIT (1974) Very Rev. Robert B. Flannery, Canonical Pastor; Rev. Pattinikuttige Kingsley Nonis, Sacramental Min.; Sr. Carol Karnitsky, SSCM, Parish Life Coord.
Office: 300 N. Pine St., 62918. Tel: 618-985-2900; 618-925-5099. Email: holyspirit300@frontier.com.
Catechesis/Religious Program—Tel: 618-985-8348. Students 75.

CASEYVILLE, ST. CLAIR CO., ST. STEPHEN (1893) Very Rev. C. Raymond Schultz; Rev. Anthony O. Onyango, Parochial Vicar.
Res.: 901 S. Main St., P.O. Box 458, 62232. Tel: 618-397-0666; Fax: 618-397-4430. Email: ststephenoffice@charterinternet.com. Web: www.ststephencaseyville.org.
Catechesis/Religious Program—Email: ststephencarolyn@charterinternet.com. Students 52.

CENTRALIA, MARION CO., ST. MARY (1857) [CEM] Rev. Justin Olisaemeka (Nigeria), Admin.
Rectory—645 S. Lincoln Blvd., 62801. Tel: 618-532-5041; Fax: 618-532-4758. Email: parish@stmarycentralia.org.
Church Office: 424 E. Broadway, 62801. Tel: 618-532-6291.
School—Tel: 618-532-3473; Fax: 618-532-5180. Mrs. Helen Donsbach, Prin. Lay Teachers 6; Students 103.
Catechesis/Religious Program—Sr. Angela J. Schrage, A.S.C., D.R.E. Students 33.

CENTREVILLE, ST. CLAIR CO., IMMACULATE CONCEPTION (1858) [CEM] Closed. For inquiries for parish records contact the chancery.

CHESTER, RANDOLPH CO., ST. MARY HELP OF CHRISTIANS (1842) [CEM] Rev. Eugene H. Wojcik.
Res.: 911 Swanwick St., 62233. Tel: 618-826-2444; Fax: 618-826-2444.
School—Tel: 618-826-3120; Fax: 618-826-3486. Mrs. Janelle Robinson, Prin. Email: stmarychester@hotmail.com. Web: www.stmaryschester.com. Lay Teachers 10; Preschool 26; Students (K-8) 79.
Catechesis/Religious Program—Tel: 618-826-2526. Ms. Cheryl Gross, D.R.E. Students 22.

CHRISTOPHER, FRANKLIN CO., ST. ANDREW (1905) [CEM] Rev. Peter D. Balili (Philippines), Admin.
Res.: 412 E. Washington St., 62822. Tel: 618-724-4114; Fax: 618-724-4114. Email: standrew@11.net. Web: www.standrewandmary.org.
Catechesis/Religious Program—Elaine Polbinski, D.R.E. Students 42.

COBDEN, UNION CO., ST. JOSEPH (1883) [CEM] Rev. Uriel Salamanca Cipagauta; Deacon Patrick Patterson.
Res.: 101 Centennial St., P.O. Box 237, 62920. Tel: 618-893-2276. Email: stjoseph2005@verizon.net.
Catechesis/Religious Program—Tel: 618-893-2368. Ms. Sherri Haddick, C.R.E. Students 102.

COLUMBIA, MONROE CO., IMMACULATE CONCEPTION OF THE B.V.M. (1846) [CEM] Rev. Msgr. Carl E. Scherrer.
Res.: 117 E. Madison, 62236. Tel: 618-281-5105; Fax: 618-281-6848. Web: www.ics-columbia-il.us.
School—321 S. Metter, 62236. Tel: 618-281-5353; Fax: 618-281-6044. Email: mkish@htc.net. Web: www.icscolumbia.org. Mr. Michael Kish, Prin. Lay Teachers 19; Students 274.
Catechesis/Religious Program—Students 174.

COULTERVILLE, RANDOLPH CO., ST. ANTHONY, Closed. For inquiries for parish records contact the chancery.

DAHLGREN, HAMILTON CO., ST. JOHN NEPOMUCENE (1893), (German), [CEM] Rev. Slawomir Ptak (Poland), Admin.
Church: 7th & Main Sts., P.O. Box 220, 62828. Tel: 618-736-2878; 618-643-3552. Email: catholic@hamiltoncom.net. Web: www.hamiltoncom.net/~catholic.
Res.: Rte. 3, Box 170, Mc Leansboro, 62859. Tel: 618-648-2490.
Catechesis/Religious Program—Ms. Amy Wade, D.R.E. Students 25.

DAMIANSVILLE, CLINTON CO., ST. DAMIAN (1861), (German—Hispanic), [CEM] Rev. John J. Joyce.
One W. Main St., 62215. Tel: 618-248-5134; Fax: 618-248-5134. Email: stdamians@wisperhome.com.
Res.: 202 N. Broadway, Albers, 62215. Tel: 618-248-5112; Fax: 618-248-5112.
Catechesis/Religious Program—Students 83.

DU QUOIN, PERRY CO., SACRED HEART OF JESUS (1863) [CEM] Rev. Nicholas G. Junker.
Res.: 17 N. Walnut St., 62832. Tel: 618-542-3423; Fax: 618-542-5061. Email: sacredheartduquoin@gmail.com.
Catechesis/Religious Program—Students 38.

DUBOIS, WASHINGTON CO., ST. CHARLES BORROMEO (1877) [CEM] Rev. Oliver Nwachukwu, Admin.
Res.: 223 S. 3rd. St., P.O. Box 6, 62831. Tel: 618-787-2781; Fax: 618-787-2171. Email: nwaodike@yahoo.com.
Catechesis/Religious Program—Judy Pieszchalski, C.R.E. Students 16.

DUPO, ST. CLAIR CO., SACRED HEART OF JESUS (1914) Rev. Paul R. Wienhoff.
100 S. 3rd St., P.O. Box 35, 62239. Tel: 618-286-3224.
Catechesis/Religious Program—Tel: 618-337-4548. Students 21.

EAST ST. LOUIS, ST. CLAIR CO.
1—ST. AUGUSTINE OF HIPPO (2006) Rev. Carroll Mizicko, O.F.M.
408 Columbia Pl., East Saint Louis, 62205. Email: staugustineofhippo@sbcglobal.net.
Catechesis/Religious Program—Mrs. Eleanor Gregory, C.R.E. Students 40.
Chapel—Sister Thea Bowman Chapel 8313 Church Ln., East Saint Louis, 62203. Tel: 618-397-0316.
2—IMMACULATE CONCEPTION (1895), (Lithuanian), Rev. Kenneth J. York, Admin.
1509 Baugh Ave., East Saint Louis, 62205. Tel: 618-874-0162.

ELDORADO, SALINE CO., ST. MARY (1900) [CEM] Rev. Ignatius Okonkwo.
Parish Center/Office: 1158 N. 2nd St., 62930. Tel: 618-273-6947; Fax: 618-273-3134. Email: stmarys1@clearwave.com.
Catechesis/Religious Program—Students 65.

ELIZABETHTOWN, HARDIN CO., ST. JOSEPH (1897) [CEM] Rev. Ignatius Okonkwo.
Res.: IL 146-185 E Rd., Box 140, 62931-9711. Tel: 618-285-3332.
Catechesis/Religious Program—Tel: 618-287-4824. Students 14.

ELLIS GROVE, RANDOLPH CO., DIVINE MATERNITY OF THE B.V.M. (1933) Rev. Benjamin Stern, Admin.
Res.: 7362 Shawneetown Tr., 62241. Tel: 618-859-3541.
Catechesis/Religious Program—Students 46.

ENFIELD, WHITE CO., ST. PATRICK (1830), (Irish), [CEM] Rev. Stephen A. Rudolphi.
St. Polycarp Church & Office: 209 Fourth St., Carmi, 62821. Tel: 618-382-7732. Email: wccath@frontier.com.
Catechesis/Religious Program—Tel: 618-963-2431. Students 9.

EQUALITY, GALLATIN CO., ST. JOSEPH (1873) [CEM] Rev. Steven L. Beatty.
Mailing Address: P.O. Box 99, 62934. Tel: 618-276-4252. Email: stjoe@shawneelink.com. Web: www.gallatincountycatholics.org.
Res.: P.O. Box 190, Ridgway, 62979. Tel: 618-272-7059; Fax: 618-272-5400.
Catechesis/Religious Program—Students 9.

EVANSVILLE, RANDOLPH CO., ST. BONIFACE (1860) [CEM] Rev. Benjamin Stern.
Res.: 1007 Olive St., 62242. Tel: 618-853-4435; Fax: 618-853-4435. Email: stboniface1860@hotmail.com.
Catechesis/Religious Program—Students 40.

FAIRFIELD, WAYNE CO., ST. EDWARD (1881) Rev. Michael Mbonu, Admin.
Res.: 300 N.W. 5th St., 62837. Tel: 618-847-7931; Fax: 618-842-7393. Email: stedseb@fairfieldwireless.net.
Catechesis/Religious Program—Ms. Peggy Garrison, C.R.E. Students 31.

FAIRMONT CITY, ST. CLAIR CO., HOLY ROSARY (1922) Rev. David M. Wilke, Pastor.
Res.: 2716 N. 42nd St., 62201. Tel: 618-274-3486; Fax: 618-274-1814.
Catechesis/Religious Program—Students 200.

FAIRVIEW HEIGHTS, ST. CLAIR CO., HOLY TRINITY CATHOLIC CHURCH (1951) Very Rev. C. Raymond Schultz; Rev. Anthony O. Onyango, Parochial Vicar; Deacons Arthur Hampton; Tom Powers.
505 Fountains Pkwy., 62208.
Rectory—901 S. Main St., P.O. Box 458, Caseyville, 62232. Tel: 618-628-8825; Fax: 618-628-8866. Web: www.holytrinityil.org.
School—504 Fountains Pkwy., 62208. Tel: 618-628-7395; Fax: 618-628-1570. Mr. Michael Oslance, Prin. Teachers 13; Students 246.
Catechesis/Religious Program—Email: scoonan@holytrinityil.org. Mrs. Sharon Coonan, Dir. Faith Formation. Students 99.

FAYETTEVILLE, ST. CLAIR CO., ST. PANCRATIUS (1837) [CEM] Revs. Kenneth J. York; Elmar Mauer, O.M.I, Sacramental Min.
Res.: 2213 N. 2nd St., 62258. Tel: 618-677-2717.
Catechesis/Religious Program—Students 19.

FLORA, CLAY CO., ST. STEPHEN (1854) [CEM] Rev. Martin E. Ohajunwa (Nigeria), Pastoral Admin.
Res.: 812 N. Main St., 62839. Tel: 618-662-6261; Fax: 618-662-8121. Email: ststephen_flora@yahoo.com. Web: www.floracatholic.com.
Catechesis/Religious Program—Tel: 618-662-8121. Students 32.

FREEBURG, ST. CLAIR CO., ST. JOSEPH (1857) [CEM] Rev. Mark D. Reyling.
Res.: 9 N. Alton St., 62243. Tel: 618-539-3209; Fax: 618-539-4772. Web: www.stjoefreeburg.org.
School—(Grades K-8), 2 N. Alton St., 62243. Tel: 618-539-3930; Fax: 618-539-0254. Email: office@stjosephfreeburg.org. Web: www.stjosephfreeburg.org. Mrs. Charlotte Vielweber, Prin.; Mrs. Karen Kuester, Librarian. Teachers 13; Students 75.
Catechesis/Religious Program—Students 161.

GERMANTOWN, CLINTON CO., ST. BONIFACE (1837) [CEM] Rev. Msgr. James A. Buerster; Deacon Richard Bagby.
Res.: 402 Munster St., Box 280, 62245. Tel: 618-523-4271; Fax: 618-523-4263. Email: stboniface@charter.net.
Catechesis/Religious Program—Email: stbonifaceff@charter.net. Students 426.

GRAND CHAIN, PULASKI CO., ST. CATHERINE (1891) [CEM] Rev. John Agbasiere, S.M.M.M. (Nigeria).
517 N. Walnut St., Box 67, Mound City, 62963. Tel: 618-748-9113; Fax: 618-748-9260.
Catechesis/Religious Program—

HARRISBURG, SALINE CO., ST. MARY (1907) [CEM] Rev. Ignatius Okonkwo.
2000 W. Poplar St., 62946.
Res.: 1158 N. 2nd St, Eldorado, 62930.

Office: 2000 W. Poplar St., 62946. Tel: 618-253-7408; Fax: 618-252-7874. Email: stmaryhb@shawneelink.net.
Catechesis/Religious Program—Tel: 618-252-7874. Students 56.

HECKER, MONROE CO., ST. AUGUSTINE OF CANTERBURY (1824) [CEM] Rev. Von C. Deeke, Admin.
Res.: 925 Centreville Ave., Caseyville, 62220. Tel: 618-234-5264; Fax: 618-473-9141. Email: staug@htc.net.

HERRIN, WILLIAMSON CO., OUR LADY OF MOUNT CARMEL (1900) [CEM] Rev. Msgr. Kenneth J. Schaefer.
Res.: 316 W. Monroe St., 62948. Tel: 618-942-3114; Fax: 618-988-1375. Email: olmc@live.com.
School—Tel: 618-942-4484; Fax: 618-942-2864. Ms. Cheryl Patterson-Dreyer, Prin. Lay Teachers 18; Students 287.
Catechesis/Religious Program—Students 115.

JOHNSTON CITY, WILLIAMSON CO., ST. PAUL (1904) Rev. Msgr. Kenneth J. Schaefer; Sr. Catherine Wellinghoff, A.S.C., Parish Life Coord.
1103 Washington Ave., 62951. Tel: 618-983-5073. Email: stpaulcc@gmail.com.
Catechesis/Religious Program—Students 18.

KASKASKIA, RANDOLPH CO., IMMACULATE CONCEPTION (1675), (French—Native American), [CEM], (Independent Mission), Mailing Address: 6450 Klein Ln., St. Mary's, MO 63673. Tel: 618-366-2633; Fax: 618-826-2667. Email: elyons@pdwrup.net.

KINMUNDY, MARION CO., ST. ELIZABETH ANN SETON (1878) Rev. Robert J. Zwilling.
Mailing Address: 812 W. Main St., Salem, 62881. Tel: 618-548-0899; Fax: 618-548-0269. Email: sttheresaparish@hotmail.com. Web: www.stelizabethkinmundy.com.
Catechesis/Religious Program—N. Madison St., 62854. Tel: 618-245-6221. Ms. Mary Kay Sigrist, D.R.E. Students 7.

LAWRENCEVILLE, LAWRENCE CO., ST. LAWRENCE (1909) [JC] Rev. Bernardine Nganzi (Uganda).
Res.: 1006 Collins, 62439. Tel: 618-943-5255; Fax: 618-943-5255.
Catechesis/Religious Program—Students 41.

LEBANON, ST. CLAIR CO., ST. JOSEPH (1862) [CEM] Rev. Msgr. James E. Margason, Canonical Pastor; Rev. Eugene J. Neff, Sacramental Min.; Deacon Peter Cerneka III; Mrs. Brenda Pehle, Parish Life Coord.
901 N. Alton St., 62254. Tel: 618-537-2221; 618-537-2575; Fax: 618-537-0147. Email: lebstjoe@sbcglobal.net.
Catechesis/Religious Program—Students 31.

LIVELY GROVE, WASHINGTON CO., ST. ANTHONY (1868) [CEM] Rev. Christian Reuter, O.F.M., Sacramental Min.
Church: 6101 St. Anthony Church Rd., Oakdale, 62268. Tel: 618-824-6271.
Catechesis/Religious Program—Students 22.

MADONNAVILLE, MONROE CO., IMMACULATE CONCEPTION (1833) Revs. Osang Idagbo, C.M. (Nigeria); Dale A. Maxfield.
Mailing Address: 5676 LL Rd., Waterloo, 62298. Tel: 618-935-2247.
Catechesis/Religious Program—

MARION, WILLIAMSON CO., ST. JOSEPH (1940) Rev. Msgr. Thomas D. Flach.
Res.: 600 N. Russell St., 62959. Tel: 618-993-3194; Fax: 618-997-9391. Email: rgm13@midamer.net. Web: www.stjosephmarion.org.
Catechesis/Religious Program—Tel: 618-997-7373. Mr. William T. Harper III, D.R.E. Students 127.

MARYDALE, CLINTON CO., ST. TERESA OF AVILA (1919) Revs. George A. Mauck, Canonical Pastor; Lawrence M. Nickels, O.F.M., Sacramental Min.; Deacons Charles Litteken, Admin.; John Hempen.
18021 Marydale Rd., Carlyle, 62231. Tel: 618-594-3266. Email: stteressa@tincans.net.
Catechesis/Religious Program—Students 44.

MASCOUTAH, ST. CLAIR CO., HOLY CHILDHOOD OF JESUS (1857) [CEM] Rev. Msgr. Jerome D. Hartlein; Rev. Abraham O. Adejoh.
Res.: 104 N. Independence St., P.O. Box 160, 62258. Tel: 618-566-2958; Fax: 618-566-4447. Email: hcc@holychildhoodchurch.com. Web: www.holychildhoodchurch.com.
School—215 N. John St., 62258. Tel: 618-566-2922; Fax: 618-566-2720. Email: hcs@holychildhoodschool.com. Web: www.holychildhoodschool.com. Mr. Ronald Karcher, Prin. Lay Teachers 11; Students 145.
Catechesis/Religious Program—Students 109.

MCLEANSBORO, HAMILTON CO., ST. CLEMENT (1881), (German), [CEM] Rev. Slawomir Ptak (Poland), Admin.
Res.: 103 N. Hancock, Mc Leansboro, 62859. Tel: 618-643-3552; 618-648-2490; Fax: 618-643-3112. Email: catholic@hamiltoncom.net. Web: www.hamiltoncom.net/~catholic.
Catechesis/Religious Program—Tel: 618-643-4400. Students 60.

METROPOLIS, MASSAC CO., ST. ROSE OF LIMA (1872) Rev. Christopher Michael Mujule (Uganda).
Res.: 315 E. Third St., 62960-2229. Tel: 618-524-9006. Email: stroseoflimametropolis@comcast.net. Web: www.strosemetropolis.com.
Catechesis/Religious Program—405 E. Third St., 62960. Tel: 618-524-8202. Ms. Marjorie J. Hawes, C.R.E. Students 23.

MILLSTADT, ST. CLAIR CO., ST. JAMES (1851) [CEM] Rev. Msgr. Marvin C. Volk; Deacon Ronald Karcher.
Res.: 405 W. Madison St., 62260. Tel: 618-476-3513; Fax: 618-476-1281. Email: stjrectory@htc.net.
School—Tel: 618-476-3510. Email: michele.bell@stjamesmillstadt.com. Web: www.stjamesmillstadt.com. Cheryl Dunnells, Prin. Sisters 1; Lay Teachers 10; Students 114.
Catechesis/Religious Program—Tel: 618-476-1923. Students 130.

MODOC, RANDOLPH CO., ST. LEO (1893) [CEM] Very Rev. Daniel J. Jurek.
5895 St. Leo Rd., 62261. Tel: 618-284-3314; Fax: 618-284-3314. Mailing Address: 802 Middle St., P.O. Box 365, Prairie du Rocher, 62277-0365.
Catechesis/Religious Program—Students 18.

MOUND CITY, PULASKI CO., CHURCH OF THE IMMACULATE CONCEPTION-ST. MARY (1863) [CEM] Rev. John Agbasiere, S.M.M.M. (Nigeria).
Res.: 517 N. Walnut St., P.O. Box 67, 62963. Tel: 618-748-9113; Fax: 618-748-9260. Email: rcchurch-pastorstmpc@yahoo.com.
Catechesis/Religious Program—Students 7.

MOUNT CARMEL, WABASH CO., ST. MARY (1836) [CEM] Rev. William J. Rowe; Deacon Charles Speaks.
Res.: 125 W. Fifth St., 62863. Tel: 618-262-5337; Fax: 618-262-5333. Email: smsparish@hotmail.com.
School—417 Chestnut St., 62863. Tel: 618-263-3183; Fax: 618-263-3596. Mrs. Alice Wirth, Prin. Lay Teachers 13; Students 128.
Catechesis/Religious Program—Students 16.

MOUNT VERNON, JEFFERSON CO., ST. MARY (1871) [CEM] Very Rev. John C. Iffert.
Res.: 115 N. 14th St., 62864. Tel: 618-244-1559; Fax: 618-244-1793. Email: saintmary@mvn.net. Web: www.saintmary.mvn.net.
School—1416 Main St., 62864. Tel: 618-242-5353; Fax: 618-242-5365. Mr. Brett Heinzman, Prin. Lay Teachers 10; Students 137.
Catechesis/Religious Program—Students 100.

MURPHYSBORO, JACKSON CO., ST. ANDREW (1868) [CEM] Rev. Gary P. Gummersheimer; Deacon Don Sparling.
Res.: 724 Mulberry St., 62966. Tel: 618-687-2012; Fax: 618-684-3431.
School—723 Mulberry St., 62966. Tel: 618-687-2013; Fax: 618-684-4969. Email: e.noll1@frontier.com. Web: saintandrew-school.org. Mr. Edward Noll, Prin. Lay Teachers 16; Students 142.
Catechesis/Religious Program—Email: jonibailey@earthlink.net. Joni Beth Bailey, C.R.E. Students 38.

NASHVILLE, WASHINGTON CO., ST. ANN (1874) [CEM] Rev. Andrew J. Knopik.
Res. & Office: 631 S. Mill St., 62263. Tel: 618-327-3232; Fax: 618-327-4904.
School—Tel: 618-327-8741. Mrs. Bonnie Paszkiewicz, Prin. Lay Teachers 9; Students 85; PreK 19.
Catechesis/Religious Program—Students 80.

NEW ATHENS, ST. CLAIR CO., ST. AGATHA (1870) [CEM] Very Rev. James M. Nall.
Res.: 205 S. Market St., 62264. Tel: 618-475-2331; Fax: 618-475-3177.
School—207 S. Market St., 62264. Tel: 618-475-2170; Fax: 618-475-3177. Email: cnewbold@stagathaschool.org. Mrs. Charlotte Newbold, Prin. Lay Teachers 6; Students 61.
Catechesis/Religious Program—Tel: 618-295-2686. Students 27.

NEW BADEN, CLINTON CO., ST. GEORGE (1894) [CEM] Rev. Eugene J. Neff.
Res.: 200 N. 3rd St., 62265. Tel: 618-588-4323; Fax: 618-588-2413. Email: saintgcatholicchurch@gmail.com. Web: www.stgeorgefamily.org.
Catechesis/Religious Program—Students 109.

O FALLON, ST. CLAIR CO.

1—ST. CLARE (1867) [CEM] Rev. James E. Deiters; Deacon Dennis W. Vander Ven.
Office: 1411 Cross St., 62269.
Res.: 205 W. Third, 62269. Tel: 618-632-3562; Fax: 618-632-9036. Web: www.stclarechurch.org.
School—214 W. 3rd St., 62269. Tel: 618-632-6327; Fax: 618-632-5587. Mr. Ken Pajares, Business Mgr.; Mrs. Mary Neville, Prin. Lay Teachers 24; Students 412.
Catechesis/Religious Program—Students 182.

2—ST. NICHOLAS (1982) Rev. Msgr. William J. Hitpas; Deacon Richard H. Olson; Ann Daniels, Admin.
Res., Church & Office: 625 St. Nicholas Dr., 62269. Tel: 618-632-1997; 618-632-1797; Fax: 618-632-7703. Email: busadmin@stnicholasofallon.org. Web: www.stnicholasofallon.org.
Catechesis/Religious Program—Tel: 618-632-1137. Email: liturgy@stnicholasofallon.org. Sr. Judith McKenna, Liturgy Director. Tel: 618-632-1007; Ms. Barbara Furdek, D.R.E. Students 310.

OKAWVILLE, WASHINGTON CO., ST. BARBARA (1867) [CEM] Revs. John J. Joyce; Steven F. Poole, Sacramental Min.
Res.: 305 N. Front St., P.O. Box 106, 62271. Tel: 618-243-6236; Fax: 618-243-5270. Email: jheberer@egyptian.net.
Catechesis/Religious Program—Mrs. Holly Brown, D.R.E. Students 55.

OLNEY, RICHLAND CO., ST. JOSEPH (1857) [CEM] Rev. Jerry E. Wirth.
220 S. Elliott St., 62450.
Res.: 220 S. Elliott St., 62450. Tel: 618-392-6711; 618-392-8181; Fax: 618-395-8500. Email: stjosephchurch_olney@yahoo.com. Web: www.stjosephchurcholney.com.
School—Tel: 618-395-3081. Ms. Carol Potter, Prin. Lay Teachers 15; Students 160.
Catechesis/Religious Program—Students 41.

PADERBORN, ST. CLAIR CO., ST. MICHAEL (1843), (German), [CEM] Unassigned. In Res., Rev. James A. Voelker (Retired).
Church: 4576 Buss Branch Rd., Waterloo, 62298. Tel: 618-473-2798; Fax: 618-473-9180. Email: stmichaels4@aol.com.
Catechesis/Religious Program—Tel: 618-473-2915. Ms. Jackie Billings, C.R.E. Students 48.

PINCKNEYVILLE, PERRY CO., ST. BRUNO (1872) [CEM] Rev. Brian Barker.
Res.: 204 N. Gordon St., 62274. Tel: 618-357-5510; Fax: 618-357-6050. Web: www.stbrunoparish.org.
School—210 N. Gordon St., 62274. Tel: 618-357-8276; Fax: 618-357-6425. Mr. John W. Smith, Prin. Lay Teachers 8; Students 122.
Catechesis/Religious Program—Tel: 618-758-2055. Ms. Kathy Sprehe, D.R.E. Students 85.

PIOPOLIS, HAMILTON CO., ST. JOHN THE BAPTIST (1841) [CEM] Rev. Slawomir Ptak (Poland), Admin.
Res.: Route 3, Box 170, Mc Leansboro, 62859. Tel: 618-648-2490. Email: catholic@hamiltoncom.net. Web: www.hamiltoncom.net/~catholic.
Catechesis/Religious Program—Tel: 618-648-2586. Students 81.

POND SETTLEMENT, GALLATIN CO., ST. PATRICK (1842) Rev. Steven L. Beatty.
Mailing Address: P.O. Box 579, Shawneetown, 62984. Tel: 618-269-3318; Fax: 618-272-5400.
Catechesis/Religious Program—Tel: 618-272-7059; Fax: 618-277-7059. Students 6.

POSEN, WASHINGTON CO., OUR LADY OF PERPETUAL HELP (1901) [CEM] Rev. Bernard C. Goedde Jr.
Res.: 19824 Posen Rd., Nashville, 62263-6122. Tel: 618-327-3556; Fax: 618-327-3556.
Catechesis/Religious Program—Students 7.

PRAIRIE DU ROCHER, RANDOLPH CO., ST. JOSEPH (1721) [CEM] Very Rev. Daniel J. Jurek.
Res.: 802 Middle St., 62277. Tel: 618-284-3314; Fax: 618-284-3314.
Catechesis/Religious Program—Students 61.

RADDLE, JACKSON CO., ST. ANN (1875) Rev. Leo J. Hayes.
101 Raddle Ln., P.O. Box 157, Ava, 62907. Tel: 618-426-3321; Fax: 618-426-3321.
Catechesis/Religious Program—Tel: 618-965-3621. Students 4.

RADOM, WASHINGTON CO., ST. MICHAEL (1874), (Polish), [CEM] Rev. Jean-Marie Amevi Mondji, Pastoral Min.
Church: 52 S. Third St., P.O. Box 128, 62876. Fax: 618-485-2272. Email: stmichaelradom@hughes.net.
Res.: 52 S. Third St., P.O. Box 15, 62876. Tel: 618-485-2265.
School—136 S. 3rd St., 62876. Tel: 618-485-6461. Keith Senior, Prin. Lay Teachers 5; Students 59.

RED BUD, RANDOLPH CO., ST. JOHN THE BAPTIST (1862) [CEM] Rev. Msgr. Dennis R. Schaefer.
Res.: 515 Locust St., 62278. Tel: 618-282-3222; Fax: 618-282-6867.
School—519 Hazel St., 62278. Tel: 618-282-3215; Fax: 618-282-6790. Web: www.sjbredbud.parishesonline.com. Ms. Kristine Hill, Prin. Lay Teachers 12; Students 87.
Catechesis/Religious Program—Students 85.

RENAULT, MONROE CO., OUR LADY OF GOOD COUNSEL (1879) [CEM] Rev. Roger R. Karban, Admin.
Office: 2038 Washington St., P.O. Box 98, 62279. Tel: 618-458-7710; Fax: 618-458-7710.
Catechesis/Religious Program—Students 16.

RIDGWAY, GALLATIN CO., ST. JOSEPH (1870) [CEM] Rev. Steven L. Beatty.
Res.: 205 W. South St., P.O. Box 190, 62979. Tel: 618-272-7059; Fax: 618-272-5400. Email: stjoe@shawneelink.com. Web: www.gallatincountycatholics.org.
Catechesis/Religious Program—Students 45.

ROYALTON-ZEIGLER, FRANKLIN CO., ST. ALOYSIUS/SACRED HEART (1919) [JC] Rev. Trevor Murray; Sr.

Laura Reynolds, O.S.F., Pastoral Assoc.
Res.: 212 Pecan St., P.O. Box 100, 62983. Tel: 618-984-2146; Fax: 618-984-2146. Email: srlaura@neonds1.com.
Catechesis/Religious Program—Students 51.

RUMA, RANDOLPH CO., ST. PATRICK (1818) [CEM] Rev. Msgr. Dennis R. Schaefer; Rev. J. Clyde Grogan.
Res.: #1 Pioneer Ln.-Ruma, Red Bud, 62278. Tel: 618-282-3176; Fax: 618-282-3176. Email: stpats@htc.net.

ST. FRANCISVILLE, LAWRENCE CO., ST. FRANCIS XAVIER (1836), (French), [CEM] Rev. Bernardine Nganzi (Uganda).
Mailing Address: 1006 Collins St., Lawrenceville, 62439. Tel: 618-943-5255. Email: slfxic@shawneelink.net.
Catechesis/Religious Program—Students 14.

ST. LIBORY, ST. CLAIR CO., ST. LIBORIUS (1838) [CEM] Rev. Christian Reuter, O.F.M., Sacramental Min.; Deacon Andrew Lintker.
Res.: 911 Sparta St., P.O. Box 331, 62282. Tel: 618-768-4921; Fax: 618-768-4207.
Catechesis/Religious Program—Ms. Mona Mense, D.R.E. Students 56.

ST. ROSE, CLINTON CO., ST. ROSE (1868) [CEM] Rev. Edward F. Schaefer.
Res.: 18010 St. Rose Rd., 62230-2506. Tel: 618-526-4118; Fax: 618-526-0004. Email: belpsros@papadocs.com.
Catechesis/Religious Program—Tel: 618-526-4886. Sr. Justina Schaefer, A.S.C., D.R.E. Students 187.

ST. SEBASTIAN, WABASH CO., ST. SEBASTIAN (1871) [CEM] Rev. Michael Mbonu, Admin.
Church: 4921 N. 1400 Blvd., Mount Carmel, 62863. Tel: 618-298-2589.
Res.: 300 N.W. Fifth St., Fairfield, 62837. Tel: 618-847-7931; Fax: 618-842-7393.
Catechesis/Religious Program—Students 62.

SALEM, MARION CO., ST. THERESA OF AVILA (1868) [CEM] Rev. Robert J. Zwilling.
Res.: 719 Markland St., 62881. Tel: 618-548-5098; Fax: 618-548-0269. Email: sttheresaparish@hotmail.com. Web: www.sttheresa.com.
School—190 Ohio St., 62881. Tel: 618-548-3492; Fax: 618-548-9673. Email: rascals@ussonet.net. Web: www.sttheresagradeschool.com. Sr. Margaret Schmidt, S.S.N.D., Prin. Lay Teachers 5; Students 57.
Catechesis/Religious Program—Ms. Denise McGormack, D.R.E. Students 23.

SANDOVAL, MARION CO., ST. LAWRENCE (1871) [CEM] Rev. Justin Olisaemeka (Nigeria), Admin.
Mailing Address: P.O. Box 278, 62882.
Office: 412 N. Vine St., P.O. Box 278, 62882.
Church: 311 W. Missouri St., 62882. Tel: 618-247-3300; Fax: 618-247-3300. Email: stlawrence@frontiernet.net. Web: www.saintlawrencesandoval.org.
Catechesis/Religious Program—Students 12.

SCHELLER, JEFFERSON CO., ST. BARBARA (1898) Rev. Jean-Marie Amevi Mondji.
4281 N. Scheller Ln., 62883. Tel: 618-279-7207; Fax: 618-279-7207. Email: fatherjmdelacroix@yahoo.com.
Catechesis/Religious Program—Students 40.

SESSER, FRANKLIN CO., ST. MARY (1909) Rev. Peter D. Balili (Philippines), Admin.
Church: 100 N. Poplar St., P.O. Box 568, 62884. Tel: 618-625-5053.
Res.: 101 N. Poplar St., 62884. Tel: 618-625-5053.
Catechesis/Religious Program—Students 28.

SHAWNEETOWN, GALLATIN CO., ST. MARY (1842) [CEM] Rev. Steven L. Beatty.
Mailing Address: 655 W. Marshall St., P.O. Box 579, 62984. Tel: 618-269-3318; Fax: 618-272-5400. Email: stjoe@shawneelink.com. Web: www.gallatincountycatholics.org.
Catechesis/Religious Program—Tel: 618-272-7059. Students 19.

SHILOH, ST. CLAIR CO., CORPUS CHRISTI (1913) Rev. Msgr. James E. Margason.
Res.: 206 Rasp St., 62269. Tel: 618-632-7614; Fax: 618-632-7614.
Catechesis/Religious Program—Tel: 618-632-7614. Students 80.

SMITHTON, ST. CLAIR CO., ST. JOHN THE BAPTIST (1867) [CEM] Revs. Stan J. Konieczny; Gerald R. Hechenberger; Deacon Donald R. Deitz.
Res.: 10 S. Lincoln St., 62285-1614. Tel: 618-234-2068; Fax: 618-234-0179.
School—Tel: 618-233-0581. Web: www.stjohnschool.us. Mrs. Clarice McKay, Prin. Lay Teachers 7; Students 65.
Catechesis/Religious Program—Students 90.

SPARTA, RANDOLPH CO., OUR LADY OF LOURDES (1897) Rev. Lawrence Mariasoosai, O.M.I., Parochial Admin.
Res.: 611 W. Broadway, 62286. Tel: 618-443-2811. Web: www.ollandspv.com.
Catechesis/Religious Program—Tel: 618-443-2878. Ms. Lila Lehnherr, D.R.E. Students 48.

STONEFORT, WILLIAMSON CO., ST. FRANCIS DE SALES (1879) Rev. Thomas M. Barrett.
Mailing Address: 2020 State Rte. 146 E., P.O. Box 1325, Vienna, 62995. Tel: 618-658-4501. Students attend Vie.

STRINGTOWN, RICHLAND CO., ST. JOSEPH (1841) [CEM] Rev. Mark D. Stec.
Mailing Address: P.O. Box 10, Dundas, 62425. Tel: 618-754-3676; Fax: 618-754-3356. Email: stjoestringtown@hotmail.com. Web: www.stringtown.org.
Res.: 5761 Ingraham Ln., Newton, 62448. Tel: 618-752-5671.
Church: 6342 N. Stringtown Rd., Olney, 62450.
Catechesis/Religious Program—Tel: 618-754-3049. Ms. Donna Zwilling, C.R.E. Students 30.

TAMAROA, PERRY CO., IMMACULATE CONCEPTION (1904) Rev. Oliver Nwachukwu, Admin.
Res.: 533 W. 2nd North St., 62888. Tel: 618-496-5867. Email: immaculateconception@frontiernet.net.
Catechesis/Religious Program—Tel: 618-496-3100. Students 4.

TIPTON, MONROE CO., ST. PATRICK (1850) [CEM] Very Rev. Daniel J. Jurek, Admin. Pro Tem; Rev. John Kizhakedan, C.M.I., Sacramental Min.
Res.: 5675 LL Rd., Waterloo, 62298. Tel: 618-458-6875; Fax: 618-458-6875.
Catechesis/Religious Program—Students 7.

TODDS MILL, PERRY CO., ST. MARY MAGDALEN (1868) [CEM] Rev. Bernard C. Goedde Jr.
5047 Todds Mill Rd., Pinckneyville, 62274-2235.
Res. & Business Office: 19824 Posen Rd., Nashville, 62263-6122. Tel: 618-327-3556; Fax: 618-327-3556. Email: olph-smm@hughes.net.
Catechesis/Religious Program—

TRENTON, CLINTON CO., ST. MARY (1858), (German), [CEM] Rev. Joseph C. Rascher.
Res.: 215 W. Kentucky St., 62293. Tel: 618-224-9335; Fax: 618-224-9346. Web: www.stmarytrenton.com.
Office: 218 W. Kentucky St., 62293. Email: stmary@stmarytrenton.com. Web: www.stmarytrenton.com.
Catechesis/Religious Program—Mrs. Kim Mass, C.R.E. Students 124.

ULLIN, PULASKI CO., OUR LADY OF FATIMA (1949) [CEM] Closed. For inquiries for parish records contact the chancery.

VALMEYER, MONROE CO., SEVEN DOLORS OF THE B.V.M. (1921) Rev. Urban Osuji, C.M.
Res.: 101 S. Meyer Ave., 62295. Tel: 618-935-2247; Fax: 618-935-2410. Email: urbanosuji@yahoo.co.uk; smoffice@htc.net (Office).
Catechesis/Religious Program—Ms. Karen Limestall, D.R.E. Students 79.

VIENNA, JOHNSON CO., ST. PAUL (1895) [JC] Rev. Thomas M. Barrett.
Res.: 2020 State Rte. 146 E., 62995. Tel: 618-658-4501.
Catechesis/Religious Program—Students 18.

WALSH, RANDOLPH CO., ST. PIUS V (1905) Rev. Lawrence Mariasoosai, O.M.I.
7681 Walsh Rd., 62297. Tel: 618-853-4404. Email: stpius@accessus.net. In Res., Rev. John Kizhakedan, C.M.I.
Catechesis/Religious Program—Students 7.

WASHINGTON PARK, ST. CLAIR CO., ST. MARTIN OF TOURS, Closed. For inquiries for parish records contact the chancery.

WATERLOO, MONROE CO., SS. PETER AND PAUL (1843) [CEM] Revs. Osang Idagbo, C.M. (Nigeria), Admin.; Dale A. Maxfield, Parochial Vicar; Deacon Douglas L. Boyer, Admin.; Ms. Karen Seaborn, Pastoral Assoc.
Res.: 204 W. Mill St., 62298. Tel: 618-939-6426; Fax: 618-939-2011.
School—Tel: 618-939-7217; Fax: 618-939-5994. Ms. Lisa Buchheit, Prin. Lay Teachers 28; Students 339.
Catechesis/Religious Program—Angela Atkinson, D.R.E. Students 296.

WENDELIN, CLAY CO., HOLY CROSS (1870) [CEM] Rev. Mark D. Stec.
Res.: 5782 Ingraham Ln., Newton, 62448. Tel: 618-752-5671; Fax: 618-752-6006.
Catechesis/Religious Program—Ms. Melissa Weber, C.R.E. Students 127.

WEST FRANKFORT, FRANKLIN CO., ST. JOHN THE BAPTIST (1916) [CEM] Rev. Trevor K. Murry.
Res.: 703 E. Main St., 62896. Tel: 618-932-2828; Fax: 618-932-2828. Email: stjohnthebaptist@mchsi.com.
School—Tel: 618-937-2017; Fax: 618-937-2287. Mr. Kevin Spiller, Prin. Franciscan Sisters of Our Lady of Perpetual Help 1; Lay Teachers 6; Students 101.
Catechesis/Religious Program—Sr. Laura Reynolds, O.S.F., D.R.E. Students 10.

WILLISVILLE, PERRY CO., ST. JOSEPH (1903) [CEM] Rev. Leo J. Hayes.
Mailing Address: 606 W. George St., Ava, 62907. Tel: 618-426-3321.
Catechesis/Religious Program—Tel: 618-965-3621; Fax: 618-426-3321. Students 10.

ZEIGLER, FRANKLIN CO., SACRED HEART, Merged with St. Aloysius, Royalton to form St. Aloysius/Sacred Heart, Royalton-Zeigler.

SACRAMENTAL RECORDS LOCATED IN CHANCERY ARCHIVES:
St. Adalbert Church, East St. Louis—
St. Anthony, Coulterville—
St. Augustine Church, East St. Louis—
SS. Cyril and Methodius Church, East St. Louis—
St. Elizabeth Church, East St. Louis—
St. Henry Church, East St. Louis—
Holy Angels Church, East St. Louis—
Immaculate Conception, Centreville—
Immaculate Conception, East St. Louis—
Immaculate Conception, Kaskaskia—
St. John Francis Regis, East St. Louis—
St. John's Orphanage, Belleville—
St. Joseph Church, Wetaug—
St. Joseph, East St. Louis—
St. Martin of Tours, Washington Park—
St. Mary Church, East St. Louis—
Our Lady of Fatima, Ullin—
St. Patrick, East St. Louis—
St. Philip, East St. Louis—
Sacred Heart Church, East St. Louis—
St. Catherine Labourne, Cahokia—
St. Thomas Church, Millstadt—

Chaplains of Correctional Institutions and State Hospitals

ANNA. *Anna State Hospital*. Vacant. Attended from St. Mary Church, Anna.
CENTRALIA. *Centralia Correctional Center*, P.O. Box 1266, 62801. Rev. George A. Mauck.
CHESTER. *Chester Mental Health Center*, P.O. Box 31, 62233. Tel: 618-826-4571.
HARRISBURG. *Illinois Youth Center*, P.O. Box 300, 62946. Vacant.
INA. *Big Muddy River Correctional Center*. Very Rev. Daniel J. Jurek, V.F.
MARION. *Federal Maximum Security Prison*, P.O. Box 2000, 62959. Deacon Pat Patterson, Chap. Tel: 618-964-1441.
Veterans Hospital. Attended from St. Joseph, Marion.
MENARD. *Menard Correctional Center*, P.O. Box 711, 62259. Vacant. Tel: 618-826-5071.
VIENNA. *Dixon Springs Work Camp* 62995. Vacant.
Shawnee Correctional Center, Box 400, 62995. Rev. Christian Reuter, O.F.M.
Vienna Correctional Center. Rev. Christian Reuter, O.F.M.

Military Chaplains:
Rev.—
Gegotek, Tadeusz, U.S.N.R.

Special Assignment:
Revs.—
Geller, Charles H., Fort Stockton, TX
Kizhakedan, John, C.M.I., Prison Ministry

Leave of Absence:
Revs.—
Harbaugh, Paul E.
Hechenberger, Gerald R.
Higgins, John
Lemay, Larry
O'Guinn, Jon
Ruppert, Alan E.
Sebescak, Gary
Unverferth, Steven R.
Witte, Steven D.

Retired:
Most Rev.—
Schlarman, Stanley G., D.D., Fiat House, 113 N. Ottawa, Joliet, 60432. Tel: 618-277-6814
Rev. Msgrs.—
Baumann, Theodore J.
Blazine, James A.
Eichenseer, Donald W.
Haselhorst, Vincent
Lawler, Joseph A., V.F.
Mazuchowski, Hyacinth
Schwaegel, Joseph R., (On Leave)
Revs.—
Ancheril, Jose
Balestrieri, Edward, (On Leave)
Blaes, Donald A., 205 N. 3rd St., New Baden, 62265.
Chlopecki, Robert J., (On Leave)
Crook, David G., (On Leave)
Daly, Richard L.
Dougherty, James R.
Engelhart, Henry R.
Frerker, Jack W.
Hibner, Jerome H.

Hsu, Peter
Humphrey, Steven
Iffert, Wilbert J.
Jeffrey, James
Kastner, Edwin H., (On Leave)
Koehr, Louis
Kownacki, Raymond F.
Kreher, Albert E.
Kribs, Charles R.
Lenzini, Donald J.
Long, James T.
Lopardo, Vito R., Hincke Residence for Priests, 2620 Lebanon Ave., 62221.
Miriani, Gerald C.
Mohr, Richard G.
Peterson, Louis P., (On Leave)
Ratermann, Jerome B., (On Leave)
Rensing, William F., (On Leave)
Thoonkuzhy, Joseph (TLS)
Van Oss, James R.
Voelker, David A.
Voelker, James A.
Voss, Dennis F.
Weidert, Richard J.

Permanent Deacons:
Bach, Gerald, Sr.
Bagby, Richard
Becker, Robert H.
Boyer, Douglas
Cerneka, Peter, III
Dietz, Donald
DuBois, Omer E., (Retired)
Hampton, Arthur
Hempen, John
Karcher, Ronald
Klostermann, Linus
Lanter, Robert
Lintker, Andrew
Lippert, Robert
Litteken, Charles
Mills, George, Jr.
Munie, George J.
Netemeyer, Glennon J.
Olson, Richard H.
Patterson, Pat
Pautler, Stephen
Rickert, Dennis
Sparling, Don
Speaks, Charles
Teaff, Joseph (Retired)
Vander Ven, Dennis W.

INSTITUTIONS LOCATED IN THE DIOCESE

[A] HIGH SCHOOLS, DIOCESAN

BELLEVILLE. *Althoff Catholic High School*, 5401 W. Main St., 62226-4796. Tel: 618-235-1100; Fax: 618-235-9535. Email: althoff@norcom2000.com. Web: www.althoff.net. Mr. David L. Harris, M.S., Prin.; Rev. Sean Palas. Lay Teachers 32; Students 416.

BREESE. *Mater Dei High School*, 900 N. Mater Dei Dr., 62230. Tel: 618-526-7216; Fax: 618-526-8310. Email: mda@lcls.org. Web: www.materdeiknights.org. Mr. Dennis Litteken, Prin.; Mrs. Maria Zurliene, Asst. Prin.; Rev. Charles W. Tuttle, Dir. Institution Advancement; Ms. Carol Bandre, Librarian. Central Catholic High School for Clinton Co. Priests 1; Lay Teachers 42; Students 470.

WATERLOO. *Gibault Catholic High School*, 501 Columbia Ave., 62298. Tel: 618-939-3883; Fax: 618-939-7215. Email: russhart@gibaultonline.com. Web: www.gibaultonline.com. Mr. Russell Hart, Prin.; Ms. Michelle Posey, Librarian. Sisters 2; Teachers 27; Students 243.

[B] ELEMENTARY SCHOOLS

BREESE. *All Saints Academy*, (Grades PreK-8), 295 N. Clinton St., 62230. Tel: 618-526-4323; Fax: 618-526-2547. Email: asabooth@gmail.com. Web: www.asasaints.com. Dr. Robin Booth, Prin.; Ms. Jane Klostermann, Librarian; Ms. Marietta Kuhl, Librarian. Consolidated schools of Saint Augustine, Saint Dominic parishes, Breese, IL, and St. Anthony Parish, Beckemeyer, IL. Lay Teachers 24; Students 330.

EAST SAINT LOUIS. *Sister Thea Bowman Catholic School*, (Grades K-8), 8213 Church Ln., 62203. Tel: 618-397-0316; Fax: 618-397-0337. Email: thea_bowman@yahoo.com. Sr. Janet McCann, A.S.C., M.A., Prin. Sisters 3; Lay Teachers 10; Students 120.

FAIRVIEW HEIGHTS. *Holy Trinity Catholic School*, (Grades PreSchool-8), Consolidated schools of St. Stephen Parish, Caseyville, IL; Our Lady of the Assumption Parish, Fairview Heights, IL; St. Albert the Great and Elizabeth Seton School., 504 Fountains Pkwy., 62208. Tel: 618-628-7395; Fax: 618-628-1570. Email: htschool504@sbcglobal.net. Web: www.holytrinityfairviewheights.com. Mr. Michael Oslance, Prin. Priests 1; Lay Teachers 14; Students 219.

[C] DAY CARE CENTERS

BELLEVILLE. *St. Henry Creative Learning Center* (1980) 5303 W. Main St., 62226. Tel: 618-234-6061; Fax: 618-234-6801. Email: sthdaycare@peaknet.net. Ms. Judy Shovlin, Dir.; Ms. Mary Haas, Co-Dir. Lay Teachers 10; Children 56.

St. John Children's Home, 2620 Lebanon Ave., 62221.

Chancery Office, 222 S. Third St., 62220. Tel: 618-277-8181. Very Rev. John W. McEvilly, V.G.

St. John Day Care Center, 2620 Lebanon Ave., 62221. Tel: 618-235-6717; Fax: 618-235-8485. Email: director79@aol.com. Ms. April Jones, Dir. Lay Women 11; Children 75.

EAST SAINT LOUIS. *Catholic Day Care Center* (1973) 617 Summit Ave., 62201. Tel: 618-874-7178; Fax: 618-261-2005. Email: catholicdcc@sbcglobal.net. Nursery and Kindergarten.; Conducted by the Cordi-Marian Sisters.
2417 Ridge Ave., 62205. Tel: 618-875-1447. Email: irenejua@htctech.net. Sr. Gema Juarez, M.C.M., Dir. Brothers 2; Sisters 2; Lay Teachers 6; Children 70.

[D] GENERAL HOSPITALS

BELLEVILLE. *St. Elizabeth Hospital* (1875) 211 S. Third St., 62220-1998. Tel: 618-234-2120; Fax: 618-222-4650. Web: www.steliz.org. Maryann Reese, CEO. Hospital Sisters of the Third Order of St. Francis, Clinically Affiliated with St. Louis University School of Medicine. Sisters 4; Staff 1,493; Bed Capacity 338; Patients Assisted Annually 185,343.

BREESE. *St. Joseph Hospital* (1897) 9515 Holy Cross Ln., 62230. Tel: 618-526-4511; Fax: 618-526-8022. Email: sniemann@sjb.hshs.org; mklosterman@sjb.hshs.org. Web: www.stjoebreese.com. Mark Klosterman, CEO; Sr. Dorothy Niemann, S.C.S.C., Pastoral Care. Hospital Sisters of the Third Order of St. Francis. Sisters 2; Staff 343; Bed Capacity 85; Patients Assisted Annually 89,000.

CENTRALIA. **St. Mary's Hospital*, 400 N. Pleasant Ave., 62801. Tel: 618-436-8000; Fax: 618-436-8038. Web: www.smgsi.com. Mr. Bruce A. Merrell, Pres. Felician Sisters 4; Staff 850; Bed Capacity 180; Patients Assisted Annually 139,968.

MOUNT VERNON. **Good Samaritan Regional Health Center*, 605 N. 12th St., 62864. Tel: 618-242-4600; Fax: 618-242-3196. Web: www.smgsi.com. Mr. Mike Warren, Pres.; Mr. Jeffrey Stewart, Dir. Pastoral Care. Member of SSM Health Care. Bed Capacity 154; Staff 1,099; Patients Assisted Annually 93,804.

MURPHYSBORO. *St. Joseph Memorial Hospital*, 2 S. Hospital Dr., 62966. Tel: 618-684-3156; Fax: 618-529-0529. Web: www.sih.net. Mr. Scott Seaborn, Admin.; Sr. Clara Ternes, A.S.C., Corp. Dir. of Missions, Values & Ethics. Adorers of the Blood of Christ., A service of Southern Illinois Healthcare. Sisters 1; Total Staff 250; Bed Capacity 25; Patients Assisted Annually 16,229.

[E] HOMES FOR SENIOR CITIZENS

BELLEVILLE. *Charles and Bertha Hincke Residence for Priests and Sense Residence*, 2620 Lebanon Ave., 62221. Tel: 618-234-5722; Fax: 618-234-5792. Email: hinckehome@gmail.com. Ms. Joline Beck, Mgr. Owned by Diocese of Belleville. Guests 17; Staff 10; Bed Capacity 21.

Our Lady of the Snows Apartment Community Retirement Home, 726 Community Dr., 62223. Tel: 618-394-6400; Fax: 618-394-9051. Email: bob.mccardle@apartmentcommunity.org. Web: apartmentcommunity.org. Mr. D. Robert McCardle, Exec. Vice Pres.; Rev. Thomas Hayes, O.M.I. Independent Apartments 125; Skilled Care 57; Assisted Living 38.

[F] MONASTERIES AND RESIDENCES OF PRIESTS AND BROTHERS

BELLEVILLE. *Missionary Oblates of Mary Immaculate - St. Henry's Oblate Residence*, 200 N. 60th St., 62223. Tel: 618-233-2991. Email: sthenryomi@charter.net. Revs. Gerard Bolduc, O.M.I.; George Capen, O.M.I.; Andrew G. Chalkey, O.M.I.; William Clark, O.M.I.; John M. Ettensohn, O.M.I.; Urban Figge, O.M.I.; Thomas Hayes, O.M.I.; Michael Hussey, O.M.I.; George Kuryvial, O.M.I.; John Louis, O.M.I. (Retired); Allen J. Maes, O.M.I., Supr. Oblate Community; Elmar Mauer, O.M.I; Gerald T. McGovern; Thomas Meyer, O.M.I.; Jerry Orsino; Eugene V. Prendiville; Thomas J. Singer, O.M.I.; James E. Taylor, O.M.I.; James Wynne, O.M.I.; Clarence Zachman, O.M.I.; Bro. Andrew Lawlor, O.M.I. Priests 19; Brothers 1.

Shrine of Our Lady of the Snows, 442 S. DeMazenod Dr., 62223-1023. Tel: 618-397-6700; Fax: 618-397-1210. Email: info@snows.org. Web: www.snows.org. Revs. James Brobst, O.M.I., Area Councillor; Harold Fischer, O.M.I.; Robert Leising, O.M.I.; John R. Madigan, O.M.I.; Joseph Menker, O.M.I.; Leo Miller, O.M.I. (Retired); Vincent Ott, O.M.I.; Thomas Ovalle, O.M.I., Dir.; Joseph Pitts, O.M.I.; Boniface Wittenbrink, O.M.I. (Retired); Bros. William Johnson, O.M.I., Councillor-at-large; Thomas Ruhmann, O.M.I., Shrine District Supr. Missionary Oblates of Mary Immaculate.

EAST SAINT LOUIS. *St. Benedict the Black Friary* (2002) 404 N. 14th St., 62205. Tel: 618-482-5570; Fax: 618-482-5574. Revs. Christian Reuter, O.F.M., Diocesan Coord. of Prison Ministry; Carroll Mizicko, O.F.M., Pastor St. Augustine of Hippo.

Marianist House of Intercession Marianist Community, 641 N. 7th St., 62201. Tel: 618-271-0204; Fax: 618-261-2005. Email: mrnstes1@att.net. Bro. John Laudenbach, S.M, Contact Person.

[G] CONVENTS AND RESIDENCES FOR SISTERS

BELLEVILLE. *Hospital Sisters of St. Francis* (1844) 1031 Golfview Ct., 62223-3261. Tel: 618-538-6033; Fax: 618-538-6033. Web: www.hospitalsisters.org. Sisters 3.

Hospital Sisters of The Third Order of St. Francis (1844) 1000 Royal Heights Rd., Apt. 58, 62226. Tel: 618-233-1687; Fax: 618-233-1687. Email: sistertk1948@yahoo.com. Web: www.springfieldfranciscans.org.

Poor Clare Monastery of Our Lady of Mercy (1986) 300 N. 60th St., 62223. Tel: 618-235-4407; Fax: 618-235-4426. Web: www.poorclares-belleville.info. Sr. Mary Giovanna, P.C.C., Abbess. Sisters 9.

CAIRO. *Mary Katherine Convent, Poor Handmaids of Jesus Christ*, 725 22nd St., 62914. Tel: 618-734-0778; Fax: 618-734-0778. Email: soupkitchen618@hotmail.com. Sisters 2.

EAST ST. LOUIS. *Daughters of Charity*, 3500 Market St., East Saint Louis, 62207-1637. Tel: 618-274-2513; Fax: 618-274-2513. Email: mclifford@diobelle.org.

RUMA. *Adorers of the Blood of Christ Ruma Center*, 2 Pioneer Ln. - Ruma, Red Bud, 62278. Tel: 618-282-3848; Fax: 618-282-3266. Email: grossm@adorers.org. Web: www.adorers.org. Sr. Mildred Gross, A.S.C., Dir., Community Life & Mission. Sisters 62; Total Membership of the Province 294.

[H] RETREAT HOUSES

BELLEVILLE. *King's House Retreat and Renewal Center* (1951) 700 N. 66th St., 62223-3949. Tel: 618-397-0584; Fax: 618-397-5123. Email: info@kingsretreatcenter.org. Web: www.kingsretreatcenter.org. Rev. Mark Dean, O.M.I.; Bros. Patrick M. McGee, O.M.I., Dir.; Victor Capek, O.M.I.; Edward Driggins, O.M.I.

[I] NEWMAN CENTERS

CARBONDALE. *The Newman Catholic Student Center* Southern Illinois University, 715 S. Washington, 62901. Tel: 618-529-3311; Fax: 618-549-9401. Web: www.siucnewman.org. Mr. Tim Taylor, Dir.

[J] MISCELLANEOUS LISTINGS

BELLEVILLE. *Althoff Catholic High School Educational Endowment Trust*, 222 S. 3rd St., 62220. Tel: 618-277-8181. Mr. David L. Harris, M.S., Contact Person.

Ancient Order of Hibernians, 1520 Weil Rd., Lebanon, 62254. Tel: 618-632-4538. Mr. Gish A. Johnson Jr., Contact Person.

Ancient Order of Hibernians (LAOH), P.O. Box 23193, 62223. Tel: 618-277-9620. 16 Catherine Dr., Fairview Heights, 62208. Ms. Marcia Gilhausen, Pres.

Catholic Committee on Scouting of the Diocese of Belleville, 2243 Havenford Dr., Shiloh, 62221. Email: tderousse@charter.net. Mr. Tim DeRousse, Contact Person.

Catholic Community Foundation for the Diocese of Belleville, 222 S. 3rd St., 62220-1985. Tel: 618-277-8181.

Catholic Diocese of Belleville General Fund, 222 S. Third St., 62220.

Catholic Holy Family Society, Mary Barbara Kurtz, P.O. Box 327, 62222. Tel: 618-233-0286; Fax: 618-277-8259. Email: mbkurtz@chfsociety.org. Web: www.chfsociety.org.

Catholic Social Services of Southern Illinois, 8601 W. Main St., Ste. 201, 62223. Tel: 618-394-5900; Fax: 619-394-5909. Email: admin@cssil.org. Web: www.cssil.org. Mr. Gary Huelsmann, Exec. Dir.

Catholic War Veterans, Mailing Address: P.O. Box 325, 62222. 3535 State Rte. 159, Freeburg, 62243. Tel: 618-234-3074.

D & L Fund, NFP, 222 S. Third St., 62220. Tel: 618-277-8181; Fax: 618-277-0819. Email: dwaeltz@diobelle.org. Web: diobelle.org. Most Rev. Edward Kenneth Braxton, Ph.D., S.T.D., Pres.; Very Rev. John W. McEvilly, V.G., Sec.; James Mroczkowski, CFO.

Diocese of Belleville The Catholic Service and Ministry Appeal, 222 S. Third St., 62220. Tel: 618-277-8181.

Engaged Encounter, 2620 Lebanon Ave., 62221. Tel: 618-235-9601. Web: www.eeofs-il.org. Mr. Jerry Bach, Coord.; Ms. Ann Bach, Coord.

St. Francis Thrift Shop, 800 E. Main St., 62220. Tel: 618-233-6998. Mr. Leroy Forness, Mgr. Tel: 618-233-1669.

Minds Eye Information Service, 9541 Church Circle Dr., 62223. Tel: 618-394-6444; Fax: 618-394-6438. Ms. Marjorie Williams, Exec. Dir. Closed Circuit Radio for the blind and print disabled.

Ministry Formation Fund, NFP, 222 S. Third St., 62220. Tel: 618-277-8181; Fax: 618-277-0819. Email: dwaeltz@diobelle.org. Web: diobelle.org. Most Rev. Edward K. Braxton, Pres.; Very Rev. John W. McEvilly, V.G., Sec.; James Mroczkowski, CFO.

Missionary Association of Mary Immaculate-Missionary Oblates of Mary Immaculate, 9480 N. De Mazenod Dr., 62223-1160. Tel: 618-398-4848; Fax: 618-398-0588. Email: mami@oblatesusa.org. Web: www.oblatesusa.org. Rev. John R. Madigan, O.M.I., Oblate Dir. Serving the missions of the Missionary Oblates, the National Shrine of Our Lady of the Snows, and the Tekakwitha Indian Missions.

Property & Liability Insurance Fund, NFP, 222 S. Third St., 62220. Tel: 618-277-8181; Fax: 618-277-0819. Email: dwaeltz@diobelle.org. Web: diobelle.org. Most Rev. Edward Kenneth Braxton, Ph.D., S.T.D., Pres.; Very Rev. John W. McEvilly, V.G., Sec.; James Mroczkowski, CFO.

Secular Franciscan Order, 200 W. Harrison, 62220. Email: Fransfo@aol.com. Ms. Mary Ellen Herman, S.F.O. Tel: 618-234-4945. St. Peter Fraternity.

Serra Club of St. Clair County, P.O. Box 23017, 62223. Tel: 618-973-8116. Mr. Thomas H. Norrenberns, Pres., 2 Corrington Pl., Mascoutah, 62258.

1333 Goldfinch Dr., 62223. Tel: 618-632-7541.

TEC (Teens Encounter Christ), 2620 Lebanon Ave., 62221. Email: chairperson@bellevilletec.com. Web: www.bellevilletec.com. Ms. Carissa Cushman, Chairperson.

Victorious Missionaries, 442 S. DeMazenod Dr., 62223-1097. Tel: 618-394-6281 (Voice/TDD); Fax: 618-397-1210. Email: truhmann@snows.org. Web: www.vmusa.org. Bro. Thomas Ruhmann, O.M.I., National Dir. Spiritual Support Network for people with disabilities, chronic illness, and those who want to share the journey.

World Apostolate of Fatima, The Blue Army, U.S.A., c/o 222 S. 3rd St., 62220-1985. Very Rev. John T. Myler, S.T.D., V.F., Spiritual Advisor. Tel: 618-234-1166. Priests 3; Total Staff 45; Total Assisted 150.

AVISTON. *Daughters of Isabella, Precious Blood Circle #718*, 248 W. Elm, P.O. Box 375, 62216. Tel: 618-228-7372. Ms. Amelia Wesselmann, Diocesan Chairperson.

CARLYLE. *Carlyle Priest Center*, 222 S. Third St., 62220. 17440 Highline Rd., 62231. Contact the Chancery, Tel: 618-277-8181.

CENTRALIA. **St. Mary's - Good Samaritan, Inc.*, 400 N. Pleasant Ave., 62801. Tel: 618-436-8000. Web: www.smgsi.com. Mr. Philip Gustafson, Pres., CEO. Co-Sponsored by the Franciscan Sisters of Mary and the Felician Sisters.

St. Mary's Hospital Foundation, 400 N. Pleasant Ave., 62801. Tel: 618-436-6455; Fax: 618-241-4811.

CHRISTOPHER. *Catholic Daughters of the Americas*, 805 S. Jesse, 62822. Tel: 618-724-4364. Mrs. Frances Furlin, Diocesan Chm.

MOUNT VERNON. *Good Samaritan Regional Health Center Foundation*, 605 N. 12th St., 62864. Tel: 618-241-2326; Fax: 618-241-4811.

SCOTT AFB. *Scott Air Force Base*, Scott AFB Chapel, 375 AW/HC, 320 Ward Dr., Bldg. 1620, 62225-5256. Tel: 618-256-3303; Fax: 618-256-8010.

WATERLOO. *Worldwide Marriage Encounter*, 721 Ridge Rd., 62298. Tel: 618-939-3846. Email: hermes@htc.net. Web: www.aweekendofdiscovery.org. Mr. John Hermes, Exec. Couple; Mrs. Karen Hermes, Exec. Couple.

INCORPORATED CEMETERIES

BELLEVILLE. *Catholic Diocese of Belleville Cemetery Association* Dee Dee Murray, Contact Person. Tel: 618-397-0181. Covers: Mt. Carmel, Belleville; Immaculate Conception, Centreville; Holy Cross, Fairview Hts; St. Phillips, East St. Louis, IL

Green Mount Catholic Cemetery of the Cathedral Congregation of Belleville

BREESE. *St. Dominic Roman Catholic Cemetery of Breese*

FAIRVIEW HEIGHTS. *St. Adalbert Association (An Illinois Religious Corporation)*

O'FALLON. *Mount Calvary Cemetery of St. Clare Roman Catholic Congregation*

VILLA RIDGE. *Calvary Cemetery of St. Patrick Roman Catholic Church of Cairo*

NECROLOGY

† Dobkowski, Rev. Msgr. Paulin J., (Retired)—Died May 12, 2011

† Abell, Donald E.—Died March 24, 2011

† Gore, Robert D., (Retired)—Died Jan. 20, 2011

† Linnemann, Eugene C., (Retired)—Died March 1, 2011

† MacPherson, Walter E., (Retired)—Died July 16, 2011

† Reinhardt, Leo S., (Retired)—Died June 3, 2011

† Stauder, Paul W., (Retired)—Died Nov. 16, 2011

An asterisk (*) denotes an organization that has established tax-exempt status directly with the IRS and is not covered by the USCCB Group Ruling.

Diocese of Biloxi

(Dioecesis Biloxiiensis)

Most Reverend

ROGER P. MORIN

Bishop of Biloxi; ordained April 15, 1971; appointed Auxiliary Bishop of New Orleans and Titular Bishop of Aulon February 11, 2003; ordained April 22, 2003; appointed Bishop of Biloxi March 2, 2009; installed April 27, 2009. *Office: 1790 Popps Ferry Rd., Biloxi, MS 39532-2118.*

WALK HUMBLY AND ACT JUSTLY

Chancery Office: 1790 Popps Ferry Rd., Biloxi, MS 39532-2118. Tel: 228-702-2100; Fax: 228-702-2125.

Most Reverend

JOSEPH LAWSON HOWZE, D.D.

Bishop Emeritus of Biloxi; ordained May 7, 1959; appointed Titular Bishop of Maxita and Auxiliary of Natchez-Jackson, November 8, 1972; ordained Bishop January 28, 1973; appointed Bishop of Biloxi March 1, 1977; installed June 6, 1977; retired May 15, 2001. *Mailing Address: P.O. Box 6067, Mobile, AL 36660-0067.*

ESTABLISHED MARCH 1, 1977.

Square Miles 9,653.

Comprises 17 counties in southern Mississippi: Jackson, Harrison, Hancock, George, Stone, Pearl River, Greene, Perry, Forrest, Lamar, Marion, Walthall, Wayne, Jones, Covington, Jefferson Davis and Lawrence.

Legal Title: "Catholic Diocese of Biloxi".
For legal titles of parishes and diocesan institutions, consult the Chancery Office.

STATISTICAL OVERVIEW

Personnel	
Bishop	1
Retired Bishops	1
Priests: Diocesan Active in Diocese	36
Priests: Diocesan Active Outside Diocese	1
Priests: Retired, Sick or Absent	14
Number of Diocesan Priests	51
Religious Priests in Diocese	25
Total Priests in Diocese	76
Extern Priests in Diocese	6
Ordinations:	
Diocesan Priests	3
Transitional Deacons	1
Permanent Deacons in Diocese	32
Total Brothers	12
Total Sisters	37
Parishes	
Parishes	42
With Resident Pastor:	
Resident Diocesan Priests	29
Resident Religious Priests	11
Without Resident Pastor:	
Administered by Priests	2
Missions	9
Professional Ministry Personnel:	
Sisters	7
Lay Ministers	14
Welfare	
Homes for the Aged	7
Total Assisted	475
Special Centers for Social Services	7
Total Assisted	436,810
Other Institutions	1
Total Assisted	2,999
Educational	
Diocesan Students in Other Seminaries	9
Total Seminarians	9
High Schools, Diocesan and Parish	4
Total Students	1,170
High Schools, Private	1
Total Students	357
Elementary Schools, Diocesan and Parish	10
Total Students	2,648
Catechesis/Religious Education:	
High School Students	908
Elementary Students	3,638
Total Students under Catholic Instruction	8,730
Teachers in the Diocese:	
Brothers	3
Sisters	3
Lay Teachers	345
Vital Statistics	
Receptions into the Church:	
Infant Baptism Totals	947
Minor Baptism Totals	131
Adult Baptism Totals	123
Received into Full Communion	162
First Communions	967
Confirmations	673
Marriages:	
Catholic	137
Interfaith	97
Total Marriages	234
Deaths	645
Total Catholic Population	58,702
Total Population	800,165

Former Bishop—Most Revs. JOSEPH LAWSON HOWZE, D.D. (Retired), ord. May 7, 1959; appt. Titular Bishop of Maxita and Auxiliary of Natchez-Jackson Nov. 8, 1972; ord. Bishop Jan. 28, 1973; appt. Bishop of Biloxi March 1, 1977; installed June 6, 1977; retired May 15, 2001; THOMAS J. RODI, ord. May 20, 1978; appt. Bishop of Biloxi May 15, 2001; ord. and installed July 2, 2001; appt. Archbishop of Mobile April 2, 2008; installed June 6, 2008.

Office of the Bishop—1790 Popps Ferry Rd., Biloxi, 39532-2118. Tel: 228-702-2111.

Vicar General—Rev. Msgr. T. DOMINICK FULLAM, J.C.L., V.G., 1790 Popps Ferry Rd., Biloxi, 39532-2118. Tel: 228-702-2112.

Moderator of Curia—Rev. Msgr. T. DOMINICK FULLAM, J.C.L., V.G., 1790 Popps Ferry Rd., Biloxi, 39532-2118. Tel: 228-702-2112.

Chancery Office—1790 Popps Ferry Rd., Biloxi, 39532-2118. Tel: 228-702-2100; Fax: 228-702-2125. Office Hours: Mon.-Fri. 8:30-5; All offices are at this address unless otherwise noted.

Pastoral Services—Deacon GAYDEN R. HARPER. Tel: 228-702-2107.

Special Delegate for Matrimonial Dispensations—Rev. Msgr. JOHN R. MCGRATH, J.C.L., J.V., V.F. Tel: 228-702-2117.

Chancellor—Sr. REBECCA A. RUTKOWSKI, O.S.F. Tel: 228-702-2136.

Office for Planning and Development—Deacon ROBERTO JIMENEZ, Dir. Tel: 228-702-2100.

Marriage Tribunal—

Judicial Vicar—Rev. Msgr. JOHN R. MCGRATH, J.C.L., J.V., V.F. Tel: 228-702-2117.

Promoter of Justice—Rev. Msgr. MICHAEL J. THORNTON, J.C.L.

Tribunal Judges—Rev. Msgr. JOHN R. MCGRATH, J.C.L., J.V., V.F.; Rev. CHARLES W. NUTTER, J.C.L.

Defenders of the Bond—Rev. Msgr. T. DOMINICK FULLAM, J.C.L., V.G.; Very Rev. THOMAS S. CONWAY, V.F.; Rev. Msgr. MICHAEL J. THORNTON, J.C.L.

Pro-Synodal Judge—Rev. Msgr. JAMES P. MCGOUGH, J.C.D. (Retired).

Advocates—Rev. PATRICK J. MOCKLER; Deacons JOHN R. HENDERSON; JOHN E. JENNINGS; ROBERTO JIMENEZ.

Secretaries and Ecclesiastical Notaries (Court of First Instance)—Rev. MICHAEL TRACEY; Mrs. CLAIRE D. JONES; Mrs. JENNIFER C. DENTON.

Auditor—VACANT.

Deans—Very Revs. DENNIS J. CARVER, V.F., West Coast Deanery; PETER F. MOCKLER, V.F., Central Coast Deanery; Rev. Msgr. JOHN R. MCGRATH, J.C.L., J.V., V.F., East Central Coast Deanery; Very Revs. MICHAEL P. AUSTIN, V.F., East Coast Deanery; THOMAS S. CONWAY, V.F., Northern Deanery.

College of Consultors—Very Rev. DENNIS J. CARVER, V.F.; Rev. Msgr. T. DOMINICK FULLAM, J.C.L., V.G.; Rev. LOUIS LOHAN; Rev. Msgr. JOHN R. MCGRATH, J.C.L., J.V., V.F.; Rev. CHARLES E. MCMAHON, S.S.J.; Very Rev. PETER F. MOCKLER, V.F.; Revs. CUTHBERT R. O'CONNELL; I. ANTHONY ARGUELLES, V.F.; MICHAEL P. O'CONNOR; Rev. Msgr. MICHAEL J. THORNTON, J.C.L.

Diocesan Attorney—KEVIN J. NECAISE, Mailing Address: P.O. Box 636, Gulfport, 39502. Tel: 228-586-0933.

Department of Finance—TAMMY W. DILORENZO, CPA, Dir. Tel: 228-702-2118.

Office of Information Technology—RICHARD A. YOUNG, Dir. Tel: 228-702-2171.

Office of Human Resources—Deacon GAYDEN R. HARPER. Tel: 228-702-2107.

Catholic Foundation of the Diocese of Biloxi, Inc.—Deacon ROBERTO JIMENEZ, Exec. Dir. Tel: 228-702-2100.

Mission Office—Very Rev. MICHAEL P. AUSTIN, V.F. Tel: 228-475-0777.

Office of Communication—VACANT, 1790 Popps Ferry Rd., Biloxi, 39532-2118. Tel: 228-702-2126; Fax: 228-702-2128. Email: gulfpinecatholic@biloxidiocese.org.

"Gulf Pine Catholic Newspaper"—TERRY DICKSON, Editor. Tel: 228-702-2126; 228-702-2127; Fax: 228-702-2128. Email: gulfpinecatholic@biloxidiocese.org.

Radio Ministry—VACANT. Tel: 228-702-2126; Fax: 228-702-2128.

Department of Education—

Office of Superintendent of Catholic Schools—Dr. MIKE LADNER, Supt. Tel: 228-702-2130; 228-702-2129; Dr. RHONDA P. CLARK, Asst. Supt. Tel: 228-702-2130; 228-702-2151.

Resource Center—Mr. LEO TRAHAN; JOY LANDRY.
Office of Special Education—Dr. MIKE LADNER; Dr. RHONDA P. CLARK.
Office of Religious Education—Mr. LEO TRAHAN, Dir. Tel: 228-702-2131.
CDB Religious Education, Inc.—Mr. LEO TRAHAN, Contact Person, 1790 Popps Ferry Rd., Biloxi, 39532-2118. Tel: 228-702-2131.
Office of Youth Ministry—BRAGG MOORE, Dir. Tel: 228-702-2142.
Catholic Boy Scouts—KAREN MONJU. Tel: 228-255-2806.
Campus Ministry—Very Rev. THOMAS S. CONWAY, V.F., Dir., 3117 W. Fourth St., Hattiesburg, 39401. Tel: 601-264-5192.
Priests' Continuing Education and Retreat Programs—Rev. CUTHBERT R. O'CONNELL, 236 S. Beach Blvd., Waveland, 39576.
Ecumenical & Interreligious Affairs—Mr. LEO TRAHAN, Contact Person. Tel: 228-702-2131.
Liturgy, Office of—Very Rev. MICHAEL P. AUSTIN, V.F., Dir., Mailing Address: St. Joseph the Worker Parish, P.O. Box 8549, Moss Point, 39562-0008. Tel: 228-475-0777.
Diocesan Liturgical Commission—Very Rev. MICHAEL P. AUSTIN, V.F., Chm.; Mr. PHIL BEINING, Music Liaison; Mr. KEVIN BENEFIELD; Ms. PAULA SPEARS; Sr. MARIE FRANCIS TRAN, F.M.S.R.; Deacons WILLIAM VRAZEL; BEN WIMBERLY JR.
Catholic Charities— Legal Title: Catholic Social and Community Services, Inc. *Administrative Office: 1790 Popps Ferry Rd., Biloxi, 39532-2118.* Tel: 228-702-2137. JENNIFER WILLIAMS, L.S.W., Diocesan Dir. Tel: 228-701-0555.
Hattiesburg Regional Office—2707 McInnis Loop, Hattiesburg, 39402. Tel: 601-261-5320. POLLY SUMRALL, Office Mgr.; JANNIE GREENE, Case Mgr.
Morning Star Pregnancy Care Center and Community Outreach of Jackson County—3503 Market St., Pascagoula, 39567. Tel: 228-567-0001; 228-567-0002. Case Managers: JENNIFER STACKHOUSE; HIEN NGUYEN.
Adoption Services—NANCY LOFTUS, L.S.W., 1450 North St., Gulfport, 39507. Tel: 228-701-0555.
Disaster Relief and Recovery—NANCY LOFTUS, L.S.W., 1450 North St., Gulfport, 39507. Tel: 228-701-0555.
St. Gerard Community Outreach—MARY MCLEOD, Case Mgr.; ANNE HALE, Office Mgr., 2074 Hwy. 90, Ste. D, Bay St. Louis, 39520. Tel: 228-467-2600.
Morning Star Pregnancy Care Center and Community Outreach— (Unplanned pregnancy services) ANN RIVERA, Office Mgr., 2204 24th Ave., Gulfport, 39507. Tel: 228-864-4221.
12 Baskets Food Bank—JENNIFER KEEGAN, Dir., 333 Cowan Rd., Gulfport, 39501. Tel: 228-822-0836.
Refugee Resettlement—MAGDA LELEAUX, Dir., 800 Division St., Biloxi, 39531. Tel: 228-374-6554.
Family Life Office—Tel: 228-702-2137.
Catholic Charities Housing Association of Biloxi, Inc.—
Santa Maria Retirement Apartments; Villa Maria Retirement Apartments—Most Rev. ROGER P. MORIN, D.D., Pres.; GREG CRAPO, Contact Person. Tel: 228-702-2100.
Samaritan Housing, Inc.—Most Rev. ROGER P. MORIN, D.D., Pres.; GREG CRAPO, Contact Person. Tel: 228-702-2100.
Notre Dame de la Mer, Inc.—Most Rev. ROGER P. MORIN, D.D., Pres.; GREG CRAPO, Contact Person. Tel: 228-702-2100.
Gabriel Manor, Inc.—Most Rev. ROGER P. MORIN, D.D., Pres.; GREG CRAPO, Contact Person. Tel: 228-702-2100.
Caritas Manor, Inc.—Most Rev. ROGER P. MORIN, D.D., Pres.; GREG CRAPO, Contact Person. Tel: 228-702-2100.
Carlow Manor—Most Rev. ROGER P. MORIN, D.D., Pres.; GREG CRAPO, Contact Person. Tel: 228-702-2100.
Gabriel Manor II, Inc.—Most Rev. ROGER P. MORIN, D.D., Pres.; GREG CRAPO, Contact Person. Tel: 228-702-2100.
Apostleship of the Sea—Port of Gulfport: Deacon JOHN R. HENDERSON.
Vietnamese Apostolate—Rev. JAMES CHAU PHAM, C.Ss.R.
Prison Apostolate—Jackson County Jails: Deacon AL STOCKERT. Tel: 228-702-2107. Harrison County Jails: Deacon AL STOCKERT. Tel: 228-702-2107. Hancock County Jails: Deacon AL STOCKERT. Tel: 228-702-2107. South Mississippi Correctional Facility: Rev. Msgr. MICHAEL J. THORNTON, J.C.L.
Diocesan Boards and Committees—
Association of Priests (Diocese of Biloxi and Jackson)—Most Revs. ROGER P. MORIN, D.D., Bishop of Biloxi & Co-Chm.; JOSEPH N. LATINO, Bishop of Jackson & Co-Chm.; Rev. Msgr. MICHAEL J. THORNTON, J.C.L., Pres.; Rev. THOMAS MCGING, Sec., Treas. & Pres.-Elect. Trustees: Rev. PATRICK J. MOCKLER; Very Rev. THOMAS S. CONWAY, V.F.; Rev. CHARLES BUCCIANTINI; Rev. Msgr. PATRICK FARRELL.
Building and Real Estate Committee—Very Rev. MICHAEL P. AUSTIN, V.F., Chm.; CHUCK COLLINS; GEORGE DENMARK; KELEAL HASSIN JR.; GERALD HOPKINS; BOB MANDAL; HOPPY ALLRED; ROBERT STARKS; STEPHEN STOJCICH; WESLEY TOCHE III.
Catholic Foundation-Diocese of Biloxi—Most Rev. ROGER P. MORIN, D.D., Pres.; Rev. Msgr. T. DOMINICK FULLAM, J.C.L., V.G., Vice Pres.; Deacon ROBERTO JIMENEZ, Exec. Dir.; HENRY N. DICK III, Esq.; JOSEPH HUDSON; SALVADOR DOMINO; TED LONGO; VONRETTA J. SINGLETON; ROBERT TUCEI; WILLIAM WARD; TAMMY W. DILORENZO, CPA, Advisor.
Catholic Housing Board—Most Rev. ROGER P. MORIN, D.D., Pres.; GREG CRAPO, Sec.; Rev. Msgr. T. DOMINICK FULLAM, J.C.L., V.G.; Rev. BERNARD P. FARRELL; TAMMY W. DILORENZO, CPA; SALVADOR DOMINO; GARY YOUNG; Rev. Msgr. JOHN R. MCGRATH, J.C.L., J.V., V.F.
Finance Council—Most Rev. ROGER P. MORIN, D.D.; Rev. Msgr. T. DOMINICK FULLAM, J.C.L., V.G.; RICHARD ECKERT; JAMES FARRELL; HENRY FOX; M.C. PRINCY HARRISON; WILLIAM KEARNEY; BILLY KNIGHT SR.; JERRY L. LEVENS; JOSEPH P. HUDSON; Very Rev. PETER F. MOCKLER, V.F.; STEVE MONTAGNET JR.; JOHN P. MYERS; Deacon ROBERTO JIMENEZ.
Insurance Committee—Most Rev. ROGER P. MORIN, D.D.; Rev. Msgr. T. DOMINICK FULLAM, J.C.L., V.G.; Dr. MIKE LADNER; GREG CRAPO. Advisor: TAMMY W. DILORENZO, CPA.
Mission Board—Most Rev. ROGER P. MORIN, D.D.; Very Rev. MICHAEL P. AUSTIN, V.F.
Personnel Board—Rev. Msgr. MICHAEL J. THORNTON, J.C.L.; Very Rev. DENNIS J. CARVER, V.F.; Rev. BERNARD P. FARRELL; Rev. Msgr. T. DOMINICK FULLAM, J.C.L., V.G.; Rev. ROBERT P. HIGGINBOTHAM; Rev. Msgr. JOHN R. MCGRATH, J.C.L., J.V., V.F.
Presbyteral Council—Most Rev. ROGER P. MORIN, D.D., Pres.; Rev. Msgr. JOHN R. MCGRATH, J.C.L., J.V., V.F.; Very Revs. MICHAEL P. AUSTIN, V.F.; DENNIS J. CARVER, V.F.; THOMAS S. CONWAY, V.F.; PETER F. MOCKLER, V.F.; Rev. Msgr. T. DOMINICK FULLAM, J.C.L., V.G.; Revs. SERGIO A. BALDERAS; LOUIS LOHAN; PATRICK J. MOCKLER; MICHAEL P. O'CONNOR; JOSEPH TRUONG Q. TRINH; JOSEPH M. UKO; STEVEN WILSON, C.Ss.R.
Miscellaneous Apostolates—
Campaign for Human Development—GREG CRAPO, 1790 Popps Ferry Rd., Biloxi, 39532-2118. Tel: 228-702-3001.
Catholic Relief Services—GREG CRAPO, 1790 Popps Ferry Rd., Biloxi, 39532-2118. Tel: 228-702-3001.
Catholic University, Friends of—Rev. Msgr. T. DOMINICK FULLAM, J.C.L., V.G., 1790 Popps Ferry Rd., Biloxi, 39532-2118.
Charismatic Renewal—Rev. GEORGE R. KITCHIN, Dir., St. James Parish, 366 Cowan-Lorraine Rd., Gulfport, 39507.
Council of the St. Vincent de Paul Society—SUSAN TAYLOR, Pres. Tel: 228-388-1837.
Cursillo and Retreats—Rev. MICHAEL P. O'CONNOR, Spiritual Dir., 14595 Vidalia Rd., Pass Christian, 39571. Tel: 228-255-7560.
Deaf and Disabled, Office of the—Mr. GREGORY K. CRAPO, B.S., M.B.A, Dir., de l'Epee Deaf Center, Inc., 1450 North St., Gulfport, 39507. Tel: 228-897-2280 (Voice-TTY); 866-939-7209 (Video Phone); Fax: 228-897-2462.
Latin American Apostolate— Mission-Saltillo, Mexico, co-sponsored with Diocese of Jackson Rev. BENJAMIN PIOVAN, Parroquia San Miguel Arcangel, Av. Central 4649, Col. Vista Hermosa, Saltillo, Coah CP 25010 Mexico.
Legion of Mary—Contact: Office of Pastoral Svcs. Tel: 228-702-2107.
Permanent Diaconate Program—1790 Popps Ferry Rd., Biloxi, 39532. Tel: 228-702-2107. Deacons GAYDEN R. HARPER, Dir.; RICHARD A. HOLLINGSWORTH, Assoc. Dir. Formation; RALPH TORRELLI, Continuing Educ.
Pontifical Association of the Holy Childhood—Very Rev. MICHAEL P. AUSTIN, V.F., Dir., Mailing Address: P.O. Box 8549, Moss Point, 39563-0549. Tel: 228-475-0777.
Propagation of the Faith—Very Rev. MICHAEL P. AUSTIN, V.F., Dir., Mailing Address: P.O. Box 8549, Moss Point, 39563-0549. Tel: 228-475-0777.
Vocations—Very Rev. DENNIS J. CARVER, V.F., Dir., 22342 Evangeline Rd., Pass Christian, 39571. Tel: 228-452-4686; Rev. SERGIO A. BALDERAS, Asst. Vocations Dir. to Hispanic Seminarians, 2090 Pass Rd., Biloxi, 39531-3130. Tel: 228-388-3887.
CDB Seminarian Education, Inc.—Very Rev. DENNIS J. CARVER, V.F., Contact Person, 1790 Popps Ferry Rd., Biloxi, 39532-2118. Tel: 228-452-4686.
Victim Assistance Coordinator—Sr. MARY JO MIKE, O.S.F., 1046 Beach Blvd., Biloxi, 39530. Tel: 228-806-5677. Email: smaryjm@aol.com.
Construction Manager for the Diocese of Biloxi—STEVE LABARRE. Tel: 228-702-2148; Cell: 228-216-5222. Email: slabarre@biloxidiocese.org; JACK ROUSSO. Tel: 228-702-2149; Cell: 251-689-8483. Email: jrousso@biloxidiocese.org.

CLERGY, PARISHES, MISSIONS AND PAROCHIAL SCHOOLS

CITY OF BILOXI

(HARRISON COUNTY)

1—CATHEDRAL OF THE NATIVITY OF THE BLESSED VIRGIN MARY (1843) Rev. Msgr. John R. McGrath, Rector; Rev. Bernard J. Papania Jr.; Deacon Ben Wimberly Jr. In Res., Rev. Gregory Barras.
Res.: 870 Howard Ave., P.O. Box 367, 39533. Tel: 228-374-1717; Fax: 228-374-1773. Email: office@nativitybvmcathedral.org.
School—(Grades PreK-6), 1046 Beach Blvd., 39530. Tel: 228-432-2269; Fax: 228-432-9421. Web: www.nativitybvm.org. Sr. Mary Jo Mike, O.S.F., Prin.; Kelly Pennell, Librarian. Sisters 1; Lay Teachers 14; Students 188.
Catechesis/Religious Program— Twinned with Nativity BVM Parish. Students 82.

2—BLESSED FRANCIS XAVIER SEELOS (2005) Rev. Steven Wilson, C.Ss.R.
Mailing Address: P.O. Box 347, 39533-0347. Tel: 228-374-0117; Fax: 228-374-0118.
Res.: 724 Bradford St., 39530. Tel: 228-374-0117; Fax: 228-374-0118.
Catechesis/Religious Program—P.O. Box 347, 39533. Tel: 228-374-0117. Students 24.

3—CHURCH OF THE VIETNAMESE MARTYRS (2000), (Vietnamese), [JC] Rev. James Chau Pham, C.Ss.R.
Res.: 172 Oak St., 39530. Tel: 228-374-1116; Fax: 228-374-9344.
Catechesis/Religious Program—Tel: 228-432-7724. Students 170.

4—ST. LOUIS (1957) Closed. For inquiries for sacramental records, please see Blessed Francis Xavier Seelos, Biloxi.

5—ST. MARY (1967) Rev. Msgr. T. Dominick Fullam.
Res.: 8343 Woolmarket Rd., 39532. Tel: 228-392-7500; Fax: 228-392-4552.
Catechesis/Religious Program—Tel: 228-392-1999; Fax: 228-392-4552. Students 112.

6—ST. MICHAEL (1917) Rev. Gregory Barras.
Res.: 177 First St., P.O. Box 523, 39533. Tel: 228-435-5578; Fax: 228-435-5579. Email: stmichaelschurch@cableone.net. Web: www.stmichaelchurchbiloxi.com.
Catechesis/Religious Program—Students 24.

7—OUR LADY OF FATIMA (1957) Revs. Patrick J. Mockler; Ryan M. McCoy, Parochial Vicar. In Res., Rev. Msgr. Francis Farrell (Retired).
Res.: 2090 Pass Rd., 39531. Tel: 228-388-3887; Fax: 228-388-7069. Email: fatima@cableone.net. Web: www.fatima-biloxi.com.
School—(Grades PreK-6), 320 Jim Money Rd., 39531. Tel: 228-388-3602; Fax: 228-385-1140. Web: www.fatimafalcons.org. Elizabeth Williams, Librarian. Lay Teachers 15; Students 231.
Catechesis/Religious Program—Tel: 228-388-5737. Students 163.

8—OUR MOTHER OF SORROWS (1914), (African American), Rev. Steven Wilson, C.Ss.R.
Mailing Address: P.O. Box 347, 39533-0347.
Res.: 803 Division St., 39530. Tel: 228-435-0007; Fax: 228-435-7555.
Catechesis/Religious Program—Students 26.

9—SACRED HEART (1921) Revs. Robert P. Higginbotham; Sergio A. Balderas (Mexico).
Res.: 10446 Le Moyne Blvd., P.O. Box 6819, D'Iberville, 39540. Tel: 228-392-4526; Fax: 228-392-0684.
School—(Grades PreK-6), 10482 Le Moyne Blvd., D'Iberville, 39540. Tel: 228-392-4180; Fax: 228-392-4859. Jane Sema, Prin.; Gerri Weldon, Librarian. Lay Teachers 8; Students 127.
Catechesis/Religious Program—Tel: 228-392-4180; 228-392-5509. Sr. Julia Marie Burke, R.S.M., D.R.E. Students 163.

OUTSIDE THE CITY OF BILOXI

BASSFIELD, JEFFERSON DAVIS CO., ST. PETER (1904), (Irish), [CEM 2] [JC 2] Rev. Peter Varghese, C.M.I.; Deacon Robert Everard.
Res.: 4135 Hwy. 42, P.O. Box 10, 39421. Tel: 601-943-5104; 601-943-6688 (Office); Fax: 601-943-8055.
Catechesis/Religious Program—Tel: 601-943-6259. Amber Harvey, D.R.E. Students 51.

Mission—St. Mary's Prentiss, Jefferson Davis Co.
Mission—St. Lawrence P.O. Box 16, Monticello, Lawrence Co. 39654. Tel: 601-587-8017.

BAY ST. LOUIS, HANCOCK CO.

1—OUR LADY OF THE GULF (1847) [CEM] Rev. Michael Tracey; Deacons Eddie Renz; Mike Harris; Kathleen LeBlanc, Pastoral Assoc.
Res.: 228 S. Beach Blvd., 39520. Tel: 228-467-6509; Fax: 228-467-2960. Email: olgchurc@bellsouth.net. Web: www.olgchurch.net.
School—Holy Trinity Catholic Elementary, (Grades PreK-6), 301 Second St., 39520. Tel: 228-467-5158; Fax: 228-467-9742. Web: www.holytrinitycatholic-.net. Janet Buras, Prin. Lay Teachers 23; Students 332.
Catechesis/Religious Program—Tel: 228-467-6509. Students 59.

2—ST. ROSE DE LIMA (1924), (African American), Rev. Donald Murrin, S.V.D.
Res.: 301 S. Necaise Ave., 39520. Tel: 228-467-7347; Fax: 228-467-7740.
Catechesis/Religious Program—Tel: 228-363-1017. Mrs. Joan Thomas, D.R.E. Students 46.

CLERMONT HARBOR, HANCOCK CO., ST. ANN (1915) [CEM] Rev. George Manchapilly, C.M.I.
Res.: 5858 Lower Bay Rd., Bay Saint Louis, 39520. Tel: 228-467-5128; Fax: 228-467-5638. Email: stannscathparish@att.net.
Catechesis/Religious Program—Students 38.
Chapel—St. Joseph Chapel 5383 Hwy. 604, Pearlington, 39572. Tel: 228-342-3459; Fax: 228-533-0155.
Chapel—Holy Infant of Good Health Chapel

COLUMBIA, MARION CO., HOLY TRINITY (1959) Rev. Martin Joseph Gillespie.
Res.: 1429 N. Park Ave., 39429. Tel: 601-736-3136; Fax: 601-736-1920. Email: holytrinitycc@gmail.com. Web: www.holytrinityonline.com.
Catechesis/Religious Program—Jessica Martin, D.R.E. (Holy Trinity Catholic Church). Students 43.
Mission—St. Paul the Apostle 702 Union St., P.O. Box 470, Tylertown, Walthall Co. 39667. Tel: 601-876-6422; Fax: 601-876-6422.
Catechesis/Religious Program—Audrey Rink, D.R.E.

DELISLE, HARRISON CO.

1—MOST HOLY TRINITY PARISH (1869) Rev. David A. Hamm, S.T.; Deacon Lucien F. Moragas.
Mailing Address: 9062 Kiln DeLisle Rd., Pass Christian, 39571.
Res.: 25220 St. Stephen Rd., Pass Christian, 39571. Tel: 228-255-1294; Fax: 228-255-7479.
Catechesis/Religious Program—Melanie Walrod, D.R.E. Students 379.

2—ST. STEPHEN (1874) Closed. For inquiries for parish records see Most Holy Trinity, Pass Christian.

GAUTIER, JACKSON CO., ST. MARY (1968) Rev. Charles W. Nutter.
Res.: 809 De La Pointe Rd., 39553. Tel: 228-497-2364; Fax: 228-497-5887. Email: stmarygautier@yahoo.com.
Catechesis/Religious Program— MaryAnn Meehan, D.R.E. Students 121.

GULFPORT, HARRISON CO.

1—ST. ANN (1939) Very Rev. Peter F. Mockler.
Res.: 23529 Hwy. 53, 39503. Tel: 228-832-2560; Fax: 228-832-2560. Web: www.stannparishlizana.org.
Catechesis/Religious Program—Tel: 228-831-9452. Robert Earl Lizana, D.R.E. Students 83.
Mission—Our Lady of Chartres Big Creek Rd., Delmas Dedeaux, Harrison Co. 39503. Tel: 228-832-2560; Fax: 228-832-2560.

2—ST. JAMES (1898) [CEM] Rev. George R. Kitchin; Deacons John R. Henderson, Pastoral Assoc.; Rick Conason.
Res.: 366 Cowan Rd., 39507. Tel: 228-896-6059; Fax: 228-896-5498.
School—(Grades PreK-6), 603 West Ave., 39507. Tel: 228-896-6631; Fax: 228-896-6638. Mrs. Jennifer Broadus, Prin.; Connie Favret, Librarian. Sisters of Mercy (Ennis, Ireland) 1; Lay Teachers 18; Students 394.
Catechesis/Religious Program— Rob Russo, D.R.E. Students 151.

3—ST. JOHN THE EVANGELIST (1900) Revs. Joseph M. Uko; Gerard M. Cleary (Retired).
Res.: 2414 17th St., 39501. Tel: 228-864-2272; Fax: 228-864-2273. Email: stjohnthee@cableone.net.
High School—St. Patrick High School, 18300 Hwy. 67, 39532-8655. Tel: 228-702-0500; Fax: 228-702-0511. Email: btrosclair@biloxidiocese.org. Web: www.stpatrickhighschool.net. Bobby Trosclair, Prin. Brothers 1; Lay Teachers 37; Students 510.
Catechesis/Religious Program—Sr. Mary Kealy, P.B.V.M., D.R.E. Students 42.

4—ST. JOSEPH CATHOLIC CHURCH (Northwood Hills) (1966) Rev. George E. Murphy.
Res.: 12290 DePew Rd., 39503. Tel: 228-832-3244; 228-832-1166; Fax: 228-832-1166. Email: stjosephgulfport@bellsouth.net. Web: www.stjosephcc.com.
Catechesis/Religious Program— Mrs. Michele Stoner, D.R.E. Students 105.

5—ST. THERESE (1932), (African American), Rev. John J. McBrearty, S.S.J.
Mailing Address: P.O. Box 263, 39502.
Res.: 3521 19th St., 39501. Tel: 228-863-0624; Fax: 228-863-2531.
Catechesis/Religious Program—Sr. Carmelita Mulry, S.H.Sp., D.R.E. Students 51.

HATTIESBURG, FORREST CO.

1—HOLY ROSARY (1949), (African American), Rev. Kenneth Ramon-Landry.
Res.: 900 Dabbs St., 39401. Tel: 601-584-6528; Fax: 601-584-9533.

2—SACRED HEART (1900) [CEM] Revs. Kenneth Ramon-Landry; Jose Vazquez; Deacons Warren Goff; Tom LeBlanc, (Retired).
Res.: 313 Walnut St., P.O. Box 1027, 39401. Tel: 601-583-9404; Fax: 601-583-9486. Email: sacheartchurch@aol.com. Web: www.sacredhearthattiesburg.org.
School—(Grades PreK-6), 608 Southern Ave. - Elementary, 39401. Tel: 601-583-8683; Fax: 601-583-8684. Email: bmccrory@biloxidiocese.org. Web: www.shshattiesburg.com. Brian McCrory, Prin.; Karyn Walsh, Librarian. Lay Teachers 54; Asst. Teachers 10; Students 697.
High School—(Grades 7-12), 510 W. Pine St., 39401. Tel: 601-450-5736; Fax: 601-450-5739.
Catechesis/Religious Program—Tel: 601-583-9404; Fax: 601-583-9486. Email: jbeck02@hotmail.com. Jean Beckett, D.R.E. Students 154.

3—ST. THOMAS AQUINAS (1968), (University of Southern Mississippi-Student Parish) Very Rev. Thomas S. Conway.
Res.: 3117 W. Fourth St., 39401. Tel: 601-264-5192; Fax: 601-264-0834.
Catechesis/Religious Program—Tel: 601-270-5789. Kelly Lamunyon, D.R.E. Students 295.

KILN, HANCOCK CO., ANNUNCIATION (1869) [CEM] Very Rev. John T. Noone.
Res.: 5370 Kiln-DeLisle Rd., 39556. Tel: 228-255-1800; Fax: 228-255-1894. Email: annunciationkiln@hughes.net.
Catechesis/Religious Program—Mollie Nunez, D.R.E. Students 95.

LAUREL, JONES CO., IMMACULATE CONCEPTION (1887) Rev. Msgr. Michael J. Thornton; Revs. Anthony Doan Tran; Ignacio Jimenez Morales, Parochial Vicar; Deacons Richard Hollingsworth; David Hughes Sr.; Mrs. Suzie Middleton, Youth Min.
Res.: 833 W. Sixth St., 39440. Tel: 601-426-3473; Fax: 601-426-3890.
Catechesis/Religious Program—Tel: 601-426-3473. Students 119.

LONG BEACH, HARRISON CO., ST. THOMAS THE APOSTLE (1903) Rev. Louis Lohan.
Mailing Address: P.O. Box 1529, 39560.
Res.: 725 N. Nicholson, P.O. Box 1529, 39560. Tel: 228-863-1610; Fax: 228-868-6068. Email: stthomaschurch@cableone.net. Web: www.stthomaschurchlb.org.
School—St. Vincent de Paul Elementary, (Grades PreK-12), 4321 Espy Ave., 39560. Tel: 228-863-6876; Fax: 228-222-6003. Email: smcallister@biloxidiocese.org. Web: www.svdpcatholicschool.org. Sherry McAllister, Prin.; Susan Hughes, Librarian. Lay Teachers 38; Students 340.
Catechesis/Religious Program—Tel: 228-868-3774. Students 302.

LUMBERTON, LAMAR CO., OUR LADY OF PERPETUAL HELP (1922) [CEM] Rev. Truong Quang Trinh.
Res.: 379 W. Seneca Rd., 39455-7728. Tel: 601-796-3051 (Office); 601-796-3053 (Rectory); Fax: 601-796-3023. Email: olphst@megagate.com.
Catechesis/Religious Program—Students 14.
Mission—St. Joseph 17 Bilbo Hill, P.O. Box 202, Poplarville, Pearl River Co. 39470. Tel: 601-795-9164. Email: stjosephcat4461@bellsouth.net.

MOSS POINT, JACKSON CO., ST. JOSEPH (1950) Very Rev. Michael P. Austin; Deacons Emery E. Elder; Frank W. Martin.
Res.: 4114 First St., P.O. Box 8549, 39562-8549. Tel: 228-475-0777; Fax: 228-475-3672. Email: stjosephmoss@aol.com.
Catechesis/Religious Program—Students 79.
Mission—St. Ann P.O. Box 8549, Hurley, Jackson Co. 39562-8549. Tel: 228-588-0599; Fax: 228-588-0599.

OCEAN SPRINGS, JACKSON CO.

1—ST. ALPHONSUS (1860) Revs. Henry McInerney; Thomas White; Deacon Gregory Miller.
Res.: 502 Jackson Ave., 39564. Tel: 228-875-5419; Fax: 228-875-5410. Email: stals@cableone.net.
School—(Grades PreK-6), 504 Jackson Ave., 39564. Tel: 228-875-5329; Fax: 228-875-3584. Dr. Pamela Rogers, Prin.; Katherine Mendoza, Librarian. Lay Teachers 16; Students 163.
Catechesis/Religious Program—Tel: 228-872-2652. Pat Cronin, D.R.E. Students 208.

2—ST. ELIZABETH ANN SETON (1975) Rev. Bernard P. Farrell; Deacon Martin Finnegan.
Res.: 4900 Riley Rd., 39564. Tel: 228-875-0654; Fax: 228-875-6852. Email: office@stelseton.com.
Catechesis/Religious Program—Linda Holtorf, D.R.E. Students 310.

PASCAGOULA, JACKSON CO.

1—OUR LADY OF VICTORIES (1855) Rev. I. Anthony Arguelles.
Res.: 510 Convent St., P.O. Box 368, 39568. Tel: 228-762-1653; Fax: 228-762-2546. Email: ourladyofvictori@bellsouth.net.
Catechesis/Religious Program—Tel: 228-623-4747. Michele Hill, D.R.E. Students 21.

2—ST. PETER THE APOSTLE (1907), (African American), [CEM] Rev. Charles E. McMahon, S.S.J.
Mailing Address: P.O. Box 876, 39568.
Res.: 1715 Telephone Rd., 39567. Tel: 228-762-1759; Fax: 228-762-1709.
Catechesis/Religious Program—Lena Sanders, D.R.E.; Sr. Mary Kay Schreier, D.C., D.R.E. Students 44.

3—SACRED HEART (1962) Rev. Michael Kelleher.
Mailing Address: P.O. Box 2190, 39569. Tel: 228-762-1837; Fax: 228-762-1958.
Res.: 3702 Quinn Dr., 39581. Tel: 228-762-1837.
School—Resurrection School-Elementary, (Grades PreK-6), 3704 Quinn Dr., 39581-2356. Tel: 228-762-7207; Fax: 228-762-0611. Elizabeth K. Benefield, Prin.; Linda Wiggins, Librarian; Cathy Groff, Librarian. Lay Teachers 25; Students 336.
Catechesis/Religious Program—Students 19.

PASS CHRISTIAN, HARRISON CO.

1—HOLY FAMILY PARISH (2005, Pineville) [CEM] Very Rev. Dennis J. Carver; Rev. Thomas J. Pazheparambil; Deacon William Vrazel; Sr. Jackie Tarrant, R.S.M., Pastoral Assoc.
Mailing Address: 22342 Evangeline Dr., 39571.
Res.: 22410 Glad Acres, 39571. Tel: 228-452-4686; Fax: 228-452-5488. Web: www.holyfamilyparish.cc.
School—St. Vincent de Paul Elementary, (Grades PreK-6) Tel: 228-863-6876; Fax: 228-863-9537. Mrs. Elizabeth Fortenberry, Prin.; Susan Hewes, Librarian. Lay Teachers 48; Students 385.
Catechesis/Religious Program— Linden Williams, D.R.E.; Craig Spence, Youth Dir. Students 90.

2—OUR MOTHER OF MERCY (1911), (African American), [JC] Rev. Batholomew Enslow, S.S.J.
Res.: 216 Saucier Ave., 39571. Tel: 228-452-4514; 228-452-6309; Fax: 228-452-4514.
Catechesis/Religious Program—Tel: 228-452-4002. Students 54.

3—ST. PAUL, Closed. For inquiries for parish records contact Holy Family, Pass Christian.

4—SACRED HEART (Dedeaux) (1967) Rev. Michael P. O'Connor; Deacon Roberto Jimenez.
Res. & Office: 14595 Vidalia Rd., 39571. Tel: 228-255-3381; 228-255-7560 (Office); Fax: 228-255-7888 (Office).
Catechesis/Religious Program—Students 159.
Station—Cursillo Center, (Dedeaux), Tel: 228-255-0430.

PEARLINGTON, HANCOCK CO., ST. JOSEPH (1939) [JC] Closed. For inquiries for sacramental records, please see St. Ann, Clermont Harbor.

PICAYUNE, PEARL RIVER CO., ST. CHARLES BORROMEO (1950) Rev. Michael E. Snyder; Deacon Douglas R. McNair.
Res.: 1020 Fifth St., 39466. Tel: 601-798-4779. Email: stcborromeo@att.net. Web: www.scborromeo.org.
School—St. Charles Borromeo Catholic Elementary School, (Grades PreK-8), 1006 Goodyear Blvd., 39466. Tel: 601-799-0860; Fax: 601-798-4749. Email: stcb@att.net. Web: scborromeo.org/school. Ellen Loper, Prin. Lay Teachers 13; Students 106.
Catechesis/Religious Program—Tel: 601-749-5008 (Youth Min.); 601-799-0860 (Children's Min.); Fax: 601-798-4749. Ellen Loper, D.R.E. & Prin. Students 340.

PINEVILLE, HARRISON CO., OUR LADY OF LOURDES (Pass Christian) (1973) Closed. Please see Holy Family, Pass Christian.

VANCLEAVE, JACKSON CO., HOLY SPIRIT CATHOLIC CHURCH (1980) Rev. Thang John Pham; Deacon John E. Jennings.
Res.: 6705 Jim Ramsey Rd., 39565. Tel: 228-826-4008; Fax: 228-826-1650.
Catechesis/Religious Program—(Holy Spirit & Christ the King combined) 195.
Mission—Christ the King 10601 Daisy Vestry, Latimer, Jackson Co. 39565. Tel: 228-392-0340.

WAVELAND, HANCOCK CO., ST. CLARE (1919) Rev. Cuthbert R. O'Connell.
Res.: 236 S. Beach Blvd., P.O. Box 500, 39576. Tel: 228-467-9275; Fax: 228-467-9278. Email: stclarecatholic@yahoo.com.
Catechesis/Religious Program—Tel: 228-424-8771. Noel Phillips, D.R.E. Students 51.

WAYNESBORO, WAYNE CO., ST. BERNADETTE (1977) [JC 2] Rev. Msgr. Michael J. Thornton; Rev. Anthony

Doan Tran.
Res.: 401 Mississippi Dr., 39367. Tel: 601-735-9420.
Catechesis/Religious Program—Students 11.
Mission—Holy Trinity 911 Jackson Ave., P.O. Box 896, Leakesville, Perry Co. 39451. Tel: 601-394-6761.

WHITE CYPRESS, HANCOCK CO., ST. MATTHEW THE APOSTLE (1982) Rev. Satish Baburao Adhav (India).
Mailing Address: P.O. Box 919, Kiln, 39556.
Res.: 27074 St. Matthew Church Rd., Perkinston, 39573. Tel: 228-255-7720; Fax: 228-255-7786. Email: stshadhav@gmail.com.
Catechesis/Religious Program—Students 152.

WIGGINS, STONE CO., ST. FRANCIS XAVIER (1961) [JC] Rev. Fintan J. Kilmurray.
Res.: 1026 E. Central Ave., 39577. Tel: 601-928-2182; Fax: 601-928-2875.
Church: Tel: 601-928-2182.
Catechesis/Religious Program—Tel: 601-528-9778. Leona O'Neil, D.R.E. Students 107.
Mission—St. Lucy 125 Scott Rd., Lucedale, George Co. 39452. Tel: 601-947-9968. Deacon Curba L. Merrill.
Station—Perkinston Junior College Perkinston.

Chaplains of Public Institutions

BILOXI. *Keesler Airforce Base*. Revs. Mitchell Zygaldo, Major, John W. Schuetze, Captain.
V.A. Center. Vacant.

COLUMBIA. *Industrial and Training School*. Rev. Martin Joseph Gillespie.

GULFPORT. *Naval Const. Bn. Center*. Vacant.

HATTIESBURG. *University of Southern Mississippi*. Very Rev. Thomas S. Conway, V.F.

LEAKESVILLE. *South Mississippi Correctional Institution*. Rev. Msgr. Michael J. Thornton, J.C.L.
Unassigned Rev. Bartosz T. Kunat.

Retired:
Most Rev.—
Howze, Joseph Lawson, D.D.
Rev. Msgrs.—
Farrell, Francis
McGough, James P., J.C.D.
Mercier, Joseph
Revs.—
Cleary, Gerard M.
Fannon, Noel
Izral, John
Kelly, John J.
Kozak, Remigius A.
Lynch, Antone
McDermott, Patrick M.
O'Shaughnessy, Patrick
Phan, Dominic

Permanent Deacons:
Baglioni, Victor, (Retired)
Bradford, L. Paul, Sr., Our Lady of Fatima, Biloxi
Conason, Rick, St. James, Gulfport
Elder, Emery, St. Joseph, Moss Point
Everard, Robert, St. Peter, Bassfield
Finnegan, Martin, St. Elizabeth Seton, Ocean Springs
Gaule, Harold, (Retired)
Gilly, Michael, Our Lady of Victories, Pascagoula
Goff, Warren P., Sr., Sacred Heart, Hattiesburg
Harper, Gayden R., Our Lady of Victories, Pascagoula
Harris, Michael M., Our Lady of the Gulf, Bay St. Louis
Henderson, John R., St. James, Gulfport
Hollingsworth, Richard A., Immaculate Conception, Laurel
Hughes, David O., Immaculate Conception, Laurel
Hunter, Jack, (Retired)
Jennings, John E., Holy Spirit, Vancleave
Jimenez, Roberto, Sacred Heart, Pass Christian
Landry, Melvin J., Blessed Francis Xavier Seelos, Biloxi
LeBlanc, Tom, (Retired)
Martin, Frank W., St. Ann Mission, Hurley
McNair, Douglas R., St. Charles Borromeo, Picayune
Merrill, Curba L., St. Lucy, Lucedale
Miller, Gregory, St. Alphonsus, Ocean Springs
Miller, Tom, (Retired)
Moragas, Lucien F., Jr., Most Holy Trinity, Delisle
Renz, Edward, Our Lady of the Gulf, Bay St. Louis
Stockert, Al, St. Mary, Biloxi
Torrelli, Ralph, St. Thomas, Hattiesburg
Vancourt, Ernest, St. Thomas the Apostle, Long Beach
Vrazel, William, Holy Family, Pass Christian
Walker, Charles, (Retired)
Wimberly, Ben, Jr., Nativity B.V.M. Cathedral, Biloxi

INSTITUTIONS LOCATED IN THE DIOCESE

[A] HIGH SCHOOLS, INTERPAROCHIAL

BILOXI. *St. Patrick Catholic High School*, (Grades 7-12), (Coed), 18300 St. Patrick Rd., 39532. Tel: 228-702-0500; Fax: 228-702-0511. Email: btrosclair@biloxidiocese.org. Web: www.stpatrickhighschool.net. Bobby Trosclair, Prin.; Margaret Evans, Librarian. Lay Teachers 35; Students 475.

BAY ST. LOUIS. *Our Lady Academy*, (Grades 7-12), (Girls), 222 S. Beach Blvd., 39520-4320. Tel: 228-467-7048; Fax: 228-467-1666. Email: tiffany.lindmark@ourladyacademy.com. Web: www.ourladyacademy.com. Tiffany Lindmark, Prin.; Virginia Gex, Librarian. Sisters of Mercy 2; Lay Teachers 20; Students 221.

PASCAGOULA. *Resurrection Middle/Sr. School*, (Grades 7-12), (Coed), 520 Watts Ave., 39567. Tel: 228-762-3353; Fax: 228-769-1226. Email: kmckenna@rcseagles.com. Web: www.rcseagles.com. Kay McKenna, Prin.; Laura Thompson, Librarian; Linda Wiggins, Librarian. Lay Teachers 25; Students 224.
Resurrection Elementary School (Grades PreK-6), 3704 Quinn, 39581. Tel: 228-762-7207; Fax: 228-762-0611. Elizabeth K. Benefield, Prin.; Linda Wiggins, Librarian. Lay Teachers 30; Students 303.

[B] HIGH SCHOOLS AND ELEMENTARY SCHOOLS, PRIVATE

BAY ST. LOUIS. *St. Stanislaus College* (1854) (Grades 7-12), 304 S. Beach Blvd., 39520-4301. Tel: 228-467-9057; Fax: 228-466-2972. Email: admissions@ststan.com. Web: www.ststan.com. Bro. Bernard Couvillion, S.C., Pres.; Mr. Patrick McGrath, Prin.; John Thibodeaux, Dir. Admissions; Virginia Gex, Librarian. Brothers of the Sacred Heart., Boys boarding and day school, secondary and elementary. Brothers 6; Lay Teachers 38; Students 375.
Camp Stanislaus Tel: 228-467-9057; Fax: 228-466-2972. Boys' summer program for ages 9-15.

[C] HOUSING FOR THE ELDERLY

BILOXI. *Gabriel Manor*, 2321 Atkinson Rd., 39531. Tel: 228-388-1013; Fax: 228-388-1176. Email: gabrielmanor@bellsouth.net. Ms. Brenda Mulvaney, Mgr. Total Staff 3; Total in Residence 51.
Gabriel Manor II, Inc.
Santa Maria Retirement Apartments, 1790 Popps Ferry Rd., 39532. Tel: 228-702-2137. Mr. Gregory K. Crapo, B.S., M.B.A, Sec. Bed Capacity 209; Total Assisted Annually 250; Total Staff 3.

BAY ST. LOUIS. *Notre Dame de la Mer Retirement Apartments*, 292 Hwy. 90, 39520. Tel: 228-467-2885; Fax: 228-466-6300. Email: mftine@bellsouth.net. Ms. Michele Tine, Mgr. (2 full time, 1 part time) 3; Total in Residence 63.

GULFPORT. *Carlow Manor*, 15195 Barbara Dr., 39503. Tel: 228-539-0707; Fax: 228-539-0704. Email: carlow@bellsouth.net. Donna G. Holliman, Mgr. Bed Capacity 39; Total Assisted Annually 39; Total Staff 3.

OCEAN SPRINGS. *Samaritan House* (1987) 642 Jackson Ave., 39564. Tel: 228-875-1087; Fax: 228-872-9500. Email: samaritanhousere@bellsouth.net. Ms. Sharon Ballow, Mgr. Total Staff 2; Total in Residence 54.
Villa Maria Retirement Apartments, 921 Porter Ave., 39564. Tel: 228-875-8811; Fax: 228-875-8889. Email: villacindy@bellsouth.net. Mrs. Cindy A. Ladnier, Mgr. Total Staff 15; Total in Residence 209.

PETAL. *Caritas Manor*, 145 W. 10th Ave., 39465. Tel: 601-545-7744; Fax: 601-545-7740. Email: caritaspetal@att.net. Total Staff 2; Total in Residence 32.

[D] MONASTERIES AND RESIDENCES OF PRIESTS AND BROTHERS

BAY ST. LOUIS. *St. Augustine's Residence* (1920) 199 Seminary Dr., 39520. Tel: 228-467-6414; Fax: 228-466-4393. Very Rev. Augustine Wall, S.V.D., Rector; Revs. Thaddeus Boucree, S.V.D.; Walter Bracken, S.V.D., Chap. Retreat Center; George Gormley, S.V.D., House Fin. Admin.; Very Rev. James Pawlicki, S.V.D., Provincial Supr.; Revs. Stanley Plutz, S.V.D.; Thomas Potts, S.V.D.; Bros. Richard Chambers, S.V.D.; Matthew Connors, S.V.D.; James Heeb, S.V.D. Priests 9; Brothers 2; Permanent Staff Priests 9; Permanent Staff Brothers 2. *St. Augustine's Retreat Center* Tel: 228-467-1097; Fax: 228-466-4393. Very Rev. Augustine Wall, S.V.D., Retreat Center Supvr.
Brothers of the Sacred Heart, 114 Bookter St., 39520. Tel: 228-466-4974. Email: bgcouvillion@gmail.com. Bros. Edwardo Baldioceda, S.C., Sub-Dir.; Raymond Sylve, S.C.; Bernard Couvillion, S.C., Dir.; Dwight Kenney, S.C.; Francis Fleming, S.C.; Barry Landry, S.C.; Harold Harris, S.C. Total in Residence 7. *Media Production Center* Tel: 228-467-1097; Fax: 228-466-5618. Email: pawlicki@inaword.com.
Media Production Center "In A Word", 199 Seminary Dr., 39520. Tel: 228-467-1097; Fax: 228-466-5618. Email: editor@inaword.com. Web: www.inaword.com. Very Rev. James Pawlicki, S.V.D., Dir. & Editor.
Southern Province of St. Augustine - Provincial Offices, 199 Seminary Dr., 39520. Tel: 228-467-4322; Fax: 228-466-5618. Email: sudsouthusa@yahoo.com. Very Rev. James Pawlicki, S.V.D., Prov.; Revs. Paul Kahan, S.V.D., Vice Prov.; George Gormley, S.V.D., Treas. Society of the Divine Word. Priests 64; Brothers 4; Parishes 33; Mission Stations 5; Elementary Schools 5. *Province Development Office* Tel: 228-467-3815; Fax: 228-466-5618. Rev. Thomas Potts, S.V.D., Dir.

[E] CONVENTS AND RESIDENCES FOR SISTERS

BILOXI. *Community of Charity and Social Services, Our Lady of Fatima Convent*, 158 Beachview Ave., 39531. Tel: 228-243-0947; 228-273-0509. Email: sistercecilia@cableone.net.
Sisters of Mercy Convent, 11454 Spring Ln., 39532. Sr. Kim Marie Lajoie, R.S.M., Contact Person. Religious Sisters of Mercy of the Americas 4.

LONG BEACH. *Congregation of the Holy Rosary* (Vietnamese), 5122 N. Gates Ave., 39560. Tel: 228-863-3045. Sisters 3.
Presentation Sisters, 18091 Commission Rd., 39560. Tel: 228-864-8418; Fax: 228-864-1627. Email: pres18091@cableone.net. Web: www.tbvmunion.org. Union of the Sisters of the Presentation of the Blessed Virgin Mary.

[F] NEWMAN CENTERS

HATTIESBURG. *University of Southern Mississippi* St. Thomas Aquinas Catholic Church, 3117 W. Fourth St., 39401. Tel: 601-264-5192; Fax: 601-264-0834. Email: church@stthomas-usm.org. Web: www.stthomas-usm.org. Very Rev. Thomas S. Conway, V.F., Chap.; Rev. Godfrey Andoh, Chap.; Carrie Bell, Campus Min. Priests 2; Staff 8.

[G] MISCELLANEOUS

BILOXI. *Magnificat - Mississippi Gulf Coast Chapter*, 1501 Popps Ferry Rd., 39532. Tel: 228-392-0697. Mrs. Yvette D. Livaccari, Contact Person.

DIAMONDHEAD. *Magnificat of Diamondhead*, 883 Manini Way, 39525. Tel: 228-255-8490. Cindy Burnett, Coord.

RELIGIOUS INSTITUTES OF MEN REPRESENTED IN THE DIOCESE

For further details refer to the corresponding bracketed number in the Religious Institutes of Men or Women section.

[1100]—*Brothers of the Sacred Heart*—S.C.

[]—*Carmelites of Mary Immaculate*—C.M.I.

[]—*The Cistercian Order of the Strict Observance*—O.C.S.O.

[]—*Heralds of Good News*—H.G.N.

[]—*Missionaries of Charity Fathers*—M.C.

[0840]—*Missionary Servants of the Most Holy Trinity*—S.T.

[1070]—*Redemptorist Fathers*—C.Ss.R.

[0420]—*Society of the Divine Word*—S.V.D.

[0700]—*St. Joseph's Society of the Sacred Heart*—S.S.J.

[]—*Xaverian Brothers Congregation*—C.F.X.

RELIGIOUS INSTITUTES OF WOMEN REPRESENTED IN THE DIOCESE

[]—*Community of Charity and Social Services*—C.C.S.S.

[0760]—*Daughters of Charity of St. Vincent De Paul*—D.C.

[]—*Daughters of Our Lady of the Holy Rosary*—F.M.S.R.

[2575]—*Institute of the Sisters of Mercy of the Americas*—R.S.M.

[]—*Missionaries of the Infant Jesus of Good Health*

[3530]—*Missionary Sisters Servants of the Holy Spirit*—S.H.Sp.

[3280]—*Presentation of the Blessed Virgin Mary Sisters*—P.B.V.M.

[]—*Sisters for Christian Community*—S.F.C.C.

[]—*Sisters of Charity of Blessed Virgin Mary*—B.V.M.

[1510]—*Sisters of St. Francis*—O.S.F.

[]—*Sisters of the Blessed Sacrament*—S.B.S.

NECROLOGY

† Vollor, William J., Hattiesburg, MS Holy Rosary Parish.—Died March 2, 2011

An asterisk (*) denotes an organization that has established tax-exempt status directly with the IRS and is not covered by the USCCB Group Ruling.

Diocese of Birmingham

(Dioecesis Birminghamiensis)

Most Reverend

ROBERT J. BAKER, S.T.D.

Bishop of Birmingham; ordained March 21, 1970; appointed Bishop of Charleston July 12, 1999; ordained and installed September 29, 1999; appointed Bishop of Birmingham August 14, 2007; installed October 2, 2007.

Most Reverend

DAVID E. FOLEY, D.D.

Bishop Emeritus of Birmingham; ordained May 26, 1956; appointed Auxiliary Bishop of Richmond, Virginia May 3, 1986; ordained Bishop June 27, 1986; appointed Bishop of Birmingham March 22, 1994; installed May 13, 1994; retired May 10, 2005.

Chancery Office: Catholic Diocese of Birmingham, P.O. Box 12047, Birmingham, AL 35202-2047. Tel: 205-838-8322; Fax: 205-836-1910.

Web: www.bhmdiocese.org

ESTABLISHED JUNE 28, 1969.

Square Miles 28,091.

Comprises the Counties of North Alabama in an irregular line between the Counties (west to east) of Sumter and Choctaw and following the base of the following Counties: Marengo, Perry, Chilton, Coosa, Tallapoosa and Chambers or comprising the Counties of: Bibb, Blount, Calhoun, Chambers, Cherokee, Chilton, Clay, Cleburne, Colbert, Coosa, Cullman, DeKalb, Etowah, Fayette, Franklin, Greene, Hale, Jackson, Jefferson, Lamar, Lauderdale, Lawrence, Limestone, Madison, Marengo, Marion, Marshall, Morgan, Perry, Pickens, Randolph, St. Clair, Shelby, Sumter, Talladega, Tallapoosa, Tuscaloosa, Walker and Winston.

Legal Title: The Catholic Bishop of Birmingham in Alabama, a Corporation Sole.
For legal titles of institutions, consult the Chancery Office

STATISTICAL OVERVIEW

Personnel	
Bishop	1
Retired Bishops	1
Abbots	1
Retired Abbots	1
Priests: Diocesan Active in Diocese	61
Priests: Diocesan Active Outside Diocese	1
Priests: Retired, Sick or Absent	22
Number of Diocesan Priests	84
Religious Priests in Diocese	28
Total Priests in Diocese	112
Ordinations:	
Diocesan Priests	1
Transitional Deacons	1
Permanent Deacons in Diocese	51
Total Brothers	22
Total Sisters	118
Parishes	
Parishes	54
With Resident Pastor:	
Resident Diocesan Priests	36
Resident Religious Priests	19
Without Resident Pastor:	
Administered by Priests	2
Administered by Lay People	1
Missions	19
Professional Ministry Personnel:	
Brothers	1
Sisters	10
Lay Ministers	48
Welfare	
Catholic Hospitals	4
Total Assisted	689,500
Health Care Centers	1
Total Assisted	39,600
Specialized Homes	1
Total Assisted	20
Special Centers for Social Services	19
Total Assisted	91,500
Educational	
Diocesan Students in Other Seminaries	11
Students Religious	5
Total Seminarians	16
High Schools, Diocesan and Parish	5
Total Students	1,461
High Schools, Private	1
Total Students	153
Elementary Schools, Diocesan and Parish	18
Total Students	4,601
Elementary Schools, Private	1
Total Students	185
Non-residential Schools for the Disabled	1
Total Students	120
Catechesis/Religious Education:	
High School Students	1,534
Elementary Students	6,267
Total Students under Catholic Instruction	14,337
Teachers in the Diocese:	
Priests	4
Brothers	1
Sisters	14
Lay Teachers	380
Vital Statistics	
Receptions into the Church:	
Infant Baptism Totals	1,821
Minor Baptism Totals	180
Adult Baptism Totals	157
Received into Full Communion	414
First Communions	1,973
Confirmations	1,560
Marriages:	
Catholic	227
Interfaith	111
Total Marriages	338
Deaths	631
Total Catholic Population	90,135
Total Population	2,945,960

Former Bishops—Most Revs. JOSEPH G. VATH, ord. June 7, 1941; appt. Auxiliary Bishop of Mobile-Birmingham March 25, 1966; cons. May 26, 1966; transferred to the Diocese of Birmingham Dec. 9, 1969; died July 14, 1987; RAYMOND J. BOLAND, D.D., ord. June 16, 1957; appt. Bishop of Birmingham Feb. 2, 1988; cons. March 25, 1988; transferred to Kansas City-St. Joseph Sept. 9, 1993; DAVID E. FOLEY, D.D., ord. May 26, 1956; appt. Titular Bishop of Ottaba and Auxiliary Bishop of Richmond May 3, 1986; cons. June 27, 1986; appt. Bishop of Birmingham March 22, 1994; installed May 13, 1994; retired May 10, 2005.

Chancery Office—Catholic Diocese of Birmingham, 2121 Third Ave. N., Birmingham, 35203. Tel: 205-838-8322; Fax: 205-836-1910. *Mailing Address: P.O. Box 12047, Birmingham, 35202-2047* Web: www.bhmdiocese.org. Address all Diocesan Correspondence to the above P.O. Box unless otherwise indicated. Telephones listed below.

Office of the Bishop—WILLIAM "ZACH" SUMMERS, Sec. Tel: 205-838-8318; GERRY NABORS, Exec. Asst. Tel: 205-833-0175.

Chancellor—Very Rev. KEVIN M. BAZZEL, J.C.L.

Priests'/Presbyteral Council—Most Rev. ROBERT JOSEPH BAKER, Pres.; Very Revs. WILLIAM P. LUCAS, Chair; KEVIN M. BAZZEL, J.C.L., Vice-Chair; JOSEPH G. CULOTTA, Sec.; PATRICK P. CULLEN; JEREMIAH DEASY; MICHAEL J. DEERING, V.G.; Rev. JOHN H. HARTSFIELD; Very Revs. BRYAN K. LOWE; MICHAEL MAC MAHON; Rev. Msgrs. MARTIN M. MULLER; PAUL L. ROHLING, V.G.; MICHAEL F. SEXTON; Very Rev. GREGORY T. BITTNER, J.C.L., J.D., Observer.

Diocesan College of Consultors—Very Revs. J. THOMAS ACKERMAN; KEVIN M. BAZZEL, J.C.L.; PATRICK P. CULLEN; JOSEPH G. CULOTTA; JEREMIAH DEASY; MICHAEL J. DEERING, V.G.; WILLIAM P. LUCAS; MICHAEL MAC MAHON; Rev. Msgr. MARTIN M. MULLER; Very Rev. RAYMOND J. REMKE; Rev. Msgrs. PAUL L. ROHLING, V.G.; MICHAEL F. SEXTON.

Diocesan College of Vicars—Rev. Msgr. PAUL L. ROHLING, V.G.; Very Revs. MICHAEL J. DEERING, V.G.; GREGORY T. BITTNER, J.C.L., J.D., Judicial Vicar; KEVIN M. BAZZEL, J.C.L., Adjutant Judicial Vicar; Rev. Msgr. MICHAEL F. SEXTON, Vicar for Clergy, Southeast Deanery; Very Revs. JOSEPH G. CULOTTA, Vicar for Ecumenical & Interfaith Dialogue; RICHARD A. CHENAULT JR., Vicar for Vocations; VERNON HUGULEY, Vicar for Black Catholic Ministry; J. THOMAS ACKERMAN, Vicar for Hispanic Ministry; RICHARD E. DONOHOE, Vicar for Catholic Charities; PATRICK P. CULLEN, West Birmingham Deanery; JEREMIAH DEASY, Southwest Deanery; WILLIAM P. LUCAS, East Birmingham Deanery; MICHAEL MAC MAHON, Northeast Deanery; Rev. Msgr. MARTIN M. MULLER, Central Birmingham Deanery; Very Rev. RAYMOND J. REMKE, Northwest Deanery.

Diocesan Pastoral Council—Most Rev. ROBERT JOSEPH BAKER, Pres., Members include lay representatives of the Diocesan Deaneries, four Vicars for Deaneries, four religious and a staff representative.

Diocesan Finance Council—Most Rev. ROBERT JOSEPH BAKER, Pres.; ROGER MCLAUGHLIN, Chm. Members: Very Rev. GREGORY T. BITTNER, J.C.L., J.D.; RAY G. DYER JR., CPA; PAUL J. SHARBEL; MARY JACKA HALL; Rev. ROBERT J. SULLIVAN; JERRY HARRIS; JIM FRANKLIN; JOHN HARDIN. Staff Members: ROBERT M. SELLERS JR., CFO; GERRY NABORS, Exec. Asst., Plus members of Diocesan Committees: Audit, Investment, Property, Human Resources.

Tribunal— Please address all rogatory commissions and matrimonial matters to the Office of the Tribunal. Very Revs. GREGORY T. BITTNER, J.C.L., J.D., Judicial Vicar. Tel: 205-838-8307; KEVIN M.

BAZZEL, J.C.L., Adjutant Judicial Vicar; CYWILLA FABIJANIC, Moderator of Tribunal Chancery & Notary; MATTIE SHUMATE, Sec. & Notary.

Judges—Rev. LOUIS GIARDINO; Rev. Msgr. PAUL L. ROHLING, V.G.

Defender of the Bond—Sr. LYNN MCKENZIE, O.S.B., J.C.L.

Catholic Social Services—ALBERT MANZELLA, Exec. Dir. Tel: 205-838-8316.

Catholic Family Services—TOM COOK, D.S.W., Rgnl. Dir., 1515 12th Ave. S., Birmingham, 35205. Tel: 205-324-6561.

Catholic Family Services Offices—LAURA DINWIDDIE, M.S.W., Rgnl. Dir., 1010 Church St., Huntsville, 35804. Tel: 256-536-0073; Sr. CAROL ANN GRAY, M.H.S.H., Dir., Catholic Family Service Center, 608 37th St., Tuscaloosa, 35405. Tel: 205-759-9384; MICHELE RIVARD, M.S.W., M.S., Social Worker, 1111 E. College St., Florence, 35630. Tel: 256-768-1550.

Catholic Centers of Concern— Birmingham; Anniston; Gadsden; Hamilton; Huntsville; Eutaw; Winfield; Sulligent; Tuscaloosa.

Apostolate to the Aged—Deacon AL GERMANN, Dir., 369 Midwood Ave., Birmingham, 35228. Tel: 205-923-7108.

Engaged Encounter—DAN CATT; TERRY CATT, 2116 Bailey Brook Dr., Birmingham, 35244. Tel: 205-988-3962.

Natural Family Planning—HAROLD GRAY; CATHY GRAY, 1538 Shamrock Dr., Gardendale, 35071. Tel: 205-631-0568.

Department of Education—FRANK X. SAVAGE, Dir., Catholic Educ. & Lifelong Formation.

Catholic Schools—FRAN LAWLOR, Supt. Tel: 205-838-8303.

Religious Education—ELIZABETH SUTTON, Dir. Tel: 205-838-8312.

Apostolate with Mentally Retarded Persons—Very Rev. PATRICK P. CULLEN, Dir.; Sr. MARY VERNON GENTLE, R.S.M., Assoc. Dir., The Nazareth House, 751 Academy Dr., Bessemer, 35020. Tel: 205-424-2984; Fax: 205-426-5753. Email: mvgentle@aol.com.

Catholic Youth Ministry—DONALD SCHWARZHOFF, Dir. Tel: 205-838-8301.

Campus Ministry—JOHN MARTIGNONI, Dir. Tel: 205-776-7186. Email: jmartignoni@bhmdiocese.org.

Catholic Scouting—DONALD SCHWARZHOFF, Dir. Tel: 205-838-8301.

Toy Bowl Association—FRANK X. SAVAGE, Diocesan Contact, Mailing Address: P.O. Box 12047, Birmingham, 35202-2047. Tel: 205-838-8308.

Board of Education—FRED BIASINI, Chm. Tel: 205-967-6170.

Finance Office and Administration—

Diocesan Finance Officer—ROBERT M. SELLERS JR. Tel: 205-833-0173.

Annual Catholic Charities Appeal— Catholic Relief Services, and National and Special Collections Very Rev. RICHARD E. DONOHOE, Dir. Tel: 205-838-8309.

Human Resources—JAMES H. WARREN II, Dir. Tel: 205-838-8321.

Family Life Ministry—JOHN MARTIGNONI, Dir. Tel: 205-776-7186. Email: jmartignoni@bhmdiocese.org.

Beginning Experience—TOM GARNER. Tel: 205-969-8509.

Children's Beginning Experience—JEANNETTE CAMPISI, 936 5th Ave., N.W., Alabaster, 35007. Tel: 205-664-0401.

Cursillo Program—KEVIN KISBY-GREEN, Lay Dir., 1735 Woodland St., N.W., Cullman, 35055. Tel: 256-736-2091. Email: kisbygreen@aol.com.

Hispanic Ministries—Deacon ANDRES RODRIGUEZ, Dir. Tel: 205-838-8308.

Services to Hispanics—Sr. GABRIELA RAMIREZ, M.G.Sp.S. Tel: 205-987-4771.

Catholic Social Services Center - Hoover—Sr. GABRIELA RAMIREZ, M.G.Sp.S., Dir. Tel: 205-987-4771.

Lay Ministries Program—Sr. MARIE LEONARD, O.S.B., Dir. Tel: 205-838-8300.

Marriage Encounter—KARL BRADY; MARY BRADY. Email: kbrady0816@aol.com.

Black Catholic Ministry—JAMES WATTS, Dir.

Pro-Life Activities—JOHN MARTIGNONI, Dir. Tel: 205-776-7186.

Propagation of the Faith and Holy Childhood—Very Rev. RAYMOND J. REMKE, Dir.; ELLEN JUSTICE, Asst. Dir. Tel: 205-776-7181.

Serra Club of Birmingham—TIM HESS, Pres. Tel: 205-991-5301.

Vocations—Very Rev. RICHARD A. CHENAULT JR., Vicar; JOHN MARTIGNONI, Coord. Tel: 205-838-2184.

"One Voice"— Diocesan weekly MARY ALICE CROCKETT, Mng. Editor. Tel: 205-838-8305; ANN LANZI, Circulation, The Birmingham Catholic Press, Inc., P.O. Box 10822, Birmingham, 35202. Tel: 205-838-8305; Fax: 205-838-8319.

Retrouvaille of Alabama, Inc.—Coordinators: LEE HINES; FRAN HINES. Tel: 205-967-3458.

Diocesan Council of Catholic Women—RUTH MAYS, Pres., 84 Muirfield Circle, Oneonta, 35121. Tel: 205-274-4101.

Priests' Retirement Fund—Mr. HENRY SMITH, c/o Priests' Retirement Fund, P.O. Box 10247, Birmingham, 35202-2047. Tel: 205-833-0173.

Victim Assistance Coordinator—ALBERT MANZELLA. Email: amanzella@bhmdiocese.org.

Office of the New Evangelization and Stewardship—JOHN MARTIGNONI, Dir. Tel: 205-776-7186. Email: jmartignoni@bhmdiocese.org.

CLERGY, PARISHES, MISSIONS AND PAROCHIAL SCHOOLS

CITY OF BIRMINGHAM

(JEFFERSON COUNTY)

1—ST. PAUL'S CATHEDRAL (1871) Very Rev. Kevin M. Bazzel, Rector & Adjutant Judicial Vicar; Deacons Neal Kay; Edward W. Zieveink.
Mailing Address: P.O. Box 10044, 35202-0044. Tel: 205-251-1279; Fax: 205-251-1284.
Res.: 2120 Third Ave. N., 35203. Tel: 205-328-7209.
Catechesis/Religious Program—Students 125.
Mission—St. Stephen the Martyr and Campus Center 1515 12th Ave. S., Jefferson Co. 35205. Tel: 205-933-2508. Sr. Karen Ann Lortscher, O.S.B., Campus Min.

2—ST. ANTHONY'S (1900) Closed. For inquiries for parish records contact St. Paul Cathedral, Birmingham.

3—ST. BARNABAS (1908) Rev. J. Michael Wrigley, Admin.
Mailing Address: P.O. Box 610304, 35261. In Res., Rev. Msgr. Eugene O'Connor (Retired).
Res.: 7921 First Ave. N., 35206. Tel: 205-833-0334; 205-833-5695; Fax: 205-833-5695.
School—(Grades K-8), 7901 First Ave. N., 35206. Tel: 205-836-5385; Fax: 205-833-0272. Sr. Brenda Monahan, D.C., Prin. Lay Teachers 11; Students 132.
Mailing Address: P.O. Box 610347, 35261.
Catechesis/Religious Program—Tel: 205-836-4567. Kimberly Hemmler, C.R.E. Students 19.

4—ST. BERNARD'S (Inglenook) (1928) Closed. For inquiries for parish records contact St. Paul Cathedral, Birmingham.

5—BLESSED SACRAMENT (1910) [CEM] Rev. Jim W. Booth, Admin.
Res.: 1460 Pearson Ave., S.W., P.O. Box 110006, 35211. Tel: 205-785-9840.
Catechesis/Religious Program—Ann Noblitt, D.R.E.

6—ST. FRANCIS XAVIER (1953) Rev. Robert J. Sullivan; Very Rev. John G. McDonald; Deacon George Mickwee; Sr. Jane Bishop, O.S.B., Pastoral Assoc. In Res., Very Rev. Gregory T. Bittner, Diocesan Judicial Vicar.
Res.: P.O. Box 130669, 35213. Tel: 205-871-1153; Fax: 205-871-9831.
School—(Grades K-8) Tel: 205-871-1687; Fax: 205-871-1674. Nathan Wright, Prin. Lay Teachers 18; Students 215.
Catechesis/Religious Program—Daniel McCormick, D.R.E. Students 360.

7—HOLY FAMILY (1938), (African American), Rev. Robert Crossmyer, C.P.; Deacon Benjamin Jett. In Res., Rev. Alex Steinmiller, C.P.
Res.: 1910 19th St., 35218. Tel: 205-780-3440; Fax: 205-780-5272.
School—(Grades K-8), 1916 19th St., Ensley, 35218. Tel: 205-785-5858; Fax: 205-785-2666. William Kindall, Pres.; Chandra Farrier, Prin. Lay Teachers 12; Students 155.
Catechesis/Religious Program—Fax: 205-780-3440. Rose Sturdivant, D.R.E. Students 53.
Mission—St. Mary's (1943) 6101 Dr. Martin Luther King Dr., Fairfield, Jefferson Co. 35064. Tel: 205-923-0202 (Office); 205-780-9683 (Res.); Fax: 205-923-2276. Rev. Justin Nelson Alphonse, C.P.; Deacon Walter Henderson.
Catechesis/Religious Program—Wade White, D.R.E. Students 20.
School—St. Mary's Early Childhood Center, (Grades PreK-2), 6124 Myron Massey Blvd., Fairfield, 35064. Tel: 205-923-5161; Fax: 205-923-5166. Shilisha Logan, Prin. Lay Teachers 5; Students 45.

8—HOLY ROSARY (Gate City) (1889) Revs. Anthony D'Angelo, S.D.B.; Kenneth Germaine, S.D.B.
7414 Georgia Rd., 35212. Tel: 205-595-0652.

9—ST. JOHN BOSCO (1973) Closed. For inquiries for parish records, please contact Holy Rosary, Birmingham.

10—ST. JOSEPH'S (1921), (Italian), Rev. Guillermo Castillo DelGadillo, Admin.
Res.: 3020 Avenue K, 35218. Tel: 205-788-5721; Fax: 205-788-7146.
Catechesis/Religious Program—Antonia Casas, D.R.E. Students 24.

11—KOREAN CATHOLIC COMMUNITY, ST. LUKE HWANG (1995), (Korean), Rev. Jeong Sang-Ki.
Res.: 759 Valley St., 35226. Tel: 205-823-2301.

12—ST. MARGARET'S (1986) Closed. For inquiries for parish records contact Blessed Sacrament Parish, Birmingham.

13—ST. MARK THE EVANGELIST (1999) Very Rev. Joseph G. Culotta.
Mailing Address: P.O. Box 380396, 35238-0396. Tel: 205-980-1810; Fax: 205-980-9208.
Catechesis/Religious Program—Susan Webb, C.R.E. Students 413.

14—ST. MARK'S (1904) Closed. For inquiries for parish records contact St. Paul's Cathedral, Birmingham.

15—OUR LADY OF FATIMA (1905), (African American), Rev. Paul Oberg, S.S.J.; Deacon Douglass C. Moorer.
Res.: 708 First St. S., 35205. Tel: 205-322-1205; Fax: 205-714-5056.
School—(Grades K-8), 630 First St. S., 35205. Tel: 205-251-8395; Fax: 205-251-8393. Velda Gilyot, Prin. Sisters of The Blessed Sacrament, PA 5; Lay Teachers 14; Students 212.
Catechesis/Religious Program—Mrs. Theresa Nalls, D.R.E. Students 89.

16—OUR LADY OF LOURDES (1959) Rev. Andrew Kennedy; Deacon William F. Brandt.
Res.: 980 Huffman Rd., 35215.
Office: Tel: 205-836-2274; Fax: 205-836-5436.
Catechesis/Religious Program—Students 63.

17—OUR LADY OF SORROWS (1887) Rev. Msgr. Martin M. Muller; Revs. Jaya Prathap Duggimpudi; John Michael Adams; Sr. Pat Sullivan, M.S.B.T., Pastoral Assoc.
1730 Oxmoor Rd., 35209. Tel: 205-871-8121; Fax: 205-871-8180.
Res.: 1728 Oxmoor Rd., 35209. (Homewood)
School—(Grades K-8) Tel: 205-879-3237; Fax: 205-879-9332. Mary Jane Dorn, Prin. Lay Teachers 30; Students 484.
Catechesis/Religious Program—Tel: 205-871-1431; Fax: 205-871-1487. Suzanne Corso, D.R.E.; Christine Wright, D.R.E. Students 339.

18—OUR LADY OF THE VALLEY (1974) Rev. Msgr. Paul L. Rohling; Rev. Anthony J. Weis; Sr. Madeline Contorno, O.S.B., Pastoral Assoc.; Deacon Bob Martin; Rev. Michael J. White, Pastor Emeritus (Retired).
Res.: 5514 Double Oak Ln., 35242. Tel: 205-991-5488; Fax: 205-991-5181.
Church: Tel: 205-991-5488; Fax: 205-991-5181.
School—(Grades K-8) Tel: 205-991-5963; Fax: 205-991-1251. Sandra Roden, Prin.; Susan Natter, Librarian. Lay Teachers 48; Students 411.
Catechesis/Religious Program—Tel: 205-991-5489; Fax: 205-991-5181. Deacon Dan Whitaker, D.R.E. Students 442.

19—OUR LADY QUEEN OF THE UNIVERSE (1955), (African American), Rev. Jose Brahmakulam Chacko.
Res.: 961 Center St. N., 35204. Tel: 205-328-7729; Fax: 205-328-7703.
Catechesis/Religious Program—Carol Washington, D.R.E. Students 52.
Mission—Sacred Heart 3401 27th Ct. N., Collegeville, Jefferson Co. 35207. Tel: 205-252-8909.

20—ST. PETER THE APOSTLE (1962) Revs. Thomas M. Kelly; Joy Nellisary; Deacons Sam Anzalone; Christopher J. Rosko. In Res., Rev. John Robinson.
Res.: 2061 Patton Chapel Rd., 35216. Tel: 205-822-4480; Fax: 205-822-4534.
Catechesis/Religious Program—Tel: 205-823-4480, Ext. 24. Marcella Stobert, D.R.E. Students 363.

21—PRINCE OF PEACE (1984) Rev. John Fallon; Very Rev. J. Thomas Ackerman, Coord., Hispanic Ministry; Deacons Andres Eduardo Rodriguez Tejeda; Jose Vasquez. In Res., Rev. Henry McDaid (Retired).
Church & Mailing Address: 4600 Preserve Pkwy., Birmingham (Hoover), 35226. Tel: 205-822-9125; Fax: 205-822-9127.
Res.: 10-A Shades Crest Rd., 35226. Tel: 205-682-0460.
School—(Grades PreK-8) Tel: 205-824-7886; Fax: 205-827-2093. Connie Angstadt, Prin. Lay Teachers 35; Students 360.
Catechesis/Religious Program—Tel: 205-822-9125; Fax: 205-822-9127. Megan Everett, D.R.E. Students 742.

22—SACRED HEART (1955) See separate listing. See Our Lady Queen of the Universe, Birmingham for details.

23—ST. STANISLAUS (1914) Very Rev. Vernon Huguley.
Mailing Address: 904 Indiana St., 35224. Tel:

205-785-9625.
Catechesis/Religious Program—Students 9.
24—ST. STEPHEN THE MARTYR (1991) See separate listing. Now a mission of Cathedral of St. Paul, Birmingham.
25—ST. THERESA'S, Closed. For inquiries for parish records contact St. Paul's Cathedral, Birmingham.
26—OUR LADY OF LAVANG PARISH @ ST. JOHN BOSCO CHURCH (2005) Rev. John Duc Vu.
142 52nd Pl. N., 35212. Tel: 205-599-2124.

OUTSIDE THE CITY OF BIRMINGHAM

ADAMSVILLE, JEFFERSON CO., ST. PATRICK'S (1983) [CEM] Very Rev. Vernon Huguley.
301 Shamrock Tr., 35005.
Res.: 404 Brian Dr., 35005. Tel: 205-674-7090.
Church: Tel: 205-798-5326; Fax: 205-798-5330.
Catechesis/Religious Program—Students 64.
Family Life Center—Tel: 205-798-0372.

ALEXANDER CITY, TALLAPOOSA CO., ST. JOHN THE APOSTLE (1948) Rev. Joseph Thekkethala, Admin.
Res.: 454 N. Central Ave., 35010. Tel: 256-234-3631; Fax: 256-234-3789.
Catechesis/Religious Program—Tel: 256-329-8204; Fax: 256-234-3789. Marty Rittmann, D.R.E. Students 35.
Mission—St. Mark (1994) 460 Country Club Rd., P.O. Box 98, Ashland, Clay Co. 36251. Tel: 256-354-3598. P.O. Box 98, Ashland, 36251.

ANNISTON, CALHOUN CO.
1—ALL SAINTS (1939) B. Dianne Green, Parish Dir.
Mailing Address: P.O. Box 4862, 36204. 1112 W. 15th St., 36201. Tel: 256-237-9230; Fax: 256-237-9230.
Catechesis/Religious Program—Rose Munford, D.R.E.
2—SACRED HEART OF JESUS (1886) Very Rev. Bryan K. Lowe.
Res.: P.O. Box 5010, 36205. Tel: 256-237-3011; Fax: 256-241-2048.
School—(Grades K-12), 16 Morton Rd., Fort McClellan, 36205. Tel: 256-237-4231; Fax: 256-241-2353. Charles Maniscalco, Prin. Lay Teachers 24; Students 200.
Catechesis/Religious Program—Carla Keith, D.R.E. Students 124.

ASHLAND, CLAY CO., ST. MARK'S, See separate listing. See St. John the Apostle, Alexander City for details.

ATHENS, LIMESTONE CO., ST. PAUL'S (1959) Rev. Charles Alookaran.
Mailing Address: P.O. Box 998, 35612.
Res.: 1900 Hwy. 72 W., 35611. Tel: 256-232-4191.
Catechesis/Religious Program—Elizabeth Niedzwiecki, D.R.E. Students 238.

BESSEMER, JEFFERSON CO.
1—ST. ALOYSIUS CHURCH (1886) Very Rev. Patrick P. Cullen; Stephanie Gerson, Pastoral Assoc.
Mailing Address: 751 Academy Dr., 35022. Tel: 205-424-2984; Fax: 205-426-5753.
Res.: Tel: 205-424-1839.
School—(Grades K-8) Tel: 205-425-0045; Fax: 205-425-0046. Stephanie Burke, Prin.; Marian Campbell, Librarian. Lay Teachers 21; Students 150.
Catechesis/Religious Program—Students 30.
2—ST. FRANCIS OF ASSISI (1940), (African American), Rev. Paul Asih, M.S.P. In Res., Rev. Raphael Obatama.
Res.: 2400 Seventh Ave. N., 35020.
Catechesis/Religious Program—2410 7th Ave. N., 35020. Tel: 205-428-4758; Fax: 205-428-4751. Students 19.

CLANTON, CHILTON CO., CHURCH OF THE RESURRECTION Rev. Bruce Bumbarger, M.SS.CC.
300 First Ave., 35045. Tel: 205-755-5498; Fax: 205-755-5498.
Catechesis/Religious Program—Marsha Gentle, D.R.E.

CULLMAN, CULLMAN CO., SACRED HEART (1877), (German), [CEM] Revs. Patrick Egan, O.S.B.; John O'Donnell, O.S.B.; Deacons William Roberson; Mike Branch.
Res.: 217 Second St., S.E., P.O. Box 1085, 35056. Tel: 256-734-3730; Fax: 256-734-3476.
School—(Grades K-6), 112 2nd Ave. S.E., 35055. Tel: 256-734-4563; Fax: 256-734-5882. Earnest Hauk, Prin. Lay Teachers 13; Students 128.
Catechesis/Religious Program—Fharis Richter, D.R.E. Students 150.
Mission—St. Boniface [CEM] P.O. Box 1085, Cullman Co. 35056.

DECATUR, MORGAN CO.
1—ST. ANN'S (1870) [JC], For more information please see Annunciation of the Lord, Decatur.
2—ANNUNCIATION OF THE LORD (2003) Very Rev. Raymond J. Remke; Sr. Teresa Walsh, C.S.J., Pastoral Assoc.; Deacon Javier Ramirez.
Res.: 3910 Spring Ave., S.W., 35603. Tel: 256-353-2667; Fax: 256-353-8994.
School—(Grades PreK-8) Tel: 256-353-6543; Fax: 256-353-0705. Christine Wright, Prin.; Vicki Large, Librarian. Lay Teachers 11; Students 105.
Catechesis/Religious Program—Jan Gile, D.R.E. Students 134.

DEMOPOLIS, MARENGO CO., ST. LEO (1936) Rev. Lawrence E. Shinnick.
Res.: 306 S. Main Ave., P.O. Box 937, 36732. Tel: 334-289-2767; Fax: 334-289-6085.
Catechesis/Religious Program—Diane Busby, D.R.E. Students 44.
Mission—Our Lady of Lourdes 8 Erwin Woods Dr., Greensboro, Hale Co. 37644.
Mission—St. Mary (1948) 274 Wilson Ave., Eutaw, Greene Co. 35462. (African American)

EUTAW, GREENE CO., ST. MARY (1948), (African American), See separate listing. See St. Leo, Demopolis for details.

FAIRFIELD, JEFFERSON CO., ST. MARY (1943) See separate listing. See Holy Family, Birmingham for details.

FLORENCE, LAUDERDALE CO.
1—ST. JOSEPH'S (1898) Rev. Andrew A. Sullivan; Kathie Franck, Pastoral Min.
Res.: 1111 E. College St., 35630. Tel: 256-764-3303; 256-767-9069 (Rectory); Fax: 256-718-0208.
School—(Grades K-8) Tel: 256-766-1923; 256-766-1955; Fax: 256-766-1713. Kelley Dewberry, Prin. Lay Teachers 21; Students 204.
Catechesis/Religious Program—Students 77.
2—ST. MICHAEL (1873) [CEM] Rev. Edward P. Markley, O.S.B.
Res.: 2751 County Rd. 30, 35634. Tel: 256-764-1885; Fax: 256-764-8933.
Catechesis/Religious Program—Karen Holden, D.R.E., (High School). Students 70.

FORT PAYNE, DE KALB CO., OUR LADY OF THE VALLEY (1959) Rev. Mark T. Spruill, Admin.
Church & Mailing Address: 2910 Gault Ave., N., 35967. Tel: 256-845-4774; Fax: 256-845-4708.
Catechesis/Religious Program—Students 277.

GADSDEN, ETOWAH CO.
1—ST. JAMES (1912) Rev. E. Gray Bean.
Mailing Address: P.O. Box 38, 35902.
Res.: 225 Carleen St., 35901. Tel: 256-546-5339.
Church: 622 Chestnut St., 35901. Tel: 256-546-2975; Fax: 256-546-2930.
School—(Grades K-8) Tel: 256-546-0132; Fax: 256-546-0134. John Parker, Prin. Lay Teachers 14; Students 181.
Catechesis/Religious Program—Sandra Ashley, C.R.E. Students 215.
2—ST. MARTIN DE PORRES, Closed. For inquiries for parish records contact St. James, Gadsden.

GARDENDALE, JEFFERSON CO., ST. ELIZABETH ANN SETON (1976) Very Rev. Michael J. Deering; Margaret Wiley, Pastoral Assoc.
Mailing Address: 334 Main St., P.O. Box 1027, 35071. Tel: 205-631-9398 (Office); Fax: 205-631-5781.
Res.: 205 Powell Dr., P.O. Box 1027, 35071. Tel: 205-631-8582.
Catechesis/Religious Program—Fax: 205-631-5781. Jeanne Busby, D.R.E.; Jim Jernigan, D.R.E. Students 96.
Mission—St. Henry [CEM] 211 5th St., Warrior, Jefferson Co. 35180.

GUNTERSVILLE, MARSHALL CO., ST. WILLIAM (1952) Rev. Timothy Pfander; Deacon Edwin M. Santos.
929 Gunter Ave., 35976. Tel: 256-582-4245 (Office); 256-572-3796 (Hispanic Min); Fax: 256-582-7954.
Res.: 1002 Blount Ave., 35976.
Catechesis/Religious Program—Ms. Cecilia Hall, D.R.E. Students 451.
Mission—Chapel of the Holy Cross 1534 Whitesville Rd., Albertville, Marshall Co. 35950. Tel: 256-891-0550.

HUNTSVILLE, MADISON CO.
1—GOOD SHEPHERD (1981) Rev. Louis Giardino; Deacons Ron Puent; Helmut Sassenfeld.
Res.: 13550 Chaney Thompson Rd. S.E., 35803-2326. Tel: 256-882-1844; Fax: 256-882-1841.
Catechesis/Religious Program— Katherine Maxwell, D.R.E. Students 351.
2—HOLY SPIRIT (1965) Very Rev. Michael Mac Mahon; Revs. Bryan W. Jerabek, (On Sabbatical); Vincent Bresowar; Deacons Samuel Dias; Lawrence E. Sisterman; Michael P. Sudnik.
Res.: 625 Airport Rd. S.W., 35802. Tel: 256-881-4781; Fax: 256-881-5510.
School—(Grades K-8) Tel: 256-881-4852; Fax: 256-881-4904. James Bell, Prin.; Carrie Turner, Librarian. Lay Teachers 28; Students 423.
Catechesis/Religious Program—Tel: 256-881-0345. Mrs. Tracy Finke, D.R.E. Students 297.
3—ST. JOSEPH'S (1952) [CEM] Revs. Gary New, S.D.S.; Patrick Nelson, S.D.S.
Res.: 2300 Beasley Ave., N.W., 35816. Tel: 256-534-8459; Fax: 256-534-8450.
School—Holy Family School, (Grades K-8) Tel: 256-539-5221; Fax: 256-533-0747. Mary Tomaine, Prin. Sisters of the Divine Savior 1; Lay Teachers 17; Students 169.
Catechesis/Religious Program—Tel: 256-534-1310. Carmen Amato, D.R.E. Students 73.
4—ST. MARY OF THE VISITATION (1861) Rev. Glen W. Sayers, S.D.S.; Deacon James G. Bodine.
Res.: 222 N. Jefferson St., 35801. Tel: 256-536-6349; Fax: 256-536-6349.
Catechesis/Religious Program—Tel: 256-536-6760. Beth Ann Ryan, D.R.E. Students 75.
5—OUR LADY QUEEN OF THE UNIVERSE (1965) Rev. Joy Chalissery; Deacon Daniel Melchoir.
Mailing Address: P.O. Box 3268, 35810.
Res.: 3701 Grizzard, 35810. Tel: 256-852-0788.
Church: 2421 Shady Lane Dr., N.W., 35810. Fax: 256-852-0199.
Catechesis/Religious Program—Susan Turner, D.R.E. Students 110.

JACKSONVILLE, CALHOUN CO., ST. CHARLES BORROMEO (1964) Rev. James R. Macey.
Church: 308 Seventh St., N.E., 36265. Tel: 256-435-3238; Fax: 256-435-4942.
Res.: 400 Seventh St., N.E., 36265. Tel: 256-435-1307.
Catechesis/Religious Program—Peggy Sugar, D.R.E. Students 44.
Mission—St. Joachim c/o 308 7th St., N.E., Piedmont, Calhoun Co. 36265. Deacon Donald Ash.

JASPER, WALKER CO., ST. CECILIA (1964) Rev. David Buchanan.
Mailing Address: 2159 Hwy. 195, 35503.
Res.: Tel: 205-384-4800 (Office); Fax: 205-384-1009.
Catechesis/Religious Program—Teresa Collins, D.R.E. Students 72.

LANETT, CHAMBERS CO., HOLY FAMILY (1915) [CEM] Rev. Antoo Alappat, Admin.
Res.: 705 N. Third Ave., 36863-0325. Tel: 334-644-4405; Fax: 706-645-6783.
Catechesis/Religious Program—Students 20.
Mission—Immaculate Conception 1256 Main St., Roanoke, Randolph Co. 36274. Tel: 334-853-4418.

LEEDS, JEFFERSON CO., ST. THERESA'S (1951) Rev. James J. Naughton, S.D.B.; Deacon Silverio Rubio Roman.
Res.: 1390 Ashville Ct., P.O. Box 525, 35094. Tel: 205-699-8534; Fax: 205-702-4010.
Catechesis/Religious Program—Mrs. Kristin Sessions, D.R.E. Students 84.

LIVINGSTON, SUMTER CO., ST. FRANCIS OF ASSISI (1972), Administered by The Catholic Church in West Central Alabama. Rev. Lawrence E. Shinnick.
Mailing Address: P.O. Box 1035, 35470. Tel: 334-289-2767; Fax: 334-289-0544.
Church: Hwy. 28 E., 35470.
Catechesis/Religious Program—Grace Neel, D.R.E. Students 2.

MADISON, MADISON CO., ST. JOHN THE BAPTIST (1973) Revs. Philip N. O'Kennedy; Roy Runkle; Deacons Dan Laurita; Darrell Diem; Carmelo Graffagnini; Lawrence Howell.
Res.: 1059 Hughes Rd., 35758. Tel: 256-722-0130; Fax: 256-722-0303.
School—(Grades K-8), 1057 Hughes Rd., 35758. Tel: 256-722-0772; Fax: 256-722-0151. Sherry Lewis, Prin.; Rosemary Terry, Librarian. Lay Teachers 26; Students 441.
Catechesis/Religious Program—Tel: 256-722-8590. Greg Thompson, D.R.E. Students 620.

MONTEVALLO, SHELBY CO., ST. THOMAS THE APOSTLE (1951) Rev. Raymond A. Dunmyer; Deacon William P. Alexiou.
Res. & Mailing Address: 80 St. Thomas Way, 35115. Tel: 205-663-3936; Fax: 205-663-3929.
Catechesis/Religious Program—Pat Shoop, D.R.E. Students 321.

MOULTON, LAWRENCE CO., RESURRECTION CATHOLIC CHAPEL (1993) Unassigned.
Res.: 7363 Alabama Hwy. 33, 35650. Tel: 256-905-0330; Fax: 256-905-0330 (Call First).
Catechesis/Religious Program—Students 8.

ONEONTA, BLOUNT CO., CORPUS CHRISTI (1983) Rev. John H. Hartsfield; Deacon Paul I. Mullen.
Res.: 115 Androse Dr., 35121. Tel: 205-274-0343.
Church: 32015 State Hwy. 75, 35121. Tel: 205-625-6078; Fax: 205-625-6078.
Catechesis/Religious Program—Charlene Makofsky, C.R.E. Students 168.

PELL CITY, ST. CLAIR CO., OUR LADY OF THE LAKE (1969) Rev. Msgr. Michael F. Sexton; Deacon Terrence L. Rumore.
Mailing Address: Hwy. 231 S., P.O. Box 388, Cropwell, 35054.
Res.: 117 Ingram Lane, Cropwell, 35054. Tel: 205-525-5161 (Church); Fax: 205-525-5162.
Catechesis/Religious Program—Parma Boyle, D.R.E. Students 165.

RUSSELLVILLE, FRANKLIN CO., GOOD SHEPHERD CHURCH (1973) Rev. James A. Hedderman.
Res.: 1700 N. Jackson Ave., P.O. Box 878, 35653. Tel: 256-332-4861.
Catechesis/Religious Program—Students 152.

SCOTTSBORO, JACKSON CO., ST. JUDE (1971) Rev. Alan C. Mackey; Deacon Jerome P. Raispis.
Res.: 17205 Hwy. 35, 35768. Tel: 205-574-6156.

Catechesis/Religious Program—Carol Miller, C.R.E. Students 30.

SYLACAUGA, TALLADEGA CO., ST. JUDE (1947) Rev. Thomas F. Woods.
Res.: 310 W. Bay St., P.O. Box 111, 35150. Tel: 256-245-7741.
Catechesis/Religious Program—Students 22.
Mission—Holy Name of Jesus 4th St., S.W. at 5th Ave., Childersburg, Talladega Co. 35044.

TALLADEGA, TALLADEGA CO., ST. FRANCIS OF ASSISI (1951) [CEM] Rev. Thomas F. Woods.
Res.: 722 East St. S., P.O. Box 1142, 35161. Tel: 256-362-5372.
Catechesis/Religious Program—Cindi Greene, D.R.E. Students 10.

TRUSSVILLE, JEFFERSON CO., HOLY INFANT OF PRAGUE (1941) Very Rev. William P. Lucas; Deacons Ed Pruet; E. Lee Robinson Sr.
Res.: 8090 Gadsden Hwy., P.O. Box 43, 35173. Tel: 205-655-2541; Fax: 205-661-9231.
Catechesis/Religious Program—Terry Pruet, D.R.E. Students 250.

TUSCALOOSA, TUSCALOOSA CO.

1—ST. FRANCIS OF ASSISI UNIVERSITY PARISH (1929) Rev. Gerald Holloway; Very Rev. Richard A. Chenault Jr.; Deacons J. Adrian Straley; William J. Remmert; Susan Nelms, Campus Min.
Res.: 811 Fifth Ave., 35401. Tel: 205-758-5672; Fax: 205-758-5673.
Catechesis/Religious Program—Nancy Woodbury, D.R.E. Students 145.
Mission—St. Robert 407 2nd St., S.W., Reform, Pickens Co. 35481. Tel: 205-375-2638.

2—HOLY SPIRIT (1961) Very Rev. Jeremiah Deasy; Deacons Francis N. Viselli Jr.; Frank R. Slapikas; J. Adrian Straley.
Res.: 733 James I. Harrison Jr. Pkwy. E., 35405. Tel: 205-553-9733; Fax: 205-553-7014.
School—(Grades K-6), 711 James I. Harrison Jr. Pkwy. E., 35405. Tel: 205-553-9630; Fax: 205-553-8880. Sr. Elaine Sebera, R.S.M., Pres. (Grades PreK-12). Tel: 205-553-5606; Judith H. Halli, Prin. (Grades 7-12). Tel: 205-553-5606; Felicia Corona, Prin. (Grades PreK-6). Lay Teachers 45; Students 530.
Catechesis/Religious Program—Mary Jane Wagner, D.R.E. Students 94.
Mission—St. John c/o Rev. Jeremiah Deasy at Holy Spirit, 8th & Lurleen Wallace Blvd., Tuscaloosa Co. 35401.

TUSCUMBIA, COLBERT CO., OUR LADY OF THE SHOALS (1869) [CEM] Rev. Patrick Don Bosco Forsythe.
Church & Res.: 200 E. Commons St. N., 35674. Tel: 256-383-7207 (Church); 256-381-2699 (Res.); Fax: 256-383-7883.
Catechesis/Religious Program—Kathy Yordy, D.R.E. Students 82.

WINFIELD, MARION CO., HOLY SPIRIT (1965) Rev. Show Reddy Kasu, Admin.
2710 U.S. Hwy. 43 N., 35594. Tel: 205-487-3616; Fax: 205-487-3616.
Catechesis/Religious Program—Teresa Gray, D.R.E. Students 63.
Mission—Holy Family 423 19th St., N.W., Fayette, Fayette Co. 35555. Tel: 205-932-6242.
Mission—Our Lady of Guadalupe 485 Layne Hill Dr., Haleyville, Winston Co. 35565. Tel: 205-487-3616.

On Special or Other Diocesan Assignment:
Most Rev.—
Marino, Joseph, Apostolic Nuncio to Bangladesh, U.N. Rd. 2, Baridhana, P.O. Box 6003, Dhaka 1212 Bangladesh.
Rev.—
O'Donnell, John, O.S.B., 112 Second Ave., S.E., Cullman, 35055.

On Duty Outside the Diocese:
Revs.—
Fisher, Albert, Chap., St. Joseph's Hospital, 9 Brackenston Sq., Savannah, GA 31406.
Reynolds, Jeffrie S. (Retired), 2159 S. McKenzie, #290, Foley, 36535. Tel: 352-228-3138

Absent on Leave:
Revs.—
Klauck, Michael
Stone, Francis Mary, M.F.V.A.
Summitt, James A.

Retired:
Rev. Msgr.—
O'Connor, Eugene
Very Rev.—
Tierney, Patrick J., V.F., 10162 151st St., Orland Park, IL 60462.
Revs.—
Blazak, Camillus, 533 Alexian Way #111, Signal Mountain, TN 37377.
Brennan, Matthew. Tel: 205-525-4711
Keiser, Raymond W., 3011 Massey Rd., Apt. E, Vestavia, 35216.
McDaid, Henry, 10-B Shades Crest Rd., 35226. Tel: 205-989-4060
Murrin, Raymond J., 18 Merrion Ct., Ailesbury Rd., Dublin 4, Ireland.
Muscolino, Frank J., 2600 Arlington Ave., Apt. 52, 35205. Tel: 205-933-5252
O'Donoghue, Patrick, Haleyville, St. Anne's Rd., Killarney, County Kerry, Ireland.
Regan, Desmond, 2724 Hanover Cir. S., 35205.
Reynolds, Jeffrie S., 2159 S. McKenzie, #290, Foley, 36535. Tel: 352-228-3138
Sheehan, J. Peter, 653 S.E. Lakeview Dr., Sebring, FL 33870. Tel: 863-471-0378
Thorsen, Henry, 700 Connell Dr., Pensacola, FL 32507. Tel: 850-469-0919
Underwood, Joseph, 6520 Court K, 35228. Tel: 205-925-8329
White, Michael J., Pastor Emeritus, Our Lady of the Valley, 837 Greystone Highlands Dr., 35242-2651. Tel: 205-408-1034

Permanent Deacons:
Alexiou, William P., St. Thomas the Apostle, Montevallo
Anzalone, J.S., St. Peter the Apostle, Birmingham
Ash, Donald J., St. Joachim, Piedmont
Bodine, James G., St. Mary's, Huntsville
Branch, Michael E., Sacred Heart of Jesus, Cullman
Brandt, William F., Our Lady of Lourdes, Birmingham
Cova, Michael A., St. John the Apostle, Alexander City
DeBlieux, John D., Holy Spirit, Winfield; Holy Family, Fayette
Dias, Sam A., Holy Spirit, Huntsville
Diem, Darrell, St. John the Baptist, Madison
Germann, Aloysius A., (Retired)
Graffagnini, Carmelo, St. John the Baptist, Madison
Henderson, Walter J., St. Mary, Fairfield
Howell, Lawrence, (Retired)
Hunkele, Thomas H., Holy Family, Lanett
Iovino, Frank, Prince of Peace, Birmingham
Jett, Benjamin, Holy Family, Birmingham
Joly, Walter Jerome, (On Leave)
Kay, G. Neal, Cathedral of St. Paul, Birmingham
Laremore, Robert, (Retired)
Larsen, Alf B., St. Joseph, Huntsville
Laurita, Dan, St. John the Baptist, Madison
Machus, Paul, (Retired)
Martin, Robert A., Jr., Our Lady of the Valley, Birmingham
Mickwee, George, St. Francis Xavier, Birmingham
Moorer, Douglass C., Our Lady of Fatima, Birmingham
Motherway, Gerald, Holy Family, Birmingham
Mullen, Paul I., Corpus Christi, Oneonta
Pruet, Ed, Holy Infant of Prague, Trussville
Puent, Ron, Good Shepherd, Huntsville
Raispis, Jerome P., (Retired)
Ramirez, Javier, Annunciation of the Lord, Decatur
Remmert, William J., St. Francis University Parish, Tuscaloosa
Ritchey, Seraphim (NTN), St. George the Great Martyr, Birmingham
Roberson, William, Sacred Heart, Cullman
Robinson, E. Lee, Sr., Holy Infant of Prague, Trussville
Rodriguez, Ramon D., Annunciation of the Lord, Decatur
Roman, Silverio Rubio, St. Theresa, Leeds
Rosko, Christopher J., St. Peter the Apostle, Birmingham
Rumore, Terrence L., Our Lady of the Lake, Pell City
Santos, Edwin M., St. William, Guntersville
Sassenfeld, Helmut, Good Shepherd, Huntsville
Sisterman, Lawrence E., Holy Spirit, Huntsville
Slapikas, Frank R., Holy Spirit, Tuscaloosa
Stagg, James A., Archdiocese of Atlanta
Steltemeier, R. William
Stephens, Joseph R., Jr., St. Elias (Marionite Rite), Birmingham
Straley, J. Adrian, Holy Spirit, Tuscaloosa
Sudnik, Michael P., Holy Spirit, Huntsville
Tejeda, Andres Eduardo Rodriguez, Prince of Peace, Birmingham
Vazquez, Jose R., Hispanic Ministry, Prince of Peace, Birmingham
Viselli, Francis N., Jr., Holy Spirit, Tuscaloosa
Wehby, Samuel J., St. Elias, Birmingham
Whitaker, Dan, Our Lady of the Valley, Birmingham
Zieverink, Edward Walter, Jr., Cathedral of St. Paul, Birmingham

INSTITUTIONS LOCATED IN THE DIOCESE

[A] HIGH SCHOOLS, DIOCESAN

BIRMINGHAM. *John Carroll Catholic High School*, 300 Lakeshore Pkwy., P.O. Box 19907, 35209. Tel: 205-940-2400; Fax: 205-945-7429. Web: www.jcchs.org. Very Rev. John G. McDonald, Prin. Priests 1; Deacons 1; Sisters 4; Lay Teachers 50; Students 624.
Sacred Heart Catholic High School Lay Teachers 18; Students 235.

FORT MCCLELLAN. *Sacred Heart Catholic High School*, 16 Morton Rd., Fort Mc Clellan, 36205. Tel: 265-237-4231; Fax: 256-237-4231. Email: principal@sacredheartcardinals.org. Charles Maniscalco, Prin. Lay Teachers 18; Students 235.

HUNTSVILLE. *Pope John Paul II Catholic High School*, 7301 Old Madison Pike, 35806. Tel: 256-430-1760; Fax: 256-430-1766. Email: vaquila@jp2falcons.org. Web: www.chsfalcons.org. Rev. Vincent Bresowar, Chap.; Vince Aquila, Prin.; Kathy Smith, Librarian. Priests 1; Lay Teachers 37; Students 397.

TUSCALOOSA. *Holy Spirit Catholic High School*, (Grades 7-12), 601 James I. Harrison Jr. Pkwy. E., 35405. Tel: 205-553-5606; Fax: 205-556-7103. Email: jhalli@holyspirit-al.com. Web: www.holyspirit-al.com. Judi Halli, Prin. Lay Teachers 27; Students 250.

[B] HIGH SCHOOLS, PRIVATE

BIRMINGHAM. *Holy Family Cristo Rey Catholic High School*, 2001 19th St. Ensley, 35218. Tel: 205-787-9937; Fax: 205-787-8530. Web: www.hfcristorey.org. Rev. Alex Steinmiller, C.P., Pres.; Robert Larcher, Prin. Passionist Community of Chicago, IL. Priests 1; Lay Teachers 11; Students 172.

CULLMAN. *St. Bernard Preparatory School*, (Grades 7-12), 1600 St. Bernard Dr., SE, 35055. Tel: 256-739-6682; Fax: 256-734-2925. Email: sbprep@hiwaay.net. Web: www.stbernardprep.com. Rev. Joel W. Martin, O.S.B., Pres.; John Tekulve, Headmaster. Priests 3; Brothers 3; Lay Teachers 21; Students 153.

[C] ELEMENTARY SCHOOLS, PRIVATE

BIRMINGHAM. *St. Rose of Lima Academy*, (Grades K-8), 1401 22nd St. S., 35205. Tel: 205-933-0549; Fax: 205-933-0591. Email: smseton@saintroseacademy.com. Web: www.saintroseacademy.com. Sr. Mary Seton, Prin.; Peter Rataj, Librarian. Dominican Sisters of Nashville, TN. Sisters 5; Staff 10; Lay Teachers 12; Students 189.

[D] GENERAL HOSPITALS

BIRMINGHAM. *St. Vincent's Health System*, 810 St. Vincent's Dr., 35205. Tel: 205-939-7184; Fax: 205-930-2284. Email: Rhonda.Buzbee@stvhs.com. Web: www.stvhs.com. John O'Neil, Pres. & CEO. Ascension Health Sisters 3.
St. Vincent's Birmingham, P.O. Box 12407, 35202-2407. Tel: 205-939-7000; Fax: 205-930-2157. Email: dona.bush@stvhs.com. Web: www.stvhs.com. 810 St. Vincent's Dr., 35205. Ascension Health Total Staff 1,940; Nurses 723; Patients Assisted Annually 457,000; Bed Capacity 409.
St. Vincent's East, 50 Medical Park E. Dr., 35235. Tel: 205-838-3000; Fax: 205-838-3326. Email: nancy.lawrence@stvhs.com. Web: www.stvhs.com. Andy Davis, Pres. & COO. Ascension Health Total Staff 1,381; Nurses 194; Total Assisted Annually 190,000; Bed Capacity 282.
St. Vincent's Blount, 150 Gilbreath Dr., Oneonta, 35121. Tel: 205-274-3000; Fax: 205-274-3002. Email: Michelle.Brown@stvhs.com. Web: www.stvhs.com. Sean Tinney, Pres. Rural Facilities. Ascension Health Total Staff 195; Nurses 40; Total Assisted Annually 41,000; Bed Capacity 40.
St. Vincent's St. Clair, 2850 Dr. John Haynes Dr., Pell City, 35125. Tel: 205-338-3301; Fax: 205-814-2145. Email: Joanna.Murphree@stvhs.com. Web: www.stvhs.com. Sean Tinney, Pres. Rural Facilities. Ascension Health Total Staff 159; Nurses 56; Total Assisted Annually 1,500; Bed Capacity 82.

HUNTSVILLE. *Holy Name of Jesus Medical Center, Inc.*, 8305 Whitesburg Way, Apt. 305, Box 18173, 35804. Tel: 256-880-7064; Fax: 256-534-3141. Sr. Helen Gaffney, M.S.B.T., Pres. & CEO.

[E] MONASTERIES AND RESIDENCES OF PRIESTS AND BROTHERS

BIRMINGHAM. *Franciscan Missionaries of the Eternal*

Word, A Public Association of the Christian Faithful, 5821 Old Leeds Rd., 35210. Tel: 205-271-2937; Fax: 205-271-2949. Web: www.franciscanmissionaries.com. Revs. Anthony Mary Stelten, M.F.V.A., Community Servant; Joseph M. Wolfe, M.F.V.A.; Mark Mary Cristina, M.V.F.A.; Miguel Marie Soeherman, M.F.V.A., Community Vicar; Dominic Mary Garner, M.F.V.A. Professed 15; Total in Residence 17.

St. John Vianney Residence for Priests, 2724 Hanover Cir., 35205. Tel: 205-933-8078; Fax: 205-933-8097.

CULLMAN. *St. Bernard Abbey* (Corporate Title: Benedictine Society of Alabama, Inc.), 1600 St. Bernard Dr., S.E., 35055. Tel: 256-734-8291; Fax: 256-734-3885. Email: abcletus@stbernardprep.com. Web: www.stbernardabbey.com. Rt. Revs. Cletus D. Meagher, O.S.B., Abbot; Victor J. Clark, O.S.B., Retired Abbot (Retired); Revs. Edward P. Markley, O.S.B.; Marcus J. Voss, O.S.B.; Very Rev. Kevin D. McGrath, O.S.B.; Revs. Joel W. Martin, O.S.B.; Howard R. Moussier, O.S.B.; John O'Donnell, O.S.B.; Patrick Egan, O.S.B.; Bede Marcy, O.S.B.; Jacob Amos, O.S.B. Total Priests of Abbey 11; Brothers 20.

[F] CONVENTS AND RESIDENCES OF SISTERS

BIRMINGHAM. *Sister Servants of the Eternal Word*, Casa Maria Retreat House, 3721 Belmont Rd., 35210. Tel: 205-956-6760; Fax: 205-951-0386. Sr. Mary Gabriel, Supr.

CULLMAN. *Sacred Heart Monastery*, 916 Convent Rd., 35055. Tel: 256-734-4622; 256-734-2199; Fax: 256-255-0048. Email: sjmf@shmon.org. Sr. Janet Marie Flemming, O.S.B., Prioress. Benedictine Sisters. Professed Sisters 40.

HANCEVILLE. *Our Lady of the Angels Monastery, Inc. and Shrine of the Most Blessed Sacrament*, 3222 County Rd. 548, 35077. Tel: 205-271-2917; Fax: 205-795-5702. Web: www.olamshrine.com. Sisters M. Angelica, P.C.P.A., Abbess Emerita; Mary Catherine, Vicar. Poor Clare Nuns of Perpetual Adoration. Sisters 19; Novices 4; Postulants 3.

[G] DIOCESAN SOCIAL SERVICE

BIRMINGHAM. *Catholic Center of Concern* (Div. of Catholic Charities), 712 Fourth Ct. W., 35204. Tel: 205-786-4388; Fax: 205-786-6321. P.O. Box 12701, 35202. Email: czamboni@cssbhm.org. Sr. Cecilia Zamboni, M.C. Consolata Missionary Sisters. Total Staff 6; Total Assisted 20,000; Volunteer Hours 6,000.

Catholic Family Services, 1515 12th Ave., S., 35205. Tel: 205-324-6561; Fax: 205-323-0475. Email: tcook@cfsbhm.org. Web: www.cfsbhm.org. Thomas Cook, D.S.W., Dir. Total Staff 6; Total Assisted 1,095.

ANNISTON. *All Saints Interfaith Center of Concern*, 1029 W. 15th St., 36201. Tel: 256-236-7793; Fax: 256-236-7793. Email: sisterjane.coc@att.net. Sr. Jane O'Connor, M.S.B.T., Dir. Tel: 256-238-1365. Total Staff 3; Total Assisted 14,000.

EUTAW. *Consolata Apostolate*, 331 Boligee St., P.O. Box 538, 35462. Tel: 205-372-3497; Fax: 205-372-3497. Total Staff 2; Total Assisted 9,454.

FLORENCE. *Catholic Family Services*, 1111 E. College St., 35630. Tel: 256-768-1550. Michele Rivard, M.S.W., M.S., Social Worker. Total Assisted 342.

GADSDEN. *Catholic Center of Concern*, 612 Chestnut St., 35901. Tel: 866-546-4883; Fax: 256-547-1730. Total Assisted 15,601.

HAMILTON. *Christian Center of Concern*, P.O. Box 973, 35570. Tel: 205-921-3470. Rev. Timothy Pfander, Dir. Total Assisted 1,694.

HUNTSVILLE. *Catholic Center of Concern*, 1010 Church St., N.W., P.O. Box 745, 35804. Tel: 256-536-0041; Fax: 256-534-3141. Email: shgcctr@knology.net. Sr. Helen Gaffney, M.S.B.T., Dir. Total Assisted 4,306.

Catholic Family Services, 1010 Church St., N.W., P.O. Box 745, 35804. Tel: 256-536-0073; Fax: 256-534-3141. Email: cfshsv@knology.net. Web: www.cfsbhm.org. Laura Dinwiddie, M.S.W., Regl. Dir. Total Staff 3; Total Families Served 885.

SULLIGENT. *Christian Center of Concern*, P.O. Box 1154, 35586. Tel: 205-698-7197. Rev. Timothy Pfander, Dir. Total Staff 6; Total Assisted 1,029.

WINFIELD. *Christian Center of Concern*, 197 State Hwy. 253, 35594. Tel: 205-487-6230. Rev. Timothy Pfander, Dir.; Judy Sobrak, Bookkeeper. Total Assisted 3,641.

[H] CAMPUS MINISTRY

BIRMINGHAM. *The Chapel of St. Stephen the Martyr Campus Center* 1515 12th Ave. S., 35205. Tel: 205-933-2500; Fax: 205-939-1500. Email: saintst@bellsouth.com. Very Rev. Kevin M. Bazzel, J.C.L.; Sr. Karen Ann Lortscher, O.S.B., Campus Min. Parish Serves: University of Alabama at Birmingham, Samford University, Birmingham-Southern College. Total Staff 2; Students 100.

FLORENCE. *University of North Alabama* St. Joseph's Church, 1111 E. College St., 35630. Tel: 256-764-3303; Fax: 256-718-0208. Email: stjoseph@catholichill.com. Rev. Andrew A. Sullivan.

HUNTSVILLE. *Campus Ministry - University of Alabama in Huntsville c/o St. Joseph*, 2300 Beasley Ave., 35805. Tel: 256-534-8459; Fax: 256-534-8450. Email: stjoseph52@aol.com. Rev. Gary New, S.D.S., Contact Person.

JACKSONVILLE. *Jacksonville State University* St. Charles Church, 308 Seventh St., N.E., 36265. Tel: 256-435-3238; Fax: 256-435-4942. Email: stcharlesoffice@bellsouth.net. Rev. James R. Macey. Total Staff 2; Total in Program 15.

MONTEVALLO. *University of Montevallo* St. Thomas the Apostle Catholic Campus Ministry, 80 St. Thomas Way, 35115. Tel: 205-663-3936; Fax: 205-663-3929. Rev. Raymond A. Dunmyer.

TALLADEGA. *Talladega College Catholic Campus Ministry St. Francis of Assisi*, P.O. Box 1142, 35160. Tel: 256-362-5372. Rev. Thomas F. Woods.

TUSCALOOSA. *Diocesan Campus Ministry Office St. Francis University Parish*, 811 Fifth Ave., 35401. Tel: 205-758-5672; Fax: 205-758-5673. Email: frgerald@stfrancisuofa.com. Web: stfrancisuofa.com. Rev. Gerald Holloway. Total Staff 1; Total in Residence 1.

University of Alabama in Tuscaloosa St. Francis University Parish, 811 Fifth Ave., 35401. Tel: 205-758-5672; Fax: 205-758-5673. Email: office@stfrancisuofa.com. Web: stfrancisuofa.com. Rev. Gerald Holloway, Campus Min. Total Staff 2; Total in Residence 1.

[I] MISCELLANEOUS LISTINGS

BIRMINGHAM. *St. Barnabas Regional School Educational Foundation*, 7921 First Ave. N., 35206. Tel: 205-833-0334; Fax: 205-833-0270.

Bruno Family's Catholic Diocesan Trust, P.O. Box 12047, 35202-2047. Tel: 205-838-8322; Fax: 205-836-1910. Email: gnabors@bhmdiocese.org. Web: www.bhmdiocese.org.

Casa Maria Retreat House, 3721 Belmont Rd., 35210. Tel: 205-956-6760; Fax: 205-951-0386. Sr. Mary Gabriel, Dir.

Catholic Housing of Birmingham, Inc., P.O. Box 12047, 35202. Tel: 205-838-8311; Fax: 205-836-1910. 2121 3rd Ave. N., 35203. William M. Moran, Pres.; Rev. Msgr. Paul L. Rohling, V.G.

Congregation of the Passion: Holy Family Community, Inc. (House of Religious Men), 1910 19th St., Ensley, 35218. Tel: 205-780-3440; Fax: 205-780-5272. Email: rcrossmyer@aol.com. Revs. Robert Crossmyer, C.P., Local Supr.; Alex Steinmiller, C.P. Corporation for Holy Family Church, and Holy Family Elementary, Birmingham, and St. Mary's Church, Fairfield, St. Mary Elementary, Fairfield.

Contemplative Outreach Birmingham, 106 Red Stick Rd., Pelham, 35124. Tel: 205-991-6964. Email: tschached@bellsouth.net. Web: www.bham.net/cobweb. Diana Tschache, Coord.; Aloysius Golden, Area Contact Person. Tel: 205-592-3930.

The Fatima Educational Foundation, 708 First St. S., 35205. Tel: 205-322-1205. Web: olf.schoolinsites.com. Rev. Paul Oberg, S.S.J., Contact Person; Velda Gilyot, Prin.

St. Francis Xavier Catholic School Education Foundation, 2 Xavier Cir., 35213. Tel: 205-871-1687; Fax: 205-871-1674. Email: jnwrightiii@hotmail.com. Web: www.saintfrancisxavierschool.com. Nathan Wright, Prin. & Contact Person.

Holy Family Educational Foundation, 1910 19th St., 35218. Tel: 205-780-3440; Fax: 205-782-5272. Email: lmlang@bellsouth.net. Web: www.passionist.org. Melva Langford, Bd. Chair.

Holy Name of Jesus Hospital Trust (Senior Citizen Housing), c/o Regions Bank, P.O. Box 11426, 35202. Tel: 205-326-7219; Fax: 205-581-7433. Email: sidney.roebuck@regions.com. Sidney O. Roebuck Jr., Trustee, Vice Pres. & Senior Trust Officer, Regions Bank. Total Assisted 350.

John Carroll Catholic High School Educational Foundation, Inc., 300 Lakeshore Pkwy., 35209. Tel: 205-940-2400; Fax: 205-945-7429. Web: www.jcchs.org.

Ladies of Charity of Central Alabama, 1437 Ferncliff Cir., 35213. Tel: 205-421-9704. Email: marlygil@aol.com.

Magnificat: Mary, Woman of Faith Chapter, P.O. Box 660136, 35266-0136. Tel: 205-979-7645. Email: carolinamaenza@gmail.com. Web: www.magnificat-birminghamal.org. Carolina Maenza, Coord.

Our Lady of Sorrows Educational School Foundation, 1728 Oxmoor Rd., 35209. Tel: 205-871-8121; Fax: 205-871-8180.

Our Lady of the Valley Educational Foundation, 5514 Double Oak Ln., 35242. Tel: 205-991-5488; Fax: 205-991-5181. Email: olvchurch@olvsch.com.

St. Peter's Endowment Foundation, 2061 Patton Chapel Rd., 35216. Email: stpeterapostle@bellsouth.net. Rev. Thomas M. Kelly. Total Assisted 149; Total Staff 35.

St. Thomas More Society of Metro Birmingham, 2001 Park Pl. N., Ste. 400, 35203. Tel: 205-639-5300. Email: jwhitaker@wmslawfirm.com. G. Rick DiGiorgio, Chm.; John Whitaker, Pres.

Tuxedo Junction Catholic Community, Inc., 1910 19th St., Ensley, 35218. Tel: 205-780-3440; Fax: 205-780-5272.

Villa Maria I, 500 82nd St. S., 35206. Tel: 205-836-7839; Fax: 205-836-0664. Judy Murphree, Mgr. Total Staff 7; Total in Residence 63.

Villa Maria II, 500 82nd St. S., 35206.

St. Vincent's Foundation, 2800 University Blvd., Ste. 304, 35205. Tel: 205-939-7825; Fax: 205-930-2525. Web: www. stvfoundation.org. William M. Moran, Pres.; Jeffrey Scott Powell, Dir. Devel.; Jacqueline Godby Gardner, Dir. Capital Campaign.

BESSEMER. *St. Aloysius Educational Foundation*, 751 Academy Dr., 35022. Tel: 205-424-2984; Fax: 205-426-5753. Email: staloysius@bellsouth.net. Very Rev. Patrick P. Cullen.

CULLMAN. *Benedictine Manor Retirement Home, Inc.*, 200 Janeway Dr., 35055. Tel: 256-739-2853; Fax: 256-739-2860 (Call First). Email: benedictinemanor@att.net. Web: www.shmon.org. Sr. Virginia Rohling, O.S.B., Dir. Resident Capacity 35.

Benedictine Sisters Retreat Center, 916 Convent Rd., 35055-2019. Tel: 256-734-8302; Fax: 256-255-0048 (Call First). Email: retreats@shmon.org. Web: www.shmon.org. Sr. Therese Haydel, O.S.B., Dir. Bed Capacity 72; Total Staff 7.

St. Bernard Abbey Foundation, 1600 St. Bernard Dr., S.E., 35055. Tel: 256-734-8291; Fax: 256-734-3885. Web: www.stbernardabbey.com. Rt. Rev. Cletus Meagher, O.S.B., Chm.

St. Bernard Preparatory School Educational Foundation, 1600 St. Bernard Dr., S.E., 35055. Tel: 256-739-6682; Fax: 256-734-2925. Email: frmarcus@stbernardprep.com. Web: www.stbernardprep.com. Rt. Rev. Cletus Meagher, O.S.B., Chm.

Sacred Heart Monastery of Cullman, Alabama Foundation, 916 Convent Rd., 35055-2019. Tel: 256-734-4622; 256-734-3835; Fax: 256-255-0048. Web: www.shmon.org. Sr. Janet Marie Flemming, O.S.B., Prioress.

DECATUR. *St. Ann's Educational Foundation*, 3910 A Spring Ave., 35603. Tel: 256-353-2667; Fax: 256-353-8994. Email: parish@annunlord.com. Web: www.saintanndecatur.org. Christine Wright.

FLORENCE. *St. Joseph School Foundation, Florence*, 115 Plum St., 35630. Tel: 256-766-1923. Email: ceckleck@aol.com.

Society of St. Vincent de Paul, St. Joseph Conference, 659 S. Poplar St., 35630-6818. Tel: 256-718-0901; Fax: 256-718-0901. Email: stvincent2007@bellsouth.net. Rev. Andrew A. Sullivan, Spiritual Advisor; Roberta Bergner, Treas.

GADSDEN. *St. James Educational Foundation*, 700 Albert Rains Blvd., 35901. Tel: 256-546-0132; Fax: 256-546-0134. Email: jparker@st.jamesgadsden.org. Total Staff 22.

HUNTSVILLE. *Holy Spirit Regional School Foundation*, 625 Airport Rd., 35802. Tel: 256-881-4852, Ext. 137; Fax: 256-881-4904. Email: foundation89@comcast.net. Web: www.hstigers.org. Lee Dumbacher, Admin.

Society of St. Vincent dePaul, District Council of Huntsville, 625 Airport Rd., 35802. Tel: 256-883-0157. Email: hsvsvdp@knology.net. John Wolfsberger, Pres., District Council of Huntsville; Deacon Sam A. Dias, Spiritual Advisor; Patricia Schuessler, Treas.

St. Vincent De Paul Thrift Store, 2140 Jonathan Dr., 35810-3453. Tel: 256-851-8881. Patricia Schuessler, Mgr.

MADISON. *St. John's Educational Foundation*, 1055 Hughes Rd., 35758. Tel: 256-722-0130; Fax: 256-722-0303. Rev. Philip N. O'Kennedy.

PLEASANT GROVE. *Queen of Heaven Radio, Inc.*, P.O. Box 483, 35127. Tel: 205-744-4456; Fax: 205-744-4457.

TUSCALOOSA. *The Harrison Family Endowment Trust for the Benefit of Holy Spirit School*, 711 James I. Harrison Jr. Pkwy. E., 35405. Tel: 205-553-9630; Fax: 205-553-8880. Web: holyspirit-al.com. Very Rev. Jeremiah Deasy.

RELIGIOUS INSTITUTES OF MEN REPRESENTED IN THE DIOCESE

For further details refer to the corresponding bracketed number in the Religious Institutes of Men or Women section.

[0200]—*Benedictine Monks*—O.S.B.
[1000]—*Congregation of the Passion*—C.P.
[]—*Franciscan Missionaries of the Eternal Word*—M.F.V.A.
[]—*Incanatio Consecratio Missio*—(I.C.M.)
[1120]—*Missionaries of the Sacred Hearts of Jesus and Mary*—M.SS.CC.
[1190]—*Salesians of Don Bosco*—S.D.B.
[1200]—*Society of the Divine Savior*—S.D.S.
[0700]—*St. Joseph's Society of the Sacred Heart* (Baltimore, MD)—S.S.J.

RELIGIOUS INSTITUTES OF WOMEN REPRESENTED IN THE DIOCESE

[0230]—*Benedictine Sisters of Pontifical Jurisdiction*—O.S.B.
[0260]—*Blessed Sacrament Sisters*—S.B.S.
[0720]—*Consolata Missionary Sisters*—M.C.
[0760]—*Daughters of Charity of St. Vincent de Paul*—D.C.
[0820]—*Daughters of the Holy Spirit*—D.H.S.
[1070-03]—*Dominican Sisters* (Adrian, MI)—O.P.
[1070-07]—*Dominican Sisters* (Nashville, TN)—O.P.
[1845]—*Guadalupan Missionaries of the Holy Spirit*—M.G.Sp.S.
[2720]—*Mission Helpers of the Sacred Heart*—M.H.S.H.
[2790]—*Missionary Servants of the Most Blessed Trinity*—M.S.B.T.
[3210]—*Poor Clares of Perpetual Adoration*—P.C.P.A.
[]—*Sister Servants of the Eternal Word*—S.S.E.W.
[2575]—*Sisters of Mercy of the Americas*—R.S.M.
[1650]—*Sisters of St. Francis of Philadelphia*—O.S.F.
[3840]—*Sisters of St. Joseph of Carondelet*—C.S.J.
[1030]—*Sisters of the Divine Savior*—S.D.S.
[3320]—*Sisters of the Presentation of the B.V.M.*—P.B.V.M
[4048]—*Society of Sisters Faithful Companions of Jesus*—F.C.J.

NECROLOGY

† Egan, Rev. Msgr. Brian J., (Retired)—Died Jan. 25, 2011

An asterisk (*) denotes an organization that has established tax-exempt status directly with the IRS and is not covered by the USCCB Group Ruling.

Diocese of Bismarck

(Dioecesis Bismarckiensis)

Most Reverend

DAVID D. KAGAN, D.D., P.A., J.C.L.

Bishop of Bismarck; ordained June 14, 1975; named Prelate of Honor November 14, 1994; Protonotary Apostolic May 21, 2011; appointed Bishop of Bismarck October 19, 2011; installed November 30, 2011.

NIHIL AMORI CHRISTI PRAEPONERE

Chancery Office: *420 Raymond St., P.O. Box 1575, Bismarck, ND 58502-1575.* Tel: 701-223-1347; Fax: 701-223-3693.

Most Reverend

PAUL A. ZIPFEL, D.D.

Bishop Emeritus of Bismarck; ordained March 18, 1961; appointed Titular Bishop of Walla Walla and Auxiliary Bishop of St. Louis May 16, 1989; consecrated June 29, 1989; appointed Bishop of Bismarck December 31, 1996; installed February 20, 1997; retired October 19, 2011. *Res.: University of Mary, 7500 University Dr., Bismarck, ND 58504-9634.*

ESTABLISHED DECEMBER 31, 1909.

Square Miles 34,268.

Comprises the Counties of Adams, Billings, Bowman, Burke, Burleigh, Divide, Dunn, Emmons, Golden Valley, Grant, Hettinger, McKenzie, McLean, Mercer, Morton, Mountrail, Oliver, Renville, Sioux, Slope, Stark, Ward and Williams in the State of North Dakota.

For legal titles of parishes and diocesan institutions, consult the Chancery Office.

STATISTICAL OVERVIEW

Personnel	
Bishop	1
Retired Bishops	1
Abbots	1
Priests: Diocesan Active in Diocese	41
Priests: Diocesan Active Outside Diocese	4
Priests: Retired, Sick or Absent	21
Number of Diocesan Priests	66
Religious Priests in Diocese	19
Total Priests in Diocese	85
Extern Priests in Diocese	14
Ordinations:	
Diocesan Priests	2
Transitional Deacons	1
Permanent Deacons	4
Permanent Deacons in Diocese	77
Total Brothers	20
Total Sisters	78
Parishes	
Parishes	98
With Resident Pastor:	
Resident Diocesan Priests	32
Resident Religious Priests	13
Without Resident Pastor:	
Administered by Priests	52
Administered by Deacons	1
Pastoral Centers	1
Professional Ministry Personnel:	
Sisters	2
Lay Ministers	35
Welfare	
Catholic Hospitals	4
Total Assisted	354,819
Homes for the Aged	6
Total Assisted	617
Special Centers for Social Services	4
Total Assisted	500
Other Institutions	1
Total Assisted	120
Educational	
Diocesan Students in Other Seminaries	17
Total Seminarians	17
Colleges and Universities	1
Total Students	2,971
High Schools, Diocesan and Parish	3
Total Students	663
Elementary Schools, Diocesan and Parish	10
Total Students	1,620
Catechesis/Religious Education:	
High School Students	1,529
Elementary Students	5,127
Total Students under Catholic Instruction	11,927
Teachers in the Diocese:	
Priests	3
Sisters	4
Lay Teachers	206
Vital Statistics	
Receptions into the Church:	
Infant Baptism Totals	950
Minor Baptism Totals	100
Adult Baptism Totals	36
Received into Full Communion	110
First Communions	870
Confirmations	980
Marriages:	
Catholic	208
Interfaith	120
Total Marriages	328
Deaths	551
Total Catholic Population	60,411
Total Population	281,619

Former Bishops—Most Revs. VINCENT DE PAUL WEHRLE, O.S.B., D.D., appt. Bishop of Bismarck, April 9, 1910; cons. May 19, 1910; retired Dec. 11, 1939; named Titular Bishop of Teos by Pope Pius XII; died Nov. 2, 1941; VINCENT J. RYAN, D.D., L.L.D., appt. March 19, 1940; cons. May 28, 1940; died Nov. 10, 1951; LAMBERT A. HOCH, D.D., L.L.D., appt. Jan. 23, 1952; cons. March 25, 1952; transferred to Diocese of Sioux Falls, Dec. 5, 1956; died June 27, 1990; HILARY B. HACKER, D.D., appt. Bishop, Dec. 29, 1956; retired June 28, 1982; died Nov. 6, 1990; JOHN F. KINNEY, D.D., J.C.D., appt. June 28, 1982; Episcopal Ord. Jan. 25, 1977; installed Aug. 23, 1982; transferred to Diocese of St. Cloud, July 6, 1995; PAUL A. ZIPFEL, D.D. (Retired), ord. March 18, 1961; appt. Titular Bishop of Walla Walla and Auxiliary Bishop of St. Louis May 16, 1989; cons. June 29, 1989; appt. Bishop of Bismarck Dec. 31, 1996; installed Feb. 20, 1997; retired Oct. 19, 2011.

Moderator of the Curia—Rev. JOHN G. GUTHRIE.

Vicar General—Rev. JOHN G. GUTHRIE.

Chancery Office—420 Raymond St., P.O. Box 1575, Bismarck, 58502-1575. Tel: 701-223-1347; Fax: 701-223-3693.

Chancellor—Deacon JOEL MELARVIE.

Center for Pastoral Ministry Office—520 N. Washington St., P.O. Box 1137, Bismarck, 58502-1137. Tel: 701-222-3035.

Office of Canonical Services (Marriage Tribunal)—520 N. Washington St., P.O. Box 1137, Bismarck, 58502-1137. Tel: 701-222-3035. Marriage papers are sent to this office.

Judicial Vicar—Rev. GENE E. LINDEMANN, J.C.L., Dir.

Defensor Vinculi—Rev. DAVID L. ZIMMER, J.C.L.

Promoter of Justice—Rev. DAVID L. ZIMMER, J.C.L.

Pro-Synodal Judges—Revs. MARVIN J. KLEMMER (Retired); BRUCE D. KREBS; GENE LINDEMANN, J.C.L.; Ms. MARY TARVER, J.C.L. Ponens..

Associate Judges—Revs. KEITH N. STREIFEL; DAVID RICHTER; SHANNON G. LUCHT; CHAD GION.

Auditor—HELEN SCHERR-BOURGOIS.

Notary—SANDRA BREINER.

Presbyteral Council—Revs. GENE E. LINDEMANN, J.C.L., Chm.; BRUCE D. KREBS, Sec.; DENNIS R. SCHAFER; DANIEL J. BERG; JOHN G. GUTHRIE, Ex Officio; SHANNON G. LUCHT, Treas.; Rt. Rev. BRIAN WANGLER, O.S.B., M.A.; Revs. THOMAS E. KRAMER, Vice Chm. (Retired); PAUL D. BECKER.

Diocesan Corporate Board—Most Rev. DAVID D. KAGAN, Pres.; Revs. JOHN G. GUTHRIE, Vice Pres.; DANIEL J. BERG; JAMES B. BRAATEN; Deacon JOEL MELARVIE, Sec.

Diocesan Finance Council—Most Rev. DAVID D. KAGAN, Pres.; Revs. JOHN G. GUTHRIE, Chm.; JAMES B. BRAATEN; DANIEL J. BERG; MIKE SCHWINDT; MARVIN HEINERT, Consultant; THOMAS BAIR, Consultant; TIM CONLIN; KEVIN DVORAK; JIM LONG; BRIAN RUMMEL; GREG VETTER; MICHAEL T. SCHMITZ. Ex Officio: LAURA J. HUBER; Deacon JOEL MELARVIE; RON SCHATZ.

Diocesan Offices and Directors

Archives—Deacon JOEL MELARVIE, Mailing Address: P.O. Box 1575, Bismarck, 58502-1575. Tel: 701-223-1347.

Boy Scouts—

National Catholic Committee on Scouting—Deacon HARVEY HANEL, 1918 Grandview Lane, Bismarck, 58503-0849.

Catholic Campaign For Human Development—Mr. RONALD SCHATZ, Dir., Mailing Address: P.O. Box 1137, Bismarck, 58502-1137. Tel: 701-222-3035.

Catholic Charities North Dakota—LARRY BERNHARDT, Exec. Dir., 5201 Bishops Blvd., Ste. B, Fargo, 58104-7605. Tel: 701-235-4457. Other Locations: 919 7th St. S., Ste. 607, Bismarck, 58504-5881. Tel: 701-255-1793. 216 S. Broadway, Ste. 103, Minot, 58701-3852. Tel: 701-852-2854.

Catholic Relief—Mr. RONALD SCHATZ, Dir., Mailing Address: P.O. Box 1137, Bismarck, 58502-1137. Tel: 701-222-3035.

Office of Vocations—Rev. THOMAS J. RICHTER, Dir., Mailing Address: P.O. Box 1137, Bismarck, 58502-1137. Tel: 701-222-3035.

Vicar for Presbyters—Rev. JAMES B. BRAATEN, Mailing Address: 1905 S. 3rd St., Bismarck, 58504-7118. Tel: 701-223-3606.

Office of Worship—Rev. GENE E. LINDEMANN, J.C.L., Interim Dir., Mailing Address: P.O. Box 1575, Bismarck, 58502-1575. Tel: 701-223-1347.

Continuing Education for Clergy—Rev. AUSTIN VETTER, 105 1st St., S.E., Minot, 58701-3901. Tel: 701-838-1026.

Newspaper— "Dakota Catholic Action" Deacon JOEL MELARVIE, Editor, Mailing Address: P.O. Box

1575, Bismarck, 58502-1575. Tel: 701-223-1347.

North Dakota Catholic Conference—CHRISTOPHER DODSON, 103 S. 3rd St., Ste. 10, Bismarck, 58501-3800. Tel: 701-223-2519; Fax: 701-223-6075.

Permanent Diaconate Office—

Vicar for Deacons—Rev. THOMAS J. RICHTER, Mailing Address: P.O. Box 1137, Bismarck, 58502-1137. Tel: 701-222-3035.

Director of Deacons—DAVID FLECK, Mailing Address: P.O. Box 1137, Bismarck, 58502-1137. Tel: 701-222-3035.

Priests' Benefit Association—Most Rev. DAVID D. KAGAN, Pres.; Revs. KENNETH G. PHILLIPS, Vice Chm.; CHARLES A. HEIDT, Treas. (Retired); DAVID G. MORMAN; JAMES B. BRAATEN, Chm.; DAVID RICHTER; RUSSELL P. KOVASH; LAURA J. HUBER, Agent of Record.

Priests' Personnel Board—Revs. CHAD GION, Chm.; PATRICK A. SCHUMACHER, S.T.L., Sec.; DAVID L. ZIMMER, J.C.L.; RUSSELL P. KOVASH; THOMAS J. RICHTER, Ex Officio; Most Rev. DAVID D. KAGAN, Ex Officio.

Propagation of the Faith—Mr. RONALD M. SCHATZ, Mailing Address: P.O. Box 1137, Bismarck, 58502-1137. Tel: 701-222-3035.

Communications Office—Deacon JOEL MELARVIE, Dir., Mailing Address: P.O. Box 1575, Bismarck, 58502-1575. Tel: 701-223-1347.

Faith Formation and Education—BETTY E. GREFF, Dir., Mailing Address: P.O. Box 1137, Bismarck, 58502-1137. Tel: 701-222-3035. Email: bgreff@bismarckdiocese.com.

Provision for the Future—LAURA J. HUBER, Contact Person, 520 N. Washington St., P.O. Box 1137, Bismarck, 58502-1137. Tel: 701-222-3035. Email: lhuber@bismarckdiocese.com.

Stewardship and Resource Development Office—Mr. RONALD SCHATZ, Dir., Mailing Address: P.O. Box 1137, Bismarck, 58502-1137. Tel: 701-222-3035. Email: rschatz@bismarckdiocese.com.

Planned Giving—Mr. MIKE KIEDROWSKI, Dir., Mailing Address: P.O. Box 1137, Bismarck, 58502-1137. Tel: 701-222-3035. Email: mkiedrowski@bismarckdiocese.com.

Youth Ministry—KENNETH H. ROSHAU, Dir., 11010 41st St., S.W., Dickinson, 58601-9512. Tel: 701-290-4137. Email: kroshau@bismarckdiocese.com.

Search Program—KENNETH H. ROSHAU, 11010 41st St., S.W., Dickinson, 58601-9512. Tel: 701-290-4137. Email: kroshau@bismarckdiocese.com.

Victim Assistance Coordinator—Deacon JOEL MELARVIE, Mailing Address: P.O. Box 1575, Bismarck, 58502-1575. Tel: 701-223-1347. Email: jmelarvie@bismarckdiocese.com.

Finance Officer—LAURA J. HUBER, Mailing Address: P.O. Box 1137, Bismarck, 58502-1137. Tel: 701-222-3035. Email: lhuber@bismarckdiocese.com.

Family Ministry—JOYCE MCDOWALL, Dir., Mailing Address: P.O. Box 1137, Bismarck, 58502-1137. Tel: 701-222-3035. Email: jmcdowall@bismarckdiocese.com.

Parish Planning—Deacon LYNN CLANCY, Mailing Address: P.O. Box 1137, Bismarck, 58502-1137. Tel: 701-222-3035. Email: lclancy@bismarckdiocese.com.

Risk Management—ROMAN WEILER, Dir., Mailing Address: P.O. Box 1137, Bismarck, 58502-1137. Tel: 701-222-3035. Email: rweiler@bismarckdiocese.com.

Ecumenism—VACANT.

Respect Life—AMANDA ELLERKAMP. Tel: 701-590-2837.

Native American Ministry—Mr. RONALD SCHATZ, Mailing Address: P.O. Box 1137, Bismarck, 58502-1137. Tel: 701-222-3035.

CLERGY, PARISHES, MISSIONS AND PAROCHIAL SCHOOLS

CITY OF BISMARCK

(BURLEIGH COUNTY)

1—CATHEDRAL OF THE HOLY SPIRIT (1945) [JC] Revs. John G. Guthrie; Brian P. Gross, Parochial Vicar; Deacons Richard Fettig; Gary Mizeur; Ralph von Ruden; Wilfred Wolf, (Retired).
Mailing Address: 519 Raymond St., 58501. Tel: 701-223-1033; Fax: 701-223-1438. Email: cathchrch@bismarckdiocese.com. Web: www.cathedralparish.com.
School—508 Raymond St., 58501. Tel: 701-223-5484; Fax: 701-223-5485. Leann Binde, Prin. Lay Teachers 16; Students 227.
Catechesis/Religious Program—Tel: 701-222-2259. Marie Gabel, D.R.E. Students 338.

2—SAINT ANNE (1957) [JC] Revs. Edwin P. Wehner; Jason R. Signalness, Parochial Vicar; Deacons Wayne Jundt; Joe Krupinsky; Mary Ann Meyer, Business & Operations Mgr.
Res.: 1321 Braman Ave., 58501. Tel: 701-223-1549; Fax: 701-250-9214. Web: www.stannesbismarck.org.
School—(Grades PreK-8) Tel: 701-223-3373. Web: www.st-anneschool.org. Cori Hilzendeger, Prin.; Sheila Krogstad, Librarian. Lay Teachers 14; Students 210.
Catechesis/Religious Program—Tel: 701-224-0847. Marilyn Geiger, C.R.E. Students 351.

3—ASCENSION (1974) [JC] Rev. James B. Braaten; Deacons Ray Grabar, (Retired); Tony J. Finneman; Doyle F. Schulz.
Res.: 1905 S. Third St., 58504-7118. Tel: 701-223-3606; Fax: 701-223-5783. Email: ascension@midconetwork.com. Web: ascensionbismarck.org.
Catechesis/Religious Program—Tel: 701-223-5783. Brian Hefer, D.R.E. Students 269.

4—CORPUS CHRISTI (1964) [JC] Rev. Paul D. Becker; Sr. Ivo Schoch, Pastoral Assoc.; Deacons Harry M. Deichert, (Retired); Michael Fix; Joseph J. Mathern, (Retired); Rex McDowell; John Tharaldsen.
Res.: 1919 N. Second St., 58501. Tel: 701-255-4600 (Church); Fax: 701-255-4616.
Catechesis/Religious Program—Tel: 701-255-3104. Tara Brooke, D.R.E.; Tracy Kraft, D.R.E. Students 496.

5—ST. MARY (1877) [JC] Rev. Gene E. Lindemann; Deacons Tony Dworshak, (Retired); Terry Glatt, Outreach Min.; Harvey Hanel; Kenneth Klein; Michael Marback; Steve Braus, Admin.; Diane Huck, Pastoral Min.; Lila Steffes, Bookkeeper; Diane Grotewold, Music Min.; Mary Vandal, Sec.
Res.: 816 E. Broadway, 58501. Tel: 701-223-5562; Fax: 701-530-0864. Email: smpf@stmarysparishfamily.net. Web: stmarysbismarck.org.
School—(Grades PreSchool-8), 807 E. Thayer Ave., 58501. Tel: 701-223-0225; Fax: 701-250-9918. Email: tony.fladeland@sendit.nodak.edu. Tony Fladeland, Prin. Lay Teachers 14; Students 234.
Catechesis/Religious Program—Email: sheila@stmarysparishfamily.net. Sheila Gilbertson, Faith Formation. Students 177.

OUTSIDE THE CITY OF BISMARCK

ALEXANDER, MCKENZIE CO., OUR LADY OF CONSOLATION (1907), Served from Watford City. Rev. John M. Pfeifer.
c/o Epiphany, P.O. Box 670, Watford City, 58854-0670. Tel: 701-842-3791.

ALMONT, MORTON CO., ST. MARY, QUEEN OF PEACE (1907), Served from New Salem. Rev. Amalraj Roche (India).
c/o St. Pius V, P.O. Box C, New Salem, 58563-0429. Tel: 701-843-7061.
Catechesis/Religious Program—

ALPHA, GOLDEN VALLEY CO., MOST HOLY REDEEMER (1919) Closed. For inquiries for parish records contact the chancery.

AMIDON, SLOPE CO., SS. PETER & PAUL (1918) Closed. For inquiries for parish records contact the chancery.

BEACH, GOLDEN VALLEY CO., ST. JOHN THE BAPTIST (1909) [CEM] Rev. Russell P. Kovash; Bro. Samuel Larson, S.D.S.; Deacons Donald Nistler; James Wosepka.
Res.: 162 2nd Ave., S.E., Box 337, 58621-0337. Tel: 701-872-4153; Fax: 701-872-4733.
Catechesis/Religious Program—Walt Losinski, D.R.E.; Shelly Hauck, D.R.E. Students 73.

BELFIELD, STARK CO., ST. BERNARD (1910) [CEM] Rev. Shannon G. Lucht.
Res.: P.O. Box 38, 58622. Tel: 701-575-4295; Fax: 701-575-8457. Email: stbernardbelfield@ndsupernet.com.
Catechesis/Religious Program—Tel: 701-575-4099. Diane Procive, D.R.E. (High School). Students 65.

BENTLEY, HETTINGER CO., SACRED HEART (1920) Closed. For inquiries for parish records contact the chancery.

BERTHOLD, WARD CO., ST. ANN (1903), Served from Stanley. Rev. Mike Millard.
c/o Queen of the Most Holy Rosary, P.O. Box 159, Stanley, 58784-0159. Tel: 701-628-2323.
Catechesis/Religious Program—Rhonda Hanson, D.R.E. Students 17.

BEULAH, MERCER CO.

1—ST. BENEDICT (1911) Closed. For inquiries for parish records contact the chancery.

2—ST. JOSEPH (1915), (German—Russian), [CEM] Rev. Johnson Kuriappilly; Deacon Daniel Wallach. 115 3rd St., N.E., 58523. Email: stjoseph.office@midconetwork.com. Web: sanjoscommunity.org. Mailing Address: P.O. Box 146, 58523.
Res.: 508 1st Ave., N.E., 58523. Tel: 701-873-5397; Fax: 701-873-5614. Email: stjoseph.pastor@midconetwork.com. Web: radical4gospel.com.
Catechesis/Religious Program—Tel: 701-873-5006; Fax: 701-873-5614. Email: stjoseph.ccd@midconetwork.com; stjoseph.youth@midconetwork.com. Students 122.

BLAISDELL, MOUNTRAIL CO., ST. MARGARET (1912) Closed. For inquiries for parish records contact the chancery.

BOWBELLS, BURKE CO., ST. JOSEPH (BOWBELLS) (1905), (German—Scandinavian), Rev. Selvaraj Periannan, M.S.F.X. (India).
Res.: 409 E. Division, P.O. Box 488, Kenmare, 58746. Tel: 701-385-4311; Fax: 701-385-4321.
Church: 102 3rd St., N.W., 58721. Tel: 701-377-2611 (Parish Center).
Catechesis/Religious Program— Combined with St. Agnes Students 1.

BOWMAN, BOWMAN CO., ST. CHARLES (1910) Rev. David G. Morman.
Res.: 202 First Ave. S.W., 58623. Tel: 701-523-5292; Fax: 701-523-5415.
Catechesis/Religious Program—Tel: 701-523-5415. Tobiann Andrews, D.R.E. (Grades 1-6); Barbi Narum, D.R.E. (Grades 7-12). Students 126.

BRADDOCK, EMMONS CO., ST. KATHERINE (1908), Served from Linton. Rev. David Richter.
c/o St. Anthony, 613 N. Broadway, Linton, 58552-7311. Tel: 701-254-4588.
Catechesis/Religious Program—Students 8.

BRISBANE, GRANT CO., HOLY INFANT JESUS (1911) Closed. For inquiries for parish records contact the chancery.

BURLINGTON, WARD CO., ST. FRANCIS OF ASSISI (1889) Closed. For inquiries for parish records contact the chancery.

BUTTE, MCLEAN CO., HOLY GHOST (1939) Closed. For inquiries for parish records contact the chancery.

CANNON BALL, SIOUX CO., ST. ELIZABETH (1897), Served from Fort Yates. Rev. Basil Atwell, O.S.B.
c/o St. Peter, P.O. Box 394, Fort Yates, 58538-0394. Tel: 701-854-3473.

CARSON, GRANT CO., ST. THERESA THE CHILD JESUS (1920) [JC] Rev. Daniel J. Berg.
204 2nd Ave., N.E., 58529.
Res.: 421 Court St., Flasher, 58535-7216. Tel: 701-597-3570; 701-597-3228; Fax: 701-597-3228.
Catechesis/Religious Program—Tel: 701-597-3228. Students 30.

CARTWRIGHT, MCKENZIE CO., ST. JOSEPH (1913) Closed. For inquiries for parish records contact the chancery.

CENTER, OLIVER CO., ST. MARTIN (1914) [CEM 3] [JC] Rev. Amalraj Roche (India).
Res.: 322 2nd St. E., P.O. Box 2766, 58530. Tel: 701-794-3329; Fax: 701-794-3601.
Catechesis/Religious Program—Tel: 701-794-3191. Judith McNulty, D.R.E. Students 40.

COLUMBUS, BURKE CO., ST. MICHAEL (1905) Closed. For inquiries for parish records contact the chancery.

CROSBY, DIVIDE CO., ST. PATRICK (1912) [CEM 4] [JC 2] Rev. Biju Chitteth (India).
Res.: 205 1st. St. N.W., P.O. Box 89, 58730. Tel: 701-965-6537; Fax: 701-965-6537.
Catechesis/Religious Program—Tel: 701-965-6674. Students 13.

CROWN BUTTE, MORTON CO., ST. VINCENT (1896) [CEM] Deacon Steve M. Brannan; Nancy J. Brannan, Pastoral Assoc.
Res.: 2119 S. 3rd St., 58504.
Catechesis/Religious Program—Students 26.

DE LACS, WARD CO., ST. VINCENT DE PAUL (1912) Closed. For inquiries for parish records contact the chancery.

DICKINSON, STARK CO.

1—ST. JOSEPH (1902), (German—Russian), [CEM] Rev. Keith N. Streifel; Deacons Terry B. Quintus; Al Schwindt.
Res.: 240 E. Broadway, 58601. Tel: 701-483-2223; Fax: 701-483-0648. Email: stjoseph@ndsupernet.com.
Catechesis/Religious Program—Kris Quintus, D.R.E. Students 111.

2—ST. PATRICK (1885) Rev. Todd Kreitinger; Deacons Anton Wanner; Ron Keller.
Res.: 229 Third Ave. W., 58601. Tel: 701-483-6700; Fax: 701-483-6702. Email: stpatrick@goesp.com.
Catechesis/Religious Program—Tel: 701-225-8831; Fax: 701-225-8831. Jessica Emter, D.R.E. Students 100.

3—QUEEN OF PEACE CHURCH (1973) [JC] Revs. Jeffrey Zwack; Joshua J. Ehli, Parochial Vicar.
Office: 725 12th St. W., 58601-3516. Tel: 701-483-2134; 701-483-2991 (Res.); Fax: 701-483-1379. Web: www.queenofpeacedickinson.org.
Catechesis/Religious Program—Sr. Phoebe Schwartze, O.S.B., D.R.E. Students 164.

4—ST. WENCESLAUS (1912), (Bohemian), [CEM] [JC] Rev. Patrick A. Schumacher; Deacons Eugene F. Morman, (Retired); Raymond Jilek, (Retired); Robert Stockert; Robert Zent; Sarah Bengtson, Pastoral Asst.
Res.: 525 Third St. E., 58601. Tel: 701-225-3972;

Fax: 701-225-4146.
School—515 3rd St. E., 58601. Tel: 701-225-9463; 701-483-6083; Fax: 701-225-0474. Kelly Koppinger, Supt.; Mr. Carter Fong, Prin. High Sch. & Jr. High; Peggy Mayer, Elem. Prin. Lay Teachers 11; Students 118.
See Dickinson Catholic School, Dickinson under High Schools Interparochial and Parish located in the Institution section.
Catechesis/Religious Program—Nicole Berg, Rel. Educ. Coord. Students 211.

DODGE, DUNN CO.
1—ST. MARTIN (1908) Closed. For inquiries for parish records contact the chancery.
2—PRECIOUS BLOOD (1920) Closed. For inquiries for parish records contact the chancery.

DONNYBROOK, WARD CO., ST. ANTHONY (1902), Served from Kenmare. Rev. Selvaraj Periannan, M.S.F.X. (India).
c/o St. Agnes, P.O. Box 488, Kenmare, 58746-0488. Tel: 701-385-4311.
Catechesis/Religious Program—Deb Zettinger, D.R.E.; Andrea Hager, D.R.E. Combined with St. Agnes Students 6.

DOUGLAS, WARD CO., HOLY CROSS (1908) Closed. For inquiries for parish records contact the chancery.

DRISCOLL, BURLEIGH CO., ST. ANTHONY (1906) Closed. For inquiries for parish records contact the chancery.

EMMONS, EMMONS CO.
1—ST. BERNARD (1884) Closed. For inquiries for parish records contact the chancery.
2—ST. JOSEPH (1918) Closed. For inquiries for parish records contact the chancery.

ENDRES, MCLEAN CO., ST. ADOLPH (1906) Closed. For inquiries for parish records contact the chancery.

EPPING, WILLIAMS CO., ST. MARY (1915) Closed. For inquiries for parish records contact the chancery.

FALLON, MORTON CO., SS. PETER & PAUL (1907) Closed. For inquiries for parish records contact the chancery.

FAYETTE, DUNN CO., ST. EDWARD (1914) Closed. For inquiries for parish records contact the chancery.

FLASHER, MORTON CO., ST. LAWRENCE (1912) [CEM] Rev. Daniel J. Berg.
Res.: 421 Court St., 58535-7216. Tel: 701-597-3570; Fax: 701-597-3228. Email: stlwrnce@westriv.com.
Catechesis/Religious Program—Tel: 701-597-3228. Students 96.

FORT RICE, MORTON CO. , IMMACULATE CONCEPTION (1908) Closed. For inquiries for parish records contact the chancery.

FORT YATES, SIOUX CO., ST. PETER - CATHOLIC INDIAN MISSION (1878), (Native American), [CEM], (Standing Rock Indian Reservation) Rev. Basil Atwell, O.S.B.; Bro. George Maufort, S.D.S.
Res.: P.O. Box 394, 58538. Tel: 701-854-3473; Fax: 701-854-3474.
School—St. Bernard Mission School, (Grades K-7) Tel: 701-854-7413. Sr. Richarde Wolf, S.S.N.D., Prin. Lay Teachers 3; Students 70.
Catechesis/Religious Program—Tel: 701-854-3447.

FORTUNA, DIVIDE CO., ST. BERNARD (1918) Closed. For inquiries for parish records contact the chancery.

FOXHOLM, WARD CO., ST. MARY (1887) [CEM] [JC] Rev. Tomy Joseph, M.S.F.X.
Res.: 17901 128th Ave. N.W., 58718-9643. Tel: 701-468-5925.
Catechesis/Religious Program—Tel: 701-468-5648. Students 80.

GARRISON, MCLEAN CO., ST. NICHOLAS (1905) Rev. Joseph John Kandathiparambil (India).
Res.: 235 Second St. N.E., P.O. Box 870, 58540. Tel: 701-463-2327; Fax: 701-463-2323.
Catechesis/Religious Program—Students 59.

GAYLORD, STARK CO., OUR LADY OF LOURDES (1910) Closed. For inquiries for parish records contact the chancery.

GLADSTONE, STARK CO., ST. THOMAS (1903), Served from Richardton. Rev. Boniface Muggli, O.S.B.
c/o St. Mary, 332 2nd St. N., Richardton, 58652-7141. Tel: 701-974-3569.
Catechesis/Religious Program—Dennise Miller, D.R.E. Twinned with St. Mary's, Richardton. Students 2.

GLEN ULLIN, MORTON CO.
1—ST. JOSEPH (1918), Served from Glen Ullin. Rev. Arul Joseph Irudamoney.
c/o Sacred Heart, P.O. Box 609, 58631-0609. Tel: 701-348-3527. 5210 62nd Ave., 58631.
Catechesis/Religious Program— Twinned with Sacred Heart, Glen Ullin. Students 5.
2—SACRED HEART OF JESUS (1883), (German—Russian), [CEM 2] Rev. Arul Joseph Irudamoney.
Res.: 204 E. Ash Ave., Box 609, 58631-0609. Tel: 701-348-3518. Email: aruljoe@gmail.com.
Catechesis/Religious Program—Tel: 701-348-3527. Mrs. Lisa Staiger, Coord.; Mrs. Darla Geiss, Coord. Students 72.

GLENBURN, RENVILLE CO., ST. PHILOMENA (1948), (German—Scandinavian), [CEM] Rev. Tomy Joseph, M.S.F.X.
Res.: 310 3rd Ave. N., P.O. Box 68, 58740. Tel: 701-362-7571; Fax: 701-362-7571.
Catechesis/Religious Program—Kelly Zelinski, D.R.E. Students 18.

GOLVA, GOLDEN VALLEY CO., ST. MARY'S GOLVA (1906) [CEM], Served from Beach. Rev. Russell P. Kovash.
c/o St. John the Baptist, P.O. Box 337, Beach, 58621-0337. Tel: 701-872-4153.
Catechesis/Religious Program—Walt Losinski, D.R.E. (Grades 7-12); Shelly Hauck, D.R.E. (Grades K-6). High School twinned with St. John, Beach. Students 19.

GRASSNA, EMMONS CO., HOLY TRINITY (1900) Closed. For inquiries for parish records contact the chancery.

GRASSY BUTTE, MCKENZIE CO., ST. PETER CANSIUS (1927) Closed. For inquiries for parish records contact the chancery.

GRENORA, WILLIAMS CO., ST. BONIFACE (1912) [CEM 2] [JC] Rev. Raymond A. Aydt.
Church: P.O. Box 37, 58845. Tel: 701-694-3743.
Res.: 118 Fifth St. W., Williston, 58801. Tel: 701-572-6732.
Catechesis/Religious Program—Tel: 701-694-6560. Nicole Berg, D.R.E. Students 12.

HAGUE, EMMONS CO.
1—ST. ALOYSIUS (1899) Closed. For inquiries for parish records contact the chancery.
2—ST. MARY (1890), (German—Russian), [CEM 2] Rev. Paul Eberle.
Church: P.O. Box 156, 58542. Tel: 701-336-7456.
Res.: Box 322, Strasburg, 58573. Tel: 701-336-7172.
Catechesis/Religious Program—Tel: 701-336-7102. Kathleen Kramer Nagel, D.R.E. Students 27.

HALEY, BOWMAN CO., ST. STANISLAUS (1908) Closed. For inquiries for parish records contact the chancery.

HALLIDAY, DUNN CO., ST. PAUL (1952) [CEM] [JC], (Quasi-Parish) Rev. Darnis Selvanayakam, M.S.F.X. (India).
Res.: 152 3rd Ave. N.W., P.O. Box 299, Killdeer, 58640. Tel: 701-764-5357; Fax: 701-764-6246. Email: stjosephs@ndsupernet.com.
Catechesis/Religious Program—Students 3.

HANKS, WILLIAMS CO., OUR LADY OF GOOD COUNSEL (1918) Closed. For inquiries for parish records contact the chancery.

HAYMARSH, MORTON CO., ST. CLEMENT (ORATORY) (1887), Served from Hebron. Rev. Arul Joseph Irudamoney.
c/o St. Ann, P.O. Box 12, Hebron, 58638-0012. Tel: 701-878-4658.
Catechesis/Religious Program— Twinned with St. Ann's. Students 2.

HAYNES, ADAMS CO., ST. PETER (1908) Closed. For inquiries for parish records contact the chancery.

HAZELTON, EMMONS CO., ST. PAUL (1905) Rev. David Richter; Deacon Kenneth Wolbaum.
Church: 372 Harold St., 58544. Tel: 701-254-4588.
Res.: 613 N. Broadway St., Linton, 58552.
Catechesis/Religious Program—Tel: 701-782-6281. Charlotte Beastrom, D.R.E. Students 36.

HAZEN, MERCER CO., ST. MARTIN (1914), (German—Russian), [CEM] Rev. Johnson Kuriappilly.
Mailing Address: 101 3rd Ave., S.W., P.O. Box 387, 58545. Tel: 701-748-2121. Email: stmhazen@westriv.com.
Res.: 508 1st. Ave. N.E., P.O. Box 146, Beulah, 58523. Tel: 701-566-8011; Fax: 701-873-5614.
Catechesis/Religious Program— LuAnn Woeste, D.R.E. Students 95.

HEBRON, MORTON CO., ST. ANN (1906), (German), [CEM 3] Rev. Irudamoney Arul Joseph.
Res.: 204 Park St. S., Box 12, 58638. Tel: 701-878-4658.
Catechesis/Religious Program—Irene Wehri, D.R.E. Students 51.

HETTINGER, ADAMS CO., HOLY TRINITY (1916), (German), [CEM] [JC] Rev. Joseph Chipson (India).
Res.: 405 3rd St. N., 58639. Tel: 701-567-2772.
Catechesis/Religious Program—Kasey Tuhy, D.R.E. Tel: 701-567-5272. Students (includes missions) 39.

HIRSCHVILLE, STARK CO., ST. PHILIP (1908) Closed. For inquiries for parish records contact the chancery.

HUFF, MORTON CO., ST. MARTIN (1911), Served from Mandan. Rev. Chad Gion.
c/o Spirit of Life, Box 247, Mandan, 58554. Tel: 701-663-8842.
Catechesis/Religious Program—Students 10.

KENMARE, WARD CO., ST. AGNES (1901), (Scandinavian—German), [CEM] Rev. Selvaraj Periannan, M.S.F.X. (India).
Res.: 409 E. Division, P.O. Box 488, 58746. Tel: 701-385-4311; Fax: 701-385-4321.
Catechesis/Religious Program—Tel: 701-386-2403. Deb Zeltinger, D.R.E.; Andrea Hager, D.R.E. Students 30.

KENNEDY, BOWMAN CO., ST. HELENA (1912) Closed. For inquiries for parish records contact the chancery.

KILLDEER, DUNN CO., ST. JOSEPH (1917) [CEM] [JC 2] Rev. Darnis Selvanayakam, M.S.F.X. (India).
Res.: 152 3rd Ave., N.W., P.O. Box 299, 58640. Tel: 701-764-5357; Fax: 701-764-6246. Email: stjoseph@ndsupernet.com.
Catechesis/Religious Program—Tel: 701-764-5886. Sarah McFadden, D.R.E. Students 75.

LANSFORD, BOTTINEAU CO., ST. JOHNS (1949), Served from Mohall. Rev. Gary Benz.
c/o St. Jerome, P.O. Box 457, Mohall, 58761-0457. Tel: 701-756-6601.
Catechesis/Religious Program—Shannon Moberg, D.R.E. Students 11.

LEFOR, STARK CO., ST. ELIZABETH (1898) [CEM] Rev. Patrick Moore, O.S.B.
5043 100D Ave. S.W., 58641.
Rectory—10 - 5th & Mckenzie, New England, 58647. Email: stmarysne@ndsupernet.com.
Parish Office: 437 Main St., P.O. Box 369, New England, 58647-0369.
Catechesis/Religious Program—Anne Wolf, D.R.E. Attend St. Mary's program Students 4.

LIGNITE, BURKE CO., ST. MARY (1920) Closed. For inquiries for parish records contact the chancery.

LINTON, EMMONS CO.
1—ST. ANTHONY (1909) [CEM] Rev. David Richter; Deacon Kenneth Wolbaum.
Res.: 613 N. Broadway, 58552-7311. Tel: 701-254-4588; Fax: 701-254-4588.
Catechesis/Religious Program—Susan Schumacher, D.R.E.; Denice Kautz, D.R.E. Students 147.
2—ST. MICHAEL (1916), Served from Strasburg. Rev. Paul Eberle.
c/o SS. Peter & Paul, P.O. Box 322, Strasburg, 58573-0322. Tel: 701-336-7172.
Catechesis/Religious Program—Rosie Vetter, D.R.E. Students 32.

MAKOTI, WARD CO., ST. ELIZABETH (1948), Served from Parshall. Rev. Roger A. Synek.
4th & Edwards St., 58756. *c/o St. Bridget*, P.O. Box 519, Parshall, 58770-0519. Tel: 701-862-3484.
Catechesis/Religious Program—Students 6.

MANDAN, MORTON CO.
1—CHRIST THE KING (1957) [CEM] Rev. Kenneth G. Phillips; Deacon Dennis Rohr.
Res.: 505-10th Ave., N.W., 58554-2552. Tel: 701-663-8842; Fax: 701-667-1730. Web: christthekingmandan.org.
School—Tel: 701-663-6200; Fax: 701-667-1730. Lay Teachers 13; Students 115.
Catechesis/Religious Program—Andrea Helbing, D.R.E.; Sandra Breiner, Sacramental Prep. Students 106.
2—ST. JOSEPH (1879) [CEM] Rev. Shane Campbell; Deacons Peter Hoffman, (Retired); Larry Dorrheim, (Retired); Randall Frohlich.
Res.: 108 Third St. N.E., 58554. Tel: 701-663-9562; Fax: 701-663-6522. Email: stjosephmandan@goesp.com. Web: www.stjosephmandan.com.
School—(Grades K-6), 110 Collins Ave., 58554. Tel: 701-663-9563; Fax: 701-663-0183. Josephine Greff, Librarian. Lay Teachers 14; Students 145.
Catechesis/Religious Program—Michele Himmelspach, D.R.E. Students 160.
3—SPIRIT OF LIFE (1978) Revs. Chad Gion; William A. Ruelle, Parochial Vicar; Deacon Joel Melarvie.
Mailing Address: 801 1st St. S.E., 58554. Web: myspiritoflife.com.
Res.: 809 First St. S.E., 58554. Tel: 701-663-1660; Fax: 701-667-2021.
Catechesis/Religious Program—Students 310.

MANDAREE, DUNN CO., ST. ANTHONY, (Native American), [CEM] Rev. Stephen Kranz, O.S.B.
Res.: Fr. Berthold Reservation, 9385 BIA Rte. 12, 58757-9269. Tel: 701-759-3412; Fax: 701-759-3412 (Call first). Email: skranz@restel.net.
Catechesis/Religious Program—Students 45.

MARMARTH, SLOPE CO., ST. MARY (1915), Served from Bowman. Rev. David G. Morman.
c/o St. Charles, 202 1st Ave., S.W., Bowman, 58623-4216. Tel: 701-523-5292.
Catechesis/Religious Program—Students 3.

MAX, MCLEAN CO., IMMACULATE CONCEPTION (1908), Served from Garrison. Rev. Joseph John Kandathiparambil (India).
c/o St. Nicholas, P.O. Box 870, Garrison, 58540-0870. Tel: 701-463-2327.
Catechesis/Religious Program—Peggy Bingham, D.R.E. Students 26.

MEDORA, BILLINGS CO. , ST. MARY (MEDORA) (1886) [CEM], Served from Beach. Rev. Russell P. Kovash.
c/o St. John the Baptist, P.O. Box 337, Beach, 58621-0337. Tel: 701-872-4153.
Catechesis/Religious Program—Walt Losinski, D.R.E.; Shelly Hauck, D.R.E. Twinned with St.

John the Baptist, Beach.

MENOKEN, BURLEIGH CO., ST. HILDEGARD (1947) [JC] Rev. Joshua K. Waltz.
Res.: 17200 Hwy. 10, 58558-9604. Tel: 701-673-3177; Fax: 701-673-3177. Email: sthildegard@bektel.com.
Catechesis/Religious Program—Tel: 701-673-3488. Denise Richter, D.R.E. Students 73.

MINER, GRANT CO., MARY IMMACULATE (1912) Closed. For inquiries for parish records contact the chancery.

MINOT, WARD CO.

1—ST. JOHN THE APOSTLE (1961) Rev. David L. Zimmer; Deacon Charles Kramer.
Mailing Address: 2600 Central Ave. W., 58701.
Res.: 109-25th St. N.W., 58703-2862. Tel: 701-839-7076; Fax: 701-839-2553. Email: stjohnchurch@srt.com. Web: www.stjohnminot.com.
Catechesis/Religious Program—Monica Perry, D.R.E. Teachers 16; Students 198.

2—ST. LEO (1886), (German), [CEM] Revs. Austin Vetter; Christopher J. Kadrmas, Parochial Vicar. In Res., Rev. Justin P. Waltz.
Res.: 305 1st. St., S.E., 58701. Tel: 701-838-1026; Fax: 701-852-4683.
Catechesis/Religious Program— Brian Rodgers, D.R.E. Students 223.

3—OUR LADY OF GRACE (1959) Rev. Bruce D. Krebs; Deacon Steven F. Streitz.
Mailing Address: 707 16th Ave., S.W., 58701.
Res.: 715 16th Ave., S.W., 58701. Tel: 701-839-6834; 701-852-3002; Fax: 701-837-1080.
Catechesis/Religious Program—Darlene Demars, D.R.E., (Grades K-5); Barb Johnson, D.R.E., (Grades 6-12). Students 335.

4—ST. THERESE THE LITTLE FLOWER (1954) [JC] Rev. Frederick R. Harvey; Linda Aleshire, Parish Sec.
Res.: 800 University Ave. W., 58703. Tel: 701-838-1520; Fax: 701-838-1520. Email: lfp@brhs.com. Web: littleflowerminot.com.
See Little Flower Elementary, Minot under Miscellaneous located in the Institution section.
Catechesis/Religious Program—Tel: 701-839-8567. Deb Carroll, D.R.E. (Approximate) 60.

MOHALL, RENVILLE CO., ST. JEROME (1906) [CEM] [JC] Rev. Gary Benz, Parochial Admin.
Res.: 303 E. Main St., P.O. Box 457, 58761-0457. Tel: 701-756-6601; Fax: 701-756-6901.
Catechesis/Religious Program—Students 29.

MORTON, MORTON CO., SS. PETER & PAUL (1904) Closed. For inquiries for parish records contact the chancery.

MOTT, HETTINGER CO., ST. VINCENT DE PAUL (1907) [CEM] Rev. Charles A. Zins; Deacons Ervin Schneider; David M. Crane.
Res.: 408 Iowa Ave., 58646. Tel: 701-824-2651; Fax: 701-824-2651.
Catechesis/Religious Program—Students 71.

NEW ENGLAND, HETTINGER CO., ST. MARY (1910) [CEM] Rev. Patrick Moore, O.S.B.; Deacon Victor F. Dvorak.
Rectory—10 - 5th & McKenzie, 58647. Tel: 701-579-4312; Fax: 701-579-4874. Email: stmarysne@ndsupernet.com.
Parish Office: 437 Main St., P.O. Box 369, 58647.
Catechesis/Religious Program—Anne Wolf, D.R.E. Students 70.

NEW HRADEC, DUNN CO., SS. PETER AND PAUL (1898), Served from Belfield. Rev. Shannon G. Lucht.
c/o St. Bernard, P.O. Box 38, Belfield, 58622-0038. Tel: 701-575-4295.

NEW LEIPZIG, GRANT CO., ST. JOHN THE BAPTIST (1911), Served from Mott. Rev. Charles A. Zins.
c/o St. Vincent de Paul, 408 Iowa Ave., Mott, 58646-7260. Tel: 701-824-2651.
Catechesis/Religious Program—Students 7.

NEW SALEM, MORTON CO., ST. PIUS V (1912) [CEM] Rev. Amalraj Roche (India).
Mailing Address: 202 N. 3rd. St., P.O. Box C, 58563-0429.
Res.: 213 N. 3rd St., P.O. Box C, 58563-0429. Tel: 701-843-7144. Email: stpiusv@westriv.com.
Catechesis/Religious Program—Tel: 701-843-7061. Students 94.

NEW TOWN, MOUNTRAIL CO., ST. ANTHONY (1954), (Native American), [CEM 4] [JC] Rev. Roger A. Synek; Deacon Daniel Barone.
Mailing Address: *c/o St. Bridget*, P.O. Box 519, Parshall, 58770-0519.
Res.: 206 Eagle Dr., P.O. Box 519, Parshall, 58770-0519. Tel: 701-862-3484.
Catechesis/Religious Program—Students 71.

NOONAN, DIVIDE CO. , ST. LUKE (1914), Served from Crosby. Rev. Biju Chitteth (India).
c/o St. Patrick, P.O. Box 89, Crosby, 58730-0089. Tel: 701-965-6537.
Catechesis/Religious Program—

ODENSE, MORTON CO., ST. JOHN (1905) Closed. For inquiries for parish records contact the chancery.

PARSHALL, MOUNTRAIL CO., ST. BRIDGET (1917), (German—Norwegian), [CEM 4] [JC 3] Rev. Roger A. Synek.
Res.: 12 First Ave., N.E., P.O. Box 519, 58770-0519. Tel: 701-862-3484. Email: stbridget@restel.com.
Catechesis/Religious Program—Tel: 701-862-3484. Students 25.

PLAZA, MOUNTRAIL CO., SACRED HEART (1910), Served from Parshall. Rev. Roger A. Synek.
4th Ave. & Reserve St., 58771. *c/o St. Bridget*, P.O. Box 519, Parshall, 58770-0519. Tel: 701-862-3484.
Catechesis/Religious Program—Students 6.

PORCUPINE, SIOUX CO., ST. JAMES (1897), Served from Fort Yates. Rev. Basil Atwell, O.S.B.
c/o St. Peter, P.O. Box 394, Fort Yates, 58538-0394. Tel: 701-854-3473.

PORTAL, BURKE CO., ST. JOHN THE BAPTIST (1900), Served from Crosby. Rev. Biju Chitteth (India).
c/o St. Patrick, P.O. Box 89, Crosby, 58730-0089. Tel: 701-965-6537.
Catechesis/Religious Program—Students 6.

POWERS LAKE, BURKE CO., ST. JAMES (1910), Served from Tioga. Rev. Benny D. Putharayil (India).
c/o St. Thomas the Apostle, P.O. Box 667, Tioga, 58852-0667. Tel: 701-664-2445.
Catechesis/Religious Program—Jane Streifel, D.R.E. Students 12.

RALEIGH, GRANT CO., ST. GERTRUDE (1913) [CEM] Rev. Daniel J. Berg.
Mailing Address: 421 Court St., Flasher, 58535-7216. Fax: 701-597-3228.
Church: 7785 St. Gertrude Ave., 58564. Tel: 701-597-3570.
Catechesis/Religious Program—Tel: 701-597-3228. Students 3.

RAY, WILLIAMS CO., ST. MICHAEL (1903), Served from Tioga. Rev. Benny D. Putharayil (India).
c/o St. Thomas the Apostle, P.O. Box 667, Tioga, 58852-0667. Tel: 701-664-2445.
Catechesis/Religious Program—Rebecca Jungemann, D.R.E. Students 14.

REEDER, ADAMS CO., SACRED HEART (1908), Served from Hettinger. Rev. Joseph Chipson (India).
c/o Holy Trinity, 405 3rd St. N., Hettinger, 58639-7125. Tel: 701-567-2772.
Catechesis/Religious Program— Twinned with Sacred Heart, Scranton.

REGENT, HETTINGER CO., ST. HENRY (1913) [JC] Rev. Charles A. Zins; Deacon Don J. Gion.
Res.: 150 W. Fifth, P.O. Box 155, 58650-0155. Tel: 701-563-4595.
Catechesis/Religious Program— Twinned with St. Vincent's, Mott. Students 21.

RHAME, BOWMAN CO., ST. MEL (1914), Served from Bowman. Rev. David G. Morman.
Catechesis/Religious Program—Theresa Fischer, D.R.E. Students 18.

RICHARDTON, STARK CO., ST. MARY (1895) [CEM] Rev. Boniface Muggli, O.S.B.
332 2nd St. N., 58652-7141. Web: www.marychurch.org.
Res.: 418 N. 3rd Ave. W., 58652. Tel: 701-974-3569. Web: www.marychurch.org.
Catechesis/Religious Program—Dennise Miller, D.R.E. (Grades K-12). Students 78.

RIVERDALE, MCLEAN CO., ST. JOHN (1947) Closed. For inquiries for parish records contact the chancery.

ROSENTHAL, EMMONS CO., SACRED HEART (1907) Closed. For inquiries for parish records contact the chancery.

ROSS, MOUNTRAIL CO., ST. FRANCIS (1911) Closed. For inquiries for parish records contact the chancery.

RYDER, WARD CO., ST. CHARLES (1907) Closed. For inquiries for parish records contact the chancery.

ST. ANTHONY, MORTON CO., ST. ANTHONY (1894), Served from Mandan. Rev. Chad Gion.
c/o Spirit of Life, Box 247, Mandan, 58554. Tel: 701-663-1660.
Catechesis/Religious Program—Jonathan Marohl, D.R.E. Students 23.

SCRANTON, BOWMAN CO., SACRED HEART (1928), Served from Hettinger. Rev. Joseph Chipson (India).
c/o Holy Trinity, 405 3rd St. N., Hettinger, 58639-7125. Tel: 701-567-2772.
Catechesis/Religious Program—Joanne Bartfolmy, C.C.D. Coord. Students 36.

SELFRIDGE, SIOUX CO., ST. PHILOMENA (1919), (German—Russian), [CEM] Rev. Basil Atwell, O.S.B.
Res.: P.O. Box 394, Fort Yates, 58538-0394. Tel: 701-854-3473; Fax: 701-854-3474.
Catechesis/Religious Program—

SENTINEL BUTTE, GOLDEN VALLEY CO., ST. MICHAEL (1891) Closed. For inquiries for parish records contact the chancery.

SHEFFIELD, STARK CO., ST. PIUS (1912) Closed. For inquiries for parish records contact the chancery.

SHERWOOD, RENVILLE CO., ST. JAMES (1911), Served from Mohall. Rev. Gary Benz.
c/o St. Jerome, 303 E. Main St., P.O. Box 457, Mohall, 58761-0457. Tel: 701-756-6601.
Catechesis/Religious Program—Trudi Southam, D.R.E. Students 30.

SHIELDS, MORTON CO., ST. GABRIEL (1912) Closed. For inquiries for parish records contact the chancery.

SOLEN, SIOUX CO., SACRED HEART (1913), Served from Ft. Yates. Rev. Basil Atwell, O.S.B.
c/o St. Peter, P.O. Box 394, Fort Yates, 58538-0394. Tel: 701-854-3473.

SOUTH HEART, STARK CO., ST. MARY (1923) [CEM] Rev. Shannon G. Lucht.
Res.: P.O. Box 189, 58655. Tel: 701-677-5886.
Catechesis/Religious Program—Tel: 701-575-4838. Students 71.

STANLEY, MOUNTRAIL CO., QUEEN OF THE MOST HOLY ROSARY (1908) [JC] Rev. Glen Michael Millard.
Res.: 425 1st St. S.E., P.O. Box 159, 58784. Tel: 701-628-2323. Email: mikemillardeagl@hotmail.com.
Catechesis/Religious Program—Tel: 701-628-3405. Students 70.
Mission—St. Ann Berthold, 58718. Tel: 701-453-3660.

STARK, STARK CO., ST. STEPHEN (1900) [CEM], Served from Richardton. Rev. Boniface Muggli, O.S.B.
c/o St. Mary, 332 2nd St. N., Richardton, 58652-7141. Tel: 701-974-3569.
Catechesis/Religious Program—Dennise Miller, D.R.E. Twinned with St. Mary's, Richardton. Students 6.

STRASBURG, EMMONS CO., STS. PETER AND PAUL (1889), (German—Russian), [CEM] Rev. Paul Eberle.
Res.: P.O. Box 322, 58573-0322. Tel: 701-336-7172.
Catechesis/Religious Program—Tel: 701-336-4607. Kathleen Kramer Nagel, D.R.E. Students 83.

TAYLOR, STARK CO., ST. PETER (1883) Closed. For inquiries for parish records contact the chancery.

TIOGA, WILLIAMS CO., ST. THOMAS (1914) [JC] Rev. Benny D. Putharayil (India).
Res.: 213 N. Gilbertson St., P.O. Box 667, 58852. Tel: 701-664-2445; Fax: 701-664-3531.
Catechesis/Religious Program—Students 28.

TOLLEY, WARD CO., SS. PETER & PAUL (1906) Closed. For inquiries for parish records contact the chancery.

TRENTON, WILLIAMS CO., ST. JOHN THE BAPTIST (1890), Served from Williston. Rev. Dennis R. Schafer.
c/o St. Joseph, P.O. Box K, Williston, 58802-1115. Tel: 701-572-6731.
Catechesis/Religious Program—Students 57.

TURTLE LAKE, MCLEAN CO., ST. CATHERINE (1913), Served from Underwood. Rev. Frank J. Schuster.
Catechesis/Religious Program—Lynn Schwalk, D.R.E. Students 25.

TWIN BUTTES, DUNN CO., ST. JOSEPH (1951), Served from Mandaree. Rev. Stephen Kranz, O.S.B.
c/o St. Anthony, 9385 BIA Rte. 12, Mandaree, 58757-9269. Tel: 701-759-3412.
Catechesis/Religious Program—Students 20.

UNDERWOOD, MCLEAN CO., ST. BONAVENTURE (1913) [CEM] Rev. Frank J. Schuster.
Res.: 503 Grant Ave., 58576. Tel: 701-442-5229; Fax: 701-442-5259. Email: stbonaventureschurch@westriv.com.
Catechesis/Religious Program—Students 31.

WASHBURN, MCLEAN CO., ST. EDWIN'S CHURCH (1903), Served from Underwood. Rev. Frank J. Schuster.
c/o St. Bonaventure, P.O. Box 240, Underwood, 58576-0240. Tel: 701-442-5229.
Catechesis/Religious Program—Jill Grumbo, D.R.E. Students 60.

WATFORD CITY, MCKENZIE CO., EPIPHANY (1915) Rev. John M. Pfeifer.
Res.: 112 6th Ave., N.E., P.O. Box 670, 58854. Tel: 701-842-3505.
Catechesis/Religious Program—Tel: 701-842-3791; 701-444-5150. Leah Voll, D.R.E. Students 59.

WHITE EARTH, MOUNTRAIL CO., ST. FRANCIS OF ASSISI (1894) Closed. For inquiries for parish records contact the chancery.

WHITE SHIELD, MCLEAN CO., SACRED HEART (1953), Served from Garrison. Rev. Joseph John Kandathiparambil (India).
c/o St. Nicholas, P.O. Box 870, Garrison, 58540-0870. Tel: 701-463-2327.
Catechesis/Religious Program—Students 14.

WILDROSE, DIVIDE CO., SACRED HEART OF JESUS (1916) Closed. For inquiries for parish records contact the chancery.

WILLA, STARK CO., ST. PLACIDUS (1903) Closed. For inquiries for parish records contact the chancery.

WILLISTON, WILLIAMS CO., ST. JOSEPH (1901) [JC] Revs. Dennis R. Schafer; Joseph Pathil Anthony (India).
124 Sixth St. W., P.O. Box K, 58802.
Res.: 524 First Ave. W., P.O. Box K, 58802. Tel: 701-572-6731; Fax: 701-572-4203. Email: stjoech@nemontel.net.
School—Tel: 701-572-6384; Fax: 701-774-0998. Ben Schafer, Prin. Lay Teachers 13; Students 197.
Catechesis/Religious Program—Tel: 701-572-0201. Email: stjoedre@nemont. Kristal Schmit, D.R.E. Students 174.

WILTON, MCLEAN CO., SACRED HEART (1906) [CEM] [JC] Unassigned.212 4th St. N., P.O. Box 128,

58579-0128.
Catechesis/Religious Program—Tel: 701-734-6799. Misty Schafer, D.R.E. Students 30.

WING, BURLEIGH CO., ST. IGNATIUS (1914) Closed. For inquiries for parish records contact the chancery.

Chaplains of Public Institutions

BISMARCK. *North Dakota State Penitentiary* 58504. Tel: 701-328-6357. Deacon Jim Fritz.

MANDAN

On Duty Outside the Diocese:
Revs.—
Brown, Phillip J., S.S., Rector, Theological College, The Catholic University of America, 401 Michigan Ave. NE., Washington, DC 20017-1010.
Deichert, Joseph, 180 Kuntz Ave. #15A W/HC, Hickam AFB, HI 96853-5419.
Kuss, Allen R., St. Paul Seminary, 2260 Summit Ave., St. Paul, MN 55105-1010.

Graduate Studies:
Rev.—
Schneider, Nick L., Casa Santa Maria, Via dell Umilta 30, Rome 00187 Italy.

Retired:
Rev. Msgr.—
Walsh, Gerald J., 3037 W. Avenida Destino, Tucson, AZ 85746-8268.
Revs.—
Bova, Eugene R., 360 Pinon Rd., Bailey, CO 80421-1837.
Cervinski, Paul, P.O. Box 1425, New Town, 58763-1425.
Cosgrove, William P., c/o St. Theresa of Lisieux, P.O. Box 435, Patagonia, AZ 85624-0435.
Dignan, Thomas L., 211 W. Sutton Sq., Stafford, TX 77477-4715.
Dukart, George, 1021 N. 26th St., Room 55, 58501-3109.
Eckroth, Leonard A., P.O. Box 116, Bowbells, 58721-0116.
Heidt, Charles A., 4199 13th St., N.W., Lot #28, Garrison, 58540-9423.
Kautzman, Jerome G., Emmaus Place, 1020 N. 26th St., Apt. 5, 58501-3186.
Klemmer, Marvin, 1020 N. 25th St. #4, 58501-3186.
Kramer, Thomas E., Emmaus Place, 1020 N. 26th St., Apt. 7, 58501-3187.
Leary, Albert R., P.O. Box 329, Strasburg, 58573-0329.
O'Leary, John P., Emmaus Place, 1020 N. 26th St., Apt. 1, 58501-3186.
Paluck, Casimir S., P.O. Box 283, South Heart, 58655-0283.
Rushford, William A., Emmaus Place, 1020 N. 26th St., Apt. 2, 58501-3186.
Schneider, Henry W., 1900 28th St. S.W., Minot, 58701-8135.
Schumacher, Jacob J., Emmaus Place, 1020 N. 26th St., Apt. 6, 58501-3186.
Wald, Kenneth J., 601 24th Ave., S.W. #319, Minot, 58701-1501.
Walter, Chris B., 1900 28th St. S.W., #154, Minot, 58701-8135.

Permanent Deacons:
Barone, Daniel, St. Anthony, New Town
Brannan, Steve M., St. Vincent de Paul, Crown Butte
Clancy, Lynn, (Retired)
Crane, David M., St. Vincent de Paul, Mott
Cunningham, Patrick M., (In Seminary)
Dangel, Robert A., (Unassigned)
Dean, Dennis L., St. John, Lansford
Deichert, Harry M., (Retired)
Dorrheim, Larry L., (Retired)
Due, Keith, St. Edward, Washburn
Dukart, Herman, (Retired)
Dvorak, Victor F., St. Mary, New England
Fettig, Richard H., Cathedral of the Holy Spirit, Bismarck
Finneman, Tony, Ascension, Bismarck
Fischer, Leonard, St. Charles, Bowman
Fix, Michael, Corpus Christi, Bismarck
Frohlich, Randall, St. Joseph, Mandan
Gayzur, Hans, St. Theresa the Little Flower, Minot
Gion, Donald J., St. Henry, Regent
Glatt, Terry, St. Mary, Bismarck
Grabar, Ray A., (Retired)
Grabowska, Lonnie, Corpus Christi, Bismarck
Haga, James A., St. Joseph, Williston
Hanel, Harvey, St. Mary, Bismarck
Helbing, Douglas, Christ the King, Mandan
Hoffman, Peter, (Retired)
Hogan, Ronald, (Unassigned)
Jilek, Raymond, (Retired)
Johnson, Ed J., Sr., Rolla, ND
Johnson, Ward A., (Retired)
Jundt, Wayne M., Saint Anne, Bismarck
Keller, Ronald, St. Patrick, Dickinson
Klein, Kenneth M., St. Mary, Bismarck
Kordonowy, Leonard J., (Retired)
Kramer, Charles L., St. John the Apostle, Minot
Krupinsky, Joseph M., Saint Anne, Bismarck
Marback, Michael, St. Mary, Bismarck
Martin, Morris E., (Retired)
Mathern, Joseph J., (Retired)
Mattson, Joseph M., Holy Trinity, Hettinger
Mays, Stephen B., (Retired)
McDowall, Rexford R., Corpus Christi, Bismarck
Melarvie, Joel D., Spirit of Life, Mandan
Mizeur, Gary, Cathedral of the Holy Spirit, Bismarck
Morman, Eugene F., (Retired)
Nistler, Donald R., (Retired)
Nistler, James A., (Retired)
Olson, Robert C., (Retired)
Quintus, Terry B., St. Joseph, Dickinson
Ressler, James V., (Retired)
Riehl, Emil J., (Retired)
Ringwall, Kris, Queen of Peace, Dickinson
Rohr, Dennis, Christ the King, Mandan
Rustand, Gerald T., (Unassigned)
Schmit, Kenneth, St. Charles, Bowman
Schneider, Ervin H., St. Vincent de Paul, Mott
Schulz, Doyle, Ascension, Bismarck
Schwindt, Alvin W., St. Joseph, Dickinson
Stockert, Ralph F., (Retired)
Stockert, Robert, St. Wenceslaus, Dickinson
Streitz, Steven F., Our Lady of Grace, Minot
Tharaldsen, John, Corpus Christi, Bismarck
Volk, Jerome, Queen of Peace, Dickinson
Von Ruden, Ralph, Cathedral of the Holy Spirit, Bismarck
Wallach, Daniel, St. Joseph, Beulah
Wanner, Anton, Jr., St. Patrick, Dickinson
Wesolowski, Edwin A., St. Mary, Bismarck
Wingenbach, Bob A., St. Joseph, Mandan
Woiwode, Mike, St. Leo, Minot
Wolbaum, Kenneth J., St. Katherine, Braddock
Wolberg, Ronald R., Queen of Peace, Dickinson
Wolf, Wilfred P., (Retired)
Wosepka, James, St. John the Baptist, Beach
Zent, Robert, St. Wenceslaus, Dickinson
Ziman, Edward J., (Retired)

INSTITUTIONS LOCATED IN THE DIOCESE

[A] SEMINARIES, RELIGIOUS OR SCHOLASTICATES

RICHARDTON. *Assumption Abbey* (1893) P.O. Box A, 58652. Tel: 701-974-3315; Fax: 701-974-3317. Email: monks@assumptionabbey.com. Web: www.assumptionabbey.com. Rt. Revs. Brian Wangler, O.S.B., M.A., Abbot; Lawrence Wagner, O.S.B., Abbot (Retired); Rev. Valerian Odermann, O.S.B., Ph.D., Teacher & Chap.; Bro. Basil Kirsch, O.S.B., Prior; Revs. Claude Seeberger, O.S.B., M.A., Chap.; Gerald Ruelle, O.S.B. (Retired); Raymond Dietlein, O.S.B. (Retired); Stephen Kranz, O.S.B.; Damian Dietlein, O.S.B., S.T.L., Seminary Prof.; Sebastian Schmidt, O.S.B., Subprior; Denis Fournier, O.S.B., Ph.D., Archivist; Francis Wehri, O.S.B., M.A., Rector, (Overseas); Terrence Kardong, O.S.B., M.A.; Victor Feser, O.S.B., Ph.D., Teacher; Odo Muggli, O.S.B., Business Mgr.; Daniel Maloney, O.S.B., M.A., Chap. & Teacher; Philip Vanderlin, O.S.B., Prior, (Overseas); Francis dos Remedios, O.S.B. (Retired); Julian Nix, O.S.B., Hospital Chap.; Hugo L. Blotsky, O.S.B.; Efraim Villegas, O.S.B., Pastoral Work, (Overseas); Boniface Muggli, O.S.B.; Gonzalo Blanco, O.S.B., (Overseas); Thomas Wordekemper, O.S.B., Chap.; Nicolas Cano, O.S.B., Headmaster, (Overseas); James Kilzer, O.S.B., Asst. Business Mgr.; Basil Atwell, O.S.B.; Manuel Cely, Supr., (Overseas); Warren Heidgen, O.S.B., Chap.; Benedict Fischer, O.S.B., Teacher; Carlos Suarez, O.S.B., (Overseas); Bro. Aaron Jensen, O.S.B., Librarian; Rev. Patrick Moore, O.S.B., Resigned Abbot. Priests 31; Brothers 24; Monks 56.

[B] COLLEGES AND UNIVERSITIES

BISMARCK. *University of Mary* (1959) 7500 University Dr., 58504-9652. Tel: 701-255-7500; Fax: 701-255-7687. Email: marauder@umary.edu. Web: www.umary.edu. Rev. James P. Shea, Ph.L., Pres.; Dr. Diane Fladeland, Vice Pres. Academic Affairs; Revs. Victor Feser, O.S.B., Ph.D.; Benedict Fischer, O.S.B., Chap.; Daniel Maloney, O.S.B., M.A.; Valerian Odermann, O.S.B., Ph.D.; Cheryl Bailey, Librarian. Priests 5; Sisters 9; Lay Teachers 96; Students 2,971.

[C] HIGH SCHOOLS, INTERPAROCHIAL AND PARISH

BISMARCK. *St. Mary's Central High School*, 1025 N. Second St., 58501. Tel: 701-223-4113; Fax: 701-223-8629. Email: smchs@smchs.org. Web: www.smchs.org. Tom Eberle, Prin.; Rev. Joshua K. Waltz, Chap. & Instructor; Connie Tschider, Librarian. Priests 1; Lay Teachers 27; Students 349.

DICKINSON. *Dickinson Catholic Schools*, (Grades PreK-12), P.O. Box 1177, 58601. Tel: 701-483-6092; Fax: 701-483-1450. Email: kelly.koppinger@sendit.nodak.edu. Web: www.dickinsoncatholicschools.com. Kelly Koppinger, Supt.; Mr. Carter Fong, Prin. (Trinity High Sch.); Rachel Ebach, Librarian (Trinity High Sch.); Peggy Mayer, Prin. (Trinity Elem. Sch. East & West); Sandra Peterson, Librarian (Trinity Elem. Sch. East & West). Priests 1; Sisters 1; Lay Teachers 41; K-12 Students 513; Pre-K Students 51.

Trinity High School (1961) (Grades 7-12), 810 Empire Rd., P.O. Box 1177, 58602-1177. Tel: 701-483-6081; Fax: 701-483-1450. Email: carter.j.fong@sendit.nodak.edu. Web: www.trinityhighschool.com. Mr. Carter Fong, Prin.; Rev. Joshua J. Ehli, Chap.; Rachel Ebach, Librarian. Priests 1; Sisters 1; Lay Teachers 22; Total Staff 21; Students 243.

MINOT. *Bishop Ryan High School* (1958) 316 11th Ave. N.W., 58703-2260. Tel: 701-852-4004; Fax: 701-839-4651. Email: terry.voiles@brhs.com. Web: www.minotcatholic.org. Terry Voiles, Supt.; Darwin Routledge, Prin.; Cindy Lientz, Librarian. Priests 1; Teachers 27; Students (Grades 6-12) 232.

[D] GENERAL HOSPITALS

BISMARCK. *St. Alexius Medical Center* (1885) P.O. Box 5510, 58506-5510. Tel: 701-530-7000; Fax: 701-530-7284. Web: www.st.alexius.org. Gary P. Miller, Admin. & CEO; Sr. Renee Zastoupil, Dir. Pastoral Care. Sisters of St. Benedict. Priests 2; Sisters 4; Bed Capacity 306; Total Staff 2,221; Patients Assisted Annually 243,389.

DICKINSON. *St. Joseph's Hospital and Health Center*, 30 W. Seventh St., 58601. Tel: 701-456-4271; Fax: 701-456-4800. Web: stjoeshospital.org. Reed E. Reyman, Pres. & CEO. Nurses 148; Total Staff 364; Bed Capacity 25; Patients Assisted Annually 38,430.

GARRISON. *Garrison Memorial Hospital*, 407 3rd Ave. S.E., 58540. Tel: 701-463-2275; Fax: 701-463-6569. Email: dmattern@primecare.org. Web: garrisonmh.com. Dean Mattern, Admin. Sisters of St. Benedict (Bismarck) 2; Nurses 48; Bed Capacity 50; Total Staff 145; Patients Assisted Annually 13,000.

WILLISTON. *Mercy Medical Center - Affiliate of Catholic Health Initiatives*, 1301 15th Ave. W., 58801. Tel: 701-774-7400; Fax: 701-774-7479. Web: www.mercy-williston.org. Matthew Grimshaw, Pres. & CEO. Bed Capacity 35; Patients Assisted Annually 60,000; Total Staff 454.

Mercy Medical Foundation, 1301 15th Ave. W., 58801. Tel: 701-774-7404; Fax: 701-774-7479. Email: warrensundet@catholichealth.net. Web: www.mercy-williston.org. Bed Capacity 35; Patients Assisted Annually 60,000; Total Staff 454.

[E] SPECIAL CARE FACILITIES

DICKINSON. *Benedictine Living Communities, Inc. dba St. Benedicts Health Center* 851 Fourth Ave. E., 58601. Tel: 701-456-7242; Fax: 701-456-7250. Email: Jon.frantsvog@bhshealth.org. Web: www.saint-benedicts.org. Jon Frantsvog, Admin. Operated by Benedictine Living Communities, Inc. Bed Capacity 164; Total Staff 250; Total Assisted Annually 164.

Benedictine Living Communities, Inc. dba Benedict Court (2003) 830 2nd Ave. E., 58601. Tel: 701-456-7242; Fax: 701-456-7250. Email: Jon.frantsvog@bhshealth.org. Web: www.benedict-court.org. Jon Frantsvog, Admin. & Contact Person. Bed Capacity 26; Total Assisted Annually 26; Total Staff 10.

GARRISON. *Benedictine Living Communities, Inc. dba Benedictine Living Center of Garrison* (1969) 609 4th Ave., N.E., P.O. Box 219, 58540. Tel: 701-463-2226; Fax: 701-463-2650. Email: scott.foss@bhshealth.org. Scott Foss, Admin. Operated by Benedictine Health System Long Term Care, Inc. Bed Capacity 52; Total Staff 75; Total Assisted Annually 70; Assisted-Living Capacity 18.

[F] PROTECTIVE INSTITUTIONS

SENTINEL BUTTE. *Home On The Range* (1950) 16351 I-94, 58654-9500. Tel: 701-872-3745; Fax: 701-872-3748. Email: jayhotr@gmail.com. Web: www.hotrnd.com. Mr. Jay Johnson, M.S.W., L.I.C.S.W., Exec. Dir.; Rev. Russell P. Kovash, Chap. Total Staff 77; Total Assisted 107; Bed Capacity 54.

[G] HOMES FOR AGED

BISMARCK. *Emmaus Place*, 1020 N. 26th St., 58501. Tel: 701-258-2618. Revs. Jerome G. Kautzman (Retired); Marvin J. Klemmer (Retired); Thomas E. Kramer (Retired); John P. O'Leary (Retired); William A. Rushford (Retired); Jacob J. Schumacher (Retired). Priests retirement home. Total Staff 6; Total Assisted Annually 8; Total in Residence 8.

Marillac Manor (1977) 1016 N. 28th St., 58501. Tel: 701-258-8702; Fax: 701-250-4898. Email: awilz@mohs.org. Web: medcenterone.com. Kirk Greff, Admin. Retirement Apartments 77; Total Staff 5; Total in Residence 85.

**Medcenter One St. Vincent's Care Center* (1943) 1021 N. 26 St., 58501-3199. Tel: 701-323-1999; Fax: 701-323-1989. Email: kgreff@mohs.org. Kirk Greff, Admin. Sisters of St. Benedict 1; Total Staff 180; Resident Patients 101; Total Assisted Annually 170; Bed Capacity 101.

[H] CONVENTS AND RESIDENCES FOR SISTERS

BISMARCK. *Annunciation Monastery* (1947) 7520 University Dr., 58504-9653. Tel: 701-255-1520; Fax: 701-255-1440. Web: www.annunciationmonastery.org. Sr. Nancy Miller, O.S.B., Prioress; Rev. Daniel Maloney, O.S.B., M.A., Resident Chap. Motherhouse and Novitiate of the Benedictine Sisters of the Annunciation, B.M.V. Professed Sisters 53.

RICHARDTON. *Sacred Heart Monastery*, 8969 Hwy. 10 W., P.O. Box 364, 58652. Tel: 701-974-2121; Fax: 701-974-2124. Email: busoffice@sacredheartmonastery.com. Web: www.sacredheartmonastery.com. Sr. Paula Larson, Prioress & Pres. Motherhouse and Novitiate of the Sisters of the Order of St. Benedict. Professed Sisters 25.

[I] MISCELLANEOUS

BISMARCK. *Benedictine Living Communities - Bismarck, Inc. aka St. Gabriel's Community* 4580 Coleman St., 58503. Tel: 701-751-4224; Fax: 701-751-4225. Email: steven.przybilla@bhshealth.org. Web: www.stgabrielscommunity.org. Steven Przybilla, Admin. Skilled Nursing Beds 72; Transitional Care Beds 24.

**Bismarck Guild*, 2520 Domino Dr., 58503-0825.

The St. Mary's Central High School Endowment for Operations and Tuition Aid for Students at SMCHS, 1025 N. 2nd St., 58501. Tel: 701-223-4113; Fax: 701-223-8629.

World Apostolate of Fatima, 2114 N. 3rd St., 58501. Tel: 701-222-0185; 701-391-1172; Fax: 701-223-9486. Email: shirlein@bis.midco.net. Shirlein Vetter, Pres.

DICKINSON. *Subiaco Manor* (1990) 2441 10th Ave. W. #10, 58601. Tel: 701-483-2350. Email: subiacomgr@ndsupernet.com. Sr. Carol Axtmann, O.S.B., Resident Mgr. Sponsored by the Benedictine Sisters of Sacred Heart Monastery in Richardton. Total Staff 1; Total in Residence 11.

MINOT. *Minot Catholic Schools Corporation* (1994) 316 11th Ave., N.W., 58703-2299. Tel: 701-852-4004; Fax: 701-837-8914. Email: terry.voiles@brhs.com. Web: www.minotcatholic.org. Terry Voiles, Supt. Full- and part-time staff members 55.

Bishop Ryan High School, 316 11th Ave., N.W., 58703-2260. Tel: 701-838-3355; Fax: 701-839-4651. Email: terry.voiles@brhs.com. Web: www.minot-catholic.org. Terry Voiles, Supt.; Mary Hemphill, Prin.; Rev. Justin P. Waltz, Chap. & Instructor. Priests 1; Lay Teachers 23; Students (Grades 6-12) 232.

Little Flower Elementary (Grades 6-12), 800 University Ave. W., 58703. Tel: 701-839-5882; Fax: 701-839-8567. Gary Volk, Prin. Lay Teachers 11; Students 136.

RICHARDTON. *Benedictine Sponsorship Board*, 8969 Hwy. 10 W., P.O. Box 364, 58652-0364. Tel: 701-974-2121; Fax: 701-974-2124. Email: spaula@sacredheartmonastery.com. Web: www.sacredheartmonastery.com. Sr. Paula Larson, Pres. & Contact Person.

PIA Tegler Benedictine Foundation, 8969 Hwy. 10 W., P.O. Box 364, 58652-0364. Tel: 701-974-2121; Fax: 701-974-2124. Email: busoffice@sacredheartmonastery.com. Web: www.sacredheartmonastery.com. Sisters Michael Emond, O.S.B., Pres.; Phoebe Schwartze, O.S.B., Vice Pres.; Marie Hunkler, O.S.B., Sec. & Treas.

Sacred Heart Benedictine Foundation, 8969 Hwy. 10 W., P.O. Box 364, 58652-0364. Tel: 701-974-2121; Fax: 701-974-2124. Email: busoffice@sacredheartmonastery.com. Web: www.sacredheartmonastery.com. Sr. Paula Larson, Pres.

Sacred Heart Mission, 418 3rd Ave. W., 58652-7100. Tel: 701-974-3315; Fax: 701-974-3317. Email: odo@assumptionabbey.com. Rev. Odo Muggli, O.S.B., Sec. & Treas.

SENTINEL BUTTE. *Home On The Range Foundation* (1999) 16351 I-94, 58654. Tel: 701-872-3745; Fax: 701-872-3748. Email: jayhotr@gmail.com. Web: www.hotrnd.com. Rev. David G. Morman, Pres.

RELIGIOUS INSTITUTES OF MEN REPRESENTED IN THE DIOCESE

For further details refer to the corresponding bracketed number in the Religious Institutes of Men or Women section.

[0200]—*Benedictine Monks* (Richardton, ND)—O.S.B.

[]—*Missionary Society of St. Francis Xavier* (Chennai, India)—M.S.F.X.

[1200]—*Society of the Divine Savior* (Milwaukee, WI)—S.D.S.

RELIGIOUS INSTITUTES OF WOMEN REPRESENTED IN THE DIOCESE

[0230]—*Benedictine Sisters of Pontifical Jurisdiction* (Bismarck; Richardton, ND; Duluth, MN)—O.S.B.

[2970]—*School Sisters of Notre Dame* (Mankato Prov.)—S.S.N.D.

[]—*Sisters of Mary of the Presentation* (Valley City, ND)—S.M.P.

NECROLOGY

† Krank, Michael T., (Retired)—Died Nov. 28, 2010

An asterisk (*) denotes an organization that has established tax-exempt status directly with the IRS and is not covered by the USCCB Group Ruling.

Diocese of Boise

(Dioecesis Xylopolitana)

Most Reverend

MICHAEL P. DRISCOLL, M.S.W., D.D.

Bishop of Boise; ordained May 1, 1965; appointed Titular Bishop of Massita and Auxiliary Bishop of Orange December 19, 1989; consecrated March 6, 1990; appointed Bishop of Boise January 19, 1999; installed March 18, 1999. *Res.: 1501 Federal Way, Boise, ID 83705.*

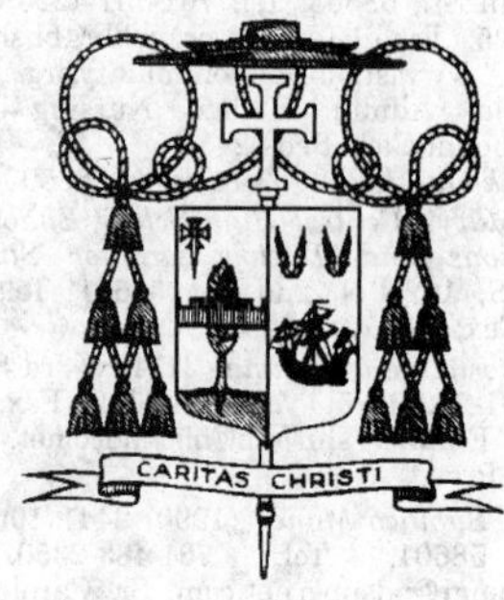

Chancery Office: 1501 Federal Way, Boise, ID 83705. Tel: 208-342-1311; Fax: 208-342-0224.

Email: mwilske@rcdb.org

ESTABLISHED AS A VICARIATE-APOSTOLIC MARCH 3, 1868.

Square Miles 83,557.

Erected a Diocese by His Holiness Pope Leo XIII, August 26, 1893

Comprises the State of Idaho, with a Total Population of 1,532,200.

Legal Title: "Roman Catholic Diocese of Boise". For legal titles of parishes and diocesan institutions, consult the Chancery Office.

STATISTICAL OVERVIEW

Personnel	
Bishop	1
Priests: Diocesan Active in Diocese	48
Priests: Diocesan Active Outside Diocese	6
Priests: Retired, Sick or Absent	29
Number of Diocesan Priests	83
Religious Priests in Diocese	15
Total Priests in Diocese	98
Extern Priests in Diocese	6
Ordinations:	
Permanent Deacons	1
Permanent Deacons in Diocese	70
Total Brothers	5
Total Sisters	75
Parishes	
Parishes	52
With Resident Pastor:	
Resident Diocesan Priests	39
Resident Religious Priests	2
Without Resident Pastor:	
Administered by Priests	9
Administered by Deacons	2
Missions	28
Pastoral Centers	28
Professional Ministry Personnel:	
Brothers	5
Sisters	75
Lay Ministers	51
Welfare	
Catholic Hospitals	4
Total Assisted	552,297
Day Care Centers	4
Total Assisted	160
Special Centers for Social Services	19
Total Assisted	410,000
Educational	
Diocesan Students in Other Seminaries	8
Total Seminarians	8
High Schools, Diocesan and Parish	1
Total Students	680
Elementary Schools, Diocesan and Parish	13
Total Students	2,286
Catechesis/Religious Education:	
High School Students	2,313
Elementary Students	5,902
Total Students under Catholic Instruction	11,189
Teachers in the Diocese:	
Sisters	1
Lay Teachers	209
Vital Statistics	
Receptions into the Church:	
Infant Baptism Totals	2,672
Minor Baptism Totals	287
Adult Baptism Totals	216
Received into Full Communion	307
First Communions	2,298
Confirmations	1,219
Marriages:	
Catholic	404
Interfaith	137
Total Marriages	541
Deaths	808
Total Catholic Population	172,434
Total Population	1,567,582

Former Bishops—Rt. Revs. LOUIS LOOTENS, D.D., ord. June 14, 1851; appt. first Vicar-Apostolic of Idaho, March 3, 1868; cons. Bishop of Castabala, Aug. 9, 1868; resigned July 16, 1876; died Jan. 13, 1898; ALPHONSE JOSEPH GLORIEUX, D.D., ord. Aug. 17, 1867; appt. second Vicar-Apostolic of Idaho, Feb. 27, 1885; cons. Titular Bishop of Apolonia, April 19, 1885; appt. first Bishop of the Diocese of Boise, Aug. 26, 1893; died Aug. 25, 1917; DANIEL MARY GORMAN, D.D., LL.D., ord. June 24, 1892; cons. May 1, 1918; died June 9, 1927; Most Revs. EDWARD JOSEPH KELLY, D.D., ord. June 2, 1917; cons. March 6, 1928; died April 21, 1956; JAMES J. BYRNE, D.D., S.T.D., ord. June 3, 1933; appt. Titular Bishop of Etenna and Auxiliary of St. Paul, July 2, 1947; cons. July 2, 1947; transferred to Boise June 16, 1956; appt. Archbishop of Dubuque, March 19, 1962; retired Aug. 23, 1983; died Aug. 2, 1996; SYLVESTER WILLIAM TREINEN, D.D., ord. June 11, 1946; appt. May 19, 1962; cons. July 25, 1962; retired Aug. 17, 1988; died Sept. 30, 1996; TOD D. BROWN, D.D., ord. May 1, 1963; appt. Dec. 27, 1988; ord. and installed April 3, 1989; appt. Bishop of Orange, June 30, 1998.

Executive Secretary to Bishop/Administration—BARBARA BIRD.

Vicars General—Rev. Msgrs. JOSEPH DA SILVA, V.G.; DENNIS WASSMUTH, V.G.

Administrative Assistant to Vicar General—CYNTHIA TALBOY.

Chancery Office—1501 Federal Way, Boise, 83705. Tel: 208-342-1311; Fax: 208-342-0224.

Chancellor—Ms. MARCELLA M. WILSKE, M.A., M.S.

Assistant to the Chancellor—CAROLINE CARTHY-WICKHAM.

Office of Cultural Ministries—Ms. CHRISTINE KING, Dir., 1501 Federal Way, Boise, 83705. Tel: 208-342-1311.

Coordinator of Multicultural Ministries—SANTIAGO ROBLES.

Notaries—DOVE MIZELL; Ms. MARCELLA M. WILSKE, M.A., M.S.; CYNTHIA TALBOY.

Diocesan Tribunal—1501 Federal Way, Boise, 83705. Tel: 208-344-1344; Fax: 208-342-0224. (Direct all correspondence here.)

Director—MARK L. RAPER, J.C.L., M.C.L.

Staff Canonist—VACANT.

Judicial Vicar—Very Rev. HENRY CARMONA, J.C.L., J.V.

Adjutant Judicial Vicars—Revs. WILLIAM C. CROWLEY; GERALD FUNKE, J.C.L.

Promoters of Justice—Very Rev. JOSEPH F. MCDONALD III, J.C.L., V.F.; MARK L. RAPER, J.C.L., M.C.L.

Notaries—Rev. Msgr. DENNIS WASSMUTH, V.G.; MARK L. RAPER, J.C.L., M.C.L.; COLLEEN CUNNINGHAM; MARISELA BACA; CAROLINE CARTHY-WICKHAM.

Judges—Very Rev. HENRY CARMONA, J.C.L., J.V.; Revs. WILLIAM C. CROWLEY; W. THOMAS FAUCHER, J.C.L., V.U.; GERALD FUNKE, J.C.L.; JAIRO RESTREPO, J.C.L.; MARK L. RAPER, J.C.L., M.C.L.; Rev. JOHN MORGAN.

Defenders of the Bond—Rev. Msgr. ANDREW SCHUMACHER (Retired); Rev. JAIRO RESTREPO, J.C.L.; MARK L. RAPER, J.C.L., M.C.L.

College of Consultors—Very Revs. JOSEPH F. MCDONALD III, J.C.L., V.F.; DENNIS C. DAY, V.F.; LESLIE P. KISH, V.F.; Rev. TIMOTHY M. RITCHEY; Very Revs. JOSEPH F. SCHMIDT (Retired); BENJAMIN UHLENKOTT, V.U.; CALVIN L. BLANKINSHIP JR., V.F.; Rev. JULIO VICENTE; Rev. Msgr. ANDREW SCHUMACHER (Retired); Very Rev. RAUL R. COVARRUBIAS, V.F.

Ex Officio—Rev. Msgrs. DENNIS WASSMUTH, V.G.; JOSEPH DA SILVA, V.G.

Deans—Very Revs. DENNIS C. DAY, V.F., Northern Deanery; RAUL R. COVARRUBIAS, V.F., Eastern Deanery; CALVIN L. BLANKINSHIP JR., V.F., Western Deanery; BENJAMIN UHLENKOTT, V.U., West Central Deanery; JOSEPH F. MCDONALD III, J.C.L., V.F., Southern Deanery; LESLIE P. KISH, V.F., North Central Deanery.

Presbyteral Council— See College of Consultors.

Priest Personnel Commission—Rev. TIMOTHY M. RITCHEY; Very Revs. BRADLEY NEELY, V.F.; BENJAMIN UHLENKOTT, V.U.; Rev. FRANCISCO FLORES; Very Rev. RAUL R. COVARRUBIAS, V.F.; Revs. CALEB VOGEL; PAUL WANDER; JUSTIN BRADY; Rev. Msgrs. DENNIS WASSMUTH, V.G., Ex Officio; JOSEPH DA SILVA, V.G., Ex Officio.

Finance Council—Rev. Msgrs. DENNIS WASSMUTH, V.G., Chm.; JOSEPH DA SILVA, V.G., Ex Officio; TOM ZABALA; SANDRA DALTON; LARRY HELLHAKE; TOM GILLESPIE; STANLEY WELSH; ALAN WINKLE; SUSAN COPPLE; GLENN SCHUMACHER; Ms. MARCELLA M. WILSKE, M.A., M.S.; CHARLES LAWRENCE, Officer; Most Rev. MICHAEL P. DRISCOLL, D.D., M.S.W., Ex Officio.

Building Commission—Rev. Msgr. DENNIS WASSMUTH, V.G., Chm.; Deacon JACK PELOWITZ; DAVID DAVIES; MICHAEL JONES; JAMES MESPLAY; PETER ROCKWELL; PATRICIA NORBERG; BRIAN ELSWORTH; RONDA JALBERT; TOM MANNSCHRECK; LARRY HELHAKE.

Priest Retirement Committee—Rev. Msgr. DENNIS WASSMUTH, V.G., Chm.; Revs. JOSEPH MUHA (Retired); TIMOTHY M. RITCHEY; JOHN WORSTER; Very Rev. RAUL R. COVARRUBIAS, V.F.; Rev. FRANCISCO FLORES, 1501 Federal Way, Boise, 83705. Tel: 208-342-1311.

Ex Officio—Rev. Msgr. JOSEPH DA SILVA, V.G.

Diocesan Offices and Directors

Apostleship of Prayer—VACANT.

Bureau of Information— *"Idaho Catholic Register" 1501 Federal Way, Boise, 83705.*

Catholic Campaign for Human Development—Ms.

MARCELLA M. WILSKE, M.A., M.S., 1501 Federal Way, Ste. #400, Boise, 83705-5925.

Catholic Charities of Idaho, Inc.—LANDIS ROSSI, Exec. Dir.; ERICA MEDALEN, Assoc. Dir.; Most Rev. MICHAEL P. DRISCOLL, D.D., M.S.W., Pres.; LYNNE JOHNSON, Admin. Mgr., 1501 Federal Way, Boise, 83705. Tel: 208-345-6031; Fax: 208-345-5674.

Catholic Communications Center—MICHAEL BROWN, 1501 Federal Way, Ste. 400, Boise, 53705.

Catholic Relief Services—Ms. MARCELLA M. WILSKE, M.A., M.S., 1501 Federal Way, Ste. 400, Boise, 83705.

Catholic Scouts—DAVID L. DAVIS, Chm., 142 N. 9th St., Pocatello, 83201. Tel: 208-232-2098; Rev. ROGER LACHANCE, V.F., M.A., Chap., St. Pius X, 625 E. Haycraft, Coeur d'Alene, 83815. Tel: 208-765-5108.

Catholic Daughters of the Americas—MARY KAY RUSSELL. Email: maryk@russellmining.com.

Catholic Schools—ROBERT SOBOTTA SR., Supt., 1501 Federal Way, Ste. 400, Boise, 83705.

Catholic Hospitals—VACANT, 1501 Federal Way, Ste. 400, Boise, 83705. Tel: 208-342-1311.

Catholic Liturgical Commission—LETITIA THORNTON, Chm. Email: tthornton@rcdb.org; MARISELLA WILSKE, M.A., M.S.; Deacon GERALD PERA; KATHY SELLS; ELWOOD KLEAVER; LARRY HARRISON; Rev. MARCOS SANCHEZ; Rev. Msgr. DENNIS WASSMUTH, V.G.; Deacons RICHARD KULLECK; RICK BONNEY.

Censor Librorum—Rev. Msgr. ANDREW SCHUMACHER (Retired), 3213 Fifth St., Unit I, Lewiston, 83501. Tel: 208-746-3362.

Charismatic Renewal—VACANT.

Children, Youth and Adult Protection Coordinator—Dr. ROBERT FONTAINE. Tel: 208-350-7555.

Priest Retirement Plan— Direct Inquiries to the Chancery, *1501 Federal Way, Ste. 400, Boise, 83705.*

Cursillo Movement—MICHELLE RAYMOND, Region XII Coord. (English); ARTEMIO PEREZ, Region XII Coord. (Spanish), 3973 N. 3300 E., Twin Falls, 83301. Tel: 208-404-9987; Rev. MAURICIO MEDINA, Spiritual Dir. - Spanish (Retired), 931 Eastland Dr. N., Twin Falls, 83301. Tel: 208-734-2432.

Development/Stewardship Office—JIM HUGHES, Dir., 1501 Federal Way, Ste. 400, Boise, 83705. Tel: 208-342-1311; Fax: 208-342-0224; Cell: 208-861-2202.

Diocesan Pastoral Council—FRAN GOLDING, Pres.

Ecumenical Commission—Rev. Msgr. JOSEPH DA SILVA, V.G., 11511 Lake Hazel Rd., Boise, 83709.

Parish Life and Faith Formation—Mr. MICHAEL BENTON, Dir.; PATRICIA THOMAS, Events Coord.; VERONICA CHILDERS, Admin. Asst./Resource Ctr., 1501 Federal Way, Boise, 83705. Tel: 208-342-1311.

Parish Life & Faith Formation West, West Central Deanery's—MICHAEL BENTON.

Parish Life & Faith Formation North, North Central Deanery's—Sr. MEG SASS, O.S.B.

Parish Life & Faith Formation Southern & Eastern Deanery's—VACANT.

Finance Officer—CHARLES LAWRENCE.

Human Resources—Dr. ROBERT FONTAINE.

Idaho Council of Catholic Women—ETHEL ROURKE, Pres.

Idaho Catholic Foundation—Most Rev. MICHAEL P. DRISCOLL, D.D., M.S.W., Pres.

Knights of Columbus—BRIAN SIMER, State Deputy; Rev. JUSTIN BRADY, State Chap.

Campus Ministry—MICHAEL BENTON, Dir. Campus Min., 1501 Federal Way, Ste. 400, Boise, 83705. Tel: 208-342-1311.

Newspaper— "Idaho Catholic Register" Most Rev. MICHAEL P. DRISCOLL, D.D., M.S.W., Publisher; MICHAEL BROWN, Exec. Editor; ANN BIXBY, Advertising/Business/Circulation; LORETTA GOSSI, Sec., Library, 1501 Federal Way, Ste. 400, Boise, 83705. Tel: 208-342-1311.

Deacon Life and Ministry—Deacons GARY MCSWAIN, Dir., 625 E. Haycraft, Coeur d'Alene, 83815. Tel: 208-667-9233; JAMES KELLY, 1323 Johnson St., Boise, 83705. Tel: 208-343-9619.

Deacon and Lay Formation Director—Deacon RICHARD KULLECK, 1501 Federal Way, Ste. 400, Boise, 83705. Tel: 208-342-1311.

Prison Ministry—Rev. JESUS CAMACHO, 322 S. Manville St., Boise, 83705. Tel: 208-429-9196.

Propagation of the Faith—Ms. MARCELLA M. WILSKE, M.A., M.S., 1501 Federal Way, Ste. 400, Boise, 83705.

Diocesan Respect Life Coordinator—Deacon PIERCE MURPHY.

St. Vincent de Paul Society—Rev. GERALD FUNKE, J.C.L., Diocesan Spiritual Dir., 1515 8th St., S., Nampa, 83651. Tel: 208-466-7031.

State Trustee—MIKE GALLAGHER. Tel: 208-376-0690.

Vocations—Revs. CALEB VOGEL, Dir. Recruitment; ROBERT P. COOK, Dir. Seminarians, 1501 S. Federal Way, Ste. 400, Boise, 83705. Tel: 208-342-1311.

CLERGY, PARISHES, MISSIONS AND PAROCHIAL SCHOOLS

CITY OF BOISE

(ADA COUNTY)

1—CATHEDRAL OF ST. JOHN THE EVANGELIST (1906) Very Rev. Henry Carmona, Rector; Rev. Jose T. Ramirez, Parochial Vicar; Deacons Ken Hiner; Tom Dominick; Jack Pelowitz; Stephen Germain; Ms. Bobbi Dominick, Pastoral Assoc.
Res.: 775 N. 8th St., 83702. Tel: 208-342-3511; 208-342-3512; Fax: 208-342-1564.
School—St. Joseph's School, (Grades K-8), 825 W. Fort St., 83702. Tel: 208-342-4909; Fax: 208-342-0997. Ms. Antonia Bicandi, Prin. Lay Teachers 22; Students 334.
Catechesis/Religious Program—Jackie Hopper, D.R.E. Students 310.

2—ST. MARK'S (1970) Revs. Steven Rukavina; Bruno Mgaya; Deacons Ralph Pierce; James Bowen; Joseph Rodriguez; Mike Lowe; Diana Tetreault, Pastoral Assoc.; Phyllis Sawyer, Pastoral Assoc.
7960 Northview, 83704.
School—(Grades K-8), 7503 Northview, 83704. Tel: 208-375-6654; Fax: 208-375-9471. Dan Maloney, Prin.; Dorthy Sammortino, Librarian. Lay Teachers 15; Students 329.
Catechesis/Religious Program—Students 346.

3—ST. MARY'S (1937) Revs. W. Thomas Faucher; Jesus Camacho; Arnie Miller; Deacons William Petzak; Francis Hess; Jorge Gonzalez.
Res.: 2612 W. State St., 83702. Tel: 208-344-2597; Fax: 208-344-9337. Email: rharlow@stmarysboise.org. Web: www.stmarysboise.org.
School—(Grades K-8), 2620 W. State St., 83702. Tel: 208-342-7476; Fax: 208-345-5154. Marianne White, Prin.; Tammy Morrison, Librarian. Lay Teachers 13; Students 193.
Catechesis/Religious Program—Students 295.

4—OUR LADY OF THE ROSARY (1947) Rev. Msgr. Dennis Wassmuth; Deacons Michael Dessert; Pierce Murphy; Chuck Skoro; Mike Servatius.
Res.: 1500 E. Wright, 83706. Tel: 208-343-9041; Fax: 208-343-2644.
Catechesis/Religious Program—Rosie Skoro, D.R.E. Students 250.
Chapel—Idaho City, St. Joseph's
Chapel—Boise, St. Paul's Student Center

5—ST. PAUL'S, Closed. See Our Lady of the Rosary, Boise for details.

6—RISEN CHRIST CATHOLIC COMMUNITY (1992) [CEM] Rev. Msgr. Joseph da Silva; Rev. Chase R. Hasenoehrl, Parochial Vicar; Deacons Richard Kulleck; C. J. Harris.
Res.: 11511 W. Lake Hazel Rd., 83709. Tel: 208-362-6584; Fax: 208-362-9545.
Catechesis/Religious Program—Mark Henry, D.R.E. Students 193.

7—SACRED HEART (1952) Rev. Robert P. Cook; Deacons James R. Kelly; Rick Bonney; Jude Gary; Michael Eisenbeiss.
Mailing Address: 811 S. Latah St., 83705-0127. Tel: 208-344-8311; Fax: 208-343-1876.
School—(Grades PreK-8), 3901 Cassia St., 83705. Tel: 208-344-9738; Fax: 208-343-1939. Brock Carpenter, Prin.; Jane Collins, Librarian. Sisters 1; Lay Teachers 12; Students 155.
Catechesis/Religious Program—Deborah Fischer, D.R.E. (K-6); Roger Graefe, D.R.E. (Youth 7- 12); Carol Mcgee, D.R.E. (Adult). Students 115.

OUTSIDE THE CITY OF BOISE

ABERDEEN, BINGHAM CO., BLESSED SACRAMENT, Merged with St. Mary, American Falls to form Presentation of the Lord, Aberdeen.

AMERICAN FALLS, POWER CO.

1—ST. MARY, Merged with Blessed Sacrament, Aberdeen to form Presentation of the Lord, Aberdeen.

2—PRESENTATION OF THE LORD Rev. Carlos Camargo, Admin.
P.O. Box 117, 83211. Tel: 208-220-0868; Fax: 208-226-1125.
Catechesis/Religious Program—Zulma Ceana, D.R.E. Students 183.
Chapel—Pingree, St. John
Chapel—St. Mary 376 Roosevelt, 83211. Tel: 208-226-5217.
Chapel—Aberdeen, Blessed Sacrament 667 S. 4th W., Aberdeen, 83210.

ARCO, BUTTE CO., ST. ANN'S, See separate listing. See St. Charles, Salmon for details.

BLACKFOOT, BINGHAM CO., ST. BERNARD'S Rev. Jose de Jesus Gonzalez, Admin.
Res.: 584 W. Sexton St., 83221. Tel: 208-785-1935; Fax: 208-785-7382.
Catechesis/Religious Program—Students 216.
Chapel—Blessed Kateri Tekakwitha Sheepskin Rd., Fort Hall, 83203.

BONNERS FERRY, BOUNDARY CO., ST. ANN'S (1800) Rev. Carlos Perez, Admin.; Deacon Joseph Nicholas.
Res.: 6712 El Paso, 83805. Tel: 208-267-2852; Fax: 208-267-8222. Email: st-anns@peoplepc.com.
Catechesis/Religious Program—Students 48.

BUHL, TWIN FALLS CO., IMMACULATE CONCEPTION Rev. Jorge E. Garcia.
Res.: 1701 Poplar, Box 626, 83316. Tel: 208-543-9878; 208-543-5136 (Office); Fax: 208-543-5714.
Catechesis/Religious Program—Patricia Beltran, D.R.E. Students 118.
Station—Hagerman, St. Catherine's Hagerman. Tel: 208-837-6592.

BURLEY, CASSIA CO., ST. THERESE LITTLE FLOWER (1938) Revs. Marcos Sanchez, Admin.; Marcos Sanchez, Parochial Vicar.
Res.: 1550 Oakley, 83318. Tel: 208-678-5453; Fax: 208-678-5479.
1601 Oakley Ave., 83318.
Catechesis/Religious Program—Melissa Santana, D.R.E. Students 132.

CALDWELL, CANYON CO.

1—ST. MARY'S, Merged to form Our Lady of the Valley, Caldwell.

2—OUR LADY OF THE VALLEY Revs. Francisco Flores; Adrian Vazquez, Parochial Vicar; Deacon Humberto Almeida.
Office: 1122 W. Linden St., 83605. Tel: 208-459-3653; Fax: 208-454-8789.
Catechesis/Religious Program—Students 650.
Chapel—Homedale, St. Hubert's

CHUBBUCK, BANNOCK CO., ST. PAUL'S, Merged with St. Anthony's, Pocatello and St. Joseph, Pocatello to form Holy Spirit Catholic Community, Pocatello.

COEUR D'ALENE, KOOTENAI CO.

1—ST. JOAN OF ARC Rev. Carlos S. Casavantes, F.S.S.P.
773 N. 11th St., 83814. Tel: 208-660-6036.

2—ST. PIUS X Revs. Roger LaChance; Francisco H. Godinez, Parochial Vicar; Deacons Gary McSwain; Leonard Trueworthy.
Res.: 625 E. Haycraft, 83815. Tel: 208-765-5108; Fax: 208-664-5325.
Catechesis/Religious Program—Deacon Gary McSwain, D.R.E. Students 170.

3—ST. THOMAS (1890) Rev. William C. Crowley.
Res.: 919 E. Indiana Ave., 83814. Tel: 208-664-9259; Fax: 208-667-8321.
Catechesis/Religious Program—John Kastelic, D.R.E. Students 90.
St. Thomas Parish Center—406 N. 10th St., 83814.

COTTONWOOD, IDAHO CO., ST. MARY'S (1890) [CEM] Rev. Richard S. Haldane.
Mailing Address: 503 Garrett St., P.O. Box 425, 83522-0425. Tel: 208-962-3214; Fax: 208-962-5477. Church: 508 Church St., 83522-0425.
Catechesis/Religious Program—Heather Uhlenkott, D.R.E. (Children); Joe Seubert, D.R.E. (Adults). Students 150.
Chapel—Keuterville, Holy Cross

COUNCIL, ADAMS CO., ST. JUDE STATION, See separate listing. See St. Agnes, Weiser for details.

DESMET, BENEWAH CO., SACRED HEART (1842) Rev. Jerry D. Graham, S.J.; Sr. Dolores Ellwart, S.P., Pastoral Assoc.; Deacon Nick Vietri.
Res.: Box 306, 83824. Tel: 208-274-5871; Fax: 208-274-3015.
Catechesis/Religious Program—Students 88.
Station—Plummer, Our Lady of Perpetual Help Plummer.
Station—Worley, St. Michael's Worley.

EAGLE, ADA CO., ST. MATTHEW, Merged with Holy Spirit, Meridian to form Holy Apostles, Meridian.

EMMETT, GEM CO., SACRED HEART Rev. Oscar Jaramillo; Deacon Alan Shaber.
Res.: 211 E. First Street, 83617. Tel: 208-365-4320; Fax: 208-365-0754.
Catechesis/Religious Program—Students 88.
Station—Garden Valley, St. Jude Garden Valley.

FERDINAND, IDAHO CO., ASSUMPTION (1900) Rev. Richard S. Haldane.
Mailing Address: P.O. Box 425, Cottonwood, 83522-0425.
Catechesis/Religious Program—Joe Seubert, D.R.E. (Adults); Heather Uhlenkott, D.R.E. (Children). Twinned with St. Mary's, Cottonwood.

FRUITLAND, PAYETTE CO., CORPUS CHRISTI CATHOLIC CHURCH (1999) Very Rev. Calvin L. Blankinship Jr.; Deacons Harley Salazar; Juan Tamayo.
Mailing Address: 900 N.W. 7th St., 83619.
Res.: 1104 Partridge St., 83619. Tel: 208-452-5778; Fax: 208-452-6778.

Catechesis/Religious Program—Students 175.
GARDEN VALLEY, BOISE CO., ST. JUDE'S, See separate listing. See Sacred Heart, Emmett for details.
GENESEE, LATAH CO., ST. MARY STATION, See St. Mary's, Moscow for details.
Res.: 138 N. Jackson, P.O. Box 36, 83832. Tel: 208-882-4813; Fax: 208-883-0608.
Catechesis/Religious Program—Kristy Mayer, D.R.E.; Marnie Zenner, D.R.E. Students 25.
GLENNS FERRY, ELMORE CO., OUR LADY OF LIMERICK STATION (1892), See Our Lady of Good Counsel, Mountain Home for details.
Res.: 21 W. Arthur St., Box 216, 83623. Tel: 208-366-7721.
Catechesis/Religious Program—
GOODING, GOODING CO., ST. ELIZABETH'S Very Rev. Michael St. Marie, Priest Mod.; Rev. John Koelsch, Sacramental Min. (Retired); Deacons Javier Leiga; John McKinley, Parish Life Dir.
Res.: Box 147, 83330-0147. Tel: 208-934-5634; Fax: 208-934-4910. Email: stelizabethgooding@yahoo.com.
Catechesis/Religious Program—Bridget Arkoosh, D.R.E.; Maria Garcia, D.R.E. (Gooding). Students 74.
Station—Wendell, St. Anthony's P.O. Box 811, Wendell, 83355.
GRANDVIEW, OWYHEE CO., ST. HENRY CHAPEL, See Our Lady of Good Counsel, Mountain Home for details.
GRANGEVILLE, IDAHO CO., SS. PETER AND PAUL (1892) Very Rev. Bradley Neely; Deacon Don Sokolowski.
Office: 625 Lake St., 83530.
Res.: 622 S.W. 1st St., 83530. Tel: 208-983-0403; Fax: 208-983-0115.
School—330 S. B St., 83530. Tel: 208-983-2182. Teresa Groom, Prin. Lay Teachers 4; Students 61.
Catechesis/Religious Program—Students 68.
Station—Nez Perce, Holy Trinity P.O Box 65, Nez Perce, 83543. Tel: 208-937-2300.
Chapel—White Bird, Sacred Heart, See Sts. Peter & Paul, Grangeville for details.
GREENCREEK, IDAHO CO., ST. ANTHONY'S (1900) [CEM] Rev. Richard S. Haldane.
Res.: P.O. Box 425, Cottonwood, 83522.
Catechesis/Religious Program—(Included in St. Mary's) Patricia Schmidt, D.R.E.; Joe Seubert, D.R.E. (Adults); Heather Uhlenkott, D.R.E. (Children).
HAGERMAN, GOODING CO., ST. CATHERINE'S, See separate listing. See Immaculate Conception, Buhl for details.
HAILEY, BLAINE CO., ST. CHARLES BORROMEO (1881) Rev. Joseph F. McDonald III.
Res.: 313 1st. Ave. S., Box 789, 83333. Tel: 208-788-3024; Fax: 208-788-0726. Email: stcharles@qwestoffice.net.
Catechesis/Religious Program—Students 178.
Chapel—Fairfield, Immaculate Conception
HOMEDALE, OWYHEE CO., ST. HUBERT, Merged with St. Mary's, Caldwell and Sacred Hearts of Jesus and Mary, Parma to form Our Lady of the Valley, Caldwell.
HORSESHOE BEND, BOISE CO., OUR LADY QUEEN OF ANGELS CHAPEL, See separate listing. See Holy Apostle, Meridian for details.
IDAHO CITY, BOISE CO., ST. JOSEPH'S CHAPEL, See separate listing. See Our Lady of the Rosary, Boise for details.
IDAHO FALLS, BONNEVILLE CO.
1—BLESSED JOHN PAUL II PARISH Very Rev. Raul R. Covarrubias; Rev. Jairo Restrepo, Parochial Vicar; Deacons Alvaro Ponce; Wence Rodriquez; Eric Shaber; Chris Reilly.
Res.: 145 E. 9th St., 83404. Tel: 208-522-4366; Fax: 208-523-3827.
School—(Grades PreSchool-8), 161 Ninth St., 83404. Tel: 208-522-7781; Fax: 208-522-7782. Marilyn Reilly, Prin. Lay Teachers 10; Students 132.
Catechesis/Religious Program—Mary Haley, D.R.E.; Mary Lou Hart, D.R.E. Students 725.
Chapel—Shelley, Our Lady of Guadalupe
Station—Roberts, St. Anthony's Roberts.
Station—Mud Lake, St. Ann's Mud Lake.
2—CHRIST THE KING, Merged with Holy Rosary, Idaho Falls to form Blessed John Paul II Parish, Idaho Falls.
3—HOLY ROSARY, Merged with Christ the King, Idaho Falls to form Blessed John Paul II Parish, Idaho Falls.
JEROME, JEROME CO., ST. JEROME'S Rev. Ronald Wekerle; Deacons John Baumbach; Marino Perea, Pastoral Assoc.
Res.: 216 2nd Ave. E., Box 169, 83338. Tel: 208-324-8794; Fax: 208-324-4141.
Catechesis/Religious Program—Generations of Faith Students 178.
KAMIAH, LEWIS CO., ST. CATHERINE OF SIENA (1964) Unassigned.
Res.: 407 7th St., Box 685, 83536-0685. Tel: 208-935-2130; Fax: 208-935-2130.
Catechesis/Religious Program—Students 33.
KELLOGG, SHOSHONE CO., ST. RITA'S Rev. Thomas Loucks.
Res.: 27 Kellogg Ave., 83837-2626. Tel: 208-784-7361; Fax: 208-784-7361.
Catechesis/Religious Program—Students 6.
KEUTERVILLE, IDAHO CO., HOLY CROSS, Merged with St. Mary's, Cottonwood.
LEWISTON, NEZ PERCE CO.
1—ALL SAINTS CATHOLIC PARISH - OUR LADY OF LOURDES CHURCH Very Rev. Leslie P. Kish; Rev. Julio Vicente, Parochial Vicar; Deacon Fred Schmidt.
Church & Res.: 2015 13th Ave., 83501. Tel: 208-743-6101 (Church); Fax: 208-743-5301. Email: ourladyoflourdes@cableone.net. Web: www.lewistoncatholics.org.
Catechesis/Religious Program—Students 192.
2—ALL SAINTS CATHOLIC PARISH - ST. STANISLAUS CHURCH Very Rev. Leslie P. Kish; Rev. Julio Vicente, Parochial Vicar.
Res.: 633 5th Ave., 83501. Tel: 208-743-7331; Fax: 208-746-7134.
School—All Saints Catholic School, (Grades PreSchool-6) Denise Hammrich, Prin. Lay Teachers 18; Students 156.
Catechesis/Religious Program—(Included in Our Lady of Lourdes) Heidi Munoz, D.R.E. Students 277.
3—ALL SAINTS CATHOLIC PARISH - ST. JAMES CHURCH (1970) Very Rev. Leslie P. Kish; Rev. Julio Vicente, Parochial Vicar.
Office: 1519 Ripon Ave., 83501. Tel: 208-743-8231; Fax: 208-798-8407. Web: www.allsaintslewiston.org.
Catechesis/Religious Program—(Included in Our Lady of Lourdes)
Station—Lapwai, Sacred Heart 203 Birch Ave., Lapwai, 83840. Tel: 208-843-2562; Fax: 208-843-2562.
MCCALL, VALLEY CO., OUR LADY OF THE LAKE (1916) Rev. Msgr. Dennis Wassmuth, Admin.; Rev. John Gathungu, Parochial Vicar.
Res.: 501 Cross Rd., Box 821, 83638. Tel: 208-634-5474; Fax: 208-634-5475.
Catechesis/Religious Program—Students 23.
Station—St. Katharine Drexel, Cascade
Chapel—Riggins, St. Jerome's
MERIDIAN, ADA CO.
1—HOLY APOSTLES (1998) [CEM] Revs. Len MacMillan; Dat Vu, Parochial Vicar; Deacons Ralph Flager; Gerald Pera; Charles Rasmussen; Malherbe Desert; Patty Blazek, Pastoral Assoc.
Res.: Box 708, 83680. Tel: 208-888-1182; Fax: 208-884-1800. Web: www.holyapostlesmeridian.net.
Holy Apostles Columbarium— (2008), [CEM]
Catechesis/Religious Program—Mary Ossenkop, D.R.E.; Robert Barros-Bailey, Youth Min.; Rusty Bang, Youth Min. Students 789.
Chapel—Horseshoe Bend, Our Lady Queen of Angels
2—HOLY SPIRIT, Merged Sacramental records are at Holy Apostles, Meridian.
MOSCOW, LATAH CO.
1—ST. AUGUSTINE'S, (Catholic Center) Rev. Caleb Vogel; Katie Goodson, Campus Min.
Res.: 628 Deakin Ave., P.O. Box 3457, 83843. Tel: 208-882-4613.
Station—Potlatch, St. Mary's P.O. Box 143, Potlatch, 83855.
2—ST. MARY'S (1882) Revs. Bradley Neely, Priest Mod.; Brian T. May, Parochial Vicar; Deacons George Canney, Parish Life Dir.; Verne Geidl.
Res.: 618 E. First St., Box 9106, 83843. Tel: 208-882-4813; Fax: 208-883-0608.
School—(Grades K-6), 412 N. Monroe, 83843. Tel: 208-882-2121. Sr. Margaret Johnson, O.S.U., Prin. Lay Teachers 7; Students 120.
Nursery & Preschool—St. Rose, 412 N. Howard, 83843. Tel: 208-882-4014; Fax: 208-882-0970. Owned by the Ursuline Nuns, affiliated with St. Mary's School.
Catechesis/Religious Program—Students 100.
Station—Genesee, St. Mary's Genessee.
MOUNTAIN HOME AIR FORCE BASE, ELMORE CO., ST. MARY'S, Unassigned.
Res.: 366 FW/HC, 420 Gunfighter Ave., Mountain Home A F B, 83648. Tel: 208-828-6417; Fax: 208-828-4570.
Catechesis/Religious Program—Students 150.
MOUNTAIN HOME, ELMORE CO., OUR LADY OF GOOD COUNSEL Very Rev. Benjamin Uhlenkott; Rev. Eladio Vieyra, Parochial Vicar.
Res.: 115 N. 4th St. E., Box 310, 83647. Tel: 208-587-3046; Fax: 208-587-5114.
Catechesis/Religious Program—Tenille Rudeen, D.R.E. Students 270.
Station—Bruneau, St. Bridget Bruneau.
Station—Glenns Ferry, Our Lady of Limerick Glenn's Ferry.
Chapel—Grand View, St. Henry's
NAMPA, CANYON CO.
1—OUR LADY OF GUADALUPE CHAPEL, Closed. See St. Paul's, Nampa for details.
2—ST. PAUL'S (1898) [CEM] Revs. Gerald Funke; German Osorio, Parochial Vicar; Deacons Michael Collins; Jose Luis Granados; Sisters Maria del la Luz Cabrera, H.M.R.F., Pastoral Assoc. & Hispanic Ministry; Pilar Casillas, H.M.R.F., Pastoral Assoc. & Hispanic Ministry.
Res.: 1515 8th St. S., 83651. Tel: 208-466-7031; Fax: 208-467-7203.
School—(Grades PreSchool-8) Tel: 208-467-3601; Fax: 208-467-6485. Randy McCormick, Prin. Lay Teachers 12; Students 157.
Catechesis/Religious Program—Students 375.
Station—Melba, St. Joseph
Chapel—Silver City, Our Lady of Tears
Chapel—Oreana, Our Lady Queen of Heaven
NEW PLYMOUTH, PAYETTE CO., ST. ALOYSIUS, Merged to form Corpus Christi Catholic Community, Fruitland.
NEZPERCE, LEWIS CO., HOLY TRINITY, See SS. Peter and Paul, Grangeville for details.
Res.: 506 Willow St., Box 65, Nez Perce, 83543. Tel: 208-937-2300.
Catechesis/Religious Program—
OREANA, OWYHEE CO., QUEEN OF HEAVEN CHAPEL, See separate listing. See St. Paul's, Nampa for details.
OROFINO, CLEARWATER CO., ST. THERESA'S (1926) Rev. Sipho Mathabela, Parochial Vicar.
Res.: 446 Brown Ave., Box 1169, 83544. Tel: 208-476-5121.
Catechesis/Religious Program—Students 19.
Chapel—Pierce, Our Lady of Woodland
PARMA, CANYON CO., SACRED HEARTS OF JESUS AND MARY, Merged with St. Mary's, Caldwell and St. Hubert's, Homedale to form Our Lady of the Valley, Caldwell.
PAYETTE, PAYETTE CO., HOLY FAMILY, Merged with St. Aloysius, New Plymouth to form Corpus Christi, Fruitland.
POCATELLO, BANNOCK CO.
1—ST. ANTHONY'S, Merged with St. Joseph, Pocatello and St. Paul, Chubbuck to form Holy Spirit Catholic Community, Pocatello.
2—HOLY SPIRIT CATHOLIC COMMUNITY (2003) Revs. John Worster; Reginald Nwauzor, Parochial Vicar; Kathy Barkdull, Pastoral Assoc.
Res.: 524 N. 7th Ave., 83201. Tel: 208-232-1196; Fax: 208-234-1624. Web: www.holyspirit.org.
School—(Grades PreK-8), 540 N. 7th Ave., 83205. Tel: 208-232-5763; Fax: 208-232-7142. Nancy Corgiat, Prin. Lay Teachers 19; Students 189.
Catechesis/Religious Program—Students 127.
St. John's Catholic Student Center—920 E. Lovejoy St., I.S.U., Box 8129, 83209-0001. Tel: 208-233-0880; Fax: 208-233-5745.
Chapel—Pocatello, St. Anthony of Padua Chapel 504 N. 7th Ave., 83201.
Chapel—Pocatello, St. Joseph Chapel 439 N. Hayes St., 83204.
Chapel—Chubbuck, St. Paul Chapel 820 W. Chubbuck Rd., 83202.
3—ST. JOSEPH'S, Merged with St. Anthony, Pocatello and St. Paul, Chubbuck to form Holy Spirit Catholic Community, Pocatello.
POST FALLS, KOOTENAI CO., ST. GEORGE'S (1917) Revs. Timothy M. Ritchey; Colman J. Nolan, S.T.; Deacons Timothy Penberthy; Michael Pentony.
Res.: Box 10, 83854-0010. Tel: 208-773-4715; Fax: 208-777-1549.
Catechesis/Religious Program—Rosemary McDougall, D.R.E. Students 126.
Chapel—Rathdrum, St. Stanislaus
Chapel—Spirit Lake, St. Joseph
POTLATCH, LATAH CO., ST. MARY'S STATION, See separate listing. See St. Augustine's, Moscow for details.
PRIEST RIVER, BONNER CO., ST. CATHERINE'S Rev. G. Peter Fernando, Admin.
Res.: P.O. Box 445, 83856. Tel: 208-448-2127.
Catechesis/Religious Program—Students 8.
Station—St. Blanche Priest Lake.
RATHDRUM, KOOTENAI CO., ST. STANISLAUS CHAPEL, See separate listing. See St. George, Post Falls for details.
RUPERT, MINIDOKA CO., ST. NICHOLAS (1908) Rev. Justin Brady; Deacons Paul Henscheid; Orville Rathe.
Res.: 802 F St., Box 115, 83350-0115. Tel: 208-436-3781; Fax: 208-436-0628. Email: stnich@pmt.org.
School—(Grades K-5), P.O. Box 26, 83350. Tel: 208-436-6320. Diane Brumley, Prin. Lay Teachers 8; Students 104.
Catechesis/Religious Program—Students 169.
ST. ANTHONY, FREMONT CO., MARY IMMACULATE Rev. Camilo Garcia Delgado, Admin.
Res.: 328 W. First N., P.O. Box 527, 83445. Tel: 208-624-7459; Fax: 208-624-7479.
Catechesis/Religious Program—Arcelia Gatica, D.R.E.; Pilar Hernandez, D.R.E. (St. Patricks). Students 108.

Station—Rexburg, St. Patrick's Rexburg.
Station—Driggs, Good Shepherd Driggs.
Chapel—Island Park, Chapel of the Pines Island Park.

SAINT MARIES, BENEWAH CO., ST. MARY IMMACULATE (1912) Revs. Timothy M. Ritchey, Admin.; Jack de Verteuil, Parochial Vicar; Deacon Floyd Turner.
Res.: 921 W. Jefferson Ave., P.O. Box 335, St. Maries, 83861. Tel: 208-245-2977; Fax: 208-245-3143. Web: www.stmariescatholic.com.
Catechesis/Religious Program—Students 25.
Station—Harrison, Our Lady of Perpetual Help Pine St., Harrison, 83833.

SALMON, LEMHI CO., ST. CHARLES (1908) Revs. Paul Wander; Evarist T. Shiyo, Parochial Vicar.
Mailing Address: 505 Hope Ave., P.O. Box 550, 83467.
Res.: 342 Lost River, P.O. Box 161, Arco, 83213. Tel: 208-756-2432; Fax: 208-756-1190.
Catechesis/Religious Program—Kate Curet, D.R.E. (Jr. High & High School); Kathy Tracy, D.R.E. (Elementary). Students 32.
Station—Arco, St. Ann Box 161, Arco, 83213. Tel: 208-521-3035.
Station—Challis, St. Louise P.O. Box 572, Challis, 83226.
Station—Mackay, St. Barbara Box 452, Mackay, 83251. Tel: 208-527-3035.
Chapel—Leadore, St. Joseph P.O. Box 550, 83467.

SANDPOINT, BONNER CO., ST. JOSEPH'S (1907) Very Rev. Dennis C. Day.
Res.: 601 S. Lincoln, P.O. Box 279, 83864-0279. Tel: 208-263-3720; Fax: 208-265-4974. Web: www.st-joseph-church.net.
Catechesis/Religious Program—Sandra Babin, D.R.E. Students 100.
Chapel—Clark Fork, Sacred Heart

SHOSHONE, LINCOLN CO., ST. PETER'S Very Rev. Michael St. Marie, Priest Mod.; Rev. John Koelsch, Sacramental Min. (Retired); Deacons Javier Leiga; John McKinley, Parish Life Dir.
Res.: 215 W. B St., Box 336, 83352. Tel: 208-886-2002; 208-934-5634.
Catechesis/Religious Program— Twinned with St. Elizabeth's, Gooding.

SODA SPRINGS, CARIBOU CO., GOOD SHEPHERD CATHOLIC COMMUNITY (1910) Rev. Robert C. Irwin, Admin.
Res.: 99 W. Center, 83276. Tel: 208-547-3200; Fax: 208-547-3200.
Catechesis/Religious Program—Students 44.
Chapel—Montpelier, Blessed Sacrament Montpelier.
Chapel—Soda Springs, St. Mary's
Chapel—Preston, St. Peter's Preston.
Chapel—Lava Hot Springs, Our Lady of Lourdes Lava Hot Springs.

SUN VALLEY, BLAINE CO., OUR LADY OF THE SNOWS (1970) Rev. Joseph F. McDonald III.
Res.: Sun Valley Rd., Box 1650, 83353. Tel: 208-622-3432; Fax: 208-622-4348. Email: parishoffice@ourladyofthesnowssunvalley.net. Web: www.ourladyofthesnowssunvalley.net.
Catechesis/Religious Program—Students 80.

TWIN FALLS, TWIN FALLS CO.
1—ST. EDWARD THE CONFESSOR (1920) Very Rev. Michael St. Marie; Rev. Mariusz Majewski, Parochial Vicar; Deacons Lloyd LeClair, (Retired); James Herrett; John Hurley.
Res.: 212 7th Ave. E., 83301-6321. Tel: 208-733-3907; Fax: 208-733-3935.
School—(Grades K-5), 139 Sixth Ave. E., 83301-6316. Tel: 208-734-3872; Fax: 208-734-1214. Clint Evans, Prin. Lay Teachers 12; Students 154.
Catechesis/Religious Program—Students 221.
2—ST. EDWARD'S, Merged with Our Lady of Guadalupe, Twin Falls to form St. Edward The Confessor, Twin Falls.
3—OUR LADY OF GUADALUPE, Merged with St. Edward's, Twin Falls to form St. Edward The Confessor, Twin Falls.

WALLACE, SHOSHONE CO., ST. ALPHONSUS Rev. Thomas Loucks.
Res.: 214 Pine St., 83873. Tel: 208-752-3551. Email: alphonsus@frontier.com.
Catechesis/Religious Program—Students 29.
Chapel—Mullan, St. Michael's

WEISER, WASHINGTON CO., ST. AGNES (1878) Revs. Victor Jagerstatter, Admin.; Thomas Keller; Deacons Francis Wander, (Retired); Ignacio Cornejo.
Res.: 214 E. Liberty, P.O. Box 87, 83672. Tel: 208-549-0088; Fax: 208-549-1080. Email: saintagnes@qwestoffice.net.
Catechesis/Religious Program—Students 190.
Station—Cambridge, Holy Rosary P.O. Box 335, Cambridge, 83610-0335. Tel: 208-257-3559.
Station—Council, St. Jude the Apostle 2054 Hwy. 95 N., Council, 83612. Tel: 208-253-6470.

WENDELL, GOODING CO., ST. ANTHONY'S, See separate listing. See St. Elizabeth's, Gooding for details.

Chaplains of Public Institutions

BOISE. *Elks Rehabilitation*, 204 Fort Pl., 83702. Vacant. Attended by St. John's Cathedral, 775 N. 8th St., Boise, ID 83702. Tel: 208-342-3511.
St. Luke's Medical Center, 190 E. Bannock, 83712. Vacant. Attended by St. John Cathedral, 775 N. 8th St., Boise, ID, 83702. Tel: 208-342-3511.
VA Hospital, 5th St. & Fort St., 83401. Vacant. Attended by St. John Cathedral, 775 N. 8th St., Boise, ID, 83702. Tel: 208-342-3511.

COEUR D'ARLENE. *St. Joan of Art Chapel*, 773 N. 11th St., Coeur d'Alene, 83814. Tel: 208-660-6036. Revs. Carlos S. Casavantes, F.S.S.P., David J. Kermra, F.S.S.P., Parochial Vicar.

COTTONWOOD. *Monastery of St. Gertrude*, HC 3 Box 121, 83522-9408. Tel: 208-962-3224. Rev. Meinrad Schallberger, O.S.B.

On Duty Outside the Diocese:
Revs.—
Legerski, John, Bishop Manogue High School, 110 Bishop Manogue Dr., Reno, NV 89511.
Ramirez, Jorge, St. Patrick's Church, Dio of Kansas - St. Joseph.
Segatta, Bruno
Stravinskas, Peter M.J., Newman House, 5401 S. 33rd St., Omaha, NE 68107.
Velez, Carlos, St. Phillips, 702 Beltram N.W., Bemidji, MN 56601.
Zuletta, Nondier, Columbia, Diocese of California.

Retired:
Rev. Msgrs.—
Morgan, John W.
O'Donovan, Timothy John, 1802 W. Ontario St., Sand Point, 83864-6380.
Schumacher, Andrew, 3213 S. M St., Unit 1, Lewiston, 83501.
Very Rev.—
Schmidt, Joseph F.
Revs.—
Caulfield, Sean, 505 7th Ave., Lewiston, 83501.
Dennis, Patrick
DiLoreto, Anthony, 524 N. 7th Ave., Pocatello, 83201.
Dohman, William, J.C.L., 5972 Via Casitas Ave., Carmichael, CA 95608-6541.
Dolan, Raymond, M.H. Station, Box 217, Staten Island, NY 10303.
Fernandez, Marcellus
Fraser, Donald D.
Garatea, Juan M.
Koelsch, John
Medina, Mauricio, 931 Eastland Dr. N., Twin Falls, 83301.
Muha, Joseph, 2711 N. 29th St., 83703.
O'Sullivan, John, 700 E. Fairview, #116, Meridian, 83642-3315.
Pu, Matthew, P.O. Box 9012, 83707.
Riffle, David
Riffle, Donald J.
Scarcello, Michael S., 3427 W. Scarcello Rd., Rathdrum, 83858-3427.
Taylor, Gordon A., P.O. Box 161, Arco, 83213.
Taylor, William
Terriquez, Enrique, V.F.

Permanent Deacons:
Almeida, Humberto, Our Lady of the Valley, Caldwell
Arndt, Ralph, (Retired)
Aslett, Devon H., St. Peter, Shoshone; St. Elizabeth's, Gooding; St. Anthony's, Wendell
Baumbach, John, St. Jerome's, Jerome
Bonney, Richard, Sacred Heart, Boise
Booth, William, (Retired)
Bowen, James E., St. Mark's, Boise
Canney, George, St. Mary's, Moscow; St. Mary's, Genesee
Collins, Michael, St. Paul's, Nampa
Cornejo, Ignacio, St. Agnes, Weiser
Davies, Christopher, All Saints, Lewiston
Desert, Malherbe, Holy Apostles, Meridian
Dessert, Michael, Our Lady of the Rosary, Boise
Dominick, Thomas, St. John's Cathedral, Boise
Duggan, Bill, (On Duty Outside the Diocese)
Eisenbeiss, Michael, Sacred Heart, Boise
Finan, Charles, St. Pius X, Coeur d'Alene
Flager, Ralph, Holy Apostles, Meridian
Gary, Jude, Sacred Heart, Boise
Geidl, Verne, St. Mary's, Moscow
Germain, Stephen, St. John's Cathedral
Gonzalez, Jorge, St. Mary's, Boise
Granados, Jose Luis, St. Paul's, Nampa
Hamm, Richard, (Retired)
Harris, C. J., Risen Christ Catholic Community, Boise
Henscheid, Paul, St. Nicholas, Rupert
Herrett, James, St. Edward's, Twin Falls
Hess, Francis, St. Mary's, Boise
Hiner, Kenneth, (Retired)
Hurley, John, St. Edwards
Jacobs, Gary, St. Thomas, Coeur D'Alene
Kelly, James, Sacred Heart, Boise
Kelso, Richard
Kreilcamp, Ben, (Retired)
Kulleck, Richard, Risen Christ, Boise
Le Clair, Lloyd, (Retired)
Leija, Javier, St. Elizabeth's, Gooding
Lowe, Michael, St. Mark's, Boise
McKinley, John D., Jr., St. Elizabeth's, Gooding; St. Peters, Shoshone
McSwain, Gary, St. Pius X, Coeur d'Alene
Murphy, Pierce, Our Lady of the Rosary, Boise
Nicholas, Joseph, St. Ann's, Bonners Ferry
Pearhill, Scott, Holy Spirit Catholic Community
Pelowitz, Jack, St. John's Cathedral, Boise
Pemberthy, Timothy, St. Georges, Post Falls
Pera, Gerald D., Holy Apostles, Meridian
Perea, Marino, St. Jerome, Jerome
Petzak, William, St. Mary, Boise
Pierce, Ralph, St. Mark, Boise
Ponce, Alvaro, Catholic Community, Idaho Falls
Rasmussen, Charles, Holy Apostles, Meridian
Rathe, Orville, St. Nicholas, Rupert
Reilly, Christopher, Catholic Community, Idaho Falls
Rodriguez, Wence, Catholic Community, Idaho Falls
Rodriquez, Joseph, St. Marks's, Boise
Rueda, Reynaldo, St. Bernard's, Blackfoot
Salazar, Harley, Corpus Christi, Fruitland
Schmidt, Fred, All Saints, Lewiston
Servatius, Michael, Our Lady of the Rosary, Boise
Shaber, Alan, Sacred Heart, Emmett
Shaber, Eric, Catholic Community, Idaho Falls
Skoro, Chuck, Our Lady of the Rosary, Boise
Sokolowski, Don, SS. Peter & Paul, Grangeville
Solbrig, Charles W., (Retired)
Souza, Edward, (On Duty Outside the Diocese)
Tamayo, Juan, (Retired)
Trueworthy, Leonard, (Retired)
Turner, Floyd, St. Mary Immaculate, St. Maries
Vietri, Nick, Sacred Heart Indian Mission, DeSmet
Wander, Francis, (Retired)

INSTITUTIONS LOCATED IN THE DIOCESE

[A] HIGH SCHOOLS, INTER-PAROCHIAL

BOISE. *Bishop Kelly High School*, 7009 Franklin Rd., 83709-0922. Tel: 208-375-6010; Fax: 208-375-3626. Robert Wehde, Prin. Lay Teachers 43; Students 680.

COEUR D'ALENE. *Holy Family Catholic School of Coeur d'Alene*, (Grades PreSchool-8), 3005 Kathleen Ave., 83815. Tel: 208-765-4327; Fax: 208-664-2903. Karen Durgin, Prin. Lay Teachers 14; Students 202.

[B] GENERAL HOSPITALS

BOISE. *Saint Alphonsus Health System, Inc.*, 1055 N. Curtis Rd., 83706. Tel: 208-367-2000; Fax: 208-367-3966. Sally Jeffcoat, Pres.
Saint Alphonsus Regional Medical Center, Inc. (1894) *Saint Alphonsus Heal System*, 1055 N. Curtis Rd., 83706-1370. Tel: 208-367-2121. Sally Jeffcoat, Pres. & CEO.
Saint Alphonsus Regional Medical Center, Inc.
Saint Alphonsus Building Company, Inc.
Saint Alphonsus Health System, Inc. Sisters of the Holy Cross 4; Bed Capacity 387; Patients Assisted Annually 301,070.

COTTONWOOD. *St. Mary's Hospital*, 701 Lewiston St., P.O. Box 137, 83522. Tel: 208-962-3251; Fax: 208-962-3722. Ms. Casey Meza, Admin.; Rev. Meinrad Schallberger, O.S.B., Chap.; Sr. Janet Barnard, O.S.B., Dir., Mission Svc. Sponsored by Sisters of St. Benedict, Duluth, MN. Sisters 1; Bed Capacity 25; Patients Assisted Annually 10,000.

LEWISTON. *St. Joseph Regional Medical Center*, 415 6th St., P.O. Box 816, 83501-0816. Tel: 208-743-2511; Fax: 208-799-5528. Timothy P. Sayler, Pres. & CEO. Nursing Education is in affiliation with Lewis-Clark State College and with Walla-Walla Community College, Clarkston Branch. Total Staff 980; Bed Capacity 161; Patients Assisted Annually 126,810.

NAMPA. *Saint Alphonsus Medical Center - Nampa Inc., Saint Alphonsus Health System, Inc.*, 1055 N. Curtis Rd., 83706. Tel: 208-463-5000. Mr. Karl Keeler, Pres. & CEO; Rev. Mark Bekkedahl, Vice Pres. Mission Integration; Sr. Alice Marie Schmid, O.P.; Jim Hoff, Dir. Spiritual Care Resources &

Chap. Sisters 1; Bed Capacity 152; Patients Assisted Annually 114,417.

[C] MONASTERIES AND RESIDENCES OF PRIESTS AND BROTHERS

JEROME. *Monastery of the Ascension*, 541 E. 100 S., 83338. Tel: 208-324-2377; Fax: 208-324-2377. Revs. Boniface Lautz, O.S.B.; Norbert Novak, O.S.B.; Meinrad Schallberger, O.S.B.; Andrew Baumgartner, O.S.B., Subprior; Hugh Feiss, O.S.B.; Eugene Esch, O.S.B.; Ezekiel Lotz, O.S.B.; Paul Montez, O.S.B.; Rt. Rev. Kenneth C. Hein, O.S.B., Prior (Retired); Bros. Sylvester Sonnen, O.S.B.; Selby Coffman, O.S.B.; Tobiah Urrutia, O.S.B.; Jose Echanove, O.S.B.
The Benedictine Monks of Idaho, Inc. The Benedictine Monks of Idaho, Inc.

LEMHI. *Hermitage of St. Joseph*, Box 37, 83465. Bro. Maurice Mansfield, H.M.C. Hermits of Mt. Carmel.

[D] CONVENTS AND RESIDENCES OF SISTERS

COTTONWOOD. *Monastery of St. Gertrude, Motherhouse and Novitiate*, 465 Keuterville Rd., 83522-5183. Tel: 208-962-3224; Fax: 208-962-7212. Rev. Meinrad Schallberger, O.S.B., Chap.; Sisters Clarissa Goeckner, O.S.B., Prioress; Bernadette Stang, O.S.B., Asst. Prioress. Sisters of St. Benedict 54.

MESA. *Marymount Hermitage, Inc., Hermit Sisters of Mary*, 2150 Hermitage Ln., 83643-5005. Tel: 208-256-4354 (msg. only). Email: marymount@ctcweb.net. Web: www.marymount-hermitage.org. Sr. Mary Beverly Greger, H.S.M., Supr. Sisters 1.

[E] RETREAT HOUSES

BOISE. *Nazareth*, 4450 N. Five Mile Rd., 83713-2709. Tel: 208-375-2932; Fax: 208-376-5787. Web: www.nazarethretreatcenter.org. Marjorie DiLorenzo, Dir.; Fred DiLorenzo, Dir.

COTTONWOOD. *Spirit Center*, 465 Keuterville Rd., 83522-5183. Tel: 208-962-2000; Fax: 208-962-2003. Mary Schmidt, Admin.

[F] CAMPUS MINISTRY

BOISE. *Boise State University, St. Paul's Catholic Center* 1915 University Dr., 83706. Tel: 208-343-2128; Fax: 208-367-1110. Email: chuck@stpaulsboise.org. Deacon Charles L. Skorro, Coord. Campus Ministry.

CALDWELL. *The College of Idaho c/o Our Lady of The Valley*, 1122 W. Linden St., 83605. Tel: 208-459-3653; Fax: 208-454-8789. Rev. Francisco Flores.

COEUR D'ALENE. *North Idaho College* St Pius X, 625 E. Haycraft, 83815. Tel: 208-765-5108; Fax: 208-664-5325. Email: frlachance@roadrunner.com. Rev. Roger LaChance, V.F., M.A.

LEWISTON. *Lewis Clark State College* St. Stanislaus, 633 5th Ave., 83501. Tel: 208-743-7331; Fax: 208-746-7134. Very Rev. Leslie P. Kish, V.F., Pastor.

MOSCOW. *St. Augustine Catholic Center* 628 Deakin Ave., Box 3457, 83843-1911. Tel: 208-882-4613; Fax: 208-882-0810. Email: auggiesecretary@moscow.com. Rev. Caleb Vogel. (Serving University of Idaho)

POCATELLO. *Idaho State University, St. John's Catholic Student Center* 920 E. Lovejoy, I.S.U., Box 8129, 83209. Tel: 208-233-0880; Fax: 208-233-5745. Email: stjohns@isu.edu. Web: www.bannockcatholic.net. Jennifer Seaich, Dir.

TWIN FALLS. *College of Southern Idaho* 212 7th Ave. E., 83301-6321. Tel: 208-733-3907; Fax: 208-734-4145. Very Rev. Michael St. Marie, V.F. Attended by St. Edward the Confessor, Twin Falls.

[G] MISCELLANEOUS

BOISE. *Catholic Charities of Idaho, Inc.*, 1501 S. Federal Way, Ste. 450, 83705. Tel: 208-345-6031; Fax: 208-350-7499. Landis Rossi, Exec. Dir.; Most Rev. Michael P. Driscoll, D.D., M.S.W., Pres. Bd. of Dirs.; Lynne Johnson, Admin. Mgr.
Society of St. Vincent de Paul - Southwest Idaho District Council, 3217 W. Overland Rd., 83705. Web: svdpid.org. Mike Gallagher, Pres.
St. Vincent de Paul Society, St. Mark's Conference, 7960 Northview, 83704. Tel: 208-853-2593. Rebecca Echols, Pres.
St. Vincent de Paul Society, Our Lady of the Rosary Conference, 1500 E. Wright St., 83706-5358. Tel: 208-343-9041. Melinda Runkle, Pres.
St. Vincent de Paul Society Thrift Stores, 6464 W. State St., 83703. Tel: 208-853-4921; Fax: 208-853-4935. Email: vickyrowell@svdpid.org. Vicky Rowell, Store Dir.
St. Vincent de Paul Society St. John's Conference., 775 N. 8th St., 83702. Tel: 208-331-2208. Nonie McWhorter, Pres.
St. Vincent de Paul Society Sacred Heart Conference. Sharon Eisenbeiss, Pres.
St. Vincent de Paul Society Risen Christ Conference. Margarita Santos, Pres.

CALDWELL. *Society of St. Vincent de Paul* Society of St. Vincent de Paul, 17281 Ustick Rd., 83607. Tel: 208-459-7658. Paul Hubb, Pres.

COEUR D'ALENE. **St. Vincent de Paul Salvage Bureau* St. Thomas Conference., 201 E. Harrison Ave., 83814. Tel: 208-664-3095; Fax: 208-664-1772. John Bruning, Pres.; Jeff Conroy, Exec. Dir.

EAGLE. *Mercy Housing Northwest - Idaho, Inc.*, 540 N. Eagle Rd., #117, 83616. Tel: 208-939-6838; Fax: 208-939-9480.
Mercy Properties II, Inc., 83616.
Mercy Idaho Properties, Inc., 83616.
Mercy Twin Falls, Inc., 83616.
Mercy Moscow, Inc., 83616.
Mercy Southeast Idaho, Inc., 83616.
Eagle Senior Village, Inc., 83616.
Mercy Independence Hill, Inc.

LEWISTON. **Lewis and Clark District Council of St. Vincent de Paul*, 365 W. Shiloh Dr., 83501. Colleen Stevens, Board Pres.

MERIDIAN. **Holy Apostles Conference*, 2189 W. Grassy Branch Dr., 83646. Tel: 208-888-1182. Jack Crane, Pres.

NAMPA. **Our Lady of Guadalupe Conference*, c/o 1501 S. Federal Way, Ste. 400, 83705. Tel: 208-442-3089.

RELIGIOUS INSTITUTES OF MEN REPRESENTED IN THE DIOCESE

For further details refer to the corresponding bracketed number in the Religious Institutes of Men or Women section.

[]—*Apostolic Life Community of Priests*—A.L.C.P.
[0200]—*Benedictine Monks*—O.S.B.
[]—*Hermits of Mt. Carmel*—H.M.C.
[0690]—*Jesuit Fathers* (Oregon Prov.)—S.J.
[0840]—*Missionary Servants of the Most Holy Trinity*—S.T.
[1065]—*Priestly Fraternity of St. Peter*—F.S.S.P.

RELIGIOUS INSTITUTES OF WOMEN REPRESENTED IN THE DIOCESE

[0230]—*Benedictine Sisters of Pontifical Jurisdiction*—O.S.B.
[1920]—*Congregation of the Sisters of the Holy Cross*—C.S.C.
[1070-21]—*Dominican Sisters*—O.P.
[]—*Hermit Sisters of Mary*—H.S.M.
[1250]—*Institute of the Franciscan Sisters of the Eucharist*—F.S.E.
[2575]—*Institute of the Sisters of Mercy of the Americas*—R.S.M.
[]—*Missionary Sisters of the Sacred Heart of the Rosary of Fatima*—H.M.R.F.
[3340]—*Sisters of Providence*—S.P.
[3830]—*Sisters of St. Joseph*—C.S.J.
[1990]—*Sisters of the Holy Names of Jesus and Mary*—S.N.J.M.
[]—*Society of Sisters of the Church*—S.S.C.
[4110]—*Ursuline Nuns* (Western Prov.)—O.S.U.

NECROLOGY

† King, Rev. Msgr. George L., Orofino, ID St. Theresa's.—Died Nov. 25, 2010
† Finucane, Robert, (Retired)—Died March 16, 2011
† Sprute, Merlyn, (Retired)—Died Dec. 1, 2010

An asterisk (*) denotes an organization that has established tax-exempt status directly with the IRS and is not covered by the USCCB Group Ruling.

Archdiocese of Boston

(Archidioecesis Bostoniensis)

His Eminence

SEÁN PATRICK CARDINAL O'MALLEY, O.F.M.CAP.

Archbishop of Boston; ordained priest August 29, 1970; ordained Coadjutor Bishop of St. Thomas in the Virgin Islands August 2, 1984; succeeded to the See, October 16, 1985; Named sixth Bishop of Fall River, MA June 16, 1992; installed August 10, 1992; Named fourth Bishop of Palm Beach, FL September 3, 2002; installed October 19, 2002; Named ninth Bishop and sixth Metropolitan Archbishop of Boston July 1, 2003; installed July 30, 2003; Named Cardinal Priest with the title of Santa Maria della Vittoria, in the consistory of March 24, 2006. *Office: 66 Brooks Dr., Braintree, MA 02184-3839*. Tel: 617-782-2544; Fax: 617-779-3820. *Res.: Cathedral of the Holy Cross, 75 Union Park St., Boston, MA 02118*. Tel: 617-542-5682; Fax: 617-542-5926.

Chancery Office: 66 Brooks Dr., Braintree, MA 02184-3839. Tel: 617-254-0100; Fax: 617-779-4571.

Web: www.bostoncatholic.org

Most Reverend

WALTER JAMES EDYVEAN

Titular Bishop of Aeliae, Auxiliary Bishop of Boston, Vicar General and Regional Bishop-West; ordained priest December 16, 1964; ordained Bishop September 14, 2001. *Office: 5 Wilson St., Natick, MA 01760*. Tel: 508-647-0296; Fax: 508-647-1542. *Res.: Saint Patrick Rectory, 44 E. Central St., Natick, MA 01760*. Tel: 508-647-1860.

Most Reverend

JOHN ANTHONY DOOHER

Titular Bishop of Theveste, Auxiliary Bishop of Boston, Vicar General and Regional Bishop-South; ordained priest May 21, 1969; ordained Bishop December 12, 2006. *Office: 236 Pleasant St., Weymouth, MA 02190-2599*. Tel: 781-337-4413; Fax: 781-337-3625. *Res.: Saint Jerome Rectory, 632 Bridge St., Weymouth, MA 02191*. Tel: 781-335-2038; Fax: 781-340-7165.

Most Reverend

ROBERT FRANCIS HENNESSEY

Titular Bishop of Tigias, Auxiliary Bishop of Boston, Vicar General and Regional Bishop-Central; ordained priest May 20, 1978; ordained Bishop December 12, 2006. *Office: 841 E. Broadway, Boston, MA 02127-2302*. Tel: 617-269-4001; Fax: 617-269-4006. *Res.: Saint James the Greater Rectory, 135 Harrison Ave., Boston, MA 02111*. Tel: 617-542-8498; Fax: 617-542-2708.

Most Reverend

ARTHUR LEO KENNEDY

Titular Bishop of Tmidana, Auxiliary Bishop of Boston, Vicar General & Rector of Saint John Seminary; ordained priest December 17, 1966; ordained Bishop September 14, 2010. *Office & Res.: 127 Lake St., Brighton, MA 02135-3898*. Tel: 617-254-2610; Fax: 617-787-2336.

Most Reverend

PETER JOHN UGLIETTO

Titular Bishop of Thubursicum, Auxiliary Bishop of Boston, Vicar General and Regional Bishop-North; ordained priest May 21, 1977; ordained Bishop September 14, 2010. *Office: 99 Margin St., Peabody, MA 01960*. Tel: 978-531-1013; Fax: 978-531-5312. *Res.: Saint Patrick Rectory, 9 Pomeworth St., Stoneham, MA 02180-2025*. Tel: 781-438-0960; Fax: 781-438-6809.

Most Reverend

JOHN PATRICK BOLES

Titular Bishop of Nova Sparsa; ordained priest February 2, 1955; ordained Bishop May 21, 1992; retired October 12, 2006. *Office: 841 E. Broadway, Boston, MA 02127-2302*. Tel: 617-269-4001; Fax: 617-269-4006. *Res.: Saint Mary of the Assumption Rectory, 5 Linden St., Brookline, MA 02445-7311*. Tel: 617-734-0444; Fax: 617-734-3001.

Most Reverend

FRANCIS XAVIER IRWIN

Titular Bishop of Ubaza and Vicar General; ordained priest February 2, 1960; ordained Bishop September 17, 1996; retired October 15, 2009. *Res.: Saint Raphael Rectory, 38 Boston Ave., Medford, MA 02155*. Tel: 781-488-5444; Fax: 781-483-3375.

Most Reverend

EMILIO SIMEON ALLUE, S.D.B.

Titular Bishop of Croe and Vicar General; ordained priest December 22, 1966; ordained Bishop September 17, 1996; retired June 30, 2010. *Res.: Saint Theresa of Avila Rectory, 10 Saint Theresa Ave., Boston, MA 02132*. Tel: 617-325-1300; Fax: 617-325-0380.

Square Miles 2,465.

Created a Diocese April 8, 1808; Made Metropolitan Archdiocese February 12, 1875.

Comprises the Counties of Essex, Middlesex, Norfolk, Suffolk and Plymouth (the towns of Marion, Mattapoisett and Wareham excepted) in the Commonwealth of Massachusetts.

For legal titles of parishes and archdiocesan agencies and institutions, consult the Chancery Office.

STATISTICAL OVERVIEW

Personnel	
Cardinals	1
Auxiliary Bishops	5
Retired Bishops	3
Retired Abbots	1
Priests: Diocesan Active in Diocese	370
Priests: Diocesan Active Outside Diocese	28
Priests: Diocesan in Foreign Missions	4
Priests: Retired, Sick or Absent	297
Number of Diocesan Priests	699
Religious Priests in Diocese	505
Total Priests in Diocese	1,204
Extern Priests in Diocese	54
Ordinations:	
Diocesan Priests	6
Transitional Deacons	1
Permanent Deacons	13
Permanent Deacons in Diocese	265
Total Brothers	151
Total Sisters	1,760
Parishes	
Parishes	289
With Resident Pastor:	
Resident Diocesan Priests	273
Resident Religious Priests	16
Missions	1
New Parishes Created	1
Closed Parishes	3
Professional Ministry Personnel:	
Sisters	36
Lay Ministers	241
Welfare	
Catholic Hospitals	8
Total Assisted	708,219
Health Care Centers	3
Total Assisted	7,511
Homes for the Aged	15
Total Assisted	2,832
Residential Care of Children	1
Total Assisted	921
Day Care Centers	11
Total Assisted	1,110
Specialized Homes	21
Total Assisted	1,722
Special Centers for Social Services	43
Total Assisted	206,000
Other Institutions	3
Total Assisted	35,410
Educational	
Seminaries, Diocesan	3
Students from This Diocese	61
Students from Other Diocese	93
Diocesan Students in Other Seminaries	2
Seminaries, Religious	1
Students Religious	33
Total Seminarians	96
Colleges and Universities	6
Total Students	24,900
High Schools, Diocesan and Parish	3
Total Students	1,150
High Schools, Private	29
Total Students	15,155
Elementary Schools, Diocesan and Parish	79
Total Students	24,067
Elementary Schools, Private	9
Total Students	2,264
Non-residential Schools for the Disabled	2
Total Students	139
Catechesis/Religious Education:	
High School Students	26,624
Elementary Students	97,419
Total Students under Catholic Instruction	191,814
Teachers in the Diocese:	
Priests	7
Brothers	31
Sisters	91
Lay Teachers	3,177
Vital Statistics	
Receptions into the Church:	
Infant Baptism Totals	13,390
Minor Baptism Totals	2,434
Adult Baptism Totals	250
Received into Full Communion	255
First Communions	16,786
Confirmations	13,305
Marriages:	
Catholic	2,409
Interfaith	603
Total Marriages	3,012
Deaths	14,426
Total Catholic Population	1,807,002
Total Population	3,764,587

Former Bishops—His Eminence JOHN LEFEVRE CARDINAL DE CHEVERUS, ord. Dec. 18, 1790; appt. first Bishop of Boston, April 8, 1808; ord. Bishop Nov. 1, 1810; Apostolic Administrator of New York, NY (1810-1815); transferred to Montauban, May 3, 1823; appt. Archbishop of Bordeaux Oct. 2, 1826; named Cardinal, Feb. 1, 1836 (died before receiving red hat and titular church); died July 19, 1836; Most Revs. BENEDICT J. FENWICK, S.J., ord. June 11, 1808; appt. second Bishop of Boston, May 10, 1825; ord. Bishop Nov. 1, 1825; died Aug. 11, 1846; JOHN BERNARD FITZPATRICK, ord. June 13, 1840; appt. Titular Bishop of Callipolis and Coadjutor of Boston, Nov. 21, 1843; ord. Bishop March 24, 1844; Succeeded as third Bishop of Boston, Aug. 11, 1846; died Feb. 13, 1866; JOHN JOSEPH WILLIAMS, D.D., ord. May 17, 1845; appt. Titular Bishop of Tripolis and Coadjutor of Boston, Jan. 8, 1866; ord. fourth Bishop of Boston, March 11, 1866; named first Archbishop of Boston, Feb. 12, 1875; died Aug. 30, 1907; His Eminence WILLIAM HENRY CARDINAL O'CONNELL, ord. June 7, 1884; appt. third Bishop of Portland, Maine, Feb. 8, 1901; ord. Bishop May 19, 1901; appt. Titular Archbishop of Constantia and Coadjutor with right of succession to the Archbishop of Boston, Feb. 8, 1906; appt. fifth Bishop and second Archbishop of Boston, April 30, 1907; named Cardinal, Nov. 27, 1911, Titular Church, San Clemente; died April 22, 1944; RICHARD JAMES CARDINAL CUSHING, ord. May 26, 1921; appt. Titular Bishop of Mela and Auxiliary of Boston, June 10, 1939; ord. Bishop June 29, 1939; appt. sixth Bishop and third Archbishop of Boston, Sept. 25, 1944; named Cardinal December 15, 1958, Titular Church, Santa Susanna; died Nov. 2, 1970; HUMBERTO SOUSA CARDINAL MEDEIROS, ord. June 15, 1946; appt. second Bishop of Brownsville, Texas April 14, 1966; ord. Bishop June 9, 1966; named seventh Bishop and fourth Archbishop of Boston, Sept. 8, 1970; installed Oct. 7, 1970; named Cardinal March 5, 1973, Titular Church, Santa Susanna; died Sept. 17, 1983; BERNARD FRANCIS CARDINAL LAW, ord. priest May 21, 1961; appt. fourth Bishop of Springfield-Cape Girardeau Oct. 22, 1973; ord. Bishop of Springfield-Cape Girardeau Dec. 5, 1973; appt. eighth Bishop and fifth Archbishop of Boston Jan. 11, 1984; installed March 23, 1984; named Cardinal Priest May 25, 1985; Titular Church, Santa Susanna; resigned Dec. 13, 2002; named Archpriest of the Patriarchal Basilica of St. Mary Major, Rome, Italy, May 27, 2004; resigned Nov. 4, 2011.

Vicars General—Most Revs. EMILIO S. ALLUE, S.D.B.; JOHN P. BOLES; JOHN A. DOOHER; WALTER J. EDYVEAN, S.T.D.; ROBERT F. HENNESSEY; FRANCIS X. IRWIN; ARTHUR L. KENNEDY; PETER J. UGLIETTO; Rev. Msgr. ROBERT P. DEELEY, V.F., J.C.D.

Regional Bishops and Vicars—

Central Region—Most Rev. ROBERT F. HENNESSEY. Tel: 617-269-4001; Fax: 617-269-4006. Vicariate I: Very Rev. BRIAN M. CLARY, V.F., Saint Mary of the Assumption, Brookline. Tel: 617-325-3322; Fax: 617-325-2145. Vicariate II: Very Rev. ROBERT E. CASEY, V.F., Gate of Heaven and St. Brigid, South Boston. Tel: 617-268-2122; Fax: 617-268-2666. Vicariate III: Very Rev. KEVIN J. O'LEARY, V.F., Cathedral of the Holy Cross, Boston. Tel: 617-542-5682; Fax: 617-542-5926. Vicariate IV: Very Rev. WALTER A. CARREIRO, V.F., St. Anthony of Padua, Cambridge. Tel: 617-547-5593; Fax: 617-547-1505.

Merrimack Region—Very Rev. ARTHUR M. COYLE. Tel: 978-399-0000; Fax: 978-399-0123. Vicariate I: Very Rev. PAUL E. RITT, V.F., St. John the Evangelist, Chelmsford. Tel: 978-251-8571; Fax: 978-251-7873. Vicariate II: Very Rev. BRIAN E. MAHONEY, V.F., St. Francis of Assisi, Dracut. Tel: 978-851-7331; Fax: 978-858-0544. Vicariate III: Very Rev. JOHN W. DELANEY, V.F., St. Michael, North Andover. Tel: 978-686-4050; Fax: 978-686-5408. Vicariate IV: Very Rev. TIMOTHY A. HARRISON, V.F., Immaculate Conception, Newburyport. Tel: 978-887-5505; Fax: 978-887-8201.

North Region—Most Rev. PETER J. UGLIETTO. Tel: 978-531-1013; Fax: 978-531-5312. Vicariate I: Very Rev. JOHN E. FARRELL, V.F., Our Lady of the Assumption, Lynnfield. Tel: 781-598-4313; Fax: 781-598-0055. Vicariate II: Very Rev. JOHN E. MACINNIS, V.F., St. John the Baptist, Peabody. Tel: 978-531-0002; Fax: 978-531-5199. Vicariate III: Very Rev. THOMAS F. NESTOR, V.F., St. Eulalia, Winchester. Tel: 781-729-8220; Fax: 781-729-0919. Vicariate IV: Very Rev. TERENCE J. MORAN, V.F., Saint Rose of Lime, Chelsea. Tel: 617-884-0030; Fax: 617-884-0957.

South Region—Most Rev. JOHN A. DOOHER. Tel: 781-337-4413; Fax: 781-337-3625. Vicariate I: Very Rev. KEVIN M. SEPE, V.F., St. Francis of Assisi, Braintree. Tel: 781-843-1332; Fax: 781-848-0976. Vicariate II: Very Rev. DANIEL J. RILEY, V.F., Sacred Heart, Weymouth. Tel: 781-337-6333; Fax: 781-337-9192. Vicariate III: Very Rev. JOSEPH K. RAEKE, V.F., Saint Edith Stein, Brockton. Tel: 508-697-9538; Fax: 508-279-1859. Vicariate IV: Very Rev. CHARLES J. HIGGINS, V.F., St. Joseph, Kingston. Tel: 781-585-6679; Fax: 781-645-1337.

West Region—Most Rev. WALTER J. EDYVEAN, S.T.D. Tel: 508-647-0296; Fax: 508-647-1542. Vicariate I: Very Rev. MICHAEL W. MACEWEN, V.F., Immaculate Conception, Marlborough. Tel: 508-358-2985; Fax: 508-358-3415. Vicariate II: Very Rev. ROBERT L. CONNORS, V.F., St. Patrick, Watertown. Tel: 617-926-3680; Fax: 781-235-4620. Vicariate III: Very Rev. DAVID C. MICHAEL, V.F., St. Joseph, Needham. Tel: 508-785-0305; Fax: 508-785-0432. Vicariate IV: Very Rev. JOHN P. CULLOTY, V.F., St. Timothy, Norwood. Tel: 508-533-6500; Fax: 508-533-1236.

Vicar General and Moderator of the Curia—Rev. Msgr. ROBERT P. DEELEY, V.F., J.C.D., 66 Brooks Dr., Braintree, 02184-3839. Tel: 617-254-0100; Fax: 617-746-5920. Email: vicar_general@rcab.org.

Assistant to the Moderator of the Curia—Very Rev. BRYAN K. PARRISH, V.F., 66 Brooks Dr., Braintree, 02184-3839. Tel: 617-254-0100; Fax: 617-746-5920.

Assistant to the Moderator of the Curia for Canonical Affairs—Rev. ROBERT J. OLIVER, B.H., S.T.D., J.C.D., 66 Brooks Dr., Braintree, 02184-3839. Tel: 617-746-5635; Fax: 617-746-5920. Email: peters_j@rcab.org.

Archives—Mr. ROBERT JOHNSON-LALLY, Archivist, 66 Brooks Dr., Braintree, 02184-3839. Tel: 617-746-5797; Fax: 617-746-4561.

Pontifical Association of the Holy Childhood—

Pontifical Society for the Propagation of the Faith—

Pontifical Society of Saint Peter the Apostle—Rev. RODNEY J. COPP, J.C.L., Dir., 66 Brooks Dr., Braintree, 02184-3839. Tel: 617-779-3865. Email: officestaff@propfaithatboston.org.

Metropolitan Tribunal

Ecclesiastical Court of the Archdiocese of Boston—66 Brooks Dr., Braintree, 02184-3839. Tel: 617-746-5900; Fax: 617-779-4566.

Judicial Vicar of the Archdiocese—Very Rev. MARK O'CONNELL, J.C.D.

Archdiocesan Judges—Tribunal Court: Rev. Msgr. MICHAEL S. FOSTER, J.C.D.; Very Rev. MARK O'CONNELL, J.C.D.; Rev. JOSEPH F. MOZER JR., J.C.L.; Sr. MARGARET L. SULLIVAN, C.S.J., J.C.L.; Ms. MARIA GALINDEZ-BIANCO, J.C.L., J.D. Associates: Revs. JOSEPH M. HENNESSEY, J.C.L.; ROBERT W. OLIVER, B.H., S.T.D., J.C.D.

Court Advocate/Petitioner—Rev. WLODZIMIERZ SOBOLEWSKI, C.R.

Court Advocate/Respondent—Rev. PETER G. GORI, O.S.A., J.C.D.

Defenders of the Bond—Revs. JAMES G. BURKE, J.C.L.; RODNEY J. COPP, J.C.L.; AIDAN J. WALSH, J.C.L.

Promoter of Justice—Rev. RODNEY J. COPP, J.C.L.

Notary—Ms. MARSHA A. STATEN.

Staff—Ms. ROSE GRENIER; Ms. ELLEN OBSHATKIN; Ms. JULIANNE SHANKLIN; Ms. MARSHA A. STATEN.

Canonical Affairs Committee—Very Rev. MARK O'CONNELL, J.C.D., Chm.; Most Rev. WALTER J. EDYVEAN, S.T.D.; Revs. JAMES G. BURKE, J.C.L.; RODNEY J. COPP, J.C.L.; PETER G. GORI, O.S.A., J.C.D.; Very Rev. JAMES J. LAUGHLIN, J.C.L., V.F.; Revs. JOSEPH F. MOZER JR., J.C.L.; WALTER J. WOODS, S.T.D.; Sr. MARGARET L. SULLIVAN, C.S.J., J.C.L.

Presbyteral Council—His Eminence SEAN CARDINAL O'MALLEY, O.F.M.Cap.; Most Revs. EMILIO S. ALLUE, S.D.B.; JOHN P. BOLES; JOHN A. DOOHER; WALTER J. EDYVEAN, S.T.D.; ROBERT F. HENNESSEY; FRANCIS X. IRWIN; ARTHUR L. KENNEDY; PETER J. UGLIETTO; Rev. Msgrs. FRANCIS H. KELLEY, V.F.; FRANCIS J. MCGANN (Retired); DENNIS F. SHEEHAN; Very Revs. EDWIN D. CONDON (Retired); ARTHUR M. COYLE; RICHARD M. ERIKSON, V.G.; THOMAS S. FOLEY, V.F.; PAUL E. RITT, V.F.; Revs. IGNACIO D. BERRIO; ROBERT M. BLANEY, V.F.; MARK J. COIRO; ARNOLD F. COLETTI; Very Rev. ROBERT L. CONNORS, V.F.; Revs. DONALD R. DELAY; STEPHEN S. DONOHOE, M.Div.; MATHIAS DOYLE, O.F.M.; GEORGE F. EMERSON (Retired); GEORGE P. EVANS, M.Div., S.T.D.; DANIEL J. FINN; PETER G. GORI, O.S.A., J.C.D.; THOMAS GRIFFITHS, S.V.D.; MICHAEL A. HOBSON; HERBERT J. JONES, O.Carm.; J. MICHAEL LAWLOR; THOMAS A. KOPP, J.C.L.; MICHAEL D. LINDEN, S.J.; PATRICK J. MCLAUGHLIN; VINCENT P. MELLONE; ANTHONY G. NGUYEN; GERARD PETRINGA; LAWRENCE E. PRATT (Retired); PETER F. QUINN; JOHN J. RONAGHAN; NICHOLAS A. SANELLA; MICHAEL L. STEELE; WILLIAM G. WILLIAMS.

College of Consultors—His Eminence SEAN CARDINAL O'MALLEY, O.F.M.Cap.; Most Revs. EMILIO S. ALLUE, S.D.B.; JOHN P. BOLES; JOHN A. DOOHER; WALTER J. EDYVEAN, S.T.D.; ROBERT F. HENNESSEY; FRANCIS X. IRWIN; ARTHUR L. KENNEDY; PETER J. UGLIETTO; Rev. Msgrs. ROBERT P. DEELEY, V.F., J.C.D.; WILLIAM J. FAY; Very Rev. ARTHUR M. COYLE; Rev. GEORGE F. EMERSON (Retired).

Finance Council—President: His Eminence SEAN CARDINAL O'MALLEY, O.F.M.Cap. Members: Rev. Msgr. ROBERT P. DEELEY, V.F., J.C.D.; Sr. JOAN DUFFY, C.S.J.; Mr. JOHN J. CONNORS JR.; Mr. JOHN A. KANEB; Mr. PETER S. LYNCH; Mr. WILLIAM F. MCCALL; Mr. JOHN MCCARTHY; Mr. JAMES P. MCDONOUGH; Mr. SEAN P. MCGRATH; Mr. JOHN A. MCNIECE; Mr. JAMES MOONEY; Mr. ROBERT J. MORRISSEY; Mr. GILES MOSHER; Mr. PAUL W. SANDMAN; Ms. MARY RYAN.

Archdiocesan Pastoral Council—President: His Eminence SEAN CARDINAL O'MALLEY, O.F.M.Cap. Ex Officio: Rev. Msgr. ROBERT P. DEELEY, V.F., J.C.D.; Very Rev. ARTHUR M. COYLE. Appointed: Revs. LEONARD F. O'MALLEY; FRANK J. SILVA; Deacon PHILIP H. LAFOND; Bro. JOHN F. KERR, C.F.X.; Sisters SUZANNE FONDINI, M.F.I.C.; MARK LOUIS RANDALL, O.Carm.; Mr. PETER A. BAILEY; Mr. KEVIN M. CASEY; Mr. VINCENT J. DEBAGGIS; Mr. KEVIN DELEHANTY; Mr. ARMAND J. DI LANDO; Mr. ROBERT GADBOIS; Mr. MARK GARVEY; Mr. MICHAEL F. GILROY; Dr. EDWARD GOTGART; Mr. JOHNNY IP; Mr. TIMOTHY J. KELLEY; Mr. JOSEPH KOSCIUSZEK; Mr. HERB LYNCH, Attorney; Mr. JOHN F. MORAN; Mr. PHILLIP MORAN; Mr. JOHN T. MULCAHY; Mr. THOMAS J. NUTTALL; Mr. THONG PHAMDUY; Mr. PETER POUND; Mr. JIM SULLIVAN; Mr. PHILIP J. WALSH; Ms. ANDREA S. ALBERTI; Ms. SANDRA BISHOP; Ms. NANCY D. CIRONE; Ms. ELLEN H. CONNELL; Ms. JANE DEVLIN; Ms. PATRICIA M. DINNEEN; Ms. ANTONIA GARCIA-VEGA; Ms. NANCY HARRINGTON; Ms. PATRICIA MEUSE; Ms. SHARON M. MOORE; Ms. LINDA RILEY; Ms. SUZANNE ROBOTHAM; Ms. BETTY SNIEGOSKI; Ms. BUFFY WALSH.

Administration and Financial Services—Mr. JAMES P. MCDONOUGH, Sec. & Chancellor, 66 Brooks Dr., Braintree, 02184-3839. Tel: 617-746-5670; Fax: 617-779-4571. Email: jpm@rcab.org.

Cemeteries—Mr. ROBERT VISCONTI, Dir., 175 Broadway, Malden, 02148-6097. Tel: 781-322-6300; Fax: 781-322-3801. Email: rvisconti@rcab.org. Web: ccemetery.org.

Finance and Technology—VACANT, Dir., 66 Brooks Dr., Braintree, 02184-3839. Tel: 617-746-5878; Fax: 617-779-4564.

Human Resources—CAROL GUSTAVSON, Dir., 66 Brooks Dr., Braintree, 02184-3839. Tel: 617-746-5829; Fax: 617-779-4571. Email: carol_gustavson@rcab.org.

Parish Services and Risk Management—Mr. JOSEPH F. MCENNESS, Dir., 66 Brooks Dr., Braintree, 02184-3839. Tel: 617-746-5740; Fax: 617-779-4510. Email: jmcenness@rcab.org.

Planning and Projects—Mr. KEVIN KILEY, Dir., 66 Brooks Dr., Braintree, 02184-3839. Tel: 617-746-5671; Fax: 617-746-5456. Email: peter_silva@rcab.org.

Planning Office for Urban Affairs—Ms. LISA ALBERGHINI, Dir., 84 State St., Boston, 02109. Tel: 617-350-8885; Fax: 617-350-8889. Email: lba@poua.org.

Health Benefit Trust, Insurance and Pension Trusts, Caritas Christi Retirement Plan—His Eminence SEAN P. CARDINAL O'MALLEY, O.F.M.Cap.; Rev. Msgr. ROBERT P. DEELEY, V.F., J.C.D.; Very Rev. JOSEPH K. RAEKE, V.F.; Mr. ROBERT GUYON; Mr. JAMES P. MCDONOUGH; Mr. WILSON D. ROGERS, Esq.; Mr. DAVID WOONTON; Ms. HELEN DRINAN; Ms. ANNA-MARIE FERRARO. Plan Administrator: Mr. JAMES M. WALSH. Plan Manager: Ms. MARY REGAN. Attorney for the Trust: LINDA SHERMAN, Consultants: JP Morgan Compensation and Benefit Strategies for the pension plans and Mercer for the health plan.

Insurance Advisory Committee—Chair: Mr. JAMES P. MCDONOUGH. Members: Mr. JOHN P. RIORDON; Mr. JAMES M. WALSH; Mr. EDWARD WAYSTACK. Consultant: Mr. JOSEPH F. MCENNESS.

Massachusetts Catholic Self Insurance Group—President: Mr. JAMES P. MCDONOUGH. Treasurer: Mr. JAMES M. WALSH. Directors: Mr. ROBERT CANTWELL; Mr. STEVEN FISCHER; Mr. JOSEPH P. WELCH. Counsel: TIMOTHY M. MCCRYSTAL, Esq. Clerk: Rev. CHARLES J. HIGGINS. Administrator: Mr. JOSEPH F. MCENNESS.

Investment Advisory Committee—Chair: Deacon CHARLES I. CLOUGH; Rev. Msgr. ROBERT P. DEELEY, V.F., J.C.D.; Mr. GERALD CURTIS; Mr. JAMES J. MAHONEY; Mr. JAMES P. MCDONOUGH; Mr. THOMAS M. O'NEIL; Mr. THOMAS STAKEM; Ms. MAUREEN E. CULLINANE; Ms. KATHLEEN HEGENBART.

Audit Committee—Chair: Mr. JOHN MCCARTHY. Members: Mr. JOSEPH FINN; Mr. JAMES F. O'CONNOR.

Archdiocesan Building Commission—Chair: Mr. JAMES P. MCDONOUGH. Members: Revs. JOSEPH A. ANTONELLIS; WILLIAM D. COUGHLIN; BRIAN F. MANNING; ROBERT G. MCMILLAN, S.J.

Consultants: Mr. RAFIK AYOUB; Mr. ROBERT A. CASSIDY.

Delegate for Religious—Sr. MARIAN BATHO, C.S.J., Sec., 66 Brooks Dr., Braintree, 02184-3839. Tel: 617-746-5637; Fax: 617-746-5754. Email: sr_marian_batho@rcab.org.

Airport Chaplaincy—Rev. RICHARD A. UFTRING, Chap., Logan International Airport, Boston, 02128. Tel: 617-567-2800. Email: fatherrichard@massport.com.

Office of Black Catholics—Ms. LORNA DESROSES, 66 Brooks Dr., Braintree, 02184-3839. Tel: 617-746-5810; Fax: 617-746-5614. Email: ldesroses@rcab.org.

Black Catholic Choir—Ms. RUTH VILLARD. Tel: 617-288-2252.

African-American—Ms. LORNA DESROSES. Tel: 617-746-5810.

Cape Verdean—Rev. EGIDIO ALVES DOS SANTOS. Tel: 617-445-7615.

Congolese—Ms. JACQUELINE KALONJI. Tel: 781-599-6662.

Eritrean—Rev. ABAYNEH GEBREMICHAEL. Tel: 508-583-1121.

Ethiopian—Rev. ABAYNEH GEBREMICHAEL. Tel: 508-583-1121.

Ghanaian—Mr. PATRICK SOSSOU. Tel: 617-323-6458.

Haitian—Rev. GABRIEL MICHEL. Tel: 617-298-0080.

Kenyan—Rev. MICHAEL KUMO. Tel: 978-459-0713.

Nigerian—Rev. ANSELM NWAGBARA. Tel: 617-445-8915.

Ugandan—Mr. HENRY NDAWULA. Tel: 781-935-0610.

Boston Catholic Directory—Rev. ROBERT M. O'GRADY, Mng. Editor, 66 Brooks Dr., Braintree, 02184-3839. Tel: 617-746-5873; Fax: 617-779-4560. Email: rmogrady@thebostonpilot.com.

Campus Ministry—Rev. RICHARD F. CLANCY, Dir., 66 Brooks Dr., Braintree, 02184-3839. Tel: 617-746-5856; Fax: 617-782-0213. Email: father_richard_clancy@rcab.org.

Boston—

Boston University—Rev. PAUL D. HELFRICH, B.H., Campus Min., 211 Bay State Rd., Boston, 02215. Tel: 617-353-3632; Fax: 617-358-2049. Email: frpaul@bu.edu. Web: bu.edu.

Emerson College—Ms. KRISTELLE ANGELLI, Campus Min., 120 Boylston St., Boston, 02116. Tel: 617-783-3924. Email: volservice@aol.com.

Emmanuel College—VACANT, Campus Min., 400 The Fenway, Boston, 02115. Tel: 617-735-9780; Fax: 617-735-9877. Web: emmanuel.edu.

Northeastern University—Bro. JOSEPH DONOVAN, B.H., Campus Min., 68 Saint Stephen St., Boston, 02115. Tel: 617-373-8964. Email: jj.donovan@neu.edu. Web: northeastern.edu.

Babson Park—

Babson College—VACANT, Campus Min., Galvin Family Chapel, Babson Park, 02457-0310. Tel: 781-239-5623. Web: babson.edu.

Bridgewater—

Bridgewater State College—Ms. JENNIFER SPARROW, Campus Min., 122 Park Ave., Bridgewater, 02324. Tel: 508-531-1346. Email: gatorfan@gmail.com. Web: bridgew.edu.

Cambridge—

Harvard University—Rev. MICHAEL E. DREA, Campus Min., 20 Arrow St., Cambridge, 02138. Tel: 617-868-6585. Email: mdrea@stpaulparish.org. Web: harvard.edu.

Massachusetts Institute of Technology—Rev. RICHARD F. CLANCY, Campus Min., 40 Massachusetts Ave., Cambridge, 02139-4312. Tel: 617-253-2981; Fax: 617-253-3260. Email: frclancy@mit.edu.

Chestnut Hill—

Boston College—Rev. TONY PENNA, Dir., McElroy 233, Chestnut Hill, 02467-3805. Tel: 617-552-3475; Fax: 617-552-3473. Email: ministry@bc.edu. Web: bc.edu.

Dorchester—

Laboure College—Rev. JOHN J. STAGNARO, Campus Min., 2120 Dorchester Ave., Dorchester, 02124-5698. Tel: 617-296-8300; Fax: 617-296-7947. Email: jstagnaro@labourecollege.org. Web: labourecollege.org.

University of Massachusetts-Boston—Ms. JENNIFER SPARROW, Campus Min., Harbor Campus, Dorchester, 02125-3393. Tel: 617-287-5839; Fax: 617-287-5815. Email: gatorfan@gmail.com. Web: umb.edu.

Framingham—

Framingham State College—Ms. HAI OK HWANG, M.Div., Campus Min., 100 State St., Framingham, 01701-9101. Tel: 508-626-4610; Fax: 508-626-4939. Email: hhwang@frc.mass.edu. Web: frc.mass.edu.

Lowell—

University of Massachusetts-Lowell—Ms. BERNADINE KENSINGER, Campus Min., Mailing Address: Box 360, Lowell, 01853-0360. Tel: 978-934-5032. Email: bernadine_kensinger@uml.edu. Web: uml.edu.

Medford—

Tufts University—Ms. LYNN COOPER, M.Div., Campus Min., Three The Green, Medford, 02155-5300. Tel: 781-391-7272; Fax: 617-571-5269. Email: lynn.cooper@tufts.edu. Web: tufts.edu.

Milton—

Curry College—VACANT, Spiritual Life Coord., Curry College, Milton, 02186. Tel: 617-333-2289; Fax: 617-333-2014. Web: curry.edu.

North Andover—

Merrimack College—Sr. MARY ELLEN DOW, S.N.D., Campus Min., Grace J. Palmisano Center, North Andover, 01845. Tel: 978-837-5450; Fax: 978-837-5004. Email: maryellendow@merrimack.edu. Web: merrimack.edu.

Salem—

Salem State College—Rev. GERARD R. MCKEON, S.J., Campus Min., Interfaith Office, 352 Lafayette St., Salem, 01970. Tel: 978-542-6074.

Waltham—

Bentley College—Rev. CLAUDE GRENACHE, A.A., B.A., S.T.B., S.T.L., Campus Min., 175 Forest St., Waltham, 02452-4705. Tel: 781-891-2754; Fax: 781-891-2839. Email: cgrenache@bentley.edu. Web: bentley.edu.

Brandeis University—Rev. WALTER H. CUENIN, Campus Min., Mail Stop 205, Waltham, 02454-9110. Tel: 781-736-3574; Fax: 781-736-3577. Email: whcuenin@hotmail.com.

Wellesley—

Wellesley College—Sr. NANCY CORCORAN, C.S.J., Campus Min., Chaplaincy Center, Wellesley, 02481. Tel: 781-283-2688. Email: ncorcora@wellesley.edu. Web: wellesley.edu.

Weston—

Regis College—Sr. ROSEMARY MULVIHILL, R.S.M., Campus Min., 235 Wellesley St., Weston, 02493-1571. Tel: 781-768-7063; Fax: 781-768-8339. Email: rosemary.mulvihill@regiscollege.edu. Web: regiscollege.edu.

Catholic Charitable Bureau of the Archdiocese of Boston, Inc.—His Eminence SEAN PATRICK CARDINAL O'MALLEY, O.F.M.Cap., Archbishop of Boston; Rev. J. BRYAN HEHIR, Pres., 51 Sleeper St., Boston, 02110. Tel: 617-482-5440; Fax: 617-451-0337. Email: info@ccab.org. Web: www.rcab.org.

Community Service Centers and Divisions— El Centro del Cardenal; Greater Boston Catholic Charities; Haitian Multi-Service Center; Laboure Center; Merrimack Valley Catholic Charities; Catholic Charities North; Catholic Charities South; Catholic Charities West; Behavioral Health Division; Child Care Division; Refugee and Immigration Services Division.

Catholic Charities Senior Management—JENNIFER MENDELSOHN, CFO; Rev. PHILLIP B. EARLEY, Sec. & Gen. Counsel; DEBORAH KINCADE RAMBO, L.I.C.S.W., Vice Pres. Programs; JOSEPH BURNIEIKA, Vice Pres. External Affairs; DAVID I. WALSH, Chief Information Officer; CAROL REILLY, Dir. Human Resources; KENNETH P. BINDER, Vice Pres. Devel.; JUDITH WHITMARSH, Dir. Public Policy; BRIDGET RYAN SNELL, Dir. Mktg. & Public Rels.; BARRY VERONESI, Controller; DANIEL DORMER, Dir. Real Estate.

Greater Boston Catholic Charities—VIVIAN SOPER, L.I.C.S.W., Dir.; BETH CHAMBERS, Dir. Community Svcs. Services: Basic Needs Emergency Services, Sunset Point Camp, Youth Empowerment, Family Stabilization, Foster Grandparents, Friendly Visitor and Elderly Outreach, Healthy Families, Housing and Transitional Living, Adoption Search. 185 Columbia Rd., Dorchester, 02121. Tel: 617-506-6600; Fax: 617-474-1009.

Greater Boston Catholic Charities at Somerville—270 Washington St., Somerville, 02143. Tel: 617-625-1920; Fax: 617-629-2246.

Teen Center at St. Peter's—278 Bowdoin St., Dorchester, 02122. Tel: 617-506-6600; Fax: 617-282-3483.

Sunset Point Camp—2 10th St., Hull, 02045. Tel: 781-925-0710; Fax: 781-925-3840.

Saint Ambrose Family Shelter—Tel: 617-288-7675; Fax: 617-288-7037.

Brigid's Crossing—Tel: 978-454-0081; Fax: 978-454-0210.

Robert McBride House—Tel: 617-236-8319; Fax: 617-236-8219.

Seton Manor—Tel: 617-277-7133; Fax: 617-227-7288.

Genesis II—Tel: 617-332-9905; Fax: 617-964-4354.

Nazareth Residence for Mothers and Children—Tel: 617-541-0100; Fax: 617-541-8781.

St. Patrick's Shelter for Homeless Women—Tel: 617-628-3015; Fax: 617-629-2246.

Caritas Saint Mary Women and Children's Center—Ms. JUDITH BECKLER, Exec. Dir., 90 Cushing Ave., Boston, 02125. Tel: 617-436-8600; Fax: 617-288-8961. Email: jbeckler@smwic.org. Web: smwic.org. Region: Central.

Laboure Center—Sr. MARYADELE ROBINSON, D.C., M.S.W., Dir., 275 W. Broadway, South Boston, 02127. Tel: 617-268-9670; Fax: 617-268-3088 Services: Basic Needs Emergency Services, Pregnancy Counseling, T.E.A.M., Youth Tutoring Youth, Family Intervention, Visiting Nurse Services.

Metro Boston—

El Centro del Cardenal—DEBORAH KINCADE RAMBO, L.I.C.S.W., Interim Dir.; ROBERT HIBBARD, Dir. Adult Educ.; EDWARD CASTRO, Dir. Youth Educ.; BETH CHAMBERS, Dir. Community Svcs. Services: Basic Needs Emergency Services, Adult Basic Education, English for Employment, English for Speakers of Other Languages, Career Pathways, Alternative High School (Diploma), Pa'lante (English and Spanish GED), Parenting Support. 76 Union Park St., Boston, 02118. Tel: 617-542-9292; Fax: 617-542-6912.

Haitian Multi-Service Center—VIVIAN SOPER, L.I.C.S.W., Interim Dir. Services: Basic Needs Emergency Services, Outpatient Counseling, Sante Manman se Sante Petite, Elder Services, Adult Education ESOL Classes, Health and Human Services Management Certificate Program. 185 Columbia Rd., Dorchester, 02121. Tel: 617-506-6600; Fax: 617-474-1009.

Merrimack Valley Catholic Charities—VIRGINIA DOOCEY, Dir. Services: Basic Needs Emergency Services, Outpatient Counseling, Latino Outreach, Young Parents Program, Grandparents as Parents, Parent Aide Program, Adoption Search. 354 Merrimack St., Bldg. 1, Rm. 305, Lawrence, 01843. Tel: 978-685-5930; Fax: 978-685-0329.

Merrimack Valley Catholic Charities at Lowell—70 Lawrence St., Lowell, 01852. Tel: 978-452-1421; Fax: 978-454-9968.

Open Hand Food Pantry—16 Ashland St., Haverhill, 01830. Tel: 978-372-2828.

Food Pantry of Merrimack Valley—174 Central St., Lowell, 01852. Tel: 978-454-9946.

Merrimack Valley Young Parents Program—45 Merrimack St., Ste. 225, Lowell, 01852. Tel: 978-459-2387; Fax: 978-459-2801.

Catholic Charities North—VIRGINIA DOOCY, M.A., Dir. Services: Basic Needs Emergency Services, Education and Parenting Skills Center, Teenstart, Youthworks, The Asian Center, Office Works, Companions to the Aging, Fathers Support, Young Parents, Pregnancy Counseling, Parent Aide, Family Preservation, Healthy Families, Adoption Search.

Catholic Charities North at Lynn—55 Lynn Shore Dr., Lynn, 01902. Tel: 781-593-2312; Fax: 781-581-3270.

Catholic Charities North at Salem—280 Washington St., Salem, 01970. Tel: 978-740-6923; Fax: 978-745-1863.

Catholic Charities North at Gloucester—74 Pleasant St., Gloucester, 01930. Tel: 978-283-3055.

Healthy Families North Shore—117 Franklin St., Lynn, 01902. Tel: 781-593-4515; Fax: 781-593-4615.

Asian Center—12 Orchard St., Lynn, 01905. Tel: 781-593-2312; Fax: 781-581-3270.

Haverhill Area Healthy Families—191 Merrimack St., Haverhill, 01830. Tel: 978-521-6265.

Catholic Charities South—DAVID PHILLIPS, Dir. Services - Basic Needs Emergency Services, Nursing Assistant Training, ESOL, Youth Tracking and Mentoring, SOAR, Pregnancy Counseling, Parent Support Program, Adoption Search. 686 N. Main St., Brockton, 02301. Tel: 508-587-0815; Fax: 508-580-0837.

Nursing Assistant Home Health Aide Training Program—250 Thatcher St., Mater Dei Bldg., Brockton, 02302. Tel: 508-587-0815; Fax: 508-580-0837.

Thrifty Pilgrim Thrift Shop—36 Cordage Park Cir., Plymouth, 02360. Tel: 508-746-6133.

Catholic Charities West—BETH CHAMBERS, Dir. Community Svcs. Services: Basic Needs Emergency Services. 126 Main St., Rm. 6, Milford, 01757. Tel: 508-478-9632.

Behavioral Health - Family Counseling & Guidance Center—DEBORAH KINCADE RAMBO, Interim Dir.

Brockton Clinic—686 N. Main St., Brockton, MA 01923. Tel: 508-587-0815; Fax: 508-586-9446.

Driver Alcohol Education—686 N. Main St., Brockton, 01923. Tel: 508-587-0815.

Danvers Clinic—152 Sylvan St., Danvers, 01923. Tel: 978-774-6820; Fax: 978-777-4242.

Refugee and Immigration Services—MARJEAN PERHOT, Dir., 275 W. Broadway, South Boston, 02210. Tel: 617-451-7979; Fax: 617-629-5768.

Refugee Resettlement—275 W. Broadway, South

Boston, 02210. Tel: 617-451-7979.

Refugee Employment Services—275 W. Broadway, South Boston, 02210. Tel: 617-451-7979.

Community Interpreter Services—275 W. Broadway, South Boston, 02210. Tel: 617-451-7979; Fax: 617-629-5768. Email: cis_request@ccab.org.

Immigration Legal Services—275 W. Broadway, South Boston, 02210. Tel: 617-451-7979.

Child Care—MARY ANN ANTHONY, M.S., Dir., Child Care Division Office: c/o Nazareth, 19 Saint Joseph St., Jamaica Plain, 02130. Tel: 617-524-9595; Fax: 617-832-7448.

Child Care Sites—Lynn Child Care, JANET MACDOUGALL, Dir. Child Care Svcs.; BEVERLY PRIFTI, (Peabody) - Family Child Care Dir., 37 N. Federal St., Lynn, 01905. Tel: 781-598-2759; Fax: 781-581-9740. *Peabody Child Care*, CHUCK JOHNSON, Dir. Child Care Svcs.; BEVERLY PRIFTI, (Peabody) - Family Child Care Dir.; NADINE LADA, Preschool Prog. Dir.; RALPH LAMONDA, School-Age Prog. Dir., 13 Pulaski St., Peabody, 01960. Tel: 978-532-6860; Fax: 978-531-7429. *Cambridge/Somerville/Malden*, RICHARD MURPHY, Dir. Child Care Svcs.; SHARON RICHARDSON-O'CONNELL, Family Child Care Dir., 187 Central St., Somerville, 02145. Tel: 617-623-8555; Fax: 617-623-5014. *Cambridge Children's Center*, CINDY GREEN, Dir. Child Care Svcs., 21C Walden Square Rd., Cambridge, 02140. Tel: 617-876-0503; Fax: 617-497-6464. *Malden High Teen Parent Child Care*, DIANA MAKHLOUF, Dir. Child Care Svcs., 77 Salem St., Malden, 02148. Tel: 781-397-1556; Fax: 781-322-4309. *Malden Early Education & Learning Program*, DIANA MAKHLOUF, Prog. Dir., 77 Salem St., Malden, 02148. Tel: 781-397-1556; Fax: 781-322-4309. *Laboure Child Care Center*, PEGGY KELLY, Dir. Child Care Svcs., 275 W. Broadway, Boston, 02127. Tel: 617-464-8533; Fax: 617-269-1386. *Yawkey Konbit-Kreyol Center for Early Education & Care*, Sr. ESTHER GARCIA, S.A., Dir. Child Care Svcs., 185 Columbia Rd., Dorchester, 02121. Tel: 617-506-6600. *Nazareth Child Care Center*, PAMELA J. PENTON, Dir. Child Care Svcs., 19 Saint Joseph St., Jamaica Plain, 02130. Tel: 617-522-4040; Fax: 617-983-0460. *Caritas Saint Mary Women and Children's Center*, Ms. JUDITH BECKLER, Exec. Dir., 90 Cushing Ave., Boston, 02125. Tel: 617-436-8600; Fax: 617-288-8961. Email: jbeckler@smwic.org. Web: smwic.org.

Education—Dr. MARY GRASSA O'NEILL, Sec., Catholic School Office, 66 Brooks Dr., Braintree, 02184-3839. Tel: 617-779-3604; Fax: 617-746-5702.

Catholic School Office—66 Brooks Dr., Braintree, 02184-3839. Tel: 617-779-3601; Fax: 617-746-5702. Web: catholicschoolsboston.org.

Superintendent of Schools—Dr. MARY GRASSA O'NEILL.

Associate Superintendent for Administration/Finance—Mr. JAMES M. WALSH. Email: walsh_j@rcab.org.

Associate Superintendent for Academic Excellence—Mr. WILLIAM MCKERSIE. Email: william_mckersie@rcab.org.

Deputy Director for Academic Excellence—Mr. CHRIS FLIEGER. Email: cflieger@rcab.org.

Associate Superintendent for Government Funded Programs—Mr. JOHN SHEEHAN. Email: sheehan_j@rcab.org.

Special Assistant to the Superintendent (Interim)—Dr. IRENE MCCARTHY. Email: mccart_i@rcab.org.

Network Administrator—Ms. NANCY MORRISON. Email: nmorrison@rcab.org.

Administrative Assistants—Ms. BARBARA DEVINE. Email: devine_b@rcab.org; Ms. NINA MAYO. Email: mayo_n@rcab.org.

Executive Assistant—Mrs. ROBIN MOBLEY. Email: robin-marie_mobley@rcab.org.

Catholic Television—Rev. ROBERT P. REED, Dir., Mailing Address: 34 Chestnut St., Box 9196, Watertown, 02471-9196. Tel: 617-923-0220. Email: reed@catholictv.org. Web: catholictv.com.

Archdiocesan Cemeteries—

The Catholic Cemetery Association of the Archdiocese of Boston, Inc.—Mr. ROBERT VISCONTI, Exec. Dir., 175 Broadway, Malden, 02148-6097. Tel: 888-919-7926; 781-322-6300; Fax: 781-322-3801. Web: ccemetery.org.

Boston—Saint Francis de Sales, 313 Bunker Hill St., Boston, 02129-1826. Pastoral Region Central.

Andover—Sacred Heart, Corbett Rd., Andover, 01810. Pastoral Region Merrimack.

Arlington—Saint Paul, 30 Broadway, Arlington, 02179-5523. Pastoral Region North.

Beverly—Saint Mary, 106 Brimbal Ave., Beverly, 01915-1936. Pastoral Region North.

Cambridge—North Cambridge Catholic, 244 Rindge Ave., Cambridge, 02140-2526. Pastoral Region Central.

Framingham—Saint George, 177 Cherry St., Framingham, 01706. Pastoral Region West.

Gloucester—Calvary, 151 Eastern Ave., Gloucester, 01930. Pastoral Region North. Oak Hill, 55 Poplar St., Gloucester, 01930. Pastoral Region North.

Haverhill—Saint James, 360 Primrose St., Haverhill, 01830-3198. Pastoral Region Merrimack. Saint Joseph, 892 Hilldale Ave., Haverhill, 01830. Pastoral Region Merrimack. St. Patrick, 395 N. Broadway, Haverhill, 01830. Pastoral Region Merrimack.

Lynn—Saint Jean, 134 Broadway, Lynn, 01904-1868. Pastoral Region North. Saint Joseph, 134 Broadway, Lynn, 01904-1868. Pastoral Region North. Saint Mary, 190 Lynnfield St., Lynn, 01904. Pastoral Region North.

Malden—Holy Cross, 175 Broadway, Malden, 02148-6097. Pastoral Region North. Saint Mary, 304 Fellsway E., Malden, 02148. Pastoral Region North.

Marblehead—Star of the Sea, 140 Lafayette St., Marblehead, 01947. Pastoral Region North.

Marlborough—Immaculate Conception, Beach St., Marlborough, 01752. Pastoral Region West. Saint Mary, Beach St., Marlborough, 01752. Pastoral Region West.

Salem—Saint Mary, 226 North St., Salem, 01970-1645. Pastoral Region North.

Stoneham—Saint Patrick, 120 Elm St., Stoneham, 02180. Pastoral Region North.

Waltham—Calvary, 250 High St., Waltham, 02154-5914. Pastoral Region West.

Watertown—Catholic Mount Auburn, 64 Cottage St., Watertown, 02472-1516. Pastoral Region West. Saint Patrick, Belmont St., Watertown, 02472. Pastoral Region West.

Winchester—Calvary, 686 Washington St., Winchester, 01890. Pastoral Region North.

Boston—Saint Augustine, 225 Dorchester Ave., Boston, 02127. Tel: 617-268-1230. Parish: Saint Monica and Saint Augustine Parish. Region: Central.

Abington—Saint Patrick, 455 Plymouth St., Abington, 02351. Tel: 781-982-8974. Parish: Saint Bridget Parish. Region: South.

Amesbury—Saint Joseph, 6 Allen's Court, Amesbury, 01913. Tel: 978-388-0330. Parish: Holy Family Parish. Region: Merrimack.

Avon—Saint Michael, 87 N. Main St., Avon, 02322. Tel: 508-586-7210. Parish: Saint Michael Parish. Region: South.

Ayer—Saint Mary, 31 Shirley St., Ayer, 01432. Tel: 978-772-2414. Parish: Saint Mary Parish. Region: Merrimack.

Bridgewater—Saint Thomas Aquinas, 103 Center St., Bridgewater, 02324. Tel: 508-697-9528. Parish: Saint Thomas Aquinas Parish. Region: South.

Brockton—Calvary, 331 Main St., Brockton, 02301. Tel: 508-586-4840 Parish: Saint Patrick Parish. Region: South. *Saint Patrick, 331 Main St., Brockton, 02301*. Tel: 508-586-4840. Parish: Saint Patrick Parish. Region: South.

Canton—Saint Mary, 700 Washington St., Canton, 02021. Tel: 781-828-0090. Parish: Saint John the Evangelist Parish. Region: South.

Concord—Saint Bernard, 70 Monument Square, Concord, 01742. Tel: 978-369-7442. Parish: Holy Family Parish. Region: West.

Danvers—Annunciation, 24 Conant St., Danvers, 01935. Tel: 978-774-0340 Parish: Saint Mary of the Annunciation Parish. Region: West. *Saint Mary, 24 Conant St., Danvers, 01935*. Tel: 978-774-0340. Parish: Saint Mary of the Annunciation Parish. Region: West.

Dedham—Saint Mary, 420 High St., Dedham, 02026. Tel: 781-326-0550. Parish: Saint Mary Parish. Region: West.

Foxborough—Saint Mary, 58 Carpenter St., Foxborough, 02035. Tel: 508-543-7726. Parish: Saint Mary Parish. Region: West.

Framingham—Saint Stephen, 221 Concord St., Framingham, 01702. Tel: 508-875-4788 Parish: Saint Stephen Parish. Region: West. *Saint Tarcisius, Winthrop St., Framingham, 01702*. Tel: 508-875-8623 Parish: Saint Tarcisius Parish. Region: West.

Franklin—Saint Mary, Beaver St., Franklin, 02038. Tel: 508-528-6826. Parish: Saint Mary Parish. Region: West.

Hingham—Saint Paul, 147 North St., Hingham, 02043. Tel: 781-749-0587. Parish: Saint Paul Parish. Region: South.

Holliston—Saint Mary, Washington St., Holliston, 01746. Tel: 508-429-4427. Parish: Saint Mary Parish. Region: West.

Hopkinton—Saint John the Evangelist, 20 Church St., Hopkinton, 01748. Tel: 508-435-3313. Parish: Saint John the Evangelist Parish. Region: West.

Kingston—Saint Joseph, Elm St., Kingston, 02364. Tel: 781-585-6679. Parish: Saint Joseph Parish. Region: South

Lawrence—Saint Mary, 29 Barker St., Lawrence, 01841. Tel: 978-682-8181. Parish: Our Lady of Good Counsel Parish. Region: Merrimack.

Lowell—Holy Trinity, 140 Boston Rd., Lowell, 01852. Tel: 978-452-2564 Parish: Holy Trinity Parish. Region: Merrimack. *Saint Mary, 384 Stevens St., Lowell, 01851*. Tel: 978-458-8464 Parish: Saint Margaret Parish. Region: Merrimack. *Saint Patrick, 384 Stevens St., Lowell, 01851*. Tel: 978-458-8464 Parish: Saint Margaret Parish. Region: Merrimack.

Maynard—Saint Bridget, One Percival St., Maynard, 01754. Tel: 978-897-2171. Parish: Saint Bridget Parish. Region: West.

Middleborough—Saint Mary, Wood St., Middleboro, 02346. Tel: 508-947-0444. Parish: Sacred Heart Parish. Region: South.

Needham—Saint Mary, 270 Elliot St., Newton, 02462. Tel: 781-235-1841. Parish: Mary Immaculate of Lourdes Parish. Region: West.

Newburyport—Saint Mary, Green St., Newburyport, 01950. Tel: 978-462-2724. Parish: Immaculate Conception Parish. Region: Merrimack.

North Andover—Holy Sepulchre, 114 S. Broadway, Lawrence, 01843. Tel: 978-683-9416. Parish: Saint Patrick Parish. Region: Merrimack.

Pepperell—Saint Joseph, Jersey St., Pepperell, 01463. Tel: 978-433-9725. Parish: Saint Joseph Parish. Region: Merrimack.

Plymouth—Saint Joseph, 86 Court St., Plymouth, 02360. Tel: 508-746-0663. Parish: Saint Peter Parish. Region: South.

Quincy—Saint Mary, 95 Crescent St., Quincy, 02169. Tel: 617-773-0120. Parish: Saint Mary Parish. Region: South.

Randolph—Saint Mary, 211 N. Main St., Randolph, 02368. Tel: 781-961-9323. Parish: Saint Mary Parish. Region: South.

Rockland—Holy Family, 403 Union St., Rockland, 02370. Tel: 781-878-2306. Parish: Holy Family Parish. Region: South.

Shirley—Saint Anthony of Padua, 12 Phoenix St., Shirley, 01464. Tel: 978-425-4588. Parish: Saint Anthony of Padua Parish. Region: Merrimack.

Stoughton—Holy Sepulchre, Central St., Stoughton, 02072. Tel: 781-344-2073. Parish: Immaculate Conception Parish. Region: South.

Walpole—Saint Francis, Diamond St., Walpole, 02081. Tel: 508-668-4700. Parish: Blessed Sacrament Parish. Region: West.

Wayland—Saint Zepherin, 99 Main St., Wayland, 01778. Tel: 508-653-8013. Parish: Saint Zepherin Parish. Region: West.

Westford—Saint Catherine of Alexandria, 107 N. Main St., Westford, 01886. Tel: 978-692-6353. Parish: Saint Catherine of Alexandria Parish. Region: Merrimack.

Weymouth—Saint Francis Xavier, 234 Pleasant St., Weymouth, 02190. Tel: 781-337-3144. Parish: Saint Francis Xavier Parish. Region: South.

Whitman—Saint James, School St., Whitman, 02382. Tel: 781-447-4421. Parish: Holy Ghost Parish. Region: South.

Private Cemeteries—

Boston—Mount Benedict Cemetery, 409 Corey St., West Roxbury, 02132. Tel: 617-323-8389 Owner: Boston Catholic Cemetery Association. Region: Central. *Mount Calvary Cemetery, 366 Cummins Hwy., Roslindale, 02131*. Tel: 617-325-0883 Owner: Boston Catholic Cemetery Association. Region: Central. *New Calvary Cemetery, 800 Harvard St., Mattapan, 02126*. Tel: 617-296-2339 Owner: Boston Catholic Cemetery Association. Region: Central. *Saint Joseph Cemetery, 990 Lagrange St., West Roxbury, 02132*. Tel: 617-327-1010 Owner: Holyhood Cemetery Association. Region: Central. *Saint Mary Cemetery, Bernard St., Dorchester, 02124*. Tel: 617-325-6830 Owner: Boston Catholic Cemetery Association. Region: Central. *Saint Michael Cemetery, 500 Canterbury St., Forest Hills, 02131*. Tel: 617-524-1036. Owner: Saint Michael Cemetery Association. Region: Central.

Brookline—Holyhood Cemetery, Heath St., Brookline, 02467. Tel: 617-327-1010. Owner: Holyhood Cemetery Association. Region: Central.

Chelmsford—Saint Joseph Cemetery, 96 Riverneck Rd., Chelmsford, 01824-2941. Tel: 978-458-4851. Owner: Saint Joseph Cemetery, Inc. Region: Merrimack.

Charismatic Renewal—Mr. VINCENT CERASUOLO, Dir. & Liaison, 30 Pond St., Waltham, 02451-4514. Tel: 781-891-3592; Fax: 781-874-9467. Email: staff@crsboston.org.

Chrism—Ms. CELIA SIROIS, Coord., 236 Pleasant St., Weymouth, 02190-2507. Tel: 781-331-5194; Fax:

781-337-3225.

Clergy Services Group—66 Brooks Dr., Braintree, 02184-3839.

Clergy Personnel—Rev. MICHAEL B. MEDAS, M.S.W., Dir. Tel: 617-779-3685; Fax: 617-746-5614; Deacon PATRICK E. GUERRINI, Asst. Dir. Tel: 617-746-5658; Fax: 617-746-5498. Email: deacon_patrick_guerrini@rcab.org.

Pastoral Care of Clergy—Very Rev. EDWIN D. CONDON, Vicar (Retired). Tel: 617-746-5601; Fax: 617-779-4570. Email: edwinduxb@aol.com.

Priests' Recovery Program—Very Rev. BRIAN M. CLARY, V.F., Dir., 5 Linden Pl., Brookline, 02445-7311. Tel: 617-473-0444; Fax: 617-734-3001. Email: frbrian2002@yahoo.com.

Senior Priests—60 William Cardinal O'Connell Way, Boston, 02114-2729. Tel: 617-723-3976; Fax: 617-523-0092. Deacon PATRICK E. GUERRINI, Asst. Dir. Tel: 617-746-5658; Fax: 617-746-5614. Email: deacon_patrick_guerrini@rcab.org.

Clergy Personnel Board—Ex Officio: Rev. Msgr. ROBERT P. DEELEY, V.F., J.C.D.; Very Rev. THOMAS S. FOLEY, V.F.; Rev. ROBERT J. DEEHAN. Designated: Rev. Msgr. DENNIS F. SHEEHAN; Very Rev. JOHN E. MACINNIS, V.F. Elected: Rev. Msgrs. PETER V. CONLEY, V.F., Block I; GEORGE F. CARLSON, Block II; Rev. GEORGE P. EVANS, M.Div., S.T.D., Block III; Very Rev. KEVIN M. SEPE, V.F., Block IV; Revs. JAMES M. MAHONEY, M.Div., Block V; GEORGE C. HINES, Block VI.

Communications and Public Affairs—Mr. TERRENCE C. DONILON, Sec., 66 Brooks Dr., Braintree, 02184-3839. Tel: 617-746-5775; Fax: 617-779-4572. Email: tdonilon@rcab.org.

Cor Unum Meal Center—Ms. DIANE JARVIS, Dir., 191 Salem St., Lawrence, 01843-1427. Tel: 978-688-8900; Fax: 978-681-5808. Email: corunummealcenter@comcast.net. Web: www.corunummealcenter.org.

Courage—Rev. JOHN M. SULLIVAN, Spiritual Dir., 46 Myrtle St., Melrose, 02176-3827. Tel: 781-665-0152; Fax: 781-665-2750. Email: info@bostoncourage.org.

Cursillo—Rev. JOHN E. SASSANI, Spiritual Dir., 66 Brooks Dr., Braintree, 02184-3839. Tel: 617-779-3640; Fax: 617-779-4570. Email: jsassani@ourladys.com; Ms. MARYANN MCLAUGHLIN, Lay Dir. Tel: 617-779-3640; Fax: 617-779-4570. Email: maryann_mclaughlin@rcab.org.

Office of the Deaf Apostolate—66 Brooks Dr., Braintree, 02184-3839. Tel: 617-997-8025; Fax: 617-746-5614. Web: www.deafcatholic.org.

Director—Rev. JEREMY P. ST. MARTIN. Tel: 617-746-5645 (Work); 617-997-8025 (Text); 774-217-3000 (Video Phone). Email: frjeremy@deafcatholic.org.

Assistant Director of the Office of the Deaf Apostolate—Rev. SHAWN P. CAREY. Email: frshawn@deafcatholic.org; frshawn@sprint.blackberry.net (Emergency)Tel: 866-572-8386 (Video Phone); 781-267-7109 (Video Phone).

Interpreters / Coordinators—Mrs. JENNY CORBIN. Email: jenny.corbin@deafcatholic.org; Miss CELIA MOJICA. Tel: 617-746-5815 (Work). Email: mojica.celia@deafcatholic.org.

Assistant Coordinator of the Deaf Senior Wellness Program—Mrs. MARY BROOKS. Tel: 617-746-5815 (Work). Email: mary.k.brooks@deafcatholic.org. Mass in American Sign Language and Deaf Senior Wellness Program take place at Sacred Heart Parish, 1317 Centre St., Newton, MA 02459. Tel: 617-969-2248.

American Sign—

Bellingham—Saint Blaise. Tel: 508-966-1258.

Boston—Cathedral of the Holy Cross. Tel: 617-542-5682.

Danvers—New England Home for the Deaf. Tel: 978-774-0445.

Hopkington—Saint John the Evangelist. Tel: 508-435-3313.

Middleborough—Sacred Heart. Tel: 508-947-0444.

Newton—Sacred Heart. Tel: 617-969-2248.

Stoneham—Saint Patrick. Tel: 781-438-0960.

Whitman—Holy Ghost. Tel: 781-447-4421.

Disabilities—Ms. KAREN MURRAY, 66 Brooks Dr., Braintree, 02184-3839. Tel: 617-746-5679; Fax: 617-779-4570. Email: kmurray@rcab.org.

Divine Worship and Spiritual Life—66 Brooks Dr., Braintree, 02184-3839. Tel: 617-779-3640; Fax: 617-779-4570. Rev. JONATHAN M. GASPAR, Dir. Divine Worship. Tel: 617-746-5880. Email: jgaspar@rcab.org.

Ecumenical and Interreligious Affairs—66 Brooks Dr., Braintree, 02184-3839. Tel: 617-435-0019; Fax: 617-783-5642.

EnCourage—Rev. ALBERT A. SYLVIA, Spiritual Dir., 558 South Ave., Weston, 02493. Tel: 781-899-5500; Fax: 781-899-9057.

Ethnic Ministries—Sr. MARY CORRIPIO, S.N.D., Dir., 66 Brooks Dr., Braintree, 02184-3839. Tel: 617-746-5818; Fax: 617-746-5614. Email: mcorripio@rcab.org; Ms. LINDA RUSSO. Tel: 617-746-5794. Email: lrusso@rcab.org.

Brazilian—Rev. EDUARDO MARQUES. Tel: 617-783-2121.

Cambodian—Deacon AN ROS. Tel: 978-459-0561.

Chinese—Ms. LAURA CHAN. Tel: 781-438-4772.

Filipino—Rev. CELESTINO V. PASCUAL. Tel: 617-726-1947.

French—Office of Cultural Diversity. Tel: 617-746-5818.

German—Rev. HARRY J. KAUFMAN. Tel: 617-268-2122.

Hmong—Dr. PAULE VERDET. Tel: 617-965-2499.

Indian—Ms. DEEPA PRABHU. Tel: 781-724-5179.

Irish—Sr. MARGUERITE KELLY, M.F.I.C. Tel: 617-479-7404.

Italian—Rev. ANTONIO NARDOIANNI, O.F.M. Tel: 617-523-2110.

Japanese—Office of Cultural Diversity. Tel: 617-746-5794.

Korean—Rev. DOMINIC JUNG, C.PP.S. Tel: 617-244-9685.

Lithuanian—Rev. STEPHEN P. ZUKAS. Tel: 617-268-0353.

Polish—Rev. ANDRZEJ URBANIAK, O.F.M.Conv. Tel: 617-268-4355.

Portuguese—Very Rev. WALTER A. CARREIRO, V.F. Tel: 617-547-5593.

Vietnamese—Rev. HOANG V. LE. Tel: 617-265-5302.

Health Care—

Caritas Christi Health Care Corporation—Dr. RALPH DE LA TORRE, M.D., Pres., 736 Cambridge St., Boston, 02135-2997. Tel: 617-789-5050; Fax: 617-789-2124. Email: patricia.prichette@caritaschristi.org. Web: caritaschristi.org.

Hispanic Apostolate—Most Rev. EMILIO S. ALLUE, S.D.B., Vicar Gen. Tel: 617-746-5916; Fax: 617-746-5614. Email: bishop_emilio@rcab.org; Mr. FERNANDO FERNANDEZ-ARELLANO, Coord. Programs, 66 Brooks Dr., Braintree, 02184-3839. Tel: 617-746-5816; Fax: 617-746-5614. Email: fernando_fernandez@rcab.org.

Boston—Cathedral of the Holy Cross. Tel: 617-542-5682. *Saint Anthony Shrine*. Tel: 617-542-6440. *Saint Francis Chapel*. Tel: 617-437-7117.

Hispanic Ministry Sites—

Brighton—Saint Columbkille. Tel: 617-782-5774.

Charlestown—Saint Mary-Saint Catherine of Siena. Tel: 617-242-4664.

Dorchester—Holy Family. Tel: 617-445-9553. *Saint Ambrose*. Tel: 617-265-5302. *Saint Christopher*. Tel: 617-436-7273.

East Boston—Madonna Queen Shrine. Tel: 617-569-2100. *Most Holy Redeemer*. Tel: 617-567-3227. *Our Lady of the Assumption*. Tel: 617-567-1223.

Jamaica Plain—Our Lady of Lourdes. Tel: 617-524-0434. *Saint Thomas Aquinas*. Tel: 617-524-0240.

Roslindale—Sacred Heart. Tel: 617-325-3322.

Roxbury—Our Lady of Perpetual Help-Mission Church. Tel: 617-445-2600. *Saint Mary of the Angels*. Tel: 617-445-1524. *Saint Patrick*. Tel: 617-445-7645.

South Boston—Saint Monica and Saint Augustine. Tel: 617-268-1230.

Brockton—Saint Patrick. Tel: 508-586-4840.

Cambridge—Saint Mary of the Annunciation. Tel: 617-547-0120.

Chelsea—Saint Rose of Lima. Tel: 617-889-2774.

Everett—Saint Anthony of Padua. Tel: 617-387-0310. *Immaculate Conception*. Tel: 617-389-5660.

Framingham—Saint Stephen. Tel: 508-875-4788.

Haverhill—Saint James. Tel: 978-372-8537.

Lawrence—Corpus Christi. Tel: 978-685-1711. *Saint Mary of the Assumption*. Tel: 978-685-1111. *Saint Patrick*. Tel: 978-683-9416.

Lowell—Saint Patrick. Tel: 978-459-0561.

Lynn—Saint Joseph. Tel: 781-599-7040.

Marlborough—Immaculate Conception. Tel: 508-485-0016.

Newton—Saint Ignatius Loyola Church. Tel: 617-552-6100.

Peabody—Saint John the Baptist. Tel: 978-531-0002.

Revere—Immaculate Conception. Tel: 781-289-0735.

Salem—Immaculate Conception. Tel: 978-745-6303.

Somerville—Saint Ann. Tel: 617-625-1904. *Saint Benedict*. Tel: 617-625-0029.

Waltham—Saint Mary. Tel: 781-891-1730.

Woburn—Saint Charles Borromeo. Tel: 781-933-0300.

Holy Name Societies—Mr. ROBERT QUAGAN, 35 Cass St., Boston, 02132-4411. Tel: 617-325-5905. Email: rquagan@comcast.net.

Hospital Chaplain Ministry—Deacon JAMES F. GREER, Dir., 66 Brooks Dr., Braintree, 02184-3839. Tel: 617-746-5843; Fax: 617-746-5754.

Boston—

Arbour Hospital—49 Robinwood Ave., Boston, 02130. Tel: 617-522-4400. Pastoral Care: Our Lady of Lourdes, Jamaica Plain

Beth Israel Deaconess Medical Center—330 Brookline Ave., Boston, 02215. Tel: 617-667-4205. Pastoral Care: Rev. BRUCE N. TEAGUE.

Boston Medical Center - Harrison Avenue Campus—818 Harrison Ave., Boston, 02118. Tel: 617-414-7560. Pastoral Care: Sr. MARYANNE RUZZO, S.C.

Boston Medical Center - Newton Street Campus—One Medical Center Pl., Boston, 02118-2393. Tel: 617-638-6851. Pastoral Care: Rev. ROGER BOURGEA, S.M.

Brigham and Women's Hospital—75 Francis St., Boston, 02115-6195. Tel: 617-732-7480; Fax: 617-232-2746. Pastoral Care: Sr. KATHLEEN GALLIVAN, S.N.D.

Caritas Carney Hospital—2100 Dorchester St., Boston, 02124-5666. Tel: 617-296-4000; Fax: 617-296-9513. Pastoral Care: Sr. PAULA TINLIN, S.N.D.

Caritas Saint Elizabeth Medical Center—736 Cambridge St., Boston, 02135-2997. Tel: 617-789-3228; Fax: 617-789-2281. Pastoral Care: Ms. CHERYL AMRICH.

Children's Hospital—300 Longwood Ave., Boston, 02115. Tel: 617-355-4775. Pastoral Care: Ms. MARIA CATALDO-CUNNIFF.

Dana Farber Cancer Institute—44 Binney St., Boston, 02115. Tel: 617-632-3000.

Faulkner Hospital—1153 Centre St., Boston, 02130. Tel: 617-983-7000, Ext. 1556. Pastoral Care: Ms. REGINA CLARE GAVIN.

Franciscan Children's Hospital—30 Warren St., Boston, 02135. Tel: 617-779-1645. Pastoral Care: Sr. JEAN MULLOY, C.S.J.

Hebrew Rehabilitation Center—1200 Centre St., Boston, 02131. Tel: 617-361-5249. Pastoral Care: Sacred Heart, Roslindale and Holy Name, West Roxbury

Jewish Memorial Hospital—59 Townsend St., Boston, 02119. Tel: 617-989-8315. Pastoral Care: Saint Patrick and Saint Mary of the Angels, Roxbury

Kindred Hospital Boston—1515 Commonwealth Ave., Brighton, 02135. Tel: 617-254-1100. Pastoral Care: Saint Columbkille, Brighton

Lemuel Shattuck Hospital—170 Morton St., Boston, 02130. Tel: 617-522-8110. Pastoral Care: Our Lady of Lourdes, Jamaica Plain

Massachusetts General Hospital—55 Fruit St., Boston, 02114. Tel: 617-724-3226; Fax: 617-726-2220. Pastoral Care: Mr. MICHAEL MCELHINNY.

New England Baptist Hospital—91 Parker Hill Ave., Boston, 02120. Tel: 617-754-5160. Pastoral Care: Rev. ANDREW ALBERT, S.M.

New England Medical Center—750 Washington St., Boston, 02111. Tel: 617-636-5896. Pastoral Care: Rev. JAMES SHAUGHNESSEY, S.J.

Shriners Burns Institute—51 Blossom St., Boston, 02114. Tel: 617-722-3000. Pastoral Care: Saint Joseph and Saint Leonard of Port Maurice, Boston

Spaulding Rehabilitation Hospital—125 Nashua St., Boston, 02114-1198. Tel: 617-572-2780; Fax: 617-573-2419. Pastoral Care: Ms. JOAN HORGAN.

Veterans Administration Health Care System - West Roxbury—1400 VRW Pkwy., Boston, 02132. Tel: 617-323-7700. Pastoral Care: Rev. CLAUDIUS NOWINSKI, M.S.

Veterans Administration Health Care System - Jamaica Plain—150 S. Huntington Ave., Boston, 02130. Tel: 857-364-5065. Pastoral Care: Rev. PHILIP SALOIS, M.S.

Ayer—

Nashoba Valley Medical Center—200 Groton St., Ayer, 01432. Tel: 978-772-2414. Pastoral Care: Saint Constance Gagnon, S.U.S.C.

Bedford—

Veterans Administration Health Care System - Bedford—200 Spring Rd., Bedford, 01730. Tel: 781-687-2384. Pastoral Care: Rev. SEBASTIAN A. UGOCHUKWU.

Belmont—

McLean Hospital—115 Mill St., Belmont, 02178. Tel: 617-855-2000. Pastoral Care: Saint Luke, Belmont and local parishes

Beverly—

Beverly Hospital—75 Herrick St., Beverly, 01915. Tel: 978-922-3000, Ext. 2790. Pastoral Care: Mr. JOHN KWIATEK.

Braintree—

Health South Braintree Hospital—250 Pond St., Braintree, 02184. Tel: 781-348-2500. Pastoral Care: Saint Francis of Assisi

Northeast Specialty Hospital—2001 Washington St., Braintree, 02185. Tel: 781-952-2254. Pastoral Care: Saint Clare, Braintree

Brockton—

Brockton Hospital—680 Centre St., Brockton, 02302. Tel: 508-941-7000, Ext. 2550. Pastoral Care: Sr. BARBARA HARRINGTON, O.P.

Caritas Good Samaritan Medical Center—235 N.

Pearl St., Brockton, 02301. Tel: 508-427-2376. Pastoral Care: Rev. RICHARD W. VISBISKY.
McLean Hospital Brockton—940 Belmont St., Brockton, 02402. Tel: 508-894-8420. Pastoral Care: Our Lady of Lourdes, Brockton
Veterans Administration Health Care System - Brockton—930 Belmont St., Brockton, 02402. Tel: 508-583-4500. Pastoral Care: Rev. HENRY P. NICHOLS (Retired).
Brookline—
Bournewood Health System—300 South St., Brookline, 02146. Tel: 617-469-0300. Pastoral Care: Saint Mary of the Assumption, Brookline
Burlington—
Lahey Clinic—41 Mall Rd., Burlington, 01805. Tel: 781-744-8800. Pastoral Care: Mr. WILLIAM W. HOUGHTON.
Cambridge—
Cambridge Hospital—1493 Cambridge St., Cambridge, 02139. Tel: 617-665-1000. Pastoral Care: Local Cambridge Parishes
Mount Auburn Hospital—330 Mt. Auburn St., Cambridge, 02238. Tel: 617-499-5206. Pastoral Care: Ms. MARY HARRISON.
Youville Lifecare—1575 Cambridge St., Cambridge, 02138-4398. Tel: 617-758-5495. Pastoral Care: Mr. ROBERT SHORT.
Canton—
Massachusetts Hospital School—Randloph St., Canton, 02121. Tel: 781-828-2440. Pastoral Care: Saint Gerard Mejella, Canton
Chelsea—
Quigley Memorial Hospital—91 Crest St., Chelsea, 02150. Tel: 617-889-7146. Pastoral Care: Rev. PATRICK F. HEALY, O.M.I.
Concord—
Emerson Hospital—Rte. 2 ORNAC, Box 9120, Concord, 01742-9120. Tel: 978-287-3015. Pastoral Care: Ms. GEORGIA GOJMERAC-LEINER.
Everett—
Whidden Memorial Hospital—103 Garland St., Everett, 02149. Tel: 617-381-7202. Pastoral Care: Sr. THERESA CARLOW, S.N.D.
Framingham—
Metro West Medical Center - Framingham Campus—115 Lincoln St., Framingham, 01701-9167. Tel: 508-383-1007. Pastoral Care: Sr. URSULA TISDALL, O.S.F.
Gloucester—
Addison Gilbert Hospital—298 Washington St., Gloucester, 01930. Tel: 978-283-4000. Pastoral Care: Holy Family and Our Lady of Good Voyage, Gloucester
Haverhill—
Merrimack Valley Hospital—140 Lincoln Ave., Haverhill, 01830. Tel: 978-374-2000. Pastoral Care: Saint John the Baptist, Haverhill and local parishes
Whittier Rehabilitation Hospital—76 Summer St., Haverhill, 01830. Tel: 978-372-8000. Pastoral Care: Saint James, Haverhill
Lawrence—
Lawrence General Hospital—One General St., Lawrence, 01842. Tel: 978-683-4000. Pastoral Care: Ms. ARLENE LARSEN.
Lowell—
Lowell General Hospital—295 Varnum Ave., Lowell, 01854. Tel: 978-937-6418. Pastoral Care: Mrs. CAROL GAGNE.
Saints Memorial Medical Center—One Hospital Dr., Lowell, 01852. Tel: 978-458-1411; Fax: 978-934-8526. Pastoral Care: Ms. CATHERINE SEELEY.
Lynn—
Northshore Medical Center - Lynn—500 Lynnfield St., Lynn, 01904. Tel: 781-477-3955. Pastoral Care: Rev. ROBERT G. LABRIE.
Marlborough—
Marlborough Hospital—155 Union St., Marlborough, 01752. Tel: 508-958-3536. Pastoral Care: Immaculate Conception, Marlborough and local parishes
Medford—
Lawrence Memorial Hospital—170 Governor's Ave., Medford, 02155. Tel: 781-306-6665. Pastoral Care: Ms. ROSEMARY BURKE.
Melrose—
Melrose Wakefield Hospital—585 Lebanon St., Melrose, 02176. Tel: 781-979-3011. Pastoral Care: Rev. WILLIAM F. LUCEY (Retired).
Methuen—
Caritas Holy Family Medical Center—70 East St., Methuen, 01844. Tel: 978-687-0156. Pastoral Care: Mr. WILLIAM SWEENEY JR.
Milton—
Milton Hospital—92 Highland St., Milton, 02186. Tel: 617-696-4600, Ext. 1801. Pastoral Care: Ms. VIRGINIA ALLEN.
Natick—
Metro West Medical Center - Natick Campus—67 Union St., Natick, 01760. Tel: 508-650-7331. Pastoral Care: Saint Patrick, Natick and local parishes
Needham—
Beth Israel Deaconess Hospital - Needham—148 Chestnut St., Needham, 02192. Tel: 781-453-3000. Pastoral Care: Needham Parishes
Newburyport—
Anna Jacques Hospital—25 Highland Ave., Newburyport, 01950. Tel: 978-463-1000. Pastoral Care: Immaculate Conception, Newburyport and local parishes
Newton—
Newton Wellesley Hospital—2014 Washington St., Newton, 02462. Tel: 617-243-6634. Pastoral Care: Ms. ANN LOMUTO.
Norwood—
Caritas Norwood Hospital—800 Washington St., Norwood, 02062. Tel: 781-278-6045. Pastoral Care: Bro. GERALD PACIELLO, O.F.M.
Peabody—
Kindred Hospital Northshore—15 King St., Peabody, 01960. Tel: 978-531-2900. Pastoral Care: Saint John the Baptist, Peabody
Plymouth—
Jordan Hospital—275 Sandwich St., Plymouth, 02360. Tel: 508-830-2626. Pastoral Care: Ms. KAREN FARRELL.
Quincy—
Quincy Hospital—114 Whitwell St., Quincy, 02169. Tel: 617-376-5501. Pastoral Care: Ms. KATHLEEN HALLEE.
Salem—
Northshore Medical Center Salem—57 Highland Ave., Salem, 01970. Tel: 978-741-1215, Ext. 7698. Pastoral Care: Ms. JANE KORINS.
Somerville—
Somerville Hospital—230 Highland Ave., Somerville, 02143. Tel: 617-666-4400. Pastoral Care: Saint Catherine of Genoa, Somerville and local parishes
Stoughton—
New England Sinai Hospital—150 York St., Stoughton, 02072. Tel: 617-344-0600; Fax: 617-297-1302. Pastoral Care: Sr. ELLEN REILLY, S.N.D.
Tewksbury—
Tewksbury Hospital—365 East St., Tewksbury, 01876. Tel: 978-851-7321, Ext. 2889. Pastoral Care: Ms. PATRICIA HARDY.
Waltham—
Fernald Development Center—200 Trapelo Rd., Waltham, 02452-6302. Tel: 781-894-3600. Pastoral Care: Rev. WILLIAM T. LEONARD.
Westwood—
Westwood Lodge Hospital—45 Clapboardtree St., Westwood, 02090. Tel: 781-762-7764. Pastoral Care: Saint Margaret Mary, Westwood
Weymouth—
South Shore Hospital—55 Fogg Rd., Weymouth, 02190. Tel: 781-340-8589. Pastoral Care: Deacon CHARLES P. WEBB.
Winchester—
Winchester Hospital—41 Highland Ave., Winchester, 01890. Tel: 781-756-2295. Pastoral Care: Ms. MARY BETH MORAN.
Woburn—
Health South - New England Rehabilitation Hospital—Two Rehabilitation Way, Woburn, 01801. Tel: 781-935-5050. Pastoral Care: Saint Barbara, Woburn
Wrentham—
Wrentham Development Center—131 Emerald St., Wrentham, 02093. Tel: 508-384-3114; Fax: 617-779-1119. Email: jvischetti@fhfc.org. Web: fhf-c.org. Pastoral Care: Saint Mary, Wrentham. Region Central.

Institutional Advancement—VACANT, Sec. Advancement & Chief Devel. Officer, 66 Brooks Dr., Braintree, 02184-3839. Tel: 617-779-3700; Fax: 617-779-3731; VACANT, Mgr. Gift Processing & Donor Rels. Tel: 617-779-3708; Fax: 617-779-3721; Ms. JUDY CHOHARIS, Senior Gifts Processor. Tel: 617-779-3707; Fax: 617-779-3721. Email: jchoharis@rcab.org; Mr. DAMIEN DEVASTO, Chief Leadership Giving Officer. Tel: 617-779-3703; Fax: 617-779-3721. Email: ddevasto@rcab.org; VACANT, Catholic Appeal Mgr. Tel: 617-779-3711; Fax: 617-779-3721; VACANT, Leadership Giving Officer. Tel: 617-779-3712; Fax: 617-779-3721; VACANT, Gift Processing Assoc. Tel: 617-779-3705; Fax: 617-779-3721; VACANT, Sr. Oper. Assoc. & Parish Stewardship Coord. Tel: 617-779-3706; Fax: 617-779-3731; VACANT, Dir. Digital Communications & New Media. Tel: 617-779-3705; Fax: 617-779-3721; VACANT, Oper. Assoc. Tel: 617-779-3709; Fax: 617-779-3731.

The Catholic Foundation Board of Trustees—Mr. CRAIG B. GIBSON, Pres.; Ms. JANE MANCINI PULIAFICO, Vice Pres. Trustees: His Eminence SEAN CARDINAL O'MALLEY, O.F.M.Cap.; Very Rev. RICHARD M. ERIKSON, V.G.; Rev. Msgrs. PAUL V. GARRITY, V.F.; WILLIAM M. HELMICK; CORNELIUS M. MCRAE; FRANCIS V. STRAHAN, V.F.; Revs. RODNEY J. COPP, J.C.L.; PAUL B. O'BRIEN; BRYAN K. PARRISH, V.F.; GEORGE L. SZAL, S.M.; WALTER J. WALDRON; Deacon DANIEL C. NELSON; R. STEPHEN BARRETT; MARY CORCORAN; JACK DUNN; JANICE JUDGE FOX; Mr. CRAIG B. GIBSON; KEVIN GILL; JOHN J. GRIFFIN; MICHAEL HALLORAN; CHRISTOPHER HAUGHEY; PHILIP HAUGHEY; RICHARD HORAN; JEFFREY J. KANEB; Mr. SCOT LANDRY; JANE MANCINI PULIAFICO; JAMES P. MCDONOUGH; JOANN MCGRATH; JOHN A. MCNEICE; JAMES F. MOONEY; MANUEL PIRES; Mr. JOHN M. RILEY; JACK J. SHAUGHNESSY; MARSHALL SLOANE.

Jewish Relations—Very Rev. DAVID C. MICHAEL, V.F., Dir., 4750 Washington St., Boston, 02132. Tel: 617-323-4410; Fax: 617-323-0423.

Labor Guild—Rev. PATRICK SULLIVAN, C.S.C., Dir., 85 Commercial St., Weymouth, 02188. Tel: 781-340-7887; Fax: 781-340-5885. Email: laborguild@aol.com. Web: www.laborguild.com.

L'Arche Irenicon, Inc.—SWANNA CHAMPLIN, Exec. Dir., Mailing Address: Box 1177, Haverhill, 01831. Tel: 978-374-6928; Fax: 978-373-9097. Email: office@larcheirenicon.org.

League of Catholic Women—Ms. MARY SULLIVAN, Pres., 39 Washington Park Rd., Braintree, 02184. Tel: 781-843-6616.

*Legatus Boston—66 Brooks Dr., Braintree, 02184-3839*Web: legatus.org.

Legion of Mary—Mr. JAMES KJELLANDER, Pres., 75 Union Park St., Boston, 02118-2141. Tel: 617-542-5682; Fax: 617-542-5926.

Life Resources— Residential and Community Services to Adolescents. Ms. LYNNE MARIE BIELECKI, Pres., 100 River St., Braintree, 02184-2021. Tel: 781-849-7751; Fax: 781-849-7754. Email: lbielecki@liferesourcesinc.org. Web: www.liferesourcesinc.org.

The Listening Place—Rev. ALFONSE FERREIRA, O.F.M., Dir., 36 Michigan Ave., Lynn, 01902-1934. Tel: 781-592-7396; Fax: 781-595-6724.

Liturgies in Other Languages—
American Sign—
Boston—Cathedral of the Holy Cross. Tel: 617-542-5682.
Bellingham—Saint Blaise. Tel: 508-966-1258.
Danvers—New England Home for the Deaf. Tel: 978-774-0445.
Hopkington—Saint John the Evangelist. Tel: 508-435-3313.
Middleborough—Sacred Heart. Tel: 508-947-0444.
Newton—Sacred Heart. Tel: 617-969-2248.
Stoneham—Saint Patrick. Tel: 781-438-0960.
Whitman—Holy Ghost. Tel: 781-447-4421.
Amharic—
Boston—Cathedral of the Holy Cross. Tel: 617-542-5682.
Chinese—
Boston—Saint James the Greater. Tel: 617-542-8498.
Congolese French—
Lynn—Saint Mary. Tel: 781-598-4907.
Haitian Creole—
Brockton—Christ the King. Tel: 508-586-1575.
Cambridge—Saint John the Evangelist. Tel: 617-547-4880.
Chelsea—Our Lady of Grace. Tel: 617-884-0030.
Dorchester—Saint Matthew. Tel: 617-436-3590.
Everett—Immaculate Conception. Tel: 617-389-5660.
Lynn—Saint Mary. Tel: 781-598-4907.
Mattapan—Saint Angela Merici. Tel: 617-298-0080.
Somerville—Saint Ann. Tel: 617-625-1904.
Igbo (Nigerian)—
Roxbury—Saint Katherine Drexel. Tel: 617-445-8915.
Italian—
Boston—Saint Leonard of Port Maurice. Tel: 617-523-2110.
Cambridge—Saint Francis of Assisi. Tel: 617-876-6754.
East Boston—Sacred Heart. Tel: 617-567-5776.
Everett—Saint Anthony of Padua. Tel: 617-387-0310.
Lawrence—Corpus Christi. Tel: 978-685-1711.
Khmer (Cambodian)—
Lowell—Saint Patrick. Tel: 978-459-0561.
Kiswahili (Kenyan)—
Lowell—Saint Michael. Tel: 617-846-7400.
Quincy—Sacred Heart. Tel: 978-459-0713.
Winthrop—Saint John the Evangelist. Tel: 617-328-8666.
Korean—
Newton—Saint Philip Neri. Tel: 617-244-9685.
Lithuanian—
Lawrence—Corpus Christi. Tel: 978-685-1711.
South Boston—Saint Peter. Tel: 617-268-0353.
Polish—
Chelsea—Saint Stanislaus. Tel: 617-889-0261.
Hyde Park—Saint Adalbert. Tel: 617-361-0565.

Lawrence—Corpus Christi. Tel: 978-685-1711.
Lowell—Holy Trinity. Tel: 978-452-2564.
Salem—Saint John the Baptist. Tel: 978-744-1278.
South Boston—Our Lady of Czestochowa. Tel: 617-268-4355.
Portuguese (Brazilian)—
Allston—Saint Anthony of Padua. Tel: 617-782-0775.
Cambridge—Saint Anthony of Padua. Tel: 617-547-5593.
East Boston—Madonna Queen Shrine. Tel: 617-569-2100.
Everett—Saint Anthony of Padua. Tel: 617-387-0310.
Framingham—Saint Tarcisius. Tel: 508-875-8623.
Gloucester—Holy Family. Tel: 978-281-4820.
Hudson—Saint Michael. Tel: 978-562-2552.
Lowell—Holy Family. Tel: 978-453-2134.
Marlborough—Immaculate Conception. Tel: 508-485-0016.
Maynard—Saint Bridget. Tel: 978-897-2171.
Peabody—Our Lady of Fatima. Tel: 978-532-0272.
Plymouth—Saint Mary. Tel: 508-746-0426.
Rockland—Holy Family. Tel: 781-878-0160.
Somerville—Saint Anthony of Padua. Tel: 617-625-4530.
Stoughton—Immaculate Conception. Tel: 781-344-2073.
Woburn—Saint Charles Borromeo. Tel: 781-933-0300.
Portuguese (Cape Verdean)—
Brockton—Saint Edith Stein. Tel: 508-586-6491.
Dorchester—Saint Peter. Tel: 617-265-1132.
Roxbury—Saint Patrick. Tel: 617-445-7645.
Scituate—Saint Mary of the Nativity. Tel: 781-545-3335.
Portuguese (European)—
Cambridge—Saint Anthony of Padua. Tel: 617-547-5593.
Framingham—Saint Tarcisius. Tel: 508-875-8623.
Gloucester—Our Lady of Good Voyage. Tel: 978-283-1490.
Hudson—Saint Michael. Tel: 978-562-2552.
Lawrence—Corpus Christi. Tel: 978-685-1711.
Lowell—Saint Anthony of Padua. Tel: 978-452-1506.
Peabody—Our Lady of Fatima. Tel: 978-532-0272.
Stoughton—Immaculate Conception. Tel: 781-344-2073.
Spanish—
Boston—Cathedral of the Holy Cross. Tel: 617-542-5682. *Saint Anthony Shrine*. Tel: 617-542-6440. *Saint Francis Chapel*. Tel: 617-437-7117.
Brighton—Saint Columbkille. Tel: 617-782-5774.
Brockton—Saint Patrick. Tel: 508-586-4840.
Cambridge—Saint Mary of the Annunciation. Tel: 617-547-0120.
Charlestown—Saint Mary-Saint Catherine of Siena. Tel: 617-242-1750.
Chelsea—Saint Rose of Lima. Tel: 617-889-2774.
Dorchester—Holy Family. Tel: 617-445-9553. *Saint Ambrose*. Tel: 617-265-5302. *Saint Christopher*. Tel: 617-436-7273.
East Boston—Madonna Queen Shrine. Tel: 617-569-2100. *Most Holy Redeemer*. Tel: 617-567-3227. *Oud Lady of the Assumption*. Tel: 617-567-1223.
Everett—Saint Anthony of Padua. Tel: 617-387-0310.
Framingham—Saint Stephen. Tel: 508-875-4788.
Haverhill—Saint James. Tel: 978-372-8537.
Jamaica Plain—Our Lady of Lourdes. Tel: 617-524-0434.
Lawrence—Corpus Christi. Tel: 978-685-1711. *Saint Mary of the Assumption*. Tel: 978-685-1111. *Saint Patrick*. Tel: 978-683-9416.
Lowell—Saint Patrick. Tel: 978-459-0561.
Lynn—Saint Joseph. Tel: 781-599-7040.
Marlborough—Immaculate Conception. Tel: 508-485-0016.
Newton—Saint Ignatius Loyola. Tel: 617-552-6100.
Peabody—Saint John the Baptist. Tel: 978-531-0002.
Revere—Immaculate Conception. Tel: 781-289-0735.
Roslindale—Sacred Heart. Tel: 617-325-3519.
Roxbury—Our Lady of Perpetual Help. Tel: 617-445-1524. *Saint Mary of the Angels*. Tel: 617-445-1524. *Saint Patrick*. Tel: 617-445-7645.
Salem—Immaculate Conception. Tel: 978-745-6303.
Somerville—Saint Ann. Tel: 617-625-1904. *Saint Benedict*. Tel: 617-625-0029.
South Boston—Saint Monica and Saint Augustine. Tel: 617-269-6760.
Waltham—Saint Mary. Tel: 781-891-1730.
Woburn—Saint Charles Borromeo. Tel: 781-933-0300.
Tagalog—
Malden—Saint Joseph. Tel: 781-324-0402.
Quincy—Saint John the Baptist. Tel: 617-773-1021.
West Roxbury—Holy Name. Tel: 617-325-4865.
Tigrinya—
Boston—Cathedral of the Holy Cross. Tel: 617-542-5682.
Vietnamese—Chelsea, Saint Rose of Lima. Tel: 617-889-2774. *Dorchester, Saint Ambrose*. Tel: 617-265-5302. *East Boston, Sacred Heart*. Tel: 617-567-5776. *Haverhill, Saint James*. Tel: 978-372-8537. *Lawrence, Saint Patrick*. Tel: 978-683-9416. *Lowell, Saint Patrick*. Tel: 978-459-0561. *Malden, Sacred Heart*. Tel: 781-324-0728. *Randolph, Saint Bernadette*. Tel: 781-963-1327.

Maria Droste Services—Sr. LORRAINE BERNIER, R.G.S., Admin., 1354 Hancock St., Quincy, 02169. Tel: 617-471-5686; Fax: 617-471-6622. Email: mariadroste@verizon.net.

Marian Devotions—Rev. WILLIAM R. CARROLL, Spiritual Dir., 46 Myrtle St., Melrose, 02176-3827. Tel: 781-665-0152; Fax: 781-665-2750.

Marriage Ministry—Ms. KARI COLELLA, Coord. Tel: 617-746-5801; Fax: 617-783-5642. Email: kari_colella@rcab.org.

Massachusetts Catholic Conference—VACANT, Exec. Dir., 150 Staniford St., Boston, 02114-2511. Tel: 617-367-6060; Fax: 617-367-2767.

Natural Family Planning—Ms. MARY FINNIGAN, Coord. Tel: 617-746-5803; Fax: 617-746-5782. Email: mary_finnigan@rcab.org.

New Ecclesial Movements—
New Evangelization of Youth and Young Adults—Rev. MATTHEW M. WILLIAMS, Dir., 66 Brooks Dr., Braintree, 02184-3839. Tel: 617-746-5752; Fax: 617-779-4572. Email: fr.matt@rcab.org.

Notre Dame Education Center—50 W. Broadway, Boston, 02127-1093. Tel: 617-268-1912; Fax: 617-464-7924. Email: ndecboston@aol.com.

Notre Dame Mission Center—Sr. RUTH DUFFY, S.N.D., Dir., 30 Jeffreys Neck Rd., Ipswich, 01938. Tel: 978-682-6441; Fax: 978-356-3552. Email: ndcimps@aol.com. Web: sndden.org.

Notre Dame Education Center—Sr. MARY MURPHY, S.N.D., Ph.D., Dir., 301 Haverhill St., Lawrence, 01842-9998. Tel: 978-682-6441; Fax: 978-974-8940. Email: sndmemurphy@aol.com.

Outreach and Cultural Diversity—VACANT, 66 Brooks Dr., Braintree, 02184-3839. Tel: 617-746-5818; Fax: 617-746-5614.

Parish Life and Leadership—Very Rev. THOMAS S. FOLEY, V.F., Sec. & Episcopal Vicar, 66 Brooks Dr., Braintree, 02184-3839. Tel: 617-746-5834; Fax: 617-779-4576. Email: reverendthomas_foley@rcab.org.

Pastoral Centers—
Brazilian Pastoral Centers—
Saint Anthony of Padua Social Action—43 Holton St., Allston, 02134. Tel: 617-783-2121.
Centro Bom Samaritano—Good Samaritan Center, 116 Concord St., Ste. 3, Framingham, 01702. Tel: 508-628-3721; Fax: 508-875-6358. Email: centrobomsamaritano@hotmail.com.
Centro Comunitario Scalabrini—Sr. ELISETE TERESIHNA SIGNOR, M.S.C.S., 63 Oakes St., Everett, 02149. Tel: 617-387-0822.
Chinese Pastoral Center—Sr. MADELINE GALLAGHER, M.H.S.H., 78 Tyler St., Boston, 02111-1831. Tel: 617-482-2949; Fax: 617-482-2949.
Irish Pastoral Center—Sr. MARGUERITE KELLY, M.F.I.C., 953 Hancock St., Quincy, 02170-2322. Tel: 617-479-7404; Fax: 617-479-0541. Email: ipcboston@yahoo.com.
Other Pastoral Centers—
Our Lady's Guild House—ANDREA BEALL, 20 Charlesgate W., Boston, 02215-2703. Tel: 617-536-3000; Fax: 617-536-8508.
Salesian Boys and Girls Club—Rev. JOHN NAZZARO, S.D.B., 150 Byron St., Boston, 02128. Tel: 617-667-6626; Fax: 617-567-0418.
Don Guanella Center—Sr. RHONDA BROWN, D.S.M.P., 37 Nichols St., Chelsea, 02150-1225. Tel: 617-889-0179.

Pastoral Planning—Rev. DAVID COUTERIER, O.F.M.Cap., Dir., 66 Brooks Dr., Boston, 02135-3193. Tel: 617-746-5865; Fax: 617-746-5614. Email: reverenddavid_couturier@rcab.org.

Pauline Books and Media—Sr. DONNA GIAIAMO, F.S.P., Dir., 885 Providence Hwy., Dedham, 02026. Tel: 781-326-5385; Fax: 781-461-1013. Email: dedham@paulinemedia.com. Web: pauline.org.

Pauline Center for Media Studies—Sr. MARY SOPHIE STEWART, F.S.P., Dir., 50 Saint Paul's Ave., Boston, 02130-3491. Tel: 617-522-8911; Fax: 617-522-4081. Web: pauline.org.

Pilgrimages—Rev. MICHAEL E. DREA, Coord., 29 Mount Auburn St., Cambridge, 02138. Tel: 617-491-8400; Fax: 617-354-7092.

The Pilot—Mr. ANTONIO ENRIQUE, Editor, 66 Brooks Dr., Braintree, 02184-3839. Tel: 617-746-5890; Fax: 617-779-4563. Email: aenrique@thebostonpilot.com. Web: thebostonpilot.com.

Pregnancy Help— Supporting women in crisis pregnancies. MARY B. GIRARD, R.N., Dir. 77 Warren St., Ste. 251, Brighton Marine Mental Health Center; Caritas Saint Elizabeth Medical Center, Boston, MA 02135Tel: 888-771-3914 (Toll Free In State); 617-782-5151; Fax: 617-782-1662.
Metro-West—5 Wilson St., Natick, 01760. Tel: 508-651-0753; Fax: 508-651-0754. Email: help@pregnancyhelpboston.org. Web: pregnancyhelpboston.org.

Prison Ministry—Deacon JAMES F. GREER, Interim Dir., 66 Brooks Dr., Braintree, 02184-3839. Tel: 978-746-5842; Fax: 617-742-5754. Email: jgreer@rcab.org.
State Facilities—
Bay State Correctional Facility—Rev. THOMAS F. STANTON, Chap., 28 Clark St., Norfolk, 02056. Tel: 508-668-1687.
Bridgewater State Hospital—Ms. PEG NEWMAN, Coord., 20 Administration Rd., Bridgewater, 02324. Tel: 508-279-4500.
Longwood Treatment Center—Ms. PEG NEWMAN, Coord., Two Administration Rd., Bridgewater, 02324. Tel: 508-279-3500.
Massachusetts Correctional Institution - Cedar Junction—Rev. THOMAS F. STANTON, Chap., Rte. 1A, Norfolk, 02056. Tel: 508-660-8000.
Massachusetts Correctional Institution - Concord—Rev. GEORGE WILLIAMS, S.J., Chap., 965 Elm St., Concord, 01742. Tel: 978-405-6100.
Massachusetts Correctional Institution - Framingham—Sr. MAUREEN CLARK, C.S.J., Coord., Mailing Address: Box 9007, Framingham, 01701-9007. Tel: 508-532-5100.
Massachusetts Correctional Institution - Norfolk—Ms. MARY BETH ROBINSON, Coord., 2 Clark St., Norfolk, 02056. Tel: 508-660-5900.
Massachusetts Correctional Institution - Plymouth—Deacon THOMAS HANLON, Mailing Address: Box 207, Carver, 02355-0207. Tel: 508-295-2647.
Massachusetts Correctional Institution - Shirley—Deacon ARTHUR F. ROGERS JR., Coord., Mailing Address: Box 1218, Shirley, 01464-1218. Tel: 978-425-4341.
Massachusetts Treatment Center—Deacon THOMAS HANLON, Coord., 30 Administration Rd., Bridgewater, 02324. Tel: 508-279-8100.
Northeast Correctional Center—Rev. GEORGE WILLIAMS, S.J., Chap., Barretts Mill Rd., Concord, 01742. Tel: 978-369-4120.
Old Colony Correction Center—VACANT, One Administration Rd., Bridgewater, 02324. Tel: 508-879-6000.
Pondville Correctional Center—Ms. MARY BETH ROBINSON, Coord., Mailing Address: Box 146, Norfolk, 02056-0146. Tel: 508-660-3924.
Shattuck Hospital Correctional Unit—180 Morton St., Boston, 02130. Tel: 617-522-7585.
South Middlesex Correctional Center—Sr. MAUREEN CLARK, C.S.J., Coord., 135 Western Ave., Framingham, 01701-0850. Tel: 508-879-1241.
County Facilities—
Essex County Correctional Facility—Deacon CARROLL H. TAYLOR, Coord., 20 Manning Ave., Middleton, 01949. Tel: 978-750-1900.
Middlesex County - House of Correction—Deacon WILLIAM R. EMERSON, Coord., 269 Treble Cove Rd., Billerica, 01821. Tel: 978-667-1711.
Middlesex County Jail—Deacon WILLIAM R. EMERSON, 40 Thorndike St., Cambridge, 02146. Tel: 617-494-4410.
Suffolk County Jail—200 Nashua St., Boston, 02118. Tel: 617-635-1100.
Norfolk County Correctional Facility—Rev. ROBERT M. JONES, S.V.D., Chap., 200 West St., Dedham, 02026. Tel: 781-329-3705.
Plymouth County Correctional Center—VACANT, 20 Long Pond Rd., Plymouth, 02360. Tel: 508-830-6200.
Suffolk County - House of Correction—VACANT, 20 Brandston St., Boston, 02118. Tel: 617-635-1000.
Youth Facilities—
Metro Youth Service Center—Rev. JOSEPH J. BAGGETTA, Chap., 425 Harvard St., Boston, 02124-2737. Tel: 617-727-6603.

Private Associations of Christ's Faithful—
Foyer of Charity—Rev. MATTHEW BRADLEY, Dir., 74 Hollett St., Scituate, 02066. Tel: 781-545-1080; Fax: 240-332-5826. Email: fb@foyerofcharity.org. Web: foyerofcharity.org.
Little Brothers of Saint Francis—785 Parker St., Boston, 02120-3021. Tel: 617-442-2556. Web: littlebrothersofstfrancis.org.
Marian Community—Sr. MARGARET CATHERINE SIMS, C.S.J., Dir., 154 Summer St., Medway, 02053-0639. Tel: 508-533-5377; Fax: 508-533-2877. Web: mariancommunity.org.

Professional Standards and Oversight—66 Brooks Dr., Braintree, 02184-3839. Tel: 617-782-2544; Fax: 617-779-3820.

Background Screening—Mrs. ANN LALLY, 66 Brooks Dr., Braintree, 02184-3839. Tel: 617-746-5840; Fax: 617-779-4565.

Delegate for Investigations—Mr. JAY CROWLEY, Delegate, 66 Brooks Dr., Braintree, 02184-3839. Tel: 617-746-5639; Fax: 617-746-5696.

Pastoral Support and Outreach—Ms. BARBARA THORP, Dir., 25 Braintree Hill Office Park, Ste. 300, Braintree, 02184. Tel: 866-244-9603 (Toll Free); 781-794-2581 (Local); Fax: 781-794-2584. Email: barbara_thorp@pastoralsupportandoutreach.org. Web: www.rcab.org/oha/homepage.htm.

Project Hope— Little Sisters of the Assumption Family Health Services, Inc. Sr. MARGARET LEONARD, L.S.A., Exec. Dir., 550 Dudley St., Roxbury, 02119. Tel: 617-442-1880; Fax: 617-238-0473. Email: mleonard@prohope.org.

Project Rachel— Post-Abortion Reconciliation and Healing. Mrs. MARIANNE P. LUTHIN, Dir., 5 Wilson St., Natick, 01760. Tel: 508-651-3100; Fax: 508-651-0754. Email: help@projectrachelboston.com. Web: projectrachelboston.com. Est. 1986.

Pro-Life Office—Mrs. MARIANNE P. LUTHIN, Dir., 5 Wilson St., Natick, 01760. Tel: 508-651-1900; Fax: 508-651-0754. Email: prolifeoffice@rcab.org. Web: bostoncatholic.org/prolifeoffice.aspx.

Public Association of Christ's Faithful—

Association of Saint Francis De Sales—Ms. CATHERINE CULLEN, Area Dir., 10 Wright Ln., Duxbury, 02332. Tel: 781-934-7228. Email: kateycullen@msn.com. Web: desalesassociation.org.

Brotherhood of Hope—194 Summer St., Somerville, 02143-2525. Tel: 617-623-9592; Fax: 617-625-1837. Email: info@brotherhoodofhope.org. Web: brotherhoodofhope.org.

Franciscans of the Primitive Observance—Bro. JOHN M. SWEENEY, F.P.O., 30 Trinity St., Lawrence, 01841.

Radio—Rev. ROBERT P. REED, Dir., Mailing Address: 34 Chestnut St., Box 9196, Watertown, 02471-9196. Tel: 617-923-0220.

Regina Cleri—Mr. STEPHEN J. GUST, Dir., 60 William Cardinal O'Connell Way, Boston, 02114-2729. Tel: 617-523-1861; Fax: 617-720-0585. Email: sgust@reginacleri.org.

Religious Education—Ms. SUSAN LANG ABBOTT, Dir.; Ms. SUSAN J. KAY, Asst. Dir. Catechetical Leadership; Ms. M. PILAR LATORRE, Assoc. Dir. Hispanic Catechesis, 66 Brooks Dr., Braintree, 02184-3839. Tel: 617-779-3625; Fax: 617-746-5702.

Respect Life Education Office—KATHLEEN DARDIS, Asst. Dir., 66 Brooks Dr., Braintree, 02184-3839. Tel: 617-746-5684; Fax: 617-747-5702. Email: respectlifeed@rcab.org. Web: respectlifeeducation.com.

Saint Ann's Home, Inc.—Mr. DENIS GRANDBOIS, Pres. & CEO, 100-A Haverhill St., Methuen, 01844. Tel: 978-685-5276; Fax: 978-688-4932. Email: dgrandbois@st.annshome.org. Web: st.annshome.org.

Society of Saint James the Apostle—24 Clark St., Boston, 02109-1127. Tel: 617-742-4715; Fax: 617-723-7389.

Society of Saint Vincent de Paul—EDWARD J. RESNICK, Controller, 18 Canton St., Stoughton, 02072. Tel: 781-344-3100; Fax: 617-341-4560. Email: execdir@svdpboston.com. Web: svdpboston.com.

Seaport Chaplaincy—Rev. RICHARD A. UFTRING, Chap., Logan International Airport, Boston, 02128. Tel: 617-567-2800. Email: fatherrichard@massport.com.

Secular Institutes—

Oblate Missionaries of Mary Immaculate—Ms. PAULINE LABBE, Dir., 9 Bayberry Dr., Atkinson, NH 03811. Tel: 603-362-9960. Email: pjlabbe1@juno.com.

Caritas Christi—Ms. ANNE M. RYAN, Sec., 537 Winter St., Framingham, 01702-5632. Tel: 508-875-7990. Email: aryan1211@aol.com. Web: ccinfo.org.

Secular Augustinians—205 Hampshire St., Lawrence, 01841. Tel: 978-685-1111; Fax: 978-686-5555. Rev. JORGE A. REYES, O.S.A., Dir., 205 Hampshire St., Lawrence, 01841. Tel: 978-685-1111; Fax: 978-686-5555.

Secular Carmelites—Ms. LORETTA L. GALLAGHER, O.D.C.S., 36 Virginia Ln., Newburyport, 01950. Tel: 978-462-1057. Email: lorluceri@yahoo.com.

Lay Dominicans—Mr. RAYMOND A. DIBONA, O.P., Dir., 45 Trafford St., Quincy, 02169. Tel: 617-472-4446. Email: kmcaldwell@verizon.net.

Secular Franciscans—Ms. JACQUELYN D. WALSH, Regl. Min., 102 Everett Cir., Stoughton, 02072-5101. Tel: 781-344-7719. Email: jackiesfo@juno.com.

Social Services—

Catholic Relief Services—Rev. J. BRYAN HEHIR, 66 Brooks Dr., Braintree, 02184-3839. Tel: 617-746-5733; Fax: 617-779-4571. Email: bryan-hehir@harvard.edu.

Labor Guild—Rev. PATRICK SULLIVAN, C.S.C., Dir., 85 Commercial St., Weymouth, 02188. Tel: 781-340-7887; Fax: 781-340-5885. Email: laborguild@aol.com. Web: www.laborguild.com.

Life Resources— Residential and Community Services to Adolescents Ms. LYNNE MARIE BIELECKI, Pres., 100 River St., Braintree, 02184-2021. Tel: 781-849-7751; Fax: 781-849-7754. Email: lbielecki@liferesourcesinc.org. Web: www.liferesourcesinc.org.

L'Arche Irenicon, Inc.—SWANNA CHAMPLIN, Exec. Dir., Mailing Address: Box 1177, Haverhill, 01831. Tel: 978-374-6928; Fax: 978-373-9097. Email: office@larcheirenicon.org.

Pregnancy Help— Supporting women in crisis pregnancies. MARY B. GIRARD, R.N., Dir. 77 Warren St., Ste. 251, Brighton Marine Mental Health Center; Caritas Saint Elizabeth Medical Center, Boston, MA 02135Tel: 888-771-3914 (Toll Free In State); 617-782-5151; Fax: 617-782-1662.

Metro-West—5 Wilson St., Natick, 01760. Tel: 508-651-0753; Fax: 508-651-0754. Email: help@pregnancyhelpboston.org. Web: pregnancyhelpboston.org.

Project Rachel— Post-Abortion Reconciliation and Healing. Mrs. MARIANNE P. LUTHIN, Dir., 5 Wilson St., Natick, 01760. Tel: 508-651-3100; Fax: 508-651-0754. Email: help@projectrachelboston.com. Web: projectrachelboston.com. Est. 1986.

Pro-Life Office—Mrs. MARIANNE P. LUTHIN, Dir., 5 Wilson St., Natick, 01760. Tel: 508-651-1900; Fax: 508-651-0754. Email: prolifeoffice@rcab.org. Web: bostoncatholic.org/prolifeoffice.aspx.

Respect Life Education Office—KATHLEEN DARDIS, Asst. Dir., 66 Brooks Dr., Braintree, 02184-3839. Tel: 617-746-5684; Fax: 617-747-5702. Email: respectlifeed@rcab.org. Web: respectlifeeducation.com.

Saint Ann's Home, Inc.—Mr. DENIS GRANDBOIS, Pres. & CEO, 100-A Haverhill St., Methuen, 01844. Tel: 978-685-5276; Fax: 978-688-4932. Email: dgrandbois@st.annshome.org. Web: st.annshome.org.

Related Services—

Cor Unum Meal Center—Ms. DIANE JARVIS, Dir., 191 Salem St., Lawrence, 01843-1427. Tel: 978-688-8900; Fax: 978-681-5808. Email: corunummealcenter@comcast.net. Web: www.corunummealcenter.org.

The Listening Place— Counseling and Spiritual Services. Rev. ALFONSE FERREIRA, O.F.M., Dir., 36 Michigan Ave., Lynn, 01902-1934. Tel: 781-592-7396; Fax: 781-595-6724.

Maria Droste Services— Counseling Service. Sr. LORRAINE BERNIER, R.G.S., Admin. & Interim Dir., 1354 Hancock St., Rm. 203, Quincy, 02169. Tel: 617-471-5686; Fax: 617-471-6622. Email: mariadroste@verizon.net.

Project Hope— Little Sisters of the Assumption Family Health Services, Inc. Sr. MARGARET LEONARD, L.S.A., Exec. Dir., 550 Dudley St., Roxbury, 02119. Tel: 617-442-1880; Fax: 617-238-0473. Email: mleonard@prohope.org.

Society of Saint Vincent De Paul—PAUL MCNEIL, Exec. Dir.; EDWARD J. RESNICK, 18 Canton St., Stoughton, 02072. Tel: 781-344-3100; Fax: 781-341-4560. Email: exdir@svdpboston.com. Web: www.svdpboston.com.

Specialized Catholic Organizations—

Ancient Order of Hibernians - Ladies Auxiliary—VACANT, 18 Beach Rd., Salisbury, 01953-1436. Tel: 978-465-3334; Fax: 978-465-5524. Email: starsea@seacoast.com. Web: laoh.massboard.org.

Ancient Order of Hibernians—Mr. RICHARD J. THOMPSON, Pres., 7 Derby Rd., Watertown, 02472. Tel: 617-924-9765. Email: rthomp521@comcast.net. Web: massaoh.org.

Archdiocesan Union of Holy Name Societies—Mr. ROBERT QUAGAN, 35 Cass St., Boston, 02132-4411. Tel: 617-325-5905. Email: rquagan@comcast.net.

Casa Monte Cassino—11 Tileston St., Boston, 02113. Tel: 617-227-1613; Fax: 617-227-1613. Email: casamontecassino@earthlink.net. Web: casamontecassino.org.

Catholic Alumni Club—Mr. THOMAS LITRENTA, Pres., 40 Nowell Rd., Melrose, 02176-1242. Tel: 617-261-9600. Email: cachubbub@yahoo.com. Web: caci.org.

Catholic Association of Foresters—Mr. JOHN F. ANDERSON, Treas., 132 Forbes Rd., Braintree, 02184-2693. Tel: 781-848-8221; Fax: 781-848-0311. Email: john@catholicforesters.org. Web: catholicforesters.org.

Catholic Daughters of the Americas—Ms. JOYCE A. FLEMING, Regent, 62 Cushing St., Medford, 02155. Tel: 781-391-1069. Email: jatfleming@comcast.net.

Catholic Lawyers Guild—HON. JOSEPH R. NOLAN, Pres., 100 Cambridge St., Boston, 02114. Tel: 617-723-1100.

Cor Unum Meal Center—Ms. DIANE JARVIS, Dir., 191 Salem St., Lawrence, 01843-1427. Tel: 978-688-8900; Fax: 978-681-5808. Email: corunummealcenter@comcast.net. Web: corunummealcenter.org.

Daughters of Isabella—Ms. THERESA LEWIS, Regent, 72 Seabreeze Dr., South Dartmouth, 02748. Tel: 508-993-5085.

Equestrian Order of the Holy Sepulchre of Jerusalem—Mr. JOHN J. MONAHAN, Lieutenant, 340 Main St., Worcester, 01608. Tel: 508-752-3311; Fax: 508-752-3531. Email: eohsjne@aol.com.

Guild of the Infant Savior—Ms. SHARON DEEHAN, Pres., 162 Pineridge Rd., North Andover, 01845. Tel: 978-683-9846. Email: sdeehan@comcaset.net.

Healing and Restoration Ministry—1545 Tremont St., Boston, 02120. Tel: 617-442-2008; Fax: 617-442-2845.

International Order of the Alhambra—Mr. CORNELIUS M. MURPHY, Sec., 15 Carolina St., Medford, 02155-4806. Tel: 781-396-1979.

Knights of Columbus—470 Washington St., Norwood, 02062-0194. Tel: 781-551-0628; Fax: 781-551-0490. Email: mastatekofc@verizon.net. Web: massachusettsstatekofc.org.

Knights of Peter Claver—Mr. MEYER CHAMBERS, Grand Knight, 32 Courtney Rd., Boston, 02132-1044. Tel: 617-552-1298; Fax: 617-552-3044. Email: meyer.chambers.1@bc.edu. Web: kofpc.org.

League of Catholic Women—Ms. MARY SULLIVAN, Pres., 39 Washington Park Rd., Braintree, 02184. Tel: 781-843-6616.

*Legatus Boston—66 Brooks Dr., Braintree, 02184-3839*Web: legatus.org.

Legion of Mary—Mr. JAMES KJELLANDER, Pres., 75 Union Park St., Boston, 02118-2141. Tel: 617-542-5682; Fax: 617-542-5926.

Magnificat Joy of Boston—Ms. LOUISE SCIPIONE, Coord., 42 Packard Rd., Stoughton, 02072. Tel: 781-344-6616.

Maria Droste Services—Sr. LORRAINE BERNIER, R.G.S., Admin., 1354 Hancock St., Quincy, 02169. Tel: 617-471-5686; Fax: 617-471-6622. Email: mariadroste@verizon.net.

Nocturnal Adoration Society—Mr. GEORGE J. HALLETT, Pres., 45 Courtland Cir., Milton, 02186-4303. Tel: 617-698-6321. Email: geojoshal@aol.com.

Pax Christi USA—Rev. WILLIAM T. KREMMELL, Advisor (Retired), 27 Bainbridge Rd., Reading, 01867-1810. Tel: 781-944-0330; Fax: 781-944-1266. Email: pax_2_you@yahoo.com.

Pieta—Ms. BARBARA WATERS, Coord., 66 Enoch Pond Rd., Wrentham, 02093-1391. Tel: 508-384-6663. Email: hanknann@verizon.net.

Pro Maria Committee—Ms. IRENE TREMBLAY, Dir., 112 Norris Rd., Tyngsborough, 01879. Tel: 978-649-1813. Email: irene_tremblay@hotmail.com.

Pro Parvulis—Ms. BEVERLY C. BAKER, Treas., 286 Turtle Pond Pkwy., Boston, 02136-1224.

Project Hope—Sr. MARGARET LEONARD, L.S.A., Exec. Dir., 550 Dudly St., Boston, 02119. Tel: 617-442-1880; Fax: 617-238-0473. Email: mleonard@prohope.org. Web: prohope.org.

Serra Boston—Leaders: BRIAN GALLAGHER; LORETTA GALLAGHER, 36 Virginia Ln., Newburyport, 01950. Tel; 978-462-1057. Email: information@serraboston.org. Web: serraboston.org.

Seton Club—Ms. JOSEPH WELLER, Pres., 14 Summer St., Saugus, 01906-2139. Tel: 781-233-2497; Fax: 781-231-5569.

Simon of Cyrene Society—Sr. MARGARET YOUNGCLAUS, S.N.D., Dir., Mailing Address: Box 54, Boston, 02127-0054. Tel: 617-268-8393. Email: sndbol@aol.com. Web: simonofcyrene.com.

Society of Saint Vincent de Paul—EDWARD J. RESNICK, Controller, 18 Canton St., Stoughton, 02072. Tel: 781-344-3100; Fax: 617-341-4560. Email: execdir@svdpboston.com. Web: svdpboston.com.

The Gathering Place—Sr. PATRICIA BRENNAN, R.G.S., Dir., 3 Common St., Waltham, 02451-4401. Tel: 781-647-0012; Fax: 781-647-0055. Email: gather1997@aol.com. Web: thegatheringplace@homestead.com.

The Listening Place—Rev. ALFONSE FERREIRA, O.F.M., Dir., 36 Michigan Ave., Lynn, 01902-1934. Tel: 781-592-7396; Fax: 781-595-6724.

Women Affirming Life—Ms. FRANCES X. HOGAN, Pres., Mailing Address: Box 35532, Boston, 02135-0532. Tel: 617-254-2277; Fax: 617-254-2299.

World Apostolate of Fatima—Ms. LYNN KENN, Pres.,

Mailing Address: Box 308, East Bridgewater, 02333-0308. Tel: 508-378-7431. Email: elk314@comcast.net.

Special Needs—

Braintree— Cardinal Cushing Centers, Inc. Mr. RON SHEPHERD, Prin., 85 Washington St., Braintree, 02184. Tel: 781-848-6250; Fax: 781-848-0640. Web: www.coletta.org/cardinal/braintree/braintree.htm. Email: rshepherd@coletta.org.

Hanover— Cardinal Cushing Centers, Inc. Mrs. ROBERTA PULASKI, Dir. Educ., 405 Washington St., Hanover, 02339. Tel: 781-826-6371; Fax: 781-826-1559. Web: www.coletta.org/cardinal/hanoverprogs/hanover.htm. Email: rpulaski@coletta.org.

Spiritual Life—66 Brooks Dr., Braintree, 02184-3839. Tel: 617-779-3640; Fax: 617-779-4570. Ms. MARYANN MCLAUGHLIN, Dir. Spiritual Life. Tel: 617-779-3641. Email: mmclaugh@rcab.org; Sr. ANNE D'ARCY, C.S.J., Assoc. Dir. Spiritual Life. Tel: 617-779-3648; Fax: 617-779-4570. Email: sdarcy@rcab.org; Revs. DANIEL O'CONNELL, Assoc. Dir. Spiritual Life. Tel: 617-779-3643; Fax: 617-779-4570. Email: roconnell@rcab.org; JOHN E. SASSANI, Assoc. Dir. Spiritual Life. Tel: 617-527-7560, Ext. 215; Fax: 617-779-4570. Email: jsassani@ourladys.com; Ms. PATRICIA DEBAISE, Administrative Asst. Tel: 617-779-3645; Fax: 617-779-4570. Email: patricia_debaise@rcab.org.

*ARISE: Together in Christ—*Ms. MARYANN MCLAUGHLIN, Archdiocesan Coord. Tel: 617-779-3640; Fax: 617-779-4570. Email: mmclaugh@rcab.org; Ms. ANN M. CUSSEN, Oper. Asst. Tel: 617-779-3640; Fax: 617-779-4570. Email: ann_cussen@rcab.org.

*Vocations—*Revs. DANIEL F. HENNESSEY, Dir., 66 Brooks Dr., Braintree, 02184-3839. Tel: 617-746-5949; Fax: 617-779-5470. Email: reverend_daniel_hennessey@rcab.org; MICHAEL C. HARRINGTON, Assoc. Dir. Tel: 617-746-5939; Fax: 617-779-5470. Email: michael_harrington@rcab.org; ALONSO E. MACIAS, Assoc. Dir. Tel: 617-746-5987; Fax: 617-779-5470. Email: reverend_alonso_macias@rcab.org.

CLERGY, PARISHES, MISSIONS AND PAROCHIAL SCHOOLS

BOSTON

(SUFFOLK COUNTY)

1—CATHEDRAL OF THE HOLY CROSS (1788) Very Rev. Kevin J. O'Leary, Admin.; Mr. Robert V. Travers, Pastoral Assoc.; Deacon Ricardo M. Mesa. In Res., His Eminence Sean P. O'Malley, O.F.M.Cap.; Rev. Msgr. Robert P. Deeley; Revs. Robert T. Kickham; Jonathan M. Gaspar.
Res.: 75 Union Park St., Boston, 02118. Tel: 617-542-5682; Fax: 617-542-5926. Email: cathedral2@rcab.org. Web: www.holycrossboston.com.
School—Cathedral Grammar School, 595 Harrison Ave., Boston, 02118. Tel: 617-422-0042. Sr. Dorothy Burns, C.S.J., Prin. Sisters 2; Lay Teachers 13; Students 201.
See Cathedral High School under High Schools, Archdiocesan in the Institution section.
Catechesis/Religious Program—
Convent—Mission Helpers of Sacred Heart, 286 Shuwmut Ave., Boston, Suffolk Co. 02118. Tel: 617-542-1143.

2—ST. ADALBERT (1913), (Polish), Rev. Andrzej Urbaniak, O.F.M.Conv., Admin.
Res.: 1450 River St., Hyde Park, 02136-2150. Tel: 617-361-0565; Fax: 617-361-7788. Email: stadalberts@homeofpeace.org.

3—ALL SAINTS (1894), All Saints, Roxbury was suppressed. This parish's records are located at St. Patrick, Boston.

4—ST. AMBROSE (1914) Revs. Daniel J. Finn; Tinh Van Nguyen, Parochial Vicar; Joseph Chinh Nguyen (Vietnam), Parochial Vicar; Sr. Mary Damien Powers, O.S.M., Pastoral Assoc.; Deacon Marcio O. Fonseca. In Res., Rt. Rev. John J. Ahern; Revs. Richard C. Conway; Huy H. Nguyen; Thomas F. Bouton.
Res.: 240 Adams St., Dorchester, 02122-1380. Tel: 617-265-5302; Fax: 617-265-0886. Email: stambroseparish@comcast.net.

5—ST. ANDREW (1918), St. Andrew the Apostle, Forest Hills was suppressed. This parish's records are located at Sacred Heart, Boston.

6—ST. ANGELA MERICI (1907) Rev. William P. Joy; Mr. Joseph E. Dorlus, Pastoral Assoc.
Res.: 1544 Blue Hill Ave., Mattapan, 02126. Tel: 617-298-0080; Fax: 617-298-2388. Email: rectory@stangelaparish.org. Web: www.stangelaparish.org.

7—ST. ANN (1889) Rev. Sean M. Connor. In Res., Rev. John J. Connelly.
Res.: 243 Neponset Ave., Dorchester, 02122-3239. Tel: 617-825-6180. Email: saintanneponset@gmail.com. Web: www.saintanneponset.com.
*Convent—*241 Neponset Ave., Dorchester, 02122. Tel: 617-288-1202.

8—ST. ANN (1945), St. Ann, Back Bay was suppressed. This parish's records are located at St. Cecilia, Boston.

9—ST. ANNE (1919) Rev. William F. Joyce. In Res., Rev. William F. Sweeney, S.S.C.
Res.: 79 W. Milton St., Readville, 02136-1929. Tel: 617-361-3443; Fax: 617-361-6690.
*Convent—*85 W. Milton St., Readville, 02136. Tel: 617-361-8224.

10—ST. ANTHONY OF PADUA (1896) Revs. Francis M. Glynn; Jose E. Marques (Brazil), Parochial Vicar. In Res., Revs. Walter H. Cuenin; Paul E. Kilroy.
Res.: 43 Holton St., Allston, 02134-1397. Tel: 617-782-0775; Fax: 617-782-2008. Email: glynnfrank@hotmail.com.

11—ST. AUGUSTINE (1868), St. Augustine, South Boston was suppressed. This parish's records are located at St. Monica and St. Augustine, Boston.

12—BLESSED MOTHER TERESA OF CALCUTTA (2004) Rt. Rev. John J. Ahern; Revs. Richard C. Conway, Parochial Vicar; Huy H. Nguyen, Parochial Vicar.
Mailing Address & Res.: 240 Adams St., Dorchester, 02122. Tel: 617-436-2190; Fax: 617-282-5428. Email: bmtdorchester@gmail.com. Web: www.motherteresadorchester.org.

13—BLESSED SACRAMENT (1891), Blessed Sacrament, Jamaica Plain was suppressed. This parish's records are located at Our Lady of Lourdes, Boston.

14—ST. BRENDAN (1929) Rev. John J. Connolly. In Res., Revs. John M. McCarthy (Ireland); Brian F. McMahon.
Res.: 15 Rita Rd., Dorchester, 02124-5321. Tel: 617-436-0310; Fax: 617-436-1386. Email: stbrndn@gis.net.
*School—*29 Rita Rd., Dorchester, 02124-5321. Tel: 617-282-3388. Ellen Leary, Prin. Lay Teachers 12; Students 209.
*Catechesis/Religious Program—*Tel: 617-825-8622. Jean Curley, D.R.E.

15—ST. BRIGID (1908) Very Rev. Robert E. Casey; Rev. Robert J. Blaney, Parochial Vicar; Bro. Stephen Fahrig, O.M.V., Pastoral Assoc. In Res., Rev. C. Paul Rouse (Retired).
Res.: 841 E. Broadway, South Boston, 02127-2302. Tel: 617-268-2122; Fax: 617-268-2666. Email: stbrigidparish@aol.com. Web: www.stbrigidparish.com.
School—South Boston Catholic Academy, 866 E. Broadway, Boston, 02127-2302. Tel: 617-268-2356.
*Catechesis/Religious Program—*James Fowkes, D.R.E.
*Convent—*100 N St., South Boston, 02127.

16—ST. CATHERINE OF SIENA (1887), St. Catherine of Siena, Charlestown was suppressed. This parish's records are located at St. Mary - St. Catherine of Siena, Boston.

17—ST. CECILIA (1888) Rev. John J. Unni; Mr. Mark Donohoe, Pastoral Assoc. In Res., Rev. Thomas A. Mahoney.
Res.: 30 St. Cecilia St., Boston, 02115-3132. Tel: 617-536-4548; Fax: 617-536-1781. Email: info@stceciliaboston.org. Web: www.stceciliaboston.org.

18—ST. CHRISTOPHER (1956) Rev. George A. Carrigg, Admin.; Ms. Louise Tardif, Pastoral Assoc.
Res.: 263 Mt. Vernon St., Dorchester, 02125-3182. Tel: 617-436-7273; Fax: 617-265-2704. Web: www.stchristopherchurch.org.
Catechesis/Religious Program—

19—ST. COLUMBKILLE (1871) Rev. Msgr. William P. Fay; Rev. Daniel P. Moloney, Parochial Vicar. In Res., Revs. Carney E. Gavin; Bostjan Toplikar (Slovenia); Sebastian Chukwudi Madike (Nigeria).
Res.: 321 Market St., Brighton, 02135-2126. Tel: 617-782-5774; Fax: 617-782-7283. Email: office@brightoncatholic.org. Web: www.brightoncatholic.org.
*School—*25 Arlington St., Brighton, 02135-2199. Tel: 617-254-3110. Michael A. McCarthy, Prin. Sisters 4; Lay Teachers 10; Students 200.
*Catechesis/Religious Program—*Christopher Carmody, D.R.E.

20—CONGREGATION OF SAINT ATHANASIUS Rev. Richard S. Bradford, Admin.
Res.: 767 W. Roxbury Pkwy., Boston, 02132-2121. Tel: 617-325-5232; Fax: 617-325-5232. Web: www.locator.net.

21—ST. FRANCIS DE SALES (1859) Rev. Daniel J. Mahoney. In Res., Rev. Martin Okwir (Uganda).
Res.: 303 Bunker Hill St., Charlestown, 02129-1826. Tel: 617-242-0147; Fax: 617-242-3026. Email: stfran303@aol.com. Web: www.stfrancisdesalescharlestown.com.

22—ST. FRANCIS DE SALES-ST. PHILIP (1867), St. Francis de Sales, Roxbury was suppressed. This parish's records are located at St. Katherine Drexel, Boston.

23—ST. GABRIEL (1934), St. Gabriel, Brighton was suppressed. This parish's records are located at St. Columbkille, Boston.

24—GATE OF HEAVEN (1862) Very Rev. Robert E. Casey; Rev. Robert J. Blaney, Parochial Vicar; Bro. Stephen Fahrig, O.M.V., Pastoral Assoc.
Res.: 841 E. Broadway, South Boston, 02127-2302. Tel: 617-268-3344; Fax: 617-268-2666. Email: gateofheavensb@aol.com. Web: www.gateofheavenparish.com.
School—South Boston Catholic Academy, 866 E. Broadway, South Boston, 02127. Tel: 617-268-2316. Sr. Patricia McCarthy, C.S.J., Prin. Sisters 3; Lay Teachers 17; Students 483.
*Catechesis/Religious Program—*James Fowkes, D.R.E.

25—ST. GREGORY (1863) Rev. Vincent E. Daily (Retired). In Res., Revs. Richard F. Clancy; Laurence J. Borges (Retired).
Res.: 2223 Dorchester Ave., Dorchester, 02124-5607. Tel: 617-298-2460; Fax: 617-298-9232. Email: stgregoryparish@gmail.com. Web: www.stgregoryparish.com.
*School—*2214 Dorchester Ave., Dorchester, 02124. Tel: 617-296-1210. Margaret Donovan, Prin. Lay Teachers 18; Students 225.
*Catechesis/Religious Program—*Elizabeth Labbe, D.R.E.

26—HOLY FAMILY (1995) Rt. Rev. John J. Ahern; Revs. Richard C. Conway, Parochial Vicar; Huy H. Nguyen, Parochial Vicar.
Mailing Address: 240 Adams St., Dorchester, 02122. Tel: 617-445-9553. Email: stpeterparishdorchester@gmail.com.
School—St. Kevin, 516 Columbia Rd., Dorchester, 02125. Tel: 617-825-3883. Sr. Paula Kelley, S.C.H., Prin.
*Catechesis/Religious Program—*336 Saratoga St., East Boston, 02128. Tel: 617-567-6509; Fax: 617-567-2561.

27—HOLY NAME (1927) Rev. Msgr. George F. Carlson; Rev. Oscar J. Pratt, Parochial Vicar; Fran M. Hauck, Pastoral Assoc. In Res., Very Rev. Richard M. Erikson.
Res.: 1689 Centre St., West Roxbury, 02132-1292. Tel: 617-325-4865; Fax: 617-325-5571. Email: holyname.parish@verizon.net. Web: www.holynameparish.com.
*School—*525 W. Roxbury Pkwy., West Roxbury, 02132-1292. Tel: 617-325-9338. Linda Workman, Prin. Sisters 2; Lay Teachers 40; Students 572.
*Convent—*525 W. Roxbury Pkwy., West Roxbury, 02132. Tel: 617-325-5089.

28—HOLY TRINITY (1844), (German), Rev. John J. Connolly, Admin.
Res.: 140 Shawmut Ave., Boston, 02118-2227. Tel: 617-426-6142; Fax: 617-426-5409. Email: htparish@aol.com. Web: www.holytrinitygerman.org.
*Catechesis/Religious Program—*Patti Strom, D.R.E.

29—ST. JAMES THE GREATER (1854) Very Rev. Kevin J. O'Leary, Admin.; Rev. Peter H. Shen (China), Parochial Vicar. In Res., Most Rev. Robert F. Hennessey; Rev. Joseph J. Baggetta.
Res. & Parish: 135 Harrison Ave., Boston, 02111. Tel: 617-542-8498; Fax: 617-542-2708. Email: bccc.stjames@gmail.com. Web: www.rc.net/boston/bccc-stjames.
*Catechesis/Religious Program—*Susan Ho, D.R.E.; Teresa Yuen, D.R.E.

30—ST. JOHN CHRYSOSTOM (1952) Rev. William S. Dunn; Sr. Maureen Taaffe, S.C.N., Pastoral Assoc.
Res.: 4740 Washington St., West Roxbury, 02132. Tel: 617-323-4410; Fax: 617-323-0423. Email: stjohnoffice1@msn.com. Web: www.stjohnchrysostom02132.org.
Catechesis/Religious Program—

31—ST. JOHN THE BAPTIST (1921), St. John the Baptist, East Boston was suppressed. This parish's records are located at Sacred Heart, Boston.

32—ST. JOHN-ST. HUGH (1901), St. John-St. Hugh was suppressed. This parish's records are located at St. Katherine Drexel, Boston.

33—ST. JOSEPH (1845), St. Joseph, Roxbury was suppressed. This parish's records are located at St. Patrick, Boston.

34—ST. JOSEPH (1862), St. Joseph, East Boston was suppressed. This parish's records are located at St. Joseph-St. Lazarus, Boston.

35—ST. JOSEPH (1938), St. Joseph, Hyde Park was suppressed. This parish's records are located at St. Angela Merici, Boston.

36—ST. JOSEPH (1862) Rev. Daniel C. O'Connell.
68 William Cardinal O'Connell Way, Boston, 02114-2709. Tel: 617-523-4342; Fax: 617-523-8459.

Email: st.josephs01@verizon.net. Web: www.stjosephboston.com. In Res., Rev. Robert P. Reed.
Catechesis/Religious Program—Denise Tompkins, D.R.E.

37—St. Joseph-St. Lazarus (1892) Rev. Miroslaw Kowalczyk, F.D.P.
Res.: 59 Ashley St., East Boston, 02128. Tel: 617-569-0406; Fax: 617-569-8212. Email: orioneparish@gmail.com.
School—St. Mary Star of the Sea, 58 Moore St., East Boston, 02128. Tel: 617-567-6609. Joan Lawrence, Prin.
Catechesis/Religious Program—Maria Zolla, D.R.E.

38—St. Kevin (1945), St. Kevin, Dorchester was suppressed. This parish's records are located at Holy Family, Boston.

39—St. Lazarus (1892), St. Lazarus, East Boston was suppressed. This parish's records are located at St. Joseph-St. Lazarus, Boston.

40—St. Leo (1902), St. Leo, Dorchester was suppressed. This parish's records are located at St. Angela Merici, Boston.

41—St. Leonard of Port Maurice (1873), (Italian), Revs. Antonio Nardoianni, O.F.M./I.C.; Claude Scrima, O.F.M./I.C., Parochial Vicar. In Res., Rev. Michael MacInnis, O.F.M./I.C.
Res.: 14 N. Bennett St., Boston, 02113-1913. Tel: 617-523-2110; Fax: 617-367-0456. Email: stleonardboston@gmail.com. Web: www.saintleonardchurchboston.org.
School—St. John, 9 Moon St., Boston, 02113-1913. Tel: 617-227-3143. Sr. Eileen Harvey, C.S.J., Prin.
Chapel—St. Mary 150 Endicott St., Boston, 02113.

42—St. Margaret (1893), St. Margaret, Dorchester was suppressed. This parish's records are located at Blessed Mother Teresa of Calcutta, Boston.

43—St. Mark (1905) Revs. Daniel J. Finn; Paschal Mugerwa (Uganda), Parochial Vicar; Sr. Helen Roberts, O.S.F., Pastoral Assoc.
Res.: 20 Roseland St., Dorchester, 02124. Tel: 617-825-2852; Fax: 617-825-0514. Email: judy.stmarks@comcast.net. Web: www.stmarkparish.com.
School—197 Centre Ave., Dorchester, 02124. Tel: 617-282-2577. Edward Butler, Prin. Sisters 7; Lay Teachers 15; Students 512.
Catechesis/Religious Program—Kathy Wall, D.R.E.; Mary Swanton, D.R.E.

44—St. Mary, St. Mary, North End was suppressed. This parish's records are located at St. Leonard of Port Maurice, Boston.

45—St. Mary (1828), St. Mary, Charlestown was suppressed. This parish's records are located at St. Mary - St. Catherine of Siena, Boston.

46—St. Mary - St. Catherine of Siena (2006) Rev. James J. Ronan; Sr. Nancy Citro, S.N.D., Pastoral Assoc. In Res., Revs. Jerome F. Gillespie; John P. Kearns.
Res.: 49 Vine St., Charlestown, 02129. Tel: 617-242-4664; Fax: 617-242-0016. Web: www.stmarystcatherine.org.
Catechesis/Religious Program—Sr. Kathleen Carven, S.C., D.R.E.

47—St. Mary of the Angels (1904) Rev. Alonso E. Macias (Mexico); Deacons Jesus M. Ortiz; Luciano Herrera; Ms. Jen Roy, Pastoral Assoc.
Res.: 377 Walnut Ave., Roxbury, 02119. Tel: 617-445-1524; Fax: 617-442-6455. Email: stmaryoftheangels@msn.com. Web: www.stmaryoftheangelsroxbury.org.
Catechesis/Religious Program—Tel: 617-524-0913.

48—St. Mary, Star of the Sea (1864), St. Mary Star of the Sea, East Boston was suppressed. This parish's records are located at St. Joseph-St. Lazarus, Boston.

49—St. Matthew (1900) Revs. William P. Joy; Jean Gabriel Charles (Haiti), Parochial Vicar.
Res.: 33 Stanton St., Dorchester, 02124-3716. Tel: 617-436-3590; Fax: 617-287-2741. Web: www.stmatthewdorchester.org.
School—29 Stanton St., Dorchester, 02124. Tel: 617-825-7955. Mary Lanata, Prin. Sisters 2; Lay Teachers 10; Students 247.
Catechesis/Religious Program—Josette Rameau, D.R.E.

50—St. Monica (1907), St. Monica, South Boston was suppressed. This parish's records are located at St. Monica and St. Augustine, Boston.

51—St. Monica-St. Augustine (1907) [CEM] Rev. Robert R. Kennedy.
Res.: 70 Devine Way, South Boston, 02127. Tel: 617-268-1230; Fax: 617-269-3831. Email: stmonicastaugustine@hotmail.com.

52—Most Holy Redeemer (1844) Rev. Thomas S. Domurat; Deacons Antonio M. Perea; Pedro LaTorre. Member Central Catholic School of East Boston. In Res., Rev. Alexander J. Keenan.
Res.: 65 London St., East Boston, 02128-1924. Tel: 617-567-3227; Fax: 617-569-6950.
See East Boston Central Catholic School under Sacred Heart, 69 London St., East Boston.
Catechesis/Religious Program—Angelina Monge, D.R.E.

53—Most Precious Blood (1880) Rev. Peter P. Nolan, C.S.Sp.
Res.: 43 Maple St., Hyde Park, 02136-2755. Tel: 617-364-9500; Fax: 617-364-2590. Email: ppnmpb@aol.com. Web: www.mostpreciousbloodhydepark.com.
Catechesis/Religious Program—Joseph Shaughnessy, D.R.E.

54—Our Lady of Czestochowa (1893), (Polish), Revs. Andrzej Urbaniak, O.F.M.Conv.; Wieslaw Ciemiega, O.F.M.Conv. (Poland), Parochial Vicar. In Res., Rev. Janusz Chmielecki, O.F.M.Conv.
Res.: 655 Dorchester Ave., South Boston, 02127. Tel: 617-268-4355; Fax: 617-268-4599. Email: parish@ourladyofczestochowa.com. Web: www.ourladyofsczestochowa.com.
Convent—666 Dorchester Ave., Boston, 02127.

55—Our Lady of Kazan, Our Lady of Kazan, South Boston was suppressed. This parish's records are located at St. Vincent de Paul, Boston.

56—Our Lady of Lourdes (1908) Rev. Alonso E. Macias (Mexico); Deacons Jesus M. Ortiz; Luciano Herrera.
97 South St., Jamaica Plain, 02130-2370.
Res.: 45 Brookside Ave., Jamaica Plain, 02130-2370. Tel: 617-524-0434; Fax: 617-524-1888. Email: ololjppastor@lourdes.comcastbiz.net. Web: www.ourladyoflourdesjpma.org.
School—54 Brookside Ave., Jamaica Plain, 02130. Tel: 617-524-6136. Janice C. Wilson, Prin. Sisters 2; Lay Teachers 10; Students 220.
Catechesis/Religious Program—Lourdes Ortiz, D.R.E.

57—Our Lady of Mt. Carmel (1905), (Italian), Our Lady of Mt. Carmel, East Boston was suppressed. This parish's records are located at Sacred Heart, Boston.

58—Our Lady of Ostrobrama, Our Lady of Ostrobrama, West End was suppressed. This parish's records are located at Archives, Boston.

59—Our Lady of Perpetual Help (1868) Revs. Raymond Collins, C.Ss.R.; Philip Dabney, C.Ss.R., Parochial Vicar; John Furey, C.Ss.R., Parochial Vicar. In Res., Revs. John C. Devin, C.Ss.R.; John J. Hennessey, C.Ss.R.; Philip A. Cabasino, C.Ss.R.; Denis Sweeney, C.Ss.R.
Res.: 1545 Tremont St., Boston, 02120-2909. Tel: 617-445-2600; Fax: 617-445-1857. Web: www.themissionchurchboston.com.
School—(Grades 1-6), 94 St. Alphonsus St., Boston, 02120. Tel: 617-442-2660. Maura Bradley, Prin. Sisters 4; Lay Teachers 3; Students 152.
Catechesis/Religious Program—Alyson Perry, D.R.E.

60—Our Lady of Pompeii, Our Lady of Pompeii, South End was suppressed. This parish's records are located at Archives, Boston.

61—Our Lady of the Assumption (1869) Rev. Oscar Martin Dominguez (NEW). Member East Boston Central Catholic School Consortium.
Res.: 404 Sumner St., East Boston, 02128. Tel: 617-567-1223. Email: olaboston@gmail.com.
See East Boston Central Catholic School under Sacred Heart, 69 London St., East Boston.

62—Our Lady of the Presentation (1909), Our Lady of the Presentation, Brighton was suppressed. This parish's records are located at St. Columbkille, Boston.

63—Our Lady of the Rosary, Our Lady of the Rosary, South Boston was suppressed. This parish's records are located at St. Vincent de Paul, Boston.

64—Our Lady of Victories (1880), (French), Revs. Joseph J. McLaughlin, S.M.; Philip E. Parent, S.M., Parochial Vicar. In Res., Revs. Gerard A. Demers, S.M.; Edward Sheehan, S.M. (Retired).
Res.: 27 Isabella St., Boston, 02116-5216. Tel: 617-426-4448; Fax: 617-426-1884. Email: olvbboston@yahoo.com. Web: www.olvboston.com.

65—St. Patrick (1836) Revs. Walter J. Waldron; Egidio Alves dos Santos (Cape Verde), Parochial Vicar; Carlos A. Lopez (Puerto Rico), Parochial Vicar; Sisters Gerard Ndagano, I.H.M.R., Pastoral Assoc.; Christine Smith, S.B.S., Pastoral Assoc.; Luisa Vasconcelos, F.I.C., Pastoral Assoc.; Maria Macedo, F.I.C., Pastoral Assoc.; Antonia Soares, F.I.C., Pastoral Assoc.; Laura Lopes, F.I.C., Pastoral Assoc. In Res., Rev. Russell W. Best.
Res.: 10 Magazine St., Roxbury, 02119-2706. Tel: 617-445-7645; Fax: 617-445-6166. Email: stpatrickrox@comcast.net.
School—131 Mt. Pleasant Ave., Roxbury, 02119. Tel: 617-427-3881. Mary Lanata, Prin. Religious Brother 1; Sisters 4; Lay Teachers 17; Students 251.

66—St. Paul (1907), St. Paul, Dorchester was suppressed. This parish's records are located at Holy Family, Boston.

67—St. Peter (1872) Rt. Rev. John J. Ahern; Revs. Richard C. Conway, Parochial Vicar; Huy H. Nguyen, Parochial Vicar.
Res.: 240 Adams St., Dorchester, 02122-1834. Tel: 617-265-1132; Fax: 617-265-0463. Email: stpeterparishdorchester@gmail.com.

68—St. Peter (1904), (Lithuanian), Rev. Stephen P. Zukas.
Res.: 50 Orton Marotta Way, South Boston, 02127-2006. Tel: 617-268-0353; Fax: 617-268-2585. Email: klebonas@me.com. Web: www.stpeterparishboston.com.
Catechesis/Religious Program—Mrs. Aldona Lingertat, D.R.E.; Mrs. Glorija Adonkaitis, D.R.E.

69—SS. Peter and Paul (1844), SS. Peter and Paul, South Boston was suppressed. This parish's records are located at St. Vincent de Paul, Boston.

70—St. Philip, St. Philip, Roxbury was suppressed. This parish's records are located at St. Katherine Drexel, Boston.

71—St. Richard, St. Richard, Roxbury was suppressed. This parish's records are located at St. Patrick, Boston.

72—Sacred Heart (1873) Very Rev. Wayne L. Belschner; Deacon Anthony J. Constantino. In Res., Rev. John R. McLaughlin.
Res.: 303 Paris St., East Boston, 02128-3063. Tel: 617-567-5776; Fax: 617-567-3042. Email: mtalluto@yahoo.com. Web: www.rc.net/boston/sacredhearteast.
School—East Boston Central Catholic School Consortium, 69 London St., East Boston, 02128. Tel: 617-567-7456. Mary Ann Manfredonia, Prin. Sisters 1; Lay Teachers 12; Students 229.
Catechesis/Religious Program—See Holy Family, Boston, Tel: 617-567-6509. Sharon A. Rozzi, D.R.E.

73—Sacred Heart (1888), (Italian), Sacred Heart, North End was suppressed. This parish's records are located at St. Leonard of Port Maurice, Boston.

74—Sacred Heart (1893) Rev. Msgr. Francis H. Kelley; Rev. John M. Mendicoa, Parochial Vicar; Mr. John Scanlon, Pastoral Assoc.; Ms. Kathy Sherrod, Pastoral Assoc.
Res.: 169 Cummins Hwy., Roslindale, 02131-3739. Tel: 617-325-3322; Fax: 617-325-2145. Email: sacredheartparish@sh-roslindale.org. Web: www.sh-roslindale.org.
School—1035 Canterbury St., Roslindale, 02131. Tel: 617-323-2500. Sr. Gail Ripley, C.S.J., Prin. Sisters 2; Lay Teachers 15; Students 464.
Catechesis/Religious Program—Caroline Quiles, D.R.E.

75—St. Stephen Rev. Msgr. Timothy F. O'Leary (Wales), Admin.
24 Clark St., Boston, 02109-9923. Tel: 617-523-1230; Fax: 617-723-7389. Email: info@socstjames.com. In Res., Rev. Patrick J. Universal (Retired).

76—St. Stephen, St. Stephen, North End was suppressed. This parish's records are located at St. Leonard of Port Maurice, Boston.

77—St. Theresa of Avila (1895) Rev. Msgr. William M. Helmick; Rev. Richard S. Bradford, Parochial Vicar; Sr. Virginia Kelleher, C.S.J., Pastoral Assoc. In Res., Most Rev. Emilio S. Allue, S.D.B.; Rev. Raymond G. Helmick, S.J.
Res.: 10 St. Theresa Ave., West Roxbury, 02132-3416. Tel: 617-325-1300; Fax: 617-325-0380. Email: sttheresarectory@msn.com. Web: www.rc.net/boston/st_theresa.
School—40 St. Theresa Ave., West Roxbury, 02132. Tel: 617-323-1050. Jane Gibbons, Prin. Sisters 2; Lay Teachers 20; Students 589.
Catechesis/Religious Program—Ann Barden, D.R.E.; Diane Flynn, D.R.E.; Jennifer McKiernan, D.R.E.
Convent—20 Pine Lodge Rd., West Roxbury, 02132. Tel: 617-325-9171.

78—St. Thomas Aquinas (1869) Rev. Alonso E. Macias (Mexico); Deacons Jesus M. Ortiz; Luciano Herrera.
Res.: 97 South St., Jamaica Plain, 02130. Tel: 617-524-0240; Fax: 866-339-5148. Email: stthosq@comcast.net.
Catechesis/Religious Program—Ms. Nancy Thompson, D.R.E.

79—St. Vincent de Paul (1872) Rev. Joseph M. White; Ms. Nicole Feeley, Pastoral Assoc.
Res.: 363 E St., South Boston, 02127. Tel: 617-268-8100; Fax: 617-268-1277. Email: stvincentdepaul@comcast.net. Web: www.stvincentdepaulparish.org.

80—St. William (1909), St. William, Dorchester was suppressed. This parish's records are located at Blessed Mother Teresa of Calcutta, Boston.

OUTSIDE THE CITY OF BOSTON

Abington, Plymouth Co.

1—St. Bridget (1863) [JC] Revs. James M. Mahoney; Tamiru F. Atraga, Parochial Vicar; Deacon James V. McLaughlin. In Res., Rev. Joseph G. Arsenault.
Res.: 455 Plymouth St., 02351-1889. Tel: 781-878-0900; Fax: 781-878-6566. Web:

www.rc.net/boston/saintbridget/.
School—Joseph F. Cirigliano, Prin. Lay Teachers 11; Students 249.
Catechesis/Religious Program—Tel: 781-878-5950. Anne Fennell, D.R.E.

2—ST. NICHOLAS (1964), St. Nicholas, Abington was suppressed. This parish's records are located at St. Edith Stein, Brockton.

ACTON, MIDDLESEX CO., ST. ELIZABETH OF HUNGARY (1945) Rev. Walter J. Woods; Mr. Stephen J. Ryan, Pastoral Assoc.
Res.: 89 Arlington St., 01720-2503. Tel: 978-263-4305; Fax: 978-263-9014. Email: office@seoh.org. Web: www.seoh.org.
Catechesis/Religious Program—Barbara M. Dane, D.R.E.; Cindy K. Harrington, D.R.E.; Mr. James Flanagan, D.R.E.

AMESBURY, ESSEX CO.

1—HOLY FAMILY (1998) [CEM] Revs. Louis R. Palmieri; Michael J. Farrell, Parochial Vicar; Deacon Raymond E. Doucette.
Office & Rectory: 9 Sparhawk St., 01913. Tel: 978-388-0330; Fax: 978-388-8840. Email: parishoffice@hfamesbury.com. Web: www.hfamesbury.com.
Catechesis/Religious Program—Tel: 978-388-3477. Doreen A. Keller, D.R.E.

2—ST. JOSEPH, St. Joseph, Amesbury was suppressed. This parish's records are located at Holy Family, Amesbury.

3—SACRED HEART, Sacred Heart, Amesbury was suppressed. This parish's records are located at Holy Family, Amesbury.

ANDOVER, ESSEX CO.

1—ST. AUGUSTINE (1866) [CEM] Revs. Peter G. Gori, O.S.A.; Richard T. O'Leary, O.S.A., Parochial Vicar. In Res., Revs. Fritz J. Cerullo, O.S.A.; Richard L. Foley, O.S.A.
Res.: 43 Essex St., 01810-3748. Tel: 978-475-0050; Fax: 978-475-3078. Email: info@staugustineparish.org. Web: www.staugustineparish.org.
School—26 Central St., 01810. Tel: 978-475-2414. Ann Kendall, Prin. Sisters 1; Lay Teachers 28; Students 493.
Catechesis/Religious Program—Tel: 978-475-7612; Fax: 978-475-9825. Bridget Rao, D.R.E.
Mission—St. Joseph's (1881) Ballardville.
Convent—Sisters of Notre Dame, 47 Essex St., Essex Co. 01810. Tel: 978-475-0087.

2—ST. ROBERT BELLARMINE (1961) Rev. Richard T. Conway.
Res.: 198 Haggetts Pond Rd., 01810-4218. Tel: 978-683-8922; Fax: 978-689-8878. Web: www.saintroberts.net.
Catechesis/Religious Program—Amanda Roberts, D.R.E.

ARLINGTON, MIDDLESEX CO.

1—SAINT AGNES (1872) Revs. Brian M. Flatley; John J. Graham, Parochial Vicar.
Res.: 51 Medford St., 02474-3197. Tel: 781-648-0220; Fax: 781-643-7883. Email: parish@saintagnes.net. Web: www.saintagnes.net.
School—39 Medford St., 02474. Tel: 781-643-9031. Sr. Patricia Randall, R.S.M., Prin. Religious 3; Lay Teachers 20; Students 400.
High School—Arlington Catholic High School, 16 Medford St., 02474. Tel: 781-646-7770. Stephen J. Biagioni, Prin. Religious 10; Lay Teachers 40; Students 800.
Catechesis/Religious Program—Tel: 781-646-5579. Ms. Joyce Patriacca, D.R.E.

2—ST. CAMILLUS (1950) Rev. James E. O'Leary. In Res., Revs. Robert M. O'Grady; Joseph F. Byrne (Retired).
Res.: 1175 Concord Tpke., 02476-7262. Tel: 781-643-3132; Fax: 781-643-8228. Email: stcamillus@verizon.net.
Catechesis/Religious Program—Catherine Robinson, D.R.E.; John Flahery, D.R.E.

3—ST. JAMES THE APOSTLE (1914), St. James the Apostle, Arlington was suppressed. This parish's records are located at St. Camillus, Arlington.

4—ST. JEROME (1934), St. Jerome, Arlington was suppressed. This parish's records are located at St. Agnes, Arlington.

ASHLAND, MIDDLESEX CO., ST. CECILIA (1885) Rev. Richard P. Cornell.
Res.: 54 Esty St., 01721-2126. Tel: 508-881-1107; Fax: 508-881-8606. Email: business.stcecilia@comcast.net. Web: www.saintcecilia.org.
Catechesis/Religious Program—Tel: 508-881-6107. Janet Wilkinson, D.R.E.; Jason Giombetti, D.R.E.

AVON, NORFOLK CO., ST. MICHAEL (1908) [CEM] Rev. Thomas C. Boudreau.
Res.: 87 N. Main St., 02322-1286. Tel: 508-586-7210; Fax: 508-586-7211. Email: stmichaelavon@comcast.net.
Catechesis/Religious Program—Carol Prance, D.R.E.

AYER, MIDDLESEX CO., ST. MARY (1858) [CEM] Rev. Edmond M. Derosier; Sr. Joan Guertin, S.U.S.C., Pastoral Assoc.
31 Shirley St., 01432-1219. Tel: 978-772-2414; Fax: 978-772-0727. Email: office@stmarysayer.net. Web: www.stmarysayer.org.
Catechesis/Religious Program—

BEDFORD, MIDDLESEX CO., ST. MICHAEL (1931) Rev. Mark S. Sheehan. In Res., Rev. Isaac Ebo Mensah (Ghana).
Res.: 90 Concord Rd., 01730. Tel: 781-275-6318; Fax: 781-271-9879. Email: office@saintmichaelparishbedford.org. Web: www.saintmichaelparishbedford.org.
Catechesis/Religious Program—Tel: 781-275-6324; Fax: 781-271-0133. Patricia Marks, D.R.E.

BELLINGHAM, NORFOLK CO.

1—ASSUMPTION (1927), Assumption, Bellingham was suppressed. This parish's records are located at St. Blaise, Bellingham.

2—ST. BLAISE (1962) Rev. Albert M. Faretra.
Res. & Office: 1158 Main St., 02019-1597. Tel: 508-966-1258; Fax: 508-966-0310. Web: www.saintblaise.org.
Catechesis/Religious Program—Cheryl Langevin, D.R.E.

3—ST. BRENDAN (1945) Rev. David J. Mullen; Senior Deacon Robert T. Hackett.
Res.: 384 Hartford Ave., 02019-1217. Tel: 508-966-0260; Fax: 508-966-4404. Email: fr.mullen.saintbrendan@verizon.net. Web: www.saintbrendansparish.org.
Catechesis/Religious Program—Gladys Griffin, D.R.E.

BELMONT, MIDDLESEX CO.

1—ST. JOSEPH (1900) Rev. Thomas A. Mahoney.
Res.: 345 Waverley St., 02478-2418. Tel: 617-484-0279; Fax: 617-489-5423. Email: frfaretra@stjoseph.belmont.ma.us. Web: www.stjoseph.belmont.ma.us.
Catechesis/Religious Program—Tel: 617-484-1770. Ann Marie Mahoney, C.R.E.

2—ST. LUKE (1919) Rev. Gerard Petringa; Sr. Kathleen Moran, C.S.J., Pastoral Assoc.
Res.: 132 Lexington St., 02478. Tel: 617-484-1996; Fax: 617-484-7831. Email: stlukebelmont@verizon.net. Web: www.stlukesbelmont.org.
Catechesis/Religious Program—Tel: 617-484-9357. Robert Flaherty, D.R.E.

3—OUR LADY OF MERCY (1926), Our Lady of Mercy, Belmont was suppressed. This parish's records are located at St. Luke, Belmont.

BEVERLY, ESSEX CO.

1—ST. ALPHONSUS (1917), St. Alphonsus, Beverly was suppressed. This parish's records are located at St. Mary Star of the Sea, Beverly.

2—ST. JOHN THE EVANGELIST (1955) Rev. Msgr. William F. Cuddy, Admin.
Res.: 552 Cabot St., 01915. Tel: 978-922-5542; Fax: 978-921-4563. Email: stjohnrc@parishmail.com. Web: www.stjohnchurchbeverly.com.
School—111 New Balch St., 01915. Tel: 978-922-0048. Karen P. McCarthy, Prin.
Catechesis/Religious Program—Jean Sword, D.R.E. (Elem. School); Jude Odimone Milan, D.R.E. (High School).

3—ST. MARGARET (1905) Revs. David J. Barnes, Admin.; Ixon Chateau, Parochial Vicar.
Res.: 672 Hale St., 01915-2119. Tel: 978-927-0069; Fax: 978-927-9359. Email: casstmargbf@comcast.net.
Catechesis/Religious Program—Miss Mary Murray, D.R.E.

4—ST. MARY STAR OF THE SEA (1870) Revs. David J. Barnes; Ixon Chateau, Parochial Vicar.
Res.: 253 Cabot St., 01915-4597. Tel: 978-922-0113; Fax: 978-922-8501. Web: www.stmarystar.org.
School—13 Chapman St., 01915. Tel: 978-927-3259. Patricia Diglio, Prin.
Catechesis/Religious Program—Christine O'Brien, D.R.E.
Convent—St. Mary, 15 Chapman St., 01915-4597.

BILLERICA, MIDDLESEX CO.

1—ST. ANDREW (1868) Rev. James T. Kelly; Ms. Adrienne Cullen, Pastoral Assoc.
Res.: 45 Talbot Ave., 01862-1414. Tel: 978-663-3624; Fax: 978-670-1433. Email: pastor@saintandrewbillericacom. Web: www.saintandrewbillerica.com.
Catechesis/Religious Program—Tel: 978-667-9024. Ann Marie Huff, D.R.E.

2—ST. MARY (1937) Rev. Francis E. Sullivan; Deacon Allan R. Shanahan.
Res.: 796 Boston Rd., 01821. Tel: 978-663-2215; Fax: 978-663-0127. Email: parish@stmarybillerica.com. Web: www.stmarybillerica.com.
Catechesis/Religious Program—Roberta Breen, D.R.E.; James J. Spinale, D.R.E.

3—ST. THERESA OF LISIEUX (1945) Revs. Shawn W. Allen; F. Augustin Anda Gomez, Parochial Vicar; Deacon Phillip T. DiBello. In Res., Rev. John J. McCormick (Retired).
Res.: One Grace Ave., 01821-2504. Tel: 978-663-8816; Fax: 978-663-0577. Email: rectory_parish@sttheresaparishbillerica.com. Web: www.sttheresaparishbillerica.com.
Catechesis/Religious Program—Stephanie Tuzzolo, D.R.E.; Lorraine Ronan, D.R.E.; Theresa Grejdus, D.R.E.; Carol Roncari, D.R.E.

BRAINTREE, NORFOLK CO.

1—ST. CLARE (1959) Rev. Paul S. Sughrue; Deacon Michael J. Cavanaugh.
Res.: 1244 Liberty St., 02184-8299. Tel: 781-848-7480; Fax: 781-356-8380. Email: stclare1@verizon.net.
Catechesis/Religious Program—Tel: 781-848-7481. Gilbert Capone, D.R.E.

2—ST. FRANCIS OF ASSISI (1903) Very Rev. Kevin M. Sepe; Rev. Gregory G. Vozzo, Parochial Vicar; Linda M. Muldoon, Pastoral Assoc. In Res., Very Rev. Mark O'Connell.
Res.: 856 Washington St., 02184-6464. Tel: 781-843-1332; Fax: 781-848-0976. Email: parish@sfab.org. Web: www.sfab.org.
School—850 Washington St., 02184. Tel: 781-848-0842. Victoria DeBenedictis, Prin.
Catechesis/Religious Program—Margaret L. Donaher, D.R.E.

3—ST. THOMAS MORE (1938) Rev. James J. McCarthy; Ms. Janelle Snarsky, Pastoral Assoc.
Res.: 8 Hawthorn Rd., 02184-1402. Tel: 781-843-1980; Fax: 781-843-7110. Web: www.stmparish.org.
Catechesis/Religious Program—Tel: 781-843-2142. Anne Vail, D.R.E.; Jerry Hubbard, D.R.E.

BRIDGEWATER, PLYMOUTH CO., ST. THOMAS AQUINAS (1848) [CEM] Revs. William D. Devine; John A. D'Arpino, Parochial Vicar; Deacon Gerald P. Ryan.
Res.: 103 Center St., 02324-1397. Tel: 508-697-9528; Fax: 508-279-1859. Email: stthomasaquinas@comcast.net. Web: www.stthomasaquinas.com.
Catechesis/Religious Program—Tel: 508-697-3652; Fax: 508-697-8907. Ms. Francine Bell, D.R.E.

BROCKTON, PLYMOUTH CO.

1—ST. CASIMIR (1898), (Lithuanian), Unassigned.
Res.: 21 Sawtell Ave., 02302. Tel: 508-586-2226; Fax: 508-559-2761.

2—CHRIST THE KING (2004) Very Rev. Joseph K. Raeke; Revs. Arlin Jean-Louis, O.M.I., Parochial Vicar; Carlos D. Suarez, Parochial Vicar; Sr. Alice M. Arsenault, S.U.S.C., Pastoral Assoc.; Deacons Philip H. LaFond; Christopher Z. Connelly.
Res.: 71 E. Main St., 02302-3122. Tel: 508-586-1575; Fax: 508-586-9393. Web: www.ctkp.org.
Catechesis/Religious Program—Judy A. Sullivan, D.R.E.; Joseph Sanon, D.R.E.
Convent—45 Erie Ave., 02302. Tel: 508-559-7642.

3—ST. COLMAN OF CLOYNE (2004), St. Colman of Cloyne, Brockton was suppressed. This parish's records are located at Christ the King, Brockton.

4—ST. EDITH STEIN (2003) Very Rev. Joseph K. Raeke; Revs. Carlos D. Suarez, Parochial Vicar; Egidio Alves dos Santos (Cape Verde), Parochial Vicar; Deacons Christopher Z. Connelly; Philip H. LaFond; Sisters Eugenia DaSilva, F.I.C., Pastoral Assoc.; Djai, Pastoral Assoc.
Res.: 71 E. Main St., 02301-2461. Tel: 508-586-6491; Fax: 508-587-1796. Email: saintedithstein@gmail.com. Web: www.stedithsteinparish.org.
Catechesis/Religious Program—Tel: 508-588-7032. Mary Ann Yezukevich, D.R.E.

5—ST. EDWARD (1897), St. Edward, Brockton was suppressed. This parish's records are located at St. Edith Stein, Brockton.

6—ST. MARGARET (1902), St. Margaret, Brockton was suppressed. This parish's records are located at Our Lady of Lourdes, Brockton.

7—OUR LADY OF LOURDES (1931) Very Rev. Joseph K. Raeke; Rev. Carlos D. Suarez, Parochial Vicar; Deacon Christopher Z. Connelly; Ms. Jeanne Lafond, Pastoral Assoc.
439 West St., 02301. Tel: 508-586-4715; Fax: 508-584-6257. Email: our.loudes@comcast.net. Web: ourladyoflourdes-brockton.com.

8—OUR LADY OF OSTROBRAMA (1914), Our Lady of Ostrobrama, Brockton was suppressed. This parish's records are located at St. Edith Stein, Brockton.

9—ST. PATRICK (1856) Rev. Jose M. Abalon (NEW).
Res.: 335 Main St., 02301-5396. Tel: 508-586-4840; Fax: 508-941-0639. Email: stpatrickbrockton@yahoo.com.

10—SACRED HEART (1891), Sacred Heart, Brockton was suppressed. This parish's records are located at Christ the King, Brockton.

BROOKLINE, NORFOLK CO.

1—ST. AIDAN (1911), St. Aidan, Brookline was suppressed. This parish's records are located at St. Mary of the Assumption, Brookline.

2—INFANT JESUS (1938), Infant Jesus, Brookline was

suppressed. This parish's records are located at St. Mary of the Assumption, Brookline.

3—INFANT JESUS-ST. LAWRENCE (Chestnut Hill) (1999), Infant Jesus-St. Lawrence, Brookline was suppressed. This parish's records are located at St. Mary of the Assumption, Brookline.

4—ST. LAWRENCE (1898), St. Lawrence, Brookline was suppressed. This parish's records are located at St. Mary of the Assumption, Brookline.

5—ST. MARY OF THE ASSUMPTION (1852) Very Rev. Brian M. Clary; Rev. Robert J. Congdon, Parochial Vicar; Deacon James A. Manzi.
Res.: 5 Linden Pl., 02445-7311. Tel: 617-734-0444; Fax: 617-734-3001. Web: www.stmarybrookline.com.
School—67 Harvard St., 02445. Tel: 617-566-7184. Maureen Jutras, Prin.
Catechesis/Religious Program—Julianne J. Shanklis, D.R.E.

BURLINGTON, MIDDLESEX CO.

1—ST. MALACHY (1964) Rev. John M. Capuci.
Res.: 99 Bedford St., 01803. Tel: 781-272-5111; Fax: 781-270-9407. Email: office@saint-malachy.org. Web: www.saint-malachy.org.
Catechesis/Religious Program—Donald P. Nealon, D.R.E.; Susan Hurton, D.R.E.; Ms. Anna Molettieri, D.R.E.

2—ST. MARGARET (1945) Rev. Joseph P. Robinson; Deacon Richard F. Bilotta.
Res.: 111 Winn St., 01803. Tel: 781-272-3111; Fax: 781-272-9204. Email: tinapeg2@verizon.net. Web: www.saintmargaretschurch.net.
Catechesis/Religious Program—Tel: 781-935-7373. Mary Murgo, D.R.E.

CAMBRIDGE, MIDDLESEX CO.

1—ST. ANTHONY OF PADUA (1902), (Portuguese), Very Rev. Walter A. Carreiro; Rev. James M. Achadinha, Parochial Vicar. In Res., Revs. Cristiano G. Borro Barbosa (Brazil); Leonel V. Batista (Portugal).
Res.: 400 Cardinal Medeiros Ave., 02141-1411. Tel: 617-547-5593; Fax: 617-547-1505. Email: stanthony.camb@verizon.net. Web: www.stanthony-cambridge.com.
Catechesis/Religious Program—Mariazinha Sousa, D.R.E.

2—BLESSED SACRAMENT (1905), Blessed Sacrament, Cambridge was suppressed. This parish's records are located at St. Mary of the Annunciation, Cambridge.

3—ST. FRANCIS OF ASSISI (1917), (Italian), Rev. Norbert DeAmato, O.F.M. (Retired); Ms. Joan DeGuglielmo, Pastoral Assoc.
Res.: 42 Sciarappa St., 02141. Tel: 617-876-6754; Fax: 617-876-6753. Email: st_francis_42@yahoo.com.

4—ST. HEDWIG (1907), St. Hedwig, Cambridge was suppressed. This parish's records are located at Archives, Boston.

5—IMMACULATE CONCEPTION (1910), (Lithuanian), Immaculate Conception, Cambridge was suppressed. This parish's records are located at Sacred Heart, Cambridge.

6—IMMACULATE CONCEPTION (1926), Immaculate Conception, Cambridge was suppressed. This parish's records are located at St. John the Evangelist, Cambridge.

7—ST. JOHN THE EVANGELIST (1893) Revs. Charles E. Collins; Arlin Jean-Louis, O.M.I., Parochial Vicar; Deacon Alfred J. Geneus. In Res., Revs. Robert E. Nee (Retired); Thomas L. Leclerc, M.S.
Res.: 2254 Massachusetts Ave., 02140-1837. Tel: 617-547-4880; Fax: 617-441-8028. Email: info@stjohncambridge.org. Web: www.stjohncambridge.org.
Catechesis/Religious Program—Maureen Megnia, D.R.E.

8—ST. MARY OF THE ANNUNCIATION (1867) Revs. Gabriel Troy; James C. Butts, S.D.V., Parochial Vicar; Deacon Stanley A. Straub.
Res.: 134 Norfolk St., 02139. Tel: 617-547-0120; Fax: 617-547-0232. Email: parishinfo@stmaryoftheannunciation.com. Web: www.stmaryoftheannunciation.com.
Catechesis/Religious Program—Tel: 617-547-0145. Maria Bermudez, D.R.E.

9—OUR LADY OF PITY (1892), Our Lady of Pity, Cambridge was suppressed. This parish's records are located at St. John the Evangelist, Cambridge.

10—ST. PATRICK (1908), St. Patrick, Cambridge was suppressed. This parish's records are located at Sacred Heart, Cambridge.

11—ST. PAUL (1875) Revs. Michael E. Drea; James W. Savage, Parochial Vicar. In Res., Revs. Matthew J. Westcott; George S. Salzmann, O.S.F.S.
Res.: 29 Mt. Auburn St., 02138-6097. Tel: 617-491-8400; Fax: 617-354-7092. Email: info@stpaulparish.org. Web: www.stpaulparish.org.
School—Boston Archdiocesan Choir School, Tel: 617-868-8658. Jennine D. Zito, Prin.
Catechesis/Religious Program—Ms. Patty Lee, D.R.E.

12—ST. PETER (1848) Rev. Leonard F. O'Malley; Deacon Thomas L. O'Donnell; Ms. Anna Molettieri, Pastoral Assoc.
Res.: 31 Buckingham St., 02138-2297. Tel: 617-547-4235; Fax: 617-547-1525. Email: office@saintpetercambridge.org. Web: www.saintpetercambridge.org.
School—96 Concord Ave., 02138. Tel: 617-547-0101. Mrs. Mary Jo Keaney, Prin. Sisters 5; Lay Teachers 7; Students 201.
Catechesis/Religious Program—Kathryn Smith, D.R.E.

13—SACRED HEART (1842) Rev. John P. Tackney.
Res.: 49 Sixth St., 02141-1594. Tel: 617-547-0399; Fax: 617-441-8648. Email: sacredheartofj@msn.com.
Catechesis/Religious Program—

CANTON, NORFOLK CO.

1—ST. GERARD MAJELLA (1960) Rev. John L. Sullivan; Ms. Ellie George, Pastoral Assoc.
Res.: 1860 Washington St., 02021. Tel: 781-828-3420; Fax: 781-828-2520. Email: welcome@saintgerard.org. Web: www.saintgerard.org.
Catechesis/Religious Program—Eleanor George, D.R.E.

2—ST. JOHN THE EVANGELIST (1861) Rev. Michael F. McLellan. In Res., Rev. Msgr. Charles J. Bourque (Retired); Rev. John F. Reardon.
Res.: 700 Washington St., 02021-3036. Tel: 781-828-0090; Fax: 781-828-2480. Web: www.stjohncanton.org.
School—696 Washington St., 02021-3036. Tel: 781-828-2130. Charlotte Kelly, Prin. Sisters 1; Lay Teachers 25; Students 261.
Catechesis/Religious Program—Tel: 781-828-5130. Mrs. Lorraine M. Wright, D.R.E.

CARLISLE, MIDDLESEX CO., ST. IRENE (1960) Revs. Thomas P. Donohoe; Romain Rurangirwa (Rowanda), Parochial Vicar; Deacons Dean C. Bulpett; Charles A. Ferraro.
Res.: 187 East St., 01741-1104. Tel: 978-369-3940; Fax: 978-287-1440. Email: stirene@comcast.net. Web: www.stirenes.org.
Catechesis/Religious Program—Georgia Winfrey, D.R.E.

CARVER, PLYMOUTH CO., OUR LADY OF LOURDES (1950) Rev. Anthony J. Medairos; Deacon Paul D. Coughlin. Parish Office: 130 Main St., 02330-0068. Tel: 508-866-4000; Fax: 508-866-5588. Email: ololcarver@comcast.net. Web: www.ourladyoflourdescarver.parishesonline.com.
Catechesis/Religious Program—Tel: 508-866-9211. Linda Cedrone, D.R.E.

CHELMSFORD, MIDDLESEX CO.

1—ST. JOHN THE EVANGELIST (1893) Very Rev. Paul E. Ritt; Rev. Richard G. Curran, Parochial Vicar. In Res., Rev. Francis B. Leonard (Retired).
Res.: 115 Middlesex St., 01863-2030. Tel: 978-251-8571; Fax: 978-251-7873. Email: sje.church@parishmail.com. Web: www.saintjhonchelmsford.org.
Catechesis/Religious Program—Tel: 978-251-4310. Ms. Debra Anderson, D.R.E.

2—ST. MARY (1931) Revs. Stephen S. Donohoe; Thomas B. Corcoran, Parochial Vicar.
Res.: 25 North Rd., 01824-2767. Tel: 978-256-2374; Fax: 978-256-0122. Web: www.saint-mary.org.
Catechesis/Religious Program—Ms. Heather Hannaway, D.R.E.

CHELSEA, SUFFOLK CO.

1—OUR LADY OF GRACE (1913) Very Rev. James J. Barry; Ms. Linda DeCristoforo, Pastoral Assoc.
Res.: 59 Nichols St., 02150-1225. Tel: 617-884-0030; Fax: 617-884-0957. Email: ologparish@comcast.net. Web: www.olgp.net.
Catechesis/Religious Program—Fax: 617-884-2482. Sr. Kathy Stark, D.R.E.

2—OUR LADY OF THE ASSUMPTION (1907), Our Lady of the Assumption, Chelsea was suppressed. This parish's records are located at Saint Rose of Lima, Chelsea.

3—ST. ROSE OF LIMA (1849) Very Rev. Terence J. Moran; Revs. Succes Jeanty (Mexico), Parochial Vicar; Cao Xuan Thanh, C.M.C., Parochial Vicar; Sr. Orquidea Sosa, H.M.C.J., Pastoral Assoc.; Deacons Luis F. Rivera; Alejandro Iraola.
Res.: 601 Broadway, 02150-2998. Tel: 617-889-2774; Fax: 617-889-2854. Email: strosechelsea@hotmail.com.
School—580 Broadway, 02150-2998. Tel: 617-884-2626. Mary Ann Babineau, Prin. Sisters 8; Lay Teachers 10; Students 423.
Catechesis/Religious Program—Marie Horgan, D.R.E. (English); Sor Ynocencia, D.R.E. (Spanish); Danha Nguyen, D.R.E. (Vietnamese).

4—ST. STANISLAUS (1905), (Polish), Rev. Andrew T. Grelak.
Res.: 163 Chestnut St., 02150. Tel: 617-889-0261; Fax: 617-466-2107. Email: stanislaus61@comcast.com.

COHASSET, NORFOLK CO., ST. ANTHONY OF PADUA (1886) Rev. John R. Mulvehill; Deacon Paul S. Rooney.
Res.: 129 S. Main St., 02025. Tel: 781-383-0219; Fax: 781-383-2988 (Rectory). Email: stanthonycoh@aol.com. Web: www.saintanthonycohasset.org.
Catechesis/Religious Program—Tel: 781-383-0630. Virginia Macleod, D.R.E.

CONCORD, MIDDLESEX CO.

1—ST. BERNARD (1863), St. Bernard, Concord was suppressed. This parish's records are located at Holy Family, Concord.

2—HOLY FAMILY (2004) Rev. Austin H. Fleming; Deacons Charles I. Clough; Gregory J. Burch; Sr. Rose Marie Lipke, C.D.P., Pastoral Assoc.
Res.: 70 Monument Sq., 01742. Tel: 978-369-7442; Fax: 978-371-0853. Email: holyfamily@holyfamilyconcord.org. Web: www.holyfamilyconcord.org.
Catechesis/Religious Program—Sandra Meuller, D.R.E.; Helen Cushman, D.R.E.

3—OUR LADY HELP OF CHRISTIANS (1907), Our Lady Help of Christians, Concord was suppressed. This parish's records are located at Holy Family, Concord.

DANVERS, ESSEX CO.

1—ST. MARY OF THE ANNUNCIATION (1871) [CEM] Rev. Gerard L. Dorgan; Mr. Dominic Margaglione, Pastoral Assoc. In Res., Rev. Msgr. Frederick J. Murphy (Retired).
Res.: 24 Conant St., 01923-2968. Tel: 978-774-0340; Fax: 978-774-9407. Email: stmarydanvers@comcast.net. Web: www.stmarychurchdanvers.org.
School—14 Otis St., 01923. Tel: 978-774-0307. Molly Kelley, Prin.
Catechesis/Religious Program—Tel: 978-774-8605. John J. Dillon, D.R.E.; Judy DiGennaro, D.R.E.

2—ST. RICHARD OF CHICHESTER (1963) Rev. Bruce G. Flannagan; Deacon Edward P. Elibero.
Res.: 90 Forest St., 01923-1806. Tel: 978-774-7575; Fax: 978-774-9543. Web: www.stricharddanvers.org.
School—St. Mary of the Annunciation School, 20 Otis St., 01923-1806. Tel: 978-774-0307. Molly Kelley, Prin.
Catechesis/Religious Program—Doreen Verda, D.R.E.

DEDHAM, NORFOLK CO.

1—ST. MARY (1866) [CEM] Revs. William T. Kelly; Paul V. Sullivan, Parochial Vicar; Deacon Louis W. Sheedy; Sr. Barbara Lavin, O.P., Pastoral Assoc. In Res., Revs. Joseph F. Mozer Jr.; Michael C. Harrington.
Res.: 420 High St., 02026-2892. Tel: 781-326-0550; Fax: 781-326-1809. Email: secretary@stmaryonline.net. Web: www.stmaryonline.net.
Catechesis/Religious Program—Tel: 781-329-5488. Sr. Anne Michael Hannigan, S.N.D., D.R.E.

2—ST. SUSANNA (1960) Rev. Stephen S. Josoma; Deacon Laurence J. Bloom; Ms. Mary Scanlon, Pastoral Assoc.
Res.: 262 Needham St., 02026-7009. Tel: 781-329-9575; Fax: 781-329-5966. Email: saintsusanna@hotmail.com. Web: www.saintsusanna.org.
Catechesis/Religious Program—Nancy Leoncini, D.R.E.

DOVER, NORFOLK CO., MOST PRECIOUS BLOOD (1959) Very Rev. John J. Grimes.
30 Centre St., 02030-0812. Tel: 508-785-0305; Fax: 508-785-0432. Email: mpb.dover@verizon.net. Web: www.mostpreciousbloodchurch.org.
Catechesis/Religious Program—Tel: 508-785-9909 (Grades 6-12); 508-785-1217. Ann Carroll, D.R.E. (Grades 1-5); Regina O'Connor, D.R.E. (Grades 6-12).

DRACUT, MIDDLESEX CO.

1—ST. FRANCIS OF ASSISI (1963) Very Rev. Brian E. Mahoney; Deacon John C. Hunt; Ms. Kathleen Long, Pastoral Assoc. Tel: 978-453-4460.
Parish Office: 115 Wheeler Rd., 01826-4254. Tel: 978-452-6611; Fax: 978-452-0772. Web: www.saintfrancis.net.
Catechesis/Religious Program—

2—STE. MARGUERITE D'YOUVILLE (2001) Revs. Marc J. Bishop; Garcia Breneville (Haiti), Parochial Vicar; Deacon Everett F. Penney; Ms. Joan Donnelly, Pastoral Assoc.
Res.: 158 Mammoth Rd., Lowell, 01854. Tel: 978-957-0322; Fax: 978-957-5266. Email: stmar@comcast.net. Web: www.stmar.org.
School—St. Louis, 77 Boisvert St., Lowell, 01850. Tel: 978-458-7594. Sr. Irene Martineau, S.A.S.V., Prin.
Convent—85 Boisvert St., Lowell, 01850. Tel: 978-454-5742.

3—ST. MARY OF THE ASSUMPTION (1909), St. Mary of the Assumption, Dracut was suppressed. This parish's records are located at St. Marguerite d'Youville, Dracut.

4—ST. THERESE (1927), St. Therese, Dracut was suppressed. This parish's records are located at St.

Marguerite d'Youville, Dracut.

DUXBURY, PLYMOUTH CO., HOLY FAMILY (1945) Revs. Robert J. Deehan; Sean M. Maher, Parochial Vicar; Deacons Arthur J. Keefe; Daniel R. Burns.
Church: 601 Tremont St., 02332-4450. Tel: 781-934-5055; Fax: 781-934-5796. Email: office@holyfamilyduxbury.org. Web: www.holyfamilyduxbury.org.
Catechesis/Religious Program—Tel: 781-934-6839. Mrs. Catherine Kelleher, D.R.E.

EAST BRIDGEWATER, PLYMOUTH CO., ST. JOHN THE EVANGELIST (1903) Rev. Walter F. Keymont; Deacon Joseph J. Hopgood.
Res.: 210 Central St., 02333-1998. Tel: 508-378-4207; Fax: 508-378-7317. Email: stjohnebridge@comcast.net. Web: www.stjohneb.org.
Catechesis/Religious Program—Tel: 508-378-1521. Mrs. Nancy Smith, D.R.E. (Pre-K-K); Richard Grasso, D.R.E. (Gr. 1); Pam LeBlanc, D.R.E. (Gr. 2); Carolyn Sullivan, D.R.E. (Gr. 8-11).

EVERETT, MIDDLESEX CO.

1—ST. ANTHONY OF PADUA (1927), (Italian), Revs. Dominic Rodighiero, C.S.; Armando Gomez Gama, C.S., Parochial Vicar; Deacon Thomas W. Marchant.
Res.: 38 Oakes St., 02149. Tel: 617-387-0310; Fax: 617-387-1229.
School—54 Oakes St., 02149. Tel: 617-389-2448. Maria Giggie, Prin. Sisters 2; Lay Teachers 8; Students 213.
Catechesis/Religious Program—Doris DiTullio, D.R.E. (Gr. 1-6 English). Tel: 617-387-4806; Maria Sentance, D.R.E. (Gr. 7-10 English); Maybell Montano, D.R.E. (Spanish).

2—IMMACULATE CONCEPTION (1885) Rev. Gerald J. Osterman; Marie Philomene Pean, Pastoral Assoc.
Res.: 489 Broadway, 02149-3603. Tel: 617-389-5660; Fax: 617-389-2456. Web: www.parishesonline.com/iceverett.
Catechesis/Religious Program—Janine Keller, D.R.E. (Gr. 3-5). Tel: 617-710-4963; Richard Randazzo, D.R.E. (Gr. 6-10); Fran Foley, D.R.E. (Gr. 1 & 2).

3—ST. JOSEPH (1912), St. Joseph, Everett was suppressed. This parish's records are located at Immaculate Conception, Everett.

4—ST. THERESE (1927), St. Therese, Everett was suppressed. This parish's records are located at Immaculate Conception, Everett.

FOXBOROUGH, NORFOLK CO., ST. MARY (1859) Revs. Stephen J. Madden; Brian P. Smith, Parochial Vicar; Deacon Paul M. Kline.
Res.: 83 Central St., 02035. Tel: 508-543-7726; Fax: 508-543-7728. Email: st.mary@foxboro.comcastbiz.net. Web: www.stmarysfoxboro.org.
Catechesis/Religious Program—Tel: 508-543-4577. Geraldine Saegh, D.R.E.; Catherine Briggs, D.R.E.; Elaine L'Etoile, D.R.E.

FRAMINGHAM, MIDDLESEX CO.

1—ST. BRIDGET (1878) Rev. Msgr. Francis V. Strahan; Rev. Mark J. DeAngelis, Parochial Vicar.
Res.: 15 Wheeler Ave., 01702-2902. Tel: 508-875-5959; Fax: 508-875-1270. Email: strahan@stbridgetparish.org. Web: www.stbridgetparish.org.
School—832 Worcester Rd., 01702. Tel: 508-875-0181. Roseanne Mungovan, Prin. Lay Teachers 19; Students 344.
Catechesis/Religious Program—Gail Barbato, D.R.E. (Gr. K-5); Marguerite Tibbert, D.R.E. (Gr. 6-10).

2—ST. GEORGE (1847) Rev. John M. Rowan; Sr. Ann Marie McAndrews, S.N.D., Pastoral Assoc.
Res.: 74 School St., 01701. Tel: 508-877-5130; Fax: 508-877-3080. Web: www.churchofstgeorge.org.
Catechesis/Religious Program—Paula Dolliver, D.R.E.; Leslee Willitts, D.R.E.

3—ST. JEREMIAH (1958), St. Jeremiah, Framingham was suppressed. This parish's records are located at St. George, Framingham.

4—ST. STEPHEN (1883) [CEM] Revs. Francisco J. Anzoategui, Team Ministry; Albert H. Stankard, Team Ministry; Mr. Enrique Mendez, Pastoral Assoc.; Deacons Pedro L. Torres; Alfredo Nieves.
Res.: 221 Concord St., 01702. Tel: 508-875-4788; Fax: 508-875-2577. Email: ststephenchurch1@verizon.net. Web: www.ststephenparish.org.
Catechesis/Religious Program—James J. Drummey, D.R.E.; Maria Nieves, D.R.E. Students 300.

5—ST. TARCISIUS (1907), (Italian), [CEM] Revs. Rinaldo Vecchiato, C.S.; Lino Ayala Garcia, C.S., Parochial Vicar; Deacons Manoel de Souza (Brazil); Edwin J. Robinson.
Res.: 35 Cedar St., 01702-6925. Tel: 508-875-8623; Fax: 508-875-6358. Email: sttarcis@aol.com.
School—560 Waverly St., 01702. Tel: 508-872-8188. Mary Ellen Wyman, Prin.
Catechesis/Religious Program—Marie Jutkiewicz, D.R.E.; Peter DeFazio, D.R.E.

FRANKLIN, NORFOLK CO., ST. MARY (1877) [CEM] Revs. Brian F. Manning; Frank D. Campo, Parochial Vicar; Ms. Nan Rafter, Pastoral Assoc.
Res.: One Church Sq., 02038-1896. Tel: 508-528-0020; Fax: 508-528-1641. Email: parishpublishing@stmarysfranklin.org. Web: www.stmarysfranklin.org.
Catechesis/Religious Program—Isabel Coyne, D.R.E.; Karen Ackles, D.R.E.

GEORGETOWN, ESSEX CO., ST. MARY (2006) Rev. Robert A. Poitras; Deacon Paul A. Dow.
Res.: 94 Andover St., 01833-0396. Tel: 978-352-2024; Fax: 978-352-2308. Email: rectory@parishmail.com. Web: www.saintmaryparish.org.
Catechesis/Religious Program—Tel: 978-352-6540. Mary Williams, D.R.E.

GLOUCESTER, ESSEX CO.

1—ST. ANN (1855), St. Ann, Gloucester was suppressed. This parish's records are located at Holy Family, Gloucester.

2—HOLY FAMILY (2005) Revs. John G. Kiley; Matthew E. Green, L.C., Parochial Vicar; Deacons Daniel A. Dunn; William F.X. Kane; Ms. Anna Matturro, Pastoral Assoc.
Res.: 60 Prospect St., 01930. Tel: 978-281-4820; Fax: 978-281-4964. Email: info@holyfamilycapeann.org. Web: www.holyfamilycapeann.org.
Catechesis/Religious Program—Dawn Alves, D.R.E.; Ms. Kathleen McCabe, D.R.E.

3—OUR LADY OF GOOD VOYAGE (1889), (Portuguese), Rev. Eugene L. Alves.
Res.: 142 Prospect St., 01930-3714. Tel: 978-283-1490; Fax: 978-283-0787. Email: olgv@comcast.net.
Catechesis/Religious Program—Tel: 978-283-8597. Sisters Mitrina, C.S.J., D.R.E.; Sebastian, C.S.J., D.R.E.

4—ST. PETER (1928), St. Peter, Gloucester was suppressed. This parish's records are located at Holy Family, Gloucester.

5—SACRED HEART (1946), Sacred Heart, Gloucester was suppressed. This parish's records are located at Holy Family, Gloucester.

GROTON, MIDDLESEX CO.

1—ST. JAMES (1945), St. James the Apostle, Groton was suppressed. This parish's records are located at Sacred Heart-St. James, Groton.

2—SACRED HEART, Sacred Heart, Groton was suppressed. This parish's records are located at Sacred Heart-St. James, Groton.

3—SACRED HEART-ST. JAMES (2003) Merged with St. Joseph in Pepperell to form Our Lady of Grace, Pepperell.

GROVELAND, ESSEX CO., ST. PATRICK (1946), St. Patrick, Groveland was suppressed. This parish's records are located at Sacred Hearts, Haverhill.

HALIFAX, PLYMOUTH CO., OUR LADY OF THE LAKE (1945) Rev. Stephen M. Healy.
P.O. Box 35, Monponsett, 02350-0035.
Res.: 580 Monponsett St., 02338-0035. Tel: 781-293-7971; Fax: 781-293-7969. Email: ollc350@aol.com. Web: www.ourladyofthelakehalifax.org.
Catechesis/Religious Program—Tel: 781-294-4571. Patsy Gillespie, D.R.E.; Carolyn Sullivan, D.R.E.

HAMILTON, ESSEX CO., ST. PAUL (1922) Rev. J. Michael Lawlor; Ms. Mary Elizabeth Reilly, Pastoral Assoc.
Res.: 50 Union St., 01982. Tel: 978-468-2337; Fax: 978-468-6538. Email: stpaulsparish@verizon.net. Web: www.churchofsaintpaul.net.
Catechesis/Religious Program—Tel: 978-468-3617. Jeanne Abbott, D.R.E.

HANOVER, PLYMOUTH CO., ST. MARY OF THE SACRED HEART (1907) Revs. Christopher J. Hickey; Ted K. Kofitse (Ghana), Parochial Vicar. In Res., Rev. Martin P. Connor (Retired).
Res.: 392 Hanover St., 02339. Tel: 781-826-4303; Fax: 781-826-5203. Email: mgallagher@stmaryshanover.com. Web: www.stmaryshanover.com.
Catechesis/Religious Program—Tel: 781-826-2351; Fax: 781-829-9271. Kathy Gallo, D.R.E.

HANSON, PLYMOUTH CO., ST. JOSEPH THE WORKER (1956) Revs. John M. Hannon; Michael J. McNamara, Parochial Vicar; Deacon John F. Alexander.
Res.: One Maquan St., 02341-1714. Tel: 781-293-3581; Fax: 781-294-1052. Email: j.worker@comcast.net. Web: www.stjosephtheworker.org.
Catechesis/Religious Program—Robin Muise, D.R.E.; Kevin Mossman, D.R.E.; Mary Lewek, D.R.E.

HAVERHILL, ESSEX CO.

1—ALL SAINTS (1998) Revs. Timothy E. Kearney; Michael K. Harvey, Parochial Vicar. In Res., Rev. Arnold E. Kelley (Retired).
Res.: 120 Bellevue Ave., 01832. Tel: 978-372-7721; Fax: 978-372-2085. Email: aspsec@verizon.net.
School—St. Joseph, 56 Oak Ter., 01832. Tel: 978-521-4256. Carol J. Simone, Prin.
Catechesis/Religious Program—Tel: 978-373-5473. Maureen Cartier, D.R.E.
St. Joseph's Early Childhood Ed. Center—100 Bellevue Ave., 01832. Tel: 978-372-0111.

2—ST. GEORGE (1961), St. George, Haverhill was suppressed. This parish's records are located at All Saints, Haverhill.

3—ST. JAMES (1859) Revs. Robert W. Murray; John J. Walsh, S.J., Parochial Vicar; Deacon Jose N. Agudelo; Senior Deacon Leo A. Martin. In Res., Rev. Mabvuto Felix Phiri (Zambia).
Res.: 6 Cottage St., 01830-4920. Tel: 978-372-8537; Fax: 978-373-1505. Email: stjamesrcc@hotmail.com. Web: stjameshaverhill.net.
Catechesis/Religious Program—Larry N. Webster, D.R.E.

4—ST. JOHN THE BAPTIST (1955) Revs. Robert W. Murray; John J. Walsh, S.J., Parochial Vicar; Deacon Thomas A. Anthony.
Res.: 6 Cottage St., 01830. Tel: 978-372-8537; Fax: 978-373-1505. Email: stjohn@parishmail.com. Web: www.stjohnhaverhill.org.

5—ST. JOSEPH (1876), St. Joseph, Haverhill was suppressed. This parish's records are located at All Saints, Haverhill.

6—ST. MICHAEL (1910), St. Michael, Haverhill was suppressed. This parish's records are located at All Saints, Haverhill.

7—ST. RITA (1932), St. Rita, Haverhill was suppressed. This parish's records are located at All Saints, Haverhill.

8—SACRED HEARTS (2007) Revs. Robert W. Conole; Timothy E. Kearney, Admin.; Benjamin T. LeTran, Parochial Vicar.
48 S. Chestnut St., 01835.
Res.: 6 Carleton Ave., 01835. Tel: 978-373-1281; Fax: 978-374-3043. Web: www.sacredheartsparish.com.
School—31 S. Chestnut St., 01835. Tel: 978-372-5451. Kathleen Blain, Prin. Sisters 1; Lay Teachers 9; Students 247.
Catechesis/Religious Program—Bridget Lacefield, D.R.E.

HINGHAM, PLYMOUTH CO.

1—ST. PAUL (1871) [CEM] Very Rev. James F. Rafferty; Deacon John A. Sullivan; Ms. Patricia Mikus, Pastoral Assoc.
Res.: 147 North St., 02043-3995. Tel: 781-749-0587; Fax: 781-749-8053. Email: stpaulparishhingham@gmail.com. Web: www.stpaulhingham.net.
School—18 Fearing Rd., 02043. Tel: 781-749-2407. Bro. Richard J. Lunny, C.F.X., Prin. Lay Teachers 9; Students 253; Religious 1.
Catechesis/Religious Program—Tel: 781-749-5568. Judy Tetreault-Murphy, D.R.E.

2—RESURRECTION OF OUR LORD AND SAVIOR JESUS CHRIST (1957) Rev. Kenneth B. Quinn.
Res.: 1057 Main St., 02043-3995. Tel: 781-749-3577; Fax: 781-740-0689. Email: resparish@comcast.net.
Catechesis/Religious Program—Janet Hickey, D.R.E.

HOLBROOK, NORFOLK CO., ST. JOSEPH (1887) Rev. John A. Currie; Deacon John F. Boyle; Sr. Catherine Joseph McDonough, D.C., Pastoral Assoc. In Res., Rev. Matthew M. Williams.
Res.: 153 S. Franklin St., 02343. Tel: 781-767-0605; Fax: 781-767-5225. Email: bulletin.sjp@comcast.net. Web: www.stjosephholbrook.org.
School—143 S. Franklin St., 02343. Tel: 781-767-1544. Anne F. Clough, Prin. Sisters 2; Lay Teachers 14; Students 290.
Catechesis/Religious Program—Tel: 781-767-0536. Maura Burke, D.R.E.
Convent—143 S. Franklin St., 02343. Tel: 781-767-4641.

HOLLISTON, MIDDLESEX CO., ST. MARY (1870) [CEM] Rev. Mark J. Coiro; Deacons Martin E. Breinlinger; Philip M. Caruso.
Res.: 8 Church St., 01746. Tel: 508-429-4427; Fax: 508-429-3324. Email: st.marys2@verizon.net. Web: www.stmarysholliston.com.
Catechesis/Religious Program—Tel: 508-429-6076. Andrea DeMayo, D.R.E.

HOPKINTON, MIDDLESEX CO., ST. JOHN THE EVANGELIST (1866) [CEM] Revs. Paul T. Clifford; Shawn P. Carey, Parochial Vicar; Deacon Michael M. Mott; Ms. Marie Buckley, Pastoral Assoc.
Res.: 20 Church St., 01748-1836. Tel: 508-435-3313; Fax: 508-435-5651. Email: stjohnshopkinton@verizon.net. Web: www.stjohnshopkinton.com.
Catechesis/Religious Program—Tel: 508-435-3313, Ext. 208. Carol Zani, D.R.E.; Ken Lysik, D.R.E.; Elaine Mitsock, D.R.E.

HUDSON, MIDDLESEX CO.

1—CHRIST THE KING (1927), Christ the King, Hudson was suppressed. This parish's records are located at St. Michael, Hudson.

2—ST. MICHAEL (1870) [CEM] Rev. Ronald G. Calhoun; Deacon Daniel F. Crimmins; Ms. Carmen Giombetti, Pastoral Assoc.
Res.: 21 Manning St., 01749-2315. Tel: 978-562-2552; Fax: 978-568-1761. Email: parish@stmikes.org. Web: www.stmikes.org.
School—198 Main St., 01749. Tel: 978-562-2917. Patricia E. Delaney, Prin. Lay Teachers 18; Students 201.
High School—Hudson Catholic High School, 198 Main St., 01749. Tel: 978-562-6701. Caroline P. Flynn, Prin. Lay Teachers 19; Students 201.
Catechesis/Religious Program—Tel: 978-562-7174. Ms. Karen Levelle, D.R.E.

HULL, PLYMOUTH CO., ST. MARY OF THE ASSUMPTION (1938) Rev. Joseph M. Mazzone; Deacon James G. Theriault.
Res.: 208 Samoset Ave., 02045-0565. Tel: 781-925-0680; Fax: 781-925-0685. Web: www.stmaryhull.com/church/.
Catechesis/Religious Program—Lisa H. Scarry, D.R.E.

IPSWICH, ESSEX CO.

1—ST. JOSEPH (1889), St. Joseph, Ipswich was suppressed. This parish's records are located at Our Lady of Hope, Ipswich.

2—OUR LADY OF HOPE (1997) Rev. Thomas E. Keyes; Deacon Carl M. Roberts; Ms. Elisa St. Clair, Pastoral Assoc. Tel: 978-356-2522.
Res.: One Pineswamp Rd., 01938-2922. Tel: 978-356-3944; Fax: 978-356-9592. Email: rectory@ipswichcatholics.org. Web: www.ipswichcatholics.org.
Catechesis/Religious Program—Tel: 978-356-2522. Nancy Salah, D.R.E.

3—SACRED HEART (1908), Sacred Heart, Ipswich was suppressed. This parish's records are located at Our Lady of Hope, Ipswich.

4—ST. STANISLAUS (1910), St. Stanislaus, Ipswich was suppressed. This parish's records are located at Our Lady of Hope, Ipswich.

KINGSTON, PLYMOUTH CO., ST. JOSEPH (1908) [CEM] Very Rev. Charles J. Higgins; Deacon Kevin J. Winn.
272 Main St., 02364-1922.
Res.: 268 Main St., 02364-1922. Tel: 781-585-6679; Fax: 781-645-1337. Email: stjosephkingstonma@comcast.net. Web: www.stjosephkingston.com.
Catechesis/Religious Program—Tel: 781-585-6372. Margart M. Hall, D.R.E.; Ms. Ann M. Cussen, D.R.E.

LAKEVILLE, PLYMOUTH CO., SAINTS MARTHA AND MARY (1958) Rev. Francis E. Daley; Deacon Richard J. Brennan.
Res.: 354 Bedford St., 02347-2107. Tel: 508-947-2107; Fax: 508-947-6543. Email: saintsmarthaandmary@comcast.net. Web: www.saintsmarthaandmary.com.
Catechesis/Religious Program—Sr. Rachel Labonville, C.S.C., D.R.E.

LAWRENCE, ESSEX CO.

1—ST. ANNE, St. Anne, Lawrence was suppressed. This parish's records are located at St. Patrick, Lawrence.

2—ASSUMPTION OF THE BLESSED VIRGIN, Assumption of the Blessed Virgin, Lawrence was suppressed. This parish's records are located at St. Mary of the Assumption, Lawrence.

3—ASUNCION DE LA VIRGEN MARIA (1993), (Hispanic), Asuncion de la Virgen Maria, Lawrence was suppressed. This parish's records are located at St. Mary of the Assumption, Lawrence.

4—ST. AUGUSTINE (1935), St. Augustine, Lawrence was suppressed. This parish's records are located at Our Lady of Good Counsel, Methuen.

5—CORPUS CHRISTI (2004) Rev. Francis X. Mawn; Deacon Julio C. Vargas.
Res.: 35 Essex St., 01840. Tel: 978-685-1711; Fax: 978-691-5927. Email: pastor@corpuschristilawrence.org. Web: www.corpuschristilawrence.org.
Catechesis/Religious Program—Mary Crow, D.R.E.

6—ST. FRANCIS (1903), St. Francis, Lawrence was suppressed. This parish's records are located at Corpus Christi, Lawrence.

7—HOLY ROSARY (1904), Holy Rosary, Lawrence was suppressed. This parish's records are located at Corpus Christi, Lawrence.

8—HOLY TRINITY (1905), Holy Trinity, Lawrence was suppressed. This parish's records are located at Corpus Christi, Lawrence.

9—IMMACULATE CONCEPTION, Immaculate Conception, Lawrence was suppressed. This parish's records are located at St. Mary of the Assumption, Lawrence.

10—ST. LAURENCE O'TOOLE, St. Laurence O'Toole, Lawrence was suppressed. This parish's records are located at St. Mary of the Assumption, Lawrence.

11—ST. MARY, St. Mary, Lawrence was suppressed. This parish's records are located at St. Mary of the Assumption, Lawrence.

12—ST. MARY OF THE ASSUMPTION (2004) Revs. Carlos E. Urbina, O.S.A.; John F. Dello Russo, O.S.A., Parochial Vicar; Deacons Jesus Castillo; Alvaro Arsenio Frias (Democratic Republic of Congo).
Res.: 300 Haverhill St., 01840. Tel: 978-685-1111; Fax: 978-686-5555. Web: www.stmaryassumption-lawrence.org.
School—301 Haverhill St., 01840. Tel: 978-685-2091. Vina Troianello, Prin. Sisters 2; Lay Teachers 8; Students 171.
Catechesis/Religious Program—Felix Duran, D.R.E.

13—ST. MARY-IMMACULATE CONCEPTION, St. Mary-Immaculate Conception, Lawrence was suppressed. This parish's records are located at St. Mary of the Assumption, Lawrence.

14—ST. PATRICK (1872) [CEM] Revs. Paul B. O'Brien; Israel J. Rodriguez, Parochial Vicar.
Res.: 118 S. Broadway, 01843-1427. Tel: 978-683-9416; Fax: 978-681-5808. Web: www.saintpatrickparish.com.
School—101 Parker St., 01843. Tel: 978-683-5822. Sr. Lucy Veilleux, S.C.I.M., Prin. Sisters 8; Lay Teachers 17; Students 500.
Catechesis/Religious Program—Ms. Diane Jarvis, D.R.E.

15—SS. PETER AND PAUL (1907), SS. Peter and Paul, Lawrence was suppressed. This parish's records are located at Corpus Christi, Lawrence.

16—SACRED HEART (1905), Sacred Heart, Lawrence was suppressed. This parish's records are located at St. Patrick, Lawrence.

LEXINGTON, MIDDLESEX CO.

1—ST. BRIGID (1848) Revs. Arnold F. Colletti; Hoang V. Le, Parochial Vicar; Ms. Beverly Good, Pastoral Assoc.; Ms. Mary Peterson, Pastoral Assoc.
Res.: 2001 Massachusetts Ave., 02421-4812. Tel: 781-862-0335; Fax: 781-862-1409. Email: shepherd@lexingtoncatholic.org. Web: www.lexingtoncatholic.org.
Catechesis/Religious Program—George Begin, D.R.E. (Gr. 1-8). Tel: 781-862-8724; Megan Chenaille, D.R.E. (Gr. 9-12).

2—SACRED HEART (1931) Revs. Arnold F. Coletti; Hoang V. Le, Parochial Vicar; Ms. Beverly Good, Pastoral Assoc.; Ms. Mary Peterson, Pastoral Assoc.
Res.: 2001 Massachusetts Ave., 02421-4812. Tel: 781-862-4646; Fax: 781-862-1409. Email: shepherd@lexingtoncatholic.org. Web: www.lexingtoncatholic.org.
Catechesis/Religious Program—Tel: 781-861-8385, Ext. 19. George Begin, D.R.E.

LINCOLN, MIDDLESEX CO., ST. JOSEPH (1946), St. Joseph, Lincoln was suppressed. This parish's records are located at St. Julia, Weston.

LITTLETON, MIDDLESEX CO., ST. ANNE (1945) Rev. Richard L. Casey.
Res.: 75 King St., 01460-1528. Tel: 978-486-4100; Fax: 978-952-6303. Email: stannes.rectory@verizon.net. Web: www.rc.net/boston/stanne.
Catechesis/Religious Program—Jacquelyn Butterfield, D.R.E.; Michelle Hatch, D.R.E.

LOWELL, MIDDLESEX CO.

1—ST. ANTHONY OF PADUA (1901), (Portuguese), Rev. Charles J. Hughes, Admin.; Mr. Victor Melo, Pastoral Assoc.
Res.: 893 Central St., 01852-3407. Tel: 978-452-1506; Fax: 978-458-9662. Email: st.anthony@comcast.net. Web: www.stanthony.portoinc.com.

2—HOLY FAMILY (2003) Rev. Donald G. Lozier, O.M.I.; Sr. Joan Gregoire, S.N.D., Pastoral Assoc. In Res., Rev. Norman E. Parent, O.M.I.
Res.: 122 Andrews St., 01852-5006. Tel: 978-453-2134; Fax: 978-453-0933. Email: holyfamilylowell@yahoo.com.
Catechesis/Religious Program—Richard Ouellette, D.R.E.

3—HOLY TRINITY (1904), (Polish), [CEM] Rev. Msgr. Stanislaw Kempa; Deacon Stephen M. Papik.
Res.: 340 High St., 01852-2760. Tel: 978-452-2564; Fax: 978-452-4679. Web: www.holytrinitylowell.org.
Catechesis/Religious Program—Robert Mullin, D.R.E.

4—IMMACULATE CONCEPTION (1869) Rev. Nicholas A. Sannella; Ms. Claire Couillard, Pastoral Assoc.
Res.: 3 Fayette St., 01852. Tel: 978-458-1474; Fax: 978-446-0790. Email: iclowell@yahoo.com. Web: iclowell.org.
School—218 E. Merrimack St., 01852. Tel: 978-454-5339. Catherine Fiorino, Prin. Sisters 1; Lay Teachers 8; Students 175.
Catechesis/Religious Program—Katherine Gendron, D.R.E.; Susan Hurton, D.R.E.

5—ST. JEAN BAPTISTE, St. Jean Baptist, Lowell was suppressed. This parish's records are located at St. Marguerite d'Youville, Dracut.

6—SAINT JEANNE D'ARC (1922), Saint Jeanne d'Arc, Lowell was suppressed. This parish's records are located at St. Rita, Lowell.

7—ST. JOSEPH (1908), St. Joseph, Lowell was suppressed. This parish's records are located at Immaculate Conception, Lowell.

8—ST. LOUIS DE FRANCE (1904), St. Louis de France, Lowell was suppressed. This parish's records are located at St. Marguerite d'Youville, Dracut.

9—ST. MARGARET (1910) [CEM] Rev. Raymond P. Benoit, Admin.; Deacon Barry V. Lloyd.
Res.: 374 Stevens St., 01851. Tel: 978-454-5143; Fax: 978-458-8472. Email: dmcandrews@parishmail.com. Web: www.stmargaretlowell.org.
School—486 Stevens St., 01851. Tel: 978-453-8491. Sr. Loretta Fleming, S.N.D., Prin. Sisters 1; Lay Teachers 19; Students 382.
Catechesis/Religious Program—Tel: 978-459-4481. Paula Nalavich, D.R.E.; Pamela Quinn, D.R.E.

10—ST. MARIE (1931), St. Marie, Lowell was suppressed. This parish's records are located at Holy Family, Lowell.

11—ST. MICHAEL (1883) Revs. Albert L. Capone; Thomas P. Rossi, Parochial Vicar; Deacon Roland E. Leduc; Lisa K. Crowley, Pastoral Assoc.
Res.: 543 Bridge St., 01850-2098. Tel: 978-459-0713; Fax: 978-453-1123. Email: stmichaels@comcast.net. Web: www.saint-michael.com.
School—21 Sixth St., 01850. Tel: 978-453-9511. Mary Frances Chisholm, Prin. Lay Teachers 26; Students 392.
Catechesis/Religious Program—Tel: 978-458-1617. Nicole Walsh, D.R.E.; Jean Haumann, D.R.E.

12—NOTRE DAME DE LOURDES (1908), Notre Dame de Lourdes, Lowell was suppressed. This parish's records are located at St. Margaret, Lowell.

13—NUESTRA SENORA DEL CARMEN (1990), Nuestra Senora del Carmen, Lowell was suppressed. This parish's records are located at St. Patrick, Lowell.

14—ST. PATRICK (1831) Revs. Paul Ouellette, O.M.I.; Daniel Crahen, O.M.I., Parochial Vicar; Tuan Ngoc Pham, O.M.I., Parochial Vicar; Deacon Peter An Ros; Sisters Luz Vera, M.S.S., Pastoral Assoc.; Guadalupe Grance, M.S.S., Pastoral Assoc.
Res.: 282 Suffolk St., 01854-4297. Tel: 978-459-0561; Fax: 978-446-0266. Email: stpatricklowell@comcast.net. Web: www.stpatricklowell.org.
Catechesis/Religious Program— Sr. Luzelana Vera, M.S.S., D.R.E.

15—ST. PETER (1841), St. Peter, Lowell was suppressed. This parish's records are located at Holy Family, Lowell.

16—ST. RITA (1910) Revs. Marc J. Bishop; Garcia Breneville (Haiti), Parochial Vicar. In Res., Very Rev. Arthur M. Coyle.
Res.: 158 Mammoth Rd., 01854-2619. Tel: 978-452-4812; Fax: 978-459-8969. Email: saintritalowell01854@yahoo.com. Web: www.parishesonline.com.
School—St. Jeanne d'Arc, 68 Dracut St., 01854. Tel: 978-453-4114. Sr. Precille Malo, Prin.
Catechesis/Religious Program—Gail Irish, D.R.E.

17—SACRED HEART (1884), Sacred Heart, Lowell was suppressed. This parish's records are located at Holy Family, Lowell.

LYNN, ESSEX CO.

1—ST. FRANCIS OF ASSISI, St. Francis of Assisi, Lynn was suppressed. This parish's records are located at Holy Family, Lynn.

2—HOLY FAMILY (1922), (Italian), Rev. Gregory Mercurio; Deacon John M. Bresnahan.
Res.: 26 Bessom St., 01902. Tel: 781-599-7200; Fax: 781-599-2202. Web: holyfamilychurchlynn.net.
Catechesis/Religious Program—Tel: 781-596-2390; Fax: 781-599-2202. Catherine M. Raymond, D.R.E.

3—ST. JOHN THE BAPTIST (1886), St. John the Baptist, Lynn was suppressed. This parish's records are located at St. Mary, Lynn.

4—ST. JOSEPH (1874) Revs. James E. Gaudreau; Victor D. Marino Barragan (Brazil), Parochial Vicar; Senior Deacons Finley H. Chisholm; Lawrence R. McManus.
Res.: 40 Green St., 01902-2905. Tel: 781-599-7040; Fax: 781-598-7439.
Convent—43 Green St., 01902. Tel: 781-581-7848. Sisters of St. Joseph 2.

5—ST. MARY (1862) Revs. Brian L. Flynn; Michael M. Ferraro, Parochial Vicar; Gabriel Loremus (Haiti), Parochial Vicar; Deacon Timothy F. Dempsey.
Res.: 8 S. Common St., 01902-4489. Tel: 781-598-4907; Fax: 781-599-2088. Email: rectory@saintmaryslynn.org. Web: www.stmaryslynn.org.
High School—35 Tremont St., 01902. Tel: 781-595-7885. Carl DiMaiti, Prin. Lay Teachers 30; Students 650.

6—ST. MICHAEL (1906), (Polish), St. Michael, Lynn was suppressed. This parish's records are located at Sacred Heart, Lynn.

7—ST. PATRICK (1906), St. Patrick, Lynn was suppressed. This parish's records are located at St. Mary, Lynn.

8—ST. PIUS FIFTH (1912) Revs. Cornelius J. Mullaney, Team Ministry; Joseph M. Rossi, Team Ministry; Sr. Patricia Shea, S.N.D., Pastoral Assoc.
Res.: 215 Maple St., 01904-2799. Tel: 781-595-7487; Fax: 781-595-7270. Email: officeadministrator@stpiusvlynn.org. Web: www.stpiusvlynn.org.
School—28 Bowler St., 01904. Tel: 781-593-8292. Paul Maestranzi, Prin. Sisters 3; Lay Teachers 25; Students 511.
Catechesis/Religious Program—Tel: 781-581-3503; Fax: 781-595-7270. Deborah E. Bartlett, D.R.E.

9—SACRED HEART (1894) Rev. Mark G. Derrane; Ms. Frances Taylor, Pastoral Assoc.; Deacon Richard P. Field Jr.
Res.: 571 Boston St., 01905-2160. Tel: 781-593-8047; Fax: 781-599-4040. Email: shparishsecretary@gmail.com. Web: www.sacredheart01905.com.
School—581 Boston St., 01905-2160. Tel: 781-592-7581. Joanne Eagan, Prin. Sisters 1; Lay Teachers 8; Students 261.
Catechesis/Religious Program—Tel: 781-592-1963.

LYNNFIELD, ESSEX CO.

1—ST. MARIA GORETTI (1960) Rev. Thomas J. Powers.
Res.: 112 Chestnut St., 01940-2405. Tel: 781-334-2367; Fax: 781-334-9819. Email: office@stmaria.org. Web: www.stmaria.org.
Catechesis/Religious Program—Hazel Kochocki, D.R.E.

2—OUR LADY OF THE ASSUMPTION (1937) Very Rev. John E. Farrell; Rev. Linus Mendis (Sri Lanka), Parochial Vicar.
Res.: 17 Grove St., 01940. Tel: 781-598-4313; Fax: 781-598-0055. Email: dyer_1116@yahoo.com. Web: www.olalynnfield.org.
School—34 Grove St., 01940. Tel: 781-599-4422. Dr. Joan Shea-Desmond, Prin. Sisters 2; Lay Teachers 16; Students 457.
Catechesis/Religious Program—Judith Dixon, D.R.E.

MALDEN, MIDDLESEX CO.

1—IMMACULATE CONCEPTION (1854) Very Rev. Richard J. Mehm; Revs. Joseph F. Keville, Parochial Vicar; Mark D. Barr, Parochial Vicar; Deacon Mark E. Rumley. In Res., Revs. James B. Canniff (Retired); Richard T. Bakker, S.M.A.
Res.: 10 Fellsway E., 02148-5313. Tel: 781-324-4941; Fax: 781-397-8571. Web: www.icmalden.com.
Catechesis/Religious Program—Tel: 781-324-5518. Sr. Margo Shea, C.S.J., D.R.E.

2—ST. JOSEPH (1902) Revs. William J. Minigan; John F. Mulloy, Parochial Vicar; Ms. Buffy Walsh, Pastoral Assoc.
Res.: 790 Salem St., 02148. Tel: 781-324-0402; Fax: 781-324-1790. Email: stjosephs2@comcast.net. Web: www.stjosephparishmalden.com.
Catechesis/Religious Program—Tel: 781-324-2444. David Wilcox, D.R.E.

3—ST. PETER (1972), St. Peter, Malden was suppressed. This parish's records are located at Immaculate Conception, Malden.

4—SACRED HEARTS (1890) Rev. Daniel J. Hickey.
Res.: 297 Main St., 02148-7414. Tel: 781-324-0728; Fax: 781-324-2714. Email: sh.parish@verizon.net. Web: www.sacredheartsparish.org.
School—30 Irving St., 02148. Tel: 781-324-6584. Susan M. Degnan, Prin. Lay Teachers 20; Students 400.
Catechesis/Religious Program—Susan Evans, D.R.E.

MANCHESTER BY THE SEA, ESSEX CO.

1—ST. JOHN THE BAPTIST (1931) Rev. John W. Gentleman; Ms. Jean Fecteau, Pastoral Assoc.
Res.: 62 School St., 01944-1342. Tel: 978-768-6284; Fax: 978-526-4335. Email: shsjparishes@comcast.net. Web: www.stjohnessex.parishesonline.com.
Catechesis/Religious Program—Valerie Shippen, D.R.E.

2—SACRED HEART (1905) Rev. John W. Gentleman; Ms. Jean Fecteau, Pastoral Assoc.
Res.: 62 School St., 01944-1342. Tel: 978-526-1263; Fax: 978-526-4335. Email: shsjparishes@comcast.net. Web: www.sacredheartmanchester.parishonline.com.
Catechesis/Religious Program—Valerie Shippen, D.R.E.

MARBLEHEAD, ESSEX CO., OUR LADY, STAR OF THE SEA (1859) Rev. Michael L. Steele; Deacon John E. Whipple.
Res.: 85 Atlantic Ave., 01945. Tel: 781-631-0086; Fax: 781-631-5668. Email: sosrectory@verizon.net. Web: www.staroftheseamarblehead.org.
Catechesis/Religious Program—Tel: 781-631-8340. Jude Odimone-Milan, D.R.E. (Gr. 1-4); Helen Haas, D.R.E. (Gr. 5-8).

MARLBOROUGH, MIDDLESEX CO.

1—ST. ANN (1921), St. Ann, Marlborough was suppressed. This parish's records are located at Immaculate Conception, Marlborough.

2—IMMACULATE CONCEPTION (1854) Very Rev. Michael W. MacEwen; Revs. Andreas R. Davison, Parochial Vicar; Ignacio D. Berrio (Colombia), Parochial Vicar; Deacon Robert I. Hoaglund.
Res.: 17 Washington Ct., 01752. Tel: 508-485-0016; Fax: 508-480-9644. Email: icmarlboro42@verizon.net. Web: www.icmarlboro.org.
School—25 Washington Ct., 01752. Tel: 508-460-3401. Martha McCook, Prin. Lay Teachers 14; Students 257.
Catechesis/Religious Program—Tel: 508-481-7535. Jennifer McKiernan, D.R.E.
Mission—St. Ann

3—ST. MARY (1870), St. Mary, Marlborough was suppressed. This parish's records are located at Immaculate Conception, Marlborough.

4—ST. MATTHIAS (1963) Rev. Francis P. O'Brien; Deacon Douglas P. Peltak.
Res.: 409 Hemenway St., 01752-6710. Tel: 508-460-9255; Fax: 508-480-8801. Email: admin@stmattpar.org. Web: www.stmattpar.org.
Catechesis/Religious Program—Karen McNamara, D.R.E.

MARSHFIELD, PLYMOUTH CO.

1—ST. ANN BY THE SEA (1945) Rev. John F. Carmichael.
Res.: 591 Ocean St., 02050. Tel: 781-834-4953; Fax: 781-834-7472. Email: info@stanns.net. Web: www.stanns.net.
Catechesis/Religious Program—Tel: 781-834-8223. Martha McLaughlin, D.R.E.

2—ST. CHRISTINE (1945) Rev. Thomas J. Walsh; Mary Doolan, Pastoral Assoc.; Doretha Gurry, Pastoral Assoc.; Deacon Paul F. Bankowski.
Res.: 1295 Main St., 02050-2029. Tel: 781-834-6003; Fax: 781-834-4263. Email: stchristinespsh@aol.com. Web: saintchristines.org.
Catechesis/Religious Program—Tel: 781-837-0088. Jean Godin, D.R.E.
Mission—St. Theresa's, Plymouth Co.

3—OUR LADY OF THE ASSUMPTION (1949) Rev. Mark E. Ballard.
Res.: 40 Canal St., 02050. Tel: 781-834-6252; Fax: 781-834-8338. Email: assumchrch@verizon.net. Web: www.assumptionparish.com.
Catechesis/Religious Program—Tel: 781-837-3662; Fax: 781-834-5694. Mary Forrester, D.R.E.

MAYNARD, MIDDLESEX CO.

1—ST. BRIDGET (1881) [CEM] Revs. John P. Prusaitis; Jean P. Aubin, Parochial Vicar; Deacon John W. Pepi.
Res.: One Percival St., 01754-1699. Tel: 978-897-2171; Fax: 978-897-5358. Web: www.saintbridgetmaynard.com.
Catechesis/Religious Program—Tel: 978-897-4612. Joan Ferguson, D.R.E.

2—ST. CASIMIR (1912), St. Casimir, Maynard was suppressed. This parish's records are located at St. Bridget, Maynard.

MEDFIELD, NORFOLK CO., ST. EDWARD THE CONFESSOR (1892) Rev. Leroy E. Owens; Deacon Frederick B. Horgan.
Res.: 133 Spring St., 02052-2513. Tel: 508-359-2633; Fax: 508-359-1846. Email: mail@stedward-ma.org. Web: www.steward-ma.org.
Catechesis/Religious Program—Tel: 508-359-5853. Terry Ferraris, D.R.E.

MEDFORD, MIDDLESEX CO.

1—ST. CLEMENT (1912) Revs. Dennis A. Dever; David M. O'Leary, Parochial Vicar.
Res.: 71 Warner St., 02155. Tel: 781-396-3922; Fax: 781-396-2506. Email: stclementmedford@comcast.net.
School—589 Boston Ave., 02155. Tel: 781-396-3488. Robert G. Chevrier, Prin. Sisters of St. Joseph 2; Lay Teachers 17; Students 240.
High School—579 Boston Ave., 02155. Tel: 781-393-5600. Robert G. Chevrier, Prin. Sisters 2; Lay Teachers 3; Students 150.
Catechesis/Religious Program—Tel: 781-396-3322. Carla Garofalo, D.R.E.

2—ST. FRANCIS OF ASSISI (1921) Rev. Joseph R. Foster; Deacon Robert F. Breen.
Res.: 441 Fellsway W., 02155. Tel: 781-396-3400; Fax: 781-396-3254. Email: saintfrancischurch@comcast.net. Web: www.stfrancismedford.com.
Catechesis/Religious Program—Tel: 781-395-4042; Fax: 781-306-0044. Margaret Aranyosi, D.R.E.

3—ST. JAMES (1919), St. James, Medford was suppressed. This parish's records are located at St. Joseph, Medford.

4—ST. JOSEPH (1883) Revs. Patrick J. McLaughlin, Admin.; Joseph Diem, Parochial Vicar.
Res.: 114 High St., 02155-3882. Tel: 781-396-0423; Fax: 781-391-2919. Email: stjosephparishmedfordma@msn.com. Web: www.stjoesmedford.org.
School—132 High St., 02155. Tel: 781-396-3636. Sr. Maureen Joseph Hunt, Prin. Sisters 5; Lay Teachers 14; Students 342.
Catechesis/Religious Program—Tel: 781-395-1784. Phyllis Patten, D.R.E.
Convent—2520 Mystic Valley Pkwy., 02155. Tel: 781-396-5670.

5—ST. RAPHAEL (1905) Revs. Kevin G. Toomey; Paul F. Coughlin, Parochial Vicar.
Res.: 38 Boston Ave., 02155-6722. Tel: 781-488-5444; Fax: 781-483-3375. Web: www.saintraphaelparish.org.
School—516 High St., 02155. Tel: 781-483-3373. Jean B. Murphy, Prin. Lay Teachers 19; Students 399.
Catechesis/Religious Program—Tel: 781-483-1139. Dr. Ginny McCabe, D.R.E.

6—SACRED HEART (1937), Sacred Heart, Medford was suppressed. This parish's records are located at St. Clement, Somerville.

MEDWAY, NORFOLK CO., ST. JOSEPH (1885) Rev. Msgr. Timothy J. Moran.
Res.: 2 Barber St., 02053. Tel: 508-533-6500; Fax: 508-533-1236.
Catechesis/Religious Program—145 Holliston St., 02053-1954. Tel: 508-533-7771; Fax: 508-533-0604. Sharon Moore, D.R.E.

MELROSE, MIDDLESEX CO.

1—INCARNATION OF OUR LORD AND SAVIOR JESUS CHRIST (1958) Rev. Stephen M. Boyle; Linda Swett, Pastoral Assoc.
Res.: 429 Upham St., 02176. Tel: 781-662-8844; Fax: 781-662-9340. Email: l.rectory@comcast.net. Web: www.incarnationmelrose.org.
Catechesis/Religious Program—Linda Swett, D.R.E.

2—ST. MARY OF THE ANNUNCIATION (1894) Revs. John M. Sullivan; William R. Carroll, Parochial Vicar; Sr. Mary Samson, S.H.C.J., Pastoral Assoc. In Res., Rev. Bernard J. Shea.
Res.: 46 Myrtle St., 02176-3827. Tel: 781-665-0152; Fax: 781-665-2750. Web: www.stmarysmelrose.org.
School—4 Myrtle St., 02176. Tel: 781-665-5037. Cynthia Boyle, Prin. Lay Teachers 27; Students 405.
Catechesis/Religious Program—9 Herbert St., 02176. Tel: 781-665-3707. Ms. Sheila Hurley, D.R.E.

MERRIMAC, ESSEX CO.

1—HOLY REDEEMER (2006) Rev. George E. Morin.
Res.: 4 Green St., 01860-1921. Tel: 978-346-8604; Fax: 978-346-9970.
Catechesis/Religious Program—Doreen O'Leary, D.R.E.

2—NATIVITY (1891), Nativity, Merrimac was suppressed. This parish's records are located at Holy Redeemer, Merrimac.

METHUEN, ESSEX CO.

1—ST. LUCY (1958) Rev. Richard T. Burton; Sr. Rina Brunetti, P.M., Pastoral Assoc.
Res.: 254 Merrimack St., 01844. Tel: 978-686-3311; Fax: 978-686-5343. Email: stlucy254@comcast.net. Web: www.saint-lucy.org.
Catechesis/Religious Program—Tel: 978-794-0383. Kevin Fitzgerald, D.R.E.

2—ST. MONICA (1917) Revs. Patrick S. Armano; David W. Gunter, Parochial Vicar; Deacons John B. Pierce; Andrew J. Goldy. In Res., Rev. Richard M. O'Brien.
Res.: 214 Lawrence St., 01844-3852. Tel: 978-683-1193; Fax: 978-686-0249. Email: stmonica@verizon.net.
School—212 Lawrence St., 01844. Tel: 978-686-1801. Beth Ingeneri, Prin. Sisters 4; Lay Teachers 12; Students 522.
Catechesis/Religious Program—Tel: 978-686-9573; Fax: 978-738-8898. Claire Tebeau, D.R.E. (Gr. K-5); Laurene Costello, D.R.E. (Gr. 6-8); Wendy Adams, D.R.E. (Gr. 9-10).
Convent—212 Lawrence St., 01844. Tel: 978-682-2448.

3—OUR LADY OF GOOD COUNSEL (2000) Rev. Christopher J. Casey; Deacon Steven J. Murphy.
Res.: 22 Plymouth St., 01844-4299. Tel: 978-686-3984; Fax: 978-686-8300. Email: olgcparish@comcast.net. Web: www.olgcmethuen.com.
School—526 Lowell St., Lawrence, 01841. Tel: 978-682-9761. Maureen Cocchiaro, Prin. Sisters 1; Lay Teachers 9; Students 206.
Catechesis/Religious Program—Tel: 978-686-3985; Fax: 978-686-8300. Mark Friedrich, D.R.E.; Mark Houle, D.R.E.

4—OUR LADY OF MOUNT CARMEL (1937), Our Lady of Mount Carmel, Methuen was suppressed. This parish's records are located at St. Monica, Methuen.

5—ST. THERESA (1936), St. Theresa, Methuen was suppressed. This parish's records are located at Our Lady of Good Counsel, Methuen.

MIDDLEBOROUGH, PLYMOUTH CO., SACRED HEART (1885) Revs. Richard P. Crowley; John T. Swencki, Parochial Vicar; Ms. Holly Clark, Pastoral Assoc.; Deacon George M. Gabriel. In Res., Rev. Daniel J. Crowley (Retired).
Res.: 340 Centre St., 02346-2102. Tel: 508-947-0444; Fax: 508-947-4333. Email:

info@sacredheartstrose.org. Web: www.sacredheartstrose.org.
Catechesis/Religious Program—M. Judith West, D.R.E. Tel: 508-947-2050; Fax: 508-947-2364; Michelle Sylvie, D.R.E. Tel: 508-923-1151; Lori Handerhan, D.R.E.

MIDDLETON, ESSEX CO., ST. AGNES (1945) Rev. Michael A. Hobson; Deacon John W. Wise.
Res.: 22 Boston St., 01949-2199. Tel: 978-774-1958; Fax: 978-774-1964. Email: stagnes@parishmail.com. Web: www.saintagnesparish.parishesonline.com.
Catechesis/Religious Program—Tel: 978-777-3404. Sr. Mildred Rothwell, O.S.F., D.R.E.

MILLIS, NORFOLK CO., ST. THOMAS THE APOSTLE (1937) Rev. Henry G. Chambers.
Res.: 111 Exchange St., 02054-1273. Tel: 508-376-2621; Fax: 508-376-4308. Email: stthomasmillis@comcast.net.
Catechesis/Religious Program—Helen Boucher, D.R.E.; Annmarie Fontecchio, D.R.E.

MILTON, NORFOLK CO.

1—ST. AGATHA (1922) Revs. Peter J. Casey; Mark W. Murphy, Parochial Vicar; Mary Gallagher, Pastoral Assoc.; Deacon Daniel F. Sullivan.
Res.: 432 Adams St., 02186-4399. Tel: 617-698-2439; Fax: 617-698-1517. Email: rectory@stagathaparish.org. Web: www.stagathaparish.org.
School—440 Adams St., 02186. Tel: 617-696-3548. Maureen C. Simmons, Prin. Sisters 2; Lay Teachers 15; Students 377.
Catechesis/Religious Program—Sr. Susan Czaplick, S.S.N.D., D.R.E.

2—ST. ELIZABETH (1946) Rev. Aidan J. Walsh. In Res., Rev. Michael B. Medas.
Res.: 350 Reedsdale Rd., 02186-3999. Tel: 617-696-6688; Fax: 617-698-4864. Email: office@stelizabethmilton.org. Web: www.stelizabethmilton.org.
Catechesis/Religious Program—Tel: 617-698-5763. Sr. Mary K. Walsh, C.S.T., D.R.E.

3—ST. MARY OF THE HILLS (1931) Rev. Arthur J. Wright; Harold J. Feldmann, Pastoral Assoc.
Res.: 29 St. Mary's Rd., 02186-2024. Tel: 617-696-0120; Fax: 617-696-7044. Email: smhrectory@aol.com. Web: www.saintmaryofthehills.org.
School—250 Brook Rd., 02186. Tel: 617-698-2464. Mrs. Andrea Tavaska, Prin. Sisters 2; Lay Teachers 14; Students 307.
Catechesis/Religious Program—Tel: 617-696-6117. Madeline Feldmann, D.R.E.

4—ST. PIUS TENTH (1954) Rev. Peter P. Nolan, C.S.Sp., Admin.
Res.: 865 Brush Hill Rd., 02186-1209. Tel: 617-333-0401; Fax: 617-364-2590. Email: piusx.miltonma@verizon.net.
Catechesis/Religious Program—Sheila Farley, D.R.E.

NAHANT, ESSEX CO., ST. THOMAS AQUINAS (1902) Revs. Thomas S. Rafferty; Wallace E. Blackwood, Parochial Vicar.
Res.: 248 Nahant Rd., 01908-1340. Tel: 781-581-0023; Fax: 781-598-8860. Email: nahantrectory@comcast.net. Web: www.stthomasnahant.com.
Catechesis/Religious Program—Tel: 781-595-7942. Kathy Marini, D.R.E.

NATICK, MIDDLESEX CO.

1—ST. LINUS (1950) Rev. Msgr. J. Robert Giggi; Donna McIntosh, Pastoral Assoc.; Deacon Herbert C. Hanson.
Res.: 119 Hartford St., 01760. Tel: 508-653-5505; Fax: 508-655-4577. Web: www.stlinusparish.com.
Catechesis/Religious Program—Tel: 508-653-6005. Cynthia Giardina, D.R.E.; Laura McLarnon, D.R.E.

2—ST. PATRICK (1858) Revs. Brian R. Kiely; David C. Goodrow, Parochial Vicar; Hal N. Obayashi, Parochial Vicar; Ms. Jean Lorrey, Pastoral Assoc. In Res., Most Rev. Walter J. Edyvean.
Res.: 44 E. Central St., 01760. Tel: 508-653-1093; Fax: 508-650-2922. Email: stpatsparish@comcast.net. Web: www.stpatsnatick.org.
Catechesis/Religious Program—Lisa Correia, D.R.E.

3—SACRED HEART (1891), Sacred Heart, Natick was suppressed. This parish's records are located at St. Patrick, Natick.

NEEDHAM, NORFOLK CO.

1—ST. BARTHOLOMEW (1952) Rev. Philip E. McGaugh; Ms. Barbara Dury, Pastoral Assoc.
Res.: 1180 Greendale Ave., 02492-4706. Tel: 781-444-3434; Fax: 781-449-7550. Email: stbarthomew@comcast.net. Web: www.stbartholomew-needham.org.
Catechesis/Religious Program—Tel: 781-444-4343. Melisa Hughes, D.R.E.

2—ST. JOSEPH (1917) Very Rev. David C. Michael; Rev. Guy F. Sciacca, Parochial Vicar; Ms. Susan Horne, Pastoral Assoc. In Res., Rev. Msgr. Francis J. McGann (Retired).
Res.: 1382 Highland Ave., 02492-2694. Tel: 781-444-0245; Fax: 781-444-7713. Web: www.saintjoes.com.
School—Elementary School, 90 Pickering St., 02492. Tel: 781-444-4459. Paul G. Kelly, Prin. Lay Teachers 34; Students 440.

NEWBURYPORT, ESSEX CO.

1—IMMACULATE CONCEPTION (1848) Very Rev. Timothy A. Harrison; Rev. William H. McLaughlin, Parochial Vicar; Ms. Marin Fortune, Pastoral Assoc. Tel: 978-234-7405; Deacon Richard Siebert. In Res., Revs. Paul W. Berube (Retired); James M. Broderick (Retired).
Res.: 42 Green St., 01950-2502. Tel: 978-462-2724; Fax: 978-234-7399. Email: info@newburyportcatholic.org. Web: www.newburyportcatholic.org.
School—One Washington St., 01950. Tel: 978-465-7780. Mary Reardon, Prin. Sisters 2; Lay Teachers 7; Students 198.
Mission—*St. James* Plum Island.

2—ST. LOUIS DE GONZAGUE (1902), (French), St. Louis de Gonzague, Newburyport was suppressed. This parish's records are located at Immaculate Conception, Newburyport.

NEWTON, MIDDLESEX CO.

1—ST. BERNARD (1876), St. Bernard, Newton was suppressed. This parish's records are located at Corpus Christi-St. Bernard, Newton.

2—CORPUS CHRISTI (1922), Corpus Christi, Newton was suppressed. This parish's records are located at Corpus Christi-St. Bernard, Newton.

3—CORPUS CHRISTI - ST. BERNARD (2006) Rev. Frank J. Silva; Deacon Daniel C. Nelson; Mr. Thomas F. Griffin, Pastoral Assoc. In Res., Rev. Francis M. Conroy (Retired).
Res.: 1529 Washington St., 02465. Tel: 617-244-0608; Fax: 617-969-1025. Email: info@ccsbparish.org. Web: www.ccsbparish.org.
Catechesis/Religious Program—Maureen Connell, D.R.E.

4—ST. IGNATIUS LOYOLA (1926) Revs. Robert F. VerEecke, S.J.; John Allan Loftus, S.J., Parochial Vicar; Kenneth G. Loftus, S.J., Parochial Vicar; Sr. Diane Vallerio, O.S.F., Pastoral Assoc.
Res.: 28 Commonwealth Ave., 02465. Tel: 617-552-6100; Fax: 617-552-6101. Email: ignatius@bc.edu. Web: www.bc.edu/st-ignatius.
Catechesis/Religious Program—Melisa Melnyk, D.R.E.

5—ST. JOHN THE EVANGELIST (1911), St. John the Evangelist, Newton was suppressed. This parish's records are located at Our Lady Help of Christians, Newton.

6—MARY IMMACULATE OF LOURDES (1870) Very Rev. Charles J. Higgins; Rev. Michael J. Harkins, Parochial Vicar.
Res.: 270 Elliot St., 02464. Tel: 617-244-0558; Fax: 617-965-4815. Email: miol@parishmail.com. Web: www.maryimmaculatenewton.org.
Catechesis/Religious Program—Jean Johnson, D.R.E.

7—OUR LADY HELP OF CHRISTIANS (1878) Rev. John E. Sassani; Rev. Msgr. Dennis F. Sheehan, Parochial Vicar; Ms. Jennifer Sues-Vassel, Pastoral Assoc.; Deacon William B. Koffel.
Res.: 573 Washington St., 02458-1494. Tel: 617-527-7560; Fax: 617-527-1338. Email: welcome@ourladys.com. Web: www.ourladys.com.
High School—Trinity Catholic High School, 575 Washington St., 02458-1494. Tel: 617-244-1841. Kelly Surapeneni, Prin. Sisters 2; Lay Teachers 10; Students 152.
Catechesis/Religious Program—Rosemary Seibold, D.R.E.; Kara O'Malley, D.R.E. Students 363.

8—ST. PHILIP NERI (1934), St. Philip Neri was suppressed. This parish's records are located at Sacred Heart Parish, Newton.

9—SACRED HEART (1890) Revs. John J. Connelly; Jeremy P. Saint Martin, Parochial Vicar; Ms. Winifred Murphy, Pastoral Assoc. Tel: 617-969-4021. In Res., Rev. Robert P. Imbelli (NY).
Res.: 1321 Centre St., 02459-2466. Tel: 617-969-2248; Fax: 617-965-7515. Email: parish@sacredheart.ws. Web: www.sacredheart.ws;deafcatholic.org.
Catechesis/Religious Program—Michelle Solomon, D.R.E.

NORFOLK, NORFOLK CO., ST. JUDE (1949) Rev. Msgr. Peter V. Conley; Deacon David R. Ghioni. In Res., Rev. Robert Rivard, F.M.S.I.
Res.: 86 Main St., 02056. Tel: 508-528-0170; Fax: 508-528-1860. Email: stjudenorfolk@comcast.net. Web: www.stjudenorfolk.com.
Catechesis/Religious Program—Tel: 508-528-1470. Terry Ferraris, D.R.E.

NORTH ANDOVER, ESSEX CO., ST. MICHAEL (1900) Very Rev. John W. Delaney, Team Ministry; Revs. George G. Hogan, Team Ministry; Paul T. Keyes, Team Ministry; Ms. Mary Alice Rock, Pastoral Assoc.
Res.: 196 Main St., 01845-2598. Tel: 978-686-4050; Fax: 978-686-5408. Email: st-michael@comcast.net. Web: www.saint-michael.org.
School—80 Maple Ave., 01845. Tel: 978-688-9181. Susan Reidy, Prin. Sisters 1; Lay Teachers 21; Students 525.
Catechesis/Religious Program—Tel: 978-682-9484. Maryann Marinelli, D.R.E.; Ms. Mary Alice Rock, D.R.E.

NORTH READING, MIDDLESEX CO., ST. THERESA OF LISIEUX (1945) Revs. Thomas M. Gillespie; Thomas J. Reilly, Parochial Vicar; Deacon Alfred O. Balestracci; Mary Ann Thomas, Pastoral Assoc.
Res.: 63 Winter St., 01864-2282. Tel: 978-664-3412; Fax: 978-276-0034. Email: sttheresa@parishmail.com. Web: www.sttheresanreading.org.
Catechesis/Religious Program—Tel: 978-664-2962. Paula L. Colpitts, D.R.E.; Nancy Cirone, D.R.E.

NORWELL, PLYMOUTH CO., ST. HELEN MOTHER OF THE EMPEROR CONSTANTINE (1950) Rev. Thomas H. Maguire.
Res.: 383 Washington St., 02061. Tel: 781-659-2993; Fax: 781-659-7861. Email: sthelenrectory@aol.com. Web: www.sthelenchurchnorwell.org.
Catechesis/Religious Program—Mary Nedder, D.R.E.; Kathleen Mogayzel, C.R.E.

NORWOOD, NORFOLK CO.

1—ST. CATHERINE OF SIENA (1890) Rev. Msgr. Paul V. Garrity; Rev. Anthony V. Luongo, Parochial Vicar; Deacon John A. Brent; Ms. Patricia Szczebak, Pastoral Assoc. In Res., Rev. Msgr. Paul T. Ryan (Retired).
Res.: 547 Washington St., 02062-0547. Tel: 781-762-6080; Fax: 781-255-9312. Email: parish@stcatherinenorwood.org. Web: www.stcatherinenorwood.org.
School—249 Nahatan St., 02062. Tel: 781-769-5354. Gretchen Hawley, Prin. Sisters 1; Lay Teachers 40; Students 472.
Catechesis/Religious Program—Frank Connell, D.R.E. Tel: 781-254-5087; Marybeth McDonough, D.R.E. Students 759.

2—ST. GEORGE (1912), St. George, Norwood was suppressed. This parish's records are located at St. Catherine of Siena, Norwood.

3—ST. PETER (1918), St. Peter, Norwood was suppressed. This parish's records are located at Archives, Boston.

4—ST. TIMOTHY (1963) Very Rev. John P. Culloty; Deacon Joseph M. Messina. In Res., Rev. George F. Emerson (Retired).
Res.: 650 Nichols St., 02062-1099. Tel: 781-769-2522; Fax: 781-769-9362. Email: sttim@sttim.net. Web: www.sttim.net.
Catechesis/Religious Program—Tel: 781-762-4868. Judith Miley, D.R.E.; Frank Connell, Dir. Faith Formation.

PEABODY, ESSEX CO.

1—ST. ADELAIDE (1962) Revs. Raymond Van De Moortell, Team Ministry; David C. Lewis, Team Ministry.
Res.: 17 Bow St., 01960-3427. Tel: 978-535-1985; Fax: 978-535-4845. Email: saintadelaide@verizon.net. Web: www.stadelaide.com.
Catechesis/Religious Program—712 Lowell St., 01960. Tel: 978-535-5376. Angela Federico, D.R.E.

2—ST. ANN (1937) Rev. Charles R. Stanley; Deacon Richard W. Cordeau.
Res.: 136 Lynn St., 01960-6432. Tel: 978-531-1480; Fax: 978-531-6683. Email: saintannpeabody@verizon.net. Web: www.catholic-church.org/st-ann-peabody.
Catechesis/Religious Program—Tel: 978-531-5791. Ellen Fitzgerald, D.R.E.

3—ST. JOHN THE BAPTIST (1871) Very Rev. John E. MacInnis; Revs. Paul G. McManus, Parochial Vicar; Anselm Nwagbara (Nigeria), Parochial Vicar; Deacon Valentin Rivera; Senior Deacon Leo A. Martin; Sr. Nancy Rowen, S.N.D., Pastoral Assoc. In Res., Rev. Msgr. Francis G. O'Sullivan (Retired); Rev. John C. Tibakunirwa (Uganda).
Res.: 17 Chestnut St., 01960-5429. Tel: 978-531-0002; Fax: 978-531-5199. Email: parishcenter@stjohnspeabody.com. Web: www.stjohnspeabody.com.
School—19 Chestnut St., 01960-5429. Tel: 978-531-0444. Maureen J. Kelleher, Prin. Sisters 2; Lay Teachers 20; Students 510.
Catechesis/Religious Program—Tel: 978-532-1586. Karen E. Hinton, D.R.E.

4—ST. JOSEPH (1927), St. Joseph, Peabody was suppressed. This parish's records are located at Archives, Boston.

5—OUR LADY OF FATIMA (1965), (Portuguese), Rev. Christopher Gomes.
Res.: 35 Newcastle Rd., 01960-1999. Tel: 978-532-0272; Fax: 978-977-2991. Email: ourladyoffatima@verizon.net. Web: www.rc.net/boston/fatima.

Catechesis/Religious Program—Ms. Frances Taylor, D.R.E.

PEMBROKE, PLYMOUTH CO., ST. THECLA (1964) Rev. Joseph S. McCarthy (Retired); Deacons John A. Sullivan; Howard C. League.
Res.: 145 Washington St., 02359. Tel: 781-826-9786; Fax: 781-826-3484. Email: sttheclaparish@msn.com. Web: www.stthecla.org.
Catechesis/Religious Program—Tel: 781-826-8042. Mary K. Doller, D.R.E.

PEPPERELL, MIDDLESEX CO.

1—ST. JOSEPH (1870) Merged with Sacred Heart-St. James in Groton to form Our Lady of Grace, Pepperell.

2—OUR LADY OF GRACE (2009) Rev. Paul L. Ring; Deacon Michael J. Markham; Ms. Jeanne Shanley-DiPietro, Pastoral Assoc.
28 Tarbell St., 01463. Tel: 978-433-5737; Fax: 978-433-9566. Email: parishoffice@ourladyofgracema.org. Web: www.ladyofgracema.org.

PLAINVILLE, NORFOLK CO., ST. MARTHA (1953) Rev. Thomas J. Stanton; Deacon Bertrand H. Guerin.
P.O. Box 1745, 02762.
Res.: 219 South St., 02762. Tel: 508-699-8543; Fax: 508-699-6677. Email: stmarthaoffice@gmail.com. Web: www.saintmarthaschurch.org.
Catechesis/Religious Program—Sharon Guerin, D.R.E.

PLYMOUTH, PLYMOUTH CO.

1—BLESSED KATERI TEKAKWITHA (1982) Rev. James E. Braley; Deacon James F. Greer.
Res.: 126 S. Meadow Rd., 02360. Tel: 508-747-1568; Fax: 508-747-0616. Email: office@blessedkateri.com. Web: www.blessedkateri.com.
Catechesis/Religious Program—Tel: 508-747-1568. Joyce Hokanson, D.R.E.

2—ST. BONAVENTURE (1950) Rev. Kenneth C. Overbeck; Sr. Jeremy Horgan, C.S.J., Pastoral Assoc. Tel: 508-224-4454.
Box 996, Manomet, 02345-0996.
Res.: 807 State Rd., Manomet, 02345-0996. Tel: 508-224-3636; Fax: 508-224-5889. Email: stbonaventure@parishmail.com. Web: www.stbonaventureplymouth.org.
Church: 799 State Rd., 02362.
Catechesis/Religious Program—Tel: 508-224-3636. Rachel Patnaude, D.R.E.
Mission—St. Catherine's Chapel 95 White Horse Rd., White Horse Beach, 02381.

3—ST. MARY (1915) Rev. Joseph T. MacCarthy. In Res., Rev. Paul F. Bailey (Retired).
Res.: 313 Court St., 02360-4336. Tel: 508-746-0426; Fax: 508-747-5886. Email: jevans@stmarysplymouth.org. Web: www.stmarysplymouth.org.
Catechesis/Religious Program—Kathleen Liolios, D.R.E.

4—ST. PETER (1876) Revs. William G. Williams; Robert T. Milling, Parochial Vicar; Deacon John A. Hulme.
Res.: 81 Court St., 02360. Tel: 508-746-0663; Fax: 508-747-1071. Email: stpeterparish@comcast.net. Web: www.stpetersplymouth.com.
Catechesis/Religious Program—Tel: 508-746-8268. Elizabeth Adey, D.R.E.

QUINCY, NORFOLK CO.

1—ST. ANN (1922) Rev. John J. Ronaghan; Sr. Patricia Boyle, C.S.J., Pastoral Assoc.; Deacon Joseph E. MacDonald. In Res., Rev. Thomas C. Foley (Retired); Very Rev. Francis J. Cloherty; Rev. Paul J. Aveni.
Res.: 757 Hancock St., 02170. Tel: 617-479-5400; Fax: 617-479-0955. Email: stannquincy@comcast.net. Web: www.stannquincy.org.
Catechesis/Religious Program—One St. Ann Rd., 02170. Tel: 617-479-2385. Nancy White, D.R.E.; Joseph DelRosso, D.R.E.

2—ST. BONIFACE (1956), St. Boniface, Quincy was suppressed. This parish's records are located at Holy Trinity, Quincy.

3—ST. ELIZABETH ANN SETON (2001), St. Elizabeth Ann Seton, Quincy was suppressed. This parish's records are located at Holy Trinity, Quincy.

4—HOLY TRINITY (2005) Rev. Paul J. Aveni, Admin.; Deacons John R. Menz; William F. Maloney.
Rectory—227 Sea St., 02169. Tel: 617-479-9200; Fax: 617-479-5766. Email: office@htpquincy.org. Web: holytrinityquincy.tripod.com.
Catechesis/Religious Program—Denise Gleason, D.R.E.

5—ST. JOHN THE BAPTIST (1863) Revs. Richard E. Cannon; Robert J. Cullen, Parochial Vicar; Deacon Paul A. Lewis. In Res., Very Rev. Thomas S. Foley.
Res.: 21 Gay St., 02169-6602. Tel: 617-773-1021; Fax: 617-773-5608. Email: stjohns@stjohnsquincy.org. Web: www.stjohnsquincy.org.
Catechesis/Religious Program—Ms. Joanne Curry, D.R.E.

6—ST. JOSEPH (1917) Rev. Vincent P. Doolan; Deacon Leo J. Donoghue.
Res.: 556 Washington St., 02169-7216. Tel: 617-472-6321; Fax: 617-471-8849. Email: stjoesquincy@comcast.net. Web: www.stjosephsquincy.com.
Catechesis/Religious Program—550 Washington St., 02169-7216. Ellen Curran, D.R.E.

7—ST. MARY (1840) Rev. David P. Callahan.
Res.: 115 Crescent St., 02169-4040. Tel: 617-773-0120; Fax: 617-786-9199.
Catechesis/Religious Program—Tel: 617-773-0515. Ellen March, D.R.E.; Margaret L. Donaher, D.R.E.

8—MOST BLESSED SACRAMENT (1915), Most Blessed Sacrament, Quincy was suppressed. This parish's records are located at Holy Trinity, Quincy.

9—OUR LADY OF GOOD COUNSEL (1938), Our Lady of Good Counsel, Quincy was suppressed. This parish's records are located at Holy Trinity, Quincy.

10—SACRED HEART (1903) Revs. John W. O'Brien; Raymond P. Kiley, Parochial Vicar. In Res., Rev. Bryan K. Parrish.
Res.: 386 Hancock St., 02171-2414. Tel: 617-328-8666; Fax: 617-773-2522. Email: office@sacredheartquincy.org. Web: www.sacredheartquincy.org.
Catechesis/Religious Program—Marjory O'Day, D.R.E.

11—STAR OF THE SEA (1945), Star of the Sea, Quincy was suppressed. This parish's records are located at Sacred Heart, Quincy.

RANDOLPH, NORFOLK CO.

1—ST. BERNADETTE (1937) Rev. Linh T. Nguyen; Sr. Ann Shea, D.C., Pastoral Assoc.; Deacon Thomas P. Burke.
Res.: 1026 N. Main St., 02368. Tel: 781-963-1327; Fax: 781-963-0198. Email: stbernadetteparish@comcast.net. Web: www.saintbernadette.us.
Catechesis/Religious Program—Laura Donovan, D.R.E.; Sandy Messia, D.R.E.; Jen Rajani, D.R.E.

2—ST. MARY (1851) Revs. Ronald D. Coyne; Garrett J. Barry, Parochial Vicar; Deacon James H. Eames. In Res., Rev. Vincent R. Maffei (Retired).
Res.: 211 N. Main St., 02368. Tel: 781-963-4141; Fax: 781-963-0884. Email: stmary@stmaryrandolph.org. Web: www.stmaryrandolph.org.
Catechesis/Religious Program—Tel: 781-961-5009. Patricia O'Connor, D.R.E.

READING, MIDDLESEX CO.

1—ST. AGNES (1904) Revs. Stephen B. Rock; Edward T. Malone, Parochial Vicar.
Res.: 186 Woburn St., 01867-3599. Tel: 781-944-0490. Email: stagnes@stagnesreading.org. Web: www.stagnesreading.org.
Catechesis/Religious Program—Tel: 781-944-4552; Fax: 781-944-4403. Eileen A. McGrath, D.R.E.

2—ST. ATHANASIUS (1961) Rev. Darin V. Colarusso; Deacon Neil J. Sumner.
Rectory—300 Haverhill St., 01867-1810. Tel: 781-944-0330; Fax: 781-944-1266. Email: stathanasius@parishmail.com. Web: www.rc.net/boston/stathanasius.
Catechesis/Religious Program—Jennifer Campagna, Dir. Faith Formation.

REVERE, SUFFOLK CO.

1—ST. ANTHONY OF PADUA (2001) Revs. George J. Butera, Admin.; Udayakumar Xavariapitchai (India), Parochial Vicar; Deacon Joseph A. Belmonte.
Res.: 250 Revere St., 02151-4618. Tel: 781-289-1234; Fax: 781-289-6394. Email: saintanthonysrevere@gmail.com. Web: www.saintanthonysrevere.org.
Catechesis/Religious Program—Mary Belliveau, D.R.E.

2—IMMACULATE CONCEPTION (1888) Revs. George L. Szal, S.M.; Carlos F. Flor (NEW), Parochial Vicar.
Res.: 22 Lowe St., 02151. Tel: 781-289-0735; Fax: 781-286-1124. Email: icrevere@comcast.net.
School—125 Winthrop Ave., 02151. Tel: 781-284-0519. Josephine Felice, Prin. Sisters 1; Lay Teachers 10; Students 269.
Catechesis/Religious Program—Tel: 781-289-8126.

3—ST. JOHN VIANNEY (1950), St. John Vianney, Revere was suppressed. This parish's records are located at St. Anthony of Padua Revere.

4—ST. MARY OF THE ASSUMPTION (1947) Very Rev. James J. Barry.
Res.: 670 Washington Ave., 02151. Tel: 781-284-5252; Fax: 781-284-5801. Email: stmaryrevere@verizon.net.
Catechesis/Religious Program—Irene Hunt, D.R.E.

5—OUR LADY OF LOURDES (1905), Our Lady of Lourdes, Revere was suppressed. This parish's records are located at Immaculate Conception, Revere.

6—ST. THERESA (1937), St. Theresa, Revere was suppressed. This parish's records are located at St. Anthony of Padua, Revere.

ROCHESTER, PLYMOUTH CO., ST. ROSE OF LIMA (1980), St. Rose of Lima, Rochester was suppressed. This parish's records are located at Sacred Heart, Middleborough.

ROCKLAND, PLYMOUTH CO., HOLY FAMILY (1882) [CEM] Revs. James F. Hickey; James O'Driscoll, Parochial Vicar; Darci Donizetti da Silva (Brazil), Parochial Vicar; Sr. Anne Conway, C.S.J., Pastoral Assoc.; Ms. Teresa D. Smith, Pastoral Assoc.
Res.: 403 Union St., 02370-1799. Tel: 781-878-0160; Fax: 781-871-6389. Web: www.holyfamilyrockland.org.
School—6 Del Prete Ave., 02370. Tel: 781-878-1154. Ann Marie Manning, Prin. Religious 3; Lay Teachers 14; Students 315.
Catechesis/Religious Program—Tel: 781-871-1244. Helen Ulich, D.R.E.

ROCKPORT, ESSEX CO., ST. JOACHIM (1849), St. Joachim, Rockport was suppressed. This parish's records are located at Holy Family, Gloucester.

ROWLEY, ESSEX CO., ST. MARY (1945), St. Mary, Rowley was suppressed. This parish's records are located at St. Mary, Georgetown.

ROXBURY, SUFFOLK CO., ST. KATHARINE DREXEL (2005) Revs. Gerald J. Osterman, Admin.; Anselm Nwagbara (Nigeria), Parochial Vicar; Jude T. Osunkwo (Nigeria), Parochial Vicar; Deacon John W. McHugh; Sisters Mary Hart, R.G.S., Pastoral Assoc.; Christine Smith, S.B.S., Pastoral Assoc.; Mr. Tipp Harris, Pastoral Assoc.
Rectory—26 Lawrence Ave., 02120. Tel: 617-445-8915; Fax: 617-445-1652.

SALEM, ESSEX CO.

1—ST. ANNE (1901), (French), Rev. George J. Dufour.
Res.: 290 Jefferson Ave., 01970-2895. Tel: 978-744-1930; Fax: 978-745-1190. Email: stannesalem@aol.com. Web: www.stannesalem.com.
Catechesis/Religious Program—Tel: 978-745-8915. Karen Moran, D.R.E.

2—IMMACULATE CONCEPTION (1826) Revs. Timothy J. Murphy; Paul G. McManus, Parochial Vicar; Mary Louise Daly, Pastoral Assoc.; Deacon Pablo Morel. In Res., Rev. Edward M. Keohan (Retired).
Res.: 30 Union St., 01970-3709. Tel: 978-745-6303; Fax: 978-744-4382. Email: office@icsalem.com. Web: www.icsalem.com.
Catechesis/Religious Program—

3—ST. JAMES (1850) Rev. John E. Sheridan; Ms. Andre Schwartz, Pastoral Assoc.; Senior Deacon Norman P. LaPointe. In Res., Revs. Lawrence J. Rondeau (Retired); Robert G. Labrie; Louis D. Bourgeois (Retired).
Res.: 161 Federal St., 01970-3297. Tel: 978-745-9060; Fax: 978-745-0561. Email: stjamessalem@aol.com. Web: www.stjamessalem.homestead.com.
Catechesis/Religious Program—Tel: 978-744-2230. Diane Santos, D.R.E.

4—ST. JOHN THE BAPTIST (1903), (Polish), Rev. Msgr. Stanislaw Parfienczyk.
Res.: 28 St. Peter St., 01970. Tel: 978-744-1278; Fax: 978-744-2093. Email: stjohnsalem@verizon.net. Web: www.stjohnsalem.org.
Catechesis/Religious Program—Teresa Prochorska, D.R.E.

5—ST. JOSEPH (1873), St. Joseph, Salem was suppressed. This parish's records are located at St. James, Salem.

6—ST. MARY (1918), St. Mary, Salem was suppressed. This parish's records are located at Immaculate Conception, Salem.

7—ST. THOMAS THE APOSTLE (1927) Very Rev. John E. MacInnis; Rev. Anselm Nwagbara (Nigeria), Parochial Vicar; Bro. Thomas Petitte, F.M.S., Pastoral Assoc.
Res.: One Margin St., Peabody, 01960-1999. Tel: 978-531-0224; Fax: 978-531-6517. Email: stthomas344p@comcast.net. Web: www.stthomasparish.net.
Catechesis/Religious Program—Nancy O'Brine, D.R.E.

SALISBURY, ESSEX CO., STAR OF THE SEA (1947) Revs. Louis R. Palmieri; Michael J. Farrell, Parochial Vicar.
Mailing Address: 9 Sparhawk St., Amesbury, 01913.
Res.: 18 Beach Rd., 01952-2007. Tel: 978-465-3334; Fax: 978-388-8840. Email: starsea11@verizon.net.

SAUGUS, ESSEX CO.

1—BLESSED SACRAMENT (1917) Revs. Daniel P. McCoy, Admin.; Michael J. Kearney, Parochial Vicar; Deacon Francis M. Gaffney. In Res., Rev. Albert J. Sallese (Retired).
Res.: 14 Summer St., 01906-2139. Tel: 781-233-2497; Fax: 781-231-3569. Web: www.blessedsacramentparish.org.
Catechesis/Religious Program—Tel: 781-231-3699. Donna G. Zinna, D.R.E.

2—ST. MARGARET (1949) Revs. Daniel P. McCoy, Admin.; Michael J. Kearney, Parochial Vicar.
Res.: 431 Lincoln Ave., 01906-3917. Tel: 781-233-1040; Fax: 781-233-7135. Web: www.stmargaretssaugus.org.

Catechesis/Religious Program—Carol Nadeau, D.R.E.

SCITUATE, PLYMOUTH CO.

1—ST. FRANCES XAVIER CABRINI (1960), St. Frances Xavier Cabrini, Scituate was suppressed. This parish's records are located at St. Mary of the Nativity, Scituate.

2—ST. MARY OF THE NATIVITY (1921) Rev. Kenneth V. Cannon; Deacon Martin W. Henry; Ms. Jane Kuklis, Pastoral Assoc.
Res.: One Kent St., 02066-4215. Tel: 781-545-3335; Fax: 781-544-3678. Email: Akeefe@stmaryscituate.org. Web: www.stmaryscituate.org.
Catechesis/Religious Program—Fax: 781-544-3678. Rosemary Lonborg, D.R.E. (Grades K-5); Ms. Jane Kuklis, D.R.E. (Grades 6-10).

SHARON, NORFOLK CO., OUR LADY OF SORROWS (1906) Rev. Scott A. Euvrard; Deacon Michael A. Iwanowicz.
Res.: 59 Cottage St., 02067-2132. Tel: 781-784-2265; Fax: 781-784-2540. Web: www.olossharonma.parishesonline.com.
Catechesis/Religious Program—Tel: 781-784-5091. Tami C. Ellis, D.R.E.

SHERBORN, MIDDLESEX CO., ST. THERESA OF LISIEUX (1945) Very Rev. John J. Grimes; Elizabeth Yon, Pastoral Assoc.
P.O. Box 176, 01770.
Res.: 35 S. Main St., 01770. Tel: 508-653-6253; Fax: 508-651-1318. Email: fr.grimes@st-theresa.sherborn.org. Web: www.st-theresa.sherborn.org.
Catechesis/Religious Program—Regina O'Connor, D.R.E.

SHIRLEY, MIDDLESEX CO., ST. ANTHONY OF PADUA (1905) [CEM] Rev. Edmond M. Derosier; Senior Deacon Raymond A. Gagnon; Sr. Joan Guertin, S.U.S.C., Pastoral Assoc.
P.O. Box 595, 01464.
Res.: 14 Phoenix St., 01464. Tel: 978-425-4588; Fax: 978-425-2033. Web: stanthonychurchshirley.org.
Catechesis/Religious Program—Tel: 978-425-0980. Donna Vaira, D.R.E.

SOMERVILLE, MIDDLESEX CO.

1—ST. ANN (1881) Revs. Brian J. McHugh; Jason W. Worthley, Parochial Vicar; Deacon Joseph Breyere Guerrier.
50 Thurston St., 02145.
Rectory—179 Summer St., 02143-2501. Tel: 617-625-1904; Fax: 617-625-7043. Email: parish@stannsomerville.org. Web: www.stannsomerville.org.

2—ST. ANTHONY OF PADUA (1915), (Italian), Rev. Ademir Guerini, C.S., Admin.
Res.: 12 Properzi Way, 02143-3226. Tel: 617-625-4530; Fax: 617-625-2457. Email: stanthonysomer@aol.com.
Catechesis/Religious Program—

3—ST. BENEDICT (1911) Rev. Robert J. Carr; William Jackson, Pastoral Assoc. Tel: 857-204-8332.
Res.: 25 Arlington St., 02145-3235. Tel: 617-625-0029; Fax: 866-571-8983. Email: stbenedictsomerville@gmail.com. Web: www.stbenedictsomerville.com; www.asembleasanbenito.com.
Catechesis/Religious Program—Tel: 617-825-4333. Daisy Gomez, D.R.E. Tel: 617-825-4333.

4—ST. CATHERINE OF GENOA (1891) Revs. Brian J. McHugh; Jason W. Worthley, Parochial Vicar; Deacon Joseph Breyere Guerrier. In Res., Rev. Harry J. Kaufman.
Res.: 179 Summer St., 02143-2501. Tel: 617-666-2087; Fax: 617-666-5470. Email: parishsec@stcofg.com. Web: www.stcatherinesomerville.com.
School—192 Summer St., 02143-2501. Tel: 617-666-9116. Marian Burns, Prin. Sisters 2; Lay Teachers 9; Students 225.
Catechesis/Religious Program—

5—ST. JOSEPH (1869) Revs. Henry J. Jennings; Charles Madi-Okin, Parochial Vicar; Sr. Marie Saint Joseph Santry, S.N.D., Pastoral Assoc.
Res.: 264 Washington St., 02143-3313. Tel: 617-666-4140; Fax: 617-628-0557. Email: stjoe1869@verizon.net.
Catechesis/Religious Program—John J. Piantedosi, D.R.E.

6—ST. POLYCARP (1927), St. Polycarp, Somerville was suppressed. This parish's records are located at St. Ann, Somerville.

STONEHAM, MIDDLESEX CO., ST. PATRICK (1868) Revs. William T. Schmidt; Mario J. Orrigo, Parochial Vicar; Sr. Marylou A. Cassidy, C.S.J., Pastoral Assoc.; Deacons J. Robert Turner; Cyril T. O'Neil. In Res., Most Rev. Peter John Uglietto.
Res.: 9 Pomeworth St., 02180-2025. Tel: 781-438-0960; Fax: 781-435-0075. Email: stpatstone@aol.com. Web: www.catholic-church.org/st-patricks.
School—20 Pleasant St., 02180. Tel: 781-438-2593. Arthur Swanson, Prin. Lay Teachers 10; Students 223.
Catechesis/Religious Program—Tel: 781-438-1093. Marie Kopf, D.R.E.

STOUGHTON, NORFOLK CO.

1—IMMACULATE CONCEPTION (1872) Revs. Joseph P. McDermott; Francisco C. Silva (Brazil), Parochial Vicar.
Res.: 122 Canton St., 02072-2204. Tel: 781-344-2073; Fax: 781-344-2979. Email: immaculateconception@verizon.net.
Catechesis/Religious Program—Tel: 781-341-0611. Alice Bachant, D.R.E.

2—ST. JAMES (1962) Rev. John E. Kelly.
Res.: 560 Page St., 02072. Tel: 781-344-9121; Fax: 781-341-9323. Email: saintjamesstoughton@comcast.net.
Catechesis/Religious Program—Tel: 781-297-7582. Mrs. Mary Ann Caldwell, D.R.E.

3—OUR LADY OF THE ROSARY (1958), Our Lady of the Rosary, Stoughton was suppressed. This parish's records are located at St. James, Stoughton.

STOW, MIDDLESEX CO., ST. ISIDORE (1961) Rev. David A. Doucet; Deacons Charles A. Cornell; Robert F. Brady. In Res., Rev. Luke U. Odor (Nigeria).
Res.: 429 Great Rd., 01775-1101. Tel: 978-897-2710; Fax: 978-461-0577. Email: info@stisidorestow.org. Web: www.stisidorestow.org.
Catechesis/Religious Program—Tel: 978-897-9790. Nancy Dome, D.R.E.

SUDBURY, MIDDLESEX CO.

1—ST. ANSELM (1963), St. Anselm, Sudbury was suppressed. This parish's records are located at Our Lady of Fatima, Sudbury.

2—OUR LADY OF FATIMA (1955) Very Rev. Michael J. Bova Conti; Deacon John D. Nicholson.
Res.: 160 Concord Rd., 01776-2353. Tel: 978-443-2647; Fax: 978-443-6264. Email: psecretary@fatimasudbury.org. Web: www.fatimasudbury.org.
Catechesis/Religious Program—Tel: 978-443-9166. Susan Murphy, D.R.E.

SWAMPSCOTT, ESSEX CO., ST. JOHN THE EVANGELIST (1905) Revs. Thomas S. Rafferty; Wallace E. Blackwood, Parochial Vicar; Deacon Andrew J. Acampora.
Res.: 174 Humphrey St., 01907-2512. Tel: 781-593-2544; Fax: 781-593-3616. Email: stjohnsswampscott@gmail.com. Web: www.stjohnswampscott.com.
Catechesis/Religious Program—Tel: 781-599-4711. Mr. A. Joseph Hunt, D.R.E.

TEWKSBURY, MIDDLESEX CO., ST. WILLIAM (1935) Revs. Andrew Knop, O.M.I.; John J. Hogan, O.M.I., Parochial Vicar; Michael Powell, O.M.I., Parochial Vicar; Deacon Gerard J. Hardy. In Res., Rev. J. George Croft, O.M.I.
Res.: 1351 Main St., 01876-2039. Tel: 978-851-7331; Fax: 978-858-0544. Email: stwilliamsrectory@comcast.net. Web: www.home.catholicweb.com/stwilliams.
Catechesis/Religious Program—Deborah M. Albano, D.R.E.

TOPSFIELD, ESSEX CO., ST. ROSE OF LIMA (1945) Very Rev. Mark A. Mahoney.
Res.: 17 Prospect St., 01983-0458. Tel: 978-887-5505; Fax: 978-887-8201. Email: stroselima1@verizon.net. Web: www.strosetopsfield.org.
Catechesis/Religious Program—Tel: 978-882-0882. Mary I. Connor, D.R.E.; Kathleen A. Yanchus, D.R.E.

TOWNSEND, MIDDLESEX CO., ST. JOHN THE EVANGELIST (1945) Mr. Edward Kelly, Pastoral Assoc.
Res.: One School St., 01469-0533. Tel: 978-597-2291; Fax: 978-597-3401. Email: saintjohns@comcast.net. Web: www.stjohnsoftownsend.com.
Catechesis/Religious Program—Tel: 978-597-2183. Kathleen Twombly, D.R.E.

TYNGSBOROUGH, MIDDLESEX CO., ST. MARY MAGDALEN (2004) Rev. Ronald L. Saint Pierre; Deacon David A. Brooks.
P.O. Box 100, 01879.
Res.: 93 Lakeview Ave., 01879. Tel: 978-649-7315; Fax: 978-649-3796. Email: saintmarymagdalen@verizon.net. Web: www.stmarymagdalenparish.com.
Catechesis/Religious Program—Cathy Kennedy, D.R.E.

WAKEFIELD, MIDDLESEX CO.

1—ST. FLORENCE (1947) Rev. Vincent J. Gianni.
Res.: 49 Butler Ave., 01880-5199. Tel: 781-245-2711; Fax: 781-245-4512. Email: stflo@comcast.net. Web: www.stflorence.org.
Catechesis/Religious Program—Deanna Kerns, D.R.E.

2—ST. JOSEPH (1854) Rev. Ronald A. Barker.
Res.: 173 Albion St., 01880-3224. Tel: 781-245-5770; Fax: 781-246-2423. Email: office@stjosephwakefield.org. Web: www.stjosephwakefield.org.
School—15 Gould St., 01880-2700. Tel: 781-245-2081. Ms. Maria Morris, Prin. Sisters 1; Lay Teachers 15; Students 235.
Catechesis/Religious Program—Tel: 781-245-1930. Molly DiTonno, D.R.E.

3—MOST BLESSED SACRAMENT (1931) Rev. William D. Coughlin; Deacon Frank A. Valeri.
Res.: 11 Grove St., 01880-4222. Tel: 781-245-2080; Fax: 781-245-7981. Email: mbsparish1@aol.com. Web: www.mbsparishwakefield.com.
Catechesis/Religious Program—Tel: 781-245-4669; 781-245-3414. Christine Carlson, D.R.E.; Laurine Kohler, D.R.E.

WALPOLE, NORFOLK CO.

1—BLESSED SACRAMENT (1874) Revs. Timothy J. Kelleher, Team Ministry; Emile R. Boutin, Team Ministry; Deacon Reynold G. Spadoni; Marie A. Martin, Pastoral Assoc.; William Dittrich, Pastoral Assoc.
Res.: 796 East St., 02081. Tel: 508-668-4700 (Parish); Fax: 508-668-3554 (Parish). Web: www.blessedsacrament.org.
School—808 East St., 02081. Tel: 508-668-2336. Russ W. Wilson, Prin. Lay Teachers 30; Students 440.
Catechesis/Religious Program—
Convent—808 East St., 02081. Tel: 508-668-6693.

2—ST. MARY (1931) Rev. Donald R. Delay.
Res.: 176 Washington St., 02032-0131. Tel: 508-668-4974; Fax: 508-668-3083. Email: stmarys176@msn.com.
Catechesis/Religious Program—Tel: 508-668-6853. Thomas Connor, D.R.E.; Judith Connor, D.R.E.

WALTHAM, MIDDLESEX CO.

1—ST. CHARLES BORROMEO (1909) Rev. Rodney J. Copp.
Res.: 30 Taylor St., 02453-5299. Tel: 781-893-0330; Fax: 781-893-2060. Email: stcharleswaltham@yahoo.com. Web: www.stcharleswaltham4lpi.com.
Catechesis/Religious Program—Tel: 781-893-1438. Carol A. Gill, D.R.E.

2—ST. JOSEPH (1894), St. Joseph, Waltham was suppressed. This parish's records are located at St. Mary Waltham.

3—ST. JUDE (1949) Rev. William T. Leonard; Deacon Alfred E. Santosuosso.
Res.: 147-R Main St., 02453-6622. Tel: 781-893-3100; Fax: 781-893-2424. Email: stjude1@comcast.net. Web: www.cnet/boston/st-jude.
School—175 Main St., 02453-6622. Tel: 781-899-3644. Sr. Katherine Martin, S.N.D., Prin. Sisters 2; Lay Teachers 8; Students 199.
Catechesis/Religious Program—Tel: 781-891-5718. Barbara A. Keville, D.R.E.

4—ST. MARY (1839) Revs. Michael L. Nolan; Gabino Olivia Macias (Mexico), Parochial Vicar; Deacon Eduardo R. Mora. In Res., Rev. Daniel F. Hennessey.
Res.: 133 School St., 02451-4599. Tel: 781-891-1730; Fax: 781-209-0555. Email: stmarywaltham@gmail.com. Web: www.stmarywaltham.org.
Catechesis/Religious Program—Tel: 781-893-0917. Marjorie Harris, D.R.E.

5—OUR LADY, COMFORTER OF THE AFFLICTED (1930) Rev. James M. DiPerri; Deacon Robert N. Johnson. In Res., Rev. William J. English (Retired).
Res.: 857 Trapelo Rd., 02452-4841. Tel: 781-894-3481; Fax: 781-894-0021. Email: parish@olca.org. Web: www.olca.org.
School—*Our Lady's Academy*, 920 Trapelo Rd., 02452-4841. Tel: 781-899-0353. Chandra Mino, Prin. Lay Teachers 8; Students 180.

6—SACRED HEART (1922), (Italian), Rev. Dennis Wheatley, O.F.M.; Friar Damian J. Johnson, O.F.M., Pastoral Assoc.
Res.: 311 River St., 02453. Tel: 781-899-0469; Fax: 781-899-0081. Email: sacredheart311@aol.com. Web: www.sacredheart311.org.
Catechesis/Religious Program—Tel: 781-893-8461. Bernadette Scalese, D.R.E.

WATERTOWN, MIDDLESEX CO.

1—ST. PATRICK (1847) Very Rev. Robert L. Connors; Rev. Martin G. Dzengeleski, Parochial Vicar; Ms. Carol Salerno, Pastoral Assoc.
Res.: 25 Chestnut St., 02472-2337. Tel: 617-926-9680; Fax: 617-926-3715. Email: parishoffice@stpatswatertown.org. Web: www.stpatswatertown.org.
Catechesis/Religious Program—Tel: 617-926-3441; Fax: 617-926-3715. Sandy Clancy, D.R.E.

2—SACRED HEART (1893) Rev. Joseph L. Curran; Sr. Mary Claire Kirkpatrick, O.P., Pastoral Assoc. In Res., Rev. John J. Stagnaro.
Res.: 770 Mt. Auburn St., 02472-1567. Tel: 617-924-9110; Fax: 617-926-3341.
Catechesis/Religious Program—Judy Gilreath, D.R.E.

3—ST. THERESA OF THE CHILD JESUS (1927), St. Theresa of the Child Jesus, Watertown was suppressed. This parish's records are located at St. Patrick, Watertown.

WAYLAND, MIDDLESEX CO.

1—ST. ANN (1945) Very Rev. James J. Laughlin; Sr. Roberta Rzeznik, S.N.D., Pastoral Assoc.
Res.: 124 Cochituate Rd., 01778-2610. Tel: 508-358-2985; Fax: 508-358-3415. Email: parish@saintann.org. Web: www.saintann.org.
Catechesis / Religious Program—Jane Asber, D.R.E. Tel: 508-358-2985, Ext. 13.

2—GOOD SHEPHERD PARISH (2011) Very Rev. James J. Laughlin; Deacon Geoffrey W. Higgins; Sr. Roberta Rzeznik, S.N.D., Pastoral Assoc.
99 Main St., 01778. Tel: 508-650-3445; Fax: 508-655-6948. Email: parish@goodshepherdwayland.org. Web: www.goodshepherdwayland.org.

3—ST. ZEPHERIN (1889) Very Rev. James J. Laughlin; Sr. Roberta Reznik, S.N.D., Pastoral Assoc.
Res.: 124 Cochituate Rd., 01778-2610. Tel: 508-653-8013; Fax: 508-655-6948. Email: stzepherin@comcast.net. Web: www.stzepherin.org.
Catechesis / Religious Program—Sr. Frances Thomas, D.R.E.

WELLESLEY, NORFOLK CO.

1—ST. JAMES THE GREAT (1947), St. James the Great, Wellesley was suppressed. This parish's records are located at St. Paul, Wellesley.

2—ST. JOHN THE EVANGELIST (1890) Very Rev. Thomas F. Powers; Deacon Thomas A. Smith; Sr. Evelyn Ronan, S.N.D., Pastoral Assoc. In Res., Rev. J. Bryan Hehir.
Res.: 9 Glen Rd., 02481-1600. Tel: 781-235-0045; Fax: 781-235-6990. Email: st-johns@comcast.net. Web: www.stjohnwellesley.org.
School—9 Ledyard St., 02481. Tel: 781-235-0300. Carol Roncari, Prin. Sisters 2; Lay Teachers 5; Students 187.
Catechesis / Religious Program—Tel: 781-235-5337. Linda Messore, D.R.E.; Jane Leonard, D.R.E.; Christine Tierney, D.R.E.

3—ST. PAUL (1922) Very Rev. Richard W. Fitzgerald; Rev. Mark J. Riley, Parochial Vicar; Deacon Paul M. Cloonan. In Res., Rev. Msgr. Joseph G. Lind (Retired).
Res.: 502 Washington St., 02482-5907. Tel: 781-235-1060; Fax: 781-235-4620. Email: stpauloffice1@verizon.net. Web: www.stpaulwellesley.com.
School—10 Atwood St., 02482. Tel: 781-235-1510. Karen McLaughlin, Prin. Sisters 1; Lay Teachers 7; Students 184.
Catechesis / Religious Program—Tel: 781-235-5012. Kathleen Curley, D.R.E.

WEST BRIDGEWATER, PLYMOUTH CO., ST. ANN (1938) Rev. Edward D. McCabe; Deacon Brendan A. Fitzgerald.
Res.: 103 N. Main St., 02379-0427. Tel: 508-586-4880; Fax: 508-586-3876. Email: stanns@comcast.net. Web: stannswb.com.
Catechesis / Religious Program—Maria Lallemand, D.R.E.

WEST NEWBURY, ESSEX CO., ST. ANN (1945), St. Ann, West Newbury was suppressed. This parish's records are located at Holy Redeemer, Merrimac.

WESTFORD, MIDDLESEX CO., ST. CATHERINE OF ALEXANDRIA (1922) [CEM] Revs. Peter F. Quinn; David P. White, Parochial Vicar; Ms. Majorie Hicks, Pastoral Assoc.; Deacon Richard T. Joy.
Res.: 107 N. Main St., 01886. Tel: 978-692-6353; Fax: 978-392-0644. Email: denise@stcatherineparish.org. Web: www.westford.com/stcatherines.
Catechesis / Religious Program—Diahne Goodwin, D.R.E.

WESTON, MIDDLESEX CO., ST. JULIA (1919) Revs. George P. Evans; Joseph M. Hennessey, Parochial Vicar; Deacon Guy C. Saint Sauveur; Susan Bayard, Pastoral Assoc.
Res.: 374 Boston Post Rd., 02493-1581. Tel: 781-899-2611; Fax: 781-899-8046. Email: stjulia@stjulia.org. Web: www.stjulia.org.
Catechesis / Religious Program—Tel: 781-899-2611. Sr. Marie LaBollita, S.C., D.R.E.
Mission—St. Joseph 142 Lincoln Rd., Lincoln, Middlesex Co. 01773.

WESTWOOD, NORFOLK CO.

1—ST. DENIS (1949) Rev. James G. Burke. In Res., Rev. William C. Burckhart (Retired).
Res.: 157 Washington St., 02090-1336. Tel: 781-326-5858; Fax: 781-326-1232. Web: www.stdeniswestwood.com.
Catechesis / Religious Program—Mary Campion, D.R.E.; Kathleen A. Burton, D.R.E.

2—ST. MARGARET MARY (1931) Revs. Stephen J. Linehan; William C. Palladino, Parochial Vicar; Deacon Joseph E. Holderried; Ms. Dorothy R. Ruggiero, Pastoral Assoc.
Res.: 845 High St., 02090-0386. Tel: 781-326-1071; Fax: 781-329-1879. Email: info@stmmparish.org. Web: www.saintmmparish.org.
Catechesis / Religious Program—Karlene Duffy, D.R.E.

WEYMOUTH, NORFOLK CO.

1—ST. ALBERT THE GREAT (1950) Rev. Paul R. Soper. In Res., Rev. Stephen J. Malloy.
Res.: 1130 Washington St., 02189-1932. Tel: 781-337-8778; Fax: 781-335-5850. Email: parishoffice1130@verizon.net. Web: www.atgweymouth.org.
Catechesis / Religious Program—John J. Hammel, D.R.E.

2—ST. FRANCIS XAVIER (1859) [CEM] Revs. Eugene P. Sullivan; Richard S. DeVeer, Parochial Vicar; Deacon Joseph A. Canova.
Res.: 261 Pleasant St., 02190. Tel: 781-337-2171; Fax: 781-331-4192. Email: sfxprsh@aol.com. Web: www.stfrancisxavier.org.
School—234 Pleasant St., 02190. Tel: 781-335-6868. Sr. Teresa Vesey, C.S.J., Prin. Religious 1; Lay Teachers 18; Students 471.
Catechesis / Religious Program—Marjorie Kearney, D.R.E.; Barbara Spink, D.R.E.

3—IMMACULATE CONCEPTION (1871) Rev. William F. Salmon; Deacons Francis J. Corbett; Stephen M. Buttrick.
Res.: 1199 Commercial St., 02189. Tel: 781-337-0380; Fax: 781-340-3979. Email: icwey@comcast.net. Web: www.icweymouth.org.
Catechesis / Religious Program—Tel: 781-337-3024. Ruthann Sinibaldi, D.R.E. Tel: 781-335-3902.

4—ST. JEROME (1928) Rev. Robert M. Blaney; Deacons Timothy J. Maher; Joseph V. Vitello. In Res., Most Rev. John A. Dooher; Rev. Msgr. Peter T. Martocchio (Retired).
Res.: 632 Bridge St., 02191. Tel: 781-335-2038; Fax: 781-340-7165. Email: office@saintjeromeparish.org. Web: www.saintjeromeparish.org.
School—598 Bridge St., 02191. Tel: 781-335-1235. Kathleen Shea, Prin. Sisters 1; Lay Teachers 9; Students 234.
Catechesis / Religious Program—Tel: 781-335-2786. Sr. Barbara Joyce, C.S.J., D.R.E.

5—SACRED HEART (1871) Very Rev. Daniel J. Riley; Rev. Andrew T. Lee, Parochial Vicar; Deacon Kenneth N. Ryan.
Res.: 55 Commercial St., 02188-2604. Tel: 781-337-6333; Fax: 781-337-9192. Email: p.heart@comcast.net. Web: www.sacredheartweymouth.org.
School—75 Commercial St., 02188-2604. Tel: 781-335-6010. Mary R. Ferrucci, Prin. Sisters 2; Lay Teachers 7; Students 165.
Catechesis / Religious Program—Jean Duke, D.R.E.; Susan McLeod, D.R.E.

WHITMAN, PLYMOUTH CO., HOLY GHOST (1897) Rev. Jason M. Makos; Deacon Joseph T. Nickley.
Res.: 518 Washington St., 02382. Tel: 781-447-4421; Fax: 781-447-1375. Email: info@holyghostwhitman.org. Web: www.holyghostwhitman.org.
Catechesis / Religious Program—Tel: 781-447-3135. Ann Lawrence, D.R.E.

WILMINGTON, MIDDLESEX CO.

1—ST. DOROTHY (1954) Revs. Phillip B. Earley; Paul G. Flammia, Parochial Vicar; Deacons Clifford D. King; Joseph M. Fagan Jr.
Res.: 126 Middlesex Ave., 01887-2723. Tel: 978-658-3550; Fax: 978-658-2008. Web: www.saintdorothys.20m.com.
Catechesis / Religious Program—Mary E. Medeiros, D.R.E.

2—ST. THOMAS OF VILLANOVA (1919) Revs. Phillip B. Earley; Paul G. Flammia, Parochial Vicar; Deacons Clifford D. King; Joseph M. Fagan Jr.
Res.: 126 Middlesex Ave., 01887-2723. Tel: 978-658-4665; Fax: 978-658-4670. Web: www.stthomasvillanova.com.
Catechesis / Religious Program—Marilyn Mandosa, D.R.E.

WINCHESTER, MIDDLESEX CO.

1—ST. EULALIA (1966) Very Rev. Thomas F. Nestor; Ms. Louise Cocuzzo, Pastoral Assoc.
Res.: 38 Ridge St., 01890-3633. Tel: 781-729-8220; Fax: 781-729-0919. Email: steulalia@verizon.net. Web: www.steulalia.org.
Catechesis / Religious Program—Barbara Penkala, D.R.E.; Donna DiFonzo, D.R.E.

2—IMMACULATE CONCEPTION (1931), Immaculate Conception, Winchester was suppressed. This parish's records are located at St. Mary, Winchester.

3—ST. MARY (1876) Revs. Richard C. Messina; Richard C. Beaulieu, Parochial Vicar; Ms. Melissa Behrle, Pastoral Assoc.; Salvatore Caraviello, Pastoral Assoc.
Res.: 158 Washington St., 01890. Tel: 781-729-0055; Fax: 781-721-6542. Email: stmarywinchester@comcast.net. Web: www.stmary-winchester.org.
School—162 Washington St., 01890-2173. Tel: 781-729-5515. Steven B. Ultrino, Prin. Lay Teachers 20; Students 198.
Catechesis / Religious Program—Tel: 781-729-1965.

WINTHROP, SUFFOLK CO.

1—HOLY ROSARY (1953) Rev. Thomas A. DiLorenzo, Admin.
Rectory—993 Shirley St., 02152-2535. Tel: 617-846-1210; Fax: 617-539-4402. Web: www.holyrosaryparish.net.
Church: 1015 Shirley St., 02152-2535.
Catechesis / Religious Program—Deborah Tewksbury, D.R.E.

2—ST. JOHN THE EVANGELIST (1907) Rev. Charles E. Bourke; Deacon Vincent J. Leo; Sr. Jane Iannaccone, S.P., Pastoral Assoc. In Res., Rev. Richard A. Uftring.
Res.: 320 Winthrop St., 02152-3127. Tel: 617-846-7400; Fax: 617-539-0627. Web: www.stjohnswinthrop.org.
Catechesis / Religious Program—Tel: 617-846-3100. Geraldine Butters, D.R.E.

WOBURN, MIDDLESEX CO.

1—ST. ANTHONY OF PADUA (1945) Revs. Richard J. Shmaruk; John R. Carroll, Parochial Vicar.
Rectory—80 Elm St., 01801-1855. Tel: 781-933-1323; Fax: 781-937-3233. Email: st_anthony_parish@verizon.net.
Catechesis / Religious Program—Sandra Strong, D.R.E.

2—ST. BARBARA (1954) Revs. Vincent P. Mellone; Gerard E. Reid (Jamaica), Parochial Vicar.
Res.: 138 Cambridge Rd., 01801-4772. Tel: 781-933-4130; Fax: 781-932-2536.
Catechesis / Religious Program—Tel: 781-935-0529. Barbara Jeannotte, D.R.E.

3—ST. CHARLES BORROMEO (1862) Revs. Timothy J. Shea; Arthur T. MacKay, Parochial Vicar; Deacons Philip P. Hardcastle; Manuel A. Rosario. In Res., Rev. Patrick J. Kelly (Retired).
Res.: 280 Main St., 01801. Tel: 781-933-0300; Fax: 781-932-7581. Web: www.saintcharleschurch.net.
School—Tel: 781-935-4635. Rita Masotta, Prin. Lay Teachers 25; Students 350.
Catechesis / Religious Program—Cliff Garvey, D.R.E.

4—ST. JOSEPH (1906) Rev. Harold E. LeBlanc.
Res.: 22 Central St., 01801-4616. Tel: 781-938-0473; Fax: 781-938-7818.
Catechesis / Religious Program—Tel: 781-937-6392. Donna Ingham, D.R.E.

WRENTHAM, NORFOLK CO., ST. MARY (1928) Revs. George C. Hines; William P. Lohan, Parochial Vicar; Deacon Kenneth W. Oles.
Res.: 130 South St., 02093-0326. Tel: 508-384-3373; Fax: 508-384-5747. Email: stmary414@verizon.net. Web: www.stmarywrentham.squarespace.com.
Catechesis / Religious Program—Tel: 508-384-7922. Roberta Oles, D.R.E.

Absent on Leave. For contact information please call or write: Clergy Personnel Office, 66 Brooks Dr., Braintree, MA 02184-3839; Tel: 617-779-3685:

Revs.—
Antonellis, Joseph A.
Parise, Michael
Shoemaker, David A.
Sullivan, William M.

Awaiting Assignment. For contact information please call or write Clergy Personnel Office, 66 Brooks Dr., Braintree, MA 02184-3839; Tel. 617-779-3685:

Rev.—
Gillespie, Jerome F.

Health Leave. For contact information please call or write: Clergy Personnel Office, 66 Brooks Dr., Braintree, MA 02184-3839; Tel: 617-779-3685:

Revs.—
Ajemian, David J.
Bouton, Thomas F.
Jacques, Roger N.
Keenan, Alexander J.
Malloy, Stephen J.
McCarthy, Sean M.
Thuma, Clifton M.

Military & VA Chaplains. For contact information please call or write: Clergy Personnel Office, 66 Brooks Dr., Braintree, MA 02184-3839; Tel: 617-779-3685:

Revs.—
Butler, Timothy A.
Cordery, Robert J.
Hurley, Paul K.
Kennedy, William M.
Monagle, Robert J.
Raux, Redmond P.
Yanju, Henry M.

On Duty Outside the Archdiocese. For contact information please call or write: Clergy Personnel Office, 66 Brooks Dr., Braintree, MA 02184-3839; Tel: 617-779-3685:

Rev. Msgrs.—

Abruzzese, John A.
McInerny, Paul B.
Russell, Paul F.
Revs.—
Beauregard, Andrew F., F.P.O.
Donahue, Richard T.
Driscoll, Joseph J.
Galvin, John P., D.Th.
Giroux, Peter, F.P.O.
Grant, Benedict, F.P.O.
Helfrich, Paul D., B.H.
Kim, Carlos C.
Marcham, David S.
McNeil, John R. (Retired)
Medio, Joseph Paul, F.P.O.
Pucciarelli, George W.
Sullivan, Robert E.

Permanent Disability. For contact information please call or write: Clergy Personnel Office, 66 Brooks Dr., Braintree, MA 02184-3839; Tele: 617-799-3685:
Revs.—
Best, Russell W.
Carroll, Edward G.
Fraser, Gerald C.
McGrade, Kevin M.
McNulty, Martin J.
Moran, James F.
Scanlan, William J.

Senior Priests. For contact information please call or write: Clergy Personnel Office, 66 Brooks Dr., Braintree, MA 02184-3839; 617-779-3685:
Rev. Msgrs.—
Abucewicz, John A. (Retired), Box 363, Durham, NH 03824-0363.
Alves, Joseph T. (Retired), 60 William Cardinal O'Connell Way, Boston, 02114-2729.
Bourque, Charles J., V.F. (Retired), 700 Washington St., Canton, 02021-3036.
Boyle, Robert J. (Retired), 60 William Cardinal O'Connell Way, Boston, 02114-2729.
Brady, Roger J. (Retired), 81 Hartwell Rd., Bedford, 01730-2408.
Connell, Andrew F. (Retired), 275 Flaggler Dr., Box 756, Marshfield, 02050-0756.
Contons, Albert J. (Retired), P.O. Box 1025, Humarock, 02047-1025.
Coppenrath, Leonard A. (Retired), 1573 Cambridge St., Cambridge, 02138-4370.
Fichtner, Robert C. (Retired), 24 Beal Rd., Waltham, 02453-6644.
Forster, William J. (Retired), 36 Glover Dr., Revere, 02151-4915.
Glynn, William F. (Retired), 290 Kingstown Way, Unit 228, Duxbury, 02332-4640.
Lind, Joseph G. (Retired), 502 Washington St., Wellesley, 02482-5907.
Martocchio, Peter T. (Retired), 632 Bridge St., Weymouth, 02191-1845.
McDonough, John P. (Retired), One Pond St., Apt. 4H, Winthrop, 02152-1080.
McGann, Francis J. (Retired), 1382 Highland Ave., Needham, 02492-2614.
McGrath, Laurence W., M.Div., M.A., M.S. (Retired), 34 Bunerk Hill Rd., Auburn, NH 03032-3528.
McManus, Paul J. (Retired), 1573 Cambridge St., Cambridge, 02138-4370.
McNamara, Eugene P. (Retired), 1573 Cambridge St., Cambridge, 02138-4370.
Murphy, Frederick J. (Retired), 24 Conant St., Danvers, 01923-2988.
O'Sullivan, Francis G. (Retired), 17 Chestnut St., Peabody, 01960-6498.
Palladino, Alfonso G. (Retired), 46 Myrtle St., Melrose, 02176-3827.
Roche, William H. (Retired), 60 William Cardinal O'Connell Way, Boston, 02114-2729.
Ryan, Paul T. (Retired), 547 Washington St., Norwood, 02062-0547.
Tierney, James E. (Retired), 60 William Cardinal O'Connell Way, Boston, 02114-2729.
Very Rev.—
Condon, Edwin D. (Retired), 225 Lincoln St., Unit E2, Duxbury, 02332-3627.
Revs.—
Ahearn, Richard F. (Retired), 1573 Cambridge St., Cambridge, 02138-4370.
Bailey, Paul F. (Retired), 313 Court St., Plymouth, 02360-4336.
Bartley, David J. (Retired), 190 Bridge St., Apt. 3202, Salem, 01970-7409.
Beksha, Francis W. (Retired), 6 Cassidy Ln., Medway, 02053-1235.
Bertelli, Ameilio James (Retired), 4 Payson St., Lexington, 02421-7924.
Berube, Paul W. (Retired), 42 Green St., Newburyport, 01950-2647.
Bilicky, Louis S. (Retired), 24 Rickey Dr., Maynard, 01754-1052.
Blute, Robert H. (Retired), 60 William Cardinal O'Connell Way, Boston, 02114-2729.
Boivin, Henry P. (Retired), 660 Union St., Unit 3D, 02184-4130.
Borges, Laurence J. (Retired)
Bourgault, Ronald L. (Retired), 100 Salisbury Rd., Franklin, NH 03235-2501.
Bourgeois, Louis D. (Retired)
Brennan, Gerard M. (Retired), 60 William Cardinal O'Connell Way, Boston, 02114-2729.
Brennan, James F. (Retired), 60 William Cardinal O'Connell Way, Boston, 02114-2729.
Broderick, James M. (Retired), 42 Green St., Newburyport, 01950-2647.
Brown, Arthur A. (Retired), 45 Clipper Ln., Box 625, Falmouth, 02540.
Browne, Robert M. (Retired), 2 Park Ln., Gloucester, 01930-3924.
Brudzynski, Peter F. (Retired), 316 Angelico Dr., Nokomis, FL 34275-7446.
Buckley, Thomas W. (Retired), 198 Centre St., Abington, 02351-2208.
Butler, Allan L. W. (Retired), 27 Vaughan Ave., Whitman, 02382-1307.
Butler, James P. (Retired), 11 Courtney St. (#8), Fall River, 02720-6740.
Butler, Richard J. (Retired), 5 Linden Pl., Brookline, 02445-7801.
Butler, Robert J. (Retired), 432 Adams St., Milton, 02186-4399.
Byrne, Joseph F. (Retired), 41 Cooper Rd., Falmouth, 02540.
Calter, Arthur M. (Retired), 60 William Cardinal O'Connell Way, Boston, 02114-2729.
Campbell, William W. (Retired), 117 Heather Ln., N Falmouth, 02556.
Canniff, James B. (Retired), 10 Fellsway E., Malden, 02148-5313.
Carrigg, William J. (Retired), Cranberry Village, 27 Adams Cir., Carver, 02330-1611.
Carroll, James M., V.F. (Retired)
Clifford, Donald P. (Retired), 125 Lakeview Blvd., Plymouth, 02360.
Clougherty, Paul L. (Retired), 2969 Flint Dr., S., Clearwater, FL 33759-2577.
Connolly, John G. (Retired), 36 Belmont Rd., Apt. E22, West Harwich, 02671-1357.
Connor, Martin P., S.T.L. (Retired), 392 Hanover St., Hanover, 02339.
Conroy, Francis M. (Retired), 1529 Washington St., Newton, 02465.
Conroy, Philip M. (Retired), 66 Brooks Dr., 02184-3839.
Cormier, Leo G. (Retired), 90 Flower Ln., Dracut, 01826-4650.
Cormier, Roger C. (Retired), 45 S. Meadow Village, Unit 5, Carver, 02330-1802.
Costello, Robert B. (Retired), P.O. Box 92, Nahant, 01908-0092.
Craig, Richard J. (Retired), 209 E. Side Dr., Box 310, Alton Bay, NH 03810-0310.
Crowley, Daniel J. (Retired), 340 Center St., Middleboro, 02346-2102.
Cunney, Henry M. (Retired), 1008 Paradise Rd., Unit 1B, Swampscott, 01907-1303.
Curley, Terence P. (Retired)
Curran, Paul E. (Retired), 60 William Cardinal O'Connell Way, Boston, 02114-2729.
Curtin, Eugene P. (Retired), 60 William Cardinal O'Connell Way, Boston, 02114-2729.
Daily, Vincent E. (Retired), 1573 Cambridge St., Cambridge, 02138-4370.
Daniele, Anthony J. (Retired), 444 Centre St., Milton, 02186-4198.
Darcy, James F. (Retired), 60 William Cardinal O'Connell Way, Boston, 02114-2729.
DeAdder, James W., S.T.D., Ph.D., J.C.D. (Retired), 60 William Cardinal O'Connell Way, Boston, 02114-2729.
Degnan, James F. (Retired), 60 William Cardinal O'Connell Way, Boston, 02114-2729.
Desmond, Hubert E. (Retired), 51 Broad Reach, Apt. M56A, Weymouth, 02191-2266.
Desrosiers, Philip J. (Retired), P.O. Box 8149, Lynn, 01904-0149.
Doherty, Henry F. (Retired), 12 Sachem Village Rd., P.O. Box 31, West Dennis, 02670-0031.
Doherty, Robert J. (Retired), 13991 Amarilis Ct., Fort Pierce, FL 34951-4201.
Donovan, John L. (Retired), 60 William Cardinal O'Connell Way, Boston, 02114-2729.
Doyle, John L. (Retired), 83 Long Ave., Framingham, 01702-5735.
Drennan, Lawrence J. (Retired), 61 Broad Reach, T81B, Weymouth, 02191-2288.
Driscoll, Arthur J. (Retired), 57 Sylvan St., Unit 7A, Danvers, 01923-2747.
Driscoll, Richard A. (Retired), 69 Washington St., Apt. 11, Topsfield, 01983-1743.
DuFour, Louis C. (Retired), P.O. Box 731, Seabrook, NH 03874-0731.
Emerson, George F. (Retired), 650 Nichols St., Norwood, 02062-1099.
English, William J. (Retired)
Fagan, Joseph K., M.Div. (Retired), 60 William Cardinal O'Connell Way, Boston, 02114-2729.
Fahey, James L. (Retired), 35 Sawyer Rd., Hampstead, NH 03841.
Fallon, John F. (Retired), 60 William Cardinal O'Connell Way, Boston, 02114-2729.
Fallon, John J. (Retired), 60 William Cardinal O'Connell Way, Boston, 02114-2729.
Ferreira, Jose S. (Retired), 6 McDewell Ave., Apt. 8, Danvers, 01923-3340.
Fitzpatrick, John P. (Retired), P.O. Box 130, Bennington, NH 03442-0130.
Flynn, Arthur C. (Retired), 45 Folly Pond Rd., Apt. 24, Beverly, 01915-5384.
Flynn, George R. (Retired), Apartado 18-0825, Lima, Peru.
Foley, Thomas C. (Retired), 757 Hancock St., Quincy, 02170-2722.
Franz, Paul R. (Retired), 19877 N. Emmerson Dr., Maricopa, AZ 85239-9400.
Gallagher, Edward L. (Retired), 10036 Connell Rd., San Diego, CA 92131-1430.
Gallagher, John E. (Retired), P.O. Box 465, Farmington, ME 04938-0465.
Garrity, Francis D. (Retired), 22 Weatherly Dr., Salem, 01970-6647.
Gaudet, Joseph A. (Retired), 39 Revere St., Everett, 02149-3524.
Geary, Edward P. (Retired), 61 Adamson St., Boston, 02134-1321.
Girardin, Peter T. (Retired), 2616 Fenwood Rd., Houston, TX 77005-3436.
Gomes, Ronald A. (Retired)
Gosselin, Richard R. (Retired), 3 Hudson St., Apt. 3, Methuen, 01844.
Goulet, Raymond O. (Retired), 31 Simpson Rd., Marlborough, 01752-1532.
Groden, Michael F. (Retired)
Guerrette, William J. (Retired), P.O. Box 2, Rumney, NH 03266-0002.
Harrington, James J. (Retired), 2 Raymond St., Manchester, 01944-1613.
Horrigan, Kevin P. (Retired)
Janiunas, Albin F. (Retired), 19 Maple Ave., Cambridge, 02139-1115.
Kane, Joseph M. (Retired), 60 William Cardinal O'Connell Way, Boston, 02114-2729.
Keane, John F. (Retired), 7 Bay Rd., P.O. Box 372, West Yarmouth, 02673-5803.
Kelley, Arnold E. (Retired), 120 Bellevue Ave., Haverhill, 01832.
Kelley, Laurence E. (Retired), 22 Elm St., Scituate, 02066-4009.
Kelly, John P. (Retired), 186 Highland Ave., Somerville, 02143.
Kelly, Patrick J. (Retired), 280 Main St., Woburn, 01801-5094.
Keohan, Edward M. (Retired), 15 Hawthorne Blvd., Salem, 01970-3709.
King, Edward L. (Retired), 180 Water St., Haverhill, 01830.
King, Philip J. (Retired), 1573 Cambridge St., Cambridge, 02138-4370.
Kirke, Eugene K. (Retired), 24 Clark St., Boston, 02109-1127.
Koen, Stephen A. (Retired), 3 Indian Mound Ln., Falmouth, 02540.
Kremmell, William T. (Retired)
Lanergan, James F. (Retired), P.O. Box 547, Manomet, 02345-0547.
LaRaia, Joseph P. (Retired), 243 Franklin Rd., Box 297, Salisbury, NH 03268.
Lawson, Harold F. (Retired), 60 William Cardinal O'Connell Way, Boston, 02114-2729.
Leonard, Francis B. (Retired), 115 Middlesex St., Chelmsford, 01824.
Leonard, John F. (Retired), 43 Hill St., Newburyport, 01950-3952.
Lizio, John R. (Retired), 933 Central St., Framingham, 01701-4872.
Logue, Charles D. (Retired), 44 Ethelma Rd., Chatham, 02633-1508.
Lucey, William F. (Retired), 106 Church St., Boston, 02132-1052.
Lukas, Joseph S. (Retired), 1200 Liberty St., 02184-8212.
Lynch, Leo X. (Retired), 60 William Cardinal O'Connell Way, Boston, 02114-2729.
MacDonald, Paul V. (Retired), 90 Oakmere St., Boston, 02132-5531.
MacKenzie, William M. (Retired), 115 Eagle Dr., Rochester, NH 03868.
Maffei, Vincent R. (Retired), 211 N. Main St., Randolph, 02368-1745.
Magni, Daniel M. (Retired)
Mansfield, John L. (Retired), 60 William Cardinal O'Connell Way, Boston, 02114-2729.
Martel, Leo E. (Retired), 32 Kings Dr., Raymond,

Martin, Joseph I. (Retired), 24 Clark St., Boston, 02109-1127.
McConnell, William J. (Retired), 60 William Cardinal O'Connell Way, Boston, 02114-2729.
McCormick, John J. (Retired), One Grace Ave., Billerica, 01821-2504.
McElroy, John W. (Retired), 6 Lakeview Ln., Palm Coast, FL 32137-1490.
McGowan, Frederick R. (Retired), 2C Greenleaf Park, Merrimac, 01860-1833.
McGowan, James J. (Retired)
McLaughlin, Edward J. (Retired), 103 Center St., Bridgewater, 02324-1397.
McLaughlin, Richard P. (Retired), 14 Boston Ave., Somerville, 02144-2302.
McPartland, Paul G. (Retired), 50 Monument Ave., Boston, 02129-3324.
McQuade, Richard E. (Retired), 10 Buttonwood Ln., Scituate, 02066-1107.
Meade, Maurice P. (Retired), 411 Franklin St., #201, Cambridge, 02139.
Medeiros, Antonio S. (Retired), 131 Winston St., Acushnet, 02745.
Meskell, David B. (Retired), 30 Cambridge St., Winchester, 01890-3730.
Moran, Richard S. (Retired), 23 Spruce St., Malden, 02148-4416.
Morris, John S. (Retired), 505 Mill St., #269, Worcester, 01602-2482.
Mottau, Robert S. (Retired), 20 Devens St., Apt. 404, Boston, 02129-3725.
Moynihan, T. Joseph (Retired), 151 Coolidge Ave., #610, Watertown, 02472-2867.
Mulligan, Paul F. (Retired), 60 William Cardinal O'Connell Way, Boston, 02114-2729.
Murphy, H. Joseph (Retired), 42 Melody Ln., Waltham, 02454.
Murray, John A. (Retired), 53 George St., Watertown, 02472-3343.
Murray, Thomas F. (Retired), 37 Gia Ln., Mashpee, 02649-3755.
Naughton, Thomas J. (Retired), 29 St. Mary's Rd., Milton, 02186-2022.
Nee, Robert E. (Retired)
Nichols, Henry P. (Retired)
Nichols, John J. (Retired), Capella South 1104, Goat Island, Newport, RI 02840-1582.
Noonan, Mark L., Ph.D. (Retired), 78 Bucks Creek Rd., Chatham, 02633.
O'Brien, Frederick W. (Retired), 60 William Cardinal O'Connell Way, Boston, 02114-2729.
O'Connor, Maurice J. (Retired), 750 Whittenton St., Unit 723, Taunton, 02780-1353.
O'Connor, William J. (Retired), P.O. Box 414, Marshfield, 02050-0414.
O'Donnell, John F. (Retired), 61 Williams Way, Goffstown, NH 03045-6615.
O'Hara, Francis A. (Retired), 257 Acapesket Rd., East Falmouth, 02536-6021.
O'Meara, Gerard J. (Retired), 24 Clark St., Boston, 02109-1127.
O'Regan, Hugh H., V.F. (Retired), 101 Seth Parker Rd., Centerville, 02632-2166.
Oliviera, Joel D. (Retired), 155 Fort St., East Providence, RI 02914-5139.
Pearsall, William T. (Retired), 60 William Cardinal O'Connell Way, Boston, 02114-2729.
Perron, Richard J. (Retired), 419 Lafayette St., Salem, 01970-5337.
Phinn, Paul A. (Retired), 265 Walker St., Box 331, Falmouth, 02541-0331.
Poirier, Vincent J. (Retired), 206 Linden Ponds Way, OW614, Hingham, 02043-3767.
Pollis, Robert G. (Retired), 60 William Cardinal O'Connell Way, Boston, 02114-2729.
Pratt, Lawrence E. (Retired), 112 Old Wharf Rd, E-3, Dennis Port, 02639-2230.
Regan, Michael J. (Retired), 60 William Cardinal O'Connell Way, Boston, 02114-2729.
Reilly, Thomas J. (Retired), 26 Centerville Way, Plymouth, 02360.
Riley, James H. (Retired), 66 Emerald Dr., Lynn, 01904-1255.
Rondeau, Lawrence J. (Retired), 161 Federal St., Salem, 01970-3297.
Rothwell, Joseph T. (Retired), 130 Dorchester St., Boston, 02127-2699.
Rouse, C. Paul (Retired), P.O. Box 347, Boston, 02127-0003.
Ruggeri, Joseph A. (Retired), 224 Grosbeak Ln., Naples, FL 34114-3013.
Sallese, Albert J. (Retired), 1158 Main St., Bellingham, 02019-1597.
Santerre, Richard R. (Retired), 1573 Cambridge St., Cambridge, 02138-4370.
Schatzel, John E. (Retired), P.O. Box 601, Bryantville, 02327-0601.
Serena, Edward T. (Retired), 40 South Meadow Village, Unit 6, Carver, 02330-1802.
Shea, John J. (Retired), 500 Ocean St., Marshfield, 02050-5007.
Sheehy, Charles I. (Retired), 60 William Cardinal O'Connell Way, Boston, 02114-2729.
Smyth, Joseph P. (Retired), 46 Laurel Ct., Nashua, NH 03062-4461.
Soucy, Robert P. (Retired), 112 Old Wharf Rd., E-3, Dennis Port, 02639-2230.
Sullivan, E. Paul (Retired), 822 Orleans Rd., Harwich, 02645-3037.
Sullivan, Lawrence F. (Retired), 102 Brooksby Village Dr., Apt. 3, Peabody, 01960.
Svirskas, Joseph J. (Retired), 3 Pleasant Ave., South Hamilton, 01982-1752.
Sweeney, Frederick E. (Retired), 49 Ocean Ave., Box 1111, York, ME 03909-1111.
Thomas, Robert W. (Retired), 3115 Corrib Dr., Tallahassee, FL 32309-3307.
Toomey, John M. (Retired), 60 William Cardinal O'Connell Way, Boston, 02112-2729.
Vartzelis, George D. (Retired), 1573 Cambridge St., Cambridge, 02138-4370.
Verrill, O. Wendell, V.F. (Retired), 91 Wompatuck Rd., Hingham, 02043-1175.
Von Euw, Vincent P. (Retired), 130 Dorchester St., Boston, 02127-2642.
Waldron, Robert J. (Retired), 75 Chase St., Box 77, West Harwich, 02671-0077.
Wasnewski, Richard P. (Retired), 46 Village St., Medway, 02053-1048.
Wetterholm, Lawrence E. (Retired), 60 William Cardinal O'Connell Way, Boston, 02114-2729.
Wyndham, Thomas F. (Retired), 9 Settlers Ter., Box 801, Eastham, 02642-0801.

Society of St. James the Apostle. For contact information please call or write: Society of Saint James the Apostle, 24 Clark St., Boston, MA 02109-1127; Tel: 617-742-4715:

Revs.—
McCarthy, Jeremiah J.
O'Sullivan, Raymond S.
Oates, Thomas F.
Tynan, Desmond A.

Unassigned. For contact information please call or write: Clergy Personnel Office, 66 Brooks Dr., Braintree, MA 02184-3839; Tel: 617-779-3685:

Revs.—
Clark, James B.
D'Onofrio, Joseph J.
LeBlanc, Keith P.
Picardi, John M.
Randone, Michael C.
Sullivan, Robert J.
Tighe, Leonard J.
Twomey, Daniel F.
Ventura, William N.

Permanent Deacons:
Acampora, Andrew J., St. John the Evangelist, Swampscott
Agudelo, Jose N., St. James, Haverhill
Alexander, John F., St. Joseph the Worker, Hanson
Anthony, Thomas A., St. John the Baptist, Haverhill
Arsenault, Joseph G., St. Francis of Assisi, Braintree
Balestracci, Alfred O., St. Theresa of Lisieux, North Reading
Bankowski, Paul F., St. Christine, Marshfield
Beatrice, Lee A., (Unassigned)
Belmonte, Joseph A., St. Anthony of Padua, Revere
Bilotta, Richard F., St. Margaret, Burlington
Biron, R. Donald, (Lend Lease)
Bloom, Laurence J., St. Susanna, Dedham
Bortz, John E., Saint Mary, Chelmsford
Bower, Charles H., Sacred Heart, Middleborough
Boyle, John F., St. Joseph, Holbrook
Brady, Robert F., St. Isidore, Stow
Breen, Robert F., St. Francis of Assisi, Medford
Breinlinger, Martin E., St. Mary's, Holliston
Brennan, Richard J., Sts. Martha and Mary, Lakeville
Brent, John A., St. Catherine of Siena, Norwood
Bresnahan, John M., Holy Family, Lynn
Bulpett, Dean C., St. Irene, Carlisle
Burch, Gregory J., Holy Family, Concord
Burke, Thomas P., St. Bernadette, Randolph
Burns, Daniel R., Formation Dir., Office for Permanent Diaconate
Buttrick, Stephen M., Immaculate Conception, Weymouth
Cabral, John F., (Unassigned)
Cabrera, Crescencio A., (Lend Lease)
Camacho, Teodoro, (Lend Lease)
Canova, Joseph A., St. Francis Xavier, Weymouth
Carey, John J., (Lend Lease)
Caruso, Philip M., St. Mary, Holliston
Casillas, Luis R., (Lend Lease)
Castillo, Jesus, St. Mary of the Assumption, Lawrence
Cavanaugh, Michael J., St. Clare, Braintree
Cloonan, Paul M., St. Paul, Wellesley
Clough, Charles I., Holy Family, Concord
Constantino, Anthony J., Sacred Heart, East Boston
Corbett, Francis J., Immaculate Conception, Weymouth
Cordeau, Richard W., St. Ann, Peabody
Cornell, Charles A., St. Isidore, Stowe
Crimmins, Daniel F., St. Anne, Littleton
Delio, Richard P., (Unassigned)
Dello Russo, Francis B., St. Patrick, Stoneham
Dempsey, Timothy F., St. Mary, Lynn
DiBello, Phillip T., St. Theresa of Lisieux, Billerica
Donoghue, Leo J., St. Joseph, Quincy
Doucette, Raymond E., Holy Family, Amesbury
Dow, Paul A., Our Lady of the Assumption, Lynnfield
Dunn, Daniel A., Holy Family, Gloucester
Dzuris, Robert W., St. Rita, Lowell
Eames, James H., St. Mary, Randolph
Elibero, Edward P., St. Richard of Chichester, Danvers
Fagan, Joseph M., Jr., St. Thomas of Villanova, Wilmington
Farguheson, Wood Rowe, St. Joseph, Salem
Fenton, Jack H., (Lend Lease)
Ferraro, Charles A., St. Irene, Carlisle
Ferrazzi, Charles J., (Unassigned)
Field, Richard P., Jr., (Unassigned)
Fitzgerald, Brendan A., (Unassigned)
Fonseca, Marcio O., St. Ambrose, Dorchester
Gabriel, George M., Sacred Heart, Middleborough
Gaffney, Francis M., Blessed Sacrament, Saugus
Gagne, Ronald D., (Unassigned)
Gallant, Robert J., (Leave of Absence)
Gardyna, Henry A., (Health Leave)
Gaudreau, Robert J., (Unassigned)
Geneus, Alfred J., Saint John the Evangelist, Cambridge; Haitian Community
Ghioni, David R., St. Jude, Norfolk
Goldy, Andrew J., (Health Leave)
Greer, James F., Blessed Kateri Tekakwitha, Plymouth
Grimley, Edward J., (Lend Lease)
Guerin, Bertrand H., St. Martha, Plainville
Guerrini, Patrick E., Asst. Dir., Office for Permanent Diaconate
Hanson, Herbert C., St. Linus, Natick
Hardcastle, Philip P., St. Charles Borromeo, Woburn
Hardin, Howard P., (Unassigned)
Hardy, Gerard J., St. William, Tewksbury
Henry, Martin W., St. Mary of the Nativity, Scituate
Herrera, Luciano, Our Lady of Lourdes, Jamaica Plain
Hickey, C. Michael, (Unassigned)
Hidalgo, Nelson J., St. Joseph, Lynn
Hoaglund, Robert I., (Unassigned)
Holderried, Joseph E., St. Margaret Mary, Westwood
Horgan, Frederick B., St. Edward the Confessor, Medfield
Hulme, John A., St. Peter, Plymouth
Hunt, John C., St. Francis of Assisi, Dracut
Hwang, Augustine J., Sacred Heart, Newton
Iraola, Alejandro, St. Rose of Lima, Chelsea
Iwanowicz, Michael A., Our Lady of Sorrows, Sharon
Johnson, Robert N., Our Lady Comforter of the Afflicted, Waltham
Jones, Paul S., Our Lady of Lourdes, Carver
Joy, Richard T., St. Catherine of Alexandria, Westford
Kane, William F.X., Holy Family, Gloucester
Keefe, Arthur J., Holy Family, Duxbury
Kerns, William E., St. Florence, Wakefield
Kerrigan, James V., St. Barbara, Woburn
King, Clifford D., St. Thomas, Wilmington
Koffel, William B., Our Lady Help of Christians, Newton
Kramich, Robert A., Holy Family, Gloucester
L'Italien, George G., (Unassigned)
LaFond, Philip H., Christ the King, Brockton
LaTorre, Pedro, (Unassigned)
Laws, Brian H., St. Anne, Littleton
Leduc, Roland E., St. Michael, Lowell
Lewis, Paul A., St. John the Baptist, Quincy
Lloyd, Barry V., St. Margaret, Lowell
MacDonald, Joseph E., St. Benedict, Somerville
Maloney, William F., Holy Trinity, Quincy
Manzi, James A., St. Paul, Hamilton
Markham, Michael J., Our Lady of Grace, Pepperell
Martinez, Orlando, (Unassigned)
Martino, Richard C., (Lend Lease)
McCarthy, Daniel E., (Unassigned)
McCarty, William J., (Lend Lease)
McGuffie, Jacques A., St. Patrick, Roxbury
McHugh, Francis W., Most Holy Redeemer, East Boston
McHugh, John W., St. Katherine Drexel, Roxbury

McLaughlin, James V., St. Bridget, Abington
McLaughlin, Richard B., Hanscom AFB, Bedford
Menendez, Silvio J., (Lend Lease)
Menz, John R., Holy Trinity, Quincy
Mesa, Ricardo M., Cathedral of the Holy Cross, Boston
Messina, Joseph M., St. Timothy, Westwood
Miles, Walter J., (Unassigned)
Mills, Chester P., (Unassigned)
Montes, Eddy M., (Health Leave)
Mora, Eduardo R., St. Mary, Waltham
Morel, Pablo, St. Joseph, Lynn
Morey, Russell W., (Unassigned)
Mott, Michael M., St. John the Evangelist, Hopkinton
Murphy, Steven J., (Health Leave)
Nagle, William V., St. Joseph, Kingston
Naveo, Jose D., (Unassigned)
Nelson, Daniel C., Corpus Christi-Saint Bernard, Newton
Nguyen, Hon H., St. Ambrose, Dorchester
Nicholson, John D., Our Lady of Fatima, Sudbury
Nickley, Joseph T., Jr., Holy Ghost, Whitman
Nieves, Alfredo, St. Stephen, Framingham
O'Neil, Cyril T., St. Patrick, Stoneham
Oles, Kenneth W., St. Mary, Wrentham
Ortiz, Jesus M., Our Lady of Lourdes, Jamaica Plain
Papik, Stephen M., Holy Trinity, Lowell
Patino, Jorge A., (Unassigned)
Patrick, Alexander J., (Unassigned)
Peltak, Douglas P., St. Matthias, Marlborough
Penney, Everett F., St. Marguerite D'Youville, Dracut
Pepi, John W., St. Bridget, Maynard
Perea, Antonio M., Most Holy Redeemer, East Boston
Perez, Jose, (Unassigned)
Pierce, John B., St. Monica, Methuen
Quiles, Francisco M., (Lend Lease)
Radford, Richard F., (Lend Lease)
Ramrath, Joseph R., (Unassigned)
Reilly, Christopher P., St. Mary of the Sacred Heart, Hanover
Rivera, Luis F., St. Rose of Lima, Chelsea
Rivera, Valentin, St. John the Baptist, Peabody
Rivero, Victor R., Most Holy Redeemer, East Boston
Rizzuto, Anthony P., (Unassigned)
Roberts, Carl M., Our Lady of Hope, Ipswich
Robinson, Edwin J., St. Tarcisius, Framingham
Rodrigues, Pedro M., St. Anthony of Padua, Somerville
Rodriguez, Diego N., (Lend Lease)
Rogers, Arthur F., Jr., Prison Ministry
Rooney, Paul S., St. Anthony of Padua, Cohasset
Ros, Peter An, St. Patrick, Lowell
Rosario, Manuel A., St. Charles Borromeo, Woburn
Rumley, Mark E., Immaculate Conception, Malden
Ryan, Gerald P., St. Thomas Aquinas, Bridgewater
Ryan, Kenneth N., Sacred Heart, Weymouth
Saint Hilaire, Norman R., (Unassigned)
Saint Sauveur, Guy C., St. Michael, Bedford
Santosuosso, Alfred E., St. Jude, Waltham
Shanahan, Allan R., St. Mary, Billerica
Sheedy, Louis W., St. Mary, Dedham
Shrader, David J., (Lend Lease)
Sicuso, Anthony C., (Leave of Absence)
Siebert, Richard, Immaculate Conception, Newburyport
Smith, Thomas A., St. John the Evangelist, Wellesley
Spadoni, Reynold G., Blessed Sacrament, Walpole
Specht, Paul V., St. Patrick, Lawrence
Spiri, Guy J., St. Stephen, Framingham
Stenstrom, Eugene V., St. Mary, Plymouth
Straub, Stanley A., St. Mary of the Annunciation, Cambridge
Sullivan, Charles E., Office of the Regional Bishop-South
Sullivan, Daniel F., St. Agatha, Milton
Sullivan, John A., St. Thecla Parish, Pembroke
Sumner, Neil J., St. Athanasius, Reading
Taylor, Carroll H., Prison Ministry
Theriault, James G., St. Mary of the Assumption, Hull
Torres, Pedro L., St. Stephen, Framingham
Tremblay, Francis R., St. Timothy, Norwood
Turner, J. Robert, St. Patrick, Stoneham
Valeri, Frank A., Most Blessed Sacrament, Wakefield
Vandi, Dennis, (Unassigned)
Vargas, Julio C., Corpus Christi, Lawrence
Velasquez, Edin, Most Holy Redeemer, East Boston
Vitale, Paul D., (Lend Lease)
Vitello, Joseph V., St. Jerome, Weymouth
Webb, Charles P., St. Thomas More, Braintree
Wheeler, Raymond A., (Lend Lease)
Whipple, John E., Our Lady, Star of the Sea, Marblehead
Wildes, William H., (Lend Lease)
Wise, John W., St. Agnes, Middleton

Senior Deacons:
Senior Deacons—
Abercrombie, J. Scott
Alence, Robert W.
Alicea, Francisco
Amerault, Robert P.
Bubello, Charles M.
Callahan, James C.
Capomaccio, John J.
Chisholm, Finley H.
Connor, John P.
Counihan, Eugene A.
Creutz, Edward F.
Crump, James M.
D'Ambrosio, Francis D.
Delaney, Joseph L.
Ego, John J.
Gagnon, Raymond A.
Guerrios, Francisco
Hackett, Robert T.
Hanlon, Thomas H.
Hardy, John W.
Heffernan, Francis X.
Jennette, John F.
Juliano, Anthony J.
Kaelin, Gerard J.
LaBrache, Leo F.
Lacey, Neil F.
LaPointe, Norman P.
Lauture, Albert
Leavitt, James P.
MacDonald, Joseph P.
MacKinnon, William J.
Mannion, John J., Prison Ministry
Marchant, Thomas W.
Markey, Paul G.
Martin, Leo A.
McManus, Lawrence R.
Murphy, Alfred L.
Pugsley, Stanley G.
Quigley, Edward M.
Quiles, Jesus M.
Salenius, John D.
Sanchez, Tomas E.
Watson, John W.
Welch, Henry M.
Yanikoski, Florian F.

INSTITUTIONS LOCATED IN THE ARCHDIOCESE

[A] SEMINARIES, ARCHDIOCESAN

BOSTON. *St. John Seminary* (1884) 127 Lake St., Brighton, 02135. Tel: 617-254-2610; Fax: 617-787-2336. Web: www.sjs.edu. Revs. Arthur L. Kennedy, Ph.D., Rector; Raymond Van De Moortell, Th.M., M.Div., Ph.D., M.L.I.S., Librarian; Joseph F. Scorzello, M.Div., S.T.L., Ph.D.; Stephen E. Salocks, S.S.L., M.Div., Dean, Faculty; Romanus Cessario, O.P., S.T.D., S.T.L.; Peter P. Gojuk, O.M.V., Coord., Spiritual Dir.; Philip E. Merdinger, M.A., Spiritual Dir.; Christopher K. O'Connor, M.Div., M.A., Ph.L, Vice Rector; Michael B. Medas, M.S.W., Dir. Supervised Ministries; Robert W. Oliver, B.H., S.T.D., J.C.D.; Rev. Msgr. James P. Moroney, B.A., S.T.L.; Rev. Derek J. Borek, M.Div., S.T.L., Dean of Students; Kathleen Heck, B.A., J.D., Dir. Communications & Devel.; Dr. J. David Franks, Ph.D., Prof.; Sr. Mary Veronica Sabelli, R.S.M., Ph.D., Prof.; Mrs. Aldona Lingertat, Ph.D., Dir. Master of Arts in Ministry; Dr. J. David Franks, Ph.D., Co-Assoc. Dir. Master of Arts in Ministry; Dr. Angela Franks, Co-Assoc. Dir. Master of Arts in Ministry; Sr. Mary Cora Uryase, R.S.M., Ph.D.; Dr. Janet Hunt. Priests 21; Sisters 2; Lay Teachers 14; Students 180; Total Enrollment 180.

WESTON. *Blessed John XXIII National Seminary* (1964) 558 South Ave., 02493. Tel: 781-899-5500; Fax: 781-899-9057. Email: seminary@blessedjohnxxiii.edu. Web: www.blessedjohnxxiii.edu. Very Rev. Peter J. Uglietto, M.Div., S.T.L., S.T.D., Rector & Pres.; Revs. James M. DiPerri, M.A., M.Div., J.C.L.; Paul E. Fitzpatrick, S.M., S.T.L., S.T.D.; Joseph K. Fagan, M.Div. (Retired); Gregory J. Hoppough, C.S.S., M.Div., S.T.L., S.T.D., M.A.; Thomas F. Schmitt, S.T.L., Dean of Students; Paul E. Miceli; William B. Palardy, Ph.D., Academic Dean; Leo M. Manglaviti, S.J.; Dr. Anthony W. Keaty; Dr. Leonard Maluf, S.T.D.; Sr. Jacqueline Miller, S.S.A., Librarian. A Major National Seminary open to men over thirty studying for the diocesan and religious priesthood. Priests 9; Lay Teachers 2; Students 65.

[B] SEMINARIES, RELIGIOUS OR SCHOLASTICATES

BOSTON. *Oblate Provincialate*, 2 Ipswich St., 02215-3607. Tel: 617-536-4141; Fax: 617-536-7016. Email: omv.office@verizon.net. Web: www.omvusa.org. Rev. David Nicgorski, O.M.V., Prov.; Bro. Luigi Falbo, O.M.V., Treas. St. Ignatius Province of the Oblates of the Virgin Mary, Inc.
Priests of the Province on Special Assignment:
Philippines: Revs. Lino Estadilla, O.M.V.; Nnamdi Monevne, O.M.V.; Gregory Short, O.M.V.; Mark Yavarone, O.M.V. (Philippines).

Our Lady of Grace Seminary, 1105 Boylston St., 02215-3604. Tel: 617-266-5999; Fax: 617-247-7576. Web: www.omvusa.org. Revs. David N. Beauregard, O.M.V., Dean of Studies; Timothy M. Gallagher, O.M.V., Formation Staff; Gregory Staab, O.M.V., Formation Staff; Peter Grover, O.M.V., Supr.; Peter P. Gojuk, O.M.V., Formation Staff; Jeremy Paulin, O.M.V., Vocation Dir. St. Ignatius Province of the Oblates of the Virgin Mary, Inc. Priests 6; Lay Teachers 2; Students 8.

CHESTNUT HILL. *The Ecclesiastical Faculty at Boston College* (known as Weston Jesuit, an academic department within the Boston College School of Theology and Ministry), 140 Commonwealth Ave., 02467. Tel: 617-552-6501; Fax: 617-552-0811. Email: stm@bc.edu. Web: www.bc.edu/stm. Revs. William P. Leahy, S.J., Ph.D., Pres.; Richard J. Clifford, S.J., Dean. Priests 12; Sisters 1; Lay Teachers 5; Students 133.

Redemptoris Mater Archdiocesan Missionary Seminary, 774 Boylston St., 02467-2501. Tel: 617-879-9813; 617-879-9814; Fax: 617-879-0170. Revs. Antonio F. Medeiros, Rector; Roderick A. Crispo, O.F.M., Spiritual Dir.; Emanuele DeNigris (WDC), Vice Rector.

DANVERS. *Xavier Center* House of Formation., 21 Spring St., 01923. Tel: 978-777-1326. Bro. John D. Hamilton, C.F.X., Dir. Xaverian Brothers, USA. Brothers Professed 3.

FRAMINGHAM. *Sylva Maria* (1952) 567 Salem End Rd., 01702-5599. Tel: 508-879-6711; Fax: 508-879-7667. Email: sonsboston@gmail.com. Web: www.sonsofmary.com. Revs. Robert Rivard, F.M.S.I.; John Wallace, F.M.S.I. House and Novitiate of the Sons of Mary, Health of the Sick. Priests 4; Brothers 4.
Council: Revs. John Murphy, F.M.S.I., Coord.; John Coss, F.M.S.I., Councilor; Bro. Kevin Courtney, F.M.S.I.

[C] COLLEGES AND UNIVERSITIES

BOSTON. *Caritas Laboure College, Inc.* (1892) 2120 Dorchester Ave., 02124. Tel: 617-296-8300; Fax: 617-296-7947. Web: www.laboure.edu. Joseph W. Mc Nabb, Ph.D., Pres.; Andrew Calo, Librarian. Two year college for nursing and allied health. Member of Caritas Christi Health Care System. Priests 1; Lay Teachers 75; Students 578; Total Enrollment 680.

Emmanuel College, 400 The Fenway, 02115. Tel: 617-735-9715; Fax: 617-735-9877. Email: hatten@emmanuel.edu. Web: www.emmanuel.edu. Sr. Janet Eisner, S.N.D., Ph.D., Pres. Sisters of Notre Dame de Namur; Rev. Stephen Bayle, Co-Dir. Campus Ministry; Sr. Margaret Cummins, S.N.D., Dir. Campus Ministry. Priests 1; Sisters 3; Lay Teachers 49; Students 1,856.

CHESTNUT HILL. **Boston College* (1863) (Coed), 02467. Tel: 617-552-8000. Web: www.bc.edu. Rev. William P. Leahy, S.J., Ph.D., Pres.; Cutberto Garza, Ph.D., Provost; Thomas Wall, Univ. Librarian. Priests 35; Sisters 4; Lay Teachers 698; Students 14,640.

College of Arts and Sciences (1863) Tel: 617-552-2393; Fax: 617-552-1383. David Quigley, Ph.D., Dean. Students 6,119.

Summer Session Tel: 617-552-3900; Fax: 617-552-3199. Rev. James A. Woods, S.J., Dean. Students 3,667.

Graduate School of Arts and Sciences (1925) Tel: 617-552-3268; Fax: 617-552-3700. David Quigley, Ph.D., Dean. Students 872.

School of Law (1929) Tel: 617-552-4340; Fax: 617-552-2851. Vincent Rougeau, J.D., Interim Dean. Students 817.

Woods College of Advancing Studies (1929) Tel: 617-552-3900; Fax: 617-552-3199. Rev. James A. Woods, S.J., Dean. Students 779.

Graduate School of Social Work (1936) Tel: 617-552-4020; Fax: 617-552-2374. Alberto Godenzi, Ph.D., Dean. Students 513.

Carroll School of Management (1938) Tel: 617-552-8420; Fax: 617-552-2593. Andrew C. Boynton, Ph.D., Dean. Students 1,930.

Carroll Graduate School of Management (1957) Tel: 617-552-8420; Fax: 617-552-2593. Andrew C. Boynton, Ph.D., Dean. Students 888.

Connell School of Nursing (1947) Tel: 617-552-4250;

Fax: 617-552-0745. Susan Gennaro, D.S.N., Dean. Students 377.

Lynch School of Education (1952) Tel: 617-552-4200; Fax: 617-552-0812. Maureen Kenny, Ph.D., Interim Dean. Students 673.

Connell Graduate School of Nursing (1994) Tel: 617-552-4250; Fax: 617-552-0745. Susan Gennaro, D.S.N., Dean. Students 331.

Lynch Graduate School of Education (1994) Tel: 617-552-4200; Fax: 617-552-0812. Maureen Kenny, Ph.D., Interim Dean. Students 1,003.

The School of Theology and Ministry (2008) Tel: 617-552-6501; Fax: 617-552-0811. Rev. Mark S. Massa, S.J., Dean; Esther Griswold, Librarian. Students 338.

NORTH ANDOVER. *Merrimack College*, 315 Turnpike St., 01845-5800. Tel: 978-837-5000; Fax: 978-837-5222. Web: www.merrimack.edu. Christopher F. Hopey, Ph.D., Pres.; Josephone Modica-Napolitano, Ph.D., Interim Provost; Michael Accardi, Vice Pres., Inst. Advancement; Kristin Greene, Vice Pres. Enrollment Mgmt.; Alexa Abowitz, Vice Pres., Admin. & Counsel to College; Rev. James Wenzel, O.S.A., Coord. Augustinian Values for Campus Life, Res.: St. Ambrose Friary, 196 Elm St., Andover, 01810. Tel: 978-475-8485; Fax: 978-409-1072; Donna Swartwout, Ph.D., Dean of Campus Life; Rev. Keith Hollis, O.S.A., Dir. Campus Ministry. Priests 6; Lay Teachers 139; Students (Full-Time) 2,000; Continuing Education 139.

Our Mother of Good Counsel Monastery (1947) Tel: 978-837-5213; Fax: 978-837-5269. In Res. Revs. Edward J. Enright, O.S.A., Prof. & Prior Austin House; Raymond F. Dlugos, O.S.A., Vice Pres. Mission & Student Affairs & Prior St. Ambrose Friary; William F. Waters, O.S.A., Campus Min. & Treas. St. Ambrose Friary.

SWAMPSCOTT. *Marian Court College*, Little's Point Rd., 01907. Tel: 781-595-6768; Fax: 781-595-3560. Email: info@mariancourt.edu. Web: www.mariancourt.edu. Dr. Ghazi Darkazalli, Ph.D., Pres. & C.E.O.; Maribeth Forbes, C.F.O.; Dr. Denise Hammon, Dean Academic Affairs, Faculty & Student Svcs.; Michele Ahouse, Vice Pres. Inst. Advancement & Enrollment. Sisters 1; Lay Teachers 20; Lay Staff 25; Students 300.

WESTON. *Regis College* (1927) 235 Wellesley St., 02493-1571. Tel: 781-768-7000; Fax: 781-768-8339. Email: postmaster@regiscollege.edu. Web: www.regiscollege.edu. Mary Jane England, M.D., Pres.; Sr. Rosemary Mulvihill, R.S.M., Campus Min.; Lynn Triplett, Librarian Dir. Sisters of St. Joseph 7; Lay Teachers 179; Students 2,018.

[D] HIGH SCHOOLS, PRIVATE

BOSTON. *Boston College High School*, 150 Morrissey Blvd., 02125. Tel: 617-929-9495; Fax: 617-929-9459. Email: rperry@sjnen.org. Web: www.bchigh.edu/. Revs. Ronald V. Perry, S.J., Rector; Joseph T. Bennett, S.J. Tel: 617-929-9482; Herbert J. Cleary, S.J.; Robert R. Dorin, S.J.; Jon D. Fuller, S.J.; Charles J. Healey, S.J.; James J. Hosie, S.J. Tel: 617-929-9488; Thomas J. Kenny, S.J., Campus Min.; Gerard R. McKeon, S.J.; James W. O'Neil, S.J. Tel: 617-929-9452; Martin G. Shaughnessy, S.J.; Bro. Donald J. Murray, S.J. Tel: 617-436-3900. Priests 11; Brothers 1; Sisters 1; Lay Teachers 128; Students 1,600.

Cathedral High School, Inc., 74 Union Park St., 02118. Tel: 617-542-2325; Fax: 617-542-1745. Web: www.cathedralhighschool.net. Thomas P. Arria Jr., Headmaster; Rashaun J. Martin, Prin.; Richard Smyth, Librarian. Brothers 1; Sisters 6; Lay Teachers 22; Staff 18; Students 296.

Catholic Memorial School, (Grades 7-12), (Boys), 235 Baker St., 02132-4395. Web: www.catholicmemorial.org. Paul E. Sheff, Pres.; Richard F. Chisholm, Prin. Congregation of Christian Brothers. Brothers 4; Lay Teachers 65; Boys 800.

Cristo Rey Boston High School Corporate Work Study Program, Inc., 100 Savin Hill Ave., 02125. Tel: 617-825-2580; Fax: 617-825-2613. Email: jthielman@cristoreyboston.org. Jeff Thielman, Contact Person.

Cristo Rey Boston High School, Inc., 100 Savin Hill Ave., 02125. Tel: 617-825-2580; Fax: 617-825-2613. Email: jthielman@cristoreyboston.org. Jeff Thielman, Pres. & Contact Person; Rev. Jose Medina, F.S.C.B., Prin. Priests 2; Lay Teachers 18; Students 313.

Mount Saint Joseph Academy, 617 Cambridge St., 02134-2460. Tel: 617-254-8383 (School Office); 617-783-4747 (Guidance Office); Fax: 617-254-0240. Email: kathleen.fraser@mountsaintjosephacademy.org. Web: www.mountsaintjosephacademy.org. Kathleen Fraser, Prin.; Linda Walkins, Librarian. Sponsored by Sisters of St. Joseph of Boston. Sisters 4; Lay Teachers 20; Girls 200.

BRAINTREE. *Archbishop Williams High School, Inc.* (1949) 80 Independence Ave., 02184. Tel: 781-843-3636; Fax: 781-843-3782. Email: mlsadowski@awhs.org. Web: www.awhs.org. Mary Louise Sadowski, Prin.; Dr. Carmen Mariano, Pres.; Joanna Sands, Librarian. Sisters 1; Teachers 42.

BROCKTON. *Cardinal Spellman High School, Inc.* (1958) 738 Court St., 02302. Tel: 508-583-6875; Fax: 508-580-1977. Email: cshs@spellman.pvt.k12.ma.us. Web: www.spellman.com. John F. McEwan, Ed.D., Pres., Chief Admin. & Contact Person; Dorothy Lynch, Prin.; Diane McDonough, Librarian. Sisters of St. Joseph. Brothers 1; Sisters 1; Lay Teachers 48; Students 690.

CAMBRIDGE. *Matignon High School, Inc.*, 1 Matignon Rd., 02140. Tel: 617-876-1212; Fax: 617-661-3905. Web: www.matignon-hs.org. Thomas F. Galligani, Headmaster; Joseph DiSarcina, Prin.; Patricia D'Angelo, Vice Prin. College Preparatory. Religious 1; Lay Staff 50; Students 445.

DANVERS. *St. John's Preparatory School* (1907) 01923. Tel: 978-774-1050; Fax: 978-774-5069. Email: ehardiman@stjohnsprep.org. Web: www.stjohnsprep.org. Edward Hardiman, Headmaster; Keith Crowley, Ph.D., Prin. Day Students. Brothers 5; Lay Teachers 104; Boys 1,260.

DEDHAM. *Ursuline Academy* (1946) (Grades 7-12), 85 Lowder St., 02026-4299. Tel: 781-326-6161; Fax: 781-326-4898. Email: mkeaney@ursulineacademy.net. Web: www.ursulineacademy.net. Mrs. Rosann Whiting, Pres.; Mrs. Mary Jo Keaney, Prin.; Amity Johnson, Librarian. Operated by Ursuline Convent. Ursuline Nuns. College Prep School for Girls. Sisters 4; Lay Teachers 44; Total Staff 67; Girls 398.

EVERETT. *Pope John XXIII High School, Inc.* (1966) 888 Broadway, 02149. Tel: 617-389-0240; Fax: 617-389-2201. Email: info@popejohnhs.org. Web: www.popejohnhs.org. Kathleen Donovan, Pres.; Mary Ann DiMarco, Prin.; Maria Touet, Librarian. Sisters 1; Lay Teachers 19; Students 250; Staff 12.

FRAMINGHAM. *Marian High School, Inc.*, 273 Union Ave., 01702. Tel: 508-875-7646; Fax: 508-875-0838. Email: mbaril@marianhigh.org. Web: www.marianhigh.org. Sr. Catherine Clifford, C.S.J., Prin. & Chief Admin.; Mary Condon, Librarian. Sisters 3; Lay Teachers 24; Students 304.

HINGHAM. *Notre Dame Academy* (1853) 1073 Main St., 02043. Tel: 781-749-5930; Fax: 781-749-8366. Email: president@ndahingham.com. Web: www.ndahingham.com. Sr. Barbara Barry, S.N.D., Pres.; Kathleen Colin, Prin.; Patricia Bologna, Librarian. Girls 600; Lay Teachers 55; Sisters 5; Total Staff 100.

KINGSTON. *Sacred Heart High School*, 399 Bishops Hwy., 02364-2098. Tel: 781-585-7511; Fax: 781-585-7063; 781-585-1249. Email: info@sacredheartkingston.com. Web: www.sacredheartkingston.com. Mr. John Enos III, Prin.; Mrs. Marilyn Rennie-Stanton, Asst. Prin. Academics; Mrs. Anne Marie League, Asst. Prin., Student Svcs & Dir. Intermediate School. Sisters 8; Lay Teachers 49; Students 470.

LAWRENCE. *Central Catholic High School of Lawrence, Inc.*, 300 Hampshire St., 01841. Tel: 978-682-0260; Fax: 978-685-2707. Email: dkeller@centralcatholic.net. Web: www.centralcatholic.net. Bro. Thomas P. Long, F.M.S., Pres.; Doreen A. Keller, Prin.; Kristina Keleher, Librarian. Conducted by the Marist Brothers of the Schools. Religious 8; Lay Teachers 80; Students 1,355.

Notre Dame High School of Lawrence, Inc. (2004) 301 Haverhill St., 01840. Tel: 978-689-8222; Fax: 978-689-8728. Sr. Mary Murphy, S.N.D., Ph.D., Pres.; Dr. Thomas Ryan, Prin.; James Compagna, Dir. of Curriculum; Sr. Margaret Mary Mohr, M.F.I.C., Librarian. Sisters 5; Lay Teachers 20; Students 270.

LOWELL. *Lowell Catholic High School, Inc.*, 530 Stevens St., 01851. Tel: 978-452-1794. Email: ed2000@tiac.net. Mr. Edward J. Quinn, Prin. Sisters 2; Lay Teachers 18; Students 280.

MALDEN. *Malden Catholic High School*, 99 Crystal St., 02148. Tel: 781-322-3098; Fax: 781-397-0573. Email: tyrrelle@maldencatholic.org. Web: www.maldencatholic.org. Edward C. Tyrrell, Headmaster; Bro. Thomas Pucclo, C.F.X., Prin.; Karen Davidson-Heller, Librarian. Xaverian Brothers. Brothers 3; Lay Teachers 48; Boys 600.

METHUEN. *Presentation of Mary Academy* (1958) 209 Lawrence St., 01844. Tel: 978-682-9391; Fax: 978-975-3595. Web: www.pmamethuen.org. Sr. Susan Frederick, P.M., Pres.; Rose Maria Redman, Prin. Sisters of the Presentation of Mary. Sisters 4; Lay Teachers 21; Total Staff 31; Co-ed 200.

MILTON. *Fontbonne Academy* (1954) 930 Brook Rd., 02186. Tel: 617-696-3241; Fax: 617-696-7688. Web: www.fontbonneacademy.org. Mary Ellen Barnes, Prin.; Florence Lathrop, Librarian. Sisters of St. Joseph 5; Lay Teachers 35; Students 300.

NEEDHAM. *St. Sebastian's School, Inc.*, (Grades 7-12), 1191 Greendale Ave., 02492. Tel: 617-449-5200; Fax: 617-449-5630. Web: www.stsebs.org. Mr. William L. Burke III, Headmaster; Revs. John F. Arens; John U. Paris. Priests 2; Lay Teachers 59; Boys 375.

NEWTON. *Country Day School of the Sacred Heart*, (Grades 5-12), 785 Centre St., 02158. Tel: 617-244-4246; Fax: 617-965-5313. Email: alazure@newtoncountryday.org. Web: www.newtoncountryday.org. Sr. Barbara Rogers, R.S.C.J., Prin.

Boston Academy of the Sacred Heart Religious of the Sacred Heart 1; Lay Teachers 70; Girls 380.

Mount Alvernia High School, (Grades 7-12), 790 Centre St., 02458. Tel: 617-964-4766 (Convent); 617-969-2260 (School); Fax: 617-969-4246. Email: MAHSinfo@mountalverniahs.org. Web: mountalverniahs.org. Eileen McLaughlin, Head of School; Patricia Daley, Asst. Head of School; Lauren Bagnell, Devel. Dir.; Susan Akie, Librarian. Missionary Franciscan Sisters of the Immaculate Conception. Sisters 5; Lay Teachers 26; Total Staff 39; Girls 240.

PEABODY. *Bishop Fenwick High School, Inc.* (1959) 99 Margin St., 01960. Tel: 978-587-8300; Fax: 978-587-8309. Email: bfhs@fenwick.org. Web: www.fenwick.org. Sr. Catherine Fleming, S.N.D., Prin., Chief Admin. & Contact Person; Alison Connelly, Librarian. Sisters 3; Lay Teachers 56; Students 563.

READING. *Austin Preparatory School*, (Grades 6-12), 101 Willow St., 01867. Tel: 781-944-4900; Fax: 781-944-7530. Email: pmoran@austinprepschool.org. Web: www.austinprepschool.org. Mr. Paul J. Moran, Headmaster; Rev. Kenneth Healey, S.M.; James Morris; Jay Zimmerman, Librarian. Priests 2; Lay Teachers 61; Administrators 10; Students 687.

TYNGSBOROUGH. *Academy of Notre Dame* (1854) 01879. Tel: 978-649-7611; Fax: 978-649-2909. Web: www.ndatyngsboro.org. Sr. Patricia Conner, S.N.D., Prin.; Kathy Arsneault, Librarian. Sisters of Notre Dame de Namur 1; Faculty 27; Girls 174; Lay Teachers 26; Religious 1.

WESTWOOD. *Xaverian Brothers High School* (1963) 800 Clapboardtree St., 02090. Tel: 781-326-6392; Fax: 781-320-0458. Email: admin@xbhs.com. Web: www.xbhs.com. Bro. Daniel Skala, C.F.X., Headmaster; Domenic Lalli, Prin. Xaverian Brothers. Brothers 3; Lay Teachers 77; Boys 950.

[E] ELEMENTARY SCHOOLS, ARCHDIOCESAN

DANVERS. *St. Mary of the Annunciation School*, 14 Otis St., 01923. Tel: 978-774-0307; Fax: 978-750-4852. Email: khunter@stmaryschooldanvers.org. Web: stmaryschooldanvers.org. Katherine Hunter, Prin. (Grades PreK-8 & Extended Day Care); Annamaria Ferrante, Librarian. Sisters of Notre Dame de Namur 1; Lay Teachers 33; Students 425.

[F] MONTESSORI SCHOOLS

HAVERHILL. *The Merrimack Montessori School*, 55 Saltonstall Rd., 01830. Tel: 978-374-6103; Fax: 978-469-0730. Email: megale_99@yahoo.com. Web: www.merrimackmontessorischool.org. Mary E. Gale, Head of School. (For boys and girls: Pre-primary 24 months-3 yr; Primary 3-6 yr.; Lower Elem. 1st-3rd grade; before & after school programs.) Lay Teachers 11; Students 85.

MARLBOROUGH. *St. Anne Montessori School* (1964) 720 Boston Post Rd. E., 01752. Tel: 508-597-1416. Web: www.stannemontessori.org. Kathleen Finn, Dir. (For boys and girls aged 3-6) Religious 2; Lay Teachers 4; Students 72.

NEWTON. *Walnut Park Montessori School*, 47 Walnut Park, 02458. Tel: 617-969-9208; Fax: 617-969-6408. Email: walnutpk@gis.net. Web: www.walnutparkmontessori.org. Ms. Mary Rockett, Head of School; Sr. Alice Mary Brady, C.S.J., Librarian. Religious 5; Lay Teachers 14; Students 127.

WENHAM. *Notre Dame Children's Class* (1967) 74 Grapevine Rd., 01984. Tel: 508-468-1340; Fax: 508-468-0166. Email: notredcc@aol.com. Web: sndden.org/ndcc. Sisters Barbara Beauchamp, S.N.D., Dir.; Susan Raymo, S.N.D., Co-Dir. Religious 2; Lay Teachers 3; Primary Class 20; Preschool 48.

[G] ELEMENTARY SCHOOLS, PRIVATE

BOSTON. *St. Columbkille School, Inc.*, 25 Arlington St., 02135. Mary E. Battles, Prin.

Mother Caroline Academy (1993) 515 Blue Hill Ave.,

Dorchester, 02121. Tel: 617-427-1177; Fax: 617-427-7788. Email: info@mcaec.org. Web: www.mcaec.org. Ed Hudner, Pres.; Michelle Albert, Co-Prin.; Betty Brown, Co-Prin.

Mother Caroline Academy for Girls, Inc. Sisters 1; Lay Teachers 13; Students 54.

Nativity Preparatory School, (Grades 5-8), 39 Lamartine St., Jamaica Plain, 02130. Tel: 857-728-0031; Fax: 857-728-0037. Email: jwronskisj@nativityboston.org. Web: www.nativityboston.org. Rev. John C. Wronski, S.J., Exec. Dir.

Nativity Boston, Inc., A Jesuit Middle School. Priests 1; Lay Teachers 11; Boys 60.

BRAINTREE. *Cardinal Cushing Centers,* 85 Washington St., 02184. Tel: 617-848-6250; Fax: 617-848-0640. Email: PLarson@Coletta.org. Web: www.Coletta.org.

St. Coletta's and Cardinal Cushing Schools of MA, Inc., Day School for multiple handicapped, developmentally delayed children, ages 4-22 years. Lay Teachers 9; Students 33.

BROCKTON. *Trinity Catholic Academy, Inc.*, 37 Erie Ave., 02302. Tel: 508-583-6237; Fax: 508-583-6260. Mr. Anthony Luizzi, Reg. Dir.; Marie Masaitis, Prin. Lower Campus; Cynthia McNally, Prin. Upper Campus; Jane Clifford, Librarian Lower Campus; Theresa Ballard, Librarian Upper Campus.

CHESTNUT HILL. *Mount Alvernia Academy,* 20 Manet Rd., 02467. Tel: 617-527-7540; Fax: 617-527-7995. Email: jsullivan@mtalverniaacad.org. Web: www.mtalverniaacad.org. Barbara M. Plunkett, Prin. Lay Teachers 27; Students 335; Personnel 49.

DORCHESTER. *Pope John Paul II Catholic Academy Inc.*, 2214 Dorchester Ave., 02124. Tel: 617-265-0019; Fax: 617-298-2926. Russ W. Wilson, Regional Dir. Religious 2; Lay Teachers 77.

GROTON. *Country Day School of the Holy Union* (1949) 14 Main St., 01450. Tel: 978-448-5646; Fax: 978-448-2392. Email: cdsgroton@yahoo.com. Web: www.cdsgroton.org. Sr. Yvette Ladurantaye, S.U.S.C., Prin. Holy Union Sisters 1; Lay Teachers 21; Students 230.

HANOVER. *Cardinal Cushing Centers, Inc.*, 400 Washington St., 02339. Tel: 781-826-6371; Fax: 781-826-1559. Email: skozaryn@coletta.org. Lawrence Sauer, Vice Pres. Student Prog. & Svcs.; Jean Rogers, Vice Pres. Community & Adult Svcs. Lay Staff 550; Students 125.

KINGSTON. *Sacred Heart Elementary School and Early Childhood Center,* (Grades PreSchool-6), (Day School), 329 Bishops Hwy., 02364. Tel: 617-585-2114; Fax: 617-585-6993. Ann Taylor, Prin. (Preschool - 6); Lisa Green, Early Childhood Dir.; Carrie Mathias, Librarian. Sisters of Divine Providence 4; Lay Teachers 30; (K-6) 430; Preschool 72.

Sacred Heart Pre-Primary School, 363 Bishops Hwy., 02364-2035. Tel: 781-585-3545; Fax: 781-422-5224. Sr. Angela Provost, C.D.P., Dir. Religious 1; Lay Teachers 3; Students 64.

LAWRENCE. *Blessed Stephen Bellesini, O.S.A., Academy, Inc.* (2002) 94 Bradford St., 01840-1003. Tel: 978-989-0004; Fax: 978-989-9404. Email: office@bellesiniacademy.org. Web: www.bellesiniacademy.org. Ms. Julie DiFilippo, Exec. Dir. Total Staff 8; Students 60.

Lawrence Catholic Academy of Lawrence, Massachusetts, Inc., 101 Parker St., 01843.

LOWELL. *Franco-American Private School* (1908) 357 Pawtucket St., 01854. Tel: 978-458-0308; Fax: 978-458-0308. Email: faslowell@comcast.net. Web: www.francoamericanschool.org. Sisters Lorraine Richard, S.C.Q., Prin.; Jane Holland, S.C.Q., Asst. Prin. Religious 2; Lay Teachers 17; Students 250.

MARLBOROUGH. *Our Lady Thrift Shop* (1973) 197 Pleasant St., 01752. Tel: 508-485-0740; Fax: 508-481-0663. Email: chretienne@verizon.net. Sr. Ida M. Devoe, S.S.Ch., Officer of the Board. Religious 5.

NEWTON. *Jackson School Elementary,* (Grades K-6), 200 Jackson Rd., 02458-1428. Tel: 617-969-1537; Fax: 617-244-8596. Email: info@jacksonschool.org. Web: www.jacksonschool.org. Mrs. Susan G. Niden, Prin. Sisters 9; Lay Teachers 22; Staff 5; Students 255.

Jackson Walnut Park Educational Collaborative, Inc., (Grades PreSchool-6), 47 Walnut Park St., 02458. Tel: 617-686-0105; 617-969-9208; Fax: 617-969-6908. Email: victoria.londergan@cojboston.org. Web: www.jacksonschool.org. Victoria N. Londergan, Pres.; Mrs. Susan G. Niden, Prin. (Elementary); Mary Reckett, Prin. (Pre-School); Sr. Diane Neumyer, C.S.J., Librarian. Sisters (Jackson) 8; Lay Teachers (Jackson) 17; Sisters (Walnut Park) 4; Lay Teachers (Walnut Park) 19.

TYNGSBOROUGH. *Academy of Notre Dame at Tyngsboro,* 180 Middlesex Rd., 01879. Tel: 978-649-7611; Fax: 978-649-2909. Email: mduke@ndatyngsboro.org. Web: www.ndatyngsboro.org. Sr. Mary Duke, S.N.D., Prin.; Kathy Smith, Librarian. Sisters of Notre Dame de Namur 2; Lay Teachers 26; Students 435.

QUINCY. *Quincy Catholic Academy of Quincy, Massachusetts, Inc.*, 370 Hancock St., 02171.

[H] SPECIAL SCHOOLS

METHUEN. *St. Ann's Home Special Needs School,* 100 A. Haverhill St., 01844. Tel: 978-682-5276; Fax: 978-688-4932. Email: dgrandbois@st.annshome.org. Web: www.st.annshome.org. Mr. Denis Grandbois, Exec. Dir. Ungraded special needs school for emotionally disturbed and behaviorally disordered children. Lay Teachers 38; Psychotherapists 20; Counselors 120; Administrators 11; Staff 23; Residential Students 103; Day Students 68; Bed Capacity 150; Total Staff 260.

PEABODY. *Holy Childhood Nursery & Kindergarten* (1854) 5 Wheatland St., 01960. Tel: 978-531-4733; Fax: 978-531-2468. Email: carmelite@verizon.net. Web: www.carmelitepreschool.com. Sr. Kathleen A. Bettencourt, O.Carm., Coord. & Co-Dir. Sisters 5; Lay Teachers 6; Students 90.

WATERTOWN. *Rosary Academy Learning Center* (1981) 2 Rosary Dr., 02472. Tel: 617-923-1935; Fax: 617-923-2993. Email: ralc1@verizon.net. Web: www.rosaryacademy.net. Sr. Judith Ward, S.N.D., Dir.; Mrs. Eileen Edmondson, Assoc. Dir. Dominican Sisters of Peace., Preschool & Day Care. Sisters 1; Lay Teachers 6; Students 26.

[I] CATHOLIC CHARITIES

BOSTON. *Catholic Charitable Bureau of the Archdiocese of Boston, Inc.* (1903) 51 Sleeper St., 02210. Tel: 617-482-5440; Fax: 617-451-0337. Email: info@ccab.org. Web: www.ccab.org. Ms. Deborah Kincade Rambo, L.I.C.S.W., Pres. Social Service Agency Total Clients Served (Across Eastern Massachusetts) 200,000.

El Centro Del Cardenal/Catholic Charities, 76 Union Park St., 02118. Tel: 617-542-9292; Fax: 617-542-6912. Ms. Elisabeth Zweig-Snippe, Contact Person.

Yawky Center for Early Ed & Care Catholic Charities, 185 Columbia Rd., 02121. Tel: 617-506-6930; Fax: 617-929-0453. Email: esther_garcia@ccab.org. Web: www.ccab.org. Sr. Esther Garcia, S.A., Dir. Community Based Agency of the Catholic Charitable Bureau of the Archdiocese of Boston, Inc.; Day Care. Franciscan Sisters of the Atonement 2.

[J] FAMILY COUNSELING AND GUIDANCE CENTERS

BROCKTON. *Catholic Charities South* A Division of Catholic Charities, 686 N. Main St., 02301. Tel: 508-587-0815; Fax: 508-580-0837. Email: lisa_lodge@ccab.org. Web: ccab.org.

Local Clinics:

North Shore-Danvers, 140 Commonwealth Ave., Ste. 202, Danvers, 01923. Tel: 978-774-6820; Fax: 978-777-4242.

Brockton, 686 N. Main St., 02301. Tel: 508-587-0815; Fax: 508-580-0837.

[K] SOCIETY OF ST. VINCENT DE PAUL

STOUGHTON. *Society of St. Vincent DePaul, Central Office,* 18 Canton St., 02072. Tel: 781-344-3100; Fax: 781-341-4560. Email: ejresnick@svdpboston.com. Web: svdpboston.com. Edward J. Resnick, Exec. Dir.

[L] CHILD CARE AGENCIES

BOSTON. *Nazareth Child Care Center,* 19 St. Joseph St., Jamaica Plain, 02130. Tel: 617-522-4040; Fax: 617-983-0460. Email: pam-penton@ccab.org. Pamela J. Penton, Dir.

Catholic Charities dba Nazareth Child Care Center Capacity 83; Total Staff 18.

Nazareth Residence for Mothers and Children, 91 Regent St., 02119. Tel: 617-541-0100; Fax: 617-541-8781. Email: nazareth_residence@ccab.org. Sr. Mary Farren, R.G.S., Program Dir. Home for homeless mothers and children who are HIV positive. Capacity 8; Total Staff 10; Total in Residence 22.

METHUEN. *St. Ann's Home, Inc.*, 100A Haverhill St., 01844. Tel: 978-682-5276; Fax: 978-688-4932. Email: dgrandbois@st.annshome.org. Web: www.st.annshome.org. Mr. Denis Grandbois, Exec. Dir.; Mrs. Sharon Cutter, Business Mgr. Total in Residence 105; Day Students 66; Total Staff 245; School Children 145.

Residential Treatment Center Tel: 978-692-5276; Fax: 978-688-4932. Children 165.

[M] GUIDANCE CENTERS

BOSTON. *St. Mary Women and Children's Center* (1993) 90 Cushing Ave., 02125. Tel: 617-436-8600; Fax: 617-288-8961. Email: jbeckler@smwcc.org. Web: www.smwcc.org. Ms. Judith Beckler, Pres. Provides residential, education and training programs for women and children who are homeless or living in poverty. Patients Assisted Annually 250; Total Staff 100.

Salesian Boys & Girls Club (Central Unit), 150 Byron St., 02128. Tel: 617-567-6626; Fax: 617-568-3851. Email: sbgclub@juno.com. Web: www.salesianclub.com. Salesians of St. John Bosco. Total Assisted 1,750; Total Staff 16.

Orient Heights Unit, 145-150 Bryon St., 02128. Tel: 617-567-6626. Rev. John Nazzaro, S.D.B., Exec. Dir., Club Admin. & Rector Salesian Staff: Revs. Richard Putnam, S.D.B.; Richard Cressman, S.D.B.; Bro. Robert Metell, S.D.B.

BRAINTREE. *Life Resources, Inc.*, 100 River St., 02184. Tel: 781-849-7751; Fax: 781-849-7754. Web: www.liferesourcesinc.org. Michelle M. Nickerson, Pres.

Life Resources/Alpha-Omega, 140 Adams St., 02184. Tel: 781-848-5510; Fax: 781-380-7565. Web: www.liferesourcesinc.org. A long term residence for 20 adolescent boys.

BROCKTON. *Phaneuf Youth Treatment Center,* 104 Market St., 02301. Tel: 508-584-0500. Short term residence for 16 adolescent males.

LAKEVILLE. *Bishop Joseph John Ruocco House,* 22 Highland Rd., 02347. Tel: 508-947-2823; Fax: 508-947-0305. Web: liferesourcesinc.org. Short term residence for 16 female adolescents. To provide comprehensive life skill services to residents and their families.

[N] INFORMATION - CONFERENCE CENTERS

BOSTON. *Paulist Center,* 5 Park St., 02108. Tel: 617-742-4460; Fax: 617-720-5756. Email: fiveparkst@aol.com. Web: www.paulistboston.com. Revs. Frank Desiderio, C.S.P., M.A. Theology, M.A. Communication, Dir.; Broderick M. Walsh, C.S.P., M.Div., Assoc. Dir.; Susan Rutkowski, M.Div., Pastoral Min., Family Rel. Educ. & Social Justice; Patricia Simpson, M.Div., Admin.; Michael Kurley, Pastoral Min., Liturgy & Music.

BROCKTON. *Chapel of Our Savior-Catholic Pastoral and Information Center* (1961) 475 Westgate Dr., 02301-1819. Tel: 508-583-8357; Fax: 508-586-5510. Revs. Gerald DiGiralamo, S.A., Dir.; Malcolm Martin, S.A. (Retired); Robert Langone, S.A.; Daniel O'Shea, S.A.; Bros. Thomas Banacki, S.A.; Louis Marek, S.A.; Savio McNeice, S.A. Priests 4; Brothers 3.

[O] GENERAL HOSPITALS

BOSTON. *Caritas Carney Hospital, Inc.*, 2100 Dorchester Ave., 02124-5666. Tel: 617-723-1100. Mr. Wilson D. Rogers Jr., Esq., Contact Person.

Caritas St. Elizabeth's Medical Center of Boston, Inc., 736 Cambridge St., Brighton, 02135. Tel: 617-789-3000; Fax: 617-789-3007. Email: shagop@aol.com. Web: www.cchcs.org. Dr. Ralph de la Torre, M.D., CEO, Caritas Christi; Mr. John J. Holiver, Pres., St. Elizabeth; Revs. Robert J. Caprio, O.F.M., Dir. Spiritual Care Dept.; Charles E. Salamone; Sr. Mary Anne Gallagher, O.S.F.; Rev. Anselm Nwagbara (Nigeria); Sisters Shirley Nugent, S.C.N.; Mary Olsen, C.S.J.; Timothy Duff; Martha Sullivan; Ms. Cheryl Amrich. Priests 3; Total Staff 10; Bed Capacity 350; Bassinets (NICU level 3) 20; Nursery Beds 30; Patients Assisted Annually 118,223.

BROCKTON. *Caritas Good Samaritan Medical Center, Inc.*, 235 N. Pearl St., 02401. Tel: 508-427-3000; 508-427-3151; 508-427-2602. Mr. Steven R. Gordon, Pres.; Rev. Richard W. Visbisky, Chap. & Dir. of Pastoral Care; Pauline Heal, (Congregational). A Caritas family hospital. Total Assisted 193,388; Total Staff 1,302; Sisters of Charity of Nazareth 1; Sisters of Jesus Crucified and the Sorrowful Mother 1; Holy Union Sisters 1.

Caritas Good Samaritan Cancer Center, Inc.

Caritas Good Samaritan Occupational Health Services, Inc.

LOWELL. *Saints Memorial Health System, Inc.*, One Hospital Dr., 01852. Tel: 978-458-1411; Fax: 978-458-8369. Email: info@stmmc.org. Web: www.saints-memorial.org. Thom Clark, Pres. & CEO. Sisters of Charity of Ottawa. Bed Capacity 218; Total Assisted 214,000; Total Staff 1,352.

METHUEN. *Caritas Holy Family Hospital, Inc.* (1984) 70 East St., 01844-4597. Tel: 978-687-0151; Fax: 978-688-7689. Web: www.holyfamilyhosp.org. Lester Schindel, Pres. & CEO; Rev. Richard O'Brien, Chap. Affiliating Hospital for: St. Anselm's Collegiate School of Nursing; Northern Essex Community College; UMass, Lowell; Salem State College; New Hampshire Technical School; Massachusetts Bay Community College;

Northeastern University; Rivier College; Greater Lawrence Vocational School. Bed Capacity 222; Bassinets 28; Patients Assisted Annually 230,000; Total Staff 1,575; Priests 1.

Caritas Holy Family Hospital Auxiliary (1947) 70 East St., 01844-4597. Tel: 978-687-0156, Ext. 2301; Fax: 978-688-7689.

Caritas Holy Family Hospital Men's Guild (1950) 70 East St., 01844-4597. Tel: 978-687-0156, Ext. 2362; Fax: 978-688-7689.

[P] SPECIAL HOSPITALS

BOSTON. *Franciscan Hospital for Children*, 30 Warren St., Brighton, 02135. Tel: 617-254-3800; Fax: 617-779-1119. Email: fch@fhfc.org. Web: www.fhfc.org. Mr. Paul Della Rocco, Pres. & CEO. General Pediatrics, Rehabilitation, Special Education, Mental Health Services & Home Care. Bed Capacity 100; Number under care 59,000; Day Program 90; Total Staff 650.

[Q] SOCIAL SERVICES

BOSTON. *Chinese Catholic Pastoral Center*, 78 Tyler St., 02111-1831. Tel: 617-482-2949; Fax: 617-482-2949.

Little Sisters of the Assumption, Family Health Service, Inc. (1981) (Project Hope), 550 Dudley St., 02119. Tel: 617-442-1880; Fax: 617-238-0473. Email: mleonard@prohope.org. Web: www.prohope.org. Project Hope is a multi-service agency at the forefront of efforts in Boston to move families beyond homelessness and poverty. It provides low-income women with children with access to education, jobs, housing and emergency child care services; fosters their personal transformation; and works for broader systems change. Total Assisted 1,000; Total Staff 54; Sisters 2.

CAMBRIDGE. **Helping Hands of St. Marguerite, Inc.*, 799 Concord Ave., 02138. Tel: 617-492-1023; Fax: 617-492-1025. Email: ddougherty@helpinghands-homecare.org. Web: www.helpinghands-homecare.org. Daniel Dougherty, Exec. Dir. Covenant Health Systems, Tewksbury, MA., Personal care, housekeeping and companion services to individuals and families in their own homes, in assisted living residences or in retirement communities.

LAWRENCE. **M.I. Adult Day Health Center, Inc.*, 189 Maple St., 01841. Tel: 978-682-6321; Fax: 978-975-0050. Email: gerard_foley@gmail.com. Web: www.mihcs.com. *Covenant Health Systems*, 100 Ames Pond Dr., Ste. 102, Tewksbury, 01876. Gerard Foley, Pres. & CEO. Covenant Health Systems, Tewksbury, MA., Adult day health care for senior citizens; also, bilingual/bicultural (Spanish) adult day health care. Total in Residence 70; Total Staff 12.

**M.I. Transportation, Inc.*, 189 Maple St., 01841. Tel: 978-682-7575; Fax: 978-691-5374. Email: gerard_foley@gmail.com. Web: www.mihcs.com. *Covenant Health Systems*, 100 Ames Pond Dr., Ste. 102, Tewksbury, 01876. Covenant Health Systems, Tewksbury, MA. Total Assisted 75; Total Staff 5.

**Mary Immaculate Adult Day Health Center, Inc.*, 189 Maple St., 01841. Tel: 978-685-6321; Fax: 978-975-0050. Email: gerard_foley@mihcs.com. Web: www.mihcs.com. Gerard Foley, Pres. & CEO. Covenant Health Systems, Lexington, MA

[R] PROTECTIVE INSTITUTIONS

BOSTON. *St. Mary's Women and Infants Center*, 90 Cushing Ave., 02125. Center for pregnant women.; (See Guidance Centers for more information.)

[S] HOMES FOR AGED-RESIDENTS & NURSING

BOSTON. *Don Orione Nursing Home*, 111 Orient Ave., East Boston, 02128-1006. Tel: 617-569-2100; Fax: 617-561-1138. Email: rgovoni@donorionehome.org. Revs. Miroslaw Kowalczyk, F.D.P.; Gino Marchesani, F.D.P., Chap. Sons of Divine Providence (Don Orione Fathers) 5; Guests 110; Total Assisted 185; Total Staff 230.

Marian Manor (1954) 130 Dorchester St., South Boston, 02127. Tel: 617-268-3333; Fax: 617-268-4589. Email: joe@marianmanor.org. Web: www.marianmanor.org. Sr. Mark Louis, Admin.; Rev. Herbert J. Cleary, S.J., Chap. Priests 1; Carmelite Sisters for the Aged and Infirm 10; Total Staff 520; Guests 366.

BROCKTON. *St. Joseph Manor Health Care Inc.* (1965) 215 Thatcher St., 02302. Tel: 508-583-5834; Fax: 508-583-8551. Email: christopher.kenney@sjmbrockton.org. Web: www.sjmbrockton.org. *Covenant Health Systems*, 100 Ames Pond Dr., Ste. 102, Tewksbury, 01876. Tel: 978-654-6363; Fax: 978-851-0828. Christopher Kenney, CEO & Admin. A member of Covenant Health Systems, Tewksbury, MA. Sisters of Jesus Crucified and the Sorrowful Mother 5; Residents 118; Total Staff 202.

Adult Day Health Center Tel: 508-583-8313; Fax: 508-588-7384. Total Assisted Per Day 60; Total Staff 12.

CAMBRIDGE. *Sancta Maria Nursing Facility* (1948) *Covenant Health Systems*, 100 Ames Pond Dr., Ste. 102, Tewksbury, 01876. Tel: 978-654-6363; Fax: 978-851-0828. 799 Concord Ave., 02138. Tel: 617-868-2200; Fax: 617-864-2801. Sr. Mary Mark, D.M., Admin. Daughters of Mary of the Immaculate Conception., An affiliate of Covenant Health Systems, Tewksbury, MA. Sisters 4; Residents 141; Bed Capacity 141; Total Staff 217.

**Youville Hospital & Rehabilitation Center, Inc.*, 1575 Cambridge St., 02138-4398. Tel: 617-876-4344; Fax: 617-547-5501. Email: leaheyd@youville.org. Web: www.youville.org. Mr. Daniel Leahey, Pres. & CEO; Mr. Robert Short, Sr. Dir., Mission & Pastoral Care; Rev. Martin Okwir (Uganda), Chap.; Bruce Aguilar, Chap.; Janice Matter, Chap. Covenant Health Systems, Tewksbury, MA. Priests 1; Bed Capacity 180; Patients Assisted Annually 2,340; Total Staff 650.

**Youville House, Inc.*, 1573 Cambridge St., 02138-4398. Tel: 617-491-1234; Fax: 617-491-8838. Email: joannecparsons@youvillehouse.org. Web: www.youvilleassistedliving.com. Joanne C. Parsons, CEO. Covenant Health Systems, Tewksbury, MA., Youville House is an assisted living residence. Total in Residence 92; Total Apartments 95; Residents Assisted Annually 120; Total Staff 85.

FRAMINGHAM. *Carmel Terrace* (1995) 933 Central St., 01701. Tel: 508-788-8000; Fax: 508-626-1603. Web: www.carmelterrace.org. Sr. Jeanette D. Lindsay, O.Carm., Dir. Carmelite Sisters for the Aged and Infirm 3; Apartments for Assisted Living of the Elderly 69; Total Assisted 75; Total Staff 38.

St. Patrick Manor, Inc., 863 Central St., 01701. Tel: 508-879-8000; Fax: 508-626-1604. Web: www.stpatricksmanor.org. Sr. Maureen McDonough, O.Carm., Admin. Carmelite Sisters for the Aged and Infirm 30; Total Staff 460.

IPSWICH. *St. Julie Billiart Residential Care Center, Inc.* (2002) 30 Jeffreys Neck Rd., 01938. Tel: 978-356-4381; Fax: 978-356-1380. Email: lee.pakstis@sndden.org. Lee Pakstis, Admin. Total Staff 45; Bed Capacity 54; Total Assisted Annually 58.

LAWRENCE. *M.I. Residential Community II, Inc.*, 191 Maple St., 01841. Tel: 978-685-6321; Fax: 978-975-0050. Email: gerard_foley@gmail.com. Web: www.mihcs.com. Gerard Foley, Pres. & CEO. Covenant Health Systems, Tewksbury, MA., Independent & assisted living for elderly and handicapped. Units 106; Total in Residence 120; Total Staff 35.

M.I. Residential Community, Inc., 189 Maple St., 01841. Tel: 978-685-6321; Fax: 978-975-0050. Email: gerard_foley@gmail.com. Web: www.mihcs.com. *Covenant Health Systems*, 100 Ames Pond Dr., Ste. 102, Tewksbury, 01876. Gerard Foley, Pres. & CEO. Convenant Health Systems, Tewksbury, MA., "Marguerite's House" Assisted Living Facility-106 Units. Units 106; Total in Residence 121; Total Staff 35.

Mary Immaculate Nursing Restorative Center, 172 Lawrence St., 01841. Tel: 978-685-6321; Fax: 978-975-0050. Email: gerard_foley@gmail.com. Web: www.mihcs.com. *Covenant Health Systems*, 100 Ames Pond Dr., Ste. 102, Tewksbury, 01876. Tel: 978-654-6363; Fax: 978-851-0828. Gerard Foley, Pres. & CEO. Convenant Health Systems, Tewksbury, MA., Multi-level Skilled Nursing Facility; Unit of Mary Immaculate Health Care Services. Residents 250; Total Staff 300.

MI Management, Inc., 172 Lawrence St., 01841. Tel: 978-685-6321; Fax: 978-975-0050. Email: barbara_grant@gmail.com. Web: www.mihcs.com. Gerard Foley, Pres. & CEO. Convenant Health Systems, Tewksbury, MA., Management company for all Mary Immaculate Facilities.

LEXINGTON. *Youville Place, Inc.* (1997) 10 Pelham Rd., 02421-8408. Tel: 781-861-3535; Fax: 781-862-4289. Email: joannecparsons@youvillehouse.org. Web: youvilleplace.org. *Covenant Health Systems*, 100 Ames Pond Dr., Ste. 102, Tewksbury, 01876. Joanne C. Parsons, CEO. Covenant Health Systems, Tewksbury, MA., Assisted Living Facility.

LOWELL. *D'Youville Life and Wellness Community, Inc.*, 981 Varnum Ave., 01854. Tel: 978-569-1000; Fax: 978-453-3561. Email: nprendergast@dyouville.org. Web: www.dyouville.org. Ms. Naomi M. Prendergast, CEO; Cynthia Dobrzynski, Dir. Mission & Values. Sisters of Charity of Ottawa (Grey Nuns of the Cross). Sisters 5; Total Assisted 208; Total Staff 375; Adult Day Health Care Capacity 23.

MARLBOROUGH. *Marie Esther Health Center, Inc.* (1993) 720 Boston Post Rd. E., 01752. Tel: 508-485-3791; 508-460-1951; Fax: 508-229-2294. Email: ecaron@sistersofsaintanne.org. Total Assisted 72; Total Staff 58.

SOMERVILLE. *Jeanne Jugan Pavilion*, 190 Highland Ave., 02143. Tel: 617-776-4420; Fax: 617-625-6720. Email: smmothersuperior@littlesistersofthepoor.org. 186 Highland Ave., 02143. Apartments for the Elderly 27; Residents 29; Total Staff 1.

Jeanne Jugan Residence, 186 Highland Ave., 02143. Tel: 617-776-4420; Fax: 617-623-0707. Email: smmothersuperior@littlesistersofthepoor.org. Little Sisters of the Poor 14; Residents 111; Senior Citizen Total in Residence 84; Total Staff 105.

WALTHAM. *Maristhill Nursing and Rehabilitation Center* (1969) 66 Newton St., 02453-6063. Tel: 781-893-0240; Fax: 781-894-6330. Email: cfenn@maristhill.org. Web: www.maristhill.org. Ms. Carolyn Fenn, Pres. & CEO. Covenant Health Systems, Tewksbury, MA.

[T] PERSONAL PRELATURES

CAMBRIDGE. *Opus Dei, Prelature of the Holy Cross and Opus Dei*, 25 Follen St., 02138. Tel: 617-354-3204; Fax: 617-868-0349. Web: www.opusdei.org. Revs. Thomas J. Lamb; David J. Cavanagh.

NEWTON. *Prelature of the Holy Cross and Opus Dei*, 481 Hammond St., 02167. Tel: 617-738-7348; Fax: 617-739-6001. Web: www.opusdei.org. Revs. Jose P. Ruisanchez; Richard W. Rieman; Salvador S. Vahi; Thomas J. Lamb.

[U] MONASTERIES AND RESIDENCES OF PRIESTS AND BROTHERS

BOSTON. *Assumptionist Center* (1989) 330 Market St., 02135. Tel: 617-783-0400; Fax: 617-783-8030. Email: despinosa@assumptio.org. Web: www.assumption.us. Revs. Donald Espinosa, A.A., Provincial Treas.; Claude Grenache, A.A., B.A., S.T.B., S.T.L., Campus Minister, Bentley/Supr.; Vincent Machozi, A.A.; Roland Guilmain, A.A. Total in Residence 12.

Assumption Guild, Inc.: Revs. Donald Espinosa, A.A.; Camillus Thibault, A.A. *Assumption Guild*, 330 Market St., Brighton, 02135. Tel: 617-783-0495; Fax: 617-783-8030. Email: assumptionguild@yahoo.com. Web: masscardsaa-.com. Rev. Gerard Messier, A.A., Hospital Chap.

Serving Abroad: Revs. Gary Perron, A.A., Parroquia Emperatrix de America, Mercaderes 99, 03900 Mexico D.F., Mexico. Tel: 525-593-2002; Fax: 525-651-2000; Leo Brassard, A.A., Haktari Songdang, 600-2 Hakgyio-Ri Hakgyio-Myon, Hamp Yong-Gun, Jeollan Amdo 525-812 Korea, South. Tel: 011-061-323-1337; Fax: 011-061-323-1337; Richard Brunelle, A.A., Novice Master, Austin House, P.O. Box 13230, Arusha, Tanzania. Tel: 011-255-57-2443; Luc Martel, A.A., Assumptionist Community, P.O. Box 58488, Nairobi 0200 Kenya. Tel: 011-254-2-567-698; Fax: 011-254-2-570-303; Very Rev. Richard Lamoureux, A.A., Supr. General, Padri Assunzionisti, Via San Piov 55, Rome 00165 Italy.

Carmelite Monastery (1942) 166 Foster St., 02135-3902. Tel: 617-787-5056; Fax: 617-783-1396. Revs. Paul Fohlin, O.C.D., Prior; Leonard Copeland, O.C.D.; Kevin Culligan, O.C.D., B.A., M.A., M.S., Ph.D.; Mark-Joseph DeVelis, O.C.D.; Terrence Dougherty, O.C.D.; Anthony Haglof, O.C.D.; Lawrence F. Sullivan, O.C.D.; Bro. Augustine Wharf, O.C.D. Discalced Carmelite Friars. Priests 7; Brothers 1; Total in Residence 8.

St. Christopher Friary, 18 N. Bennet St., 02113. Tel: 617-742-4190; Fax: 617-742-1676. Bro. Robert Artman, O.F.M., Health Care Dir.; Revs. Robert J. Caprio, O.F.M.; Norbert DeAmato, O.F.M. (Retired); John C. DiMauro, O.F.M. (Retired); Januarius Izzo, O.F.M. (Retired); Kieran Monahan, O.F.M.; Richard Passeri, O.F.M. (Retired); Roland Petinge, O.F.M. (Retired); Aubert Marie Picardi, O.F.M.; Berard Tufo, O.F.M. (Retired); Emery Parillo, O.F.M. (Retired); Bros. Charles Trebino, O.F.M.; James T. Welch, O.F.M. Brothers 1; Priests 8.

St. Francis of Assisi Friary (2008) (The Province of St. Mary of the Capuchin Order, White Plains, NY), 46 Brookside Ave., Jamaica Plain, 02130-2370. Tel: 617-522-6469. Web: www.capuchin.org. Rev. Brendan P. Buckley, O.F.M.Cap., Pastor & Guardian; Bro. James M. Peterson, O.F.M.Cap., J.D., J.C.L., Vicar; Revs. John Rathschmidt, O.F.M.Cap., Ph.D., Dir. of Formation; David B. Couturier, O.F.M.Cap., Ph.D., D.Min. Student Friars 3.

Little Brothers of St. Francis, 785-789 Parker St., 02120. Tel: 617-442-2556. Web: www.littlebrothersofstfrancis.org. Bro. Didacus-Maria Etrata, L.B.S.F., Servant General.

Little Brothers of St. Francis Franciscan Fraternity of Peace and Love, Inc., Regional

Fraternity and Novitiate. Brothers 5.

Loyola House, 300 Newbury St., 02115-2801. Tel: 617-424-0155; Fax: 617-424-0155. Revs. James F. Walsh, S.J., Supr.; Charles B. Connolly, S.J.; Robert G. McMillan, S.J., Treas.; James M. Shaughnessy, S.J.; John P. Spencer, S.J.; Richard J. Stanley, S.J.; George P. Winchester, S.J.; Dennis J. Yesalonia, S.J. The Society of Jesus. Priests 8; Total in Residence 8.

Marist Fathers Lourdes Residence, 698 Beacon St., 02215. Tel: 617-262-2271; Fax: 617-536-1694. Revs. Andrew Albert, S.M., Dir.; Roland Lacasse, S.M., Assoc.; Normand J. Martin, S.M., Assoc.; Albert DiIannl, S.M. Priests 4.

The Salesian Community (1945) 150 Byron St., 02128. Tel: 617-569-6551; 617-567-6626; Fax: 617-568-3851. Email: salesians@comcast.net. Web: www.salesiansociety.org. Total Assisted 2,000.

San Lorenzo Friary (2002) (The Province of St. Mary of the Capuchin Order, White Plains, New York), 15 Montebello Rd., 02130-2352. Tel: 617-983-1919; 617-983-3692; Fax: 617-983-0515. Email: yakiecap@yahoo.com. Web: www.capuchin.org. Bro. James M. Peterson, O.F.M.Cap., J.D., J.C.L., Guardian; Revs. Michael Banks, O.F.M.Cap., B.A., M.Div., M.S.Ed, Vicar & Dir., Formation; Michael Banks, O.F.M.Cap., B.A., M.Div., M.S.Ed. Student Friars 7.

The Society of Jesus of New England-Provincial Offices (1926) 85 School St., Watertown, 02472-4251. Tel: 617-607-2800; Fax: 617-607-2888. Email: nenprvsj@sjnen.org. Web: www.sjnen.org. Mailing Address: P.O. Box 9199, Watertown, 02471-9199. Very Rev. Myles N. Sheehan, S.J., Prov.; Revs. Joseph A. Appleyard, S.J., Exec. Asst.; Robert J. Daly, S.J., Asst. for Higher Educ.; Thomas J. Feely, S.J., Asst. for Formation; Charles A. Frederico, S.J., Vocation Dir.; Michael D. Linden, S.J., Asst. for Intl. Ministries; James M. Shaughnessy, S.J., Liaison for Hospital Chaplaincy Ministry; Dennis J. Yesalonia, S.J., Treas.

Priests of Province on Special Assignment: Revs. Albert A. Agresti, S.J.; Ronald J. Amiot, S.J.; Robert J. Araujo, S.J.; John J. Begley, S.J.; I. Michael Bellafiore, S.J.; Richard D. Bertrand, S.J.; B. Jeffrey Blangiardi, S.J.; Richard P. Boyle, S.J.; Robert J. Braunreuther, S.J.; Scott N. Brodeur, S.J.; Joseph J. Bruce, S.J.; Mark J. Burke, S.J.; James P. Carr, S.J.; Gregory C. Chisholm, S.J.; Thomas F. Clark, S.J.; Brian J. Conley, S.J.; Michael J. Connolly, S.J.; John T. Crabb, S.J.; John R. d'Anjou, S.J.; Andrew N. Downing, S.J.; Theodore A. Dziak, S.J.; Gerald F. Finnegan, S.J.; Thomas J. Fitzpatrick, S.J.; James J. Fleming, S.J.; Anthony J. Forte, S.J.; Andrew J. Garavel, S.J.; Francois Gick, S.J.; David H. Gill, S.J.; Julio Giulietti, S.J.; Richard K. Gross, S.J.; Robert M. Hanlon, S.J.; G. Simon Harak, S.J.; James J. Hederman, S.J.; Daniel P. Jamros, S.J.; Robert L. Keane, S.J., Chap.; John W. Keegan, S.J.; Charles F. Kelley, S.J.; Brian F. Linnane, S.J.; Daniel J. Lusch, S.J.; Frederic A. Maples, S.J.; James J. Martin, S.J.; Richard B. McCafferty, S.J.; Frederick G. McLeod, S.J.; Ronald A. Mercier, S.J.; John W. Michalowski, S.J.; John C. Monahan, S.J., Chap.; Matthew S. Monnig, S.J.; Bruce T. Morrill, S.J.; Francis J. Moy, S.J.; Thomas R. E. Murphy, S.J.; Joseph R. Palmisano, S.J.; Arthur H. Pare, S.J.; James F.X. Pratt, S.J.; Robert F. Regan, S.J.; Thomas J. Regan, S.J.; Stephen J. Sanford, S.J.; Solomon I. Sara, S.J.; Joseph J. Schad, S.J.; John R. Siberski, S.J.; Lawrence C. Smith, S.J.; Walter J. Smith, S.J.; John E. Surette, S.J.; Robert F. Taft, S.J.; Luis A. Tampe, S.J.; David O. Travers, S.J.; Terrance G. Walsh, S.J.; George T. Williams, S.J.

The Society of St. James the Apostle, Inc., 24 Clark St., 02109. Tel: 617-742-4715; Fax: 617-723-7389. Email: info@socstjames.com. Web: socstjames.com. Rev. David Costello, Dir. Founded by His Eminence Richard Cardinal Cushing, in 1958 to recruit Diocesan Priest volunteers for South America. See American Foreign Missions section for Diocesan Priests serving in Latin America. In Res. Rev. Patrick J. Universal (Retired).

ANDOVER. *St. Francis Friary*, 459 River Rd., 01810. Tel: 978-851-3391; Fax: 978-858-0675. Email: franretc@aol.com. Web: www.franrcent.org. Bro. Robert Artman, O.F.M., Guardian. Order of Friars Minor. Total in Residence 7.

Community: Revs. John C. DiMauro, O.F.M. (Retired); Robert J. Caprio, O.F.M.; Bro. Charles Trebino, O.F.M.; Revs. Richard Donovan, O.F.M.; Roland Petinge, O.F.M. (Retired).

BRIGHTON. *Blessed Peter Faber Jesuit Community, Ignatius Loyola House*, 188 Foster St., 02135-4620. Tel: 617-779-4200; Fax: 617-779-4205. Priests 34; Brothers 4; Scholastics 35. *Miguel Pro House*, 192-B Foster St., 02135-4620. Tel: 617-779-4287; Fax: 617-779-4205. Revs. Thomas Ahoussi, S.J., Student of Theology; Christopher Frechette, S.J., Faculty - Boston College School of Theology & Ministry; Jaime Alejandro Olayo Mendez, S.J., Student of Theology; Rene Mario Micallef, S.J., Doctoral Student - Boston College School of Theology & Ministry; Richard H. Roos, S.J.; Gonzalo Villagran, S.J., Doctoral Student - Boston College School of Theology & Ministry. *Alberto Hurtado House*, 194 Foster St., 02135-4620. Tel: 617-779-4285; Fax: 617-779-4205. Revs. Arnel Aquino, S.J.; Francis Alvarez, S.J., Student of Theology; Gregoire Catt, S.J., Student of Theology; Kenneth J. Hughes, S.J., Spiritual Dir. - Boston College School of Theology & Ministry; Varghese Lopez, S.J., Student of Theology; Bradley M. Schaeffer, S.J., Rector - Faber Jesuit Community. *Walter Ciszek House*, 190-A Foster St., 02135-4620. Tel: 617-779-4286; Fax: 617-779-4205. Revs. Thomas D. Stegman, S.J., Faculty - Boston College School of Theology & Ministry; Tomasz Fiedler, S.J., Student of Theology; Edward V. Vacek, S.J., On Sabbatical at Woodstock Jesuit House, Washington D.C. *Isaac Jogues House*, 196-A Foster St., 02135-4620. Tel: 617-779-4288; Fax: 617-799-4205. Revs. Daniel J. Harrington, S.J., Faculty - Boston College School of Theology & Ministry; Emmanuel Lundemba, S.J., Student of Theology; Tu Van Pham, S.J., Student of Theology; Pedro Pereira Tomas, S.J., Student of Theology; Jose Maria Valverde Viqueira, S.J. *Noel Chabanel House*, 196-B Foster St., 02135-4620. Tel: 617-779-4269; Fax: 617-779-4205. Revs. Richard J. Clifford, S.J., Prof. of Old Testament - BC School of Theology & Ministry; Cathal Doherty, S.J., Student of Theology; John Randy Sachs, S.J., Prof. of Systematic Theology Boston College School of Theology & Ministry; Cyprian Tellis, S.J., Student of Theology. *Francis Xavier House*, 190-B Foster St., 02135-4620. Tel: 617-779-4219; Fax: 617-779-4205. Revs. Thomas Massaro, S.J., Faculty - Boston College School of Theology & Ministry; Paulus Bambang Irawan, S.J., Student of Theology; Victor Hugo Miranda, S.J., Student of Theology; Damjan Ristic, Student of Theology; Jose Maria Segura Salvador, S.J., Student of Theology. *Edmund Campion House*, 192-A Foster St., 02135-4620. Tel: 617-779-4239; Fax: 617-779-4205. Revs. John Baldovin, S.J., Faculty - Boston College School of Theology & Ministry; Joseph Laramie, S.J., Student of Theology; Pedro McDade, S.J., Student of Theology.

Priests of the Assumption, Inc., 330 Market St., 02135. Tel: 617-783-0400; Fax: 617-783-8030.

BROCKTON. *Chapel of Our Savior* (1961) 475 Westgate Dr., 02301-1819. Tel: 508-583-8357; Fax: 508-586-5510. Revs. Gerald DiGiralamo, S.A., Dir.; Robert Langone, S.A.; Malcolm Martin, S.A. (Retired); Daniel O'Shea, S.A.; Bros. Savio McNeice, S.A.; Louis Marek, S.A.; Thomas Banacki, S.A. Franciscan Friars of the Atonement. Priests 4; Brothers 3.

COHASSET. *Bellarmine House*, 150 Howard Gleason Rd., 02025. Tel: 781-383-0723; Fax: 781-383-3164. Rev. Michael F. Ford, S.J., Admin. (Summer Res. for Jesuits of New England Prov.).

DANVERS. *Xavier Center* (1975) 21 Spring St., 01923. Tel: 978-777-1326. Bro. John D. Hamilton, C.F.X., Dir. of Formation, House of Formation. Xaverian Brothers, U.S.A. Brothers Professed 3.

DEDHAM. *African Mission House* Society of African Missions, Inc., 337 Common St., 02026-4030. Tel: 781-326-3288; 781-326-4670; Fax: 781-326-7627. Email: smausa-d@ix.netcom.com. Web: www.smafathers.org. Revs. Ulick Bourke, S.M.A.; Anthony Fevlo, S.M.A.; Hugh Lagan, S.M.A. Priests 1.

DUXBURY. *Society of the Divine Word*, 121 Parks St., P.O. Box M, 02331-0614. Tel: 781-585-2460; Fax: 781-585-3770. Email: miramarma@aol.com. Web: www.miramarretreat.org. Bro. Donald Champagne, S.V.D., Dir., Rector; Revs. John J. Bergin, S.V.D.; Joseph Connolly, S.V.D.; John Farley, S.V.D.; Thomas Griffith, S.V.D.; James Heiar, S.V.D.; Robert M. Jones, S.V.D.; Robert Mallonee, S.V.D.; Thomas Umbras, S.V.D. Priests 8; Brothers 1; Total Staff 26.

HINGHAM. *Glastonbury Abbey* (1954) 16 Hull St., 02043. Tel: 781-749-2155; Fax: 781-749-6236. Email: office@glastonburyabbey.org. Web: www.glastonburyabbey.org. Revs. Thomas J. O'Connor, Prior - Admin; Nicholas J. Morcone, O.S.B.; Timothy J. Joyce; Andrew M. Quillen; John P. Kelleher, O.S.B.; Gerald T. Leibenguth, O.S.B.; Bros. David K. Coakley, O.S.B., Music Dir.; James Crowley, O.S.B.; Daniel F. Walters, O.S.B., Conference Center Dir. Benedictine Monks., Benedictine Monastery. Priests 6; Brothers 3; Retreat House Capacity 32; Conference Center Capacity 180.

HOLLISTON. *Xaverian Missionaries*, 101 Summer St., P.O. Box 5857, 01746-5857. Tel: 508-429-2144; Fax: 508-429-4793. Email: holliston@xaviermissionaries.org. Web: www.xaviermissionaries.org. Revs. Giuseppe Matteucig, S.X., Supr.; Gerard Furlan, S.X.; Tony B. Lalli, S.X.; Robert S. Maloney, S.X.; Adolph J. Menendez, S.X.; Rocco N. Puopolo, S.X.; Francis Signorelli, S.X. Priests 5.

LAWRENCE. *Franciscans of Primitive Observance*, 30 Trinity St., 01841. Revs. Andrew F. Beauregard, F.P.O.; Peter Giroux, F.P.O.; Benedict Grant, F.P.O.; Sean Patrick Hurley, F.P.O.; Joseph Paul Medio, F.P.O.; John Maria Sweeney, F.P.O.; Bros. Pio Anthony Butti, F.P.O.; Michael Francis Sheehan, F.P.O.; Lawrence Mary Stamm, F.P.O.; Felix Mary Waldren, F.P.O.; James Magdalen Wartman, F.P.O. Co-Redemptrix Friary.

Marist Brothers, 26 Leeds Ter., 01843. Tel: 978-686-7411. Bros. Jerry Dowsky, F.M.S.; John Kachinsky, F.M.S.; Thomas P. Long, F.M.S. Brothers 3.

Marist Brothers Residence, 12 Sheridan St., 01841. Tel: 508-682-1163. Bros. William Lambert, F.M.S., Dir.; C. Vincent Dinnean, F.M.S.; Ernest Beland, F.M.S.; Richard Carey, F.M.S. Brothers 4.

LEXINGTON. *Priestly Fraternity of the Missionaries of St. Charles Borromeo, Inc.*, 21 Follen Rd., 02421-5921. Tel: 781-864-3427 (Rev. Colombo); 781-538-6181. Web: www.fraternityofsaintcharles.org. Revs. Stefano Colombo, F.S.C.B., Contact Person; Jose Medina, F.S.C.B.; Luca Brancolini. *House of Washington DC*, 7600 Carter Ct., Bethesda, MD 20817. Revs. Antonio Lopez, F.S.C.B.; Roberto Amoruso, F.S.C.B.; Pietro Rossotti, F.S.C.B.; Franco Soma, F.S.C.B.; Jose Maria Cortes, F.S.C.B.; Paolo Prosperi, F.S.C.B. *House of Denver, Nativity of Our Lord Parish*, 900 W. Midway Blvd., Broomfield, CO 80020-2048. Tel: 303-469-5171. Revs. Michael Carvill, F.S.C.B.; Accursio Ciaccio, F.S.C.B.; Gabriele Azzalin, F.S.C.B.

LOWELL. *Missionary Oblates of Mary Immaculate*, 27 Kirk St., 01852-1004. Tel: 978-937-9594; Fax: 978-458-3603. Email: andregarinresidence@yahoo.com.

Andre Garin Retirement Residence Tel: 978-937-9594; Fax: 978-458-3603. Email: andregarinresidence@yahoo.com. Bro. Charles Gilbert, O.M.I., Dir. Tel: 978-441-1245; Revs. Roland Couture, Asst. Dir.; Adhemar Deveau, O.M.I.; Leroy Landry, O.M.I.; Donald G. Lozier, O.M.I.; Bro. Thomas Cruise, O.M.I.

Missionary Oblates of Mary Immaculate (1847) *Northeast / Southeast Area Office*, 60 Wyman St., 01852-2841. Tel: 978-458-9912; Fax: 978-458-7274. Email: suds@omiusa.org. Web: www.omiusa.org. Revs. James E. Taggart, O.M.I., Area Councillor; George Brown, O.M.I.; Norman Comtois, O.M.I., Retreat Center; Wilfred Harvey, O.M.I., Pastoral School Chap.; John King, O.M.I., Hermitage; Roger E. Lamoureux, O.M.I.; Joseph Schwab, O.M.I. (Retired); William Sheehan, O.M.I., Preacher, Spiritual Dir.; Andre Tanguay, O.M.I. (Retired); Louis J. Villarreal, O.M.I., Preacher. Priests 94; Brothers 9; Total Staff 1; Total in Residence 6; Total Membership 103. *St. Eugene House (Residence)* (1995) 285 Andover St., 01852-1438. Tel: 978-441-0649; Fax: 978-454-0677. Revs. Charles Breault, O.M.I.; Herve Gagnon, O.M.I. (Retired); James E. Taggart, O.M.I., Area Councillor; Lucien A. Sawyer, O.M.I., Chap.; William Sheehan, O.M.I., Supr.; Bro. Augustin Cote, O.M.I., Dir. Oblate Foreign Mission Office. *Oblate Foreign Mission Office, Northeast*, 60 Wyman St., 01852-2841. Tel: 978-458-4380; Fax: 978-458-7274. Email: oblate_missions_lowell@juno.com. Bro. Augustin Cote, O.M.I., Dir.

LYNN. *Franciscan Community (Province of Immaculate Conception)*, 38 Michigan Ave., 01902. Tel: 617-592-7396; Fax: 781-595-6724. Rev. Alfonse Ferreira, O.F.M., Procurator & Guardian. *"The Listening Place" (Counseling Center)*, 36 Michigan Ave., 01902. Tel: 781-592-7396; Fax: 781-593-8805. Rev. Alfonse Ferreira, O.F.M., Dir.; Sr. Jane Hogan, O.S.F., Assoc. Dir.

MILTON. *Oblate Residence (St. Joseph House)*, 65 Fr. Carney Dr., 02186-4206. Tel: 617-698-6785; Fax: 617-698-7621. Web: www.omvusa.org. Revs. Dennis Brown, O.M.V.; John Ferrara, O.M.V.; Robert Lowrey, O.M.V.; Craig McMahon, O.M.V.; James Montanaro, O.M.V.; David Nicgorski, O.M.V.; David Yankauskas, O.M.V.; Bro. Joseph O'Connor, O.M.V. Congregation of the Oblates of the Virgin Mary. Priests 7; Brothers 1.

NEWTON. *The Jesuit Community at Boston College* (1863) 02467. Tel: 617-552-8200; Fax: 617-552-2380. Web: www.bc.edu/sj/. Very Rev. Myles N. Sheehan, S.J., Prov.; Revs. T. Frank Kennedy, S.J., Rector; Michael F. Ford, S.J., Asst. Rector & Admin.; Francis R. Herrmann, S.J., Asst. Rector; Edward M. O'Flaherty, S.J., Treas.; James A. Woods, S.J., Dean; Stanislaus Alla, S.J.; Joseph A. Appleyard, S.J.; Joseph B. Badokufa, S.J.;

Michael C. Barber, S.J.; Jimmy Bartolo, S.J.; Casey C. Beaumier, S.J.; James W. Bernauer, S.J.; Richard Blake, S.J.; Michael Boughton, S.J.; James F. Bresnahan, S.J.; James T. Bretzke, S.J.; Emmanuel Bueya, S.J.; Rolando S. Bustamante, S.J.; John Butler, S.J.; Sammy Chong, S.J.; Mario M. Cisneros, S.J.; Jeremy Clarke, S.J.; Walter J. Conlan, S.J.; James J. Conn, S.J.; James Conroy, S.J.; Robert J. Daly, S.J.; Michael F. Davidson, S.J.; Kurt Denk, S.J.; Terrence P. Devino, S.J.; Trung Hoa Dinh, S.J.; George Drury, S.J.; Joseph P. Duffy, S.J.; Harvey D. Egan, S.J.; Frederick Enman, S.J.; Michael A. Fahey, S.J.; Robert Farrell, S.J.; Charles R. Gallagher, S.J.; Gary Gurtler, S.J.; Emmanuel Gurumombe, S.J.; Charles J. Healey, S.J.; Raymond G. Helmick, S.J.; Kenneth Himes, O.F.M.; David Hollenbach, S.J.; Fidele Ingiyimbere, S.J.; Jiang Joseph, S.J.; Gregory Kalscheur, S.J.; James Keenan, S.J.; Joseph M. Kiarie, S.J.; Stephen J. Kieta, S.J.; Philip Kiley, S.J.; William P. Leahy, S.J., Ph.D., Pres.; John Allan Loftus, S.J.; Kenneth G. Loftus, S.J.; Donald A. MacMillan, S.J.; Arthur R. Madigan, S.J.; Mark S. Massa, S.J., Dean School of Theology & Ministry; Richard A. McGowan, S.J.; Paul McNellis, S.J.; Jean Messingue, S.J.; Willy Mubelo Moka, S.J.; J. Donald Monan, S.J.; William B. Neenan, S.J.; Gerard C. O'Brien, S.J.; Joseph M. O'Keefe, S.J.; Cyril Opeil, S.J.; John Paris, S.J.; Frank J. Parker, S.J.; William J. Richardson, S.J.; Richard Ross, S.J.; William C. Russell, S.J.; Gregory C. Sharkey, S.J.; Francis A. Sullivan, S.J.; Ronald K. Tacelli, S.J.; Alan Thomasset, S.J.; Robert F. VerEecke, S.J.; Andrea Vicini, S.J.; Christopher Willcock, S.J.; John C. Wronski, S.J.

PEABODY. *Our Lady of the Scapular Priory* (1970) 4 Wheatland St., 01960. Tel: 978-532-2891; Fax: 978-532-1040. Revs. Herbert J. Jones, O.Carm., Chapel Dir.; Felix Prior, O.Carm.; Mario Lopez, O.Carm.; Bro. Damien Chong, O.Carm. Priests 3; Brothers 1.

SOMERVILLE. *Brotherhood of Hope* (1980) 194 Summer St., 02143-2525. Tel: 617-623-9592; Fax: 617-625-1837. Email: bohinfo@brohope.net. Web: www.brotherhoodofhope.org. Brothers 7; Brothers Elsewhere 11; Priests 3; Total in Residence 7.

TEWKSBURY. *Oblate World/Missionary Association of Mary Immaculate*, 486 Chandler St., 01876-0680. Tel: 978-858-0434; Fax: 978-858-3661. Email: oblateworld@omires.com. Rev. James Flavin, O.M.I., Dir.

WALTHAM. *Bertoni Hall - Formation House* Bertoni Hall, 554 Lexington, 02452-3097. Tel: 781-209-3100. Web: www.stigmatines.com. Rev. Gregory J. Hoppough, C.S.S., M.Div., S.T.L., S.T.D., M.A., Admin.

Stigmatine Fathers & Brothers Provincial House, 554 Lexington St., 02452. Tel: 718-209-3100; Fax: 781-894-9785. Web: www.stigmatines.com. Very Rev. Robert S. White, C.S.S., M.Div., S.T.L., Prov.; Revs. Peter Pramonte Chinnacode, C.S.S. (Thailand); Robert Masciocchi, C.S.S. Total Staff 4.

WESTON. *Campion Health Center, Inc.*, 319 Concord Rd., 02493-1398. Tel: 781-788-6800; Fax: 781-894-5864. *Covenant Health Systems*, 100 Ames Pond Dr., Ste. 102, Tewksbury, 01876-1293. Revs. Robert J. Levens, S.J., Rector; Ronald E. Wozniak, S.J., Min.; Francis R. Allen, S.J.; Joseph F. Brennan, S.J.; Vincent M. Burns, S.J.; Albert A. Cardoni, S.J.; Joseph H. Casey, S.J.; Herbert J. Cleary, S.J.; James M. Collins, S.J.; Denis R. Como, S.J.; William J. Connolly, S.J.; Lawrence E. Corcoran, S.J.; Neil F. Decker, S.J.; John F. Devane, S.J.; Joseph D. Devlin, S.J.; James J. Dressman, S.J.; John W. Elder, S.J.; Joseph G. Fennell, S.J.; Paul P. Gilmartin, S.J.; William J. Hamilton, S.J.; John B. Handrahan, S.J.; Edward J. Hanrahan, S.J.; Philip K. Harrigan, S.J.; John J. Karwin, S.J.; James M. Keegan, S.J.; Joseph R. Laughlin, S.J.; Paul T. Lucey, S.J.; James B. Malley, S.J.; John J. Mandile, S.J.; Leo M. Manglaviti, S.J.; Stanley B. Marrow, S.J.; Paul T. McCarty, S.J.; Joseph B. McHugh, S.J.; John P. McIntyre, S.J.; Paul A. Messer, S.J.; James C. O'Brien, S.J.; Lawrence J. O'Toole, S.J.; Joseph A. Paquet, S.J.; Arthur H. Pare, S.J.; Ernest F. Passero, S.J.; Normand A. Pepin, S.J.; Anthony R. Picariello, S.J.; Donald J. Plocke, S.J.; Richard W. Rousseau, S.J.; Philip C. Rule, S.J.; Patrick J. Ryan, S.J.; James W. Skehan, S.J.; Bros. Edward P. Babinski, S.J.; Vincent M. Brennan, S.J.; H. Francis Cluff, S.J.; James J. Moran, S.J.; Cornelius C. Murphy, S.J.; Edward L. Niziolek, S.J. Priests 49; Brothers 6; Total in Community 55.

Campion Jesuit Community, 319 Concord Rd., 02493. Tel: 781-788-6800; Fax: 781-894-5864. Revs. Robert J. Levens, S.J., Rector; Ronald E. Wozniak, S.J., Min.; James R. Mattaliano, S.J., Dir., Renewal Ctr.; William A. Barry, S.J.; Stephen J. Bonian, S.J.; Harry J. Cain, S.J.; Paul E. Carrier, S.J.; Ned H. Cassem, S.J.; Robert G. Doherty, S.J.; William B. Foley, S.J.; Robert G. Gilroy, S.J.; Edward F. Howard, S.J.; William D. Ibach, S.J.; Paul C. Kenney, S.J.; Francis J. McManus, S.J.; George B. Murray, S.J.; Joseph V. Owens, S.J.; James F. Talbot, S.J.; Thomas Vallamattam, S.J.; E. Corbett Walsh, S.J.; Alfred O. Winshman, S.J.; Bros. Theodore C. Bender, S.J.; Calvin A. Clarke, S.J.

Campion Residence & Renewal Center, Inc. Priests 21; Brothers 2; Total Staff 23.

[V] CONVENTS AND RESIDENCES FOR SISTERS

BOSTON. *The Congregation of the Sisters of Our Lady of Mercy*, 241 Neponset Ave., 02122. Tel: 617-288-1202; Fax: 617-288-1177. Email: mercy@sisterfaustina.org. Web: www.sisterfaustina.org. Professed Sisters 8.

Daughters of St. Paul Inc. (1915) 50 St. Paul's Ave., 02130-3491. Tel: 617-522-8911; Fax: 617-524-8648. Email: usaprov@paulinemedia.com. Web: www.pauline.org.

Daughters of St. Paul, Inc. Novitiate, Provincialate Headquarters, and Publishing House for U.S. Prov. Community 7; Perpetually Professed Sisters 69; Novices 4; Junior Professed 2.

Pauline Book & Media Center (1988) 885 Providence Hwy., Dedham, 02026. Tel: 781-326-5385; Fax: 781-461-1013.

Franciscan Missionary Sisters for Africa (1957) (USA Headquarters and only house.), 172 Foster St., Brighton, 02135. Tel: 617-254-4343; Fax: 617-787-8007. Email: brightonsisters172@yahoo.com; connorju46@yahoo.com. Web: www.members.aol.com/sisters172/fmsa.html. Serving in Uganda, Kenya, Zambia, Zimbabwe, Sudan and South Africa. Completely a Missionary congregation. Sisters 4.

Franciscan Monastery of St. Clare, The (1906) 920 Centre St., 02130. Tel: 617-524-1760; Fax: 617-983-5205. Email: bostonpoorclares@yahoo.com. Web: www.StAnthonyShrine.org/PoorClares. Sr. Clare Frances McAvoy, O.S.C., Abbess. Franciscan Poor Clare Nuns., Solemn Vows. Cloistered Solemnly Professed 18; Extern Sisters 2.

Franciscan Sisters of the Atonement, 651 Adamst St., 02122. Tel: 617-740-0614.

Little Sisters of the Assumption Convent (1947) 65 Magnolia St., 02125. Tel: 617-442-9411. Email: mleonard@prohope.org. Web: www.littlesisters.org.

Little Sisters of the Assumption

Missionary Sisters of St. Columban, 73 Mapleton St., 02135. Tel: 617-782-5683; Fax: 617-789-3569. Email: columbansbrighton@verizon.net. Web: columbansistersusa.com. Sr. Margaret Holleran, S.C.C., U.S. Area Coord.

Missionary Sisters of Saint Columban Professed Sisters 8.

Monastery of Discalced Carmelites (1890) 61 Mt. Pleasant Ave., 02119. Tel: 617-442-1411; Fax: 617-442-0203. Email: bostoncarmel@juno.com. Web: www.carmelitesofboston.org. Sr. Bernadette Therese, O.C.D., Prioress. Cloistered. Professed 8; Novices 2.

Motherhouse of the Sisters of St. Joseph of Boston (1873) 637 Cambridge St., 02135. Tel: 617-783-9090; Fax: 617-783-8246. Email: bostoncsj@csjboston.org. Web: www.csjboston.org. Admin. Offices - 637 Cambridge St. Total in Residence 78.

Sister Disciples of the Divine Master (1924) Convent and Eucharistic Center, 43 West St., 02111. Tel: 482-682-0978; 482-423-2629; Fax: 482-682-3779. Email: sddmboston@aol.com. Web: www.pddm.us. Sr. Josephine Fallon, Supr. Sisters 12.

Sisters of Notre Dame de Namur (Boston Province Offices), 351 Broadway, Everett, 02149-3425. Tel: 617-387-2500; Fax: 617-387-1303. Email: boadministrator@sndden.org. Web: www.sndden.org/boston. Total in Community 196. Provincial Team: Sisters Edie Daly, S.N.D.deN., Prov. Admin.; Barbara Metz, S.N.D.deN., Prov. Admin.; Maureen Marr, S.N.D.deN., Prov. Admin.; Anne M. Donovan, S.N.D.deN., Treas.

Sisters of the Eucharistic Heart of Jesus, E.H.J. Sisters, 59 Richmere Rd., Mattapan, 02126. Tel: 617-296-0167; Cell: 617-767-9097; Fax: 617-296-0167. Email: ehjsistersboston@verizon.net; ehjsistersboston@netzero.net; conyewuche@yahoo.com. Web: www.ehjsrsboston.org.

Sisters of the Good Shepherd, 35 Tyndale St., 02131. Tel: 617-469-2492; Fax: 617-469-9857. Email: smhrgs@verizon.net. Sisters 3.

ANDOVER. *Monastery of St. Clare*, 445 River Rd., 01810-4213. Tel: 978-683-7599; Fax: 978-683-6085. Sr. Therese Marie Lacroix, O.S.C., Abbess. Poor Clare Nuns. Cloistered Solemnly Professed 12; Extern Perpetually Professed 2; Novices 1.

BRIGHTON. *Franciscan Missionaries of Mary* (1990) 284 Foster St., Boston, 02135. Tel: 617-787-1505; Fax: 617-787-1982. Email: nkloanfmm@yahoo.com. Sr. Lois A. Pereira, F.M.M., Prov.

(1990) 3305 Wallace Ave., Bronx, NY 10467-6599. Tel: 718-547-4693; Fax: 718-547-4607. Sr. Lois A. Pereira, F.M.M., Prov.

BROCKTON. *Our Lady of Sorrows Convent*, 261 Thatcher St., 02302-3997. Tel: 508-588-5070; Fax: 508-580-6770. Email: mjv@cjcbrockton.org. Web: www.cjcbrockton.org. Sr. Mary Valliere, C.J.C., Gen. Supr. Poor Sisters of Jesus Crucified and the Sorrowful Mother. Sisters 25.

CAMBRIDGE. *Sancta Maria Convent*, 799 Concord Ave., 02138. Tel: 617-868-2200, Ext. 2950 (Convent); 617-868-2200, Ext. 2100 (Office); Fax: 617-864-2801.

CHELSEA. *Don Guanella Center, Inc., Daughters of St. Mary of Providence* (1982) 37 Nichols St., 02150. Tel: 617-889-0179; Fax: 617-889-3363. Email: dgcenter.chelsea2@verizon.net. Web: www.donguanellacenter.com. Sr. Rhonda Brown, D.S.M.P., Dir. of Center. Family Support Respite for Developmentally Handicapped Women (ages 18 & older). Sisters 2; Families 70; Total Staff 12.

DANVERS. *Discalced Carmelite Monastery* (1958) 15 Mt. Carmel Rd., 01923-3796. Tel: 978-774-3008; Fax: 978-774-7409. Sr. Teresa Benedicta of the Cross, O.C.D., Prioress. Total in Residence 14.

DEDHAM. *Ursuline Convent, Inc.*, 65 Lowder St., 02026-4205. Tel: 781-326-3158; Fax: 781-326-4428. Email: nestabeaudoin@verizon.net. Sr. Mercedes Videira, O.S.U., Prioress. Sisters 7.

Ursuline Provincialate (1947) 45 Lowder St., 02026-4200. Tel: 781-326-7296; Fax: 781-326-7296. Email: provosu@verizon.net. Sr. Angela Krippendorf, O.S.U., Prov. Ursulines of the Roman Union, Northeastern Province 29.

IPSWICH. *Sisters of Notre Dame de Namur Generalate Office*, 30 Jeffrey's Neck Rd., 01938. Tel: 978-356-2159; Fax: 978-356-1034. Email: connell@sndden.org. Web: www.sndden.org. Sr. Lorraine Connell, S.N.D.deN., Gen. Treas.

Casa Generalizia di Suore di Nostra Signora di Namur, Via Raffaello Sardiello, 20, Rome 00165 Italy. Tel: 39-06-6641-8704; Fax: 39-06-6641-8709. Sr. Teresita Weind, S.N.D.deN., Gen. Moderator. (Generalate)

The Sisters of Notre Dame de Namur Congregational Mission Office, Inc., 30 Jeffrey's Neck Rd., 01938. Tel: 978-356-2159; Fax: 978-356-1034.

Sisters of Notre Dame de Namur (Provincial Residence) (1804) 30 Jeffreys Neck Rd., 01938-1308. Tel: 978-380-1372; Fax: 978-356-9759. Email: mary.farren@sndden.org. Web: www.sndden.org. Sisters 82; Total Staff 71. Provincial Leadership Team: Sisters Mary M. Farren, S.N.D.deN., Prov. Admin.; Mary Boretti, S.N.D.deN., Prov. & Admin.; Andrea Walsh, S.N.D.deN., Prov. & Admin.

KINGSTON. *Congregation of the Sisters of Divine Providence* (1851) Providence House, 363 Bishops Hwy., 02364. Tel: 781-585-7707; Fax: 781-422-5236. Email: cdpward@comcast.net. Sr. Claudia Ward, C.D.P., Area Asst.

LEXINGTON. *Congregation of Armenian Catholic Sisters of Immaculate Conception, Inc.*, 6 Eliot Rd., 02173. Tel: 781-863-5962; Fax: 781-862-8479. Sisters 3.

Grey Nuns Area Offices, 10 Pelham Rd., Ste. 1000, 02421-8499. Tel: 781-674-7401; Fax: 781-861-9641. Email: srjuneketterer@sgmlex.org. Web: www.grey-nuns. Headquarters (U.S.A. Region) of the Sisters of Charity of Montreal. "Grey Nuns". *General Administration*, 138 Rue Saint-Pierre, Montreal QC H2Y 2L7 Canada. Tel: 514-842-9411; Fax: 514-842-7855. Sr. June Ketterer, S.G.M., Area Coord. Sisters 3.

LOWELL. *St. Joseph Provincial House*, 559 Fletcher St., 01854-3434. Tel: 978-458-4472; Fax: 978-441-1452. Email: prleblanc2@comcast.net. Web: www.soeursdelachariteottawa.com. Sr. Pauline Leblanc, S.C.O., Prov. Supr. Sisters of Charity of Ottawa (Grey Nuns of the Cross); D'Youville Senior Care Center, Lowell; Saints Medical Center, Lowell. Sisters 22.

MARLBOROUGH. *Sisters of St. Anne, Provincialate* (1850) 720 Boston Post Rd. E., 01752. Tel: 508-481-4934; Fax: 508-481-4939. Email: sydargy@hotmail.com. Web: www.ssacong.org. Headquarters of American Province. Sisters 104.

Community of the Sisters of Saint Anne Tel: 508-481-4934; Fax: 508-481-4939. *St. Anne Convent*, 720 Boston Post Rd. E., 01752. Tel: 508-485-3791; Fax: 508-481-4939. Sisters 50.

Sisters of St. Chretienne (1807) 197 Pleasant St., 01752-1169. Tel: 508-485-0740; Fax: 508-481-0663. Email: chretienne@verizon.net. Web: www.sistersofstchretienne.org. Sr. Jeannette

Desorcy, S.S.Ch., Local Coord. House of Retirement. Sisters 31.

Sisters of St. Chretienne, 207 Pleasant St., 01752-1169. Tel: 508-229-3505; Fax: 508-481-0663.

Sisters of the Good Shepherd, 406 Hemenway St., 01752. Tel: 508-485-8610; Fax: 508-460-6372. Sr. Theresa Marie O'Leary, Contact Person & Pastoral Care. Sisters 29.

METHUEN. *Presentation of Mary*, 209 Lawrence St., 01844. Tel: 978-687-1369; Fax: 978-975-1998. Email: prov.methuen@verizon.net. Web: www.presmarymethuen.org. Sr. Cecile Plasse, P.M., Prov. Supr. Presentation of Mary Academy. Sisters 95; Total in Residence 77.

MILTON. *Holy Union Sisters* (1826) *Province Office*, 444 Centre St., P.O. Box 410, 02186-0006. Tel: 617-696-8765; Fax: 617-696-8571. Web: www.holyunionsisters.org. Sisters Mary Catherine Burns, S.U.S.C., Province Mission Team; Paula Coelho, S.U.S.C., Province Mission Team; Maryellen Ryan, S.U.S.C., Province Mission Team.

NEWTON. *Immaculate Conception Provincialate* (1873) 790 Centre St., 02458-2530. Tel: 617-527-1004; Fax: 617-527-2528. Email: mfic@mficusa.org. Web: www.mficusa.org. Missionary Franciscan Sisters of the Immaculate Conception. Total in Residence 3; Total Staff 4.

Mt. Alvernia Convent (1873) 790 Centre St., 02458-2530. Tel: 617-969-4766; Fax: 617-527-2528. Email: mtalverniaconvent@comcast.net. Web: www.mficusa.org. Sisters 15; Staff 3.

SOMERVILLE. *Medical Missionaries of Mary, Inc.* (1937) 179 Highland Ave., 02143. Tel: 617-666-3223; Fax: 617-666-1877. Email: mmmsomerville@comcast.net. Web: www.mmmusa.org. Medical Missionaries of Mary Motherhouse, Beechgrove, Drogheda, Ireland. Professed Sisters 10.

WALTHAM. *Marist Missionary Sisters*

Missionary Sisters of the Society of Mary, Inc., S.M.S.M. Provincial Offices, 349 Grove St., 02453-6018. Tel: 781-893-0149; Fax: 781-899-6838. Email: maristsmsm@aol.com. Web: www.maristmissionarysmsm.org. *Residence for Senior Sisters*, 62 Newton St., 02453-6058. Tel: 781-893-3960. Sisters 32.

Marillac Residence, 125 Oakland St., Wellesley, 02481-5338. Sisters 12.

Bethany Health Care Centre, 97 Bethany Rd., Framingham, 01702-7296. Tel: 508-872-6750. Sisters 5.

Maristhill Nursing Home, 66 Newton St., 02453-6058. Sisters 2.

Other Local Communities: 21 Beech St., Belmont, 02478-1299. Tel: 617-489-3587. Sisters 6. 4 Craig St., Framingham, 01701-7664. Tel: 508-877-7371. Sisters 3. 357 Grove St., 02453-6018. Tel: 781-899-3839. Sisters 5. 88 Lexington St., 02452.

Religious of Christian Education, Inc., 68 Lafayette St., Apt. A, 02453-6829. Tel: 781-899-6292; Fax: 781-899-6293. Email: yvettetrce@aol.com. Sr. Yvette Rivard, R.C.E., Contact Person.

Sisters of the Good Shepherd, 83-85 Lake St., 02451. Tel: 781-891-7688; Fax: 617-471-6622. Email: elishmcpar@verizon.net. Sr. Elish McPartland, R.G.S., Contact Person.

WATERTOWN. *Rosary Manor*, One Rosary Dr., 02472. Tel: 617-924-1717; Fax: 617-924-8118. Email: liztop@juno.com. Sr. Mary Elizabeth Thompson, O.P., Coord. Total in Residence 17.

WELLESLEY. *Elizabeth Seton Residence, Inc.*, 125 Oakland St., 02481. Tel: 781-237-2161; Fax: 781-431-2589. Email: ptedesco@schalifax.org. Web: www.Elizabethseton.org. Ms. Phyllis A. Tedesco, Admin. Sisters of Charity of St. Vincent de Paul, Halifax, Nova Scotia, Canada., 84 Bed Skilled Nursing & Rehab Facility. Medicare-Medicaid Certified.

Marillac Residence, Inc., 125 Oakland St., 02481-5338. Tel: 781-997-1165; Fax: 781-237-8152. Email: crowleyk28@aol.com. Web: www.schalifax.ca. Sr. Kathleen Crowley, S.C. Sisters of Charity (Halifax).

Mount St. Vincent Retirement Community, 125 Oakland St., 02481-5338. Tel: 781-997-1165; Fax: 781-237-8152. Email: crowleyk28@aol.com. Web: www.schalifax.com. Sr. Kathleen Crowley, S.C., Community Leadership Team. Sisters of Charity (Halifax).

Sisters of Charity (Halifax) (1849) (Boston Office), 125 Oakland St., 02481. Tel: 781-997-1355; Fax: 781-997-1358. Email: smclaughlin@schalifax.ca; aregan@schalifax.ca. Web: www.schalifax.ca. Sisters Sally McLaughlin, S.C.H., Congregational Councilor; Ann Regan, Congregational Councilor; Marjory Gallagher, Congregational Councillor & Sec.

Sisters of Charity (Halifax) Corporate Mission, Inc., 125 Oakland St., 02481. Tel: 781-997-1357. Email: bostreasurer@schalifax.org. Web: www.schalifax.ca. Sr. Donna Geernaert, S.C., Congregational Leader.

Sisters of Charity (Halifax) Supporting Corporation (1977) 125 Oakland St., 02481-5338. Tel: 781-997-1126; Fax: 781-235-8068. Sr. Donna Geernaert, S.C., Congregational Leader.

WRENTHAM. *St. Chretienne Provincialate* (1807) 297 Arnold St., 02093-1798. Tel: 508-384-7841; 508-384-8066; Fax: 508-507-3634. Email: ssch@tiac.net. Web: sistersofstchretienne.org. Sisters of St. Chretienne. Sisters 3; Total in Residence 3.

Mount St. Mary's Abbey (1949) 300 Arnold St., 02093. Tel: 508-528-1282; Fax: 508-528-5360. Email: sisters@msmabbey.org. Web: www.msmabbey.org. Sr. Maureen McCabe, O.C.S.O., Abbess.

The Cistercians of the Strict Observance in Massachusetts, Inc. The Cistercian Nuns of the Strict Observance (Trappistines). Professed Sisters 45; Total in Residence 46.

[W] RETREAT HOUSES

COHASSET. *St. Joseph Retreat Center*, 339 Jerusalem Rd., 02025. Tel: 781-383-6024; 781-383-6029. Email: retreat.center@csjboston.org. Web: www.csjretreatcenter.org. Sr. Joan M. McCarthy, C.S.J., Dir. Sisters of St. Joseph 2.

DUXBURY. *Miramar Retreat Center*, 121 Parks St., P.O. Box M, 02331-0614. Tel: 781-585-2460; Fax: 781-585-3770. Email: miramarma@aol.com. Web: www.miramarretreat.org. Rev. Thomas Umbras, S.V.D., Dir., Rector. Total in Residence 10; Total Staff 25.

GLOUCESTER. *Eastern Point Retreat House*, Gonzaga, 37 Niles Pond Rd., 01930. Tel: 978-283-0013; Fax: 978-282-1989. Email: office@easternpoint.org. Web: www.easternpoint.org. Revs. James P. Carr, S.J., Dir.; Joseph McHugh, S.J.; Richard J. Stanley, S.J.; Paul M. Sullivan, S.J.; Sr. Madeline Tiberii, S.S.J. Priests 4; Sisters 1; Total Staff 5.

SCITUATE. *Foyer of Charity* (1977) 74 Hollett St., 02066. Tel: 781-545-1080. Email: info@foyerofcharity.com. Web: www.foyerofcharity.com. Rev. Matthew Bradley, Dir. Total in Residence 2; Total Staff 6.

WALTHAM. *Espousal Retreat House and Conference Center*, 554 Lexington St., 02452. Tel: 781-209-3120; Fax: 781-893-0291. Email: espousaladmin@gmail.com. Web: www.espousal.org. Rev. Robert Masciocchi, C.S.S., Dir. Stigmatine Fathers and Brothers., Weekend and Weekly Retreats, Days-Evenings of Recollection. Total in Residence 2; Total Staff 10.

WESTON. *Campion Renewal Center* (1975) 319 Concord Rd., 02493-1398. Tel: 781-419-1337; Fax: 781-894-5864. Email: acopponi@campioncenter.org. Web: www.campioncenter.org. Rev. James R. Mattaliano, S.J., Dir. & Staff Member. Total in Residence 2; Total Staff 2.

[X] RETIREMENT RESIDENCES FOR PRIESTS AND BROTHERS

BOSTON. *Saint Anthony Residence*, 103 Arch St., 02110-1102. Tel: 617-542-6454; Fax: 617-778-5882. Revs. Bernardine Kessing, O.F.M. (Retired); Thomas R. Hartle, O.F.M.; Vianney Devlin, O.F.M., Vicar (Retired); Carmel F. Miotke, O.F.M. (Retired); Jude Murphy, O.F.M., (Retired); Cyril Seaman, O.F.M. (Retired); Bros. Albert Aldrich, O.F.M., (Retired); Nathnael Necaster, O.F.M., (Retired); Brian J. Hart, O.F.M.; Richard James, O.F.M., (Retired); Gerald Paciello, O.F.M., Chap.; Charles F. Gilmartin, O.F.M., (Retired). (For Retired Franciscan Friars.) Priests 11; Brothers 4; Retired 14; Total in Residence 15.

Regina Cleri Residence, 60 William Cardinal O'Connell Way, 02114. Tel: 617-523-1861; Fax: 617-720-0585. Email: sgust@reginacleri.org. Mr. Stephen J. Gust, Exec. Dir. Residence for Retired Archdiocesan Priests. Priests 57; Sisters 3.

TEWKSBURY. *Immaculate Heart of Mary Residence*, 486 Chandler St., 01876-2899. Tel: 978-851-7258; Fax: 978-851-0952. Revs. T. Francis Bagan, O.M.I.; Charles Beausoleil, O.M.I.; Marcel Bolduc, O.M.I.; Richard Bolduc, O.M.I.; Chester J. Cappucci, O.M.I.; Raymond Crowe, O.M.I.; Francis Demers, O.M.I.; Normand A. Fillion, O.M.I.; Gerald Flater, O.M.I.; James Flavin, O.M.I.; Francis X. Gorham, O.M.I.; Richard Harr, O.M.I.; Patrick F. Healy, O.M.I.; Charles Heon, O.M.I.; Andre Houle, O.M.I.; Albert P. Martineau, O.M.I.; Richard McAlear, O.M.I.; John F. Mc Hugh, O.M.I.; George McLean, O.M.I.; William McSweeney, O.M.I.; Daniel Nassaney, O.M.I.; Daniel O'Leary, O.M.I.; Raymond Steen, O.M.I.; Bros. Joseph Gagne, O.M.I.; James H. Lucas, O.M.I.; Paul Ricard, O.M.I.; Lorenzo Williams, O.M.I. Priests 23; Brothers 4.

WALTHAM. *Stigmatine Fathers and Brothers*, St. Joseph's Hall, 554 Lexington St., 02452. Tel: 781-209-3100; Fax: 781-209-3070. Web: www.stigmatines.com. Revs. Paul D. Burns, C.S.S.; Joseph M. Connolly, C.S.S. (Retired); James Cunningham, C.S.S. (Retired); Leonard Ferrecchia, C.S.S. (Retired); James E. Flanagan, C.S.S. (Retired); Henry Linse, C.S.S. (Retired); David F. Gallagher, C.S.S. (Retired); Donald Higgins, C.S.S. (Retired); Nicholas Spagnolo, C.S.S. (Retired). Priests 9.

[Y] RESIDENCES FOR MEN AND WOMEN

BOSTON. *St. Helena House*, 89 Union Park St., 02118. Tel: 617-426-2922; Fax: 617-542-3460. James A. Smith, Property Mgr. Seniors, low income & disabled persons. Residents 99.

Our Lady's Guild House - Residence for Women, 20 Charlesgate W., 02215. Tel: 617-536-3000; Fax: 617-536-8508. Andrea Beall, Admin. Residents 133.

BRIGHTON. *Archdiocesan Central High Schools, Inc.*, 66 Brooks Dr., 02184-3839. Tel: 617-746-5855; Fax: 617-782-0213. His Eminence Sean Cardinal O'Malley, O.F.M.Cap.

[Z] PUBLIC ORATORIES AND CHAPELS

BOSTON. *St. Anthony Shrine* 100 Arch St., 02110. Tel: 617-542-6440; Fax: 617-542-4225. Email: info@StAnthonyShrine.org. Web: www.StAnthonyShrine.org. Revs. James Patrick Kelly, O.F.M., Guardian & Exec. Dir.; Raphael Bonanno, O.F.M.; Brian Cullinane, O.F.M.; Charles Finnegan, O.F.M.; Richard C. Flaherty, O.F.M.; Fergus Healey, O.F.M.; John P. Hogan, O.F.M.; Barry J. Langley, O.F.M.; Paul Lostritto, O.F.M.; Raymond Mann, O.F.M.; Myron McCormick, O.F.M.; Emeric Meier, O.F.M.; Philip O'Shea, O.F.M.; Gene Pistacchio, O.F.M.; Ronald Stark, O.F.M.; Flavian A. Walsh, O.F.M.; Bros. Gregory Day, O.F.M.; Thomas Donovan, O.F.M.; Justus Frazier, O.F.M.; Richard James, O.F.M.; John Jaskowiak, O.F.M.; John Maganzini, O.F.M.; James McIntosh, O.F.M.; Daniel Murray, O.F.M. Priests 18; Brothers 9.

Chapel of Our Lady of Lourdes 698 Beacon St., 02215. Tel: 617-536-2761; Fax: 617-526-1694. Marist Fathers. Priests 4.

Marist Fathers Residence Tel: 617-262-2271; Fax: 617-536-1694. Revs. Andrew Albert, S.M., Dir.; Roland Lacasse, S.M., Assoc.; Normand J. Martin, S.M., Assoc. In Res. Rev. Albert DiIanni, S.M., Ph.D.

Chapel of the Holy Spirit Paulist Center, 5 Park St., 02108. Tel: 617-742-4460; Fax: 617-720-5756. Email: fiveparkst@aol.com. Web: www.paulistboston.com. Rev. Frank Desiderio, C.S.P., M.A. Theology, M.A. Communication, Dir.; Patricia Simpson, M.Div., Admin.; Susan Rutkowski, M.Div., Pastoral Min., Family Religious Educ. & Social Justice; Michael Kurley, Pastoral Min. Liturgy & Music; Rev. Broderick M. Walsh, C.S.P., M.Div. Paulist Fathers.

St. Clement Archdiocesan Eucharistic Shrine 1105 Boylston St., 02215. Tel: 617-266-5999; Fax: 617-247-7576. Email: petergrover@juno.com. Web: www.omvusa.org. Revs. Peter Grover, O.M.V., Dir. of Shrine; David N. Beauregard, O.M.V. St. Ignatius Province of the Oblates of the Virgin Mary. Priests 2.

St. Francis Chapel Prudential Center Plaza, 800 Boylston St., #1001, 02199. Tel: 617-437-7117; Fax: 617-437-8420. Email: st.francis@chapel.as. Web: www.stfrancischapel.org. Revs. Robert Lowrey, O.M.V.; David Yankauskas, O.M.V.; Gregory Staab, O.M.V.; Christopher W. Uhl, O.M.V. St. Ignatius Province of the Oblates of the Virgin Mary. Priests 4.

Madonna Queen Shrine 150 Orient Ave., 02128. Tel: 617-569-2100; Fax: 617-569-8701. Email: madonna_orione@hotmail.com. Revs. Marcelo Boschi, F.D.P., Rector; Miguel Alvamir Goncalves, Vice-Rector. Don Orione Fathers.

Our Lady of the Airways Chapel First Floor, Tower Bldg., Logan International Airport, 02128. Tel: 617-567-2800; Fax: 617-569-6950. Email: fatherrichard@assport.com. Rev. Richard A. Uftring.

BROCKTON. *Chapel of Our Saviour* 475 Westgate Dr., 02301-1819. Tel: 508-583-8357; Fax: 508-586-5510. Revs. Gerald DiGiralamo, S.A., Dir.; Robert Langone, S.A.; Malcolm Martin, S.A. (Retired); Daniel O'Shea, S.A.; Bros. Thomas Banacki, S.A.; Louis Marek, S.A.; Savio McNiece, S.A. Priests 4; Brothers 3.

HOLLISTON. *Our Lady of Fatima Shrine* 101 Summer St., P.O. Box 5857, 01746-5857. Tel: 508-429-2144; Fax: 508-429-4793. Email: holliston.sx@gmail.com. Web: www.xaviermissionaries.org. Rev. Francis Signorelli, S.X. Xaverian Missionaries.

LOWELL. *St. Joseph the Worker Shrine* 37 Lee St., 01852-1103. Tel: 978-458-6346; 978-459-9522; 800-287-9522 (Gift Shop); Fax: 978-441-0963; 978-323-0763 (Gift Shop). Email: info@

stjosephshrine.org. Web: www.stjosephshrine.org.

Andre Garin Residence, 27 Kirk St., 01852-1103. Tel: 978-454-6004; Fax: 978-458-3603. Revs. Terrence E. O'Connell, O.M.I., Dir.; Patrick J. Hollywood, O.M.I.; Eugene Tremblay, O.M.I.; Martin Walsh, O.M.I.; Norman E. Parent, O.M.I.

PEABODY. *St. Theresa Carmelite Chapel* North Shore Mall, 01960. Tel: 978-531-6145; Fax: 978-531-1359. Email: hjones@carmelnet.org. Revs. Herbert J. Jones, O.Carm., Dir.; Mario Lopez, O.Carm.; Felix Prior, O.Carm.; Bro. Damien Chong, O.Carm. Priests 3; Brothers 1.

[AA] CAMPUS MINISTRY

BOSTON. *The Catholic Center at Boston University* 211 Bay State Rd., 02215. Tel: 617-353-3632; Fax: 617-358-2049. Email: catholic@bu.edu. Web: www.bu.edu/CATHOLIC. Rev. Clifton M. Thuma, Chap.; Bros. Patrick Reilly, B.H.; Samuel Gunn, B.H.; Parker Jordan, B.H., Assoc. Campus Min.; Sr. Olga Yaqob.

Emmanuel College Campus Ministry (1919) 400 The Fenway, 02115. Tel: 617-735-9703. Web: emmanuel.edu. Sr. Margaret Cummins, S.N.D.

University of Massachusetts at Boston Campus Ministry

Harbor Campus, Dorchester, 02125. Tel: 617-287-5839. Email: maggie.cahill@umb.edu.

BRIDGEWATER. *Bridgewater State College Catholic Center* 122 Park Ave., 02325. Tel: 508-531-1346; Fax: 508-531-6188. Email: mnolan@bridgew.edu. Web: www.bridgew.edu/depts/cathcntr/. Rev. Michael Nolan, Campus Min.

CAMBRIDGE. *Harvard Catholic Center* 29 Mount Auburn St., 02138. Tel: 617-491-8400; Fax: 617-354-7092. Email: mdrea@stpaulparish.org. Web: www.stpaulparish.org. Revs. Michael E. Drea, Senior Chap. Email: frdreaharvard@gmail.com; George S. Salzmann, O.S.F.S., Graduate Chap.; Matthew J. Westcott, Undergrad Chaplain; Andrew Griswold, Business Mgr.

Massachusetts Institute of Technology Catholic Community 40 Massachusetts Ave., W-11, 02139. Tel: 617-253-2981; Fax: 617-253-3260. Email: catholic@mit.edu. Web: www.web.mit.edu/tcc/. Rev. Richard F. Clancy; Cyndi Aimo. Total Staff 2.

FRAMINGHAM. *Framingham State College Campus Ministry* 100 State St., 01701. Tel: 508-626-4610; Fax: 508-626-4939. Email: pgojuk@frc.mass.edu. Ms. Hai Ok Hwang, M.Div., Chap.

LOWELL. *The Catholic Center U Mass, Lowell* 52 Colonial Ave., 01854. Tel: 978-454-0151. Email: Catholic_Center@uml.edu; Kenneth_Apuzzo@uml.edu. Web: www.uml.edu/student-services/ministry/catholic/. Bro. Kenneth Apuzzo, Campus Min. Total in Residence 4; Total Staff 1.

MEDFORD. *Tufts Interfaith Center Tufts University Catholic Chaplaincy* 58 Winthrop St., 02155-5300. Tel: 617-627-3427. Email: lynn.cooper@tufts.edu. Web: www.tufts.edu/chaplaincy. Ms. Lynn Cooper, M.Div., Catholic Chap. Total Staff 1; Total Assisted Annually 2,800.

NEWTON. *Boston College Campus Ministry* 140 Commonwealth Ave., Chestnut Hill, 02467. Tel: 617-552-3475; Fax: 617-552-3044. Email: ministry@bc.edu. Web: www.bc.edu/ministry. Total in Residence 6; Total Staff 14.

McElroy 233, Chestnut Hill, 02467. Tel: 617-552-3475; Fax: 617-552-3044. Email: ministry@bc.edu. Web: www.bc.edu/ministry.

NORTH ANDOVER. *Merrimack College Campus Ministry Center* 315 Turnpike St., 01845. Tel: 978-837-5450; Fax: 978-837-5004. Revs. Keith Hollis, O.S.A., Dir.; William F. Waters, O.S.A., Campus Min.; Mr. Brian Suehs-Vassel, Campus Min. Priests 1; Total Assisted 2,000; Total Staff 5.

SALEM. *Salem State College, Catholic Campus Ministry* 352 Lafayette St., 01970. Tel: 978-542-6074; Fax: 978-744-2757. Email: gmckeon@salemstate.edu. Rev. Gerard R. McKeon, S.J.

WALTHAM. *Bentley University Spiritual Life Center* (1917) 175 Forest St., 02452-4705. Tel: 781-891-2435; Fax: 781-891-2839. Email: mdilorenzo@bentley.edu. Web: www.bentley.edu. Maria DiLorenzo, B.A., M.A., Dir. Spiritual Life Center, Catholic Advisor.

Brandeis University Catholic Chaplaincy Mail stop 205, P.O. Box 549110, 02454-9110. Tel: 781-736-3574; Fax: 781-736-3577. Email: cuenin@brandeis.edu. Rev. Walter H. Cuenin.

WELLESLEY. *Babson College Campus Ministry* 9 Glen Rd., 02181. Tel: 617-235-1200. Sr. Frances Sheehey, O.S.F., Campus Coord.

Wellesley College - Office of Religious and Spiritual Life 02481. Tel: 781-283-2688; Fax: 781-283-3676. Email: ncorcora@wellesley.edu. Sr. Nancy Corcoran, C.S.J., Catholic Chap. & Dir. Newman Catholic Ministry.

WESTON. *Regis College Office of Campus Ministry* 235 Wellesley St., 02493. Tel: 781-768-7027; 781-768-7028; 781-768-7029; Fax: 781-768-8339. Email: ministry@regiscollege.edu. Web: www.regiscollege.edu. Sr. Elizabeth Conway, C.S.J., Dir. of Spiritual Life; Dawn Doucette, Dir. of Social Outreach; Rev. Paul E. Kilroy, Chap.

[BB] FOUNDATIONS, FUNDS & TRUSTS

BOSTON. *Chancery Office*, 66 Brooks Dr., 02184-3839. Tel: 617-254-0100; Fax: 617-783-4564. Web: www.rcab.org. Also see Miscellaneous Section for additional listings.

The Cardinal Medeiros Trust Tel: 617-254-0100.

Cardinal Cushing General Hospital Foundation, Brockton

The Carney Hospital Foundation, Inc., 2100 Dorchester Ave., 02124. Tel: 617-296-1788. J. Barry Driscoll, Pres.; Paul J. Kingston, Vice Pres.; Daniel J. McDevitt, Sec.; William F. Henderson, Exec. Dir. (Formerly The New Caritas Christi Hospital, Inc.)

The Catholic Cemetery Association Perpetual Care Trust, 66 Brooks Dr., 02184-3839.

**Catholic Schools Foundation, Inc.* Tel: 617-254-0100; Fax: 617-783-6366. (Formerly St. Anthony's Scholarship Fund, Inc.).

Clergy Benefit Trust Tel: 617-254-0100; Fax: 617-783-2947.

Clergy Fund Society Tel: 617-254-0100; Fax: 617-783-2947.

Clergy Medical-Hospitalization Trust Tel: 617-254-0100; Fax: 617-783-2947.

Archdiocese of Boston Clergy Retirement/Disability Trust Tel: 617-254-0100; Fax: 617-783-2947.

Family Counseling Endowment Fund, Inc., 141 Tremont St., 02111. Tel: 617-482-4355.

Marist Capital Trust Fund

c/o Financial Admin., The Missionary Sisters of the Society of Mary, Inc., 349 Grove St., Waltham, 02154. Tel: 617-893-0149. Sr. Virginia Fornasa, S.M.S.M., Trustee; John E. McCormack.

Metropolitan Boston Dialysis Center, Inc., 736 Cambridge St., Brighton, 02135.

Mission Promotion Missionary Sisters of the Society of Mary.

c/o Mission Promoter, 349 Grove St., Waltham, 02453. Tel: 781-893-0149.

Roman Catholic Archdiocese of Boston Health Benefit Trust Tel: 617-746-5680; Fax: 617-783-4564. Mr. James M. Walsh, Admin.

Roman Catholic Archdiocese of Boston Insurance Trust Tel: 617-746-5640; Fax: 617-783-4564. Mr. James M. Walsh, Admin. Benefit Office.

Roman Catholic Archdiocese of Boston Pension Trust Tel: 617-746-5640; Fax: 617-746-4564. Mr. James M. Walsh, Admin. Benefit Office.

Roman Catholic Archdiocese of Boston Long Term Disability Trust Tel: 617-746-5640; Fax: 617-783-4564. Mr. James M. Walsh, Admin.

Roman Catholic Archdiocese of Boston Common Investment Fund Tel: 617-746-5680; Fax: 617-783-4564.

Roman Catholic Archdiocese of Boston Fixed Income Investment Fund Tel: 617-746-5680; Fax: 617-783-4564.

St. Charles Borromeo Educational Foundation, Inc.

Sacred Heart Trust Fund, c/o Society of Jesus, Trustee, 761 Harrison Ave., 02118. Tel: 617-536-5604. Bro. H. Francis Cluff, S.J.

St. Elizabeth's Hospital Foundation, Inc., 159 Washington St., Brighton, 02135.

Caritas Holy Family Hospital Foundation, Inc.

Catholic Foundation of the Archdiocese of Boston, 66 Brooks Dr., 02184-3839. Tel: 617-746-5621; Fax: 617-783-6366. Mr. James Mooney, Pres.

The Xaverian Brothers Northeastern Community Support Charitable Trust Fund, 704 Brush Hill Rd., Milton, 02186.

Benefit Trust for Non-Incardinated Priests Tel: 617-254-0100; Fax: 617-783-2947.

Benefit Trust for Non-Incardinated Priest Duly Assigned for Service in the Archdiocese of Boston

St. Mary's High School Foundation, Inc., 66 Brooks Dr., 02184-3839. Tel: 617-746-5680. David W. Smith, Contact Person.

Clergy Assistance Trust, 66 Brooks Dr., 02184-3839. Tel: 617-746-5615; Fax: 617-783-2947.

Massachusetts Catholic Self-Insurance Group, Inc., 66 Brooks Dr., 02184-3839. Tel: 617-746-5740; Fax: 517-746-5421. Email: Joseph_McEnness@rcab.org. Mr. Joseph F. McEnness, Admin.; Timothy M. McCrystal, Esq., Counsel.

Board of Directors: Very Rev. Charles J. Higgins, V.F., Clerk; James P. McDonough, Pres.; Mr. John Straub, Treas.; Mr. John M. Riley; Mr. Joseph P. Welch; Mr. William LaBroad; Mr. Neil Buckley.

FRAMINGHAM. *Senior Religious Trust Fund of Marist Fathers of Boston*, 518 Pleasant St., 01701-2898. Tel: 508-879-7223; Fax: 508-879-0719.

IPSWICH. *Blin Charitable Trust* (1995) 30 Jeffrey's Neck Rd., 01938. Tel: 978-380-1372; Fax: 978-356-9759. Email: mary.farren@sndden.org. Web: www.sndden.org. Sisters of Notre Dame de Namur.

LOWELL. *D'Youville Senior Care Foundation, Inc.*, 981 Varnum Ave., 01854. Tel: 978-569-1000; Fax: 978-569-1070. Email: dmain@dyouville.org. Web: dyouville.org.

Saints Memorial Medical Center Foundation, P.O. Box 367, 01853-0367. Tel: 978-934-8334; Fax: 978-934-8479. Email: fund.kec@tmmc.org. Web: www.saints-memorial.org. Thom Clark, Pres. & CEO; Kevin E. Coughlin, Vice Pres.; D. Harold Sullivan, Chm.

METHUEN. *Caritas Holy Family Hospital Foundation, Inc.*, 70 East St., 01844-4597. Tel: 978-687-0151; Fax: 978-688-7689. Email: nmallen@cchcs.org. Web: www.holyfamilyhosp.org. Mrs. Noreen V. Mallen, Exec. Dir.

NEEDHAM. *St. Joseph Parish School Fund, Inc., Needham*, 1382 Highland Ave., 02492. Tel: 781-444-0245; Fax: 781-444-7713. John Brennan, Treas.

[CC] MISCELLANEOUS

BOSTON. *Caritas Christi Retirement Plan and Trust*, 66 Brooks Dr., 02184-3839. Tel: 617-746-5830; Fax: 617-779-4567. Carol Gustavson, Plan Admin. Governing Board: His Eminence Sean Cardinal O'Malley, O.F.M.Cap.; Very Rev. Joseph K. Raeke, V.F.; Rev. Msgr. Robert P. Deeley, V.F., J.C.D.; Very Rev. Bryon Parrish; Rev. Robert T. Kickham; James P. McDonough.

Caritas Christi-A Catholic Health Care System, 736 Cambridge St., 02135. Tel: 617-789-2500; Fax: 617-789-2124. Web: www.caritaschristi.org. Dr. Ralph de la Torre, M.D., Pres. & CEO. Caritas Christi, Boston; Cardinal Cushing General Hospital Foundation, Inc., Brockton; Caritas Carney Hospital Foundation, Inc., Boston; Caritas Carney Hospital, Inc., Boston, Caritas Carney Medical Group, Inc., Boston*; Caritas Christi Network Services, Inc.; Caritas Christi Diagnostic Support Services, Inc., Boston*; Caritas Christi Network Services, Inc., Boston; Caritas Christi Physician Network, Inc., Boston*; Caritas Christi Support Services, Inc., Boston; Caritas Excell Clinical Laboratories, Inc., Boston*; Caritas Good Samaritan Cancer Center, Inc.; Caritas Good Samaritan Hospice, Inc., Boston; Caritas Good Samaritan Medical Center, Inc., Brockton, MA*; Caritas Good Samaritan Medical Practice Corporation, Brockton*; Caritas Good Samaritan Occupational Health Services, Inc., Brockton*; Caritas Holy Family Hospital Foundation, Inc., Methuen; Caritas Holy Family Hospital, Inc., Methuen; Caritas Home Care, Inc., Boston*; Laboure College, Inc., Boston; Caritas Norwood Hospital, Inc., Norwood; Caritas Por Cristo, Inc., Boston*; Caritas Southwood Hospital, Inc., Norfolk; Caritas St. Elizabeth's Hospital Foundation, Inc., Boston; Caritas St. Elizabeth's Medical Center of Boston, Inc., Boston; Caritas St. Elizabeth's Realty Corp., Boston*; Caritas St. John of God Hospital, Inc., Boston; Caritas St. Joseph Nursing Care Center, Inc., Boston; Caritas Valley Regional Health System, Inc., Methuen; Caritas Valley Regional Medical Services Corporation, Methuen; Caritas Valley Regional Support Services, Inc., Methuen; Greater Lawrence Mental Health Center, Inc., Lawrence; Neponset Valley Hospice, Inc., Norwood*; Norfolk-Bristol Homemaker Services, Inc., Norwood*; NVHS Coverage Associates, Inc., Norwood*; NVHS Management Services, Inc., Norwood*; Caritas Christi Retirement Plan and Trust, Boston; Caritas Medical Trust; Caritas Holy Family Hospital Auxiliary, Methuen; Caritas Holy Family Hospital Men's Guild, Methuen.

Caritas Good Samaritan Hospice, Inc., 310 Allston St., 02135. Tel: 617-566-6242; Fax: 617-566-3055. Web: caritaschristi.org. Mr. Leo P. Smith, L.I.C.S.W., Exec. Dir. & Contact Person.

The Catholic Lawyers Guild of the Archdiocese of Boston, Inc., One Lewis Wharf, 02110. Tel: 617-722-8175; Fax: 617-723-1180. Hon. Joseph R. Nolan, Pres.

Corporation for the Sponsored Ministries of the Sisters of St. Joseph of Boston (2000) 637 Cambridge St., 02135-2800. Tel: 617-746-2190; Fax: 617-746-2194. Email: suzanne.kearney@csjboston.org. Web: www.csjboston.org. Suzanne M. Kearney, Exec. Dir.

CSJ Ministries Connection, Inc. (2004) 637 Cambridge St., 02135-2800. Tel: 617-746-2191; Fax: 617-746-2194. Email: josephine.perico@csjboston.org. Web: www.csjboston.org. Sr. Josephine Perico, C.S.J., Admin. Coord.

Equestrian Order of the Holy Sepulchre of Jerusalem (1099)

Northeastern Lieutenancy, c/o Rev. Jonathan Gaspar, Pastoral Ctr., 66 Brooks Dr., 02184-3839.

**KOLBE Association, Inc.*, 66 Brooks Dr., 02184-3839. Tel: 617-746-5425. Email: rev.michael.medas@sjs.edu. His Eminence Sean

Cardinal O'Malley, O.F.M.Cap., Episcopal Moderator; Rev. Michael B. Medas, M.S.W., Exec. Dir.

Lanteri Charitable Trust, 1105 Boylston St., 02215-3660. Tel: 617-536-4141; Fax: 617-536-7016. Email: wbrownomv@aol.com. Laurence Flynn, Admin.

League of Catholic Women of the Archdiocese of Boston, St. Mary of the Sacred Heart, 392 Hanover St., Hanover, 02339. Tel: 781-826-4303. Mrs. John F. O'Donoghue Jr., Pres.; Rev. Martin P. Connor, S.T.L., Spiritual Dir. (Retired).

Lourdes Bureau, 698 Beacon St., 02215. Tel: 617-536-2761; Fax: 617-536-1694. Marist Fathers., Official Representatives in America for the Shrine of Lourdes, France.

Medaille Corporation, 637 Cambridge St., 02135. Tel: 617-783-9090; Fax: 617-783-8246. Email: bostoncsj@csjboston.org. Web: www.csjboston.org. Sisters Mary L. Murphy, C.S.J., Pres.; Maureen Doherty, C.S.J., Treas.

Most Holy Name of Jesus Federation of Poor Clare Monasteries in the Eastern Region of the United States (1959) Monastery of Saint Clare, 920 Centre St., 02130. Tel: 617-524-1760; Fax: 617-983-5205. Email: bostonpoorclares@yahoo.com. Sr. Clare Frances McAvoy, O.S.C., Pres. Solemn Vows 124; Simple Professed 8.

PACE - Parents Alliance for Catholic Education, 14 Beacon St., Ste. 102, 02108. Tel: 617-723-9890; Fax: 617-723-9892. Email: fkalisz@paceorg.net. Web: www.paceorg.net. Frederick M. Kalisz Jr., Exec. Dir.

Pontifical Mission Societies in the Archdiocese of Boston The Society for the Propagation of the Faith, The Holy Childhood Association, The Society of Saint Peter Apostle & The Missionary Union of Priests and Religious, Mailing Address & Office: Pastoral Center, 66 Brooks Dr., 02184-3839. Tel: 617-542-1776; Fax: 617-542-1778. Email: info@propfaithboston.org. Rev. Rodney J. Copp, J.C.L., Archdiocesan Dir. Total Staff 10.

Sancta Maria House, Inc. (1972) 11 Waltham St., 02118-2162. Tel: 617-423-4366. Rev. Msgr. William H. Roche, Pres. (Retired).

St. Vincent Pallotti Center for Apostolic Development of Boston, Inc., 66 Brooks Dr., 02184-3839. Tel: 617-783-3924. Email: VolService@aol.com. Web: www.pallotticenterboston.org.

**Women Affirming Life, Inc.*, P.O. Box 35532, 02135. Tel: 617-254-2277; Fax: 617-254-2299. Email: mail@affirmlife.com. Web: www.affirmlife.com. Frances X. Hogan, Pres.

ARLINGTON. *Fidelity House*, 25 Medford St., 02474-3105. Tel: 781-648-2005; Fax: 781-648-4604. Email: Fidelityhouse@rcn.com. Web: www.fidelityhouse.org. Edward F. Woods, Dir. Purpose: A community center sponsored by the Saint Agnes Parish providing quality services primarily for youth development with flexible and diverse services for people of all ages.

BRAINTREE. *The Fund for Catholic Schools, Inc. dba Campaign for Catholic Schools* 66 Brooks Dr., 02184. Tel: 617-262-5600; Fax: 617-262-5601. Email: campaignforcatholicschools@rcab.org. Web: campaignforcatholicschools.org. Kathleen F. Driscoll, Pres.; Mary Flynn Myers, Vice Pres. Devel.

BRIGHTON. *Boston Inter-Community Ministries, Inc.*, 637 Cambridge St., 02135. Tel: 617-746-2041. Sr. Ellen Powers, C.S.J., Contact Person.

The Literacy Connection (1987) 637 Cambridge St., 02135. Tel: 617-746-2100; Fax: 617-783-8246. Sr. Patricia Andrews, C.S.J., Dir.

CAMBRIDGE. **The Youville House, Inc.*, 1575 Cambridge St., 02138-4398. Tel: 617-876-4344. Email: leaheyd@youville.org. Web: www.youville.org. Mr. T. Richard Quigley, Pres. & CEO; Ms. Marsha V. Whelan, Vice Pres. Mission Integration; Revs. William L. Mulligan, S.J., Chap.; Jennifer Casstevens, Chap.; Ms. Patricia Kennedy, Dir. of Pastoral Care Svcs. & Chap.; Elizabeth Walsh, Chap. Member of Youville Lifecare, Inc. Priests 1; Sisters of Charity (Grey Nuns) 3; Assisted Living Units 95.

EVERETT. *Notre Dame Volunteer Corporation*, 351 Broadway, 02149. Tel: 617-387-2500; Fax: 617-387-1303. Email: dalye@sndden.org. Web: www.sndeN.org. Sisters Judith Clemens, S.N.D.deN., Pres.; Barbara English, S.N.D.deN., Treas.; Edie Daly, S.N.D.deN., Contact Person.

FRAMINGHAM. *Bethany Health Care Center, Inc.*, 97 Bethany Rd., 01702-7237. Tel: 508-872-6750; Fax: 508-875-5425. Email: jacquelyn.mccarthy@csjboston.org. Web: www.bethanyhealthcare.org. Sr. Jacquelyn McCarthy, C.S.J., CEO & Admin. Congregation of Sisters of St. Joseph of Boston. An affiliate of Covenant Health Systems, Tewksbury., Skilled Nursing Facilityand Residential Living Bed Capacity 169.

Bethany Hill School, Inc., 89 Bethany Rd., 01702. Tel: 508-875-1117; Fax: 508-875-2288. Email: dakcsj@aol.com. Sponsored by the Sisters of St. Joseph of Boston., 41 units of educational housing for low-income people with a variety of needs.

IPSWICH. *Cuvilly Arts and Earth Center, Inc.* (1983) 10 Jeffrey Neck Rd., 01938. Tel: 508-356-4288. Email: cuvilly@verizon.net. Web: cuvilly.org. Sr. Patricia Rolinger, S.N.D.deN., M.A., Exec. Dir. Total Assisted 100; Total Staff 12.

JAMAICA PLAIN. *Daughters of St. Paul Defined Pension Plan & Trust*, 50 St. Paul's Ave., 02130. Email: snancy@paulinemedia.com. Sr. Nancy Usselmann, F.S.P., Contact Person.

LAWRENCE. **Greater Lawrence Mental Health Center, Inc.*, 30 General St., 01841. Tel: 978-683-3128; Fax: 978-686-7856. Jeffrey Fox, Exec. Dir.

Notre Dame Education Center (1992) (Adult Literacy), 354 Merrimack St., Ste. 210, 01843. Tel: 978-682-6441; Fax: 978-974-9840. Email: executivedirector@ndeclawrence.com. Sr. Eileen T. Burns, S.N.D., Exec. Dir. Sisters of Notre Dame de Namur., ESOL, Citizenship, LEAD, Computer, Spanish, Nursing Assistant Program, GED. Sisters 2; Adults 504; Total Staff 10.

Notre Dame High School Corporate Internship Program, Inc. (2004) 207 Hampshire St., 01841. Tel: 978-689-8222; Fax: 978-689-1967. Sr. Mary Murphy, S.N.D., Ph.D., Pres.

LOWELL. *Saints Medical Center Inc.*, Saints Medical Center, One Hospital Dr., 01852. Tel: 978-458-1411. Email: sguimond@saintsmedicalcenter.com. Web: www.saintsmedicalcenter.com. Mr. Stephen Guimond, CEO.

MALDEN. *The Catholic Cemetery Association of the Archdiocese of Boston, Inc.*, 175 Broadway, 02148. Tel: 781-322-6300; Fax: 781-322-3801. Email: cemetery_contactus@rcab.org. Web: www.ccemetery.org. Robert Visconti, Exec. Dir; David W. Smith, Sec.

METHUEN. *Caritas Holy Family Hospital Men's Guild* (1950) 70 East St., 01844-4597. Tel: 978-687-0156, Ext. 2362; Fax: 978-688-7689. Web: www.holyfamilyhosp.org. Lester Schindel, Pres. & CEO.

Caritas Valley Regional Health System, Inc. (1945) 70 East St., 01844-4597. Tel: 978-687-0151; Fax: 978-688-7689. Web: www.holyfamilyhosp.org.

Caritas Holy Family Hospital, Inc. (1984) Tel: 978-687-0151; Fax: 978-688-7689.

Caritas Holy Family Hospital Auxiliary (1947) Tel: 978-687-0156, Ext. 2301; Fax: 978-688-7689.

Caritas Holy Family Hospital Men's Guild (1950) Tel: 978-687-0156, Ext. 2362; Fax: 978-688-7689.

Caritas Holy Family Hospital Foundation, Inc. (1987) Tel: 978-687-0156, Ext. 2104; Fax: 978-688-7689.

Caritas Valley Regional Support Services, Inc. (1984) Tel: 978-687-0151; Fax: 978-688-7689.

Caritas Valley Regional Medical Services Corporation (1995) 70 East St., 01844. Tel: 978-687-0151; Fax: 978-682-9908.

Caritas Valley Regional Ventures, Inc.

Greater Lawrence Mental Health Center, Inc

NEEDHAM. *St. Sebastian's School Fund, Inc.*, 1191 Greendale Ave., 02492. Tel: 781-449-5200. John J. Doherty, Contact Person & Business Mgr.

NEWTON. *Catholic Purchasing Services, Inc.* (1985) 580 Washington St., 02458. Tel: 617-965-4343; Fax: 617-965-5430. Email: RJW@catholicpurchasing.org. Web: catholicpurchasing.org. Mr. Richard J. Wasilauskas, Pres.

QUINCY. *The Good Shepherd: Maria Droste Services*, 1354 Hancock St., Ste. 209, 02169. Tel: 617-471-5686; Fax: 617-471-6622. Email: mariadroste@verizon.net. Sr. Lorraine Bernier, R.G.S.

Madonna Hall Total Staff 6; Volunteers 16; Total Assisted 290.

SCITUATE. *Mass Times Trust dba Masstimes.org* 91 Surfside Rd., 02066. Mr. Robert A. Hummel, Trustee.

TEWKSBURY. *Covenant Health Systems, Inc.*, 100 Ames Pond, Ste. 102, 01876. Tel: 978-654-6363; Fax: 978-851-0828. Email: info@covenanths.org. Web: www.covenanths.org. David R. Lincoln, Pres. & CEO. Sponsored organizations: Youville Hospital and Rehabilitation Center, Tewksbury, MA; Youville Life-care, Inc., Tewksbury, MA; Youville House Assisted Living Residence, Cambridge, MA; St. Joseph Healthcare, Nashua, NH; St. Joseph Hospital, Nashua, NH; Souhegan Home and Hospice Care, Inc., Nashua, NH; St. Joseph Hospital DH Family Medicine, Nashua, NH; St. Mary's Health System, Lewiston, ME; St. Mary's Regional Medical Center, Lewiston, ME; St. Mary's d'Youville Pavilion, Lewiston, ME; Neighborhood Housing Initiative, Lewiston, ME; St. Mary's Clinical Services, Lewiston, ME; St. Mary's Residences, Lewiston, ME; Mary Immaculate Health/Care Services, Lawrence, MA; Mary Immaculate Nursing/Restorative Center, Lawrence, MA; Mary Immaculate Residential Community, I, II, and II, Lawrence, MA; Mary Immaculate Adult Care, Lawrence, MA; Mary Immaculate Management, Lawrence, MA: Mary Immaculate Transportation, Lawrence, MA; Marguerite's House, Lawrence, MA; CHS of Waltham, dba Maristhill Nursing and Rehabilitation Center, Waltham, MA; St. Joseph Manor Health Care, Brockton, MA; Fanny Allen Corp., Colchester, VT; Fanny Allen Holdings, Inc., Colchester, VT; CHS of Worcester, dba St. Mary's Health Care Center, Worcester, MA; St. Andre Healthcare Facility, Biddeford, ME: St. Mary's Villa Nursing Home, Elmhurst Township, PA; St. Mary's Villa Personal Care Residence, Elmhurst Township, PA; Youville Place Assisted Living Residence, Lexington, MA; Helping Hands of St. Marguerite, Cambridge, MA; St. Joseph Healthcare, Bangor, ME.; Affiliate organizations: Sancta Maria Nursing Facility, Cambridge, MA; Mont Marie Health Care Center, Holyoke, MA; Bethany Health Care Center, Framingham, MA; D'Youville Senior Care Center, Lowell, MA; Notre Dame duLac, Worcester, MA; Notre Dame Long Term Care Center, Worcester, MA.

**Youville Lifecare, Inc.* (1895) *Covenant Health Systems*, 100 Ames Pond Dr., Ste 102, 01876. John Ahle, CFO. Covenant Health Systems, Tewksbury, MA

WALTHAM. **Marist Missionary Sisters Senior Religious Trust*, 349 Grove St., 02453. Tel: 781-893-0149; Fax: 781-899-6838. Email: maristsmsm@aol.com. Web: www.maristmissionarysmsm.org.

WATERTOWN. *St. Joseph Hall, Inc.*, 2 Rosary Dr., 02472-1732. Tel: 617-924-6559; Fax: 617-923-0953. Sr. Marie Jeanne Surette, O.P., Chm. Brd. of Dir. Tel: 859-262-5769; Robyn Rufo, Property Mgr.

RELIGIOUS INSTITUTES OF MEN REPRESENTED IN THE ARCHDIOCESE

For further details refer to the corresponding bracketed number in the Religious Institutes of Men or Women section.

[0130]—*Assumptionists*—A.A.
[1040]—*The Augustinians* (Villanova, PA)—O.S.A.
[0200]—*Benedictine Monks*—O.S.B.
[1350]—*Brothers of St. Francis Xavier*—C.F.X.
[0330]—*Brothers of the Christian Schools* (Long Island, New England Provs.)—F.S.C.
[0470]—*The Capuchin Friars* (Prov. of Mary)—O.F.M.Cap.
[0270]—*Carmelite Fathers & Brothers* (Prov. of Most Pure Heart of Mary)—O.Carm.
[0310]—*Congregation of Christian Brothers* (Eastern Prov.)—C.F.C.
[1210]—*Congregation of the Missionaries of St. Charles*—C.S.
[1000]—*Congregation of the Passion* (St. Paul of the Cross Prov.)—C.P.
[1140]—*Congregation of the Sacred Hearts of Jesus and Mary*—SS.CC.
[0480]—*Conventual Franciscans* (Buffalo, NY)—O.F.M.Conv.
[0260]—*Discalced Carmelite Friars*—O.C.D.
[0520]—*Franciscan Friars* (Assumption of B.V.M., Holy Name, Immaculate Conception Provs.)—O.F.M.
[0530]—*Franciscan Friars of the Atonement*—S.A.
[0670]—*Hospitaller Brothers of St. John of God*—O.H.
[0690]—*Jesuit Fathers and Brother* (New England Prov.)—S.J.
[0770]—*The Marist Brothers* (Poughkeepsie, NY)—F.M.S.
[0780]—*Marist Fathers* (Boston Prov.)—S.M.
[0800]—*Maryknoll*—M.M.
[]—*Mekhitarist Fathers*—C.M.V.D.
[0720]—*The Missionaries of Our Lady of La Salette* (Eastern Prov.)—M.S.
[0910]—*Oblates of Mary Immaculate* (Eastern, St. John the Baptist Provs.)—O.M.I.
[0430]—*Order of Preachers-Dominicans* (Prov. of St. Joseph)—O.P.
[1030]—*Paulist Fathers*—C.S.P.
[0610]—*Priests of the Congregation of Holy Cross* (Eastern Prov.)—C.S.C.
[1070]—*Redemptorist Fathers* (Baltimore Prov.)—C.SS.R.
[1190]—*Salesians of Don Bosco* (Prov. of St. Philip)—S.D.B.
[0110]—*Society of African Missions*—S.M.A.
[0420]—*Society of Divine Word* (Sacred Heart Prov.)—S.V.D.
[0850]—*Society of Missionaries of Africa*—M.Afr.
[0370]—*Society of St. Columban* (American Region)—S.S.C.
[0410]—*Sons of Divine Providence*—F.D.P.
[1270]—*Sons of Mary Missionary Society*—F.M.S.I.

[1280]—*Stigmatine Fathers and Brothers* (Rome, Italy)—C.S.S.
[1360]—*Xaverian Missionary Fathers*—S.X.

RELIGIOUS INSTITUTES OF WOMEN REPRESENTED IN THE ARCHDIOCESE

[1810]—*Bernardine Franciscan Sisters*—O.S.F.
[0330]—*Carmelite Sisters for the Aged and Infirm*—O.Carm.
[0670]—*Cistercian Nuns of the Strict Observance*—O.C.S.O.
[0270]—*Congregation of Bon Secours*—C.B.S.
[3110]—*Congregation of Our Lady of the Retreat in the Cenacle*—R.C.
[]—*Congregation of the Armenian Catholic Sisters of the Immaculate Conception, Inc.*
[1920]—*Congregation of the Sisters of the Holy Cross*—C.S.C.
[0760]—*Daughters of Charity of St. Vincent de Paul*—D.C.
[0860]—*Daughters of Mary of the Immaculate Conception*—C.M.
[0420]—*Discalced Carmelite Nuns*—O.C.D.
[1070-03]—*Dominican Sisters*—O.P.
[1070-13]—*Dominican Sisters*—O.P.
[1115]—*Dominican Sisters of Peace*—O.P.
[1170]—*Felician Sisters*—C.S.S.F.
[1370]—*Franciscan Missionaries of Mary*—F.M.M.
[1320]—*Franciscan Missionary Sisters for Africa* (Co. Louth, Ireland)—O.S.F.
[1180]—*Franciscan Sisters of Allegany, New York*—O.S.F.
[1470]—*Franciscan Sisters of St. Joseph*—F.S.S.J.
[1840]—*Grey Nuns of the Sacred Heart*—G.N.S.H.
[2070]—*Holy Union Sisters*—S.U.S.C.
[0410]—*Institute of the Sisters of Our Lady of Mt. Carmel*—O.Carm.
[2290]—*Little Missionary Sisters of Charity*—L.M.S.C.
[2310]—*Little Sisters of the Assumption*—L.S.A.
[2320]—*Little Sisters of the Holy Family*—P.S.S.F.
[2340]—*Little Sisters of the Poor*—L.S.P.
[2420]—*Marist Missionary Sisters-Missionary Sisters of the Society of Mary*—S.M.S.M.
[2470]—*Maryknoll Sisters of St. Dominic*—M.M.
[2480]—*Medical Missionaries of Mary*—M.M.M.
[1360]—*Missionary Franciscan Sisters of the Immaculate Conception*—O.S.F.
[2790]—*Missionary Servants of the Most Blessed Trinity*—M.S.B.T.
[2880]—*Missionary Sisters of St. Columban*—S.S.C.
[2800]—*Missionary Sisters of the Most Sacred Heart of Jesus of Hiltrup*—M.S.C.
[3030]—*Oblates of the Most Holy Redeemer*—O.SS.R.
[3760]—*Order of St. Clare*—O.S.C.
[0950]—*Pious Society Daughters of St. Paul*—D.S.P.
[3240]—*Poor Sisters of Jesus Crucified and the Sorrowful Mother*—C.J.C.
[3410]—*Religious of Christian Education*—R.C.E.
[2070]—*Religious of the Holy Union of the Sacred Hearts*—S.U.S.C.
[2970]—*School Sisters of Notre Dame*—S.S.N.D.
[3550]—*Servants of the Immaculate Heart of Mary*—S.C.I.M.
[0980]—*Sisters Disciples of the Divine Master*—P.D.D.M.
[0490]—*Sisters of Charity of Montreal-Grey Nuns*—S.G.M.
[0500]—*Sisters of Charity of Nazareth*—S.C.N.
[0560]—*Sisters of Charity of Quebec-Grey Nuns*—S.C.Q.
[0590]—*Sisters of Charity of Saint Elizabeth, Convent Station*—S.C.
[0640]—*Sisters of Charity of St. Vincent de Paul, Halifax*—S.C.
[0540]—*Sisters of Charity, At Ottawa-Grey Nuns of the Cross*—S.C.O.
[0990]—*Sisters of Divine Providence*—C.D.P.
[2580]—*Sisters of Mercy of the Union in the United States of America*—R.S.M.
[3000]—*Sisters of Notre Dame de Namur*—S.N.D.deN.
[3360]—*Sisters of Providence of Saint Mary-Of-The-Woods, Indiana*—S.P.
[3950]—*Sisters of Saint Mary of Namur*—S.S.M.N.
[3720]—*Sisters of St. Anne*—S.S.A.
[3750]—*Sisters of St. Chretienne*—S.S.Ch.
[1650]—*Sisters of St. Francis of Philadelphia*—O.S.F.
[3830]—*Sisters of St. Joseph*—C.S.J.
[3815]—*Sisters of Ste. Jeanne D'Arc*—S.J.A.
[0150]—*Sisters of the Assumption B.V.*—S.A.S.V.
[1830]—*Sisters of the Good Shepherd*—R.G.S.
[3310]—*Sisters of the Presentation of Mary*—P.M.
[1490]—*Sisters of the Third Franciscan Order*—O.S.F.
[1705]—*Sisters of the Third Order of St. Francis of Assisi*—O.S.F.
[4060]—*Society of the Holy Child Jesus*—S.H.C.J.
[4070]—*Society of the Sacred Heart*—R.S.C.J.
[4110]—*Ursuline Nuns* (Eastern Prov.)—O.S.U.

ARCHDIOCESAN CEMETERIES

ARLINGTON. *St. Paul*
BEVERLY. *St. Mary*
CAMBRIDGE. *North Cambridge Catholic*
CHARLESTOWN. *St. Francis de Sales*
HAVERHILL. *St. James, St. Joseph & St. Patrick*
LOWELL. *St. Patrick*
LYNN. *St. Mary, St. Joseph & St. Jean Baptiste*
MALDEN. *Holy Cross & St. Mary*
MARBLEHEAD. *Star of the Sea*
SALEM. *St. Mary*
SAXONVILLE. *St. George*
STONEHAM. *St. Patrick*
WALTHAM. *Calvary*
WATERTOWN. *Mount Auburn & St. Patrick*
WOBURN. *Calvary*

PRIVATE CATHOLIC CEMETERIES

CHELMSFORD. *St. Joseph Cemetery, Inc.*, 96 Riverneck Rd., 01824-2942. Tel: 978-458-4851; Fax: 978-441-3958. Email: stjosephcemetery@stjc1894.com. Web: stjc1894.com. Rev. Charles Breault, O.M.I., Dir. & Contact Person; Clare Taddeo, Asst. Dir. & Contact Person.

NECROLOGY

† Sypek, Rev. Msgr. Stanislaus T., Boston, MA St. Adalbert.—Died Oct. 2, 2011
† Brady, Richard J., (Retired)—Died March 30, 2011
† Burns, John F., (Retired)—Died July 9, 2011
† DePietro, Arthur J., (Retired)—Died Oct. 31, 2011
† Fleming, Thomas J., (Retired)—Died Dec. 23, 2011
† Francis, Paul R., (Retired)—Died Oct. 16, 2011
† Gillis, Edward F., (Retired)—Died Nov. 24, 2011
† Grant, Frederick A., (Retired)—Died Nov. 1, 2011
† Haley, William J., (Retired)—Died May 14, 2011
† Keane, Thomas F., (Retired)—Died June 4, 2011
† Kelleher, Robert N., (Retired)—Died Nov. 18, 2011
† Kelley, Edward T., (Retired)—Died Aug. 10, 2011
† Leonard, Clyde A., (Retired)—Died Oct. 5, 2011
† Lyons, James D., (Retired)—Died May 29, 2011
† McAskill, Kenneth F., (Retired)—Died Nov. 9, 2011
† McCune, James L., (Retired)—Died Dec. 7, 2011
† Morgan, Thomas B., (Retired)—Died May 6, 2011
† Murphy, Charles J., (Retired)—Died June 11, 2011
† Pied, Wilfrid L., (Retired)—Died May 29, 2011
† Regan, Francis A., (Retired)—Died Oct. 23, 2011
† Sheehan, Daniel J., (Retired)—Died July 2, 2011
† Weber, Charles P., (Retired)—Died Nov. 2, 2011

An asterisk (*) denotes an organization that has established tax-exempt status directly with the IRS and is not covered by the USCCB Group Ruling.

Diocese of Bridgeport

(Dioecesis Bridgeportensis)

ESTABLISHED AUGUST 6, 1953.

Square Miles 633.

Corporate Title: The Bridgeport Roman Catholic Diocesan Corporation.

Comprises all of Fairfield County in the State of Connecticut.

For legal titles of parishes and diocesan institutions, consult the Chancery at The Catholic Center.

(VACANT SEE)

Chancery: The Catholic Center, 238 Jewett Ave., Bridgeport, CT 06606-2892. Tel: 203-372-4301; Fax: 203-371-8698.

Web: www.bridgeportdiocese.org

STATISTICAL OVERVIEW

Personnel	
Priests: Diocesan Active in Diocese	160
Priests: Diocesan Active Outside Diocese	13
Priests: Diocesan in Foreign Missions	3
Priests: Retired, Sick or Absent	64
Number of Diocesan Priests	240
Religious Priests in Diocese	31
Total Priests in Diocese	271
Extern Priests in Diocese	31
Ordinations:	
Diocesan Priests	1
Permanent Deacons in Diocese	103
Total Sisters	343
Parishes	
Parishes	87
With Resident Pastor:	
Resident Diocesan Priests	71
Resident Religious Priests	4
Without Resident Pastor:	
Administered by Priests	11
Administered by Deacons	1
Professional Ministry Personnel:	
Sisters	343
Welfare	
Catholic Hospitals	1
Total Assisted	215,000
Health Care Centers	2
Total Assisted	22,405
Homes for the Aged	15
Total Assisted	1,165
Day Care Centers	5
Total Assisted	322
Specialized Homes	1
Total Assisted	41
Special Centers for Social Services	19
Total Assisted	487,000
Other Institutions	5
Total Assisted	338
Educational	
Seminaries, Diocesan	1
Students from This Diocese	14
Diocesan Students in Other Seminaries	21
Total Seminarians	35
Colleges and Universities	3
Total Students	12,366
High Schools, Diocesan and Parish	5
Total Students	2,326
High Schools, Private	2
Total Students	1,189
Elementary Schools, Diocesan and Parish	32
Total Students	7,628
Elementary Schools, Private	21
Total Students	548
Non-residential Schools for the Disabled	2
Total Students	20
Catechesis/Religious Education:	
High School Students	3,170
Elementary Students	43,770
Total Students under Catholic Instruction	71,052
Teachers in the Diocese:	
Priests	13
Sisters	16
Lay Teachers	854
Vital Statistics	
Receptions into the Church:	
Infant Baptism Totals	4,212
Adult Baptism Totals	175
Received into Full Communion	602
First Communions	5,320
Confirmations	5,228
Marriages:	
Catholic	1,002
Interfaith	83
Total Marriages	1,085
Deaths	2,708
Total Catholic Population	410,834
Total Population	916,289

Former Bishops—His Eminence LAWRENCE J. CARDINAL SHEHAN, D.D., ord. Dec. 23, 1922; cons. Dec. 12, 1945 as Auxiliary Bishop of Baltimore; installed as first Bishop of Bridgeport, Dec. 1, 1953; transferred to Archdiocese of Baltimore, July 10, 1961; created Cardinal, Feb. 22, 1965; died Aug. 26, 1984; Most Revs. WALTER W. CURTIS, S.T.D., ord. Dec. 8, 1937; appt. Auxiliary Bishop of Newark and Titular Bishop of Bisica in Tunis; cons. Sept. 24, 1957; appt. Bishop of Bridgeport, Sept. 23, 1961; installed Nov. 20, 1961; retired June 28, 1988; died Oct. 18, 1997; EDWARD M. EGAN, J.C.D., ord. Dec. 15, 1957; appt. Titular Bishop of Allegheny and Auxiliary Bishop of New York, April 1, 1985; cons. May 22, 1985; appt. Bishop of Bridgeport, Nov. 8, 1988; installed Dec. 14, 1988; appt. Archbishop of New York, May 11, 2000; installed June 19, 2000; created Cardinal Feb. 21, 2001; WILLIAM E. LORI, ord. May 14, 1977; appt. Titular Bishop of Bulla and Auxiliary of Washington April 20, 1995; appt. Bishop of Bridgeport Jan. 23, 2001; installed March 19, 2001; appt. Archbishop of Baltimore March 20, 2012.

Vicars General—Rev. Msgrs. J. PETER CULLEN, P.A., V.G.; WILLIAM J. SCHEYD, P.A., V.G.; THOMAS J. DRISCOLL, P.A., V.G., 238 Jewett Ave., Bridgeport, 06606-2892.

Episcopal Vicar for Administration—Rev. Msgr. JERALD A. DOYLE, Ph.D., J.C.D.

Chancery—The Catholic Center, 238 Jewett Ave., Bridgeport, 06606-2892. Tel: 203-372-4301; Fax: 203-371-8698. Office Hours: Mon.-Fri. 8:30-4:30.

Chancellor—Mrs. ANNE O. MCCRORY, Esq., Catholic Center, 238 Jewett Ave., Bridgeport, 06606-2892. Tel: 203-416-1356.

Secretary to the Bishop—Rev. JOSEPH A. MARCELLO.

Episcopal Vicar for Religious—VACANT.

Episcopal Vicar for Clergy—Rev. Msgr. KEVIN T. ROYAL, S.T.L., Dir.

Episcopal Vicar for Haitians—Rev. G. FRANTZ DESRUISSEAUX, J.C.L.

Episcopal Vicar for Hispanics—Rev. GUSTAVO A. FALLA.

Chief Finance Officer—Mr. NORMAN R. WALKER, CFO.

Diocesan Tribunal—The Catholic Center, 238 Jewett Ave., Bridgeport, 06606-2892. Tel: 203-416-1423.

Judicial Vicar—Rev. Msgr. JERALD A. DOYLE, Ph.D., J.C.D.

Adjutant Judicial Vicar—Rev. Msgr. J. JAMES CUNEO, J.C.D.

Judges—Rev. Msgrs. WILLIAM A. GENUARIO, P.A., J.C.D. (Retired); THOMAS J. DRISCOLL, P.A., V.G.; Revs. MICHAEL A. BOCCACCIO; ROBERT V. BIROSCHAK, J.C.L.; Sr. ELIZABETH MCDONOUGH, O.P., J.C.D.; Revs. MICHAEL SKROGKY, J.C.D.; WILLIAM M. QUINLAN, J.C.L.; WILLIAM F. VERRILLI, J.C.L.

Defenders of the Bond—Revs. RICHARD F. FUTIE, J.C.D.; ALFRED F. PECARIC, S.T.L.

Promoter of Justice—Rev. G. FRANTZ DESRUISSEAUX, J.C.L.

Notaries—MARY A. MOLLOY; KERRY PERILLE.

Diocesan Legal Services—R. SCOTT BEACH, Esq., Day Pitney, LLP, One Canterbury Green, Stamford, 06901.

Diocesan Censors—Rev. Msgrs. LAURENCE R. BRONKIEWICZ, S.T.D.; THOMAS J. DRISCOLL, P.A., V.G.; CHRISTOPHER J. WALSH, Ph.D., S.T.D.

Diocesan Consultors—Rev. Msgrs. J. PETER CULLEN, P.A., V.G.; LOUIS A. DEPROFIO, P.A. (Retired); THOMAS J. DRISCOLL, P.A., V.G.; Rev. THOMAS P. THORNE; Rev. Msgrs. WILLIAM J. SCHEYD, P.A., V.G.; WALTER C. ORLOWSKI; ANDREW G. VARGA; ANICETO VILLAMIDE; ROBERT E. WEISS; DARIUSZ J. ZIELONKA; JERALD A. DOYLE, Ph.D., J.C.D.

Presbyteral Council—VACANT, Presider; Rev. Msgrs. WILLIAM J. SCHEYD, P.A., V.G., Vice Chm.; J. PETER CULLEN, P.A., V.G.; LOUIS A. DEPROFIO, P.A. (Retired); JERALD A. DOYLE, Ph.D., J.C.D.; THOMAS J. DRISCOLL, P.A., V.G.; Revs. CYRUS BARTOLOME; DAVID W. BLANCHFIELD; ROBERT J. CROFUT; Rev. Msgr. KEVIN T. ROYAL, S.T.L.; Revs. ROBERT M. KINNALLY; MICHAEL P. LYONS; Rev. Msgr. WALTER C. ORLOWSKI; Revs. DENNIS MASON, O.F.M.Conv.; LEONEL S. MEDEIROS; J. BARRY FUREY; REGINALD D. NORMAN; FRANCIS T. HOFFMANN; PAWEL M. HREBENKO; IAN JEREMIAH; JOSEPH A. MARCELLO; PAUL G. MURPHY; THOMAS P. THORNE.

Finance Council—Rev. Msgrs. WILLIAM J. SCHEYD, P.A., V.G.; J. PETER CULLEN, P.A., V.G.; THOMAS J. DRISCOLL, P.A., V.G.; Mrs. ANNE O. MCCRORY, Esq.; Mr. NORMAN R. WALKER; CAROL JAMES; Mr. WILLIAM H. BESGEN; Mr. MICHAEL F. HOBEN; Mr. MICHAEL O'ROURKE; Mr. BRIAN YOUNG; Mr. PHILLIP D. AMEEN; Mr. DENNIS NALLY; Mr. JOSEPH D. ROXE; Mr. WILLIAM J. TOTTEN.

Parochial Examiners—Revs. DAVID W. BLANCHFIELD; ROBERT J. CROFUT; PAUL G. MURPHY; Rev. Msgr. WALTER C. ORLOWSKI; Rev. J. BARRY FUREY.

Territorial Vicars—Vicariate I (Stamford, Darien, Glenbrook, Greenwich, Byram, Riverside): Rev.

FRANCIS T. HOFFMANN, St. Catherine of Siena Rectory, 4 Riverside Ave., Riverside, 06878. Tel: 203-637-3661. Vicariate II (Norwalk, New Canaan, Wilton, Weston, Westport): Rev. THOMAS P. THORNE, 98 Riverside Ave., Westport, 06880. Tel: 203-227-5161; Fax: 203-227-1206. Vicariate III (Fairfield, Easton, West Bridgeport): Rev. J. BARRY FUREY, Assumption Rectory, 545 Stratfield Rd., Fairfield, 06825. Tel: 203-333-9055. Vicariate IV (East Bridgeport, Stratford, Trumbull, Monroe, Shelton): Rev. NICHOLAS S. PAVIA, St. Joseph Rectory, 50 Fairmont Pl., Shelton, 06484. Tel: 203-924-8611. Vicariate V (Bethel, Brookfield, Danbury, Georgetown, Newtown, New Fairfield, Redding, Ridgefield, Sherman): Rev. COREY V. PICCININO, St. Mary Rector, 26 Dodgingtown Rd., Bethel, 06801-2241. Tel: 203-744-5777.

Office for Clergy and Religious—Rev. Msgr. KEVIN T. ROYAL, S.T.L., Episcopal Vicar for Clergy Personnel; Deacon ANTHONY J. DETJE, Asst. to Dir.; Sr. NANCY STRILLACCI, A.S.C.J., Bishop's Delegate for Rel.

The Catholic Center—238 Jewett Ave., Bridgeport, 06606. Tel: 203-372-4301; Fax: 203-372-9835. Web: www.bridgeportdiocese.org.

Services-Business Office—The Catholic Center, 238 Jewett Ave., Bridgeport, 06606-2892. Mr. NORMAN R. WALKER, CFO; Ms. TERESA NUNES, Diocesan Financial Dir.; Mr. ROBERT LEBLANC, Dir. Property Mgmt. Tel: 203-416-1419.

Members of the Clergy Personnel Committee—Rev. Msgr. KEVIN T. ROYAL, S.T.L.; Revs. COREY V. PICCININO; DAVID W. BLANCHFIELD; LEONEL S. MEDEIROS.

Office for the Continuing Education of Clergy—Rev. Msgr. KEVIN T. ROYAL, S.T.L.; Revs. FRANCIS T. HOFFMAN; SAMUEL V. SCOTT; ROBERT A. UZZILIO (Retired).

Office of Vocations—Rev. ROBERT M. KINNALLY, 238 Jewett Ave., Bridgeport, 06606. Tel: 203-416-1512; Fax: 203-612-9832. Email: frkinnally@diobpt.org. Assistant Vocation Directors: Revs. LEONEL S. MEDEIROS; JOSEPH A. MARCELLO.

Priest Vocation Advisory Board—Rev. Msgrs. J. PETER CULLEN, P.A., V.G.; JERALD A. DOYLE, Ph.D., J.C.D.; THOMAS J. DRISCOLL, P.A., V.G.; WILLIAM J. SCHEYD, P.A., V.G.; Revs. LEONEL S. MEDEIROS; JOSEPH A. MARCELLO; GUSTAVO A. FALLA; ROBERT J. CROFUT; G. FRANTZ DESRUISSEAUX, J.C.L.; ROBERT M. KINNALLY; PAWEL M. HREBENKO; RICHARD D. MURPHY; EDICSON OROZCO; JOSEPH A. PRINCE; Rev. Msgr. KEVIN T. ROYAL, S.T.L.; Rev. ROLANDO TORRES; Rev. Msgr. ANICETO VILLAMIDE.

Office of the Permanent Diaconate—Deacons ANTHONY J. DETJE, Dir.; JOHN J. MORANSKI, Asst. Dir. Diaconate Formation.

Office for Ecumenical and Interreligious Affairs—Rev. SAMUEL V. SCOTT, Dir., St. John Fisher Residence, 894 Newfield Ave., Stamford, 06905-2518. Fax: 203-461-9876.

Diocesan Office of Divine Worship—VACANT.

Pastoral Services—Mr. DAMIEN O'CONNOR, The Catholic Center, 238 Jewett Ave., Bridgeport, 06606-2892. Tel: 203-416-1334; Fax: 203-373-1418. Email: doconnor@diobpt.org.

Family Life Ministry Diocesan Office—238 Jewett Ave., Bridgeport, 06606-2892. Tel: 203-416-1442; Fax: 203-371-8698. Sr. MARY CONCEPTA, Dir. Ministry Programs include Post Abortion Support and Pro-Life Ministry. Respect Life Ministry, Catholic Center, 238 Jewett Ave., Bridgeport, 06606-2892. Tel: 203-416-1444; Fax: 203-371-8698. Please call Martha Dombroski regarding Marriage Preparation. Tel: 203-416-1440.

Ministry for People With Developmental Disabilities—238 Jewett Ave., Bridgeport, 06606. Tel: 203-416-1502; Fax: 203-371-8698. Please call Michelle Mara regarding Catechise & Sacramental Preparation for People with Developmental Disabilities.

Youth Ministry—Sr. ERIKA SCHEELJE. Tel: 203-416-1449. Email: srscheelje@diobpt.org.

Formation—VACANT, Dir.

Adult Formation—Ms. GINO DONNARUMMO. Tel: 203-416-1446. Email: gdonnarummo@diobpt.org.

Religious Education—Mrs. CAROL PINARD. Tel: 203-416-1441. Email: cpinard@diobpt.org.

Catholic Scouts—VACANT.

Bridgeport Diocesan Schools, Corp.—238 Jewett Ave., Bridgeport, 06606. Tel: 203-416-1375; Fax: 203-372-1961. Dr. MARGARET A. DAMES, Ed.D., Supt. Schools, 238 Jewett Ave., Bridgeport, 06606-2892. Tel: 203-416-1375; Fax: 203-372-1961. Email: mdames@diobpt.org; Mr. JOHN COOK, Deputy Supt. Schools. Tel: 203-416-1417; Sr. MARY GRACE WALSH, A.S.C.J., Ph.D., Deputy Supt. Schools. Tel: 203-416-1397; Mr. MARTIN TRISTINE, Asst. to Supt. Tel: 203-416-1377. Email: mtristine@diobpt.org; JENNIFER MITCHELL, Dir. Devel., Communication & Mktg. Tel: 203-416-1378.

Special Education—Dr. CANDY LOMBARDO, Special Educ., The Catholic Center, 238 Jewett Ave., Bridgeport, 06606-2892. Tel: 203-416-1375; Fax: 203-372-1961.

Catholic Charities of Fairfield County, Inc.—Mr. ALBERT BARBER, Exec. Dir., Catholic Center, 238 Jewett Ave., Bridgeport, 06606-2892. Tel: 203-416-1307; 203-416-1333. Email: abarber@ccfc-ct.org.

Diocesan Offices and Directors

Ethnic and Cultural Services—Mr. MICHAEL TINTRUP, Sec., 238 Jewett Ave., Bridgeport, 06606-2892. Tel: 203-416-1305; Fax: 203-372-5045.

Aging, Diocesan Task Force—VACANT.

Archives—Deacon WILLIAM J. BISSENDEN, Archivist. Tel: 203-416-1354.

African Americans, Apostolate of—Rev. REGINALD D. NORMAN, The Catholic Center, 238 Jewett Ave., Bridgeport, 06606.

Catholic Lawyers—Rev. Msgr. J. JAMES CUNEO, J.C.D., Spiritual Moderator; LEOPOLD DEFUSCO, Esq., Coord., St. Thomas More Society of Fairfield Co., 238 Jewett Ave., Bridgeport, 06606-2892. Tel: 203-374-2590.

Catholic Physicians Guild—Dr. THOMAS G. FLYNN, Coord., 39 Old Studio Rd., New Canaan, 06840. Tel: 203-966-1959.

Catholic Women, Council of—Mrs. MARIE WALSH, 63 Glenbrook Rd,. Apt. 7A, Stamford, 06902. Tel: 203-358-8598. District Spiritual Directors: Rev. Msgr. ERNEST T. ESPOSITO, D.Min., (Bridgeport) (Retired), Catholic Center, 238 Jewett Ave., Bridgeport, 06606. Tel: 203-416-1443; Fax: 203-371-8698; Rev. MARTIN S. IGOE, (Greenwich) (Retired), Sacred Heart Parish, 95 Henry St., Greenwich, 06830. Tel: 203-531-8730; Fax: 203-531-8794.

Cemeteries—RAY CAPO, Dir., 238 Jewett Ave., Bridgeport, 06606-2892. Tel: 203-416-1494; Fax: 203-374-7588. Email: rcapo@diobpt.org.

Communications—Mr. BRIAN D. WALLACE, Dir., 238 Jewett Ave., Bridgeport, 06606-2892. Tel: 203-416-1464; Fax: 203-374-2044. Email: fcc@diobpt.org. Web: www.bridgeportdiocese.com; Rev. MARK CONNOLLY, Diocesan Dir., Radio & Television (Retired), Mailing Address: P.O. Box 7466, Greenwich, 06836. Tel: 203-316-9394.

Connecticut Catholic Conference—MICHAEL C. CULHANE, 134 Farmington Ave., Hartford, 06105. Tel: 203-524-7882.

Cursillos of Fairfield County, Inc.—Rev. Msgr. ANICETO VILLAMIDE, Advisor for Spanish Language, St. Peter Rectory, 695 Colorado Ave., Bridgeport, 06605. Tel: 203-366-5611.

Deaf, Apostolate for—Rev. PETER A. DEMARCO, Moderator (Retired), Res.: Catherine Dennis Keefe Queen of the Clergy, 274 Strawberry Hill Ave., Stamford, 06902. Tel: 203-358-9906. Email: pdem243377@aol.com.

Development, Office of—Mr. JEFF MACHI, Exec. Dir. Devel., 238 Jewett Ave., Bridgeport, 06606-2892. Tel: 203-416-1324.

Fairfield Foundation of the Diocese of Bridgeport, Inc.—MICHELLE JONES DELMHORST, Pres., 238 Jewett Ave., Bridgeport, 06606-2892. Tel: 203-416-1400.

Inner-City Foundation for Charity and Education—Mr. RICHARD T. STONE, Dir., 238 Jewett Ave., Bridgeport, 06606-2892. Tel: 203-416-1363; Fax: 203-371-8698. Email: innercity.foundation@snet.net.

Catholic Ministry for the Elderly—VACANT.

Haitian American Catholic Center of Greater Stamford—Rev. JEAN-RONY PHILIPPE, 93 Hope St., Stamford, 06906. Tel: 203-406-0343; Fax: 203-406-0347.

Support Services, Office of—LOUISE STEWART-SPAGNUOLO, Dir., 238 Jewett Ave., Bridgeport, 06606-2892. Tel: 203-416-1402; Fax: 203-371-0875. Email: lsspagnuolo@diobpt.org.

Insurance Office—JOSEPH G. BURTON, Claims & Risk Mgr., Catholic Mutual Group, 238 Jewett Ave., Bridgeport, 06606. Tel: 203-416-1310; Fax: 203-371-6139. Email: jburton@catholicmutual.org.

Nurses, Council of Catholic—Rev. STEPHEN J. GLEESON, Dir., St. Stephen Rectory, 6949 Main St., Trumbull, 06611. Tel: 203-268-6217; Fax: 203-268-9861.

Official Newspapers— "The Fairfield County Catholic", (Biweekly) VACANT, Publisher; Mr. BRIAN D. WALLACE, Dir., 238 Jewett Ave., Bridgeport, 06606. Tel: 203-416-1464; Fax: 203-374-2044. Web: www.bridgeportdiocese.com; Mrs. PATRICIA HENNESSY, Asst. Editor. Tel: 203-416-1460; Fax: 203-374-2044. Email: phennessy@diobpt.org.

Pilgrimages, Office of Diocesan—Rev. Msgr. WILLIAM J. LOUGHLIN (Retired), Catherine Dennis Keefe Queen of the Clergy Retired Priests' Residence, 274 Strawberry Hill Ave., Stamford, 06902. Tel: 203-358-9906.

Pontifical Association of the Holy Childhood—Rev. FREDERICK L. SAVIANO, Dir., The Catholic Center, 238 Jewett Ave., Bridgeport, 06606-2892. Tel: 203-416-1447; Fax: 203-371-8698.

Portuguese-Speaking People, Apostolate for—VACANT.

Propagation of the Faith—Rev. FREDERICK L. SAVIANO, Dir., The Catholic Center, 238 Jewett Ave., Bridgeport, 06606-2892. Tel: 203-416-1447; Fax: 203-371-8698. Email: frsaviano@diobpt.org.

Boy Scouts and Girl Scouts—VACANT.

Retired Priests—Rev. Msgr. LOUIS A. DEPROFIO, P.A., Dir. (Retired); VICKEY HICKEY, Admin., The Catherine Dennis Keefe Queen of the Clergy Retired Priests' Residence, 274 Strawberry Hill Ave., Stamford, 06904. Tel: 203-358-9906; Fax: 203-358-9524.

Office of Safe Environment—Ms. ERIN NEIL, Dir., 238 Jewett Ave., Bridgeport, 06606. Tel: 203-416-1406. Email: eneil@diobpt.org.

Victims Assistance Coordinators—Mr. MICHAEL TINTRUP. Tel: 203-241-0987. Email: mtintrup@diobpt.org; Ms. ERIN NEIL, M.S.W., 238 Jewett Ave., Bridgeport, 06606. Tel: 203-650-3265. Email: eneil@diobpt.org.

CLERGY, PARISHES, MISSIONS AND PAROCHIAL SCHOOLS

CITY OF BRIDGEPORT

(FAIRFIELD COUNTY)

1—ST. AUGUSTINE CATHEDRAL (1842) Revs. Gustavo A. Falla; Sean R. Kulacz; John J. Gomez; Ha Dinh Dang; Deacon Santos Garcia.
Res.: 359 Washington Ave., 06604. Tel: 203-368-6777; Fax: 203-368-6386.
See St. Augustine Cathedral, Bridgeport under Elementary Schools, Regional located in the Institution section.
Catechesis/Religious Program—Students 285.

2—ST. AMBROSE (1928) Rev. John Stronkowski; Deacon Kenneth J. Ruge. In Res., Rev. Churchill Penn.
Res.: 1596 Boston Ave., 06610. Tel: 203-333-1336; Fax: 203-330-9085. Email: stambrose@optonline.net.
See St. Ambrose, Bridgeport under Elementary Schools, Regional located in the Institution section.
Catechesis/Religious Program—Students 64.
Station—Bishop Curtis Homes 525 Palisade Ave. Tel: 203-366-4333.
Station—Success Park Success Ave.

3—ST. ANDREW (1961) Revs. Eugene R. Szantyr; Hyginus Agu. In Res., Rev. William F. Verrilli.
Res.: 435 Anton St., 06606. Tel: 203-374-6171; Fax: 203-372-7709.
See St. Andrew, Bridgeport under Elementary Schools, Regional located in the Institution section.
Catechesis/Religious Program—Tel: 203-374-8118. Susan Baldwin, D.R.E. Students 190.

4—ST. ANN (1922) [CEM] Rev. Peter J. Towsley.
Res.: 481 Brewster St., 06605. Tel: 203-368-1607; Fax: 203-336-4233. Email: admin@stannblackrock.com. Web: www.stannblackrock.com.
See St. Ann, Bridgeport under Elementary Schools, Regional located in the Institution section.
Catechesis/Religious Program—Students 50.

5—ST. ANTHONY OF PADUA, Merged with St. Peter, Bridgeport. See separate listing.

6—BLESSED SACRAMENT (1917) Rev. Reginald D. Norman, Admin.; Deacons Ricardo Martinez; Donald P. Foust; Joseph Mihalek, Pastoral Assoc.
Res.: 275 Union Ave., 06607. Tel: 203-333-1202; Fax: 203-368-3502. Email: blessedsacramentrc@sbcglobal.net. Web: blessedsacramentrc.parishesonline.net.
Catechesis/Religious Program—Students 40.

7—ST. CHARLES BORROMEO (1902) Revs. Edicson Orozco; Rogerio Silva Perri.
Res.: 391 Ogden St., 06608. Tel: 203-333-2147; Fax: 203-330-8316.
Catechesis/Religious Program—Tel: 203-576-1629. Students 276.

8—SS. CYRIL AND METHODIUS (1907), (Slovak), Rev. Msgr. Joseph W. Pekar.
Res.: 79 Church St., 06608. Tel: 203-333-7003.

9—ST. GEORGE (1907), (Lithuanian), Rev. Julio Lopresti, I.V.E.
Res.: 443 Park Ave., 06604. Tel: 203-335-1797; Fax: 203-334-6359. Email: stgeorge.church@sbcglobal.net.
Catechesis/Religious Program—Tel: 203-330-8409. Email: c-damaris@sersdoras.org. Web: www.ss/musa.org. Sr. Blessed Sacrament, S.S.V.M., D.R.E. Students 205.

10—HOLY ROSARY (1903), (Italian), Deacon Donald P. Foust, Admin.

Res.: 365 E. Washington Ave., 06608. Tel: 203-334-2447; Fax: 203-335-5334.
Catechesis/Religious Program—Students 3.

11—St. John Nepomucene, Closed. For inquiries for parish records contact Holy Name of Jesus, Stratford.

12—St. Joseph's, Closed. May 23, 1988. For inquiries for parish records contact St. Patrick, Bridgeport.

13—St. Mary (1857), (Spanish), [CEM] Rev. Msgr. Matthew Bernelli; Deacon Reynaldo Olavarria.
Res.: 25 Sherman St., 06608. Tel: 203-334-8811; Fax: 203-334-8574. Email: stmarychurchbpt@optonline.net. Web: www.stmarychurchbridgeport.com.
Catechesis/Religious Program—Students 147.

14—St. Michael The Archangel (1899), (Polish), [CEM] Rev. Stefan Morawski, O.F.M.Conv.
Res.: 310 Pulaski St., 06608. Tel: 203-334-1822; Fax: 203-696-0078. Web: www.smaparish.com.
Catechesis/Religious Program—Students 125.

15—Our Lady of Fatima (1962), (Portuguese), Rev. Joseph De Brito Alves (Portugal), Admin.; Deacon Gabriel A. Pereira.
Res.: 429 Huntington Rd., 06608. Tel: 203-333-7575; Fax: 203-333-7575.
Catechesis/Religious Program—Tel: 203-929-1085. Students 122.

16—Our Lady of Good Counsel (1955) [CEM] Revs. Eugene R. Szantyr, Admin.; Seraphim Ralph Rohlman.
Res.: 163 Ortega Ave., 06606. Tel: 203-372-3533.
Catechesis/Religious Program— Noreen Franklin, D.R.E. Students 8.

17—St. Patrick Church (1889) Rev. Norman J. Guilbert; Deacons William J. Bissenden; Alix Africot. In Res., Rev. Bernardo C. Rodriguez.
Res. & Business Office: 170 Thompson St., 06604-2816. Tel: 203-335-0106; Fax: 203-335-0107. Email: stpats@optonline.net. Web: www.stpatrickbridgeport.com.
Church: 851 North Ave., 06606.
Catechesis/Religious Program—Email: mgruce@optonline.net. Marcia Gruce, D.R.E. Students 63.
Station—Connecticut State Correctional Institution
Station—St. Vincent Medical Center, Tel: 203-576-6000.
Station—Northbridge Health Care Center, Tel: 203-336-0232.

18—St. Peter (1900), (Spanish), [CEM] Rev. Msgr. Aniceto Villamide; Rev. Jose Rebaque, S.A.C., Temp. Parochial Vicar; Deacons Domingo Reveron; Luis Torres.
Res.: 695 Colorado Ave., 06605. Tel: 203-366-5611; Fax: 203-335-1924.
See St. Peter, Bridgeport under Elementary Schools, Regional located in the Institution section.
Catechesis/Religious Program—Tel: 203-334-5681; Fax: 203-333-1590. Sr. Aida Ramirez, M.S.S., D.R.E. Students 260.

19—St. Raphael (1925), (Italian), Revs. Alfonso Picone, Admin.; Grazioso Artuso; Giandomenico Flora, Parochial Vicar; Deacon Joseph Melita.
Res.: 162 Oak St., 06604. Tel: 203-333-3161; Fax: 203-368-1727.
See St. Raphael, Bridgeport under Elementary Schools, Regional located in the Institution section.
Catechesis/Religious Program—Students 95.
Convent—671 Oak St., 06604. Tel: 203-335-9817; Fax: 203-336-9205.
Chapel—St. Margaret's Shrine 2539 Park Ave., 06604. Tel: 203-368-4425.

OUTSIDE THE CITY OF BRIDGEPORT

Bethel, Fairfield Co., St. Mary (1882) [CEM] Revs. Corey V. Piccinino; Cyrus Bartolome; Edward J. McAuley, (Diocese of Tororo); Deacons Michael Oles; John DeRoin; Joseph Gill.
Church & Office: 26 Dodgingtown Rd., 06801. Tel: 203-744-5777; Fax: 203-744-3740. Email: stmaryoffice@comcast.net. Web: www.stmarybethel.org.
See St. Mary, Bethel under Elementary Schools, Regional located in the Institution section.
Catechesis/Religious Program—24 Dodgingtown Rd., 06801. Tel: 203-743-4557. Email: meferri@aol.com. Mary Ferri, D.R.E. Students 687.
Convent—Tel: 203-743-6985.

Brookfield, Fairfield Co.

1—St. Joseph (1941) Revs. George F. O'Neill; Henry Hoffmann, Parochial Vicar; Deacons William J. Shaughnessy; Peter J. Kuhn.
Res.: 159 Whisconier Rd., 06804. Tel: 203-775-1035; Fax: 203-775-1684. Web: www.stjosephbrookfield.com.
See St. Joseph, Brookfield under Elementary Schools, Regional located in the Institution section.
Catechesis/Religious Program—Tel: 203-775-1035. Andrea Woronick, D.R.E. Students 681.

2—St. Marguerite Bourgeoys (1982) [CEM] Revs. George S. Sankoorikal; Francis Luke; Deacons Richard A. Fenton; Anthony J. Detje.
Res.: 138 Candlewood Lake Rd., 06804. Tel: 203-775-5117; Fax: 203-775-9254.
Catechesis/Religious Program—Tel: 203-775-2644. Carole Harris, D.R.E. Students 429.

Danbury, Fairfield Co.

1—St. Gregory the Great (1960) Revs. Angelo S. Arrando; Otoniel Lizcano; Raymond M. Scherba; Deacons Robert Blankschen; William D. Murphy; Daniel N. Myott; Paul B. Pilkington; Richard P. Kovacs.
Res.: 85 Great Plain Rd., 06811. Tel: 203-797-0222; Fax: 203-743-7049. Email: frarrando@aol.com. Web: www.danbury.org/stgreg.
See St. Gregory the Great, Danbury under Elementary Schools, Regional located in the Institution section.
Catechesis/Religious Program—Tel: 203-743-5168. Mrs. Mary Ann Hauser, D.R.E. Students 406.

2—Immaculate Heart of Mary (1980), (Portuguese), [CEM] Rev. Jose Brito Martins; Deacon Jose Rodrigues Cabral.
Res.: 149 Deer Hill Ave., 06811. Tel: 203-797-1821; Fax: 203-743-9146. Email: heartofmary@sbcglobal.net.
Catechesis/Religious Program— Helena Andrade, D.R.E. Students 100.

3—St. Joseph (1905) Revs. Michael F. Dogali; David W. Franklin. In Res., Revs. Joseph Jojayya Dasari (India); Raymond K. Petrucci.
Res.: 8 Robinson Ave., 06810. Tel: 203-748-8177; Fax: 203-748-2010. Web: www.stjosephsdanbury.com.
See St. Joseph, Danbury under Elementary Schools, Regional located in the Institution section.
Catechesis/Religious Program—Tel: 203-778-1920; Fax: 203-730-0026. Sherry Morris, D.R.E. Students 363.

4—Our Lady of Guadalupe (1985), (Spanish), [CEM] Revs. Hector Leon; Jose Montoya (Colombia).
Res.: 29 Golden Hill Rd., 06811-4629. Tel: 203-743-1021; Fax: 203-798-8143.
Catechesis/Religious Program—Students 311.

5—St. Peter (1851) [CEM] Rev. Gregg D. Mecca; Rev. Msgr. Pedro D. Diniz (Brazil), Ministry to Brazilian Community; Deacon John Buchholz. In Res., Revs. Paul F. Merry; Joseph M. Joaquin (Retired).
Res.: 104 Main St., 06810. Tel: 203-743-2707; Fax: 203-794-1928. Email: office@stpeterdanb.org. Web: www.stpeterdanb.org.
See St. Peter-Sacred Heart School, Danbury under Elementary Schools, Diocesan located in the Institution section.
Catechesis/Religious Program—Tel: 203-743-1048; Fax: 203-797-9471. Joanne Durkin, D.R.E. (K-8). Students 297.

6—Sacred Heart of Jesus (1925) Rev. Dennis Mason, O.F.M.Conv.; Deacon John F. Esterheld. In Res., Rev. Brad Heckathorne, O.F.M.Conv.
Parish Center & Res.: 46 Stone St., 06810. Tel: 203-948-9029; Fax: 203-748-9168. Email: sacred_heart@snet.net. Web: www.sacredhrtchurch.org.
See Sacred Heart, Danbury under Elementary Schools, Regional located in the Institution section.
Catechesis/Religious Program—Tel: 203-743-0689. Email: sh-dre@snet.net. Students 95.

Darien, Fairfield Co.

1—St. John (1895) [CEM] Rev. Msgr. Frank C. McGrath; Rev. Francisco Gomez, Parochial Vicar; Deacon William K. Rowe.
Res.: 1986 Post Rd., 06820. Tel: 203-655-1145; Fax: 203-655-1048. Email: stjohn2@oponline.net. Web: www.stjohndarien.com.
Catechesis/Religious Program—Tel: 203-655-8020. Email: religiousedsj@optonline.net. John Cunningham, D.R.E.; Lisa Ioli, D.R.E. Students 590.

2—St. Thomas More (1966) Revs. Paul G. Murphy; Robert J. Post.
Res. & Parish Office: 374 Middlesex Rd., 06820. Tel: 203-655-3303; Fax: 203-655-6478. Email: stmdarienct@aol.com. Web: www.stmdarienct.org.
Catechesis/Religious Program—374 Middlesex Rd., 06820. Tel: 203-655-3077; Fax: 203-655-8901. Email: stmdariened@aol.com. Mary Ellen O'Connor, Interim D.R.E.; Janis Pataky, Youth Min. (Gr. 6-12); Maria Oliveira, Dir. PreSchool. Students 916.

Easton, Fairfield Co., Notre Dame (of Easton) (1956) [CEM] Rev. Msgr. Thomas J. Driscoll; Rev. Milan Dimic; Deacons Harold J. Lynch; Gerald F. Sabol.
Res.: 640 Morehouse Rd., 06612. Tel: 203-268-5838; Fax: 203-459-4940. Email: notredame@optonline.net. Web: www.notredameofeaston.org.
Church: 655 Morehouse Rd., 06612-1334.
Catechesis/Religious Program—Tel: 203-261-5596; Fax: 203-459-4940. Patricia Steccato, D.R.E. Students 487.

Fairfield, Fairfield Co.

1—St. Anthony of Padua (1927) Rev. John P. Baran; Deacon Donald J. Ross.
Res.: 149 S. Pine Creek Rd., 06824. Tel: 203-259-0358; Fax: 203-259-5112.
Catechesis/Religious Program— Eleanor W. Sauers, D.R.E. Students 195.

2—St. Emery (1932), (Hungarian), (Franciscan), (United with St. Stephen's of Bridgeport 1897-1971) Rev. Louis M. Pintye, O.F.M.; Deacon Rudolph P. Trankovich.
Office/Friary: 838 King's Hwy. E., 06825-5418. Tel: 203-334-0312; Fax: 203-579-9423. Email: ssemerstep@aol.com. Web: www.stemerys.com.
Catechesis/Religious Program—Students 12.
Convent—Congregation of Notre Dame, 105 Biro St., 06825-5418. Tel: 203-334-3913. Congregation of Notre Dame 3.

3—Holy Cross (1913), (Slovenian), Rev. Alfred F. Pecaric.
Res.: 750 Tahmore Dr., 06825. Tel: 203-372-4595; Fax: 203-372-4668. Email: holy_cross_church@sbcglobal.net.
Catechesis/Religious Program—Tel: 203-373-0466. Students 48.

4—Holy Family (1938) Revs. Guido G. Montanaro; Walter J. Seekamp; Deacons Joseph De Biase; Stephen Sebestyen.
Res.: 700 Old Stratfield Rd., 06825. Tel: 203-336-1835; Fax: 203-336-0342.
Catechesis/Religious Program—Tel: 203-336-1835; Fax: 203-336-0342. Students 170.

5—Our Lady of the Assumption (1922) [CEM] Revs. J. Barry Furey; Joseph Sidera, C.S.C.; Deacons Raymond J. Chervenak; Kevin Moore.
Res.: 545 Stratfield Rd., 06825. Tel: 203-333-9065; Fax: 203-333-2562. Email: ola.fairfield@sbcglobal.net. Web: www.assumption-fairfield.org.
School—605 Stratfield Rd., 06825. Tel: 203-334-6271; Fax: 203-382-0399. Email: schoolbulldogs@aol.com. See separate listing under Elementary Schools in the Institution section.
Catechesis/Religious Program—Tel: 203-367-1108; Fax: 203-367-0927. Frank Macari, D.R.E.; Alice Kilcullen-McFarland, C.R.E. Students 518.
Parish Center—591 Stratfield Rd., 06825. Tel: 203-336-3419.

6—St. Pius X (1955) [CEM] Revs. Michael F. Dogali; Samuel S. Kachuba; Michael Lantowski, Dir. Music. In Res., Rev. Msgr. Ernest T. Esposito (Retired).
Res.: 834 Brookside Dr., 06824. Tel: 203-255-6134; Fax: 203-255-5232. Email: jdonnelly@st-pius.org. Web: www.st-pius.org.
Catechesis/Religious Program—Tel: 203-259-4800; Fax: 203-255-5232. Email: dcamillo@st-pius.org. Diane Camillo, D.R.E. Students 957.

7—St. Thomas Aquinas (1876) [CEM] Revs. Victor T. Martin; Roger F. McDonough; Deacons Daniel Ianniello; Patrick Toole; Sr. Catherine Leonard, C.N.D., Pastoral Asst.
Res.: 1719 Post Rd., 06824. Tel: 203-255-1097; Fax: 203-256-8177. Email: stthoaq@aol.com.
See St. Thomas Aquinas, Fairfield under Elementary Schools, Regional located in the Institution section.
Catechesis/Religious Program—Tel: 203-255-1984; Fax: 203-256-9305. Email: stthoaqccd@aol.com. Sr. Monica Leonard, C.N.D., D.R.E. Students 890.

Georgetown, Fairfield Co., Sacred Heart (1881) Revs. David C. Leopold; Colin J. McKenna.
Res.: 30 Church St., Box 388, 06829. Tel: 203-544-8345. Email: sacredheartgtn@aol.com. Web: www.sacredheartct.org.
Catechesis/Religious Program—Tel: 203-544-8423. Email: sacredheart.rel.edu@sbcglobal.net. Students 334.

Greenwich, Fairfield Co.

1—St. Agnes (1963) Rev. James A. McDevitt; Deacon John M. Linsenmeyer.
Res.: 247 Stanwich Rd., 06830. Tel: 203-869-5396; Fax: 203-625-0596. Email: stagnesgreenwich@aol.com. Web: www.stagnesre.org.
Catechesis/Religious Program—Students 35.

2—St. Mary (1874) [CEM] Rev. Msgr. Francis C. Wissel; Revs. John J. Inserra; Richard J. Gemza; Deacon Paul Tupper.
Res.: 178 Greenwich Ave., 06830. Tel: 203-869-9393; Fax: 203-869-1032. Email: stmaryparish@verizon.net. Web: www.stmaryparishgreenwich.org.
Catechesis/Religious Program—Tel: 203-869-9250; Fax: 203-625-4760. Email: saintmre@verizon.net. Students 258.

3—St. Michael the Archangel (1963) [CEM] Rev. Msgr. J. Peter Cullen; Revs. Ciprian Bejan (Romania); Shawn W. Cutler; Deacon Russell T. Rigg.
Res.: 469 North St., 06830. Tel: 203-869-5421; Fax: 203-869-0169.
Catechesis/Religious Program—Tel: 203-661-3088; Fax: 203-869-0169. Email: srceline@optonline.net.

Sr. Celine M. Flynn, S.S.N.D., D.R.E. Students 630.
Mission—St. Timothy's 1034 North St., Fairfield Co. 06831. Tel: 203-869-5421; Fax: 203-869-0169.

4—ST. PAUL (1902) [CEM] Rev. Frank A. Winn.
Res.: 84 Sherwood Ave., 06831. Tel: 203-531-8741; Fax: 203-532-1414. Email: stpgreenwichct@aol.com. Web: www.stpaulgreenwich.org.
Catechesis/Religious Program—Tel: 203-531-4265. Rosie Pennella, D.R.E. Students 452.

5—ST. ROCH (1938) Very Rev. Canon Matthew Mauriello; Rev. Carlos Rodriques.
Res.: 10 St. Roch Ave., 06830-6234. Tel: 203-869-4176; Fax: 203-618-0341. Email: strochcatholic@verizon.net.
Catechesis/Religious Program—Jane Kowaleski, D.R.E. Students 137.

6—SACRED HEART (1890) [CEM] Rev. Bose Raja Selvaraj (India).
Res.: 95 Henry St., 06830. Tel: 203-531-8730; Fax: 203-531-8794. Email: sacredheartqrn@optonline.net.
Catechesis/Religious Program—Tel: 203-531-4772. Laurie Palastro, C.R.E. Students 100.

MONROE, FAIRFIELD CO., ST. JUDE (1973) Rev. Msgr. John B. Sabia; Revs. Joseph J. Karcsinski; Michael P. Novajosky; Deacon John DiTaranto.
Res.: 707 Monroe Tpke., 06468. Tel: 203-261-6404; Fax: 203-261-7507. Email: parishoffice@saintjudechurch.net. Web: www.stjudechurch.net.
See St. Jude, Monroe under Elementary Schools, Regional located in the Institution section.
Catechesis/Religious Program—Tel: 203-261-6788. Mrs. Jean Paul, D.R.E. Students 1,166.

NEW CANAAN, FAIRFIELD CO., ST. ALOYSIUS (1896) Rev. Msgr. William J. Scheyd; Revs. William G. Carey; Ian Jeremiah; Deacons William A. Santulli; Stephen W. Pond. In Res., Rev. Bernard A. Keefe (Retired).
Res.: 40 Maple St., 06840. Tel: 203-966-0020; Fax: 203-972-7691. Email: office@starcc.com. Web: www.starcc.com.
See St. Aloysius, New Canaan under Elementary Schools, Regional located in the Institution section.
Catechesis/Religious Program—Tel: 203-966-4555. Students 1,135.

NEW FAIRFIELD, FAIRFIELD CO., ST. EDWARD THE CONFESSOR (1954) Revs. Nicholas A. Cirillo; Jeffrey W. Couture; Henry J. Hoffman; Deacon David Vaughn.
Res.: 21 Brush Hill Rd., 06812. Tel: 203-746-7298; Fax: 203-746-4856. Web: www.saintedwardchurch.org.
Catechesis/Religious Program—Tel: 203-746-4270. Kathryn LaRegina, C.R.E. Students 1,188.

NEWTOWN, FAIRFIELD CO., ST. ROSE OF LIMA (1859) [CEM] Rev. Msgr. Robert E. Weiss; Revs. Luke Suarez; Jose Ignacio A. Ortigas; Deacons Thomas F. Curran; Donald Naiman; Norman Roos; Daniel O'Connor.
Res.: 46 Church Hill Rd., 06470. Tel: 203-426-1014; Fax: 203-426-6222.
Catechesis/Religious Program—38 Church Hill Rd., 06470. Tel: 203-426-2333; Fax: 203-426-8074. Pam Arsenault, D.R.E. Students 1,584.

NORWALK, FAIRFIELD CO.

1—ST. JEROME (1960) [CEM] Revs. David W. Blanchfield; Joseph Palacino (Retired). In Res., Rev. Michael Hoag, S.J.
Church: 23 Half Mile Rd., 06851. Tel: 203-847-5349; Fax: 203-846-0238.
Catechesis/Religious Program—Tel: 203-846-2111. Email: reachstjerome@optonline.net. Web: www.stnorwalkst.org. Students 385.

2—ST. JOSEPH (South Norwalk) (1895) Revs. Gilbert P. D'Souza; Jaime Marin-Cardona; Deacon William O. Murphy. In Res., Rev. G. Frantz Desruisseaux.
Res.: 85 S. Main St., 06854. Tel: 203-838-4171; Fax: 203-899-0007. Email: stjosono@aol.com.
Catechesis/Religious Program—Tel: 203-866-1225. Mrs. Dora Deandrade, C.R.E. Students 379.
Convent—14 Chestnut St., 06854. Tel: 203-866-9452.

3—ST. LADISLAUS (1907), (Hungarian), [CEM] Rev. Michael J. Bachman. In Res., Rev. Stephen J. Balint.
Res.: 25 Cliff St., 06854. Tel: 203-866-1867; Fax: 203-866-7830.
Catechesis/Religious Program—Students 16.

4—ST. MARY (1848) [CEM] Revs. Greg J. Markey; Richard G. Cipolla; Deacon Stephan A. Genovese. In Res., Rev. Paul N. Check.
Res.: 669 West Ave., 06850. Tel: 203-866-5546; Fax: 203-866-0464. Web: www.stmarynorwalk.net.
Catechesis/Religious Program—Tel: 203-866-7429; Fax: 203-866-0127. Mrs. Jacqueline Juhasz, D.R.E. Students 442.

5—ST. MATTHEW (1957) Rev. Msgr. Walter C. Orlowski; Rev. Sudhir D'Souza; Deacon David M. Sochacki.
Res.: 216 Scribner Ave., 06854. Tel: 203-838-3788; Fax: 203-838-8195. Email: stmattparish@hotmail.com. Web: www.stmatthewnorwalk.com.
Catechesis/Religious Program—Tel: 203-838-0231; Fax: 203-838-4195. Michele Scholl, D.R.E.; Lori Paladino, D.R.E.; Jean Des Rockeas, D.R.E. Students 780.

6—ST. PHILIP (1964) Rev. Michael A. Boccaccio; Sr. Mary Ann McPartland, C.N.D., Pastoral Assoc.; Deacons Frank J. Chiappetta; Paul J. Reilly; John W. Mahon.
Res.: One Fr. Conlon Pl., 06851. Tel: 203-847-4549 (Office); Fax: 203-847-4148.
Catechesis/Religious Program—Tel: 203-847-4286. Mrs. Doris Chiappetta, Dir. Faith Formation. Students 218.

7—ST. THOMAS THE APOSTLE (1935) Revs. Robert J. Crofut; Junil Pereira, I.M.S. In Res., Rev. Paul Sankar.
Res.: 203 East Ave., 06855. Tel: 203-866-3141; Fax: 203-866-1219. Email: stthomasnorwalk@optonline.net.
Malta House—5 Prowitt St., 06855. Tel: 203-857-0088; Fax: 203-857-0018.
Catechesis/Religious Program—208 East Ave., 06855. Tel: 203-866-1189; Fax: 203-866-1219. Email: stthomasfuture@sbcglobal.net. Mrs. Jeanne Bisson, D.R.E. Students 118.

REDDING, FAIRFIELD CO., ST. PATRICK (1879), (Irish), Rev. Joseph Cervero; Deacon William C. Timmel. In Res., Rev. Miroslav Stachurski.
Res.: 169 Black Rock Tpke., P.O. Box 119, Redding Ridge, 06876. Tel: 203-938-2253; Fax: 203-938-3396. Email: stpatrickreading@sbcglobal.net.
Catechesis/Religious Program—Tel: 203-664-1387. Email: rdaureli@sbcglobal.net. Pam Davis, C.R.E. Students 225.

RIDGEFIELD, FAIRFIELD CO.

1—ST. ELIZABETH SETON (1976) Rev. Joseph A. Prince; Deacon Robert Morris.
Res.: 520 Ridgebury Rd., 06877. Tel: 203-438-7292; Fax: 203-438-0600. Email: stsetonparish@comcast.net.
Catechesis/Religious Program—Tel: 203-438-9707; Fax: 203-438-7947. Gigi Pekala, C.R.E.; Marie Trebing, C.R.E. Students 502.

2—ST. MARY (1882) [CEM] Rev. Msgr. Laurence R. Bronkiewicz, Pastor; Revs. Russell A. Augustine, Parochial Vicar; Peter K. Smolik, Parochial Vicar; Deacons Robert A. Salvestrini; Henry Hein; Gerald H. Lambert.
Res.: 31 Bryon Ave., 06877. Tel: 203-438-6538; Fax: 203-438-4406. Web: www.smcr.org.
School—183 Highridge Ave., 06877. Tel: 203-438-7288; Fax: 203-431-8742. Ms. Anna O'Rourke, Prin. See separate listing under Elementary Schools in the Institution Section.
Catechesis/Religious Program—Tel: 203-438-7335; Fax: 203-438-6876. Sr. Joan Brennan, D.R.E. Students 1,415.

RIVERSIDE, FAIRFIELD CO., ST. CATHERINE OF SIENA Rev. Msgr. Alan F. Detscher; Rev. Francis T. Hoffmann; Deacons Renato Berzolla; Robert Henrey; Vincent J. Heidenreich. In Res., Rev. Stephen J. DeLuca.
Res.: 4 Riverside Ave., 06878. Tel: 203-637-3661; Fax: 203-637-8934. Email: scsrectory@aol.com. Web: www.stcath.org.
Catechesis/Religious Program—6 Riverside Ave., 06878. Tel: 203-637-3661, Ext. 338; Fax: 203-637-2089. Marcella Abatemarco, D.R.E. Students 830.

SHELTON, FAIRFIELD CO.

1—ST. JOSEPH (1906) Rev. Msgr. Christopher J. Walsh; Revs. Nicholas S. Pavia; Marcel St. Jean, Parochial Vicar; Deacons Jeffrey J. Kingsley; Anthony Conti.
Res.: 50 Fairmont Pl., 06484. Tel: 203-924-8611; Fax: 203-924-9446. Email: stjoseph.rectory@snet.net. Web: www.sjcshelton.org.
See St. Joseph School, Shelton under Elementary Schools, Regional located in the Institution section.
Catechesis/Religious Program—Tel: 203-924-9677. Mrs. Patricia Heller, D.R.E. Students 420.
Convent—Apostles of the Sacred Heart of Jesus, 420 Coram Ave., 06484. Tel: 203-924-1449.

2—ST. LAWRENCE (1955) [CEM] Rev. Michael K. Jones; Miroslav Stachurski; Deacons Joseph Filingeri; Frank J. Masso.
Res.: 505 Shelton Ave., 06484. Tel: 203-929-5355; Fax: 203-929-8939. Email: stlawrpar1@aol.com. Web: www.diobptstlawrenceparish.net.
School—Tel: 203-929-4422; Fax: 203-929-3669. Email: sis@snet.net. Martha Reitman, Prin. See separate listing located in Shelton under Elementary Schools in the Institution section.
Catechesis/Religious Program—Tel: 203-929-8421. Mrs. Karen O'Keefe, C.R.E. Students 824.

3—ST. MARGARET MARY (1963) [CEM] Rev. Msgr. Thomas J. Whalen; Rev. Nello Barachini (Retired).
Res.: 380 Long Hill Ave., 06484. Tel: 203-924-4929; Fax: 203-924-1849.
Catechesis/Religious Program—Tel: 203-924-2679. Mrs. Carol D'Amico, D.R.E. Students 195.

SHERMAN, FAIRFIELD CO., HOLY TRINITY (1985) [CEM] Rev. Alfred A. Riendeau Jr.
Res.: 15 Rte. 37 Center, P.O. Box 97, 06784. Tel: 860-354-1414; Fax: 860-355-9439.
Catechesis/Religious Program—Tel: 860-355-1483; Fax: 860-355-9439. Mrs. Michele Curnan, D.R.E. Students 215.

STAMFORD, FAIRFIELD CO.

1—THE BASILICA OF SAINT JOHN THE EVANGELIST (1854) [CEM] Rev. Msgr. Stephen M. Di Giovanni; Rev. Terrence P. Walsh, Parochial Vicar. In Res., Rev. Albert Audette (Retired).
Res.: 279 Atlantic St., 06901. Tel: 203-324-1553; Fax: 203-359-2660. Email: stjc@optonline.net. Web: stjohnsstamford.com.
Catechesis/Religious Program—Students 239.

2—ST. BENEDICT (1930), (Slovak), Merged with Our Lady of Montserrat, Stamford to form Saint Benedict and Our Lady of Montserrat, Stamford.

3—SAINT BENEDICT - OUR LADY OF MONTSERRAT (2000) [CEM] Revs. Arthur Mollenhauer; John Jairo Perez; Rolando Torres.
Mailing Address: One St. Benedict Cir., 06902. Tel: 203-327-7250; 203-323-7379; Fax: 203-323-0798. Email: myparish@optonline.net.
Catechesis/Religious Program—Tel: 203-353-1733. Students 160.

4—ST. BRIDGET OF IRELAND (1963) Rev. Gill C. Babeu.
Res.: 278 Strawberry Hill Ave., 06902. Tel: 203-324-2910; Fax: 203-363-0135. Email: bridgetct@aol.com. Web: www.stbridgetofireland.org.
Catechesis/Religious Program—Tel: 203-357-8157. Mr. Albert J Griffith, D.R.E. Students 127.

5—ST. CECILIA (1926) [CEM] Rev. David J. Riley.
Res.: 1184 Newfield Ave., 06905-1496. Tel: 203-322-1562; Fax: 203-968-1550.
School—Tel: 203-322-6505; Fax: 203-322-6835. See separate listing under Elementary Schools in the Institution section.
Catechesis/Religious Program—Tel: 203-329-8783; Fax: 203-595-0519. Students 351.

6—ST. CLEMENT OF ROME (1928) Rev. Joseph J. Malloy.
Res.: 535 Fairfield Ave., 06902. Tel: 203-348-4206; Fax: 203-316-8131. Email: stclement@optonline.net.
Catechesis/Religious Program—Tel: 203-348-1233; Fax: 203-316-8131. Kay Hendrick, D.R.E. Students 84.

7—ST. GABRIEL (1963) Rev. Cyprian P. LaPastina; Deacons Larry Buzzeo; Jose Viola.
Res.: 914 Newfield Ave., 06905. Tel: 203-322-7426; Fax: 203-968-6266. Email: gabe914@aol.com.
See St. Gabriel, Stamford under Elementary Schools, Regional located in the Institution section.
Catechesis/Religious Program—Tel: 203-329-1978. Maryanne Didelot, Asst. D.R.E. Students 191.

8—HOLY NAME OF JESUS (1903), (Polish), Rev. Eugene Kotlinsky, C.M.
Res.: 4 Pulaski St., 06902. Tel: 203-323-4967; Fax: 203-327-2229.
Catechesis/Religious Program—Tel: 203-359-3618; Fax: 203-323-4546. Sr. Joanna McCloskey, S.M.M.I., D.R.E. Students 170.

9—HOLY SPIRIT (1962) [CEM] Rev. Robert J. Hyl; Deacon Paul J. Jennings.
Res.: 403 Scofieldtown Rd., 06903-4009. Tel: 203-322-3722; Fax: 203-322-0543. Email: holyspiritparish@aol.com.
See Holy Spirit, Stamford under Elementary Schools, Regional located in the Institution section.
Catechesis/Religious Program— Mrs. Patricia LaValle, D.R.E. Students 167.

10—ST. LEO (1960) [CEM] Revs. James D. Grosso; Leszek P. Szymaszek. In Res., Rev. William M. Quinlan.
Res.: 24 Roxbury Rd., 06902. Tel: 203-322-1669; 203-329-8884; Fax: 203-461-9761.
Catechesis/Religious Program—Tel: 203-348-0052; Fax: 203-357-9639. Mrs. Eileen Towne, D.R.E. Students 700.

11—ST. MARY (1907) [CEM] Revs. Arthur Mollenhauer; John Jairo Perez, Parochial Vicar; Rolando Torres, Parochial Vicar.
Res.: 566 Elm St., 06902. Tel: 203-324-7321; Fax: 203-323-9407. Email: amollenhauer@optimum.net. Web: www.stmarystamford.org.
Catechesis/Religious Program—Tel: 203-348-5196. Phyllis Taylor, D.R.E. & Office Mgr. Students 185.

12—ST. MAURICE (1935) [CEM] Rev. Albert G. Pinciaro; Deacon Ralph Hammock. In Res., Rev. Ayub Mwampela.
Res.: 358 Glenbrook Rd., 06906-2198. Tel: 203-324-3434; Fax: 203-964-8023. Email: stmauricegb@optonline.net. Web: www.stmauricegb.org.
Catechesis/Religious Program—Tel: 203-348-8768; Fax: 203-964-8023. Email: stmauricedff@optonline.net. Mrs. Deborah Ruffin, D.R.E. Students 140.

13—OUR LADY OF MONTSERRAT (1984), (Spanish),

Merged with St. Benedict, Stamford to form Saint Benedict and Our Lady of Montserrat, Stamford.

14—OUR LADY STAR OF THE SEA (1964) Rev. Msgr. Edward R. Surwilo; Deacon Gauthier Vincent.
Res.: 1200 Shippan Ave., 06902. Tel: 203-324-4634; Fax: 203-348-9963. Web: ourladystaroftheseastamford.org.
See Our Lady Star of the Sea, Stamford under Elementary Schools, Regional located in the Institution section.
Catechesis/Religious Program—Dee Fumega, C.R.E. Students 145.
Convent—1216 Shippan Ave., 06902. Tel: 203-569-0310.

15—SACRED HEART (1920), (Italian), [CEM] Revs. Richard F. Futie; Martin P. deMayo. In Res., Rev. Carlos R. Rodrigues.
Res.: 37 Schuyler Ave., 06902. Tel: 203-324-9544; Fax: 203-324-9202.
Catechesis/Religious Program—Tel: 203-541-3977. Students 95.

STRATFORD, FAIRFIELD CO.

1—HOLY NAME OF JESUS (1923), (Slovak), Rev. Andrew G. Marus; Deacon Michael Saranich. In Res., Rev. Msgr. J. James Cuneo.
Res.: 1950 Barnum Ave., 06614. Tel: 203-375-5815; Fax: 203-375-5954.
School— See separate listing under Elementary Schools, Regional in the Institution section.
Catechesis/Religious Program—Tel: 203-378-7407. Sr. Madonna Figura, S.S.C.M., D.R.E. Students 190.
Convent—2 Mary Ave., 06614. Tel: 203-378-1203.

2—ST. JAMES (1886) Revs. Thomas F. Lynch; Bruce Roby; Deacons John Barton; Timothy Bolton; Thomas Masaryk.
Res.: 2110 Main St., 06615. Tel: 203-375-5887; Fax: 203-378-1562. Web: www.stjamesstratford.com.
See St. James, Stratford under Elementary Schools, Regional located in the Institution section.
Catechesis/Religious Program—Students 303.

3—ST. MARK (1960) Revs. Donald A. Guglielmi; Martin P. deMayo; Birendra Soreng (India), Parochial Vicar; Deacons T. Emmet Murray; F. Paul Kurmay.
Res.: 500 Wigwam Ln., 06614. Tel: 203-377-0444; Fax: 203-386-8071. Web: www.stmarkstratford.com.
See St. Mark, Stratford under Elementary Schools, Regional located in the Institution section.
Catechesis/Religious Program—Tel: 203-377-3158. Mrs. Patricia Nettleton, D.R.E. Students 510.

4—OUR LADY OF GRACE (1954) [CEM] Rev. Msgr. William F. Schultz; Deacon Robert W. McLaughlin. In Res., Rev. Msgr. Jerald A. Doyle.
Res.: 497 Second Hill Ln., 06614-2595. Tel: 203-377-0928; Fax: 203-377-5235. Web: www.olgstratford.com.
Parish Center—345 Second Hill Ln., 06614-2595. Tel: 203-375-2005 (Hall and gym); 203-375-6610 (Preschool).
Catechesis/Religious Program—Tel: 203-375-6133. Mrs. Denise L. Bartelson, C.R.E. (Pre School Dir.). Students 233.

5—OUR LADY OF PEACE (1948) Rev. Richard D. Murphy.
Office: 10 Ivy St., 06615. Tel: 203-377-4863; Fax: 203-378-5253. Email: ourlady@sbcglobal.net.
Res.: 230 Park Blvd., 06615.
Catechesis/Religious Program—Tel: 203-378-3053. Sr. Carolyn Stoe, S.S.N.D., D.R.E. Students 101.

TRUMBULL, FAIRFIELD CO.

1—ST. CATHERINE OF SIENA (1955) [CEM] Rev. Msgr. Richard J. Shea; Revs. Christopher J. Samele; Peter J. Lynch; Deacon Ronald Landru.
Res.: 200 Shelton Rd., 06611. Tel: 203-377-3133; Fax: 203-377-1023. Email: marymurphy@st.catherinetrumbull.com. Web: www.stcatherinetrumbull.com.
See St. Catherine of Siena, Trumbull under Elementary Schools, Regional located in the Institution section.
Catechesis/Religious Program—220 Shelton Rd., 06611. Tel: 203-377-3133, Ext. 22. Students 541.

2—CHRIST THE KING (1962) [CEM] Rev. Lawrence F. Carew.
Res.: 4700 Madison Ave., 06611. Tel: 203-268-8695; Fax: 203-268-9265. Email: ctkparish@aol.com.
Catechesis/Religious Program—Tel: 203-261-2583. Students 338.

3—ST. STEPHEN (1953) Rev. Stephen J. Gleeson; Deacons Gary Carpenter; John S. Moranski.
Res.: 6948 Main St., 06611-1340. Tel: 203-268-6217; Fax: 203-268-9861. Email: ststephen@ststephentc.org. Web: www.ststephentc.org.
Catechesis/Religious Program—Tel: 203-268-6860. Liz Harakal, D.R.E. Students 526.

4—ST. THERESA (1934) [CEM] Revs. Brian P. Gannon; Michael F. Flynn, Parochial Vicar; Karol J. Ksiazek; Deacon Salvatore Clarizio. In Res., Rev. Peter A. Cipriani.
Res.: 5301 Main St., 06611. Tel: 203-261-3676; Fax: 203-268-8723.
See St. Theresa, Trumbull under Elementary Schools located in the Institution section.
Catechesis/Religious Program—19 Rosemond Ter., 06611. Tel: 203-261-4706; Fax: 203-445-9108. Mrs. Denise Heady, D.R.E. Students 745.
Convent—

WESTON, FAIRFIELD CO., ST. FRANCIS OF ASSISI (1955) Rev. Michael L. Dunn; Deacon Donald W. Brunetto.
Res.: 35 Norfield Rd, P.O. Box 1025, 06883. Tel: 203-227-1341; Fax: 203-226-1154. Web: www.sfaparish.com.
Catechesis/Religious Program—Tel: 203-226-9474. Email: jlacorte@sfaparish.com. Students 289.

WESTPORT, FAIRFIELD CO.

1—CHURCH OF THE ASSUMPTION (1876) [CEM] Revs. Thomas P. Thorne; Lawrence A. Larson; Frank Matto, Music Dir. In Res., Rev. Robert M. Kinnally.
Res.: 98 Riverside Ave., 06880. Tel: 203-227-5161; Fax: 203-227-1206. Web: www.assumption-westport.org.
Catechesis/Religious Program—Tel: 203-226-5448. Cathy Romano, D.R.E. Students 592.

2—ST. LUKE (1957) Rev. Msgr. Andrew G. Varga; Sr. Maureen Fleming, S.S.N.D., Coord. Pastoral Outreach Activities; Deacons Brian J. Kelly; Lance C. Fredricks.
Res.: 84 Long Lots Rd., 06880. Tel: 203-227-7245; Fax: 203-226-8063. Web: www.stlukewestport.com.
Catechesis/Religious Program—49 N. Turkey Hill Rd., 06880. Tel: 203-226-0729; Fax: 203-226-5446. Lorraine M. Morrong, C.R.E. Students 230.

WILTON, FAIRFIELD CO., OUR LADY OF FATIMA (1953) Revs. Michael C. Palmer; James C. Vattakunnel; Deacon Thomas J. McManus.
Res.: 229 Danbury Rd., 06897. Tel: 203-762-3928; Fax: 203-834-1261. Email: ourlady229@aol.com. Web: www.olfwilton.org.
See Our Lady of Fatima, Wilton under Elementary Schools, Regional located in the Institution section.
Catechesis/Religious Program—225 Danbury Rd., 06897. Tel: 203-762-9080. Email: angels225@aol.com. Web: www.olfreligioused.org. Mrs. Kathleen Rooney, D.R.E. Students 1,033.

Chaplains of Public Institutions

BRIDGEPORT. *Bridgeport Community Correctional Facility*, 1106 North Ave., 06604. Tel: 203-579-6131. Rev. Bernardo C. Rodriguez, Chap.
Bridgeport Health Care, 600 Bond St., 06610. Tel: 203-384-6400. Rev. George Maslar, O.F.M.Conv., Chap.
Bridgeport Hospital, 267 Grant St., 06610. Tel: 203-384-3311. Rev. Remigius Nwabichie.

DANBURY. *Danbury Area Mental Health Authority*, 64 West St., 06810. Tel: 203-778-1640, Ext. 247. Vacant.
Danbury Hospital, 24 Hospital Ave., 06810. Tel: 203-797-7912. Rev. Raymond K. Petrucci, Chap.
Federal Correctional Institution 06811. Tel: 203-743-6471. Sr. Anne Marie Raftery, O.S.F., Dir. of Pastoral Care.

GREENWICH. *Greenwich Hospital* 06830. Tel: 203-863-3000. Revs. Stephen J. DeLuca, Chap., Ayub Mwampela, Chap.

NORWALK. *Norwalk Hospital* 06856. Tel: 203-852-2000.

STAMFORD. *Stamford Hospital* 06902. Tel: 203-325-7584. Rev. Msgr. Peter P. Dora.

On Duty Outside the Diocese:
Rev. Msgrs.—
Green, Thomas J., J.C.D., Catholic University of America, Dept. of Canon Law, Washington, DC 20017.
Millea, William V., Via della Nocetta 63, Rome 00164 Italy.
Potter, Joseph D. (Retired)
Revs.—
Boyd, Robert J., 32 W. Franklin Ave., Pequannock, NJ 07440.
Daigle, David, CHC, USN, LTJG Chap, Ch01, USS Iwo Jima (LHD-7), Fpo, AE 09574-1664.
Devore, Daniel B., 9 Arbor Club Dr., Ponte Vedra, FL 32082.
Kloster, David, 641 Walking Gait, San Antonio, TX 78240.
Lincon, Joseph, St. Anthony, 908 E. Olive St., Longview, TX 75601.
McCall, Edward
McDevitt, James A., St. John the Evangelist Rectory, 250 Twenty-first St., Brooklyn, NY 11215.
Posluszny, Francis, Parroquia San Juan Apostal, APTO 735, Chiclayo, Peru.
Powers, Thomas, North American College 00120 Vatican City State.
Smolko, John F. (Retired), 9808 Dale Dr., Upper Marlboro, MD 20772.
Talar, Charles J.T., 9845 Memorial Dr., Houston, TX 77024.
Tracy, David W., University of Chicago, The Divinity School, 1025 E. 58th St., Chicago, IL 60637.

Leave of Absence:
Revs.—
Bohorquez, Hernan D.
Gray, Sherman
Haber, Thomas N.
Madden, Michael J.
Morrissey, Robert
Olbrys, Mariusz

Retired:
Rev. Msgrs.—
Birge, George D.
Caldas, Constantino R.
DeProfio, Louis A., P.A.
Esposito, Ernest T., D.Min.
Genuario, William A., P.A., J.C.D.
Grieco, Nicholas V.
Hossan, John B.
Howley, Edward J.
Kohut, Joseph J.
Loughlin, William J.
Nagle, William A.
Potter, Joseph D.
Rousseau, Stanlislaus B.
Sanders, John C.
Scull, Edward J.
Watts, Roger J.
Revs.—
Audette, Albert
Barachini, Nello
Brady, Philip W.
Breen, James J.
Calabro, Nicholas J.
Carey, William F.
Colohan, Edward A.
Connolly, Mark
Coyne, Edwin J.
DeMarco, Peter A.
Dennehy, Martin J.
Dytkowski, Louis M.
Fernandez, Jose A.
Gay, James A.
Giuliani, John B.
Gregori, Emidio O.
Grise, Clifford J.
Hitchcock, Martin B.
Howell, David W.
Hribsek, Aloysius J.
Igoe, Martin S.
Joaquin, Joseph M.
Kennelly, Daniel
Knurek, Dennis A.
Koziol, Stanley N.
Maty, Robert J.
Palacino, Joseph
Parampath, Joseph K., J.C.D.
Punnakunnel, John (India)
Saba, Joseph J.
Smolko, John F.
Szlezak, Emeric
Usenza, Robert J.
Uzzilio, Robert A.
Watts, Albert W.
Wright, Addison G., S.S.

Permanent Deacons:
Africot, Alix, St. Patrick, Bridgeport
Barton, Jack, St. James, Stratford
Berger, Rob, (On Duty Outside Diocese)
Berzolla, Renato L., St. Catherine, Riverside
Bissenden, William J., St. Patrick, Bridgeport
Blankschen, Robert, St. Gregory, Danbury
Blier, Roland, (Retired), St. Thomas More, Darien
Bolton, Timothy, St. James, Stratford
Brown, James, St. Lawrence, Huntington
Brunetto, Donald W., St. Francis, Weston
Buchholz, John, St. Mary, Bethel
Buzzeo, Michael L., St. Gabriel, Stamford
Cabral, Jose R., Immaculate Heart of Mary, Danbury
Cahill, William, (Leave of Absence)
Calabrese, Robert P., (On Duty Outside Diocese)
Carpenter, Gary E., St. Stephen, Trumbull
Chervenak, Raymond J., Assumption, Fairfield
Chiappetta, Frank, St. Philip, Norwalk
Clarizio, Salvatore, Ph.D., St. Theresa, Trumbull
Conti, Anthony, St. James, Stratford
Curran, Thomas F., St. Rose, Newtown
De Biase, Joseph, Holy Family, Fairfield
DeRoin, John, St. Mary, Bethel
Detje, Anthony, St. Marguerite Bourgeoys, Brookfield
DiTaranto, John, St. Jude, Monroe
Dwyer, F. Robert, (Retired)
Dzujna, Andrew W., St. Mark, Stratford
Esterheld, John, Sacred Heart, Danbury

Farley, Joseph J., (Retired)
Fenton, Richard A., St. Marguerite Bourgeoys, Brookfield
Filingeri, Joseph, St. Lawrence, Huntington
Finch, Dean W., St. Jerome, Norwalk
Foust, Donald P., Blessed Sacrament, Bridgeport; Holy Rosary, Bridgeport
Foyt, Frank, St. Elizabeth Seton, Ridgefield
Fredricks, Lance C., St. Luke, Westport
Gagne, Joseph, Our Lady of Peace, Stratford
Garcia, Santos, St. Augustine, Bridgeport
Genovese, Stephan A., St. Mary, Norwalk
Grant, Terence J., (On Duty Outside Diocese)
Hammock, Ralph, St. Maurice, Stamford
Heidenreich, Vincent J., St. Catherine, Riverside
Hein, Henry R., St. Mary, Ridgefield
Henrey, Robert, St. Catherine of Siena, Riverside
Herman, H. Paul, (On Duty Outside of Diocese)
Howe, Louis F., (Leave of Absence)
Ianniello, Daniel, St. Thomas Aquinas, Fairfield
Jennings, Paul J., Holy Spirit, Stamford
Kelly, Brian J., Ph.D., St. Luke, Westport
Kingsley, Jeffrey J., St. Joseph, Shelton
Koniers, William A., St. Pius, Fairfield
Kovacs, Richard P., St. Gregory the Great, Danbury
Kuhn, Peter J., St. Joseph, Brookfield
Kurmay, Paul F., St. Mark, Stratford
Landry, Ronald, St. Catherine of Siena, Trumbull
Linsenmeyer, John M., St. Agnes, Greenwich
Lynch, Harold J., Notre Dame, Easton
Mack, Thomas, (On Duty Outside the Diocese)
Mahon, John W., St. Philip, Norwalk
Malloy, Wayne E., St. John, Darien
Martinez, Ricardo, Blessed Sacrament, Bridgeport
Masaryk, Thomas, St. James, Stratford
Masso, Frank J., St. Lawrence, Huntington
McLaughlin, Robert W., Our Lady of Grace, Stratford
McMancus, Thomas J., Our Lady of Fatima, Wilton
Melita, Joseph, St. Raphael, Bridgeport
Molnar, Joseph, (Leave of Absence)
Moore, Kevin, Assumption, Fairfield
Moran, Manuel, (Leave of Absence)
Moranski, John J., St. Stephens, Trumbull
Morris, Robert, St. Elizabeth Seton, Ridgefield
Murphy, William D., St. Gregory the Great, Danbury
Murphy, William O., St. Joseph, Norwalk
Murray, Emmet, St. Mark, Stratford
Myott, Daniel N., St. Gregory the Great, Danbury
Naiman, Donald, St. Rose, Newtown
Nelson, Thomas E., (Leave of Absence)
Newton, Philip J., (On Duty Outside Diocese)
O'Connor, Daniel, St. Rose, Newtown
Olavarria, Reynaldo, St. Mary, Bridgeport
Oles, Michael, St. Mary, Bethel
Pereira, Gabriel, Our Lady of Fatima, Bridgeport
Pierre-Louis, Augustin, (On Duty Outside Diocese)
Pilkington, Paul B., St. Gregory, Danbury
Pond, Stephen W., St. Aloysius, New Canaan
Reilly, Paul, St. Philip, Norwalk
Reveron, Domingo, St. Peter, Bridgeport
Rigg, Russ, St. Michael the Archangel, Greenwich
Rivera, Ramon, (On Duty Outside the Diocese)
Rodriguez, Miguel, (On Duty Outside the Diocese)
Roos, Norman, St. Rose, Newtown
Ross, Donald J., St. Anthony of Padua, Fairfield
Rowan, Joseph L., (Retired)
Rowe, William K., (Retired)
Ruge, Kenneth J., (Leave of Absence)
Sabol, Gerald, Notre Dame, Easton
Salvestrini, Robert A., St. Mary, Ridgefield
Santulli, William A., St. Aloysius, New Canaan
Saranich, Michael, Holy Name, Stratford
Saymon, Richard F., (Leave of Absence)
Seith, Thomas K., (Retired)
Shaughnessy, William J., St. Joseph, Brookfield
Shine, Mark T., St. Matthew, Norwalk
Smythe, Bradford, St. Joseph, Shelton
Sochacki, David M., (On Duty Outside Diocese)
Stanley, Thomas, (Leave of Absence)
Stenbey, Richard, (On Duty Outside the Diocese)
Stroud, Kenneth, (Retired)
Sullivan, Timothy A., St. Joseph Manor, Trumbull
Tetreault, Fred, (Leave of Absence)
Timmel, William C., St. Patrick, Redding
Toole, Patrick, St. Thomas Aquinas, Fairfield
Torres, Luis, St. Peter, Bridgeport
Trankovich, Rudolph P., St. Emery, Fairfield
Tucci, Bruce, (Leave of Absence)
Tugman, John H., (On Duty Outside the Diocese)
Tupper, Paul, St. Mary, Greenwich
Vaughn, David J., St. Peter, Danbury
Vincent, Gauthier, Our Lady Star of the Sea, Stamford
Viola, Jose, St. Gabriel, Stamford
Volpe, James, (Retired)
Wolfer, Michael K., (Retired)

INSTITUTIONS LOCATED IN THE DIOCESE

[A] SEMINARIES, DIOCESAN

STAMFORD. *St. John Fisher Seminary Residence* (1989) 894 Newfield Ave., 06905. Tel: 203-322-5331; Fax: 203-461-9876. Email: frkinnally@diobpt.org. Web: bridgeportvocations.org. Revs. Robert M. Kinnally, Rector; Nicholas A. Cirillo, Spiritual Dir.; Robert M. Kinnally. Priests 5; Deacons 1; Lay Teachers 5; Lay Staff 4.

[B] COLLEGES AND UNIVERSITIES

BRIDGEPORT. *St. Vincent's College* (1991) 2800 Main St., 06606. Tel: 203-576-5318; Fax: 203-576-5893. Email: nmusante@stvincentscollege.edu. Web: www.stvincentscollege.edu. Martha K. Shouldis, Ed.D., Pres. & CEO; Joanne R. Wolfertz, Ed.D., Vice Pres. Dean; John Gleckler, C.P.A., Interim CFO; Janice Faye, Dir. Admin. Svcs.; Joseph Macionus, M.P.A., Registrar; Susan Capasso, C.G.C., Ed.D., Dean, Academic Svcs.; Joseph Marrone, M.S., Dir., Admissions. Lay Teachers 46; Students 510.

FAIRFIELD. **Fairfield University* (Coed), 1073 N. Benson Rd., 06824-5195. Tel: 203-254-4910; Fax: 203-254-4221. Web: www.fairfield.edu. Revs. Jeffrey P. von Arx, S.J., Ph.D., Pres.; Paul D. Holland, S.J.; Charles H. Allen, S.J., Exec. Asst. to Pres.; George E. Collins, S.J., Coord., Missions Identity Progs.; Paul J. Fitzgerald, S.J., Sr. Vice Pres. Academic Affairs; Mr. Robert C. Russo, Univ. Registrar; Mr. Mark J. Guglielmoni, Dir. Human Resources; Dr. Donald E. Gibson, Dean Dolan School of Business; Dr. Suzanne Campbell, Dean School of Nursing; Dr. Robbin Crabtree, Dean, Arts & Sciences & Dean Univ. College; Dr. Jack Beal, Dean School of Engineering; Susan Franzosa, Dean, Graduate School of Educ. & Allied Professions; Mary Frances Malone, Assoc. Academic Vice Pres.; Judith M. Dobai, Vice Pres. Enrollment & Mgmt.; Elizabeth Boguet, Dean, Academic Engagement; Joseph Defeo, Assoc. Dean of Students & Dir. Student Devel.; Mr. Mark C. Reed, Vice Pres. Admin. & Chief of Staff; Mr. Thomas Pellegrino, Assoc. Vice Pres. Student Affairs; Rama Sudhakar, Vice Pres. Mktg. & Communications; Mr. James D. Fitzpatrick, Asst. Vice Pres., Students Affairs; Dr. Susan Birge, Asst. Vice Pres. & Dir., Counseling Svcs. & Psychological Svcs.; William Johnson, Assoc. Dean, Students & Dir. Student Diversity Progs.; Mr. Matthew Dinnan, Sr. Assoc. Dean, Students Activities; Rev. Michael J. Doody, S.J., Dir. Campus Ministry; Ms. Carolyn Rusiackas, Assoc. Univ. Chap.; Conor L. O'Kane, Assoc. Dir. Campus Ministry; Ms. Stephanie Frost, Vice Pres. Advancement; Ms. Janet Canepa, Dir. Alumni Rels.; David W. Frassinelli, Assoc. Vice Pres., Facilities Mgmt.; Julie L. Dolan, Vice Pres. Finance & Admin. and Treas.; Mr. Kenneth R. Fontaine, Controller; Revs. Francis T. Hannafey, S.J., Assoc. Prof., Religious Studies; Mark P. Scalese, S.J., M.F.A., Assoc. Prof., Visual & Performing Arts; James J. Mayzik, S.J., Dir. Media Ctr., Asst. Prof. New Media & Dir. Ignatian Res. College; Richard J. Ryscavage, S.J., Dir. for Center of Faith & Public Life; Fredy Cesar Maldonado, S.J., Asst. Prof. Modern Languages & Literature; Douglas Peduti, S.J., Asst. Prof., Philosophy; Ms. Ann K. Stehney, Dir. Inst. Research; Joan Overfield, Univ. Librarian & Dir. Library Svcs. The Society of Jesus. College of Arts and Sciences; Dolan School of Business; University College; School of Nursing; School of Engineering; Graduate School of Education & Allied Professions; Graduate Program in Financial Management; Graduate Program in Nursing; Masters in Business Administration; Graduate Programs in Engineering and Masters in American Studies and Mathematics.; (See separate listing for Fairfield College Prep). Jesuits 13; Priests 13; Lay Teachers 248; Students 5,146; Personnel (not including faculty) 546.

**Sacred Heart University*, 5151 Park Ave., 06825-1000. Tel: 203-371-7999; Fax: 203-365-7652. Web: www.sacredheart.edu. John Petillo, Pres.; Dr. Thomas Forget, Vice Pres. for Academic Affairs; Mr. James M. Barquinero, Vice Pres. Enrollment Planning & Student Affairs; Mr. Michael J. Kinney, Sr. Vice Pres. Finance & Admin. Coeducational and Comprehensive University. Courses offered year round, day & evening. Priests 2; Sisters 2; Lay Teachers 480; Students 5,800.

[C] HIGH SCHOOLS, DIOCESAN

BRIDGEPORT. *Kolbe-Cathedral High School* (1963) 33 Calhoun Pl., 06604. Tel: 203-335-2554; Fax: 203-335-2556. Email: cougars@kolbecaths.org. Web: www.kolbecaths.org. Mrs. Jo Anne Jakab, Prin.; Mrs. Lisa Matson, Asst. Prin.; Rev. F. John Ringley, Spiritual Dir.; Susan D'Amato, Librarian. Priests 1; Lay Teachers 24; Administrators 2; Students 325.

DANBURY. *Immaculate High School* (1962) 73 Southern Blvd., 06810. Tel: 203-744-1510; Fax: 203-744-1275. Email: info@immaculatehs.org. Web: immaculatehs.org. Kathleen Casey, Pres.; Mr. Joseph Carmen, Prin.; Mrs. Mary Ann Foncello, Asst. Principal. Priests 1; Lay Teachers 32; Students 362.

FAIRFIELD. *Notre Dame Catholic High School*, 220 Jefferson St., 06825. Tel: 203-372-6521; Fax: 203-374-0387. Email: info@notredame.org. Web: www.notredame.org. Rev. William F. Sangiovanni, Pres.; Mr. Christopher Cipriano, Prin.; Mr. Carl Philipp, Asst. Prin.; Rev. Peter A. Cipriani, Chap.; Mrs. Tracie Marko, Librarian & Media Specialist. Priests 2; Lay Teachers 45; Students 555.

STAMFORD. *Trinity Catholic High School*, 926 Newfield Ave., 09605. Tel: 203-322-3401; Fax: 203-322-5330. Email: TCHS1@JUNO.COM. Web: www.trinitycatholic.org. Kevin Burke, Pres.; Mrs. Diane Warzoha, Asst. Prin.; Mrs. Connie McGoldrick, Admissions Coord.; Rev. Nicholas A. Cirillo, Spiritual Dir.; Mr. Tracy Nichols, Athletic Dir.; Mrs. Mary D'Aquila, Reach Out; Mrs. Lorraine Castelluccio, Librarian. (Formerly Stamford Catholic High School); Records for Central Catholic High School, Norwich, and St. Mary's High School, Greenwich, located at Trinity. Priests 1; Lay Teachers 42; Students 465.

TRUMBULL. *St. Joseph High School* (1962) 2320 Huntington Tpke., 06611-5099. Tel: 203-378-9378; Fax: 203-378-7306. Web: www.sjcadets.org. Mr. William J. Fitzgerald, Ph.D., M.Div., Pres.; Mr. Kenneth Mayo, Prin.; Mrs. Nancy DiBuono, Asst. Prin.; Mrs. Suzanne Siano, Dir. Guidance; Rev. Christopher J. Samele; Mr. James Olayos, Esq., Dir. Athletics; Mr. Paul Bernetsky, Advancement Dir.; Mrs. Maureen Anderson, Dir. Students Activities; Mr. Martin Dempsey, Dean of Students; Mrs. Margaret Marino, Admissions Dir.; Sr. Gabriela DaVila, Dir. Campus Ministry; Mrs. Christine Woods, Registrar; Mrs. Laurene Collins, Registrar; Mrs. Joanne Rodgerson, Bursar; Mrs. Linda Batten, Dir. Finance; Mrs. Michele Kraszna, Alumni Dir.; Mr. Brian Highland, Librarian. Priests 1; Sisters 1; Lay Teachers 65; Students 831.

[D] SPECIAL SCHOOLS, DIOCESAN

FAIRFIELD. *St. Catherine Academy*, (Grades K-12), 760 Tahmore Dr., 06825. Tel: 203-540-5381; Fax: 203-540-5383. Email: srmuldoon@diobpt.org. Web: www.stcatherineacademy.org. Helen Burland, Pres.; Sr. Marilyn Muldoon, O.S.U., Prin. & Admin. Sisters 4; Lay Teachers 2; Students 19.

[E] HIGH SCHOOLS, PRIVATE

FAIRFIELD. *Fairfield College Preparatory School* (1942) 1073 N. Benson Rd., 06824. Tel: 203-254-4200; Fax: 203-254-4108. Email: rperrotta@fairfieldprep.org. Web: www.fairfieldprep.org. Dr. Robert A. Perrotta, Ed.D., J.D., Prin.; Revs. John J. Hanwell, S.J., Pres. Fairfield Prep.; William J. Eagan, S.J., Chm. Theology Dept.; George A. Gallarelli, S.J., Guidance; Laurence D. Ryan, S.J., Chap.; Paul D. Holland, S.J.; Mr. Harold Davis, Librarian. Society of Jesus of New England., A preparatory day school for boys, established in 1942. Priests 5; Lay Teachers 81; Students 908.

GREENWICH

See Convent of the Sacred Heart, Greenwich under Elementary Schools, Private located in the Institution section.

[F] ELEMENTARY SCHOOLS DIOCESAN

BRIDGEPORT. *Cathedral Education Cluster*, The Catholic Center, 238 Jewett Ave., 06606. Tel: 203-416-1370; Fax: 203-372-0020. Email: rgaits@bcess.com. Web: www.cathedralcluster.org.

St. Ambrose (Grades PreK-8), 461 Mill Hill Ave., 06610. Tel: 203-368-2835; Fax: 203-366-0599. Mrs. Margaret Carabelli, Prin. Servants of the Immaculate of Mary 2; Lay Teachers 11; Students 222.

St. Andrew (Grades PreK-8), 395 Anton St., 06606. Tel: 203-373-1552; Fax: 203-373-0641. Mrs. Maria O'Neill, Prin. Lay Teachers 10; Students 238.

St. Ann (Grades PreK-8), 521 Brewster St., 06605. Tel: 203-334-5856; Fax: 203-333-8263. Mrs. Theresa Tillinger, Prin. Daughters of the Holy Spirit 1; Lay Teachers 14; Students 210.

St. Augustine Cathedral (Grades PreK-8), 63 Pequonnock St., 06604-3599. Tel: 203-366-6500; Fax: 203-362-2934. Mrs. Mary M. Daley, Prin. Lay Teachers 10; Students 220.

St. Peter (Grades K-8), 659 Beechwood Ave., 06605. Tel: 203-333-2048; Fax: 203-333-2878. Miss Suzanna Zello, Prin. Sisters of the Company of the Savior 2; Lay Teachers 12; Students 160.

St. Raphael (Grades PreK-8), 324 Frank St., 06604. Tel: 203-333-6818; Fax: 203-336-9205. Sr. Deborah Lopez, A.S.C.J., Prin. Apostles of the Sacred Heart 3; Lay Teachers 9; Students 211.

DANBURY. *Bridgeport Diocesan Schools Corporation*, 238 Jewett Ave., 06606. Tel: 203-416-1380.

St. Gregory the Great School (Grades K-8), 85 Great Plain Rd., 06811. Tel: 203-748-1217; Fax: 203-748-6508. Web: st.gregoryschool.org. Sr. Mary John O'Rourke, O.S.U., Prin. Lay Teachers 12; Students 288.

St. Joseph (Grades PreK-8), 370 Main St., 06810. Tel: 203-748-6615; Fax: 203-748-6508. Web: www.sjsdanbury.org. Mrs. Lisa Lanni, Prin. Lay Teachers 23; Students 330.

St. Peter-Sacred Heart School (Grades N-8), 98 Main St. & 17 Cottage St., 06810. Tel: 203-748-2895; Fax: 203-748-5684. Web: www.stpetersacredheart.org. Mrs. Mary McCormack, Prin. Lay Teachers 15; Students 154.

St. Joseph School (Grades K-8), 5 Obtuse Hill Rd., Brookfield, 06804. Tel: 203-775-2774; Fax: 203-775-5810. Web: www.sjsbrookfield.org. Mrs. Rosemarie Forte, Prin. Lay Teachers 25; Students 211.

St. Rose of Lima School (Grades PreK-8), 40 Church Hill Rd., Newtown, 06470. Tel: 203-426-5102; Fax: 203-426-5374. Web: www.stroseschool.com. Mrs. Mary Maloney, Prin. Religious 2; Lay Teachers 38; Students 451.

FAIRFIELD. *Bridgeport Diocesan Schools Corporation*, (Grades PreK-8), 238 Jewett Ave., 06606. Tel: 203-416-1380.

Our Lady of the Assumption/Holy Family Catholic School (Grades PreK-8), 605 Stratfield Rd., 06825. Tel: 203-334-6271; Fax: 203-382-0399. Web: www.olahf.org. Ms. Gerri Desio, Prin.; Mrs. Jean Blaze, Asst. Prin. Lay Teachers 17; Students 195.

St. Thomas Aquinas (Grades PreK-8), 1719 Post Rd., 06824. Tel: 203-255-0556; Fax: 203-255-0596. Web: www.stannline.net. Ms. Patricia Brady, Prin.; Mrs. Clare Stafstrom, Librarian. Lay Teachers 25; Students 398.

GREENWICH. *Bridgeport Diocesan Schools Corporation*, 238 Jewett Ave., 06606. Tel: 203-416-1380.

Greenwich Catholic School, 471 North St., 06830. Tel: 203-869-4000; Fax: 203-869-3405. Email: pkopas@diobpt.org. Web: www.gcsct.org. Mrs. Pat Kopas, Prin.; Mrs. Dianne Davenport, Librarian. Lay Teachers 37; Students 440.

NORWALK. *Bridgeport Diocesan Schools Corporation*, 238 Jewett Ave., 06606. Tel: 203-416-1380.

All Saints Catholic Elementary School (Grades Day Care-8), 139 W. Rocks Rd., 06851. Tel: 203-847-3881; Fax: 203-847-8055. Web: www.ascs.net. Mrs. Linda Dunn, Prin.; Mrs. Eileen D'Andrea, Librarian. Priests 1; Sisters 1; Lay Teachers 35; Students 590.

SHELTON. *Bridgeport Diocesan Schools Corporation*, (Grades PreK-8), 238 Jewett Ave., 06606. Tel: 203-416-1380.

St. Joseph (Grades PreK-8), 430 Coram Ave., 06484. Tel: 203-924-4669; Fax: 203-922-0161. Email: vrossi@diobpt.org. Web: www.stjoesschoolshelton.org. Miss Victoria Rossi, Prin. Lay Teachers 19; Students 188.

St. Lawrence (Grades PreK-8), 503 Shelton Ave., 06484. Tel: 203-929-4422; Fax: 203-929-3669. Email: mreitman@diobpt.org. Web: www.stlawrenceshelton.com. Martha Reitman, Prin. Sisters 1; Lay Teachers 18; Students 270.

STAMFORD. *Bridgeport Diocesan Schools Corporation*, 238 Jewett Ave., 06606. Tel: 203-416-1380.

St. Aloysius School (Grades K-8), 33 South Ave., New Canaan, 06840. Tel: 203-966-0786; Fax: 203-972-6960. Email: dhoward@diobpt.org. Web: starcc.com/school/inclex.php. Dr. Donald Howard, Prin. Lay Teachers 21; Students 191.

Holy Spirit School (Grades PreK-5), 403 Scofieldtown Rd., 06903. Tel: 203-329-7148; Fax: 203-595-0858. Email: ptorchen@dioprt.org. Web: www.holyspiritschool.info. Patricia Torchen, Prin. Lay Teachers 14; Students 95.

Our Lady Star of the Sea School (Grades PreK-5), 1170 Shippan Ave., 06903. Tel: 203-348-1155; Fax: 203-324-6150. Email: gryan@diobpt.org. Web: www.ourladystaroftheseaschool.org. Sr. Anne Marie Landry, Prin. Sisters 1; Lay Teachers 17; Students 139.

Sacred Heart School (Grades PreK-8), One Schuyler Ave., 06902. Tel: 203-323-4844; Fax: 203-359-9859. Ms. Sherry Tarantino, Prin. Sisters 1; Lay Teachers 3; Students 43.

St. Cecilia School (Grades PreK-4), 1186 Newfield Ave., 06905. Tel: 203-322-6505; Fax: 203-322-6835. Email: jborchetta@diobpt.org. Web: www.stcecilia.net. Mrs. Joann Borchetta, Prin. Sisters 1; Lay Teachers 19; Students 304.

Trinity Catholic Middle School (Grades 6-8), 948 Newfield Ave., 06905. Tel: 203-322-7383; Fax: 203-322-4435. Email: rfox@diobpt.org. Web: www.trinitycatholicms.com. Mr. Richard Fox, Prin. Religious 1; Lay Teachers 21; Students 214.

STRATFORD. *Bridgeport Diocesan Schools Corporation*, (Grades PreK-8), 238 Jewett Ave., 06606. Tel: 203-416-1380.

St. James School (Grades PreK-8), One Monument Pl., 06615. Tel: 203-375-5994; Fax: 203-380-0749. Web: www.stjamesstratford.org. Mr. James Gieryng, Prin. Lay Teachers 28; Students 361.

St. Mark School (Grades PreK-8), 500 Wigwam Ln., 06614. Tel: 203-375-4291; Fax: 203-375-4833. Web: www.stmarkschool.org. Mr. Gene Holmes, Prin. Lay Teachers 21; Students 187.

TRUMBULL. *Bridgeport Diocesan Schools Corporation*, 238 Jewett Ave., 06606. Tel: 203-416-1380.

St. Jude School (Grades PreK-8), 707 Monroe Tpke., Monroe, 06468. Tel: 203-261-3619; Fax: 203-268-8748. Web: www.stjudemonroe.org. Mrs. Katherin Sniffin, Prin. Lay Teachers 16; Students 186.

St. Catherine of Siena School (Grades PreK-8), 190 Shelton Rd., 06611. Tel: 203-375-1947; Fax: 203-378-3935. Web: www.stcatherinesienatrumbull.org. Mrs. Beth Hamilton, Prin. Lay Teachers 20; Students 231.

St. Theresa School (Grades PreK-8), 55 Rosemond Ter., 06611. Tel: 203-268-3236; Fax: 203-268-7966. Web: www.sttheresaschool.org. Mr. Salvatore Vittoria, Prin. Lay Teachers 19; Students 290.

WILTON. *Bridgeport Diocesan Schools Corporation*, 238 Jewett Ave., 06606. Tel: 203-416-1380.

Our Lady of Fatima School (Grades PreK-8), 225 Danbury Rd., 06897. Tel: 203-762-8100; Fax: 203-834-0614. Mrs. Dina Monti, Prin. Lay Teachers 20; Students 192.

Saint Mary's School (Grades K-8), 183 High Ridge Ave., Ridgefield, 06877. Tel: 203-438-7288; Fax: 203-431-8742. Web: www.smsridgefield.org. Ms. Anna O'Rourke, Prin. Lay Teachers 22; Students 220.

[G] ELEMENTARY SCHOOLS, PRIVATE

GREENWICH. *Convent of the Sacred Heart*, (Grades PreSchool-12), Day School for Girls, 1177 King St., 06831. Tel: 203-531-6500; Fax: 203-531-5206. Email: sacredheart@cshgreenwich.org. Web: www.cshgreenwich.org. Pamela Juan Hayes, Head of School; Elizabeth Fernandez, Librarian; Mrs. Jayne Collins, U.S. Head; Mr. David Olson, M.S. Head; Dr. Ann Marr, L.S. Head. Sisters 4; Lay Teachers 122; Students 769.

STAMFORD. *Villa Maria Education Center*, 161 Sky Meadow Dr., 06903. Tel: 203-322-5886; Fax: 203-322-0228. Email: scarol@villamariaedu.org. Web: villamariaedu.org. Sr. Carol Ann Nawracaj, O.S.F., Exec. Dir.; Eileen Cassidy, Education Dir.; Wanda Serafino, Librarian. Bernardine Franciscan Sisters., School for Children with Learning Disabilities. Sisters 3; Lay Teachers 21; Students 64.

[H] CATHOLIC CHARITIES

BRIDGEPORT. *Catholic Charities*, Catholic Center, 238 Jewett Ave., 06606-2892. Tel: 203-416-1307; Fax: 203-372-5045. Email: abarber@ccfc-ct.org. Web: www.ccfc-ct.org. Mr. Albert Barber, Pres.

Family Directions, 238 Jewett Ave., 06606-2892. Tel: 203-416-1336; Fax: 203-373-0835. Email: azajac@ccfc-ct.org. Amy Zajac, Dir. Family Directions. Adoptions and Home Studies.

Catholic Charities, Bridgeport, 238 Jewett Ave., 06606-2892. Tel: 203-416-1318; Fax: 203-373-0835. Email: mtintrup@ccfc-cr.org. Mr. Michael Tintrup, Vice Pres.

Catholic Charities, Danbury, 30 Main St., Suite 503, Danbury, 06810. Tel: 203-743-4412; Fax: 203-744-3500. Email: emalgieri@ccfc-ct.org. Elaine Malgieri, M.S.W., L.C.S.W., District Dir.

Ways to Work Family Loan Program, 30 Main St., Ste. 503, Danbury, 06810. Tel: 203-743-4412; Fax: 203-744-3500. Email: emalgieri@ccfc-ct.org.

Catholic Charities, Norwalk, One Park St., P.O. Box 2025, Norwalk, 06851. Tel: 203-416-1318; Fax: 203-750-9651. Email: tgillin@ccfc-ct.org. Terry Gillin, Clinical Dir.

Catholic Charities, Stamford, 30 Myano Ln., Ste. 12, Stamford, 06902. Tel: 203-416-1305; Fax: 203-323-1108. Email: mtintrup@ccfc-ct.org. Mr. Michael Tintrup, Vice Pres.

Catholic Campaign for Human Development, 238 Jewett Ave., 06606. Tel: 203-416-1307.

Room to Grow School Readiness, 208 East Ave., Norwalk, 06850. Tel: 203-855-0637; Fax: 203-831-8200. Email: nowens@ccfc-ct.org. Nancy Owens, Dir.

Houses of Hospitality:

New Covenant House of Hospitality, 90 Fairfield Ave., Stamford, 06904. Tel: 203-964-8228; Fax: 203-375-0314. Email: bjenkins@ccfc-ct.org. Brian Jenkins, Dir.

Thomas Merton Center, 43 Madison Ave., 06604. Tel: 203-367-9036; Fax: 203-367-8828. Email: mgrasso@ccfc-ct.org. Mark Grasso, Dir.

St. Stephen's Emergency Food Center, 43 Madison Ave., 06604. Tel: 203-394-6881.

NEW HEIGHTS, 66 West Street, Danbury, 06810. Tel: 203-794-0819; Fax: 203-731-3260. Email: cpeters@ccfc-ct.org. Camilla Peters, Dir.

Case Management Program, 24 Grassy Plain St., Bethel, 06801. Tel: 203-748-0848; Fax: 203-796-0046. Email: scole@ccfc-ct.org. Web: www.ccfc-ct.org. Sandy Cole, Vice Pres.

Homeless Outreach Team, 24 Grassy Plain St., Bethel, 06801. Tel: 203-748-0848; Fax: 203-796-0046. Email: mconderino@ccfc-ct.org. Web: www.ccfc-ct.org. Michelle Conderino, Dir.

Senior Nutrition Program, 30 Myano Ln., Stamford, 06902. Tel: 203-324-6175; Fax: 203-323-1108. Email: cphelps@ccfc-ct.org. Cindy Phelps, B.S., Dir.

Senior Neighborhood Support Services, 18 Quintard Ter., Stamford, 06901. Tel: 203-324-2404. Sandy Cole, Vice Pres.

Catholic Charities, 238 Jewett Ave., 06606. Tel: 203-416-1338. Email: dfrederick@ccfc-ct.org. Ms. Debra Frederick, COO.

Housing Services, Catholic Center, 238 Jewett Ave., 06606-2892. Tel: 203-416-1317. Email: lbrown-gambino@ccfc-ct.org. Letticia Brown-Gambino, Dir.

Early Childhood Consultation Services, Catholic Center, 30 Main St., Danbury, 06810. Tel: 203-743-4412. Melissa Glaser, Dir., Behavioral Health & Related Svcs.

Immigration Services, Catholic Center, 238 Jewett Ave., 06606. Tel: 203-416-1313. Email: mgrasso@ccfc-ct.org. Mark Grasso, Vice Pres.

[I] DAY NURSERIES

BRIDGEPORT. *Daughters of Charity of the Most Precious Blood Day Nursery* (1908) 1490 North Ave., 06604. Tel: 203-334-7000; Fax: 203-334-7000. Email: daughtersofcharity@yahoo.com. Sr. Theresa Tremblay, D.C.P.B., Dir. Sisters 2; Lay Staff 3.

STAMFORD. *Our Lady of Grace Day Nursery*, 635 Glenbrook Rd., 06906. Tel: 203-348-5531; Fax: 203-324-9638. Email: sgesuina@aol.com. Sr. Gesuina Gencarelli, P.O.S.C., Supr. Little Workers of the Sacred Hearts.

Stepping Stones Preschool, Inc., (Grades PreSchool-K), Sacred Heart Academy, 200 Strawberry Hill Ave., 06902. Tel: 203-323-3173; 203-323-7554; Fax: 203-975-7804. Sr. Jeanne Paulella, C.S.J., Dir. Sisters of Saint Joseph.

[J] GENERAL HOSPITALS

BRIDGEPORT. *St. Joseph Medical Center Foundation, Inc.*, Diocese of Bridgeport, 238 Jewett Ave., 06606-2852.

St. Vincent's Development Corporation, 2800 Main St., 06606. Tel: 203-576-5459; Fax: 203-576-5345. Web: www.stvincents.org. Anthony Milano, Chm.; Susan L. Davis, Pres. & CEO.

St. Vincent's Health Services Corporation, 2800 Main St., 06606. Tel: 203-576-5455; Fax: 203-576-5345. Web: www.stvincents.org. Ruben Rodriguez, Chm.; Susan L. Davis, Pres. & CEO. Bed Capacity 473; Total Assisted Annually 230,000; Total Staff 3,000.

St. Vincent's Medical Center, 2800 Main St., 06606. Tel: 203-576-6000; Fax: 203-576-5345. Web: www.stvincents.org. Ruben Rodriguez, Chm.; Susan L. Davis, CEO; John Glecker, CFO; Mr. William Hoey, A.C.S.W, L.C.S.W., Vice Pres., Mission Svcs. Daughters of Charity of St. Vincent de Paul (Albany, NY). Bed Capacity 473; Total Assisted Annually 206,000; Total Staff 2,350.

St. Vincent's College Tel: 203-576-5578; Fax: 203-576-5893. Students 531.

Saint Vincent's Special Needs Center, Inc., 95 Merritt Blvd., Trumbull, 06611. Tel: 203-375-6400; Fax: 203-380-1190. Web: www.stvincentsspecialneed.org. Raymond Baldwin, Pres. & CEO. Staff 284; Total Assisted Annually 1,783.

Hall-Brooke Behavioral Health Services, 47 Long Lots Rd., Westport, 06880. Tel: 203-227-1251; Fax: 203-227-8616. Web: www.hallbrooke.org. Margaret Harby, R.N., Vice Pres. & Exec. Dir. Total Staff 300; Bed Capacity 76; Total Assisted Annually 20,670.

St. Vincent's Medical Center Foundation, 2800 Main St., 06606. Tel: 203-576-5451; Fax: 203-576-5880. Email: rbianchi@svhs-ct.org. Mr. Anthony Vallilo, Chm.; Mr. Ronald J. Bianchi, Pres. & CEO. Bed Capacity 400; Total Assisted Annually 110,000; Total Staff 1,700.

[K] SPECIAL HOSPITALS

BRIDGEPORT. *Bridgeport Diocesan Health Care Corporation*, 238 Jewett Ave., 06606. Tel: 203-372-4301; Fax: 203-372-1817.

[L] HOMES FOR AGED

BRIDGEPORT. *Augustana Homes/Bishop Curtis Homes*, 525 Palisade Ave., 06610. Tel: 203-366-4333; Fax: 203-366-4756. Mr. Alan Regan, Regl. Vice Pres. (Winn Mgmt. Corp.); Mrs. Lillian Araujo, Site Mgr. Apartments 186; Total Staff 4.

Augustana Homes/Bishop Curtis Homes (1991) 280 Jewett Ave., 06606. Tel: 203-374-5346. Mr. Alan Regan, Regl. Vice Pres. (Winn Residential Corp.); Mrs. Nilda Alamo, Site Mgr.

Augustana Homes/Bishop Curtis Homes - East Bridgeport, 264 Union Ave., 06607-1895. Mr. Alan Regan, Regl. Vice Pres. (Winn Residential Corp.). Total Assisted 48; Total Staff 2.

Roncalli Apartments, 430 Grant St., 06610. Tel: 203-384-9984. Mariann Callahan, L.P.N., Admin. Affiliate of the Roncalli Institute, Supervised Apartments for the Elderly & Handicapped.

BETHEL. *Augustana Homes/Bishop Curtis Homes*, 28 & 101 Simeon Rd., 06801. Tel: 203-743-2508; Fax: 203-743-4570. Mr. Alan Regan, Regl. Vice Pres. (Winn Residential Corp.); Anne Dennis Tapia, Property Mgr. Total Staff 12; Total Assisted 143.

DANBURY. *Augustana Homes Bishop Curtis Homes - Danbury*, 88 Main St., 06810. Tel: 203-791-8510; Fax: 203-743-2352. Mr. Alan Regan, Regl. Vice Pres. (Winn Residential Corp.). Total Assisted 46; Total Staff 2.

FAIRFIELD. *Augustana Homes/Bishop Curtis Homes*, 1677 Post Rd., 06430. Mr. Alan Regan, Regl. Vice Pres. (Winn Residential Corp.).

RIVERSIDE. *Augustana Homes of Greenwich/Bishop Curtis Homes*, 1040 E. Putnam Ave., 06878. Tel: 203-637-8065; Fax: 203-637-7432. Mr. Alan Regan, Regl. Vice Pres. (Winn Residential Corp.). Total Assisted 33; Total Staff 2.

STAMFORD. *Augustana Homes/Bishop Curtis Homes - Glenbrook*, 352 Glenbrook Rd., 06906. Tel: 203-324-5881; Fax: 203-388-8814. Mr. Alan Regan, Regl. Vice Pres. (Winn Residential Corp.). Total Assisted 35; Total Staff 2.

TRUMBULL. *Carmel Ridge*, 6454 Main St., 06611. Tel: 203-261-2229. Mr. Peter Cady, Property Mgr.

St. Joseph's Housing Corporation, Teresian Towers & Carmel Ridge Estates, 6448 Main St., 06611. Tel: 203-261-2229. Mr. Peter Cady, Property Mgr.

[M] CONVALESCENT HOMES

NORWALK. *Notre Dame Convalescent Home* (1952) 76 W. Rocks Rd., 06851. Tel: 203-847-5893; Fax: 203-849-1959. Sr. Jean Marie Raymond, S.S.T.V., Supr.; Mr. Dana Paul, Admin.; Rev. Samuel Martis (India). Sisters of St. Thomas of Villanova. Sisters 3; Patients Assisted Annually 75; Total Staff 85.

[N] MONASTIC FOUNDATIONS

WEST REDDING. *The Benedictine Grange* (1977) 06896. Tel: 203-938-3689; Fax: 203-938-3689. Email: navj@optonline.net. Rev. John B. Giuliani (Retired).

[O] RESIDENCES OF PRIESTS AND BROTHERS

BRIDGEPORT. *Instituto Verbo Encarnado*, St. George Parish, 443 Park Ave., 06604-5493. Tel: 203-335-1797; Fax: 203-334-6359. Email: st_george_church@sbcglobal.net. Rev. Julio Lopresti, I.V.E.

Provincial Offices of the Priests and Brothers of Holy Cross, Eastern Province (Province of Our Lady of Holy Cross), 835 Clinton Ave., 06604. Tel: 203-367-7252; Fax: 203-366-7886. Email: David.T.Tyson.4@nd.edu. Web: www.holycrossusa.org. Revs. David T. Tyson, C.S.C., Prov.; Thomas Bertone, C.S.C., Asst. Prov. & Vicar.

Congregation of Holy Cross - Eastern Province, Inc.

FAIRFIELD. *The Fairfield Jesuit Community-Fairfield University*, 1073 N. Benson Rd., 06824-5195. Tel: 203-256-1650; Fax: 203-255-5947. Web: www.faculty.fairfield.edu/jesuit. Revs. Jeffrey P. von Arx, S.J., Ph.D., Pres.; Charles H. Allen, S.J.; Gerhard H. Bowering, S.J. (Germany); James M. Bowler, S.J.; George E. Collins, S.J.; Denis G. Donoghue, S.J.; Michael J. Doody, S.J.; William J. Eagan, S.J.; Paul J. Fitzgerald, S.J.; George A. Gallarelli, S.J.; Francis T. Hannafey, S.J.; John J. Hanwell, S.J.; John J. Higgins, S.J.; Paul D. Holland, S.J., Rector; Fredy Cesar Maldonado, S.J., (Sabbatical); James J. Mayzik, S.J.; Douglas Peduti, S.J.; Walter R. Pelletier, S.J. (Retired); Laurence D. Ryan, S.J.; Richard J. Ryscavage, S.J.; Mark P. Scalese, S.J., M.F.A.

STAMFORD. *The Catherine Dennis Keefe Queen of the Clergy Retired Priests' Residence*, 274 Strawberry Hill Ave., 06902. Tel: 203-358-9906; Fax: 203-358-9524. Rev. Msgrs. Louis A. DeProfio, P.A. (Retired); William A. Genuario, P.A., J.C.D. (Retired); Nicholas V. Grieco (Retired); Joseph J. Kohut (Retired); William J. Loughlin (Retired); Thaddeus F. Malanowski; William A. Nagle (Retired); Stanley B. Rousseau (Retired); John C. Sanders (Retired); Revs. James E. Breen (Retired); Nicholas J. Calabro (Retired); Edward A. Colohan (Retired); Peter A. DeMarco (Retired); Clifford J. Grise (Retired); David W. Howell (Retired); Aloysius J. Hribsek (Retired); Joseph K. Parampath, J.C.D. (Retired), P.O. Box 1025, Weston, 06883. Home for Retired Priests

[P] CONVENTS AND RESIDENCES FOR SISTERS

BRIDGEPORT. *Convent of Mary Immaculate, Missionary Sisters of the Blessed Sacrament and Mary Immaculate.* Prov. Headquarters., 1111 Wordin Ave., 06605. Tel: 203-334-5681; Fax: 203-333-1590. Email: misamie.ucarvistia@sbcglobal.net. Sr. Presencion Zabata, Prov. Assisting the Apostolate to Spanish-Speaking People. Sisters 5.

Daughters of Charity of the Most Precious Blood Convent, 1482 North Ave., 06604. Tel: 203-334-7000; Fax: 203-334-7000. Email: daughtersofcharity@yahoo.com. Web: www.dcmpb.org. Sr. Theresa Tremblay, D.C.P.B., Dir.

Institute Servants of the Lord and the Virgin of Matara (1988) 153 Linden Ave., 06604-5730. Tel: 203-330-8409; Fax: 203-334-6359. Email: c.damaris@servidoras.org. Web: www.servidoras.org. Sr. Myriam Altnah, S.S.V.M., Local Supr.

Missionaries of Charity, 599 Beechwood Ave., 06604. Tel: 203-336-5626. Sr. M. Regis Devasia, M.C., Contact Person.

Sisters of the Company of the Savior, 820 Clinton Ave., 06604. Tel: 203-368-1875; Fax: 203-368-1875. Sr. Constanza Lopez, Supr. Spanish-Speaking Apostolate.

GREENWICH. *Sacred Heart Convent*, 38 Gold St., 06830. Tel: 203-531-8547. Franciscan Sisters of the Atonement 4.

MONROE. *Sisters of the Holy Family of Nazareth, C.S.F.N.* (1875) 1428 Monroe Tpke., 06468. Tel: 203-268-6560; Fax: 203-261-0866. Web: www.nazarethcsfn.org. Rev. James J. Cole, Chap. Professed 48.

NORWALK. *Regional House of Sisters of St. Thomas of Villanova* (1948) 76 W. Rocks Rd., 06851. Tel: 203-847-2885; Fax: 203-847-3740. Email: sstv_usa@sbcglobal.net. Web: www.saintthomasofvillanova.com. Sr. Alain Michel, S.S.T.V., Supr. Gen. Notre Dame Convalescent Home. Professed 3.

RIDGEFIELD. *Provincial House, Congregation de Notre Dame*, 30 Highfield Rd., Wilton, 06897. Tel: 203-762-4300; Fax: 203-762-4319. Email: rhager@cnd-m.org. Sr. Patricia McCarthy, C.N.D., Prov. Leader.

STAMFORD. *The Bernardine Sisters of the Third Order of St. Francis of Stamford, CT, Inc.*, 163 Sky Meadow Dr., 06903-3414. Tel: 203-322-5920; Fax: 203-322-5491. Email: HMCSTAM@aol.com. Sr. Maria Angela Kurczak, O.S.F., Local Min. Tel: 203-322-8721. Bernardine Sisters 11. In Res. Sisters Robertine Babula, O.S.F.; Dulceline Cieslukowski, O.S.F.; Joanne Helen Grejdus, O.S.F.; Jolancia Kozlinski, O.S.F.; Carol Ann Nawracaj, O.S.F.; Mary Cabrini Nowosielski, O.S.F.; Phyllis Marie Soja, O.S.F.; Mary Innocentia Spaniak, O.S.F.; Deborah Ann Surgot, O.S.F.

Villa Maria Education Center, 161 Sky Meadow Dr., 06903. Tel: 203-322-5886; Fax: 203-322-0228. Sr. Carol Ann Nawracaj, O.S.F., Exec. Dir. School for children with learning disabilities (Grades 1-8). Sisters 3; Lay Teachers 21; Students 63.

Dominican Sisters of Our Lady of the Springs of Bridgeport, Sacred Heart Convent, 21 Schuyler Ave., 06902-3759. Tel: 203-588-0707; 203-562-9202; 203-773-4421. Sr. Melanie Hannigan, O.P., Prioress. Tel: 203-562-9202; 203-773-4421. Total in Community 22.

Franciscan Sisters of the Immaculate Heart of Mary, 1216 Shippan Ave., 06902-7425. Tel: 203-569-0310. Email: fihmstamford@yahoo.com. Sr. Franciscal Alphonse, F.I.H.M., Supr.

Our Lady of Grace Convent, 635 Glenbrook Rd., 06906. Tel: 203-348-5531; Fax: 203-324-9638. Email: sgesuina@aol.com. Sr. Gesuina Gencarelli, P.O.S.C., Supr. Motherhouse and Novitiate of Little Workers of Sacred Hearts.

Sisters Minor of Mary Immaculate, 305 Washington Blvd., 06902. Tel: 203-323-4546. Sisters 5.

Villa Divino Amore Convent, Little Workers of the Sacred Hearts of Jesus & Mary, 117 Hope St., 06906. Tel: 203-324-2449. Sr. Enrica Capalbo, P.O.S.C., Supr.

Villa Maria Guadalupe Life Center, 159 Skymeadow Dr., 06903. Tel: 203-329-1492; Fax: 203-329-1495. Sr. Mary Karen, S.V., Supr. Beds for Retreat Center 60; Sisters in Residence 12.

STRATFORD. *Holy Spirit Convent, Daughters of the Holy Spirit* (1706) 1811 North Ave., 06614. Tel: 203-383-4377; Fax: 203-383-4377. Email: Daughters831@aol.com.

WILTON. *Lourdes Health Care Center, Inc.* (1973) 345 Belden Hill Rd., 06897-3898. Tel: 203-762-4135; Fax: 203-762-2144. Email: adm@lourdeswilton.org. Sr. Eileen Shea, S.S.N.D., Prov. Councilor; Rev. Thomas Elliot, C.S.C., Resident Chap.

School Sisters of Notre Dame (1833) 345 Belden Hill Rd., 06897. Tel: 203-762-3318; Fax: 203-762-9434. Web: www.ssnd.org. Sr. Kathleen Cornell, Prov. Supr.; Rev. Thomas Elliott, C.S.C. Tel: 203-762-3318. Priests 1; Professed 115.

[Q] SECULAR INSTITUTES

BRIDGEPORT. *The Society of Our Lady of the Way*, 584 Capitol Ave., Apt. 6, 06606. Tel: 203-579-4531. Miss Margaret Gould. A secular institute for women.

[R] FOUNDATIONS, TRUSTS AND FUNDS

BRIDGEPORT. *Fairfield Foundation of the Diocese of Bridgeport, Inc.*, 238 Jewett Ave., 06606-2892. Tel: 203-372-4301; Fax: 203-371-8698. Most Rev. William E. Lori, S.T.D., Pres.; Mrs. Nancy B. Matthews, Esq., Sec.

Inner-City Foundation For Charity & Education (1991) 238 Jewett Ave., 06606-2892. Tel: 203-416-1363; Fax: 203-372-0364. Email: innercity-foundation@snet.net. Web: www.innercityfoundation.org. Rev. Msgr. Kevin W. Wallin, Exec. Dir.; Mr. Richard T. Stone, Dir.

[S] GUEST HOUSES

DARIEN. *Convent of St. Birgitta*, 4 Rukenhage Rd., 06820. Tel: 203-655-1068; Fax: 203-655-3496. Email: convent@birgittines-us.com; conventsb@optonline.net. Web: www.birgittines-us.com. Sr. M. Eunice Kulangrathottyil, O.SS.S., Supr.; Rev. Robert F. McCormick, Chap.

[T] HOUSES OF STUDIES

BRIDGEPORT. *St. Peter's Parish, St. Maximillian Kolbe House of Studies*, 535 Colorado Ave., 06605. Tel: 203-869-1032; Fax: 203-625-4760. Email: st.m.kolbe.house@snet.net. Rev. Msgr. Francis C. Wissel, Dir.

[U] RETREAT HOUSES

BRIDGEPORT. *Queen of Saints, The Catholic Center*, 238 Jewett Ave., 06606. Tel: 203-416-1403. Retreat Facility

The Urban Center of St. Charles Parish, 1279 E. Main St., 06608. Tel: 203-333-2147; Fax: 203-330-8316.

St. Charles Outreach Program Tel: 203-333-2147; Fax: 203-330-8316. Rev. Edicson Orozco, Admin.

DARIEN. *Convent of St. Birgitta*, 4 Runkenhage Rd., 06820. Tel: 203-655-1068; Fax: 203-655-3496. Email: convent@birgittines-us.com; conventsb@optonline.net. Web: www.birgittines-us.com. Sr. M. Eunice Kulangrathottyil, O.SS.S., Supr.

MONROE. *Marian Heights Convent*, 1428 Monroe Tpke., 06468. Tel: 203-268-6540; Fax: 203-261-0866. Web: www.nazarethcsfn.org. Sisters of the Holy Family of Nazareth

STAMFORD. *Villa Maria Guadalupe Retreat Center*, 159 Sky Meadow Dr., 06903. Tel: 203-329-1492; Fax: 203-329-1495. Web: sistersoflife.org. Sr. Mary Karen Toomey, S.V., Supr. Owned by Sisters of Life Sisters of Life 8; Bed Capacity 60.

[V] CAMPUS MINISTRY

DANBURY. *Newman Center at Western CT State University* 7 Eighth Ave., 06810. Tel: 203-744-5846. Email: laskym@wcsu.edu. Rev. Michael Lasky, O.F.M.Conv., Chap.

FAIRFIELD. *Fairfield University* , (Fairfield), 1073 N. Benson Rd., 06824-5195. Tel: 203-254-4190; Fax: 203-254-4221. Ms. Ann K. Stehney, Dir. Inst. Research; Revs. Gerald R. Blaszczak, S.J., Univ. Chap.; Michael J. Doody, S.J., Dir. Campus Min.; Mrs. Carolyn M. Rusiackas, Assoc. Univ. Chap.; Conor L. O'Kane, Assoc. Dir. Campus Ministry; Wylie J. Smith, Asst. Univ. Chap.; Cristina Bowen, Campus Min.

[W] MISCELLANEOUS LISTINGS

BRIDGEPORT. *Blessed Brother Andre Charitable Trust*, 835 Clinton Ave., 06604. Tel: 203-367-7252; Fax: 203-366-7886. Email: tlooney@hcep.com; jlack@hcep.com.

St. Camillus Home Foundation, Inc., 238 Jewett Ave., 06606. Tel: 203-416-1355.

Cardinal Shehan Center, Inc., 1494 Main St., 06604.

Tel: 203-336-4468; Fax: 203-368-0901. Email: tjo@shehancenter.org. Web: shehancenter.org. Mr. Terry O'Connor, Exec. Dir.

Caroline House, Inc., 574 Stillman St., 06608. Tel: 203-334-0640; Fax: 203-334-0248. Email: thecarolinehouse@snet.net. Web: thecarolinehouse.org. Sr. Peg Regan, S.S.N.D., Exec. Dir.; Christine Matthews Paine, Devel. Dir.

The Diocesan Cemetery Care Fund, Inc., 238 Jewett Ave., 06606. Tel: 203-416-1491.

Faith in the Future Fund, Inc., 238 Jewett Ave., 06606. Tel: 203-416-1472; Fax: 203-373-6890.

Hispanic Social Ministries of Fairfield County, Inc., 238 Jewett Ave., 06606-9990. Tel: 203-366-5611; Fax: 203-335-1924. Rev. Msgr. Aniceto Villamide, Contact Person.

**McGivney Community Center, Inc.*, Mailing Address: P.O. Box 5220, 06610-0220. 338 Stillman St., 06610-0220. Tel: 203-333-2789; Fax: 203-334-1933. Email: karenking@mcgivney.org. Web: www.mcgivney.org. Karen King, Exec. Dir.

Needle Fund, Inc., 238 Jewett Ave., 06606.

The Pope John Paul II Foundation, Inc., 238 Jewett Ave., 06606. Tel: 203-416-1355.

Saint Charles Brazilian Children, 238 Jewett Ave., 06606. Tel: 203-881-1174. Email: scbc1@sbcglobal.net.

DANBURY. *Magnificat, A Ministry to Catholic Women* (2003) 6 W. Pine Dr., 06811-4316. Tel: 203-744-1856. Email: magnificatbpt@sbcglobal.net. Web: www.triumphantheart.org. Frances Hood, Coord. (Triumphant Heart of Mary Immaculate)

The Pope John Paul II Center for Health Care, Inc., 33 Lincoln Ave., 06810. Tel: 203-416-1355. Sr. Frances Smalkowski, C.F.S.N., Co-Dir. Pastoral Care. Total Staff 5.

GREENWICH. *Clemons Productions, Inc.* (1981) (In association with That's The Spirit Productions, Inc.), P.O. Box 7466, 06836. Tel: 203-316-9394; Fax: 203-316-9396. Email: clemons10@aol.com. Web: www.spirituality.org. Rev. Mark Connolly, Pres. (Retired). Tel: 203-316-9394.

Spirituality For Today (1995) Tel: 203-316-9394; Fax: 203-316-9396.

Radio Program: Thoughts for the Week (1993) Tel: 203-316-9394; Fax: 203-316-9396. Web: www.spirituality.org.

NORWALK. *Malta House, Inc.*, 5 Prowitt St., 06855-1203. Tel: 203-857-0088; Fax: 203-857-0018. Email: lgabriele@maltahouse.org.

RIVERSIDE. *The Mother Teresa of Calcutta Center*, P.O. Box 455, 06878. Tel: 203-637-7578. Email: tleogallagher@aol.com.

STAMFORD. *St. Camillus Health Center*, 494 Elm St., 06902. Tel: 203-325-0200; Fax: 203-353-0550. Web: www.stcamillushealth.org. Rev. Carlos R. Rodrigues, Chap. Total Staff 4.

St. Camillus Auxiliary Committee, 494 Elm St., 06902. Tel: 203-325-0200; Fax: 203-353-0550.

Haitian American Catholic Center (2000) 93 Hope St., 06906. Tel: 203-406-0343; Fax: 203-406-0347. Rev. Jean-Rony Philippe.

TRUMBULL. *St. Joseph's Manor*, 6448 Main St., 06611. Tel: 203-268-6204; Fax: 203-268-5271. Web: www.harborsidehealthcare.com. Rev. Msgr. Ernest T. Esposito, D.Min., Chap. (Retired); Deacon Timothy A. Sullivan, Asst. Chap. Capacity 297; Total Staff 6.

RELIGIOUS INSTITUTES OF MEN REPRESENTED IN THE DIOCESE

For further details refer to the corresponding bracketed number in the Religious Institutes of Men or Women section.

[0470]—*The Capuchin Friars* (Prov. of St. Mary)—O.F.M.Cap.

[0520]—*Franciscan Friars* (Commissariat of St. Stephen)—O.F.M.

[0650]—*Holy Ghost Fathers* (Irish Prov.)—C.S.Sp.

[]—*Instituto Verbo Encarnado*—I.V.E.

[0690]—*Jesuit Fathers and Brothers* (New England Prov.)—S.J.

[0870]—*Montfort Missionaries* (Haitian Prov.)—S.M.M.

[0610]—*Priests of the Congregation of Holy Cross* (Prov. of Our Lady of Holy Cross)—C.S.C.

[]—*The Augustinians*—O.S.A.

RELIGIOUS INSTITUTES OF WOMEN REPRESENTED IN THE DIOCESE

[0130]—*Apostles of the Sacred Heart of Jesus*—A.S.C.J.

[1810]—*Bernardine Sisters of the Third Order of St. Francis*—O.S.F.

[0280]—*Brigittine Sisters*—O.SS.S.

[]—*The Community of the Mother of God of Tenderness*—C.M.G.T.

[0710]—*Company of the Saviour*—C.S.

[4030]—*Congregation of Sisters of St. Thomas of Villanova*—S.S.T.V.

[0760]—*Daughters of Charity of St. Vincent de Paul*—D.C.

[0740]—*Daughters of Charity of the Most Precious Blood*—D.C.P.B.

[0820]—*Daughters of the Holy Spirit*—D.H.S.

[]—*Dominican Sisters*—O.P.

[]—*Dominican Sisters of Hope* (New Burgh, NY)—O.P.

[1125]—*Dominican Sisters of Our Lady of the Springs of Bridgeport*—O.P.

[1190]—*Franciscan Sisters of the Atonement*—S.A.

[]—*Franciscan Sisters of the Immaculate Heart of Mary*—F.I.H.M.

[2575]—*Institute of the Sisters of Mercy of the Americas*—R.S.M.

[]—*Institute Servants of the Lord and the Virgin of Matara*—S.S.V.M.

[2345]—*Little Workers of the Sacred Hearts of Jesus & Mary*—P.O.S.C.

[]—*Marian Community of Reconciliation*—M.C.R.

[]—*Missionaries of Charity*—M.C.

[]—*Missionary Franciscan Sisters of the Immaculate Conception*—M.F.I.C.

[]—*Missionary Sisters of the Blessed Sacrament and Mary Immaculate*—M.S.S.M.I.

[2780]—*Missionary Sisters of the Most Blessed Sacrament* (Spain)—M.SS.S.

[3430]—*Religious Teachers Filippini*—M.P.F.

[2970]—*School Sisters of Notre Dame*—S.S.N.D.

[]—*Sisters Minor of the Mary Immaculate*—S.M.M.I.

[]—*Sisters of Charity of St. Vincent de Paul of New York*—S.C.

[]—*Sisters of Life*—S.V.

[]—*Sisters of Love of the Holy Cross*—S.L.C.

[2990]—*Sisters of Notre Dame*—S.N.D.

[3000]—*Sisters of Notre Dame de Namur*—S.N.D.deN.

[3780]—*Sisters of Saints Cyril and Methodius*—SS.C.M.

[]—*Sisters of St. Joseph*—S.S.J.

[]—*Sisters of St. Joseph of Chambery*—C.S.J.

[]—*Sisters of St. Mary of Namur*—S.S.M.N.

[2980]—*Sisters of the Congregation de Notre Dame*—C.N.D.

[]—*Sisters of the Holy Cross*—C.S.C.

[1970]—*Sisters of the Holy Family of Nazareth*—C.S.F.N.

[2160]—*Sisters, Servants of the Immaculate Heart of Mary*—I.H.M.

[4070]—*Society of the Sacred Heart*—R.S.C.J.

[]—*Ursuline Nuns (Roman Union)*

[4130]—*Ursuline Sisters of the Congregation of Tildonk, Belgium*—O.S.U.C.

DIOCESAN CEMETERIES

DANBURY. *St. Peter's*, Lake Ave. Exit, 06810. Tel: 203-743-9626.

DARIEN. *St. John's*, 25 Camp Ave., 06820. Tel: 203-322-0455; Fax: 203-595-9243.

Queen of Peace, c/o St. John Cemetery, 25 Camp Ave., 06820. Tel: 203-322-0455; Fax: 203-595-9243.

GREENWICH. *St. Mary's*, 399 North St., 06830. Tel: 203-869-7026.

Putnam, 35 Parsonage Rd., 06830. Tel: 203-869-4828; Fax: 203-869-9246.

NEWTOWN. *Resurrection*, c/o Gate of Heaven Cemetery, 1056 Daniels Farm Rd., Trumbull, 06611. Tel: 203-268-5574; Fax: 203-268-2203.

NORWALK. *Assumption Green Farms*, Kings Hwy., c/o St. John Cemetery, 223 Richards Ave., 06850. Tel: 203-838-4271.

St. John's & St. Mary's, 223 Richards Ave., 06850. Tel: 203-838-4271.

STRATFORD. *St. Michael's*, 2205 Stratford Ave., 06615. Tel: 203-378-0404; Fax: 203-378-0313.

TRUMBULL. *Gate of Heaven*, 1056 Daniels Farms Rd., 06611. Tel: 203-268-5574; Fax: 203-268-2203.

NECROLOGY

† Gilmartin, Rev. Msgr. John E., (Retired)—Died Dec. 3, 2011

† Devore, Gerald T., (Retired)—Died Jan. 9, 2011

† Lalic, Paul, (Retired)—Died July 24, 2011

† Terentieff, Robert J., (Retired)—Died July 17, 2011

An asterisk (*) denotes an organization that has established tax-exempt status directly with the IRS and is not covered by the USCCB Group Ruling.

Diocese of Brooklyn

(Dioecesis Bruklyniensis)

Most Reverend

NICHOLAS DiMARZIO, Ph.D., D.D.

Seventh Bishop of Brooklyn; ordained May 30, 1970; appointed Titular Bishop of Mauriana and Auxiliary Bishop of Newark September 10, 1996; consecrated October 31, 1996; appointed Bishop of Camden June 18, 1999; installed July 22, 1999; appointed Bishop of Brooklyn August 1, 2003; installed October 3, 2003. *Office: 310 Prospect Park W., Brooklyn, NY 11215.*

Chancery Office: 310 Prospect Park W., Brooklyn, NY 11215. Tel: 718-399-5990; Fax: 718-399-5934.

Email: curia@diobrook.org

Most Reverend

THOMAS V. DAILY, D.D.

Retired Bishop of Brooklyn; ordained January 10, 1952; appointed Auxiliary to the Archbishop of Boston and Titular Bishop of Bladia December 31, 1974; consecrated February 11, 1975; appointed First Bishop of Palm Beach July 17, 1984; appointed Sixth Bishop of Brooklyn February 20, 1990; took possession April 16, 1990; installed April 18, 1990; retired August 1, 2003. *Mailing Address: 7200 Douglaston Pkwy., Douglaston, NY 11362.*

Most Reverend

JOSEPH M. SULLIVAN, M.S.W., M.P.A.

Retired Auxiliary Bishop of Brooklyn; ordained June 2, 1956; appointed Titular Bishop of Suliana October 7, 1980; episcopal ordination November 24, 1980; retired May 12, 2005. *Mailing Address: Queen of All Saints, 300 Vanderbilt Ave., Brooklyn, NY 11205-3696.*

Most Reverend

RENE A. VALERO, M.S.W.

Retired Auxiliary Bishop of Brooklyn; priestly ordination June 2, 1956; appointed Titular Bishop of Vicus Turris October 7, 1980; episcopal ordination November 24, 1980; retired October 27, 2005. *Res.: 7200 Douglaston Pkwy., Douglaston, NY 11362.*

Most Reverend

IGNATIUS A. CATANELLO, Ph.D., V.E.

Retired Auxiliary Bishop of Brooklyn; ordained May 28, 1966; appointed Titular Bishop of Deulto June 28, 1994; episcopal ordination August 22, 1994; retired September 20, 2010. *Res.: 175-20 74th Ave., Flushing, NY 11366.*

Most Reverend

OCTAVIO CISNEROS, D.D., V.E.

Auxiliary Bishop of Brooklyn; ordained May 29, 1971; appointed Titular Bishop of Eanach Duin June 6, 2006; episcopal ordination August 22, 2006. *Mailing Address: Holy Child Jesus, 111-11 86th Ave., Richmond Hill, NY 11418-1613.*

Most Reverend

GUY SANSARICQ, D.D., V.E.

Retired Auxiliary Bishop of Brooklyn; ordained June 29, 1960; appointed Titular Bishop of Glenndalocha June 6, 2006; episcopal ordination August 22, 2006; retired October 6, 2010. *Mailing Address: St. Matthew, 1123 Eastern Pkwy., Brooklyn, NY 11213-4801.*

Most Reverend

FRANK J. CAGGIANO, D.D., V.G.

Auxiliary Bishop of Brooklyn; ordained May 16, 1987; appointed Titular Bishop of Inis Cathaig June 6, 2006; episcopal ordination August 22, 2006. *Mailing Address: 310 Prospect Park W., Brooklyn, NY 11215.*

ESTABLISHED JULY 29, 1853.

Square Miles 179.

Comprises Kings and Queens Counties in the State of New York.

For legal titles of parishes and diocesan institutions, consult the Chancery Office.

STATISTICAL OVERVIEW

Personnel	
Bishop	1
Auxiliary Bishops	2
Retired Bishops	5
Priests: Diocesan Active in Diocese	276
Priests: Diocesan Active Outside Diocese	15
Priests: Diocesan in Foreign Missions	1
Priests: Retired, Sick or Absent	215
Number of Diocesan Priests	507
Religious Priests in Diocese	165
Total Priests in Diocese	672
Extern Priests in Diocese	99
Ordinations:	
Diocesan Priests	3
Transitional Deacons	8
Permanent Deacons	27
Permanent Deacons in Diocese	216
Total Brothers	124
Total Sisters	872
Parishes	
Parishes	188
With Resident Pastor:	
Resident Diocesan Priests	166
Resident Religious Priests	20
Without Resident Pastor:	
Administered by Priests	2
Welfare	
Homes for the Aged	5
Total Assisted	967
Residential Care of Children	1
Total Assisted	1,534
Day Care Centers	28
Total Assisted	4,604
Specialized Homes	32
Total Assisted	4,580
Special Centers for Social Services	92
Total Assisted	110,439
Residential Care of Disabled	25
Total Assisted	875
Other Institutions	2,857
Total Assisted	4,042
Educational	
Seminaries, Diocesan	1
Students from This Diocese	20
Diocesan Students in Other Seminaries	43
Students Religious	63
Total Seminarians	126
Colleges and Universities	3
Total Students	25,587
High Schools, Diocesan and Parish	20
Total Students	14,458
Elementary Schools, Diocesan and Parish	97
Total Students	30,755
Non-residential Schools for the Disabled	1
Total Students	72
Catechesis/Religious Education:	
High School Students	2,742
Elementary Students	38,446
Total Students under Catholic Instruction	112,186
Teachers in the Diocese:	
Priests	2
Brothers	7
Sisters	44
Lay Teachers	3,278
Vital Statistics	
Receptions into the Church:	
Infant Baptism Totals	16,259
Minor Baptism Totals	859
Adult Baptism Totals	605
Received into Full Communion	47
First Communions	11,874
Confirmations	10,034
Marriages:	
Catholic	1,895
Interfaith	264
Total Marriages	2,159
Deaths	8,293
Total Catholic Population	1,440,000
Total Population	4,735,422

Former Bishops—Rt. Revs. JOHN LOUGHLIN, D.D., First Bishop of Brooklyn; ord. Oct. 18, 1840; cons. Oct. 30, 1853; died Dec. 28, 1891; CHARLES E. MCDONNELL, D.D., Second Bishop of Brooklyn; ord. May 19, 1878; cons. April 25, 1892; died Aug. 8, 1921; Most Revs. THOMAS E. MOLLOY, D.D., Third Bishop of Brooklyn; ord. Sept. 19, 1908; cons. Second Auxiliary Bishop of Brooklyn, Oct. 3, 1920; appt. Bishop of Brooklyn, Nov. 21, 1921; installed Feb. 15, 1922; died Nov. 26, 1956; BRYAN J. MCENTEGART, D.D., LL.D., Fourth Bishop of Brooklyn; ord. Sept. 8, 1917; appt. Bishop of Ogdensburg, June 5, 1943; cons. Aug. 3, 1943; appt. Rector of the Catholic University of America, Washington, DC, June 26, 1953; appt. Titular Bishop of Aradi, Aug. 19, 1953; appt. Bishop of Brooklyn, April 16, 1957; installed June 13, 1957; retired and appt. Titular Archbishop of Gabii, July 17, 1968; died Sept. 30, 1968; FRANCIS J. MUGAVERO, D.D., Fifth Bishop of Brooklyn; ord. May 18, 1940; Bishop of Brooklyn; appt. July 15, 1968; cons. Sept. 12, 1968; installed Sept. 12, 1968; retired Feb. 20, 1990; died July 12, 1991; THOMAS V. DAILY, D.D., ord. Jan. 10, 1952; appt. Auxiliary to the Archbishop of Boston and Titular Bishop of Bladia Dec. 31, 1974; cons. Feb. 11, 1975; appt. First Bishop of Palm Beach July 17, 1984; appt. Sixth Bishop of Brooklyn Feb. 20, 1990; took possession April 16, 1990; installed April 18, 1990; retired Aug. 1, 2003.

Central Offices—310 Prospect Park W., Brooklyn, 11215. Tel: 718-399-5900. Office Hours: Mon.-Fri. 8:30-5.

Vicar General and Moderator of the Curia—Most Rev. FRANK J. CAGGIANO, D.D., S.T.D., V.G., 310 Prospect Park W., Brooklyn, 11215. Tel: 718-399-5995; Fax: 718-399-5965.

Regional Bishop of Brooklyn—Most Rev. GUY SANSARICQ, D.D., St. Matthew, 1123 Eastern Pkwy., Brooklyn, 11213-4801. Tel: 718-774-6747.

Regional Bishop of Queens—Most Rev. OCTAVIO CISNEROS, D.D., Immaculate Conception Center, 7200 Douglaston Pkwy., Douglaston, 11362.

Episcopal Vicars-Territorial—Brooklyn: Rev. Msgr. STEVEN A. FERRARI, V.E., Immaculate Heart of Mary, 2805 Fort Hamilton Pkwy., Brooklyn, 11218. Tel: 718-871-1310. Queens: Rev. Msgr. PAUL R. SANCHEZ, V.E., Resurrection-Ascension, 61-11 85th St., Rego Park, 11374. Tel: 718-424-5212.

Vicar for Black Catholic Concerns—VACANT.

Vicar for Canonical Affairs—Rev. Msgr. ANTHONY HERNANDEZ, J.C.L., 310 Prospect Park W., Brooklyn, 11215. Tel: 718-399-5990.

Secretariat for Financial Administration/Econome—Rev. Msgr. MICHAEL J. REID, Vicar, 310 Prospect Park W., Brooklyn, 11215. Tel: 718-965-7300.

Secretariat for Catholic Education and Formation—Sr. ANGELA GANNON, C.S.J., Sec., 310

Prospect Park W., Brooklyn, 11215. Tel: 718-281-9618.

Secretariat for Communications—Rev. Msgr. KIERAN E. HARRINGTON, V.E., Vicar, 1712 10th Ave., Brooklyn, 11215. Tel: 718-499-6461.

Secretariat for Development—Rev. Msgr. JAMIE J. GIGANTIELLO, Vicar, 310 Prospect Park W., Brooklyn, 11215. Tel: 718-965-7300.

Secretariat for Human and Information Resources—Deacon EDWARD S. GAINE, Sec., 310 Prospect Park W., Brooklyn, 11215. Tel: 718-965-7362.

Human Resources Office—310 Prospect Park W., Brooklyn, 11215. Tel: 718-965-7300; Fax: 718-965-7363.

Spiritual Director of the Cathedral Seminary Residence—Very Rev. JOSEPH G. FONTI, S.T.L., Vicar, 7200 Douglaston Pkwy., Douglaston, 11362. Tel: 718-281-9491.

Vicar for Clergy, Consecrated Life and Apostolic Organizations—Rev. Msgr. RAYMOND F. CHAPPETTO, Our Lady of the Snows, 258-15 80th Ave., Floral Park, 11004. Tel: 718-347-6070; Fax: 718-343-3221.

Special Assistant to Vicar for Clergy—Rev. RAYMOND RODEN, 23-25 Newtown Ave., Astoria, 11102. Tel: 718-728-0880.

Vicar for Higher Education—Rev. Msgr. JOHN STRYNKOWSKI, 250 Cathedral Pl., Brooklyn, 11201. Tel: 718-852-4002.

Vicar for Hispanic Concerns—Most Rev. OCTAVIO CISNEROS, D.D., Immaculate Conception Center, 7200 Douglaston Pkwy., Douglaston, 11362. Tel: 718-281-9677.

Vicar for Human Services—Rev. Msgr. ALFRED P. LOPINTO, V.E., St. Helen, 157-10 83rd St., Howard Beach, 11414. Tel: 718-738-1616.

Vicar for Migrant and Ethnic Apostolates—Rev. Msgr. RONALD T. MARINO, V.E., 1258 65th St., Brooklyn, 11219. Tel: 718-236-3000.

Finance Officer—Mr. JOHN J. BORGIA, CFO & Treas., 310 Prospect Park W., Brooklyn, 11215. Tel: 718-965-7300; Mr. MARTIN J. MCMANUS, CPA, Comptroller. Tel: 718-965-7300, Ext. 1401; Fax: 718-965-7371.

Parish Services Corp.—Rev. Msgr. DAVID L. CASSATO, M.Div., M.S.Ed., Pres.; Mr. JOHN J. BORGIA, Vice Pres.; Rev. Msgr. PETER V. KAIN, Bd. of Dir.; Mr. MARTIN J. MCMANUS, CPA, Treas.; BRIAN T. COSGROVE, Sec., 310 Prospect Park W., Brooklyn, 11215. Tel: 718-965-7300; Fax: 718-965-7382.

Peter Turner Insurance Co.—7 Hanover Square, New York, 10004. Mr. JOHN J. BORGIA, Exec. Vice Pres.; Mr. MARTIN J. MCMANUS, CPA, Treas.; BRIAN T. COSGROVE, Sec. Board of Directors: Rev. Msgrs. DAVID L. CASSATO, M.Div., M.S.Ed.; PETER V. KAIN; Mr. JOHN G. DOLAN; Ms. SUZANNE B. HOLOHAN; Mr. SEAN KANE, Esq.; Mr. KEVIN KEARNEY, Esq., Counsel.

Rocklyn Asset Corp.—COLEEN A. CERIELLO, Exec. Dir.; Mr. ROBERT DADONA, Head Capital Improvements. Tel: 718-965-7300; Fax: 718-965-7353.

Chancery Office—310 Prospect Park W., Brooklyn, 11215. Tel: 718-399-5990; Fax: 718-399-5934.

Chancellor—Rev. Msgr. ANTHONY HERNANDEZ, J.C.L.

Vice Chancellors—Revs. ROBERT V. MUCCI, J.C.L.; PETER J. PURPURA, J.C.L.

Assistant Chancellor—VACANT.

Diocesan Archivist—JOSEPH W. COEN, C.A., Mailing Address: 310 Prospect Park W., Brooklyn, 11215. Tel: 718-965-7300, Ext. 1001.

Censors of Books—Most Rev. FRANK J. CAGGIANO, D.D., S.T.D., V.G.; Rev. Msgr. PETER I. VACCARI, S.T.L.; Revs. BRYAN D. PATTERSON; JOHN P. CUSH, B.A., S.T.L., Cathedral Preparatory Seminary, 56-25 92nd St., Elmhurst, 11373.

Assistant to the Bishop—Deacon JAMIE VARELA. Tel: 718-399-5970; Fax: 718-399-5975.

Tribunal—7200 Douglaston Pkwy., Douglaston, 11362. Tel: 718-229-8131; Fax: 718-631-1339.

Officialis-Judicial Vicar—Rev. Msgr. STEVEN J. AGUGGIA, J.C.L.

Vice Officiale-Associate Judicial Vicar—Revs. PETER J. PURPURA, J.C.L.; REINALDO A. SALDARRIAGA, J.C.D.

Diocesan Judges—Revs. DARIUSZ PIOTR BLICHARZ, J.C.D.; ROBERT V. MUCCI, J.C.L.; Rev. Msgrs. OTTO L. GARCIA, J.C.D., V.G.; ANDREW J. VACCARI, J.C.L.

Defenders of the Marriage Bond—Rev. Msgrs. JOHN J. BROWN, S.T.L., J.C.L.; JOSEPH C. MULQUEEN, J.C.L. (Retired); Revs. WITOLD MROZIEWSKI, J.C.D.; WILLIAM M. HOPPE, J.C.L.

Promoters of Justice—Revs. WILLIAM M. HOPPE, J.C.L.; WITOLD MROZIEWSKI, J.C.D.

Presiding Judge of the Appellate Court—Rev. Msgr. ROBERT J. THELEN, S.T.L., KCHS.

Attorneys and Counselors at Canon Law—Rev. Msgrs. STEVEN J. AGUGGIA, J.C.L.; OTTO L. GARCIA, J.C.D., V.G.; ANDREW J. VACCARI, J.C.L.; JOSEPH C. MULQUEEN, J.C.L. (Retired); ROBERT J. THELEN, S.T.L., KCHS; JOHN J. BROWN, S.T.L., J.C.L.; Revs. WITOLD MROZIEWSKI, J.C.D.; PETER J. PURPURA, J.C.L.; REINALDO A. SALDARRIAGA, J.C.D.; DARIUSZ PIOTR BLICHARZ, J.C.D.; ROBERT V. MUCCI, J.C.L.; WILLIAM M. HOPPE, J.C.L.

Religious, Episcopal Delegate for—Sr. MARYANN SETON LOPICCOLO, S.C., 310 Prospect Park W., Brooklyn, 11215. Tel: 718-399-5900.

Office of Legislative Affairs—Rev. Msgr. KIERAN E. HARRINGTON, V.E.

Cemeteries—STEPHEN COMANDO, Dir.

Education, Offices— (See Institutions located in the Diocese for details)

Diocesan Insurance Committee—310 Prospect Park W., Brooklyn, 11215. Tel: 718-965-7300; Fax: 718-965-7382. BRIAN T. COSGROVE, Dir. Insurance. Tel: 718-965-7300, Ext. 1351; Rev. CHRISTOPHER C. TURCZANY; Rev. Msgrs. DAVID L. CASSATO, M.Div., M.S.Ed.; JOSEPH P. NAGLE; PETER V. KAIN; Rev. PATRICK J. WEST; GINA DAVI. Tel: 718-965-7300, Ext. 1352.

Mediation and Arbitration, Board of—Rev. Msgr. EDWARD B. SCHARFENBERGER, S.T.L., J.C.L., Exec. Sec., Mailing Address: 310 Prospect Park W., Brooklyn, 11215.

Office of Priestly Life & Ministry—Immaculate Conception Center, 7200 Douglaston Pkwy., Douglaston, 11362. Tel: 718-229-8001, Ext. 315; Fax: 718-352-2490. Email: jfonti@diobrook.org. Very Rev. JOSEPH G. FONTI, S.T.L., Dir.

Ministerial Development Program—Very Rev. JOSEPH G. FONTI, S.T.L. Tel: 718-229-8001.

Newspaper "The Tablet"—ED WILKINSON, Editor, 1712 10th Ave., Brooklyn, 11215. Tel: 718-499-9705.

Office for Clergy Personnel—Deacon JULIO BARRENECHE, 310 Prospect Park W., Brooklyn, 11215. Tel: 718-399-5941; Fax: 718-399-5940.

Assignment Board—Rev. Msgr. RONALD T. MARINO, V.E.; Deacon JULIO BARRENECHE; Revs. THOMAS F. VASSALOTTI; THOMAS F. LEACH; Rev. Msgrs. STEVEN A. FERRARI, V.E.; PAUL R. SANCHEZ, V.E.; Rev. MICHAEL A. CARRANO; Rev. Msgrs. RAYMOND F. CHAPPETTO, (Facilitator); MICHAEL J. REID; ANTHONY HERNANDEZ, J.C.L.

Mission Office—Rev. TERRENCE J. MULKERIN (Retired), Office, 310 Prospect Park W., Brooklyn, 11215. Tel: 718-965-7300.

Office of Communications & Public Policy—Rev. Msgr. KIERAN E. HARRINGTON, V.E., Dir., 1712 10th Ave., Brooklyn, 11215. Tel: 718-499-6461.

Retirement Board (Priests)—Most Rev. IGNATIUS CATANELLO, D.D., Ph.D., V.E., Chm. (Retired), Mailing Address: 7200 Douglaston Pkwy., Douglaston, 11362.

Victim Assistance Coordinator—Sr. ELLEN PATRICIA FINN, O.P., M.Ed., L.M.S.W. Tel: 718-722-6050. Email: srepfinn@ccbq.org.

Safe Environment, Office of—7200 Douglaston Pkwy., Douglaston, 11362. Tel: 718-281-9672; Fax: 718-281-9673.

Vocations, Office of—Rev. KEVIN P. ABELS, B.A., M.Div., Dir.

Consultative Bodies

Presbyteral Council—Most Revs. OCTAVIO CISNEROS, D.D.; GUY SANSARICQ, D.D.; Rev. Msgr. PETER V. KAIN, Exec. Sec.; Most Rev. FRANK J. CAGGIANO, D.D., S.T.D., V.G.; Rev. Msgrs. THOMAS G. CASERTA, M.A., M.Div., D.Min.; KEVIN B. NOONE, V.E.; Rev. JAMES H. SWEENEY; Rev. Msgr. PETER W. ZENDZIAN; Revs. RUSSELL GOVERNALE, O.F.M.Conv.; THOMAS F. LEACH; GERALD J. FITZSIMMONS, S.M.M.; GORDON P. KUSI; Rev. Msgr. ANTHONY HERNANDEZ, J.C.L.

Diocesan Budget Committee—Rev. Msgr. MICHAEL J. REID; Mr. JOHN J. BORGIA; Mr. MARTIN J. MCMANUS, CPA.

Diocesan Consultors—Most Rev. FRANK J. CAGGIANO, D.D., S.T.D., V.G.; Rev. RICHARD J. BEUTHER; Rev. Msgr. RAYMOND F. CHAPPETTO; Rev. JAMES E. DEVLIN; Rev. Msgr. VINCENT FULLUM; Rev. JOSEPH R. GRIMALDI, J.C.L.; Rev. Msgrs. ANTHONY HERNANDEZ, J.C.L.; PETER V. KAIN; Revs. WILLIAM F. KRLIS; CHRISTOPHER M. O'CONNOR; Rev. Msgr. MICHAEL J. REID, Exec. Sec.

Diocesan Finance Council—Rev. Msgr. MICHAEL J. REID; Mr. ROBERT COUGHLAN; Mr. BRENDAN J. DUGAN; Mr. JOSEPH E. GEOGHAN; Mr. PETER LABBAT; Dr. FRANK MACCHIAROLA; Mr. JAMES J. MINOGUE; Mr. THOMAS MITCHELL; Rev. Msgrs. SEAN G. OGLE; ROBERT J. PAWSON; Justice JOSEPH P. SULLIVAN; Ms. MAUREEN SCANNELL BATEMAN.

Diocesan Diaconal Council—Deacons JOHN SUCICH, Co Chm.; JULIO BARRENECHE; ARTHUR CUTTER; STANLEY J. GALAZIN; SALVATORE V. LICATA; JOHN WARREN; JORGE A. GONZALEZ; THOMAS DAVIS; FRANK J. D'ACCORDO; MANUEL L. RODRIGUEZ; GREGORY KANDRA; THOMAS J. DEVANEY.

Diocesan Pastoral Council—WILLIAM KEARNS, Pres.; Most Rev. FRANK J. CAGGIANO, D.D., S.T.D., V.G., Bishop's Liaison.

Commissions and Offices for Pastoral Services

Alcoholism Committee—Rev. Msgr. THOMAS M. HAGGERTY (Retired).

Art and Architecture Commission—Revs. FRANK C. TUMINO, Dir.; ROBERT B. ADAMO; ROBERT J. ARMATO; HILAIRE BELIZAIRE; Mr. GREGORY JACK, Office: Immaculate Conception Center, 7200 Douglaston Pkwy., Douglaston, 11362. Tel: 718-281-9612; Fax: 718-281-9613.

Catholic Charities—ROBERT SIEBEL, M.S.W., Exec. Dir., 191 Joralemon St., Brooklyn, 11201. Tel: 718-722-6000 (See Institutions located in the Diocese for details).

Catholic Migration and Refugee Office— (See Institutions located in the Diocese for details)

Catholic Migration Services, Inc.—Rev. PATRICK J. KEATING, Dir. Tel: 718-236-3000.

Chaplains and Uniformed Services, Official—Police Department: Rev. ROBERT J. ROMANO, M.Div.; Rev. Msgr. DAVID L. CASSATO, M.Div., M.S.Ed. Fire Department: Rev. Msgr. JOHN DELENDICK; Rev. JOSEPH M. HOFFMAN. Sanitation Department: Rev. Msgr. ROBERT J. THELEN, S.T.L., KCHS. BMT Holy Name Society: Rev. Msgr. WILLIAM J. FLOOD (Retired).

Diocesan Liturgy Office—Revs. JOHN J. O'CONNOR, Assoc. Dir.; FRANK C. TUMINO, Exec. Sec., St. Thomas the Apostle, 87-19 88 Ave., Woodhaven, 11421. Tel: 718-847-1353; Fax: 718-849-3776.

Diocesan Real Estate Board—Rev. Msgr. JOHN DELENDICK; Revs. JOSEPH R. GRIMALDI, J.C.L.; WILLIAM F. KRLIS; COLEEN A. CERIELLO; COLLEEN LEFFERTS.

Diocesan Food Service—Mr. JAMES AUSTIN, Dir., 7200 Douglaston Pkwy., Douglaston, 11362. Tel: 718-229-8001, Ext. 531.

Diaconate Formation Office—Deacon JORGE A. GONZALEZ, Dir., 310 Prospect Park W., Brooklyn, 11215.

Ecumenical and Interreligious Affairs, Diocesan Commission for—Rev. Msgr. GUY A. MASSIE, Exec. Sec.

Committee for Eastern Orthodox-Catholic Relations—Rev. Msgr. STEVEN J. AGUGGIA, J.C.L., Chm.

Committee for Catholic-Protestant Relations—Rev. Msgr. JOHN STRYNKOWSKI.

Committee for Catholic-Jewish Relations—Rev. Msgr. GUY A. MASSIE.

Catholic Muslim Dialogue—Rev. Msgr. GUY A. MASSIE, Chm.

Catholic Hindu/Buddhist Dialogue—Rev. ABRAHAM MATTHEW, Chm.

Home School Association—VACANT.

Liturgical Commission—Rev. FRANK C. TUMINO, Exec. Dir.

Office of Music Ministry—Immaculate Conception Center, 7200 Douglaston Pkwy., Douglaston, 11362. Tel: 718-281-9612; Fax: 718-281-9613.

Music Commission—Rev. FRANK C. TUMINO, Exec. Sec.; Mr. EMMANUEL BOLOGNA, Co Chair; Ms. JESSICA TRANZILLO-SMITH, Co Chair, Immaculate Conception Center, 7200 Douglaston Pkwy., Douglaston, 11362. Tel: 718-281-9612; Fax: 718-281-9613.

Pastoral Care of the Sick Office— (See Institutions located in the Diocese for details)

Pastoral Communications, Office of—Mr. CHRISTOPHER QUINN, Gen. Mgr. TVC, 1712 10th Ave., Brooklyn, 11215. Tel: 718-499-9705 Legal Title: Trans Video Communications, Inc.

Pastoral Institute—GERRY PORTORELLA, Dir., 7200 Douglaston Pkwy., Douglaston, 11362. Tel: 718-631-4267.

Pilgrimage Office—Rev. GERARD J. SAUER, Dir., 7200 Douglaston Pkwy., Douglaston, 11362. Tel: 718-965-7313. Email: pilgrimages@rcdob.org.

Prison Ministries Office— (See listing under Catholic Charities)

Office of Faith Formation—Mr. THEODORE J. MUSCO, Dir., Diocese of Brooklyn, 310 Prospect Park W., Brooklyn, 11215.

Family Life Office—Mrs. ANA PUENTE, Dir., 310 Prospect Park W., Brooklyn, 11215.

Coordinator of Childhood Faith Formation—VACANT.

Coordinator of Adolescent and Young Adult Faith Formation—VACANT.

Coordinator of Adult Faith Formation—PAUL MORISI, 310 Prospect Park W., Brooklyn, 11215.

Coordinator of Catholic School Faith Formation and Catechist Formation—VACANT.

Coordinator of RCIA—Sr. ALICE MICHAEL, S.U.S.C.

Coordinator of Marriage and Family Ministry—Mrs. ANA PUENTE.

Coordinator of Respect Life Education—VACANT.

CYO (Catholic Youth Organization)—7200 Douglaston Pkwy., Douglaston, 11362. Tel: 718-229-8001. Deacon JOSEPH CATANELLO, Dir.

Pastoral Planning Office—Mr. ROBERT CHOINIERE, Dir.; ELLEN RHATIGAN, Mailing Address: 310 Prospect Park W., Brooklyn, 11215. Tel: 718-399-5900.

Apostolic Organizations

Catholic Youth Organization, Diocesan—Deacon JOSEPH CATANELLO, 7200 Douglaston Pkwy., Douglaston, 11362. Tel: 718-229-8001.

Charismatic Groups, Catholic—

Charismatic Renewal (English-speaking) of the Diocese of Brooklyn—JOSEPHINE CACHIA, Dir.; JOSEPHINE MCNALLY, Sec., 240 Jay St., Brooklyn, 11201. Tel: 718-260-9111; Fax: 718-260-9121.

Renouveau Charismatique of the Diocese of Brooklyn— (serving the Haitian Charismatics of the Diocese) Rev. Msgr. JOSEPH P. MALAGRECA, Dir., 2530 Church Ave., Brooklyn, 11226. Tel: 718-469-5900; Fax: 718-469-5901.

Renovacion Carismatica of the Diocese of Brooklyn— (serving the Hispanic Charismatics of the Diocese) Rev. Msgr. JOSEPH P. MALAGRECA, Dir., 2530 Church Ave., Brooklyn, 11226. Tel: 718-469-5900; Fax: 718-469-5901.

Confraternity of the Guard of Honor and Confraternity of the Holy Hour—VACANT.

Confraternity of the Precious Blood—Rev. Msgr. AUSTIN P. BENNETT, J.C.D., P.A., Dir. (Retired), 5300 Fort Hamilton Pkwy., Brooklyn, 11219. Tel: 718-436-1120.

Courage Ministry—Rev. Msgr. WALTER C. MURPHY (Retired), Immaculate Conception Center, 7200 Douglaston Pkwy., Douglaston, 11362. Tel: 718-229-1748 (Hotline).

Guilds—

Accountant—Rev. Msgr. WALTER C. MURPHY, Dir. (Retired).

Catholic Cemetery Guild—Rev. Msgr. MICHAEL J. REID, Moderator.

Lawyers—Rev. Msgrs. EDWARD B. SCHARFENBERGER, S.T.L., J.C.L., Kings Co.; GREGORY C. WIELUNSKI, J.C.D., Queens Co.

Physicians—VACANT.

Teachers—Rev. Msgr. THOMAS F. NOONAN, Dir. (Retired).

Holy Name Society—Rev. DENNIS J. FARRELL, Moderator.

Marriage Encounter—Coordinators: JOHN TORIO; TONI TORIO. Tel: 718-746-8979.

National Council of Catholic Women—CLAIRE DUNNE, Pres.

Legion of Mary—Rev. Msgrs. VINCENT F. FULLAM, Dir. (Retired); JOSEPH R. ROSA, Spanish Curia (Retired); Deacon JEAN BAPTISTE BOURSIQUOT, Haitian Curia; VACANT, Korean Curia; VACANT, Flushing Curia; Revs. CHARLES REPOLE, O.F.M.Cap., N.W. Queens Curia (Retired); JOSEPH MARRIN, C.Ss.R., Bay Ridge Curia, 82-00 35th Ave., Jackson Heights, 11372. Tel: 718-429-2333.

Nocturnal Adoration Society—Rev. JOHN MADURI.

St. John's Priests Relief Society—Rev. Msgr. GEORGE M. SCHUSTER, Pres. (Retired).

Apostleship of Prayer—Rev. Msgr. VINCENT A. KEANE (Retired).

CLERGY, PARISHES, MISSIONS AND PAROCHIAL SCHOOLS

CITY OF NEW YORK

BOROUGH OF BROOKLYN

1—ST. AGATHA'S (1912) Revs. Francisco J. Walker; Lewis H. Maynard (Retired); Bai Lianjiang; Sr. Anne Burke, Pastoral Assoc.
Res.: 702 48th St., 11220. Tel: 718-436-1080; Fax: 718-436-8870.
School—736 48th St., 11220. Tel: 718-435-3137; Fax: 718-437-7505. Ms. Alice Rios, Prin. Religious 1; Lay Teachers 11; Students 204.
Catechesis/Religious Program—Ms. Susan Lehman, D.R.E. Students 272.

2—ST. AGNES (1878) Merged with Saint Peter-Paul-Our Lady of Pilar, Brooklyn to form Saint Paul and Saint Agnes, Brooklyn

3—ALL SAINTS (1867), (Spanish), Merged with Our Lady of Montserrate-St. Ambrose, Brooklyn to form All Saints, Brooklyn.

4—ALL SAINTS (2008) Rev. William Chacon (Costa Rica); Deacon Carlos A. Martinez. In Res., Rev. David P. Bertolotti.
Res.: 115 Throop Ave., 11206-4415. Tel: 718-388-1951; Fax: 718-388-7712. Email: allsaints11206@gmail.com.
Our Lady of Montserrate Chapel—Additional Worship Site: 134 Vernon Ave., 11206-4415.
Catechesis/Religious Program—Awilda Martinez, D.R.E. (All Saints); Elsie Torres, C.R.E. (Our Lady of Montserrate Chapel). Students 209.

5—ST. ALPHONSUS, Merged 1976. Records at St. Anthony of Padua-St. Alphonsus.

6—ST. AMBROSE, Merged 1978. Records at Our Lady of Monserrate-St. Ambrose.

7—ST. ANDREW THE APOSTLE (1971) Rev. Msgr. Guy A. Massie; Deacon Gregory Dixon.
Res.: 6713 Ridge Blvd., 11220. Tel: 718-680-1010; Fax: 718-680-3160. Email: standrewrc@gmail.com. Web: saintandrewtheapostle.net.
Catechesis/Religious Program—Tel: 718-836-4679; Fax: 718-680-3160. Christine Kemp, D.R.E. Students 264.

8—ST. ANN-ST. GEORGE (1860) Closed. For inquiries for parish records contact the chancery.

9—ANNUNCIATION OF THE BLESSED VIRGIN MARY (1863), (Lithuanian), Rev. Msgr. Joseph P. Calise, Admin.; Rev. Michael J. Lynch, Parochial Vicar.
Mailing Address: 275 N. Eighth St., 11211. Tel: 718-384-0223; Fax: 718-384-5838.
Church: 259 N. 5th St., 11211.
Catechesis/Religious Program—

10—ST. ANSELM (1922) Rev. Msgrs. John W. Maloney; Michael J. Phillips (Retired); Revs. Martin R. Kull, Parochial Vicar; Anthony Alimnonu, Parochial Vicar; Andrew M. Kim, Parochial Vicar; Deacon Thomas Davis. Brooklyn, NY St. Anselm
Res.: 356 82nd St., 11209. Tel: 718-238-2900; Fax: 718-238-2902. Email: revmaloney@aol.com. Web: www.starcc.net.
School—365 83rd St., 11209. Tel: 718-745-7643; Fax: 718-745-0086. Mrs. Linda Addonisio, Prin. Lay Teachers 24; Students 354.
Catechesis/Religious Program—Tel: 718-745-0077. Sisters Anne Bernadette, M.S.B.T., D.R.E.; Regina Corde, O.P., Pastoral Assoc. Tel: 718-836-0708. Students 113.
Missionary Cenacle—351 83rd St., 11209. Tel: 718-836-0957. Missionary Servants of the Most Blessed Trinity 2.

11—ST. ANTHONY OF PADUA-ST. ALPHONSUS (1856) Revs. Robert W. Czok (Retired); Dagoberto Noguera, Parochial Vicar; Roy Jacob, Parochial Vicar.
Res.: 862 Manhattan Ave., 11222. Tel: 718-383-3339; Fax: 718-383-6958. Email: ant862@aol.com.
Catechesis/Religious Program—Tel: 718-383-6935. Rose Accetta, D.R.E. Students 164.

12—ASSUMPTION OF THE BLESSED VIRGIN MARY (1842), (Lithuanian), Rev. James W. King. In Res., Rev. Peter Mahoney.
Res.: 64 Middagh St., 11201. Tel: 718-625-1161; Fax: 718-625-7223. Email: fr.jamesking@gmail.com. Web: www.assumptionparish.net.
Catechesis/Religious Program—Students 54.

13—ST. ATHANASIUS (1913) Rev. Msgr. David L. Cassato; Revs. Ronald M. D'Antonio, Parochial Vicar; Gabriel Toro-Rivas, Parochial Vicar; Deacon Dante Colandrea; Mr. Alvoro Chavarriaga, Pastoral Assoc.; Mr. Paul Kim, Pastoral Assoc.
Res.: 2154 61st St., 11204. Tel: 718-236-0124; Fax: 718-236-4960. Email: stathanasiusny@hotmail.com. Web: www.stathanasius.brooklyn.org.
School—6120 Bay Pkwy., 11204. Tel: 718-236-4791; Fax: 718-621-1423. Email: sta6120@aol.com. Mrs. Lorraine Garone-Tesoro, Prin. Lay Teachers 15; Students 306.
Catechesis/Religious Program—Tel: 718-331-8811; Fax: 718-331-2582. Mrs. Nicoletta Milo, D.R.E. Students 501.
Convent—2201 62nd St., 11204. Tel: 718-236-2680.
Chapel—St. Augustine Yu Chin-gil Chapel 2115 61st St., 11204. Tel: 718-729-0132; Fax: 718-729-0132.

14—ST. AUGUSTINE (1870) Rev. Thomas W. Ahern. In Res., Revs. Agnelo Pinto, (St. Boniface, Winnipeg, Canada); Charles P. Keeney; Lucien Charlot (Retired).
Res.: 116 Sixth Ave., 11217. Tel: 718-783-3132; Fax: 718-638-4669. Email: staugustinerc@verizon.net. Web: www.staugustineparkslope.org.
Catechesis/Religious Program—Students 90.

15—ST. BARBARA (1893) Rev. Joseph M. Hoffman; Deacon Fausto Duran.
Res.: 138 Bleecker St., 11221. Tel: 718-452-3660; Fax: 718-452-1279. Email: fr.fg@hotmail.com. Web: www.stbarbarascatholicchurch.com.
Catechesis/Religious Program—139 Menaham St., 11221. Tel: 718-453-1406. Ms. Angie Lee Vasquez, D.R.E. Students 335.

16—ST. BENEDICT'S, Closed. For inquiries for parish records contact the chancery.

17—ST. BERNADETTE (1935) Rev. Msgr. Thomas G. Caserta; Rev. Joseph A. Gancila, Parochial Vicar; Deacons Anthony P. Martucci; Frank DiMichele. In Res., Rev. Joseph K. Dolan (Retired).
Res.: 8201 13th Ave., 11228. Tel: 718-837-3400; Fax: 718-236-5883. Email: aquin79@aol.com. Web: www.shrinechurchofst bernadette.com.
School—1313 83rd St., 11228. Tel: 718-236-1560; Fax: 718-236-3364. Email: stbernadette83@yahoo.com. Web: www.stbernadette-school.org. Sr. Joan DiRienzo, M.P.F., Prin. Sisters (Religious Teachers Filippini) 2; Lay Teachers 21; Students 370.
Catechesis/Religious Program—Tel: 718-232-7733. Students 187.

18—ST. BERNARD, Closed. For inquiries for parish records contact the chancery.

19—ST. BERNARD OF CLAIRVAUX (1961) Revs. Ralph J. Caputo; Winson Parekkat; Deacon Frank J. D'Accordo; Mr. James Millen, Music Dir.
Res.: 2055 E. 69th St., 11234. Tel: 718-763-5533; Fax: 718-763-0224. Email: ralphmystery@aol.com.
School—2031 E. 69th St., 11234. Tel: 718-241-6040; Fax: 718-241-7258. Kathleen Buscemi, Prin. Lay Teachers 20; Students 335.
Catechesis/Religious Program—Tel: 718-444-4674; Fax: 718-241-7258. Students 341.

20—ST. BLAISE, Merged with St. Francis of Assisi in 1980. Records at St. Francis of Assisi-St. Blaise.

21—BLESSED SACRAMENT (1891) Rev. Francis T. Shannon.
Res.: 198 Euclid Ave., 11208. Tel: 718-827-1200; Fax: 718-827-2422. Email: devinemaster2@aol.com.
School—187 Euclid Ave., 11208. Tel: 718-235-4863; Fax: 718-235-1132. Marylou Celmer, Prin. Lay Teachers 14; Students 286.
Catechesis/Religious Program—Tel: 718-277-3231; Fax: 718-277-3231. Students 679.

22—ST. BONIFACE (1854) Revs. Joel M. Warden, C.O., Parochial Vicar; Anthony Andreassi, C.O., Parochial Vicar; Deacon William Powers, (Retired); Christopher Smith, Business Mgr. In Res., Rev. Mark J. Lane, C.O.; Very Rev. Dennis M. Corrado, C.O., Provost, Brooklyn Oratory; Rev. Michael J. Callaghan, C.O.; Bro. James Simon, C.O.
Res.: 109 Willoughby St., 11201. Tel: 718-875-2096; Fax: 718-875-4678. Email: info@oratory-church.org. Web: www.oratory-church.org.
Catechesis/Religious Program—Email: eileen.randig@oratory-church.org. Eileen Randig, D.R.E. Students 192.

23—ST. BRENDAN (1907) Rev. Frank W. Spacek; Rev. Msgr. Rocco D. Villani, Parochial Vicar (Retired); Stephen T. Rzonca, Pastoral Assoc. In Res., Rev. Kevin P. Cavalluzzi.
Res.: 1525 E. 12th St., 11230. Tel: 718-339-2828; Fax: 718-339-5951. Email: stbrendanbklyn@yahoo.com.
Catechesis/Religious Program—Tel: 718-377-6932; Fax: 718-377-6374. Students 60.
Convent—1526 E. 13th St., 11230. Tel: 718-998-2032.

24—ST. BRIGID (1887) Rev. Msgr. James J. Kelly; Rev. Emlio Melendez, Parochial Vicar. In Res., Rev. John H. Wilkinson (Retired).
Res.: 409 Linden St., 11237. Tel: 718-821-1690; Fax: 718-386-4302. Email: sheamusk@aol.com.
School—438 Grove St. E., 11237. Tel: 718-821-1477; Fax: 718-821-1079. Mrs. Shelia Smith-Gonzalez, Prin. Lay Teachers 14; Students 268.
Catechesis/Religious Program—Tel: 718-821-6401. Jacqueline Perez, D.R.E. Students 1,100.

25—ST. CASIMIR, (Polish), Merged with Our Lady of Czestochowa in 1980. Records at Our Lady of Czestochowa-St. Casimir.

26—ST. CATHARINE OF ALEXANDRIA (1902) Revs. Frederick Cintron; Francis Kwame Asagba, Parochial Vicar; Deacon Gustavo Medina; Sr. Barbara Mullen, Pastoral Assoc. In Res., Rev. Dariusz Piotr Blicharz, Parochial Vicar.
Res.: 1119 41st St., 11218. Tel: 718-436-5917; Fax: 718-871-5140. Email: frcintron59@hotmail.com.
Catechesis/Religious Program—Tel: 718-436-2471. Mrs. Grace Olavarria, D.R.E. Students 277.

27—THE CATHEDRAL-BASILICA OF ST. JAMES (Jay St. at Tillary) (1822) Rev. Msgr. John Strynkowski; Joseph B. Smith, Music Dir. In Res., Rev. Kevin P. Cavalluzzi.
Office: 240 Jay St., 11201. Fax: 718-852-9452. Email: secretary@brooklyncathedral.net. Web: www.brooklyncathedral.net.
Res.: 250 Cathedral Pl., 11201. Tel: 718-852-4002 (Office); 718-855-6390 (Rectory); Fax: 718-852-9452. Email: jjscath@mail.com.

28—ST. CATHERINE OF GENOA (1911) Rev. Charles Akoto Oduro (Ghana).
Res.: 520 Linden Blvd., 11203. Tel: 718-282-7162; Fax: 718-282-5568. Email: stcatherineofgenoa@hotmail.com. Web: www.stcatherineofgenoachurchonline.com.
Catechesis/Religious Program—Tel: 718-469-7505. Marie Rose Terlonge, D.R.E. Students 31.

29—ST. CECILIA (1871), Merged with St. Nicholas, Brooklyn & St. Francis of Paola, Brooklyn to form Divine Mercy Roman Catholic Church, Brooklyn. Revs. James J. Krische, Parochial Vicar; Kenneth J. Grande; Deacon Carlos Valderama. In Res., Rev. Richard E. Long.

Res.: 84 Herbert St., 11222. Tel: 718-389-0010; Fax: 718-389-5090. Email: parish@stcecilia-bklyn.org. Web: www.stcecilia-bklyn.org.
Catechesis/Religious Program—1-15 Monitor St., 11222. Tel: 718-389-2546. Students 38.

30—ST. CHARLES BORROMEO (1849) Rev. Edward P. Doran.
Res.: 21 Sidney Pl., 11201. Tel: 718-625-1177; Fax: 718-624-1627. Email: stcharlesbklyn@aol.com.
Catechesis/Religious Program—Maureen Pond, D.R.E. Students 60.

31—ST. COLUMBA (1967) Revs. Francis J. Hughes; Peter Dery Gbaalo; Deacon Lawrence Coyle. In Res., Rev. Charles J. Matonti (Retired).
Res.: 2245 Kimball St., 11234. Tel: 718-338-6265; Fax: 718-377-6440. Email: stcolumbac@aol.com.
Catechesis/Religious Program—Tel: 718-253-8840. Deacon Fred Ritchie, D.R.E. Students 176.

32—ST. COLUMBKILLE, Closed. Parochial records are located at SS. Cyril and Methodius. Became a mission in 1939.

33—SS. CYRIL AND METHODIUS (1917), (Polish), Revs. Tadeusz Maciejewski, C.M.; Joseph Wisniewski, C.M., Parochial Vicar.
Res.: 150 Dupont St., 11222. Tel: 718-389-4424; Fax: 718-389-4191. Email: parish@cyrilandmethodius.org. Web: www.cyrilandmethodius.org.
Catechesis/Religious Program—Tel: 718-349-7732. Students 209.

34—DIVINE MERCY ROMAN CATHOLIC CHURCH (2011) 219 Conselyea St., 11211.

35—ST. DOMINIC (1972) Revs. John Tino; Anthony Iroh (Nigeria), Parochial Vicar; Deacon Paul P. Morin.
Res.: 2001 Bay Ridge Pkwy., 11204. Tel: 718-259-4636; Fax: 718-259-3066. Email: saintdominicrectoryoffice@gmail.com.
Catechesis/Religious Program—Tel: 718-621-0422. Students 162.

36—ST. EDMUND (1922) Rev. Edward G. Brophy; Deacon Ronald Rizzuto. In Res., Rev. Anthony V. Dell'Anno (Retired).
Res.: 2450 Ocean Ave., 11229-3509. Tel: 718-743-0102; Fax: 718-891-7834. Email: stedmund@aol.com.
School—1902 Avenue T, 11229. Tel: 718-648-9229. Email: saintedmundelem@gmail.com. Ms. Mariann Solano, Prin. Lay Teachers 22; Students 261.
High School—Denis Maloney Institute/St. Edmund Preparatory High School, 2474 Ocean Ave., 11229. Tel: 718-743-6100; Fax: 718-743-5243. Mr. John Lorenzetti, Prin.; Allison McGinnis, Asst. Prin.; Sr. Barbara Doyle, C.S.J., Campus Min. Sisters 2; Lay Teachers 44; Students 750.
Catechesis/Religious Program—Tel: 718-743-8107; Fax: 718-891-7834. Ms. Jenny Valeri, D.R.E. Students 63.

37—ST. EDWARD, Merged with St. Michael Archangel in 1942. St. Michael Archangel-St. Edward merged with Sacred Heart in 2008 to form Mary of Nazareth, Brooklyn.

38—ST. EPHREM (1921) Rev. Msgr. Peter V. Kain; Revs. Theophilus Joseph, Parochial Vicar; William A. With, Parochial Vicar; Deacon Anthony Stucchio; Thomas Marchesiello, Music Dir.; Michele James, Business Mgr.
Res.: 929 Bay Ridge Pkwy., 11228. Tel: 718-833-1010; Fax: 718-921-5232. Email: stephremrectory@aol.com.
School—7415 Ft. Hamilton Pkwy., 11228. Tel: 718-833-1440; Fax: 718-745-5301. Email: stephremschool@aol.com. Web: stephremsch.org. Annamarie Bartone, Prin. Servants of the Immaculate Heart of Mary 3; Lay Teachers 19; Students 313.
Catechesis/Religious Program—Tel: 718-745-7486; Fax: 718-745-2302. Email: stephremreled@verizon.net. Rita Lavin O'Connell, D.R.E. Students 243.
Convent—935 Bay Ridge Pkwy., 11228. Tel: 718-833-1555.

39—EPIPHANY (1905) Merged with SS. Peter and Paul, Brooklyn. For inquiries for parish records please see SS. Peter and Paul, Brooklyn.

40—ST. FINBAR (1880) Revs. Michael L. Gelfant; Christopher V. Ruggles, Parochial Vicar; Deacons Anthony Favale; Francis G. Mateo. In Res., Deacon John E. Hull.
Res.: 138 Bay 20th St., 11214. Tel: 718-236-3312; Fax: 718-236-3750. Email: stfinbarchurch@yahoo.com. Web: www.stfinbarbrooklyn.org.
Catechesis/Religious Program—Tel: 718-837-3935. Sr. Eileen Sweeney, O.S.F., D.R.E. Students 276.
Convent—131 Bay 19 St., 11214. Tel: 718-259-4439.

41—ST. FORTUNATA (1934) Rev. Vincent F. Miceli; Sr. Anna Celentano, C.S.J.B., Pastoral Assoc.; Deacons Osborn Miranda; Eugene Okafoe. In Res., Rev. Hyacinth I. Ikemelu (Nigeria), Pastor Emeritus.
Res.: 2609 Linden Blvd., 11208. Tel: 718-647-2632; Fax: 718-647-1321. Email: stfortunatachurch@netzero.net.
Catechesis/Religious Program—Sr. Loretta M. Florio, C.S.J.B., D.R.E. Students 184.

42—FOURTEEN HOLY MARTYRS, Merged with St. Martin of Tours in 1976. Records at St. Martin of Tours-Fourteen Holy Martyrs.

43—ST. FRANCES CABRINI (1963) Rev. Gaetano J. Sbordone; Vacant, Parochial Vicar.
Church, Office & Rectory: 1562 86th. St., 11228. Tel: 718-236-9165; Fax: 718-331-8139.
Catechesis/Religious Program—21 Bay 11th St., 11228. Tel: 718-232-4228. Sara Nespoli, D.R.E. Students 119.

44—ST. FRANCES CABRINI CHAPEL, Closed. For inquiries for parish records please see Sacred Heart of Jesus and Mary and St. Stephen.

45—ST. FRANCES DE CHANTAL (1891) Revs. Canon Andrzej Kurowski, S.A.C.; Marian Wierzchowski, S.A.C., Parochial Vicar; Antoni Zemula, S.A.C., Parochial Vicar.
Res.: 1273 58th St., 11219. Tel: 718-436-6407; Fax: 718-854-2761. Email: francesdechantal@verizon.net. Web: www.francesdechantal.org.
Catechesis/Religious Program—

46—ST. FRANCIS IN THE FIELDS, Closed. For inquiries for parish records contact the chancery.

47—ST. FRANCIS OF ASSISI-ST. BLAISE (1898) Revs. Juan J. Gonzalez, S.M.; Maciej J. Pawlowski, S.M., Parochial Vicar; James F. McGoldrick, Parochial Vicar.
Res.: Tel: 718-756-2015; Fax: 718-756-1773. Email: sfa-stb@optonline.net.
Church: 319 Maple St., 11225.
School—400 Lincoln Rd., 11225. Tel: 718-778-3700; Fax: 718-778-7877. Email: office@sfabrooklyn.org. Web: www.sfabrooklyn.org. Sr. Theresa Scanlon, C.S.J., Prin. Religious Teachers 2; Lay Teachers 17; Students 280.
Catechesis/Religious Program—335 Maple St., 11225. Tel: 718-778-1302. Ms. Myrmonde Dorismonde, D.R.E. Students 97.

48—ST. FRANCIS OF PAOLA (1918), (Italian), Merged with St. Nicholas, Brooklyn & St. Cecilia, Brooklyn to form Divine Mercy Roman Catholic Church, Brooklyn. Revs. Matteo Rizzo; Kenneth J. Grande; Deacon John P. Orlandello.
Res.: 219 Conselyea St., 11211. Tel: 718-387-0256; Fax: 718-384-0068. Email: paola219c@yahoo.com.
Catechesis/Religious Program— Suzanne O'Connor, D.R.E. Students 30.

49—ST. FRANCIS XAVIER (1886) Rev. William J. Rueger; Sr. Helene Conway, C.S.J., Pastoral Assoc.; Deacon James Ramos; Michael Kaminski, Music Dir. In Res., Rev. Mark Burke.
Res.: 225 Sixth Ave., 11215. Tel: 718-638-1880; Fax: 718-638-2839. Email: franxrc@gmail.com. Web: www.stfxbrooklyn.org.
School—763 President St., 11215. Tel: 718-857-2559; Fax: 718-857-5391. Email: sfxparkslope@att.net. Web: www.sfxparkslope.com. Sr. Kathleen Sullivan, C.S.J., Prin. Lay Teachers 15; Students 221.
Catechesis/Religious Program—Tel: 718-857-2903. Email: hacreled@aol.com. Sr. Helene Conway, C.S.J., D.R.E. Students 185.

50—ST. GABRIEL THE ARCHANGEL (1901) Merged with Saint John Cantius, Brooklyn to form St. Mary, Mother of the Church, Brooklyn

51—ST. GEORGE, Closed. For inquiries for parish records contact the chancery.

52—GOOD SHEPHERD (1927) Revs. James E. Devlin; Michael J. McGee, Parochial Vicar; Anthony M. Ozele, Parochial Vicar; Deacon Christopher A. Wagner; Mr. Michael Fontana, Music Dir. In Res., Rev. Msgr. Thomas F. Brady (Retired).
Res.: 1950 Batchelder St., 11229. Tel: 718-998-2800; Fax: 718-382-5428. Email: gsrcc@aol.com. Web: www.goodshepherdrcc.org.
School—1943 Brown St., 11229. Tel: 718-339-2745; Fax: 718-645-4513. Web: www.goodshepherdbklyn.org. Mr. Anthony Paparelli, Prin. Lay Teachers 8; Students 311.
Catechesis/Religious Program—Tel: 718-375-0899. Elvira Anselmo, D.R.E. Students 470.

53—ST. GREGORY THE GREAT (1905), Merged with St. Matthew. Rev. Caleb A. Buchanan, Admin. In Res., Most Rev. Guy Sansaricq.
Res.: 224 Brooklyn Ave., 11213-2505. Tel: 718-773-0100; Fax: 718-773-4198.
School—991 St. Johns Pl., 11213-2532. Tel: 718-774-3330; Fax: 718-774-3332. Rudolph Cyrus-Charles, Prin. Lay Teachers 11; Students 351.
Catechesis/Religious Program—Tel: 718-773-0100; Fax: 718-773-4198. Students 30.

54—GUARDIAN ANGEL (1885) Revs. Adnel T. Burgos; Janusz Dymek, Parochial Vicar; Deacon Manuel Zelaya.
Res.: 2978 Ocean Pkwy., 11235. Tel: 718-266-1561; Fax: 718-372-1603. Email: guardianangel@verizon.net. Web: www.guardianangelchurch.com.
Catechesis/Religious Program—Tel: 718-372-1967. Olga Ortiz, D.R.E. Students 230.

55—HOLY CROSS (1848) Rev. Msgr. Joseph P. Malagreca; Rev. Jean-Francois Nixon, Parochial Vicar.
Res.: 2530 Church Ave., 11226. Tel: 718-469-5900; Fax: 718-469-5901.
Catechesis/Religious Program—Tel: 718-941-5066. Catherine Hayes, D.R.E. Students 245.

56—HOLY FAMILY (1880) Merged with St. Thomas Aquinas to form Holy Family-St. Thomas Aquinas. For inquiries and parish records see Holy Family-St. Thomas Aquinas.

57—HOLY FAMILY (1880) Revs. John J. Amann; Edward R. P. Kane, Parochial Vicar; Jean Augustin Francois, Parochial Vicar. In Res., Revs. John J. Gildea; Vitalis N. Opara (Nigeria).
Res.: 9719 Flatlands Ave., 11236. Tel: 718-257-4423; Fax: 718-257-4806. Email: hfamilyr@aol.com. Web: www.holyfamilycanarsie.org.
Catechesis/Religious Program—Tel: 718-257-8016; Fax: 718-272-2279. Brendan Egonu, D.R.E. Students 191.

58—HOLY FAMILY (1905), (Slovak), Merged with St. Anthony-St. Alphonsus. Rev. Walter Thelapilly, C.M.I. (India).
Res.: 21 Nassau Ave., 11222. Tel: 718-388-5145; Fax: 718-387-1877. Email: frwaltercmi@hotmail.com. Web: www.hfschurch.org.

59—HOLY FAMILY-SAINT THOMAS AQUINAS (2008) Rev. Jesus Cuadros; Deacon John A. Flannery. In Res., Rev. Msgr. Leo J. White (Retired).
Res.: 249 Ninth St., 11215. Tel: 718-768-9471; Fax: 718-788-3390. Email: dn249@aol.com. Web: www.stthomasaquinaschurch.org.
Holy Family Church—Additional Worship Site: 205 14th St., 11215.
Catechesis/Religious Program—Sr. Doryne M. Bermoy, F.L.P., D.R.E. Students 165.

60—HOLY INNOCENTS (1910) Revs. Pascal Louis; Bony Monastere, Parochial Vicar.
Res.: 279 E. 17th St., 11226. Tel: 718-469-9500; Fax: 718-941-4931. Email: agranil406@yahoo.com. Web: www.holyinnocentsbrooklyn.org.
Catechesis/Religious Program— Nancy Gerard, D.R.E. Students 285.

61—HOLY NAME (1878) Revs. James K. Cunningham; Felix Quarshie, Parochial Vicar; James H. Sweeney, Parochial Vicar; Deacons Abel Torres; Thomas J. Devaney; Felipe Almendarez. In Res., Revs. Austin Emen; Terrence J. Mulkerin (Retired); Antonios Fanous.
Res.: 245 Prospect Park W., 11215. Tel: 718-768-3071; Fax: 718-369-2039. Email: frjimholyname@aol.com. Web: www.holynamebrooklyn.org.
School—241 Prospect Park W., 11215. Tel: 718-768-7629; Fax: 718-768-3007. Web: www.hnjbklyn.org. Email: hnjcaccamo@yahoo.com. Joan E. Caccamo, Prin. & D.R.E. Lay Teachers 18; Students 244.
Catechesis/Religious Program—241 Prospect Park W., 11215. Tel: 718-768-7629; Fax: 718-768-3007. Students 65.

62—HOLY ROSARY (1889), (African American), Merged with Our Lady of Victory & St. Peter Claver, Brooklyn to form Saint Martin de Porres, Brooklyn

63—HOLY SPIRIT Revs. Heebong Nam; Jose E. Lopez, Parochial Vicar; Deacon Wilfredo Hernandez. In Res., Rev. Charlse Ugochukwu.
Res.: 1712 45th St., 11204. Tel: 718-436-5565; Fax: 718-436-5586. Email: holyspiritparishbp@hotmail.com.
Catechesis/Religious Program—Mrs. Martha Castro, D.R.E. Students 125.
Convent—1679 47th St., 11204.

64—ST. IGNATIUS (1908), Merged with St. Francis of Assisi-St. Blaise. Revs. Carlos Quijano, S.J., Admin.; Michael Corcoran; John J. Podziadlo; Deacon Berthal Beaubrun.
Res.: 1101 Carroll St., 11225. Tel: 718-774-2102; Fax: 718-774-5821.
Catechesis/Religious Program— Lorraine Pierre, D.R.E. Students 45.

65—IMMACULATE CONCEPTION OF THE BLESSED VIRGIN MARY (1853) Closed. For inquiries and parish records, see Most Holy Trinity - St. Mary, Brooklyn.

66—IMMACULATE HEART OF MARY (1893) Rev. Robert B. Adamo; Sr. Mary Ann Ambrose, C.S.J., Pastoral Assoc.; Deacons James D. Noble, Safe Environment Coord.; John Cantirino. In Res., Rev. Msgr. Steven A. Ferrari.
Res.: 2805 Ft. Hamilton Pkwy., 11218. Tel: 718-871-1310; Fax: 718-633-1866. Email: ihmpastor@verizon.net. Web: www.ihmbrooklyn.org.
School—3002 Ft. Hamilton Pkwy., 11218. Tel: 718-438-7373; Fax: 718-853-5994. Web: www.ihmaryschool.org. Ms. Maureen Rooney, Prin. Lay Teachers 24; Students 208.
Catechesis/Religious Program—Tel: 718-854-7326. Students 240.

67—ST. JEROME (1901) Revs. Jean-Miguel Aguste, Admin.; Hugues Berrette, Parochial Vicar; Deacon

Magloire Marcel.
Res.: 2900 Newkirk Ave., 11226. Tel: 718-462-0224; Fax: 718-462-7753. Email: stjeromechurch@hotmail.com.
School—465 E. 29th St., 11226. Tel: 718-462-0211; Fax: 718-462-1828. Marie Clobette Jean-Louis, Prin. Lay Teachers 11; Students 297.
Catechesis/Religious Program—Paul Norman, D.R.E. Students 170.
Convent—455 E. 29th St., 11226. Tel: 718-856-3323.

68—ST. JOHN CANTIUS (1902) Merged with Saint Gabriel the Archangel, Brooklyn to form St. Mary Mother of the Church, Brooklyn (2007).

69—ST. JOHN THE BAPTIST (1868) Revs. Emmet J. Nolan, C.M.; Astor Rodriguez, C.M., Parochial Vicar.
Res.: 75 Lewis Ave., 11206. Tel: 718-455-6864; Fax: 718-452-3738. Email: scorcnado@stjohnthebaptistrcc.org. Web: www.stjohnthebaptistrcc.org.
Additional Worship Site:—
Our Lady of Good Counsel—915 Putnam Ave., 11221.
Catechesis/Religious Program—Eugenia Ortiz, D.R.E. Students 111.

70—ST. JOHN THE EVANGELIST (1849), Merged with St. Rocco, Brooklyn to form Saint John the Evangelist-Saint Rocco Roman Catholic Church, Brooklyn. Rev. Johnson Chanassery, O.C.D., Parochial Vicar.
Res.: 250 21st St., 11215. Tel: 718-768-3751; Fax: 718-768-4689. Email: johnevangelist@verizon.net.
Catechesis/Religious Program—Students 89.

71—SAINT JOHN THE EVANGELIST-SAINT ROCCO ROMAN CATHOLIC CHURCH (2011) 250 21st St., 11215.

72—ST. JOHN'S CHAPEL, Closed. For inquiries for parish records please see Queen of all Saints Church.

73—ST. JOSEPH (1850) Rev. Msgr. Kieran E. Harrington, Admin.; Rev. Jorge Ortiz, Parochial Vicar; Bro. Vincenzo Cartilicchia.
Res.: 856 Pacific St., 11238. Tel: 718-783-4500; Fax: 718-398-2410. Email: kharrington@diobrook.org.
Catechesis/Religious Program—Students 69.

74—ST. JOSEPH PATRON OF THE UNIVERSAL CHURCH (1921), (Scalabrini Fathers) Rev. Jairo Ariel Alfonso, C.S., Parochial Vicar.
Res.: 185 Suydam St., 11221. Tel: 718-386-0175; Fax: 718-484-3176. Web: www.stjosephpatronny.com.
See St. Frances Cabrini Catholic Academy, Brooklyn under Consolidated Elementary Schools (Regional) located in the Institution section.
Catechesis/Religious Program—Students 597.

75—ST. JUDE SHRINE CHURCH (1961) Rev. Msgr. John Delendick; Sr. Mary Stievfater, Pastoral Assoc.
Res.: 1677 Canarsie Rd., 11236. Tel: 718-763-6300; Fax: 718-531-9655. Email: uncjed@aol.com.
See Our Lady of Trust School-St. Jude Campus, Brooklyn under Consolidated Elementary Schools (Regional) located in the Institution section
Catechesis/Religious Program—Tel: 718-241-4030. Ms. Helen Teifer, D.R.E. Students 145.

76—ST. LAURENCE (1964) Rev. Frank A. Black.
Res.: 1020 Van Siclen Ave., 11207. Tel: 718-649-0545; Fax: 718-649-1606. Email: st.laurence1020@gmail.com. Web: www.stlaurencercchurch.com.
Catechesis/Religious Program—Email: judinawilson@att.net. Ms. Judina Wilson, D.R.E. Students 68.

77—ST. LEONARD OF PORT MAURICE, Closed. 1978. Records at St. Joseph, Patron of the Universal Church.

78—ST. LOUIS, Closed. Became a Mission of St. Lucy in 1939. Parochial records are at St. Lucy-St. Patrick's, 285 Willoughby Ave., 11205. Tel: 718-622-8748; Fax: 718-622-6330.

79—ST. LUCY-ST. PATRICK (1843), Merged with Mary of Nazareth. Rev. Robert P. Vitaglione.
Res.: 285 Willoughby Ave., 11205. Tel: 718-625-5115; Fax: 718-625-2918.
Catechesis/Religious Program—Students 111.

80—ST. MALACHY (1854) Merged with Saint Michael the Archangel, Brooklyn to form Saint Michael-Saint Malachy, Brooklyn

81—ST. MARGARET MARY (1920) Rev. Joseph R. Grimaldi, Admin.
215 Exeter St., 11235-3725. Tel: 718-891-3100; Fax: 718-891-9677.

82—ST. MARK (1861) Revs. Joseph R. Grimaldi; Joseph Vella, Parochial Vicar; Christopher C. Turczany; Cyril F. Doody (Retired). In Res., Revs. Andrew Dunyo; Joseph P. Quigley (Retired).
Res.: 2609 E. 19th St., 11235. Tel: 718-891-3100; Fax: 718-891-9677. Email: stmarkrccbklyn@aol.com. Web: www.stmarkparish.org.
Church: Ocean Ave. & Ave. Z, 11235.
School—2602 E. 19th St., 11235. Tel: 718-332-9604; Fax: 718-332-3872. Email: stmarkschool9@hotmail.com. Web: www.stmarkschoolbklyn.org. Mrs. Caroline Donnelly, Prin. Religious 1; Lay Teachers 16; Students 278.
Catechesis/Religious Program—Tel: 718-769-6311. Joann Pino, D.R.E. Students 116.

83—SAINT MARTIN DE PORRES (2007) Rev. Msgr. Paul W. Jervis; Revs. Christopher L. Coleman; Caleb A.P. Buchanan, Parochial Vicar; Deacon Balfour A. Thompson.
Office: 583 Throop Ave., 11216. Email: stmartindeporresparish@gmail.com. Web: www.stmartindeporresparish.org.
Catechesis/Religious Program—Tel: 718-574-5772; Fax: 718-919-2265. Students 17.
Worship Sites:—
Our Lady of Victory—583 Throop Ave., 11216.
Holy Rosary—172 Bainbridge St., 11233.
St. Peter Claver—29 Peter Claver Pl., 11238.
Convent—Missionaries of Charity, 262 Macon St., 11216.
Convent—Daughters of Divine Love

84—ST. MARTIN OF TOURS-OUR LADY OF LOURDES (1906), (1872) Rev. John Jaime Tobon; Deacon Pedro V. Leon, Pastoral Assoc.
Res.: 1288 Hancock St., 11221. Tel: 718-443-8484; Fax: 718-443-2968. Web: www.stmartinbrooklyn.parishesonline.com.
Catechesis/Religious Program— Held at St. Elizabeth Seton School (751 Knickerbocker Ave., Brooklyn, NY 11221). Students 400.
Chapel—Our Lady of Lourdes Chapel 89 Furman Ave., 11207.

85—ST. MARY MOTHER OF JESUS (1889) Rev. Msgr. Andrew J. Vaccari; Rev. Robert V. Mucci, Parochial Vicar; Deacon Bryan Amore. In Res., Rev. Benjamin Elias.
Res.: 2326 84th St., 11214. Tel: 718-372-4000; Fax: 718-372-4002. Email: smmj@broadviewnet.net. Web: www.smmjparishesonline.com.
See St. Mary Mother of Jesus-St. Frances Cabrini Academy, Brooklyn under Consolidated Elementary Schools (Regional) located in the Institution section.
Catechesis/Religious Program—Tel: 718-449-8263; Fax: 718-265-6209. Mrs. Maria Beyra, D.R.E. Students 187.

86—MARY MOTHER OF THE CHURCH (2007) Revs. Jose A. Orellana, I.V.E.; Elio Sosa, Parochial Vicar; Deacon Rafael Marte.
Church: *St. Gabriel the Archangel*, 749 Linwood St., 11208. Tel: 718-257-0612; Fax: 718-257-5258. Email: joseagustinorellana@ive.org. Web: www.marymotherofthechurch.us.
Catechesis/Religious Program—666 Essex St., 11208. Tel: 718-649-0450; Fax: 718-649-0450. Angelus Crowell, D.R.E. Students 225.
Worship Site: *St. John Cantius*, 479 New Jersey Ave., 11207. Tel: 718-342-2679; Fax: 718-342-4878. Email: jcantius@aol.com.

87—MARY OF NAZARETH (2008), Merged with St. Lucy-St. Patrick. Rev. Robert P. Vitaglione.
Res & Office: 41 Adelphia St., 11205. Tel: 718-625-5115; Fax: 718-625-2918.
Worship Sites:—
Sacred Heart—41 Adelphi St., 11205.
St. Edward—108 St. Edward's St., 11205.
Catechesis/Religious Program—Students 126.

88—ST. MARY OF THE ANGELS, (Lithuanian), Closed. For inquiries for parish records contact the chancery.

89—MARY QUEEN OF HEAVEN (1927) Rev. Msgr. Jamie J. Gigantiello; Rev. Ilyas Gill, O.F.M. (Pakistan); Sr. Joan J. Holmberg, S.C., Pastoral Assoc.; Deacon Jean Baptiste Boursiquot. In Res., Rev. Msgr. John A. Burns, Pastor Emeritus (Retired).
Res.: 1395 E. 56th St., 11234. Tel: 718-763-2330; Fax: 718-763-6592. Email: mqhchurch@aol.com. Web: www.mqhchurch.net.
School—1326 E. 57th St., 11234. Tel: 718-763-2360; Fax: 718-763-7540. Email: mqhsec@optonline.net. Sr. Donna Murphy, O.P., Prin. Lay Teachers 11; Students 322.
Catechesis/Religious Program—Tel: 718-763-2590. Mary Casatelli, D.R.E. Students 142.
Convent—Sisters of St. Dominic, 1304 E. 57th St., 11234. Tel: 718-891-7451.

90—ST. MARY STAR OF THE SEA (1851) Rev. Christopher T. Cashman.
Res.: 467 Court St., 11231. Tel: 718-625-2270; Fax: 718-624-9017. Email: smss1851@aol.com.
Catechesis/Religious Program—Tel: 718-625-1717. Students 12.

91—ST. MATTHEW (1886) Revs. Andrew L. Struzzieri; Victor O. Ubaka, Parochial Vicar; Deacons Florencio Cruz; Dennis A. DaCosta; James J. Lacy; Mickey Cutter. In Res., Rev. Saint-Martin Estiverne.
Res.: 1123 Eastern Pkwy., 11213. Tel: 718-774-6747; Fax: 718-953-4895. Email: stmatthew1123@aol.com. Web: www.stmatthewromancatholicchurch.org.
Catechesis/Religious Program—1351 Lincoln Pl., 11213. Steven J. Horka, D.R.E. Students 379.

92—ST. MICHAEL (1860) Merged with Saint Malachy, Brooklyn to form Saint Michael-Saint Malachy, Brooklyn

93—ST. MICHAEL ARCHANGEL AND ST. EDWARD THE CONFESSOR (1891) Merged with Sacred Heart to form Mary of Nazareth, Brooklyn.

94—ST. MICHAEL - SAINT MALACHY (2007) Rev. Pablo Ruani; Deacon Carlos Garcia.
Church: *St. Michael*, 284 Warwick St., 11207. Fax: 718-647-2384. Email: stmichael284@yahoo.com.
Res.: 225 Jerome St., 11207. Tel: 718-647-1818.
Catechesis/Religious Program—Sr. Maria Virgo Offerens, D.R.E. Students 258.
Convent—129 Van Siclen Ave., 11207. Tel: 718-647-2751.

95—ST. MICHAEL (1870) Revs. Kevin J. Sweeney; Manuel Rodriguez; Stephen P. Lynch, Parochial Vicar; Deacons Julio C. Mejia; Hector S. Blanco. In Res., Rev. Msgr. Youssef Bochra Nasri.
Res.: 352 42nd St., 11232. Tel: 718-768-6065; Fax: 718-768-3336. Email: stmichaelarc42@verizon.net. Web: www.stmichaelssunsetpark.com.
Catechesis/Religious Program—Tel: 718-788-3442. Ines Cordero, D.R.E. Students 370.

96—MOST HOLY TRINITY - SAINT MARY (1841) Revs. Santo Cricchio, O.F.M.Conv.; Timothy Dore, O.F.M-.Conv.; Dariusz Barna, O.F.M.Conv. (Poland).
Res.: 138 Montrose Ave., 11206. Tel: 718-384-0215; Fax: 718-384-3030. Email: mhtbrooklyn@yahoo.com. Web: www.mhtbrooklyn.org.
Catechesis/Religious Program—Tel: 718-486-6276. Sr. Karen Landermenn, O.P., D.R.E. Students 175.

97—MOST PRECIOUS BLOOD (1927) Rev. Msgr. Joseph Rosa; Revs. John Maduri; Joseph Attard, Parochial Vicar.
Res.: 70 Bay 47th St., 11214. Tel: 718-372-8022; Fax: 718-996-6575. Email: mpb11214@aol.com.
Catechesis/Religious Program—Rosemarie Paccione, D.R.E. Students 50.

98—NATIVITY OF OUR BLESSED LORD, Merged with St. Peter Claver in 1973. Records at St. Peter Claver Church.

99—ST. NICHOLAS (1865), Merged with St. Francis of Paola, Brooklyn & St. Cecilia, Brooklyn to form Divine Mercy Roman Catholic Church, Brooklyn. Rev. Kenneth J. Grande.
Res.: 26 Olive St., 11211. Tel: 718-388-1420; Fax: 718-388-9516. Email: stnicholasrcc@msn.com.
Catechesis/Religious Program—Amilia Castro, C.R.E. Students 93.
Convent—312 De Voe St., 11211.

100—OUR LADY HELP OF CHRISTIANS (1927) Revs. Peter J. Rayder; Joey Francisco, Parochial Vicar; Deacon Michael J. Troy. In Res., Rev. Msgr. John J. Bracken; Bro. James Smith.
Res.: 1315 E. 28th St., 11210. Tel: 718-338-5242; Fax: 718-258-5341. Email: olhcbrooklyn@gmail.com. Web: www.olhcbrooklyn.org.
See Midwood Catholic Academy, Brooklyn under Consolidated Elementary Schools (Regional) in the Institution Section.
Catechesis/Religious Program—Tel: 718-377-6932. Stephen T. Rzonca, D.R.E. Students 68.

101—OUR LADY OF ANGELS (1891) Rev. Msgr. Kevin B. Noone; Revs. Richard Lewkiewicz, Parochial Vicar; Rodnev Lapommeray, Parochial Vicar; Deacons Ed Gaine; Charles R. Hurley; Gloria Florez, Pastoral Assoc. In Res., Revs. Arputham Arulsamy; Kenneth J. Calder (Retired).
Res.: 7320 Fourth Ave., 11209. Tel: 718-836-7200; Fax: 718-238-2466. Email: ola.bayridge@verizon.net. Web: www.ourladyofangelsparish.org.
Catechesis/Religious Program—Tel: 718-748-6553. Ann O'Brien, D.R.E. Students 225.

102—OUR LADY OF CHARITY (1903), (African American), Merged with St. Matthew, Brooklyn. For inquiries for parish records please see St. Matthew, Brooklyn.

103—OUR LADY OF CONSOLATION (1909), (Polish), Revs. Wlodzimierz R. Las, S.D.S. (Poland); Ludwik Kolodziej, Parochial Vicar; Andrzej Kujawa, S.D.S, Parochial Vicar.
Res.: 184 Metropolitan Ave., 11211. Tel: 718-388-1942; Fax: 718-388-8993. Email: olconsolation@verizon.net. Web: www.mbpbrooklyn.com.
Catechesis/Religious Program—Students 142.

104—OUR LADY OF CZESTOCHOWA-ST. CASIMIR (1896), (Polish), Revs. Witold Mroziewski; Thomas Shepanzyk, Parochial Vicar.
Res.: 183 25th St., 11232. Tel: 718-768-5724; Fax: 718-768-4996. Email: parishoffice@olcsc.org.
Catechesis/Religious Program—Students 283.

105—OUR LADY OF GOOD COUNSEL (1886) Merged with St. John the Baptist, Brooklyn. For inquiries for parish records please see St. John the Baptist, Brooklyn.

106—OUR LADY OF GRACE (1935), (Italian), Revs. Thomas F. Leach; Edward A. Cassar, Parochial Vicar; Deacon Philip Siani. In Res., Rev. Dominick

F. Cutrone, Pastor Emeritus (Retired).
Res.: 430 Avenue W, 11223. Tel: 718-627-2020; Fax: 718-336-8033. Email: tfjl430@aol.com. Web: www.ologchurch.com.
School—385 Avenue W, 11223. Tel: 718-375-2081; Fax: 718-376-7685. Email: olgie385@aol.com. Mrs. Joan McMaster, Prin. Lay Teachers 13; Students 289.
Catechesis/Religious Program—Tel: 718-375-0404. Phyllis Niwinski, D.R.E. Students 135.

107—OUR LADY OF GUADALUPE (1906), (Italian—Spanish), Rev. Msgr. Robert Romano; Revs. Thomas R. Gilbert, Parochial Vicar; Andrew Kofi Soley, Prochial Vicar; Deacon John J. LaGreca.
Res.: 7201 Fifteenth Ave., 11228. Tel: 718-236-8300; Fax: 718-236-8119. Email: olguadalupebulletin@yahoo.om.
School—1518 73rd St., 11228. Tel: 718-236-5587; Fax: 718-236-5587. Ms. Diana C. Meringolo, Prin. Lay Teachers 19; Students 285.
Catechesis/Religious Program—Tel: 718-331-4003. Students 174.

108—OUR LADY OF LORETO (1894) Merged with Our Lady of the Presentation.

109—OUR LADY OF LOURDES (1872) Merged with St. Martin of Tours, Brooklyn. For inquiries for parish records please see St. Martin of Tours, Brooklyn.

110—OUR LADY OF MERCY (1961), Merged with Our Lady of the Presentation-Our Lady of Loreto, Brooklyn to form Our Lady of the Presentation-Our Lady of Mercy Roman Catholic Church, Brooklyn. Rev. Edward J. Mason; Sr. Bernadette M. Sassone, Pastoral Assoc.; Deacons Victorino Ellgio; Fabio E. Tavarez.
Office: 680 Mother Gaston Blvd., 11212. Tel: 718-346-3166; Fax: 718-346-5776. Email: jjgildea@verizon.net.
Catechesis/Religious Program—Sr. Bernadette M. Sassone, D.R.E. Students 150.

111—OUR LADY OF MERCY, Closed. in 1908. Second church at Schermerhorn & Bond closed April, Debevoise Place & DeKalb Ave. For inquiries for parish records contact the chancery.

112—OUR LADY OF MIRACLES (1936) Revs. Gerald Dumont; Calonge Lemaine; Deacon Ernst Paul; Patrick David, Music Dir.
Res.: 757 E. 86th St., 11236. Tel: 718-257-2400; Fax: 718-257-4634. Email: kawolv@hotmail.com.
See Our Lady of Trust School at Our Lady of Miracles Campus, Brooklyn under Consolidated Elementary Schools (Regional) located in the Institution section.
Catechesis/Religious Program—Tel: 718-649-1006. Sr. Doryne M. Bermoy, F.L.P., D.R.E. Students 125.

113—OUR LADY OF MONSERRATE-ST. AMBROSE (1954) Merged with All Saints, Brooklyn.

114—OUR LADY OF MOUNT CARMEL SHRINE CHURCH (1887), (Italian), Rev. Msgr. Joseph P. Calise; Rev. Michael Lynch, Parochial Vicar; Deacon Edward F. O'Connell; Giuditta Coccia, A.O., Pastoral Assoc. & Italian Apostolate. In Res., Rev. Msgr. Thomas M. Haggerty (Retired).
Res.: 275 N. Eighth St., 11211. Tel: 718-384-0223; Fax: 718-384-5838. Email: olmcn8th@yahoo.com. Web: www.olmcfeast.com.
Catechesis/Religious Program—Rosemarie Walsh, D.R.E. Students 132.

115—OUR LADY OF PEACE (1899), (Italian), Revs. Patrick D. Boyle; Orlando Ruiz, Parochial Vicar.
Res.: 522 Carroll St., 11215. Tel: 718-624-5122; Fax: 718-852-6149. Email: olp1899@aol.com.
Catechesis/Religious Program— Lillian Flores, D.R.E. Students 115.
Convent—Hermanas Franciscanas de la Immaculada, 209 First St., 11215. Tel: 718-624-6720; Fax: 718-625-7657.

116—OUR LADY OF PERPETUAL HELP BASILICA (1893) Revs. Joseph Tizio, C.Ss.R.; Norman S. Bennett, C.Ss.R.; Peter Cao, C.Ss.R. (Vietnam); Luis A. Caro, C.Ss.R. (Chile); Ruskin Piedra, C.Ss.R.; Pierce Kenny, C.Ss.R.; Charles McDonald; John McKenna; Sr. Lucille Aliperti, C.S.J., Dir. Adult Faith Formation; Deacons Abdon Mejia (Peru), Pastoral Assoc.; Jesus Soto. In Res., Revs. John Gauci, C.Ss.R.; Thomas F. Hickey, C.Ss.R.; John J. Travers, C.Ss.R.
Res.: 526-59th St., 11220. Tel: 718-492-9200; Fax: 718-439-8528. Email: jctizio@aol.com. Web: www.olphbklyn.org.
School—5902 6th Ave., 11220. Tel: 718-492-8067; Fax: 718-439-8081. Mr. Vincent Tannacore, Prin. Religious 1; Lay Teachers 14; Students 243.
Catechesis/Religious Program—Tel: 718-439-4795. Maritza Mejia, D.R.E. Students 545.

117—OUR LADY OF REFUGE (1911) Revs. Michael A. Perry; Rony Mendes, Parochial Vicar; Sr. Sylvia J. Obrigewitsch, Pastoral Assoc.
Res.: 2020 Foster Ave., 11210. Tel: 718-434-2090; Fax: 718-859-7411. Email: olrefuge@aol.com.
Catechesis/Religious Program—Jennifer Baptiste, D.R.E. Students 174.

118—OUR LADY OF SOLACE (1900) Revs. Patrick J. West; Giovani Romero Bermudez, Parochial Vicar.
Res.: 2866 W. 17th St., 11224. Tel: 718-266-1612; Fax: 718-946-3651. Email: frpatrickwest@olsbrooklyn.com. Web: www.olsbrooklyn.com.
Catechesis/Religious Program—Email: rec@olsbrooklyn.com. Mr. Augusto Lucero, D.R.E. Students 297.

119—OUR LADY OF SORROWS, Merged with St. Leonard in 1942. Parochial records are at St. Joseph Patron of the Universal Church.

120—OUR LADY OF THE PRESENTATION-OUR LADY OF MERCY ROMAN CATHOLIC CHURCH (2011) 1677 St. Marks Ave., 11233.

121—OUR LADY OF THE PRESENTATION-OUR LADY OF LORETO (1887), (African American—Hispanic), Merged with Our Lady of Mercy, Brooklyn to form Our Lady of the Presentation-Our Lady of Mercy Roman Catholic Church, Brooklyn. Revs. James H. Sweeney; Edward J. Mason; Deacons Jaime Varela; Ricardo Reyes.
Res.: 1677 St. Marks Ave., 11233-4813. Tel: 718-345-2604; Fax: 718-345-4639. Email: olpres@optimum.net.
Additional Worship Site:—
Our Lady of Loreto—Church: 124 Sackman St., 11233.
Catechesis/Religious Program—Students 93.

122—OUR LADY OF THE ROSARY OF POMPEII (1900), (Hispanic), Revs. Frank Amato, S.A.C.; Carlos A. Cardoso, Parochial Vicar; Bernard Carman.
Res.: 225 Seigel St., 11206. Tel: 718-497-0614; Fax: 718-366-3236. Email: olopompeii@hotmail.com.
Catechesis/Religious Program—Students 83.

123—OUR LADY OF VICTORY (1868) Merged with Holy Rosary & St. Peter Claver, Brooklyn to form Saint Martin de Porres, Brooklyn

124—ST. PATRICK (1849) Rev. Msgr. Joseph P. Nagle; Revs. Mark Simmons, Parochial Vicar; Anthony Banye; Andre Bain, Parochial Vicar; James Massa; Deacon John E. Hull; Sr. Jeanne Elaine Matullo, O.P., Pastoral Assoc.
Res.: 9511 Fourth Ave., 11209. Tel: 718-238-2600; Fax: 718-238-1508. Email: parish@stpatrickbayridge.org. Web: www.stpatrickbayridge.org.
School—401 97th St., 11209. Tel: 718-833-0124; Fax: 718-238-6840. Mrs. Andrea D'Emic, Prin. Lay Teachers 21; Students 269.
Catechesis/Religious Program—Miss Nicole Marie Fiore, D.R.E. Tel: 718-238-2600, Ext. 104. Students 446.

125—ST. PATRICK'S, Merged with St. Lucy's in 1974. Records at St. Lucy-St. Patrick's.

126—SAINT PAUL AND SAINT AGNES ROMAN CATHOLIC CHURCH (2007) Rev. Robert M. Powers, Admin.; Deacons Jaime Cobham; Louis Gonzalez; Leroy P. Branch; Sr. Innocencia Lipari, Pastoral Assoc.
Tel: 718-625-1717; Fax: 718-625-1929. Email: peterpaulagnes@aol.com.
Worship Sites:—
St. Agnes—433 Sackett St., 11231.
St. Paul—234 Congress St., 11201.
Catechesis/Religious Program—William Gorman, D.R.E. Students 70.

127—SS. PETER AND PAUL (1843) Rev. Manuel de Jesus Rodriguez; Deacon Juan Carattini.
Church: 82 S. 2nd St., 11211.
Res.: 71 S. Third St., 11211. Tel: 718-388-9576; Fax: 718-388-0714. Email: saintspeterandpaul@gmail.com.
Additional Worship Site:—
Epiphany—Church: 96 S. 9th St., 11211.
Catechesis/Religious Program—Tel: 718-387-1041. Sr. Jesus Maria Doliente, S.S.V.M., D.R.E. Students 340.

128—ST. PETER CLAVER (1921) Merged with Our Lady of Victory & Holy Rosary, Brooklyn to form Saint Martin de Porres, Brooklyn

129—ST. PETER-ST. PAUL-OUR LADY OF PILAR (1836) Merged with Saint Agnes, Brooklyn to form Saint Paul and Saint Agnes, Brooklyn

130—QUEEN OF ALL SAINTS (1879) Rev. Joseph A. Ceriello. In Res., Most Rev. Joseph M. Sullivan (Retired).
Res.: 300 Vanderbilt Ave., 11205. Tel: 718-638-7625; 718-638-7626; Fax: 718-638-7393. Email: office@qasrcc.org. Web: www.qasrcc.org.
School—300 Vanderbilt Ave., 11205. Tel: 718-857-3114; Fax: 718-857-0632. Theresa Attianese, Prin. Lay Teachers 16; Students 210.
Catechesis/Religious Program—Ralphetta Johnson-Moses, D.R.E. Students 90.

131—REGINA PACIS VOTIVE SHRINE (1951), For personnel see St. Rosalia., 1230 65th St., 11219. Tel: 718-236-0909; Fax: 718-236-5357. Email: rosalia1230@aol.com.

132—RESURRECTION (1924) Revs. Dennis J. Farrell; Edwin Okey Nwabugwu, Parochial Vicar.
Res.: 2331 Gerritsen Ave., 11229. Tel: 718-743-7234; 718-743-7235; Fax: 718-743-0152. Email: revdj43@aol.com. Web: www.resurrectionrcchurch.com.
Catechesis/Religious Program—2335 Gerritsen Ave., 11229. Tel: 718-891-0888. Mrs. Angela Parente, D.R.E. Students 205.

133—RESURRECTION CATHOLIC COPTIC CHAPEL (1985) Rev. Msgr. Youssef Bochra Nasri, (Coptic Catholic Patriarchate).
Mailing Address: 352 42nd St., 11232. Tel: 718-965-0422; Fax: 718-768-3336.
Church: 328 14th St., 11215. Tel: 718-499-6946.

134—ST. RITA (1913), (Spanish), Rev. Luis Fernando Laverde Saldarriaga (Colombia), Admin.; Deacons Felix Mejia; Ronald Ronacher; Andy Rosa.
Res.: 275 Shepherd Ave., 11208. Tel: 718-647-4910; Fax: 718-827-2767. Email: strita275@hotmail.com.
Catechesis/Religious Program—Mrs. Annemarie Ronacher, D.R.E. Students 174.

135—ST. ROCCO (1902), Merged with St. John the Evangelist, Brooklyn to form Saint John the Evangelist-Saint Rocco Roman Catholic Church, Brooklyn. Rev. Msgr. Faustino Cordero.
Res.: 216 27th St., 11232. Tel: 718-768-9798; Fax: 718-768-7742. Email: strcchurch@aol.com. Web: www.saintroccochurch.com.
Catechesis/Religious Program— Karen Salinas-Reyes, D.R.E. Students 132.

136—ST. ROSALIA-REGINA PACIS (1904) Rev. Msgr. Ronald T. Marino; Revs. Vincentius Toan Do, Parochial Vicar; John J. Granados, Parochial Vicar; Sr. Anna O'Brien, Pastoral Assoc.; Deacons Ramon C. Pons; John J. Dolan.
Res.: 1230 65th St., 11219. Tel: 718-236-0909; Fax: 718-236-5357. Email: reginarectory@aol.com. Web: www.reginarectory.com.
Regina Center, Inc.—1258 65th St., 11219. Tel: 718-232-4340.
Catechesis/Religious Program—Tel: 718-236-0909, Ext. 40. Elizabeth Mathew, D.R.E. Students 196.
Mission—Regina Pacis Votive Shrine, Kings Co.

137—ST. ROSE OF LIMA (1870) Revs. Lukasz Pawel Trocha; Jose Lopez, Parochial Vicar.
Res.: 269 Parkville Ave., 11230. Tel: 718-434-8040; Fax: 718-421-4223. Email: stroseoflimabkln@aol.com. Web: www.stroseoflimabrooklyn.org.
Catechesis/Religious Program—Sr. Maureen Sullivan, C.S.J., D.R.E. Students 119.
Convent—Sisters of St. Joseph, 250 Newkirk Ave., 11230. Tel: 718-859-5722.

138—SACRED HEART (1871) Merged with St. Michael Archangel and St. Edward the Confessor to form Mary of Nazareth, Brooklyn.

139—SACRED HEART CHAPEL (1996) Closed. For inquiries for parish records contact the Chancery.

140—SACRED HEART MISSION (1942) Closed. For inquiries for parish records contact the Chancery.

141—SACRED HEARTS OF JESUS AND MARY AND ST. STEPHEN (1866), (Italian), Revs. Anthony J. Sansone; Antonio Camora.
Res.: 108 Carroll St., 11231. Tel: 718-596-7750; Fax: 718-260-9233. Email: anthonyjajs22550@aol.com.
Church: Summit & Hicks Sts., 11231.
Catechesis/Religious Program—Tel: 718-596-0880. Sr. Rosalind Picciano, C.S.J., D.R.E. Students 115.

142—ST. SAVIOUR (1905) Revs. Daniel S. Murphy; Timothy P. Tighe, C.S.P., Parochial Vicar; John P. Cush, Parochial Vicar; Deacon William Williamsen. In Res., Rev. Robert Frueh.
Res.: 611 Eighth Ave., 11215. Tel: 718-768-4055; 718-768-7983; Fax: 718-768-4872. Email: stsaviourchurch@aol.com. Web: www.saintsaviourchurch.org.
School—701 Eighth Ave., 11215. Tel: 718-768-8000. Ms. Maura Lorenzen, Prin. Sisters 1; Lay Teachers 27; Students 401.
High School—588 Sixth St., 11215. Tel: 718-768-4406; Fax: 718-369-2688. Sr. Valeria Belanger, S.S.N.D., Prin. Students 358.
Catechesis/Religious Program—Tel: 718-768-4055; Fax: 718-768-4872. Ms. Sue Walsh, D.R.E. Students 178.
Convent—590 6th St., 11215.

143—SS. SIMON AND JUDE (1897) Revs. Gregory A. Stankus; Arthur G. Minichello, Parochial Vicar; Sr. Ann Elizabeth DiLiberti, O.P., Pastoral Assoc.; Deacon Carlo Mellace, Parish Life Coord.
Res.: 185 Van Sicklen St., 11223. Tel: 718-375-9600; Fax: 718-375-6642. Email: rectoryssj@optonline.net.
Catechesis/Religious Program—294 Avenue T, 11223. Tel: 718-372-0733. Email: rel.ed@stsimonandjude.org. Sara Nespoli, D.R.E. Students 153.

144—ST. STANISLAUS KOSTKA (1896), (Polish), Revs. Marek W. Sobczak, C.M.; Jan Urbaniak, C.M., Parochial Vicar; Jaroslaw Robert Lawrenz, C.M., Parochial Vicar; Jan Szylar, C.M., Parochial Vicar; Joseph Szpilski, C.M., Parochial Vicar.
Res.: 607 Humboldt St., 11222. Tel: 718-388-0170;

Fax: 718-384-5290. Email: ststankc@nyc.rr.com. Web: www.ststanskostka.org.
Catechesis/Religious Program—Tel: 718-388-0170. Krzysztof Gospodarzec, D.R.E. Students 351.

145—ST. STANISLAUS MARTYR, Merged with Holy Family (14th St.) in 1979. Records at Holy Family, 14th St., between Sixth and Seventh Aves.

146—ST. STEPHEN, Merged with Sacred Hearts in 1941. Parochial records are at Sacred Hearts-St. Stephen Church, Carroll St.

147—ST. SYLVESTER (1923) Revs. Anthony F. Raso; James L. Hughes; Deacon Jose L. Oviedo.
Res.: 416 Grant Ave., 11208. Tel: 718-647-1995; Fax: 718-348-4035.
Catechesis/Religious Program— Carmen Perez, D.R.E. Students 133.

148—ST. TERESA OF AVILA (1874) Revs. Saint Charles Borno; Anthony Bature (Nigeria).
Res.: 563 Sterling Pl., 11238. Tel: 718-622-6500; Fax: 718-622-2234. Email: stteresaofavilobrooklyn@gmail.com. Web: www.stteresaofavilobrooklyn.org.
Catechesis/Religious Program—Students 56.

149—ST. THERESE OF LISIEUX (1926), (The Little Flower) Revs. Hilaire Belizaire; Joseph Bruno, Parochial Vicar; Deacon Jocelyn Rameau.
Res.: 1281 Troy Ave., 11203. Tel: 718-451-1500; Fax: 718-451-1502. Email: stthereselis@aol.com. Web: www.sttherеselisieux.org.
Catechesis/Religious Program—Tel: 718-451-1671; Fax: 718-451-1671. Frances McCormick, D.R.E. Students 100.

150—ST. THOMAS AQUINAS (1884) Merged with Holy Family to become Holy Family-St. Thomas Aquinas. For inquiries and parish records see Holy Family-St. Thomas Aquinas.

151—ST. THOMAS AQUINAS (1885) Revs. Thomas V. Doyle; Antonius P. Gopaul, Parochial Vicar; Sr. Theresa Agliardi, R.S.M., Pastoral Assoc. In Res., Rev. Msgr. Austin P. Bennett (Retired).
Res.: 1550 Hendrickson St., 11234. Tel: 718-253-4404. Email: tvdbrook@aol.com.
Catechesis/Religious Program—Tel: 718-253-4404, Ext. 31; Fax: 718-338-7757. Kevin McCuthcan, D.R.E. Students 191.

152—TRANSFIGURATION (1874) Rev. Msgr. Anthony Hernandez; Deacons Israel Rosario; German Martinez.
Res.: 263 Marcy Ave., 11211. Tel: 718-388-8773; Fax: 718-388-8774. Email: amnl968@gmail.com. Web: www.transfigurationrcc.org.
Catechesis/Religious Program—Sr. Maryann Ricioppo, D.R.E. Students 127.
Southside Mission for Social Services—280 Marcy Ave., 11211. Tel: 718-388-3784. John Mulhern, Dir.

153—ST. VINCENT DE PAUL, Closed. For inquiries for parish records contact the chancery.

154—ST. VINCENT FERRER (1923) Rev. Msgr. Joseph A. Nugent; Deacon Mauclair Simon.
Res.: 1603 Brooklyn Ave., 11210-3495. Tel: 718-859-0041; 718-859-9009; Fax: 718-859-9032. Email: saintferrer@aol.com.
Church: E. 37th St. & Glenwood Rd., 11210.
Catechesis/Religious Program—Students 80.

155—VISITATION OF THE BLESSED VIRGIN MARY (1854) Revs. Claudio Antecini; Johannes S.A.G. Siegert, Parochial Vicar; Sr. Frauke Tinat, Pastoral Assoc.; Deacon Emon G. Murray. In Res., Bros. Giovanni Sveglati; Matej Kurbei; Marcelo Melgar; Martin Aguilar Cano.
Res.: 98 Richards St., 11231. Tel: 718-624-1572; Fax: 718-722-7748. Email: visitationbvm1854@gmail.com.
Catechesis/Religious Program—Sylvia Dobles, D.R.E.

*BOROUGH AND COUNTY OF QUEENS

1—ST. ADALBERT (1892), (Polish), Revs. Russell Governale, O.F.M.Conv.; Herman Czaster, O.F.M.Conv., Parochial Vicar.
Res.: 52-29 83rd St., Elmhurst, 11373. Tel: 718-639-0212; Fax: 718-651-1705.
School—52-17 83rd St., Elmhurst, 11373. Tel: 718-424-2376; Fax: 718-639-0465. Sr. Kathleen Maciej, C.S.F.N., Prin. Sisters 3; Lay Teachers 24; Students 395.
Catechesis/Religious Program—Tel: 718-565-8227. Mary Anne Page, D.R.E. Students 129.
Office for Pastoral Care of the Sick—

2—ST. ALOYSIUS (1892) Revs. George Poltorek, S.A.C.; Marek Rudecki, S.A.C., Parochial Vicar; Gizela Sterbenz, Sec.
Res.: 382 Onderdonk Ave., Ridgewood, 11385. Tel: 718-821-0231; Fax: 718-628-7304. Email: saloysius@nyc.rr.com.
Catechesis/Religious Program—Tel: 718-417-6327. Students 415.
Pastoral Care Office—Tel: 718-963-7689.

3—AMERICAN MARTYRS (1948) Rev. Frank L. Schwarz; Deacon Stanley J. Galazin. In Res., Rev. William F. Sweeney.
Res.: 79-43 Bell Blvd., Oakland Gardens, 11364. Tel: 718-464-4582; Fax: 718-464-5488. Email: americanmartyrs@aol.com.
Catechesis/Religious Program—Tel: 718-464-6411. Ms. Susan Templin, D.R.E. Students 165.

4—ST. ANASTASIA (1915) Rev. Msgrs. George J. Ryan; Anthony F. Sherman, Parochial Vicar. In Res., Rev. Matteo Rizzo.
Res.: 45-14 245th St., Douglaston, 11362. Tel: 718-631-4454; Fax: 718-631-1774. Email: info@stanastasia.info. Web: www.stanastasia.info.
Catechesis/Religious Program—Tel: 718-225-5191. Janine Kramer, D.R.E. Students 259.

5—ST. ANDREW AVELLINO (1914) Rev. Joseph T. Holcomb; Rev. Msgr. Michael J. Brennan, Parochial Vicar; Deacon George Borbeau. In Res., Revs. Matthew J. Diamond (Retired); Wilfred F. Dewan, C.S.P. (Retired).
Res.: 35-60 158th St., Flushing, 11358. Tel: 718-359-0417; Fax: 718-539-2830.
School—35-50 158th St., Flushing, 11358. Tel: 718-359-7887; Fax: 718-359-2295. Debora A. Hanna, Prin. Lay Teachers 21; Students 303.
Catechesis/Religious Program—Tel: 718-445-7012. Mrs. Maria Tortorella, D.R.E. Students 261.

6—ST. ANN (1927) Revs. Edward M. Kachurka; Samuel Ebulley Afful (Ghana), Parochial Vicar; Deacon Salvatore V. Licata. In Res., Rev. George A. Pfundstein (Retired).
Res.: 142-30 58th Ave., Flushing, 11355-5314. Tel: 718-886-3890; Fax: 718-358-4964. Email: stannrcc1@aol.com. Web: www.stannflushing.4lpi.com.
Catechesis/Religious Program—142-25 58th Rd., Flushing, 11355. Tel: 718-359-8019. Sr. Patricia A. Anglin, O.P., D.R.E. Students 61.

7—ST. ANTHONY OF PADUA (1937) Revs. William A. Smith; Christopher Ezeoke, Parochial Vicar; Deacons Ruben G. Siavichay; Patrick M. Flanagan.
Res.: 133-25 128th St., South Ozone Park, 11420-3303. Tel: 718-843-7410; 718-843-3356; Fax: 718-659-1478. Email: stanthonyofpaduaqueens@gmail.com.
Catechesis/Religious Program—Mr. Mark Kruse, D.R.E. Students 63.

8—ASCENSION (1945) Revs. Jovito B. Carongay Jr.; Kyrian C. Echekwu, Parochial Vicar; Peter Chici Osuagwa, Parochial Vicar; Martin Egubuogu, Parochial Vicar.
Res.: 86-13 55th Ave., Elmhurst, 11373. Tel: 718-335-2626; Fax: 718-335-4181. Email: ascensionrc@aol.com. Web: www.churchoftheascension.org.
Catechesis/Religious Program—Maria Gallo, D.R.E. Students 160.

9—ST. BARTHOLOMEW (1906) Revs. Richard J. Beuther; John J. Gildea, Parochial Vicar; Joyce Ellen Lubofsky, Pastoral Assoc.; Sr. Susan Sabol, C.S.J., Pastoral Assoc.; Deacon William Contreras.
Res.: 43-22 Ithaca St., Elmhurst, 11373. Tel: 718-424-5400; Fax: 718-899-5257. Email: stbartrcch@aol.com.
School—44-15 Judge St., Elmhurst, 11373. Tel: 718-446-7575. Jeannette Boursiquot-Charles, Prin. Lay Teachers 15; Students 262.
Catechesis/Religious Program—44-15 Judge St., Elmhurst, 11373. Tel: 718-898-0096. Joyce Ellen Lubofsky, D.R.E. Students 413.

10—ST. BENEDICT JOSEPH LABRE (1892), (Spanish), Revs. Philip J. Pizzo; Thomas Muthukatti (Retired); Deacon Manuel I. Martinez. In Res., Rev. Msgr. Cornelius T. Kneafsey (Retired).
Res.: 94-40 118th St., South Richmond Hill, 11419. Tel: 718-849-4048; Fax: 718-846-0732. Email: sbjl1892@nycrr.com.
Catechesis/Religious Program—Tel: 718-849-0246. Sr. Maria Rijpkema, D.R.E. Students 111.

11—ST. BENEDICT, THE MOOR (1932), (African American), Merged with St. Bonaventure to form St. Bonaventure-St. Benedict the Moor RC Church.

12—BLESSED SACRAMENT (1929) Rev. Patrick G. Burns.
Res.: 34-43 93rd St., Jackson Heights, 11372. Tel: 718-639-3888; Fax: 718-478-5536. Email: blessacjh@aol.com. Web: www.blessedsacramentjacksonheights.
Catechesis/Religious Program—93-15 35th Ave., Jackson Heights, 11372. Tel: 718-639-6159. Students 946.
Convent—93-11 35th Ave., Jackson Heights, 11372. Tel: 718-639-1545.

13—BLESSED TRINITY ROMAN CATHOLIC CHURCH (2008) Rev. Msgrs. Michael J. Curran; Ronald Newland, Senior Priest; Revs. Michael C. Gribbon, Parochial Vicar; Francis JoJo Obu-Mends, Parochial Vicar; Deacons Bernard M. Deschler; Richard G. Lee; James F. Ruoff; Sr. Mary Beata, Music Dir. In Res., Rev. John F. Cullinane, P.E., Senior Active Priest (Retired).
Res.: 204-25 Rockaway Point Blvd., Rockaway Point, 11697. Tel: 718-634-6357; Fax: 718-634-6222. Email: blessedtrin@aol.com. Web: www.parishofblessedtrinity.org.
Additional Worship Sites:—
St. Thomas More-St. Edmund—Church: 204-25 Rockaway Point Blvd., Rockaway Point, 11697.
St. Genevieve—Church: 6 Beach 178th St., Rockaway Point, 11697.
Catechesis/Religious Program—Suzanne O'Connor, D.R.E. Students 219.

14—BLESSED VIRGIN MARY, HELP OF CHRISTIANS (1854) Revs. Noel Moynihan, C.S.Sp.; Edmund Brendan Duggan, C.S.Sp., Parochial Vicar; Deacon Leopold Montes. In Res., Rev. Bohuo Seo.
Res.: 70-31 48th Ave., Woodside, 11377. Tel: 718-672-4848; Fax: 718-457-4055. Email: bvmwoodside11377@aol.com. Web: www.stmarysofwinfield.com.
Catechesis/Religious Program—Tel: 718-672-4784. Patricia Wise, D.R.E. Students 451.

15—ST. BONAVENTURE (1932) Merged with St. Benedict, the Moor to form St. Bonaventure-St. Benedict the Moor RC Church.

16—ST. BONAVENTURE-ST. BENEDICT THE MOOR RC CHURCH (2008) Revs. Gordon P. Kusi (Ghana); James Asare; Deacon Pascual Olivas.
Res.: 114-58 170th St., Jamaica, 11434. Tel: 718-526-0040; Fax: 718-526-4825. Email: sst.bonaventure-benedictthemoor@yahoo.com.
Catechesis/Religious Program—Mrs. Angela M. Lewis, D.R.E. Students 80.

17—SAINT CAMILLUS-SAINT VIRGILIUS (2008) Revs. Richard J. Ahlemeyer; James M. Dunne, Pastor Emeritus (Retired); Thomas Asante.
Res.: 99-15 Rockaway Beach Blvd., Rockaway Beach, 11694. Tel: 718-634-8229; Fax: 718-634-8193. Email: stcamstvirg@aol.com. Web: www.stcstv.com.
Additional Worship Site:—
St. Virgilius—Church: 210 Noel Rd., Broad Channel, 11693. Tel: 718-634-5680; Fax: 718-424-1538.
School—*St. Camillus*, 185 Beach 99th St., Rockaway Beach, 11694. Tel: 718-634-5260; Fax: 718-634-8253. Sr. Agnes White, C.S.J., Prin. Lay Teachers 12; Students 179.
Catechesis/Religious Program—Tel: 718-634-8229 (St. Camillus); 718-634-6237 (St. Virgilius). Sr. Mary Ann Kollmer, O.P., D.R.E. Students 207.

18—ST. CATHERINE OF SIENNA (1920) Merged with St. Pascal Baylon, to form Our Lady of Light Roman Catholic Church.

19—CHRIST THE KING (1933) Rev. Jeffry T. Dillon; Deacons Winston M. Mayers; Lamont A. Blake; Mary Doyle, Pastoral Assoc. In Res., Rev. Slawomir Sobiech.
Res.: 145-39 Farmers Blvd., Springfield Gardens, 11434. Tel: 718-528-6010; Fax: 718-949-3255. Email: christthekingsg@aol.com. Web: www.christthekingsg.org.
Catechesis/Religious Program—Tel: 718-528-6010. Email: mdoylectk@verizon.net. Mary Doyle, D.R.E. Students 94.

20—ST. CLARE (1924) Revs. Kevin F. McBrien; Alonzo Q. Cox, Parochial Vicar; Deacon Christopher E. Barber.
Res.: 137-35 Brookville Blvd., Rosedale, 11422. Tel: 718-341-1018; Fax: 718-276-2001. Email: stclareqns@aol.com. Web: www.stclareqns.com.
School—137-25 Brookville Blvd., Rosedale, 11422. Tel: 718-528-7174; Fax: 718-528-4389. Email: stclareschool@nyc.rr.com. Web: www.stclarerosedale.com. Mrs. Mary Rafferty-Basile, Prin. Sisters 1; Lay Teachers 16; Students 309.
Catechesis/Religious Program—Tel: 718-527-6153. Lorena DeFilippis, D.R.E. Students 185.

21—ST. CLEMENT POPE (1908) Revs. Jeffry T. Dillon; Michael S. Udoh, Parochial Vicar; Bro. Dennis Wermert, S.C., Pastoral Assoc.; Deacon Nathaniel J. Smith.
Res.: 141-11 123rd Ave., South Ozone Park, 11436. Tel: 718-529-0273; Fax: 718-529-3089.
Catechesis/Religious Program—120-09 141st St., Jamaica, 11436. Tel: 718-641-1915; Fax: 718-738-0588. Sr. Patience Quayson, D.R.E. Students 46.

22—CORPUS CHRISTI (1937) Revs. Peter D. Gillen; Jose Francisco Herrera; Alex L. Ramos, Parochial Vicar; Deacon Juan J. Zhagnay; Mr. Paul Canestro, Pastoral Assoc. In Res., Rev. John O'Neill, I.V.Dei.
Res.: 31-30 61st St., Woodside, 11377. Tel: 718-278-8114; Fax: 718-278-3619. Email: c.corpuschristi@verizon.net.
School—31-29 60th St., Woodside, 11377. Tel: 718-721-2484; Fax: 718-721-4579. Email: ccsprincipal01@nsm.com. Mr. Robert Dinardo, Prin. Lay Teachers 15; Students 174.
Catechesis/Religious Program—Email: cc11414@optonline.net. Mr. Paul Canestro, D.R.E. Students 157.

23—ST. ELIZABETH (1873) Revs. Robert F. Barclay; Maurice Mmegbuadimma, Parochial Vicar; Rafael Gomez (Colombia); Sr. Mary Jareth, R.S.M., Pastoral Assoc.; Deacon Manuel Rodriquez.
Res.: 94-20 85th St., Ozone Park, 11416-1237. Tel:

718-296-4900; Fax: 718-296-1140.
Catechesis/Religious Program—Students 137.

24—ST. FIDELIS (1856), (Irish—German), Revs. William A. McLaughlin; Joseph Vu, Parochial Vicar; Deacons John Reichert; Daniel P. Donnelly. In Res., Rev. Frank Mann.
Res.: 123-06 14th Ave., College Point, 11356. Tel: 718-445-6164; Fax: 718-445-1623. Email: stfidelisol@gmail.com. Web: www.stfidelis.org.
School—124-06 14th Ave., College Point, 11356. Tel: 718-539-2628. Web: www.stfidelis.org. Ms. Diana Silvestri, Prin. Lay Teachers 14; Students 194.
Catechesis/Religious Program—Tel: 718-539-1249. Anna Klidas, D.R.E. & Dir. School Devel. Students 270.
St. Fidelis Mother and Child Residence—Tel: 718-353-4749.

25—ST. FRANCIS DE SALES (1906) Rev. Msgr. John J. Brown; Revs. Thomas G. D'Albro; John Wtulich; Deacon Vincent M. LaGamba.
Res.: 129-16 Rockaway Beach Blvd., Belle Harbor, 11694. Tel: 718-634-6464; Fax: 718-634-0716. Email: dbrennastfrancisdesalesparish@aol.com. Web: www.stfrancisdesalesparish.org.
School—219 Beach 129th St., Belle Harbor, 11694. Tel: 718-634-2775; Fax: 718-634-6673. Sr. Patricia Chelius, C.S.J., Prin. Religious 1; Lay Teachers 26; Students 526.
Catechesis/Religious Program—Tel: 718-945-6911. Dr. Virginia Clark, D.R.E. Students 394.

26—ST. FRANCIS OF ASSISI (1930) Rev. Msgr. Ralph J. Maresca; Rev. Matthew U. Obiekezie (Nigeria), Parochial Vicar.
Res.: 21-17 45 St., Astoria, 11105. Tel: 718-728-7801; Fax: 718-728-7853. Email: chsecy@sfaschool.org. Web: www.stfrancisofassisiastoria.com.
School—21-18 46th St., Astoria, 11105. Tel: 718-726-9405; Fax: 718-721-2577. Ms. Anne Stefano, Prin. Lay Teachers 19; Students 307.
Catechesis/Religious Program—Tel: 718-278-0259. Mr. Richard Pipchinski, D.R.E. Students 142.

27—ST. GABRIEL (1923) Revs. Gioacchino Basile; Celestine Anyanwu (Nigeria); Robert J. Sadlack, Parochial Vicar.
Res.: 26-26 98th St., East Elmhurst, 11369. Tel: 718-639-0474; Fax: 718-639-2810. Email: stgabriel2626@aol.com.
Catechesis/Religious Program—Ms. Nelly Gitierrez, D.R.E. Students 177.

28—ST. GENEVIEVE, (German—Irish), Merged with St. Thomas More-St. Edmund to form Blessed Trinity Roman Catholic Church, Rockaway Point, NY. Records are at Blessed Trinity Roman Catholic Church.

29—ST. GERARD MAJELLA (1907) Revs. Josephjude C. Gannon; Joseph Tharackal; James A. Kuroly; Aloysius Enemali; Deacons Guillermo Gomez; Joseph H. Dass; Laurence O. McMaster.
Res.: 188-16 91st Ave., Hollis, 11423-2520. Tel: 718-468-6565; Fax: 718-468-3136. Email: stgerardm@verizon.net.
Catechesis/Religious Program—Tel: 718-468-1166, Ext. 22. Carmen Macchio, D.R.E. Students 124.

30—ST. GERTRUDE (1911) Merged with St. Mary Star of the Sea to form St. Mary Star of the Sea and St. Gertrude. Parish records at St. Mary Star of the Sea and St. Gertrude.

31—ST. GREGORY THE GREAT (1936) Revs. Joseph L. Cunningham; William R. Dulaney; Johnson Nedungadan, C.M. (India); Deacons Arthur Cutter; Robert Zeuner. In Res., Rev. James J. Krische.
Res.: 242-20 88th Ave., Bellerose, 11426. Tel: 718-347-3707; Fax: 718-347-0583. Email: stgregoffice@aol.com. Web: www.saintgregorythegreat.com.
School—244-44 87th Ave., Bellerose, 11426. Tel: 718-343-5053; Fax: 718-347-1142. Ms. Joanne Aldorisio, Prin. Lay Teachers 19; Students 328.
Catechesis/Religious Program—Tel: 718-347-0525. Regina Joyce, D.R.E. Students 261.
Convent—88-19 Cross Island Pkwy., Bellerose, 11426. 242-11 88th Rd., Bellerose, 11426.

32—ST. HELEN (1960) Rev. Msgr. Alfred P. LoPinto; Rev. Robert E. Keighron, Parochial Vicar; Deacons Armand D'Accordo, Pastoral Assoc.; Richard E. Elrose, Pastoral Assoc. In Res., Rev. Msgr. Joseph C. Pfeiffer, Pastor Emeritus (Retired).
Res.: 157-10 83rd St., Howard Beach, 11414. Tel: 718-738-1616; Fax: 718-835-5144. Web: www.sthelen.org.
School—83-09 157th Ave., Howard Beach, 11414. Tel: 718-835-4155; Fax: 718-848-8722. Ms. Kathy Bollinger, Prin. Lay Teachers 18; Students 237.
Catechesis/Religious Program—Tel: 718-835-6216. Ms. Sandra Pepitone, D.R.E. Students 326.

33—HOLY CHILD JESUS (1910) Most Rev. Octavio Cisneros; Revs. Thomas M. Catania, Parochial Vicar; Francis A. Colamaria, Admin.; Reinaldo A. Saldarriaga (Colombia), Parochial Vicar; Francisco J. Ares; Deacons Dean Tully; Raul S. Elias; Jeremiah W. Schwarz.
Res.: 111-11 86th Ave., Richmond Hill, 11418. Tel: 718-847-1860; Fax: 718-847-2696. Email: hcjchurch@aol.com. Web: www.holychildjesuschurch.org.
School—111-02 86th Ave., Richmond Hill, 11418. Tel: 718-849-3988; Fax: 718-850-2842. Martin C. Abruzzo, Prin. Lay Teachers 21; Students 404.
Catechesis/Religious Program—Tel: 718-805-5771. Students 325.

34—HOLY CROSS (1913), (Polish), Rev. Msgr. Peter W. Zendzian; Revs. Grzegorz Stasiak (Poland), Parochial Vicar; Ryszard Koper (Poland), Parochial Vicar.
Res.: 61-21 56th Rd., Maspeth, 11378-2498. Tel: 718-894-1387; Fax: 718-416-9245.
Catechesis/Religious Program—Mrs. Jolanta Neubauer, D.R.E. Students 347.

35—HOLY FAMILY (1940) Rev. Casper J. Furnari; Deacon Joseph V. Catanello; Sr. Nora McNiff, Pastoral Assoc. In Res., Most Rev. Ignatius Catanello (Retired); Rev. Msgr. Joseph L. Stafford (Retired); Revs. Louis D. Aufiero (Retired); James F. Fraser (Retired).
Res.: 175-20 74th Ave., Flushing, 11366-1529. Tel: 718-969-2448; Fax: 718-591-6166. Email: pastor@hfsflushing.org. Web: www.hfsflushing.org.
School—74-15 175th St., Flushing, 11366. Tel: 718-969-2124; Fax: 718-380-2183. Mary Scheer, Prin. Sisters of St. Joseph 3; Lay Teachers 14; Students 243.
Catechesis/Religious Program—Tel: 718-591-6438. Barbara Makolin, D.R.E. Students 138.
Convent—175-11 75 Ave., Flushing, 11366.

36—HOLY TRINITY (1965) Rev. Joseph R. Gibino. In Res., Rev. Emmanuel Nartey.
Res.: 14-51 143rd St., Whitestone, 11357. Tel: 718-746-7730; Fax: 718-767-1368. Email: holytrinityrcchurch@verizon.net. Web: www.holytrinityrcparish.org.
School—14-45 143rd St., Whitestone, 11357. Tel: 718-746-1479; Fax: 718-746-4793. Eleanor Menna, Prin. Lay Teachers 14; Students 261.
Catechesis/Religious Program—Email: holytrinityfaithformation@verizon.net. Donna Marie Spoto, D.R.E. Students 201.

37—IMMACULATE CONCEPTION (1924) Revs. Jed Sumampong, C.P.; Theophane Cooney, C.P., Parochial Vicar; John Douglas, C.P., Parochial Vicar; Sr. Karen Cavanagh, C.S.J., Pastoral Assoc.; Deacons Ramon G. Diaz; Daniel R. Rodriguez.
Res.: 86-45 Edgerton Blvd., Jamaica, 11432. Tel: 718-739-0880; Fax: 718-657-0543. Email: ICCJamaica@aol.com. Web: www.immconjam.org.
School—179-14 Dalny Rd., Jamaica, 11432. Tel: 718-739-5933; Fax: 718-523-7436. Ms. Dorothea Breen, Prin. Lay Teachers 24; Students 467.
Catechesis/Religious Program—86-16 Midland Pkwy., Jamaica, 11432. Tel: 718-291-3080. Students 155.

38—IMMACULATE CONCEPTION (1924) Rev. Msgr. Fernando A. Ferrarese; Revs. Liju Augustine, C.M.I., Parochial Vicar; Allan Basilio (Philippines), Parochial Vicar; Joseph Gaspar D. Hugo (Philippines), Parochial Vicar; Sr. Bridget McGettigan, Pastoral Assoc. In Res., Rev. Msgrs. Vincent F. Fullam, Senior Priest (Retired); Charles P. Boccio, Pastor Emeritus (Retired).
Res.: 21-47 29th St., Astoria, 11105. Tel: 718-728-1613; Fax: 718-956-9229. Email: pastor@ic-astoria.org.
School—21-63 29th St., Astoria, 11105. Tel: 718-728-1969; Fax: 718-728-3374. Email: principal@icsastoria.org. Web: www.ic-astoria.org. Eileen Harnischfeger, Prin. Lay Teachers 17; Students 263.
Catechesis/Religious Program—Tel: 718-956-4494. Marylyn Crum, D.R.E. Students 363.
Convent—21-60 31st St., Long Island City, 11105. Fax: 718-959-9229.

39—INCARNATION (1927) Revs. John J. O'Connor; August P. Iantosca; Deacons Francois Innocent; Franklin Munoz; Clemenceau Pierre-Antoine; Robinson Despeignes; Luis R. Lopez.
Res.: 89-43 Francis Lewis Blvd., Queens Village, 11427. Tel: 718-465-8534; Fax: 718-465-3834. Email: joconnor@incrcc.org. Web: www.incrcc.org.
School—89-15 Francis Lewis Blvd., Queens Village, 11427. Tel: 718-465-5066; Fax: 718-464-4128. Email: principal@incrcc.org. Mrs. Satti Marchan, Prin. Religious 4; Lay Teachers 13; Students 324.
Catechesis/Religious Program—Sr. Joan Klimski, O.P., D.R.E. Students 123.

40—SS. JOACHIM AND ANNE (1896) Revs. Robert M. Robinson; Jean M. Delva, Parochial Vicar. In Res., Rev. Jean-Pierre Ruiz.
Res.: 218-26 105th Ave., Queens Village, 11429. Tel: 718-465-0124; Fax: 718-479-3548. Email: ssjaqville@aol.com.
School—218-19 105th Ave., Queens Village, 11429. Tel: 718-465-2230; Fax: 718-468-5698. Linda Freebes, Prin. Sisters of Notre Dame de Namur 1; Lay Teachers 23; Students 515.
Catechesis/Religious Program—Lisa Sampson, D.R.E. Students 234.

41—ST. JOAN OF ARC (1920) Rev. Msgr. Otto L. Garcia; Revs. Stephen Valdazo, Parochial Vicar; Anthony Sikandar Chanan, Parochial Vicar; Deacon Jorge E. Castillo; Sr. Maryann McHugh, C.S.J., Pastoral Assoc.
Res.: 82-00 35th Ave., Jackson Heights, 11372. Tel: 718-429-2333; Fax: 718-672-5881. Email: joanofarcqueens@aol.com. Web: www.sjany.org.
School—35-27 82nd St., Jackson Heights, 11372. Tel: 718-639-9020; Fax: 718-639-5428. Email: sjaschool@juno.com. Web: www.sjaschoolny.com. John Fruner, Prin. Sisters 1; Lay Teachers 21; Students 503.
Catechesis/Religious Program—Tel: 718-478-5593; Fax: 718-651-8485. Email: sjareled@netzero.com. Noemi Fitzgerald, D.R.E. Students 483.

42—ST. JOHN VIANNEY (1967) Revs. Antonius Ho, C.S.J.B. (Taiwan); Victor Cao, C.S.J.B., Parochial Vicar; Deacon John McGreevey; Sr. Monica Gan, C.S.T., Pastoral Assoc. In Res., Revs. Hugo Bedoya (Retired); Edward Zhang, C.S.J.B.
Res.: 140-10 34th Ave., Flushing, 11354. Tel: 718-762-7920; Fax: 718-460-8032. Email: stjv@msn.com.
Catechesis/Religious Program—Tel: 718-961-5092. Eileen Nesi, D.R.E. Students 148.

43—ST. JOSAPHAT (1910), (Polish), Rev. Andrzej Wojciech Klocek; Deacon Robert P. Lonergan. In Res., Rev. James J. Meszaros, Senior Priest (Retired).
Res.: 34-32 210th St., Bayside, 11361. Tel: 718-229-1663; Fax: 718-229-8018. Email: stjosaphats@aol.com.
Catechesis/Religious Program—Students 40.

44—ST. JOSEPH (1904), (Polish), Rev. Krystian J. Piasta, O.F.M.
Parish Office/Parish House: 108-43 Sutphin Blvd., Jamaica, 11435-5445. Tel: 718-739-4781; Fax: 718-658-5447. Email: stjll435@yahoo.com. Web: www.stjjamaica.org.
Catechesis/Religious Program—Students 18.

45—ST. JOSEPH (1877) Revs. John P. Harrington; Robert J. Armato, Parochial Vicar; Lawrence Gellel, S.J., Parochial Vicar; Deacon Felipe J. Alvarez. In Res., Rev. William C. Farrugia (Retired).
Res.: 43-19 30th Ave., Long Island City, 11103. Tel: 718-278-1611; Fax: 718-956-3589. Email: rectory@stjosephlic.org. Web: www.stjosephlic.org.
School—28-46 44th St., Astoria, 11103. Tel: 718-728-0724; Fax: 718-728-6142. Web: www.stjosephsch.org. Luke Nawrocki, Prin. Lay Teachers 23; Students 381.
Catechesis/Religious Program—Tel: 718-545-7338. Email: sjreled@gmail.com. Loretta Rosas, D.R.E. Students 264.

46—ST. KEVIN (1926) Rev. Msgr. D. Joseph Finnerty; Rev. Louis J. DeGaetano, Parochial Vicar; Mr. Thomas Sexton, Music Dir. In Res., Rev. Michael Parisi (Retired).
Res.: 45-21 194th St., Flushing, 11358. Tel: 718-357-8888; Fax: 718-357-3671. Email: stkevinsrcc@aol.com. Web: stkevins.org.
School—45-50 195th St., Flushing, 11358. Tel: 718-357-8110; Fax: 718-357-2519. Sue Ann Roye, Prin.; Mr. John Gillooly, Dir. Bldgs. & Grounds. Religious 1; Lay Teachers 15; Students 201.
Catechesis/Religious Program—Tel: 718-357-5317. Agnes Rus, D.R.E. Students 185.

47—ST. LEO (1903), (Hispanic—Italian), Revs. William M. Hoppe; Carlos A. Agudelo, Parochial Vicar; Diego Villegas, Parochial Vicar.
Res.: 104-05 49th Ave., Corona, 11368. Tel: 718-592-7569; Fax: 718-271-6726. Email: saintleo@earthlink.net. Web: www.saintleoparish.com.
School—104-19 49th Ave., Corona, 11368. Tel: 718-592-7050; Fax: 718-592-0787. Mrs. Maureen Blaine, Prin. Lay Teachers 20; Students 379.
Catechesis/Religious Program—Tel: 718-699-8565. Mr. Conrado Hernandez, D.R.E. Students 315.
Mission—Our Lady of Mount Carmel Corona. 103-56 52nd Ave., Corona, Queens Co. 11368. Tel: 718-592-7569.

48—ST. LUKE (1870) Rev. Msgr. John C. Tosi; Revs. David J. Dettmer, Parochial Vicar; Vincent G. Chirichella, Parochial Vicar; Sr. Catherine T. Reilly, O.P., Pastoral Assoc.
Res.: 16-34 Clintonville St., Whitestone, 11357. Tel: 718-746-8102; Fax: 718-746-3589. Email: stlukewhitestone@aol.com. Web: www.stlukewhitestone.org.
School—16-01 150th Pl., Whitestone, 11357. Tel: 718-746-3833; Fax: 718-747-2101. Mrs. Barbara Reiter, Prin. Lay Teachers 29; Students 494.
Catechesis/Religious Program—Tel: 718-746-3409. Sr. Katherine Burke, C.S.J., D.R.E. Students 475.

49—ST. MARGARET (1860) Rev. Msgr. Steven J. Aguggia; Revs. William A. With; Joseph F. Wilson,

Parochial Vicar; Sr. Bridget Olwell, O.S.U., Pastoral Assoc.; Deacon Michael J. Brainerd; Ann Winkler, Pastoral Assoc. In Res., Rev. Msgr. Nicholas W. Sivillo (Retired).
Res.: 66-05 79th Pl., Middle Village, 11379. Tel: 718-326-1911; Fax: 718-326-1883. Email: stmargaretmv@gmail.com. Web: www.stmargaretmv.org.
School—66-10 80th St., Middle Village, 11379. Tel: 718-326-0922. Sr. Rena Perrone, O.P., Prin. Sisters of St. Dominic 1; Lay Teachers 14; Students 323.
Catechesis/Religious Program—Tel: 718-381-4048. Dolores Voyer, D.R.E. Students 294.

50—ST. MARGARET MARY (1961) Merged with Our Lady of Mount Carmel in 2007. Parish records at Our Lady of Mount Carmel.

51—ST. MARY (1868) Rev. Ralph E. Barile. In Res., Rev. Msgr. Joseph C. Mulqueen (Retired).
Res.: 10-08 49th Ave., Long Island City, 11101. Tel: 718-786-0705; Fax: 718-482-7115. Email: stmarylic@aol.com.
Catechesis/Religious Program—Students 60.

52—ST. MARY GATE OF HEAVEN (1904) Revs. Gerald J. Fitzsimmons, S.M.M.; Hugh Gillespie, Parochial Vicar; Richard Magararu, S.M.M., Parochial Vicar; Bro. Paul Llorens, S.M.M., Pastoral Assoc.; Deacons Richard Gilligan; Timothy McBride; Ramon Cruz; Frances Franzke, Business Mgr. In Res., Very Rev. Matthew J. Considine, S.M.M.; Rev. Peter D'Abele, S.M.M.
Res.: 101-25 104th St., Ozone Park, 11416. Tel: 718-847-5957; Fax: 718-846-6489. Email: pa381@rcdob.org. Web: www.smghparish.org.
School—104-06 101st Ave., Ozone Park, 11416. Tel: 718-846-0689; Fax: 718-846-1059. Patrick Scannell, Prin. Religious 1; Lay Teachers 23; Students 503.
Catechesis/Religious Program—Tel: 718-849-9329. Ann Farrell, D.R.E. Students 300.

53—ST. MARY MAGDALENE (1913) Revs. Jeffry T. Dillon; Cosmas Nzeabalu, Parochial Vicar; Deacons Lee C. Williams; Ernest F. Hart; Sisters Maryellen Kane, C.S.J., Pastoral Assoc.; Kathleen Hickey, Pastoral Assoc.
Res.: 218-12 136th Ave., Springfield Gardens, 11413. Tel: 718-949-4311; Fax: 718-528-7208.
Catechesis/Religious Program—Students 101.

54—ST. MARY STAR OF THE SEA (1857) Merged with St. Gertrude to form St. Mary Star of the Sea and St. Gertrude.

55—ST. MARY STAR OF THE SEA AND ST. GERTRUDE (2008) Rev. Jean Y. Pierre, Parochial Vicar; Rev. Msgr. John J. Bracken; Deacons Michael C. Moss; Adalberto Montero. In Res., Revs. Frederick Anawonah (Nigeria); Charles H. White (Retired).
Res.: 1920 New Haven Ave., Far Rockaway, 11691. Tel: 718-327-1133; Fax: 718-327-3276. Email: info@saintsmaryandgertrude.org. Web: www.saintsmaryandgertrude.org.
Additional Worship Site:—
St. Gertrude—Church: 336 Beach 38th St., Far Rockaway, 11691.
Catechesis/Religious Program—Mr. Conrado Hernandez, D.R.E. Students 330.

56—MARY'S NATIVITY (1926) Revs. Richard W. Conlon; Anacleto Asebius, Parochial Vicar. In Res., Rev. Msgr. Edward J. Bottino, Pastor Emeritus (Retired); Rev. Joseph F. Wiseman (Retired).
Res.: 46-02 Parsons Blvd., Flushing, 11355. Tel: 718-359-5996; Fax: 718-939-6737. Email: marysnativity@aol.com. Web: www.marysnativitychurch.info.
Church & Convent: Jasmine Ave. & Parsons Blvd., Flushing, 11355. Tel: 718-445-7180.
Catechesis/Religious Program—Email: marysnativityccd@verizon.net. Mrs. Barbara Devito, D.R.E. Students 112.

57—ST. MATTHIAS (1908) Rev. Msgr. Edward B. Scharfenberger; Revs. Richard J. Bretone, Parochial Vicar; Wladyslaw Z. Kubrak, Parochial Vicar; Silvaster Sarihaddula, Parochial Vicar; Bro. Michael Loerch, O.F.M.Cap.; Deacons John Sands; Lawrence Mule.
Res.: 58-15 Catalpa Ave., Ridgewood, 11385. Tel: 718-821-6447; 718-821-6448; 718-821-6449; Fax: 718-821-6876.
School—58-25 Catalpa Ave., Ridgewood, 11385. Tel: 718-381-8003; Fax: 718-381-5319. Miss Barbara Wehnes. Religious 4; Lay Teachers 18; Students 408.
Catechesis/Religious Program—Tel: 718-386-1077; Fax: 718-821-6876. Students 383.

58—ST. MEL (1941) Revs. Christopher C. Turczany; Italo Barozzi, Parochial Vicar; Gerard J. Sauer; Coleman J. Costello, Senior Priest (Retired); Francis Igboanugo. In Res., Bro. Lawrence Larmann, O.S.F.
Res.: 28-20 154th St., Flushing, 11354. Tel: 718-886-0201; 718-886-0881; Fax: 718-886-0882. Email: stmel2820@aol.com. Web: www.saintmel.org.
School—154-24 26th Ave., Flushing, 11354. Tel: 718-539-8211. Mrs. Diane Competello, Prin. Sisters 1; Lay Teachers 26; Students 349.
Catechesis/Religious Program—Tel: 718-461-9840; Fax: 718-886-0882. Bro. Lawrence Larmann, O.S.F., D.R.E.; Ms. Paula Migliore, D.R.E. Students 167.

59—ST. MICHAEL (1833) Rev. Msgr. Edward V. Wetterer; Revs. Anthony I. Ezekwe, Parochial Vicar; Moises Madrid; Freddi A. Rosales, Parochial Vicar; Sr. Maureen Jessnik, Pastoral Asst.
Res.: 136-76 41st Ave., Flushing, 11355. Tel: 718-961-0295; Fax: 718-961-1403. Email: stmicheall833@aol.com. Web: www.stmichaelflushingonline.org.
School—136-58 41st Ave., Flushing, 11355. Tel: 718-961-0246. Email: rogonesms@aol.com. Mrs. Maureen Rogone, Prin. Religious 2; Lay Teachers 10; Students 201.
Catechesis/Religious Program—138-25 Barclay Ave., Flushing, 11355. Tel: 718-961-0312. Luz May, D.R.E. Students 330.

60—ST. MONICA, (Jamaica), Closed. For inquiries for parish records contact the chancery.

61—MOST PRECIOUS BLOOD (1922) Revs. William F. Krlis; Peter Onyibuchi Nwadimkoa, Parochial Vicar; James Rodriguez, Parochial Vicar; Gabriel A. Ahiara Kwen, Parochial Vicar; Jean Gerard Laquerre; Jorge Dinguis, Parochial Vicar; Deacon Giacomo Panessa.
Res.: 32-23 36th St., Long Island City, 11106. Tel: 718-278-3337; Fax: 718-278-4354. Email: williamkrlis@yahoo.com.
School—32-52 37th St., Long Island City, 11103. Tel: 718-278-4081; Fax: 718-278-3089. Barbara DeMaio, Prin. Lay Teachers 23; Students 335.
Catechesis/Religious Program—Tel: 718-721-9850. Mrs. Cecelia Uriguen, D.R.E. Students 320.
Convent—32-16 36th St., Long Island City, 11106. Tel: 718-278-4706.

62—NATIVITY OF THE BLESSED VIRGIN MARY (1925), Merged with St. Stanislaus Bishop & Martyr, Ozone Park to form Nativity of the Blessed Virgin Mary-St. Stanislaus Bishop & Martyr Roman Catholic Church, Ozone Park. Revs. Paul C. Palmiotto; Angelo B. Pezzullo (Retired); Andrezej Salwowski, Parochial Vicar; Paul M. Gyamfi, Parochial Vicar; Deacon Edward J. Guster Jr.
Res.: 101-41 91st St., Ozone Park, 11416-2227. Tel: 718-845-3691; Fax: 718-845-8978. Email: nativityststans@verizon.net.
Catechesis/Religious Program—101-41 91st St., Ozone Park, 11416. Tel: 718-461-9840. Elizabeth Perretta, D.R.E. Students 282.

63—NATIVITY OF THE BLESSED VIRGIN MARY-SAINT STANISLAUS BISHOP AND MARTYR ROMAN CATHOLIC CHURCH (2011) 101-41 91st St., Ozone Park, 11416.

64—ST. NICHOLAS OF TOLENTINE (1916) Revs. Thomas G. Pettei, Admin.; Abraham P. Mathew; Anthony Nzegwu (Nigeria); Deacon Lionel Knight. In Res., Rev. John J. Costello.
Res.: 150-75 Goethals Ave., Jamaica, 11432. Tel: 718-969-3226; Fax: 718-380-0345. Email: tgpettei@hotmail.com. Web: www.iamsnt.org.
School—80-22 Parsons Blvd., Jamaica, 11432. Tel: 718-380-1900; Fax: 718-591-6977. Anne Badalamenti, Prin. Lay Teachers 18; Students 301.
Catechesis/Religious Program—150-85 Goethals Ave., Jamaica, 11432. Tel: 718-591-6536. Monica Gonzalez, D.R.E. Students 148.

65—OUR LADY OF CHINA CHAPEL (1978) Attended by St. John Vianney, Flushing Rev. Antonius Ho, C.S.J.B. (Taiwan); Sr. Monica Gan, C.S.T., Pastoral Assoc.
Office: 54-09 92nd St., Elmhurst, 11373. Tel: 718-699-1929; Fax: 718-592-5981. Email: olcny@msn.com. Web: olc.faithweb.com.
School—Ming Yuan Chinese School, 54-17 90th St., Elmhurst, 11373. Tel: 718-271-3944. 6201 8th Ave., 11219. Tel: 718-439-3656. Bro. Peter Li, C.S.J.B., Prin.
Catechesis/Religious Program—Tel: 718-961-5092; Fax: 718-460-8032.

66—OUR LADY OF FATIMA (1948) Rev. Msgrs. Michael J. Brennan; John E. Mahoney; Revs. Yovanny Acosta; Eugene F. Donnelly (Retired); George L Dinguis. In Res., Rev. Msgr. Edward J. Breen, Pastor Emeritus (Retired); Revs. James Fedigan; Patrick J. Frawley.
Res.: 25-02 80th St., Jackson Heights, 11370. Tel: 718-899-2801; Fax: 718-429-6404. Email: olfatima11370@msn.com. Web: www.olfparish.catholicweb.com.
School—25-38 80th St., Jackson Heights, 11370. Tel: 718-429-7031; Fax: 718-899-2811. Mrs. Cassie Zelic, Prin. Lay Teachers 32; Students 683.
Catechesis/Religious Program—25-56 80th St. Tel: 718-457-3457. Patricia Anton, D.R.E. Students 188.
Convent—25-56 80th St., Jackson Heights, 11370. Tel: 718-747-3457.

67—OUR LADY OF GRACE (1924) Rev. Anthony M. Rucando; Deacon Alexander Breviario.
Res.: 100-05 159th Ave., Howard Beach, 11414. Tel: 718-843-6218; Fax: 718-738-8208. Email: olghowardbeach@nyc.rr.com. Web: www.olghowardbeach.org.
Catechesis/Religious Program—Tel: 718-835-2165; Fax: 718-835-4524. Mrs. Anne Coghlan, D.R.E. Students 382.

68—OUR LADY OF HOPE (1960) Revs. Michael A. Carrano; Arthur A. Candreva, I.V.Dei, Parochial Vicar; Peter J. Purpura, Parochial Vicar; Deacon Robert F. Lavanco.
Res.: 61-27 71st St., Middle Village, 11379. Tel: 718-429-5438; Fax: 718-429-2764. Email: macarrano@juno.com. Web: www.ourladyofhopeparish.org.
School—61-21 71st St., Middle Village, 11379. Tel: 718-458-3535. Ms. Michele Krebs, Prin. Religious 1; Lay Teachers 32; Students 622.
Catechesis/Religious Program—Tel: 718-335-8394. Karen Colletti, D.R.E. Students 353.

69—OUR LADY OF LIGHT ROMAN CATHOLIC CHURCH (2008) Rev. William G. Smith; Rev. Msgr. Francis Yaw Tawiah; Deacons Albert Saldana; Luis C. Taylor; Freddy Torres; Florence McKinley, Music Min.
Res.: 118-22 Riverton St., St. Albans, 11412. Tel: 718-528-1220; Fax: 718-528-7907. Email: info@ourladyoflightparish.com. Web: www.ourladyoflightparish.com.
Rectory—112-43 198th St., St. Albans, 11412. Tel: 718-468-3511; Fax: 718-479-2303.
Additional Worship Sites:—
St. Catherine of Sienna—Church: 118-22 Riverton St., St. Albans, 11412.
St. Pascal Baylon—Church: 112-43 198th St., St. Albans, 11412.
Catechesis/Religious Program—Mary Harris, D.R.E.; Sr. Mary Jane Rolston, O.P., D.R.E. Students 81.

70—OUR LADY OF LOURDES (1924) Rev. Msgr. Robert J. Pawson; Rev. Michael G. Tedone, Parochial Vicar; Deacons Ricardo Moreno; Walter C. Zimmermann; Joseph C. Denzler. In Res., Rev. Msgr. John F. Casey (Retired); Rev. Amarilho Checon, S.J.
Res.: 92-96 220th St., Queens Village, 11428. Tel: 718-479-5111; Fax: 718-479-0826.
School—92-80 220th St., Queens Village, 11428. Tel: 718-464-1480; Fax: 718-740-4091. Web: www.ollqv.org. Sr. Josephine Barbiere, C.S.J., Prin. Religious 1; Lay Teachers 22; Students 330.
Catechesis/Religious Program—Tel: 718-740-4090. Joanne Russo, D.R.E. Students 260.

71—OUR LADY OF MERCY (1930) Rev. Msgr. John A. McGuirl; Revs. John J. Cremins (Retired); Raphael Munday-Kukana, Parochial Vicar; Deacons Edward Smolinski; John F. Killian. In Res., Rev. Msgr. Gerald J. Langelier, Pastor Emeritus (Retired).
Res.: 70-01 Kessel St., Forest Hills, 11375. Tel: 718-268-6143; Fax: 718-544-3764. Email: office@mercyhills.org. Web: www.mercyhills.org.
School—70-25 Kessel St., Forest Hills, 11375. Tel: 718-793-2086; Fax: 718-897-2144. Email: principal@mercyhills.org. Linda Dougherty, Prin. Lay Teachers 20; Students 337.
Catechesis/Religious Program—70-20 Juno St., Forest Hills, 11375. Tel: 718-261-6285. Web: www.olm-religioused.com. Sr. Ann Barbara DeSiano, I.H.M., D.R.E. Students 125.

72—OUR LADY OF MOUNT CARMEL (1841) Rev. Msgr. Sean G. Ogle; Revs. Josephtan Pham, Parochial Vicar; Peter Nguyen, C.S.J.B., Parochial Vicar. In Res., Revs. Frank M. Lynch; Raymond Roden.
Res.: 23-25 Newtown Ave., Long Island City, 11102. Tel: 718-278-1834; Fax: 718-278-0998. Email: church@mountcarmelastoria.org. Web: www.mountcarmelastoria.org.
Additional Worship Site:—
St. Margaret Mary—Church: 9-18 27th Ave., Long Island City, 11102.
Catechesis/Religious Program—Fax: 718-278-0998. Zilia Hirsch, D.R.E. Students 218.

73—OUR LADY OF PERPETUAL HELP (1923) Revs. Vincent M. Daly; John Garkowski, Parochial Vicar; Donald M. Berran (Retired); Sr. Margaret Sweeney, C.S.J., Pastoral Assoc.; Deacon Jorge L. Alvarado. In Res., Rev. Donald M. Berran (Retired).
Res.: 111-50 115th St., South Ozone Park, 11420. Tel: 718-843-1212; Fax: 718-843-3554. Email: olphchurchqns@hotmail.com.
School—111-10 115th St., South Ozone Park, 11420. Tel: 718-843-4184; Fax: 718-843-6838. Mrs. Frances DeLuca, Prin. Religious 1; Lay Teachers 41; Students 644.
Catechesis/Religious Program—Tel: 718-641-6165. Mr. Timothy Carroll, D.R.E. Students 138.

74—OUR LADY OF SORROWS (1876) Revs. Thomas J. Healy; Manuel Ros (Retired); Walter G. Lawson, Parochial Vicar; Juan Ruiz, Parochial Vicar; Deacons Jose F. Tineo; Daniel Magana.
Res.: 104-11 37th Ave., Corona, 11368. Tel: 718-424-7554; Fax: 718-424-4910. Email: olsrectory@nyc.rr.com.

School—35-34 105th St., Corona, 11368. Tel: 718-426-5517; Fax: 718-651-5682. Email: khanrahan@olscorona.org. Sr. Katherine Hanrahan, C.S.J., Prin. Lay Teachers 17; Students 296.
Catechesis/Religious Program—Tel: 718-651-5682. Email: olsccd@aol.com. Aurora De La Cruz, D.R.E. Students 1,351.

75—OUR LADY OF THE ANGELUS (1938) Revs. John Mendonca; Daniel Ayala, Parochial Vicar; Deacons Edwin Cancel; Julio C. Murillo. In Res., Rev. Jose Cadusale (Philippines).
Res.: 63-63 98th St., Rego Park, 11374. Tel: 718-897-4444; Fax: 718-897-1453. Email: pola@nyc.rr.com. Web: www.ola63.org.
School—98-05 63rd. Dr., Rego Park, 11374. Tel: 718-896-7220; Fax: 718-896-5723. Email: olarcschool@aol.com. Web: www.ourladyoftheangelus.com. Joan M. Armstrong, Prin. Religious 1; Lay Teachers 15; Students 228.
Catechesis/Religious Program—Tel: 718-896-4388. Sr. Jo Ann Schwarz, S.C., D.R.E. Students 145.

76—OUR LADY OF THE BLESSED SACRAMENT (1930) Rev. Robert J. Whelan; Deacons George Bourbeau, Safe Environment Coord.; Ernesto A. Avallone. In Res., Rev. Msgr. William J. Flood (Retired).
Res.: 34-24 203rd St., Bayside, 11361. Tel: 718-229-5929; Fax: 718-229-3354. Email: secretary@olbschurch.org. Web: www.olbschurch.org.
School—34-45 202nd St., Bayside, 11361. Tel: 718-229-4434; Fax: 718-229-5820. Joan Kane, Prin. Religious 1; Lay Teachers 26; Students 399.
Catechesis/Religious Program—Tel: 718-225-6179. Sr. Carla Lorenz, P.B.V.M., D.R.E. Students 187.

77—OUR LADY OF THE CENACLE (1922) Revs. Robert P. Morales; Jose Francisco Herrera; Deacon Eduardo Sencion. In Res., Rev. Pablo Sans (Retired).
Res.: 136-06 87th Ave., Richmond Hill, 11418. Tel: 718-291-2540; Fax: 718-291-6211. Email: ourladyofthecenacle@verizon.net.
Catechesis/Religious Program—Mrs. Sharon Robayo, D.R.E.; Mrs. Marie J. Nondesir, D.R.E. Students 160.

78—OUR LADY OF THE MIRACULOUS MEDAL (1917) Rev. Msgr. Edward A. Ryan; Rev. Soju Varghese, Parochial Vicar; Deacon James E. Maloney. In Res., Rev. Msgr. George M. Schuster, Pastor Emeritus (Retired).
Res.: 62-81 60th Pl., Ridgewood, 11385. Tel: 718-366-3360; Fax: 718-456-0564. Email: olmm11385@aol.com. Web: www.olmmchurch.org.
See Notre Dame Catholic Academy, Ridgewood under Consolidated Elementary Schools (Regional) located in the Institution section
Catechesis/Religious Program—Tel: 718-456-3275. Mary Macchiaroli, D.R.E. Students 241.

79—OUR LADY OF THE SKIES CHAPEL (1955) Rev. Krystian J. Piasta, O.F.M.
Kennedy International Airport Terminal: JFK International Airport, Terminal 4, Jamaica, 11430. Tel: 718-656-5348; Fax: 718-656-8162. Email: jfkchapel@gmail.com. Web: www.jfkchapel.org.

80—OUR LADY OF THE SNOWS (1948) Rev. Msgr. Raymond F. Chappetto; Rev. Patrick H. O. Longalong, Parochial Vicar; Deacons Henry J. Smith; Matthew Oellinger; Steven Borheck; John Warren; Mrs. Regina Moreno, Pastoral Assoc. In Res., Rev. Bartholomew Okonkwo.
Res.: 258-15 80th Ave., Floral Park, 11004. Tel: 718-347-6070; Fax: 718-343-3221. Email: church@olsnows.org. Web: www.olsnows.org.
School—79-33 258th St., Floral Park, 11004. Tel: 718-343-1346; Fax: 718-343-7303. Web: www.ourladyofsnowsschool.org. Sr. Roberta Oberle, C.S.J., Prin. Religious 1; Lay Teachers 26; Students 487.
Catechesis/Religious Program—Tel: 718-347-3511. Email: rel.ed@olsnows.org. Mrs. Regina Moreno, D.R.E. Students 260.

81—OUR LADY QUEEN OF MARTYRS (1917) Rev. Msgr. Joseph A. Funaro; Rev. Francis J. Passenant, Parochial Vicar; Deacons William McNamara; Gregory Kandra; Mr. Dennis Paptelli, Pastoral Assoc. In Res., Rev. Jan Czudek, Parochial Vicar.
Res.: 110-06 Queens Blvd., Forest Hills, 11375. Tel: 718-268-6251; Fax: 718-793-2584. Email: pastorolqm@aol.com. Web: www.ourladyqueenofmartyrs.org.
School—72-55 Austin St., Forest Hills, 11375. Tel: 718-263-2622; Fax: 718-263-0063. Email: olqmschool@aol.com. Web: www.olqmschool.com. Mrs. Ann Zuschlag, Prin. Lay Teachers 20; Students 336.
Catechesis/Religious Program—Tel: 718-263-0907. Email: olqmreled@verizon.net. Students 318.

82—ST. PANCRAS (1904) Rev. Msgr. Gregory C. Wielunski; Rev. Dariusz Strzelecki, Parochial Vicar; Deacon James E. Maloney.
Res.: 72-22 68th St., Glendale, 11385. Tel: 718-821-2323; Fax: 718-417-8021. Email: gwielunski@saintpancras.org. Web: www.saintpancras.org.
School—68-20 Myrtle Ave., Glendale, 11385. Tel: 718-821-6721; Fax: 718-418-8991. Mr. Philip Ciani, Prin. Lay Teachers 16; Students 232.
Catechesis/Religious Program—Tel: 718-479-0590. Email: fotopeg@aol.com. Margaret Walter, D.R.E. Students 253.
Convent—72-21 68th St., 72-25 68th St., Glendale, 11385.

83—ST. PASCAL BAYLON (1930), (African American), Merged with St. Catherine of Sienna to form Our Lady of Light Roman Catholic Church.

84—ST. PATRICK (1869) Rev. William F. Krlis; Rev. Msgr. Raymond J. Kelly (Retired); Rev. Jorge Dinguis, Parochial Vicar; Deacon Carlos A. Trochez. In Res., Revs. Charles F. Gilley, I.V.Dei.; Alexander G. Abugel.
Res.: 39-38 29th St., Long Island City, 11101. Tel: 718-729-6060; Fax: 718-729-1276. Email: stpatrick@yahoo.com. Web: www.stpatrick.org.
Catechesis/Religious Program—Tel: 718-937-1239; Fax: 718-706-0565. Sr. Flora Marinelli, C.S.J., D.R.E. Students 164.

85—ST. PAUL CHONG HA-SANG ROMAN CATHOLIC CHAPEL (2006), (Korean), Revs. Gabriel Lee; Seung-Je Pancratius Kim, Parochial Vicar; Dong-Jin Samuel Kim, Parochial Vicar; Joseph R. Veneroso, M.M.; Deacon Paul M. Chin.
Office: 32-15 Parsons Blvd., Flushing, 11354. Tel: 718-321-7676; Fax: 718-321-7005.
Catechesis/Religious Program—Students 305.
Convent—Olivetan Benedictine Sisters, 32-15 Parsons Blvd., Flushing, 11354.

86—ST. PAUL THE APOSTLE (1964) Rev. Darrell Da Costa.
Res. & Office: 98-16 55 Ave., Corona, 11368. Tel: 718-271-1000; Fax: 718-760-3496. Email: stpaulcorona@verizon.net. Web: www.stpaulcorona.com.
Catechesis/Religious Program—Students 260.

87—ST. PIUS V (1908) Rev. Jose Francisco Herrera.
Res.: 106-12 Liverpool St., Jamaica, 11435. Tel: 718-739-3731; Fax: 718-739-7086. Email: stpiusvjamaica@aol.com.
Catechesis/Religious Program—Students 150.

88—ST. PIUS X (1960) Rev. Msgr. Thomas A. Graham; Rev. Louis N. Uzoh.
Res.: 148-10 249th St., Rosedale, 11422. Tel: 718-525-9099; Fax: 718-276-2467. Email: stpiusxrestore@aol.com.
Catechesis/Religious Program—Marilyne Jean, D.R.E. Students 50.

89—PRESENTATION OF THE BLESSED VIRGIN MARY (1886) Revs. Christopher M. O'Connor; Domingo Collado, Parochial Vicar; Deacon Jose Armanso Lizama. In Res., Rev. Msgr. John O'Brien.
Res.: 88-19 Parsons Blvd., Jamaica, 11432. Tel: 718-739-0241; Fax: 718-739-2753. Email: pbvmchurch@msn.com. Web: www.presentationbvmjamaica.org.
Providence House III—159-23 89th Ave., Jamaica, 11432. Tel: 718-739-1348.
Youth Ministry Office—88-13 Parsons Blvd., Jamaica, 11432. Tel: 718-739-2003; Fax: 718-526-8153.
Catechesis/Religious Program—Ms. Beverley Madar, D.R.E. Students 343.

90—QUEEN OF ANGELS (1953) Revs. Brian P. Dowd; Ricardo A. Pepez, Parochial Vicar; Mr. Juan Rodriguez, Pastoral Assoc. In Res., Rev. Sebastian Many.
Res.: 44-04 Skillman Ave., Long Island City, 11104. Tel: 718-392-0011; 718-392-0012; Fax: 718-472-2625.
Catechesis/Religious Program—Tel: 718-937-5174. Students 130.

91—QUEEN OF PEACE (1939) Rev. James L. Tighe; Mercedes Lopez, Admin. Asst.; Deacon Jose M. Fernandez.
Res.: 141-36 77th Ave., Flushing, 11367. Tel: 718-380-5031; Fax: 718-969-2025. Email: queenofpeacerectory@verizon.net. Web: queenofpeacechurch.org.
Catechesis/Religious Program—Gregory J. Bizzoco Jr., D.R.E. Students 99.
Convent—Tel: 718-380-4293.

92—ST. RAPHAEL (1868) Rev. Jerome Jecewicz.
Res.: 35-20 Greenpoint Ave., Long Island City, 11101. Tel: 718-729-8957; Fax: 718-729-5238. Web: www.saintraphaellic.org.
School—48-25 37th St., Long Island City, 11101. Tel: 718-784-0482; Fax: 718-482-0214. Web: www-.straphaelschoollic.com. Sr. Maureen Ahlemeyer, P.B.V.M., Prin. Lay Teachers 14; Students 164.
Catechesis/Religious Program—Sr. Christine Scherer, D.W., D.R.E. Students 62.

93—RESURRECTION-ASCENSION (1926) Rev. Salvatore J. Amato. In Res., Rev. Msgr. Paul R. Sanchez.
Res.: 61-11 85th St., Rego Park, 11374. Tel: 718-424-5212; Fax: 718-639-8679. Email: rachsch@aol.com. Web: www.rachurch.org.
School—85-25 61st Rd., Rego Park, 11374. Tel: 718-426-4963; Fax: 718-426-0940. Joann Heppt, Prin. Lay Teachers 19; Students 267.
Catechesis/Religious Program—Tel: 718-533-7898. Ms. Joyce Mennona, D.R.E. Students 122.

94—ST. RITA (1900) Revs. Jose Carlos Da Silva; Robert Ambalathingal, O.C.D., Parochial Vicar; Sr. M. Erlinda Pimo, I.S.S.M., Pastoral Assoc.
Res.: 36-25 11th St., Long Island City, 11106. Tel: 718-361-1884; Fax: 718-786-4573. Web: www.stritalic.org.
Catechesis/Religious Program—Tel: 718-361-1884; Fax: 718-786-4573. Students 215.

95—ST. ROBERT BELLARMINE (1939) Rev. Msgr. Martin T. Geraghty; Revs. Godofredo Felicitas (Philippines), Parochial Vicar; Mark E. Soh, Parochial Vicar; Deacon Andrew Ciccaroni, Pastoral Assoc. In Res., Rev. Henry A. Lang (Retired).
Res.: 56-15 213th St., Bayside, 11364. Tel: 718-229-6465; Fax: 718-229-8126. Email: srb@nyc.rr.com. Web: www.stroberts.org.
School—56-10 214th St., Bayside, 11364. Tel: 718-225-8795; Fax: 718-423-5612. Ms. Angela M. Fazio, Prin. Sisters 1; Religious 1; Lay Teachers 13; Students 269.
Catechesis/Religious Program—Tel: 718-225-3181. Students 198.

96—ST. ROSE OF LIMA (1886) Rev. Msgr. James F. Spengler; Revs. Andrzej Lukianiuk; Daniel Rajski, Parochial Vicar; Deacon Patrick Logue, Business Mgr.
Res.: 130 Beach 84th St., Rockaway Beach, 11693. Tel: 718-634-7394; Fax: 718-634-6591. Web: www.stroseoflimarb.org.
School—154 Beach 84th St., Rockaway Beach, 11693. Tel: 718-474-7079; Fax: 718-634-0524. Mrs. Theresa Andersen, Prin. Sisters 2; Lay Teachers 26; Students 449.
Catechesis/Religious Program—Tel: 718-945-4850. Email: job616@aol.com. Students 137.

97—SACRED HEART Revs. Bryan D. Patterson; Donelson Thevenin, Parochial Vicar; Deacons Paul Dorsinville; Roy Dudley; Francois G. Cajoux; Marcus A. Mordan. In Res., Rev. Joseph M. Nolan (Retired).
Res.: 115-58 222nd St., Cambria Heights, 11411. Tel: 718-528-0577; Fax: 718-341-0253. Email: shcambria@aol.com. Web: www.sacredheartny.com.
School—115-50 221st St., Cambria Heights, 11411. Tel: 718-527-0123; Fax: 718-527-1204. Email: sacredheartch@gmail.com. Mrs. Yvonne-Therese Russell Smith, Prin. Lay Teachers 20; Students 347.
Catechesis/Religious Program—Students 59.

98—SACRED HEART (1931) Revs. John J. Fullum; Binoy George, Parochial Vicar; Sr. Margaret Mary Raibaldi, C.S.J., Pastoral Assoc.; Deacon Peter Stamm; Mr. Charles Nicholson, Mus. Dir. In Res., Rev. Romano Zanon.
Res.: 83-17 78th Ave., East Glendale, 11385. Tel: 718-821-6434; Fax: 718-497-2881. Email: sacredheartglendale@earthlink.net. Web: www.sacredheartrccglendale.org.
School—84-05 78th Ave., East Glendale, 11385. Tel: 718-456-6636; Fax: 718-456-0286. Ms. Joanne Gangi, Prin. Lay Teachers 19; Students 305.
Catechesis/Religious Program—Tel: 718-386-5616. Mrs. Laura Ciraolo, D.R.E.; Mrs. Sandra Hutter, D.R.E. Students 384.

99—SACRED HEART OF JESUS (1878) Revs. Thomas F. Brosnan; Martin Asiedu-Peprah, Parochial Vicar; Deacon William McNamara; Sr. Kathleen Masterson, R.S.M., Pastoral Assoc.
Res.: 215-35 38th Ave., Bayside, 11361. Tel: 718-428-2200; Fax: 718-428-5840. Email: sacredheartrectory2@verizon.net. Web: www.sacredheartbayside.net.
School—216-33 38th Ave., Bayside, 11361. Tel: 718-631-4804; Fax: 718-631-5738. Mr. Dennis J. Farrell, Prin. Lay Teachers 29; Students 480.
Catechesis/Religious Program—Tel: 718-631-1307. Mrs. Georgette Lyons, D.R.E. Students 222.

100—ST. SEBASTIAN (1894) Rev. Msgr. Michael J. Hardiman; Revs. Michael J. McHugh, Parochial Vicar; Joy Alookaran (India), Parochial Vicar; Thaddeus Abraham, Parochial Vicar; Deacon Stephen Damato. In Res., Rev. Daniel Suh.
Res.: 39-63 57th St., Woodside, 11377. Tel: 718-429-4442; Fax: 718-429-7581. Email: administration@stsebastianwoodside.org. Web: www.stsebastianwoodside.org.
School—39-68 58th St., Woodside, 11377. Tel: 718-429-1982; Fax: 718-446-7225. Mrs. JoAnn Dolan, Prin. Sisters of Charity (Halifax) 1; Lay Teachers 24; Students 435.
Catechesis/Religious Program—39-66 58th St., Woodside, 11377. Tel: 718-899-3341. Ms. Sonia Casanova, D.R.E. Students 363.

101—ST. STANISLAUS BISHOP AND MARTYR (1923), (Polish), Merged with Nativity of the Blessed Virgin Mary, Ozone Park to form Nativity of the Blessed Virgin Mary-St. Stanislaus Bishop & Martyr Roman Catholic Church, Ozone Park. Revs. Paul C. Palmiotto; Andrezej Salwowski, Parochial Vicar; Angelo B. Pezzullo, Parochial Vicar (Retired).

Res.: 88-10 102nd Ave., Ozone Park, 11416. Tel: 718-845-3691; Fax: 718-843-8978. Email: nativityststans@verizon.net.

Catechesis/Religious Program—Elizabeth Perretta, D.R.E. Students 48.

102—ST. STANISLAUS KOSTKA (1872) Revs. Paul A. Wood; Joseph Palackal, C.M.I. (India), Parochial Vicar; Deacon David J. Corciari. In Res., Rev. Msgr. Algimantas A. Bartkus.

Res.: 57-15 61st St., Maspeth, 11378-2713. Tel: 718-326-2185; Fax: 718-416-2108. Email: ststanislauskostka@catholicweb.com.

School—61-17 Grand Ave., Maspeth, 11378. Tel: 718-326-1585; Fax: 718-326-1745. Web: www.ststans-school.org. Sr. Rose Torma, C.S.J., Prin. Religious 1; Lay Teachers 19; Students 221.

Catechesis/Religious Program—Students 156.

103—ST. TERESA (1928) Rev. Msgr. Denis M. Herron; Deacons Martin Soraire; Roberto Abundo. In Res., Rev. Msgr. Perfecto Vasquez.

Res.: 50-20 45th St., Woodside, 11377. Tel: 718-784-2123; Fax: 718-706-6797. Web: www.saintteresachurch.org.

Catechesis/Religious Program—Tel: 718-937-4819. Sr. Mary Jane Kelly, O.P., D.R.E. Students 376.

104—ST. TERESA OF AVILA (1929) Rev. Richard Hoare; Deacon Louis Panico.

Res.: 109-26 130th St., South Ozone Park, 11420. Tel: 718-529-3587; Fax: 718-529-0324.

School—Tel: 718-641-1316; Fax: 718-843-0769. Ms. Loretta Rybacki, Prin. Religious 1; Lay Teachers 13; Students 272.

Catechesis/Religious Program—Tel: 718-641-5710. Douglas M. Blaine, D.R.E. Students 116.

105—ST. THOMAS APOSTLE (1910) Revs. Frank C. Tumino; John Francis, Parochial Vicar; Rafael Gomez (Colombia); Deacon Jose A. Contreras.

Res.: 87-19 88th Ave., Woodhaven, 11421. Tel: 718-847-1353; Fax: 718-849-3776. Email: sthomasapostlewdhvn@nyc.rr.com. Web: www.stawoodhaven.org.

School—87-49 87th St., Woodhaven, 11421. Tel: 718-847-3904; Fax: 718-847-3513. Cathleen Quinn, Prin. Sisters 1; Lay Teachers 15; Students 203.

Catechesis/Religious Program—Tel: 718-441-8409. Sr. Helene Jakubowski, R.S.M., D.R.E. Students 160.

106—ST. THOMAS MORE-ST. EDMUND (1937) Merged with St. Genevieve to form Blessed Trinity Roman Catholic Church, Rockaway Point, NY. Records are at Blessed Trinity Roman Catholic Church.

107—TRANSFIGURATION (1908), (Lithuanian), Revs. Paul A. Wood; Vytautas Volertas, Parochial Vicar.

Res.: 64-14 Clinton Ave., Maspeth, 11378. Tel: 718-326-2236; Fax: 718-326-2249. Email: transfiguration@catholicweb.com. Web: transfiguration.catholicweb.com.

Catechesis/Religious Program—Students 78.

108—ST. VIRGILIUS (1914) Merged with St. Camillus in 2008 to form St. Camillus-St. Virgilius.

Chaplains of Public Institutions

BROOKLYN. *Bernard Fineson Development Center*. Vacant.

Beth Israel Medical Center/Kings Hgwy. Elaine Chan.

Metropolitan Detention Center. Vacant.

Brookdale Hospital Medical Center. Angela DiPaola.

Brooklyn Development Center. Vacant.

The Brooklyn Hospital. Rev. John O'Leary.

Coney Island Hospital. Rev. Joseph P. Quigley (Retired).

Downstate Medical Center. Rev. St. Martin Estiverne (Haiti), Chap.

Kings County Hospital Center. Rev. Souvenir Jean Paul, S.M.

Kingsboro Psychiatric Center. Rev. Robert Frueh, M.S.

Long Island College Hospital. Has an interfaith Chap.

Lutheran Medical Center. Rev. Augustine Emeh (Nigeria).

Maimonides Medical Center of Brooklyn. Rev. St. Martin Estiverne (Haiti).

Methodist Hospital. Rev. Sherif S.I. Fanous.

Woodhull Medical & Mental Health Center. Rev. David P. Bertolotti.

Wyckoff Heights Hospital. Rev. Francisco J. Ares.

QUEENS. *Creedmoor Psychiatric Center*. Revs. Paul Chenot, C.P., August P. Iantosca.

Elmhurst General Hospital. Rev. Alan Briceland, S.J.

Flushing Hospital and Medical Center. Rev. Bryan J. Carney, Chap.

Jamaica Hospital - Trump Pavilion. Rev. James Nunes, M.S.

St. John's Episcopal Hospital. Rev. Frederick Anawonah (Nigeria).

Long Island Jewish Hospital. Sr. Faustina Quayson, H.H.C.J., Rev. Barthlomew I. Okonkwo (Nigeria), Chap.

The Mount Sinai Hospital of Queens. Rev. Jean G. Laguerre (Haiti).

N.Y. Hospital Medical Center of Queens. Rev. Bryan J. Carney, Chap., Sr. Rosarine Quinn, C.S.J.

Peninsula Hospital Center. Rev. Frederick Anawonah (Nigeria).

Queens Hospital Center--Pastoral Care Office. Rev. Jose Cadusale (Philippines).

Veterans Affairs Extended Care Center, St. Albans, NY. Rev. Andrew Sioleti, O.F.M. Conv.

Military Chaplains:

Revs.—

Finley, James F., US Navy, Command Chap. (Retired), US Marine Corps. Air Station, Box 99100, Yuma, AZ 85369-9100.

Hirten, Timothy J., US Airforce Base, 436 AW/HC, Dover Afb, DE 19902.

Krische, James J., U.S. Army

Released from Diocesan Assignment:

Rev. Msgrs.—

Harris, Robert M., M.S.W., M.Phil., M.A., St. Vincent's Residence, 66 Boerum Pl., 11201.

Maksymowicz, John H., Apostolic Nunciature, 3339 Massachusetts Ave., N.W., Washington, DC 20008.

Marchese, Richard E., Apostolic Nunciature, 3339 Massachusetts Ave., N.W., Washington, DC 20008.

Sarno, Robert J., Congregation for the Causes of Saints, Piazza Pio XII, 10 00120 Vatican City State. (Europe)

Vaccari, Peter I., S.T.L., Immaculate Conception Seminary, W. Neck Rd., Lloyd Harbor, Huntington, 11743.

Revs.—

Bellantonio, Albert, P.O. Box 382, Tannersville, PA 18372.

Bordeleau, Beau-Pierre G., 512 W. River Rd., Apt. 219, Hooksett, NH 03106.

Buonanno, Vito A., Basilica of the National Shrine of the Immaculate Conception, 400 Michigan Ave. N.E., Washington, DC 20017.

Caccavale, Charles, Seminary of the Immaculate Conception, Huntington, 11743.

Costello, John J., Dir. Pastoral Formation, Pontifical North American College 00120 Vatican City State. (Europe)

DeSanctis, Peter A., Our Lady of the Isle Church, 5 Prospect Ave., P.O. Box 3027, Shelter Island Heights, 11965.

Fermeglia, Charles, Our Lady of Pillar, 540 Kelly St., Half Moon Bay, CA 94019.

Frawley, Patrick J., Fidelis Care, 95-25 Queens Blvd., Rego Park, 11374.

Himes, Michael J., Dept. of Theology, Boston College, Chestnut Hill, MA 02167-3806.

Lauder, Robert E., Bishop Mugavero Residence, 7200 Douglaston Pkwy., Douglaston, 11362.

Machalski, Thomas C., Jr., M.S.Ed., J.C.L., SS. Cyril and Methodius Seminary, 3535 Indian Tr., Orchard Lake, MI 48324.

Penta, Leo J., Catholic University of Applied Sciences, Kopenicker Allee 39-57, Berlin, Germany.

Ruiz, Jean-Pierre, S.T.D., SS. Joachim & Anne, 218-26 105th Ave., Queens Village, 11429.

Valencia, Carlos D., 4519 W. 171 St., Lawndale, CA 90260.

Vesey, John E., M.M., Northeastern University, Foreign Affairs Office, Shenyang 110004 China.

Zuk, Richard P., P.O. Box 1214, Saranac Lake, 12983.

Graduate Studies:

Revs.—

Bruno, Michael J. S.
Champoli, Daniel
Keating, Patrick J.
Kuroly, James A.
Pham, Cuong M.
Suh, Daniel
Swartvagher, Marc E., S.T.L.

On Leave/Unassigned:

Revs.—

Abugel, Alexander G.
Brown, Charles L.
Ercolano, Anthony S.
Espinal, David
Espinosa, David F.
Gillen, Peter D.
Greene, Michael M.
Guiry, Robert W.
Hand, Kenneth J.
Hannan, James G.
Hauser, John G.
Javier, Nazareno
Klein, Dennis D.
Lazar, John E.
Lukianiuk, Andrzej
Miller, John C.
Miller, Joseph A.
Perez, Jose
Piro, Gerald J.
Reynolds, James J.
Rizzo, Matteo
Steinhauser, Michael G.
Stewart, Edward R.
Wulinski, Stanley F.

Retired:

Rev. Msgrs.—

Angles, Sebastian, 2601 Muscatello St., Orlando, FL 32821.

Arella, Gerard, Bishop Mugavero Residence, 7200 Douglaston Pkwy., Douglaston, 11362.

Basler, Howard B., 156-06 46th Ave., Flushing, 11355.

Bednartz, August C., Bishop Mugavero Residence, 7200 Douglaston Pkwy., Douglaston, 11362.

Bennett, Austin P., J.C.D., P.A., 1550 Hendrickson St., 11234.

Boccio, Charles P., 336 N. Birch Rd., #7A, Fort Lauderdale, FL 33304.

Bottino, Edward J., Mary's Nativity, 46-02 Parsons Blvd., Flushing, 11355.

Brady, Thomas F., Good Shepherd, 1950 Batchelder St., 11229.

Breen, Edward J., Our Lady of Fatima, 25-02 80 St., Jackson Heights, 11370.

Burns, John A., 1395 E. 56th St., 11234.

Bynon, Joseph P., Bishop Mugavero Residence, 7200 Douglaston Pkwy., Douglaston, 11362.

Cantley, Michael J., Bishop Mugavero Residence, 7200 Douglaston Pkwy., Douglaston, 11362.

Casey, John F., Our Lady of Lourdes, 92-96 220th St., Queens Village, 11428.

Collini, Celsus O., 141-36 77th Ave., Kew Gardens Hills, 11367.

Cooney, James J., B.A., M.A., Bishop Mugavero Residence, 7200 Douglaston Pkwy., Douglaston, 11362.

Darbouze, Rollin, 18338 Winter Garden Ave., Port Charlotte, FL 33948.

Deas, George T., Bishop Mugavero Residence, 7200 Douglaston Pkwy., Douglaston, 11362.

Dietz, Conrad R., Bishop Mugavero Residence, 7200 Douglaston Pkwy., Douglaston, 11362.

Dunn, Richard F., 54 Elm Ct., New Hyde Park, 11040.

Ecker, Robert J., 300 Second St., Coronado, CA 92118.

Feldhaus, Eugene A., Bishop Magavero Residence, 7200 Douglaston Pkwy., Douglaston, 11362.

Flanagan, Thomas J., P.O. Box 804, Hampton Bays, 11946.

Flood, William J., Our Lady of the Blessed Sacrament, 34-24 203rd St., Bayside, 11361.

Foley, Matthew F., P.O. Box 91T, Bethel, 12720.

Fullam, Vincent F., Immaculate Conception, 21-47 29 St., Astoria, 11105.

Gotimer, James E., 239 W. 21 St., New York, 10011.

Gradilone, Thomas J., Bishop Mugavero Residence, 7200 Douglaston Pkwy., Douglaston, 11362.

Haggerty, Thomas M., Our Lady of Mount Carmel, 275 N. 8th St., 11211.

Hartmann, John F., 141 State St., Guilford, CT 06437.

Hinch, Lawrence E., Bishop Mugavero Residence, 7200 Douglaston Pkwy., Douglaston, 11362.

Hunt, James A., Bishop Mugavero Residence, 7200 Douglaston Pkwy., Douglaston, 11362.

Keane, Vincent A., 7200 Douglaston Pkwy., Douglaston, 11362.

Kelly, Raymond J., S.T.L., Bishop Mugavero Residence, 7200 Douglaston Pkwy., Douglaston, 11362.

Keppler, John F., Bishop Mugavero Residence, 7200 Douglaston Pkwy., Douglaston, 11362.

King, James P., Bishop Mugavero Residence, 7200 Douglaston Pkwy., Douglaston, 11362.

Kneafsey, Cornelius T., St. Benedict Joseph Labre, 94-40 118 St., Richmond Hill, 11418.

Kutner, Raymond W., J.C.D., 605 Oaks Dr., Pompano Beach, FL 33069.

Langelier, Gerald J., Our Lady of Mercy, 70-01 Kessel St., Forest Hills, 11375.

Mulqueen, Joseph C., J.C.L., St. Mary, 10-08 49 Ave., Long Island City, 11101.

Murphy, Walter C., Bishop Mugavero Residence, 7200 Douglaston Pkwy., Douglaston, 11362.

Noonan, Thomas F., St. Edmund, 2460 Ocean Ave., 11229.

O'Brien, John H., 88-19 Parsons Blvd., Jamaica, 11432.

O'Toole, Patrick F., 13105 S.W. 16 Ct., Apt. L413, Pembroke Pines, FL 33027.

Pfeiffer, Joseph C., 157-10 83rd St., Howard Beach, 11414. 157-10 83rd St., Howard Beach, 11414.

Phillips, Michael J., St. Anselm, 356 82nd St., 11209.

Powis, John J., 138 Bleeker St., 11221.

Reilly, Philip J., Monastery of the Precious Blood, 5400 Fort Hamilton Pkwy., 11219.

Rodgers, William J., Queen of Peace Residence, 110-30 221st St., Queens Village, 11429.
Rosa, Joseph R., 70 Bay 47th St., 11214.
Ryan, James W., Queen of Peace Residence, 110-30 221 St., Queens Village, 11429.
Schuster, George M., Our Lady of the Miraculous Medal, 62-81 60th Pl., Ridgewood, 11385.
Sivillo, Nicholas W., St. Margaret, 66-05 79th Pl., Middle Village, 11379.
Stafford, Joseph L., Holy Family, 175-20 74 Ave., Flushing, 11366.
Vazquez, Perfecto, St. Teresa, 50-20 45th St., Woodside, 11377.
Villani, Rocco D., St. Brendan, 1525 East 12th St., 11230.
Waldron, John E., Bishop Mugavero Residence, 7200 Douglaston Pkwy., Douglaston, 11362.
White, Leo J., St. George's Cathedral, Westminster Bridge Rd., London SW1 7HY England.

Revs.—
Aufiero, Louis D., Holy Family Church, 175-20 74th Ave., Flushing, 11366.
Badia, Leonard F., Ph.D., 4810 N.W. 4th St., Apt. C., Delray Beach, FL 33445.
Bedoya, Hugo, St. John Vianney, 140-10 34th Ave., Flushing, 11354.
Berran, Donald M., 111-50 115 St., South Ozone Park, 11420.
Blauvelt, Robert, Bishop Mugavero Residence, 7200 Douglaston Pkwy., Douglaston, 11362.
Boyd, James A., 7462 Hanford Pl., San Diego, CA 92111.
Brady, Edmund P., Our Lady of Mount Carmel, 23-25 Newtown Ave., Astoria, 11102.
Byrne, Hugh A., Bishop Mugavero Residence, 7200 Douglaston Pkwy., Douglaston, 11362.
Byrnes, Francis J., Bishop Mugavero Residence, 7200 Douglaston Pkwy., Douglaston, 11362.
Byrnes, John W., Queen of Peace Residence, 110-30 221 St., Queens Village, 11429.
Calder, Kenneth J., Our Lady of Angels, 7320 Fourth Ave., 11209.
Casey, Anthony C., Queen of Peace Residence, 110-30 221st St., Queens Village, 11429.
Cestaro, Joseph A., 111 W. 71st St., Apt. 11B, New York, 10023.
Charlot, Lucien, St. Augustine, 116 Sixth Ave., 11217.
Costello, Coleman J., Bishop Mugavero Residence, 7200 Douglaston Pkwy., Douglaston, 11362.
Cowan, George R., Bishop Mugavero Residence, 7200 Douglaston Pkwy., Douglaston, 11362.
Coyle, Eugene P., 7200 Douglaston Pkwy., Douglaston, 11362.
Cremins, John J., Our Lady of Mercy, 70-01 Kessel St., Forest Hills, 11375.
Cullinane, John F., P.E., Blessed Trinity, 204-25 Rockaway Point Blvd., Rockaway Point, 11697.
Cutrone, Dominick F., Our Lady of Grace, 430 Ave. W., 11223.
Czok, Robert W., St. Rose of Lima, 130 Beach 84 St., Rockaway Beach, 11693.
De Laura, Felice J., 81-23 189th St., Jamaica, 11423.
Dell'Anno, Anthony V., St. Edmund, #2460 Ocean Ave., 11229.
Denzer, Joseph W., Bishop Mugavero Residence, 7200 Douglaston Pkwy., Douglaston, 11362.
Devine, James T., Bishop Mugavero Residence, 7200 Douglaston Pkwy., Douglaston, 11362.
Diamond, Matthew J., St. Andrew Avellino, 35-60 158th St., Flushing, 11358.
Diffley, Patrick J., 8000 Shore Front Pkwy., Apt. 6B, Rockaway Beach, 11693.
Dolan, Joseph, 8201 13 Ave., 11228.
Dolan, Thomas D., 7200 Douglaston Pkwy., Douglaston, 11362.
Donnelly, Eugene F., 25-02 80th St., Jackson Heights, 11370.
Doody, Cyril F., 27 Parkway Dr., Sag Harbor, 11963.
Dunne, James M., St. Camillus-St. Virgilius, 99-15 Rockaway Beach Blvd., Rockaway Beach, 11693.
Early, William F., 53-91 Outlook Point, San Diego, CA 92124.
Estrada, Sabino, 39-76 57th St., #3D, Woodside, 11377.
Farrugia, William C., 20-51 26th St., Astoria, 11105.
Fernando, Joachim (Sri Lanka), 91 Basiyawatta, Negumbo, Sri Lanka.
Finley, James F., 21686 Eric Rd Apt. E, Lexington Park, MD 20653.
Fraser, James F., 175-20 74th Ave., Flushing, 11366.
Gallo, Vincent, 32 Beach 219th St., Breezy Point, 11697.
Grzelak, Thaddeus A., 4662 Brisa Dr., Palmdale, CA 93551.
Guarracino, Ralph, Mount Saint Mary Cemetery, 172-00 Booth Memorial Ave., Flushing, 11365.
Gural, Marion A., 123 Henry Rd., Southampton, 11968.
Gurrieri, John A., Bishop Mugavero Residence, 7200 Douglaston Pkwy., Douglaston, 11362.
Heffernan, James F., 485 Sheafe Rd., Wappingers Falls, 12590.
Kehoe, Charles B., Rose Garden Villa, Unit 202, 5510 S.W. 4th Pl., Cape Coral, FL 33914.
Keohane, Daniel G., Bishop Mugavero Residence, 7200 Douglaston Pkwy., Douglaston, 11362.
Kiernan, Edward J., 43 Highland Rd., Southampton, 11968.
Kirby, Martin F., M.A., 31-30 74 St., Jackson Heights, 11372.
Kirrane, James A., Chapin Home for the Aging, 165-01 Chapin Pkwy., Jamaica, 11432.
Labita, Francis J., Bishop Mugavero Residence, 7200 Douglaston Pkwy., Douglaston, 11362.
Lang, Henry A., 56-15 213th St., Bayside Hills, 11364.
Leone, James M., P.O. Box 426, Mastic Beach, 11951.
Lutjen, George J., 71-08 72nd Pl., Glendale, 11385.
Lynch, Francis, Our Lady of Mt. Carmel, 23-25 Newtown Ave., Astoria, 11361.
Maloney, John P., 209-10 41st Ave., Apt. 2R, Bayside, 11361.
Matonti, Charles J., St. Columba, 2245 Kimball St., 11234.
Maynard, Lewis H., St. Agatha, 702 48th St., 11220.
McGovern, Eugene F., Bishop Mugavero Residence, 7200 Douglaston Pkwy., Douglaston, 11362.
McShane, John A., 7200 Douglaston Pkwy., Douglaston, 11362.
Meszaros, James J., St. Josaphat, 34-32 210th St., Bayside, 11361.
Mitchell, Walter A., 1329 Surf Ave., 11224.
Mulkerin, Terrence J., Holy Name of Jesus, 245 Prospect Park W., 11215.
Muthukatti, Thomas, St. Benedict Joseph Labre Church, 94-40 118th St., South Richmond Hill, 11419.
Nadine, Jerome E., P.O. Box 2982, Fallbrook, CA 92088.
Newell, John J., 94 Rose Ave., Floral Park, 11001.
Nolan, Joseph M., 115-58 222nd St., Cambria Heights, 11411.
O'Donoghue, Kevin J., Bishop Mugavero Residence, 7200 Douglaston Pkwy., Douglaston, 11362.
Ossa, Pedro N., St. Martin of Tours, 1288 Hancock St., 11221.
Parisi, Michael R., St. Kevin, 45-21 194th St., Flushing, 11358.
Pasciuto, Joseph C., 451 Abingdon Ave., Staten Island, 10308.
Pezzullo, Angelo B., Nativity of the Blessed Virgin Mary, 101-41 91st St., Ozone Park, 11416.
Pfundstein, George A., St. Ann, 142-30 58th Ave., Flushing, 11355.
Pomilio, Matthew J., 175-20 Wexford Ter., Jamaica, 11432.
Quigley, Joseph P., St. Mark, 2609 E. 19th St., 11235.
Ros, Manuel, Our Lady of Sorrows, 104-11 37th Ave., Corona, 11368.
Sabatos, Daniel C., 9 Lenore Dr., White Plains, 10607.
Salerno, Emilio J., 118 Lake Emerald Dr. #104, Oakland Park, FL 33309.
Sans, Pablo, 136-06 87th Ave., Richmond Hill, 11416.
Schmidt, Jerome J., Bishop Mugavero Residence, 7200 Douglaston Pkwy., Douglaston, 11362.
Schmidt, Raymond F., 507 Barberry Ln., New Windsor, 12553.
Smith, Edward J., 241-16 Rushmore Ave., Douglaston, 11362.
Smith, LeRoy J., 1605 S. US1 Apt. #B304, Jupiter, FL 33477.
Sommermeyer, Gary H., 622 A. Heritage Village, Southbury, CT 06488.
Suran, Joaquin, 555 North Ave., #3B, Fort Lee, NJ 07024.
Termine, Vincent J., 93 Goldeneye Rd., Kiawah Island, SC 29455.
Tivenan, John J., 6128 Hadley Commons Dr., Riverview, FL 33578.
Varano, Andrew R., 1238 Avenue V., 11229.
Vendetti, Michael A., 94-26 Sutter Ave., Ozone Park, 11417.
Verrengio, Rocco F., P.O. Box 61321, Staten Island, 10306.
Visich, Eduard C., 5510 N. Ocean Dr., Singer Island, FL 33404.
Vivona, Anthony, 388 Avenue S Apt. 2F, 11223-2955.
Walker, Gerard T., 8 N. William St., East Patchogue, 11772.
Wei, Luke, 2886 Fernley Dr. E., West Palm Beach, FL 33415.
Weiscopf, Daniel J., 2720 Surf Avve., 11224.
White, Charles H., St. Mary Star of the Sea, 1920 New Haven Ave., Far Rockaway, 11691.
Wilkinson, John H., St. Brigid, 409 Linden St., 11237.
Wiseman, Joseph F., 46-02 Parsons Blvd., Flushing, 11355.
Zaccagnigno, Raffaele, Via Federico Paolini 115, Scala D. int. 11, 00122 Ostia Lido, Rome, Italy.
Zanon, Romano A., Sacred Heart, 83-17 78th Ave., Glendale, 11385.

Permanent Deacons:
Abundo, Roberto S., St. Teresa, Woodside
Agnant, Ronald Y., Holy Innocents, Brooklyn
Aigbojie, Edward A., St. Martin Porres, Brooklyn
Alayu, Perlito B., Diocese of Orlando
Alick, Alejandro, Inactive
Almendarez, Felipe, Holy Name of Jesus, Brooklyn
Almodovar, Ismael, Diocese of Orlando
Alvarado, Jorge L., Our Lady of Perpetual Help, South Ozone Park
Alvarez, Felipe J., St. Joseph, Long Island City
Alvia, Humberto R., (Diocese of Venice)
Amore, Bryan J., St. Mary Mother of Jesus, Brooklyn
Arcand, Dennis A., Diocese of Savannah
Aris, Anthony J., (Inactive)
Arteaga, Emilio S., St. Agatha, Brooklyn
Avallone, Ernesto A., Our Lady of the Blessed Sacrament, Bayside
Baez, Angel, (Inactive)
Barahona, Manuel S., Our Lady of Mount Carmel, Astoria
Barber, Christopher E., St. Clare, Rosedale
Barreneche, Julio C., St. Kevin, Flushing
Beaubrun, Berthal, (Retired)
Bichotte, Joseph, (Retired)
Blake, Lamont A., Christ the King, Springfield Gardens
Blanco, Hector S., Our Lady of Perpetual Help, Brooklyn
Bobadilla, Antonio, Archdiocese of Santo Domingo, Dominican Republic
Borheck, Steven J., Our Lady of the Snows, N. Floral Park
Bourbeau, George A., Our Lady of the Blessed Sacrament, Bayside
Boursiquot, Jean B., (Retired)
Brainerd, Michael J., St. Margaret, Middle Village
Branch, Leroy P., St. Paul & St. Agnes, Brooklyn
Breviario, Alexander, Our Lady of Grace, Howard Beach
Bugay, Josefino Y., (Inactive)
Caceres, Ycelso, (Inactive)
Cajiao, Henry, Diocese of St. Petersburg
Cajoux, Francois G., Sacred Heart Cambria Hts.
Calvo, Juan, (Retired)
Campisi, Joseph, (Retired)
Cancel, Edwin, Our Lady of the Angelus, Rego Park
Cantirino, John, Immaculate Heart of Mary, Brooklyn
Carattini, Juan M., SS. Peter and Paul, Brooklyn
Cardona, Ramon, Diocese of Mayaguez, PR
Casares, Gabriel, (Leave of Absence)
Castillo, Jorge E., St. Joan of Arc, Jackson Heights
Catanello, Joseph V., Holy Family, Flushing
Cederroth, Charles J., Diocese of Trenton
Cepin, Concepcion, St. Joseph Patron, Brooklyn
Chin, Paul M., St. Paul Chong Ha-Sang Chapel, Flushing
Ciccaroni, Andrew, St. Robert Bellarmine, Bayside
Cobham, Jaime A., St. Paul & St. Agnes, Brooklyn
Coffey, John P., (Retired)
Colandrea, Dante, St. Athanasius, Brooklyn
Colon, Rafael, (Inactive)
Contreras, Jose A., St. Thomas the Apostle, Woodhaven
Contreras, William de Jesus, St. Bartholomew, Elmhurst
Corciari, David J., St. Stanislaus Kostka, Maspeth
Coyle, Lawrence J., St. Columba, Brooklyn
Cruz, Florencio, (Retired)
Cruz, Rafael, Archdiocese of Miami
Cruz, Ramon, St. Mary Gate of Heaven, Ozone Park
Cutter, Arthur, St. Gregory the Great, Bellerose
D'Accordo, Armand C., St. Helen, Howard Beach
D'Accordo, Frank J., Saint Bernard, Brooklyn
Da Costa, Dennis A., (Retired)
Damato, Stephen T., St. Sebastian, Woodside
Daniel, Gordon V., (Inactive)
Dass, Joseph H., St. Gerard Majella, Hollis
Davis, Thomas G., St. Anselm, Brooklyn
De Tucci, Frank A., Inactive
DeBiase, Vincent, (Retired)
DeLeon, Andres, Our Lady of Mount Carmel, Brooklyn
Dennehy, John P., (Inactive)
Denzler, Joseph C., Our Lady of Lourdes, Queens Village
Deschler, Bernard M., (Retired)

Despeignes, Robinson, Incarnation, Queens Village
Devaney, Thomas J., Holy Name of Jesus, Brooklyn
Diaz, Rafael, (Retired)
Diaz, Ramon G., Immaculate Conception, Jamaica
DiMichele, Frank, St. Bernadette, Brooklyn
Dixon, Gregory D., St. Andrew the Apostle, Brooklyn
Dolan, John J., St. Rosalia-Regina Pacis, Brooklyn
Donnelly, Daniel P., St. Fidelis, College Point
Dorsinville, Paul C., Sacred Heart, Cambria Heights
Dudley, Roy A., (Retired)
Duncan, Isaac, (Retired)
Dupuy, Eulogio S., (Retired)
Duran, Fausto, P.D., St. Barbara, Brooklyn
Duran, Juan R., Archdiocese of Minneapolis
Elias, Raul S., Holy Child Jesus, Richmond Hill
Elijio, Victorino P., Our Lady of Presentation - Our Lady of Presentation
Elrose, Richard E., St. Helen, Howard Beach
Espinal, Luis J., (Inactive)
Favale, Anthony, St. Finbar, Brooklyn
Felix, Antoine, (Inactive)
Fernandez, Jose M., Queen of Peace, Kew Gardens Hills
Fernandez, Justo I., (Inactive)
Flaim, Fabio, (Retired)
Flanagan, Patrick M., St. Anthony of Padua, Ozone Park
Flannery, John A., (Retired)
Francis, John J., (Retired)
Gaine, Edward S., Our Lady of Angels, Brooklyn
Galazin, Stanley J., American Martyrs, Bayside, Dir. Immaculate Conception Center, Douglaston
Garamella, Robert, Diocese of Rockville Centre
Garcia, Carlos, St. Malachy, Brooklyn
Garcia, Jimmy, Diocese of Fort Worth, Texas
George, Roy N., St. Matthew, Brooklyn
Germain, Moliere, (Retired)
Gilligan, Richard J., St. Mary Gate of Heaven, Ozone Park
Gomez, Guillermo D., St. Gerard Majella, Hollis
Gonzales, Rafael, Diocese of Orlando
Gonzalez, Jorge A., Dir. Diaconate Formation Office
Gonzalez, Louis A., St. Paul & St. Agnes, Brooklyn
Gordon, Daniel, (Inactive)
Griffin, Arthur J., Transfiguration, Maspeth
Guster, Edward J., Jr., Nativity of the Blessed Virgin Mary, Ozone Park
Hart, Ernest F., St. Mary Magdalene, Springfield Gardens
Hernandez, Rafael, Diocese of Orlando
Hernandez, Rene, St. Mary Star of the Sea and St. Gertrude, Far Rockaway
Hernandez, Wilfredo, Holy Spirit, Brooklyn
Hili, Saviour, St. Francis of Assisi, Long Island City
Horne, Wilfred N., (Retired)
Huckemeyer, Edward J., (On Leave)
Hull, John E., St. Patrick, Brooklyn
Hurley, Charles R., Our Lady of Angels, Brooklyn
Innocent, Francois, (Retired)
Kandra, Gregory, Our Lady Queen of Martyrs, Forest Hills
Kelly, William V., St. Athanasius, Brooklyn
Kennedy, James F., Diocese of St. Petersburg, FL
Killian, John F., Our Lady of Mercy, Forest Hills
Knight, Lionel A., (Retired)
Krebs, Jerome H., (Retired)
Lacy, James J., (Retired)
LaGamba, Vincent M., St. Francis De Sales, Belle Harbor
LaGreca, John J., Our Lady of Guadalupe, Brooklyn
Landron, Jaime, (Retired)
Lavanco, Robert F., Our Lady of Hope, Middle Village
Lee, Richard G., (Retired)
Leon, Pedro V., St. Martin of Tours, Brooklyn
Licata, Salvatore V., (Retired)
Lima, Ramon, St. Raphael, Long Island City
Lizama, Jose Armanso, Presentation of the Blessed Virgin Mary, Jamaica
Logue, Patrick J., St. Rose of Lima, Rockaway Beech
Lonergan, Robert P., St. Josaphat, Bayside
Lopez, Eduvigis, (Inactive)
Lopez, Hiram, Archdiocese of New York
Lopez, Luis R., Incarnation, Queens Village
Lopez, Marco V., Our Lady of Fatima, Jackson Heights
Magana, Daniel, Our Lady of Sorrows, Corona
Maldonado, Andres, Diocese of Ponce, PR
Malone, William F., Diocese of Trenton, NJ
Maloney, James E., Our Lady of The Miraculous Medal, Ridgewood
Marcel, Magloire, St. Jerome, Brooklyn
Marchello, Andrew A., (Retired)
Marley, Daniel J., (Retired)
Marte, Rafael, St. Mary Mother of the Church, Brooklyn
Martinez, Carlos A., All Saints, Brooklyn
Martinez, German, Transfiguration, Brooklyn
Martinez, Manuel I., St. Benedict Joseph Labre, Richmond Hill
Martucci, Anthony P., St. Bernadette, Brooklyn
Mateo, Francis G., St. Finbar, Brooklyn
Mayers, Winston M., (Retired)
Mazza, Nicholas, (Retired)
McBride, Timothy, St. Mary Gate of Heaven, Ozone Park
McGreevey, John F., (Retired)
McGuire, Joseph P., (Retired)
McMaster, Laurence O., St. Gerard Majella, Hollis
McNamara, William, Sacred Heart, Bayside
Medina, Gustavo, St. Catharine of Alexandria, Brooklyn
Mejia, Abdon (Peru), (Retired)
Mejia, Felix, St. Rita, Brooklyn
Mejia, Julio C., St. Michael, Brooklyn
Mejia, Rafael A., Diocese of Orlando
Mellace, Carlo V., SS. Simon and Jude Brooklyn
Miller, Leon F., (Diocese of San Jose, CA)
Miranda, Osborne, St. Fortunata, Brooklyn
Montero, Adalberto, St. Mary Star of Sea & St. Gertrude, Far Rockaway
Montes, Leopoldo R, Blessed Virgin Mary Help of Christians, Woodside
Morales, Julio A., Diocese of Orlando
Morano, Frank A., St. Frances Cabrini, Brooklyn
Mordan, Marcus A., Sacred Heart, Cambria Heights
Moreno, Ricardo, Our Lady of Lourdes, Queens Village
Morin, Paul P., St. Dominic, Brooklyn
Moss, Michael C., St. Mary Star of the Sea, Far Rockaway
Mule, Lawrence C., St. Matthias, Ridgewood
Munoz, Franklin G., Incarnation, Queens Village
Murillo, Julio C., Our Lady of the Angelus, Rego Park
Murphy, John J., (Retired)
Noble, James D., Immaculate Heart of Mary, Brooklyn
O'Connell, Edward F., Our Lady of Mount Carmel, Brooklyn
Occhiuto, Joseph J., (Inactive)
Oellinger, Matthew J., Our Lady of the Snows, North Floral Park
Oggeri, William, (Retired)
Olivas, Pascual B., St. Bonaventure, Jamaica
Orlandello, John P., Divine Mercy, Brooklyn
Orozco, Fernando, St. Paul the Apostle, Corona
Oviedo, Jose L., St. Sylvester, Brooklyn
Page, Thomas J., St. Adalbert, Elmhurst
Panessa, Giacomo, Most Precious Blood, Astoria
Panico, Louis J., St. Teresa of Avila, South Ozone Park
Park, Julio, (Retired)
Park, Kyuchon J., (Inactive)
Pascal, Orlando, Archdiocese of NY
Paul, Ernst, Our Lady of Miracles, Brooklyn
Pavlyshin, Peter, (Diocese of Venice)
Perez, Richard, (Retired)
Piaubert, Joseph C., Holy Innocents, Brooklyn
Pierre-Antoine, Clemenceau, Incarnation, Queens Village
Pittie, Francis M., St. Rose of Lima, Brooklyn
Pons, Ramon C., St. Rosalia-Regina Pacis, Brooklyn
Pouso, Roberto J., (Inactive)
Rameau, Jean J., St. Therese of Lisieux, Brooklyn
Ramirez, Manuel, (Inactive)
Ramos, James, St. Francis Xavier, Brooklyn
Ramos, Jose A., (Diocese of Orlando)
Reichert, John P., (Retired)
Reyes, Ricardo, Our Lady of the Presentation, Brooklyn
Ritchie, Frederick V., St. Columba, Brooklyn
Rivera, Hector R., Archdiocese of San Juan, PR
Rizzo, Giovanni A., (Retired)
Rizzuto, Ronald, St. Edmund, Brooklyn
Roberts, Lionel V., Diocese of St. Petersburg, FL
Rodriguez, Daniel R., Immaculate Conception, Jamaica
Rodriguez, Manuel L., St. Elizabeth, Ozone Park
Roman, Luis A., (Inactive)
Ronacher, Ronald M., St. Rita, Brooklyn
Rosa, Andy, St. Rita, Brooklyn
Rosario, Israel, Transfiguration, Brooklyn
Ruiz, José D., Diocese of Ponce, PR
Ruoff, James F., Blessed Trinity, Rockaway Point
Russo, Anthony J., (Retired)
Ryan, Kevin F., (Retired)
Saldana, Albert, Our Lady of Light, St. Albans
Sampson, Harold S., St. Rose of Lima, Rockaway Beach
Sands, John E., St. Matthias, Ridgewood
Sawney, Ira, Florida
Schwarz, Jeremiah W., Holy Child Jesus, Richmond Hill
Sclafani, Leonard A., Holy Trinity, Whitestone
Sencion, Eduardo, Our Lady of the Cenacle, Richmond Hill
Siani, Philip J., Our Lady of Grace, Brooklyn
Siavichay, Ruben G., St. Anthony of Padua, South Ozone Park
Simon, Mauclair, St. Vincent Ferrer, Brooklyn
Sinisi, Henry C., (On Leave)
Smith, Charles J., Diocese of Trenton
Smith, Henry J., (Retired)
Smith, Nathaniel J., St. Clement Pope, South Ozone Park
Smith, Ramon, (On Leave)
Smolinski, Edward A., (Retired)
Soraire, Martin D., St. Teresa, Woodside
Soto, Jesus, Our Lady of Perpetual Help, Brooklyn
Stamm, Peter, Sacred Heart, Glendale
Stucchio, Anthony, St. Ephrem, Brooklyn
Sucich, John R., St. Francis of Assisi, Long Island City
Svebel, Harry A., (Retired)
Tavarez, Fabio E., Our Lady of Presentation - Our Ladyof Mercy, Brooklyn
Taylor, Luis C., Our Lady of Light, St. Albans
Thompson, Balfour A., St. Martin de Porres, Brooklyn
Tierney, John A., Diocese of Albany
Tineo, Jose F., Our Lady of Sorrows, Corona
Tokarcsik, George M., Pennsylvania
Torres, Abel, Holy Name, Brooklyn
Torres, Freddy, Our Lady of Light, St. Albans
Trochez, Carlos A., St. Patrick, Brooklyn
Troy, Michael J., (Retired)
Tully, Dean T., Holy Child Jesus, Richmond Hill
Uzoigwe, Okafor C., St. Fortunata, Brooklyn
Valderama, Carlos, Divine Mercy, Brooklyn
Valle Valle, Esteban, Archdiocese of San Juan, PR
Van de Ven, Theodore, Diocese of Rockville Centre
Van Wassenhove, Raymond J., Diocese of Peoria
Varela, Jamie, (Assistant to the Bishop), Our Lady of the Presentation & Our Lady of Mercy, Brooklyn
Vargas, Juan R., (Diocese of Orlando)
Vega, Rogelio, Most Holy Trinity and St. Mary, Brooklyn
Vicinanza, Michael W.
Wagner, Christopher A., St. Bernard, Brooklyn
Warner, Lester, St. Gabriel, East Elmhurst
Warren, John, Our Lady of the Snows, Floral Park
Williams, Lee C., (Retired)
Williamsen, William, (Retired)
Yepes, Elias H., St. Michael, Flushing
Zelaya, Manuel, Guardian Angel, Brooklyn
Zeuner, Robert J., St. Gregory the Great, Bellerose
Zhagnay, Juan J., Corpus Christi, Woodside
Zimmermann, Walter C., (Retired)

INSTITUTIONS LOCATED IN THE DIOCESE

[A] PASTORAL CENTERS

DOUGLASTON. *Immaculate Conception Center* (1968) 7200 Douglaston Pkwy., 11362-1997. Tel: 718-281-9526; Fax: 718-229-2658. Email: sgalazin@diobrook.org. Deacon Stanley J. Galazin, Dir.; Mr. Howard Maresca, Asst. Dir. Bldg. Svcs. & Maintenance.

[B] SEMINARIES, DIOCESAN

DOUGLASTON. *Cathedral Seminary Residence of the Immaculate Conception*, 7200 Douglaston Pkwy., 11362. Tel: 718-229-8001; Fax: 718-281-9536. Rev. Msgrs. Robert J. Thelen, S.T.L., KCHS, Rector; Conrad R. Dietz, Philosophy Prof. (Retired); Revs. Fred Marano, B.A., M.A., Spiritual Dir.; Marc E. Swartvagher, S.T.L., Academic Dean, Philosophy Prof.; Very Rev. Joseph G. Fonti, S.T.L., Assoc. Spiritual Dir.; Revs. Luis Saldana, S.T.L., Vice Rector; Brian Barr, M.Div., Dean, Discipline; Joseph Kelly, D.Min., M.A., M.Div., Spiritual Dir. Residence for college level and post college level candidates for Priesthood. Priests 12; Lay Teachers 5; Seminarians 77.

ELMHURST. *Cathedral Preparatory Seminary of the Immaculate Conception*, 56-25 92nd St., 11373. Tel: 718-592-6800; Fax: 718-592-5574. Email: frmarano@cathedralprepseminary.com. Revs. Fred Marano, B.A., M.A., Rector & Prin.; John P. Cush, B.A., S.T.L., Spiritual Dir. & Dir. Devel.; James A. Kuroly, B.A., M.A., Dir. Recruitment. Priests 3; Lay Teachers 13; Seminarians 178.

[C] COLLEGES AND UNIVERSITIES

BROOKLYN. **St. Francis College*, 180 Remsen St., 11201. Tel: 718-522-2300; Fax: 718-624-6692. Web: www.sfc.edu. Mr. Brendan J. Dugan, Pres.; James Smith, Librarian. Priests 1; Brothers 5; Sisters 1; Students 2,728; Total Staff 83.

**St. Joseph's College*, 245 Clinton Ave., 11205. Tel: 718-940-5300; Fax: 718-636-7245. Email: fburns@sjcny.edu. Web: www.sjcny.edu. Under supervision of Board of Trustees. Administrators 6; Faculty 3; Total Staff 60; Lay Teachers 57; Students 1,505.

Branch Campus, 155 W. Roe Blvd., Patchoque, 11772. Tel: 631-687-5100; Fax: 631-654-1782. Web: www.sjcny.edu. Sisters Elizabeth A. Hill, C.S.J., M.A., J.D., Pres.; Mary Florence Burns, C.S.J., Ph.D., Asst. to Pres.; Nancy J. Connors, M.S., Vice Pres. Institute Advancement; John Roth, M.B.A., CFO; Kenneth McCollum, Ph.D., CIO; Sr. Loretta McGrann, C.S.J., Ph.D., Provost; Richard Greenwald, Ph.D., Academic Dean, School of Arts & Sciences, Brooklyn Campus; Doris Stratmann, M.A., Academic Dean, School of Arts & Sciences, Patchogue Campus; Thomas G. Travis, Ph.D., Vice Pres. & Dean, School of Professional Graduate Educ.; William Meng, Ph.D., Dir., McEntegart Library. Administrators 3; Sisters 11; Lay Teachers 108; Students 4,359.

QUEENS. *St. John's University* (1870) 8000 Utopia Pkwy., 11439. Tel: 718-990-6161; Fax: 718-990-5723. Email: admhelp@stjohns.edu. Web: www.stjohns.edu. Rev. Donald J. Harrington, C.M., B.A., M.Div., Th. M., Pres. Sponsored by the Vincentian Priests and Brothers Eastern Province of the Congregation of the Mission. Priests 7; Sisters 1; Lay Teachers 640; Queens Campus Enrollment 18,783; Total Enrollment (Undergrad. and Graduate of Queens, Manhattan and Staten Island Campuses, and Rome) 21,354.

Officers of Administration: Martha Hirst, Senior Vice Pres., Opers. & Treas.; Dr. Julia A. Upton, R.S.M., Provost; Rev. James J. Maher, C.M., B.A., M.Div., D.Min., Th.M., Exec. Vice Pres., Mission & Student Svcs.; Beth M. Evans, Vice Pres. Enrollment Mgmt.; Michael A. Simons, Dean Law School; Dr. Jeffrey Fagen, Dean, St. John's College; Dr. Dorothy E. Habben, Ph.D., Vice Pres. & Univ. Sec.; Mary Harper Hagan, Senior Vice Pres. Human Resources & Strategic Planning IR; Joseph E. Oliva Esq., Gen. Counsel; Dr. Victoria Schoaf, Dean, Tobin College of Business; Dr. Kathleen Voute MacDonald, Dean, College of Professional Studies; Dr. Kathryn T. Hutchinson, Ph.D., Vice Pres., Student Affairs; Dr. Robert Mangione, Ed.D., R.Ph., Dean, College of Pharmacy & Allied Health Professions; Dr. Jerrold Ross, Dean, School of Educ., & Academic Vice Pres., Staten Island; Robert Wile, Senior Vice Pres. & Chief of Staff to Pres.; Theresa Maylone, Interim Dean Libraries & Univ. Librarian.

Bread & Life Soup Kitchen

[D] CAMPUS MINISTRY

Campus Ministers and Ministry Centers 250 Cathedral Pl., 11201. Tel: 718-852-4002. Rev. Msgr. John Strynkowski, Vicar Higher Educ.; Revs. Richard E. Long. Tel: 718-434-1900 Brooklyn College; Paul A. Wood. Tel: 718-793-3130 Queens College; Stephen P. Lynch, Pratt Institute of Technology; Charles P. Keeney. Tel: 718-488-3359 Long Island University; Bro. Thomas Grady, O.S.F. Tel: 718-489-5345 St. Francis College; Revs. Michael G. Tedone. Tel: 718-423-0002 Queensborough Community College; James Mahar St. John's University; Sr. Susan Wilcox, C.S.J., St. Joseph X College; Revs. Kevin P. Cavalluzzi. Tel: 718-522-2105 Polytechnic University & NY Technical College; Cristobal Martin, Id.M. Tel: 718-361-1884 La Guardia Community College; Andre Bain, Kingsborough Community College; Josephjude C. Gannon, York College. Legal Titles & Corporations: Newman Apostolate, Inc.

[E] CATHOLIC EDUCATION OFFICES

BROOKLYN. *Office of Faith Formation*, 310 Prospect Park W., 11230. Tel: 718-281-9544. Email: tmusco@diobrook.org. Web: www.dioceseofbrooklyn.org/OFF. Mr. Theodore J. Musco, Dir., Office of Faith Formation; Sr. Alice Michael, S.U.S.C., Coord. Childhood Faith Formation; Mrs. Ana Puente, Coord. Marriage & Family Ministry; Paul Morisi, Coord. Youth & Young Adult Ministry.

Office of the Superintendent of Schools, 310 Prospect Park W., 11215. Tel: 718-965-7300. Web: www.dioceseofbrooklyn.org/catholic-ed. Thomas Chadzutko, Ed.D., Supt. Priests 1; Brothers 25; Sisters 97; Total Enrollment 43,721.

Diocese of Brooklyn Education Offices Legal Titles & Corporations: Department of Education, Diocese of Brooklyn; Henry M. Hald High School Association; Saint John's Preparatory School, Brooklyn.

MIDDLE VILLAGE. *Catholic Youth Organization*, 66-25 79th Pl., 11379. Tel: 718-281-9549; Fax: 718-281-9557.

[F] HIGH SCHOOLS, DIOCESAN

BROOKLYN. *Bishop Loughlin Memorial High School* (Coed), 357 Clermont Ave., 11238. Tel: 718-857-2700; Fax: 718-398-4227. Email: dcronin@blmhs.org. Web: www.bishoploughlin.org. Bro. Dennis Cronin, F.S.C., Pres.; James Dorney, Prin.; Nancy McKeever, Asst. Prin.; Nicole Maxwell, Dean; John Flack, Dean. Legal Corp.: Henry M. Hald Assoc. Brothers of the Christian Schools 4; Sisters 2; Lay Teachers 50; Students 876.

[G] HIGH SCHOOLS, PRIVATE

BROOKLYN. *Bishop Ford Central Catholic High School* (Coed), 500 19th St., 11215. Tel: 718-360-2500; Fax: 718-360-2595. Email: brancato11@aol.com. Web: www.bishopfordhs.org. Mr. Raymond P. Nash, Pres.; Mr. Frank V. Brancato, Prin.; Mr. Rocco V. Grella, Asst. Prin.; Mr. Sam Sued, Asst. Prin.; Mrs. Marta Parfrey, Librarian. Brothers 2; Sisters 1; Lay Teachers 55; Students 800.

Bishop Kearney High School (Girls), 2202 60th St., 11204-2599. Tel: 718-236-6363; Fax: 718-236-7784. Email: principal@bishopkearneyhs.org. Web: www.bishopkearneyhs.org. Sisters Thomasine Stagnitta, C.S.J., Prin.; Barbara Lynch, C.S.J., Librarian. Sisters of St. Joseph (Brentwood Community) 13; Lay Teachers 32; Students 600.

Catherine McAuley (Girls), 710 E. 37th St., 11203. Tel: 718-462-7282; Fax: 718-462-7284. Sr. Margaret Dempsey, R.S.M., Pres.; Ms. Peggy Lake, Co-Prin.; Ms. Josephine Valente, Co-Prin. Sisters of Mercy 3; Lay Teachers 15; Students 200.

Cristo Rey Brooklyn High School, 2-12 Aberdeen St., 11207. Tel: 718-455-3555; Fax: 718-455-3556. Robert Catell, Bd. Chm.; William Henson, Pres.; Edward Davey, Dir. Corp. Work Study; Marie Bathelmy, Dir., Admissions; Jenny Dolan, Prin.; Keisha Baptiste, Dean, Students. Lay Teachers 12; Staff 12; Total Staff 24; Enrollment 200.

Fontbonne Hall Academy (Girls), 9901 Shore Rd., 11209. Tel: 718-748-2244; Fax: 718-745-3841. Email: crepeau@fontbonne.org. Web: www.fontbonne.org. Sisters Dolores F. Crepeau, C.S.J., Prin.; Margaret Kelly, C.S.J., Librarian. Sisters of St. Joseph (Brentwood Community) 5; Lay Teachers 41; Students 526.

St. Joseph (Girls), 80 Willoughby St., 11201-5265. Tel: 718-624-3618; Fax: 718-624-2792. Email: admin@sjhsbridge.org. Web: www.sjhsbridge.org. Sr. Joan Gallagher, C.S.J., Prin.; Mrs. Miranda Cruz, Librarian. Sisters of St. Joseph (Brentwood Community) 6; Other Religious 1; Lay Teachers 32; Students 308.

Nazareth Regional (Coed), 475 E. 57th St., 11203. Tel: 718-763-1100, Ext. 225; Fax: 718-629-5382. Web: www.nazarethrhs.org. Providencia Quiles, Prin. Lay Teachers 25; Students 350.

Xaverian (Boys), 7100 Shore Rd., 11209. Tel: 718-836-7100; Fax: 718-836-7114. Email: ralesi@xaverian.org. Web: www.xaverian.org. Mr. Robert Alesi, Pres.; Deacon Kevin McCormack, Prin.; Mr. Michael Wilson, Asst. Prin. Discipline & Opers.; Edward Mayrose, Dir. of Alumni Rels.; Ms. Vincenza Milkie, Librarian; Ms. Maria Rodriguez, Asst. Prin. Student Support; Ms. Sandra Mummolo, Asst. Prin. Curriculum & Instruction. Priests 1; Xaverian Brothers 1; Deacons 2; Lay Teachers 89; Students 1,200.

Queens

ASTORIA

St. John Preparatory School (1870) (Coed), 21-21 Crescent St., 11105-3398. Tel: 718-721-7200; Fax: 718-545-9385. Web: www.stjohnsprepschool.org. Mr. William A. Higgins, B.A., M.A., M.S., Prin.; Revs. James Rodriguez, Chap.; Liju Augustine, Chap.; Valerie Bove, Librarian. Priests 3; Sisters 3; Lay Teachers 55; Students 900.

BRIARWOOD

Archbishop Molloy (Coed), 83-53 Manton St., 11435. Tel: 718-441-2100; Fax: 718-849-8251. Email: president@molloyhs.org. Web: www.molloyhs.org. Bro. Thomas Schady, F.M.S., Prin. Brothers 14; Sisters 2; Lay Teachers 68; Students 1,530.

COLLEGE POINT

St. Agnes Academic High School (Girls), 13-20 124 St., 11356-1814. Tel: 718-353-6276; Fax: 718-353-6068. Email: jmartin@stagneshs.org. Web: stagneshs.org. Sr. Joan Martin, O.P., Prin.; Mrs. Darlene O'Neill-Gerasoulis, Librarian. Sisters of St. Dominic (Amityville) 10; Lay Teachers 21; Students 300.

EAST ELMHURST

Monsignor McClancy (1956) (Boys), 71-06 31st Ave., 11370. Tel: 718-898-3800; Fax: 718-898-3929. Bro. Joseph Holthaus, S.C., Pres.; Mr. James P. Carey, Prin. Brothers 12; Lay Teachers 30; Boys 539.

FLUSHING

Holy Cross High School (1955) (Boys), 26-20 Francis Lewis Blvd., 11358. Tel: 718-886-7250; Fax: 718-886-7257. Email: info@holycrosshs.org. Web: www.holycrosshs.org. Rev. Walter Jenkins, C.S.C., Pres.; Mr. Joseph Giannuzzi, Prin.; Mrs. Denise Fox, Librarian. Brothers of Holy Cross 6; Lay Teachers 51; Students 875; Holy Cross Fathers 1.

FRESH MEADOWS

St. Francis Preparatory School (Coed), 6100 Francis Lewis Blvd., 11365. Tel: 718-423-8810; Fax: 718-224-2108. Email: 21stcentury@sfponline.org. Web: www.sfponline.org. Bro. Leonard Conway, O.S.F., Prin.; Rev. William F. Sweeney, Chap.; Mr. Frank Trubiano, Librarian. Priests 1; Franciscan Brothers 6; Sisters 5; Lay Teachers 137; Students 2,650; Personnel 66.

JAMAICA ESTATES

The Mary Louis Academy (College Preparatory) (Girls), 176-21 Wexford Ter., 11432. Tel: 718-297-2120; Fax: 718-739-0037. Web: www.tmla.org. Sr. Kathleen McKinney, C.S.J., Prin.; Mrs. Marie Whelan, Librarian. Sisters of St. Joseph (Brentwood Community) 18; Lay Teachers 78; Students 948.

MIDDLE VILLAGE

Christ the King Regional High School (Coed), 68-02 Metropolitan Ave., 11379. Tel: 718-366-7400; Fax: 718-366-1165. Email: info@ctkrhs.org. Web: www.ctkrhs.org. Peter J. Mannarino, Prin.; Michael W. Michel, Pres.; Mr. Steven Giusto, Dir. Admissions; Carolann Timpone, Asst. Prin.; Rebecca Tibbetts, Asst. Prin.; Mr. Anthony Allison, Asst. Prin.; Veronica Arbitello, Asst. Prin.; Marie Weisner, Librarian; Rev. Frank W. Spacek, School Chap.; Sr. Elizabeth Graham, Campus Min. Sisters 1; Lay Teachers 45; Students 1,000.

[H] HIGH SCHOOLS PAROCHIAL

BROOKLYN. *Denis Maloney Institute/St. Edmund Preparatory High School* (Coed), 2474 Ocean Ave., 11229. Tel: 718-743-6100; Fax: 718-743-5243. Email: jlorenzetti@stedmundprep.org. Web: www.stedmundprep.org. Mr. John P. Lorenzetti, Prin.; Kevin Raphael, Asst. Prin.; Johanna Motta, Librarian. Deacons 2; Sisters 1; Lay Teachers 55; Students 750.

St. Saviour High School (Girls), 588 6th St., 11215. Tel: 718-768-4406; Fax: 718-369-2688. Email: belanger.sv@stsaviour.org. Web: www.stsaviour.org. Sisters Valeria Belanger, S.S.N.D., Prin.; Anne Lally, C.S.J., Campus Min.; Michael McDuffie, Librarian; Mrs. Margaret Bernstein, Asst. Prin. Priests 1; Sisters 2; Lay Teachers 26; Students 230.

[I] SPECIAL SCHOOLS

BROOKLYN. *Catherine Laboure Special Education Program*, Dept. of Educ., 21 Bay 11th St., 11228. Tel: 718-449-1857; Fax: 718-449-0212. Web: www.dioceseofbrooklyn.org. Mrs. Margaret Sacca, Exec. Dir. Program for mentally challenged students ages 5-21 and learning disabled students grades 4-8. Lay Teachers and Staff 37; Students 72.

St. Francis de Sales School for the Deaf (1960) 260 Eastern Pkwy., 11225. Tel: 718-636-4573; Fax: 718-636-4577. Email: school@sfdesales.org. Web: www.sfdesales.org. Maria Bartolillo, Dir. Infant through Elementary Grades (8th Grade). Sisters 2; Lay Teachers 39; Students 100.

St. Francis De Sales School for the Deaf Development Fund, 260 Eastern Pkwy., 11225. Tel: 718-636-4573; Fax: 718-636-4577. Email: school@sfdesales.org.

Ryken Educational Center, Inc., 7100 Shore Rd., 11209. Tel: 718-759-5758; Fax: 718-759-5744. Email: wslow@xaverian.org. William Slow, Dir.

SPRINGFIELD GARDENS. *Martin de Porres School*, 136-25 218th St., 11413-2226. Tel: 718-525-3414; Fax: 718-525-0982. Email: mdpschool@metrocon.com. Web: www.mdp.org. Mr. Edward Dana, Exec. Dir.; Mr. Eon Parks, Dir. Educ. Svcs.; Paulette Chobot, Residence Dir.; Atef Aiken, Prin. Specialized day school for emotionally challenged children, ages 6-21. Brothers 5; Administrators 15; Teachers 45; Asst. Teachers 45; Classroom Aides 45; Residential Case Workers 24; Counselors 35; Support Personnel 40; Total Staff 250; Capacity 480.

Additional Sites:

Martin de Porres High School, 147-65 249th St., Rosedale, 11422. Tel: 718-525-5550; Fax: 718-525-5440. Ms. Karel Lancaster, Prin.

Martin de Porres Academy for Career Development, 621 Elmont Rd., Elmont, 11003. Tel: 516-616-0580; Fax: 516-616-0582. Mr. David Robinson, Prin.

Martin de Porres Group Residence, 101-25 104th St., Ozone Park, 11416. Tel: 718-850-0191; Fax: 718-850-0192. Paulette Chobot, Residence Dir. Day & residential school for emotionally challenged youth.

Martin De Porres Youth Center, 136-25 218th St., 11413. Tel: 718-233-2536; Fax: 800-472-0716. Bro. Raymond R. Blixt, F.S.C., M.A., Exec. Dir.

[J] CONSOLIDATED ELEMENTARY SCHOOLS (REGIONAL)

BROOKLYN. *Brooklyn Jesuit Prep* (2003) 560 Sterling Pl., 11238. Tel: 718-638-5884; Fax: 718-638-5284. Web: www.nynativity.org. Rev. Jack Podsiadlo, S.J., Pres.; Brian Chap, Prin.; Ms. Patricia Gauvey, Librarian. Brothers 1; Lay Teachers 10; Students 85.

Saint Catherine of Genoa-Saint Therese of Lisieux Catholic Academy, (Grades K-8), 4410 Avenue D, 11203.

St. Frances Cabrini Catholic Academy, 181 Suydam St., 11221. Tel: 718-386-9277; Fax: 718-386-9064. Email: principal@stfrancescabrinischool.org. Mr. Przemyslaw Murczkiewicz, Prin.; Elizabeth Rose, Librarian. Lay Teachers 12; Students 280.

Holy Angels Academy, 337 74th St., 11209.

Saints Joseph & Dominic Catholic Academy of Williamsburg, 140 Montrose Ave., 11206. Tel: 718-384-1101; Fax: 718-384-6567. Email: ssjdacademy@ssjda.org. Evette Ngadi, Prin. Lay Teachers 11; Students 277.

St. Mary Mother of Jesus-St. Frances Cabrini Academy, 8401 23rd Ave., 11214. Tel: 718-372-0025; Fax: 718-265-6498. Email: smmjbk@aol.com. Dr. Vincent Bellafiore, Prin. Lay Teachers 17; Students 273.

Midwood Catholic Academy, 1501 Hendrickson St., 11234. Tel: 718-377-1800; Fax: 718-377-6374. Web: www.midwoodcatholicacademy.org. Mrs. Elena Heimbach, Prin. Lay Teachers 17; Students 381.

Our Lady of Trust School at Our Lady of Miracles Campus, 744 E. 87 St., 11236. Tel: 718-649-0271; Fax: 718-272-0442. Arlene Barcia, Prin.

Our Lady of Trust School-St. Jude Campus, 1696 Canarsie Rd., 11236. Tel: 718-241-6633. Arlene Barcia, Prin. Lay Teachers 14; Students 428.

Queen of the Rosary Catholic Academy, 287 Powers St., 11211. Tel: 718-388-7992; Fax: 718-388-7543. Sr. Joan Losson, O.P., Prin. Full-time teachers 20; Part-time teachers 6.

Salve Regina Catholic Academy, (Grades K-8), 237 Jerome St., 11207.

St. Stanislaus Kostka Catholic Academy, (Grades PreK-8), 12 Newell St., 11222. Tel: 718-383-1970; Fax: 718-383-1711. Ms. Christina Cieloszczyk, Prin. Lay Teachers 12.

Visitation Academy, 8902 Ridge Blvd., 11209. Tel: 718-680-9452; Fax: 718-680-4441. Email: dobsc261@impresso.com. Web: www.visitationacademy.net. Sr. Mary Pauline Baulis, V.H.M., R.N., Supr. & Pres.; Mrs. Arlene Figaro, Prin. Sisters of the Visitation 5; Lay Teachers 13; Girls 179.

DOUGLASTON. *Divine Wisdom Catholic Academy*, 45-11 245th St., 11362.

FLUSHING. *Most Holy Redeemer Catholic Academy*, (Grades K-8), 146-28 Jasmine Ave., 11355.

HOWARD BEACH. *Ave Maria Catholic Academy*, (Grades K-8), 158-20 101st St., 11414.

OZONE PARK. *Divine Mercy Catholic Academy*, 101-60 92nd St., 11416. Tel: 718-845-3074; Fax: 718-845-5068. Web: www.dmcacademy.com. Sr. Francis Marie Wystepek, C.S.F.N., Prin. Elementary Campus N-8. Sisters 1; Full-time lay teachers 11; Part-time lay teachers 2; Lay Staff 4; Aides 2.

St. Elizabeth Catholic Academy, 9401 85th St., 11416. Tel: 718-641-6990; Fax: 718-323-5010. Mr. William G. Ferguson, Prin.; Mrs. Donna Allocca, Librarian. Full-time lay teachers 13.

RIDGEWOOD. *Notre Dame Catholic Academy of Ridgewood*, (Grades K-8), Bleeker & 61st St., 11385.

[K] CATHOLIC CHARITIES

BROOKLYN. *Catholic Charities*, Central Office, 191 Joralemon St., 11201. Tel: 718-722-6000; Fax: 718-722-6096. Email: lhunte@ccbq.org. Web: www.ccbq.org. Most Rev. Nicholas A. DiMarzio, Ph.D., D.D.; Rev. Msgr. Alfred P. LoPinto, V.E., Episcopal Vicar for Human Svcs.; Robert Siebel, M.S.W., CEO; Sr. Ellen Patricia Finn, O.P., M.Ed., L.M.S.W., Deputy Exec. Dir.; Alan Wolinetz, C.F.O.; Emmie Glynn Ryan, Esq., Dir. Legal Affairs & Chief Compliance Officer; Thaddeus B. Taberski, M.S.W., M.B.A., Exec. Dir. Catholic Charities Neighborhood Services, Inc.; Donna Corrado, Exec. Sec. & COO-Catholic Charities Neighborhood Services, Inc.; Gladys Rodriguez, C.S.W., Vice Pres. Family Svcs.; Robert Marquez, Vice Pres. Early Childhood Svcs.; Janice Aris, Vice Pres. Developmental Disabilities; Patricia Bowles, Vice Pres. Behavioral Health Svcs., Chief Privacy Officer; Judith Kleve, Vice Pres. Svcs. for Older Adults; Mary Hurson, Admin. Family Svcs.; Rev. Peter Mahoney, Assoc. Dir. Evaluation; Anne Fitzgerald, Ph.D., Dir. Quality Assurance; Barbara Conley, M.S.W., Dir. Planning & Child Welfare Liaison; John Tynan, M.U.P., Dir. Housing Devel.; Nina Valmonte, Dir. Parish & Community Svcs. and Campaign for Human Devel.; Jacqueline Gibbons, Dir. Human Resources; Brian Gavin, Dir. Office of Devel. & Communications; Patrick Mahon, Dir. Computer Svcs.; Catherine Nicolini, Ph.D., Dir. Training; Richard Abrahamsen, Controller; Frank Paterno, Chief Information Officer & Chief Security Officer; Sr. Ellen Patricia Finn, O.P., M.Ed., L.M.S.W., Pres. Tel: 718-722-6050.

Parish & Community Outreach & Services, 191 Joralemon St., 7th Fl., 11201. Tel: 718-722-6115. Nina Valmonte, Dir. The Catholic Charities Community Centers provide outreach to and support for parishes and communities, direct social services, and open the door to the Catholic Charities network of programs & services. Direct Services: emergency food; limited financial assistance; support groups; GED/English as a Second Language; advocacy for public benefits; case management; immigration information & referral; and employment counseling. Outreach: assist with parish/cluster pastoral planning; sharing Catholic Social Teaching; community organizing; and leadership development.

Brooklyn East Community Center, 191 Joralemon St., 11201. Tel: 718-722-6001; Fax: 718-722-6254. Erin Carman, Community Center Dir.; Patrick Callaghan, Community Project Dir. Tel: 718-722-6109. Caseworkers are out-stationed in various neighborhoods in Brooklyn East. Call for the nearest satellite site.

Brooklyn West Community Center, 191 Joralemon St., 1st Fl., 11201. Tel: 718-722-6001; Fax: 718-722-6254. Erin Carman, Community Center Dir.; Sara Suman, Community Project Dir. Tel: 718-722-6046.

Our Lady of Angels Human Service Center, 336 73rd St., 11209. Tel: 718-680-6344; Fax: 718-680-0331.

Queens North Community Center, 23-40 Astoria Blvd., Astoria, 11102. Tel: 718-726-9790; Fax: 718-728-8817. Debbie Hampson, Community Center Dir.; Josefa Castro, Community Project Dir.

Queens South Community Center, 23-40 Astoria Blvd., Astoria, 11102. Tel: 718-217-1238; Fax: 718-479-8791. Debbie Hampson, Community Center Dir.; Sheldon Peters, Community Project Dir. Caseworkers are out-stationed in various neighborhoods in Queens South. Call for the nearest satellite site.

Advocate for Persons with Disabilities Services, 191 Joralemon St., 7th Fl., 11201. Tel: 718-722-6232. Rev. James P. Bradley, Program Coord.

Bereavement Services, 191 Joralemon St., 7th Fl., 11201. Tel: 718-722-6214. Ingrid Seunarine, Dir. Co-sponsored by Catholic Charities, Catholic Cemeteries, Catholic Cemeteries Guild and St. Vincent de Paul Society.

Restorative Justice, 191 Joralemon St., 7th Fl., 11201. Tel: 718-722-6113.

Services for Pregnant Women, 191 Joralemon St., 7th Fl., 11201. Tel: 718-722-6121.

Comprehensive Human Services:

Catholic Charities Neighborhood Services, Inc., 191 Joralemon St., 11201. Tel: 718-722-6000; Fax: 718-722-6096. Robert Siebel, M.S.W., CEO; Donna Corrado, Exec. Sec. & COO; Thaddeus B. Taberski, M.S.W., M.B.A., Exec. Dir.; Fidel F. Del Valle Esq, Pres. of Board; Mary Ann Dantuono Esq., Vice Pres.

CCNS - Older Adult Services: Judith Kleve, Vice Pres. Tel: 718-722-6095.

Alzheimers Adult Day Care, 157-16 65th Ave., Flushing, 11357. Tel: 718-358-3541; Fax: 718-961-4712.

Bayside Senior Center and Bayside Senior Center Transportation Program, 221-15 Horace Harding Expwy., Bayside, 11364. Tel: 718-225-1144; Fax: 718-229-7320.

South Brooklyn Alzheimer's Adult Care Program, 5701 Avenue H., 11234. Tel: 718-241-7711; 718-241-1936.

Benson Ridge Senior Services Assistance Center, 6825 5th Ave., 11220. Tel: 718-236-3205; Fax: 718-837-1957.

Hillcrest Senior Center, 168-01B Hillside Ave., Jamaica, 11432. Tel: 718-297-7171; Fax: 718-657-2247.

Pete McGuinness Senior Center, 715 Leonard St., 11222. Tel: 718-383-1940; Fax: 718-383-1960.

Northside Senior Center, 179 N. 6th St., 11211. Tel: 718-387-2316; Fax: 718-387-3235.

The Bay Senior Center, 3643 Nostrand Ave., 11229. Tel: 718-648-2053; Fax: 718-648-7213.

Catherine Sheridan Senior Center, 35-24 83rd St., Jackson Heights, 11372. Tel: 718-458-4600; Fax: 718-458-5665.

Glenwood Senior Center, 5701 Avenue H, 11234. Tel: 718-241-7711; Fax: 718-241-1936.

Narrows at the Lodge, 7711 18th Ave., 11214. Tel: 718-621-1081; Fax: 718-621-1407.

Narrows Senior Center, 1230 63rd St, 11219. Tel: 718-232-3211; Fax: 718-232-0512.

Ozone Park Senior Center, 103-02 101st Ave., Ozone Park, 11416. Tel: 718-847-2100; Fax: 718-847-2166.

Project Independence, 183-16 Jamaica Ave., Hollis, 11423. Tel: 718-217-0126; Fax: 718-217-0495.

Peter J. Della Monica Center for Seniors, 23-56 Broadway, Astoria, 11106. Tel: 718-626-1500; Fax: 718-278-4432.

Seaside Senior Center, 90-01 Rockaway Beach Blvd., Rockaway Beach, 11693. Tel: 718-634-4047; Fax: 718-634-6853.

Sheepshead Bay Supportive Services (NORC), 3677 Nostrand Ave. #3-A, 11229. Tel: 718-769-3579; Fax: 718-769-4155.

Southwest Queens Senior Services, 186-16 Jamaica Ave., 2nd Fl., Hollis, 11423. Tel: 718-217-0126; Fax: 718-217-0495.

Steinway Senior Center, 20-43 Steinway St., Astoria, 11105. Tel: 718-728-8472; Fax: 718-278-5301.

St. Charles Jubilee Senior Center, 55 Pierrepont St., 11201. Tel: 718-855-0326; Fax: 718-852-5415.

St. Louis Senior Center, 230 Kingston Ave., 11213. Tel: 718-771-7945; Fax: 718-467-2524.

Woodhaven-Richmond Hill Senior Center, 87-25 118th St., Richmond Hill, 11418. Tel: 718-846-2877; Fax: 718-847-9089.

CCNS Home Delivered Meals Program, 103-02 101st Ave., Ozone Park, 11416. Tel: 718-847-2168; Fax: 718-847-2166.

CCNS NE Queens Home Delivered Meals Program, 168-01B Hillside Ave., Jamaica, 11432. Tel: 718-357-4903; Fax: 718-357-5731.

Northeast Queens Friendly Visiting Program, c/o Hillcrest Senior Center, 168-01 Hillside Ave., Jamaica, 11432. Tel: 718-357-4903; Fax: 718-357-5731.

CCNS - Child Care & Head Start Programs: Robert Marquez, Vice Pres. Tel: 718-722-6105; Dr. Thomasine Watson-Smith, Dir. Head Start. Tel: 718-722-6236.

Coney Island Child Care Center, 2757 W. 33rd St., 11224. Tel: 718-946-8759; Fax: 718-266-6879.

Farragut Child Care Center, 32 Navy St., 11201. Tel: 718-875-7555; Fax: 718-596-9649.

Joseph Di Marco Child Care Center, 36-49 11th St., Long Island City, 11106. Tel: 718-786-1166; Fax: 718-706-7198.

Joseph Di Marco Family Day Care, 36-49 11th St., Long Island City, 11106. Tel: 718-786-7309; Fax: 718-786-7044.

J.F. Kennedy Child Care Center, 103-15 Farragut Rd., 11236. Tel: 718-272-8751; Fax: 718-272-6035.

Msgr. Andrew Landi DayCare, 21-20 35th Ave., Long Island City, 11106. Tel: 718-784-2856; Fax: 718-784-9612.

John Oravecz Child Care Center, 25 Nassau Ave., 11222. Tel: 718-782-2727; Fax: 718-782-5166.

Queensbridge Early Childhood Development Center, 38-11 27th St., Long Island City, 11101. Tel: 718-937-7640; Fax: 718-392-7928.

R.F. Kennedy Child Care Center, 741 Flushing Ave., 11206. Tel: 718-782-0766; Fax: 718-782-0767.

Vincent J. Caristo Child Care Center, 5901 13th Ave., 11219. Tel: 718-853-8300; Fax: 718-871-8186.

Madeline Jones Head Start, 3415 Neptune Ave., 11224. Tel: 718-266-5962; Fax: 718-266-5891.

Padre Kennedy Head Start, 288 Berry St., 11211. Tel: 718-387-3679; Fax: 718-599-3319.

St. Joseph's Head Start, 300 Vernon Ave., 11206. Tel: 718-455-5900; Fax: 718-455-7513.

Sunset Park Head Start, 4222 4th Ave., 11232. Tel: 718-768-1012; Fax: 718-768-1607.

Sunset Park Family Day Care, 4222 4th Ave., 11232. Tel: 718-788-3035; Fax: 718-788-4056.

St. Margaret Mary Head Start, 9-16 27th Ave., Astoria, 11102. Tel: 718-721-8065; Fax: 718-721-7454.

Therese Cervini Head Start and Annex, 35-33 105th St., Corona, 11368. Tel: 718-478-2169; Fax: 718-478-3993.

Therese Cervini Family Day Care, 35-33 104th St., 3rd Fl., Corona, 11368. Tel: 718-334-0806; Fax: 718-334-0809.

St. Malachy Child Development Center, 220 Hendrix St., 11207. Tel: 718-647-1015; Fax: 718-647-1042.

St. Malachy Head Start, 220 Hendrix St., 11207. Tel: 718-647-0966; Fax: 718-647-1042.

Colin Newell Head Start, 161-06 89th Ave., Jamaica, 11432. Tel: 718-523-1888; Fax: 718-523-2354.

Caritas Training Center, 191 Joralemon St., 13th Fl., 11201. Tel: 718-722-6032; Fax: 718-722-6031.

CCNS - Behavioral Health Services: Patricia Bowles, Vice Pres. Tel: 718-722-6146; Fax: 718-722-6062; Ellen Wagman, Assoc. Dir.

Casa Betsaida, 267 Hewes St., 11211. Tel: 718-218-7890; Fax: 718-218-8264.

Brooklyn Community Living Program, 1900B Ralph Ave., 11234. Tel: 718-253-1366; Fax: 718-253-5890.

Central Brooklyn Supported Housing, 1900B Ralph Ave., 11234. Tel: 718-253-1366; Fax: 718-253-5890.

Brooklyn Supported Housing, 1900B Ralph Ave., 11234. Tel: 718-253-1366; Fax: 718-253-5890.

Corona - Elmhurst Guidance Center, 91-14 37th Ave., Jackson Heights, 11372. Tel: 718-779-1600; Fax: 718-803-0895.

Corona Elmhurst - PROS, 91-14 37th Ave., Jackson Heights, 11372. Tel: 718-779-1600; Fax: 718-396-6189.

Flatbush Addiction Treatment Center, 1463 Flatbush Ave., 11210. Tel: 718-951-9009; Fax: 718-951-9719.

Bohan-Denton Flatlands Guidance Center, 2037 Utica Ave., 11234. Tel: 718-377-5755; Fax: 718-377-0752.

Glendale Mental Health Clinic, 67-29 Myrtle Ave., 2nd Fl., Glendale, 11385. Tel: 718-456-7001; Fax: 718-456-9470.

Jamaica Continuing Day Treatment, 165-15 88th Ave., Jamaica, 11432. Tel: 718-291-4848; Fax: 718-291-5485.

Partnership of Hope, Intensive Case Management, 29 Chapel St., Ste. 901, 11201. Tel: 718-398-0153; Fax: 718-623-2531.

Bethlehem/Blended Case Management, 29 Chapel St., Ste. 901, 11201. Tel: 718-398-0153; Fax: 718-623-2531.

Queens Community Living Program, 35-24 83rd St., Jackson Heights, 11372. Tel: 718-639-0700; Fax: 718-639-7684.

Queens Supported Housing, 35-24 83rd St., Jackson Heights, 11372. Tel: 718-639-0700; Fax: 718-639-7684.

Rockaway PROS, 13-29 Beach Channel Dr., Far Rockaway, 11691. Tel: 718-337-6850; Fax: 718-868-3782.

Rockaway Mental Health Clinic, 13-29 Beach Channel Dr., Far Rockaway, 11691. Tel: 718-337-6800; Fax: 718-337-0940.

Woodside Mental Health Clinic, 61-20 Woodside Ave., Woodside, 11377. Tel: 718-779-1234; Fax: 718-779-7775.

Supported SRO at Mercy Gardens, 249 Classon Ave., 11205. Tel: 718-399-8141; Fax: 718-399-3208.

The Open Door Club, 2037 Utica Ave., 11234. Tel: 718-377-7757; Fax: 718-951-1318.

Monica House, 161-01 89th Ave., Jamaica, 11432. Tel: 718-262-8190; Fax: 718-739-4331.

Woodside Mobile Outreach Team, 61-20 Woodside Ave., Woodside, 11377. Tel: 718-779-1234; Fax: 718-779-7775.

World of Work - Queens, 91-14 37th Ave., Jackson Heights, 11372. Tel: 718-779-1600; Fax: 718-396-6189.

World of Work - Brooklyn, 2037 Utica Ave., 11234. Tel: 718-758-9491; Fax: 718-758-9497.

Circle of Hope, 195 Bay 19th St., 2nd Fl., 11214. Tel: 718-338-4716; Fax: 718-338-5383.

Peer Advocacy Program, 13-29 Beach Channel Dr., Far Rockaway, 11691. Tel: 718-337-0504; Fax: 718-868-2059.

Supported SRO at Caring Communities:

St. Joseph's, 683 Dean St., 11238. Tel: 718-857-2266; Fax: 718-857-5866.

Most Holy Trinity, 157 Graham Ave., 11206. Tel: 718-963-3956; Fax: 718-963-4028.

Our Lady of Good Counsel, 800-826 Madison St., 11221. Tel: 718-452-3600; Fax: 718-452-4910.

CCNS - Services for People with Developmental Disabilities: Janice Aris, Vice Pres. Tel: 718-722-6081.

Peter J. Connolly Residence, 15 Willow St., 11201. Tel: 718-625-5590; Fax: 718-625-4856.

Adessa House, 101-38 92 St., Ozone Park, 11416. Tel: 718-848-1940; Fax: 718-323-1250.

Alhambra Day Habilitation, 11-29 Catherine St., 11211. Tel: 718-388-5900; Fax: 718-388-3927.

Caldwell Home, 121-01 116th Ave., South Ozone Park, 11420. Tel: 718-845-1200; Fax: 718-323-1267.

Carmel Residence, 277 N. 8th St., 11211. Tel: 718-388-6109; Fax: 718-599-6519.

Cribbin House, 218-20 104th Ave., Queens Village, 11429. Tel: 718-776-4190; Fax: 718-464-4849.

Dawson Manor IRA, 94-17 84th St., Ozone Park, 11416. Tel: 718-296-1172; Fax: 718-296-1247.

Donald Savio Residence, 104-22 48th Ave., Corona, 11368. Tel: 718-699-7800; Fax: 718-699-3773.

James Fitzpatrick Residence, 240 McKinley Ave., 11208. Tel: 718-647-7070; Fax: 718-647-6458.

Garfield Manor, 305 Garfield Pl., 11215. Tel: 718-622-2100; Fax: 718-622-3850.

Golden Residence, 225 Brooklyn Ave., 11213. Tel: 718-953-4444; Fax: 718-953-0622.

Graci Residence, 132-14 90th St., Ozone Park, 11417. Tel: 718-848-1970; Fax: 718-323-7349.

Home & Community Based Services, 183-16 Jamaica Ave., 2nd Fl., Hollis, 11423. Tel: 718-943-7713; Fax: 718-943-7716. 6825 5th Ave., 2nd Fl., 11220. Tel: 718-253-4477; Fax: 718-253-0545.

Helen Owen Carey Residence, 174 Java St., 11222. Tel: 718-383-2451; Fax: 718-383-1488.

Long Island City Day Habilitation, 36-40 37th St., Long Island City, 11101. Tel: 718-215-2183; Fax: 718-215-2172.

McLees House, 112-16 200th St., St. Albans, 11412. Tel: 718-217-0285; Fax: 718-217-9491.

Mugavero Manor, 145-16 Farmers Blvd., Springfield Gardens, 11434. Tel: 718-712-9054; Fax: 718-723-2877.

Mulrooney Manor, 479 E. 29th St., 11226. Tel: 718-287-7553; Fax: 718-826-2519.

Senior F.U.N., 415 Bleeker St., 11237. Tel: 718-417-5316; Fax: 718-417-5317.

Jeanne Noel Hower Manor, 156 Midwood St., 11225. Tel: 718-282-8045; Fax: 718-469-2874.

Mary Wayrick Residence, 90-37 189th St., Hollis, 11423. Tel: 718-464-4090; 718-464-0962 (TTY); Fax: 718-468-8919.

Straus Residence, 3730 Shore Pkwy., 11235. Tel: 718-769-8836; Fax: 718-368-0418.

Supportive Living Apartments, 1615 8th Ave., 11226. Tel: 718-930-0820.

Mullaney Apts., 4301 8th Ave., 11232. Tel: 718-437-4285; Fax: 718-854-5945.

Circle of Hope Brooklyn and Queens, 2520 Flatbush Ave., Ste. 10, 11234. Tel: 718-338-4716; Fax: 718-338-5383.

CCNS - Family Services: Gladys Rodriguez, Vice Pres. Tel: 718-722-6185.

Family Services: Gladys Rodriguez, Vice Pres. Tel: 718-722-6185; Mary Hurson, Admin. Tel: 718-722-6023.

East New York/Brownsville Support Center, 1165 Rockaway Ave., 11236. Tel: 718-385-2043; Fax: 718-385-2179.

Project Bridge, 52 Wilson Ave., 11237. Tel: 718-628-1905; Fax: 718-628-3783.

After School Plus at PS 50 (OST), 143-26 101st St., Jamaica, 11435. Tel: 718-228-7802; Fax: 718-526-7261.

Queens WIC Programs, 161-10 Jamaica Ave., 3rd Fl., Ste. 306, Jamaica, 11432. Tel: 718-657-2580; Fax: 718-657-2590. 4271 55th Pl., Woodside, 11377. Tel: 718-715-7001; Fax: 718-943-7013.

Queens North Community Centers Leaders in Training/GED, 23-40 Astoria Blvd., Astoria, 11102. Tel: 718-726-9790; Fax: 718-728-8817. Includes 21st Century Follow Up, NYCALI and Young Adult Internship Program (YAIP).

Project Bridge Healthy Families/Fidelis, 52 Wilson Ave., 11237.

21st Century Leaning Center/OST at P.S. 106, 1314 Putnam Ave., 11221. Tel: 718-574-0261, Ext. 1055; Fax: 718-574-1054.

OST H.S. and Transition to H.S., 284 Baltic St., 11201. Tel: 718-694-9741; Fax: 718-694-9745.

Man Up/Fatherhood Initiative, 440 Watkins St., 11201. Tel: 718-875-4367.

Brighter Tomorrows/21st Century and Healthy Families at SS Joseph & Dominic Catholic Academy, 140 Montrose Ave., 11206. Tel: 718-218-7049; Fax: 718-218-7051.

Bedford Hills The Children's Center L.E.A.P. Program; Nursery Program; Teen Program., 241 Harris Rd., Bedford Hills, 10507. Tel: 914-241-3100, Ext. 4050; Fax: 914-962-3659.

Brownsville Family Support Center, 1165 Rockaway Ave., 11236. Tel: 718-385-2043; Fax: 718-385-2179.

East New York Family Support Center, 1165 Rockaway Ave., 11236. Tel: 718-385-2043; Fax: 718-385-2179.

Jamaica Family and Youth Center, 87-80 Merrick Blvd., 2nd Fl., Jamaica, 11432. Tel: 718-526-5151; Fax: 718-526-6776.

Refugee Resettlement Program, 191 Joralemon St., 4th Fl., 11201. Tel: 718-722-6009; Fax: 718-722-6073.

Jamaica Family & Rehabilitation, 87-80 Merrick Blvd., 2nd Fl., Jamaica, 11432. Tel: 718-327-3471; Fax: 718-327-3474.

Far Rockaway Family Treatment Rehabilitation, 1329 Beach Channel Dr., Far Rockaway, 11691. Tel: 718-327-3471; Fax: 718-327-3474.

Housing Development and Management Services Catholic Charities:

Catholic Charities Progress of Peoples Development Corporation Tel: 718-722-6041; Fax: 718-722-6045. Robert Siebel, M.S.W., CEO; John Tynan, M.U.P., Dir.

Progress of Peoples Management Corporation Tel: 718-722-6138; Fax: 718-722-6134. Robert Siebel, M.S.W., Pres.; Thomas Catlaw, Dir.; Alla Eleon, Controller.

Housing Corporations:

Bellerose Senior HDFC, Inc., 191 Joralemon St., 11201. Tel: 718-722-6050; Fax: 718-479-6612.

Bethlehem Community HDFC Inc., 191 Joralemon St., 11201. Tel: 718-722-6000; Fax: 718-722-6045.

Bishop Boardman Senior HDFC, 191 Joralemon St., 11201. Tel: 718-722-6050; Fax: 718-965-3577.

Bishop Francis J. Mugavero Senior HDFC, 191 Joralemon St., 11201. Tel: 718-722-6050; Fax: 718-643-6492.

Casa Betsaida HDFC, 191 Joralemon St., 11201. Tel: 718-722-6000.

Casa Betsaida-Home for people with AIDS

Catherine Sheridan HDFC, Inc., 191 Joralemon St., 11201. Tel: 718-722-6050; Fax: 718-274-2333.

St. Teresa of Avila Senior HDFC, 191 Joralemon St., 11201. Tel: 718-722-6050.

Sr. Lucian Senior HDFC, 191 Joralemon St., 11201. Tel: 718-722-6050; Fax: 718-381-9407.

Caring Communities Associates HDFC, Inc., 191 Joralemon St., 11201. Tel: 718-722-6050; Fax: 718-857-5866.

Mary Star of the Sea Senior HFDC, 191 Joralemon St., 11201. Tel: 718-722-6050; Fax: 718-858-7265.

Pierrepont HDFC, 191 Joralemon St., 11201. Tel: 718-722-6000; Fax: 718-722-6096.

Mary Immaculate, Inc., 191 Joralemon St., 11201. Tel: 718-722-6000; Fax: 718-722-6096.

Mary Immaculate HDFC, Inc., 191 Joralemon St., 11201. Tel: 718-722-6000; Fax: 718-722-6096.

Mount Carmel Senior HDFC, 191 Joralemon St., 11201. Tel: 718-722-6050; Fax: 718-722-6045.

O.L. Loreto Family Housing Development Fund Corporation, 191 Joralemon St., 11201. Rev. Msgr. Alfred P. LoPinto, V.E., Pres.; Jeanne M. Diulio, Sec.; Richard Abrahamsen, Treas.

Pope John Paul II Senior HDFC, 191 Joralemon St., 11201. Tel: 718-722-6050; Fax: 718-748-4425.

Pierrepont House for the Elderly, Inc., 191 Joralemon St., 11201. Tel: 718-722-6050; Fax: 718-852-3352.

Queens Rehab Corp., 191 Joralemon St., 11201. Tel: 718-722-6000; Fax: 718-722-6045.

St. Brendan Senior HDFC, 191 Joralemon St., 11201. Tel: 718-722-6050; Fax: 718-645-7180.

St. Lucy/St.Patrick HDFC, 191 Joralemon St., 11201. Tel: 718-722-6050; Fax: 718-722-6045.

Msgr. John P. O'Brien Senior HDFC, 191 Joralemon St., 11201. Tel: 718-722-6050; Fax: 718-972-9265.

St. Paul the Apostle Senior HDFC, 191 Joralemon St., 11201. Tel: 718-722-6050; Fax: 718-722-6045.

St. Theresa of Avila Senior Housing Development Fund Corporation, 191 Joralemon St., 11201. Tel: 718-722-6086. Jeanne M. Diulio, Asst. Dir., Office of Legal Affairs.

Sunset Park HFDC, Inc., 191 Joralemon St., 11201. Tel: 718-722-6050; Fax: 718-871-2407.

Msgr. Thomas Campbell Senior HDFC, 191 Joralemon St., 11201. Tel: 718-722-6050; Fax: 718-545-0817.

Families Together HDFC, Inc., 191 Joralemon St., 11201. Tel: 718-722-6000; Fax: 718-722-6045.

Msgr. Edward T. Burke Senior HDFC, 191 Joralemon St., 11201. Tel: 718-722-6050; Fax: 718-859-3314.

Holy Spirit Senior HDFC, 191 Joralemon St., 11201. Tel: 718-722-6050; Fax: 718-854-8521.

The Msgr. Joseph F. Stedman Residence HDFC, 191 Joralemon St., 11201. Tel: 718-722-6050; Fax: 718-722-6134.

161-01 89th Avenue Corp., 191 Joralemon St., 11201. Tel: 718-262-8190; Fax: 718-739-4331.

101-105 South Eighth Street Apartments Housing Development Fund Corporation, 191 Joralemon St., 11201. Tel: 718-722-6050; Fax: 718-722-6096.

176 South Eighth Street Apartments Housing Development Fund Corporation, 191 Joralemon St., 11201. Tel: 718-722-6050; Fax: 718-722-6096.

72 Lewis Avenue, Apartments Housing Development Fund Corporation, 191 Joralemon St., 11201. Tel: 718-722-6050.

Our Lady of Fatima Apartments HDFC, Inc., 191 Joralemon St., 11201. Tel: 718-722-6050; Fax: 718-507-1214.

The David Minkin Residence HDFC, Inc., 191 Joralemon St., 11201. Tel: 718-722-6050; Fax: 718-438-0052.

Emmaus of the Diocese of Brooklyn, Inc., 191 Joralemon St., 11201. Tel: 718-722-6000; Fax: 718-722-6096.

St. Pius V Senior HDFC, 191 Joralemon St., 11201. Tel: 718-722-6050; Fax: 718-722-6045.

O.L. Loreto Family Housing Development Fund Corporation, 191 Joralemon St., 11201. Tel: 718-722-6000; Fax: 718-722-6096. Rev. Msgr. Alfred P. LoPinto, V.E., Pres.

Affiliated Agencies:

Ss. Joachim & Anne Residence, 2720 Surf Ave., 11224. Tel: 718-714-4800; Fax: 718-714-0874. Claude Ritman, Admin.

Anthonian Hall, Inc., 191 Joralemon St., 11201. Tel: 718-722-6000; Fax: 718-722-6096. Sr. Ellen Patricia Finn, O.P., M.Ed., L.M.S.W., Treas.; Most Rev. Joseph M. Sullivan, D.D., M.S.W., M.P.A., V.E., Treas. (Retired).

Catholic Guild for the Blind, Diocese of Brooklyn, Inc., 191 Joralemon St., 11201. Tel: 718-722-6000; Fax: 718-722-6096. Robert Siebel, M.S.W., Pres.

Mary's Hall, Inc., 191 Joralemon St., 11201. Tel: 718-722-6000; Fax: 718-722-6096. Most Rev. Joseph M. Sullivan, D.D., M.S.W., M.P.A., V.E., Pres. (Retired).

Family Home Care Services:

Care at Home for the Diocese of Brooklyn, Inc., 269 37th St., 11232-2409. Tel: 718-907-4711; Fax: 718-965-7010.

Family Home Care Services of Brooklyn and Queens, Inc., 241 37 St., 11232. Tel: 718-832-0550; Fax: 718-907-8750. Rose Marie Borg, Exec. Dir.

Flowers With Care/Catholic Charities Neighborhood Services, Diocese of Brooklyn, Inc., 23-40 Astoria Blvd., Astoria, 11102. Tel: 718-726-9790; Fax: 718-728-8817. Email: fwcareysc@yahoo.com. Catherine Nicolini, Ph.D., Exec. Dir.

Flowers with Care Youth Services GED Program, NYCALI, Out of School Youth (OSY) & 21st Century After School Program, 23-40 Astoria Blvd., Astoria, 11102. Tel: 718-726-9790; Fax: 718-728-8817.

Youth Employment Program: L.I.F.E. (Looking Into Future Employment), 200 Gold St., 11201. Tel: 718-875-8801; Fax: 718-875-4367.

Big Brothers/Big Sisters, 200 Gold St., 11201. Tel: 718-875-8801; Fax: 718-875-4367.

Choosing Abstinence with Peers (CAPS), 200 Gold St., 11201. Tel: 718-875-8801; Fax: 718-875-4367.

Healthy Families, 200 Gold St., 11201. Tel: 718-875-8801; Fax: 718-875-4367.

Man-Up Fatherhood Program, 200 Gold St., 11201. Tel: 718-875-8801; Fax: 718-875-4367.

Northwest Brooklyn Parenting Project: Reaching Families One Parent at a Time, 200 Gold St., 11201. Tel: 718-875-8801; Fax: 718-875-4367.

Redford Hills The Children's Center, 247 Harris Rd., Bedford Hills, 10507. Tel: 914-241-3100, Ext. 4050; Fax: 914-248-7588.

Redford Hills Teen Program, 247 Harris Rd., Bedford Hills, 10507. Tel: 917-241-3100; Fax: 914-248-7588.

Brighter Tomorrows - 21st Century at St. John the Baptist, 82 Lewis Ave., 11206. Tel: 718-453-1000; Fax: 718-453-1860.

Child Welfare Programs:

Office of Child Welfare, 191 Joralemon St., 11201. Tel: 718-722-6091; Fax: 718-722-6096. Barbara Conley, M.S.W., Dir.

Catholic Child Care Society, 191 Joralemon St., 11201. Tel: 718-722-6091; Fax: 718-722-6096.

HeartShare Human Services of NY, 12 Metro Tech Center, 11201. Tel: 718-422-4200. William R. Garinello, Pres./CEO. Tel: 718-522-4506; Carol Smith-Njiri, Senior Vice Pres. Tel: 718-422-4216. (Formerly Catholic Guardian Society/Diocese of Brooklyn).

Little Flower Children's Services of New York, Corporate Office: 186 Joralemon St., 11201. Tel: 718-875-3500. Long Island Office: N. Wading River Rd., Wading River, 11792. Tel: 516-929-6200. Queens Office: 89-12 162nd St., Queens, 11439. Tel: 718-526-9150. Grace G. LoGrande, LMSW, Exec. Dir.

Mercy Home for Children, 273 Willoughby Ave., 11205. Tel: 718-832-1075. Sr. Catherine Crumlish, R.S.M., Exec. Dir.

MercyFirst, Brooklyn Office: 6301 12th Ave., 11219. Long Island Office: 525 Convent Rd., Syosset, 11791. Tel: 516-921-0808. Gerard McCaffery, Exec. Officer.

Providence House, Inc. (1979) *Administrative Office*, 703 Lexington Ave., 11221. Tel: 718-455-0197; Fax: 718-455-0692. Web: www.providencehouse.org. Sr. Janet Kinney, C.S.J., Exec. Dir.

Providence House 1 (1979) 2518 Church Ave., 11226. Tel: 718-284-6688; Fax: 718-284-4890.

Providence House 2 (1982) 388 Prospect Ave., 11215. Tel: 718-369-9140; Fax: 718-369-9158.

Providence House 3 (1983) 159-23 89th Ave., Jamaica, 11432. Tel: 718-739-1348; Fax: 718-526-6315.

Providence House 4 (1986) 89 Sickles Ave., New Rochelle, 10801. Tel: 914-632-4177; Fax: 914-235-5766.

Providence House 5 (1986) 396 Lincoln Rd., 11225. Tel: 718-778-1310; Fax: 718-493-5932.

Providence House 6 (1988) 2876 W. 17 St., 11224. Tel: 718-996-3386.

Providence House 7, 701 Lexington Ave., 11221. Tel: 718-574-6847; Fax: 718-455-0457.

Permanent Housing (1995) 85 & 87 Sickles Ave., New Rochelle, 10801.

SCO Family of Services, 1 Alexander Pl., Glen Cove, 11542. Tel: 561-671-1253; 718-895-8670 (Tie Line); 718-935-9466 (Brooklyn); 718-526-7533 (Queens); Fax: 516-671-2899. Gail B. Nayowith, Exec. Dir.

Madonna Heights Services, 151 Burr Ln., P.O. Box 8020, Dix Hills, 11746. Tel: 516-643-8800; Fax: 516-491-4440.

St. John's Residence & School for Boys, 144 Beach 111th St., Rockaway Park, 11694. Tel: 718-945-2800. Bro. Thomas N. Trager, S.M., Exec. Dir.; Rev. Paul J. Landolfi, S.M., Chap.

St. Vincent's Services, Inc., 66 Boerum Pl., 11201. Tel: 718-522-3700. Rev. Msgr. Robert M. Harris, M.S.W., M.Phil., M.A., Pres./CEO; Henry J. Ford, Vice Pres.

Other Affiliated Agencies:

Ecclesial Consultants, Inc., 191 Joralemon St., 11201. Tel: 718-722-6000; Fax: 718-722-6096. Most Rev. Joseph M. Sullivan, D.D., M.S.W., M.P.A., V.E., Dir. (Retired); Rev. Msgrs. Emmet Fagan (RVC), Dir.; Charles J. Fahey (SY), Dir. A management service for Church agencies and organizations.

Ferrini Welfare League, 98-21 101 Ave., Ozone Park, 11416. Tel: 718-845-0539.

Italian Board of Guardians, 7808 18 Ave., 11214. Tel: 718-232-4242; Fax: 718-232-6402. Rev. Msgr. Fernando A. Ferrarese, Moderator; Maria Patalano, Exec. Dir.; Mrs. Beatrice Rizzo, Exec. Sec.

**Society of St. Vincent de Paul in Diocese of Brooklyn, Long Island, New York*, Central Office, 191 Joralemon St., 11201. Tel: 718-625-1400; Fax: 718-625-1421. Most Rev. Thomas V. Daily, D.D., Spiritual Advisor; Mr. Joseph Martino, Pres.

District Council of Kings, 191 Joralemon St., 11201. Tel: 718-625-1400; Fax: 718-625-1421. Rev. Msgr. Raymond J. Kelly, S.T.L., Spiritual Advisor (Retired); Mr. Carlos Harris, Pres.

District Council of Queens, 191 Joralemon St., 11201. Tel: 718-625-1400; Fax: 718-625-1421. Mr. Vito Buccaria, Pres.

After School Plus Program at P.S. 50, 143-26 101st Ave., Jamaica, 11435. Tel: 718-228-7802; Fax: 718-526-7261.

[L] SPECIAL CARE FACILITIES

BROOKLYN. *St. Jerome's Health Services Corp. dba Holy Family Home* 1740 84th St., 11214. Tel: 718-259-8240; Fax: 718-259-9180. Sr. Teresita R. Samson, S.F.P., Dir. Pastoral Care Dept.; Josef Hirsch, LNHA, Dir. & Admin. Affiliated with Saint Vincent Catholic Medical Centers of New York. Bed Capacity 200; Total Staff 266.

[M] CHILD CARE AGENCIES

BROOKLYN. *St. Francis Home for Boys*, 132 Eagle St., 11222. Tel: 718-349-1157; Fax: 718-349-1558. Email: info@sfhbrooklyn.com. Web: www.sfhbrooklyn.com. Rev. Benedict J. Groeschel, C.F.R., Exec. Dir.; Mr. Joseph Campo, Dir. Residents 7.

Good Shepherd Services, 441 Fourth Ave., 11215. Tel: 718-788-0666; Fax: 718-965-0365. Email: plomonaco@goodshepherd.org. Web: www.GoodShepherds.org. Sr. Paulette LoMonaco, R.G.S., Exec. Dir. Provides a comprehensive range of neighborhood family services to individuals & youth from the South Brooklyn community. Services include educational support, counseling, after school programs, a domestic violence shelter, crisis intervention, & advocacy services to children & families.

HeartShare Human Services of New York, Roman Catholic Diocese of Brooklyn, 12 Metro Tech Center, 29th Fl., 11201. Tel: 718-422-4200; Fax: 718-522-4506. Email: info@heartshare.org. Web: www.heartshare.org. William R. Guarinello, M.S., Pres. & CEO. Children and Family Services: Foster Boarding Home Program, Adoption Program, Family Services Centers, School-Based Beacon Program, Youth Services, Services for People with HIV/AIDS. Programs for the Developmentally Disabled: Group Homes, Supportive Apartments, Preschool Program (Early Childhood Centers), School Age Program, Respite & Recreation Program, Day Services/Day Habilitation Programs, Case Management, Family Support Services

Children and Family Services:

Adoption & Foster Care Services-Brooklyn Office, 191 Joralemon St., 6th Fl., 11201. Tel: 718-422-4216; Fax: 718-422-4229.

Adoption & Foster Care Services-Queens Office, 90-04 161st St., Jamaica, 11432. Tel: 718-739-5000; Fax: 718-739-6828.

Family Service Centers:

Bensonhurst-Bay Ridge Kiwanis Club Family Services, 138 Bay 20th St., 11214. Tel: 718-234-1717; Fax: 718-331-1541.

East Brooklyn Family Services, 3005 Glenwood Rd., 11210. Tel: 718-434-7900; Fax: 718-434-6715.

Family Services at P.S. 288, 2865 W. 19th St., 11224. Tel: 718-372-0580; Fax: 718-372-0634.

School-Based Beacon Programs:

McKinley Beacon Program-I.S. 259, 7301 Fort Hamilton Pkwy., 11228. Tel: 718-836-3620; Fax: 718-836-3683.

Beacon Program at P.S. 288, 2950 W. 25th St., 11224. Tel: 718-714-0103; Fax: 718-714-6738.

Youth Services/Summer Camps:

New Youth Services:, 2947 W. 28th St., 11224. Tel: 718-449-2897; Fax: 718-449-0235.

PS 102 One World After School Program, 211 72nd St., 11209. Tel: 718-567-2365; Fax: 718-567-2367.

Services for People with HIV/AIDS:

Community Follow-Up Program, 2865 W. 19th St., 11224. Tel: 718-372-0580; Fax: 718-372-0634.

Residential Housing Program, 123 Linden Blvd., 2nd Fl., 11226. Tel: 718-647-0118; Fax: 718-647-9763.

Developmental Disabilities Services:

12 Metro Tech Center, 29th Fl., 11201. Tel: 718-422-3306; 718-422-3304; Fax: 718-422-3324.

Adult Day Habilitation Services:

Bay Ridge Day Habilitation Program, 347 74th St., 2nd Fl., 11209. Tel: 718-745-7117; Fax: 718-745-3741.

Brooklyn Day Habilitation Program, 177 Livingston Ave., 2nd Fl., 11201. Tel: 718-797-2020; Fax: 718-237-8958.

Queens Day Habilitation Program, 61-58 Springfield Blvd., Bayside, 11364. Tel: 718-281-0480; Fax: 718-281-0478.

Aiello Day Habilitation Program, 163 MacDonough St., 11216. Tel: 718-443-5071; Fax: 718-443-5741.

Hoffman Day Habilitation Program, 62-10 Northern Blvd., Woodside, 11377. Tel: 718-899-2752; Fax: 718-899-9365.

Lavin Day Habilitation Program, 347 74th St., 11209. Tel: 718-745-7117; Fax: 718-745-3741.

Partnering with Autistic Citizens (PACT) Day Habilitation Program, 177 Livingston Ave., 2nd Fl., 11201. Tel: 718-797-2020, Ext. 8051; Fax: 718-237-8958.

Union Turnpike Day Habilitation Program, 159-05 Union Tpke., Fresh Meadows, 11366. Tel: 718-969-0419; Fax: 718-969-0983.

Staten Island PACT Day Habilitation Program, 1424 Richmond Ave., 2nd Fl., Staten Island, 10314. Tel: 718-698-2737; Fax: 718-698-2739.

Kaleidoscope Program, 177 Livingston St., 2nd Fl., 11201. Tel: 718-797-2020, Ext. 8047.

Early Childhood Services:

Angels on the Bay Early Childhood Evaluation Center, 162-30 Cross Bay Blvd., Howard Beach, 11414. Tel: 718-323-2877; Fax: 718-323-2897.

Governor Mario and Matilda Raffa Cuomo First Step Early Childhood Center, 115-15 101st. Ave., Richmond Hill, 11419. Tel: 718-441-5333; Fax: 718-805-0657.

Lefferts/Liberty Kiwanis First Step Early Childhood Center, 82-12 151st Ave., Howard Beach, 11414. Tel: 718-848-0300; Fax: 718-835-2862.

Dolly and Frank Russo, Sr. First Step Early Childhood Center, 118-01/03 101st Ave., Richmond Hill, 11419. Tel: 718-805-7117; Fax: 718-805-7124.

Heart Share First Step Early Childhood Center, 1825 Bath Ave., 11214. Tel: 718-238-4637; Fax: 718-238-9584.

Respite/Recreation Programs:

Family Support Services Program, 12 Metro Tech Center, 29th Fl., 11201. Tel: 718-422-3271; Fax: 718-855-5821.

School Age Program

Medicaid Service Corporation, 12 Metro Tech Ctr., 29th Fl., 11201. Tel: 718-422-3336; Fax: 718-422-3324.

Supported Apartment Program:

12 Metro Tech Center, 29th Fl., 11201. Tel: 718-422-5923; Fax: 718-422-3324.

Marian and Anthony Attardi Residence

Thomas J. Cuite Residence

James and Kathleen Buckley Residence

Clermont Residence

Clinton Residence

Doonan-Drake Residence

Antonetta Ferraro Residence

Msgr. Thomas G. Hagerty Residence

Hart Street Residence

Carol and James Scibelli Residence

Maureen Moore Residence

Lillian and John Sharkey, Sr. Residence

Helen and John Sharkey Residence

Rita P. Short Residence

35th Ave. Residence, 172-07 35th Ave., Flushing, 11358. Tel: 718-961-7673; Fax: 718-961-7753.

Clare and Frank Torre Residence

Dr. Catherine White Residence

Maureen and Vincent Curatola Residence

Josephine and Joseph Abatemarco Residence

Lydia and Napoleon Giannattasio Residence

Ann and Charles Subbiondo Residence

Affiliate Programs:

Heartshare Wellness Ltd., 177 Livingston Ave. Cellar Level, 11201. Tel: 718-855-7707; Fax: 718-855-7717.

Energy Programs, 12 Metro Tech Center, 29th Fl., 11201. Tel: 718-422-4211; Fax: 718-522-4506.

The Heart Share School, 1825 Bath Ave., 11214. Tel: 718-621-1614; Fax: 718-621-1649.

Little Flower Children and Family Services, 186 Joralemon St., 11201-4326. Tel: 718-875-3500; Fax: 718-260-8863. Email: info@lfchild.org. Web: www.LittleFlowerNY.org. Grace G. LoGrande, LMSW, Exec. Dir.; Kevin Kundmueller, CFO; Sr. Agnes Palczynski, C.S.F.N., Sister Supr.; George Grigg, Supt. Foster Care, Adoption & Post Adoption Services, Services for Adult MR/DD clients; Residential Treatment Center, U.F.S.D., & Family Day Care at Wading River, NY; Teen Mothers & Infants in Foster Homes. Lay Teachers 25.

Mercy Home for Children (1865) 273 Willoughby Ave., 11205. Tel: 718-832-1075; Fax: 718-832-7612. Email: info@mercyhomeny.org. Web: www.mercyhomeny.org. Sr. Catherine Crumlish, R.S.M. Under the sponsorship of the Sisters of Mercy.; Six Intermediate Care Facilities (Residences & Individual Residential Alternatives) for adolescents & adults who are developmentally disabled: Visitation Residence; Harold Warren Residence; de Porres Residence; Littlejohn Residence; Santulli Residence; Kevin Keating Residence; 7 IRA Residences; Chrys Residence; Gail Addeo Residence; Rev. Michael J. McGivney Residence; Augusta Residence, Frank's Residence, and St. Joseph's Residence, Mary E. Casey Residence. Three all day Saturday Recreation Programs, for adolescents and adults with developmental disabilities and children with autism, we offer MSC Services for families and the individuals. In Home Respite Services; James P. Slattery, Mercy Creative Arts Program, Mercy-Mitsui Creative Arts Program. Sisters 5; Total Staff 305; Residents 109; Saturday Programs 36; MSC Families 75; Saturday Creative Arts Center 65; In Home Respite 5.

MercyFirst, 6301 12th Ave., 11219. Tel: 718-232-1500; Fax: 718-232-0331. Web: www.mercyfirst.org. Gerard McCaffery, Pres. & CEO. Residential services provided in campus and group home settings, including diagnostic/group emergency foster care, non-secure detention, hard to place (JD and clinically intensive), abuse treatment and prevention, mother/child, and OMH programs.; Family Foster Care/Adoption, Aftercare and Preventive Services programs provide services in Nassau, Queens and Brooklyn. Children in Care 3,452; Bed Capacity 194; Total Staff 547.

Residential Programs:

McAuley Residence for Mother and Child (Agency Operated Boarding Home), Tel: 718-469-0360; Fax: 718-940-0406.

Virginia Group Residence for Mother and Child Tel: 718-369-3812; Fax: 718-369-5891.

Preventive Programs:

Montague Center, 186 Montague St., 11201. Tel: 718-522-0504; Fax: 718-522-9028.

Gerard C. Durr Center, 333 Avenue X, 11223. Tel: 718-375-7444; Fax: 718-375-2444.

Rockaway Center, 230 Beach 102 St., Ste. 1-A, Rockaway Park, 11694. Tel: 718-318-6167; Fax: 718-634-6691.

St. Vincent's Services, Inc. (1869) (Formerly St. Vincent's Home for Boys and St. Vincent's Hall, Inc.), 66 Boerum Pl., 11201. Tel: 718-522-3700; Fax: 718-875-8536. Web: www.svs.org. Rev. Msgr. Robert M. Harris, M.S.W., M.Phil., M.A., Pres. & CEO. Services includes: Family Foster Boarding Homes & Adoption and Post Adoption Services, Pediatric AIDS Program, Specialized Preventive Program for Medically Fragile Children, Primary Care Medical Clinic for children and adolescents, Group Foster Home Services, Comunity Based Homes for children with psychiatric needs, Residences for the Developmentally Disabled, NYS Licensed Alcohol and Substance Abuse Outpatient Treatment Program for youth and adults, NYS Licensed Outpatient Mental Health Clinics for children, adolescents and adults. Sisters 3; Priests 2; Employees 470.

Office Program Centers:
66 Boerum Pl., 11201.
205 Montague St., 11201.
333 Atlantic Ave., 11201.
1310 Rockaway Pkwy. (Canarsie), 11236.
89-31 161st St., Jamaica, 11432.
56 Bay St., Staten Island, 10301.
148 Bay St., Staten Island, 10301.

GLEN COVE. *SCO Family of Services*, 1 Alexander Pl., 11542. Tel: 516-671-1253; 718-895-2555; Fax: 516-671-2899. Email: gnayowith@sco.org. Web: www.sco.org. Gail B. Nayowith, Exec. Dir.; Mary Hall, Dir. of Intake and Placement. Residential Treatment Center for the profoundly & severely mentally retarded, Intermediate Care Facilities, Group Homes for Adolescent Teenage Boys and Girls, Teen Mother-Child Residence Program, Homeless Program for Teenage RS, Preventive Programs (3), EFBH Network, Therapeutic Foster Boarding Homes, Residential Treatment Facility, Article 81/89 Schools (4), Foster Care, Adoption, Homeless Shelters (5), Single Stop, Beacon Programs, After School Programs, Employment and Education Services, Nurse Family Partnership and Parent Child Home Programs, Crisis Respite, Home & Community Based Waiver Services, Madonna Heights Services, Family Dynamics, Center for Family Life. Children 5,000.

ROCKAWAY PARK. *St. John's Residence for Boys, Inc.*, 144-Beach 111 St., 11694. Tel: 718-945-2800, Ext. 200; Fax: 718-945-4662. Email: stjohnsresidence@aol.com. Bro. Thomas N. Trager, S.M., Exec. Dir. Conducted by the Brothers of Society of Mary (Marianists). Residential care for adolescent boys. Non-Secure Detention/Residential Treatment Center. Brothers 5; Residents 43.

[N] GROUP HOMES FOR RETARDED CHILDREN

SPRINGFIELD GARDENS. *Martin De Porres Group Homes* (1974) 136-25 218th St., 11413. Tel: 718-527-0606; Fax: 718-723-1528. Email: phiro@nyc.rr.com. Web: mdp.org. Bro. Philip Rofrano, F.S.C., L.C.S.W., Exec. Dir. Bed Capacity 15; Total Assisted Annually 26; Total Staff 20.

[O] RESIDENCES FOR THE AGED

BROOKLYN. *SS. Joachim & Anne Residence, Inc. dba Saints Joachim + Anne Nursing and Rehabilitation Center* 2720 Surf Ave., 11224. Tel: 718-714-4800; Fax: 718-266-1743. Claude Ritman, Exec. Dir. Bed Capacity 200; Total Assisted Annually 68,542; Total Staff 300.

BAYSIDE. *Ozanam Hall of Queens Nursing Home, Inc.* (1971) 42-41 201st St., 11361. Tel: 718-423-2000; Fax: 718-224-7598. Email: jcraymond@ozanamhall.org. Web: www.ozanamhall.org. Sr. M. Joseph Catherine Raymond, O.Carm., Admin.; Rev. James M. Kelly, C.M., M.A., Chap. Carmelite Sisters for the Aged and Infirm. Sisters 15; Residents 432; Bed Capacity 432; Total Assisted Annually 1,024; Total Staff 637.

QUEENS VILLAGE. *Queen of Peace Residence* (1869) 110-30 221st St., 11429. Tel: 718-464-1800; Fax: 347-626-2181. Sr. Celine Therese Vadukkoot, L.S.P.; Rev. Msgr. William J. Rodgers, Chap. (Retired).

Home for the Aged, Little Sisters of the Poor Sisters 20; Bed Capacity 81; Total Assisted Annually 81; Total Staff 110. In Res. Rev. Msgr. James W. Ryan (Retired); Revs. John W. Byrnes (Retired); Anthony C. Casey (Retired); Charles Repole, O.F.M.Cap. (Retired); Robert Skurla (Retired).

[P] SETTLEMENT ASSOCIATIONS

GLENDALE. *Catholic Kolping Society*, 65-04 Myrtle Ave., 11385. Tel: 718-456-7727. Evelyn H. Blatz, Pres.

Catholic Kolping Society (Katholischer Gesellen Verein) of Brooklyn, Inc.

[Q] CATHOLIC MIGRATION AND REFUGEE OFFICES

BROOKLYN. *Catholic Migration & Refugee Office* (1971) 1258 65th St., 11219. Tel: 718-236-3000; Fax: 718-256-9707. Web: www.catholicmigration.org. Apostolate Coordinators.

Arabic Speaking Apostolate (2003) Tel: 718-965-0422. Rev. Sherif S.I. Fanous, Coord. Tel: 718-965-0422. Email: antonios@catholic.org.

Brazilian Apostolate Tel: 718-361-1884; Fax: 718-786-4573. Rev. Jose Carlos Da Silva, Coord.

Chinese Apostolate-Queens Tel: 718-961-0714; Fax: 718-460-8032. Rev. Antonius Ho, C.S.J.B. (Taiwan), Coord.

Chinese Apostolate-Brooklyn Tel: 718-236-0909; Fax: 718-236-5357. Rev. Vincentius Toan Do, Asst. Tel: 718-236-0909; Fax: 718-236-5357.

Czech/Slovak Apostolate Tel: 718-268-6251; Fax: 718-793-2584. Rev. Antonin Kocurek, Coord.

Croatian Apostolate

Filipino Apostolate Tel: 718-229-6465; Fax: 718-229-8126. Rev. Godofredo Felicitas (Philippines), Co-ord.

Ghanaian Apostolate Tel: 718-282-7162; Fax: 718-282-5568. Rev. Charles Akoto Oduro (Ghana), Coord.

Haitian Apostolate Tel: 718-528-0577; Fax: 718-341-0253 1. Rev. Donelson Thevenin, Coord.

Indian Latin Rite Apostolate Tel: 718-361-1884; Fax: 718-786-4573. Rev. Robert Ambalathingal, O.C.D.

Indonesian Apostolate

Irish Apostolate Tel: 718-672-4848; Fax: 718-457-4055. Rev. Edmund Brendan Duggan, C.S.Sp., Coord.

Italian Apostolate Tel: 347-545-0549. Deacon Vincent M. LaGamba, Coord.

Korean Apostolate Tel: 718-436-5565; Fax: 718-436-5586. Rev. Heebong Nam, Coord.

Lithuanian Tel: 718-326-2236; Fax: 718-326-2249. Rev. Vytautas Volertas, Coord.

Nigerian Apostolate Tel: 718-969-3226; Fax: 718-380-0345. Rev. Anthony Nzegwu (Nigeria).

Pakistani Apostolate Tel: 718-763-2330; Fax: 718-763-6592. Rev. Ilyas Gill, O.F.M. (Pakistan), Coord.

Polish Apostolate Tel: 718-768-5724; Fax: 718-768-4996. Rev. Witold Mroziewski, J.C.D., Coord.

Russian Apostolate Rt. Rev. Roman V. Russo, Coord.

Vietnamese Apostolate Tel: 718-278-1834; Fax: 718-278-0998. Rev. Peter H. Nguyen, Coord.

West Indian Apostolate Tel: 718-574-5772; Fax: 718-919-2265. Rev. Caleb A. Buchanan, Coord.

Apostleship of the Sea Tel: 718-596-7750; Fax: 718-260-9233. Rev. Antonio Camora.

Resources, Inc., 1258 65th St., 11219. Tel: 718-236-3000; Fax: 718-256-9707. Michael Campo, Mgr. Maintenance Dept.; Mr. James Casale, Business Devel.

Catholic Immigrant Ministries, Inc., 1258 65th St., 11219. Tel: 718-236-3000; Fax: 718-256-9707.

Catholic Migration Services, Inc., 1258 65th St., 11219. Tel: 718-236-3000; Fax: 718-256-9707.

[R] MONASTERIES AND RESIDENCES OF PRIESTS AND BROTHERS

BROOKLYN. *Brothers of the Christian Schools*, 1214-1216 Beverley Rd., 11218. Tel: 718-857-4311; Fax: 718-857-7576. Bros. John Bassett, F.S.C.; Peter Bonventre, F.S.C.; David Carroll, F.S.C.; Ralph Darmento, F.S.C.; Robert Ferguson, F.S.C.; Richard Grieco, F.S.C.; William Kemmerer, F.S.C. Brothers 7.

Carmelites of Mary Immaculate, Inc., 862 Manhattan Ave., 11222. Tel: 718-383-3339; Fax: 718-383-5968. Email: cmiusa@hotmail.com. Web: www.cmiusa.org. Revs. Sojan Anthony Madathil, Coord. Gen. & Procurator for Missions; Roy Jacob, Parochial Vicar, 1006 St. Elizabeth St., St. Martinville, LA 70582.

St. Francis Monastery-Generalate Offices of Franciscan Brothers, 135 Remsen St., 11201-4212. Tel: 718-858-8217; Fax: 718-858-8306. Email: generalate@gmail.com. Web: www.franciscanbrothers.org. Bros. William Boslet, O.S.F., M.A., Supr. Gen.; Kevin Smith, O.S.F., 1st Councilor; Richard Contino, O.S.F., 2nd Councilor; Joshua Di Mauro, O.S.F., 3rd Councilor; Jeremy Sztabnik, O.S.F., 4th Councilor. Brothers 73.

St. John the Baptist Rectory (1868) 75 Lewis Ave., 11206. Tel: 718-455-6864; Fax: 718-452-3738. Rev. Emmet J. Nolan, C.M. In Res. Revs. Thomas J. Hynes, C.M.; Biju Chittooparamban, C.M., B.A., B.Th., M.A.

Res.: *Our Lady of Good Counsel Rectory*, 915 Putnam Ave., 11221.

St. Michael's Friary, 225 Jerome St., 11207. Tel: 718-827-6990; Fax: 718-827-5789. Rev. Michael Greco, O.F.M.Cap., Dir. Capuchin Postulancy Program & Guardian; Bros. Mario Guerrero, O.F.M.Cap., Fraternity Vicar; Timothy Jones, O.F.M.Cap., Dir. Vocation Ministry; Michael Loerch, O.F.M.Cap. Priests 1; Postulants 4; Brothers 3.

Oratory of Saint Philip Neri, Congregation Pontifical Rite (1988) 109 Willoughby St., 11201. Tel: 718-875-2096; Fax: 718-875-4678. Email: creekhaven4952@gmail.com. Web: Brooklyn-oratory.org. Very Rev. Dennis M. Corrado, C.O., Provost; Revs. Mark J. Lane, C.O.; Joel M. Warden, C.O.; Anthony Andreassi, C.O.; Michael J. Callaghan, C.O.; Bro. James Simon, C.O. Priests 5; Brothers 1.

Redemptorist Fathers of New York, Inc.-Baltimore Province (1969) 7509 Shore Rd., 11209. Tel: 718-833-1900; Fax: 718-630-5666. Web: www.redemptorists.net. Very Rev. Kevin J. Moley, C.Ss.R., Prov. Supr.; Revs. Lawrence E. Lover, C.Ss.R., J.C.D., Cannon Lawyer; Francis Gargani, C.Ss.R., Supr.; Carl W. Hoegerl, C.Ss.R., Prov. Archivist; Robert M. Pagliari, Ph.D., Asst. Procurator & Sec.; Edmund Faliskie, C.Ss.R., Procurator; Joseph F. Jones, C.Ss.R., Vicar. Provincial Residence for Redemptorist Fathers and Brothers Priests 10.

ASTORIA. *Our Lady of China Chapel*, 54-09 92nd St., Elmhurst, 11373. Tel: 718-699-1929; Fax: 718-460-8032. Email: olcny@msn.com. Web: olc.faithweb.com. Revs. Antonius Ho, C.S.J.B. (Taiwan), Dir.; Dehua Zhang, C.S.J.B., Assoc.

DOUGLASTON. *Bishop Mugavero Residence*, 7200 Douglaston Pkwy., 11362. Tel: 718-229-8001, Ext. 411; Fax: 718-428-3070. Email: moellinger@rcdob.org. Deacon Matthew Oellinger, Coord., Office of Sr. Priests In Res. Most Revs. Thomas V. Daily, D.D. (Retired); Rene A. Valero, D.D., M.S.W., V.E. (Retired); Rev. Msgrs. Gerard Arella (Retired); Joseph P. Bynon (Retired); Michael J. Cantley (Retired); James J. Cooney, B.A., M.A. (Retired); George T. Deas (Retired); Conrad R. Dietz (Retired); Richard F. Dunn (Retired), 54 Elm Ct., New Hyde Park, 11040; Eugene A. Feldhaus (Retired); Thomas J. Gradilone (Retired); Lawrence E. Hinch (Retired); Vincent A. Keane (Retired); Raymond J. Kelly, S.T.L. (Retired); John F. Keppler (Retired); James P. King (Retired); Walter C. Murphy (Retired);

James A. Hunt (Retired); August C. Bednartz (Retired); John E. Waldron (Retired); Revs. Robert Blauvelt (Retired); Hugh A. Byrne (Retired); Coleman J. Costello (Retired); George R. Cowan (Retired); Eugene P. Coyle (Retired); Joseph W. Denzer (Retired); James T. Devine (Retired); Daniel G. Keohane (Retired); Eugene McGovern (Retired); John A. McShane (Retired); Kevin J. O'Donoghue (Retired); James J. Reynolds; Jerome J. Schmidt (Retired); Francis J. Labita (Retired); Francis J. Byrnes (Retired); John A. Gurrieri (Retired); Thomas D. Dolan (Retired).

ELMHURST. *Congregation of St. John the Baptist of China*, 54-17 90th St., 11373. Tel: 718-271-3944; Fax: 718-271-3215. Email: csjbny@catholic.org. Web: csjb.faithweb.com. Revs. Antonius Ho, C.S.J.B. (Taiwan), Regl. Supr.; Dehua Zhang, C.S.J.B.; Victor Cao, C.S.J.B.; Ambrose Khong, C.S.J.B. Priests 4; Brothers 2.

JAMAICA. *Saint Charles House of Studies*, 168-41 84th Ave., 11432. Tel: 718-351-8808; Fax: 718-667-4598. Rev. Matthew Didone, C.S., Prov. Supr.

Immaculate Conception Monastery (1936) 86-45 Edgerton Blvd., 11432. Tel: 718-739-6502; Fax: 718-739-7770. Email: pgrace@cpprov.org. Web: www.passionists.us. Revs. Peter Grace, C.P., Rector; Richard A. Nalepa, C.P., Vice-Rector; Quentin Amrhein, C.P. (Retired); Lawrence Bellew, C.P. (Retired); Jerome Bracken, C.P., Seminary Prof.; Alberto Cabrera, C.P., Hispanic Min.; Paul Chenot, C.P., Chap.; Christopher Cleary, C.P., Asst. Dir. Retreat House; Theophane Cooney, C.P., Asst. Pastor; Neil Davin, C.P., Officialis; James Earley, C.P. (Retired); Daniel Free, C.P. (Retired); Henry Free, C.P. (Retired); Mario Gallipoli, C.P., Mission Preacher; Thomas Griffiths, C.P. (Retired); Joseph D. Guzinski, C.P., Confraternity Dir.; Stephen Haslach, C.P., Confessor; Angelo Iacovone, C.P. (Retired); Thomas Joyce, C.P., Pastor Emeritus (Retired); Owen Lally, C.P., Charismatic Min.; Richard Leary, C.P. (Retired); John Michael Lee, C.P., Dir. Retreat House; Julian Morgan, C.P. (Retired); Gilbert Otieno Omolo, C.P., Hospital Chap.; Dominic Papa, C.P., Vice-Postulator; Kenan Peters, C.P., Mission Preacher; Isaias Powers, C.P. (Retired); John Powers, C.P., Author & Preacher; Salvatore Riccardi, C.P., Asst. Pastor; Lawrence Rywalt, C.P., Gen. Sec.; Richard Scheiner, C.P., Confessor; Roy Srampical, C.P., Missionary; Jed Sumampong, C.P. Immaculate Conception Church; Theodore Walsh, C.P., Mission Preacher; Michael Greene, C.P., Associate Retreat Dir.; Bonaventure Moccia, C.P., Sec., Translator; Paul Zilonka, C.P., Provincial Consultor; Bros. Anselm Catalucci, C.P., (Retired); Conrad Federspiel, C.P., (Retired); Philip Maggiulli, C.P., (Retired); August Parlavechio, C.P., Devel.; Angelo Sena, C.P., Receptionist; G. Bernard Johnson, Librarian; James Gillette, de familia; Maurice X. Hayes, Sacristan. Priests 38; Brothers 6. *Passionist Benefactor's Society* Tel: 718-739-9337; Fax: 718-206-9284. Email: pgrace@cpprov.org. Web: www.icmonastery.org.

Reverend John B. Murray, CM, House (1958) *St. John's University*, 8000 Utopia Pkwy., 11439. Tel: 718-990-6744; Fax: 718-990-5724. Email: flanagap@stjohns.edu. Revs. Peter J. Albano, C.M., Ph.D., Visiting Prof., Philosophy; Tri Minh Duong, C.M., B.A., M.Div., M.A., Asst. Supr. & Campus Min.; Henry M. Bradbury, C.M., B.A., S.T.L., General Min.; Michael J. Callaghan, C.M., Ph.D., B.A., M.Div., M.A.T., Assoc. Prof. English; Dang Kim Doai, C.M., Student/ Grad. Studies; James F. Dorr, C.M., Gen. Ministry; Patrick S. Flanagan, C.M., B.S., M.Div., Ph.D., Supr. & Asst. Prof. Theology & Rel. Studies; Peter D. Goldbach, C.M., B.A., S.T.L.; Patrick J. Griffin, C.M., B.S., M.Div., Th.M, M.A., Ph.D., Dir. Gen., Daughters of Charity; James M. Kelly, C.M., M.A., Chap. Ozanam Nursing Home; Astor Rodriguez, C.M., B.S., Vocation Dir.; Hung Van Le (Peter), C.M. (Vietnam), Grad. Student (Paris Province); Tri Sunaring Widiatmoko (Indonesia), Grad. Student (Indonesian Province).

St. Vincent's House, 84-15 Kendrick Pl., 11432. Tel: 718-990-7900; Fax: 718-990-7933. Email: kettelbj@stjohns.edu. Revs. John H. McKenna, C.M., B.A., M.A., S.T.D.; Joseph V. Daly, C.M., B.A., M.A., M.S.; Donald J. Harrington, C.M., B.A., M.Div., Th. M.; John A. Kettelberger, C.M., Th.M., Supr.; James J. Maher, C.M., B.A., M.Div., D.Min., Th.M.; Michael D. Whalen, C.M., B.A., M.Div., Th.M., M.A., S.T.L., S.T.D. Vincentian Fathers.

JAMAICA ESTATES. *Paulist Fathers - Generalate*, 86-11 Midland Pkwy., 11432. Tel: 718-291-5995; Fax: 718-291-6646. Email: mcgarry@paulist.org. Web: www.paulist.org. Revs. Michael B. McGarry, C.S.P., Pres.; Lawrence A. Rice, C.S.P., First Consultor; John J. Foley, C.S.P., Vice Pres. Paulist Priests at Paulist Foundations Outside the U.S. Revs. Gregory Apparcel, C.S.P., Via Venti Settembre 15, Rome 00187 Italy. Tel: 011-3906-488-2748; Fax: 011-3906-474-0236; John F. Duffy, C.S.P., Via Venti Settembre 15, Rome 00187 Italy. Tel: 011-3906-488-2748; Fax: 011-3906-474-0236; James A. Haley, C.S.P., 659 Markham St., Toronto ON M6G 2M1 Canada. Tel: 416-534-4219; Fax: 416-534-2328; Stephen E. Bossi, C.S.P., 659 Markham St., Toronto ON M6G 2M1 Canada. Tel: 416-534-4219; Fax: 416-534-2328; Paul A. Lannon, C.S.P., 659 Markham St., Toronto ON M6G 2M1 Canada. Tel: 416-534-4219; Fax: 416-534-2328; Thomas R. Marshall, C.S.P., 659 Markham St., Toronto ON M6G 2M1 Canada. Tel: 416-534-4219; Fax: 416-534-2328; James F. McCabe, C.S.P., 659 Markham St., Toronto ON M6G 2M1 Canada. Tel: 416-534-4219; Fax: 416-534-2328; Thomas P. Murphy, C.S.P., 659 Markham St., Toronto ON M6G 2M1 Canada. Tel: 416-534-4219; Fax: 416-534-2328; Deacon Richard J. Boudreau, C.S.P., 659 Markham St., Toronto ON M6G 2M1 Canada. Tel: 416-534-4219; Fax: 416-534-2328 On Special Assignment in the U.S. Revs. Thomas A. Kane, C.S.P.; Justin J. McCormick, C.S.P. Retired Revs. Robert W. Baer, C.S.P. (Retired); Wilfred A. Brimley, C.S.P. (Retired); Wilfred F. Dewan, C.S.P. (Retired); William J. Dougherty, C.S.P. (Retired); Philip W. Hart, C.S.P. (Retired); William J. Kenney, C.S.P. (Retired); Joachim Lally, C.S.P. (Retired); Kenneth H. McGuire, C.S.P. (Retired); Louis F. McKernan, C.S.P. (Retired); Ernest C. Mort, C.S.P. (Retired); James R. O'Gara, C.S.P. (Retired); Robert F. Quinn, C.S.P. (Retired); Robert T. Scott, C.S.P. (Retired).

LONG ISLAND CITY. *Holy Ghost Fathers of Ireland*, 48-49 37th St., 11101. Tel: 718-729-5273; Fax: 718-729-6949. Email: tbasquel@aol.com. Web: www.irishspiritans.ie. Very Rev. Thomas Basquel, C.S.Sp., Prov. Delegate; Revs. James Delaney, C.S.Sp. (Retired); Noel P. O'Meara, C.S.Sp.

OZONE PARK. *Montfort Missionaries Provincialate (Missionaries of the Company of Mary)* (1705) 101-18 104th St., 11416. Tel: 718-849-5885; Fax: 718-849-7518. Email: montfort.secretariat@gmail.com. Web: montfortusa.org. Very Rev. Matthew J. Considine, S.M.M.; Revs. Peter D'Abele, S.M.M., Ozone Park, NY; Donald LaSalle, S.M.M., Ozone Park, NY; Richard Magararu, S.M.M., Ozone Park, NY; Richard Schebera, S.M.M. Priests 8.

Priests of Province Serving Abroad: Revs. Alonzo Lazo, S.M.M., Chontales, Nicaragua; Harry Flores Morales, S.M.M., Chontales, Nicaragua; Thomas D. Poth, S.M.M., Chontales, Nicaragua; Delegation Supr.

QUEENS VILLAGE. *DePaul Residence*, 80-14 217th St., 11427. Tel: 718-766-7344; Fax: 718-468-2903. Revs. Stephen C. Bicsko, C.M.; Michael J. Cummins, C.M.; Richard J. Devine, C.M.; Joseph P. Foley, C.M.

ROCKAWAY PARK. *Franciscan Missionary Brothers of North America New York*, 99-07 Rockaway Beach Blvd., 11694. Tel: 718-634-6476; Fax: 718-634-5833. Email: franciscanbi@verizon.net. Bro. Jose Valliara, C.M.S.F., Supr. General.

SOUTH OZONE PARK. *Sacred Heart Provincialate* (NY Province), 141-11 123 Ave., 11436-1426. Tel: 718-322-3309; Fax: 718-529-6004. Email: nyprovince@verizon.net. Bro. Joseph Rocco, S.C., Prov. Brothers 5.

SPRINGFIELD GARDENS. *Martin De Porres Brothers Community*, 136-01 219th St., 11413. Tel: 718-525-3414; Fax: 718-525-0982. Email: rrbfsc@mdp.org. Web: www.mdp.org. Bros. Raymond R. Blixt, F.S.C., M.A., Exec. Dir., Martin de Porres Youth Center; Philip Rofrano, F.S.C., L.C.S.W., Exec., Martin de Porres Group Homes; Kevin Finn, F.S.C., M.A., Dir. of Community. Brothers 4. In Res. Bro. Peter Iorlano, F.S.C., M.A.

[S] CONVENTS AND RESIDENCES FOR SISTERS

BROOKLYN. *The Congregation of the Daughters of Mary, Brooklyn*, 332 E. 32nd St., 11226. Tel: 718-856-3323; Fax: 718-703-0980. Sr. Juvenia Joseph, Supr. of House.

Discalced Carmelite Nuns (2004) 361 Highland Blvd., 11207. Tel: 718-235-0422; Fax: 718-235-0542.

Franciscan Sisters of the Poor, Congregational Office, 133 Remsen St., 11201. Tel: 718-643-1919; Fax: 718-643-9710. Email: sfp@franciscansisters.org. Web: www.franciscansisters.org. Sr. Tiziana Merletti, S.F.P., Congregation Min.

Missionaries of Charity, Contemplative/Our Lady of Lourdes Convent (1982) 34 Aberdeen St., 11207. Tel: 718-443-2868. Sisters M. Linda Chacko, M.C.; M. Joy Zanin, M.C.; M. John Soulis, M.C.; Margaret Mary Arias, M.C.; M. Raphaelita Francis, M.C.; M. Faustina Soumas, M.C.; M. Bernadette Viola, M.C.; Teresa of Avila Fosc, M.C.; Sebastina Kadenturu, M.C.; Irene Waruguru, M.C.; M. Gemma Chong, M.C. Sisters 11.

Monastery of the Sisters Adorers of the Precious Blood, 5300 Ft. Hamilton Pkwy., 11219-4037. Tel: 718-438-6371; Fax: 718-438-6381. Rev. Msgrs. Austin P. Bennett, J.C.D., P.A., Exec. Dir. Confraternity of the Precious Blood (Retired); Philip J. Reilly, Chap. (Retired). Sisters 5.

Confraternity of the Precious Blood, 5300 Ft. Hamilton Ave., 11219-4035. Tel: 718-436-1120; Fax: 718-854-6058. Rev. Msgr. Austin P. Bennett, J.C.D., P.A., Exec. Dir. (Retired). Staff 5.

Sisters of Mercy of the Americas, Mid-Atlantic Community (1855) 273 Willoughby Ave., 11205-1487. Tel: 718-622-5840; Fax: 718-398-7866. Web: www.mercymidatlantic.org. Sr. Patricia Vetrano, R.S.M., Pres. Sisters 1,007.

Sisters of the Good Shepherd, 348 Ninth St., 11215. Tel: 718-499-9212. Sisters 2.

Provincial Office, 25-30 21st Ave., Astoria, 11105. Tel: 718-278-1155. Sr. Ellen Kelly, Prov. Officer.

Sisters of the Visitation of Brooklyn, NY (1855) 8902 Ridge Blvd., 11209. Tel: 718-745-5151; Fax: 718-745-3680. Email: srp2srr@aol.com. Web: www.visitationsisters.org/mona/bro_main.asp. Sr. Mary Pauline Baulis, V.H.M., R.N., Supr. Professed Sisters 17.

ASTORIA. *Provincialate of the Sisters of the Good Shepherd* (1834) 25-30 21st Ave., 11105. Tel: 718-278-1155; Fax: 718-278-1158. Email: ekelly@nygoodshepherd.org. Web: goodshepherdsistersna.com. Sr. Ellen Kelly, Prov.; Irene Liber, Admin. Asst.

Sisters of the Good Shepherd, Province of New York

Sisters of the Good Shepherd, 61-03 56th Ave., Maspeth, 11378. Tel: 718-418-0280; Fax: 718-418-0282. Sisters 6.

JAMAICA. *The Congregation of the Sisters of Jesus the Savior*, 171-17 110th Ave., 11433. Tel: 718-526-0973; Fax: 718-526-0973. Sisters Mary Fidelis Ezemaduka, S.J.S., Regional Coord.; Maria Gemma Njeze, S.J.S., Community Supr.; Christiana Nwachukwu, S.J.S., Bursar.

Ursuline Sisters of Tildonk, Glengarda, 81-15 Utopia Pkwy., 11432-1308. Tel: 718-591-0681; Fax: 718-969-4275. Email: ctalia@tildonkursuline.org. Web: www.tildonkursuline.org. Sr. Catherine Talia, O.S.U., Prov. Supr.

QUEENS VILLAGE. *St. Ann's Novitiate, Little Sisters of the Poor* (1902) 110-39 Springfield Blvd., P.O. Box 280356, 11428. Tel: 718-464-4920; Fax: 718-479-3126. Email: nvmothersuperior@littlesistersofthepoor.org. Web: www.littlesistersofthepoor.org. Sr. Mary Richard, L.S.P., Supr. & Mistress of Novices; Rev. Msgr. James Pereda, C.R.C., Chap. Sisters 5; Novices 12; Postulants 6.

Little Sisters of the Poor, Provincial Residence, 110-30 221st St., 11429. Tel: 718-464-1800; Fax: 347-626-2181. Email: provincialbklyn@littlesistersofthepoor.org. Web: www.littlesistersofthepoor.org. Sr. Margaret Regina Halloran, l.s.p., Prov. Sisters 120.

RIDGEWOOD. *Convent of the Sisters of Mary Reparatrix*, 62-67 60 Pl., 11385. Tel: 718-456-4242; 718-386-1107 (Altar Bread Department); Fax: 718-386-2254. Email: smrnyc@covad.net. Web: www.smr.org. Sr. Pat Mullen, S.M.R., Local Leader. Sisters 2.

ROCKAWAY PARK. *Stella Maris Convent, Sisters of St. Joseph*, 140 Beach 112th St., 11694-2497. Tel: 718-634-1886.

[T] EVANGELIZATION AND RENEWAL CENTERS

BROOKLYN. *Jesus of Nazareth Diocesan Retreat Center*, 475 E. 57th St., 11203. Tel: 347-710-0010; Fax: 347-710-0014. Deacon Carlos Garcia, Dir.

JAMAICA. *Bishop Molloy Retreat House* (1924) 86-45 Edgerton Blvd., 11432. Tel: 718-739-1229; Fax: 718-739-3421. Web: www.bishopmolloy.org. Revs. John Michael Lee, C.P., Retreat Dir.; Michael Greene, C.P., Assoc. Passionist Fathers.

[U] SECULAR INSTITUTES

FLUSHING. *The Institute of the Apostolic Oblates/Pro Sanctity* (1950) 45-30 195th St., 11358. Tel: 718-649-0324; Fax: 718-272-5012. Email: apostolicoblates@verizon.net. Web: www.prosanctity.org. Agnes Rus, Local Moderator.

FOREST HILLS. *Asociacion Misioneros Contemplativos Laicos* (Lay Association of Contemplative Missionaries), 3543 84th St., Apt. 308, Jackson Heights, 11372. Tel: 718-592-5458. Antonio Alvarez, Representative; Ana Luisa Ortega, Treas.

[V] MISCELLANEOUS LISTINGS

BROOKLYN. *Aid to the Church in Need, Inc.*, 725 Leonard St., 3rd Fl., 11222-0384. Tel: 718-609-0939; Fax: 718-609-0938. Web: www.churchinneed.org.

Alive in Hope Foundation of the Diocese of Brooklyn (1998) 310 Prospect Park West, 11215. Tel: 718-965-7375; Fax: 718-965-7341. Email: info@aliveinhope.org. Web: www.aliveinhope.org.

Casa Betsaida Housing Development Fund Corp., 191 Joralemon St., 11201. Tel: 718-722-6086. Jeanne M. Diulio, Asst. Dir., Office of Legal Affairs.

Casa Betsaida-Home for people with AIDS, 267 Hewes St., 11211. Tel: 718-218-7890; Fax: 718-218-8264. Email: cbetsaidainc@aol.com. Rev. Msgr. Anthony Hernandez, J.C.L., Chm. Bd. Total Staff 16; Total Assisted 67.

The Cathedral Club of Brooklyn, P.O. Box 315, 11209-0315. Tel: 718-809-2440; Fax: 646-720-1183. Web: www.cathedralclubbrooklyn.org. James B. McHugh, Board Member.

Churches United Corp., 247 Hewes St., 11211. Tel: 718-388-3774; Fax: 718-388-3784. Web: churchesunitedcorp.org.

Compostela Fund of the Roman Catholic Diocese of Brooklyn (2002) 310 Prospect Park W., 11215. Tel: 718-965-7300; Fax: 718-965-7311. Email: mreid@diobrook.org. Rev. Msgr. Michael J. Reid, Vicar for Financial Admin.

St. Elizabeth Ann Seton Charitable Trust, 310 Prospect Park West, 11215. Tel: 718-399-5995; Fax: 718-399-5965.

**Federation of Oases of Koinonia John the Baptist*, 205 14th St., 11215. Tel: 718-624-1572; Fax: 718-722-7748.

Franciscan Brothers Charitable Trust (1999) 135 Remsen St., 11201. Tel: 718-858-8217; Fax: 718-858-8306. Email: generalate@gmail.com. Web: www.francisanbrothers.org. Richard T. Arkwright, Trustee; Robert Schaefer, Trustee; Michael Henning, Trustee.

Franciscan Sisters of the Poor Charitable Trust, 133 Remsen St., 11201. Tel: 718-643-1919; Fax: 718-643-9710. Email: sfp@franciscansisters.org. Web: www.franciscansisters.org. Sr. Tiziana Merletti, S.F.P., Congregation Min.

Franciscan Sisters of the Poor Communities, Inc., 133 Remsen St., 11201. Tel: 718-643-1919; Fax: 718-643-9710.

The Futures in Education Foundation, Inc., 310 Prospect Park West, 11215. Tel: 718-965-7308; Fax: 718-965-7341. Email: info@futuresineducation.org. Web: www.futuresineducation.org.

Good Shepherd Charitable Trust, 310 Prospect Park W., 11215.

Heart's Home USA, 108 Saint Edwards St., 11205. Tel: 718-522-2121; Fax: 718-522-2922. Email: info@heartshomeusa.org. Web: www.heartshomeusa.org. Laetitia Palluat de Besset, Pres.

HeartShare Human Services of NY - Clermont Residence, 26 Clermont Ave., 11205. Tel: 718-834-9317; Fax: 718-834-9364. Miss Sharon Bewry, Resident Mgr. Residence for Developmentally Disabled Adults.

St. John Vianney Fund Charitable Trust, 310 Prospect Park West, 11215.

St. John's Bread & Life Program, Inc., 795 Lexington Ave., 11221. Tel: 718-443-2240; 718-574-0058; Fax: 718-455-7796. Mr. Anthony Butler, Exec. Dir.; Sr. Kathleen Byrne, S.C., Mobile Soup Kitchen Dir. (Soup Kitchen, Employment Counseling, HIV/AIDS Support Group/Food Pantry, Counseling, Referrals and Advocacy)

Juan Neumann Center (Immigration Services), 545 60th St., 11220. Tel: 718-439-8160; Fax: 718-439-8685.

**The Maura Clarke Ita Ford Center* (1993) 75 Lewis Ave., 11206. Tel: 718-452-0167; Fax: 718-452-5173. Email: mcifcenter@mcifc.org. Web: www.mcifc.org. Janet Marcic, Dir.

Mercy Home Foundation, 273 Willoughby Ave., 11205. Tel: 718-832-1075; Fax: 718-832-7612. Sr. Virginia Farnan, Contact Person.

Mercy Medical Mission (Sisters of Mercy Mid-Atlantic Community), 273 Willoughby Ave., 11205.

National Center of the Haitian Apostolate, 332 E. 32nd St., 11226. Tel: 718-856-3323; Fax: 718-703-0980. Web: snaa.org. Rev. Yvon Pierre, Exec. Dir.

Rocklyn Asset Corporation, 310 Prospect Park W., 11215.

Rocklyn Ecclesiastical Corporation, 310 Prospect Park W., 11215.

The Roman Catholic Pontifical Lay Association Memores Domini, 218 76th St., 11209. Tel: 718-833-3992. Email: asala218@gmail.com.

Men's House (1993) 218 76 St., 11209. Tel: 718-833-3992. Email: chris.vath@gmail.com. Christopher H. Vath, Head of the House.

Women's House (1993) 10 Kraft Ave., Bronxville, 10708. Tel: 916-395-0019. Email: mariacerny@yahoo.com. Elvira Parravicini, Head of the House.

Ryken Educational Center, Inc., 7100 Shore Rd., 11209. Tel: 718-759-5758; Fax: 718-759-5744. Email: wslow@xaverian.org. William Slow, Dir.

Saint Vincent DePaul Charitable Trust, 310 Prospect Park W., 11215.

Society of the Immaculate Conception of Brooklyn (Missionary Society), 310 Prospect Park W., 11215. Tel: 718-965-7326; Fax: 718-965-7325. Email: tmulkerin@rcdob.org. Rev. Terrence J. Mulkerin, Exec. Dir. (Retired). (Missionary Society)

ASTORIA. *Good Shepherd Volunteers*, 25-30 21st Ave., 11105. Tel: 718-943-7489; Fax: 718-777-1928. Peter Altman, Exec. Dir.

HandCrafting Justice, Inc. (1997) 25-30 21st Ave., 11105. Tel: 718-204-0909; Fax: 718-777-1928. Email: hcj@handcraftingjustice.org. Web: www.handcraftingjustice.org. Sr. Maureen McGowan, R.G.S., Prog. Dir.

BAYSIDE. *Ozanam Geriatric Foundation* (1997) 42-41 201 St., 11361. Tel: 718-971-2020; Fax: 718-971-2025. Email: jcraymond@ozanamhall.org. Web: www.ozanamhall.org.

BRIARWOOD. *Archbishop Molloy High School Charitable Trust*, 85-53 Manton St., 11435. Tel: 718-441-9210; Fax: 718-846-3202.

FLUSHING. *Pro Sanctity Movement* (1947) 45-30 195th St., 11358. Tel: 718-649-0324; Fax: 718-272-5012. Email: prosanctitynewyork@verizon.net. Web: www.nyprosanctity.org. Angela DiPaola, Dir.; Rev. Msgr. Steven J. Aguggia, J.C.L., Spiritual Advisor.

**Women Helping Women* (1981) P.O. Box 580086, 11358-0086. Tel: 718-539-9111; Fax: 718-961-3322. Email: whwcol@earthlink.net.

HOLLIS HILLS. *Glencara, Inc.* (1996) 86-05 218th St., 11427. Tel: 718-454-9804; Fax: 718-454-9804. Email: sfoley@nyc.rr.com. Sisters Louise Cullen, R.S.M., Board of Directors. Tel: 631-968-8859; Sean Foley, R.S.M., Pres. Tel: 718-454-9804; Patricia A. Hartigan Esq. Tel: 718-343-4450; Sisters Francene Horan, R.S.M., Sec.; Francis Marie Sheridan, R.S.M., Board of Directors; Eileen Trainor, 2nd Vice Pres. Tel: 718-452-0167; Regina Williams, Treas. Tel: 516-873-9191, Ext. 104.

JACKSON HEIGHTS. **Eternal Flame of Hope Ministries, Inc.*, c/o Rev. Richard J. Bretone, 74-18 Ditmars Blvd., 11370. Tel: 718-274-4919. Rev. Richard J. Bretone, Spiritual Dir.

Preachers of Christ and Mary, 93-11 35th Ave., 11372. Tel: 347-294-1452. Sr. Oneida Franco Vargas, P.C.M., Asst., Rel. Educ. Prog.

LONG ISLAND CITY. *Hour Children* (1995) 13-07 37th Ave., 11101. Tel: 718-443-4724; Fax: 718-433-4728. Email: sisterterese@hourchildren.org. Web: www.hourchildren.org. Sr. Teresa Fitzgerald, C.S.J., Exec. Dir. Families Capacity 60; Total Staff 42; Total Assisted Annually (Includes work inside prisons) 3,000; Volunteers 60.

World Compassion Link, P.O. Box 4279, 11104-9808. Tel: 718-729-5273. Email: omearanoel@gmail.com; wcljd54@yahoo.com. Web: worldcompassionlink.org. 48-49 37th St., 11101. Tel: 718-729-5273. Rev. Noel P. O'Meara, C.S.Sp., Pres.; Very Rev. Thomas Basquel, C.S.Sp., Vice Pres.; Rev. James Delaney, C.S.Sp., Dir. Devel. & Treas. (Retired).

MIDDLE VILLAGE. *National Italian Apostolate Conference* (1968) 66-05 79th Pl., 11379. Tel: 718-326-1911; Fax: 718-326-1883. Email: niac.america@gmail.com. Rev. Msgr. Steven J. Aguggia, J.C.L., Exec. Dir.

REGO PARK. *Lifeway Network, Inc.*, 85-10 61st Rd., 11374. Tel: 718-779-8075; Fax: 718-651-5645.

RIDGEWOOD. *Friends of RADIO MARIA, Inc.* (1992) 70-05 Fresh Pond Rd., 11385. Tel: 718-417-0550; Fax: 718-417-5188. Email: info.nyi@radiomaria.us. Web: www.radiomaria.org. Rev. Walter Tonelotto, C.S., Dir.

ROCKAWAY PARK. *Franciscan Missionary Brothers of North America, NY* (1901) 99-07 Rockaway Beach Blvd., 11694. Tel: 718-634-6476; Fax: 718-634-5833. Email: franciscanbi@netzero.net. Bro. Joseph Karimalayil, C.M.S.F., Ph.D., Pres. & Supr. General.

WOODHAVEN. *School Sisters of Notre Dame Educational Center*, 87-04 88th Ave., 11421. Tel: 718-738-0588; Fax: 718-322-5515. Email: ssndec@aol.com. Sr. Catherine Feeney, S.S.N.D., Exec. Dir. Staff 5; Total Assisted 80.

RELIGIOUS INSTITUTES OF MEN REPRESENTED IN THE DIOCESE

For further details refer to the corresponding bracketed number in the Religious Institutes of Men or Women section.

[1350]—*Brothers of St. Francis Xavier* (Sacred Heart Prov.)—C.F.X.
[0330]—*Brothers of the Christian Schools*—F.S.C.
[0600]—*Brothers of the Congregation of Holy Cross*—C.S.C.
[1100]—*Brothers of the Sacred Heart*—S.C.
[0470]—*The Capuchin Friars* (Prov. of St. Mary)—O.F.M.Cap.
[0275]—*Carmelites of Mary Immaculate*—C.M.I.
[]—*Congregation of St. John the Baptist of China, Inc.*—C.S.J.B.
[1330]—*Congregation of the Mission - Philadelphia (Vincentians)*—C.M.
[1330]—*Congregation of the Mission (Vincentian Fathers)*—C.M.
[1210]—*Congregation of the Missionaries of St. Charles*—C.S.
[]—*Congregation of the Missionary Brothers of St. Francis of Assisi*—C.M.S.F.
[1000]—*Congregation of the Passion* (Prov. of St. Paul of the Cross)—C.P.
[0480]—*Conventual Franciscans* (Polish Prov.)—O.F.M.Conv
[0490]—*Franciscan Brothers of Brooklyn*—O.S.F.
[]—*Franciscan Province of Immaculate Conception*—O.F.M.
[0650]—*Holy Ghost Fathers*—C.S.Sp.
[]—*Institute of the Incarnate Word*—I.V.E.
[0690]—*Jesuit Fathers and Brothers* (New York Prov.)—S.J.
[]—*Lasalette Missionaries*—M.S.
[0770]—*The Marist Brothers*—F.M.S.
[0780]—*The Marist Fathers*—S.M.
[0870]—*Montfort Missionaries (Missionaries of the Company of Mary)*—S.M.M.
[1330]—*New England Province of the Congregation of the Mission (Vincentian)*—C.M.
[0950]—*Oratorians* (Brooklyn)—C.O.
[0990]—*Pallottine*—S.A.C.
[]—*Pallottine* (Polish Prov.)—S.A.C.
[1030]—*Paulist Fathers*—C.S.P.
[1070]—*The Redemptorists*—C.SS.R.
[1200]—*Salvatorian Fathers*—S.D.S.
[0690]—*Society of Jesus*—S.J.
[0760]—*Society of Mary (Marianists)* (New York Prov.)—S.M.
[0990]—*Society of the Catholic Apostolate*—S.A.C.
[1200]—*Society of the Divine Savior*—S.D.S.
[1350]—*Xaverian Brothers U.S.A., Inc.*—C.F.X.

RELIGIOUS INSTITUTES OF WOMEN REPRESENTED IN THE DIOCESE

[0340]—*Carmelite Sisters of Charity*—C.C.V.
[0330]—*Carmelite Sisters of the Aged and Infirm*—O.Carm.
[2980]—*Congregation of Notre Dame*—C.N.D.
[2950]—*Congregation of Notre Dame de Sion*—N.D.S.
[]—*Congregation of Olivetan Benedictine Sisters* (Korea)—O.S.B.
[2230]—*Congregation of the Infant Jesus*—C.I.J.
[3832]—*Congregation of the Sisters of St. Joseph*—C.S.J.
[0760]—*Daughters of Charity of St. Vincent de Paul*—D.C.
[]—*Daughters of Divine Love*—D.D.L.
[]—*Daughters of Mary*—F.de.M.
[]—*Daughters of Mary Mother of Mercy*—D.M.M.M.
[]—*Daughters of Our Lady of the Garden*—F.M.H.
[0960]—*Daughters of Wisdom*—D.W.
[0420]—*Discalced Carmelite Nuns*—O.C.D.
[1070-11]—*Dominican Congregation of Our Lady of the Rosary (Sparkill Dominicans)*—O.P.
[1070-05]—*Dominican Sisters* (Amityville, NY)—O.P.
[1105]—*Dominican Sisters of Hope*—O.P.
[1115]—*Dominican Sisters of Peace*—O.P.
[1400]—*Franciscan Missionary Sisters of the Sacred Heart*—F.M.S.C.
[]—*Franciscan Sisters of St. Bernadette*—F.S.S.B.
[]—*Franciscan Sisters of the Immaculate (Honduras)*—H.F.I.
[1440]—*Franciscan Sisters of the Poor*—S.F.P.
[1840]—*Grey Nuns of the Sacred Heart*—G.N.S.H.
[]—*Handmaids of the Divine Redeemer* (Ghana)—H.D.R.
[]—*Handmaids of the Holy Child Jesus* (Nigeria)—H.H.C.J.
[]—*Hermanas Predicadoras de Cristo y Maria* (Columbia)—P.C.M.
[2070]—*Holy Union Sisters*—S.U.S.C.
[]—*Idente Missionaries*—M.Id
[2340]—*Little Sisters of the Poor*—L.S.P.
[2710]—*Missionaries of Charity*—M.C.

[2710]—*Missionaries of Charity (Contemplative)*—M.C.

[]—*Missionary Congregation Sisters Servants of the Holy Spirit*—S.Sp.S.

[2790]—*Missionary Servants of the Most Blessed Trinity*—M.S.B.T.

[]—*Missionary Sisters of the Immaculate Conception*—M.F.I.C.

[]—*Missionary Sisters of the Precious Blood* (Canada)—C.P.S.

[4190]—*Order of Visitation*—V.H.M.

[3465]—*Religious of the Sacred Heart of Mary*—R.S.H.M.

[3430]—*Religious Teachers Filippini*—M.P.F.

[2970]—*School Sisters of Notre Dame*—S.S.N.D.

[]—*Servants of the Lord and the Virgin of Matara* (Argentina)—S.S.V.M.

[0110]—*Sisters Adorers of the Most Precious Blood*—A.P.B.

[0650]—*Sisters of Charity of St. Vincent de Paul of New York*—S.C.

[0640]—*Sisters of Charity of St. Vincent de Paul, Halifax*—S.C.

[]—*Sisters of Jesus the Savior* (Nigeria)—S.J.S.

[]—*Sisters of Mary Immaculate* (Kenya)—S.M.I.

[2575]—*Sisters of Mercy of the Americas* (Mid-Atlantic Community)—R.S.M.

[2990]—*Sisters of Notre Dame*—S.N.D.

[3000]—*Sisters of Notre Dame de Namur*—S.N.D.deN.

[3820]—*Sisters of St. John the Baptist*—C.S.J.B.

[3830-05]—*Sisters of St. Joseph*—C.S.J.

[]—*Sisters of St. Joseph (Philadelphia)*—S.S.J.

[3830-01]—*Sisters of St. Joseph of Boston*—C.S.J.

[1830]—*Sisters of the Good Shepherd*—R.G.S.

[1970]—*Sisters of the Holy Family of Nazareth* (Immaculate Heart of Mary Prov.)—C.S.F.N.

[]—*Sisters of the Immaculate Heart of Mary* Kongmoon, China—I.H.M.

[]—*Sisters of the Korean Martyrs*—S.B.K.M.

[3320]—*Sisters of the Presentation of the B.V.M.* (Newburgh)—P.B.V.M.

[2160]—*Sisters, Servants of the Immaculate Heart of Mary*—I.H.M.

[2460]—*Society of Mary Reparatrix*—S.M.R.

[4130]—*Ursuline Sisters of the Congregation of Tildonk, Belgium*—O.S.U.

[4190]—*Visitation Nuns*—V.H.M.

CATHOLIC CEMETERIES

MIDDLE VILLAGE. *Saint John's Cemetery* Operating: St. Johns's Cemetery (Middle Village); Holy Cross Cemetery (Brooklyn); Mount St. Mary Cemetery (Flushing); St. Charles/Resurrection Cemetery (Farmingdale), 80-01 Metropolitan Ave., 11379. Tel: 718-894-4888; Fax: 718-326-2033. Web: www.ccbklyn.org. Stephen Comando, Exec. Dir.

PARISH CEMETERIES

BROOKLYN. *Trinity*, Tel: 718-894-4888. Most Holy Trinity Parish, Brooklyn.

AMITYVILLE. *Most Holy Trinity* Most Holy Trinity Parish, Brooklyn.

ROCKAWAY. *St. Mary Star of the Sea Cemetery*, Far Rockaway, 11691. Tel: 718-894-4888 (Office); Fax: 718-326-4105.

NECROLOGY

† Donovan, Rev. Msgr. Thomas F., (Retired)—Died March 31, 2011

† Kennedy, Rev. Msgr. Louis J., (Retired)—Died Aug. 13, 2011

† McCourt, Rev. Msgr. Robert R., (Retired)—Died June 21, 2011

† Saporito, Rev. Msgr. Cosmo G., (Retired)—Died March 11, 2011

† Anastasio, Thomas, (Retired)—Died Sept. 17, 2011

† Duran, Ernesto, (Retired)—Died Jan. 6, 2011

† Keane, Edward M., (Retired)—Died Feb. 4, 2011

† Kelly, Thomas F., (Retired)—Died Jan. 16, 2011

† Mariano, John M., (Retired)—Died Feb. 28, 2011

† Pfaff, Joseph A., Glendale, NY Sacred Heart.—Died May 12, 2011

† Rogers, Gary P., Brooklyn, NY St. Thomas Aquinas.—Died July 19, 2011

† Sheridan, Matthew W., (Retired)—Died March 7, 2011

An asterisk (*) denotes an organization that has established tax-exempt status directly with the IRS and is not covered by the USCCB Group Ruling.

Diocese of Brownsville

(Dioecesis Brownsvillensis)

Most Reverend

DANIEL E. FLORES, S.T.D.

Bishop of Brownsville; ordained January 30, 1988; appointed Auxiliary Bishop of Detroit and Titular Bishop of Cozyla October 28, 2006; consecrated November 29, 2006; appointed Bishop of Brownsville December 9, 2009; installed February 2, 2010. *Mailing Address: P.O. Box 2279, Brownsville, TX 78522-2279.*

Most Reverend

RAYMUNDO J. PEÑA, D.D.

Retired Bishop of Brownsville; ordained May 25, 1957; appointed Titular Bishop of Trisipa and Auxiliary of San Antonio October 16, 1976; consecrated December 13, 1976; appointed Bishop of El Paso April 29, 1980; installed June 18, 1980; appointed Bishop of Brownsville May 23, 1995; installed August 6, 1995; retired December 9, 2009. *Mailing Address: P.O. Box 2279, Brownsville, TX 78522-2279.*

ESTABLISHED JULY 10, 1965.

Square Miles 4,296.

Comprises the four Counties of Cameron, Hidalgo, Starr and Willacy in the State of Texas.

For legal titles of parishes and diocesan institutions, consult the Chancery.

Chancery: 1910 University Blvd., P.O. Box 2279, Brownsville, TX 78522-2279. Tel: 956-542-2501; Fax: 956-542-6751.

Web: www.cdob.org

Email: cdob@cdob.org

STATISTICAL OVERVIEW

Personnel	
Bishop	1
Retired Bishops	1
Priests: Diocesan Active in Diocese	66
Priests: Diocesan Active Outside Diocese	3
Priests: Retired, Sick or Absent	12
Number of Diocesan Priests	81
Religious Priests in Diocese	29
Total Priests in Diocese	110
Extern Priests in Diocese	8
Ordinations:	
Diocesan Priests	3
Transitional Deacons	4
Permanent Deacons in Diocese	91
Total Brothers	16
Total Sisters	103
Parishes	
Parishes	69
With Resident Pastor:	
Resident Diocesan Priests	50
Resident Religious Priests	14
Without Resident Pastor:	
Administered by Priests	5
Missions	45
Pastoral Centers	2
Professional Ministry Personnel:	
Brothers	2
Sisters	5
Lay Ministers	50
Welfare	
Health Care Centers	1
Total Assisted	137
Homes for the Aged	2
Total Assisted	256
Day Care Centers	1
Total Assisted	17
Special Centers for Social Services	6
Total Assisted	139,944
Other Institutions	4
Total Assisted	9,539
Educational	
Seminaries, Diocesan	1
Students from This Diocese	8
Diocesan Students in Other Seminaries	26
Total Seminarians	34
High Schools, Private	3
Total Students	968
Elementary Schools, Diocesan and Parish	8
Total Students	2,292
Elementary Schools, Private	3
Total Students	912
Catechesis/Religious Education:	
High School Students	8,497
Elementary Students	28,374
Total Students under Catholic Instruction	41,077
Teachers in the Diocese:	
Priests	4
Brothers	6
Sisters	12
Lay Teachers	297
Vital Statistics	
Receptions into the Church:	
Infant Baptism Totals	8,846
Minor Baptism Totals	624
Adult Baptism Totals	290
Received into Full Communion	901
First Communions	8,238
Confirmations	3,924
Marriages:	
Catholic	1,354
Interfaith	91
Total Marriages	1,445
Deaths	2,695
Total Catholic Population	1,074,477
Total Population	1,264,091

Former Prelates—Rt. Revs. DOMINIC MANUCY, Titular Bishop of Delma and Vicar Apostolic of Brownsville; cons. Dec. 8, 1874; transferred to Mobile, March 9, 1884; reappointed to Vicariate Apostolic of Brownsville, Feb. 1, 1885; died Dec. 4, 1885; PETER VERDAGUER, Titular Bishop of Aulon and Vicar Apostolic of Brownsville; cons. Nov. 9, 1890; died Oct. 26, 1911; CLAUDE JAILLET, O.P., Administrator of Vicariate Apostolic of Brownsville, 1911-1913.

Former Bishops—Most Rev. ADOLPH MARX, D.D., J.C.D., first Bishop of Brownsville, ord. May 2, 1940; appt. Titular Bishop of Citrus and Auxiliary Bishop of Corpus Christi, July 6, 1956; cons. Oct. 9, 1956; appt. first Bishop of Brownsville, July 19, 1965; installed Sept. 2, 1965; died in Cologne, Germany Nov. 1, 1965; His Eminence HUMBERTO CARDINAL MEDEIROS, D.D., second Bishop of Brownsville, appt. April 14, 1966; cons. June 9, 1966; installed Bishop of Brownsville, June 29, 1966; appt. Archbishop of Boston, Sept. 8, 1970; installed Archbishop of Boston, Oct. 7, 1970; created Cardinal, March 5, 1973; died Sept. 17, 1983; Most Revs. JOHN J. FITZPATRICK, D.D., third Bishop of Brownsville, ord. Dec. 13, 1942; appt. Auxiliary Bishop of Miami, June 24, 1968; cons. Aug. 28, 1968; appt. Bishop of Brownsville, April 27, 1971; installed May 27, 1971; retired Nov. 30, 1991; died July 15, 2006; ENRIQUE SAN PEDRO, S.J., S.T.D., S.S.L., fourth Bishop of Brownsville, ord. March 18, 1957; appt. Auxiliary Bishop of Galveston-Houston April 1, 1986; cons. June 29, 1986; appt. Coadjutor Bishop of Brownsville, Aug. 13, 1991; installed Sept. 26, 1991; succeeded to the See, Nov. 30, 1991; died July 17, 1994; RAYMUNDO J. PENA, D.D., fifth Bishop of Brownsville, ord. May 25, 1957; appt. Titular Bishop of Trisipa and Auxiliary of San Antonio Oct. 16, 1976; cons. Dec. 13, 1976; appt. Bishop of El Paso April 29, 1980; installed June 18, 1980; appt. Bishop of Brownsville May 23, 1995; installed Aug. 6, 1995; retired Dec. 9, 2009.

Office of the Bishop—Most Rev. DANIEL E. FLORES, S.T.D., 1910 University Blvd., P.O. Box 2279, Brownsville, 78522-2279. Tel: 956-550-1510; Fax: 956-550-1565. Email: bishopflores@cdob.org.

Vicar General—Rev. Msgr. ROBERT E. MAHER, V.G. Email: rmaher@cdob.org; St. Joseph Parish, 122 W. Fay, Edinburg, 78539. Tel: 956-383-3728; Fax: 956-383-8630. Email: stjoseph-edinburg@catholic.org.

Deans/Deaneries—Brownsville Deanery: Rev. MICHAEL J. AMESSE, O.M.I. Tel: 956-546-3178. Harlingen Deanery: Rev. WILLIAM T. PENDERGHEST, SS.CC. Tel: 956-423-6341. McAllen-Edinburg Deanery: Rev. Msgr. GUSTAVO BARRERA. Tel: 956-686-0251. Mission Deanery: Rev. ROY LEE SNIPES, O.M.I. Tel: 956-585-2623. Pharr Deanery: Rev. GERALD W. FRANK. Tel: 956-783-1196. Rio Grande City Deanery: Rev. JEAN OLIVIER M. SAMBU. Tel: 956-423-6341. San Benito Deanery: Rev. SAMUEL ARIZPE. Tel: 956-399-3247. Weslaco Deanery: Rev. GREGORY T. LABUS. Tel: 956-565-1141.

Development Office—Ms. ROSIE RODRIGUEZ, Dir., 700 N. Virgen de San Juan Blvd., San Juan, 78589. Tel: 956-781-5323; Fax: 956-784-5096. Email: rrodriguez@cdob.org.

Stewardship Office—VACANT, Dir.

Judicial Department and Diocesan Tribunal—Very Rev. A. OLIVER ANGEL, J.C.L., Judicial Vicar. Email: oangel@cdob.org; Ms. ANNITA GONZALEZ,

Ecclesiastical Notary & Advocate Facilitator, 700 N. Virgen de San Juan Blvd., San Juan, 78589. Tel: 956-784-5070; Fax: 956-784-5087. Email: agonzalez@cdob.org.

Presiding Judge—Very Rev. A. OLIVER ANGEL, J.C.L.

Promoter of Justice—Rev. Msgr. GUSTAVO BARRERA.

Procurators and Advocates—Ms. ANNITA GONZALEZ, Coord.

Court Expert—Sr. NORMA PIMENTEL, M.J., L.P.C.

Associate Judges—Revs. JOSE RENE ANGEL, J.C.L.; THOMAS G. KULLECK.

Defenders of the Bond—Rev. Msgr. GUSTAVO BARRERA, First Instance. Email: gcbarrera@rgv.rr.com; Rev. JOSE RENE ANGEL, J.C.L., Second Instance.

Office of the Chancellor—1910 University Blvd., P.O. Box 2279, Brownsville, 78522-2279. Tel: 956-542-2501; Fax: 956-542-6751. Rev. Msgr. HEBERTO M. DIAZ JR., Chancellor. Email: hdiaz@cdob.org; Revs. JORGE A. GOMEZ, Vice Chancellor. Email: jogomez@cdob.org; THOMAS G. KULLECK, Historical Archivist. Email: tkulleck@cdob.org.

Moderator of the Curia/Brownsville/San Juan—Rev. Msgr. HEBERTO M. DIAZ JR., 1910 University Blvd., P.O. Box 2279, Brownsville, 78522-2279. Tel: 956-542-2501; Fax: 956-542-6751. Email: hdiaz@cdob.org.

Office for Pastoral Planning—Mr. LUIS ZUNIGA, Dir. Tel: 956-542-2501, Ext. 356. Email: lzuniga@cdob.org.

Diocesan Relations—700 N. Virgen de San Juan Blvd., San Juan, 78589. Tel: 956-781-5323; Fax: 956-784-5082. Mrs. BRENDA NETTLES RIOJAS, Dir. Email: bnrpr@cdob.org.

Fiscal Office—1910 University Blvd., P.O. Box 2279, Brownsville, 78522-2279. Tel: 956-542-2501, Ext. 336; Fax: 956-550-1563. Mr. JACK GRAHAM, Comptroller. Email: jgraham@cdob.org.

Information Technology—1910 University Blvd., P.O. Box 2279, Brownsville, 78522-2279. Tel: 956-542-2501, Ext. 340; Fax: 956-542-6751. *700 N. Virgen de San Juan Blvd., San Juan, 78589.* Tel: 956-784-5004; Fax: 956-784-5097. Mr. ALBERTO ZAVALA, Dir. Tel: 956-550-1540. Email: azavala@cdob.org.

Human Resources Office—1910 University Blvd., P.O. Box 2279, Brownsville, 78522-2279. Tel: 956-542-2501, Ext. 345; Fax: 956-550-1561. Mrs. GENOVEVA TREVINO, Dir. Email: gtrevino@cdob.org.

Insurance and Priest Pensions—1910 University Blvd., P.O. Box 2279, Brownsville, 78522-2279. Tel: 956-542-2501, Ext. 357; Fax: 956-550-1586. Mrs. PATRICIA GOMEZ, Insurance Admin. Tel: 956-550-1557. Email: pgomez@cdob.org.

Building/Property/Construction Management—700 N. Virgen de San Juan Blvd., San Juan, 78589. Tel: 956-781-5323; Fax: 956-784-5096. Mr. JAVIER SOLIS, Dir. Email: jsolis@cdob.org.

Vicar for Priests—Rev. PATRICK K. SEITZ, St. Pius X Parish, 600 S. Oklahoma Ave., Weslaco, 78596. Tel: 956-968-7471; Fax: 956-969-3040.

Office of Permanent Deacons—Rev. EDOUARD ATANGANA, S.T.L., Dir., 700 N. Virgen de San Juan Blvd., San Juan, 78589. Tel: 956-784-5007.

Vicar for Religious—Rev. THOMAS LUCZAK, O.F.M., Sacred Heart Parish, P.O. Box 370, McAllen, 78505-0370. Tel: 956-686-7711; Fax: 956-686-2028; Sr. NORMA PIMENTEL, M.J., L.P.C., Asst. Tel: 956-702-4088; Fax: 956-782-0418.

Campaign for Human Development—Rev. Msgr. HEBERTO M. DIAZ JR., 1910 University Blvd., P.O. Box 2279, Brownsville, 78522-2279. Tel: 956-542-2501; Fax: 956-542-6751.

Catholic Relief Services—VACANT.

Immigration Counseling Services—700 N. Virgen de San Juan Blvd., San Juan, 78589. Tel: 956-784-5057; Fax: 956-784-5096. Mrs. SANTA ACUNA, Coord. Email: sacuna@cdob.org.

Division for Education and Formation—

Media Resource-Library—Sr. MAUREEN CROSBY, S.S.D., Dir. Tel: 956-787-8571. Email: mcrosby@cdob.org.

San Juan Diego Lay Ministry Institute—Mr. LUIS ZUNIGA, Coord. Tel: 956-784-5011; Fax: 956-784-5086. Email: lzuniga@cdob.org.

Catholic Schools Office—700 N. Virgen de San Juan Blvd., San Juan, 78589-3042. Tel: 956-787-8571. Mrs. LISETTE ALLEN, Supt. Email: lallen@cdob.org.

Family Life Office—700 N. Virgen de San Juan Blvd., San Juan, 78589-3042. Tel: 956-784-5012. Mrs. LYDIA PESINA, Dir. Email: lpesina@cdob.org.

Office of Catechesis—700 N. Virgen de San Juan Blvd., San Juan, 78589-3042. Tel: 956-781-5323.

Division for Health Care Ministries—

Coordinator—Rev. EDOUARD ATANGANA, S.T.L., 700 N. Virgen de San Juan Blvd., San Juan, 78589. Tel: 956-784-5007; Fax: 956-784-5088.

Respect for Life Ministry—Sr. NANCY BOUSHEY, O.S.B., Mailing Address: P.O. Box 1501, Rio Grande City, 78582. Tel: 956-486-2680. Email: sanbenito@granderiver.net.

Diocesan Attorney—Mr. DAVID GARZA, 680 E. St. Charles St., Brownsville, 78520. Tel: 956-541-4914; Fax: 956-542-7403.

Presbyteral Council—Board Members: Most Rev. DANIEL E. FLORES, S.T.D.; Revs. SAMUEL ARIZPE; RICHARD L. LIFRAK, SS.CC.; Rev. Msgr. JUAN NICOLAU, Ph.D., S.T.L.; Revs. WILLIAM T. PENDERGHEST, SS.CC.; JEAN OLIVIER M. SAMBU; JOSE LUIS GARCIA; AMADOR GARZA; ALFONSO M. GUEVARA; AGLAYDE RAFAEL VEGA; ERNESTO MAGALLON; MARIO A. CASTRO. Ex Officio Members: Rev. Msgrs. ROBERT E. MAHER, V.G.; HEBERTO M. DIAZ JR.

Catholic Foundation of the Rio Grande Valley Board—Most Rev. DANIEL E. FLORES, S.T.D.; Mr. ALONZO BELTRAN; Rev. Msgr. HEBERTO M. DIAZ JR.; Mr. JACK GRAHAM; Ms. DELIA CHAVEZ; Deacon ANTONIO M. ARTEAGA, C.F.P., C.T.F.A.; Mr. JOE D. TREVINO; Mr. RICK FLORES.

College of Consultors—Most Rev. DANIEL E. FLORES, S.T.D.; Revs. PATRICK K. SEITZ; RUBEN DELGADO; Rev. Msgrs. HEBERTO M. DIAZ JR.; GUSTAVO BARRERA; ROBERT E. MAHER, V.G.

Diocesan Finance Council—Most Rev. DANIEL E. FLORES, S.T.D.; Ms. LILY G. DE LA ROSA; Mr. NOE GARZA; Rev. Msgr. GUSTAVO BARRERA; Mr. BOB ELLIOT; Mr. RUBEN BOSQUEZ; Dr. CHARLES ELLARD; Mr. HUGH EMERSON; Ms. EDNA MARTINEZ.

Priests' Assignment Board—Most Rev. DANIEL E. FLORES, S.T.D.; Revs. EDOUARD ATANGANA, S.T.L.; AMADOR GARZA; PATRICK K. SEITZ; FRANCISCO J. SOLIS; Rev. Msgr. HEBERTO M. DIAZ JR.

Propagation of the Faith—VACANT, 1910 University Blvd., P.O. Box 2279, Brownsville, 78522-2279. Tel: 956-542-2501.

Church in Latin America—VACANT, 1910 University Blvd., P.O. Box 2279, Brownsville, 78522-2279. Tel: 956-542-2501.

Victim Assistance and Safe Environment Coordinator—Mr. WALTER LUKASZEK, L.M.S.W., I.P.R. Tel: 956-784-5066; Cell: 956-457-0010. Email: wlukaszek@cdob.org; walukaszek@gmail.com.

CLERGY, PARISHES, MISSIONS AND PAROCHIAL SCHOOLS

CITY OF BROWNSVILLE

(CAMERON COUNTY)

1—IMMACULATE CONCEPTION CATHEDRAL (1849) Revs. Michael J. Amesse, O.M.I., Rector; Jose R. Torres, O.M.I.; Deacon Roberto Cano. In Res., Revs. Armand Matthew, O.M.I.; Pasquale Lanese, O.M.I. (Retired).
Res.: 1218 E. Jefferson St., P.O. Box 311, 78522. Tel: 956-546-3178; Fax: 956-546-1284.
Catechesis/Religious Program—Mrs. Alondra Guerrero, D.R.E. Students 201.
Mission—St. Thomas 155 E. Jefferson St., Cameron Co. 78520.
Mission—Sacred Heart 602 E. Elizabeth St., Cameron Co. 78520.

2—CHRIST THE KING (1953) Rev. Jose Luis Garcia.
2255 Southmost Rd., 78521. Tel: 956-546-1982; Fax: 956-546-7120. In Res., Rev. Michael Gnanaraj.
Catechesis/Religious Program—Tel: 956-546-5147. Mrs. Elva Reyes, D.R.E. Students 343.
Mission—San Juan Diego de Guadalupe Valle Escondido 4180 S. Browne, Cameron Co. 78521.

3—CHURCH OF THE GOOD SHEPHERD (1968) Rev. Mario A. Castro; Deacon Alvino C. Olvera.
Res.: 2645 Tulipan St., 78521. Tel: 956-542-5142; Fax: 956-542-5278.
Catechesis/Religious Program—Mrs. Arabella Garcia, D.R.E. Students 521.

4—ST. EUGENE DE MAZENOD (1996) Rev. Timothy W. Paulsen, O.M.I.
Res.: 5409 Austin Rd., 78521. Tel: 956-831-9923; Fax: 956-831-3110. Email: frtimpaulsenomi@aol.com.
Catechesis/Religious Program—Ms. Eva Guerra, C.R.E. (Grades 1-5); Ms. Belinda Rodriguez, C.R.E. (Grades 6-12). Students 327.

5—HOLY FAMILY (1966) Rev. Jorge A. Gomez.
Mailing Address: 2405 E. Tyler, 78520.
Church: 2308 E. Tyler, 78520. Tel: 956-546-6975; Fax: 956-550-8884. Email: holy_family_brw@cdob.org.
Catechesis/Religious Program—Tel: 956-574-9873. Ms. Cindy Gonzalez, C.R.E. Students 360.

6—ST. JOSEPH (1953) Rev. Oscar O. Siordia; Deacon Francisco Garza.
Res. & Mailing Address: 555 W. St. Francis St., 78520. Tel: 956-542-2709; Fax: 956-542-2275.
Catechesis/Religious Program—Tel: 956-546-4894. Students 258.

7—ST. LUKE (1974) Rev. Fernando Gonzalez; Deacons George M. Terrazas; Javier A. Garcia.
Res.: 2800 Rockwell Dr., 78521. Tel: 956-541-1480; Fax: 956-542-8043. Email: saint-luke@cdob.org.
School—(Grades PreK-8), 2850 Price Rd., 78521. Tel: 956-544-7982; Fax: 956-544-4874. Web: www-.stlukes.org. Mrs. Ana E. Gomez, Prin.; Ms. Patty Garza, Librarian. Lay Teachers 26; Students 351.
Catechesis/Religious Program—Mrs. Helen Vargas, D.R.E. Students 550.

8—MARY, MOTHER OF THE CHURCH (1967) Rev. Msgr. Heberto M. Diaz Jr.; Rev. Alejandro F. Flores; Deacons John P. Kinch; Juan Pablo Navarro; Luis Zuniga.
Res.: 1914 Barnard Rd., 78520-8247. Tel: 956-546-3800; Fax: 956-546-1589.
School—Preschool & Day Care Center: Little Saints Day Care, (2 yr. olds) Students 17.
School—(Grades PreK-6), 1300 Los Ebanos Blvd., 78520. Tel: 956-546-1805; Fax: 956-546-0787. Ms. Judy Faulk, Prin.; Mrs. Blanca Chavez, Librarian. Religious 1; Lay Teachers 26; Students 459.
Catechesis/Religious Program—Mrs. Betty Bonnet, D.R.E. Students 735.

9—OUR LADY OF GOOD COUNSEL (1966) Revs. Thomas L. Pincelli; Thomas G. Kulleck, Weekend Duties.
1055 Military Hwy., 78520. Tel: 956-541-8341; Fax: 956-548-0229.
Catechesis/Religious Program—Rosario Figueroa, D.R.E. Students 447.

10—OUR LADY OF GUADALUPE (1928) Rev. Francisco Acosta; Deacon Bruno Cedillo.
Mailing Address: P.O. Box 4900, 78523.
Res.: 1200 E. Lincoln St., 78521. Tel: 956-542-4823; Fax: 956-542-5944.
Catechesis/Religious Program—Tel: 956-542-3619. Sr. Arminda Rangel, M.J., D.R.E. Students 361.

11—THE PARISH OF THE LORD OF DIVINE MERCY (2005) Rev. Rodolfo Franco.
Office & Rectory: 1393 E. Alton Gloor, Ste. 11, 78526. Tel: 956-544-2112; Fax: 956-544-2208.
Catechesis/Religious Program—Students 674.
Mission—San Pedro 7602 Old Military Rd., San Pedro, Cameron Co. Tel: 956-542-2596; Fax: 956-546-8080. Mailing Address: P.O. Box 1658, Olmito, 78575. Rev. Hector J. Cruz, S.M.
Mission—Our Heavenly Father 9178 Tomas Cortez Jr. St., Olmito, Cameron Co. 78575. Tel: 956-350-5190; Fax: 956-350-5207. Mailing Address: P.O. Box 249, Olmito, 78575. Rev. Eduardo Gomez.

12—SAN FELIPE DE JESUS (1996) Revs. Hector J. Cruz, S.M.; Joel Grissom, S.M., Parochial Vicar.
Mailing Address: P.O. Box 8093, 78526-8093.
Office: 2218 Carlos Ave., 78526. Tel: 956-982-2007; Fax: 956-541-4177.
Res.: 2511 Dennis, 78526.
Church: 2215 Rancho Viejo Ave., 78526.
Catechesis/Religious Program—Tel: 956-982-2035. Ms. Dominga Torres, C.R.E. Students 414.

OUTSIDE THE CITY OF BROWNSVILLE

ALAMO, HIDALGO CO., RESURRECTION (1926), (Formerly St. Joseph/Our Lady of Fatima) Rev. Emmanuel Bialoncik, O.F.M.
Res.: 312 N. 9th St., 78516. Tel: 956-787-2963; Fax: 956-787-6788.
Catechesis/Religious Program—Rosemary Rodriguez, C.R.E. Students 1,105.

ALTON, HIDALGO CO., SAN MARTIN DE PORRES (1967) Rev. Julian Becerril, O.de.M.; Deacons Antonio M. Arteaga; Armandin Villarreal.
Mailing Address: 106 S. Alton Blvd., PMB 9023, 78573. Tel: 956-585-8001; Fax: 956-585-0715.
Res.: 621 W. Main St., 78573.
Catechesis/Religious Program—Tel: 956-585-3125. Students 500.
Mission—Capilla Santa Cecilia Monte Cristo, Hidalgo Co., TX.
Mission—Centro Catolico San Juan Diego El Flaco, Hidalgo Co., TX.

DONNA, HIDALGO CO., ST. JOSEPH (1928) Revs. Alberto T. Trevino Jr., M.S.F.; Franciscus Asisi Eka Yuantoro, M.S.F.; Deacons Eduardo Ovalle; Juan Barbosa.
Res.: 306 S. D Salinas Blvd., 78537. Tel: 956-464-3331; Fax: 956-464-6808.
Catechesis/Religious Program—Tel: 956-464-3472; Fax: 956-464-7373. Mrs. Liza G. Tobias, D.R.E. Students 844.
Mission—Christ the King 1/2 Mile S. FM 493, Colonia Nueva, Hidalgo Co.

EDCOUCH, HIDALGO CO., ST. THERESA OF THE INFANT JESUS (1948) Rev. Ernesto Magallon; Deacon Gilberto Perez.
Res.: 200 P. Salazar, P.O. Box 307, 78538. Tel: 956-262-1347; Fax: 956-262-1348.
Catechesis/Religious Program—Mr. Juan Jose

Meave, D.R.E. Students 299.
Mission—Our Lady of Guadalupe 200 N. Laurel, La Villa, Hidalgo Co. 78562.

EDINBURG, HIDALGO CO.

1—HOLY FAMILY (1967) Rev. Eusebio Martinez; Deacon Ruben Lopez.
Res.: 1302 E. Champion, 78539-4864. Tel: 956-383-5472; Fax: 956-383-5034.
Catechesis/Religious Program—Tel: 956-383-4593. Ms. Susie de la Garza, D.R.E. Students 621.

2—ST. JOSEPH (1948) Rev. Msgr. Robert E. Maher; Deacons Irineo Gonzalez Jr.; Ramiro Davila Jr.; Silvestre J. Garcia.
Res.: 122 W. Fay St., 78539. Tel: 956-383-3728; Fax: 956-383-8630. Email: stjoseph-edinburg@catholic.org.
School—(Grades PreK-8), 119 W. Fay St., 78539. Tel: 956-383-3957; Fax: 956-318-0681. Web: stjoseph-edinburg.org. Sr. Kathleen Murray, D.C., Prin.; Ms. Lupita Davila, Librarian. Lay Teachers 22; Students 255.
Catechesis/Religious Program—Mrs. Ann Ameling, D.R.E. Students 614.

3—SACRED HEART (1927) Revs. Robert Charlton, SS.CC.; Richard L. Lifrak, SS.CC.; Deacons Jose A. Solis; Gilberto Lopez. In Res., Rev. Alfredo Garcia, SS.CC.
Res.: 215 N. 16th Ave., 78541. Tel: 956-383-3253; Fax: 956-383-7311. Email: sacredheartedg@sbcglobal.net.
Catechesis/Religious Program—Tel: 956-383-4631. Students 1,194.
Mission—Capilla de San Jose 4101 Flores St., Hidalgo Co. 78541. Tel: 956-386-1235. Ms. Susan Mercado, D.R.E.

EL RANCHITO, CAMERON CO., ST. IGNATIUS (1967) Rev. Martin de la Cruz.
24380 W. U.S. Hwy. 281, San Benito, 78586. Tel: 956-399-2022; Fax: 956-399-1213.
Catechesis/Religious Program—Ms. Maria Valdez, D.R.E. Students 376.
Mission—Our Lady of Lourdes La Paloma, Cameron Co.
Mission—Sacred Heart Las Rucias, Cameron Co.

ELSA, HIDALGO CO., SACRED HEART (1948) Rev. Ruben Delgado; Deacon Gerardo J. Rosa. In Res., Rev. Emmanuel Kwofie.
Res.: 1100 N. Broadway, P.O. Box 6, 78543. Tel: 956-262-1406; Fax: 956-262-4265.
Catechesis/Religious Program—Ms. Maria E. Martinez, D.R.E. Students 803.
Mission—Christ the King Monte Alto, Hidalgo Co. 78538.
Mission—Holy Cross Catechetical Center, Mile 15

ESCOBARES, STARR CO., SACRED HEART (1967) Rev. Francisco J. Solis; Deacon Rodolfo C. Salinas.
Mailing Address: P.O. Box 1180, Roma, 78584.
Res.: 4987 Old Escobares Hwy. 83, Roma, 78584. Tel: 956-849-1741; Fax: 956-847-1502.
Catechesis/Religious Program—Mr. Rolando Munoz, D.R.E. Students 327.
Mission—Santa Rosa de Lima 4201 Old Hwy. 83 (7 Miles E. of Roma), La Rosita, Starr Co.
Mission—Our Lady of Guadalupe 1155 N. FM 649 (13 Miles N. of Roma), El Sauz, Starr Co.

HARLINGEN, CAMERON CO.

1—ST. ANTHONY (1940) Rev. Lawrence J. Klein; Deacon Paulo Escobar.
Res.: 209 S. 10th, 78550. Tel: 956-428-6111; Fax: 956-428-4276. Email: stanthonychurch2@aol.com.
School—(Grades PreK-8), 1015 E. Harrison St., 78550. Tel: 956-423-2486; Fax: 956-412-0084. Mr. Chester Arizmendi, Prin.; Mrs. Belinda Casarez, Librarian. Lay Teachers 21; Students 222.
Catechesis/Religious Program—Tel: 956-428-2476; Fax: 956-425-8969. Mrs. Mary Kyser, D.R.E. Students 448.

2—IMMACULATE HEART OF MARY (1927) Rev. Msgr. Pedro Briseno.
Office: 412 S. C St., 78550. Tel: 956-423-0855; Fax: 956-421-1071. Email: immaculateheartofmary@hotmail.com. Web: heartofmarytexas.org.
Rectory—505 S. "C" St., 78550.
Catechesis/Religious Program—Students 339.

3—OUR LADY OF THE ASSUMPTION (1958) Rev. Horacio Chavarria; Deacon Catarino Villanueva Jr.
1313 W. Buchanan St., 78550. Tel: 956-423-4670; Fax: 956-423-5970. In Res., Rev. George A. Gonzalez.
Catechesis/Religious Program—Tel: 956-423-1765. Ms. Yzenia Huerta, D.R.E. Students 1,143.
Mission—San Felipe 1706 Rangerville Rd., Cameron Co. 78550.

4—QUEEN OF PEACE (1967) Revs. William T. Penderghest, SS.CC.; Alphonsus McHugh, SS.CC.; Deacon Genaro Ibarra.
Res.: 1509 New Combes Hwy., 78550. Tel: 956-423-6341; Fax: 956-423-2864. Email: qp_secretary@rgv.rr.com; queen-of-peace@cdob.org.
Catechesis/Religious Program—Tel: 956-425-2830. Ms. Maria T. Hernandez, D.R.E. Students 448.

HIDALGO, HIDALGO CO., SACRED HEART (1967) Rev. Mario Alberto Aviles, C.O.
Res.: 208 E. Camelia Ave., P.O. Box 579, 78557. Tel: 956-843-2463; Fax: 956-843-2187.
Catechesis/Religious Program—Mrs. Elisa Garza, D.R.E. Students 502.

LA FERIA, CAMERON CO., ST. FRANCIS XAVIER (1930) Rev. Gabriel I. Ezeh; Deacons Hugo De la Cruz; Jose G. Gonzalez.
Mailing Address: P.O. Box 116, 78559.
Office: 502 S. Canal St., P.O. Box 116, 78559. Tel: 956-797-2666; Fax: 956-797-3387. Email: stfrancislaferia@aol.com.
Church: 500 S. Canal St., 78559.
Catechesis/Religious Program—Tel: 956-797-5568. Mrs. San Juana Betancourt, D.R.E. Students 610.

LA GRULLA, STARR CO., HOLY FAMILY (1967) Rev. Terrence Gorski, O.F.M.; Deacon Benito Saenz Jr.
Mailing Address: P.O. Box 67, 78548.
Res.: 107 W. Private Lazaro Solis St., 78548. Tel: 956-487-3365; Fax: 956-487-4727.
Catechesis/Religious Program—Ms. Maria Guzman, D.R.E.; Ms. Martina Garcia, C.R.E.; Ms. Irma Garcia, C.R.E. Students 224.
Mission—Cristo Rey N. FM 2360, Cristo Rey, Starr Co.
Mission—Our Lady of the Peace FM 1430, La Casita, Starr Co.

LA JOYA, HIDALGO CO., OUR LADY, QUEEN OF ANGELS (1960) Revs. Jaime V. Torres; Miguel Angel Ortega; Deacon Alberto X. Chapa.
Res.: 916 S. Leo Ave., 78560. Tel: 956-585-5223; Fax: 956-585-4878.
Catechesis/Religious Program—Rosie Gonzalez, D.R.E. Students 421.
Mission—St. Mary Magdalene Abram, Hidalgo Co.
Mission—St. Anthony Penitas, Hidalgo Co.
Mission—St. Michael Los Ebanos, Hidalgo Co.
Mission—St. William Sullivan City, Hidalgo Co.

LOS FRESNOS, CAMERON CO., ST. CECILIA (1964) Rev. Esteban Hernandez; Deacon Augusto Chapa Jr.
Res.: 606 W. Ocean Blvd., 78566. Tel: 956-233-5619; Fax: 956-233-5565.
Catechesis/Religious Program—Tel: 956-233-5213. Mrs. Letty Villarreal, D.R.E. Students 537.

LYFORD, WILLACY CO., PRINCE OF PEACE (1967) Rev. Aglayde Rafael Vega.
Res.: 8413 Park Ave., P.O. Box 460, 78569. Tel: 956-347-3580; Fax: 956-347-3649.
Catechesis/Religious Program—Students 230.
Mission—Santa Monica FM 1018 & 1420, Santa Monica, Willacy Co.
Mission—St. Martin 345 Martin Cavazos St., P.O. Box 247, Sebastian, Willacy Co. 78594.

MCALLEN, HIDALGO CO.

1—HOLY SPIRIT (1981) Rev. Msgr. Louis L. Brum; Deacons Carlos S. Trevino; Alvin H. Gerbermann; David Espinoza; Reynaldo I. Florez; Crawford A. Higgins.
Res.: 2201 Martin Ave., 78504. Tel: 956-631-5295; Fax: 956-631-5460.
Catechesis/Religious Program—Tel: 956-664-2518. Students 1,399.

2—ST. JOSEPH THE WORKER (1967) Rev. Alfonso M. Guevara; Deacons Alejandro Gamboa; Rodolfo Sepulveda Jr.
Office: 2315 Ithaca St., 78501. Tel: 956-682-1351; Fax: 956-618-3317.
Church: 900 S. 23rd St., 78501.
Catechesis/Religious Program—Tel: 956-686-6871. Students 702.

3—SAINT JUAN DIEGO CUAUHTLATOATZIN (2002) Rev. Carlos Zuniga; Deacon Salvador Rojas.
Mailing Address & Office: 3408 Idela Ave., 78503. Tel: 965-682-5155; Fax: 956-682-5472. Email: sjdparish2002@aol.com.
Church: 3413 Helena Ave., 78503.
Catechesis/Religious Program—Maricela Garcia, C.R.E. & Youth Min. Students 496.

4—OUR LADY OF PERPETUAL HELP (1967) Rev. Msgr. Juan Nicolau; Deacon Agapito L. Cantu. In Res., Rev. Ignacio Tapia.
Res.: 2209 Kendlewood Ave., 78501. Tel: 956-682-4238; Fax: 956-682-0289. Email: olph2209@yahoo.com.
Catechesis/Religious Program—Tel: 956-682-3663. Ms. Pura Reyna, C.R.E. Students 790.

5—OUR LADY OF SORROWS (1941) Rev. Msgr. Gustavo Barrera; Rev. Mishael J. Koday; Deacons John F. Schwarz; Raymond L. Thomas Jr.
Res.: 1108 W. Hackberry St., 78501-4304. Tel: 956-686-0251; Fax: 956-686-0322. Email: parish@oladyofsorrows.org. Web: www.oladyofsorrows.org.
School—(Grades PreK-8), 1100 Gumwood, 78501. Tel: 956-686-3651; Fax: 956-686-1996. Mr. Rolando J. Garza, Prin.; Joseph O'Brien, Asst. Prin.; Patricia Espinosa, Librarian Mgr. Religious 1; Lay Teachers 29; Students 594.
Catechesis/Religious Program—Mrs. Janie Barragan, D.R.E.; Mrs. Letty Huggins, Asst. D.R.E. Students 1,080.

6—SACRED HEART (1917) Revs. Thomas Luczak, O.F.M.; Hilary J. Brzezinski, O.F.M.; Deacon Jose Luis Mendoza. In Res., Bro. Mario Nagy, O.F.M.
Res.: 306 S. 15th St., P.O. Box 370, 78505-0370. Tel: 956-686-7711; Fax: 956-686-2028.
Catechesis/Religious Program—Ms. Sandra Kent, D.R.E. Students 447.

MCCOOK, HIDALGO CO., IMMACULATE CONCEPTION (1950) Rev. Jose Rene Angel.
28212 FM 2058, Edinburg, 78541. Tel: 956-842-3663.

MERCEDES, HIDALGO CO.

1—OUR LADY OF MERCY (1909) Rev. Gregory T. Labus; Deacon Roberto Cantu.
Res.: 322 S. Vermont Ave., P.O. Box 805, 78570. Tel: 956-565-1141; Fax: 956-565-1640.
Catechesis/Religious Program—Students 288.

2—SACRED HEART CHURCH (1969) Rev. Eduardo Ortega.
920 Anacuitas, 78570. Tel: 956-565-0271; Fax: 956-565-0272.
Res.: 600 N. Washington, 78570.
Catechesis/Religious Program—Miss Maria Celeste Garcia, D.R.E. Students 633.

MISSION, HIDALGO CO.

1—OUR LADY OF GUADALUPE (1899) [CEM] Revs. Roy Lee Snipes, O.M.I.; James E. Pfeifer, O.M.I.; Deacons Guillermo "Bill" Castaneda Jr.; Francisco R. Flores.
Res.: 620 Dunlap St., P.O. Box 1047, 78572-1047. Tel: 956-585-2623; Fax: 956-584-5856. Email: olgparish@sbcglobal.net. Web: olgmissiontexas.org.
School—(Grades PreK-6), 611 N. Dunlap St., 78572. Tel: 956-585-6445; Fax: 956-584-3055. Sr. Cynthia A. Mello, S.S.D., Prin. Religious 3; Lay Teachers 8; Students 107.
Catechesis/Religious Program—Tel: 956-585-1376. Sr. Maria Guadalupe Cortes, M.C.P., D.R.E. Students 976.
Chapel—La Lomita

2—OUR LADY OF ST. JOHN OF THE FIELDS (1967) Rev. Francisco Castillo; Deacons Daniel Zamora; Pedro (Peter) Requenez Jr.
Res.: 1052 Washington St., 78572. Tel: 956-585-2325; Fax: 956-585-7270.
Catechesis/Religious Program—Tel: 956-581-1289. Mrs. Ana Maria Middlebrook, D.R.E. Students 477.

3—OUR LADY OF THE HOLY ROSARY (1968) Very Rev. A. Oliver Angel; Deacons Eduardo Reyna; Israel Sagredo.
Res.: 923 Matamoros St., P.O. Box 1439, 78572. Tel: 956-581-2193; Fax: 956-581-1906.
Catechesis/Religious Program—Mrs. Olga Gomez, D.R.E. Students 312.

4—ST. PAUL (1915) Rev. Gregory M. Kuczmanski; Deacon Robert Ledesma.
Res.: 1119 Francisco Ave., 78572. Tel: 956-585-2701; Fax: 956-581-4801.
Catechesis/Religious Program—Tel: 956-585-2486. Mrs. Cindy Schaefer, D.R.E. Students 757.

5—SAN CRISTOBAL MAGALLANES & COMPANIONS (2004) Rev. Ignacio Tapia; Deacon Ronaldo M. "Mitch" Chavez.
Mailing Address: 3805 Plantation Blvd., Ste. 5, 78572. Tel: 956-580-4551; Fax: 956-519-3537. Email: sancristobalmagallanes@gmail.com.
Catechesis/Religious Program—Ms. Maria Guadalupe Segura, D.R.E. Students 313.
Mission—Our Lady of Fatima 6634 El Camino Real, Hidalgo Co. 78572.
Mission—Our Lady of Lourdes 2 1/2 Miles S. Conway, Hidalgo Co. 78572.

PHARR, HIDALGO CO.

1—ST. ANNE, MOTHER OF MARY (1973) Rev. Genaro Henriquez.
801 E. Juarez, 78577. Tel: 956-787-8122; Fax: 956-787-8272. Email: stanne710@sbcglobal.net.
Res.: 309 N. First, 78577.
Catechesis/Religious Program—Tel: 956-787-5139. Janie Leal, C.R.E. Students 374.

2—ST. FRANCES XAVIER CABRINI (1999) Rev. Edouard Atangana; Deacon Jesus Antonio Osorio.
Church: 8001 S. Cage Blvd., 78577. Tel: 956-787-3554; Fax: 956-283-1354. Email: st-frances-cabrini@cdob.org. Web: madrecabrini.org.
Catechesis/Religious Program—Carmen Lopez, D.R.E. Students 619.

3—ST. JUDE THADDEUS (1951) Very Rev. Leo Francis Daniels, C.O.; Revs. Jose E. Losoya, C.O.; Jose Juan Ortiz, C.O.
Res.: 505 S. Ironwood, P.O. Box 1688, 78577-1630. Tel: 956-781-2489; Fax: 956-783-4614.
School—Oratory Academy of St. Philip Neri, (Grades PreK-8), 1407 W. Moore Rd., 78577. Tel: 956-781-3056; Fax: 956-787-1516. Rev. Mario Alberto Aviles, C.O., Prin.; Mrs. G. Yvonne Perez, Pres.; Revs. Jose E. Losoya, C.O., Vice Prin.; Jose Juan Ortiz, C.O., Librarian. Religious Teachers 4; Lay Teachers 37; Students 519.

School—Oratory - Athenaeum for University Preparation, (Grades 9-12), 1407 W. Moore Rd., 78577. Rev. Mario Alberto Aviles, C.O., Prin.; Mrs. G. Yvonne Perez, Pres.; Revs. Jose E. Losoya, C.O., Vice Prin.; Jose Juan Ortiz, C.O., Librarian. Religious Teachers 4; Lay Teachers 13; Students 207.
Catechesis/Religious Program—Tel: 956-781-3521. Mrs. Sochil J. Duran, D.R.E. Students 540.
4—ST. MARGARET MARY (1927) Rev. Msgr. Luis Javier Garcia.
Res.: 122 W. Hawk Ave., 78577. Tel: 956-787-8563; Fax: 956-702-4509.
Catechesis/Religious Program—Tel: 956-787-0832; Fax: 956-787-5385. Students 193.
PORT ISABEL, CAMERON CO., OUR LADY STAR OF THE SEA (1927) Rev. James C. Erving, O.M.I. In Res., Rev. Harry Schuckenbrock, O.M.I.
Res.: 705 S. Longoria St., 78578. Tel: 956-943-1297; Fax: 956-943-1422.
Catechesis/Religious Program—Tel: 956-943-6392. Mrs. Rosa Gonzalez, D.R.E. Students 482.
Mission—Laguna Heights Chapel Garfield St., Laguna Heights, Cameron Co. 78578.
PROGRESO, HIDALGO CO., HOLY SPIRIT (1969) Rev. Raymond Nwachukwu.
Res.: 210 Watts Ave., P.O. Box 216, 78579. Tel: 956-565-6856; Fax: 956-565-3462.
Catechesis/Religious Program—Tel: 956-565-1572. Mrs. Matilde Lopez, D.R.E. Students 244.
Mission—St. Margaret Ann Military Hwy. 281, Santa Maria, Cameron Co. 78592.
Mission—Cristo Rey Military Hwy. 281, Bluetown, Cameron Co. 78592.
RAYMONDVILLE, WILLACY CO.
1—ST. ANTHONY (1907) Rev. Juan Victor Heredia.
Res.: 464 S. First St., 78580. Tel: 956-690-4078; Fax: 956-690-4078.
2—OUR LADY OF GUADALUPE (1927) Rev. George Kerketta; Deacon Juan Francisco Gonzalez.
Res.: 693 N. Third St., 78580. Tel: 956-689-2408; Fax: 956-689-1687.
Catechesis/Religious Program—Students 380.
Mission—St. Patrick 1 Mile S. of 186 on Hwy. 1015, Lasara, Willacy Co. 78561.
Mission—St. Frances Xavier Cabrini 1 Block off 490 & 493, Hargill, Hidalgo Co. 78549.
Mission—St. Anne, Mother of Mary Bay Blvd. & Paloma, San Perlita, Hidalgo Co. 78590.
RIO GRANDE CITY, STARR CO.
1—IMMACULATE CONCEPTION (1880) [CEM] Revs. Jean Olivier M. Sambu; Marco Antonio Reynoso, Parochial Vicar.
Res.: 101 E. Third St., P.O. Box 1, 78582. Tel: 956-487-2317; Fax: 956-488-8133.
School—(Grades PreK-8), 305 N. Britton Ave., 78582. Tel: 956-487-2558; Fax: 956-487-6478. Mrs. Rubirita Urbina, Prin.; Ms. Donis Garza, Librarian. Religious 2; Lay Teachers 14; Students 248.
Catechesis/Religious Program—Araceli Barrientos, C.C.E. Coord. Students 919.
Mission—Sacred Heart Old US Hwy. 83, Los Garcias Ranch, Starr Co.
2—ST. PAUL THE APOSTLE (2009) Rev. Eduardo Villa.
Mailing Address: P.O. Box 269, Garciasville, 78547. Office: 5547 E. Hwy. 83, 78582. Tel: 956-488-8349; Fax: 956-488-8085.
Church: 5752 E. Hwy. 83, 78582.
RIO HONDO, CAMERON CO., ST. HELEN (1943) Rev. Rigobert Poulang Mot; Deacon Jose Guerra.
Res.: 228 Huisache, P.O. Box 451, 78583. Tel: 956-748-2327; Fax: 956-748-0089. Email: saint-helen@cdob.org.
Catechesis/Religious Program—Virginia Salinas, C.R.E. Students 290.
Mission—St. Vincent de Paul 2513 Lozano Rd., Lozano, Cameron Co. 78568.
ROMA, STARR CO., OUR LADY OF REFUGE (1853) Rev. Francisco J. Solis; Deacon Amando Pena Jr.
Res.: 4 St. Eugene de Mazenod Ave., P.O. Box 156, 78584. Tel: 956-849-1455; Fax: 956-849-2257.
Catechesis/Religious Program—Tel: 956-849-7155. Mrs. Maria Teresa Garcia, D.R.E. Students 741.
Mission—Holy Trinity 4 Miles S. FM 2098, Falcon Heights, Starr Co. 78545. Tel: 956-437-9238.
Mission—St. Joseph Iglesia St., Salineno, Starr Co. 78585. Tel: 956-353-8397.
Mission—Holy Family 202 S. Francesca Ave., Los Saenz, Starr Co. 78584. Tel: 956-849-1127.
Mission—Lamb of God Church St., Fronton, Starr Co. 78584. Tel: 956-849-2199.
SAN BENITO, CAMERON CO.
1—ST. BENEDICT (1912) Rev. Ignacio Luna; Deacon Manuel Sanchez.
Res.: 351 S. Bowie, P.O. Box 1780, 78586. Tel: 956-399-2353; Fax: 956-399-5701.
Catechesis/Religious Program—Tel: 956-399-5975. Students 435.
2—OUR LADY, QUEEN OF THE UNIVERSE (1960) Rev. Isaac Emeka Erondu.
Office & Mailing Address: 121 Garrison Dr., 78586. Tel: 956-399-2865; Fax: 956-399-2045.
Church: 1425 N. Sam Houston, 78586.
Catechesis/Religious Program—Miss Estefana Garcia, D.R.E. Students 361.
Mission—St. Joseph 1001 W. Hwy. 77, Cameron Co. 78586. Tel: 956-399-2615.
3—ST. THERESA (1954) Rev. Samuel Arizpe; Deacon Benito Flores.
Res.: 1300 Combes St., P.O. Box 1839, 78586. Tel: 956-399-3247; Fax: 956-276-0142.
Catechesis/Religious Program—Ms. Estela de la Fuente, D.R.E. Students 652.
SAN CARLOS, HIDALGO CO., ST. JOSEPH THE WORKER (1970) Rev. Salvador Ramirez; Deacon Hector Perez.
Res.: 8310 Highland Ave., Edinburg, 78542. Tel: 956-383-5880; Fax: 956-383-0420.
Catechesis/Religious Program—Tel: 956-381-1888. Students 598.
Mission—St. Anne San Manuel 22 Miles N. 281, San Manuel, Hidalgo Co.
Mission—St. Theresa Faysville Faysville, Hidalgo Co. Tel: 956-318-5135.
SAN ISIDRO, STARR CO., ST. ISIDORE (1964) Rev. Jose Rene Angel.
5160 FM 1017, P.O. Box 60, 78588. Tel: 956-481-3392; Fax: 956-481-3869.
Catechesis/Religious Program—Mrs. Manuelita Olivarez, D.R.E. Students 94.
SAN JUAN, HIDALGO CO.
1—BASILICA OF OUR LADY OF SAN JUAN DEL VALLE-NATIONAL SHRINE Revs. Amador Garza, Rector; Juan Rogelio Gutierrez, Asst. to Rector; Efiri Matthias Selemobri, M.S.P., Asst. to Rector; Manuel Alfredo Razo; Mr. Pablo H. Villescas, Admin.; Deacons Julio Castilleja; Jesus P. Galvan; Nicolas E. Trujillo.
Res.: 400 Virgen de San Juan Blvd., 78589. Tel: 956-787-0033; Fax: 956-787-2908.
2—ST. JOHN THE BAPTIST (1949) Revs. Gerald W. Frank; Joaquin Zermeno, Parochial Vicar; Deacons Rene Villalon Sr.; Graciano A. Rodriguez.
Mailing Address: 216 W. First St., P.O. Box 1269, 78589. Tel: 956-783-1196; Fax: 956-702-7447. Email: sjtbchurch@sbcglobal.net. Web: sjtbchurch.myplaceofworship.org.
Catechesis/Religious Program—Tel: 956-783-1068. Ms. Estela Salazar, C.R.E. Students 1,160.
Mission—Immaculate Conception 901 Church St., 78589.
SANTA ROSA, CAMERON CO., ST. MARY (1967) Rev. Juan Pablo Davalos; Deacon Gerardo Aguilar.
Res.: 101 San Antonio Ave., P.O. Box 365, 78593. Tel: 956-636-1211; Fax: 956-636-2941.
Catechesis/Religious Program—Mrs. Rosie Aguilar, D.R.E. Students 150.
WESLACO, HIDALGO CO.
1—ST. JOAN OF ARC (1929) Rev. Lee DaCosta.
Res.: 109 S. Illinois Ave., 78596. Tel: 956-968-3670; Fax: 956-968-1872.
Catechesis/Religious Program—Tel: 956-968-6812. Mr. Joshua Salinas, D.R.E. Students 429.
2—ST. PIUS X (1955) Revs. Patrick K. Seitz; Luis Fernando Sanchez; Deacon Jesus E. Aguayo.
Res.: 600 S. Oklahoma Ave., 78596. Tel: 956-968-7471; Fax: 956-969-3040.
Catechesis/Religious Program—Tel: 956-968-0317. Mr. John Trevino, D.R.E. Students 943.
3—SAN MARTIN DE PORRES (1967) Revs. Patrick K. Seitz; Gustavo Obando; Paul Roman, F.S.S.P.; Deacons Juan Mitch Delgado; Jose G. Garza; Oscar Garcia; Gilberto Guardiola Jr.
Res.: 901 N. Texas Blvd., 78596. Tel: 956-968-2691; Fax: 956-968-1473.
School—(Grades PreK-3), 905 N. Texas Blvd., 78596. Tel: 956-973-8642; Fax: 956-973-0522. Sr. Helen Rottier, C.S.J., Prin.; Ms. Adelina Olivo, Librarian. Religious 2; Lay Teachers 9; Students 59.
Catechesis/Religious Program—Tel: 956-968-1979. Mr. Oscar Dayaon, D.R.E. Students 1,617.
Mission—St. Jude Chapel, Hidalgo Co.
Mission—Nuestra Senora de Guadalupe Corpus Christi Dr., Expressway Heights, Hidalgo Co.

Chaplains of Public Institutions

BROWNSVILLE. *Jail Ministry*, 955 W. Price Rd., 78520. Tel: 956-541-0220. Mr. Jaime Gomez, Coord., Mr. Victor Villegas, Jail Min., Rev. George A. Gonzalez.
Valley Baptist Health Systems-Brownsville, 1040 W. Jefferson St., 78520. Tel: 956-698-4452. Rev. Michael Gnanaraj. Email: ranjithagmich@yahoo.com, Mr. Paulo Segoviano.
Valley Regional Medical Center, 100 Alton Gloor Blvd., Unit #100A, 78526. Tel: 956-350-7124. Rev. Michael Gnanaraj, Sr. Esther F. Rodriguez, O.P. Email: esther.rodriguez@hcahealthcare.com.
EDINBURG. *Doctor's Hospital at Renaissance*, 5501 S. McColl Rd., 78539. Tel: 956-661-7100. Rev. Emmanuel Kwofie, Rev. Msgr. Agostinho S. Pacheco (Retired), Sisters Therese Ann Ridge, I.W.B.S. Email: zonestar44@hotmail.com, Mary Lucy Ugo, D.D.L. Email: l.ugo@dhr-rgv.com, Deacon Reynaldo I. Flores, Ms. Melida Salinas, Ms. Norma Linda Walters.
Edinburg Children's Hospital, 1102 W. Trenton Rd., 78539. Tel: 956-388-6800. Mr. Carlos Salinas.
Edinburg Regional Hospital, 1102 W. Trenton Rd., 78539. Tel: 956-388-6634. Rev. Francois Tsanga, S.C., Mr. Carlos Salinas.
HARLINGEN. *Harlingen Medical Center*, 5501 S. Expressway 77, 78550. Tel: 956-365-1844. Deacon Jesus H. Reyes.
Valley Baptist Health System-Harlingen, 2101 Pease St., 78550. Tel: 956-389-1194. Sr. Aurora P. Sibug, Obl. O.S.B.
MCALLEN. *McAllen Heart Hospital*, 1900 S. "D" St., 78503. Tel: 956-994-2107. Rev. Francois Tsanga, S.C., Deacons Larry Hildebrand. Email: larry.hildebrand@uhsrgv.com, Rene Villalon Sr.
McAllen Medical Hospital, 301 W. Expwy. 83, 78503. Tel: 956-632-4388. Rev. Francois Tsanga, S.C., Deacons Larry Hildebrand. Email: larry.hildebrand@uhsrgv.com, Rene Villalon Sr.
Rio Grande Regional Hospital, 101 E. Ridge Rd., 78503. Tel: 956-632-6616. Mr. Ruben Wong. Email: paipe49@aol.com.
MISSION. *Mission Hospital*, 900 S. Bryan Rd., 78572. Tel: 956-323-1273. Mr. Jerry Garcia. Email: gegarcia@missionrmc.org.
RIO GRANDE CITY. *Starr County Memorial Hospital*, P.O. Box 78, 78582. Tel: 956-487-5561, Ext. 2206. Vacant.
WESLACO. *Knapp Medical Center*, 1401 E. 8th St., 78596. Tel: 956-968-4564. Rev. Emmanuel Kwofie. Email: ekwofie@cdob.org.

On Assignment Outside the Diocese:
Revs.—
Carolan, Craig G., Diocese of Saginaw, 5800 Weiss St., Saginaw, MI 48603-2762.
Figueroa, Honecimo
Lopez, Lionel, Belen Jesuit Preparatory School, 500 S.W. 127th Ave., Miami, FL 33184. Tel: 305-223-8600
Mestas, Leonard J., Jerry L. Pettis Memorial Hospital, 11201 Benton St., Loma Linda, CA 92357.

On Leave:
Revs.—
Robles, Juan Pablo
Villalon, Jose M., Jr.
Villareal, Carlos A.
Zuniga, Carlos

Retired:
Rev. Msgrs.—
DaVola, F. Robert, St. Paul, 1119 Francisco Ave., Mission, 78572.
Doherty, Patrick J., St. John Vianney, P.O. Box 747, San Juan, 78589.
Pacheco, Agostinho S., P.O. Box 5548, McAllen, 78502.
Revs.—
Azcoiti, Vicente, St. John Vianney, P.O. Box 747, San Juan, 78589.
Cabanas, Jaime R., St. John Vianney, P.O. Box 747, San Juan, 78589.
Escobedo, Armando, 615 Palo Blanco St., Mission, 78572.
Gomez, Frank, Mount Carmel Home, 4130 S. Alameda, Corpus Christi, 78411.
Lanese, Pasquale, O.M.I., P.O. Box 311, 78522. Tel: 956-546-3178
Mateos, Tomas, St. John Vianney, P.O. Box 747, San Juan, 78589.

Permanent Deacons:
Aguayo, Jesus E., St. Pius X, Weslaco
Aguilar, Gerardo, St. Mary, Santa Rosa
Arteaga, Antonio M., San Martin de Porres, Alton
Barbosa, Juan, St. Joseph, Donna
Borja, Gilberto, (Retired)
Cano, Roberto, Immaculate Conception Cathedral, Brownsville
Cantu, Agapito L., Our Lady of Perpetual Help, McAllen
Cantu, Roberto, Our Lady of Mercy, Mercedes
Castaneda, Guillermo "Bill", Jr., Our Lady of Guadalupe, Mission
Castilleja, Julio, Basilica of Our Lady of San Juan del Valle-National Shrine, San Juan
Castro, Jose R., (Retired)
Cedillo, Bruno, Our Lady of Guadalupe, Brownsville
Chapa, Alberto X., Our Lady, Queen of Angels, La Joya
Chapa, Augusto, Jr., St. Cecilia, Los Fresnos
Chavez, Ronaldo M. "Mitch", San Cristobal Magallanes & Companions, Mission

Crixell, Alfred V., (Retired)
Davila, Ramiro, Jr., St. Joseph, Edinburg
De la Cruz, Hugo, St. Francis Xavier, La Feria
Delgado, Juan Mitch, San Martin de Porres, Weslaco
Diaz, Inocencio, (Inactive)
Escobar, Paulo, St. Anthony, Harlingen
Espinoza, David, Holy Spirit, McAllen
Flores, Alejandro, (Retired)
Flores, Benito, St. Theresa, San Benito
Flores, Francisco R., Our Lady of Guadalupe, Mission
Florez, Reynaldo I., Holy Spirit, McAllen
Galvan, Jesus P., Basilica of Our Lady of San Juan del Valle National-Shrine, San Juan
Gamboa, Alejandro, St. Joseph the Worker, McAllen
Garcia, Ismael, (Retired)
Garcia, Javier A., St. Luke, Brownsville
Garcia, Oscar, San Martin de Porres, Weslaco
Garcia, Silvestre J., St. Joseph, Edinburg
Garza, Francisco, St. Joseph, Brownsville
Garza, Jose G., San Martin de Porres, Weslaco
Gerbermann, Alvin H., Holy Spirit, McAllen
Gonzales, Ignacio R., (Retired)
Gonzales, Juan F., Our Lady of Guadalupe, Raymondville
Gonzalez, Irineo, Jr., St. Joseph, Edinburg
Gonzalez, Jose G., St. Francis Xavier, La Feria
Gonzalez, Leopoldo, (Retired)
Guardiola, Gilberto, Jr., San Martin de Porres, Weslaco
Guerra, Jose, St. Helen, Rio Hondo
Higgins, Crawford A., Holy Spirit, McAllen
Hildebrand, Larry, South Texas Health System, McAllen
Ibarra, Genaro, Queen of Peace, Harlingen
Kinch, John P., Mary, Mother of the Church, Brownsville
Leal, Ramon G., (Retired)
Ledesma, Robert, St. Paul, Mission
Lopez, Gilberto, Sacred Heart, Edinburg
Lopez, Ruben, Holy Family, Edinburg
Mendoza, Jose Luis, Sacred Heart, McAllen
Merino, Reynaldo Q., St. Anne, Mother of Mary, Pharr
Munoz, Andres, (Retired)
Navarro, Juan Pablo, Mary, Mother of the Church, Brownsville
Oden, Louis, (Retired)
Olvera, Alvino C., Good Shepherd, Brownsville
Osorio, Jesus Antonio, St. Frances Xavier Cabrini, Pharr
Ovalle, Eduardo, St. Joseph, Donna
Pena, Amando, Jr., Our Lady of Refuge, Roma
Perez, Gilberto, St. Theresa of the Infant Jesus, Edcouch
Perez, Hector, St. Joseph the Worker, San Carlos
Requenez, Pedro (Peter), Jr., Our Lady of St. John of the Fields, Mission
Reyes, Jesus H., Harlingen Medical Center
Reyna, Eduardo, Our Lady of the Holy Rosary, Mission
Rodriguez, Arturo, (Retired)
Rodriguez, Graciano A., St. John the Baptist, San Juan
Rojas, Salvador, Sr., St. Juan Diego Cuauhtlatoatzin, McAllen
Rosa, Gerardo J., Sacred Heart, Elsa
Saenz, Benito, Jr., Holy Family, Grulla
Sagredo, Israel, Our Lady of the Holy Rosary, Mission
Saldana, Enrique, (Retired)
Saldivar, Salvador G., (Retired)
Salinas, Rodolfo C., Sacred Heart, Escobares
Sanchez, Manuel, St. Benedict, San Benito
Sanchez, Pedro F., (Medical Leave)
Schwarz, John F., Our Lady of Sorrows, McAllen
Sepulveda, Rodolfo, Jr., St. Joseph the Worker, McAllen
Solis, Heriberto, (Retired)
Solis, Jose A., Sacred Heart, Edinburg
Terrazas, George M., St. Luke, Brownsville
Thomas, Raymond L., Jr., Our Lady of Sorrow, McAllen
Trevino, Carlos S., Holy Spirit, McAllen
Trevino, Felipe, (Retired)
Trevino, Heriberto A., (Retired)
Trujillo, Nicolas E., Basilica of Our Lady of San Juan del Valle, National Shrine, San Juan
Valenzuela, Juan, (Retired)
Villalon, Rene, Sr., St. John the Baptist, San Juan
Villanueva, Catarino, Jr., Our Lady of the Assumption, Harlingen
Villarreal, Armandin, San Martin de Porres, Alton
Zamora, Daniel, Our Lady of St. John of the Fields, Mission
Zuniga, Luis, Mary, Mother of the Church, Brownsville

INSTITUTIONS LOCATED IN THE DIOCESE

[A] SEMINARIES

OLMITO. *The Saint Joseph and Saint Peter Seminary*, 7600 Old Military Rd., 78520. Tel: 956-504-2220. Mailing Address: P.O. Box 1658, 78575. Revs. Eduardo Gomez, Dir.; Ignacio Tapia, Dir., Vocations & Seminarians, Office of Vocations, 700 N. Virgen de San Juan Blvd., San Juan, 78589. Tel: 956-784-5060; Eduardo Villa, Spiritual Dir.; Jorge A. Gomez, Asst. Spiritual Dir.

[B] HIGH SCHOOLS, PRIVATE

BROWNSVILLE. *St. Joseph Academy*, (Grades 7-12), 101 St. Joseph Dr., 78520. Tel: 956-542-3581; Fax: 956-542-4748. Email: president@sja.us. Web: www.sja.us. Bro. Richard Sharpe, F.M.S., Pres.; Ms. Lucy A. Williams, Prin.; Pamela Quantz, Librarian. Marist Brothers, United States Religious 6; Lay Teachers 48; Students 742.

MISSION. *San Juan Diego Catholic Regional High School dba Juan Diego Academy* Mailing Address: P.O. Box 3888, 78573. Tel: 956-583-2752; Fax: 956-583-3782. Web: juandiegoacademy.org. 5208 S. FM 494, 78572. Sr. Marcella Ewers, D.C., Pres.; Mr. Bob Schmidt, Prin. Lay Teachers 3; Students 19.

PHARR. *Oratory Athenaeum for University Preparation*, 1407 W. Moore Rd., 78577. Tel: 956-781-3056; Fax: 956-787-1516. Email: maviles@mail.oratoryschools.org; yperez@mail.oratoryschools.org. Web: www.oratoryschools.org. Very Rev. Leo Francis Daniels, C.O., Rector; Rev. Mario Alberto Aviles, C.O., Prin.; Mrs. G. Yvonne Perez, Pres.; Revs. Jose E. Losoya, C.O., Vice Prin.; Jose Juan Ortiz, C.O., Librarian. Religious 4; Lay Teachers 13; Students 207.

[C] JUNIOR AND ELEMENTARY SCHOOLS, PRIVATE

BROWNSVILLE. *Guadalupe Regional Middle School*, (Grades 6-8), 1214 E. Lincoln St., 78521. Tel: 956-504-5568; Fax: 956-504-9393. Email: guadalupe678@gmail.com; guadalupeprincipal@gmail.com. Web: guadalupe.schoolfusion.us. Mr. Michael Motyl, Pres.; Mrs. Kathy Stapleton, Prin. Religious 4; Lay Teachers 7; Students 86.

Incarnate Word Academy, (Grades PreK-8), (Convent Academy of the Incarnate Word), 244 Resaca Blvd., 78520-7436. Tel: 956-546-4486; Fax: 956-504-3960. Web: www.iw-academy.org. Ms. Christina Moreno, Prin. (6-8); Sisters Marilyn Springs, I.W.B.S., Prin., (PreK-5); Irma Gonzalez, I.W.B.S., Campus Dir.; Mrs. Eva Cuellar, Librarian; Miss Magda Garza, Devel. Dir. Sisters of the Incarnate Word and Blessed Sacrament. Religious 4; Lay Teachers 18; Students 309.

St. Luke School, (Grades PreK-8), 2850 E. Price Rd., 78521. Tel: 956-544-7982; Fax: 956-544-4874. Email: slschool@sbcglobal.net. Web: www.stlukecs.org. Mrs. Ana E. Gomez, Prin.; Ms. Patty Garza, Librarian. Lay Teachers 26; Students 351.

St. Mary Catholic School, (Grades PreK-6), 1300 Los Ebanos Blvd., 78520. Tel: 956-546-1805; Fax: 956-546-0787. Email: jfaulk@stmarys-cs.org. Web: stmarys-cs.org. Ms. Judy Faulk, Prin.; Mrs. Blanca Chavez, Librarian. Religious 1; Lay Teachers 26; Students 459.

EDINBURG. *St. Joseph School*, (Grades PreK-8), 119 W. Fay, 78539. Tel: 956-383-3957; Fax: 956-318-0681. Email: kmurray@stjoseph-edinburg.org. Web: www.stjoseph-edinburg.org. Sr. Kathleen Murray, D.C., Prin.; Ms. Lupita Davila, Librarian. Religious 1; Lay Teachers 26; Students 255.

HARLINGEN. *St. Anthony School*, (Grades PreK-8), 1015 E. Harrison, 78550. Tel: 956-423-2486; Fax: 956-412-0084. Email: saintanthonyeagles@yahoo.com. Web: www.saintanthonyeagles.com. Mr. Chester Arizmendi, Prin.; Mrs. Belinda Casarez, Librarian. Lay Teachers 21; Students 222.

MCALLEN. *Our Lady of Sorrows School*, (Grades PreK-8), 1100 Gumwood, 78501. Tel: 956-686-3651; Fax: 956-686-1996. Email: rolando.garza@olssnet.org. Web: www.olschool.org. Mr. Rolando J. Garza, Prin.; Joseph O'Brien, Asst. Prin.; Patricia Espinosa, Librarian. Religious 1; Lay Teachers 29; Students 594.

MISSION. *Our Lady of Guadalupe School*, (Grades PreK-6), 611 N. Dunlap St., 78572. Tel: 956-585-6445; Fax: 956-584-3055. Email: olgprincipal@sbcglobal.net. Sr. Cynthia A. Mello, S.S.D., Prin.; Ms. Mary Lovig, Librarian. Religious 3; Lay Teachers 8; Students 107.

PHARR. *Oratory Academy of St. Philip Neri*, (Grades PreK-8), 1407 W. Moore Rd., 78577. Tel: 956-781-3056; Fax: 956-787-1516. Email: maviles@mail.oratoryschools.org. Web: www.oratoryschools.org. Very Rev. Leo Francis Daniels, C.O., Rector; Revs. Mario Alberto Aviles, C.O., Prin.; Jose E. Losoya, C.O., Vice Prin.; Mrs. G. Yvonne Perez, Pres.; Rev. Jose Juan Ortiz, C.O., Librarian. Religious 4; Lay Teachers 37; Students 519.

RIO GRANDE CITY. *Immaculate Conception School*, (Grades PreK-8), 305 N. Britton Ave., 78582. Tel: 956-487-2558; Fax: 956-487-6478. Mrs. Rubirita Urbina, Prin.; Ms. Donis Garza, Librarian. Religious 2; Lay Teachers 14; Students 248.

WESLACO. *San Martin de Porres School*, (Grades PreK-3), 905 N. Texas Blvd., 78596. Tel: 956-973-8642; Fax: 956-973-0522. Sr. Helen Rottier, C.S.J., Prin.; Ms. Adelina Olivo, Librarian. Religious 2; Lay Teachers 9; Students 59.

[D] CATHOLIC CHARITIES OF THE RIO GRANDE VALLEY

BROWNSVILLE. *Catholic Charities of the Rio Grande Valley Brownsville Office*, 955 W. Price Rd., 78520. Tel: 956-541-0220; Fax: 956-544-7580.

SAN JUAN. *Catholic Charities of the Rio Grande Valley San Juan Main Office*, 700 N. Virgen de San Juan Blvd., 78589. Tel: 956-702-4088; Fax: 956-782-0418. Email: npimentel@cdob.org. Mailing Address: P.O. Box 1306, 78589.

Catholic Charities of the Rio Grande Valley Executive Board: Most Rev. Daniel E. Flores, S.T.D.; Rev. Msgrs. Robert E. Maher, V.G.; Heberto M. Diaz Jr. Board of Directors: William Anderson; Silvia Castillo; Terri Drefke; Letty Garza; Perla Hickson; Minnie Lucio.

[E] HOMES FOR THE AGED

BROWNSVILLE. *Mother of Perpetual Help Nursing Home, Inc.*, 519 E. Madison St., 78520. Tel: 956-546-6745; Fax: 956-546-0711. Martin S. Casas, Admin. Owner: Sisters of the Holy Spirit and Mary Immaculate.; Chapel attended from Immaculate Conception Cathedral. Bed Capacity 38.

SAN JUAN. *San Juan Nursing Home, Inc.*, 300 N. Nebraska Ave., 78589. Tel: 956-787-1771; Fax: 956-787-8091. Web: sjnhrgv.org. Ms. Sandra Basaldua, LNFA, Admin. Bed Capacity 122. Board of Directors: Most Rev. Daniel E. Flores, S.T.D.; Letty Garza; Graciela Garza; Alma R. Garza; Mr. Crawford Higgins; Rev. Msgr. Robert E. Maher, V.G.

[F] RESIDENCES FOR PRIESTS AND BROTHERS

BROWNSVILLE. *Congregation of Christian Brothers*, Mailing Address: *Guadalupe Regional Middle School*, 1214 E. Lincoln St., 78521. Tel: 956-986-0614; Fax: 956-504-9393. *Our Lady of Guadalupe Parish Rectory*, 1200 E. Lincoln St., 78521. Bros. J. David Concannon; Leonard Anthony Quinn; Arthur Williams. Brothers 3.

Marist Brothers, 32995 Henderson Rd., Los Fresnos, 78566. Tel: 956-254-2020. Bros. Paul U. Phillipp, Supr.; Francis Klug; Thomas J. Lee; Albert Phillipp, F.M.S.; John A. Allen; Sumner Herrick. Brothers 6.

Marist Brothers, 1780 Westminster Rd., 78521. Tel: 956-504-6532. Bros. George Dicarluccio, F.M.S., Dir.; Richard Sharpe, F.M.S.; Francis Garza, F.M.S. Brothers 3.

PHARR. *Pharr Oratory of St. Philip Neri of Pontifical Right*, P.O. Box 1698, 78577. Tel: 956-843-8217; Fax: 956-843-2946. Very Rev. Leo Francis Daniels, C.O., Provost; Revs. Jose E. Losoya, C.O., Vicar; Mario Alberto Aviles, C.O., Sec. & Treas.; Jose Juan Ortiz, C.O.

RAYMONDVILLE. *Priests of the Sacred Heart*, Rte. 2, Box 788, 78580. Tel: 956-689-6428; Fax: 956-689-3583. Priests 2.

[G] CONVENTS AND RESIDENCES FOR SISTERS

BROWNSVILLE. *Dominican Sisters of Charity of the Presentation*, 934 W. St. Charles St., 78520. Tel: 956-542-7225. Sisters 4.

Incarnate Word and Blessed Sacrament, 200 Resaca Blvd., 78520. Tel: 956-546-1685. Sisters 6.

Missionaries of Jesus, 1501 W. Adams, 78520. Tel: 956-542-2180. Web: www.missionariesofjesus.org. Sisters 5.

Sisters of the Holy Spirit and Mary Immaculate, 519 E. Madison, 78520. Tel: 956-546-2414. Sisters 1.

ALAMO. **Saint Joseph and Saint Rita Monastery of the Capuchin Poor Clare Nuns*, 725 E. Bowie St., 78516. Tel: 956-781-1044. Mailing Address: P.O. Box 1099, 78516. Sisters Martha Alicia Garcia Torres, O.S.C.Cap., Abbess; Beatriz Ayala Juarez, O.S.C.Cap., Treas.; Luz Maria Leyva Duarte,

O.S.C.Cap., Sec. & Counselor. Sisters 5.

EDINBURG. *Incarnate Word and Blessed Sacrament*, 609 Baltic Ave., 78539. Tel: 956-383-6870. Mailing Address: P.O. Box 2063, 78540. Sisters 2.

PALMVIEW. *Daughters of Mary Mother of Mercy*, 237 S. Green Rd., 78573. Tel: 956-867-0993. Sisters 3.

PENITAS. *Missionary Sisters of the Immaculate Heart of Mary*, P.O. Box 1017, 78576. Tel: 956-585-5488; Fax: 956-519-9123. Email: fatimasantiago.1@juno.com. 18110 Queen Palm Dr., 78576. Sisters 4.

Projecto Desarrollo Humano Ministry Tel: 956-580-9726.

PROGRESO. *Sisters of St. Dorothy*, P.O. Box 147, 78579. Tel: 956-565-9430; Fax: 956-825-9511. Sisters 5.

RIO GRANDE CITY. *Benedictine Sisters of the Good Shepherd*, P.O. Box 1501, 78582. Tel: 956-486-2680; Fax: 956-486-2680. Email: francesosb@gmail.com. Sisters 3.

SAN JUAN. *Missionaries of Jesus*, 700 N. Oblate Dr., 78589. Tel: 956-455-1484. Web: www.missionariesofjesus.org. Sisters 2.

[H] RETREAT HOUSES

SAN JUAN. *St. Eugene de Mazenod Christian Renewal Center*, P.O. Box 747, 78589. Tel: 956-787-0033; Fax: 956-787-2908. Santos Esquivel, Contact Person.

[I] BASILICA

SAN JUAN. *The Basilica of Our Lady of San Juan del Valle-National Shrine*, 400 N. Virgen de San Juan Blvd., 78589. Tel: 956-787-0033; Fax: 956-787-2908. Rev. Amador Garza, Rector; Mr. Pablo H. Villescas, Admin.; Revs. Juan Rogelio Gutierrez, Asst. to Rector; Efiri Matthias Selemobri, M.S.P., Asst. to Rector; Deacons Julio Castilleja; Jesus P. Galvan; Mrs. Petra Ruiz, Mgr. Tel: 956-787-0033, Ext. 223.

Religious Gift & Book Store Tel: 956-787-0033, Ext. 265. Mrs. Janie Guajardo, Mgr.

[J] CAMPUS MINISTRY

EDINBURG. *Campus & Young Adult Ministry* Mr. Miguel Santos, Dir.

Campus Ministry

University of Texas Pan American (UTPA), 1615 W. Kuhn St., 78539. Tel: 956-383-0133. Joe Garcia, Campus Min.; Most Rev. Raymundo J. Pena, D.D., Chap.

University of Texas at Brownsville/Texas Southmost College (UTB/TSC), 1910 University Blvd., 78520. Tel: 956-541-9697. Yarid Gonzalez, Campus Min.; Rev. Jorge A. Gomez, Chap.

[K] MISCELLANEOUS

BROWNSVILLE. **Bishop Enrique San Pedro Ozanam Center, Inc.*, 656 N. Minnesota Ave., 78521. Tel: 956-831-6331; Fax: 956-831-8577. Victor Maldonado, Dir.

Catholic Engaged Encounter, 700 N. Virgen de San Juan Blvd., San Juan, 78589. Tel: 956-781-5323. 1304 W. Russell Rd., Edinburg, 78541. Tel: 956-381-1135. Roel Zamora, Contact Person; Estela Zamora, Contact Person.

Catholic Foundation of the Rio Grande Valley, 1910 University Blvd., 78520-4998. Tel: 956-542-2501; Fax: 956-542-6751. Rev. Msgr. Heberto M. Diaz Jr., Vice Chm. & Contact Person.

The Guadalupe Regional Middle School Endowment, 1214 Lincoln St., 78521. Tel: 956-504-5568; Fax: 956-504-9393. Sr. Mary Ann Korczynski, I.W.B.S., Chm.

The St. Joseph Academy Endowment, 101 St. Joseph Dr., 78520. Tel: 956-542-3581; Fax: 956-541-4495. Email: president@sja.us. Bro. Richard Sharpe, F.M.S., Contact Person.

Movimiento Familiar Cristiano: Federacion Este (Brownsville/Harlingen/Los Fresnos), 6818 Blue Spruce St., 78526. Tel: 956-203-4258; 956-561-4037. Emiliano Juarez, Contact Person; Lorenza Juarez, Contact Person.

**Proyecto Juan Diego, Inc.*, Mailing Address: P.O. Box 8038, 78526. 2216 Eduardo Ave., 78526. Tel: 956-542-2334; 956-542-2488; Fax: 956-542-5055. Email: phylispeters@gmail.com. Sisters Phylis Peters, D.C., Exec. Dir.; Marcella Ewers, D.C., Chairperson.

Texas Historical Preservation Foundation, P.O. Box 2279, 78522-2279. Tel: 956-542-2501; Fax: 956-542-6751. Mr. Jack Graham, Contact Person.

Villa Maria Language Institute, 224 Resaca Blvd., 78520-7436. Tel: 956-546-7196; Fax: 956-546-1731. Sr. Irma Gonzalez, I.W.B.S., Campus Dir.

ALAMO. *ARISE-South Tower*, 330 W. San Bernardino, P.O. Box 778, 78516. Tel: 956-783-8517; Fax: 956-783-5498. Ms. Emilia Vega, Pres.

ARISE Support Center, 1417 S. Tower Rd., P.O. Box 778, 78516. Tel: 956-783-6959; Fax: 956-783-0274. Email: arisesotex@arisesotex.org. Web: www.arisesotex.org. Mrs. Lourdes Flores, Pres. *ARISE Support Center*

EDINBURG. *ARISE-Muñiz*, 3917 Jam Sq., 78542. Tel: 956-782-4041; Fax: 956-782-6430. Ms. Andrea Landeras, Pres.

Movimiento Familiar Cristiano: Federacion Oeste (McAllen/Edinburg/Pharr), 2211 Carla Marie Way, 78542. Tel: 956-383-8419; 956-867-0728; 956-867-0729. Jesse Zurita, Contact Person; Angie Zurita, Contact Person.

HARLINGEN. *Encuentro Matrimonial: East*, 514 N. K, 78550. Tel: 956-428-5370; 956-792-6467. Mr. Manuel Lugo, Contact Person; Mrs. Gabriela Lugo, Contact Person.

**RGV Educational Broadcasting, Inc.*, P.O. Box 2147, 78551. Tel: 956-421-4111; Fax: 956-421-4150. Web: www.kmbh.org. Mr. Robert M. Gutierrez Jr., Pres. & CEO.

Worldwide Marriage Encounter, 1642 Hamilton, 78550. Tel: 956-536-8284. Email: robleandsons@sbcglobal.net. Jesse Robles, Contact Person; Terry Robles, Contact Person.

LA JOYA. *Boy Scouts*, P.O. Box 365, Santa Rosa, 78593. Tel: 956-636-1211. Rev. Juan Pablo Davalos.

MCALLEN. *Comfort House Services, Inc.*, 617 Dallas Ave., 78501. Tel: 956-687-7367; Fax: 956-630-6423. Email: chsi@att.net. Ms. Maria Botello, Admin. AIDS Education & Outreach; Palliative Care to the Terminally Ill. Bed Capacity 10.

Encuentro Matrimonial: West, 3912 Kerria Ave., 78504. Tel: 956-534-1463; 956-624-4973. Eduardo Cuellar, Contact Person; Maggie Cuellar, Contact Person.

MERCEDES. *La Merced Charitable Trust*, 413 S. Virginia, 78570. Tel: 956-565-2622; Fax: 956-565-4185. Email: rmedrano@cdob.org.
Housing Board: Rev. Gerald W. Frank; Mr. Alfredo Huerta, Trustee; Mr. Robert A. Calvillo, Trustee; Mr. Jose Luis Gonzalez, Trustee; Ms. Estella L. Trevino, Trustee.

MISSION. *El Rosario Charitable Trust*, 119 Retama, 78572. Tel: 956-585-5051; Fax: 956-585-9938. Email: rmedrano@cdob.org.

Fraternity of Our Lady of Guadalupe Secular Franciscan Order, 2600 W. Mile 7 Rd., 78574. Tel: 956-519-9504. Rev. Tomas Mateos, Spiritual Asst.

PHARR. *ARISE-Las Milpas*, 125 E. Denny, 78577. Tel: 956-783-9293; Fax: 956-783-2099. Ms. Andrea Olvera, Pres.

SAN BENITO. *La Posada Providencia*, 1610 Marydale Rd., 78586. Tel: 956-399-3826; Fax: 956-399-2898. Email: srmfranciscdp@hotmail.com. Web: www.lppshelter.org. Sisters Zita Telkamp, C.D.P., Dir.; Therese Cunningham, S.H.Sp., Mentor/ESL Teacher. A non-profit emergency shelter for indigent immigrants and asylum seekers. They reside in the shelter as they wait for their legal cases to adjudicate before U.S. Immigration Court.

WESLACO. *Movimiento Familiar Cristiano: Federacion Weslaco (Weslaco/Donna/Mercedes)*, 5125 Mile 12 N., Mercedes, 78570. Tel: 956-607-7665; 956-376-0122. Astolfo Gracia, Contact Person; Martha Gracia, Contact Person.

Natural Family Planning, 600 S. Oklahoma Ave., 78596. Tel: 956-969-3079; 956-968-7142.

RELIGIOUS INSTITUTES OF MEN REPRESENTED IN THE DIOCESE

For further details refer to the corresponding bracketed number in the Religious Institutes of Men or Women section.

[0310]—*Congregation of Christian Brothers*—C.F.C.
[1140]—*Congregation of the Sacred Hearts*—SS.CC.
[0520]—*Franciscan Friars*—O.F.M.
[0770]—*Marist Brothers*—F.M.S.
[0780]—*Marist Fathers*—S.M.
[0630]—*Missionaries of the Holy Family*—M.S.F.
[]—*Missionary Servants of the Cross*—M.S.C.
[0854]—*Missionary Society of St. Paul of Nigeria*—M.S.P.
[0910]—*Oblates of Mary Immaculate*—O.M.I.
[0950]—*Oratorians of St. Philip Neri*—C.O.
[0970]—*Orden de la Merced*—O.de.M.
[1065]—*Priestly Fraternity of St. Peter*—F.S.S.P.
[1130]—*Priests of the Sacred Heart*—S.C.J.
[0370]—*Society of St. Columban*—S.S.C.

RELIGIOUS INSTITUTES OF WOMEN REPRESENTED IN THE DIOCESE

[0230]—*Benedictine Sisters of Crookston*—O.S.B.
[]—*Benedictine Sisters of the Good Shepherd (Monastery)*—O.S.B.
[]—*Capuchin Poor Clares*—O.S.C.Cap.
[0760]—*Daughters of Charity of St. Vincent de Paul*—D.C.
[0793]—*Daughters of Divine Love*—D.D.L.
[]—*Daughters of Mary Mother of Mercy*—D.M.M.M.
[1100]—*Dominican Sisters of Charity of the Presentation of the Blessed Virgin*—O.P.
[1115]—*Dominican Sisters of Peace*—O.P.
[1070-3]—*Dominican Sisters of Sinsinawa, Wisconsin*—O.P.
[]—*Dominican Sisters of St. Thomas Aquino*—O.P.
[1415]—*Franciscan Sisters of Mary*—F.S.M.
[1310]—*Franciscan Sisters of Little Falls, Minnesota*—O.S.F.
[]—*Misioneras Catequistas de los Pobres*—M.C.P.
[1150]—*Misioneras Eucaristicas Franciscanas*—M.E.F.
[]—*Missionaries of Jesus*—M.J.
[]—*Missionary Benedictine Sisters of Tutzin* (Norfolk, NE)—Obl. O.S.B.
[2690]—*Missionary Catechists of Divine Providence*—M.C.D.P.
[2750]—*Missionary Sisters of the Immaculate Heart of Mary*—I.C.M.
[]—*Missioneras del Espiritu Santo Y la Sagrada Familia*—M.E.S.S.F.
[2970]—*School Sisters of Notre Dame* (Prov. of Dallas)—S.S.N.D.
[]—*Sisters of Charity*—S.C.
[0990]—*Sisters of Divine Providence*—C.D.P.
[2575]—*Sisters of Mercy of the Americas* (South Central Community)—R.S.M.
[3840]—*Sisters of St. Joseph of Carondelet* (Province of St. Paul, MN)—C.S.J.
[3790]—*Sisters of St. Dorothy*—S.S.D.
[1705]—*Sisters of St. Francis of Assisi*—O.S.F.
[3840]—*Sisters of St. Joseph of Carondelet* (Province of St. Louis, MO)—C.S.J.
[2050]—*Sisters of the Holy Spirit and Mary Immaculate*—S.H.Sp.
[2205]—*Sisters of the Incarnate Word and Blessed Sacrament*—I.W.B.S.
[3320]—*Sisters of the Presentation of the Blessed Virgin Mary*—P.B.V.M.
[]—*Sisters of the Secular Franciscan Order*—S.F.O.
[4120-04]—*Ursuline Sisters of Cleveland, OH*—O.S.U.

NECROLOGY

† Garcia, Ricardo, Brownsville, TX Mary, Mother of the Church.—Died Feb. 21, 2011
† O'Malley, John A., (Retired)—Died Feb. 21, 2011
† Ortiz, Benedicto, (Retired)—Died May 14, 2011

An asterisk (*) denotes an organization that has established tax-exempt status directly with the IRS and is not covered by the USCCB Group Ruling.

Diocese of Buffalo

(Dioecesis Buffalensis)

Most Reverend

EDWARD U. KMIEC, D.D., S.T.L.

Bishop of Buffalo ordained December 20, 1961; appointed Titular Bishop of Simidicca and Auxiliary Bishop of Trenton August 26, 1982; consecrated November 3, 1982; appointed Bishop of Nashville October 13, 1992; installed December 3, 1992; appointed Bishop of Buffalo August 12, 2004; installed October 28, 2004. *Res.: 77 Oakland Pl., Buffalo, NY 14222-1241.*

Most Reverend

BERNARD J. MCLAUGHLIN, D.D., V.G.

Retired Auxiliary Bishop of Buffalo; ordained December 21, 1935; appointed Auxiliary Bishop of Buffalo and Titular Bishop of Mottola December 28, 1968; consecrated January 6, 1969; retired January 15, 1988. *Res.: 204 Knoche Rd., Tonawanda, NY 14150.*

Most Reverend

EDWARD M. GROSZ, D.D.

Auxiliary Bishop of Buffalo; ordained May 29, 1971; appointed November 22, 1989; consecrated February 2, 1990. *Res.: Blessed Sacrament Parish, 1035 Delaware Ave., Buffalo, NY 14209-1605.*

ESTABLISHED APRIL 23, 1847

Square Miles 6,357.

Incorporated under the laws of the State of New York October 30th, 1897. Re-incorporated by special act passed April 5, 1951, Chapter 568 of the laws of 1951.

Corporate Title: The Diocese of Buffalo, N.Y.

Comprises the Counties of Erie, Niagara, Genesee, Orleans, Chautauqua, Wyoming, Cattaraugus and Allegany in the State of New York.

For legal titles of parishes and diocesan institutions, consult the Chancery Office.

Chancery Office: 795 Main St., Buffalo, NY 14203. Tel: 716-847-5500; Fax: 716-847-5557.

Web: www.buffalodiocese.org

Email: dob@buffalodiocese.org

STATISTICAL OVERVIEW

Personnel	
Bishop	1
Auxiliary Bishops	1
Retired Bishops	1
Priests: Diocesan Active in Diocese	179
Priests: Diocesan Active Outside Diocese	9
Priests: Retired, Sick or Absent	135
Number of Diocesan Priests	323
Religious Priests in Diocese	109
Total Priests in Diocese	432
Extern Priests in Diocese	10
Ordinations:	
Diocesan Priests	2
Transitional Deacons	3
Permanent Deacons	2
Permanent Deacons in Diocese	124
Total Brothers	36
Total Sisters	880
Parishes	
Parishes	164
With Resident Pastor:	
Resident Diocesan Priests	132
Resident Religious Priests	12
Without Resident Pastor:	
Administered by Priests	16
Administered by Deacons	2
Administered by Religious Women	1
Administered by Pastoral Teams, etc.	1
Missions	1
Pastoral Centers	3
New Parishes Created	2
Closed Parishes	7
Professional Ministry Personnel:	
Brothers	1
Sisters	41
Lay Ministers	112
Welfare	
Catholic Hospitals	4
Total Assisted	1,411,218
Health Care Centers	1
Total Assisted	950
Homes for the Aged	8
Total Assisted	3,548
Day Care Centers	2
Total Assisted	85
Specialized Homes	3
Total Assisted	6,048
Special Centers for Social Services	5
Total Assisted	610,559
Residential Care of Disabled	4
Total Assisted	31
Other Institutions	1
Total Assisted	11,945
Educational	
Seminaries, Diocesan	1
Students from This Diocese	20
Students from Other Diocese	1
Diocesan Students in Other Seminaries	4
Seminaries, Religious	1
Total Seminarians	24
Colleges and Universities	7
Total Students	18,071
High Schools, Private	15
Total Students	5,143
Elementary Schools, Diocesan and Parish	51
Total Students	10,851
Elementary Schools, Private	4
Total Students	731
Non-residential Schools for the Disabled	1
Total Students	325
Catechesis/Religious Education:	
High School Students	8,457
Elementary Students	24,072
Total Students under Catholic Instruction	67,674
Teachers in the Diocese:	
Priests	36
Brothers	15
Sisters	70
Lay Teachers	1,823
Vital Statistics	
Receptions into the Church:	
Infant Baptism Totals	3,836
Minor Baptism Totals	145
Adult Baptism Totals	143
Received into Full Communion	199
First Communions	4,722
Confirmations	4,790
Marriages:	
Catholic	1,024
Interfaith	394
Total Marriages	1,418
Deaths	6,064
Total Catholic Population	633,123
Total Population	1,544,203

Former Bishops—Rt. Revs. JOHN TIMON, C.M., D.D., ord. Sept. 23, 1826; cons. Oct. 17, 1847; died April 16, 1867; STEPHEN V. RYAN, C.M., D.D., ord. June 24, 1849; cons. Nov. 8, 1868; died April 10, 1896; JAMES EDWARD QUIGLEY, D.D., ord. April 13, 1879; cons. Bishop of Buffalo, Feb. 24, 1897; promoted to the Archdiocese of Chicago, Feb. 19, 1903; died July 10, 1915; CHARLES HENRY COLTON, D.D., ord. June 10, 1876; cons. Aug. 24, 1903; died May 9, 1915; His Eminence DENNIS CARDINAL DOUGHERTY, D.D., ord. May 31, 1890; cons. Bishop of Nueva Segovia, June 14, 1903; transferred to the Diocese of Jaro, April 19, 1908; transferred to the Diocese of Buffalo, Dec. 6, 1915; promoted to Archdiocese of Philadelphia, May 1, 1918; created Cardinal, March 7, 1921; died May 31, 1951; Most Revs. WILLIAM TURNER, D.D., ord. Aug. 13, 1893; cons. March 30, 1919; died July 10, 1936; JOHN A. DUFFY, D.D., ord. June 13, 1908; cons. Bishop of Syracuse, June 29, 1933; transferred to the Diocese of Buffalo, April 14, 1937; died Sept. 27, 1944; His Eminence JOHN CARDINAL O'HARA, C.S.C., ord. Sept. 9, 1916; appt. Military Delegate of the Armed Forces and Titular Bishop of Mylasa, Dec. 11, 1939; cons. Jan. 15, 1940; transferred to Buffalo, March 10, 1945; installed May 8, 1945; promoted to the Archdiocese of Philadelphia, Nov. 23, 1951; created Cardinal, Dec. 15, 1958; died Aug. 28, 1960; Most Revs. JOSEPH A. BURKE, D.D., ord. Aug. 3, 1912; cons. Titular Bishop of Vita and Auxiliary, June 29, 1943; promoted to the See, Feb. 9, 1952; died Oct. 16, 1962; JAMES A. MCNULTY, D.D., ord. July 12, 1925; cons. Oct. 7, 1947; Titular Bishop of Methone and Auxiliary Bishop of Newark, NJ; appt. Bishop of Paterson, NJ April 9, 1953; transferred to Buffalo, Feb. 12, 1963; died Sept. 4, 1972; EDWARD D. HEAD, D.D., ord. Jan. 27, 1945; appt. Titular Bishop of Ardstratha and Auxiliary of New York, Jan. 27, 1970; cons. March 19, 1970; appt. Bishop of Buffalo, Jan. 17, 1973; installed March 19, 1973; retired June 12, 1995; died March 29, 2005; HENRY J. MANSELL, D.D., ord. Dec. 19, 1962; appt. Titular Bishop of Marazane and Auxiliary of New York Nov. 24, 1992; ord. Jan. 6, 1993; appt. Bishop of Buffalo April 18, 1995; installed June 12, 1995; promoted to Archbishop of Hartford Oct. 20, 2003.

Vicars General—Most Rev. EDWARD M. GROSZ, D.D., V.G.; Rev. Msgr. DAVID S. SLUBECKY, J.C.L., S.T.L., V.G.

Chancery Office—795 Main St., Buffalo, 14203. Tel: 716-847-5500; Fax: 716-847-5557. Email: dob@buffalodiocese.org. Office Hours: Mon.-Fri. 9-4:30.

Moderator of the Curia—Rev. Msgr. DAVID S. SLUBECKY, J.C.L., S.T.L., V.G.

Chancellor—Rev. Msgr. PAUL A. LITWIN, J.C.L.

Secretary to Diocesan Bishop and Vice Chancellor—Rev. Msgr. DAVID G. LIPUMA.

Diocesan Tribunal—795 Main St., Buffalo, 14203. Tel: 716-847-8769; Fax: 716-847-8772. Email: tribunal@buffalodiocese.org. Send all rogatory commissions to the Tribunal.

Judicial Vicar—Rev. Msgr. SALVATORE MANGANELLO, J.C.L., S.T.L.

Adjunct Judicial Vicar—Rev. PAUL P. SABO.

Defenders of the Bond—Revs. EDWARD R. CZARNECKI; FRANCIS X. MAZUR; GREGORY M. FAULHABER, S.T.D.; DENNIS A. FRONCZAK.

Advocates—Deacon DANIEL E. BRICK ESQ.; Revs. RICHARD S. DIGIULIO (Retired); ROBERT W. VOGT (Retired).

Promoter of Justice—Rev. Msgr. W. JEROME SULLIVAN, J.C.D. (Retired).

Judges—Rev. JAMES M. AUGUSTYN (Retired); Rev. Msgr. VINCENT J. BECKER (Retired); Rev. JOSEPH KLOS, J.C.L.; Rev. Msgr. SALVATORE MANGANELLO, J.C.L., S.T.L.; Revs. HENRY A. ORSZULAK; PAUL P. SABO.

Auditor—Rev. ROBERT W. ZILLIOX.

Notaries—NICOLE BALL; LUCILLE BUCZEK.

Consultors, College of—Most Rev. EDWARD M. GROSZ, D.D., V.G.; Rev. Msgrs. DAVID S. SLUBECKY, J.C.L., S.T.L., V.G.; JAMES E. WALL; W. JEROME SULLIVAN, J.C.D. (Retired); ROBERT E. ZAPFEL, S.T.D.; Revs. PETER J. DRILLING, Th.D.; JACOB C. LEDWON; PETER J. KARALUS; RONALD W. SAMS, S.J.; Rev. Msgr. JOSEPH J. SICARI.

Council of Priests—Most Revs. EDWARD U. KMIEC, D.D., S.T.L.; EDWARD M. GROSZ, D.D., V.G.; Rev. Msgr. DAVID S. SLUBECKY, J.C.L., S.T.L., V.G.; Revs. JAMES D. CIUPEK; JOHN J. CULLEN; PETER J. DRILLING, Th.D.; JOSEPH A. GULLO; JAMES G. JUDGE; PETER J. KARALUS; JOHN J. MATTIMORE, S.J.; JACEK P. MAZUR; F. PATRICK MELFI; RICHARD A. REINA, M.Div., M.S.W., M.C.Sp.; TODD M. REMICK; MICHAEL R. ROCK, O.de.M.; EUGENE P. ULRICH; JAMES VACCO, O.F.M., M.A.; Rev. Msgr. FRANCIS G. WELDGEN (Retired); Revs. MARK J. WOLSKI; ROBERT A. WOZNIAK; Rev. Msgr. ROBERT E. ZAPFEL, S.T.D.; Revs. RICHARD E. ZAJAC; RONALD W. SAMS, S.J.; JACOB C. LEDWON; Rev. Msgrs. JOSEPH J. SICARI; W. JEROME SULLIVAN, J.C.D. (Retired); JAMES E. WALL; Rev. JAMES A. WALTER.

Finance Council—Most Revs. EDWARD U. KMIEC, D.D., S.T.L.; EDWARD M. GROSZ, D.D., V.G.; Rev. Msgrs. PAUL J.E. BURKARD; ANGELO M. CALIGIURI (Retired); JAMES F. CAMPBELL; Mr. GEORGE J. EBERL; Rev. Msgr. FREDERICK D. LEISING; Rev. JOHN R. GAGLIONE; Rev. Msgr. WILLIAM J. GALLAGHER; Rev. CZESLAW M. KRYSA; Rev. Msgr. THOMAS F. MALONEY; Rev. FABIAN J. MARYANSKI; Mr. CHARLES A. MENDOLERA, Ex Officio; Rev. Msgr. J. THOMAS MORAN; Mr. PATRICK F. REILLY; Rev. Msgr. DAVID S. SLUBECKY, J.C.L., S.T.L., V.G., Chm.; Mr. STEVEN D. TIMMEL, Ex Officio; Rev. MARK J. WOLSKI; Rev. Msgrs. ROBERT E. ZAPFEL, S.T.D.; PAUL A. LITWIN, J.C.L.; Mr. JOSEPH F. KAPSIAK; Mr. DAVID ROGERS; Mr. JAY MCWATTERS, CPA.

Vicariates—

Vicars—Revs. RONALD P. SAJDAK, Northwest-Central Buffalo; FABIAN J. MARYANSKI, Southeast Buffalo; Rev. Msgr. ROBERT E. ZAPFEL, S.T.D., Northern Erie; Rev. THOMAS J. QUINLIVAN, Eastern Erie; Rev. Msgr. PAUL J.E. BURKARD, Southern Erie; Revs. SEAN E. DIMARIA, Allegany; DENNIS A. FRONCZAK, Tri-County; GREGORY J. DOBSON, Southern Cattaraugus; DENNIS G. RITER, Chautauqua; ARTHUR E. MATTULKE, Genesee-Wyoming; ROBERT S. HUGHSON, Western Niagara; RICHARD A. CSIZMAR, Eastern Niagara-Orleans.

The Diocese of Buffalo, N.Y.— A corporation under the laws of the State of New York. Most Revs. EDWARD U. KMIEC, D.D., S.T.L., Pres.; EDWARD M. GROSZ, D.D., V.G., Vice Pres.; Rev. Msgrs. DAVID S. SLUBECKY, J.C.L., S.T.L., V.G., Vice Pres.; PAUL A. LITWIN, J.C.L., Sec.

Diocesan Offices and Directors

All offices are located at: 795 Main St., Buffalo, NY 14203. Tel: 716-847-8700; Fax: 716-847-5557 (Unless otherwise noted).

Apostleship of Prayer—Rev. RICHARD M. I. POBLOCKI, Dir., 20 Peoria Ave., Cheektowaga, 14206.

Apostleship of the Sea—Rev. Msgr. JOHN I. DUCETTE, Dir. (Retired), Res.: 8121 Valle Dr., Apt. C3, Niagara Falls, 14304.

Archives—Sr. JEAN THOMPSON, O.S.F. Tel: 716-847-5567.

Bishop's Committee for Christian Home and Family—Mrs. NANCY SCHERR, Moderator. Tel: 716-847-2210.

Boy Scouts—Rev. MICHAEL J. PUTICH, O.F.M. Tel: 716-823-2358; Mr. JAMES S. SMYCZYNSKI, Committee Chm.

Buildings and Properties—MICHAEL J. SULLIVAN, Dir. Tel: 716-847-8750; Fax: 716-847-8756.

Camp Turner—JOHN MANN, Steward, 9150 Asp Rd. #3, Salamanca, 14779. Tel: 716-354-4555; Fax: 716-354-2055. Email: campturner@gmail.com.

Catechumenate Office—Mrs. PAULA PENEPENT, Dir. Tel: 716-847-8760; Fax: 716-847-5593.

Catholic Charities—Sr. MARY MCCARRICK, O.S.F., Dir. & Pres.; DENNIS C. WALCZYK, CEO, 741 Delaware Ave., Buffalo, 14209. Tel: 716-218-1400; Fax: 716-856-2005.

Catholic Charities Appeal—Sr. MARY MCCARRICK, O.S.F., Dir., Office: 741 Delaware Ave., Buffalo, 14209. Tel: 716-218-1400.

Catholic Medical Association—Rev. RICHARD E. ZAJAC, Moderator, 2157 Main St., Buffalo, 14214. Tel: 716-862-1224.

Daybreak TV Productions—CLAIRE RUNG, Exec. Producer. Tel: 716-847-8734.

Catholic Relief Services—741 Delaware Ave., Buffalo, 14209. Tel: 716-856-4494.

Chautauqua Catholic Community, Chautauqua Institution—Rev. TODD M. REMICK, Spiritual Dir. & Diocesan Liaison.

Council of Catholic Men—Rev. PAUL P. SABO, Moderator.

Council of Catholic Women—Mrs. BERNICE S. DINSMORE, Exec. Sec.

Cemeteries—CARMEN A. COLAO, Dir., Mt. Olivet Cemetery, 4000 Elmwood Ave., Kenmore, 14217. Tel: 716-873-6500; Fax: 716-873-3247.

Censors--Board of Diocesan Censors of Books and Vigilance for the Faith—Rev. Msgrs. SAMUEL J. FAIOLA, S.T.D. (Retired); THOMAS E. CRANE (Retired); ROBERT E. ZAPFEL, S.T.D.; Rev. PETER J. DRILLING, Th.D.

Charismatic Renewal Program—Rev. RICHARD S. DIGIULIO, Dir. (Retired).

Clergy Personnel Board—Rev. JAMES A. WALTER, Coord. Tel: 716-847-5537; Rev. Msgrs. RICHARD L. WETTER (Retired); JAMES G. KELLY; Revs. RICHARD A. CSIZMAR; MICHAEL G. UEBLER; RONALD P. SAJDAK.

Communications—KEVIN A. KEENAN, Dir. Tel: 716-847-8719; Fax: 716-847-8722.

Diocesan Directory—GREGG PRINCE. Tel: 716-847-8719.

Public Relations, Assistant Director for Communications—KRISTINA M. CONNELL. Tel: 716-847-8749.

Assistant Director of Communications for Radio—GREGG PRINCE. Tel: 716-847-8744.

Computer Services (Diocesan)—JAMES C. KAVANAGH, Dir. Tel: 716-847-5500.

Continuing Education for Clergy—Co-Directors: Rev. Msgrs. JAMES E. WALL; RICHARD W. SIEPKA, M.A., S.T.L.

Cursillo Movement—Deacon MICHAEL D. QUINN, Spiritual Dir. Tel: 716-515-8725; Mr. DONALD APPENHEIMER, Lay Dir.

Deaf Ministry—Rev. CONRAD P. STACHOWIAK, Chap., 130 Como Park Blvd., South Cheektowaga, 14227.

Advancement Office—RICHARD C. SUCHAN, Exec. Dir., The Foundation of the Roman Catholic Diocese of Buffalo and Diocesan Advancement. Tel: 716-847-8370; JAMES MCNAMARA, Advancement Oper. Mgr.

Due Process—Rev. Msgr. SALVATORE MANGANELLO, J.C.L., S.T.L., Chm., Catholic Center. Tel: 716-847-8769; Fax: 716-847-8772.

Ecumenism—Rev. FRANCIS X. MAZUR, Diocesan Liaison.

Catholic Education—Mrs. CAROL A. KOSTYNIAK, Sec. Educ., 795 Main St., Buffalo, 14203-1250. Tel: 716-847-5520; Fax: 716-847-5593; ROSEMARY J. HENRY, Ph.D., Supt. Catholic Schools. Tel: 716-847-5512; Mrs. ELIZABETH SCHANBACHER, Asst. Supt., Educational Technology. Tel: 716-847-5519; Mrs. PATRICIA TRIMPER, Asst. Supt., Curriculum, Instruction & Assessment. Tel: 716-847-5517; Mr. CHRISTIAN RISO, Asst. Supt. Govt. Programs & Special Projects. Tel: 716-847-5504; BARBARA MAROTTO, Professional Devel. Coord. Tel: 716-847-5507; Mr. BRIAN KISZEWSKI, Dir. Athletics. Tel: 716-866-5081; Mrs. NANCY DIBERARDINO, Athletic Coord. Tel: 716-847-5504.

Eucharistic Adoration—Deacon MICHAEL P. MCKEATING. Tel: 716-847-5548.

Evangelization Committee—Mrs. KATHLEEN B. HEFFERN, M.A.T. Tel: 716-847-5531; Fax: 716-847-2206.

Family Life—Mrs. NANCY SCHERR, Dir. Tel: 716-847-2210; Fax: 716-847-2206.

Finance Office—Mr. STEVEN D. TIMMEL. Tel: 716-847-5500; Fax: 716-847-5557.

Guild for the Blind, Inc.—Office: 741 Delaware Ave., Buffalo, 14209. Tel: 716-218-1400, Ext. 205.

Bishop's Representative for Health Care—Rev. Msgr. ROBERT E. ZAPFEL, S.T.D. Tel: 716-835-8905.

Office of Cultural Diversity—Mrs. MILAGROS RAMOS, Dir. Tel: 716-847-2217; Fax: 716-847-2206.

Holy Name Society—Rev. PAUL P. SABO, Moderator; RAYMOND ZIENTARA, Exec. Dir. Diocesan Union of Holy Name Societies. Tel: 716-847-2202.

Hospital Chaplains—Rev. RICHARD H. AUGUSTYN, Dir. Hospital Ministry, 100 High St., Buffalo, 14203. Tel: 716-859-5600.

Human Resources—Sr. SHAWN CZYZYCKI, C.S.S.F., Dir. Tel: 716-847-8376.

Insurance Services—JOHN SCHOLL, Dir. Tel: 716-847-8394; Fax: 716-847-5538.

Internal Audit—BRUCE C. EVERT, Dir. Tel: 716-847-5500. Email: audit@buffalodiocese.org.

Legion of Mary—Rev. MICHAEL H. BURZYNSKI, Ph.D., Spiritual Dir. Tel: 716-892-5746.

Liaison for Retired Priests—Rev. Msgr. W. JEROME SULLIVAN, J.C.D. (Retired). Tel: 716-480-9550.

Lifelong Faith Formation—Mrs. MARY BETH COATES, M.S., MAPM, Diocesan Dir. Lifelong Faith Formation. Tel: 716-847-5505; Ms. ELAINE DANKOWSKI, Assoc. Dir. Sacramental Catechesis. Tel: 716-847-5516; Mrs. SHARON URBANIAK, Assoc. Dir. People with Spec. Needs. Tel: 716-847-5514; Mr. CHRISTOPHER HANLEY, Assoc. Dir. Adult & Intergenerational Catechesis. Tel: 716-847-5521; Sr. JULIE UHRICH, O.S.F., Regl. Dir., Allegany, Southern Cattaraugus and Southern Chautauqua Counties, 25 Orchard St., Cuba, 14727. Tel: 585-968-5776.

Liturgical Commission—KAREN L. PODD, Chm.

Newman Club Chaplains—Rev. PATRICK J. ZENGIERSKI, Ph.D., Mailing Address: Vicar Campus Ministry and Newman Club Centers, 1219 Elmwood Ave., Buffalo, 14222. Tel: 716-882-1080.

Newspaper— "Western New York Catholic" KEVIN A. KEENAN, Editor in Chief. Tel: 716-847-8719; RICK FRANUSIAK, Mng. Editor. Tel: 716-849-8738; Fax: 716-847-8722.

Parish Life—Mrs. KATHLEEN B. HEFFERN, M.A.T., Dir. Tel: 716-847-5531; Fax: 716-847-2206. Email: parish-life@buffalodiocese.org; Mr. DENNIS G. MAHANEY, Assoc. Dir. Tel: 716-847-8393.

Pastoral Council—HANZILA GENEIVE JOHNSON, Exec. Chm.

Peace and Justice (Diocesan Commission)—Sr. M. JEAN SLIWINSKI, C.S.S.F., Chm., 55 Westfield Ave., Depew, 14043.

Permanent Diaconate—Deacons THADDEUS P. MAY, Dir., Christ the King Seminary, 711 Knox Rd., P.O. Box 607, East Aurora, 14052. Tel: 716-652-4308; GREGORY L. FEARY, Dir. Formation. Tel: 716-681-3484.

Priests, Vicar for—Rev. Msgr. JAMES E. WALL, 711 Knox Rd., P.O. Box 607, East Aurora, 14052-0607. Tel: 716-652-5047.

Pro-Life Activities—CHERYL M. CALIRE, Dir. Tel: 716-847-2205; Fax: 716-847-2206. Email: pro-lifeoffice@buffalodiocese.org.

Propagation of the Faith—Rev. RONALD P. SAJDAK. Tel: 716-847-8773.

Purchasing (Diocesan)—CHARLES MUSSEN. Tel: 716-847-8711; Fax: 716-847-8702. Email: dpd@buffalodiocese.org.

Research and Planning—Sr. REGINA MURPHY, S.S.M.N. Tel: 716-847-5539; Fax: 716-847-5557. Email: rmurphy@buffalodiocese.org.

Safe Environment—DONALD R. BLOWEY JR., Prog. Dir. Tel: 716-847-5532; Fax: 716-847-5593.

Worship, Office Of—Rev. CZESLAW M. KRYSA, Dir. Tel: 716-847-5545; Fax: 716-847-2206; ALAN D. LUKAS, M.Mus., Dir. Music, Mailing Address: Christ the King Seminary, P.O. Box 607, East Aurora, 14052-0607. Tel: 716-652-6565; Fax: 716-652-8903.

Vicar for Religious—Sr. JEAN THOMPSON, O.S.F., Vicar. Tel: 716-847-5529.

Victim Assistance Coordinator—MARY ANN C. DEIBEL-BRAUN, L.C.S.W. Tel: 716-895-3010. Email: maryann.deibel-braun@ccwny.org.

Vocations—Rev. WALTER J. SZCZESNY, M.Div., Dir. Tel: 716-847-5535; Fax: 716-847-2206. Email: vocations@buffalodiocese.org.

Youth and Young Adult Ministry—KATHRYN M. GOLLER, Dir. Tel: 716-847-8789; Fax: 716-847-8797. Email: youth@buffalodiocese.org.

CLERGY, PARISHES, MISSIONS AND PAROCHIAL SCHOOLS

CITY OF BUFFALO

(ERIE COUNTY)

1—ST. JOSEPH CATHEDRAL (1851) Rev. Msgr. James F. Campbell, Rector. In Res., Rev. Msgr. David S. Slubecky.
Res.: 50 Franklin St., 14202. Tel: 716-854-5855; Fax: 716-854-5861.
See Catholic Academy of West Buffalo, Buffalo under Regional and Consolidated Elementary Schools located in the Institution section.

2—ALL SAINTS (1911) Rev. Angelo M. Chimera.
Res.: 127 Chadduck Ave., 14207-1531. Tel: 716-875-8183; Fax: 716-875-6597.
Catechesis/Religious Program—Ronald Szczerbiak, D.R.E.

3—ST. ANTHONY OF PADUA (1891), (Italian), Rev. Secondo Casarotto, C.S.; Deacon Carmelo Gaudioso.
Res.: 160 Court St., 14202. Tel: 716-854-2563; Fax: 716-854-2564.
See Catholic Academy of West Buffalo, Buffalo under Regional and Consolidated Elementary Schools located in the Institution section.

4—ASSUMPTION (1888) [CEM] Rev. Richard Jedrzejewski. In Res., Rev. Msgr. John M. Ryan (Retired); Rev. Thomas P. Taton (Retired).
Res.: 435 Amherst St., 14207. Tel: 716-875-7626; Fax: 716-447-1027. Email: blackrockrcc@broadviewnet.net. Web: www.broadviewnet.net/assumption.
See Our Lady of Black Rock Regional School, Buffalo under Regional and Consolidated Elementary Schools located in the Institution section.
Catechesis/Religious Program—Tel: 716-873-7187. Mary Lou Wyrobek, D.R.E.

5—ST. BERNARD (1906) Rev. Francis J. Chmielewski, Sr. Parochial Vicar.
Res.: 414 S. Ogden, 14206. Tel: 716-822-8856; Fax: 716-822-7799. Email: ustbernardch@roadrunner.com.
Catechesis/Religious Program—St. Bernard Parish Hall, 1988 Clinton St., 14206.

6—BLESSED SACRAMENT (1887) Rev. Paul R. Bossi. In Res., Most Rev. Edward M. Grosz.
Res.: 1035 Delaware Ave., 14209-1605. Tel: 716-884-0053; Fax: 716-884-2279. Email: frpaulb@blsacbflo.org. Web: www.blsacbflo.org.
See Catholic Academy of West Buffalo, Buffalo under Regional and Consolidated Elementary Schools located in the Institution section.
Catechesis/Religious Program—Maureen Meyers, D.R.E.

7—BLESSED TRINITY (1906) Rev. George L. Reger.
Res.: 317 Leroy Ave., 14214. Tel: 716-833-0301; Fax: 716-834-4711. Email: blessedtrinitychurch@gmail.com.
See The NativityMiguel Middle School of Buffalo, Buffalo under Elementary Schools, Private located in the Institution section.

8—ST. CASIMIR ORATORY (1890), (Polish), Rev. Czeslaw M. Krysa, Rector.
Res.: 414 S. Ogden St., 14206. Tel: 716-822-8856; Fax: 716-822-7799.
Catechesis/Religious Program—1833 Clinton St., 14206. Tel: 716-826-9338.

9—ST. CLARE (2007) Rev. Steven J. Pavignano, O.F.M.; Bro. Maurice V. Swartout, O.F.M., Pastoral Assoc.
Office: 193 Elk St., 14210-1499. Tel: 716-823-2358; Fax: 716-826-2168. Email: stclareparish@gmail.com.
Res.: *St. Patrick Friary*, 102 Seymour St., 14210.

10—SS. COLUMBA-BRIGID (1888) Rev. Roy T. Herberger. Tel: 716-852-2076.
Res.: 418 N. Division St., 14204. Tel: 716-852-3331; Fax: 716-852-3331.
See The NativityMiguel Middle School of Buffalo, Buffalo under Elementary Schools, Private located in the Institution section.

11—CORONATION OF THE BLESSED VIRGIN MARY (1950), (Vietnamese), Rev. Andrew Tu Minh Nguyen; Deacon Robert W. Badaszewski.
Res.: 348 Dewitt St., 14213. Tel: 716-882-2650.
See Our Lady of Black Rock, Buffalo under Regional and Consolidated Elementary Schools located in the Institution section.
Catechesis/Religious Program—Tel: 716-882-6360. Mr. Frank Antonnucci, D.R.E.

12—CORPUS CHRISTI (1898), (Polish), Rev. Mariusz Dymek, O.S.P.P.E., Admin.
Res.: 199 Clark St., 14212-1407. Tel: 716-896-1050; Fax: 716-896-1595. Web: www.corpuschristibuffalo.org.

13—HOLY ANGELS (1852) Rev. James M. Fee, O.M.I. In Res., Revs. Richard Sudlik, O.M.I.; Quilin Bouzi, O.M.I.; Stephen Vasek, O.M.I.; Arthur King, O.M.I.
Res.: 348 Porter Ave., 14201-1034. Tel: 716-885-3767; Fax: 716-882-8211. Email: holyangelschurchbuffalo@yahoo.com.
See Catholic Academy of West Buffalo, Buffalo under Regional and Consolidated Elementary Schools located in the Institution section.
Catechesis/Religious Program—Ana Castellano, C.R.E.

14—HOLY CROSS (1914) Rev. Msgr. David M. Gallivan. In Res., Rev. Paul Ladda (Tanzania).
Res.: 345 Seventh St., 14201. Tel: 716-847-6930; Fax: 716-847-6934. Email: rectory@holycrossbuffalo.com. Web: www.holycrossbuffalo.com.
See Catholic Academy of West Buffalo, Buffalo under Regional and Consolidated Elementary Schools located in the Institution section.
Catechesis/Religious Program—Jodi Miller, D.R.E.

15—HOLY SPIRIT (1910) Rev. Joseph D. Wolf; Sr. Katherine Marie Bogner, S.S.M.N., Pastoral Assoc.
Parish Center: 85 Dakota Ave., 14216. Tel: 716-875-9478.
Res.: 91 Dakota Ave., 14216. Tel: 716-875-8102; Fax: 716-875-4186.
Catechesis/Religious Program—Tel: 716-875-9478. Ms. Karen Adamski, D.R.E.

16—ST. JOHN KANTY (1892), (Polish), (Linked with St. Stanislaus and St. Adalbert) Rev. Thaddeus Nicholas Bocianowski.
Office: 101 Swinburne St., 14212. Tel: 716-893-0412; Fax: 716-893-9864. Email: stjohnkanty121212@roadrunner.com.
Res.: 123 Townsend St., 14212.
Oratory—St. Adalbert 212 Stanislaus St., 14212.

17—ST. JOSEPH-UNIVERSITY (1850) Rev. Jacob C. Ledwon; Sr. Jeremy Midura, C.S.S.F., Pastoral Assoc.; Patricia Bubar Spear, Pastoral Assoc.; Deacons Thaddeus V. Pijacki; Paul C. Emerson.
Res.: 3269 Main St., 14214. Tel: 716-833-0298; Fax: 716-833-7339. Email: ledwon@buffalo.edu. Web: www.stjosephbuffalo.com.
School—(Grades PreK-8), 3275 Main St., 14214. Tel: 716-835-7395; Fax: 716-833-6550. Web: www.sjsbuffalo.org. Sr. M. Fredrica Polanski, C.S.S.F., Dir. Educ.; M. Anne Wojick, Dir. Curriculum & Community Partnerships; Susan Gent, Librarian. Felician Sisters 2; Lay Teachers 17; Students 186.
Catechesis/Religious Program—Tel: 716-837-2971. Diane M. Brennan, Dir. Faith Formation.

18—ST. KATHARINE DREXEL (2007) Rev. James M. Monaco.
Res.: 118 Schiller St., 14206. Tel: 716-895-6813; Fax: 716-891-4609. Web: stkatharinedrexel.net.
Catechesis/Religious Program—

19—ST. LAWRENCE (1929) Deacons Paul F. Weisenburger, Co-Pastoral Admin.; Joseph A. Pasquella; Mary Weisenburger, Co-Pastoral Admin. In Res., Rev. Joseph F. Moreno.
Res.: 1520 E. Delavan Ave., 14215. Tel: 716-892-2471; Fax: 716-892-1315. Email: stlawrencechurchinfo@verizon.net. Web: www.stlawrencebuffalo.org.
Catechesis/Religious Program—

20—ST. LOUIS (1829) Rev. Msgr. Salvatore Manganello.
Res.: 35 Edward St., 14202. Tel: 716-852-6040; Fax: 716-853-9225. Email: stlouischurch@verizon.net. Web: www.stlouisrcchurch.org.
See Catholic Academy of West Buffalo, Buffalo under Regional and Consolidated Elementary Schools located in the Institution section.
Catechesis/Religious Program—Nancy Grant, Dir., Faith Formation.

21—ST. MARGARET (1916) Rev. Msgr. James G. Kelly; Deacon Terrance P. Harter.
Res.: 1395 Hertel Ave., 14216. Tel: 716-876-5318; Fax: 716-875-9068. Email: stmargaretparish@aol.com.
School—(Grades PreK-8) Tel: 716-876-8885; Fax: 716-876-7553. Mr. William M. Fleckenstein Jr., Prin. Lay Teachers 14; Students 121.
Catechesis/Religious Program—Tel: 716-876-6122. Catharine Mazzarini, D.R.E.

22—ST. MARK (1908) Rev. Joseph S. Rogliano. (Linked with St. Rose of Lima)
Res.: 401 Woodward Ave., 14214. Tel: 716-836-1600; Fax: 716-835-7941.
School—(Grades K-8) Tel: 716-836-1191; Fax: 716-836-0391. Lydia Brenner, Prin. Sisters of St. Joseph 1; Lay Teachers 28; Students 398.
Catechesis/Religious Program—Joanne Yakovac, D.R.E.
Convent—223 Summit Ave., 14214. Tel: 716-837-9055.

23—ST. MARTIN DE PORRES (1993), (African American), Rev. Ronald P. Sajdak; Deacon Ronald Walker; Sr. Philip Marie, S.S.J., Pastoral Assoc.; Joan Ersing, Pastoral Assoc.
Office: 555 Northampton St., 14208. Tel: 716-883-7729; Fax: 716-886-4101.
See The NativityMiguel Middle School of Buffalo, Buffalo under Elementary Schools, Private located in the Institution section.
Catechesis/Religious Program—

24—ST. MARTIN OF TOURS (1926), (Linked with St. Thomas Aquinas) Rev. James G. Judge; Rev. Msgr. Fred R. Voorhes, Sr. Parochial Vicar; Deacons Michael D. Quinn; John H. Burke. In Res., Rev. Barry J. Allaire.
Res.: 1140 Abbott Rd., 14220. Tel: 716-823-7077; Fax: 716-995-0300. Email: info@stmartinbuffalo.com. Web: www.stmartinbuffalo.com.
See South Buffalo Catholic School, Buffalo under Regional and Consolidated Elementary Schools located in the Institution section.
Catechesis/Religious Program—Joint program with St. Thomas Aquinas.

25—ST. MICHAEL (1851) Revs. Ronald W. Sams, S.J.; John G. Sturm, S.J.; Richard J. Hoar, S.J.; H. James Roleke, S.J.; Peter J. Murray, S.J.; Thomas P. Green, S.J.; Edmund W. Nagle, S.J.; William P. Poorten, S.J.; Bro. James Dennehy, S.J. In Res., Rev. John J. Mattimore, S.J.
Res.: 651 Washington St., 14203. Tel: 716-854-6726; Fax: 716-854-4616. Email: rsams@roadrunner.com.
See Catholic Academy of West Buffalo, Buffalo under Regional and Consolidated Elementary Schools located in the Institution section.

26—OUR LADY OF CHARITY (2010), Parish with two sites: St. Ambrose and Holy Family Rev. Msgr. David M. Lee.
Office, Res. & St. Ambrose Church: 65 Ridgewood Rd., 14220. Tel: 716-822-5962; Fax: 716-822-0966.
Holy Family Church: 1885 S. Park Ave., 14220.
See South Buffalo Catholic School under Regional & Consolidated Elementary schools.
Catechesis/Religious Program—Ms. Denise McKenzie, D.R.E.

27—OUR LADY OF HOPE (2008) Revs. Mitch Byeck, O.M.I.; Quilin Bouzi, O.M.I., Parochial Vicar; Ronald Thaler, Pastoral Assoc.
Res.: 18 Greenwood Pl., 14213. Tel: 716-885-2469; Fax: 716-885-3385.
Church: Lafayette Ave. & Grant St., 14213.
See Catholic Academy of West Buffalo, Buffalo under Regional and Consolidated Elementary Schools located in the Institution section.
Catechesis/Religious Program—Tel: 716-882-6360. Frank Antonucci, C.R.E.

28—OUR LADY OF PERPETUAL HELP (1897) Rev. Donald J. Lutz.
Res.: 115 O'Connell Ave., 14204. Tel: 716-852-2671.
Catechesis/Religious Program—

29—ST. ROSE OF LIMA (1925) Rev. Joseph S. Rogliano. (Linked with St. Mark)
Res.: 401 Woodward Ave., 14214.
Church: 500 Parker Ave., 14216. Tel: 716-834-6688; Fax: 716-834-6689. Email: saintrose2@verizon.net. Web: www.stroselima.net.
Catechesis/Religious Program—Tel: 716-833-4100. Mrs. Mary Frances Mc Crorey, D.R.E.

30—ST. STANISLAUS (1873), (Polish), [CEM] Rev. Thaddeus Nicholas Bocianowski. (Linked with St. John Kanty)
Res.: 123 Townsend St., 14212. Tel: 716-854-5511; Fax: 716-854-0170. Email: ststansbm@adelphia.net. Web: www.ststanislauschurch.com.
Catechesis/Religious Program—

31—ST. TERESA (1897) Rev. James B. Cunningham; Deacon Robert A. Dobmeier.
Church, Res. & Office: 1974 Seneca St., 14210-2396. Tel: 716-822-0608; Fax: 716-826-3795. Email: teresa14210@yahoo.com.
See South Buffalo Catholic School, Buffalo under Regional and Consolidated Elementary Schools location in the Institution section.
Catechesis/Religious Program—Tel: 716-822-1660.

32—ST. THOMAS AQUINAS (1920), (Linked with St. Martin of Tours) Rev. James G. Judge; Rev. Msgr. Fred R. Voorhes, Sr. Parochial Vicar.
Res.: 450 Abbott Rd., 14220-1796. Tel: 716-822-1250; Fax: 716-822-2594.
See South Buffalo Catholic School, Buffalo under Regional and Consolidated Elementary Schools located in the Institution section.
Catechesis/Religious Program—

OUTSIDE THE CITY OF BUFFALO

AKRON, ERIE CO., ST. TERESA OF AVILA (1859) [CEM] Rev. Msgr. Robert J. Williamson.
Res.: 5771 Buell St., P.O. Box 168, 14001. Tel: 716-542-9103; Fax: 716-542-2444. Email: stteresasofakron@verizon.net. Web: www.stteresasofakron.com.
Catechesis/Religious Program—Tel: 716-542-9717; Fax: 716-542-2444. Sr. Mary Ruth Warejko, C.S.S.F., D.R.E.

ALBION, ORLEANS CO., HOLY FAMILY (2008) [CEM] Rev. Richard A. Csizmar; Deacon James L. Collichio.
Res.: 106 S. Main St., 14411. Tel: 585-589-4243; Fax: 585-589-0734.
Catechesis/Religious Program—Tel: 585-589-5236. Miss Nancy J. Sedita, D.R.E.

ALDEN, ERIE CO., ST. JOHN THE BAPTIST (1850) [CEM]

Rev. James D. Ciupek; Deacon Richard J. Mahaney; Sr. Ellen McCarthy, S.S.J., Pastoral Assoc.
Res.: 2021 Sandridge Rd., 14004. Tel: 716-937-6959; Fax: 716-937-0075. Web: www.stjohnalden.com.
School—(Grades PreK-8), 2028 Sandridge Rd., 14004. Tel: 716-937-9483; Fax: 716-937-9794. Email: stjohnschool@stjohnalden.com. Ms. Marilynn Camp, Prin. Lay Teachers 17; Students 159.
Catechesis/Religious Program—Tel: 716-937-3448. Email: reled@stjohnalden.com. Michael Denz, Dir. Faith Formation.

ALLEGANY, CATTARAUGUS CO., ST. BONAVENTURE (1854) Rev. James Vacco, O.F.M.; Peggy Reitz, Pastoral Assoc.
Res.: 95 E. Main St., 14706. Tel: 716-373-1330; Fax: 716-373-4220. Web: www.stbonasparish.org.
See Southern Tier Catholic, Olean under Regional and Consolidated Elementary Schools located in the Institution section.
Catechesis/Religious Program—Holly Keenan, D.R.E.

ALFRED/ALMOND, ALLEGANY CO., SS. BRENDAN AND JUDE (1992), (Linked with Blessed Sacrament, Andover) Rev. Sean E. DiMaria; Mr. Chris Yarnal, Campus Min.; Deacon Michael A. Gomola.
St. Brendan Oratory & Res.: 11 S. Main St., Box G, Almond, 14804. Tel: 607-276-5304.
Catechesis/Religious Program—
Chapel—St. Jude Parish Office: Lower College Dr., 14802. Tel: 607-587-9411; Fax: 607-587-9431. Email: stjude.alfred@gmail.com. Web: www.ssbjparish.net.

AMHERST, ERIE CO.

1—ST. GREGORY THE GREAT (1958) Revs. Joseph C. Gatto; Francis Lombardo, O.F.M.Conv.; Paul S. Salemi; David I. Richards; Deacons Kevin J. Smith; John D. Leardon; Michael G. Bochiechio; Daniel U. Golinski.
Res.: 260 St. Gregory Ct., Williamsville, 14221-2635. Tel: 716-688-5678; 716-688-5679; Fax: 716-688-2315. Web: www.stgregs.org.
School—(Grades PreK-8), 250 St. Gregory Ct., Williamsville, 14221. Tel: 716-688-5323; Fax: 716-688-6629. Mrs. Patricia Freund, Prin. Sisters 1; Lay Teachers 43; Students 631.
Catechesis/Religious Program—Tel: 716-688-5760; Fax: 716-639-8251. Mrs. Joan Rischmiller, D.R.E.

2—ST. LEO THE GREAT (1953) Rev. Msgr. Robert E. Zapfel; David Ehrke, Business Mgr.; Dawn Iacano, AFF/Outreach.
Res.: 885 Sweet Home Rd., 14226. Tel: 716-835-8905; Fax: 716-835-8997. Email: office@stleothegreatamherst.com. Web: stleothegreatamherst.com.
School—(Grades PreK-8) Tel: 716-832-6340. Mrs. Carolyn Kraus, Prin. Lay Teachers 16; Students 153.
Catechesis/Religious Program—Tel: 716-833-8359. Mary Beth Lalka, D.R.E.

ANDOVER, ALLEGANY CO., BLESSED SACRAMENT (1855) [CEM], Linked with SS. Brendan & Jude Parish, Alfred/Almond. Rev. Sean E. DiMaria; Deacon Michael A. Gomola.
Res.: 11 S. Main St., Box G, Almond, 14804. Tel: 607-276-5304; Fax: 607-587-9431. Email: fathersean1@gmail.com.
Catechesis/Religious Program—

ANGOLA, ERIE CO., MOST PRECIOUS BLOOD (1871) [CEM] Rev. John S. Kwiecien.
Res.: 22 Prospect St., 14006. Tel: 716-549-0420; Fax: 716-549-0425. Email: rectory@mpbangola.org. Web: www.mpbangola.org.
Catechesis/Religious Program—

ARCADE, WYOMING CO., ST. MARY (2007) [CEM], Parish with two sites: St. Mary, Arcade; St. Mary, East Arcade. Rev. Joseph A. Gullo.
Office & Res.: 417 Main St., 14009-1195. Tel: 585-492-5330; Fax: 585-492-1047. E. Arcade Site: 6785 E. Arcade Rd., 14009-9617.
See St. Aloysius Regional School, Springville under Regional and Consolidated Elementary Schools located in the Institution section.
Catechesis/Religious Program—

ATHOL SPRINGS, ERIE CO., ST. FRANCIS OF ASSISI (1929) Rev. Ross Syracuse, O.F.M.Conv.
Res.: S-4263 St. Francis Dr., P.O. Box 182, 14010. Tel: 716-627-2710; Fax: 716-627-5263. Email: fr.ross@verizon.net. Web: www.stfrancischurch.us.
Catechesis/Religious Program—Tel: 716-627-3357. Jean Hymes, C.R.E.

ATTICA, WYOMING CO., SS. JOACHIM & ANNE (2008) [CEM] Rev. Karl E. Loeb.
Res.: 50 East Ave., 14011. Tel: 585-591-1228; Fax: 585-591-1614. Email: esaintvincentd@rochester.rr.com.
Varysburg Site: 2311 Attica Rd., Varysburg, 14167.
Catechesis/Religious Program—Tel: 585-591-8611. Email: sbeck85@rochester.rr.com. Scott Beck, C.R.E. (Attica); Paula Beck, C.R.E. (Attica); Don Gregoire, C.R.E. (Varysburg).

BARKER, NIAGARA CO., OUR LADY OF THE LAKE (2009) [CEM], Parish with two sites: Barker; Lyndonville. Rev. James F. Hassett.
Office & Res.: 1726 Quaker Rd., 14012. Tel: 716-795-3331; Fax: 716-795-3919. Email: ourladyofthelakeparish@gmail.com.
Lyndonville Site: 38 Lake Ave., Lyndonville, 14098. Tel: 585-765-9722.
Catechesis/Religious Program—Tel: 716-795-3459; 585-682-3988.

BATAVIA, GENESEE CO.

1—ASCENSION (2008) [CEM] Rev. David R. Glassmire; Deacon Walter T. Szczesny.
Res.: 15 Sumner St., 14020. Tel: 585-343-1796; Fax: 585-343-0919.
St. Anthony Site: 122 Liberty St., 14020.
Catechesis/Religious Program—

2—RESURRECTION (2008) [CEM] Revs. Ivan R. Trujillo; Robert E. Waters, Sr. Parochial Vicar; Deacons C. Thomas Casey; Henry E. Moscicki.
Res.: 303 E. Main St., 14020. Tel: 585-343-5800; Fax: 585-345-9525. Email: ivantrujillo1@rochester.rr.com.
St. Mary's Site: 18 Elliott St., 14020.
School—St. Joseph School, (Grades PreK-8), 2 Summit St., 14020. Tel: 585-343-6154; Fax: 585-343-8911. Web: sjsbatavia.org. Mrs. Karen Green, Prin. Lay Teachers 20; Students 268.
Catechesis/Religious Program—Sr. M. Francine Fasano, R.S.M., D.R.E.; Deacon Henry E. Moscicki, D.R.E.

BELFAST, ALLEGANY CO., ST. PATRICK (1859) [CEM], (Linked with St. Patrick, Fillmore, and Our Lady of the Angels, Cuba) Rev. Dennis J. Mancuso.
Res. & Mailing Address: 109 W. Main St., P.O. Box 198, Fillmore, 14735.
Church: 18 E. Hughes St., 14711. Tel: 585-567-2282; Fax: 585-567-4172.
Catechesis/Religious Program—

BELMONT, ALLEGANY CO., HOLY FAMILY OF JESUS, MARY & JOSEPH (1861) Deacon Frank W. Pasquale, Pastoral Admin.; Rev. Sean E. DiMaria, Sacramental Min.
Office: 5 Milton St., 14813. Tel: 585-268-7272; Fax: 585-268-9128.
Catechesis/Religious Program—
Oratory—St. Joseph (1844) Cottage Bridge Rd., Scio, Allegany Co. 14880. Tel: 585-268-7272; Fax: 585-268-7272.

BEMUS POINT, CHAUTAUQUA CO., ST. MARY OF LOURDES (2008) Rev. Todd M. Remick; Deacon Samuel G. Puleo.
Bemus Point Site: 41 Main St., P.O. Box 500, 14712. Tel: 716-386-2400; Fax: 716-386-5562.
Mayville Site: 24 E. Chautauqua St., Mayville, 14757. Tel: 716-753-2332; Fax: 716-753-3836.
See Catholic Academy of the Holy Family, Jamestown under Regional and Consolidated Elementary Schools located in the Institution section.
Catechesis/Religious Program—Tracy Nelson, D.R.E.; Dayle Loutzenhiser, D.R.E.

BERGEN, GENESEE CO., ST. BRIGID (1861) [CEM], (Linked with Our Lady of Mercy, LeRoy) Rev. Michael R. Rock, O.de.M.
Res.: 44 Lake St., Le Roy, 14482. Tel: 585-768-6543; Fax: 585-768-7093.
Church: 18 Gibson St., 14416.
Catechesis/Religious Program— Combined with Our Lady of Mercy, LeRoy.

BLASDELL, ERIE CO., OUR MOTHER OF GOOD COUNSEL (1905) Revs. Lawrence E. Burns; Edward R. Czarnecki; Deacon Michael T. Dulak.
Res.: 3688 S. Park Ave., 14219. Tel: 716-822-2630; Fax: 716-821-5980.
Catechesis/Religious Program—Alice Appenheimer, D.R.E.

BOLIVAR, ALLEGANY CO., ST. MARY (1903) [CEM] Deacon Frank W. Pasquale, Pastoral Admin.; Rev. Sean E. DiMaria, Sacramental Min.
Church: 111 Wellsville St., 14715. Tel: 585-928-1024; Fax: 585-928-1024. Email: qualery1@yahoo.com.
Catechesis/Religious Program—Mary Snyder, D.R.E.

BOSTON, ERIE CO., ST. JOHN THE BAPTIST (1869) [CEM] Rev. Robert J. Hora.
Res.: 6895 Boston Cross Rd., 14025-9601. Tel: 716-941-3549; Fax: 716-941-3030. Email: rjhora@roadrunner.com.
Catechesis/Religious Program—Tel: 716-941-6363.
Oratory—St. Mary 8175 E. Eden Rd., East Eden, Erie Co. 14057.

BOWMANSVILLE, ERIE CO., SACRED HEART (1920) [CEM], (Linked with Nativity of the Blessed Virgin Mary, Clarence) Rev. Msgr. Joseph J. Sicari.
Res.: 5337 Genesee St., 14026-1098. Tel: 716-683-2375; Fax: 716-683-0412. Email: sheartshrine@aol.com. Web: www.catholicweb.com.
Catechesis/Religious Program—Tel: 585-894-0154.

CANASERAGA, ALLEGANY CO., ST. MARY (1855) [CEM] Rev. John J. Cullen.
Mailing Address: P.O. Box 189, 14822. Tel: 607-545-8601.
Catechesis/Religious Program—

CATTARAUGUS, CATTARAUGUS CO., ST. MARY (1863), (Linked with St. Joseph, Gowanda) Revs. Daniel P. Walsh; Joseph F. Moreno, Sacramental Min.; Mr. Robert Hebert, Pastoral Assoc.
Res.: 36 Washington St., 14719. Tel: 716-257-9351. Email: jeanbobo3@roadrunner.com.
Catechesis/Religious Program—

CHEEKTOWAGA, ERIE CO.

1—ST. ALOYSIUS GONZAGA (1940) Rev. Msgr. Peter J. Popadick. In Res., Rev. James R. Bastian.
Res.: 157 Cleveland Dr., 14215. Tel: 716-833-1715; Fax: 716-837-5703. Email: stalschurch@aol.com.
Catechesis/Religious Program—Tel: 716-836-9657.
Convent—130 Highview Rd., 14215. Tel: 716-834-1889. Email: stalscon@yahoo.com.

2—INFANT OF PRAGUE (1946) Rev. Raymond G. Corbin; Deacon Daniel H. Mackowiak.
Res.: 921 Cleveland Dr., 14225. Tel: 716-634-3660; Fax: 716-634-3661. Email: infantofpragueparish@roadrunner.com. Web: www.iopparish.org.
Catechesis/Religious Program—Sr. M. Antonita Sikorski, C.S.S.F., D.R.E.

3—ST. JOHN GUALBERT (1917), (Polish), Rev. Michael H. Burzynski; Deacon Edward S. Walek. In Res., Rev. Patrick Gardocki, O.F.M. (Poland).
Res.: 83 Gualbert Ave., 14211. Tel: 716-892-5746; Fax: 716-897-3906.
Catechesis/Religious Program—Tel: 716-897-2619. Mrs. Karen Pszczolkowski, Assoc. D.R.E.; Lea Bethge, Assoc. D.R.E.

4—ST. JOSAPHAT (1906), (Polish), Rev. Richard M. I. Poblocki.
Res.: 20 Peoria Ave., 14206. Tel: 716-893-1086; Fax: 716-893-1099. Email: sjrectory@roadrunner.com. Web: www.st-josaphat.com.
Catechesis/Religious Program—

5—OUR LADY HELP OF CHRISTIANS (1890) [CEM], (National Historic Site) Rev. Richard A. Jesionowski.
Res.: 4125 Union Rd., 14225. Tel: 716-634-3420; 716-634-3428; Fax: 716-634-3464.
See Mary Queen of Angels School, Cheektowaga under Regional and Consolidated Elementary Schools located in the Institution section.
Catechesis/Religious Program—Tel: 716-632-3532; Fax: 716-895-6359. Denise Seeley, D.R.E.

6—OUR LADY OF CZESTOCHOWA (1922), (Polish), Rev. Harry F. Szczesniak.
Res.: 23 Willowlawn Pkwy., 14206. Tel: 716-822-5590; Fax: 716-822-5597.
Catechesis/Religious Program—Tel: 716-826-3497.

7—ST. PHILIP THE APOSTLE (1967) Revs. David J. Borowiak; James W. Kirkpatrick Jr.; Deacon Walter N. Fudala.
Res.: 950 Losson Rd., 14227. Tel: 716-668-8370; Fax: 716-668-3824. Email: loaves@roadrunner.com.
Catechesis/Religious Program—Tel: 716-668-3344. Mary Ann Mercurio, D.R.E.; Judy Kogut, D.R.E.

8—QUEEN OF MARTYRS (1946) Rev. Louis S. Klein. In Res., Rev. John J. Sardina.
Res.: 180 George Urban Blvd., 14225-3095. Tel: 716-892-1746; Fax: 716-892-3005.
See Mary Queen of Angels School, Cheektowaga under Regional and Consolidated Elementary Schools located in the Institution section.
Catechesis/Religious Program—Tel: 716-895-2162. Rita Sandage, D.R.E.

9—RESURRECTION (1944) Rev. Conrad P. Stachowiak; Deacon Thaddeus P. May.
Res.: 130 Como Park Blvd., 14227. Tel: 716-683-3712; Fax: 716-685-4487.
Catechesis/Religious Program—

CLARENCE, ERIE CO.

1—NATIVITY OF THE BLESSED VIRGIN MARY (1954) Rev. Msgr. Frederick D. Leising; Rev. John J. Leising, Sr. Parochial Vicar; Kathy Fonte, Pastoral Assoc.; Maureen M. Orgek, Business Mgr.
Res.: 4375 Harris Hill Rd., Williamsville, 14221. Tel: 716-632-8838; Fax: 716-632-7898. Email: pastor@nativityharrishill.org. Web: www.nativityharrishill.org.
School—(Grades PreK-8), 8550 Main St., Williamsville, 14221. Tel: 716-633-7441. Email: natofmary@yahoo.com. Web: www.nativityofmary-school.com. Mrs. Cherie M. Ansuini, Prin. Lay Teachers 18; Students 202.
Catechesis/Religious Program—8550 Main St., Williamsville, 14221. Tel: 716-634-3130. Email: nativityreligiouseducation2004@yahoo.com. Mrs. Mary Ann Hoag, D.R.E.

2—OUR LADY OF PEACE (1922) Rev. Thomas D. Doyle.
Res.: 10950 Main St., 14031. Tel: 716-759-8554; Fax: 716-759-8537. Email: olpclarence@roadrunner.com. Web: www.olpclarence.com.
Catechesis/Religious Program—

CORFU, GENESEE CO., ST. MAXIMILIAN KOLBE PARISH (2009) [CEM], Parish with two sites: Corfu; East Pembroke. Rev. Robert J. Orlowski.

Office & Res.: 18 W. Main St., P.O. Box 278, 14036. Tel: 585-599-4833; Fax: 585-599-2833. Email: stmaxkolbe09@yahoo.com.
East Pembroke Site: P.O. Box 219, East Pembroke, 14056. Tel: 585-762-9006; Fax: 585-762-9036.
Catechesis/Religious Program—

CUBA, ALLEGANY CO., OUR LADY OF THE ANGELS (1850) [CEM] Rev. Dennis J. Mancuso.
Res.: 50 South St., 14727. Tel: 585-968-2885; Fax: 585-968-0123. Email: ourlady@localnet.net.
See Southern Tier Catholic, Olean under Regional and Consolidated Elementary Schools located in the Institution section.
Catechesis/Religious Program—

DARIEN CENTER, GENESEE CO., IMMACULATE HEART OF MARY (2008) [CEM] Rev. Joseph A. Fiore.
Office: 10675 Allegany Rd., 14040-9701. Tel: 585-547-3547; Fax: 585-547-3660.
Bennington Center Site: 1230 Clinton St., Attica, 14011. Tel: 585-591-0176; Fax: 585-591-4818.

DEPEW, ERIE CO.

1—BLESSED MOTHER TERESA OF CALCUTTA (1897/2009) [CEM] Rev. Lawrence P. Damian.
Res.: 496 Terrace Blvd., 14043. Tel: 716-683-2746; Fax: 716-683-3121. Email: FRLPD@yahoo.com.
Catechesis/Religious Program—Koreen Scalfaro, C.R.E.
Convent—Felician Nuns, 55 Westfield Ave., 14043. Tel: 716-685-1114.

2—ST. MARTHA (2011) Rev. Bartholomew W. Lipiec; Deacons Timothy E. Chriswell; James J. Trzaska. In Res., Rev. Robert W. Zilliox.
Res.: 10 French Rd., 14043-2129. Tel: 716-684-6342; Fax: 716-684-1853. Email: olbsparish@juno.com. Web: www.olbsdepew.org.
School—(Grades K-8), 20 French Rd., 14043. Tel: 716-685-2544; Fax: 716-685-9103. Sr. M. Janita Krawczyk, C.S.S.F., Prin.; Mrs. Karen Bauer, Librarian. Felician Sisters 2; Lay Teachers 14; Students 157.
Catechesis/Religious Program—Tel: 716-685-2546. Sr. Catherine Taberski, S.S.M.N., D.R.E.; Mrs. Katie Mescall, C.R.E.

DUNKIRK, CHAUTAUQUA CO.

1—BLESSED MARY ANGELA PARISH (2008), (Polish), [CEM], Parish with two sites. Revs. Matt Mieczyslaw Nycz; Jan Trela, Parochial Vicar, (Poland); Sr. M. Rachel Mikolajczak, C.S.S.F., Pastoral Assoc. & D.R.E.
St. Hyacinth Site: 295 Lake Shore Dr. E., 14048.
Office at St. Hedwig Site: 324 Townsend St., 14048-3131. Tel: 716-366-2307; Fax: 716-366-6335. Email: bmangela_office@roadrunner.com.
See Northern Chautauqua Catholic School under Regional & Consolidated Elementary Schools.
Catechesis/Religious Program—296 Lake Shore Dr. E., 14048. Tel: 716-366-5707; Fax: 716-366-1192. Grades K-5.
Catechesis/Religious Program—105 Doughty St., 14048. Tel: 716-445-4779. Grades 6-12.

2—ST. ELIZABETH ANN SETON (1975) [CEM] Rev. Dennis G. Riter. In Res., Rev. Walter Werbicki.
Res.: 328 Washington Ave., 14048. Tel: 716-366-1750; Fax: 716-366-4398. Email: st.elizannseton@verizon.com.
See Northern Chautauqua Catholic, Dunkirk under Regional and Consolidated Elementary Schools located in the Institution section.
Catechesis/Religious Program—Tel: 716-366-2827. Email: reledseas@yahoo.com. Wendy Kachermeyer, C.R.E.

3—HOLY TRINITY (1908) [CEM] Rev. Joseph A. Zalacca.
Res.: 1032 Central Ave., 14048. Tel: 716-366-2306; Fax: 716-366-4738. Email: allarewelcome@holytrinitydunkirk.com. Web: www.holytrinitydunkirk.com.
See Northern Chautauqua Catholic, Dunkirk under Regional and Consolidated Elementary Schools located in the Institution section.
Catechesis/Religious Program—Tel: 716-366-0499. Roberta Coniglio, D.R.E.; Donna Seyedian, D.R.E.

EAST AURORA, ERIE CO., IMMACULATE CONCEPTION (1901) [CEM] Rev. Robert W. Wardenski; Deacon Donald C. Weigel Jr.
Res.: 520 Oakwood Ave., 14052. Tel: 716-652-6400; Fax: 716-652-7168.
School—(Grades K-8), 510 Oakwood Ave., 14052. Tel: 716-652-5855; Fax: 716-805-0192. Ms. Karen Adamski, Prin. Lay Teachers 16; Students 211.
Catechesis/Religious Program—Tel: 716-655-0067. Sr. Judith Beiswanger, O.S.F., D.R.E.

EDEN, ERIE CO., IMMACULATE CONCEPTION (1908) [CEM] Rev. Walter P. Grabowski. (Linked with Holy Spirit, North Collins)
Res.: 8791 S. Main St., 14057. Tel: 716-992-3933; Fax: 716-992-2201. Email: icceden@verizon.net. Web: www.icceden.org.
Catechesis/Religious Program—Email: iccreligioused@aol.com. Sharon Reed, D.R.E.

EGGERTSVILLE, ERIE CO., ST. BENEDICT (1920) Revs. Joseph D. Porpiglia; Paul P. Sabo, Sr. Parochial Vicar; Deacon William J. Hynes. In Res., Rev. Joseph G. Fifagrowicz (Retired).
Res.: 1317 Eggert Rd., 14226. Tel: 716-834-1041; Fax: 716-835-5949. Email: frporpiglia@saintbenedicts.com. Web: www.saintbenedicts.com.
School—(Grades PreK-8), 3980 Main St., Amherst, 14226. Tel: 716-835-2518; Fax: 716-834-4932. Molly Halady, Prin.; Judy Eberle, Librarian; Mary Carroll, Librarian. Lay Teachers 18; Students 178.
Catechesis/Religious Program—Tel: 716-836-6444. Matt Smith, D.R.E.

ELLICOTTVILLE, CATTARAUGUS CO., HOLY NAME OF MARY (1850) [CEM] Rev. Ronald B. Mierzwa.
Res.: 22 Jefferson St., P.O. Box 543, 14731. Tel: 716-699-2592; Fax: 716-699-8439. Email: hnameofmary@roadrunner.com.
Catechesis/Religious Program—
Oratory—St. Pacificus Chapel Hill Rd., Humphrey, Cattaraugus Co. 14778.

ELMA, ERIE CO.

1—ANNUNCIATION OF THE BLESSED VIRGIN MARY (1905) [CEM] Rev. Eugene P. Ulrich; Deacons Joseph P. Mercurio; James J. Jaworski, Pastoral Assoc. for Admin.; Dennis W. Kapsiak; Deborah Kennan, Pastoral Assoc. for Ministry.
Res.: 7580 Clinton St., 14059. Tel: 716-683-5254; Fax: 716-681-5668.
School—(Grades PreK-8) Tel: 716-681-1327; Fax: 716-685-6380. Sr. Marilyn Ann Dudek, C.S.S.F., Prin. Lay Teachers 19; Students 82; Preschool Students 40.
Catechesis/Religious Program—Tel: 716-683-5515. Sr. Lori High, S.S.M.N., D.R.E.

2—ST. GABRIEL (1925) Rev. Daniel J. Palys; Sr. Joseph Marie Marczak, C.S.S.F., Pastoral Assoc.; Ann Bauman, Pastoral Assoc.
Res.: 5271 Clinton St., 14059-7617. Tel: 716-668-4017; Fax: 716-656-0616. Email: stgabriel5271@roadrunner.com. Web: www.stgabes.net.
Catechesis/Religious Program—Tel: 716-668-2070. Email: pbloom7@gmail.com. Paul J. Bloom, D.R.E.

FALCONER, CHAUTAUQUA CO., OUR LADY OF LORETO (1912), (Linked with St. Patrick, Randolph) Rev. Joseph P. Janaczek.
Res.: 309 W. Everett St., 14733. Tel: 716-665-4253; Fax: 716-664-9223.
See Holy Family Catholic School, Jamestown under Regional and Consolidated Elementary Schools located in the Institution section.
Catechesis/Religious Program—Tel: 716-665-3764. Mrs. Deborah C. Ognibene, C.R.E.

FARNHAM, ERIE CO., ST. ANTHONY'S (1904) [CEM] Rev. James W. Fliss.
Mailing Address: P.O. Box A-9, 14061.
Res.: 421 Commercial St., 14061. Tel: 716-549-1159.
Catechesis/Religious Program—Tel: 716-549-2867; Fax: 716-549-7742. Theresa L. White, D.R.E.

FILLMORE, ALLEGANY CO., ST. PATRICK (1881) [CEM], (Linked with St. Patrick, Belfast, and Our Lady of the Angels, Cuba) Rev. Dennis J. Mancuso.
Res.: 109 W. Main St., P.O. Box 198, 14735. Tel: 585-567-2282; Fax: 585-567-4172.
Catechesis/Religious Program—

FRANKLINVILLE, CATTARAUGUS CO., ST. PHILOMENA (1906) [JC] Rev. Robert Marino, Admin.
Res.: 26 N. Plymouth Ave., 14737. Tel: 716-676-3629; Fax: 716-676-2104.
Catechesis/Religious Program—Tel: 716-676-2123.

FREDONIA, CHAUTAUQUA CO.

1—ST. ANTHONY (1905) Rev. Carlton J. Westfield.
Res.: 42 Orchard St., 14063. Tel: 716-679-4050; 716-679-4096 (Office); Fax: 716-672-8576 (Office); 716-679-0326 (Res.). Email: fr.westfield@yahoo.com.
Cassadaga Site: *Immaculate Conception*, 88 N. Main St., Cassadaga, 14718.
See Northern Chautauqua Catholic, Dunkirk under Regional and Consolidated Elementary Schools located in the Institution section.
Catechesis/Religious Program—Joanne Catalano, C.R.E.

2—ST. JOSEPH (1899) Rev. Charles J. Zadora; Deacons Michael C. Lemieux; Matthew A. Hens.
Res.: 145 E. Main St., 14063. Tel: 716-679-4116; Fax: 716-679-1352 (1-5 P.M.).
See Northern Chautauqua Catholic, Dunkirk under Regional and Consolidated Elementary Schools located in the Institution section.
Catechesis/Religious Program—(Intergenerational - 70 households), Tel: 716-672-2647. Email: jbradley@stjosephfredonia.org.

FRENCH CREEK, CHAUTAUQUA CO., CHRIST OUR HOPE (2008) [CEM] Rev. Jozef W. Dudzik.
Church & Office: 1762 French Creek Mina Rd., Clymer, 14724-9660. Tel: 716-355-8891; Fax: 716-355-2576.
Sherman Site: 119 Miller St., Sherman, 14781.
See Holy Family Catholic School, Jamestown under Regional and Consolidated Elementary Schools located in the Institution section.
Catechesis/Religious Program—

GETZVILLE, ERIE CO., ST. PIUS X (1958) Rev. James C. O'Connor; Deacon Brian C. Walkowiak. In Res., Rev. James L. Fugle.
Res.: 1700 N. French Rd., P.O. Box 162, 14068-0162. Tel: 716-688-9143; Fax: 716-688-1203. Email: tkpiusx@aol.com. Web: www.stpiusxgetzville.org.
Catechesis/Religious Program—Tel: 716-688-5417; Fax: 716-688-0068.

GOWANDA, ERIE CO., ST. JOSEPH (1898) [CEM], (Linked with St. Mary, Cattaraugus) Rev. Daniel P. Walsh; Deacon Thomas A. McDonnell.
Res.: 26 Erie Ave., 14070. Tel: 716-532-5100; Fax: 716-532-4096.
School—(Grades PreK-8) Tel: 716-532-2520; Fax: 716-532-4172. Mr. Patrick J. Brady, Prin. Lay Teachers 10; Students 84.
Catechesis/Religious Program—Tel: 716-257-5486. Wilma Parry, C.R.E.

GRAND ISLAND, ERIE CO., ST. STEPHEN (1862) [CEM] Revs. Paul M. Nogaro; Lynn M. Shumway, Sr. Parochial Vicar.
Res.: 2100 Baseline Rd., 14072. Tel: 716-773-7647; Fax: 716-773-5792. Email: ststephenswny@roadrunner.com. Web: www.ststephenswny.com.
School—(Grades PreK-8), 2080 Baseline Rd., 14072. Tel: 716-773-4347; Fax: 716-773-1438. Email: school@ststephensgi.org. Web: www.ststephensgi.org. Mrs. Donna Ende, Prin. Lay Teachers 17; Students 191.
Catechesis/Religious Program—Tel: 716-773-2002. Angela Diebold, D.R.E.

HAMBURG, ERIE CO.

1—ST. MARY OF THE LAKE (1948) Rev. Arthur J. Smith; Sr. Paula Zelazo, F.S.S.J., Pastoral Assoc.
Res. & Church: 4737 Lake Shore Rd., 14075. Tel: 716-627-3123; Fax: 716-627-7062. Email: stmary@smolc.org.
School—(Grades PreK-8) Tel: 716-627-7700; Fax: 716-627-1255. Mrs. Kristine Hider, Prin.; Sr. Regis Zboch, F.S.S.J., Librarian. Franciscan Sisters of St. Joseph 1; Lay Teachers 16; Students 150.
Catechesis/Religious Program—Tel: 716-627-7150. Patricia Jerzewski, D.R.E.

2—SS. PETER AND PAUL (1844) [CEM] Revs. Mark J. Wolski; Sebastian C. Pierro; Deacons Carlton M. Koester; Roy P. Dibb.
Res.: 66 E. Main St., 14075. Tel: 716-649-2765; Fax: 716-649-5218. Web: www.sspeterandpaulhamburg.org.
School—(Grades PreK-8), 68 E. Main St., 14075. Tel: 716-649-7030; Fax: 716-312-9313. Mr. Patrick Riester, Prin.; Anne Marie Maggio, Librarian. Lay Teachers 23; Students 251.
Catechesis/Religious Program—Tel: 716-649-0231. Mary Ann Senchyne, D.R.E.; Mario Vinti, C.R.E.

HOLLAND, ERIE CO., ST. JOSEPH (1890) [CEM 2] Rev. Dennis A. Fronczak.
Res.: 46 N. Main St., 14080-9509. Tel: 716-537-9434; Fax: 716-537-9988. Email: stjholland@roadrunner.com. Web: www.stjholland.org.
Catechesis/Religious Program—Tel: 716-655-2841; Fax: 716-537-9988. Cheryl Zielen-Ersing, D.R.E.

HOLLEY, ORLEANS CO., ST. MARY (1866) [CEM], Linked with St. Mark, Kendall. Rev. Mark J. Noonan.
Res.: 11 S. Main St., 14470-1107. Tel: 585-638-6718; Fax: 585-638-3210. Email: smysmk@yahoo.com. Web: www.forministry.com/usnyrcathsmr1/.
Catechesis/Religious Program—Dorothy Covell, D.R.E.

JAMESTOWN, CHAUTAUQUA CO.

1—HOLY APOSTLES (2008) [CEM 2] Rev. Dennis W. Mende; Deacon Samuel Pellerito.
Res.: 508 Cherry St., 14701. Tel: 716-664-5703; Fax: 716-664-5288. Email: sspp@netsync.net. Web: www.holyapostlesparish.org.
St. John Site: 270 Newton Ave., 14701.
See Holy Family Catholic School, Jamestown under Regional and Consolidated Elementary Schools located in the Institution section.
Catechesis/Religious Program—Tel: 716-484-8958; Fax: 716-484-8958.

2—ST. JAMES (1910) [CEM] Rev. Darrell G. Duffy; Deacon Michael Lennon, Financial Admin.
Res.: 27 Allen St., 14701. Tel: 716-487-0125; Fax: 716-661-3677.
See Holy Family Catholic School, Jamestown under Regional and Consolidated Elementary Schools located in the Institution section.
Catechesis/Religious Program—Tel: 716-664-4237. Email: faithform@windstream.net. Joanne Zdrojewski, C.R.E.
Oratory—Our Lady of Victory 6 Institute St., Frewsburg, 14738.

KENDALL, ORLEANS CO., ST. MARK (1984) Attended by St. Mary, Holley. Rev. Mark J. Noonan.
Office & Res.: 11 S. Main St., Holley, 14470-1107. Tel: 585-638-6718; Fax: 585-638-3210. Email:

smysmk@yahoo.com. Web: www.forministry.com/usnyrcathsmcsm.
Catechesis/Religious Program—Tel: 585-659-8631. Dorothy Covell, D.R.E.

KENMORE, ERIE CO.

1—ST. ANDREW (1944) Rev. Msgr. Richard W. Siepka; Deacon Stephen J. Swinarski; Theresa Bornholdt, Pastoral Assoc. In Res., Rev. Vincent J. Ferraro, Chap.
Res.: 1525 Sheridan Dr., 14217. Tel: 716-873-6716; Fax: 716-873-2214. Email: standrewkenmore@roadrunner.com. Web: standrewsrcchurch.org.
School—(Grades PreK-8), 1545 Sheridan Dr., 14217. Tel: 716-877-0422; Fax: 716-877-3973. Mrs. Susan Ferrio, Prin.; Cheryl Greene, Librarian. Lay Teachers 25; Students 244.
Catechesis/Religious Program—Tel: 716-877-3034. Maryanne Snyder, D.R.E.
Mission—St. Andrew Kim 9 O'Hara Rd., Tonawanda, Erie Co. 14150.

2—ST. JOHN THE BAPTIST (1836) [CEM] Revs. Michael J. Parker; David E. Tourville, Parochial Vicar.
Res.: 1085 Englewood Ave., 14223-1982. Tel: 716-873-1122; Fax: 716-873-3305.
School—(Grades PreK-8) Tel: 716-877-6401; Fax: 716-877-9139. Web: www.stjohnskenmore.com. Cynthia Jacobs, Prin.; Rosemary Leaper, Librarian. Lay Teachers 26; Students 294.
Catechesis/Religious Program—Tel: 716-877-0474. Catherine Salzman, D.R.E.; Andrea Cammarata, Youth Min.

3—ST. PAUL (1897) Rev. Jay W. McGinnis; Deacon Richard Parker.
Res.: 33 Victoria Blvd., 14217. Tel: 716-875-2730; Fax: 716-877-3874.
Catechesis/Religious Program—Tel: 716-873-9429.

LACKAWANNA, ERIE CO.

1—ST. ANTHONY (1917) Sr. Barbara Riter, S.S.M.N., Pastoral Admin.; Rev. Henry A. Orszulak, Sacramental Min.
Res.: 306 Ingham Ave., 14218-2511. Tel: 716-823-0782; Fax: 716-827-1381. Email: bizmgrstanthonys@roadrunner.com.
Catechesis/Religious Program—Tel: 716-827-8384.

2—OUR LADY OF BISTRICA (1917), (Croatian), Rev. Christopher Coric, O.F.M.Conv. (Croatia).
Res.: 1619 Abbott Rd., 14218. Tel: 716-822-0818; Fax: 716-823-1553.
Catechesis/Religious Program—

3—OUR LADY OF VICTORY NATIONAL SHRINE (1854) Rev. Msgr. Paul J.E. Burkard; Revs. Romulus Rosolowski, O.F.M.Conv.; David D Baker.
Res.: 767 Ridge Rd., 14218. Tel: 716-828-9444; Fax: 716-828-9429. Email: olvrectory@olv-bvs.org. Web: ourladyofvictory.org.
School—(Grades PreK-8) Tel: 716-828-9434; Fax: 716-828-9383. Email: olv@adelphia.net. Sr. Ellen O'Keefe, Prin. Sisters 4; Lay Teachers 14; Students 198.
Catechesis/Religious Program—Tel: 716-828-9437. Email: religioused@olv-bvs.org. Carmel Zomeri, D.R.E.

4—QUEEN OF ANGELS (2008), (Polish), Rev. John F. Kasprzak.
Res.: 144 Warsaw St., 14218. Tel: 716-826-0880; Fax: 716-828-1867.

LAKE VIEW, ERIE CO., BLESSED JOHN PAUL II (1922/2011) Rev. Peter J. Karalus; Sr. Sharon Erickson, R.S.M., Pastoral Assoc.; Deacons Mark J. Hooper; Neal M. Linnan. (Linked with St. Vincent, North Evans)
Res.: 2052 Lake View Ave., P.O. Box 115, 14085. Tel: 716-627-2910; Fax: 716-627-7972. Email: parish@blessedjpiiparish.org. Web: www.blessedjpiiparish.org.
See Southtowns Catholic, Lakeview under Regional and Consolidated Elementary Schools located in the Institution section.
Catechesis/Religious Program—Tel: 716-627-9397. Mrs. Barbara Manley, D.R.E.

LAKEWOOD, CHAUTAUQUA CO., SACRED HEART (1912) [JC] Rev. Msgr. Joseph M. Dowdell.
Res.: 380 E. Fairmount Ave., 14750-2197. Tel: 716-763-2815; Fax: 716-763-5646. Email: mail@sacredheartlakewood.org. Web: www.sacredheartlakewood.org.
Panama Site: Our Lady of the Snows Church,: Panama, 14767.
See Holy Family Catholic School, Jamestown under Regional and Consolidated Elementary Schools located in the Institution section.
Catechesis/Religious Program—Marilyn Wozneak, Pastoral Assoc. & D.R.E.

LANCASTER, ERIE CO.

1—ST. MARY OF THE ASSUMPTION (1850) [CEM] Rev. Paul W. Steller.
Res.: 1 St. Mary's Hill, 14086-2094. Tel: 716-683-6445; Fax: 716-684-8446.
School—(Grades PreK-8) Tel: 716-683-2112; Fax: 716-683-2134. Email: driscollj@smeschool.org. Miss Jane Driscoll, Prin. Sisters of Third Order of St. Francis 1; Lay Teachers 20; Students 291.
Catechesis/Religious Program—2 St. Mary's Hill, 14086. Tel: 716-683-8564; Fax: 716-693-2134. Mrs. Elaine Driscoll, D.R.E.

2—OUR LADY OF POMPEII (1909/2008) Rev. Leon J. Biernat; Sr. M. Joyce Frances King, C.S.S.F., Pastoral Assoc.; Deacons Gregory L. Feary; John P. Gaulin.
Res.: 158 Laverack Ave., 14086. Tel: 716-683-6522; Fax: 716-685-8066. Email: ladyofpompeii@yahoo.com. Web: www.olpparish.com.
School—(Grades K-8) Tel: 716-684-4664; Fax: 716-684-4699. Mrs. Diane Liptak, Prin. Lay Teachers 15; Students 84.
Catechesis/Religious Program—Michael Denz, D.R.E.

LANGFORD, ERIE CO., EPIPHANY OF OUR LORD (1851/2006) [CEM] Rev. Robert J. Schober.
Res.: 10893 Sisson Hwy. (Langford), North Collins, 14111. Tel: 716-337-2686; Fax: 716-337-0028. Email: epiphanyparish@gmail.com.
See St. Aloysius Regional School, Springville under Regional and Consolidated Elementary Schools located in the Institution section.
Catechesis/Religious Program—Tel: 716-337-2686, Ext. 6.

LEROY, GENESEE CO., OUR LADY OF MERCY (2008) [CEM], (Linked with St. Brigid Parish, Bergen) Revs. Michael R. Rock, O.de.M.; Timothy Brady, O.de.M., Parochial Vicar; Deacon David C. Ehrhart.
Res.: 44 Lake St., Le Roy, 14482. Tel: 585-768-6543; Fax: 585-768-7093. Email: frmike@ourladyofmercyleroy.org. Web: www.ourladyofmercyleroy.org.
School—Holy Family Regional School, (Grades K-8) Tel: 585-768-7390; Fax: 585-768-6680. Mr. Kevin Robertson, Prin.; Mrs. Amy Drake, Librarian. Lay Teachers 13; Students 109.
Catechesis/Religious Program—Tel: 585-768-6720.
Oratory—St. Joseph 27 Lake St., Le Roy, 14482.

LEWISTON, NIAGARA CO., ST. PETER (1851) Rev. Michael P. Zuffoletto.
Res.: 620 Center St., 14092. Tel: 716-754-4118; Fax: 716-754-4120. Email: stpeterlewiston@wny.twcbc.com. Web: www.stpeterlewiston.net.
School—(Grades PreK-8), 140 N. 6th St., 14092. Tel: 716-754-4470; Fax: 716-754-0167. Web: www-.stpeterrc.org. Mr. Denis Coakley, Prin.; Mrs. Sandra Jordan, Librarian. Lay Teachers 17; Students 129.
Catechesis/Religious Program—Tel: 716-754-2812; Fax: 716-754-0167. Email: reled@adelphia.net.

LIMESTONE, CATTARAUGUS CO., ST. PATRICK (1875) [CEM], (Linked with Our Lady of Peace, Salamanca) Rev. F. Patrick Melfi; Deacon Michael L. Anderson.
Res.: 5823 Church St., 14753. Tel: 716-925-8596; Fax: 716-925-7319. Email: stpatrickslimestone@yahoo.com.
Catechesis/Religious Program—

LOCKPORT, NIAGARA CO.

1—ALL SAINTS (2008) [CEM] Rev. Joseph E. Vatter; Deacon Donald R. Watkins Jr.; Sr. Rene Ruberto, S.S.M.N., Pastoral Assoc. In Res., Revs. Gerald L. Bartko, O.S.F.S.; Francis M. Schimscheiner, O.S.F.S.
Office: 76 Church St., 14094. Tel: 716-433-3707; Fax: 716-438-5608. Email: allsaintslockport@verizon.net. Web: www.allsaintslockport.org.
See DeSales Catholic School, Lockport under Regional and Consolidated Elementary Schools located in the Institution section.
Catechesis/Religious Program—Tel: 716-434-3194; 716-433-5792. Sally Sayward, D.R.E.
Oratory—St. Joseph 391 Market St., 14094.
Worship Site: St. Mary—5 Saxton St., 14094.

2—ST. JOHN THE BAPTIST (1834) Revs. James A. Waite; Joseph C. Dumphrey, O.S.F.S.
Res.: 168 Chestnut St., 14094. Tel: 716-433-8118; Fax: 716-433-3562. Web: stjohnslockport.org.
See DeSales Catholic School, Lockport under Regional and Consolidated Elementary Schools located in the Institution section.
Catechesis/Religious Program—Tel: 716-433-5792. Sally Sayward, D.R.E.

MEDINA, ORLEANS CO., HOLY TRINITY (2008) [CEM] Rev. Daniel J. Fawls.
Res.: 211 Eagle St., 14103. Tel: 585-798-0112; Fax: 585-798-2834.
Middleport Site: 21 Vernon St., Middleport, 14105.
Catechesis/Religious Program—Tel: 585-798-5399.

NEWFANE, NIAGARA CO., ST. BRENDAN ON THE LAKE (2008) [CEM] Rev. Robert A. Wozniak; Deacon David H. Harvey.
Res.: 3455 Ewings Rd., Box 87, 14108-0087. Tel: 716-778-9822; Fax: 716-778-8786. Email: office@stbrendanonthelake.org. Web: www.stbrendanonthelake.org.
Wilson Site: 359 Lake St., Wilson, 14172.
Catechesis/Religious Program—Ms. Mary Palmer, C.R.E.
Oratory—St. Charles Borromeo 5972 Main St., Olcott, 14126.

NIAGARA FALLS, NIAGARA CO.

1—DIVINE MERCY (2008), (Linked with St. Mary of the Cataract, Niagara Falls) Rev. Jacek P. Mazur; Deacon David P. Slish.
Office: 2437 Niagara St., 14303. Tel: 716-285-3604; Fax: 716-282-2297.
Res.: 259 Fourth St., 14303. Tel: 716-282-0059; 716-284-6641.
Catechesis/Religious Program—

2—HOLY FAMILY OF JESUS, MARY AND JOSEPH (2008), (Italian), [CEM] Rev. Duane R. Klizek. In Res., Revs. John L. Graden, O.S.F.S.; Stewart M. Lindsay, O.S.F.S.; Bros. Fred Chiappone, O.S.F.S.; John Ventresca, O.S.F.S.
Office: 1413 Pine Ave., 14301. Tel: 716-282-1379; Fax: 716-285-3704. Web: www.holyfamilyrcchurch.org.
Res.: 2486 Grand Ave., 14301.
Catechesis/Religious Program—Mrs. Rae Pullo, D.R.E.

3—ST. JOHN DE LA SALLE (1907) Rev. Slawomir Siok, S.A.C.
Office & Res.: 8477 Buffalo Ave., 14304. Tel: 716-283-2238; Fax: 716-283-7973. Email: stjohndelasalle@juno.com. Web: www.stjohndelasalle.org.
Catechesis/Religious Program—Tel: 716-283-2238, Ext. 307.

4—ST. MARY OF THE CATARACT (1847), (Linked with Divine Mercy, Niagara Falls) Rev. Jacek P. Mazur. In Res., Bro. Francis Murray, O.S.F.S.
Res.: 259 Fourth St., 14303. Tel: 716-282-0059; Fax: 716-282-3372. Email: stmaryniagara@aol.com. Web: stmaryofthecataract.com.
Catechesis/Religious Program—

5—ST. RAPHAEL (2008) Rev. Ivan Skenderovic.
Res.: 3840 Macklem Ave., 14305. Tel: 716-282-5583; Fax: 716-282-0453. Email: st.raphael_parish@verizon.net.
Catechesis/Religious Program—Tel: 716-282-0795; Fax: 716-282-2447. Maria Gleason, C.R.E.

6—ST. VINCENT DE PAUL (2008) Rev. Robert S. Hughson.
Res.: 1040 Cayuga Dr., 14304. Tel: 716-283-2715; Fax: 716-283-5635. Email: r.s.hughson@roadrunner.com.
Prince of Peace Site: 1055 N. Military Rd., 14304.
St. Leo Site: 2748 Military Rd., 14304.
Catechesis/Religious Program—Tel: 716-297-5010.

NORTH COLLINS, ERIE CO., HOLY SPIRIT (1951) [CEM 2] Rev. Walter P. Grabowski. (Linked with Immaculate Conception, Eden)
Office: 2017 Halley Rd., 14111. Tel: 716-337-3701; Fax: 716-337-3803. Email: hschurch@roadrunner.com.
Catechesis/Religious Program—Marge Awald, D.R.E.

NORTH TONAWANDA, NIAGARA CO.

1—ST. JUDE THE APOSTLE (2007) Rev. Edward F. Jost; Deacons Daniel E. Brick Esq.; Gary C. Terrana.
Office: 1510 Kingston Ave., 14120. Tel: 716-694-0540; Fax: 716-694-8943. Email: stjudetheapostle@roadrunner.com.
Catechesis/Religious Program—Tel: 716-694-4540.

2—OUR LADY OF CZESTOCHOWA (1903), (Polish), Rev. Gary J. Szczepankiewicz; Deacon Paul J. Schnettler.
Ministry Center: 57 Center Ave., 14120. Tel: 716-693-3822; Fax: 716-693-3882. Web: www.ntolc.org.
Res.: 64 Center Ave., 14120.
Catechesis/Religious Program—Tel: 716-694-3644.

OAKFIELD, GENESEE CO., ST. PADRE PIO (2009) [CEM], Merged parish with two sites. Rev. Arthur E. Mattulke. In Res., Rev. Patrick T. O'Keefe.
Res.: 56 Maple Ave., 14125. Tel: 585-948-5344; Fax: 585-948-8239. Email: office@padrepiony.org.
Elba Site: 65 S. Main St., Elba, 14058-0185. Tel: 716-757-6891; Fax: 716-757-2472.
Catechesis/Religious Program—
Oratory—St. Patrick Lewiston Rd. at Knowlesville Rd., Wheatville, Genesee Co. 14013. Tel: 585-948-5344; Fax: 585-948-8239.

OLEAN, CATTARAUGUS CO.

1—ST. JOHN (1896) Rev. Edward J. Sheedy.
Res.: 931 N. Union St., 14760. Tel: 716-372-5313; Fax: 716-373-0919. Email: stjohnsofolean@verizon.net.
See Southern Tier Catholic, Olean under Regional and Consolidated Elementary Schools located in the Institution section.
Catechesis/Religious Program—Tel: 716-372-6633; Fax: 716-795-3919.
Oratory—Transfiguration 1102 Walnut St, Cattaraugus Co. 14760.

2—ST. MARY OF THE ANGELS (1876) Rev. Gregory J. Dobson; Deacon Richard F. Matthews.
Res.: 202 S. Union St., 14760. Tel: 716-372-4841; Fax: 716-372-5905. Email: ram@smaolean.org. Web:

www.smaolean.org.
See Southern Tier Catholic, Olean under Regional and Consolidated Elementary Schools located in the Institution section.
Catechesis/Religious Program—Tel: 716-372-4841, Ext. 24. Sr. Regina G. Aman, C.R.E.
Oratory—Oratory of the Sacred Heart 43 Maple Ave., Portville, 14770.

ORCHARD PARK, ERIE CO.

1—ST. BERNADETTE (1957) Rev. Paul D. Seil; Deacons Edward R. Howard; Lawrence P. Markowski.
Res.: 5930 S. Abbott Rd., 14127-4516. Tel: 716-649-3090; Fax: 716-649-0211.
School—(Grades K-8) Tel: 716-649-3369. Mr. Corey Pecorella, Prin. Lay Teachers 15; Students 192.
Catechesis/Religious Program—Tel: 716-648-1720. Georgette Jebb, D.R.E.

2—ST. JOHN VIANNEY (1958) Rev. Msgr. William J. Gallagher.
Res.: 2950 Southwestern Blvd., 14127. Tel: 716-674-9133; Fax: 716-674-9134. Email: sjv2950@yahoo.org.
School—(Grades PreK-8) Tel: 716-674-9232; Fax: 716-674-9248. Email: sjvoffice@yahoo.com. Web: stjohnvianney.com. Teresa A. Siuta, Prin.; Sr. Francianne Zielezinski, C.S.S.F., Librarian & Computer Tech. Sisters 1; Lay Teachers 17; Students 192.
Catechesis/Religious Program—Tel: 716-674-9145. Christine Lawrence, D.R.E.

3—NATIVITY OF OUR LORD (1908) [CEM] Rev. Bernard U. Nowak; Deacons Gary P. Andelora; Dennis P. Conroy.
Res.: 26 Thorn Ave., 14127. Tel: 716-662-9339; Fax: 716-662-2195.
School—(Grades PreK-8) Tel: 716-662-7572. Ruth Frost, Prin. Sisters of St. Francis of Penance and Christian Charity 1; Lay Teachers 18; Students 195.
Catechesis/Religious Program—Tel: 716-662-2169. Mary Barone, D.R.E.

4—OUR LADY OF THE SACRED HEART (1920) Rev. Adolph M. Kowalczyk; Deacons William J. Walkowiak; Frank S. Polizzi; Robert T. Ciezki.
Res.: 3148 Abbott Rd., 14127. Tel: 716-824-2935; Fax: 716-827-7643. Email: rectory@olshop.org. Web: www.olshop.org.
School—(Grades PreK-8), 3144 Abbott Rd., 14127. Tel: 716-824-8208; Fax: 716-824-8799. Email: olshschool@aol.com. Web: www.ourladyofthesacredheart.com. Christopher Gordon, Prin. Sisters of Mercy 1; Lay Teachers 13; Students 162.
Catechesis/Religious Program—Tel: 716-824-8209. Paula White, C.R.E.; Lynn Lipczynski, C.R.E.

PAVILION, GENESEE CO., MARY IMMACULATE (1865/2010) [CEM] Rev. Richard J. Cilano. (Merged parish with two sites: Pavilion and East Bethany)
Office: 5865 Ellicott St., East Bethany, 14054. Tel: 585-343-4537; Fax: 585-250-4213.
Res.: 11095 Saint Mary St., P.O. Box 442, 14525. Tel: 585-584-7031; Fax: 585-584-8628. Email: stmarys@rochester.rr.com.
Catechesis/Religious Program—

PENDLETON, NIAGARA CO., GOOD SHEPHERD (1847/2009) [CEM], Parish with two sites: Pendleton; Clarence. Rev. Daniel A. Young; Deacon Robert Bauer.
Office & Res.: 5442 Tonawanda Creek Rd., North Tonawanda, 14120-9699. Tel: 716-625-8594; Fax: 716-625-8365. Web: www.goodshepherd-staugustine.org.
Clarence Center Site: *St. Augustine Campus*, 8700 Goodrich Rd., Clarence Center, 14032.
Catechesis/Religious Program—Tel: 716-625-8817. Email: good.shepherd5442@gmail.com. Michele Ranke, C.R.E.

PERRY, WYOMING CO., ST. ISIDORE (2008) [CEM] Rev. Richard W. Blazejewski; Deacon Daniel J. McGuire.
Res.: 8 Park St., 14530. Tel: 585-237-2625; Fax: 585-237-0150.
Catechesis/Religious Program—

RANDOLPH, CATTARAUGUS CO., ST. PATRICK (1853) [CEM], (Linked with Our Lady of Loreto, Falconer) Rev. Joseph P. Janaczek.
Res.: 309 W. Everett St., Falconer, 14733. Tel: 716-665-4253; Fax: 716-664-9223. Email: st.patrickschurch@live.com.
See Catholic Academy of the Holy Family, Jamestown under Regional and Consolidated Elementary Schools located in the Institution section.
Catechesis/Religious Program—

RANSOMVILLE, NIAGARA CO., IMMACULATE CONCEPTION (1891) Rev. Joseph P. Badding; Deacon Paul S. Stankiewicz.
Office: 4671 Townline Rd., Rte. 429, 14131-9740. Tel: 716-731-4822; Fax: 716-731-4911.
Res.: 4720 Plank Rd., Lockport, 14094.
Catechesis/Religious Program—Tel: 716-731-5387.

RUSHFORD, ALLEGANY CO., ST. MARK (1948) Rev. Francis J. Jann (Retired).
Mailing Address: P.O. Box 37, 14777. Tel: 585-365-9977; Fax: 585-437-5332.
Res.: 7693 State Rte. 243, Caneadea, 14717.
Catechesis/Religious Program—284 Broad St., Salamanca, 14779.

SALAMANCA, CATTARAUGUS CO., OUR LADY OF PEACE (2007), (Linked with St. Patrick, Limestone) Rev. F. Patrick Melfi; Deacon Michael L. Anderson.
Res.: 79 River St., 14779-1414. Tel: 716-945-2666; Fax: 716-945-0676.
Catechesis/Religious Program—

SANBORN, NIAGARA CO., HOLY FAMILY (1953), (Tuscarora Native Americans) Rev. Peter M. Calabrese, C.R.S.P.
Res.: 1023 Swan Rd., P.O. Box 167, Youngstown, 14174-0167. Tel: 716-754-7489; Fax: 716-754-9130. Email: pmccrsp@fatimashrine.com.
Church: 5180 Chew Rd., 14132. Tel: 716-523-9114.
Catechesis/Religious Program—

SARDINIA, ERIE CO., ST. JUDE (1953) Rev. Alfons M. Osiander.
Res.: 12820 Genesee Rd., P.O. Box 267, 14134-0267. Tel: 716-496-7535; Fax: 716-496-7535.
See St. Aloysius Regional School, Springville under Regional and Consolidated Elementary Schools located in the Institution section.
Catechesis/Religious Program—Tel: 716-496-5419.

SILVER CREEK, CHAUTAUQUA CO., OUR LADY OF MT. CARMEL (1882/2008) [CEM], Parish with two sites. Rev. Daniel F. Fiebelkorn.
Res.: 165 Central Ave., 14136. Tel: 716-934-2233; Fax: 716-934-6216.
Forestville Site: 11 Center St., Forestville, 14062.
See Northern Chautauqua Catholic, Dunkirk under Regional and Consolidated Elementary Schools located in the Institution section.
Catechesis/Religious Program—Tel: 716-934-4891.

SLOAN, ERIE CO., ST. ANDREW (1915) Rev. Fabian J. Maryanski.
Res.: 34 Francis Ave., 14212. Tel: 716-892-0425; Fax: 716-892-3092.
Catechesis/Religious Program—Sr. M. Therese Chmura, C.S.S.F., Dir. Faith Formation.
Convent—Felician Sisters, 17 Gierlach St., 14212. Tel: 716-893-1007.

SNYDER, ERIE CO., CHRIST THE KING (1926) Rev. John R. Gaglione. In Res., Rev. Joseph Klos.
Res.: 30 Lamarck Dr., 14226. Tel: 716-839-1430; Fax: 716-839-1433. Web: www.ctksnyder.com.
School—(Grades PreK-8), 2 Lamarck Dr., 14226. Tel: 716-839-0473; Fax: 716-568-8198. Samuel T. Zalacca, Prin. Lay Teachers 22; Students 259.
Catechesis/Religious Program—Tel: 716-839-0946.

SPRINGBROOK, ERIE CO., ST. VINCENT (1850) [CEM] Rev. James A. Walter; Deacons Richard F. Mackiewicz; Peter Walders; Lawrence D. Eschbach.
Res.: 6441 Seneca St., P.O. Box 290, 14140. Tel: 716-652-3972; Fax: 716-655-3048. Web: www.stvincentsspringbrook.4lpi.com.
School—(Grades K-8) Tel: 716-652-8697. Mrs. Lisa Meegan, Prin.; Debbie Bonk, Librarian. Lay Teachers 12; Students 166.
Catechesis/Religious Program—Tel: 716-652-7242. Susan Denz, D.R.E.

SPRINGVILLE, ERIE CO., ST. ALOYSIUS (1853) [CEM], (Linked with St. John the Baptist, West Valley) Rev. Lawrence F. Cobel.
Res.: 190 Franklin St., 14141-1199. Tel: 716-592-2701; Fax: 716-592-4347.
See St. Aloysius Regional School, Springville under Regional and Consolidated Elementary Schools located in the Institution section.
Catechesis/Religious Program—Tel: 716-592-4869; Fax: 716-592-4869.
Convent—Sisters of St. Francis, 71 W. Main St., 14141. Tel: 716-592-7601.

STRYKERSVILLE, WYOMING CO., ST. JOHN NEUMANN (2008) [CEM] Rev. Matthew J. Zirnheld.
Res.: 3854 Main St., P.O. Box 9, 14145-0009. Tel: 585-457-3222.
Sheldon Site: 991 Centerline Rd., 14145-9553. Tel: 585-457-9437; Fax: 585-535-0477.
Catechesis/Religious Program—
Oratory—St. Patrick 1468 Main St., Java Center, 14082.

SWORMVILLE, ERIE CO., ST. MARY (1849) [CEM] Revs. Robert M. Yetter; Gary R. Kibler Sr., Parochial Vicar; Deacons Paul Snyder; Gary M. Hoover.
Res.: 6919 Transit Rd., Box 460, 14051. Tel: 716-688-9380; Fax: 716-688-6025. Email: stmaryswormville@roadrunner.com. Web: www.stmaryswormville.org.
School—(Grades PreK-8) Tel: 716-689-8424; Fax: 716-689-8424. Web: www.stmaryschoolswormville.org. Sisters Sheila Anne Burke, O.S.F., Prin.; Suzanne Hitzges, O.S.F., Librarian. Sisters of the Third Order of St. Francis 2; Lay Teachers 17; Students 200.
Catechesis/Religious Program—Tel: 716-688-0599; Fax: 716-639-8891. Email: reled14051@roadrunner.com.

TONAWANDA, ERIE CO.

1—ST. AMELIA (1953) Rev. Msgr. Thomas F. Maloney; Rev. Ryszard S. Biernat; Sr. Helen Buscarino, F.M.D.C., Pastoral Assoc.; Brian Ruh, Pastoral Assoc.; Judy Reitz, Pastoral Assoc. In Res., Rev. Donald L. Measer (Retired).
Res.: 210 St. Amelia Dr., 14150. Tel: 716-836-0011; Fax: 716-832-5439. Web: www.stamelia.com.
School—(Grades PreK-8), 2999 Eggert Rd., 14150. Tel: 716-836-2230; Fax: 716-832-9700. Email: office@stameliaschool.org. Web: www.stameliaschool.org. James Mule, Prin. Sisters 1; Lay Teachers 36; Students 538.
Catechesis/Religious Program—Tel: 716-833-8647. Elaine Volker, C.R.E.

2—ST. ANDREW KIM (1993), Mission for Korean Catholics. Rev. Cheong-il Bak, Admin.
Mailing Address: 9 O'Hara Rd., 14150. Tel: 716-693-7116; Fax: 716-693-1600. Web: www.bukoca.cyworld.com.
Catechesis/Religious Program—

3—BLESSED SACRAMENT (1929) Rev. William J. Quinlivan; Sr. M. Lucette Kinecki, C.S.S.F., Pastoral Assoc. In Res., Rev. Msgr. Leo F. McCarthy (Retired).
Res.: 263 Claremont Ave., 14223. Tel: 716-834-4282; Fax: 716-834-9573. Web: www.bsacramentchurch.com.
Catechesis/Religious Program—Tel: 716-832-6161. Josephine Palumbo, D.R.E.

4—ST. CHRISTOPHER (1928) Revs. Charles E. Slisz; Steven A. Jekielek, Parochial Vicar; Deacons Francis A. Zwack; David P. McDermott; Thomas R. Healey.
Church & Parish Office: 2660 Niagara Falls Blvd., 14150-1499. Tel: 716-692-2660; Fax: 716-693-5639. Email: rectory@saintchris.org. Web: www.stchris.org.
Res. & Outreach: *St. Edmund Campus*, 530 Ellicott Creek Rd., 14150.
School—(Grades PreK-8) Tel: 716-693-5604; Fax: 716-693-5127. Email: school@saintchris.org. Mrs. Jenny Bainbridge, Prin. Lay Teachers 29; Students 472.
Catechesis/Religious Program—Tel: 716-694-4310. Email: reled@saintchris.org.

5—ST. FRANCIS OF ASSISI (1852) [CEM] Rev. Michael G. Uebler.
Res.: 73 Adam St., 14150. Tel: 716-693-1150; Fax: 716-693-2025.
School—(Grades PreK-8) Tel: 716-692-7886. Colleen Politowski, Prin. Lay Teachers 19; Students 183.
Catechesis/Religious Program—Tel: 716-694-5342.

6—ST. TIMOTHY (1960) Rev. Dennis F. Fronckowiak; Deacon Gordon J. Steinagle.
Res.: 565 E. Park Dr., 14150. Tel: 716-875-9430; Fax: 716-931-5237. Email: sttimothyrcchurc@aol.com.
Catechesis/Religious Program—

WARSAW, WYOMING CO., ST. MICHAEL (1858) [CEM] Rev. James W. Hartwell; Deacon John J. Kelly.
Res.: 171 N. Main St., 14569. Tel: 585-786-2400; Fax: 585-786-3977. Web: stmichaelswarsaw.com.
Catechesis/Religious Program—

WELLSVILLE, ALLEGANY CO., IMMACULATE CONCEPTION (1850) [CEM], Providing Sacramental Ministry to St. Mary, Bolivar. Revs. Sean E. DiMaria; Thomas J. Roman, Parochial Vicar; Deacon Michael A. Gomola.
Res.: 6 Maple Ave., 14895. Tel: 585-593-4834; Fax: 585-593-7167. Email: icclynv@roadrunner.com.
Immaculate Conception School of Allegany County. See Regional and Consolidated Schools located in the Institution section.
Catechesis/Religious Program—Tel: 585-593-4834; Fax: 585-593-5846. Mrs. Mary Ann Newark, D.R.E.

WEST FALLS, ERIE CO., ST. GEORGE (Jewettville) (1942/2008) Rev. Pascal D. Ipolito.
Res.: 74 Old Glenwood Rd., 14170. Tel: 716-652-3153; Fax: 716-687-1336. Email: info@stgeorgercchurch.org.
Catechesis/Religious Program—Tel: 716-652-0126.

WEST SENECA, ERIE CO.

1—BLESSED JOHN XXIII (2008) Rev. Dennis G. Wolf; Marianne Hubert, Pastoral Assoc.
Office: 36 Flohr Ave., 14224. Tel: 716-823-1090; Fax: 716-825-4376.
Catechesis/Religious Program—Tel: 716-825-5053. Sharon Voigt, D.R.E.

2—FOURTEEN HOLY HELPERS (1864) [CEM] Rev. David A. Bellittiere; Deacon Thomas E. Scherr. In Res., Rev. Robert M. Mock.
Res.: 1345 Indian Church Rd., 14224. Tel: 716-674-2374; Fax: 716-675-4864.
School—(Grades PreK-8), 1339 Indian Church Rd., 14224. Tel: 716-674-1670. MaryJo Aiken, Prin.; Mrs. Susan Gerard, Librarian. Lay Teachers 20; Students 185.
Catechesis/Religious Program—Tel: 716-674-2180. Cindy Tippett, D.R.E.

3—QUEEN OF HEAVEN (1955) Revs. Thomas J. Quinlivan; Daniel J. Serbicki, Parochial Vicar; Deacon John M. Ruh.
Res.: 4220 Seneca St., 14224. Tel: 716-674-3468; Fax: 716-674-3475.
School—(Grades PreK-8), 839 Mill Rd., 14224. Tel:

716-674-5206; Fax: 716-674-2793. Miss Barbara Ryan, Prin. Lay Teachers 20; Students 221.
Catechesis/Religious Program—Tel: 716-675-3714. Barbara Maloney, D.R.E.; Elaine Kishbaugh, C.R.E.

WEST VALLEY, CATTARAUGUS CO., ST. JOHN THE BAPTIST (1904) [CEM], (Linked with St. Aloysius, Springville) Rev. Lawrence F. Cobel.
Res.: 5381 Depot St., P.O. Box 315, 14171-0315. Tel: 716-942-3259; Fax: 716-942-3259.
See St. Aloysius Regional School, Springville under Regional and Consolidated Elementary Schools located in the Institution section.
Catechesis/Religious Program—Tel: 716-942-6874. Janet Vant, D.R.E.

WESTFIELD, CHAUTAUQUA CO., ST. DOMINIC (2008) [CEM 2] Revs. Marius Walter, O.S.B.; Sean Duggan, O.S.B.; Deacon William J. Boneberg.
Office & Westfield Site: 15 Union St., 14787-1494. Tel: 716-326-2816; Fax: 716-326-4863. Email: stdominic@fairpoint.net.
Brocton Site: 12 Central Ave., Brocton, 14716-0675.
Catechesis/Religious Program—Tel: 716-326-3003. Alicia E. Quagliana, C.R.E.

WILLIAMSVILLE, ERIE CO., SS. PETER AND PAUL (1836) [CEM 2] Rev. Jerome E. Kopec; Mr. Robert Grinewich, Pastoral Assoc.
Office & Res.: 17 Grove St., 14221. Tel: 716-632-2559; Fax: 716-204-0329.
School—(Grades PreK-8), 5480 Main St., 14221. Tel: 716-632-6146; Fax: 716-626-0971. Mrs. Marianne Maines, Prin. Lay Teachers 27; Students 409.
Catechesis/Religious Program—Tel: 716-632-2678. Roberta Spencer, D.R.E.; Casey Hanley, Sacramental Coord.

YOUNGSTOWN, NIAGARA CO., ST. BERNARD'S (1946) [CEM] Rev. Msgr. J. Thomas Moran.
Res.: 218 Hinman St., 14174. Tel: 716-745-7460; Fax: 716-745-1359.
Catechesis/Religious Program—Mrs. Donna Parent, D.R.E.

Chaplains of Public Institutions

BUFFALO. *Buffalo Fire Department and Erie County Emergency Services*. Revs. Joseph Bayne, O.F.M.Conv., Arthur J. Smith, Asst. Chap.
Buffalo General Hospital. Revs. Patrick O. Fernandes, Richard H. Augustyn.
Erie County Medical Center. Rev. Francis X. Mazur.
Hope House. Deacon Terry P. Harter.
Millard Fillmore Hospital. Sr. Mary Lou Schnitzer, S.S.J.
Roswell Park Memorial Institute. Rev. Raymond G. Corbin, Deacons Neal M. Linnan, David R. Velasquez.
Sheehan Memorial Emergency Hospital. Rev. Roy T. Herberger.
Veterans Hospital. Revs. Christopher Coric, O.F.M-.Conv. (Croatia), Patrick Gardocki, O.F.M. (Poland), Michael J. Putich, O.F.M.
Women and Children's Hospital. Sr. Brenda Whelan, R.S.M., Deacon Gary P. Andelora.

ALBION. *Albion Correctional Facility*.
Orleans Correctional Facility. Deacons Thomas Bringenberg Jr., Heinz H. Friedman, Chap.

ALDEN. *Erie County Correctional Facility*, 11581 Walden Ave., 14004. Tel: 716-937-9101. Rev. Robert Moreno (STF).
Erie County Home, 11580 Walden Ave., 14004. Tel: 716-937-5693. Rev. Robert Moreno (STF), Deacon Joseph A. Pasquella.
Wende Correctional Facility. Rev. Thomas D. Doyle, Chap., Deacons Gordon J. Steinagle, Timothy J. Maloney.

AMHERST. *Millard Fillmore Suburban Hospital*. Rev. Stepan Kuklich (STF), Chap., Sr. Mary Lou Schnitzer, S.S.J., Deacons Paul L. Snyder III, Daniel U. Golinski.

ATTICA. *Attica Correctional Facility*. Rev. Ivan R. Trujillo, Sr. Rosalind Rosolowski, C.S.S.F.
Wyoming Correctional Facility. Deacon Brian C. Walkowiak.

BATAVIA. *Crossroads House*. Deacon David C. Ehrhart.
Genesee County Nursing Home. Deacon Walter T. Szczesny.
U.S. Department of Immigration & Naturalization Federal Detention Center. Rev. John J. Mattimore, S.J., Chap.
United Memorial Medical Center. Rev. Richard J. Cilano.

COLLINS. *Collins Correctional Facility*. Rev. John S. Kwiecien, Deacons John H. Burke, Peter J. Walders.

CUBA. *Cuba Memorial Hospital and Adult Day Care Facility*. Deacon Michael R. Bray.

GOWANDA. *Gowanda Correctional Facility*. Deacons Carlos W. Ramos, Timothy J. Maloney, Chap.
Tri-County Hospital. Deacon Frederick M. Johnson Jr.

LAKEVIEW. *Lakeview Shock Incarceration Correctional Facility*. Revs. Stepan Kuklich (STF), Walter Werbicki.

LANCASTER. *Elderwood Health Care*. Deacon Samuel G. Puleo.

LOCKPORT. *Niagara Hospice*. Deacon Michael J. Canzoneri.
Lockport Presbyterian Home. Deacon David H. Harvey.

NIAGARA FALLS. *Niagara Falls Memorial Medical Center*. Deacon Gary C. Terrana, Chap.

OLEAN. *Olean General Hospital*. Deacon Michael L. Anderson, Sr. Dana Hollis, O.S.F.

TOWN OF NIAGARA. *Police and Fire Departments*. Deacon Benjamin R. Marino.

WESTFIELD. *Absolute Center for Nursing & Rehabilitation*. Deacon William J. Boneberg.

WEST SENECA. *Seneca Heath Care Center*. Deacon John M. Ruh.
WNY Children's Psychiatric Center. Deacon Carlton M. Koester.

WILLIAMSVILLE. *Gateway - Longview Residence for Youth*. Deacon Michael G. Bochiechio.
Park Creek Senior Living Community. Sr. Mary Lou Schnitzer, S.S.J.

On Duty Outside the Diocese:
Revs.—
Bordonaro, Richard D., 26340 Soboba St., P.O. Box 5268, Hemet, CA 92544.
Furlong, Richard V., 17 Jethol Dr., Assonet, MA 02702.
Mack, John P., St. Michael University, Toronto, Canada
Nielsen, Kenneth M., Kentwood Village Apts., 246 Kentwood Blvd., Brook, NJ 08724.
Wild, Robert A., Madonna House, Combermere ON Canada.
Zaczynski, Piotr F., St. Joseph Parish, 606 E. Fourth St., Sault Sainte Marie, MI 49783.
Zilliox, Robert W., c/o St. Paul's College, 3015 4th St., N.E., Ste. 112, Washington, DC 20017-1199.

Military Chaplains:
Revs.—
Kelly, John E., USN, CHC, NWS Charleston, Base Chapel, 2316 Redbank Rd., Ste. 100, Goose Creek, SC 29445.
Koester, Timothy J., NAVSTA Pearl Harbor, 800 Ticonderoga St., Pearl Harbor, HI 96860.

Absent on Leave:
Revs.—
Bagienski, Ronald A., (Med.)
Bialkowski, David W.
Budez, Jorge H.
Elis, Patrick H.
Juran, Michael P., (Med.)
Moss, Robert D., (Med.)
Stelmach, Jerome J., (Med.)
Swartz, Michael R.

Awaiting Assignment:
Rev. Msgr.—
Sicari, Joseph J.
Revs.—
Allaire, Barry J.
Venne, Samuel J.

Retired:
Rev. Msgrs.—
Ayoub, S. Paul, 10689 Camarelle Cr., Fort Myers, FL 33913.
Becker, Vincent J., 3532 Rte. 77, Varysburg, 14167.
Belzer, Paul J., 368 Everett Pl., Tonawanda, 14150.
Biniszkiewicz, Leonard E., Bishop Head Residence, 10 Rosary Ave., Lackawanna, 14218.
Boruszewski, Joseph A., 29 Tamark Ct., Upper, Cheektowaga, 14227.
Braun, Francis, Sheehan Residence, 330 Linwood Ave., 14209.
Bugman, John H., 107 Parkhaven Dr., Amherst, 14228.
Cahill, Richard M., 1825 Alberta Dr., Clearwater, FL 33756.
Caligiuri, Angelo M., O'Hara Residence, 69 O'Hara Rd., Tonawanda, 14150-6224.
Caligiuri, Anthony J., O'Hara Residence, 69 O'Hara Rd., Tonawanda, 14150-6227.
Clody, Albert W., 308 Edgewater Dr., Westfield, 14787.
Connelly, James N., O'Hara Residence, 69 O'Hara Rd., Apt. 3, Tonawanda, 14150-6227.
Crane, Thomas E., O'Hara Residence, 69 O'Hara Rd., Tonawanda, 14150-6227.
DelVecchio, Michael E., P.O. Box 22, Orchard Park, 14127.
Ducette, John I., 8121 Valle Dr., Apt. C 3, Niagara Falls, 14304.
Engelhardt, Herbert G., 5539 Broadway, Apt. 155, Lancaster, 14086-2223.
Faiola, Samuel J., S.T.D., 72B Lexington Ct., Lockport, 14094-5365.
Gill, Richard, 103 E. 7th St., Dunkirk, 14048-2650.
Golombek, Robert K., 800 W. Ferry St., 14222.
Green, Gerard L., 9686 Oak Grove Dr., Angola, 14006-8904.
Hammerl, Leo E., O'Hara Residence, 69 O'Hara Rd., Tonawanda, 14150-6227.
Higgins, Grant J., 170 Countryside Ln., Apt. #4, Orchard Park, 14127.
Jasinski, Anthony J., Bishop Head Residence, 10 Rosary Ave., Lackawanna, 14218.
Juenker, Paul R., McAuley Residence, 1503 Military Rd., Kenmore, 14217.
Kopacz, Matthew S., 9993 Trevett Rd., Boston, 14025-9743.
Lichtenthal, James J., 9335 SE 177th Simon's Ln., The Villages, FL 32162.
Lorenzetti, Dino J., O'Hara Residence, 69 O'Hara Rd., Tonawanda, 14150-6227.
Madsen, John W., Conniff Residence, 68 Cowing St., Depew, 14043.
McCarthy, Leo F., 263 Claremont Ave., Kenmore, 14223.
Myszka, Daniel J., 391 Bristol St., 14206-3721.
Neu, Leon M., Bishop Head Residence, 10 Rosary Ave., Lackawanna, 14218.
O'Neill, Kevin T., 1170 Indian Church Rd., West Seneca, 14224.
Ronald, Roy K., 200 Boncroft Dr., West Seneca, 14224-2829.
Ryan, John M., 435 Amherst St., 14207-2891.
Scanlan, Edward J., 4421 Lower River Rd., Stella Niagara, 14144.
Schwinger, William A., Mercy Skilled Nursing Home, 55 Melroy Ave. #415, Lackawanna, 14218.
Sciera, Ronald P., P.O. Box 553, 14240-0553.
Skupien, Francis M., Bishop Head Residence, 10 Rosary Ave., Lackawanna, 14218.
Sobierajski, Edward J., O'Hara Residence, 69 O'Hara Rd., Tonawanda, 14150-6299.
Stengel, Paul F., Bishop Head Residence, 10 Rosary Ave., Lackawanna, 14218.
Sullivan, W. Jerome, J.C.D., Msgr. Conniff Residence, 68 Cowing St., Depew, 14043.
Wangler, Donald R., 7360 Rochester Rd., Lockport, 14094-1626.
Wangler, William O., P.O. Box 38, Frewsburg, 14738.
Weldgen, Francis G., 6955 Maple Dr., Wheatfield, 14120.
Wendzikowski, Mecislaus S., 142 Phyllis Ave., 14215-2826.
Wetter, Richard L., O'Hara Residence, 69 O'Hara Rd., Tonawanda, 14150-6227.
Whitney, Paul J., 5B Lexington Ct., Lockport, 14094.
Wright, Rupert A., 8610 Appleton Ct., East Amherst, 14051.
Yiengst, George B., 73 Reiman St. - Upper, 14206.
Yunk, Michael J., 47 Linwood Ave., 14221-6501.
Zeitler, John W., Sheehan Residence, 330 Linwood Ave., 14209.

Revs.—
Amico, Charles R., Ph.D., S.T.D., Christ the King Seminary, P.O. Box 607, East Aurora, 14052-0607.
Augustyn, James M., Bishop Head Residence, 10 Rosary Ave., Lackawanna, 14218.
Bartnik, James T., Autumn View Health Care Facility, 4650 Southwestern Blvd., Hamburg, 14075.
Becker, Donald, 13831 Eagle Ridge Lakes Dr. #103, Fort Myers, FL 33912.
Beiter, Robert G., Msgr. Conniff Residence, 68 Cowing St., Depew, 14043.
Biesinger, Robert J., Sheehan Residence, 330 Linwood Ave., 14209-1689.
Bigelow, William R., 9226 Lakeside Dr., Angola, 14006.
Bosack, Albert J., Bishop Head Residence, 10 Rosary Ave., Lackawanna, 14218.
Carlo, Joseph C., O'Hara Residence, 69 O'Hara Rd., Tonawanda, 14150.
Conoscenti, Frederick M., 169 Grand Oaks Way, Apt. 201, Naples, FL 34110.
Coveny, Richard C., Bishop Head Residence, 10 Rosary Ave., Lackawanna, 14218. (11/15-6/15): 1533 Tropic Terrace, North Fort Myers, FL 33903.
Cusimano, Salvatore J., O'Hara Residence, 69 O'Hara Rd., Tonawanda, 14150-6227.
Della Neve, Louis, 6A Lexington Ct., Lockport, 14094-5365.
DiGiulio, Richard S., Msgr. Conniff Residence, 68 Cowing St., Depew, 14043.
Dissek, Jerome M., 14929 Front Beach Rd., Panama City Beach, FL 32413.
Dolinic, Louis S., Msgr. Conniff Residence, 68 Cowing St., Depew, 14043.
Donohue, Raymond A.J., P.O. Box 24, Fredonia, 14063.

Dudek, Stanislaw, Msgr. Conniff Residence, 68 Cowing St., Depew, 14043.
Enright, James C., 15 Clark St., Auburn, 13021.
Fafinski, Donald S., 137 Serval St., Dunkirk, 14048.
Faraci, Douglas F., 132 Wilmington Ave., Tonawanda, 14150.
Fifagrowicz, Joseph G., St. Benedict Parish, 1317 Eggert Rd., Eggertsville, 14226.
Fox, John J., P.O. Box 852, Amherst, 14226-1297.
Friel, Mark M., Sheehan Residence, 330 Linwood Ave., 14209-1689.
Gagliardo, Anthony F., 1301 Wynkoop Dr., Colorado Springs, CO 80909.
Gresock, Thomas G., 749 Gilmore St., North Tonawanda, 14120.
Griffin, David G., 5904 Shoreham Dr., Lake View, 14085.
Grimmer, James A., Tonawanda Manor, 111 Ensminger Rd., #219, Tonawanda, 14150.
Haran, James E., St. Elizabeth Home, 5539 Broadway, Lancaster, 14086.
Hatrick, Brian M., 5114 Maple Grove Rd., Friendship, 14739.
Hinton, Frederick M., Kenmore Village Apts., 657 Colvin Blvd., Apt 706, Kenmore, 14217.
Ingalls, Fred D., c/o 795 Main St., 14203.
Jann, Francis J., P.O. Box 37, Rushford, 14777-0037.
Kasinski, James J., 164 Mead St., Apt. 2, North Tonawanda, 14120.
Kasprzyk, James H., P.O. Box 80033, Simpsonville, SC 29680.
Kaukus, Edwin J., 3640 N.E. 16th Ave., Oakland Park, FL 33334.
Kemp, Thomas L., 58 Lake St., Le Roy, 14482.
Kuhlmann, John L., 50 Fairmont St., Jamestown, 14701.
Mahar, Raymond J., Sheehan Residence, 330 Linwood Ave., 14209-1689.
Martlock, Loville N., P.O. Box 10, Jemez Springs, NM 87025-0010.
Massar, Richard A., Bishop Head Residence, 10 Rosary Ave., Lackawanna, 14218.
Matuszak, Walter L., Msgr. Conniff Residence, 68 Cowing St., Depew, 14043.
McArtney, Robert J., 1358 McKinley Pkwy., Lackawanna, 14218.
McCarthy, Thomas J., 540 Birchwood St., Apt. 3, West Seneca, 14224.
McGarry, William C., Our Lady of Peace Home, 5285 Lewiston Rd., Lewiston, 14092-1942.
McTigue, Norman P., 1088 Delaware Ave., #13B, 14209.
Measer, Donald L., St. Amelia, 210 St. Amelia Dr., Tonawanda, 14150-7126.
Mergenhagen, John J., P.O. Box 36, South Wales, 14139-0036.
Milby, Lawrence M., 24 Golden Sq., Westminster, London, United Kingdom W1F9JR.
Mitka, John J., Msgr. Conniff Residence, 68 Cowing St., Depew, 14043.
O'Hara, Michael D., 15 Clough Ave., Arcade, 14009.
Orsolits, Norbert F., P.O. Box 91, Springville, 14141.
Pavlock, Martin L., 247 State St., Jamestown, 14701.
Peter, David J., 2420 First St., Grand Island, 14072.
Rodriguez, Antonio L., Bishop Head Residence, 10 Rosary Ave., Lackawanna, 14218.
Rog, Theodore C., Bishop Head Residence, 10 Rosary Ave., Lackawanna, 14218.
Rossello, Nicholas A., 118 Old Niagara Rd., Apt. 3, Lockport, 14094-1520.
Russell, Raymond R., St. Francis of Williamsville, 147 Reist St., 14221.
Schroeder, Edward H., Sheehan Residence, 330 Linwood Ave., 14209.
Siracuse, Guy F., Brothers of Mercy, 10570 Bergtold Rd., Clarence, 14031.
Slomba, Eugene S., 3246 E. River Rd., Grand Island, 14072.
Stolinski, Robert A., Sheehan Residence, 330 Linwood Ave., 14209.
Sullivan, F. Norman, 8281 Lower East Hill Rd., Colden, 14033.
Swiatek, Emil P., Msgr. Conniff Residence, 68 Cowing St., Depew, 14043.
Taton, Thomas P., 435 Amherst St., 14207.
Tuyn, William R., P.O. Box 607, East Aurora, 14052.
Uschold, Raymond F., Bishop Head Residence, 10 Rosary Ave., Lackawanna, 14218.
Vogt, Robert W., 229 Moulton Dr., Longs, SC 29568.
Werth, Charles M., 65-35 Yellowstone Blvd., Apt. 5G, Forest Hills, 11375.
Wood, Robert W., 127 W. Winspear, 14214.
Wopperer, Thomas J., 1 W. Beach Rd., Dunkirk, 14048.
Zancan, Robert D., 12127 Mall Blvd., #A410, Victorville, CA 92392-7666.
Zmozynski, Francis J., 8 Tanglewood Dr., Lancaster, 14086.

Permanent Deacons:
Amantia, Philip J., Sr.
Andelora, Gary P.
Anderson, Michael L.
Badaszewski, Robert W.
Barr, Joseph M.
Bauer, Robert A.
Bochiechio, Michael G.
Boneberg, William J.
Boyd, Jimmie L., Sr.
Bray, Michael R.
Brick, Daniel E., Esq.
Bringenberg, Thomas B.
Burke, John H.
Canzoneri, Michael J.
Carmody, Paul F.
Casey, Christopher T.
Chriswell, Timothy E.
Ciezki, Robert T.
Collichio, James L.
Comerford, Michael V., Jr.
Conroy, Dennis P.
Crimi, Victor P.
Dibb, Roy P.
Dobmeier, Robert A.
Dulak, Michael T.
Ehrhart, David C.
Emerson, Paul C.
Eschbach, Lawrence D.
Eschrich, Paul C.
Feary, Gregory L., Jr.
Forcucci, Thomas M.
Foster, Norman E.
Friedman, Heinz H.
Fudala, Walter N.
Gaudioso, Carmelo
Gaulin, John P.
Golinski, Daniel U.
Gomola, Michael A.
Griesbaum, Charles J., Jr.
Harter, Terrance P.
Harvey, David H.
Healey, Thomas R.
Hens, Matthew A.
Hooper, Mark J.
Hoover, Gary M.
Howard, Edward R.
Hynes, William J.
Jacobi, Robert J.
Jaworski, James J.
Jerome, David R.
Johnson, Frederick M., Jr.
Kapsiak, Dennis W.
Kelly, John J.
Klein, George L.
Koester, Carlton M.
Leardon, John D.
Lemieux, Michael C.
Lennon, Michael
Licata, Thomas C.
Linnan, Neal M.
Mackiewicz, Richard F.
Mackowiak, Daniel H.
Mahaney, Richard J.
Maloney, Timothy J.
Marino, Benjamin R.
Markowski, Lawrence P.
Matthews, Richard F.
May, Thaddeus P.
McDermott, David P.
McDonnell, Thomas A.
McGuire, Daniel G.
McKeating, Michael P.
Mercurio, Joseph P.
Miranda, Roberto G.
Molnar, Alexander S.
Moscicki, Henry E.
Moses, Robert J.
Nowak, Mark F.
O'Connell, Edward G.
Parker, Richard W.
Pasquale, Francis W., Jr.
Pasquella, Joseph A.
Pellerito, Samuel
Penksa, Daniel M.
Pijacki, Thaddeus V.
Polizzi, Frank S.
Puleo, Samuel G.
Quinn, Michael D.
Radlinski, Donald E.
Ramos, Carlos W.
Ruh, John M.
Scherr, Thomas E.
Schnettler, Paul J.
Schultz, Thomas E.
Setera, John T.
Shaughnessey, Frank J.
Slish, David P.
Smith, Kevin J.
Snyder, Paul L., III
Stahl, Raymond H.
Stando, Matthew
Stankiewicz, Paul S.
Steffen, Franklyn C.
Steinagle, Gordon J.
Stone, John J.
Swinarski, Stephen J.
Szczesny, Walter T.
Terrana, Gary C.
Thomann, Bernard M.
Trzaska, James J.
Velasquez, David R.
Walders, Peter J.
Walek, Edward S.
Walker, Ronald
Walkowiak, Brian C.
Walkowiak, William J.
Watkins, Donald R., Jr.
Weigel, Donald C., Jr.
Weisenburger, Paul F.
Wetter, Donald A.
Wick, John G.
Willis, William W.
Zielinski, John R.
Zwack, Francis A.

INSTITUTIONS LOCATED IN THE DIOCESE

[A] SEMINARIES

EAST AURORA. *Christ the King Seminary* (1857) *Graduate School of Theology*, 711 Knox Rd., P.O. Box 607, 14052. Tel: 716-652-8900; Fax: 716-652-8903. Email: cksacad@cks.edu. Web: www.cks.edu. Interdiocesan Theologate. Owned and operated by the Diocese of Buffalo. Seminarians are assigned by the Bishop of any diocese for preparation for ordination to Priesthood.

Administration and Faculty: Revs. Peter J. Drilling, Th.D., Pres. & Rector; Gregory M. Faulhaber, S.T.D., Vice Rector; Richard A. Reina, M.Div., M.S.W., M.C.Sp., Dir. Spiritual Formation; Walter J. Szczesny, M.Div., Dir. Seminarians; Deacons Thaddeus P. May, Dir. Deacon Personnel; Gregory L. Feary, Dir. Diaconal Formation; Mr. Dennis Castillo, Ph.D., Academic Dean; Mr. Douglas George, M.A.P.M., Dir. Lay Formation; Mrs. Nancy Ehlers, Dir. Business Affairs; Mrs. Teresa Lubienecki, B.A., M.L.S., Dir. Library; Mr. Michael Sherry, Exec. Dir. Opers.

Faculty: Revs. Charles R. Amico, Ph.D., S.T.D. (Retired); Joseph F. Burke, S.J., Ph.D.; Peter J. Drilling, Th.D.; Gregory M. Faulhaber, S.T.D.; Robert L. Gebhard, M.Div.; Richard A. Reina, M.Div., M.S.W., M.C.Sp.; Gabriel Scarfia, O.F.M., S.T.D.; Xavier Seubert, O.F.M., S.T.D.; Paul L. Varuvel, S.T.D.; Sr. Marion Moeser, O.S.F., Ph.D.; Dennis Castillo, Ph.D.; Kathleen M. Castillo, M.A., Dir. Field Educ.; Alan D. Lukas, M.Mus., Dir. of Music.

Adjunct Faculty: Rev. Msgrs. David M. Lee; Paul A. Litwin, J.C.L.; Revs. Joseph C. Gatto, S.T.D.; Czeslaw M. Krysa; Alfons M. Osiander, Th.D.

[B] SEMINARIES, RELIGIOUS

LEWISTON. *St. Anthony M. Zaccaria Seminary, The Barbabite Fathers of Lewiston, NY, Inc.*, 981 Swann Rd., P.O. Box 167, Youngstown, 14174-0167. Tel: 716-754-7448; Fax: 716-754-9130. Email: BarnabitesUSA@fatimashrine.com. Web: www.fatimashrine.com. Revs. Peter M. Calabrese, C.R.S.P., Supr.; Julio M. Ciavaglia, C.R.S.P., Local Vicar; Richard M. Delzingaro, C.R.S.P., Chancellor; Joseph M. Gariolo, C.R.S.P.; Paul M. Keeling, C.R.S.P., Treas. Priests 5; Total Staff 6.

[C] COLLEGES AND UNIVERSITIES

BUFFALO. *Canisius College* (1870) 2001 Main St., 14208-1098. Tel: 716-883-7000; Fax: 716-888-2525. Email: info@canisius.edu. Web: www.canisius.edu. Mr. John J. Hurley, Pres.; Revs. Michael F. Tunney, S.J., Dir., Mission & Identity; John P. Bucki, S.J., Dir. Campus Ministry; Dr. Ellen O. Conley, Vice Pres. for Student Affairs; Mr. Craig T. Chindemi, Vice Pres. for Institutional Advancement; Patrick E. Richey, Vice Pres., Business & Finance & Treas.; Dr. Richard Wall, Interim Vice Pres. for Academic Affairs; Dr. David W. Ewing, Dean College of Arts & Sciences; Dr. Antone F. Alber, Dean Wehle School of Business; Dr. Michael Pardales, Dean School of Educ. & Human Svcs.; Dr. Joel A. Cohen, Dir., Assoc. Vice Pres. for Library & Information Svcs.; Dr. Khalid W. Bibi, Exec. Dir. Office of Professional Studies.

Priests 6; Lay Teachers 227; Total Enrollment 5,055.

D'Youville College (1908) 320 Porter Ave., 14201. Tel: 716-829-8000; Fax: 716-829-7780. Email: Brayjd@dyc.edu. Web: www.dyc.edu. Sr. Denise A. Roche, G.N.S.H., Ph.D., Pres.; Rev. Patrick T. O'Keefe, Dir. Campus Ministry; Rand Bellavia, Librarian. Grey Nuns of the Sacred Heart. Sisters 2; Lay Teachers 270; Total Staff 205; Students 3,100.

Trocaire College (1958) *Main Campus*, 360 Choate Ave., 14220. Tel: 716-826-1200; Fax: 716-828-6107. Email: hurleyp@trocaire.edu. Web: www.trocaire.edu. Extension Center: 6681 Transit Rd., Williamsville, 14221. Tel: 716-827-4300; Fax: 716-634-6139. Paul B. Hurley Jr., Ph.D., Pres.; Thomas J. Mitchell, M.A., Vice Pres. Academic Affairs; Richard N. Bernecki, M.B.A., Vice Pres. Fin. & Admin.; Michael C. LaFever, Ed.D., Dean Prog. Devel. & Enrollment Mgmt.; Tony Funigiello, Dean Student Affairs; Richard T. Linn, Ph.D., Dean Research, Assessment & Planning; Marian Meyers, Ed.D., Dean of Academic Affairs, Nursing Studies; John A. Vecchio, M.B.A., Vice Pres. Inst. Advancement; Maria Povlock, M.S., Dir. Admissions; Kathy Popielski, B.S., Dir. Communications; Judith K. Schwartz, M.L.S., Librarian; Rev. Robert M. Mock, Assoc. Dean of Academic Affairs, Non-Nursing Studies; Sr. Margaret Mary Gorman, R.S.M., M.S., Dir. Mission Svc.; Jackie Bryant, Web & Social Media Editor. A private career-oriented Catholic College established by the Sisters of Mercy in 1958. Priests 1; Sisters 8; Lay Teachers 152; Students 1,479; Total Staff 83.

Villa Maria College of Buffalo (1960) 240 Pine Ridge Rd., 14225-3999. Tel: 716-896-0700; 716-961-1805; Fax: 716-896-0705. Email: admissions@villa.edu. Web: www.villa.edu. Sr. Marcella Marie Garus, C.S.S.F., Pres. Sisters 16; Lay Teachers 80; Students 457; Total Staff 148.

HAMBURG. *Hilbert College* (1957) 5200 S. Park Ave., 14075. Tel: 716-649-7900; Fax: 716-558-6380. Email: czane@hilbert.edu. Web: www.hilbert.edu/. Cynthia A. Zane, Ed.D., Pres. Lay Teachers 102; Students 1,117; Total Staff 150.

NIAGARA UNIVERSITY. *Niagara University* (1856) Lewiston Rd., 14109. Tel: 716-285-1212; Fax: 716-286-8355. Web: www.niagara.edu. Rev. Joseph L. Levesque, C.M., Pres.; Bonnie Rose, Ph.D., Exec. Vice Pres. & Vice Pres. Academic Affairs; Timothy M. Downs, Ph.D., Vice Pres., Academic Affairs; Michael S. Jaszka, Vice Pres. for Admin.; Kevin P. Hearn, Ed.D., Vice Pres., Student Life; Donald P. Bielecki, Vice Pres. for Institutional Advancement; Judith A. Willard, Ph.D., Asst. to the Pres. for Planning; Nancy E. McGlen, Ph.D., Dean College of Arts & Sciences; Tenpao Lee, Ph.D., Acting Dean, College of Business Admin.; Debra A. Colley, Ph.D., Dean College of Educ.; Michael J. Konopski, Dean of Enrollment Mgmt.; Gary Praetzel, Ph.D., Dean College of Hospitality & Tourism Mgmt.; Jon Jay Stockslader, Dir. Ctr. for Continuing & Community Educ.; Patricia G. Kinner, Dir. Academic Support; David M. Schoen, Dir. Library; Maureen Salfi, Dir. Financial Aid; John B. Stranges, Ph.D., Univ. Prof.; Mati Ortiz, Dir., Campus Activities; Carrie McLaughlin, Dean of Students; Lori Soos, Dir. Health Svcs.; David Blackburn, Dir. Multicultural Student Affairs; Monica Romeo, Dir. Counseling Svcs.; Kimberly J. Zukowski, Dir., Residence Life; Arthur Cardella, Dir., Alumni Rels.; Thomas J. Burns, Assoc. Vice Pres. for Public Rels., Communications & Marketing; Robert Pfeil, Dir. Human Resources; Stephanie A. Cole, Esq., Gen. Counsel; Revs. Joseph G. Hubbert, C.M., Assoc. Prof. Rel. Studies & Supr. of Vincentian Community; Kevin G. Creagh, C.M., Ed.D., Assoc. Vice Pres., Campus Ministry; Bruce J. Krause, C.M., Campus Min.; John W. Gouldrick, C.M., Asst. to the Pres. for Mission Devel.; Stephen J. Denig, C.M., Assoc. Prof., Educ.; Bro. Martin J. Schneider, C.M., Coord. of Commencement & Asst. to Dir. of Theatre & Fine Arts. Priests 2; Sisters 1; Lay Teachers 155; Students 4,182.

ST. BONAVENTURE. *St. Bonaventure University* (1858) 3261 W. State Rd., Saint Bonaventure, 14778. Tel: 716-375-2000; Fax: 716-375-2055. Web: www.sbu.edu. Franciscan Friars, Province of the Holy Name, Order of Friars Minor., School of Arts and Sciences, School of Educ., School of Business, School of Journalism & Mass Communication; School of Franciscan Studies and the Franciscan Institute; Graduate Studies. Priests 12; Brothers 7; Sisters 4; Lay Teachers 205; Students 2,519.

Administration: Sr. Margaret Carney, O.S.F., S.T.D., Pres.; Michael J. Fischer, Ph.D., Vice Pres. Academic Affairs & Provost; Brenda McGee, B.S., Senior Vice Pres. Finance & Admin.; Dr. Emily F. Sinsabaugh, Vice Pres. Univ. Rels.; Peggy Y. Burke, Ed.D., Dean Graduate Studies; Wolfgang Natter, Ph.D., Dean, School of Arts & Sciences; Bro. F. Edward Coughlin, O.F.M., Ph.D., Dir., Franciscan Institute & Dean, School of Franciscan Studies; Brian McAllister, Interim Dean, School of Business; Peggy Y. Burke, Ed.D., Dean School of Educ.; Pauline Hoffmann, Ph.D., Interim Dean, Russel J. Jandoli School of Journalism & Mass Communication; David DiMattio, Ph.D., Dean, Clare College; Monica Emery, Dir., Admissions; Ann Lehman, M.B.A., Registrar & Dir. Inst. Research & Planning; Nichole J. Gonzalez, B.A., Dir. Residence Life; Joseph V. Flanagan, M.S., Dir. Alumni Svcs.; Francine Schaefer, Interim Dir., Human Resources; Margaret T. Bryner, M.S., Dir. Higher Educ. Opportunities Prog. (HEOP); Jean T. Ehman, M.A., Dir. The Teaching & Learning Ctr.; Kimberly S. Young, Dir. Leadership Prog.; Alice F. Sayegh, M.S., Dir. Intl. Studies; Michael Hoffman, B.S., Exec. Dir. of Technology Svcs.; Paul J. Spaeth, M.L.S., M.A., Dir. Library; Constance F. Whitcomb, M.S.Ed., Dir. Career Devel.; Rev. Francis DiSpigno, O.F.M., M.Div., Exec. Dir., Univ. Ministries.

[D] HIGH SCHOOLS, PRIVATE

BUFFALO. *Bishop Timon-St. Jude High School* (1946) 601 McKinley Pkwy., 14220. Tel: 716-826-3610; Fax: 716-824-5833. Web: www.bishoptimon.com. Mr. Thomas J. Sullivan, Prin. Owned and operated by Bishop Timon Board of Trustees. Priests 1; Lay Teachers 27; Students 262; Total Staff 35.

Canisius High School (1870) 1180 Delaware Ave., 14209. Tel: 716-882-0466; Fax: 716-883-1870. Email: knight@canisiushigh.org. Web: www.canisiushigh.org. Mr. John M. Knight, Pres.; Mr. Timothy Fitzgerald, Prin.; Revs. Frederick G. Betti, S.J.; Joseph W. Lux, S.J.; William J. McCurdy, S.J.; Robert J. Pecoraro, S.J.; John J. Ryan, S.J.; Eugene A. Zimpfer, S.J. Society of Jesus. Priests 5; Lay Teachers 64; Students 814; Total Staff 98.

Holy Angels Academy (1861) 24 Shoshone Dr., 14214-1097. Tel: 716-834-7120; Fax: 716-834-7128. Email: jkaczor@holyangelsacademy.org. Web: www.holyangelsacademy.org. Mrs. Joan Thomas, Pres.; Mrs. Kathleen Tedesco, Prin.; Marie Clark, Librarian. Grey Nuns of the Sacred Heart 2; Lay Teachers 36; Religious 1; Students 224; Total Staff 50.

St. Joseph's Collegiate Institute (1861) 845 Kenmore Ave., 14223-3195. Tel: 716-874-4024; Fax: 716-874-4956. Email: rscott@sjci.com. Web: www.sjci.com. Robert T. Scott, A.F.S.C., Pres.; Mr. Jeffery Hazel, Prin.; Rev. James C. Croglio, Chap. of School and Brothers' Community; Mr. Thomas Zabawa, Vice Prin., Academic Affairs; Bros. Christopher Belleman, F.S.C., Vice Prin. Student Affairs; Peter Henderson, F.S.C., Community Dir.; Joseph Reed, F.S.C.; Luke Wittmann, F.S.C.; Deacons Gregory L. Feary; William J. Hynes; William J. Walkowiak; Rev. James R. Bastian; Mr. Steven Koniarczyk, Librarian. Brothers of the Christian Schools. (De La Salle Christian Brothers). Priests 2; Deacons 3; Brothers 4; Lay Teachers 46; Students 722; Total Staff 77.

Mt. Mercy Academy (1904) 88 Red Jacket Pkwy., 14220. Tel: 716-825-8796; Fax: 716-825-0976. Email: pgaske@mtmercy.org. Web: www.mtmercy.org. Sr. Mary Ellen Twist, R.S.M., Pres.; Mrs. Margaret Staszak, Prin.; Michele Kujawinski, Librarian. Sisters of Mercy. Students 260; Total Staff 53.

Nardin Academy High School (1857) 135 Cleveland Ave., 14222. Tel: 716-881-6262; Fax: 716-881-0086. Email: rreeder@nardin.org. Web: www.nardin.org. Mrs. Marsha Sullivan, Pres.; Rebecca R. Reeder, Prin.; Karen Roslowski, Librarian. Lay Teachers 50; Girls 471.

AMHERST. *Buffalo Academy of the Sacred Heart*, 3860 Main St., 14226. Tel: 716-834-2101; Fax: 716-834-2944. Email: Info@sacredheartacademy.org. Web: www.sacredheartacademy.org. Jennifer Demert, Headmistress; Lynn Biniskiewicz, Librarian. Sisters of St. Francis of Penance and Christian Charity. Sisters 6; Lay Teachers 41; Students 397; Total Staff 78.

ATHOL SPRINGS. *St. Francis High School* (1927) 4129 Lake Shore Rd., 14010-0185. Tel: 716-627-1200; Fax: 716-627-4610. Email: frmichaels@stfrancishigh.org. Web: stfrancishigh.org. Rev. Michael Sajda, O.F.M.Conv., Pres.; Mr. Thomas Braunscheidel, Prin.; Revs. Justin Ross, O.F.M.Conv.; Mark David Skura, O.F.M.Conv.; Bros. Brian Newbigging, O.F.M.Conv.; Nicholas Romeo, O.F.M.Conv.; Mrs. Aga Chen, Librarian. St. Anthony Province of the Order of Friars Minor Conventual. Priests 3; Brothers 2; Lay Teachers 40; Total Staff 66; Students 516.

BATAVIA. *Notre Dame High School of Batavia*, 73 Union St., 14020. Tel: 585-343-2783; Fax: 585-343-7323. Email: ndhs@ndhsbatavia.com. Web: www.ndhsbatavia.com. Dr. Joseph Scanlan, Prin.; Mr. Mike Rapone, Asst. Prin. & Athletic Dir.; Miss Jennifer Kleparek, Librarian. Owned and operated by Notre Dame Board of Trustees. Lay Teachers 18; Students 184; Total Staff 25.

HAMBURG. *Immaculata Academy*, 5138 S. Park Ave., 14075. Tel: 716-649-6161; Fax: 716-646-1782. Email: jmonaco@immaculataacademy.com. Sr. M. Paulette Tirone, F.S.S.J., Pres.; Mrs. Jill A. Monaco, Prin.; Mrs. Sharon Moore, Librarian. Franciscan Sisters of St. Joseph. Sisters 3; Lay Teachers 25; Students 205; Total Staff 19.

KENMORE. *Mount St. Mary Academy* (1927) 3756 Delaware Ave., 14217. Tel: 716-877-1358; Fax: 716-877-0548. Email: driggie@mt-st-marys.org. Web: mt-st-marys.org. Mrs. Dawn M. Riggie, Prin. Owned and operated by the Mt. St. Mary Academy Board of Trustees. Sisters 2; Lay Teachers 31; Girls 283.

LANCASTER. *St. Mary's High School*, 142 Laverack Ave., 14086. Tel: 716-683-4824; Fax: 716-683-4996. Email: lancer@smhlancers.org. Web: www.smhlancers.org. Rebecca L. Kranz, Prin.; Emily Sityar, Librarian. Owned and operated by St. Mary's Board of Trustees. Lay Teachers 30; Students 380; Total Staff 55.

NIAGARA FALLS. *Niagara Catholic High School* (1975) 520-66th St., 14304. Tel: 716-283-8771; Fax: 716-283-8774. Email: rdifrancesco@niagaracatholic.org. Web: www.niagaracatholic.org. Robert M. DiFrancesco, Prin.; Rev. Gerald L. Bartko, O.S.F.S.; Deacon Daniel H. Mackowiak, Campus Min. Owned and operated by Niagara Catholic Board of Trustees. Priests 1; Deacons 1; Lay Teachers 13; Students 131.

OLEAN. *Archbishop Walsh High School*, 208 N. 24th St., 14760-1985. Tel: 716-372-8122; Fax: 716-372-6707. Email: archbishopwalsholean@yahoo.com. Web: www.mywalsh.com. Dr. Emily F. Sinsabaugh, Pres.; Mr. Thomas McGlinn, Prin. Owned and operated by Archbishop Walsh Board of Trustees. Lay Teachers 11; Students 68; Total Staff 20.

TONAWANDA. *Cardinal O'Hara High School*, 39 O'Hara Rd., 14150. Tel: 716-695-2600; Fax: 716-692-8697. Email: mholzerland@cardinalohara.org. Web: www.cardinalohara.com. Mary Holzerland, Prin.; Angelo Sciandra, Asst. Prin. Owned and operated by Cardinal O'Hara Board of Trustees. Lay Teachers 24; Students 247.

[E] ELEMENTARY SCHOOLS, PRIVATE

BUFFALO. *Nardin Academy* (1857) 135 Cleveland Ave., 14222. Tel: 716-881-6262; Fax: 716-881-4190. Email: msullivan@nardin.org. Web: www.nardin.org. Rebecca Reeder, High School Prin.; Margaret Abels, Elementary Prin.; Kristin Whitlock, Montessori Prin. (Montessori-Grade 12) Sisters 1; Lay Teachers 110; Students 926; Elementary & Montessori 455.

The NativityMiguel Middle School of Buffalo, (Grades 5-8), St. Monica Campus: 26 Wright Ave., 14215. Tel: 716-852-6854; Fax: 716-852-8410. Email: es88@buffalodiocese.org. St. Augustine Campus: 21 Davison Ave., 14215. Tel: 716-836-5188; Fax: 716-836-5189. Nancy M. Langer, Pres.; Rev. Edward J. Durkin, S.J., Prin. Priests 1; Sisters 1; Lay Teachers 7; Students 85; Total Staff 14.

LEWISTON. *Sacred Heart Villa School*, (Grades PreK-5), 5269 Lewiston Rd., 14092. Tel: 716-284-8273; 716-285-9257 (school); Fax: 716-284-8273. Email: sacredhrtv@yahoo.com. Web: www.shvilla.org. Sr. Elizabeth Domin, S.S.H.J., Prin. Sisters 8; Lay Teachers 1; Students 36.

STELLA NIAGARA. *Stella Niagara Education Park*, (Grades PreK-8), 4421 Lower River Rd., 14144. Tel: 716-754-4314; Fax: 716-754-2964. Sr. Margaret Sullivan, O.S.F., Prin. Sisters of St. Francis of Penance and Christian Charity Sisters 4; Lay Teachers 22; Students 160.

[F] ELEMENTARY SCHOOLS, SPECIAL

BUFFALO. *Cantalician Center for Learning, Inc.* (1955) 3233 Main St., 14214. Tel: 716-833-5353; Fax: 716-833-0108. Email: tscofidio@cantalician.org. Web: www.cantalician.org. Terese M. Scofidio, Exec. Dir.; Anne Spisiak, Dir. Community Svcs.; Sr. Paul Marie Baczkowski, C.S.S.F., Dir. Educ. Program for individuals with disabilities: Infant, Toddler and Preschool; Elementary and Secondary. Day programs for adult individuals with disabilities & day habilitation for retired, disabled adults. Employment opportunities for adults with disabilities through contract work and supported employment programs. Daycare, infant through pre-school. Sisters 1; Lay Staff 231; Students 475; Total Staff 232.

[G] REGIONAL AND CONSOLIDATED ELEMENTARY SCHOOLS

BUFFALO. *Catholic Academy of West Buffalo*, (Grades PreK-8), 1069 Delaware Ave., 14209-1605. Tel: 716-885-6111; Fax: 716-885-6452. Email: gglenn@cawb.org. Sr. Gail Glenn, S.S.J., Prin.; Mrs. Geraldine Kizielewicz, Assoc. Prin.; Christine Traum, Librarian. Sisters 2; Lay Teachers 16; Students 223; Total Staff 24.

Our Lady of Black Rock, (Grades PreK-8), 16 Peter St., 14207. Tel: 716-873-7497; Fax: 716-447-9926. Email: es15@buffalodiocese.org. Mrs. Martha J. Eadie, Prin.; Sharon Leising, Librarian. Lay Teachers 14; Students 120; Total Staff 18.

South Buffalo Catholic School, (Grades PreK-8), A regional school with three sites: Trinity Catholic Academy 16 Hayden St., Buffalo; Notre Dame Academy, 1125 Abbott Rd., Buffalo, NY; and Ambrose Catholic Academy, 260 Okell St., Buffalo, NY., 260 Okell St., 14220. Tel: 716-822-4546; Fax: 716-822-2576. Laura Kazmierczak, Prin. Ambrose Catholic Academy; Kimberly Suminski, Prin. Notre Dame Academy; Dolores C. Oakes, Prin. Trinity Academy; Rev. James G. Judge, Canonical Admin. Lay Teachers 50; Students 674.

CHEEKTOWAGA. *Mary Queen of Angels Catholic School* (2003) (Grades PreK-8), 170 Rosewood Ter., 14225. Tel: 716-895-6280; Fax: 716-895-6359. Email: mabagwell@mqangels.com. Web: www.mqangels.com. MaryAlice Bagwell, Prin.; Rev. Msgr. Kevin T. O'Neill, Canonical Admin. (Retired). (Regional School) Lay Teachers 19; Students 201.

DUNKIRK. *Northern Chautauqua Catholic School* (1989) (Grades PreK-8), 336 Washington Ave., 14048. Tel: 716-366-0630; Fax: 716-366-5101. Email: es37@buffalodiocese.org; ncc_principal@nccschool.us. Kathy Y. Moser, Prin. Lay Teachers 17; Students 172; Total Staff 25.

JAMESTOWN. *Catholic Academy of the Holy Family* (1887) (Grades PreK-8), 1135 N. Main St., 14701-3199. Tel: 716-483-3245; Fax: 716-661-3662. Email: es47@buffalodiocese.org. Web: www.holyfamilyjamestown.org. Mr. Samuel Pellerito, Prin.; Rev. Dennis W. Mende, Canonical Admin.; Paula Slagle, Librarian. Lay Teachers 15; Students 91; Total Staff 25.

LAKE VIEW. *Southtowns Catholic*, (Grades PreK-8), 2052 Lakeview Rd., Box 86, 14085. Tel: 716-627-5011; Fax: 716-627-5335. Email: jmacdonald@southtownscatholic.org. Web: www.southtownscatholic.org. Judith M. MacDonald, Prin. Lay Teachers 21; Students 210; Total Staff 31.

LOCKPORT. *DeSales Catholic School*, (Grades PreK-8), 6914 Chestnut School, 14094. Tel: 716-433-6422; Fax: 716-434-4002. Email: desalesp@desalescatholicschool.org. Web: www.desalescatholicschool.org. Dr. Scott C. Fike, Ph.D., Prin. Sisters 1; Lay Teachers 31; Students 420; Total Staff 52.

NIAGARA FALLS. *Catholic Academy of Niagara Falls* (Two sites) Rev. Stephen J. Denig, C.M., Canonical Admin.

St. Dominic Savio Middle School Campus (Grades 6-8), 504 66th St., 14303. Tel: 716-215-1461; Fax: 716-215-1465. Email: es62@buffalodiocese.org. Rose Mary Buscaglia, Prin. Lay Teachers 12; Students 114.

Catholic Academy of Niagara Falls Elementary Campus (Grades PreK-5), 1055 N. Military Rd., 14304. Tel: 716-283-1455; Fax: 716-283-1355. Mrs. Jeannine M. Fortunate, Prin. Lay Teachers 20; Students 134.

OLEAN. *Southern Tier Catholic School*, (Grades PreK-8), 206 N. 24th St., 14760. Tel: 716-372-2891; Fax: 716-373-1175. Web: www.wnystcs.org. Mr. Thomas McGlinn, Prin.; Rev. Gregory J. Dobson, Canonical Admin.; Jennifer Witzigman, Librarian. Lay Teachers 16; Students 136; Total Staff 23.

SPRINGVILLE. *St. Aloysius Regional School*, (Grades K-8), 186 Franklin St., 14141-1112. Tel: 716-592-7002; Fax: 716-592-7002. Email: office@staloysiusregional.com. Web: www.staloysiusregional.com. Mr. Scott Kapperman, Prin. Lay Teachers 14; Students 91.

WELLSVILLE. *Immaculate Conception School of Allegany County*, 24 Maple Ave., 14895. Tel: 585-593-5840; Fax: 585-593-5846. Email: es80@buffalodiocese.org. Web: www.icc-ics.com. Nora A. Burdick, Prin.; Cyndi Stanton, Librarian; Rev. Sean E. DiMaria, Canonical Admin. Sisters of Mercy 1; Lay Teachers 16; Students 166.

[H] CATHOLIC CHARITIES

BUFFALO. *The Catholic Charities of the Diocese of Buffalo* (1923) 741 Delaware Ave., 14209. Tel: 716-218-1400; Fax: 716-856-2005. Serving the eight counties of Western New York.

Appeal Administration and Publicity Offices Sr. Mary McCarrick, O.S.F., Diocesan Dir.

Agency Administration Dennis C. Walczyk, CEO.

Delta Development of Western New York, Inc. Tel: 716-847-1635; Fax: 716-856-7201. Bernadette Harlan, Dir. See separate listing in the Miscellaneous section.

The Msgr. Carr Institute, 76 W. Humboldt Pkwy., 14214. Tel: 716-835-9745; Fax: 716-835-6785. See separate listing in the Miscellaneous section.

[I] ORPHANAGES AND INFANT HOMES

BUFFALO. *German Roman Catholic Orphan Home*, 795 Main St., 14203. Inactive.

[J] PROTECTIVE INSTITUTES

BUFFALO. *St. Adalbert's Response to Love Center, Inc.*, 130 Kosciuszko St., 14212. Tel: 716-894-7030; Fax: 716-891-5474. Web: www.responsetolovecenter.org. Sr. Mary Johnice Rzadkiewicz, C.S.S.F., Dir. Total Assisted Annually 1,089.

The Franciscan Center, Inc., 1910 Seneca St., 14210-1842. Tel: 716-822-8017; Fax: 716-822-8537. Web: www.franciscancenterinc.org. Rev. Joseph Bayne, O.F.M.Conv., Exec. Dir. Transitional Shelters for Adolescent Males 16-20: Transitional Indep. Living Program, Supported Residence. Total Assisted 409; Total Staff 12.

LACKAWANNA. *Baker Victory Services* (1851) (formerly known as Baker Hall, Our Lady of Victory Infant Home, St. Joseph Orphanage and St. John's Protectory), 780 Ridge Rd., 14218. Tel: 716-828-9500; 888-287-1160; Fax: 716-828-9526. Email: webmaster@olv-bvs.org. Web: www.bakervictoryservices.org. Rev. Msgr. Paul J.E. Burkard, Pres. of Board; James J. Casion, CEO; Alan Nelson, Vice Pres. Admin. Svcs. Bakery Victory Services assists children, adults and families in need through preventative, outpatient, educational, and residential programs, including international and domestic adoptions, foster care, early childhood education, and a dental clinic, as well as programs for individuals with developmental disabilities and young people who are emotionally, behaviorally, or mentally challenged. Staff 1,102; Total Assisted 26,636.

Baker Victory Healthcare Center Tel: 716-828-9334; Fax: 716-828-9355. Web: www.bakervictoryservices.org.

[K] GENERAL HOSPITALS

BUFFALO. *Catholic Health System, Inc.* (1998) *Seton Professional Bldg.*, 2121 Main St., Ste. 300, 14214. Tel: 716-862-2400; Fax: 716-862-2468. Email: webmaster@WNYCHS.org. Web: www.chsbuffalo.org. Joseph D. McDonald, Pres. & CEO. Bed Capacity 1,700; Patients Assisted Annually 1,263,030; Total Staff 8,123.

McAuley Mercy Corporation, 2121 Main St., Ste. 300, 14214. Sr. Sally Maloney, R.S.M., M.A., Chairperson. A holding company for Mercy Home Care of Western New York. Sponsored by the Catholic Health System, Inc.

Mercy Hospital (1904) 565 Abbott Rd., 14220. Tel: 716-862-2410; Fax: 716-862-2468. Email: cjurlaub@chsbuffalo.org. *c/o Catholic Health System*, 2121 Main St., Ste. 300, 14214. Mr. C. J. Urlaub, Pres. & CEO; Kathy Guarino, Chief Nursing Officer. Sponsored by the Catholic Health System, Inc. Sisters of Mercy 1; Patients Assisted Annually 430,364; Bed Capacity 473; Total Staff 2,237.

Sisters Hospital Foundation, Inc., 2130 Main St., 14214. Tel: 716-862-1990; Fax: 716-835-8643. Email: asnyder@chsbuffalo.org. Web: www.sistershospitalfoundation.org. *c/o Catholic Health System*, 2121 Main St., Ste. 300, 14214. Anne E. Snyder, Chief Devel. Officer.

Sisters of Charity Hospital of Buffalo, NY (1849) Main Street Campus: 2157 Main St., 14214. Tel: 716-862-1000; Fax: 716-862-1899. Email: pbergman@chsbuffalo.org. Web: www.chsbuffalo.org. *c/o Catholic Health Systems*, 2121 Main St., Ste. 300, 14214. Peter U. Bergmann, Pres. & CEO. Sponsored by the Catholic Health System, Inc. Daughters of Charity of St. Vincent de Paul 10; Bed Capacity 413; Patients Assisted Annually 659,788; Total Staff 2,314.

St. Joseph Campus, 2605 Harlem Rd., 14225. Tel: 716-891-2400; Fax: 716-891-2616.

CHEEKTOWAGA. *McAuley-Seton Home Care* (1988) 14 Appletree Business Park, 14227. Tel: 716-685-4870; Fax: 716-651-9613. Email: jmarkiew@chsbuffalo.org. *c/o Catholic Health Systems*, 2121 Main St., Ste. 300, 14214. Joyce Markiewicz, Pres. & CEO. McAuley Seton - 10039; Mercy Home - 1655; Sisters Long Term - 251 11,945; McAuley Seton 312; Mercy Home 242; Sisters Long Term 10 564.

KENMORE. *Kenmore Mercy Foundation Inc.* (1980) 2950 Elmwood Ave., 14217. Tel: 716-447-6204; Fax: 716-447-6052. Email: smcdonou@chsbuffalo.org. Web: www.kenmoremercyfoundation.org. *c/o Catholic Health Systems*, 2121 Main St., Ste. 300, 14214. Shari McDonough, Exec. Dir.

Kenmore Mercy Hospital, 2950 Elmwood Ave., 14217. Tel: 716-447-6100; Fax: 716-447-6090. *c/o Catholic Health Systems*, 2121 Main St., Ste. 300, 14214. James M. Millard, Pres. & CEO; Sr. Ellen McClure, O.S.J., Vice Pres. Mission Integration. Sponsored by the Catholic Health System, Inc. Bed Capacity 184; Total Staff 922; Outpatient Visits 150,810; Admissions 7,556.

LEWISTON. *Mount St. Mary's Hospital of Niagara Falls*, 5300 Military Rd., 14092-1997. Tel: 716-297-4800; Fax: 716-298-2333 (Gen.); 716-298-2001 (Pres.). Web: www.msmh.org. Judith A. Maness, Pres. & CEO; Rev. Stewart M. Lindsay, O.S.F.S., Chap.; Sisters Grace Marie Dunn, D.C., Vice Pres. for Mission; Margaret Tuley, D.C., Board Pres.; Jeraldine Fritz, D.C., Chap.; Judith Terrameo, O.S.F., Chap.; Christine Steigerwald, O.S.F., Chap. Ascension Health, St. Louis, MO. Capacity 175; Patients Assisted Annually 162,700; Total Staff 877.

[L] HEALTH CARE FACILITIES

BUFFALO. *St. Francis of Buffalo, Inc.* Formerly known as St. Francis Hospital., 291 North St., 14201. Tel: 716-923-4816; Fax: 716-604-1820. Email: cjk@chsbuffalo.org. c/o Catholic Health Systems, 2121 Main St., Ste. 300, 14214. Christine J. Kluckhohn, Pres. & CEO.

LOCKPORT. *Niagara Homemaker Services, Inc. dba Mercy Home Care of Western New York* 310 S. Transit Rd., 14094. Tel: 716-434-2388. c/o Catholic Health System, 2121 Main St., Ste. 300, 14214.

[M] HOMES FOR AGED

BATAVIA. *St. Luke Manor*, 2121 Main St., Ste. 300, 14214.

CLARENCE. *Brothers of Mercy Housing Co., Inc.*, 10500 Bergtold Rd., 14031. Tel: 716-759-2122; Fax: 716-759-8030. Email: len@brothersofmercy.org. Web: www.brothersofmercy.org. Leonard Krufka, Admin.; Bro. Jude Holzfoerster, F.M.M., Pres. Apartments 100; Total in Residence 100; Total Staff 6.

Brothers of Mercy Nursing & Rehabilitation Center, 10570 Bergtold Rd., 14031. Tel: 716-759-6985; Fax: 716-759-6223. Email: valerie@brothersofmercy.org. Web: www.brothersofmercy.org. Ms. Valerie Kane, Admin.; Bro. Jude Holzfoerster, F.M.M., Pres.; Rev. John J. Sardina, Chap. Bed Capacity 240; Total Assisted Annually 950; Staff 500. In Res. Bro. Fidelis Verrall, F.M.M.

Brothers of Mercy Sacred Heart Home, Inc., 4520 Ransom Rd., 14031. Tel: 716-759-2644; Fax: 716-759-6433. Email: marion@brothersofmercy.org. Web: www.brothersofmercy.org. Marion Hummell, Admin.; Bro. Jude Holzfoerster, F.M.M., Pres. of Bd.; Rev. John J. Sardina, Chap. Total Assisted Annually 106; Total Staff 50.

DUNKIRK. *St. Vincent's Home for the Aged*, 319 Washington Ave., 14048. Tel: 716-366-2066; Fax: 716-366-0545. Email: dsmith@chsbuffalo.org. *c/o Catholic Health Systems*, 2121 Main St., Ste. 300, 14214. Deborah A. Smith, Admin. Total Assisted 51; Total Staff 28.

KENMORE. *McAuley Residence*, 1503 Military Rd., 14217. Tel: 716-447-6600; Fax: 716-447-6620. Email: tkristal@chsbuffalo.org. *c/o Catholic Health Systems*, 2121 Main St., Ste. 300, 14214. Tova Kristal, Admin. Residential Health Care Facility; Sponsored by the Catholic Health System, Inc. Bed Capacity 160; Total Assisted 1,050; Total Staff 280.

LANCASTER. *St. Elizabeth's Home* (1958) 5539 Broadway, 14086. Tel: 716-683-5150; Fax: 716-683-4049. Email: jhumes@chsbuffalo.org. *c/o Catholic Health Systems*, 2121 Main St., Ste. 300, 14214. Judith Humes, Admin. Felician Sisters 1; Residents 117; Total Assisted 147; Total Staff 71.

LEWISTON. *Our Lady of Peace, Inc. dba Our Lady of Peace Nursing Care Residence* 5285 Lewiston Rd., 14092. Tel: 716-298-2900; Fax: 716-298-2800. Ronald F. Zito, Exec. Dir.; Sisters Margaret Tuley, D.C., Chairperson; Eleanor Marie Shea, D.C., Chap.; Rev. Duane R. Klizek, Chap. Total Assisted Annually 700.

LOCKPORT. *St. Clare Manor*, c/o Catholic Health System, 2121 Main St., Ste. 300, 14214.

NIAGARA FALLS. *St. Mary Manor*, c/o Catholic Health System, 2121 Main St., Ste. 300, 14214.

OLEAN. *S. Joseph Manor*, c/o Catholic Health System, 2121 Main St., Ste. 300, 14214.

ORCHARD PARK. *Father Baker Manor* (1994) 6400 Powers Rd., 14127. Tel: 716-667-0001; Fax: 716-667-0028. Email: sguenthe@chsbuffalo.org. Web:

www.chsbuffalo.org. *c/o Catholic Health Systems*, 2121 Main St., Ste. 300, 14214. Mark Wheeler, Admin. Nursing facility sponsored by the Catholic Health System, Inc. Bed Capacity 160; Total Assisted 830; Total Staff 280.

SILVER CREEK. *St. Columbans on the Lake, Home for the Aged* (1970) 2546 Lake Rd., 14136. Tel: 716-934-4515; Fax: 716-934-3919. Email: ccolleary@stcolumbanshome.org. Web: www.stcolumbanshome.org. Sr. Corona Colleary, S.S.C., Admin. Bed Capacity 50; Columban Sisters 10; Total Staff 30; Total Assisted Annually 150. In Res. Revs. Peter J. Cronin, S.S.C.; Thomas M. Walsh, S.S.C.

WILLIAMSVILLE. *St. Francis of Williamsville*, 147 Reist St., 14221. Tel: 716-633-5400; Fax: 716-663-6404. Email: dcrispel@chsbuffalo.org. Web: www.chsbuffalo.org. *c/o Catholic Health Systems*, 2121 Main St., Ste. 300, 14214. Darlene Jones Crispell, Admin.

St. Francis of Williamsville, Skilled Nursing Facility Residents 142; Total Assisted 489; Total Staff 222.

[N] MONASTERIES AND RESIDENCES OF PRIESTS AND BROTHERS

BUFFALO. *Bishop's Residence*, 77 Oakland Pl., 14222-2041. Tel: 716-883-7707; Fax: 716-883-7702. Most Rev. Edward U. Kmiec, D.D., S.T.L.; Rev. Msgrs. David G. LiPuma, Bishop Sec. & Vice Chancellor; Paul A. Litwin, J.C.L., Chancellor.

Canisius Jesuit Community Inc., 2001 Main St., 14208. Tel: 716-883-7000; Fax: 716-886-6506. Email: tunneym@canisius.edu. Web: www.canisius.edu. Revs. Michael F. Tunney, S.J., Rector; Frederick G. Betti, S.J.; Joseph E. Billotti, S.J.; John P. Bucki, S.J.; Joseph F. Burke, S.J., Ph.D.; Thomas A. Colgan, S.J.; Paul J. Dugan, S.J.; Edward J. Durkin, S.J.; Robert A. Haus, S.J. (Retired); Daniel P. Jamros, S.J.; Frank LaRocca, S.J.; Daniel J. Lusch, S.J.; Joseph W. Lux, S.J.; Patrick J. Lynch, S.J.; William J. McCurdy, S.J.; Martin X. Moleski, S.J.; Paul W. Nochelski, S.J.; Michael H. Pastizzo, S.J.; Robert J. Pecoraro, S.J.; James M. Pribek, S.J.; George A. Restrepo, S.J.; John J. Ryan, S.J.; David F. White, S.J.; Eugene A. Zimpfer, S.J.; Bro. Christopher Derby, S.J.

The Canisius Jesuit Community, Inc.

The Eudists - Congregation of Jesus and Mary (1642) 1088 Delaware Ave., Apt. 9G, 14209. Tel: 716-886-4594. Email: bobperelli@roadrunner.com. Rev. Robert J. Perelli, C.J.M., D.Min. Total in Residence 1.

St. Patrick Friary, 102 Seymour St., 14210. Tel: 716-856-5790; Fax: 716-898-8097. Revs. John W. Alderson, O.F.M.; Steven J. Pavignano, O.F.M.; Francis Pompei, O.F.M., Guardian; Bros. Timothy S. Dauenhauer, O.F.M.; Vianney Justin, O.F.M.; Michael G. Oberst, O.F.M.; Maurice V. Swartout, O.F.M.

Sheehan Residence for Priests Residence for retired priests., 330 Linwood Ave., 14209-1689. Tel: 716-884-9679; Fax: 716-881-3268. Sr. Virginia Balk, O.S.F., Admin.; Rev. Msgrs. Francis Braun (Retired); John W. Zeitler (Retired); Revs. Robert J. Biesinger (Retired); Mark M. Friel (Retired); Raymond J. Mahar (Retired); Robert A. Martin (Retired); Edward H. Schroeder (Retired); Robert A. Stolinski (Retired).

ATHOL SPRINGS. *St. Francis of Assisi Friary* (1927) 4129 Lake Shore Rd., 14010-0185. Tel: 716-627-5762; Fax: 716-627-4610. Email: frmichaels@stfrancishigh.org. Web: www.stfrancishigh.org. Revs. Joseph Bayne, O.F.M.Conv.; Michael Sajda, O.F.M.Conv., Guardian & Pres.; Francis Lombardo, O.F.M.Conv.; Mark David Skura, O.F.M.Conv.; Justin Ross, O.F.M.Conv.; Bros. Nicholas Romeo, O.F.M.Conv.; Brian Newbigging, O.F.M.Conv. Faculty Residence for St. Francis High School Priests 5; Brothers 2; Total in Residence 7.

St. Maximilian Kolbe Friary, P.O. Box 454, 14010. Tel: 716-627-2710; Fax: 716-627-5263. Email: frdaniel@localnet.com. Revs. Romulus Rosolowski, O.F.M.Conv.; Innocent Kurkowski, O.F.M.Conv. (Retired); Ronald Sermak, O.F.M.Conv.; Marcel Sokalski, O.F.M.Conv.; Ross Syracuse, O.F.M.Conv.; Bro. William Surdyka, O.F.M.Conv. Priests 5; Total in Residence 6.

CLARENCE. *Regional Motherhouse of Brothers of Mercy*, 4520 Ransom Rd., 14031. Tel: 716-759-8341; Fax: 716-759-7243. Email: jude@brothersofmercy.org. Web: www.brothersofmercy.org. Bro. Jude Holzfoerster, F.M.M., Regl. Supr.; Rev. John J. Sardina, Chap.

Brothers of Mercy, Inc. Brothers 11.

DEPEW. *Msgr. Conniff Residence*, 68 Cowing St., 14043. Tel: 716-393-3595; Fax: 716-393-3597. Revs. Robert G. Beiter (Retired); Richard S. DiGiulio (Retired); Louis S. Dolinic (Retired); Stanislaw Dudek (Retired); Walter L. Matuszak (Retired); John J. Mitka (Retired); Emil P. Swiatek (Retired); Rev. Msgrs. W. Jerome Sullivan, J.C.D. (Retired); John W. Madsen (Retired).

LACKAWANNA. *Bishop Head Residence* (2002) 10 Rosary Ave., 14218. Tel: 716-824-4644; Fax: 716-824-4844. Diane J. Wulf, Admin.; Rev. Msgrs. Leonard E. Biniszkiewicz (Retired); Anthony J. Jasinski (Retired); Leon M. Neu (Retired); Kevin T. O'Neill (Retired); Francis M. Skupien (Retired); Paul F. Stengel (Retired); Revs. James M. Augustyn (Retired); Albert J. Bosack (Retired); Richard C. Coveny (Retired); Richard A. Massar (Retired); L. Antonio Rodriguez (Retired); Theodore C. Rog (Retired); Raymond F. Uschold (Retired).

LEROY. *Order of the BVM of Mercy/Mercedarian Friars*, Mercygrove, 7758 E. Main Rd., Le Roy, 14482-9701. Tel: 585-768-7110; Fax: 585-768-4803. Web: www.orderofmercy.org. Revs. Eugene Costa, O.de.M., Novice Master; Michael R. Rock, O.de.M., Pastor Our Lady of Mercy & St. Brigid; Timothy Brady, O.de.M., Local Supr. & Parochial Vicar; Bros. Matthew J. Levis, O.de.M., Pastoral Assoc.; Martin Jarowsinski, O.de.M., Community Devel. Office; James Chia, O.de.M. United States headquarters for the community. Novitiate formation community. Total in Community: Professed Religious 5.

St. Raymond Nonnatus Novitiate (1948) Order of the BVM of Mercy.; Residence for religious serving Our Lady of Mercy and St. Brigid Parishes., Mercygrove, 7758 E. Main Rd., Le Roy, 14482-9701. Tel: 585-768-7110; Fax: 585-768-4803. Web: www.orderofmercy.org. Revs. Eugene Costa, O.de.M., Novice Master; Timothy Brady, O.de.M., Supr. & Parochial Vicar; Michael R. Rock, O.de.M., Pastor; Bros. Matthew J. Levis, O.de.M., Pastoral Assoc.; Martin Jarowsinski, O.de.M., Community Devel. Office.

NIAGARA UNIVERSITY. *Vincentian Community at Niagara University*, Vincentian Residence, 14109-2209. Tel: 716-286-8110; Fax: 716-286-8766. Email: jhubbert@niagara.edu. Bro. Martin J. Schneider, C.M.; Revs. Kevin G. Creagh, C.M., Ed.D.; Stephen J. Denig, C.M.; John W. Gouldrick, C.M.; Joseph G. Hubbert, C.M., Supr.; Bruce J. Krause, C.M.; Joseph L. Levesque, C.M. Total in Residence 8.

NORTH TONAWANDA. *Society of the Catholic Apostolate, Infant Jesus Delegature*, 3452 Niagara Falls Blvd., P.O. Box 563, 14120-0563. Tel: 716-694-4313; Fax: 716-743-5430. Revs. John Posiewala, S.A.C., Supr. & Prov. Delegate; Severyn J. Koszyk, S.A.C.; George C. Maj, S.A.C.

ST. BONAVENTURE. *St. Bonaventure Friary* (1856) 14778. Tel: 716-375-2416; Fax: 716-375-2424. Email: skellogg@sbu.edu. Web: www.sbu.edu. Revs. David D. Blake, O.F.M., Ph.D.; Michael D. Calabria, O.F.M., M.A., Vicar; Francis DiSpigno, O.F.M., M.Div., Guardian; David Flood, O.F.M., Ph.D.; Robert Karris, O.F.M., Th.D.; Peter Schneible, O.F.M., Ph.D.; James Vacco, O.F.M., M.A.; Allen Weber, O.F.M., Ph.D.; Bros. F. Edward Coughlin, O.F.M., Ph.D.; David Haack, O.F.M., Ph.D.; Robert Lentz, O.F.M., B.A.; Basil J. Valente, O.F.M., M.T.S. Fathers 10; Brothers 5.

TONAWANDA. *Maryknoll House; Maryknoll Fathers & Brothers*, 73 Adam St., 14150. Tel: 716-213-0000; Fax: 716-875-0005. Email: buffalo@maryknoll.org. Web: www.maryknoll.org. Mr. Paul Bork, Dir. Total in Residence 1; Total Staff 2.

O'Hara Residence (1995) 69 O'Hara Rd., 14150-6227. Tel: 716-743-0037; Fax: 716-743-8772. Rev. Msgrs. Angelo M. Caligiuri (Retired); Anthony J. Caligiuri (Retired); James N. Connelly (Retired); Thomas E. Crane (Retired); Rev. Salvatore J. Cusimano (Retired); Rev. Msgrs. Leo E. Hammerl (Retired); Dino J. Lorenzetti (Retired); Edward J. Sobierajski (Retired); Richard L. Wetter (Retired); Rev. Joseph C. Carlo (Retired). Total in Residence 10; Total Staff 7.

WILLIAMSVILLE. *Consolata Fathers*, 35 Brompton Rd., P.O. Box 570, 14221. Tel: 716-634-5678; 716-634-3793. Revs. John N. Reuther, I.M.C., Admin.; James Kingori, I.M.C. (Kenya).

[O] CONVENTS AND RESIDENCES FOR SISTERS

BUFFALO. *Discalced Carmelite Monastery of St. Teresa of the Child Jesus* (1920) 75 Carmel Rd., 14214. Tel: 716-837-6499; Fax: 716-837-3517. Sr. Mother Miriam of Jesus, O.C.D., Prioress. Cloistered Professed Sisters 11; Extern Professed Sisters 2; Novices 1; Postulants 1.

Holy Name Province - Provincial Motherhouse Tel: 716-754-4312, Ext. 9764; Fax: 716-754-7657. Email: office@franciscans-stella-niagara.org. Web: www.franciscans-stella-niagara.org.

Sisters of St. Francis of Holy Name Province, Inc., 4421 Lower River Rd., Stella Niagara, 14144-1001. Tel: 716-754-4312, Ext. 9764; Fax: 716-754-7657. Email: office@franciscans-stella-niagara.org. Sr. Edith Wyss, O.S.F., Prov. Min.

Center of Renewal, Inc., 4421 Lower River Rd., Stella Niagara, 14144. Tel: 716-754-7376; Fax: 716-754-1223. Email: hospitality@center-of-renewal.org. Web: www.center-of-renewal.org. Sr. Edith Wyss, O.S.F., Prov. Min.

Francis Center, 335 24th St., Niagara Falls, 14303. Tel: 716-234-2050; Fax: 716-282-3783. Email: bneumeister14301@yahoo.com. Sr. Edith Wyss, O.S.F., Prov. Min.

Stella Niagara Education Park, Inc., 4421 Lower River Rd., Stella Niagara, 14144. Tel: 716-754-4314; Fax: 716-754-2964. Email: snepoffice@yahoo.com. Web: www.stellaniagara.org. Sr. Edith Wyss, O.S.F., Prov. Min.

The Stella Niagara Education Park Endowment Foundation, 4421 Lower River Rd., Stella Niagara, 14144. Tel: 716-754-4314; Fax: 716-754-2964. Email: snepoffice@yahoo.com. Web: www.stellaniagara.org. Sr. Edith Wyss, O.S.F., Prov. Min.

The Sisters of St. Francis Retirement Fund, 4421 Lower River Rd., Stella Niagara, 14144. Tel: 716-876-3426; Fax: 716-754-7657. Email: bernbeck@gmail.com. Sr. Edith Wyss, O.S.F., Prov. Min.

The Providence Fund, 4421 Lower River Rd., Stella Niagara, 14144. Tel: 716-754-4312, Ext. 9643; Fax: 716-754-7657. Email: mauraosf@yahoo.com. Sr. Edith Wyss, O.S.F., Prov. Min.

Buffalo Academy of the Sacred Heart, Inc., 3860 Main St., 14226-3398. Tel: 716-834-2101; Fax: 716-834-2944. Email: jdemert@sacredheartacademy.org. Web: www.sacredheartacademy.org.

Immaculate Heart of Mary Convent (1900) Villa Maria, 600 Doat St., 14211. Tel: 716-892-4141; Fax: 716-892-4177. Email: ihmcon@feliciansisters.org. Web: www.feliciansna.org. Sisters M. Kevin Szeluga, C.S.S.F., Local Min.; Mary Christopher Moore, C.S.S.F., Provincial Min. Felician Sisters 166.

Monastery of Our Lady of the Rosary (1905) 335 Doat St., 14211-2199. Tel: 716-892-0066; Fax: 716-892-8846. Email: bufprioress@opnuns.org. Sr. Mary Emmanuel, O.P., Prioress; Rev. Thomas B. Confer, O.P., Chap.

Dominican Nuns of the Perpetual Rosary, Buffalo, NY Professed Nuns 20.

Sisters of Mercy of the Americas-New York, Pennsylvania, Pacific West Community, Inc., 625 Abbott Rd., 14220. Tel: 716-826-5051; Fax: 716-826-1518. Email: nhoff@mercynyppaw.org. Web: www.mercynyppaw.org. Sr. Nancy Hoff, R.S.M., Pres. Vowed Members 463; Associates 414.

Mercy Center, Residence for Sisters: 625 Abbott Rd., 14220. Tel: 716-825-5531; Fax: 716-826-1518.

Sisters of Social Service of Buffalo (1923) 296 Summit Ave., 14214-1936. Tel: 716-834-0197; Fax: 716-834-6168. Email: sssbuf@verizon.net. Web: www.sistersofsocialservicebuffalo.org. Sr. Teresina Joo, S.S.S., District Moderator. Sisters 7.

Other Convents:

Generalate, Bathori Laszlo u 10, Budapest H-1029 Hungary. Tel: 011-361-275-7057; Fax: 011-361-391-6229. Email: sss.gen@hcbc.hu. Sr. Agnes Pataki, S.S.S., Gen. Moderator.

Sara House, 42 Linden Ave., 14214-1502. Tel: 716-836-0685. Sisters 3.

Bethany House, 152 Kinsey Ave., Kenmore, 14217-1949. Tel: 716-873-6179. Sisters 1.

Sisters of St. Mary of Namur (1819) St. Mary Center, St. Mary Center, 241 Lafayette Ave., 14213. Tel: 716-884-8221; Fax: 716-884-6598. Email: ssmnprov@verizon.net. Web: www.ssmn.us. Sisters Caroline Smith, S.S.M.N., Prov. Supr.; Marian Baumler, S.S.M.N., Prov. Councillor. Provincial House of the Sisters of St. Mary of Namur. Professed Sisters 81.

Annunciation Convent, 245 Lafayette Ave., 14213. Tel: 716-885-6252.

Sisters of St. Mary, 160 Lovering Ave., 14216. Tel: 716-873-9002.

Sisters of St. Mary, 165 University Ave., 14214. Tel: 716-833-8532.

Sisters of St. Mary, 8691 Supervisor Ave., Colden, 14033. Tel: 716-941-6359.

Sisters of St. Mary, 3100 Elmwood Ave., Kenmore, 14217. Tel: 716-873-8011.

Sisters of St. Mary, 104 Garden St., Lockport, 14094. Tel: 716-433-3966.

Sisters of St. Mary, 2484 River Rd., Niagara Falls, 14304.

ALLEGANY. *Franciscan Sisters of Allegany, New York, Inc.* (1859) 115 E. Main St., 14706. Tel: 716-373-0200; Fax: 716-372-5774. Email: fsa@fsallegany.org. Web: www.alleganyfranciscans.org. Sr. M. Avril Chin Fatt, O.S.F., Congregational Min.

St. Elizabeth Motherhouse (1859) 115 E. Main St.,

14706. Tel: 716-373-0200; Fax: 716-372-5774. Email: fsa@fsallegany.org. Web: www.alleganyfranciscans.org. Sisters M. Avril Chin Fatt, O.S.F., Congregational Min. & Pres.; Jean Hayes, O.S.F., Local Min. Sisters 79.

CLARENCE. *Congregation of the Sisters of St. Joseph Generalate*, Administrative Offices, 10324 Main St., 14031. Tel: 716-759-6454; Fax: 716-759-6415. Web: www.ssjbuffalo.org. Sr. Jean Marie Zirnheld, S.S.J., Pres. Professed Sisters 89.

Sisters of St. Joseph, Clarence Residence, 4975 Strickler Rd., 14031. Tel: 716-759-6893; Fax: 716-759-2488. Email: ssjbuffalo@msn.com. Sr. Margaret Manzella, S.S.J., Admin. Total in Residence 43.

HAMBURG. *Immaculate Conception Convent*, 5229 S. Park Ave., 14075. Tel: 716-649-1205; Fax: 716-202-4940. Web: www.franciscansistersofsaintjoseph.org. Rev. Mark David Skura, O.F.M.Conv., Chap.; Sr. Anne Marie Hudzina, F.S.S.J., Gen. Min. Motherhouse of the Franciscan Sisters of St. Joseph Sisters in Residence 60; Sisters in Diocese 67.

LEROY. *Sisters of Our Lady of Mercy (SOLM) (Mercedarians)* (1864) 27 Lake St., Le Roy, 14482. Tel: 585-768-8053. Email: Mercy@Rochester.rr.com. Sr. Rosaria Savarimuthu, S.O.L.M., Supr. Sisters 4.

LEWISTON. *Sisters of the Sacred Heart of Jesus (S.S.H.J.)*, 5269 Lewiston Rd., 14092. Tel: 716-284-8273; Fax: 716-284-8273. Email: sacredhrtv@yahoo.com. Sr. M. Terenzia Guidice, S.S.H.J., Supr. Sisters at Sacred Heart Villa School & Convent 10.

SILVER CREEK. *Missionary Sisters of St. Columban, St. Columban's on the Lake* (1924) 2546 Lake Rd., 14136. Tel: 716-934-4515; Fax: 716-934-3919. Email: sisters@stcolumbanshome.org. Web: www.columbansisters.org. Sr. Corona Colleary, S.S.C., U.S. Area Coord. Professed Sisters 10.

WEST SENECA. *Sisters of Charity of St. Vincent de Paul of Zagreb, Croatia*, 171 Knox Ave., 14224. Tel: 716-825-5859. Email: milosrdnice@roadrunner.com. Sr. Bogumila Kutlesa, M.V.Z., Supr.

Sisters of Charity of St. Vincent de Paul of Zagreb, Croatia - U.S.A. Delegacy Headquarters Professed Sisters 3.

WILLIAMSVILLE. *Sisters of St. Francis of the Neumann Communities, Western New York Region, St. Mary of the Angels Convent*, 201 Reist St., 14221. Tel: 716-632-2155; Fax: 716-632-0339. Sisters Roberta Smith, O.S.F., Gen. Councilor; Beatrice Leising, O.S.F., Regl. Co-Min. Professed Sisters in the Region 99.

[P] RETREAT HOUSES

DERBY. *St. Columban Center* (1947) 795 Main St., 14203. 6892 Lake Shore Rd., P.O. Box 816, 14047-0816. Adjunct property of Christ the King Seminary.

WEST CLARKSVILLE. *Mount Irenaeus, Franciscan Mountain Retreat & Holy Peace Friary* (1982) P.O. Box 100, 14786. Tel: 585-973-2470; Fax: 585-973-2400. Email: mmarc@sbu.edu. Web: www.mounti.com. Revs. Daniel P. Riley, O.F.M., M.A., Pres. & Guardian; John C. Coughlin, O.F.M., M.Div.; Bro. Joseph A. Kotula, O.F.M., Ph.D., Vicar; Revs. Louis M. McCormick, O.F.M., D.Min.; Robert Struzynski, O.F.M.; Bro. Kevin Kriso, O.F.M. Order of Friars Minor Holy Name Province. Total in Residence 6.

[Q] CAMPUS MINISTRY AND NEWMAN CENTERS

BUFFALO. *Buffalo State College* 1219 Elmwood Ave., 14222. Tel: 716-882-1080; Fax: 716-882-6914. Email: bscnewmancenter@yahoo.com. Web: www.buffalostate.edu/orgs/newmanct. Rev. Patrick J. Zengierski, Ph.D., Dir. & Vicar Campus Ministry; Sr. Candice Tucci, O.S.F., Campus Min.; Carmen Schaff, Campus Min.; Alesandra Mercedes, Peer Min.; Nathan Rey, Peer Min.

Canisius College, Campus Ministry Office 2001 Main St., 14208. Tel: 716-888-2420; Fax: 716-888-3144. Email: campmin@canisius.edu. Web: www.canisius.edu/camp-minist/. Revs. John P. Bucki, S.J., Dir.; Thomas A. Colgan, S.J., Assoc. Campus Minister; Ms. Luanne Firestone, Assoc. Campus Min.; Ms. Susan Fischer, Assoc. Campus Min.; Ms. Sarah Signorino, Assoc. Campus Min.; Mr. Joseph VanVolkenburg, Assoc. Campus Min.; Mr. Scott Paeplow, Dir. Music.

D'Youville College 320 Porter Ave., 14201. Tel: 716-829-7672; Fax: 716-829-7760. Rev. Patrick T. O'Keefe, Dir. Campus Min.; Rev. Janice Mahle.

State University of New York at Buffalo (Main St. South Campus) St. Joseph University Parish, 3269 Main St., 14214. Tel: 716-833-0298; Fax: 716-833-7339. Web: www.buffalocatholic.com. Rev. Jacob C. Ledwon, Dir.; Mr. Michael Hayes, Campus Min.

Trocaire College 360 Choate Ave., 14220. Tel: 716-827-2489; Fax: 716-825-0416. Sr. Marie Andre Main, R.S.M., Dir. Campus Min.

Villa Maria College 240 Pine Ridge Rd., 14225. Tel: 716-896-0700; Fax: 716-896-0705. Web: www.villa.edu. Frank Antonucci, Dir.

ALFRED. *Alfred University and Alfred State College Campus Ministry* Lower College Dr., P.O. Box 1154, 14802. Tel: 607-587-9411; Fax: 607-587-9431. Email: stjude.alfred@gmail.com. Mr. Chris Yarnal, Dir. Campus Ministry.

Niagara University Campus Ministry, P.O. Box 2016, Niagara University, 14109. Tel: 716-286-8400; Fax: 716-286-8477. Email: ministry@niagara.edu. Web: www.niagara.edu/ministry. Revs. Kevin G. Creagh, C.M., Ed.D., Dir. Campus Ministry; Bruce J. Krause, C.M., Campus Min.; Ms. Monica Saltarelli, Campus Min.; Ms. Kristina Schliesman, Campus Min.

AMHERST. *State University of New York at Buffalo (North Campus) Newman Center* 495 Skinnersville Rd., 14228. Tel: 716-636-7495; Fax: 716-568-0692. Email: prspat@buffalo.edu. Web: www.newman.buffalo.edu. Rev. Msgr. J. Patrick Keleher, Dir.; Ms. Katie Koch, Campus Min.; Mr. Ed Koch, Campus Min.

FREEDONIA. *Newman Center At SUNY - Fredonia* 222 Temple St., Fredonia, 14063. Tel: 716-679-4686; Fax: 716-679-3486. Nathan Kropp, M.S., M.A., Dir. Campus Ministry.

HAMBURG. *Hilbert College, Campus Ministry Office* 5200 S. Park Ave., 14075. Tel: 716-649-7900; Fax: 716-649-0702. Barbara Bonanno, Dir.; Deacon Dennis P. Conroy.

ST. BONAVENTURE. *St. Bonaventure University* P.O. Box AR, 14778. Tel: 716-375-2600; Fax: 716-375-2618. Revs. Francis DiSpigno, O.F.M., M.Div., Exec. Dir., Univ. Ministries; John C. Coughlin, O.F.M., M.Div.; Louis M. McCormick, O.F.M., D.Min.; Daniel P. Riley, O.F.M., M.A.; Robert Struzynski, O.F.M.; Bros. Joseph A. Kotula, O.F.M., Ph.D.; Kevin Kriso, O.F.M.

[R] CAMPS AND COMMUNITY CENTERS

SALAMANCA. *Camp Turner* (Coed)., Office: P.O. Box 264, 14779. Tel: 716-354-4555; Fax: 716-354-2055. Email: campturner@gmail.com. Web: www.campturner.com. John Mann, Dir.

[S] MISCELLANEOUS

BUFFALO. *Catholic Health System Infusion Pharmacy, Inc. dba Catholic Health Infusion Pharmacy* 6350 Transit Rd., Depew, 14043. Tel: 716-685-4870; Fax: 716-681-3483. *c/o Catholic Health Systems*, 2121 Main St., Ste. 300, 14214. Joyce Markiewicz, Pres. & CEO. A Catholic Health System organization.

Catholic Health System Program of All-Inclusive Care for the Elderly, Inc. (CHS PACE), Seton Professional Building, 2121 Main St., Ste. 300, 14214. Thomas Schifferli, Exec. Dir. Total Assisted Annually 80; Staff 18.

Catholic Union Store (1899) 795 Main St., 14203. Tel: 716-847-8715; Fax: 716-847-8702. Email: cus@buffalodiocese.org.

St. Clare Apartments Housing Development Fund Company, Inc. Low income housing for the elderly age 62 and over., c/o Delta Development of Western New York, 525 Washington St., 14203. Tel: 716-847-1635; Fax: 716-856-7201. Email: bernadette.harlan@ccwny.org. Web: www.deltadevelopmentwny.com. Bernadette Harlan, Exec. Dir. Residents 39; Staff 2.

Delta Development of Western New York, Inc., c/o Delta Development of WNY, Inc., 525 Washington St., 14203. Tel: 716-847-1635; Fax: 716-856-7201. Bernadette Harlan, Exec. Dir.; Sr. Mary McCarrick, O.S.F., Pres., Catholic Charities. Staff 6.

50-60 Kosciuzko Street Housing Development Fund Company, Inc. Special Purpose Housing for the chronically mentally ill., *c/o Delta Development of WNY, Inc.*, 525 Washington St., 14203. Tel: 716-847-1635; Fax: 716-856-7201. Email: bernadette.harlan@ccwny.org. Web: www.deltadevelopmentwny.com. Bernadette Harlan, Exec. Dir. Residents 5; Staff 2.

The Foundation of the Roman Catholic Diocese of Buffalo, NY, Inc., 795 Main St., 14203-1250. Tel: 716-847-8370; Fax: 716-847-5589. Email: devoffice@buffalodiocese.org. Web: www.FRCDB.org. Richard C. Suchan, Exec. Dir.

Franciscan Mystery Players, Inc., 102 Seymour St., 14210. Tel: 315-415-3739. Web: www.mysteryplay.org. Rev. Francis Pompei, O.F.M., Dir.

Gerard Place Housing Development Fund Company, Inc., 2515 Bailey Ave., 14215. Tel: 716-897-9948; Fax: 716-897-9953. Email: gerardhdfc@aol.com. Web: www.gerardplace.org. David Zapfel, M.S., Dir.

Immaculate Heart of Mary Home for Children, Inc. (1896) 600 Doat St., 14211. Tel: 716-892-4141; Fax: 716-892-4177. Web: www.feliciansna.org.

St. Joseph Investment Fund, Inc., 795 Main St., 14203. Tel: 716-847-5500. Email: dslubecky@buffalodiocese.org. Rev. Msgr. David S. Slubecky, J.C.L., S.T.L., V.G., Pres.

Kolping Catholic Young Men's Association of Buffalo, NY dba Kolping Society of Buffalo 1145 Cleveland Dr., 14225. Tel: 716-632-7360. Willi Evelt, Pres.; Rev. Msgr. John W. Zeitler, Mod. (Retired).

La Casa De Los Tainos Housing Development Fund Company, Inc., c/o Delta Development of WNY, Inc., 525 Washington St., 14203. Tel: 716-847-1635; Fax: 716-856-7201. Email: bernadette.harlan@ccwny.org. Web: www.deltadevelopmentwny.com. Bernadette Harlan, Exec. Dir. Low income housing for the elderly age 62 & over. Residents 49; Staff 2.

Monsignor Adamski Village Housing Development Fund Company, Inc., 123 Townsend St., 14212. Tel: 716-854-5510; Fax: 716-854-0170.

Monsignor Adamski Village, Inc., 855 Williams St., 14206. 123 Townsend St., 14212. Facility for elderly and handicapped persons of low income.

The Monsignor Carr Institute, 76 W. Humboldt Pkwy., 14214. Tel: 716-835-9745; Fax: 716-835-6785. Web: www.ccwny.org. Brian T. O'Herron, M.Ed., M.B.A., Dir. Msgr. Carr Institute; Bruce Pace, Ph.D., Dir. Children's Mental Health Clinics. Licensed outpatient mental health and substance abuse treatment, community outreach team, senior advocacy and socialization, marriage counseling, school-based drug prevention, adult psychosocial club, abstinence until marriage education. Also licensed outpatient mental health children's clinics serving seriously emotionally disturbed children and providing collateral services for families. Total Assisted 5,600.

Monsignor Kirby Apartments Housing Development Fund Company, Inc., c/o Delta Development of WNY, Inc., 525 Washington St., 14203. Tel: 716-847-1635, Ext. 3029; Fax: 716-856-7201. Email: bernadette.harlan@ccwny.org. Web: www.deltadevelopmentwny.com. Bernadette Harlan, Exec. Dir. Low income housing for the elderly age 62 and over. Total in Residence 39; Total Staff 2.

Mount St. Mary's Housing Development Fund Company, Inc., c/o Delta Development of WNY, Inc., 525 Washington St., 14203. Tel: 716-847-1635; Fax: 716-856-7201. Email: bernadette.harlan@ccwny.org. Web: www.deltadevelopmentwny.com. Bernadette Harlan, Exec. Dir. Total in Residence 39; Staff 2.

Nazareth Nursing Home, 291 North St., 14201. *c/o Catholic Health Systems*, 2121 Main St., Ste. 300, 14214.

NyPPaW Fides, Inc., 625 Abbott Rd., 14220. Tel: 716-826-5051; Fax: 716-826-1518. Sr. Jo Anne Courneen, R.S.M., Chair.

158 Chenango Street Housing Development Fund Company, Inc. dba St. John Bosco Apartments c/o Delta Development of WNY, Inc., 525 Washington St., 14203. Tel: 716-847-1635; Fax: 716-856-7201. Email: bernadette.harlan@ccwny.org. Web: www.deltadevelopmentwny.com. Bernadette Harlan, Exec. Dir. Low income housing for the elderly age 62 and over. Staff 2; Residents 12.

Our Lady of Victory Community Housing Development Organization, Inc., c/o Catholic Health Systems, 2121 Main St., Ste. 300, 14214. Tel: 716-923-4802; Fax: 716-604-1805. Email: agb@chsbuffalo.org. Christine J. Kluckhohn, Pres.

Our Lady of Victory Renaissance Corporation, c/o Catholic Health Systems, 2121 Main St., Ste. 300, 14214. Tel: 716-923-4816; Fax: 716-604-1820. Email: cjk@chsbuffalo.org. Christine J. Kluckhohn, Pres., OLV Renaissance.

Our Mother of Good Counsel Housing Development Fund Co., Inc., c/o Delta Development of WNY, Inc., 525 Washington St., 14203. Tel: 716-847-1635; Fax: 716-856-7201. Email: bernadette.harlan@ccwny.org. Web: www.deltadevelopmentwny.com. Bernadette Harlan, Exec. Dir. Housing for mobility impaired & elderly of low income. Total in Residence 39; Total Staff 2.

St. Rita's Home, Inc. (1940) 600 Doat St., 14211. Tel: 716-892-4141; Fax: 716-892-4177. Web: www.feliciansna.org.

Salesian Studios, 152 Plymouth Ave., 14201-1214. Tel: 716-886-6597. Rev. Thomas Ribits, O.S.F.S.

Santa Maria Towers Housing Development Fund Company, Inc., c/o Delta Development of WNY, Inc., 525 Washington St., 14203. Tel: 716-847-1635; Fax: 716-856-7201. Email:

bernadette.harlan@ccwny.org. Web: www.deltadevelopmentwny.com. Bernadette Harlan, Exec. Dir. Housing for mobility impaired and elderly of low income. Total in Residence 114; Staff 5.

Timon Towers Housing Development Fund Company, Inc., c/o Delta Development of WNY, Inc., 525 Washington St., 14203. Tel: 716-847-1635; Fax: 716-856-7201. Email: bernadette.harlan@ccwny.org. Web: deltadevelopmentwny.com. Bernadette Harlan, Exec. Dir. Low income housing for the mobility impaired and elderly. Total Staff 5; Total in Residence 124.

St. Timothy's Park Villa Housing Development Fund Company, Inc., c/o Delta Development of WNY, Inc., 525 Washington St., 14203. Tel: 716-847-1635; Fax: 716-856-7201. Email: bernadette.harlan@ccwny.org. Web: www.deltadevelopmentwny.com. Bernadette Harlan, Exec. Dir. Low income housing for the elderly age 62 and over. Total in Residence 49; Total Staff 2.

Western New York Catholic Healthcare Corporation, 2121 Main St., Ste. 300, 14214.

Wheatfield Housing Development Fund Company, Inc., c/o Delta Development of WNY, Inc., 525 Washington St., 14203. Tel: 716-847-1635; Fax: 716-856-7201. Email: bernadette.harlan@ccwny.org. Web: www.deltadevelopmentwny.com. Bernadette Harlan, Exec. Dir. Low income housing for the elderly age 62 and over. Apartments 49; Staff 2.

ALLEGANY. *Canticle Farm, Inc.*, 115 E. Main St., 14706. Tel: 716-373-0200; Fax: 716-373-3554. Email: canticleoffice@yahoo.com. Liselle Esposito, Bd. Chairperson; Sr. Joyce Ramage, O.S.F., Pres.

Dr. Lyle F. Renodin Foundation, Inc., 115 E. Main St., 14706. Tel: 716-373-0200; Fax: 716-372-5774. Web: www.alleganyfranciscans.org. Linda Pepperdine, Pres.; Laura Whitford, Chm.

St. Elizabeth Mission Society, Inc. (1947) 115 E. Main St., 14706. Tel: 716-373-1130; Fax: 716-373-9324. Email: stelizmission@fsallegany.org. Web: www.fsallegany.org. Sr. M. Chris Doherty, O.S.F., Dir.

AMHERST. *Victorious Missionaries*, 911B Robin Rd., 14228. Tel: 716-639-7542. Miss Carol A. Buchla, Pres. & Natl. Representative. A spiritual and social movement for the disabled and chronically ill.

ATHOL SPRINGS. *Fr. Justin Rosary Hour*, 4190 St. Francis Dr., P.O. Box 454, 14010. Tel: 716-627-3861; Fax: 716-926-8501. Email: rosaryhour@yahoo.com. Web: www.rosaryhour.com. Jerry Kornowicz, Office Mgr. A prayer and catechetical program in Polish and English aired over various radio stations and internet, conducted by St. Anthony of Padua Province of the Order of Friars Minor Conventual. Priests 1; Lay Staff 5; Total Staff 6.

KENMORE. *Catholic Cemeteries of the Roman Catholic Diocese of Buffalo, Inc.*, 4000 Elmwood Ave., 14217. Tel: 716-873-6500; Fax: 716-873-3247. Email: cathcemsbflo@buffalodiocese.org. Web: www.buffalocatholiccemeteries.org. Carmen A. Colao, Dir. Cemeteries: Assumption, Grand Island; Gate of Heaven, Lewiston; Holy Cross, Lackawanna; Holy Sepulchre, Cheektowaga; Mount Olivet, Kenmore; Queen of Heaven, Lockport.

K M H Homes, INC., 1503 Military Rd., 14217. Tel: 716-447-6600. *c/o Catholic Health Systems*, 2121 Main St., Ste. 300, 14214. James M. Millard, CEO & Pres. A holding company of the Catholic Health System.

LACKAWANNA. *Mother of Divine Grace Housing Development Fund Company, Inc.* (1991) 780 Ridge Rd., 14218. Tel: 716-828-9500; Fax: 716-828-9526. Email: baker@buffnet.net. Web: www.bakervictoryservices.org. James J. Casion, CEO. Sponsored by Baker Victory Services., Purpose: To provide housing for persons of low income, particularly handicapped mentally retarded and developmentally disabled adults. Total in Residence 10; Total Staff 11.

Nativity Housing Development Fund Company, Inc. (1992) 780 Ridge Rd., 14218. Tel: 716-828-9500; Fax: 716-828-9526. Email: baker@buffnet.net. Web: www.bakervictoryservices.org. James J. Casion, CEO. Sponsored by Baker Victory Services., Purpose: To provide housing for persons of low income, particularly handicapped mentally retarded and developmentally disabled adults. Total in Residence 10; Total Staff 9.

Our Lady of Peace Housing Development Fund Company, Inc. (2000) 780 Ridge Rd., 14218. Tel: 716-828-9500; Fax: 716-828-9526. Email: baker@buffnet.net. Web: www.bakervictoryservices.org. James J. Casion, CEO. Sponsored by Baker Victory Services., Purpose: To provide housing for persons of low income, particularly handicapped mentally retarded and developmentally disabled adults. Total in Residence 6; Total Staff 10.

Our Lady of Victory Homes of Charity (1851) 780 Ridge Rd., 14218. Tel: 716-828-9648; Fax: 716-828-9643. Email: baker@buffnet.net. Web: www.OurLadyofVictory.org. Richard L. Heist, Exec. Dir.; Rev. Msgr. Paul J.E. Burkard, Exec. Vice Pres. & Treas.

Our Lady of Victory Homes of Charity
Society for the Protection of Destitute Roman Catholic Children at Buffalo, NY
Father Baker's, (Formerly Association of Our Lady of Victory); Includes the following Institutions: Baker Victory Services 716-828-9500 or 1-888-287-1160 (Formerly Baker Hall, Our Lady of Victory Infant Home, St. Joseph Orphanage and St. John's Protectory). Total Assisted Annually 5,489; Total Staff 67.

LEWISTON. *Basilica of the National Shrine of Our Lady of Fatima, Inc.* 1023 Swann Rd., P.O. Box 167, Youngstown, 14174-0167. Tel: 716-754-7489; Fax: 716-754-9130. Email: office@fatimashrine.com. Web: www.fatimashrine.com. Revs. Julio M. Ciavaglia, C.R.S.P., Rector & Shrine Dir.; Paul M. Keeling, C.R.S.P., Assoc. Dir. & Treas.; Peter M. Calabrese, C.R.S.P., Assoc. Dir.; Richard M. Delzingaro, C.R.S.P. Priests 4; Total Staff 18.

NIAGARA UNIVERSITY. *Our Lady of Angels Association* (1918) P.O. Box 1918, 14109-1918. Tel: 716-754-0035; Fax: 716-754-0137. Email: novena@niagara.edu. Web: www.ourladyofangels.net. Deborah Korzak, Dir. of Devel. Development Office for the Congregation of the Mission, Eastern Province. Total Staff 6.

NORTH TONAWANDA. *Shrine of the Infant Jesus* 3452 Niagara Falls Blvd., P.O. Box 563, 14120-0563. Tel: 716-694-4313; Fax: 716-743-5430. Administered by the Pallottine Fathers.

STELLA NIAGARA. *DeSales Resources and Ministries, Inc.* (1980) 4421 Lower River Rd., 14144-1001. Tel: 716-754-4948; 800-782-2270; Fax: 716-754-4948. Email: desales@desalesresource.org. Web: www.desalesresource.org. Rev. John L. Graden, O.S.F.S., Dir.; Joanne Kinney, Admin.; Laura Imerese, Business Mgr. Total Staff 3.

WILLIAMSVILLE. *St. Francis Asylum Corporation of the City of Buffalo, Sisters of St. Francis*, 201 Reist St., 14221. Web: www.sosf.org.

[T] CLOSED AND MERGED PARISHES

BUFFALO. *St. Adalbert* (1886) Closed.

St. Agatha (1921) Closed in merger to form Our Lady of Charity Parish. Records at Our Lady of Charity.

St. Agnes (1883) Closed in merger to form St. Katharine Drexel Parish. Records at St. Katharine Drexel Parish.

St. Ambrose (1930) Name changed when merged with St. Agatha and Holy Family Parishes to form Our Lady of Charity Parish. Records at Our Lady of Charity.

St. Ann Merged into SS. Columba-Brigid Parish. Currently a temporary second site for SS. Columba-Brigid. Records at SS. Columba-Brigid.

Annunciation Name changed when merged with Nativity and Our Lady of Loretto Parishes to form Our Lady of Hope Parish at the Annunciation site. Records at Our Lady of Hope.

St. Bartholomew Closed in merger with Blessed Trinity Parish. Records at the Catholic Center, 795 Main St., Buffalo, NY 14203. Tel: 716-847-5567.

St. Benedict the Moor Closed in merger to form St. Martin de Porres Parish. Records at the Catholic Center, 795 Main St. Buffalo, NY 14203. Tel: 716-847-5567.

St. Boniface Closed in merger to form St. Martin de Porres Parish. Records at the Catholic Center, 795 Main St. Buffalo, NY 14203. Tel: 716-847-5567.

St. Brigid Closed in merger with St. Columba Parish to form SS. Columba-Brigid Parish. Records at SS. Columba-Brigid Parish.

St. Elizabeth of Hungary (1906) Closed in merger with Assumption Parish. Records at Assumption Parish.

St. Florian (1917) Closed in a merger with All Saints Parish. Records at All Saints Parish.

St. Francis of Assisi Name changed when merged with St. Agnes and Visitation of the B.V.M. parishes to form St. Katharine Drexel Parish at the St. Francis of Assisi site. Records at St. Katharine Drexel Parish.

St. Francis Xavier (1849) Closed in a merger with Assumption Parish. Records at Assumption Parish.

St. Gerard (1902) Closed in merger with Blessed Trinity Parish. Records at Blessed Trinity Parish.

Holy Apostles SS. Peter and Paul (1909) Closed in merger to form St. Clare Parish. Records at St. Clare Parish.

Holy Family (1902) Merged with St. Agatha and St. Ambrose Parishes to form Our Lady of Charity Parish using both the St. Ambrose and Holy Family sites. Records at Our Lady of Charity.

Holy Name of Jesus Closed. Merged into St. John Gualbert Parish. Records at St. John Gualbert Parish.

Immaculate Conception (1849) Closed when merged into Holy Cross Parish. Records at Holy Cross Parish.

Immaculate Heart of Mary (1946) Closed in merger with St. Aloysius Gonzaga Parish, Cheektogawa. Records at St. Aloysius Gonzaga.

St. James (1916) Closed in merger with Blessed Trinity Parish. Records at Blessed Trinity Parish.

St. Joachim Closed. Records at the Catholic Center, 795 Main St. Buffalo, NY 14203. Tel: 716-847-5567.

St. John the Baptist (1867) Closed. Records at Assumption Parish.

St. John the Evangelist (1906) Closed in merger with St. Theresa Parish. Records at St. Theresa.

St. Luke Closed. Records at the Catholic Center, 795 Main St. Buffalo NY 14203. Tel: 716-847-5567.

St. Mary of Sorrows (1872) Closed & merged into SS Columba-Brigid Parish. Records at SS. Columba-Brigid Parish.

St. Matthew Closed in a merger to form St. Martin de Porres Parish. Records at the Catholic Center, 795 Main St. Buffalo, NY 14203. Tel: 716-847-5567.

St. Monica Closed. Records at the Catholic Center, 795 Main St. Buffalo, NY 14203. Tel: 716-847-5567.

The Nativity of the Blessed Virgin (1898) Closed in merger with Annunciation and Our Lady of Loretto parishes to form Our Lady of Hope Parish. Records at Our Lady of Hope.

Our Lady of Loretto (1940) Closed in merger with Annunciation and Nativity parishes to form Our Lady of Hope Parish. Records at Our Lady of Hope.

Our Lady of Lourdes Closed in merger to form St. Martin de Porres Parish. Records at the Catholic Center, 795 Main St. Buffalo, NY 14203. Tel: 716-847-5567.

Precious Blood (1899) Closed in merger to form St. Clare Parish. Records at St. Clare Parish.

Queen of Peace (1920) Closed. Merged into St. John Gualbert Parish. Records at St. John Gualbert Parish.

Queen of the Most Holy Rosary Closed. Records at the Catholic Center 795 Main St. Buffalo, NY 14203. Tel: 716-847-5567.

SS. Rita & Patrick (1854) Closed in merger to form St. Clare Parish. Records at St. Clare Parish.

St. Stephen Name changed when merged with SS. Rita and Patrick, Holy Apostles SS. Peter & Paul, St. Valentine and Precious Blood Parishes to form St. Clare Parish at the St. Stephen site. Records at St. Clare Parish.

Transfiguration Closed. Records at the Catholic Center, 795 Main St. Buffalo, NY 14203. Tel: 716-847-5567.

St. Valentine (1920) Closed in merger to form St. Clare Parish. Records at St. Clare Parish.

St. Vincent de Paul Closed. Merged into Blessed Trinity Parish. Records at the Catholic Center, 795 Main St. Buffalo, NY 14203. Tel: 716-847-5567.

The Visitation of the B.V.M. (1898) Closed in merger to form St. Katharine Drexel Parish. Records at St. Katharine Drexel Parish.

ALBION. *St. Joseph* Name changed when merged with St. Mary Assumption to form Holy Family Parish. Records at Holy Family.

St. Mary Assumption (1891) Closed after merging with St. Joseph Parish to form Holy Family Parish at the St. Joseph site. Records at Holy Family.

ANGELICA. *Sacred Heart* (1848) Closed in merger to form Holy Family of Jesus, Mary & Joseph Parish in Belmont. Records at Holy Family of Jesus, Mary & Joseph Parish.

ARCADE. *SS. Peter & Paul* Name changed when merged with St. Mary, East Arcade and Blessed Sacrament, Delevan to form St. Mary Parish in Arcade and using both the Arcade and East Arcade sites. Records at St. Mary Parish, Arcade.

ATTICA. *St. Vincent de Paul* Name changed when merged with St. Joseph Parish in Varysburg to form SS. Joachim & Anne Parish using both the Attica and Varysburg sites. Parish records at SS. Joachim and Anne Parish in Attica.

BARKER. *St. Patrick* (1865) Name changed with merged with St. Joseph Parish, Lyndonville, to form Our Lady of the Lake Parish. Both the

Barker and Lyndonville sites are used. Records at Our Lady of the Lake, Barker.

BATAVIA. *St. Anthony* (1908) Merged with Sacred Heart Parish to form Ascension Parish using both sites. Records at Ascension Parish.

St. Joseph Name changed when merged with St. Mary to form Resurrection Parish using both sites. Records at Resurrection Parish.

St. Mary (1906) Merged with St. Joseph to form Resurrection Parish using both sites. Records at Resurrection Parish.

Sacred Heart Named changed when merged with St. Anthony Parish to form Ascension Parish using both sites. Records at Ascension Parish.

BELMONT. *St. Mary* Named changed when merged with St. Joseph, Scio and Sacred Heart, Angelica to form Holy Family of Jesus, Mary & Joseph at the Belmont site. Records at Holy Family of Jesus, Mary & Joseph.

BEMUS POINT. *Our Lady of Lourdes* Named changed when merged with St. Mary, Mayville to form St. Mary of Lourdes Parish using both sites. Records at St. Mary of Lourdes, Bemus Point.

BENNINGTON CENTER. *Sacred Heart of Jesus* (1872) Merged with Our Lady of Good Counsel, Darien Center to form Immaculate Heart of Mary Parish using both sites. Records at Immaculate Heart of Mary, Bennington Center.

BLISS. *St. Joseph* (1907) Closed in merger to form St. Isidore Parish, Perry & Silver Springs. Records at St. Isidore Parish, Perry.

BRANT. *Our Lady of Mt. Carmel* (1906) Closed in merger with St. Anthony, Farnham. Records at St. Anthony, Farnham.

BROCTON. *St. Patrick* (1922) Merged with St. James Major, Westfield and St. Thomas More, Ripley to form St. Dominic Parish using the Westfield and Brocton sites. Records at St. Dominic, Brocton.

CASSADAGA. *Immaculate Conception* Merged with St. Anthony, Fredonia using both sites. Records at St. Anthony, Fredonia.

CHEEKTOWAGA. *Most Holy Redeemer* (1913) Closed in merger with St. Lawrence Parish, Buffalo. Records at St. Lawrence Parish.

Mother of Divine Grace (1946) Closed in merger with Infant of Prague, Cheektowaga. Records at Infant of Prague.

CHERRY CREEK. *St. Elizabeth* Closed. Records at St. Joseph, Gowanda.

CLARENCE CENTER. *St. Augustine* (1949) Merged with Good Shepherd, Pendleton, using both sites. Records at Good Shepherd, Pendleton.

COLDEN. *Our Lady of the Sacred Heart* (1912) Closed in merger with St. George Parish, West Falls. Records at St. George, West Falls.

COLLINS CENTER. *St. Frances Cabrini* (1955) Closed in merger to form Epiphany of Our Lord Parish, Langford. Records at Epiphany of Our Lord Parish.

CORFU. *St. Francis of Assisi* (1898) Name changed when merged with Holy Name of Mary, East Pembroke, to form St. Maximilian Kolbe Parish, using both sites. Records at St. Maximilian Kolbe, Corfu.

CRITTENDEN. *St. Patrick* (1857) Closed in merger with St. Francis of Assisi, Corfu. Records at St. Maximilian Kolbe, Corfu.

DARIEN CENTER. *Our Lady of Good Counsel* (1911) Name changed when merged with Sacred Heart of Jesus, Bennington Center to become Immaculate Heart of Mary using both sites. Records at Immaculate Heart of Mary, Darien Center.

DAYTON. *St. Paul of the Cross* Closed. Records at St. Joseph Parish, Gowanda.

DELEVAN. *Blessed Sacrament* (1947) Closed in merger to form St. Mary Parish, Arcade. Records at St. Mary Parish, Arcade.

DEPEW. *Our Lady of the Blessed Sacrament* (1965) Name changed when merged with St. Barnabas to form St. Martha Parish located at Our Lady of the Blessed Sacrament site. Records at St. Martha Parish.

St. Augustine (1909) Closed in merger with St. James, Depew, to become Blessed Mother Teresa of Calcutta Parish. Records at Blessed Mother Teresa of Calcutta, Depew.

St. Barnabas (1960) Closed in merger to form St. Martha Parish, Depew. Records at St. Martha Parish.

St. James (1897) Name changed when merged with St. Augustine, Depew to form Blessed Mother Teresa of Calcutta, Depew located at the St. James site. Records at Blessed Mother Teresa of Calcutta, Depew.

SS. Peter and Paul (1896) Closed in merger with Our Lady of Pompeii, Lancaster. Records at Our Lady of Pompeii, Lancaster.

DUNKIRK. *St. Hedwig* (1902) Merged with St. Hyacinth Parish to form Blessed Mary Angela Parish, but using both sites. Records at Blessed Mary Angela Parish, St. Hyacinth site.

St. Hyacinth (1875) Name changed when merged with St. Hedwig to form Blessed Mary Angela Parish, but using both sites. Records at Blessed Mary Angela Parish, St. Hyacinth site.

EAST ARCADE. *St. Mary's* (1846) Merged with SS. Peter & Paul, Arcade to form St. Mary Parish, Arcade using both sites. Records at St. Mary, Arcade.

EAST BENNINGTON. *Our Lady Help of Christians* Closed in merger with Darien Center. Records at Immaculate Heart of Mary, Bennington Center.

EAST BETHANY. *Immaculate Conception* (1954) Merged with St. Mary, Pavilion, to form Mary Immaculate Parish using both sites. Records at Mary Immaculate, East Bethany.

EAST EDEN. *St. Mary* (1835) Merged with St. John the Baptist Parish, Boston. St. Mary Church became an oratory of St. John the Baptist. Records at St. John the Baptist.

EAST OTTO. *St. Isidore* Closed in merger with St. Mary Cattaraugus. Records at St. Mary Cattaraugus.

EAST PEMBROKE. *Holy Name of Mary* (1868) Merged with St. Francis of Assisi, Corfu, to form St. Maximilian Kolbe Parish, using both sites. Records at Oakfield site.

EDEN. *St. Mary of the Immaculate Conception* (1858) Closed in merger to form Epiphany of Our Lord Parish, Langford. Records at Epiphany of Our Lord.

ELBA. *Our Lady of Fatima* (1947) Merged with St. Cecilia, Oakfield, to form St. Padre Pio Parish using both sites. Records at St. Padre Pio, Oakfield.

FORESTVILLE. *St. Rose of Lima* (1850) Merged with Our Lady of Mt. Carmel, Silver Creek. Both sites are used. Records at Our Lady of Mt. Carmel, Forestville site.

FRENCH CREEK. *St. Matthias* Name changed when merged with St. Isaac Jogues, Sherman to form Christ Our Hope Parish using both sites. Records at the French Creek site.

FREWSBURG. *Our Lady of Victory* (1950) Merged into St. James Parish, Jamestown. The church became an oratory of St. James Parish. Records at St. James, Jamestown.

FRIENDSHIP. *Sacred Heart* Closed when merged into Our Lady of the Angels, Cuba. Records at Our Lady of the Angels, Cuba.

GASPORT. *St. Mary* (1968) Closed in merger with St. John Parish in Lockport. Records at St. John Parish.

HINSDALE. *St. Helen* (1947) Closed in merger with St. John Parish in Olean. Records at St. John Parish, Olean.

HULBERTON. *St. Rocco* Closed. Records at St. Mary, Holley.

HUMPHREY. *St. Pacificus* (1855) Merged with Holy Name of Mary, Ellicottville, and became an oratory. Records at Holy Name of Mary, Ellicottville.

JAMESTOWN. *St. John* Merged with SS. Peter & Paul to form Holy Apostles Parish using both sites. Records at Holy Apostles, SS. Peter & Paul site.

SS. Peter & Paul Name changed when merged with St. John to form Holy Apostles Parish. Records at Holy Apostles, SS. Peter & Paul site.

JAVA CENTER. *St. Patrick* (1838) Merged with parishes in Sheldon, Strykersville & North Java to form St. John Neumann Parish. St. Patrick church became an oratory of St. John Neumann. Records at St. John Neumann, Strykersville.

KNAPP CREEK. *Sacred Heart, Mission of St. Bonaventure Parish Allegany* Closed. Records at St. Mary of the Angels, Olean.

LACKAWANNA. *Assumption* (1918) Closed. Records at the Catholic Center, 795 Main St. Buffalo, NY 14203. Tel: 716-847-5567.

St. Barbara (1903) Closed in merger to form Queen of Angels Parish. Records at Queen of Angels.

St. Hyacinth (1910) Closed in merger to form Queen of Angels Parish. Records at Queen of Angels.

St. Michael the Archangel Name changed when merged with St. Barbara, St. Hyacinth & Our Lady of Grace (Woodlawn) parishes to form Queen of Angels Parish at St. Michael's site. Records at Queen of Angels.

Queen of All Saints (1949) Closed in merger with St. Anthony Parish. Records at St. Anthony, Lackawanna.

LAKE VIEW. *Our Lady of Perpetual Help* (1922) Name changed when merged with St. Vincent, North Evans, to form Blessed John Paul II Parish at the Lake View site. Records at Blessed John Paul II.

LANGFORD. *St. Martin* Name changed when merged with parishes in New Oregon and Collins Center to form Epiphany of Our Lord Parish at the Langford site. Records at Epiphany of Our Lord.

LE ROY. *St. Joseph* (1907) Merged with St. Peter Parish & St. Anthony, Lime Rock to form Our Lady of Mercy Parish. St. Joseph Church is an oratory of Our Lady of Mercy; records at Our Lady of Mercy.

St. Peter Name changed when merged with St. Joseph, LeRoy & St. Anthony in Lime Rock to form Our Lady of Mercy Parish at St. Peter's site. Records at Our Lady of Mercy.

LIME ROCK. *St. Anthony* (1907) Closed when merged with St. Joseph & St. Peter parishes in LeRoy to form Our Lady of Mercy Parish. Records at Our Lady of Mercy.

LITTLE VALLEY. *St. Mary* (1874) Closed in merger with St. Mary, Cattaraugus. Records at St. Mary, Cattaraugus.

LOCKPORT. *St. Anthony* (1928) Closed in merger to form All Saints Parish, Lockport. Records at All Saints, Lockport.

St. Joseph (1912) Merged with St. Anthony & St. Patrick parishes to form All Saints Parish and became an oratory of All Saints. Records at All Saints.

St. Mary (1859)

St. Patrick Name changed when merged with St. Anthony & St. Joseph parishes to form All Saints Parish at the St. Patrick site. Records at All Saints.

LYNDONVILLE. *St. Joseph* (1962) Merged with St. Patrick, Barker, to form Our Lady of the Lake Parish, using both the Barker and Lyndonville sites. Records at Our Lady of the Lake, Barker.

MACHIAS. *Holy Family* (1948) Closed in merger with St. Philomena, Franklinville. Records at St. Philomena Franklinville.

MAYVILLE. *St. Mary* (1925) Merged with Our Lady of Lourdes, Bemus Point to form St. Mary of Lourdes Parish using both sites. Records at St. Mary of Lourdes, Mayville.

MEDINA. *St. Mary* Name changed when merged with Sacred Heart, Medina & St. Stephen, Middleport to form Holy Trinity Parish using the St. Mary & St. Stephen sites. Records at Holy Trinity, Medina.

Sacred Heart (1910) Closed when merged with St. Mary, Medina & St. Stephen, Middleport to become Holy Trinity Parish. Records at Holy Trinity, Medina.

MIDDLEPORT. *St. Stephen* (1854) Merged with St. Mary & Sacred Heart, Medina to form Holy Trinity Parish using the St. Mary & St. Stephen sites. Records at Holy Trinity, Medina.

NEWFANE. *St. Bridget* Name changed when merged with Our Lady of the Rosary, Wilson & St. Charles Borromeo, Olcott to form St. Brendan on the Lake Parish using the Newfane and Wilson sites. Records at St. Brendan on the Lake, Newfane.

NIAGARA FALLS. *Prince of Peace* Name changed when merged with St. Leo Parish to form St. Vincent de Paul Parish using both sites. Records at St. Vincent de Paul.

St. Charles Borromeo (1970) Closed in merger with St. John de LaSalle Parish. Records at St. John de LaSalle.

St. George (1915) Closed in merger to form Divine Mercy Parish. Records at Divine Mercy.

Holy Trinity (1902) Closed in merger to form Divine Mercy Parish. Records at Divine Mercy.

St. Joseph Name changed when merged with Our Lady of Mt. Carmel to form Holy Family of Jesus, Mary & Joseph Parish using both sites. Records at Holy Family of Jesus, Mary & Joseph, St. Joseph site.

St. Leo (1957) Merged with Prince of Peace to form St. Vincent de Paul Parish using both sites. Records at St. Vincent de Paul.

Our Lady of Lebanon (1914) Closed in merger to form Divine Mercy Parish. Records at Divine Mercy.

Our Lady of Mount Carmel (1949) Merged with St. Joseph Parish to form Holy Family of Jesus, Mary & Joseph Parish using both sites. Records at Holy Family of Jesus, Mary & Joseph, St. Joseph site.

Our Lady of the Rosary (1906) Closed in merger to form Divine Mercy Parish. Records at Divine Mercy.

Sacred Heart (1854) Closed when merged with St. Teresa Parish to form St. Raphael Parish. Records at St. Raphael.

St. Stanislaus Kostka Name changed when merged with four other parishes to form Divine Mercy Parish at the St. Stanislaus site. Records at Divine Mercy.

St. Teresa of the Infant Jesus Name changed when merged with Sacred Heart Parish to form St. Raphael Parish at the St. Teresa site. Records at St. Raphael.

NORTH EVANS. *St. Vincent* (1914)

NORTH JAVA. *St. Nicholas* (1890) Closed in merger to form St. John Neumann Parish. Records at St. John Neumann, Strykersville.

NORTH TONAWANDA. *St. Albert the Great* Name changed when merged with Ascension Parish to form St. Jude the Apostle Parish. Records at St. Jude the Apostle.

Ascension (1887) Closed in merger to form St. Jude the Apostle Parish. Records at St. Jude the Apostle.

St. Joseph (1947) Closed in merger with Our Lady of Czestochowa Parish. Records at Our Lady of Czestochowa.

OAKFIELD. *St. Cecilia* (1906) Name changed when merged with Our Lady of Fatima, Elba, to form St. Padre Pio Parish. Both sites used. Records at St. Padre Pio, Oakfield.

OLCOTT. *St. Charles Borromeo* (1912) Merged with parishes in Wilson & Newfane to form St. Brendan on the Lake Parish. Summer oratory of St. Brendan on the Lake. Records at St. Brendan on the Lake, Newfane.

OLEAN. *Transfiguration* (1902) Merged with St. Helen, Hinsdale, and St. John, Olean, at St. John's site. Became an oratory of St. John. Records at St. John, Olean.

PANAMA. *Our Lady of the Snows* (1946) Merged into Sacred Heart Parish, Lakewood but Panama site is still used. Records at Sacred Heart, Lakewood.

PAVILION. *St. Mary* (1865) Name changed when merged with Immaculate Conception, East Bethany to form Mary Immaculate, East Bethany. Both sites are used. Records at Mary Immaculate, East Bethany.

PERRY. *St. Joseph* Name changed when merged with St. Stanislaus, Perry, St. Mary, Silver Springs & St. Joseph, Bliss to form St. Isidore Parish using the St. Joseph, Perry & St. Mary, Silver Springs sites. Records at St. Isidore, Perry.

St. Stanislaus Kostka (1910) Closed in merger to form St. Isidore Parish. Records at St. Isidore, Perry.

PERRYSBURG. *St. Joan of Arc* (1950) Closed in merger with St. Joseph, Gowanda. Records at St. Joseph, Gowanda.

PORTAGEVILLE. *Assumption B.V.M.* (1849) Closed in merger with St. Mary, Silver Springs. Records at St. Isidore, Perry.

PORTVILLE. *Sacred Heart* (1909) Merged with St. Mary of the Angels, Olean and became an oratory. Records at St. Mary of the Angels, Olean.

RIPLEY. *St. Thomas More* (1941) Closed in merger to form St. Dominic Parish, Westfield. Records at St. Dominic, Westfield.

SALAMANCA. *Holy Cross* Name changed when merged with St. Patrick to form Our Lady of Peace Parish temporarily using both sites. Records at Our Lady of Peace, Holy Cross site.

St. Patrick (1868) Merged with Holy Cross to form Our Lady of Peace Parish. Records at Our Lady of Peace.

SCIO. *St. Joseph* (1844) Merged with two other parishes to form Holy Family of Jesus, Mary & Joseph Parish, Belmont. Oratory of Holy Family of Jesus, Mary & Joseph, Belmont. Records at Holy Family of Jesus, Mary & Joseph, Belmont.

SHELDON. *St. Cecilia* (1848) Merged with parishes in Strykersville, North Java & Java Center to form St. John Neumann Parish using the Sheldon & Strykersville sites. Records at St. John Neumann, Strykersville.

SHERIDAN. *St. John Bosco* (1949) Closed in merger with Our Lady of Mt. Carmel, Silver Creek. Records at Our Lady of Mt. Carmel.

SHERMAN. *St. Isaac Jogues* (1947) Merged with St. Matthias, French Creek to form Christ Our Hope Parish using both sites. Records at Christ Our Hope, French Creek.

SILVER SPRINGS. *St. Mary* (1892) Merged with parishes in Perry & Bliss to form St. Isidore Parish using both the Perry & Silver Springs sites. Records at St. Isidore, Perry.

SINCLAIRVILLE. *St. John the Evangelist* (1940) Closed in merger with Immaculate Conception, Cassadaga. Records at St. Anthony Parish, Fredonia.

SOUTH BYRON. *St. Michael* (1892) Closed in merger with St. Brigid, Bergen. Records at Our Lady of Mercy, LeRoy.

SOUTH DAYTON. *St. John Fisher* (1946) Closed in merger with St. Joseph Parish, Gowanda. Records at St. Joseph, Gowanda.

STRYKERSVILLE. *St. Mary, Queen of the Rosary* Name changed when merged with parishes in Sheldon, North Java & Java Center to form St. John Neumann Parish using the Sheldon & Strykersville sites. Records at St. John Neumann, Strykersville.

TONAWANDA. *St. Edmund* (1965) Closed as a worship site in merger with St. Christopher Parish, Tonawanda. Site used for outreach ministry. Records at St. Christopher Parish.

VANDALIA. *St. John the Baptist* (1900) Merged with St. Bonaventure Parish, Allegany & became an oratory of St. Bonaventure. The oratory closed in 2011. Records at St. Bonaventure, Allegany.

VARYSBURG. *St. Joseph* (1910) Merged with St. Vincent de Paul, Attica to form SS. Joachim & Anne Parish using both the Attica & Varysburg sites. Parish records at SS. Joachim & Anne Parish, Attica.

WEST SENECA. *St. Bonaventure* (1918) Closed in merger with St. William to form Blessed John XXIII Parish. Records at Blessed John XXIII Parish, West Seneca.

St. Catherine of Siena (1967) Closed in merger with Queen of Heaven Parish, West Seneca. Records at Queen of Heaven.

St. William Name changed when merged with St. Bonaventure Parish to form Blessed John XXIII Parish at St. William's site. Records at Blessed John XXIII Parish, West Seneca.

WESTFIELD. *St. James Major* Name changed when merged with churches in Brocton & Ripley to form St. Dominic Parish, Westfield. Records at St. Dominic, Westfield.

WHEATVILLE. *St. Patrick* (1882) Merged into St. Cecilia, Oakfield and became an oratory of St. Cecilia. Records at St. Cecilia.

WHITESVILLE. *St. John of the Cross* (1949) Closed in merger with Immaculate Conception, Wellsville. Records at Immaculate Conception.

WILSON. *Our Lady of the Rosary* (1920) Merged with St. Brigid, Newfane & St. Charles Borromeo, Olcott to form St. Brendan on the Lake Parish using the Newfane & Wilson sites. Records at St. Brendan on the Lake, Newfane.

WOODLAWN. *Our Lady of Grace* (1940) Closed in merger to form Queen of Angels Parish, Lackawanna. Records at Queen of Angels.

RELIGIOUS INSTITUTES OF MEN REPRESENTED IN THE DIOCESE

For further details refer to the corresponding bracketed number in the Religious Institutes of Men or Women section.

[0200]—*Benedictine Monks*—O.S.B.
[0810]—*Brothers of Mercy*—F.M.M.
[0330]—*Brothers of the Christian Schools* (District of Eastern N. America.)—F.S.C.
[0160]—*Clerics Regular of St. Paul*—C.R.S.P.
[1330]—*Congregation of the Mission* (Eastern Prov.)—C.M.
[0390]—*Consolata Missionaries*—I.M.C.
[0480]—*Conventual Franciscans* (St. Anthony of Padua)—O.F.M.Conv.
[0450]—*The Eudists - Congregation of Jesus and Mary*—C.J.M.
[0520]—*Franciscan Friars* (Holy Name Prov.)—O.F.M.
[0690]—*Jesuit Fathers and Brothers* (New York Prov.)—S.J.
[0800]—*Maryknoll* (Buffalo)—M.M.
[1210]—*Missionaries of St. Charles-Scalabrinians*—C.S.
[0910]—*Oblates of Mary Immaculate* (Eastern Prov.)—O.M.I.
[0920]—*Oblates of St. Francis De Sales*—O.S.F.S.
[0970]—*Order of Our Lady of Mercy* (Le Roy)—O.deM.
[0430]—*Order of Preachers-Dominicans* (Prov. of St. Joseph)—O.P.
[1010]—*Pauline Fathers*—O.S.P.P.E.
[0370]—*Society of St. Columban*—S.S.C.
[0990]—*Society of the Catholic Apostolate* (Christ the King Prov.)—S.A.C.
[0560]—*Third Order Regular of St. Francis*—T.O.R.

RELIGIOUS INSTITUTES OF WOMEN REPRESENTED IN THE DIOCESE

[]—*Catechetical Sisters of Arogymatha - The Society of Sisters of Our Lady of Good Health*—C.S.A.
[]—*Christ the Light Sisters (Christu Jyothi Sisters)*—C.J.S.
[0760]—*Daughters of Charity of St. Vincent de Paul*—D.C.
[]—*Daughters of Mary Mother of Mercy*—D.M.M.M.
[]—*Daughters of Our Lady of the Holy Rosary* (Vietnam)—F.M.S.R.
[]—*Daughters of Our Lady of the Visitation* (Vietnam)—F.M.V.
[]—*Daughters of St. Francis of Assisi* (South Africa)—F.S.F.
[0420]—*Discalced Carmelite Nuns*—O.C.D.
[1050]—*Dominican Contemplative Sisters*—O.P.
[1170]—*Felician Sisters*—C.S.S.F.
[1180]—*Franciscan Sisters of Allegany, New York*—O.S.F.
[]—*Franciscan Sisters of St. Bernadette* (Tanzania)—F.S.S.B.
[1470]—*Franciscan Sisters of St. Joseph*—F.S.S.J.
[1280]—*Franciscan Sisters of the Immaculate Conception*—O.S.F.
[1840]—*Grey Nuns of the Sacred Heart*—G.N.S.H.
[]—*Immaculate Heart of Mary* (Tanzania)—B.M.
[]—*Immaculate Heart Sisters of Africa*—I.H.S.A.
[2575]—*Institute of the Sisters of Mercy of the Americas*—R.S.M.
[2480]—*Medical Missionaries of Mary*—M.M.M.
[2830]—*Missionary Sisters of Our Lady of Mercy*—M.O.M.
[2880]—*Missionary Sisters of St. Columban*—S.S.C.
[3040]—*Oblate Sisters of Providence*—O.S.P.
[]—*Servants of Mary the Queen* (Zimbabwe)—A.M.R.
[0570]—*Sisters of Charity of Seton Hill S.C.*
[0630]—*Sisters of Charity of St. Vincent de Paul of Zagreb*—V.Z.
[3000]—*Sisters of Notre Dame de Namur* (Ohio Prov.)—S.N.D.deN.
[2670]—*Sisters of Our Lady of Mercy (Mercedarians)*—S.O.L.M.
[3950]—*Sisters of Saint Mary of Namur*—S.S.M.N.
[4090]—*Sisters of Social Service*—S.S.S.
[1630]—*Sisters of St. Francis of Penance and Christian Charity*—O.S.F.
[1805]—*Sisters of St. Francis of the Neumann Communities*—O.S.F.
[1660]—*Sisters of St. Francis of the Providence of God*—O.S.F.
[3830-06]—*Sisters of St. Joseph* (Buffalo, NY)—S.S.J.
[3830-13]—*Sisters of St. Joseph* (Baden, Pa)—C.S.J.
[3658]—*Sisters of the Sacred Heart of Jesus*—S.S.H.J.

NECROLOGY

† Fisher, Rev. Msgr. Edward T., (Retired)—Died June 29, 2011
† Kozminski, Rev. Msgr. Maximilian M., (Retired)—Died Dec. 29, 2011
† Mack, Rev. Msgr. Robert A., (Retired)—Died Dec. 1, 2011
† Fimbel, Duane G., (Retired)—Died Sept. 3, 2011
† Illig, A. Mark—Died Dec. 21, 2011
† Keppeler, Richard J., (Retired)—Died Dec. 26, 2011
† Lex, Henry V., (Retired)—Died May 23, 2011
† Lutostanski, Anthony, (Retired)—Died March 13, 2011
† Schreck, Paul C., (Retired)—Died Nov. 10, 2011

Diocese of Burlington

(Dioecesis Burlingtonensis)

Most Reverend

SALVATORE R. MATANO, D.D., S.T.L., J.C.D.

Bishop of Burlington; ordained December 17, 1971; appointed Coadjutor Bishop of Burlington March 3, 2005; ordained April 19, 2005; succeeded November 9, 2005. *Mailing Address: 55 Joy Dr., South Burlington, VT 05403.*

Most Reverend

KENNETH A. ANGELL, D.D.

Bishop Emeritus of Burlington; ordained May 26, 1956; appointed Auxiliary Bishop of Providence August 9, 1974; consecrated October 7, 1974; transferred to Bishop of Burlington October 6, 1992; installed November 9, 1992; retired November 9, 2005. *Mailing Address: 55 Joy Dr., South Burlington, VT 05403.* Fax: 802-658-0436.

ESTABLISHED JULY 29, 1853.

Square Miles 9,135.

Comprises the State of Vermont.

For legal titles of parishes and diocesan institutions, consult the Chancery Office.

Chancery Office: 55 Joy Dr., South Burlington, VT 05403. Tel: 802-658-6110; Fax: 802-658-0436.

Web: www.vermontcatholic.org

STATISTICAL OVERVIEW

Personnel	
Bishop	1
Retired Bishops	1
Priests: Diocesan Active in Diocese	47
Priests: Diocesan Active Outside Diocese	2
Priests: Retired, Sick or Absent	42
Number of Diocesan Priests	91
Religious Priests in Diocese	36
Total Priests in Diocese	127
Extern Priests in Diocese	17
Ordinations:	
Diocesan Priests	1
Permanent Deacons in Diocese	49
Total Brothers	23
Total Sisters	95
Parishes	
Parishes	76
With Resident Pastor:	
Resident Diocesan Priests	52
Resident Religious Priests	11
Without Resident Pastor:	
Administered by Priests	13
Missions	35
Pastoral Centers	1
New Parishes Created	1
Closed Parishes	1
Professional Ministry Personnel:	
Sisters	7
Lay Ministers	12
Welfare	
Homes for the Aged	4
Total Assisted	290
Special Centers for Social Services	1
Total Assisted	3,493
Educational	
Diocesan Students in Other Seminaries	11
Students Religious	2
Total Seminarians	13
Colleges and Universities	2
Total Students	2,879
High Schools, Diocesan and Parish	2
Total Students	465
Elementary Schools, Diocesan and Parish	9
Total Students	1,329
Elementary Schools, Private	2
Total Students	353
Catechesis/Religious Education:	
High School Students	1,412
Elementary Students	4,319
Total Students under Catholic Instruction	10,770
Teachers in the Diocese:	
Priests	4
Lay Teachers	251
Vital Statistics	
Receptions into the Church:	
Infant Baptism Totals	764
Minor Baptism Totals	83
Adult Baptism Totals	74
Received into Full Communion	105
First Communions	911
Confirmations	905
Marriages:	
Catholic	236
Interfaith	96
Total Marriages	332
Deaths	1,384
Total Catholic Population	118,000
Total Population	625,000

Former Bishops—Rt. Revs. LOUIS DE GOESBRIAND, D.D., ord. July 13, 1840; cons. Oct. 30, 1853; died Nov. 3, 1899; JOHN S. MICHAUD, D.D., ord. June 7, 1873; cons. Coadjutor Bishop with right of succession June 29, 1892; succeeded to Nov. 3, 1899; died Dec. 22, 1908; Most Revs. JOSEPH J. RICE, D.D., ord. Sept. 29, 1894; cons. April 14, 1910; died April 1, 1938; MATTHEW F. BRADY, D.D., ord. June 10, 1916; cons. Oct. 26, 1938; transferred to Manchester, NH, Nov. 11, 1944; died Sept. 20, 1959; EDWARD F. RYAN, D.D., ord. Aug. 10, 1905; cons. Jan. 3, 1945; died Nov. 3, 1956; ROBERT F. JOYCE, D.D., ord. May 26, 1923; cons. Auxiliary Bishop Oct. 28, 1954; installed Diocesan Bishop Feb. 26, 1957; retired Jan. 24, 1972; died Sept. 2, 1990; JOHN A. MARSHALL, D.D., ord. Dec. 19, 1953; cons. and installed Jan. 25, 1972; transferred to Springfield, MA, Dec. 27, 1991; died July 3, 1994; KENNETH A. ANGELL, D.D., ord. May 26, 1956; appt. Auxiliary Bishop of Providence Aug. 9, 1974; cons. Oct. 7, 1974; transferred to Bishop of Burlington Oct. 6, 1992; installed Nov. 9, 1992; retired Nov. 9, 2005.

Vicars General—Rev. Msgrs. JOHN J. MCDERMOTT, V.G., J.C.L., Vicar Gen. & Chancellor; PETER A. ROUTHIER, V.G., Vicar Gen., 55 Joy Dr., South Burlington, 05403. Tel: 802-658-6110; Fax: 802-658-0436.

Vicar for Clergy—Rev. Msgr. RICHARD G. LAVALLEY, St. Francis Xavier Parish, 3 St. Peter St., Winooski, 05404.

Chancery Office—Rev. Msgr. JOHN J. MCDERMOTT, V.G., J.C.L., Chancellor; Rev. DANIEL E. WHITE, Moderator of the Curia & Vice Chancellor, 55 Joy Dr., South Burlington, 05403. Tel: 802-658-6110; Fax: 802-658-0436 Office Hours: Mon.-Fri. 9-12 & 1-5.

Finance Office—Mr. MARTIN A. HOAK, Diocesan Finance Officer, 55 Joy Dr., South Burlington, 05403. Tel: 802-658-6110; Fax: 802-658-6113.

Secretary to the Most Rev. Bishop—Rev. DANIEL E. WHITE, 55 Joy Dr., South Burlington, 05403. Tel: 802-658-6110.

Office of the Tribunal—55 Joy Dr., South Burlington, 05403. Tel: 802-658-6110; Fax: 802-658-0436.

Judicial Vicar—Rev. DANIEL J. JORDAN, J.C.L.

Case Director—Mrs. BRENDA TRUE.

Judges—Rev. Msgr. JOHN R. MCSWEENEY, J.C.L. (Retired); Revs. THOMAS V. MATTISON, J.C.L.; DANIEL J. JORDAN, J.C.L.; JOHN MAHONEY JR., J.C.L.

Promoter of Justice—Rev. Msgr. JOHN J. MCDERMOTT, V.G., J.C.L.

Defenders of the Bond—Revs. ROGER L. CHARBONNEAU; JOHN G. FELTZ; Rev. Msgr. JOHN J. MCDERMOTT, V.G., J.C.L.

Advocate—Rev. Msgr. PETER A. ROUTHIER, V.G.

Notaries—Revs. ROGER L. CHARBONNEAU; JOHN G. FELTZ; Mrs. BRENDA TRUE.

Diocesan Administrative Board—Most Rev. SALVATORE R. MATANO, D.D., S.T.L., J.C.D., Pres.; Rev. Msgrs. JOHN J. MCDERMOTT, V.G., J.C.L.; PETER A. ROUTHIER, V.G., Ex-Officio, Clerk; REID C. MAYO (Retired); Rev. DANIEL E. WHITE; Mr. SCOTT BEAUDIN; Mr. ARNOLD G. LANGBO; Mr. MARTIN A. HOAK, Finance Officer & D.A.B. Consultant.

Diocesan Consultors—Rev. Msgrs. REID C. MAYO (Retired); PETER A. ROUTHIER, V.G.; JOHN J. MCDERMOTT, V.G., J.C.L.; Revs. JUSTIN J. BAKER; BERNARD E. GAUDREAU; DANIEL J. RUPP; DANIEL E. WHITE.

Deans—Rev. Msgr. RICHARD G. LAVALLEY; Revs. BENEDICT C. KIELY; YVON J. ROYER; DANIEL J. RUPP; PATRICK J. FORMAN; JUSTIN J. BAKER; THOMAS V. MATTISON, J.C.L.; THOMAS L. MOSHER; MAURICE J. ROY; MICHAEL W. DEFORGE; RICHARD C. O'DONNELL.

Canon 1742 Panel of Pastors—Rev. Msgr. REID C. MAYO (Retired); Revs. WILLIAM R. BEAUDIN; CHARLES R. DANIELSON; MICHAEL W. DEFORGE; BERNARD E. GAUDREAU; JEROME MERCURE; DANIEL J. RUPP; MAURICE J. ROY; YVON J. ROYER.

Diocesan Offices and Directors

Apostolate for the Handicapped—Office of Catholic Formation, Special Needs Ministry, 55 Joy Dr., South Burlington, 05403. Tel: 802-658-6110.

Development Office—Mr. RICHARD A. FISCHER, 55 Joy Dr., South Burlington, 05403. Tel: 802-658-6110.

The Blue Army (World Apostolate of Fatima)—Rev. SEAN P. DOWLING, Chap., St. Raphael, 21 E. Main St., Poultney, 05764; TONIA BARBIN, Pres., 54 Starbird Rd., Unit F, Jericho, 05465.

Catholic Committee on Scouting—NORBERT VOGEL, Treas., 205 Biscayne Heights, Colchester, 05446. Tel: 802-862-1756. Email: norb_vogl@hotmail.com; DAVID ELY, Chm., 175 Elmwood Ave., Burlington, 05401. Tel: 802-862-5109.

Building Commission—Chancery Office: 55 Joy Dr., South Burlington, 05403. Tel: 802-658-6110.

Vermont Catholic Charities, Inc.—Mr. LAWRENCE ASSELL, Exec. Dir., Central Office, 55 Joy Dr., South Burlington, 05403. Tel: 802-658-6110; Fax: 802-860-0451. Rutland Office, 24 Center St., Rutland, 05701. Tel: 802-773-3379; Fax: 802-773-7550.

Bishop de Goesbriand Appeal for Human Development—55 Joy Dr., South Burlington, 05403. Tel: 802-658-6110; Fax: 802-860-0451.

Catholic Daughters of The Americas—Rev. PATRICK J. FORMAN, Chap., Corpus Christi Parish, 49 Winter St., St. Johnsbury, 05819-2144. Tel: 802-748-8129.

Catholic Relief Services—VACANT, 55 Joy Dr., South Burlington, 05403. Tel: 802-658-6110; Fax: 802-860-0451.

Catholic Golden Age—Rev. DANIEL J. JORDAN, J.C.L., Christ the King Parish, 305 Flynn Ave., Burlington, 05401. Tel: 802-862-5784.

Censor Librorum—Rev. RICHARD L. VANDERWEEL, S.S.E., 351 North Ave., P.O. Box 489, Burlington, 05402-0489. Tel: 802-658-6110.

Charismatic Renewal—Rev. LANCE W. HARLOW, Mailing Address: Immaculate Heart of Mary Parish, P.O. Box 1047, Williston, 05495. Tel: 802-878-4513; Deacon DANIEL PUDVAH, 12 Edgewood Ave., Barre, 05641. Tel: 802-479-9407.

Superintendent of Catholic Schools—Ms. MONA FAULKNER, Office of Catholic Schools, 55 Joy Dr., South Burlington, 05403. Tel: 802-658-6110.

Diocesan Archives—Rev. Msgr. JOHN J. MCDERMOTT, V.G., J.C.L., 55 Joy Dr., South Burlington, 05403. Tel: 802-658-6110.

Media Relations—Rev. DANIEL E. WHITE, 55 Joy Dr., South Burlington, 05403. Tel: 802-658-6110.

Daughters of Isabella—Rev. YVON J. ROYER, Chap., St. Peter Parish, 85 S. Maple St., Vergennes, 05491-0324. Tel: 802-877-2367.

Diocesan Cemetery—Resurrection Park, South Burlington, 05403. Mr. PETER WELLS, Insurance and Facilities Office, 55 Joy Dr., South Burlington, 05403. Tel: 802-658-6110.

Diocesan Finance Council—Ex Officio Members: Most Rev. SALVATORE R. MATANO, D.D., S.T.L., J.C.D., Chm.; Rev. Msgrs. PETER A. ROUTHIER, V.G.; JOHN J. MCDERMOTT, V.G., J.C.L. Board Members: WILLIAM E. BOND; MAYNARD MCLAUGHLIN; Mr. MARK KELLEY, Bishop's Delegate; Rev. BRIAN J. CUMMINGS, S.S.E.; Mr. J. PAUL GIULIANI, Esq.; Mr. MICHAEL HENRY. Consultants: Rev. DANIEL E. WHITE; Mr. MARTIN A. HOAK, Finance Officer.

Diocesan Director of Facilities and Insurance—Mr. PETER WELLS, 55 Joy Dr., South Burlington, 05403. Tel: 802-658-6110.

Diocesan Director of Human Resources—Ms. EILEEN O'ROURKE, 55 Joy Dr., South Burlington, 05403. Tel: 802-658-6110.

Ecumenical Commission—Rev. Msgr. PETER A. ROUTHIER, V.G.; Mr. JAMES G. CASE, 1818 Richmond Rd., Hinesburg, 05461; Rev. THOMAS V. MATTISON, J.C.L.

Diocesan Board of Catholic Education—Contact: Office of Catholic Schools, 55 Joy Dr., South Burlington, 05403. Tel: 802-658-6110.

Office of Marriage, Family Life/Respect Life—Ms. MARIE ANTUNES, M.A., Mailing Address: 55 Joy Dr., South Burlington, 05403. Tel: 802-658-6111.

Liturgical Commission—Rev. Msgr. PETER A. ROUTHIER, V.G., 55 Joy Dr., South Burlington, 05403. Tel: 802-658-6110.

House of Discernment—Rev. JON-DANIEL SCHNOBRICH, Dir., The Catholic Center at UVM, 390 S. Prospect St., Redstone Campus, Burlington, 05401. Tel: 802-862-8403; Fax: 802-865-9480.

Knights of Columbus—Rev. KARL A. HAHR, All Saints Rectory, 152 Main St., Richford, 05476.

Marriage Encounter, Vermont—JOHN FORCIER; DIANE FORCIER, 15 Mariner Heights, Colchester, 05446. Tel: 802-657-3083.

Diocesan Master of Ceremonies—Rev. DANIEL E. WHITE, 55 Joy Dr., South Burlington, 05403. Tel: 802-658-6110; Fax: 802-658-0436.

Office of Continuing Education for Clergy—Rev. BENEDICT C. KIELY, Dir., Mailing Address: Blessed Sacrament Parish, P.O. Box 27, Stowe, 05672. Tel: 802-253-7536; Fax: 802-253-4445.

Office of Safe Environment Programs—Mr. KEVIN P. SCULLY, Dir.; JEANNE MITIGUY BRUNO, Programs Devel. Admin.

The Review Board—Dr. WILLIAM CUNNINGHAM, Chm.; Rev. Msgr. JOHN J. MCDERMOTT, V.G., J.C.L.; Rev. RENE J. BUTLER, M.S.; GEORGE ASHLINE, Ph.D.; THERESE M. CORSONES, J.D.; DALE D. STAFFORD, M.D.; MARY FRAN STAFFORD. Ex Officio/ Consultant: Rev. Msgr. PETER A. ROUTHIER, V.G.; Mr. KEVIN P. SCULLY.

Victim's Advocacy Board—Rev. Msgrs. JOHN J. MCDERMOTT, V.G., J.C.L.; PETER A. ROUTHIER, V.G.; Mr. KEVIN P. SCULLY.

National Shrine of the Immaculate Conception, Washington—Rev. ROGER L. CHARBONNEAU, St. John the Baptist Parish, P.O. Box 563, Enosburg Falls, 05450. Tel: 802-933-4464.

Office of Catholic Formation—Mrs. DOROTHY BAREWICZ, Dir.; Ms. ELIZABETH DOHERTY, Asst. Mgr., 55 Joy Dr., South Burlington, 05403.

Office of Diocesan Pastoral Planning—Rev. Msgr. JOHN J. MCDERMOTT, V.G., J.C.L., Dir., Mailing Address: 55 Joy Dr., South Burlington, 05403. Tel: 802-658-6110.

Office of Permanent Diaconate Ministry—Rev. DANIEL E. WHITE, Spiritual Dir., 55 Joy Dr., South Burlington, 05403; Deacon CHRISTOPHER KEOUGH, 120 N. Twin Oaks, South Burlington, 05403. Tel: 802-860-7471. Email: cpkeough@comcast.net.

Institute for Catholic Enrichment and Lay Apostolate Formation—Rev. Msgr. JOHN J. MCDERMOTT, V.G., J.C.L., Dir.; Mrs. DOROTHY BAREWICZ, Asst. Dir., Mailing Address: 55 Joy Dr., South Burlington, 05403. Tel: 802-658-6110.

Diocesan Presbyteral Council—Members Ex Officio: Most Rev. SALVATORE R. MATANO, D.D., S.T.L., J.C.D., Bishop of Burlington; Rev. Msgrs. PETER A. ROUTHIER, V.G.; JOHN J. MCDERMOTT, V.G., J.C.L., Chancellor; Rev. DANIEL E. WHITE, Moderator of the Curia & Vice Chancellor. Elected Members: Revs. DONALD J. RAVEY (Retired); PATRICK J. FORMAN; THOMAS L. MOSHER; JUSTIN J. BAKER; EMMANUEL AJANMA; RICHARD C. O'DONNELL; MICHAEL REARDON, S.D.V.; LEOPOLD J. BILODEAU; BERNARD E. GAUDREAU; DANIEL J. RUPP; MAURICE J. ROY; WILLIAM R. BEAUDIN; THOMAS V. MATTISON, J.C.L.; RICHARD W. TINNEY.

Magazine— "Vermont Catholic" Most Rev. SALVATORE R. MATANO, D.D., S.T.L., J.C.D., Publisher; Mrs. PATRICIA GORE, Editor, Editorial & Business Office, 55 Joy Dr., South Burlington, 05403. Tel: 802-658-6110; Fax: 802-658-3866.

Priests' Benefit Fund—VACANT, 55 Joy Dr., South Burlington, 05403. Tel: 802-658-6110.

Prison Ministry—Deacon DENNIS MOORE, 55 Joy Dr., South Burlington, 05403. Tel: 802-658-6110.

Propagation of the Faith—Rev. ROGER L. CHARBONNEAU, Dir., 55 Joy Dr., South Burlington, 05403. Tel: 802-658-6110.

Office of Catholic Schools—Ms. MONA FAULKNER, Supt. of Schools.

Vermont Cursillo—Ms. JUDY HUSSEY, 1847 River Rd., Orleans, 05860. Tel: 802-899-2518; Rev. JEROME MERCURE, Spiritual Dir., St. Andrew, 109 South St., Waterbury, 05676.

Vocations and Seminarians—Revs. DANIEL E. WHITE, Dir., 55 Joy Dr., South Burlington, 05403. Tel: 802-658-6110; Fax: 802-658-0436; JON-DANIEL SCHNOBRICH, Asst. Dir., The Catholic Center at UVM: Redstone Campus, 390 S. Prospect St., Burlington, 05401. Tel: 802-862-8403; Fax: 802-865-9480.

CLERGY, PARISHES, MISSIONS AND PAROCHIAL SCHOOLS

CITY OF BURLINGTON

(CHITTENDEN COUNTY)

1—CATHEDRAL OF THE IMMACULATE CONCEPTION (1830) Rev. Msgr. Peter A. Routhier, Rector; Deacon William Glinka.
Mailing Address: 20 Pine St., Burlington, 05401.
Res.: 85 Elmwood Ave., Burlington, 05401. Tel: 802-658-4333.
Catechesis/Religious Program—(Combined with St. Joseph's Co-Cathedral, Burlington)., Tel: 802-862-3258. Students 11.

2—CHRIST THE KING-ST. ANTHONY (2007), Parish includes Christ the King, Burlington & St. Anthony, Burlington. Revs. Daniel J. Rupp; Daniel J. Jordan; Deacons Timm Taylor; Louis A. Meunier.
Mailing Address: 136 Locust St., Burlington, 05401-4849.
Res.: 305 Flynn Ave., Burlington, 05401-4849. Tel: 802-862-5784; Fax: 802-651-3021.
School—(Grades PreK-8) Tel: 802-862-6696; Fax: 802-658-6553. Ms. Paulette Thibault, Prin.; Aida Cadrecha, Librarian. Lay Teachers 30; Students 252.
Catechesis/Religious Program—Students 77.

3—ST. JOSEPH'S CO-CATHEDRAL (1850) [CEM] Rev. Msgr. Peter A. Routhier, Rector; Rev. Dallas T. St. Peter. In Res., Rev. Daniel E. White.
Res.: 85 Elmwood Ave., Burlington, 05401. Tel: 802-863-2388; Fax: 802-863-2380.
Catechesis/Religious Program—Tel: 802-862-0512. Mary Beth Herbert, D.R.E. Students 55.

4—ST. MARK'S (1940) Rev. William P. Giroux; Deacon Timothy Gibbo.
Res.: 1251 North Ave., Burlington, 05408. Tel: 802-864-7686; Fax: 802-651-9391.
Catechesis/Religious Program—Lauren P. Buckley, D.R.E. Students 106.
Convent—Franciscan Sisters of the Atonement, 21 Dodds Ct., Burlington, 05408. Tel: 802-862-8288.

OUTSIDE THE CITY OF BURLINGTON

ALBURGH, GRAND ISLE CO., ST. AMADEUS (1886) [CEM 2] Rev. Lawrence P. Ridgley.
Res.: P.O. Box 49, 05440. Tel: 802-796-3481; Fax: 802-796-3481.
Catechesis/Religious Program—Carol Cleland, D.R.E. Students 26.
Mission—St. Joseph Isle La Motte, Grand Isle Co.

ARLINGTON, BENNINGTON CO., ST. MARGARET MARY (1946) [CEM] Closed. See Christ Our Savior Parish, Manchester Center.

BARRE, WASHINGTON CO., ST. MONICA (1892) Revs. Leopold J. Bilodeau; Emmanuel Ajanma; Deacons David Bisson; Daniel Pudvah.
Res.: 79 Summer St., 05641. Tel: 802-479-3253; Fax: 802-479-3154.
School—Central Vermont Catholic School - St. Monica Campus, (Grades PreSchool-8) Tel: 802-476-5015; Fax: 802-476-0861. Ms. Patricia M. O'Mahoney, Prin. Lay Teachers 15; Students 127.
Catechesis/Religious Program—Tel: 802-476-4020; Fax: 802-479-3154. Antoinette Quinonez, D.R.E. Students 171.

BARTON, ORLEANS CO., MOST HOLY TRINITY (2003), Parish includes St. Paul, Barton, St. Theresa, Orleans & St. John Vianney, Irasburg. Rev. Timothy Naples.
Res.: 85 St. Paul Ln., 05822. Tel: 802-525-3711; Fax: 802-525-1292.
School—St. Paul School, (Grades K-8) Tel: 802-525-6578; Fax: 802-525-3869. Mr. Anthony Fontana, Prin. Lay Teachers 8; Students 94.
Catechesis/Religious Program—Students 47.

BELLOWS FALLS, WINDHAM CO., ST. CHARLES (1871) [CEM] Rev. Maria Lazar.
Res.: 31 Cherry Hill St., 05101. Tel: 802-463-3128; Fax: 802-463-8179. Email: 1wharlow@sover.net.
Catechesis/Religious Program—Students 55.

BENNINGTON, BENNINGTON CO., SACRED HEART ST. FRANCIS DE SALES (1995) Revs. William H. Kelley, C.S.C.; John Britto Antony, C.S.C., Parochial Victor.
Parish Office—238 Main St., 05201. Tel: 802-442-3141; Fax: 802-442-3142.
School—The School of Sacred Heart St. Francis de Sales, (Grades PreK-8), 307 School St., 05201. Tel: 802-442-2446; Fax: 802-442-3584. Mr. David B. Estes, Prin.; Marcia Hendery, Librarian; Kathy Murphy, Librarian. Lay Teachers 10; Students 145.
Catechesis/Religious Program—Tel: 802-447-0223. Janet Lucy, D.R.E. Students 112.

BETHEL, WINDSOR CO.

1—OUR LADY OF THE VALLEY PARISH (2010), Parish includes: St. Anthony, Bethel & St. Elizabeth, Rochester. Rev. Kenneth Ekekwe, Admin.
221 Church St., P.O. Box 63, 05032. Tel: 802-234-9916; Fax: 802-234-9020.
Catechesis/Religious Program—Students 9.

BRADFORD, ORANGE CO., OUR LADY OF PERPETUAL HELP (1945) Rev. Vincent Onunkwo; Deacon Kelly Fitzpatrick.
Res.: 113 Upper Plain, 05033. Tel: 802-222-5268; Fax: 802-222-5171.
Catechesis/Religious Program—Students 55.
Mission—St. Francis of Assisi Norwich, Windsor Co.
Mission—St. Eugene Wells River, Orange Co.
Mission—Our Lady of Light South Strafford, Orange Co.

BRANDON, RUTLAND CO., ST. MARY'S (1867) [CEM 2] Rev. Albert G. Baltz; Deacon Gary Griffin.
Res.: 38 Carver St., 05733. Tel: 802-247-6351; Fax: 802-247-6396.
Catechesis/Religious Program—Students 51.
Mission—St. Agnes Leicester, Addison Co.

BRATTLEBORO, WINDHAM CO., ST. MICHAEL (1855) [CEM] Rev. Richard C. O'Donnell.
Res.: 47 Walnut St., 05301. Tel: 802-257-5101; Fax: 802-257-5102.
School—(Grades PreK-8) Tel: 802-254-6320; Fax: 802-254-5229. Mrs. Elaine Beam, Prin. Lay Teachers

6; Students 96.
Catechesis/Religious Program—Students 210.

BRISTOL, ADDISON CO., ST. AMBROSE (1893) [CEM] Rev. Yvon J. Royer.
Res.: 11 School St., 05443. Tel: 802-453-2488; Fax: 802-453-7712.
Catechesis/Religious Program—Students 55.

CAMBRIDGE, LAMOILLE CO., ST. MARY (1914) Rev. Charles R. Danielson.
312 N. Main St., P.O. Box 129, 05444. Tel: 802-644-5073; Fax: 802-644-2546.
Catechesis/Religious Program—Students 30.

CASTLETON, RUTLAND CO., ST. JOHN THE BAPTIST (1899) Rev. Henry P. Furman.
Res.: 45 North Rd., P.O. Box 128, 05735. Tel: 802-468-5706; Fax: 802-468-2777.
Catechesis/Religious Program—Tel: 802-468-2155. Luis Bauzo, D.R.E. Students 19.

CHARLOTTE, CHITTENDEN CO., OUR LADY OF MOUNT CARMEL (1858) [CEM] Rev. David G. Cray, S.S.E.
Res.: 2894 Spear St., P.O. Box 158, 05445. Tel: 802-425-2637; Fax: 802-425-2671.
Catechesis/Religious Program—Students 107.

CHESTER, WINDSOR CO., ST. JOSEPH (1946) Rev. James E. Zuccaro, Admin.
Res.: 96 S. Main St., P.O. Box 1129, 05143. Tel: 802-875-2610; Fax: 802-875-2745.
Catechesis/Religious Program—Students 24.
Station—St. Joseph Chapel Londonderry.

COLCHESTER, CHITTENDEN CO.

1—HOLY CROSS (1950) [CEM] Rev. Julian Asucan; Deacon Ivan O. Hawk III.
Res.: 416 Church Rd., 05446. Tel: 802-863-3002; Fax: 802-862-5687.
Catechesis/Religious Program—Peggy Hawk, D.R.E. Students 145.

2—OUR LADY OF GRACE (1966) Rev. Peter P. O'Leary.
Res.: 800 Main St., 05446. Tel: 802-878-5987; Fax: 802-878-9308.
Catechesis/Religious Program—Students 96.

DERBY LINE, ORLEANS CO., ST. EDWARD (1946) [CEM] Revs. Michael Reardon, S.D.V.; Shiju Chittattukkara, S.D.V.; Thomas Naduviledathu, S.D.V.; Deacon John P.E. Gratton.
Res.: 250 Main St., P.O. Box 397, 05830. Tel: 802-873-3522; Fax: 802-873-3299.
St. Edward's Pre-School—Tel: 802-873-4570; Fax: 802-334-8877. Theresa Forbes, Dir. Lay Teachers 4; Students 20.
Catechesis/Religious Program—(Combined with St. Mary Star of the Sea, Newport). Students 96.
Mission—St. Benedict Labre West Charleston, Orleans Co.

ENOSBURG FALLS, FRANKLIN CO., ST. JOHN THE BAPTIST (1874) [CEM] Rev. Roger L. Charbonneau.
Res.: P.O. Box 563, 05450. Tel: 802-933-4464; Fax: 802-933-4225.
Catechesis/Religious Program—Students 92.

ESSEX CENTER, CHITTENDEN CO., ST. PIUS X (1957) Rev. Richard W. Tinney; Deacon Gerald Scilla.
Res.: 20 Jericho Rd., Essex Junction, 05452-2707. Tel: 802-878-5997; Fax: 802-878-7793.
Catechesis/Religious Program—Tel: 802-878-1182. Michelle Scilla, D.R.E.; Andrew Coulter, D.R.E. Students 245.

ESSEX JUNCTION, CHITTENDEN CO., HOLY FAMILY-ST. LAWRENCE (2006) [CEM], Parish includes Holy Family, Essex Junction & St. Lawrence, Essex Junction. Rev. Charles H. Ranges, S.S.E.
Res.: 4 Prospect St., 05452. Tel: 802-878-5331; Fax: 802-878-5332.
Catechesis/Religious Program—Tel: 802-878-5331, Ext. 202. Mr. John McMahon, D.R.E. Students 195.

FAIRFAX, FRANKLIN CO., ST. LUKE (1943) [CEM] Revs. John G. Feltz; Soosai Raj Cruz; Deacon Stephen J. Ratte.
Res.: 17 Huntville Rd., P.O. Box 7, 05454-0007. Tel: 802-849-6205; Fax: 802-849-6078.
Catechesis/Religious Program—Students 107.

FAIRFIELD, FRANKLIN CO., ST. PATRICK (1858) [CEM] Rev. Leonidas B. Laroche; Deacon Gabriel Liegey Jr.
Res.: 116 Church Rd., P.O. Box 18, 05455. Tel: 802-827-3203; Fax: 802-827-9940.
Catechesis/Religious Program—Students 75.
Mission—St. Anthony-St. George East Fairfield, Franklin Co.

FAIR HAVEN, RUTLAND CO., OUR LADY OF SEVEN DOLORS (1866) [CEM] Rev. James A. Lawrence, Admin.
Res.: 10 Washington St., 05743. Tel: 802-265-3135.
Catechesis/Religious Program—Tel: 802-265-8045. Michael Gadway, D.R.E.; Marcia Gadway, D.R.E. Students 35.
Mission—St. Matthew of Avalon West Castleton, Rutland Co.
Mission—St. Frances Cabrini West Pawlet, Rutland Co. 05775.

GRANITEVILLE, WASHINGTON CO., ST. SYLVESTER (1895) [CEM] Revs. Leopold J. Bilodeau, Admin.; Andrzej Bednarowicz, Parochial Vicar.
Res.: 217 Church Hill Rd., 05654. Tel: 802-476-3913.
Catechesis/Religious Program—Students 25.
Mission—St. Cecilia & St. Frances Cabrini East Barre, Washington Co.

HARDWICK, CALEDONIA CO., MARY QUEEN OF ALL SAINTS PARISH (1902) [CEM 2], St. Norbert, Hardwick; St. Michael, Greensboro Bend & Our Lady of Fatima, Craftsbury were suppressed. Mary Queen of All Saints was erected. Parish includes St. Norbert, Hardwick; St. Michael, Greensboro Bend & Our Lady of Fatima, Craftsbury. Rev. Absolon Florcnosos.
Res.: 193 S. Main St., 05843. Tel: 802-472-5544; Fax: 802-472-5543.
Catechesis/Religious Program—Students 52.

HINESBURG, CHITTENDEN CO., ST. JUDE THE APOSTLE (1946) Rev. David G. Cray, S.S.E.
Res.: 10759 Rte. 116, P.O. Box 69, 05461-0069. Tel: 802-482-2290; Fax: 802-482-5263.
Catechesis/Religious Program—Students 106.

ISLAND POND, ESSEX CO., ST. JAMES THE GREATER (1871) [CEM] Rev. Francis E. Connors.
Res.: 146 Middle St., P.O. Box 407, 05846. Tel: 802-723-4312.
Catechesis/Religious Program—Students 6.
Mission—St. Bernard Norton, Essex Co.

LUDLOW, WINDSOR CO., ANNUNCIATION OF THE BLESSED VIRGIN MARY (1885) Rev. Romanus Igweonu.
Res.: 7 Depot St., 05149. Tel: 802-228-3451; Fax: 802-228-7012.
Catechesis/Religious Program—Students 32.
Mission—Holy Name of Mary Proctorsville, Windsor Co.

MANCHESTER CENTER, BENNINGTON CO., CHRIST OUR SAVIOR PARISH (1896), St. Paul, Manchester Center; St. Jerome, East Dorset & Holy Trinity, Danby were suppressed. Christ Our Savior was erected. Parish includes St. Paul, Manchester Center & St. Margaret Mary, Arlington. Rev. Thomas V. Mattison.
Res.: 398 Bonnet St., 05255. Tel: 802-362-1380; Fax: 802-366-1168.
Catechesis/Religious Program—Students 132.

MIDDLEBURY, ADDISON CO., ASSUMPTION OF THE BLESSED VIRGIN MARY (1855) [CEM] Rev. William R. Beaudin.
Res.: 326 College St., 05753. Tel: 802-388-2943; 802-388-4444; Fax: 802-989-7150.
School—St. Mary's, (Grades PreK-6), 86 Shannon St., 05753. Tel: 802-388-8392. Mrs. Angela Pohlen, Prin. Lay Teachers 13; Students 77.
Catechesis/Religious Program—Students 120.
Mission—St. Bernadette/St. Genevieve Shoreham, Addison Co.

MIDDLETOWN SPRINGS, RUTLAND CO., ST. ANNE (1963) Rev. Sean P. Dowling, Admin.
Res.: 21 E. Main St., P.O. Box 1064, Poultney, 05764-1107.
Catechesis/Religious Program—(Combined with St. Raphael's, Poultney).

MILTON, CHITTENDEN CO., ST. ANN (1866) [CEM] Revs. John G. Feltz; Soosai Raj Cruz; Deacon Paul Garrow.
Res.: 41 Main St., P.O. Box 1, 05468. Tel: 802-893-2487; Fax: 802-893-3701.
Catechesis/Religious Program—Students 164.

MONTPELIER, WASHINGTON CO., ST. AUGUSTINE (1850) [CEM] Rev. Michael E. Augustinowitz; Deacons Regis E. Cummings; Walter Brenneman Jr.; Gesualdo Schneider.
Res.: 16 Barre St., 05602. Tel: 802-223-5285; Fax: 802-223-3621.
Catechesis/Religious Program—Students 140.
Mission—North American Martyrs (1963) Marshfield, Washington Co.

MORRISVILLE, LAMOILLE CO., PARISH OF THE HOLY NAME OF JESUS (2008) [CEM], Parish includes Holy Cross, Morrisville, St. Gabriel, Eden, St. Theresa, Hyde Park & St. John the Apostle, Johnson. Rev. Francis R. Prive; Deacon Thomas F. Cooney.
Res.: P.O. Box 339, 05661. Tel: 802-888-3318; Fax: 802-888-6177.
Catechesis/Religious Program—Students 78.

NEWPORT, ORLEANS CO., ST. MARY STAR OF THE SEA (1873) [CEM] Revs. Michael Reardon, S.D.V.; Shiju Chittattukkara, S.D.V.; Thomas Naduviledathu, S.D.V.
Res.: 191 Clermont Ter., 05855. Tel: 802-334-5066; Fax: 802-334-5067.
Catechesis/Religious Program—Tel: 802-334-6240. Dennis De La Bruere, D.R.E.; Aline De La Bruere, D.R.E.; Ann Gonyaw, Youth Min. & D.R.E. Students 75.

NORTH BENNINGTON, BENNINGTON CO., ST. JOHN THE BAPTIST (1885) [CEM] Revs. William H. Kelley, C.S.C.; John Britto Antony, C.S.C.; Deacon David O'Brien.
Res.: 3-5 Houghton St., P.O. Box 219, 05257. Tel: 802-447-7504; Fax: 802-442-6620.
Catechesis/Religious Program—Eileen M. Flynn, D.R.E. Students 47.

NORTH TROY, ORLEANS CO., ST. VINCENT DE PAUL (1939) [CEM] Unassigned.
Res.: P.O. Box 109, Troy, 05868. Tel: 802-988-2608; Fax: 802-988-2608.
Catechesis/Religious Program—Helene Croteau, D.R.E. Students 12.

NORTHFIELD, WASHINGTON CO., ST. JOHN THE EVANGELIST (1865) [CEM] Rev. Kevin E. Rooney.
Res.: 206 Vine St., 05663. Tel: 802-485-8313; Fax: 802-485-3043.
Catechesis/Religious Program—Students 54.
Mission—St. Edward Williamstown, Orange Co.

ORWELL, ADDISON CO., ST. PAUL (1886) [CEM] Rev. Henry P. Furman.
Res.: c/o P.O. Box 128, Castleton, 05735-0128. Tel: 802-468-5706; Fax: 802-468-2777.
Catechesis/Religious Program—Tel: 802-948-2408. Students 19.

PITTSFORD, RUTLAND CO., ST. ALPHONSUS LIGUORI (1893) [CEM] Rev. Richard Crawley, O.F.M.Cap.
Res.: 2918 U.S. Rte. 7, 05763-9499. Tel: 802-483-2301; Fax: 802-483-2136.
Catechesis/Religious Program—Lisa Adamsen, D.R.E. Students 56.

POULTNEY, RUTLAND CO., ST. RAPHAEL (1884) [CEM] Rev. Sean P. Dowling, Admin.
Res.: 21 E. Main St., P.O. Box 1064, 05764-1107. Tel: 802-287-5703.
Catechesis/Religious Program—Students 49.

PROCTOR, RUTLAND CO., ST. DOMINIC (1888) [CEM] Rev. Thomas R. Houle, O.F.M.Cap.
Church: 45 South St., 05765.
Catechesis/Religious Program—Marie Baccei, D.R.E. Students 27.

PUTNEY, WINDHAM CO., OUR LADY OF MERCY (1931) Rev. Frederick E. McLachlan, S.S.E.; Deacons Jerome Driscoll; Richard Anderberg. In Res., Rev. Francis X. McMahon, S.S.E. (Retired).
Res.: 52 Old Depot Rd., P.O. Box 246, 05346. Tel: 802-387-5861; Fax: 802-387-2154.
Catechesis/Religious Program—Students 23.
Mission—St. Edmund of Canterbury Saxtons River, Windham Co.
Mission—Chapel of the Snows Stratton Mountain, Windham Co.
Mission—Our Lady of the Valley Townshend, Windham Co.

RANDOLPH, ORANGE CO., OUR LADY OF THE ANGELS (2008) Rev. John M. Milanese.
Res.: 43 Hebard Hill Rd., P.O. Box 428, 05060. Tel: 802-728-5251; Fax: 802-728-9922.
Catechesis/Religious Program—Students 20.

READSBORO, BENNINGTON CO., ST. JOACHIM (1895) Rev. James T. Holden, Admin.
Res.: P.O. Box 158, 05350-9738. Tel: 802-423-5267; Fax: 802-423-5267.
Catechesis/Religious Program—Students 18.
Mission—St. John Bosco Stamford, Bennington Co.

RICHFORD, FRANKLIN CO., ALL SAINTS (1899) [CEM] Rev. Karl A. Hahr; Deacon Clifford Chagnon.
Res.: 152 Main St., 05476. Tel: 802-848-7741; Fax: 802-848-3150.
Catechesis/Religious Program—Students 46.
Mission—Our Lady of Lourdes East Berkshire, Franklin Co.
Mission—St. Isidore Montgomery Center, Franklin Co.

RICHMOND, CHITTENDEN CO., OUR LADY OF THE HOLY ROSARY (1860) [CEM 2] Rev. Lance W. Harlow.
Res.: 64 W. Main St., P.O. Box 243, 05477. Tel: 802-434-2521.
Catechesis/Religious Program—Jill Danilich, D.R.E. Students 90.

RUTLAND, RUTLAND CO.

1—CHRIST THE KING (1907) Revs. Justin J. Baker; James C. Dodson.
Res.: 66 S. Main St., 05701. Tel: 802-773-6820; Fax: 802-775-1054.
Catechesis/Religious Program—Students 131.

2—IMMACULATE HEART OF MARY (1869) [CEM] Rev. Remigius Bukuru Ntahondi.
Res.: 18 Lincoln Ave., 05701. Tel: 802-775-0846; Fax: 802-775-9640.
Catechesis/Religious Program—Tel: 802-775-0845. Cindy Tuomisto, D.R.E. Students 175.

3—ST. PETER (1855) [CEM] Rev. Thomas R. Houle, O.F.M.Cap. In Res., Rev. Richard Crawley, O.F.M.Cap.
Res.: 134 Convent Ave., 05701. Tel: 802-775-1994; Fax: 802-775-0178.
Catechesis/Religious Program—Students 10.

ST. ALBANS, FRANKLIN CO.

1—HOLY ANGELS (1872) [CEM] Revs. Maurice J. Roy; Daniel Lokanga; Deacon Duane Langlois.
Res.: 246 Lake St., 05478. Tel: 802-524-2585; Fax: 802-524-2586.
Catechesis/Religious Program—Students 319.
Mission—Ascension Georgia, Franklin Co.

2—IMMACULATE CONCEPTION (1847) [CEM] Rev. Brian J. O'Donnell, Admin.; Deacon Gabriel Gagne.
Res.: 45 Fairfield St., 05478. Tel: 802-527-7775; Fax: 802-527-1667.

Catechesis/Religious Program—Tel: 802-524-9416. Kathy Rogers, C.R.E. (PreK-10). Students 78.

SAINT JOHNSBURY, CALEDONIA CO.

1—CORPUS CHRISTI PARISH Revs. Patrick J. Forman; Dwight Baker; Deacons Bruce Burk; Raymond J. Desilets; Bernier L. Mayo; Peter Gummere; David Baker; Alfred Toborg.

Res.: 49 Winter St., 05819. Tel: 802-748-8129; Fax: 802-748-8120.

Catechesis/Religious Program—506 Summer St., 05819. Tel: 802-748-9256 (PreK-8). Marie Hagan, D.R.E. (PreK-8); Debra Priest, D.R.E. (High School). Students 143.

SHELBURNE, CHITTENDEN CO., ST. CATHERINE OF SIENA (1906) [CEM] Rev. Michael W. DeForge.

Res.: 72 Church St., P.O. Box 70, 05482. Tel: 802-985-2373; Fax: 802-985-9181. Email: info@shelburnecatholic.org.

Catechesis/Religious Program—Marie Cookson, D.R.E. Students 135.

SHELDON SPRINGS, FRANKLIN CO., ST. ANTHONY (1906) [CEM 2] Rev. Roger L. Charbonneau.

Res.: 102 Shawville Rd., P.O. Box 97, 05485-0097.

Catechesis/Religious Program—(Combined with St. John, Enosburg Falls).

Mission—St. Mary [CEM] 145 Square Rd., Franklin, Franklin Co. 05457.

SOUTH BURLINGTON, CHITTENDEN CO., ST. JOHN VIANNEY (1940) Rev. Bernard E. Gaudreau; Deacons Joseph Lane; Anthony Previti; Christopher Keough. In Res., Rev. Timothy Sullivan.

Res.: 160 Hinesburg Rd., 05403. Tel: 802-864-4166; Fax: 802-863-6065.

Catechesis/Religious Program—Tel: 802-864-4166, Ext. 204. Christine Guarino, Confirmation Coord.; Lauren Patterson, D.R.E. Students 234.

SOUTH HERO, GRAND ISLE CO., ST. ROSE OF LIMA (1895) Rev. Lawrence P. Ridgley.

Res.: 501 Rte. 2, 05486. Tel: 802-372-4092; Fax: 802-372-4770.

Catechesis/Religious Program—Students 37.

Mission—St. Joseph Grand Isle, Grand Isle Co.

SPRINGFIELD, WINDSOR CO., MATERNITY OF THE BLESSED VIRGIN MARY (1900) [CEM] Rev. Peter Y. Williams.

Res.: 40 Summer St., 05156. Tel: 802-885-3400; Fax: 802-885-2250.

Catechesis/Religious Program—Eileen Kendall, C.R.E. Students 85.

STOWE, LAMOILLE CO., BLESSED SACRAMENT (1954) Rev. Benedict C. Kiely.

Res.: 728 Mountain Rd., P.O. Box 27, 05672. Tel: 802-253-7536; Fax: 802-253-4445.

Catechesis/Religious Program—Tel: 802-253-7536, Ext. 13. Victoria Colyer, D.R.E. Students 64.

SWANTON, FRANKLIN CO., NATIVITY OF THE BLESSED VIRGIN MARY-ST. LOUIS (2008) [CEM], Parish includes Nativity of the Blessed Virgin Mary, Swanton & St. Louis, Highgate Center. Rev. Thomas D. Nadeau, Admin.

Res.: 65 Canada St., 05488. Tel: 802-868-4517; 802-868-4262; Fax: 802-868-9202.

Catechesis/Religious Program—Students 153.

TROY, ORLEANS CO., SACRED HEART OF JESUS (1931) [CEM] Unassigned.

Res.: P.O. Box 109, 05868. Tel: 802-988-2608; Fax: 802-988-2608.

Catechesis/Religious Program—Pauline Couture, D.R.E. Tel: 802-744-2733; Sara Leblanc, D.R.E. Tel: 802-744-6259. Students 48.

Mission—St. Ignatius Loyola Lowell, Orleans Co.

UNDERHILL CENTER, CHITTENDEN CO., ST. THOMAS (1856) [CEM 3] Rev. Charles R. Danielson; Deacon Peter Brooks.

Res.: 6 Green St., P.O. Box 3, 05490-0003. Tel: 802-899-4632; Fax: 802-899-5120.

Catechesis/Religious Program—Tel: 802-899-4770. Laura Lynch Wells, Coord. Students 133.

VERGENNES, ADDISON CO., ST. PETER (1881) [CEM] Rev. Yvon J. Royer.

Res.: 85 S. Maple St., P.O. Box 324, 05491-0924. Tel: 802-877-2367; Fax: 802-877-1063.

Catechesis/Religious Program—Kathleen Krayewsky, D.R.E. Students 65.

WALLINGFORD, RUTLAND CO., ST. PATRICK (1910) [CEM] Revs. Justin J. Baker; James C. Dodson.

Res.: 218 N. Main St., P.O. Box 99, 05773-0099. Tel: 802-446-2161.

Catechesis/Religious Program—(Christ the King Parish) Students 14.

WATERBURY, WASHINGTON CO., ST. ANDREW (1869) [CEM] Rev. Jerome Mercure.

Res.: 109 S. Main St., 05676. Tel: 802-244-7734; Fax: 802-244-7934.

Catechesis/Religious Program—Dianne Bilodeau, D.R.E. Students 101.

Mission—Our Lady of the Snows Waitsfield, Washington Co.

Mission—St. Patrick Moretown, Washington Co.

WEST RUTLAND, RUTLAND CO.

1—ST. BRIDGET (1857) [CEM 2] Rev. Vincent J. Coppola, C.S.C., Admin.

Res.: 28 Church St., 05777. Tel: 802-438-2490; Fax: 802-797-8099.

Catechesis/Religious Program—Students 40.

2—ST. STANISLAUS KOSTKA (1904), (Polish), [CEM] Rev. Vincent J. Coppola, C.S.C.

Mailing Address: 23 Barnes St., 05777.

Res.: 28 Church St., 05777. Tel: 802-438-2490.

Catechesis/Religious Program—Students 2.

WHITE RIVER JUNCTION, WINDSOR CO., ST. ANTHONY (1869) [CEM 2] Revs. Kenneth Thibodeau, S.M.; Kenneth Ridgeway, S.M.; Deacon John P. Guarino.

Res.: 15 Church St., 05001. Tel: 802-295-2225; Fax: 802-296-6008.

Religious Education Center—53 Church St., 05001. Tel: 802-295-6607.

Catechesis/Religious Program—Roisin Viens, D.R.E.; Eileen Urquhart, D.R.E.; Kelli Kehoe, D.R.E.; Dorothy Moffitt, D.R.E. Students 70.

WILLISTON, CHITTENDEN CO., IMMACULATE HEART OF MARY (1951) Rev. Lance W. Harlow.

Res.: 7417 Williston Rd., P.O. Box 1047, 05495. Tel: 802-878-4513.

Catechesis/Religious Program—Students 139.

WILMINGTON, WINDHAM CO., OUR LADY OF FATIMA (1959) Rev. Cyrain G. Cabuenas, Admin.

Res.: 96 E. Main St., P.O. Box 188, 05363. Tel: 802-464-7329; Fax: 802-464-9483.

Catechesis/Religious Program—Students 34.

WINDSOR, WINDSOR CO., ST. FRANCIS OF ASSISI (1886) [CEM] Rev. Raymond Vaillancourt, M.S.

Res.: 30 Union St., P.O. Box 46, 05089. Tel: 802-674-2157; Fax: 802-674-9416.

Catechesis/Religious Program—Joyce K. Corbin, D.R.E. Students 68.

WINOOSKI, CHITTENDEN CO.

1—ST. FRANCIS XAVIER (1868) [CEM] Rev. Msgr. Richard G. LaValley; Deacon John F. Place. In Res., Rev. Bernard W. Bourgeois.

Res.: 3 St. Peter St., Ste. 2, 05404. Tel: 802-655-2290; Fax: 802-655-3036.

School—(Grades PreK-8) Tel: 802-655-2600; Fax: 802-655-3096. Mr. Jesse Gaudette, Prin.; Mr. Eric Becker, Vice Prin.; Kathryn LaVigne, Admin. Sisters 1; Lay Teachers 23; Students 223.

Catechesis/Religious Program—Students 92.

Convent—Our Lady of Providence, Tel: 802-655-2395; Fax: 802-655-3888.

St. Vincent de Paul Center—Tel: 802-655-3006.

Extension Program—Tel: 802-655-4660.

2—ST. STEPHEN (1882) [CEM] Rev. Msgr. Wendell H. Searles, Admin. (Retired).

Res.: 115 Barlow St., 05404. Tel: 802-655-0318; Fax: 802-655-4779.

Catechesis/Religious Program—Jeffrey Badillo, D.R.E. Students 24.

WOODSTOCK, WINDSOR CO., OUR LADY OF THE SNOWS (1894) Rev. Thomas L. Mosher.

Res.: 7 South St., P.O. Box 397, 05091-0397. Tel: 802-457-2322; Fax: 802-457-7056.

Catechesis/Religious Program—Britney Koetsier, Rel. Educ. Coord. Students 62.

Mission—Our Lady of the Mountains Killington, Rutland Co.

Chaplains of Public Institutions

BURLINGTON. *Fletcher Allen Health Care* 05401. Tel: 802-656-2770. Revs. John Nwagbaraocha, D.S., Fidelis Agughara, Timothy Sullivan.

WATERBURY. *State Hospital*. Rev. Jerome Mercure.

WHITE RIVER JUNCTION. *Veterans Administration Hospital*. Rev. Joseph L. O'Keefe.

On Duty Outside the Diocese:

Rev.—

Dowd, Barry G., Mary Queen of the Universe Shrine, 8300 Vineland Ave., Orlando, FL 32821.

Unassigned:

Rev.—

Austin, Luke P.

Retired:

Rev. Msgrs.—

Mayo, Reid C., 265 Morrison Rd., Barre, 05641.

McSweeney, John R., J.C.L., 125 Kennedy Dr., Unit #36, 05403. Tel: 802-863-6017

Rivard, Roland J., 50 Winding Brook Dr., 05403.

Revs.—

Beauregard, James E., Birchwood Terrace Healthcare, 43 Starr Farm Rd., Burlington, 05408.

Davignon, Charles P., 62 Davingnon Ln., Brownington, 05860.

Depeaux, Bernard F., J.C.L., 351 North Ave., P.O. Box 489, Burlington, 05402-0489. Tel: 802-658-6110

Haskin, Jay C., M.Ch.A., 86 Westview Heights Dr., #5-2, Stowe, 05672. Tel: 802-373-4219

Herbert, John J., The Loretto Home, 59 Meadow St., Rutland, 05701. Tel: 802-773-8840

Holland, Francis M., Our Lady of Providence Convent, 47 W. Spring St., Winooski, 05404.

Kennedy-Warley, David G., 17028 N. Pinion Ln., Sun City, AZ 85373.

Krempa, Adam J., West Rutland, 05777.

LaFlamme, Julien J., 239 Rte. 67 W., North Bennington, 05257. Tel: 802-442-9974

LaMothe, Philip R., 386 Stephenson Rd., Apt. 1, Lowell, 05847.

Laplante, Jean-Paul, 64 N. Elm St., St. Albans, 05478.

LaVallee, Pierre A., #67 Manor Woods, 100 Kennedy Dr., 05403. Tel: 802-658-6343

Lively, Joseph A., 257 Peacham Pond Rd., Marshfield, 05658. Tel: 802-426-3847

McCarthy, Joseph, Starr Farm Nursing Home, 98 Starr Farm Rd., Burlington, 05408.

Morgan, William P., 2609 Roy Mountain Rd., P.O. Box 76, Barnet, 05821. Tel: 802-633-2870

Ragis, Gerald, 2215 The Terraces, Shelburne, 05482. Tel: 802-985-0707

Ravey, Donald J., 152 Allen Rd., #234, 05403. Tel: 802-497-1687

Romano, Joseph E., 320 Richmond Hill Rd., Cheshire, MA 01225. Tel: 413-743-0817

Rousseau, Peter A., The Arbors, 687 Harbor Rd., Shelburne, 05482.

Roy, Donald J., Spanish Lake Mobile Home Park, 1102 Captiva St., Nokomis, FL 34275.

Shea, James M., 792 Capri Isles Blvd., Venice, FL 34292. Tel: 941-416-2455

Whalen, Robert B., P.O. Box 59, Poultney, 05764. Tel: 802-287-9758

Permanent Deacons:

Anderberg, Richard, Our Lady of the Valley, Townshend

Baker, David, Corpus Christi, St. Johnsbury

Bisson, David, St. Monica, Barre

Blicharz, John, Bellows Falls

Brenneman, Walter, St. Augustine, Montpelier

Brooks, Peter T., St. Thomas, Underhill Ctr.

Brown, William J., III, (On Duty Outside the Diocese)

Burk, Bruce, St. John, St. Johnsbury

Chagnon, Clifford, All Saints, Richford

Cooney, Thomas F., Holy Cross, Morrisville

Cummings, Regis E., St. Augustine, Montpelier

Desilets, Raymond J., Corpus Christi, St. Johnsbury

Driscoll, Jerome, Chapel of the Snows, Stratton Mountain

Fitzpatrick, Kelly, Our Lady of Perpetual Help, Bradford

Gagne, Gabriel, St. Mary; St. Albans

Garrow, Paul, St. Ann, Milton

Gibbo, Timothy, St. Mark, Burlington

Glinka, William, Cathedral of the Immaculate Conception, Burlington

Gratton, John P.E., St. Benedict, West Charleston

Griffin, Gary, St. Mary, Brandon

Griffin, Gary, St. Mary, Brandon

Guarino, John P., St. Anthony, White River Junction

Gummere, Peter, Corpus Christi, St. Johnsbury

Hawk, Ivan O., III, Holy Cross, Colchester

Keough, Christopher, St. John Vianney, South Burlington

Krawczyk, Eugene, (Outside the Diocese)

Lane, Joseph W., Sr., St. John Vianney, South Burlington

Langlois, Duane, Holy Angels, St. Albans

Liegey, Gabriel M., Jr., St. Patrick, Fairfield

Lissandrello, Paul (On Duty Outside the Diocese)

Mayo, Bernier L., Corpus Christi, St. Johnsbury

Mello, Paul (On Duty Outside the Diocese)

Meunier, Louis A., St. Anthony and Christ the King, Burlington

Meyers, Vincent, St. Raphael, Poultney

Moore, Dennis, Ascension, Georgia

Moran, Robert J., St. Anne, Middletown Springs

O'Brien, David, St. John the Baptist, North Bennington

Place, John F., St. Francis Xavier, Winooski

Previti, Anthony, St. John Vianney, South Burlington

Pudvah, Daniel, St. Monica, Barre

Ramey, Jon, (On Duty Outside the Diocese)

Ratte, Stephen J., St. Luke, Fairfax

Rock, James E., (On Duty Outside the Diocese)

Schneider, Gesualdo, St. Augustine, Montpelier

Scilla, Gerald, St. Pius X, Essex Ctr.

Taylor, Timm, St. Anthony; Christ the King, Burlington

Toborg, Alfred, Corpus Christi, St. Johnsbury

Vincelette, Alan, (Retired)

INSTITUTIONS LOCATED IN THE DIOCESE

[A] COLLEGES AND UNIVERSITIES

COLCHESTER. *St. Michael's College*, One Winooski Park, 05439. Tel: 802-654-2000; 802-654-2476; Fax: 802-654-2780. Web: www.smcvt.edu. Dr. John J. Neuhauser, Pres.; William H. Gallagher, Chm. of the Bd.; Ms. Lisa Powlison, Asst. to Pres.; Ms. Marilyn Cormier, Dir. Community Rels.; Dr. Karen A. Talentino, Vice Pres. Academic Affairs; Mr. Michael D. Samara, Vice Pres. Student Affairs; Mr. Patrick Gallivan, Vice Pres. Institutional Advancement; Rev. Brian J. Cummings, S.S.E., Dir. Campus Ministry; Mr. Jerry E. Flanagan, Vice Pres. Enrollment & Mktg.; Mr. John D. Sheehey, Registrar; Dr. Edward Mahoney, Dir. Graduate Theology & Pastoral Ministry Prog.; Jerome P. Monachino, Dir., Liturgical Music; Michael J. New, Vice Pres. Human Resources; Revs. Raymond J. Doherty, S.S.E., Campus Min.; Richard N. Berube, S.S.E., Local Supr.; Joseph M. McLaughlin, S.S.E., Prof.; John K. Payne, Dir. Library & Information Svcs. Priests 2; Lay Teachers 150; Students 2,500.

RUTLAND. **College of St. Joseph in Vermont*, 71 Clement Rd., 05701-3899. Tel: 802-773-5900; Fax: 802-776-5258. Email: fmiglorie@csj.edu. Web: www.csj.edu. Dr. Frank G. Miglorie Jr., Ed.D., Pres.; Doreen McCullough, Librarian. Lay Teachers 13; Students 379.

[B] CENTRAL HIGH SCHOOLS, DIOCESAN AND PAROCHIAL

RUTLAND. *Mount St. Joseph Academy - Rutland Catholic Schools*, 127 Convent Ave., 05701. Tel: 802-775-0151; Fax: 802-775-0424. Email: principal@msjvermont.org. Web: www.msjvermont.org. Mr. Paolo Zancanaro, Prin.; Constance Whalen, Guidance Dir.; Donna Butman, Librarian; Rev. James C. Dodson. Sisters of St. Joseph. Priests 1; Lay Teachers 17; Students 95.

SOUTH BURLINGTON. *Rice Memorial High School*, 99 Proctor Ave., 05403. Tel: 802-862-6521; Fax: 802-864-9931. Email: bourgeois@rmhsvt.org. Web: www.rmhsvt.org. Rev. Bernard W. Bourgeois, M.A., M.Div., Prin.; Brian Ricca, Assoc. Prin. for Academics; Lloyd Hulbard, Assoc. Prin. Student Life; Ann Kenney, Librarian. Priests 2; Lay Teachers 30; Students 370.

[C] ELEMENTARY SCHOOLS, PAROCHIAL

BURLINGTON. *Christ The King*, (Grades PreSchool-8), 136 Locust St., 05401. Tel: 802-862-6696; Fax: 802-658-6553. Web: www.cksvt.org. Ms. Paulette Thibault, Prin.; Aida Cadrecha, Librarian. Lay Teachers 20; Students 259.

Mater Christi School, (Grades PreK-8), 50 Mansfield Ave., 05401. Tel: 802-658-3992; Fax: 802-863-1196. Email: pjette@mcschool.org. Web: www.mcschool.org. Mr. Paul Jette, Prin.; Kristen King, Librarian. Sisters 1; Lay Teachers 23; Students 233.

BARRE. *Central Vermont Catholic School*, (Grades PreK-8), 79 Summer St., 05641. Tel: 802-476-5015; Fax: 802-476-0861. Email: pattiecvcs@yahoo.com. Ms. Patricia M. O'Mahoney, Prin. Lay Teachers 15; Students 127.

BARTON. *St. Paul's*, (Grades PreK-8), 54 Eastern Ave., 05822. Tel: 802-525-6578; Fax: 802-525-3869. Email: stpaulsprincipalfontana@gmail.com. Mr. Peter T. Close, Prin. Priests 1; Teaching Principal 1; Lay Teachers 6; Students 89.

BENNINGTON. *The School of Sacred Heart St. Francis de Sales*, (Grades PreK-8), 307 School St., 05201. Tel: 802-442-2446; Fax: 802-442-2344. Email: estesdb@comcast.net. Web: www.sacredheartbennington.org. Mr. David B. Estes, Prin.; Marcia Hendery, Librarian; Kathy Murphy, Librarian. Lay Teachers 10; Students 145.

BRATTLEBORO. *St. Michael School*, (Grades PreSchool-8), 48 Walnut St., 05301. Tel: 802-254-6320; Fax: 802-254-5229. Email: principal@smsvt.info. Mrs. Elaine Beam, Prin. Lay Teachers 6; Students 98.

MIDDLEBURY. *St. Mary School*, (Grades PreK-6), 86 Shannon St., 05753. Tel: 802-388-8392; Fax: 802-388-8392. Email: smsprincipal@saintmarysvt.org. Mrs. Angela Pohlen, Prin. Lay Teachers 13; Students 73.

MORRISVILLE. *Bishop John A. Marshall School*, (Grades PreK-8), 680 La Porte Rd., 05661. Tel: 802-888-4758; Fax: 802-888-3137. Email: cwilson@bjams.org. Web: www.bjams.org. Mrs. Carrie Wilson, Prin.; Jennifer Wileman, Librarian; Dianne Ianni, Librarian. Lay Teachers 19; Students 120.

RUTLAND. *Christ the King - Rutland Catholic Schools*, (Grades PreK-8), 60 S. Main St., 05701. Tel: 802-773-0500; Fax: 802-773-0554. Email: cwincowski@cksrutland.org. Web: www.cksrutland.com. Mrs. Carol H. Wincowski, Prin.; Lila Millard, Librarian. Sisters 1; Lay Teachers 14; Students 160.

SAINT JOHNSBURY. *Good Shepherd School*, (Grades PreK-8), 121 Maple St., 05819. Tel: 802-751-8223; Fax: 802-751-8111. Email: khaskins@gscsvt.org. Mrs. Karen Haskins, Co-Prin.; Mrs. Linda Hartwell, Co-Prin.; Mrs. Karen Haskins, Librarian. Lay Teachers 11; Students 174.

WINOOSKI. *St. Francis Xavier*, (Grades PreK-8), 5 St. Peter St., 05404. Tel: 802-655-2600; Fax: 802-655-3096. Email: gaudette_stfrancis@yahoo.com. Web: www.edline.net/pages/sfxwinooski. Mr. Jesse Gaudette, Prin.; Mr. Eric Becker, Vice Prin.; Kathryn LaVigne, Admin. & Dir. Early Educ.; Mrs. Kathleen Finn, Librarian. Sisters 1; Lay Teachers 23; Students 223.

[D] HOMES FOR AGED

BURLINGTON. *St. Joseph/Kervick Home*, 243 N. Prospect St., 05401. Tel: 802-864-0264; Fax: 802-864-5640. Mr. Lawrence Assell, Dir.; Deacon Christopher Keough. Managed by Vermont Catholic Charities. Guests 40.

DERBY LINE. *Michaud/Kervick Home*, 47 Herrick Rd., 05830. Tel: 802-873-3152; Fax: 802-873-9206. Web: www.vermontcatholic.org. Mr. Lawrence Assell, Dir.; Ward Nolan, Admin. Managed by Vermont Catholic Charities. Guests 29.

RUTLAND. *St. Joseph/Kervick Residence*, 131 Convent Ave., 05701. Tel: 802-775-5133; Fax: 802-747-0167. Deacon Gary Griffin, Admin.; Mr. Lawrence Assell, Dir.; Rev. John W. Hamilton, Resident Chap. (Retired). Managed by Vermont Catholic Charities. Guests 51.

Loretto/Kervick Home, 59 Meadow St., 05701. Tel: 802-773-8840; Fax: 802-773-9638. Deacon Gary Griffin, Admin.; Mr. Lawrence Assell, Dir.; Rev. John J. Herbert, Resident Chap. (Retired). Managed by Vermont Catholic Charities. Guests 55.

[E] MONASTERIES AND RESIDENCES OF PRIESTS AND BROTHERS

ARLINGTON. *Carthusian Foundation in America, Inc., Charterhouse of the Transfiguration*, 1084 Ave Maria Way, 05250. Tel: 802-362-2550; Fax: 802-362-3584. Email: carthusians_in_america@chartreuse.info. Web: transfiguration.chartreux.org. Revs. Johan de Bruijn, O.Cart. (Holland), Librarian; Philip Dahl, O.Cart. (Norway), Sacristan; Lorenzo Maria Tolentino de la Rosa Jr., O.Cart. (Philippines), Prior; Mary Joseph Kim, O.Cart. (Korea, South), Novice Master. Carthusian Foundation, Association Fraternelle Romande. Choir Monks: Solemn Professed 4; Converse Brothers: Solemn Professed 4; Choir Monks: Simple Professed 1; Converse Brothers: Simple Professed 1; Perpetual Donates 1; Novices 1; Aspirant 1; Postulants 2.

COLCHESTER. *Society of St. Edmund* (Edmundite Generalate), 270 Winooski Park, 05439. Tel: 802-654-3400; Fax: 802-654-3409. Email: generalate@aol.com. Web: www.sse.org. Very Rev. Michael P. Cronogue, S.S.E., Supr. Gen.; Revs. Edward J. Dubriske, S.S.E. (Venezuela); Philippe Simonnet, S.S.E. (France). Central Offices, Society of Saint Edmund. *Society of St. Edmund*, P.O. Box 272, 05439. Tel: 802-654-2000; Fax: 802-654-3409. Revs. Richard N. Berube, S.S.E., Supr. & Treas. Gen.; Paul E. Couture, S.S.E.; Brian J. Cummings, S.S.E.; Raymond J. Doherty, S.S.E.; Joseph M. McLaughlin, S.S.E.; Richard L. Vanderweel, S.S.E.; John T. Scully, S.S.E.; David Theroux, S.S.E.; Bro. Thomas Berube, S.S.E. (Edmundite Community at St. Michael's College) *Edmundite House of Formation*, 25 Millham Ct., 05403. Tel: 802-497-0893; Fax: 802-654-3409. Rev. Marcel R. Rainville, S.S.E., Dir. Formation. Residents 4.

WESTON. *Priory of Benedictine Monks*, 58 Priory Hill Rd., 05161-6400. Tel: 802-824-5409; Fax: 802-824-3573. Email: brothers@westonpriory.org. Web: www.westonpriory.org. Very Rev. Richard Iaquinto, O.S.B., Prior; Revs. Peter Claude Anctil, O.S.B.; Robert J. Kiernan, O.S.B.; Mark Ronald Nicolosi, O.S.B.; John Hammond, O.S.B. Priests 5; Brothers 9.

[F] CONVENTS AND RESIDENCES OF SISTERS

BURLINGTON. *Sisters of Mercy of the Americas-Northeast Community*, 100 Mansfield Ave., 05401. Tel: 802-863-6835; Fax: 802-863-1486. Email: mread@mercyne.org. Sr. Marianne Read, R.S.M., M.Ed., C.A.E.S., Life & Ministry Admin. Residence for Sisters and Life Ministry Office. Sisters 26.

LOWELL. *The Carmelite Nuns of Vermont, Inc., St. Joseph's Carmelite Monastery*, 386 Stephenson Rd., 05847. Tel: 802-744-2346. Sr. Diane Gauthier, O.C.D., Vicaress. Sisters 5.

NEWPORT. *Sacred Heart Convent* (Daughters of Charity of the Sacred Heart), 119 Clermont Ter., 05855. Tel: 802-334-7058. Sisters 3.

WESTFIELD. *Monastery of the Immaculate Heart of Mary*, 4103 VT Rte. 100, 05874. Tel: 802-744-6525; Fax: 802-744-6236. Sisters Laurence A. M. Couture, O.S.B., Prioress; Maria-Magdalen Grumm, O.S.B., Subprioress & Novice Mistress; Rev. Dom Lawrence Brown, O.S.B., Resident Chap., Monk of Clear Creek, OK. Benedictine Cloistered Nuns, Congregation of Solesmes. Professed Nuns 11; Temporary Professed 2.

WINOOSKI. *Missionary Sisters of Our Lady of Africa (M.S.O.L.A.)*, 47 W. Spring St., 05404. Tel: 802-655-2395; Fax: 802-655-1830. Email: heintzmarie@gmail.com. Sr. Marie Heintz, Contact Person. Sisters 7.

Religious Hospitallers of St. Joseph (1636) 47 W. Spring St., 05404-1319. Tel: 802-655-2395; Fax: 802-654-3976. Sr. Adrienne Desjardins, R.H.S.J., Supr. Sisters 7.

Sisters of Providence, 47 W. Spring St., 05404. Tel: 802-655-2395; Fax: 802-861-2968. Email: olopr@aol.com. Sr. Carmen Proulx, S.P., Supr. Sisters 23.

[G] NEWMAN CENTERS

BURLINGTON. *University of Vermont-The Catholic Center at UVM* 390 S. Prospect St., Redstone Campus, 05401. Tel: 802-862-8403; Fax: 802-865-9480. Email: catholiccenteruvm@gmail.com. Web: www.uvmcatholic.com. Rev. Jon-Daniel Schnobrich, Dir. In Res. Rev. Msgr. John J. McDermott, V.G., J.C.L.

Castleton State College *St. John Rectory*, P.O. Box 128, Castleton, 05735. Tel: 802-468-5706; Fax: 802-468-2777. Rev. Henry P. Furman, Chap.

Goddard College (Plainfield) Attended by St. Augustine, 16 Barre St., Montpelier, 05602. Tel: 802-223-5285; Fax: 802-223-3621. Rev. Michael E. Augustinowitz.

Green Mountain College St. Raphael Rectory, Main St., Poultney, 05764. Tel: 802-287-5703. Rev. Sean P. Dowling.

Johnson State College (Johnson) P.O. Box 339, Morrisville, 05661. Tel: 802-888-3318; Fax: 802-888-6177. Attended by Holy Cross, Morrisville

Lyndon State College Lyndonville, 05851. Tel: 802-626-5267; Fax: 802-656-3324.

Middlebury College St. Mary Rectory, 326 College St., Middlebury, 05753. Tel: 802-388-2943; Fax: 802-388-6023. Rev. William R. Beaudin.

Norwich Newman Apostolate Norwich University, Northfield, 05663. Tel: 802-862-8403; Fax: 802-865-9480. Rev. Msgr. Richard G. LaValley, Co-Chap.; Rev. Michael W. DeForge, Co-Chap.

Vermont Technical College Sts. Donatian and Rogatian Rectory, 25 S. Pleasant St., Randolph, 05060. Tel: 802-728-3227; Fax: 802-728-3570. Rev. John M. Milanese, Chap.

[H] MISCELLANEOUS

BURLINGTON. *Mercy Connections, Inc.*, 255 S. Champlain St., Ste. 8, 05401. Tel: 802-846-7062; Fax: 802-846-7237. Email: dfleming@mercyconnections.org. Web: www.mercyconnections.org. Betsy Ferries, Exec. Dir.

BRATTLEBORO. *Neringa, Inc.*, 600 Liberty Hwy., Putnam, CT 06260. Tel: 978-582-5592. Email: info@neringa.org. Web: www.neringa.org. Dainora Kupcinskas, Asst. Exec. Dir.

COLCHESTER. *Fanny Allen Corporation*, 101 College Pkwy., 05446. Tel: 781-862-1634. Sponsored by Covenant Health Systems, Lexington, MA.

Fanny Allen Holdings, Inc., 790 College Pkwy., 05446. Tel: 802-847-6448; Fax: 802-847-6434. Email: ellen.kane@vtmednet.org. Ellen Kane, Pres. Fanny Allen Holdings, Inc. oversees property that it owns in Colchester, Vermont, leases to Fletcher Allen Health Care for use as a hospital and seeks to promote its Catholic identity. Fanny Allen Corporation operates a Community Fund that supports charitable organizations serving the poor, the sick and the most vulnerable.

ISLE LA MOTTE. *St. Anne's Shrine* 05463. Tel: 802-928-3362; Fax: 802-928-3305. Email: fstanne@pslift.com. Web: www.saintannesshrine.org. Rev. Brian J. Cummings, S.S.E., Spiritual Dir. Conducted by Fathers of Society of St. Edmund; Open May 15-Oct. 15.

RANDOLPH. *Prelature of the Holy Cross and Opus Dei*, Wynnview Center, R.D. 1, Sunset Hill, 05060. Tel: 802-728-5414; Fax: 802-728-3334. Web: www.opusdei.org.

RELIGIOUS INSTITUTES OF MEN REPRESENTED IN THE DIOCESE

For further details refer to the corresponding bracketed number in the Religious Institutes of Men or Women section.

[0200]—*Benedictine Monks*—O.S.B.

[]—*Capuchin Friars of North America*—O.F.M., Cap.

[0780]—*Marist Fathers*—S.M.

[0720]—*The Missionaries of Our Lady of La Salette* (Prov. of the Immaculate Heart of Mary)—M.S.

[0280]—*Order of Carthusians*—O.Cart.

[0610]—*Priests of the Congregation of Holy Cross* (Eastern Prov.)—C.S.C.

[]—*Society of Jesus*—S.J.

[0440]—*Society of Saint Edmund*—S.S.E.

RELIGIOUS INSTITUTES OF WOMEN REPRESENTED IN THE DIOCESE

[0170]—*Benedictine Cloistered Nuns of the Congregation of Solesmes*—O.S.B.

[0750]—*Daughters of the Charity of the Sacred Heart of Jesus*—F.C.S.C.J.

[0820]—*Daughters of the Holy Spirit*—D.H.S.

[0420]—*Discalced Carmelite Nuns*—O.C.D.

[1190]—*Franciscan Sisters of the Atonement*—S.A.

[2820]—*Missionary Sisters of Our Lady of Africa*—M.S.O.L.A.

[3440]—*Religious Hospitallers of Saint Joseph*—R.H.S.J.

[1930]—*Sisters of Holy Cross*—C.S.C.

[2575]—*Sisters of Mercy*—R.S.M.

[3000]—*Sisters of Notre Dame de Namur*—S.N.D.deN.

[3350]—*Sisters of Providence*—S.P.

[]—*Sisters of St. Joseph Society, Inc.*—S.S.J.

DIOCESAN CEMETERIES

SOUTH BURLINGTON. *Resurrection Park Cemetery*, 55 Joy Dr., 05403. Mr. Peter Wells, Dir. Facilities & Insurance.

NECROLOGY

† Ball, Rev. Msgr. Thomas J., Burlington, VT Cathedral of the Immaculate Conception.—Died April 19, 2011

† Chant, William S., (Retired)—Died Dec. 12, 2010

† Pray, Joseph N., (Retired)—Died June 15, 2011

† Von Fauer, Stephen C., (Retired)—Died Sept. 18, 2011

An asterisk (*) denotes an organization that has established tax-exempt status directly with the IRS and is not covered by the USCCB Group Ruling.

Diocese of Camden

(Dioecesis Camdensis)

Most Reverend

JOSEPH A. GALANTE, D.D., J.C.D.

Bishop of Camden; ordained May 16, 1964; appointed Titular Bishop of Equilum and Auxiliary Bishop of San Antonio October 13, 1992; consecrated December 11, 1992; appointed Bishop of Beaumont April 5, 1994; installed Bishop of Beaumont May 9, 1994; appointed Coadjutor Bishop of Dallas November 23, 1999; installed January 14, 2000; appointed Bishop of Camden March 23, 2004; installed April 30, 2004.

Chancery Office: Camden Diocesan Center, 631 Market St., P.O. Box 708, Camden, NJ 08101. Tel: 856-756-7900; Fax: 856-963-2655.

ESTABLISHED DECEMBER 9, 1937.

Square Miles 2,691.

Legal Corporate Title: "The Diocese of Camden, New Jersey."

Comprises six Counties in the State of New Jersey--viz., Atlantic, Camden, Cape May, Cumberland, Gloucester and Salem.

For legal titles of parishes and diocesan institutions, consult the Chancery Office.

STATISTICAL OVERVIEW

Personnel	
Bishop	1
Priests: Diocesan Active in Diocese	129
Priests: Diocesan Active Outside Diocese	11
Priests: Diocesan in Foreign Missions	1
Priests: Retired, Sick or Absent	135
Number of Diocesan Priests	276
Religious Priests in Diocese	42
Total Priests in Diocese	318
Extern Priests in Diocese	21
Ordinations:	
Diocesan Priests	3
Permanent Deacons	10
Permanent Deacons in Diocese	146
Total Brothers	12
Total Sisters	269
Parishes	
Parishes	82
With Resident Pastor:	
Resident Diocesan Priests	72
Resident Religious Priests	3
Without Resident Pastor:	
Administered by Priests	7
Administered by Pastoral Teams, etc.	1
Missions	4
New Parishes Created	22
Closed Parishes	34
Professional Ministry Personnel:	
Lay Ministers	47
Welfare	
Catholic Hospitals	1
Total Assisted	315,649
Health Care Centers	3
Total Assisted	18,573
Homes for the Aged	6
Total Assisted	1,613
Day Care Centers	4
Total Assisted	474
Special Centers for Social Services	7
Total Assisted	4,627
Other Institutions	2
Total Assisted	186,521
Educational	
Diocesan Students in Other Seminaries	9
Total Seminarians	9
High Schools, Diocesan and Parish	7
Total Students	4,269
High Schools, Private	3
Total Students	1,560
Elementary Schools, Diocesan and Parish	35
Total Students	7,831
Non-residential Schools for the Disabled	1
Total Students	741
Catechesis/Religious Education:	
Elementary Students	24,957
Total Students under Catholic Instruction	39,367
Teachers in the Diocese:	
Priests	11
Brothers	6
Sisters	38
Lay Teachers	967
Vital Statistics	
Receptions into the Church:	
Infant Baptism Totals	5,018
Adult Baptism Totals	465
Received into Full Communion	245
First Communions	5,332
Confirmations	5,026
Marriages:	
Catholic	787
Interfaith	255
Total Marriages	1,042
Total Catholic Population	511,822
Total Population	1,443,274

Former Bishops—Most Revs. BARTHOLOMEW J. EUSTACE, S.T.D., First Bishop of Camden; consecrated March 25, 1938; died Dec. 11, 1956; JUSTIN J. MCCARTHY, S.T.D., LL.D., Second Bishop of Camden; cons. June 17, 1954; appt. to Camden, Jan. 27, 1957; died Dec. 26, 1959; CELESTINE J. DAMIANO, D.D., Third Bishop of Camden; cons. Feb. 11, 1953; transferred to Camden, Jan. 24, 1960, with the personal title of Archbishop; died Oct. 2, 1967; GEORGE H. GUILFOYLE, D.D., J.D., ord. March 25, 1944; appt. Titular Bishop of Marazanae and Auxiliary Bishop of New York, Oct. 17, 1964; cons. Nov. 30, 1964; appt. Fourth Bishop of Camden, Jan. 2, 1968; installed March 4, 1968; retired May 22, 1989; died June 11, 1991; JAMES T. MCHUGH, S.T.D., ord. May 25, 1957; appt. Titular Bishop of Morosbisdo and Auxiliary Bishop of Newark, Nov. 20, 1987; cons. Jan. 25 1988; appt. Fifth Bishop of Camden, May 13, 1989; installed June 20, 1989; appt. Coadjutor Bishop of Rockville Centre, Dec. 7, 1998; installed Third Diocesan Bishop, Jan. 4, 2000; died Dec. 10, 2000; NICHOLAS A. DIMARZIO, Ph.D., D.D., ord. May 30, 1970; appt. Titular Bishop of Mauriana and Auxiliary Bishop of Newark, Sept. 10, 1996; cons. Oct. 31, 1996; appt. Sixth Bishop of Camden June 8, 1999; installed July 22, 1999; appt. Bishop of Brooklyn, Aug. 1, 2003; installed Oct. 3, 2003.

Diocesan Offices

Camden Diocesan Center—631 Market St., Camden, 08102. Tel: 856-756-7900; Fax: 856-963-2655. Some offices are listed at separate locations.

The Diocese of Camden— A corporation under the laws of the State of New Jersey.

Officers—Most Rev. JOSEPH ANTHONY GALANTE, D.D., J.C.D., Pres.; Rev. Msgr. ROGER E. MCGRATH, Ph.D., Vice Pres.; Rev. ROBERT E. HUGHES, Sec.

Diocesan Bishop—Most Rev. JOSEPH ANTHONY GALANTE, D.D., J.C.D., 631 Market St., Camden, 08102. Tel: 856-583-2808; Fax: 856-963-5777. Email: jgalante@camdendiocese.org.

Vicars General—Rev. Msgrs. JOHN H. BURTON, V.G., St. Isidore, 1655 Magnolia Rd., Vineland, 08360. Tel: 856-691-9077; Fax: 856-692-3305; ROBERT T. MCDERMOTT, V.G., Saint Joseph Pro-Cathedral, 2907 Federal St., Camden, 08102. Tel: 856-964-2776; Fax: 856-964-0044; ROGER E. MCGRATH, Ph.D., Vicar Gen. & Moderator of the Curia, 631 Market St., Camden, 08102. Tel: 856-583-2802; Fax: 856-338-0376.

Chancellor—Rev. ROBERT E. HUGHES, 631 Market St., Camden, 08102. Tel: 856-583-2803; Fax: 856-338-0376.

Vice Chancellors—Rev. JAMES L. BARTOLOMA, J.C.L. Tel: 856-583-2811; Fax: 856-338-0376; Rev. Msgr. DOMINIC J. BOTTINO, J.C.L., 631 Market St., Camden, 08102. Tel: 856-583-6162; Fax: 856-756-0113.

Assistant Vice Chancellors—Deacons MICHAEL J. CARTER. Tel: 856-583-2804; Fax: 856-338-0376; FELIX T. MIRIANDA, 631 Market St., Camden, 08102. Tel: 856-583-6162; Fax: 856-756-0113.

Judicial Vicar—Rev. DAVID J. KLEIN, J.C.L., 631 Market St., Camden, 08102. Tel: 856-583-6162; Fax: 856-756-0113.

Vicar for Clergy—Rev. TERRY M. ODIEN, 631 Market St., Camden, 08101. Tel: 856-583-2854; Fax: 856-966-5957.

Vicar for Hispanics—Rev. Msgr. VICTOR S. MURO, Divine Mercy Parish, 23 W. Chestnut Ave., Vineland, 08360. Tel: 856-691-9181; Fax: 856-794-9029.

Delegate for Men Religious—Bro. THOMAS OSORIO, O.H., Saint John of God Monastery, 1145 Delsea Dr., Westville Grove, 08093. Tel: 856-848-4700, Ext. 1163; Fax: 856-848-2154.

Delegate for Temporalities and Diocesan Finance Officer—WILLIAM J. MURRAY, 631 Market St., Camden, 08102. Tel: 856-583-2828; Fax: 856-963-2655.

Delegate for Women Religious—Sr. MARY J. GARRITY, I.H.M., 631 Market St., Camden, 08102. Tel: 856-583-2841; Fax: 856-338-0826.

Delegate of Lifelong Faith Formation—Sr. ROSEANN QUINN, S.S.J., 631 Market St., Camden, 08102. Tel: 856-583-6124; Fax: 856-225-0096.

Delegate for Inter-Parochial Affairs—Rev. Msgr. WILLIAM A. HODGE, V.F., St. Nicholas of Tolentine, 1409 Pacific Ave., Atlantic City, 08401. Tel: 609-344-1040; Fax: 609-344-3103.

Delegate for Hispanic Ministry—ANDRES ARANGO, 631 Market St., Camden, 08102. Tel: 856-583-6181; Fax: 856-583-6185.

Diocesan Tribunal

Diocesan Tribunal—15 N. 7th St., Camden, 08102. Tel: 856-583-6162; Fax: 856-756-0113.

Judicial Vicar—Rev. DAVID J. KLEIN, J.C.L. Tel: 856-583-6162.

Adjutant Judicial Vicars—Rev. Msgr. DOMINIC J. BOTTINO, J.C.L.; Rev. JOSEPH A. SALERNO, J.C.L. (Retired).

Judges—Rev. Msgr. DOMINIC J. BOTTINO, J.C.L.; Revs. JAMES L. BARTOLOMA, J.C.L.; DAVID J. KLEIN, J.C.L.; JOSEPH A. SALERNO, J.C.L. (Retired).

Defenders of the Bond—Deacon W. LEO MCBLAIN; Rev. Msgr. THOMAS F. SHARKEY, J.C.D. (Retired); Revs. ROBERT J. KANTZ, J.C.L.; JOSEPH A. SALERNO, J.C.L. (Retired).

Procurator-Advocate—VACANT.

Auditors—Rev. WALTER A. NORRIS, Esq.; Deacon FELIX MIRANDA; Mr. ROD J. HERRERA, L.C.S.W.

Notaries—DIANE GABLE; Mrs. CATHERINE GOLDY.

Councils—

Presbyteral Council—Most Rev. JOSEPH A. GALANTE, D.D., J.C.D., Presider; Revs. JOSEPH P. CAPELLA, Exec. Sec.; JOSEPH T. SZOLACK, M.Div., Recording Sec.

Appointed Members—Rev. Msgr. JOSEPH V. DIMAURO; Revs. ANTHONY J. MANUPPELLA, V.F.; THOMAS A. NEWTON; JOHN J. VIGNONE; MATTHEW J. HILLYARD, O.S.F.S.

Elected Members—

Representatives by Ordination Seniority—Revs. PAUL D. HARTE; JOSEPH P. CAPELLA; NICHOLAS DUDO.

Representative for Retired Priests—Rev. Msgr. HARRY J. JORDAN (Retired).

Deanery Representatives—Rev. Msgr. MICHAEL J. DOYLE; Rev. JAMES O. DABROWSKI; Rev. Msgr. THOMAS J. MORGAN, V.G.; Revs. RAYMOND P. GORMLEY, V.F.; JOSEPH J. ADAMSON, V.F.; DAVID A. GROVER; JOSEPH T. SZOLACK, M.Div.; PETER M. SAPORITO; Rev. Msgrs. JOHN T. FREY; WILLIAM A. HODGE, V.F.; Revs. PERRY A. CHERUBINI; EDWARD F. NAMIOTKA.

International Priests Representatives—Revs. COSME R. DE LA PENA; SANJAI DEVIS, V.C.; CESAR REBOLLEDO RAMIREZ.

Ex Officio Members—Rev. Msgr. JOHN H. BURTON, V.G.; Rev. ROBERT E. HUGHES; Rev. Msgrs. ROBERT T. MCDERMOTT, V.G.; ROGER E. MCGRATH, Ph.D.; Rev. TERRY M. ODIEN.

Priests Personnel Board—Ex Officio Members: Rev. Msgr. JOHN H. BURTON, V.G.; Rev. ROBERT E. HUGHES; Rev. Msgrs. ROBERT T. MCDERMOTT, V.G.; ROGER E. MCGRATH, Ph.D.; Revs. THOMAS A. NEWTON; TERRY M. ODIEN. Elected Members: Revs. JOSEPH A. CAPELLA; PERRY A. CHERUBINI; JOHN A. DELDUCA; PAUL D. HARTE; THOMAS R. KIELY; JOSEPH T. SZOLACK, M.Div.

Continuing Education & Spiritual Formation of Priests (CESF)—Revs. JOHN E. BRUNI; ANTHONY R. DIBARDINO, Chm.; RICO DUCLE; GERARD C. MARABLE; WILLIAM F. MOORE; VINCENT ORUM, A.J.; MICHAEL M. ROMANO; JOHN A. ROSSI; MATTHEW J. HILLYARD, O.S.F.S.; JAMES H. KING; WALTER A. NORRIS, Esq.; LAWRENCE E. POLANSKY; JON P. THOMAS. Ex Officio Members: Rev. Msgr. JOHN H. BURTON, V.G.; Rev. ROBERT E. HUGHES; Rev. Msgrs. ROBERT T. MCDERMOTT, V.G.; ROGER E. MCGRATH, Ph.D.; Rev. TERRY M. ODIEN.

Advanced Studies for Priests—Rev. TERRY M. ODIEN, Vicar. Tel: 856-583-2854.

Liaison with Retired Priests—Rev. ROBERT V. SMITH (Retired). Tel: 856-751-2010.

Consultant for Clergy Health and Wellness—Rev. THOMAS A. NEWTON.

Delegate for Men Religious—Bro. THOMAS OSORIO, O.H., St. John of God Monastery, 1145 Delsea Dr., Westville Grove, 08093. Tel: 856-227-1436, Ext. 21.

Permanent Diaconate—Deacon LEO MCBLAIN. Tel: 856-583-2857.

Office of Vocations—Tel: 856-583-2858; Fax: 856-966-5957. Rev. MICHAEL M. ROMANO; Rev. Msgr. ROGER E. MCGRATH, Ph.D., Dir. Seminarians.

Vocation Advisory Board—Revs. THOMAS J. BARCELLONA; NICHOLAS DUDO; DAVID J. KLEIN, J.C.L.; Rev. Msgr. ROGER E. MCGRATH, Ph.D.; Revs. WILLIAM F. MOORE; JOSEPH LUONG T. PHAM; JOSEPH T. SZOLACK, M.Div.; Deacon JOSEPH B. CHANDLER; Mrs. CLARE MCNAMEE; Rev. Msgr. THOMAS J. MORGAN, V.G., Consultant.

Amicus—Rev. Msgr. JOHN T. FREY, Chap. Tel: 856-547-0564.

Serra Clubs International—Cape/Atlantic Counties: Mr. THOMAS HALPIN, Pres. Tel: 609-513-2037; Rev. JOSEF A. WAGENHOFFER, V.F., Chap. (Retired).

Diocesan Historian—Rev. JAMES F. BETZ.

College of Consultors—Members: Rev. Msgr. JOHN H. BURTON, V.G.; Revs. JOSEPH P. CAPELLA; PERRY A. CHERUBINI; Rev. Msgr. JOSEPH V. DIMAURO; Revs. DAVID J. KLEIN, J.C.L.; ANTHONY J. MANUPPELLA, V.F.; Rev. Msgrs. ROBERT T. MCDERMOTT, V.G.; ROGER E. MCGRATH, Ph.D., Exec. Sec.; THOMAS J. MORGAN, V.G.; Revs. THOMAS A. NEWTON; TERRY M. ODIEN; JOHN J. VIGNONE; Rev. Msgrs. WILLIAM QUINN (Retired); WILLIAM P. BRENNAN, V.F.; JAMES R. TRACY, Ph.D., V.F. (Retired). Consultants: Revs. DAVID A. GROVER; PAUL D. HARTE; EDWARD F. NAMIOTKA; JOSEPH LUONG T. PHAM; JOSEPH T. SZOLACK, M.Div.

Diocesan Finance Council—Rev. Msgr. WILLIAM A. HODGE, V.F.; Rev. JOSEPH E. PERRAULT; Deacon JOHN WERNER; JOHN FINLEY; THOMAS GRANITE; ED RADETICH.

Information Technology Services—JOSEPH D. TORRIERI JR., Dir. Tel: 856-583-2888.

Office of Propagation of the Faith and Diocesan Missions—Rev. GEORGE C. SEITER, Dir. Tel: 856-583-2835; Fax: 856-966-5957.

Campaign for Human Development—Rev. KENNETH P. HALLAHAN, Coord. Tel: 856-228-4331.

Office of Development—JAMES J. LANAHAN, Dir. Tel: 856-583-6134; Fax: 856-338-0766.

House of Charity-Bishop's Annual Appeal—MARIANN GILBRIDE, Dir. Tel: 856-583-6128.

Planned Giving—JAMES J. LANAHAN. Tel: 856-583-6134.

Office of Stewardship—RUSSELL DAVIS, Dir. Tel: 856-583-6102.

South Jersey Scholarship Fund—JAMES J. LANAHAN. Tel: 856-583-6134.

Major Gifts—HEATHER CAPPUCCIO, Dir. Tel: 856-583-6161.

Communications and Community Relations—

Office of Communications—PETER FEUERHERD, Dir. Tel: 856-583-2851; Fax: 856-338-0826; MARIA D'ANTONIO, Asst. Tel: 856-583-2853.

Diocesan Newspaper— "The Catholic Star Herald" Mailing Address: 15 N. 7th St., Camden, 08102. Tel: 856-583-6198; Fax: 856-756-7938. PETER FEUERHERD, Assoc. Publisher. Tel: 856-583-2851; CARL D. PETERS, Mng. Editor. Tel: 856-583-6147; CYNTHIA E. SOPER, Business Mgr. Tel: 856-583-6142; PAUL J. WORTHINGTON, Advertising Mgr. Tel: 856-583-6166.

Office of Community Relations—Rev. Msgr. MICHAEL T. MANNION, S.T.L., Dir., 4824 Camden Ave., Pennsauken, 08110. Tel: 856-662-2723.

Cemeteries—LARRY READER, Acting Dir. Tel: 856-583-2821.

Facilities—ART BASCIANO, E.A.I.A., Diocesan Architect & Dir. Tel: 856-583-2844; THOMAS BECHARD, Diocesan Engineer. Tel: 856-583-2845; JOSEPH MARTIN, Diocesan Center. Cell: 856-278-4686; Tel: 856-583-2870.

Administrative and Financial Services—

Diocesan Finance Officer & Bishop's Delegate for Temporalities—WILLIAM J. MURRAY. Tel: 856-583-2828.

Temporal Services—Mr. LAWRENCE J. READER, Exec. Dir. Tel: 856-583-4121.

Business Solutions—MARIANNE LINKA, Dir. Tel: 856-583-2820.

Financial Services—EDWARD J. LOCASALE, CPA, Dir. Tel: 856-583-2822; Fax: 856-963-2655.

Diocesan Liability Insurance Program—CATHY JAMES. Tel: 856-583-2871.

Diocesan Self-Insurance Plan (DSIP) & Pension Funds—WILLIAM J. MURRAY. Tel: 856-583-2828.

Budgeting/Parish Review & Support—CAROLYN THOMPSON, Dir. Tel: 856-583-2830; MICHAEL R. PORTER, Analyst. Tel: 856-583-2832.

Comptroller—LISA M. CILIBERTO, CPA, Comptroller. Tel: 856-583-2827.

Human Resources—JOHN RAFTERY, Dir. Tel: 856-583-2867; CANDY NEWHOUSE, Health Insurance. Tel: 856-583-2313.

Office of Pastoral Planning—Sr. ANTOINE T. LAWLOR, I.H.M., D.Min., Dir. Pastoral Priorities. Tel: 856-583-2842; LAWRENCE FARMER, Dir. Mergers. Tel: 856-583-2840; LISA WATSON, Asst. Dir. Pastoral Planning. Tel: 856-583-2843.

Real Estate—KENNETH MCILVAINE, Consultant. Tel: 856-583-2861.

Safe Environment for Children, Youth and Adults—Mr. ROD J. HERRERA, L.C.S.W., Dir. Tel: 856-583-6114; Fax: 856-583-1045.

Safe Environment Training (CAP)—Tel: 856-583-6165.

Victim Assistance Coordinator—BARBARA ANN GONDEK, L.C.S.W. Tel: 800-964-6588.

Catholic Schools—

Executive Director, Catholic Schools—NICHOLAS REGINA. Tel: 856-583-6013; Fax: 856-756-0225.

Superintendent of Schools—MARY P. BOYLE, M.Ed. Tel: 856-583-6103.

Assistant Superintendent of Schools—Sr. ROSE DIFLURI, I.H.M. Tel: 856-583-6110.

Parent-Teachers Association—Rev. Msgr. JAMES P. CURRAN, Moderator. Tel: 856-456-0052; PATRICIA WIRBICK, Pres. Tel: 856-456-4839.

Lifelong Faith Formation

Diocesan Delegate for Lifelong Faith Formation—Sr. ROSEANN QUINN, S.S.J. Tel: 856-583-6124; Fax: 856-225-0096; LINDA K. ROBINSON, Assoc. Dir. Tel: 856-583-6116; Sr. SONIA AVI, I.H.M., Assoc. Dir. for Hispanics. Tel: 856-583-6113; Fax: 856-756-0297.

Associate Director for Black Catholics—CORLIS SELLERS. Tel: 856-583-6184; Fax: 856-756-0297.

Delegate for Hispanic Ministry Commission—ANDRES ARANGO. Tel: 856-583-6181; Fax: 856-583-6185.

Evangelization—ANDRES ARANGO, Dir. Tel: 856-583-6181; Fax: 856-583-6185.

Lay Ministry Formation—LINDA K. ROBINSON, Dir. Tel: 856-583-6116.

Registrar/Bilingual—KATHIA ARANGO. Tel: 856-583-6135.

Black Catholic Ministry Commission—CORLIS SELLERS. Tel: 856-583-6184.

Racial Justice Commission—CORLIS SELLERS, Coord. Tel: 856-583-6184.

Ministry with the Deaf and Persons with Disabilities—Sr. BERNADETTE MCMENAMIN, S.S.J., Co Dir. Tel: 856-583-6111; KATE SLOSAR, Co Dir. Tel: 856-583-6150; 856-283-3962 (Video Phone); Fax: 856-756-0297.

Offsite Office—Holy Saviour, Westmont. Tel: 856-833-6045.

Faith and Family Life Formation—Sr. KATHLEEN BURTON, S.S.J., Dir. Tel: 856-583-6131; MARY LOU HUGHES, Assoc. Dir. Faith Formation. Tel: 856-583-6132; Fax: 856-541-9644.

Project Rachel—Sr. KATHLEEN BURTON, S.S.J. Tel: 856-583-6131; Fax: 856-541-9644; LAWRENCE M. DIPAUL. Tel: 856-583-6119; Fax: 856-225-0096.

Youth, Young Adult & Campus Ministries—GREGORY A. COOGAN, Dir. Tel: 856-583-6122; Fax: 856-583-6185.

Scouting—JOSEPH BRENNAN. Tel: 856-428-2645.

Campus Ministries—

Rutgers University—Rev. MICHAEL J. MCCUE, O.S.F.S., Campus Min. Tel: 215-582-1666; Fax: 856-757-0438.

Rowan University—ANN POLO, Dir. Tel: 856-881-2554; Deacon KEVIN HEIL, Campus Min. Tel: 856-881-3474; Fax: 856-881-4163; Rev. PHILLIP M. JOHNSON, Univ. Parish Chap. Tel: 856-881-5642; Fax: 856-881-4183.

Richard Stockton College of New Jersey—LOIS DARK, Dir.; Rev. THOMAS R. KIELY, Chap., 235 S. Pomona Rd., Pomona, 08240. Tel: 609-804-0200; Fax: 609-804-9135.

Life and Justice Ministries—LAWRENCE M. DIPAUL, Dir. Tel: 856-583-6119; Fax: 856-225-0096.

Worship and Christian Initiation—STEPHEN F. OBARSKI, Dir. Tel: 856-583-6146; Fax: 856-338-6186.

Diocesan Director of Music Ministries—DAMARIS THILLET. Tel: 856-583-6172; Fax: 856-583-6186.

Diocesan Gospel Choir—RITA BOSTIC, Coord. Tel: 856-767-1837.

Liturgical Art and Architectural Commission—Rev. Msgr. JOHN H. BURTON, V.G., Chm. Tel: 856-691-9077; Rev. ROBERT E. HUGHES. Tel: 856-228-1616; STEPHEN F. OBARSKI. Tel: 856-583-6146.

Charismatic Renewal—Deacon JOSEPH A. GAROZZO, Diocesan Moderator. Tel: 856-467-0792.

Hispanic Charismatic Renewal—KATHIA ARANGO, Diocesan Coord. Tel: 856-583-6135.

English Cursillo—Deacon JOSEPH A. GAROZZO, Spiritual Advisor. Tel: 856-467-0792.

Ecumenical and Inter-Religious Affairs—Rev. JOSEPH D. WALLACE, Coord. Tel: 609-522-2709.

CLERGY, PARISHES, MISSIONS AND PAROCHIAL SCHOOLS

CITY OF CAMDEN

(CAMDEN COUNTY)

1—THE PARISH OF THE CATHEDRAL OF THE IMMACULATE CONCEPTION, CAMDEN, N.J. (2010) Revs. Matthew J. Hillyard, O.S.F.S., Rector; Michael J. McCue, O.S.F.S., Parochial Vicar; Deacons E. Michael Henry, (Retired); Felix Tito Miranda; Samuel Soto; Jose Rene Zayas. In Res., Rev. Francis J. Blood, O.S.F.S.; Bro. Michael O'Neill McGrath, O.S.F.S.

Rectory—642 Market St., 08102-1183. Tel: 856-964-1580; Fax: 856-757-0438. Email: smackey@camdendiocese.org. Web: www.oblates.org/dsw.

Churches—

Cathedral of the Immaculate Conception, Camden—

Holy Name, Camden—522 State St., 08102.

Our Lady of Mount Carmel and Fatima, Camden—832 S. 4th St., 08103.

School—Holy Name School, 5th & Vine Sts., 08102. Tel: 856-365-7930; Fax: 856-365-8041. Mrs. Patricia Quinter, Prin.

DeSales Service Works—Tel: 215-582-1666. Email: dsw@oblates.org.

Hopeworks 'N Camden—Tel: 856-365-4673. Rev. Jeffrey Putthoff, S.J., Dir.

2—ST. ANTHONY OF PADUA ROMAN CATHOLIC CHURCH, CAMDEN, N.J. (1945), (Hispanic), Revs. William J. Weiksnar, O.F.M.; Hugh Macsherry, O.F.M.; Bro. Karl F. Koenig, O.F.M.

Res.: 2818 River Ave., 08105. Tel: 856-963-5884; Fax: 856-635-1286. Web: www.stanthonycamden.org.

School—(Grades K-8) Tel: 856-966-6791; Fax: 856-966-1616. Anna Mae Muryasz, Prin. Lay Teachers 14; Students 204.

Catechesis/Religious Program—Students 109.

3—ST. BARTHOLOMEW'S R.C. CHURCH, CAMDEN, N.J. (1940), (African American), Merged with the Church of St. Joan of Arc, Camden to form St. Josephine Bakhita Parish, Camden.

4—THE CHURCH OF ST. JOAN OF ARC, WEST COLLINGSWOOD, N.J. (1920) Merged with St. Bartholomew's R.C. Church, Camden to form St. Josephine Bakhita Parish, Camden.

5—THE CHURCH OF SACRED HEART (1885), Records for St. George kept at Sacred Heart, Camden. Records for Sts. Peter and Paul kept at the Cathedral of the Immaculate Conception, Camden. Records for St. John the Baptist kept at St. Joseph Pro-Cathedral, Camden. Rev. Msgr. Michael J. Doyle; Rev. Dennis W. Bajkowski.
Res.: 1739 Ferry Ave., 08104. Tel: 856-966-6700; Fax: 856-756-0102.
School—(Grades K-8), Fourth & Jaspers Sts., 08104. Tel: 856-963-1341; Fax: 856-963-3551. Miss Janet Williams, Prin. Lay Teachers 13; Students 224.
Catechesis/Religious Program—Students 32.

6—THE CHURCH OF THE HOLY NAME, CAMDEN, N.J. (1913), (Hispanic), Merged with The Church of the Immaculate Conception, Camden & Our Lady of Mount Carmel/Church of Our Lady of Fatima, Camden to form The Parish of the Cathedral of the Immaculate Conception, Camden.

7—THE CHURCH OF THE IMMACULATE CONCEPTION, CAMDEN, N.J. (1864) [CEM] Merged with The Church of the Holy Name, Camden & Our Lady of Mount Carmel/Church of Our Lady of Fatima, Camden to form The Parish of the Cathedral of the Immaculate Conception, Camden.

8—ST. JOSEPH CATHOLIC CHURCH, EAST CAMDEN, N.J. (PRO-CATHEDRAL) (1893) Rev. Msgr. Robert T. McDermott; Rev. Joel Arciga Camarillo; Deacon Omar M. Aguilar; Sr. Veronica Roche, O.S.F.S., Pastoral Min.; Jim Steinitz, Business Admin.; Genevieve Jordan, Dir., Romero Ctr.; Kristin Prinn, Dir. Youth Ministry.
Res.: 2907 Federal St., 08105. Tel: 856-964-2776; Fax: 856-964-0044. Email: bmcder@comcast.net. Web: www.sjprocathedral.org.
School—(Grades K-8) Tel: 856-964-4336; Fax: 856-964-1080. Mrs. Frances Montgomery, Prin. Lay Teachers 18; Students 263.
St. Joseph Child Development Center, Inc.—17 Church St., 08105. Tel: 856-963-9202; Fax: 856-963-8940. Betty Mitchell, Dir. Children 75.
Catechesis/Religious Program—Tel: 856-964-2776, Ext. 501 6. Berta Machado, C.R.E. Tel: 856-964-2776, Ext. 502. Students 209.

9—ST. JOSEPHINE BAKHITA PARISH, CAMDEN, N.J. (2010) Rev. Gerard C. Marable; Deacon Thomas E. Jennings.
Rectory—751 Kaighns Ave., 08103-2499. Tel: 856-365-0573; Fax: 856-365-0744.
Churches—
St. Bartholomew, Camden—
St. Joan of Arc, Camden—3107 Alabama Rd., 08104-3198.
Catechesis/Religious Program—Students 38.

10—ST. JOSEPH'S CATHOLIC CHURCH, CAMDEN, N.J. (1892), (Polish), [CEM] Rev. Pawel Kryszkiewicz.
Res.: 1010 Liberty St., 08104. Tel: 856-963-1285; Fax: 856-963-2466. Web: www.stjoenj.net.

11—OUR LADY OF MOUNT CARMEL, CAMDEN, N.J./ CHURCH OF OUR LADY OF FATIMA, CAMDEN, N.J., (Hispanic—Italian), Merged with The Church of the Immaculate Conception, Camden & The Church of the Holy Name, Camden to form The Parish of the Cathedral of the Immaculate Conception, Camden.

OUTSIDE THE CITY OF CAMDEN

ABSECON, ATLANTIC CO., CHURCH OF SAINT ELIZABETH ANN SETON, ABSECON, N.J. (1975) Revs. Perry A. Cherubini; Cosme R. de la Pena; Deacon Joseph Becker.
Res.: 591 New Jersey Ave., 08201. Tel: 609-641-1480; Fax: 609-641-7396.
See Assumption Regional School, Galloway under Regional Schools, Elementary located in the Institution section.
Catechesis/Religious Program—Tel: 609-641-7043; Fax: 609-641-5709. Students 325.
Mission—St. Andrew Kim Korean Catholic Mission, Inc. 702 S. New Rd., 08201. Rev. Sung Heum (John) Kim, Admin.

ATCO, CAMDEN CO.

1—CHRIST THE REDEEMER PARISH, ATCO, N.J. Rev. Thomas J. Barcellona; Deacons Charles McAleer; Nicholas P. Ludovich.
Rectory—318 Carl Hasselman Dr., 08004-1997. Tel: 856-767-0719; Fax: 856-753-7917. Email: assumptionatco@yahoo.com. Web: www.assumptionparishatco.com.
Churches—
Assumption, Atco—
St. Anthony, Waterford—
Blessed John the Twenty-Third, Blue Anchor—
St. Lucy, Blue Anchor—
Sacred Heart, Cedar Brook—
School—Assumption School, 2122 Cooper Rd., 08004. Tel: 856-767-0569; 856-768-8910. Sr. Helene Cooke, I.H.M., Prin.
Catechesis/Religious Program—Tel: 856-767-3414. Theresa Budniak, D.R.E. Students 485.

2—THE CHURCH OF THE ASSUMPTION, ATCO, N.J. (1947) Merged with Parish of Blessed John the Twenty-Third, Blue Anchor; St. Lucy Church, Blue Anchor; Sacred Heart Church, Cedarbrook; and St. Anthony's Church, Waterford to form Christ the Redeemer Parish, Atco.

ATLANTIC CITY, ATLANTIC CO.

1—CHURCH OF ST. NICHOLAS, ATLANTIC CITY, N.J. (1855) Rev. Msgr. William A. Hodge. In Res., Rev. Robert B. Matysik.
Res.: 1409 Pacific Ave., 08401. Tel: 609-344-1040; Fax: 609-344-7975.
Catechesis/Religious Program—Students 8.

2—THE CHURCH OF THE HOLY SPIRIT, ATLANTIC CITY, N.J. (1908) Closed. For sacramental records see Our Lady Star of the Sea, Atlantic City. Rev. Robert E. Hughes.

3—ST. MICHAEL'S CHURCH, ATLANTIC CITY, N.J. (1904), (Italian), Rev. Jeffrey T. Cesarone, O.Praem, Admin.
Res.: 10 N. Mississippi Ave., 08401. Tel: 609-344-8536; Fax: 609-344-5304.

4—ST. MONICA'S CATHOLIC CHURCH, ATLANTIC CITY, N.J. (1925) Rev. Yvans Jazon, Admin.; Deacon Angel Ramos Vega.
Res.: 108 N. Pennsylvania Ave., 08401. Tel: 609-345-1786; Fax: 609-344-5090.
Catechesis/Religious Program—Students 28.

5—OUR LADY, STAR OF THE SEA, ATLANTIC CITY, N.J. (1894) Revs. Joseph Luong T. Pham; Jaime E. Hostios.
Res.: 2651 Atlantic Ave., 08401. Tel: 609-345-1878; Fax: 609-348-0248. Email: olss2651@aol.com. Web: www.olssparish.com.
School—(Grades PreK-8), 15 N. California Ave., 08401. Tel: 609-345-0648; Fax: 609-344-6735. Sr. Mary Shamus Zehrer, R.S.M., Prin. & Supr. Sisters 4; Lay Teachers 8; Students 225.
Catechesis/Religious Program—Tel: 609-340-0116. Students 315.
Convent—Sisters of Mercy, 15 N. California Ave., 08401. Tel: 609-347-0434.

AUDUBON, CAMDEN CO., CHURCH OF THE HOLY MATERNITY, AUDUBON, NJ (1957) Merged with Church of the Sacred Heart, Mount Ephraim to form Emmaus Catholic Community, Mount Ephraim.

AVALON, CAPE MAY CO.

1—ST. BRENDAN THE NAVIGATOR PARISH, AVALON, N.J. (2010) Rev. Msgr. John T. Frey; Deacon William Lauth. In Res., Rev. Cornelius F. Lambert (Retired); Rev. Msgr. William Quinn (Retired); Rev. Thomas R. Kiely.
Rectory—5012 Dune Dr., 08202-1333. Tel: 609-967-3746; Fax: 609-967-8172. Email: marisstella@comcast.net.
Churches—
Maris Stella, Avalon—
St. Paul, Stone Harbor—
Catechesis/Religious Program—Tel: 609-967-3017. Sr. Patricia Tomlin, D.R.E. Students 60.

2—THE CHURCH OF MARIS STELLA, AVALON, N.J. (1961) Merged with St. Paul's Church, Stone Harbor to form St. Brendan the Navigator, Avalon.

BARRINGTON, CAMDEN CO., CHURCH OF ST. FRANCIS DE SALES, BARRINGTON, N.J. (1955) Merged with The Church of Mary, Mother of the Church, Bellmawr & St. Gregory's Church, Magnolia to form Parish of Saint Rita, Bellmawr.

BELLMAWR, CAMDEN CO.

1—THE CHURCH OF MARY, MOTHER OF THE CHURCH, BELLMAWR, N.J. (1965) Merged with Church of St. Francis de Sales, Barrington & St. Gregory's Church, Magnolia to form Parish of Saint Rita, Bellmawr.

2—THE CHURCH OF THE ANNUNCIATION BVM, BELLMAWR, N.J. (1951) Closed. For inquiries for parish records please see St. Joachim Parish, Bellmawr, NJ.

3—ST. JOACHIM PARISH, BELLMAWR, N.J. Rev. Piotr Szamocki; Deacons Gerard V. DeMuro; Timothy M. Sullivan.
Worship Sites—
Annunciation, Bellmawr—
Saint Maurice, Brook Lawn—
Saint Anne, Westville—
Rectory—601 Browning Rd., 08031-1804. Tel: 856-931-6307; Fax: 856-931-0166.
Catechesis/Religious Program—Tel: 856-931-8590. Sr. Jean Miriam Alfonsi, I.H.M., D.R.E.
Convent—Annunciation Convent, 603 W. Browning Rd., 08031. Tel: 856-931-7192.

4—PARISH OF SAINT RITA, BELLMAWR, N.J. Rev. Carmel F. Polidano; Deacon Leonard P. Carlucci.
20 Braisington Ave., 08031-1204.
Rectory—20 Braisington Ave., 08031-1204. Tel: 858-931-0204; Fax: 856-933-5120.
Churches—
Mary, Mother of the Church, Bellmawr—
St. Francis de Sales, Barrington—
St. Gregory, Magnolia—
Catechesis/Religious Program—Students 165.
Convent—424 E. Browning Rd., 08031. Tel: 856-931-8973.
Convent—230 Evesham Ave. E., Magnolia, 08049.

BERLIN, CAMDEN CO.

1—CHURCH OF OUR LADY OF MOUNT CARMEL, BERLIN, N.J. (1903) [CEM] Merged with St. Edward's R.C. Church, Pine Hill to form Saint Simon Stock Parish, Berlin.

2—SAINT SIMON STOCK PARISH, BERLIN, N.J. (2009) [CEM] Revs. James O. Dabrowski; Jose Manjakunnel; Deacons Joseph Beebe; John D. Rich Jr.
Worship Sites—
O.L. Mt. Carmel, Berlin—
St. Edward, Pine Hill—
Parish Office: 178 W. White Horse Pike, 08009-2023. Tel: 856-767-2115; Fax: 856-767-8791.
Rectory—1 Maple Ave., 08009. Email: www.olmcweb@catholic.org. Web: www.stsimonstock.net.
See Our Lady of Mt. Carmel, Berlin under Regional Schools, Elementary located in the Institution section.
Catechesis/Religious Program—Tel: 856-767-1537; Fax: 856-767-3304. Students 431.

BLACKWOOD, CAMDEN CO.

1—ST. AGNES' CHURCH, BLACKWOOD TERRACE, N.J. (1946) Merged with The R.C. Church of St. Jude, Blackwood to form Our Lady of Hope Parish, Blackwood.

2—OUR LADY OF HOPE PARISH, BLACKWOOD, N.J. (2010) Revs. Mark R. Cavagnaro; Stephen J. Rapposelli, Parochial Vicar; John A. DelDuca; Kenneth P. Hallahan; Deacons Robert P. Foley; Michael J. Harkins; John Werner.
Rectory—701 Little Gloucester Rd., 08012-3311. Tel: 856-228-4331; 856-228-3171; Fax: 856-227-0743. Email: saadmin@comcast.net. Web: www.stagnes2000.com.
Churches—
St. Agnes, Blackwood—
St. Jude, Blackwood—
See Our Lady of Hope Regional School, Blackwood under Regional Schools, Elementary located in the Institution section.
Convent—Tel: 856-227-8658.

3—THE R.C. CHURCH OF ST. JUDE, GLOUCESTER TOWNSHIP, N.J. (1961) Merged with St. Agnes' Church, Blackwood to form Our Lady of Hope Parish, Blackwood.

BLUE ANCHOR, CAMDEN CO., PARISH OF BLESSED JOHN THE TWENTY-THIRD, BLUE ANCHOR, N.J. (1925), (Italian), [CEM] Merged with The Church of the Assumption, Atco; St. Lucy Church, Blue Anchor; Sacred Heart Church, Cedarbrook; & St. Anthony's Church, Waterford to form Christ the Redeemer Parish, Atco.

BRIDGETON, CUMBERLAND CO.

1—THE CHURCH OF ST. TERESA AVILA, BRIDGETON, N.J. (1961) Merged with The Church of the Immaculate Conception, Bridgeton; Saint Michael's Roman Catholic Church, Cedarville; St. Mary's Church, Rosenhayn; & St. Anthony's Church, Port Norris to form The Parish of the Holy Cross, Bridgeton.

2—THE CHURCH OF THE IMMACULATE CONCEPTION, BRIDGETON, N.J. (1874) [CEM] Merged with The Church of St. Teresa Avila, Bridgeton; Saint Michael's Roman Catholic Church, Cedarville; St. Mary's Church, Rosenhayn; & St. Anthony's Church, Port Norris to form The Parish of the Holy Cross, Bridgeton.

3—THE PARISH OF THE HOLY CROSS, BRIDGETON, N.J. (2010) Revs. Ariel Hernandez; Daniel A. DiNardo, Parochial Vicar; William Kelly, O.Praem., Parochial Vicar; Deacons C. J. Achee; Carmen Bischer; William Johnson; Christopher D. Nichols; Donald W. Rogozenski; Arnaldo A. Santos.
Rectory—46 Central Ave., 08302-2305. Tel: 856-455-2323; Fax: 856-455-7291.
Churches—
St. Anthony, Port Norris—
Immaculate Conception, Bridgeton—
St. Mary, Rosenhayn—
St. Michael, Cedarville—
St. Teresa Avila, Bridgeton—
Catechesis/Religious Program—Students 432.
Convent—64 North St., 08302. Tel: 856-455-9960. Missionary Daughters of the Most Pure Virgin Mary.
Station—NJ State Medium Security Prison, Bayside Prison Rte. 47, Leesburg, 08327. Tel: 856-785-0040, Ext. 5458.
Station—Ancora Bayside Prison Winslow Twp.

BRIGANTINE, ATLANTIC CO., ST. THOMAS' CATHOLIC CHURCH, BRIGANTINE, N.J. (1958) Revs. William S.

Vandegrift; Alfred Mungujakisa; Deacon Leonard W. Long.
Res.: 331 8th St. S., 08203. Tel: 609-266-2123; Fax: 609-266-6416.
Catechesis/Religious Program—Tel: 609-266-3154. Students 250.
Convent—4101 Brigantine Ave., 08203. Tel: 609-266-4153. Sisters of St. Joseph of Chestnut Hill

BROOKLAWN, CAMDEN CO., ST. MAURICE'S CHURCH, BROOKLAWN, N.J. (1955) Closed. For inquiries for parish records please see St. Joachim Parish, Bellmawr, N.J.

BUENA BOROUGH, ATLANTIC CO., QUEEN OF ANGELS PARISH, BUENA BOROUGH, N.J. (2001) [CEM] Merged with St. Rose of Lima Church, Newfield & St. Mary Church, Malaga to form Our Lady of the Blessed Sacrament Church, Newfield.

CAPE MAY COURT HOUSE, CAPE MAY CO., THE CHURCH OF OUR LADY OF THE ANGELS, CAPE MAY COURT HOUSE, N.J. (1956) Revs. John A. O'Leary; Christopher M. Mann, C.F.R.; Deacons Ralph A. Catanese; George M. Ferland, (Retired). In Res., Rev. Joseph P. Varghese, V.C.
Res.: 106 Mechanic St., 08210. Tel: 609-465-5245. Email: office@ourladyoftheangels.net. Web: www.ourladyoftheangels.net.
Parish Center: 35 Mechanic St., 08210. Tel: 609-465-5432; Fax: 609-465-7647.
See Bishop McHugh Regional School, Cape May Court House under Regional Schools, Elementary located in the Institution section.
Catechesis/Religious Program—Students 190.

CAPE MAY, CAPE MAY CO., THE CHURCH OF OUR LADY STAR OF THE SEA, CAPE MAY (1878) [CEM] Revs. Francis W. Danella, O.S.F.S.; Thomas J. McGee, O.S.F.S.; Edward T. Fitzpatrick, O.S.F.S.
Res.: 520 Lafayette St., 08204. Tel: 609-884-5311; Fax: 609-884-0162. Web: www.ladystarofthesea.org.
See Cape Trinity Catholic School, N. Wildwood under Regional Schools, Elementary located in the Institution section.
Catechesis/Religious Program—Tel: 609-884-5312. Students 37.
Convent—516 Lafayette St., 08204. Tel: 609-884-7736. Sisters of St. Joseph of Chestnut Hill
Chapel—Cape May Point, St. Agnes, (Summer)

CARNEYS POINT, SALEM CO.

1—THE CHURCH OF CORPUS CHRISTI, CARNEYS POINT, N.J. (1966) Merged with Church of the Queen of the Apostles, Pennsville; St. James' Church, Penns Grove; & St. Mary's Catholic Church, Salem to form Saint Gabriel the Archangel Parish, Carneys Point.

2—SAINT GABRIEL THE ARCHANGEL PARISH, CARNEYS POINT, N.J. (2010) [CEM] Revs. Paul D. Harte; Robert Ngageno, Parochial Vicar; Deacons Kevin L. Laughlin; Robert M. Fanelli. In Res., Rev. Rene L. Canales.
Rectory—369 Georgetown Rd., Carney's Point, 08069-2598. Tel: 856-299-3833; Fax: 856-299-3887.
Churches—
Corpus Christi, Carneys Point—
St. James, Pennsgrove—
St. Mary, Salem—
Queen of the Apostles, Pennsville—
Catechesis/Religious Program—Annette LaSala, D.R.E. Students 334.

CEDARVILLE, CUMBERLAND CO., ST. MICHAEL'S ROMAN CATHOLIC CHURCH (1942) Merged with The Church of St. Teresa Avila, Bridgeton; The Church of the Immaculate Conception, Bridgeton; St. Mary's Church, Rosenhayn; & St. Anthony's Church, Port Norris to form The Parish of the Holy Cross, Bridgeton.

CHERRY HILL, CAMDEN CO.

1—THE CATHOLIC COMMUNITY OF CHRIST OUR LIGHT, CHERRY HILL, N.J. (2009) Revs. Thomas A. Newton; Jon-Peter Thomas; Deacons W. Leo McBlain; Joseph F. Seaman. In Res., Rev. Terry M. Odien.
Rectory—402 Kings Hwy. N., 08034-1091. Tel: 856-667-2440; Fax: 856-482-0332. Churches,
Saint Peter Celestine, Cherry Hill—
Queen of Heaven, Cherry Hill—
School—Resurrection Catholic School, (Grades PreK-8) Tel: 856-667-3034; Fax: 856-667-9160. Sr. Lydia Etter, O.S.F., Prin.
Catechesis/Religious Program—Students 700.
Convent—402A N. Kings Hwy., 08034. Tel: 856-667-0395. Sisters of St. Joseph

2—THE CHURCH OF ST. PETER CELESTINE, CHERRY HILL, N.J. (1961) Merged with Church of the Queen of Heaven, Cherry Hill to form The Catholic Community of Christ Our Light, Cherry Hill.

3—THE CHURCH OF ST. PIUS X, CHERRY HILL, N.J. (1961) Merged with The Church of the Holy Rosary, Cherry Hill to form Holy Eucharist Parish, Cherry Hill.

4—THE CHURCH OF THE HOLY ROSARY, CHERRY HILL, N.J. (1958) Merged with The Church of St. Pius X, Cherry Hill to form Holy Eucharist Parish, Cherry Hill.

5—CHURCH OF THE QUEEN OF HEAVEN, CHERRY HILL, N.J. (1955) Merged with The Church of St. Peter Celestine, Cherry Hill to form The Catholic Community of Christ Our Light, Cherry Hill.

6—THE CHURCH OF ST. THOMAS MORE, CHERRY HILL, NEW JERSEY (1968) Rev. Msgr. Thomas J. Morgan; Deacon John H. Harrington Jr.; Rev. George Donkor Tang.
Res.: 1439 Springdale Rd., 08003. Tel: 856-424-3212; Fax: 856-424-2411. Email: sthomasmore@comcast.net. Web: www.stthomasmorenj.org.
Catechesis/Religious Program—Students 221.

7—HOLY EUCHARIST PARISH, CHERRY HILL, N.J. (2009) Revs. George C. Seiter; Michael J. Coffey, Senior Priest; Deacons Anthony D. Malatesta; Peter J. Powell; Michael F. Scott. In Res., Rev. Timothy E. Byerley.
Res.: 344 Kresson Rd., 08034. Tel: 856-429-1330; Fax: 856-429-8679.
Churches—
Holy Rosary, Cherry Hill— 08003.
St. Pius X, Cherry Hill— 08003.
See Christ the King Regional School, Haddonfield under Regional Schools, Elementary located in the Institution section.
Catechesis/Religious Program—Tel: 856-428-9207. Students 520.

8—ST. MARY'S R.C. CHURCH, DELAWARE TOWNSHIP, N.J. (1961) Rev. Msgr. Thomas J. Morgan; Revs. Edward J. Maher; Michael M. Romano; Deacon Michael L. Welsh; Ms. Kathleen G. Rando, Pastoral Assoc.
Res.: 2001 Springdale Rd., 08003. Tel: 856-424-1454; Fax: 856-424-8270. Email: stmarycherryhill@verizon.net. Web: www.stmaryofcherryhill.org.
Catechesis/Religious Program—Tel: 856-424-2679. Students 400.

CLAYTON, GLOUCESTER CO., ST. CATHERINE'S ROMAN CATHOLIC CHURCH, CLAYTON, N.J. (1943) Merged with R.C. Church of the Nativity, Franklinville to form Parish of St. Michael the Archangel, Franklinville.

COLLINGS LAKES, ATLANTIC CO., CHURCH OF OUR LADY OF THE LAKES, COLLINGS LAKES, N.J. (1976) Rev. John A. Cavagnaro.
Res.: 19 Malaga Rd., 08094. Tel: 609-561-8313; Fax: 609-561-8374.
See Notre Dame Regional School, Newfield under Regional Schools, Elementary located in the Institution section.
Catechesis/Religious Program—Students 82.

COLLINGSWOOD, CAMDEN CO.

1—BLESSED TERESA OF CALCUTTA PARISH, COLLINGSWOOD, N.J. (2010) Rev. John D. Bohrer, Admin.; Deacon James H. Rocks. In Res., Revs. Albert E. Harshaw; Dominic J. Mtenga Ngayaku.
Rectory—809 Park Ave., 08108-3147. Tel: 856-858-0298; Fax: 856-858-2796.
Churches—
Holy Saviour, Westmont—
St. John, Collingswood—
School—Good Shepherd Regional School, (Grades PreK-8), 100 Lees Ave., 08108. Tel: 856-858-1562; Fax: 856-858-2943. Mr. Donald W. Garecht, Prin. Lay Teachers 15; Students 191.
Catechesis/Religious Program—Tel: 856-854-1516. Patricia Lipperini, D.R.E. Students 420.

2—ST. JOHN'S CATHOLIC CHURCH, COLLINGSWOOD, N.J. (1919) Merged with The Church of the Holy Saviour, Westmont to form Blessed Teresa of Calcutta Parish, Collingswood.

3—MOST PRECIOUS BLOOD PARISH, COLLINGSWOOD, N.J. (2011) Revs. Richard J. Lodge; Mike Steve Ezeatu; Deacon William C. Robinson.
Res.: 445 White Horse Pike, West Collingswood, 08107. Tel: 856-854-0364; Fax: 856-869-5129.

DELAIR, CAMDEN CO., ST. VERONICA'S R.C. CHURCH, TOWNSHIP OF PENNSAUKEN, NEW JERSEY (1961) Merged with St. Cecilia Church, North Merchantville & St. Edward's R.C. Church, Pine Hill to form Mary, Queen of All Saints, Pennsauken.

DEPTFORD, GLOUCESTER CO., THE CHURCH OF ST. JOHN VIANNEY, GLOUCESTER COUNTY, N.J. (1971) Merged with St. Margaret's Church, Woodbury Heights to form Infant Jesus Parish, Woodbury Heights.

EGG HARBOR CITY, ATLANTIC CO., ST. NICHOLAS' CHURCH, EGG HARBOR CITY (1864) Revs. Nicholas Dudo; Armando Rodrigaez Montoya, Part Time; Deacons Michael H. Guerrieri; Jose M. Cruz.
Res.: 525 St. Louis Ave., 08215-2224. Tel: 609-965-0350; Fax: 609-804-1313. Email: stnicholaschurch@comcast.net. Web: stnicholashc.org.
Catechesis/Religious Program—

EGG HARBOR TOWNSHIP, ATLANTIC CO., THE CHURCH OF SAINT KATHARINE DREXEL, MCKEE CITY, NEW JERSEY (2000) Rev. John J. Vignone; Deacon Richard S. Maxwell.
6077 W. Jersey Ave., 08234. Tel: 609-645-7313; Fax: 609-645-9680. Email: office@skd-parish.org. Web: www.skd-parish.org.
Catechesis/Religious Program—Students 525.

ELMER, SALEM CO., ST. ANN'S CATHOLIC CHURCH, ELMER, N.J. (1961) Merged with Church of the Holy Name of Jesus, Mullica Hill & St. Joseph's Catholic Church, Woodstown to form Catholic Community of the Holy Spirit, Mullica Hill.

FRANKLINVILLE, GLOUCESTER CO.

1—PARISH OF ST. MICHAEL THE ARCHANGEL, FRANKLINVILLE, N.J. (2010) Rev. Jaromir Michalak; Deacon Matthew J. Hanrahan.
Rectory—49 W. North St., Clayton, 08312. Tel: 856-881-9155; Fax: 856-881-9166.
Churches—
St. Catherine, Clayton—
Nativity, Franklinville—Delsea Dr.
School—(Grades PreK-8), 51 W. North St., Clayton, 08312. Tel: 856-881-0067. Miss Janice Bruni, Prin. Lay Teachers 25; Students 310.
Catechesis/Religious Program—Tel: 856-694-1703. Ronald Bonner, D.R.E. Students 255.

2—R.C. CHURCH OF THE NATIVITY, FRANKLINVILLE, N.J. (1961) Merged with St. Catherine's Roman Catholic Church, Clayton to form Parish of St. Michael the Archangel, Franklinville.

GALLOWAY, ATLANTIC CO., THE CHURCH OF THE ASSUMPTION (1938) Revs. Michael Dudo; Robert J. D'Imperio; Deacons James J. Teeney, (Retired); Francis A. Cerullo.
Res.: 146 S. Pitney Rd., Bldg. 1, 08205. Tel: 609-652-0008; Fax: 609-652-0883.
See Assumption Regional School, Galloway under Regional Schools, Elementary located in the Institution section.
Catechesis/Religious Program—Students 411.

GIBBSBORO, CAMDEN CO., ST. ANDREW THE APOSTLE'S R.C. CHURCH, GIBBSBORO, N.J. (1963) Rev. Msgr. Louis A. Marucci; Revs. Howard E. Muhlbaier; Allen B. Lovell; Deacons Vincent A. Okoro; William M. Slaven.
Res.: 27 Kresson-Gibbsboro Rd., 08026. Tel: 856-784-3878; Fax: 856-435-7508. Email: andrewapos@aol.com. Web: www.standrewsrc.com.
See Our Lady of Mt. Carmel, Berlin under Regional Schools, Elementary located in the Institution section.
Catechesis/Religious Program—Tel: 856-783-0550. Students 805.

GIBBSTOWN, GLOUCESTER CO.

1—ST. CLARE OF ASSISI PARISH, GIBBSTOWN, N.J. (2010) Revs. David A. Grover; Grace Manano, Parochial Vicar; Deacons Pablo Berrios; John D. Colanero; Joseph A. Garozzo; James Kiley, (Retired); Robert Willson; Mrs. Kimberly Koorneef, Business Mgr. In Res., Rev. Francis P. Gaffney (Retired).
Office & Mailing Address: 140 Broad St., Swedesboro, 08085. Tel: 856-467-0037; Fax: 856-467-0038.
Rectory—313 Memorial Ave., 08027-1317. Tel: 856-423-0007; Fax: 856-423-1445.
See Guardian Angels Regional School, Gibbstown under Regional Schools, Elementary located in the Institution section.
Convent—320 Memorial Ave., 08027. Tel: 856-423-8680; Fax: 856-423-8681. Franciscan Missionary Sisters of the Infant Jesus

2—ST. MICHAEL'S CHURCH, GIBBSTOWN, N.J. (1940) Merged with St. Joseph's Church, Swedesborough & St. John's Church, Paulsboro to form St. Clare of Assisi Parish, Gibbstown.

GLASSBORO, GLOUCESTER CO.

1—ST. BRIDGET'S CATHOLIC CHURCH, GLASSBORO, N.J. (1887), (Italian), [CEM], (University Parish) Revs. Matthew Weber; Fabio Jose Fernandez; Phillip M. Johnson; Deacons Joseph W. Loungo; Kevin C. Heil; Samuel Soto.
Res.: 125 Church St., 08028. Tel: 856-881-2753; Fax: 856-881-9697. Email: bridget125@comcast.net. See School under Parish of St. Michael the Archangel, Franklinville.
Catechesis/Religious Program—Students 125.
Convent—212 Ellis St., 08028. Tel: 856-881-4604. Franciscan Missionary Sisters of the Immaculate Heart of Mary

2—THE CHURCH OF OUR LADY OF LOURDES, GLASSBORO, N.J. (1966) Merged with Our Lady Queen of Peace R.C. Church, Pitman, N.J. to form Mary, Mother of Mercy Parish, Glassboro, N.J.

3—MARY, MOTHER OF MERCY PARISH, GLASSBORO, N.J. (2011) Revs. James A. Casadia; Jason T. Rocks; Joseph J. Adamson; Deacons Nicholas Mortelliti; Michael J. Carter; John J. Luko Jr.
Worship Sites—
Our Lady of Lourdes, Glassboro—
Our Lady Queen of Peace, Pitman—

Res.: 500 Greentree Rd., 08028-1427. Tel: 856-881-0909; Fax: 856-881-5457.

GLOUCESTER, CAMDEN CO., ST. MARY'S CHURCH, GLOUCESTER (1848) [CEM] Rev. Msgr. James P. Curran (RIC); Deacons Frank Crosson; David W. Murnane.
Res.: 426 Monmouth St., 08030. Tel: 856-456-0052; Fax: 856-456-1837. Email: stmaryrectory@comcast.net. Web: www.stmarysgloucester.org.
Catechesis/Religious Program—Students 115.

HADDON HEIGHTS, CAMDEN CO., CHURCH OF ST. ROSE, HADDON HEIGHTS, N.J. (1896) Revs. E. Joseph Byerley; Jerry A. Gomez; Deacons Douglas R. Crawford; Brian T. Ayscue. In Res., Rev. Alfred J. Hewett (Retired).
Res.: 300 Kings Hwy., 08035-1397. Tel: 856-547-0564; Fax: 856-547-7311. Email: principal@strosenj.com. Web: www.strosenj.com.
School—(Grades K-8) Tel: 856-546-6166; Fax: 856-546-6601. Email: stroseprincipal@yahoo.com. Denise Winterberger, Prin.; Kathleen Dudgan, Advancement Vice Pres.; Marguerite Crowell, Librarian. Dominican Sisters of Hope 2; Lay Teachers 21; Students 386.
Catechesis/Religious Program—Tel: 856-546-0564, Ext. 103; Fax: 856-547-7311. Students 130.

HADDON TOWNSHIP, CAMDEN CO.
1—THE CHURCH OF ST. VINCENT PALLOTTI, HADDON TOWNSHIP, N.J. (1963) Merged with St. Aloysius, Oaklyn to form St. Joseph the Worker Parish, Haddon Township, N.J.
2—ST. JOSEPH THE WORKER PARISH, HADDON TOWNSHIP, N.J. (2011) Revs. Walter A. Norris; Frederick G. Link; Deacon Emil A. Ralbusky. In Res., Rev. Andzej C. Kielkowski, S.D.S.; Rev. Msgr. Louis A. Marucci.
Worship Sites—
St. Vincent Pallotti, Haddon Township—
St. Aloysius, Oaklyn—
Rectory—901 Hopkins Rd. Ste A, Haddonfield, 08033-3099. Tel: 856-858-1313; Fax: 856-869-9010.
Catechesis/Religious Program—Anita D'Imperio, D.R.E. Tel: 856-854-2352. Students 252.

HADDONFIELD, CAMDEN CO., CHURCH OF CHRIST THE KING, HADDONFIELD, N.J. (1927) Rev. Msgrs. William P. Brennan; Roger E. McGrath; Deacons Thomas F. O'Brien; Thomas J. Hafner, (Retired).
Res.: 200 Windsor Ave., 08033. Tel: 856-429-1600; Fax: 856-429-2734. Email: ckp@christ-the-king-parish.org. Web: www.christ-the-king-parish.org.
See Christ the King Regional School, Haddonfield under Regional Schools, Elementary located in the Institution section.
Catechesis/Religious Program—Students 613.

HAMMONTON, ATLANTIC CO.
1—ST. ANTHONY OF PADUA ROMAN CATHOLIC CHURCH, HAMMONTON, N.J. (1964) Merged with St. Joseph's Church, Hammonton & St. Martin de Porres Roman Catholic Church, Hammonton to form Saint Mary of Mount Carmel Parish, Hammonton.
2—ST. JOSEPH'S CHURCH, HAMMONTON, N.J. (1886) [CEM] Merged with St. Anthony of Padua Roman Catholic Church, Hammonton & St. Martin de Porres Roman Catholic Church, Hammonton to form Saint Mary of Mount Carmel Parish, Hammonton.
3—ST. MARTIN DE PORRES ROMAN CATHOLIC CHURCH, HAMMONTON, N.J. (1962) Merged with St. Anthony of Padua Roman Catholic Church, Hammonton & St. Joseph's Church, Hammonton to form Saint Mary of Mount Carmel Parish, Hammonton.
4—SAINT MARY OF MOUNT CARMEL PARISH, HAMMONTON, N.J. (2010) [CEM] Revs. Thomas S. Donio; Ronald S. Falotico, Parochial Vicar; Deacons Ismael Perez Tavarez; George R. VanLeer. In Res., Rev. Joachim Oforchukwu, C.S.Sp. (Nigeria).
Rectory—226 French St., 08037. Tel: 609-704-5945; Fax: 609-704-7249.
Church: 220 Third St., 08037.
Churches—
St. Anthony, Hammonton—
St. Joseph, Hammonton—
St. Martin de Porres, Hammonton—
See St. Joseph Regional Elementary School, Hammonton under Regional Schools, Elementary located in the Institution Section
Catechesis/Religious Program—Sr. Gina Piazza, D.R.E. Students 444.
Convent—219 N. 3rd St., 08037.

LINDENWOLD, CAMDEN CO.
1—CHURCH OF ST. LAWRENCE, LAUREL SPRINGS, N.J. (1896) Merged with The R.C. Church of St. Luke, Stratford & Our Lady of Grace, R.C. Church, Somerdale to form Our Lady of Guadalupe, Lindenwold.
2—OUR LADY OF GUADALUPE PARISH, LINDENWOLD, N.J. (2009) Rev. Joseph P. Capella. In Res., Revs. Wilson Kidangan Paulose; James L. Bartoloma.
Rectory—100 South Ave., 08021-1696. Tel: 856-627-2222; 856-627-7522; Fax: 856-627-8210. Churches,
St. Lawrence, Lindenwold—
St. Luke, Stratford—
Our Lady of Grace—
School—John Paul II Regional School, 55 Warwick Rd., Stratford, 08084. Tel: 856-783-3088; Fax: 856-783-9302. Mrs. Helen Persing, Prin.
Catechesis/Religious Program—Students 415.

LINWOOD, ATLANTIC CO., THE CHURCH OF OUR LADY OF SORROWS, LINWOOD, N.J. (1965) Rev. Malcolm MacLeod, M.SS.CC.
Res.: 724 Maple, 08221. Tel: 609-927-1154; Fax: 609-927-0398. Email: ourladyofsorrowslinwoodnj@verizon.net. Web: www.ourladyofsorrows.us/.
Catechesis/Religious Program—Tel: 609-927-0121. Students 426.

LONGPORT, ATLANTIC CO., CHURCH OF THE EPIPHANY, LONGPORT, N.J. (1954) Merged with Church of the Blessed Sacrament, Margate & St. James Catholic Church, Ventnor to form Holy Trinity Parish, Margate.

MAGNOLIA, CAMDEN CO., ST. GREGORY'S CHURCH, MAGNOLIA, N.J. (1955) Merged with Church of St. Francis de Sales, Barrington & The Church of Mary, Mother of the Church, Bellmawr to form Parish of Saint Rita, Bellmawr.

MALAGA, GLOUCESTER CO., ST. MARY'S ROMAN CATHOLIC CHURCH OF MALAGA, N.J. (1961) Merged with St. Rose of Lima, Newfield, Queen of Angels, Buena Borough to form Our Lady of the Blessed Sacrament, Newfield.

MANTUA, GLOUCESTER CO., R.C. CHURCH OF THE INCARNATION, TOWNSHIP OF MANTUA, NEW JERSEY (1956) Revs. Kenneth J. Johnston; Thanh Q. Pham; Deacons John Schiavo, (Retired); Joseph J. Izzo.
Res.: 240 Main St., 08051. Tel: 856-468-1314; Fax: 856-468-4886.
See St. Margaret School, Woodbury Heights under Regional Schools, Elementary located in the Institution section.
Catechesis/Religious Program—Tel: 856-468-7566. Students 1,100.

MARGATE, ATLANTIC CO.
1—HOLY TRINITY PARISH, MARGATE, N.J. (2010) Revs. Joseph R. Ferrara; James P. Rush, Pastor Emeritus; Krzysztof Wtorek, Parochial Vicar; Deacons Agatino A. Garufi, (Retired); Paul R. Bubeck Jr.
Rectory—11 N. Kenyon Ave., Margate City, 08402-1593. Tel: 609-822-7105; Fax: 609-822-3817.
Churches—
Blessed Sacrament, Margate—
Epiphany, Longport—
St. James, Ventnor—
Catechesis/Religious Program—Students 200.
Convent—St. Joseph Convent, 14 N. Jerome Ave., Margate City, 08402. Tel: 609-822-9243.

MARMORA, CAPE MAY CO.
1—CHURCH OF THE RESURRECTION, MARMORA, N.J. (1975) Merged with St. Casimir's R.C. Church, Woodbine, N.J. & St. Elizabeth's Church, Goshen to form The Parish of St. Maximilian Kolbe, Marmora, N.J.
2—THE PARISH OF ST. MAXIMILIAN KOLBE, MARMORA, N.J. (2011) Rev. Msgr. Peter M. Joyce.
Res.: 200 W. Tuckahoe Rd., 08223. Tel: 609-390-0664; Fax: 609-390-8717.

MAYS LANDING, ATLANTIC CO.
1—CHURCH OF ST. VINCENT DE PAUL, MAYS LANDING, N.J. (1906) [CEM] Merged with St. Bernard Mission, Dorothy to form St. Vincent de Paul Parish, Mays Landing.
2—ST. VINCENT DE PAUL PARISH, MAYS LANDING, N.J. (2010) Rev. Edward F. Heintzelman; Very Rev. Anthony Patrizio; Deacon Richard Wigglesworth.
Mailing Address: 114 Rte. 50, 08330-1707.
Rectory—5061 Harding Hwy., 08330-1707. Tel: 609-625-2124; Fax: 609-625-8718. Web: www.vincentdepaul.org/index.ofm.
Churches—
St. Bernard, Dorothy—
St. Vincent de Paul, Mays Landing—
School—(Grades PreK-8), 5809 Main St., 08330. Tel: 609-625-1565; Fax: 609-625-4703. Miss Linda Pirolli, Prin.
Catechesis/Religious Program—Students 217.
Convent—Sisters of St. Joseph of Chestnut Hill, 5807 Main St., 08330. Tel: 609-625-1566.

MERCHANTVILLE, CAMDEN CO., ST. PETER'S CATHOLIC CHURCH, MERCHANTVILLE, N.J. (1903) Revs. Anthony J. Manuppella; David Rivera; David V. Minniti (Retired); Deacon Joseph P. McHugh, (Retired).
Res.: 43 W. Maple Ave., 08109. Tel: 856-663-1373; Fax: 856-488-0647. Web: www.stpeterrcc.com.
School—Tel: 856-665-5789; Fax: 856-665-4943. Mrs. Antonia Taylor, Prin. PreK3-8 Lay Teachers 17; Students 303.
Catechesis/Religious Program—Tel: 856-663-4490. Sheila O'Boyle, C.R.E. Students 205.
Convent—55 W. Maple Ave., 08109. Tel: 856-662-0473. Franciscan Sisters Missionaries of the Heart of Jesus and Mary Immaculate

MILLVILLE, CUMBERLAND CO.
1—THE CHURCH OF ST. JOHN BOSCO, MILLVILLE, N.J. (1966) Merged with The Church of St. Mary Magdalen, Millville to form The Parish of All Saints, Millville.
2—THE CHURCH OF SAINT MARY MAGDALEN, MILLVILLE (1864) [CEM] Merged with The Church of St. John Bosco, Millville to form The Parish of All Saints, Millville.
3—THE PARISH OF ALL SAINTS, MILLVILLE, N.J. (2010) [CEM] Rev. Paul A. Olszewski; Deacons Hipolito Lagares; Severno S. Nasuti Jr.; Russell O. Davis. In Res., Revs. Sergio Bicomong; Cesar A. Rebolledo Ramiriz, O.F.M.; Joseph A. Salerno (Retired).
Rectory—621 Dock St., 08332-2939. Tel: 856-825-0021; Fax: 856-825-4338.
Churches—
St. John Bosco, Millville—
Saint Mary Magdalen, Millville—
School—St. Mary Magdalen Regional School, (Grades K-8), 7 W. Powell St., 08332. Tel: 856-825-3600; Fax: 856-825-9119. Email: advancement@smmrs.org. Web: www.smmrs.org. Sr. Rosa Maria Ojeda, M.D.P.V.M., Prin. Sisters 2; Lay Teachers 17; Students 189.
Catechesis/Religious Program—Tel: 609-617-5461. Lisa Caso, D.R.E. Students 100.
Convent—Missionary Daughters of the Most Pure Virgin Mary, 3 W. Powell St., 08332. Tel: 856-825-4338. Sr. Rosa Maria Ojeda, M.D.P.V.M., Supr.

MOUNT EPHRAIM, CAMDEN CO.
1—CHURCH OF THE SACRED HEART, MT. EPHRAIM, N.J. (1939) Merged with Church of the Holy Maternity, Audubon to form Emmaus Catholic Community, Mount Ephraim.
2—EMMAUS CATHOLIC COMMUNITY, MT. EPHRAIM, N.J. (2010) Rev. Msgr. Leonard G. Scott; Deacon William V. Norquist.
Mailing Address: 11 N. Black Horse Pike, 08059-1395.
Rectory—431 W. Nicholson Rd., Audubon, 08106. Tel: 856-547-0444; Fax: 856-547-0045.
Churches—
Holy Maternity, Audubon—
Sacred Heart, Mt. Ephraim—
Catechesis/Religious Program—Students 200.

MULLICA HILL, GLOUCESTER CO.
1—CATHOLIC COMMUNITY OF THE HOLY SPIRIT, MULLICA HILL, N.J. (2010) [CEM 2] Revs. Anthony R. DiBardino; Antony Savari Muthu; John P. Picinic, S.A.C., Parochial Vicar; Deacons Robert M. Fanelli; Steven T. Theis; Joseph H. Webb.
Rectory—17 Earlington Ave., 08062-9418. Tel: 856-478-2294; Fax: 856-478-4120. 51 Broad St., Woodstown, 08098. Tel: 856-769-0004.
Churches—
St. Ann, Elmer—
Holy Name of Jesus, Mullica Hill—
St. Joseph, Woodstown—
Catechesis/Religious Program—Students 1,120.
2—CHURCH OF THE HOLY NAME OF JESUS, MULLICA HILL, N.J. (1901) [CEM] Merged with St. Ann's Catholic Church, Elmer & St. Joseph's Catholic Church, Woodstown to form Catholic Community of the Holy Spirit, Mullica Hill.

NATIONAL PARK, GLOUCESTER CO., ST. MATTHEW'S CATHOLIC CHURCH, NATIONAL PARK, N.J. (1915) Merged with Church of the Most Holy Redeemer, Westville Grove & St. Patrick's Church, Woodbury to form Holy Angels Parish, Woodbury. For inquiries for parish records contact Catholic Community of the Holy Spirit, Mullica Hill.

NEWFIELD, GLOUCESTER CO.
1—OUR LADY OF THE BLESSED SACRAMENT, NEWFIELD, N.J. (2011) Revs. Allain B. Caparas; John E. Bruni, Parochial Vicar; Sigfrido Troche, M.SS.CC., Parochial Vicar; Deacons Anthony M. Jadick; Joseph A. Perella.
Worship Sites—
Saint Rose of Lima, Newfield—
St. Mary, Malaga—
Queen of Angels, Buena Borough—
Our Lady of Victories, Landisville—
Saint Michael, Minotola—
Rectory—104 Catawba Ave., 08344-9512. Tel: 856-213-6259; Fax: 856-213-6279.
School—Notre Dame Regional School, 108 Church St., 08344. Tel: 856-697-3456; 856-697-0155; Fax: 856-697-8540. Dr. Mary Alimenti, Prin.
Convent—Villa Rossello, 1009 Main St., 08344. Tel: 856-697-2008; Fax: 856-697-2983.
Shrine—St. Padre Pio Shrine 401 N. Harding Hwy., Box 203, Landisville, 08326.
2—ST. ROSE'S CATHOLIC CHURCH (1922) Merged with Queen of Angels, Buena Borough & St. Mary, Malaga to form Our Lady of the Blessed Sacrament, Newfield.

NORTH CAPE MAY, CAPE MAY CO.
1—THE CHURCH OF ST. JOHN OF GOD, NORTH CAPE MAY, N.J. (1966) Merged with St. Raymond's

Catholic Church, Villas to form The Parish of Saint John Neumann, North Cape May.

2—THE PARISH OF SAINT JOHN NEUMANN, NORTH CAPE MAY, N.J. (2010) Revs. Ernest R. Soprano; Robert J. Fritz; Deacon Gary F. Tankard, (Retired). In Res., Rev. Msgr. Timothy A. Ryan (Retired).
Rectory—680 Town Bank Rd., 08204-4413. Tel: 609-884-1656; Fax: 609-898-0673.
Churches—
St. John of God, North Cape May—
St. Raymond, Villas—
Catechesis/Religious Program—Tel: 609-886-7640. Sr. Kathleen Nuckols, I.H.M., D.R.E. Students 204.
Convent—25 E. Ocean Ave., Villas, 08251. Tel: 609-886-3663.

NORTHFIELD, ATLANTIC CO.

1—THE CHURCH OF ST. BERNADETTE, NORTHFIELD, N.J. (1966) Merged with St. Peter's Catholic Church, Pleasantville to form St. Gianna Beretta Molla Parish, Northfield.

2—ST. GIANNA BERETTA MOLLA PARISH, NORTHFIELD, N.J. (2010) Rev. Patrick J. Brady; Deacons Luis E. Correa; George Del Rossi.
Rectory—1421 New Rd., 08225-1103. Tel: 609-646-5611; Fax: 609-484-8345.
Churches—
St. Bernadette, Northfield—
St. Peter, Pleasantville—
Catechesis/Religious Program—Tel: 609-484-0249. Betsy Doyle, D.R.E. Students 389.

OAKLYN, CAMDEN CO., ST. ALOYSIUS CATHOLIC CHURCH, OAKLYN, N.J. (1935) Merged with St. Vincent Pallotti, Haddon Township to form St. Joseph the Worker Parish, Haddon Township, N.J.

OCEAN CITY, CAPE MAY CO.

1—ST. AUGUSTINE'S CATHOLIC CHURCH, OCEAN CITY, N.J. (1894) Merged with The Church of Our Lady of Good Counsel, Ocean City, N.J. and The Church of St. Frances Cabrini, Ocean City, N.J. to form Saint Damien Parish, Ocean City, N.J.

2—THE CHURCH OF ST. FRANCES CABRINI, OCEAN CITY, N.J. (1966) Merged with St. Augustine's Catholic Church, Ocean City, N.J. and The Church of Our Lady of Good Counsel, Ocean City, N.J. to form Saint Damien Parish, Ocean City, N.J.

3—THE CHURCH OF OUR LADY OF GOOD COUNSEL, OCEAN CITY, N.J. (1961) Merged with St. Augustine's Catholic Church, Ocean City, N.J. and The Church of St. Frances Cabrini, Ocean City, N.J. to form Saint Damien Parish, Ocean City, N.J.

4—SAINT DAMIEN PARISH, OCEAN CITY, N.J. Revs. Edward R. Kolla; Michael P. Rush; Massimo S. Fasciglione; Deacons Mark J. Gallagher; Joseph P. Orlando; Vincent E. Trainor.
1310 Ocean Ave., 08226-3295. Tel: 609-399-0648; Fax: 609-399-0063. In Res., Rev. Alvaro Diaz.
Worship Sites—
Saint Augustine, Ocean City—
Our Lady of Good Counsel, Ocean City—
St. Francis of Assisi, Ocean City—

PAULSBORO, GLOUCESTER CO., ST. JOHN'S CHURCH, PAULSBORO, N.J. (1904) Merged with St. Michael's Church, Gibbstown & St. Joseph's Church, Swedesborough to form St. Clare of Assisi Parish, Gibbstown.

PENNS GROVE, SALEM CO., ST. JAMES' CHURCH, PENNSGROVE, N.J. (1901) Merged with The Church of Corpus Christi, Carneys Point; Church of the Queen of the Apostles, Pennsville; & St. Mary's Catholic Church, Salem to form Saint Gabriel the Archangel Parish, Carneys Point.

PENNSAUKEN, CAMDEN CO.

1—ST. CECILIA'S CHURCH, NORTH MERCHANTVILLE, N.J. (1939) Merged with St. Veronica's R.C. Church, Delair & St. Edward's R.C. Church, Pine Hill, to form Mary, Queen of All Saints, Pennsauken.

2—MARY, QUEEN OF ALL SAINTS, PENNSAUKEN, N.J. (2009) Rev. William F. Moore; Rev. Msgr. Michael T. Mannion; Rev. Rico Ducle; Deacon Miguel A. Rivera Sr., (Retired).
Rectory—4824 Camden Ave., 08110-1921. Tel: 856-662-2723; Fax: 856-486-2089. Email: maryqueenofallsaints@comcast.net. Web: www-.maryqueenofallsaints.org. Churches,
Saint Cecilia, Pennsauken—
Saint Veronica, Delair—
Little Angels Child Care Center—48th St. & Camden Ave., 08110. Tel: 856-662-9228. Vickie Caracciolo, Dir.
School—St. Cecilia School, (Grades K-8), 4851 Camden Ave., 08110. Tel: 856-662-0149; Fax: 856-662-7460. Email: stceciliaschool@yahoo.com. Sr. Alicia Perna, S.S.J., Prin.; Mrs. Denise Carpenter, Librarian. Lay Teachers 17; Students 243.
Catechesis/Religious Program—Monica Smith, D.R.E. Students 90.

3—ST. STEPHEN'S R.C. CHURCH, PENNSAUKEN TOWNSHIP, N.J. (1952) Rev. Daniel M. Rocco; Deacons Ernest Picknally; Anthony Cioe.
Res.: 6306 Browning Rd., 08109. Tel: 856-662-9338; Fax: 856-662-4679.
School—(Grades PreK-8) Tel: 856-662-5935; Fax: 856-662-6128. Email: principal@ststephenspennsauken.com. Web: www.ststephenspennsauken.com. Mrs. Patricia Higgins, Prin. Lay Teachers 10; Students 202.
Catechesis/Religious Program—Students 32.
Convent—6300 Browning Rd., 08109. Tel: 856-665-5227. Sisters of St. Joseph of Chestnut Hill

PENNSVILLE, SALEM CO., CHURCH OF THE QUEEN OF THE APOSTLES, PENNSVILLE, N.J. (1955) Merged with The Church of Corpus Christi, Carneys Point; St. James' Church, Penns Grove; & St. Mary's Catholic Church, Salem to form Saint Gabriel the Archangel Parish, Carneys Point.

PINE HILL, CAMDEN CO., ST. EDWARD'S R.C. CHURCH, PINE HILL, NEW JERSEY (1953) Merged with Church of Our Lady of Mount Carmel, Berlin to form Saint Simon Stock Parish, Berlin.

PITMAN, GLOUCESTER CO., OUR LADY QUEEN OF PEACE R.C. CHURCH, PITMAN N.J. (1940) Merged with The Church of Our Lady of Lourdes, Glassboro, N.J. to form Mary, Mother of Mercy Parish, Glassboro, N.J.

PLEASANTVILLE, ATLANTIC CO., ST. PETER'S CATHOLIC CHURCH, PLEASANTVILLE, N.J. (1896) Merged with The Church of St. Bernadette, Northfield to form St. Gianna Beretta Molla Parish, Northfield.

ROSENHAYN, CUMBERLAND CO., ST. MARY'S CHURCH, ROSENHAYN, N.J. (1914) [CEM] Merged with The Church of St. Teresa Avila, Bridgeton; The Church of the Immaculate Conception, Bridgeton; Saint Michael's Roman Catholic Church, Cedarville; & St. Anthony's Church, Port Norris to form The Parish of the Holy Cross, Bridgeton.

RUNNEMEDE, CAMDEN CO.

1—CHURCH OF ST. MARIA GORETTI, RUNNEMEDE, N.J. (1965) Merged with Church of St. Teresa of the Infant Jesus, Runnemede to form Holy Child Parish, Runnemede.

2—CHURCH OF ST. TERESA OF THE INFANT JESUS, RUNNEMEDE, N.J. (1927) Merged with Church of St. Maria Goretti, Runnemede to form Holy Child Parish, Runnemede.

3—HOLY CHILD PARISH, RUNNEMEDE, N.J. (2010) Revs. Raymond P. Gormley; Joseph F. Ganiel, Parochial Vicar; Joseph-Cuong M. Pham, Parochial Vicar; Deacons A. Kenneth Bandiera; George R. Liss.
Rectory—13 E. Evesham Rd., 08078-1700. Tel: 856-939-1681; Fax: 856-939-3878.
Churches—
St. Maria Goretti, Runnemede—
St. Teresa, Runnemede—
See St. Teresa School, Runnemede under Regional Schools, Elementary located in the Institution section.
Catechesis/Religious Program—Students 275.
Convent—42 Ardmore Ave., 08078. Tel: 856-939-5508. Sisters, Servants of the Immaculate Heart of Mary

SALEM, SALEM CO., ST. MARY'S CATHOLIC CHURCH, SALEM (1848) [CEM] Merged with The Church of Corpus Christi, Carneys Point; Church of the Queen of the Apostles, Pennsville; & St. James' Church, Penns Grove to form Saint Gabriel the Archangel Parish, Carneys Point.

SEA ISLE CITY, CAPE MAY CO., ST. JOSEPH'S CATHOLIC CHURCH, SEA ISLE CITY, N.J. (1884) Rev. Joseph A. Perreault; Deacons Liam C. O'Clisham; Joseph A. Murphy.
Res.: 126-44th St., 08243. Tel: 609-263-8696; Fax: 609-263-7884. Email: info@stjosephsic.org. Web: www.stjosephsic.org.
Catechesis/Religious Program—Tel: 609-263-2087. Students 100.
Convent—25-59th St., 08243. Tel: 609-263-6228. Sisters of Mercy of the Americas

SEWELL, GLOUCESTER CO., CHURCH OF THE HOLY FAMILY, WASHINGTON TOWNSHIP (1974) Revs. Robert E. Hughes; Sanjai Devis, V.C.; Deacons Gerald Jablonowski; Joseph A. Kain Sr.
Res.: 226 Hurffville Rd., 08080. Tel: 856-228-1616; Fax: 856-228-6332. Email: office@churchoftheholyfamily.org. Web: www.churchoftheholyfamily.org.
See Our Lady of Hope Regional School, Blackwood under Regional Schools, Elementary located in the Institution section.
Catechesis/Religious Program—Tel: 856-228-2215; Fax: 856-401-1817. Students 1,200.

SICKLERVILLE, CAMDEN CO.

1—THE CHURCH OF ST. CHARLES BORROMEO, WASHINGTON TOWNSHIP, N.J. (1965) Revs. Michael J. Matveenko; Vincent Orum, A.J.; John A. Rossi; Mrs. Mary Ann Exler, Pastoral Assoc.; Deacons Joseph B. Chandler; Joseph Buccilli, Business Mgr.; Lawrence S. Farmer.
Res.: 176 Stagecoach Rd., 08081. Tel: 856-629-0411; Fax: 856-629-9109. Email: parishcenterscb@comcast.net. Web: www.saint-charles-borromeo.org.
See Our Lady of Hope Regional School, Blackwood under Regional Schools, Elementary located in the Institution section.
Catechesis/Religious Program—Tel: 856-228-5694. Mrs. Mary Ann Exler, D.R.E. Students 1,017.

2—CHURCH OF ST. JOHN NEUMANN, SICKLERVILLE, N.J. (1977) Merged with St. Mary's Church, Williamstown to form Our Lady of Peace Parish, Williamstown.

SOMERDALE, CAMDEN CO., OUR LADY OF GRACE, R.C. CHURCH, SOMERDALE, NEW JERSEY (1954) Merged with Church of St. Lawrence, Lindenwold & The R.C. Church of St. Luke, Stratford to form Our Lady of Guadalupe Parish, Lindenwold.

SOMERS POINT, ATLANTIC CO., ST. JOSEPH'S CHURCH, SOMERS POINT, N.J. (1946) Revs. Edward F. Namiotka; Robert J. Gregorio.
Res.: 606 Shore Rd., 08244. Tel: 609-927-3568; Fax: 609-653-8707.
School—St. Joseph Regional School, (Grades PreK-8) Tel: 609-927-2228; Fax: 609-927-7834. Sr. Frances Kane, S.S.J., Prin.; Mrs. Jan Hutton, Librarian. Regionalized with Our Lady of Sorrows Parish, Linwood; Saint Damien, Ocean City. Sisters 6; Lay Teachers 30; Students 537.
Catechesis/Religious Program—Tel: 609-927-3302. Students 362.
Convent—Sisters of St. Joseph of Chestnut Hill, 580 Shore Rd., 08244. Tel: 609-926-9127.

STONE HARBOR, CAPE MAY CO., ST. PAUL'S CHURCH, STONE HARBOR, N.J. (1911) Merged with The Church of Maris Stella, Avalon to form St. Brendan the Navigator Parish, Avalon.

STRATFORD, CAMDEN CO., THE R.C. CHURCH OF ST. LUKE, STRATFORD, N.J. (1961) Merged with Church of St. Lawrence, Lindenwold & Our Lady of Grace, R.C. Church, Somerdale to form Our Lady of Guadalupe, Lindenwold.

SWEDESBORO, GLOUCESTER CO., ST. JOSEPH'S CHURCH, SWEDESBOROUGH (1854) [CEM 2] Merged with St. Michael's Church, Gibbstown & St. John's Church, Paulsboro to form St. Clare of Assisi Parish, Gibbstown.

TURNERSVILLE, CAMDEN CO., THE CHURCH OF SAINTS PETER AND PAUL, WASHINGTON TOWNSHIP, N.J. (1973) Revs. Edward J. Lipinski; Danilo Quiray; Calogero N. LaVerde; Deacons John A. Contino; Michael A. D'Ariano; Eugene L. McLeer, (Retired).
Res.: 362 Ganttown Rd., P.O. Box 1022, 08012. Tel: 856-589-3366; Fax: 856-256-1964. Email: sspp.fin@verizon.net. Web: www.peterandpaulchurch.org.
See Our Lady of Hope Regional School, Blackwood under Regional Schools, Elementary located in the Institution section.
Catechesis/Religious Program—Students 650.

VENTNOR, ATLANTIC CO., ST. JAMES CATHOLIC CHURCH, VENTNOR, N.J. (1922) Merged with Church of the Epiphany, Longport & Church of the Blessed Sacrament, Margate to form Holy Trinity Parish, Margate.

VILLAS, CAPE MAY CO., ST. RAYMOND'S CATHOLIC CHURCH, WILDWOOD VILLAS, N.J. (1937) Merged with The Church of St. John of God, North Cape May to form The Parish of Saint John Neumann, North Cape May.

VINELAND, CUMBERLAND CO.

1—THE CATHOLIC CHURCH OF THE SACRED HEART, VINELAND, N.J. (1874), (Italian), Merged with The Church of Saint Isidore the Farmer, Vineland, N.J. to form Christ the Good Shepherd Parish, Vineland, N.J.

2—CHRIST THE GOOD SHEPHERD PARISH, VINELAND, N.J. (2011) Rev. Msgr. John H. Burton.
1655 Magnolia Rd., 08361.

3—THE CHURCH OF ST. FRANCIS OF ASSISI, VINELAND, N.J. (1961) Merged with The Parish of the Immaculate Heart of Mary, La Parroquia Del Inmaculado Corazon De Maria, Vineland to form Divine Mercy, Vineland.

4—THE CHURCH OF SAINT ISIDORE THE FARMER, VINELAND, N.J. (1962) Merged with The Catholic Church of the Sacred Heart, Vineland, N.J. to form Christ the Good Shepherd Parish, Vineland, N.J.

5—DIVINE MERCY, VINELAND, N.J. (2009) Rev. Msgrs. Victor S. Muro; Dominic J. Bottino; Deacons Charles J. Girard; Thomas S. Moleski; Bernardino Quiles; Roberto P. Rodirgues. In Res., Rev. Jones Kukatla.
Rectory—23 W. Chestnut Ave., 08360-5303. Tel: 856-691-9181; Fax: 856-794-9029.
Churches—
St. Francis of Assisi, Vineland—
Immaculate Heart of Mary, Vineland—
Catechesis/Religious Program—Tel: 856-691-9181, Ext. 13. Students 340.
Convent—Daughters of Mercy, Tel: 856-691-8129.
Pope John Paul II Retreat Center—Tel: 856-691-2299; Fax: 856-691-5522.

6—ST. MARY'S (1887) [CEM] Merged with Our Lady

of Pompeii, Vineland to form St. Padre Pio Parish, Vineland.

7—OUR LADY OF POMPEII (1909) Merged with St. Mary's, Vineland to form St. Padre Pio Parish, Vineland.

8—ST. PADRE PIO PARISH, VINELAND, N.J. (2003) Revs. Peter M. Saporito; Jerold G. Anthony.
Rectory—4680 Dante Ave., 08361-6810. Tel: 856-691-7526; Fax: 856-692-2686.
Church: *St. Mary's*, 736 S. Union Rd., 08360.
Church: *Our Lady of Pompeii*, 4680 Dante Ave., 08361.
School—St. Mary Regional School, (Grades PreK-8), 735 S. Union Rd., 08360. Tel: 856-692-8537; Fax: 856-692-5034. Sr. Margaret Curcio, D.M., Prin.; Lori Yeager, Librarian. Faculty 28; Students 245.
Catechesis/Religious Program—Students 175.

9—THE PARISH OF THE IMMACULATE HEART OF MARY, LA PARROQUIA DEL INMACULADO CORAZON DE MARIA, VINELAND, NEW JERSEY, Merged with The Church of St. Francis of Assisi, Vineland to form Divine Mercy, Vineland.

WATERFORD, CAMDEN CO., ST. ANTHONY'S CHURCH, WATERFORD, N.J. (1966) Merged with The Church of the Assumption, Atco; Parish of Blessed John the Twenty-Third, Blue Anchor; St. Lucy Church, Blue Anchor; & Sacred Heart Church, Cedarbrook to form Christ the Redeemer Parish, Atco.

WEST COLLINGSWOOD, CAMDEN CO., CHURCH OF THE TRANSFIGURATION, WEST COLLINGSWOOD, N.J. (1950) Merged with The Immaculate Heart of Mary, Woodlynne, N.J. to become Most Precious Blood Parish, Collingswood, N.J.

WESTMONT, CAMDEN CO., THE CHURCH OF THE HOLY SAVIOUR, WESTMONT, N.J. (1928) Merged with St. John's Catholic Church, Collingswood to form Blessed Teresa of Calcutta Parish, Collingswood.

WESTVILLE GROVE, GLOUCESTER CO., CHURCH OF THE MOST HOLY REDEEMER, WESTVILLE GROVE, N.J. (1958) Merged with St. Matthew's Catholic Church, National Park & St. Patrick's Church, Woodbury to form Holy Angels Parish, Woodbury.

WESTVILLE, GLOUCESTER CO., ST. ANNE'S CHURCH, WESTVILLE, N.J. (1921) Closed. For inquiries for parish records please see St. Joachim Parish, Bellmawr, N.J.

WILDWOOD CREST, CAPE MAY CO., THE CHURCH OF THE ASSUMPTION B.V.M., WILDWOOD CREST, N.J. (1961) Merged with St. Ann's Church, Wildwood to form Notre Dame de la Mer Parish, Wildwood.

WILDWOOD, CAPE MAY CO.

1—ST. ANN'S CHURCH, WILDWOOD, N.J. (1895) Merged with The Church of the Assumption of the B.V.M., Wildwood Crest to form Notre Dame de la Mer Parish, Wildwood.

2—NOTRE DAME DE LA MER PARISH, WILDWOOD, N.J. (2010) Revs. Michael J. Field, In Solidum Team Mod.; Joseph D. Wallace, In Solidum Team Mem.; Gustavo Agudelo, In Solidum Team Mem.; Deacon Joseph R. Pierce.
Office: 1500 Central Ave., Ste. 100, North Wildwood, 08260-4943. Tel: 609-522-2709; Fax: 609-522-9375.
Churches—
Assumption of the Blessed Virgin Mary, Wildwood Crest—
St. Ann, Wildwood—
School—Cape Trinity Regional School, (Grades PreK-8), 1500 Central Ave. Ste. 300, North Wildwood, 08260. Tel: 609-522-2704; Fax: 609-522-5329. Sr. Sheila Murphy, S.S.J., Prin.; Mrs. Jennifer Flud, Librarian. Sisters 1; Lay Teachers 17; Students 214.
Catechesis/Religious Program—Tel: 609-827-9587. Mrs. Sandra Borkowski, C.R.E. Students 180.
Convent—2900 Pacific Ave., 08260. Tel: 609-522-5721.

WILLIAMSTOWN, GLOUCESTER CO., ST. MARY'S CHURCH, WILLIAMSTOWN, N.J. (1906) [CEM] Merged with Church of St. John Neumann, Sicklerville to form Our Lady of Peace Parish, Williamstown.
Our Lady of Peace Parish, Monroe Township, N.J.— (2009)Revs. Cadmus D. Mazzarella; Victorino B. Coronado, C.I.C.M.; Christopher M. Markellos; Deacons John J. Leyden, (Retired); John Kacy; Michael McDonaugh; Albert A. LaMonaca Jr.
Office: 32 Carrol Ave., 08094-1713. Tel: 856-629-6142; Fax: 856-875-2097. Email: olopp@olopp.org. Web: www.olopp.org.
Rectory—640 S. Main St., 08094. Tel: 856-262-1358. Churches,
Saint Mary, Williamstown—
School—32A Carrol Ave., 08094. Tel: 856-629-6190; Fax: 856-728-1437. Mrs. Patricia Mancuso, Prin. Lay Teachers 35; Students 572.
Catechesis/Religious Program—Tel: 856-629-0614. Students 1,100.

WOODBINE, CAPE MAY CO., ST. CASIMIR'S R.C. CHURCH, WOODBINE, N.J. (1939) [CEM] Merged with Church of the Resurrection, Marmora, N.J. & St. Elizabeth's, Goshen to form The Parish of St. Maximilian Kolbe, Marmora, N.J.

WOODBURY HEIGHTS, GLOUCESTER CO.

1—INFANT JESUS PARISH, WOODBURY HEIGHTS, N.J. (2010) Revs. Joseph T. Szolack; James H. King; Felipe Doldan, Parochial Vicar; Deacons Nicholas A. Danze; Robert M. Kenney.
Rectory—334 Beech Ave., 08097-1317. Tel: 856-848-0047; Fax: 856-384-8123.
Churches—
St. John Vianney, Deptford—
St. Margaret, Woodbury Heights—
See St. Margaret Regional School, Woodbury Heights under Regional Schools, Elementary located in the Institution Section.
Catechesis/Religious Program—
Convent—745 Third St., 08097. Tel: 856-848-6049. Sr. Gloria Louise Levari, F.M.I.J., Supr.

2—ST. MARGARET'S CHURCH, WOODBURY HEIGHTS, N.J. (1961) Merged with The Church of St. John Vianney, Deptford to form Infant Jesus Parish, Woodbury Heights.

WOODBURY, GLOUCESTER CO.

1—HOLY ANGELS PARISH, WOODBURY, N.J. (2010) Rev. Msgr. Joseph V. DiMauro; Revs. Thomas S. Capperella, Parochial Vicar; Robert J. Kantz, Parochial Vicar; Deacons James N. Hogan; Paul M. Parchinski; William J. Rumaker, (Retired). In Res., Rev. Alfred Onyutha.
Rectory—64 Cooper St., 08096-4618. Tel: 856-845-0123; Fax: 856-845-7409. Email: mail@holyangels.org. Web: www.holyangelsnj.org.
Churches—
St. Matthew, National Park—
Most Holy Redeemer, Westville Grove—
St. Patrick, Woodbury—
School—Holy Trinity Regional School, 1215 Delsea Dr., Westville Grove, 08093. Tel: 856-848-6826; Fax: 856-251-0344. Dr. Kevin J. Laughlin Sr., Prin.
Catechesis/Religious Program—Family Faith Formation: 211 Cooper St., 08096. Tel: 856-853-6681. Sr. Joan Burzichelli, Dir. Faith Formation. Students 614.
Mission—St. Yi Yun Il John Korean Catholic Mission 1219 Delsea Dr., Westville Grove, 08093-9632. Tel: 856-848-6779; Fax: 856-848-6208. Rev. Sung Heum (John) Kim, Admin.

2—ST. PATRICK'S CHURCH, WOODBURY (1877) Merged with Church of the Most Holy Redeemer, Westville Grove & St. Matthew's Catholic Church, National Park to form Holy Angels Parish, Woodbury.

WOODLYNNE, CAMDEN CO., THE IMMACULATE HEART OF MARY, WOODLYNNE, N.J. (1949), (Vietnamese), Merged with Church of the Transfiguration, West Collingswood, N.J. to form Most Precious Blood Parish, Collingswood, N.J.

WOODSTOWN, SALEM CO., ST. JOSEPH'S CATHOLIC CHURCH, WOODSTOWN, N.J. (1895) [CEM] Merged with Church of the Holy Name of Jesus, Mullica Hill & St. Ann's Catholic Church, Elmer to form Catholic Community of the Holy Spirit, Mullica Hill.

Chaplains of Public Institutions

ANCORA. *New Jersey State Psychiatric Hospital*, Tel: 609-561-1700. Rev. Joachim Oforchukwu, C.S.Sp. (Nigeria), Chap.

BRIDGETON. *Southwoods State Prison, Immaculate Conception*, 08302. Rev. Robert P. Weber, Ph.D., Chap. (Retired).

CAPE MAY. *United States Coast Guard, Command Chaplain's Office*, 1 Munro Ave., 08204-5001. Tel: 609-898-6974. Rev. Miles J. Barrett.

DELMONT. *Southern State Correctional Facility*, Tel: 856-785-1300, Ext. 6389. Rev. Robert P. Weber, Ph.D. (Retired).

FAIRTON. *Federal Correctional Institution*, P.O. Box 280, 08320. Tel: 856-227-1436. Rev. Sergio Bicomong, Chap.

LAKELAND. *Camden County Hospital at Lakeland*, St. Joseph's Chapel, Blackwood Post Office, 08012. Tel: 856-227-3000, Ext. 444. Rev. Glenn R. Hartman.

LEESBURG. *New Jersey State Medium Security Prison* 08327. Tel: 856-785-0040. Rev. William James Bleiler (Retired).

VINELAND. *Vineland State School*.
Chaplaincy, St. Isidore, 08362. Tel: 856-691-9077.

WOODBINE. *State Colony*.
Chaplaincy, St. Casimir's Church, 304 Clay St., 08270. Tel: 609-861-3771.

On Duty Outside the Diocese:
Rev. Msgrs.—
Checchio, James F., Pontifical North American College 00120 Vatican City State.
Daiber, Sean J., Central Mailing Address, Paroguia de Sao Jose Rua 90 N. 40, Setor Sul, Caiza Postal 716, 74,000 Goiania Goias, Brazil. Brazilian Missions
Pokusa, Joseph W., J.C.D., Apostolic Nunciature, 3339 Massachusetts Ave. N.W., Washington, DC 20008. Tel: 202-333-7121
Revs.—
Amabile, Patsy L., Our Lady of Lourdes, Islip, NY 11751.
Betz, James F., CMR 419, Box 444, Apo, AE 09102.
Hubbs, Timothy L., Chap. (Major), 900 Army-Navy Dr., Apt. 1531, Arlington, VA 22202.
Idler, Peter M., 631 Market St., 08102.
Kocik, Francis W., 191 Hawley St., Binghamton, NY 13901.
McLaughlin, Peter A., St. Michael, 19 N. Palafax St., P.O. Box 12423, Pensacola, FL 32582. Tel: 850-438-4985
Murphy, Ronan B., 631 Market St., 08102.
Nwoga, Laserian, 16505 Lookout Hollow Cir., #738, Selma, TX 78154.
Orsi, Michael P., Ave Maria School of Law, 1025 Commons Cir., Naples, FL 34119.
Sinatra, Robert L., Casa Santa Maria, Rome, Italy.

On Sick Leave:
Revs.—
Bakey, Christopher T.
Bradley, Hugh J.
Stabeno, John M.

On Leave of Absence:
Revs.—
McLaverty, Albert J.
Melendez, Daniel J.
Spagnola, Michael G.
Tabone, Marcel M.
Witcoskie, Stanley L.

Inactive:
Revs.—
Santos, Walter Guasp
Trinh, Paul H.

Retired:
Rev. Msgrs.—
Alleyne, Edward D., St. Mary's Catholic Home, 210 St. Mary's Dr., Cherry Hill, 08003-5217. Tel: 856-449-7503
Budney, David F., 315 Ryder Cup Cir., Unit 106, St. Augustine, FL 32092. Tel: 904-940-3390
Carr, James A., Sacred Heart Residence for Priests, 200 St. Mary's Dr., Cherry Hill, 08003.
Casey, John H., 104 Wood Ln., Sparta, TN 38583.
Chiarilli, Patrick S., Clayton Mews, 865 N. Delsea Dr., Box 102, Clayton, 08312.
Clarke, John A., 112 Franklin Dr., Mullica Hill, 08062. Tel: 856-371-1933
Coyne, Michael J., P.O. Box 95, Leeds Point, 08220.
Fitzsimmons, Eugene J., J.C.D., 125 Pine Valley Rd., Cherry Hill, 08034.
Fitzsimmons, Thomas B., 6105 Central Ave., P.O. Box 116, Sea Isle City, 08243. Tel: 609-522-2709
Flynn, Thomas M., Sacred Heart Residence, 200 St. Mary's Dr., Cherry Hill, 08003. Tel: 856-751-8109
Gallagher, John Gerald, Blessed Sacrament, 15 Shea Pl., New Rochelle, NY 10801. Tel: 904-823-0975
Graham, William P., V.F., 414 Erie Ave., Carney's Point, 08069. Tel: 856-534-7976
Herron, Joseph P., P.O. Box 615, Longport, 08403.
Jordan, Harry J., Sacred Heart Residence, 200 St. Mary's Dr., Cherry Hill, 08003. Tel: 856-874-1959
Kernan, Eugene J., 91 Geneva Ave., Westmont, 08108.
Kloskowski, Stanley E., c/o 27 Fleetwood Dr., Hamilton Square, 08690.
Mannion, Martin J., 11 45th Cove, Brigantine, 08203.
Martin, Andrew E., Nazareth House, 300 Cuthbert Blvd., Cherry Hill, 08002. Tel: 609-513-1709
McIntyre, Thomas J., 14 Ealey Ct., Glassboro, 08028.
O'Connor, Paul, c/o 19 Mascoma St., Quincy, MA 02170.
O'Leary, Cornelius P., 25098 Jaclyn Ave., Moreno Valley, CA 92557-5703. Tel: 909-242-6939
O'Neill, Felix M., 717 S. Columbus Blvd., Apt. 518, Philadelphia, PA 19147. Tel: 215-925-7001
OMearain, Ciaran P., P.O. Box 26, Gibbsboro, 08026.
Quinn, William, St. Paul, 9910 Third Ave., Stone Harbor, 08247. Tel: 609-368-3091
Rock, Russell L., Sacred Heart Residence for Priests, 200 St. Mary's Dr., Cherry Hill, 08003.
Ryan, Timothy A., 680 Town Bank Rd., North Cape May, 08204.
Sharkey, Thomas F., J.C.D., 3 Catherine Pl., Northfield, 08225.
Sprecace, Francis A., 856 Palermo Rd., St.

Augustine, FL 32086.
Stoerlein, Joseph G., 97 Hobart Ave., Absecon, 08201.
Tracy, James R., Ph.D., V.F., Mary, Mother of Mercy, 500 Green Tree Rd., Glassboro, 08028. Tel: 856-881-0909

Revs.—
Anderson, Arthur T., Sacred Heart Residence for Priests, 200 St. Mary's Dr., Cherry Hill, 08003.
Annino, Sebastian V., Sacred Heart Residence for Priests, 200 St. Mary's Dr., Cherry Hill, 08003.
Barry, James F., P.O. Box 618, 08270.
Battisti, Lewis A., V.F., Garden Lake Park #128, 1402 S. Rte. #9, Cape May Court House, 08210.
Beebe, David E., Country Club Estates, 248 Rte. 40, A-8, Newfield, 08344. Tel: 856-358-0262
Bleiler, William James, Holy Cross, 46 Central Ave., Bridgeton, 08302. Tel: 609-478-6213
Bober, Marjan L., 791 Burman Ln., N.E., Palm Bay, FL 32905.
Bolcar, Andrew J., Sacred Heart Residence for Priests, 200 St. Mary's Dr., Cherry Hill, 08003-2517. Tel: 856-424-2035
Bourke, John F., 4 Twig Ct., Willingboro, 08046. Tel: 609-871-3890
Burns, Joseph, Villa Raffaella, 917 S. Main St., Pleasantville, 08232.
Cairone, A. Robert, Sacred Heart Residence, 200 St. Mary's Dr., Cherry Hill, 08003.
Carey, Stephen, Templetuohy, Thurles, County Tipperary, Ireland.
Carlone, Carmen A., V.F., 130 Southhampton Dr., Smithville, 08205.
Carpinelli, Vincent G., V.F., P.O. Box 429, Avalon, 08202.
Collins, William F., 216 Leeds Ave., Bellmawr, 08031.
Conaty, Charles, 66 Meadowridge Rd., Galloway, 08205. Tel: 609-221-2138
Dante, Neal F., 5001 Pleasant Mill Rd., Hammonton, 08037. Tel: 609-965-0464
Dunphy, Robert J., 60 Summit Rd., Portsmouth, RI 02871.
Eckert, William F., 181 Elm St., Pittsfield, MA 01201.
Fleming, John M., 161 Kamal Pkwy., Cape Coral, FL 33904. Tel: 609-369-6324
Forbes, Richard L., Sacred Heart North, 250 St. Mary's Dr., Cherry Hill, 08003. Tel: 609-425-8653
Gaffney, Francis P., J.C.L., Villa Raffaella, 917 S. Main St., Pleasantville, 08232.
Gannon, Bernard J., Sacred Heart South, 230 St. Mary's Dr., Cherry Hill, 08003. Tel: 856-424-2035
Gomes, Robert M., 1023 McTavish Way, Palm Harbor, FL 34684.
Gramigna, Francis J., 6015 Black Horse Pike, #51, Egg Harbor Twp., 08046. Tel: 609-871-3890
Hadyka, Richard J., 5 Williams Way, Ocean View, 08230.
Hart, William H., Sacred Heart Residence, 200 St. Mary's Dr., Cherry Hill, 08003.
Hayden, Joseph M., 2354 Mulligan Dr., Lakeland, FL 33810. Tel: 863-815-2541; 863-604-0272
Hegarty, Michael P., Sacred Heart North, 250 St. Mary's Dr., Cherry Hill, 08003.
Hewett, Alfred J., St. Rose of Lima, 300 Kings Hwy., Haddon Heights, 08035-1397. Tel: 609-547-0564
Hope, Abbott J., St. Mary Catholic Home, 210 St. Mary's Dr., Cherry Hill, 08003.
Jones, J. Overton, 447 N. Tennessee Ave., Atlantic City, 08401.
Jurkowski, Joseph V., Sacred Heart South, 230 St. Mary's Dr., Cherry Hill, 08003.
Karczewski, Julian A., Our Lady's Multi-Care Center, 1100 Clematis Ctr., Pleasantville, 08232.
Killeen, John C., St. Mary, 2001 Springdale Rd., Cherry Hill, 08003. Tel: 856-424-1454
Kolton, Stanislaus J., 117 Brown Ave., Spring Lake, 07762-1017. Tel: 908-449-6364
Kunzman, Richard T., 5089 Greenbriar Dr., Fort Myers, FL 33919. Tel: 239-931-7957
Lambert, Cornelius F., St. Brendan, 5012 Dune Dr., Avalon, 08202. Tel: 609-967-3345
Lavin, Wayne Patrick, Sacred Heart Residence, 200 St. Mary's Dr., Cherry Hill, 08003.
Longo, Robert, O.F.M.Cap., 1762 Crown Point Rd., Apt. 674, Thorofare, 08086. Tel: 856-848-2422
Lyons, Edward D., 1402 Massachusetts Ave., Somers Point, 08244. Tel: 609-927-1669
McBride, Henry J., Sacred Heart Residence, 200 St. Mary's Dr., Cherry Hill, 08003.
McCabe, Patrick A., 10 S. Wrenn Pl., Foxfire Village, NC 27281.
Meaney, Brendan J., Sacred Heart Residence, 200 St. Mary's Dr., Cherry Hill, 08003.
Messina, Joseph, 1209 Burrough's Mill Cir., Cherry Hill, 08002.
Minniti, Anthony L., 208A Hillcrest Ave., Collingswood, 08108.
Minniti, David V., Saint Peter, 43 W. Maple Ave., Merchantville, 08109-5141. Tel: 856-663-1373
O'Neill, Brian E., Sacred Heart Residence for Priests, 200 St. Mary's Dr., Cherry Hill, 08003. Tel: 609-980-6095
Pierce, William M., 118 S. 21st St., Apt. 718, Philadelphia, PA 19103.
Ploude, Thomas E., Summer Fields, 511 Shadow Creek Ln., Williamstown, 08094.
Romanowski, Jerome C., 168 Ellmtowne Blvd., Hammonton, 08037. Tel: 609-870-6073
Rosinski, Edward B., 39 Central Ave., Audubon, 08106.
Rush, Joseph E., 178 Berlin Rd., Gibbsboro, 08026.
Ryan, William F., 1401 S. Rte. 9, Lot 50, Cape May Court House, 08210.
Salerno, Joseph A., J.C.L., All Saints, 621 Dock St., Millville, 08332. Tel: 856-825-0021
Selleck, John P., St. Dominic Rectory, 5012 Whitaker St., Panama City, FL 32404.
Smith, Robert V., Sacred Heart Residence, 200 St. Mary's Dr., Cherry Hill, 08003. Tel: 856-751-1951
Sobolewski, Edward F., 2528 Tilton Rd., L51, Egg Harbor Township, 08234. Tel: 609-440-3776
Stoegbauer, Conrad H., Villa Raffaella, 917 S. Main St., Pleasantville, 08232.
Stout, O. Hugh, Sacred Heart Residence, 200 St. Mary's Dr., Cherry Hill, 08003. Tel: 856-751-2010
Sugrue, John F., Villa Rafaella, 917 S. Main St., Pleasantville, 08232.
Tovar, Ireneo Lopez, 121 Country Club Dr., Tower II, Apt. 403, Lake Placid, FL 33852.
Tracey, Thomas S., Manor at St. Mary's, 220 St. Mary's Dr., Cherry Hill, 08003.
Tumosa, John Joseph, 1905 3rd St., Philadelphia, PA 19148. Tel: 215-465-2620
Voltaggio, Fred, 303 W. Beach Ave., Brigantine, 08203. Tel: 609-923-9649
Wade, Edward C., Queen of Peace, 3011 Telephone Rd., Houston, TX 77023.
Wagenhoffer, Josef A., V.F., 1604 Bay Dr., Pleasantville, 08232. Tel: 609-504-1305
Ward, John P., 1334 Wilson Rd., Waldorf, MD 20602.
Weber, Robert P., Ph.D., 824 Stokes Ave., Collingswood, 08108. Tel: 856-513-5085
Wise, Paul C., 119 S. New Hampshire Ave., Atlantic City, 08401.
Yori, Robert O., 13 W. 4th St., Hazleton, PA 18201. Tel: 570-454-3476

Permanent Deacons:
Achee, C. J.
Aguilar, Omar M.
Andreacchio, Robert A.
Ayscue, Brian T.
Bandiera, A. Kenneth
Becker, Joseph F.
Beebe, Joseph F.
Berrios, Pablo
Berstecher, John L.
Bischer, Carmen M.
Bubeck, Paul R., Jr.
Buccilli, Joseph C.
Carlucci, Leonard P.
Carter, Michael J.
Catanese, Ralph A.
Cerullo, Francis A.
Chandler, Joseph B.
Cioe, Anthony
Colanero, John D.
Como, Anthony C., (Retired)
Contino, John A.
Correa, Luis E.
Costello, Joseph A., (Retired)
Crawford, Douglas R.
Crosson, Francis W.
Cruz, Jose M.
D'Ariano, Michael A.
Danze, Nicholas A.
Davis, Russell O.
Del Rossi, George C.
Deliberis, William J.
DeMuro, Gerard V.
Ellis, Raymond V., (Retired)
Engel, Francis J., (Retired)
Fanelli, Robert M.
Farmer, Lawrence S.
Ferland, George M., (Retired)
Foley, Robert P.
Gallagher, Mark J.
Gallimore, John R., (Retired)
Ganci, Joseph A., (Retired)
Garozzo, Joseph A.
Garufi, Agatino A., (Retired)
Giordano, Philip E.
Girard, Charles J.
Guaracini, Frank, Jr.
Guerrieri, Michael H.
Hafner, Thomas J., (Retired)
Hanrahan, Matthew J.
Harkins, Michael J.
Harrington, John H., Jr.
Heil, Kevin C.
Henry, E. Michael, (Retired)
Hogan, James N.
Iannuzzi, William P., (Retired)
Izzo, Joseph J.
Jablonowski, Gerard J.
Jadick, Anthony M.
Jennings, Thomas E.
Johnson, William G.
Kacy, John J.
Kain, Joseph A., Sr.
Kearney, J. Brian, (Retired)
Kenney, Robert M.
Kiley, James W., (Retired)
Lagares, Hipolito
LaMonaca, Albert A., Jr.
Latini, Vincent
Laughlin, Kevin L.
Lauth, William
Lee, Paul K.
Leyden, John J., (Retired)
Liss, George R.
Long, Leonard W.
Lopes, Joseph S.
Loungo, Joseph W.
Ludovich, Nicholas P.
Luko, John J., Jr.
Malatesta, Anthony D.
Maxwell, Richard S.
McAleer, Charles L., Sr.
McBlain, W. Leo
McCarthy, Richard F., (Retired)
McDonaugh, Michael L.
McHugh, Joseph P., (Retired)
McLeer, Eugene L., (Retired)
Miranda, Felix Tito
Moleski, Thomas S.
Mortelliti, Nicholas V.
Murnane, David W.
Murphy, Joseph A.
Nasuti, Samuel S., Jr.
Nguyen, Kim T.
Nichols, Christopher D.
Norquist, William V.
O'Brien, Thomas F.
O'Clisham, Liam C.
Okoro, Vincent A.
Orlando, Joseph P.
Parchinski, Paul M.
Pepe, Frank J., (Retired)
Perella, Joseph A.
Peters, William L.
Peterson, George J., (Retired)
Picknally, Ernest F.
Pierce, Joseph R.
Porowicz, Alfred T., (Retired)
Powell, Peter J.
Quiles, Bernardino S., (Senior)
Radziak, Raymond R.
Ralbusky, Emil A.
Ramos Vega, Angel R.
Reiss, Charles C., (Retired)
Rich, John D., Jr.
Rivera, Miguel A., Sr., (Retired)
Riviello, Albert J., (Retired)
Robinson, William C.
Rocks, James H.
Rodirgues, Roberto P.
Rogozenski, Donald W.
Rumaker, William J., (Retired)
Sampson, Richard T.
Santos, Arnaldo A.
Schiavo, John A., (Retired)
Scott, Michael F.
Seaman, Joseph F.
Slaven, William M.
Smith, James O.
Soto, Samuel
Sullivan, Timothy M.
Tankard, Gary F., (Retired)
Tavarez, Ismael P.
Teeney, James J., (Retired)
Theis, Steven T.
Tobin, Charles A.
Trainor, Vincent E.
Van Leer, George R.
Velez, Aladino
Watts, William L., (Retired)
Webb, Joseph H.
Welsh, Michael L.
Werner, John F.
Wigglesworth, Richard J., (Retired)
Willson, Robert F.
Zayas, Jose Rene

INSTITUTIONS LOCATED IN THE DIOCESE

[A] HIGH SCHOOLS, DIOCESAN

ABSECON. *Holy Spirit High School, Absecon, N.J.*, 500 S. New Rd., 08201. Tel: 609-646-3000; Fax: 609-646-1770. Email: holyspirithighschool@yahoo.com. Web: www.holyspirithighschool.com. Miss Susan W. Dennen, Prin.; Mrs. Joann Malecki, Librarian. Priests 2; Sisters of Mercy 1; Lay Teachers 37; Students 610.

CHERRY HILL. *Camden Catholic High School, Cherry Hill, N.J.* (1887) 300 Cuthbert Rd., 08002. Tel: 856-663-2247; Fax: 856-661-0632. Email: camdencatholic@aol.com. Web: www.camdencatholic.org. Mr. Jeffrey Nick, Pres.; Mr. Thomas J. Kiely, Prin.; Lindsey Perry, Librarian. Priests 2; Sisters of Mercy 1; Lay Teachers 51; Students 750; Staff 7.

HADDONFIELD. *Paul VI High School, Haddon Township, N.J.* (1966) 901 Hopkins Rd., Ste. B, 08033. Tel: 856-858-4900; Fax: 856-858-6832. Email: principal@pvihs.org. Web: pvihs.org. Mr. Michael Chambers, Pres.; Sr. Marianne McCann, M.P.F., Prin.; Rev. Michael M. Romano; Mrs. Michelle Anastasia, Librarian. Priests 1; Religious Teachers Filippini 3; Franciscan Missionary Sisters 1; Lay Teachers 68; Students 1,123.

HAMMONTON. *St. Joseph High School Hammonton, NJ, Inc.*, 328 Vine St., 08037. Tel: 609-561-8700; Fax: 609-561-8701. Mrs. Lynn Domenico, Prin. Religious 3; Lay Teachers 26; Students 378.

[B] HIGH SCHOOLS, PAROCHIAL

GLOUCESTER. *Gloucester Catholic High School, Inc.*, 333 Ridgeway St., 08030. Tel: 856-456-4400; Fax: 856-456-0506. Email: Pmurphy@gchsrams.org. Web: www.gchsrams.org. Mr. John T. Colman, Prin.; Katharine Coughlin, Public Rels. Priests 1; Lay Teachers 40; Students 685.

NORTH WILDWOOD. *Wildwood Catholic High School*, 1500 Central Ave., 08260. Tel: 609-522-7257; Fax: 609-522-2453. Web: wildwoodcatholic.org. Mr. Anthony Degatano, Prin.; Mr. Kevin Quinn, Dir. Devel. Lay Teachers 13; Students 152.

VINELAND. *Sacred Heart High School* (1927) 15 N. East Ave., 08360. Tel: 856-691-4491; Fax: 856-563-1644. Web: www.shhslions.com. Rev. Msgr. John H. Burton, Rector; Mrs. Diane Tucker, Prin. Priests 3; Lay Teachers 20; Students 203.

[C] HIGH SCHOOLS, PRIVATE

NEWFIELD. *Our Lady of Mercy Academy* (1962) 1001 Main Rd., 08344. Tel: 856-697-2008; Fax: 856-697-2887. Email: srgrace@olmanj.org. Web: www.olmanj.org. Sr. Grace Marie, D.M., Prin. Daughters of Our Lady of Mercy. Sisters 2; Lay Teachers 21; Students 150.

PENNSAUKEN. *Bishop Eustace Prep School* (1954) 5552 Rte. 70, 08109-4798. Tel: 856-662-2160, Ext. 211; Fax: 856-662-0802. Web: www.eustace.org. Rev. Robert Nolan, S.A.C.; Bro. James Beamesderfer, S.A.C., Headmaster & Local Community Supr.; Mr. Cyril J. Bleistine, Prin.; A. Nancy Croce, Librarian. Society of the Catholic Apostolate, Province of the Immaculate Conception. Priests 1; Brothers 1; Lay Teachers 70; Students 740.

RICHLAND. *St. Augustine Preparatory School*, 611 N. Cedar Ave., P.O. Box 279, 08350. Tel: 856-697-2600; 856-697-2612 (Monastery); Fax: 856-697-8389. Email: fr.galetto@hermits.com. Web: www.hermits.com. Revs. Donald F. Reilly, O.S.A., Pres.; Ronald A. Hamaday, O.S.A.; Francis J. Horn, O.S.A., J.C.D., Headmaster; Bro. David Graber, M.SS.CC.; Revs. Patrick B. McStravog, Asst., Pres.; Stephen M. Curry, O.S.A.; Francis X. Devlin, O.S.A. Order of St. Augustine, Province of St. Thomas of Villanova. Priests 7; Brothers 1; Lay Teachers 52; Students 682.

[D] REGIONAL SCHOOLS, ELEMENTARY

BERLIN. *Our Lady of Mt. Carmel Regional School*, (Grades PreK-8), One Cedar Ave., 08009. Tel: 856-767-1751; Fax: 856-767-1293. Email: olm@hotmail.com. Web: www.olmc-school.org. Donato Monforto, Prin. Serving St. Simon Stock, Berlin; St. Andrew, Gibbsboro; Mater Ecclesiae, Bellmawr. Lay Teachers 17; Students 238.

BLACKWOOD. *Our Lady of Hope Regional School*, (Grades PreK-8), 420 S. Black Horse Pike, 08012. Tel: 856-227-4442; 856-227-8558; Fax: 856-227-7115. Email: ourladyofhope@snip.net. Web: www.ourladyofhopecatholicschool.org. Sr. Paula Marie Randow, O.S.F., Prin.; Mr. John T. Cafagna, Asst. Prin. Serving Our Lady of Hope, Blackwood; SS. Peter & Paul, St. Charles Borromeo, & Holy Family, Washington Township. Sisters of St. Francis of Philadelphia 1; Lay Teachers 26; Students 469.

CAPE MAY COURT HOUSE. *The Bishop James T. McHugh Regional School, Inc.*, (Grades PreK-8), 2221 Rte. 9 N, 08210. Tel: 609-624-1900; Fax: 609-624-9696. Mrs. Laura Tomlin, Prin.; Sr. Thomas Marie Rakus, Librarian. Sisters 2; Lay Teachers 15; Students 214.

COLLINGSWOOD. *Good Shepherd Regional School*, (Grades PreK-8), 100 Lees Ave., 08108. Tel: 856-858-1562; Fax: 856-858-2943. Email: goodshepherdprincipal@comcast.net. Web: www.goodshepherdcollingswood.org. Mr. Donald W. Garecht, Prin. Serving Blessed Teresa, Collingswood; St. Aloysius, Oaklyn; Transfiguration, W. Collingswood; Holy Saviour, Westmont; St. Vincent Pallotti, Haddon Township. Sisters 1; Lay Teachers 11; Students 167; PreK 51.

GALLOWAY. *Assumption Regional School*, (Grades PreK-8), 146 S. Pitney Rd., 08205. Tel: 609-652-7134; Fax: 609-652-2544. Email: mschurtz@arcsgalloway.org. Web: www.arcsgalloway.org. Mary Ellen Schurtz, Prin.; Rose Faiss, Librarian. Serving Assumption, Galloway; St. Elizabeth Ann Seton, Absecon; St. Nicholas, Egg Harbor City. Lay Teachers 21; Students 350.

GIBBSTOWN. *Guardian Angels Regional School*, (Grades PreK-8) Sr. Jerilyn Einstein, F.M.I.J., Prin. Sisters 3; Lay Teachers 11; Students 288.

Gibbstown Campus (Grades PreK-3), 150 S. School St., 08027. Tel: 856-423-9440; Fax: 856-423-9441. Email: gars@comcast.net.

Paulsboro Campus (Grades 4-8), 717 Beacon Ave., Paulsboro, 08066. Tel: 856-423-9401.

HADDONFIELD. *Christ the King Regional School*, (Grades PreK-8), 164 Hopkins Ave., 08033. Tel: 856-429-2084; Fax: 856-429-4959. Web: www.ckrs.org. Mrs. Maureen DiBella, Prin.; Mary Stiltz, Librarian. Serving Christ the King, Haddonfield; Holy Eucharist, Cherry Hill. Lay Teachers 21; Students 307.

HAMMONTON. *St. Joseph Regional Elementary School*, (Grades PreK-8), 133 N. 3rd St., 08037. Tel: 609-704-2400; Fax: 609-561-4940. Web: www.stjosephprek8.org. Sr. Helen Sanchez, M.P.F., Prin.; Mrs. Susan Sigloch, Librarian. Serving St. Mary of Mt. Carmel, Hammonton. Religious Teachers Filippini 2; Lay Teachers 25; Students 328.

NEWFIELD. *Notre Dame Regional School, Inc.*, (Grades PreK-3), 108 Church St., 08344. Tel: 856-697-0155 (Newfield, Grades PK-1-4, K-3); 856-697-3456 (Landisville, Grades 4-8, PK 2-4); Fax: 856-697-8540 (Newfield); 856-697-5114 (Landisville). Email: notredameregional@comcast.net. Web: www.ndrschool.org. Dr. Mary Alimenti, Prin.; Lucille Doyle, Librarian. Serving Queen of Angels, Landisville; Our Lady of the Lakes, Collings Lakes; St. Rose, Newfield; St. Mary, Malaga. Lay Teachers 21; Students 254.

RUNNEMEDE. *St. Teresa Regional School*, (Grades PreK-8), 27 E. Evesham Rd., 08078. Tel: 856-939-0333; Fax: 856-939-1204. Email: sscanlon@stteresaschool.org. Web: www.holychildparish.net. Sr. Patricia Scanlon, I.H.M., Prin. Serving Open Enrollment Sisters Servants of the Immaculate Heart of Mary 2; Lay Teachers 16; Students 181.

Convent, 18 Ardmore Rd., 08078. Tel: 856-939-5508.

VINELAND. *Bishop Schad Regional School*, (Grades PreK-8), 922 E. Landis Ave., 08360. Tel: 856-691-4490; Fax: 856-691-5579. Email: mainofc@bsrschool.org. Web: www.bsrschool.org. Dr. Patrice DeMartino, Prin.; Terry Smith, Librarian. Serving Sacred Heart, St. Isidore; St. Francis, Immaculate Heart of Mary Lay Teachers 20; Students 255.

St. Mary's Regional School, (Grades PreK-8), 735 Union Rd., 08360. Tel: 856-692-8537; Fax: 856-692-5034. Email: mainoffice@smrschool.org. Web: www.smrschool.org. Steven P. Hogan, Prin.; Tarah Sawyer, Librarian. Serving St. Padre Pio, East Vineland. Lay Teachers 21; Students 215.

WOODBURY HEIGHTS. *St. Margaret Regional School* (1963) 773 Third St., 08097. Tel: 856-845-5200; Fax: 856-845-2405. Email: principal@stmargarets-rs.org. Web: www.stmargarets-rs.org. Sisters Michele DeGregorio, F.M.I.J., Prin.; Gloria Louise Levari, F.M.I.J., Supr. Serving Infant Jesus, Woodbury Heights; Incarnation, Mantua. Sisters 4; Lay Teachers 20; Students 603.

[E] SCHOOLS FOR SPECIAL CHILDREN

WESTVILLE GROVE. *Archbishop Damiano School/St. John of God Community Services* (1965) 1145 Delsea Dr., 08093. Tel: 856-848-4700; Fax: 856-848-3965. Ms. Muncie Buckalew, Exec. Dir. Brothers 3; Sisters 1; Lay Teachers 35; Students 1,000; Total Staff 250.

[F] CATHOLIC FOUNDATIONS

CAMDEN. *Diocese of Camden Trusts, Inc.* (2001) 631 Market St., 08102. Martin F. McKernan Jr., Esq., Contact Person. Priests 2; Lay Staff 1.

Francis, Elizabeth and Edward Roger Welsh Scholarship Trust, 631 Market St., 08102. Tel: 856-583-2835; Fax: 856-963-2655. Rev. Msgr. Roger E. McGrath, Ph.D., Advisory Committee Chair.

The Frank J. and Rosina W. Suttill Catholic Foundation, 631 Market St., 08102. Tel: 856-583-2806. Rev. Msgr. Roger E. McGrath, Ph.D.

The Sharkey Family Charitable Trust, 631 Market St., 08102. Tel: 856-583-2802. Rev. Msgr. Roger E. McGrath, Ph.D., Treas.

The Tuition Assistance Fund, Inc., 631 Market St., 08102. Tel: 856-583-6125; Fax: 856-338-0766. Email: jlanahan@camdendiocese.org. James J. Lanahan, Sec.

[G] GENERAL HOSPITALS

CAMDEN. *Our Lady of Lourdes Health Care Services, Inc.*, 1600 Haddon Ave., 08103. Tel: 856-757-3500; Fax: 856-757-3611. Web: www.lourdesnet.org. Alexander J. Hatala, Pres. & CEO. Bed Capacity 636; Total Staff 3,313; Patients Assisted Annually 308,199.

Our Lady of Lourdes Medical Center (Formerly Our Lady of Lourdes Hospital)(Parent Corporation: Our Lady of Lourdes Health Care Services, Inc.), 1600 Haddon Ave., 08103. Tel: 856-757-3500; Fax: 856-757-3611. Franciscan Sisters of Allegany.

Our Lady of Lourdes Health Foundation, Inc., 1600 Haddon Ave., 08103. Tel: 856-824-3485; Fax: 856-705-1370.

Lourdes Cardiovascular Foundation, Inc., 1600 Haddon Ave., 08103. Tel: 856-482-4950; Fax: 856-482-4960.

Osborn Family Health Center Inc., 1600 Haddon Ave., 08103. Tel: 856-757-3700; Fax: 856-365-7972.

Our Lady of Lourdes School of Nursing, 1600 Haddon Ave., 08103. Tel: 856-757-3629; Fax: 856-757-3758. Web: www.lourdesnursingschool.org.

Our Lady of Lourdes Medical Center Auxiliary, 1600 Haddon Ave., 08103. Tel: 856-705-1373; Fax: 856-705-1370.

Lourdes Ancillary Services, Inc., 1600 Haddon Ave., 08103. Tel: 856-757-3500; Fax: 856-757-3611.

Lourdes Dialysis at Innova, Inc., 1600 Haddon Ave., 08103. Tel: 856-757-3776; Fax: 856-968-6585. Parent Corp: Our Lady of Lourdes Health Care System, Inc.

Life at Lourdes, Inc., 1600 Haddon Ave., 08103. Tel: 856-675-3663; Fax: 856-675-3666. Parent Corp: Our Lady of Lourdes Health Care Services, Inc.

[H] NURSING HOMES

CHERRY HILL. *St. Mary's Catholic Home, Cherry Hill, N.J.* (1952) 210 St. Mary's Dr., 08003. Tel: 856-874-5300; Fax: 856-424-5143. Email: maureen.kogelman@camdendiocese.org. Maureen Kogelman, L.N.H.A., Admin.; Rev. James J. Durkin, Chap. Little Servant Sisters of the Immaculate Conception. Sisters 4; Total Staff 250; Total Assisted Annually 326; Bed Capacity 215.

NEWFIELD. *The Mater Dei Nursing Home, Newfield, New Jersey* (1967) 176 Rte. 40, 08344. Tel: 856-358-2061; Fax: 856-358-0403. Rev. Antony Savari Muthu. Sisters of Mary Immaculate 5; Bed Capacity 64; Total Staff 104; Total Assisted Annually 97.

PLEASANTVILLE. *Our Lady's Multi-Care Center, Inc.*, 1100 Clematis Ave., 08232. Tel: 609-646-2450; Fax: 609-646-7569. Anna Tosti, L.N.H.A., Admin.; Sr. Normita Nunez, H.S.M., Supr.; Rev. Augustine Peter Arul, M.SS.CC., Chap. Hospitaler Sisters of Mercy. Sisters 5; Bed Capacity 214; Patients Assisted Annually 300; Total Staff 225.

Villa Raffaella, 917 S. Main St., 08232. Tel: 609-645-9300; Fax: 609-645-9600. Senior Assisted Living Community, Hospitaler Sisters of Mercy. Total Staff 20; Bed Capacity 55.

VINELAND. *Bishop McCarthy Residence*, 1045 E. Chestnut Ave., 08360. Tel: 856-692-2850; Fax: 856-696-5770. Email: sr.lucia.maroor@camdendiocese.org. Sr. Lucia Maroor, L.N.H.A., Admin.; Rev. Jones Kukatla, Chap. Hospitaler Sisters of Mercy. Sisters 4; Bed Capacity 182; Patients Assisted Annually 315.

[I] HOME CARE

EGG HARBOR TOWNSHIP. *Holy Redeemer Home Care*, 6550 Delilah Rd., Ste. 501, 08234. Tel: 609-761-0300; 800-788-3029; Fax: 609-761-0294. A subsidiary of Holy Redeemer Health System, Inc.

SWAINTON. *Holy Redeemer Home Care*, 1801 Rte. 9 N., Cape May Court House, 08210. Tel: 609-465-2082; 800-745-4693; Fax: 609-463-6121. Web: www.holyredeemer.com. Donald Friel, Exec. Vice Pres. Sponsor: Sisters of the Holy Redeemer, C.S.R., A subsidiary of the Holy Redeemer, C.S.R.;

A Medicare Certified Home Health Agency serving patients in their own homes. A Medicare Certified Hospice Program providing services for terminally ill patients and their families.

Atlantic County Office, 6550 Delilah Rd., Ste. 501, Egg Harbor Township, 08234. Tel: 609-761-0300; 800-788-3029; Fax: 609-761-0294.

[J] HOUSING FOR AGED

CAPE MAY. *Victorian Towers, Inc.* (1973) 608 Washington St., 08204. Tel: 609-884-5883; Fax: 609-884-5625.

CHERRY HILL. *The Manor at St. Mary's* (1991) 220 St. Mary's Dr., 08003. Tel: 856-874-5400; Fax: 856-874-5363. Sr. MaryAnn Marshall, L.S.I.C., R.N., Admin. Total in Residence 76; Total Staff 60.

Marian Residence, 1000 Cropwell Rd., 08003. Tel: 856-424-1131; 856-424-1962; Fax: 856-424-5333. Little Sister Servants of the Immaculate Conception Total in Residence 2; Total Staff 1; Bed Capacity 5.

Village Apartments of Cherry Hill, NJ, Inc., 1845 Haddon Ave., 08103. Tel: 856-424-7913; Fax: 856-424-9211. Email: villageapartments@camdendiocese.org. Total in Residence 148; Total Staff 8.

NORTH CAPE MAY. *Haven House at St. John of God, Inc.*, 676 Townbank Rd., 08204. Tel: 609-884-4548; Fax: 609-884-4313.

PENNSAUKEN. *Stonegate at St. Stephen, Inc.*, 1 Stonegate Dr., 08109. Tel: 856-342-4125; Fax: 856-342-4172. Curtis H. Johnston Jr., Sec. & Contact Person.

WEST DEPTFORD. *Shepherd's Farm Senior Housing, Inc.*, 981 Grove Rd., 08086. Tel: 856-342-4125; Fax: 856-342-4172.

[K] CHILD CARE CENTERS

CAMDEN. *St. Joseph's Child Development Center, Inc.*, 17 Church St., 08105. Tel: 856-963-9202; Fax: 856-963-8940. Email: stjosephcdc@yahoo.com. Betty Mitchell, Dir.; Jim Steinitz, Admin. Staff 13; Children 75.

CHERRY HILL. *Blessed Edmund Early Childhood Education Center* (1996) 1000 Cropwell Rd., 08003. Tel: 856-424-3063; Fax: 856-424-3064. Email: blessededmund@verizon.net. Sr. M. Elizabeth Potuczko, Dir. Sisters 5; Lay Teachers 5; Children 140.

[L] MONASTERIES AND RESIDENCES OF PRIESTS AND BROTHERS

CAMDEN. *Dominican Sisters of the Perpetual Rosary Chaplain's Residence*, 1500 Haddon Ave., 08103. Tel: 856-635-1179. Rev. Anthony I. Cataudo, O.P., Chap. Tel: 856-365-4427; Sr. Mary Elizabeth, O.P., Prioress.

CHERRY HILL. *Sacred Heart Residence for Priests, Inc.*, 200 St. Mary's Dr., 08003. Tel: 856-751-2010; Fax: 856-489-8999. Rev. Msgr. Harry J. Jordan, Dir. (Retired). *Sacred Heart North*, 250 St. Mary's Dr., 08003. Tel: 856-424-1741; Fax: 856-424-2896. Rev. Msgr. Harry J. Jordan, Dir. (Retired). *Sacred Heart South*, 230 St. Mary Dr., 08003. Tel: 856-424-2035. Rev. Msgr. Harry J. Jordan, Dir. (Retired).

LINWOOD. *Villa Pieta. Missionaries of the Sacred Hearts of Jesus & Mary*, 2249 Shore Rd., P.O. Box 189, 08221. Tel: 609-927-5600; Fax: 609-927-5262. Email: mssccusa@aol.com. Revs. Robert Malagesi, M.SS.CC., Rector; Frederick Clement, M.SS.CC.; Peter DiTomasso, M.SS.CC.; Robert McDade, M.SS.CC.; John Perdue, M.SS.CC., Vice Rector; Augustine Peter Arul, M.SS.CC.; Bro. David Graber, M.SS.CC.

MARGATE. *Franciscan Friary* Holy Name Province., 118 S. Mansfield Ave., 08402-2516. Tel: 609-822-9552; Fax: 609-822-0601. Email: margate1@comcast.net. Total Staff 2.

OCEAN CITY. *Augustinian Friars*, St. Rita of Cascia Cottage, 823 5th St., 08226. Tel: 609-398-1299. Rev. Joseph S. Mostardi, O.S.A., Guestmaster. Tel: 610-574-3544.

Ocean Rest Summer School and Retreat House, 3045 Central Ave., 08226. Tel: 609-399-6480. Mailing Address: 444-A Rte. 35 S., Eatontown, 07724. Tel: 732-380-7926; Fax: 732-380-7937. Email: oceanrest@fscdena.org. Bro. Edward Hofmann, F.S.C., Dir. Brothers of Christian Schools Summer School and Retreat House.

WESTVILLE GROVE. *Hospitaller Order of St. John of God* (1965) 1145 Delsea Dr., 08093. Tel: 856-848-4700; Fax: 856-848-7305. Web: www.sjogbrothers.com. Bro. Thomas Osorio, O.H., Prior. Brothers 3.

[M] CONVENTS AND RESIDENCES FOR SISTERS

CAMDEN. *Monastery of the Dominican Nuns of the Perpetual Rosary*, 1500 Haddon Ave., 08103. Tel: 856-342-8340. Rev. Anthony I. Cataudo, O.P., Chap. Sisters 4.

ATLANTIC CITY. *St. John's Retreat House*, 128 S. Dover Ave., 08401. Tel: 609-317-4399; Fax: 609-317-4399. Sr. Maria Silvia Giraldo, Supvr. Little Servant Sisters of the Immaculate Conception. Sisters 3.

CHERRY HILL. *Franciscan Missionary Sisters of the Infant Jesus, Inc.*, U.S. Province and Novitiate: 1215 Kresson Rd., 08003. Tel: 856-428-8834; Fax: 856-428-5599. Email: fmijusdel@yahoo.com. Sr. Angela Pia Camillotti, F.M.I.J., Delegate Supr. Sisters 16.

Little Servant Sisters of the Immaculate Conception (1942) Provincialate and Novitiate., 1000 Cropwell Rd., 08003. Tel: 856-424-1962; Fax: 856-424-5333. Email: lsic.prov.@verizon.net. Web: www.littleservantsisters.com. Sr. Dorota Baranowska, L.S.I.C., Prov. Professed Sisters 24; Postulants 2; Novices 1.

ELMER. *The Sisters of Mary Immaculate of Nyeri, Inc.*, 400 State St., 08318. Tel: 856-358-4030. Email: gachiriben@yahoo.com. Sr. Bernadette Gachiri, S.M.I., Pres. & Contact Person.

MOUNT EPHRAIM. *St. Clare Convent, Franciscan Sisters of Allegany*, 136 Glover Ave., 08059. Tel: 856-208-1055.

NEWFIELD. *Villa Rossello* Provincial House and Novitiate of Daughters of Our Lady of Mercy., 1009 Main Rd., 08344. Tel: 856-697-2983; Fax: 856-697-8595. Email: dmnewfield@yahoo.com. Sr. Daniel Marie, D.M., Prov. Sisters 17.

PLEASANTVILLE. *Hospitaler Sisters of Mercy Novitiate*, 917 S. Main St., 08232. Tel: 609-677-1407; Fax: 609-645-9600. Email: villaraffaella@msn.com; hospitaler@verizon.net.

Hospitaler Sisters of Mercy Convent, 909 S. Main St., 08232. Tel: 609-677-1407; Fax: 609-645-9600. Email: hospitaler@verizon.net. Sisters 9.

Hospitaler Sisters of Mercy - Our Lady's Residence Convent, 1100 Clematis Ave., 08232. Tel: 609-272-0672. Sisters 4.

SEA ISLE CITY. *The Sisters of St. Francis of Philadelphia*, 55th & Landis Ave., 08243. Tel: 610-558-7676; Fax: 610-558-6122. Email: roconnor@osfphila.org. Web: www.osfphila.org.

STONE HARBOR. *Villa Maria by the Sea* (1937) 11101 First Ave., 08247. Tel: 609-368-3621; 609-368-5290; Fax: 609-368-0315. Summer retreat house for Sisters Servants of the Immaculate Heart of Mary. (Immaculata, PA)

VENTNOR. *The Benedictine Sisters of Elizabeth, NJ*, 114 S. Troy Ave., 08406. Tel: 609-823-9843.

Holy Family, Seaside Convent, 496 Western Hwy., Blauvelt, NY 10913. Tel: 609-822-5127; Fax: 845-359-5773. Email: choward@opblauvelt.org. Sisters of St. Dominic (Blauvelt, NY).

VINELAND. *Bishop McCarthy Residence Convent*, 1045 E. Chestnut Ave., 08360. Tel: 856-691-0740; Fax: 856-696-5770. Email: hsm856@aol.com. Sr. Lucia Maroor, L.N.H.A., Supr. Hospitaler Sisters of Mercy 5.

[N] RETREAT HOUSES

CAPE MAY POINT. *Marianist Family Retreat Center*, 417 Yale Ave., Box 488, 08212-0488. Tel: 609-884-3829; Fax: 609-884-0545. Email: mfrc@capemaymarianists.org. Web: www.capemaymarianists.org. Rev. Timothy Dwyer, S.M., Chap.; Mr. Anthony Fucci, Center Dir.; Bros. Albert Koch, S.M., (Retired); Edward Unferdorfer, S.M., (Retired).

VINELAND. *Pope John Paul II Retreat Center*, 414 S. 8th St., 08360. Tel: 853-692-8992. Email: sccpjIIrc@aol.com. Rev. Msgr. Victor S. Muro, Dir.

[O] APOSTOLIC CENTERS

CAMDEN. *Padre Pio Shrine, Buena Borough, N.J., Inc.*, 401 N. Harding Hwy., Box 203, Landisville, 08326-0203.

BERLIN. *Mater Ecclesiae Mission* 261 Cross Keys Rd., 08009-9431. Tel: 856-753-3408; Fax: 856-753-2671. Email: rector@materecclesiae.org. Web: www.materecclesiae.org. Revs. Robert C. Pasley, Rector; Glenn R. Hartman.

HADDON HEIGHTS. **Collegium Center for Faith and Culture*, 314 White Horse Pike, 08035. Tel: 856-904-1834. Email: info@collegiumcenter.org. Web: www.collegiumcenter.org. Rev. Timothy E. Byerley, Dir.

[P] FAMILY SERVICES AND COMMUNITY CENTERS OF CATHOLIC CHARITIES

CAMDEN. *Catholic Charities, Diocese of Camden, Inc.* Administrative Office, 1845 Haddon Ave., 08103. Tel: 856-342-4100; Fax: 856-342-4180. Web: www.catholiccharitiescamden.org. Kevin H. Hickey, Exec. Dir., Catholic Charities.

Catholic Charities - Camden County, 1845 Haddon Ave., 08103. Tel: 856-342-4100; Fax: 856-342-4180.

Catholic Charities - Atlantic County, 9 N. Georgia Ave., Atlantic City, 08401. Tel: 609-345-3448; Fax: 609-345-7180.

Catholic Charities - Cape May County, Village Shoppes, 1304 Rte. 47 S., Rio Grande, 08242. Tel: 609-886-2662; Fax: 609-886-3583.

Catholic Charities - Cumberland County, 810 Montrose St., Vineland, 08360. Tel: 856-691-1841; Fax: 856-692-6575.

Catholic Charities - Salem County, 114 State St., Penns Grove, 08069. Tel: 856-299-1296; Fax: 856-299-4010.

Catholic Charities - Gloucester County, 1200 N. Delsea Dr., Ste. One, Westville, 08093. Tel: 856-845-9200; Fax: 856-845-8905.

Counseling Center - Cumberland, 810 Montrose St., Vineland, 08360. Tel: 856-691-6084; Fax: 856-691-6179.

Counseling Center - Cape May, Village Shoppes, 1304 Rte. 47 S., Rio Grande, 08242. Tel: 609-886-2662; Fax: 609-886-3583.

Counseling Center - Camden, 1845 Haddon Ave., 08103. Tel: 866-682-2166; Fax: 856-342-4180. Sylvia Loumeau, L.C.S.W., Dir.

Counseling Center - Gloucester, 1200 Delsea Dr., Ste. One, Westville Grove, 08093. Tel: 856-845-9200; Fax: 856-845-8905. Sylvia Loumeau, L.C.S.W., Dir.

Guadalupe Family Services Inc., 509 State St., 08102. Tel: 856-365-8081; Fax: 856-365-8247. Sr. Helen Cole, S.S.J., L.C.S.W., Dir.

[Q] CAMPUS MINISTRIES

CAMDEN. *Rutgers University* c/o 642 Market St., 08102. Tel: 215-582-1666. Email: dsw@oblates.org. Rev. Michael J. McCue, O.S.F.S., Chap.

GLASSBORO. *Rowan University* Newman Center, 1 Redmond Ave., 08028. Tel: 856-881-5642; Fax: 856-881-4183. Ann Polo, Dir.; Deacon Kevin Heil, Campus Min.; Rev. Phillip Johnon, Univ. Parish Chap.

POMONA. *Richard Stockton College of New Jersey* (1969) 235 Pomona Rd., 08240. Tel: 609-804-0200; Fax: 609-804-9135. Lois Dark, Dir.; Rev. Thomas R. Kiely, Chap.

[R] MEDICAL CLINICS

CAMDEN. *St. John the Baptist Pre-Natal Clinic, Incorporated* (1969) 6th St. & Erie St., 08102. Tel: 856-757-9540; Fax: 856-757-9541. Patricia A. Chico, L.P.N., B.A., Admin. Patients Assisted Annually 1,750.

Saint Luke's Catholic Medical Services, Inc., 511 State St., 08102. Tel: 856-365-4642; Fax: 856-365-0539. Email: violetta.olavarria@camdendiocese.org. Lesly A. D'Ambola, D.O., Medical Dir. Patients Assisted Annually 5,969; Total Staff 7.

[S] LEGAL SERVICES

CAMDEN. **Camden Center for Law and Social Justice, Inc.* (1994) 509 State St., 08102. Tel: 856-583-2950; Fax: 856-541-8826. Email: jdecristofaro@cclsj.org. Jeffrey S. DeCristofaro, Esq., Dir. Clients Assisted Annually 5,000; Total Staff 7.

Camden Center for Law and Social Justice, Inc. Immigration Services & Legal Assistance to the Poor, 126 N. Broadway, 08103. Tel: 856-583-2950; Fax: 856-583-2955. 509 State St., 08103. Tel: 856-966-8896; Fax: 856-583-2955. 9 N. Georgia Ave., Atlantic City, 08401. Tel: 609-348-2111; Fax: 609-348-4125.

[T] MISCELLANEOUS

CAMDEN. *Benedict's Place, Inc.*, 1845 Haddon Ave, 08103.

Catholic Partnership Schools, Camden, N.J., Inc., 808 Market St., 08102. Tel: 856-338-0966; Fax: 856-338-0965. Sr. Karen Dietrich, S.S.J., Ph.D., Exec. Dir.

The Diocesan Housing Services Corporation of The Diocese of Camden, Incorporated, 1845 Haddon Ave., 08103. Tel: 856-342-4125; Fax: 856-342-4172. Email: diocesanhousing@camdendiocese.org. Curtis H. Johnson Jr., Exec. Dir.

**Hopeworks N Camden, Inc.*, 543 State St., 08102. Tel: 856-365-4673; Fax: 856-365-8734. Email: info@hopeworks.org. Web: www.hopeworks.org. Rev. Jeffrey Putthoff, S.J., Exec. Dir.

Village at St. Peter's Inc., 1845 Haddon Ave., 08103. Curtis H. Johnson Jr., Sec.

CAPE MAY. *Soul Mates for Jesus, Inc.*, 1027 Virginia Ave., 08204.

BLACKWOOD. *Pius X Spiritual Life Center*, 1840 Peter Cheeseman Rd., 08012. Tel: 856-227-7565. In Res. Rev. David J. Klein, J.C.L.; Most Rev. Joseph Anthony Galante, D.D., J.C.D.

CHERRY HILL. *St. Mary's Auxiliary, Inc.*, 210 St. Mary's Dr., 08003. Tel: 856-874-5300. Pat Romano, Pres. Tel: 856-795-1466.

HAINESPORT. *Domicilium Corporation (Davenport Village)*, 301 Davenport Ave., 08036. Tel: 609-702-0138; Fax: 609-702-5817. Email: davenport@pennrose.com.

NORTH CAPE MAY. *Christ Child Society, Cape May County Chapter*, P.O. Box 882, 08204. Tel: 609-602-7682. Phyllis Laswell, Contact Person.

RELIGIOUS INSTITUTES OF MEN REPRESENTED IN THE DIOCESE

For further details refer to the corresponding bracketed number in the Religious Institutes of Men or Women section.

[]—*Apostles of Jesus Missionaries* (East Africa)—A.J.
[0140]—*The Augustinians* (Province of St. Thomas of Villanova, Villanova, PA)—O.S.A.
[0330]—*Brothers of the Christian Schools*—F.S.C.
[0275]—*Carmelites of Mary Immaculate*—C.M.I.
[0650]—*Congregation of the Holy Ghost*—C.S.Sp.
[0520]—*Franciscan Friars* (Prov. of the Most Holy Name of Jesus)—O.F.M.
[]—*Franciscan Friars of the Renewal*—C.F.R.
[0670]—*Hospitaller Brothers of St. John of God*—O.H.
[0690]—*Jesuit Fathers and Brothers*—S.J.
[]—*Missionaries of St. Charles Scalabrinian*—C.S.
[1120]—*Missionaries of the Sacred Hearts of Jesus and Mary*—M.SS.CC.
[]—*Norbertines*—O.Praem.
[0920]—*Oblates of St. Francis De Sales* (Wilmington-Philadelphia)—O.S.F.S.
[0430]—*Order of Preachers-Dominicans* (St. Joseph Prov., New York)—O.P.
[1190]—*Salesians of St. John Bosco*—S.D.B.
[0760]—*Society of Mary*—S.M.
[0990]—*Society of the Catholic Apostolate*—S.A.C.
[1200]—*Society of the Divine Saviour*—S.D.S.
[]—*Vincentian Congregation* (India)—V.C.

RELIGIOUS INSTITUTES OF WOMEN REPRESENTED IN THE DIOCESE

[]—*Daughter of the Heart of Mary*
[0890]—*Daughters of Our Lady of Mercy*—D.M.
[0900]—*Daughters of Our Lady of the Sacred Heart*—F.D.N.S.C.
[1105]—*Dominican Sisters of Hope*—O.P.
[1050]—*Dominican Sisters of the Perpetual Rosary (contemplative)*—O.P.
[]—*Franciscan Missionaries Sisters of the Immaculate Heart of Mary*—F.M.I.H.M.
[1365]—*Franciscan Missionary Sisters of the Infant Jesus*—F.M.I.J.
[1180]—*Franciscan Sisters of Allegany, New York*—O.S.F.
[]—*Franciscan Sisters, Missionaries of the Hearts of Jesus and Mary Immaculate*—S.F.M.
[]—*Hospitaler Sisters of Mercy* (Pleasantville, NJ)—H.S.M.
[2300]—*Little Servant Sisters of the Immaculate Conception*—L.S.I.C.
[2490]—*Medical Mission Sisters*—M.M.S.
[2717]—*Missionary Daughters of the Most Pure Virgin Mary*—M.D.P.V.M.
[2575]—*Religious Sisters of Mercy of the Americas* (Mid-Atlantic Community)—R.S.M.
[3430]—*Religious Teachers Filippini* (Morristown, NJ)—M.P.F.
[0600]—*Sisters of Charity of St. Joan of Antida*—S.C.S.J.A.
[0660]—*Sisters of Christian Charity*—S.C.C.
[]—*Sisters of Mary Immaculate of Nyeri, Kenya*—S.M.I.
[1490]—*Sisters of Saint Francis of the Neumann Communities*
[3893]—*Sisters of Saint Joseph of Chestnut Hill, Philadelphia*—S.S.J.
[1650]—*Sisters of St. Francis of Philadelphia*—O.S.F.
[3890]—*Sisters of St. Joseph of Peace*—C.S.J.P.
[2170]—*Sisters, Servants of the Immaculate Heart of Mary* (Immaculata)—I.H.M.
[2160]—*Sisters, Servants of the Immaculate Heart of Mary* (Scranton)—I.H.M.

CEMETERIES

Camden Diocesan Center, 631 Market St., 08102. Larry Reader, Acting Dir. Tel: 856-583-2821.

ATLANTIC COUNTY

DOROTHY
St. Bernard Cemetery Tel: 609-625-2123. (Holy Cross Cemetery, Rte. 40, Mays Landing)

HAMMONTON
Holy Sepulchre Cemetery Tel: 609-704-5945. (St. Mary of Mt. Carmel)

LANDISVILLE
Our Lady of Victories Cemetery Tel: 856-691-1290 (Call Sacred Heart Cemetery).

MAYS LANDING
Holy Cross Cemetery & Mausoleum, Rte. 40, 08330. Tel: 609-625-2123.

PLEASANT MILLS
Our Lady of the Assumption Cemetery Closed, (Call Holy Cross Cemetery, Mays Landing, 609-625-2123)

CAMDEN COUNTY

BELLMAWR
St. Mary's Cemetery & Mausoleum Tel: 856-931-1570.

BERLIN
Gate of Heaven Cemetery Tel: 856-767-3354.

CEDARBROOK
Sacred Heart Cemetery Tel: 856-767-0719. (Christ the Redeemer, Atco)

CHEWS LANDING
St. Joseph's Cemetery (St. Joseph, Camden), Tel: 856-228-7588.

CHERRY HILL
Calvary Cemetery & Mausoleum Tel: 856-663-3345.

CAPE MAY COUNTY

CLERMONT
Resurrection Cemetery Tel: 609-624-1284.

COLD SPRINGS
St. Mary's Cemetery & Mausoleum Tel: 609-624-1284.

GOSHEN
St. Elizabeth's Cemetery Tel: 609-624-1284.

WOODBINE
St. Casimir's Cemetery Tel: 609-624-1284.

CUMBERLAND COUNTY

BRIDGETON
St. Mary's Cemetery Tel: 856-455-2323. (Holy Cross)

EAST VINELAND
St. Mary's Cemetery Tel: 856-691-7526. (Padre Pio)
Our Lady of Pompeii Cemetery Tel: 856-691-7526. (Padre Pio)

MILLVILLE
Holy Cross Cemetery Tel: 856-825-0021. (All Saints, Millville)

ROSENHAYN
St. Mary's Cemetery Tel: 856-455-2323. (Holy Cross, Bridgeton)

VINELAND
Sacred Heart Cemetery & Mausoleum Tel: 856-691-1290.

GLOUCESTER COUNTY

GLASSBORO
St. Bridget's Cemetery Tel: 856-881-2753. (St. Bridget Church)

MULLICA HILL
Holy Name Cemetery Tel: 856-478-2294. (Catholic Community of the Holy Spirit)

NEWFIELD
All Saints Cemetery Tel: 856-697-1098.

SWEDESBORO
St. Joseph's Cemetery Tel: 856-767-3354.

WILLIAMSTOWN
St. Mary's Cemetery Tel: 856-767-3354.

SALEM COUNTY

SALEM
St. Mary's Cemetery Tel: 856-299-3833. (St. Gabriel Church, Carneys Point)

WOODSTOWN
St. Joseph's Cemetery Tel: 856-478-2294. (Catholic Community of the Holy Spirit, Mullica Hill)

NECROLOGY

† Joynes, Rev. Msgr. Joseph P., (Retired)—Died Aug. 6, 2011
† Kennedy, Rev. Msgr. Edward J., (Retired)—Died March 13, 2011
† Finnerty, Peter F., (Retired)—Died May 21, 2011
† Pastore, Peter J., (Retired)—Died April 16, 2011
† Sullivan, Brendan V., (Retired)—Died April 30, 2011
† Weaver, Patrick J.—Died May 31, 2011

An asterisk (*) denotes an organization that has established tax-exempt status directly with the IRS and is not covered by the USCCB Group Ruling.

Diocese of Charleston

(Dioecesis Carolopolitana)

Most Reverend

ROBERT E. GUGLIELMONE

Bishop of Charleston; ordained April 8, 1978; appointed Bishop of Charleston January 24, 2009; installed March 25, 2009. *Office: 119 Broad St., P.O. Box 818, Charleston, SC 29402.*

Most Reverend

DAVID B. THOMPSON, D.D., J.C.L.

Retired Bishop of Charleston; ordained May 27, 1950; appointed Coadjutor Bishop of Charleston April 22, 1989; ordained May 24, 1989; succeeded to Bishop of Charleston February 22, 1990; retired July 13, 1999. *Res.: 4479 Downing Pl., Mount Pleasant, SC 29466.* Tel: 843-971-2810.

Chancery Office: 119 Broad St., P.O. Box 818, Charleston, SC 29402. Tel: 843-853-2130; Fax: 843-724-6387.

Web: www.catholic-doc.org

Email: smakowski@catholic-doc.org

ESTABLISHED JULY 11, 1820.

Square Miles 31,055.

Comprises the State of South Carolina.

For legal titles of parishes and diocesan institutions, consult the Chancery Office.

STATISTICAL OVERVIEW

Personnel	
Bishop	1
Retired Bishops	1
Priests: Diocesan Active in Diocese	59
Priests: Diocesan Active Outside Diocese	6
Priests: Retired, Sick or Absent	21
Number of Diocesan Priests	86
Religious Priests in Diocese	43
Total Priests in Diocese	129
Extern Priests in Diocese	33
Ordinations:	
Diocesan Priests	3
Religious Priests	1
Transitional Deacons	2
Permanent Deacons in Diocese	124
Total Brothers	20
Total Sisters	119
Parishes	
Parishes	92
With Resident Pastor:	
Resident Diocesan Priests	48
Resident Religious Priests	15
Without Resident Pastor:	
Administered by Priests	29
Administered by Professed Religious Men	2
Administered by Religious Women	2
Completely Vacant	1
Missions	23
Pastoral Centers	1
Professional Ministry Personnel:	
Brothers	4
Sisters	18
Lay Ministers	134
Welfare	
Catholic Hospitals	3
Total Assisted	313,244
Homes for the Aged	1
Total Assisted	26
Special Centers for Social Services	9
Total Assisted	20,561
Educational	
Diocesan Students in Other Seminaries	11
Total Seminarians	11
High Schools, Diocesan and Parish	2
Total Students	1,103
High Schools, Private	2
Total Students	646
Elementary Schools, Diocesan and Parish	28
Total Students	5,368
Catechesis/Religious Education:	
High School Students	1,697
Elementary Students	12,180
Total Students under Catholic Instruction	21,005
Teachers in the Diocese:	
Priests	4
Brothers	3
Sisters	25
Lay Teachers	599
Vital Statistics	
Receptions into the Church:	
Infant Baptism Totals	2,882
Minor Baptism Totals	303
Adult Baptism Totals	137
Received into Full Communion	412
First Communions	3,348
Confirmations	2,372
Marriages:	
Catholic	418
Interfaith	226
Total Marriages	644
Deaths	1,253
Total Catholic Population	196,658
Total Population	4,625,364

Former Bishops—Rt. Revs. JOHN ENGLAND, D.D., first Bishop; cons. Sept. 21, 1820; died April 11, 1842; WILLIAM CLANCY, D.D., cons. Dec. 21, 1834, Coadjutor; made Vicar-Apostolic of British Guiana, April 12, 1837; died June 19, 1847; IGNATIUS A. REYNOLDS, D.D., second Bishop; cons. March 19, 1844; died March 6, 1855; PATRICK N. LYNCH, D.D., third Bishop; cons. March 14, 1858; died Feb. 26, 1882; HENRY P. NORTHROP, D.D., fourth Bishop; consecrated Titular-Bishop of Rosalia and Vicar-Apostolic of North Carolina, Jan. 8, 1882; transferred to Charleston, by brief dated Jan. 27, 1883; died June 7, 1916; WILLIAM T. RUSSELL, D.D., fifth Bishop; cons. March 15, 1917; died March 18, 1927; Most Revs. EMMET M. WALSH, D.D., sixth Bishop; cons. Sept. 8, 1927; transferred to Youngstown, Ohio, as Coadjutor Bishop, Sept. 8, 1949; JOHN J. RUSSELL, D.D., seventh Bishop; cons. March 14, 1950; transferred to Bishop of Richmond, July 10, 1958; PAUL J. HALLINAN, D.D., eighth Bishop; cons. Oct. 28, 1958; transferred to Archbishop of Atlanta, Feb. 21, 1962; FRANCIS F. REH, S.T.L., J.C.D. (Retired), ninth Bishop; cons. June 29, 1962; appt. Titular Bishop of Macriana in Mauretania and Rector of North American College, Rome, Italy, Sept. 5, 1964; transferred to Saginaw, Dec. 18, 1968; installed Feb. 26, 1969; retired April 29, 1980; ERNEST L. UNTERKOEFLER, D.D., J.C.D., S.T.L., tenth Bishop; ord. May 18, 1944; appt. Titular Bishop of Latopolis and Auxiliary Bishop of Richmond, Dec. 13, 1961; cons. Feb. 22, 1962; appt. Bishop of Charleston, Dec. 12, 1964; resigned Feb. 22, 1990; died Jan. 4, 1993; DAVID B. THOMPSON, D.D., J.C.L. (Retired), eleventh Bishop; ord. May 27, 1950; appt. Coadjutor Bishop of Charleston April 22, 1989; ord. May 24, 1989; succeeded to Bishop of Charleston Feb. 22, 1990; retired July 13, 1999; ROBERT J. BAKER, twelfth Bishop; ord. March 21, 1970; appt. Bishop of Charleston July 13, 1999; cons. Sept. 29, 1999; appt. Bishop of Birmingham Aug. 14, 2007; installed Oct. 2, 2007.

Curia—Rev. Msgr. RICHARD D. HARRIS, V.G.; Sr. SANDRA MAKOWSKI, S.S.M.N., J.C.L.; Rev. Msgr. CHARLES H. ROWLAND, P.A., J.C.L.; Very Rev. RONALD R. CELLINI, V.F.; Mr. JOHN L. BARKER, CFO; Sr. CANICE ADAMS, SS.C.M.; JACQUALINE KASPROWSKI; CAROLINE WEISBERG.

Vicar General's Office—Rev. Msgr. RICHARD D. HARRIS, V.G., Vicar Gen. Tel: 843-853-2130, Ext. 207; KATHRYN DANNELLY, Exec. Administrative Asst. to the Vicar Gen., 3512 Devine St., Columbia, SC 29205. Tel: 803-540-1920. Email: kdannelly@catholic-doc.org; Deacon JOSEPH CAHILL, Task Force Coord. (Chancery West). Tel: 843-402-9115, Ext. 54. Email: joe@catholic-doc.org.

Chancellor—Sr. SANDRA MAKOWSKI, S.S.M.N., J.C.L., 119 Broad St., P.O. Box 818, Charleston, 29402. Tel: 843-853-2130, Ext. 201; ANDREA A. CRAWFORD, Administrative Asst. to the Office of Matrimonial Concerns. Tel: 843-853-2130, Ext. 202. Email: andrea@catholic-doc.org.

Chancery West—1662 Ingram Rd., Charleston, 29407. Tel: 843-402-9115; Fax: 843-402-9071; 843-402-7724 (Christian Formation and The Office of Research and Planning).

Diocesan Web Page—Web: www.catholic-doc.org.

Archives—BRIAN P. FAHEY, M.L.I.S., Archivist. Tel: 843-577-1017; Fax: 843-724-6387. Email: bfahey@catholic-doc.org; MELISSA J. BRONHEIM, M.L.I.S., Asst. Archivist. Tel: 843-724-8372. Email: mbronheim@catholic-doc.org; CHARLES WUJCIK, Clerical Asst. Tel: 843-724-8372. Email: cwujcik@catholic-doc.org.

Bishop's Office—JOSEPH OHENS, Exec. Asst. to Bishop. Tel: 843-853-2130; ANDREA A. CRAWFORD, Administrative Asst. Tel: 843-853-2130, Ext. 202. Email: andrea@catholic-doc.org; JONATHAN FRENCH, Admin. Asst. Tel: 843-853-2130. Email: jfrench@catholic-doc.org.

Office of Finance—Mr. JOHN L. BARKER, CFO. Tel: 843-402-9115, Ext. 11. Email: jbarker@catholic-doc.org; CRISTINA G. NATIVIDAD, Exec. Administrative Asst. to CFO. Tel: 843-402-9115, Ext. 30. Email: cnatividad@catholic-doc.org; AMANDA BREEN, Administrative Asst. Tel: 843-402-9115, Ext. 12. Email: abreen@catholic-doc.org; STEPHANIE POSDA, Bldg. & Renovations Coord. Tel: 843-402-9115, Ext. 46. Email: sposda@catholic-doc.org; PAT SULLIVAN, Process Analyst. Tel: 843-402-9115, Ext. 31. Email: psullivan@catholic-doc.org; TERRI BRISSON, Dir. Financial Svcs. Tel: 843-402-9115, Ext. 37. Email: tbrisson@catholic-doc.org; JUN ZHANG, Treasury Analyst. Tel: 843-402-9115, Ext. 85; Fax: 843-402-9071 (Chancery West). Email: junzhang@catholic-doc.org; DEBBY CARDENAS, Financial Analyst I. Tel: 843-402-9115, Ext. 33. Email: dcardenas@catholic-doc.org; JOYCE KIERNAN, Financial Analyst II. Tel: 843-402-9115, Ext. 48. Email: jkiernan@catholic-doc.org; TAMRA BOWMAN, Accounting Technician. Tel: 843-402-9115, Ext. 42. Email: tbowman@catholic-doc.org; SALLY MIRANDA, Accountant I. Tel: 843-402-9115, Ext. 34. Email: smiranda@catholic-doc.org; ELIZABETH HUGHES, Accounting Mgr. Tel: 843-402-9115, Ext. 22. Email: ehughes@catholic-doc.org.

Bishop's Residence and Chancery Maintenance—DONALD GLOVER, Mgr. Bishop's Residence & Chef. Tel: 843-327-1212. Email: dglover@catholic-doc.org; REGINA GREEN, Housekeeper. Tel: 843-609-6653; WADE MCDANIEL, Maintenance. Tel: 843-853-2130, Ext. 232; EDDIE WOODS, Maintenance & Mechanical Technician (Chancery West). Tel: 843-402-9115, Ext. 36. Email: ewoods@catholic-doc.org.

Presbyteral Council—Most Rev. ROBERT E. GUGLIELMONE; Rev. Msgrs. RICHARD D. HARRIS, V.G.; LAWRENCE B. MCINERNY, J.C.L.; CHESTER M. MOCZYDLOWSKI; CHARLES H. ROWLAND, P.A., J.C.L.; Very Rev. RONALD R. CELLINI, V.F.; Very Rev. Msgr. JOSEPH F. HANLEY, V.F.; Very Revs. C. ALEXANDER MCDONALD, V.F.; JAY SCOTT NEWMAN, J.C.L., V.F.; KARL ROESCH, O.S.B., V.F.; Revs. RAYMOND J. CARLO; D. ANTHONY DROZE; MICHAEL C. OKERE; TEOFILO TRUJILLO; DENNIS B. WILLEY; GREGORY B. WILSON.

Campus Ministry— (See Christian Formation)

Canonical Consultant—Rev. Msgr. THOMAS X. HOFMANN, J.C.L. Tel: 843-724-8363.

Carter-May Home—JANINE BAUDER, Admin., 1660 Ingram Rd., Charleston, 29407. Tel: 843-556-8314 (Main); 843-402-5460 (Office); Fax: 843-556-6879.

Office of Information Technology—MARK T. HOUPT, Dir. Tel: 843-402-9115, Ext. 24. Email: mthoupt@catholic-doc.org.

Continuing Education for Priests—Rev. Msgr. EDWARD D. LOFTON, 11001 Dorchester Rd., Summerville, 29485. Tel: 843-875-5002; Fax: 843-875-4884.

Office of Tribunal—Mailing Address: P.O. Box 818, Charleston, 29402. Tel: 843-724-8363. Rev. Msgrs. CHARLES H. ROWLAND, P.A., J.C.L., Judicial Vicar; THOMAS X. HOFMANN, J.C.L., Adjutant Judicial Vicar; MARY E. MCKENZIE, Moderator of the Tribunal Chancery; LUCINDA BRYAN, Procurator, Advocate & Case Analyst; JACKELINE NIEDERHEITMANN, Hispanic Desk Case Analyst & Ecclesiastical Notary; MEG WALTER, Procurator, Advocate & Case Analyst; Deacon THOMAS J. BARONOWSKI, Procurator & Advocate; Revs. BRYAN P. BABICK, SL.L., Procurator & Advocate; GABRIEL J. SMITH, Procurator & Advocate; CHARLES WUJCIK, Ecclesiastical Notary, Sec. & Tribunal Archival Records Technician. Phone inquiries are accepted Mon.-Thurs. 10:30-11:30 am & 1:30-4 pm and Fri. 10:30-11:30 am & 1:30-3:30 pm. All petitions for a sanatio, declarations of invalidity, and other questions related to divorced persons should be sent to the Office of Tribunal. All other prenuptial matters, requests for dispensations and permissions should be sent to the: Office for Matrimonial Concerns and Dispensations, P.O. Box 818, Charleston, SC 29402. Tel: 843-853-2130, ext. 202.

Judges—Most Rev. DAVID B. THOMPSON, D.D., J.C.L. (Retired); MARY E. MCKENZIE.

Defenders of the Bond—Revs. EDWARD W. FITZGERALD, J.C.L.; C. THOMAS MILES; Sr. SANDRA MAKOWSKI, S.S.M.N., J.C.L.; Dr. MARGARET POLL CHALMERS, J.C.D., J.D.; Sr. CHRISTINA MURPHY, S.N.D.deN.; Deacon J. WESCOAT SANDLIN, Esq.

Promoter of Justice—Rev. C. THOMAS MILES.

College of Consultors—Rev. Msgrs. RICHARD D. HARRIS, V.G.; CHARLES H. ROWLAND, P.A., J.C.L.; JOSEPH F. HANLEY JR., V.F.; Very Revs. RONALD R. CELLINI, V.F.; C. ALEXANDER MCDONALD, V.F.; KARL J. ROESCH, O.S.B., V.F.; JAY SCOTT NEWMAN, J.C.L., V.F.

Deans—Rev. Msgr. JOSEPH F. HANLEY JR., V.F., Coastal Deanery. Tel: 843-556-0801; Fax: 843-556-2851. Email: blessac@bellsouth.net; Very Revs. RONALD R. CELLINI, V.F., Lowcountry Deanery. Tel: 843-815-3100. Email: info@sgg.cc; C. ALEXANDER MCDONALD, V.F., Midlands Deanery. Tel: 803-788-0811; Fax: 803-788-1501. Email: frmcdonald@sc.twcbc.com; KARL J. ROESCH, O.S.B., V.F., Pee Dee Deanery. Tel: 843-332-7773; Fax: 843-332-2812. Email: jroeschjr@roadrunner.com; JAY SCOTT NEWMAN, J.C.L., V.F., Piedmont Deanery. Tel: 864-271-8422.

Family Life Services—Rev. JAMES L. LEBLANC, Vicar Family Life, Mailing Address: St. Andrew Catholic Church, 3501 N. Kings Hwy., Ste. 102, Myrtle Beach, 29577. Tel: 843-448-5930; Fax: 843-448-3947; KATHY SCHMUGGE, Dir., 2879 Hwy. 160 W., PMB #4336, Fort Mill, 29708. Tel: 803-547-5063. Email: kschmugge@catholic-doc.org; CHRISTY BROWN, Post Abortion Ministry Coord. Tel: 803-554-6088. Email: grace4healing@gmail.com; KELLI BALL, NFP Coord., Mailing Address: Diocese of Charleston, NFP Coord., P.O. Box 2, Lexington, 29071. Email: kelliball@yahoo.com.

Finance Council—Rev. Msgr. RICHARD D. HARRIS, V.G.; Mr. JOHN L. BARKER, CFO; JOSEPH J. KEENAN; CHRISTINA MYERS; SCOTT CRACRAFT; WILLIAM C. ROBINSON; DANIEL P. FANNING; EUGENE J. ZURLO; WILLIAM CONDY; DARRYL REYNA; PERRY KEITH WARING; CRISTINA G. NATIVIDAD, Recorder.

Office of Ethnic Ministries—Ms. KATHLEEN MERRITT, Dir., 204 Douthit St., A1, Greenville, 29601. Tel: 864-242-2233, Ext. 214; Fax: 864-331-2631. Email: kathleen@catholic-doc.org; MICHAEL TRAN, Asst. Dir. Tel: 864-704-6559. Email: mtran@catholic-doc.org; PATRICIA WEGMAN, Administrative Asst. Tel: 864-242-2233, Ext. 209. Email: pwegman@catholic-doc.org.

Vicar for African-American Catholics—Rev. PAUL M. WILLIAMS, O.F.M., 1303 McLees Rd., Anderson, 29621. Tel: 864-225-5341.

Vicar for Hispanic Ministry—Rev. TEOFILO TRUJILLO, 2252 Woodruff Rd., Simpsonville, 29681. Tel: 864-288-4884.

Vicar for Vietnamese Ministry—Rev. DAVID Q. PHAN, O.F.M., 307 Gower St., Greenville, 29611-4930. Tel: 864-233-7717.

Bishop's Missionary Support Committee—Rev. Msgr. EDWARD D. LOFTON, Mailing Address: St. Theresa the Little Flower, 11001 Dorchester Rd., Summerville, 29485.

Building & Renovation Advisory Committee—Rev. Msgr. RICHARD D. HARRIS, V.G., Chm.; Mr. JOHN L. BARKER; Deacon JOSEPH CAHILL; JOSEPH DEPALMA; LAWRENCE FLOOD; ROSS KUYKENDALL; JIM POSDA; WILLIAM ROBERTS; FRANK SZEWCZAK; MATTHEW DWYER; STEPHANIE POSDA, Coord. Tel: 843-402-9115, Ext. 46. Email: sposda@catholic-doc.org.

Catholic Charities—

Main Office—CAROLINE WEISBERG, Dir. Tel: 803-708-5146; Fax: 843-402-9071. Email: cweisberg@catholic-doc.org; JENNIFER ELKINS, Coord. Tel: 843-402-9115, Ext. 15. Email: jelkins@catholic-doc.org.

Elderly Services—JANINE BAUDER, Admin., Carter May Home/St. Joseph Residence, 1660 Ingram Rd., Charleston, 29407. Tel: 843-556-8314; Fax: 843-556-6879.

Coastal Deanery—HELEN O'LEARY, Regl. Coord., St. John Church, 3921 St. John's Ave., North Charleston, 29405. Tel: 843-308-9361; Fax: 843-744-2792. Email: holeary@catholic-doc.org.

Immigration Services—EMILY GUERRERO, Immigration Svcs. Supvr., 1145 Six Mile Rd., Mount Pleasant, 29466. Tel: 843-388-0089; Fax: 843-849-0943. Email: eguerrero@catholic-doc.org.

Lowcountry Deanery—PAMELA RICE, Regl. Coord., 1662 Ingram Rd., Charleston, 29407. Tel: 843-812-3078. Email: price@catholic-doc.org.

Midlands Deanery—MARY TRIVISONNO, Regl. Coord., Mailing Address: P.O. Box 7245, Columbia, 29202. Tel: 803-254-9776; Fax: 803-252-7605. Email: mtriv@catholic-doc.org.

Pee Dee Deanery—DARYL KANGARLOO, Regl. Coord. & Senior Care Mgmt. Coord., 537-B Hwy. 90, Conway, 29526. Tel: 843-234-1999; Fax: 843-234-3132. Email: dkangarloo@catholic-doc.org.

Piedmont Deanery—Deacon GABRIEL CUERVO, Regl. Coord. & Coord. Hispanic Outreach, Mailing Address: 204 Douthit St., Ste. A1, Greenville, 29601. Tel: 864-242-2233, Ext. 208; Fax: 864-242-1387. Email: gcuervo@catholic-doc.org.

Catholic Women, Council of—Very Rev. FABIO REFOSCO, C.O., Moderator, Mailing Address: The Rock Hill Oratory, P.O. Box 11586, Rock Hill, 29731-1586. Tel: 803-327-2097.

Cemeteries—WARREN STUCKEY, Dir. Cemeteries. Email: wstuckey@catholic-doc.org. Holy Cross Cemetery; PAMELA PAQUETTE, Administrative Asst., Holy Cross Cemetery. Tel: 843-795-2111; Fax: 843-576-4925; JIMMY LYLES, Supvr., St. Lawrence Cemetery. Tel: 843-723-8228.

Charismatic Renewals and Prayer Groups—Deacon JACK L. CROCKER, D.D.S., Diocesan Liaison, 220 Cirrus Ln., Gilbert, 29054. Tel: 803-356-3042. Email: jcrocker3@windstream.net.

Chief Financial Officer—Mr. JOHN L. BARKER. Tel: 843-402-9115, Ext. 12. Email: jbarker@catholic-doc.org. (Chancery West).

Counseling Services—MARA CALDERON, Ph.D., Licensed Clinical Psychologist. Tel: 843-402-9115, Ext. 17 Services in English and Spanish.

Divine Worship & Sacraments, Vicar for—Rev. BRYAN P. BABICK, SL.L., Vicar. Tel: 843-853-2130, Ext. 215. Email: frbabick@catholic-doc.org.

Catholic Schools Office—Mrs. SANDRA LEATHERWOOD, Asst. to Supt. of Schools. Email: sleatherwood@catholic-doc.org; KIMBERLY HOPKINS, Coord. Tel: 843-402-9115, Ext. 19. Email: khopkins@catholic-doc.org.

Catechesis & Christian Initiation for Parishes and Schools—Sr. PAMELA SMITH, S.S.C.M., Dir. Tel: 843-402-9115, Ext. 35. Email: psmith@catholic-doc.org; CATHY ROCHE, Administrative Asst. Tel: 843-402-9115, Ext. 18. Email: cathy@catholic-doc.org.

Youth & Young Adult Ministry Office—JERRY WHITE, Dir. Tel: 843-402-9115, Ext. 38; Fax: 843-402-7724. Email: jerry@catholic-doc.org. (Chancery West); VACANT, Assoc. Dir. Young Adult Ministry. Tel: 843-670-2586. Email: jerry@catholic-doc.org; RHINA MEDINA, Jr. Assoc. Dir. Hispanic Youth Ministry, Mailing Address: P.O. Box 23689, Columbia, 29224. Tel: 843-696-9846. Email: rmedina@catholic-doc.org; AMANDA PARHAM, Administrative Asst. Tel: 843-402-9115, Ext. 20.

Campus Ministry—JAMES GROVE, Dir. Catholic Campus Ministry, Mailing Address: c/o St. Patrick, P.O. Box 20726, Charleston, 29413. Tel: 843-937-5993. Email: cofcatholics@aol.com.

Holy Childhood Association—Rev. Msgr. EDWARD D. LOFTON, Dir., Mailing Address: St. Theresa, The Little Flower, 11001 Dorchester Rd., Summerville, 29485. Tel: 843-875-5002; Fax: 843-875-4884.

Human Resources—MARY LOUISE HUDSON, Dir. Tel: 843-402-9115, Ext. 21. Email: mlhudson@catholic-doc.org; RIITTA WIDELSKI, Sr. Generalist & Benefits Specialist. Tel: 843-402-9115, Ext. 56. Email: rwidelski@catholic-doc.org. (Chancery West); JAMIE ZBYROWSKI, Administrative Asst. Tel: 843-402-9115, Ext. 47. Email: jzbyrowski@catholic-doc.org.

Insurance—TRACY BATES, Claims/Risk Mgr., Catholic Mutual, 901 Island Park Dr., Ste. 205, Charleston, 29492. Tel: 843-884-9696; Fax: 843-884-9979. Email: tbates@catholicmutual.org; CINDY ACUFF, Asst. Tel: 843-884-9776. Email: cacuff@catholicmutual.org.

Investment Council—Rev. Msgr. RICHARD D. HARRIS, V.G.; Mr. JOHN L. BARKER; SCOTT CRACRAFT; JOSEPH J. KEENAN; WILLIAM C. ROBINSON; CRISTINA G. NATIVIDAD, Recorder.

Marian Programs—Rev. STANLEY SMOLENSKI, S.P.M.A., Dir., 300 Ashton Ave., Kingstree, 29556. Tel: 843-355-3527.

Diocesan Master of Ceremonies—Rev. BRYAN P. BABICK, SL.L. Tel: 843-853-2130, Ext. 215. Email: frbabick@catholic-doc.org.

Ministry for People with Disabilities—Office of Social Ministry. Tel: 843-402-9115, Ext. 15; Fax: 843-402-9071 (Chancery West).

Newspaper— "The Catholic Miscellany" Tel: 843-724-8375. DEIRDRE C. MAYS, Editor. Tel: 843-724-8375. Email: editor@catholic-doc.org; AMY WISE TAYLOR, Staff Writer. Tel: 843-853-6302. Email: ataylor@catholic-doc.org; STEPHANIE STOCKTON, Advertising Mgr. Tel: 843-724-6383. Email: sstockton@catholic-doc.org; PEGGY CARLILE, Circulation Coord. Tel: 843-724-8375; Fax: 843-724-8368. Email: pcarlile@catholic-doc.org; CHRISTINA LEE KNAUSS, Staff Writer. Tel: 803-238-7610. Email: cknauss@catholic-doc.org.

Office of Child Protection Services—Rev. TITUS FULCHER, Dir., 119 Broad St., Charleston, 29402. Tel: 843-853-2130, Ext. 209; 843-270-0727. Email: frtitus@catholic-doc.org; frtitus@comcast.net; BONNIE SIGERS, Safe Environment Mgr. Tel: 843-853-2130, Ext. 210. Email: bsigers@catholic-doc.org; JENNA WEBB, Coord. Tel: 843-853-2130, Ext. 216. Email: jwebb@catholic-doc.org; DEBBIE TOMAK, Administrative Asst. Tel: 843-853-2130, Ext. 206. Email: dtomak@catholic-doc.org.

Propagation of the Faith—Rev. Msgr. EDWARD D. LOFTON, Dir.; HELENA MONIZ, Coord., 11001 Dorchester Rd., Summerville, 29485. Tel: 843-875-5002; Fax: 843-875-4884. Email: propagation@sttheresachurch.com.

Office of Publications and Information—DEIRDRE C. MAYS, Dir., 119 Broad St., Charleston, 29402. Tel: 843-724-8375; Fax: 843-724-8368. Email: editor@catholic-doc.org; STEPHANIE STOCKTON, Video

Producer. Tel: 843-724-6383; Fax: 843-724-8368. Email: sstockton@catholic-doc.org; PEGGY CARLILE, Administrative Asst. Tel: 843-724-8375; Fax: 843-724-8368. Email: pcarlile@catholic-doc.org.

Respect Life— (Please see Catholic Charities Regional Offices)

Vocations—Rev. JEFFREY KIRBY, S.T.L., Vicar. Email: frkirby@charlestonvocations.com; RHETT B. WILLIAMS, Bilingual Administrative Asst. Email: rhett@charlestonvocations.com; NANCY M. TRAUTMAN, Administrative Asst. (Seminarians). Email: nancy@charlestonvocations.com.

The Drexel House - Catholic Residence for Men—34 Wentworth St., Charleston, 29401. Tel: 843-727-6727; Fax: 843-723-5760. Rev. JEFFREY KIRBY, S.T.L., Dir.; RHETT B. WILLIAMS, Pres. Email: rhett@charlestonvocations.com.

Bishop's Missionary League—Mailing Address: P.O. Box 818, Charleston, 29402. Tel: 843-853-2130, Ext. 0.

Cursillo Movement—GABRIEL TIMPANO, Lay Dir., 256 Tall Pines Way, Unit 6-2B, Pawleys Island, 29585. Tel: 843-543-0138. Email: gtimpano@sc.rr.com. Web: www.southcarolinacursillo.org; Deacon ANDRE J.P. GUILLET, Spiritual Advisor (Chancery West).

Diaconate, Office of—Rev. EDWARD FITZGERALD, J.C.L., Dir.; Deacon ANDRE J.P. GUILLET, Asst. to Dir. of the Diaconate. Tel: 843-402-9115, Ext. 77. Email: aguillet@catholic-doc.org; CATHY ROCHE, Administrative Asst., 1662 Ingram Rd., Charleston, 29407. Tel: 843-402-9115, Ext. 18. Email: cathy@catholic-doc.org.

Campaign for Human Development—Office of Social Ministry. Tel: 843-402-9115, Ext. 15; Fax: 843-402-9071. (Chancery West)

Office of Stewardship & Mission Advancement—MATTHEW DWYER, Dir. Stewardship & Devel. Tel: 843-853-2130, Ext. 213. Email: mdwyer@catholic-doc.org; LILIA CORREA, Bilingual Annual Appeal Administrative Asst. Tel: 843-853-2130, Ext. 212. Email: lilia@catholic-doc.org; JOHN BEYER, Administrative Asst. Tel: 843-853-2130, Ext. 211. Email: jbeyer@catholic-doc.org.

Personnel Committee—Very Revs. RONALD R. CELLINI, V.F., Chm.; C. ALEXANDER MCDONALD, V.F.; Rev. PAUL M. WILLIAMS, O.F.M.; Rev. Msgrs. RICHARD D. HARRIS, V.G.; JOSEPH F. HANLEY JR., V.F.; Very Revs. KARL J. ROESCH, O.S.B., V.F.; JAY SCOTT NEWMAN, J.C.L., V.F.; Rev. TEOFILO TRUJILLO.

Priests' Retirement—Rev. FRANCIS J. TRAVIS, Vicar, Our Lady of Perpetual Help, 1709 Lyttleton St., Camden, 29020. Tel: 803-432-6131. Email: ftravis@aol.com.

Priest Retirement Committee—Mr. JOHN L. BARKER, Chm.; Rev. Msgr. RICHARD D. HARRIS, V.G.; Rev. JAMES L. LEBLANC; Rev. Msgr. EDWARD D. LOFTON; Rev. JOHN M. ZIMMERMAN; SCOTT CRACRAFT; JOSEPH J. KEENAN; CRISTINA G. NATIVIDAD, Recorder.

Scouting Programs—Rev. JEFFREY KIRBY, S.T.L., Scout Chap., The Drexel House, 34 Wentworth St., Charleston, 29401. Tel: 800-660-4102. Email: frkirby@charlestonvocations.com; JIM WEISKIRCHER, Scout Chm., 745 Glenridge Rd., Spartanburg, 29301. Tel: 864-706-0768. Email: weiskircher1@charter.net.

Sites & Boundaries Committee—Rev. Msgr. RICHARD D. HARRIS, V.G.; Mr. JOHN L. BARKER. Email: jbarker@catholic-doc.org. (Chancery West).

Office of Research and Planning—HEATHER CLARK, Admin. Asst. Tel: 843-402-9115, Ext. 44; Fax: 843-402-7724. Email: hclark@catholic-doc.org.

Vietnamese Apostolate— (See Office of Ethnic Ministries)

African-American Catholics— (See Office of Ethnic Ministries)

Administrator for Ecumenical & Interreligious Affairs—Very Rev. C. ALEXANDER MCDONALD, V.F.; MELISSA WALKER, Admin., Mailing Address: P.O. Box 247, Chapin, 29036. Tel: 803-345-7407. Email: ecumenical@pal-metto.com.

Education, Dept. of— (See Christian Formation)

Hispanic Ministry— (See Office of Ethnic Ministries)

Office of Black Catholic Ministry— (See Office of Ethnic Ministries)

Vicar for Priests—Very Rev. RONALD R. CELLINI, V.F., Vicar; LARRY PAPINEAU, Coord. Tel: 843-853-2130, Ext. 208; Fax: 843-958-2162. Email: lpapineau@catholic-doc.org.

Victim Assistance Coordinator—LUISA STOREN, 886 Johnnie Dodds Blvd., Mount Pleasant, 29464. Tel: 843-856-0748; 800-921-8122 (Toll Free); Fax: 843-856-0753; 800-923-8122 (Toll Free).

Seminary Admissions Board—Rev. JEFFREY KIRBY, S.T.L., Vicar for Vocations; Rev. Msgr. RICHARD D. HARRIS, V.G.; Very Rev. RONALD R. CELLINI, V.F.; Revs. TEOFILO TRUJILLO; PATRICK TUTTLE, O.F.M.; Deacon JOSEPH F. CAHILL; Ms. MARY ANN FEY, L.P.C.; Mr. KEVIN HALL, Esq.; Mr. KEITH F. KISER; Dr. STEPHEN PLATTE, M.D.

Volunteers, Office of—Deacon JEROME P. REMKIEWICZ, Diocesan Volunteer Prog. Admin., 34 Wentworth St., Charleston, 29401. Tel: 843-723-5758; Fax: 843-723-5760.

Youth Ministry— (See Christian Formation)

Office of Media Relations—MARIA A. ASELAGE, Dir., 119 Broad St., Charleston, 29401. Tel: 843-853-2130, Ext. 218.

CLERGY, PARISHES, MISSIONS AND PAROCHIAL SCHOOLS

GREATER CHARLESTON

(CHARLESTON COUNTY)

1—CATHEDRAL OF ST. JOHN THE BAPTIST (1821) Rev. Msgr. Steven L. Brovey, Rector; Rev. Jeremi Wodecki, Parochial Vicar; Deacons Charles Olimpio; Jerome P. Remkiewicz.
Mailing & Res. Address: 120 Broad St., 29401. Tel: 843-937-8504 (Res.); 843-724-8395; Fax: 843-724-6386 (Parish). Email: cathedral@charlestoncatholiccathedral.org. Web: www.catholic-doc.org/cathedral.
See Charleston Catholic School, Charleston under Sacred Heart, Charleston for details.
Catechesis/Religious Program—Students 192.

2—ST. BENEDICT (1999) Rev. Msgr. Chester M. Moczydlowski.
Church: 950 Darrell Creek Tr., Mount Pleasant, 29466. Tel: 843-216-0039; Fax: 843-971-6789. Email: office@stbenedictparish.org. Web: www.stbenedictparish.org.
Catechesis/Religious Program—Students 250.

3—BLESSED SACRAMENT (1944) Rev. Msgr. Joseph F. Hanley Jr.; Rev. Venance Max Kishe, Parochial Vicar; Deacon James R. Moore.
Res.: 9 St. Teresa Dr., 29407. Tel: 843-556-0801; Fax: 843-556-2851. Email: blesssac@bellsouth.net. Web: www.blsac.org.
School—Blessed Sacrament School, (Grades K-8), 7 St. Teresa Dr., 29407. Tel: 843-766-2128; Fax: 843-766-2154. Email: chabless@bellsouth.net. Web: www.scbss.org. Roseann Tracy, Interim Prin.; Bonnie Perry, Librarian. Lay Teachers 26; Students 409.
Catechesis/Religious Program—Students 152.
Convent—0 Moore Dr., 29407. Tel: 843-766-5120.

4—CHRIST OUR KING (1971) Rev. Msgr. James A. Carter; Rev. Bryan P. Babick, Parochial Vicar; Deacons Joseph Cahill; Andre J.P. Guillet.
1149 Russell Dr., Mount Pleasant, 29464. Tel: 843-884-5587; Fax: 843-884-7086. Web: www.christourking.com.
School—Christ Our King Stella Maris School, (Grades K-8), 1183 Russell Dr., Mount Pleasant, 29464. Tel: 843-884-4721; Fax: 843-971-7850. Web: www.coksm.org. Jean Moschella, Prin. Lay Teachers 41; Students 600.
Catechesis/Religious Program—Students 455.

5—CHURCH OF CHRIST THE DIVINE TEACHER (1968) Rev. Dennis B. Willey; Deacon Peter Curcio.
Mailing Address: *The Catholic Chaplaincy to the Citadel*, The Citadel, MSC 58, 29409-0058. Tel: 843-953-7693. Email: willeyd1@citadel.edu. Web: www.citadel.edu/catholic.

6—CHURCH OF THE HOLY SPIRIT (1938) [CEM] Rev. Msgr. Charles H. Rowland; Rev. Jose Gabrie Rodriguez Cruz, Parochial Vicar; Deacon Mario Cardenas.
3871 Betsy Kerrison Pkwy., Johns Island, 29455. Tel: 843-768-0357; Fax: 843-793-2958. Email: hschrch@bellsouth.net. Web: www.holyspiritjohnsisland.com.
Catechesis/Religious Program—Students 11.

7—CHURCH OF THE NATIVITY (1959) Rev. S. Thomas Kingsley.
1061 Folly Rd., 29412. Tel: 843-795-3821; Fax: 843-795-2714. Email: nativityc@bellsouth.net.
School—Nativity School, (Grades K-8), 1125 Pittsford Cir., 29412. Tel: 843-795-3975; Fax: 843-795-7575. Email: pedwards@nativity-school.com. Ms. Patti Dukes, Prin.; Paula Hart, Librarian. Lay Teachers 12; Students 113.
Catechesis/Religious Program—Mrs. Mary L. Smith, D.R.E. Students 62.

8—DIVINE REDEEMER (1956) Rev. Edward W. Fitzgerald; Deacon Donald R. Dashnaw.
Office & Mailing Address: 1106 Fort Dr., Hanahan, 29410-2053. Tel: 843-553-0340; Fax: 843-533-0346. Email: office@divineredeemerchurch.org. Web: www.divineredeemerchurch.org.
School—Divine Redeemer Catholic School, (Grades K-8), 1104 Fort Dr., Hanahan, 29410-2053. Tel: 843-553-1521; Fax: 843-553-7109. Email: secretary@divineredeemerschool.com. Web: www.divineredeemerschool.com. Peggy Vice, Prin. Lay Teachers 12; Students 113.
Catechesis/Religious Program—Students 62.

9—ST. JOHN (1929) Rev. Msgr. Joseph F. Hanley Jr., Canonical Pastor; Bro. Edward E. Bergeron, C.F.C., Parish Life Facilitator.
Mailing Address: 3921 St. John's Ave., North Charleston, 29405-7158. Tel: 843-744-6201; Fax: 843-744-2792. Email: parishoffice@saintjohncatholicsc.org. Web: www.saintjohncatholicsc.org.
School—St. John Catholic School, (Grades K-8) Tel: 843-744-3901; Fax: 843-744-3689. Email: schooloffice@saintjohncatholicsc.org. Ms. Carole Anne White, Prin.; Janet Deaver, Librarian. Lay Teachers 8; Students 60.
Catechesis/Religious Program— Sr. Leonie Marie Maigret, S.N.D., D.R.E. Students 8.

10—ST. JOSEPH (1966) Rev. Gabriel J. Smith.
Mailing Address & Res.: 1695 Wallenberg Blvd., 29407. Tel: 843-566-4611; Fax: 843-566-4612. Email: info@saintjosephchas.com. Web: www.saintjosephchas.com.
Catechesis/Religious Program—Students 65.

11—ST. JOSEPH'S, Closed. For inquiries for parish records please contact Diocesan Archive, P.O. Box 818, Charleston, SC 29402. Tel: 843-724-8372.

12—ST. MARY OF THE ANNUNCIATION (1789) [CEM] Rev. Msgr. Steven L. Brovey, Admin.; Deacon Jerome P. Remkiewicz.
89 Hasell St., 29401. Tel: 843-722-7696; Fax: 843-577-5036. Email: stmarys1789@bellsouth.net. Web: www.catholic-doc.org/saintmarys/.
Catechesis/Religious Program—Students 53.

13—OUR LADY OF MERCY (1928), (African American), Rev. Henry N. Kulah (Ghana).
Mailing Address: c/o St. Patrick, P.O. Box 20726, 29413.
Res.: 77 America St., 29403. Tel: 843-723-6066; Fax: 843-853-8114.
See Charleston Catholic School, Charleston under Sacred Heart, Charleston for details.
Catechesis/Religious Program—

14—ST. PATRICK (1837), (African American), [CEM] Rev. Henry N. Kulah (Ghana).
Res.: 134 St. Phillip St., P.O. Box 20726, 29413. Tel: 843-723-6066; Fax: 843-853-8114. Email: stpat@bellsouth.net.
See Charleston Catholic School, Charleston under Sacred Heart, Charleston for details.
Catechesis/Religious Program—

15—ST. PETER'S, Closed. For inquiries for parish records contact St. Patrick, P.O. Box 20726, Charleston, SC 29413.

16—SACRED HEART (1920) Rev. Dennis B. Willey.
Office: 888 King St., 29403-4139. Tel: 843-722-7018; Fax: 843-579-9604. Email: sacredheartchas@aol.com.
School—Charleston Catholic School, (Grades K-8), 888-A King St., 29403-4139. Tel: 843-577-4495; Fax: 843-577-6916. Web: www.charlestoncatholic.com. Fred S. McKay Jr., Prin. Religious 3; Lay Teachers 15; Students 175.
Catechesis/Religious Program—Angela M. Prince, D.R.E. Students 2.

17—STELLA MARIS (1845) Rev. Msgr. Lawrence B. McInerny; Rev. Johnbosco Duraisamy, Parochial Vicar; Deacons Walter S. Pezanowski; Gerald W. Grismore; R. Michael Osbourne.
Mailing Address: P.O. Box 280, Sullivan's Island, 29482.
1204 Middle St., Sullivan's Island, 29482. Tel: 843-883-3108 (Office); 843-882-8031 (Rectory); Fax: 843-883-3160. Email: flmsmrc@bellsouth.net. Web: www.catholic-doc.org/stellamaris.
Catechesis/Religious Program—Christian Formation/CCD, Tel: 843-883-9040. Students 229.

18—ST. THOMAS THE APOSTLE (1966) Rev. Andrew Riley, Admin.; Deacon Frank T. Petrusak.
Church: 6650 Dorchester Rd., North Charleston, 29418. Tel: 843-552-2223; Fax: 843-552-6329. Web: www.catholic-doc.org/stthomas.
Catechesis/Religious Program—Students 159.

OUTSIDE OF THE CITY OF CHARLESTON

ABBEVILLE, ABBEVILLE CO., SACRED HEART (1885) Rev. Allam Marreddy (India), Admin.
Mailing Address: P.O. Box 812, 29620.
206 N. Main St., 29620. Tel: 864-366-5150; Fax: 864-366-5150. Email: sacredheart@wctel.net.
Catechesis/Religious Program—Students 2.
Station—McCormick Correctional Institution McCormick.

AIKEN, AIKEN CO.

1—ST. GERARD (1943) Rev. Donald S. Abbott.
Res.: 640 Edrie St., N.E., 29801. Tel: 803-649-3030; Fax: 803-649-3030. Email: stgerardscatholi@bellsouth.net.
Catechesis/Religious Program—

2—ST. MARY HELP OF CHRISTIANS (1853) [CEM] Revs. Gregory Wilson; Maximo E. Tria, Parochial Vicar;

Robert J. Waters (SC); Deacon Robert A. Pierce.
Mailing Address: P.O. Box 438, 29802.
203 Park Ave. S.E., 29802. Tel: 803-649-4777; Fax: 803-642-6421. Email: stmaryaikn@aol.com. Web: www.stmarys-aiken.org.
School—St. Mary Help of Christians Catholic School, (Grades PreK-8), 118 York St., 29801. Tel: 803-649-2071; Fax: 803-643-0092. Email: office@stmaryhoc.net. Web: smhoc.info. Marguerite B. Wertz, Prin. Lay Teachers 26; Students 236.
Catechesis/Religious Program—Students 461.

ANDERSON, ANDERSON CO.
1—ST. JOSEPH (1868) Rev. Paul M. Williams, O.F.M.; Deacons Henry L. Fulmer, O.F.M.; Charles Hanrahan.
1303 McLees Rd., 29621. Tel: 864-225-5341; Fax: 864-225-6432.
School—St. Joseph Catholic School, (Grades K-7), 1200 Cornelia Rd., 29621. Tel: 864-908-3746. Mary Ann Wheeler, Prin.; Francene Galbally, Librarian. Lay Teachers 11; Students 90.
Catechesis/Religious Program—Students 105.
2—ST. MARY OF THE ANGELS (1943) Rev. Aubrey McNeil, O.F.M.
Res. & Mailing Address: 1821 White St., 29624. Tel: 864-226-8621; Fax: 864-226-2536.
Catechesis/Religious Program—Tel: 864-226-3881. Students 67.

BARNWELL, BARNWELL CO., ST. ANDREW (1831) Revs. James N. Dubrouillet; Artur Przywara, Parochial Vicar.
Mailing Address: *c/o Holy Trinity*, 2202 Riverbank Dr., Orangeburg, 29118. Tel: 803-259-7593.
Church: 110 Madison St., 29812.
Catechesis/Religious Program—Dana Depew, C.R.E. Students 12.
Mission—Sacred Heart Blackville, Barnwell Co.
Mission—St. Theresa Springfield, Orangeburg Co.

BATESBURG-LEESVILLE, LEXINGTON CO., ST. JOHN OF THE CROSS (1959) Rev. Gustavo Corredor, Parochial Vicar.
Res.: 320 W. Columbia Ave., P.O. Box 2279, 29070-2279. Tel: 803-532-1208; Fax: 803-532-1208.
Catechesis/Religious Program—Tel: 803-532-6777. Email: jhayden545@gmail.com. Students 186.

BEAUFORT, BEAUFORT CO., ST. PETER (1846) [CEM] Revs. Paul D. MacNeil, Admin.; Cesar Augusto Torres Pinzon, I.M.E.Y., Parochial Vicar; Deacon Edward Peitler.
Church: 70 Lady's Island Dr., 29907. Tel: 843-522-9555; Fax: 843-522-0667. Email: stpeters@stpeters-church.org. Web: www.stpeters-church.org
School—St. Peter Catholic School, (Grades K-8) Tel: 843-522-2163; Fax: 843-522-6513. Email: stpetersschool@stpeters-church.org. Web: www.stpeters-church.org/school. Christopher A. Trott, Prin. Sisters 1; Lay Teachers 15; Students 154.
Catechesis/Religious Program—Students 139.
Mission—Holy Cross St. Helena Island, Beaufort Co. Tel: 843-838-2195.

BLUFFTON, BEAUFORT CO., ST. GREGORY THE GREAT (1960) [CEM] Very Rev. Ronald R. Cellini; Revs. Jose-Hugo Ruiz-Marentes, O.F.M., Parochial Vicar; David Nerbun, Parochial Vicar; Deacons Gregory W. Sams; Dennis Burkett; Walt Hollis; Richard D'Angelo; James Graham; John McCabe.
Mailing Address: 333 Fording Island Rd., 29909. Tel: 843-815-3100; Fax: 843-815-3150. Email: info@sgg.cc. Web: www.sgg.cc.
Res.: 232 Pinckney Colony Rd., 29909. Tel: 843-757-5558.
School—St. Gregory the Great Catholic School, (Grades PreK-7), 323 Fording Island Rd., 29909. Tel: 843-815-9988; Fax: 843-815-6137. Sr. Canice Adams, SS.C.M., Prin.; Ms. Ann Caruso, Librarian. Lay Teachers 23; Students 225.
Catechesis/Religious Program—Students 345.
Chapel—St. Andrew 220 Pinckney Colony Rd., 29909. Tel: 843-757-6057.

BLYTHEWOOD, RICHLAND CO., TRANSFIGURATION (1998) Rev. Andrew Trapp, Admin.
Office & Mailing Address: 9720 Wilson Blvd., 29016. Tel: 803-735-0512; Fax: 803-735-1742. Email: transfiguration@bellsouth.net. Web: www.catholic-doc.org/transfiguration.
306 N. Pines Rd., 29016.
Catechesis/Religious Program—Students 100.

CAMDEN, KERSHAW CO., OUR LADY OF PERPETUAL HELP (1914) Revs. Francis J. Travis; Jose Rodolfo Lache Avila (Colombia), Parochial Vicar.
1709 Lyttleton St., 29020. Tel: 803-432-6131; Fax: 803-432-3440. Email: olph@bellsouth.net. Web: ourlady.catholicweb.com.
Catechesis/Religious Program—Tel: 803-432-8808. Students 119.

CHAPIN, LEXINGTON CO., OUR LADY OF THE LAKE (1989) [CEM] Rev. Andrew J. Vollkommer; Deacons Joseph P. Biviano; Charles LaRosa; Gregory Weigold.
Mailing Address: 195 Amicks Ferry Rd., P.O. Box 549, 29036. Tel: 803-345-3962; Fax: 803-345-8933. Email: andrewjv@ollchapin.org. Web: www.ollchapin.org.
Res.: 2 Oak Stand Ct., Irmo, 29063. Tel: 803-781-8767.
Catechesis/Religious Program—Students 360.

CHERAW, CHESTERFIELD CO., ST. PETER (1842) [CEM] Rev. David Michael, Admin.
Parish & Mailing Address: 602 Market St., 29520. Tel: 843-537-7351. Email: stpeterscatholic@gmail.com.
Catechesis/Religious Program—
Mission—St. Denis Bennettsville, Marlboro Co.
Mission—St. Ernest [CEM] Pageland, Chesterfield Co.

CHESTER, CHESTER CO., ST. JOSEPH (1854) Rev. David A. Runnion.
110 West End, P.O. Box 869, 29706. Tel: 803-377-4695; Fax: 803-581-7848. Email: stjoseph@truvista.net.
Catechesis/Religious Program—

CLEMSON, PICKENS CO., ST. ANDREW (1935) Revs. H. Gregory West; Bernard Okokon, Parochial Vicar.
200 Edgewood Ave., P.O. Box 112, 29633. Tel: 864-654-1757; Fax: 864-654-2950. In Res., Rev. John W. McDowell, O.F.M.
Catechesis/Religious Program—Attended by St. Paul's & St. Andrew Students 206.
Mission—St. Paul the Apostle 170 Bountyland Rd., Seneca, Oconee Co. 29672. Tel: 864-882-8551; 864-882-7115 (Hispanic Ministry).
Mission—St. Francis of Assisi 103 W. Mauldin St., Walhalla, Oconee Co. 29691. Tel: 864-638-2984.
Station—Campus Ministry-Clemson University, Tel: 864-654-7804.

COLUMBIA, LEXINGTON CO., OUR LADY OF THE HILLS (1972) Revs. David R. Whitman; Jose Rodolfo Lache Avila (Colombia), Parochial Vicar; Sr. Christina Murphy, S.N.D.deN., Pastoral Assoc.; Deacons Charles R. DiRusso; Dennis N. Jones; Stephen Burdick.
Mailing Address: 120 Marydale Ln., 29210. Email: oloh@sc.rr.com. Web: www.ourladyofthehillssc.org.
Catechesis/Religious Program—Students 341.

COLUMBIA, RICHLAND CO.
1—GOOD SHEPHERD (1984) Rev. William D. Ladkau.
Mailing Address: P.O. Box 1298, 29202. Tel: 803-765-1334; Fax: 803-765-2208.
809 Calhoun, 29202.
Res.: 1625 Granby Rd., Cayce, 29033.
Catechesis/Religious Program—Students 15.
2—ST. JOHN NEUMANN (1977) Very Rev. C. Alexander McDonald.
Mailing Address: P.O. Box 23689, 29224.
100 Polo Rd., 29223. Tel: 803-788-0811; Fax: 803-788-1501. Email: lschmidt@sc.twcbc.com. Web: www.stjohnneumannsc.com.
School—St. John Neumann Catholic School, (Grades K-6), 721 Polo Rd., 29223. Tel: 803-788-1367; Fax: 803-788-7330. Web: www.sjncatholic.com. Barbara Cole, Prin.; Ms. Karen Zimmerman, Librarian. Lay Teachers 35; Students 367.
Catechesis/Religious Program— Mrs. Cherie Smith, D.R.E. Students 276.
3—ST. JOSEPH (1948) Rev. Msgr. Richard D. Harris; Rev. S. Matthew Gray, Parochial Vicar; Deacons Charles P. Poole Jr.; Malcolm Skipper.
Office: 3512 Devine St., 29205. Tel: 803-254-7646; Fax: 803-799-7607. Email: stjoedoc@aol.com. Web: www.stjosephcolumbia.org.
Rectory—136 High Hampton, 29209.
Church: 3600 Devine St., 29205.
School—St. Joseph Catholic School, (Grades K-6), 3700 Devine St., 29205. Tel: 803-254-6736; Fax: 803-540-1913. Web: www.stjosdevine.com. Ms. Roselyn Tindall, Prin.; Nicholas Cole, Librarian. Ursuline Nuns of the Congregation of Paris 1; Lay Teachers 27; Students 319.
Catechesis/Religious Program—Tel: 803-540-1906. Students 185.
4—SAINT MARTIN DE PORRES (1935) Revs. Michael C. Okere (Nigeria), Admin.; Bernard Oniwe, O.P.; Deacons Carl Johnson; Henry L. Fulmer, O.F.M.
2229 Hampton St., 29204. Tel: 803-254-6862; Fax: 803-799-4720. Email: deporres@yahoo.com.
Rectory—2505 Treeside Dr., 29204. Tel: 803-376-6027. Email: pw4ofm@aol.com. Web: stmartinofcolumbia.org.
School—St. Martin de Porres Catholic School, (Grades K-6), 2225 Hampton Rd., 29204. Tel: 803-254-5477; Fax: 803-254-7335. Web: www.saintmartindeporres.org. Sr. Roberta Fulton, S.S.M.N., Prin. Lay Teachers 11; Students 85.
Catechesis/Religious Program—Students 76.
Station—Correctional Institutions in the Greater Columbia Area
5—ST. PETER (1824) [CEM 3] Rev. Msgr. Leigh A. Lehocky; Rev. Bernard Kyara; Deacons Charles M. Easterling; Ronald J. Anderson; John Stetar; David Thompson.
Mailing Address: P.O. Box 1896, 29202. Email: stpeters@visitstpeters.org. Web: www.visitstpeters.org.
Res.: 2125 Raven Tr., West Columbia, 29169. Tel: 803-791-0552.
Church: 1529 Assembly St., 29201. Tel: 803-779-0036; Fax: 803-799-2438.
School—St. Peter's Catholic School, (Grades K-6), 1035 Hampton St., 29201. Tel: 803-252-8285; Fax: 803-254-4736. Web: www.stpeters-catholic-school.org. Kathy Prestor, Prin. Lay Teachers 18; Students 110.
Catechesis/Religious Program—Students 305.

CONWAY, HORRY CO., ST. JAMES (1945) Revs. Timothy M. Lijewski; John E. Silver (OG) (Retired); Deacon Jeffrey P. Mevissen.
Church, Office & Mailing Address: 1071 Academy Dr., 29526. Tel: 843-347-5168; Fax: 843-347-1212. Email: stjames@stjamesconway.org. Web: stjamesconway.org.
Catechesis/Religious Program—Students 181.

DILLON, DILLON CO., ST. LOUIS (1943) Rev. Marcian Thet-Kyaw (Burma), Admin.
Mailing Address: 607 N. 4th Ave., 29536.
Church: 207 E. Roosevelt St., 29536. Tel: 843-774-0255 (Office); Fax: 843-774-0255. Email: stlouiscatholicc@bellsouth.net.
Catechesis/Religious Program—Students 6.
Mission—Infant Jesus 4534 Hwy. 501 N., P.O. Box 520, Marion, Marion Co. 29571. Tel: 843-423-1823; Fax: 843-423-3987. Email: lauren.denitto@yahoo.com.

EDGEFIELD, EDGEFIELD CO., ST. MARY OF THE IMMACULATE CONCEPTION (1856) [CEM] Rev. Noel Tria (Philippines), Canonical Mod./Admin.
Office: 302 Jeter St., 29824. Tel: 803-637-6248; Fax: 803-637-6241. Email: stmarysc@bellsouth.net.
Church: 305 Buncombe St., 29824.
Catechesis/Religious Program—Students 17.

FLORENCE, FLORENCE CO.
1—ST. ANNE (1940) [JC] Rev. John M. Zimmerman, Admin.; Deacons James H. Johnson; Robert C. Gerald Jr.
113 S. Kemp St., 29506. Tel: 843-661-5012 (Church Office); Fax: 843-673-2680. Email: stannesec@sc.twcbc.com.
Catechesis/Religious Program—Students 40.
2—ST. ANTHONY (1872) Revs. Robert E. Morey; Richard Jackson, Parochial Vicar; Deacons Reginald A.T. Armstrong; Jeffery Pierfy.
Mailing Address: P.O. Box 5327, 29501.
Church: 2536 W. Hoffmeyer Rd., 29502. Tel: 843-665-5853 (Rectory); 843-662-5674; Fax: 843-662-4800. Email: art.dalupang@saintanthony.com. Web: www.saintanthony.com.
School—St. Anthony Catholic School, (Grades K-8) Tel: 843-662-1910; Fax: 843-662-5335. Email: stanthonyfl0@aol.com. Mr. Frank Cottone, Prin.; Patty Long, Librarian. Priests 1; Lay Teachers 18; Students 136.
Catechesis/Religious Program—Students 136.

FOLLY BEACH, CHARLESTON CO., OUR LADY OF GOOD COUNSEL (1950) Rev. Jesuprathap Narichetti (India), Admin.
Mailing Address: P.O. Box 1257, 29439. Email: office@olgc-follybeach.org. Web: www.olgc-follybeach.org.
56 Center St., 29439. Tel: 843-588-2336; Fax: 843-588-3478.
Catechesis/Religious Program—Students 5.

FORT MILL, YORK CO., ST. PHILIP NERI (1993) [CEM] Revs. John P. Giuliani, C.O.; Joseph Francis Pearce, C.O., Parochial Vicar; Deacons Jon Dwyer; Steven Rhodes.
Church: 292 Munn Rd., 29715. Tel: 803-548-7282; Fax: 803-547-2999. Email: stphilipneri@comporium.net. Web: www.saintphilipneri.org.
Catechesis/Religious Program—Students 781.
Mission—Our Lady of Grace 8286 Charlotte Hwy., Indian Land, 29707. Tel: 803-283-4969.

GAFFNEY, CHEROKEE CO., SACRED HEART (1955) Rev. Michael F. McCafferty.
205 Sams St., 29340. Tel: 864-489-9453; Fax: 864-489-9150.
Catechesis/Religious Program—Students 102.

GARDEN CITY, HORRY CO., ST. MICHAEL (1975) Revs. Raymond J. Carlo; William Hearne, Parochial Vicar; Deacons Charlie Fiore; Robert Starr; Robert Jones.
572 Cypress Ave., 29576. Tel: 843-651-3737; Fax: 843-651-6316. Email: pastor@saintmichaelsc.org.
School—St. Michael Catholic School, (Grades PreK-8) Tel: 843-651-6795; Fax: 843-651-6803. Mrs. Miriam James, Prin. Lay Teachers 15; Students 155.
Catechesis/Religious Program—Students 378.

GEORGETOWN, GEORGETOWN CO.
1—ST. CYPRIAN (1950), (African American—Hispanic), Rev. Ronald J. Farrell; Sr. Susan Pugh, Parish Life Facilitator.
Center & Mailing Address: 1905 Front St., P.O. Box 2037, 29442. Tel: 843-546-1470; Fax: 843-527-2139.

Email: stcyprian2@hotmail.com.
Catechesis/Religious Program—Students 23.
2—ST. MARY OUR LADY OF RANSOM (1899) [JC], (Our Lady of Ransom) Rev. Ronald J. Farrell.
Mailing Address: 317 Broad St., 29440. Tel: 843-546-7416; Fax: 843-546-7003. Email: smolor@scctv.net. Web: www.stmaryourladyofransom.com.
Res.: 810 Highmarket St., 29440. Tel: 843-527-1087.
Catechesis/Religious Program—Students 56.
GLOVERVILLE, AIKEN CO., OUR LADY OF THE VALLEY (1954) Rev. Peter Clarke (Retired).
Mailing Address: P.O. Box 419, 29828. Tel: 803-593-2241; Fax: 803-593-2241. Email: olv@atlanticbbn.net.
2429 Augusta Rd., 29828.
Parish Community Center—Tel: 803-593-2623; Fax: 803-593-2678.
Catechesis/Religious Program—Students 34.
Convent—Horsecreek Valley Convent, P.O. Box 358, 29828. Tel: 803-593-9862. Daughters of Charity 4.
GOOSE CREEK, BERKELEY CO., IMMACULATE CONCEPTION (1976) Revs. Nicholas Capetola, C.R.M.; H. Nestor Abog Jr., C.R.M., Parochial Vicar; Deacons Lawrence Roberts; Joseph A. Anonie; Daniel McNerny.
510 St. James Ave., 29445. Tel: 843-553-1386 (Rectory); 843-572-1270 (Office); Fax: 843-572-3128. Email: immaculateconceptiongc@gmail.com.
Catechesis/Religious Program—Students 332.
GREENVILLE, GREENVILLE CO.
1—ST. ANTHONY OF PADUA (1939), (African American), Revs. Patrick Tuttle, O.F.M.; David Q. Phan, O.F.M., Parochial Vicar; Deacons Winston C. Wright; James Williams; Henry Dillard.
307 Gower St., 29611. Tel: 864-233-7717; Fax: 864-233-2852. Email: anthonyofm@yahoo.com. Web: www.newstanthony.com.
School—St. Anthony of Padua Catholic School, (Grades K-5), 309 Gower St., 29611. Tel: 864-271-0167; Fax: 864-271-2936. Sr. Catherine Noecker, O.S.F., Prin. Sisters of St. Francis of Williamsville 3; Lay Teachers 11; Students 93.
Catechesis/Religious Program—Students 126.
2—ST. MARY (1852) Very Rev. Jay Scott Newman; Rev. Ikechi Korie, O.P., Parochial Vicar; Deacons George Tierney; Diego Ferro; John Heuser; John F. Karandisevsky.
Mailing Address & Res.: 111 Hampton Ave., 29601. Tel: 864-271-8422; Fax: 864-370-9880. Email: churchoffice@stmarysgvl.org. Web: www.stmarysgvl.org.
School—St. Mary's Catholic School, (Grades K-8), 101 Hampton Ave., 29601. Tel: 864-271-3870; Fax: 864-271-0159. Sr. Mary John Slonkosky, O.P., Prin.; Linda Hilley, Librarian. Dominicans 4; Lay Teachers 15; Students 278.
Catechesis/Religious Program—Students 254.
3—OUR LADY OF THE ROSARY (1952) Revs. Dwight Longenecker, Admin.; David Q. Phan, O.F.M., Vietnamese Ministry; Deacon Raymond Perham.
3710 Augusta Rd., P.O. Box 8396, 29604. Tel: 864-422-1648; Fax: 864-277-5969. Email: church.office@ourladyoftherosary.net. Web: www.ourladyoftherosary.net.
School—Our Lady of the Rosary Catholic School, (Grades K-8), 2 James Dr., 29605. Tel: 864-277-5350; Fax: 864-277-7745. Email: info@olrschool.net. Mr. John Harrington, Prin.; Robin Calamia, Librarian. Lay Teachers 15; Students 178.
Catechesis/Religious Program—Students 148.
GREENWOOD, GREENWOOD CO., OUR LADY OF LOURDES (1920) Revs. James M. Crowley; Henry Wilson Rodriguez Echavarria, C.H.S., Spanish Min.
Office & Mailing Address: 915 Mathis Rd., 29649. Tel: 864-223-8410; Fax: 864-223-7555. Email: pastor@olol.org. Web: www.olol.org.
Res.: 120 Colonial Dr., 29649. Tel: 864-223-3003.
Catechesis/Religious Program—Email: tomrel@embarqmail.com. Students 253.
GREER, GREENVILLE CO., BLESSED TRINITY (1974) Revs. Oscar Borda Rojas (Colombia), Admin.; Henry Wilson Rodriguez Echavarria, C.H.S., Spanish Ministry.
901 River Rd., 29652-1371. Tel: 864-879-4225; Fax: 864-879-4261. Email: blessedtrinityca@bellsouth.net.
Catechesis/Religious Program—Students 227.
HARTSVILLE, DARLINGTON CO.
1—ST. JOSEPH'S, Closed. For inquiries for parish records contact St. Mary the Virgin Mother, 363 N. 5th St., Hartsville, SC 29550.
2—ST. MARY THE VIRGIN MOTHER (1941) Very Rev. Karl J. Roesch, O.S.B., Admin.; Deacons John S. Larkin; Brian Laws.
Res.: 115 Church St., 29550. Tel: 843-332-7773; Fax: 843-332-2812. Email: stmary2@ymail.com.
Church: 363 N. 5th St., 29550.
Catechesis/Religious Program—Students 56.
Mission—St. Joseph the Worker 1308 N. Main St., Darlington, Darlington Co. 29540.
HILTON HEAD ISLAND, BEAUFORT CO.
1—ST. FRANCIS BY THE SEA (1984) [CEM] Revs. Michael J. Oenbrink; John Paul Reddy Pentareddy, Parochial Vicar; Sr. Kathleen Kane, S.S.M.N., Pastoral Assoc.; Deacons Gerald Hand; Matthew Houle; Joseph J. Nazarro; Patrick Sheehan.
Res.: 45 Beach City Rd., 29926-2423. Tel: 843-681-6350; Fax: 843-689-5502. Email: office@stfrancishhi.org. Web: www.stfrancishhi.org.
School—St. Francis Catholic School, (Grades PreK-8) Tel: 843-681-6501; Fax: 843-689-3725. Web: www.sfcshhi.org. Mike Rockers, Prin. Lay Teachers 8; Students 232.
Catechesis/Religious Program—Tel: 843-681-6350, Ext. 248. Students 227.
2—HOLY FAMILY (1966) Rev. Arturo O. Dalupang (Philippines); Deacon John DeWolfe.
24 Pope Ave., 29928. Tel: 843-785-2895; Fax: 843-842-7494. Email: pastor@holyfamilyhhi.org. Web: www.holyfamilyhhi.org.
Catechesis/Religious Program—Email: education@holyfamily.hhi.org. Students 206.
JOANNA, LAURENS CO., ST. BONIFACE (1949) Rev. Francisco Cruz (Colombia), Admin.
Office: 403 N. Main St., P.O. Box 188, 29351. Tel: 864-697-6745; Fax: 864-697-6745.
Catechesis/Religious Program—Students 12.
Mission—Holy Spirit (1963) 1040 W. Main St., P.O. Box 864, Laurens, Laurens Co. 29360. Tel: 864-984-2880; Fax: 864-984-2880.
KINGSTREE, WILLIAMSBURG CO., ST. ANN (1947) Rev. Matthew Bulala (Tanzania), Admin.; Deacon Harold Jackson.
Mailing Address: P.O. Box 529, 29556. 107 Hirsch St., 29556. Tel: 843-536-0440; Fax: 843-353-1354. Email: stannkingstree@gmail.com.
Church & Mailing Address: 303 Main St., P.O. Box 529, 29556.
Center—908 Thorne Ave., 29556. Tel: 843-354-9415; Fax: 843-354-9093.
Res.: 120 Hirsch St., P.O. Box 529, Kingtree, 29556.
Catechesis/Religious Program—Students 7.
Convent—908 Thorne Ave., 29556. Felician Sisters 2.
LAKE CITY, FLORENCE CO., ST. PHILIP THE APOSTLE (1952) [JC] Rev. Matthew Bulala (Tanzania), Admin.
120 Westover St., P.O. Box 399, 29560. Tel: 843-394-8343.
Catechesis/Religious Program—Fax: 843-394-1814. Students 20.
Mission—St. Patrick the Apostle Church St., Johnsonville, Florence Co. 29555. P.O. Box 399, 29560.
LANCASTER, LANCASTER CO., ST. CATHERINE (1948) Rev. David A. Runnion.
720 W. Meeting St., 29720. Tel: 803-283-3362; Fax: 803-283-3363. Email: stcstm@comporium.net.
Catechesis/Religious Program—Students 46.
Mission—St. Michael 310 Chester Ave., Great Falls, Chester Co. 29055.
LEXINGTON, LEXINGTON CO., CORPUS CHRISTI (1977) Rev. Emmanuel Andinam (Nigeria); Deacons Dale Palmer; Coleman T. Parks; Jack Crocker.
2350 Augusta Hwy., 29072. Tel: 803-359-4391; Fax: 803-359-8885. Web: www.catholic-doc.org/corpuschristi.
Catechesis/Religious Program—Students 437.
MCCORMICK, MCCORMICK CO., GOOD SHEPHERD, P.O. Box 1468, 29835. Tel: 843-852-4722; Fax: 843-852-4722.
MONCKS CORNER, BERKELEY CO., ST. PHILIP BENIZI (1965) Rev. Edgardo Enverga, C.R.M.
1404 Old Hwy. 52 S., 29461. Tel: 843-761-3777 Main Line; 843-771-5740; 843-771-7643; Fax: 843-761-0905. Email: diane@spbcc.org; mary@spbcc.org. Web: spbcc.org.
Catechesis/Religious Program—Students 80.
Mission—Our Lady of Peace 224 Murray's Ferry Rd., Bonneau, Berkeley Co. 29431.
MURPHY VILLAGE, EDGEFIELD CO., ST. EDWARD (1964) Rev. Cherian Thalakulam, C.M.I. (India).
Mailing Address: P.O. Box 6340, North Augusta, 29861.
1370 Edgefield Rd., 29860. Tel: 803-279-1837; Fax: 803-279-9655.
Catechesis/Religious Program—Students 159.
MYRTLE BEACH, HORRY CO., ST. ANDREW (1946) Revs. James L. LeBlanc; Casmir Maduakor, Parochial Vicar; Deacons Robert Barlow; George Ferland.
Parish Administration Office—3501 N. King Hwy. Ste. 102, 29577. Tel: 843-448-5930; Fax: 843-448-3947. Email: standrewmb@sc.rr.com. Web: standrewcatholicchurch.org.
Church: 37th Ave. N. & Hwy. 17 (Kings Hwy.), 29577.
School—St. Andrew Catholic School, (Grades K-8), 3601 N. Kings Hwy., 29577. Tel: 843-448-6062; Fax: 843-626-8644. Email: mhalasz@standrewschoolmb.org. Mrs. Mary M. Halasz, Prin.; Cheryl Sedota, Librarian. Lay Teachers 16; Students 240.
Catechesis/Religious Program—Students 295.
NEWBERRY, NEWBERRY CO., ST. MARK (1956) [JC] Rev. Francisco Cruz (Colombia), Admin.; Deacon Gerald Loignon Jr.
928 Boundary St., 29108. Tel: 803-276-6446; Fax: 803-276-0856.
Catechesis/Religious Program—Students 72.
NORTH AUGUSTA, AIKEN CO., OUR LADY OF PEACE (1948) Rev. Jacob Joseph, C.M.I.; Deacon Bob Hookness.
856 Old Edgefield Rd., P.O. Box 6605, 29861-6605. Tel: 803-279-0315; Fax: 803-279-5247. Web: www.ourlady.ws.
School—Our Lady of Peace School, (Grades K-8) Tel: 803-279-8396; Fax: 803-279-7167. Karen Wilcox, Prin.; Ms. Nancy Mack, Librarian. Lay Teachers 14; Students 119.
Catechesis/Religious Program—Students 185.
NORTH MYRTLE BEACH, HORRY CO., OUR LADY STAR OF THE SEA (1964) Revs. D. Anthony Droze; Jose Orlando Cheverria Jimenez (Colombia), Spanish Ministry; Deacons Robert Tyson; Chester Gormon; Andrew Stoshak; Peter Casamento.
Office: 1100 Eighth Ave. N., 29582. Tel: 843-249-2356; Fax: 843-249-8514. Email: olss@sc.rr.com. Web: olssnmb.com.
Res.: 1010 8th Ave. N., 29582. Tel: 843-361-5948.
School—Holy Trinity Catholic School, 1760 Living Stones Ln., Longs, 29568. Tel: 843-390-4108; Fax: 843-390-4097. Email: htcs@sccoast.net. Web: www.holytrinitylongs.com. Sheila Durante, Prin.
Catechesis/Religious Program—Students 145.
Mission—Catholic Church of the Resurrection 204 Heritage Rd., Loris, Horry Co. 29569. Tel: 843-281-6421.
ORANGEBURG, ORANGEBURG CO.
1—CHRIST THE KING, Closed. For inquiries for parish records contact Holy Trinity, 2202 Riverbank Dr., N.W. 29118-4044. Tel: 803-534-8177.
2—HOLY TRINITY (1917) Revs. James N. Dubrouillet; Artur Przywara, Parochial Vicar.
Office: 2202 Riverbank Dr., 29118-4044. Tel: 803-534-8177; Fax: 802-535-0012. Email: holytrin@sc.rr.com. Web: www.masstransit.com/sc/trinity.
Catechesis/Religious Program—Students 90.
Mission—St. Mary Allendale, Barnwell Co.
PAWLEYS ISLAND, GEORGETOWN CO., PRECIOUS BLOOD OF CHRIST (1986) [CEM] Rev. Patrick J. Stenson, M.S.C., Admin.
Office: 1633 Waverly Rd., 29585. Tel: 843-237-3428; Fax: 843-237-2293. Web: www.pbocchurch.com.
Catechesis/Religious Program—Students 180.
PICKENS, PICKENS CO., HOLY CROSS (1965) Rev. Emmanuel Efiong (Nigeria), Admin.
Church: 558 Hampton Ave., 29671. Fax: 864-878-0028. Email: holycros@bellsouth.net.
Catechesis/Religious Program—Students 45.
Mission—St. Luke 4408 Hwy. 86, Easley, Anderson Co. 29642. Tel: 864-855-9039; Fax: 864-855-9038. Deacons Eugene Egendoerfer; Anthony J. Cassandra.
RIDGELAND, JASPER CO., ST. ANTHONY (1963) Rev. Robert F. Higgins.
Mailing Address: P.O. Box 548, 29936.
10128 S. Jacob Smart Blvd., 29936. Tel: 843-726-3606; Fax: 843-726-3606.
Catechesis/Religious Program—Students 40.
Mission—St. Mary 703 5th St. E., Hampton, Hampton Co. 29924. Tel: 803-941-4019.
Mission—St. Anthony 1 Charles St., Hardeeville, Jasper Co. 29927. Tel: 843-784-2943. Rev. Francis J. Gillespie, Admin.; Deacon Albert Schito.
ROCK HILL, YORK CO.
1—ST. ANNE (1919) Rev. Elbano Munoz, C.O.; Very Rev. Fabio Refosco, C.O., Parochial Vicar; Deacons Ray Moore; Guillermo Nunez; Jim Hyland.
Office & Mailing Address: 1694 Bird St., 29730. Tel: 803-329-2662; Fax: 803-329-2190. Email: parishoffice@saintanne.com. Web: www.saintanne.com.
Res.: 434 Charlotte Ave., P.O. Box 11586, 29731. Tel: 803-327-2097.
School—St. Anne Catholic School, (Grades K-8), 1698 Bird St., 29730. Tel: 803-324-4814; Fax: 803-324-0189. Mr. Anthony Perrini, Prin. Lay Teachers 22; Students 243.
Catechesis/Religious Program—Students 429.
2—ST. MARY (1946) Revs. Agustin Guzman, C.O., Admin.; Joseph A. Wahl, C.O., Canonical Pastor; Bro. David Boone, C.O., Parish Life Facilitator; Sr. Mary John Nguyen, F.M.S.R., Parish Life Facilitator.
Bannon Hall, 902 Crawford Ave., P.O. Box 11982, 29731. Tel: 803-329-1008; Fax: 803-329-3799. Email: stmary@comporium.net. Web: www.catholic-doc.org/stmaryrh/index.html.
Catechesis/Religious Program—Students 71.
Convent—916 Crawford Rd., 29730. Tel: 803-327-7450. Daughters of Our Lady of the Holy Rosary.
St. Martin de Porres Parish Center—911 Crawford Rd., 29730.
SANTEE, ORANGEBURG CO., ST. ANN (2004) Rev. Samuel Oloyede, Admin.; Deacon Robert C. Kronyak.

Mailing Address: P.O. Box 250, 29142.
Church: 2205 State Park Rd., 29142. Tel: 803-854-5075; Fax: 803-485-8592.
Catechesis/Religious Program—Students 25.
Chapel—St. Ann Chapel of Ease Rte. 176, Holly Hill, 29059.

SIMPSONVILLE, GREENVILLE CO.
1—ST. ELIZABETH ANN SETON (1972) Rev. Patrick E. Cooper.
Mailing Address: P.O. Box 672, Mauldin, 29662-0672. Tel: 864-263-3445; Fax: 864-263-3428.
Res.: 117 Ivy Dr., 29680-6124. Tel: 864-963-4892.
Church: 8 Gillin Dr., 29680-6108.
Catechesis/Religious Program—Students 128.
Good Shepherd, McCormick—
2—ST. MARY MAGDALENE (1989) Revs. Teofilo Trujillo; Philip Gillespie, Parochial Vicar; Daniel Papineau, Parochial Vicar; Deacons Matthew A. Mannino; Gabriel Cuervo.
Church & Office: 2252 Woodruff Rd., 29681. Tel: 864-288-4884; Fax: 864-297-5804. Web: smmcc.org.
Catechesis/Religious Program—Tel: 864-288-4884, Ext. 205. Students 1,200.

SPARTANBURG, SPARTANBURG CO.
1—JESUS OUR RISEN SAVIOR (1978) Revs. Frank Palmieri, C.R.M.; Oscar Borda Rojas (Colombia), Spanish Speaking Ministry; Teodoro Kalaw, C.R.M., Parochial Vicar; Deacons Robert M. Sturm, Parish Life Facilitator; Paul F. Shook.
2575 Reidville Rd., 29301. Tel: 864-576-1164; 864-574-8117 (Rectory); Fax: 864-576-0860. Web: www.jors.cc.
Catechesis/Religious Program—Nancy Chandler, D.R.E. Students 450.
2—ST. JOSEPH'S, Closed. For inquiries for parish records contact St. Paul the Apostle, Spartanburg.
3—ST. PAUL THE APOSTLE (1881) Rev. Timothy M. Gahan; Deacon Robert L. Mahaffey Jr.
161 N. Dean St., 29302. Tel: 864-582-0674; Fax: 864-582-0716. Web: www.st-paultheapostle.org.
School—St. Paul the Apostle Catholic School, (Grades K-8), 152 Alabama St., 29302. Tel: 864-582-6645; Fax: 864-582-1225. Patricia Lanthier, Prin.; Mary Lee, Librarian. Lay Teachers 16; Students 143.
Catechesis/Religious Program—Tel: 864-585-1858; Fax: 864-582-0716. Students 206.

SUMMERTON, CLARENDON CO., ST. MARY (1914) Rev. Samuel Oloyede, Admin.; Deacon Charles Michael Walsh.
12 N. Cantey St., P.O. Box 1110, 29148. Tel: 803-485-2925; Fax: 803-485-8592.
Catechesis/Religious Program—Tel: 803-478-5182. Students 16.
Mission—Our Lady of Hope Mission 2451 Raccoon Rd., Manning, Clarendon Co. 29102. Mailing Address: P.O. Box 1110, 29148.

SUMMERVILLE, DORCHESTER CO.
1—ST. JOHN THE BELOVED (1898) Rev. Msgr. E. Christopher Lathem; Rev. Christopher Oranyelli, O.P.
28 Sumter Ave., 29483. Tel: 843-873-0631; Fax: 843-873-1431. Email: schurchrectory@sc.rr.com. Web: www.stjohnthebelovedcatholic.org.
School—Summerville Catholic School, (Grades K-8), 226 Black Oak Blvd., 29483. Tel: 843-873-9310; Fax: 843-873-5709. Lisa Tanner, Prin. Sisters 1; Lay Teachers 21; Students 210.
Catechesis/Religious Program—Students 210.
2—ST. THERESA THE LITTLE FLOWER (1984) Rev. Msgr. Edward D. Lofton; Deacons Shane Graham; Eugene Phillips.
11001 Dorchester Rd., 29485. Tel: 843-875-5002; 843-875-6911; Fax: 843-875-4884. Email: office@sttheresachurch.com.
Catechesis/Religious Program—Students 142.
Station—Charleston Detention Center

SUMTER, SUMTER CO.
1—CATHOLIC COMMUNITY OF SUMTER (1911) [CEM], (formerly St. Anne) Revs. Thomas Burke, C.Ss.R.; James Burke, C.Ss.R., Parochial Vicar; Deacons Billy J. Ellis; Michael Kulungowski.
216 E. Liberty St., 29150. Tel: 803-773-3524; Fax: 803-778-1644. Web: stannesumtersc.org.
School—St. Anne Catholic School, (Grades K-8), 11 S. Magnolia St., 29150. Tel: 803-775-3632; Fax: 803-938-9074. Ms. Kristi Doyle, Prin. Lay Teachers 18; Students 180.
Catechesis/Religious Program—Students 100.
2—CATHOLIC COMMUNITY OF SUMTER (1939), (formerly St. Jude) Revs. James Burke, C.Ss.R.; Charles Donovan, C.Ss.R., Parochial Vicar; Peter E. Sousa, C.Ss.R., Parochial Vicar; Deacon Lawrence Corum.
611 W. Oakland Ave., P.O. Box 1589, 29151. Tel: 803-773-9244; Fax: 803-775-6913. Email: stjudeschur@sc.rr.com. Web: stjudesumtersc.org.
Catechesis/Religious Program—Tel: 803-778-6404. Students 94.

TAYLORS, GREENVILLE CO., PRINCE OF PEACE (1975) Revs. Christopher Smith, Admin.; Richard Tomlinson, Parochial Vicar; Deacon Bob Smith.
1209 Brushy Creek Rd., 29687-4103. Tel: 864-268-4352; Fax: 864-322-2239. Email: stephanie.stewart@princeofpeacetaylors.org. Web: www.princeofpeacesc.org.
School—Prince of Peace Catholic School, (Grades K-8) Tel: 864-331-2145; Fax: 864-331-2153. Dr. Michael Pennell, Prin. Child Development Center
Catechesis/Religious Program—Tel: 864-331-3919. Students 218.

UNION, UNION CO., ST. AUGUSTINE (1967) Rev. Michael F. McCafferty; Deacon William Bower.
Mailing Address: P.O. Box 507, 29379. Tel: 864-427-7240; Fax: 864-427-7240.
103 E. South St., 29379.

WALTERBORO, COLLETON CO.
1—ST. ANTHONY (1917) [CEM] Rev. Jeffrey A. Kendall.
925 S. Jefferies Blvd., 29488. Tel: 843-549-5230; Fax: 843-549-9176.
Catechesis/Religious Program—Students 53.
Mission—St. James the Greater [CEM] 3087 Ritter Rd., Colleton Co. 29488.
2—ST. JOSEPH, Closed. For inquiries for parish records contact St. Anthony.

WARD, SALUDA CO., ST. WILLIAM (1895) [CEM] Rev. Noel Tria (Philippines), Canonical Mod./Admin.; Deacon John P. Klein, Parish Life Facilitator.
1199 Ridge Spring Hwy., 29166. Tel: 864-445-7215; Fax: 864-445-1150. Email: stwill@pbtcomm.net.
Catechesis/Religious Program—Students 51.

WINNSBORO, FAIRFIELD CO., ST. THERESA (1968) Rev. Andrew Trapp.
321 Bypass, P.O. Box 1004, 29180.
Catechesis/Religious Program—Aldeane Brock, D.R.E. Students 7.

YONGES ISLAND, CHARLESTON CO., ST. MARY (1911) Rev. Anthony Benjamine (India), Admin.
4255 State Hwy. 165, 29449. Tel: 843-889-8549; Fax: 843-889-8549.
Catechesis/Religious Program—Students 9.
Mission—Sts. Frederick & Stephen P.O. Box 602, Edisto Island, Charleston Co. 29438. Tel: 843-869-0124; Fax: 843-869-0124.

YORK, YORK CO., DIVINE SAVIOUR (1938) Rev. Adilso Coelho, C.O.; Deacon Henry Bernal.
Mailing Address: P.O. Box 341, 29745. Email: divinesaviour@yahoo.com.
232 Herndon Ave., 29745. Tel: 803-684-3431; Fax: 803-684-3431. Web: www.divinesaviour.org.
Catechesis/Religious Program—Students 142.
Mission—All Saints P.O. Box 5443, Lake Wylie, York Co. 29710. Tel: 803-831-9095; Fax: 803-831-9096. Email: allsaintsparish@bellsouth.net. Web: www.allsaintscatholicmission.org.

Chaplains of Public Institutions

LEXINGTON. *Correctional Institutions in the Greater Columbia Area*, 4214 Grand St., 29203. Tel: 803-786-7177. Mr. Roland L. Thomas.

Graduate Studies:
Rev.—
Miles, Thomas, St. Paul University, Ottawa, ON

Military Chaplains:
Revs.—
Linsky, Gary S., U.S. Air Force
Spencer, Robert A., U.S. Navy

Absent On Leave:
Revs.—
Bush, Carson
Coffey, John P.
Congro, Basil P.
Davino, Michael J.
Morrison, Thomas F.
Robinson, Ralph C.
Watters, Timothy J.

Retired:
Most Rev.—
Thompson, David B., D.D., J.C.L., 4479 Downing Pl., Mount Pleasant, 29466.
Rev. Msgr.—
Gorski, J. Donald, 43155 Portola Ave., SPC 120, Palm Desert, CA 92260-2547.
Revs.—
Clarke, Peter, S.T.D., 35 Murphy St., North Augusta, 29860.
Day, Charles J., 134 Bumble Cir., Mauldin, 29662.
Fix, Robert H., 7142 Woodrow St., Rm. #10, Irmo, 29063.
Kennedy, Ernest E., 105 Driftwood Dr., Bonneau, 29431.
LaBrecque, Frederick, S.T.L., 4265 Villas Dr., Unit 909, Little River, 29566.
Leonard, Eugene A., 347 W. Pointe, Spartanburg, 29301.
Masad, Frederick F., P.O. Box 23099, Columbia, 29224.
McCaffrey, Edmund M., Ph.D.
Parker, James, 2 Riverdale Dr., 29407.
Seitz, Paul F.X., 1660 Ingram Rd., 29407.
Snopek, Charles J., 190 Walcott Dr., Lyman, 29365.
Ward, Jerome A., O.M.I., 5001 Bedfordshire Dr., Fort Worth, TX 76135.

Permanent Deacons:
Anderson, Ronald J., St. Peter, Columbia
Anonie, Joseph A., Immaculate Conception Church, Goose Creek
Armstrong, Reginald, St. Anthony, Florence
Arnold, Mark, (On Duty Outside the Diocese)
Ball, James, All Saints Mission, Lake Wylie
Baranoski, Thomas, St. Joseph, Charleston
Barlow, Robert, St. Andrew, Myrtle Beach
Beeler, Michael A., St. Peter, Beaufort
Benval, Henry, Divine Savior, York
Biviano, Joseph P., Our Lady of the Lake Church, Chapin
Bower, William, St. Augustine, Union
Brown, John H., (Retired)
Burdick, Steve, Our Lady of the Hills, Columbia
Burkett, Dennis, St. Gregory the Great, Bluffton
Cahill, Joseph F., Christ Our King Church, Mount Pleasant
Campana, Richard, Sr., St. Andrew, Clemson; St. Francis Mission, Walhalla; St. Paul the Apostle Mission, Seneca
Cardenas, Mario, Holy Spirit, Johns Island
Carmody, Joseph E., (Retired)
Cassamento, Peter, Our Lady Star of the Sea, North Myrtle Beach
Cassandra, Anthony J., St. Luke, Easley
Collins, James, Church of the Resurrection, Loris
Cooper, Charles, St. Francis by the Sea, Hilton Head Island
Corum, Lawrence, St. Jude, Sumter
Crocker, Jack L., D.D.S., Corpus Christi, Lexington
Cuervo, Gabriel, St. Mary Magdalene, Simpsonville
Curcio, Peter A., Christ the Divine Teacher, Charleston
D'Angelo, V. Richard, (Retired)
Dashnaw, Donald R., Ph.D., Ed.D., (Retired)
Davis, Thomas E., (On Duty Outside the Diocese)
DeNitto, Donald, Church of the Infant Jesus, Marion
DeWolfe, John, Holy Family, Hilton Head
Dillard, Henry, (Retired)
DiRusso, Charles R., Our Lady of the Hills, Columbia
Dotson, Robert E., (Retired)
Drinkwater, Oscar, (Retired)
Dwyer, Jon E., St. Philip Neri, Fort Mill
Easterling, Charles M., (Retired)
Efken, Donald C., (Retired)
Egendoerfer, Eugene, St. Luke, Easley
Ellis, Billy J., St. Anne, Sumter
Ferland, George, St. Andrew, Myrtle Beach
Ferro, Diego, St. Mary, Greenville
Fiore, Charlie, St. Michael, Garden City
Flenke, Richard, Our Lady Star of the Sea, North Myrtle Beach
Gerald, Robert C., Jr., St. Anne, Florence
Gorman, Chester E., Our Lady of the Sea, North Myrtle Beach
Graham, James, St. Gregory the Great, Bluffton
Graham, Shane, St. Theresa the Little Flower, Summerville
Grismore, Gerald W., Stella Maris, Sullivan's Island
Guillet, Andre J.P., Christ Our King, Mount Pleasant
Hand, Gerald, St. Francis by the Sea, Hilton Head
Hanrahan, Charles, St. Joseph, Anderson
Hanson, David, St. Michael, Garden City
Hanvey, Samuel E., (Retired)
Heuser, John, St. Mary, Greenville
Hollis, Walter W., St. Gregory the Great, Bluffton
Hookness, Robert, Our Lady of Peace, North Augusta
Houle, Matthew, (Serving Out of State)
Hyland, James P., St. Anne, Rock Hill
Jackson, Harold I., St. Ann, Kingstree
Johnson, Carl, St. Martin de Porres, Columbia
Johnson, James H., St. Ann, Florence
Jones, Dennis N., Our Lady of the Hills, Columbia
Jones, Robert, St. Andrew, Myrtle Beach
Karandisevsky, John F., (Retired)
Kronyak, Robert C., St. Ann, Holly Hill
Kulungowski, Michael, St. Anne, Sumter
La Rosa, P. Charles, Jr., Sts. Frederick & Stephen Mission, Edisto Island
LaCombe, William, St. Peter, Beaufort
Larkin, John S., St. Mary, the Virgin Mother, Hartsville
Laws, Brian, St. Anthony, Hardeeville
Loignon, Gerald, Jr., St. Mark, Newberry
Mahaffey, Robert L., Jr., St. Paul the Apostle, Spartanburg
Mahefky, Paul, (On Duty Outside the Diocese)

Mannino, Matthew A., St. Mary Magdalene, Simpsonville
McCabe, John, St. Gregory the Great, Bluffton
McDonald, Thomas F., (Retired)
McNerny, Daniel, Immaculate Conception, Goose Creek
Mevissen, Jeffrey P., St. James, Conway
Meyer, Philip M.
Moore, James R., Blessed Sacrament, Charleston
Moore, Oliver R., St. Anne, Rock Hill
Murtaugh, Richard J., Jr., St. Elizabeth Ann Seton, Mauldin
Nazzaro, Joseph J., St. Francis by the Sea, Hilton Head
Nunez, Guillermo, St. Anne, Rock Hill
Olimpio, Charles, Cathedral of St. John the Baptist, Charleston
Osbourne, R. Michael, Stella Maris, Sullivan's Island
Palmer, Orean D., Corpus Christi, Lexington
Parks, Coleman T., Corpus Christi, Lexington
Pecko, Harry, (Retired)
Peitler, Edward, St. Peter, Beaufort
Perham, Raymond, Our Lady of the Rosary, Greenville
Petrusak, Frank T., (Retired)
Pezanowski, Walter S., Stella Maris, Sullivan's Island
Pierce, Robert A., St. Mary Help of Christians, Aiken
Pierfy, Jeffery, St. Anthony, Florence
Poole, Charles P., Jr., (Retired)
Ramirez, Jorge V., St. Thomas the Apostle, North Charleston
Remkiewicz, Jerome P., Cathedral of St. John the Baptist/St. Mary, Charleston
Rhodes, Steven, St. Philip Neri, Fort Mill
Richardson, David W., Melkite Community
Roberts, Lawrence, Immaculate Conception, Goose Creek
Roseborough, Donald, (On Duty Outside the Diocese)
Sams, Gregory W., St. Gregory the Great, Bluffton
Sandlin, J. Wescoat, St. John the Beloved, Summerville
Schito, Albert, St. Anthony, Hardesville
Sheehan, Patrick, St. Francis by the Sea, Hilton Head Island
Shook, Paul F., (Retired)
Skipper, Malcolm, Our Lady of the Lake, Chapin
Smith, Robert, Prince of Peace, Taylors
Starr, Robert, St. Michael, Garden City
Stetar, John, St. Peter, Columbia
Stoshak, Andrew, Our Lady Star of the Sea, North Myrtle Beach
Sturm, Robert M., Jesus, Our Risen Savior, Spartanburg
Thompson, David, St. Peter, Columbia
Tierney, George, St. Mary, Greenville
Tyson, Robert, (Retired)
Walczak, Gary, Prince of Peace, Taylors
Walsh, Charles Michael, St. Mary; Our Lady of Hope, Manning
Waters, Robert J., St. Mary Help of Christians, Aiken
Weigold, Gregory, Our Lady of the Lake, Chapin
West, James L., (On Duty Outside the Diocese)
William, W. James, II, St. Anthony of Padua, Greenville
Wright, Winston C., St. Anthony of Padua, Greenville

INSTITUTIONS LOCATED IN THE DIOCESE

[A] HIGH SCHOOLS, DIOCESAN

CHARLESTON. *Bishop England High School*, 363 Seven Farms Dr., 29492-7534. Tel: 843-849-9599; Fax: 843-849-9221. Email: dheld@behs.com. Web: www.behs.com. Michael Bolchoz, Prin.; Cindi Haviland, Librarian. Lay Teachers 62; Students 730.

COLUMBIA. *Cardinal Newman School*, (Grades 7-12), 4701 Forest Dr., 29206. Tel: 803-782-2814; Fax: 803-782-9314. Email: jkasprowski@cnhs.org. Web: www.cnhs.org. Jacqualine Kasprowski, Prin.; Kathleen Cole, Librarian. Priests 1; Sisters 1; Lay Teachers 51; Students 427.

[B] HIGH SCHOOLS, PRIVATE

GREENVILLE. *St. Joseph's Catholic School* (1993) (Grades 6-12), 100 St. Joseph's Dr., 29607. Tel: 864-234-9009; Fax: 864-234-5516. Email: info@sjcatholicschool.org. Web: www.sjcatholicschool.org. Mr. Keith F. Kiser, Headmaster. Lay Teachers 54; Total Staff 78; Students 611.

SUMTER. **St. Francis Xavier High School* (1997) 15 School St., 29150. Tel: 803-773-0210; Fax: 803-775-0119. Email: sfxhs@sc.rr.com. Web: www.sfxhs.com. Susan Lavergne, Prin.; Ilknur Leverich, Librarian. Lay Teachers 8; Students 42.

[C] GENERAL HOSPITALS

CHARLESTON. **Bon Secours St. Francis Xavier Hospital* (1882) 2095 Henry Tecklenburg Dr., 29414. Tel: 843-402-1000; Fax: 843-402-1945. Email: allen.carroll@rsfh.com. Web: www.rsfh.com. Mr. Allen P. Carroll, CEO. Sponsored by Bon Secours Ministries. Bed Capacity 204; Total Staff 1,096; Patients Assisted Annually 127,321.

Sisters of Charity Providence Hospitals, 2435 Forest Dr., Columbia, 29204. Tel: 803-256-5313; Fax: 803-296-5765. Email: George.Zara@providencehospitals.com.

GREENVILLE. *Bon Secours St. Francis Health System, Inc.*, One St. Francis Dr., 29601. Tel: 864-255-1000; Fax: 864-255-1137. Web: www.stfrancishealth.org.

St. Francis Hospital, Inc. Tel: 864-255-1000; Fax: 864-255-1137. Mark Nantz, CEO; Elizabeth Keith, Senior V.P. Mission. Sisters of Bon Secours 2; Bed Capacity 338; Total Staff 2,954; Patients Assisted Annually 197,968.

[D] HOMES FOR AGED

CHARLESTON. *Carter-May Home Assisted Living & St. Joseph Residence for Retired Priests*, 1660 Ingram Rd., 29407. Tel: 843-556-8314; Fax: 843-556-6879. Email: janine@catholic-doc.org. Mrs. Janine N. Bauder, Admin. Bed Capacity 25; Total Staff 25; Total Assisted Annually 26.

[E] MONASTERIES AND RESIDENCES OF PRIESTS AND BROTHERS

MONCKS CORNER. *Mepkin Abbey* (1949) (Trappist Monks), 1098 Mepkin Abbey Rd., 29461-4796. Tel: 843-761-8509; Fax: 843-761-6719. Email: community@mepkinabbey.org. Web: www.mepkinabbey.org. Rt. Revs. Stanislaus Gumula, O.C.S.O., Abbot; Christian Aidan Carr, O.C.S.O. (Retired); Revs. Kevin V. Walsh, O.C.S.O, Contact Person & Novice Dir.; Leonard A. Cunningham, O.C.S.O.; Aelred Hagan, O.C.S.O.; Guerric Frederick A. Heckel; Feliciano Manalili, O.C.S.O.; Richard G. McGuire, O.C.S.O.; Bros. Stephen Petronek, O.C.S.O.; John Corrigan, Cellarer. Professed Monks 16; Priests 8; Postulants 1; Novices 2; Total in Community 19.

ROCK HILL. *Oratory of St. Philip Neri, Congregation of the Oratory of Pontifical Rite*, 434 Charlotte Ave., P.O. Box 11586, 29731. Tel: 803-327-2097; Fax: 803-327-6264. Email: rhoratory@comporium.net. Web: www.rockhilloratory.org. P.O. Box 11586, 29731-1586. Tel: 803-327-2097; Fax: 803-327-6264. Very Rev. Fabio Refosco, C.O., Provost; Revs. Edward P. McDevitt, C.O.; Joseph A. Wahl, C.O.; John P. Giuliani, C.O.; Agustin Guzman, C.O.; James Moran, C.O.; Halbert Weidner, C.O., Ph.D.; Joseph Francis Pearce, C.O.; Adilso Coelho, C.O.; Elbano Munoz, C.O.; Bros. David Boone, C.O.; Joseph Guyon, C.O., Deputy; John F. Kummer, C.O., Deputy; Paul Nguyen, C.O.; Josemaria Schlubach, C.O.; Joseph Wilkerson, C.O.; Michael Young, C.O. Fathers 10; Brothers 5; Seminarians 2.

[F] CONVENTS AND RESIDENCES FOR SISTERS

CHARLESTON. *Daughters of St. Paul Convent*, 243 King St., 29401. Tel: 843-577-0175; Fax: 843-577-9833. Email: charleston@paulinemedia.com. Web: www.pauline.org. Sr. Deborah Dunevant, Local Supr. Sisters 4.

Sisters of Charity of Our Lady of Mercy (1829) 424 Ft. Johnson Rd., P.O. Box 12410, 29422. Tel: 843-795-6083; Fax: 843-795-6083. Email: olm@comcast.com. Sr. Bridget Sullivan, O.L.M., Gen. Supr. Tel: 843-795-2866. Professed Sisters in Community 19.

ST. HELENA ISLAND. *Franciscan Center*, 85 Mattis Rd., U.S. Hwy. 21, P.O. Box 682, 29920. Tel: 843-838-3924; Fax: 843-838-2152. Email: franctr@islc.net. Web: www.islc.net/~franctr. Sisters of St. Francis of Philadelphia, Glen Riddle-Aston, PA 2.

TRAVELERS REST. *Monastery of St. Clare*, 37 McCauley Rd., 29690. Tel: 864-834-8015; Fax: 864-834-5402. Email: development@poorclaresc.com. Web: www.poorclaresc.com. Sr. Mary Connor, O.S.C., Abbess. Franciscan Poor Clare Nuns. Cloistered Nuns in Solemn Vows 15; Extern in Perpetual Vows 1; Novices 2.

[G] CATHOLIC CHARITIES

CHARLESTON. *Catholic Charities of the Diocese of Charleston*, 1662 Ingram Rd., 29407. Tel: 843-402-9115, Ext. 15; Fax: 843-402-9071. Web: www.supportcatholiccharities.org.

Coastal Regional Office, 3921 St. John's Ave., North Charleston, 29405-7158. Tel: 843-308-9361; Fax: 843-744-6204. Email: holeary@catholic-doc.org. Helen O'Leary, Regl. Coord.

Midlands Regional Office, P.O. Box 7245, Columbia, 29202-7245. Tel: 803-254-9776; Fax: 803-252-7605. Email: mgohean@catholic-doc.org. Mary Trivisonno, Regl. Coord.

Pee Dee Regional Office, 537-B Hwy. 90, Conway, 29526. Tel: 843-234-1999; Fax: 843-234-3132. Daryl Kangarloo, Regl. Coord.

Piedmont Regional Office, 204 Douthit St., Ste. A1, Greenville, 29601. Tel: 864-242-2233; Fax: 864-242-1387. Deacon Gabriel Cuervo, Regl. Coord.

Lowcounty Regional Office, Pamela Rice, Regl. Coord. & Prison Ministry, 1662 Ingram Rd., 29407. Tel: 843-812-3078. Email: price@catholic-doc.org. Deborah Riley, Regl. Coord.

Echo House-Inner City Apostolate (1967) 1911 Hackermann Ave., North Charleston, 29405. Tel: 843-554-7319; Fax: 843-225-8090.

[H] CAMPUS MINISTRIES

CHARLESTON. *Catholic Campus Ministry at the College of Charleston c/o St. Patrick*, 134 St. Phillip St., 29403. Tel: 843-937-5993. Email: cofcatholics@aol.com.

Charleston Southern University P.O. Box 118087, 29423-8087. Tel: 843-863-7081. Email: emcdermo@csuniv.edu. Dr. Eugene McDermott, Ph.D., Faculty Advisor.

The Citadel Office of the Catholic Chaplain, The Citadel, MSC 58, 29409-0058. Tel: 843-953-7692; Fax: 843-953-4811. Web: citadel.edu/catholic.

AIKEN. *University of South Carolina, Aiken Extension c/o St. Mary Help of Christians*, P.O. Box 438, 29802. Tel: 803-649-4777.

BEAUFORT. *University of South Carolina, Beaufort Extension St. Peter*, 70 Lady's Island Dr., 29907. Tel: 843-522-9555. Rev. Timothy D. Tebalt.

CLEMSON. *Clemson University, Southern Wesleyan University & TriCounty Technical College* P.O. Box 112, 29633. 209 Sloan St., 29633. Tel: 864-654-7804; 864-654-1757; 864-654-9670; Fax: 864-654-2950. Email: csa@clemson.edu. Web: www.clemson.edu/~csa. Mr. Fred Mercadante, Campus Min.

Clemson University - Catholic Campus Ministry at St. Andrew's Church and the Catholic Student Association.

CLINTON. *Presbyterian College c/o St. Mark*, 928 Boundary St., Newberry, 29108. Tel: 803-276-6446; Fax: 803-276-0856.

COLUMBIA. *Allen University, Benedict College* c/o St. Martin de Porres Church, 2229 Hampton St., 29204. Tel: 803-254-6862; Fax: 803-799-4720. Email: deporres@yahoo.com. Rev. Paul M. Williams, O.F.M.

St. Thomas More Center 1610 Greene St., 29201. Tel: 803-799-5870; Fax: 803-765-0800. Email: stmcola@gmail.com. Web: www.stthomasmoreusc.org. Rev. Marcin Zahuta (Poland), Chap. & Campus Min.

CONWAY. *Coastal Carolina University Catholic Campus Ministry*, P.O. Box 261954, 29528. Tel: 843-349-2026; Fax: 843-349-2127.

FLORENCE. *Francis Marion University c/o St. Ann Church*, 113 S. Kemp St., 29506. Tel: 843-661-5012; Fax: 843-673-2680. Rev. John M. Zimmerman.

GAFFNEY. *Limestone College c/o Sacred Heart Church*, 407 Grace St., 29340. Tel: 864-489-9453; Fax: 864-489-9150. Email: sacredheart@marisao.com. Rev. Francisco Cruz (Colombia).

GREENVILLE. *Furman University Campus Ministry St. Mary's Catholic Church*, 111 Hampton Ave., 29601. Tel: 864-271-8422; Fax: 864-370-9880. Email: churchoffice@stmarysgvl.org. Web: www.stmarysgvl.org. Very Rev. Jay Scott Newman, J.C.L., V.F.; Dan Sloughter, Faculty Advisor. Students 300.

GREENWOOD. *Lander University c/o Our Lady of Lourdes*, 915 Mathis Rd., 29646. Tel: 864-223-8410; Fax: 864-223-7555. Email: frtebalt@olol.org. Rev. Timothy D. Tebalt.

HARTSVILLE. *Coker College c/o St. Mary the Virgin Mother*, 363 N. Fifth St., 29550. Tel: 843-332-7773; 843-332-3136; Fax: 843-332-2812. Email: stmary2@ymail.com. Very Rev. Karl J. Roesch, O.S.B., V.F.

ORANGEBURG. *South Carolina State University & Claflin College* P.O. Box 1691, 29116. Tel: 803-534-8177; Fax: 803-535-0012.

ROCK HILL. *Winthrop University, York Co. Tech Center*

434 Charlotte Ave., Box 11586, 29731. Tel: 803-327-2097; Fax: 803-327-6264.

SPARTANBURG. *Converse College, Wofford College, USC - Upstate c/o St. Paul the Apostle*, 161 N. Dean St., 29302. Tel: 864-582-0674; Fax: 864-582-0716. Web: www.st-paultheapostle.org. Rev. Teodoro Kalaw, C.R.M.

[I] RETREAT CENTERS

EDISTO ISLAND. **Sea of Peace House of Prayer* (1995) 542 Palmetto Pointe Rd., 29438. Tel: 843-869-0513. Email: sharonculhane@bellsouth.net. Web: www.seaofpeacehouseofprayer.org.

[J] MISCELLANEOUS

CHARLESTON. *The Barry Charitable Trust*, 424 Ft. Johnson Rd., P.O. Box 12410, 29422. Tel: 843-795-2866; Fax: 843-795-6083.

**Catholic Radio Association*, 121 Broad St., 29401. Tel: 843-853-2300. Web: www.catholicradioassociation.org. Stephen Gajdosik, Pres.; Douglas Sherman, Chm.

Catholic Stewardship Charitable Trust of South Carolina, 1662 Ingram Rd., 29407.

Our Lady of Mercy Community Outreach Services, Inc./Neighborhood House, 77 America St., 29403. Tel: 843-853-8329; Fax: 843-853-8329. Email: neighborhoodhse@bellsouth.net; srpat@bellsouth.net. Sponsored by the Sisters of Charity of Our Lady of Mercy. Total Assisted Annually 47,810.

Pauline Books & Media, 243 King St., 29401. Tel: 843-577-0175; Fax: 843-577-9833. Email: charleston@paulinemedia.com. Web: www.pauline.org. Daughters of St. Paul.

AIKEN. **Society of St. Vincent de Paul*, 190 Hunting Hills Dr., 29803. Tel: 803-641-3875. Email: greg_flach@bellsouth.net. Greg Flach, Diocesan Council Pres.; Tom Berg, Piedmont District Council Pres.; Marilyn Gray, Midlands District Council Pres.

BLUFFTON. *John Paul II Catholic School*, 333 Fording Island Rd., 29909. Dr. Helen Ryan, Acting Prin. & Contact Person.

COLUMBIA. **Family Honor, Inc.* (1987) 2927 Devine St., Ste. 130, 29205. Tel: 803-929-0858; Fax: 803-771-2379. Email: famhonor@aol.com. Web: www.familyhonor.org. Brenda Cerkez, Exec. Dir.

Healthy Learners, 2749 Laurel St., 29204. Tel: 216-696-5560; Fax: 216-696-2204. Web: www.CSAHealthSystems.org. Sr. Judith Ann Karam, C.S.A., Pres. & CEO.

Providence Hospitals Development Foundation, Mailing Address: 2435 Forest Dr., 29204. Tel: 803-256-5313. Email: george.zara@providencehospitals.com. George A. Zara, Pres. & CEO.

Sisters of Charity Foundation of South Carolina, 2711 Middleburg Dr., Ste. 115, 29204-2413. Tel: 803-254-0230; Fax: 803-748-0444. Email: scfsc@sistersofcharitysc.com. Web: www.sistersofcharitysc.com.

GREENVILLE. *Bon Secours St. Francis Foundation*, 1 St. Francis Dr., 29601. Tel: 864-255-1040; Fax: 864-679-8879. Erik Whaley, C.F.R.E., Contact Person.

JOHNS ISLAND. *Our Lady of Mercy Community Outreach Services, Inc.* (1989) 1684 Brownswood Rd., 29455. Tel: 843-559-4109; Fax: 843-559-8819. Email: info@olmoutreach.org. Web: olmoutreach.org. P.O. Box 607, 29457. Tel: 843-559-4109; Fax: 843-558-8819. Sponsored by Sisters of Charity of Our Lady of Mercy. Total Staff 25; Outreach Center 9,693; Wellness Center 3,834; Total Assisted Annually 11,000.

KINGSTREE. *Felician Center, Inc.*, 908 Thorne Ave., 29556. Tel: 843-354-9415; Fax: 843-354-9093. Sr. Johnna Ciezobka, Pres.

Shrine of Our Lady of South Carolina-Our Lady of Joyful Hope 313 E. Main St., Hwy. 261, 29556. Tel: 843-355-3527. Email: frss@ftc-i.net. Web: www.ourladyofsouthcarolina.net. Mailing Address: 300 Ashton Ave., 29556-4036. Rev. Stanley Smolenski, S.P.M.A., Office of the Shrine Dir. Administered by the Diocese of Charleston, 330 Main St., Charleston, SC 29556.

MYRTLE BEACH. *St. Elizabeth Ann Seton High School Association*, 3501 N. Kings Hwy., Ste. 102, 29577. Tel: 843-448-5930; Fax: 843-448-3947. Rev. James L. LeBlanc, Pres.

RELIGIOUS INSTITUTES OF MEN REPRESENTED IN THE DIOCESE

For further details refer to the corresponding bracketed number in the Religious Institutes of Men or Women section.

[0100]—*Adorno Fathers*—C.R.M.
[]—*Apostles of Jesus*—A.J.
[0200]—*Benedictines*—O.S.B.
[]—*Carmelites of Mary Immaculate*—C.M.I.
[0350]—*Cistercians Order of the Strict Observance-Trappist*—O.C.S.O.
[]—*Congregation of Christian Brothers*—C.F.C.
[]—*Crusaders of the Holy Spirit*—C.H.S.
[]—*Dominicans*—O.P.
[0520]—*Franciscan Friars* (Prov. of the Most Holy Name)—O.F.M.
[]—*Misioneros de Yarmul*—I.M.E.Y.
[1110]—*Missionaries of the Sacred Heart*—M.S.C.
[0950]—*Oratorians*—C.O.
[1050]—*Pontifical Institute of Foreign Missions*—P.I.M.E.
[1070]—*Redemptorist Fathers* (Richmond Vice Prov.)—C.SS.R.

RELIGIOUS INSTITUTES OF WOMEN REPRESENTED IN THE DIOCESE

[0270]—*Congregation of Bon Secours*—C.B.S.
[1730]—*Congregation of the Sisters of the Third Order of St. Francis* (Oldenburg, IN)—O.S.F.
[0760]—*Daughters of Charity of St. Vincent de Paul*—D.C.
[0960]—*Daughters of Wisdom* (American Prov.)—D.W.
[1070-11]—*Dominican Sisters* (Sparkill, NY)—O.P.
[1070-13]—*Dominican Sisters* (Adrian, MI)—O.P.
[1070-07]—*Dominican Sisters* (Nashville, TN)—O.P.
[]—*Dominican Sisters* (Ann Arbor, MI)—O.P.
[1170]—*Felician Sisters*—C.S.S.F.
[]—*Missionary Servants of the Most Blessed Trinity*—M.S.B.T.
[3760]—*Order of St. Clare*—O.S.C.
[0950]—*Pious Daughters of St. Paul*—F.S.P.
[2970]—*School Sisters of Notre Dame*—S.S.N.D.
[]—*Sisters for Christian Community*—S.F.C.C.
[0500]—*Sisters of Charity of Nazareth*—S.C.N.
[0510]—*Sisters of Charity of Our Lady of Mercy*—O.L.M.
[0580]—*Sisters of Charity of St. Augustine*—C.S.A.
[1620]—*Sisters of St. Francis of the Newman Communities*—O.S.F.
[2575]—*Sisters of Mercy of the Americas* (Chicago, IL; Pittsburgh, PA)—R.S.M.
[3000]—*Sisters of Notre Dame* (Baltimore, MD)—S.N.D.deN.
[2990]—*Sisters of Notre Dame* (Toledo, OH)—S.N.D.
[3950]—*Sisters of Saint Mary of Namur*—S.S.M.N.
[3780]—*Sisters of Saints Cyril and Methodius*—SS.C.M.
[1650]—*Sisters of St. Francis of Philadelphia*—O.S.F.
[1570]—*Sisters of St. Francis of the Holy Family*—O.S.F.
[3840]—*Sisters of St. Joseph of Carondelet* (Prov. of St. Louis)—C.S.J.
[]—*Sisters of the Sacred Heart of Jesus* (Mexico)—H.C.J.S.
[4120-03]—*Ursuline Nuns, of the Congregation of Paris*—O.S.U.

DIOCESAN CEMETERIES

CHARLESTON. *Holy Cross and St. Lawrence*, 604 Ft. Johnson Rd., 29412. Tel: 843-795-2111; Fax: 843-576-4925. Mr. Warren R. Stuckey Jr., Dir.

NECROLOGY

† Roth, Rev. Msgr. Joseph R.—Died May 15, 2011
† Juya, Filemon—Died June 30, 2011
† Sorce, John J., (Retired)—Died July 29, 2011

An asterisk (*) denotes an organization that has established tax-exempt status directly with the IRS and is not covered by the USCCB Group Ruling.

Diocese of Charlotte

(Dioecesis Carolinana)

Most Reverend

PETER J. JUGIS, J.C.D.

Bishop of Charlotte; ordained June 12, 1983; appointed Bishop of Charlotte August 1, 2003; episcopal ordination October 24, 2003.

CARITAS CHRISTI URGET NOS

Chancery: P.O. Box 36776, Charlotte, NC 28236. Tel: 704-370-6299; Fax: 704-370-3379.

Web: charlottediocese.org

Email: chancery@charlottediocese.org

ESTABLISHED JANUARY 12, 1972.

Square Miles 20,470.

Comprises the Counties of Alexander, Alleghany, Anson, Ashe, Avery, Buncombe, Burke, Cabarrus, Caldwell, Catawba, Cherokee, Clay, Cleveland, Davidson, Davie, Forsyth, Gaston, Graham, Guilford, Haywood, Henderson, Iredell, Jackson, Lincoln, Macon, Madison, McDowell, Mecklenberg, Mitchell, Montgomery, Polk, Randolph, Richmond, Rockingham, Rowan, Rutherford, Stanley, Stokes, Surry, Swain, Transylvania, Union, Watauga, Wilkes, Yadkin and Yancey in the State of North Carolina.

For legal titles of parishes and diocesan institutions, consult the Chancery.

STATISTICAL OVERVIEW

(Editor's Note: 2012 statistical information was not received)

Personnel	
Bishop	1
Retired Bishops	1
Abbots	1
Retired Abbots	1
Priests: Diocesan Active in Diocese	74
Priests: Diocesan Active Outside Diocese	2
Priests: Retired, Sick or Absent	36
Number of Diocesan Priests	112
Religious Priests in Diocese	48
Total Priests in Diocese	160
Extern Priests in Diocese	5
Ordinations:	
Diocesan Priests	4
Permanent Deacons in Diocese	103
Total Brothers	11
Total Sisters	123
Parishes	
Parishes	73
With Resident Pastor:	
Resident Diocesan Priests	56
Resident Religious Priests	17
Missions	19
Pastoral Centers	2
Professional Ministry Personnel:	
Brothers	2
Sisters	18
Lay Ministers	619
Welfare	
Health Care Centers	16
Total Assisted	56,000
Homes for the Aged	2
Total Assisted	180
Day Care Centers	13
Total Assisted	1,000
Specialized Homes	4
Total Assisted	640
Special Centers for Social Services	4
Total Assisted	29,927
Residential Care of Disabled	1
Total Assisted	125
Other Institutions	1
Educational	
Diocesan Students in Other Seminaries	12
Total Seminarians	12
Colleges and Universities	1
Total Students	1,734
High Schools, Diocesan and Parish	2
Total Students	1,941
Elementary Schools, Diocesan and Parish	16
Total Students	5,598
Catechesis/Religious Education:	
High School Students	2,841
Elementary Students	24,030
Total Students under Catholic Instruction	36,154
Teachers in the Diocese:	
Sisters	6
Lay Teachers	627
Vital Statistics	
Receptions into the Church:	
Infant Baptism Totals	3,233
Minor Baptism Totals	329
Adult Baptism Totals	293
Received into Full Communion	628
First Communions	5,587
Confirmations	3,615
Marriages:	
Catholic	639
Interfaith	312
Total Marriages	951
Deaths	1,107
Total Catholic Population	174,689
Total Population	4,801,606

Former Bishops—Most Revs. MICHAEL J. BEGLEY, D.D., ord. May 26, 1934; appt. Nov. 30, 1971; cons. first Bishop of Charlotte Jan. 12, 1972; retired 1984; died Feb. 9, 2002; JOHN F. DONOGHUE, D.D., ord. June 4, 1955; appt. Nov. 6, 1984; cons. Dec. 18, 1984; appt. Archbishop of Atlanta June 22, 1993; cons. Aug. 19, 1993; died Nov. 11, 2011; WILLIAM G. CURLIN, D.D. (Retired), ord. May 25, 1957; appt. Auxiliary Bishop of Washington Nov. 2, 1988; cons. Dec. 20, 1988; appt. Bishop of Charlotte, Feb. 22, 1994; installed April 13, 1994; retired Sept. 10, 2002.

Chancery—P.O. Box 36776, Charlotte, 28236. Tel: 704-370-6299; Fax: 704-370-3379.

Vicar General, Chancellor, and Moderator of the Curia—Rev. Msgr. MAURICIO W. WEST, P.O. Box 36776, Charlotte, 28236. Tel: 704-370-3326; Fax: 704-370-3379.

Vice Chancellor—Rev. Msgr. ANTHONY J. MARCACCIO, St. Pius Tenth Church, 2210 N. Elm St., Greensboro, 27408.

Chief Financial Officer—WILLIAM G. WELDON, CPA, 1123 S. Church St., Charlotte, 28203. Tel: 704-370-3313.

Controller—STELLA NELL, 1123 S. Church St., Charlotte, 28203. Tel: 704-370-3312.

Diocesan Properties and Risk Management—Deacon GUY A. PICHE, Dir., 1123 S. Church St., Charlotte, 28203. Tel: 704-370-3304.

Human Resources and Employee Benefits—TERRI WILHELM, 1123 S. Church St., Charlotte, 28203. Tel: 704-370-3338.

Diocesan Tribunal—1123 S. Church St., Charlotte, 28203. Tel: 704-370-3293. LISA D. SARVIS, Head Tribunal.

Judicial Vicar—Very Rev. JOHN T. PUTNAM, J.C.L.; JOY BARNES, S.I.M., Advocate; DEBBIE M. WRIGHT, Auditor; JACINTA LEWIS, Sec. & Notary.

Education—Very Rev. ROGER K. ARNSPARGER, V.F., Vicar, 1123 S. Church St., Charlotte, 28203. Tel: 704-370-3210; Fax: 704-370-3291.

Diocesan Consultors—Rev. Msgrs. MAURICIO W. WEST; ANTHONY J. MARCACCIO; RICHARD BELLOW; Rev. PAUL GARY; Very Revs. JOHN T. PUTNAM, J.C.L.; ROGER K. ARNSPARGER, V.F.; CHRISTOPHER A. ROUX; JULIO DOMINGUEZ.

Diocesan Offices and Directors

Airport Chaplain—Deacon GEORGE A. SZALONY, 1123 S. Church St., Charlotte, 28203. Tel: 704-370-3344; Fax: 704-370-3378.

Archives—VACANT, Dir., 1123 S. Church St., Charlotte, 28203. Tel: 704-370-3215; Fax: 704-370-3378.

Boy Scouts—Deacon JAMES R. JOHNSON, St. Charles Borromeo Church, 714 W. Union St., Morganton, 28655. Tel: 828-437-3461.

Campus Ministry—Ms. MARY WRIGHT, Dir., 1123 S. Church St., Charlotte, 28203. Tel: 704-370-3212; Fax: 704-370-3378.

Communications—DAVID HAINS, Dir., 1123 S. Church St., Charlotte, 28203. Tel: 704-370-3336; Fax: 704-370-3382.

Evangelization & Lay Ministry—Dr. FRANK VILLARONGA, Dir., 1123 S. Church St., Charlotte, 28203. Tel: 704-370-3274; Fax: 704-370-3291.

Office of Faith Formation—Very Rev. ROGER K. ARNSPARGER, V.F., Dir.; Dr. CRIS VILLAPANDO, Prog. Dir., 1123 S. Church St., Charlotte, 28203. Tel: 704-370-3246; Fax: 704-370-3378.

Youth Ministry—PAUL KOTLOWSKI, 1123 S. Church St., Charlotte, 28203. Tel: 704-370-3211.

Development—JAMES K. KELLEY, Dir.; BARBARA GADDY, Assoc. Dir., 1123 S. Church St., Charlotte, 28203. Tel: 704-370-3301; 704-370-3302; Fax: 704-370-3378.

Foundation of the Roman Catholic Diocese of Charlotte, Inc., The—JAMES KELLEY, Exec. Dir., 1123 S. Church St., Charlotte, 28203. Tel: 704-370-3301.

Hispanic Ministry—Rev. FIDEL C. MELO, Dir., 1123 S. Church St., Charlotte, 28203. Tel: 704-370-3269; Fax: 704-370-3291.

Hmong Ministry—Deacon PE NHIA CHA LEE, Coord., 1123 S. Church St., Charlotte, 28203. Tel: 828-584-6012.

Human Resources—TERRI WILHELM, Dir., 1123 S. Church St., Charlotte, 28203. Tel: 704-370-3338; 704-370-3339; Fax: 704-370-3378.

Korean Catholic Cultural Center—Revs. GITAE LEE, Dir., 7109 Robinson Church Rd., Charlotte, 28215. Tel: 704-531-8417; Fax: 704-531-1843; YOUNGCHEOL KIM, 2516 Glen Meadow Dr., Greensboro, 27455. Tel: 336-282-8663.

African-American Ministry—Mrs. SANDRA P. MURDOCK, Dir., 1123 S. Church St., Charlotte, 28203. Tel: 704-370-3267; Fax: 704-370-3378.

Media Resource Center—Sr. PATRICIA DURBIN, R.S.M., 1123 S. Church St., Charlotte, 28203. Tel: 704-370-3242.

Cathedral Publishing Corporation—Mailing Address: P.O. Box 37267, Charlotte, 28237. Tel: 704-370-6299. *1123 S. Church St., Charlotte, 28203.* Tel:

704-370-3336.

Newspaper: "Catholic News Herald"—PATRICIA L. GUILFOYLE, Editor, Mailing Address: P.O. Box 37267, Charlotte, 28237. Tel: 704-370-3333; 704-370-3334; Fax: 704-370-3382.

Permanent Diaconate—Rev. Msgr. MAURICIO W. WEST, Coord.; Deacon RONALD F. STEINKAMP, Dir., Mailing Address: P.O. Box 36776, Charlotte, 28236. Tel: 704-370-6299; Fax: 704-370-3379.

Planning and Research—GEORGE COBB, OblSB, Dir., 1123 S. Church St., Charlotte, 28203. Tel: 704-370-3328; Fax: 704-370-3378.

Propagation of the Faith—Rev. MARK S. LAWLOR, 1123 S. Church St., Charlotte, 28203. Tel: 704-370-6299; Fax: 704-370-3378.

School—JANICE RITTER, Ed.D., Ph.D., Supt., 1123 S. Church St., Charlotte, 28203. Tel: 704-370-3271; Fax: 704-370-3291.

Mecklenburg Area Catholic Schools—1123 S. Church St., Charlotte, 28203. Tel: 704-370-3270; Fax: 704-370-3291.

Prison Ministry— Contact Permanent Diaconate Office: *1123 S. Church St., Charlotte, 28203.* Tel: 704-370-3344; Fax: 704-370-3378.

Social Services—GERARD A. CARTER, Ph.D., Exec. Dir., 1123 S. Church St., Charlotte, 28203. Tel: 704-370-3228.

Campaign for Human Development—JOSEPH PURELLO, Prog. Dir., 1123 S. Church St., Charlotte, 28203. Tel: 704-370-3283; Fax: 704-370-3277.

Justice and Peace—JOSEPH PURELLO, Dir., 1123 S. Church St., Charlotte, 28203. Tel: 704-370-3225; Fax: 704-370-3277.

Victim Assistance Coordinator—DAVID W. HAROLD, A.C.S.W. Tel: 336-714-3202. Email: dwharold@charlottediocese.org.

Vocations—Rev. CHRISTOPHER M. GOBER, 1123 S. Church St., Charlotte, 28203.

Worship—Dr. LARRY STRATEMEYER, St. Patrick Cathedral, 1621 Dilworth Rd., E., Charlotte, 28203. Tel: 704-334-2283; Fax: 704-377-6403.

CLERGY, PARISHES, MISSIONS AND PAROCHIAL SCHOOLS

CITY OF CHARLOTTE

(MECKLENBURG COUNTY)

1—ST. PATRICK CATHEDRAL (1939), (Phelan Memorial) Very Rev. Christopher A. Roux, Rector; Rev. Richard DeClue; Deacons Nicholas Fadero, (Retired); Carlos A. Medina Sr.; Brian P. McNaulty. In Res., Rev. James A. Ebright.
Res.: 1621 Dilworth Rd., E., 28203. Tel: 704-334-2283; Fax: 704-377-6403. Email: stpatrickcharlotte@charlottediocese.org. Web: www.stpatricks.org.
Catechesis/Religious Program—Tel: 704-334-2283, Ext. 427. Quentin Salerno, D.R.E.; Jonathan Gareis, Youth Min. Students 287.

2—ST. ANN (1955) Rev. Timothy S. Reid; Sisters Judy Monahan, S.S.J., Pastoral Assoc.; Helene G. Nagle, S.S.J., Stewardship Coord.
Church & Res.: 3635 Park Rd., 28209. Tel: 704-523-4641; Fax: 704-527-8671. Email: stanncharlotte@charlottediocese.org. Web: stanncharlotte.org.
Catechesis/Religious Program—Students 165.
Convent—3430 Willow Oak Rd., 28209. Tel: 704-523-0331.

3—ST. GABRIEL (1957) Revs. Francis J. O'Rourke (Retired); J. Patrick Cahill, Parochial Vicar; Deacons Bernard Wenning Jr., (Retired); Mark Diener; Curtiss Todd, (Retired); Robert Gettelfinger, (Retired); Guido Pozo; Lawrence P. O'Toole.
Res.: 2940 Brookridge Ln., 28211. Tel: 704-366-1607; Fax: 704-362-5049. Email: StGabrielCharlotte@charlottediocese.org.
Catechesis/Religious Program—Tel: 704-366-2738. Susan Krasniewski, D.R.E. Tel: 704-362-5047, Ext. 271; Lisa Gilkey, Asst. Dir. Faith Formation; Denise Gruender, Youth Min. Students 1,064.

4—ST. JOHN NEUMANN (1977) Rev. Patrick T. Hoare; Deacons John N. Parrish; James Gorman. In Res., Rev. Peter T. Pham.
Res.: 8451 Idlewild Rd., 28227. Tel: 704-536-6520; Fax: 704-536-3147. Email: stjohnneumanncharlotte@charlottediocese.org. Web: www.4sjnc.org.
Catechesis/Religious Program—Tel: 704-535-4197. Irene Kilzer, Youth Min. Students 484.

5—ST. JOSEPH CHURCH Rev. Tri Vinh Troung.
4929 Sandy Porter Rd., 28273. Tel: 704-588-9022; 704-504-0907 (Rectory); Fax: 704-588-3149. Email: stjosephcharlotte@charlottediocese.org. Web: stjosephcharlotte.charlottediocese.org.
Catechesis/Religious Program—Duc Chu, D.R.E.; Bang Duong, Youth Min. Students 175.

6—ST. LUKE (1987) Rev. Paul Gary; Sr. Veronica Grover, S.H.C.J., Pastoral Assoc.; Deacons Jeffrey S. Evers; Rafael J. Torres.
Office: 13700 Lawyers Rd., 28227. Tel: 704-545-1224; Fax: 704-545-7288. Email: stlukeminthill@charlottediocese.org. Web: www.stlukechurch.net.
Rectory—13773 Thompson Rd., 28227. Tel: 704-246-7151.
Catechesis/Religious Program—Tel: 704-545-0065. Martha Hannah, D.R.E.; Cheryl Finch, Youth Min. Students 739.

7—ST. MATTHEW (1986) Rev. Msgr. John J. McSweeney; Revs. Patrick D. Toole, Parochial Vicar; Robert R. Conway, Parochial Vicar; Sisters Jeanne Marie Kienast, R.S.M., Pastoral Assoc.; Eileen C. McLoughlin, M.S.B.T., Pastoral Assoc.; Deacons James Hamrlik; William G. Griffin; Mark J. King; Darren S. Bitter; Paul H. Herman.
Office: 8015 Ballantyne Commons Pkwy., 28277. Tel: 704-543-7677; Fax: 704-542-7244. Email: stmatthewcharlotte@charlottediocese.org. Web: www.stmatthewcatholic.org.
Catechesis/Religious Program—Tel: 704-541-8362; Fax: 704-542-7244. Patricia Tomlinson, D.R.E.; Katie Dunne, Youth Min. Students 3,963.

8—OUR LADY OF CONSOLATION (1955) Rev. Martin A. Schratz, O.F.M.Cap.; Bro. Doug Soik, O.F.M.Cap., Pastoral Assoc.
Mailing Address: 1235 Badger Ct., 28206-1400. Email: olccharlotte@charlottediocese.org.
Church: 2301 Statesville Ave., 28206. Tel: 704-375-4339; Fax: 704-375-8039.
Catechesis/Religious Program— Felicia Johnson, D.R.E.; Nanette Lide, Youth Min. Students 97.
Mission—St. Helen 341 Dallas-Spencer Mountain Rd., Spencer Mountain, Gaston Co. 28059. Web: sthelenspencermnt.charlottediocese.org.
Catechesis/Religious Program—Barbara Gardin, D.R.E.

9—OUR LADY OF GUADALUPE CHURCH Revs. Vincent H. Finnerty, C.M.; Abel Osorio, C.M., Parochial Vicar; Karina Romero, Business Mgr.; Haydee Garcia, Pastoral Assoc.
6212 Tuckaseegee Rd., 28214. Tel: 704-391-3732; Fax: 704-391-6594. Email: olgcharlotte@charlottediocese.org. Web: olgcharlotte.charlottediocese.org. In Res., Rev. Joseph Elzi, C.M.
Catechesis/Religious Program—Adilia Rodriguez, D.R.E. Students 810.

10—OUR LADY OF THE ASSUMPTION (1949) Rev. Philip J. Scarcella (MET); Deacons Stephen J. Horai, (Retired); Peter Duca; Kevin Williams; Luis Flores; David S. Reiser.
Res.: 4207 Shamrock Dr., 28215. Tel: 704-535-9965; Fax: 704-535-3621. Email: olacharlotte@charlottediocese.org. Web: www.rc.net/charlotte/ola/.
Catechesis/Religious Program—Tel: 704-535-3310. Rigoberto Canaca, Youth Min.; Tammy Williams, Youth Min. Students 600.

11—ST. PETER (1851) Revs. Patrick F. Earl, S.J.; Thomas P. McDonnell, S.J.
Res.: 507 S. Tryon St., 28202. Fax: 704-358-0050. Email: stpetercharlotte@charlottediocese.org. Web: www.stpeterscatholic.org.
Catechesis/Religious Program—Tel: 704-332-2901. Students 136.

12—ST. THOMAS AQUINAS (1978) Revs. Remo DiSalvatore, O.F.M.Cap.; Stanley Kobel, O.F.M.Cap.; Stephen M. Hoyt, O.F.M.Cap.; Deacons Mark D. Nash; James H. Witulski.
Res.: 9230 Sandburg Ave., 28213. Tel: 704-549-1607; Fax: 704-549-1614. Email: stthomascharlotte@charlottediocese.org. Web: www.stacharlotte.com.
Catechesis/Religious Program—Tel: 704-549-5160; Fax: 704-503-5060. Michelle Hollis, D.R.E.; Sisters M. Anastacia Pagulayan, O.P., Assoc. D.R.E.; Gloria Camitan, O.P., Asst. D.R.E. Students 585.
Convent—1216 Ogden Pl., 28213. Tel: 704-503-4934.

13—ST. VINCENT DE PAUL (1965) Revs. Mark S. Lawlor; Joshua A. Voitus, Parochial Vicar; Deacon John Kopfle.
Res.: 6828 Old Reid Rd., 28210. Tel: 704-554-7088; Fax: 704-554-0490. Email: stvincentcharlotte@charlottediocese.org. Web: stvincentdepaulchurch.com.
Catechesis/Religious Program—Tel: 704-554-1622. Aida Tamayo, C.R.E.; Ruben A. Tamayo, Youth Min. Students 568.

OUTSIDE THE CITY OF CHARLOTTE

ALBEMARLE, STANLY CO., OUR LADY OF THE ANNUNCIATION (1934) Rev. Peter L. Fitzgibbons.
Res.: 416 N. Second St., 28001. Tel: 704-982-2910; Fax: 704-982-0881. Email: olaalbemarle@charlottediocese.org. Web: olaalbemarle.charlottediocese.org.
Catechesis/Religious Program—Tel: 704-982-1048. Cyndi Norton, D.R.E.; Renee Asciutto, Youth Min.; Adam Storms, Youth Min. Students 110.

ANDREWS, CHEROKEE CO., HOLY REDEEMER (1962) Rev. Brandon H. Jones.
Res.: 214 Aquone Rd., 28901-9776. Tel: 828-321-4463. Email: holyredeemerandrews@charlottediocese.org. Web: www.holyredeemerandrews.charlottediocese.org.
Mission—Prince of Peace 704 Talluah Rd., Rte. 129 S., Robbinsville, Graham Co. 28771. Email: princeofpeacerobbinsville@charlottediocese.org. Web: princeofpeacerobbinsville.charlottediocese.org.
Catechesis/Religious Program—Irene Weber, D.R.E. Students 23.

ARDEN, BUNCOMBE CO., ST. BARNABAS (1964) Rev. Adrian Porras; Deacons Michael L. Stout; Rudy J. Triana.
Mailing Address: P.O. Box 38, 28704. Tel: 828-684-6098; Fax: 828-684-6152. Email: stbarnabasarden@charlottediocese.org. Web: www.saintbarnabasarden.org.
Res.: 109 Crescent Hill Rd., 28704.
Catechesis/Religious Program—Miss Sheryl Peyton, D.R.E.; Mary AnnPoli, Youth Min. Students 288.

ASHEBORO, RANDOLPH CO., ST. JOSEPH (1948) Rev. Philip Kollithanath.
512 W. Wainman Ave., 27203-5342. Tel: 336-629-0221; Fax: 336-629-6968. Email: stjosephasheboro@charlottediocese.org. Web: www.stjoenc.org.
Res.: 308 S. Park St., 27203. Tel: 336-629-0450.
Catechesis/Religious Program—Sue Donnelly, Dir. Faith Formation; Patrick Holyfield, Youth Min. Students 257.

ASHEVILLE, BUNCOMBE CO.

1—BASILICA OF ST. LAWRENCE (1869) Very Rev. Wilbur N. Thomas, V.F.; Rev. C. Morris Boyd; LuWinn Rutherford, Pastoral Assoc.; Andrew Davis, Dir. Music Min.; Deacon Richard G. Voelgele.
Mailing Address: P.O. Box 1850, 28802.
Church Office: 97 Haywood St., 28801. Tel: 828-252-6042; Fax: 828-254-0414. Email: stlawrenceasheville@charlottediocese.org. Web: www.saintlawrencebasilica.org.
Catechesis/Religious Program—Mrs. Elizabeth Girton, D.R.E. Students 177.

2—ST. EUGENE (1957) Rev. J. Patrick Cahill; Deacon Michael Zboyovski Sr.; Sr. M. Anita Sheerin, R.S.M., Pastoral Assoc.
Office & Mailing Address: 72 Culvern St., 28804. Tel: 828-254-5193; Fax: 828-254-5797. Email: steugeneasheville@charlottediocese.org. Web: www.steugene.org.
Catechesis/Religious Program—Tracy Jedd, D.R.E. Students 200.

BELMONT, GASTON CO., QUEEN OF THE APOSTLES (1965) Rev. Francis T. Cancro; Sr. Bernadette McNamara, R.S.M., Pastoral Assoc.; Deacon William H. Wilson; Chrissy Glisson, Music Dir.
Church: 503 N. Main St., 28012. Tel: 704-825-9600; Fax: 704-825-1413. Email: QofABelmont@charlottediocese.org. Web: www.queenoftheapostles.org.
Res.: 2121 Ferncliff Ln., Cramerton, 28012. Tel: 704-825-9907.
Catechesis/Religious Program—Tel: 704-825-9600, Ext. 26. Kelly Munsee, D.R.E. Students 270.

BISCOE, MONTGOMERY CO., OUR LADY OF THE AMERICAS Rev. Ricardo Sanchez; Linda Webb, Music Dir.
Mailing Address: P.O. Box 519, Candor, 27229. 298 Farmers Market Rd., 27209. Tel: 910-974-3051; Fax: 910-974-4156. Email: olabiscoe@charlottediocese.org.
Catechesis/Religious Program—Mary Wallace, D.R.E.; Jorge Chavez, D.R.E.; Kathy Anderson, D.R.E.; Tom Swiecce, D.R.E. Students 314.

BOONE, WATAUGA CO., ST. ELIZABETH (1954) Rev. David Brzoska.
Office & Mailing Address: 259 Pilgrim's Way, 28607. Tel: 828-264-8338; Fax: 828-262-3721. Email: stelizabethboone@charlottediocese.org. Web: www.stehc.org.
Res.: 333 Poplar Hill Dr., 28607. Tel: 828-264-4503.
Catechesis/Religious Program—Ellisa Miller, D.R.E. Students 107.
Mission—Epiphany 163 Galax Ln., Blowing Rock, 28607.

BOONVILLE, YADKINVILLE CO., DIVINE REDEEMER (DIVINO REDENTOR) (2004) Rev. Jose Enrique Gonzalez-Gaytan; Deacon Michael Langsdorf.
Res.: 209 Lon Ave., 27011. Tel: 336-367-7067; Fax: 336-367-7954.
Catechesis/Religious Program— Carolina Martinez, D.R.E.; Victor Gonzalez, D.R.E.; Mary Langsdorf, Youth Min. Students 565.

BREVARD, TRANSYLVANIA CO., SACRED HEART (1949) Rev. Carl Del Giudice; Deacons John J. Burke Jr.; Patrick Crosby.
Res.: 100 Brian Berg Ln., 28712. Tel: 828-883-9572; Fax: 828-883-9587. Email: sacredheartbrevard@charlottediocese.org. Web: sacredheartcatholicchurchbrevardnc.org.
Catechesis/Religious Program— Myriam Gonzalez, D.R.E. Students 65.
Mission—St. Jude 3011 U.S. Hwy. 64 E., Sapphire, 28774. Tel: 828-743-5717; Fax: 828-743-5157. Email: stjudesapphirevalley@charlottediocese.org. Web: charlottediocese.org/stjudesapphirevalley. Rev. Dean Cesa.
Catechesis/Religious Program—Tess Cowan, D.R.E.

BRYSON CITY, SWAIN CO., ST. JOSEPH (1941) Rev. Shawn O'Neal.
Mailing Address: P.O. Box 727, 28713. Tel: 828-488-6766. Email: stjosephbrysoncity@charlottediocese.org. Web: www.stjosephbryson.org.
Office: 316 Main St., 28713.
Rectory—234 Arlington Ave., 28713.
Catechesis/Religious Program—Kathy Posey, D.R.E.; Kim Holt, Asst. D.R.E.; Barbara Hart, Youth Min. Students 15.
Mission—Our Lady of Guadalupe 82 Lambert Branch Rd., Cherokee, Swain Co. 28719. Tel: 828-497-9755. Email: olgcherokee@charlottediocese.org.

CANDLER, BUNCOMBE CO., ST. JOAN OF ARC (1928) Rev. Frank J. Seabo.
Church: 768 Ashbury Rd., 28715. Tel: 828-670-0051; Fax: 828-670-0052. Email: stjoanasheville@charlottediocese.org. Web: www.stjoanofarcasheville.catholicweb.com.
Catechesis/Religious Program— Tim Kelly, D.R.E. Students 54.

CLEMMONS, FORSYTH CO., HOLY FAMILY (1980) Very Rev. Michael J. Buttner.
Office: P.O. Box 130, 27012. Tel: 336-778-0600. Email: holyfamilyclemmons@charlottediocese.org. Web: www.holyfamilyclemmons.com.
Res.: 2890 Knobb Hill Dr., 27012. Tel: 336-608-4368.
Church: 4820 Kinnamon Rd., Winston-Salem, 27103. Fax: 336-766-2918.
Catechesis/Religious Program—Tel: 336-766-0600, Ext. 214. Ms. Peggy Schumacher, D.R.E.; Margaret McGrath, Youth Min. Students 644.

CONCORD, CABARRUS CO., ST. JAMES (1869) Revs. J. Joseph Dionne, C.Ss.R.; Joseph Fonseca, C.Ss.R., Parochial Vicar; Oscar E. Rojas Paniagua, C.Ss.R; Deacons Kenneth L. Drummer; Martin Ricart III.
Mailing Address: P.O. Box 123, 28025-0123. Tel: 704-720-0600; Fax: 704-720-0610. Email: stjamesconcord@charlottediocese.org. In Res., Rev. Vang Cong Tran, C.Ss.R.
Res.: 137 Manor Ave. S.W., 28025. Tel: 704-720-0608.
Church: 139 Manor Ave., S.W., 28025.
Catechesis/Religious Program— Patti Andruzzi, D.R.E.; Kelli Olszewski, Youth Min. Students 767.

DENVER, LINCOLN CO., HOLY SPIRIT (1988) Rev. Carmen Malacari; Deacon James Atkinson.
Church: 537 N. Hwy. 16, 28037-9235. Tel: 704-483-6448; Fax: 704-483-6898. Email: holyspiritdenver@charlottediocese.org. Web: www.holyspiritnc.org.
Res.: 6789 Hawks Nest Ln., Stanley, 28164-0123. Tel: 704-820-0153.
Catechesis/Religious Program— Kate D'Amato, Faith Formation Coord. Students 344.

EDEN, ROCKINGHAM CO., ST. JOSEPH OF THE HILLS (1938) Rev. Joseph Long Dinh.
Church & Res.: 316 Boone Rd., 27288. Tel: 336-623-2661; Fax: 336-635-0619. Email: stjosepheden@charlottediocese.org.
Catechesis/Religious Program—Tel: 336-573-8997. Bill Griffin, D.R.E. Students 74.

FOREST CITY, RUTHERFORD CO., IMMACULATE CONCEPTION (1950) Rev. Herbert Burke; Deacon Andrew Cilone.
Church: 1024 W. Main St., 28043. Tel: 828-245-4017. Email: immconcepforestcity@charlottediocese.org. Web: charlottediocese.org/immconceptionforestcity.
Catechesis/Religious Program—Students 196.

FRANKLIN, MACON CO., ST. FRANCIS OF ASSISI (1953) Rev. Tien H. Duong.
Church: 299 Maple St., 28734. Tel: 828-524-2289; Fax: 828-369-0809. Email: stfrancisfranklin@charlottediocese.org. Web: www.stfrancisofassisifranklin.org.
Catechesis/Religious Program—Tel: 828-369-8131. Fred Carl Stickney, D.R.E. Students 147.
Mission—Our Lady of the Mountains 315 N. 5th St., Highlands, 28741. Tel: 828-526-2418. Email: olmountainshighlands@charlottediocese.org. Web: www.ourladyofthemountains.net. Rev. Dean Cesa.

GASTONIA, GASTON CO., ST. MICHAEL (1903) Very Rev. Roger K. Arnsparger; Deacons John P. Weisenhorn, (Retired); Arthur J. Kingsley.
Res.: 1038 Sherwood Ave., 28052.
Church: 708 St. Michael's Ln., 28052-6198. Tel: 704-867-6212; Fax: 704-867-6379. Email: stmichaelgastonia@charlottediocese.org. Web: www.stmichaelsgastonia.org.
School—(Grades PreK-8) Tel: 704-865-4382; Fax: 704-864-5108. Web: www.smsgastonia.com. Joseph Puceta, Prin. Lay Teachers 19; Students 211.
Catechesis/Religious Program—Tel: 704-867-6212, Ext. 114. Students 260.

GREENSBORO, GUILFORD CO.

1—ST. BENEDICT (1901) Rev. James Duc H. Duong; Deacon David Boissey Sr.
Church: 109 W. Smith St., 27401. Tel: 336-272-0303. Email: stbenedictgreensboro@charlottediocese.org. Web: stbenedictgreensboro.charlottediocese.org.
Catechesis/Religious Program—Kathy Perry, D.R.E.; Lynne McGrath, Youth Min. Students 55.

2—ST. MARY (1928) Revs. Michael Manh Nguyen, C.M.; John P. Timlin, C.M.; Deacons Vincent Shaw Jr.; Pierre M. K'Briuh.
Mailing Address: P.O. Box 21012, 2742.
Res.: 812 Duke St., 27401. Tel: 336-272-8650; Fax: 336-272-3594. Email: stmarygreensboro@charlottediocese.org. Web: www.stmarysgreensboro.org.
Catechesis/Religious Program—Genevieve Weech, D.R.E. Students 408.

3—OUR LADY OF GRACE (1952), (Ethel Clay Price Memorial) Revs. Fidel C. Melo; John J. Eckert; Christopher J. Davis; Deacons Timothy Rohan, (Retired); Paul A. Teich, (Retired); Tony Pynes; Jim Toner.
Mailing Address: 201 S. Chapman St., 27403-1611.
Res.: 207 S. Chapman St., 27403. Tel: 336-275-5376. Email: olggreensboro@charlottediocese.org. Web: www.olgchurch.org.
Church: 2205 W. Market St., 27403. Tel: 336-274-6520; Fax: 336-274-7326.
School—(Grades K-8) Tel: 336-275-1522; Fax: 336-279-8824. Email: olgsch@olgsch.org. Web: www.olgsch.org. Cheryl Whitaker, Prin. Lay Teachers 27; Students 358.
Catechesis/Religious Program— James D. McCullough, D.R.E.; Katie Tang, Youth Min. Students 316.

4—ST. PAUL THE APOSTLE (1974) Rev. John A. Allen; Deacons Gordon L. Forester, (Retired); Larry Lisk; Michael J. Martini; Colleen Assai, Community Outreach Coord.
Res.: 2741 Horsepen Creek Rd., 27410. Tel: 336-294-4696 (Office); Fax: 336-294-6149. Email: stpaulgreensboro@charlottediocese.org. Web: www.stpaulcc.org.
Catechesis/Religious Program— Jeannine Martin, D.R.E.; Susan Rabold, Youth Min. Students 415.

5—ST. PIUS THE TENTH (1960) Rev. Msgr. Anthony J. Marcaccio; Mr. Tracy Earl Welliver, Pastoral Assoc.; Mrs. Patricia Spivey, Pastoral Assoc.; Deacons Philip Cooper; William S. Shaw; Ronald F. Steinkamp.
Mailing Address: P.O. Box 13588, 27415-3588.
Office: 220 State St., 27408. Tel: 336-272-4681; 336-272-8598; Fax: 336-274-8112. Email: stpiusgreensboro@charlottediocese.org. Web: www.stpiusxnc.com.
Res.: 2326 N. Elm St., 27408. Tel: 336-271-3068.
School—(Grades K-8), 2200 N. Elm St., 27408. Tel: 336-273-9865; Fax: 336-273-0199. Anne Knapke, Prin.; Ann Flynt, Asst. Prin. Lay Teachers 29; Students 468.
Catechesis/Religious Program—Dave Wils, Youth Min. Students 497.
Catholic Campus Connection (Thea House)—1009 Bluford St., 27401. Tel: 336-272-5868.

HAMLET, RICHMOND CO., ST. JAMES (1910) Rev. Jean-Pierre Swamunu Lhoposo, C.I.C.M.
Mailing Address: P.O. Box 1208, 28345. Tel: 910-582-0207; Fax: 910-582-7121. Email: stjameshamlet@charlottediocese.org. Web: stjameshamlet.charlottediocese.org.
Church: 1018 W. Hamlet Ave. (US Hwy. 74), 28345.
Catechesis/Religious Program—Email: stjameshamlet@charlottediocese.org. Cecilia Wilson, D.R.E. Students 97.
Mission—Sacred Heart 205 Rutherford St., Wadesboro, Anson Co. 28710. Web: sacredheart-wadesboro.charlottediocese.org.

HENDERSONVILLE, HENDERSON CO., IMMACULATE CONCEPTION (1912) Rev. John Salvas, O.F.M.Cap.; Bro. Michael Molloy, O.F.M.Cap.; Feliciano Botello, Pastoral Assoc.
Parish Office—208 7th Ave., W., 28791-3602. Tel: 828-693-6901; Fax: 828-697-1656. Email: ImmConcepHendersonville@charlottediocese.org. Web: www.immaculateconceptionchurch.com.
Res.: 717 Buncombe St., 28791-3609. Tel: 828-692-0550.
School—Immaculata, (Grades K-8), 711 Buncombe St., 28791-3609. Tel: 828-693-3277; Fax: 828-696-3677. Carole Breerwood, Prin.; Gail McCaslin, Asst. Prin. Lay Teachers 18; Students 139.
Catechesis/Religious Program—Tel: 828-697-7420. Sandy Donecho, D.R.E.; Emily Sevier, Youth Min. Students 361.

HICKORY, CATAWBA CO., ST. ALOYSIUS (1913) Revs. Robert M. Ferris; Gabriel S. Carvajal-Salazer; Deacons Thomas A. Rasmussen; Ronald R. Caplette, (Retired); Kathy Sucoop, Pastoral Assoc.
921 2nd St. N.E., 28601. Fax: 828-327-3376.
Res.: 862 First St., 28601. Tel: 828-327-2341. Email: staloysiushickory@charlottediocese.org. Web: www.staloysiushickory.org.
Catechesis/Religious Program—Students 777.

HIGH POINT, GUILFORD CO.

1—CHRIST THE KING (1940) Rev. Gnanapragasam Mariasoosai.
Res.: 1601 E. Kivett Dr., 27260. Tel: 336-884-0244. Email: christkinghighpoint@charlottediocese.org. Web: charlottediocese.org.christkinghighpoint.
Church: 1505 E. Kivett Dr., 27260-5455.
Catechesis/Religious Program—Jill Frentz, D.R.E.; Nancy Lautz, Youth Min. Students 74.

2—IMMACULATE HEART OF MARY (1947) Revs. Vincent E. Smith, O.S.F.S.; Joseph C. Zuschmidt, O.S.F.S.; James F. Byrne, O.S.F.S.; Deacons Thomas Kak, (Retired); Walter Haarsgaard.
Mailing Address: 605 Barbee Ave., 27262. Email: ihmhighpoint@charlottediocese.org. Web: www.ihmchurch.org.
Church: 4145 Johnson St., 27265. Tel: 336-869-7739; Fax: 336-869-1059.
Res.: 3821 Oak Forest Dr., 27265. Tel: 336-886-4847.
School—(Grades K-8), 500 Montlieu Ave., 27262. Tel: 336-887-2613; Fax: 336-884-1849. Web: www.ihm-school.com. Wanda Garrett, Prin. Lay Teachers 23; Students 252.
Catechesis/Religious Program—Tel: 336-885-5210. Students 438.

HUNTERSVILLE, MECKLENBURG CO., ST. MARK (1997) Rev. Msgr. Richard Bellow; Rev. David P. Miller, Parochial Vicar; Deacons Louis A. Pais; Ronald D. Sherwood.
Church & Res.: 14740 Stumptown Rd., 28078. Tel: 704-948-0231; 980-253-1605 (Res.); Fax: 704-948-8018. Email: stmarkhuntersville@charlottediocese.org. Web: www.stmarknc.org.
Catechesis/Religious Program—Tel: 704-948-1306. Donna Smith, D.R.E.; Tim Flynn, Youth Min. Students 1,280.

JEFFERSON, ASHE CO., ST. FRANCIS OF ASSISI (1962) Rev. James A. Stuhrenberg.
Mailing Address: P.O. Box 1, 28640. Tel: 336-246-9151; Fax: 336-246-3141. Email: stfrancisjefferson@charlottediocese.org. Web: stfrancisjefferson.charlottediocese.org.
Church: 326 E. Main St., 28640.
Catechesis/Religious Program—Patrick Hession, D.R.E.; Chuck Spanbauer, Youth Min. Students 63.
Mission—St. Frances of Rome 29 Highland Dr., Sparta, 28675. Tel: 336-372-8846. Email: stfrancissparta@charlottediocese.org. Web: www.sfor-sparta.org. Mailing Address: P.O. Box 367, Sparta, 28675.

KANNAPOLIS, CABARRUS CO., ST. JOSEPH CHURCH Rev. Alvaro A. Riquelme, C.Ss.R.; Deacon Myles Decker.
108 Saint Joseph St., 28081. Tel: 704-932-4607; Fax: 704-932-0566. Email: stjosephchurch@ctc.net. Web: www.saintjosephcatholic.org.
Rectory—137 Manor Ave., Concord, 28026. Tel: 704-720-0608.
Catechesis/Religious Program—Kelly Whitley, D.R.E. Students 175.

KERNERSVILLE, FORSYTH CO., HOLY CROSS (1973) Rev. Paul Dechant, O.S.F.S.; Deacons Eugene J. Gillis, (Retired); Timothy Ritchey.
Church: 616 S. Cherry St., 27284. Tel: 336-996-5109; Fax: 336-996-5669. Email: holycrosskernersville@charlottediocese.org. Web: www.holycrossnc.org.
Child Developmental Center—Tel: 336-996-5144; Fax: 336-996-5115. Cathie Reel, Dir.
Catechesis/Religious Program— Marie Kinney, D.R.E.; Mario Rojas, Youth Min. Students 457.

LENOIR, CALDWELL CO., ST. FRANCIS OF ASSISI (1936) Very Rev. Julio Dominguez; Deacon A. Stephen Pickett.
Res.: 323 Sharon Ave., N.W., 28645.
Church: 328-B Woodsway Ln., N.W., 28645-4356. Tel: 828-754-5281; Fax: 828-754-5281. Email: stfrancislenoir@charlottediocese.org. Web: www.stfrancislenoir.com.
Catechesis/Religious Program—Amy Tauv, D.R.E.; Ivan Cruz, Youth Min. Students 157.

LEXINGTON, DAVIDSON CO., OUR LADY OF THE ROSARY (1944) Rev. Albert J. Gondek, O.S.F.S.; Sr. Katherine Francis French, S.P., Pastoral Assoc.
Church & Res.: 619 S. Main St., 27292-3238. Tel: 336-248-2463; 336-236-2161 (Res.); Fax: 336-238-3241. Email: olrosarylexington@charlottediocese.org.

Web: www.olr-nc.org.
Catechesis/Religious Program—Sr. Betty Paul, S.P., Youth Min.; Guillermo Razo, Youth Min. Students 180.

LINCOLNTON, LINCOLN CO., ST. DOROTHY (1944) Rev. Matthew R. Buettner.
Res.: 601 N. Grove St., 28092-9801.
Church: 148 St. Dorothy Ln., 28092-9801. Tel: 704-735-5575; Fax: 704-735-3113. Email: stdorothylincolnton@charlottediocese.org. Web: www.stdorothys.org.
Catechesis/Religious Program—Margaret Barrett, D.R.E.; Scarlet Casey, Youth Min.; Marian Clark, Youth Min. Students 218.

MAGGIE VALLEY, HAYWOOD CO., ST. MARGARET OF SCOTLAND (1968) Rev. Richard R. Benonis (PH) (Retired); Deacon Gerald P. LaPointe, (Retired).
Mailing Address: P.O. Box 1359, 28751-1359. Tel: 828-926-0106; Fax: 828-926-0855.
Church: 37 Murphy Dr., 28751. Email: stmargaretmaggievalley@charlottediocese.org. Web: www.catholicretreat.org/stmargaret.htm.
Catechesis/Religious Program—Betsy McLeod, D.R.E. Students 40.

MARS HILL, MADISON CO., ST. ANDREW THE APOSTLE (1985) Rev. Frederick H. Werth.
Mailing Address: P.O. Box 1406, 28754-1406. Tel: 828-689-3719. Email: standrewmarshill@charlottediocese.org. Web: standrewmarshill.charlottediocese.org.
Res. & Church: 149 Brook St., 28754-1406.
Catechesis/Religious Program—Fax: 828-689-3719. Ann Stowe, D.R.E. Students 58.
Mission—Sacred Heart 20 Summit St., Burnsville, Yancey Co. 28714. Email: sacredheartburnsville@charlottediocese.org. Web: sacredheartburnsville.charlottediocses.org.

MOCKSVILLE, DAVIE CO., ST. FRANCIS OF ASSISI (1958) Rev. F. Starczewski; Deacon John O. Zimmerle.
Church: 862 Yadkinville Rd., 27028. Tel: 336-751-2973; Fax: 336-751-9929. Email: stfrancismocksville@charlottediocese.org. Web: www.stfrancismocksville.com.
Catechesis/Religious Program— Nancy Gerrety, D.R.E. Students 138.

MONROE, UNION CO., OUR LADY OF LOURDES (1945) Rev. Thomas Kessler; Deacons Roland R. Geoffroy; Sidney Huff, (Retired).
Church: 725 Deese St., 28112. Tel: 704-289-2773; Fax: 704-283-7210. Email: ollourdesmonroe@charlottediocese.org. Web: ollourdesmonroe.charlottediocese.org.
Catechesis/Religious Program— Sandy Sawyer, Dir. of Faith Formation. Students 538.

MOORESVILLE, IREDELL CO., ST. THERESE (1946) Revs. Vincent C. Curtin, S.J.; Joseph B. Kappes, S.J.; Donald M. Ward Jr., S.J.; Deacon John E. Sims; Donna Pfenfer, Pastoral Assoc.
Church: 217 Brawley School Rd., 28117. Tel: 704-664-3992; Fax: 704-660-6321. Email: sttheresemooresville@charlottediocese.org. Web: www.sainttherese.net.
Catechesis/Religious Program—Tel: 704-664-7762; Fax: 704-664-2045. Carmen Sanjuan, Dir. of Faith Formation. Students 1,181.

MORGANTON, BURKE CO., ST. CHARLES BORROMEO (1947) Very Rev. Kenneth L. Whittington; Deacons James R. Johnson; Pe nhia cha Lee; John Martino; Edward A. Konarski.
Church: 728 W. Union St., 28655. Tel: 828-437-3108; Fax: 828-437-6262. Email: stcharlesmorganton@charlottediocese.org. Web: stcharlesmorganton.charlottediocese.org.
Catechesis/Religious Program— Terri Martino, D.R.E.; Denise Hussey, Youth Min. Students 245.
Mission—Our Lady of the Angels P.O. Box 1006, Marion, 28752. 258 N. Garden St., Marion, McDowell Co. 28752. Tel: 828-652-8690; Fax: 828-559-0678. Email: olamarion@charlottediocese.org. Web: olamarion.charlottediocese.org. Rev. Carl E. Kaltreider.

MOUNT AIRY, SURRY CO., HOLY ANGELS (1921) Rev. Eric Kowalski; Deacon Paul Liotard, (Retired).
Church & Res.: 1208 N. Main St., Mt. Airy, 27030. Tel: 336-786-8147. Email: holyangelsmountairy@charlottediocese.org. Web: holyangelsmountairy.charlottediocese.org.
Catechesis/Religious Program—Linda Gallasetti-Simmons, D.R.E. Students 128.

MURPHY, CHEROKEE CO., ST. WILLIAM (1952) Very Rev. George M. Kloster; Deacon Carl Hubbel.
Mailing Address: P.O. Box 546, 28906.
Church & Res.: 765 Andrews Rd., 28906. Tel: 828-837-2000; Fax: 828-835-9889. Email: stwilliammurphy@charlottediocese.org. Web: www.st-william.net.
Catechesis/Religious Program— Michelle Calascione, D.R.E. Students 81.
Mission—Immaculate Heart of Mary U.S. Hwy. 64 W., Hayesville, Clay Co. 28904. Email: ihmhayesville@charlottediocese.org. Web: www.ihmhayesville.com.

NEWTON, CATAWBA CO., ST. JOSEPH (1978) Rev. James M. Collins; Deacon Scott D. Gilfillan.
Church: 720 W. 13th St., 28658-3899. Tel: 828-464-9207; Fax: 828-464-9880. Email: stjosephnewton@charlottediocese.org. Web: www.stjosephrcc.org.
Holy Family Parish Center—Tel: 828-465-2878.
Catechesis/Religious Program—Kathy Mulligan, D.R.E. Students 180.

NORTH WILKESBORO, ST. JOHN BAPTIST DE LASALLE (1952) Very Rev. John D. Hanic; Deacon Harold Markle, (Retired); Sr. Janice McQuade, S.S.J., Pastoral Assoc.
Church & Res.: 275 C.C. Wright School Rd., 28659. Tel: 336-838-5562. Email: stjohnnwilkesboro@charlottediocese.org. Web: stjohnnwilkesboro.charlottediocese.org.
Catechesis/Religious Program—Tel: 336-670-2792. Mary Sorel, D.R.E. Students 171.
Mission—St. Stephen 101 Hawthorne, Elkin, Surry Co. 28621. Tel: 336-835-3007. Email: ststephenelkin@charlottediocese.org. Web: ststephenelkin.charlottediocese.org.

REIDSVILLE, ROCKINGHAM CO., HOLY INFANT (1961) Rev. Joseph W. Mack; Deacon Gerald W. Potkay.
Mailing Address: P.O. Box 1197, 27323-1197.
Church & Res.: 1042 Freeway Dr., P.O. Box 1197, 27323. Tel: 336-342-1448. Email: holyinfantreidsville@charlottediocese.org. Web: www.holyinfantreidsvillenc.com.
Catechesis/Religious Program—Susan McHugh, Youth Min. Students 128.

SALISBURY, ROWAN CO., SACRED HEART (1882) Very Rev. John T. Putnam; Rev. Benjamin A. Roberts; Deacon James Mazur; Sr. Mary Robert Williams, R.S.M., Pastoral Assoc.
Church Office: 375 Lumen Christie Ln., 28147. Tel: 704-633-0591; Fax: 704-647-0126. Email: sacredheartsalisbury@charlottediocese.org. Web: www.salisburycatholic.org.
Res.: 1721 Colony Rd., 28144. Tel: 704-637-3068.
School—(Grades K-8), 385 Lumen Christi Ln., 28147. Tel: 704-633-2841; Fax: 704-633-6033. Francisco J. Cardelle, Prin.; Katie Meseroll, Asst. Prin.; Frances Rash, Librarian. Religious 3; Lay Teachers 19; Students 188.
Catechesis/Religious Program—Students 340.
Convent—Dominican Sisters of St. Catherine of Siena, 425 W. Council St., 28144. Tel: 704-636-4070.

SHELBY, CLEVELAND CO., ST. MARY'S (1935) Rev. Michael T. Kottar.
Church & Res.: 818 McGowan Rd., 28150. Tel: 704-487-7697; Fax: 704-487-0187. Email: stmaryshelby@charlottediocese.org. Web: stmaryshelbync.parishesonline.com.
Catechesis/Religious Program—Maureen Westlund, Faith Formation Coord. Students 149.
Mission—Christ the King 714 Stone St., Kings Mountain, Cleveland Co. 28086. Email: christkingkingsmountain@charlottediocese.org.

SPRUCE PINE, MITCHELL CO., ST. LUCIEN (1940) Rev. Christopher M. Gober.
Mailing Address: P.O. Box 688, 28777-0688.
Church: 695 Summit Ave., 28777. Tel: 828-765-2224; Fax: 828-765-2238. Email: stlucienspruce pine@charlottediocese.org. Web: stlucienspruce pine.charlottediocese.org.
Mission—St. Bernadette 2085 State Hwy. 105, Linville, Avery Co. 28646. Tel: 828-898-6900. Email: stbernadettelinville@charlottediocese.org. Web: www.stbernadettelinville.org. Rev. Christopher M. Gober; Deacon R. Alexander Lyerly.
Catechesis/Religious Program— Margaret Haskell, D.R.E. (St. Lucien); Will Havron, D.R.E. (St. Bernadette); Bobbie Havron, D.R.E. (St. Bernadette). Students 49.

STATESVILLE, IREDELL CO., ST. PHILIP THE APOSTLE (1898) Rev. Kurt M. Fohn; Deacons Charles Brantley, (Retired); Matthew Reilly.
Mailing Address: P.O. Box 882, 28687-0882.
Office: Tel: 704-872-2579; Fax: 704-872-2579. Email: stphilipstatesville@charlottediocese.org. Web: stphilipapostle.com.
Res.: 1019 Harmony Dr., 28677. Tel: 704-904-5718.
Church: 525 Camden Dr., 28677.
Catechesis/Religious Program—Tel: 704-872-2579; Fax: 704-872-2579. Jeanine Marsilia, D.R.E. (St. Philip); Elizabeth Cronan, D.R.E. (Holy Trinity). Students 270.
Mission—Holy Trinity 1039 NC Hwy. 90 W., Taylorsville, Alexander Co. 28681. Tel: 828-632-8009; Fax: 828-632-8009. Email: holytrinitytaylorsville@charlottediocese.org. Web: holytrinitytaylorsville.charlottediocese.org. Rev. James M. Byer.

SWANNANOA, BUNCOMBE CO., ST. MARGARET MARY (1936) Rev. Matthew Leonard; Deacon Ralph R. Eckoff, (Retired).
Office: Tel: 828-686-8833; Fax: 828-686-8832.
Res.: 67 Beech Glen Dr., Black Mountain, 28711. Tel: 828-686-5300. Email: stmargaretswannanoa@charlottediocese.org. Web: www.stmargaretmarycatholic.org.
Catechesis/Religious Program— Bea Madden, D.R.E. Students 62.

SYLVA, JACKSON CO., ST. MARY (1955) Rev. H. Alejandro Ayala.
Res.: 141 Dillsboro Rd., 28779. Tel: 828-631-0576. Email: stmarysylva@charlottediocese.org. Web: stmarysylva.charlottediocese.org.
Church: 22 Barlett St., 28779.
Catechesis/Religious Program— Isabella Harcourt, D.R.E. Students 35.

THOMASVILLE, DAVIDSON CO., OUR LADY OF THE HIGHWAYS (1953) Rev. James M. Turner, O.S.F.S.; Deacon Wayne Adams.
Church & Res.: 943 Ball Park Rd., 27360. Tel: 336-475-2667; Fax: 336-476-3337. Email: olhighwaysthomasville@charlottediocese.org. Web: olhighwaysthomasville.charlottediocese.org.
Catechesis/Religious Program—Kathy Laskis, Dir. Faith Formation. Students 331.

TRYON, POLK CO., ST. JOHN THE BAPTIST (1911) Rev. Patrick J. Winslow; Deacon Joseph Fugere Jr.
Rectory—38 Doubleday Rd., 28782.
Church: 180 Laurel Ave., 28782. Tel: 828-859-9574; Fax: 828-859-5932. Email: stjohntryon@charlottediocese.org. Web: www.stjohntryon.com.
Catechesis/Religious Program—Tel: 828-859-5932. Theresa Finch, D.R.E. Students 72.

WAYNESVILLE, HAYWOOD CO., ST. JOHN THE EVANGELIST (1926) Rev. Lawrence M. LoMonaco.
Church & Res.: 234 Church St., 28786. Tel: 828-456-6707. Email: stjohnwaynesville@charlottediocese.org. Web: webpages.charter.net/stjohnswnc.
Catechesis/Religious Program— Mary Finn, D.R.E. Students 105.
Mission—Immaculate Conception 42 Newfound Rd., Canton, Haywood Co. 28716. Web: webpages.charter.net/stjohnswnc.

WINSTON-SALEM, FORSYTH CO.

1—ST. BENEDICT THE MOOR (1940) Rev. Lawrence W. Heiney.
Church & Res.: 1625 E. Twelfth St., 27101. Tel: 336-725-9200; Fax: 336-722-4264. Email: stbenedictwinstonsalem@charlottediocese.org. Web: stbenedictwinstonsalem.charlottediocese.org.
Mission—Good Shepherd P.O. Box 1149, King, Stokes Co. 27021. Web: goodshepherdking.charlottediocese.org. 105 Good Shepherd Dr., King, 27021.
Catechesis/Religious Program—Judith Murphy, D.R.E. Students 261.

2—ST. LEO THE GREAT (1891) Revs. Brian J. Cook; Lucas Rossi; Deacon Robert DeSautels.
Res.: 334 Springdale Ave., 27104. Tel: 336-724-5314. Email: stleowinstonsalem@charlottediocese.org. Web: www.stleocatholic.com.
Church: 335 Springdale Ave., 27104. Tel: 336-724-0561; Fax: 336-724-7036.
School—(Grades PreK-8), 333 Springdale Ave., 27104. Tel: 336-748-8252; Fax: 336-748-9005. Mrs. Georgette Schraeder, Prin. Sisters of St. Joseph 1; Lay Teachers 35; Students 284.
Catechesis/Religious Program—Tel: 336-724-0561. Lauren Gardner, D.R.E.; Jennifer Eklund, Youth Min. Students 388.
Convent—1975 Georgia Ave., 27104. Tel: 336-723-3639.

3—OUR LADY OF MERCY (1954) Revs. William Robinson, O.F.M.Conv.; Joseph Barry Angelini, O.F.M.Conv.; Deacon Joseph Schumacher, (Retired). In Res., Rev. Charles Jagodzinski, O.F.M.Conv.
Church & Office: 1730 Link Rd., 27103. Tel: 336-722-7001; Fax: 336-722-0465. Email: olmwinstonsalem@charlottediocese.org. Web: www.olmnc.org.
Friary: 1147 Lockland Ave., 27103. Tel: 336-724-6806.
School—(Grades K-8) Tel: 336-722-7204; Fax: 336-725-2294. Email: admin@ourladyofmercyschool.org. Web: www.ourladyofmercyschool.org. Sr. Geri Rogers, S.S.J., Prin.; Shirley Shaw, Asst. Prin. Sisters of St. Joseph 1; Lay Teachers 20; Students 212.
Catechesis/Religious Program—Tel: 336-722-7001, Ext. 26. Sr. Kathleen Ganiel, O.S.F., D.R.E. Students 376.
Convent—2141 New Castle Dr., 27103. Tel: 336-774-3956.
Mission—Our Lady of Fatima 211 W. 3rd St., Forsyth Co. 27101. Tel: 336-723-8238; Fax: 336-723-8290. Email: olfwinstonsalem@charlottediocese.org.

Special Assignment:
Rev. Msgr.—
West, Mauricio W., Vicar Gen. & Chancellor

Very Rev.—
Roux, Christopher A.
Rev.—
Hoover, John P.

On Duty Outside the Diocese:
Revs.—
Choquet, Alexei H.
Mulligan, Joseph V.
Osorio, Louis
Pagel, John M.
Wilderotter, Paul C.

Graduate Studies:
Rev.—
Kauth, Matthew K.

Military Chaplains:
Rev.—
Fitzgibbons, Peter L., U.S. Army

Unassigned:
Revs.—
Hanson, Richard N.
Tarasi, Carlo D.

Absent On Leave:
Revs.—
Baker, Donald P.
DeAguilar, Arturo
Hanic, Jonathan
Kuhn, Dennis R.
Schneider, John
Tice, Cecil
Williamson, Thomas

Absent on Medical Leave:
Revs.—
Hokanson, Richard P.
Williams, W. Ray

Retired:
Most Rev.—
Curlin, William G., D.D., 3005 Markworth Ave., 28203.
Rev. Msgrs.—
Kerin, Joseph A., 2410 Old Steine Rd., Apt. 803, 28269.
Kovacic, Anthony, 107 Penny Rd., Apt. #1008, High Point, 27260.
Showfety, Joseph, 7-A Fountain Manor Dr., Greensboro, 27405.
Walsh, Thomas R., 12 N. 6th St., Allegany, NY 14706.
Revs.—
Ayathupadam, Joseph, 114 White Branch Ct., Fort Mill, SC 29715.
Cahill, James, P.O. Box 1856, Sylva, 28779-1856.
Cintula, Francis M., 45 S.E. 13th St., A-1, Boca Raton, FL 33432.
Clements, Thomas P., P.O. Box 5086, Statesville, 28687.
Evans, William Morris, P.O. Box 665, Cashiers, 28717-0665.
Hawker, James, 133 Cmdr. Shae Blvd., Unit 807, Quincy, MA 02171.
Hoover, Conrad, D.Min., 1300 Reece Rd., Apt. 505, 28209.
Hourihan, Raymond B., 507 Fulton St., Elmira, NY 14904.
Latsko, Andrew, St. Mary of Providence Center, 227 Isabella Rd., Elverson, PA 19520.
Manley, Bernard A., Pennybyrn at Maryfield, 107 Penny Rd., Apt. 1017, High Point, 27260.
McCue, Richard T., 50 Brookside Dr., Apt. D2, Exeter, NH 03833-1653.
Meehan, Gabriel, 805 Foxwood Ct. S.W., Lenoir, 28645.
Reese, Charles T., 800 Bay Dr., No. 25, Niceville, FL 32578.
Sheridan, Edward J., 6860 Greedy Hwy., Hickory, 28602.
Solari, James K., 109 Penny Rd., 219E, High Point, 27260.
Sullivan, D. Edward, Autumn House East, 2618 E. Market St., York, PA 17402-2411.
Tuller, John, St. Ann's House, 2161 Leonard St., N.W., Grand Rapids, MI 49504.
Waters, Joseph, Pennybyrn at Maryfield, 107 Penny Rd., Apt. 1020, High Point, 27260.

Permanent Deacons:
Adams, Wayne, Our Lady of the Highways, Thomasville
Atkinson, James, Holy Spirit, Denver
Barone, John
Bitter, Darren S., St. Matthew, Charlotte
Boissey, David, Sr., St. Benedict, Greensboro
Brantley, Charles, (Retired), St. Philip the Apostle, Statesville
Burke, John J., Jr., (Retired), (Living Outside the Diocese)
Caplette, Ronald R., (Retired), St. Aloysius, Hickory
Cilone, Andrew, Immaculate Conception, Forest City
Cooper, Philip, St. Pius X, Greensboro
Crosby, Patrick, Sacred Heart, Brevard
Decker, Myles, St. Joseph, Kannapolis
DeSautels, Charles, St. Leo, Winston-Salem
Diener, Mark, Our Lady of the Assumption, Charlotte
Dotson, Robert E.
Drummer, Kenneth L., St. James the Greater, Concord
Duca, Peter, Our Lady of the Assumption, Charlotte
Eckoff, Ralph R., (Retired), St. Margaret Mary, Swannanoa
Evers, Jeffrey S., St. Luke, Charlotte
Flores, Louis, Our Lady of the Assumption, Charlotte
Forester, Gordon L., (Retired), St. Paul the Apostle, Greensboro
Fugere, John, St. John the Baptist, Tryon
Geoffroy, Roland R., Our Lady of Lourdes, Monroe
Gettlefinger, Robert, (Retired), (Unassigned)
Gilfillan, Scott D., St. Joseph, Newton
Gillis, Eugene J., (Retired), Holy Cross, Kernersville
Gorman, James, St. John Neumann, Charlotte
Griffin, William G., St. Matthew, Charlotte
Haarsgard, Walter, Immaculate Heart of Mary, High Point
Hamrlik, James, St. Matthew, Charlotte
Haslett, Bruce H., (Living Outside of Diocese)
Heine, Charles, (Unassigned)
Herman, Paul, St. Matthew, Charlotte
Hickey, Gerald P., (Retired), St. Vincent de Paul, Charlotte
Horai, Stephen J., (Retired), Our Lady of the Assumption, Charlotte
Hubbell, Carl, St. William, Murphy
Huff, Sidney, (Retired), Our Lady of Lourdes, Monroe
Johnson, James R., St. Charles, Morganton
K'Briuh, Pierre M., St. Mary, Greensboro
Kak, Thomas, (Retired), Immaculate Heart of Mary, High Point
King, David E., Maryfield Pennybyrn, High Point
King, Mark J., St. Matthew, Charlotte
Kingsley, Arthur J., St. Michael, Gastonia
Knight, Charles, (Living Outside the Diocese)
Konarski, Edward A., St. Charles Borromeo, Morganton
Kopfle, John, St. Vincent de Paul, Charlotte
La Pointe, Gerard P. St. Margaret, Maggie Valley
Langsdorf, Michael, Divine Redeemer, Boonville
Leahy, Michael, (Unassigned)
Lee, Pe nhia cha, St. Charles Borromeo, Morganton
Liotard, Paul, (Retired), Holy Angels, Mount Airy
Lisk, Larry, St. Paul the Apostle, Greensboro
Lyerly, R. Alexander, St. Bernadette, Linville
Mack, Joseph H., Jr., (Retired), (Living Outside Diocese)
Markle, Harold, (Retired), St. John Baptiste de la Salle, North Wilkesboro
Martini, Michael J., St. Paul the Apostle, Greensboro
Martino, John, St. Charles Borromeo, Morganton
Mazur, James, Sacred Heart, Salisbury
McNulty, Brian P., St. Patrick, Charlotte
Medina, Carlos A., Sr., St. Patrick, Charlotte
Murphy, Robert, St. Mark, Huntersville
Nash, Mark D., St. Thomas Aquinas, Charlotte
O'Madigan, Dennis T., (Retired), (Unassigned)
Pais, Louis, St. Mark, Huntersville
Parrish, John N., St. John Neumann, Charlotte
Piche, Guy, Chap., Catholic Conference Center, Hickory; St. Helen, Spencer Mountain
Pickett, A. Stephen, St. Francis, Lenoir
Potkay, Gerald, Holy Infant, Reidsville
Pozo, Guido, Our Lady of the Assumption, Charlotte
Pynes, Tony, Our Lady of Grace, Greensboro
Rasmussen, Thomas, St. Aloysius, Hickory
Reilly, Matthew, St. Phillip The Apostle, Statesville
Ricart, Martin, III, St. James the Greater, Concord
Ritchey, Timothy, Holy Cross, Keunersville
Rodriguez, Edwin, St. Mark, Huntersville
Rohan, Timothy, (Retired), Our Lady of Grace, Greensboro
Schumacher, Joseph N., (Retired), Our Lady of Mercy, Winston-Salem
Shaw, Vincent H., Jr., St. Mary, Greensboro
Shaw, William S., St. Pius Tenth, Greensboro
Sherwood, Ronald D., St. Mark, Huntersville
Sims, John E., St. Therese, Mooresville
Smith, Joseph T., (Retired), (Unassigned)
Steinkamp, Ronald F., St. Pius Tenth, Greensboro
Stout, Michael L., St. Barnabas, Arden
Szalony, George A., St. Ann, Charlotte
Teich, Paul A., (Retired), Our Lady of Grace, Greensboro
Todd, Curtiss, (Retired), Our Lady of the Assumption, Charlotte
Toner, Jim, Our Lady of Grace, Greensboro
Torres, Rafael J., St. Luke, Charlotte
Triana, Rudy J., (Unassigned)
Voegele, Richard, Bascilica of St. Lawrence, Asheville
Weisenhorn, John P., (Retired), St. Michael, Gastonia
Wenning, Bernard W., Jr., (Retired), St. Gabriel, Charlotte
Williams, Kevin, Our Lady of the Assumption, Charlotte
Wilson, William H., Queen of the Apostles, Belmont
Witulski, James H., St. Thomas Aquinas, Charlotte
Zandy, Richard J., St. Andrew the Apostle, Mars Hill
Zboyovski, Michael J., Sr., St. Eugene, Asheville
Zimmerle, John O., St. Francis of Assisi, Mocksville

INSTITUTIONS LOCATED IN THE DIOCESE

[A] COLLEGES AND UNIVERSITIES

BELMONT. **Belmont Abbey College*, 100 Belmont-Mount Holly Rd., 28012-1802. Tel: 704-461-6700; Fax: 704-461-6748. Email: donaldbeagle@bac.edu. Web: belmontabbeycollege.edu. Rt. Rev. Placid D. Solari, O.S.B., Chancellor; William Thierfelder, Ed.D., Pres.; Carson Daly, Ph.D., Academic Dean; Rev. David G. Brown, O.S.B., Registrar; Wayne Scroggins, Vice Pres. Admin. & Finance; Donald Beagle, Dir. Library. (Coed) Liberal Arts Senior College. Priests 1; Sisters 1; Lay Teachers 137; Students 1,711.

The Ecumenical Institute of Wake Forest University and Belmont Abbey College Tel: 704-825-6748; Fax: 704-825-6743.

Sacred Heart College, 101 Mercy Dr., 28012-4805. Tel: 704-829-5100; Fax: 704-829-5137. Sr. Rosalind Picot, R.S.M., Pres. Sisters of Mercy., College ceased academic operation, effective August 1987. Corporation intact.

[B] HIGH SCHOOLS

CHARLOTTE. *Christ the King Catholic High School, MACS*, 1123 S. Church St., 28203. Tel: 704-799-4400; Fax: 704-799-4404. Dan Dolan, Prin.

KERNERSVILLE. *Bishop McGuinness Catholic High School*, 1725 N.C. Hwy. 66 S., 27284. Tel: 336-564-1010; Fax: 336-564-1060. Email: grepass@bmhs.us. Web: www.bmhs.us. George L. Repass, M.Ed., Prin.; Tracy A. Shaw, M.Ed., Asst. Prin. & Dir., Studies; Sr. Anne Thomas Taylor, Dean of Students; Lyndall Cantrell, Librarian. Sisters of St. Joseph 2; Lay Teachers 41; Students 547.

[C] ELEMENTARY SCHOOLS, INTERPAROCHIAL

ASHEVILLE. *Asheville Catholic School*, (Grades PreK-8), 12 Culvern St., 28804. Tel: 828-252-7896; Fax: 828-252-5708. Email: info@ashevillecatholic.org. Web: www.ashevillecatholic.org. Cecilia Rosello, Prin.; Shonra McManus, Librarian. Lay Teachers 16; Students 193.

[D] REGIONAL SCHOOLS

CHARLOTTE. *Mecklenburg Area Catholic Schools (M.A.C.S.)*, (Grades PreK-12), Catholic School System of Nine Schools., 1123 S. Church St., 28203. Tel: 704-370-3214; Fax: 704-370-3292. Web: www.charlottediocese.org/catholicschools. Janice Ritter, Ed.D., Ph.D., Interim Supt.

Charlotte Catholic High School (Bishop Hafey Memorial), 7702 Pineville-Matthews Rd., 28226. Tel: 704-543-1127; Fax: 704-543-1217. Web: www.gocougars.org. Gerald A. Healy, Prin.; Randy Belk, Dean of Students; Steve Carpenter, Asst. Prin.; Angela Montague, Asst. Prin.; Lynn Hidell, Librarian. Lay Teachers 105; Students 1,429.

Charlotte Catholic High School Athletic Association Tel: 704-543-1127; Fax: 704-543-1217.

Charlotte Catholic High School Alumni Association Tel: 704-543-9118; Fax: 704-543-1217.

Charlotte Catholic High School Home School Association Tel: 704-543-1127; Fax: 704-543-1217.

Holy Trinity Middle School (Grades 6-8), 3100 Park Rd., 28209. Tel: 704-527-7822; Fax: 704-525-7288. Kevin Parks, Prin.; Sheena Zawistowicz, Dean of Students; Deb Robinson, Asst. Prin.; Kevin Glossner, Asst. Prin.; Kathleen Murray, Librarian. Lay Teachers 66; Students 921.

St. Matthew School (Grades PreK-5), 11525 Elm Ln., 28277. Tel: 704-544-2070; Fax: 704-544-2184. Kevin O'Herron, Prin.; Kathy McKinney, Asst.

Prin.; Debra Lee, Librarian. Lay Teachers 40; Students 627.

Our Lady of the Assumption School (Grades PreK-6), 4225 Shamrock Dr., 28215. Tel: 704-531-0067; Fax: 704-531-7633. Allana-Rae Ramkissaen, Prin.; Sandra Brighton, Asst. Prin. Lay Teachers 18; Students 132.

St. Ann School (Grades PreK-5), 600 Hillside Ave., 28209. Tel: 704-525-4938; Fax: 704-525-2640. Peggy Mazzola, Prin.; Lisa Horton, Asst. Prin. Lay Teachers 19; Students 204.

St. Gabriel School (Grades PreK-5), 3028 Providence Rd., 28211. Tel: 704-366-2409; Fax: 704-362-5063. Sharon Broxterman, Prin.; Michelle Snoke, Asst. Prin.; Ellen Chase, Librarian. Lay Teachers 40; Students 565.

St. Mark School (Grades K-5), 14750 Stumptown Rd., Huntersville, 28078. Tel: 704-766-5000; Fax: 704-875-6377. Debbie Butler, Prin.; Crystal Koury, Asst. Prin.; Lisa Rox, Librarian. Lay Teachers 50; Students 751.

St. Patrick School (Grades K-8), 1125 Buchanan St., 28203. Tel: 704-333-3174; Fax: 704-333-3178. Debbie Mixer, Prin.; Kelly Parks, Asst. Prin.; Lisa Lehmuller, Librarian. Lay Teachers 28; Students 320.

[E] GENERAL HOSPITALS

ASHEVILLE. *Sisters of Mercy Services Corporation*, 1201 Patton Ave., 28806. Tel: 828-281-1303; Fax: 828-254-4102. Email: sharon@somsc.org. Web: www.somsc.org. P.O. Box 16367, 28816-0367. Tim Johnston, Pres. & CEO.

Sisters of Mercy Urgent Care, Inc., 1201 Patton Ave., 28806-0367. Tel: 828-210-2121; Fax: 828-254-4102. Web: www.urgentcares.org. P.O. Box 16367, 28816-0367. Patients Assisted Annually 54,000; Total Staff 51.

[F] SPECIAL CARE FACILITIES

BELMONT. **Holy Angels Services, Inc.*, 6600 Wilkinson Blvd., 28012. Tel: 704-825-4161; Fax: 704-825-0553. Email: info@holyangelsnc.org. Web: www.holyangelsnc.org. Mailing Address: P.O. Box 710, 28012. Mrs. Regina P. Moody, M.Ed., Pres. & CEO. Residential and developmental programs and svcs. for children and adults with mental retardation and physical disabilities. Sisters of Mercy 2; Capacity (All Programs) 125.

Morrow Center (Children 0-20)

Little Angels Child Development Center On-site integrated day care.

Great Adventures Social Club Adults with mental retardation.

South Point Adult group home.

Lakewood Adult group home.

McAuley Residence ICF/MR Group Homes Bed Capacity 48.

Cherubs Cafe, Gifts & Candy Bouquets Tel: 704-825-0414; Fax: 704-825-0553. (Age 18+); Job coaching, work options.

Supported Living (Age 18+)

Camp Hope Recreational opportunities for individuals with developmental disabilities.

Carrabaun Adult group home.

Gary Home Adult group home. Total Assisted Annually 125.

[G] CATHOLIC SOCIAL SERVICES

CHARLOTTE. *Catholic Social Services of the Diocese of Charlotte, Inc.*, The Pastoral Center: 1123 S. Church St., 28203. Tel: 704-370-3228; Fax: 704-370-3298. Email: gacarter@charlottediocese.org. Web: www.cssnc.org. Gerard A. Carter, Ph.D., Exec. Dir.

Area Offices:

Catholic Social Services-Western Regional Office, 50 Orange St., Asheville, 28801. Tel: 828-255-0146; Fax: 828-253-7339. Michele Sheppard, Dir.

Catholic Social Services-Charlotte Regional Office, 1123 S. Church St., 28203. Tel: 704-370-3262; Fax: 704-370-3377. Sharon Davis, Dir.

Catholic Social Services-Piedmont and Triad Office, 627 W. Second St., Winston-Salem, 27101. Tel: 336-727-0705; Fax: 336-714-3232. Diane Bullard, Dir.

Catholic Social Services-Refugee Resettlement Office, 1123 S. Church St., 28203. Tel: 704-370-3262; Fax: 704-370-3377. Cira Ponce, Refugee Resettlement Dir.

Special Ministries:

Office of Justice and Peace, 1123 S. Church St., 28203. Tel: 704-370-3225; Fax: 704-370-3377. Joseph Purello, Dir.

Catholic Social Services-Office of Economic Opportunity, 27 Hatchett St., Murphy, 28906. Tel: 828-835-3535; Fax: 828-835-9794. Claudie Burchfield, Prog. Dir.

[H] HOME HEALTH CARE

ROSMAN. **Frances Warde Health Service*, 9526 Rosman Hwy., 28772. Tel: 828-884-7990; Fax: 828-966-9609. Email: jdewarrsm@juno.com. Sr. Jacqueline Dewar, R.S.M., Business Mgr. Sisters 2; Total Assisted 1,500; Staff 1.

[I] NURSING HOMES

HIGH POINT. *Maryfield Nursing Home*, 1315 Greensboro Rd., 27260. Tel: 336-821-4000; Fax: 336-886-4036. Email: sisterlucy@pbmccrc.com. Web: www.pennybyrnatmaryfield.com. Sr. Lucy Hennessy, S.M.G., Chm. of the Board. Poor Servants of the Mother of God 5; Bed Capacity 125.

Pennybyrn at Maryfield Tel: 336-886-2444; Fax: 336-886-4036. Apartments 131; Cottages 49; Assisted Living 48.

[J] MONASTERIES AND RESIDENCES OF PRIESTS AND BROTHERS

BELMONT. *Belmont Abbey*, 100 Belmont-Mount Holly Rd., 28012-1802. Tel: 704-461-6675; Fax: 704-461-6242. Email: AbbotPlacid@bac.edu. Web: belmontabbey.org. Rt. Revs. Placid D. Solari, O.S.B., Abbot; Oscar C. Burnett, O.S.B., Prior (Retired); Revs. David G. Brown, O.S.B.; Matthew T. McSorley, O.S.B.; Kenneth A. Geyer, O.S.B.; David R. Kessinger, O.S.B.; Kieran A. Neilson, O.S.B.; Francis P. Forster, O.S.B.; Arthur J. Pendleton, O.S.B.; Christopher A. Kirchgessner, O.S.B.; Agostino Fernandez, O.S.B.; Bros. Tobiah Abbott, O.S.B.; Elias Correa-Torres, O.S.B.; Paul Shanley, O.S.B.; Edward Mancuso, O.S.B.; Emmanuel Slobodzian, O.S.B.; Anthony Swofford, O.S.B., Subprior; Andrew Spivey, O.S.B.

Southern Benedictine Society of North Carolina, Inc. Abbots 2; Monk Priests of Abbey 9; Priests in Residence 8; Brothers 7.

MOORESVILLE. *Jesuit Community*, 217 Brawley School Rd., 28117-9103. Tel: 704-664-3992; Fax: 704-660-6321. Email: vcurtin@gmail.com. Revs. Vincent C. Curtin, S.J.; Patrick Earl, S.J.; William J. Lynch, S.J.; Thomas P. McDonnell, S.J.; Francis X. Reese, S.J.; Donald M. Ward Jr., S.J.

Jesuit Community in Western North Carolina

STONVILLE. *Franciscan Friary*, 477 Grogan Rd., Stoneville, 27048. Tel: 336-573-3751; Fax: 336-573-3752. Rev. Louis Canino, O.F.M., Dir.

[K] CONVENTS AND RESIDENCES FOR SISTERS

CHARLOTTE. *Missionaries of Charity*, 1625 Glenn St., 28205. Tel: 704-531-2943. Ministry for poor. Sisters 4.

Sisters of Mercy of the Americas, South Central Community, Inc., Carmel House, 11427 Olde Turnbury Ct., 28277. Tel: 704-542-0951; Fax: 704-542-0951. Sisters Kathy Green, R.S.M., Pres.; Paulette Williams, R.S.M., Sec./Treas., Sisters of Mercy, N.C. Administration

St. Joseph Adoration Monastery, 3452 Willow Oak Rd., 28209. Tel: 704-999-7895. Email: nuns@stjosephmonatery.com. Web: www.stjosephmonastery.com. Sr. Dolores Maries, Abbess. Total in Community 8.

ASHEVILLE. *Sisters of Mercy of the Americas, South Central Community, Inc.*, Sisters of Mercy Convent, 2 Sunset Walk, 28804. Tel: 828-232-0084; Fax: 828-254-4102. Email: smg@somsc.org. Web: www.urgentcares.org. Sisters 3; Health Care 1; Parish 1; Retired 1.

BELMONT. *Sisters of Mercy of the Americas, South Central Community, Inc.*, Sacred Heart Convent, 100 Mercy Dr., 28012-4805. Tel: 704-829-5100; Fax: 704-829-5137. Email: maray@mercysc.org. Web: www.mercysc.org. Sr. Mary Andrew Ray, R.S.M., Coord. Connected with the Sacred Heart Convent are Holy Angels, Inc., House of Mercy, Inc., and Catherine's House, Inc. Sisters in Scared Heart Convent 35.

Sisters of Mercy of the Americas, South Central Community, Inc., Mercy Administration Center: 101 Mercy Dr., 28012-2898. Tel: 704-829-5260; Fax: 704-829-5267. Web: www.mercysc.org.

HAMPTONVILLE. *Sisters of Mercy of the Americas, South Central Community, Inc., Well of Mercy*, 181 Mercy Ln., 27020-7199. Tel: 704-539-5449; Fax: 704-539-4487. Email: mercy@yadtel.net.

HIGH POINT. *Congregation of the Sisters of Charity of St. Vincent De Paul*, St. Vincent Convent, 1225 Elon Pl., 27263. Tel: 336-884-1442; Fax: 336-884-4545. Email: scvsisters@northstate.net. Sr. Archana, S.C.V., Supr.

Poor Servants of the Mother of God Inc., 1315 Greensboro Rd., 27260. Tel: 336-821-4000; Fax: 336-886-4036. Email: sisterlucy@pbmccrc.com. Sr. Lucy Hennessy, S.M.G., Mission Leader.

MATTHEWS. *Sisters of Mercy of the Americas, South Central Community, Inc., Coolock House*, 1510 Kirkbridge Ct., 28105. Tel: 704-847-5363; Fax: 704-847-5363. Email: therese_galligan@yahoo.com. Parish and Bereavement Ministry. Sisters of Mercy of the Americas 2.

VALE. *Maryvale Motherhouse*, 2522 June Bug Rd., 28168. Tel: 704-276-2626; Fax: 704-276-2626. Sr. Mary Louis, Foundress and Supr. Congregation of Our Lady Help of the Clergy, (Maryvale Sisters). Parish ministry, day-care center, spiritual/retreat center. Sisters 5.

WINSTON-SALEM. *Sisters of St. Joseph of Chestnut Hill, PA, Our Lady of Mercy Convent*, 2141 New Castle Dr., 27103. Tel: 336-774-3956; Fax: 336-725-2294.

Sisters of St. Joseph of Chestnut Hill, PA, St. Leo Convent, 1975 Georgia Ave., 27104. Tel: 336-723-3639.

[L] CAMPUS MINISTRY CENTERS

CHARLOTTE. *Diocesan Office of Campus Ministry* Ms. Mary Wright, Diocesan Dir., Campus Ministry.

University of North Carolina-Charlotte Catholic Campus Ministry House, 9408 Sandburg Ave., 28213-0565. Tel: 704-717-7104. Email: ccmuncc@gmail.com. Sr. Eileen Spanier, G.N.S.H., Catholic Campus Min.

University of North Carolina-Asheville/Mars Hill College Catholic Campus Ministry, UNC-Asheville, P.O. Box 8067, Asheville, 28814. Tel: 828-226-3809. Email: ashevilleccm@gmail.com. Gloria Schweizer, Catholic Campus Min.

Belmont Abbey College 100 Belmont-Mount Holly Rd., Belmont, 28012. Tel: 704-461-5094. Patricia Stevenson, Dir. Campus Ministry. Email: triciastevenson@bac.edu.

Appalachian State University 232 Faculty St., Boone, 28607. Tel: 828-264-7087; Fax: 828-262-0970. Erin Leonard, Catholic Campus Min.

Western Carolina University Catholic Student Center, P.O. Box 2766, Cullowhee, 28723-0364. Tel: 828-293-7472; Fax: 828-262-3721. Email: wcucatholic@gmail.com. Matthew Newsome, Catholic Campus Min.

Davidson College Catholic Campus Ministry, Campus Box 7181, Davidson, 28035-7181. Tel: 704-894-2423. Email: kasoos@davidson.edu. Karen Soos, Catholic Campus Min.

NC Agricultural and Technical State University & Bennett College 1009 Bluford St., Greensboro, 27401. Tel: 336-272-5868. Email: theahouse@bellsouth.net. Alberta Hairston, Catholic Campus Min.

University of North Carolina-Greensboro, Greensboro College & Guilford College UNG-G ACM Center, P.O. Box 26170, Greensboro, 27402-6170. Tel: 336-334-5130. Email: ccmuncg@gmail.com.

Wake Forest University and Winston-Salem University P.O. Box 7204, Reynolda Station, Winston-Salem, 27109. Tel: 336-758-5018. Rev. Charles Jagodzinski, O.F.M.Conv., Catholic Campus Min.

[M] RETREAT CENTERS

STONEVILLE. **St. Francis Springs Prayer Center*, 477 Grogan Rd., 27048. Tel: 336-573-3751; Fax: 336-573-3752. Email: fransprings@aol.com. Web: www.stfrancissprings.com. Rev. Louis Canino, O.F.M.

[N] REFLECTION CENTERS

HAMPTONVILLE. *Well of Mercy Inc.*, 181 Mercy Ln., 27020. Tel: 704-539-5449; Fax: 704-539-4487. Email: mercy@yadtel.net. Sisters Brigid McCarthy, R.S.M., Co-Dir.; Donna Marie Vaillancourt, R.S.M., Co-Dir. Retreats and psycho-spiritual development programs.

MAGGIE VALLEY. *Living Waters Catholic Reflection Center*, 103 Living Waters Ln., 28751. Tel: 828-926-3833; Fax: 828-926-1997. Email: lwcrc@bellsouth.net. Web: www.catholicretreat.org. Sr. Frances Maries Grady, S.C.L., Dir. Retreats, days of recollection, and continuing educ.

[O] HISPANIC MINISTRY

CHARLOTTE. *Diocesan Hispanic Ministry*, 1123 S. Church St., 28203. Tel: 704-370-3269; Fax: 704-370-3291. Email: fmelo@charlottediocese.org. Rev. Fidel C. Melo, Dir. Hispanic Ministry.

[P] CONFERENCE CENTERS

HICKORY. *Catholic Conference Center*, 1551 Trinity Ln., 28602-9247. Tel: 828-327-7441; 888-536-7441 (Toll Free); Fax: 828-327-0872. Email: info@catholicconference.org. Web: www.catholicconference.org. Deacon Guy A. Piche, Dir. & Chap.

[Q] MISCELLANEOUS

CHARLOTTE. *Catholic Diocese of Charlotte Housing Corp.*, 1123 S. Church St., 28203. Tel: 704-370-3248; Fax: 704-971-4312. Email: jvwidelski@

charlottediocese.org. Rev. Msgr. Mauricio W. West, Pres.; Gerald C. Carter, Ph.D., Vice Pres.; William G. Weldon, CPA, Treas.; Jerry Widelski, Dir. Develops housing facilities and services for individuals and families with special needs.

MACS Education Foundation, 1123 S. Church St., 28203. Tel: 704-370-3303; Fax: 704-370-3398. Web: charlottediocese.org/edu-foundation-macs.

**Room at the Inn, Inc.*, 3737 Weona Ave., 28209. Tel: 704-525-4673; Fax: 704-521-2751. Email: iroomattheinn@rati.org. Web: www.rati.org. Jeannie Wray, Exec. Dir. Room at the Inn-Charlotte, 3737 Weona Ave., Charlotte, NC 28209. Tel: 704-525-4673. Long-term maternity and aftercare services for single, pregnant women, with their babies.

Sisters of Mercy of North Carolina Foundation, Inc., 2115 Rexford Rd., Ste. 314, 28211. Tel: 704-366-0087; Fax: 704-366-8850. Web: www.somncfdn.org. Edward J. Schlicksup, Pres.; Sr. Mary Jerome Spradley, R.S.M., Bd. Chairperson.

Triad Catholic Schools Foundation, 1123 S. Church St., 28203. Tel: 800-560-6311; 704-370-3303; Fax: 704-370-3398.

ASHEVILLE. *Catherine McAuley Mercy Foundation, Inc.*, 1201 Patton Ave., 28806. Tel: 828-281-2598; Fax: 828-254-4102. Email: sharon@somsc.org. Mailing Address: P.O. Box 16367, 28816-0367.

BELMONT. **Catherine's House*, 400 Mercy Dr., P.O. Box 1633, 28012. Tel: 704-825-9599; Fax: 704-825-2734. Email: patsyfuller@catherineshouse.org. Web: www.catherineshouse.org. Stan Patterson, Pres. & CEO. Transitional housing for women and women with children who are homeless.

Holy Angels Foundation, Inc., 6600 Wilkinson Blvd., 28012. Tel: 704-825-4161; Fax: 704-825-0401. Mailing Address: P.O. Box 710, 28012.

Holy Angels, Inc., 6600 Wilkinson Blvd., 28012. P.O. Box 710, 28012.

House of Mercy, Inc., 701 Mercy Dr., 28012. Tel: 704-825-4711; Fax: 704-825-9976. Email: hse4mercy@aol.com. Web: www.thehouseofmercy.org. P.O. Box 808, 28012. Stan Patterson, Pres. & CEO. Provides a home for persons living with AIDS in the advanced stages who have no other housing alternative in an 11 county region. Bed Capacity 6.

Mercy Community Housing North Carolina (MCHNC), 6531 Wilkinson Blvd., 28012. Tel: 404-873-3887; Fax: 877-693-2333. Email: pgrant@mercyhousing.org. Web: www.mercyhousing.org. Paula Grant, Vice Pres.

Mercy Housing, South East, Inc., 6531 Wilkinson Blvd., 28012. Tel: 404-873-3887; Fax: 877-693-2333. Email: pgrant@mercyhousing.org. Web: www.mercyhousing.org. Purpose: provide housing and supportive services to low income, special needs populations and seniors.

Mercy Place Belmont, 6531 Wilkinson Blvd., 28012. Tel: 404-873-3887; Fax: 877-698-2333. Paula Grant, Vice Pres.; Patricia O'Roark, Legal Affairs Mgr. Provides housing and support services for very low-income seniors.

Sisters of Mercy of the Americas, South Central Community, Inc., 101 Mercy Dr., 28012-2898. Tel: 704-829-5260; Fax: 704-829-5267. Email: support@mercysc.org. Web: www.mercysc.org. Sr. Kathy Green, R.S.M., Pres.

South Central FIDES, Inc., 101 Mercy Dr., 28012. Tel: 704-829-5260; Fax: 704-829-5267.

COLFAX. *Room At The Inn of the Carolinas, Inc.*, P.O. Box 484, 27235. Tel: 336-996-3788 (NC); 843-815-9911 (SC); Fax: 336-996-7567. Web: www.roominn.org. O. Albert Hodges, Pres.

GASTONIA. *Charlotte Catholic Women's Group*, 708 St. Michael's Ln., 28052. Email: jlgranzow@windstream.net. Web: www.charlottecatholicwomensgroup.org. Linda Granzow, Pres.

**Seton Media House, Inc.*, 1520 S. York St., 28053. Email: setonhouse@aol.com. P.O. Box 269, 28053. Richard G. Hoefling, Pres. & CEO; Stephen M. Wilfong, Exec. Dir. Purpose: Distribution of printed materials reflective of Catholic teaching to Catholic schools, and religious educ. programs at no cost to students, family or school.

GREENSBORO. *Franciscan Center*, 233 N. Greene St., 27401. Tel: 336-273-2554; Fax: 336-273-2441. Email: fransprings@aol.com. Web: www.stfrancissprings.com. Rev. Louis Canino, O.F.M., Dir.

Society of St. Vincent De Paul, 201 S. Chapman St., 27403. Tel: 336-272-0336. Financial assistance, furniture and appliances.

SALISBURY. *Cursillos in Christianity*, 218 W. Thomas St., 28144. Butch Mayer, Contact Person.

RELIGIOUS INSTITUTES OF MEN REPRESENTED IN THE DIOCESE

For further details refer to the corresponding bracketed number in the Religious Institutes of Men or Women section.

[0200]—*Benedictine Monks* (Belmont, NC)—O.S.B.
[]—*Benedictine Monks* (St. Meinrad, IN)—O.S.B.
[0470]—*The Capuchin Friars Province of the Stigmata*—O.F.M.Cap.
[1330]—*Congregation of the Mission* (Eastern Prov.)—C.M.
[0480]—*Conventual Franciscans* (Union City, NJ)—O.F.M.Conv
[0520]—*Franciscan Friars* (New York, NY)—O.F.M.
[0690]—*Jesuit Fathers and Brothers* (Maryland Prov.)—S.J.
[]—*Jesuit Fathers and Brothers* (Detroit Province)—S.J.
[0920]—*Oblates of St. Francis De Sales* (Wilmington-Philadelphia)—O.S.F.S.
[1070]—*Redemptorist Fathers* (Baltimore Prov.)—C.Ss.R.
[0560]—*Third Order Regular of St. Francis* (Pittsburgh, PA)—T.O.R.

RELIGIOUS INSTITUTES OF WOMEN REPRESENTED IN THE DIOCESE

[2980]—*Congregation de Notre Dame*—C.N.D.
[3080]—*Congregation of Our Lady, Help of the Clergy*—C.L.H.C.
[]—*Congregation of the Immaculate Heart of Mary*—C.I.C.M.
[1110]—*Dominican Sisters of St. Catherine of Siena*—O.P.
[]—*Grey Nuns of the Sacred Heart*—G.N.S.H.
[2470]—*Maryknoll Sisters*—M.M.
[2710]—*Missionaries of Charity*—M.C.
[]—*Missionary Servants of the Most Blessed Trinity*—M.S.B.T.
[]—*Poor Clares of Perpetual Adoration*—P.C.P.A.
[3640]—*Poor Servants of the Mother of God*—S.M.G.
[]—*School Sisters of Notre Dame*—S.S.N.D.
[]—*School Sisters of St. Francis* (Milwaukee, WI)—O.S.F.
[]—*Sisters of Charity* (Leavenworth, KS)—S.C.L.
[0590]—*Sisters of Charity of Saint Elizabeth, Convent Station*—S.C.
[]—*Sisters of Charity of Saint Vincent de Paul*—S.C.V.
[]—*Sisters of Mercy of the Americas* (South Central Community, Inc.)—R.S.M.
[]—*Sisters of Mercy of the Americas* (Mid-Atlantic Community)—R.S.M.
[]—*Sisters of Mercy of the Americas* (West Midwest Community)—R.S.M.
[]—*Sisters of Providence*—S.P.
[]—*Sisters of St. Joseph of Carondelet* (Rochester, MN)—C.S.J.
[]—*Sisters of St. Francis* (Tiffin, OH)—O.S.F.
[]—*Sisters of St. Francis* (Philadelphia, PA)—O.S.F.
[3893]—*Sisters of St. Joseph* (Chestnut Hill, PA)—S.S.J.
[4060]—*Society of the Holy Child Jesus* (Drexel Hill)—S.H.C.J.

NECROLOGY

† Kimbrough, Conrad, (Retired)—Died July 5, 2011

An asterisk (*) denotes an organization that has established tax-exempt status directly with the IRS and is not covered by the USCCB Group Ruling.

Diocese of Cheyenne

(Dioecesis Cheyennensis)

Most Reverend

PAUL D. ETIENNE, D.D., S.T.L.

Bishop of Cheyenne; ordained June 27, 1992; appointed Bishop of Cheyenne October 19, 2009; Episcopal Ordination and installed December 9, 2009. *Res.: P.O. Box 1468, Cheyenne, WY 82003-1468.*

Most Reverend

JOSEPH HART, D.D.

Retired Bishop of Cheyenne; ordained May 1, 1956; appointed July 1, 1976; appointed Titular Bishop of Timida Regia; Episcopal Ordination August 31, 1976; installed June 12, 1978; retired September 26, 2001. *Res.: P.O. Box 1468, Cheyenne, WY 82003.*

Chancery Office: 2121 Capitol Ave., P.O. Box 1468, Cheyenne, WY 82003-1468. Tel: 307-638-1530; Fax: 307-637-7936.

Web: www.dioceseofcheyenne.org

Email: dmcintyre@dioceseofcheyenne.org

ESTABLISHED AUGUST 2, 1887.

Square Miles 97,548.

Comprises the State of Wyoming and Yellowstone National Park.

For legal titles of parishes and diocesan institutions, consult the Chancery Office.

STATISTICAL OVERVIEW

Personnel	
Bishop	1
Retired Bishops	1
Priests: Diocesan Active in Diocese	38
Priests: Diocesan Active Outside Diocese	1
Priests: Retired, Sick or Absent	16
Number of Diocesan Priests	55
Religious Priests in Diocese	5
Total Priests in Diocese	60
Extern Priests in Diocese	6
Permanent Deacons in Diocese	22
Total Brothers	1
Total Sisters	19
Parishes	
Parishes	32
With Resident Pastor:	
Resident Diocesan Priests	27
Resident Religious Priests	3
Missions	39
Professional Ministry Personnel:	
Sisters	3
Lay Ministers	35
Welfare	
Homes for the Aged	2
Total Assisted	102
Residential Care of Children	1
Total Assisted	242
Special Centers for Social Services	4
Total Assisted	14,859
Educational	
Diocesan Students in Other Seminaries	12
Total Seminarians	12
Elementary Schools, Diocesan and Parish	7
Total Students	961
Catechesis/Religious Education:	
High School Students	907
Elementary Students	3,015
Total Students under Catholic Instruction	4,895
Teachers in the Diocese:	
Sisters	2
Lay Teachers	91
Vital Statistics	
Receptions into the Church:	
Infant Baptism Totals	942
Minor Baptism Totals	124
Adult Baptism Totals	117
Received into Full Communion	122
First Communions	862
Confirmations	846
Marriages:	
Catholic	134
Interfaith	97
Total Marriages	231
Deaths	563
Total Catholic Population	54,129
Total Population	563,626

Former Bishops—Rt. Revs. MAURICE F. BURKE, D.D., cons. Oct. 28, 1887; transferred to the See of St. Joseph, MO, June 19, 1893; died March 17, 1923; THOMAS M. LENIHAN, D.D., cons. Feb. 24, 1897; died Dec. 15, 1901; Most Revs. JAMES J. KEANE, D.D., cons. Bishop of Cheyenne Oct. 28, 1902; raised to the archiepiscopal dignity and transferred to Archdiocese of Dubuque, Aug. 11, 1911; died Aug. 2, 1929; PATRICK A. MCGOVERN, D.D., LL.D., ord. Aug. 18, 1895; assistant at the Pontifical Throne; appt. Jan. 19, 1912; cons. April 11, 1912; died Nov. 8, 1951; HUBERT M. NEWELL, D.D., LL.D., ord. June 15, 1930; appt. Coadjutor Aug. 2, 1947; cons. Sept. 24, 1947; succeeded to the See Nov. 8, 1951; retired Jan. 3, 1978; died Sept. 8, 1987; HUBERT JOSEPH HART, D.D., ord. May 1, 1956; appt. Titular Bishop of Timida Regia July 1, 1976; cons. Aug. 31, 1976; installed June 12, 1978; retired Sept. 26, 2001; DAVID L. RICKEN, D.D., J.C.L., ord. Sept. 12, 1980; appt. Coadjutor Bishop of Cheyenne Dec. 14, 1999; Episcopal Ordination Jan. 6, 2000; succeeded to See Sept. 26, 2001; installed Bishop of Green Bay Aug. 28, 2008.

Chancery Office—2121 Capitol Ave., P.O. Box 1468, Cheyenne, 82003-1468. Tel: 307-638-1530; Fax: 307-637-7936.

Vicar General—Very Rev. MICHAEL CARR.

Chancellor—CAROL DELOIS, Mailing Address: P.O. Box 1468, Cheyenne, 82003-1468. Tel: 307-638-1530; Fax: 307-637-7936.

Judicial Vicar—Rev. THOMAS E. CRONKLETON JR., J.C.D., Mailing Address: P.O. Box 1468, Cheyenne, 82003-1468. Tel: 307-638-1530; 866-790-0014; Fax: 307-637-7936.

Adjutant Judicial Vicar—Rev. THOMAS R. KADERA, J.C.L., Mailing Address: P.O. Box 1468, Cheyenne, 82003-1468.

Vicar for Retired and Disabled Clergy—VACANT.

College of Consultors—Most Rev. PAUL D. ETIENNE, D.D., S.T.L.; Very Rev. MICHAEL CARR; Revs. THOMAS E. CRONKLETON JR., J.C.D.; ANDREW D. DUNCAN; Very Revs. CARL GALLINGER; JAMES HEISER; Rev. GLEN SZCZECHOWSKI.

Presbyteral Council—Most Rev. PAUL D. ETIENNE, D.D., S.T.L.; Very Rev. MICHAEL CARR; Rev. THOMAS E. CRONKLETON JR., J.C.D.; Very Rev. VERNON CLARK; Rev. ROBERT L. FOX; Very Rev. CARL GALLINGER; Revs. WILLIAM HILL III; RAY RODRIGUEZ; ROBERT SPAULDING; STEVEN MATTHEW TITUS; PHILIP C. WAGNER.

Vicars Forane—Very Revs. AUGUST KOEUNE, Casper Deanery; CARL GALLINGER, Cheyenne Deanery; SAMUEL HAYES, Rock Springs Deanery; JAMES HEISER, Sheridan Deanery; VERNON F. CLARK, Thermopolis Deanery.

Finance Officer—Mr. LOREN SCHILLINGER, Finance Officer, Mailing Address: P.O. Box 1468, Cheyenne, 82003-1468. Tel: 307-638-1530; Fax: 307-637-7936.

Finance Council—Most Rev. PAUL D. ETIENNE, D.D., S.T.L. Ex Officios, Voting: Rev. GARY RUZICKA; The Honorable MIKE SULLIVAN; Mr. HOWARD BAKER; Rev. THOMAS E. CRONKLETON JR., J.C.D.; Very Rev. MICHAEL CARR. Appointed Members, Voting: JARED BLACK; WILLIAM DOWNES; FRANK ROTELLINI; CHUCK HARKINS, Chm.; LYNNE BOOMGAARDEN; FRED HARRISON.

Diocesan Pastoral Council—Most Rev. PAUL D. ETIENNE, D.D., S.T.L.; Very Rev. MICHAEL CARR; ED BOENISCH; Deacon KIM CARROLL; D. J. CUNNINGHAM; ALBERTO ENRIQUEZ; BETSY FLAHERTY; Sr. RUTH ANN HEHN, S.C.L.; LARRY HELL; JOHN MCMAHAN; Rev. Msgr. JAMES O'NEILL (Retired); JIM PEW; MARGE ST. CLAIR; GEORGE TUCKER.

Tribunal Office— All marriage correspondence are to be directed to: *Mailing Address: The Tribunal Office, P.O. Box 1468, Cheyenne, 82003-1468.* Tel: 307-638-1530; 866-790-0014; Fax: 307-637-7936.

Judicial Vicar—Rev. THOMAS E. CRONKLETON JR., J.C.D.

Adjutant Judicial Vicar—Rev. THOMAS R. KADERA, J.C.L.

Tribunal Case Instructor—CONNIE KASSAHN.

Ecclesiastical Notary—LINDA ROBBINS.

Promoter of Justice—Rev. Msgr. CHARLES F. TAYLOR, J.C.D. (Retired).

Judges—Very Rev. MICHAEL CARR; Revs. THOMAS E. CRONKLETON JR., J.C.D.; THOMAS R. KADERA, J.C.L.

Defenders of the Bond—Very Revs. SAMUEL HAYES; CARL GALLINGER; Revs. DAVID L. DEIBEL, J.D.,

J.C.L.; JOHN GRIFFITHS, J.C.D.

Advocates—SUSAN SIMON; BONNIE BAUMBERGER; Deacon EDWARD MCCARTHY; PAT MCCARTHY; DORENE MCINTYRE; Deacon KIM CARROLL; Very Rev. JAMES HEISER; Rev. RANDALL J. OSWALD; Sr. GLADYS NOREEN, O.S.B.

Diocesan Administrative Offices and Boards

Development—Mr. MATTHEW N. POTTER, C.F.P., C.I.M.A., Dir.; TAMMY SKALA, Exec. Asst., Mailing Address: P.O. Box 1468, Cheyenne, 82003-1468. Tel: 307-638-1530; 866-790-0014.

Education Office—Deacon VERNON DOBELMANN, Supt. Catholic Schools & Dir. Pastoral Ministries, Mailing Address: P.O. Box 1468, Cheyenne, 82003. Tel: 307-638-1530; Fax: 307-637-7936; JOANN ANDERSON, Media Consultant, St. Rose of Lima, 605 E. 22nd Ave., Torrington, 82240. Tel: 307-532-5556; Fax: 307-534-2329.

Diocesan Schools Advisory Group—Most Rev. PAUL D. ETIENNE, D.D., S.T.L.; Deacon VERNON DOBELMANN, Supt. Catholic Schools; Revs. CARL BEAVERS; DEMITRO PENASCOZA; Very Rev. JAMES HEISER; Revs. GARY RUZICKA; JAMES SCHUMACHER; LINDA MARCOS, Prin. Holy Spirit School; STEVEN GRESBACK, Prin. St. Margaret School; JANET MATERI, Prin. St. Mary's School; CYNDY NOVOTNY, Prin. St. Anthony Tri-Parish Catholic School; TOM WILHELM, Prin. St. Laurence O'Toole School; MARY LEGLER, Prin. Holy Name School; MELANIE SYLTE, Prin. John Paul II School.

Pastoral Ministries—Deacon VERNON DOBELMANN, Dir.; AMY LARSEN, Asst. Dir., Mailing Address: P.O. Box 1468, Cheyenne, 82003-1468. Tel: 307-638-1530; Fax: 307-637-7936.

Beginning Experience for Divorced or Widowed—CURTIS WEST, Mailing Address: P.O. Box 9953, Casper, 82609. Tel: 307-463-2677.

Marriage Encounter—MIKE WINGERT; ANN WINGERT, 2005 Apache St., Cheyenne, 82009. Tel: 307-637-0441.

Natural Family Planning—Deacon VERNON DOBELMANN; AMY LARSEN.

Respect Life Catholic Pro-Life Ministry—Deacon VERNON DOBELMANN; AMY LARSEN.

Retrouvaille, Ministry for Hurting Marriages—Deacon VERNON DOBELMANN; AMY LARSEN.

Newspaper "Wyoming Catholic Register"—

Stewardship Committee—Most Rev. PAUL D. ETIENNE, D.D., S.T.L.; Very Revs. MICHAEL CARR; CARL GALLINGER; Deacons DOUGLAS VLCHEK; KIM CARROLL; DORENE MCINTYRE; DONNA CUIN; D. J. CUNNINGHAM.

Vocation Office—Rev. WILLIAM HILL III, Dir., Mailing Address: St. Paul's Newman Center, 1800 E. Grand Ave., Laramie, 82070. Tel: 307-745-5461; Fax: 307-742-0521.

Youth Office—Deacon VERNON DOBELMANN, Dir. Pastoral Ministries; AMY LARSEN, Asst. Dir. Pastoral Ministries, Mailing Address: P.O. Box 1468, Cheyenne, 82003-1468. Tel: 307-638-1530; Fax: 307-637-7936.

Other Diocesan Boards, Councils and Programs

Diocese of Cheyenne, Board of Directors—Most Rev. PAUL D. ETIENNE, D.D., S.T.L.; Rev. GARY RUZICKA; Mr. HOWARD BAKER; The Honorable MIKE SULLIVAN.

Living & Giving in Christ: Diocesan Appeal—Mr. LOREN SCHILLINGER, Mailing Address: P.O. Box 1468, Cheyenne, 82003-1468. Tel: 307-638-1530; Fax: 307-637-7936.

Boy Scouts—WILL HILL, 1025 Falls Court, Riverton, 82501. Tel: 307-332-2688.

Building Committee—Most Rev. PAUL D. ETIENNE, D.D., S.T.L.; ROGER BAALMAN, A.I.A., Chm.; Rev. GARY RUZICKA; BOB ADAMS; CAROL DELOIS; JOHN STEIL; HERBERT W. STOUGHTON, Ph.D.; Mr. LOREN SCHILLINGER, Sec.; Mr. GENE ROCCABRUNA, P.E.

Catholic Relief Services—

Clergy Continuing Education Grants—Very Rev. CLIFFORD JACOBSON, 1000 Butler Spaeth Rd., Gillette, 82716. Tel: 307-682-3319; Fax: 307-682-6386.

Confraternity of Christian Doctrine—Deacon VERNON DOBELMANN, Mailing Address: P.O. Box 1468, Cheyenne, 82003-1468. Tel: 307-638-1530.

Council of Religious—Sr. RUTH ANN HEHN, S.C.L.

Cursillo Board—CHARLIE RANDO, 5150 Roundtop Dr., Cheyenne, 82009-5053.

Permanent Diaconate—Deacon KEN PITLICK, Dir., 736 Houston, Newcastle, 82701.

Diaconate Program, Permanent—Deacon ROLLAND RABOIN, Mailing Address: 4525 Rd. 66, Torrington, 82240. Tel: 307-532-1571.

Housing—JUNE THRONBURG, Admin., St. Anthony Manor, 211 E. 6th, Casper, 82601. Tel: 307-237-0843; Sr. RUTH ANN HEHN, S.C.L., Admin., Holy Trinity Manor, 2516 E. 18th St., Cheyenne, 82001. Tel: 307-778-8850.

Information Office—

June Priests' Retreat—Rev. GLEN SZCZECHOWSKI, Coord., Mailing Address: P.O. Box 818, Powell, 82435. Tel: 307-754-2480.

Liturgical Commission—VACANT.

Propagation of the Faith—Deacon VERNON DOBELMANN, Mailing Address: P.O. Box 1468, Cheyenne, 82003-1468.

Pastoral Ministries—Deacon VERNON DOBELMANN, Dir.; AMY LARSEN, Asst. Dir., Mailing Address: P.O. Box 1468, Cheyenne, 82003-1468. Tel: 307-638-1530; Fax: 307-637-7936.

St. Joseph's Society for Priests (Clergy Mutual Benefit Society)—Most Rev. PAUL D. ETIENNE, D.D., S.T.L.; Revs. THOMAS OGG, Pres. (Retired); CARL BEAVERS; KARL MILLIS; WILLIAM HILL III; STEVEN MATTHEW TITUS; THOMAS E. CRONKLETON JR., J.C.D., Sec.; DAVID ERICKSON; Rev. Msgr. EUGENE SULLIVAN (Retired); Mr. LEO RILEY, Admin.; Mr. MATTHEW N. POTTER, C.F.P., C.I.M.A., Dir. Devel.

Victim Assistance Coordinator—Deacon ROLLAND RABOIN. Tel: 307-532-4586. Email: rraboin@vistabeam.com.

CLERGY, PARISHES, MISSIONS AND PAROCHIAL SCHOOLS

CITY OF CHEYENNE

(LARAMIE COUNTY)

1—ST. MARY'S CATHEDRAL (1868) [CEM] Revs. Gary Ruzicka; Steven Matthew Titus; Robert Spaulding; Deacons Al Lancaster; Vernon Dobelmann.
Mailing Address: P.O. Box 1268, 82003-1268. Tel: 307-635-9261; Fax: 307-635-5723. Web: www.stmarycathedral.com.
School—Janet Materi, Prin. Lay Teachers 18; Students 180.
Catechesis/Religious Program—Tel: 307-637-4009; 307-635-9261. Becky Hart, D.R.E. (Grades PreK-5); Vicki Yeoman, D.R.E. (Grades 6-8); Chris Martinez, Youth Dir. (Grades 9-12). Students 339.

2—HOLY TRINITY (1957) Rev. Thomas E. Cronkleton Jr.; Deacon David Zelenka. In Res., Revs. James Doudican (Retired); Kevin Koch; Jan Santich.
Res.: 1836 Hot Springs Ave., 82003-5337. Tel: 307-632-5872; Fax: 307-632-1810. Web: www.holytrinitycheyenne.org.
Catechesis/Religious Program—Cameron Smith, Dir. Faith Formation. Students 315.

3—ST. JOSEPH'S (1929), (Hispanic), Rev. Raymond B. Moss; Deacon Patrick Bradley.
Mailing Address: P.O. Box 1141, 82003-1141. Tel: 307-634-4625; Fax: 307-635-4700. Web: www.stjosephscheyenne.org.
Office: 314 E. Sixth St., 82007.
Res.: 515 House, 82007. Tel: 307-638-3133.
Church: 300 E. 6th St., 82007.
Catechesis/Religious Program—Tel: 307-634-4625, Ext. 103. Eva Estorga, D.R.E. Students 95.

OUTSIDE CITY OF CHEYENNE

BUFFALO, JOHNSON CO., ST. JOHN THE BAPTIST (1885), (Basque), Rev. Peter Johnson.
Res.: 532 N. Lobban, 82834. Tel: 307-684-7268; Fax: 307-684-5490. Email: frpete@bresnan.net.
Catechesis/Religious Program—Tel: 307-684-7440; Fax: 307-684-5490. Carol Gagliano, D.R.E. Students 108.
Mission—St. Mary Clearmont, Johnson Co. 82834.
Mission—St. Hubert Kaycee, Johnson Co. 82834.

CASPER, NATRONA CO.

1—ST. ANTHONY OF PADUA (1903) Rev. Lucas K. Simango (Zambia); Deacons Don Stewart; David Johnson.
Office: 604 S. Center, 82601. Tel: 307-266-2666; Fax: 307-266-4127. Email: shepherd@bresnan.net. Web: www.stanthonyscasper.org.
School—St. Anthony Tri-Parish School, 1145 W. 20th St., 82604. Tel: 307-234-2873; Fax: 307-235-4946. Email: sasprincipal@bresnan.net. Web: www.stanthonytri-parishschool.net. Cyndy Novotny, Prin. Lay Teachers 24; Students (K-9) 305; Preschool 58.
Catechesis/Religious Program—Email: stanthonyRE@bresnan.net. Kellei Hennessey, C.R.E.; Dean Menardi, Youth Min. Students 78.

2—OUR LADY OF FATIMA (1954) Rev. Robert L. Fox; Deacon Ed McCarthy.
Res.: 1401 CY Ave., 82604. Tel: 307-265-5586; Fax: 307-266-2958. Email: church@fatimaincasper.org.
Catechesis/Religious Program—Tel: 307-473-2076. Carol O'Hearn, C.R.E. Students 121.

3—SAINT PATRICK'S (1963), (Irish), Very Rev. August Koeune; Rev. Msgr. James O'Neill (Retired); Deacon Russ Humphreys.
Office: 400 Country Club Rd., Box 50397, 82605-0397. Tel: 307-235-5535; 307-266-2495; Fax: 307-237-7244. Web: www.stpatricks-casper.com.
Catechesis/Religious Program—Email: samsc@tribcsp.com. Sam Carrick, D.R.E. Students 139.

CODY, PARK CO., ST. ANTHONY (1942) Very Rev. Vernon F. Clark; Deacon Lee Pico.
Res.: 1333 Monument Dr., 82414-3406. Tel: 307-587-3388; Fax: 307-587-3383. Email: info@stanthonycody.org. Web: www.stanthonycody.org.
Catechesis/Religious Program—Tel: 307-587-2567; Fax: 307-587-3383. Rick Moser, D.R.E. Students 155.
Mission—Tel: 307-587-3388. Sunday Services at Old Faithful, Lake Lodge, Canyon, and Mammoth in summer only.
Mission—St. Therese 1406 State, Meeteetse, Park Co. 82433.
Mission—Our Lady of the Valley 35 Rd. 1 AXW, Clark, Park Co. 82435.

DOUGLAS, CONVERSE CO., ST. JAMES (1907) Rev. John Savio.
Mailing Address: P.O. Box 1500, 82633-1500. Tel: 307-358-2338; Fax: 307-358-8498. Email: stjames@communicomm.com.
Catechesis/Religious Program—Kathi Cox, D.R.E. Students 100.
Mission—Our Lady of Lourdes, Tel: 307-358-2338.

EVANSTON, UINTA CO., ST. MARY MAGDALEN (1878) [JC] Rev. Jaime Bueno (Colombia).
Mailing Address: Box 163, 82931-0163. Tel: 307-789-2189; Fax: 307-789-2788. Email: stmmagdalen@questoffice.net. Web: www.stmmagdalen.com.
Catechesis/Religious Program—Students 75.
Mission—St. Helen P.O. Box 183, Fort Bridger, Uinta Co. 82933. Tel: 307-782-6190.
Catechesis/Religious Program—Tel: 307-787-6590. Students 10.

GILLETTE, CAMPBELL CO., ST. MATTHEW'S (1926) [JC] Very Rev. Clifford Jacobson; Rev. Timothy James Martinson, Parochial Vicar.
Res.: 1000 Butler Spaeth Rd., 82716. Tel: 307-682-3319; Fax: 307-682-6386. Email: stmatthews@stmatthewswy.org. Web: www.stmatthewswy.org.
School—John Paul II Catholic School, (Grades PreSchool-6) Tel: 307-686-4114; Fax: 307-682-6368. Web: www.johnpauliicatholicschool.com. Melanie Sylte, Prin. Lay Teachers 8; Students (K-6) 86; Students (Preschool) 70.
Catechesis/Religious Program—Students 306.
Mission—Blessed Sacrament 624 Wright Blvd., Wright, Campbell Co. 82732. Tel: 307-464-0809.
Mission—St. Patrick 216 N. Belle Fourche, Moorcroft, Crook Co. 82721. Tel: 307-756-9478.

GLENROCK, CONVERSE CO., ST. LOUIS (1920) [JC] Rev. George E. Von Kaenel, S.J.
Mailing Address: P.O. Box 27, 82637-0027. Tel: 307-436-9529. Email: chstlou@vcn.com.
Catechesis/Religious Program—Students 39.

GREEN RIVER, SWEETWATER CO., IMMACULATE CONCEPTION (1884) [JC] Rev. Thomas Sheridan; Deacon Wes Nash.
Mailing Address: P.O. Box 70, 82935-0070. Tel: 307-875-2441; Fax: 307-875-0274. Email: icc@wyoming.com.
Catechesis/Religious Program—Michele Harris, D.R.E. Students 124.

GREYBULL, BIG HORN CO., SACRED HEART (1919) Rev. Raymond P. Rodriguez.
Mailing Address: P.O. Box 231, 82426-0231. Tel: 307-765-2438; Fax: 307-765-2249. Email: shcg@tctwest.net.
Catechesis/Religious Program—Students 45.
Mission—St. Philip Ave. D, Basin, Big Horn Co. 82410. Fax: 307-765-2478.

GUERNSEY, PLATTE CO., ST. ANTHONY'S (1969) Very Rev. Michael Carr.
Res.: 96 N. Kansas, P.O. Box 430, 82214-0430. Tel: 307-836-2586. Email: stanthonyguernsey@embarqmail.com.
Catechesis/Religious Program—Lori Ibarra, D.R.E. Students 13.

JACKSON, TETON CO., OUR LADY OF THE MOUNTAINS (1955) [JC] Revs. Randall J. Oswald; Florante E. Marcelo; Deacons Robert J. Miller; Doug Vlchek; Bill Hill.
Mailing Address: P.O. Box 992, 83001-0992. Tel: 307-733-2516; Fax: 307-739-1478. Email: tamra@olmcatholic.org. Web: www.olmcatholic.org.
Catechesis/Religious Program—Tel: 307-733-7919. Email: chris.owens@wyoming.com. Students 220.
Mission—Holy Family P.O. Box 231, Afton, Lincoln Co. 83110. Tel: 307-886-0731. Web: www.holyfamilywy.org.
Chapel—Sacred Heart Chapel, (Grand Teton National Park)Web: www.olmcatholic.org.

KEMMERER, LINCOLN CO., ST. PATRICK'S (1901), (Italian—Slovak), [JC] Rev. Philip Vaske.
Mailing Address: Box 311, 83101-0311. Tel: 307-877-4573; Fax: 307-877-3354. Email: stpatricks@hamsfork.net.
Catechesis/Religious Program—Students 50.
Mission—St. Dominic
Mission—La Barge Catholic Community Center

LANDER, FREMONT CO., HOLY ROSARY (1882) [JC] Rev. David Erickson. In Res., Rev. Robert K.C. Siu (HON) (Retired).
Res.: 163 Leedy Rd., P.O. Box 1047, 82520-1047. Tel: 307-332-4952; Fax: 307-332-6141. Email: jmb4hr@gmail.com.
Catechesis/Religious Program—Tel: 307-332-4803. Michael Lewis, D.R.E. Students 68.
Mission—Ascension
Mission—St. Brendan Jeffrey City, Freemont Co.

LARAMIE, ALBANY CO.
1—ST. LAURENCE O'TOOLE (1872) [JC] Rev. James Schumacher; Deacons John Deti; Alfred Franco.
Mailing Address: 617 S. Fourth St., 82070-1045. Tel: 307-745-3115; Fax: 307-745-3131. Email: slotoole@bresnan.net. Web: www.stlaurenceotoole.org.
School—(Grades K-6), 608 S. Fourth St., 82070. Tel: 307-742-6363; Fax: 307-745-3131. Tom Wilhelm, Prin. Lay Teachers 6; Students 51.
Catechesis/Religious Program—Students 66.
2—ST. PAUL'S NEWMAN CENTER (1957) Very Rev. Carl Gallinger; Juli Smith, Dir. Campus Ministry.
Mailing Address: Parish, 1800 E. Grand Ave., 82070-4316. Tel: 307-745-5461; Fax: 307-742-0521. Email: newman@newmancenter.org. Web: www.newmancenter.org.
Catechesis/Religious Program—Students 71.

LOVELL, BIG HORN CO., ST. JOSEPH'S (1979) Rev. Glen Szczechowski.
Church: 1141 Shoshone Ave., P.O. Box 185, 82431-0185. Tel: 307-548-2282; Fax: 307-548-2395. Email: stjoseph@tctwest.net.
Catechesis/Religious Program—Students 19.

LUSK, NIOBRARA CO., ST. LEO'S (1911), (German—Irish), [JC] Very Rev. Michael Carr.
Res.: 900 W. Fifth St., Box 959, 82225-0959. Tel: 307-334-2702; Fax: 307-334-3161. Email: stleochurch@gmail.com.
Catechesis/Religious Program—Kristi Hart, D.R.E. & Parish Sec. Students 22.

NEWCASTLE, WESTON CO., CORPUS CHRISTI (1890) [JC] Rev. Philip C. Wagner; Deacons Kenneth Pitlick, Pastoral Assoc. & Sec.; Peter Kim Carroll, Pastoral Assoc.
Res.: 19 W. Winthrop, 82701. Tel: 307-746-4219; Fax: 307-746-9909. Email: corpus@rtconnect.net.
Catechesis/Religious Program—Students 69.
Mission—St. Paul P.O. Box 28, Sundance, Crook Co. 82729. Tel: 307-283-2383; Fax: 307-283-2383.
Catechesis/Religious Program—Students 21.
Mission—St. Anthony P.O. Box 177, Upton, Weston Co. 82730.
Catechesis/Religious Program—Students 38.
Mission—St. Matthew's 26 Hunter, Hulett, Crook Co. 82720.
Catechesis/Religious Program—Students 30.

PINE BLUFFS, LARAMIE CO., ST. PAUL'S (1913) Rev. Killian Muli (Kenya).
Mailing Address: P.O. Box 97, 82082-0097.
Rectory—307 Beech St., 82082-0097. Tel: 307-245-3761. Email: stpaulschurch@RTconnect.net.
Church: 501 E. 4th St., 82082.
Catechesis/Religious Program—Pam Miller, D.R.E. Students 24.
Mission—St. Joseph Albin, Laramie Co.
Mission—St. Peter 316 4th St., Carpenter, Laramie Co. 82054.

PINEDALE, SUBLETTE CO., OUR LADY OF PEACE (1940) Rev. Peter James Mwaura; Deacon Daniel Kostelc.
Mailing Address: P.O. Box 70, 82941-0070. Tel: 307-367-2359; Fax: 307-367-3553.
Church: 112 S. Sublette, 82941.
Catechesis/Religious Program—Jennifer Hayward, D.R.E. (K-12). Students 65.
Mission—St. Anne Big Piney, Sublette Co. 83113. Tel: 307-276-3227.
Catechesis/Religious Program—Students 36.

POWELL, PARK CO., ST. BARBARA (1910) Rev. Glen Szczechowski.
Res.: 115 E. Third, P.O. Box 818, 82435-0818. Tel: 307-754-2480; Fax: 307-754-5018. Email: stbarb@tctwest.net.
Catechesis/Religious Program—Tel: 307-754-3361. Tom Spiering, D.R.E.; Janet Spiering, D.R.E. Students 109.
Mission—St. Joseph's Lovell, 82431.

RAWLINS, CARBON CO., ST. JOSEPH'S (1867) [JC] Very Rev. Samuel Hayes; Deacon Jesus P. Juarez.
Mailing Address: P.O. Box 68, 82301-0068. Tel: 307-324-4631; Fax: 307-324-3288. Email: cachurcsaj@qwestoffice.net.
Catechesis/Religious Program—Tel: 307-324-4033. Joan Reeves, D.R.E. Students 100.
Mission—Our Lady of the Sage P.O. Box 116, Baggs, Carbon Co. 82321. Tel: 307-383-6100.

RIVERTON, FREMONT CO., ST. MARGARET'S (1908) Rev. Demitro Penascoza (Philippines).
Res.: 622 E. Park, 82501. Tel: 307-856-3757; Fax: 307-856-8533. Email: stmargchurch@wyoming.com.
School—(Grades PreK-5), 220 N. 7th E., 82501. Tel: 307-856-5922. Steven Gresback, Prin. Lay Teachers 10; Students 67.
Catechesis/Religious Program—Tel: 307-856-1277. Evan Diquette, D.R.E.; Judy Ray, D.R.E. Students 54.
Mission—St. Joseph 211 Wyoming St., Shoshoni, Fremont Co. 82649. Tel: 307-876-2760.
Mission—Our Lady of the Woods 4 S. Riverton St., P.O. Box 1134, Dubois, Fremont Co. 82513. Tel: 307-455-2533.
Mission—St. Edward Kinnear Rectory, 11350 US Hwy. 26, Kinnear, Fremont Co. 82516. Tel: 307-856-5502.

ROCK SPRINGS, SWEETWATER CO.
1—SS. CYRIL AND METHODIUS (1910) Consolidated with Our Lady of Sorrows Church, Rock Springs to form Holy Spirit Catholic Community.
2—HOLY SPIRIT CATHOLIC COMMUNITY (1887) Revs. Carl Beavers; Joey Buencamino; Deacon Charles Lux.
Mailing Address: 116 Broadway, 82901. Tel: 307-362-2611; Fax: 307-382-4911. Email: info@theholyspiritparish.com.
Res.: 633 Bridger Ave., 82901. Tel: 307-362-3493.
School—Holy Spirit Catholic School, Tel: 307-362-6077; Fax: 307-362-2177. Email: hscsoffice@wyoming.com. Linda Marcos, Prin. Sisters 2; Lay Teachers 6; Students 72.
Catechesis/Religious Program—Tel: 307-362-2611; Fax: 307-382-4911. Email: charlescatterall@theholyspiritparish.com. Students 199.
Mission—St. Vivian Superior, Sweetwater Co.
Mission—St. Anthony Wamsutter, Sweetwater Co.
Mission—St. Christopher Eden, Sweetwater Co. 82926.
3—OUR LADY OF SORROWS, Consolidated with SS. Cyril and Methodius to form Holy Spirit Catholic Community.

SAINT STEPHENS, FREMONT CO., ST. STEPHEN'S (1884), (Native American), [CEM], Indian Mission for the Shoshone and Arapaho Indians. St. Stephen's Indian Mission, Inc. Revs. John Gaffney, S.O.L.T.; Eckley Macklin, S.O.L.T.; Carlito Saballo, S.O.L.T.; Sisters Florence Petsch, O.S.F., Pastoral Assoc.; Teresa Frawley, O.S.F., Pastoral Assoc.; Monica Suhayda, C.S.J., Pastoral Assoc.
Mailing Address: 33 St. Stephens Rd., Box 250, 82524-0250. Tel: 307-856-5937; Fax: 307-856-3853. Email: ssimf@wyoming.com. Web: www.ssimf.com/.
Catechesis/Religious Program—Tel: 307-856-7806. Jean Watt, D.R.E. Students 41.
Mission—St. Joseph Box 8358, Ethete, Fremont Co. 82520. Tel: 307-332-4415.
Mission—Blessed Sacrament

SARATOGA, CARBON CO., ST. ANN'S (1957) Rev. Karl Millis.
Mailing Address: P.O. Box 667, 82331-0667. Tel: 307-326-5444. Email: stanns@union-tel.com ktcmillis@union-tel.com.
Catechesis/Religious Program—Gail Ford, D.R.E. Students 26.
Mission—St. Joseph Hanna, Carbon Co. 82327. Tel: 307-325-6434.

SHERIDAN, SHERIDAN CO., HOLY NAME (1885) [JC] Very Rev. James Heiser; Revs. Ronald Stolcis; Michael Ehiemere.
Mailing Address: 9 S. Connor, 82801. Tel: 307-672-2848; Fax: 307-672-5105. Email: holynamechurch@fiberpipe.net. Web: www.holynamesheridan.org.
School—121 S. Connor, 82801. Tel: 307-672-2021; Fax: 307-673-4474. Web: www.hncswy.org. Mary Legler, Prin. Lay Teachers 19; Students 130.
Catechesis/Religious Program—Tel: 307-672-2848, Ext. 17. Students 145.
Mission—Our Lady of the Pines 34 Wagon Box Rd., Story, Sheridan Co. 82842.
Mission—St. Edmund 310 Historic Hwy. 14, Ranchester, Sheridan Co. 82839.

THERMOPOLIS, HOT SPRINGS CO., ST. FRANCIS (1906) Rev. Hugo L. Blotsky, O.S.B.
Mailing Address: 815 Arapahoe, P.O. Box 272, 82443-0272. Tel: 307-864-2674. Email: stfrancis@rtconnect.net.
Catechesis/Religious Program—Fax: 307-864-2458. Sharon Cordingly, C.R.E.; Kent Cordingly, C.R.E. Students 31.

TORRINGTON, GOSHEN CO., ST. ROSE (1906) Very Rev. Michael Carr; Deacon Rolland Raboin.
Mailing Address: 605 E. 22nd Ave., 82240. In Res., Rev. Andrew Duncan.
Res.: 700 E. 22nd Ave., 82240. Tel: 307-532-5556; Fax: 307-534-2329. Email: strosetorrington@yahoo.com.
Catechesis/Religious Program—Russell Dockins, D.R.E. Students 102.

WHEATLAND, PLATTE CO., ST. PATRICK'S (1891) [JC] Rev. Thomas R. Kadera.
Res.: 1009 Ninth St., 82201. Tel: 307-322-2070. Email: stpatrickchurch@qwestoffice.net.
Catechesis/Religious Program—Tel: 307-322-4213. Students 65.
Mission—Mary Queen of Heaven 401 5th St., Chugwater, Platte Co. 82201.

WORLAND, WASHAKIE CO., ST. MARY MAGDALEN (1949) [JC] Rev. Ray Rodriguez.
Mailing Address: 1099 Charles Ave., 82401-0901. Tel: 307-347-2820; Fax: 307-347-2450. Email: stmarym@rtconnect.net. Web: www.worland.com/magdalen.
Catechesis/Religious Program—Students 189.

Chaplains of Public Institutions

CHEYENNE. *U.S. Veterans Administration Hospital 1*, 90 MW/HC, F.E. Warren AFB, 82005. Vacant.
EVANSTON. *Wyoming State Hospital*. Vacant.
LUSK. *Wyoming Women's Center (Correctional Facility)*. Very Rev. Michael Carr.
RAWLINS. *Wyoming State Penitentiary*, P.O. Box 468, 82301-0068. Tel: 307-324-4631. Rev. Karl Millis.
SHERIDAN. *U.S. Veterans Administration Hospital*. Vacant.

In Res.:
Revs.—
Duncan, Andrew, St. Rose of Lima, 605 E. 22nd Ave., Torrington, 82240.
Gibbons, Joseph Marie of Jesus, M. Carm., Monks of the Most Blessed Virgin Mary of Mt. Carmel, 35 Rd. AFW, Powell, 82435.
Koch, Kevin, Holy Trinity, 1836 Hot Springs Ave., 82001.
Schneider, Daniel Mary, M. Carm., Prior, Monks of the Most Blessed Virgin Mary of Mt. Carmel, 35 Rd. AFW, Powell, 82435.
Siu, Robert K.C. (HON) (Retired), Holy Rosary Church, P.O. Box 1047, Lander, 82520-1047.
Wright, Michael Mary of the Trinity, M. Carm., Monks of the Most Blessed Virgin Mary of Mt. Carmel, 35 Rd. AFW, Powell, 82435.

Retired:
Rev. Msgrs.—
O'Neill, James, P.O. Box 50397, Casper, 82605-0397. Tel: 307-235-5535
Sullivan, Eugene, 1416 Trent Ct., 82009.
Taylor, Charles F., J.C.D., P.O. Box 710, Kemmerer, 83101.
Revs.—
Chleborad, Gerald, 6388 S. Grape Ct., Centennial, CO 80121.
Colibraro, Daniel, P.O. Box 1368, Casper, 82602-1368.
Colibraro, Philip, P.O. Box 2025, Casper, 82602-2025.
Daley, Joseph A., 2919 Bass Ave., Cody, 82414.
Doudican, James, 1836 Hot Springs Ave., 82001-5337.
Fahey, Thomas C., Chap., Victory Noll Sisters, 1900 W. Park Dr., Box 109, Huntington, IN 46750.
Fraher, Joseph P., 412 Kearney St., Laramie, 82070.
Gianola, William, 650 Mooring Line Dr., Naples, FL 34102.
Murray, John, 604 S. Center, Casper, 82601.
Ogg, Thomas, P.O. Box 101, Ten Sleep, 82442.
Reid, Malcolm, 120 W. Pine St., Rawlins, 82301.
Santich, Jan Joseph, Holy Trinity, 1836 Hot Springs Ave., 82001.
Wright, John A., 639 Ave. H #22, Powell, 82435.

Permanent Deacons:
Bradley, Patrick, UMC Chap.; St. Joseph, Cheyenne
Carroll, Kim, Corpus Christi, Newcastle
Deti, John, St. Laurence O'Toole, Laramie
Dobelmann, Vernon, St. Mary, Cheyenne (St. Mary's Cathedral)
Franco, Alfred, Immaculate Conception, Green River
Hill, Bill, Our Lady of the Mountains, Jackson
Hruska, Randy, Holy Family, Afton
Humphreys, Russ, St. Patrick's Church, Casper
Johnson, David, St. Anthony, Casper
Juarez, Jesus, St. Joseph, Rawlins
Kostelc, Daniel, Pinedale
Lancaster, Al, St. Mary's Cathedral, Cheyenne
Lux, Charles, Holy Spirit, Rock Springs
McCarthy, Ed, Our Lady of Fatima, Casper
Miller, Robert J., Our Lady of the Mountains, Jackson
Nash, Wes, Immaculate Conception, Green River

Pico, Lee, St. Anthony, Cody, Yellowstone National Park
Pitlick, Ken, Corpus Christi, Newcastle
Raboin, Rolland, St. Rose of Lima, Torrington
Stewart, Don, St. Anthony's Church, Casper
Vlchek, Douglas, Our Lady of the Mountains, Jackson
Zelenka, David, Holy Trinity, Cheyenne

INSTITUTIONS LOCATED IN THE DIOCESE

[A] PROTECTIVE INSTITUTIONS

TORRINGTON. *St. Joseph's Children's Home* (1930) Box 1117, 82240-1117. Tel: 307-532-4197; Fax: 307-532-8405. Email: bmayor@stjoseph-wy.org. Web: www.stjoseph-wy.org. Robert C. Mayor, Exec. Dir.; Travis Lenz, Prin. Children 62; Total Staff 150; Total Assisted 242.

[B] COLLEGES AND UNIVERSITIES

LANDER. **Wyoming Catholic College*, P.O. Box 750, 82520. Tel: 307-332-2930; Fax: 307-332-2918. Email: info@wyomingcatholiccollege.com. Web: www.wyomingcatholiccollege.com. Rev. Robert W. Cook, Pres.; Mr. Patrick Owens, Librarian. Priests 2; Lay Teachers 16.

[C] HOUSING FOR THE ELDERLY (LOW INCOME)

CHEYENNE. *Holy Trinity Manor* (1989) 2516 E. 18th St., 82001. Tel: 307-778-8850; Fax: 307-634-2451. Email: rhehn@archdiocesanhousing.org; holytrinitymanor@archdiocesanhousing.org. Sr. Ruth Ann Hehn, S.C.L., Site Mgr. Total Staff 1; Total in Residence 30; Total Assisted 40.

CASPER. *St. Anthony Manor* (1983) 211 E. Sixth St., 82601. Tel: 307-237-0843; Fax: 307-237-3516. Email: stanthonymanor@archdiocesanhousing.org. Rev. Lucas K. Simango (Zambia); June Thronburg, Site Mgr. Total Staff 6; Total in Residence 64; Total Assisted Annually 61.

[D] MONASTERIES AND RESIDENCES FOR PRIESTS AND BROTHERS

POWELL. *Monks of the Most Blessed Virgin Mary of Mt. Carmel* (2004) 31 Road AFW, 82435. Tel: 307-645-3310; Fax: 307-645-3085. Web: www.carmelitemonks.org. Revs. Daniel Mary Schneider, M. Carm., Prior; Michael Mary of the Trinity Wright, M. Carm., Novice Master; Joseph Marie of Jesus Gibbons, M. Carm., Vocations Dir. Priests 3; Novices 4; Postulants 3; Temporary Vows 3; Perpetual Vows 5.

SAINT STEPHENS. *St. Stephens Mission* (1884) 33 St. Stephens Rd., 82524. Tel: 307-856-7806; Fax: 307-856-3853. Email: frtonyblount@hotmail.com. Revs. Anthony Blount, S.O.L.T.; John Gaffney, S.O.L.T.; Eckley Macklin, S.O.L.T.; Carlito Saballo, S.O.L.T.; Sisters Florence Petsch, O.S.F., Pastoral Assoc.; Teresa Frawley, O.S.F., Pastoral Assoc.; Monica Suhayda, C.S.J., Pastoral Assoc.; Maria Amata Aumell, S.O.L.T., Youth Ministry; Mary Aloysius of Jesus Kim, S.O.L.T., Youth Ministry; Bro. Kyle Hoesley, S.O.L.T., Youth Ministry. Total Staff 15.

[E] CONVENTS AND RESIDENCES FOR SISTERS

DAYTON. *Benedictine Sisters of Perpetual Adoration, San Benito Monastery*, P.O. Box 510, 82836-0520. Tel: 307-655-9013. Email: sanbenito@vcn.com. Web: www.benedictinesisters.org/b6.html. Sr. Josetta Grant, O.S.B., Supr. Sisters 6.

[F] CAMPUS MINISTRY

CASPER. *St. Francis Newman Center* (1984) 1732 S. Elm St., 82601. Tel: 307-266-2666; Fax: 307-266-4127. 9: 604 S. Center, 82601. Rev. Lucas K. Simango (Zambia), Dir. Total Staff 4.

LARAMIE. *St. Paul's Newman Center, University Catholic Community (University of Wyoming)* 1800 E. Grand Ave., 82070-4316. Tel: 307-745-5461; Fax: 307-742-0521. Email: newman@newmancenter.org. Web: www.newmancenter.org. Very Rev. Carl Gallinger. Total Staff 8.

POWELL. *NorthWest College John Henry Newman Center, St. Barbara Church*, P.O. Box 818, 82435. Tel: 307-754-9220; Fax: 307-754-5018. Email: stbarb@bresnan.net. Rev. Glen Szczechowski; Malinda Hetzel, Coord. Attended by St. Barbara, Powell. Students 28.

[G] MISCELLANEOUS LISTINGS

CHEYENNE. *Catholic Charities of Wyoming, Inc.*, P.O. Box 907, 82003. Tel: 307-637-0554; Fax: 307-632-2346. P.O. Box 1026, Torrington, 82240. Most Rev. Paul D. Etienne, D.D., S.T.L.; Very Rev. Michael Carr, Vice Pres.; Merit Thomas, Sec. & Treas.; Ann Norwood, Bd. Member; Rev. Robert L. Fox, Bd. Member; Robert C. Mayor, Agency Dir.

Holy Trinity Youth Education Trust, c/o Fr. Thomas E. Cronkleton, Jr., 1836 Hot Springs Ave., 82001-5337. Tel: 307-632-5872; Fax: 307-632-1810.

Mall at St. Vincent DePaul (1998) *c/o St. Mary Cathedral*, P.O. Box 1268, 82003. Tel: 307-432-0253. Mary Genereux, Mgr. Total Staff 5.

St. Mary's School Foundation, P.O. Box 1268, 82003. Tel: 307-635-9261; Fax: 307-635-5723. Email: gruzicka@stmarycathedral.com. Rev. Gary Ruzicka; Janet Materi, Prin.

The Wyoming Catholic Ministries Foundation, P.O. Box 227, 82003. Tel: 307-638-2558; Fax: 307-637-7936. Email: development@wyocmf.org. Board of Directors Most Rev. Paul D. Etienne, D.D., S.T.L.; William N. Willingham; Esther McGann; Mr. Matthew N. Potter, C.F.P., C.I.M.A., Exec. Dir.; Gay Woodhouse; Stuart Palmer; Harry Flavin; Mike Lovelett; Jim Magana.

CASPER. *St. Anthony Tri-Parish School Foundation*, 1145 W. 20th St., 82604. Tel: 307-234-2873; Fax: 307-235-4946. Email: sasfoundation@bresnan.net. Web: www.stanthonytri-parishschool.net. Very Rev. August Koeune; Cyndy Novotny, Prin.; Paula Gillette, Contact Person.

**Holy Cross Center, Inc.* (1982) (Food Bank), 1030 N. Lincoln, 82601. Tel: 307-577-1041. Kitty Carr, Dir. Operated by Holy Cross Center, Inc. 25 Volunteers 3; Total Assisted 14,442.

Knights of Columbus Charitable Trust for Seminarian Education and Priests' Retirement (1991) 604 S. Center, 82601. Tel: 307-266-2666. Email: dstewart@bresnan.net. Deacon Don Stewart, Chm. & Trustee.

**Mother Seton Housing, Inc.* (1989) 910 N. Durbin, P.O. Box 1557, 82602. Tel: 307-577-8026; Fax: 307-577-0125. Email: setonh@tribcsp.com. Pam Kozola, Exec. Dir. Emergency & Transitional Housing for Homeless Single Parents and Children.

Shelter, 324 E. H St., P.O. Box 1557, 82602. Tel: 307-577-8026; Fax: 307-577-0125. Total Assisted 60; Individuals 417.

St. Vincent De Paul Thrift Store (1965) 301 E. H St., 82601. Tel: 307-237-2607. Amanda Perrotta, Mgr.

LARAMIE. *St. Laurence School Foundation*, 608 S. 4th, 82070. Tel: 307-742-6363; Fax: 307-745-3131. Email: twilhelm@stlos.com. Web: stlos.com. Tom Wilhelm, Prin.; Rev. James Schumacher, Contact Person.

ROCK SPRINGS. *Rock Springs Catholic School Foundation*, 116 Broadway St., 82901. Tel: 307-362-2611; Fax: 307-382-4911. Email: info@theholyspiritparish.com. Rev. Carl Beavers; Linda Marcos, Prin.

SAINT STEPHENS. *St. Stephens Indian Mission Foundation* (1974) P.O. Box 278, St. Stephens, 82524-0278. Tel: 307-856-6797; Fax: 307-857-1802. Email: ssimf@wyoming.com. Ronald Mamot, Dir.

RELIGIOUS INSTITUTES OF MEN REPRESENTED IN THE DIOCESE

For further details refer to the corresponding bracketed number in the Religious Institutes of Men or Women section.

[0200]—*Benedictine Monks*—O.S.B.
[]—*Congregation of the Mission*—C.M.
[0690]—*Jesuit Fathers and Brothers Jesus*—S.J.
[]—*Monachi Carmelitarm*—M.Carm.
[0975]—*Society of Our Lady of the Most Holy Trinity*—S.O.L.T.

RELIGIOUS INSTITUTES OF WOMEN REPRESENTED IN THE DIOCESE

[0230]—*Benedictine Sisters of Pontifical Jurisdiction*—O.S.B.
[1070-03]—*Dominican Sisters* (Sinsinawa)—O.P.
[]—*Dominican Sisters of Hope*—O.P.
[3130]—*Our Lady of Victory Missionary Sisters*—O.L.V.M.
[1680]—*School Sisters of St. Francis* (Milwaukee, WI)—O.S.F.
[0480]—*Sisters of Charity of Leavenworth, Kansas*—S.C.L.
[1650]—*Sisters of St. Francis of Philadelphia*—O.S.F.
[3830]—*Sisters of St. Joseph*—C.S.J.

DIOCESAN CEMETERIES

CHEYENNE. *Olivet Cemetery* Rev. Gary Ruzicka.

NECROLOGY

(No Deaths)

An asterisk (*) denotes an organization that has established tax-exempt status directly with the IRS and is not covered by the USCCB Group Ruling.

Archdiocese of Chicago

(Archidioecesis Chicagiensis)

His Eminence

FRANCIS CARDINAL GEORGE, O.M.I., PH.D., S.T.D.

Archbishop of Chicago; Profession of Perpetual Vows September 8, 1961; ordained December 21, 1963; appointed Bishop of Yakima July 10, 1990; Episcopal Ordination and Installation September 21, 1990; appointed Archbishop of Portland in Oregon April 30, 1996; installed May 27, 1996; appointed Archbishop of Chicago April 8, 1997; installed May 7, 1997; created Cardinal Priest February 21, 1998. *Res.: 1555 N. State Pkwy., Chicago, IL 60610.*

Archbishop Quigley Center & Cardinal Meyer Center: P.O. Box 1979, Chicago, IL 60690-1979. Tel: 312-534-8200.

Web: www.archchicago.org

Most Reverend

TIMOTHY J. LYNE

Retired Auxiliary Bishop of Chicago; ordained May 1, 1943; appointed Auxiliary Bishop of Chicago and Titular Bishop of Vamalla October 31, 1983; consecrated December 13, 1983; retired January 24, 1995. *Res.: Holy Name Cathedral, 730 N. Wabash, Chicago, IL 60611.* Tel: 312-787-8040; Fax: 312-787-9113.

Most Reverend

THAD J. JAKUBOWSKI

Retired Auxiliary Bishop of Chicago; ordained May 3, 1950; appointed Auxiliary Bishop of Chicago and Titular Bishop of Plestia February 16, 1988; consecrated April 11, 1988; retired January 24, 2003. *Res.: 6002 W. Berteau Ave., Chicago, IL 60634-1630.* Tel: 773-202-7720; Fax: 773-202-7725.

Most Reverend

JOHN R. GORMAN

Retired Auxiliary Bishop of Chicago and Titular Bishop of Catula; ordained May 1, 1952; appointed February 16, 1988; consecrated April 11, 1988; retired January 24, 2003. *Res.: Our Lady of the Woods, 10731 W. 131st St., Orland Park, IL 60462.* Tel: 708-361-4754.

Most Reverend

RAYMOND E. GOEDERT

Retired Auxiliary Bishop of Chicago; ordained May 1, 1952; appointed Auxiliary Bishop of Chicago and Titular Bishop of Tamazeni July 8, 1991; consecrated August 29, 1991; retired January 24, 2003. *Res.: 1555 N. State Pkwy., Chicago, IL 60610.* Tel: 312-534-8271.

Most Reverend

GEORGE J. RASSAS

Auxiliary Bishop of Chicago; ordained May 2, 1968; appointed Auxiliary Bishop of Chicago and Titular Bishop of Reperi December 1, 2005; consecrated February 2, 2006. *Mailing Address: 200 N. Milwaukee Ave., Ste. 200, Libertyville, IL 60048-2250.* Tel: 847-549-0160; Fax: 847-549-0163.

Most Reverend

FRANCIS J. KANE

Auxiliary Bishop of Chicago; ordained May 14, 1969; appointed Auxiliary Bishop of Chicago and Titular Bishop of Sault Sainte Marie in Michigan January 24, 2003; consecrated March 19, 2003. *Mailing Address: 1641 W. Diversey Pkwy., Chicago, IL 60614.* Tel: 773-388-8670; Fax: 773-388-8676.

Most Reverend

JOHN R. MANZ

Auxiliary Bishop of Chicago; ordained May 12, 1971; appointed Auxiliary Bishop of Chicago and Titular Bishop of Mulia January 13, 1996; consecrated March 5, 1996. *Mailing Address: 1400 S. Austin Blvd., Cicero, IL 60804.* Tel: 708-329-4040; Fax: 708-222-8854.

Most Reverend

JOSEPH N. PERRY

Auxiliary Bishop of Chicago; ordained May 24, 1975; appointed Auxiliary Bishop of Chicago and Titular Bishop of Lead May 5, 1998; consecrated June 29, 1998. *Mailing Address: P.O. Box 733, South Holland, IL 60473-0733.* Tel: 708-339-2474; Fax: 708-339-2477.

Most Reverend

ANDREW P. WYPYCH

Auxiliary Bishop of Chicago; ordained April 29, 1979; appointed Auxiliary Bishop of Chicago and Titular Bishop of Naraggara June 13, 2011; Episcopal ordination August 10, 2011. *2330 W. 118th St., Chicago, IL 60643.* Tel: 773-779-8440; Fax: 773-779-8469.

Most Reverend

ALBERTO ROJAS

Auxiliary Bishop of Chicago; ordained May 24, 1997; appointed Auxiliary Bishop of Chicago and Titular Bishop of Marazanae June 13, 2011; Episcopal ordination August 10, 2011. *1850 S. Throop St., Chicago, IL 60608.* Tel: 312-243-4655; Fax: 312-243-4970.

ESTABLISHED NOVEMBER 28, 1843; CREATED 1880.

Square Miles 1,411.

Comprises the Counties of Cook and Lake in the State of Illinois.

Legal Title: The Catholic Bishop of Chicago, a Corporation Sole.
For legal titles of institutions, consult The Pastoral Center.

STATISTICAL OVERVIEW

Personnel	
Cardinals	1
Auxiliary Bishops	6
Retired Bishops	4
Priests: Diocesan Active in Diocese	539
Priests: Diocesan Active Outside Diocese	31
Priests: Diocesan in Foreign Missions	2
Priests: Retired, Sick or Absent	219
Number of Diocesan Priests	791
Religious Priests in Diocese	710
Total Priests in Diocese	1,501
Extern Priests in Diocese	161
Ordinations:	
Diocesan Priests	10
Religious Priests	11
Transitional Deacons	13
Permanent Deacons	12
Permanent Deacons in Diocese	654
Total Brothers	250
Total Sisters	1,781
Parishes	
Parishes	356
With Resident Pastor:	
Resident Diocesan Priests	274
Resident Religious Priests	55
Without Resident Pastor:	
Administered by Priests	27
Missions	11
Pastoral Centers	8
New Parishes Created	1
Closed Parishes	2
Professional Ministry Personnel:	
Brothers	6
Sisters	58
Lay Ministers	724
Welfare	
Catholic Hospitals	18
Total Assisted	2,811,758
Health Care Centers	2
Total Assisted	17,500
Homes for the Aged	41
Total Assisted	5,717
Residential Care of Children	2
Total Assisted	2,662
Day Care Centers	9
Total Assisted	1,798
Specialized Homes	6
Total Assisted	466
Special Centers for Social Services	100
Total Assisted	760,236
Residential Care of Disabled	6
Total Assisted	1,388
Educational	
Seminaries, Diocesan	2
Students from This Diocese	82
Students from Other Diocese	114
Diocesan Students in Other Seminaries	1
Seminaries, Religious	1
Students Religious	103
Total Seminarians	186
Colleges and Universities	6
Total Students	50,928
High Schools, Diocesan and Parish	7
Total Students	1,082
High Schools, Private	33
Total Students	23,741
Elementary Schools, Diocesan and Parish	213
Total Students	60,707
Elementary Schools, Private	2
Total Students	972
Non-residential Schools for the Disabled	5
Total Students	450
Catechesis/Religious Education:	
High School Students	6,925
Elementary Students	83,760
Total Students under Catholic Instruction	228,751
Teachers in the Diocese:	
Priests	26
Brothers	23
Sisters	86
Lay Teachers	6,757
Vital Statistics	
Receptions into the Church:	
Infant Baptism Totals	32,914
Adult Baptism Totals	1,585
Received into Full Communion	1,208
First Communions	26,433
Confirmations	21,745
Marriages:	
Catholic	5,036
Interfaith	969
Total Marriages	6,005
Deaths	12,920
Total Catholic Population	2,323,000
Total Population	5,956,555

Former Bishops—Rt. Revs. WILLIAM QUARTER, D.D., cons. March 10, 1844; died April 10, 1848; JAMES O. VAN DE VELDE, D.D., cons. Feb. 11, 1849; transferred to Natchez, July 29, 1853; died Nov. 13, 1855; ANTHONY O'REGAN, D.D., cons. July 25, 1854; resigned 1858; died Nov., 1866; JAMES DUGGAN, D.D., cons. Bishop of Antigone, and Coadjutor to the Archbishop of St. Louis, May 1, 1857; transferred to Chicago, Jan. 21, 1859; hospitalized, 1869; died March 27, 1899; THOMAS FOLEY, D.D., Coadjutor-Bishop and Administrator of the diocese; cons. Bishop of Pergamus, Feb. 27, 1870; died Feb. 19, 1879; Most Revs. PATRICK A. FEEHAN, D.D., First Archbishop of Chicago; cons. Bishop of Nashville, Nov. 1, 1865; promoted to Chicago, Sept. 10, 1880; died July 12, 1902; JAMES EDWARD QUIGLEY, D.D., Archbishop of Chicago; ord. April 12, 1879; cons. Bishop of Buffalo, Feb. 24, 1897; promoted to Archbishop of Chicago, Jan. 8, 1903; died July 10, 1915; His Eminence GEORGE CARDINAL MUNDELEIN, Archbishop of Chicago; ord. June 8, 1895; cons. Titular Bishop of Loryma and Auxiliary Bishop of Brooklyn, Sept. 21, 1909; promoted to the See of Chicago, Dec. 9, 1915; created Cardinal Priest, March 24, 1924; died Oct. 2, 1939; SAMUEL CARDINAL STRITCH, Archbishop of Chicago; ord. May 21, 1910; appt. Bishop of Toledo, Aug. 10, 1921; promoted to Archbishop of Milwaukee, Aug. 26, 1930; transferred to Archbishop of Chicago, Dec. 27, 1939; created Cardinal Priest Feb. 18, 1946; elevated to the Roman Curia, Sacred Congregation for the Propagation of the Faith, March 1, 1958; died in Rome, May 27, 1958; ALBERT CARDINAL MEYER, Archbishop of Chicago; ord. July 11, 1926; appt. Bishop of Superior, Feb. 18, 1946; promoted to Archbishop of Milwaukee, July 21, 1953; transferred to Archbishop of Chicago, Sept. 19, 1958; created Cardinal Priest, Dec. 24, 1959; died April 9, 1965; JOHN CARDINAL CODY, S.T.D., D.D., Archbishop of Chicago; ord. Dec. 8, 1931; appt. Auxiliary Bishop of St. Louis, May 14, 1947; cons. July 2, 1947; promoted to Coadjutor of St. Joseph, Jan. 27, 1954; transferred to Kansas City-St. Joseph, Aug. 29, 1956; promoted to Coadjutor Archbishop of New Orleans, Aug. 14, 1961; acceded to the See of New Orleans, Nov. 8, 1964; transferred to the Archdiocese of Chicago, June 16, 1965; created Cardinal Priest in the Consistory, June 26, 1967; died April 25, 1982; JOSEPH CARDINAL BERNARDIN, D.D., Archbishop of Chicago; ord. April 26, 1952; appt. Auxiliary Bishop of Atlanta, March 9, 1966; cons. April 26, 1966; appt. Archbishop of Cincinnati, Nov. 21, 1972; appt. Archbishop of Chicago, July 10, 1982; installed Aug. 25, 1982; created Cardinal Priest, Feb. 2, 1983; died Nov. 14, 1996.

Vicar General—Rev. Msgr. JOHN F. CANARY.

Episcopal Vicars—Most Revs. GEORGE J. RASSAS, Vicariate I (Deaneries A, B, C, D, E, F); FRANCIS J. KANE, Vicariate II (Deaneries A, B, C, D, E, F); ALBERTO ROJAS, Vicariate III (Deaneries A, B, D, E); JOHN R. MANZ, Vicariate IV (Deaneries A, B, C, D, E); ANDREW P. WYPYCH, Vicariate V (Deaneries A, BE, BW, C, D, E); JOSEPH N. PERRY, Vicariate VI (Deaneries A, B, C, D).

Deans—Revs. RONALD J. LEWINSKI, S.T.L., Deanery I-A; PATRICK J. RUGEN, S.T.L., M.Div., M.A., Deanery I-B; MICHAEL G. MCGOVERN, Deanery I-C; EDWARD R. FIALKOWSKI, Deanery I-D; JOHN W. DEARHAMMER, Deanery I-E; EDWARD B. PANEK, Deanery I-F; MICHAEL A. WULSCH, Deanery II-A; JAMES L. BARRETT, Deanery II-B; Rev. Msgr. JAMES T. KACZOROWSKI, Deanery II-C; Revs. KENNETH C. SIMPSON, B.S., M.Div., D.Min., Deanery II-D; RONALD N. KALAS, Deanery II-E (Retired); STEPHEN F. KANONIK, Deanery II-F; MICHAL OSUCH, C.R., Deanery III-A; NICHOLAS R. DESMOND, Deanery III-B; THOMAS E. CIMA, Deanery III-C; LAWRENCE R. DOWLING, Deanery III-D; DONALD J. NEVINS, Deanery III-E; PAUL G. SEAMAN, Deanery IV-A; CLAUDIO HOLZER, C.S., Deanery IV-B; MARK A. BARTOSIC, Deanery IV-C; ROBERT J. LOJEK, Deanery IV-D; ROBERT J. CLARK, Deanery IV-D; ANTHONY B. PIZZO, O.S.A., Deanery V-A; THADDEUS J. BOJCZUK, Deanery V-B; THOMAS P. CONDE, M.Div., S.T.B., M.B.A., Deanery V-C; WILLIAM T. CORCORAN, Ph.D., Deanery V-D; EDWARD F. UPTON, Deanery V-E; DAVID A. JONES, Deanery VI-A; JAMES E. FLYNN, Deanery VI-B; CARL J. QUEBEDEAUX, C.M.F., Deanery VI-C; MICHAEL A. NACIUS, Deanery VI-D.

College of Consultors—Revs. KENNETH A. BUDZIKOWSKI; PAUL C. BURAK; JOHN COLLINS; Rev. Msgr. ROBERT J. DEMPSEY; Revs. LAWRENCE R. DOWLING; ROBERT M. FEDEK; EDWARD R. FIALKOWSKI; MICHAEL P. KNOTEK; MICHAEL G. MCGOVERN; EDWARD M. MIKOLAJCZYK; CARL MORELLO; Rev. Msgr. PATRICK J. POLLARD.

Presbyteral Council—Revs. JEREMY THOMAS, Chm.; JOSE CARMEN MENDEZ IZQUIERDO, Vice Chm.; JOHN T. NOGA, Treas.; LOUIS TYLKA, Sec.

Administrative Council—Rev. Msgr. JOHN F. CANARY; Mr. JIMMY M. LAGO; Most Revs. GEORGE J. RASSAS; FRANCIS J. KANE; JOHN R. MANZ; JOSEPH N. PERRY; ALBERTO ROJAS; ANDREW P. WYPYCH; Rev. THOMAS A. BAIMA, M.B.A., S.T.D.; Rev. Msgr. MICHAEL M. BOLAND; Mr. RAYMOND P. COUGHLIN; Ms. COLLEEN H. DOLAN; Dr. CAROL L. FOWLER; Rev. Msgr. RICHARD P. HYNES; Mr. KEVIN J. MARZALIK; Sr. MARY PAUL MCCAUGHEY, O.P.

Finance Council—Vice Chairmen: Rev. Msgr. JOHN F. CANARY; Mr. EDWARD J. WEHMER; Mr. JIMMY M. LAGO; Mr. H. PATRICK HACKETT JR. Members: Mr. WILLIAM L. BAX; Mr. JOHN BRENNAN; Ms. BETSY BOHLEN; Mr. JOHN W. CROGHAN; Mr. GENO FERNANDEZ; Mr. EDWIN H. FUTA; Mr. WARD R. HAMM; Mr. CHARLES W. MAUNEY JR.; Mr. OLIVER NICKLIN; Revs. MARTIN E. O'DONOVAN; MICHAEL D. PLACE, S.T.D.; Rev. Msgr. R. GEORGE SARAUSKAS; Mr. TIMOTHY SULLIVAN; Mr. SCOTT C. SWANSON.

Pastoral Council—Mr. THOMAS KINASZ, Chm.; Mr. CLARK MCCAIN, Vice Chm.

Women's Committee—Ms. BETSY BOCCIO-HUNT, Chm.; TERESA PENNIX-GILL, Vice Chair; Ms. RITA KATTNER, D.Min., Dir., Office for Councils. Tel: 773-534-8364.

Youth Council—DAVID BOBRO, Co Chair; JACQUELINE OROZCO, Co Chair.

Consejo Pastoral Arquidiocesano Hispano - Americano—Dr. JAIME BASCUNAN, M.S., D.Min., Chm.; Rev. MARCO A. MERCADO, Dir. Office for Hispanic Catholics. Tel: 312-534-1080.

Provincial Offices

Catholic Conference of Illinois—ROBERT F. GILLIGAN, 65 E. Wacker Pl., Ste. 1620, Chicago, 60601. Tel: 312-368-1066; Fax: 321-368-1090. Web: catholicconferenceofillinois.org.

Provincial Court of Appeals—Rev. JOHN P. LUCAS, 20 N. Wacker Dr., Ste. 3420, Chicago, 60606. Tel: 312-553-4080; Fax: 312-553-4085. Email: johnplucas43@yahoo.com.

Archdiocesan Offices

Archdiocesan Departments can be contacted through the Archbishop Quigley Center, 835 N. Rush St., Chicago, IL 60611-2030 or the Cardinal Meyer Center, 3525 S. Lake Park Ave., Chicago, IL 60653-1402 (street & package delivery addresses). Address all mail to P.O. Box 1979, Chicago, IL 60690-1979. Tel: 312-534-8200.

Office of the Archbishop—Rev. DANIEL A. FLENS, Priest Sec. to the Archbishop. Tel: 312-534-8219; Mrs. MARIE FELLER-KNOLL, Special Asst. Tel: 312-534-8299; Mrs. MARY HALLAN FIORITO, Exec. Asst. Tel: 312-534-8211.

The Chancery— See Office of the Chancellor.

The Metropolitan Tribunal— See Office for Canonical Services.

Vicar General

Vicar General—Rev. Msgr. JOHN F. CANARY, Archbishop Quigley Center, 835 N. Rush St., Chicago, 60611-2030. Tel: 312-534-8271.

Vicar for Priests—Revs. JOHN COLLINS; KENNETH A. BUDZIKOWSKI, 980 N. Michigan Ave., Ste. #1525, Chicago, 60611. Tel: 312-642-1837; Fax: 312-642-4933.

Commission on the Mission and Life of Diocesan Priests—Rev. JOHN COLLINS, Chm., 980 N. Michigan Ave., Ste. #1525, Chicago, 60611. Tel: 312-642-1837.

Diocesan Priests' Placement Board—Revs. JAMES J. DONOVAN JR., Exec. Sec. Tel: 312-534-5270; Fax: 312-534-5281; ROBERT L. TUZIK, Special Consultant. Tel: 312-534-5278.

Archbishop's Delegate for Extern and International Priests—Rev. JEREMIAH M. BOLAND, Archbishop's Delegate. Tel: 312-534-5237; Fax: 312-534-0357.

Mundelein Seminary/University of St. Mary of the Lake—Rev. Msgr. DENNIS J. LYLE, S.T.D., Rector & Pres.; Revs. THOMAS R. FRANZMAN, M.Div., Provost; THOMAS A. BAIMA, M.B.A., S.T.D., Vice Rector Academic Affairs; RONALD A. HICKS, D.Min., Dean of Formation, 1000 E. Maple Ave., Mundelein, 60060. Tel: 847-566-6401.

St. Joseph College Seminary at Loyola University—Very Rev. PETER SNIEG JR., S.T.L., Rector & Pres., 6551 N. Sheridan Rd., Chicago, 60626. Tel: 773-973-9700.

Bishop Abramowicz Seminary—Very Rev. MAREK KASPERCZUK, Rector, 750 N. Wabash Ave., Chicago, 60611-2514. Tel: 312-915-0598; 312-640-1065; Fax: 312-640-1066.

Casa Jesus—Very Rev. OCTAVIO MUNOZ, Rector, 750 N. Wabash, Chicago, 60611-2514. Tel: 312-640-1065; Fax: 312-640-1066.

The Tuite Program at St. Joseph College Seminary—Very Rev. PETER SNIEG JR., S.T.L., Dir., 6551 N. Sheridan Rd., Chicago, 60626. Tel: 773-973-9700; Fax: 773-973-9758.

Archdiocesan Vocations—Rev. BRIAN T. WELTER, M.Div., Dir. Tel: 312-534-8298; Fax: 312-867-0357. Email: vocations@archchicago.org. Web: www.chicagopriest.org.

Chaplaincies/Chaplain Affairs—Rev. Msgr. JOHN F. CANARY, Liaison. Tel: 312-534-8271.

Chicago Airports Catholic Chaplaincy—Rev. MICHAEL G. ZANIOLO, S.T.L., C.A.C., Chap., Mailing Address: P.O. Box 66353, Chicago, 60666-0353. Tel: 773-686-2636; Fax: 773-686-0130. Email: ordchapel@aol.com. Web: www.airportchapels.org.

Fire Department Chaplain—Rev. THOMAS A. MULCRONE, Chap., 1140 W. Jackson Blvd., Chicago, 60607. Tel: 312-738-9246.

Police Department Chaplain—Revs. DANIEL J. BRANDT, Dir.; THOMAS R. NANGLE, Chap. Emeritus, 1140 W. Jackson Blvd., Chicago, 60607. Tel: 312-738-7588; Fax: 312-738-2825.

Ecumenical and Interreligious Affairs, Office for—Sisters JOAN MCGUIRE, O.P., Dir. Tel: 312-534-5325; MARY ELLEN COOMBE, N.D.S., Assoc. Dir. Tel: 312-534-5324.

Institute for Catholic Jewish Education—Sr. MARY ELLEN COOMBE, N.D.S., Dir. Tel: 312-251-8800, Ext. 316.

Office of the Chancellor

Chancellor—Mr. JIMMY M. LAGO, Archbishop Quigley Center, 835 N. Rush St., Chicago, 60611-2030. Tel: 312-534-8220; Fax: 312-534-5381.

Department Directors—Rev. Msgr. RICHARD P. HYNES, Parish Life & Formation; Mr. RAYMOND P. COUGHLIN, Stewardship & Devel.; Rev. Msgr. MICHAEL M. BOLAND, Human Svcs.; Mr. KEVIN J. MARZALIK, Financial Svcs.; Ms. COLLEEN H. DOLAN, Communication & Pub. Rels.; Dr. CAROL L. FOWLER, Personnel Svcs.; Sr. MARY PAUL MCCAUGHEY, O.P., Catholic Schools.

Racial Justice—Sr. ANITA P. BAIRD, D.H.M., Dir.; Ms. ALICIA JUAREZ, Assoc. Dir., Cardinal Meyer Center, 3525 S. Lake Park Ave., Chicago, 60616. Tel: 312-534-8336.

Legal Services—Mr. JOHN C. O'MALLEY, Dir. Tel: 312-534-5379.

Information Technology—Ms. ELLEN M. ANDERSON, Dir. Tel: 312-534-5330; Fax: 312-534-5346; Mr. GANG CHEN, Mgr. Applications Svcs. Tel: 312-534-8331; Fax: 312-534-5346; Mr. HUGH O'NEILL, Mgr. Technical Svcs. Tel: 312-534-5249; Fax: 312-534-5346.

Research & Planning—Ms. JEAN WELTER, Dir. Tel: 312-534-8345; Fax: 312-534-8766.

Archives and Records—Mr. JOHN J. TREANOR, Vice Chancellor Archives & Records, 711 W. Monroe St., Chicago, 60661. Tel: 312-831-0711; Fax: 312-831-0610.

Office of Canonical Services

Canonical Services—Very Rev. DANIEL A. SMILANIC, J.C.D., Vicar, Archbishop Quigley Center, 835 N. Rush St., Chicago, 60611-2030. Tel: 312-534-8206; Fax: 312-534-5307. Associate Vicars: Rev. Msgr. RICHARD T. SAUDIS. Tel: 312-534-8382; Revs. WILLIAM H. WOESTMAN, O.M.I., J.C.D. Tel: 312-534-8362; FRANCIS Q. KUB. Tel: 312-534-8382. Email: fkub@archchicago.org; JEFFREY S. GROB, J.C.D., Archbishop's Delegate to Review Bd. Tel: 312-534-5256. Email: jgrob@archchicago.org; Deacon DANIEL G. WELTER, J.D., Actuarius. Tel: 312-534-8283. Email: dwelter@archchicago.org; SUZETTE CASH, Administrative Asst. Tel: 312-534-8207; Fax: 312-534-8314.

Metropolitan Tribunal

Metropolitan Tribunal—Tel: 312-534-8280; Fax: 312-534-8314.

Judicial Vicar—Very Rev. MICHAEL A. HACK, J.C.D. Tel: 312-534-8255. Email: tribunal@archchicago.org.

Adjutant Judicial Vicar—Very Rev. DANIEL A. SMILANIC, J.C.D. Tel: 312-534-8206.

Applications Coordinator—GLENDA MCFADDEN. Tel: 312-534-8253.

Promoter of Justice—Rev. WILLIAM H. WOESTMAN, O.M.I., J.C.D.

Judges—Very Rev. MICHAEL A. HACK, J.C.D.; Sr. JOYCE HOBEN, S.N.D.; Revs. JOHN M. GRIFFITHS, J.C.D.; JOHN C. HERGENROTHER; Rev. Msgr. PATRICK R. LAGGES, J.C.D.; Very Rev. DANIEL A. SMILANIC, J.C.D.; Revs. WOJCIECH A. MARAT, J.C.D.; DAVID M. HYNOUS, O.P.; MICHAEL BRADLEY, J.C.L.; ALEC J. WOLFF; Sr. CHRISTINE KUB, O.P., J.C.L.; MONICA MAVRIC DE BELTRAMI,

Esq.; Mr. RAPHAEL FRACKIEWICZ, J.C.D.; Ms. RENATA BABICZ, J.U.D.

Defenders of the Bond—Revs. WILLIAM H. WOESTMAN, O.M.I., J.C.D.; RIGOBERTO GAMEZ, J.C.D.; MACIEJ GALLE, J.C.L.; Mr. OLEGARIO CASTILLO, J.C.L.

Delegate of the Archbishop for Privilege Cases—Rev. JOSEPH C. MOL.

Auditors—SUSAN MILLER; Sr. BARBARA KOSINSKA, M.Ch.R.

Advocates—Revs. JOSEPH C. MOL; RIGOBERTO GAMEZ, J.C.D.; Sr. DIONETTE WERNER, C.S.S.F.; LUIS FLORES, J.C.L.; Rev. WOJCIECH A. MARAT, J.C.D.

Department of Parish Life and Formation

Department of Parish Life and Formation—Rev. Msgr. RICHARD P. HYNES, Dir., Cardinal Meyer Center, 3525 S. Lake Park Ave., Chicago, 60653-1402. Tel: 312-534-8388; Mr. ROBERT BENNETT, Prog. Asst. Tel: 312-534-8385; Ms. PATTY MONTES, Sec. Tel: 312-534-8389; Fax: 312-534-3856. Web: www.archchicago.org/dplf; Ms. NANCY POLACEK, Coord. Strategic Pastoral Plan. Tel: 312-534-5316; Ms. TIMONE DAVIS, ReCiL. Tel: 312-534-8308.

Office for Catechesis and Youth Ministry—MARIA H. "MARUJA" SEDANO, Dir. Associate Directors: CATHY WALZ; KRISTEN HEMPSTEAD. Tel: 312-534-3700; Fax: 312-534-3801. Web: www.catechesis-chicago.org; JUAN CASTILLO, Catechetical Ministry Coord.

Vicariate Catechetical Coordinators—

Vicariate I—PAT REDINGTON.

Vicariate II—AMANDA THOMPSON.

Vicariate III—LIBIA PAEZ-HOWARD.

Vicariate IV—JUAN CARLOS FARIAS GONZALEZ.

Vicariate V—VACANT.

Vicariate VI—LOIS DEFELICE.

Vicariate Youth Coordinators—

Vicariate I—JOANNE WALCZYNSKI Web: www.catechesis-chicago.org.

Vicariate II—DARIUS VILLALOBOS.

Vicariate III—JESUS "CHUY" DELEON.

Vicariate IV—LISA BORIS.

Vicariate V—MARIA "COOKY" PEREZ-ERACI.

Vicariate VI—VACANT.

Youth Ministry—JACEK CHABA.

Jegen Center for Catechetical Media & Research—Sr. JUDITH DIETERLE, S.S.L., Coord. Tel: 312-534-3700; Fax: 312-534-3801. Web: www.jegen.org.

Special Religious Education (SPRED)—Rev. JAMES H. MCCARTHY, Dir. Emeritus (Retired), 2956 S. Lowe, Chicago, 60616. Tel: 312-842-1039; Fax: 312-842-4449; Sisters MARY THERESE HARRINGTON, S.H.; SUSANNE GALLAGHER, S.P.

Office for Mission Education and Animation—Sr. MADGE KARECKI, S.S.J.-T.O.S.F., Dir. Tel: 312-534-3318; Mr. TOMASZ MARKOWSKI, Coord. Multi-Cultural Parish Evangelization. Tel: 312-534-8297.

Family Ministries—Mr. FRANCIS P. HANNIGAN, Dir. Associate Directors: VALENTIN ARAYA; ELSIE RADTKE. Tel: 312-534-8351; Fax: 312-534-3858. Web: www.familyministries.org; KIM HAGARTY, Asst. Dir.

Marriage Preparation—Mr. FRANCIS P. HANNIGAN. Tel: 312-534-8340.

Marriage Education—Mr. FRANCIS P. HANNIGAN. Tel: 312-534-8340.

Annulment Support Ministry—ELSIE RADTKE. Tel: 312-534-8391.

Hispanic Family Ministries—VALENTIN ARAYA, Contact. Tel: 312-534-8240.

Natural Family Planning—MARIA GARCIA, Contact. Tel: 312-534-5298 (Spanish); 312-534-8273 (English).

Divorce Ministry—ELSIE RADTKE. Tel: 312-534-8353.

Divine Worship, Office for—Mr. TODD WILLIAMSON, Dir.; Ms. MARGARET (GOSIA) CZELUSNIAK, Administrative Asst.; Mr. JOSE CASTILLO, Dir. Hispanic Programming; Sr. RENE SIMONELIC, O.S.F., Dir. Gen. Programming; Ms. JACKIE MOYENO, Prog. Assoc.; Rev. ROBERT L. TUZIK, Consultant & Special Projects; Ms. ANNA BELLE O'SHEA, Dir. Liturgies & Music. Tel: 312-534-5153; Fax: 312-534-5158. Web: www.odw.org.

Young Adult Ministry/Singles—Rev. JOHN C. CUSICK, Dir.; Dr. KATHERINE F. DEVRIES, Assoc. Dir., 711 W. Monroe St., Chicago, 60661. Tel: 312-466-9473; Fax: 312-466-9474. Web: www.yamchicago.org.

Office for Peace & Justice—Mr. SCOTT MCLARTY. Tel: 312-534-5383; Fax: 312-787-1554.

Catholic Campaign for Human Development/Parish Sharing—CAROL SMITH, Prog. Dir.

Office of Immigrant Affairs and Immigration Education—Ms. ELENA SEGURA, Dir.

St. Toribio Immigrant Center—MARCO LOPEZ, Dir., 2434 S. California Ave., Chicago, 60608. Tel: 773-376-1276; Fax: 773-376-9678.

Catholic Relief Services and Justice Education—Ms. ADRIENNE CURRY, Prog. Dir.

Office for Mission Education and Animation, Propagation of the Faith, Holy Childhood Association—Sr. MADGE KARECKI, S.S.J.-T.O.S.F., Dir. Tel: 312-534-3318.

Respect Life/Pro-Life Office—MARGIE MANCZKO BREEN, Interim Dir. & Prog. Mgr. Tel: 312-534-5355; Fax: 312-534-1554.

Project Rachel—Tel: 312-337-1962; 800-456-4673 (800-456-HOPE).

Chastity Education Initiative—Tel: 312-534-5355.

Jail Ministry/Kolbe House—Rev. ARTURO PEREZ-RODRIGUEZ, Dir., 2434 S. California, Chicago, 60608. Tel: 773-247-0070; Fax: 773-247-0665.

Councils, The Archdiocesan Office for—Ms. RITA KATTNER, D.Min., Dir.

Parish Pastoral Councils—Ms. RITA KATTNER, D.Min., Dir. Tel: 312-534-8364; Fax: 312-534-3883.

Christ Renews His Parish—Ms. RITA KATTNER, D.Min., Spiritual Dir. Tel: 312-534-8364.

Amate House/Young Adult Volunteer Program—Deacon JOHN V. LUCAS, Exec. Dir., 3600 S. Seeley, Chicago, 60609. Tel: 773-376-2445. Web: www.amatehouse.org.

Ethnic Offices—Mr. ANDREW LYKE, Dir., Office for Black Catholics. Tel: 312-534-8377; Fax: 312-534-5207; Mrs. TERESITA L. NUVAL, Dir., Office for Asian Catholics. Tel: 312-534-8305; Fax: 312-534-5207; Revs. CASIMIR GARBACZ, S.V.D., Dir., Office for European Catholics. Tel: 312-534-8352; Fax: 312-534-5207; MARCO A. MERCADO, Dir., Office for Hispanic Catholics. Tel: 312-534-1080; Fax: 312-534-3459.

Vicariate Hispanic Coordinators—

Vicariate I—GRACIELA CONTRERAS, 200 N. Milwaukee Ave., Ste. 212, Libertyville, 60048. Tel: 847-549-0164.

Vicariate V—YENISSE ROMAN, 2330 W. 118th St., Chicago, 60643. Tel: 773-881-2100.

Centro Espiritu Santo - Vicariate V—YENISSE ROMAN, Dir., 2330 W. 118th St., Chicago, 60643. Tel: 773-881-2100; Fax: 773-779-8469.

Vicariate VI—VACANT.

Hispanic Young Adult Ministry—Mr. JORGE RIVERA, 1838 S. Throop St., Chicago, 60608. Tel: 312-534-1080.

Ethnic Apostolates—

Kateri Center (American Indian Ministry of the Archdiocese of Chicago)—GEORGINA ROY, Dir., Kateri Center, 3938 N. Leavitt St., Chicago, 60618. Tel: 773-561-6155.

Haitian Catholic Apostolate—7851 S. Jeffery Blvd., Chicago, 60649. Tel: 773-721-6365.

Indochinese Catholic Center—Rev. PETER HUNG, Dir. (Retired), 4827 N. Kenmore, Chicago, 60640. Tel: 773-784-1932.

Archdiocesan Council of Catholic Women (ACCW)—CHRISTINE SCHUMANN, Pres. Tel: 312-534-8325.

Archdiocesan Council of Catholic Men—Rev. JOHN C. CUSICK, 711 W. Monroe St., Chicago, 60661. Tel: 312-466-9473; Fax: 312-466-9474.

Department of Stewardship and Development

Department of Stewardship and Development—Mr. RAYMOND P. COUGHLIN, Dir., Archbishop Quigley Center, 835 N. Rush St., Chicago, 60611-2030. Tel: 312-534-7910; Ms. PATRICIA A. CONDON, Senior Administrative Asst. Tel: 312-534-7935; Fax: 312-534-7354.

Vicariate Stewardship Coordinators—Mr. MICHAEL J. GLEASON. Tel: 312-534-7830; Ms. LEA DECANAY. Tel: 312-534-7713.

Development Services—Ms. BARBARA SHEA COLLINS. Tel: 312-534-7944.

Wills, Trusts, Estates & Planned Giving/Annuities—Mr. RICHARD S. GOODE, Dir. Tel: 312-534-7848.

Major Gifts—Mr. PETER CULLEN-CONWAY, Dir. Tel: 312-534-7929.

Major Gifts Officer, Catholic Schools—Mr. WILLIAM BOOTH. Tel: 312-534-8486.

Benefactor Relations Coordinator—Ms. MARY ANN PERROTTI. Tel: 312-534-7928.

Department of Human Services

Director—Rev. Msgr. MICHAEL M. BOLAND, 721 N. LaSalle St., Chicago, 60654-3574. Tel: 312-655-7460; Fax: 312-655-0219.

Catholic Charities of Chicago—Rev. Msgr. MICHAEL M. BOLAND, Admin., Pres. & CEO; Mr. J. ANTONIO FERNANDEZ, Sr. Vice Pres. Oper.; Ms. CYNTHIA D. SMETANA, CFO; Ms. KATHY DONAHUE, Sr. Vice Pres. Programs; JOHN J. RYAN, Chief of Staff. Associate Administrators: Revs. RICHARD E. BULWITH; RICHARD JAKUBIK; GERARD P. KELLY, C.M.; CHARLES T. RUBEY (Retired); WAYNE F. WATTS; Deacon MANUEL DORANTES, 721 N. LaSalle St., Chicago, 60654-3574. Tel: 312-655-7000 Central Intake Phone; 800-244-0505 (Refer to Catholic Charities section under the Institutions located in the Archdiocese for further listings).

Maternity Fund—NORENE CHESEBRO, 721 N. LaSalle St., Chicago, 60654-3574. Tel: 312-655-7596.

Office for Persons with Disabilities—Rev. CHARLES T. RUBEY, Dir. (Retired), 721 N. LaSalle St., Chicago, 60654-3574. Tel: 312-655-7280.

Catholic Office of the Deaf—Rev. JOSEPH A. MULCRONE, Dir.; Ms. MARGARET SWATEK, D.R.E., Cardinal Meyer Center, 3525 S. Lake Park Ave., Chicago, 60653-1402. Tel: 312-534-7899; 312-534-8368 TTY; Fax: 312-534-0394. Email: cathdeafch@archchicago.org. Web: www.deafchurchchicago.parishesonline.com.

Health/Hospital Affairs—Rev. WILLIAM P. GROGAN, Cardinal's Delegate for Hospitals. Tel: 312-534-8339; Rev. Msgr. MICHAEL M. BOLAND, Cardinal's Delegate for Nursing Homes & Senior Svcs. Tel: 312-655-7460; Fax: 312-655-0219.

Bio Ethics Commission—Rev. WILLIAM P. GROGAN, Chair. Tel: 312-534-8339.

Mercy Home for Boys and Girls—Rev. SCOTT DONAHUE, Pres. & CEO, 1140 W. Jackson, Chicago, 60607. Tel: 312-738-9240.

Office for Persons with Disabilities—Rev. CHARLES T. RUBEY (Retired), 721 N. LaSalle St., Chicago, 60654-3574. Tel: 312-655-7280.

Department of Financial Services

Director—Mr. KEVIN J. MARZALIK, Archbishop Quigley Center, 835 N. Rush St., Chicago, 60611-2030. Tel: 312-534-8218.

Facilities and Construction—Mr. C. GREGORY VEITH, Mgr. Tel: 312-534-8342.

Controller's Operations—Ms. CHRISTINE DUSZYNSKI, Controller. Tel: 312-534-5266.

Risk Management - Property & Casualty—Mr. DON TURLEK, Mgr. Tel: 312-534-8295; Fax: 312-534-8302.

Real Estate—Mr. THOMAS KENNEDY, Dir. Tel: 312-534-8221.

Parish Operations—TAFFIE IWANICKI, Oper. Mgr. Tel: 312-534-5312.

Vicariate I—DENNIS ROBAK. Tel: 312-534-5364. Vicariate Office. Tel: 847-549-0165.

Vicariate II—JOSEPH LANGE. Tel: 312-534-5321. Vicariate Office. Tel: 773-388-8673.

Vicariate III—JESSE ESTRADA. Tel: 312-534-5323. Vicariate Office. Tel: 312-243-1135.

Vicariate IV—PATRICIA POMYKALSKI. Tel: 312-534-5384. Vicariate Office. Tel: 708-329-4050.

Vicariate V—ERICH BANGERT. Tel: 312-534-5318. Vicariate Office. Tel: 773-239-4559.

Vicariate VI—PAMELA GUTTER. Tel: 312-534-5342. Vicariate Office. Tel: 708-333-6132.

Catholic Cemeteries—Rev. Msgr. PATRICK J. POLLARD, CCCE, Archdiocesan Dir.; Mr. ROMAN SZABELSKI, CCCE, Exec. Dir., 1400 S. Wolf Rd., Hillside, 60162. Tel: 708-449-6100; Fax: 708-449-3419.

Bereavement Ministry—MARTHA BURKE TRESSLER. Tel: 708-423-0471.

Department of Communications and Public Relations

Department of Communications and Public Relations—Ms. COLLEEN H. DOLAN, Dir., Archbishop Quigley Center, 835 N. Rush St., Chicago, 60611-2030. Tel: 312-534-8289; Fax: 312-534-5306.

Office of Media Relations—Ms. SUSAN BURRITT, Dir. Communications. Tel: 312-534-8233.

Office of Radio & Television—Mr. JIM DISCH, Dir. Tel: 312-534-8277.

School Marketing and Communications—RYAN BLACKBURN, Dir. Tel: 312-534-5334; Fax: 312-534-5295.

New World Publications—DAWN VIDMAR, Gen. Mgr., Cardinal Meyer Center, 3525 S. Lake Park Ave., Chicago, 60653-1402. Tel: 312-534-7777; Fax: 312-534-7310.

Catholic New World—JOYCE DURIGA, Editor. Tel: 312-534-7577.

Hispanic Communications—ALEJANDRO CASTILLO, Dir. Tel: 312-534-7880; Fax: 312-534-7310.

Chicago Catolico—ALEJANDRO CASTILLO, Gen. Mgr. Tel: 312-534-7880.

KATOLIK— The Polish language newspaper of the Archdiocese. ALICJA POZYWIO, News Editor. Tel: 312-534-7294.

Department of Personnel Services

Director—Dr. CAROL FOWLER, Archbishop Quigley Center, 835 N. Rush St., Chicago, 60611-2030. Tel: 312-534-8349.

Human Resources—FRED VAN DEN HENDE, Dir. Tel: 312-534-5352.

Lay Ecclesial Ministry, Office for—CAROL A. WALTERS, Dir. Tel: 312-534-5263; Fax: 312-534-5281.

Office of Conciliation—RALPH BONACCORSI, Exec. Dir. Email: concil@archchicago.org.

Office of Ministerial Evaluation—KATHLEEN LEGGDAS, Dir. Tel: 312-534-5265; Fax: 312-534-5281.

Religious, Office for—Sisters JOAN MCGLINCHEY, M.S.C., Dir. Tel: 312-534-8360; KATHLEEN MCNULTY, O.S.F., Asst. Dir. Tel: 312-534-3877; MARGARET COLEMAN, O.S.F., Retirement Collection. Tel: 312-534-8234; ELYSE RAMIREZ, O.P., Coord. Rel. Vocation Ministries. Tel: 312-534-5240.

Priests' Retirement and Mutual Aid Association (PRMAA)—Mr. ALEX BECKER, Exec. Dir., 4951 Harrrison St., Hillside, 60162. Tel: 708-449-8026; Fax: 708-449-8148.

Vicars for Senior Priests—Most Revs. TIMOTHY J. LYNE (Retired). Tel: 312-787-8040; Fax: 312-787-9113; THAD J. JAKUBOWSKI, D.D. Tel: 773-202-7720; Fax: 773-202-7725; Rev. EDWARD D. GRACE. Tel: 312-534-1837; Rev. Msgr. JOHN A. KUZINSKAS, Asst. Vicar (Retired).

Vicar for the Diaconate Community—Rev. MICHAEL P. AHLSTROM, 816 Marengo, Forest Park, 60130. Tel: 708-366-8900; Fax: 708-366-8968; Deacons DENNIS L. COLGAN, Assoc. Dir. Diaconate Community; ENRIQUE ALONSO, Assoc. Dir. Hispanic Diaconate Community.

Office for Protection of Children and Youth—Ms. JAN SLATTERY, Dir., 737 N. Michigan Ave., Ste. 900, Chicago, 60611-2956. Tel: 312-751-5319; Fax: 312-751-8307.

Assistance Ministry—TOM THARAYIL, Dir. Tel: 312-751-8267; Fax: 312-751-8307.

Child Abuse Investigations and Review—Ms. LEAH R. MCCLUSKEY, Dir. Tel: 312-751-5205; Fax: 312-751-5279. Email: lmccluskey@archchicago.org.

Safe Environment—MYRA FLORES, Coord. Tel: 312-751-5238; Fax: 312-751-5307.

Cardinal Stritch Retreat House—Deacon RICHARD F. HUDZIK, Dir., 1300 Stritch Dr., P.O. Box 455, Mundelein, 60060-0455. Tel: 847-566-6060; Fax: 847-566-6082.

Department of Catholic Schools

Department of Catholic Schools—Sr. MARY PAUL MCCAUGHEY, O.P., Supt., Archbishop Quigley Center, 835 N. Rush St., Chicago, 60611-2030. Tel: 312-534-5210; Fax: 312-534-5392; MARY KEARNEY, Assoc. Supt. Tel: 312-534-5255.

Other Archdiocesan Agencies

Food Service Professionals, Archdiocese—Mr. JOHN KOUBEK, Dir., 5150 Northwest Hwy., Chicago, 60638. Tel: 773-385-5100; Fax: 773-385-6025. Web: www.fspro.com.

Liturgy Training Publications (LTP)—JOHN A. THOMAS, Dir., 3943 S. Racine Ave., Chicago, 60690. Tel: 773-486-8970; Fax: 773-486-7094. Orders: Tel: 800-933-2800; Fax: 800-933-7094. Email: orders@ltp.org; DEANNA KEEFE, Mktg. & Sales Fulfillment Mgr. Email: dkeefe@ltp.org. Web: www.ltp.org.

CLERGY, PARISHES, MISSIONS AND PAROCHIAL SCHOOLS

CITY OF CHICAGO

(COOK COUNTY)

1—HOLY NAME CATHEDRAL (1849) Rev. Msgr. Daniel G. Mayall, Rector & Pastor of Parish; Revs. John P. Boivin; Matthew Ross Compton; Thomas G. Aschenbrener; Deacons Michael McCloskey; Stan Strom; Mrs. Ann Klocke, Pastoral Assoc.; Ms. Pat Still, Pastoral Asst.; Mary Ann Hoban, Coord. of Ministry of Care; H. Ricardo Ramirez, Dir. Music; Mr. David C. Jonies, Assoc. Dir. Music; Mr. Andrew Skura, Comptroller; Mr. Alex Lucio, Stewardship Coord.; Laura Grazioli, Pastor's Sec.; Scott LaMorte, Devel. Dir. In Res., Most Rev. Timothy J. Lyne, Pastor Emeritus & Auxiliary Bishop of Chicago (Retired); Rev. Msgr. Michael M. Boland; Revs. William J. Moriarity; Louis J. Cameli; William H. Woestman, O.M.I.; Brian T. Welter.
Rectory—730 N. Wabash Ave., 60611. Tel: 312-787-8040; Fax: 312-787-9113. Web: www.holynamecathedral.org.
Cardinal's Residence—1555 N. State Pkwy., 60610. His Eminence Francis Cardinal George, O.M.I., Archbishop of Chicago; Most Rev. Raymond E. Goedert, Auxiliary Bishop (Retired); Rev. Msgr. John F. Canary, Vicar Gen.; Rev. Daniel A. Flens, Sec. to the Archbishop.
Seminary Formation House-Casa Jesus—750 N. Wabash, 60611. Tel: 312-640-1065. Very Rev. Octavio Munoz, Rector.
Seminary Formation House-Bishop Abramowicz Seminary—Tel: 312-915-0598; Fax: 312-640-1066. Very Rev. Marek Kasperczuk (Poland), Rector.
Catechesis/Religious Program—Tel: 312-787-8040. Ms. Sharon Kinsley, D.R.E. Students 120.
Convent—Oblate Sisters of Jesus the Priest, Tel: 312-787-8040; Fax: 312-787-9113.

2—ST. ADALBERT Rev. Michael S. Michelini; Deacon Juan Dominguez. In Res., Rev. Antoni Bradlo, C.Ss.R.
Res.: 1650 W. 17th St., 60608-0194. Tel: 312-226-0340; Fax: 312-266-0194.
Catechesis/Religious Program—Students 79.

3—ST. ADRIAN Rev. Thomas J. Mescall; Deacon Ruben Aguilar.
Res.: 7000 S. Fairfield Ave., 60629. Tel: 773-434-3223; Fax: 773-434-6380. Email: stadrian@archchicago.org.
Church: 70th and S. Washtenaw Ave., 60619.
Catechesis/Religious Program—Students 125.

4—ST. AGATHA Revs. Lawrence R. Dowling; Thomas P. Walsh; Deacon Gregory Shumpert.
Res.: 3147 W. Douglas Blvd., 60623. Tel: 773-522-3050; Fax: 773-522-3842.
School—Saint Agatha Catholic Academy, (Preschool-3rd Grade Campus): 3151 W. Douglas Blvd., 60623-1898. Tel: 773-762-1809; Fax: 773-762-9781. (4th-8th Grade Campus): 3800 W. Lexington St., 60624-3648. Tel: 773-638-6555; Fax: 773-638-0070. Lay Teachers 10; Students 200.
Catechesis/Religious Program—Students 89.

5—ST. AGNES OF BOHEMIA Revs. Donald J. Nevins; Martin D. Ibarra; Robert Sprott, O.F.M.; Sr. Bertha Lopez, Human Services & Rel. Educ. Coord.; Deacon Angel Favila.
Res.: 2651 S. Central Park Ave., 60623. Tel: 773-522-0142; Fax: 773-522-0172. Email: stagnescentral@archchicago.org. Web: www.stagnesofbohemia.org.
School—2643 S. Central Park Ave., 60623. Tel: 773-522-0143; Fax: 773-522-0132. Ms. Kathleen M. Duffy, Prin. Lay Teachers 23; Students 440.
Catechesis/Religious Program—Tel: 773-277-5446. Students 610.
Convent—Misioneras de San Pio X, 2658 S. Central Park Ave., 60623. Tel: 773-762-3229.

6—ST. AILBE Revs. Lawrence M. Duris; Andrew Charles Smith Jr.; Deacon Bruce T. McElrath.
Res.: 9015 S. Harper Ave., 60619. Tel: 773-374-2345; Fax: 773-374-7096. Email: stailbe@aol.com.
School—9037 S. Harper Ave., 60619. Tel: 773-734-1386; Fax: 773-734-1440. Paul D. Houser, Prin. Lay Teachers 12; Students 144.
Catechesis/Religious Program—Students 205.

7—ALL SAINTS-ST. ANTHONY Rev. John W. Parker; Deacon Duke Vemich.
Res.: 518 W. 28th Pl., 60616. Tel: 312-842-2744; Fax: 312-842-2791.
See Bridgeport Catholic Academy, Chicago under Consolidated Elementary Schools, located in the Institution section.
Catechesis/Religious Program—Students 51.

8—ST. ALOYSIUS Rev. Nicholas R. Desmond; Deacons Adolfo Lopez; Dennis Ramos; William Smyser; Ramon Navarro.
Res.: 2300 W. Le Moyne St., 60622. Tel: 773-278-4808; Fax: 773-278-4898. Email: parish@staloysiusparish.org. Web: www.staloysiusparish.org.
Catechesis/Religious Program—Students 120.

9—ST. ALPHONSUS, (German), Revs. James F. Hurlbert; Shawn Gould; Steven Bauer.
Res.: 1429 W. Wellington Ave., 60657. Tel: 773-525-0709; Fax: 773-525-3238. Email: stalparish@aol.com. Web: www.stalphonsuschgo.org.
School—Alphonsus Academy and Center for the Arts, Tel: 773-348-4629; Fax: 773-348-4829. Dr. Megan Stanten-Anderson, Prin. Students 369.
Catechesis/Religious Program—Catherine Crino, D.R.E. Students 128.

10—ST. AMBROSE Rev. Freddy Washington, C.S.Sp.
Res.: *Congregation of the Holy Ghost (Spiritans)*, 1012 E. 47th St., 60653. Tel: 773-624-3695; Fax: 773-624-3697.

11—ST. ANDREW Revs. Sergio Romo; John A. Farry, Pastor Emeritus (Retired); Arokia D. Savarimuthu, A.L.C.P./O.S.S.; Deacon David Reyes.
Res.: 3546 N. Paulina St., 60657. Tel: 773-525-3016; Fax: 773-525-4124. Web: www.saintandrewchicago.com.
School—1710 W. Addison, 60613. Tel: 773-248-2500; Fax: 773-248-2709. Lay Teachers 29; Students 396.
Catechesis/Religious Program—Students 100.

12—ST. ANGELA, Closed. Consult Archives and Records Center for parish and school records.

13—ST. ANN Rev. Felipe Vaglienty; Deacon Rodrigo Silva.
Res.: 1840 S. Leavitt St., 60608. Tel: 312-733-7486; Fax: 312-733-5681.
School—2211 W. 18th Pl., 60608. Tel: 312-829-4153. Mr. Brian K. Morten, Prin. Lay Teachers 14; Students 220.
Catechesis/Religious Program—Students 120.

14—ANNUNCIATA (1941) Revs. Paul M. Cullen, O.S.M.; Dennis Kriz, O.S.M.; Mr. Mike Schnabel, Business Mgr. In Res., Rev. Conrad M. Borntrager, O.S.M.
Res.: 11128 S. Avenue G, 60617. Tel: 773-221-1040; Fax: 773-221-1556. Email: annunciata@archchicago.org. Web: www.annunciataonline.com.
School—3750 E. 112th St., 60617. Tel: 773-375-5711; Fax: 773-375-5704. Mrs. Carol A. Miceli, Prin. Lay Teachers 14; Students 183.
Catechesis/Religious Program—Students 190.

15—ST. ANSELM Rev. Abelardo Gabriel, S.V.D., Admin. In Res., Rev. Donald J. Ehr, S.V.D.
Res.: 6045 S. Michigan Ave., 60637. Tel: 773-493-5959; Fax: 773-363-1887.
Catechesis/Religious Program—Students 37.

16—ST. ANTHONY OF PADUA (1903) Rev. Mark J. Krylowicz.
Res.: 11533 S. Prairie Ave., 60628. Tel: 773-468-1200; Fax: 773-468-1922. Email: saintanthony@ameritech.net.
Catechesis/Religious Program—Students 136.

17—ASSUMPTION Rev. Arturo Perez Rodriguez.
Res.: 2434 S. California Ave., 60608. Tel: 773-247-6644; Fax: 773-247-0665.
Convent—2831 W. 24th St. Blvd., 60623. Tel: 773-247-1100.
Kolbe House—Web: www.kolbehouseministry.org. Rev. Arturo Perez-Rodriguez, Dir. Catholic Prison Ministry.
Catechesis/Religious Program—Students 158.

18—ASSUMPTION OF THE B.V.M./ST. CATHERINE OF GENOA, Closed. Consult Archives and Records Center for parish and school records.

19—ASSUMPTION OF THE BLESSED VIRGIN MARY Rev. Joseph Chamblain, O.S.M. In Res., Revs. John M. Pawlikowski, O.S.M.; David M. Brown, O.S.M.; Damian M. Charbonneau, O.S.M.; Michael Doyle, O.S.M.
Res.: 323 W. Illinois St., 60654-7812. Tel: 312-644-0036; Fax: 312-644-1838. Email: parishoffice@assumption-chgo.org.

20—ST. BARBARA Revs. Dennis A. Ziomek; Andrew Beltowski (Poland).
Res.: 2859 S. Throop St., 60608. Tel: 312-842-7979; Fax: 312-842-7978. Email: stbarbara@stbarbarachicago.org. Web: www.stbarbarachicago.org.
School—Tel: 312-326-6243; Fax: 312-842-7960. Mrs. Dorene A. Hurckes, Prin. Lay Teachers 13; Students 179.
Catechesis/Religious Program—Students 5.

21—ST. BARNABAS Revs. William E. Malloy; Raymond J. Tillrock, Pastor Emeritus (Retired); John G. Hetland; Anthony M. Leahy (Retired); Deacons James Temple; William Sullivan; James L. Conway; Andrew Neu; Ms. Kitty T. Ryan, Pastoral Assoc. & Liturgy Dir. In Res., Revs. James J. Donovan Jr.; William G. Kenneally, Senior Priest (Retired); Carl J. Markelz, O.Carm.
Res.: 10134 S. Longwood Dr., 60643. Tel: 773-779-1166; Fax: 773-445-9671. Web: www.stbarnabasparish.org.
School—10121 S. Longwood Dr., 60643. Tel: 773-445-7711; Fax: 773-445-9815. Mrs. Lenore Barnes, Prin. Lay Teachers 24; Students 455.
Catechesis/Religious Program—Tel: 773-445-3450. Students 197.

22—ST. BARTHOLOMEW Revs. Jason A. Malave; George F. Cerny, Pastor Emeritus (Retired); Tirso S. Villaverde; Mr. Jesus Flores, Lay Min.; Mrs. Leonor Navarro, Lay Min.; Mrs. Nancy Kleiber, Lay Min.; Mr. Faustino Santiago, Lay Min.; Ms. Cyndee Zbtlut, Music Dir. In Res., Revs. Eduardo Pinzon, S.J. (Retired); Michael A. Goergen (Retired); Hippolytus Njoku, S.M.M.M.
Res.: 4949 W. Patterson Ave., 60641. Tel: 773-286-7871; Fax: 773-286-4808. Web: www.stbartholomew.net.
School—4941 W. Patterson Ave., 60641. Tel: 773-282-9373; Fax: 773-282-4757. Mr. Martin Graham-McHugh, Prin. Lay Teachers 14; Students 265.
Catechesis/Religious Program—Maria Arrez, C.R.E. Students 446.

23—ST. BASIL/VISITATION Revs. Clement O. Oyafemi; Balthazar Ndyomugaloe.
Res.: 843 W. Garfield Blvd., 60621. Tel: 773-846-3570; Fax: 773-783-3348. Email: basvis@aol.com.
School—Visitation School, 900 W. Garfield Blvd., 60609. Tel: 733-373-5200; Fax: 733-373-5201. Sr. Jean Matijosaitis, O.P., Prin. Sisters 5; Lay Teachers 15; Students 186.
Catechesis/Religious Program—Students 14.

24—ST. BEDE THE VENERABLE Revs. Jose de Jesus Medina, Admin.; Juan Carlos Arrieta Correa; Deacon Pablo Perez.
Res.: 8200 S. Kostner Ave., 60652. Tel: 773-884-2000; Fax: 773-582-0026. Web: www.stbedechicago.org.
School—4440 W. 83rd St., 60652. Tel: 773-884-2020; Fax: 773-582-3366. Lay Teachers 22; Students 470.
Catechesis/Religious Program—Tel: 773-884-2038;

Fax: 773-884-2037. Students 206.
25—ST. BENEDICT (1902) Revs. Robert W. Beaven; Joseph Pillai; Deacon Philip Bertolani.
Res.: 2215 W. Irving Park Rd., 60618. Tel: 773-588-6484; Fax: 773-588-4927. Email: sbparish@stben.com. Web: www.stbenedict.com.
School—3920 N. Leavitt St., 60618. Tel: 773-463-6797; Fax: 773-463-0782. Ms. Rachel A. Bernhardt, Prin. Lay Teachers 42; Students 556.
High School—3900 N. Leavitt St., 60618. Tel: 773-539-0066; Fax: 773-539-3397. Sisters 2; Lay Teachers 22; Students 163.
Catechesis/Religious Program—Mary S. Wiegus, D.R.E. Students 166.
26—ST. BENEDICT THE AFRICAN (EAST) Rev. David A. Jones; Sisters Mary Pokorny, Pastoral Min.; Joanne Delehanty, Pastoral Min.
Res.: 340 W. 66th St., 60621. Tel: 773-873-4464; Fax: 773-873-1992.
School—Academy of St. Benedict the African Total Students for 2 Sites 200.
Stewart Site—6547 S. Stewart, 60636. Tel: 773-994-6100.
Catechesis/Religious Program—Students 75.
27—ST. BENEDICT THE AFRICAN (WEST) (1989) Very Rev. Paul De Porres Whittington, O.P.
Res.: 1818 W. 71st St., 60636. Tel: 773-925-5071; Fax: 773-925-7071.
School—Academy of St. Benedict the African
Laflin Site—6020 S. Laflin St., 60636. Tel: 773-776-3316; Fax: 773-776-3715.
Stewart Site—6547 S. Stewart St., 60636. Tel: 773-994-6100; Fax: 773-994-1433.
Catechesis/Religious Program—Students 138.
28—BLESSED ALOJZIJE STEPINAC CROATIAN MISSION Rev. Ivica Majstorovic, O.F.M., Admin. (Independent Mission)
Res.: 6346 N. Ridge, 60660. Tel: 773-262-0535; Fax: 773-262-4603. Email: bastepinacchicago@sbcglobal.net.
Catechesis/Religious Program—Suzana Culjak, D.R.E. Students 36.
29—BLESSED SACRAMENT Revs. Thomas Smithson, S.S.S.; Michael J. Boehm; Deacons Dismas Fernandez; Rudolf Hess. In Res., Rev. Rudsend Paragas, S.S.S.; Rev. Msgr. Richard O'Donnell; Revs. John Christman, S.S.S.; Anthony Marshall, S.S.S.
Office: 3528 S. Hermitage Ave., 60609-1217. Tel: 773-523-3917; Fax: 773-247-9285.
Catechesis/Religious Program—
30—BLESSED SACRAMENT-MILLARD, Closed. Consult Archives and Records Center for parish and school records.
31—ST. BONAVENTURE, Closed. Consult Archives and Records Center for parish and school records. See Section W-Miscellaneous for oratory listing.
32—ST. BRIDE (1893) Rev. Robert J. Roll. In Res., Rev. W. James Clavey.
Res.: 7811 S. Coles Ave., 60649. Tel: 773-731-8822; Fax: 773-721-0673. Email: stbride@archchicago.org. Web: www.st-bride.org.
Catechesis/Religious Program—Students 25.
33—ST. BRONISLAVA Rev. Ricardo Castillo; Deacon Faustino Ramos.
Res.: 8708 S. Colfax Ave., 60617. Tel: 773-734-0776; Fax: 773-734-1429. Email: jesusp@saintbronislava.com.
Catechesis/Religious Program—Students 146.
34—ST. BRUNO Rev. Antoni Bury; Deacon Sal Villa. In Res., Rev. Emil Cudak (Poland).
Res.: 4751 S. Harding Ave., 60632. Tel: 773-523-3467; Fax: 773-523-4253. Email: stbruno@comcast.net. Web: www.stbrunochicago.org.
School—4839 S. Harding Ave., 60632. Tel: 773-847-0697; Fax: 773-847-1620. Mrs. Katrina A. McDermott, Prin. Lay Teachers 14; Students 204.
Catechesis/Religious Program—Students 129.
35—ST. CAJETAN Revs. Frank A. Kurucz; William A. Burke, Pastor Emeritus; Phillip T. Owen; Thomas R. McCarthy, O.S.A.; Peter McGarry, O.Carm.
Parish Center Office—2445 W. 112th St., 60655. Tel: 773-474-7800; Fax: 773-474-7878.
Res.: 11234 S. Artesian Ave., 60655. Tel: 773-238-4100.
School—2447 W. 112th St., 60655. Tel: 773-233-8844. Mrs. Terry Reger, Prin. Lay Teachers 26; Students 355.
Catechesis/Religious Program—Students 132.
36—ST. CAMILLUS Revs. Waclaw L. Lech, O.C.D.; Pawel P. Furdzik, O.C.D.; Jacek Chodzynski, O.C.D.
Res.: 5426 S. Lockwood Ave., 60638. Tel: 773-767-8183; Fax: 773-284-3812.
Catechesis/Religious Program—Students 518.
37—CHRIST THE KING (1936) Revs. Thomas P. Conde; Joseph Woseitz. In Res., Rev. Msgr. Michael J. Adams (Retired).
Res.: 9235 S. Hamilton Ave., 60643-6360. Tel: 773-238-4877; Fax: 773-238-4963. Web: www.ckchicago.org.
School—9240 S. Hoyne Ave., 60643-6303. Tel: 773-779-3329; Fax: 773-779-3390. Ms. Maureen R. Aspell, Prin. Lay Teachers 24; Students 310.
Catechesis/Religious Program—Mrs. Irene Friend, D.R.E. Students 65.
38—CHRIST THE REDEEMER BYZANTINE BIELARUSIAN, Closed. Consult Archives and Records Center for parish records.
39—ST. CHRISTINA Revs. Lawrence J. Sullivan; Karol Tybor; Thomas J. Purtell (Retired); Deacons Thomas Ryan; Stanley Rakauskas.
Res.: 11005 S. Homan Ave., 60655. Tel: 773-779-7181; Fax: 773-238-2942.
School—3333 W. 110th St., 60655. Tel: 773-445-2969; Fax: 773-445-0444. Mrs. Mary E. Stokes, Prin. Lay Teachers 26; Students 568.
Catechesis/Religious Program—3333 W. 110th St., 60655. Tel: 773-445-9539. Students 417.
40—ST. CLARE OF MONTEFALCO Rev. Michael Sullivan, O.F.M.Cap.
Res.: 5443 S. Washtenaw Ave., 60632. Tel: 773-436-4422; Fax: 773-476-1888. Email: st.clare@sbcglobal.net.
Catechesis/Religious Program—Tel: 773-434-5599. Students 207.
41—ST. CLEMENT Revs. Kenneth C. Simpson; Manuel Dorantes; Joseph O'Brien (Retired). In Res., Rev. Bill Wilson.
Res.: 642 W. Deming Pl., 60614. Tel: 773-281-0371; Fax: 773-281-2509. Email: feedback@stclementchurch.org. Web: www.stclementchurch.org.
School—2524 N. Orchard St., 60614. Tel: 773-348-8212; Fax: 773-348-4712. Ms. Melissa Dan, Prin. Lay Teachers 34; Students 459.
Catechesis/Religious Program—Tel: 773-281-0371, Ext. 14. Students 185.
42—ST. CLOTILDE Rev. John B. Atoyebi. In Res., Rev. Joseph O. Awoyale.
Res.: 8430 Calumet Ave., 60619. Tel: 773-874-1022; Fax: 773-874-1736.
Catechesis/Religious Program—Sr. Theresa Ocloo, E.H.J., D.R.E.
43—ST. COLUMBA (1884) Revs. James F. Nallen; Kilian J. Knittel (Retired).
Res.: 13323 S. Greenbay Ave., 60633. Tel: 773-646-2660; Fax: 773-646-6821.
44—ST. COLUMBANUS Revs. Michael P. Knotek; William E. Vanecko, Senior Priest (Retired); Deacon William McKinnis.
Res.: 331 E. 71st St., 60619. Tel: 773-224-1022; Fax: 773-224-1477.
School—7120 S. Calumet, 60619. Tel: 773-224-3811; Fax: 773-224-3810. Mrs. Sandra E. Wilson, Prin. Lay Teachers 12; Students 243.
Catechesis/Religious Program—Students 35.
45—ST. CONSTANCE (1916) Revs. Thaddeus Dzieszko; Ryszard Gron (Poland); Maciej Galle; Deacons James Schiltz; George Gniech, Pastoral Assoc. In Res., Rev. Wladyslaw Podeszwik (Poland) (Retired).
Res.: 5843 W. Strong St., 60630. Tel: 773-545-8581; Fax: 773-545-0227. Email: church@stconstance.org. Web: www.stconstance.org.
School—5841 W. Strong St., 60630. Tel: 773-283-2311; Fax: 773-283-3515. Mrs. Eva M. Panczyk, Prin. Lay Teachers 13; Students 129.
Catechesis/Religious Program—Sr. Elzbieta Barnowska, M.C.H.R., D.R.E. 81 English; 351 Polish. Students 140.
46—ST. CORNELIUS Revs. Daniel R. Fallon; Edwin D. Pacocha (Retired); Deacons Carl D. Olson; Edward Condon.
Res.: 5205 N. Lieb Ave., 60630. Tel: 773-283-5222; Fax: 773-283-8484.
School—Tel: 773-283-2192; Fax: 773-283-1377. Ms. Christina Bowman, Prin. Lay Teachers 13; Students 193.
Catechesis/Religious Program—Students 100.
47—CORPUS CHRISTI Rev. Raphael Ezeh, M.S.P.
Corpus Christi Friary—4920 King Dr., 60615-2306. Tel: 773-285-7720; Fax: 773-285-2572.
Catechesis/Religious Program—Students 20.
48—ST. DANIEL THE PROPHET Revs. John T. Noga; Slawomir Kurc (Poland); Michael E. Flynn; Deacon Richard Voytas.
Parish Office & Res.: 5300 S. Natoma Ave., 60638. Tel: 773-586-1223; Fax: 773-583-1238. Email: stdaniel1@attglobal.net.
School—Tel: 773-586-1225; Fax: 773-586-1232. Mrs. Mary F. Porod, Prin. Lay Teachers 27; Students 642.
Catechesis/Religious Program—Tel: 773-229-8794. Students 147.
49—ST. DENIS Rev. Theodore L. Ostrowski.
Res.: 8301 S. St. Louis Ave., 60652. Tel: 773-434-3313; Fax: 773-776-3922. Email: stdenis@archchicago.org.
Catechesis/Religious Program—Students 58.
50—ST. DOROTHY Rev. Robert J. Miller; Deacon Wallace Harris.
Res.: 450 E. 78th St., 60619. Tel: 773-651-7000; Fax: 773-651-0969.
School—7740 S. Eberhart Ave., 60619. Tel: 773-783-0555; Fax: 773-783-3736. Mr. Robert J. Zeegers, Prin. Sisters of the Presentation of the Blessed Virgin Mary 1; Lay Teachers 14; Students 217.
Catechesis/Religious Program—Tel: 773-651-7000; Fax: 773-651-0969. Joycelyn A. King, D.R.E. Students 29.
51—ST. EDWARD Revs. Michael J. Cronin; James D. Beath; John J. Donohue (Retired). In Res., Revs. Joseph C. Taylor (Retired); James P. McIlhone.
Res.: 4350 W. Sunnyside Ave., 60630-4146. Tel: 773-545-6496; Fax: 773-545-1136.
School—4343 W. Sunnyside Ave., 60630-4146. Tel: 773-736-9133; Fax: 773-736-9280. Dominican Sisters (Springfield, IL) 4; Lay Teachers 22; Students 336.
Catechesis/Religious Program—Students 148.
52—ST. ELIZABETH Rev. Richard Andrus, S.V.D.
Res.: 50 E. 41st St., 60653. Tel: 773-373-8638; Fax: 773-268-2640. Email: stelizabethchicago@sbcglobal.net.
School—4052 S. Wabash, 60653. Tel: 773-548-4100; Fax: 773-373-8642. Mrs. Danielle D. Graham-Harris, Prin. Sisters 2; Lay Teachers 13; Students 218.
Catechesis/Religious Program—Students 231.
Convent—4117 S. Michigan, 60653. Tel: 773-373-8630.
53—EPIPHANY Revs. Daniel Long; Stephen F. Lesniewski.
Res.: 2524 S. Keeler Ave., 60623. Tel: 773-521-1112; Fax: 773-521-4394. Web: www.epiphanychicago.org.
School—4223 W. 25th St., 60623. Tel: 773-762-1542. Mr. David S. Burke, Prin. Lay Teachers 13; Students 196.
Catechesis/Religious Program—Students 255.
54—ST. ETHELREDA, Closed. Consult Archives and Records Center for parish records. (See St. Kilian parish for school information).
55—ST. EUGENE Revs. George Koeune; Philip J. Grib, S.J.; Jerome Twarog; James J. O'Brien, M.A. (Retired); Deacons James Cozzo Jr.; Edward O'Leary.
Res.: 7958 W. Foster Ave., 60656-1651. Tel: 773-775-6659; Fax: 773-775-2832. Email: churchoffice@st-eugene.org. Web: www.st-eugene.org.
School—7930 W. Foster Ave., 60656-1651. Tel: 773-763-2235; Fax: 773-763-2775. Dr. Patricia M. Brown, Prin. Lay Teachers 17; Students 295.
Catechesis/Religious Program—Students 132.
56—ST. FELICITAS Rev. Gregory A. Rom; Sr. Kathleen Smith, Pastoral Assoc.; Deacon John Cook. In Res., Rev. John Bosco Mujuni (Uganda).
Res.: 1526 E. 84th St., 60619. Tel: 773-734-2300; Fax: 773-731-5381.
Catechesis/Religious Program—Students 15.
57—ST. FERDINAND (1927) Revs. Zdzislaw J. Torba; Robert M. Pajor; Michak Rosa; Albert G. Judy, O.P.; Raymond E. O'Connor, C.M.F.; Mariusz P. Stefanowski; Deacons Irwin Hotcaveg; Ron Weiner; Mr. Marcin Wojtulewicz, Fin. Mgr.
Res.: 5900 W. Barry Ave., 60634. Tel: 773-622-5900; Fax: 773-622-5903. Web: www.saintferdinand.org.
High School—Notre Dame High School, 3115 N. Mason Ave., 60634. Tel: 773-622-9494; Fax: 773-622-8511. Email: dpiekarski@ndhs4girls.org. Web: www.ndhs4girls.org. Denise Piekarski, Prin.; Dr. Lucine Mastalerz, Pres.; Mr. Bill Barnum, Info Tech Mgr. Sisters of Notre Dame de Namur. Lay Teachers 18; Girls 150.
School—3131 N. Mason Ave., 60634. Tel: 773-622-3022; Fax: 773-622-2807. Dr. Lucine Mastalerz, Prin. Lay Teachers 18; Students 272.
Catechesis/Religious Program—Tel: 773-622-5900, Ext. 366. Sr. Anna Strycharz, M.Ch.R., D.R.E. Students 1,419.
Convent—5936 W. Barry Ave., 60634. Tel: 773-889-7979. Missionary Sisters of Christ the King for Polonia 4.
58—ST. FIDELIS, Closed. Consult Archives and Records Center for parish and school records.
59—FIVE HOLY MARTYRS Revs. Wojciech Baryski, S.Ch.; Wieslaw Berdowicz, S.Ch.
Res.: 4327 S. Richmond St., 60632. Tel: 773-254-3636; Fax: 773-254-3609. Email: fiveholymartyrs@yahoo.com.
School—Pope John Paul II School, Five Holy Martyrs Campus, 4325 S. Richmond St., 60632. Tel: 773-523-6161; Fax: 773-254-9194. Lay Teachers 13; Students 190.
Catechesis/Religious Program—Students 58.
60—ST. FLORIAN (1905) Revs. James A. Mezydlo; William J. Lisowski (Retired).
Res.: 13145 S. Houston Ave., 60633. Tel: 773-646-4877; Fax: 773-646-5965. Email: stflorian@archchicago.org. Web: florian.hegewisch.net.
School—13110 S. Baltimore Ave., 60633. Tel: 773-646-2868; Fax: 773-646-2891. Ms. Deborah J. Poturalski, Prin. Lay Teachers 11; Students 115.
Catechesis/Religious Program—Students 71.
61—ST. FRANCIS BORGIA (1949) Revs. Richard Milek; Piotr Gnoinski; Alessandro DiTaddeo; Deacons Robert Cnota; Casimir Fronczek; Ralph Hinch;

William Lehman, (Retired). In Res., Revs. Joseph A. Mulcrone; Robert I. Grib, S.J.
Res.: 8033 W. Addison St., 60634. Tel: 773-625-1118; Fax: 773-625-1110. Web: www.stfrancisborgiachicago.org.
School—Tel: 773-589-1000; Fax: 773-589-0781. Mrs. Connie J. Kohler, Prin. Lay Teachers 12; Students 261.
Catechesis/Religious Program—Tel: 773-625-1705; Fax: 773-625-1774. Students 115.
Convent—3521 N. Panama St., 60634. Tel: 773-625-8063.

62—ST. FRANCIS DE SALES Revs. Edilberto Ramon; Bernardo Lozano Hernandez.
Res.: 10201 S. Ewing Ave., 60617. Tel: 773-734-1383; Fax: 773-734-3022.

63—ST. FRANCIS OF ASSISI, (Hispanic), Revs. Francisco Liporace, I.V.E.; Ruben Rios, I.V.E., Parochial Vicar; Deacons J. Zeferino Ochoa; Manuel Rodriguez.
Res.: 813 W. Roosevelt Rd., 60608. Tel: 312-226-7575; Fax: 312-226-6283.
Catechesis/Religious Program—Tel: 312-226-7575; Fax: 312-226-6283. Students 570.

64—ST. FRANCIS OF ASSISI Rev. Lawrence M. Choate, O.S.M., Admin.; Deacon Sabino Sanchez.
Res.: 932 N. Kostner, 60651. Tel: 773-235-3132; Fax: 773-486-7726.
Catechesis/Religious Program—Students 90.

65—ST. GABRIEL (1880) Revs. James E. Merold (Retired); Richard C. Creagh.
Res.: 4522 S. Wallace St., 60609. Tel: 773-268-9595; Fax: 773-268-9586. Email: saintgabes@saintgabes.com. Web: www.saintgabes.com.
Church: 45th St. & Lowe Ave., 60609. Fax: 773-268-9568.
School—607 W. 45th St., 60609. Tel: 773-268-6636; Fax: 773-268-2501. Mr. Theodore H. Morgan, Prin. Lay Teachers 16; Students 184.
Catechesis/Religious Program—Students 90.

66—ST. GALL Rev. Gary M. Graf; Deacons Michael Slajchert; Albert Herrera; John Bumbul; Raymundo Diaz DeLeon. In Res., Rev. Marco A. Mercado.
Res.: 5511 S. Sawyer Ave., 60629. Tel: 773-737-3113; Fax: 773-737-0272.
School—5515 S. Sawyer Ave., 60629. Tel: 773-737-3454. Ms. Janie C. Flores, Prin. Lay Teachers 15; Students 287.
Catechesis/Religious Program—Students 875.

67—ST. GELASIUS, Closed. Consult Archives and Records Center for parish and school records.

68—ST. GENEVIEVE Revs. Salvador Den Hallegado; Thomas F. Maher, Pastor Emeritus (Retired); Norman H. Mosan-Rosero; Eugenio F. Bernas; Sr. Jean Michael Rafferty, S.P., Pastoral Assoc.; Deacon Miguel A. Valle.
Res.: 4835 W. Altgeld St., 60639. Tel: 773-237-3011; Fax: 773-237-3043.
School—4854 W. Montana St., 60639. Tel: 773-237-7131; Fax: 773-237-7265. Mrs. Marie B. Neis, Prin. Lay Teachers 15; Students 171.
Catechesis/Religious Program—Tel: 773-637-6086; Fax: 773-237-3043. Students 326.

69—ST. GEORGE, (Slovenian), Most Rev. Joseph N. Perry, Admin.; Revs. Phillip C. Kiley; Pascal K. Kamanzi, S.X.
Res.: 9546 S. Ewing Ave., 60617. Tel: 773-734-0554; Fax: 773-734-3327.
Catechesis/Religious Program—Tel: 773-734-1383. Students 96.

70—ST. GERTRUDE Revs. Dominic J. Grassi; William G. Kenneally, Pastor Emeritus (Retired); Dr. Peter Buttitta, Dir. Ministries. In Res., Rev. Michael Bradley.
Res.: 1420 W. Granville Ave., 60660. Tel: 773-764-3621; Fax: 773-761-4164. Email: stgertrude1420@sbcglobal.net. Web: www.stgertrudechicago.org.
School—Northside Catholic Academy, 6216 N. Glenwood Ave., 60660. Tel: 773-743-6277; Fax: 773-743-6174. Lay Teachers 22; Students 450.
Catechesis/Religious Program—Students 79.

71—GOOD SHEPHERD Revs. Donald J. Nevins; Donald J. Lund, Pastor Emeritus (Retired); Deacon Martin Enciso. In Res., Most Rev. John R. Manz; Rev. Sergio de la Torre Carrillo.
Res.: 2719 S. Kolin Ave., 60623. Tel: 773-762-2322; Fax: 773-762-4885.
Catechesis/Religious Program—Students 390.

72—ST. GREGORY, THE GREAT Revs. Paul H. Wachdorf; Brian J. Fischer; Sr. Barbara Quinn, S.N.D.deN., Pastoral Assoc.; Scott Snider, Pastoral Assoc. In Res., Rev. John P. Moulder.
Office: 5545 N. Paulina St., 60640.
Res.: 1634 W. Gregory St., 60640. Tel: 773-561-3546; Fax: 773-728-3827. Email: info@stgregory.net. Web: www.stgregory.net.
High School—1677 W. Bryn Mawr Ave., 60660. Tel: 773-907-2100; Fax: 773-907-2120. Lay Teachers 17; Students 200.
Catechesis/Religious Program—Students 85.

73—ST. HEDWIG Revs. Stanislaw Jankowski, C.R.; Tomasz Wojciechowski, C.R. In Res., Revs. Marcelo de Jesusmaria, C.R.; Eugene Szarek, C.R.; Deacons Gilberto Cintron; Daniel Cabrera.
Res.: 2226 N. Hoyne Ave., 60647. Tel: 773-486-1660; Fax: 773-486-1684. Email: sthedwig@sbcglobal.net. Web: www.sthedwigrcchurch-bucktown.org.
Catechesis/Religious Program—Students 24.

74—ST. HELEN Rev. Waldemar Stawiarski.
Res.: 2315 W. Augusta Blvd., 60622. Tel: 773-235-3575; Fax: 773-235-3810. Email: sthelen@archchicago.org. Web: www.sthelenparish.net.
School—2347 W. Augusta Blvd., 60622. Tel: 773-486-1055. Mrs. Marianne I. Johnson, Prin. Lay Teachers 20; Students 366.
Catechesis/Religious Program—Fax: 773-235-3810. Students 75.

75—ST. HELENA OF TGHE CROSS Revs. Honoratus C. Mwageni (Rwanda); Leo Tinkatumire; Deacons Daniel Sutton; Tommy West; Clayton Kort.
Res.: 10121 S. Parnell Ave., 60628. Tel: 773-779-2243; Fax: 773-779-2749.
School—10115 S. Parnell Ave., 60628. Tel: 773-238-5432; Fax: 773-238-6026. Ms. Marylou Piazza, Prin. Lay Teachers 9; Students 188.
Catechesis/Religious Program—

76—ST. HENRY Revs. Dominic Vinh Van Ha; Bernard C. White (Retired); Deacon Duc Van Nguyen.
Res.: 6335 N. Hoyne Ave., 60659. Tel: 773-764-7413; Fax: 773-764-5994.
Catechesis/Religious Program—Students 65.

77—ST. HILARY (1926) Revs. William A. Eddy; Robert G. Darow, Pastor Emeritus (Retired); Roger J. Caplis, Pastor Emeritus (Retired); Arthur J. Olsen; Deacons Donald Wehling; Daniel G. Welter.
Res.: 5600 N. Fairfield Ave., 60659. Tel: 773-561-3474; Fax: 773-561-1129.
School—5614 N. Fairfield Ave., 60659. Tel: 773-561-5885; Fax: 773-561-6409. Mr. Michael G. Neis, Prin. Lay Teachers 22; Students 299.
Catechesis/Religious Program—Students 80.

78—HOLY ANGELS Rev. John B. Atoyebi; Deacons Leroy Gill Jr.; Mervin O. Johnson.
Res.: 615 E. Oakwood Blvd., 60653. Tel: 773-624-5375; Fax: 773-624-8393. Email: holyangelschurch@comcast.net. Web: www.holyangels.com.
School—750 E. 40th St., 60653. Tel: 772-624-0727; Fax: 773-538-9683. Priests 2; Sisters 3; Lay Teachers 22; Students 300.
Catechesis/Religious Program—Sr. Theresa Ocloo, E.H.J., D.R.E.

79—HOLY CROSS/IMMACULATE HEART OF MARY Revs. Bruce L. Wellems, C.M.F.; Mark J. Brummel, C.M.F.; Jose Marino Novoa, C.M.F.; Hector M. Navalo, C.M.F.; Vito E. Mikolaitis (Retired). In Res., Rev. George Ruffolo, C.M.F.
Res.: 4557 S. Wood St., 60609. Tel: 773-376-3900; Fax: 773-376-8929. Email: hcihm@claret.org. Web: www.hcihm.org.
Catechesis/Religious Program—Students 397.

80—HOLY FAMILY Rev. Jeremiah M. Boland, Admin.; Deacon Rudolph Kotleba, (Retired).
Res.: 1080 W. Roosevelt Rd., 60608. Tel: 312-492-8442; Fax: 312-492-8430. Web: www.holyfamilychurchchicago.org.
Catechesis/Religious Program—Students 30.

81—HOLY INNOCENTS Rev. Philip E. Cyscon; Very Rev. Marek Kasperczuk (Poland).
Res.: 743 N. Armour St., 60622. Tel: 312-666-3675; Fax: 312-666-0714. Email: holyinnocents743@aol.com.
Catechesis/Religious Program—1448 W. Superior St., 60622. Tel: 312-243-9887; Fax: 312-243-4524. Students 225.
Bishop Abramowicz Seminary—1447 W. Superior St., 60622. Tel: 312-455-0598.

82—HOLY NAME OF MARY Rev. James F. Flynn.
Res.: 11159 S. Loomis St., 60643. Tel: 773-238-6800; Fax: 773-238-7304.
Mission—Sacred Heart 11652 S. Church St., Cook Co. 60643. Tel: 773-233-3955.
Catechesis/Religious Program—

83—HOLY ROSARY Rev. Michael V. Kalck; Deacon Jorge Rozo.
Res.: 612 N. Western Ave., 60612. Tel: 773-278-4820; Fax: 773-278-3770. Web: www.holyrosaryonwesternave.org.
Catechesis/Religious Program—Students 81.

84—HOLY ROSARY-113TH, Closed. Consult Archives and Records Center for parish and school records.

85—HOLY TRINITY, (Croatian), Closed. For inquiries for parish records contact Archives and Records Center.

86—HOLY TRINITY MISSION, (Polish), Revs. Andrzej Maslejak, S.Ch.; Bogdan Molenda, S.Ch. In Res., Rev. Thadeusz Baniowski, S.Ch.
Res.: 1118 N. Noble St., 60642. Tel: 773-489-4140; Fax: 773-489-5918. Email: parafia@trojcowo.com. Web: www.trojcowo.com.
Catechesis/Religious Program—Students 252.

87—ST. HYACINTH BASILICA Revs. Michal Osuch, C.R.; Francis Rog, C.R.; Steven Bartczyszyn, C.R.; Adam Piasecki, C.R. (Poland); Stanislaw Lasota, C.R. (Poland).
Res.: 3636 W. Wolfram St., 60618. Tel: 773-342-3636; Fax: 773-342-3638. Web: www.sthyacinthbasilica.org.
School—3640 W. Wolfram St., 60618. Tel: 773-342-7550; Fax: 773-384-0581. Ms. Annmarie N. Mahay, Prin. Lay Teachers 12; Students 126.
Catechesis/Religious Program—Students 495.

88—ST. IGNATIUS Revs. Joseph M. Jackson; Elias K. Kithuri; Deacons Raul Mora; Rogelio Soto. In Res., Revs. William P. Grogan; Jackson Colon; Patrick J. McAteer, S.J.
Res.: 6559 N. Glenwood Ave., 60626. Tel: 773-764-5936; Fax: 773-764-4360.
Catechesis/Religious Program—Students 95.

89—IMMACULATE CONCEPTION Revs. Eric Meyer, C.P.; Ronan Newbold, C.P.; Sr. Judy David, S.S.J.-T.O.S.F., Pastoral Assoc.
Res.: 7211 W. Talcott Ave., 60631. Tel: 773-775-3833; Fax: 773-631-1024. Web: www.icparish.net.
School—7263 W. Talcott Ave., 60631. Tel: 773-775-0545; Fax: 773-775-3822. Bernadette Felicione, Prin. Lay Teachers 30; Students 488.
Catechesis/Religious Program—Tel: 773-775-0545, Ext. 216. Students 226.

90—IMMACULATE CONCEPTION (1912), (Lithuanian), Revs. Thomas R. Koys; Armando Morales-Martinez; Edward J. Maxa (Retired); Deacon Roberto Rivas.
Res.: 2745 W. 44th St., 60632-1999. Tel: 773-523-1402; Fax: 773-523-8465. Email: ftkoys@aol.com. Web: www.imcc-chicago.org.
See Pope John Paul II School, Five Holy Martyrs Campus under Five Holy Martyrs, Chicago.
Catechesis/Religious Program—Students 400.

91—IMMACULATE CONCEPTION OF THE BLESSED VIRGIN MARY (1859) Revs. Patrick J. Lee; Ronald Galt (Scotland).
Res.: 1431 N. North Park Ave., 60610. Tel: 312-944-1230; Fax: 312-944-0673. Web: sjicparish.org.
Catechesis/Religious Program—Mrs. Alice Doering, D.R.E.

92—IMMACULATE CONCEPTION OF THE BLESSED VIRGIN MARY Rev. Ricardo Castillo; Deacons Abraham Chavez; Jose M. Sandoval.
Parish Office and Rectory—2944 E. 88th St., 60617. Tel: 773-768-2100.
Church: 88th & Commercial Ave., 60617.
School—8739 S. Exchange, 60617. Tel: 773-375-4674. Sr. Claudia Carrillo, Prin. Students 167.
Catechesis/Religious Program—Tel: 773-221-1423. Jose Delgadillo, D.R.E. Students 125.

93—IMMACULATE HEART OF MARY Revs. James A. Heneghan; Livinus Anweting (Nigeria).
Res.: 3834 N. Spaulding, 60618. Tel: 773-478-1157; Fax: 773-267-6884. Email: FatherJim_ihm@comcast.net. Web: ihm.archchicago.org.
Catechesis/Religious Program—Tel: 773-478-1157, Ext. 16. Students 207.

94—IMMACULATE HEART OF MARY VICARIATE, Closed. See Holy Cross/Immaculate Heart of Mary.

95—SAINT ITA (1900) Revs. David P. Pavlik; Laurence F. Maddock, Pastor Emeritus (Retired); Daniel J. Cassidy; Rodolfo Gaytan Ramirez.
Res.: 1220 W. Catalpa Ave., 60640. Tel: 773-561-5343; Fax: 773-561-5609. Email: stita@archchicago.org.
School—Northside Catholic Academy, 5525 N. Magnolia Ave., 60640. Tel: 773-271-2008; Fax: 773-271-3101. Email: dsullivan@ncaweb.org. Web: www.northsidecatholic.org. Lay Teachers 37; Students 446.
Catechesis/Religious Program—Students 226.

96—ST. JAMES (1855) Rev. Edward Linton, O.S.B.; Deacon Terrence C. Collins.
Mailing Address: 2907 S. Wabash Ave., 60616.
Res.: 2942 S. Wabash Ave., 60616. Tel: 312-842-1919; Fax: 312-842-3612. Web: www.stjameswabash.org.
Catechesis/Religious Program—Students 7.

97—ST. JAMES Revs. Andrzej A. Bartos; John L. Wodniak, Pastor Emeritus (Retired); Jose Antonio Murcia Abellan (Poland); Krzysztof Pankanin (Poland) (Extern); Deacons Salvador Sanchez; Orlando Perez.
Res.: 5730 W. Fullerton Ave., 60639. Tel: 773-237-1474; Fax: 773-237-1546.
Catechesis/Religious Program—Tel: 773-237-1474; Fax: 773-237-1546. Students 740.
Convent—2441 N. Menard Ave., 60639. Tel: 773-637-9187. Missionary Sisters of Christ the King for Polonia 2.

98—ST. JANE DE CHANTAL Revs. Edward J. Cronin, Admin.; Paul B. Marszalek, Pastor Emeritus (Retired); Jon M. Wachala; Deacon Ron Morowczynski.
Res.: 5252 S. Austin Ave., 60638. Tel: 773-767-2411;

Fax: 773-767-2769.
School—5201 S. McVicker Ave., 60638. Tel: 773-767-1130; Fax: 772-767-1387. Ms. Nancy A. Andrasco, Prin. Lay Teachers 13; Students 261.
Catechesis/Religious Program—Students 82.

99—ST. JEROME Revs. Jeremy Thomas; Harold A. Bonin, Pastor Emeritus (Retired); Luis Valerio Romero; Deacons Fritz Jean-Pierre; Raymond Ward, (Retired); Elisco Ramos; Francisco Marin; Victor J. LaCoursiere.
Res.: 1709 W. Lunt Ave., 60626. Tel: 773-262-3170; Fax: 773-262-2834. Email: stjerome-lunt@archchicago.org.
Catechesis/Religious Program—1706 W. Morse Ave., 60626. Tel: 773-262-9880; Fax: 773-262-2834. Students 358.

100—ST. JEROME (1912), (Croatian), Revs. Jozo Grbes, O.F.M.; Ivan M. Strmecki, O.F.M.
Res.: 2823 S. Princeton Ave., Cardinal Stepinac Way, 60616. Tel: 312-842-1871; Fax: 312-842-6427. Email: grbes@aol.com. Web: www.stjeromecroatian.org.
School—2801 S. Princeton Ave., 60616. Tel: 312-842-7668; Fax: 312-842-6427. Mr. Christopher J. Caban, Prin. Lay Teachers 10; Students 213.
Catechesis/Religious Program—2716 S. Princeton Ave., 60616. Tel: 312-842-4077. Students 43.

101—ST. JOACHIM Revs. Robert J. Gilbert; Raphael A. Makori; Deacon Roscoe B. Dixon Jr.
Res.: 700 E. 91st St., 60619. Tel: 773-488-4488; Fax: 773-994-8945. Email: stjoachim@sbcglobal.net.

102—ST. JOHN BERCHMANS Revs. Wayne F. Watts; William B. Gubbins, Pastor Emeritus (Retired); Deacons Jorge Cabrera; Guillermo Mendizabal. In Res., Rev. A. Paul Reicher (Retired).
Res.: 2517 W. Logan Blvd., 60647. Tel: 773-486-4300; Fax: 773-252-5346. Email: info@stjohnberchmans.org. Web: www.stjohnberchmans.org.
School—2511 W. Logan Blvd., 60647. Tel: 773-486-1334; Fax: 773-486-1782. Mrs. Margaret A. Roketenetz, Prin. Lay Teachers 23; Students 239.
Catechesis/Religious Program—Students 99.

103—ST. JOHN BOSCO (1934) Revs. Timothy Zak, S.D.B.; Gregory Fishel, S.D.B.; Louis Aineto, S.D.B.; Bro. Charles Thenier, S.D.B.; Deacon Ronald Swiatek.
Res.: 2250 N. McVicker Ave., 60639. Tel: 773-622-4620; Fax: 773-622-5040.
Catechesis/Religious Program—2310 N. McVicker Ave., 60639. Tel: 773-836-2413. Sr. Lourdes Ramirez, D.R.E. Students 650.

104—ST. JOHN CANTIUS Revs. C. Frank Phillips, C.R.; Albert Tremari, S.J.C.; Scott Haynes, S.J.C.; Brendan Gibson, S.J.C.; Bartholomew Juncer, S.J.C.
Res.: 825 N. Carpenter St., 60622. Tel: 312-243-7373; Fax: 312-243-4545. Web: www.cantius.org.
Catechesis/Religious Program—Judith Keefe, D.R.E. Students 50.

105—ST. JOHN DE LA SALLE Rev. Avitus L. Rukuratwa. In Res., Revs. John M. Collins; Bernard Okafor.
Res.: 10205 King Dr., 60628. Tel: 773-785-2022.
School—St. John de la Salle Catholic Academy, Tel: 773-785-2331. Mr. Charles Carroll, Prin. Lay Teachers 12; Students 218.
Catechesis/Religious Program—Students 8.

106—ST. JOHN FISHER (1948) Revs. Robert J. Kyfes; Thomas J. Purtell, Pastor Emeritus (Retired); Marion Soprych; Deacons Raymond Reilly; Thomas Siska; Robert Carroll.
Res.: 10234 S. Washtenaw Ave., 60655. Tel: 773-445-6565; Fax: 773-445-1644.
School—10200 S. Washtenaw Ave., 60655. Tel: 773-445-4737; Fax: 773-233-3012. Sr. Jean Anne McGrath, C.S.J., Prin. Sisters of St. Joseph (LaGrange, IL) 1; Lay Teachers 33; Students 705.
Catechesis/Religious Program—Tel: 773-238-1851. Elena Chermak, D.R.E. Students 190.

107—ST. JOSAPHAT (1883) Revs. Richard J. Prendergast; Michael A. Gabriel; Deacon David J. Keene.
Res.: 2311 N. Southport Ave., 60614. Tel: 773-327-8955; Fax: 773-327-2047. Email: mail@stjosaphatparish.org. Web: www.stjosaphatparish.org.
School—2245 N. Southport Ave., 60614. Tel: 773-549-0909; Fax: 773-549-3127. Ms. Coleen M. Canon, Prin. Lay Teachers 28; Students 362.
Catechesis/Religious Program—Dr. Margaret Hanrahan, D.R.E. Students 82.

108—ST. JOSEPH (1846) Rev. Patrick J. Lee. In Res., Rev. Ronald Galt (Scotland).
Res.: 1107 N. Orleans St., 60610. Tel: 312-787-7174; Fax: 312-787-9825. Web: www.sjicparish.org.
Catechesis/Religious Program—Students 115.

109—ST. JOSEPH (1887) Revs. Hugo Leon Londono, M.S.C.; Jon M. Wachala; Dario E. Moreno, M.S.C.
Res.: 4821 S. Hermitage Ave., 60609. Tel: 773-254-2366; Fax: 773-254-2640.
Catechesis/Religious Program—Students 390.

110—ST. JULIANA Revs. Stephen F. Kanonik; Philip J. Dressler, Pastor Emeritus (Retired); Donald J. Ahearn, Pastor Emeritus (Retired); Krzysztof Paluch; Ms. Pam Francisco, Pastoral Assoc. & D.R.E.; Deacons Robert Ryan; Edward Dolan. In Res., Rev. Roger J. Caplis (Retired).
Office: 7200 N. Osceola, 60631. Tel: 773-631-4127; Fax: 773-631-4150.
Res.: 7158 N. Osceola Ave., 60631. Tel: 773-631-4386; Fax: 773-631-4150.
School—7400 W. Touhy, 60631. Tel: 773-631-2256. Lay Teachers 30; Students 549.
Catechesis/Religious Program—Students 342.

111—ST. KEVIN Rev. Pedro Campos.
Res.: 10509 S. Torrence Ave., 60617. Tel: 773-721-2563; Fax: 773-721-2208.
Catechesis/Religious Program—Tel: 708-862-1087; Fax: 773-721-2563. Students 175.

112—ST. KILIAN Rev. Francis Ibanga, M.S.P.; Deacon Warren Allen.
Res.: 8725 S. May St., 60620. Tel: 773-651-4000; Fax: 773-651-5876.
School—St. Ethelreda, 8734 S. Paulina St., 60620. Tel: 773-238-1757; Fax: 773-238-6059. Lay Teachers 12; Students 220.
Catechesis/Religious Program—Students 20.

113—ST. LADISLAUS (1914) Revs. Jacek Wrona (Poland); William J. Lisowski, Pastor Emeritus (Retired); Jan Mucha (Poland); Andrzej Bartosz (Poland).
Res.: 5345 W. Roscoe St., 60641. Tel: 773-725-2300; Fax: 773-725-6042. Email: stladislaus@sbcglobal.net. Web: www.stladislauschurch.org.
School—3330 N. Lockwood Ave., 60641. Tel: 773-545-5600; Fax: 773-545-5676. Mrs. Linda L. Brusky, Prin. Sisters of the Holy Family of Nazareth (Des Plaines, IL) 1; Lay Teachers 13; Students 161.
Catechesis/Religious Program—Tel: 773-545-5809; Fax: 773-545-4340. Students 217.
Convent—5330 W. Henderson St., 60641. Tel: 773-545-1811; Fax: 773-545-4340.

114—ST. LAURENCE, Closed. Consult Archives and Records Center for parish and school records.

115—ST. LEO THE GREAT, Closed. Consult Archives and Records Center for parish and school records.

116—ST. MALACHY + PRECIOUS BLOOD Rev. Matthew Eyerman; Deacons Mario Avila; David Castaneda; Dexter Watson.
Res.: 2248 W. Washington Blvd., 60612. Tel: 312-733-1068; Fax: 312-491-9164. Email: stmalachy@sbcglobal.net.
School—2252 W. Washington Blvd., 60612. Tel: 312-733-2252; Fax: 312-733-5703. Ms. Mary B. Miller, Prin. Sisters 1; Lay Teachers 14; Students 245.
Catechesis/Religious Program—Students 250.

117—ST. MARGARET MARY Rev. James L. Barrett; Deacon Neba Ambe. In Res., Revs. Donatus Chukwu (Nigeria); Harold B. Murphy (Retired).
Res.: 2324 W. Chase Ave., 60645. Tel: 773-764-0615; Fax: 773-764-0641.
School—Tel: 773-764-0641; Fax: 773-764-1095. Ms. Margaret M. Finnegan, Prin. Lay Teachers 15; Students 191.
Catechesis/Religious Program—Students 91.

118—ST. MARGARET OF SCOTLAND Most Rev. Joseph N. Perry, Admin.; Revs. Daniel J. Mallette (Retired); Claude Souffrant, S.J.
Res.: 9837 S. Throop St., 60643. Tel: 773-779-5151; Fax: 773-779-6198.
School—9833 S. Throop St., 60643. Tel: 773-238-1088; Fax: 773-238-1049. Mr. Rickey F. Harris, Prin. School Sisters of Notre Dame 2; Lay Teachers 13; Students 177.
Shelter—St. Margaret of Scotland-Heartland. Tel: 773-371-2500; Fax: 773-371-2515. Students 35.
Catechesis/Religious Program—Students 55.

119—ST. MARK Rev. Elmer Romero; Deacons Jorge Gutierrez; Antonio Villalobos; Antonio Navarro; Kenneth Velasquez, Pastoral Assoc. In Res., Most Rev. Enrique Rivera Hernandez (Puerto Rico).
Res.: 1048 N. Campbell Ave., 60622. Tel: 773-342-1516; Fax: 773-342-1372. Email: stmarkparish@comcast.net.
Catechesis/Religious Program—Francisco Cardona, D.R.E.

120—ST. MARTIN DE PORRES Rev. Maurizio Binaghi, M.C.C.J.; Deacons Anthony Llorens; William Pouncy. In Res., Rev. Paul J. Ewers, M.C.C.J.
Res.: 5112 W. Washington Blvd., 60644. Tel: 773-287-0206; Fax: 773-261-2344.

121—ST. MARY MAGDALENE Revs. Freddy Washington, C.S.Sp.; Clement Uchendu, C.S.Sp. In Res. Congregation of the Holy Ghost (Spiritans), Rev. James C. Okoye, C.S.Sp.
Res.: 8426 S. Marquette Ave., 60617. Tel: 773-768-1700; Fax: 773-734-8518.
Catechesis/Religious Program—Students 125.

122—ST. MARY OF PERPETUAL HELP Rev. Donald R. Craig.
Res.: 1039 W. 32nd St., 60608. Tel: 773-927-6646; Fax: 773-523-4565. Email: stmaryph@aol.com.
Catechesis/Religious Program—Students 40.

123—ST. MARY OF THE ANGELS Revs. Hilary F. Mahaney; Joseph P. Landauer; Charles M. Ferrer; Deacon Glenn Tylutki.
Res.: 1850 N. Hermitage Ave., 60622. Tel: 773-278-2644; Fax: 773-278-8904. Email: info@stmaryoftheangels.net. Web: www.stmaryoftheangels.net.
School—1810 N. Hermitage Ave., 60622. Tel: 773-486-0119; Fax: 773-486-0996. Ms. Elizabeth M. Dolack, Prin. Lay Teachers 15; Students 172.
Catechesis/Religious Program—Students 175.

124—ST. MARY OF THE ASSUMPTION (1886), Closed 6/30/2011 & merged with Queen of Apostles, Riverdale.

125—ST. MARY OF THE LAKE (1901) Rev. James J. Kastigar; Deacons Paul Spalla; Ubaldo Munoz. In Res., Revs. Daniel J. Collins (Retired); Paul A. Choorathottiyil.
Res.: 4200 N. Sheridan Rd., 60613. Tel: 773-472-3711; Fax: 773-327-2899. Web: www.smolchicago.com.
School—1026 W. Buena Ave., 60613. Tel: 773-281-0018; Fax: 773-281-0112. Ms. Christine M. Boyd, Prin. Lay Teachers 11; Students 281.
Catechesis/Religious Program—Students 94.

126—ST. MARY OF THE WOODS (1952) Revs. Patrick G. Cecil; Leo T. Mahon, Pastor Emeritus (Retired); Michael J. Owen; Deacons William Mages; James Thompson; Marcia Mahoney, Pastoral Assoc. & D.R.E. In Res., Rev. Donald J. Headley (Retired).
Res.: 7033 N. Moselle Ave., 60646. Tel: 773-763-0206; Fax: 773-763-4968. Email: smowparish@sbcglobal.net. Web: www.smow.org.
School—Tel: 773-763-7577; Fax: 773-763-4293. Mr. Patrick J. Kelly, Prin. Lay Teachers 27; Students 436.
Catechesis/Religious Program—Students 235.

127—ST. MARY, STAR OF THE SEA (1948) Rev. John J. McDonnell; Rev. Msgr. Michael J. Adams, Pastor Emeritus (Retired); Revs. James D. Beath; Victor Correa-Roballo (Colombia); Deacons Jesse Navarro; Jesus Ochoa; Gregory Serratore. In Res., Rev. Charles Balskus (Retired).
Res.: 6435 S. Kilbourn Ave., 60629. Tel: 773-767-1246; Fax: 773-735-3894. Email: stmary-sea@archchicago.org. Web: stmarystarofthesea.archchicago.org.
School—6424 S. Kenneth Ave., 60629. Tel: 773-767-6160. Mrs. Evelyn M. Califfe, Prin. Lay Teachers 16; Students 259.
Catechesis/Religious Program—Tel: 773-767-7078; Fax: 773-767-7077. Therese A. Navarro, D.R.E. Students 325.

128—MATERNITY OF THE BLESSED VIRGIN MARY Revs. Thomas Pelton; Kevin M. Birmingham, Pastor Emeritus; Deacons Jorge Garcia; Felipe Gonzalez; Floro Hita; Milton Rodriguez; Jose Vazquez.
Res.: 3647 W. North Ave., 60647. Tel: 773-772-9401; Fax: 773-772-7454.
School—1537 N. Lawndale Ave., 60651. Tel: 773-227-1140; Fax: 773-227-2939. Mr. Daniel C. Fleming, Prin. Lay Teachers 12; Students 165.
Catechesis/Religious Program—Students 263.

129—ST. MATTHIAS Rev. John J. Sanaghan; Deacon Rolando Merced.
Res.: 2310 W. Ainslie St., 60625. Tel: 773-506-2191; Fax: 773-506-2418.
School—4910 N. Claremont Ave., 60625. Tel: 773-784-0999; Fax: 773-784-3601. Ms. Sandria F. Desapio, Prin. Lay Teachers 20; Students 292.
Catechesis/Religious Program—Students 138.

130—ST. MAURICE, Closed. Consult Archives and Records Center for parish and school records.

131—ST. MICHAEL ARCHANGEL, (Italian), Closed. Consult Archives and Records Center for parish records.

132—ST. MICHAEL IN OLD TOWN (1852) Revs. Thomas Santa, C.Ss.R.; Thomas Donaldson, C.Ss.R.; Kenneth Sedlak, C.Ss.R.; Joseph J. Morin, C.Ss.R. In Res., Revs. John Paul Andree, C.Ss.R.; Anthony Judge, C.Ss.R.; Arturo Uribe, C.Ss.R.; John Kuehner, C.Ss.R.; John Phelps, C.Ss.R.; James Keena, C.Ss.R.; Maurice J. Nutt, C.Ss.R.; Gregory Schmitt, C.Ss.R.
Res.: 1633 N. Cleveland Ave., 60614. Tel: 312-642-2498; Fax: 312-642-9283. Email: stmichael@st-mikes.org. Web: www.st-mikes.org.
Catechesis/Religious Program—Tel: 312-943-4767. Mrs. Mary Catherine Meek, D.R.E. Students 61.

133—ST. MICHAEL THE ARCHANGEL Revs. Robert R. Perez; Guido Gutierrez. In Res., Rev. John S. Breslin.
Res.: 8237 S. Shore Dr., 60617. Tel: 773-734-4921; Fax: 773-734-8723. Email: info@stmichaelchicago.org. Web: www.stmichaelchicago.org.
School—8231 S. Shore Dr., 60617. Tel: 773-221-0212; Fax: 773-734-8732. Ms. Bridget M. Agnew, Prin. Lay Teachers 10; Students 169.
Catechesis/Religious Program—Students 49.

134—ST. MICHAEL THE ARCHANGEL, (Slovak), Revs. Thomas E. Cima; John E. Tilford.

Res.: 4821 S. Damen Ave., 60609. Tel: 773-523-1248; Fax: 773-523-0955. Email: sma48@ameritech.net.
Catechesis/Religious Program—Students 255.

135—ST. MONICA Revs. Fred W. Tomzik; George W. Klein, Pastor Emeritus (Retired); Andrew Izyk; Deacons Ken Jenney, Pastoral Assoc.; Ron Gronek; Edward Podgorski. In Res., Revs. William M. Holbrook (Retired); James J. O'Brien, M.A. (Retired).
Office: 5136 N. Nottingham Ave., 60656. Tel: 773-763-1661; Fax: 773-763-4917.
Res.: 5135 N. Mont Clare Ave., 60656.
School—Tel: 773-631-7880; Fax: 773-631-3266. Raymond Coleman, Prin.; Christopher Haruska, Asst. Prin. Lay Teachers 26; Students 417.
Catechesis/Religious Program—Tel: 773-631-7810; Fax: 773-763-4917. Christine Perenchio, D.R.E. Students 361.

136—NATIVITY OF OUR LORD (1868) Revs. Joseph W. Altman; Thomas Joyce, C.M.F., Senior Priest; Deacons Francis Henry; Erik Zeimys. In Res., Rev. Michael Flynn, O.Carm.; Rev. Msgr. Richard P. Hynes.
Res.: 653 W. 37th St., 60609. Tel: 773-927-6263; Fax: 773-847-0600. Email: fatherdan@nativitybridgeport.org. Web: www.nativitybridgeport.org.
See Bridgeport Catholic Academy, Chicago under Consolidated Elementary Schools, located in the Institution section.
Catechesis/Religious Program—Students 110.

137—NATIVITY OF THE BLESSED VIRGIN MARY Rev. Jaunius Kelpsas (Lithuania), Admin.; Rev. Msgr. John A. Kuzinskas, Pastor Emeritus (Retired); Deacon Vitas Paskauskas. In Res., Rev. Thomas J. Mescall.
Res.: 6812 S. Washtenaw Ave., 60629. Tel: 773-776-4600; Fax: 773-776-0677.
School—6820 S. Washtenaw Ave., 60629. Tel: 773-476-0571; Fax: 773-476-0065. Mr. Robert Gawlik, Prin. Lay Teachers 5; Students 93.
Convent—6804 S. Washtenaw Ave., 60629. Tel: 773-476-5135.

138—ST. NICHOLAS OF TOLENTINE (1909) Revs. Jose Sequeira; Francisco Ortega Munoz; Deacon Pablo Perez.
Res.: 3721 W. 62nd St., 60629. Tel: 773-735-1121; Fax: 773-735-1135. Email: stnicholas-tolentine@archchicago.org. Web: www.stnicksparish.org.
School—3743 W. 62nd St., 60629. Tel: 773-735-0772; Fax: 773-735-5414. Ms. Mariagnes Menden, Prin. Lay Teachers 10; Students 231.
Catechesis/Religious Program—Tel: 773-284-2635. Students 28.

139—NOTRE DAME DE CHICAGO (1864) Rev. Msgr. Patrick J. Pollard; Revs. A. Paul Reicher, Pastor Emeritus (Retired); JoAndre Beltran; Megan Mio, Pastoral Assoc. In Res., Most Rev. Alberto Rojas; Rev. Dennis R. Karamitis, S.J.; Very Rev. Michael A. Hack; Rev. Robert L. Tuzik.
Res.: 1335 W. Harrison St., 60607-3318. Tel: 312-243-7400; Fax: 312-243-7614. Email: nddechgo@aol.com. Web: www.nddc.archchicago.org.
School—Children of Peace School, 1900 W. Taylor St., 60612. Tel: 312-243-8186; Fax: 312-243-8479. Ms. Arlene E. Redmond, Prin.
School—Holy Trinity School for the Deaf, Tel: 312-243-0785.
Catechesis/Religious Program—Students 100.

140—OLD ST. MARY Revs. Michael J. Kallock, C.S.P.; Richard Sparks, C.S.P.
Res.: 1500 S. Michigan, 60605. Tel: 312-922-3444; Fax: 312-922-3447. Web: www.oldstmarys.com.
School—1532 S. Michigan Ave., 60605. Tel: 312-386-1560; Fax: 312-386-1560. Web: www.osmschool-.com. Dr. Mary L. Calihan, Prin. Students 203.
Catechesis/Religious Program—Students 62.

141—OLD ST. PATRICK'S (1846) Revs. Thomas J. Hurley; John C. Cusick. In Res., Rev. John J. Wall.
Res.: 700 W. Adams St., 60661. Tel: 312-648-1021; Fax: 312-648-9025. Web: www.oldstpats.org.
Shrine—Shrine of Our Lady of Pompeii, Tel: 312-421-3757; Fax: 312-421-3756.
Catechesis/Religious Program—Bea Cunningham, D.R.E. Students 555.

142—OUR LADY GATE OF HEAVEN (1848) Rev. Mel Hermanns, O.F.M.Cap.
Res.: 2338 E. 99th St., 60617. Tel: 773-375-3059; Fax: 773-375-3046. Email: OL-GateOfHeaven@archchicago.org.
Catechesis/Religious Program—Students 26.

143—OUR LADY HELP OF CHRISTIANS, Closed. Consult Archives and Records Center for parish and school records.

144—OUR LADY OF AGLONA, (Latvian), Closed. Consult Archives and Records Center for mission records.

145—OUR LADY OF FATIMA Rev. Nestor Saenz (Peru).
Res.: 2751 W. 38th Pl., 60632. Tel: 773-927-2421; Fax: 773-247-1737. Email: ol-fatima@archchicago.org.
Catechesis/Religious Program—Sr. Yesenia Saldarriaga, C.R.E. Students 246.

146—OUR LADY OF GOOD COUNSEL, Closed. Consult Archives and Records Center for parish and school records.

147—OUR LADY OF GRACE Rev. George L. Schopp; Sr. Florence Norton, S.P., Pastoral Assoc.; Deacons James Kwasigroch; Enrique Alonso; Ernesto Robles; Juan Ramirez. In Res., Rev. Lawrence E. Gorski.
Res.: 2455 N. Hamlin Ave., 60647. Tel: 773-772-5900; Fax: 773-276-4469.
School—2446 N. Ridgeway Ave., 60647. Tel: 773-342-0170; Fax: 773-342-5305. Dominican Sisters (Springfield, IL) 7; Lay Teachers 9; Students 190.
Catechesis/Religious Program—Students 53.

148—OUR LADY OF GUADALUPE Revs. Carl J. Quebedeaux, C.M.F.; Thomas Moran, C.M.F.; Deacons Raul Nunez; Jose M. Estrada; Ramon Jimenez. In Res., Revs. Severino Lopez, C.M.F.; Ferdinand Okorie, C.M.F.; Manuel Villalobos, C.M.F.
Res.: 3200 E. 91st, 60617. Tel: 773-768-0793; Fax: 773-768-3245. Email: olg@claretians.org.
School—9050 S. Burley, 60617. Tel: 773-768-0999; Fax: 773-768-0529. Mr. Michael Hughes, Prin. Lay Teachers 11; Students 204.
Shrine—National Shrine of St. Jude, Tel: 312-236-7782; Fax: 312-236-7230. (Claretian Missionaries)
Catechesis/Religious Program—9049 S. Brandon, 60617. Tel: 773-734-0605. Students 434.

149—OUR LADY OF LOURDES Revs. Michael J. Shanahan; Manuel G. Padilla; Deacon Daniel Patino. In Res., Rev. Richard E. Bulwith.
Res.: 4640 N. Ashland Ave., 60640. Tel: 773-561-2141; Fax: 773-561-9853. Email: ol-lourdes-ashland@archchicago.org. Web: www.ololchicago.parishesonline.com.
Catechesis/Religious Program—Students 325.

150—OUR LADY OF LOURDES, Closed. Consult Archives and Records Center for parish and school records.

151—OUR LADY OF MERCY Revs. Joseph P. Tito; Donald J. Headley, Pastor Emeritus (Retired); Jorge L. Estrada; Deacons Manuel R. Del Llano; Robert Janega; Aurelio Garcia; Ms. Theresita Perez, Dir. Evangelization & Formation.
Res.: 4432 N. Troy St., 60625. Tel: 773-588-2620; Fax: 773-866-1838. Email: ol-mercy@archchicago.org. Web: www.olmchicago.com.
Catechesis/Religious Program—4414 N. Troy St. (2nd door bell), 60625. Tel: 773-588-1637; Fax: 773-588-1638. Students 650.

152—OUR LADY OF MOUNT CARMEL Revs. Thomas E. Srenn; Thomas I. Healy, Pastor Emeritus (Retired); Phillip F. Cioffi; John N. Dondapati, A.L.C.P./O.S.S.; Deacons Edmund Gronkiewicz; Thomas Lambert; Richard Johnson.
Office: 708 W. Belmont, 60657. Tel: 773-525-0453; Fax: 773-525-9438. Email: olmcinfo@aol.com. Web: www.mt-carmel.org.
Res.: 690 W. Belmont, 60657.
School—720 W. Belmont Ave., 60657. Tel: 773-525-8779; Fax: 773-525-7810. Mr. Shane P. Staszcuk, Prin. Lay Teachers 21; Students 248.
Catechesis/Religious Program—Students 42.

153—OUR LADY OF PEACE Rev. Mark Kalema; Deacon Rameau Buissereth.
Res.: 7851 S. Jeffery Blvd., 60649. Tel: 773-768-0105; Fax: 773-721-3835.
Catechesis/Religious Program—Students 40.

154—OUR LADY OF POMPEII, See separate listing. See Old St. Patrick, Shrine of Our Lady of Pompeii

155—OUR LADY OF SORROWS, BASILICA OF Revs. Christopher M. Krymski, O.S.M.; Robert J. Warsey, O.S.M.; Deacon Davis Fair. In Res., Revs. Vidal M. Martinez, O.S.M.; John R. LeMay, O.S.M.
Res.: 3121 W. Jackson Blvd., 60612. Tel: 773-638-0159; Fax: 773-638-3036. Email: olsparish@olsparish-chicago.org. Web: www.ols-chicago.org.
Catechesis/Religious Program—Students 22.

156—OUR LADY OF TEPEYAC Revs. Rigoberto Gamez-Alfonso (Colombia); Ernesto Vargas Cuellar (Colombia); Deacons Ramon Echevarria; Jesse Blanco.
Res.: 2226 S. Whipple St., 60623. Tel: 773-521-8400; Fax: 773-521-4890.
School—2235 S. Albany, 60623. Tel: 773-522-0024; Fax: 773-522-4577. Lay Teachers 13; Students 172.
High School—2228 S. Whipple St., 60623. Tel: 773-522-0023; Fax: 773-522-0508. Sisters 1; Lay Teachers 15; Students 176.
Catechesis/Religious Program—Tel: 773-277-0320. Students 388.

157—OUR LADY OF THE SNOWS Rev. Stanley G. Rataj; Deacon Francisco Foti.
Res.: 4858 S. Leamington Ave., 60638. Tel: 773-582-2266; Fax: 773-582-3363.
School—4810 S. Leamington Ave., 60638. Tel: 773-735-4810; Fax: 773-582-3363. Mrs. Joyce M. Willenborg, Prin. Lay Teachers 10; Students 163.
Catechesis/Religious Program—Tel: 773-582-4904. Students 139.

158—OUR LADY OF VICTORY Rev. Robert M. Fedek; Deacons Robert Leck; Michael Ahern. In Res., Rev. Abraham M. Jacob (SYM).
Res.: 5212 W. Agatite Ave., 60630. Tel: 773-286-2950; Fax: 773-286-8579. Web: www.olvchicago.org.
School—4434 N. Laramie, 60630. Tel: 773-283-2229; Fax: 773-283-0842. Sr. M. Zachary Sergeena, O.P., Prin. Students 209.
Catechesis/Religious Program—Mary Beth Frystak, D.R.E. Students 113.

159—OUR LADY, MOTHER OF THE CHURCH (1966) Rev. Richard J. Klajbor.
Res.: 8747 W. Lawrence Ave., 60656. Tel: 773-625-3369; Fax: 773-625-0226.
Catechesis/Religious Program—Jackie Froehlich, D.R.E. Students 173.

160—ST. PANCRATIUS (1924) Rev. Bronislaw Chmiel.
Res.: 4025 S. Sacramento Ave., 60632. Tel: 773-523-5666; Fax: 773-523-3115.
Catechesis/Religious Program—Students 19.

161—ST. PASCAL Revs. Paul G. Seaman; Pawel Zemczak; Deacons Eugene Dorgan; Thomas Stubstad; J. Frank Marquez. In Res., Rev. Thomas M. Dore (Retired).
Res.: 3935 N. Melvina Ave., 60634. Tel: 773-725-7641; Fax: 773-725-9368. Email: StPascal@archchicago.org. Web: www.stpascal.org.
School—6143 W. Irving Park Rd., 60634. Tel: 773-736-8806; Fax: 773-725-3461. Ms. Denise H. Akana, Prin. Lay Teachers 14; Students 152.
Ciezadlo Center—3954 N. Meade Ave., 60634. Tel: 773-545-9453.
Catechesis/Religious Program—Tel: 773-725-7641, Ext. 22. Students 96.

162—ST. PAUL (1876) Rev. Michael P. Enright; Deacon Juan J. Gomez.
Res.: 2127 W. 22nd Pl., 60608. Tel: 773-847-7622; Fax: 773-847-8687.
School—2114 W. 22nd Pl., 60608. Tel: 773-847-6078; Fax: 778-847-2118. Dr. Roy J. Pletsch, Prin. Sisters 2; Lay Teachers 10; Students 119.
Catechesis/Religious Program—Students 115.

163—SS. PETER AND PAUL Rev. Pascal Bigirimana, Admin. (Extern). In Res., Rev. Bruno T. Kaharuza.
Res.: 12433 S. Halsted St., 60628. Tel: 773-785-1200.

164—SS. PETER AND PAUL, Closed. Consult Archives and Records Center for parish and school records.

165—ST. PETER CANISIUS, Closed. Consult Archives and Records Center for parish and school records.

166—ST. PETER'S Rev. Kurt Hartrich, O.F.M.
St. Peter's Friary—110 W. Madison St., 60602. Tel: 312-372-5111; Fax: 312-853-2361. Email: stpeter-madison@archchicago.org. Web: stpetersloop.org. (For complete listing of residents see Section N Residences of Priests and Brothers.) Priests 14; Brothers 6.

167—ST. PHILIP NERI Rev. Thomas G. Belanger; Deacon Willie Cooper; Odessa Foster, Pastoral Assoc. In Res., Most Rev. Joseph N. Perry; Rev. William H. Sheridan (Retired).
Res.: 2132 E. 72nd St., 60649. Tel: 773-363-1700; Fax: 773-363-1718.
School—2110 E. 72nd St., 60649. Tel: 773-288-1138; Fax: 773-288-8252. Ms. Linda Sauders, Prin. Lay Teachers 3; Students 91.
Catechesis/Religious Program—Lay Teachers 94.

168—ST. PHILOMENA Rev. Jesus Puentes (Colombia), Admin.; Deacons Francisco Ramos; Benjamin Diaz.
Res.: 1921 N. Kedvale Ave., 60639. Tel: 773-489-1100; Fax: 773-489-1088.
Catechesis/Religious Program—Tel: 773-342-3462. Students 471.

169—ST. PIUS V Revs. Brendan A. Curran, O.P.; Matthias R. Mueller, O.P. In Res., Revs. Charles W. Dahm, O.P.; Mark Paraday, O.P.
Office: 1919 S. Ashland Ave., 60608. Tel: 312-226-6161. Web: www.stpiusvparish.org.
Res.: 1914 S. Ashland Ave., 60608. Tel: 312-829-1931; Fax: 312-226-7265.
School—1919 S. Ashland Ave., 60608. Tel: 312-226-1590. Mrs. Nancy Nasko, Prin. Lay Teachers 13; Students 208.
Catechesis/Religious Program—Sisters 138.
Shrine—Shrine of St. Jude Thaddeus, Tel: 312-226-0020; Fax: 312-226-6440. Web: www.shrineofsaint-jude.com.

170—PRECIOUS BLOOD, Closed. Consult Archives and Records Center for parish and school records.

171—PRESENTATION, Closed. Consult Archives and Records Center for parish and school records.

172—ST. PRISCILLA Revs. Idzi Stacherczak; Daniel K. Kusa.
Res.: 6949 W. Addison St., 60634. Tel: 773-545-8840; Fax: 773-545-8919.
Catechesis/Religious Program—Tel: 773-685-3785. Students 97.

173—ST. PROCOPIUS Rev. Sean A. O'Sullivan, S.J. (Ireland); Deacon Candelario Rodriguez. In Res.,

Rev. John P. Foley, S.J.
Res.: 1641 S. Allport St., 60608. Tel: 312-226-7887; Fax: 312-226-0812.
School—Tel: 312-421-5135; Fax: 312-492-8368. Lay Teachers 14; Students 232.
Catechesis/Religious Program—Students 341.

174—PROVIDENCE OF GOD Rev. Alejandro Garrido.
Res.: 717 W. 18th St., 60616. Tel: 312-226-2929; Fax: 312-226-3694. Email: providence@archchicago.org. Web: www.providenceofgod.com.
Catechesis/Religious Program—1814 S. Union, 60616. Students 192.

175—QUEEN OF ALL SAINTS BASILICA Rev. Msgr. John Pollard; Revs. Thomas J. Campana; Simon F. Braganza (India); Deacons Michael Monnelly; William Malloy; Sr. Ann Kathleen McDonnell, B.V.M., Pastoral Assoc. In Res., Rev. Msgr. Wayne Prist (Retired); Revs. Richard Conyers, C.S.C.; Edward D. Grace.
Res.: 6280 N. Sauganash Ave., 60646. Tel: 773-736-6060; Fax: 773-736-6099. Web: qasparish.org.
School—Tel: 773-736-0567. Ms. Stephanie M. DiPrima, Prin. Sisters 3; Lay Teachers 25; Students 582.
Catechesis/Religious Program—Students 336.

176—QUEEN OF ANGELS (1909) Rev. Msgr. James T. Kaczorowski; Deacon Bienvenido Nieves. In Res., Rev. John M. Griffiths.
Parish Office—4412 N. Western Ave., 60625. Tel: 773-539-7510; Fax: 773-539-3408. Email: parish@queenofangelschicago.org. Web: parish.queenofangelschicago.org.
Res.: 2330 W. Sunnyside Ave., 60625.
School—4520 N. Western Ave., 60625. Tel: 773-769-4211; Fax: 773-769-4289. Mrs. Julia B. Kelly, Prin. Lay Teachers 27; Students 414.
Catechesis/Religious Program—Students 180.

177—QUEEN OF THE UNIVERSE Revs. Victor Zuniga, M.S.P.; Alejandro Medina Vasquez, M.S.P.
Res.: 7114 S. Hamlin Ave., 60629. Tel: 773-582-4662; Fax: 773-581-3313. Email: quniverseparish@yahoo.com.
School—7130 S. Hamlin Ave., 60629. Tel: 773-582-4266; Fax: 773-585-7254. Ms. Jessica Lopez, Prin. Lay Teachers 14; Students 210.
Catechesis/Religious Program—Students 74.

178—ST. RENE GOUPIL Revs. Thomas R. Kasputis; Peter P. Paurazas (Retired); Deacon Salvatore Lema.
Res.: 6949 W. 63rd Pl., 60638. Tel: 773-229-8523; Fax: 773-229-1252. Email: strenec6949@earthlink.net. Web: www.strenegoupilchicago.com.
School—6340 S. New England Ave., 60638. Tel: 773-586-4414; Fax: 773-586-3747. Paula Calvert, Prin. Lay Teachers 13; Students 226.
Catechesis/Religious Program—Students 86.

179—RESURRECTION Revs. Paul J. Kalchik; Thomas A. Tivy (Retired); Fernando Zuleta; Deacons Paul Bovyn; Uriol Rodriguez; Efrain Lopez; Juan Gonzalez; Francisco Rivera.
Business Office—3043 N. Francisco Ave., 60618. Tel: 773-478-9705; Fax: 773-478-1387.
Catechesis/Religious Program—Students 175.

180—ST. RICHARD Revs. Thomas A. Bernas; Jon M. Wachala; Deacon Lawrence J. Chyba.
Office: 5030 S. Kostner Ave., 60632.
Res.: 5032 S. Kostner Ave., 60632. Tel: 773-585-1221; Fax: 773-585-4959.
School—5025 S. Kenneth Ave., 60632. Tel: 773-582-8083; Fax: 773-582-8330. Ms. Patricia A. Adduci, Prin. Lay Teachers 19; Students 346.
Catechesis/Religious Program—Students 73.

181—ST. RITA OF CASCIA Revs. Anthony B. Pizzo, O.S.A.; David Vargas-Grajales, O.S.A.; Deacon David D. Andrade; Jenny Meehan, Pastoral Assoc. In Res., Revs. Michael J. Slattery, O.S.A.; Bernard R. Danber, O.S.A.; Edward J. Kersten, O.S.A.; Christopher C. Steinle, O.S.A.
Res.: 6243 S. Fairfield Ave., 60629. Tel: 773-434-9600; Fax: 773-434-9668. Email: ritaparishosa@ameritech.net.
Catechesis/Religious Program—Students 236.

182—ST. ROBERT BELLARMINE Revs. Neil E. Fackler; Michael A. Goergen (Retired); Deacon Antonio Delgado. In Res., Rev. L. Scott Donahue.
Res.: 4646 N. Austin Ave., 60630-3157. Tel: 773-777-2666; Fax: 773-777-2770. Web: www.srb-chicago.org.
School—6036 W. Eastwood Ave., 60630. Tel: 773-725-5133; Fax: 773-777-2770. Mrs. Carrie A. Mijal, Prin. Sisters 5; Lay Teachers 15; Students 239.
Catechesis/Religious Program—Tel: 773-286-0956. Students 155.

183—ST. ROMAN Rev. Walter Yepes.
Res.: 2311 S. Washtenaw Ave., 60608. Tel: 773-247-6645; Fax: 773-927-1610.
Catechesis/Religious Program—Students 384.

184—ST. SABINA Revs. Michael L. Pfleger; Thulani D. Magwaza.
Res.: 1210 W. 78th Pl., 60620. Tel: 773-483-4300; Fax: 773-483-7583.
School—7801 S. Throop St., 60620. Tel: 773-483-5000; Fax: 773-483-7583. Mrs. Helen Dumas, Prin. Dominican Sisters (Sinsinawa, WI) 1; Sisters (Congregation of Mother of Carmel) 3; Lay Teachers 14; Students 306.
Catechesis/Religious Program—Students 201.

185—SACRED HEART, (Croatian), Rev. Stephen Bedenikovic, O.F.M.
Res.: 2864 E. 96th St., 60617. Tel: 773-768-1423; Fax: 773-768-3750.
School—2906 E. 96th St., 60617. Tel: 773-773-3728; Fax: 773-768-5034. Mr. Stephen J. Adams, Prin. School Sisters of St. Francis 3; Lay Teachers 8; Students 150.
Catechesis/Religious Program—Students 26.

186—SACRED HEART MISSION OF HOLY NAME OF MARY Rev. James F. Flynn.
Res.: 11652 S. Church St., 60643. Tel: 773-233-3955.
Catechesis/Religious Program—Students 36.

187—SANTA LUCIA-SANTA MARIA INCORONATA Rev. Nicholas A. Marro, C.S.
Res.: 3022 S. Wells St., 60616. Tel: 312-842-6115; Fax: 312-842-0103. Email: bersantalucia@hotmail.com.
School—3017 S. Wells St., 60616. Tel: 312-326-1839; Fax: 312-326-1945. Geraldine Maratea, Prin. Lay Teachers 12; Students 145.
Catechesis/Religious Program—Students 34.

188—SANTA MARIA ADDOLORATA (1903) Revs. Jesus Reyes, C.S.; Gino Dalpiaz, C.S.; Deacons Arthur DeLuna; Luis Perez. In Res., Most Rev. Lawrence P. Sabatini, C.S.
Res.: 528 N. Ada St., 60642. Tel: 312-421-3122; Fax: 312-421-4814. Email: santamariaaddolorata@yahoo.com.
Catechesis/Religious Program—Students 141.

189—ST. SIMON THE APOSTLE Revs. Lyle Gundrum, O.F.M.Cap.; Francis Q. Kub; Laura L. Zbella, Pastoral Assoc. In Res., Rev. August Sewbert, O.F.M.Cap.
Res.: 5157 S. California Ave., 60632. Tel: 773-436-1045; Fax: 773-436-4684. Email: stsimonchurch@comcast.net. Web: www.stsimontheapostle.org.
Catechesis/Religious Program—Students 378.

190—ST. STANISLAUS KOSTKA, (Polish—Spanish), Rev. Anthony Bus, C.R.; Deacons Nicolas Flores; Miguel Garcia.
Res.: 1351 W. Evergreen Ave., 60622. Tel: 773-278-2470; Fax: 773-278-2471.
School—1255 N. Noble St., 60622. Tel: 773-278-4560; Fax: 773-278-9097. Ms. Marjorie Hill, Prin. Sisters 1; Lay Teachers 16; Students 188.
Catechesis/Religious Program—Students 119.

191—ST. STANISLAUS, BISHOP AND MARTYR Revs. Anthony Dziorek, C.R.; Richard Balazs, C.R.; Deacon Mitchell Szady.
Res.: 5352 W. Belden Ave., 60639. Tel: 773-237-5800; Fax: 773-237-7029.
Catechesis/Religious Program—Students 38.

192—ST. STEPHEN, KING OF HUNGARY Revs. Nicholas R. Desmond, Admin.; Sandor Siklodi.
Res. & Office: 2015 W. Augusta Blvd., 60622-6062. Tel: 773-486-1896; Fax: 773-486-1902.
Catechesis/Religious Program—Students 7.

193—ST. SYLVESTER (1884) Rev. Paul Stein; Deacons Sigifredo Ortiz; Emiliano Rodriguez.
Res.: 2915 W. Palmer St., 60647. Tel: 773-235-3646; Fax: 773-489-0974.
School—3027 W. Palmer Blvd., 60647. Tel: 773-772-5222; Fax: 773-722-0352. Mr. Daniel F. Bennett, Prin. Lay Teachers 14; Students 250.
Catechesis/Religious Program—Tel: 773-772-9082. Students 495.

194—ST. SYMPHOROSA AND SEVEN SONS Rev. Thaddeus J. Bojczuk; Rev. Msgr. Francis N. Maniola, Pastor Emeritus (Retired); Revs. Norman J. Trela; Mariusz J. Nawalaniec (Poland).
Res.: 6135 S. Austin Ave., 60638. Tel: 773-767-1523; Fax: 773-767-6135.
School—6125 S. Austin Ave., 60638. Tel: 773-585-6888; 773-585-6804; Fax: 773-585-8411. Ms. Margaret Mary Kowalczyk, Prin. Lay Teachers 17; Students 325.
Catechesis/Religious Program—Students 238.

195—ST. TARCISSUS (1926) Revs. Michael J. Salazzo; Daniel P. McCarthy; Krzysztof D. Ciaston; Leonard J. Felczak (Retired); John J. Grace (Retired); Michael Leonard (Ireland); Deacon Gregory M. Bzdon.
Res.: 6020 W. Ardmore Ave., 60646. Tel: 773-763-8228; Fax: 773-774-8461. Email: mail_sttars@sbcglobal.net. Web: www.sttars.org.
School—6040 W. Ardmore Ave., 60646. Tel: 773-763-7080; Fax: 773-775-3593. Mr. Roy C. Hecker, Prin. Lay Teachers 23; Students 375.
Catechesis/Religious Program—Students 173.

196—ST. TERESA OF AVILA Rev. Frank J. Latzko; Deacon Hector Rivera.
Parish Office: 1930 N. Kenmore, 60614-4139. Tel: 773-528-6650; Fax: 773-871-6766. Email: secretary@stteresaparish.org. Web: www.st-teresa.net.
Cardinal Bernardin Early Childhood Center—1651 W. Diversey Pkwy., 60614. Tel: 773-975-6330; Fax: 773-975-6339. Web: www.cbecc.org. Sr. Barbara Jean Ciszek, C.S.J., Prin.
Catechesis/Religious Program—Students 136.

197—ST. THADDEUS Rev. Frank M. Sasso.
Res.: 9540 S. Harvard Ave., 60628. Tel: 773-568-7077; Fax: 773-928-5447.
Catechesis/Religious Program—Students 12.

198—ST. THECLA Revs. Gene J. Dyer; Gerald E. Rogala (Retired); Wojciech A. Marat (Poland); Deacons John Rottman; Robert Cnota; Steven Wagner.
Res.: 6725 W. Devon Ave., 60631. Tel: 773-792-3077; Fax: 773-792-3820. Email: parish@saintthecla.org. Web: www.saintthecla.org.
School—6323 N. Newcastle Ave., 60631. Tel: 773-763-3380; Fax: 773-763-6151. Mrs. Carol Styka, Prin. Lay Teachers 17; Students 239.
Catechesis/Religious Program—Students 140.

199—ST. THERESE CATHOLIC CHINESE CHURCH Rev. Dong Ping, F.L.
Res.: 218 W. Alexander St., 60616. Tel: 312-842-6777; Fax: 312-567-1389.
School—247 W. 23rd St., 60616. Tel: 312-326-2837; Fax: 312-326-6068. Mrs. Phyllis Cavallone-Jurek, Prin. Sisters 4; Lay Teachers 17; Students 296.
Catechesis/Religious Program—Students 269.

200—ST. THOMAS APOSTLE Revs. Elias O'Brien, O.Carm.; Michael Mulhall, O.Carm.; Kevin McBrien, O.Carm.
Res.: 5472 S. Kimbark Ave., 60615. Tel: 773-324-2626; Fax: 773-753-7415. Web: www.stahydepark.org.
School—5467 S. Woodlawn Ave., 60615. Tel: 773-667-1142; Fax: 773-753-7434. Ms. Marianne Scheidt, Prin. Lay Teachers 20; Students 171.
Catechesis/Religious Program—Students 65.

201—ST. THOMAS MORE Revs. Charles V. Fanelli; Juan C. Gavancho; Marek Sitar; Deacon George Borha. In Res., Revs. John P. Frawley (Retired); John F. McGrath (Retired).
Res.: 2825 W. 81st St., 60652. Tel: 773-436-4444; Fax: 773-778-9087. Email: stmrc@comcast.net.
Convent—8120 S. California, 60652. Tel: 773-737-9440. Congregation of the Mother of Carmel 6; Sinsinwa Dominicans 1.
Catechesis/Religious Program—Students 17.

202—ST. THOMAS OF CANTERBURY (1916) Rev. Daniel F. Costello; Deacon Antonio Rodriguez. In Res., Rev. Trinh Peter Hung, Senior Priest.
Res.: 4827 N. Kenmore Ave., 60640. Tel: 773-878-5507.
School—Tel: 773-271-8655; Fax: 773-271-1624. Ms. Christine M. Boyd, Prin. Lay Teachers 9; Students 264.
Catechesis/Religious Program—

203—ST. TIMOTHY Revs. Peter Fernandes, S.F.X. (India); Harold B. Murphy (Retired).
Res.: 6326 N. Washtenaw Ave., 60659. Tel: 773-262-6600; 773-262-6665; Fax: 773-262-9214. Email: sttimothy@archchicago.org. Web: www.sttimothychgo.com.
Catechesis/Religious Program—Fax: 773-262-9214. Students 50.

204—TRANSFIGURATION OF OUR LORD Revs. Alfredo J. Salera; John J. Rudnik, Pastor Emeritus (Retired); Americo Dalbello.
Res.: 2609 W. Carmen Ave., 60625. Tel: 773-561-7953; Fax: 773-561-7635. Email: transofourlordcc@aol.com.
Catechesis/Religious Program—Karyn McGovern, D.R.E. Students 185.

205—ST. TURIBIUS Rev. William E. Lego, O.S.A.; Rev. Msgr. Joseph L. Mroczkowski (Retired); Rev. John J. Dowling, O.S.A.
Res.: 5646 S. Karlov Ave., 60629. Tel: 773-581-2730; Fax: 773-581-5396.
School—4120 W. 57th St., 60629. Tel: 773-585-5150; Fax: 773-585-5328. Felician Sisters 3; Lay Teachers 11; Students 232.
Catechesis/Religious Program—Sr. Mary Beth Bromer, C.S.S.F., D.R.E. Students 213.

206—ST. VIATOR (1888) Revs. Charles G. Bolser, C.S.V.; Christopher J. Glancy, C.S.V.
Res.: 4170 W. Addison St., 60641. Tel: 773-286-4040; Fax: 773-286-4122.
School—4140 W. Addison St., 60641. Tel: 773-545-2173; Fax: 773-794-1697. Ms. Kathleen Kowalski, Prin. Lay Teachers 17; Students 204.
Catechesis/Religious Program—Students 157.

207—ST. VINCENT DE PAUL (1875) Rev. Christopher S. Robinson, C.M.; Deacon Dean G. Vaeth.
Res.: 1010 W. Webster Ave., 60614. Tel: 773-325-8610; Fax: 773-325-8626. Email: info@stvdep.org. Web: www.stvdep.org.

208—ST. WALTER Revs. Peter J. Heidenrich; Charles W. Watkins, Admin.; Deacon James Deiters.

Res.: 11722 S. Oakley Ave., 60643. Tel: 773-779-1515; Fax: 773-779-0381. Email: stwalterchgo@aol.com. Web: www.stwalter.com.
School—11741 S. Western Ave., 60643. Tel: 773-445-8850; Fax: 773-445-0277. Sisters 5; Lay Teachers 13; Students 230.
Catechesis/Religious Program—Students 247.

209—ST. WENCESLAUS Rev. Jacek Praski, C.R.; Deacons Feliciano Crespo; Jamie Rios. In Res., Revs. John H. Nowak, C.R.; Jerzy Matuszak.
Res.: 3400 N. Monticello Ave., 60618. Tel: 773-588-1135; Fax: 773-588-3735.
Catechesis/Religious Program—Students 124.

210—ST. WILLIAM (1916) Revs. Robert J. Lojek; Edmond Aristil, C.S.Sp. (Haiti); Deacons Dennis Colgan; Edward Simola; Juan Ponce De Leon.
Res.: 2600 N. Sayre Ave., 60707. Tel: 773-637-6565; Fax: 773-637-7042. Email: stwilliam@archchicago.org. Web: www.stwilliamelmwoodpark.parishesonline.com.
School—2559 N. Sayre Ave., 60707. Tel: 773-637-5130; Fax: 773-745-4208. Mr. Laszio G. Katona, Prin. Lay Teachers 13; Students 163.
Catechesis/Religious Program—Students 100.

OUTSIDE THE CITY OF CHICAGO

ALSIP, COOK CO., ST. TERRENCE Rev. Edward J. Barrett; Deacon Richard Miska.
Res.: 4300 W. 119th Pl., 60803. Tel: 708-597-0970; Fax: 708-597-9118. Email: stterrence@comcast.net. Web: www.stterrence.org.
Catechesis/Religious Program—Tel: 708-597-0754. Students 403.

ANTIOCH, LAKE CO.

1—ST. PETER Revs. Michael F. McMahon; Ronald H. Anglim, Pastor Emeritus (Retired); Dean F. Semmer; Deacons Robert A. Gagnon; Paul M. Neurauter; Jonathan Thompson.
Res.: 557 W. Lake St., 60002. Tel: 847-395-0274; Fax: 847-395-4553. Email: administration@stpeterantioch.org. Web: www.stpeterantioch.org.
School—900 St. Peter St., 60002. Tel: 847-395-0037; Fax: 847-395-2532. Ms. Christine Mors, Prin. Lay Teachers 14; Students 210.
Catechesis/Religious Program—559 Elizabeth, 60002. Tel: 847-395-0246; Fax: 847-395-2532. Students 462.

2—ST. RAPHAEL THE ARCHANGEL Revs. John A. Jamnicky; Ronald C. Lewandowski, Senior Priest (Retired).
40000 N. U.S. Hwy. 45, Old Mill Creek, 60046. Tel: 847-395-3474; Fax: 847-395-3552. Email: rectory@straphaelcatholic.org. Web: www.straphaelcatholic.org.
Catechesis/Religious Program—Students 191.

ARGO, COOK CO., ST. BLASE (1924) Revs. Wojciech Kwiecien; Jan F. Kaplan.
Res.: 6101 S. 75th Ave., 60501. Tel: 708-458-0007; Fax: 708-458-0276. Email: stblase@archchicago.org.
Catechesis/Religious Program—Tel: 708-458-0246 (Spanish & English); 708-458-8772 (Polish); Fax: 708-458-8554 (Spanish & English); 708-458-9560 (Polish). Students 1,236.

ARLINGTON HEIGHTS, COOK CO.

1—ST. EDNA (1965) Revs. Jerome J. Jacob; Benedykt M. Pazdan; Deacons James Gaughan; James Pauwels; Gregory M. Beeber; Joseph Yannotta. In Res., Revs. John J. Hurley, Pastor Emeritus (Retired); Eugene J. Faucher (Retired).
Res.: 2525 N. Arlington Heights Rd., 60004. Tel: 847-398-3362; Fax: 847-394-5226. Email: parishmanager@stedna.org. Web: www.stedna.org.
Catechesis/Religious Program—Students 124.

2—ST. JAMES Revs. William J. Zavaski; Krzysztof A. Kulig; Joji Thanugundla (India); Deacons Matt Hennessy; Paul Schmidt; Pierce Sheehan; Tom Morgan; Matt Hahn; William Reinert; Thomas Westerkamp; Marianne Dilsner, Pastoral Assoc.
Office: 820 N. Arlington Heights Rd., 60004. Tel: 224-345-7200; Fax: 224-345-7220. Email: parishoffice@stjamesah.org. Web: www.stjamesah.org.
School—Tel: 224-345-7145; Fax: 224-345-7140. Judy Pappas, Prin. Lay Teachers 33; Students 494.
Catechesis/Religious Program—Melody Devine, D.R.E. Students 699.

3—MISION SAN JUAN DIEGO Rev. Claudio Diaz Jr.; Deacon Miguel Vargas.
Res.: 2323 North Wilke Rd., 60004. Tel: 847-590-9332; Fax: 847-590-9333.
Catechesis/Religious Program—Students 400.

4—OUR LADY OF THE WAYSIDE Revs. Edward R. Fialkowski; Peter B. McQuinn; Deacons Thomas Corcoran; Donald Grossnickle; Brendan Foley; Donna Cunningham, Pastoral Assoc. In Res., Rev. Daniel J. Brady (Retired).
Res.: 432 W. Park St., 60005. Tel: 847-253-5353; Fax: 847-253-7175. Web: www.olwparish.org.
School—Tel: 847-253-0050; Fax: 847-253-0543. Mr. David W. Wood, Prin. Lay Teachers 36; Students 575.
Catechesis/Religious Program—432 S. Mitchell, 60005. Tel: 847-398-5011; Fax: 847-253-0050. Students 596.

BARRINGTON, LAKE CO., ST. ANNE Revs. Bernard J. Pietrzak; John W. Dewes, Pastor Emeritus (Retired); Thomas Bishop; Fred Licciardi, C.PP.S.; Deacons James Crane; Robert Powers; James Condill; Robert C. Brauch; William T. Karstenson; Sr. Lauretta Leipzig, Pastoral Assoc.
Res.: 120 N. Ela St., 60010. Tel: 847-382-5300; Fax: 847-382-5363.
School—319 E. Franklin St., 60010. Tel: 847-381-0311; Fax: 847-381-0384. School Sisters of St. Francis 6; Lay Teachers 29; Students 450.
Catechesis/Religious Program—Students 861.

BARTLETT, COOK CO., ST. PETER DAMIAN Rev. Walter J. Takuski; Deacons David Sattler; Robert F. Esposito.
Res.: 109 S. Crest Ave., 60103. Tel: 630-837-5411; Fax: 630-837-9424. Email: info@stpeterdamian.org. Web: www.stpeterdamian.org.
Catechesis/Religious Program—Tel: 630-830-2295. Students 638.

BELLWOOD, COOK CO., ST. SIMEON Rev. Kombo L. Peshu. In Res., Rev. Joseph Ekpo; Deacons Victor Chairez; Sergio Lopez.
Res.: 430 Bohland Ave., 60104. Tel: 708-547-6868; Fax: 708-547-7075.
Catechesis/Religious Program—Students 80.

BERWYN, COOK CO.

1—ST. LEONARD Rev. Roger A. Corrales-Diaz; Deacons Peter Morrissey; Jose Cisneros.
Res.: 3318 S. Clarence Ave., 60402. Tel: 708-484-0015; Fax: 708-484-6982.
School—3322 S. Clarence Ave., 60402. Tel: 708-749-3666; Fax: 708-749-7981. Ms. Maureen A. Wilson, Prin. Lay Teachers 12; Students 223.
Catechesis/Religious Program—Tel: 708-795-5919. Students 160.

2—ST. MARY OF CELLE Revs. William J. Stenzel; Orlando Flores; Deacons Philip Gianatasio; Asuncion Valadez.
Res.: 1428 Wesley Ave., 60402. Tel: 708-788-0876; Fax: 708-788-0242. Email: smcrectory@sbcglobal.net. Web: www.stmaryofcelle.org.
Catechesis/Religious Program—Tel: 708-795-6460; Fax: 708-749-2120. Students 161.

3—ST. ODILO Revs. Anthony J. Brankin; Elvio C. Baldeon Lope. In Res., Rev. Msgr. Richard T. Saudis; Rev. Thomas J. Kaveney (Retired).
Res.: 2244 East Ave., 60402. Tel: 708-484-2161; Fax: 708-788-0565. Web: www.saintodilo.org.
School—2301 S. Clarence Ave., 60402. Tel: 708-484-0755; Fax: 708-484-0088. William Donegan, Prin. Sisters of Charity B.V.M. 2; Lay Teachers 12; Students 206.
Catechesis/Religious Program—Students 126.
Shrine—Poor Souls, Tel: 708-484-2161; Fax: 708-788-0565.

BLUE ISLAND, COOK CO.

1—ST. BENEDICT Rev. Ismael Sandoval; Deacons Juan Limon; Abundio Valadez. In Res., Rev. Marco J. Cardenas, C.M.F.
Res.: 2339 York St., 60406. Tel: 708-385-8510; Fax: 708-371-2631.
School—2324 New St., 60406. Tel: 708-385-2016; Fax: 708-385-4490. Mrs. Susan A. Rys, Prin. Lay Teachers 14; Students 192.
Catechesis/Religious Program—Students 238.
Mission—St. Peter Claver 14125 Claire Blvd., Robbins, Cook Co. 60472. Tel: 708-389-2434; Fax: 708-389-2434.

2—ST. DONATUS (1909) Rev. Diego Cadavid, Admin.; Deacon Miguel Luevano.
Res.: 1939 Union St., 60406. Tel: 708-385-2890; Fax: 708-385-4708.
Catechesis/Religious Program—12905 Division St., 60406. Tel: 708-388-7886. Ernesto Vargas, D.R.E. Students 380.

3—ST. ISIDORE Most Rev. Joseph N. Perry, Admin.; Revs. Eze Venantius Umunnakwe, C.S.Sp. (Extern); Casimir Eke, C.S.Sp. (Extern).
Res.: 1811 W. Burr Oak Ave., 60406. Tel: 708-388-0807; Fax: 708-388-5077.

BRIDGEVIEW, COOK CO., ST. FABIAN Revs. Peter J. Cyscon; Robert J. Kash, Pastor Emeritus (Retired); Jan Bukowski, COr (Poland); Deacons Charles Tipperreiter; Kevin O'Donnell; Ronald Zielinski.
Res.: 8300 S. Thomas Ave., 60455. Tel: 708-599-1110; Fax: 708-599-0673. Email: stfabian65@sbcglobal.net. Web: www.saint-fabian.org.
Catechesis/Religious Program—7450 83rd St., 60455. Tel: 708-458-6150; Fax: 708-458-2398. Students 949.

BROOKFIELD, COOK CO.

1—ST. BARBARA Revs. Robert G. Casey; Bolivar G. Molina-Ramirez; Sr. Margaret Halligan, C.S.J., Pastoral Assoc.; Deacons John Debnar; Dave Brencic. In Res., Rev. Michael P. Ahlstrom.
Res.: 4008 Prairie Ave., 60513. Tel: 708-485-2900; Fax: 708-387-0103. Email: stbarbaraprairie@archdiocese.org. Web: www.stbarbaraparish.com.
School—8900 Windemere Ave., 60513. Tel: 708-485-0806; Fax: 708-485-2343. Ms. Janet Erazmus, Prin. Lay Teachers 14; Students 134.
Catechesis/Religious Program—Tel: 708-485-4610. Students 241.

2—CZECH MISSION OF SAINTS CYRIL AND METHODIUS Rev. Dusan Hladik (Czech Republic).
Res.: 9415 Rochester Ave., 60513. Tel: 708-656-7472; Cell: 708-533-1050; Fax: 708-656-7472. Web: www.velehradchicago.home.comcast.net.
Catechesis/Religious Program—

BUFFALO GROVE, LAKE CO., ST. MARY, [CEM] Revs. Marc W. Reszel; Richard E. Sztorc; Deacons Eugene Kukla, Senior Deacon; Gary Long, Senior Deacon; William J. Krueger, Senior Deacon. In Res., Rev. Denis Carneiro (India).
Res.: 10 N. Buffalo Grove Rd., 60089. Tel: 847-541-1450; Fax: 847-541-2443. Web: www.stmarybg.org.
School—50 N. Buffalo Grove Rd., 60089. Tel: 847-459-6270; Fax: 847-537-2810. Ms. Nicole A. Raftery, Prin. Lay Teachers 20; Students 331.
Catechesis/Religious Program—Tel: 847-537-9423; Fax: 847-808-0548. Students 563.

BURBANK, COOK CO., ST. ALBERT THE GREAT Revs. Michael L. Zoufal; Joseph P. Lynch (Retired); Ryszard Czerniak, S.Ch.; Deacon Irvin Bryce.
Res.: 5555 W. State Rd., 60459. Tel: 708-423-0321; Fax: 708-425-4329.
School—5535 W. State Rd., 60459. Tel: 708-424-7757. Mrs. Marilyn E. Kurowski, Prin. Lay Teachers 13; Students 169.
Catechesis/Religious Program—Tel: 708-636-0406. Students 267.

BURNHAM, COOK CO., MOTHER OF GOD Rev. Edmund F. Guz, Pastor Emeritus (Retired).
Res.: 14207 S. Green Bay Ave., 60633. Tel: 708-862-8777; Fax: 708-891-1349.

CALUMET CITY, COOK CO.

1—ST. ANDREW THE APOSTLE (1992) Rev. Jacek A. Dada (Poland); Deacon Robert Banet.
Res.: 768 Lincoln Ave., 60409. Tel: 708-862-4165; Fax: 708-862-4124. Email: a.rectory@comcast.net. Web: www.saintandrewparish.com.
Catechesis/Religious Program—Tel: 708-862-4165. Students 75.

2—OUR LADY OF KNOCK Revs. Patrick M. Lyons; Donald J. Fenske, Pastor Emeritus (Retired); Sr. Alban Hermes, O.P., Pastoral Assoc.; Deacons Edward Ryan; Thomas Knetl.
Res.: 501 163rd St., 60409. Tel: 708-862-3011; Fax: 708-862-9618.
School—Christ Our Savior, (Inter-Parish School), Tel: 708-333-8173; Fax: 708-339-3336. Web: www.christoursaviorcatholicschool.org.
Catechesis/Religious Program—Tel: 708-868-1711. Students 70.

3—ST. VICTOR Revs. Leonard A. Dubi; Alejandro Jesus Marca Mansilla, O.C.D.; Deacon Dan Ragonese.
Res.: 553 Hirsch Ave., 60409. Tel: 708-891-8920; Fax: 708-891-8929. Email: stvictorcc@sbcglobal.net. Web: www.stvictorcc.org.
School—Christ Our Savior, (Inter-Parish School), Tel: 708-333-8173; Fax: 708-333-3247.
Catechesis/Religious Program—Students 135.

CALUMET PARK, COOK CO., SEVEN HOLY FOUNDERS Most Rev. Joseph N. Perry, Admin.; Revs. Deusdedit Byomuhangi; Rogelio Banvelas Castro; Deacon Tomas Herrera.
Res.: 12400 S. Ada St., 60827. Tel: 708-385-8459; Fax: 708-385-2143.
Catechesis/Religious Program—Tel: 708-385-8498. Students 40.

CHICAGO HEIGHTS, COOK CO.

1—ST. AGNES Revs. John S. Siemianowski; William T. O'Mara, Senior Priest (Retired); Deacons Thomas Nowak; David Brothers; Charlene Klabacha, Pastoral Assoc.
Res.: 1501 Chicago Rd., 60411. Tel: 708-709-2694; Fax: 708-709-2693. Web: www.stagnes-parish.org.
School—Mr. Matthew T. Lungaro, Prin. Lay Teachers 16; Students 280.
Catechesis/Religious Program—Students 130.

2—ST. KIERAN Rev. Joseph T. Cook; Deacons Eugene La Belle; David Dutko; Emil Vasek.
Res.: 724 W. 195th St., 60411. Tel: 708-755-0074; Fax: 708-754-2246. Web: www.stkieranchurch.org.
School—700 W. 195th St., 60411. Tel: 708-754-8999; Fax: 708-754-9007. Mr. Anthony G. Simone, Prin. Lay Teachers 12; Students 104.
Catechesis/Religious Program—Tel: 708-754-0484; Fax: 708-754-0484. Students 69.

3—ST. PAUL Rev. Rene Mena Beltran, M.Div.; Deacons Juan L. Garza; Joseph Kudra.
Res.: 206 E. 25th St., 60411. Tel: 708-754-3120; Fax: 708-754-0076.
Catechesis/Religious Program—Tel: 708-754-7720. Students 500.

CHICAGO RIDGE, COOK CO., OUR LADY OF THE RIDGE Revs. Wayne A. Svida; George O. Omwando; Deacons Terris Albano; Edwin Hill; John Orzechowski; Robert J. Landuyt.
Res.: 10811 S. Ridgeland Ave., 60415. Tel: 708-425-3800; Fax: 708-425-2792.
School—10859 S. Ridgeland Ave., 60415. Tel: 708-424-4409. Sr. Stephanie Marie Kondik, O.S.F., Prin. Lay Teachers 11; Students 180.
Catechesis/Religious Program—Tel: 708-424-4949. Students 242.

CICERO, COOK CO.

1—ST. ANTHONY OF PADUA Rev. Sergio Solis; Deacon Gilberto Mercado.
Res.: 1515 S. 50th Ave., 60804. Tel: 708-652-0231; Fax: 708-652-0228.
St. Anthony Center—1510 S. 49th Ct., 60804. Tel: 708-652-0231; Fax: 708-652-0228.
Catechesis/Religious Program—Students 446.

2—ST. FRANCES OF ROME Revs. Mark A. Bartosic; Sergio Mena-Mena; Deacon Javier Pineda. In Res., Rev. Alfred Tumwesigye.
Res.: 1428 S. 59th Ct., 60804. Tel: 708-652-2140; Fax: 708-652-6513.
School—1401 S. Austin Blvd., 60804. Tel: 708-652-2277. Web: www.sfr-school.org. Ms. Patricia Huizar, Prin. Lay Teachers 15; Students 244.
Catechesis/Religious Program—Tel: 708-656-8632. Students 93.

3—ST. MARY OF CZESTOCHOWA (1895), (Polish—Spanish), Revs. Radoslaw Jaszczuk, C.Ss.R.; Waldemar Wieladek, C.Ss.R.; Zbigniew Pienkos, C.Ss.R.
Res.: 3010 S. 48th Ct., 60804. Tel: 708-652-0948; Fax: 708-652-0646. Email: parish@stmaryofczestochowa.org. Web: stmaryofczestochowa.org.
Catechesis/Religious Program—Tel: 708-652-0948; Fax: 708-652-0646. Students 77.

4—MARY, QUEEN OF HEAVEN (1911) Revs. James W. Schulz, S.J.; Hugo Morales; Deacon Armando Herrera.
Res.: 5300 W. 24th St., 60804. Tel: 708-863-6608; Fax: 708-863-2349.
Catechesis/Religious Program—Students 104.

5—OUR LADY OF CHARITY (1954) Revs. Mark A. Bartosic; Sergio Mena-Mena; Wilfred Bwezani Phiri (Zambia); Deacon Antonio Ponce.
Res.: 3600 57th Ct., 60804-4235. Tel: 708-863-1207; Fax: 708-863-1209. Email: office@olc-church.org.
School—3620 57th Ct., 60804. Tel: 708-652-0262; Fax: 708-652-0601. Web: www.olc-school.org. Ms. Katie Molson, Prin. Lay Teachers 14; Students 229.
Catechesis/Religious Program—Students 40.

6—OUR LADY OF THE MOUNT Rev. Adan Sandoval Duron; Deacon Flavio V. Gonzalez.
Res.: 2414 S. 61st Ave., 60804. Tel: 708-652-2791; Fax: 708-863-6014.
Catechesis/Religious Program—Students 100.

COUNTRY CLUB HILLS, COOK CO., ST. EMERIC Revs. Martin T. Marren; John J. Rochford, Pastor Emeritus (Retired); Deacons James Detloff, Senior Deacon; Philip DuBrownik.
Res.: 4330 W. 180th St., 60478. Tel: 708-798-0757; Fax: 708-798-0799. Email: stemeric@comcast.net. Web: stemeric-countryclubhills.e-paluch.com.
Catechesis/Religious Program—Tel: 708-799-4430; Fax: 708-798-0799. Students 69.

DEERFIELD, LAKE CO., HOLY CROSS Revs. Vincent F. Costello; John M. Thinnes, Pastor Emeritus (Retired); Deacons Edward Melton; Kevin Garvey; Jerome Kasimatis; James Carroll; Mary Ann Spina, Pastoral Assoc. In Res., Rev. Dennis Stafford.
Res.: 724 Elder Ln., 60015. Tel: 847-945-0430; Fax: 847-945-7651. Web: www.holycrossparish.net.
School—720 Elder Ln., 60015. Tel: 847-945-0135; Fax: 847-945-0705. Ms. Janice M. Divincenzo, Prin. Lay Teachers 21; Students 276.
Catechesis/Religious Program—Tel: 847-945-0581; Fax: 847-945-0582. Mrs. Becky Phillips, D.R.E. & Youth Ministry. Students 425.

DES PLAINES, COOK CO.

1—ST. MARY Revs. Lawrence Collins; Paul F. Rosemeyer, Pastor Emeritus (Retired); Martin E. Bedoya.
Res.: 794 Pearson St., 60016. Tel: 847-824-8144; Fax: 847-824-3906. Email: stmary-pearson@archchicago.org. Web: www.stmary-dp.org.
School—Our Lady of Destiny, 1880 Ash St., 60018. Tel: 847-827-2900. Linda Chorazy, Prin. Lay Teachers 15; Students 197.
Catechesis/Religious Program—Tel: 847-298-1435; Fax: 847-824-3906. Students 372.

2—ST. PAUL CHONG HASANG Rev. Simeon Ho Chan Cha (Korea, South), Dir.
Res.: 725 Dursey Ln., 60016. Tel: 847-699-6334; Fax: 847-699-1281. Email: stpaul-mission@archchicago.org. Web: www.stpaulchong.org.
Catechesis/Religious Program—Students 195.

3—ST. STEPHEN PROTOMARTYR Rev. Noel Beltran Reyes; Deacons Donald J. Telposky; Anthony Towey; William H. Warmouth; Ivan Lazcano.
1267 Everett Ave., 60018-2398. Tel: 847-824-2026; Fax: 847-824-3842. Email: ststephen@sbcglobal.net. Web: www.ststephen-desplaines.org. In Res., Rev. Michael G. Zaniolo.
School—Our Lady of Destiny, 1880 Ash St., 60018-2343. Tel: 847-827-2900; Fax: 847-827-0475. Lay Teachers 14; Students 171.
Catechesis/Religious Program—Tel: 847-297-3844; Fax: 847-824-3842. Students 85.

4—ST. ZACHARY (1961) Revs. John S. Plotkowski; Augustine Mahonge; Deacons John J. Smith; Sam Pincich; David Brezinski; Michael E. Wundsam. In Res., Rev. Lawrence F. Springer (Retired).
Res.: 567 W. Algonquin Rd., 60016. Tel: 847-956-7020; Fax: 847-981-1448. Email: parishoffice@saintzachary.org. Web: www.saintzachary.org.
School—Fax: 847-758-1064. Ms. Catherine Determann, Prin. Lay Teachers 15; Students 186.
Catechesis/Religious Program—Tel: 847-956-1175. Students 280.

ELK GROVE VILLAGE, COOK CO.

1—ST. JULIAN EYMARD Rev. Leon J. Rezula; Deacon Ted Czarnecki.
Res.: 601 Biesterfield Rd., 60007. Tel: 847-956-0130; Fax: 847-956-0189.
Catechesis/Religious Program—Tel: 847-593-8938. Students 502.

2—QUEEN OF THE ROSARY Rev. Edward Pelrine; Deacon Lawrence J. Smith. In Res., Rev. Robert L. Ebrom.
Res.: 750 Elk Grove Blvd., 60007. Tel: 847-437-0403; Fax: 847-437-8461. Email: sqrm59@comcast.net. Web: www.qotr.org.
School—690 Elk Grove Blvd., 60007. Tel: 847-437-3322; Fax: 847-437-3290. Lay Teachers 19; Students 323.
Catechesis/Religious Program—680 Elk Grove Blvd., 60007. Tel: 847-437-3346; Fax: 847-431-8961. Students 269.

ELMWOOD PARK, COOK CO., ST. CELESTINE Revs. Jeffrey S. Grob; Artur J. Sowa; Patrick J. O'Malley (Retired); Deacon Michael DeLarco. In Res., Rev. Bernard C. White (Retired).
Res.: 3020 N. 76th Ct., 60707. Tel: 708-453-2555; Fax: 708-462-0560. Web: www.stcelestine.org.
School—3017 N. 77th Ave., 60707. Tel: 708-453-8234; Fax: 708-452-0237. Mrs. Jeanine L. Rocchi, Prin. Lay Teachers 24; Students 436.
Catechesis/Religious Program—Students 178.

EVANSTON, COOK CO.

1—ST. ATHANASIUS Revs. Thomas A. Libera; Henan Cuevas.
Res.: 1615 Lincoln St., 60201. Tel: 847-328-1430; Fax: 847-328-1809. Web: www.stathanasius-evanston.org.
School—2510 Ashland Ave., 60201. Tel: 847-864-2650; Fax: 847-475-7385. Mrs. Susan A. Castagna, Prin. Lay Teachers 29; Students 365.
Catechesis/Religious Program—Students 149.

2—ST. MARY Revs. Gregory Sakowicz; Antony A. Joseph; Deacon Dennis R. Robak. In Res., Rev. Kenneth A. Budzikowski.
Parish Center—Res.: 1012 Lake St., 60201. Tel: 847-864-0333; Fax: 847-864-0354. Email: stmary1012@stmaryparish-evanston.org. Web: www.stmaryparish-evanston.org.
School—Tel: 847-475-5678; Fax: 847-475-5683. Consolidated with St. Nicholas Parish to form Pope John XXIII School. See St. Nicholas for further details.
Catechesis/Religious Program—Students 100.

3—ST. NICHOLAS Revs. William Tkachuk; Robert H. Oldershaw, Pastor Emeritus (Retired); James R. Halstead, O.S.A.; Richard Vega; Deacon Mario Tamayo; Suzanne Lefevre, Business Mgr.; Mr. David Philippart, Liturgy Director.
Res.: 806 Ridge Ave., 60202. Tel: 847-864-1185; Fax: 847-864-7810. Email: stnicks@nickchurch.org. Web: www.nickchurch.org.
School—1120 Washington, 60202. Tel: 847-475-5678; Fax: 847-475-5683. Mrs. Rosalie Musiala, Prin. Consolidated with St. Mary Parish to form Pope John XXIII School. Lay Teachers 28; Students 316.
Catechesis/Religious Program—Students 331.

EVERGREEN PARK, COOK CO.

1—ST. BERNADETTE Revs. Gary M. Miller; Joseph W. Seitz, Senior Priest (Retired).
Res.: 9343 Francisco Ave., 60805. Tel: 708-422-8995; Fax: 708-422-8699. Web: stbernardettechurch.org.
School—9311 S. Francisco Ave., 60805. Tel: 708-422-6429; Fax: 708-422-6484. Dominican Sisters (Springfield, IL) 1; Lay Teachers 11; Students 127.
Catechesis/Religious Program—Tel: 708-425-7697. Students 124.

2—MOST HOLY REDEEMER Revs. James M. Hyland; Richard J. Dempsey, Pastor Emeritus (Retired); William J. Devine, Pastor Emeritus (Retired); Matthew Nemchausky; Deacons Alfred Antonsen; Mark Phelan. In Res., Revs. Albert R. Adamich (Retired); Joseph F. Hardy.
Res.: 9525 S. Lawndale Ave., 60805. Tel: 708-425-5354; Fax: 708-346-8182. Web: www.mostholyredeemer.org.
School—9536 S. Millard Ave., 60805. Tel: 708-422-8280; Fax: 708-422-4193. Lay Teachers 24; Students 422.
Catechesis/Religious Program—Tel: 708-346-8185. Students 334.

3—QUEEN OF MARTYRS Revs. Edward M. Mikolajczyk; George Panthananickal, C.M.I.
Res.: 10233 S. Central Park, 60805-3799. Tel: 708-423-8110; Fax: 708-423-7372.
School—3550 W. 103rd St., 60655. Tel: 708-422-1540; Fax: 708-422-1811. Mr. Michael E. Krsek, Prin. Lay Teachers 25; Students 438.
Catechesis/Religious Program—Tel: 708-422-1647. Students 153.

FLOSSMOOR, COOK CO., INFANT JESUS OF PRAGUE Revs. Michael A. Nacius; Ronald P. Stake; William J. Flaherty (Retired); Deacon Samuel E. Howard.
Res.: 1131 Douglas Ave., 60422. Tel: 708-799-5400.
School—1101 Douglas Ave., 60422. Mr. Daniel G. Smith, Prin. Lay Teachers 28; Students 462.

FOREST PARK, COOK CO., ST. BERNARDINE Revs. George Velloorattil; Patrick M. Wangai; Deacon John Walters. In Res., Rev. Abraham Kaduthodil.
Res.: 7246 Harrison St., 60130. Tel: 708-366-0839; Fax: 708-366-3136. Email: saintbernardine@juno.com. Web: www.stbern.com.
School—815 Elgin Ave., 60130. Tel: 708-366-6890; Fax: 708-366-8015. Mr. Robert A. Mass, Prin. Lay Teachers 11; Students 137.
Catechesis/Religious Program—Tel: 708-366-3553. Students 72.

FRANKLIN PARK, COOK CO., ST. GERTRUDE Revs. Eryk Czarnecki (Poland); Alfred P. Corbo, Pastor Emeritus (Retired); Enrique Francisco, Garcia Lozada; Deacons Robert Murphy; Michael Principe.
Res.: 9613 Schiller Blvd., 60131. Tel: 847-455-1100; Fax: 847-455-1209.
Catechesis/Religious Program—9617 Schiller Blvd., 60131. Tel: 847-455-5810. Students 308.

GLENVIEW, COOK CO.

1—ST. CATHERINE LABOURE Revs. Paul Maina Waithaka; Robert G. Mair, Pastor Emeritus (Retired); James P. Murphy, Pastor Emeritus (Retired); Lorenzo Gamboa Cadena; Deacons Ray Gavin; Frank Beil; Alan Sedivy.
Res.: 3535 Thornwood Ave., 60026. Tel: 847-729-1414; Fax: 847-729-5184. Email: sc13535@att.net. Web: www.stcatherinelaboure.com.
School—3425 Thornwood Ave., 60026. Tel: 847-724-2240; Fax: 847-724-5805. Mrs. Laurie A. Konicek, Prin. Lay Teachers 22; Students 312.
Catechesis/Religious Program—Students 280.

2—OUR LADY OF PERPETUAL HELP Revs. Thomas E. Hickey; John E. Flavin, Pastor Emeritus (Retired); Jacek A. Jura; Patrick Tyrrell, S.J. (Ireland); Gerald G. Walsh; Elliott Richard Dees; Deacons James Revord; David Kalina. In Res., Rev. Lawrence P. McBrady.
Res.: 1775 Grove St., 60025. Tel: 847-729-1525; Fax: 847-729-0623. Email: OL-Help@archchicago.org. Web: www.olphglenview.org.
School—1123 Church St., 60025. Tel: 847-724-6990; Fax: 847-724-7025. School Sisters of St. Francis 3; Lay Teachers 64; Students 949.
Catechesis/Religious Program—Tel: 847-998-5289; Fax: 847-729-6194. Students 1,057.

GLENWOOD, COOK CO., ST. JOHN Rev. John J. Sullivan; Jamae Myers, Pastoral Assoc.
Res.: 301 S. Cottage Grove Ave., 60425. Tel: 708-758-5098; Fax: 708-758-0408. Web: www.rc.net/chicago/stjohn.
Catechesis/Religious Program—Students 125.

GRAYSLAKE, LAKE CO., ST. GILBERT (1930) Revs. Eugene J. Nowak; Samson Ngatia Mukundi; Deacon Richard Globis.
Res.: 301 E. Belvidere Rd., 60030. Tel: 847-223-4731; Fax: 847-223-5840. Web: www.stgilbert.org.
School—231 E. Belvidere Rd., 60030. Tel: 847-223-8600. Mrs. Alison O'Connor, Prin. Lay Teachers 34; Students 664.
Catechesis/Religious Program—Tel: 847-223-3071; Fax: 847-223-6545. Students 703.

GURNEE, LAKE CO., ST. PAUL THE APOSTLE Revs. Raymond Clennon, O.Carm.; Farrell J. Kane, O.Carm.; Deacons Michael Penich; Mark J. Purdome.
Res.: 6401 Gages Lake Rd., 60031. Tel: 847-918-0600; Fax: 847-918-0640. Email: stpaultheapostle@sbcglobal.net. Web: www.stpaul-gurnee.com.
Catechesis/Religious Program—Tel: 847-816-8677; Fax: 847-918-0640. Students 1,653.

HANOVER PARK, COOK CO., ST. ANSGAR (1968) Revs. Eduardo Garcia-Ferrer; John W. Tapper, Pastor

Emeritus (Retired); Deacons Oscar Monterroso; John Szarek.
Res.: 2040 Laurel Ave., 60133. Tel: 630-837-5553; Fax: 630-837-9847. Email: ansgar@sbcglobal.net.
Catechesis/Religious Program—Students 168.

HARVEY, COOK CO.

1—ASCENSION-ST. SUSANNA Rev. Thadeo E. Mgimba; Deacons Thomas R. Carvlin; Henry Burke Jr. In Res., Rev. Stephen O. Abaukaka.
Res.: 15234 Myrtle Ave., 60426. Tel: 708-333-0931; Fax: 708-333-3281. Email: pastor@ascstsus.org.
Catechesis/Religious Program—Students 20.

2—ST. JOHN THE BAPTIST, (Polish), Rev. Edward Romanski (Poland), Admin.
Res.: 15746 Union Ave., 60426. Tel: 708-333-0184; Fax: 708-333-0861.
Catechesis/Religious Program—Students 90.

HARWOOD HEIGHTS, NORRIDGE, COOK CO., ST. ROSALIE Revs. Bogdan Olzacki, O.S.P.P.E., Parish Admin.; Arnis G. Suleimanovs, O.S.P.P.E.
Res.: 4401 N. Oak Park Ave., Harwood Heights-Norridge, 60706. Tel: 708-867-8817; Fax: 708-867-8615.
Catechesis/Religious Program—6750 W. Montrose, Harwood Hts., 60706. Tel: 708-867-4588; Fax: 708-867-0774. Students 89.

HAZEL CREST, COOK CO., ST. ANNE Rev. Ralph H. Zwirn; Deacons John Leonas, (Retired); Herman Benthey; Steven Moore; William Churilla; George Brooks.
Res.: 16802 S. Lincoln St., 60429. Tel: 708-355-1792; Fax: 708-335-1953. Web: www.saintannecc.org.
Early Learning Center—(Grades PreK-Day Care), 16777 Dixie Hwy., 60429. Tel: 708-335-4831. Students 82.
Catechesis/Religious Program—Tel: 708-335-2286. Students 34.

HICKORY HILLS, COOK CO., ST. PATRICIA Revs. Marcel J. Pasciak; Frank J. Burek; Gerald F. Mulcahy (Retired); Deacons Charles Keegan; Norbert Weitendorf.
Res.: 9050 S. 86th Ave., 60457. Tel: 708-598-5222; Fax: 708-598-5280.
School—9000 S. 86th Ave., 60457. Tel: 708-598-8200; Fax: 708-598-8233. Dr. Robert F. Smith, Prin. Sisters of the Holy Family of Nazareth (Des Plaines, IL) 1; Lay Teachers 13; Students 221.
Catechesis/Religious Program—Tel: 708-599-1221; Fax: 708-598-8233. Students 339.

HIGHLAND PARK, LAKE CO., IMMACULATE CONCEPTION Revs. Kenneth Anderson; Terrance A. McCartyy, Pastor Emeritus; Joseph Nam H. Dao; Deacons Louis Vignocchi; Luis R. Lara; Stewart Adams; John Baier; Dr. Bradley R. Nitschke, Music Min.; Deacon Robert Ochsner, Business Mgr.; Jim Walsh, Youth Min. In Res., Rev. Alec J. Wolff.
Res.: 770 Deerfield Rd., 60035. Tel: 847-433-0130; Fax: 847-433-0669. Email: parishinfo@icparish.org. Web: www.icparish.org.
Catechesis/Religious Program—Tel: 847-433-2224. Students 243.

HIGHWOOD, LAKE CO., ST. JAMES Revs. Thomas F. Baldonieri; Ronald E. Scarlata, Pastor Emeritus (Retired); James F. O'Malley, Pastor Emeritus (Retired); Deacons Ellsworth Cordesman; Roger Mullaney; Luis R. Lara; James Gallagher; Bruno Pagliai. In Res., Rev. John E. Mulvihill.
Res.: 134 North Ave., 60040. Tel: 847-433-1494; Fax: 847-433-2011.
School—140 North Ave., 60040. Tel: 847-432-2277; Fax: 847-432-1321. Web: www.stjamesschoolhwd.org. Mrs. Deborah E. Dedeo, Prin. Lay Teachers 14; Students 158.
Catechesis/Religious Program—Tel: 847-432-2570. Mrs. Judy Cullen, D.R.E. Students 145.

HILLSIDE, COOK CO., ST. DOMITILLA Rev. Timothy R. Fiala; Deacons Angelo Marotto; Kenneth Bell; Joseph Siranovic.
Res.: 4940 Washington St., 60162. Tel: 708-449-8430; Fax: 708-449-2009.
School—601 Hillside Ave., 60162. Tel: 708-449-7420. Sisters 3; Lay Teachers 8; Students 69.
Catechesis/Religious Program—Tel: 708-449-1558. Students 64.

HOFFMAN ESTATES, COOK CO., ST. HUBERT Rev. Robert C. Rizzo; Deacons Richard Lawson; Thomas Hayden; Steven Baldasti; Allen Tatara.
Res.: 729 Grand Canyon St., 60169. Tel: 847-885-7700; Fax: 847-885-4631.
School—255 Flagstaff Ln., 60169. Tel: 847-885-7702; Fax: 847-885-0604. Mr. Vito DeFrisco, Prin. Lay Teachers 30; Students 521.
Catechesis/Religious Program—Tel: 847-855-7703. Students 395.

HOMETOWN, COOK CO., OUR LADY OF LORETTO (1951) Rev. Thomas S. Cabala.
Res.: 8925 S. Kostner Ave., 60456. Tel: 708-424-7471; Fax: 708-424-7588. Web: www.ourladyloretto.net.
Catechesis/Religious Program—Tel: 708-499-0832. Students 99.

HOMEWOOD, COOK CO., ST. JOSEPH Revs. Richard J. Kozak; James M. Sayers, Pastor Emeritus (Retired); Daniel Jarosewic; Deacons Jack O'Leary; George Maddock; Daniel Dietsch.
Res.: 17951 Dixie Hwy., 60430. Tel: 708-798-0622; Fax: 708-798-6137. Web: www.parishofstjoseph-homewood.org.
School—17949 Dixie Hwy., 60430. Tel: 708-798-0467; Fax: 708-957-5659. Lay Teachers 14; Students 189.
Catechesis/Religious Program—Tel: 708-798-6311. Patricia Hoffman, D.R.E. Students 294.

INDIAN CREEK, LAKE CO., ST. MARY OF VERNON (1978) Revs. Joseph C. Curtis; John P. Finnegan, Pastor Emeritus (Retired); Deacons Mark R. Zwolski; James Wogan; Philip Pagnotta Jr.; John Glenn; Maureen Evers, Pastoral Assoc.
Res.: 236 U.S. Hwy. 45, 60061. Tel: 847-362-1005; Fax: 847-362-6375. Email: smv@maryofvernon.org. Web: www.maryofvernon.org.
Catechesis/Religious Program—Tel: 847-362-0653. Students 608.

INGLESIDE, LAKE CO., ST. BEDE Rev. Timothy J. Fairman; Deacons John McMahon; James Devine; Lawrence Spohr; Gregory Zeifest. In Res., Revs. Robert J. Fitzpatrick, Pastor Emeritus (Retired); John F. Krebs, Pastor Emeritus (Retired).
Res.: 36455 N. Wilson Rd., 60041. Tel: 847-587-2251; Fax: 847-973-1765. Web: www.stbedechurch.com.
School—36399 N. Wilson Rd., 60041. Tel: 847-587-5541; Fax: 847-587-2713. Ms. Kathy E. Petroshius, Prin. Lay Teachers 17; Students 270.
Catechesis/Religious Program—Tel: 847-587-2301. Students 286.

INVERNESS, COOK CO., HOLY FAMILY Rev. Terence M. Keehan; Marsha Adamczyk, Pastoral Assoc.; Deacon Robert S. Antiss.
Res.: 2515 W. Palatine Rd., 60067. Tel: 847-359-0042; Fax: 847-359-0639. Email: staff@holyfamilyparish.org. Web: www.holyfamilyparish.org.
School—Holy Family Catholic Academy Dr. Gretchen Ludwig, Prin. Teachers 22; Students 342.
Catechesis/Religious Program—Tel: 847-359-0572. Students 971.

LA GRANGE, COOK CO.

1—ST. CLETUS Revs. Robert J. Clark; Charles G. Gallagher, Pastor Emeritus (Retired); Edgar Rodriguez; Kenneth Baker; Deacon Jesus Casas.
Res.: 600 W. 55th St., 60525. Tel: 708-352-6209; Fax: 708-352-6774.
School—700 W. 55th St., 60525. Tel: 708-352-4820; Fax: 708-352-0788. Mr. Jeffrey S. Taylor, Prin. Lay Teachers 28; Students 431.
Catechesis/Religious Program—Tel: 708-352-2383. Students 404.

2—ST. FRANCIS XAVIER Revs. John R. Hoffman; Robert A. Bacchi; William E. Killeen; James T. O'Connor, Senior Priest (Retired); Susan D. Matthews, Pastoral Assoc.; Allen Sterwalt, Music Dir.; Deacon Andrew Allison.
Res.: 124 N. Spring Ave., 60525. Tel: 708-352-0168; Fax: 708-352-4904. Email: SFXinLG@sfx-lg.org. Web: www.sfx-lg.org.
School—145 N. Waiola Ave., 60525. Tel: 708-352-2175; Fax: 708-352-2057. Ms. Debra E. Rodde, Prin. Lay Teachers 39; Students 631.
Catechesis/Religious Program—Tel: 708-352-4555. Terri Simeoni, D.R.E. Students 1,077.

LA GRANGE PARK, COOK CO., ST. LOUISE DE MARILLAC (1955) Revs. Denis Condon; John C. Hergenrother, Pastor Emeritus; Joseph J. Wojcik; Deacons Michael McLynn; Kevin L. Reynolds.
Res.: 1144 Harrison Ave., 60526. Tel: 708-352-7388; Fax: 708-352-0714. Email: parishoffice@stlouisedemarillac.com. Web: www.stlouisedemarillac.com.
School—Tel: 708-352-2202; Fax: 708-352-6654. Ms. Kelly M. Zawisza, Prin. Lay Teachers 13; Students 145.
Youth Ministry—1144 Harrison Ave., 60526. Tel: 708-352-7388; Fax: 708-352-0714.
Catechesis/Religious Program—1125 Harrison Ave., 60526. Tel: 708-482-8814. Students 255.

LAKE FOREST, LAKE CO.

1—ST. MARY Revs. Michael G. McGovern; Donald C. Woznicki; Matthew Kowalski, O.S.B.; Deacons James L. Kenney; Joseph G. Krakora; Richard F. Hudzik. In Res., Rev. Stephen E. Grunow.
Res.: 175 E. Illinois Rd., 60045. Tel: 847-234-0205; Fax: 847-234-9860. Email: information@churchofstmary.org. Web: www.churchofstmary.org.
School—185 E. Illinois Rd., 60045. Tel: 847-234-0371; Fax: 847-234-9593. Dr. Venette Biancalara, Prin. Lay Teachers 40; Students 543.
Catechesis/Religious Program—Tel: 847-234-0090; Fax: 847-234-2755. Students 521.

2—ST. PATRICK Revs. Laurence J. Dunn; William J. McNulty, Pastor Emeritus (Retired); Deacons Frank DeFrank; John V. Lucas; Raymond C. Loman.
Res.: 991 S. Waukegan Rd., 60045. Tel: 847-234-1401; Fax: 847-234-1433. Web: www.stpatrick-lakeforest.org.
Catechesis/Religious Program—Tel: 847-234-2179; Fax: 847-234-2313. Students 507.

LAKE VILLA, LAKE CO., PRINCE OF PEACE (1955) Revs. Richard M. Yanos; David R. Straub; Deacons Timothy Leonard; Jeff Barton; Joseph LaFleur; Christopher Savage; Jim Minor. In Res., Rev. Daniel F. Sullivan (Retired).
Res.: 135 S. Milwaukee Ave., 60046. Tel: 847-356-7915; Fax: 847-265-1678. Web: www.princeofpeacelv.org.
School—Tel: 847-356-6111; Fax: 847-356-6121. Mrs. Elizabeth A. Brown, Prin. Lay Teachers 14; Students 255.
Catechesis/Religious Program—Tel: 847-356-5850; Fax: 847-265-1678. Students 281.

LAKE ZURICH, LAKE CO., ST. FRANCIS DE SALES (1949) Rev. David Ryan; Deacons Robert Arvidson; George Flaherty.
Res. & Rectory: 227 E. Main St., 60047.
Church: 135 S. Buesching Rd., 60047. Tel: 847-438-6622; Fax: 847-438-6638. Web: www.stfrancislz.org.
School—11 S. Buesching Rd., 60047. Tel: 847-438-7921; Fax: 847-438-7114. Roy Rash, Prin.; Sr. Michael Marie, C.S.F.N., Asst. Prin. Lay Teachers 27; Students 497.
Catechesis/Religious Program—Tel: 847-726-4850; Fax: 847-438-7114. Kathy Brady-Murfin, D.R.E. Students 828.

LANSING, COOK CO., ST. ANN Rev. William M. McFarlane; Deacon James Detloff.
Parish Office—3010 Ridge Rd., 60438. Tel: 708-895-6700; Fax: 708-895-6877. Email: stannch@comcast.net.
Res.: 3026 Ridge Rd., 60438. Tel: 708-895-6700; Fax: 708-895-6877.
School—3014 Ridge Rd., 60438. Tel: 708-895-1661; Fax: 708-865-6923. Ms. Donna A. Lamoureux, Prin. Lay Teachers 13; Students 243.
Catechesis/Religious Program—Tel: 708-895-5970. Ms. Barbara Antoskiewicz, D.R.E. Students 153.

LEMONT, COOK CO.

1—ST. ALPHONSUS Rev. Brian Ardagh.
Res.: 210 E. Logan, 60439. Tel: 630-257-2414; Fax: 630-257-2476. Email: stals-lemont@comcast.net. Web: www.st-als.org.
School—St. Alphonsus-St. Patrick Consolidated, (Grades K-8), Admin. Office: 20 W. 145 Davey Rd., 60439. Tel: 630-783-2220. Sisters 1; Lay Teachers 19; Students 338.
Catechesis/Religious Program—Tel: 630-257-2371; Fax: 630-257-2381. Students 419.

2—BLESSED JURGIS MATULAITIS MISSION Rev. Antanas Saulaitis, S.J.
Mailing Address: 14915-127th St., Unit 101, 60439. In Res., Rev. Msgr. Ignatius L. Urbonas (GRY) (Retired).
Lithuanian Catholic Mission—14911 127th St., 60439-7417. Tel: 630-257-5613; Fax: 630-257-5695. Email: matulaitismission@sbcglobal.net. Web: www.matulaitismission.com.
Catechesis/Religious Program—Students 782.

3—SS. CYRIL AND METHODIUS (1884) Revs. Lawrence M. Lisowski; Marcin Szczypula; Deacons Norbert Lesnieski, (Retired); Michael Ciciura.
Res.: 608 Sobieski St., 60439. Tel: 630-257-2776; Fax: 630-257-9372. Email: rectory@stcyril.org. Web: www.stcyril.org.
School—607 Sobieski St., 60439. Tel: 630-257-6488; Fax: 630-257-6465. Lay Teachers 24; Students 474.
Catechesis/Religious Program—Tel: 630-257-9314; Fax: 630-257-9805. Students 595.

4—ST. JAMES AT SAG BRIDGE, [CEM] Rev. Edward D. Gleeson; Pamela Stafford, Music Min.; Deacon John M. Wilkinson.
Res.: 10600 South Archer Ave., 60439-9344. Tel: 630-257-7000; Fax: 630-257-7912.
Catechesis/Religious Program—Students 53.

5—ST. PATRICK (1839) Revs. Kurt D. Boras; Richard J. Shannon, Pastor Emeritus (Retired); Deacon Joseph Winblad.
Res.: 200 Illinois St., 60439. Tel: 630-257-6134; Fax: 630-257-0401. Email: stpatricklemont@sbcglobal.net.
School—St. Alphonsus-St. Patrick Consolidated, (Grades PreK-8), Admin. Office: 20 W. 145 Davey Rd., 60439. Tel: 630-783-2220; Fax: 630-783-2230. Lay Teachers 14; Students 239.
Catechesis/Religious Program—Tel: 630-257-8012; Fax: 630-257-0401. Students 188.

6—SLOVENIAN CATHOLIC MISSION (1994), (Dedicated to Bl. A.M. Slomsek) Rev. Metod Ogorevc, O.F.M.; Deacon John Vidmar.
Res.: 14246 Main St., P.O. Box 608, 60439-0608. Tel: 630-257-2068; Fax: 630-257-2359.

LIBERTYVILLE, LAKE CO., ST. JOSEPH Revs. John E. Hennessey; Kenneth Kiepura; John Trout, S.P.S.; Deacons David Tiemeier; George Kashmar.

Res.: 121 E. Maple Ave., 60048. Tel: 847-362-2073; Fax: 847-362-6821. Email: info@stjoseph-libertyville.org. Web: www.stjoseph-libertyville.org.
School—221 Park Pl., 60048. Tel: 847-362-0730; Fax: 847-362-8130. Mr. Charles J. Lynch, Prin. Lay Teachers 28; Students 495.
Catechesis/Religious Program—116 Hurlburt Ct., 60048. Tel: 847-362-5797; Fax: 847-362-6821. Students 1,172.

LYONS, COOK CO., ST. HUGH Revs. Robert J. Burnell; James T. O'Conner, Pastor Emeritus; Edward S. Stockus, Pastor Emeritus (Retired).
Res.: 7939 W. 43rd St., 60534. Tel: 708-447-3108; Fax: 708-447-9870. Email: sthughlyon@sbcglobal.net.
Catechesis/Religious Program—Tel: 708-447-5711. Students 66.

MARKHAM, COOK CO., ST. GERARD MAJELLA Revs. Thadeo E. Mgimba; Daniel J. Sullivan, Pastor Emeritus (Retired).
Res.: 16130 Clifton Park, 60426. Tel: 708-331-8400; Fax: 708-596-0770.
Catechesis/Religious Program—Students 21.

MATTESON, COOK CO., ST. LAWRENCE O'TOOLE (1959) Rev. Michael Novick; Deacons Rossini Alcos; John Rangel; Edward Winter; William A. Doerr.
Res.: 4101 St. Lawrence Ave., 60443. Tel: 708-748-6090; Fax: 708-748-4055. Web: www.slotoole.org.
School—Tel: 708-748-6090; Fax: 708-747-4099. Mr. Patricia N. Hofkamp, Prin. Lay Teachers 13; Students 200.
Catechesis/Religious Program—Tel: 708-748-6090. Students 74.

MAYWOOD, COOK CO.

1—ST. EULALIA Rev. Jose Carmen Mendez Izquierdo; Deacons Giulio Camerini; George Lambert, (Retired); Philip White; Dwight Sullivan.
Res.: 1851 S. 9th Ave., 60153. Tel: 708-343-6120.
Catechesis/Religious Program—Students 45.

2—ST. JAMES, Closed. Consult Archives and Records Center for parish and school records.

MELROSE PARK, COOK CO.

1—ST. CHARLES BORROMEO Revs. Jorge Bravo Martinez, C.S.; Anderson L. Hammes, C.S.; August Feccia, C.S.; Deacon Freddy Palacios.
Res.: 1637 N. 37th Ave., 60160. Tel: 708-343-7646; Fax: 708-343-3527.
Catechesis/Religious Program—Modesta Soto-Martinez, D.R.E.

2—OUR LADY OF MOUNT CARMEL, (Italian), Revs. Claudio Holzer, C.S.; Fernando Cuevas, C.S.
Res.: 1101 N. 23rd Ave., 60160. Tel: 708-344-4140; Fax: 708-344-0902. Email: olmcmp@yahoo.com.
Catechesis/Religious Program—Modesta Martinez, D.R.E. Students 54.

3—SACRED HEART Rev. Erwin J. Friedl; Deacons Raymond Behrendt; Norberto Ojeda; Michael K. Barnish. In Res., Revs. Benedict Ezeoke (Nigeria); Herbert J. Meyr (Retired).
Res.: 819 N. 16th Ave., 60160. Tel: 708-344-0757; Fax: 708-344-5906. Email: parish@shsparish.org. Web: www.shsparish.org.
School—815 N. 16th Ave., 60160. Tel: 708-681-0240; Fax: 708-681-0454. Mrs. Barbara J. Ciconte, Prin. Sisters of the Third Order of St. Francis of the Holy Family 1; Lay Teachers 12; Students 144.
Catechesis/Religious Program—Students 150.
Convent—1503 W. Rice St., 60160. Tel: 708-344-6940.

MIDLOTHIAN, COOK CO., ST. CHRISTOPHER (1922) Revs. Mark J. Walter; Laurent Mhagama; Deacons Joseph Brady, Pastoral Assoc. (Retired); Michael Smith.
Res.: 4130 W. 147th St., 60445. Tel: 708-388-8190; Fax: 708-388-0072. Email: stchris@stchristopherparish.com. Web: www.stchristopherparish.com.
School—14611 S. Keeler Ave., 60445. Tel: 708-385-8776; Fax: 708-385-8102. Mr. Michael B. Johnson, Prin. Sisters 1; Lay Teachers 14; Students 191.
Catechesis/Religious Program—Tel: 708-388-4040. Students 185.

MORTON GROVE, COOK CO., ST. MARTHA Revs. Dennis B. O'Neill; Eugene J. Faucher, Pastor Emeritus (Retired); Deacon Peter Meehan.
Res.: 8523 Georgiana Ave., 60053. Tel: 847-965-0262; Fax: 847-965-2535. Email: stmarthachurch@yahoo.com. Web: www.saintmarthachurch.org.
Catechesis/Religious Program—Tel: 847-965-6861. Students 183.

MT. PROSPECT, COOK CO.

1—ST. CECILIA Revs. Michael A. Olivero; Daniel J. Brady, Pastor Emeritus (Retired).
Res.: 700 S. Meier Rd., 60056. Tel: 847-437-6208; Fax: 847-437-2520. Email: stcecilia@archchicago.org. Web: www.stceciliamtprospect.org.
Catechesis/Religious Program—Tel: 847-437-6310; Fax: 847-437-5730. Students 168.

2—ST. EMILY Revs. Ronald W. Navoy; Dennis M. Zalecki; Gail Goleas, Pastoral Assoc.; Barbara Stempien, Business Mgr.; Charlotte Schiller, Music Dir.; Gregg Belgard, Youth Min. In Res., Rev. John W. Roller (Retired).
Office: 1400 E. Central Rd., 60056.
Res.: 101 N. Horner Ln., 60056. Tel: 847-824-5049; Fax: 847-297-0358. Web: www.stemily.org.
School—1400 E. Central Rd., 60056. Tel: 847-296-3490; Fax: 847-296-1155. Sisters of the Holy Family of Nazareth 1; Lay Teachers 21; Students 316.
Catechesis/Religious Program—Tel: 847-299-5865. Students 441.

3—ST. RAYMOND DE PENAFORT Revs. Steven G. Dombrowski; Nhat Hong Le (Vietnam); Sr. Dee Peppard, Pastoral Assoc.; Deacon John Lorbach.
Res.: 301 S. I Oka St., 60056. Tel: 847-253-8600; Fax: 847-253-0023. Email: pmc@st-raymond.org. Web: www.st-raymond.org.
School—300 S. Elmhurst Ave., 60056. Tel: 847-253-8555; Fax: 847-253-8939. Mr. Andrew Galus, Prin. Lay Teachers 31; Students 582.
Catechesis/Religious Program—Tel: 847-253-8600, Ext. 150. Students 589.

4—ST. THOMAS BECKET (1969) Rev. Edward B. Panek.
Res.: 1321 Burning Bush Ln., 60056. Tel: 847-827-9220; Fax: 847-827-0370.
Catechesis/Religious Program—Tel: 847-296-9051. Students 58.

MUNDELEIN, LAKE CO.

1—ST. MARY OF THE ANNUNCIATION (1864) (Fremont Center) Revs. Ronald J. Lewinski; Nathaniel Payne; Deacons Robert A. Poletto; Michael O'Malley; Gary L. Kupsak.
Res.: 22333 W. Erhart Rd., 60060. Tel: 847-223-0010; Fax: 847-223-5960. Email: parish@stmota.org. Web: www.stmaryfc.org.
School—(Grades PreK-5), 22277 W. Erhart Rd., 60060. Tel: 847-223-4021; Fax: 847-223-3489. Ms. Eileen M. Sullivan, Prin. Lay Teachers 11; Students 130.
See Frassati Catholic Academy(Grades 6-8) located at Transfiguration, Wauconda.
Catechesis/Religious Program—Students 616.

2—SANTA MARIA DEL POPOLO (1935) Revs. David Arcila, O.C.D.; James W. Kinn, Pastor Emeritus (Retired); Gerald K. O'Reilly; Deacons John Simmons; Dave Auld; Efrain Flores; Felipe Vasquez.
Res.: 116 N. Lake St., 60060. Tel: 847-949-8300; Fax: 847-949-2339. Web: www.smdpparish.org.
School—126 N. Lake St., 60060. Tel: 847-990-6866; Fax: 847-566-1096. Mrs. Patricia Strang, Prin. Lay Teachers 10; Students 79.
See Frassati Catholic Academy(Grades 6-8) located at Transfiguration, Wauconda.
Catechesis/Religious Program—Tel: 847-990-6865. Students 162.
Convent—133 N. Lincoln Ave., 60060. Tel: 847-566-7343.

NILES, COOK CO.

1—ST. ISAAC JOGUES Revs. Andrew E. Luczak; Camillus Janas, O.F.M.; Deacons Robert C. O'Keefe; Paul Stanton; Rod Ranola.
Res.: 8149 Golf Rd., 60714. Tel: 847-967-1060; Fax: 847-967-1070.
Catechesis/Religious Program—Tel: 847-966-1180; Fax: 847-966-0159. Students 153.

2—ST. JOHN BREBEUF Revs. Michael G. Meany; Robert S. Banzin, Pastor Emeritus (Retired); Krzysztof Janczak; Andrzej Nowicki; Deacons Andrew J. Beierwaltes; Kevin D. Hill; Lawrence Skaja; Mariusz J. Kosla.
Res.: 8307 N. Harlem Ave., 60714. Tel: 847-966-8145; Fax: 847-966-0014.
School—8301 Harlem Ave., 60714. Tel: 847-966-3266; Fax: 847-966-5351. Mrs. Margaret Whitman, Prin. Sisters 2; Lay Teachers 24; Students 349.
Catechesis/Religious Program—Tel: 847-966-3269. Students 351.

3—OUR LADY OF RANSOM (1960) Revs. Thomas M. Enright; Christopher M. Gustafson; Deacons Charles O'Donnell; James Fruge.
Ministry Center—Parish Office: 8624 W. Normal, 60714. Tel: 847-823-2550; Fax: 847-823-4291. Web: www.olransom.org.
Catechesis/Religious Program—Tel: 847-696-2994. Students 193.

NORRIDGE, COOK CO., DIVINE SAVIOR (1955) Rev. Richard J. LoBianco.
Res.: 7740 W. Montrose, 60706. Tel: 708-456-9000; Fax: 708-456-7838. Email: dsavior@aol.com. Web: www.divinesaviornorridge.org.
School—Academy of St. Priscilla at Divine Savior, (Grades PreK-2) Tel: 708-452-0323; Fax: 708-452-0494. Email: elem.acadpriscilla@archchicago.org. Web: www.stpriscillaacademy.org.
Catechesis/Religious Program—Students 230.

NORTH CHICAGO, LAKE CO., QUEEN OF PEACE, Merged with Holy Family, Waukegan & Immaculate Conception B.V.M. to form Most Blessed Trinity, Waukegan.

NORTH RIVERSIDE, COOK CO., MATER CHRISTI Revs. Louis Tylka; M. Cyril Nemecek, Pastor Emeritus; Deacon Ronald Pilarski.
Res.: 2431 S. 10th Ave., 60546. Tel: 708-442-5611; Fax: 708-442-1306. Web: www.materchristichurch.com.
Catechesis/Religious Program—2400 S. 10th Ave., 60546. Students 114.
Shrine—Mother of Mothers

NORTHBROOK, COOK CO.

1—ST. NORBERT (1899) Revs. Robert P. Heinz; William J. Vollmer. In Res., Rev. Richard J. Mueller (Retired).
Res.: 1809 Walters Ave., 60062. Tel: 847-272-7090; Fax: 847-272-7771. Email: rectory@stnorbertparish.org. Web: www.stnorbertparish.org.
School—1817 Walters Ave., 60062. Tel: 847-272-0051; Fax: 847-272-5274. Kim Rich, Prin. Lay Teachers 26; Students 274.
Catechesis/Religious Program—Tel: 847-272-3086; Fax: 847-513-6761. Students 599.

2—OUR LADY OF THE BROOK Revs. Thomas A. Moran; Robert G. Herne, Pastor Emeritus (Retired); Ananda R. Isukala; Deacons Dennis F. McAllister; Perry Duderstadt.
Res.: 3700 W. Dundee Rd., 60062. Tel: 847-272-5686; Fax: 847-498-0899. Email: rectory@olbparish.org. Web: www.olbparish.org.
Catechesis/Religious Program—Tel: 847-272-5131; Fax: 847-498-0899. Justin Huyck, C.R.E. Students 223.

NORTHFIELD, COOK CO., ST. PHILIP THE APOSTLE Rev. Msgr. Robert J. Dempsey; Deacon Robert Puhala. In Res., Rev. George W. Klein (Retired).
Res.: 1962 Old Willow Rd., 60093. Tel: 847-446-8383; Fax: 847-446-8338. Email: office@stphilipparish.org. Web: www.stphilipparish.org.
Catechesis/Religious Program—1962 Old Willow Rd., 60093. Tel: 847-446-8390. Students 142.

NORTHLAKE, COOK CO., ST. JOHN VIANNEY, CURE OF ARS Revs. Thomas Refermat; Luke E. Winkelmann; Deacons John Zurawski; James Sinacore.
Res.: 46 N. Wolf Rd., 60164. Tel: 708-562-0500; Fax: 708-562-1824. Email: sjvchurch@comcast.net. Web: www.freewebs.com/sjvchurch.
School—27 N. Lavergne Ave., 60164. Tel: 708-562-1466; Fax: 708-562-0142. Ms. Linda A. Andrejek, Prin. Lay Teachers 11; Students 196.
Catechesis/Religious Program—Tel: 708-562-1466, Ext. 120. Students 192.

OAK FOREST, COOK CO., ST. DAMIAN (1961) Revs. Joseph T. Noonan; Phi Nguyen; Christopher Kituli; Deacons Len Steinbeigle, (Retired); Thomas Hipelius; William Stearns; John Rex; Guy J. Grabiec. In Res., Rev. Francis G. Scanlan (Retired).
Office: 5250 W. 155th St., 60452. Email: stdamian@hotmail.com.
Res.: 5220 W. 155th St., 60452. Tel: 708-687-1370; Fax: 708-687-1377.
School—5300 W. 155th St., 60452. Tel: 708-687-4230; Fax: 708-687-8347. Colleen Domke, Prin. Lay Teachers 27; Students 524.
Catechesis/Religious Program—Tel: 708-687-7788; Fax: 708-687-1735. Students 429.

OAK LAWN, COOK CO.

1—ST. CATHERINE OF ALEXANDRIA Revs. Patrick J. Henry; William J. Lion, Pastor Emeritus (Retired); George P. McKenna, Pastor Emeritus (Retired); Stanley Stuglik; Sr. Annmarie Klasky, C.S.S.F., Pastoral Assoc.
Res.: 4100 W. 107th St., 60453. Tel: 708-425-2850; Fax: 708-425-2313.
School—10621 S. Kedvale Ave., 60453. Tel: 708-425-5547; Fax: 708-425-3701. Lay Teachers 25; Students 471.
Catechesis/Religious Program—Tel: 708-425-5747; Fax: 708-425-3701. Students 130.

2—ST. GERALD (1934) Revs. Lawrence J. Malcolm; Michael A. Moczko.
Parish Office—9310 S. 55th Ct., 60453. Tel: 708-422-0234; Fax: 708-422-0822. Web: www.stgerald.com.
Res.: 9349 S. Central Ave., 60453. Tel: 708-422-0234; Fax: 708-422-0822.
School—9320 S. 55th Ct., 60453. Tel: 708-422-0121; Fax: 708-422-9216. Lay Teachers 22; Students 390.
Catechesis/Religious Program—Tel: 708-423-0458. Students 248.

3—ST. GERMAINE (1962) Revs. Michael J. Furlan; William O. Goedert, Pastor Emeritus (Retired); Brian Kean; Deacons John Flanagan; Joseph Gonzalez; John L. Malone; Carol Conway, Pastoral Assoc.
Mailing Address: 9711 S. Kolin, 60453.
Res.: 4240 W. 98th St., 60453. Tel: 708-636-5060; Fax: 708-636-8007.
School—9735 S. Kolin, 60453. Tel: 708-425-6063. Mr. Kevin Reedy, Prin. Lay Teachers 18; Students 328.
Catechesis/Religious Program—Marion Krucek, D.R.E. Students 278.

4—ST. LINUS (1955) Revs. William T. Corcoran;

Joseph E. Auer, Pastor Emeritus (Retired); Marcin J. Bulinski; Deacons Edward Gadomski; Richard Feltes; Robert L. Cislo. In Res., Revs. Orlando Martins (Portugal); Gene F. Smith.
Res.: 10300 S. Lawler Ave., 60453. Tel: 708-422-2400; Fax: 708-422-2707. Web: www.saintlinusreligiouseducation.org; www.stlinusschool.org.
School—10400 S. Lawler Ave., 60453. Tel: 708-425-1656; Fax: 708-425-1802. Dr. Michael P. Stritch, Prin. Lay Teachers 23; Students 383.
Catechesis/Religious Program—Tel: 708-636-4373. Students 206.

5—ST. LOUIS DE MONTFORT Revs. Mark P. Canavan; Daniel W. Tomich; Deacons Michael Karnoski; William Sullivan.
Res.: 8808 S. Ridgeland, 60453. Tel: 708-599-5300; Fax: 708-599-2678. Email: stlouismonfort@archchicago.org. Web: www.sldmchurch.com.
School—Tel: 708-599-5781; Fax: 708-599-5782. Ms. Holly Gross, Prin. Lay Teachers 17; Students 266.
Catechesis/Religious Program—8840 S. Ridgeland, 60453. Tel: 708-591-5787. Students 151.

OAK PARK, COOK CO.

1—ASCENSION (1907) Revs. Lawrence R. McNally; Robert A. Cross, Pastor Emeritus (Retired); Deacons Roger Vandervest; Lendell Richardson; Joseph A. Walsh.
Parish Office: 808 S. East Ave., 60304. Tel: 708-848-2703; Fax: 708-848-2773. Email: ascensionchurch@comcast.net. Web: www.ascensionchurch.com.
School—601 Van Buren, 60304. Tel: 708-386-7282; Fax: 708-524-4796. Ms. Mary Jo Burns, Prin. Lay Teachers 28; Students 481.
Catechesis/Religious Program—Tel: 708-848-3099. Students 431.

2—ST. CATHERINE OF SIENA-ST. LUCY Revs. Daniel Whiteside; John J. Carolan, Pastor Emeritus (Retired); James Hargadon, Pastoral Assoc.
Res.: 38 N. Austin Blvd., 60302. Tel: 708-386-8077; Fax: 708-386-5190.
School—27 Washington Blvd., 60302. Tel: 708-386-5286; Fax: 708-386-7328. Sr. Marion Cypser, R.S.M., Prin. Sisters of Mercy 1; Lay Teachers 9; Students 207.
Catechesis/Religious Program—Students 49.

3—ST. EDMUND Revs. John W. McGivern; Joseph B. Ruiz, Pastor Emeritus (Retired); Sr. Madeleva Deegan, R.S.M., Pastoral Assoc.; Deacon Thomas M. Dwyer. In Res., Rev. John P. Lucas.
Res.: 188 S. Oak Park Ave., 60302. Tel: 708-848-4417; Fax: 708-848-0049.
School—200 S. Oak Park Ave., 60302. Tel: 708-386-5131; Fax: 708-386-5616. Mr. Michael P. Sweeney, Prin. Lay Teachers 13; Students 151.
Catechesis/Religious Program—Tel: 708-848-7220. Students 130.

4—ST. GILES (1927) Revs. Carl Morello; Thomas M. Dore, Pastor Emeritus (Retired); Deacons John A. Henricks; Gerald Zych; Loretto J. Madonia. In Res., Rev. Edward P. Salmon (Retired).
Office: 1025 Columbian Ave., 60302. Tel: 708-383-3430; Fax: 708-383-8644. Email: stgiles@stgilesparish.org. Web: www.stgilesparish.org.
Res.: 1045 Columbian Ave., 60302.
School—1034 Linden Ave., 60302. Tel: 708-383-6279; Fax: 708-383-9952. Mrs. Susan M. Poetzel, Prin. Lay Teachers 28; Students 480.
Catechesis/Religious Program—Tel: 708-383-4185; Fax: 708-383-8669. Students 405.

ORLAND HILLS, COOK CO., ST. ELIZABETH SETON Revs. Richard M. Homa; William T. O'Mara, Pastor Emeritus (Retired); Stanislaw Kuca; Deacons Frank Gildea; Joseph Bishop. In Res., Rev. William B. Gubbins (Retired).
Res.: 9300 W. 167th St., 60477. Tel: 708-403-0101; Fax: 708-403-0105. Web: www.steseton.com.
School—Cardinal Joseph Bernardin, 9250 W. 167th St., 60477. Tel: 708-403-6525; Fax: 708-403-8621. Mary Iannueilli, Prin. Inter-Parish School serving St. Elizabeth Seton, St. Francis of Assisi, St. Julie Billiart and St. Stephen, Deacon and Martyr.
Catechesis/Religious Program—Tel: 708-403-0101; Fax: 708-403-9810. Students 650.

ORLAND PARK, COOK CO.

1—ST. FRANCIS OF ASSISI Revs. Edward F. Upton; John Zurek; Deacons Joseph Truesdale; Daniel Carroll; Michael J. Pindelski.
Res.: 15050 S. Wolf Rd., 60467. Tel: 708-460-0042; Fax: 708-460-0136. Email: parishoffice@assisiparish.org. Web: www.assisiparish.org.
Catechesis/Religious Program—15010 S. Wolf Rd., 60467. Tel: 708-460-0155; Fax: 708-460-5086. Mary Kay Burberry, D.R.E. Students 1,195.

2—ST. MICHAEL Revs. Paul C. Burak; Edward McLaughlin, Pastor Emeritus (Retired); Michael G. Foley; Carlos Rodriguez; Sr. Marietta Umlor, C.S.C., Pastoral Assoc.; Deacons Michael McDonough; Thomas Bartholomew; Tony Cocco; Jim Janicek; Saul Vazquez. In Res., Rev. William J. Finnegan (Retired).
Res.: 14310 Highland Ave., 60462. Tel: 708-349-0903; Fax: 708-349-6015. Email: info@saintmike.com. Web: www.saintmike.com.
School—14355 Highland Ave., 60462. Tel: 708-349-0068; Fax: 708-349-2658. Lay Teachers 30; Students 596.
Catechesis/Religious Program—14345 Highland Ave., 60462. Tel: 708-349-0769; Fax: 708-873-4643. Students 451.

3—OUR LADY OF THE WOODS Revs. Michael W. O'Connell; William J. Finnegan, Pastor Emeritus (Retired); Deacon John Macarol; Ellen Stanley, Pastoral Assoc. In Res., Most Rev. John R. Gorman, Emeritus Auxiliary Bishop (Retired).
Res.: 10731 W. 131st St., 60462. Tel: 708-361-4754; Fax: 708-361-5965. Email: olwparish@aol.com. Web: www.ourladyofthewoods.org.
Catechesis/Religious Program—Tel: 708-361-9435. Colleen Walery, D.R.E. Students 710.

PALATINE, COOK CO.

1—ST. THERESA Rev. Richard M. Zborowski; Rev. Msgr. John P. McNamara, Pastor Emeritus (Retired); Revs. Grzegorz P. Gorczyca; Jacek Nowak, S.Ch.; Deacons Stephen Norys; Richard Pizzato; Lou Riccio; Lawrence R. Schumacher; Gail McCusker, Business Mgr.; Bob Moffett, Dir. Music. In Res., Rev. Paul F. Rosemeyer (Retired).
Res.: 455 N. Benton, 60067. Tel: 847-358-7760; Fax: 847-202-8941. Web: www.sttheresachurch.org.
Church: 465 N. Benton, 60067. Tel: 847-358-7760.
Pauline Center/Ministry Center—455 N. Benton, 60067. Tel: 847-359-2846.
School—445 N. Benton, 60067. Tel: 847-359-1820; Fax: 847-705-2084. Mr. Milton M. Kobus, Prin. Lay Teachers 31; Students 540.
Catechesis/Religious Program—Tel: 847-358-2846. Elizabeth Vogt, D.R.E. Students 564.

2—ST. THOMAS OF VILLANOVA Revs. Thomas R. Rzepiela; Wojciech Jan Oleksy; Deacons Thomas J. Maloney; Thomas Dunne; Len Marturano; Richard Willer; Mark Duffey; John Breit. In Res., Rev. Raymond A. Yadron, Pastor Emeritus (Retired).
Office: 1201 E. Anderson Dr., 60074. Tel: 847-358-6999; Fax: 847-934-4919. Email: stovparish@stov.org. Web: www.stov.org.
School—1141 E. Anderson Dr., 60074. Tel: 847-358-2110; Fax: 847-776-1435. Mr. John A. La Roche, Prin. Lay Teachers 16; Students 182.
Catechesis/Religious Program—Tel: 847-358-2386. Students 532.

PALOS HEIGHTS, COOK CO.

1—ST. ALEXANDER (1959) Revs. Martin E. Michniewicz; Patrick J. O'Neill; Deacons Timothy Keating; James Horton.
Res.: 7025 W. 126th St., 60463. Tel: 708-448-4861; Fax: 708-448-0039. Email: alchurch1@comcast.net. Web: www.saintalsparish.org.
School—126th St. at 71st Ave., 60463. Tel: 708-448-0408; Fax: 708-448-5947. Mrs. Catherine Biel, Prin. Lay Teachers 23; Students 353.
Catechesis/Religious Program—Tel: 708-448-6624. Students 449.

2—INCARNATION Revs. Ronald J. Mass; Robert E. Dovick, Pastor Emeritus (Retired); Arkadiusz Falara; Deacon James Langwell; Kathryn L. McNicholas, Pastoral Assoc. In Res., Rev. Edward McLaughlin (Retired); Rev. Msgr. R. George Sarauskas.
Res.: 5757 W. 127th St., 60463. Tel: 708-597-3180; Fax: 708-597-2452. Email: church@incarnationcatholic.com. Web: www.incarnationcatholic.com.
School—Tel: 708-385-6250; Fax: 708-597-0588. Mrs. Maria E. Hawk, Prin. Lay Teachers 15; Students 225.
Catechesis/Religious Program—Tel: 708-388-4004; Fax: 708-597-0588. Students 232.

PALOS HILLS, COOK CO., SACRED HEART Revs. Patrick M. Tucker; Robert F. McGinnity, Pastor Emeritus (Retired); Grzegorz Wojcik; Deacons Richard Werner; Thomas J. Rzendzian. In Res., Rev. Robert G. Herne (Retired).
Res.: 8245 W. 111th St., 60465. Tel: 708-974-3336; Fax: 708-974-3556.
Catechesis/Religious Program—Tel: 708-974-3900; Fax: 708-974-3922. Sharon Allison, D.R.E. Students 260.

PARK FOREST, COOK CO., ST. IRENAEUS (1948) Rev. Terrance Johnson.
Res.: 78 Cherry St., 60466. Tel: 708-748-6891; Fax: 708-748-7998.
Catechesis/Religious Program—Tel: 708-748-7997. Students 97.

PARK RIDGE, COOK CO.

1—MARY, SEAT OF WISDOM (1955) Revs. Gerald T. Gunderson; Ronald N. Kalas, Pastor Emeritus (Retired); Andrew Liaugminas (MET); Richard Grek, C.R. In Res., Rev. Theodore Stone (Retired).
Res.: 920 Granville Ave., 60068. Tel: 847-825-3153; Fax: 847-825-3484. Email: mswrectory@maryseatofwisdom.org. Web: www.mswparish.org.
School—1352 S. Cumberland, 60068. Tel: 847-825-2500; Fax: 847-825-1943. Mrs. Judith A. Schutter, Prin. Lay Teachers 28; Students 443.
Catechesis/Religious Program—Tel: 847-825-8763; Fax: 847-825-8658. Students 341.

2—ST. PAUL OF THE CROSS (1911) Revs. Britto Berchmans; John P. Chrzan; Charles E. Musula; Deacons Aloysius J. Memmel; Robert T. Bulger. In Res., Very Rev. Daniel A. Smilanic.
Res.: 320 S. Washington St., 60068. Tel: 847-825-7605; Fax: 847-825-5186. Web: www.spc-church.org.
School—140 S. Northwest Hwy., 60068. Tel: 847-825-6366; Fax: 847-825-2466. Mrs. Lorelei A. Bobroff, Prin. Lay Teachers 37; Students 695.
Catechesis/Religious Program—215 S. Ridge Ter., 60068. Tel: 847-692-2758. Anna Mae Parkhill, D.R.E. Students 1,302.

POSEN, COOK CO., ST. STANISLAUS BISHOP AND MARTYR Rev. Pius Eusebius Kokose, C.S.Sp. (Ghana); Deacon Daniel Dutkiewicz.
Res.: 14414 McKinley Ave., 60469. Tel: 708-597-4910; Fax: 708-597-4841.
Catechesis/Religious Program—Students 149.

PROSPECT HEIGHTS, COOK CO., ST. ALPHONSUS LIGUORI Revs. Curtis Lambert; Richard J. Maginot, Pastor Emeritus (Retired); John W. Hurley; Deacons Norbert Ciesil; Calvin Blickle Jr.
Res.: 411 N. Wheeling Rd., 60070. Tel: 847-255-7452; Fax: 847-255-7520. Email: saintalphonsus@hotmail.com. Web: www.saintalphonsus.com.
School—Tel: 847-255-5538. Mr. Fred Muehleman, Prin. Lay Teachers 18; Students 235.
Catechesis/Religious Program—Tel: 847-255-9490. Students 246.

RIVER FOREST, COOK CO.

1—ST. LUKE (1887) Revs. Kenneth J. Fischer; Robert P. Marchwiany; Deacons Terrance Norton; John O'Neill; Paul Faherty; Robert Slobig; Roman Revering. In Res., Rev. Leroy A. Wickowski (Retired).
Res.: 528 Lathrop Ave., 60305-1835. Tel: 708-771-8250; Fax: 708-771-8809. Email: stlukeparish@stlukeparish.org. Web: www.stlukeparish.org.
School—519 Ashland Ave., 60305-1824. Tel: 708-366-8587; Fax: 708-366-3831. Mrs. Barbara A. Rasinski, Prin. Lay Teachers 24; Students 347.
Catechesis/Religious Program—Tel: 708-771-5959; Fax: 708-771-5960. Students 231.

2—ST. VINCENT FERRER Revs. Herbert C. Hayek, O.P.; Dennis C. Woerter, O.P.; Very Rev. Michael G. Kyte, O.P.; Deacons John Gaughan; Jerome J. Trakszelis. In Res., Revs. John J. O'Malley, O.P.; Kevin O'Rourke, O.P.; Kevin R. Fane, O.P.; Peter J. Hereley, O.P.; Albert G. Judy, O.P.; Michael A. Garcia, O.P.; Andrew M. McAlpin, O.P.; John Fabian, O.P.
Res.: 1530 Jackson Ave., 60305. Tel: 708-366-7090; Fax: 708-366-7092. Web: www.svfparish.org.
Church: 1530 Jackson Ave., 60305.
School—1515 Lathrop Ave., 60305. Tel: 708-771-5905; Fax: 708-771-7114. Dr. Charles F. Terry, Prin. Lay Teachers 16; Students 244.
Catechesis/Religious Program—1527 Lathrop, 60305. Tel: 708-366-7090, Ext. 144. Students 130.

RIVER GROVE, COOK CO., ST. CYPRIAN Revs. Eugene W. Gratkowski; Thomas M. Powers, Pastor Emeritus (Retired); Deacon James Platt, (Retired).
Res.: 2601 Clinton St., 60171. Tel: 708-453-4800; Fax: 708-453-6141. Email: stcyprianchurch@netzero.net. Web: www.stcyprian.org.
School—2561 Clinton St., 60171. Tel: 708-453-6300; Fax: 708-453-6141. Sr. Kathleen Klinger, O.P., Prin. Religious 1; Lay Teachers 10; Students 114.
Catechesis/Religious Program—Tel: 708-453-5719; Fax: 708-453-6141. Students 93.

RIVERDALE, COOK CO.

1—ST. MARY QUEEN OF APOSTLES Rev. John L. Harvey; Deacon Gerald Hahn.
Res.: 207 W. 145th St., 60827. Tel: 708-849-4901; Fax: 708-849-5903. Email: qofa207@att.net.
School—Christ Our Savior, (Inter-Parish School), Tel: 708-333-8173. Web: www.christoursaviorcatholicschool.org.

2—QUEEN OF APOSTLES (1953), Closed 6/30/2011 & merged with St. Mary of the Assumption, Chicago to form St. Mary Queen of Apostles.

RIVERSIDE, COOK CO., ST. MARY Revs. Thomas P. May; Leon R. Wagner, Pastor Emeritus (Retired); Michal Lewon; Sr. Margaret Sannasardo, B.V.M., Pastoral Assoc.; Deacons Thomas W. Coffey; Robert Boharic. In Res., Rev. Thomas Heskin, O.S.M.
Res.: 126 Herrick Rd., 60546. Tel: 708-447-1020; Fax: 708-447-3309. Email: maryriver@stmaryriverside.org. Web: www.stmaryriverside.org.

School—97 Herrick Rd., 60546. Tel: 708-442-5747; Fax: 708-442-0125. Ms. Diane M. Simonaitis, Prin. Lay Teachers 24; Students 399.
Catechesis/Religious Program—Tel: 708-447-6812. Barbara Outly, D.R.E. Students 390.

ROLLING MEADOWS, COOK CO., ST. COLETTE Rev. Peter Galek; Deacons John Connor; Antero Santos.
Res.: 3900 S. Meadow Dr., 60008. Tel: 847-394-8100; Fax: 847-394-8102.
School—Tel: 847-392-4098; Fax: 847-392-8155. Ms. Valarie Zemko, Prin. Lay Teachers 16; Students 173.
Catechesis/Religious Program—Students 291.

ROSEMONT-DES PLAINES, COOK CO., OUR LADY OF HOPE Revs. John W. Clemens; William D. Mannion, Pastor Emeritus (Retired); Deacon James J. Ernst. In Res., Rev. Msgr. Kenneth Velo.
Res.: 9711 W. Devon Ave., 60018. Tel: 847-825-4673; Fax: 847-825-4631.
Catechesis/Religious Program—Students 132.

ROUND LAKE, LAKE CO., ST. JOSEPH Revs. Timothy J. O'Malley; Armando Ramirez-Ruiz (Mexico); Deacons David Bresemann; Joel Ruiz.
Res.: 114 N. Lincoln Ave., 60073. Tel: 847-546-3610; Fax: 847-546-3449. Web: www.stjosephrl.org.
School—118 N. Lincoln Ave., 60073. Tel: 847-546-1720. Ms. Jeanne Petkus, Prin. Lay Teachers 15; Students 205.
Catechesis/Religious Program—Tel: 847-546-3554. Diane Raihle, D.R.E. Students 761.

SAUK VILLAGE, COOK CO., ST. JAMES Revs. David B. Krolczyk; David J. Simonetti.
Res.: 22400 S. Torrence Ave., 60411-5144. Tel: 708-757-2170; Fax: 708-757-2176.
Catechesis/Religious Program—Tel: 708-757-2174; Fax: 708-757-2176. Students 215.
Convent—21903 Orion St., 60411. Tel: 708-758-5431.

SCHAUMBURG, COOK CO.

1—CHURCH OF THE HOLY SPIRIT Revs. John W. Dearhammer; George J. Kane, Pastor Emeritus (Retired); Sr. Marianne Supan, O.P., Pastoral Assoc.; Deacons Wayne Beyer; Mario Contreras; Mike Enger; Sung Han; Xavier Carrera; Raymond Doud.
Res.: 1451 W. Bode Rd., 60194. Tel: 847-882-7580; Fax: 847-882-1845. Email: pastor@churchoftheholyspirit.org. Web: www.churchoftheholyspirit.org.
Catechesis/Religious Program—Tel: 847-882-7584. Students 136.

2—ST. MARCELLINE (1968) Rev. Harold B. Stanger; Deacons Joe Garcia; Thomas LaMantia; Michael Filipucci; Paul Migala; Don Maiers.
Res.: 822 Springinsguth Rd., 60193. Tel: 847-524-4429; Fax: 847-524-4597. Email: stmarcelline@stmarcelline.com. Web: www.stmarcelline.com.
Catechesis/Religious Program—Students 302.

3—ST. MATTHEW Rev. Joseph Glab, C.R.; Deacon Thomas Duszynski; Ms. Milissa Bartold, Pastoral Assoc.
Res.: 1001 E. Schaumburg Rd., 60194. Tel: 847-891-1220; Fax: 847-891-3140. Web: www.saintmatthewparish.org.
Catechesis/Religious Program—1005 Schaumburg Rd., 60194. Tel: 847-891-8408; Fax: 847-891-4291. Students 477.

SCHILLER PARK, COOK CO.

1—ST. BEATRICE (1926) Revs. Robert Schultz; Raymond P. Devereux (Retired); John J. Bresnahan (Retired).
Res.: 4157 Atlantic Ave., 60176. Tel: 847-678-0138; Fax: 847-678-3974.
Catechesis/Religious Program—Students 62.

2—ST. MARIA GORETTI (1962) Rev. James F. Blazek.
Res.: 3929 N. Wehrman Ave., 60176. Tel: 847-678-3988; Fax: 847-678-3901.
School—Tel: 847-678-2560; Fax: 847-678-2919. Ms. Christine Weiner, Prin. Lay Teachers 13; Students 246.
Catechesis/Religious Program—Students 69.

SKOKIE, COOK CO.

1—ST. JOAN OF ARC Revs. James P. Kehoe; James F. Moriarty, Pastor Emeritus (Retired).
Res.: 9248 N. Lawndale Ave., Evanston, 60203-1509. Tel: 847-673-0409; Fax: 847-673-9626. Email: sja60203@aol.com. Web: www.saintjoanofarc.net.
School—Tel: 847-679-0660; Fax: 847-673-0689. Ms. Carrie J. Bergeson, Prin. Lay Teachers 10; Students 229.
Catechesis/Religious Program—Students 90.

2—ST. LAMBERT Rev. Richard T. Simon; Deacons John C. O'Leary; Richard H. Moritz. In Res., Rev. James F. Heyd.
Res.: 8148 Karlov Ave., 60076. Tel: 847-673-5090; Fax: 847-677-5135. Email: saintlambert@aol.com. Web: www.stlambert.org.
Catechesis/Religious Program—Tel: 847-329-1201. Students 142.

3—ST. PETER Revs. Michael A. Wulsch; Andrew Wawrzyn; Deacon James Wills; Sr. Kathleen Maloney, O.S.B., Pastoral Assoc. In Res., Rev. Peter Raposo.
Res.: 8116 Niles Center Rd., 60077. Tel: 847-673-1492; Fax: 847-673-6979.
School—8140 Niles Center Rd., 60077. Tel: 847-673-0918; Fax: 847-673-6469. Mr. Sante M. Iacovelli, Prin. Lay Teachers 14; Students 150.
Catechesis/Religious Program—Tel: 847-679-1202; Fax: 847-673-6469. Students 190.

SOUTH HOLLAND, COOK CO.

1—HOLY GHOST (1962) Revs. Anthony M. Talarico; Richard J. Feller, Pastor Emeritus (Retired); Deacon James Renwick.
Res.: 700 E. 170th St., 60473. Tel: 708-333-7011; Fax: 708-333-1996.
School—Christ Our Savior, (Inter-Parish School), Tel: 708-333-8173.
Catechesis/Religious Program—Tel: 708-333-7011. Students 18.

2—ST. JUDE THE APOSTLE Revs. Ignatius I. Anaele; John J. Powers, Pastor Emeritus (Retired); Deacons Herbert Drazba; Arthur Nylen; Mel Stasinski; Timothy Springer.
Res.: 880 E. 154th St., 60473. Tel: 708-333-3550; Fax: 708-339-3336. Email: apostljude@aol.com. Web: www.stjudetheapostle.org.
School—Christ Our Savior Catholic School, Inter-Parish school serving St. Andrew, Our Lady of Knock, St. Victor, Holy Ghost, St. Jude and Queen of Apostles., 900 E. 154th St., 60473-1106. Tel: 708-333-8173.
Catechesis/Religious Program—Tel: 708-225-1180. Students 40.

STICKNEY, COOK CO., ST. PIUS X (1954) Revs. Anthony L. Markus; Neil Van Dyke, Pastor Emeritus (Retired); Deacons Marvin Kocar; Russell Ramirez; Frank Mamolella.
Res.: 4314 S. Oak Park Ave., 60402. Tel: 708-484-7951; Fax: 708-749-8518. Email: spxparish@aol.com.
Catechesis/Religious Program—4300 S. Oak Park Ave., 60402. Tel: 708-788-6090. Students 145.

STREAMWOOD, COOK CO., ST. JOHN THE EVANGELIST (1962) Revs. Theodore Schmitt; William J. Moriarity, Pastor Emeritus; Piotr Gnoinski; Deacons Earl Dahl; James Furey; Robert DeFiore; Larry Rybicki; Jozef S. Mika.
Res.: 540 S. Park Blvd., 60107. Tel: 630-837-6500; Fax: 630-483-3153.
School—513 Parkside Cir., 60107. Fax: 630-289-3026. Mrs. Mary Ellyn Billmeyer, Prin. Lay Teachers 11; Students 206.
Catechesis/Religious Program—Tel: 630-837-1060. Students 357.

SUMMIT, COOK CO., ST. JOSEPH Revs. Robert Stuglik; Thomas E. Lamping; Deacons Ben Michalowski; Richard Tryjfaczkam.
Res.: 7240 W. 57th St., 60501. Tel: 708-458-0501.
School—5641 S. 73rd Ave., 60501. Tel: 708-458-2927. Lay Teachers 13; Students 226.
Catechesis/Religious Program—Students 168.

TINLEY PARK, COOK CO.

1—ST. GEORGE (1934) Revs. Kenneth J. Fleck; William J. Curran; Franciszek Florczyk (Poland); Deacons John Ficker; Joseph Panek; Gregory Bartos; Peter Manning. In Res., Rev. Blaise Coelho.
Res.: 6707 W. 175th St., 60477. Tel: 708-532-2243; Fax: 708-532-2055. Web: www.stgeorge60477.org.
School—6700 W. 176th St., 60477. Tel: 708-532-2626; Fax: 708-532-2025. Mr. Edward Weston, Prin. Mantellate Sisters 1; Lay Teachers 15; Students 300.
Catechesis/Religious Program—6670 W. 176th St., 60477. Tel: 708-532-8211; Fax: 708-532-3372. Nancy Bishop, CRE. Students 384.

2—SAINT JULIE BILLIART Revs. Steven M. Lanza; Michael F. Wheaton; Deacons Michael Kiley; Richard Miska, Business Mgr.; Edward Pluchar; William Lubben; Sr. Gael Gensler, Pastoral Assoc.; Deanne Tumpich, Music Dir.; Sheila Pluchar, Youth Min.; Mary Alice Roth, Liturgy Director.
Res.: 7399 W. 159th St., 60477. Tel: 708-429-6767; Fax: 708-429-6788. Web: www.stjulie.org.
Catechesis/Religious Program—Tel: 708-429-1044. Patricia Kmak, D.R.E. Students 684.

3—ST. STEPHEN, DEACON AND MARTYR (1999) Revs. James Finno; Grzegorz Warmuz; Deacons Joseph Stalcup Sr.; Kenneth Zawadzki; William Engler; Charles McFarland; Peter Van Merkestyn; William Schultz.
Res.: 17500 S. 84th Ave., 60487. Tel: 708-342-2400; Fax: 708-342-1545. Email: karen@ststephentinley.com. Web: www.ststephentinley.com.
Catechesis/Religious Program—Mary Jeanne Pazin, D.R.E. Students 1,478.

VOLO, LAKE CO., ST. PETER Revs. James E. Isaacon, S.J.C., Admin.; Anthony Rice, S.J.C.
Mailing Address: 27551 Volo Village Rd., 60073.
Res.: 27570 Volo Village Rd., 60073. Tel: 815-385-5496. Email: stpetervolo@juno.com. Web: www.stpetervolo.org.
Catechesis/Religious Program—Students 136.

WADSWORTH, LAKE CO., ST. PATRICK Revs. Fred Pesek Jr.; George J. Dyer, Pastor Emeritus (Retired); Deacons Thomas F. Adams; Louis Abboud; William Gibbons; Edward Tomkowiak; David Egan; David Wagner; Dennis Brown, Pastoral Assoc.; Jeremy N. Carter; Bernie Oberdick, Music Dir.
Mailing Address: 15000 Wadsworth Rd., 60083.
Res.: 15040 Wadsworth Rd., 60083. Tel: 847-244-4161; Fax: 847-336-0630. Web: www.stpatrickwadsworth.org.
School—15020 Wadsworth Rd., 60083. Tel: 847-623-8446; Fax: 847-623-3119. Marcella Bosnak, Prin.; Barb Cegieliski, Vice Prin. Lay Teachers 26; Students 633.
Catechesis/Religious Program—Tel: 847-236-9131; Fax: 847-336-0630. John Devine, Youth Min. Students 155.

WAUCONDA, LAKE CO., TRANSFIGURATION Revs. Ronald J. Gollatz; Juan Pablo Avila-Ibarra; Deacons Marion Omiatek; Feliks Pezowicz; Jose Mancilla.
Res.: 316 W. Mill St., 60084. Tel: 847-526-2400; Fax: 847-526-2961. Email: parish@transfig-wauconda.org. Web: www.transfig-wauconda.org.
School—Tel: 847-526-6311; Fax: 847-526-4637. Mrs. Tina M. Vakiljnejad, Prin. Lay Teachers 12; Students 156.
School—Frassati Catholic Academy, (Grades 6-8), Ministry of St. Mary of the Assumption; Santa Maria del Popolo, Mundelein., Tel: 847-487-5600; Fax: 847-487-5611. Email: elem.frassatica@archchicago.org. Web: www.frassaticatholicacademy.org. Dr. Dianne Vida, Prin.; Rev. Ronald J. Lewinski, Pres.
Catechesis/Religious Program—Tel: 847-526-6400. Students 504.

WAUKEGAN, LAKE CO.

1—ST. ANASTASIA Revs. Aloysius Funtila; Edward S. Maraczewski, Pastor Emeritus (Retired).
Res.: 624 Douglas Ave., 60085. Tel: 847-623-2875; Fax: 847-623-4882.
School—Tel: 847-623-8320; Fax: 847-623-0556. Mrs. Lourdes G. Mon, Prin. Lay Teachers 14; Students 288.
Catechesis/Religious Program—Students 120.

2—ST. BARTHOLOMEW, Merged with St. Joseph. See Holy Family for details.

3—ST. DISMAS Revs. Patrick J. Rugen; John M. Ryan, Pastor Emeritus (Retired); Deacons Anthony Sacramento; Victor Ruiz; Bruce Peters.
Res.: 2600 Sunset Ave., 60087. Tel: 847-623-5050; Fax: 847-623-5292. Web: www.stdismasparish.net.
Catechesis/Religious Program—2226 McAree Rd., 60087. Tel: 847-244-9510. Students 138.

4—HOLY FAMILY, Merged with Immaculate Conception B.V.M., Waukegan to form Most Blessed Trinity, Waukegan.

5—IMMACULATE CONCEPTION B.V.M., Merged with Holy Family, Waukegan to form Most Blessed Trinity, Waukegan.

6—ST. JOSEPH, Merged with St. Bartholomew, Waukegan. See Holy Family for details.

7—MOST BLESSED TRINITY Revs. Daniel F. Hartnett, S.J.; Nestor Torres (Colombia); Benjamin Arevalos Lupercia; Jose Gabriel Torres Garzon; Deacons Marcellino Hernandez; Dennis Mudd; Gary Munda; Irwin Boppart; Pedro Martinez; Stephen I. Rynkiewicz.
450 Keller Ave., 60085-5030.
School—Academy of Our Lady, 510 Grand Ave., 60085. Tel: 847-623-4110; Fax: 847-599-0477. Lay Teachers 16; Students 17.
Catechesis/Religious Program—Students 179.

WESTCHESTER, COOK CO.

1—DIVINE INFANT Revs. Michael J. Wanda; Gerald P. Joyce, Pastor Emeritus (Retired); Thomas Winikates.
Res.: 1601 Newcastle Ave., 60154. Tel: 708-865-8071; Fax: 708-865-8032. Web: dnn.archchicago.org/divineinfant.
School—Tel: 708-865-0122; Fax: 708-865-9495. Mr. Leonard J. Gramorossa, Prin. Lay Teachers 13; Students 168.
Catechesis/Religious Program—Students 158.

2—DIVINE PROVIDENCE Revs. Thomas E. Unz; John C. Rosemeyer, Pastor Emeritus (Retired); Rev. Msgr. John V. Dolciamore, Pastor Emeritus (Retired); Deacons Jerry Fox; Edward DeLorenzo.
Res.: 2550 S. Mayfair Ave., 60154. Tel: 708-562-3364; Fax: 708-562-3134. Email: pastor@dprov.org. Web: www.dprov.org.
School—2500 S. Mayfair Ave., 60154. Tel: 708-562-2258; Fax: 708-562-9171. Mr. Jerry M. Spatara, Prin. Lay Teachers 11; Students 195.
Catechesis/Religious Program—Tel: 708-562-3422; Fax: 708-562-3134. Students 137.

WESTERN SPRINGS, COOK CO., ST. JOHN OF THE CROSS (1960) Revs. David P. Dowdle; Joseph F. McDonnell, Pastor Emeritus (Retired); Darrio L. Boscutti; Filbert Ngwila; Deacons Thomas McGorey; Joseph Pepitone; John E. Schopp IV. In Res., Rev. Deusdedit Byomuhangi (Extern).

Res.: 5005 Wolf Rd., 60558. Tel: 708-246-4404; Fax: 708-246-4566.
School—705 51st St., 60558. Tel: 708-246-4454; Fax: 708-246-9010. Mrs. Kathleen A. Govman, Prin. Lay Teachers 34; Students 657.
Catechesis/Religious Program—51st St. & Wolf Rd., 60558. Tel: 708-246-6760; Fax: 708-246-9010. Students 1,316.

WHEELING, COOK CO., ST. JOSEPH THE WORKER Revs. Michael J. Bonner, S.V.D.; Jerzy Gawlik, S.V.D.; Krzysztof B. Pipa, S.V.D.; Deacons Martin Carrillo; Steve Stecker.
Res.: 181 W. Dundee Rd., 60090. Tel: 847-537-2740; Fax: 847-537-7914.
Polska Parafialna Szkola Im. Juliusza Slowackiego, NFP—Web: www.juliuszlowacki.com.
Catechesis/Religious Program—Tel: 847-537-4182. Students 367.

WILLOW SPRINGS, COOK CO., OUR LADY, MOTHER OF THE CHURCH POLISH MISSION Revs. John Muc, O.Cist., Dir.; Michael Blicharski, O.Cist.; Ludwik Zyla, O.Cist.
Mailing Address: Box 334, Argo, 60501.
Church: 116 Hilton St., 60480-0479. Tel: 708-467-0436; Fax: 708-467-0479. Email: cistercianfathers@yahoo.com.
Catechesis/Religious Program—

WILMETTE, COOK CO.
1—ST. FRANCIS XAVIER Revs. William J. Sheridan; Edward F. Harnett, Pastor Emeritus (Retired); Przemyslaw Wojcik; Sr. Joyce Shanabarger, O.S.F., Pastoral Assoc.; Dr. Patty Jane Pelton, Pastoral Assoc.; Deacon Robert Kerls. In Res., Rev. Richard Jakubik.
Office: 524 Ninth St., 60091-2714. Tel: 847-256-4250; Fax: 847-256-4254. Email: sfxparish@comcast.net. Web: www.sfxparish.org.
School—808 Linden Ave., 60091-2714. Tel: 847-256-0644; Fax: 847-256-0753. Daniel G. McKenna, Prin. Lay Teachers 28; Students 359.
Catechesis/Religious Program—Tel: 847-251-6730; Fax: 847-256-4254. Sr. Mary Ann Casey, O.P., Dir. PREP Prog. Students 409.
2—ST. JOSEPH Revs. Robert F. Tonelli; Henry C. Kricek; Gosbertus Rwezahura; Deacon Derald Shinkle. In Res., Rev. Jacek A. Jura.
Res.: 1747 Lake Ave., 60091. Tel: 847-251-0771; Fax: 847-251-7715.
School—1740 Lake Ave., 60091. Tel: 847-256-7870. Laura Clark, Prin. Lay Teachers 23; Students 334.
Catechesis/Religious Program—Tel: 847-851-3734. Ms. Dana McKenna, D.R.E. Students 408.

WINNETKA, COOK CO.
1—SS. FAITH, HOPE AND CHARITY Revs. Martin E. O'Donovan; Paul G. Stemn; Deacons Michael Cavanaugh; Barry Schliesmann; Susan Martin, Pastoral Assoc. In Res., Rev. William J. Flaherty (Retired).
Res.: 191 Linden St., 60093. Tel: 847-446-7646; Fax: 847-446-7630. Web: www.faithhope.org.
School—180 Ridge Ave., 60093. Tel: 847-446-0031; Fax: 847-446-9064. Mrs. Mary C. Rehfield, Prin. Sisters 1; Lay Teachers 32; Students 359.
Catechesis/Religious Program—200 Ridge Rd., 60093. Tel: 847-446-1828; Fax: 847-446-2145. Students 550.
2—SACRED HEART Revs. Robert J. Heidenreich; Robert Ferrigan, Pastor Emeritus (Retired); Collins Kisaka Nyache; Deacons Michael McNulty; John Fay; Gerald M. Keenan.
Res.: 1077 Tower Rd., 60093. Tel: 847-446-0856; Fax: 847-501-5311. Email: sh@shparish.com. Web: www.shparish.com.
Parish Center—1090 Gage St., 60093. Tel: 847-446-0856.
School—1095 Gage St., 60093. Tel: 847-446-0005. Sr. Kathleen Donnelly, O.P., Prin. Lay Teachers 31; Students 291.
Catechesis/Religious Program—Tel: 847-446-6535; Fax: 847-446-1969. Students 504.

ZION-BEACH PARK, LAKE CO., OUR LADY OF HUMILITY Revs. Thomas Hoffman; David J. Mulvihill, Pastor Emeritus (Retired); Deacons James Askew; Michael Mercure; Robert Ochsner.
Res.: 10655 W. Wadsworth Rd., 60099-3558. Tel: 847-872-8778; Fax: 847-872-8780. Email: olhch@yahoo.com. Web: ourladyofhumility.org.
School—10601 Wadsworth Rd., 60099. Tel: 847-746-3722; Fax: 847-731-2870. Patrick Browne, Prin. Lay Teachers 15; Students 277.
Catechesis/Religious Program—Tel: 847-746-3744; Fax: 847-872-8780. Students 287.

Syro-Malabar Rite

BELLWOOD, COOK CO., SYRO-MALABAR CATHOLIC MISSION OF THE ARCHDIOCESE OF CHICAGO, See separate listing. Under the Diocese of St. Thomas Syro-Malabar.

CHICAGO, COOK CO., KNANITE SYRO-MALABAR CATHOLIC MISSION OF THE ARCHDIOCESE OF CHICAGO, See separate listing. Under the Diocese of St. Thomas Syro-Malabar.

Malankara Rite

CHICAGO, COOK CO., SYRO-MALANKARA CATHOLIC MISSION OF THE ARCHDIOCESE OF CHICAGO
Divine Liturgy-Ascension Church—1208 Ashland Ave., Evanston, 60202. Tel: 847-332-1794; Fax: 847-424-0889. Rev. Saji George Mukkoot, Dir. In Res., Rev. Thomas Kuttiyanickal, S.A.C.

Chaplains of Public Institutions

CHICAGO. *Chicago Airports Catholic Chaplaincy*, P.O. Box 66353, 60666. Rev. Michael G. Zaniolo, S.T.L., C.A.C.
Hines V.A. Hospital. Revs. James Burnett (DAV), Benjamin Chinnappan (India) (MO), Terry L. Langford, Leoncio S. Santiago.
John H. Stroger, Jr. Hospital of Cook County, Tel: 312-864-1246. Revs. Eugene J. Nevins, S.J., Dir., James Chambers, S.J., Robert E. Finn, S.J., Sr. Marie Louise Jilk, S.Sp.S.

NORTH CHICAGO. *Veterans Affairs Medical Center*. Rev. William F. Vander Heyden (GB).

OAK FOREST. *Oak Forest Hospital*, 4700 W. 159th St., 60452. Tel: 708-687-2035. Rev. Wayne H. Wurst.

On Duty Outside the Archdiocese:
Rev. Msgrs.—
Brankin, Patrick M., St. Theresa, P.O. Box 297, Collinsville, OK 74021-0297.
Dobes, George E., J.C.L., 3370 S. 2nd St., Arlington, VA 22204-1709.
Trisco, Robert F., Hist.Eccl.D. (Retired), Curley Hall, Catholic University of America, Washington, DC 20064.
Revs.—
Kiley, J. Cletus, Pres. & CEO, Faith & Politics Institute, 110 Maryland Ave., N.E., Ste. 504, Washington, DC 20002.
Lorenz, Matthais E., 5531 E. Lake Dr., #31C, Lisle, 60532.

Military Chaplains:
Revs.—
Barkemeyer, John F., c/o Mr. & Mrs. Barkemeyer, 120 Fourth St., Wilmette, 60091.
Carlson, Kenneth F., M.Div., c/o 17020 Como Ave., Lockport, 60441.
Doering, Christopher, HQ. RC. South-HSC 82nd Airborne Div., Apo, AE 09355.
Foley, Matthew E., 145 Curling Stone Pl., Alpharetta, GA 30022-5274.
Greschel, Mark, 3731 Laguna Vista Dr., #2, Fayetteville, NC 28311.
Hannigan, John T., 409 Waters Cove, Stafford, VA 22554-3981.
Keener, Robert J., 3534 W. 198th St., Flossmoor, 60422. USN
Kilian, Waldemar A., Chap., Naval Station Command, 2601A Paul Jones St., Great Lakes, 60088. USN
Kloak, David G., ForceChaplain III, Marine Expeditionary Force Unit 35605, Fpo, AP 96606-5605.
Nguyen, Hoang H., 300 E. Poplar Ave., Fairchild Air Force Base, WA 99011.
Simpson, Brian L., 10098 Benning Rd., Columbia, SC 29207-5307.

Missionary Work:
Revs.—
Cleary, Philip C., 5503 Danbury Cir., Lake In The Hills, 60156.
Hays, Kevin W., Missionary Society of St. James the Apostle, 24 Clark St., Boston, MA 02109.

Other Assignments:
Revs.—
Becker, Charles P., P.O. Box 633, Wauconda, 60084.
Behnke, Robert C., 2825 W. 81st St., 60652.
Brennan, Patrick J., St. Thomas the Apostle, 1500 Brookdale, Naperville, 60563.
Coleman, Robert P., 5802 Bullock Freeway, C1-9-292, Laredo, TX 78041.
Egan, Gerard P., Hancock Bldg., 175 E. Delaware, Apt. 4810, 60611.
Galivan, James F., 1039 W. 32nd St., 60608.
Gilligan, Michael J., Ph.D., S.T.L., San Rocco Oratory of St. Agnes, 315 E. 22nd St & San Rocco Pl., Chicago Hts., 60411.
Henseler, Philip E., Holy Family Villa, 12220 S. Will-Cook Rd., Orland Park, 60462-4898.
Hergenrother, John C., W7585 Ethelyn Dr., Delavan, WI 53115-2698.
Heyd, James F., Priests for Life, Maryville, 1150 N. River Rd., Des Plaines, 60016.
Kleiber, Kenneth R., 15202 N. 40th St., #223-2, Phoenix, AZ 85032-4652.
Laz, Medard P., P.O. Box 300415, 60630.
Lefebure, Leo D., Our Lady of Victory, 4835 MacArthur Blvd. N.W., Washington, DC 20007.
Lewanski, Gary J., 3525 W. 55th Pl., 60629.
Lupton, Brendan P., Catholic University of America, 3015 4th St., N.E., Washington, DC 20017-1199.
Marin, Moises, 980 N. Michigan Ave., Ste. 1525, 60611.
Martinez Solis, Jesus E., St. Columbkille, 6315 S. Main St., Los Angeles, CA 90003.
McNalis, John P., 3219 W. Dickens, 60647.
McQuaid, Thomas W., 100 N. Hermitage #914, 60612.
Munoz-Capetillo, Octavio, Casa Jesus, 750 N. Wabash, 60611.
Nangle, Thomas R., Police Chaplaincy, 1140 W. Jackson, 60607.
Nguyen, Joseph Thai, 7800 Carousel Ln., Richmond, VA 23294.
Nguyen, Phien T., St. Callistus, 12921 Lewis St., Garden Grove, CA 92840.
Parrish, L. Jerome, c/o 2610 E. 78th St., 60649.
Patte, Steven W., 980 N. Michigan Ave., #1525, 60611.
Quinlan, James V., 3050 N.E. 47th Ct., Fort Lauderdale, FL 33308.
Riley, Dennis S., 7801 S. Ingleside Ave., 60619-3215.
Sanchez-Espinoza, Juan, 980 N. Michigan Ave., Ste. 1525, 60611.
Spiess, Kevin J., 1401 Burr Oak Rd., #202B, Hinsdale, 60521.
Stake, Ronald P., Nsa Bahrain, Psc 451, Box 90, Fpo, AE 09834-2800.
Stefanski, Gery W., 902 Oakton, Unit 1A, Evanston, 60202.
Strus, Walter A., 1039 W. 32nd St., 60608.
Zimmer, William E., 5758 W. Potomoac Ave., 60651-1132.

Retired:
Rev. Msgrs.—
Adams, Michael J., Christ the King, 9235 S. Hamilton Ave., 60620.
Coughlin, Daniel P., 5100 N. Marine Dr. #27M, 60640.
Dolciamore, John V., J.C.L., S.T.L., University of St. Mary of the Lake, 1000 E. Maple Ave., Mundelein, 60060-1174.
Kuzinskas, John A., Holy Family Villa, 12220 S. Will-Cook Rd., Palos Park, 60464-7332.
Mahon, Leo T., St. Mary of the Woods, 7033 N. Moselle Ave., 60646.
Maniola, Francis N., 6135 S. Austin, 60638.
McNamara, John P., Bishop Lyne Home, 12230 S. Will-Cook Rd., Palos Park, 60464.
Meyer, Charles R., M.A., S.T.D., Mundelein Seminary, University of St. Mary of the Lake, Mundelein, 60060.
Mroczkowski, Joseph L., 1501 Hoffman St., Hammond, IN 46327.
O'Donnell, Richard J., 3528 S. Hermitage, 60609.
Prist, Wayne, Queen of All Saints, Chicago, 6280 N. Sauganash Ave., 60646.
Revs.—
Adamich, Albert R., Most Holy Redeemer, 9525 S. Lawndale Ave., Evergreen Park, 60042.
Ahearn, Donald J., St. Juliana, 7142 N. Osceola, 60063.
Alcantara, Miguel B., Abby Manor, 7450 Waukegan Ave., #209, Niles, 60714.
Anglim, Ronald H., 7231 S. Wolf Rd. F6, Indian Head Park, 60525.
Auer, Joseph E., Bishop Lyne Home, 12210 S. Will-Cook Rd., Palos Park, 60464-7332.
Baldwin, John F., CHC, USN, 1002 Fontana Dr., Alameda, CA 94502.
Balskus, Charles, St. Mary, Star of the Sea, 6435 S. Kilbourn Ave., 60629-5599.
Banzin, Robert S., 5100 Marine Dr., #13 M, 60640.
Bonin, Harold A., St. Jerome, 1709 W. Lunt Ave., 60623-3212.
Bowler, Michael J., 3211 S. Racine Ave., 2nd. Fl. Front, 60608.
Brady, Daniel J., 432 W. Park St., Arlington Heights, 60005.
Bresnahan, John J., 1675 Mill St., Apt. 504, Des Plaines, 60018.
Broccolo, Gerard T., 1011 S. Valentia St., #135, Denver, CO 80231.
Burke, William A., Bishop Lyn Home, 12230 S. Will-Cook Rd., Palos Park, 60464.
Caplis, Roger J., P.O. Box 656, Williams Bay, WI 53191-0656.
Carolan, John J., St. Catherine of Siena-St. Lucy, 38 N. Austin Blvd., Oak Park, 60302.
Cassidy, John M., St. Benedict Nursing and Rehab. Center, 6930 W. Touhy Ave., Niles, 60714.
Cerny, George F., Holy Family Villa, 12220 S. Will-Cook Rd., Orland Park, 60462-4898.
Chen, Anthony K., St. Martin De Porres Hospital, 565, Sec. 2, Daya Rd., Chiayi City 600, Taiwan.
Clements, George H., 10226 S. Trumbull St., Evergreen Park, 60805.
Colleran, James A., 8627 Wapalo Rd., Marshall, IN 47859.
Collins, Daniel J., 4200 N. Sheridan Rd., 60613.

Corbo, Alfred P., 321 Bryn Mawr, Itasca, 60143.
Corcoran, Edward G., P.O. Box 28232, San Diego, CA 92128.
Costello, William J., 632 Pinehurst Ct., Twin Lakes, WI 53181.
Cowell, Raymond, Paraoquia Nuest, Sen De Fatima, El Pari Casilla 919, Santa Cruz, Bolivia.
Cross, Robert A., 700 Ashland, River Forest, 60305.
Darow, Robert G., 5901 N. Sauganash Ln., 60646.
Dempsey, Richard J., 11022 S. Fairfield Ave., 60655.
Devereux, Raymond P., 923 Forest Ave., River Forest, 60305.
Devine, William J., P.O. Box 53, Worth, 60482.
Dewes, John W., St. Anne, 120 N. Ela St., Barrington, 60010.
Donohue, John J., 282 Woodstone Cir., Buffalo Grove, 60089-6701.
Dore, Thomas M., St. Pascal, 3935 N. Melvina Ave., 60634-2527.
Dovick, Robert E., Alvernia Manor, 13950 Main St., Lemont, 60439.
Dressler, Philip J., 7142 N. Osceola Ave., 60631.
Durkin, Eugene F., Holy Name Cathedral, 730 N. Wabash Ave., 60611.
Dyer, George J., 890 Audubon Way Bw-T12, Lincolnshire, 60069.
Falkenthal, Thomas W., Apostleship/Seaport Everglades, 1835 N.E. Miami Gardens Dr., #294, P.O. Box 55001, North Miami Beach, FL 33179.
Farry, John A., St. Andrew, 3546 N. Paulina St., 60657.
Faucher, Eugene J., St. Edna, 2525 N. Arlington Heights Rd., Arlington Heights, 60004.
Felczak, Leonard J., 4325 S. Spaulding, 60632.
Feller, Richard J., 1201 Bonita, Park Ridge, 60068.
Fenske, Donald J., Our Lady of Knock, 501 163rd St., Calumet City, 60409.
Ferrigan, Robert, 1340 N. Dearborn, Unit 17A, 60610.
Finnegan, John P., 660 Chandler Rd., Gurnee, 60031.
Finnegan, William J., 14327 Highland Ave., Orland Park, 60462.
Fitzpatrick, Robert J., St. Bede Parish, 36455 N. Wilson Rd., Ingleside, 60041-9609.
Flaherty, William J., 191 Linden St., Winnetka, 60093-3832.
Flavin, John E., St. Benedict Nursing and Rehab., 6930 Touhy Ave., Niles, 60714.
Frawley, John P., 2825 W. 81st St., 60652-2722.
Gallagher, Charles G., St. Cletus, 600 W. 55th St., La Grange, 60525.
Gallagher, James R., 2108 S. Scoville, Berwyn, 60402.
Gerrity, Raymond J., 917 S. 8th Ave., #2, LaGrange, 60525.
Goedert, William O., St. Germaine, 4240 W. 98th St., Oak Lawn, 60453.
Goergen, Michael A., 4949 W. Patterson Ave., 60641.
Grace, James N., 1833 E. Wildberry Dr., Glenview, 60025.
Grace, John J., St. Benedict Home, 6930 Touhy, Niles, 60714.
Greeley, Andrew M., 175 E. Delaware Pl., 60611.
Gubbins, William B., 9440 Seton Pl., Orland Park, 60459.
Guz, Edmund F., 14207 S. Green Bay Rd., Burnham, 60633.
Harnett, Edward F., St. Francis Xavier, 524 Ninth St., Wilmette, 60091.
Headley, Donald J., St. Mary of the Woods, 7033 N. Moselle Ave., 60646.
Healy, Thomas I., St. Bonaventure Oratory, 1641 W. Diversey Pkwy., 60614.
Herne, Robert G., Sacred Heart Parish, 8245 W. 111th St., Palos Hills, 60465.
Hung, Peter, St. Thomas of Canterbury, 4827 N. Kenmore Ave., 60634-2527.
Hurley, John J., St. Edna, 2525 N. Arlington Hts. Rd., Arlington Hts., 60004.
Huske, Leonard G., 347 Daffodil Ln., Matteson, 60443.
Ivers, Victor J., St. Benedict Home, 6930 W. Touhy Ave., Niles, 60714.
Jabusch, Willard F., 5040 Warren St., Apt. 404, Skokie, 60077.
Janik, Bruno, Ul. Cegielniana 18/E/24, Rzeow 35-068 Poland.
Jasinski, Raymond J., Rosary Hill Nursing Home, 9000 W. 81st St., Justice, 60458.
Joslyn, James W., 9935 S. Clifton Park, Evergreen Park, 60805.
Joyce, Gerald P., Divine Infant, 1601 Newcastle Ave., Westchester, 60154.
Kalas, Ronald N., 7258 W. Gregory, 60656.
Kane, George J., 1700 Cambourne, Schaumburg, 60194.
Kash, Robert J., Bishop Lyne Home, 12230 S. Will-Cook Rd., Palos Park, 60464.
Kastigar, John J., 1774 Lexington Dr., Sierra Vista, AZ 85635.
Kaveney, Thomas J., St. Odilo, 2244 S. East Ave., Berwyn, 60402.
Kenneally, William G., 10427 S. Hoyne, 60643.
Kinn, James W., 6318 243rd Ct., Salem, WI 53168.
Kissane, Maurice J., 21663 Howell Dr., Cassopolis, MI 49031.
Klein, George W., St. Philip the Apostle, 1962 Old Willow Rd., Northfield, 60093.
Knittel, Kilian J., P.O. Box 9408, Michigan City, IN 46361.
Kouba, Charles J., St. Benedict Home, 6930 W. Touhy Ave., Niles, 60714.
Krebs, John F., Resurrection Retirement Community, 7260 W. Peterson Ave. Apt. E-511, 60631.
Laske, Kenneth S., 4032 W. Nelson St., 60641.
Lee, Joseph, 6157 N. Leavitt St., 60659.
Lewandowski, Ronald C., 24961 87th St., #3, Salem, WI 53168.
Lion, William J., Catherine of Alexandria, 4100 W. 107th St., Oak Lawn, 60453.
Lisowski, William J., 15714 Old Orchard Ct., Orland Park, 60462.
Lund, Donald J., 726 Westmore Rd., Davis, 61019.
Lynch, Joseph P., 14130 Green Valley Dr., Orland Park, 60462.
Maddock, Laurence F., S.T.L., St. Joseph Seminary College at Loyola University, 6551 N. Sheridan Rd., 60626.
Maginot, Richard J., St. Benedict Home, 6930 W. Touhy Ave., W4, Niles, 60714.
Maher, Thomas F., Resurrection Life Center, 7370 W. Talcott Ave., 60631.
Mair, Robert G., c/o Thomas Place, 2200 Patriot Blvd., Glenview, 60026.
Mallette, Daniel J., St. Margaret of Scotland, 9837 S. Throop St., 60643.
Maloney, Edward J., 7417 Channahon Ct., Fox Lake, 60020.
Mannion, William D., 5100 N. Marine Dr., #15A, 60640.
Maraczewski, Edward S., 1516 E. Lowden Ln., Mount Prospect, 60056.
Marszalek, Paul B., Bishop Lyne Residence, 12230 S. Will-Cook Rd., Palos Park, 60464-7332.
Martin, Richard J., 10806 S. Trumbull, 60655.
Maxa, Edward J., 2745 W. 44th St., 60632-1999.
McCarthy, James H., SPRED, 2953 S. Lowe Ave., 60616.
McCarthy, Terrence A., 1301 N. Western Ave., #320, Lake Forest, 60045.
McCarthy, Warren J., 1080 W. Irving Park Rd., Roselle, 60172.
McDonnell, Joseph F., 17 W. 706 Butterfield Rd., Oakbrook Terrace, 60181.
McGinnity, Robert F., Sacred Heart, 8245 W. 111th St., Palos Hills, 60465.
McGlinn, Robert J., St. Hyacinth, 1414 W. Becher St., Milwaukee, WI 53215.
McGrath, John F., St. Thomas More, 2825 W. 81st St., 60652.
McKenna, Edward J., P.O. Box 648, Beverly Shores, IN 46301-0648.
McKenna, George P., Bishop Lyne Home, 12230 S. Will-Cook Rd., Palos Park, 60464.
McLaughlin, Edward, Incarnation, 5757 W. 127th St., Palos Heights, 60463.
McNulty, William J., 1433 Perry St., #402, Des Plaines, 60016.
Merold, James E., St. Gabriel, 4522 S. Wallace St., 60609.
Meyr, Herbert J., 1706 N. Broadway, Melrose Park, 60130.
Mikolaitis, Vito E., Bishop Lyne Home, 12230 Will-Cook Rd., Palos Park, 60464.
Millea, Thomas V., P.O. Box 48623, Niles, 60714.
Moriarty, James F., Bishop Lyne Home, 12230 Will-Cook Rd., Palos Park, 60464.
Mueller, Richard J., 1809 Walters Ave., Northbrook, 60062.
Mulcahy, Gerald F., 8225 Concord Ln., Apt. C, Justice, 60458.
Mulvihill, David J., J.C.D., Ph.D., St. Benedict Nurs & Rehab, 6930 W. Touhy Ave., Rm. 21, Niles, 60714-4522.
Murphy, Harold B., St. Margaret Mary, 2324 W. Chase Ave., 60645.
Murphy, James P., 1623 Ashland, Apt. 5E, Des Plaines, 60016.
Murray, John W., 1804 N. Riverwoods Dr., Melrose Park, 60160.
Nemecek, Cyril, 2333 S. 8th Ave., North Riverside, 60546.
Nicola, John J., Belle Meade, 400 Waters Dr., Apt. D1-13, Southern Pines, NC 28387.
Novak, Robert J., Addolorata Villa, 553 McHenry Rd., Apt. 271, Wheeling, 60090.
O'Brien, James J., M.A., St. Monica, 5136 N. Nottingham Ave., 60656-3696.
O'Brien, Joseph, 300 N. State St., #2627, 60610.
O'Connor, James T., 447 N. Dover Ave., LaGrange Park, 60526.
O'Malley, James F., Bishop Timothy J. Lyne Residence for Retired Priests, 12230 S. Will-Cook Rd., Palos Park, 60464.
O'Malley, Patrick J., M.A., S.T.L., Mundelein Seminary, University of St. Mary of the Lake, 1000 E. Maple, Mundelein, 60060.
O'Mara, William T., 9765 Cambridge Cir., Mokena, 60448.
Oldershaw, Robert H., St. Nicholas, 2244 Sherman Ave., Evanston, 60201.
Ouletta, James F., N2020 County Rd. H., S., Lot 206, Lake Geneva, WI 53147.
Pacocha, Edwin D., 2712 N. Western Ave., 60647.
Pastick, Joseph A., 191 Astaire Ln., Apt 212, Spring Hill, FL 34609.
Paurazas, Peter P., St. Patricia, 9050 S. 86th Ave., Hickory Hills, 60457.
Peng, John B., c/o Stephanie Leung, 6833 N. Minnetonka, 60646.
Powers, John J., St. Jude the Apostle, 880 E. 154th St., South Holland, 60473.
Powers, Thomas M., St. Benedict Nurs and Rehab Center, 6930 W. Touhy Ave., Niles, 60714.
Price, John R., 6054 W. 64th Pl., 60638.
Purtell, Thomas J., St. Christina, 11005 S. Homan Ave., 60655.
Reicher, A. Paul, St. John Berchmans, 2517 W. Logan Blvd., 60647.
Roache, James P., P.O. Box 58, Lyons, WI 53148-0058.
Rochford, John J., Bishop Lyne Home, 12230 S. Will-Cook Rd., Palos Park, 60464.
Rodell, Jeremiah J., Devonshire, 1700 Robin Ln., Apt. 424, Lisle, 60532.
Rogala, Gerald E., 500 Lakeview Ave., Apt. 1A, Highwood, 60040.
Roller, John W., 1400 E. Central Rd., Mount Prospect, 60056.
Rosemeyer, John C., 2550 Mayfair Ave., Westchester, 60154.
Rosemeyer, Paul F., St. Theresa, 467 Benton, Palatine, 60067.
Rudcki, Stanley R., 7712 W. Oak Ridge Ct., #2B, Palos Heights, 60463.
Rudnik, John J., Transfiguration, 2609 W. Carmen Ave., 60625.
Ruiz, Joseph B., Holy Redeemer, 9525 S. Lawndale Ave., Evergreen Park, 60805.
Ryan, John M., 26 N. Pistakee Lake Rd., #2A, Fox Lake, 60020.
Salmon, Edward P., 1045 Columbian Ave., Oak Park, 60302.
Sayers, James M., 155 Vintage Cir., Apt. 204, Naples, FL 34119.
Scanlan, Francis G., St. Damian, 5220 W. 155th St., 60452.
Scarlata, Ronald E., 1302 Franciscan Way, Joliet, 60435.
Schlax, Charles H., Nazarethville, 300 N. River Rd., Des Plaines, 60016.
Schouten, Francis L., 3755 W. 112th Pl., 60655.
Schroeder, Richard F., 7216 Oxford Cir., Fox Lake, 60020.
Seitz, Joseph W., 9131 S. Sacramento, Evergreen Park, 60805.
Shannon, Richard J., 709 79th St., Unit 107, Darien, 60561.
Sheridan, William H., 2132 E. 72nd St., 60649.
Smith, Gene F., St. Linus, 10300 S. Lawles Ave., Oak Lawn, 60453.
Springer, Lawrence F., 567 W. Algonquin Rd., Des Plaines, 60016.
Stockus, Edward S., 10508 S. Keeler, Oak Lawn, 60453.
Stone, Theodore, 355 S. Crescent, Park Ridge, 60068.
Sullivan, Daniel F., 129 E. Mill St., Apt. 203, Wauconda, 60084.
Sullivan, Daniel J., 3217 W. 184th St., Homewood, 60430.
Szabelski, Joseph R., Queen of Peace Retirement Center, 24955 N. Hwy. 12, Lake Zurich, 60047.
Tapper, John W., Mayslake Village, 1725 35th St., #2231, Oak Brook, 60523.
Taylor, Joseph C., 4350 W. Sunnyside Ave., 60630.
Thinnes, John M., 2200 Patriot Blvd., Unit 330, Glenview, 60026.
Tillrock, Raymond J., 5346 S. Cornell, Apt. 201, 60615.
Tivy, Thomas A., 951 N. Willard Ct., Unit 404, 60642.
Tuite, Howard A., 700 S. Paulina, #922, 60612.
Van Dyke, Neil, St. Pius X, 4313 S. Oak Park Ave., Stickney, 60402.
Vanecko, William E., St. Columbus, 331 E. 71st St., 60619.
Vita, Mariano L., 2949 Glacier Tr., Porter, IN 46304.

Vitro, Thomas J., P.O. Box 932, Lake Geneva, WI 53147.
Wagner, Leon R., 2435 Seabrook Island Rd., John Island, SC 29455.
Walsh, Michael J., Bishop Lyne Home, 12230 S. Will-Cook Rd., Palos Park, 60464.
Welsh, William P., 8340 Callie Ave., #314, Morton Grove, 60053.
White, Bernard C., 3020 N. 76th Ct., Elmwood Park, 60707.
Wickowski, Leroy A., St. Luke, 528 Lathrop Ave., River Forest, 60305.
Winters, Martin N., Benedictine Monastery of Our Lady of Sorrows, 5800 W. 147th St., 60452.
Wodniak, John L., 135 Castle Rock Ln., Bloomingdale, 60108.
Wojcik, Richard J., S.T.L., M.C.G., Mundelein Seminary of the University of St. Mary of the Lake, 1000 E. Maple, Mundelein, 60060.
Yadron, Raymond A., 1152 E. Anderson Dr., Palatine, 60074.
Zake, Louis J., Ph.D., 310 S. Michigan Ave., Unit 704, 60604.

Permanent Deacons:
Abboud, Louis, St. Patrick, Wadsworth
Adams, Stewart, Immaculate Conception, Highland Park
Adams, Thomas F., St. Patrick, Wadsworth
Aguilar, Ruben, St. Adrian, Chicago
Ahern, Michael, Our Lady of Victory
Albano, Terris, Our Lady of the Ridge, Chicago Ridge
Alcos, Rossini, St. Lawrence O'Toole, Matteson
Allen, Warren, (Retired), St. Kilian, Chicago
Allison, Andrew, St. Francis, LaGrange
Alonso, Enrique, Our Lady of Grace, Chicago; Office of the Diaconate
Alvarez, Ignacio, St. Turibius, Chicago
Alvarez, Jose, (Retired), St. Aloysius, Chicago
Ambe, Neba, St. Margaret Mary, Chicago
Amberg, John, (Retired), Frankfort, IL
Anderberg, Russell F., (Retired), Summerfield, FL
Andrade, David D., St. Rita of Cascia, Chicago
Annoreno, Ausgust, Our Lady Mother of the Church, Chicago
Antiss, Robert S., Holy Family, Inverness
Antonsen, Larry, Most Holy Redeemer, Evergreen Park
Arndt, John, (Retired), Evanston, IL
Arvidson, Robert, St. Francis de Sales, Lake Zurich
Askew, James, Our Lady of Humility, Beach Park/Zion
Auld, David D., Santa Maria del Popolo, Mundelein
Avila, Mario, St. Malachy & Precious Blood, Chicago
Ayala, Efrain, (Retired), Downers Grove, IL
Baier, John, Immaculate Conception, Highland Park
Baldasti, Steven, St. Hubert, Hoffman Estates
Banet, Robert, St. Andrew the Apostle, Calumet City
Barnish, Michael K., Sacred Heart, Melrose Park
Bartholomew, Thomas, St. Michael, Orland Park
Barton, Jeffrey, Prince of Peace, Lake Villa
Bartos, Gregory, St. George, Tinley Park
Battisto, John, Our Lady of Mount Carmel, Melrose Park
Baum, Richard, (Retired), Cary, IL
Beeber, Gregory M., St. Edna, Arlington Heights
Behrendt, Raymond J., Sacred Heart, Melrose Park
Beierwaltes, Andrew J., St. John Brebeuf, Niles
Beil, Frank, St. Catherine Laboure, Glenview
Belanger, James, (Retired), Niles, IL
Bell, Kenneth, St. Domitilla, Hillside
Benthey, Herman, St. Anne, Hazel Crest
Bergquist, Bernard, (Retired), Cheswick, PA
Bertolani, Philip, St. Benedict, Chicago
Beyer, Wayne, Church of Holy Spirit, Schaumburg
Bishop, Joseph, St. Elizabeth Seton, Orland Hills
Blais, Emile, (Retired), Chicago, IL
Blanco, Jesus, Our Lady of Tepeyac, Chicago
Blickle, Calvin, Jr., St. Alphonsus Ligouri, Prospect Heights
Bohannon, Morris E., (Retired), Creve Coeur, MO
Boharic, Robert, St. Mary, Riverside
Boppart, Irwin, Most Blessed Trinity, Waukegan
Borha, George, St. Thomas More, Chicago
Bovyn, Paul, Resurrection, Chicago
Bowns, Loren T., St. Irenaeus, Park Forest
Brady, Joseph, St. Christopher, Midlothian
Brauch, Robert, St. Anne, Barrington
Breit, John, St. Thomas of Villanova, Palatine
Brencic, David, St. Barbara, Brookfield
Bresemann, David, St. Joseph, Round Lake
Bretz, Michael, St. Mary, Des Plaines
Brezinski, David, St. Zachary, Des Plaines
Brooks, George, J.D., St. Anne, Hazel Crest
Brothers, David, St. Agnes, Chicago Heights
Brown, Dennis G., St. Patrick, Wadsworth
Bryce, Irvin, St. Albert the Great, Burbank
Buissereth, Rameau, Haitian Catholic Apostolate & Our Lady of Peace, Chicago
Bulger, Robert, St. Paul of the Cross, Park Ridge
Bumbul, John, St. Gall, Chicago
Burke, Henry, Ascension/St. Susanna, Harvey
Burt, John D., (Retired), Chicago, IL
Bzdon, Gregory M., St. Tarcissus, Chicago
Cabrera, Daniel, St. Hedwig
Cabrera, Jorge, St. John Berchmans, Chicago
Camerini, Guilio, Our Lady of Mt. Carmel, Melrose Park
Carerra, Xavier, Holy Spirit, Schaumburg
Carrillo, Martin, St. Joseph the Worker, Wheeling
Carrizales, Maximiliano, (Retired), Chicago, IL
Carroll, Daniel, St. Francis of Assisi, Orland Park
Carroll, James, Holy Cross, Deerfield
Carroll, Robert O., Jr., St. John Fisher, Chicago
Carter, Jeremy N., St. Patrick, Wadsworth
Carvlin, Thomas, Ascension/St. Susanna, Harvey
Casas, Jesus, St. Cletus, La Grange
Cascino, Joseph, Jr., Huntley, IL
Castaneda, David, St. Malachy & Precious Blood, Chicago
Cavanaugh, Michael, Ss. Faith, Hope and Charity, Winnetka
Centeno, Benito, (Retired), Pompano Beach, FL
Chairez, Victor, St. Simeon, Bellwood
Chausse, Joseph, (Retired), Office for the Deaf, Chicago
Chavez, Abraham, Immaculate Conception, 88th, Chicago
Chrastka, Joel, (Retired), Berwyn, IL
Christensen, Thomas, St. Turibius, Chicago
Churilla, William, St. Anne, Hazelcrest
Chyba, Lawrence J., St. Richard, Chicago
Ciciura, Michael, Ss. Cyril and Methodius, Lemont
Ciesil, Norbert, St. Alphonsus, Prospect Heights
Cintron, Gilberto, St. Hedwig, Chicago
Cislo, Robert L., St. Linus, Oak Lawn
Cisneros, Jose, St. Leonard, Berwyn
Cnota, Robert, St. Thecla, Chicago
Cocco, Anthony, St. Michael, Orland Park
Coffey, Thomas W., St. Mary, Riverside
Coleman, Alfred, II, St. Basil/Visitation, Chicago
Colgan, Dennis L., St. William; Office of the Diaconate, Chicago
Collins, Terrence C., St. James (Wabash), Chicago
Condill, James, St. Anne, Barrington
Condon, Edward, St. Cornelius, Chicago
Connor, John, St. Colette, Rolling Meadows
Contreras, Mario, Church of the Holy Spirit, Schaumburg
Conway, James, St. Barnabas, Chicago
Cook, John, St. Felicitas
Cooper, Willie, (Retired), Chicago, IL
Corcoran, Thomas, Our Lady of the Wayside, Arlington Heights
Cordesman, Ellsworth, (Retired), Lake Forest, IL
Cornejo, Salvador, (Retired), Chicago, IL
Cozzo, James, St. Eugene, Chicago
Crane, Walter James, St. Ann, Barrington
Crespo, Feliciano, St. Wencelaus, Chicago
Cunalata, Oswaldo, (Retired), Elmhurst, IL
Czarnecki, Thaddeus, St. Julian Eymard, Elk Grove Village
Dahl, Earl, St. John the Evangelist, Streamwood
Dahn, James C., Our Lady, Mother of the Church, Chicago
Damian, Eugene P., (Retired), Spring Grove, IL
Daum, Donald, (Retired), Oak Lawn, IL
Davis, James, (Retired), Forest Park, IL
Deabel, Raymond, St. James Hospital, Chicago Heights
Debnar, John, St. Barbara, Brookfield
DeFiore, Robert, St. John the Evangelist, Streamwood
DeFrank, Frank, St. Patrick, Lake Forest
Dehler, Thomas, (Retired), O'Fallon, MI
Deiters, James, St. Walter, Chicago
Del Llano, Manuel, Our Lady of Mercy, Chicago
DeLarco, Michael, St. Celestine, Elmwood Park
Delgado, Antonio, St. Robert Bellarmine, Chicago
Delisi, Leonard, (Retired), Lansing, IL
DeLorenzo, Edward, Divine Providence, Westchester
DeLuna, Arthur, Sta. Maria Addolorata, Chicago
Detloff, James, St. Emeric, Country Club Hills
Devine, James, St. Bede, Ingleside
DeVita, Frank, (Retired), Westchester, IL
Diaz, Benjamin, St. Philomena, Chicago
Diaz De Leon, Raymundo, St. Gall, Chicago
DiCanio, Vito W., St. Emily, Mt. Prospect
Dietsch, Daniel, St. Joseph, Homewood
Disparte, Philip, O'Hare Airport Chapel
Dixon, Roscoe B., Jr., St. Joachim, Chicago
Doerr, William A., St. Lawrence O'Toole, Matteson
Dolan, Edward, St. Juliana, Chicago
Dominguez, Juan, St. Adalbert, Chicago
Donovan, Timothy, Old St. Mary's, Chicago
Dorgan, Eugene J., St. Pascal, Chicago
Doud, Raymond, Church of the Holy Spirit, Schaumburg
Drazba, Herbert, St. Jude the Apostle, South Holland
Dubrownik, Phillip, St. Emeric, Country Club Hills
Duderstadt, Peery, Our Lady of the Brook, Northbrook
Duffey, Mark, St. Thomas of Villanova, Palatine
Dulen, John, (Retired), Buffalo Grove, IL
Dunn, William, Jr., (Retired), Elkhorn, WI
Dunne, Thomas, St. Thomas of Villanova, Palatine
Duszynski, Thomas, St. Matthew, Schaumburg
Dutkiewicz, Daniel, St. Stanislaus and Martyr, Posen
Dutko, David, St. Kieran, Chicago Heights
Dwyer, Thomas M., St. Edmund, Oak Park
Echevarria, Ramon, Our Lady of Tepeyac, Chicago
Egan, David, St. Patrick, Wadsworth
Encisco, Martin, Good Shepherd, Chicago
Ende, Gilbert, (Lemont Nursing Home)
Enger, Michael, Church of the Holy Spirit, Schaumburg
Engler, William, St. Stephen, Deacon & Martyr, Tinley Park
Ernst, James, Our Lady of Hope, Rosemont
Esposito, Robert F., St. Peter Damian, Bartlett
Estrada, Jose M., Our Lady of Guadalupe, Chicago
Ewers, Thomas, (Retired), Chicago
Faherty, Paul, St. Luke, River Forest
Fair, Davis, Our Lady of Sorrows Basilica, Chicago
Favila, Angel, St. Agnes of Bohemia, Chicago
Fay, John, Sacred Heart, Winnetka
Feltes, Richard, St. Linus, Oak Lawn
Fernandez, Dismas, Blessed Sacrament, Chicago
Ficker, John, St. George, Tinley Park
Filipucci, Michael, St. Marcelline, Schaumburg
Fitterer, George, (Retired), Evergreen, CO
Flaherty, George, St. Francis DeSales, Lake Zurich
Flam, Richard, (Retired), Tuscon, AZ
Flanagan, John, St. Germaine, Oak Lawn
Flewellen, James, (Retired), Chicago, IL
Flores, Nicolas, St. Stanislaus Kostka, Chicago
Flores-Zamora, Efrain, Santa Maria del Popolo, Mundelein
Foley, Brendan, Our Lady of the Wayside, Arlington Heights
Foti, Francisco, Our Lady of the Snows, Chicago
Fox, Gerald, Divine Providence, Westchester
Fronczek, Casimir, Office of the Deaf, Chicago
Fruge, James, Our Lady of Ransom, Niles
Furey, James P., St. John the Evangelist, Streamwood
Gadomski, Edward, St. Linus, Oak Lawn
Gagnon, Robert, St. Peter, Antioch
Gallagher, James, St. James, Highwood
Garcia, Aurelio, Our Lady of Mercy, Chicago
Garcia, Joe, St. Marcelline, Schaumburg
Garcia, Jorge, Maternity BVM, Chicago
Garcia, Miguel, St. Stanislaus Kostka, Chicago
Garvey, Kevin, Holy Cross, Deerfield
Garza, Juan L., St. Paul, Chicago Heights
Gaughan, James, St. Edna, Arlington Hts.
Gaughan, John, St. Vincent Ferrer, River Forest
Gavin, Raymond, St. Catherine Laboure, Glenview
Gianatasio, Philip, St. Mary of Celle, Berwyn
Gibbons, William, St. Patrick, Wadsworth
Gilbert, Paul, (Retired), Tinley Park
Gildea, Francis, St. Elizabeth Seton, Orland Park
Gill, Leroy, Jr., Holy Angels, Chicago
Glenn, John, St. Mary of Vernon, Indian Creek
Globis, Richard J., St. Gilbert, Grayslake
Gniech, George, St. Constance, Chicago
Gomez, Juan J., St. Paul, Chicago
Gonzalez, Felipe, Maternity, B.V.M., Chicago
Gonzalez, Joseph, St. Germaine, Oak Lawn
Gonzalez, Juan, Resurrection, Chicago
Gonzalez, Oscar, St. Pius V, Chicago
Grabiec, Guy J., St. Damian, Oak Forest
Graham, William, St. Cecilia, Mount Prospect
Gronek, Ronald, St. Monica, Chicago
Gronkiewicz, Edmund, Our Lady of Mount Carmel, Chicago
Grossnickle, Donald R., Our Lady of the Wayside, Arlington Heights
Gutierrez, Jorge, St. Mark, Chicago
Hahn, Gerald E., St. Mary Queen of Apostles, Riverdale
Hahn, Matthew, St. James, Arlington Heights
Han, Sung, Church of the Holy Spirit, Schaumburg
Haro, Vincente, St. Clare of Montefalco, Chicago
Harris, Wallace, St. Dorothy, Chicago
Hayden, Thomas L., St. Hubert, Hoffman Estates
Heckathorne, Eugene, (Retired), Kadoka, SD
Hennessy, Matthew, St. James, Arlington Heights
Henricks, John, St. Giles, Oak Park
Henry, Francis, Nativity of Our Lord, Chicago
Hernandez, Marcelino, Most Blessed Trinity, Waukegan
Herrera, Albert, St. Gall, Chicago
Herrera, Armando, Mary Queen of Heaven, Chicago

Herrera, Marcial, St. Francis De Sales, Chicago
Herrera, Tomas, Seven Holy Founders, Calumet Park
Hess, Rudolf, Blessed Sacrament, Chicago
Hill, Edwin, Our Lady of the Ridge, Chicago Ridge
Hill, Kevin D., St. John Brebeuf, Niles
Hinch, Ralph, Office of the Deaf, Chicago
Hipelius, Thomas, St. Damian, Oak Forest
Hita, Floro, Maternity BVM, Chicago
Horton, James, St. Alexander, Palos Heights
Hotcaveg, Irwin E., St. Ferdinand, Chicago
Howard, Samuel E., (Retired), Infant Jesus of Prague, Flossmoor
Huber, Charles, Des Plaines
Hudzik, Richard F., St. Mary, Lake Forest
Hyde, Thomas, St. Symphorosa, Chicago
Janega, Robert, Our Lady of Mercy
Janicek, James, St. Michael, Orland Park
Jannotta, Anthony, St. Thomas Becket, Mt. Prospect
Jean-Pierre, Fritz, St. Jerome, Chicago
Jeffrey, August, (Retired), Wonder Lake, IL
Jenney, Kenneth, Jr., St. Monica, Chicago
Jimenez, Ramon, Our Lady of Guadalupe, Chicago
Johnson, Mervin O., Holy Angels, Chicago
Johnson, Richard, Our Lady of Mount Carmel, Chicago
Joynt, William, (Retired), Elgin, IL
Kalina, David J., Our Lady of Perpetual Help, Glenview
Kalivoda, Bill, Addolorata Villa, Wheeling
Karnoski, Michael, St. Louis de Montfort, Oak Lawn
Karstenson, William T., St. Anne, Barrington
Kashmar, George, St. Joseph, Libertyville
Kasimatis, Jerome, Holy Cross, Deerfield
Keating, Timothy, St. Alexander, Palos Heights
Keegan, Charles, St. Patricia, Hickory Hills
Keenan, Gerald M., Sacred Heart, Winnetka
Keene, David J., St. Josaphat, Chicago
Kenney, James, St. Mary, Lake Forest
Kerls, Robert, St. Francis Xavier, Wilmette
Kiley, Michael E., St. Julie Billart, Tinley Park
Knetl, Thomas, Our Lady of Knock, Calumet City
Kocar, Marvin, St. Pius X, Stickney
Kort, Clayton, St. Helena of the Cross, Chicago
Kosla, Mariusz J., St. John Brebeuf, Niles
Kotleba, Rudolf, Holy Family, Chicago
Kozloski, Stanley, (Retired), Gilberts, IL
Krakora, Joseph, St. Mary, Lake Forest
Krueger, William J., St. Mary, Buffalo Grove
Kudra, Joseph, St. Paul, Chicago, Heights
Kukla, Eugene, St. Mary, Buffalo Grove
Kupsak, Gary L., St. Mary of the Annunciation, Mundelein
Kush, Michael G., (Retired), Deltona, FL
Kwasigroch, James, Our Lady of Grace, Chicago
La Belle, Eugene, St. Kieran, Chicago Heights
La Cosse, Robert, (Retired), Marquette, MI
LaCoursiere, Victor J., St. Jerome, Chicago
LaFleur, Joseph, Prince of Peace, Lake Villa
Lagges, Peter, (Retired), Des Plaines, IL
LaMantia, Thomas, St. Marcelline Schaumburg
Lambert, George, St. Eulalia, Maywood
Lambert, Thomas, Our Lady of Mt. Carmel, Chicago
Landuyt, Robert J., Our Lady of the Ridge, Chicago Heights
Langwell, James E., Incarnation, Palos Heights
Lara, Luis R., St. James, Highwood
Lawson, Richard, St. Hubert, Hoffman Estates
Lazcano, Ivan, St. Stephen Protomartyr, Des Plaines
Leck, Robert, Our Lady of Victory, Chicago
Lehman, William B., St. Francis Borgia, Chicago
Lekan, Louis, (Retired), Lindenhurst, IL
Lema, Salvatore, St. Rene Goupil, Chicago
Leonard, Timothy, Prince of Peace, Lake Villa
Leonas, John, (Retired), Manteno
Leone, Charles C., (Retired), Deerfield Beach, FL
Lesnieski, Norbert, SS. Cyril & Methodius, Lemont
Limon, Juan, St. Benedict, Blue Island
Lisowski, Thaddeus, (Retired), Park Ridge, IL
Llorens, Anthony, St. Martin de Porres, Chicago
Loman, Raymond C., St. Patrick, Lake Forest
Long, Gary, St. Mary, Buffalo Grove
Lopez, Adolfo, St. Aloysius, Chicago
Lopez, Efrain, Resurrection, Chicago
Lopez, Sergio, St. Simeon, Bellwood
Lorbach, John, St. Raymond de Penafort, Mt. Prospect
Lubben, William, St. Julie Billiart, Tinley Park
Lucas, John V., St. Patrick, Lake Forest
Luevano, Miguel, St. Donatus, Blue Island
Macarol, John, Our Lady of the Woods, Orland Park
Maddock, George, St. Joseph, Homewood
Madonia, Loretto, St. Giles, Oak Park
Mages, William, St. Mary of the Woods, Chicago
Maiers, Donald R., St. Marcelline, Schaumburg
Maldonado, Meliquides, (Retired), Chicago, IL
Malloy, William, Queen of All Saints Basilica
Malone, John, St. Germaine, Oak Lawn
Maloney, Thomas J., St. Thomas of Villanova, Palatine
Mamolella, Frank, St. Pius X, Stickney
Mancilla-Martinez, Jose, Transfiguration, Wauconda
Manning, Peter, St. George, Tinley Park
Marin, Francisco, St. Jerome, Chicago
Marotto, Angelo, St. Domitilla, Hillside
Marquez, J. Frank, (Retired), St. Pascal, Chicago
Marrero, Jose, (Retired), Chicago, IL
Marszalek, Theodore D., Our Lady, Mother of the Church, Chicago
Martinez, Francisco, (Retired), McAllen, TX
Martinez, Pedro, Most Blessed Trinity, Waukegan
Marturano, Leonard, St. Thomas of Villanova, Palatine
Maune, William, (Retired), St. Irenaeus, Park Forest
McAllister, Dennis F., Our Lady of the Brook, Northbrook
McCloskey, Michael, Holy Name Cathedral, Chicago
McDonough, Michael, St. Michael, Orland Park
McElrath, Bruce, Chicago, IL
McFarland, Charles, St. Stephen, Deacon and Martyr, Tinley Park
McGorey, Thomas, St. John of the Cross, Western Springs
McGuire, Terrence, St. Alphonsus, Lemont
McKinnis, William, St. Columbanus, Chicago
McLynn, Michael, St. Louis de Marillac, La Grange Park
McMahon, John, St. Bede, Ingleside
McNulty, Michael, Sacred Heart, Winnetka
Meehan, Peter, St. Martha, Morton Grove
Meehan, Thomas, (Retired), Hometown, IL
Melton, Edward, Holy Cross, Deerfield
Memmel, Aloysius, St. Paul of the Cross, Park Ridge
Mendez, Genaro, St. Anastasia, Waukegan
Mendieta, Raul, (Retired), Chicago
Mendizabal, Guillermo, St. John Berchmans, Chicago
Mercado, Gilberto, St. Anthony of Padua, Cicero
Merced, Rolando, Transfiguration of Our Lord
Mercure, Michael, Our Lady of Humility, Zion-Beach Park
Metallo, Arthur, (Retired), St. Francis Hospital, Evanston
Michalowski, Benedict, St. Joseph, Summit
Migala, Paul, St. Marcelline, Schaumberg
Mika, Jozef S., St. John the Evangelist, Streamwood
Minor, James R., Prince of Peace, Lake Villa
Miska, Richard, St. Terrence, Alsip
Monnelly, Michael, Queen of All Saints, Chicago
Monterroso, Oscar, St. Ansgar, Hanover Park
Moore, Steven, St. Anne, Hazel Crest
Mora, Raul, St. Ignatius, Chicago
Moran, Charles, (Retired), Streamwood
Moreno, Eusebio, St. Anastasia, Waukegan
Morgan, Thomas, St. James, Arlington Heights
Moritz, Richard H., St. Lambert, Skokie
Morowczynski, Romuald, St. Jane de Chantal, Chicago
Morris, Robert, II, St. Cajetan, Chicago
Morrissey, Henry, St. Leonard, Berwyn
Mudd, Dennis, Most Blessed Trinity, Waukegan
Mullaney, Roger, St. James, Highwood
Munda, Gary, Most Blessed Trinity, Waukegan
Munoz, Romeo, (Retired), Scottsdale, AZ
Munoz, Ubaldo, St. Mary of the Lake, Chicago
Murphy, Robert, St. Gertrude, Franklin Park
Murray, Michael, (Retired), Northbrook, IL
Navarro, Antonio, St. Mark, Chicago
Navarro, Jesse, St. Mary, Star of the Sea, Chicago
Navarro, Ramon, St. Aloysius, Chicago
Navolio, John, (Retired), Chicago, IL
Neiman, Harold, St. Sabina, Chicago
Neu, Andrew, St. Barnabas
Neurauter, Paul, St. Peter, Antioch
Newhall, Redondo, (Retired), Chicago, IL
Nguyen, Duc Van, St. Henry, Chicago
Nieves, Bienvenido, Queen of Angels, Chicago
Nimietz, James, (Retired), Chicago, IL
Nolan, John, St. Julian Eymard, Elk Grove Park
Norton, Terrence, St. Luke, River Forest
Norys, Stephen, St. Theresa, Palatine
Nowak, Thomas, St. Agnes, Chicago Heights
Nunez, Raul, Our Lady of Guadalupe, Chicago
Nylen, Arthur A., St. Jude the Apostle, South Holland
O'Donnell, Charles, Our Lady of Ransom, Niles
O'Donnell, Kevin, St. Fabian, Bridgeview
O'Keefe, Robert C., St. Isaac Jogues, Niles
O'Leary, Edward, St. Eugene, Chicago
O'Leary, John A., St. Joseph, Homewood
O'Leary, John C., St. Lambert, Skokie
O'Malley, James, Chicago Airports Catholic Chaplaincy
O'Malley, Michael, St. Mary of the Annunciation, Mundelein
O'Neill, John, St. Luke, River Forest
Ochoa, J. Zeferino, St. Francis of Assisi, Chicago
Ochoa, Jesus, St. Mary, Star of the Sea, Chicago
Ochsner, Robert, Our Lady of Humility, Beach Park & Zion
Ojeda, Norberto, Sacred Heart, Melrose Park
Olson, Carl, St. Cornelius, Chicago
Ontiveros, Philip, St. Julian Eymard, Elk Grove Village
Ortega, Ignacio, (Retired), Fondulac, IL
Ortiz, Eddies, Schaumburg
Ortiz, Sigifredo, St. Sylvester, Chicago
Orzechowski, John, Our Lady of the Ridge, Chicago Ridge
Pagliai, Bruno, St. James, Highwood
Pagnotta, Philip, Jr., St. Mary of Vernon, Indian Creek
Palacios, Freddy, St. Charles Borromeo, Melrose Park
Panek, Joseph, St. George, Tinley Park
Paskauskas, Vitas, Nativity, B.V.M.
Patino, Daniel, Our Lady of Lourdes
Patino, Felix, St. Clare of Montefalco, Chicago
Pauwels, James, St. Edna, Arlington Heights
Pena, Leonardo, Area Hispanic Ministry
Penich, Michael, Jr., St. Paul the Apostle, Gurnee
Pepitone, Joe, St. John of the Cross, Western Springs
Perez, Carlos, (Retired), Streamwood, IL
Perez, Luis, Santa Maria Addolorata, Chicago
Perez, Miguel, (Retired), Chicago
Perez, Orlando, St. James, Chicago
Perez, Pablo, St. Bede the Venerable, Chicago
Perkowitz, John, (Retired), Niles, IL
Peters, Bruce, St. Dismas, Waukegan
Peterson, George A., (Retired), Prospect Heights, IL
Pezowicz, Feliks, Transfiguration, Wauconda
Phelan, Mark, Most Holy Redeemer, Evergreen Park
Pilarski, Ronald, Mater Christi, North Riverside
Pincich, Samuel, St. Zachary, Des Plaines
Pindelski, Michael J., St. Francis of Assisi, Orland Park
Pineda, Javier, St. Frances of Rome, Cicero
Pizzato, Richard, St. Theresa, Palatine
Platt, James, St. Cyprian, River Grove
Pluchar, Edward, St. Julie Billiart, Tinley Park
Podgorski, Edward, St. Monica, Chicago
Poletto, Robert, St. Mary, Mundelein
Ponce, Antonio, Our Lady of Charity, Cicero
Ponce De Leon, Juan, St. William, Chicago
Porter, John, (Retired), St. Joseph's Home for the Elderly, Palatine
Pouncy, William, St. Martin de Porres, Chicago
Powers, Robert, St. Anne, Barrington
Principe, Michael, St. Gertrude, Schiller Park
Puhala, Robert, St. Philip the Apostle, Northfield
Purdome, Mark J., St. Paul the Apostle, Gurnee
Quackenbush, Edward, (Retired), Lake Villa, IL
Ragonese, Dan, St. Victor, Calumet City
Rakauskas, Stanley, St. Christina, Chicago
Ramirez, Juan, Our Lady of Grace, Chicago
Ramirez, Rosalio, St. Pius X, Stickney
Ramos, Dennis, St. Aloysius, Chicago
Ramos, Eliseo, St. Jerome
Ramos, Faustino, St. Bronislava, Chicago
Ramos, Francisco, St. Philomena, Chicago
Rangel, John, St. Lawrence O'Toole, Matteson
Ranola, Rodrigo, St. Isaac Jogues, Niles
Reilly, Raymond, St. John Fisher, Chicago
Reinert, William, St. James, Arlington Heights
Renk, Dennis A., (Retired), Zion, IL
Renwick, James, Holy Ghost, South Holland
Revering, Roman, (Retired), St. Luke School
Revord, James, Our Lady of Perpetual Help, Glenview
Rex, John, St. Damian, Oak Forest
Reyes, David, St. Andrew, Chicago
Reynolds, Kevin L., St. Louise De Marillac, Lagrange Park
Riccio, Louis, St. Theresa, Palatine
Richardson, John, (Retired), Zion, IL
Richardson, Lendell, Ascension, Oak Park
Richardson, Leonard M., St. Sabina, Chicago
Riffner, Joseph, (Retired), Chicago, IL
Rios, Jamie, St. Wenceslaus, Chicago
Rittenhouse, Daniel, St. Alphonsus, Lemont
Rivas, Roberto, Immaculate Conception, Chicago
Rivera, Francisco, Resurrection, Chicago
Rivera, Hector, St. Teresa of Avila, Chicago
Robak, Dennis R., St. Mary, Evanston
Robles, Ernesto, Our Lady of Grace, Chicago
Roccasalva, Joseph, St. Cajetan, Chicago
Rodriguez, Antonio, St. Thomas of Canterbury, Chicago
Rodriguez, Candelario, St. Procopius, Chicago
Rodriguez, Emiliano, St. Sylvester, Chicago
Rodriguez, Manuel, (Retired), St. Francis of Assisi, Chicago

Rodriguez, Milton, Maternity of B.V.M., Chicago
Rodriguez, Santiago, (Retired), Mesa, AZ
Rodriguez, Uriol, Resurrection, Chicago
Rodriguez, Wilmer, (Retired), Cicero
Roman, Francisco, (Retired), Chicago, IL
Romano, Michael, St. Joseph Hospital, Chicago
Rosa, Abraham, (Retired), Springhill, FL
Rottman, John, St. Thecla
Rozo, Jorge, Holy Rosary, Chicago
Rueth, William, (Retired), New Lennox, IL
Ruiz, Angel, (Retired), Magate, FL
Ruiz, Joel, St. Joseph, Round Lake
Ruiz, Victor, St. Dismas, Waukegan
Ryan, Edward, Our Lady of Knock, Calumet City
Ryan, Robert E., Sr., St. Juliana, Chicago
Ryan, Thomas, St. Christina, Chicago
Rybicki, Lawrence, St. John the Evangelist, Streamwood
Rynkiewicz, Stephen I., Most Blessed Trinity, Waukegan
Rzendzian, Thomas J., Sacred Heart, Palos Hills
Sacramento, Anthony, St. Dismas, Waukegan
Sanchez, Sabino, St. Francis of Assisi, Chicago
Sanchez, Salvador, St. James, Fullerton Ave., Chicago
Sandoval, Jose M., Immaculate Conception
Sanford, James, (Retired), Des Plaines, IL
Santos, Antero, St. Colette, Rolling Meadows
Sassetti, Robert C., (Retired), River Forest, IL
Sattler, David, St. Peter Damian, Bartlett
Savage, Christopher, Prince of Peace, Lake Villa
Scarbalis, Edward, (Retired), Waukegan, IL
Schiltz, James, St. Constance, Chicago
Schliesmann, Barry, SS. Faith, Hope and Charity, Winnetka
Schmidt, Paul, St. James, Arlington Heights
Schopp, John E., IV, St. John of the Cross, Western Springs
Schultz, Ronald, (Retired), Calumet City
Schultz, William, St. Stephen, Deacon and Martyr, Tinley Park
Schumacher, Lawrence R., St. Theresa, Palatine
Sedano, Pedro, Our Lady of Mount Carmel, Melrose Park
Sedivy, Alan, St. Catherine LaBoure, Glenview
Serna, Ramiro, St. Clare of Montefalco, Chicago
Serratore, Gregory, St. Mary Star of Sea, Chicago
Sheehan, Patrick P., St. James, Arlington Heights
Shinkle, Derald, St. Joseph, Wilmette
Shumpert, Gregory, St. Agatha
Silva, Rodrigo, St. Ann, Chicago
Simmons, John, Santa Maria del Popolo, Mundelein
Simola, Edward, St. William, Chicago
Sinacore, James M., St. John Vianney, Northlake
Siranovic, Joseph, St. Domitilla, Hillside
Siska, Thomas, St. John Fisher, Chicago
Skaja, Lawrence, St. John Brebeuf, Niles
Slajchert, Michael, St. Gall, Chicago
Slobig, Robert, St. Luke, River Forest
Smith, John J., St. Zachary, Des Plaines
Smith, Lawrence J., Queen of the Rosary, Elk Grove Village
Smith, Michael E., St. Christopher, Midlothian
Smyser, William, St. Aloysius, Chicago
Soria, Carlos, (Retired), Chicago, IL
Soto, Rogelio, St. Ignatius, Chicago
Soto, Santos, (Retired), Chicago
Spalla, Paul, St. Mary-of-the-Lake, Chicago
Spitizzeri, Fred, (Retired), Niles, IL
Spohr, Lawrence, St. Bede, Ingleside
Springer, Timothy, St. Jude the Apostle, South Holland
Stalcup, Joseph, Sr., St. Stephen, Tinley Park
Stanton, Paul, St. Isaac Jogues, Niles
Stasinski, Melvin, St. Jude the Apostle, South Holland
Stearns, William, St. Damian, Oak Forest
Stecker, Stephen, St. Joseph the Worker, Wheeling
Steinbeigle, Francis, St. Damian, Oak Forest
Strom, Stanley, Holy Name Cathedral, Chicago
Stubstad, Thomas, St. Pascal, Chicago
Sullivan, Dwight, St. Eulalia, Maywood
Sullivan, William, St. Barnabas, Chicago
Sullivan, William, St. Louis de Montfort, Oak Lawn
Sutton, Daniel, (Retired), Oak Lawn, IL
Swiatek, Ronald, St. John Bosco, Chicago
Swiech, Edward, (Retired), Lake Zurich, IL
Szady, Mitchell, (Retired), St. Stanislaus B & M, Chicago
Szarek, John, St. Ansgar, Hanover Park
Tamayo, Mario, St. Nicholas, Evanston
Tatara, Allen, St. Hubert, Hoffman Estates
Telle, Paul, (Retired), Park City, IL
Telposky, Donald, St. Stephen Protomartyr, Des Plaines
Temple, James, St. Barnabas, Chicago
Thompson, James, St. Mary of the Woods, Chicago
Thompson, Johnathan, St. Peter, Antioch
Tiemeier, David, St. Joseph, Libertyville
Tipperreiter, Charles, St. Fabian, Bridgeview
Tomkowiak, Edward, St. Patrick, Wadsworth
Towey, Anthony, St. Stephen Protomartyr, Des Plaines
Trakszelis, Jerome J., St. Vincent Ferrer, River Forest
Trevino, Luis, Chicago-O'Hare International Airport
Truesdale, Joseph, St. Francis of Assisi, Orland Park
Tryjefaczek, Richard, St. Joseph, Summit
Tylutki, Glenn, St. Mary of the Angels, Chicago
Uroza, Jose, (Retired), Schiller Park, IL
Vaeth, Dean G., St. Vincent de Paul, Chicago
Valadez, Abundio, St. Benedict, Blue Island
Valadez, Asuncion, St. Mary of Celle, Berwyn
Valdivia, Juan, (Retired)
Valencia, Juan, Epiphany, Chicago
Valentin, Jose, (Retired), Buffalo Grove
Valle, Miguel A., St. Genevieve, Chicago
Van Merkestyn, Peter, St. Stephen, Deacon and Martyr, Tinley Park
Vandervest, Roger, Ascension, Oak Park
Vargas, Miguel, Mision San Juan Diego, Arlington Heights
Vasek, Emil, St. Kieran, Chicago Heights
Vazquez, Gilberto, Santa Maria Del Popolo, Mundelein
Vazquez, Jose, Maternity B.V.M., Chicago
Vazquez, Saul, St. Michael, Orland Park
Velasco, Benito, (Retired), Joliet, IL
Vellurattil, Matthew, St. Ladislaus
Vemich, Duke, All Saints-St. Anthony, Chicago
Vidmar, John, Bl. A.M. Slomsek Slovenian Catholic Mission, Lemont
Vignocchi, Louis, Immaculate Conception, Highland Park
Villa, Salvatore, St. Bruno, Chicago
Villalobos, Antonio, St. Mark, Chicago
Villasenor, Faustino, St. Mary, Des Plaines
Virruso, Christopher, Our Lady, Mother of the Church, Chicago
Voytas, Richard, St. Daniel the Prophet, Chicago
Wagner, David, St. Patrick, Wadsworth
Wagner, Steve J., St. Thecla, Chicago
Walsh, Joseph A., Ascension, Oak Park
Walters, John, St. Bernardine, Forest Park
Ward, Raymond, St. Jerome, Chicago
Warfield, Richard, Little Company of Mary Hospital
Warmouth, William H., St. Stephen Protomartyr, Des Plaines
Wasielak, Peter G., (Retired), Tucson, AZ
Watson, Dexter, St. Malachy & Precious Blood, Chicago
Wehling, Donald, St. Hilary, Chicago
Weiner, Ronald, St. Ferdinand, Chicago
Weitendorf, Norbert, St. Patricia, Hickory Hills
Welter, Daniel G., J.D., St. Hilary, Chicago
Werner, Richard, Sacred Heart, Palos Hills
West, Tommy, St. Helena of the Cross, Chicago
Westerkamp, Thomas, St. James, Arlington Heights
White, Philip, St. Eulalia, Maywood
Wilkinson, John M., St. James at Sag Bridge, Lemont
Willer, Richard, St. Thomas of Villanova, Palatine
Wills, James, St. Peter, Skokie
Winblad, Joseph, St. Patrick, Lemont
Winter, Edward, St. Lawrence O'Toole, Matteson
Wogan, James, St. Mary of Vernon, Indian Creek
Wundsam, Michael E., St. Zachary, Des Plaines
Yannotta, Joseph, St. Edna, Arlington Heights
Zadruzny, Wieslaw, (Retired), Chicago, IL
Zanardo, Ronald, (Retired), Inverness, IL
Zaragoza, Luis, Inverness, IL
Zawadzki, Kenneth, St. Stephen, Deacon & Martyr, Tinley Park
Zeifest, Gregory, St. Bede, Ingleside
Zeimys, Erik, Nativity of Our Lord, Chicago
Zeller, John, Schaumburg, IL
Zielinski, Ronald, St. Fabian, Bridgeview
Zima, Robert, (Retired), Lake in the Hills
Zimmerman, Edward, (Retired), Oak Brook Terrace, IL
Zurawski, John, St. John Vianney, Northlake
Zwolski, Mark, St. Mary of Vernon, Indian Creek
Zych, Gerald, St. Giles, Oak Park

INSTITUTIONS LOCATED IN THE ARCHDIOCESE

[A] SEMINARIES, ARCHDIOCESAN

CHICAGO. *St. Joseph College Seminary*, The Seminary College at Loyola University, 6551 N. Sheridan Rd., 60626. Tel: 773-973-9700; Fax: 773-973-9718. Email: psnieg@luc.edu. Web: www.stjoseph.luc.edu. Priests 4; Lay Teachers 6; Enrollment 34.

Seminary Administration: Very Rev. Peter Snieg Jr., S.T.L., Pres. Rector & Dean of Formation; Revs. Pawel Komperda, Dir. of Admissions; Laurence F. Maddock, S.T.L., Spiritual Dir. (Retired); Duy Cao, D.Min. (Cand.), Dir. Liturgy; Thomas Regan, S.J., Academic Dean; Michael G. Scherschel, Asst. Vocation Dir.

Part-Time Faculty: Rev. Britto Berchmans, Ph.D., Communications; Mr. Alberto Bertozzi, Philosophy; Dr. Brian DuSell, D.M.A., Music Instructor; Revs. Timothy R. Fiala, S.T.L., Theology; Henry C. Kricek, M.A., S.T.L., Philosophy; Dr. William Joseph Napiwocki, Ph.D., Latin Instructor.

Administrative Staff: Mrs. Yuvanka Zavala-Juarez, B.A., Business Mgr.; Mrs. Diana Kozojed, Dir., Institutional Advancement Office; Mrs. Dawn Zamora, Office of Institutional Advancement; Ms. Harriet McCullough, Grant Writer; Bro. Clement Burger, C.S.C., Night Receptionist.

MUNDELEIN. *University of St. Mary of the Lake/ Mundelein Seminary*, 1000 E. Maple Ave., 60060-1174. Tel: 847-566-6401; Fax: 847-566-7330. Email: rector@usml.edu. Web: www.usml.edu. Priests 31; Sisters 1; Lay Teachers 9; Students 165.

Administration: Rev. Msgr. Dennis J. Lyle, S.T.D., Rector, Pres.; Revs. James Presta, S.T.L., S.T.D., M.Div., Vice Rector for Seminary Admin.; Thomas A. Baima, M.B.A., S.T.D., Vice Rector for Academic Affairs; Thomas R. Franzman, M.Div., Provost; Ronald A. Hicks, D.Min., Dean of Formation; John G. Lodge, S.S.L., S.T.D., Pres., Ecclesiastical Faculty; Martin Zielinski, M.Div., Ph.D., Vice Pres. Ongoing Formation; Mr. John Lehocky, C.P.A., M.B.A., Vice Pres. Finance; Mr. Stanley C. Rys, M.B.A., Vice Pres. Facilities; Mr. Mark J. Teresi, CFRE, Vice Pres. Institutional Advancement; Rev. Nathaniel Payne, M.Div., Canonical Recorder.

Faculty: Revs. Peter Damian Akpunonu, S.S.L., S.T.D., Prof., (Extern); Thomas A. Baima, M.B.A., S.T.D., Prof.; Martin Barnum, D.Min., Assoc. Dean of Formation; Dr. Melanie Barrett, S.T.L., Ph.D., S.T.D. (Cand.), Asst. Prof; Revs. Robert E. Barron, M.A. (Phil.), S.T.D., Prof.; August J. Belauskas, M.A., S.T.L., Assoc. Dean of Formation; Jacque B. Beltran, S.T.B., D.Min. (Cand.), Assoc. Dean of Formation; Patrick J. Boyle, S.J., M.A., Ph.L., S.T.L., Ph.D., Assoc. Prof.; Ms. Linda Cerabona, M.A., Dir. of Music; Revs. Christopher Ciomek, D.Min. (Cand.), Assoc. Dean of Formation; Emery de Gaal, Dipl. Theol., Ph.D., Chairperson & Assoc. Prof, (Extern); Vincent Bataille, O.S.B., Spiritual Dir.; Rev. Msgr. John V. Dolciamore, J.C.L., S.T.L., Professor Emeritus (Retired); Mr. Thomas Dougherty, B.A., Dir., ESL; Revs. Kevin J. Feeney, M.A.S., D.Min. (Cand.), Assoc. Dean of Formation; Thomas R. Franzman, M.Div., Chief Campaign & Stewardship Officer; Michael J.K. Fuller, S.T.D. (RCK), Chairperson & Asst. Prof.; W. Scott Hebden, S.T.D., Asst. Prof.; Sr. Sara Butler, M.S.B.T., S.T.L., Ph.D., Paluch Prof. Theology; Rev. Lawrence R. Hennessey, M.A., S.T.L., Ph.D., Prof.; Dr. Paul Hilliard, Ph.D., Asst. Prof.; Revs. Ronald T. Kunkel, S.T.D. (Cand.), Instructor; John G. Lodge, S.S.L., S.T.D., Assoc. Prof.; Rev. Msgr. Dennis J. Lyle, S.T.D., Assoc. Prof.; Rev. Douglas A. Martis, Ph.D., S.T.D., Dir. & Assoc. Prof.; Dr. Christopher McAtee, D.Min., Asst. Academic Dean; Dr. Denis R. McNamara, Ph.D., Asst. Dir., Liturgical Institute; Rev. Msgr. Charles R. Meyer, M.A., S.T.D., Prof. Emeritus (Retired); Dr. Elizabeth Nagel, S.S.D., Prof.; Rev. Edward T. Oakes, S.J., Ph.D., Assoc. Prof.; Ms. Lorraine Olley, M.A.Div., M.A.L.S., Library Dir.; Revs. Patrick J. O'Malley, M.A., S.T.L., Spiritual Dir. (Retired); Ronald A. Hicks, D.Min., Dean of Formation; Robert L. Schoenstene, M.A., S.S.L. (JOL), Assoc. Prof.; Daniel S. Siwek, S.T.L., Instructor; John S. Szmyd, M.Div., S.T.B., Assoc. Dean of Formation & Dir. of Liturgy; Raymond J. Webb, S.T.D., Ph.D., Prof., Dir. Pastoral Internships; Mrs. Kathleen Wiskus, M.A., D.Min., Assoc. Dean of Formation & Asst. Prof.; Revs. Richard J. Wojcik, S.T.L., M.C.G., Prof. Emeritus (Retired); Martin Zielinski, M.Div., Ph.D., Assoc. Prof.; James Presta, S.T.L., S.T.D., M.Div., Asst. Prof.

Convent Tel: 847-970-4827; Fax: 847-566-7330. Sr. Miriam Vazquez, Supr. Oblate Sisters of Jesus the Priest 4.

The Liturgical Institute, 1000 E. Maple Ave., 60060. Tel: 847-837-4542; Fax: 847-837-4545. Web: www.liturgicalinstitute.org. Rev. Douglas A. Martis, Ph.D., S.T.D., Dir.; Dr. Denis R. McNamara, Ph.D., Asst. Dir.

Ministerial and Continuing Education, 1000 E. Maple Ave., 60060-1174. Tel: 847-970-4860; Fax: 847-970-4818. Rev. Thomas A. Baima, M.B.A., S.T.D., Archbishop's Liaison Formation Progs.

Deacon Formation Program, 1000 E. Maple Ave., 60060-1174. Tel: 847-837-4563; Fax: 847-837-4565. Deacon Robert Puhala, Dir.; Rev. Dennis Stafford,

Dir. Spiritual Formation; Anne Chrzan, Assoc. Dir.
Instituto De Liderazgo Pastoral (Hispanic Programs for Lay Ministry and Permanent Diaconate), 1000 E. Maple Ave., 60060-1174. Tel: 847-837-4556; Fax: 847-837-4565. Ms. Nelly Lorenzo, M.Div., Dir.; Rev. Carlos Monsalve, O.C.D. (Colombia), Dir. Spiritual Formation; Luz Alvarez, Assoc. Dir. Instituto de Liderazgo Pastoral; Rebecca Villanueva, Assoc. Dir. Instituto de Liderazgo Pastoral.
Lay Ministry Formation Programs, 1000 E. Maple Ave., 60060-1174. Tel: 847-837-4550; Fax: 847-837-4565. Ms. Linda Couri, M.S.W., Dir.
Conference Center, 1000 E. Maple Ave., 60060-1174. Tel: 847-837-4505; Fax: 847-837-4505. Rev. Thomas R. Franzman, M.Div., Dir.; Carol Rose, Mgr. Guest Svcs.; Richard Arnold, Mgr. Event Planning.
Ongoing Formation, 1000 E. Maple Ave., 60060-1174. Tel: 847-837-4558; Fax: 847-837-4565. Rev. Martin Zielinski, M.Div., Ph.D., Dir.; Ms. Megan Diechl, Assoc. Dir.
Feehan Memorial Library Ms. Lorraine Olley, M.A.Div., M.A.L.S., Library Dir.

[B] SEMINARIES, RELIGIOUS OR SCHOLASTICATES

CHICAGO. *Catholic Theological Union*, 5401 S. Cornell Ave., 60615. Tel: 773-371-5400; Fax: 773-324-8490. Email: presoffice@ctu.edu. Web: www.ctu.edu. Major Seminary. Serving the following: Franciscans, Servites, Passionists, Augustinians, Norbertines, Society of the Divine Word, Missionaries of the Precious Blood, Claretians, Crosier Fathers, Spiritans, Missionaries of the Sacred Heart, Viatorians, Comboni Missionaries, Franciscans Capuchins, Congregation of the Blessed Sacrament, Columban Missionaries, Redemptorist Fathers, Xaverian Missionaries, Maryknoll Missionaries, Conventual Franciscans, Scalabrinians Priests 12; Sisters 5; Lay Teachers 7; Lay Administrators 11; Non-Catholic Clergy 2; Students 439.
Administration: Rev. Donald Senior, C.P., S.T.D., Pres.; Sr. Barbara Reid, O.P., Ph.D., Vice Pres. & Academic Dean; Mr. Michael W. Connors, C.P.A., Vice Pres. Admin. & Finance; Ms. Anne Marie Tirpak, Dir. Devel. Office; Ms. Kathy Van Duser, Dir. Admissions & Recruitment; Ms. Vanessa White, M.T.S., Dir. Tolton Prog.; Ms. Sheila McLaughlin, Dir. Bernardin Center; Sr. Maria Hughes, A.S.C., Dir. Institute of Rel. Formation; Rev. Msgr. Patrick R. Lagges, J.C.D., Dir. Hesburgh Sabatical Prog.; Melody McMahon, Dir. Library Svcs.; Mrs. Maria de Jesus Lemus, Registrar; Carlos Salmeron, Dir. Romero Prog.; Ms. Keiren O'Kelly, M.Div., Dir. Continuing & Distance Educ. & Dir MAPS Prog.; Mr. Terrence Stadler, Assoc. Dir. Emmaus Prog.; Ms. Elizabeth White, Dir., Mktg. & Communs.; Sr. Sallie Latkovich, C.S.J., Dir. Biblical Study & Travel Progs. & Dir. Summer Institute.
Faculty: Mr. Michel Andraos, Ph.D., Assoc. Prof. Cross Cultural Ministry & Dir. M.Div Prog.; Mr. Scott C. Alexander, Ph.D., Assoc. Prof of Islam & Dir. Catholic Muslim-Studies; Rev. Claude-Marie Barbour, S.T.D., Prof. World Mission; Sr. Dianne Bergant, C.S.A., Ph.D., Prof. Old Testament Studies; Rev. Stephen B. Bevans, S.V.D., Prof. Mission & Culture; Sr. Laurie A. Brink, O.P., Asst. Prof. of Biblical Studies; Ms. Carmen Nanko-Fernandez, D.Min., Dir. Dr. in Ministry Prog.; Mr. Richard E. McCarron, Ph.D., Assoc. Prof. Liturgy; Revs. Richard Fragomeni, Ph.D., Assoc. Prof. Liturgy & Preaching; Edward Foley, O.F.M.Cap., Prof. Liturgy & Music; Sr. Mary Frohlich, R.S.C.J., Ph.D., Assoc. Prof. Spirituality & Dir. M.A. Prog.; Revs. Anthony Gittins, C.S.Sp., Ph.D., Prof. Catholic Missiology; vanThanh Nguyen, S.V.D., Asst. Prof. New Testament; James C. Okoye, C.S.Sp., Prof. of Biblical Studies; Gilbert Ostdiek, O.F.M., S.T.D., Prof. of Liturgy; John M. Pawlikowski, O.S.M., Ph.D., Dir. Catholic-Jewish Studies, Prof. of Ethics; Sisters Barbara Reid, O.P., Ph.D., Vice Pres. & Academic Dean, Prof. New Testament Studies; Dawn Nothwehr, O.S.F., Ph.D., Prof. Catholic Theological Ethics; Revs. Robert Schreiter, C.PP.S., Th.D., Prof. Systematic Theology; Roger P. Schroeder, S.V.D., Prof. Cross-Cultural Ministry; Donald Senior, C.P., S.T.D., Pres. & Prof. of New Testament Studies; Gilberto Cavazos-Gonzales, O.F.M., S.L.T., Assoc. Prof. Spirituality & Dir. Hispanic Ministry Prog.; Rabbi David Sandmel, Ph.D., Crown-Ryan Chair, Assoc. Prof., Jewish Studies; Ms. Eileen Crowley, Ph.D., Asst. Prof., Word & Worship; Ms. C. Vanessa White, D.Min., Asst. Prof. Spirituality & Dir. Augustus Tolton Prog.

[C] COLLEGES AND UNIVERSITIES

CHICAGO. *De Paul University*, One E. Jackson Blvd., 60604. Tel: 312-362-8000; Fax: 312-362-6606. Web: www.depaul.edu. Revs. Dennis H. Holtschneider, C.M., Pres.; John T. Richardson, C.M., Chancellor; Edward R. Udovic, C.M., Senior Exec. Univ. Mission, Sec.; Dr. Helmut P. Epp, Provost; Mr. Robert L. Kozoman, Exec. Vice Pres. Sponsored by the Congregation of the Mission (Vincentian Fathers and Brothers)., Campuses: Downtown, Lincoln Park, Oak Forest, O'Hare, Naperville, Rolling Meadows. Faculty 955; University Staff 1,636; Students 25,398.
Administrative Officers of the University: Mr. Jose D. Padilla, Vice Pres. and General Counsel; Mr. Jeff Bethke, Treas.; Mr. James R. Doyle, Vice Pres. Student Affairs; Ms. Bonnie Frankel, Vice Pres., Fin.; Mr. Robert Janis, Vice Pres. Facilities Operations; Dr. David Kalsbeek, Senior Vice Pres. Enrollment Mgmt. & Mktg.; Mr. Robert McCormick, Dir. Information Svcs.; Mr. William Seithel, Vice Pres. Human Resources; Ms. Jay Braatz, Senior Exec., Presidential Opers.; Ms. Mary C. Finger, Senior Vice Pres., Advancement; Mr. David Lively, Vice Pres. Devel.; Mr. J. D. Bindenagel, Vice Pres. Community, Government & Intl. Affairs; Ms. Elizabeth Ortiz, Vice Pres. Institutional Diversity & Equity; Mrs. Patricia O'Donoghue, Vice Pres. Alumni Engagement & Outreach; Rev. Edward R. Udovic, C.M., Sr. Exec. Univ. Mission & Vice Pres. Teaching & Learning Resources.
College of Liberal Arts and Sciences, 990 W. Fullerton Ave., Ste. 4200, 60614. Tel: 773-325-7310; Fax: 773-325-7304. Dr. Charles S. Suchar, Dean.
College of Law, 931 Lewis Center, 25 E. Jackson Blvd., 60604. Tel: 312-362-8701; Fax: 312-362-5826. Gregory Mark, Dean.
College of Commerce, Kellstadt Graduate School of Business, 7103 DePaul Center, One E. Jackson Blvd., 60604. Tel: 312-362-6783; Fax: 312-362-6677. Dr. Ray Whittington, Dean.
College of Communication, 14 E. Jackson Blvd., Ste. 1800, 60604. Tel: 312-362-8000; Fax: 312-362-7584. Dr. Jacqueline Taylor, Dean.
School of Music, 200 Music Bldg., 804 W. Belden, 60614. Tel: 773-325-7260; Fax: 773-325-7263. Dr. Donald E. Casey, Dean.
School for New Learning, 14 E. Jackson Blvd., 60604. Tel: 312-362-8001; Fax: 312-362-8809. Dr. Marisa Alicea, Dean.
College of Computing and Digital Media, CDM Center 401, 243 S. Wabash Ave., 60604-2302. Tel: 312-362-8381; Fax: 312-362-6116. Dr. David Miller, Dean.
College of Science and Health, 1110 W. Belden Ave. Ste. 403 McGowan S., 60614. Tel: 773-325-8300. Dr. Jerry Cleland, Dean.
The Theatre School, 214 Theatre School Bldg., 2135 N. Kenmore Ave., 60614. Tel: 773-325-7917; Fax: 773-325-7920. Mr. John Culbert, Dean.
College of Education, 458 Schmitt Academic Center, 60614. Tel: 773-325-7740; Fax: 773-325-7713. Dr. Paul Zionts, Dean.
Jesuit Community at Loyola University Chicago, 6324 N. Kenmore, 60660. Tel: 773-508-8800; Fax: 773-508-2098. Web: www.luc.edu. Revs. Paul Tango Abomo, S.J.; Michael Agliardo, S.J.; Mark W. Andrews, S.J.; Ranieri Araujo, S.J.; Robert J. Araujo, S.J.; Peter J. Bernardi, S.J.; Robert L. Bireley, S.J.; Mark G. Bosco, S.J.; Robert J. Braunreuther, S.J.; William A. Clark, S.J.; Edil Calero Cortez, S.J.; William E. Creed, S.J.; John D. Cunningham, S.J.; Justin Daffron, S.J.; Stefano Del Bove, S.J.; Patrick Dorsey, S.J.; Michael J. Garanzini, S.J., Pres.; Kevin Gillespie, S.J.; Brendan Horan, S.J.; Charles Jurgensmeier, S.J.; John J. Kilgallen, S.J.; Steven E. Kimmons, S.J.; Stephen T. Krupa, S.J.; Tuan Le, S.J.; Jeremiah W. Lynch, S.J.; Patrick J. McAteer, S.J.; John M. McManamon, S.J.; Jose A. Mesa, S.J.; Stephen F. Mitten, S.J.; Keith F. Muccino, S.J.; Kafarhire Murhula, S.J.; James G. Murphy, S.J.; John J. O'Callaghan, S.J., S.T.D.; Thomas E. Oguagua, S.J.; Peter Otieno Omollo, S.J.; T. Jerome Overbeck, S.J.; Brian G. Paulson, S.J., Rector; Thomas J. Regan, S.J.; Donald F. Rowe, S.J.; Stephen Schloesser, S.J.; David J. Stagaman, S.J.; John E. Surette, S.J.; Robert J. Thesing, S.J.; Thomas H. Tobin, S.J.
The Jesuit Community Corporation at Loyola University Priests 45; Brothers 2; Sisters 5; Lay Staff 2,011; Students 15,816.
**Loyola University-Chicago*, 6631 N. Sheridan Rd., 60660. Tel: 312-915-6000; 773-274-3000; Fax: 312-915-8501. Web: www.luc.edu.
Loyola University of Chicago, Illinois Total University Enrollment 15,951; Total Full-Time Faculty 737; Total Staff 1,493.
President's Office, 820 N. Michigan Ave., 60611. Tel: 312-915-6400; Fax: 312-915-6414. Web: www.luc.edu. Michael R. Quinlan, Bd. Chm.; Rev. Michael J. Garanzini, S.J., Pres.; Dr. Paul K. Whelton, M.D., M.Sc., Pres. & CEO, Loyola Univ. Medical Center; Mr. Jonathan Heintzelman, Vice Pres. Advancement; Dr. Robert Kelly, Vice Pres. Student Devel.; Dr. John Hardt, Asst. to the Pres. Mission & Identity; Dr. John Pelissero, Provost; Mr. Philip D. Hale, Vice Pres., Public Affairs; Mr. Phil Kosiba, Vice Pres., Facilities; Mr. Tom Kelly, Vice Pres. Human Resources; Dr. Richard S. Hurst, Dir. Inst. Research; Mr. Paul Roberts, Assoc. Provost Enrollment Mgmt., Graduate & Professional Enrollment Mgmt.; Ms. Lori Greene, Dir. Undergraduate Admissions; Mr. Eric Weems, Dir. Student Financial Assistance; Ms. Claire Korinek, Dir. Registration & Records; Ms. Diane Hullinger, Asst. Dir. Registration and Records; Mr. Romando Nash, Dir. Residence Life; Dr. Robert Seal, Dean of Libraries; Ms. Kelly M. Shannon, Vice Pres. University Mktg. & Communications; Mr. Eugene Grotbeck, University Controller; Mr. William Laird, Vice Pres. Finance & CFO; Mr. Wayne Magdziarz, Vice Pres. & Chief of Staff; Mrs. Ellen Kane Munro, Vice Pres. & Gen. Counsel.
The following are the Schools and Colleges which compose the University:
The College of Arts and Sciences (1870) 6525 N. Sheridan Rd., 60626. Tel: 773-508-3500; Fax: 773-508-3514. Dr. Francis Fennell, Dean.
The School of Law (1908) 25 E. Pearson St., 60611. Tel: 312-915-7120; Fax: 312-915-7201. David Yellen, Dean.
The Stritch School of Medicine (1909) 2160 S. First Ave., Maywood, 60153. Tel: 708-216-3223; Fax: 708-216-4305. Dr. Richard Gamelli, Dean.
School of Social Work (1914) 820 N. Michigan Ave., 60611. Tel: 312-915-7005; Fax: 312-915-7645. Rev. Kevin Gillespie, S.J., Interim Dean.
School of Professional Studies, 820 N. Michigan Ave., 60611. Tel: 312-915-6501; Fax: 312-915-6508. Dr. Jeffrey Rosen, Dean.
The School of Business Administration (1922) 820 N. Michigan Ave., 60611. Tel: 312-915-6113; Fax: 312-915-6118. Mr. Abol Jalilvand, Dean.
The Graduate School (1926) 6525 N. Sheridan Rd., 60626. Tel: 773-508-3396; Fax: 773-508-2460. Dr. Samuel Attoh, Dean.
The School of Nursing (1935) 6525 N. Sheridan Rd., 60626. Tel: 773-508-3249; Fax: 773-508-3241. Dr. Vicki Keough, Dean.
The School of Education (1969) 820 N. Michigan Ave., 60611. Tel: 312-915-6800; Fax: 312-915-6660. Dr. David Prasse, Dean.
School of Communication (2008) 820 N. Michigan Ave., 60611. Tel: 312-915-6548; Fax: 312-915-8593. Dr. Donald Heider, Dean.
St. Joseph's Seminary, 6551 N. Sheridan Rd., 60626. Tel: 773-973-9700; Fax: 773-973-9718. Rev. David J. Stagaman, S.J., Academic Dean.
Saint Xavier University, 3700 W. 103rd St., 60655-3105. Tel: 773-298-3000; Fax: 773-779-9061. Web: www.sxu.edu. Christine M. Wiseman, J.D., Pres. Sponsorship: Institute of the Sisters of Mercy of the Americas., Campus locations: Chicago, Orland Park & Chicago Bar Association. Priests 1; Sisters 7; Faculty 206; Staff 465; Students 5,000.
Administrative Officers of the University: Angela Durante, Ph.D., Provost; Steven J. Murphy, Ed.D., Vice Pres., University Advancement; John P. Pelrine Jr., M.P.S., Vice Pres., Student Affairs; Robert C. Tenczar Jr., B.A., M.B.A., Vice Pres., University Rels.; Kathleen Carlson, Ph.D., Vice Pres. Student Recruitment & Enrollment Planning; Sr. Susan M. Sanders, R.S.M., Ph.D., Vice Pres., Admin. & Planning, Sec. of the Corp.; Raymond P. Catania, M.B.A, C.P.A., CFP, CFO; Kathleen A. Rinehart, J.D., Gen. Counsel. Email: rinehart@sxu.edu.
College of Arts and Sciences Tel: 773-298-3091; Fax: 773-298-3872. Kathleen Alaimo, Ph.D., Dean.
School of Nursing Tel: 773-298-3701; Fax: 773-298-3704. Gloria Jacobson, R.N., Ph.D., Dean. Email: jacobson@sxu.edu.
Graham School of Management Tel: 773-298-3600; Fax: 773-298-3610. James D. Brodzinski, Ph.D., Dean.
School of Education Tel: 773-298-3200; Fax: 773-298-3201. S. Beverly Gulley, Ph.D., Dean.
School for Continuing and Professional Studies Tel: 708-802-6205; Fax: 708-802-6202. Leslie M. Petty, Ed.D., Dean.
The Bishop John R. Gorman Institute Tel: 708-802-6200; Fax: 708-802-6202.

RIVER FOREST. *Dominican University (Formerly Rosary College)*, 7900 W. Division St., 60305. Tel: 708-366-2490; Fax: 708-524-5990. Email: webmaster@email.dom.edu. Web: www.dom.edu. Dr. Donna M. Carroll, Pres.; Sr. Elwyn McHale, O.P., Prioress; Dr. Cheryl Johnson-Odim, Provost & Vice Pres. Academic Affairs; Ms. Amy McCormack, Senior Vice Pres. Finance & Admin.
Dominican University Dominican Sisters of Sinsinawa, WI. Priests 1; Sisters 3; Total Enrollment 3,690; Faculty 155; Staff 214.
Rosary College of Arts and Sciences at Dominican University Tel: 708-524-6816; Fax: 708-524-5990. Dr. Jeffrey Carlson, Dean.
Brennan School of Business Tel: 708-524-6810; Fax: 708-524-6939. Dr. Arvid Johnson, Dean.

School of Education Tel: 708-524-6922; Fax: 708-524-6665. Dr. Colleen Reardon, Dean.
Graduate School of Library and Information Science Tel: 708-524-6845; Fax: 708-524-6657. Dr. Susan Roman, Dean.
Graduate School of Social Work Tel: 708-366-3463; Fax: 708-366-3446. Dr. Mark Rodgers, Dean.
School of Continuing Studies Tel: 708-714-9056; Fax: 708-714-9126. Mr. Matt Hlinak, Assistan Provost.

[D] HIGH SCHOOLS, PRIVATE

CHICAGO. *Brother Rice High School*, 10001 S. Pulaski Rd., 60655-3356. Tel: 773-429-4300; Fax: 773-779-5239. Email: kburns@brrice.org. Web: www.brotherrice.org. Bro. Karl J. Walczak, C.F.C., Pres.; Mr. James P. Antos, Prin.; Ms. Beverly Buciak, Librarian. Congregation of Christian Brothers. Priests 1; Brothers 6; Lay Teachers 53; Students 842.
Christ the King Jesuit College Preparatory School, 5088 W. Jackson Blvd., 60644. Tel: 773-261-7505; Fax: 773-261-7507. Email: cdevron@ctkjesuit.org. Web: www.ctkjesuit.org. Rev. Christopher Devron, S.J., Pres.; Brendan Conroy, Prin. Participant in the Cristo Rey Work/Study Program, Inc. Priests 1; Sisters 3; Lay Teachers 18; Students 270.
Cristo Rey Jesuit High School, Inc., 1852 W. 22nd Pl., 60608. Tel: 773-890-6800; Fax: 773-890-6801. Email: jgartland@cristorey.net. Web: www.cristorey.net. Rev. James G. Gartland, S.J., Pres.; Patricia Garrity, Prin.; Diane Madrid-Limon, Librarian. Priests 2; Sisters 1; Brothers 1; Scholastics 2; Lay Teachers 26; Students 535.
Cristo Rey Work/Study Program, Inc., 1852 W. 22nd Pl., 60608. Tel: 773-890-6800; Fax: 773-890-6880. Carlos De La Rosa, Dir.
De La Salle Institute
De La Salle Institute Brothers of the Christian Schools.
Institute Campus for Young Men, 3455 S. Wabash Ave., 60616. Tel: 312-842-7355; Fax: 312-842-4142. Email: webmaster@dls.org. Web: www.dls.org. Rev. Paul E. Novak, O.S.M., Pres.; Mr. James Krygier, Prin. Brothers 2; Lay Teachers 55; Students 673.
Lourdes Hall Campus for Young Women, 1040 W. 32nd Pl., 60608. Tel: 773-650-6800; Fax: 773-650-9722. Email: webmaster@dls.org. Web: www.dl-s.org. Rev. Paul E. Novak, O.S.M., Pres.; Ms. Diane Brown, Prin. Sisters 3; Lay Teachers 30; Students 434.
St. Francis de Sales High School, 10155 S. Ewing Ave., 60617. Tel: 773-731-7272; Fax: 773-731-7888. Email: info@sfdshs.org. Web: www.sfdshs.org. Mary Kay Ramirez, Prin. Lay Teachers 22; Students 220.
Gordon Tech High School, 3633 N. California Ave., 60618-4602. Tel: 773-539-3600; Fax: 773-539-9158. Email: noberfell@gordontech.org. Web: www.gordontech.org. Ms. Kelly Jones, Pres.; Rev. Joseph Malczyk, C.R., Campus Min.; Bro. Ed Jaszkowski, C.R., Maintenance Engineer; Carl Hagman, Prin.; Anthony Mill Spaugh, Librarian. Priests 1; Brothers 1; Lay Teachers 26; Students 445. In Res. Revs. Martin Bratek, C.R.; Edward Jaskula, C.R.; Joseph Korabik, C.R.
**Hales Franciscan High School, Inc.*, 4930 Cottage Grove Ave., 60615. Tel: 773-285-8400; Fax: 773-285-7025. Robert Anderson, Pres.; Ms. Avis Wright, Acting Prin.; Friar Johnpaul Cafiero, O.F.M., D.Min., M.A., M.Div., Dir. Campus Ministry; Revs. Phil D. Hogan, O.F.M., Coord. Student Activities & Special Programs; David Rodriguez, O.F.M., M.F.A., Fine Arts & Theology Chair; Bro. Fred Smith, O.F.M., Mgr. Bookstore. Priests 3; Brothers 1; Lay Teachers 28; Students 400.
Hales Services, Inc., 4930 S. Cottage Grove, 60615. Tel: 773-285-8400, Ext. 255; Fax: 773-285-7025. Sylvia Lottie, Dir.
Holy Trinity High School, 1443 W. Division St., 60642. Tel: 773-278-4212; Fax: 773-278-0144. Email: arog@holytrinity-hs.org. Web: www.holytrinity-hs.org. Mr. Timothy Bopp, Pres.; Ms. Anne Rog, Prin. Brothers of Holy Cross. Priests 2; Sisters 2; Lay Teachers 29; Students 275.
St. Ignatius College Prep, 1076 W. Roosevelt Rd., 60608-1594. Tel: 312-421-5900; Fax: 312-421-7124. Email: michael.caruso@ignatius.org. Web: www.ignatius.org. Revs. Michael P. Caruso, S.J., Pres.; Patrick A. Fairbanks, S.J., Rector; Dr. Catherine A. Karl, Ph.D., Prin.; Revs. Richard W. Anderson, S.J., Faculty Chap.; Ross Pribyl, S.J.; Ms. Carla Hickey, Librarian. Priests 1; Lay Teachers 93; Students 1,384; Sisters 1.
St. Ignatius Jesuit Community, 1025 W. Taylor, 60607. Tel: 312-829-2297; Fax: 312-829-9552. Revs. Richard W. Anderson, S.J., High School Counselor; Louis E. Busemeyer, S.J., Assoc. Pastor; Michael P. Caruso, S.J., High School Pres.; Glen Chun, S.J., Vocation Promoter; James J. Creighton, S.J., Hospital Chap.; John R. Crocker, S.J., Retreat Dir.; Patrick A. Fairbanks, S.J., Rector; Philip J. Grib, S.J., Assoc. Pastor; Robert I. Grib, S.J., Assoc. Pastor; Joel Medina, S.J., Hospital Chap.; Eugene J. Nevins, S.J., Hospital Chap.; Ross Pribyl, S.J., High School English Teacher; James F. Riley, Consultor to Prov.; James F. Vorwoldt, S.J., Artist; Bro. John L. Moriconi, S.J., Sec. to Prov. Priests 16.
Josephinum Academy, 1501 N. Oakley Blvd., 60622. Tel: 773-276-1261; Fax: 773-292-3963. Email: martha.roughan@josephinum.org. Web: www.josephinum.org. Sr. Martha Roughan, R.S.C.J., Prin.; Nancy Rowley, Librarian.
Josephinum, Inc., Middle School and High School (Grades 6-12) Sisters 3; Lay Teachers 19; Girls 150.
Leo High School, 7901 S. Sangamon, 60620. Tel: 773-224-9600; Fax: 773-224-3856. Email: admin@leohighschool.org. Web: www.leohighschool.org. Philip Mesina, Prin. Boys 322.
Maria High School (Formerly St. Casimir Academy), 6727 S. California Ave., 60629. Tel: 773-925-8686; Fax: 773-925-8885. Email: maria-hs@archchicago.org. Web: www.mariahighschool.org. Wendy Lynn, Pres.; Margaret Hayes, Prin.; Pamela Hovan, Librarian. Sisters of St. Casimir. Sisters 1; Lay Teachers 21; Students 207.
Marist High School, 4200 W. 115th St., 60655-4306. Tel: 773-881-5300; Fax: 773-881-0595. Email: laurencell.karen@marist.net. Web: www.marist.net. Bro. Patrick McNamara, F.M.S., Pres.; Larry N. Tucker, Prin. Brothers 5; Sisters 1; Lay Teachers 113; Students 1,797.
Marist Brothers Tel: 773-881-5300; Fax: 773-881-0595. Larry N. Tucker, Prin.
Mother McAuley Liberal Arts High School, 3737 W. 99th St., 60655. Tel: 773-881-6500; Fax: 773-881-6562. Email: cmelone@mothermcauley.org. Web: www.mothermcauley.org. Dr. Christine M. Melone, Pres. & Prin.; Ms. Patricia McGreal, Librarian. Sisters of Mercy. Sisters 4; Lay Teachers 93; Students 1,356.
Mt. Carmel High School, 6410 S. Dante Ave., 60637. Tel: 773-324-1020; Fax: 773-324-9235. Email: cmarkelz@mchs.org. Web: www.mchs.org. Carmelites.
Res.: 6401 S. Harper Ave., 60638. Revs. Benjamin Aguilar, O.Carm.; Carl J. Markelz, O.Carm., Prin.; Daniel Carroll, O.Carm. (Retired); Mark Kwiecien, O.Carm.; Peter McGarry, O.Carm. Carmelites in Residence 5; Lay Teachers 65; Students 850.
St. Patrick High School, 5900 W. Belmont Ave., 60634. Tel: 773-282-8844; Fax: 773-282-2361. Web: www.stpatrick.org. Bro. Konrad Diebold, F.S.C., Pres.; Dr. Joseph Schmidt, Prin.; Mr. Jeffrey Troxell, Asst. Prin.; Ms. Marilyn Wenzel, Librarian.
St. Patrick High School Brothers of the Christian Schools. Brothers 3; Lay Teachers 61; Students 816.
Resurrection College Prep High School, 7500 W. Talcott Ave., 60631. Tel: 773-775-6616; Fax: 773-775-0611. Email: hs.resurrection@archchicago.org. Web: www.reshs.org. Dr. Lynne Saccaro, Pres. & Prin.; Mrs. Teresa Hamlin, Librarian. Sisters of the Resurrection. Sisters 4; Lay Teachers 50; Girls 643.
St. Rita of Cascia High School, 7740 S. Western Ave., 60620. Tel: 773-925-6600; Fax: 773-925-2451. Email: strita@stritahs.com. Web: www.stritahs.com. Rev. Thomas R. McCarthy, O.S.A., Pres.; Brendan Conroy, Prin.; Mrs. Robyn Kurnat, Librarian.
St. Rita of Cascia High School Corporation, (See Section N for Monastery listing) Priests 4; Brothers 1; Sisters 2; Lay Teachers 45; Students 711.
St. Rita of Cascia High School Foundation, 7740 S. Western Ave., 60620. Tel: 773-925-6600; Fax: 773-925-2451. Email: mgallagher@stritahs.com. Mike Gallagher, CFO.
St. Rita of Cascia High School Facilities, Inc., 7740 S. Western Ave., 60620. Tel: 773-925-6600; Fax: 773-925-2451.
St. Scholastica Academy, 7416 N. Ridge Blvd., 60645. Tel: 773-764-5715; Fax: 773-764-0304. Web: www.scholastica.us. Loretta A. Namovic, Pres.; Ms. Colleen Brewer, Prin.; Mr. Russell Kracke, Librarian. Sisters 4; Lay Teachers 29; Students 250.
Convent, 7430 N. Ridge Blvd., 60645. Tel: 773-764-2413; Fax: 773-761-5131.
ARLINGTON HEIGHTS. *St. Viator High School*, 1213 E. Oakton St., 60004. Tel: 847-392-4050; Fax: 847-392-8305. Email: megan@saintviator.com. Web: www.saintviator.com. Revs. Robert M. Egan, C.S.V., Pres.; Corey D. Brost, C.S.V.; Arnold E. Perham, C.S.V.; John E. Van Wiel, C.S.V.; Bros. James E. Leonard, C.S.V.; Daniel J. Lydon, C.S.V.; Rob Robertson, C.S.V.; Daniel J. Tripamer, C.S.V.; Eileen Manno, Prin.; Cheryl Quinn, Librarian. Clerics of St. Viator. Priests 4; Brothers 4; Lay Teachers 89; Students 1,000.
BURBANK. *St. Laurence High School, Inc.*, 5556 W. 77th St., 60459. Tel: 708-458-6900; Fax: 708-458-6908. Email: vikings@stlaurence.com. Web: www.stlaurence.com. Thomas J. Ondria, Pres.; James C. Muting Jr., Prin.; Laura Baldwin, Librarian. Congregation of Christian Brothers. Priests 1; Brothers 3; Lay Teachers 43; Students 687.
Queen of Peace High School (Girls)., 7659 S. Linder Ave., 60459. Tel: 708-458-7600; Fax: 708-458-5734. Email: info@queenofpeacehs.org. Web: www.queenofpeacehs.org. Anne O'Malley, Pres.; Ms. Mary Kay Nickels, Prin.; Ms. Natalie Formica, Asst. Prin. Student Svcs.; Ms. Barbara Smith, Asst. Prin. & Dir. Technology Integration. Lay Teachers 24; Students 361.
CHICAGO HEIGHTS. *Marian Catholic High School*, 700 Ashland Ave., 60411. Tel: 708-755-7565; Fax: 708-756-9758. Email: mchsinfo@marianchs.com. Web: www.marianchs.com. Sisters Judine Hilbing, O.P., Pres.; Kathleen Anne Tait, O.P., Prin.; Mrs. Susan Silander, Librarian. Dominican Sisters (Springfield, IL). Sisters 13; Lay Teachers 85; Students 1,505.
LAGRANGE PARK. *Nazareth Academy*, 1209 W. Ogden Ave., La Grange Park, 60526. Tel: 708-354-0061; Fax: 708-354-0109. Email: dtracy@nazarethacademy.com. Web: www.nazarethacademy.com. Mrs. Deborah Tracy, Prin.; Mr. Dennis Moran, Pres.; Vera Beggs, Librarian. Congregation of St. Joseph. Sisters 2; Lay Teachers 47; Students 803.
LAKE FOREST. *Woodlands Academy of the Sacred Heart*, 760 E. Westleigh Rd., 60045-3298. Tel: 847-234-4300; Fax: 847-234-4348. Email: info@woodlandsacademy.org. Web: www.woodlandsacademy.org. Mr. Gerald Grossman, Head of School; Ms. Madonna L. Edmunds, Prin.; Ms. Ellen Hines, Librarian. Religious of Sacred Heart. Lay Teachers 32; Students 171.
LEMONT. *Mt. Assisi Academy*, 13860 Main St., 60439. Tel: 630-257-7844; Fax: 630-257-6362. Sr. Mary Francis Werner, O.S.F. Sisters of St. Francis of Christ the King. Sisters 5; Lay Teachers 30; Students 219.
MUNDELEIN. *Carmel Catholic High School*, One Carmel Pkwy., 60060. Tel: 847-566-3000; Fax: 847-566-8465. Email: (name)@carmelhs.org. Web: www.carmelhs.org. Judith Mucheck, Ph.D., Pres.; Lynne Strutzel, M.A., Prin.; Greg Hirsch, Chm. Bd. Dirs.; Eric Franklin, Librarian. Sisters 3; Lay Teachers 79; Students 1,362.
NILES. *Notre Dame College Prep.* (Boys), 7655 Dempster St., 60714. Tel: 847-965-2900; Fax: 847-965-2975. Web: www.nddons.org. Revs. John P. Smyth, Pres.; Raymond F. Klees, Exec. Vice Pres.; Ms. Paula Waters, Exec. Chair; Mr. Charles McNulty, CFO; Mr. Daniel Tully, Prin.; Mr. Scott L. Dutton, Asst. Prin. Academics; Mr. Timothy M. Jarotkiewicz, Asst. Prin. Student Life; Mr. Richard Balentine, Dir. Campus Ministry; Ms. MaryAnn Malartsik, Business Mgr.; Mr. Michael Hennessey, Dir. Athletics; Rev. Richard Conyers, C.S.C.; Mrs. Veronica Price, Librarian. Priests 3; Sisters 1; Lay Teachers 56; Students 835.
OAK PARK. *Fenwick High School*, 505 Washington Blvd., 60302. Tel: 708-386-0127; Fax: 708-386-3052. Email: admin@fenwickfriars.com. Web: www.fenwickfriars.com. Rev. Richard C. LaPata, O.P., Assoc. Dir. Devel. & Alumni; Richard Borsch, Assoc. Prin. & Dir. of Student Svcs.; Peter Groom, Prin.; Revs. William J. Bernacki, O.P.; Joseph Ekpo; DePorres C. Durham, O.P., Pres.; Michael A. Winkels, O.P.; Bros. Timothy Combs, O.P.; R. Douglas-Adam Greer, O.P.; Ms. Mary Pat Ryan, Librarian. Dominican Order. Dominican Order Priests 4; Dominican Brothers 2; Diocesan Priests 1; Lay Teachers 84; Students 1,218.
RIVER FOREST. *Trinity High School*, 7574 W. Division St., 60305. Tel: 708-771-8383; Fax: 708-488-2014. Web: www.trinityhs.org. Sr. Michelle Germanson, O.P., Pres.; Antonia C. Bouillette, Prin.; Molly Klownen, Librarian. Dominican Sisters (Sinsinawa, WI). Sisters 1; Lay Teachers 44; Students 519.
RIVER GROVE. *Guerin College Preparatory High School*, 8001 Belmont Ave., 60171. Tel: 708-453-6233; Fax: 708-453-6296. Email: nnolan@guerinprep.org. Web: www.guerinprep.org. Sr. Nancy Nolan, S.P., Pres.; Mrs. Bonnie Brown, Prin.; Bro. John Ptaszek, C.S.C., Librarian. Sisters of Providence. Sisters 9; Lay Teachers 61; Students 700.
SOUTH HOLLAND. *Seton Academy*, 16100 Seton Dr.,

60473-1899. Tel: 708-333-6300; Fax: 708-333-1534. Email: seton@seton-academy.org. Web: www.seton-academy.org. Marianne Lynch, Prin.; Earl McKay, Dean; Elizabeth Starczewski, Campus Min. Lay Teachers 18; Students 250.

WAUKEGAN. *St. Martin de Porres High School*, 515 S. Martin Luther King Jr. Ave., 60085. Tel: 847-623-5500; Fax: 847-623-5604. Email: pkendall@smdpwaukegan.org. Web: www.smdpwaukegan.org. Mr. G. Preston Kendall, Pres.; Mr. Michael Odiotti, Prin.; Sr. Judy Seiberlich, O.P., Asst. Prin.; Arthur Jones, Dean Students. Lay Teachers 19; Students 247.

SMDP Work Study, Inc., 501 S. Martin Luther King Jr. Ave., 60085. Tel: 847-244-6895; Fax: 847-244-8237. Email: pkendall@smdpwaukegan.org. Web: www.smdpwaukegan.org. Jim Dippold, Campus Min.

WESTCHESTER. *St. Joseph High School*, 10900 W. Cermak Rd., 60154-4299. Tel: 708-562-4433; Fax: 708-562-4459. Email: ronald.hoover@stjoeshs.org. Web: stjoeshs.org. Mr. David McCreery, Pres.; Mr. Ronald Hoover, Prin. Brothers of the Christian Schools. Lay Teachers 35; Students 600.

WILMETTE. *Loyola Academy*, 1100 Laramie Ave., 60091-1021. Tel: 847-256-1100; Fax: 847-251-4031. Web: www.goramblers.org. Revs. Patrick E. McGrath, S.J., Pres.; Richard H. McGurn, S.J.; James S. Prehn, S.J., Jesuit Supr.; Mr. Patrick Mahoney, Athletic Dir.; Mrs. Beth Waid-Prince, Asst.Prin. for Academics; Ms. Margaret Culhane, Dean of Students; Dr. Kathryn Baal, Prin.; Mr. Terence K. Brennan, Vice Pres. & CFO; David Behof, Registrar/Institutional Researcher; Geryl Cerney, Controller; Vicki Siegelman, Librarian. Priests 6; Brothers 1; Lay Teachers 185; Students 2,000.

Regina Dominican High School, 701 Locust Rd., 60091. Tel: 847-256-7660; Fax: 847-256-3726. Email: mpachucki@rdhs.org. Web: www.rdhs.org. Sr. Mary Margaret Pachucki, O.P., Pres. Email: mpachucki@rdhs.org. Sisters of St. Dominic (Adrian, MI)., (Catholic School for Women) Sisters 3; Lay Teachers 33; Students 325.

[E] ELEMENTARY SCHOOLS, PRIVATE

CHICAGO. *St. Angela School*, 1332 N. Massasoit Ave., 60651-1108. Tel: 773-626-2655; Fax: 773-626-8156.

Chicago Jesuit Academy, at Resurrection Campus, 5058 W. Jackson Blvd., 60644-4324. Tel: 773-638-6103; Fax: 773-638-6107. Email: info@cjacademy.org. Web: www.cjacademy.org. Revs. Richard H. McGurn, S.J., Jesuit Dir.; Richard L. Millbourn, S.J., Jesuit Dir.; Patrick E. McGrath, S.J., Jesuit Dir.; Matthew Lynch, Pres.; Mr. Thomas Beckley, Prin.; Mr. David Diehl, Dean, Students; Ms. Catherine Cassidy, Vice Pres. Operations & Devel. Operated by the Chicago Detroit Province of the Society of Jesus. Full-scholarship, college-prep Roman Catholic, Jesuit middle school for boys of modest economic backgrounds from Chicago's west side; serving 97, 5th, 6th, 7th & 8th grade boys; 12-student learning groups; extended academic day; 11-month school year; prepares young men for success in the college-prep high schools, universities and community leadership; high school scholarship support available for alumni. Total Staff 23; Total Assisted Annually 142.

The Frances Xavier Warde School, 120 S. Des Plaines St., 60661-3515. Tel: 312-466-0700; Fax: 312-466-0711. Email: fxw@fxw.org. Web: www.fxw.org. Ms. Mary Reiling, Head of School. Email: reilingm@fxw.org; Mrs. Erin Horne, Prin., Old St. Patrick Campus (Grades K-3); D. Michael Veitch, Prin. Holy Name Campus (Grades 4-8). Lay Teachers 85; Students 895.

Sacred Heart Schools (Academy of the Sacred Heart for Girls, Hardey Prep. for Boys), (Grades K-8), 6250 N. Sheridan Rd., 60660-1730. Tel: 773-262-4446; Fax: 773-262-6178. Email: sacred.heart@shschicago.org. Web: www.shschicago.org. Mr. Nat Wilburn, Head Schools; Mrs. Mary Ann Ligon, Head of Lower School, (Grades 3-5); Mrs. Christine Elliott, Head of Middle School, (Grades 6-8); Ms. Meg Steele, Head of Primary School, (Grades K-2); Mrs. Jean Brunder, Library Media Specialist. Religious of the Sacred Heart. Lay Teachers 81; Students 690.

San Miguel Febres Cordero School, Inc., 819 Leamington Ave., 60651. Tel: 773-890-0233 (Administrative Office); Fax: 773-261-2250 (Administrative Office). Email: info@sanmiguelchicago.org. Web: www.sanmiguelchicago.org. Michael Anderer-McClelland, Pres., Exec. Dir. & Prin Gary Comer Campus; Tad Smith, Prin. Back of the Yards Campus. Operated by DeLaSalle Christian Brothers. Gratuitous Catholic Middle School with two campuses for at risk youth; adult education (ESL, financial mgmt., and computer skills); after school and evening youth development programs, ages 11-18; parenting skills classes. Mentoring, tutoring retreat opportunities, and support to graduates who study in high school. Total Staff 37; Children 355; Families 350.

LEMONT. *Everest Academy of Lemont, Inc.*, 11550 Bell Rd., 60439. Tel: 630-243-1995; Fax: 630-243-1988. Email: cgamache@everestlemont.com. Web: www.everestadvantage.com. Rev. Jose F. Ortega, L.C., Sec. & Treas.; Christine M. Gamache, Prin. Total Staff 11; Priests 2; Lay Teachers 10; Total Assisted Annually 94.

[F] CONSOLIDATED ELEMENTARY SCHOOLS

CHICAGO. *Bridgeport Catholic Academy*, 3700 S. Lowe, 60609. Tel: 773-376-6223. Mrs. Lillian Buckley, Prin. Serving the following parishes: All Saints-St. Anthony (518 W. 28th Pl.); Nativity of Our Lord (653 W. 37th St.). Lay Teachers 10; Students 200.

[G] CATHOLIC CHARITIES

CHICAGO. *Catholic Charities of the Archdiocese of Chicago-Archdiocesan Offices*, 721 N. LaSalle St., 60654. Tel: 312-655-7000; Fax: 312-655-0219. Web: catholiccharities.net. Administration: Rev. Msgr. Michael M. Boland, Administrator, Pres. & CEO; Mr. J. Antonio Fernandez, Sr. Vice Pres. Operations; Rev. Charles T. Rubey, Assoc. Dir. Programs (Retired); Ms. Kathy Donahue, Sr. Vice Pres. Programs; Ms. Cynthia Smetana, CFO; Revs. Richard E. Bulwith, Assoc. Admin.; Charles T. Rubey (Retired); Wayne F. Watts, Assoc. Admin.; John J. Ryan, Chief of Staff; Michele Bianchi, Sr. Vice Pres. of Human Resources & General Counsel.

Development, 721 LaSalle St., 60654. Tel: 312-655-7289; Fax: 312-655-0605. Judith M. Silekis, Dir.

Facilities Operations, 721 N. LaSalle St., 60654. Tel: 312-655-7435; Fax: 312-266-7146. Sandra DeSico, Dir.

Finance, 721 N. LaSalle St., 60654. Tel: 312-655-7326; Fax: 312-266-4276. Elida Hernandez, Dir.

Human Resources, 721 N. LaSalle St., 60654. Tel: 312-655-7538; Fax: 312-654-0849. Michele Bianchi, Senior Vice Pres.

Government Relations, 721 N. LaSalle, 60654. Tel: 312-655-7314; Fax: 312-266-6556. Laurie Barretto, Dir.

Legal and Compliance Services, 721 N. LaSalle, 60654. Tel: 312-655-7538; Fax: 312-654-0849. Michele Bianchi, General Counsel.

Board Relations, 721 N. LaSalle St., 60654. Tel: 312-655-7171; Fax: 312-930-0425. Anne Grosklaus, Dir.

Communications, 721 N. LaSalle St., 60654. Tel: 312-655-7010; Fax: 312-930-0425. Kristin Ortman, Dir.

Research and Quality Improvement, 721 N. LaSalle, 60654. Tel: 312-655-7592; Fax: 312-266-2142.

Cook County Regional Services:

Chicago Services, 721 N. LaSalle St., 60654. Tel: 312-655-7700; Fax: 312-948-6974. Arlene Jackson-Ervin, Regl. Svcs. Rep.

North Suburban Services, 1717 Rand Rd., Des Plaines, 60016. Tel: 847-376-2100; Fax: 847-390-8214. Mary Beth Hartmann, Regl. Svcs. Rep.

Northwest Suburban Services, 1717 Rand Rd., Des Plaines, 60016. Tel: 847-376-2100; Fax: 847-390-8214. Mary Insprucker, Regl. Svcs. Rep.

South Suburban Services, 16100 Seton Dr., South Holland, 60473. Tel: 708-333-8379, Ext. 222; Fax: 708-333-9519. Frederick Shannon, Regl. Svc. Rep.

Southwest Suburban Services, 7000 W. 111th St., Worth, 60482. Tel: 708-586-1355; Fax: 708-430-0502. Jeff Sims, Regl. Svc. Rep.

West Suburban Services, 1400 S. Austin Blvd., Cicero, 60804. Tel: 708-329-4022; Fax: 708-222-1491. Esmeralda Zepeda, Regl. Svc. Rep.

Lake County Regional Services:

Joseph Cardinal Bernardin Center for Lake County Services, 671 S. Lewis Ave., Waukegan, 60085. Tel: 847-782-4000; Fax: 847-782-1040. Teresa Denny, Community Liaison & Business Mgr.

Community Development and Outreach Services:

Office, 721 N. La Salle, 60654. Tel: 312-655-7508; Fax: 312-642-9716. Angel Gutierrez, Vice Pres.

Commodity and Food Supplemental Program (CFSP), 4940 W. Flournoy, 60644. Tel: 773-378-6643; Fax: 773-261-0536. Eliu Irizarry, Prog. Dir.

Immunization Linkage Program, 721 N. La Salle, 60654. Tel: 312-655-7330; Fax: 312-642-9716. Shelly Baldwin, Program Dir.

Lunch-N-More Catering and Food Service Enterprise, 6212 S. Sangamon St., 60621. Tel: 773-808-2962.

Mother and Child Food and Nutrition Program (MAC), 4940 W. Flournoy, 60644. Tel: 773-378-3127; Fax: 773-261-0536. Eliu Irizarry, Prog. Dir.

Mother and Child Food and Nutrition (MAC) Warehouse, 1965 W. Pershing Rd., 60608. Tel: 773-523-0299. Emil Atoyebi, Program Dir.

Senior Mother and Children Nutrition Program (SMCNP), 4940 W. Flournoy St., 60644. Tel: 773-378-3127.

Seniors Farmers Market Nutrition Program (SFMNP), 4940 W. Flournoy St., 60644. Tel: 773-379-5268. Yolanda James, Contact Person.

Women, Infants and Children (WIC) Food and Nutrition Centers Program, 4624 W. Diversey, 60639. Tel: 312-951-7672; Fax: 773-205-1271. William Abi Rached, Program Dir. WIC Warehouse; 4500 W. Chicago Ave., Chicago, IL 60651; WIC Food Centers: 416 E. 43rd St., Chicago, IL 60653; 6202 S. Halsted St., Chicago, IL 60621; 2310 W. Roosevelt Rd., Chicago, IL 60608; 5332 S. Western, Chicago, IL 60609; 3110 W. Armitage, Chicago, IL 60647; 1643 W. Cermak Rd., Chicago, IL 60608; 1734 W. Chicago Ave., Chicago, IL 60622; 3932 W. Madison St., Chicago, IL 60624; 5125 W. Chicago, Chicago, IL 60651; 1802 E. 71st St., Chicago IL 60649; 11255 S. Michigan Ave., Chicago, IL 60628; 4622 W. Diversey Ave., Chicago, IL 60639; 8959 S. Commercial Ave., Chicago, IL 60617; 2400 S. Kedzie Ave., Chicago, IL 60623 and 1106 W. 79th St., Chicago, IL 60620.

Family and Parish Support Services:

Office, 651 W. Lake St., 60661. Tel: 312-651-2007; Fax: 312-648-1034. Eileen Higgins, Vice Pres.; Bob Haennicke, Assoc. Vice Pres.; Maureen Murphy, Assoc. Vice Pres.

Addiction Consultation and Educational Services, 651 W. Lake St., 60661. Tel: 312-655-7453. Mary Ellen Flynn, Prog. Dir.

Casa Catalina, 4533-37 S. Ashland Ave., 60609. Tel: 773-376-9425.

Central Information and Referral Services, 651 W. Lake St., 60661. Tel: 312-655-7700; Fax: 312-655-0678. Louis Barbosa, Prog. Dir.

Central States Institute of Addiction, 651 W. Lake St., 60661. Tel: 312-655-7530; Fax: 312-266-9027. Kevin J. Doyle, Dept. Dir.

Community Family Service Center, 1100 S. May, 60607. Tel: 312-733-5661, Ext. 1467; Fax: 312-733-5211. Sandra Villwocks, Prog. Dir.

Cooke's Manor Transitional Housing For Men, Bldg. 14 Hines VA Campus, 5th Ave. & Roosevelt Rd., Hines, 60141. Tel: 708-273-6627; Fax: 708-343-4469. Rev. Richard E. Bulwith, Chap.; Gloria Wright, Prog. Dir.

Emergency Assistance Department, 721 N. LaSalle St., 60654. Tel: 312-655-7500; Fax: 312-654-9861. Christene Dykes-Sorrells, Dept. Dir.

Community Casework and Counseling, 651 W. Lake St., 60661. Tel: 312-655-7167; Fax: 312-879-0208. Pam Davis, Prog. Dir.

Forever Free, 6212 S. Sangamon, 60621. Tel: 773-374-8165; Fax: 773-548-4522. Sharon Love Williams, Prog. Dir.

Archdiocesan AIDS Ministry Office, 651 W. Lake St., 60661. Tel: 312-948-6500; Fax: 312-879-0208. Patricia Drott, Program Dir.

Holbrook Center for Counseling and Psychotherapy, 641 W. Lake St., 60661. Tel: 312-655-7719; Fax: 312-655-0678. Linda Hoag, Dept. Dir.

Lake County HIV/AIDS Case Management, 671 S. Lewis, Waukegan, 60085. Tel: 847-782-4144; Fax: 847-782-1030. David Fries, Dept. Dir.

Immigration & Naturalization Services, 651 W. Lake St., 60661. Tel: 312-382-2707; Fax: 312-427-3130. Nancy Gavilanes, Prog. Dir.

Refugee Resettlement Program, 651 W. Lake St., 60661. Tel: 312-655-7856; Fax: 312-879-0208. Elmida Kulovic, Prog. Dir.

LOSS (Loving Outreach to Survivors of Suicide), 721 N. LaSalle St., 60654. Tel: 312-655-7283; Fax: 312-948-3340. Rev. Charles Rubey, Founder; Deborah Major, Dept.Dir.

Joseph Cardinal Bernardin Family Shelter Program, 651 W. Lake St., 60661. Tel: 312-655-7700; Fax: 773-483-5301. Terri Denny, Dept. Dir.

St. Francis de Paula Interim Housing, 7811 S. Ellis, 60619. Tel: 773-487-8615; Fax: 773-651-0582. Derrolyn Steele, Supvr.

St. Susanna Shelter Apartments, 14926 S. Honore, Harvey, 60426. Tel: 708-331-8211; Fax: 708-339-4398. Derrolyn Steele, Supvr.

Madonna House, 1114 W. Grace St. Tel: 773-327-1605; Fax: 773-248-1497. Mary Fuqua, Admin.

New Hope Apartments, 651 W. Lake St., 60661. Tel: 312-651-2007; Fax: 312-906-8265. Eileen Higgins, Dept. Dir.

Lake County Samaritan House, 671 S. Lewis Ave., Waukegan, 60085. Tel: 847-782-4000; Fax: 847-782-4133. Joyce Molett, Supvr.

North/Northwest Suburban Family Shelter Program, 1717 N. Rand Rd., Des Plaines, 60016. Tel: 847-376-2100; Fax: 847-390-8214. Millicent Ntiamoah, Dir.

Homelessness Prevention Call Center, 721 N. LaSalle St., 60610. Tel: 312-698-5070; Fax: 312-655-0678. Sandra Murray, Dept. Dir.

Legal Assistance, 651 W. Lake St., 60610. Tel: 312-948-6984; Fax: 312-475-9039. Dennis Trainor, Prog. Dir.

Streets to Home, 651 W. Lake St., 60661. Tel: 312-651-2007; Fax: 312-879-0208. Jean Kielty, Program Dir.

Veterans Employment Program, 6212 S. Sangamon, 60617. Tel: 773-808-2973; Fax: 773-808-2960. Bertel Smith, Supervisor.

Lake County Family Self-Sufficiency, 671 S. Lewis, Waukegan, 60085. Tel: 847-782-4160; Fax: 847-782-1030. Christine Edwards, Dept. Dir.

Child, Youth and Family Services:

Office, 651 W. Lake St., 60661. Tel: 312-655-8570; Fax: 312-879-0293. Laura Rios, Vice Pres.

Youth and Family Therapeutic Services, 651 W. Lake, 60661. Tel: 312-655-7984; Fax: 312-236-5384. Margaret Monahan, Dept. Dir.

Intact Family Services, 651 W. Lake St., 60661. Tel: 312-382-2505; Fax: 312-258-1839. Mary J. Henderson, Dept. Dir.

Maternity/Adoption Services, 651 W. Lake St., 60661. Tel: 312-655-7071; Fax: 312-882-1612. Norene Chesebro, Dept. Dir.

Jadonal E. Ford Center for Adolescent Parenting, 11255 S. Michigan Ave., 60628. Tel: 773-474-7227; Fax: 773-995-0125. Velma Brown-Walker, Dir.

Arts of Living Institute, 651 W. Lake St., 60661. Tel: 312-948-6003; Fax: 312-236-5384. Alice Wyatt, Prog. Dir.

Administration - Head Start Centers, 651 W. Lake St., 60661. Tel: 312-651-2061; Fax: 312-879-0293. Tasha Brown, Dept. Dir.

Administration - Child Care Centers, 651 W. Lake St., 60661. Tel: 312-948-6170; Fax: 312-879-0293. Diane Rodriguez, Prog. Dir.

Childhood Development Programs, Daycare/Head Start:

St. Blase Child Development Center, 7438 W. 61st Pl., Summit, 60501. Tel: 708-496-1193; Fax: 708-496-1246.

Chicago Lawn Child Development Center, 3001 W. 59th St., 60629. Tel: 773-925-1085; Fax: 773-925-1170.

Cordi-Marian Child Development Center, 1100 S. May St., 60607. Tel: 312-666-3787; Fax: 312-666-3562.

Grace Mission Child Development Center, 5332 S. Western Ave., 60609. Tel: 773-476-1990; Fax: 773-476-2421.

St. John of God Development Center, 5114 S. Elizabeth, 60609. Tel: 773-446-6264; Fax: 773-446-6227.

St. Joseph Child Development Center, 4800 S. Paulina, 60609. Tel: 773-927-2524; Fax: 773-927-2122.

St. Mary of Celle, 1428 S. Wesley Ave., Berwyn, 60402. Tel: 312-655-8492.

Our Lady of Lourdes Child Development Center, 1449 S. Keeler, 60623. Tel: 773-521-3126; Fax: 773-522-3753.

Our Lady of Tepeyac Child Development Center, 651 W. Lake St., 60661. Tel: 312-655-8570; Fax: 312-879-0293.

Housing Management and Development Services:

Office, 721 N. LaSalle St. 5th FL., 60654. Tel: 312-655-7490; Fax: 312-944-1550. Email: housingmanagement@catholiccharities.net. Gracia Shiffrin, Vice Pres.; Elaine Layden, Vice Pres.

Catholic Charities Housing Development Corporation, 721 N. LaSalle 5th FL., 60654. Tel: 312-655-7490; Fax: 312-944-1550. Garcia M. Shiffrin, COO.

Ailbe Assisted Housing Corporation
Ailbe Senior Housing Corporation
All Saints Senior Housing, NFP
Bernardin Senior Housing Corporation
Brendan Senior Housing Corporation
Cortland Manor Development Corporation
Frances Senior Housing Corporation
Goedert Senior Housing Corporation
Lawrence Senior Housing Corporation
Hayes Senior Housing Corporation
St. Leo Assisted Housing, NFP
St. Leo Development Association
Matthew Senior Housing Corporation
North Center Senior Housing, NFP
Northlake Senior Housing, NFP
Palos Park Senior Housing, NFP
St. Peter Claver Senior Housing Corporation
Roseland Senior Housing Corporation
Sabina Senior Housing Corporation
Tolton Senior Housing Corporation Under Development:

All Saints Residence, 11701 S. State St., 60628. Tel: 312-655-7440.

Affordable Housing Institutions:

Bishop Goedert Residence, Bldg. 53, Hines VA Campus, Hines, 60141. Tel: 708-273-6600; Fax: 708-273-6609.

Hayes Manor, 1211 W. Marquette Rd., 60636. Tel: 773-873-7400; Fax: 773-873-1709.

Matthew Manor, 251 N. Albany Ave., 60612. Tel: 773-533-0001; Fax: 773-533-0622.

Ozanam Village, 271 N. Albany Ave., 60612. Tel: 773-533-0001; Fax: 773-533-0622.

Roseland Manor, 11717 S. State St., 60628. Tel: 773-995-9000; Fax: 773-995-1310.

St. Peter Claver Courts, 14115 St. Claire Blvd., Robbins, 60472. Tel: 708-389-1570; Fax: 708-389-1571.

St. Ailbe Faith Apartments, 1244 E. 93rd St., 60619. Tel: 773-721-0903; Fax: 773-721-0920.

St. Ailbe Love Apartments, 9240 S. Kimbark Ave., 60619. Tel: 773-721-0903; Fax: 773-721-0920.

St. Ailbe Hope Apartments, 9101-9103 S. Harper, 60619. Tel: 773-721-0903; Fax: 773-721-0920.

St. Brendan Apartments, 6718 S. Racine Ave., 60636. Tel: 773-846-8600; Fax: 773-846-0873.

St. Francis of Assisi Residence, 12218 S. Will-Cook Rd., Palos Park, 60464. Tel: 630-343-1880; Fax: 630-343-1890.

St. Leo Residence for Veterans, 7750 S. Emerald Ave., 60620. Tel: 773-651-9950; Fax: 773-651-9970.

St. Sabina Elders Village, 1222 W. 79th St., 60620. Tel: 773-994-7850; Fax: 773-994-7945.

Tolton Manor, 6345 S. Stewart Ave., 60621. Tel: 773-783-7800; Fax: 773-846-0868.

Frances Manor, 1270 E. Golf Rd., Des Plaines, 60016. Tel: 847-390-1270; Fax: 847-390-9331.

Lawrence Manor, 21425 Southwick Dr., Matteson, 60443. Tel: 708-481-1200; Fax: 708-481-3168.

Bernardin Manor, 1700 Memorial Dr., Calumet City, 60409. Tel: 708-832-1700; Fax: 708-832-9160.

Donald W. Kent Residence, 100 S. Wolf Rd., Northlake, 60164. Tel: 708-409-4710; Fax: 708-409-4712.

St. Vincent de Paul Residence, 4040 N. Oakley St., 60618. Tel: 312-655-7440.

Pope John Paul II Residence, 7747 S. Emerald Ave., 60620. Tel: 773-651-9950; Fax: 773-651-9970.

Senior Services and Healthcare:

Division Office, 721 N. La Salle Dr., 60654. Tel: 312-655-7572; Fax: 312-640-1587. Wendy S. Siefert, Div. Mgr.; Dorothy Russell, Assoc. Vice Pres.

Northeast/Northwest Chicago Case Management Services, 3125 N. Knox, 60641. Tel: 773-583-9224; Fax: 773-583-2373. Magalie Oscar, Dir.

South Suburban Senior Services and Senior Activity Center, 15300 S. Lexington, Harvey, 60426. Tel: 708-596-2222; Fax: 708-596-6329. Angela Taylor, Dept. Dir.

Lake County Senior Case Management Services, 116 N. Lincoln, Round Lake, 60073. Tel: 847-546-5733; Fax: 847-546-7114. Marla Harris, Dept. Dir.

Lake County Senior Community Services & Nutrition Program Sites, 671 S. Lewis Ave., Waukegan, 60085. Tel: 847-782-4267; Fax: 847-782-4296. Barbara Gaskill, Dept. Dir.

Lake County Senior Nutrition Program Sites:

Round Lake Latino Site, 116 N. Lincoln, Round Lake, 60073. Tel: 847-740-6714.

Grayslake Senior Center, 50 Library Ln., Grayslake, 60030. Tel: 847-543-1041.

Good Shepherd Manor, 445 E. Main St., Barrington, 60010. Tel: 847-381-5030.

Barrington Area Council on Aging, 235 Lion Dr., Barrington, 60010.

North Suburban Meals on Wheels, 1700 E. Lake St., Glenview, 60025. Tel: 847-729-1300, Ext. 230.

Antioch/Lake Villa Meals on Wheels, 1625 Deep Lake Rd., Lake Villa, 60046.

Park Place, 414 S. Lewis Ave., Waukegan, 60085. Tel: 847-740-6714.

The Avalon Family Restaurant, 4821 Grand Ave., Gurnee, 60031.

Dino's Den Restaurant, 88 E. Grand Ave., Fox Lake, 60020. Tel: 847-587-6604.

Northwest Suburban Senior Services, 1801 W. Central, Arlington Heights, 60005. Tel: 847-797-5321; Fax: 847-253-9597. Ms. Cindy Gunderson, Prog. Dir.

Accolade Adult Day Care, 112 S. Humphrey, Oak Park, 60302-2704. Tel: 708-445-1300; Fax: 708-445-9595. Theresa Gates-Ross, Site Dir.

Ada S. Niles Adult Day Care, 6717 S. Elizabeth, 60639. Tel: 773-488-5400; Fax: 773-488-5878. Cristal Bridges, Site Dir.

St. Ailbe Adult Day Care, 9249 S. Avalon, 60619. Tel: 773-721-0177; Fax: 773-721-1228. Delizza Russell, Site Dir.

Ada S. Niles Senior Center and Adult Day Care Services, 653 W. 63rd St., 60621. Tel: 312-745-3307; Fax: 312-745-3330. Denise King, Senior Center Dir.

Senior Aides Employment Program Tel: 773-874-2400; Fax: 773-488-5878. Babette Woods, Supr.

Catholic Home Care, Inc., 721 N. La Salle St., 60654. Tel: 312-655-7415; Fax: 312-337-2705. Mary Ann Bibat, Dir.

St. Vincent De Paul Residence North Center Senior Satellite, 4040 N. Oakley St., 60639. Tel: 312-744-4029; Fax: 312-744-8812. Liza Martin, Senior Center Dir.

Josephine P. Argento Senior Center, 1700 N. Memorial Dr., Calumet City, 60409. Angela Taylor, Dir.

Senior Care Skilled Nursing Home:

Holy Family Villa, 12220 S. Will-Cook Rd., Palos Park, 60464-7332. Tel: 630-257-2291; Fax: 630-257-2334. Roberta Magurany, Admin.

Bishop T.J. Lyne Residence for Retired Priests, 12230 South Will-Cook Rd., Palos Park, 60464-7332. Tel: 630-257-2291; Fax: 630-257-2334. Mary Ann Bibat, Dir.; Roberta Magurany, Contact Person.

Supportive Housing:

Bishop Edwin M. Conway Residence, 1900 N. Karlov Ave., 60639. Tel: 773-252-9941; Fax: 773-525-9946. Roberta Magurany, Dir.; Gabriela Saldana, Prog. Dir.

Non-Service Area Listing:

Christ Child Society of Chicago, 1616 Sheridan Rd., Wilmette, 60091. Tel: 847-251-9253. Mrs. Jane Helmer, Contact Person.

Keenager News, 721 N. LaSalle St., 60654. Tel: 312-948-7672; Fax: 312-930-0425. Sheila Haennicke, Editor.

Mission of the Holy Cross, 721 N. LaSalle St., 60654. Tel: 312-655-7000; Fax: 312-655-0219. Rev. Msgr. Michael M. Boland.

Options for Housing, Inc. f/k/a Shelter for the Homeless, Inc., 721 N. LaSalle St., 60610. Tel: 312-655-7305. Ms. Kathy Donahue, Contact Person.

St. Josephs Carondelet Child Center, 721 N. LaSalle St., 60654.

Society of St. Vincent De Paul of Chicago, 651 N. Lake St., 60661. Tel: 312-655-7181; Fax: 312-454-0101. Web: www.svdpchicago.org. Freida Bertello, Exec. Dir.; Michael Harrington, Pres.

Affiliated Agencies:

Maryville Academy, 1150 N. River Rd., Des Plaines, 60016. Tel: 847-824-6126; Fax: 847-824-7190. Sr. Catherine M. Ryan, O.S.F., Exec. Dir.

Mercy Home for Boys & Girls, 1140 W. Jackson Blvd., 60607. Tel: 312-738-7590; Fax: 312-738-0484. Rev. Scott Donahue, Pres.

Misericordia Home, Misericordia/Heart of Mercy Center, 6300 N. Ridge, 60660. Tel: 773-973-6300; Fax: 773-973-5214. Sr. Rosemary Connelly, R.S.M., Exec. Dir.

St. Coletta's of Illinois, 18350 Crossing Dr., Tinley Park, 60477. Tel: 708-342-5200; Fax: 708-342-2579. Wayne A. Kottmeyer, Exec. Dir.

[H] RESIDENTIAL CHILD-YOUTH CARE

CHICAGO. *Mission of Our Lady of Mercy-Mercy Home for Boys and Girls*, 1140 W. Jackson Blvd., 60607. Tel: 312-738-7560; Fax: 312-738-0484. Email: mhinfo@mercyhome.org. Web: www.mercyhome.org. Rev. L. Scott Donahue, Pres. & CEO; Cheryl Murphy, CFO, Vice Pres. Facilities & Human Resources; Tom Gilardi, Vice Pres. Youth Programs; Elizabeth Mulligan, Vice Pres. The Academy; Mimi LeClair, Agency Advancement; Tim Henry, Vice Pres. Quality Improvement; Tom Scheffers, Mgr. Mission Press & Facilities; Steve Snyder, Vice Pres. Information Systems. Total Staff 309; Religious 5; Youths 400.

DES PLAINES. *Maryville Academy*, 1150 N. River Rd., 60016. Tel: 847-294-1999; Fax: 847-824-7277. Web: www.maryvilleacademy.org. Sr. Catherine M. Ryan, O.S.F., Exec. Dir.; Cheryl M. Heyden, Asst. Exec. Dir.

Maryville Academy Patients Assisted Annually 2,000.

Casa Imani Program, 951 W. Bartlett Rd., Bartlett, 60103. Tel: 630-736-4546; Fax: 630-736-7478. Susan Miller, Prog. Dir.

Children's HealthCare Center, 4015 N. Oak Park Ave., 60634. Tel: 773-205-3600; Fax: 773-205-3630. Nina Aliprandi, Div. Dir.

Crisis Nursery, 4015 N. Oak Park Ave., 60634. Tel: 773-205-3600; Fax: 773-205-3633. Amy Kendal-Lynch, Prog. Dir.

Casa Salama Program, 951 W. Bartlett Rd., Bartlett, 60103. Tel: 630-736-4587; Fax: 630-736-7485. Dr. Rocco Cimmarusti, Prog. Dir.

Fatherhood Initiative Program, 1150 N. River Rd., 60016. Tel: 847-294-1987. Don Pettway, Dir.

Madden Shelter, 1658 W. Grand Ave., 60622. Tel: 312-491-3500; Fax: 312-491-3501. Fred Smith, Prog. Dir.

Maryville CYO, 1658 W. Grand Ave., 60622. Tel: 312-491-3500; Fax: 312-491-3501. Kimberly Williams, Prog. Coord.

Maryville Jen School, 1150 N. River Rd., 60016. Tel: 847-390-3020; Fax: 847-294-1738. Dr. Craig Maki, Educ. Dir.

Saint George Program Tel: 847-294-1721; Fax: 847-294-1916. Sarah Pope, Prog. Dir.

St. Martin de Porres Program, 1150 N. River Rd., 60016. Tel: 847-294-1722; Fax: 847-294-1737. William Gorman, Prog. Dir.

Scott Nolan Acute Psychiatric Hospital, 555 Wilson Ln., 60016. Tel: 847-768-5430; Fax: 847-768-5478. Randall Autry, Hospital Admin.

Scott Nolan Mental Illness / Substance Abuse Program Tel: 847-768-5430; Fax: 847-768-5478. Mary Pernaccairo, Prog. Dir.

Scott Nolan Residential Treatment Center, 555 Wilson Ln., 60016. Tel: 847-768-5430; Fax: 847-768-5478. Elizabeth Pitts, Acting Prog. Dir.; Dr. Amit Kakkar, Clin. Dir.

[I] DAY NURSERIES, SETTLEMENTS AND SOCIAL CENTERS

CHICAGO. **Claver House of Renewal, Inc.*, 8514 S. Avalon St., 60619. Tel: 773-731-3294. Edward Chatman, Pres. Food pantry, soup kitchen, homebound senior citizen care, after-school youth recreational programs; mentoring; tutoring and scholarship assistance to elementary and high school graduates continuing studies at Catholic educational institutions. Outreach to the homeless: clothing, toys and basic toiletries for local shelters.

Marillac Social Center, 212 S. Francisco Ave., 60612. Tel: 773-722-7440; Fax: 773-722-1469. Web: Marillachouse.org. Bart Winters, CEO. Day care for children ages 15 months to 13 years; Recreation programs for ages 6 to 19 years; emergency assistance food for poor families; child abuse and neglect treatment; counseling svcs.; programs for pregnant & parenting teens and their babies; home bound elderly; svcs. for teenage mothers. Lay Teachers 26; Day Care Capacity 250.

**Port Ministries*, 5013 S. Hermitage Ave., 60609. Tel: 773-778-5955; Fax: 773-778-2451. Email: port532857@aol.com. Web: www.portministries.org. Rev. Augustin Milon, O.F.M., Founder & Pres. A Franciscan outreach to the poor and homeless; mobile soup kitchen, family transitional shelter, GED, ESL, family svcs., neighborhood gym and free clinic. Total Staff 30; Total Assisted Annually 3,000.

St. Rose Center, 4911 S. Hoyne Ave., 60609. Tel: 773-436-1433; Fax: 773-436-2280. Email: strosecenter@aol.com. Web: www.strosecenter.org. Sr. Theresa Tamburo, D.S.M.P., Admin. Day Training Program for Developmentally Impaired young adults. Sisters 2; Q.M.R.P. 2; Developmental Support Person (DSP's) 6; Work Activity Director 1; Job Coach 1; Bookkeeper 1; Secretary 1; Capacity 50.

St. Vincent de Paul Center, 2145 N. Halsted St., 60614. Tel: 312-943-6776; Fax: 312-943-2257. Email: bwinters@svdpc.org. Bart Winters, CEO. Day care for children 3 months to 13 years; family social svcs; early childhood education; pre-school and afterschool programs; family social services.; Provides case management, counseling, and emergency relief for senior citizens. Outreach to the homeless in the form of case management and other concrete services. Daughters of Charity 2; Lay Teachers 65; Capacity 468.

[J] HOSPITALS

CHICAGO. *St. Anthony Hospital* Ascension Health & Missionary Sisters of the Sacred Heart of Jesus., 2875 W. 19th St., 60623. Tel: 773-484-1000. Mr. Peter Fazio, Bd. Chm.; Mr. Guy Medaglia, Interim CEO; Sr. Benigna Morais, M.S.C., Chap.; Revs. Paschalis Agu (Africa); Benedict Ezeoke (Nigeria); David Petraitis, O.S.A.

Catholic Health Partners Services Total Staff 880; Total Nursing Beds 20; Total Licensed Beds 166; Patients Assisted Annually 101,018.

St. Bernard Hospital & Health Care Center, 326 W. 64th St., 60621. Tel: 773-962-3900; Fax: 773-602-3849. Email: elizvs@aol.com. Web: stbernardhospital.org. Sr. Elizabeth Van Straten, R.H.S.J., Pres. & CEO.

St. Bernard Hospital Religious Hospitallers of St. Joseph. Sisters 1; Total Staff 700; Bed Capacity 210; Patients Assisted Annually 120,000.

Holy Cross Hospital, 2701 W. 68th St., 60629. Tel: 773-884-9000. Web: www.holycrosshospital.org. Wayne M. Lerner, D.P.H., F.A.C.H.E., Pres. & CEO; Rev. Bernard R. Danber, O.S.A., Chap.; Sr. Agnes Chapp, Patient Visitor.

Holy Cross Hospital Sisters of St. Casimir of Chicago. Sisters 5; Licensed Beds 274; Patients Assisted Annually 180,000; Total Staff 966.

Saint Joseph Hospital, 2900 N. Lake Shore Dr., 60657. Tel: 773-665-3000; Fax: 773-665-4859. Web: www.sjh.reshealth.org. Sandra Bruce, Pres.; Ron Struxness, Group Vice Pres., Exec. Vice Pres. & CEO; Revs. Theodore Ploplis, Coord. Spiritual Svcs.; Donatus Chukwu (Nigeria); Richard O'Nyamwaro, A.J.; Deacon Michael Romano, Chap.; Sr. Alverda Bonifas, O.P., Chap.; Rabbi Norm Lewison. Sponsored by Sisters of the Holy Family of Nazareth & Sisters of the Resurrection., An Affiliate of Resurrection Health Care. Bassinets 31; Bed Capacity 402; Patients Assisted Annually 190,924.

Saints Mary and Elizabeth Medical Center, 2233 W. Division, 60622. Tel: 312-770-2000; Fax: 312-770-2392. Web: www.smemc.reshealth.org. Sandra Bruce, Pres.; Margaret McDermott, Exec. Vice Pres. & CEO; Isidro Gallegos Rodriguez, Coord., Spiritual Svcs.; Most Rev. Enrique Rivera Hernandez (Puerto Rico), Chap.; Revs. William G. Hubmann, C.PP.S., Chap.; Ihor Koshyk, Chap.; Skariya Poulose, M.S.T., Chap.; Daniel R. Steiner, Chap.; Sr. Blanche Zalewski, C.S.F.N., Chap.; Michael Doyle, Chap.; William F. Kramer, Chap. Sponsored by Sisters of the Holy Family of Nazareth & Sisters of the Resurrection., An Affiliate of Resurrection Health Care. Bed Capacity-Saint Mary Campus 325; Bed Capacity-Saint Elizabeth Campus 251; Patients Assisted Annually 93,958; Total Staff 2,115.

Mercy Hospital and Medical Center, 2525 S. Michigan Ave., 60616-2477. Tel: 312-567-2100; Fax: 312-567-6575. Web: www.mercy-chicago.org. Sr. Sheila Lyne, R.S.M., Pres. & CEO. Tel: 312-567-2580; Fax: 312-567-6575; Rev. Martin J. Hebda, Vice Pres., Spirituality & Mission. Tel: 312-567-2045; Fax: 312-328-7741. Sisters 5; Bed Capacity 479; Staffed Beds 305; Patients Assisted Annually 338,019.

Affiliates:

Mercy Health System of Chicago

Mercy Family Health Center

Mercy Services Corp.

Mercy Foundation, Inc.

Mercy Health System of Chicago Liability Self-Insurance Trust

Mercy Medical at Dearborn Station (Outpatient Physician Offices), 47 W. Polk St., 60605. Tel: 312-922-3011.

Mercy Works at Dearborn Station, 47 W. Polk St., 60605. Tel: 312-922-3011; Fax: 312-922-5860.

Mercy Medical in Chinatown (Outpatient Physician Offices), 2347 S. Wentworth, 60616. Tel: 312-842-0100.

Mercy Medical on Pulaski (Outpatient Satellite Facility), 5525 S. Pulaski Rd., 60629. Tel: 773-585-1955; 773-284-5268.

Mercy Works on Pulaski, 5635 S. Pulaski Rd., 60629. Tel: 773-284-5278; Fax: 773-585-0395.

Mercy Medical on Michigan, 2930 S. Michigan Ave., 60616. Tel: 312-808-0400.

Mercy Works on Ashland, 3316 S. Ashland, 60608. Tel: 773-254-2133.

Mercy Medical in Chatham, 8541 S. State St., 60619. Tel: 773-994-2300.

**Our Lady of the Resurrection Medical Center*, 5645 W. Addison, 60634. Tel: 773-282-7000; Fax: 773-794-7671. Web: www.olr.reshealth.org. Sandra Bruce, Pres.; Ivette Estrada, Exec. Vice Pres. & CEO; Mr. Robert Shuford, Coord., Spiritual Svcs.; Revs. Abraham M. Jacob (SYM), Chap.; Tomy Vadakevattukula, M.S.T. (India), Chap.; Sisters Sebastiana Filip, C.F.S.N., Chap.; Mary Hedwig Kuczynski, C.R., Chap.; Kathleen Ponce, Chap. Sponsored by Sisters of the Holy Family of Nazareth & Sisters of the Resurrection., An Affiliate of Resurrection Health Care. Bed Capacity 264; Patients Assisted Annually 186,187.

Resurrection Medical Center, 7435 Talcott Ave., 60631. Tel: 773-774-8000; Fax: 773-990-7626. Web: www.reshealth.org. Sandra Bruce, Pres.; Sr. Donna Marie, C.R., Exec. Vice Pres. & CEO; James Croegaert, Coord., Spiritual Svcs.; Revs. Mykola Buryadnyk, Chap.; Kevin R. Fane, O.P., Chap.; Saji George Mukkoot, Chap.; Jerome Onwughalu, C.S.Sp., Chap.; Sisters Dominic Rossell, C.R., Chap.; Agnes Chimbayo, R.S.C.J., Chap.; Mr. Habteghabr Anisera, Chap.; Michael Doyle, Chap. Sponsored by Sisters of the Holy Family of Nazareth & Sisters of the Resurrection., An Affiliate of Resurrection Health Care. Bed Capacity 360; Patients Assisted Annually 222,077; Student Nurses affiliated with Nurses-Triton College 40; Student Nurses, Oakton Community College 20; Chicago Board of Education 12.

CHICAGO HEIGHTS. *Franciscan St. James Health*, 1423 Chicago Rd., 60411. Tel: 708-756-1000; Fax: 708-756-6863. Web: www.stjameshospital.org. 20201 S. Crawford Ave., Olympia Fields, 60461. Tel: 708-747-4000; Fax: 708-503-3270. Mr. Seth C.R. Warren, Pres. & CEO; Sr. M. Madonna Rougeau, O.S.F., Vice Pres. Mission Integration; Rev. Ronald L. Kondziolka, Chap.

Franciscan Alliance, Inc. Sisters 4; Bed Capacity 476; Patients Assisted Annually 180,094; Total Staff 1,840.

St. James Community Foundation, 1423 Chicago Rd., 60411. Tel: 708-756-1000; Fax: 708-756-1000. Email: tom.senesac@ssfhs.org. Thomas W. Senesac, Treas.

Alverno Clinical Laboratories, 1423 Chicago Rd., 60411. Tel: 708-756-1000; Fax: 708-756-6863. Email: tom.senesac@ssfhs.org. Thomas W. Senesac, Vice Pres.

DES PLAINES. *Holy Family Medical Center*, 100 N. River Rd., 60016. Tel: 847-297-1800; Fax: 847-297-1863. Web: www.reshealth.org. Sandra Bruce, Pres.; John Baird, Exec. Vice Pres. & CEO; Bro. Kenney Gorman, C.F.X., Coord. Spiritual Svcs.; Revs. Stepan Kostiuk (STN), Chap.; Haldane Mysliwiec, Chap.; Mr. Richard Nash, Chap.; Sr. Bridget Zanin, M.S.C., Chap. Sponsored by Sisters of the Holy Family of Nazareth & Sisters of the Resurrection., An Affiliate of Resurrection Health Care. Bed Capacity 252; Patients Assisted Annually 98,233.

ELK GROVE VILLAGE. *Alexian Brothers Medical Center*, 800 Biesterfield Rd., 60007-3392. Tel: 847-437-5500; Fax: 847-981-5774. Email: john.werrbach@alexian.net. Web: www.alexianbrothershealth.org. John Werrbach, Pres. & CEO; Beth Collier, Chap.Coord.; James Gullickson, Mgr., Clinical Pastoral Educ.; Phyllis Harman, Chap.; Dave Sattler, Chap.; Lauren Ivory, Chap.; Revs. Peter Kunnalakattu, Chap.; Matthew Varkey, Chap.; William E. Veith, Chap. Congregation of Alexian Brothers, Immaculate Conception Province., Parent Institution: Alexian Brothers Hospital Network Licensed Beds 387; Lay Staff 2,939; Patients Assisted Annually 404,045.

EVANSTON. *Saint Francis Hospital*, 355 Ridge Ave., 60202. Tel: 847-316-4000; Fax: 847-316-7733. Web: www.sfh.reshealth.org. Sandra Bruce, Pres.; Jeffrey Murphy, Exec. Vice Pres. & CEO; Anne Murphy, Coord. Spiritual Svcs.; Revs. Thomas Kuttiyanickal, S.A.C., Chap.; Tomy Vadakevattukula, M.S.T. (India), Chap.; Eulogio Roselada, O.F.M., Chap.; Rabbi Ilene Melemad, Chap. Sponsored by Sisters of the Holy Family of Nazareth & Sisters of the Resurrection., An Affiliate of Resurrection Health Care. Bed Capacity 375; Patients Assisted Annually 200,000.

EVERGREEN PARK. *Little Company of Mary Hospital and Health Care Centers*, 2800 W. 95th St., 60805. Tel: 708-422-6200; Fax: 708-425-9756. Web: www.lcmh.org. Sr. Kathleen McIntyre, L.C.M., Bd. Chm.; Dennis Reilly, Pres.; Mary Jo Quick, Vice Pres. Mission & Spirituality; Revs. James R. Gallagher, Chap. (Retired); James Thompson, O.S.A., Chap.; Bro. Brian Boyle, Chap.; Carol Ehler, Chap.; Deacon Rick Feltes, Chap.; Sisters Christa Henrich, Chap.; Margaret Nyangreli, Chap.; Margaret Schneider, Chap.; Joellyn Skrip, Chap.; Deacon Richard Warfield, Mgr. Pastoral Care.

The Little Company of Mary Hospital and Health Care Centers Sisters of the Little Company of Mary 19; Bed Capacity 298; Bassinets 24; Patients Assisted Annually 237,452.

Affiliates:

Little Company of Mary Auxiliary, 2800 W. 95th St., 60805. Tel: 708-229-5447.

Little Company of Mary Affiliated Services, Inc., 2800 W. 95th St., 60805. Tel: 708-422-6200, Ext. 5100; Fax: 708-425-9369.

Palos Office Center, 12450 S. Harlem, Palos Heights, 60463. Tel: 708-448-1207; Fax: 708-361-8049.

Oak Lawn Care Station, 5660 W. 95th St., Oak Lawn, 60453. Tel: 708-499-2273; Fax: 708-857-3705.

Burbank Office Building, 4901 W. 79th St., Burbank, 60459. Tel: 708-424-2273; Fax: 708-857-3713.

Mary Potter Pavilion, 2850 W. 95th St., 60805. Tel: 708-229-5148.

Little Company of Mary Hospital Foundation, 2800 W. 95th St., 60805. Tel: 708-229-5022; Fax: 708-229-6525. Brian Lepacek, Exec. Dir.

Little Company of Mary Health Systems of Evergreen Park, 2800 W. 95th St., 60805. Tel: 708-422-6200, Ext. 5004. Dennis Reilly, Pres.; Sr. Jean Stickney, Treas.; Kevin Egan, Sec.

HOFFMAN ESTATES. *Alexian Brothers Behavioral Health Hospital*, 1650 Moon Lake Blvd., 60169. Tel: 847-882-1600; Fax: 847-755-8060. Web: www.alexianbrothershealth.org. Clayton Ciha, CEO & Pres.; Stan Kedzior, Dir. Mission Integration; Michele Guest, Coord. Chap. Congregation of Alexian Brothers, Immaculate Conception Province. Total Staff 591; Licensed Beds 141; Patients Assisted Annually 18,540.

Parents:

Alexian Brothers Health System Tel: 847-385-7147; Fax: 847-483-7036.

Alexian Brothers Hospital Network Tel: 847-385-7147; Fax: 847-483-7036.

St. Alexius Medical Center, 1555 Barrington Rd.,

60169. Tel: 847-843-2000; Fax: 847-490-2570. Web: www.alexianbrothershealth.org. Edward M. Goldberg, Pres. & CEO; Stan Kedzior, Dir. Mission Integration; Sisters Laura Mankivsky, M.Div., Staff Chap.; N. Noemia Silva, Staff Chap.; Revs. Domingo Hurtado-Badillo, Chap.; Mykhailo Kuzma, Chap.; Tom Thomas, M.S.F.S., Chap. Congregation of Alexian Brothers, Immaculate Conception Province. Brothers 1; Licensed Beds 339; Lay Staff 2,107; Patients Assisted Annually 263,572.

Parent Institutions:

Alexian Brothers Health System Tel: 847-385-7147; Fax: 847-483-7036.

Alexian Brothers Hospital Network Tel: 847-385-7147; Fax: 847-483-7036.

MAYWOOD. **Loyola University Medical Center aka Foster G. McGaw Hospital* 2160 S. First Ave., 60153. Tel: 708-216-9000. Web: loyolamedicine.org. Dr. Paul K. Whelton, M.D., M.Sc., Pres. & CEO; Sharon O'Keefe, B.S., R.N., M.S., Pres., LUH; Rev. John J. O'Callaghan, S.J., S.T.D., Vice Pres., Mission & Ministry; Mr. Charles E. Reiter III, Sr. Vice Pres., Gen. Counsel & Sec.; Marie Coglianese, M.P.S., Dir. Pastoral Care & Educ.; Revs. Ronald Galt (Scotland); Tuan Le, S.J.; Mr. Jerry Kaelin, M.Div., M.A., Chap. CPE Supvr., CPE Mgr.; Revs. James J. Creighton, S.J., CPE Supvr.; Monica Isaac, M.Div.; Ms. Kathleen Brannigan, M.T.S.; Revs. Matthew Eaton, M.Div.; Alin Dogaru, Romanian Catholic Diocese of U.S.; Mr. John Garrity, M.S.W., J.D.; Mr. John Grubba, M.Div., M.A.; Sisters Fran Glowinski, O.S.F.; Cyrilla Zarek, O.P., M.A.; Mrs. Ruth Jandeska, M.Div.; Mrs. Deirdre Manning-Ostry; Rev. Lee Smits, M.Div. Bed Capacity 568; Total Staff 6,000; Patients Assisted Annually 70,000.

OAK PARK. *Rush Oak Park Hospital*, 520 S. Maple Ave., 60304. Tel: 708-383-9300; Fax: 708-660-6658. Mr. Bruce M. Elegant, Pres. & CEO; Aoife Lee, Dir. Spiritual Care & Mission; Ian C. Burch, Chap.; Sylvia Fromme, Chap.

Rush Oak Park Hospital Wheaton Franciscan Sisters. Bed Capacity 175; Total Staff 708; Patients Assisted Annually 84,933.

Resurrection University Tel: 708-763-6530; Fax: 708-763-1531. Email: admissions@wcn.edu. Web: www-.wscn.edu. Rebecca Jones, D.N.Sc., R.N., C.N.A.A., B.C., Chancellor. Accredited by the Commission on Collegiate Nursing Education, Higher Learning Commission, a member of North Central Association of Colleges and Schools and approved by the Illinois Department of Financial and Professional Regulation. Degrees Offered: Bachelor of Science in Nursing (BSN), Master of Science in Nursing (MSN). Students 209.

[K] HEALTH CARE CENTERS

CHICAGO. *St. Basil Health Service - Free People's Clinic*, 1850 W. Garfield, 60609. Tel: 773-436-4758; Fax: 773-436-2749. Patients Assisted Annually 5,000.

BROADVIEW. **Proviso Family Services, Inc. dba Resurrection Behavioral Health, d.b.a. ProCare Centers* 1820 S. 25th Ave., 60160. Tel: 708-681-2324; Fax: 708-681-1289. Web: www.reshealth.org. Sandra Bruce, Pres.; Mr. Frank C. Perham, Vice Pres., Behavioral Health. Sponsored by the Sisters of the Holy Family of Nazareth & Sisters of the Resurrection., An Affiliate of Resurrection Health Care. Patients Assisted Annually 20,000.

[L] PROTECTIVE INSTITUTIONS

CHICAGO. *House of the Good Shepherd*, 1114 W. Grace St., 60613. Tel: 773-935-3434; Fax: 773-935-3523.

House of the Good Shepherd Sisters of The Good Shepherd., Shelter for abused women with children. Sisters 4; Capacity (Families) 14; Total Staff 30.

**L'Arche Chicago*, 2010 W. Carroll Ave., 60612. Tel: 312-226-1273; Fax: 708-863-1273 (Call first). Email: larchechicago@sbcglobal.net. Web: www.larchechicago.org. Alexandra Conroy, Community Leader & Dir. L'Arche is people with and without intellectual disabilities sharing life in communities of faith. Mutual relationships and trust in God is at the heart of our life together.

St. Mary of Providence, 4200 N. Austin Ave., 60634. Tel: 773-545-8300; Fax: 773-545-8035. Email: SrRitaB@sbcglobal.net. Sr. Rita Butler, Dir.; Darlene Zdanowski, Admin.; Rev. Thomas A. Mulcrone, Chap.

Daughters of St. Mary of Providence, Developmental training and residential care of developmentally disabled adults. Sisters 8; Total Staff 130; Total Assisted Annually 120; Bed Capacity 94.

Misericordia/Heart of Mercy Center, 6300 N. Ridge, 60660-1017. Tel: 773-973-6300; Fax: 773-973-5214. Web: www.misericordia.com. Sr. Rosemary Connelly, R.S.M., Exec. Dir.; Rev. John J. Clair, Asst. Exec. Dir. Children and adults with developmental disabilities. Priests 1; Sisters 13; Total Staff 990; Bed Capacity 612; Total Assisted Annually 612.

BARTLETT. *Bartlett Learning Center*, 801 Carillon Dr., 60103. Tel: 630-289-4221; Fax: 630-289-4390. Michael Meis, Prin.; Moisette McNerney, Librarian.

Barlett Learning Center, Inc. dba Clarewoods Academy and Cupertino Home. Sponsored by the Sisters of St. Joseph, Third Order of St. Francis., Operates Bartlett Learning Center Day School Program and the Cupertino Home, Warrenville, IL. Day School program serves developmentally delayed and multiple handicapped individuals ages 3 to 21. Day School Program accepts youth identified LD, BD, EMH, TMH, and TBI Speech/Language Impaired, Autistic. Community Integrated Living Arrangement Serves developmentally delayed gentlemen ages 18 to 45. Sisters 2; Lay Staff 88; Patients Assisted Annually 115.

LAKE ZURICH. *Mt. St. Joseph Home*, 24955 North Hwy. 12, 60047. Tel: 847-438-5050; Fax: 847-438-6313. Email: msjlz@aol.com. Web: mtstjosephhome.com. Sr. Gertrude Barbera, D.S.M.P., Exec. Dir.; Rev. Aloysius Romanski, O.F.M.Conv., Chap. Operated by the Daughters of St. Mary of Providence., Intermediate care for developmentally disabled women. Sisters 6; Total Staff 150; Total Assisted Annually 130.

RIVER FOREST. *Big Sisters*, P.O. Box 5728, 60305. Tel: 708-488-8893. Web: bigsistersofchicago.org. Mrs. Susan Duffy, Pres.; Mrs. Mary Alice Jovan, Past Pres.

TINLEY PARK. *St. Coletta's of Illinois, Inc.*, 18350 Crossing Dr., 60487. Tel: 708-342-5200; Fax: 708-342-2579. Web: www.stcolettas.com. Wayne A. Kottmeyer, Exec. Dir. Sponsored by the Sisters of St. Francis of Assisi. Residential care, education, job training & job placement for developmentally disabled children and adults. Capacity 187; Total Assisted Annually 400; Total Staff 320.

Divisions:

Lt. Joseph P. Kennedy Jr. School, Tinley Park Tel: 708-342-5200; Fax: 708-342-2579.

Vocational Job Training Center, Tinley Park Tel: 708-342-5200; Fax: 708-342-2579.

St. Coletta's of Illinois Foundation Tel: 708-342-5246; Fax: 708-342-2579. Email: bsiwinski@stcolettail.org. Affiliate.

[M] SENIOR CARE INSTITUTIONS

CHICAGO. *Cortland Manor Retirement Home*, 1900 N. Karlov, 60639. Tel: 773-235-3670. Maureen Scholle, Admin. Catholic Charities Housing Development Corporation. Capacity 48.

Franciscan Communities dba St. Joseph Village of Chicago 4021 W. Belmont Ave., 60641. Tel: 773-328-5500; 800-524-6126. Email: sla@ franciscancommunities.com. Web: www.stjosephvillageofchicago.com. Lora Ann Slawinski, Admin.; Rev. John H. Nowak, C.R., Chap. Sisters 8; Licensed Beds 94.

Jugan Terrace, 2300 N. Racine, 60614. Tel: 773-935-9600; Fax: 773-935-9614. Email: mschicago@ littlesistersofthepoor.org.

Little Sisters of the Poor of Chicago, Inc. Senior Housing Apts. 50.

Little Sisters of the Poor Center for the Aging, 2325 N. Lakewood Ave., 60614. Tel: 773-935-9600; Fax: 773-935-9614. Sr. Patricia Metzgar, L.S.P., Supr.

Little Sisters of the Poor of Chicago, Inc., Intermediate and skilled care facility. Sisters 10; Residents 76; Bed Capacity 76; Staff 110; Assisted Annually 100.

Resurrection Life Center, 7370 W. Talcott Ave., 60631. Tel: 773-594-7400; Fax: 773-594-7402. Web: www.seniors.reshealth.org. Sandra Bruce, Pres.; Nancy Razo, Admin.; Leszek Baczkura, Coord. Spiritual Svcs.; Sisters M. Leonette Klafeta, C.R., Chap.; Elaine Skrzypczynski, C.S.F.N., Chap. A division of Resurrection Senior Services.; Skilled intermediate and sheltered nursing care. Bed Capacity 162.

Resurrection Retirement Community, 7262 W. Peterson Ave., 60631. Tel: 773-792-7930; Fax: 773-792-8316. Web: www.reshealth.org. Sandra Bruce, Pres.; Sr. Kathleen Ann Stadler, C.S.F.N., Exec. Dir.; Leszek Baczkura, Coord., Spiritual Svcs.; Lawrence Valentine, Chap. A division of Resurrection Health Care managed by Resurrection Senior Services Independent Living Apartments 435; Assisted Living Apartments 37; Total Staff 102; Total Assisted Annually 532.

DES PLAINES. *Holy Family Nursing and Rehabilitation Center*, 2380 Dempster, 60016. Tel: 847-296-3335; Fax: 847-296-2027. Web: www.seniors.reshealth.org. Sandra Bruce, Pres.; Anthony Madl, Admin.; Leszek Baczkura, Coord. Spiritual Svcs. Sponsored by Sisters of the Holy Family of Nazareth and Sisters of the Resurrection., A division of Resurrection Senior Services; Intermediate and Skilled Nursing Facility. Licensed Bed Capacity 251.

Nazarethville, 300 N. River Rd., 60016. Tel: 847-297-5900; Fax: 847-297-0504. Web: www.nazarethville.com. Sr. M. Lucille Madura, C.S.F.N., Admin. Sponsored by the Sisters of the Holy Family of Nazareth. Total Assisted Annually 30,295. In Res. Rev. John Stephen, C.R.

EVANSTON. *Saint Francis Nursing and Rehabilitation Center*, 500 Ashbury Ave., 60202. Tel: 847-316-3320; Fax: 847-316-3337. Web: www.seniors.reshealth.org. Sandra Bruce, Pres.; Michael Kaplan, Admin.; Leszek Baczkura, Coord. Spiritual Svcs.; Lauren Ivory, Chap. Sponsored by Sisters of the Holy Family of Nazareth and Sisters of the Resurrection., A division of Resurrection Senior Services; Comprehensive nursing, rehabilitation and social services. Bed Capacity 127.

GLENVIEW. *Maryhaven Nursing and Rehabilitation Center*, 1700 East Lake Ave., 60025. Tel: 847-729-1300; Fax: 847-729-9620. Web: www.seniors.reshealth.org. Sandra Bruce, Pres.; Sara Szumski, Admin.; Leszek Baczkura, Coord. Spiritual Svcs.; Michael Stacy, Chap. Sponsored by Sisters of the Holy Family of Nazareth and Sisters of the Resurrection., A division of Resurrection Senior Services; Home for Aged, intermediate and skilled care facilities, Medicare, Therapy. Total Staff 110; Capacity 135; Total Assisted Annually 225.

JUSTICE. *Rosary Hill Home*, 9000 W. 81st St., 60458. Tel: 708-458-3040; Fax: 708-458-7230. Email: rosaryhill@sbcglobal.net. Web: www.sistersop.org. Sr. M. Natalie, O.P., Admin.; Rev. Raymond J. Jasinski (Retired). Operated by the Dominican Sisters of the Immaculate Conception. Sisters 12; Bed Capacity 60; Number under care 60; Staff 35.

LAGRANGE PARK. *Bethlehem Woods Retirement Community*, 1571 Ogden Ave., La Grange Park, 60526. Tel: 708-579-3663; Fax: 708-579-7159. Web: www.seniors.reshealth.org. Sandra Bruce, Pres.; Mary Jester, Exec. Dir.; Leszek Baczkura, Coord. Spiritual Svcs.; Timothy John Doody, Chap. Sponsored by Sisters of the Holy Family of Nazareth and Sisters of the Resurrection., A division of Resurrection Health Care managed by Resurrection Senior Services. Independent living apartments and Licensed assisted living apartments. Residents 316; Bed Capacity 334; Total Staff 100.

LEMONT. *Alvernia Manor Senior Living*, 13950 Main St., 60439. Tel: 630-257-7721; Fax: 630-257-0338. Email: info@alverniamanor.org. Web: www.alverniamanor.org. Sr. Cynthia Drozd, O.S.F., Admin. Sponsored by The School Sisters of St. Francis of Christ the King. Residents 50.

Franciscan Village, 1270 Franciscan Dr., 60439. Tel: 630-243-3400; Fax: 630-257-5823. Email: rcoon@ franciscancommunities.com. Web: www.franciscancommunities.com. Robert E. Coon, Exec. Dir. Sponsored by the Franciscan Sisters of Chicago., Continuing Care Retirement Community. Independent Living 187; Assisted Living 30; Nursing Home 127; Total Staff 207.

NILES. *Saint Andrew Life Center*, 7000 N. Newark Ave., 60714-4497. Tel: 847-647-8332; Fax: 847-647-7073. Web: www.seniors.reshealth.org. Sandra Bruce, Pres.; Ms. Anne Berg, Exec. Dir.; Leszek Baczkura, Coord. Spiritual Svcs.; Rev. Stepan Kostiuk (STN), Chap.; Sr. Kathryn Wojcik, C.R., Chap. Sponsored by Sisters of the Holy Family of Nazareth and Sisters of the Resurrection., A division of Resurrection Senior Services.; Independent living apartments, Licensed assisted living apartments and Intermediate Nursing Care. Number Under Care 164.

Saint Benedict Nursing and Rehabilitation Center, 6930 W. Touhy Ave., 60714. Tel: 847-647-0003; Fax: 847-647-1936. Web: www.seniors.reshealth.org. Sandra Bruce, Pres.; Peter E. Goschy, Admin.; Leszek Baczkura, Coord. Spiritual Svcs.; Deacon Ed O'Leary, Chap. Sponsored by Sisters of the Holy Family of Nazareth and Sisters of the Resurrection., A division of Resurrection Senior Services. Residents 99.

NORTHLAKE. *Casa San Carlo Retirement Community*, 420 N. Wolf Rd., 60164. Tel: 708-562-4300; Fax: 708-492-3526. Web: www.seniors.reshealth.org. Sandra Bruce, Pres.; Sr. M. Elizabeth Trembczynski, C.S.F.N., Exec. Dir.; Leszek Baczkura, Coord., Spiritual Svcs.; Timothy John Doody, Chap. Sponsored by Sisters of the Holy Family of Nazareth and Sisters of the Resurrection., A division of Resurrection Health Care managed by Resurrection Senior Services.;

Independent living apartments Residents 175; Bed Capacity 182; Total Staff 54.

Villa Scalabrini Nursing and Rehabilitation Center, 480 N. Wolf Rd., 60164-1667. Tel: 708-562-0040; Fax: 708-562-5180. Web: www.seniors.reshealth.org. Sandra Bruce, Pres.; Abraham Matthew, Admin.; Leszek Baczkura, Coord. Spiritual Svcs.; Sisters Maria Cigolini, M.S.C.S., Chap.; Ruth Marostica, M.S.C.S., Chap.; Rev. Abraham Kaduthodil. Sponsored by Sisters of the Holy Family of Nazareth and Sisters of the Resurrection., A division of Resurrection Senior Services.; Skilled and intermediate nursing care Staff 220; Bed Capacity 253; Residents 253.

PALATINE. *St. Joseph's Home for the Elderly*, 80 W. Northwest Hwy., 60067. Tel: 847-358-5700; Fax: 847-358-5763. Email: mspalatine@littlesistersofthepoor.org. Sr. Marguerite McCarthy, Supr.; Most Rev. Andrew J. McDonald, D.D., J.C.D. (Retired).

Little Sisters of the Poor of Palatine, Inc. Operated by the Little Sisters of the Poor. Sisters 15; Total Assisted Annually 103; Bed Capacity 101; Total Staff 111.

PALOS PARK. *Holy Family Villa*, 12220 S. Will-Cook Rd., 60464. Tel: 630-257-2291; Fax: 630-257-2334. Email: hfv12375@aol.com. Roberta Magurany, Admin. Catholic Charities, Archdiocese of Chicago. Sisters 2; Residents 99; Bed Capacity 99; Total Assisted 142; Total Staff 120.

PARK RIDGE. *Resurrection Nursing and Rehabilitation Center*, 1001 N. Greenwood, 60068. Tel: 847-692-5600; Fax: 847-692-2305. Web: www.seniors.reshealth.org. Sandra Bruce, Pres.; James R. Farlee, Admin.; Bro. Kenney Gorman, C.F.X., Coord. Spiritual Svcs.; Rev. Stepan Kostiuk (STN), Chap.; Sisters Rita Mary Ganser, C.R., Chap.; Fidelis Rolfes, S.L.W., Chap.; Dominic Doherty, Chap. Sponsored by Sisters of the Holy Family of Nazareth and Sisters of the Resurrection., A division of Resurrection Senior Services. Skilled Care Bed Capacity 295.

WHEELING. **Addolorata Villa*, 555 McHenry Rd., 60090-3899. Tel: 847-537-2900; Fax: 847-215-5805. Email: tong@franciscancommunities.com. Web: www.addoloratavilla.com. Ms. Dawn Cohn, Exec. Dir.; Mr. Brian Celerio, Admin.; Ms. Maureen Tokar, Dir. Residential Svcs.; Mr. David Matenear, M.Div., Pastoral Care Coord. Email: dmatenear@franciscancommunities.com; Rev. Antonio Ong, Dir. Mission Integration & Pastoral Care. Email: tong@franciscancommunities.com; Ms. Carol Jagielinik, Chap. Email: cjagielinik@franciscancommunities.com; Deacon Bill Kalivoda, Chap. Email: bkalivoda@franciscancommunities.com. Sponsored by the Franciscan Sisters of Chicago, a continuing care retirement community. Sisters (Servants of Mary) 5; Skilled 88; Intermediate 10; Sheltered 31; Assisted Living 39; Assisted Living - Memory Lane 22; Independent Living Apartments 100.

[N] MONASTERIES AND RESIDENCES OF PRIESTS AND BROTHERS

CHICAGO. *St. Augustine Friary*, 5413 S. Cornell Ave., 60615. Tel: 773-358-6500, Ext. 402. Email: veraosa@mac.com. Revs. Philip C. Cook, O.S.A., Prior & Treas. Email: pcook@stritahs.com; Luis A. Vera, O.S.A., Formation Dir.

In Res. Rev. Joseph G. Stobba, O.S.A.

Carmelite Priory of St. Cyril, 6401 S. Harper Ave., 60637. Tel: 773-684-0112; Fax: 773-684-4713. Web: www.mchs.org. Rev. Daniel Carroll, O.Carm. (Retired).

Residing here are all the priests who teach at Mt. Carmel High School: Revs. Carl J. Markelz, O.Carm., Prin.; Peter McGarry, O.Carm.; Benjamin Aguilar, O.Carm.; Michael Kwiecien, O.Carm.

Chicago Province of the Society of Jesus-Provincial Office, 2050 N. Clark St., 60614. Tel: 773-975-6363; Fax: 773-975-0230. Email: chgprov@jesuits-chgdet.org. Web: www.jesuits-chgdet.org. Very Rev. Timothy P. Kesicki, S.J., Prov. Chicago/Detroit Province of Society of Jesus. Email: provincial@jesuits-chgdet.org; Revs. Walter C. Deye, S.J., Chicago & Detroit Socius; James S. Prehn, S.J., Chicago & Detroit Asst. Secondary Education; Theodore G. Munz, S.J., Chicago & Detroit Asst. for Business & Finance; Paul J. Faulstich, S.J., Asst. Records & Res.; Patrick A. Fairbanks, S.J., Chicago & Detroit Asst. for Vocation Promotion; Raymond P. Guiao, S.J., Chicago & Detroit Asst. Formation.

Jesuits Serving Abroad: Revs. Richard J. Baumann, S.J., Nairobi; Keith J. Esenther, S.J., Zimbabwe; Kevin H. Flaherty, S.J., Peru; Robert J. Geisinger, S.J., Rome; Jeffrey L. Klaiber, S.J., Peru; James M. McCann, S.J., Rome; Paul R. Mueller, S.J., Rome; Lewis C. Murtaugh, S.J., Peru; Peter P. Nguyen, S.J., Toronto, Canada; James M. O'Leary, S.J., Spain; John R. Sima, S.J., Peru.

Members in U.S. not listed elsewhere: Revs. Michael W. Cooper, S.J., Safety Harbor, FL; Brian E. Daley, S.J., South Bend, IN; Denis A. Dirscherl, S.J., Fairborn, OH; Andrew N. Downing, S.J., South Bend, IN; Brian P. Dunkle, S.J., Henri de Lubac House, 1713 Burdette St., South Bend, IN 46637-5522; Matthew T. Gamber, S.J., Cincinnati, OH; Steven F. Hurd, S.J., Chicago, IL; Edward H. Konerman, S.J., Donaldson, IN; Edoth Mukasa, S.J., South Bend, IN; Paul J. Nienaber, S.J., Winona, MN; Robert J. Ochs, S.J., El Cerrito, CA; Mitchell C. Pacwa, S.J., Birmingham, AL; John S. Thiede, S.J., South Bend, IN; Robert A. Ytsen, S.J., Lake Orion, MI. *Clark Street Jesuit Residence*, 2050 N. Clark St., 60614. Tel: 773-935-3947; Fax: 773-975-0230. Revs. Paul Campbell, S.J.; Walter C. Deye, S.J.; Raymond P. Guiao, S.J. Priests 7.

Woodlawn Jesuit Community, 5554 S. Woodlawn, 60637. Tel: 773-667-1395; Fax: 773-667-2089. Revs. James M. Dixon, S.J.; Robert E. Finn, S.J.; Paul V. Mankowski, S.J.; George A. Lane, S.J.; Robert T. Sears, S.J.; Eduardo Pinzon Umana, S.J. Priests 7.

St. Clare Friary, 3407 S. Archer Ave., 60608-6817. Tel: 773-890-1238; Fax: 773-847-7409. Web: www.capuchinfranciscans.org. Revs. Mark Joseph Costello, O.F.M.Cap., Dir. Post-Novitiate Formation, Vicar Provincial; William Cieslak, O.F.M.Cap., Itinerant Preaches; William Hugo, O.F.M. Cap., Pos: Local Min., Vocation Dir, Prov. Dir. of Formation; Peter Kutch, O.F.M.Cap., Local Vicar, Asst. Dir. Post-Novitiate Formation; Kalist Tesha, O.F.M.Cap.; Bros. David Hirt, O.F.M.Cap., Temporary Professed; Tien Dinh, O.F.M.Cap., Temporary Professed; Mitchell Frantz, O.F.M.Cap., Student; Vito Martinez, O.F.M.Cap., Temporary Professed; Quan Nguyen, O.F.M.Cap., Temporary Professed; Tom Nguyen, O.F.M.Cap., Temporary Professed; Richard Reinhardt, O.F.M.Cap., Temporary Professed; Parker Tiffany, O.F.M.Cap., Temporary Professed; Stephen Greco, O.F.M. Cap., Temporary Professed; Michael Joseph Groark, O.F.M. Cap., Temporary Professed.

Claretian Missionaries, St. Jude League, Inc., 205 W. Monroe, 60606. Tel: 312-236-7782; Fax: 312-236-7230. Web: www.claretians.org. Revs. John Molyneux, C.M.F., Dir.; Mark J. Brummel, C.M.F., Dir. Editorial Offices: "U.S. Catholic" and other Claretian Publications.

Columban Fathers Mission Center, 6449 N. Magnolia Ave., 60626. Tel: 773-274-9111; Fax: 773-274-9053. Revs. John Wanaurny; Charles Duster, S.S.C.

Columban Fathers Theologate, 5103 S. Ellis Ave., 60615. Tel: 773-955-0660; Fax: 773-955-0805. Revs. Timothy Mulroy, S.S.C., Rector; Leo Distor, S.S.C., Vice Rector. Priests 2; Seminarians 14.

Comboni Missionaries Theologate (M.C.C.J.), Verona Fathers, 5512 Hyde Park Blvd., 60637. Tel: 773-667-8920. Email: chicombtheo@ameritech.net. Revs. David Bohnsack, M.C.C.J.; Archimede Fornasari, M.C.C.J., Ph.D.; Mario Malacrida, M.C.C.J. (Italy). Theology Students 2.

Congregation of Christian Brothers, Brother Rice Community, 10001 S. Pulaski Rd., 60655. Tel: 773-429-4300. Bros. Robert McGovern, C.F.C., Community Leader; Eugene O. Carty, C.F.C.; Robert E. Beckstrom, C.F.C.; Thomas J. Collins, C.F.C.; George G. Gremley, C.F.C.; Paul Ickes, C.F.C.; Donald McGovern, C.F.C.; John Toole, C.F.C.; Patrick T. Varilla, C.F.C.; Ken Wolf, C.F.C. Brothers 10.

Conventual Franciscans of St. Bonaventure Province, 6107 N. Kenmore Ave., 60660. Tel: 773-274-7681; Fax: 773-274-9751. Rev. Patrick Greenough, O.F.M.Conv., Min. Prov.

The Conventual Franciscans of Saint Bonaventure Province Corporation

The Conventual Franciscans of Saint Bonaventure Province Charitable Continuing Care Trust Fund

Franciscan Friars Educational Corporation

St. Hedwig Cemetery and Mausoleum Corporation

Franciscan Friars Retirement Corporation Sacred Heart Friary, 6107 N. Kenmore Ave., 60660. Tel: 773-764-8811. Rev. Patrick Stoffer, O.F.M. Conv., Formation Dir.; Bros. Joseph Graff; Joseph Schenk, O.F.M.Conv. (Jamaica); Joseph Wood, O.F.M.Conv., Vocation Dir. & Formation Dir.

Assigned but serving elsewhere: Revs. Francis Kiley, O.F.M.Conv.; Bernard Geiger, O.F.M.Conv., Apostolate for Family Consecration, 3375 County Rd. 36, Bloomingdale, OH 43910-7903.

Friars of the Province Serving Abroad: Revs. John Calgaro, O.F.M.Conv. (Mexico); Abraham Crisostomo, O.F.M.Conv. (Mexico); Bro. Paschal Metzger, O.F.M.Conv. (Mexico).

Croatian Franciscan Custody of the Holy Family, 4851 S. Drexel Blvd., 60615. Tel: 773-536-0552; Fax: 773-536-2094. Email: custody@sbcglobal.net; custos@croatianfranciscans.org. Web: www.croatianfranciscans.org. Rev. Paul Maslach, O.F.M., Custos, Croatia Franciscan Custody of the Holy Family. *St. Anthony's Friary*, 4848 S. Ellis Ave., 60615. Tel: 773-373-3463; Fax: 773-268-7744. Revs. Josip N. Galic, O.F.M., Guardian; Timothy Majic, O.F.M.; Ljubo Krasic, O.F.M., Vicar; Zvonimir Kutlesa, O.F.M.; Philip Pavich, O.F.M.

Croatian Franciscan Fathers, 6346 N. Ridge, 60660. Tel: 773-262-0535; Fax: 773-262-4603. Email: bastepinacchicago@sbcglobal.net. Rev. Ivica Majstorovic, O.F.M., Croatian Catholic Mission Blessed Alojzije Stepinac.

Crosier Community of Chicago, 5401 S. Cornell Ave., 60615. Tel: 773-684-6975; Fax: 773-684-8357. Rev. Thomas Enneking, O.S.C.; Bro. David Donnay, O.S.C.

DePaul Vincentian Residence, 2233 N. Kenmore Ave., 60614-3594. Tel: 773-325-8700; Fax: 773-325-8719. Rev. John E. Rybolt, C.M., Supr.; Mr. Michael Walsh, Treas.; Rev. John T. Richardson, C.M. Congregation of the Mission, Society of Priests.

Members of the Vincentian Community (Congregation of the Mission-Western Province): Bro. Leo F. Keigher, C.M.; Revs. John Era, C.M.; Daniel Hasso, C.M., (Ethiopia Province); Dennis H. Holtschneider, C.M., (Eastern Province); Ronald J. Hoye, C.M.; Jaroslav Jasso, C.M., (Ukraine Province); Firmin Mola Mbalo, C.M., (Toulouse Province); Robert R. Rohrich, C.M.; Charles F. Shelby, C.M.; Paul Sisul, C.M.; Edward J. Tomasiewicz, C.M.

Divine Word Theologate, 5342 S. University, 60615-5106. Tel: 773-288-2777 (office); 773-288-7923 (residence); Fax: 773-288-6307. Email: theologate@aol.com. Revs. Stanley Uroda, S.V.D., Rector; Quang Duc Dinh, S.V.D., Dir. Formation; vanThanh Nguyen, S.V.D., Admonitor; Roger P. Schroeder, S.V.D.; Bro. Michael Decker, S.V.D., Vice Rector & Dir. Brother Formation. Priests 8; Brothers 4; Students 22.

Edward McGuinn, S.V.D. Residence, 5045 S. Ellis Ave., 60615-2711. Tel: 773-538-0431. Revs. Stephen B. Bevans, S.V.D.; Gary L. Riebe-Estrella, S.V.D.; Mark Schramm, S.V.D.

Angels Studio, 701 W. Jackson Blvd., Ste. 111, 60661. Tel: 312-234-9838; Fax: 312-583-9561; 312-234-9839. Rev. Derek Simons, S.V.D.

Dominican Community, 1914 S. Ashland Ave., 60608. Tel: 312-829-1931; Fax: 312-226-6119. Email: bcurran@stpiusvparish.org. Revs. Charles W. Dahm, O.P.; Matthias R. Mueller, O.P.; Brendan A. Curran, O.P.

Dominicans (Provincial Office), 2005 S. Ashland Ave., 60608. Tel: 312-243-0011; Fax: 312-829-8471. Email: office@domcentral.org. Web: www.op.org/domcentral.

Dominicans, Province of St. Albert the Great, U.S.A. (Central Dominican Province) Provincial Office, 2005 S. Ashland Ave., 60608. Tel: 312-243-0011; Fax: 312-829-8471. Email: office@domcentral.org.

Provincial Staff: Very Rev. Charles E. Bouchard, O.P., Prior Prov.; Revs. Robert J. Botthof, O.P., Spiritual Dir. Shrine of St. Jude; Patrick Norris, O.P., Promoter of Social Justice; Louis Morrone, O.P., Syndic & Vicar Prov.; Andrew-Carl Wisdom, O.P., Dir. Vocations & Vocational Support; Thomas McDermott, O.P., Regent of Studies; Richard Litzau, O.P., Promoter of Dominican Laity. *St. Pius V Priory*, 1909 S. Ashland Ave., 60608. Tel: 312-226-0074; Fax: 312-226-6199. Very Revs. Charles E. Bouchard, O.P., Prior Prov.; Michael G. Kyte, O.P., Prior; Revs. Robert L. Barry, O.P.; William J. Bernacki, O.P.; John Vincent Blake, O.P.; Robert J. Botthof, O.P.; Roderick M. Brown, O.P.; Gerard B. Cleator, O.P.; John R. Dolehide, O.P.; Rapael A. Fabish, O.P.; Joseph A. Fogarty, O.P.; John M. Gambro, O.P.; Robert A. Goedert, O.P.; Wilfred G. Hoff, O.P.; David M. Hynous, O.P.; James M. Karepin, O.P.; Giles R. Klapperich, O.P.; John J. Meany, O.P.; Thomas McGonigle, O.P.; James R. Motl, O.P.; Gregory J. Moore, O.P.; Thomas A. Morrison, O.P.; Louis Morrone, O.P., Syndic & Vicar Provencial; Walter T. O'Connell, O.P.; Mark Paraday, O.P.; Andrew-Carl Wisdom, O.P.; Bros. Paul M. Byrd, O.P.; Michael McGovern, O.P.; Reginald W. Neu, O.P.

Spirituality Today Journal, Inc.; Shrine of St. Jude Thaddeus; Society for Vocational Support, Inc.; St. Dominic Mission Society; Dominican Social Action Fund; Dominican Laity; The Bolivian Trust of the Dominicans; Office for Mission Advancement

Assigned but Serving Elsewhere: Revs. Richard de Ranitz, O.P.; Thomas P. Doyle, O.P.; Francis X. Dyer, O.P.; Daniel W. Morrissey, O.P.; Frank M. Nouza, O.P.

Priests of the Province Serving Abroad: Revs. Albert G. Glade, O.P. Italy; Dominic M. Holtz, O.P. Italy; Joseph P. Kenny, O.P. Nigeria; Michael A. Mascari, O.P. Italy; Dominic J. McManus, O.P. Italy; Michael J. Monshau, O.P. Italy; Peter Otillio, O.P. Nigeria; Justus M. Pokrzewinski, O.P. Nigeria;

Edward H. Riley, O.P. Nigeria; Edward Ruane, O.P. Italy; Gilbert J. Thesing, O.P. Nigeria; Benedict T. Viviano, O.P., Switzerland; Bro. Stephen D. Lucas, O.P. Nigeria.

Franciscan House of Studies, 6107 N. Kenmore Ave., 60660. Tel: 773-764-8811; Fax: 773-274-9751. Bro. Joseph Wood, O.F.M.Conv., Formation Dir. A Formation House of Conventual Franciscan Friars.

Holy Evangelists Friary Order of Friars Minor., 4513 N. Ashland Blvd., 60651-5401. Tel: 773-878-3723; Fax: 773-878-1382. Email: rfpawell@aol.com. Friar Johnpaul Cafiero, O.F.M., D.Min., M.A., M.Div.; Revs. Robert Pawell, M.Div.; Eulogio Roselada, O.F.M. Priests 3.

Holy Name Friary, Assumption BVM Province, 3800 W. Peterson Ave., 60659-3116. Tel: 773-539-4042; Fax: 773-539-9553. Revs. Lawrence Janowski, O.F.M., Guardian; Faculty & Chap. Felician Sisters, Loyola Univ.; Nathan Jaskulski, O.F.M., Chap., Felician Sisters; Hugh Zurat, O.F.M., Chap., The Port; Camillus Janas, O.F.M., Assoc. Pastor St. Isaac Joques.

Holy Spirit Friary, Order of Friars Minor, 5225 S. Greenwood Ave., 60615-4335. Tel: 773-753-1920. Revs. Gilberto Cavazos-Gonzales, O.F.M., S.L.T., Faculty, Catholic Theological Union; Albert Haase, O.F.M., Staff, Mayslake Ministries; Phil D. Hogan, O.F.M., Faculty, Hales Franciscan High School; Gilbert Ostdiek, O.F.M., S.T.D., Faculty, Catholic Theological Union; Charles E. Payne, O.F.M., Ph.D., Adjunct Faculty, Catholic Theological Union; Bro. Charles Reid, O.F.M., Theological Student; Rev. David Rodriguez, O.F.M., M.F.A., Faculty, St. Rita of Cascia High School.

Institute of Christ the King Sovereign Priest, 6415 S. Woodlawn Ave., 60637-3817. Tel: 773-363-7409; Fax: 773-363-7824. Email: info@institute-christ-king.org. Web: www.institute-christ-king.org. Very Rev. Msgr. R. Michael Schmitz; Revs. Matthew L. Talarico, Vice Rector; Raphael Veda, Vicar. *Shrine of Christ the King Sovereign Priest* Church: 64th and Woodlawn. Res.: *Priory of the Infant Jesus*.

St. John Stone Friary, 1165 E. 54th Pl., 60615-5109. Tel: 773-684-6510; Fax: 773-684-9830. Web: www.midwestaugustinians.org. Revs. James Thompson, O.S.A., Prior; David Petraitis, O.S.A.; Reinhard J. Sternemann, O.S.A., Treas.; John Szura, O.S.A.; Bros. Fred R. Kaiser, O.S.A., Subprior; John Patrick Currier, O.S.A.; John J. Stobba, O.S.A.

St. Joseph Interprovincial Post-Novitiate Formation House (A Franciscan House of the Sacred Heart Province), 5495 S. Hyde Park Blvd., 60615. Tel: 773-363-0072; Fax: 773-363-0076. Revs. Mark Soehner, O.F.M., Guardian & Formation Staff; James Lause, O.F.M., Vicar Formation Staff; Bernard Kennedy, O.F.M., Formation Dir.; Bro. Daniel Sulmasy, O.F.M., M.D., Ph.D., Prof. Medicine & Ethics, University of Chicago, Profession Date 1985. Professed 15.

Korean Catholic Center, 4115 N. Kedvale, 60641. Tel: 773-283-3979. Rev. John Smith, S.S.C., Dir.

Lithuanian American Jesuits (Della Strada Residence and Lithuanian Youth Center), 2345 W. 56th St., 60636. Tel: 773-737-8400.

Jesuit Fathers of Della Strada Inc. Baltic Jesuits Advancement Office, 12690 Archer Ave., Lemont, 60439-6732. Tel: 630-243-6234. Email: lithjesuit@hotmail.com. Revs. Antanas Grazulis, S.J., Sec.; Antanas Saulaitis, S.J., Chap. Dir. *Blessed Jurgis Matulaitis Mission*, 14911 E. 127th St., Lemont, 60439. Tel: 630-257-5613. Priests 3. *Lithuanian Youth Center Inc.*, 5620 S. Claremont Ave., 60636. Tel: 773-778-7500.

Marist Brothers, Monastery Community, 4200 W. 115th St., 60655. Tel: 773-881-6380; Fax: 773-881-0595. Email: moran.kevin@marist.net. Web: www.marist.net. Bros. Kevin Moran, Dir.; Julian Roy; Paul Forgues; Richard Grenier; Christopher Shannon.

Marist Brothers, St. Ann Residence, 10114 S. Leavitt, 60643. Tel: 773-239-4116. Bros. Vito Aresto, Dir.; Stephen Synan; Hugh Turley, F.M.S.; Henry Hammer; Brendan Brennan.

Maryknoll Fathers & Brothers, 5128 S. Hyde Park Blvd., 60615-4217. Tel: 773-493-3367; Fax: 773-493-3427. Email: chicago@maryknoll.org. Web: society.maryknoll.org. Mr. Gregory Darr, Regnl. Dir.; Mr. Jay Weingarten, Major Gift Officer; Revs. Herman W. Cisek, M.M.; William J. Donnelly, M.M.; John W. Eybel, M.M.; Bros. Joseph Bruener, M.M.; Adrian R. Mazuchowski, M.M.

Legal Title: The Catholic Foreign Mission Society of America

Miguel Pro Jesuit Community, 1611 S. Allport St., 60608. Tel: 312-226-6496; Fax: 312-226-2915. Revs. Christopher J. Denron, S.J., Pres. Christ the King Jesuit College Preparatory School; John P. Foley, S.J., Chm. Cristo Rey Network; James G. Gartland, S.J., Pres. Cristo Rey Jesuit High School; Sean A. O'Sullivan, S.J. (Ireland), Pastor St. Procopius.

Monastery of the Holy Cross, 3111 S. Aberdeen St., 60608-6503. Tel: 773-927-7424; Fax: 773-927-5734. Email: porter@chicagomonk.org. Web: www.chicagomonk.org. Revs. Peter Funk, O.S.B., Prior; Brendan D. Creeden, O.S.B., Sub Prior Novice Master; Edward J. Glanzmann, O.S.B., Vocation Dir.; Bros. Ignatius Isaac, O.S.B., Oblate Dir. & Librarian; Augustine Jusas, O.S.B., Building Mgr.; Ezekiel Brennan, O.S.B., Formation, Guest Master. Benedictine Monks (Subiaco Congregation). Novices 1.

The Oblate House of Theology, 5535 S. Kenwood Ave., 60637. Tel: 773-493-8917. Rev. Gregory T. Cholewa, O.M.I., Caretaker.

Order of Friar Servants of Mary (Servites) United States of America Province, Inc., Servite Provincial Center, 3121 W. Jackson Blvd., 60612-2729. Tel: 773-533-0360; Fax: 773-533-8307. Email: michaelcallary@servitesUSA.org. Web: www.servite.org. Very Rev. John M. Fontana, O.S.M., Prior Prov.; Revs. Frank M. Falco, O.S.M., Prov. Councilor; Gerald M. Horan, O.S.M., Prov. Councilor; Michael M. Pontarelli, O.S.M., Prov. Councilor & Prov. Vocation Team Coord.; Luke M. Stano, O.S.M., Asst. Prov.; Lawrence M. Choate, O.S.M., Prov. Treas. & Dir. Province Devel. Office & Prov. Sacristan; Bro. Michael M. Callary, O.S.M., Prov. & Corp. Sec. & Province Mission Procurator; Revs. Conrad M. Borntrager, O.S.M., Province Archivist & Historian; Christopher M. Krymski, O.S.M., Dir. National Shrine of St. Peregrine O.S.M.; Robert J. Warsey, O.S.M., Dir. National Shrine of Our Lady of Sorrows & Dir. Marian Center; Vidal M. Martinez, O.S.M., Natl. Asst. for Servite Secular Order; John M. Topper, O.S.M., Dir., National Shrine of Our Sorrowful Mother "The Grotto", Portland, OR; Paul M. Gins, O.S.M., Province Vocation Dir. Priests 71; Brothers 11; Temporary Professed 5; Novices 2.

Servite Vocation Team Coordinator, 31520 Camino Capistrano, San Juan Capistrano, CA 92675. Tel: 714-322-5862; Fax: 773-533-8307. Email: ciaopadre@hotmail.com. Web: www.servite.org. Rev. Michael M. Pontarelli, O.S.M., Province Vocation Team Coord. *Servite Vocation Director*, 1316 N. Acacia Ave., Fullerton, CA 92831. Tel: 714-879-1971. Email: pbenizi@aol.com. Web: www.servite.org. Rev. Paul M. Gins, O.S.M., Province Vocation Dir. *Servite Secular Order*, 3121 W. Jackson Blvd., 60612-2729. Tel: 773-638-5800, Ext. 48; Fax: 773-533-8307. Email: osmsecular@aol.com. Web: www.servite.org. Rev. Vidal M. Martinez, O.S.M., National Asst. Servite Secular Order. *Servite Marian Center*, 3121 W. Jackson Blvd., 60612-2729. Tel: 773-638-5800, Ext. 37; Fax: 773-533-8307. Email: rjwarseyosm@aol.com. Web: www.servite.org. Rev. Robert J. Warsey, O.S.M., Dir. *National Shrine of Our Lady of Sorrows*, 3121 W. Jackson Blvd., 60612-2729. Tel: 773-638-0159, Ext. 102. Email: rjwarseyosm@aol.com. Web: www.ols-chicago.org. Rev. Robert J. Warsey, O.S.M., Dir. *National Shrine of St. Peregrine, O.S.M.*, 3121 W. Jackson Blvd., 60612-2729. Tel: 773-638-0189, Ext. 100. Email: chriskrymski@aol.com. Web: www.servite.org. Rev. Christopher M. Krymski, O.S.M., Dir. *Servants of Mary (Servite) Development Office*, 1439 S. Harlem Ave., Berwyn, 60402. Tel: 708-795-8885; Fax: 708-795-8892. Email: lchoate@servitedevelopment.org. Web: www.servite.org. Rev. Lawrence M. Choate, O.S.M., Dir. Devel. Office. *Monastery of Our Lady of Sorrows*, 3121 W. Jackson Blvd., 60612-2729. Tel: 773-638-5800; Fax: 773-533-8307. Web: www.servite.org. Bros. Edmund M. Baran, O.S.M.; Robert M. Fandel, O.S.M.; Joseph Fundak, O.S.M.; Bonfilius M. McGovern, O.S.M.; Revs. Lawrence M. Choate, O.S.M.; Donald M. Gantley, O.S.M.; Thomas M. Greaney, O.S.M.; Christopher M. Krymski, O.S.M.; Augustine M. Kulbis, O.S.M.; John R. LeMay, O.S.M.; Vidal M. Martinez, O.S.M.; Luke M. Stano, O.S.M.; Robert J. Warsey, O.S.M *Annunciata Priory*, 11128 S. Avenue G, 60617-6925. Tel: 773-221-1043; Fax: 773-221-1556. Bro. Brian M. Fitzpatrick, O.S.M.; Revs. Conrad M. Borntrager, O.S.M.; Paul M. Cullen, O.S.M.; Dennis Kriz, O.S.M. *Assumption Priory*, 323 W. Illinois St., 60654. Tel: 312-644-0036; Fax: 312-644-1838. Revs. David M. Brown, O.S.M.; Joseph Chamblain, O.S.M.; Damian M. Charbonneau, O.S.M.; Lawrence Michael Doyle, O.S.M.; John M. Pawlikowski, O.S.M., Ph.D. *St. Bonfilius Priory*, 3401 S. Home Ave., Berwyn, 60402-3329. Tel: 708-484-2595; Fax: 708-484-0064. Email: berwynosm@aol.com. Revs. Thomas Heskin, O.S.M.; Peter M. Rookey, O.S.M.

Passionist Community of St. Vincent Strambi, 5417 S. Cornell Ave., 60615. Tel: 773-324-2704; Fax: 773-324-2557. Email: smacdonald@passionist.org. Revs. Sebastian MacDonald, C.P., S.T.D., Supr.; Donald Senior, C.P., S.T.D., Pres., CTU; Alfred Bwana, C.P., Graduate Student; John Conley, C.P., M.Div., Asst. Supr.; Christopher Gibson, C.P., Vocation Dir.; Bro. Jeffrey Gros, F.S.C., Prof. Emeritus Lewis University.

Congregation of the Passion: St. Vincent Strambi Community Priests 5; Brothers 1.

Passionist Community-Immaculate Conception Community, 5700 N. Harlem Ave., 60631-2342. Tel: 773-631-1686; Fax: 773-631-1705. Email: arthurcp@passionist.org. Web: www.passionist.org. Rev. Arthur Carrillo, C.P., Mission Appeal Dir.; Very Rev. Donald Webber, C.P., Prov. Supr.; Revs. Michael Higgins, C.P., Development Dir.; Francis X. Keenan, C.P., Chap., Lutheran General Hospital; Eric Meyer, C.P., Pastor, Immaculate Conception Parish; Ronan Newbold, C.P., Assoc. Pastor, Immaculate Conception Parish.

Congregation of the Passion: Immaculate Conception Community Priests 6.

Passionist Provincial Office, 5700 N. Harlem Ave., 60631-2342. Tel: 773-631-6336; Fax: 773-631-8059. Email: passdw@aol.com. Web: www.passionist.org. Very Rev. Donald Webber, C.P., Prov. Supr.; Revs. Richard Burke, C.P, Consultor; John Conley, C.P., M.Div., Consultor; Joseph Moons, C.P., Prov. Asst.; John Schork, C.P., Consultor.

Congregation of the Passion: Holy Cross Province

Special Assignment: Revs. Richard Johnson, C.P., 20120 N. Key Dr., Boca Raton, FL 33498. Tel: 451-470-5828; Robert Coward, C.P., Curia Generalizia Dei Passionisti, Piazza SS. Giovanni e Paolo 13, Rome 00184 Italy. Tel: 011-39-06-772-711; Fax: 011-39-06-700-8454. Email: robertcp@passiochristi.org; John B. Ormechea, C.P., Dei Passionisti, Piazza SS. Giovanni e Paolo 13, Rome 00184 Italy. Tel: 001-39-6-072-711; Fax: 001-39-06-700-8454; John P. Day, C.P., Holy Martyrs of Japan, 8244 Highway AE, Sullivan, MO 63080. Tel: 573-627-3378; Fax: 573-627-3387. Email: frjohnpd@aol.com; Joseph Van Leeuwen, C.P., Ashram J.X.P., Pallichal Rd. - Palluruthy, Kerala 682-006 India. Tel: 001-91-0484-223-1309; Fax: 011-91-0484-222-3652. Email: joejxp@yahoo.com; Deacon James Griffin, C.P., 35090 W. Eight Mile Rd., #6, Farmington Hills, MI 48335. Tel: 901-321-3964; Fax: 901-321-3505; Rev. Tu-Jin Paul Kim, C.P.

Provincial Offices: *Stauros U.S.A.*, 5700 N. Harlem, 60631-2342. Tel: 773-631-6336; Fax: 773-631-8059. Email: arthurcp@passionist.org. Web: www.stauros.org. Rev. Arthur Carrillo, C.P. *Passionist Missions of India*, 5700 N. Harlem Ave., 60631. Tel: 773-631-6336; Fax: 773-631-8059. Email: arthurcp@passionist.org. Rev. Arthur Carrillo, C.P., Procurator. *Congregation of the Passion*, 5700 N. Harlem Ave., 60631. Tel: 773-631-6336; Fax: 773-631-8059. *Passionist Missions, Inc.*, 5700 N. Harlem Ave., 60631. Tel: 773-631-6336; Fax: 773-631-8059. Rev. Arthur Carrillo, C.P., Mission Appeals, 23335 Schoolcraft St., Detroit, MI 48223-2405. Tel: 313-531-0562; Fax: 313-535-8468. *Province Development Office*, 5700 N. Harlem Ave., 60631-2342. Tel: 847-518-8844; Fax: 847-518-0461. Rev. Michael Higgins, C.P., Exec. Dir. *Planned Giving*, 5700 N. Harlem Ave., 60631-2342. Tel: 847-518-8844; Fax: 847-518-0461. Mrs. Angela Kwasinski, Dir. Planned Giving. *Passionist Communications*, 5700 N. Harlem Ave., 60631-2342. Tel: 847-518-8844; Fax: 847-518-0461. Nancy Nickel, Dir. Communications. *Province Finance Office*, 5700 N. Harlem Ave., 60631-2342. Tel: 773-631-6336; Fax: 773-631-8059. Mr. Keith Zekind, Dir. Finance; Mrs. Susan Arvanitis, Controller; Rev. Michael Hoolahan, C.P., Province Treas. *Passionist Archives*, 5700 N. Harlem Ave., 60631-2342. Tel: 773-631-6336; Fax: 773-631-8059. Rev. Kenneth O'Malley, C.P., Ph.D., Archivist.

St. Patrick's Missionary Society, 8422 W. Windsor Ave., 60656-4252. Tel: 773-887-4741; Fax: 773-887-3654. Email: spsil@spms.org. Web: spms.org. Rev. Karl Langsdorf, S.P.S., Supr. *St. Patrick's Fathers Guilds and Associates*

St. Peter's Friary, 110 W. Madison St., 60602-4196. Tel: 312-372-5111; Fax: 312-853-2361. Web: www.stpetersloop.org. Revs. William Burton, O.F.M.; Elric Sampson; Wenceslaus Church; Bro. Sammy Danna; Revs. Thomas Ess; Charles Faso; Robert Hutmacher; Robert Karris, O.F.M.; Bros. Clarence Klingert; Thomas Krull; William Lanning; Revs. George Musial; Glenn Phillips; Bros. Herbert Rempe, Business Mgr.; Raymond Shuhert; Thinh Van Tran; Revs. Michael Luke Ubben; Arthur Anderson; Mario DiCicco, O.F.M., Confessor; Vaughn Fayle, O.F.M., D.Phil., Prof. Catholic Theological Union; Bro. Leo Geurts, O.F.M., Front Office, Book Store; Revs. Kurt Hartrich, O.F.M.; James A. Hoffman, O.F.M., Confessor, Franciscan Outreach Ministry; Bros.

Edward McKenzie, O.F.M., Deacon; Joseph Middleton, O.F.M., Front Office, Guest Master; Revs. James Perluzzi, O.F.M., Guardian, Confessor; Kenneth Cadalbo, O.F.M., Confessor; Juan Carlos Ruiz Guerrero, O.F.M, Confessor; Edward Shea, O.F.M., Vicar, Confessor. Order of Friars Minor.

Premonstratensian Fathers and Brothers (Norbertines), 4841 S. Woodlawn Ave., 60615. Tel: 773-548-8020; Fax: 773-548-8023. Web: www.norbertines.org. Rev. David Komatz, O.Praem, House Supr.; Bro. Terrence Lauerman, O.Praem. Holy Spirit House of Studies. Priests 1; Students 7.

Priests of the Sacred Heart (Dehon House of Formation), 1421 E. 53rd St., 60615-4501. Tel: 773-363-1326; Fax: 773-363-1442. Bro. Duane Lemke, S.C.J., Candidate Dir. & Supr. Priests 2; Brothers 1; Scholastics 3; College Candidates 4. *SCJ Novitiate* Tel: 773-363-1326; Fax: 773-363-1442. Revs. John Czyzynski, S.C.J., Novice Dir.; Robert W. Bossie, S.C.J.

Provincial Office of the Congregation of the Resurrection, 3601 N. California Ave., 60618-4602. Tel: 773-463-7506; Fax: 773-463-7512. Very Rev. Eugene Szarek, C.R., Prov. Supr.

Weber High School, Inc., Tel: 773-463-7506

Weber Endowment Fund, Tel: 773-463-7506

Priests serving abroad: Rev. James Gibson, C.R., Curia Generalate, Via San Sebastianello 11, Rome 00187 Italy. Tel: 011-39-06-679-5908; Fax: 011-39-06-678-4397 General Curia Rome, Italy.

Priests serving elsewhere: Revs. Gary Hogan, C.R., Prov. Councilor; Timothy Keppel, C.R., Asst. Prov.; Paul Sims, C.R., Ph.D., Prov. Councilor; Tadevsz Sosnowski, C.R., Prov. Councilor.

The Redemptorist Fathers of Chicago, 1633 N. Cleveland Ave., 60614. Tel: 312-642-2498; Fax: 312-642-9283. Email: stmichael-cleveland@archchicago.org. Web: www.st-mikes.org. Revs. Thomas Santa, C.Ss.R., Pastor, St. Michael in Old Town; Kenneth Sedlak, C.Ss.R.; Thomas Donaldson, C.Ss.R., Assoc. Pastor, St. Michael in Old Town; John Paul Andree, C.Ss.R., Mission Team; John Dowd, C.Ss.R. (Retired); Joseph J. Morin, C.Ss.R., Min., Assoc. Pastor, St. Michael in Old Town; John Kuehner, C.Ss.R., (on loan to Diocese of San Angelo, TX); Anthony Judge, C.Ss.R., Mission Team Coord.; Arturo Uribe, C.Ss.R., Mission Team; Gregory Schmitt, C.Ss.R., Mission Team; Maurice J. Nutt, C.Ss.R., Mission Team; Daniel Andree, C.Ss.R., Studies in Rome; James Keewa, C.Ss.R., Assoc.; John Phelps, C.Ss.R., Life Directions.

Redemptorist Theology Residence, 1027 E. Hyde Park Blvd., 60615-2807. Tel: 773-363-2094; Fax: 773-363-2095. Email: jpfgcssr@juno.com. Revs. J. Robert Fenili, C.Ss.R.; John P. Fahey-Guerra, C.Ss.R., Co-Dir. Formation Prog & Supr.; Tuan Anh Pham, C.Ss.R., Co-Dir. Formation Prog. & Vicar Supr.; Bros. Bruce Davidson, C.Ss.R.; Ted Dorcey, C.Ss.R.; Thanh Nguyen, C.Ss.R.; Landon Cao, C.Ss.R.; Mario Gonzalez, C.Ss.R.; Aaron Meszaros, C.Ss.R. Priests 4; Students 6.

Assigned to Community, Living in Rome: Rev. Stephen Rehrauer, C.Ss.R.

St. Rita Monastery, 7740 S. Western Ave., 60620-5867. Tel: 773-476-3879; Fax: 773-925-2451. Very Rev. Bernard C. Scianna, O.S.A., Provincial; Revs. Alfred M. Burke, O.S.A.; Edwin J. Dodge, O.S.A.; Thomas R. McCarthy, O.S.A.; John P. Tasto, O.S.A.; Ronald R. Turcich, O.S.A.; Richard A. Young, O.S.A.; Bro. Gary L. Hresil, O.S.A., Prior. (See High Schools, Private)

Sacred Heart Mission House, 4105 N. Avers Ave., 60618. Tel: 773-588-7476; Fax: 773-588-6517. Email: polmes@jezuicichicago.org. Web: www.jezuicichicago.org. Revs. Stanislaw Czarnecki, S.J., Supr. & Pres., Editor, The Messenger of The Sacred Heart in Polish language; Miroslaw Bozek, S.J. (Poland); Wieslaw Faron, S.J.; Piotr Kochanowicz, S.J., Treas.; Jerzy Karpinski, S.J.; Bro. Adam Poreba.

The Polish Messenger of The Sacred Heart, Inc. Priests 5; Brothers 1. *Jesuit Millennium Center*, 5835 W. Irving Park Rd., 60634. Tel: 773-777-7000; Fax: 773-427-0126. Email: agendajom@yahoo.com. *Jan Beyzym Society, Inc.*, 4105 N. Avers Ave., 60618. Tel: 773-588-7476; Fax: 773-588-6517. Rev. Stanislaw Czarnecki, S.J. (Polish Jesuit Foreign Missions)

Scalabrini House of Theology, 5121 S. University Ave., 60615. Tel: 773-684-5230; 773-684-1706; Fax: 773-684-5240. Email: scalajmr@hotmail.com. Revs. Jesus Reyes, C.S., Rector; Mauro Lazzarato, C.S., Animator; Gino Dalpiaz, C.S., Spiritual Dir. Priests 2; Students 8.

Viatorian Residence, 1201 W. Belden, 60614. Tel: 773-871-6245. Email: d.p.houde@viatorians.com. Web: www.viatorians.com. Revs. Thomas G. Kass, C.S.V. Tel: 773-871-3613; C. Gregory Jones, C.S.V. Tel: 773-871-6245; Thomas E. Long, C.S.V. Tel: 773-883-1003; Bro. Donald P. Houde, C.S.V. Tel: 773-871-6523. Priests 3; Brothers 1.

Vincentian Community, Congregation of the Mission, Western Province, 2210-12 N. Racine Ave., 60614. Tel: 773-325-8761; Fax: 773-348-4802. Revs. Guillermo Campuzano, C.M.; Thomas Croak, C.M.; Patrick V. Harrity, C.M.; Gerard P. Kelly, C.M.; Robert Lucas, C.M.; J. Patrick Murphy, C.M.; James Murphy, C.M.; Christopher S. Robinson, C.M.; Edward R. Udovic, C.M., Supr.; Bro. Mark Elder, C.M.

Xaverian Missionaries (S.X.), 9546 S. Ewing, 60617. Tel: 773-372-9748. Email: kaskampascox@yahoo.com. Web: www.xaviermissionaries.org. Rev. Pascal Kasanziki, S.X., Rector.

ARLINGTON HEIGHTS. *Congregation of Alexian Brothers Immaculate Conception Province, Inc.*, 3040 W. Salt Creek Ln., 60005. Tel: 847-385-7147; Fax: 847-483-7036. Web: www.alexianbrothers.org. Provincial Councilors: Bros. Theodore Loucks, C.F.A.; James Classon, C.F.A.; John Howard, C.F.A.; Lawrence Krueger, C.F.A., Treas. & Asst. Sec.; Richard Lowe, C.F.A. *Brothers of St. Alexius Health and Welfare Fund, Inc.* Tel: 847-385-7147; Fax: 847-483-7036.

Viatorian Province Center-Clerics of St. Viator, 1212 E. Euclid Ave., 60004-5747. Tel: 847-398-1354; Fax: 847-637-2145. Email: tvonbehren@viatorians.com. Web: www.viatorians.com. Very Rev. Thomas R. von Behren, C.S.V., Prov. Supr.; Revs. George J. Auger, C.S.V.; Robert F. Cooney, C.S.V.; James F. Crilly, C.S.V., 4219 Pinecrest Cir. E., Las Vegas, NV 89121; Robert E. Erickson, C.S.V.; Donald J. Fitzsimmons, C.S.V.; Donald W. Huntimer, C.S.V., 800 N. County Club Rd., Tucson, AZ 85716; Lawrence D. Lentz, C.S.V., 336 Cathedral Way, Las Vegas, NV 89109; William C. Mayer, C.S.V.; James E. Michaletz, C.S.V., 308 E. Marsile St., Bourbonnais, 60914; John W. Milton, C.S.V.; Arnold E. Perham, C.S.V.; Francis P. White, C.S.V.; Kenneth E. Yarno, C.S.V. (Retired); Deacon Dale A. Barth, C.S.V.; Bros. Carlos Ernesto Florez, C.S.V.; Leo V. Ryan, C.S.V.

Priests & Brothers of the Province Serving Abroad: Very Rev. Mark R. Francis, C.S.V., Supr. Gen., Chierici di San Viatore, Casella Postale 10793, Rome 00144 Italy. Tel: 011-39-06-529-1603; Fax: 011-39-06-529-4076; Revs. Alejandro Adame, C.S.V., Clerigos de San Viator, Apartado Aereo 140011 (Centro Chia), Bogota D.C., Colombia. Tel: 011-571-862-7060; Carlos Luis Claro, C.S.V., Clerigos de San Viator, Apartado Aereo 140011 (Centro Chia), Bogota D.C., Colombia. Tel: 011-571-862-7060; Daniel R. Hall, C.S.V.; Pedro E. Herrera, C.S.V., Clergios de San Viator, Apartado Aereo 120060, Bogota, D.C., Colombia. Tel: 011-571-676-0296; Luis E. Lopez, C.S.V., Clergios de San Viator, Apartado Aero 120060, Bogota D.C., Colombia. Tel: 011-571-676-0296; Jose Felipe Montes, C.S.V., Parroquia San Juan Maria Vianney, Transversal 18B #187-31 (Barrio Verbenal), Bogota, D.C., Colombia. Tel: 011-571-677-5915; John A. Pisors, C.S.V., Clergios de San Viator, Apartado Aereo 140011 (Centro Chia), Bogota D.C., Colombia. Tel: 011-571-862-7060; Rafael Sanabria, C.S.V., Parroquia San Juan Maria Vianney, Transversal 18B #187-31 (Barrio Verbenal), Bogota D.C., Colombia. Tel: 011-571-677-5915; Edgar Suarez, C.S.V., Parroquia San Basilio Magno, Calle 80A #101-37 (Barrio Bochica), Bogota D.C., Colombia. Tel: 011-571-229-2248; Albeyro Vanegas, C.S.V., Clerigos de San Viator, Calle 61 #4-49 (Chapinero Alto), Bogota D.C., Colombia. Tel: 011-571-255-2947; Bros. Fredy Contreras, C.S.V., Clerigos de San Viator, Calle 61 #4-49 (Chapinero Alto), Bogota, D.C., Colombia. Tel: 011-571-255-2947; Frank H. Enciso, C.S.V., Parroquia San Basilio Magno, Calle 80A #101-37 (Barrio Bochica), Bogota D.C., Colombia. Tel: 011-571-229-2248; John R. Eustice, C.S.V.; Gustavo C. Lopez, C.S.V., Clerigos de San Viator, Apartade Aereo 120060, Bogota D.C., Colombia. Tel: 011-571-676-0296; Edwin J. Ruiz, C.S.V.; Daniel M. Villalobos, C.S.V.; Carlos E. Diaz, C.S.V.

Priests & Brothers Serving Elsewhere In The Archdiocese of Chicago: Revs. Charles G. Bolser, C.S.V.; Corey D. Brost, C.S.V.; Robert M. Egan, C.S.V.; Christopher J. Glancy, C.S.V.; Bro. Donald P. Houde, C.S.V.; Revs. C. Gregory Jones, C.S.V.; Thomas G. Kass, C.S.V.; Bro. James E. Lewnard, C.S.V.; Revs. Thomas E. Long, C.S.V.; Moises L. Mesh, C.S.V.; Bros. Rob Robertson, C.S.V.; Daniel J. Tripamer, C.S.V.; Michael T. Gosch, C.S.V., Asst. Prov.; Daniel J. Lydon, C.S.V.; Rev. John E. Van Wiel, C.S.V.

Priests & Brothers Serving Elsewhere In U.S.A.: Revs. Daniel R. Belanger, C.S.V.; Edward Anderson, C.S.V., 4219 Pinecrest Cir. E., Las Vegas, NV 89121; John N. Peeters, C.S.V., 428 S. Indiana Ave., Kankakee, 60901; Donald R. Wehnert, C.S.V., 428 S. Indiana Ave., Kankakee, 60901; Robert T. Bolser, C.S.V., 2736 Legend Hollow Ct., Henderson, NV 89074; Michael P. Keliher, C.S.V., 2736 Legend Hollow Ct., Henderson, NV 89074; Patrick W. Render, C.S.V., 2736 Legend Hollow Ct., Henderson, NV 89074; Bros. John J. Dodd, C.S.V., 5710 E. Tropicana Ave., #2040, Las Vegas, NV 89122; Patrick T. Drohan, C.S.V., Villa Desderata, 3015 N. Bayview Ln., McHenry, 60051; Revs. James F. Fanale, C.S.V., 230 N. Sixth Ave., P.O. Box 470, Saint Anne, 60964; William F. Haesaert, C.S.V., 2461 E. Flamingo Rd., Las Vegas, NV 89121; Bro. Michael A. Rice, C.S.V., 2461 E. Flamingo Rd., Las Vegas, NV 89121; Revs. Richard A. Rinn, C.S.V., 2461 E. Flamingo Rd., Las Vegas, NV 89121; Thomas G. Langenfeld, C.S.V., 1932 Heritage Oaks, Las Vegas, NV 89119; Simon P. Lefebvre, C.S.V., P.O. Box 515, Aguanga, CA 92536; John E. Linnan, C.S.V., 445 Briarcliff Ln., Apt. 5, Bourbonnais, 60914; Richard J. Pighini, C.S.V., 308 E. Marsile St., Bourbonnais, 60914; Daniel J. Mirabelli, C.S.V., 1303 40th St., Rock Island, 61201; Daniel T. Nolan, C.S.V., University of Notre Dame, 120 Keenan Hall, Notre Dame, IN 46556-0366; John M. Palmer, C.S.V., 1861 Portsmouth Dr., Lisle, 60532; Erwin M. Savela, C.S.V., 1601 Barton Rd., Apt. 1206, Redlands, CA 92373; Alan M. Syslo, C.S.V., 3785 Viking Garden Cir., Las Vegas, NV 89121; Eugene J. Weitzel, C.S.V., 318 W. 6th St., Beardstown, 62618; John E. Eck, C.S.V.; Jason P. Nesbit, C.S.V.; Bro. Fredy L. Santos, C.S.V., Parroquia San Juan Maria Vianney, Transversal 18B #187-31 (Barrio Verbenal), Bogota D.C., Colombia. Tel: 011-571-677-5915.

BLUE ISLAND. *Marist Brothers*, 12212 Irving Ave., 60406. Tel: 708-385-1488. Bros. Patrick McNamara, F.M.S.; Patrick McNulty, F.M.S.; James McKnight, F.M.S.

BURBANK. *Congregation of Christian Brothers dba Christian Brothers of Ireland, Inc.* 5550 W. 87th St., 60459-2914. Tel: 773-429-4353; Fax: 773-429-4381. Bro. Patrick Hayes, C.F.C.

CICERO. *San Damiano Friary Order of Friars Minor*, 4856 W. 29th St., 60804-3611. Tel: 708-656-1022. Rev. Lawrence Jagdfeld, O.F.M.; Bro. Christopher Neuman, O.F.M.

COUNTRYSIDE. *St. Gratian Friary, Franciscan Friars*, 5536 S. Edgewood Ln., 60525-3426. Tel: 708-482-4546; Fax: 708-482-8676. Email: stgratian@aol.com. Revs. James Walton, O.F.M.; Benet Fonck, O.F.M.; Dennis Koopman, O.F.M., Guardian; Kieran Kemner, O.F.M.; Albert Haase, O.F.M.; Bro. Leon Beranek, O.F.M. Priests 5; Brothers 1.

EVANSTON. *Canisius House*, 201 Dempster St., 60201-4704. Tel: 847-475-1825; Fax: 847-475-1869. Revs. Gene D. Phillips, S.J.; Theodore G. Munz, S.J.; James S. Prehn, S.J., Supr.; Timothy P. Kesicki, S.J.

GLENVIEW. *The Redemptorists of Glenview, Illinois*, 1111 N. Milwaukee Ave., P.O. Box 6, 60025. Tel: 847-724-0425; Fax: 847-724-8953. Revs. Ramon Dompke, C.Ss.R., Treas.; Fawaz Kako, C.Ss.R.; Bros. Daniel Hall, C.Ss.R.; Paul Jorns, C.Ss.R.

HILLSIDE. *Legion of Christ*, 601 N. Hillside Ave., 60162. Tel: 708-714-7737. Email: chicago@legionaries.org. Revs. Kevin Baldwin, L.C.; John Budke, L.C., Supr.; Jacob Dumont, L.C.; Matthew Kaderabek, L.C.; Patrick Murphy, L.C.; Bros. Michael Aoyama; Ryan Carlin, L.C.; Dustin George, L.C.

LA GRANGE PARK. *Comboni Missionaries*, 1615 E. 31st St., 60526-1377. Tel: 708-354-1999; Fax: 708-354-2006. Email: cmcoffice@sbcglobal.net. Web: www.combonimissionaries.org; www.laymission-comboni.org. Revs. Dennis Conway, M.C.C.J., Supr.; Abil Nairki Modi, M.C.C.J., Ministry; John Paul Pezzi, M.C.C.J., Ministry.

LEMONT. *The Slovene Franciscan Fathers, Order of Friars Minor, Commissariat of the Holy Cross*, 14246 Main St., P.O. Box 608, 60439. Tel: 630-257-2494; Fax: 630-257-2359. Revs. Blase Chemazar, O.F.M., Pres.; Metod Ogorevc, O.F.M., Guardian; Bernardin Susnik, O.F.M.; Martin Stepanich, O.F.M.; Athanasius Lovrencic, O.F.M. Priests 5.

**Slovenian Catholic Center*, 14252 Main St., P.O. Box 634, 60439. Tel: 708-204-4390. Email: john.vidmar@synovate.com. Web: www.slovenian-center.org. Deacon John Vidmar, Bd. Member.

LIBERTYVILLE. *Marytown, Our Lady of Fatima Friary*, 1600 W. Park Ave., 60048-2593. Tel: 847-367-7800; Fax: 847-367-7831. Email: frstephen@marytown.com. Web: www.marytown.com; www.consecration.com. Bro. Juniper Kriss, O.F.M.Conv., Guardian; Revs. Stephen McKinley, O.F.M.Conv., Rector, J.I. Editorial Office for Immaculata Magazine & Prow Books; Edmond Des Forges, O.F.M.Conv., Vicar; Patrick Greenough, O.F.M.Conv., Provincial; Bros. George Searles, O.F.M. Conv.; Stanley Zabkiewicz, O.F.M.Conv. (Zambia). *Conventual Franciscan*

Friars of Marytown Tel: 847-367-7800; Fax: 847-367-7831. *National Shrine of St. Maximilian Kolbe* Tel: 847-367-7800; Fax: 847-367-7831. Conventual Franciscan Friars 13.

MATTESON. *Austin Friary*, 5245 Stoneridge Ct., 60443-2269. Tel: 708-747-2732; Fax: 708-747-3549. Revs. Terry A. Deffenbaugh, O.S.A., Prior; Michael J. O'Connor, O.S.A., Dir. Senior Care; Edward Andrews, O.S.A. (Retired); Bros. David W. Adelsbach, O.S.A.; Thomas P. Taylor, O.S.A., Sec. of Province. Priests 3; Brothers 2.

OAK PARK. *Claretian Missionaries USA Eastern Province*, 400 N. Euclid, 60302. Tel: 708-848-2076; Fax: 312-236-7756. Email: usaprovincial@claretians.org. Web: www.claretians.org. Very Rev. Rosendo Urrabazo, C.M.F., Prov. Supr.; Revs. Thomas Brummel, C.M.F.; Richard Farrell, C.M.F.; Raymond E. O'Connor, C.M.F., Supr.; Wayne Schimmelmann, C.M.F.; Bro. Richard Wilga, C.M.F. Priests 25; Scholastics 6; Brothers 5.

Claretian Formation Houses:

Claret House, 5540 S. Everett, 60637. Tel: 773-493-8119; Fax: 773-493-8411. Email: stuar@claretians.org. Revs. Theodore Cirone, C.M.F.; Jose Sanchez, C.M.F.; Ronald Stua, C.M.F.; Bro. Daniel Magner, C.M.F.

Barbastro House (Claretian Candidate House), 3525 S. Hermitage Ave., 60609. Tel: 773-801-0077. Email: joycet@claretians.org. Revs. Thomas Joyce, C.M.F., Supr.; Brian Culley, C.M.F., Dir.

Priests and Brothers living elsewhere in the Archdiocese of Chicago: Revs. Marco J. Cardenas, C.M.F.; Severino Lopez, C.M.F.; Bro. Thomas Haerle, C.M.F.; Revs. Mark J. Brummel, C.M.F., Supr.; Carl J. Quebedeaux, C.M.F.; Bruce L. Wellems, C.M.F.; Thomas Moran, C.M.F.; Manuel Villalobos, C.M.F.; Ferdinand Okorie, C.M.F.; Jose Marino Novoa, C.M.F.; Hector M. Navalo, C.M.F.; Francesco Iacona, C.M.F.

Priests living elsewhere: Revs. James F. Maloney, C.M.F., Marian Village, 15555 Mount Carmel Dr., Homer Glen, 60491. Tel: 708-226-3780; Fax: 708-226-3781; Richard Bartlett, C.M.F., Resurrection Life Center, 7370 W. Talcott, 60631; Jose Alexander Gaitan, C.M.F.; Benjamin Zomero Arrieta, C.M.F.; Bro. Oscar Mendoza, C.M.F. *Claretian Missionaries Community Support Trust*, 400 N. Euclid Ave., 60302. Tel: 708-848-2076; Fax: 708-848-2069. Very Rev. Rosendo Urrabazo, C.M.F., Pres.; Revs. Leonard Brown, C.M.F.; Mark J. Brummel, C.M.F., Treas.; Jose Sanchez, C.M.F.; Bruce L. Wellems, C.M.F., Sec.

Dominican Community of St. Martin de Porres, 204 S. Humphrey, 60302. Tel: 708-848-4271. Email: stmartin@dominicans.org. Web: www.domcentral.org. Revs. Michael A. Winkels, O.P.; James Marchionda, O.P.

Missionaries of Saint Charles, Provincial Residence, 546 N. East Ave., 60302. Tel: 708-386-4430; Fax: 708-386-4457. Web: www.scalabrinians.org. Rev. Adilso Luiz Balen, C.S., Prov.

Fathers of St. Charles Scalabrini Development Office, 546 N. East Ave., 60302. Tel: 708-848-1616; Fax: 708-848-2525. Rev. Aldo Vendramin, C.S., Dir. *Scalabrinians Community Support Corporation, Oak Park* Tel: 708-386-4430; Fax: 708-386-4457. *Scalabrinians Community Formation Corporation, Oak Park* Tel: 708-386-4430; Fax: 708-386-4457.

OLYMPIA FIELDS. *The Augustinians-Provincialate*, Augustinian Province Offices, 5401 S. Cornell Ave., 60615-5664. Tel: 773-595-4000; Fax: 773-595-4004. Email: secretary@midwestaugustinians.org. Web: www.midwestaugustinians.org. Very Revs. Bernard C. Scianna, O.S.A., Prior Prov.; Robert F. Prevost, O.S.A., Prior Gen.; Bro. Thomas Taylor, O.S.A., Prov. Sec.; Rev. Thomas R. McCarthy, O.S.A., Vocation Dir. Tel: 773-776-3044; Bro. Gary L. Hresil, O.S.A., Personnel Dir.; Revs. John D. Merkelis, O.S.A., Asst. Personnel Dir.; Michael J. Slattery, O.S.A., Province Treas. & Vicar Prov.

RIVER FOREST. *St. Thomas Aquinas Priory*, 7200 Division St., 60305. Tel: 708-771-3030; Fax: 708-714-9002. Revs. Thomas F. O'Meara, O.P., Prior; Bede R. Jagoe, O.P., Lector; Richard C. LaPata, O.P.; Jordan A. McGrath, O.P., Subprior; Richard J. Woods, O.P.; DePorres C. Durham, O.P.; Alfred A. Lopez, O.P.; Bros. Edward van Merrienboer, O.P., Treas.; Douglas Greer, O.P. Legal Subsidiaries and holdings: The Priory Press, 2005 S. Ashland Ave., Chicago, IL 60608. Tel: 312-243-0011; Fax: 312-829-8471. President: Rev. William J. Bernacki, O.P., '56, theology texts for high schools. Priests 8; Brothers 1; Deacons 1.

Living elsewhere: Bro. Joseph Kilikevich, O.P.

TECHNY. *Divine Word Residence*, 1901 Waukegan Rd., P.O. Box 6000, 60082-6000. Tel: 847-412-1100; Fax: 847-753-7456. Email: rector@techny.org. Web: www.divineword.org. Revs. Adam MacDonald, S.V.D., Rector; James Braband, S.V.D.; James Artzer, S.V.D.; Lukas Batmomolin, S.V.D.; Charles Boykins, S.V.D.; Joseph Bugner, S.V.D.; Peter DeTaVo, S.V.D.; Quang Duc Dinh, S.V.D., Rector; John Donaghey, S.V.D.; Felix Eckerman, S.V.D.; Bernard Fisher, S.V.D.; Sunny Francis, S.V.D.; Dariusz Garbaciak, S.V.D.; Kazimierz Garbacz, S.V.D.; Joseph Guidry, S.V.D.; William Halvey, S.V.D.; John Harpel, S.V.D.; Edward Herberger, S.V.D.; Janusz Horowski; Robert Kelly, S.V.D.; John Kersten, S.V.D.; John Kirby, S.V.D.; Arnold Lang, S.V.D.; August Langenkamp, S.V.D.; William Liebert, S.V.D. (Retired); Paschal LoBianco, S.V.D.; John McSherry, S.V.D.; Raymond Quetchenbach, S.V.D.; Alexander Rodlach, S.V.D.; John Rodney, S.V.D.; Charles Scanlon, S.V.D.; Charles Schneider, S.V.D.; William Seifert, S.V.D.; Peter Silvester, S.V.D.; Francis Theriault, S.V.D.; Vinh The Trinh, S.V.D.; Eric Vargas, S.V.D.; Richard Vaz, S.V.D.; Very Rev. Mark Weber, S.V.D., Prov.; Rev. Jerome Ziliak, S.V.D.; Bros. Raymond Albers, S.V.D.; Rodney Bowers, S.V.D.; Joachim Brignac, S.V.D.; Rene Gawlik, S.V.D.; Patrick Hegarty, S.V.D.; Daniel Holman, S.V.D.; Brian McLauchlin, S.V.D.; Dennis Newton, S.V.D.; Gerard Pashia, S.V.D.; Cyril Schroeder, S.V.D.; Kenneth Valois, S.V.D.; Robert Zalikowski, S.V.D.; Mathew Zemel, S.V.D.

Divine Word Techny Community Corporation, (Formerly Divine Word Seminary-St. Mary's Mission House) Retired Archbishop 1; Retired Bishop 1; Priests 39; Brothers 13.

Society of the Divine Word, Provincial Headquarters-Chicago Prov. (Province of Saint Joseph Freinademetz, S.V.D.), 1985 Waukegan Rd., P.O. Box 6038, 60082-6038. Tel: 847-412-9505; Fax: 847-412-9505. Email: provincial@uscsvd.org. Web: www.divineword.org. Very Rev. Thomas J. Ascheman, S.V.D., Prov. Supvr.; Revs. Dariusz Garbaciak, S.V.D., Prov. Treas.; James Braband, S.V.D., Sec. Education, Recruitment & Formation; Adam Oleszczuk, S.V.D., Vice Prov. *Vocation Office* Tel: 800-553-3321; Fax: 563-876-5515. Email: svdvocations@dwci.edu. Web: www.svdvocations.org. Mr. Len Uhal, National Dir. *Blessed Arnold Charitable Trust*, 1985 Waukegan Rd., P.O. Box 6067, 60082-6067. Tel: 847-272-2700; Fax: 847-753-7464. Email: dgarbaciak@uscsvd.org. Web: www.divineword.org. Rev. Dariusz Garbaciak, S.V.D., Sec. *DWTCRE Charitable Trust*, 1901 Waukegan Rd., 60082. Tel: 847-272-2700; Fax: 847-753-7464. Email: dgarbaciak@uscsvd.org. Web: www.divineword.org. Rev. Dariusz Garbaciak, S.V.D., Sec. *Divine Word Funds, Inc. S.V.D. Funds, Inc.*, P.O. Box 6067, 60082-6067. Tel: 847-272-2700; Fax: 847-753-7464. Email: dgarbaciak@uscsvd.org. Web: www.annuitysvd.org. Very Rev. Thomas J. Ascheman, S.V.D., Pres.; Rev. Dariusz Garbaciak, S.V.D., Prov. Treas. *Divine Word Novitiate*, 1945 Waukegan Rd., 60082-6000. Tel: 847-412-1444; Fax: 847-753-7456. Bro. Rodney Bowers, S.V.D., Novice Dir.; Rev. William Seifert, S.V.D., Assoc. Novice Dir. Novices 7.

WILLOW SPRINGS. *Cistercian Fathers, Our Lady Mother of the Church Polish Mission*, 116 Hilton St., 60480-1697. Tel: 708-467-0436; Fax: 708-467-0479. Email: cistercianfathers@yahoo.com. Box 334, Argo, 60501. Revs. Michael Blicharski, O.Cist.; Filip Krzemien, O.Cist.; John Muc, O.Cist.; Ludwik Zyla, O.Cist.

Cistercian Fathers, Our Lady Mother of the Church., Cistercian Priory dependant monastery of the Abbey in Szczyrzyc, Poland (Polish Congregation) est. 1982. Priests 4.

[O] CONVENTS AND RESIDENCES FOR SISTERS

CHICAGO. *Benedictine Sisters of Chicago*, St. Scholastica Monastery, 7430 N. Ridge Blvd., 60645. Tel: 773-764-2413; Fax: 773-761-5131. Email: prioress@osbchicago.org. Web: www.osbchicago.org. Sr. Patricia Crowley, O.S.B., Prioress. Sisters 44.

Congregation of the Albertine Sisters, 1550 N. Astor, 60610. Tel: 312-642-5838. Sr. Domicela Pekala, Contact Person.

Daughters of Divine Love Congregation, 2601 N. Sayre Ave., 60707. Tel: 773-622-2434 (office); 773-622-3758 (convent); Fax: 773-622-2499. Email: ddloveus@aol.com. Sr. Magdalene Etachum Ogah, D.D.L., D.D.L., Regl. Supr. A Pontifical Religious Institute.

Daughters of St. Mary of Providence, Provincialate: 4200 N. Austin Ave., 60634-1615. Tel: 773-205-1313; Fax: 773-205-1316. Email: dsmpchi@sbcglobal.net. Web: www.dsmpic.org. Sr. Patricia McCafferty, Prov.

Daughters of St. Paul, 172 N. Michigan, 60601. Tel: 312-346-4902 (convent); 312-346-4228 (center); Fax: 312-346-2587. Email: chicago@pauline.org. Web: www.pauline.org. Sr. Helen Rita Lane, F.S.P., Supr. Sisters 5.

St. Elizabeth Convent, 1356 N. Claremont Ave., 60622. Sr. Bonnie Boilini, P.H.J.C., Contact Person. Poor Handmaids of Jesus Christ.

Little Sisters of Jesus, 1529 S. Sawyer St., 60623. Tel: 773-277-5061. Email: littlesrs.chg@juno.com. Web: www.rc.net/org/littlesisters. Sisters 3.

Little Sisters of the Poor, The, 2325 N. Lakewood Ave., 60614. Tel: 773-935-9600; Fax: 773-935-9614. Sr. Patricia Metzgar, L.S.P., Supr.

Little Sisters of the Poor of Chicago, Inc. Sisters 13.

Medical Missionaries of Mary, 3410 W. 60th Pl., 60629. Tel: 773-737-3458. Email: mmmchi@sbcglobal.net. Web: www.mmmusa.org. Sisters 4.

Mercy Convent, 10044 S. Central Park, 60655. Tel: 773-238-4887; Fax: 773-238-0024. Sr. Ann Sullivan, R.S.M., Admin. Sisters 30.

Missionaries of Charity, 2325 W. 24th Pl., 60608. Tel: 773-847-8771. Sr. Drita Maris, M.C., Local Supr. Sisters 7.

Missionary Sisters of Christ the King, 4910 N. Menard Ave., 60630. Tel: 773-481-1831; Fax: 773-545-4171. Sr. Ewa Biniek, M.Ch.R., Supr. 1118 N. Noble St., 60622. Tel: 773-489-0714. Sr. Gertruda Szymanska, M.Ch.R., Supr. 5936 W. Barry Ave., 60634-5130. Tel: 773-889-7979. Sr. Anna Strycharz, M.Ch.R., Supr. 2441 N. Menard Ave., 60639-2334. Tel: 773-637-9187. Sr. Ewa Biniek, M.Ch.R., Supr. 3651 W. George St., 60618. Tel: 773-395-3520. Sr. Marta Cichon, M.Ch.R., Supr. 6101 S. 75th Ave., Summit, 60501. Tel: 708-458-8556. Sr. Dorota Domin, M.Ch.R., Supr.

Missionary Sisters of the Sacred Heart, 434 W. Deming Pl., 60614. Tel: 773-883-7302; Fax: 773-525-0513. Sr. Joaquina Costa, M.S.C., Treas.

Mother of Good Counsel Central Convent, 3800 W. Peterson Ave., 60659-3116. Tel: 773-463-3020; Fax: 773-463-3567. Email: smchristopher@feliciansisters.org. Web: www.feliciansna.org. Sr. Mary Christopher Moore, C.S.S.F., Prov. Min.

The Felician Sisters of the United States of America, Incorporated, Chicago Province, Felician Sisters: Mother of Good Counsel Convent; Our Lady of the Angels Convent; Archives; (*) Felician Services, Inc. Professed Sisters 140.

Felician Volunteers in Mission, Inc.

North American Province of the Congregation of Our Lady of the Cenacle, Inc., 513 W. Fullerton Pkwy., 60614-6428. Tel: 773-528-6300; Fax: 773-549-0554. Email: cenacleprovincialate@usa.net. Web: www.cenaclesisters.org. Sr. Evelyn Jegen, R.C., Prov. Professed Sisters 105.

Cenacle Sisters, 513 W. Fullerton Pkwy., 60614-6428. Tel: 773-528-6300; Fax: 773-528-2456. Email: csisters@cenaclechicago.org. Web: www.cenaclesisters.org. Sr. Marguerite Gautreao, S.J., Local Leader. Professed Sisters 21.

Queen of the Resurrection House of Prayer, 7430 W. Talcott Ave., 60631. Sr. M. Therese Yokiel, Supr. Sisters 23.

Religious Hospitallers of St. Joseph of Delaware, Inc., 326 W. 64th St., 60621. Tel: 773-962-3900; Fax: 773-873-8247. Email: elizvs@aol.com. Sr. Janet Wahleither, R.H.S.J., Local Contact.

Sisters of Charity of Seton Hill Generalate, Seton House International, 4933 W. Patterson Ave., 60641-3512. Tel: 773-205-1822; Fax: 773-205-1855. Email: marlenemondalek@hotmail.com. Sr. Marlene Mondalek, S.C., Gen. Supr. Seton House International

Sisters of Mercy of the Americas West Midwest Community, Inc., 10024 S. Central Park, 60655-3132. Tel: 773-779-6011; Fax: 773-779-6094. Email: info@mercywmw.org. Web: www.mercywestmidwest.org. Sr. Judith Frikker, R.S.M., Pres. Sisters 4.

Sisters of Our Lady of LaSalette, 4220 N. Sheridan Rd., 60613. Tel: 773-248-4047. Email: marijosnds@starpower.com; sr_emie@yahoo.com. Sisters Josephine S. Valenton, S.N.D.S., U.S.A. Mission in Charge; Emelita S. Sobrepena, S.N.D.S., Local Supr. Sisters (Chicago Community) 2; Sisters (Miami, FL Community) 3; Sisters (Virginia Community) 3.

Sisters of St. Casimir, Motherhouse and Novitiate, 2601 W. Marquette Rd., 60629-1817. Tel: 773-776-1324; Fax: 773-776-8755. Web: www.ssc2601.com. Sr. M. Immacula Wendt, S.S.C., Gen. Supr. Sisters 77.

Sisters of the Good Shepherd, 1114 W. Grace St., 60613. Tel: 773-935-3434; Fax: 773-935-3523. Sr. Joan Spiering, R.G.S., Community Leader. Sisters 4.

Sisters of the Holy Cross, 7422 N. Harlem, 60631-4409. Tel: 773-774-5449.

Other Residences: *Sisters of the Holy Cross*, 9964 W. 153rd St., Orland Park, 60462. Tel: 708-403-5134.

Sisters of the Resurrection Provincial House and

Novitiate, 7432 Talcott Ave., 60631. Tel: 773-792-6363; Fax: 773-792-9590. Sr. Virginia Ann Wanzek, C.R., Prov. Supr.

Sisters of the Resurrection Congregation of the Sisters of the Resurrection, Chicago Province., Attended by Passionist Fathers. Sisters 42.

Society of Helpers (1956) Provincial Office, 4721 J S. Woodlawn, 60615. Tel: 773-548-5026; Fax: 773-548-5026. Email: memooresh@sbcglobal.net. Sr. Mary Ellen Moore, Prov. Professed Sisters 30.

Other residences:

Society of Helpers, 2043 N. Humboldt Blvd., 1st Fl., 60647. Tel: 773-342-8832. *Society of Helpers*, 2043 N. Humboldt Blvd., 2nd Fl., 60647. Tel: 773-384-7707. *Society of Helpers*, 4721 J S. Woodlawn, 60615. Tel: 773-548-5026; Fax: 773-548-5026. *Society of Helpers*, 4541 S. Wood, 60609. Tel: 773-807-8561; Fax: 773-376-8929. *Society of Helpers*, 2258 S. Marshall Blvd., 60623. Tel: 773-522-9160; Fax: 773-522-9161.

Wright Hall-Sisters of Charity B.V.M., 6364 Sheridan Rd., 60660-1726. Tel: 773-761-7550; Fax: 773-761-4341. Email: sisters@wrighthall.org. Sr. Mary Donahey, B.V.M., Treas. Professed Sisters B.V.M. 25.

ARLINGTON HEIGHTS. *Missionaries of the Sacred Heart of Jesus and Our Lady of Guadalupe M.S.C.Gpe.*, 1212 E. Euclid Ave., 60004. Tel: 847-255-5616.

Sisters of the Living Word, 800 N. Fernandez Ave. B, 60004-5336. Tel: 847-577-5972; Fax: 847-577-5980. Email: slw@slw.org. Web: www.slw.org. Sr. Mary Cornille, S.L.W., Leadership. Sisters 64.

BARTLETT. *Immaculata Congregational Home*, 801 W. Bartlett Rd., 60103-4401. Tel: 630-837-4061; Fax: 630-837-0052. Email: ssj801@sbcglobal.net. Sr. Patricia Schafke, S.S.J.-T.O.S.F., Coord. Congregational Home of the Sisters of St. Joseph, T.O.S.F. Sisters in Residence 19.

BLUE ISLAND. *Mother of Sorrows Convent*, 13811 S. Western Ave., 60406. Tel: 708-385-2103; Fax: 708-824-0688. Sr. Louise Staszewski, O.S.M., Regl. Supr.

Mantellate Sisters Servants of Mary, Motherhouse of the Servants of Mary. Sisters 11.

DES PLAINES. *Monastery of Discalced Carmelites*, 949 N. River Rd., 60016. Tel: 847-298-4241; Fax: 847-298-4242. Sr. Anne of Jesus, O.C.D., Prioress. Attended by priests of the Archdiocese.

Sisters of the Holy Family of Nazareth, Holy Family Province, 310 N. River Rd., 60016. Tel: 847-298-6760; Fax: 847-803-1941. Email: skiepura@nazarethcsfn.org. Web: www.nazarethcsfn.org. Sr. Sally Marie Kiepura, C.S.F.N., Prov. Supr. Professed Sisters 328.

EVERGREEN PARK. *American Province of Little Company of Mary Sisters* (Little Company of Mary Sisters), 9350 S. California, 60805. Tel: 708-422-0130; Fax: 708-422-2212. Email: kmcintyre@lcmh.org. Web: www.lcmglobal.org. Sr. Kathleen McIntyre, L.C.M., Prov. Leader. Charitable Trust: American Province of Little Company of Mary Sisters Charitable Trust. Total in Community 19.

HOFFMAN ESTATES. *Poor Handmaids of Jesus Christ, Annunciation Convent*, 1480 Ashley Rd., 60169-4818. Tel: 847-519-1384; Fax: 847-885-2757. Email: phjcashley@aol.com. Web: www.poorhandmaids.org.

JUSTICE. *Immaculate Conception Prov. House and Novitiate of the Dominican Sisters*, 9000 W. 81st St., 60458. Tel: 708-458-3040; Fax: 708-458-7230. Email: rosaryhill@sbcglobal.net. Web: www.sistersop.org. Sr. Natalie, O.P., Prov. Vicar. Sisters 39.

LA GRANGE PARK. *Adrian Dominican Sisters, Dominican Midwest Mission Chapter*, 1515 W. Ogden Ave., 60526-1721. Tel: 708-482-5047; Fax: 708-354-9573. Email: pdulka@adriandominicans.org. Web: www.adriandominicans.org. Sr. Patricia Ann Dulka, O.P., Chapter Prioress.

Sisters of St. Joseph of La Grange, 1515 W. Ogden Ave., 60526. Tel: 708-354-9200; Fax: 708-354-9573. Email: joursler@csjoseph.org. Web: csjoseph.org. Sr. Nancy Conway, C.S.J., Pres.

Nazareth Academy, Sisters of St. Joseph Charitable Trust. Sponsored ministries include secondary education, Christ in the Wilderness (retreat center), School and tutors on Wheels, an adult literacy program, The Well (spirituality center) and Taller de Jose (outreach program), St. Joseph Press, and Ministry of the Arts. Total in Community 78.

LAKE VILLA. *Handmaids of the Precious Blood*, 724 W. Petite Lake Rd., 60046-9619. Tel: 847-356-7729; Fax: 847-356-7729. Rev. Donald Dietz, O.M.I., Chap.; Sr. Angela Rose, H.P.B, Prioress. Sisters 5.

LEMONT. *Franciscan Sisters of Chicago, General Administration Building*, 11500 Theresa Dr., 60439-2727. Tel: 630-243-3600; Fax: 630-243-3576. Email: dcollins@chicagofranciscans.com. Web: www.chicagofranciscans.org. Sr. Diane Marie Collins, Gen. Min.

Franciscan Sisters of Chicago Sisters 45; Professed Sisters 45.

Mount Assisi Convent School, Sisters of St. Francis of Christ the King, 13900 Main St., 60439-9736. Tel: 630-257-7495; Fax: 630-257-2618. Email: lemont_prov@sbcglobal.net. Sr. Therese Ann Quigney, S.S.F.C.R., Prov. Supr. Sisters 42.

Our Lady of Victory Convent, 11400 Theresa Dr., 60439-2728. Tel: 630-243-3600; Fax: 630-243-3601. Email: dcollins@chicagofranciscans.com. Web: www.chicagofranciscans.org. Sr. Diane Marie Collins, Gen. Min. General Motherhouse and Novitiate of the Franciscan Sisters of Chicago.

MELROSE PARK. *Missionary Sisters of St. Charles Borromeo* Provincialate, Novitiate and Bishop Scalabrini Community., 1414 N. 37th Ave., 60160. Tel: 708-343-2162; Fax: 708-343-6452. Email: provincialmscs@sbcglobal.net. Web: www.scalabrinian.org. Sisters Marciana Zambiasi, M.S.C.S., Prov. Supr.; Marissonia Daltoe, M.S.C.S., First Councilor & Treas.; Elizabeth Pedemal, M.S.C.S., Councilor & Sec.; Noemie E. Digo, M.S.C.S., Councilor & Prov. Coord. on Formation; Elisete Teresenna Singor, M.S.C.S., Prov. Councilor & Prov. Coord. on Apostolate. Missionary Sisters of St. Charles Borromeo (Scalabrinians). Sisters 65.

NORRIDGE. *School Sisters of Notre Dame*, 4425 N. Ozanam Ave., 60206. Tel: 708-583-2402; Fax: 708-583-2409. Email: kcornell@amssnd.org. Web: www.ssnd.org. Professed Sisters 73.

OAK FOREST. *Missionary Sisters of St. Benedict of Illinois, Inc.*, 5900 W. 147th St., 60452. Tel: 708-535-9623; Fax: 708-535-3625. Email: missionarysis@sbcglobal.net. Sr. Assumpta Wrobel, Supr. In Res. Rev. Martin N. Winters (Retired).

OAK PARK. *Daughters of the Heart of Mary*, 140 N. Euclid Ave., #401, 60302-1684. Tel: 708-386-0190; Fax: 708-383-1327. Email: ephpheta@sbcglobal.net. Web: www.dhmna.org. Sr. Marilyn Smith, D.H.M., Supr.

Ephpheta Center Sisters 3.

PALOS PARK. *Poor Clare Monastery of the Immaculate Conception of Illinois*, 12210 S. Will Cook Rd., 60464-7332. Tel: 708-361-1810; Fax: 708-361-1816. Web: www.chicagopoorclares.org. Sr. M. Teresita, P.C.C., Abbess.

TECHNY. *Provincial House of the Missionary Sisters Servants of the Holy Spirit*, 319 Waukegan Rd., P.O. Box 6026, 60082-6026. Tel: 847-441-0126; Fax: 847-441-5587. Email: provinceleader@live.com. Sr. Carol Welp, S.Sp.S., Prov. Supr. Professed Sisters 81.

Arnold Janssen Foundation

Helena Stollenwerk Foundation

WAUKEGAN. *Franciscan Missionaries of Mary*, 726 S. Lincoln Ave., 60085. Tel: 847-662-8439. Email: waukfmm@aol.com. Web: www.fmmusa.org. Sr. Sheila Lehmkwhle, F.M.M., Coord. Sisters 4.

WILMETTE. *Maria Immaculata Convent-The Province Center* The Society of the Sisters of Christian Charity, Corporation of Mallinckrodt College of the North Shore, 2041 Elmwood Ave., 60091-1431. Tel: 847-920-9341; Fax: 847-920-9346. Email: srjanice@sccwilmette.org. Web: www.sccwilmette.org. Sr. Janice Boyer, S.C.C., Prov. Supr. Sisters 5.

Sacred Heart Convent, 2221 Elmwood Ave., 60091-1435. Tel: 847-251-3770; Fax: 847-251-8040. Sr. Carolyn Eultgen, S.C.C., Supr. A home for aged and infirm Sisters of Christian Charity. Motherhouse in Wilmette, Illinois. Sisters in Residence 35.

[P] PIOUS UNIONS AND OTHER SOCIETIES

CHICAGO. **Canons Regular of Saint John Cantius*, 825 N. Carpenter St., 60642-5499. Tel: 312-243-7373; Fax: 312-243-4545. Email: pastor@cantius.org. Web: www.canons-regular.org. Revs. C. Frank Phillips, C.R., Moderator; James Isaacson, S.J.C.; Dennis Kolinski, S.J.C.; Albert Tremari, S.J.C.; Brendan Gibson, S.J.C.; Scott Haynes, S.J.C.; Bartholomew Juncer, S.J.C.; Anthony Rice, S.J.C. A public diocesan association of the Christian Faithful. Priests 8; Brothers 2; Seminarians 5; Novices 7; Juniors 4.

LIBERTYVILLE. *Marytown, U.S. National Center of the Militia of the Immaculata Movement*, Shrine of St. Maximilian Kolbe, 1600 W. Park Ave., 60048-2593. Tel: 847-367-7800; Fax: 847-367-7831. Email: frstephen@marytown.com. Web: www.marytown.com. Rev. Patrick Greenough, O.F.M.Conv., Min. Prov. & National Dir. M.I. International Latin name: Militia Immaculatae (M.I.).; An association of clergy, religious and laity dedicated to Catholic evangelization, founded 1917 in Rome by St. Maximilian Kolbe.

[Q] VISITING AND NURSING OF THE SICK IN THEIR HOMES

CHICAGO. *Catholic Home Care*, 721 N. LaSalle St., 60610. Tel: 312-655-7415. Home health agency, Medicare certified, JCAHO accredited, providing health care to individuals in their homes in Cook and Lake Counties.

Catholic Home Care Home Services, 721 N. LaSalle St., 60610. Tel: 312-655-7415. Home health agency, private duty, JCAHO accredited

MORTON GROVE. **Resurrection Home Health Services*, 5747 W. Dempster St., Ste. B, 60053-3061. Tel: 877-742-7447 (toll free); Fax: 847-568-8537. Web: www.reshealth.org. Sandra Bruce, Pres.; Mrs. Marie Cleary-Fishman, Senior Vice Pres., Performance Distinction & Home Health Svcs. Sponsored by Sisters of the Holy Family of Nazareth & Sisters of the Resurrection., An Affiliate of Resurrection Health Care. Patients Assisted Annually 72,795.

[R] SOCIETIES, CLUBS AND RESIDENCES

CHICAGO. *Kolping Center*, 5826 N. Elston, 60646. Tel: 773-792-2190; Fax: 773-792-0062. Email: chicagokolping@aol.com. Web: www.kolping.org. Rev. Paul Cao, Praeses. The Catholic Kolping Society of Chicago.

VERNON HILLS. *Equestrian Order of the Holy Sepulchre of Jerusalem* North Central Lieutenancy, 202 Annapolis Dr., 60061. Tel: 815-244-9397. Email: jwrapp@grics.net. Web: www.holysepulchre.net. H.E. John W. Rapp, KGCHS; Sir Thomas Mulligan, KGCHS, Treas.; Sir Charles H. Foos, KGCHS, Sec.

[S] RETREAT HOUSES

CHICAGO. *Ascension Guest House*, 3111 S. Aberdeen St., 60608. Tel: 773-927-7424; 888-539-4261 (toll free); Fax: 773-927-5734. Email: porter@chicagomonk.org. Web: www.chicagomonk.org.

Cenacle Retreat and Conference Center, 513 Fullerton Pkwy., 60614. Tel: 773-528-6300; Fax: 773-528-0361. Email: crcc@cenaclechicago.org; ministryoffice@cenaclechicago.org (ministry office); prayercardoffice@cenaclechicago.org (prayer enrollment office). Web: www.cenaclechicago.org. Mr. Robert J. Raccuglia, Dir.

Focolare Movement-Mariapolis Center, 5001 S. Greenwood Ave., 60615. Tel: 773-285-2746; Fax: 773-536-5054. Email: midwest@focolare.us. Web: www.focolare.us. Daytime Capacity 60; Overnight Capacity 30.

BARRINGTON. *Jesuit Retreat League of Chicago aka Bellamine Jesuit Retreat House* 420 W. County Line Rd., 60010. Tel: 847-381-1261; Fax: 847-381-4695. Email: bellarmine@bellarminehall.org. Web: www.bellarminehall.org. Jesuit Retreat House serving laity (High School, College & Adults), priests and religious. Overnight Capacity 72.

The Jesuit Retreat League of Chicago Tel: 847-381-1261; Fax: 847-381-4695. Revs. Mark W. Andrews, S.J., Supr. & Acting Dir.; Robert S. Flack, S.J.; James P. Gschwend, S.J.

DES PLAINES. *Cabrini Retreat Center* (Formerly St. Frances Cabrini Retreat House), 9430 Golf Rd., 60016. Tel: 847-297-6530; Fax: 847-297-6544. Email: info@cabrinicenter.org. Web: www.cabrinicenter.org. Nancy A. Golen, Dir.; Sr. Grace Waters, M.S.C., Mission Integration Dir.; Christy Salazar, Assoc. Dir. Retreats for youth, laity, religious and immigrants. Sponsored by the Missionary Sisters of the Sacred Heart of Jesus. Sisters 2.

LEMONT. *St. Mary's Retreat House*, 14230 Main St., P.O. Box 608, 60439. Tel: 630-257-5102; Fax: 630-257-2359. Rev. Blase Chemazar, O.F.M., Dir.

MUNDELEIN. *Cardinal Stritch Retreat House*, 1300 Stritch Dr., P.O. Box 455, 60060-0455. Tel: 847-566-6060; Fax: 847-566-6082. Email: stritch@archchicago.org. Web: www.stritchretreat.org. Deacon Richard F. Hudzik, Dir.; Ms. Eva Schopper, Office Mgr. Serves the clergy, Catholic laity and ministers of Chicago and Region VII. Retreatants during year 1,800.

TECHNY. *Techny Towers Retreat and Conference Center*, 2001 Waukegan Rd., P.O. Box 176, 60082-0176. Tel: 847-272-1100; Fax: 847-272-9363. Email: info@technytowers.org. Web: www.technytowers.org. Catherine M. Collins, Exec. Dir.; Erin Brown, Conference Mgr. A full-service conference facility used by parish groups, religious communities, nonprofit organizations and schools. Accommodations for 250 (daytime) and 125 (overnight). Chapel seats 750.

[T] NATIONAL INSTITUTIONS

CHICAGO. *Catholic Church Extension Society aka Catholic Extension* 150 S. Wacker Dr., 20th Fl., 60606-4200. Tel: 800-842-7804; Fax: 312-236-5276. Email: info@catholicextension.org. Web:

www.catholicextension.org. His Eminence Francis Cardinal George, O.M.I., Ph.D., S.T.D., Chancellor; Most Rev. William R. Houck, D.D., Pres. Emeritus (Retired); Rev. John J. Wall, Pres.; Ms. Julie Turley, Vice Pres. Devel.; Mr. Tom Gordon, COO; Mr. Kevin P. McGowan, CFO.

The Catholic Church Extension Society of the United States of America

**Catholic Guild for the Blind*, 180 N. Michigan Ave., Ste. 1700, 60601-7463. Tel: 312-236-8569; Fax: 312-236-8128. Email: guild@guildfortheblind.org. Web: www.guildfortheblind.org. Mr. David J. Tabak, Exec. Dir. Provides devotional services including large print Mass, library, scholarships for Catholic Students; the liturgy of the Hours in large print or audio cassette; the sacramental rites in large print; and large print Bibles.

Catholic Kolping Society of America-National Endowment Fund, 5826 N. Elston Ave., 60646-5544. Tel: 877-659-7237; Fax: 973-478-8049. Email: patfarkas@optonline.net. Web: www.Kopling.org. Lisa Brinkmann, Treas.

Catholic League for Religious Assistance to Poland, 1400 S. Austin Blvd., Cicero, 60804. Tel: 708-329-4040; Fax: 708-222-8854. Most Rev. Thomas J. Paprocki, D.D., J.C.D., S.T.D., Exec. Dir.; Rev. Thaddeus Dzieszko, Asst. Dir.

Catholic League for Religious Assistance to Poland

Center for the Study of Religious Life, 5401 S. Cornell Ave., 60615-5698. Tel: 773-752-2720; Fax: 773-752-2723. Email: csrl@religious-life.org. Web: www.religious-life.org. Sr. Mary Charlotte Chandler, R.S.C.J., Dir. Sponsored by the Conference of Major Superiors of Men, the Leadership Conference of Women Religious and Catholic Theological Union at Chicago to conduct interdisciplinary and intercultural reflection on U.S. religious life and serve as a resource to religious leadership.

**Friends of the Orphans*, 134 N. LaSalle St., Ste. 500, 60602. Tel: 312-386-7499; Fax: 312-658-0040. Email: info@friendsoftheorphans.org. Web: www.friendsoftheorphans.org. Jessica Carrier, Exec. Asst. Dedicated to improving the lives of orphaned, abandoned and disadvantaged children through the support of the Nuestros Pequenos Hermanos (NPH) network of orphanages in Latin America and the Caribbean.

Jan Beyzym Society, Inc., 4105 N. Avers Ave., 60618. Tel: 773-588-7476; Fax: 773-588-6517. Email: polmes@jezuicichicago.org. Web: www.jezuicichicago.org. Polish Jesuits Foreign Missions.

Lumen Christi Institute, 5735 S. University Ave., 60637-1507. Tel: 773-955-5887; Fax: 773-955-5233. Email: info@lumenchristi.org. Web: www.lumenchristi.org. Organized by Catholic scholars at the University of Chicago in 1997, The Lumen Christi Institute promotes Catholic thought and culture among students and faculty at the University of Chicago through lectures, courses, conferences and other programs. It also sponsors a national Catholic Scholars Program that works with faculty from across the nation in fields such as law, theology, philosophy and science and religion to renew Catholic thought and mentor the next generation of college teachers.

**The National Center for the Laity*, P.O. Box 291102, 60629. Tel: 773-776-9036; Fax: 773-776-9036. Email: wdroel@cs.com. Web: www.catholiclabor.org/ncl.htm. Mr. Vaile Scott, Pres. Founded in 1977, the NCL is dedicated to advancing a key insight of Vatican II: that the church is the people of God in service to the modern world. NCL publishes a newsletter, INITIATIVES, hosts conferences and retreats and maintains a speakers' bureau.

National Organization for Continuing Education of Roman Catholic Clergy, Inc., 333 N. Michigan Ave., Ste. 1205, 60601. Tel: 312-781-9450; Fax: 312-442-9709. Email: nocercc@nocercc.org. Web: www.nocercc.org. Rev. Richard L. Chiola, Ph.D. (SFD), Pres.; Mr. James H. Alphen, M.B.A., Exec. Dir. Founded in 1973, a membership association of dioceses, religious communities, and other interested organizations and individuals committed to the Church's mission to promote and support ongoing formation for priests and presbyterates. Professional and formational services include an annual convention; an annual orientation workshop; regional meetings; programs that dioceses and religious communities can host for clergy and other pastoral ministers; a quarterly newsletter; and other practical resources in diverse media.

National Religious Vocation Conference, 5401 S. Cornell, Ste. 207, 60615. Tel: 773-363-5454; Fax: 773-363-5530. Email: NRVC@nrvc.net. Web: www.nrvc.net. Bro. Paul Bednarczyk, C.S.C., Exec. Dir. A professional organization of women and men committed to vocation awareness, invitation and discernment to consecrated life as brothers, sisters and priests. In an inclusive and collaborative style we present religious life as a viable option for today's church.

Radio Maryja, 6965 W. Belmont Ave., 60634. Tel: 773-385-8472; Fax: 773-385-5631. Email: admin@radiomaryjachicago.org. Web: www.radiomaryja.pl; www.radiomaryjachicago.org. 6965 W. Belmont Ave., 60634. Redemptorist religious radio.

ARLINGTON HEIGHTS. *Foundation For Children In Need*, 800 N. Pine Ave., 60004. Tel: 847-670-1145. Email: tomchitta@hotmail.com. Web: www.fcn-usa.org. Tom Chitta, Co-founder. FCN is a Catholic lay organization established to reach out to the neediest in the rural villages of India. The main focus is to provide sponsorship help for education and health care for the poor.

EVANSTON. **Solidarity Bridge, Inc.*, 1577 Florence Ave., 60201. Tel: 847-328-7748; Fax: 547-328-6860. Email: solidbridge@aol.com. Web: www.solidaritybridge.org. Juan L. Hinojosa, Exec. Dir. Provides short term international mission opportunities utilizing secular callings as vehicles of service to the poor in partnership with local counterparts in Bolivia.

GLENVIEW. **Coalition in Support of Ecclesia Dei, Ltd.*, P.O. Box 2071, 60025-6071. Tel: 847-724-7151; Fax: 847-724-7158. Email: ecclesiadei@sbcglobal.net. Web: www.ecclesiadei.org. Mary M. Kraychy, Pres. & Exec. Dir. The Coalition assists priests, seminarians and laity in the implementation of Pope Benedict XVI's Summorum Pontificum, providing Latin-English Booklet Missals and other inspirational/educational materials (electronic media DVD's/videos) and printed material, eg. Atlar Cards).

GURNEE. **Caritas For Children, Inc.*, 5250 Grand Ave., PMB 105, 60031-1877. Tel: 888-227-4827; Fax: 414-771-3528. Email: cthoar@caritasforchildren.org. Web: www.caritasforchildren.org. Christopher T. Hoar, Contact Person. A private juridic person in the Archdiocese of Chicago, Caritas for Children promotes and supports inter-country adoptions from Poland through Catholic Charities of Chicago and provides financial assistance for the health, education and general welfare of orphaned and other disadvantaged children located worldwide under a variety of Child-Sponsorship programs in partnership with the services of Catholic Religious communities.

LA GRANGE PARK. *Dominican Leadership Conference*, 1515 W. Ogden Ave., 60526-1721. Tel: 708-482-5033. Email: sisters@domlife.org. Web: www.domlife.org/dlc. Sr. Mary Sue Kennedy, O.P., Exec. Dir.

Dominican Leadership Conference of Dominican Men and Women Religious in the United States of America

LIBERTYVILLE. **Institute on Religious Life*, P.O. Box 7500, 60048-7500. Tel: 847-573-8975; Fax: 847-573-8960. Email: IRLstaff@religiouslife.com. Web: www.religiouslife.com. Rev. Thomas Nelson, O.Praem., Nat'l. Dir.; Michael D. Wick, Exec. Dir.; M. Kathleen O'Brien, Dir. Operations. IRL promotes and supports the growth, development, and renewal of the consecrated life-particularly vowed religious life-as a gift to the Church and an evangelical witness to the world.

RIVER FOREST. **American Friends of the Ecole Biblique*, 1530 Jackson Ave., 60305. Tel: 708-366-7090. Email: ecolebibli@aol.com. Web: www.op.org/op/ebaf/index-eng.htm. Rev. Peter J. Hereley, O.P., Dir.; Judy Valentine Gerth, Mng. Dir. Tel: 847-475-4114. Organized to raise funds in the U.S. to support the work of the Ecole Biblique et Archeologique Francaise de Jerusalem and promote the dissemination of biblical scholarship and archeological research through newsletters, receptions, and seminars with biblical scholars.

TECHNY. *Divine Word Missionaries, Inc.*, 1835 Waukegan Rd., Box 6099, 60082-6099. Tel: 847-272-7600; Fax: 847-272-8572. Email: info@svdmissions.org. Web: www.svdmissions.org. Bro. Dennis Newton, S.V.D., Pres.; Rev. Richard Vaz, S.V.D., Supr. Delegate; Mr. David Gallagher, Treas.

S.V.D., Catholic Universities, Inc.

[U] MINISTRY IN HIGHER EDUCATION

CHICAGO. *Campus Ministries*, 835 N. Rush St., 60611. Tel: 312-534-8271.

Non-Catholic Institutions:

Northwestern University, Sheil Center 2110 N. Sheridan Rd., Evanston, 60201. Tel: 847-328-4648; Fax: 847-328-4660. Rev. John F. Kartje, Dir. & Chap.

University of Chicago Calvert House 5735 S. University Ave., 60637. Tel: 773-288-2311; Fax: 773-288-1124. Web: www.calvert.uchicago.edu. Rev. Msgr. Patrick R. Lagges, J.C.D., Chap. & Dir.

University of Illinois at Chicago - John Paul II Newman Center 700 S. Morgan St., 60607-3429. Tel: 312-226-1880; Fax: 312-226-2361. Web: www.jp2newman.com. Revs. Patrick M. Marshall, Chap. & Exec. Dir.; Steven Bauer, Assoc. Chap.

[V] PERSONAL PRELATURE

CHICAGO. *Midtown Residence* Prelature of the Holy Cross and Opus Dei, 1825 N. Wood St., 60622. Tel: 773-292-5450; 773-292-0660; Fax: 773-292-0996. Web: www.opusdei.org. Revs. Charles M. Ferrer; Joseph P. Landauer; Hilary F. Mahaney; C. John McCloskey; Barry Cole.

Northview University Center Prelature of the Holy Cross and Opus Dei, 7225 N. Greenview Ave., 60626. Tel: 773-465-3468; Fax: 773-465-1195. Web: www.opusdei.org. Rev. John Waiss.

Prelature of the Holy Cross and Opus Dei, 5800 N. Keating Ave., 60646. Tel: 773-283-5800; Fax: 773-202-8179. Web: www.opusdei.org. Very Rev. Peter V. Armenio, B.S., Ph.D., Vicar for the Midwest; Revs. Frank J. Hoffman; F. Javier del Castillo; Edward G. Maristany. Office of the Vicar for the Midwest.

OAK PARK. *Oak Park Study Center* Prelature of the Holy Cross and Opus Dei, 831 S. Euclid Ave., 60304. Tel: 708-383-0928; Fax: 708-386-2612. Web: www.oakparkstudy.org. Revs. Mark Mannion; James Socias.

[W] MISCELLANEOUS LISTINGS

CHICAGO. **Aid for Women, Inc.*, 8 S. Michigan Ave., Ste. 1100, 60603-3311. Tel: 312-621-1101; Fax: 312-621-1972. Email: info@aidforwomen.org. Web: www.aidforwomen.org. Susan Barrett, Exec. Dir. Dedicated to upholding the principles of Humanae Vitae and Evangelium Vitae, the organization maintains a crisis center where any pregnant woman will find help and encouragement to choose life for her unborn child through pregnancy testing, confidential counseling and referral to community resources. Long-term support is also available through a residential program, Heather's house.

Alexian Brothers Bonaventure House, 825 W. Wellington Ave., 60657. Tel: 773-327-9921; Fax: 773-327-9113. Email: information@abam.org. Web: www.abam.org. Michelle Wetzel, CEO. Congregation of Alexian Brothers, Immaculate Conception Province., Housing and supportive services for otherwise homeless persons with HIV/AIDS.

Alexian Brothers Bettendorf Place, LLC

The Aquin Guild, c/o Office for Catechesis & Youth Ministry, Cardinal Meyer Center, 3525 S. Lake Park Ave., 60653-1402. Tel: 312-534-3700; Fax: 312-534-3801. Rev. John W. Clemens, Dir. Provides spiritual direction to Catholics engaged in public and parochial education.

Aquinas Literacy Center (ESL), 3540 S. Hermitage, 60609. Tel: 773-927-0512; Fax: 773-927-8980. Email: aquinaslit@aol.com. Web: www.aquinasliteracycenter.org. Alison Altmeyer, Exec. Dir.

St. Bernard Housing Development Corp., 326 W. 64th St., 60621. Tel: 773-962-4165. Web: www.stbh.org. Charles Holland, Exec. Dir. A subsidy of St. Bernard Hospital, Chicago.

**Bethany Trust Fund*, Brown Brothers Harriman Trust Company, N.A., 150 S. Wacker Dr., Ste. 3250, 60606. Tel: 312-781-7140.

**Big Shoulders Fund*, 309 W. Washington St., Ste. 550, 60606. Tel: 312-751-8337; Fax: 773-751-5235. Web: www.bigshouldersfund.org. Joshua Hale, Exec. Dir. Provides support to the Catholic Schools in the neediest areas of inner-city Chicago.

The Bolivian Trust of the Dominicans, 1909 S. Ashland Ave., 60608-2994. Tel: 312-666-3244; Fax: 312-829-8471. Rev. Louis Morrone, O.P.

St. Bonaventure Oratory, Res.: 1641 W. Diversey Pkwy., 60614. Tel: 773-281-6588; Fax: 773-388-8676. Email: stbonaventure@archchicago.org. Rev. Thomas I. Healy (Retired).

**Brother David Darst Center for Justice and Peace, Spirituality and Education*, 2834 S. Normal Ave., 60616. Tel: 312-225-3099; Fax: 312-842-4178. Email: director@brdaviddarstcenter.org. Web: www.brdaviddarstcenter.org. Melinda Rueden, Exec. Dir.

Catholic Conference of Illinois, 65 E. Wacker Pl., Ste. 1620, 60601. Tel: 312-368-1066; Fax: 312-368-1090. Web: www.catholicconferenceofillinois.org. Mr. Robert Gilligan, Exec. Dir.

The Catholic Education Institute, c/o Hinshaw and Culbertson, 222 N. LaSalle St., 60601. Tel: 718-823-8565; Fax: 718-823-8072. Email: johnpiderit@me.com. Web: www.catholicexcellence.org. Rev. John J. Piderit, S.J., Pres.

Catholic Health Partners Services, 2875 W. 19th St.,

60623. Tel: 773-484-4300; Fax: 773-521-7902. Web: www.saintanthonyhospital.org. Sponsored by Ascension Health and the Missionary Sisters of the Sacred Heart of Jesus to operate St. Anthony Hospital.

St. Anthony Health Affiliates, 2875 W. 19th St., 60623. Tel: 773-484-4300; Fax: 773-521-7902.

Catholic Office of the Deaf, 3525 S. Lake Park Ave., 60653-1402. Tel: 312-534-7899 (Voice); 312-751-8368 (TDD); Fax: 312-534-0394. Email: cathdeafch@archchicago.org. Web: www.deafchurchchicago.parishesonline.com. Rev. Joseph A. Mulcrone, Dir.

**Central American Martyrs Center (Su Casa Catholic Worker Community)*, 5045 S. Laflin, 60609. Tel: 773-376-9263; Fax: 773-376-9241. Email: sucasacw@gmail.com. Web: www.sucasacw.org. Bro. Denis Murphy, F.S.C.

Charis Ministries, 1400 Devon Ave., Box 415, 60660. Tel: 773-508-3237; Fax: 773-508-2844. Email: charis@charisministries.org. Web: www.charisministries.org. Provides opportunities for spiritual growth utilizing the gifts of Ignatian Spirituality for adults in their 20s and 30s.

Charitable Trust of the Order of Friar Servants of Mary, United States of America Province, Inc., 3121 W. Jackson Blvd., 60612-2729. Tel: 773-533-0360; Fax: 773-533-8307. Email: michaelcallary@servitesusa.org. Web: www.servite.org.

Chicago Airports Catholic Chaplaincy, P.O. Box 66353, 60666-0353. Tel: 773-686-2636; Fax: 773-686-0130. Email: ordchapel@aol.com. Web: www.airportchapels.org. Rev. Michael G. Zaniolo, S.T.L., C.A.C., Chap.

Claret Center, 5536 S. Everett, 60637. Tel: 773-643-6259; Fax: 773-643-6929. Email: claret_center@claret.org. Web: www.claret.org. Pauline LaMothe, O.P., Admin. Resources for Counseling and Spiritual Direction.

Claretian Associates, Inc., 9108 S. Brandon Ave., 60617. Tel: 773-734-9181; Fax: 773-734-9221. Email: angelah@claretianassociates.org. Web: www.claretianassociates.org. Angela Hurlock, Exec. Dir. Organization to provide affordable housing and encourage neighborhood improvement in South Chicago.

Claretian Volunteers and Lay Missionaries, 205 W. Monroe St., 60606. Tel: 312-544-8176, Ext. 479; Fax: 312-236-7756. Email: volunteers@claretians.org. Web: www.claretianvolunteers.org. Deana Brewer, Dir.

Court of Appeals-Province of Chicago, 20 N. Wacker Dr., Ste. 3420, 60606. Tel: 312-553-4080; Fax: 312-553-4085. Email: coaprovchicago@yahoo.com. Rev. John P. Lucas, Judicial Vicar. The Court of Second Instance in matrimonial cases for the Tribunals of the Province of Chicago.

**Cristo Rey Network*, 14 E. Jackson Blvd., Ste. 1200, 60604. Tel: 312-784-7200; Fax: 312-784-7201. Email: rbirdsell@cristoreynetwork.org. Web: www.cristoreynetwork.org. Rev. John P. Foley, S.J., Exec. Chm.; Rob Birdsell, Pres.; Elizabeth Goettl, Chief Academic Officer. The Cristo Rey Network supports and helps establish Catholic high schools where students work to earn tuition and gain business experience. Each school is modeled after Cristo Rey Jesuit High School of Chicago.

Daughters of Charity Ministries of Chicago, Inc., 30 N. LaSalle St., Ste. 4100, 60602. Tel: 312-422-9140; Fax: 312-621-0297. Email: dancoyne@okeefe-law.com. Daniel W. Coyne, Registered Agent.

**DeSales Charitable Trust*, Brown Brothers Harriman Trust Company, N.A., 150 S. Wacker Dr., Ste. 3250, 60606. Tel: 312-781-7140.

**Dominican Volunteers USA*, 1914 S. Ashland Ave., 60608. Tel: 708-524-5985; Fax: 708-524-5985. Email: info@dvusa.org. Web: www.dvusa.org. Michael Chapuran, M.P.A., Exec. Dir. Dominican Volunteers USA provides full-time volunteer opportunities for lay people. Volunteers live and work with Dominican (Order of Preachers) ministries and communities across the United States, serving those who are in most need.

**Felician Services, Inc.*, 3800 W. Peterson Ave., 60659-3116. Tel: 773-463-3806; Fax: 773-463-2059. Sr. Mary Clarette Stryzewski, C.S.S.F., Pres. & CEO.

Focolare Movement, P.O. Box 53426, 60653. Tel: 773-536-7873; Fax: 773-536-5054. Email: midwest@focolare.us. Web: www.focolare.us. Work of Mary founded in Trent, Italy in 1943. International headquarters are in Rome, Italy; national formation center in New York.

Women, 5017 S. Greenwood Ave., 60615. Tel: 773-536-7873; Fax: 773-536-5054. Ms. Paloma Cabetas, Co-Dir.

Men, 7018 W. 34th St., Berwyn, 60402. Tel: 708-484-9771; Fax: 708-484-4998. Mr. Marco Desalvo, Co-Dir.

Franciscan Friars Retirement Corporation, 6107 Kenmore Ave., 60660-2797. Tel: 773-274-7681; Fax: 773-274-9751.

Franciscan Outreach Association, 1645 W. LeMoyne St., 60622. Tel: 773-278-6724; Fax: 773-278-7120. Web: www.franoutreach.org. Diana Faust, SFO, Exec. Dir. Owns & operates: Marquard Center (dining room for the homeless), Franciscan House of Mary & Joseph (shelter) and a Case Management Program for the homeless in Chicago. Total Staff 28; Bed Capacity 252; Total Assisted Annually 4,000.

General Assistance, Inc. aka Daughters of Charity International Project Services 30 N. LaSalle St., Ste. 4100, 60602. Tel: 312-422-9140; Fax: 312-621-0297. Email: dancoyne@okeefe-law.com. Daniel W. Coyne, Contact Person. Support organization for the Daughters of Charity.

**Hermitage Charitable Trust*, Brown Brothers Harriman Trust Company, N.A., 150 S. Wacker Dr., Ste. 3250, 60606. Tel: 312-781-7140.

Holy Family Church, Inc., 2050 N. Clark St., 60614. Tel: 773-975-6363; Fax: 773-975-0230. Email: treasurer@jesuits-chgdet.org.

Homebound Ministries, Inc., 3800 W. Peterson Ave., 60659. Tel: 773-463-3806. Sr. Nancy Marie Jamroz, Pres.

Ignatian Spirituality Project, 1641 S. Allport, 60608. Tel: 312-226-9184. Email: info@ispretreats.org. Web: www.ispretreats.org. The project works with the homeless through retreats and spiritual companionship in the belief that by claiming their spiritual life they can recover from addiction and other problems associated with homelessness

Ignatius Productions, Inc., 2050 N. Clark St., 60614. Tel: 773-975-6363; Fax: 773-975-0230. Web: www.fathermitchpacwa.org.

Illinois Catholic Health Association, 65 E. Wacker Pl., Ste. 1620, 60601. Tel: 312-368-0011; Fax: 312-368-1701. Email: pcacchione@il-cha.org. Web: www.il-cha.org. Patrick J. Cacchione, Exec. Dir.

The Illinois Patrons of the Arts in the Vatican Museums, c/o Archdioce of Chicago Office of Vicar General, 835 N. Rush, 60611. Tel: 312-624-8667; Fax: 312-624-8427. Email: AD612@aol.com. His Eminence Francis Cardinal George, O.M.I., Ph.D., S.T.D., Chm.; Anne Shea, Pres.

Institute for Spiritual Leadership, 5401 S. Cornell, 60615. Tel: 773-752-5962; Fax: 773-752-5964. Email: islusa@aol.com. Web: www.spiritleader.org. Lucy Abbott Tucker, Board Pres. Education Center for Spiritual Direction and Renewal.

Intercommunity Housing Corporation, c/o Edward T. Joyce & Associates, 135 S. LaSalle St., Ste. 2200, 60603. Tel: 312-641-2600. Email: ejoyce@joycelaw.com. David E. Myles, Pres.; Edward T. Joyce, Sec. The Intercommunity Housing Corporation promotes the development and establishment of affordable residential retirement housing for religious, clergy and laity; a design for 21st century living.

Italian Catholic Federation, 2825 W. 81st St., 60652. Tel: 773-436-4444; Fax: 773-778-9087. Email: info@icf.org. Web: www.icf.org. Rev. Charles V. Fanelli, Chap.

Jesuit International Missions, Inc., 2050 N. Clark St., 60614. Tel: 773-975-6870; Fax: 773-975-0230. Email: treasurer@jesuits-chgdet.org. Rev. Walter C. Deye, S.J., Asst. for Intl. Ministry.

Jesuit Seminary Association, 2050 N. Clark St., 60614. Tel: 773-975-6363; Fax: 773-975-0230. Web: www.jesuits-chgdet.org.

Kolbe House, 2434 S. California Ave., 60608. Tel: 773-247-0070; Fax: 773-247-0665. Email: khjailmin@aol.com. Revs. David A. Kelly, C.PP.S.; Arturo Perez-Rodriguez, Dir.; Deacon Pablo Perez, Jail Chap.; David Perez, Ex-Offender Intern Co-ord. Catholic jail ministry.

Loyola Press, 3441 N. Ashland Ave., 60657. Tel: 773-281-1818; Fax: 773-281-0555. Email: locke@loyolapress.com. Web: www.loyolapress.com. Teresa Locke, Pres.

Marist Volunteer Program, 4200 W. 115th St., 60655-4306. Tel: 773-881-5343; Fax: 773-881-3667. Email: maristvolunteerprogram@yahoo.com. Bro. Hugh Turley, F.M.S., Contact Person.

Martin de Porres House, 3322 Washington Blvd., 60624. Tel: 773-826-9336. Margaret Brooks, Pres.; Cathryn Peters, Vice Pres.; Claire Cummings, Sec.

Medical Missionaries of Mary, Inc., Mission Development Office, 4425 W. 63rd St., Ste. 100, 60629-5530. Tel: 773-735-3712; Fax: 773-735-4661. Email: development@mmmusa.org. Web: www.mmmusa.org. Sr. Mary Ann MacRae, M.M.M., Devel. Dir.

Mercy Circle, 10024 S. Central Park Ave., 60655. Tel: 773-779-6011. Web: www.mercycircle.org. Sr. Sheila Megley, R.S.M., Treas.

Miles Jesu, P.O. Box 267989, 60626. Tel: 773-262-0861; Fax: 773-267-1093. Email: administration@milesjesu.com. Web: www.milesjesu.com.

Women's Formation Center, 1126 W. Morse Ave., 60626. Tel: 773-262-1253; Fax: 773-262-1093. Maire Duggan, M.J., Vocation Dir.

Mother Cabrini League, 434 W. Deming Pl., 60614. Tel: 773-388-7329; Fax: 773-525-0513. Sr. Joaquina Costa, M.S.C., Dir.; Joyce Bandera, Office Supvr. The purpose of the League is to spread devotion to St. Frances Xavier Cabrini.

**Mughamba Scholarship Foundation*, 120 LaSalle St., Ste. 3800, 60602. Rev. Kombo L. Peshu, Pres.

Mundelein College, Office of the General Counsel of Loyola University-Chicago, 820 N. Michigan Ave., 60611. Tel: 312-915-6195. Email: emunro@luc.edu. Web: www.luc.edu. 6525 N. Sheridan Rd., 60626. Tel: 773-508-3029; Fax: 312-915-6208. Mr. Wayne Magdziarz, Pres. & Chm. Bd. Trustees; Ms. Ellen Kane Munro, Sec.; Philip R. Kosiba, Vice Pres. & Treas.

New World Publications, 3525 S. Lake Park Ave., 60653. Tel: 312-534-7777; Fax: 312-534-7350. Email: mail@catholicnewworld.com. Web: www.catholicnewworld.com. Ms. Colleen H. Dolan, Dir. Communications & Public Rels. & Assoc. Publisher; Dawn Vidmar, Gen. Mgr.; Joyce Duriga, Editor; Ann DeFrisco, Office Mgr. Publishers of Catholic New World; Chicago Catolico; Katolik; and the Archdiocesan Directory.

Oblates for International Pastoral aka Oblate International Pastoral Investment Trust 161 N. Clark St., Ste. 4700, 60601. Email: whitley@omigen.org. Revs. Warren A. Brown, O.M.I., Trustee; Rufus J. Whitley, O.M.I., Trustee & Admin.; Gregory Robert Gallagher, O.M.I., Trustee; Joseph Hitpas, O.M.I., Trustee; Anne VanDyke, COO.

Office for Mission Advancement Dominicans: Province of St. Albert the Great., 1909 S. Ashland Ave., 60608. Tel: 312-226-0020; Fax: 312-226-6440. Email: office@domcentral.org. Web: www.op.org.

Order of Friar Servants of Mary United States of America Province, Inc., 3121 W. Jackson Blvd., 60612-2729. Tel: 773-533-0360; Fax: 773-533-8307. Email: bromikeosm@hotmail.com; michaelcallary@servitesusa.org. Web: www.servite.org. The Order of Friar Servants of Mary-U.S.A. Province, Inc., Chicago, IL.

Pathways to Hope, Inc., 205 W. Monroe St., 60606. Tel: 312-223-1085; 866-784-5900; Fax: 312-223-0947. Web: www.pathwaystohope.com. Jennifer Reed, L.C.P.C., Exec. Dir. Pathways to Hope, established by 15 male Roman Catholic religious communities in the Midwest, provides a compassionate and appropriate pastoral response to victims of sexual misconduct by their members.

The Peace Corner, Incorporated, P.O. Box 440113, 60644. Tel: 773-261-5330; Fax: 773-261-1523. Email: thepeacecorner@yahoo.com. Web: www.thepeacecorner.org. Revs. Maurizio Binaghi, M.C.C.J., Pres. & Exec. Dir.; Rufino Ezama, M.C.C.J., Vice Pres. & Sec.; Brian Quigley, M.C.C.J., Treas. A ministry of the Comboni Missionaries of the Heart of Jesus, Inc., The Peace Corner is a youth center in the Austin neighborhood of Chicago (5022 W. Madison Ave.) serving youth in need with no distinction of faith, race and background. The Peace Corner offers a safe and caring environment for youth while providing tutoring, computer classes, GED preparation, legal counseling, job training, support groups and recreational activities.

Precious Blood Ministry of Reconciliation, P.O. Box 09379, 60609-0379. Tel: 773-579-0781; Fax: 773-579-0782. Email: nojail@aol.com. Revs. David A. Kelly, C.PP.S., Exec. Dir.; Dennis Kinderman, C.PP.S.; William Nordenbrock, C.PP.S.; Sr. Mary Louise Degenhart, A.S.C. A ministry of the Cincinnati and Kansas City provinces of the Missionaries of the Precious Blood that responds to violence and conflict in the Back of the Yards neighborhood of Chicago (5114 S. Elizabeth St.) and fosters renewal of the church through reconciliation programs, retreats and training workshops for church communities.

Resurrection Health Care, 7435 W. Talcott Ave., 60631. Tel: 773-774-8000; Fax: 773-792-9926. Web: www.reshealth.org. Sandra Bruce, Pres. & CEO; Sr. Clara Frances Kusek, C.R., Exec. Vice Pres., Mission; Deacon Robert Bulger, Mission Senior Vice Pres.; Sr. Paracleta Amrich, S.S.C.M., Dir. Clinical Pastoral Educ. The Sisters of the Holy Family of Nazareth and the Sisters of the Resurrection co-sponsor Holy Family Medical Center, Our Lady of the Resurrection Medical Center, Resurrection Medical Center, Saint Francis Hospital (Evanston), Saint Joseph Hospital and Saints Mary and Elizabeth Medical Center, in addition to other legal corporations listed below.

Other members of Resurrection Health Care:

**Proviso Family Services, Inc. dba Resurrection Behavioral Health, d.b.a. ProCare Centers* Tel:

708-681-2324; Fax: 708-681-1289.

Resurrection Development Foundation Tel: 847-813-3477; Fax: 847-813-3482.

**Partners Home Care Foundation dba Resurrection Home Health Foundation* Tel: 847-568-8536; Fax: 847-568-8537.

**Resurrection Home Health Foundation*, 7000 N. Newark, Ste. 144, Niles, 60714. Tel: 847-647-2383; Fax: 847-647-2762.

**Resurrection Home Health Services* Tel: 847-568-8536; Fax: 847-568-8537.

Resurrection Senior Services Tel: 847-813-3176; Fax: 847-813-3876.

Resurrection Services Tel: 773-774-8000; Fax: 773-792-9926.

Retirement Plan of the Order of Friar Servants of Mary-U.S.A. Province, Inc., 3121 W. Jackson Blvd., 60612-2729. Tel: 773-533-0360; Fax: 773-533-8307. Email: michaelcallary@servitesusa.org. Web: www.servite.org.

S.F.V., Inc., 1645 W. LeMoyne St., 60622. Tel: 773-278-6724; Fax: 773-278-7021. Rev. Kurt Hartrich, O.F.M., Pres. Sponsor corporation of St. Francis Village (a retirement village) in Crowley, TX.

St. Joseph Services, Inc., 30 N. LaSalle St., Ste. 4100, 60602. Tel: 312-422-9140. Email: dancoyne@okeefe-law.com. Daniel W. Coyne, Registered Agent. Supports the mission of the Daughters of Charity to serve the poor.

Serra International, 70 E. Lake St., Ste. 1210, 60601. Tel: 312-419-7411; 800-488-4008 (toll free); Fax: 312-419-8077; 800-377-7877 (toll free). Email: serra@serra.org. Web: www.serra.org. Mr. John W. Woodward, Exec. Dir., Serra International & Serra International Foundation.

USA Council of Serra International Tel: 312-201-6549; 888-777-6681 (toll free); Fax: 312-201-6548; 888-777-6803 (toll free). Email: serraus@serraus.org. Web: www.serraus.org. Mr. E.V. Verbeke, Exec. Dir.

**Society of Friends of the John Paul II Foundation*, P.O. Box 34618, 60634. Email: mskawski@earthlink.net.

**Society of Jesus Worldwide*, 2050 N. Clark St., 60614. Tel: 773-975-6363; Fax: 773-975-0230.

Taller de Jose, 3047 W. Cermak Rd., 60623. Tel: 773-542-1019; Fax: 773-542-1019. Email: info@tallerdejose.org. Web: www.tallerdejose.org. Sr. Kathy Brazda, C.S.J., Dir. Taller de Jose is a community resource center, offering accompaniment to people in need, connecting people to services and services to people. It partners with communities of Chicago to help alleviate human sufferings caused by, but not limited to hunger, domestic abuse, addictions, homelessness, sickness and violence. As a sponsored ministry of the Congregation of St. Joseph, Taller de Jose exists so that all may be one.

St. Thomas Aquinas Foundation (STAF) (St. Albert the Great Prov.), 1909 S. Ashland Ave., 60608-2994. Tel: 312-666-3244; Fax: 312-829-8471. Rev. Louis Morrone, O.P., Sec. & Treas.

United Stand Family Center, 3731 W. 62nd St., 60629. Tel: 773-585-4499; Fax: 773-585-5615. Sr. Kim Mis, C.S.S.F., Exec. Dir. Education, Prevention, Problem Identification, Consultation, and Intervention with Children and Families. Total Staff 55.

Villa Guadalupe Senior Services Corporation, 3201 E. 91st St., 60617. Tel: 773-933-0344; Fax: 773-933-0827. Angela Hurlock, Exec. Dir.; Rev. Mark J. Brummel, C.M.F., Treas. Organization to provide affordable housing and related services for Senior Citizens in South Chicago. Apartments 53; Seniors Assisted 2,500; Staff 6.

Westcourt Corporation, 5550 W. 87th St., Burbank, 60459. Tel: 773-429-4343; Fax: 773-429-4381. Bro. Patrick Hayes, C.F.C.

Zaccheus House (2002) 12242 S. Parnell, 60628. Tel: 773-568-7822; Fax: 773-287-1258. Web: www.zacchaeushouse.org. Most Rev. Joseph N. Perry, Moderator. A ministry of Deacons offering hospitality and life skills education to men in transition to stability in their lives.

ARLINGTON HEIGHTS. **Alexian Brothers Center for Mental Health*, 3350 W. Salt Creek Ln., Ste. 114, 60005. Tel: 847-952-7460; Fax: 847-222-1754. Web: www.alexiancenter.org. Mr. Scott Burgess, Exec. Dir. Congregation of Alexian Brothers, Immaculate Conception Province.

Alexian Brothers Community Services, 3040 W. Salt Creek Ln., 60005. Tel: 847-385-7147; Fax: 847-483-7036. Web: www.alexianbrothers.org. Alexian Brothers Community Services (Programs for the care of the elderly) in Chattanooga, TN and in St. Louis, MO.

Alexian Brothers Health System dba Alexian Brothers Foundation 3040 W. Salt Creek Ln., 60005. Tel: 847-385-7147; Fax: 847-483-7036. Web: www.alexianbrothers.org. Congregation of Alexian Brothers, Immaculate Conception Province.

**Alexian Brothers Health System, Inc. Investment Trust*, 3040 W. Salt Creek Ln., 60005. Tel: 847-385-7147; Fax: 847-483-7036. Web: www.alexianbrothers.org.

Alexian Brothers of America, Inc., 3040 W. Salt Creek Ln., 60005. Tel: 847-385-7147; Fax: 847-483-7036. Web: www.alexianbrothers.org. Congregation of Alexian Brothers, Immaculate Conception Province.

Alexian Brothers Senior Ministries, 3040 W. Salt Creek Ln., 60005. Tel: 847-385-7147; Fax: 847-483-7036. Web: www.alexianbrothers.org. Congregation of Alexian Brothers, Immaculate Conception Province.

Living Word Charitable Trust, 800 N. Fernandez Ave.-B, 60004-5336. Tel: 847-577-5972; Fax: 847-577-5980. Email: slw@slw.org. Web: slw.org. Michael Gibbs, Trustee.

BLUE ISLAND. *St. Francis Hospital and Health Center*, 12935 S. Gregory St., 60406.

CHICAGO HEIGHTS. *Dominican Association of Secondary Schools, Inc.*, 700 S. Ashland Ave., 60411. Tel: 708-755-7565; Fax: 708-756-9759. Web: www.dominicanschools.org. Sr. Kathleen Anne Tait, O.P., Contact Person.

DES PLAINS. *Maryville-Our Lady of Guadalupe Chapel*, 1150 N. River Rd., Des Plaines, 60016. Tel: 847-294-1806; Fax: 847-294-1841. Email: ol-guadalupe-cerrito@archchicago.org. Web: www.maryville.org. Rev. Miguel Angel Martinez, Chap.

Sisters of the Holy Family of Nazareth - U.S.A., Inc., 310 N. River Rd., Des Plaines, 60016. Tel: 847-298-6760; Fax: 847-803-1941. Email: skiepura@nazarethcsfn.org.

EVERGREEN PARK. *American Province of Little Company of Mary Sisters Charitable Trust*, 9350 S. California, 60805. Tel: 708-422-0130; Fax: 708-422-2212. Email: kmcintyre@lcmh.org. Web: www.lcmglobal.org.

Network for Mercy Education, 9318 S. Kedzie Ave., Ste. 1, 60805. Tel: 708-229-1630. Web: www.netmercyed.org.

GLENVIEW. *Redemptorist Fathers of St. Alphonsus Parish of Chicago, c/o Redemptorists of Glenview, Illinois*, 1111 N. Milwaukee Ave., P.O. Box 6, 60025. Tel: 847-724-0425; Fax: 847-724-8953.

The Redemptorists of Blessed Sacrament, c/o Redemptorists of Glenview Illinois, 1111 N. Milwaukee Ave., P.O. Box 6, 60025. Tel: 847-724-0425; Fax: 847-724-8953.

Villa Redeemer, c/o Redemptorists of Glenview, Illinois, 1111 N. Milwaukee Ave., P.O. Box 6, 60025. Tel: 847-724-0425; Fax: 847-724-8953.

GURNEE. *Assisi Homes of Gurnee, Inc.*, 3495 W. Grand Ave., 60031. Tel: 847-336-4428; Fax: 847-336-3778. Web: www.fm-inc.org. Units 60.

HOMEWOOD. **The Clare at Water Tower*, 1055 W. 175th St., Ste. 202, 60430. Tel: 708-647-6500.

Franciscan Communities, 1055 W. 175th St., Ste. 202, 60430. Tel: 708-647-6500; Fax: 708-647-6982.

**Franciscan Communities St. Mary of the Woods, Inc.*, 1055 W. 175th St., Suite 202, 60430. Tel: 708-647-6500. Web: www.franciscancommunities.org.

Franciscan Community Benefit Services, 1055 W. 175th St., Ste. 202, 60430. Tel: 708-647-3127; Fax: 708-647-6982. Email: tmalik@franciscanservices.com. Web: www.madonnafoundation4girls.org. Terry Malik, Pres. Sponsored by the Franciscan Sisters of Chicago., A charitable foundation focused on the ministry of the Franciscan Sisters of Chicago and increasing access to Catholic high schools by young women in urban areas through scholarships and program enhancement.

ITASCA. *Rainbows for All Children, Inc.*, 1360 Hamilton Pkwy, 60143. Tel: 800-266-3206; Fax: 847-952-1774. Email: info@rainbows.org. Web: www.rainbows.org. Mrs. Suzy Yehl Marta, Founder & Pres.

JUSTICE. **Pope John Paul II Eucharistic Adoration Association, Inc.*, 9000 W. 81st. St., 60458. Tel: 708-728-0840; Fax: 708-728-0840. Email: pjp2ea@sbcglobal.net. Web: www.pj2ea.org. Charles Smith, Treas.

LAGRANGE PARK. **Joyful Again*, Charlotte Hrubes, P.O. Box 1365, La Grange Park, 60526-9465. Tel: 708-354-7211. Email: joyfulagain@att.net. Web: www.joyfulagain.org. Rev. Medard P. Laz, Exec. Dir.; Charlotte Hrubes, Dir. Support program for widowed men and women.

School and Tutors on Wheels, 1515 W. Ogden Ave., La Grange Park, 60526. Tel: 708-354-9200; Fax: 708-482-5036. Web: www.schoolonwheels.com.

Sisters of St. Joseph of LaGrange Charitable Trust, 1515 W. Ogden Ave., La Grange Park, 60526-2721. Tel: 708-354-9200; Fax: 708-354-9573. Email: gsbr@juno.com.

LAKE FOREST. *Barat Education Foundation*, P.O. Box 457, 60045. Tel: 847-501-1726; Fax: 847-234-4628. Email: alumni@thebaratfoundation.org. Web: www.thebaratfoundation.org. Maureen Ryan, Exec. Dir.

**New Ethos*, 825 S. Waukegan Rd. A8 #225, 60045. Tel: 312-208-8777. Email: frdon@new-ethos.org. Web: www.new-ethos.org. Rev. Donald C. Woznicki, Exec. Dir. Collaborates with the Entertainment Industry to bring the Catholic consumer true, good & beautiful entertainment.

MELROSE PARK. **Dominican Literacy Center (ESL)*, 1503 Rice St., 60160. Tel: 708-338-0659; Fax: 708-338-0659. Email: jcurranx@yahoo.com. Sr. Judith Curran, O.P., Dir.

MUNDELEIN. *Civitas Dei Foundation*, 1000 E. Maple Ave., 60060. Tel: 847-566-6401. Rev. Lawrence R. Hennessey, M.A., S.T.L., Ph.D. The Journal is named Chicago Studies.

Foundation for Adult Catechetical Teaching Aids, 22333 W. Erhart Rd., 60060. Tel: 847-223-0010; Fax: 847-223-5960. Web: www.actafoundation.org. Revs. Ronald J. Lewinski, S.T.L., Pres.; Donald Senior, C.P., S.T.D., Treas.

NORTHBROOK. *Techny Land Corporation, NFP*, 1985 Waukegan Rd., 60062.

Techny Land Investments, 1985 Waukegan Rd., 60062.

NORTHLAKE. *Scalabrini Village*, 420-480 N. Wolf Rd., 60164. Tel: 708-562-0040; Fax: 708-562-5180.

RIVER FOREST. **Education and Intervention, Inc. dba ICAP (Inter Congregational Addictions Program)* 7777 W. Lake St., Ste. 115, 60305-1734. Tel: 708-488-9770; Fax: 708-488-9774. Email: icapsrs@sbcglobal.net. Sisters Letitia Close, Pres. & Exec. Dir.; Mary Gene Kinney, B.V.M., Master Addictions Counselor (M.A.C.).

Education and Intervention, Inc., National and International network for women religious recovering in 12 step programs; services of intervention, referral, follow-up and education to communities of women religious.

SOUTH HOLLAND. **American Catholic Press*, 16565 S. State St., 60473. Tel: 708-331-5485; Fax: 708-331-5484. Email: acp@acpress.org. Web: www.americancatholicpress.org. Rev. Michael J. Gilligan, Ph.D., S.T.L., Exec. Dir. Founded in 1967, ACP makes available resources on liturgy and liturgical music, especially for parishes and dioceses. ACP was incorporated as a nonprofit organization in 1972.

TECHNY. *Blessed Arnold Religious Charitable Trust*, 1985 Waukegan Rd., P.O. Box 6067, 60082-6067. Tel: 847-272-2700; Fax: 847-753-7464. Email: dgarbaciak@uscsvd.org. Web: www.divineword.org. Society of the Divine Word.

Divine Word Techny Community Corporation dba Divine Word Seminary/Divine Word Residence f/k/a DWTCRE Charitable Trusts 1901 Waukegan Rd., 60082. Tel: 847-272-2700; Fax: 847-753-7464. Email: tlc1670@uscsvd.org. Web: www.divineword.org. Bro. Mathew Zemel, S.V.D., Trustee; Rev. Dariusz Garbaciak, S.V.D., Sec.

WAUKEGAN. *Alexian Brothers The Harbor, c/o Bonaventure House*, 825 W. Wellington Ave., 60657. Tel: 847-782-8015; Fax: 847-782-0822. Email: infor@abam.org. Web: www.abam.org. Michelle Wetzel, CEO. Congregation of Alexian Brothers, Immaculate Conception Province., Operated by Alexian Brothers Bonaventure House, Inc.; Housing and supportive services for otherwise homeless persons with HIV/AIDS.

WILMETTE. *Loyola Recreational Facility Corp.*, 1100 Laramie, 60091-1021. Tel: 847-256-1100; Fax: 847-251-4031. Web: www.goramblers.org. Rev. Patrick E. McGrath, S.J.

Musica Pacis, Office of the Treasurer, P.O. Box 969, 60091-0969. Tel: 708-624-2559. Email: musicapacis@attglobal.net. Revs. Willard F. Jabusch, Pres. (Retired); Alec J. Wolff, Treas.

[X] CLOSED INSTITUTIONS

CHICAGO. *Archdiocese of Chicago's Joseph Cardinal Bernardin Archives and Records Center*, 711 W. Monroe St., 60661. Tel: 312-534-4400; Fax: 312-831-0610. Email: info@archchicago.org. Web: archives.archchicago.org. The following parish, school or institution records may be found at the above address unless otherwise indicated. Notations to sacramental records of closed parishes held by the Archives and Records Center should be directed to the Archives and Records Center and should specify the name of the parish. The location of records periodically changes. Inquiries for records of parishes, schools or institutions not on this list should be directed to the above address.

Academy of St. Benedict the African (May St.)

Academy of St. Benedict the African (Honore St.), 6547 S. Stewart Ave., 60621. Tel: 773-994-6100.

Academy of the Immaculate Conception (Unknown)
Academy of the Sacred Heart, Sacred Heart Schools, 6250 N. Sheridan Rd., 60660. Tel: 773-262-4446.
Academy of Our Lady aka Longwood Academy
Academy of Our Lady of Mount Carmel (Unknown) Became school for Our Lady of Mount Carmel.
Academy of St. Joseph (Unknown)
Academy of St. Scholastica Renamed St. Scholastica Academy
Academy of the Holy Child St. Anastasia School
St. Adalbert Commercial High School (Unknown)
St. Adalbert School (Archives)
St. Adrian School
St. Agatha Academy (Unknown)
St. Agatha School
Blessed Agnes Commercial High School and School, St. Agnes of Bohemia School, 2643 S. Central Park, 60623. Tel: 773-522-0143.
Blessed Agnes of Bohemia Church, St. Agnes of Bohemia Parish, 2643 S. Central Park, 60623. Tel: 773-522-0143.
St. Agnes Academy (Unknown)
St. Agnes Parish (39th St.) (Pershing Rd.)
St. Agnes School (39th St.)
St. Agnes High School (39th St.) (Unknown)
St. Albertus Academy (Waukegan) (Unknown)
Alexine Learning Center School
All Saints Parish (State St.)
All Saints School (State St.)
All Saints Parish (Wallace St.)
All Saints School (Wallace St.)
All Saints / St. Anthony School (Wallace)
St. Aloysius School
St. Aloysius Commercial High School (Boys) (Unknown)
St. Aloysius High School (Boys) (Unknown)
St. Alphonsus School (Wellington) Renamed Alphonsus Academy and Center for the Arts
St. Alphonsus School (Lemont), St. Alphonsus/St. Patrick School, 205 Cass St., Lemont, 60439. Tel: 630-257-2380; Fax: 630-257-4648.
St. Alphonsus Commercial High School (Chicago) (Unknown)
St. Alphonsus Commercial High School (Lemont) (Unknown)
Alvernia Conservatory of Music (Unknown)
Alvernia High School
St. Ambrose High School (Unknown)
St. Ambrose School (47th St.)
St. Ambrose Parish (117th St.) See St. Louis de France Parish (117th St.)
St. Andrew High School
St. Andrew Mission (Wadsworth), St. Patrick Parish, 15000 Wadsworth Rd., Wadsworth, 60083. Tel: 847-244-4161; Fax: 847-336-0630.
St. Andrew The Apostle School (Calumet City)
Angel Guardian Croatian Catholic Mission Blessed Alojzije Stepinac Croatian Catholic Mission, 6346 N. Ridge Ave., 60660. Tel: 773-262-0535; Fax: 773-262-4603.
Angel Guardian Orphanage
St. Angela Parish
St. Angela Academy (Unknown)
St. Ann Parish (Chicago Heights)
St. Ann School (Chicago Heights)
St. Ann High School (Leavitt St.)
St. Anne Hospital and St. Anne's Tuberculosis Sanitarium, Saint Elizabeth Campus, Saints Mary and Elizabeth Medical Center, 1431 N. Claremont Ave., 60622. Tel: 773-278-2000.
St. Anne's School of Nursing, Ancilla College, 9601 Union Rd., Plymouth, IN 46563. Tel: 574-936-8898; 866-262-4552 (Toll Free).
St. Anne Parish (Garfield Blvd.)
St. Anne School (Garfield Blvd.)
St. Anne School (Hazel Crest)
St. Anne Parish (Waukegan), 711 W. Monroe St., 60661. Tel: 312-534-4400; Fax: 312-831-0610.
St. Anne Mission Chapel , (Richton), St. Liborius Parish, 71 W. 35th St., Steger, 60475. Tel: 708-754-1363.
Annunciation Parish (Wabansia)
Annunciation School (Wabansia)
St. Anselm School
St. Anthony of Padua Parish (24th Pl.)
St. Anthony of Padua School (24th Pl.)
St. Anthony School (Cicero)
St. Anthony High School & Commercial High School (24th Pl.)
St. Anthony School (Prairie)
Aquinas Catholic High School
Aquinas Dominican High School
Aquinas High School
Archbishop Quigley Preparatory Seminary
Ascension Parish (Harvey), at Ascension-St. Susanna Parish, 15234 Myrtle Ave., Harvey, 60426-3194. Tel: 708-333-0931; Fax: 708-333-3281.
Ascension School (Harvey)
Ascension-St. Susanna School (Harvey)
Ascension of Our Lord Parish (Evanston)
Ascension of Our Lord School (Evanston)
Assumption School (24th St.)
Assumption Parish (Marshfield Ave.)
Assumption School (Marshfield Ave.)
Assumption BVM Parish (123rd St.)
Assumption BVM School (123rd St.)
Assumption School (Illinois St.) (Unknown)
Assumption / St. Catherine of Genoa School and Parish
St. Attracta Parish (Cicero)
St. Attracta School (Cicero)
St. Attracta-St. Valentine Church (Cicero)
St. Augustine Parish (S. Laflin)
St. Augustine School & High School
St. Beatrice School
Barat College (Lake Forest), De Paul University, 1 E. Jackson Blvd., 60604. Tel: 312-362-8850.
St. Barbara High School
St. Bartholomew Parish (Waukegan)
St. Bartholomew School (Waukegan)
St. Basil Parish, St. Basil/Visitation Parish 5443 S. Honore, 60609.
St. Basil Parish (Ukrainian Rite), St. Michael Parish (Ukrainian Rite), 12205 S. Parnell, 60628. Tel: 773-291-0168.
St. Basil School
Bellarmine School of Theology, Loyola University of Chicago, Dean of Students of the Graduate School, 820 N. Michigan Ave., 60611.
St. Benedict High School (Coed 1919-1939) (Unknown)
St. Bernard Parish (65th St.)
St. Bernard School
Bishop Quarter Boarding School for Motherless Boys
Bishop Quarter Junior Military School aka Bishop Quarter School for Little Boys
St. Blase School (Argo)
Blessed Sacrament Parish (Millard St.)
Blessed Sacrament School (Millard St.)
Blessed Sacrament / Our Lady of Lourdes School
SS. Benedict and Scholastica Academy St. Scholastica Academy
St. Bonaventure Parish, St. Alphonsus Parish, 1429 W. Wellington Ave., 60657. Tel: 773-525-0709.
St. Bonaventure School (Diversey)
St. Boniface Parish (N. Noble)
St. Boniface School (N. Noble)
St. Boniface High School (Unknown)
St. Brendan Parish (Racine)
St. Brendan School (Racine)
St. Bride School
St. Bridget Parish
St. Bridget School & High School
Bridgeport Industrial School for Boys See Illinois Industrial School for Boys
Bridgeport Catholic Academy Middle School (St. Mary of Perpetual Help Campus)
Bridgeport Catholic Academy North Campus (All Saints/St. Anthony Campus)
Bridgeport Catholic Academy South Campus (Nativity of Our Lord Campus), 711 W. Monroe St., 60661. Tel: 312-534-4400; Fax: 312-831-0610. open, Pre-2002
St. Bronislava School
Brother Candidates High School (Techny), Box 107, East Troy, WI 53120. Tel: 414-642-3300.
Cabrini Green Alternative High School
Cabrini Hospital Sacramental records - St. Anthony Hospital (Chicago); Medical records - St. Anthony Hospital
St. Callistus Parish
St. Callistus School
St. Camillus School
Cardinal Stritch High School
Carmel High School (Boys' Carmel and Girls' Carmel merged to form 1 Carmel High School), Carmel High School, One Carmel Pkwy., Mundelein, 60060-2499. Tel: 847-566-3000. (Boys and Girls)
St. Carthage Parish (73rd St.)
St. Carthage School
St. Casimir Academy, Maria High School, 6727 S. California Ave., 60629-1887. Tel: 773-925-8686.
St. Casimir Parish (Chicago Heights)
St. Casimir School (Chicago Heights)
St. Casimir Parish (Whipple St.)
St. Casimir School (Whipple St.)
St. Casimir High School, Our Lady of Tepeyac High School, 2228 S. Whipple St., 60623. Tel: 773-522-0023; Fax: 773-522-0508. (Whipple St.)
St. Catherine Academy (See Siena High School)
St. Catherine High School (See Siena High School)
Cathedral College
Cathedral High School
Chrysalis Program
Corpus Christi School
St. Catherine of Genoa Parish
St. Catherine of Genoa School
St. Catherine of Siena Parish (Oak Park), Sacramental Records: St. Catherine/St. Lucy Parish, 38 N. Austin Blvd., Oak Park, 60302. Tel: 708-386-8077; Fax: 708-386-5190.
St. Catherine of Siena School (Oak Park), School Records: St. Catherine/St. Lucy School, 27 W. Washington Blvd., Oak Park, 60302. Tel: 708-386-5286.
St. Cecilia Parish (Wells St.)
St. Cecilia School (Wells St.)
St. Charles Borromeo Parish (Hoyne Ave.)
St. Charles Borromeo School (Hoyne Ave.)
St. Charles Borromeo School (Melrose Park)
St. Charles Lwanga Parish (W. Garfield)
St. Charles Lwanga School (W. Garfield)
Christ the Redeemer Church (Byzantine Rite)
St. Clara Parish (Woodlawn Ave.)
St. Clara School (Woodlawn)
St. Clara-St. Cyril Parish (S. Woodlawn)
St. Clara-St. Cyril School
St. Clare of Montefalco School
St. Clement High School
St. Clotilde School
St. Columba Academy (Unknown)
St. Columba School (134th St.)
St. Columbanus High School (Unknown)
St. Columbkille Parish (Paulina)
St. Columbkille School & Commercial High School
Columbus Hospital Sacramental Records - Archives, Medical Records - St. Anthony Hospital
Columbus Hospital School of Nursing
St. Constance High School
Convent of the Holy Child Renamed Holy Child High School
Convent of the Sacred Heart (Chicago), Sacred Heart Schools, 6250 N. Sheridan Rd., 60660. Tel: 773-262-4446.
Convent of the Sacred Heart High School (Lake Forest), Woodlands Academy of the Sacred Heart, 760 E. Westleigh Rd., Lake Forest, 60045-3298. Tel: 847-234-4300.
Cook County Hospital (Sacramental Records)
Corpus Christi High School, Hales Franciscan High School, 4930 S. Cottage Grove, 60615. Tel: 773-285-8400.
Cuneo Hospital Medical Records - St. Anthony Hospital; Sacramental-Archives
St. Cyril College, Mt. Carmel High School.
St. Cyril Parish (Dante Ave.)
St. Cyril School
Ss. Cyril & Methodius Church & School (Hermitage Ave.)
Ss. Cyril & Methodius Church & School (Walton St.)
St. David School
St. David Parish
De Lourdes College (Des Plaines), Holy Family College, Registrar's Office, Grant Ave. & Frankford Ave., Philadelphia, PA 19114. Tel: 215-637-4851.
St. Denis School
DePaul Academy & DePaul University Academy, DePaul University, Registrar's Office, 243 S. Wabash, 60604. Tel: 312-341-8610.
DePaul High School (Unknown)
DePaul University Loop High School (Unknown)
St. Dionysius Parish (Cicero)
St. Dionysius School (Cicero)
Divine Savior School
St. Dionysius High School (Cicero) (Unknown)
St. Dominic Parish (Locust)
St. Dominic School & High School
St. Donatus School (Blue Island)
St. Elizabeth High School (41st St.) Pre-1924 - Records Unknown; Post-1924 at Archives
St. Emeric Church (Washtenaw Ave.), St. Stephen King of Hungary Parish, 2015 W. Augusta Blvd., 60622-4947. Tel: 773-486-1896; Fax: 773-486-1902.
St. Emeric School (County Club Hills)
Englewood Catholic Academy (Honore St.)
Englewood Catholic Academy (Laflin St.)
Englewood Catholic Academy (May St.)
Englewood Catholic Academy (Princeton St.)
Ephpheta School for the Deaf
St. Ethelreda Parish
St. Eulalia School
Felician College
St. Felicitas High School (Unknown)
St. Felicitas School
St. Fidelis Parish, 711 W. Monroe St., 60661. Tel: 312-534-4400; Fax: 312-831-0610.
St. Fidelis School (N. Washtenaw)
St. Finbarr Parish
St. Finbarr High School and School (Unknown)
Five Holy Martyrs School
St. Florian Commerical High School (Unknown)
St. Florian Mission , (52nd & Archer), St. Camillus, 5426 S. Lockwood Ave., 60638. Tel: 773-767-8183.
Ford City Catholic Center
Fournier Institute, DePaul University, Registrar's Office, 243 S. Wabash, 60604. Tel: 312-341-8610.
Fornier Institute Viatorian Preparatory (Lemont), Viatorian Archives, Arlington Heights, 60006.
St. Frances Xavier Cabrini Parish (Lexington St.)
St. Frances Xavier Cabrini School (Lexington St.)
St. Frances Xavier Cabrini School of Nursing

St. Francis Xavier Commercial High School (Unknown)
St. Francis de Paula Parish
St. Frances de Paula School (S. Ellis)
St. Francis de Sales School
St. Francis of Assisi Church (Kostner Ave.), 711 W. Monroe St., 60661. Tel: 312-534-4400; Fax: 312-831-0610.
St. Francis of Assisi High School (Unknown)
St. Francis of Assisi School (Kostner Ave.)
St. Francis of Assisi School (Roosevelt Ave.)
St. Francis Hospital (Blue Island) Sacramental Records - Archives
St. Francis of Assisi / Our Lady of the Angel Parish
St. Francis of Assisi Parish, 932 N. Kostner Ave., 60651. Tel: 773-235-3132. (Kostner Ave.)
St. Francis Xavier Parish (Nelson), Resurrection Parish, 2840 W. Nelson, 60618-7012. Tel: 773-478-9705; Fax: 773-478-1387.
St. Francis Xavier School (Nelson)
St. Gabriel Commercial High School St. Gabriel High School (Unknown)
St. Gabriel School (open) Records (1941-1965) at Archives
Garfield Alternative High School
St. Gelasius Parish and School
St. George Parish (Wentworth Ave.)
St. George School & Commercial High School (Lituanica Ave.)
St. George School (Wentworth Ave.)
St. George Parish (Lituanica Ave.)
St. George School (Ewing St.)
St. George High School (Evanston)
St. Gerald High School (Oak Lawn) (Unknown)
St. Gerard Majella School (Markham)
St. Gertrude High School (Franklin Park) (Unknown)
St. Gertrude School (Chicago)
St. Gertrude School (Franklin Park)
Good Counsel High School
Good Shepherd Chapel (Illinois Technical School for the Colored Girls).
Good Shepherd School
St. Gregory the Great School
Hardey Preparatory, Sacred Heart Schools, 6250 N. Sheridan Rd., 60660. Tel: 773-262-4446.
Heart of Mary High School
St. Hedwig Mission St. John Berchmans Parish, 2517 W. Logan Blvd., 60647. Tel: 773-486-4300; Fax: 773-252-5346. (Washtenaw Ave.)
St. Hedwig Orphanage (Niles)
St. Hedwig School
St. Henry School
St. Henry Commercial High School (Unknown)
Holy Child High School (Waukegan), 711 W. Monroe St., 60661. Tel: 312-534-4400; Fax: 312-831-0610.
Holy Cross Parish (65th St.)
Holy Cross School (65th St.)
Holy Cross School (Wood St.)
Holy Cross Parish (46th St.)
Holy Cross High School (River Grove) Records at Guerin College Preparatory High School (River Grove)
Holy Family Parish (North Chicago)
Holy Family Parish (Waukegan), 711 W. Monroe St., 60661. Tel: 312-534-4400; Fax: 312-831-0610.
Holy Family High School (Unknown)
Holy Family School (North Chicago)
Holy Family School (May St.)
Holy Family Academy (Division St.)
Holy Family Extension High School (Des Plaines), Sisters of Holy Family of Nazareth, Provincial Archives, 310 N. River Rd., Des Plaines, 60016. Tel: 847-298-6760.
Holy Family Orphanage (Unknown)
Holy Ghost Parish & School
Holy Ghost Academy (Techny), Convent of the Holy Spirit (Techny).
Holy Ghost School (South Holland)
Holy Guardian Angel Parish (Arthington/Cabrini)
Holy Guardian Angel School
Holy Innocents School
Holy Name Cathedral School
Holy Name Cathedral High School
Holy Name High School
Holy Name of Mary School
Holy Rosary Commercial High School (North Chicago) (Unknown)
Holy Rosary Slovak Parish (108th St.)
Holy Rosary Slovak School (108th St.)
Holy Rosary Parish and School (113th St.)
Holy Rosary Parish (North Chicago)
Holy Rosary School (North Chicago)
Holy Rosary School (Western Ave.)
Holy Trinity Parish, Holy Trinity Polish Mission, 1118 N. Noble St., 60622-4015. Tel: 773-489-4140; Fax: 773-489-5918.
Holy Trinity School (Noble St.)
Holy Trinity Parish (Wolcott)
Holy Trinity Parish (Throop)
Holy Trinity School (Throop)
Holy Trinity School (Wolcott)
Holy Trinity School (Taylor, Deaf Children)
House of the Good Shepherd
St. Hugh School (Lyons)
St. Hyacinth Mission , (Spaulding), St. Hyacinth Basilica Parish, 3636 N. Wolfram, 60618. Tel: 773-342-3636; Fax: 773-342-3638.
St. Ignatius College, St. Ignatius College Prep., 1073 W. Roosevelt Rd., 60608. Tel: 312-421-5900.
St. Ignatius School
Illinois Industrial School for Boys (Unknown)
Illinois Technical School for Colored Girls
Illinois Industrial School for Girls (Unknown)
Immaculata High School
Immaculate Conception School (Exchange Ave.; Open, 1884-1984 only)
Immaculate Conception Commercial High School (Aberdeen St.)
Immaculate Conception-St. Bridget School
Immaculate Conception Parish (Aberdeen St.)
Immaculate Conception School (Aberdeen St.)
Immaculate Conception School (44th St.)
Immaculate Conception Parish (Waukegan), 711 W. Monroe St., 60661. Tel: 312-534-4400; Fax: 312-831-0610.
Immaculate Conception School (Waukegan)
Immaculate Conception School (Highland Park)
Immaculate Conception School (North Park Ave.; Open, 1868-1986 only)
Immaculate Conception High School (Highland Park) (Unknown)
Immaculate Conception Parish, 75 N. Buffalo Grove Rd., Buffalo Grove, 60089. (Buffalo Grove) St. Mary Parish (Buffalo Grove)
Immaculate Heart of Mary High School (Westchester)
Immaculate Heart of Mary School (Spaulding Ave.)
Immaculate Heart of Mary Vicariate (Ashland)
Industrial and Manual Labor School (Unknown)
Institute of Our Lady of the Sacred Heart Renamed Academy of Our Lady (Longwood Academy)
St. Irenaeus School (Park Forest)
St. Isaac Jogues School (Niles)
St. Isidore the Farmer School (Blue Island)
St. Ita High School (Unknown)
St. Ita School
St. James Academy (Lemont) (Unknown)
St. James Parish (Strassburg or New Strassburg) (Unknown)
St. James School (Wabash Ave.)
St. James Parish & School (Maywood)
St. James Parish (Mundelein or Fremont Center), St. Mary of the Annunciation Parish, 22333 W. Erhart Rd., Mundelein, 60060. Tel: 847-223-0010; Fax: 847-223-5960.
St. James Commercial High School (Maywood) (Unknown)
St. James School (Fullerton and Menard)
St. James School (Sauk Village)
St. James High School (Wabash) (Unknown)
St. Jarlath Parish (Jackson)
St. Jarlath School (Jackson)
St. Jean Baptiste Church (33rd Pl.)
St. Jerome School (Lunt)
Jesuit School of Theology, Loyola University of Chicago, 820 N. Michigan Ave., 60611. Loyola University of Chicago, Office of the Dean of Graduate School.
Jesus, Our Brother School
St. Joachim School
St. John Bosco School
Old St. John Parish (18th St.)
Old St. John School, Christian Brothers University, 2455 Avery Ave., Memphis, TN 38112.
St. John Cantius Commercial High School (Unknown)
St. John Cantius School
St. John Chrysostom Parish and School (Bellwood)
St. John De La Salle School Renamed St. John De La Salle Academy of Fine Arts
St. John Nepomucene Church & School
St. John of God Parish & School (S. Throop)
St. John the Baptist Parish (50th Pl.)
St. John the Baptist Church (Burley Ave.)
St. John the Baptist School (50th Pl.)
St. John the Baptist School (Harvey)
St. Josaphat Commerical High School (Hermitage Ave.)
St. Josaphat School (Open pre 1961)
St. Josaphat Parish Orphanage (Unknown)
St. Joseph Bohemian Orphanage (Lisle), Maryville Academy, 1150 N. River Rd., Des Plaines, 60016. Tel: 708-824-6126; Fax: 847-824-7277. (Assumed location)
St. Joseph Commercial Business College (Waukegan)
St. Joseph Orphanage (Lisle); See St. Joseph Bohemian Orphanage (Lisle)
St. Joseph School (Wilmette); (Pre-1986 only at Archives)
St. Joseph the Worker School
St. Joseph's Institute
St. Joseph Parish (17th Pl.)
St. Joseph School (17th Pl.) (Unknown)
St. Joseph Parish and School (38th Pl.) (See St. Joseph and St. Anne Parish)
St. Joseph School (Orleans)
St. Joseph School (Hermitage)
St. Joseph High School (Hermitage Ave.), 711 W. Monroe St., 60661. Tel: 312-534-4400; Fax: 312-831-0610.
St. Joseph Commercial High School (Hermitage); Unknown
St. Joseph Parish (Chicago Heights)
St. Joseph School (Chicago Hts.)
St. Joseph School (38th) - Archives
St. Joseph Parish (Saginaw St.)
St. Joseph School (Saginaw St.)
St. Joseph's Orphan Asylum (35th St.)
St. Joseph Orphanage for Boys (destroyed by fire, post-1859 in archives)
St. Joseph Parish Orphanage (Unknown)
St. Joseph Provident Orphanage
St. Joseph Military Academy (See St. Joseph's Institute)
St. Joseph Academy (LaGrange Park) (See St. Joseph's Institute)
St. Joseph Commercial High School (Waukegan); (Unknown)
St. Joseph Parish (Waukegan)
SS. Joseph & Bartholomew Parish Renamed Holy Family Parish (Waukegan)
St. Joseph School (Waukegan)
St. Joseph & St. Anne Parish (Archives)
St. Joseph & St. Anne Commercial High School and School (Unknown)
St. Joseph Mission , (13th St.)
St. Joseph Mission School , (13th St.)
St. Joseph Servite Seminary (Elgin-St. Charles), Provincial Archives, Servite Provincial Center, 3121 W. Jackson Blvd., 60612. Tel: 773-533-0360.
St. Joseph's Academy Renamed St. Scholastica Academy
St. Joseph's Carondelet Child Center
St. Joseph's Home for the Friendless
St. Joseph Technical High School (Techny), Divine Word Missionaries, East Troy, WI 53120.
Josephinum High School renamed Josephinum Academy
St. Jude the Apostle School (South Holland)
St. Justin Martyr Parish (71st St.)
St. Justin Martyr School
St. Kevin School, 10509 S. Torrence, 60617. Tel: 773-721-2563.
St. Kilian School
Lake Shore Catholic Academy (Waukegan & North Chicago)
St. Lambert School (Skokie)
St. Laurence School and Parish
St. Leo High School, Mother Guerin Convent, 8001 Belmont Ave., River Grove, 60171. Tel: 708-453-6233.
St. Leo the Great School and Parish
St. Leonard Commercial High School (Berwyn), St. Leonard School, 3322 S. Clarence, Berwyn, 60402. Tel: 708-749-1989; Fax: 708-749-7981.
Lewis Memorial Maternity Hospital
Little Flower Parish & School see St. Therese of the Infant Jesus School
Little Flower High School
Longwood Academy see Academy of Our Lady
Loretto Academy (Adams St., 1864-1871) (Unknown)
Loretto Academy (Woodlawn)
Loretto Academy (Englewood)
Loretto Adult Center (Englewood), Kennedy King College, 6800 S. Wentworth, Rm. 3571, 60621.
Loretto Extension Service (Unknown)
Loretto High School (Englewood)
St. Louis de France Parish (117th St.)
St. Louis de France School (117th St.)
St. Louis Parish (Polk St.)
St. Louis School (Polk St.) (Unknown)
St. Louis Academy
Lourdes High School Records located at De LaSalle Institute, 3455 S. Wabash, 60616. Tel: 312-842-7355; Fax: 312-842-5640.
Loyola Academy (Chicago), 1100 N. Laramie Ave., Wilmette, 60091. Tel: 847-256-1100.
St. Lucy Parish, St. Catherine-St. Lucy Parish, 38 N. Austin Blvd., Oak Park, 60302. Tel: 708-386-8077; Fax: 708-386-5190.
St. Lucy School
St. Ludmilla Parish
St. Ludmilla School
St. Louise de Marillac High School
Madonna High School
St. Malachy High School, St. Malachy School, 2252 W. Washington, 60612. Tel: 312-733-2252; Fax: 312-733-5703.
St. Malachy Parish St. Malachy & Precious Blood Parish at St. Malachy Location.

Mallinckrodt High School
Mallinckrodt College (Wilmette) (Unknown)
St. Margaret's Home & Hospital (Unknown)
Marian School for Deaf (Unknown)
Maria Immaculata Academy (Wilmette)
St. Mark School (Cortez St.)
St. Mark the Evangelist School
Marquette Institute (Clark St.)
St. Martha School (Morton Grove)
St. Martin Parish (Princeton St.)
St. Martin de Porres Academy
St. Martin de Porres School (Jackson Blvd.)
St. Martin School & Commercial High School (Princeton)
St. Mary Academy (Libertyville) (Unknown)
St. Mary Commercial High School (Mundelein) (Unknown)
St. Mary High School (Lake Forest) (Unknown)
St. Mary High School (Highland Park) (Unknown)
St. Mary High School (Grenshaw)
St. Mary School (Des Plaines)
St. Mary School (Evanston)
St. Mary School (Riverside) (Open) (1948-1995 at Archives)
St. Mary Parish (Lemont), St Patrick Parish, 200 Illinois St., Lemont, 60439. Tel: 708-257-6134; Fax: 630-257-0401.
St. Mary Parish (Waukegan), 711 W. Monroe St., 60661. Tel: 312-534-4400; Fax: 312-831-0610.
St. Mary Center for Learning (Grenshaw)
St. Mary Alternative High School (Grenshaw) Records to 1976 at Archives. Records after 1976 or from the night school at, *Harold Washington College*, 30 E. Lake St., 60601. Tel: 312-553-6065.
St. Mary Parish and St. Mary's Mission St. Mary (Seeley); St. Mary's Mission (90th St.); (Byzantine Rite), *Annunciation Byzantine*, 14610 Will-Cook Rd., Lockport, 60441-9212. Tel: 708-645-0214.
St. Mary Magdalene School
St. Mary of Celle School (Berwyn)
St. Mary of the Assumption Parish (137th)
St. Mary of the Assumption School (137th St.) St. Mary of the Assumption Parish (137th),St. Mary Queen of Apostles Parish, 207 W. 145th St., Riverdale IL 60827708-849-4901.
St. Mary of Czestochowa School (Cicero), 711 W. Monroe St., 60661. Tel: 312-534-4400; Fax: 312-831-0610.
St. Mary of the Lake Parish (1870-1928, Ingleside); Renamed St. Bede Parish (Ingleside)
St. Mary of the Lake High School (1844-1867); Unknown, assumed destroyed
St. Mary of Mt. Carmel Parish (Hermitage St.)
St. Mary of Mt. Carmel School (Hermitage)
St. Mary of Nazareth School (Harvey)
St. Mary of Perpetual Help School, Bridgeport Catholic Academy, 3700 S. Lowe, 60609-6507. Tel: 773-376-6223; Fax: 773-376-3864.
St. Mary of Perpetual Help High School
St. Mary Queen of Apostles Parish, 207 W. 145th St., Riverdale, 60827. Tel: 708-849-4901.
St. Mary of the Woods Parish (Highland Park), Immaculate Conception Parish, 700 W. Deerfield Rd., Highland Park, 60035. Tel: 847-433-0130; Fax: 847-433-0669.
St. Mary Mission Seminary (Techny), Catholic Theological Union, 5401 S. Cornell, 60615-5698. Tel: 773-324-8000.
St. Mary Orphanage for Girls, 711 W. Monroe St., 60661. Tel: 312-534-4400; Fax: 312-831-0610. (Destroyed in fire, some records exist in St. Joseph Orphanage registers)
Mary, Queen of Heaven School (Cicero)
St. Mary's Training School, Maryville Academy, 1150 N. River Rd., Des Plaines, 60016. Tel: 847-824-6126; Fax: 847-824-7277. Several intake registers are at the archives.
St. Mary's School of Nursing (Des Plaines), Holy Family College, Registrar's Office, Grant Ave. & Frankford Ave., Philadelphia, PA 19114. Tel: 215-637-4851.
St. Mary's Academy, Christian Brothers University, 2455 Avery Ave., Memphis, TN 38112.
St. Mary's High School (Des Plaines) (Unknown)
St. Mary's Select School, Sisters of the Holy Cross, Notre Dame, IN 46556.
St. Mary's Seminary (Unknown)
Marywood High School (Evanston), *Mother Guerin Convent*, 8001 Belmont Ave., River Grove, 60171. Tel: 773-625-3278; 708-453-6233.
Mater Christi School
Mater Dolorosa Seminary (Hillside), 3121 W. Jackson Blvd., 60612.
Maternity B.V.M. Mission (92nd) Renamed St. Ailbe Parish.
St. Matthew Parish (Walnut St.)
St. Matthew Commercial High School (Unknown)
St. Matthew School (Walnut St.)
St. Matthias School
St. Maurice Parish Renamed Blessed Sacrament (Hoyne Ave.)
St. Maurice School
McKinley Park Catholic School
St. Mel Parish & St. Mel-Holy Ghost Parish
St. Mel & St. Mel-Holy Ghost School
St. Mel High School (Up to 1969)
Mendel High School
Mercy High School
Mercy Mission High School
St. Michael School (Cleveland & Hudson) (1918-1949 only)
St. Michael Central High School (Cleveland & Hudson)
St. Michael School (South Shore Dr.); (Open); Pre-1949 only at Archives.
St. Michael Parish (Wabansia St.)
St. Michael School (Wabansia St.)
St. Michael Parish (24th Pl.)
St. Michael School (24th Pl.)
St. Michael the Archangel Mission (Bellwood); Renamed St. Simeon Parish (Bellwood)
St. Michael the Archangel School
St. Michael the Archangel Commercial High School (Unknown)
St. Michael Commercial High School (South Shore Dr.)
Misericordia Hospital, Client Records & Adoption Placements: *Catholic Charities*, 651 N. LaSalle, 60611. Tel: 312-655-7073; Fax: 312-236-5172. Sacramental Records in registers of St. Agnes Parish, 39th St. and Catholic Charities.
Mission of the Holy Ghost , (Northbrook), St. Norbert Parish, 1809 Walters Ave., Northbrook, 60062. Tel: 847-272-7090; Fax: 847-272-7771.
St. Monica Parish (36th St.)
St. Monica School (36th St.) (Unknown)
St. Monica Mission (Harwood Heights); Renamed St. Rosalie Parish (Harwood Heights)
Monastery of Mt. St. Phillip Servite Novitiate, Provincial Archives, Servite Provincial Center, 3121 W. Jackson Blvd., 60612. Tel: 773-533-0360. (Granville, WI)
Montay College
Mother Theodore Guerin High School (River Grove), at Guerin College Preparatory High School, 8001 W. Belmont, River Grove, 60171. Tel: 708-453-6233; Fax: 708-453-6296.
Mother of God Parish (Waukegan)
Mother of God School & High School (Waukegan)
Mother of Sorrows Grade and High School (Blue Island)
Mount Carmel Academy (Unknown)
Mount Carmel Academy (Girls); (Part of St. Patrick Academy in Chicago, later Des Plaines), *Mother McAuley High School*, 3737 W. 99th St., 60642. Tel: 773-881-6522.
Mount Carmel School (Chicago Heights) (Served St. Rocco)
Mundelein College, Office of Registration & Records, 820 N. Michigan Ave., Room 504, 60611. Tel: 312-915-7221.
Mundelein Cathedral High School
Mundelein High School
Mundelein Seminary See University of St. Mary of the Lake (Mundelein)
Municipal Tuberculosis Sanitarium (Sacred Heart Chapel)
Nativity of Our Lord High School (Unknown)
Nativity of Our Lord School & Commercial High School
Nativity BVM Parish (Paulina St.) (Ukranian Rite: Moved to Palos Park)
Nazareth Academy (LaGrange) (Grammar School - Unknown, Renamed Our Lady of Bethelehem Academy),(High School Still open as Nazareth Academy)
St. Nicholas School (Evanston)
St. Nicholas Parish (State St.)
St. Nicholas School (State St.)
Niles College at St. Joseph Seminary, Loyola University Chicago.
Northside Catholic Academy (St. Henry Campus); (Records split between two remaining campuses); *St. Gertrude Campus*, 6216 N. Glenwood Ave., 60660. Tel: 773-743-6277. *St. Ita Campus*, 5525 N. Magnolia Ave., 60640-1306. Tel: 773-271-2008.
Notre Dame Academy (Unknown)
Notre Dame de Chicago School
Notre Dame High School for Girls (Mango Ave.) - Archives
Our Lady of Aglona, 711 W. Monroe St., 60661. Tel: 312-534-4400; Fax: 312-831-0610.
Our Lady of Bethlehem Academy
Our Lady of Fatima Mission , (Christina Ave.), St. Hyacinth Basilica Parish, 3636 N. Wolfram, 60618. Tel: 773-342-3636; Fax: 773-342-3638.
Our Lady of Fatima School (39th/Pershing Rd.)
Our Lady of the Gardens Parish
Our Lady of the Gardens School, 711 W. Monroe St., 60661. Tel: 312-534-4400; Fax: 312-831-0610.
Our Lady Gate of Heaven School
Our Lady of Good Counsel Parish (Western Ave.)
Our Lady of Good Counsel School (Western Ave.)
Our Lady of the Good Counsel Parish (Hermitage Ave.), Blessed Sacrament, 3615 S. Hoyne Ave., 60609. Tel: 773-847-3357.
Our Lady of Good Counsel School (Hermitage Ave.)
Our Lady of Guadalupe Chapel , Archives
Our Lady Help of Christians Parish
Our Lady Help of Christians School
Our Lady of Hope School (Des Plaines)
Our Lady of Hungary Parish (93rd St.)
Our Lady of Hungary School (93rd St.)
Our Lady of Knock School (Calumet City)
Our Lady of Loretto School (Hometown)
Our Lady of Lourdes School (Ashland Ave.)
Our Lady of Lourdes Commercial High School (Keeler St.)
Our Lady of Lourdes Parish (Keeler St.)
Our Lady of Lourdes School (Keeler St.)
Our Lady of Lourdes High School (Ashland Ave.); (Unknown)
Our Lady of Mercy Commercial High School (Unknown)
Our Lady of Mercy School
Our Lady of the Miraculous Medal Parish (Langley Ave.); Renamed Our Lady of the Gardens Parish
Our Lady of the Mount School (Cicero)
Our Lady of Mt. Carmel School (Melrose Park)
Our Lady of Peace School
Our Lady of Perpetual Help Vicariate (13th St.)
Our Lady of Perpetual Help Vicariate School (13th St.)
Our Lady of Providence Academy (Records destroyed in flood)
Our Lady of Ransom School
Our Lady of Solace Parish (Sangamon)
Our Lady of Solace School (Sangamon)
Our Lady of Sorrows High School (1887-1897), *Mother Guerin Convent*, 8001 Belmont Ave., River Grove, 60171.
Our Lady of Sorrows School
Our Lady of Sorrows Seminary, Servite Provincial Archives, 3121 W. Jackson, 60612. Tel: 773-638-0159; Fax: 773-638-3036.
Our Lady of the Angels Parish, 711 W. Monroe St., 60661. Tel: 312-534-4400; Fax: 312-831-0610.
Our Lady of Angels School
Our Lady of the Cross Mission Chapel St. Margaret Mary Parish, 2324 W. Chase, 60645. Tel: 773-764-0615; Fax: 773-764-0941.
Our Lady of Pompeii School
Our Lady of Pompeii Parish
Our Lady of Victory High School (Unknown)
Our Lady of Vilna Parish (23rd St.)
Our Lady of Vilna School (23rd St.), St. Paul/Our Lady of Vilna School, 2114 W. 22nd Pl., 60608. Tel: 773-847-6078; Fax: 773-847-2118.
Our Lady of the West Side School Renamed St. Agatha Catholic Academy
St. Pancratius School
St. Patrick Academy (Chicago, later Des Plaines) (Girls), *Mother McAuley High School*, 3737 W. 99th St., 60608. Tel: 773-881-6522.
St. Patrick School (Adams St.) (pre 1967, post 1967 at Frances Xavier Ward School)
St. Patrick School (Lemont), St. Alphonsus-St. Patrick School, 205 Cass St., Lemont, 60439. Tel: 630-257-2380.
St. Patrick Parish (Commercial Ave.)
St. Patrick School (Commercial Ave.)
St. Patrick Academy (Boys); at St. Patrick High School (Belmont Ave.)
St. Patrick High School (Boys, Adams St.); at St. Patrick High School (Belmont Ave.)
St. Patrick High School (Adams St.) (Girls)
St. Patrick High School (Commercial Ave.) (Unknown)
St. Paul School (Chicago Heights); (Unknown)
St. Paul School (22nd St.), St. Paul/Our Lady of Vilna School (22nd St.), 2114 W. 22nd Pl., 60608. Tel: 773-847-6078; Fax: 773-847-2118.
St. Paul Commercial High School (Unknown)
St. Paul High School (Midway)
St. Paul Parish (12th St.) (Records destroyed in 1871 fire)
St. Paul School (12th St.) - destroyed
St. Paul Select School (Unknown)
St. Paul's Home for Working Boys (Renamed Mercy Mission)
St. Peter School (Volo), St. Peter Parish, 27551 W. Hwy. 120, Round Lake, 60073. Tel: 815-385-5496; Fax: 631-514-4647.
St. Peter School (Madison) (Unknown)
St. Peter Canisius Parish, 711 W Monroe St., 60661. Tel: 312-534-4400; Fax: 312-831-0610.
St. Peter Canisius School
St. Peter Commercial High School (Skokie) (Unknown)
SS. Peter and Paul Parish (Exchange St.)
SS. Peter and Paul School (Exchange St.)
St. Peter & Paul School (Halsted St.)
SS. Peter and Paul Parish (Paulina St.), Blessed

Sacrament Parish, 3615 S. Hoyne Ave., 60609. Tel: 773-847-3357.
Ss. Peter & Paul School (Paulina St.)
SS. Peter & Paul Parish (Libertyville), St. Joseph Parish, 121 E. Maple, Libertyville, 60048. Tel: 847-362-2073; Fax: 847-362-6821.
SS. Peter & Paul High School (Exchange Ave.)
St. Peter & Paul Church (Central Park Ave.); (Byzantine Rite), St. Nicholas Parish (Byzantine Rite), 8103 Columbia Ave., Munster, IN 46321-1802. Tel: 219-838-9380.
St. Philip Benizi Parish (Maypole St.) (later named St. Mel Parish)
St. Philip Benizi School (Maypole St.) (Unknown)
St. Philip Benizi Parish (Oak St.)
St. Philip Benizi School (Oak St.)
St. Philip Evening School (Unknown)
St. Philip Basilica High School
St. Philip the Apostle School (Northfield)
St. Philomena School
St. Philomena Commercial High School
St. Pius V Commercial High School, St. Pius V School, 1919 S. Ashland, 60608. Tel: 312-226-1590; Fax: 312-226-7265.
St. Pius X School (Stickney)
Precious Blood School
Presentation Parish
Precious Blood Parish St. Malachy + Precious Blood Parish at Precious Location.
Presentation School
Presentation-Precious Blood Unit School, 2401 W. Congress, 60612. Tel: 773-421-6157.
St. Priscilla School, 711 W. Monroe St., 60661. Tel: 312-534-4400; Fax: 312-831-0610.
St. Procopius College Academy (Chicago); Renamed St. Procopius College Academy (Lisle)
St. Procopius School (open) (pre 1983)
St. Procopius High School
Providence Academy & High School (pre-1970), *Mother Guerin Convent*, 8001 Belmont Ave., River Grove, 60171. Tel: 312-625-3278.
Providence of God School and Commercial High School
Providence-St. Mel High School (No longer under the authority of the Archdiocese), 119 S. Central Park Blvd., 60624. Tel: 773-722-4600.
Queen of Peace Parish (Waukegan), 711 W. Monroe St., 60661. Tel: 312-534-4400; Fax: 312-831-0610.
Queen of Angels High School (Unknown)
Queen of Apostles Parish
St. Mary Queen of Apostles Parish, 207 W. 145th St., Riverdale, 60827. Tel: 708-849-4901.
Queen of Apostles School (Riverdale)
Quigley Preparatory Seminary North
Quigley Preparatory Seminary South
Quigley Preparatory Seminary
St. Raphael Parish (60th St.)
St. Raphael School (60th St.)
Resurrection Catholic Academy (Barry Ave.)
Resurrection Parish and School (Jackson Blvd.)
St. Rita College, St. Rita High School, 7740 S. Western Ave., 60620. Tel: 773-925-6600.
St. Rita of Cascia School
St. Rocco Parish (Chicago Heights) (For school records, see Mt. Carmel School.)
St. Roman School
St. Rosalie School (Harwood Heights)
Rosary House High School (River Forest), 7574 W. Division St., River Forest, 60305. Tel: 708-771-8383.
Rosary College, Dominican University, 7900 W. Division St., River Forest, 60305. Tel: 708-366-2490.
St. Rose of Lima Parish (W. 48th St.)
St. Rose of Lima School
Sacred Heart Parish (19th St.)
Sacred Heart School & High School (19th St.)
Sacred Heart Parish (May St.)
Sacred Heart School & High School (May St.)
Sacred Heart Parish (Oakley Blvd.)
Sacred Heart School (Oakley Blvd.)
Sacred Heart High School (Oakley) (Unknown)
Sacred Heart (Church St.), Sacred Heart Mission, 11652 S. Church St., 60643. Tel: 773-233-3955.
Sacred Heart of Jesus Parish (46th St.)
Sacred Heart of Jesus School (46th St.)
Sacred Heart of Jesus High School (46th St.)
Sacred Heart of Mary High School (Arlington Heights), St. Viator High School, 1213 E. Oakton St., Arlington Heights, 60004. Tel: 847-392-4050.
Sacred Heart Seminary (Melrose Park) (Stone Park), Scalabrini Mission Center, 3800 W. Division St., Stone Park, 60165. Tel: 708-345-8270.
St. Salomea Parish (S. Indiana)
St. Salomea School (S. Indiana)
San Callisto Mission
San Marcello Mission , (Evergreen), Immaculate Conception Parish, 1415 N. North Park, 60610. Tel: 312-944-1230; Fax: 312-944-0673.
Santa Lucia Mission , Sacramental Records:, Santa Lucia-Santa Maria Incoronata Parish, 3022 S. Wells, 60616. Tel: 312-842-6115; Fax: 312-842-0103.
Santa Lucia, 3017 S. Wells, 60616. Tel: 312-326-1839; Fax: 312-842-0103. (School Records)
Santa Maria Addolorata School
Santa Maria Incoronata Parish, Santa Lucia-Santa Maria Incoronata Parish, 3022 S. Wells, 60616. Tel: 312-842-6115. Sacramental Records:
Santa Teresita Vicariate (Palatine), Mision San Juan Diego, 35 W. Wood St., Palatine, 60067. Tel: 847-358-6337; Fax: 847-202-4603.
St. Scholastica High School Renamed St. Scholastica Academy.
St. Sebastian Parish (W. Wellington)
St. Sebastian School & High School
Servite Seminary (Hillside), Provincial Archives, Servite Provincial Center, 3121 W. Jackson Blvd., 60612. Tel: 773-533-0360.
Seven Holy Founders School (Calumet Park)
Sheil Institute
Siena High School, Mother McAuley High School, 3737 W. 99th St., 60642. Tel: 773-881-6522.
South Side Italian Mission (Alexander St.)
St. Simeon School (Bellwood)
St. Simon the Apostle School
St. Stanislaus Bishop and Martyr School (Lorel Ave.)
St. Stanislaus Bishop and Martyr School (Posen)
St. Stanislaus College, Gordon Technical High School, 3633 N. California, 60618. Tel: 773-539-3600.
St. Stanislaus Kostka High School, St. Stanislaus Kostka Elementary, 1255 N. Noble, 60622. Tel: 773-278-4560; Fax: 773-278-2471.
St. Stanislaus Parish and School (19th, renamed Sacred Heart)
St. Stephen School (22nd Pl.)
St. Stephen Protomartyr School (Des Plaines)
St. Stephen Parish (22nd Pl.)
Old St. Stephen Parish (Ohio St.)
Old St. Stephen School (Ohio St.)
St. Susanna Parish (Harvey), Ascension-St. Susanna Parish, 15234 Myrtle, Harvey, 60426-3194. Tel: 708-333-0931.
St. Susanna School (Harvey)
St. Sylvester Commercial High School
St. Thaddeus School
St. Theodore Parish (S. Paulina)
St. Theodore School
St. Therese Medical Center (Waukegan) Sacramental Records Archives
St. Teresa of Avila School
St. Therese of the Infant Jesus Parish (Wood St.)
St. Therese of the Infant Jesus School
St. Thomas Aquinas (Washington Blvd.) (Church and School)
St. Thomas More School
St. Thomas Mission , (River Forest), St. Luke Parish, 528 Lathrop, River Forest, 60305. Tel: 708-771-8250; Fax: 708-771-8809.
St. Thomas the Apostle High School, St. Thomas the Apostle School, 5467 S. Woodlawn, 60615. Tel: 773-667-1142; Fax: 773-753-7434.
St. Timothy School
Transfiguration of Our Lord School
Unity Catholic High School
Unity High School
University of St. Mary of the Lake (Chicago, 1844-1866) (Unknown, assumed destroyed)
St. Valentine Parish (Cicero)
St. Valentine School (Cicero)
St. Veronica Parish, Resurrection Parish, 2840 W. Nelson, 60618. Tel: 773-478-9705.
St. Veronica School (Whipple St.)
St. Viator High School (Addison) (Unknown)
Viatorian Preparatory School (Lemont) See Fournier Institute, Viatorian Preparatory School (Lemont)
St. Victor High School (Calumet City) (Unknown)
Villa Nazareth High School (Des Plaines)
St. Vincent de Paul School
St. Vincent de Paul Academy & St. Vincent Academy (Girls) (See DePaul High School)
St. Vincent de Paul High School Seminary (Lemont), *Vincentians Academic Archives*, 2233 N. Kenmore St., 60614. Tel: 312-362-8042.
St. Vincent Orphanage / St. Vincent Infant Hospital / St. Vincent Infant Asylum Client & School Records: Catholic Charities, Division of Services for Children and Youth, 651 N. LaSalle, Chicago, IL 60611. Tel: 312-655-7073; Sacramental Records: Holy Name Cathedral, 730 N. Wabash, Chicago, IL 60611 Tel: 312-787-8040 Fax: 312-787-9113
St. Vincent Ferrer Orphanage (Unknown)
Sacramental Records, 711 W. Monroe St., 60661. Tel: 312-534-4400; Fax: 312-831-0610.
St. Vincent Infant Hospital School of Child Care, St. Vincent de Paul Center, 2145 N. Halsted, 60614. Tel: 312-943-6776.
Visitation Parish (Garfield Blvd.), *St. Basil-Visitation Parish*, 5443 S. Honore, 60609. Tel: 773-625-6311; Fax: 773-783-3348.
Visitation Academy (Evanston) See Marywood High School. (Records destroyed in flood.)
Visitation High School
St. Vitus Parish
St. Vitus School
Weber High School, Gordon Technical High School, 3633 N. California Ave., 60618. Tel: 773-539-3600.
St. Wenceslaus School (Monticello St.)
St. Wenceslaus Parish (DeKoven St.)
St. Wenceslaus School (DeKoven St.) (Unknown)
St. Willibrord Parish (114th St.)
St. Willibrord School (114th St.)
Willibrord Catholic High School
St. Willibrord High School
St. Xavier Academy, Mother McAuley High School, 3737 W. 99th St., 60655. Tel: 773-881-6500.
Young Ladies' Seminary of the Sacred Heart Renamed Woodlands Academy of the Sacred Heart (Lake Forest)

RELIGIOUS INSTITUTES OF MEN REPRESENTED IN THE ARCHDIOCESE

For further details refer to the corresponding bracketed number in the Religious Institutes of Men or Women section.

[0120]—*Alexian Brothers*—C.F.A.
[0140]—*The Augustinians* Chicago—O.S.A.
[0200]—*Benedictine Monks*—O.S.B.
[0330]—*Brothers of the Christian Schools (Midwest Province)* (Burr Ridge, IL)—F.S.C.
[0600]—*Brothers of the Congregation of Holy Cross*—C.S.C.
[0900]—*Canons Regular of Premontre* (U.S. Circary)—O.Praem.
[]—*Canons Regular of St. John Cantius*—S.J.C.
[0400]—*Canons Regular of the Order of the Holy Cross* (Prov. of St. Odilia, Minneapolis, MN)—O.S.C.
[0470]—*The Capuchin Friars*—O.F.M.Cap.
[0270]—*Carmelite Fathers & Brothers* (Most Pure Heart of Mary)—O.Carm.
[0340]—*Cistercian Fathers* (Polish Congr.)—O.Cist.
[0360]—*Claretian Missionaries*—C.M.F.
[1320]—*Clerics of St. Viator* (Chicago, IL)—C.S.V.
[0380]—*Comboni Missionaries of the Heart of Jesus-Verona*—M.C.C.J.
[0310]—*Congregation of Christian Brothers*—C.F.C.
[0750]—*Congregation of Marianhill Missionaries*—C.M.M.
[0220]—*Congregation of the Blessed Sacrament* (Rome, Italy)—S.S.S.
[]—*Congregation of the Holy Spirit* (Eastern Prov.)—C.S.Sp.
[1330]—*Congregation of the Mission* (Western Prov.)—C.M.
[1210]—*Congregation of the Missionaries of St. Charles* (Western Prov.)—C.S.
[1000]—*Congregation of the Passion* (Western Prov.)—C.P.
[1130]—*Congregation of the Priests of the Sacred Heart*—S.C.J.
[1080]—*Congregation of the Resurrection* (Chicago Prov.)—C.R.
[0480]—*Conventual Franciscans* (St. Bonaventure, Our Lady of Consolation Provs.)—O.F.M.Conv.
[0260]—*Discalced Carmelite Friars*—O.C.D.
[0520]—*Franciscan Friars* (Sacred Heart, Assumption of B.V.M. Provs.; Commissariats of the Holy Cross, Holy Family)—O.F.M.
[0690]—*Jesuit Fathers and Brothers* (Chicago, Polish, Lithuanian Provs.)—S.J.
[0730]—*Legionnaires of Christ*—L.C.
[0740]—*Marian Fathers*—M.I.C.
[0770]—*The Marist Brothers*—F.M.S.
[0780]—*Marist Fathers*—S.M.
[0800]—*Maryknoll*—M.M.
[0830]—*Mill Hill Missionaries*—M.H.M.
[0860]—*Missionhurst Congregation of the Immaculate Heart of Mary*—C.I.C.M.
[0910]—*Oblates of Mary Immaculate*—O.M.I.
[0430]—*Order of Preachers-Dominicans*—O.P.
[1030]—*Paulist Fathers* (New York Prov.)—C.S.P.
[0610]—*Priests of the Congregation of Holy Cross* (Notre Dame, IN)—C.S.C.
[1070]—*Redemptorist Fathers* (Denver)—C.SS.R.
[1190]—*Salesians of Don Bosco*—S.D.B.
[1220]—*Servants of Charity*—S.C.
[1240]—*Servites* (Chicago, IL)—O.S.M.
[1260]—*Society of Christ*—S.Ch.
[0760]—*Society of Mary*—S.M.
[0370]—*Society of St. Columban*—S.S.C.
[1200]—*Society of the Divine Savior*—S.D.S.
[0420]—*Society of the Divine Word*—S.V.D.
[1060]—*Society of the Precious Blood* (Kansas City Prov.)—C.PP.S.
[1170]—*St. Patrick Missionary Society*—S.P.S.
[1360]—*Xaverian Missionary Fathers*—S.X.

RELIGIOUS INSTITUTES OF WOMEN REPRESENTED IN THE ARCHDIOCESE

[0100]—*Adorers of the Blood of Christ*—A.S.C.
[0230]—*Benedictine Sisters of Pontifical Jurisdiction* (Chicago, IL; Duluth, MN)—O.S.B.
[0690]—*Comboni Missionary Sisters*—C.M.S.
[3110]—*Congregation of Our Lady of the Retreat in the Cenacle*—R.C.
[1860]—*Congregation of the Handmaids of the Precious Blood*—H.P.B.
[2100]—*Congregation of the Humility of Mary*—C.H.M.
[]—*Congregation of the Mother of Carmel*—C.M.C.
[0460]—*Congregation of the Sisters of Charity of the Incarnate Word*—C.C.V.I.
[3710]—*Congregation of the Sisters of Saint Agnes*—C.S.A.
[3832]—*Congregation of the Sisters of St. Joseph*—C.S.J.
[1920]—*Congregation of the Sisters of the Holy Cross*—C.S.C.
[1780]—*Congregation of the Sisters of the Third Order of St. Francis of Perpetual Adoration*—F.S.P.A.
[1710]—*Congregation of the Third Order of St. Francis of Mary Immaculate, Joliet, IL*—O.S.F.
[1730]—*Congregation of the Third Order of St. Francis, Oldenburg, IN*—O.S.F.
[0760]—*Daughters of Charity of St. Vincent de Paul*—D.C.
[0793]—*Daughters of Divine Love*—D.D.L.
[0940]—*Daughters of St. Mary of Providence*—D.S.M.P.
[0810]—*Daughters of the Heart of Mary*—D.H.M.
[0420]—*Discalced Carmelite Nuns*—O.C.D.
[1070-03]—*Dominican Sisters*—O.P.
[1070-07]—*Dominican Sisters*—O.P.
[1070-27]—*Dominican Sisters*—O.P.
[1070-13]—*Dominican Sisters*—O.P.
[1070-10]—*Dominican Sisters*—O.P.
[1115]—*Dominican Sisters of Peace*—O.P.
[1170]—*Felician Sisters*—C.S.S.F.
[1370]—*Franciscan Missionaries of Mary*—F.M.M.
[1210]—*Franciscan Sisters of Chicago*—O.S.F.
[1230]—*Franciscan Sisters of Christian Charity*—O.S.F.
[1310]—*Franciscan Sisters of Little Falls, Minnesota*—O.S.F.
[1415]—*Franciscan Sisters of Mary*—F.S.M.
[1430]—*Franciscan Sisters of Our Lady of Perpetual Help*—O.S.F.
[1450]—*Franciscan Sisters of the Sacred Heart*—O.S.F.
[1240]—*Franciscan Sisters, Daughters of the Sacred Hearts of Jesus and Mary*—O.S.F.
[2370]—*Institute of the Blessed Virgin Mary (Loretto Sisters)*—I.B.V.M.
[2330]—*Little Sisters of Jesus*—L.S.J.
[2320]—*Little Sisters of the Holy Family*—P.S.S.F.
[2340]—*Little Sisters of the Poor*—L.S.P.
[3570]—*Mantellate Sisters, Servants of Mary of Blue Island*—O.S.M.
[2420]—*Marist Missionary Sisters*—S.M.S.M.
[2430]—*Marist Sisters Congregation of Mary*—S.M.
[2470]—*Maryknoll Sisters of St. Dominic*—M.M.
[2480]—*Medical Missionaries of Mary*—M.M.M.
[2680]—*Misericordia Sisters*—S.M.
[2710]—*Missionaries of Charity*—M.C.
[2865]—*Missionaries of the Sacred Heart of Jesus and Our Lady of Guadalupe*—M.S.C.Gpe.
[2790]—*Missionary Servants of the Most Blessed Trinity*—M.S.B.T.
[2715]—*Missionary Sisters of Christ the King for Polonia*—M.CHR.
[2900]—*Missionary Sisters of St. Charles Borromeo*—M.S.C.S.
[3990]—*Missionary Sisters of St. Peter Claver*—S.S.P.C.
[2860]—*Missionary Sisters of the Sacred Heart*—M.S.C.
[3530]—*Missionary Sisters Servants of the Holy Spirit*—S.Sp.S.
[]—*Oblate Sisters of Jesus the Priest*—O.J.S.
[3040]—*Oblate Sisters of Providence*—O.S.P.
[3130]—*Our Lady of Victory Missionary Sisters*—O.L.V.M.
[0950]—*Pious Society Daughters of St. Paul*—F.S.P.
[3230]—*Poor Handmaids of Jesus Christ*—P.H.J.C.
[3440]—*Religious Hospitallers of Saint Joseph*—R.H.S.J.
[2970]—*School Sisters of Notre Dame*—S.S.N.D.
[1680]—*School Sisters of St. Francis*—O.S.F.
[3590]—*Servants of Mary (Servite Sisters)*—O.S.M.
[3520]—*Servants of the Holy Heart of Mary*—S.S.C.M.
[0440]—*Sisters of Charity of Cincinnati, Ohio*—S.C.
[0570]—*Sisters of Charity of Seton Hill, Greensburg, Pennsylvania*—S.C.
[0630]—*Sisters of Charity of St. Vincent de Paul*—S.V.Z.
[0430]—*Sisters of Charity of the Blessed Virgin Mary*—B.V.M.
[0660]—*Sisters of Christian Charity*—S.C.C.
[0990]—*Sisters of Divine Providence*—C.D.P.
[2360]—*Sisters of Loretto at the Foot of the Cross*—S.L.
[2575]—*Sisters of Mercy of the Americas* (Chicago, IL)—R.S.M.
[3000]—*Sisters of Notre Dame de Namur*—S.N.D.deN.
[3080]—*Sisters of Our Lady Christian Doctrine*—R.C.D.
[3350]—*Sisters of Providence*—S.P.
[3360]—*Sisters of Providence of Saint Mary-of-the-Woods, IN*—S.P.
[1620]—*Sisters of Saint Francis of Millvale, Pennsylvania*—O.S.F.
[1540]—*Sisters of Saint Francis, Clinton, Iowa*—O.S.F.
[3780]—*Sisters of Saints Cyril and Methodius*—SS.C.M.
[3740]—*Sisters of St. Casimir*—S.S.C.
[1520]—*Sisters of St. Francis of Christ the King*—O.S.F.
[1640]—*Sisters of St. Francis of Perpetual Adoration*—O.S.F.
[1570]—*Sisters of St. Francis of the Holy Family*—O.S.F.
[1800]—*Sisters of St. Francis of the Third Order Regular*—O.S.F.
[3830-15]—*Sisters of St. Joseph*—C.S.J.
[3840]—*Sisters of St. Joseph of Carondelet*—C.S.J.
[3930]—*Sisters of St. Joseph of the Third Order of St. Francis*—S.S.J.-T.O.S.F.
[0260]—*Sisters of the Blessed Sacrament for Indians and Colored People*—S.B.S.
[2980]—*Sisters of the Congregation de Notre Dame*—C.N.D.
[1030]—*Sisters of the Divine Savior*—S.D.S.
[1830]—*Sisters of the Good Shepherd*—R.G.S.
[1970]—*Sisters of the Holy Family of Nazareth*—C.S.F.N.
[2140]—*Sisters of the Immaculate Conception of the Blessed Virgin Mary* (Lithuanian)
[2270]—*Sisters of the Little Company of Mary*—L.C.M.
[2350]—*Sisters of the Living Word*—S.L.W.
[3320]—*Sisters of the Presentation of the B.V.M*—P.B.V.M.
[3480]—*Sisters of the Resurrection*—C.R.
[1705]—*Sisters of the Third Order of St. Francis of Assisi*—O.S.F.
[1720]—*Sisters of the Third Order of St. Francis of the Congregation of Our Lady of Lourdes*—O.S.F.
[2150]—*Sisters, Servants of the Immaculate Heart of Mary*—I.H.M.
[1890]—*Society of Helpers*—H.H.S.
[4060]—*Society of the Holy Child Jesus*—S.H.C.J.
[4070]—*Society of the Sacred Heart*—R.S.C.J.

ARCHDIOCESAN CEMETERIES

CHICAGO. *Central Office*, Catholic Cemeteries: 1400 S. Wolf Rd., Hillside, 60162-2197. Tel: 708-449-6100; Fax: 708-449-3419. Web: www.cathcemchgo.org. Rev. Msgr. Patrick J. Pollard, Archdiocesan Dir.; Mr. Roman Szabelski, Exec. Dir.
St. Boniface
St. Casimir
St. Henry
Mt. Olivet

CALUMET CITY. *Holy Cross*
CRESTWOOD. *St. Benedict*
DES PLAINES. *All Saints*
EVANSTON. *Calvary*
EVERGREEN PARK. *St. Mary*
FOX LAKE. *St. Bede*
FREMONT CENTER. *St. Mary*
GLENWOOD. *Assumption*
HIGHLAND PARK. *St. Mary*
HILLSIDE. *Mt. Carmel*
Our Lady of Sorrows
Queen of Heaven
JUSTICE. *Resurrection*
LAKE FOREST. *St. Mary*
LEMONT. *St. Alphonsus*
SS. Cyril & Methodius
St. James, Sag Bridge
St. Patrick
LIBERTYVILLE. *Ascension*
NILES. *St. Adalbert*
Maryhill
NORTHBROOK. *Sacred Heart*
OAK FOREST. *St. Gabriel*
ORLAND PARK. *St. Michael*
PALATINE. *St. Michael the Archangel*
PARK FOREST. *St. Anne*
RIVER GROVE. *St. Joseph*
ROSENCRANS. *St. Patrick*
ROUND LAKE. *St. Joseph*
SAUK VILLAGE. *St. James*
SKOKIE. *St. Peter*
STEGER. *Calvary*
VOLO. *St. Peter*
WAUCONDA. *Transfiguration*
WAUKEGAN. *St. Mary*
WEST LAKE FOREST. *St. Patrick*
WILMETTE. *St. Joseph*
WORTH. *Holy Sepulchre*

NECROLOGY

† Cimarrusti, Rev. Msgr. Francis A., (Retired)—Died March 29, 2011
† Carroll, Gilbert A., (Retired)—Died March 20, 2011
† Cassidy, Francis P., (Retired)—Died Feb. 18, 2011
† Close, James J., (Retired)—Died Aug. 31, 2011
† Enright, John P., (Retired)—Died Feb. 14, 2011
† Fitzpatrick, Edmund J., (Retired)—Died Jan. 5, 2011
† Hanley, Lawrence F., (Retired)—Died June 1, 2011
† Hastings, William J., Chicago, IL St. William.—Died Feb. 10, 2011
† Kaminski, Thomas J., (Retired)—Died Feb. 12, 2011
† Kauzlarich, John J., (Retired)—Died Sept. 20, 2011
† Kobus, John J., (On Assignment)—Died Sept. 17, 2011
† McHugh, Thomas J., (Retired)—Died May 19, 2011
† O'Brien, John E., (Retired)—Died July 27, 2011
† Schendt, Richard L.—Died 2011
† Tlapa, Richard J., (Retired)—Died May 28, 2011
† Valker, Richard J., (Retired)—Died Oct. 27, 2011

An asterisk (*) denotes an organization that has established tax-exempt status directly with the IRS and is not covered by the USCCB Group Ruling.

Archdiocese of Cincinnati

(Archidioecesis Cincinnatensis)

Most Reverend

DENNIS M. SCHNURR, J.C.D., D.D.

Archbishop of Cincinnati; ordained July 20, 1974; appointed Bishop of Duluth January 18, 2001; ordained April 2, 2001; appointed Coadjutor Archbishop of Cincinnati October 17, 2008; installed December 7, 2008; Succeeded to the See December 21, 2009. *Office: 100 E. Eighth St., Cincinnati, OH 45202-2129.*

Most Reverend

DANIEL E. PILARCZYK, S.T.D., PH.D., D.D.

Archbishop Emeritus of Cincinnati; ordained December 20, 1959; appointed Titular Bishop of Hodelm and Auxiliary Bishop of Cincinnati November 12, 1974; consecrated December 20, 1974; appointed Archbishop of Cincinnati November 2, 1982; installed December 20, 1982; retired December 21, 2009. *Office: 100 E. Eighth St., Cincinnati, OH 45202-2129.*

Archdiocesan Offices: 100 E. Eighth St., Cincinnati, OH 45202-2129. Tel: 513-421-3131; Fax: 513-421-6225.

Web: www.catholiccincinnati.org

Most Reverend

JOSEPH R. BINZER

Auxiliary Bishop of Cincinnati; ordained June 4, 1994; appointed Titular Bishop of Subbar and Auxiliary Bishop of Cincinnati April 6, 2011; consecrated June 9, 2011. *Office: 100 E. Eighth St., Cincinnati, OH 45202-2129.*

Square Miles 8,543.

Erected Diocese June 19, 1821; Archdiocese July 19, 1850.

Comprises that part of the State of Ohio lying south of 40 degrees, 41 minutes, being the 19 Counties south of the northern line of Mercer, Auglaize, and Logan, all west of the eastern line of Logan, Champaign, Clark, Greene, Clinton, Highland and Adams Counties.

For legal titles of parishes and archdiocesan institutions, consult the Chancery Office.

STATISTICAL OVERVIEW

Personnel	
Archbishops	1
Retired Archbishops	1
Auxiliary Bishops	1
Priests: Diocesan Active in Diocese	176
Priests: Diocesan Active Outside Diocese	4
Priests: Retired, Sick or Absent	95
Number of Diocesan Priests	275
Religious Priests in Diocese	237
Total Priests in Diocese	512
Extern Priests in Diocese	14
Ordinations:	
Diocesan Priests	3
Religious Priests	1
Transitional Deacons	4
Permanent Deacons in Diocese	201
Total Brothers	122
Total Sisters	878
Parishes	
Parishes	214
With Resident Pastor:	
Resident Diocesan Priests	131
Resident Religious Priests	21
Without Resident Pastor:	
Administered by Priests	62
Professional Ministry Personnel:	
Brothers	10
Sisters	30
Lay Ministers	290
Welfare	
Catholic Hospitals	9
Total Assisted	1,564,493
Homes for the Aged	13
Total Assisted	4,044
Residential Care of Children	1
Total Assisted	1,300
Day Care Centers	1
Total Assisted	302
Special Centers for Social Services	9
Total Assisted	113,186
Residential Care of Disabled	1
Total Assisted	40
Other Institutions	4
Total Assisted	55,235
Educational	
Seminaries, Diocesan	1
Students from This Diocese	24
Students from Other Diocese	15
Diocesan Students in Other Seminaries	8
Total Seminarians	32
Colleges and Universities	4
Total Students	20,747
High Schools, Diocesan and Parish	19
Total Students	9,937
High Schools, Private	4
Total Students	3,334
Elementary Schools, Diocesan and Parish	86
Total Students	28,003
Elementary Schools, Private	7
Total Students	1,989
Catechesis/Religious Education:	
High School Students	4,797
Elementary Students	23,662
Total Students under Catholic Instruction	92,501
Teachers in the Diocese:	
Priests	12
Brothers	11
Sisters	41
Lay Teachers	2,655
Vital Statistics	
Receptions into the Church:	
Infant Baptism Totals	5,525
Minor Baptism Totals	316
Adult Baptism Totals	437
Received into Full Communion	748
First Communions	6,899
Confirmations	6,839
Marriages:	
Catholic	1,255
Interfaith	606
Total Marriages	1,861
Deaths	3,928
Total Catholic Population	477,338
Total Population	2,994,520

Former Bishops—Rt. Rev. EDWARD D. FENWICK, O.P., D.D., ord. Feb. 23, 1793; cons. Jan. 13, 1822; died Sept. 26, 1832; Most Revs. JOHN BAPTIST PURCELL, D.D., ord. May 20, 1826; cons. Oct. 13, 1833; appt. Archbishop, July 19, 1850; died July 4, 1883; WILLIAM HENRY ELDER, D.D., cons. Bishop of Natchez May 3, 1857; appt. Titular Bishop of Avar, and Coadjutor to the Archbishop of Cincinnati cum jure successionis, Jan. 30, 1880; succeeded to the See of Cincinnati, July 4, 1883; died Oct. 31, 1904; HENRY K. MOELLER, D.D., cons. Bishop of Columbus, Aug. 25, 1900; promoted to Archiepiscopal See of Areopolis and made Coadjutor to the Most Rev. William Henry Elder cum jure successionis, April 27, 1903; succeeded to the See of Cincinnati, Oct. 31, 1904; died Jan. 5, 1925; JOHN T. MCNICHOLAS, O.P., S.T.M., cons. Bishop of Duluth, MN Sept. 8, 1918; promoted to Archiepiscopal See of Cincinnati, July 8, 1925; appt. Assistant at the Pontifical Throne, Feb. 18, 1923; died April 22, 1950; KARL J. ALTER, D.D., LL.D., cons. Bishop of Toledo, June 17, 1931; appt. Assistant to the Pontifical Throne, May 30, 1950; elevated to Archbishop of Cincinnati, June 21, 1950; retired July 23, 1969; died Aug. 23, 1977; PAUL F. LEIBOLD, D.D., J.C.D., appt. Titular Bishop of Trebenna and Auxiliary of Cincinnati, April 10, 1958; cons. June 17, 1958; installed as Bishop of Evansville, June 15, 1966; transferred to Archdiocese of Cincinnati, July 23, 1969; installed Oct. 2, 1969; died June 1, 1972; His Eminence JOSEPH CARDINAL BERNARDIN, D.D., appt. Titular Bishop of Lugura and Auxiliary Bishop of Atlanta, March 9, 1966; cons. April 26, 1966; appt. Archbishop of Cincinnati, Nov. 21, 1972; installed Dec. 19, 1972; appt. Archbishop of Chicago, July 10, 1982; installed Aug. 25, 1982; created Cardinal Priest, Feb. 2, 1983; died Nov. 14, 1996; Most Rev. DANIEL E. PILARCZYK, S.T.D., Ph.D., D.D., ord. Dec. 20, 1959; appt. Titular Bishop of Hodelm and Auxiliary Bishop of Cincinnati Nov. 12, 1974; cons. Dec. 20, 1974; appt. Archbishop of Cincinnati Nov. 2, 1982; installed Dec. 20, 1982; retired Dec. 21, 2009.

Vicar General—Most Rev. JOSEPH R. BINZER, J.C.L.

Archdiocesan Department Directors—Ms. KATHLEEN DONNELLAN, Dir., Community Svcs.; Dr. JIM RIGG, Ph.D., Dir., Educational Svcs.; Rev. STEVE J. ANGI, Dir., Exec. Svcs.; Mr. RICHARD KELLY, Dir., Financial Svcs.; Rev. LEONARD C. WENKE, Dir., Pastoral Svcs.; Mr. MICHAEL E. VANDERBURGH, Dir. Stewardship Svcs.

Presbyteral Council—Most Revs. DENNIS M. SCHNURR, J.C.D., D.D.; JOSEPH R. BINZER, J.C.L.; Revs. STEVE J. ANGI; DOHRMAN W. BYERS; CHRISTOPHER C. COLEMAN; ANTHONY E. CUTCHER; TERENCE J. HAMILTON; EDWARD M. JACH, S.M.; J. DENNIS JASPERS; TIMOTHY S. KALLAHER; HAROLD W. KIST (Retired); ERIC J. KNAPP, S.J.; GREGORY J. KONERMAN; CARL J. LANGENDERFER, O.F.M.; THOMAS M. MANNEBACH; WILLIAM O'DONNELL, C.PP.S.; JAMES SHAPPELLE; LARRY R. THARP; JOHN W. TONKIN; LEONARD C. WENKE.

Vicarri Foranei (Deans)—Revs. JOSEPH A. ROBINSON, Cathedral Deanery; TIMOTHY S. BUNCH, St. Andrew Deanery; LEONARD C. WENKE, St. Francis de Sales Deanery; JEFFREY M. KEMPER, Ph.D., St. Lawrence Deanery; GEORGE JACQUEMIN, St. Margaret Mary Deanery; LARRY R. THARP,

Hamilton Deanery; WILLIAM C. WAGNER, St. Martin Deanery; LAWRENCE E. MIERENFELD, Dayton Deanery; DENNIS J. CAYLOR, J.C.L., Springfield Deanery; STEVEN L. SHOUP, Sidney Deanery; THOMAS M. MANNEBACH, St. Mary's Deanery.

Consultors—Most Rev. JOSEPH R. BINZER, J.C.L.; Revs. DOHRMAN W. BYERS; CHRISTOPHER C. COLEMAN; TERENCE J. HAMILTON; J. DENNIS JASPERS; TIMOTHY S. KALLAHER; GREGORY J. KONERMAN; THOMAS M. MANNEBACH; JAMES SHAPPELLE; LARRY R. THARP; JOHN W. TONKIN; LEONARD C. WENKE.

Archdiocesan Offices

Unless otherwise indicated, all Archdiocesan Offices and Directors are located at: *100 E. Eighth St., Cincinnati, 45202*. Tel: 513-421-3131; Fax: 513-421-6225.

Office of the Archbishop—LINDA CHOUTEAU, Exec. Sec. to the Archbishop. Tel: 513-263-6612; Fax: 513-421-7537.

Office of Mediation—VACANT. Tel: 513-421-3131, Ext. 2810.

Department of Executive Services

Director—Rev. STEVE J. ANGI.

Chancery—

Chancellor—Rev. STEVE J. ANGI, J.C.L.

Assistant Chancellor—Rev. THOMAS A. SNODGRASS, J.C.L.

Archivist—DON H. BUSKE (Special Address & Phone No. for Historical Archives Only), 212 E. Eighth St., Cincinnati, 45202. Tel: 513-621-2086.

Imprimatur Censors—Revs. CHRISTOPHER R. ARMSTRONG, J.C.D., St. Antonius, 1500 Linneman Rd., Cincinnati, 45238. Tel: 513-922-5400; EARL K. FERNANDES, S.T.D., Mt. St. Mary Seminary, 6616 Beechmont Ave., Cincinnati, 45230. Tel: 513-233-4245; RICHARD L. KLUG, S.T.L. (Retired), 3776 Francis Ave., Cincinnati, 45211. Tel: 513-662-3049; DONALD G. MCCARTHY, Ph.D. (Retired), St. Ignatius Loyola, 5222 N. Bend Rd., Cincinnati, 45247. Tel: 513-661-6565; TIMOTHY P. SCHEHR, Ph.D., Mt. St. Mary Seminary, 6616 Beechmont Ave., Cincinnati, 45230. Tel: 513-231-6139; ROBERT A. STRICKER, S.T.D. (Retired), 5560 Kirby Ave., Cincinnati, 45239. Tel: 513-541-5560; RICHARD W. WALLING, S.T.D. Coldwater Cluster (St. Anthony, St. Anthony; St. Mary, Philothea; and Holy Trinity, Coldwater) 116 E. Main St., Coldwater, 45828. Tel: 419-678-4802; JOHN E. WESSLING, S.T.D. (Retired), 10095 Wayside Dr., #259, Cincinnati, 45241. Tel: 513-779-5350; DAVID L. ZINK, M.A., Saint Nicholas Parish, P.O. Box 9, Osgood, 45351. Tel: 419-582-2531.

Communications Office—DAN ANDRIACCO, Dir.

Newspaper-"The Catholic Telegraph"—Most Rev. DENNIS M. SCHNURR, J.C.D., D.D., Publisher.

Office of Religious—Sr. MARILYN KERBER, S.N.D.deN., Dir.

Permanent Diaconate Office—BERNARD J. MERSMANN.

Victim Assistance Coordinator—SANDY KEISER, L.I.S.W. Tel: 513-263-6623. Email: skeiser@catholiccharitiesswo.org.

Tribunal-Archdiocese of Cincinnati—Tel: 513-421-3131; Fax: 513-723-1035.

Director—Sr. VICTORIA VONDENBERGER, R.S.M., J.C.L.

Judicial Vicar—Rev. MANUEL VIERA, O.F.M., J.C.L.

Adjutant Judicial Vicars—Revs. STEVE J. ANGI, J.C.L.; EDWIN F. GEARHART, J.C.L.; BARRY M. WINDHOLTZ, J.C.L.

Judges—Rev. CHRISTOPHER R. ARMSTRONG, J.C.D.; Deacon MICHAEL A. ASCOLESE; Most Rev. JOSEPH R. BINZER, J.C.L.; Rev. JAMES A. BRAMLAGE (Retired); Deacon STEVEN R. BROWN, J.C.L.; Revs. DAVID E. FAY; JOHN P. FISCHER; GERALD R. HAEMMERLE, M.A.; TIMOTHY S. KALLAHER; RAYMOND C. KELLERMAN; RICHARD L. KLUG, S.T.L. (Retired); NORMAN W. LANGENBRUNNER; THOMAS C. NOLKER; ROBERT A. OBERMEYER (Retired); R. MARC SHERLOCK; TERRANCE W. SMITH; THOMAS A. SNODGRASS, J.C.L.; LARRY R. THARP; FRANCIS W. VOELLMECKE, Ph.D. (Retired); JOHN R. WHITE, J.C.L.

Defenders of the Bond—Rev. DENNIS J. CAYLOR, J.C.L.; Sr. VICTORIA VONDENBERGER, R.S.M., J.C.L.; Rev. WILLIAM H. WYSONG, J.C.L.

Promoter of Justice—Sr. VICTORIA VONDENBERGER, R.S.M., J.C.L.

Assessors—Mrs. KELLY M. TERRY; Miss CHRISTINE M. GATELY.

Auditors—Mrs. CANDY L. ENGELKE; Mrs. PATRICIA A. KLEINER; Ms. AMI R. QUINN.

Vocations Office—Rev. KYLE E. SCHNIPPEL, Dir.; Mr. WAYNE TOPP, Asst. Dir.

Department of Community Services

Director—Ms. KATHLEEN DONNELLAN.

Archdiocesan Office of Catholic Charities—Ms. KATHLEEN DONNELLAN, Dir.

Catholic Residential Services of Archdiocese of Cincinnati with People with Mental Retardation—100 E. Eighth St., Cincinnati, 45202. Tel: 513-784-0400; Fax: 513-333-3172. Co Directors: AMY LINZ; PEGGY FRYER.

Catholic Charities of Southwestern Ohio—Ms. KATHLEEN DONNELLAN, CEO, Cincinnati Office: 100 E. Eighth St., Cincinnati, 45202. Tel: 513-241-7745.

Su Casa Hispanic Center—GIOVANNA ALVAREZ, Contact Person, 7036 Fairpark Ave., Cincinnati, 45216. Email: galvarez@catholiccharitiesswo.org. Web: www.catholiccharitiesswo.org.

Hamilton Office—140 N. Fifth St., Hamilton, 45011. Tel: 513-863-6129.

Springfield Office—701 E. Columbia St., Springfield, 45504. Tel: 937-325-8715.

Catholic Social Services of Miami Valley—LAURA ROESCH, Exec. Dir., 922 W. Riverview Dr., Dayton, 45407. Tel: 937-223-7217.

Rural Life Conference—ANTHONY STIERITZ, Dir., 1436 Needmore Rd., Dayton, 45414. Tel: 937-224-3026.

Catholic Social Action—ANTHONY STIERITZ, Dir., 100 E. 8th St., Cincinnati, 45202. Tel: 513-421-3131. Dayton Office: PAM LONG, 1436 Needmore Rd., Dayton, 45414. Tel: 937-224-3026.

Department of Educational Services

Director—Dr. JIM RIGG, Ph.D.

School Office—Dr. JIM RIGG, Ph.D., Supt., Archdiocesan Schools; Dr. LAURA MEIBERS, Deputy Supt., Archdiocesan Schools Office, 1436 Needmore Rd., Dayton, 45414. Tel: 937-223-5151.

CISE (Catholic Inner-City Schools Education) Office—Ms. CARY B. POWELL, Dir., 100 E. 8th St., Cincinnati, 45202. Tel: 513-421-3131; Fax: 513-421-6271.

Office of Evangelization and Catechesis—KENNETH GLEASON, Archdiocesan Dir., 100 E. Eighth St., Cincinnati, 45202. Tel: 513-421-3131; DAVID RILEY, Regl. Dir., Dayton Office of Evangelization and Catechesis, 1436 Needmore Rd., Dayton, 45414. Tel: 937-223-4075; VACANT, Sidney Office of Evangelization and Catechesis, 119 E. Water St., Sidney, 45365. Tel: 937-498-1192.

Department of Financial Services

Chief Financial Officer—Mr. RICHARD KELLY.

Controller—Mr. STEPHEN E. BURGER.

Senior Accountant—Mr. DANIEL R. UMBERG.

Director of Benefits and Risk Management—BARBARA A. WALSH.

Assistant Directors—Mrs. ANNIE LIPPS ZOZ, Asst. Dir. & Payroll Mgr.; Ms. ANNE MORROW, Accts. Payable & Receivable.

Cemeteries—Ms. DEBRA K. CRANE, Esq., Dir. Tel: 513-489-0300.

Office of Property Management-Central Services—GARY RAFFEL, Dir.

Office of Human Resources—BILL HANCOCK, Dir.

Department of Pastoral Services

Director—Rev. LEONARD C. WENKE.

Campus Ministry—Dr. JANE STEINHAUSER, Dir., 444 W. Third St., Dayton, 45402. (See Special Listing: Campus Ministry).

African American Catholic Ministries—Deacon ROYCE E. WINTERS, Dir.

Family Life—Ms. COLLEEN GERKE, Dir. Dayton: Ms. NOREEN WENDELN, 1436 Needmore Rd., Dayton, 45414. Tel: 937-222-0227. Northern Area: Mr. JOSH DANIS, 119 E. Water St., Sidney, 45365. Tel: 937-492-4449.

Missions—

Pontifical Mission Aid Societies—Rev. LEONARD C. WENKE.

Missions Office—Dr. MIKE GABLE, Dir.

Pastoral Council Secretariat—Rev. RAYMOND E. LARGER, Exec. Sec.

Priestly Formation—Rev. THOMAS P. DIFOLCO, Dir.

Priests' Personnel Director—Most Rev. JOSEPH R. BINZER, Dir.

Hispanic Catholic Ministry, Cincinnati—VACANT, 115 W. Seymour Ave., Cincinnati, 45216. Tel: 513-948-1760.

Hispanic Catholic Ministry, Dayton—Sr. MARIA FRANCINE STACY, S.N.D., Holy Family/Nazareth Center, 310 Allen St., Dayton, 45410. Tel: 937-258-1309.

Archdiocesan Office of Hispanic Ministry—Rev. LOUIS GASPARINI, M.C.C.J., Dir., 100 E. Eighth St., Cincinnati, 45202. Tel: 513-421-3131.

Hamilton Hispanic Ministry—Ms. DINA BEACH, 224 Dayton St., Hamilton, 45011. Tel: 513-894-6300.

Worship—Ms. KAREN KANE, Dir., 100 E. Eighth St., Cincinnati, 45202. Tel: 513-421-3131.

Youth and Young Adult—Mr. SEAN REYNOLDS, Dir., 100 E. Eighth St., Cincinnati, 45202. Tel: 513-421-3131; TIMOTHY E. COLBERT, Regl. Dir., Dayton & Northern Area: 1436 Needmore Rd., Dayton, 45414. Tel: 937-223-1001.

Department of Stewardship

Department of Stewardship—Mr. MICHAEL E. VANDERBURGH, Dir.; Mr. BRIAN C. DOYLE, Assoc. Dir.

CLERGY, PARISHES, MISSIONS AND PAROCHIAL SCHOOLS

GREATER CINCINNATI

(HAMILTON COUNTY)

1—ST. PETER IN CHAINS CATHEDRAL (1822) Rev. Barry M. Windholtz; Deacon David Klingshirn; Rev. Raymond E. Larger.
Res.: 325 W. Eighth St., 45202. Tel: 513-421-5355; Fax: 513-241-9517. Email: info@stpeterinchainscathedral.org. Web: www.stpeterinchainscathedral.org.
Church: Tel: 513-421-5354.

2—ALL SAINTS (Kenwood) (1948) Rev. J. Dennis Jaspers; Deacons Amado Lim, Pastoral Assoc.; Robert J. Leever, Asst. Pastoral Assoc.; Marianna Kuhn, Business Mgr.; Ron Miller, Music Dir.
Res.: 8939 Montgomery Rd., 45236. Tel: 513-792-4600; Fax: 513-792-4730. Web: www.allsaints.cc.
School—(Grades K-8) Tel: 513-792-4732; Fax: 513-792-7990. Mr. Daniel Stringer, Prin.; Patti Lewis, Librarian. Lay Teachers 29; Students 453.
Catechesis/Religious Program—Tel: 513-792-4603; Fax: 513-792-4730. Ginny Rush, Dir. Faith Formation; Micki Harrell, Dir. Devel. Students 195.

3—ST. ALOYSIUS GONZAGA (Bridgetown) (1866) Rev. W. Michael Hay; Deacon Jerry Schneider.
Res.: 4366 Bridgetown Rd., 45211. Tel: 513-574-4840; Fax: 513-574-4402. Email: staloysius5@fuse.net. Web: saintals.org.
School—(Grades K-8), 4390 Bridgetown Rd., 45211. Tel: 513-574-4035; Fax: 513-574-5421. James Leisring, Prin. Lay Teachers 14; Students 194.
Catechesis/Religious Program—Tel: 513-574-4840; Fax: 513-574-4402. Students 47.

4—ST. ALOYSIUS-ON-THE-OHIO (1873) Rev. Richard E. Dressman; Deacon Luis Riva Saleta.
Res.: 134 Whipple St., 45233. Tel: 513-941-3445; Fax: 513-941-2257. Web: www.saoto.org.
School—(Grades PreK-8), 6207 Portage, 45233. Tel: 513-941-7831; Fax: 513-941-5418. Mr. Richard Harrmann, Prin.; Jean Hoferer, Librarian. Lay Teachers 12; Students 105.
Catechesis/Religious Program—Tel: 513-941-3445; Fax: 513-941-2257. Students 15.

5—ST. ANN (Groesbeck) (1953) Rev. Thomas J. Dennemann; Deacon John M. Quattrone. In Res., Revs. Shawn R. Landenwitch, Faculty, LaSalle High School; Anthony J. Muller (Retired).
Res.: 2900 W. Galbraith Rd., 45239. Tel: 513-521-8440; Fax: 513-521-7221. Email: info@saintannparish.org. Web: www.saintannparish.org.
See Our Lady of Grace, Cincinnati under Consolidated Elementary Schools located in the Institution section.
Catechesis/Religious Program—Tel: 513-729-2810. Web: www.saintannparish.org/ReligiousEd/religious_education.htm. Diane C. Ferrier, D.R.E. Students 103.

6—ANNUNCIATION OF THE BLESSED VIRGIN MARY (1910) Rev. Todd Grogan.
Res.: 3547 Clifton Ave., 45220. Tel: 513-861-1295; Fax: 513-861-6789. Web: www.annunciationbvmparish.org.
School—(Grades PreK-8), 3545 Clifton Ave., 45220. Tel: 513-221-1230; Fax: 513-281-8009. Ms. Cindy Hardesty, Prin. Lay Teachers 14; Students 158.
Catechesis/Religious Program—Tel: 513-861-1295. Students 30.

7—ST. ANTHONY (Madisonville) (1858) [CEM] Rev. David A. Lemkuhl; Sr. Carol Leveque, S.C., Pastoral Assoc.
Church & Office: 6104 Desmond St., 45227. Tel: 513-271-0920; Fax: 513-271-6630. Email: office@stanthonychurch.net. Web: www.stanthonychurch.net.
Catechesis/Religious Program—Tel: 513-271-0920; Fax: 513-271-6630. Mary Ann Putman, Coord. Faith Formation. Students 34.

8—ST. ANTONINUS (1944) Revs. Christopher R. Armstrong; Lawrence J. Mick (Retired); Deacon Robert J. Schroeder, Pastoral Assoc.
Res.: 1500 Linneman Rd., 45238. Tel: 513-922-5400; Fax: 513-451-5871. Email: saintantoninus@fuse.net. Web:

www.saintantoninus.org.
School—(Grades K-8), 5425 Julmar Dr., 45238. Tel: 513-922-2500; Fax: 513-922-5519. Jack Corey, Prin.; Marilyn Ruther, Librarian. Lay Teachers 26; Students 469.
Catechesis/Religious Program—Tel: 513-922-4759. Students 36.

9—ASSUMPTION OF THE BLESSED VIRGIN MARY (Walnut Hills) (1872) Rev. Thomas Bokenkotter.
4512 Hector Ave., 45227. Tel: 513-271-0016.

10—ST. BARTHOLOMEW (1961) Rev. Patrick J. Welsh; Deacon Michael A. Ascolese; Paul Bresciani, Pastoral Assoc. Music & Liturgy; Suzanne Engel, Pastoral Assoc. for Religious Educ.; Karen Brutz, Pastoral Assoc. for Religious Educ.; Amy Staubach, Pastoral Assoc. for Youth Ministry; Sandy Hornbach, Pastoral Assoc. for Parish Life & Hospitality; Skip Borgman, Business Mgr.
Res.: 9375 Winton Rd., 45231. Tel: 513-522-3680; Fax: 513-728-3141.
See St. John Paul II Catholic, Cincinnati under Consolidated Elementary Schools located in the Institution section.
Catechesis/Religious Program—Tel: 513-728-3146, Ext. 105; Fax: 513-728-3141. Students 52.

11—ST. BERNARD (1919) Revs. James Schutte; James Shappelle, Parochial Vicar.
Res.: 740 Circle Ave., 45232. Tel: 513-541-3732; Fax: 513-541-0362. Email: stbernardwp@fuse.net.
Catechesis/Religious Program— Twinned with Mother of Christ. Students 8.

12—ST. BERNARD (Taylor's Creek) (1867) [CEM] Rev. Donald L. Siciliano.
Res.: 7130 Harrison Rd., 45247. Tel: 513-353-4207; Fax: 513-353-9600. Email: stbernard@cinci.rr.com. Web: www.stbernardtc.catholicweb.com.
School—(Grades K-8), 7115 Springdale Rd., 45247. Tel: 513-353-4224; Fax: 513-353-3958. Web: www-.stbernardtc.org. Jane Acra, Prin. Lay Teachers 13; Students 183.
Catechesis/Religious Program—Students 55.

13—ST. BONIFACE (1863) Rev. Joseph A. Robinson; Deacon Jerry Yetter; Carol Roosa, Pastoral Admin.
Res.: 1750 Chase Ave., 45223. Tel: 513-541-1563; Fax: 513-541-1514. Email: stboniface@cinci.rr.com. Web: www.stbonifacecincinnati.com.
See St. Boniface School, Cincinnati under Consolidated Elementary Schools located in the Institution section.
Catechesis/Religious Program—Students 5.

14—ST. CATHARINE OF SIENA (1903) Rev. Anthony M. Dattilo; Therese Bower Hibdon, Pastoral Min.
Res.: 2848 Fischer Pl., 45211. Tel: 513-661-0651; Fax: 513-661-0652. Web: stcatharinesiena.org.
School—(Grades K-8), 3324 Wunder Ave., 45211. Tel: 513-481-7683; Fax: 513-481-9438. Mary Ann Bernier, Prin.; Jennifer Moore, Librarian. Lay Teachers 10; Students 185.
Catechesis/Religious Program—Students 8.

15—ST. CECILIA (Oakley) (1908) Rev. Jamie Weber.
Res.: 3105 Madison Rd., 45209. Tel: 513-871-5757; Fax: 513-533-6066. Email: fr.jamie@stceciliacincinnati.org. Web: stceciliacincinnati.org.
School—(Grades K-8), 4115 Taylor Ave., 45209. Tel: 513-533-6060; Fax: 513-533-6068. Mr. Michael Goedde, Prin. Lay Teachers 12; Students 189.
Catechesis/Religious Program—Students 35.
Parish Center—4030 Gilmore Ave., 45209.

16—CHURCH OF THE ASSUMPTION (Mount Healthy) (1854) [CEM] Revs. Jerome J. Gardner, Pastoral Admin.; Thomas A. Snodgrass, Parochial Vicar; Deacons Richard J. Reder; Robert A. Staab Jr.
Res.: 7711 Joseph St., 45231. Tel: 513-521-7274; Fax: 513-521-3728. Email: rectory@assumptionmthealthy.org. Web: www.assumptionmthealthy.org.
See Our Lady of Grace, Cincinnati under Consolidated Elementary Schools located in the Institution section.
Catechesis/Religious Program—Tel: 513-728-4941. Sr. Rose Ann Menke, C.D.P., D.R.E. Students 12.

17—CHURCH OF THE RESURRECTION (2010) Rev. Dennis Chriszt, C.PP.S.; Deacon Royce E. Winters.
Church: 1619 California Ave., 45237. Tel: 513-242-0400.

18—ST. CLARE (College Hill) (1908) Rev. George Jacquemin. In Res., Rev. Robert J. Hater (Retired).
See John Paul II Catholic, Cincinnati under Consolidated Elementary Schools located in the Institution section.
Res.: 1443 Cedar Ave., 45224. Tel: 513-541-2100; Fax: 513-541-2101. Email: stclare@one.com. Web: www.saintclareparish.org.
Catechesis/Religious Program—Students 30.

19—ST. CLEMENT (St. Bernard) (1850) Revs. Fred Link, O.F.M.; James VanVurst, O.F.M.; Deacon John P. Gerke; Marty Cunningham, Music Min.
St. Clement Friary: 4536 Vine St., 45217. Tel: 513-641-3176 (Church); 513-641-2257 (Friary); Fax: 513-641-2262 (Friary); 513-641-0149 (Church Office).
School—(Grades PreK-8), 4534 Vine St., 45217. Tel: 513-641-2137; Fax: 513-242-6036. Web: www-.stcschool.org. Mr. Jeff Eiser, Prin. Tel: 513-641-2137, Ext. 802. Sisters 2; Lay Teachers 14; Students 171.
Catechesis/Religious Program—4536 Vine St., St. Bernard, 45217. Tel: 513-641-2137, Ext. 808; Fax: 513-641-0149. Lawrence Ungerer, D.R.E. Students 28.

20—CORPUS CHRISTI (1958) Rev. James W. Meade; Deacon John Corson; Pam McLaughlin, Pastoral Assoc.; William Marshall, Pastoral Assoc. & Admin., Music & Liturgy; Deacon Larry H. Day. In Res., Rev. Robert B. Buening (Retired).
Res.: 2014 Springdale Rd., 45231. Tel: 513-825-0618; Fax: 513-825-0182. Email: info@corpuschristicommunity.org. Web: corpuschristicommunity.org.
See St. John the Baptist Catholic School, Cincinnati under Consolidated Elementary Schools in the institution section.
Catechesis/Religious Program—Tel: 513-825-0182. Students 96.

21—ST. DOMINIC (Delhi Hills) (1933) Revs. Jim J. Walsh; Chris Lack; Deacon Mark A. Bardonaro.
Res.: 4551 Delhi Pike, 45238. Tel: 513-471-7741; Fax: 513-471-0363. Email: parishoffice@stdominicdelhi.org. Web: www.stdominicdelhi.org.
School—(Grades K-8), 371 Pedretti Ave., 45238. Tel: 513-251-1276; Fax: 513-251-6428. William S. Cavanaugh, Prin.; Mrs. Linda Nutter, Librarian. Lay Teachers 26; Students 454.
Catechesis/Religious Program—Tel: 513-471-7741, Ext. 481. Email: aandriaccos@stdominicdelhi.org. Students 124.

22—ST. FRANCIS DE SALES (1849) [CEM], Collaborative cluster - see St. Robert, Bellarmine. Rev. Eugene Contadino, S.M.
Res.: 1600 Madison Rd., 45206. Tel: 513-961-1945; Fax: 513-221-4907.
School—(Grades K-8) Tel: 513-961-1953; Fax: 513-961-2900. William Shula, Prin.; Sr. Charlotte Foppe, Librarian. Brothers 1; Lay Teachers 11; Students 221.
Catechesis/Religious Program— Collaborative Cluster, see St. Robert Bellarmine.

23—ST. FRANCIS SERAPH (1859) Rev. Gregory Friedman, O.F.M.; Bro. Timothy Sucher, O.F.M., Pastoral Team.
St. Francis Friary: 1615 Vine St., 45202. Tel: 513-535-2719; Fax: 513-421-9672. Web: www.sfsparish.org.
School—(Grades PreSchool-8), 14 E. Liberty St., 45202. Tel: 513-721-7778; Fax: 513-721-5445. Web: stfrancisseraph.org/School/school.html. Mrs. Kathleen Russell, Prin. Sisters 1; Lay Teachers 12; Students 163.
Catechesis/Religious Program—

24—ST. FRANCIS XAVIER (1819) Revs. Eric J. Knapp, S.J.; John P. Murphy, S.J.; M. Joseph Casey, S.J.
Res.: 607 Sycamore St., 45202. Tel: 513-721-4045; Fax: 513-723-0451. Email: stxavier1@fuse.net. Web: www.stxchurch.org.

25—ST. GABRIEL (Glendale) (1857) Rev. David E. Fay; Deacons Herman H. Bryant; Gerald A. Flamm.
Res.: 48 W. Sharon Ave., 45246. Tel: 513-771-4700; Fax: 513-612-4545. Email: gabrielglendale@fuse.net.
See St. Gabriel Consolidated School, Cincinnati under Consolidated Elementary Schools located in the Institution section.
Catechesis/Religious Program—Fax: 513-621-4545. Rose Voulgarakis, D.R.E. Students 33.

26—ST. GERTRUDE (Madeira) (1923) Revs. Andre-Joseph LaCasse, O.P.; James M. Sullivan, O.P., Novice Master; Very Rev. Basil Cole, O.P., Prior; Revs. Joseph Clement Burns, O.P.; Ezra Sullivan, O.P., Parochial Vicar; Albert Trudel, O.P., Parochial Vicor & Asst. Novice Master. In Res., Revs. Terence Quinn, O.P.; Paul Keller, O.P.
Res.: 7630 Shawnee Run Rd., 45243. Tel: 513-561-5954; Fax: 513-527-3971. Web: www.stgertrude.org.
School—(Grades K-8), 6543 Miami Ave., 45243. Tel: 513-561-8020; Fax: 513-561-7184. Web: www-.stgertrudesch.org. Sr. Mary Aquinas, O.P, Prin.; Patricia Lacker, Librarian. Dominican Sisters (Nashville, TN) 4; Lay Teachers 22; Students 386.
Catechesis/Religious Program—Tel: 513-561-8369; Fax: 513-561-8369. Students 690.

27—GOOD SHEPHERD (1973) Revs. Robert E. Schmitz; Terrance W. Smith, Parochial Vicar; Deacons Richard W. Gallenstein, Pastoral Min.; Max Schellman, Human Resources Min.; James Jones, Coord. Family Life Ministries; Stephen P. Lindner, Dir. Liturgical Ministries; Patricia Lindner, Dir. Communications; Donna Krabbe, Dir. Educ. & Formation; Teri Cunningham, Dir. Stewardship; Rick Hagee, Dir. Music Ministry; Dan Parker, Dir. Facilities; Deacon Mark Westendorf, Dir. Pastoral Care & Outreach; Sr. Deb Wischmeyer, S.N.D., Bookkeeper; Diane Griesser, Parish Sec.
Church & Mailing Address: 8815 E. Kemper Rd., 45249. Tel: 513-489-8815; Fax: 513-489-8521. Email: gs.info@good-shepherd.org. Web: www.good-shepherd.org.
Catechesis/Religious Program—Sr. Elaine Winter, S.N.D., Coord. K-6 Formation; Emily Meyer, Coord. of Youth Formation. Students 432.

28—GUARDIAN ANGELS (Mt. Washington) (1892) [CEM] Rev. Thomas M. King; Deacons Rick Novick; Robert Fey.
Res.: 6531 Beechmont Ave., 45230. Tel: 513-231-7440; Fax: 513-624-3145. Email: office@gaparish.org. Web: www.gaparish.org.
School—(Grades K-8), 6539 Beechmont Ave., 45230. Tel: 513-624-3141; Fax: 513-624-3150. Web: www.gaschool.org. William Kenney, Prin.; Mrs. Karen Lavelle, Librarian. Lay Teachers 40; Students 565.
Catechesis/Religious Program—Tel: 513-624-3146. Students 250.

29—HOLY CROSS-IMMACULATA (Mount Adams) (1859) Rev. Martin O. Moran III; Deacon Tracy W. Jamison.
Res.: 30 Guido St., 45202. Tel: 513-721-6544; Fax: 513-721-6177. Email: holymac30@fuse.net. Web: www.hciparish.org.
Catechesis/Religious Program—

30—HOLY FAMILY (Price Hill) (1883), Includes the consolidation of Our Lady of Grace, Our Lady of Perpetual Help Parishes, Blessed Sacrament and St. Michael. Rev. James G. Kiffmeyer.
Parish Office—3006 W. 8th St., 45205. Tel: 513-921-7527; Fax: 513-921-6033. Email: holyfamily@fuse.net. Web: www.holyfamilycincinnati.com.
Res.: 814 Hawthorne Ave., 45205. Tel: 513-921-7527; Fax: 513-921-6033.
School—(Grades K-8), 3001 Price Ave., 45205. Tel: 513-921-8483; Fax: 513-921-2460. Web: www.hf-school.org. Mrs. Jennifer O'Brien, Prin. Sisters 2; Lay Teachers 20; Students 171.
Catechesis/Religious Program—
Chapel—San Antonio di Padova 1950 Queen City Ave., 45214.

31—HOLY NAME (1904) Rev. Alan Hirt, O.F.M.; Sr. Elaine Becker, C.P.P.S., Pastoral Admin.
Church: 2448 Auburn Ave., 45219. Tel: 513-721-5608.
Catechesis/Religious Program—

32—HOLY TRINITY CHURCH (Norwood) (1994) Rev. Raymond C. Kellerman.
Res.: 2420 Drex Ave., 45212. Tel: 513-366-4400; Fax: 513-366-4404. Email: holytrinity1@fuse.net. Web: www.holytrinitynorwood.org.
See St. Nicholas Academy, Cincinnati under Consolidated Elementary Schools in the institution section.
Catechesis/Religious Program—Tel: 513-791-3238; Fax: 513-686-2720. Twinned with St. John the Evangelist, Cincinnati. Students 16.

33—ST. IGNATIUS OF LOYOLA (Monfort Heights) (1946) Revs. Peter T. St. George; Donald G. McCarthy (Retired); John E. Wall (Retired); Deacon Anthony Gagliarducci; Frank Posinski, Business Mgr.; Sr. Lucy Zientek, C.D.P., Pastoral Assoc.; Ms. Patty Stretch, Music Min.
Res.: 5222 North Bend Rd., 45247. Tel: 513-661-6565; Fax: 513-389-3241. Email: office@sainti.org. Web: www.sainti.org.
School—(Grades K-8) Tel: 513-389-3242; Fax: 513-389-3255. Timothy Reilly, Prin. Lay Teachers 44; Students 998.
Catechesis/Religious Program—Kris Schoettmer, C.R.E.; Liz Riesser, Junior High Youth Min. Students 140.

34—IMMACULATE HEART OF MARY (Forestville) (1944) Revs. Thomas W. Kreidler; Adam D. Puntel, Parochial Vicar; Mrs. Debbie Birck, Pastoral Assoc.; Deacons Bill Mullaney; Dave Shea; Dave Shaffer; Michael J. Cassani; J. Russell Feldkamp; Mark U. Johnson.
Res.: 7820 Beechmont Ave., 45255. Tel: 513-388-4466; Fax: 513-388-4097. Email: parish@ihom.org. Web: www.ihom.org.
School—(Grades K-8), 7800 Beechmont Ave., 45255. Tel: 513-388-4086; Fax: 513-388-3026. Email: school@ihom.org. Web: www.ihomschool.org. Mrs. Mary Hedger, Co-Prin.; Mrs. Nancy Goebel, Co-Prin. Brothers 1; Lay Teachers 34; Students 675.
Catechesis/Religious Program—Tel: 513-388-4093; Fax: 513-388-4097. Email: formation@ihom.org. Mr. Patrick Reis, Youth Min. Students 501.

35—ST. JAMES OF THE VALLEY (Wyoming) (1886) Rev. Jack W. Wehman; Deacon Conrad C. Kolis; Scott C. Dover, Business Mgr.; Mrs. Sharon Russo, Pastoral Assoc.
Res.: 411 Springfield Pk., Wyoming, 45215. Tel: 513-948-1218; Fax: 513-948-1225. Email: sdover@stjamesotv.org. Web: www.stjamesotv.com.
School—(Grades K-8) Tel: 513-821-9054; Fax: 513-821-9556. Email: jhaag@stjamesvalley.org. Web:

www.stjamesvalley.org. Mr. James Haag, Prin.; Ms. Jane Ray, Librarian. Lay Teachers 14; Students 162.
Catechesis/Religious Program—Mrs. Angela Glassmeyer, D.R.E. Students 160.

36—ST. JAMES THE GREATER (White Oak) (1843) [CEM] Revs. Thomas C. Nolker; Martin E. Bachman, Parochial Vicar; Deacons Tim A. Crooker; Paul Kluener.
Res.: 3565 Hubble Rd., 45247. Tel: 513-741-5300; Fax: 513-741-5302. Email: info@stjameswhiteoak.com. Web: www.stjameswhiteoak.com.
School—(Grades K-8), 6111 Cheviot Rd., 45247. Tel: 513-741-5333; Fax: 513-741-5312. Web: www-.stjameswo.org. Donna Beebe, Prin. Lay Teachers 35; Students 675.
Catechesis/Religious Program—Tel: 513-741-5335; Fax: 513-741-5302. Students 60.

37—ST. JOHN FISHER (Newtown) (1947) Rev. Steven P. Walter; Aimee Baer, Pastoral Assoc.
Office: 3227 Church St., 45244. Tel: 513-561-9431; Fax: 513-561-7513. Email: stjohnfisher@juno.com. Web: www.sjfchurch.org.
Catechesis/Religious Program—Students 185.

38—ST. JOHN NEUMANN (Springfield Township) (1978) Rev. Steven J. Kolde; Deacons John R. Gobbi, Pastoral Assoc.; Patrick A. Palumbo, Pastoral Assoc.; Ronald H. Risch, Pastoral Assoc.
Res.: 12191 Mill Rd., 45240. Tel: 513-742-0953; Fax: 513-742-5875.
See St. John the Baptist Catholic School, Cincinnati under Consolidated Elementary Schools located in the Institution section.
Catechesis/Religious Program—Tel: 513-742-0953; Fax: 513-742-5875. Students 127.

39—ST. JOHN THE BAPTIST (Dry Ridge) (1860) [CEM] Rev. Timothy S. Kallaher.
Res.: 5361 Dry Ridge Rd., 45252. Tel: 513-385-8010; Fax: 513-385-8080. Email: pastor@stjohns-dr.org. Web: www.stjohns-dr.org.
See St. John the Baptist Catholic School, Cincinnati under Consolidated Schools in the Institution section.
Catechesis/Religious Program—Students 95.

40—ST. JOHN THE BAPTIST (Harrison) (1851) [CEM] Revs. Jeffrey M. Kemper; Edward J. Shine (Retired); William J. Dorrmann (Retired); Deacon Donald J. Meyer Jr.
Res.: 509 Harrison Ave., Harrison, 45030. Tel: 513-367-9086; Fax: 513-367-0501. Email: parishoffice@stjb.net. Web: www.stjb.net.
School—(Grades K-8), 508 Park Ave., Harrison, 45030. Tel: 513-367-6826; Fax: 513-367-6864. Web: sjbharrison.org. Susan Meymann, Prin.; Julia Koors, Librarian. Lay Teachers 21; Students 263.
Catechesis/Religious Program—Students 214.

41—ST. JOHN THE EVANGELIST (1891) Revs. Thomas Espelage; Dale C. Peterka.
Res.: 7121 Plainfield Rd., 45236. Tel: 513-791-3238; Fax: 513-686-2720. Web: www.stjohndp.org.
See St. Nicholas Academy, Cincinnati under Consolidated Schools in the Institution section.
Catechesis/Religious Program—Laura E. Davis, Pastoral Min. Students 65.

42—ST. JOSEPH (1846), (African American), Rev. Reynaldo S. Taylor; Deacons Raphael Simmons; Dennis Edwards; Wylie G. Howell, Pastoral Assoc.; William Jefferson, Business Mgr./Parish Finance.
Res.: 224 E. 8th St., Ste. 203, 45202. Tel: 513-284-4201.
Church & Mailing Address: 745 Ezzard Charles Dr., 45203. Tel: 513-381-4526; Fax: 513-381-5244. Email: stjosephchurch@fuse.net. Web: www.stjoseph-catholicchurch.org.
School—(Grades K-8) Tel: 513-381-2126; Fax: 513-381-6513. Dionne Thompson, Prin.; Maureen Lechleiter, Librarian. Lay Teachers 14; Students 182.
Catechesis/Religious Program—Tel: 513-381-4526, Ext. 16. Sr. Rachel Richards, S.F.C.C., D.R.E. Students 8.

43—ST. JUDE THE APOSTLE (1956) Rev. Eric A. Bowman; Deacon James Sunderman, Pastoral Assoc.
Res.: 5924 Bridgetown Rd., 45248. Tel: 513-574-1230; Fax: 513-598-2109. Email: parishoffice@thestjudeparish.org. Web: www.stjudebridgetown.org.
School—5940 Bridgetown Rd., 45248. Tel: 513-598-2100; Fax: 513-598-2118. Louis Eichhold, Prin. Lay Teachers 22; Students 474.
Catechesis/Religious Program—Tel: 513-598-2100, Ext. 30; Fax: 513-598-2109. Students 111.

44—ST. LAWRENCE (Price Hill) (1868) Rev. Mark T. Watkins; Sr. Helen Julia Hahn, S.C., Pastoral Min.
Res.: 3680 Warsaw Ave., 45205. Tel: 513-921-0328; Fax: 513-921-5108. Email: rectory@stlawrenceparish.org. Web: www.stlawrenceparish.org.
School—(Grades PreSchool-8), 1020 Carson Ave., 45205. Tel: 513-921-4996. Mrs. Alma Lee Joesting, Prin. Lay Teachers 22; Students 266.
Catechesis/Religious Program—

45—ST. LEO THE GREAT (1886) Rev. James Schutte.
Mailing Address: 2573 St. Leo Pl., 45225-1960. Tel: 513-921-1044; Fax: 513-921-8048.
See St. Boniface School, Cincinnati under Consolidated Elementary Schools located in the Institution section.
Catechesis/Religious Program—Students 55.

46—ST. LOUIS (1870), (German), Rev. Steve J. Angi.
Res.: 29 E. Eighth St., 45202-2086. Tel: 513-263-6621; Fax: 513-263-6624. Web: stlouischurchcincinnati.org.

47—ST. MARGARET - ST. JOHN PARISH (2008) Rev. David A. Lemkuhl.
Mailing Address: 4100 Watterson St., 45227. Tel: 513-271-0856; Fax: 513-271-1513. Email: michelleboehle@fuse.net; marymathers@fuse.net. Web: www.smsjparish.com. In Res., Rev. William H. Cross.
Res. & Church: 4448 Berwick St., 45227. Tel: 513-271-1968.
Worship Sites:—
St. Margaret of Cortona Church—6000 Murray Rd., 45227.
St. John Vianney Church—4448 Berwick St., 45227.
School—*Prince of Peace*, (Grades K-8), 6000 Murray Rd., 45227. Tel: 513-271-8288; Fax: 513-272-1740. Web: www.princeofpeacecincinnati.org. Mr. Frank Barlag, Prin. Lay Teachers 14; Students 141.
Catechesis/Religious Program—Mary Ann Putman, Faith Formation Coord.; Nathan Etan, Youth Coord. Students 50.

48—ST. MARGARET MARY (North College Hill) (1920) Revs. Jerome J. Gardner; Thomas A. Snodgrass, Parochial Vicar.
Res.: 1830 W. Galbraith Rd., 45239. Tel: 513-521-7387; Fax: 513-521-7388. Email: mmason@zoomtown.com. Web: www.stmargaretmaryparish.org.
See Our Lady of Grace, Cincinnati under Consolidated Elementary Schools located in the Institution section.
Catechesis/Religious Program—Tel: 513-729-0222. Mrs. Wilma McGlasson, D.R.E. Students 66.

49—ST. MARTIN OF TOURS (Cheviot) (1911) Rev. Terence J. Hamilton.
Res.: 3720 St. Martin Pl., 45211. Tel: 513-661-2000; Fax: 513-661-1432.
School—(Grades K-8), 3729 Harding Ave., 45211. Tel: 513-661-7609; Fax: 513-661-8102. Mrs. Carolyn Murphy, Prin. Lay Teachers 15; Students 245.
Catechesis/Religious Program—Students 35.

50—ST. MARY (Hyde Park) (1898) Rev. Kenneth E. Schartz; Deacon Timothy M. Helmick; Ms. Mary Anne Bressler, Pastoral Assoc.; Mr. Keith Pfaller, Pastoral Assoc.; Ms. Margaret Shank, Pastoral Assoc.
Res.: 2853 Erie Ave., 45208. Tel: 513-321-1207; Fax: 513-533-5518. Email: parish@saintmaryhydepark.org. Web: www.saintmaryhydepark.org.
School—(Grades K-8), 2845 Erie Ave., 45208. Tel: 513-321-0703; Fax: 513-533-5517. Web: www.smshp.com. Miss Marianne Rosemond, Prin. Lay Teachers 24; Students 489.
Catechesis/Religious Program—Tel: 513-321-0703; Fax: 513-533-5518. Students 336.

51—ST. MATTHIAS (Forest Park) (1967) Revs. Peter Helmlinger; Paul A. Bader (Retired); Deacon Raymond George.
Res.: 1050 W. Kemper Rd., 45240. Tel: 513-851-1930; Fax: 513-589-3850.
Catechesis/Religious Program—Tel: 513-851-1930, Ext. 10; Fax: 513-589-3850. Students 11.

52—ST. MICHAEL (1919) Rev. Thomas P. DiFolco, Parochial Admin.; Deacon Kenneth J. Dehanes Sr., Pastoral Assoc.; Brian Bisig, Dir. Music; Scott Hungler, Business Mgr.
Church & Mailing Address: 11144 Spinner Ave., 45241. Tel: 513-563-6377; Fax: 513-554-3543. Web: www.saintmichaelchurch.net.
School—(Grades K-8), 11136 Oak St., 45241. Tel: 513-554-3555; Fax: 513-554-3551. Jody Farrell, Prin.; Frances Ablett, Librarian. Lay Teachers 22; Students 420.
Catechesis/Religious Program—Tel: 513-563-6377, Ext. 303. Lori Anne Fothergill, Dir. Faith Formation (Youth). Students 126.

53—ST. MONICA-ST. GEORGE PARISH NEWMAN CENTER (1993) Rev. Alan Hirt, O.F.M.
328 W. McMillan St., 45219.
Res.: 533 Howell Ave., 45220. Tel: 513-381-6400; Fax: 513-381-2540. Email: st.monica-st.george@fuse.net. Web: www.smsgparishonline.com.
Church: Tel: 513-381-6400.
Catechesis/Religious Program—Students 82.

54—MOTHER OF CHRIST (1946), (African American), Rev. James Shappelle; Vanessa Rozier, Business Mgr.
Church: 5301 Winneste Ave., 45232. Tel: 513-242-0164 (Church); 513-541-3732 (Res); Fax: 513-242-0164 (Church); 513-541-0362 (Res). Email: mocaoc@aol.com. Web: www.motherofchrist.homestead.com.
Catechesis/Religious Program—Students 18.

55—NATIVITY OF OUR LORD (Pleasant Ridge) (1917) Rev. Paul F. DeLuca.
Res.: 5935 Pandora Ave., 45213-2017. Tel: 513-531-3164; Fax: 513-458-6761. Web: www.nativity-cincinnati.org.
School—(Grades K-8), 5936 Ridge Ave., 45213-1699. Tel: 513-458-6767; Fax: 513-458-6769. Robert C. Herring, Prin. Lay Teachers 24; Students 423.
Catechesis/Religious Program—Students 58.

56—OLD ST. MARY (1842) Revs. Martin O. Moran III; Lawrence Juarez.
Res.: 123 E. 13th St., 45202. Tel: 513-721-2988; Fax: 513-721-0436. Web: www.oldstmarys.org.
Catechesis/Religious Program—

57—OUR LADY OF LOURDES (Westwood) (1927) Rev. David A. Sunberg; Deacon Thomas E. Westerfield; Sr. Carla Murar, O.S.U., Pastoral Assoc.; James G. Frede, Parish Admin. In Res., Rev. Kyle E. Schnippel.
Res.: 2832 Rosebud Dr., 45238. Tel: 513-922-0715; 513-347-2641 (Res.); Fax: 513-347-2644. Email: parish@lourdes.org. Web: www.lourdes.org.
School—(Grades K-8), 5835 Glenway Ave., 45238. Tel: 513-347-2660; Fax: 513-347-2663. Ms. Aimee Ellmaker, Prin. Lay Teachers 20; Students 350.
Catechesis/Religious Program—Tel: 513-347-2646. Carol Greulich, D.R.E. Students 65.

58—OUR LADY OF THE ROSARY (Greenhills) (1938) Rev. Peter Helmlinger; Deacons Walter A. Hucke Jr., Business Mgr.; Steven A. Ryan; Katherine A. Klich, Pastoral Assoc.
Res.: 17 Farragut Rd., 45218. Tel: 513-825-8626; Fax: 513-825-2783. Email: whucke@olr.net. Web: www.olr.net.
See John Paul II Catholic, Cincinnati under Consolidated Elementary Schools located in the Institution section.
Catechesis/Religious Program—Tel: 513-825-8626, Ext. 321. Mr. David Nissen, D.R.E. Students 138.

59—OUR LADY OF THE SACRED HEART (Reading) (1874) Rev. Ronald Williams; Angie Touvelle, Accounts Mgr.; Dick Berish, Opers. Mgr.; Michael Collins, Music Dir. & Youth Min.
Res.: 177 Siebenthaler Ave., 45215. Tel: 513-733-4950; Fax: 513-733-0973. Email: olsh@fuse.net.
Catechesis/Religious Program—Students 118.

60—OUR LADY OF THE VISITATION (Mack) (1947) Revs. Mark J. Burger; Patrick M. McMullen, Parochial Vicar; Ken Meymann, Pastoral Assoc.; Bill Tonnis, Dir. of Youth & Outreach Ministries; Carolyn Witterstaetter, Music Min.; Diane Williams, Business Mgr.; Leslee House, Accountant; Dave Feldman, Facility Mgr.
Res.: 3172 South Rd., 45248. Tel: 513-922-2056; Fax: 513-347-2238. Email: olvisititation@olvisitation.net. Web: www.olvisitation.org.
School—3180 South Rd., 45248. Tel: 513-347-2222; Fax: 513-347-2225. Mr. Terry P. Chapman, Prin. Sisters 1; Lay Teachers 41; Students 857.
Catechesis/Religious Program—Tel: 513-347-2228; Fax: 513-347-2225. Sr. Mary Tewes, O.S.B., D.R.E. Students 153.

61—OUR LADY OF VICTORY (Delhi Hills) (1842) [CEM] Rev. James G. Reutter; Deacon Charles Jenkins.
Res.: 810 Neeb Rd., 45233. Tel: 513-922-4460; Fax: 513-922-5476. Web: www.olv.org.
School—(Grades K-8), 808 Neeb Rd., 45233. Tel: 513-347-2072; Fax: 513-922-5476. Ms. Kathy Kane, Prin.; Mrs. Jenny Luchsinger, Librarian. Lay Teachers 30; Students 528.
Catechesis/Religious Program—Tel: 513-347-2071; Fax: 513-922-5476. Mr. Jonathan Schafer, D.R.E. Students 67.

62—OUR LORD, CHRIST THE KING (Mt. Lookout) (1926) Revs. Edward P. Smith; Francis W. Voellmecke (Retired); Deacon Donald Gloeckler. In Res., Rev. Leonard C. Wenke.
Res.: 3223 Linwood Ave., 45226. Tel: 513-321-4121; Fax: 513-871-3978. Email: parish@ourlordchristtheking.org. Web: www.ourlordchristtheking.org.
School—*Cardinal Pacelli*, (Grades PreK-8), 927 Ellison, 45226. Tel: 513-321-1048; Fax: 513-533-6118. Web: www.carinalpacelli.org. Kim Roy, Prin. Lay Teachers 25; Students 408.
Catechesis/Religious Program—Students 60.

63—STS. PETER AND PAUL (Reading) (1850) [CEM] Rev. David G. Howard; Deacon Tom Lynd; Mrs. Beth Pettigrew, Pastoral Assoc.
330 W. Vine St., Reading, 45215. Tel: 513-554-1010; Fax: 513-554-0190. In Res., Rev. John P. Heim, S.J.
Catechesis/Religious Program—Email: ppanzeca1@fuse.net. Web: saintspeterandpaulreading.com. Students 90.

64—RESURRECTION OF OUR LORD (1919) Rev. Robert

L. Keller.
Res.: 1744 Iliff Ave., 45205-1018. Tel: 513-471-2700; Fax: 513-471-2703.
School—(Grades K-8), 1740 Iliff Ave., 45205-1018. Tel: 513-471-6600; 513-471-6620; Fax: 513-471-2610. Kathleen Sparks, Prin. Sisters 2; Lay Teachers 11; Students 172.
Catechesis/Religious Program—

65—ST. ROBERT BELLARMINE (1927) Revs. Richard W. Bollman, S.J.; Kent A. Beausoleil, S.J.; Jeff Campbell, Dir. Social Mission. Tel: 513-745-1908; Scott Buzza, Dir. Music Min. Tel: 513-745-3270; Sue Antoinette, Dir. Youth Min. Tel: 513-745-4224; Karen Brandstetter, Pastoral Assoc. Tel: 513-745-3349.
Xavier University: 3800 Victory Pkwy., 45207-2211. Tel: 513-745-3398; Fax: 513-745-2031. Web: www.bellarminechapel.org.
Catechesis/Religious Program—Tel: 513-745-3317. Students 182.

66—ST. ROSE OF LIMA (1867) Rev. Barry M. Windholtz, Canonical Pastor; Deacon John J. Convery, Parish Admin.
Church & Mailing Address: 2501 Riverside Dr., 45202. Tel: 513-871-1162; Fax: 513-871-2851.

67—SACRED HEART (1870), (Italian), Revs. Vincent Cutrara, C.S.; Mario Rauzi, C.S.
Res.: 2733 Massachusetts Ave., 45225. Tel: 513-541-4654; Fax: 513-541-4662. Email: sacredheartcamp@yahoo.com. Web: www.sacredheartchurchcincinnati.com.
See Corryville Catholic Elementary School, Cincinnati under Consolidated Elementary Schools located in the Institution section.

68—ST. SAVIOUR (Deer Park) (1947) Rev. Timothy S. Bunch; Deacon Jerome Cain.
Res.: 4136 Myrtle Ave., 45236. Tel: 513-791-9004; Fax: 513-791-6530.
Catechesis/Religious Program—Tel: 513-791-0119. Students 86.

69—ST. SIMON THE APOSTLE (1966) Rev. Richard E. Dressman, Parochial Admin.
Res.: 825 Pontius Rd., 45233. Tel: 513-941-3656; Fax: 513-941-1562. Email: awhess@isoc.net. Web: www.stsimonparish.org.
Catechesis/Religious Program—Beth Schumacher, D.R.E. Students 160.

70—ST. STEPHEN (1867) Revs. Edward P. Smith, Canonical Pastor; Stanley H. Neiheisel (Retired); Beth Worland, Pastoral Admin.
Res.: 320 Donham Ave., 45226. Tel: 513-871-3373. Email: bethststephen@fuse.net.
Catechesis/Religious Program—Students 15.

71—ST. TERESA OF AVILA (1916) Rev. Thomas L. Bolte; Deacon Gregg Rose. In Res., Rev. George R. Schmitz (Retired).
Res.: 1175 Overlook Ave., 45238. Tel: 513-921-9200; Fax: 513-921-0307. Email: stteresa@fuse.net. Web: www.stteresa-avila.org.
School—(Grades K-8), 1194 Rulison Ave., 45238. Tel: 513-471-4530; Fax: 513-471-1254. Email: maier_m@stteresa.net. Web: www.stteresa.net. Mrs. Sharon Willmes, Prin.; Mrs. Judy Honkomp, Librarian; Mrs. Chris Artmayer, Librarian. Lay Teachers 20; Students 266.
Catechesis/Religious Program—Tel: 513-921-9200, Ext. 117. Web: www.stteresa-avila.org. Michelle Thoman, D.R.E. Students 47.

72—ST. THERESE, THE LITTLE FLOWER (Mt. Airy) (1926) Rev. Robert W. Goebel.
Res.: 5560 Kirby Ave., 45239. Tel: 513-541-5560; Fax: 513-681-2631. Email: parishoffice@littleflowerchurch.org. Web: www.littleflower-church.org.
See Our Lady of Grace, Cincinnati under Consolidated Elementary Schools located in the Institution section.
Catechesis/Religious Program—Tel: 513-541-5560. Sr. Francis Margaret Maag, C.D.P., D.R.E. Students 23.

73—ST. VINCENT DE PAUL (1861) Rev. Donald R. Rettig.
Res.: 4026 River Rd., 45204. Tel: 513-451-5714; Fax: 513-451-3830. Email: svdpcin@hotmail.com.

74—ST. VINCENT FERRER (Kenwood) (1946) Rev. George C. Kunkel.
Res.: 7754 Montgomery Rd., 45236. Tel: 513-791-9030; Fax: 513-686-1132. Web: www.svfchurch.org.
School—(Grades K-8) Tel: 513-791-6320; Fax: 513-791-3332. Email: doug.alpiger@svf-school.org. Douglas Alpiger, Prin. Lay Teachers 17; Students 177.
Catechesis/Religious Program—Tel: 513-791-6321. Karen McMichael, Dir. Faith Formation. Students 63.

75—ST. VIVIAN (1943) Rev. Paul L. Gebhardt; Kathleen Rothschild, Business Mgr.; Lynne Morris, Dir. Devel.; Deacon Larry Maag; Tim McManus, Dir. Liturgy & Music; Jeanne Stephens, Dir. Youth Ministry & Lay Pastoral Min.
Res.: 7600 Winton Rd., 45224. Tel: 513-728-4331; Fax: 513-728-4335. Email: rectory@stvivian.org. Web: www.stvivian.org.
School—(Grades PreSchool-8), 885 Denier Pl., 45224. Tel: 513-522-6858; Fax: 513-728-4336. Email: steve.zinser@stvivianschool.org. Web: www.stvivianschool.org. Steve Zinser, Prin.; Mary Hanson, Librarian. Lay Teachers 27; Students 374.
Catechesis/Religious Program—Tel: 513-728-4339; Fax: 513-728-4335. Julie Zinser, Faith Formation Coord. Students 30.

76—ST. WILLIAM (1909) Rev. Andrew J. Umberg; Deacons George Bruce; Thomas Faeth.
Res.: 4108 W. Eighth St., 45205. Tel: 513-921-0247; Fax: 513-921-2810. Email: info@saintwilliam.com. Web: www.saintwilliam.com.
School—(Grades K-8), 4125 St. William Ave., 45205. Tel: 513-471-2989; Fax: 513-471-8226. Mr. Michael Monnig, Prin.; Mrs. Julie Conway, Librarian. Sisters 2; Lay Teachers 31; Students 249.

OUTSIDE THE CITY OF CINCINNATI

AMELIA, CLERMONT CO., ST. BERNADETTE (1944) Rev. William R. Stockelman.
Res.: 1479 Locust Lake Rd., 45102-1798. Tel: 513-753-5566; Fax: 513-753-7664. Email: stbernadetteamelia@fuse.net. Web: www.stbernadetteamelia.org.
School—(Grades K-8), 1453 Locust Lake Rd., 45102-1703. Tel: 513-753-4744; Fax: 513-753-9018. Mr. Thomas Salerno, Prin. Lay Teachers 13; Students 145.
Catechesis/Religious Program—Elizabeth Himes, D.R.E. Students 80.

ARNHEIM, BROWN CO., ST. MARY (1837) [CEM] Rev. Dohrman W. Byers; Deacon Ronald S. Dvorachek; Marilyn Fryer, Pastoral Assoc.
Res.: 6647 Van Buren St., Georgetown, 45121. Tel: 937-446-2555; Fax: 937-446-2555. Email: stmaryarnheim@hughes.net.
Catechesis/Religious Program—Tel: 937-446-1854. Linda Mulvaney, D.R.E. Students 80.

BATAVIA, CLERMONT CO., HOLY TRINITY (1906) Rev. Gerard P. Hiland, Temporary Parochial Admin.; Deacon James Hennessey.
Res.: 140 N. 6th St., 45103. Tel: 513-732-2024; Fax: 513-732-0049. Email: alleluia@fuse.net.
Catechesis/Religious Program—Tel: 513-732-2024, Ext. 13. Students 11.

BEAVERCREEK, GREENE CO., ST. LUKE (1955) Rev. Terrance L. Schneider; Deacons Gerald M. Dupree; Richard D. Simpson.
Res.: 1440 N. Fairfield Rd., 45432. Tel: 937-426-1733; Fax: 937-426-3965. Email: stluke@saintlukeparish.org. Web: www.saintlukeparish.org.
School—(Grades K-8), 1442 N. Fairfield Rd., 45432. Tel: 937-426-1733; Fax: 937-426-6435. Email: suttond@stluke.cnd.pvt.k12.oh.us. Web: www.stluke.cnd.pvt.k12.oh.us. Mrs. Leslie Vondrell, Prin. Lay Teachers 23; Students 426.
Catechesis/Religious Program—1444 N. Fairfield Rd., 45432. Students 246.

BELLEFONTAINE, LOGAN CO., ST. PATRICK (1852) [CEM] Rev. Patrick L. Sheridan; Deacons Harold Dipple; Robert A. Crook.
Res.: 328 E. Patterson Ave., 43311. Tel: 937-592-1656; Fax: 937-592-0971. Web: www.catholicbellefontaine.org.
Catechesis/Religious Program—316 E. Patterson Rd., 43311. Students 109.

BETHEL, CLERMONT CO., ST. MARY (1941) Rev. Michael F. Leshney; Deacon Jerry Etienne.
Church & Mailing Address: 3398 S.R. 125, 45106. Tel: 513-734-4041; Fax: 513-734-3588. Email: michaelleshney@fuse.net. Web: www.stmaryparishfamily.org.
Catechesis/Religious Program—Tel: 513-734-3676; Fax: 513-734-3588. Students 118.

BOTKINS, SHELBY CO., IMMACULATE CONCEPTION (1865), (German), [CEM] Revs. Patrick L. Sloneker; Matthew K. Lee, Parochial Vicar.
Res.: 116 N. Mill St., P.O. Box 519, 45306. Tel: 937-693-2561; Fax: 937-693-2561.
Church: N. Main & Walnut Sts., 45306.
Catechesis/Religious Program—Students 270.

BRADFORD, MIAMI CO., IMMACULATE CONCEPTION (1875) [JC] Rev. James L. Simons.
Res.: 6925 W. U.S. Rte. 36, Covington, 45318. Tel: 937-473-2970. Email: icinbradford@woh.rr.com.
Church: 5874 N. Buckneck Rd., R.R. 2, 45308. Tel: 937-448-6220; Fax: 937-473-2476.
Catechesis/Religious Program—Tel: 937-448-6220. Students 28.

BURKETTSVILLE, MERCER CO., ST. BERNARD (1874), (St. Henry Cluster) Revs. Thomas Hemm, C.PP.S.; Benedict Magabe, C.PP.S. (Tanzania).
Mailing Address: 272 E. Main St., Box 350, Saint Henry, 45883. Web: www.sthenrycluster.com.
Church: 71 W. Main St., 45310. Tel: 419-678-4118; Fax: 419-678-8285.
St. Henry Catechetical Center—Tel: 419-678-3811. See St. Henry, St. Henry for details.
Catechesis/Religious Program—Students 123.

CAMDEN, PREBLE CO., ST. MARY (1942) Rev. Francis Tandoh, C.S.Sp., Admin.
Res.: 130 Gramont Ave., P.O. Box 17219, Dayton, 45417. Tel: 937-268-2747.
Church: 7721 N. Main St., P.O. Box 28, 45311. Tel: 937-452-3352.
Catechesis/Religious Program—Students 30.

CARTHAGENA, MERCER CO., ST. ALOYSIUS (1865), (German), [CEM], (St. Henry Cluster) Revs. Thomas Hemm, C.PP.S.; Benedict Magabe, C.PP.S. (Tanzania).
Mailing Address: P.O. Box 350, Saint Henry, 45883. Tel: 419-678-4118. Web: www.sthenrycluster.com.
Res.: 1509 Cranberry Rd., Saint Henry, 45883. Tel: 419-925-4776; Fax: 419-678-8285. Email: tomhemm@hotmail.com.
Church: 6036 State Rte. 274, 45822.
St. Henry Catechetical Center— For details call Tel: 419-678-3811.
Catechesis/Religious Program—Catherine Wenning, D.R.E. Students 33.

CASSELLA, MERCER CO., NATIVITY OF THE BLESSED VIRGIN MARY (1847) [CEM], (Marion Catholic Community) Rev. Eugene H. Schnipke, C.PP.S.
7428 State Rte. 119, Maria Stein, 45860. Tel: 419-925-4775; Fax: 419-925-1745. Email: marioncathcom@gmail.com. Web: www.marioncatholiccommunity.org.
Catechesis/Religious Program—Tel: 419-925-4017. Katie Dippold, C.R.E. Students 87.

CELINA, MERCER CO., IMMACULATE CONCEPTION OF THE BLESSED VIRGIN MARY (1864), (German), [CEM] Revs. Ken Schnipke, C.PP.S.; Kenneth G. Alt, C.PP.S.
Res.: 229 W. Anthony St., 45822. Tel: 419-586-6648; Fax: 419-586-6649.
School—(Grades PreK-6), 200 W. Wayne St., 45822-1469. Tel: 419-586-2379; Fax: 419-586-6649. Mrs. Pauline Muhlenkamp, Prin. Sisters of the Precious Blood 1; Lay Teachers 14; Students 117.
Catechesis/Religious Program—Wayne & Walnut Sts., 45822. Tel: 419-586-2370; Fax: 419-586-6649. Joyce Johnson, C.R.E.; Charlie Salway, Youth Min. Students 265.

CENTERVILLE, MONTGOMERY CO.

1—ST. FRANCIS OF ASSISI (1969) Rev. Thomas W. Schmidt; Deacons Mark Stasiak, Business Mgr.; Jack Pitts; Joyce Connell, Parish Sec.; Frances Obringer, Sec. In Res., Rev. Joseph C. Kindel.
Res.: 6245 Wilmington Pike, 45459. Tel: 937-433-1013; Fax: 937-433-1699. Web: www.sfacc.org.
Catechesis/Religious Program—Tel: 937-433-0128; Fax: 937-433-1699. Mary Ellen Singer, D.R.E. Students 418.

2—INCARNATION (1945) Revs. Lawrence E. Mierenfeld; C. Scott Wright, Parochial Vicar; Deacons Robert Zinck; Roger E. Duffy; Tim Niesel, Pastoral Assoc.; Marilyn Porcino, Pastoral Assoc.
Res.: 55 Williamsburg Ln., 45459. Tel: 937-433-1188; Fax: 937-433-3263. Web: www.incarnation-parish.com.
School—(Grades PreK-8), 45 Williamsburg Ln., 45459. Tel: 937-433-1051; Fax: 937-433-9796. Web: www.incarnation-school.com. Cheryl Reichel, Prin. Lay Teachers 48; Students 853.
Catechesis/Religious Program—Tel: 937-433-3377; Fax: 937-433-3263. Paula Weckesser, C.R.E.; Daniel Dunn, Youth & Young Adult Ministry. Students 684.

COLDWATER, MERCER CO., HOLY TRINITY (1867) [CEM], (Coldwater Cluster) Revs. Richard W. Walling; Barry J. Stechschulte, Parochial Vicar; Deacon Thomas Huff.
Mailing Address: P.O. Box 107, 45828. Email: cwcluster@coldwatercluster.org. Web: www.coldwatercluster.org.
Res.: 116 E. Main St., P.O. Box 107, 45828. Tel: 419-678-4802; Fax: 419-678-4803.
Catechesis/Religious Program—110 N. Second St., 45828. Tel: 419-678-3328. Charmaine Bettinger, D.R.E. Students 940.

COVINGTON, MIAMI CO., ST. TERESA OF THE INFANT JESUS (1950), (German—French), [JC] Rev. James L. Simons.
Res.: 6925 W. U.S. 36, 45318. Tel: 937-473-2970; Fax: 937-473-2476. Email: stteresaij@woh.rr.com.
Catechesis/Religious Program—Tel: 937-473-2970; Fax: 937-473-2476. Mrs. Elaine Christian, D.R.E. Students 67.

CRANBERRY PRAIRIE, MERCER CO., ST. FRANCIS (1858), (German), [CEM], (St. Henry Cluster) Revs. Thomas Hemm, C.PP.S.; Benedict Magabe, C.PP.S. (Tanzania).
Mailing Address: P.O. Box 350, Saint Henry, 45883. Web: www.sthenrycluster.com.
Church & Res.: 1509 Cranberry Rd., Saint Henry, 45883. Tel: 419-678-4118 (Church); 419-925-4776 (Residence); Fax: 419-678-8285. Email: tomhemm@hotmail.com.
St. Henry Catechetical Center—Catherine Wenning, D.R.E. See St. Henry, St. Henry for details. Tel:

419-678-3811. E-mail: sthenryccd@bright.net Students 52.

DAYTON, GREENE CO., QUEEN OF APOSTLES (1973) Rev. Thomas A. Schroer, S.M., Priest Coord.; Deacon Greg Cecere, Pastoral Assoc.
Church: 4400 Shakertown Rd., 45430-1057. Tel: 937-429-0510; Fax: 937-429-0510. Email: qacohio@sbcglobal.net. Web: www.qac-ohio.org.
Catechesis/Religious Program— Maggie Atkinson, D.R.E. Students 69.

DAYTON, MONTGOMERY CO.

1—ST. ADALBERT (1903), (Polish), Rev. Michael J. Holloran; Anne Rusen, Pastoral Min.
Office: 22 Notre Dame Ave., 45404. Tel: 937-228-8802.
Catechesis/Religious Program— Joint program with Holy Cross, Our Lady of the Rosary, and St. Stephen.

2—ST. ALBERT THE GREAT (1939) Revs. Thomas E. Meyer; Ned J. Brown; Deacon Jeffrey Hall.
Res.: 3033 Far Hills Ave., 45429. Tel: 937-293-1191; Fax: 937-293-1848. Email: parish@stalbertthegreat.net. Web: www.stalbertthegreat.net.
School—(Grades PreK-8), 104 W. Dorothy Ln., Kettering, 45429. Tel: 937-293-9452; Fax: 937-293-7525. Email: npsamkirry@mdeca.org. Web: www-.stalbertthegreat.net. Mr. Mike Kirry, Prin. Lay Teachers 30; Students 400.
Catechesis/Religious Program—104 Dorothy Ln., Kettering, 45429. Tel: 937-298-2402; Fax: 937-293-8292. Jean Carr, C.R.E. Students 380.

3—ST. ANTHONY OF PADUA (1913) Rev. Christopher C. Coleman; Deacon Jeffrey Hall, Pastoral Assoc. & Project Mgr.; Janet Gaier, Pastoral Assoc.; Madelon Kinzig, Music Dir.; Sidney Gnann, Business Mgr.
Res.: 830 Bowen St., 45410. Tel: 937-253-9132; Fax: 937-253-6658. Email: stabmanager@bizwoh.rr.com.
School—(Grades K-8), 1824 St. Charles Ave., 45410. Tel: 937-253-6251; Fax: 937-253-1541. David Timpone, Prin. Lay Teachers 10; Students 200.
Catechesis/Religious Program—

4—ASCENSION (1955) Rev. Christopher J. Worland; Cathy Magness, Pastoral Assoc.; Deacon Victor B. Hildebrand, Pastoral Assoc.; Christy Shanklin, Business Mgr.; Sr. Carol Gaeke, O.P., Adult Faith Formation; Joseph Ollier, Coord. Youth Min.
Res.: 2025 Woodman Dr., Kettering, 45420. Tel: 937-253-5171; Fax: 937-253-0886.
School—(Grades K-8), 2001 Woodman Dr., Kettering, 45420. Tel: 937-254-5411; Fax: 937-254-1150. Brent Devitt, Prin.; Sherry Smith, Librarian. Lay Teachers 24; Students 377.
Catechesis/Religious Program—Tel: 937-254-0622. Sue Graham, C.R.E. Students 334.

5—ST. BENEDICT THE MOOR (2005), (African American), Revs. Francis Tandoh, C.S.Sp.; Matthew Amoako-Attah, C.S.Sp.; Deacon Jacob Jernigan.
Rectory—130 Gramont Ave., P.O. Box 17219, 45417. Tel: 937-228-6123.
Office: 519 Liscum Dr., P.O. Box 17219, 45417. Tel: 937-268-6697; Fax: 937-268-6698. Email: sajares@yahoo.com. Web: www.unitedinhope.com.
See Mary Queen of Peace, Dayton under Consolidated Elementary Schools located in the Institution section.
Catechesis/Religious Program—Students 22.

6—ST. CHARLES BORROMEO (Kettering) (1962) Revs. Gerald R. Haemmerle; Timothy W. Ralston, Parochial Vicar; Deacons William Moore; Robert Collins; Brenda Tibbits, Pastoral Assoc.
Res.: 4440 Andrea, 45429.
Church: 4500 Ackerman Rd., 45429. Tel: 937-434-6081; Fax: 937-434-6251. Web: www.stcharles-kettering.org.
School—(Grades K-8), 4600 Ackerman Blvd., 45429. Tel: 937-434-4933; Fax: 937-434-6692. David Bogle, Prin. Lay Teachers 24; Students 426.
Catechesis/Religious Program—Tel: 937-434-9272. Tim Clarke, Dir. Faith Formation. Students 210.

7—CORPUS CHRISTI (1911) Rev. Joshua Otusafo, C.S.Sp., Parochial Admin.; Deacons Tom Platfoot; Skip Royer.
Mailing Address & Parish Office: 220 W. Siebenthaler Ave., 45405. Tel: 937-274-2107; Fax: 937-274-4363. Email: info@corpusmercymartyrs.org. Web: www.corpusmercymartyrs.org.
Church: 527 Forest Ave., 45405.
See Mary Queen of Peace, Dayton under Consolidated Elementary Schools located in the Institution section.
Catechesis/Religious Program—Jan Reed, Lay Ecclesial Min. Evangelization & Catechesis.

8—EMMANUEL (1837) Very Rev. Angelo Anthony, C.PP.S.; Rev. Kenneth Pleiman, C.PP.S., Parochial Vicar; Gary Geisel, Liturgy & Music Dir.
Res.: 149 Franklin St., 45402. Tel: 937-228-2013; Fax: 937-228-5354. Email: parishoffice@emmanuelcatholic.com. Web: www.emmanuelcatholic.com.
Catechesis/Religious Program—Email: jpoppdre@gmail.com. Mr. John Popp, D.R.E. Students 69.

9—ST. HELEN (1953) Revs. David E. Brinkmoeller; Satish Antony Joseph; Mary Heider, Pastoral Assoc. Liturgy & Stewardship; Deacons Susano Mascorro; Ralph O'Bleness; John Danner.
Res.: 605 Granville Pl., 45431. Tel: 937-254-6233; Fax: 937-256-6117. Email: office@sthelenparish.org. Web: www.sthelenparish.org.
School—(Grades K-8) Tel: 937-256-1761; Fax: 937-254-4614. Ms. Barbara Markus, Prin.; Jackie Skiple, Librarian. Lay Teachers 19; Students 322.
Catechesis/Religious Program—Tel: 937-256-8815. Joan Torres, Dir. Faith Formation (Adult); Matt Minix, Dir. Faith Formation (Youth). Students 141.

10—ST. HENRY (1960) Revs. Thomas M. Shearer; Ronald P. Combs; Deacon Michael Mahoney; Mary Ehret, Pastoral Assoc.
Mailing Address & Church: 6696 Springboro Rd., 45449. Tel: 937-434-9231; Fax: 937-434-6798. Email: ddavis@sthenryparish.com. Web: www.sthenryparish.com.
Res.: 6340 Blossom Park Dr., West Carrollton, 45449-3021. Email: shearer@sthenryparish.com. Web: www.sthenryparish.com.
See Bishop Leibold School, Dayton under Consolidated Elementary Schools located in the Institution section.
Catechesis/Religious Program—Students 400.

11—HOLY ANGELS (1902) Rev. Daniel J. Meyer; Sr. Annette Grisley, O.S.F., Pastoral Assoc.
Parish Office—1322 Brown St., 45409. Tel: 937-229-5911; Fax: 937-229-5919. Email: kdoran@holyangels.cc. Web: www.holyangels.cc.
Church: Brown & L Sts., 45409. Tel: 931-229-5912.
School—(Grades PreK-8) Tel: 937-229-5959; Fax: 937-229-5960. Email: bbauer@holyangels.cc. Rob Fortener, Prin. Lay Teachers 21; Students 293.
Catechesis/Religious Program—Tel: 937-229-5916. Jeanne Fairbanks, D.R.E. Students 183.

12—HOLY CROSS (1914), (Lithuanian), Rev. Michael J. Holloran.
22 Notre Dame Ave., 45404.
Catechesis/Religious Program—Tel: 937-228-8802; Fax: 937-443-0969. Students 1.

13—HOLY FAMILY (1905) Rev. Mark Wojdelski, F.S.S.P.
Mailing Address: 140 S. Findlay, 45403. Tel: 937-938-6098. Email: pastor@daytonlatinmass.org. Web: www.daytonlatinmass.org.
See Mary Queen of Peace, Dayton under Consolidated Elementary Schools located in the Institution section.
Catechesis/Religious Program— Please call office for information.

14—HOLY TRINITY (1860) [JC] Very Rev. Angelo Anthony, C.PP.S.; Rev. Kenneth Pleiman, C.PP.S., Parochial Vicar; Deacon George Zvonar; Mary C. Wlodarski, Pastoral Assoc.; Judith L. Trick, Business Mgr.
Parish Office: 272 Bainbridge St., 45402. Tel: 937-228-1223; Fax: 937-445-0232. Web: holytrinityofdayton.org.
Catechesis/Religious Program—Students 61.

15—ST. JOSEPH (1847) Very Rev. Angelo Anthony, C.PP.S.; Rev. Kenneth Pleiman, C.PP.S., Parochial Vicar.
Res.: 411 E. Second St., 45402. Tel: 937-228-9272; Fax: 937-228-6144. Email: stjosephday@sbcglobal.net.

16—ST. MARY (1859) Rev. Francis Tandoh, C.S.Sp.; Deacon William Saluke; Jim Buerschen, Business Mgr.
Rectory & Office: 310 Allen St., 45410. Tel: 937-256-5633; Fax: 937-256-7138. Email: hfsmchurches@sbcglobal.net. Web: www.stmarydayton.org.
See Mary Queen of Peace, Dayton under Consolidated Elementary Schools located in the Institution section.
Catechesis/Religious Program—Tel: 937-268-6697. Please contact parish office for more information.

17—OUR LADY OF MERCY (1928) Rev. Joshua Otusafo, C.S.Sp., Parochial Admin.; Deacons Tom Platfoot; Skip Royer.
Mailing Address & Parish Office: 220 W. Siebenthaler Ave., 45405. Tel: 937-274-2107; Fax: 937-274-4363. Email: info@corpusmercymartyrs.org. Web: www.corpusmercymartyrs.org.
Church: 533 Odlin Ave., 45405.
See Mary Queen of Peace Catholic School, Dayton under Consolidated Elementary Schools in the Institution section.
Catechesis/Religious Program—Jan Reed, Lay Ecclesial Min.Evangelization & Catechesis.

18—OUR LADY OF THE IMMACULATE CONCEPTION (1938) Revs. David E. Brinkmoeller; Satish Antony Joseph.
Res.: 2300 S. Smithville Rd., 45420. Tel: 937-252-9919; Fax: 937-252-1992. Web: www.icparishdayton.org.
School—(Grades K-8), 2268 S. Smithville Rd., 45420. Tel: 937-253-8831; Fax: 937-252-8832. Mrs. Karyn J. Hecker, Prin. Lay Teachers 12; Students 223.
Catechesis/Religious Program—Students 56.

19—OUR LADY OF THE ROSARY (1887) Rev. Michael J. Holloran.
Office & Mailing Address: 22 Notre Dame Ave., 45404. Tel: 937-228-8802; Fax: 937-443-0969. Email: olrdayton@aol.com. Web: www.olrdayton.com.
School—(Grades K-8), 40 Notre Dame Ave., 45404. Tel: 937-222-7231; Fax: 937-222-7393. Web: www.ol-r.com. Jack Loffer, Prin. Lay Teachers 11; Students 210.
Catechesis/Religious Program— Joint program with Holy Cross, Our Lady of the Rosary, and St. Stephen & St. Peter. Please see St. Peter, Huber Heights. Students 5.

20—ST. PETER (Huber Heights) (1959) Revs. Earl Francis Simone; Robert F. Hadden, Parochial Vicar; Kenneth Hummel, Parochial Vicar, (Peoria); Bro. Tim Cahill, C.PP.S.; Deacons Allen K. Miller; Norbert Nagy; John E. Gould; Timothy J. Harris; Russell O. Baldwin; Leo N. Cordonnier; Daniel J. Wade; Robert L. Basye; Ms. Joy Blaul, Dir. School of Religion.
Res.: 6161 Chambersburg Rd., 45424. Tel: 937-233-1503; Fax: 937-237-3523. Email: bulletin@saintpeterparish.org. Web: www.saintpeterparish.org.
School—(Grades PreK-8) Tel: 937-233-8710; Fax: 937-237-3974. Email: npstpeter@mdeca.org. Feliza Poling, Prin.; Mrs. Josephine Moore, Librarian. Lay Teachers 42; Students 834.
Catechesis/Religious Program—Tel: 937-237-3516; Fax: 937-233-5717. Ms. Joy Blaul, D.R.E. Students 271.

21—PRECIOUS BLOOD (1948) Rev. William O'Donnell, C.PP.S.; Deacons Richard Janowiecki; Michael F. Prier; Andrew R. Rammel; Joseph Hurr, Business Mgr. In Res., Rev. Vincent Wirtner, C.PP.S.
Res.: 4961 Salem Ave., 45416. Tel: 937-276-5954; Fax: 937-276-5956. Email: parishoffice@preciousbloodchurch.org. Web: www.preciousbloodchurch.org.
School—Mother Maria Anna Brunner School, (Grades K-8), 4870 Denlinger Rd., 45426. Tel: 937-277-2291; Fax: 937-277-2217. Web: www.brunnercatholicschool.org. Veronica Murphy, Prin.; Kay Feldmann, Librarian. Lay Teachers 24; Students 373.
Pre-School—1995 Shiloh Springs Rd., 45426. Tel: 937-854-7173; Fax: 937-854-8052.
Catechesis/Religious Program—Tel: 937-276-5954; Fax: 937-276-5955. Kristi Gaston, Coord. Children's Faith Formation. Students 119.

22—QUEEN OF MARTYRS (Northridge) (1948) Rev. Joshua Otusafo, C.S.Sp., Parochial Admin.; Deacons Tom Platfoot; Skip Royer; Jan Reed, Lay Ecclesial Min., Evangelization & Catechesis.
Mailing Address & Church Office: 220 W. Siebenthaler Ave., 45405-2240. Tel: 937-274-2107; Fax: 937-274-4363.
Church: 4134 Cedar Ridge Rd., 45414.
See Mary Queen of Peace, Dayton under Consolidated Elementary Schools located in the Institution section.
Catechesis/Religious Program—

23—ST. RITA (1922) Rev. William O'Donnell, C.PP.S.; Matt Ruttle, Pastoral Assoc.; Deacon James C. Olinger; Joseph Hurr, Business Mgr.
Res.: 5401 N. Main St., 45415. Tel: 937-278-5815; Fax: 937-275-3302. Web: www.stritadayton.org.
School—Mother Maria Anna Brunner School, (Grades K-8), 4870 Denlinger Rd., 45416. Tel: 937-277-2291; Fax: 937-277-2217. Veronica Murphy, Prin.; Kay Feldman, Librarian.
Catechesis/Religious Program—Students 16.

24—ST. STEPHEN (North Dayton) (1906), (Hungarian), Rev. Michael J. Holloran.
Parish Office—22 Notre Dame Ave., 45404-1924. Tel: 937-228-8802; Fax: 937-443-0969.
Church: 1114 Troy St., 45404.
Catechesis/Religious Program—Joint Program with Our Lady of the Rosary, St. Adalbert and Holy Cross Parishes, Dayton, Tel: 937-228-8604.

EATON, PREBLE CO., VISITATION OF THE BLESSED VIRGIN MARY (1853) Rev. J. Thomas Fitzsimmons.
Res.: 407 E. Main St., 45320. Tel: 937-456-3380; Fax: 937-456-3380. Email: church@visitationstjohn.com.
Catechesis/Religious Program—Tel: 937-456-3395. Email: ccdvisitation@msn.com. Sharon Stump, D.R.E.; Kimberly Leach, Youth Min. Students 125.

EGYPT, AUGLAIZE CO., ST. JOSEPH (1852) [CEM], Clustered with St. Augustine, Minster. Rev. Rick Nieberding, C.PP.S.
Res.: 02441 SR 364, 45865. Tel: 419-628-2614; Fax: 419-628-1078.
Catechesis/Religious Program—Tel: 419-628-3434. Clustered with St. Augustine, Minster. Students 57.

ENGLEWOOD, MONTGOMERY CO., ST. PAUL (1972) Rev. Stephen Dos Santos, C.PP.S.; Deacon Joseph Subler.
Res.: 1000 W. Wenger Rd., 45322. Tel: 937-836-7535; Fax: 937-836-1130. Web: www.stpaulenglewood.org.
Catechesis/Religious Program—Charles O. Wright, C.R.E. Students 131.

FAIRBORN, GREENE CO., MARY HELP OF CHRISTIANS (1862) [CEM] Rev. Charles F. Lang; Deacon Max Roadruck; Bill Fortener, Pastoral Assoc.
Res.: 954 N. Maple Ave., 45324-5498. Tel: 937-878-8353; Fax: 937-879-8800. Web: www.mhcparish.com.
Catechesis/Religious Program—Tel: 937-878-7325; Fax: 937-879-8800. Molly Hynes Collinsworth, D.R.E. Students 116.

FAIRFIELD, BUTLER CO., SACRED HEART OF JESUS (1957) Rev. Larry R. Tharp.
Church: 400 Nilles Rd., 45014. Tel: 513-858-4210; Fax: 513-858-4211. Web: www.sacredheart-fairfield.org.
Res.: 5202 Mississippi Dr., 45014. Tel: 513-863-5318; Fax: 513-863-5318.
School—Tel: 513-858-4215; Fax: 513-858-4218. Joseph Nagle, Prin. Lay Teachers 21; Students 402.
Catechesis/Religious Program—Tel: 513-858-4213; Fax: 513-858-4211. Students 199.

FAYETTEVILLE, BROWN CO., ST. ANGELA MERICI (2003) Rev. Henry F. Albietz.
130 Stone Alley, P.O. Box 279, 45118. Tel: 513-875-5020; Fax: 513-875-5022. Email: stangelamericiparish@cinci.rr.com. Web: www.home.catholicweb.com/stangelamerici.
Catechesis/Religious Program—130 Stone Alley, P.O. Box 279, 45118. Tel: 513-875-5020; Fax: 513-875-5022. Email: stangelamericiparish@cinci.rr.com. Web: home.catholicweb.com/stangelamerici. Rita Vilvens, C.R.E. Students 113.
Chapel—St. Patrick Chapel 45118.
Chapel—St. Martin Chapel 45118.

FORT LORAMIE, SHELBY CO., ST. MICHAEL (1838) [CEM] [JC 3] Rev. Steven L. Shoup; Ann Bollheimer, Pastoral Assoc.; Rose Meyer, Pastoral Assoc.; Kevin Musser, Youth Min. Coord.
Res.: 33 Elm St., P.O. Box 7, 45845. Tel: 937-295-3001. Email: steves@nflregion.org. Web: www.nflregion.org.
Catechesis/Religious Program—Tel: 937-295-2179; Fax: 937-295-3349. Diane Seger, D.R.E.; Kate Boeke, D.R.E. Students 619.

FORT RECOVERY, MERCER CO., MARY HELP OF CHRISTIANS (1881) [CEM], (Fort Recovery Cluster) Rev. Thomas E. Dorn; Deacon John Parker.
Mailing Address: 403 Sharpsburg Rd., 45846.
Res.: 417 Meiring Rd., 45846. Tel: 419-375-2603. Email: maryhelpccc@bright.net. Web: www.fortrecoverycatholicparishes.com.
Catechesis/Religious Program—Tel: 419-375-4153; Fax: 419-375-4154. Students 250.

FRANKLIN, WARREN CO., ST. MARY (1867) Rev. James J. Manning; Deacon Stephen Bermick III.
Church: 115 S. Main St., 45005. Tel: 937-746-5404; Fax: 937-746-5470. Email: stmaryfranklin@sbcglobal.net. Web: www.stmaryfranklin.4lpi.com.
Catechesis/Religious Program—Tel: 937-746-1404. Students 199.

FRENCHTOWN, DARKE CO., HOLY FAMILY (1846) [CEM] Rev. David P. Vincent.
Res.: 14 E. Wood St., Versailles, 45380-1440. Tel: 937-526-4945; Fax: 937-526-4893. Web: www.stdenishf.org.
Catechesis/Religious Program—Tel: 937-526-3957. Linda Meyer, C.R.E. Students 75.

FRYBURG, AUGLAIZE CO., ST. JOHN (1850), (German), [CEM 2] Rev. Oscar H. Seger; Deacon Nicholas Jurosic.
Res.: 11319 Van Buren St., Wapakoneta, 45895-8467. Tel: 419-738-6043; Fax: 419-738-4364.
Catechesis/Religious Program—Tel: 419-738-6268. Ann Limbert, D.R.E. Students 58.

GEORGETOWN, BROWN CO., ST. GEORGE (1902) Rev. Dohrman W. Byers; Deacon Ronald S. Dvorachek; Joan St. Clair, Pastoral Assoc.; Susan Caproni, Business Mgr.
Parish Office & Mailing Address: 16 N. 4th St., Ripley, 45167. Tel: 937-392-1116; Fax: 937-392-1699. Email: stsmichael-george@sbcglobal.net. Web: www.stgeorge.homestead.com.
Church: 509 E. State St. & Elm St., 45121.
Catechesis/Religious Program—Tel: 937-378-6453. Joan St. Clair, D.R.E. Students 19.

GERMANTOWN, MONTGOMERY CO., ST. AUGUSTINE (1941) Rev. Francis Tandoh, C.S.Sp.
Res.: 130 Gramont Ave., Dayton, 45417. Tel: 937-268-2747; Fax: 937-268-6698. Email: info@unitedinhope.org.
Church: 6939 Weaver Rd., 45327-9378. Tel: 937-855-2289; Fax: 937-855-2289.
Catechesis/Religious Program—Tel: 937-855-2289. Students 82.

GLYNWOOD, AUGLAIZE CO., ST. PATRICK (1857), (Irish), [CEM] Rev. Oscar H. Seger.
Church: 06959 Glynwood Rd., St. Marys, 45885. Tel: 419-738-6043; Fax: 419-738-4364.
Catechesis/Religious Program—Tel: 419-394-8458. Margaret Oen, D.R.E. Students 29.

GREENFIELD, HIGHLAND CO., ST. BENIGNUS (1856) [CEM] Rev. Michael A. Paraniuk; Patrick Hays, Business Mgr.
Res.: 204 S. Second St., P.O. Box 399, 45123. Tel: 937-981-2785; Fax: 937-981-4483. Web: stbenignus.org.
Catechesis/Religious Program—Katie Paugh, C.R.E. Students 35.

GREENVILLE, DARKE CO., ST. MARY (1853) [CEM] Rev. John R. White.
Res.: 233 W. 3rd St., 45331. Tel: 937-548-1616; Fax: 937-548-0352. Email: stmjc@bizwoh.rr.com. Web: www.stmarysgreenville.org.
School—(Grades PreK-8), 238 W. 3rd St., 45331. Tel: 937-548-2345; Fax: 937-548-0878. Email: chrisdetling@swohio.twcbc.com. Vernon Rosenbeck, Prin. Lay Teachers 10; Students 79.
Catechesis/Religious Program—Email: stmak@bizwoh.rr.com. Students 90.

HAMILTON, BUTLER CO.

1—ST. ANN (1909) Rev. Stephen J. Mondiek; Deacon George Schmidl.
Res.: 171 Washington St., 45011. Tel: 513-863-1424.
Church & Mailing Address: 646 Clinton Ave., 45015. Tel: 513-863-4963. Email: gerismith@live.com. Web: www.saintanncc.com.
School—(Grades K-8), 3064 Pleasant Ave., 45015. Tel: 513-863-0604. Web: www.stannhamilton.net. Mrs. Donna L. Weber, Prin. Lay Teachers 9; Students 144.
Catechesis/Religious Program—Tel: 513-863-4963. Students 33.

2—ST. JOSEPH (1867), (German), Revs. Stephen J. Mondiek; James H. Elsbernd, Sacramental Min.
Res. and Mailing Address: 171 Washington St., 45011. Tel: 513-863-1424; Fax: 513-863-1451. Email: jhaubner@sjcshamilton.org.
School—(Grades K-8), 925 Second St., 45011. Tel: 513-863-8758; Fax: 513-863-5772. Web: www.sjcshamilton.org. J. William Hicks, Prin. Lay Teachers 10; Students 210.
Catechesis/Religious Program—Students 3.

3—ST. JULIE BILLIART (1989) [CEM 2], (This parish is the successor in interest to St. Mary, St. Stephen and St. Veronica parishes, formerly located in Hamilton, OH.) Rev. Michael U. Pucke; Deacons William B. Renneker, Pastoral Assoc.; Thomas Strodtbeck; Mrs. Betty Meiner, Business Mgr.; Janet Poulin, Music Dir.
Church: 224 Dayton St., 45011-1634. Tel: 513-863-1040; Fax: 513-863-1132. Email: sjbparish@stjulie.net.
Catechesis/Religious Program—Mrs. Alison Smith, C.R.E. Students 205.

4—ST. PETER IN CHAINS (1894), (German), Rev. Ronald C. Haft.
Church, Mailing & Office Address: 382 Liberty Ave., 45013. Tel: 513-863-3938; Fax: 513-863-1257. Email: parishoffice@stpeterinchains.org. Web: www.stpeterinchains.org.
School—(Grades K-8), 451 Ridgelawn Ave., 45013. Tel: 513-863-0685; Fax: 513-863-1859. Email: schooloffice@stpeterinchains.org. Charlotte Sharon, Prin. Lay Teachers 14; Students 232.
Catechesis/Religious Program—382 Liberty Ave., 45013. Tel: 513-863-3938, Ext. 302. Email: valeriust@stpeterinchains.org; deatonm@stpeterinchains.org. Students 90.

HILLSBORO, HIGHLAND CO., ST. MARY (1853) [CEM] Rev. Michael A. Paraniuk; Deacon Leonard Parker, (Retired).
Res.: 212 S. High St., 45133-1445. Tel: 937-393-1742; Fax: 937-393-1742. Email: edbourdase@yahoo.com. Web: www.stmaryhillsboro.org.
School—(Grades PreSchool-4) Tel: 937-840-9932; Fax: 937-840-9932. Email: sschool35@cinci.rr.com. Web: www.stmaryofhillsboro.com. Mary Stanforth, Prin. Lay Teachers 3; Students 55.
Catechesis/Religious Program—Email: stmarycre@cinci.rr.com. Michelle Salyer, C.R.E. Students 70.

JAMESTOWN, GREENE CO., ST. AUGUSTINE (1870) Rev. John E. Krumm.
Res.: 16 Lucerne, Dayton, 45410. Tel: 937-409-9355.
Church: 44 E. Washington St., P.O. Box 189, 45335. Tel: 937-675-2601.
Catechesis/Religious Program—Gabrielle Bradds, D.R.E. Students 40.

LEBANON, WARREN CO., ST. FRANCIS DE SALES (1883) Rev. Bernard J. Weldishofer; Deacons Herschel Steward; Jay Rettig; Susan Olsen, Business Mgr.
Parish Office: 20-A DeSales Ave., 45036. Tel: 513-932-2601; Fax: 513-932-9144. Web: stfrancisdesales-lebanon.org.
Res.: 15 DeSales Ave., 45036. Tel: 513-933-0708.
Oratory— 20 DeSales Ave., 45036. Tel: 513-932-6501. Mr. Paul McLaughlin, Prin. Lay Teachers 12; Students 200.
Catechesis/Religious Program—Tel: 513-932-2601. Mike Kletzly, D.R.E.; Patrica Metzger, Music Min. Students 250.

LIBERTY TOWNSHIP, BUTLER CO., ST. MAXIMILIAN KOLBE (1989) Rev. Geoffrey D. Drew; Deacons John Paul Back; Michael W. Hinger; Michael E. Lippman.
Church & Mailing: 5720 Hamilton-Mason Rd., 45011. Tel: 513-777-4322; Fax: 513-777-7264. Email: web@saint-max.org. Web: www.saint-max.org.
Res.: 7168 St. Albans Way, Liberty Twp., 45011. In Res., Rev. Robert K. Muhlenkamp.
See St. Gabriel Consolidated School, Cincinnati under Consolidated Elementary Schools located in the Institution section.
Catechesis/Religious Program—Students 999.

LOVELAND, CLERMONT CO., ST. COLUMBAN (1859) Rev. Lawrence R. Tensi; Deacons Joseph Coll; James Miller; Jim Verhoff; Gerard J. Sasson; Harry Walker.
Office & Mailing Address: 894 Oakland Rd., 45140. Tel: 513-683-0105; Fax: 513-683-1389. Email: frontdesk@stcolumban.org. Web: www.stcolumban.org.
Res.: 885 Oakland Rd., 45140. Tel: 513-677-8084.
School—(Grades K-8), 896 Oakland Rd., 45140. Fax: 513-683-7904. Web: www.saintcolumban-school.org. Mrs. Jo Rhoten, Prin. Sisters 1; Lay Teachers 30; Students 725.
Catechesis/Religious Program—Tel: 513-683-0105; Fax: 513-683-1389. Students 460.
Convent—Sisters of Notre Dame, (Covington, KY), 896 Oakland Rd., 45140. Tel: 513-683-0255.

MARIA STEIN, MERCER CO.

1—ST. JOHN THE BAPTIST (1836) [CEM], (Marion Catholic Community) Revs. Eugene H. Schnipke, C.PP.S.; Thomas Brenberger, C.PP.S., Sr. Assoc. Pastor; Deacon Omer Bertke.
Marion Catholic Community Office: 7428 State Rte. 119, 45860. Tel: 419-925-4775; Fax: 419-925-1745. Email: marioncathcom@gmail.com. Web: www.marioncatholiccommunity.org.
Res.: 8533 State Rte. 119, 45860. Tel: 419-925-4522.
Catechesis/Religious Program—Tel: 419-925-6200; 419-925-4822. Julie Brunswick, D.R.E.; Angie Bertke, D.R.E. Students 300.

2—MOST PRECIOUS BLOOD (1903), (German), [CEM], (Marion Catholic Community) Revs. Eugene H. Schnipke, C.PP.S.; Thomas Brenberger, C.PP.S.
Office: *Marion Catholic Community Office*, 7428 State Rte. 119, 45860. Tel: 419-925-4775; Fax: 419-925-1745. Email: marioncathcom@gmail.com. Web: www.marioncatholiccommunity.org.
Res.: 8533 State Rte. 119, 45860. Tel: 419-925-4522.
Church: 35 S. Maple St., Box 26, Chickasaw, 45826-0026.
Catechesis/Religious Program—Katie Eilerman, C.R.E. Students 101.

MASON, WARREN CO., ST. SUSANNA (1938) Revs. Robert J. Farrell; Anthony G. Tozzi, Parochial Vicar; Deacons James A. Merritt; Daniel L. Rader; Karen Gottschall, Pastoral Assoc.; Chris Kreger, Pastoral Assoc.; Charlotte McManis, Business Mgr.
Church: 616 Reading Rd., 45040.
School—500 Reading Rd., 45040. Tel: 513-398-3821; Fax: 513-398-1657. Kevan Hartman, Prin. Lay Teachers 35; Students 646.
Catechesis/Religious Program—Tel: 513-398-3821. Students 1,129.

MCCARTYVILLE, SHELBY CO., SACRED HEART OF JESUS (1882) Rev. John W. Tonkin; Deacon Paul Luthman.
Res. & Mailing Address: 9333 State Rte. 119 W., Anna, 45302-9520. Tel: 937-394-3823; 419-628-2502; Fax: 937-394-2723. Email: office@sacredheartohio.org.
Catechesis/Religious Program—Barbara Riethman, C.R.E. Students 406.

MECHANICSBURG, CHAMPAIGN CO., ST. MICHAEL (1865) Rev. Lawrence M. Gearhart.
Res.: 40 Walnut St., 43044. Tel: 937-834-2664. Web: wwwchampaigncatholic.org.
Catechesis/Religious Program—Students 29.

MIAMISBURG, MONTGOMERY CO., OUR LADY OF GOOD HOPE (1852) [CEM] Rev. Thomas A. Nevels; Deacons Richard Martin; Terry Martin.
Res.: 6 S. Third St., 45342. Tel: 937-866-1432; Fax: 937-859-5035. Email: olgh2@sbcglobal.net. Web: www.olghchurch.org.
See Bishop Leibold School, Dayton under Consolidated Elementary Schools located in the Institution section.
Catechesis/Religious Program—Tel: 937-866-1492; Fax: 937-859-5035. Email: olghreled@catholicweb.com. Students 160.

MIDDLETOWN, BUTLER CO., HOLY FAMILY (1991) [JC], (This parish is the successor in interest to Holy Trinity, St. John the Baptist and St. Mary parishes, formerly located in Middletown, OH) Rev. John R.

Civille; Sr. Jean Sora, O.S.F., Pastoral Assoc.; Deacons William Krumm; Thomas Coyle, (Retired). Office: 201 Clark St., 45042. Tel: 513-422-0602; Fax: 513-424-7416. Web: www.holyfamilymiddletown.com.
See John XIII Catholic Elementary School under Consolidated Elementary Schools located in the Institution section.
Catechesis / Religious Program—Tel: 513-422-0602; Fax: 513-424-7416. Students 140.

MILFORD, CLERMONT CO., ST. ANDREW (1854) [CEM] Rev. Robert C. Waller; Deacon Timothy Schutte.
Res.: 552 Main St., 45150. Tel: 513-831-3353; Fax: 513-831-6597. Email: standy@cinci.rr.com. Web: www.standrew-milford.org.
School—St. Andrew-St. Elizabeth Seton, (Grades K-8), 555 Main St., 45150. Tel: 513-831-5277; Fax: 513-831-8436. Mr. Thomas Devolve, Prin. Consolidated. Lay Teachers 31; Students 485.
Catechesis / Religious Program—Fax: 513-831-6597. Kathy Bitzer, A.R.E. Students 215.

MILLVILLE, BUTLER CO., QUEEN OF PEACE (1941) Rev. Jeffery W. Bacon; Deacons Michael E. Mignery; Jeffrey P. Ehrnschwender.
Res.: 2550 Millville Ave., Hamilton, 45013. Tel: 513-863-4344; Fax: 513-863-4364. Email: parishoffice@qpchurch.org. Web: www.queenofpeachchurch.net.
School—(Grades PreK-8) Tel: 513-863-8705; Fax: 513-863-4310. Susan Schnell, Prin. Lay Teachers 15; Students 242.
Catechesis / Religious Program—Fax: 513-863-4364. Mary Ann Estridge, C.R.E.; Randi Hom, Youth Min. Students 83.

MINSTER, AUGLAIZE CO., ST. AUGUSTINE (1832), (German), [CEM] Rev. Rick Nieberding, C.PP.S.; Deacons John J. Schmiesing; Hal Belcher; Roger L. Klosterman.
Res.: 48 N. Hanover St., P.O. Box 93, 45865. Tel: 419-628-2614; Fax: 419-628-1078. Email: info@staugie.com. Web: www.staugie.com.
Catechesis / Religious Program—89 N. Lincoln St., P.O. Box 93, 45865. Tel: 419-628-3434; Fax: 419-628-3584. Email: augreled@staugie.com. Jane Boeke, D.R.E. Students 618.

MONROE, BUTLER CO., OUR LADY OF SORROWS (1883) Rev. Edward Pratt; Deacon Daniel Thomas; Nora Belwood, Pastoral Assoc.
Mailing Address: 330 Lebanon St., 45050. Web: www.olosmonroe.parishesonline.com.
Res.: 416 Lebanon St., 45050. Tel: 513-539-8383; Fax: 513-539-0443.
Catechesis / Religious Program—330 Lebanon St., 45050. Tel: 513-539-8061; Fax: 513-539-0443. Email: olos@cinci.rr.com. Students 147.

MONTEZUMA, MERCER CO., OUR LADY OF GUADALUPE (1904) [CEM] Rev. Rick Friebel, C.PP.S.
Res.: 6701 State Rte. 219, P.O. Box 69, 45866. Tel: 419-268-2312; Fax: 419-268-1602.
Catechesis / Religious Program—Tel: 419-268-2312. Ruth Wynk, C.R.E. Students 81.

MORROW, WARREN CO., ST. PHILIP THE APOSTLE (1965) [CEM] Rev. Ronald J. Piepmeyer; Deacon David M. Wallace.
Res.: 824 E. U.S. 22-3, 45152-9690.
Church: 944 E. U.S. 22-3, 45152-9690. Tel: 513-899-3601; Fax: 513-899-3785. Email: frron@stphilipmorrow.org. Web: www.stphilipmorrow.org.
Catechesis / Religious Program—Tel: 513-899-3601. Mrs. Mary Orite-Shea, C.R.E. Students 126.

MOUNT CARMEL, CLERMONT CO., ST. VERONICA (1949) Revs. P. Del Staigers; Patrick H. Crone (Retired); Deacon R. Daniel Murphy.
Church: 4473 Mt. Carmel-Tobasco Rd., 45244. Tel: 513-528-1622; Fax: 513-528-1622. Email: office@stveronica.org. Web: www.stveronica.org.
School—(Grades PreK-8), 4475 Mt. Carmel-Tobasco Rd., 45244. Tel: 513-528-0442; Fax: 513-528-0513. Email: school@stveronica.org. Gina Code, Prin. Sisters 1; Lay Teachers 24; Students 543.
Catechesis / Religious Program—Tel: 513-528-8723. Students 150.

MOUNT ORAB, BROWN CO., ST. MICHAEL (1944) Rev. Henry F. Albietz.
Res. & Offices: 130 Stone Alley, P.O. Box 279, Fayetteville, 45118. Tel: 513-875-5020; Fax: 513-875-5022. Email: stangelamericiparish@cinci.rr.com.
Church: 220 S. High St., 45154.
Catechesis / Religious Program—Linda Mulvaney, D.R.E. Students 19.

MOUNT REPOSE, CLERMONT CO., ST. ELIZABETH ANN SETON (1976) Rev. Michael L. Cordier; Deacon Steve R. Brown.
Res.: 5890 Buckwheat Rd., Milford, 45150. Tel: 513-575-0119; Fax: 513-575-0957. Email: easeton@cinci.rr.com. Web: www.setonmilford.org.
School—(Grades K-8), 5900 Buckwheat Rd., Milford, 45150. Tel: 513-575-0093; Fax: 513-575-1078. Mr. Thomas Devolve, Prin. Lay Teachers 27; Students 452.
Preschool—Tel: 513-575-9900; Fax: 513-575-1078. Mrs. Terri Imming, Dir. Lay Teachers 8; Students 126.
Catechesis / Religious Program—Tel: 513-575-0119; Fax: 513-575-0957. Patricia Norris, D.R.E. Students 226.

NEW BREMEN, AUGLAIZE CO., HOLY REDEEMER (1948) Rev. Thomas M. Mannebach; Deacon Gregory Bornhorst.
Church: 120 S. Eastmoor Dr., P.O. Box 67, 45869. Tel: 419-629-2543; Fax: 419-629-2543. Email: holyredeemer@nktelco.net. Web: www.holyredeemercatholicchurch.org.
Catechesis / Religious Program—Students 350.

NEW CARLISLE, CLARK CO., SACRED HEART (1950) Rev. Michael L. Bidwell; Deacon Robert Kozlowski.
Res.: 476 N. Scott St., 45344. Tel: 937-845-3121; Fax: 937-846-1223. Email: shsaintsnc@aol.com. Web: home.catholicweb.com/sacredsaints.
Catechesis / Religious Program—Tel: 937-845-1373. Melissa Elleman, C.R.E. Students 213.

NEW PARIS, PREBLE CO., ST. JOHN THE EVANGELIST (1870) [CEM] Rev. J. Thomas Fitzsimmons.
Res. & Mailing Address: 407 E. Main St., Eaton, 45320. Tel: 937-456-3380; Fax: 937-456-3380.
Church: N. Spring St., 45347.
Catechesis / Religious Program— Joint program with Visitation Parish, Eaton, OH

NEW RICHMOND, CLERMONT CO., ST. PETER (1850) [CEM] Rev. Michael F. Leshney; Deacon Ronald L. Stang.
Res.: 1192 Bethel-New Richmond Rd., 45157. Tel: 513-553-3267; Fax: 513-553-4321. Email: michaelleshney@fuse.net. Web: www.stpeternewrichmond.org.
Catechesis / Religious Program— Tina Conners, D.R.E. Students 54.

NEWPORT, SHELBY CO., SS. PETER AND PAUL (1856) [CEM] Rev. Steven L. Shoup.
Res.: 6788 State Rte. 66, P.O. Box 199, Fort Loramie, 45845. Tel: 937-295-2891; Fax: 937-295-3349. Email: bettyanne@nflregion.org. Web: www.nflregion.org.
Catechesis / Religious Program—Tel: 937-295-2536. Lisa Monnin, C.R.E. Students 79.

NORTH LEWISBURG, CHAMPAIGN CO., IMMACULATE CONCEPTION (1869) Rev. Lawrence M. Gearhart.
Res. & Mailing Address: 40 Walnut St., Mechanicsburg, 43044. Tel: 937-834-2664. Web: www.champaigncatholic.org.
Church: Corner of Elm & Winder Sts., 43060.
Catechesis / Religious Program—Students 9.

NORTH BEND, HAMILTON CO., ST. JOSEPH (1860) Rev. Michael A. Savino.
Mailing Address: P.O. Box 219, 45052. Email: stjosephnorthbend@roadrunner.com. Web: www.stjosephnorthbend.com.
Church: 25 E. Harrison Ave., 45052. Tel: 513-941-3661; Fax: 513-941-8559.
Res.: 3700 Chestnut Park, Cleves, 45002. Tel: 513-467-0450.
Catechesis / Religious Program—Mary Jo Ressel, D.R.E. Students 125.

NORTH STAR, DARKE CO., ST. LOUIS (1891) [CEM] Rev. David L. Zink.
Parish Office—P.O. Box 9, Osgood, 45351. Tel: 419-582-2531; Fax: 419-582-2015.
Church: 15 Star Rd., 45350.
Catechesis / Religious Program—Linda Wehrkamp, D.R.E. Students 192.

OSGOOD, DARKE CO., ST. NICHOLAS (1909) [CEM] Rev. David L. Zink.
Office: 128 Church St., P.O. Box 9, 45351. Tel: 419-582-2531; Fax: 419-582-2015.
Catechesis / Religious Program—Linda Kuether, D.R.E. Students 219.

OWENSVILLE, CLERMONT CO., ST. LOUIS (1856) [CEM] Rev. Gerard P. Hiland.
Res.: 255 N. Broadway, 45160. Tel: 513-732-0649; 513-732-2218 (office); Fax: 513-732-2368. Email: fatherhiland@aol.com. Web: www.stlparish.org.
School—(Grades PreK-8), 250 N. Broadway, 45160. Tel: 513-732-0636. Mrs. Margaret Noonan Hunsberger, Prin. Lay Teachers 12; Students 156.
Catechesis / Religious Program—Students 71.

OXFORD, BUTLER CO., ST. MARY CHURCH AND CATHOLIC CAMPUS MINISTRY (Miami U.) (1853) [CEM] Rev. Jeffrey P. Silver; Roberta L. Kinne, Pastoral Assoc.; Kimberly Wagner, Campus Min.; Ryan Leep, Music Dir.; Pam Burk, Business Mgr.; Tara Bowers, Sec.
Res.: 111 E. High St., 45056. Tel: 513-523-2153; Fax: 513-523-0559. Email: info@stmaryoxfordohio.org. Web: www.stmaryoxfordohio.org.
Catechesis / Religious Program—Michael Puglielli, D.R.E. Students 130.

PEEBLES, ADAMS CO., ST. MARY QUEEN OF HEAVEN (1952), (Vicariate) Rev. Theodore C. Kosse.
Church, Office & Mailing Address: *Holy Trinity*, 205 Wendell Ave., 45660. Tel: 937-544-2757; Fax: 937-544-7637.
Catechesis / Religious Program—Tel: 937-446-9294. Students 10.

PHILOTHEA, MERCER CO., ST. MARY (1851), (German), [CEM], (Coldwater Cluster) Revs. Richard W. Walling; Barry J. Stechschulte, Parochial Vicar.
Mailing Address: P.O. Box 107, Coldwater, 45828.
Res.: 120 E. Main St., P.O. Box 107, Coldwater, 45828. Tel: 419-678-4802; Fax: 419-678-4803. Email: coldwatercluster@bright.net. Web: www.coldwatercluster.org.
Catechesis / Religious Program—Sue Homan, D.R.E. Students 51.

PIQUA, MIAMI CO.
1—ST. BONIFACE (1855) Revs. Martin E. Fox; Angelo C. Caserta (Retired). Tel: 937-778-9526.
310 S. Downing St., 45356.
Res.: 528 Broadway, 45356. Tel: 937-773-0075. Web: www.stbonifacepiqua.org.
See Piqua Catholic School, Piqua under Consolidated Elementary Schools located in the Institution section.
Catechesis / Religious Program—Tel: 937-773-1656; Fax: 937-773-2665. Email: religioused@stbonifacepiqua.org. Students 53.
2—ST. MARY (1843) Revs. Martin E. Fox; Thomas J. Grilliot (Retired); Sr. Joan Clare Stewart, S.C., Pastoral Assoc.
Mailing Address & Parish Offices: 310 S. Downing St., 45356.
Res. & Church: 528 Broadway, 45356. Tel: 937-773-1327; Fax: 937-773-2665.
See Piqua Catholic School, Piqua under Consolidated Elementary Schools located in the Institution section.
Catechesis / Religious Program—Students 30.

RHINE, SHELBY CO., ST. LAWRENCE (1856), (German), [CEM] Revs. Patrick L. Sloneker; Matthew K. Lee, Parochial Vicar; Deacon Terrell Coleman.
Mailing Address & Parish Office: P.O. Box 519, Botkins, 45306.
Res.: 16053 Botkins Rd., P.O. Box 519, Botkins, 45306. Tel: 937-693-2561; Fax: 937-693-2561.
Catechesis / Religious Program—Tel: 937-693-2571. Students 103.

RIPLEY, BROWN CO., ST. MICHAEL (1840) Rev. Dohrman W. Byers; Deacon Ronald S. Dvorachek; Maureen Harvey, Pastoral Assoc. & Rel. Educ.; Susan Caproni, Business Mgr.
Church & Parish Office: 16 N. Fourth St., 45167. Tel: 937-392-1116 (Office Sec.); 937-392-1840 (Bus. Mgr.); Fax: 937-392-1699. Email: stsmichael-george@sbcglobal.net. Web: www.stmichael.homestead.com.
School—(Grades PreK-8) Tel: 937-392-4202; Fax: 937-392-4248. Web: www.stmichaelcatholic-school.org. Sr. Carol Ann Mause, O.S.F., Prin.; Melody Kokensparger, Librarian. Lay Teachers 10; Students 60.
Catechesis / Religious Program—Tel: 937-392-1335. Students 18.

ROCKFORD, MERCER CO., ST. TERESA (1936) Rev. Ken Schnipke, C.PP.S.
Church: 4227 State Rte. 707, P.O. Box 445, 45882. Tel: 419-363-2633; Fax: 419-363-2633. Email: stteresachurch@bright.net.
Catechesis / Religious Program— Annie Ford, C.R.E. Students 75.

RUSSELLS POINT, LOGAN CO., ST. MARY OF THE WOODS (1927) Rev. Harold W. Kist (Retired).
Mailing Address: P.O. Box 329, 43348-0329.
Res.: 464 Madison Ave., P.O. Box 329, 43348. Tel: 937-843-3127; Fax: 937-843-3866. Email: stmarwds@bright.net. Web: saintmaryofthewoods.com.
Catechesis / Religious Program—Tel: 937-843-4227. Dona Fischer. Students 129.
Mission—St. George Chapel Marianists of Ohio 9636 Lake Shore Dr., E., Huntsville, Logan Co. 43324. Tel: 937-842-4902.

RUSSIA, SHELBY CO., ST. REMY (1846) [CEM] Rev. Frank G. Amberger.
Res.: 108 E. Main St., 45363-9701. Tel: 937-526-3437; Fax: 937-526-5326. Email: stremy@roadrunner.com. Web: www.stremychurch.com.
Catechesis / Religious Program—Tel: 937-526-3437; Fax: 937-526-5326. Email: stremydre@roadrunner.com. Karen Rosenbeck, C.R.E. Students 353.

ST. ANTHONY, MERCER CO., ST. ANTHONY (1852), (German), [CEM], (Coldwater Cluster) Revs. Richard W. Walling; Barry J. Stechschulte, Parochial Vicar.
Mailing Address: P.O. Box 107, Coldwater, 45828. Tel: 419-678-4802; Fax: 419-678-4803.
Church: 471 St. Anthony Rd., Fort Recovery, 45846-9404.
Catechesis / Religious Program—Tel: 419-375-3013. Cindy Muhlenkamp, D.R.E. Students 85.

SAINT HENRY, MERCER CO., ST. HENRY (1839) [CEM], (St. Henry Cluster) Revs. Thomas Hemm, C.PP.S.;

Benedict Magabe, C.PP.S. (Tanzania); Deacons Jerry Buschur; Randy Balster.
Res.: 1509 Cranberry Rd., Cranberry, 45883. Tel: 419-925-4776.
Church & Mailing Address: 272 E. Main St., Box 350, 45883. Tel: 419-678-4118; Fax: 419-678-8285. Email: shclusteroffice@hotmail.com. Web: www.sthenrycluster.com.
Inter-parish Center—162 S. Walnut, 45883. Tel: 419-678-3811; Fax: 419-678-8285.
Catechesis / Religious Program—Tel: 419-678-3811. Email: sthenryccd@bright.net. Catherine Wenning, D.R.E. Students 565.

ST. JOSEPH, MERCER CO., ST. JOSEPH (1839), (German), [CEM], (Fort Recovery Cluster) Rev. Thomas E. Dorn.
Mailing Address: 403 Sharpsburg Rd., Fort Recovery, 45846. Tel: 419-375-4153. Email: maryhelpccc@bright.net. Web: www.fortrecoverycatholicparishes.com.
Church: 1689 St. Joseph Rd., Fort Recovery, 45846. Fax: 419-375-4154.
Catechesis / Religious Program—Valerie Heitkamp, D.R.E. Twinned with St. Peter Parish, St. Peter. Students 251.

ST. MARYS, AUGLAIZE CO., HOLY ROSARY (1852) [CEM] Rev. Anthony E. Cutcher.
Res.: 511 E. Spring St., 45885. Tel: 419-394-5050; Fax: 419-394-0184. Email: holyrosary@bright.net. Web: www.holyrosarychurch.us.
School—(Grades PreK-8) Tel: 419-394-5291. Web: www.holyrosaryschool.us. Lora Krugh, Prin.; Elaine Mallory, Librarian. Lay Teachers 11; Students 129.
Catechesis / Religious Program—Email: mielkecrew@yahoo.com. Nan Mielke, C.R.E. Students 150.

ST. PARIS, CHAMPAIGN CO., SACRED HEART (ST. PARIS) (1868) Rev. Gregory J. Konerman.
Res. Mailing Address & Office: 231 Washington Ave., Urbana, 43078-1728. Tel: 937-653-1375; Fax: 937-653-1383. Email: stmary@ctcn.net. Web: www.champaigncatholic.org.
Church: 121 E. Walnut St., 43072.
Catechesis / Religious Program—Tel: 937-653-1375. Twinned with St. Mary, Urbana.

ST. PETER, MERCER CO., ST. PETER (1860), (German), [CEM], (Fort Recovery Cluster) Rev. Thomas E. Dorn.
Mailing Address: 403 Sharpsburg Rd., Fort Recovery, 45846.
Church: 1477 Philothea Rd., Fort Recovery, 45846. Tel: 419-375-4153; Fax: 419-375-4154. Email: maryhelpccc@bright.net. Web: www.fortrecoverycatholicparishes.com.
Catechesis / Religious Program—Valerie Heitkamp, D.R.E. Twinned with St. Joseph Parish, St. Joseph. Students 251.

ST. ROSE, MERCER CO., ST. ROSE (1839), (German), [CEM], (Marion Catholic Community) Revs. Eugene H. Schnipke, C.PP.S.; Thomas Brenberger, C.PP.S.
Marion Catholic Community Office: 7428 State Rte. 119, Maria Stein, 45860. Tel: 419-925-4775; Fax: 419-925-1745. Email: marioncathcom@gmail.com. Web: www.marioncatholiccommunity.org.
Res.: 8533 State Rte. 119, Maria Stein, 45860. Tel: 419-925-4522.
Catechesis / Religious Program—Tel: 419-925-4641. Jackie Garman, D.R.E. Students 78.

ST. SEBASTIAN, MERCER CO., ST. SEBASTIAN (1852), (German), [CEM], (Marion Catholic Community) Revs. Eugene H. Schnipke, C.PP.S.; Thomas Brenberger, C.PP.S.
Mailing Address: 7428 State Rte. 119, Maria Stein, 45860. Tel: 419-925-4775. Email: marioncathcom@gmail.com. Web: www.marioncatholiccommunity.org.
Church: 3280 Co. Rd. 716-A, Celina, 45822.
Catechesis / Religious Program—Becky Kunkler, D.R.E. Students 51.

ST. WENDELIN, MERCER CO., ST. WENDELIN (1856) [CEM], (St. Henry Cluster) Revs. Thomas Hemm, C.PP.S.; Benedict Magabe, C.PP.S. (Tanzania).
Mailing Address: 272 E. Main St., Box 350, Saint Henry, 45883. Tel: 419-678-4118; Fax: 419-678-8285. Email: tomhemm@hotmail.com. Web: www.sthenrycluster.com.
Res.: 1509 Cranberry Rd., Saint Henry, 45883. Tel: 419-925-4776.
Church: 2980 Ft. Recovery-Minster Rd., Saint Henry, 45883.
Catechesis / Religious Program—Tel: 419-678-3811. Email: sthenryccd@bright.net. Students 43.

SHANDON, BUTLER CO., ST. ALOYSIUS (1867) [CEM] Rev. Raymond J. Leurck; Deacon Bill Brunsman.
Res.: 5484 Cinti Brookville Rd., 45063. Tel: 513-738-1014; Fax: 513-738-2084.
Church: 3350 Chapel Rd., P.O. Box 95, 45063. Tel: 513-738-1014.
Catechesis / Religious Program—Tel: 513-738-4641. Students 120.

SHARPSBURG, MERCER CO., ST. PAUL (1868) [CEM], (Fort Recovery Cluster) Rev. Thomas E. Dorn.
Mailing Address: 403 Sharpsburg Rd., Fort Recovery, 45846. Tel: 419-375-4153. Email: maryhelpccc@bright.net. Web: www.fortrecoverycatholicparishes.com.
Res.: 517 Meiring Rd., Fort Recovery, 45846. Tel: 419-375-2603; Fax: 419-375-9413.
Catechesis / Religious Program—Tel: 419-375-2308. Students 154.

SIDNEY, SHELBY CO., HOLY ANGELS (1848) Revs. Daniel J. Schmitmeyer; Daniel K. Hess, Parochial Vicar; Deacons Philip Myers; John Holthaus, Pastoral Assoc.
Res.: 324 S. Ohio Ave., 45365-3012. Tel: 937-498-2307; Fax: 937-498-2308. Email: info@holyangelssidney.com. Web: www.holyangelssidney.com.
School—(Grades K-8), 120 E. Water St., 45365-3199. Tel: 937-492-9293; Fax: 937-492-8578. Email: info@holyangelscatholic.com. Web: www.holyangelscatholic.com. Mary T. Martin, Prin.; Jill Heitmeyer, Librarian. Lay Teachers 18; Students 226.
Catechesis / Religious Program—c/o Office 121 E. Water St., 45365-3199. Tel: 937-498-0433; Fax: 937-498-1448. Email: hareligioused@hotmail.com. Susan Anderson, C.R.E. Students 221.

SOUTH CHARLESTON, CLARK CO., ST. CHARLES BORROMEO (1866) [CEM] Rev. Anthony J. Geraci.
31 S. Chillicothe St., P.O. Box F, 45368-0806. Tel: 937-462-8971; Fax: 937-462-9184. Web: www.charlesborromeo.com.
Rectory—St. Paul Rectory, 308 Phillips St., Yellow Springs, 45387-1724. Tel: 937-767-7450; Fax: 937-767-7465. Email: stpauloffice@woh.rr.com.
Catechesis / Religious Program—Fax: 937-462-9184. Students 15.

SPRINGFIELD, CLARK CO.

1—ST. BERNARD (1860), (German), [CEM] Rev. Paul F. Hurst.
Res.: 910 Lagonda Ave., 45503. Tel: 937-322-5243; Fax: 937-322-3788.
School—Catholic Central Elementary, (Grades PreK-6), *Central Offices*, 1817 N. Limestone St., 45503-2696. Tel: 937-399-5451; Fax: 937-342-0042. Ms. Mary Callahan, Prin.; Molly Mann, Librarian & Technology Coord. Lay Teachers 9; Students 190.
Catechesis / Religious Program—Tel: 937-324-2870; Fax: 937-322-3788. Trish Evans, C.R.E. Students 51.

2—ST. JOSEPH (1882) Rev. Dennis J. Caylor; Deacons John R. Collins; Norman G. Horstman.
Res.: 1041 Sundown Dr., 45503. Tel: 937-323-7097.
Church Mailing Address: 225 E. High St., 45505. Tel: 937-323-7523; Fax: 937-324-1512. Web: www.josephraphael.org.
See Catholic Central Elementary School, Springfield under St. Bernard, Springfield for details.
Catechesis / Religious Program— Twinned with St. Raphael, Springfield. Students 50.

3—ST. RAPHAEL (1849) Rev. Dennis J. Caylor; Deacons John R. Collins; Norman G. Horstman.
Res.: 1041 Sundown Dr., 45503. Tel: 937-323-7097.
Church: 225 E. High St., 45505. Tel: 937-323-7523; Fax: 937-324-1512. Web: www.josephraphael.org.
See Catholic Central Elementary School, Springfield under St. Bernard, Springfield for details.
Catechesis / Religious Program—Tel: 937-323-7523. Twinned with St. Joseph, Springfield. Students 164.

4—ST. TERESA OF THE CHILD JESUS (1931) Rev. Edwin F. Gearhart.
Res.: 137 Floral Ave., 45504.
Church: 1827 N. Limestone St., 45503. Tel: 937-342-8861; Fax: 937-399-6971. Email: stteresa.church@bizwoh.rr.com.
School—Catholic Central Elementary School, (Grades K-6) Tel: 937-399-5451; Fax: 937-342-0042. Molly Mann, Prin.; Laura Watkins, Librarian.
Catechesis / Religious Program—Tel: 937-342-8861, Ext. 16; Fax: 937-399-6971. Melanie Oliver, C.R.E. Students 43.

STONELICK, CLERMONT CO., ST. PHILOMENA (1837) [CEM] Rev. Gerard P. Hiland.
Res.: 255 N. Broadway, Box 85, Owensville, 45160.
Church & Mailing Address: 210 N. Broadway, Box 85, Owensville, 45160. Tel: 513-732-2218; Fax: 513-732-2368. Email: fatherhiland@aol.com.

TIPP CITY, MIAMI CO., ST. JOHN THE BAPTIST (1858) [CEM] Rev. R. Marc Sherlock.
Res.: 753 S. Hyatt St., 45371-1255. Tel: 937-667-3419; Fax: 937-667-9267. Email: sjbsecretary@woh.rr.com. Web: www.stjohntippcity.org.
Catechesis / Religious Program—Tel: 937-667-3419. Jennifer Melke, D.R.E. Students 344.

TRENTON, BUTLER CO., HOLY NAME (1871) [CEM] Rev. Thomas H. McCarthy, Parochial Admin.; Deacon William E. Schaefer.
Res.: 222 Hamilton Ave., 45067. Tel: 513-988-6335; Fax: 513-998-9900.
Catechesis / Religious Program—Tel: 513-988-9348. Students 75.

TROY, MIAMI CO., ST. PATRICK (1857) Revs. James S. Duell; Joseph F. Kozar, S.M.; Deacons John Carlin; Robert Knight.
Res.: 409 E. Main St., 45373. Tel: 937-335-2833; Fax: 937-335-1453. Email: stpatofficemgr@woh.rr.com. Web: www.stpattroy.org.
School—(Grades PreK-6), 420 E. Water St., 45373. Tel: 937-339-3705; Fax: 937-339-1158. Ms. Cyndi Cathcart, Prin. Lay Teachers 7; Students 134.
Catechesis / Religious Program—409 E. Main St., 45373. Students 323.

TWENTY MILE STAND, WARREN CO., ST. MARGARET OF YORK (1984) Rev. Jan Kevin Schmidt; Deacon Raymond Kroger.
Res.: 9483 Columbia Rd., Loveland, 45140. Tel: 513-683-7100; Fax: 513-683-7101. Email: feedback@stmargaretofyork.org. Web: www.stmargaretofyork.org.
School—(Grades K-8), 9495 Columbia Rd., Loveland, 45140. Tel: 513-683-9793; Fax: 513-683-8949. Email: info@smoyschool.com. Web: stmargaret-york.cnd.pvt.k12.oh.us. Dr. Tony Riegling, Prin.; Mrs. Nancy Shula, Asst. Prin. Lay Teachers 32; Students 705.
Catechesis / Religious Program—Tel: 513-683-7100, Ext. 206. Email: susangravely@stmargaretofyork.org. Susan Gravely, D.R.E. Students 602.

URBANA, CHAMPAIGN CO., ST. MARY (1853) Rev. Gregory J. Konerman; Deacon Earl Rogers Jr.
Res.: 231 Washington Ave., 43078. Tel: 937-653-1375; Fax: 937-653-1383. Email: stmary@ctcn.net. Web: www.champaigncatholic.org.
School—Catholic Central Elementary School, (Grades K-6), *Administrative Offices*, 1827 N. Limestone St., Springfield, 45503. Tel: 937-399-5451; Fax: 937-342-0042. Ms. Mary Callahan, Prin.
Catechesis / Religious Program—Students 61.

VANDALIA, MONTGOMERY CO., ST. CHRISTOPHER (1957) Rev. Francis J. Keferl; Charles O. Wright; Joan Dunn, Pastoral Assoc.
Res.: 435 E. National Rd., 45377. Tel: 937-898-3542; Fax: 937-898-1017. Email: christophervandalia@catholicweb.com. Web: www.stchristopheronline.com.
School—(Grades K-8), 405 E. National Rd., 45377. Tel: 937-898-5104; Fax: 937-454-4790. Email: spk@stchris.cnd.pvt.k12.oh.us. Web: www.stchris.cnd.pvt.k12.oh.us. Sr. Patricia Kremer, Prin.; Carrie Hartley, Librarian. Lay Teachers 23; Students 372.
Catechesis / Religious Program—Email: lslattery@catholicweb.com. Students 395.

VERSAILLES, DARKE CO., ST. DENIS (1839) [CEM] Rev. David P. Vincent.
Res.: 14 E. Wood St., 45380. Tel: 937-526-4945; Fax: 937-526-4893. Email: dvincent@bright.net. Web: www.stdenishf.org.
Catechesis / Religious Program—Tel: 937-526-3957. Linda Meyer, C.R.E. Students 518.

WAPAKONETA, AUGLAIZE CO., ST. JOSEPH (1839) [CEM] Revs. Patrick L. Sloneker; Matthew K. Lee, Parochial Vicar; Deacon Richard L. Westbay.
Office & Mailing Address: 309 Perry St., 45895. Tel: 419-738-2115; Fax: 419-738-4525. Email: stjoe@bright.net. Web: www.stjoewapak.org.
Church: 101 W. Pearl St., 45895.
Catechesis / Religious Program—Tel: 419-738-2115; Fax: 419-738-4525. Students 310.

WAYNESVILLE, WARREN CO., ST. AUGUSTINE (1876) [JC] Rev. Raymond Kammerer.
Res.: 5715 Lytle Rd., 45068. Tel: 513-897-2821; Fax: 513-897-2821.
Catechesis / Religious Program—Tel: 937-299-2772. Pat Ebright, D.R.E. Students 98.

WEST CHESTER, BUTLER CO., ST. JOHN (1880) Rev. Don J. West; Deacon Gerald L. Barney.
Res.: 9080 Cincinnati-Dayton Rd., 45069. Tel: 513-777-6433; Fax: 513-777-9741. Email: info@stjohnwc.org. Web: www.stjohnwc.org.
See St. Gabriel Consolidated School, Cincinnati under Consolidated Elementary Schools located in the Institution section.
Catechesis / Religious Program—Tel: 513-755-4974. Students 407.

WEST MILTON, MIAMI CO., TRANSFIGURATION (1950) Rev. John D. MacQuarrie.
Res.: 972 S. Miami St., 45383. Tel: 937-698-4520; Fax: 937-698-4500. Email: transcathch@woh.rr.com. Web: www.transfigurationonline.com.
Catechesis / Religious Program—Students 153.

WEST UNION, ADAMS CO., HOLY TRINITY (1950) Rev. Theodore C. Kosse.
Res.: 612 E. Mulberry St., 45693. Tel: 937-544-2757; Fax: 937-544-7637.
Catechesis / Religious Program—Tel: 937-544-2013. Email: maryann.welling@holytrinity-ac.org. Students 53.

WILLIAMSBURG, CLERMONT CO., ST. ANN (1947) Rev. Gerard P. Hiland, Temporary Parochial Admin.
Res. & Mailing Address: 140 N. Sixth St., Batavia, 45103. Tel: 513-732-2024; Fax: 513-732-0049. Email: alleluia@fuse.net.
Church: 370 S. 5th St., 45176. Tel: 513-724-7684.
Catechesis/Religious Program—Cynthia Barno, D.R.E. Students 20.

WILMINGTON, CLINTON CO., ST. COLUMBKILLE (1866) Rev. James M. Wedig; Deacons Robert G. Baker; Robert E. Meyer.
Res.: 73 N. Mulberry St., 45177-2277. Tel: 937-382-2236; Fax: 937-382-3234. Email: saintcolumbkille@yahoo.com. Web: www.stcolumbkille.org.
Catechesis/Religious Program—Tel: 937-382-1596. Students 182.

WITHAMSVILLE, CLERMONT CO., ST. THOMAS MORE (1940) Rev. William C. Wagner; Deacons Frederick J. Haas; Michael T. Thomas, Pastoral Assoc.
Res.: 800 Ohio Pike, 45245-2299. Tel: 513-752-2080 (Office); 513-753-2553 (Pastor); Fax: 513-753-2542. Email: stm@sttm.org. Web: www.sttm.org.
School—(Grades K-8), 788 Ohio Pike, 45245-2156. Tel: 513-753-2540, Ext. 122; Fax: 513-753-2554. Email: principal@sttm.org. Web: www.sttm-school.org. Mrs. Peggy Fischer, Prin. Lay Teachers 17; Students 300.
Catechesis/Religious Program—Tel: 513-753-2548; Fax: 513-753-2542. Mrs. Becky Ready, D.R.E. Students 121.

XENIA, GREENE CO., ST. BRIGID (1849) [CEM] Rev. John E. Krumm; Deacon Dennis Kall.
Church & Mailing Address: 258 Purcell Dr., 45385. Tel: 937-372-3193; Fax: 937-374-3622.
Res.: 16 Lucerne Ave., Dayton, 45410. Tel: 937-409-9355.
School—(Grades PreK-8), 312 Fairground Rd., 45385. Tel: 937-372-3222. Patricia Harner, Prin. Lay Teachers 12; Students 165.
Catechesis/Religious Program—Tel: 937-372-3222. Students 100.

YELLOW SPRINGS, GREENE CO., ST. PAUL (1856) [CEM] Rev. Anthony J. Geraci; Deacon Paul E. Richardson.
Church & Mailing Address: 308 Phillips St., 45387. Tel: 937-767-7450; Fax: 937-767-7465. Email: stpauloffice@woh.rr.com. Web: www.stpaulchurchyso.org.
Catechesis/Religious Program—Email: stpauldre@woh.rr.com. Mr. Josh Danis, C.R.E. Students 67.

Closed and Merged Parishes

GREATER CINCINNATI

1—ST. AGNES (Bond Hill) (1892), (African American), Merged with St. Andrew, St. Mark the Evangelist, and St. Martin de Porres, Cincinnati, to form Church of the Resurrection, Cincinnati. For inquiries for parish records contact the Chancery.

2—ST. ALOYSIUS CHURCH (Elmwood Place) Closed. For inquiries for parish records, contact St. Clement, (St. Bernard).

3—ST. ANDREW (1874), (African American), Merged with St. Agnes, St. Mark the Evangelist, and St. Martin de Porres, Cincinnati, to form Church of the Resurrection, Cincinnati. For inquiries for parish records contact the Chancery.

4—ST. BONAVENTURE (1869) Closed. For inquiries for parish records, contact St. Leo, Cincinnati.

5—ST. CHARLES BORROMEO CHURCH (Carthage) Closed. For inquiries for parish records, contact St. James of the Valley, (Wyoming).

6—COMMUNITY OF HOPE, Closed. For inquiries for parish records contact the chancery.

7—ST. ELIZABETH CHURCH (Norwood) Merged with St. Matthew Church, Norwood and Sts. Peter & Paul Church, Norwood to form Holy Trinity Church, Norwood. Records at Holy Trinity Church.

8—ST. GEORGE PARISH & NEWMAN CENTER, Closed. For inquiries for parish records contact St. Monica-St. George Newman Center.

9—HOLY ANGELS (1859) Merged with St. Francis de Sales, Cincinnati. Records at St. Francis de Sales.

10—ST. JEROME (1863) Closed. For inquiries for parish records contact Guardian Angels, Cincinnati.

11—ST. JOHN VIANNEY (Madison Pl.) (1949) Merged with St. Margaret of Cortona Parish, Cincinnati to form St. Margaret-St. John Parish, Cincinnati. For inquiries for parish records contact St. Margaret-St. John, Cincinnati.

12—ST. MARGARET OF CORTONA (Madisonville) (1921) Merged with St. John Vianney Parish, Cincinnati to form St. Margaret-St. John Parish, Cincinnati. For inquiries for parish records contact St. Margaret-St. John, Cincinnati.

13—ST. MARK THE EVANGELIST (1905) Merged with St. Agnes, St. Andrew, and St. Martin de Porres, Cincinnati, to form Church of the Resurrection, Cincinnati. For inquiries for parish records contact the Chancery.

14—ST. MARTIN DE PORRES (Lincoln Heights) (1935), (African American), Merged with St. Agnes, St. Andrew, and St. Mark the Evangelist, Cincinnati, to form Church of the Resurrection, Cincinnati. For inquiries for parish records contact the Chancery.

15—ST. MATTHEW CHURCH (Norwood) Merged with St. Elizabeth Church, Norwood and Sts. Peter & Paul Church, Norwood to form Holy Trinity Church, Norwood. Records at Holy Trinity Church.

16—ST. MICHAEL CHURCH (LOWER PRICE HILL), Closed. For inquiries for parish records, contact Holy Family Parish, (Price Hill).

17—OUR LADY OF GRACE (Price Hill) Consolidated with Holy Family Parish. Records at Holy Family. (Price Hill)

18—OUR LADY OF LORETTO (LINWOOD), Merged with St. Margaret of Cortona, Madisonville. For inquiries for parish records contact St. Margaret-St. John, Cincinnati.

19—OUR LADY OF PERPETUAL HELP (Sedamsville) Consolidated with Holy Family Parish, Price Hill. Records at Holy Family Parish. (Price Hill)

20—OUR LADY OF PRESENTATION (ENGLISH WOODS), Closed. For inquiries for parish records contact St. Leo the Great, Cincinnati.

21—OUR MOTHER OF SORROWS (Roselawn) (1941) Closed. For inquiries for parish records, contact Nativity of Our Lord, Cincinnati.

22—ST. PATRICK (Northside) Merged with St. Boniface, Cincinnati. See listing for details. Records at St. Boniface (Northside).

23—STS. PETER AND PAUL CHURCH (Norwood) Merged with St. Elizabeth Church, Norwood and St. Matthew Church, Norwood to form Holy Trinity Church, Norwood. Records at Holy Trinity Church.

24—ST. PIUS CHURCH (CUMMINSVILLE), Closed. For inquiries for parish records contact the chancery.

25—ST. RICHARD OF CHICHESTER (College Hill) Merged with St. Therese, the Little Flower, Cincinnati. See listing for details. Records at St. Therese, the Little Flower.

26—SAN ANTONIO DI PADOVA (FAIRMOUNT), (Italian), Refer to Holy Family (Price Hill) for records.

27—ST. THOMAS AQUINAS (NORTH AVONDALE), Closed. For inquiries for parish records, contact St. Clement, St. Bernard.

BLANCHESTER, CLINTON CO., HOLY NAME (1853) Closed. For inquiries for parish records, see St. Columbille, Wilmington.

BLUE CREEK, ADAMS CO., ST. JOSEPH, Closed. For inquiries for parish records contact Holy Trinity, West Union.

DAYTON, MONTGOMERY CO.

1—ST. AGNES (1915) Closed. For Sacramental records, please see Corpus Christi, Dayton.

2—ASSUMPTION (1949) Merged with Our Lady of Mercy, Dayton. For Sacramental records, please see Our Lady of Mercy, Dayton.

3—ST. JAMES (1919) Closed. For Sacramental records, please see St. Benedict the Moor, Dayton.

4—SACRED HEART, Closed. For inquiries for parish records contact Emmanuel, Dayton.

FAYETTEVILLE, BROWN CO., ST. PATRICK (1837) [CEM] Closed. For inquiries for parish records, see St. Angela Merici, Fayetteville.

FELICITY, CLERMONT CO., OUR MOTHER OF GOOD COUNSEL, Closed. For inquiries for parish records please see St. Mary Church, Bethel.

HAMILTON, BUTLER CO.

1—ST. MARY, Merged now known as St. Julie Billiart. Records St. Julie Billiart, Hamilton.

2—ST. STEPHEN, Merged now known as St. Julie Billiart. Records St. Julie Billiart, Hamilton.

3—ST. VERONICA, Merged now known as St. Julie Billiart. Records St. Julie Billiart, Hamilton.

MANCHESTER, ADAMS CO., ST. MARY OF THE ASSUMPTION (1878) Closed. For inquiries for parish records please contact Holy Trinity, West Union.

SAINT MARTIN, BROWN CO., SAINT MARTIN (1830) [CEM] Closed. For inquiries for parish records, see St. Angela Merici, Fayetteville.

MIDDLETOWN, BUTLER CO.

1—HOLY TRINITY, Merged now known as Holy Family.

2—ST. JOHN THE BAPTIST, Merged now known as Holy Family.

3—ST. MARY, Merged now known as Holy Family.

NEW MIAMI, BUTLER CO., ST. LAWRENCE, Closed. For inquiries for parish records please see St. Julie Billiart, Hamilton.

NEW VIENNA, CLINTON CO., ST. MICHAEL (1874) Closed. For inquiries for parish records contact St. Benignus, Greenfield.

ST. PATRICK, SHELBY CO., ST. PATRICK, Closed. For inquiries for parish records contact St. Michael, Fort Loramie.

SARDINIA, BROWN CO., ST. ELIZABETH PARISH (1955) Closed. For inquiries for parish records, contact St. Mary, Arnheim.

SPRINGFIELD, CLARK, CO., ST. MARY (1921) Closed. For inquiries for parish records please see St. Raphael, Springfield.

VERA CRUZ, BROWN CO., HOLY GHOST (VICARIATE), Closed. For inquiries for parish records contact St. Angela Merici, Fayetteville.

On Special and Archdiocesan Assignment:
Revs.—
Duffy, Patrick D., 1302 Millville Ave., Hamilton, 45013. Tel: 513-892-3239
Elsbernd, James H., 6678 Paisley Dr., 45236.
Fecko, Leonard J., 2497 Riverside Dr., 45202.
Gruenbauer, Hans H., P.O. Box 54541, 45254.
Heis, Clarence G., 1140 Clifton Hills Dr., 45220.
Kindel, Joseph C., 6245 Wilmington Pike, Centerville, 45459.
Kroeger, John, 409 Elizabeth St., 45203.
Peterka, Dale C., 7121 Plainfield Rd., 45236. Tel: 513-791-3238
Ruiz, Ryan, Casa Sant Maria, Via dell' Umilta 30, Rome 00187 Italy.
Taylor, Reynaldo S., 745 Ezzard Charles Dr., 45203.

On Duty Outside the Archdiocese:
Revs.—
McGuire, Frederick J., Blessed Trinity, 1600 54th Ave., St. Petersburg, FL 33712.
Nguyen, Linh N., St. Martha Church, 3702 Woodland Hills Dr., Kingwood, TX 77339.
Schmitmeyer, James M., P.O. Box 96, Quitaque, TX 79255.

Medical Leave of Absence:
Revs.—
Fisher, John P., 3608 State Rte. 222, Batavia, 45103.
Gaeke, Thomas M., 4578 Swigart Rd., Dayton, 45440.

Priests On Administrative Leave:
Revs.—
Cooper, Ronald C.
Feldhaus, Thomas F.
Kuhn, Thomas A.
Pater, Daniel R.
Reilly, David F.

Priests On Personal Leave:
Revs.—
Do, Tuan Anh
Reif, Bryan T.

Priests Commended to a Life of Prayer and Penance:
Revs.—
Hopp, Thomas R.
Massarella, Francis A. (Retired)

Retired:
Revs.—
Aichele, Raymond P., 2472 Picnic Woods, Lawrenceburg, IN 47025. Tel: 812-637-2490
Allison, Joseph C., 6019 Woodford Ct., #3, 45213. Tel: 513-731-5273
Axe, Thomas R., 7010 Rowan Hill Dr., #111, 45227.
Bader, Paul A., 1044 W. Kemper Rd., 45240.
Beckman, Joseph F., 6616 Beechmont Ave., 45230. Tel: 513-624-0554
Bensman, Gerald E., S.T.L., 3505 Calumet Rd. #5A, Ludlow Falls, 45339. Tel: 937-719-3917
Bensman, John L., 2860 U.S. Rte. 127, Carthagena, 45822. Tel: 419-925-4516
Birarelli, Carl A., 3618 Prado Dr., Sarasota, FL 34235. Tel: 941-355-5246
Bramlage, James A., 934 Mound St., 45203. Tel: 513-381-0327
Breaker, Donald J., 605 Ravenna St. N., Nokomis, FL 34275-2335.
Bruemmer, Joseph A., 5440 Moeller Ave., 45212. Tel: 513-351-4661
Bruening, Joseph B., 5900 Delhi Rd., Mount Saint Joseph, 45051. Tel: 513-347-5311
Buening, Robert B., Corpus Christi, 2014 Springdale Rd., 45231. Tel: 513-825-0618
Caserta, Angelo C., P.O. Box 1636, Piqua, 45356. Tel: 937-778-9526
Caserta, Charles W., 133 Douglas Dr., Lewisburg, 45338. Tel: 937-272-6761
Collins, James R., 19 Woodview Ct., 45246. Tel: 513-648-9659
Crone, Patrick H., 1201 Scottwood Dr., Batavia, 45103. Tel: 513-460-4293
Dettenwanger, Dennis, 135 Garfield Pl., #617, 45202.
Dorrmann, William J., 2472 Picnic Woods, Lawrenceburg, IN 47025. Tel: 812-637-0327
Emerick, Stephen J., 5371 S. Milford Rd. Room 86E, Milford, 45150. Tel: 513-248-8002
Flaherty, Michael T., 1312 Twin Spires Dr., Batavia, 45103. Tel: 513-843-7859

Gerdes, Harry J., Bayley Place, 928 Bayley Place Dr., 45233. Tel: 513-347-5647
Goetz, Joseph W., 1528 Turnberry Village Dr., Dayton, 45458. Tel: 937-432-6589
Hackman, Marvin R., 121 Dover Rd., Springfield, 45504. Tel: 937-390-0925
Hater, Robert J., 1443 Cedar Ave., 45224. Tel: 513-541-4611
Henz, Kenneth W., 1805 John Glenn Rd., Dayton, 45420. Tel: 937-253-2829
Hohlmayer, Louis R., 3505 Calumet Rd., #1A, Ludlow Falls, 45339. Tel: 937-698-6757
Hussey, Edmund M., 3714 Falls Circle Dr., Hilliard, 43026. Tel: 614-771-2736
Keller, Neil J., 836 N. Hill Ln., 45224. Tel: 513-522-5578
Kennedy, William M., 2853 Erie Ave., 45208. Tel: 513-321-1207
Kist, Harold W., 145 Otter Ct., Lakeview, 43331. Tel: 937-935-4376
Klug, Richard L., S.T.L., 3776 Francis Ave., 45211. Tel: 513-622-3049
Kummer, John R., 3505 Calumet Rd. #3B, Ludlow Falls, 45339. Tel: 937-698-5019
Lammeier, Francis G., 12120 Regency Run Ct. #7, 45240. Tel: 513-742-9982
Langenbrunner, Norman, 7864 Gapstow Bridge, 45231. Tel: 513-376-8191
Lutmer, Joseph H., 6940 Miami Hills Dr., 45234. Tel: 513-793-9937
Macpherson, Walter, 4830 Salem Ave. #1, Dayton, 45416.
Mattscheck, John J., 3468 Robb Ave., 45211. Tel: 513-389-9366
Mauntel, Robert J., 19 Mohave Dr., Sardinia, 45171. Tel: 937-446-3491
McCarthy, Donald G., Ph.D., 5222 N. Bend Rd., 45247. Tel: 513-661-6565
Meehan, Terence A., 3171 Bridget St., Dayton, 45418.
Meyer, Harry J., 4010 Townsely Dr., Loveland, 45140. Tel: 513-697-1048
Mick, Lawrence J., 1500 Linneman Rd., 45238. Tel: 513-922-5400
Mick, Lawrence E., 3103 Observation Tr., Dayton, 45449. Tel: 937-434-4689
Monnin, Robert J., 546 Unger Ave., Englewood, 45322. Tel: 937-540-1074
Mueller, Eugene J., 3055 Inwood Dr., 45241. Tel: 513-769-4908
Muller, Anthony J., 2900 W. Galbraith Rd., 45239. Tel: 513-521-8440
Neiheisel, Stanley H., 320 Donham St., 45226.
Nguyen, Huan Tien, 314 Township Ave., 45216. Tel: 513-225-8221
Niehaus, Francis H., P.O. Box 727, Florence, KY 41022.
Niemeier, Dennis A., 1521 Nature Trail Way, 45231. Tel: 513-648-0976
Niklas, Gerald R., 577 Lowell Ave., 45220. Tel: 513-559-1390
O'Connor, James J., 319 Mulberry Pl., Sidney, 45365. Tel: 937-492-9577
Obermeyer, Robert A., 1279 S. Waynesville Rd., Oregonia, 45054. Tel: 513-265-9641
Pater, Giles H., Ph.D., 1435 Meadowbright, 45230. Tel: 513-233-0066
Perin, Glen W., 3505 Calumet Rd., #1-B, Ludlow Falls, 45339. Tel: 937-698-6713
Porter, John E., 3505 Calumet Rd., #3A, Ludlow Falls, 45339. Tel: 937-698-5989
Raudabaugh, Joseph R., 3505 Calumet Rd. #4B, Ludlow Falls, 45339. Tel: 937-698-4821
Robisch, David C., 3 Sheldon Close, 45227. Tel: 513-271-4246
Rohrkemper, Charles, 2860 U.S. Rte. 127, Carthagena, 45822. Tel: 937-925-4516
Schmitz, George R., 1175 Overlook Ave., 45238. Tel: 513-921-9200
Seher, Philip O., 5536 Palisades Dr., 45238.
Shelander, Donald E., P.O. Box 11469, 45211.
Shine, Edward J., 212 George St., Harrison, 45030.
Smith, Elmer W., 7010 Rowan Hill Dr. #428, 45227. Tel: 513-271-2949
Stricker, Robert A., S.T.D., 5332 S. Ridge Dr. #123, 45224. Tel: 513-853-2092
Thomas, William V., 3505 Calumet Rd., #4A, Ludlow Falls, 45339. Tel: 937-698-5960
Thorsen, Robert J., 4580 E. Galbraith Rd., 45236. Tel: 513-745-9600
Trick, James F., 2860 Rte. 127, Carthagena, 45822-9591. Tel: 419-925-4516
Trippel, Edward G., 476 Riddle Rd., #612, 45220. Tel: 513-281-8001
Voellmecke, Francis W., Ph.D., 3223 Linwood Rd., 45226. Tel: 513-321-4121
Vonderhaar, Eugene F., 10560 Blocker Rd., Bradford, 45308.
Wall, John E., 5222 N. Bend Rd., 45247. Tel: 513-661-6565
Wessling, John E., S.T.D., 10095 Wayside Dr., #259, 45241. Tel: 513-779-5350
Westerhoff, Ralph A., 843 Neeb Rd. #1, 45233. Tel: 513-921-2021
Wilker, Ronald H., 7001 Cottonwood Rd., Celina, 45822. Tel: 419-268-2842
Witsken, Gary J., 5848 Bayou Ct., 45248. Tel: 513-347-0134
Wolfer, Robert R., c/o 230 Cloverhill Ter., 45238.
Wollering, Carl J., 5858 Kellog Ave., 45228. Tel: 513-231-7042

Permanent Deacons:
Ascolese, Michael A., St. Bartholomew, Cincinnati
Aufderheide, William, (Retired)
Back, John Paul, St. Maximilian Kolbe, Liberty Twp.
Baker, Robert, St. Columbkille, Wilmington
Baldwin, Russell O., St. Peter, Huber Heights
Balster, Randolph L., St. Henry Cluster Parishes
Baltes, Leonard W., (Retired)
Bardonaro, Mark A., St. Dominic, Cincinnati
Barney, Gerald L., St. John, West Chester
Basye, Robert L., St. Peter, Dayton
Belcher, Halver L., St. Augustine, Minster
Bermick, Stephen, III, St. Mary, Franklin
Bertke, Omer H., St. John the Baptist, Maria Stein
Borgerding, Jonathan P., (Retired)
Bornhorst, Gregory A., Holy Redeemer, New Bremen
Brodeur, Wilfred J., (Retired)
Brown, Martin J., Holy Rosary, St. Marys
Brown, Steven R., J.C.L., St. Elizabeth Ann Seton, Milford
Bruce, George R., St. William, Cincinnati
Brunsman, Willard, St. Aloysius, Shandon
Bryant, Herman, St. Gabriel, Cincinnati
Buschur, Jerome L., St. Henry, St. Henry
Cain, Jerome, St. Saviour, Cincinnati (Blue Ash)
Camele, David G., (Retired)
Campos, Brian M., Ascension, Dayton
Carlin, John K., St. Patrick, Troy
Cassani, Michael J., Immaculate Heart of Mary, Cincinnati
Cecere, Gregory, Queen of Apostles, Dayton
Cohen, Kim, St. Michael the Archangel, Sarasota, FL
Coleman, Terrell, St. Lawrence, Rhine; Immaculate Conception, Botkins
Coll, Joseph J., St. Columban, Loveland
Collins, John R., St. Joseph & St. Raphael, Springfield
Collins, Robert, St. Charles Borromeo, Kettering
Convery, John J., St. Rose, Cincinnati
Cordonnier, Leo N., St. Peter, Dayton
Corson, John, Corpus Christi, New Burlington
Couzins, Jerome, (Unassigned)
Coyle, Thomas J., (Retired)
Crook, Robert A., St. Patrick, Bellefontaine
Crooker, Timothy, St. James the Greater, White Oak
Danner, Jonathan M., St. Helen, Dayton
Dawson, David A., (Unassigned)
Day, Larry H., Corpus Christi, New Burlington
Deardorff, Roy L., (Retired)
Dehanes, Kenneth J., Sr., St. Michael, Sharonville
Desmond, Mark, (Unassigned)
Dipple, Harold I., St. Patrick, Bellefontaine
Duffy, Roger E., Church of the Incarnation, Centerville
Dupree, Gerald M., St. Luke, Beavercreek
Dvorachek, Ronald S., St. George, Georgetown; St. Mary, Arnheim; St. Michael the Archangel, Ripley
Edwards, Dennis, St. Joseph, Cincinnati
Ehrnschwender, Jeffrey P., Queen of Peace, Millville
Erb, Michael C., Our Lady of Visitation, Cincinnati
Etienne, Jerald F., St. Mary, Bethel
Faeth, Thomas J., St. William, Cincinnati
Feldkamp, J. Russell, Immaculate Heart of Mary, Cincinnati
Fey, Robert, Guardian Angels, Cincinnati
Fischesser, Elmer, Mercy Hospital, Fairfield
Flamm, Gerald A., St. Gabriel, Glendale
Gagliarducci, Anthony, St. Ignatius, Monfort Heights
Gallenstein, Richard W., Good Shepherd, Cincinnati
George, Raymond W., St. Matthias, Cincinnati
Geraci, James L., (Retired)
Gerke, John P., St. Clement, St. Bernard
Glassmeyer, Robert A., (Retired)
Gloeckler, Donald, Our Lord Christ the King, Cincinnati
Glynn, John T., (Retired)
Gobbi, John R., St. John Neumann, Cincinnati
Graber, Thomas H., St. Mary, Greenville
Grismer, Raymond L., (Retired)
Haas, Frederick J., St. Thomas More, Withamsville
Hall, Jeffrey, St. Albert the Great, Kettering; St. Anthony, Dayton
Harris, Timothy J., St. Peter, Huber Heights
Helmick, Timothy M., St. Mary, Hyde Park
Hennessey, James F., Holy Trinity, Batavia
Hildebrand, Victor B., Ascension, Kettering
Hinger, Michael W., St. Maximilian Kolbe, Liberty Twp.
Hobbs, Richard D., St. Mary, Franklin
Holthaus, John G., Holy Angels, Sidney
Horstman, Norman G., St. Raphael & St. Joseph, Springfield
Hucke, Walter A., Jr., Our Lady of the Rosary, Greenhills
Huff, Thomas, Holy Trinity, Coldwater
Jamison, Tracy W., Ph.D., Holy Cross-Immaculata & Old St. Mary, Cincinnati
Janowiecki, Richard J., Precious Blood, Dayton
Jenkins, Charles J., Our Lady of Victory, Cincinnati
Jernigan, Jacob, (Retired)
Johnson, Mark U., Immaculate Heart of Mary, Cincinnati
Jones, James E., Good Shepherd, Cincinnati
Jurosic, Nicholas T., St. John Fryberg; St. Patrick, Glynwood
Kall, Dennis, St. Brigid, Xenia
Keller, David R., (Leave of Absence)
Klingshirn, David, Cathedral of St. Peter in Chains, Cincinnati
Klosterman, Roger L., St. Augustine, Minster
Kluener, Paul, (Retired)
Knight, Michael R., St. Patrick, Troy
Kolis, Conrad C., St. James of the Valley, Wyoming
Kostic, Nicholas V., Jr., St. Brigid, Xenia
Kowalski, James, (Retired)
Kozlowski, Robert R., Sacred Heart, New Carlisle
Kraus, Daniel E., Ascension, Kettering
Kroger, Raymond, St. Margaret of York, Twenty Mile Stand
Krumm, William T., Holy Family, Middletown
Leever, Robert J., All Saints, Cincinnati
Leibold, Paul F., St. Philip the Apostle, Morrow
Lim, Amado L., All Saints, Cincinnati
Lippman, Michael E., St. Maximilian Kolbe, Liberty Twp.
Lochtefeld, Virgil V., (Retired)
Luthman, Paul, Sacred Heart, McCartyville
Lynd, Thomas, Sts. Peter & Paul, Reading
Maag, Lawrence A., St. Vivian, Cincinnati
Mahoney, Michael, St. Henry, Dayton
Martin, Richaed W., Our Lady of Good Hope, Miamisburg
Martin, Terrance A., Our Lady of Good Hope, Miamisburg
Martin, William, (Unassigned)
Mascorro, Susano, (Retired)
Merrell, Jeffrey, St. Peter in Chains, Hamilton
Merritt, James A., St. Susanna, Mason
Meyer, David, (Unassigned)
Meyer, Donald J., Jr., St. John the Baptist, Harrison
Meyer, Robert E., St. Columbkille, Wilmington
Mignery, Michael E., Queen of Peace, Millville
Miller, James A., St. Columban, Loveland
Moore, William F., St. Charles Borromeo, Kettering
Mullaney, William M., Immaculate Heart of Mary, Cincinnati
Murphy, Daniel R., St. Veronica, Cincinnati
Myers, Philip B., Holy Angels, Sidney
Nagy, Norbert, St. Peter, Huber Heights
Novick, Rick, Guardian Angels, Cincinnati
Obleness, Ralph F., St. Helen, Dayton
Olinger, James C., St. Rita, Dayton
Palumbo, Patrick A., St. John Neumann, Cincinnati
Parker, John G., Mary, Help of Christians, Fort Recovery
Parker, Leonard B., (Retired)
Perkins, Jeffrey M., St. Margaret of York, Twenty Mile Stand
Perry, Robert W., Our Lady, Queen of Peace, Wright Patterson Air Force Base
Petrie, William J., (Retired)
Pitts, Joseph L., Jr., St. Francis of Assisi, Centerville
Platfoot, Thomas F., Our Lady of Mercy, Queen of Martyrs, & Corpus Christi, Dayton
Prier, Michael F., Precious Blood, Dayton
Quattrone, John M., St. Ann, Groesbeck
Rader, Daniel L., St. Susanna, Mason
Rammel, Andrew R., Precious Blood, Dayton
Reder, Richard J., Assumption, Mt. Healthy
Reising, Edward B., St. Joseph, North Bend
Renneker, William B., St. Julie Billiart, Hamilton
Rettig, John M., St. Francis de Sales, Lebanon
Richardson, Paul E., St. Paul, Yellow Springs
Risch, Ronald H., St. John Neumann, Cincinnati
Riva-Saleta, Luis O., St. Aloysius on-the-Ohio, Cincinnati
Roadruck, Max, Mary Help of Christians, Fairborn
Rogers, Earl, St. Mary, Urbana
Rose, Gregory L., St. Teresa of Avila, Cincinnati
Royer, Milton W., Queen of Martyrs, Our Lady of Mercy, & Corpus Christi, Dayton

Ryan, Steven A., Our Lady of the Rosary, Greenhills
Saluke, William M., (Retired)
Sasson, Gerard J., St. Columban, Loveland
Schaefer, William E., Holy Name, Trenton
Schellman, Leon, Good Shepherd, Cincinnati
Schmidl, George L., St. Ann, Hamilton
Schmiesing, John J., St. Augustine, Minster
Schneider, Jerry R., St. Aloysius Gonzaga, Cincinnati
Schroeder, Robert J., St. Antoninus, Cincinnati
Schutte, Timothy, St. Andrew, Milford
Shaffer, David, Immaculate Heart of Mary, Anderson
Shea, David J., Immaculate Heart of Mary, Cincinnati
Simmons, Raphael, St. Joseph, Cincinnati
Simpson, Richard D., St. Luke, Beavercreek
Slattery, John M., (Unassigned)
Sonnenberg, James J., (Retired)
Srode, Walter, (Retired)
Staab, Robert A., Jr., Assumption, Mt. Healthy
Stang, Ronald L., St. Peter, New Richmond
Stasiak, Mark, St. Francis of Assisi, Centerville
Steward, Herschel R., St. Francis De Sales, Lebanon
Strodtbeck, Thomas M., St. Julie Billiart, Hamilton
Subler, Joseph, St. Paul, Englewood
Sunderman, James P., St. Jude the Apostle, Cincinnati
Thamann, John D., (Retired)
Thomas, Dan, Our Lady of Sorrows, Monroe
Thomas, Michael T., St. Thomas More, Withamsville
Vilaboy, Manuel D., (Retired)
Vu, Hoang D., Sacred Heart, Fairfield
Wade, Daniel J., St. Peter, Huber Heights
Wagner, Francis X., St. Peter in Chains Cathedral, Cincinnati
Walker, Harry S., St. Columban, Loveland
Wallace, David M., St. Philip, Morrow
Walworth, James W., Sr., Holy Angels, Dayton
Westbay, Richard L., St. Joseph, Wapakoneta
Westendorf, Mark J., Good Shepherd, Cincinnati
Westerfield, Thomas E., Our Lady of Lourdes, Cincinnati
Winters, Royce E., Church of the Resurrection, Cincinnati
Woeste, James H., St. Elizabeth Seton, Rockford, IL
Yetter, Jerry J., St. Boniface, Cincinnati
Zinck, Robert C., Jr., Incarnation, Centerville
Zvonar, George J., Holy Trinity, Dayton
Wright, Charles O., St. Christopher, Vandalia

INSTITUTIONS LOCATED IN THE ARCHDIOCESE

[A] THE ATHENAEUM OF OHIO

CINCINNATI. *The Athenaeum of Ohio* (1829) Mt. St. Mary's Seminary, 6616 Beechmont Ave., 45230. Tel: 513-231-2223; Fax: 513-231-3254. Email: ath@athenaeum.edu. Web: www.athenaeum.edu. Most Rev. Dennis M. Schnurr, J.C.D., D.D., Archbishop of Cincinnati, Chancellor, Chm. of Bd. of Trustees; Revs. Benedict O'Cinnsealaigh, S.T.D., Pres. & Rector; Earl K. Fernandes, S.T.D., Dean, Athenaeum of Ohio; Dr. Terrance Callan, Ph.D., Dean, Special Studies; Mr. Dennis K. Eagan, B.B.A., Vice Pres., Finance Admin. Incorporated March 24, 1928 by the State of Ohio and presently has three divisions: Mt. St. Mary's Seminary of the West; the Lay Pastoral Ministry Program and the Special Studies Division.

Lay Pastoral Ministry Program, 6616 Beechmont Ave., 45230. Tel: 513-231-1200; Fax: 513-231-3254. Dr. Susan McGurgan, M.A.R., Dir.; Dr. Hal Belcher, Ph.D., Prog. Coord.; Mr. Thomas Giordano, M.Div., Assoc. Dir.; Janice VonHandorf, M.A.P.M., Assoc. Dir. Special Studies Division: Dr. Terrance Callan, Ph.D., Dean; Rev. Anthony M. Brausch, Ph.L., Dir. Permanent Deacon Program; Mrs. Connie Song, M.L.S., Librarian.

The St. Gregory Seminary Trust, 100 E. Eighth St., 45202.

[B] SEMINARIES

CINCINNATI. *Mount St. Mary's Seminary of the West* (1829) (Diocesan), 6616 Beechmont Ave., 45230. Tel: 513-231-2223; Fax: 513-231-3254. Email: ath@mtsm.org. Web: www.athenaeum.edu. Rev. Benedict O'Cinnsealaigh, S.T.D., Rector; Dr. Terrance Callan, Ph.D., Dean, Spec. Studies; Rev. Earl K. Fernandes, S.T.D., Athenaeum Academic Dean; Rev. Msgr. Frank Lane, Ph.D. (COL), Spiritual Dir.; Rev. Paul A. Ruwe, M.A., Dean of Students; Mr. Thomas Giordano, M.Div., Dir. of Pastoral Internship; Rev. Anthony M. Brausch, Ph.L., Dir. of Formation; Michael E. Sweeney, M.A., Registrar; Mr. Dennis K. Eagan, B.B.A., Vice Pres., Finance & Admin.; Mr. Kevin Prendergast, Dir. Pastoral Counseling Degree; Mr. James W. Jackson, B.A., Dir. Devel. Major seminary for students in Theology. Priests 19; Sisters 2; Lay Teachers 29; Seminarians 41; Students 213. In Res. Rev. Msgr. Frank Lane, Ph.D. (COL); Revs. Joseph F. Beckman (Retired); Anthony M. Brausch, Ph.L.; David J. Endres, Ph.D.; Earl K. Fernandes, S.T.D.; J. Robert Jack, M.A.; Benedict O'Cinnsealaigh, S.T.D.; Theodore Ross, S.J., S.T.L.; Paul A. Ruwe, M.A.; Timothy P. Schehr, Ph.D.; Michael A. Seger, S.T.D.; Ken Morman, S.S.L. (TOL).

Non-Resident Faculty: Rev. Paul Keller, O.P., S.T.D.; Sr. Betty Jane Lillie, Ph.D.; Dr. Terrance Callan, Ph.D.; Dr. David Foster, Ph.D.; Mr. Anthony Dicello, M.M.; Mrs. Connie Song, M.L.S., Librarian; Mr. Kevin Prendergast; Mr. Dennis K. Eagan, B.B.A.; Mr. James W. Jackson, B.A.; Deacons Dave Shea, D.Min.; Tracy W. Jamison, Ph.D.; Dr. John Gutting, Ph.D.

[C] NOVITIATES AND HOUSES OF STUDY

CINCINNATI. *St. Anthony Shrine, Franciscan Postulancy* (1888) St. John the Baptist Province, 5000 Colerain Ave., 45223-1213. Tel: 513-541-2146; Fax: 513-541-9347. Revs. Kenan Freson, O.F.M., Liaison Sponsored Ministries; Carl J. Langenderfer, O.F.M., Dir. of Postulants & Vicar; Frank Geers, O.F.M., Assoc. Dir. of Postulants; Daniel Kroger, O.F.M., CEO-St. Anthony Messenger Press.; Frank Jasper, O.F.M., Vicar Prov.; Joseph Ricchini, O.F.M., Spiritual Dir.; Humbert Moster, O.F.M., Sacramental Min. for St. Peter/St. Mary of the Rock, IN; Bonaventure Bai, O.F.M., Chap. Good Samaritan Hosital, Cincinnati; Daniel Havron, O.F.M., Evangelizer, Parish Missions, Sacramental Min.; Bros. Gabriel Balassone, O.F.M., Porter; Gene Mayer, O.F.M., Guardian, Sec. of the Prov. Priests 9; Brothers 2; Postulants 6.

Dominican Novitiate, 7630 Shawnee Run Rd., 45243. Tel: 513-527-3972; Fax: 513-527-3973. Email: jmsullivan@op.org. Web: www.op-stjoseph.org. Rev. James M. Sullivan, O.P., Novice Master & Contact Person. Novices 21.

DAYTON. *Marianist Novitiate*, 4435 E. Patterson Rd., 45430-1095. Tel: 937-426-5721; Fax: 937-429-4686. Rev. Christopher T. Wittmann, S.M., Dir. of Novices; Bro. Charles Johnson, S.M., Asst. Dir. of Novices. Priests 3; Brothers 4; Novices 7.

[D] COLLEGES AND UNIVERSITIES

CINCINNATI. *College of Mount St. Joseph* (1920) 5701 Delhi Rd., 45233-1670. Tel: 513-244-4200; Fax: 513-244-4654. Web: www.msj.edu. Mr. Tony Aretz, Ph.D., Pres.; Anne Marie Wagner, Chief Fin. Officer; Alan deCourcy, Chief Academic Officer; Keith Weber, Chief Information Officer; Douglas Frizzell, Dean of Students; Paul Jenkins, Dir., Library Svcs.; Kathleen Lundrigan, Dir. Mktg. Coed. Chartered by the State of Ohio. Priests 1; Sisters 1; Lay Teachers 250; Students 2,324; Total Staff 264.

Xavier University (1831) 3800 Victory Pkwy., 45207. Tel: 513-745-3000; Fax: 513-745-4223. Email: vezina@xavier.edu. Web: www.xavier.edu. Revs. Michael J. Graham, S.J., Pres.; Richard W. Bollman, S.J., Pastor & Rector, Bellarmine Chapel; Dr. James Snodgrass III, Assoc. Dean College of Arts & Sciences; Dr. Debra Mooney, Assoc. Vice Pres. Mission & Identity; Dr. Hema Krishnan, Assoc. Dean Williams College of Business; Ms. Mary Alyce Orahood, Registrar; Dr. Mark Meyers, Dean College of Social Sciences, Health & Educ.; Maribeth Amyot, Sr. Vice Pres. & CFO; Dr. John F. Kucia, Admin. Vice Pres.; Dr. R. Stafford Johnson, Interim Dean Williams College of Business; Dr. Scott Chadwick, Provost & Chief Academic Officer; Mr. Gary R. Massa, Vice Pres. Univ. Rels.; Mr. David Dodd, Vice Pres. Information Resources & CIO; Dr. Kathleen Simons, Assoc. Provost Student Life & Leadership; Jackie Vezina, Contact Person; Dr. Janice Walker, Dean College of Arts & Sciences; Sheila Doran, Acting Dean Center Adult and Part-time Students. College of Arts & Sciences Enrollment 2,026; Williams College of Business Undergraduates 1,114; College of Social Sciences Enrollment 1,215; Center for Adults & Part-time Students Enrollment 185; Graduate Program Enrollment 2,405; Permanent Staff: Priests 9; Sisters 5; Faculty (Full-Time): Priests 7; Lay Teachers 334.

DAYTON. *The University of Dayton* (1850) (Coed), 300 College Park Ave., 45469-1660. Tel: 937-229-1000; Fax: 937-229-4000. Web: www.udayton.edu. Dr. Daniel J. Curran, Ph.D., Pres.; David J. O'Brien, Ph.D., Univ. Prof. Faith & Culture; Joseph E. Saliba, Ph.D., Provost (Interim); Pat G. Donnelly, Ph.D., Assoc. Provost, Faculty & Administrative Affairs; Mr. Thomas E. Burkhardt, B.S., M.S., Vice Pres. for Finance Affairs & Admin. Svcs.; Timothy J. Wabler, B.S.B., Vice Pres. & Dir. of Athletics; William Fischer, Interim Vice Pres. Student Devel. & Dean Students; Rev. James Fitz, S.M., M.Div., Rector; Mr. S. Ted Bucaro, B.A., M.A., Govt. & Regl. Rels. Dir.; Beth Keyes, Asst. Vice Pres. Facilities Mgmt; Mr. Thomas J. Westendorf, B.S., MBA, Asst. Vice Pres. & Registrar; J. Kathy McEuen Harmon, B.F.A., Asst. Vice Pres. & Dean of Admissions; Joyce Carter, B.A., Vice Pres. Human Resources; Michael McCabe, Ph.D., Vice Pres. & Exec. Dir. Research Inst.; Deborah A. Read, Vice Pres. Univ. Advancement; Sundar Kumarasamy, Vice Pres. Enrollment Mgmt.; Dr. Deborah J. Bickford, Ph.D., Assoc. Provost Academic Affairs & Learning Initiatives; Dr. Thomas D. Skill, Ph.D., Assoc. Provost & Chief Information Officer; Ms. Lisa Risimiller, B.A., M.P.A., Dir. Women's Center; Revs. Norbert C. Burns, S.M. (Retired); Gerald T. Chinchar, S.M., D.Min., Campus Min.; Christopher W. Conlon, S.M., Campus Min.; Francois Rossier, S.M., Dir., Intl. Marian Research Inst.; Joseph F. Kozar, S.M., Ph.D., Religious Studies; Paul F. Vieson, S.M. (Retired); Joseph P. Tedesco, S.M.; Thomas A. Thompson, S.M., Dir., Marian Library; Bertrand A. Buby, S.M., Ph.D. (Retired); John A. McGrath, Religious Studies; Johann B.G. Roten, S.M., S.T.D., Intl. Marian research Inst. & Marian Library; Joseph D. Massucci, Educational Leadership; David McGuigan, S.M., Univ. Chap.; Bro. Philip T. Aaron, S.M., Ph.D., (Retired); Rev. George Abmayr, S.M., (Retired); Bros. William Callahan, S.M., (Retired); Sean R. Downing, S.M., Regl. Vocation Office; William M. Fackovec, S.M., M. S.L.S., Intl. Marian Research Inst. & Marian Library; Thomas Farnsworth, S.M., Community Wellness; Raymond L. Fitz, S.M., Ph.D., Social Justice; Victor M. Forlani, S.M., M.B.A., D.B.A., Mgmt. & Mktg.; Louis Fournier, S.M., (Retired); Charles Gausling, S.M., (Retired); Donald R. Geiger, S.M., Ph.D., (Retired); Thomas Giardino, S.M., Intl. Center for Marianist Formation; John Habjan, S.M., (Retired); Robert H. Hughes, S.M., Printing & Design; Daniel L. Klco, S.M., M.S.; M. Gary Marcinowski, S.M., M.F.A. ; Raymond E. Martin, S.M., (Retired); Thomas E. Oldenski, S.M., Educational Leadership; Ronald Overman, S.M., Fin. & Admin. Svcs.; Thomas J. Pieper, S.M., Campus Min.; Daniel Stupka, S.M., (Retired); Edward E. Zamierowski, S.M., Fitz Center for Leadership in Community; Sisters Jean Frisk, I.S.S.M., M.A., S.T.L., Intl. Marian Research Inst., Marian Library; Leanne Jablonski, F.M.I., Religious Studies; Linda Lee Jackson, O.P., Campus Min.; Laura M. Leming, F.M.I., Ph.D.; Danielle M. Peters, I.S.S.M., S.T.L.; Kathleen A. Rossman, O.S.F., Campus Min.; Dennis Tisler, Educational Leadership; Nicole D. Trahan, F.M.I.; Pamela L. Thimmes, O.S.F., Ph.D.; Judith G. Martin, S.S.J., Ph.D.; Angela Ann Zukowski, M.H.S.H., D.Min., Dir., Inst. for Pastoral Initiatives; Mary Louise Foley, F.M.I.; Phyllis Gronotte, Librarian. Society of Mary (Marianists). Priests 4; Brothers 5; Sisters 3; Lay Teachers 494; Students 11,045.

College of Arts and Sciences (1882) Tel: 937-229-2611; Fax: 937-229-2615. Dr. Paul H. Benson, Ph.D., Dean; Donald L. Pair, Ph.D., Assoc. Dean for Integrated Learning & Curriculum; Dr. Mary J. Brown, Ph.D., Assoc. Dean for Fin. Information & Data Analysis; Donald J. Polzella, Ph.D., Assoc. Dean for Faculty Devel. & Graduate Prog. Professors 293; Students 3,512.

Graduate School Tel: 937-229-2390; Fax: 937-229-4545. Dr. Paul M. Vanderburgh, Ed.D., Assoc. Provost & Dean Graduate School; Dr. Bradley Duncan, Ph.D., Assoc. Dean Graduate School.

School of Business Administration (1921) Tel: 937-229-3731; Fax: 937-229-3301. Dr. Joseph F. Castellano, Ph.D., Acting Dean; Dr. Elizabeth F. Gustafson, Ph.D., Assoc. Dean; Dr. Paul D. Sweeney, Ph.D., Assoc. Dean. Professors 60; Students 1,908.

School of Education (1920) Tel: 937-229-3146; Fax: 937-229-3199. Kevin R. Kelly, Ph.D., Dean; Dr. Kathryn A. Kinnucan-Welsch, Assoc. Dean, Undergraduate Education & Community Outreach; Dr. C. Daniel Raisch, Ph.D., Assoc. Dean Admin. Professors 52; Students 2,643.

School of Engineering (1910) 45469. Tel: 937-229-2736; Fax: 937-229-2756. Dr. Tony E. Saliba, Ph.D., Dean; Dr. John G. Weber, Ph.D., Assoc. Dean & Graduate Studies; Riad S. Alakkad, Assoc. Dean & Undergraduate Studies. Professors 68; Students 2,241.

School of Law (1974) Tel: 937-229-3211; Fax: 937-229-4769. Paul E. McGreal, J.D., Dean; Richard D. Perna, J.D., Assoc. Dean for Academic Affairs.

Professors 30; Students 493.
Libraries and Information Technologies Tel: 937-229-4265.
The Marian Library/International Marian Research Institute (IMRI) (1943) Tel: 937-229-4124; Fax: 937-229-4258. Rev. Francois Rossier, S.M., Exec. Dir. Marian Library & Intl. Marian Research Inst.
Institute for Pastoral Initiatives (1971) Tel: 937-229-3126; Fax: 937-229-3130. Sr. Angela Ann Zukowski, M.H.S.H., D.Min., Dir.; Kathleen M. Webb, M.L.S., Dean of Libraries; Fred W. Jenkins, Ph.D., Assoc. Dean of Libraries, Collections Opers.
Libraries
University of Dayton (1850) 45469-1390. Tel: 937-229-4214.

SAINT MARTIN. *Chatfield College* (1971) Brown County Ursulines, 20918 State Rte. 251, St. Martin, 45118. Tel: 513-875-3344; Fax: 513-875-3912. Email: john.tafaro@chatfield.edu. Web: www.chatfield.edu. John P. Tafaro, Pres.; Dolores Berish, Librarian. Faculty 3; Adjunct Faculty 78; Staff 30; Students 433.

[E] HIGH SCHOOLS, INTER-PAROCHIAL

CINCINNATI. *Elder High School* (1922) 3900 Vincent Ave., 45205-1699. Tel: 513-921-3744; Fax: 513-921-8123. Email: otten.t@elderhs.org. Web: www.elderhs.org. Tom Otten, Prin. & Contact Person; Rev. Donald R. Rettig; Mary Ploehs, Librarian. Priests 1; Lay Teachers 65; Students 940.
LaSalle High School (1960) 3091 N. Bend Rd., 45239-7696. Tel: 513-741-3000; Fax: 513-741-2666. Web: www.cincinnatilasalle.net/. Mr. Thomas Luebbe, Prin.; Jacob McCullough, Librarian & Media Center Specialist. Priests 1; Lay Teachers 54; Students 710.
McAuley High School, 6000 Oakwood Ave., 45224. Tel: 513-681-1800; Fax: 513-681-1802. Email: sucherc@live.mcauleyhs.net. Web: www.mcauleyhs.net. Mrs. Cheryl A. Sucher, Pres. & Contact Person; Mrs. Nicole Brainard, Prin.; Mrs. Connie Kampschmidt, Asst. Prin.; Mrs. Kelly Grote, Asst. Prin.; Mrs. Becky Reilly, Librarian. Sisters of Mercy 2; Lay Teachers 51; Girls 620.
McNicholas High School, 6536 Beechmont Ave., 45230. Tel: 513-231-3500; Fax: 513-231-1351. Email: pbeckert@mcnhs.org. Web: www.mcnhs.org. Patricia A. Beckert, Prin.; Anne Jones, Librarian. Lay Teachers 47; Students 636.
Moeller High School (1959) 9001 Montgomery Rd., 45242. Tel: 513-791-1680; Fax: 513-792-3343. Email: bbalbach@moeller.org. Web: www.moeller.org. Mr. Blane Collison, Prin.; William J. Balbach, Treas. & Contact Person; Mr. William E. Hunt, Pres. Sisters of Mercy 1; Marianist Brothers 3; Lay Teachers 57; Students 930.
Mother of Mercy High School, 3036 Werk Rd., 45211. Tel: 513-661-2740; Fax: 513-661-1842. Email: info@motherofmercy.org. Web: www.motherofmercy.org. Kirsten MacDougal, Pres.; Diane H. Laake, Prin.; Linda Behen, Librarian. Lay Teachers 50; Girls 500.
Mt. Notre Dame High School, 711 E. Columbia Ave., 45215. Tel: 513-821-3044; Fax: 513-821-6068. Web: www.mndhs.org. Mr. Larry Mock, Prin.; Mrs. Kathy Derrick, Librarian. Sisters 3; Lay Teachers 60; Girls 679.
Purcell Marian High School (East Walnut Hills), 2935 Hackberry St., 45206. Tel: 513-751-1230; Fax: 513-751-1395. Web: www.purcellmarian.org. Al Early, Pres.; Robert Obert, Bus. Mgr.; Teresa Davis, Dir. Ministry; Paul Ramstetter, Prin.; Peggy Flick, Librarian. Priests 1; Brothers 1; Sisters 1; Lay Teachers 27; Students 396.
Roger Bacon High School (1928) 4320 Vine St., 45217. Tel: 513-641-1300; Fax: 513-641-0498. Email: wfarris@rogerbacon.org. Web: www.rogerbacon.org. Steve Schad, Prin.; Amy M. Wilson, Contact Person; Rev. William Farris, O.F.M., Pres.; Bro. Christopher Cahill, O.F.M., Computer Network Coord.; Rev. Mark J. Hudak, O.F.M.; Brandon Cowans, Dir. Retention Recruitment; Donna Briggs, Media Specialist & Librarian. Franciscan Friars of the Cincinnati Province of St. John the Baptist. Priests 3; Brothers 2; Lay Teachers 40; Students 400.
Seton High School (Price Hill), 3901 Glenway Ave., 45205. Tel: 513-471-2600; Fax: 513-471-0529. Email: briggerd@setoncincinnati.org. Web: www.setoncincinnati.org. Mrs. Donna Brigger, Prin.; Kathy Chevalier, Senior Dir. Devel.; Mr. Rich Klus, Assoc. Prin.; Marianne Ridiman, Dir. Admissions; Mrs. Janice Linz, Campus Min.; Ms. Monica Williams-Mitchell, Librarian. Sisters of Charity of Cincinnati 6; Lay Teachers 38; Students 557.

DAYTON. *Archbishop Alter High School* (1962) 940 E. David Rd., Kettering, 45429. Tel: 937-434-4434; Fax: 937-434-0507. Web: www.alterhs.org. Mrs. Lourdes Lambert, Prin.; Mrs. Christine Sanderman, Librarian. Priests 1; Sisters 1; Lay Teachers 50; Students 680.
Carroll High School (1961) 4524 Linden Ave., 45432. Tel: 937-253-8188; Fax: 937-258-7001. Email: msableski@carrollhs.org. Web: www.carrollhs.org. Mr. Matthew T. Sableski, Prin.; Mrs. Shirley Russ, Librarian. Lay Teachers 55; Students 789.
Chaminade Julienne Catholic High School, 505 S. Ludlow St., 45402. Tel: 937-461-3740; Fax: 937-461-6256. Web: www.cjeagles.org. Mr. Dan Meixner, Pres.; Mr. John Marshall, Prin.; Jason Unger, Asst. Prin.; Sandra Ervin, Dir. Fin. & Accounting; Mrs. Kelli Kinnear, Dir. Campus Ministry; Gina Harrington, Librarian. Conducted by the Society of Mary (Marianists) and Sisters of Notre Dame de Namur. Sisters 1; Lay Teachers 50; Students 623.

HAMILTON. *Stephen T. Badin High School* (1966) 571 New London Rd., 45013. Tel: 513-863-3993; Fax: 513-785-2844. Email: bpendergest@badinhs.org. Web: badinhs.org. Brian Pendergest, Prin.; Rev. Robert K. Muhlenkamp; Mr. Mike Memory, Technology Coord. Lay Teachers 34; Total Staff 63; Students 452.

MIDDLETOWN. *Bishop Fenwick High School*, 4855 State Rte. 122, Franklin, 45005. Tel: 513-423-0723; Fax: 513-420-8690. Web: www.fenwickfalcons.org. Mr. Michael Miller, Prin. Priests 1; Sisters 1; Lay Teachers 37; Students 558.

SIDNEY. *Lehman Catholic High School* (1970) 2400 St. Mary's Ave., 45365. Tel: 937-498-1161; Fax: 937-492-9877. Email: m.barhorst@lehmancatholic.com. Web: www.lehmancatholic.com. Mr. Michael Barhorst, Pres.; Denise Stauffer, Prin.; Rev. Daniel K. Hess. Priests 2; Sisters 1; Lay Teachers 20; Students 211.

SPRINGFIELD. *Catholic Central Jr./Sr. High School*, (Grades 7-12), 1200 E. High St., 45505-1124. Tel: 937-325-9204; Fax: 937-328-7426. Email: pfinneran@ccirish.org. Web: www.ccirish.org. Steve DeWitt, Junior High Admin.; Kenith Britt, Pres.; Mr. Patrick Finneran, Prin.; Mrs. Kelly Perry, Librarian. Lay Teachers 28; Students 368.

[F] HIGH SCHOOLS, PRIVATE

CINCINNATI. *DePaul Cristo Rey High School*, 1133 Clifton Hills Ave., 45220. Tel: 513-861-0600; Fax: 513-861-0900. Web: www.depaulcristorey.org. Sr. Jeanne Bessette, O.S.F., Pres. & Contact Person; Mr. Andrew Farfsing, Prin.; Lisa Claytor, Dir. Corp Work Study; Renee Hargrove, Dir. Bus. Admin.; Keianna Matthews, Dir. Admissions; Darrick Murphy, Dir. Technology. Sponsored by Sisters of Charity of Cincinnati Sisters 1; Lay Teachers 5; Students 85.
The Summit Country Day School Please see The Summit Country Day school located under Elementary Schools, Private., 2161 Grandin Rd., 45208-3300. Tel: 513-871-4700; Fax: 513-533-5373. Web: www.summitcds.org. Richard Wilson, Head of School. Priests 1; Lay Teachers 113; Students 387.
St. Ursula Academy, 1339 E. McMillan St., 45206. Tel: 513-961-3410; Fax: 513-961-3856. Email: lkramer@saintursula.org. Web: www.saintursula.org. Lelia Kramer, Pres.; Judy O'Donnell, Prin.; Jill Herald, Librarian. Lay Teachers 59; Girls 662.
Ursuline Academy of Cincinnati (1896) Senior High School., 5535 Pfeiffer Rd., 45242. Tel: 513-791-5791; Fax: 513-791-3170. Email: pwilson@ursulineacademy.org. Web: www.ursulineacademy.org. Rev. John E. Wessling, S.T.D. (Retired); Sharon Redmond, Pres.; Thomas Barhorst, Prin.; Ms. Mary Bender, Asst. Prin.; Julie Burwrinkle, Librarian. Ursuline Sisters of Brown Co. Saint Martin, OH. Priests 1; Sisters 2; Lay Teachers 69; Girls 723.
St. Xavier High School, 600 W. North Bend Rd., 45224. Tel: 513-761-7600; Fax: 513-842-1610. Web: www.stxavier.org. Mr. David B. Mueller, Prin.; Rev. Timothy A. Howe, S.J., Pres.; Mr. William Sandquist Jr., Asst. Prin.; Revs. Edward L. Pigott, S.J., Rector; Dennis P. Ahern, S.J., Alumni Chap.; Francis J. Daly, S.J., Adult Faith Coord.; Mr. Dan Hogan, Chief Information Officer; Julie Conlon, Librarian. Priests 6; Sisters 1; Lay Teachers 125; Students 1,565.

[G] CONSOLIDATED ELEMENTARY SCHOOLS

CINCINNATI. *St. Boniface School* (1867) (Grades K-8), 4305 Pitts Ave., 45223. Tel: 513-541-5122; Fax: 513-541-3939. Email: fightmaster_j@stbonnie.org. Web: www.stbonifaceschool.net. Sr. Ann Gorman, R.S.M., Prin. Assoc. Admin; Mr. Jason Fightmaster, Contact Person; Mrs. Diane Stroud, B.A., M.A., Librarian. Serving the parishes of St. Boniface, St. Leo and Mother of Christ, Cincinnati. Sisters 4; Lay Teachers 15; Students 200.
Corryville Catholic Elementary School, (Grades PreSchool-8), 108 Calhoun St., 45219. Tel: 513-281-4856; Fax: 513-281-6497. Email: smith-ma@corryvillecatholic.org. Sr. Marie Smith, S.N.D.deN., Prin. & Contact Person. Consolidated school serving the parishes of Holy Name, St. Andrew, Assumption, Sacred Heart and Monica-St. George. Sisters 6; Lay Teachers 12; Students 189.
St. Gabriel Consolidated School, (Grades K-8), 18 W. Sharon Ave., 45246. Tel: 513-771-5220; Fax: 513-771-5133. Email: j.epplen@stgabeschool.org. Web: www.st.gabeschool.org. Joseph Epplen, Prin. & Contact Person; Gail Motz, Librarian. Consolidated school serving the parishes of St. Gabriel, Glendale; St. John, West Chester; St. Matthias, Forest Park; St. Maximilian Kolbe, West Chester. Lay Teachers 22; Students 432.
John Paul II Catholic School (1980) (Grades K-8), 9375 Winton Rd., 45231. Tel: 513-521-0860; Fax: 513-728-3110. Email: nroach@jpiics.org. Web: www.jpiics.org. Mrs. Leanora Roach, Prin.; Mrs. Nancy Acciani, Librarian. Lay Teachers 23; Students 423.
St. John the Baptist Catholic School, (Grades PreK-8), 5375 Dry Ridge Rd., 45252. Tel: 513-385-7970; Fax: 513-699-6964. Ms. Catie Blum, Prin. Teachers 26; Students 474.
St. Nicholas Academy, (Grades K-8), 170 Siebenthaler Ave., 45215. Tel: 513-686-2727; Fax: 513-686-2729. Web: stnacademy.org. Gerard Myers, Prin.; Mrs. Jeane Perry, Librarian. An interparish elementary school sponsored by St. John the Evangelist, Deer Park, Holy Trinity, Norwood and Our Lady of the Sacred Heart, Reading parishes. Lay Teachers 25; Students 314.
Our Lady of Grace, (Grades K-8), 2940 W. Galbraith Rd., 45239. Tel: 513-931-3070; Fax: 513-931-3707. Mrs. Sally Hicks, Prin.; Karen Southerington, Librarian. Serving the parishes of St. Ann (Groesbeck), Church of the Assumption (Mount Healthy), St. Margaret Mary (North College Hill) & St. Therese, the Little Flower (Mt. Airy). Teachers 31; Students 607.

DAYTON. *Bishop Leibold School*, (Grades PreSchool-8)Web: www.bishopleiboldschool.com. Mr. Paul Beyerle, Prin. Consolidated school of St. Henry, Dayton and Our Lady of Good Hope, Miamisburg. Lay Teachers 24; Students 472.
West Campus (Grades PreSchool-3), 24 S. Third St., Miamisburg, 45342. Tel: 937-866-3021; Fax: 937-866-5680. Mr. Paul Beyerle, Prin.; Julie Wehner, Sec. (West Campus).
East Campus (Grades 4-8), 6666 Springboro Rd., 45449. Tel: 937-434-9343; Fax: 937-436-3048. Mr. Paul Beyerle, Prin.; Laura Eiken, Sec. (East Campus).
Mary Queen of Peace Catholic School, (Grades PreK-8), Gramont Campus: 138 Gramont Ave., 45417. Tel: 937-268-6391; Fax: 937-268-9775. Web: www.maryqueenofpeace.us. Homewood Campus: 200 Homewood Ave., 45405. Tel: 937-228-3091; Fax: 937-449-2440. Ms. Debra Johnson, Prin., Homewood Campus & Gramont Campus. Regional School for St. Benedict the Moor, Corpus Christi, Holy Family, St. Mary, Our Lady of Mercy and Queen of Martyrs. Lay Teachers 24; Students 400.

HAMILTON. *St. Joseph Consolidated School*, (Grades K-8), 925 S. Second St., 45011. Tel: 513-863-8758; Fax: 513-863-5772. Email: info@sjcshamilton.org. Web: www.sjcshamilton.org. J. William Hicks, Prin.; Theresa Stenger, Contact Person. Serving the parishes of St. Aloysius, Shandon and St. Joseph, Hamilton. Lay Teachers 11; Students 215; Total Staff 15.

MIDDLETOWN. *John XXIII Catholic School*, (Grades PreK-8), 3806 Manchester Rd., 45042. Tel: 513-424-1196; Fax: 513-420-8480. Web: john23middletown.org. Brenda Neu, Prin.; Mrs. Janet Lucas, Asst. Prin.; Mrs. Janet Zappia, Librarian. Serving the parishes of Holy Family, Middletown; St. Mary, Franklin; Holy Name, Trenton; Our Lady of Sorrows, Monroe. Lay Teachers 22; Students 410.

PIQUA. *Piqua Catholic School*, (Grades K-8) Sr. Mary Alice Haithcoat, Prin. & Contact Person. Serving the parishes of St. Boniface and St. Mary. Sisters 1; Lay Teachers 15; Students 209.
North St. Campus (Grades 4-8), 503 W. North St., 45356. Tel: 937-773-1564; Fax: 937-773-0380. Email: haithcoatm@piquacatholic.org. Web: www.piqua-catholic.org. Sr. Mary Alice Haithcoat, Prin.; Mary Zimmerman, Librarian.
Downing St. Campus (Grades K-3), 218 S. Downing St., 45356. Tel: 937-773-3876; Fax: 937-773-5875. Sr. Mary Alice Haithcoat, Prin.; Linda Lange,

Contact Person; Gail Breisch, Bookkeeper; Mary Zimmerman, Librarian.

[H] ELEMENTARY SCHOOLS, PRIVATE

CINCINNATI. **Queen of Angels Montessori School*, (Grades PreK-8), 4460 Berwick St., 45227. Tel: 513-271-4171; Fax: 513-271-4680. Web: www.gscmontessori.org. Daniel Teller, Prin. Students 200; Faculty 30.

The Summit Country Day School (1890) 2161 Grandin Rd., 45208-3300. Tel: 513-871-4700; Fax: 513-533-5373. Email: summitinfo@summitcds.org. Web: www.summitcds.org. Richard Wilson, Head of School; David Paulin, Treas. Priests 1; Lay Teachers 113; Students 695.

St. Ursula Villa, (Grades PreK-8), 3660 Vineyard Pl., 45226. Tel: 513-871-7218; Fax: 513-871-0082. Web: www.stursulavilla.org. Polly Duplace, Prin. & Contact Person; Susan Hall, Librarian. Sisters 1; Lay Teachers 53; Students 454.

LIBERTY TOWNSHIP. *Mother Teresa Catholic Elementary School* (1998) (Grades K-8), 7197 Mother Teresa Ln., 45044-9426. Tel: 513-779-6585; Fax: 513-779-6468. Email: sranne@mtces.org. Web: www.mtces.org. Michael Maratea, School Bd. Chm.; Noel Balster, Devel. Dir.; Sr. Anne Mary Schulz, C.PP.S., Prin.; Mr. Alex Schuster, Asst. Prin.; Pam Kleingers, Librarian. Sisters 1; Lay Teachers 19; Students 451.

[I] CHILD CARE INSTITUTIONS

CINCINNATI. *St. Joseph Infant and Maternity Home dba St. Joseph Home of Cincinnati* (1876) 10722 Wyscarver Rd., 45241. Tel: 513-563-2520; Fax: 513-563-1958. Email: mrench@sjh-cincy.com. Web: www.sjh-cincy.com. Mr. Michael J. Rench, Pres. & CEO & Contact Person. Sisters of Charity of Cincinnati, OH. Respite Beds 8; Residential 48.

St. Joseph Orphanage (1829) 5400 Edalbert Dr., 45239-7695. Tel: 513-741-3100; Fax: 513-741-5686. Email: info@sjokids.org. Web: wwwsjokids.org. Robert J. Wehr, Ph.D., Exec. Dir. Archdiocesan Children's Residential Center.

A.C.T. Child Case Management, 5400 Edalbert Dr., 45239. Tel: 513-385-1900; Fax: 513-245-7970. Robert J. Wehr, Ph.D., Exec. Dir. Employees 47; Children Served 450; Lay Teachers 8.

St. Joseph Villa, 5400 Edalbert Dr., 45239. Tel: 513-741-3100; Fax: 513-741-5686. Residential Treatment and Education and Day Treatment and Foster Care Service for Children 6-18. Total Staff 110; Total Assisted 400.

Altercrest, 274 Sutton Rd., 45230. Tel: 513-231-5010; Fax: 513-231-8651. Robert J. Wehr, Ph.D., Exec. Dir.; Joseph Cassiere, Assoc. Exec. Dir. Comprehensive services for adolescents including Community Transition Programs, Special Education, Outpaitent, Day Treatment & Residential Mental/Behavioral Healthcare. Total Staff 65; Total Assisted Annually 350.

C.A.R.E. Child Case Management, 6975 Dixie Hwy., Ste. A, Fairfield, 45014. Tel: 513-887-2100; Fax: 513-887-2101. Robert J. Wehr, Ph.D., Exec. Dir. Total Staff 17; Children Served 300.

Dayton Foster Care, 3131 S. Dixie Dr., Ste. 220, Moraine, 45439. Tel: 937-643-0398; Fax: 937-643-9961. Total Staff 14; Total Assisted 100.

[J] SPECIAL SCHOOLS

CINCINNATI. *St. Rita School for the Deaf* (1915) (Grades PreK-12), 1720 Glendale-Milford Rd., 45215. Tel: 513-771-7600; Fax: 513-326-8264. Email: gernst@srsdeaf.org. Web: www.srsdeaf.org. Mr. Gregroy R. Ernst, Exec. Dir.; Rev. William H. Wysong, J.C.L. Residential and day school for deaf and hard of hearing children. Franciscan Sisters of Mary 1; Lay Teachers 30; High School Students 36; Elementary Students 68; Preschool 81.

[K] GENERAL HOSPITALS

CINCINNATI. *The Good Samaritan Hospital of Cincinnati, Ohio*, Mailing Address: 619 Oak St., 3 S., 45206. Tel: 513-569-6739; Fax: 513-569-6358. 375 Dixmyth Ave., 45220. Tel: 513-862-1400; Fax: 513-862-3435. Web: www.trihealth.com. Mr. John Prout, Pres. & CEO; David Dornheggen, COO; Frank Nation, Mgr. Pastoral Care. Tel: 513-862-2281; Fax: 513-862-7050. Catholic Health Initiative (CHI). Bassinets 69; Bed Capacity 592; Patients Assisted Annually 230,000; Total Staff 3,500.

Registered Training College of Nursing Tel: 513-862-2631; Fax: 513-862-3572. Students 313.

Mercy Hospital Anderson dba Mercy Health-Anderson Hospital 7500 State Rd., 45255. Tel: 513-624-4500; Fax: 513-624-3299. Web: www.e-mercy.com. Mailing Address: 4600 McAuley Pl., 6th Fl., 45242. LeeAnn Liska, Interim Pres. Sisters of Mercy. Bed Capacity 193; Patients Assisted Annually 174,588; Total Staff 1,172.

Mercy Hospitals West dba Mercy Health-Western Hills Hospital 3131 Queen City Ave., 45238. Tel: 513-389-5000; Fax: 513-389-9141. Web: www.e-mercy.com. Mailing Address: 4600 McAuley Pl., 6th Flr., 45242. Michael Stephens, Pres. & Mkt. Leader; Don Rohling, Senior Vice Pres. Mission Integration; Rev. Bruno Kremp, O.F.M., Chap.; Sr. Elaine Merkel, O.S.F., Chap.; Immanuel Krishman, Chap. A member of the Mercy Health Partners. Sisters 1; Bed Capacity 261; Patients Assisted Annually 131,815; Total Staff 770.

Mercy Hospitals West dba Mercy Health-Mt. Airy Hospital 2446 Kipling Ave., 45239. Tel: 513-853-5000; Fax: 513-853-9141. Web: www.e-mercy.com. Mailing Address: 4600 McAuley Pl., 6th Flr., 45242. Michael Stephens, Pres. & Mkt. Leader; Don Rohling, Senior Vice Pres. Mission Integration; Sr. Donna DeMange, O.S.F., Chap.; Grace Forsyth, Chap.; Susan Mackall, Chap. A member of the Mercy Health Partners. Bed Capacity 269; Patients Assisted Annually 89,962; Total Staff 830.

BATAVIA. *The Sisters of Mercy Of Clermont County, Ohio dba Mercy Health-Clermont Hospital* 3000 Hospital Dr., 45103. Tel: 513-732-8200; Fax: 513-732-8537. Web: www.e-mercy.com. Mailing Address: 4600 McAuley Pl., 6th Flr., 45242. Gayle H. Heintzelman, Pres. & CEO; Don Rohling, Senior Vice Pres. Mission Integration; Irene Behling, Dir. Mission Svcs.; Kay O'Rourke. Bed Capacity 166; Patients Assisted Annually 125,021; Total Staff 701.

DAYTON. *Good Samaritan Hospital* (1932) 2222 Philadelphia Dr., 45406. Tel: 937-734-2612. Web: www.goodsamdayton.org. Mr. Mark Shaker, Pres. & CEO. Affiliate with Catholic Health Initiative. Bed Capacity 560; Patients Assisted Annually 300,000; Total Staff 3,200.

FAIRFIELD. *Sisters of Mercy of Hamilton Ohio dba Mercy Health-Fairfield Hospital* 3000 Mack Rd., 45014. Tel: 513-870-7000; Fax: 513-870-7065. Web: www.e-mercy.com. Mailing Address: 4600 McAuley Pl., 6th Fl., 45242. Thomas S. Urban, Pres. & CEO; Sr. Sharon Wiedmar, R.S.M., Dir. Mission Svcs. Bed Capacity 221; Total Assisted Annually 203,304; Total Staff 1,439.

[L] HEALTH CARE SYSTEMS

CINCINNATI. *Catholic Health Partners*, 615 Elsinore Pl., 45202. Tel: 513-639-2800; Fax: 513-639-2700. Web: www.health-partners.org. Mr. Michael D. Connelly, Pres. & CEO. 24 hospitals, 23 acute care, and 1 specialty, 13 long-term care facilities, HUD: 15 facilities, 606 units; low-income tax credit housing: 2 facilities, 181 units, 5,246 licensed hospital beds, Total Staff 32,480 (Total System). Catholic Health Partners is co-sponsored by the Sisters of Mercy, South Central Community; Sisters of Mercy, Mid-Atlantic Community; Covenant Health Systems, Sisters of the Humility of Mary, Franciscan Sisters of the Poor. Bed Capacity 3,856; Total Assisted Annually 6,751,664.

Mercy Health Partners of Southwest Ohio dba Mercy Health 4600 McAuley Pl. 6th Fl., 45242. Tel: 513-981-6000; Fax: 513-981-6133. Web: www.e-mercy.com. James E. May, Pres. & CEO. Total Staff 1,069.

DAYTON. *The Heart Institute of Dayton*, 2200 Philadelphia Dr., Ste. 510, 45406. Tel: 937-734-8660; Fax: 937-567-4130. Web: www.thidayton.org. Mr. Josh Lader, Exec. Dir.

Samaritan Health Partners, 2222 Philadelphia Dr., 45406. Tel: 937-734-2612. Web: www.goodsamdayton.org. Affiliate of Catholic Health Initiative.

SPRINGFIELD. *Community Mercy Health Partners*, One S. Limestone St., Ste.700, P.O. Box 688, 45501-0688. Tel: 937-328-7000; Fax: 937-328-6214. Web: www.communitymercy.org. Mark Wiener, Pres. & CEO.

Mercy Memorial Hospital, 904 Scioto St., Urbana, 43078. Tel: 937-484-6112; Fax: 937-484-6105. Bed Capacity 25; Staff 142; Total Assisted Annually 55,858.

Springfield Regional Medical Center (1950) 100 Medical Center Dr., 45504. Tel: 937-523-1000. Bed Capacity 284; Staff 1,778; Total Assisted Annually 253,945.

Mercy St. John's Center, 100 W. McCreight Ave., 45504. Tel: 937-399-9910; Fax: 937-399-9449. Day care center for adults. Four Levels of Care: 1. Adult Day (Petticrew Ctr.); 2. High Functioning Unit (The Gardens); 3. Intermediate Unit (The Bridge); 4. End Stage (The Rainbow). Skilled & intermediate long-term care facility for all ages, Alzheimer's unit, ventilator unit. Bed Capacity 89; Staff 140; Total Assisted Annually 472.

Oakwood Village, 1500 Villa Rd., 45503. Tel: 937-390-9000; Fax: 937-390-9333. Web: www.oakwoodvillage.com. Jamie J. Houseman, Admin. Total Assisted Annually 326; Bed Capacity 248; Total Staff 208.

Mercy McAuley Center, 906 Scioto St., Urbana, 43078. Tel: 937-653-5432; Fax: 937-652-2072. Mark Wiener, Regl. Pres. & CEO. Residents 129; Bed Capacity 129; Total Staff 194; Total Assisted Annually 221.

Mercy Siena Woods, 6125 N. Main St., Dayton, 45415. Tel: 937-278-8211. Retirement Community, nonsectarian. A member of Catholic Healthcare Partners. Specialized Alzheimer's Center, Skilled Nursing Center. Assisted living and Independent Cottages. Sponsored by the Religious Sisters of Mercy since 1943. Sisters 2; Bed Capacity 99; Total Assisted Annually 179; Total Staff 130.

Mercy Siena Gardens, 6105 N. Main St., Dayton, 45415. Tel: 937-279-6879; Fax: 937-279-6885. Web: www.mercysiena.com. Bed Capacity 65; Total Staff 88; Total Assisted Annually 30.

[M] SENIOR RESIDENCES

CINCINNATI. *Archbishop Leibold Home for the Aged*, 476 Riddle Rd., 45220-2493. Tel: 513-281-8001; Fax: 513-281-4943. Email: mscincinnati@littlesistersofthepoor.org. Rev. Cyprian Berens, O.F.M., Chap. (Retired); Sr. Francis King, Supr. The Little Sisters of the Poor. Sisters 11; Residents 95; Total Staff 120; Bed Capacity 95; Total Assisted 108.

St. Margaret Hall, 1960 Madison Rd., 45206-1896. Tel: 513-751-5880; Fax: 513-751-9813. Email: contact@stmargarethall.com. Web: www.stmargarethall.com. Janet Murphy, Admin. & Contact Person. Carmelite Sisters for the Aged and Infirm 6; Residents 135; Total Staff 210.

Mercy Franciscan Senior Health and Housing Services Inc. dba Mercy Health-St. Theresa 7010 Rowan Hill Dr., 45227. Tel: 513-271-7010; Fax: 513-527-0143. Web: www.e-mercy.com. Mailing Address: 4600 McAuley Pl., 6th Flr., 45242. Jason Niehaus, Pres.; Kendra Couch, Exec. Dir.; Deacon Jerry Schneider. Bed Capacity 192; Residents 117; Total Assisted 538; Total Staff 157.

Mercy Franciscan Senior Health and Housing Services, Inc. dba Mercy Health-Terrace 100 Compton Rd., 45215. Tel: 513-761-9036; Fax: 513-761-5199. Web: www.e-mercy.com. Mailing Address: 4600 McAuley Pl., 6th Flr., 45242. Jason Niehaus, Pres. & Exec. Dir.; Rachel Wirth, Exec. Dir.; Joan Owens, Pastoral Care. Licensed Beds 185; Total Assisted 512; Total Staff 174; Residents 147.

Mercy Franciscan Senior Health and Housing Services, Inc. dba Mercy Health-West Park 2950 West Park Dr., 45238. Tel: 513-451-8900; Fax: 513-451-3728. Web: www.e-mercy.com. Mailing Address: 4600 McAuley Pl., 6th Flr., 45242. Jason Niehaus, Pres.; Kendra Couch, Exec. Dir. Bed Capacity 341; Total Assisted Annually 670; Total Staff 270; Residents 268.

Sisters of Charity Senior Care Corp. dba Bayley 990 Bayley Place Dr., 45233. Tel: 513-347-5500; Fax: 513-347-5553. Web: www.bayleylife.org. Adrienne Walsh, Pres. & CEO. Also includes Bayley Adult Day Program and Bayley Village. Total Assisted Living 85; Independent Cottages 78; Health Care 110; Licensed Nursing 110; Total Staff 292.

CENTERVILLE. **St. Leonard*, 8100 Clyo Rd., 45458. Tel: 937-433-0480; Fax: 937-439-7165. Web: www.stleonard.net. Timothy C. Dressman, Exec. Dir. & Contact Person; Rev. Loren Connell, O.F.M., Chap. A facility of the Sylvania Franciscan Health, sponsored by the Sisters of St. Francis, Sylvania, OH. A residence for Senior Citizens. Residents 700; Total Staff 360; Bed Capacity 663.

DAYTON. *Mercy Siena Springs I* (1984) 6215 N. Main St., 45415. Tel: 937-279-6114; Fax: 937-279-6870. Sponsored by the Sisters of Mercy., Apartments, Independent Living for the Elderly. Residents 45; Total Staff 5.

Mercy Siena Springs II (2001) 6217 N. Main St., 45415. Tel: 937-279-6114; Fax: 937-279-6870. Residents 34; Total Staff 3.

HAMILTON. *Mercy Franciscan Senior Health and Housing Services, Inc. dba Mercy Health-Schroder* 1302 Millville Ave., 45013. Tel: 513-867-4100; Fax: 513-867-1415. Web: www.e-mercy.com. Mailing Address: 4600 McAuley Pl., 6th Flr., 45242. Jason Niehaus, Pres.; Marcie Calvert, Exec. Dir. A Facility of the Mercy Health Partners of Southwest Ohio. Sponsored by the Catholic Healthcare Partners. Premier short-term rehabilitation program. Bed Capacity 173; Total Assisted 572; Total Staff 152; Residents 109.

[N] MONASTERIES AND RESIDENCES OF PRIESTS AND BROTHERS

CINCINNATI. *Brother Juniper Friary*, 4344 Sullivan Ave., 45217-1747. Tel: 513-898-0569. Rev. Donald A. Miller, O.F.M., Ph.D., Vocation Dir.; Bros. Chris

Cahill, O.F.M., Faculty, Roger Beacon High School; David Crank, O.F.M., Dir. Office for Sr. Friars In Res.

Brothers of the Poor of St. Francis, 7831 Ayerdayl Ln., 45255. Tel: 513-924-0111; Fax: 513-321-3777. Email: hibrothers@fuse.net. Bro. Edward Kesler, C.F.P., Contact Person. Brothers of the Poor of St. Francis.

The Catholic Foreign Mission Society of America, Inc., 6930 Greenfield Dr., 45224-1626. Tel: 513-681-7888. Email: mklcin@maryknoll.org. Web: www.maryknoll.org. Revs. Leslie F. Blowers, M.M., Regl. Dir.; Peter L. Chabot, M.M. Maryknoll Fathers.

St. Clare Friary, 5831 Saranac Ave., 45224. Tel: 513-541-0488; Fax: 513-541-2424. Revs. Patrick McCloskey, O.F.M.; David Kohut, O.F.M.; Bro. Robert Lucero, O.F.M.

St. Clement Friary (1850) 4536 Vine St., 45217. Tel: 513-641-2257; Fax: 513-641-2262. Email: vincedel@franciscan.org. Revs. Fred Link, O.F.M., Pastor; Louis Bartko, O.F.M. (Retired); Joel Byrne, O.F.M. (Retired); William Farris, O.F.M., Pres., Roger Bacon High School; Howard Hudepohl, O.F.M., Chap., Mercy Franciscan Terrrace; James Van Vurst, O.F.M., Vicar, Assoc. Pastor; Valentine Young, O.F.M., Teacher, Roger Bacon High School; Bros. Conrad F. Rebmann, O.F.M., (Retired); Louis Lamping, O.F.M., (Retired); Joseph Haley, O.F.M., Fraternal Svc.; Bernard Jennings, O.F.M., (Retired); Kenneth Beetz, O.F.M., Maintenance; Stephen Richter, O.F.M., (Retired); Phillips Robinette, O.F.M., Assoc. Archivist; Kevin Schroder, O.F.M., St. Anthony Messenger; Vincent Delorenzo, O.F.M., Mission Office/Guardian, Prov. Councilor. St. John the Baptist Province. Residence for Retired Friars, Pastor of St. Clement Parish and other Friars. Priests 6; Brothers 9.

Comboni Missionaries (Verona Fathers)-Comboni Mission Center, 1318 Nagel Rd., 45255-3120. Tel: 513-474-4997; Fax: 513-474-0382. Email: info@combonimissionaries.org. Web: www.combonimissionaries.org. Revs. Manuel Baeza Gama, M.C.C.J., Prov.; Brian Quigley, M.C.C.J., Dir. of Mission Office & Prov. Treas.; Mario Ongaro, M.C.C.J. (Retired); Cindy Browne, Mgr. & Editor, CPN Newsletter; Mgr., Justice & Peace Resource Ctr.; Jeanie Stephens, Devel. Dir.; Revs. Kenneth Gerth, M.C.C.J.; William J. Jansen, M.C.C.J.; Ms. Mary Bertolini, Dir. Communications; Rev. Ruffino Ezama, M.C.C.J., Mission Promotion. Houses Comboni Missionaries of the Heart of Jesus, Inc., The Offices of the Province of North America, including the Office of the Provincial. Priests 8.

De Sales Crossings Marianist Community, 1600 Madison Rd., 45206-1815. Tel: 513-961-1945; 513-961-2257; Fax: 513-221-4907. Bros. Giancarlo Bonutti, S.M., Dir. of Community; Robert A. Politi, S.M.; Robert N. Wiethorn, S.M.; William I. Grundish, S.M.; J. Mitchell Schweickart, S.M.; Rev. Eugene Contadino, S.M., B.A., M.A., Ph.D.; Bros. Michael A. Murphy, S.M.; Michael J. O'Grady, S.M. Priests 1; Brothers 7.

Faber Jesuit Community, 790 Clinton Springs Ave., 45229. Tel: 513-961-7700; Fax: 513-569-4587. Email: faberjes@cinci.rr.com. Revs. J. Peter Carey, S.J.; John M. Ferone, S.J.; Joseph D. Folzenlogen, S.J., Supr.; Charles A. Hofmann, S.J.; Peter Sharkey, S.J. 6818 Buckingham Pl., 45227. Bros. Donald H. Bengert, S.J.; John P. Martin, S.J.; Robert W. Schneider, S.J. Priests 6; Brothers 3.

St. Francis Seraph Friary, 1615 Vine St., 45202-6400. Tel: 513-721-4700; Fax: 513-421-9672. Email: sjbsec@franciscan.com. Web: www.franciscan.org. Revs. Hilarion Kistner, O.F.M., Educ. Homily Helps, Assoc. Chap, The Christ Hospital; Jeffrey Scheeler, O.F.M., Prov. Min.; Mr. David O'Brien, CFO; Revs. Page Polk, O.F.M., Assoc. Dir.; Gregory Friedman, O.F.M., Pastor, St. Francis Seraph; Simeon Cleves, O.F.M., Chap., Christ Hospital; Thomas Speier, O.F.M., Part-time Sacramental Min. at St. Monica - St. George Parish and Newman Ctr.; Part-time Word Ministry; Manuel Viera, O.F.M., J.C.L., Arch Judical Vicar; Damian Cesanek, O.F.M., Sacramental Ministry, Asst. Chap. at Christ Hospital, Cincinnati; Frank Jasper, O.F.M., Prov. Vicar/Treas.; Daniel J. Anderson, O.F.M., Admin. Asst. to Prov.; John Bok, O.F.M., Co-Dir. Friar Works Office; Ms. Colleen Cushard, Co-Dir. Friar Works Office; Sr. Donna Graham, O.S.F., Office of Justice, Peace and Integrity of Creation; Ms. Toni Cashnelli, Dir. Communications; Bros. Gene Mayer, O.F.M., Prov. Sec.; Daniel Barrett, O.F.M., Parochial & Fraternal Assistance; John Carey, O.F.M., Assoc., Mission Office; Timothy Sucher, O.F.M., Guardian, Pastoral Assoc.; John Barker, O.F.M., Graduate Studies; Brian Maloney, O.F.M., (Sabbatical); Vincent Delorenzo, O.F.M., Dir. Franciscan Mission Office; Cletus Riederer, O.F.M., Fraternal Assistance. Provincial Headquarters of the Province of St. John the Baptist of the Order of Friars Minor. Priests 8; Brothers 6.

Friars of the Province Serving Abroad: Revs. Harold Geers, O.F.M., 69 San Pedro Bautista St., San Francisco del Monte, 1104 Quezon City, Philippines. Tel: 011-63-02-373-2973; Fax: 011-63-02-373-2972; James M. Bok, O.F.M.; Joseph Hund, O.F.M.; Max Langenderfer, O.F.M.; Bros. Philip Wilhelm, O.F.M., Sanctuario de San Antonio, Forbes Park, Makati, P.O. Box 3215 MCC, Metro Manila 1299 Philippines. Tel: 011-63-02-843-8830; Fax: 011-63-02-843-9223; Roger Covero, O.F.M., Balay Piksalabukan Friary, Josefina St., Zamboanga del Sur, Philippines; Louis Zant, O.F.M., St. Joseph Friary, P.O. Box 66, Savanna-la-mar, Westmoreland. Tel: 876-955-2648; Thomas Gerchak, O.F.M.

Friars on Special Assignment in the U.S.A.: Revs. Arthur Espelage, O.F.M., J.C.D., Marriage Tribunal, Diocese of Venice, FL; Matthias Crehan, O.F.M., Chap., Veteran's Affairs Med. Ctr., Phoenix, AZ; Robert Bruno, O.F.M., Senior Staff Chap./USAF Academy; Francis S. Tebbe, O.F.M., (Sabbatical); Jeremy Harrington, O.F.M., (On Special Assignment) Commissary & Guardian Franciscans for the Holy Land); Charles Smiech, O.F.M., Retreat Ministry; Rock Travnikar, O.F.M., Coord. Pastoral Svcs. for Rocky Creek Village, FL; Francis Wendling, O.F.M., Prayer Ministry, MO; Loren Connell, O.F.M., Chap. St. Leonard Senior Community, OH; Paul Walsman, O.F.M., Preaching, Food for the Poor, FL; Bros. Andrew Stettler, O.F.M., Christian Svc. Prog., LA; Giovanni Ried, O.F.M., Christian Svc. Prog., LA; Josef Anderlohr, O.F.M., Prayer Ministry.

Friars in Retirement Homes in the Archdiocese of Cincinnati: Revs. Cyprian Berens, O.F.M., Chap. (Retired), Archbishop Leibold Home for the Aged, 476 Riddle Rd., 45220-2493. Tel: 513-281-8001; Fax: 513-281-4943; John Boehman, O.F.M. (Retired); Curt Lanzrath, O.F.M. (Retired); Theobald Hattrup, O.F.M. (Retired), Archbishop Leibold Home for the Aged, 476 Riddle Rd., 45220-2493. Tel: 513-281-8001; Fax: 513-281-4943; Bert Heise, O.F.M.; Donald E. Holtgrewe, O.F.M.; Joseph Rigali, O.F.M.; Noel William, O.F.M. (Retired), Archbishop Leibold Home for the Aged, 476 Riddle Rd., 45220-2493. Tel: 513-281-8001; Fax: 513-281-4943; Valens J. Waldschmidt, O.F.M. (Retired), Archbishop Leibold Home for the Aged, 476 Riddle Rd., 45220-2493. Tel: 513-281-8001; Fax: 513-281-4943; Gil Wohler, O.F.M.; Bros. Donald Rewers, O.F.M.; Joel Soldenski, O.F.M.

St. Gertrude Priory, 7630 Shawnee Run Rd., 45243. Tel: 513-561-5954; Fax: 513-527-3971. Web: www.stgertrude.org. Very Rev. Basil Cole, O.P., Prior; Revs. James M. Sullivan, O.P., Novice Master; Andre-Joseph LaCasse, O.P., Pastor; Joseph Clement Burns, O.P.; Randall Erza Sullivan, O.P., Assoc.; Guy Albert Trudell, O.P., Asst. Novice Master; Paul Keller, O.P., S.T.D., Asst. Prof. Mount St. Mary's Seminary; Terence Quinn, O.P.

Headquarters of Glenmary Home Missioners (1939) P.O. Box 465618, 45246-5618. Tel: 513-874-8900; Fax: 513-874-1690. Email: info@glenmary.org. Web: www.glenmary.org. Also known as The Home Missioners of America. 4119 Glenmary Trace, Fairfield, 45014. Tel: 513-874-8900; Fax: 513-874-1690. Revs. Chet Artysiewicz, G.H.M., Pres.; Neil Pezzulo, G.H.M., 1st Vice Pres.; Bro. Jack Henn, G.H.M., 2nd Vice Pres.; Revs. Dan Dorsey, G.H.M., Novitiate Dir.; Dominic R. Duggins, G.H.M., Dir. of Devel.; Bros. David Henley, G.H.M., Dir. of Vocations; Dennis Craig, G.H.M., Dir. Senior & Disabled Members.

Senior Members: Revs. Ed Gorny, G.H.M. (Retired); Robert Dalton, G.H.M. (Retired); David Glockner, G.H.M. (Retired); Laurence Goulding, G.H.M. (Retired); August Guppenberger (Retired); Del Holmes, G.H.M. (Retired); Charles Hughes, G.H.M. (Retired); James Kelly, G.H.M. (Retired); Richard Kreimer, G.H.M. (Retired); Fid Levri, G.H.M. (Retired); George Mathis, G.H.M. (Retired); Gerald Peterson, G.H.M. (Retired); Robert Rademacher, G.H.M. (Retired); Frank Ruff, G.H.M. (Retired); Francis Schenk, G.H.M. (Retired); Leo Schloemer, G.H.M. (Retired); Wil Steinbacher, G.H.M. (Retired); Bros. Robert Hoffman, G.H.M., (Retired); Terry O'Rourke, G.H.M., (Retired); Mike Springer, G.H.M., (Retired); Bernie Stern, G.H.M., (Retired); Ken Woods, G.H.M., (Retired).

Jesuit Community at Xavier University, Jesuit Community Residence, 3844 Victory Pkwy., 45207. Tel: 513-745-3591; Fax: 513-745-3858. Revs. Kent A. Beausoleil, S.J., Asst. Pastor, Bellarmine Chapel; Campus Min., Xavier Univ.; Joseph A. Bracken, S.J.; Albert J. Bischoff, S.J.; Richard W. Bollman, S.J., Parish Priest, Bellarmine Chapel; Robert Bueter, S.J., Adjunct Prof. & Assoc. Dir. of Center for Catholic Educ.; Bro. Darrell J. Burns, S.J., Mission & Identity, Activities Coord.; Revs. Eugene Carmichael, S.J.; Michael J. Graham, S.J.; Robert E. Hurd, S.J.; Thomas P. Kennealy, S.J.; J. Leo Klein, S.J.; John J. LaRocca, S.J., Rector; Thomas A. Ryan, S.J.; Benjamin J. Urmston, S.J.; William Verbryke, S.J.; Joseph Wagner, S.J.; Cyril Whitaker, S.J.; George B. Wilson, S.J.; Mr. Matt Dunch, S.J.; Mr. Jim Riordan, S.J. Members of the Jesuit Community (Society of Jesus, S.J.). Priests 17; Brothers 1; Scholastics 1.

Jesuit Community at St. Xavier High School, Jesuit Community, 7361 View Pl., 45224. Tel: 513-761-5522; Fax: 513-761-0514. Revs. Dennis P. Ahern, S.J.; Francis J. Daly, S.J.; Timothy A. Howe, S.J.; Edward L. Pigott, S.J., Rector; John P. Heim, S.J.; Richard Millbourn, S.J.; Denis A. Dirscherl, S.J.; Paul O'Connor, S.J.

St. John the Baptist Friary, 10722 Wyscarver Rd., 45241-3083. Tel: 513-769-1613; Fax: 513-769-1650. Email: johnpbok@gmail.com. Revs. Paul Desch, O.F.M.; John Bok, O.F.M., Local Min.; Bruno Kremp, O.F.M.; Edward Lammert, O.F.M.; Bill Reichel, O.F.M.; Anthony Walter, O.F.M.; Warren Zeisler, O.F.M.; Bros. Martin Humphreys, O.F.M., (Retired); Dominic Lococo, O.F.M., Vicar; Allan Schmitz, O.F.M.

Marianist Community, 1516 Elm St., #1, 45202. Tel: 513-687-5518. Bro. Michael A. Murphy, S.M. Brothers 1.

Pleasant Street Friary (1969) 1723 Pleasant St., 45202-6413. Tel: 513-621-0599; Fax: 513-621-0599. Email: gregf1723@gmail.com. Revs. Gregory Friedman, O.F.M.; Mark J. Hudak, O.F.M.; Daniel J. Anderson, O.F.M.; Jack R. Wintz, O.F.M.; Murray L. Bodo, O.F.M. In Res. Rev. John Quigley, O.F.M.

CARTHAGENA. *St. Charles*, Society of the Precious Blood: 2860 U.S. Rte. 127, 45822. Tel: 419-925-4516; Fax: 419-925-4800. Web: ma.noacsc.org/stcharl. Revs. James C. Seibert, C.PP.S., Dir.; Norbert Adelman, C.PP.S (Retired); George Albers, C.PP.S. (Retired); John Behen, C.PP.S. (Retired); Thomas Beischel, C.PP.S. (Retired); James Bender, C.PP.S. (Retired); John L. Bensman (Retired); Joseph Brown, C.PP.S. (Retired); Harry M. Cavanaugh, C.PP.S. (Retired); Robert Conway, C.PP.S. (Retired); Lawrence Cyr, C.PP.S. (Retired); Bernard Diekhoff, C.PP.S. (Retired); William Dineen, C.PP.S. (Retired); James Dugal, C.PP.S. (Retired); Linus Evers, C.PP.S. (Retired); John Falter, C.PP.S. (Retired); Albert Fey, C.PP.S. (Retired); George Fey, C.PP.S. (Retired); Henry Frantz, C.PP.S. (Retired); Dominic Gerlach, C.PP.S. (Retired); Leonard Goettemoeller, C.PP.S (Retired); Lawrence Heiman, C.PP.S. (Retired); Alvin Herber, C.PP.S. (Retired); John Herber, C.PP.S.; John Hoying, C.PP.S. (Retired); Vincent Hoying, C.PP.S. (Retired); William Hoyng, C.PP.S. (Retired); Edward Joyce, C.PP.S. (Retired); Leonard A. Kistler, C.PP.S. (Retired); Timothy Knepper, C.PP.S; William Kramer, C.PP.S. (Retired); Frederick Lang, C.PP.S. (Retired); Rev. Msgr. Vincent L. Lengerich (GRY) (Retired); Revs. James McCabe, C.PP.S. (Retired); James Miller, C.PP.S. (Retired); Bernard Mullen, C.PP.S. (Retired); Charles Mullen, C.PP.S. (Retired); Alfred Naseman, C.PP.S., Retreat & Renewal; Louis Osterhage, C.PP.S. (Retired); Daniel Raible, C.PP.S. (Retired); Ernest W. Ranly, C.PP.S. (Retired); Albert Reed, C.PP.S. (Retired); Richard R. Riedel, C.PP.S. (Retired); Robert Reinhart, C.PP.S. (Retired); Charles Rohrkemper (Retired); Gary Scherer, C.PP.S. (Retired); Louis Schmit, C.PP.S. (Retired); James Schrader, C.PP.S; Kenneth J. Schroeder, C.PP.S.; Emil Schuwey, C.PP.S. (Retired); John Spatt, C.PP.S. (Retired); James F. Trick (Retired); Paul W. Wohlwend, C.PP.S. (Retired); Bro. Jude Brown, C.PP.S., Librarian. Priests 54; Brothers 8. In Res. Revs. Joseph Hinders, C.PP.S. (Retired); Ralph Verdi, C.PP.S.

DAYTON. *Marianist Community*, 100 Chambers St., 45409. Tel: 937-627-8998. Rev. Christopher W. Conlon, S.M., Dir.; Bros. Philip Aaron, S.M.; M. Gary Marcinowski, S.M., M.F.A. ; Thomas E. Oldenski, S.M. Priests 1; Brothers 3. *Marianist Community*, Meyer Hall, 4435 E. Patterson Rd., 45430-1095. Tel: 937-426-7852; Fax: 937-426-7858. Rev. John Putka, S.M., Ph.D.; Bros. A. Joseph Barrish, S.M.; Hugh Bihl, S.M.; Donald R. Geiger, S.M., Ph.D.; Joseph Mariscalco, S.M.; Donald Neff, S.M.; Donald Smith, S.M., Dir.; Jeffrey Sullivan, S.M. Priests 1; Brothers 7. *Marianist Community, Novitiate*, 4435 E. Patterson Rd., 45430-1095. Tel: 937-426-5721; Fax: 937-429-4686. Revs. Michael Lisbeth, S.M., Dir. & Master of Novices; Christopher T. Wittmann, S.M.; D'Cruz Nicholas, S.M.; Bros. Charles Johnson, S.M., Asst.

Dir. of Novices; John Lemker, S.M.; John Somerville, S.M.; Patrick Tonry, S.M. *Marianist Community*, 141 Washington St., 45402-2530. Tel: 937-224-9978. Revs. John A. McGrath; Kenneth Sommer; Bros. James Brown, S.M.; Victor M. Forlani, S.M., M.B.A., D.B.A.; Bernard Hartman, S.M.; Paul Jablinski, S.M.; Anthony Pistoni; Fred Stovall, S.M.; Edward E. Zamierowski, S.M., Dir. Priests 2; Brothers 7. *Marianist Community*, 312 Stonemill Rd., 45409-2543. Tel: 937-627-1553. Revs. Gerald T. Chinchar, S.M., D.Min.; Bertrand A. Buby, S.M., Ph.D. (Retired); David McGuigan, S.M.; Bros. Raymond Fitz, S.M., Dir.; Daniel L. Klco, S.M., M.S.; Blaise Mosengo, S.M. Priests 3; Brothers 3. *Marianist Community*, 121 Sawmill Rd., 45409-2524. Tel: 937-222-4928. Rev. Norbert C. Burns, S.M. (Retired); Bros. James Facette; Alex J. Tuss, S.M., Ph.D., Dir.; Lawrence Cada, S.M. Priests 1; Brothers 3. *Marianist Community*, 1903 Trinity Ave., 45409-2445. Tel: 937-293-9744. Rev. Francois Rossier, S.M.; Bros. Thomas Giardino, S.M., Dir.; Robert H. Hughes, S.M.; Robert Jones, S.M.; Patrick Wanderi Kagai; Daniel Osino Odero; Claude Gerard Sery, S.M. Priests 1; Brothers 6.

Marianist Community, Alumni Hall, University of Dayton, 45469-0300. Revs. George Abmayr, S.M.; Paul F. Vieson, S.M. (Retired); Robert E. Hughes, S.M.; Anthony Jansen, S.M.; Joseph F. Kozar, S.M., Ph.D., Dir.; Johann B.G. Roten, S.M., S.T.D.; Thomas A. Thompson, S.M.; Bros. William Fackovec, S.M.; Charles Gausling, S.M.; John Habjan, S.M.; James Moran, S.M.; Ronald Overman, S.M.; David Schmitz, S.M.; Daniel Stupka, S.M.; Louis Fournier, S.M. Priests 7; Brothers 8. *Mercy Siena Gardens*, 6105 N. Main St., 45415-3110. Revs. James R. McKay, S.M.; Robert Backherns, S.M.; Bros. William Callahan, S.M.; Francis Deibel. Tel: 937-279-9803; Robert Johns, S.M.; Raymond Martin, S.M.; Paul Quinn. Tel: 937-274-9597; Donald Schaaf. Tel: 937-275-4257. Priests 2; Brothers 6. *Mercy Siena Woods, Nursing Care*, 6125 N. Main St., 45415-3110. Revs. Francis J. Kenney, S.M.; Thomas Stanley, S.M.; Bros. Charles Roggemann; Donald Winfree. Tel: 937-278-8211, Ext. 6405. Priests 2; Brothers 2. *Mercy Siena Support Community*, Old Dublin Ct., 45415-3194. Tel: 937-274-4626. Revs. Edward M. Jach, S.M.; Nicholas Rufo; Thomas A. Schroer, S.M., Dir.; Bro. Kenneth Thompson, S.M. Priests 3; Brothers 1. *Mercy Siena Village*, 6045 N. Main St., 45415. Tel: 937-238-4323. Bros. Francis Smith, S.M.; Bernard Zalewski, S.M. *Marianist Community*, 301 Kiefaber St., 45409. Tel: 937-627-8091. Rev. James Fitz, S.M.; Bros. Sean R. Downing, S.M.; Thomas Farnsworth, S.M.; Thomas J. Pieper, S.M., Dir.; Charles Wanda, S.M. Brothers 4; Priests 1. *Marianist Network for the Arts* Tel: 937-320-5450; Fax: 937-429-3195. Religious 3; Total Staff 3. *North American Center for Marianist Studies* Tel: 937-429-2521; Fax: 937-429-3195. Religious 2; Total Staff 14. *Marianist Mission*, 119 Franklin St., 45402-2599. Tel: 937-222-4641; 800-348-4732; Fax: 937-222-3038. Religious 5; Total Staff 60. *Marianist Environmental Education Center* Tel: 937-429-3582; Fax: 937-429-3195. Religious 2; Total Staff 6.

Provincial Office of the Cincinnati Province of the Society of the Precious Blood, 431 E. Second St., 45402-1764. Tel: 937-228-9263; Fax: 937-228-6878. Email: prodirsec@cpps-preciousblood.org. Web: www.cpps-preciousblood.org. Very Rev. Larry J. Hemmelgarn, C.PP.S., Prov. Dir.; Bro. Joseph J. Fisher, C.PP.S., Treas.; Revs. Vincent Wirtner, C.PP.S., Dir. Vocations; Jeffrey Kirch, C.PP.S., Prov. Sec.; Benjamin Berinti, C.PP.S., Retreat & Renewal; Benedict Magabe, C.PP.S. (Tanzania), Parish Assignment; Alfons Minja, C.PP.S., Parish Assignment; JayaBabu Nuthulapati, C.PP.S.; Andrew O'Reilly, C.PP.S., Retreat & Renewal; Clarence Williams, C.PP.S., Admin.; Bros. James Ballmann, C.PP.S.; Benjamin Basile, C.PP.S.; Terrence Nufer, C.PP.S.; Jerry Schwieterman, C.PP.S.; Antonio Sison, C.PP.S., Teaching.

Members of the Provincial Council: Very Rev. Larry J. Hemmelgarn, C.PP.S., Provincial; Revs. Benjamin Berinti, C.PP.S., Vice Prov.; Thomas Hemm, C.PP.S., 1st Councilor; Bro. Robert Reuter, C.PP.S., 2nd Councilor; Revs. Anthony Fortman, C.PP.S., 3rd Councilor; Ken Schnipke, C.PP.S., 4th Councilor; Jeffrey Kirch, C.PP.S., 5th Councilor.

Military: Rev. John S. Srode, C.PP.S., PSC 41 Box 3003, Apo, AE 09464-2801.

Priests of the Province Serving Abroad: Very Rev. Barry J. Fischer, C.PP.S., Retreat & Renewal, Viale di Porta Ardeatina, 66, Rome 1-00154 Italy. Tel: 011-39-06-574-1656; Fax: 011-39-06-574-2874.

Foreign Mission: Revs. William J. Beuth, C.PP.S., Parroguia Sangre de Cristo, Apartado Postal 2483, 01901 Guatemala City, Guatemala. Tel: 011-502-6640-2600; Fax: 011-502-6640-2686; Joseph F. Deardorff, C.PP.S., Nuestra Senora de la Luz, Apartado 2348, Lima, 100, Peru. Tel: 011-51-1-536-4592; Fax: 011-51-1-537-5107; Gerald G. Dreiling, C.PP.S., Apartado 07-0148, Lima 07, Peru. Tel: 011-51-1-539-5285; Fax: 011-51-1-546-0285; Edgar Jutte, C.PP.S., Iglesia Del Sagrado Corazon de Jesus, Calzada San Lorenzo 749, Col San Juan Xalpa, Iztapalapa 09850DF Mexico. Tel: 011-525-55-614-9022; John Falter, C.PP.S. (Retired), Parroguia Sangre de Cristo, Casilla 194, Purranque, Chile. Tel: 011-56-64-351-340; James E. Gaynor, C.PP.S., San Francisco de Borja, Apartado Aereo, 85182, Carrera, 20 N. 52-23, Bogata, D.C., Colombia. Tel: 011-57-1-345-8466; Fax: 011-57-1-346-6388; James Bender, C.PP.S. (Retired), Parroquia Cristo Rey, Apartado 36, La Oroya, Peru. Tel: 011-51-1-64-39-1675; Fax: 011-51-1-64-39-1675; Donald J. Thieman, C.PP.S., N.S. de la P. Sangre, Casilla 163 Correo 55, Santiago, Chile. Tel: 011-56-2-274-4584; Fax: 011-56-2-341-4279.

In Residences Not Listed Elsewhere: Revs. James E. Franck, C.PP.S., 5788 Thornton Ave., Newark, CA 94560. Tel: 510-797-0241; John Franck, C.PP.S, 2625 Vermont Ave., Los Angeles, CA 90007. Tel: 323-731-2464; Fax: 323-731-6186; Jeffrey R. Keyes, C.PP.S., 5788 Thornton Ave., Newark, CA 94560. Tel: 510-797-0241; Ernest Krantz, C.PP.S., 3950 Columbia Ave., Columbia, PA 17512. Tel: 219-922-2859; David A. Kelly, C.PP.S., 4835 S. Marshfeld Ave., 2nd Fl., Chicago, IL 60609. Tel: 773-927-1664; Dennis Kinderman, C.PP.S., 1936 W. 48th St. - Rear, P.O. Box 09379, Chicago, IL 60609. Tel: 773-579-0781; Fax: 773-579-0782; Fred Licciardi, C.PP.S., 120 N. Ela St., Barrington, IL 60010. Tel: 847-382-5300; Fax: 847-382-5363; Donald Davison, C.PP.S., 2222 E. Third St., Bloomington, IN 47401-5305. Tel: 812-336-6846; Leon Flaherty, C.PP.S., 1410 Baxter Ave., Superior, WI 54880. Tel: 715-392-8511; Robert Hunt, C.PP.S., 14037 Fairway Island Dr., Apt. 226, Orlando, FL 32837-5250. Tel: 407-251-0909; Edward Joyce, C.PP.S. (Retired), 22866 Montalvo Rd., Laguna Niguel, CA 92677-2740. Tel: 714-493-2800; Jeffrey Kirch, C.PP.S., Chicago, IL; William Nordenbrock, C.PP.S., P.O. Box 09379, Chicago, IL 60609-0379. Tel: 773-579-0781; Fax: 773-579-0782; Mark Peres, C.PP.S., Chicago, IL; Joseph Rodak, C.PP.S., Our Lady of Good Counsel Church, 4423 Pearl St., Cleveland, 44109-4266. Tel: 216-749-2324; Fax: 216-741-7183; Robert Schreiter, C.PP.S.; Alphonse Spilly, C.PP.S., 652 Stewart Ct., Whiting, IN 46394-1464. Tel: 219-473-4351; Jerome P. Stack, C.PP.S., Whiting, IN; Jerome Steinbrunner, C.PP.S.; Michael Winkowski, C.PP.S., 8046 Shady Dr., Walkerton, IN 46574. Tel: 574-586-7408; Bros. Brian Boyle, C.PP.S., 5332 S. Woodlawn, Apt. 3, Chicago, IL 60615. Tel: 773-752-0672; Fax: 773-752-0676; Timothy Cahill, C.PP.S., 1114 Troy St., 45404-2719. Tel: 973-223-8306; Joseph J. Fisher, C.PP.S.; Nicholas Renner, C.PP.S; Matthew Schaefer, C.PP.S; Jerome Schulte, C.PP.S., 4880 Denlinger Rd., 45426-2012. Tel: 937-278-3265.

HUNTSVILLE. *St. George Chapel of Marianist Community* (1953) 9636 Lakeshore Dr., E., 43324-9520. Tel: 937-842-4902. Email: pbredus@yahoo.com. Bros. Paul F. Bredestege, S.M., Dir. & Contact Person; William A. Deanhofer, S.M.; Rev. James A. Russell, S.M. Priests 1; Brothers 2.

[O] CONVENTS AND RESIDENCES FOR SISTERS

CINCINNATI. *St. Clare Convent, Franciscan Sisters of the Poor* U.S. Area Office Franciscan Sisters of the Poor, 60 Compton Rd., 45215. Tel: 513-761-9040; Fax: 513-761-6703. Email: sfpusarea@fuse.net. Web: www.franciscansisters.org. Sisters Joanne Schuster, S.F.P., Congregation Councilor & Contact Person; Karen Hartman, S.F.P., Community Min. Sisters 20.

Dominican Sisters of Hope, 4027 Fawnhill Ln., 45205. Tel: 513-621-5899. Email: gaia916@juno.com. Dominican Sisters of Hope 3.

Franciscan Monastery of St. Clare (Poor Clares) (1990) 1505 Miles Rd., 45231-2427. Tel: 513-825-7177; Fax: 513-825-4071. Email: contactsisters@fuse.net. Web: www.poorclarescincinnati.org. Sr. Ann Bartko, O.S.C., Abbess. Sisters 10.

McAuley Convent (1964) 1768 Cedar Ave., 45224-2802. Tel: 513-681-2100; Fax: 513-354-5051. Sisters of Mercy 35.

Provincial House, Health Center of Sisters of Notre Dame de Namur, 699 E. Columbia Ave., 45215-3945. Tel: 513-821-7448; Fax: 513-821-7476. Web: www.sndohio.org. Sisters Carol Lichtenberg, S.N.D.deN., Prov.; Elizabeth Marie Bowyer, S.N.D.deN., Local Mod.; Donna Wisowaty, S.N.D.deN., Admin. Sisters 80.

Sisters of Charity of Cincinnati, Ohio (1952) 5900 Delhi Rd., 45051. Tel: 513-347-5201; Fax: 513-347-5228. Email: j.cook@srcharitycinti.org. Web: www.srcharitycinti.org. Sr. Joan Elizabeth Cook, S.C., Pres. Sisters in Congregation 390; Sisters in Archdiocese 297.

Ursulines of Cincinnati (1910) 1339 E. McMillan St., 45206-2164. Tel: 513-961-3410, Ext. 140; Fax: 513-872-7177. Email: ursofcinti@juno.com. Ursuline Sisters., Sisters of this community sponsor one high school, one elementary school, counseling, social service, communications, adult education and parish work. Sisters 13.

DAYTON. *Sisters of the Precious Blood Generalate* (1834) 4000 Denlinger Rd., 45426. Tel: 937-837-3302; Fax: 937-837-8825. Email: sisters@preciousbloodsistersdayton.org. Web: www.preciousbloodsistersdayton.org. Sisters Joyce Lehman, C.PP.S., Pres.; Nancy Kinross, C.PP.S., Vice Pres. & Councilor & Sec.; Linda Pleiman, C.PP.S., Councilor; Cecilia Taphorn, C.PP.S., Councilor & Treas.; Mary Yarger, C.PP.S., Councilor; Noreen Jutte, C.PP.S., Archivist.

Sisters of the Precious Blood, Salem Heights Convent, 4960 Salem Ave., 45416-1797. Tel: 937-278-0871; Fax: 937-278-8722. Email: shadmin@preciousbloodsistersdayton.org. Web: www.preciousbloodsistersdayton.org. Sisters Judy Kroeger, C.PP.S, Admin.; Nadine Kaschalk, C.PP.S., Coord. Sr. Svcs. Sisters 50.

SAINT MARTIN. *Ursulines of Brown County* (1845) 20860 State Rte. 251, St. Martin, 45118. Tel: 513-875-2020; Fax: 513-875-2311. Web: www.ursulinesofbc.org. Sr. Lucia Castellini, O.S.U., Congregational Min. Ursuline Order, Congregation of Paris. Sisters 27.

[P] RESIDENCES FOR ADULTS AND YOUTHS

CINCINNATI. *Friars Club*, 1615 Vine St., 45202. Tel: 513-381-5432; Fax: 513-381-7909. Email: atimmons@friarsclubinc.org. Web: www.friarsclubinc.org. Michael L. Besl, Board Chair; Annie Timmons, Exec. Dir. Total Staff 3; Total Assisted Annually 600.

[Q] RETREAT HOUSES, CONFERENCE AND RENEWAL CENTERS

CINCINNATI. **Our Lady of the Holy Spirit Center*, 5440 Moeller Ave., 45212. Tel: 513-351-9800; Fax: 513-351-9885. Web: www.olhsc.org. Mr. Tom Leibel, Dir.

DAYTON. *Bergamo Center for Lifelong Learning* (1967) 4400 Shakertown Rd., 45430-1075. Tel: 937-426-2363; Fax: 937-426-1090. Email: info@bergamocenter.org. Web: www.bergamocenter.org. Mr. Dick Flack, Exec. Dir.; Kevin Kozlowski, Dir. Youth Programs; Barbara Kozlowski, Prog. Dir.; Patricia O'Grady, Dir. Conference Svcs. & Guest Rels.

MILFORD. *Jesuit Spiritual Center at Milford*, 5361 S. Milford Rd., 45150-9746. Tel: 513-248-3500; Fax: 513-248-3503. Email: rreder@jesuitspiritualcenter.com. Web: www.jesuitspiritualcenter.com. Revs. George W. Traub, S.J.; Thomas A. Ryan, S.J.; Richard P. Reder, Exec. Dir. & Contact Person; Jennifer Verkamp, Chm. Bd.

[R] CAMPUS MINISTRY AND NEWMAN CENTERS

CINCINNATI. *College of Mount St. Joseph Mission and Ministry* (1920) 5701 Delhi Rd., 45233-1670. Tel: 513-244-4844; Fax: 513-244-4594. Email: andrea_stiles@mail.msj.edu. Web: www.msj.edu. Andrea Stiles, Dir. Mission & Min.; Kate Romolo, Coord. Campus Min.

University of Cincinnati Newman Center 328 W. McMillan St., 45219-1224. Tel: 513-381-6400; Fax: 513-381-2540. Email: smsgnewman@gmail.com. Web: www.smsgonline.com. Rev. Alan Hirt, O.F.M.; Sr. Leslie Keener, C.D.P., Campus Min.; Mrs. Jill Kreinbrink, Music Min.; Ms. Linda Martin, Business Mgr.; Ms. Ann Boltz, Pastoral Assoc.; Michael Schreiner, Campus Min.

Xavier University Dorothy Day Center for Faith & Justice 3800 Victory Pkwy., 45207-2141. Tel: 513-745-3567; Fax: 513-745-1959. Email: minning@xavier.edu. Web: www.xavier.edu/cfj. Mr. David Johnson, Exec. Dir.; Mr. Scot Buzza, Coord. Liturgical Music & Univ. Events; Ms. Katie Minning, Sec.; Mr. Tim Dunn, Asst. Dir., Faith & Min.; Rev. Albert J. Bischoff, S.J., Campus Min.; Ms. Deanna Martin, Assoc. Dir.; Angela Gray, Assoc. Dir., Svc. & Justice; Molly Robertshaw, Asst. Dir., Svc. & Justice; Greg Carpinello, Asst. Dir. Liturgy & Min.; Ms. Andrea Bardelmeier, Asst. Dir., Ecumenical & Multi-Faith; Mr. Jim Riordan, S.J., Asst. Dir., Faith & Justice; Dominique Brown, Coord., Svc. & Justice.

DAYTON. *Sinclair Community College Campus Ministry* 444 W. Third St., 45402. Tel: 937-512-2768. Email: jane.steinhauser@sinclair.edu. Web: www.sinclaircampusministry.org. Dr. V. Jane Steinhauser, Archdiocesan Dir. of Campus Ministry.

University of Dayton Campus Ministry 300 College Park, 45469-0408. Tel: 937-229-3339; Fax: 937-229-2035. Email: campus-ministry@udayton.edu.

Web: www.ministry.udayton.edu. Rev. Crystal Sullivan, Dir. Tel: 937-229-3339; Rev. Gerald T. Chinchar, S.M., D.Min., Campus Min. Catechetical Prog. & Priest On Call. Tel: 937-229-2725; Jennifer Morin-Williamson, Residence Hall Campus Min. Marycrest; Sr. Kathleen Rossman, O.S.F., Campus Min. Sophomore/VWK. Tel: 937-229-4587; Bro. Thomas Pieper, S.M., Campus Min. Stuart Hall/Marianist Hall. Tel: 937-229-2211; Nick Cardilino, Assoc. Dir. Campus Ministry, Dir. Center of Social Concern & Coord. Community Outreach & Svc. Clubs. Tel: 937-229-2576; Sue Terbay, Sec. Center of Social Concern. Tel: 937-229-2524; Bridget Ebbert, Campus Min., Sophomore/South Quad/Founders. Tel: 937-229-1754; Terri Lauer, Admin. Sec. to Campus Min. Tel: 937-229-3339; Mary Niebler, Assoc. Dir. of C.S.C. & Coord. of Cross Cultural Immersions. Tel: 937-229-2012; Kelly Bohrer, Coord. for Community Outreach & Svc. Clubs; Mr. James Pera, Campus Min. Liturgical Music. Tel: 937-229-2019; Kelly Adamson, Assoc. Dir. Campus Min., Dir. Res. Life Min. & Admin. Tel: 937-229-2574; Sr. Linda Lee Jackson, O.P., Neighborhood Faith Communities Coord. Tel: 937-229-3570; Rev. David McGuigan, S.M., Univ. Chap., Campus Min. for Law School; Kathy Sales, Sacristan Immaculate Conception Chapel; Rev. LaKendra Hardware, Campus Min. Interdenominational Min. & Marianist Hall; Allison Leigh, Asst. Dir. Retreats & Faith Communities. Tel: 937-229-2010; Teri Dickison, Asst. to Dir. Campus Min.

FAIRBORN. *Catholic Campus Ministry* (1968) 3650 Colonel Glenn Hwy., 45324-2096. Tel: 937-426-1836; Fax: 937-426-3490. Email: edward.burns@wright.edu. Web: www.raidercatholics.com. Rev. Edward M. Burns, Dir. Catholic Campus Ministry; Jenna Connor, Campus Min.; Ms. Joan Marquis, Campus Min.; Allyson Michal, Music Min.

OXFORD. *Miami University Catholic Campus Ministry* 111 E. High St., 45056. Tel: 513-523-2153; Fax: 513-523-0559. Email: info@stmaryoxfordohio.org. Web: www.stmaryoxfordohio.org. Rev. Jeffrey P. Silver; Roberta L. Kinne, Pastoral Assoc.; Michael Puglielli, D.R.E.; Kimberly Wagner, Campus Min.; Ryan Leep, Music Dir.; Pam Burk, Business Mgr.

WILMINGTON. *Wilmington College Campus Ministry* 73 N. Mulberry St., 45177. Tel: 937-382-2236; Fax: 937-382-3234. Email: saintcolumbkille@yahoo.com. Web: www.stcolumbkille.org. Rev. James M. Wedig. Pastoral care available through St. Columbkille Parish.

[S] COMMUNITY CENTERS

CINCINNATI. *Healthy Moms & Babes, Inc.* (1985) 2270 Banning Rd., Ste. 200, 45239. Tel: 513-591-5600; Fax: 513-591-5604. Email: office@healthymomsandbabes.org. Web: www.healthymomsandbabes.org. Kathleen Brogle, M.S.W., Pres. & CEO. Annual Participants 3,500; Staff 15.

Mercy Franciscan Social Ministries, Inc. dba Mercy Franciscan at St. John 1800 Logan St., 45202. Tel: 513-981-5800; Fax: 513-981-5899. Web: www.e-mercy.com. Mailing Address: 4600 McAuley Pl., 6th Fl., 45242. Ericka Copeland, Exec. Dir. Provides emergency assistance, temporary shelter for families, job training classes, shared housing for seniors, a senior center and program for male responsibility. Total Staff 21; Total Assisted 25,789.

HAMILTON. *Mercy Franciscan at St. Raphael, Inc.*, Mailing Address: 4600 McAuley Pl., 45242. 610 High St., 45011. Tel: 513-603-8222; Fax: 513-893-1814. Web: www.e-mercy.com. Don Rohling, Senior Vice Pres. Mission Integration; Terry Lee Perdue, Interim Exec. Dir. Total Assisted 25,474; Total Staff 7.

[T] FOUNDATIONS AND ENDOWMENTS

CINCINNATI. *Community Support Charitable Trust* (1987) 1615 Vine St., 45202. Tel: 513-721-4700; Fax: 513-287-8488. David P. O'Brien, Admin.; Revs. Kenan Freson, O.F.M., Trustee; Jeremy Harrington, O.F.M., Trustee; Bro. Vincent Delorenzo, O.F.M., Trustee.

Community Support Charitable Trust for the Province of St. John the Baptist of the Order of Friars Minor

Friars Club Foundation, Inc., 1615 Vine St., 45202. Tel: 513-721-4700; Fax: 513-287-8488. Mr. Thomas Klinedinst Jr., Trustee & Pres.; Mr. David O'Brien, Trustee & Treas.; Mr. John O'Connor, Vice Pres., Sec. & Trustee.

Good Samaritan Hospital Foundation of Cincinnati, Inc., 375 Dixmyth Ave., 45220-2489. Tel: 513-862-3786; Fax: 513-862-1355. Email: mary_rafferty@trihealth.com. Web: www.gshfoundation.com. Mary L. Rafferty, Contact Person.

Mercy Health Partners of Southwest Ohio Foundation dba Mercy Health Foundation 4600 Mc Auley Pl., 6th Fl., 45242. Tel: 513-981-6329; Fax: 513-981-6104. Web: www.e-mercy.com. Todd E. Lindley, Pres. A Subsidiary of Mercy Health Partners of Southwest Ohio. Total Staff 10.

Roger Bacon High School Endowment, 4320 Vine St., 45217. Tel: 513-641-1300; Fax: 513-641-0498. Email: wfarris@rogerbacon.org. Web: www.rogerbacon.org. Rev. William Farris, O.F.M., Pres. & Contact Person; Steve Schad, Prin.

SC Ministry Foundation, Inc. (1986) 345 Neeb Rd., 45233. Tel: 513-347-1122; Fax: 513-347-1017. Email: dsmiley@scministryfdn.org. Web: www.scministryfdn.org. Sr. Sally Duffy, S.C., Pres. & Exec. Dir.

Sisters of Charity of Cincinnati-Charitable Trust (1988) 5900 Delhi Rd., 45051. Tel: 513-347-5201; Fax: 513-347-5228. Email: j.cook@srcharitycinti.org. Web: www.srcharitycinti.org. Sr. Joan Elizabeth Cook, S.C., Pres. A designated trust fund to primarily support older and infirmed members of the congregation.

Sisters of Notre Dame De Namur, Ohio Province, Charitable Trust, 701 E. Columbia Ave., 45215-3999. Tel: 513-761-7636; Fax: 513-761-6159. Email: ohprovoff@ohsnd.org. Web: www.sndohio.org. Sr. Carol Lichtenberg, S.N.D.deN., Prov.; Virginia Chasteen, Contact Person.

The Summit Country Day School Foundation (1994) 2161 Grandin Rd., 45208. Tel: 513-871-4700; Fax: 513-871-6558. Email: paulin_d@summitcds.org. George Thurner, Pres.; Tom Theobald, Chm.; David Paulin, Sec. & Treas.

Ursulines of Cincinnati, Ohio Charitable Trust, 1339 E. McMillan St., 45206-2164. Tel: 513-961-3410, Ext. 139; Fax: 513-872-7177. Email: ursofcinti@juno.com. Sr. Mary Jerome Buchert, O.S.U.

DAYTON. *Community Support Charitable Trust* (1994) 431 E. Second St., 45402. Tel: 937-228-9263; Fax: 937-228-6878. Revs. Kenneth F. Pleiman, C.PP.S., Trustee; Thomas Brenberger, C.PP.S., Chm. & Trustee; Scott T. Kramer, C.PP.S., Trustee; Bros. Joseph J. Fisher, C.PP.S., Admin. & Trustee; Thomas R. Bohman, C.PP.S., Trustee; Mr. John York, Trustee; Ms. Cynthia Hill, Trustee.

**Good Samaritan Hospital Foundation-Dayton* (1973) 2222 Philadelphia Dr., 45406. Tel: 937-734-4483; Fax: 937-734-4154. Email: msmartens@gshdayton.org. Web: www.gshfoundationdayton.org. Marc S. Martens, Pres. & Exec. Officer. Affiliate of Catholic Health Initiatives and Samaritan Health Partners.

FAIRFIELD. *Glenmary Home Missioners Charitable Trust*, 4119 Glenmary Trace, 45014. Tel: 513-874-8900; Fax: 513-874-1690. Rev. Dominic R. Duggins, G.H.M., Sec. & Trustee; Bros. Dennis Craig, G.H.M., Trustee (Retired); Jack Henn, G.H.M., Trustee; Teresa Heckenmueller, Trustee; John Monroe, Trustee.

[U] MISCELLANEOUS LISTINGS

CINCINNATI. *St. Andrew Kim Korean Catholic Community* (1980) 3171 Struble Rd., 45251. Tel: 513-322-3183. Email: zmsqkdn@gmail.com. Web: www.cincinnatikoreancatholic.org. Rev. Huengwoo Lee, Chap. & Admin.

St. Anthony Messenger (1893) 28 W. Liberty St., 45202. Tel: 513-241-5615; Fax: 513-241-0399. Email: st.anthony@americancatholic.org. Web: www.americancatholic.org. Thomas A. Shumate, Contact Person; Rev. Daniel Kroger, O.F.M. Operated by the St. John the Baptist Province of the Franciscan Friars.

St. Anthony Messenger Press and Franciscan Communications, 28 W. Liberty St., 45202. Tel: 513-241-5615; Fax: 513-241-0399. Email: stanthony@americancatholic.org. Web: www.americancatholic.org. Thomas A. Shumate, Contact Person; Rev. Daniel Kroger, O.F.M.

Catholic Alumni Club (Cincinnati Chapter), 5618 Karen Ave., 45248.

Catholic Cursillo of Cincinnati (1962) P.O. Box 317655, 45231. Tel: 513-931-7382. Email: kkluener@fuse.net. Web: www.cincinnati-cursillo.org. Ken Kluener, Lay Dir.; Deacon William Krumm, Spiritual Advisor.

Catholic Healthcare Partners Housing Development, 615 Elsinore Pl., 45202. Tel: 513-639-2800; Fax: 513-639-2810. Web: www.health-partners.org. Scott Schitter, Dir.

**The Catholic Social Workers National Association Foundation*, P.O. Box 498531, 45249. Tel: 317-416-8285. Web: www.cswna.org. Kathleen Neher, Pres. & Contact Person.

Cincinnati Catholic Women's Association (1917) 958 Marion Ave., 45229. Tel: 513-961-3566. Web: cincinnaticatholicwomen.org. Carol Helmick, Pres.

Claver Jesuit Ministry, 3838 Llewellyn Ave., 45223-2352. Tel: 513-681-8500; Fax: 513-681-4503. Email: clavermin@fuse.net. Web: home.fuse.net/clavermin. Rev. Joseph D. Folzenlogen, S.J., Dir.

The Comboni Lay Missionaries Association, 1318 Nagel Rd., 45255-3120. Tel: 513-474-4997; Fax: 513-474-0382. Email: info@laymission-comboni.org. Web: www.combonimissionaries.org; www.laymission-comboni.org. Mr. Thomas Drexler, Pres.; Mr. Chuck Carey, Vice Pres.; Mr. Paul Wheeler, Dir.; Ms. JoAnne Harbert, Assoc. Dir.; Ms. Opal Easter-Smith, Treas.; Mrs. Gisela Grundges-Andraos, Sec.

The Comboni Missionaries Auxiliary, Inc., 1318 Nagel Rd., 45255-3120. Tel: 513-474-4997; Fax: 513-474-0382. Email: info@combonimissionaries.org. Web: www.combonimissionaries.org. Sandi Smith, Pres.; Jane Mentzel, Vice Pres.; Marie Rose Obert, Sec.; Velma Bishak, Treas.; Rev. Brian Quigley, M.C.C.J., Spiritual Advisor.

**The Couple to Couple League International* (1971) P.O. Box 111184, 45211. 4290 Delhi Pk., 45238. Tel: 513-471-2000; Fax: 513-557-2449. Email: ccli@ccli.org. Web: www.ccli.org. Michael D. Manhart, Ph.D., Exec. Dir.; Don Regan, Business Mgr.

De Paul Cristo Rey Work Study Program Corporation, 1133 Clifton Hills Ave., 45220. Tel: 513-347-5201; Fax: 513-347-5228. Web: www.depaulcristorey.org. Sr. Jeanne Bessette, O.S.F., Pres.; Lisa Claytor, Dir.

St. Dymphna Ministry, c/o Summit Behavioral Healthcare, 1101 Summit Rd., 45237. Tel: 513-948-3727. Res.: 476 Riddle Rd., 45220. Tel: 513-961-4422. Rev. Valens J. Waldschmidt, O.F.M. (Retired).

**Embrace the Children*, 2086 Buttersbridge Ct., 45230. Tel: 513-614-8501.

St. Francis Seraph Ministries, 1615 Vine St., 45202. Tel: 513-533-2719; Fax: 513-721-1152; 513-421-9672. Web: www.sfsministry.org. Mr. Cliff Cavanaugh, Contact Person.

Franciscan Central Purchasing (1965) St. Clement Friary, 4536 Vine St., 45217. Tel: 513-641-2257; Fax: 513-641-2262. Rev. Maynard Tetreault, O.F.M., Dir.

Franciscan Missionary Union, 1615 Vine St., 45202. Tel: 513-721-4700, Ext. 3222; Fax: 513-421-9672. Email: missionoffice@franciscan.org. Web: www.franciscan.org. Bro. Vincent Delorenzo, O.F.M., Exec. Dir.; Marilyn Wilson, Sec. & Contact Person.

Franciscans Network, 4820 Glenway Ave., 45238. Tel: 513-238-3226. Email: franciscansnetwork@cinci.rr.com. Web: www.franciscansnetwork.org. Diane H. Laake, Contact Person; Revs. John Quigley, O.F.M., Bd. of Trustees; Murray L. Bodo, O.F.M., Bd. of Trustees; Alan Hartman, S.F.O., Bd. of Trustees.

Good Samaritan College of Nursing and Health Science, 375 Dixmyth Ave., 45220. Tel: 513-862-2631; Fax: 513-862-3572. Email: morey.cohen@email.gscollege.edu. Web: www.trihealth.com; www.gscollege.edu. Morris Cohen, Pres.; Donna S. Nienaber, Sec.

Hispanic Ministry at St. Charles Borromeo, Archdiocese of Cincinnati, 115 W. Seymour Ave., 45216. Tel: 513-948-1760; Fax: 513-948-1823. Email: hispanicministry@catholiccincinnati.org. Web: www.archdiocese-cinti.org. Rev. Jorge Ochoa, M.C.C.J., Chap. & Mod.

Jesuit Advancement Office, 607 Sycamore St., 45202. Tel: 513-751-6688; Fax: 513-723-0451. Email: mmaxwell@jesuits-chgdet.org. Web: www.jesuits-chgdet.org. Mark E. Maxwell, Dir. of Major Gifts.

Living Monuments of Reparation, P.O. Box 29372, 45229. Tel: 248-620-2542; Fax: 248-625-3526. Rev. Herbert J. Raterman, S.J., Dir.

Marian Center of Cincinnati, 5365 Cleves Warsaw, 45238. Tel: 513-922-1250; Fax: 859-441-0641. Mr. Robert E. Hater, Lay Dir.; Lois A. Hater, Sec.

St. Mark's Chaplaincy for the Extraordinary Form, 530 Liberty Hall, No. 2, 45202. Tel: 513-393-9872. Web: www.restorestmarks.org. Ashley Paver, Pres.

**Mercy Neighborhood Ministries, Inc.*, 1602 Madison Rd., 45206. Tel: 513-751-2500; Fax: 513-221-5498. Web: www.mercyneighborhoodministries.org. Suzanne M. Kathman, Exec. Dir.

Ministers of Service, 745 Ezzard Charles, 45203. Tel: 513-381-0630; Fax: 513-742-9096. Email: church3824@cs.com. Mr. Jack D. McWilliams, Dir. The Ministers of Service Program, which began in 1979, provides training in urban ministry, primarily but not exclusively for African American laypersons. The Ministers of Service Program focuses on parish/community ministry to prepare laypersons to take active roles in church ministry.

**Natural Family Planning International Inc.*, Mailing Address: P.O. Box 11216, 45211. 2911 Werk Rd., 45211-7018. Tel: 513-661-7396; Fax: 513-661-7396. Web: www.nfpandmore.org. Mr. John F. Kippley, Pres.; Sheila Kippley, Sec. & Treas.

New Jerusalem Community, 745 Derby Ave., 45232.

Tel: 513-541-4748; Fax: 513-541-4748. Email: njcommunity@juno.com. Mary Heimert, Leadership Council; Debby Carrico, Leadership Council; Barb Gutting, Admin. & Coord. Community Life.

**Pregnancy Center West, Inc.*, 4900 Glenway Ave., 45238. Tel: 513-244-5700; Fax: 513-244-2886. Web: www.pc-west.org. Mrs. Rachel Renner, Exec. Dir.

**Presentation Ministries, Inc.*, 3230 McHenry Ave., 45211. Tel: 513-662-5378. Email: pubsandtapes@presentationministries.com. Web: www.presentationministries.com. Deacon George Schmidl, Pres. & Contact Person.

**St. Rita Comprehensive Communication Resources*, 1720 Glendale Milford Rd., 45215. Tel: 513-771-7600. Web: www.apraxiaeducation.org. Mr. Ronald Stoerker, Pres.

**Ruah Woods*, 6675 Wesselman Rd., 45248. Tel: 513-407-8672; Fax: 513-417-8955. Web: www.ruahwoods.org. Leslie Kuhlman, Exec. Dir.

Secular Franciscan Order, 4012 Ryland, Springfield, 45503. Tel: 937-399-7531; Fax: 937-493-0269. Email: sfo-pax@mindspring.com. Steve White, S.F.O. Regl. Min., (Cincinnati, OH); Rose Mary Menetrey, S.F.O. Regl. Councilor. Holy Trinity Regional Fraternity, Inc.; Founded by St. Francis of Assisi before A.D. 1215.

Seton Family Center, 712 Purcell Ave., 45205. Tel: 513-471-9169; Fax: 513-471-9159. Email: info@setonfamilycenter.org. Web: www.setonfamilycenter.org. Dr. Helmut R. Roehrig, Pres. Exec. Dir.; Pam Shannon, Bd. Chair; Sisters Mary Jo Gasdorf, S.C., Vice Chair; Jacqueline Kowalski, S.C., Foundress. Sponsored by: Sisters of Charity of Mt. St. Joseph., Purpose: Individual and Family Therapy, Children's Play Therapy and Diagnostic Services.

The Company of St. Ursula - USA, 2718 Hackberry St., Flr. 1, 45206. Tel: 513-961-0667; Fax: 513-961-0667. Web: www.companyofstursula.org. Ms. Mary-Cabrini Durkin, Pres.

**The Dynamic Catholic Institute, Inc.*, 2330 Kemper Ln., 45206. Tel: 513-221-7700; Fax: 513-221-7710. Web: www.dynamiccatholic.com. Mr. G. Shane Giblin, Dir. Devel.

Ursuline Education Services, 2330 Victory Pkwy., Ste. 800, 45206. Tel: 513-221-5300. Email: jwimberg@ursuline-education.com. Web: www.ursuline-education.com. Ms. Judith Wimberg, Exec. Dir.; Sr. Patricia Homan, O.S.U., Representative. U.E.S. is a service to all Ursuline Schools.

Vietnamese Catholic Community of Our Lady of Lavang, 314 Township Ave., 45216. Tel: 513-242-2933. Rev. Chau Pham, Temporary Chap. & Mod.

St. Xavier Church Property Corporation, 607 Sycamore St., 45202. Tel: 513-721-4045; Fax: 513-723-0451. Rev. Eric J. Knapp, S.J., Contact Person & Trustee; Very Rev. Timothy P. Kesicki, S.J., Pres.

CARTHAGENA. *The Society of the Precious Blood Senior Housing Corporation*, 2860 U.S. Rte. 127, 45822. Tel: 419-925-4516; Fax: 419-925-4800. Email: frjseibert@email.com. Rev. James C. Seibert, C.PP.S., Pres. & Contact Person.

CENTERVILLE. *St. Leonard Faith Community*, 8100 Clyo Rd., 45458. Tel: 937-435-3626; Fax: 937-435-3626. Email: faithcomm4@sbcglobal.net. Web: www.stleonardfaithcommunity.com. Rev. Loren Connell, O.F.M., Moderator/Chap.

St. Leonard Foundation, 8100 Clyo Rd., 45458. Tel: 937-436-6382; Fax: 937-432-6504. Web: www.stleonard.net. Jill Harris, Pres. & Contact Person.

DAYTON. *Catholic Alumni Club (Dayton Chapter)*, P.O. Box 3612, 45401-3612. Tel: 937-252-7035. Email: jwildenj516@yahoo.com. Jennifer Gladski, Contact Person; Rev. Daniel J. Meyer, Chap., 218 K St., 45409.

Catholic Vietnamese Community of Dayton, 217 W. Fourth St., 45402. Tel: 937-224-3904. Email: sacredheartdayton@yahoo.com. Rev. Hung M. Tran, Chap. & Admin.

Samaritan Behavioral Health, Inc. (2002) 601 Edwin C. Moses Blvd. 4th Fl., 45417. Tel: 937-734-8333; Fax: 937-734-8336. Email: smcgatha@gshdayton.org. Web: www.sbhihelp.org. Sue McGatha, Pres. & CEO. Samaritan Behavioral Health, Inc. is a community-based provider of mental health and drug and alcohol services.

FAIRBORN. *National Diaconate Institute for Continuing Education, Inc.*, 330 Chatham Dr., 45324. Tel: 937-879-5332. Web: www.ndice.org. Max J. Roadruck Jr., Past Pres.

MARIA STEIN. *Maria Stein Shrine of the Holy Relics* (1846) 2291 St. Johns Rd., 45860. Tel: 419-925-4532; Fax: 513-925-5044. Email: director@mariasteinshrine.org. Web: www.mariasteinshrine.org. Sr. Barbara Ann Hoying, C.PP.S., Mission Effectiveness/Pastoral Activities Min.; Donald C. Rosenbeck, Admin. Includes The National Marian Shrine of the Holy Relics, The Heritage Museum, and The Pilgrim Gift Shop.

MOUNT SAINT JOSEPH. *Archivists for Congregations of Women Religious, ACWR National Office*, 5900 Delhi Rd., Mount St. Joseph, 45051. Tel: 513-347-4080. Email: acwr@juno.com. Web: www.archivistsacwr.org. Purpose: Professional Preservation of the archives of Roman Catholic women religious congregations and collaboration with historians in making known the lives and works of women religious.

RELIGIOUS INSTITUTES OF MEN REPRESENTED IN THE ARCHDIOCESE

For further details refer to the corresponding bracketed number in the Religious Institutes of Men or Women section.

[0460]—*Brothers of the Poor of St. Francis*—C.F.P.
[0380]—*Comboni Missionaries of the Heart of Jesus (Verona)*—M.C.C.J.
[0650]—*Congregation of the Holy Spirit* (Eastern Province)—C.S.Sp.
[0520]—*Franciscan Friars* (Province of St. John the Baptist, Cincinnati and Province of the Assumption, Franklin, WI)—O.F.M.
[0570]—*Glenmary Home Missioners*—G.H.M.
[0690]—*Jesuit Fathers and Brothers* (Chicago Province)—S.J.
[0800]—*Maryknoll*—M.M.
[1210]—*Missionaries of St. Charles (Scalabrinians)*—C.S.
[0430]—*Order of Preachers (Dominicans)* (St. Joseph Province)—O.P.
[0760]—*Society of Mary (Marianists)* (United States Province)—S.M.
[1060]—*Society of the Precious Blood* (Cincinnati Province)—C.PP.S

RELIGIOUS INSTITUTES OF WOMEN REPRESENTED IN THE ARCHDIOCESE

[0230]—*Benedictine Sisters of Pontifical Jurisdiction* (Beech Grove, IN; Villa Hills, KY)—O.S.B.
[0330]—*Carmelite Sisters for the Aged and Infirm*—O.Carm.
[1000]—*Congregation of Divine Providence of Kentucky*—C.D.P.
[0870]—*Congregation of the Daughters of Mary Immaculate (Marianist Sisters)*—F.M.I.
[3832]—*Congregation of the Sisters of St. Joseph*—C.S.J.
[1920]—*Congregation of the Sisters of the Holy Cross*—C.S.C.
[1730]—*Congregation of the Sisters of the Third Order of St. Francis, Oldenburg, IN*—O.S.F.
[1710]—*Congregation of the Third Order of St. Francis of Mary Immaculate, Joliet, IL*—O.S.F.
[1070-07]—*Dominican Sisters* (Adrian, MI)—O.P.
[1070-16]—*Dominican Sisters* (Nashville, TN)—O.P.
[1070-17]—*Dominican Sisters* (Elkins Park, PA)—O.P.
[1070-15]—*Dominican Sisters of Hope*—O.P.
[1070-13]—*Dominican Sisters of Peace* (Columbus, OH)—O.P.
[1415]—*Franciscan Sisters of Mary* (Bridgetown, MO)—F.S.M.
[1430]—*Franciscan Sisters of Our Lady Perpetual Help* (St. Louis, MO)—O.S.F.
[1440]—*Franciscan Sisters of the Poor*—S.F.P.
[2340]—*Little Sisters of the Poor*—L.S.P.
[2470]—*Maryknoll Sisters of St. Dominic*—M.M.
[2720]—*Mission Helpers of the Sacred Heart*—M.H.S.H.
[3760]—*Order of St. Clare-Poor Clares*—O.S.C.
[3230]—*Poor Handmaids of Jesus Christ*—P.H.J.C.
[0440]—*Sisters of Charity of Cincinnati, Ohio*—S.C.
[0500]—*Sisters of Charity of Nazareth* (KY)—S.C.N.
[0570]—*Sisters of Charity of Seton Hill, Greensburg, Pennsylvania*—S.C.
[1710]—*Sisters of St. Francis of Mary Immaculate* (Joliet, IL)—O.S.F.
[2575]—*Sisters of Mercy of the Americas* (South Central Community, Belmont, NC)—R.S.M.
[2630]—*Sisters of Mercy of the Holy Cross*—S.C.S.C.
[2990]—*Sisters of Notre Dame* (Covington Prov.)—S.N.D.
[3000]—*Sisters of Notre Dame de Namur*—S.N.D.deN.
[3360]—*Sisters of Providence of Saint Mary-of-the-Woods, Indiana*—S.P.
[1530]—*Sisters of St Francis of the Congregation of Our Lady of Lourdes* (Sylvania, OH)—O.S.F.
[1630]—*Sisters of St. Francis of Penance and Christian Charity, Stella Niagara, NY*—O.S.F.
[3840]—*Sisters of St. Joseph of Carondolet* (Latham, NY)—C.S.J.
[2110]—*Sisters of the Humility of Mary*—H.M.
[3260]—*Sisters of the Precious Blood* (Dayton, OH)—C.PP.S.
[2560]—*Society of Mary Reparatrix*—S.M.R.
[4120]—*Ursuline Nuns of the Congregation of Paris* (Saint Martin)—O.S.U.
[4120-01]—*Ursuline Nuns of the Congregation of Paris* (Cincinnati, OH)—O.S.U.
[4120-03]—*Ursuline Nuns of the Congregation of Paris* (Louisville, KY)—O.S.U.

CEMETERIES

CINCINNATI. *Calvary*, 1721 Duck Creek Rd., 45207. Tel: 513-961-2179; Fax: 513-961-0062. Ronald Hibbard, Supt.

Gate of Heaven, 11000 Montgomery Rd., 45242. Tel: 513-489-0300; Fax: 513-489-1817. Ms. Debra K. Crane, Esq., Dir.; Paula Rooks, Business Mgr.

St. John, 3819 W. 8th St., 45205. Tel: 513-242-4191. 4423 Vine St., 45217. Tel: 513-242-4191; Fax: 513-482-4343. Stephen E. Bittner, Pres.

St. Joseph, 3819 W. 8th St., 45205. Tel: 513-557-2306, Ext. 19 (St. Joseph Office); 513-921-3050; Fax: 513-557-2310. Stephen E. Bittner, Pres.

St. Joseph New Cemetery Association, 4500 Foley Rd., 45238. Tel: 513-251-3110; Fax: 513-251-1075. Rob Winter, Gen. Mgr.

St. Mary, 701 Ross Ave., 45217. Tel: 513-242-4191; Fax: 513-482-4343. 3819 W. 8th St., 45205. Stephen E. Bittner, Pres.

DAYTON. *The Calvary Cemetery Association*, 1625 Calvary Dr., 45409. Tel: 937-293-1221; Fax: 937-293-7316. Janet Baughman, Office Mgr.

SPRINGFIELD. *Calvary*, 3155 E. Possum Rd., 45502. Tel: 937-323-7474. James P. Matthews, Supt.

NECROLOGY

† Beatty, Michael D., Cincinnati, OH St. Simon the Apostle—Died Dec. 14, 2011
† Boeke, Anselm F., (Retired)—Died Jan. 7, 2011
† Byrne, James O., (Retired)—Died July 6, 2011
† Evers, Gerard A., (Retired)—Died Aug. 12, 2011
† Guntzelman, Louis J., (Retired)—Died June 20, 2011
† Hoying, Leo A., (Retired)—Died May 22, 2011
† Rehling, Paul L., (Retired)—Died Feb. 7, 2011

Diocese of Cleveland

(Dioecesis Clevelandensis)

Most Reverend

RICHARD GERARD LENNON

Bishop of Cleveland; ordained priest May 19, 1973; appointed Titular Bishop of Sufes and Auxiliary Bishop of Boston June 29, 2001; ordained September 14, 2001; appointed Bishop of Cleveland April 4, 2006; installed May 15, 2006. *Office: 1404 E. Ninth St., Cleveland, OH 44114.* Tel: 216-696-6525; 800-869-6525 (Ohio only); Fax: 216-696-6547.

Cathedral Square Plaza: 1404 E. Ninth St., Cleveland, OH 44114. Tel: 216-696-6525; 800-869-6525 (Ohio only); Fax: 216-621-7332.

Web: www.dioceseofcleveland.org

Email: info@dioceseofcleveland.org

Most Reverend

ANTHONY M. PILLA, D.D., M.A.

Retired Bishop of Cleveland; ordained May 23, 1959; appointed Auxiliary and Titular Bishop of Scardona June 30, 1979; consecrated August 1, 1979; named Apostolic Administrator of Cleveland July 29, 1980; appointed Bishop of Cleveland November 18, 1980; installed January 6, 1981; retired May15, 2006. *Office: 28700 Euclid Ave., Wickliffe, OH 44092.* Tel: 440-943-7600; Fax: 440-943-2428.

Most Reverend

A. EDWARD PEVEC, PH.D.

Retired Auxiliary Bishop of Cleveland; ordained April 29, 1950; appointed Auxiliary and Titular Bishop of Mercia April 13, 1982; consecrated July 2, 1982; retired September 1, 2002. *Office: Center for Pastoral Leadership, 28700 Euclid Ave., Wickliffe, OH 44092.* Tel: 216-944-1400; Fax: 440-943-7673.

Most Reverend

A. JAMES QUINN, J.C.D., J.D.

Retired Auxiliary Bishop of Cleveland; ordained May 24, 1958; appointed Auxiliary and Titular Bishop of Socia October 14, 1983; consecrated December 5, 1983; retired June 14, 2008. *Office: 2345 Bassett Rd., Westlake, OH 44145.* Tel: 440-250-9271; Fax: 440-835-5895.

Most Reverend

ROGER W. GRIES, O.S.B.

Auxiliary Bishop of Cleveland; ordained May 16, 1963; appointed Auxiliary and Titular Bishop of Presidio April 3, 2001; consecrated June 7, 2001. *Office: 1230 Ansel Rd., Cleveland, OH 44109.* Tel: 216-721-0676; Fax: 216-721-0903.

ESTABLISHED APRIL 23, 1847.

Square Miles 3,414.

Comprises, since July 22, 1943, eight counties in the north-central part of the State of Ohio, namely Ashland, Cuyahoga, Geauga, Lake, Lorain, Medina, Summit and Wayne Counties.

For legal titles of parishes and diocesan institutions, consult the Chancery Office.

STATISTICAL OVERVIEW

Personnel	
Bishop	1
Auxiliary Bishops	1
Retired Bishops	3
Abbots	1
Retired Abbots	1
Priests: Diocesan Active in Diocese	266
Priests: Diocesan Active Outside Diocese	6
Priests: Diocesan in Foreign Missions	3
Priests: Retired, Sick or Absent	117
Number of Diocesan Priests	392
Religious Priests in Diocese	90
Total Priests in Diocese	482
Extern Priests in Diocese	6
Ordinations:	
Diocesan Priests	5
Religious Priests	2
Transitional Deacons	3
Permanent Deacons in Diocese	220
Total Brothers	51
Total Sisters	1,025
Parishes	
Parishes	174
With Resident Pastor:	
Resident Diocesan Priests	154
Resident Religious Priests	10
Without Resident Pastor:	
Administered by Priests	3
Administered by Professed Religious Men	1
Administered by Religious Women	1
Administered by Pastoral Teams, etc.	5
Missions	1
Pastoral Centers	1
Professional Ministry Personnel:	
Brothers	7
Sisters	51
Lay Ministers	222
Welfare	
Catholic Hospitals	5
Total Assisted	650,000
Health Care Centers	1
Total Assisted	527
Homes for the Aged	24
Total Assisted	5,334
Residential Care of Children	1
Total Assisted	223
Day Care Centers	5
Total Assisted	392
Specialized Homes	4
Total Assisted	535
Special Centers for Social Services	17
Total Assisted	148,956
Residential Care of Disabled	1
Total Assisted	167
Other Institutions	2
Total Assisted	42,245
Educational	
Seminaries, Diocesan	2
Students from This Diocese	51
Students from Other Diocese	10
Students Religious	6
Total Seminarians	57
Colleges and Universities	3
Total Students	7,268
High Schools, Diocesan and Parish	6
Total Students	3,006
High Schools, Private	15
Total Students	9,978
Elementary Schools, Diocesan and Parish	94
Total Students	31,400
Elementary Schools, Private	10
Total Students	2,398
Non-residential Schools for the Disabled	1
Total Students	121
Catechesis/Religious Education:	
High School Students	3,662
Elementary Students	33,070
Total Students under Catholic Instruction	90,960
Teachers in the Diocese:	
Priests	2
Brothers	8
Sisters	45
Lay Teachers	2,856
Vital Statistics	
Receptions into the Church:	
Infant Baptism Totals	6,210
Minor Baptism Totals	372
Adult Baptism Totals	416
Received into Full Communion	875
First Communions	8,461
Confirmations	7,661
Marriages:	
Catholic	1,551
Interfaith	806
Total Marriages	2,357
Deaths	7,672
Total Catholic Population	706,465
Total Population	2,786,680

Former Bishops—Rt. Revs. AMADEUS RAPPE, D.D., ord. March 14, 1829; cons. Oct. 10, 1847; resigned July 29, 1870; died Sept 8, 1877; RICHARD GILMOUR, D.D., ord. Aug. 30, 1852; cons. April 14, 1872; died April 13, 1891; IGNATIUS F. HORSTMANN, D.D., ord. June 10, 1865; cons. Feb. 25, 1892; died May 13, 1908; JOHN P. FARRELLY, D.D., ord. May 22, 1880; cons. May 1, 1909; died Feb. 12, 1921; Most Revs. JOSEPH SCHREMBS, S.T.D., Archbishop-Bishop of Cleveland; cons. Feb. 22, 1911; transferred to the See of Cleveland, June 16, 1921; installed Sept. 8, 1921; appt. Archbishop, March 25, 1939; died November 2, 1945; EDWARD F. HOBAN, S.T.D., Ph.D., L.L.D., Archbishop-Bishop of Cleveland; cons. Dec. 21, 1921; transferred to Cleveland as Coadjutor Bishop "cum jure successionis" Nov. 14, 1942; succeeded to See of Cleveland, Nov. 2, 1945; appt. Archbishop, July 23, 1951; died Sept. 22, 1966; CLARENCE G. ISSENMANN, S.T.D., cons. May 25, 1954; transferred to Cleveland as Coadjutor Bishop "cum jure successionis" and Titular Bishop of Filaca. Ap-Adm. Oct. 7, 1964; succeeded to See of Cleveland, Sept. 22, 1966; retired June 5, 1974; died July 27, 1982; JAMES A. HICKEY, S.T.D., J.C.D., cons. April 14, 1967; appt. Bishop of Cleveland, June 5, 1974; installed July 16, 1974; appt. Archbishop of Washington, DC June 17, 1980; created Cardinal by Pope John Paul II in the consistory on June 28, 1988; retired Nov. 21, 2000; died Oct. 24, 2004; ANTHONY M. PILLA, ord. May 23, 1959; appt. Auxiliary and Titular Bishop of Scardona June 30, 1979; cons. Aug. 1, 1979; named Apostolic Administrator of Cleveland July 29, 1980; appt. Bishop of Cleveland Nov. 18, 1980; installed Jan. 6, 1981.

Vicars General—Most Revs. A. JAMES QUINN, J.C.D., J.D., V.G. (Retired), 2500 Elyria Ave., Lorain, 44055. Tel: 440-244-2120; 216-579-0326 (Cleveland Line); ROGER W. GRIES, O.S.B., D.D., M.Ed., St. Andrew, 1230 Ansel Rd., Cleveland, 44109. Tel: 216-721-0903; ANTHONY M. PILLA, D.D., M.A., (Bishop Emeritus) (Retired), Center for Pastoral Ministry, 28700 Euclid Ave., Wickliffe, 44092. Tel: 440-943-3928; A. EDWARD PEVEC, Ph.D. (Retired), Center for Pastoral Leadership,

28700 Euclid Ave., Wickliffe, 44092. Tel: 440-944-1400; Rev. RALPH E. WIATROWSKI, J.C.D., 9451 Brandywine Rd., Northfield, 44067-2484. Tel: 330-467-7959.

College of Consultors—Most Rev. ROGER W. GRIES, O.S.B., D.D., M.Ed.; Revs. WILLIAM G. BOUHALL; JOSEPH H. CALLAHAN; CHARLES T. DIEDRICK, M.A.; EDWARD T. ESTOK, M.A., M.Div.; WALTER J. HYCLAK; DONALD P. OLEKSIAK; THOMAS W. TIFFT, Ph.D.

Presbyteral Council—Most Rev. RICHARD G. LENNON, D.D., M.A., M.Th., Pres.; Revs. VINCENT J. HAWK; THOMAS J. BEHREND, Moderator; WILLIAM G. BOUHALL; CHARLES T. DIEDRICK, M.A.; MARK A. DINARDO; LAWRENCE JURCAK, J.C.L.; JOHN THOMAS LANE, S.S.S.; Most Rev. ROGER W. GRIES, O.S.B., D.D., M.Ed. (ex officio); Revs. ROBERT J. JASNEY; MICHAEL A. VINCENT, S.J.; EDWARD T. ESTOK, M.A., M.Div.; STEPHEN A. FLYNN; JOHN R. OLSAVSKY, J.C.L. (Retired); JOSEPH R. MAMICH; JOHN P. SEABOLD; KEVIN M. LIEBHARDT; ROBERT H. JACKSON; LORN J. SNOW, S.J.; JOHN T. MCDONOUGH (Retired); MARTIN F. POLITO; DONALD P. OLEKSIAK (ex officio); THOMAS W. TIFFT, Ph.D. (ex officio); PAUL J. ROSING, M.Div.; CHRISTOPHER H. WEBER; JAMES R. STENGER; A. JONATHAN ZINGALES, J.C.L. Presbyteral Conveners: Revs. THOMAS J. BEHREND; WILLIAM G. BOUHALL; CHARLES T. DIEDRICK, M.A.; MARK A. DINARDO; STEPHEN A. FLYNN; VINCENT J. HAWK; ROBERT H. JACKSON; MARTIN F. POLITO; LAWRENCE JURCAK, J.C.L.; LORN J. SNOW, S.J.; ROBERT J. JASANY; CHRISTOPHER H. WEBER; A. JONATHAN ZINGALES, J.C.L.

Diocesan Finance Council—RICHARD MARSH, Chm.; ANGELA CARLIN; KAREN KLEINHENZ; DOMINIC OZANNE; THOMAS J. PERCIAK; ANTHONY LANG; WILLIAM J. REIDY; MARIA COYNE; DONALD DAILEY; MICHAEL MEEHAN; THOMAS RICHLOVSKY; JANET MILLER; PATRICK MCMAHON.

Diocesan Pastoral Council—Most Rev. RICHARD G. LENNON, D.D., M.A., M.Th.; VACANT, Chm.; VACANT, Vice Chm.; RICHARD S. KRIVANKA, Exec. Sec.

Conference of Religious Leadership—Sisters MARY ELLEN BRINOVEC, O.S.U., 1564 Maple Ave., Cleveland, 44121. Tel: 440-282-0547; MARY PAT COOK, H.M., 20960 Hillard Blvd., Rocky River, 44116. Tel: 440-321-8791.

Diocese of Cleveland—Cathedral Square Plaza, 1404 E. Ninth St., Cleveland, 44114.

All Diocesan Offices are in the Cathedral Square Plaza at 1404 E. Ninth St. and may be reached at: Tel: 216-696-6525; 800-869-6525 (Ohio only); Fax: 216-781-8243.

Address dispensations and all business communication to the Chancery Office.

Chancellor—Sr. THERESE GUERIN SULLIVAN, S.P., J.C.L., Office: Cathedral Square Plaza. Fax: 216-621-7332.

Administrative Assistant to the Bishop—Rev. THEODORE MARSZAL, S.T.D., Office: 1404 E. Ninth St., 6th Fl., Cleveland, 44114.

Office for Worship—1404 E. Ninth St., 6th Fl., Cleveland, 44114. Tel: 216-696-6525, Ext. 4120. Ms. CHRISTINA RONZIO, Dir.

Tribunal—Office: 1404 E. Ninth St., Ste. 700, Cleveland, 44114-2555. Tel: 216-696-6525; 800-869-6525 (Ohio only); 800-676-4431 (Outside Ohio); Fax: 216-696-3226.

Judicial Vicar—Rev. GARY D. YANUS, J.C.D.

Adjunct Judicial Vicars—Revs. WILLIAM M. JERSE, J.C.L.; LAWRENCE JURCAK, J.C.L.; CHARLES F. STREBLER, J.C.L.

Judges—Ms. LYNETTE TAIT, J.C.L.; Rev. ROBERT M. WENDELKEN, D.Min. (Retired).

Defenders of the Bond—Revs. JOSEPH A. BACEVICE, M.Div.; A. JONATHAN ZINGALES, J.C.L.; Mr. CARL A. CALDWELL, M.A., G.C.C.L.

Judges in Second Instance—Revs. MIRKO HLADNI, J.C.L.; EDWARD J. LUCA, J.C.D. (Retired); JOHN R. OLSAVSKY, J.C.L. (Retired); WILLIAM P. O'NEILL, J.C.L. (Retired); ROBERT F. PFEIFFER, J.C.L. (Retired); ROBERT J. SANSON, J.C.D.; DAVID J. WALKOWIAK, J.C.D.; RALPH E. WIATROWSKI, J.C.D.

Associate Judges—Deacon JAMES L. AGRIPPE, (Retired); Revs. CHARLES T. DIEDRICK, M.A.; JEROME J. DUKE; JOHN R. HENGLE; EDWARD J. KORDAS; ALLAN R. LAUBENTHAL, S.T.D. (Retired); JOHN E. MANNING, M.A., M.Div.; LAWRENCE N. MARTELLO, M.A., M.Div.; THOMAS W. MCCANN (Retired); PAUL J. ROSING, M.Div.; DONALD E. SNYDER, M.Div.; CHARLES J. STOLLENWERK, M.Div.

Auditors/Assessors—Deacon THOMAS B. DAW; Mrs. ELAINE T. SHAWHAN, D.Min.; Mrs. PATRICIA DAW.

Procurators—Ms. ALICE HINKEL; Deacon DAVID PECOT; Ms. GAYLE CILIMBURG.

Promoters of Justice—Revs. A. JONATHAN ZINGALES, J.C.L.; MARK Q. FEDOR, J.C.D.

Ecclesiastical Notaries & Notary Publics—Mrs. LEE ANN CALVERT; Mrs. AMANDA L. HOCKENBERRY; Mrs. TERESA LUIKART.

Translators—Revs. BEDE KOTLINSKI, O.S.B.; AUGUSTINE PHAM VAN LAN; JOHN F. WESSEL (Retired); MICHAEL J. TROHA; RICHARD BONA.

Director of Facilities—Mr. LAWRENCE E. MURTAUGH, Cathedral Square Plaza, 4th Fl.

Archivist—Sr. THERESE GUERIN SULLIVAN, S.P., J.C.L.; PHILIP HAAS, Dir. Archives, Cathedral Square Plaza, 4th Fl.

Catholic Cemeteries Association—ANDREJ N. LAH, Pres., 10000 Miles Ave., Cleveland, 44105. Tel: 216-641-7575.

Callistian Guild—Mailing Address: P.O. Box 605125, Cleveland, 44105. Tel: 216-641-7575.

Catholic Community Foundation—Mr. PATRICK J. GRACE, Exec. Dir., 1404 E. 9th St., Ste. 810, Cleveland, 44114-1722. Tel: 216-696-6525, Ext. 5750; Fax: 216-348-0740.

Stewardship Office—1404 E. 9th St., 8th Fl., Cleveland, 44114. Mrs. MARY PAT FREY, Dir. Tel: 216-696-6525, Ext. 2120. Email: mpfrey@cdcf.org; Mrs. TERRI PRESKAR, Parish Relationship Mgr. Tel: 216-696-6525, Ext. 5090. Email: tpreskar@cdcf.org.

Central Purchasing—JAMES P. TERESI, Dir., 9000 Town Centre Dr., Broadview Heights, 44147. Tel: 440-717-9700.

Communications Department—ROBERT D. TAYEK, Dir., Media & Pub. Rel., Chancery Building. Tel: 216-696-6525, Ext. 4460.

"Catholic Universe Bulletin"—Most Rev. RICHARD G. LENNON, D.D., M.A., M.Th., Publisher; JOSEPH M. POLITO, Assoc. Publisher & CEO, 1404 E. Ninth St., 6th Fl. Tel: 216-696-6525, Ext. 5870.

Catholic Universe Bulletin Publishing Company, Inc.—JOSEPH M. POLITO, CEO, 1404 E. 9th St., 6th Fl. Tel: 216-696-6525, Ext. 5870.

Diocesan Pastoral Planning Office—RICHARD S. KRIVANKA, Dir.; DAVID DE LAMBO, Ph.D., Assoc. Dir.; ANN MARIE PERKINS, Office Coord., Office: Tel: 216-696-6525, Ext. 4210.

Mission Office, Society for the Propagation of the Faith—Rev. R. STEPHEN VELLENGA, Dir., Office: 1404 E. 9th St., Cleveland, 44114. Tel: 216-696-6525, Ext. 4240.

Pontifical Programs— Society for the Propagation of the Faith; Society of St. Peter the Apostle; Missionary Union of the Clergy; Holy Childhood Assoc.

National Programs— Latin-American Program; Lay Mission Volunteers

Diocesan Programs— Missionary Cooperation Plan; St. Francis Xavier Mission Assoc.; Cleveland Diocesan Mission, C.A.

Finance Office—JAMES P. GULICK, Finance Officer; WILLIAM R. HUDSON, Asst. Finance Officer, 1404 E. 9th St., 8th Fl., Cleveland, 44114.

Diocesan Legal Office—Bro. PATRICK T. SHEA, O.F.M., Gen. Counsel, 1404 E. 9th St., 7th Fl., Ste. 701, Cleveland, 44114.

Diocesan Building Commission—KEVIN T. BURKE, Coord., 1404 E. 9th St., 7th Fl., Cleveland, 44114.

Property/Casualty Office—KATHLEEN PIERCE, Dir., 1404 E. 9th St., 8th Fl., Cleveland, 44114.

DISC: Diocesan Insurance Service Committee—J. THOMAS HANNON, 1100 Chester Ave., Ste. 300, Cleveland, 44115.

Benefit Plans - Health Benefits, Group Life, and Pension—PALMIRA JURAS, 1404 E. 9th St., 8th Fl., Cleveland, 44114.

Human Resources Office—DONNA B. SPEAGLE, 1404 E. 9th St., 8th Fl., Cleveland, 44114.

Workers' Compensation Office—KATHLEEN PIERCE, 1404 E. 9th St., 8th Fl., Cleveland, 44114.

Diocese of Cleveland Facilities Services Corp.—formerly Catholic Charities Facilities Services Mr. LAWRENCE E. MURTAUGH, Exec. Dir., 1404 E. 9th St., 3rd Fl., Cleveland, 44114.

Secretariat for Education and Catechesis

Secretary for Education/Superintendent—MARGARET LYONS, 1404 E. 9th St., 2nd Fl., Cleveland, 44114. Tel: 216-696-6525, Ext. 1022.

Secretary for Catechetical Services—Mr. WILLIAM B. MILLER, 1404 E. 9th St., Cleveland, 44114. Tel: 216-696-6525, Ext. 2880.

Departments—

Catholic Education Endowment Trust—PEGGY LIPINSKI, 1404 E. 9th St., Cleveland, 44114. Tel: 216-696-6525, Ext. 2830.

Office of Catechetical Services—Mr. WILLIAM B. MILLER, Dir., 1404 E. 9th St., Cleveland, 44114. Tel: 216-696-6525, Ext. 2880.

Newman Campus Ministry—Mr. WILLIAM B. MILLER, Dir., 1404 E. 9th St., Cleveland, 44114. Tel: 216-696-6525, Ext. 2880.

Ministers—JOHN SZARWARK, Akron University. Tel: 216-696-6525, Ext. 3000; TONY VENTO, Case Western Reserve University. Tel: 216-421-9614, Ext. 302; Rev. VINCENT J. HAWK, Ashland University. Tel: 419-994-4396; KAREN HAHN, College of Wooster. Tel: 330-287-3718; GREGORY STEVENS, Oberlin College. Tel: 440-775-5190; MINDY KUSHLAK, Baldwin Wallace College. Tel: 440-243-4955; DEBBIE DACONE, Cleveland State University. Tel: 216-771-3630, Ext. 7145; KIRSTEN VILINSKY, Baldwin Wallace College. Tel: 440-243-4955.

Catechetical Consultants—DENISE SMITHBERGER, Southern Area Office, 1558 Creighton Ave., Akron, 44310. Tel: 330-773-7621; MARY LOU NECKEL-JAMES, 1404 E. 9th St., Cleveland, 44114. Tel: 216-696-6525, Ext. 1028.

Media Consultant—JEFF STUTZMAN, 1404 E. 9th St., Cleveland, 44114. Tel: 216-696-6525, Ext. 4330.

Office of Catholic Education—MARGARET LYONS, Sec. Educ./Supt., 1404 E. 9th St., Cleveland, 44114. Tel: 216-696-6525, Ext. 1022.

Educational Services—KATHLEEN O'BRIEN, Dir., 1404 E. Ninth St., Cleveland, 44114. Tel: 216-696-6525, Ext. 1148.

Assistant Superintendents—FRANK M. KUHAR, Eastern Area, 1404 E. Ninth St., Cleveland, 44114. Tel: 216-696-6525, Ext. 1280; ANNE MARIE WOYMA, Western Area, 1404 E. Ninth St., Cleveland, 44114. Tel: 216-696-6525, Ext. 1890; MICHELLE C. KROLL, Southern Area, 1404 E. Ninth St., Cleveland, 44114. Tel: 216-696-6525, Ext. 1290.

Elementary Schools/Accreditation—ANNE MARIE WOYMA, Asst. Supt. Elementary Schools, 1404 E. 9th St., Cleveland, 44114. Tel: 216-696-6525, Ext. 1890.

Special Projects/Voucher Programs—JUDY NAKASIAN, Coord., 1404 E. 9th St., Cleveland, 44114. Tel: 216-696-6525, Ext. 3250.

Finance—JOHN R. AHERN, Dir., 1404 E. 9th St., Cleveland, 44114. Tel: 216-696-6525, Ext. 5310.

Secondary Schools—WAYNE UEHLEIN, Assoc. Supt., 1404 E. 9th St., Cleveland, 44114. Tel: 216-696-6525, Ext. 2450.

Government Programs—MICHAEL VOINOVICH, Dir., 1404 E. 9th St., Cleveland, 44114. Tel: 216-696-6525, Ext. 3350.

Teacher Personnel Services—MELISSA HOKANSON, Dir., 1404 E. 9th St., Cleveland, 44114. Tel: 216-696-6525, Ext. 3360.

Nutrition Services/Summer Food Program—EDWARD MOREL, Dir., 1404 E. 9th St., Cleveland, 44114. Tel: 216-696-6525, Ext. 3110.

Curriculum—Dr. RUTHANN HEINTSCHEL, Coord., 1404 E. 9th St., Cleveland, 44114. Tel: 216-696-6525, Ext. 3240.

Educational Technology—DOLORES BRUNO, 1404 E. 9th St., Cleveland, 44114. Tel: 216-696-6525, Ext. 8990.

Technology—THOMAS MCBRIDE, Dir., 1404 E. 9th St., Cleveland, 44114. Tel: 216-696-6525, Ext. 3200.

Mandated Services—Consultants: JOHN KASTELIC, Representative. Tel: 216-696-6525, Ext. 3770; PAMELA OUZTS, Coord., 1404 E. 9th St., Cleveland, 44114. Tel: 216-696-6525, Ext. 5140.

Secretariat for Parish Life

Secretary—Sr. RITA MARY HARWOOD, S.N.D., 1404 E. 9th St., 3rd Fl., Cleveland, 44114. Tel: 216-696-6525, Ext. 3500.

African Ministry—Sr. RITA MARY HARWOOD, S.N.D. Tel: 216-696-6525, Ext. 3500.

Apostleship of the Sea Chaplain for the Diocese of Cleveland (Port Chaplain)—Sr. RITA MARY HARWOOD, S.N.D., Interim. Tel: 216-696-6525, Ext. 3500.

Asian Ministry—Sr. RITA MARY HARWOOD, S.N.D. Tel: 216-696-6525, Ext. 3500.

World Apostolate of Fatima, USA, Inc.— (also known as the Blue Army) *Cleveland Diocesan Division, P.O. Box 347328, Parma, 44134.* Tel: 216-641-8444, Ext. 20.

Catholic Renewal Ministries—Rev. ROBERT J. FRANCO, 35777 Center Ridge Rd., North Ridgeville, 44039-3097. Tel: 440-327-2201. Bishop's Delegate, Presentation House, 28706 Euclid Ave., #4, Wickliffe, 44092. Tel: 440-944-9445.

Central City Ministry with Poor—Rev. JAMES P. O'DONNELL, 2186 E. 35th St., Cleveland, 44115. Tel: 216-566-0531.

Diocesan Interfaith Commission—Rev. JOSEPH T. HILINSKI, Delegate. Tel: 216-696-6525, Ext. 5110.

Enthronement of the Sacred Heart—Diocesan Center, St. John Cathedral Rectory, 1007 Superior Ave., Cleveland, 44114. MARLENE R. PALUMBO, Sec. & Treas. Tel: 216-447-9375.

Ethnic Ministries— For the Pastoral Care of Migrants and Refugees and for any ethnic communities not listed below, please contact Sr. Rita Mary

Harwood, S.N.D., The Parish Life Office. Tel: 216-696-6525, Ext. 3500.

Diocesan Hispanic Office—MISAEL MAYORGA, Dir., 1404 E. 9th St., Cleveland, 44114. Tel: 216-696-6525, Ext. 4300.

Korean Catholic Apostolate—Rev. CHANG SU O, St. Andrew Kim (Korean Pastoral Center), 2310 W. 14th St., Cleveland, 44113. Tel: 216-861-4630.

Native American Ministry—Sr. RITA MARY HARWOOD, S.N.D., Dir., 1404 E. 9th St., Cleveland, 44114. Tel: 216-696-6525, Ext. 3500.

Office of Ministry to African American Catholics—VANESSA GRIFFIN CAMPBELL, Dir. Tel: 216-696-6525, Ext. 3020.

Philippine-American Ministry—Rev. RODEL ANGELES, Dir., 1007 Superior Ave., Cleveland, 44114. Tel: 216-771-6666.

Vietnamese-American Apostolate—Rev. AUGUSTINE PHAM VAN LAN, Dir., 3545 W. 54th St., Cleveland, 44102. Tel: 216-961-2713, Ext. 2540.

Office of Evangelization—TERRIE BALDWIN, Dir. Tel: 216-696-6525, Ext. 2540.

Holy Name Societies, Cleveland Diocesan Union—Rev. THOMAS A. HAREN, Spiritual Dir., 13623 Rockside Rd., Garfield Heights, 44125-5197. Tel: 216-662-8685.

Pastoral Ministry Office—Ms. KATHLEEN HAASE-FALBO, Dir., Center for Pastoral Leadership, 28700 Euclid Ave., Wickliffe, 44092. Tel: 440-943-7669.

Office for Women in Church and Society—LEANNE MAHOVLIC, Dir., 1404 E. 9th St., Cleveland, 44114. Tel: 216-696-6525, Ext. 3070.

Secretariat for Clergy and Religious

Secretary—Rev. MICHAEL K. GURNICK, M.A., M.Div., Sec. & Vicar for Clergy & Relg., 1404 E. 9th St., 2nd Fl., Cleveland, 44114.

Borromeo Seminary— See Seminaries.

Clergy Personnel Board—Rev. DONALD P. OLEKSIAK, Dir., 1404 E. 9th St., 2nd Fl., Cleveland, 44114.

Continuing Education for Formation of Ministers—Rev. JOSEPH T. HILINSKI, Dir.; Deacon PAUL KIPSFTUHL; KATHEE STERBENZ.

Permanent Diaconate Formation Office—Rev. ANTHONY J. SCHUERGER, Dir., The Center for Pastoral Leadership, 28700 Euclid Ave., Wickliffe, 44092. St. Malachi Parish, 2459 Washington Ave., Cleveland, 44133-2380.

Retirement Board—Revs. MICHAEL J. TROHA, Immaculate Conception Parish, 37935 Wright St., Willoughby, 44094-5899. Tel: 440-942-4500; JOSEPH PREVITE, St. Columbkille Parish, 6740 Broadview Rd., Parma, 44134-4898. Tel: 216-524-1987.

St. Mary Seminary— See Seminaries.

Senior Priests—Rev. ALBERT A. KRUPP, Delegate, 1404 E. 9th St., 2nd Fl., Cleveland, 44114.

Vocations Office—Rev. MICHAEL P. MCCANDLESS, M.Div., M.A., Dir., Center for Pastoral Leadership, 28700 Euclid Ave., Wickliffe, 44092.

Avilas of the Diocese of Cleveland—Mrs. MARIE BECKER, 20790 Lake Rd., Rocky River, 44116.

Parents of Priests—DONALD TRASK, Pres., 1404 E. 9th St., 2nd Fl., Cleveland, 44114.

Catholic Charities Health and Human Services

Catholic Charities Health and Human Services—Mr. PATRICK GAREAU, Pres. & CEO, 7911 Detroit Ave., Cleveland, 44102. Tel: 216-334-2901.

Catholic Charities Annual Appeal—Mr. PATRICK J. GRACE, 1404 E. Ninth St., 8th Fl., Cleveland, 44114. Tel: 216-696-6525, Ext. 5750; Fax: 216-348-0740.

Catholic Charities Parish & Community Ministries—Executive Directors: Mr. TERRENCE FLANAGAN; JOHN P. KLEE, 7911 Detroit Ave., Cleveland, 44102. Tel: 216-334-2959; Fax: 216-334-2983.

Special Ministry to the Aged—6804 Lansing Ave., Cleveland, 44105-1521. Tel: 216-441-5402; Fax: 216-441-4510. Sr. ANNA KASZUBA, S.S.M.I., Dir.

Pro Life Office—PEGGY GEROVAC, Dir., 7911 Detroit Ave., Cleveland, 44102. Tel: 216-334-2965; Fax: 216-334-2976.

Office of Ministry for Persons with Disabilities—Rev. JOSEPH D. MCNULTY, Exec. Dir., St. Augustine Church, 2486 W. 14th St., Cleveland, 44113. Tel: 216-781-5530; Fax: 216-781-1124.

Marriage and Family Office—WILLIAM BOOMER, Dir., 7911 Detroit Ave., Cleveland, 44102. Tel: 216-334-2971.

Youth and Young Adult Ministry and CYO Office—GREG MOSER, Dir., 7911 Detroit Ave., Cleveland, 44102. Tel: 216-334-1261, Ext. 32.

Migration and Refugee Services—TOM MROSKO, Dir., 7800 Detroit Ave., Cleveland, 44102. Tel: 216-939-3731.

Catholic Charities Services Corporation—3135 Euclid Ave., Rm. 202, Cleveland, 44115. MAUREEN DEE. Tel: 216-391-2030; Fax: 216-291-8946.

Catholic Charities Community Services—BERNADETTE WASHINGTON, Exec. Dir., 7911 Detroit Ave., Cleveland, 44102. Tel: 216-334-2937; Fax: 216-334-2907.

Disabilities Services—DENNIS MCNULTY, Senior Dir. Tel: 440-334-2962. OLA/St. Joseph Center, 2346 W. 14th St., Cleveland, 44113. Tel: 216-621-3451.

Emergency Assistance Services—GAYLE DOUCETTE, Dir., 1736 Superior Ave., Cleveland, 44114. Tel: 216-781-8262.

Older Adult Services—DAVE MODARSKY, Senior Dir., 7800 Detroit Ave., Cleveland, 44102. Tel: 216-939-3703; Fax: 216-631-3654.

Pastoral Care Services—Rev. KENNETH F. WALLACE, 7911 Detroit Ave., Cleveland, 44102. Tel: 216-587-8377.

Catholic Charities Housing Corporation—7911 Detroit Ave., Cleveland, 44102. MARYELLEN STAAB, Dir. Tel: 216-334-2954.

Catholic Charities Corporation—JOHN P. KLEE, Exec. Dir., 7911 Detroit Ave., Cleveland, 44102. Tel: 216-334-2959; Fax: 216-334-2983.

Diocesan Social Action Office—Sr. KATHLEEN RYAN, S.N.D., 7800 Detroit Ave., Cleveland, 44102. Tel: 216-939-3843; Fax: 216-939-3850.

Commission on Catholic Community Action—Sr. KATHLEEN RYAN, S.N.D., Dir., 7800 Detroit Ave., Cleveland, 44102. Tel: 216-939-3843; Fax: 216-939-3850.

Catholic Action Commission of Lorain County—VACANT, Dir., 320 Middle Ave., Elyria, 44035. Tel: 440-326-0316; Fax: 440-326-0314.

Catholic Commission of Lake and Geauga Counties—JEROME WALCOTT, 28700 Euclid Ave., Wickliffe, 44092. Tel: 440-943-7608.

Catholic Commission (Summit County)—KAREN LEITH, Dir., 795 Russell Ave., Akron, 44307. Tel: 330-535-2787; Fax: 330-535-9040.

Catholic Commission of Wayne, Ashland and Medina Counties—PATRICK O'BRYAN, Dir., 521 Beall Ave., P.O. Box 15, Wooster, 44691. Tel: 330-263-6176; Fax: 330-262-4633.

Campaign for Human Development—Deacon JUAN ORTIZ, Coord., 320 Middle Ave., Elyria, 44035. Tel: 440-326-0316; Fax: 440-326-0314.

Catholic Relief Services—Deacon JUAN ORTIZ, Dir., 320 Middle Ave., Elyria, 44035. Tel: 440-326-0316; Fax: 440-326-0314.

Bishop William M. Cosgrove Family Center—1736 Superior Ave., Cleveland, 44114. Tel: 216-781-8262; Fax: 216-566-9161. NICOLE EVANS, Prog. Dir.

Catholic Charities Services/Summit County—Deacon JOHN D. GREEN, Dir., 812 Biruta St., Akron, 44307. Tel: 330-762-2961; Fax: 330-762-2001. Camp Christopher, Ira & Hametown Rd., Bath, 44210. Tel: 800-CYO-CAMP; Fax: 330-762-2001.

Rose-Mary, The Johanna Grasselli Rehabilitation and Education Center—Ms. PATRICIA A. COLOMBO, Exec. Dir., 19350 Euclid Ave., Cleveland, 44102. Tel: 216-634-7400; Fax: 216-634-7483.

St. Augustine Corporation—ANDREW KOHA, Exec. Dir. & Pres., 7801 Detroit Ave., Cleveland, 44102. Tel: 216-634-7400; Fax: 216-634-7483.

The Society of St. Vincent de Paul—Cathedral Square Plaza, 1404 E. 9th St., Cleveland, 44114. Tel: 216-696-6525, Ext. 3150.

Catholic Lawyers' Guild of Cleveland— The Catholic Diocese of Cleveland Foundation.

Catholic Lawyers' Guild of Cleveland Endowment Trust— The Catholic Diocese of Cleveland Foundation.

Victim Assistance Coordinator—Mr. TERRENCE FLANAGAN. Tel: 216-334-2958. Email: tjflanagan@clevelandcatholiccharities.org.

CLERGY, PARISHES, MISSIONS AND PAROCHIAL SCHOOLS

CITY OF CLEVELAND

(CUYAHOGA COUNTY)

1—CATHEDRAL OF ST. JOHN THE EVANGELIST (1848) Revs. Theodore Marszal; Rodel Angeles; Deacons John P. Sferry Sr., Pastoral Assoc.; J. Kevin McKenna. In Res., Revs. Charles F. Strebler, Tribunal - Judical Vicar; Michael K. Gurnick, Sec. & Vicar for Clergy & Relg.
Res.: 1007 Superior Ave., N.E., 44114-2582. Tel: 216-771-6666; Fax: 216-781-5646.
Church: E. 9th St. & Superior Ave., N.E., 44114.
Catechesis/Religious Program—Students 8.

2—ST. ADALBERT (1883), For information call the Chancery.
Res.: 2347 E. 83rd St., 44104-2198. Tel: 216-881-7647; Fax: 216-881-7670.
School—2345 E. 83rd St., 44104. Tel: 216-881-6250; Fax: 216-881-9030. James Smith, Prin. Religious 1; Lay Teachers 11; Students 179.
Catechesis/Religious Program—Students 25.

3—ST. AGNES - OUR LADY OF FATIMA (1980) Rev. Robert Marva, O.F.M.Cap.; Deacon Hardin M. Martin.
Res.: 6800 Lexington Ave., 44103-3297. Tel: 216-391-1655 (Office); Fax: 216-391-7919.
Church: 6800 Lexington Ave., 44103. Tel: 216-391-1655.
Catechesis/Religious Program—Students 30.

4—ST. ALOYSIUS - ST. AGATHA (1975) Bro. Paul Hoffman, S.M., Parish Life Coord.; Rev. Theodore Cassidy, S.M.; Deacon James Paul Jr. In Res., Bros. Robert Dzubinski, S.M.; Richard Olsen, S.M.
Res.: 10932 St. Clair Ave., 44108-1939. Tel: 216-451-3262; 216-451-3263; Fax: 216-268-3830.
School—640 Lakeview Rd., N.E., 44108. Tel: 216-451-2050; Fax: 216-541-1601. Sr. Sandra Sabo, S.S.J.-T.O.S.F., Prin. Sisters 3; Lay Teachers 9; Students 121.
Catechesis/Religious Program—Students 17.

5—ST. ANDREW (1906), (Slovak), Closed. For inquiries for parish records, contact the Archives, Diocese of Cleveland.

6—ST. ANDREW KIM PASTORAL CENTER (1988), (Korean), Rev. Chang Su O, Admin.; Deacon Charles C. Shin.
Res.: 2310 W. 14th St., 44113-3613. Tel: 216-861-4630; Fax: 216-241-6366.
Catechesis/Religious Program—Students 59.

7—ANNUNCIATION (1924) Closed. For inquiries for parish records contact Blessed Trinity Parish, Cleveland.

8—ASCENSION (1946) Closed. For inquiries for parish records contact Blessed Trinity Parish, Cleveland.

9—ST. AUGUSTINE (1860) Rev. Joseph D. McNulty; Sr. Corita Ambro, C.S.J., Pastoral Assoc.; Deacons John M. Rivera, Pastoral Assoc.; Louis Woyton, Pastoral Assoc.; Mary Smith, Pastoral Assoc.; Mary Ellen Czelusniak, Pastoral Assoc.
Res.: 2486 W. 14th St., 44113-4449. Tel: 216-781-5530 (Voice & TTY); 216-781-5880 (Voice & TTY); Fax: 216-781-1124.
Catechesis/Religious Program—Mrs. Kathleen Ulintz, D.R.E. Students 482.
Convent—2432 W. 14th St., 44113. Tel: 216-579-1306.

10—ST. BARBARA (1905), (Polish), For information call the Chancery.
Res.: 1505 Denison Ave., 44109-2890. Tel: 216-741-2067.
Catechesis/Religious Program—
Convent—3855 W. 16th St., 44109. Tel: 216-661-0547.

11—ST. BENEDICT, Closed. For inquiries for parish records contact the chancery.

12—BLESSED SACRAMENT (1903) Closed. For inquiries for parish records contact the Archives of the Diocese of Cleveland.

13—BLESSED TRINITY PARISH (2010) Rev. Douglas H. Koesel; Deacons John A. Koch; Richard C. Beercheck; William M. Staab; Kathleen Corbett, Pastoral Min.; Carol Roberts, Pastoral Assoc.
14040 Puritas Ave., 44135-2822. Tel: 216-671-5890; Fax: 216-671-2320.
School—*West Park Catholic Academy*, 17720 Puritas Ave., 44135. Tel: 216-671-4314; Fax: 216-761-5277. Annemarie Rajnicek, Prin. Lay Teachers 18; Students 271.
Catechesis/Religious Program—Students 41.

14—ST. BONIFACE (1903) Rev. Augustine Pham Van Lan.
Res.: 3545 W. 54th St., 44102. Tel: 216-961-2713; 216-961-2714; Fax: 216-961-1859.
See Metro Catholic School, Cleveland under Elementary Schools, Parochial and Diocesan located in the Institution section.
Catechesis/Religious Program—
Convent—3588 W. 52nd St., 44102. Tel: 216-961-0669.

15—ST. CASIMIR (1891), (Polish), Closed. For inquiries for parish records contact the chancery.

16—ST. CASIMIR (2009) Rev. Joseph A. Bacevice.
18022 Neff Rd., 44119-2644. Tel: 216-481-3157; Fax: 216-481-3734.
Catechesis/Religious Program—Mrs. Jackie Caruso-Taylor, D.R.E. Students 11.

17—ST. CATHERINE (1898) Closed. For inquiries for parish records, contact the Archives, Diocese of Cleveland.

18—ST. CECILIA (1915) Closed. For inquiries for parish records contact the Archives of the Diocese of Cleveland.

19—ST. COLMAN (1880) Rev. Robert T. Begin; Sisters Wilma Apack, C.S.J., Pastoral Assoc.; Audrey Koch, C.S.J., Pastoral Assoc.; Mary Beth Gray, S.N.D.,

Dir. of Music; Deacon William H. Corrigan; Eileen Kelly, Outreach Ministry.
Res.: 2027 W. 65th St., 44102-4394. Tel: 216-651-0550; 216-939-9139; Fax: 216-651-1663.
Catechesis/Religious Program—Students 39.
Convent—2007 W. 65th St., 44102.

20—COMMUNITY OF ST. MALACHI (1975) Closed. For inquiries for parish records contact St. Malachi, Cleveland.; (Personal Parish)

21—CONVERSION OF ST. PAUL (1931) Closed. For inquiries for parish records contact the Archives of the Diocese of Cleveland.

22—CORPUS CHRISTI (1935) Closed. For inquiries for parish records contact Mary Queen of Peace Parish, Cleveland.

23—CRISTO REY, CAPILLA DE (1983), (Hispanic), Closed. For inquiries for parish records contact La Sagrada Familia.

24—ST. ELIZABETH OF HUNGARY (1892), (Hungarian), Rev. Andras Antal, Admin.
Mailing Address: P.O. Box 20175, 44104-0175. Tel: 216-231-0325; Fax: 216-421-0461.
Church: 9016 Buckeye Rd., 44104.
Catechesis/Religious Program—Students 12.

25—ST. EMERIC (1904 & Territorial 1964), (Magyar), For information call the Chancery.
Res.: 1860 W. 22nd St., 44113-3185. Tel: 216-861-1937.

26—EPIPHANY (1944) Closed. For inquiries for parish records contact the chancery.

27—ST. FRANCIS (1887) Closed. For inquiries for parish records contact the chancery.

28—ST. GEORGE (1895), (Lithuanian), Closed. For inquiries for parish records contact St. Casimir, Cleveland.

29—ST. HENRY (1946) Closed. For inquiries for parish records, contact the Archives, Diocese of Cleveland.

30—HOLY FAMILY (1911) Closed. For inquiries for parish records contact the chancery.

31—HOLY NAME (1854) Rev. Msgr. Richard C. Antall. In Res., Rev. Edward M. Czech (Retired).
Res.: 8328 Broadway Ave., S.E., 44105-3931. Tel: 216-271-4242; 216-271-4243; 216-271-6995; Fax: 216-271-0886.
School—Tel: 216-341-0084; Fax: 216-341-1122. Lorenzo Jones, Prin. Lay Teachers 15; Students 149.
Catechesis/Religious Program—Students 11.

32—HOLY REDEEMER (1924), (Italian), Rev. Martin F. Polito; Sr. Carmen Hocevar, O.S.U., Pastoral Assoc. In Res., Rev. Carl L. D'Agostino (Retired).
Res.: 15712 Kipling Ave., 44110-3104. Tel: 216-531-3313; 216-531-3338; Fax: 216-531-4717.
Catechesis/Religious Program—Students 15.
Convent—924 Ruple Rd., 44110. Tel: 216-481-2740.

33—HOLY ROSARY (1892), (Italian), Rev. Joseph Previte; Deacon Bruce J. Battista; Anne DeMarco, Pastoral Assoc.
Res.: 12021 Mayfield Rd., 44106-1996. Tel: 216-421-2995; Fax: 216-421-2258.
Catechesis/Religious Program—Students 134.

34—HOLY TRINITY - ST. EDWARD (1975) Closed. For inquiries for parish records contact the chancery.

35—ST. HYACINTH (1906), (Polish), Closed. For inquiries for parish records contact the chancery.

36—ST. IGNATIUS OF ANTIOCH (1902) Rev. James R. McGonegal; Sr. Dianne Piunno, S.N.D., Pastoral Assoc. In Res., Rev. Gary D. Yanus.
Res.: 10205 Lorain Ave., 44111-5435. Tel: 216-251-0300; Fax: 216-251-0302.
School—Tel: 216-671-0535; Fax: 216-671-0536. Margaret Ricksecker, Prin. Lay Teachers 20; Students 304.
Catechesis/Religious Program—Students 32.

37—IMMACULATE CONCEPTION (1865) Revs. Frank G. Godic; Albert J. Mackert, Pastor Emeritus (Retired). In Res., Rev. John J. Hayes (Retired).
Res.: 4129 Superior Ave., 44103-1179. Tel: 216-431-5900; Fax: 216-431-0463.
Catechesis/Religious Program—

38—IMMACULATE HEART OF MARY (1894), (Polish), [CEM] Revs. Ralph Hudak; Andrew Knapik, Parochial Vicar.
Res.: 6700 Lansing Ave., 44105-3797. Tel: 216-341-2734; 216-341-2735; Fax: 216-341-7200.
Catechesis/Religious Program—Students 15.
Convent—6804 Lansing Ave., 44105. Tel: 216-641-7121.

39—ST. JEROME (1919) Rev. Anthony J. Cassese; Deacon Peter Travalik.
Res.: 15000 Lake Shore Blvd., 44110-1298. Tel: 216-481-8200; Fax: 216-481-6459.
School—15100 Lake Shore Blvd., 44110. Tel: 216-486-3587; Fax: 216-486-4288. Mrs. Susan Coan, Prin. Religious 3; Lay Teachers 12; Students 166.
Catechesis/Religious Program—
Convent—15025 Ridpath Ave., 44110.

40—ST. JOHN CANTIUS (1898), (Polish), Revs. Lucjan Stokowski; Ralph A. Bodziony, Pastor Emeritus (Retired).
Res.: 906 College Ave., S.W., 44113-4494. Tel: 216-781-9095; Fax: 216-696-6065.
Catechesis/Religious Program—

41—ST. JOHN NEPOMUCENE (1902), (Bohemian), Rev. Robert J. Jasany; Sr. Karen Beargie, M.M., Pastoral Assoc.
Res.: 3785 Independence Rd., 44105-3357. Tel: 216-641-8444; 216-641-8445; Fax: 216-641-8824.
Church: Fleet Ave. & E. 50th St., 44105. Tel: 216-641-8444.
Catechesis/Religious Program—Students 36.

42—ST. JOSAPHAT (1908) Closed. For inquiries for parish records contact the chancery.

43—ST. JOSEPH (Woodland) Closed. For inquiries for parish records contact the chancery.

44—ST. JOSEPH (Collinwood) (1877) Closed. For inquiries for parish records contact St. Aloysius, Cleveland.

45—ST. LAWRENCE (1901) Closed. For inquiries for parish records contact the chancery.

46—ST. LEO THE GREAT (1948) Rev. Russell P. Lowe. In Res., Rev. James J. Vesely (Retired).
Res.: 4940 Broadview Rd., 44109-5799. Tel: 216-661-1006; 216-661-1007; 216-661-1008; Fax: 216-661-0887.
School—4900 Broadview Rd., 44109. Tel: 216-661-2120; Fax: 216-661-7125. Diane Weiss, Prin. Lay Teachers 16; Students 252.
Catechesis/Religious Program—Students 105.

47—ST. MALACHI (1865) Closed. For inquiries for parish records contact St. Malachi, Cleveland.

48—ST. MALACHI (2009) Revs. Anthony J. Schuerger; Paul J. Hritz, Pastor Emeritus (Retired).
Res.: 2459 Washington Ave., 44113-2380. Tel: 216-861-5343; 216-861-5344; Fax: 216-861-5340.
School—Urban Community School, 4909 Lorain Ave., 44102. Tel: 216-939-8330; Fax: 216-939-8324. Pamela Delly, Dir. (Intermediate Level) (See St. Wendelin listing for Primary Level) Sisters 2; Lay Teachers 25; Students 447.
Catechesis/Religious Program—Stephanie Pritts, D.R.E. Students 75.
Convent—2456 Vermont Ave., 44113. Tel: 216-781-3481.

49—ST. MARK (1945) Rev. John P. Miceli; Deacons Howard Masony; David J. Lundeen. In Res., Rev. Edward N. Schwet.
Res.: 15800 Montrose Ave., 44111-1084. Tel: 216-226-7577; Fax: 216-521-0371.
School—15724 Montrose Ave., 44111. Tel: 216-521-4115; Fax: 216-221-8664. Mrs. Karen Cocita. Lay Teachers 23; Students 383.
Catechesis/Religious Program—Students 166.

50—ST. MARY (1905), (Slovenian), Rev. John M. Kumse; Deacon David S. Kushner.
Res.: 15519 Holmes Ave., 44110-2497. Tel: 216-761-7740; 216-761-1837; Fax: 216-761-6673.
Catechesis/Religious Program—Students 48.

51—ST. MARY OF CZESTOCHOWA (1913), (Polish), Closed. For inquiries for parish records contact the chancery.

52—MARY QUEEN OF PEACE (2010) Rev. Douglas T. Brown; Deacon Patrick F. Berigan.
4423 Pearl Rd., 44109-4266. Tel: 216-749-2323; Fax: 216-741-7183.
School—Mary Queen of Peace Elementary School, 4419 Pearl Rd., 44109-4268. Tel: 216-741-3685; Fax: 216-741-5534. Mrs. Jennifer Berardinelli, Prin. Lay Teachers 14; Students 230.
Catechesis/Religious Program—Mrs. Joan Berigan, D.R.E. Students 40.

53—ST. MEL (1945) Rev. Mark Q. Fedor.
Res.: 14436 Triskett Rd., 44111-2263. Tel: 216-941-4313; 216-941-4314; Fax: 216-941-1093.
Catechesis/Religious Program—Students 37.

54—ST. MICHAEL THE ARCHANGEL (1882) Revs. James H. McCreight; Dennis R. O'Grady, Pastor Emeritus (Retired); Sr. Mary Reean Coyne, S.N.D., Pastoral Assoc.; Deacons Gonzalo Lopez; Reinaldo Sanchez; Miguel Figueroa.
Res.: 3114 Scranton Rd., 44109-1632. Tel: 216-861-6297; 216-621-3847 (Spanish).
See Metro Catholic School, Cleveland under Elementary Schools, Parochial and Diocesan located in the Institution section.
Catechesis/Religious Program—Students 118.

55—NATIVITY OF THE BLESSED VIRGIN MARY, Closed. For inquiries for parish records contact the chancery.

56—OUR LADY OF ANGELS (1922) Rev. Jerome J. Duke; Deacon Thomas J. Senn. In Res., Rev. John Lyons.
Res.: 3644 Rocky River Dr., 44111-3998. Tel: 216-252-2332; Fax: 216-252-2383.
School—Tel: 216-251-6841; Fax: 216-251-7831. Miss Kathleen A. Lynch, Prin.; Mrs. Elizabeth DeCore, Prin. Lay Teachers 26; Students 396.

57—OUR LADY OF GOOD COUNSEL (1873) Closed. For inquiries for parish records contact Mary Queen of Peace Parish, Cleveland.

58—OUR LADY OF LOURDES (1883), (Bohemian), Rev. Joseph H. Callahan; Deacon Frank Lozada.
Res.: 3395 E. 53rd St., 44127-1692. Tel: 216-641-2829; Fax: 216-641-0043.
Church: 3396 E. 55th St., 44127-1692.
Convent—3401 E. 53rd St., 44127.
Catechesis/Religious Program—Students 95.

59—OUR LADY OF MERCY (1922), (Slovak), Closed. For inquiries for parish records contact the Archives of the Diocese of Cleveland.

60—OUR LADY OF MOUNT CARMEL (East) (1936) Closed. For inquiries for parish records contact the chancery.

61—OUR LADY OF MOUNT CARMEL (West) (1926), (Italian), Revs. Richard S. Rasch, O.de.M.; Anthony M. Fortunato, O.de.M., Parochial Vicar; Jerome P. Laubacker, O.de.M. In Res., Rev. Michael Donovan, O.de.M.
Res.: 6928 Detroit Ave., 44102-3093. Tel: 216-651-5043; Fax: 216-651-6641.
School—1355 W. 70th St., 44102. Tel: 216-281-7146; Fax: 216-281-7001. Sr. Rosario Vega, H.M.S.S., Prin. Mercedarian Sisters of the Blessed Sacrament 3; Lay Teachers 13; Students 241.
Catechesis/Religious Program—Students 10.
Convent—1355 W. 70th St., 44102. Tel: 216-281-9304.

62—OUR LADY OF PEACE (1919) Rev. Gary Chmura; Deacon William E. Dirk; Sr. Margaret Ann Kelley, O.S.U., Pastoral Assoc.; Mrs. Nancy McIntosh, Pastoral Assoc. In Res., Revs. Augustine Okwuzu, S.M.M.M.; Maurice Emelu.
Res.: 12503 Buckingham Ave., 44120-1498. Tel: 216-421-4211; 216-421-4212; Fax: 216-421-1612.
Church: 12601 Shaker Blvd., 44120.
Catechesis/Religious Program—Students 36.

63—OUR LADY OF PERPETUAL HELP (1929), (Lithuanian), Closed. For inquiries for parish records contact St. Casimir, Cleveland.

64—ST. PATRICK (1853) Rev. Mark A. DiNardo; Deacon William Merriman.
Res.: 3602 Bridge Ave., 44113-3314. Tel: 216-631-6872; 216-631-6873; 216-631-6874; Fax: 216-631-0267.
School—Urban Community School, Tel: 216-939-8330; Fax: 216-939-0240. See St. Malachi listing.
Catechesis/Religious Program—Students 79.

65—ST. PATRICK (West Park) (1848) [CEM], For information call the Chancery.
Res.: 4427 Rocky River Dr., 44135-2551. Tel: 216-251-8286; 216-251-8287; Fax: 216-251-8555.
Catechesis/Religious Program—Students 40.
Convent—17712 Puritas Ave., 44135. Tel: 216-941-1088.

66—ST. PAUL (1902), (Croatian), Revs. Mirko Hladni; Zvonko Blasko.
Res.: 1369 E. 40th St., 44103-1194. Tel: 216-431-1895; Fax: 216-431-1128.
Catechesis/Religious Program—Students 84.

67—ST. PETER (1853), (German), For information call the Chancery.
Res.: 1533 E. 17th St., 44114. Tel: 216-861-1798; Fax: 216-861-1799.
Catechesis/Religious Program—Students 39.

68—SS. PHILIP AND JAMES (1950) Closed. For inquiries for parish records contact the Archives of the Diocese of Cleveland.

69—ST. PHILIP NERI (1914) Closed. For inquiries for parish records, contact the Archives, Diocese of Cleveland.

70—ST. PROCOP (1872), (Bohemian), Closed. For inquiries for parish records contact the chancery.

71—ST. ROCCO (1922), (Italian), Very Rev. Michael Contardi, O.de.M.; Revs. Paschal Rosca, O.de.M.; Paul J. Pietrzyk, O.de.M. In Res., Rev. Justin Freeman, O.de.M.; Bro. Richard Henry, O.de.M.
Res.: 3205 Fulton Rd., 44109-1495. Tel: 216-961-8331; Fax: 216-961-1845.
School—Tel: 216-961-8557; Fax: 216-961-1112. Sr. Judith Wulk, O.SS.T., Prin. Sisters of Most Holy Trinity 4; Lay Teachers 8; Students 188.
Catechesis/Religious Program—Students 35.
Convent—Tel: 216-961-2378.

72—ST. ROSE OF LIMA (1899) Closed. For inquiries for parish records contact the chancery.

73—SACRED HEART OF JESUS (1888), (Polish), Closed. For inquiries for parish records contact the Archives of the Diocese of Cleveland.

74—SAGRADA FAMILIA (1997), (Hispanic), Rev. Robert J. Reidy; Deacons Ceferino Medina; Epifanio Torres; Victor Colon; Ignacio Miranda; Frederick Simon.
Church: 7719 Detroit Ave., 44102-2811. Tel: 216-631-6817; 216-631-2888; 216-631-2889; Fax: 216-631-3305.
Catechesis/Religious Program—Students 100.

75—SAN JUAN BAUTISTA (1975), (Spanish), Closed. For inquiries for Parish Records contact La Sagrada Familia.

76—ST. STANISLAUS (1873), (Polish), Revs. Michael Surafka, O.F.M., Admin.; Placyd Kon, O.F.M.; Leonard Stunek, O.F.M. In Res., Bro. Justin Kwietniewski, O.F.M.

Res.: 3649 E. 65th St., 44105-1293. Tel: 216-341-9091; Fax: 216-341-2688.
Church: Forman Ave. & E. 65th St., 44105.
School—6615 Forman Ave., 44105. Tel: 216-883-3307; Fax: 216-883-0514. Mrs. Deborah Martin, Prin. Lay Teachers 19; Students 287.
Catechesis/Religious Program—
Convent—6615 Forman Ave., 44105. Tel: 216-341-0934.

77—ST. STEPHEN (1869), (German), Rev. S. Michael Franz; Deacon Moises Cruz.
Res.: 1930 W. 54th St., 44102-3298. Tel: 216-631-5633; Fax: 216-631-5634.
See Metro Catholic School, Cleveland under Elementary Schools, Parochial and Diocesan located in the Institution section.
Catechesis/Religious Program—Students 15.
Convent—1891 W. 57th St., 44102. Tel: 216-631-0754.

78—ST. THOMAS AQUINAS, Closed. For inquiries for parish records contact the chancery.

79—TRANSFIGURATION (1943) Closed. For inquiries for parish records contact the chancery.

80—ST. VINCENT DE PAUL (1922) Revs. John E. Manning; Robert E. Clancy; Deacon Kenneth J. Hill.
Res.: 13400 Lorain Ave., 44111-3470. Tel: 216-252-2626; Fax: 216-252-6993.
Church: Lorain Ave. & Berea Rd., 44111.
School—13442 Lorain Ave., 44111. Tel: 216-251-3932; Fax: 216-251-0455. Denise King, Prin. Lay Teachers 12; Students 182.
Catechesis/Religious Program—Students 27.

81—ST. VITUS (1893), (Slovenian), Rev. Joseph P. Boznar; Sr. Mary Avsec, S.N.D., Pastoral Assoc. In Res., Rev. Cirilo A. Nacorda.
Res.: 6019 Lausche Ave., 44103-1455. Tel: 216-361-1444; 216-361-1445; Fax: 216-361-1445.
Catechesis/Religious Program—Students 118.

82—ST. WENDELIN (1903), (Slovak), For information call the Chancery.
Res.: 2281 Columbus Rd., 44113-4230. Tel: 216-861-1141; Fax: 216-861-1141.
School—*Urban Community School*, 4909 Lorain Ave., 44102. Tel: 216-939-8330; Fax: 216-939-8360. Pam Delly, Prin. (Primary and Junior High) (See St. Malachi listing for Intermediate Level)
Catechesis/Religious Program—Students 19.
Convent—2259 Columbus Rd., 44113. Tel: 216-241-1773.

OUTSIDE THE CITY OF CLEVELAND

AKRON, SUMMIT CO.

1—ANNUNCIATION (1907) Closed. For inquiries for parish records contact Visitation of Mary, Akron.

2—ST. ANTHONY OF PADUA (1933), (Italian), Revs. James V. Ragnoni; Edward A. Burba, Parochial Vicar.
Res.: 83 Mosser Pl., 44310-3184. Tel: 330-762-7277; Fax: 330-762-2229.
School—80 E. York St., 44310. Tel: 330-253-6918; Fax: 330-376-6163. Sr. Elizabeth Szilvasi, M.P.F., Prin. Religious 2; Lay Teachers 5; Students 114.
Catechesis/Religious Program—Students 46.
Convent—93 Mosser Pl., 44310. Tel: 216-376-1735.

3—ST. BERNARD (1861) [CEM] Closed. For inquiries for parish records contact the chancery.

4—ST. BERNARD - ST. MARY PARISH (2010) Rev. Daniel J. Reed; Deacon Ramon DiMascio.
44 University Ave., 44308-1609. Tel: 330-253-5161; Fax: 330-253-6949. In Res., Rev. Norman Douglas.
School—*St. Bernard-St. Mary School*, 750 S. Main St., 44311-1094. Tel: 330-253-1233; Fax: 330-253-1473. Rosemary Capotosto, Prin. Teachers 13; Students 188.
Catechesis/Religious Program—Students 43.

5—BLESSED TRINITY (2009) Rev. Joseph A. Warner; Sr. Mercia Madigan, O.S.U., Pastoral Min.
300 E. Tallmadge Ave., 44310-2399. Tel: 330-376-5144; Fax: 330-376-5311.
Catechesis/Religious Program—Mrs. Linda Herold, D.R.E. Students 26.

6—CHRIST THE KING (1935) Closed. For inquiries for parish records contact Blessed Trinity, Akron.

7—ST. FRANCIS DE SALES (1948) Revs. G. David Bline; Anthony J. Suso, Parochial Vicar; Deacons Richard C. Butz; Raymond S. Herrick.
Res.: 4019 Manchester Rd., 44319-2193. Tel: 330-644-2225; 330-644-2226.
School—4009 Manchester Rd., 44319. Tel: 330-644-0638; Fax: 330-644-2663. Sherry Parrish, Prin. Lay Teachers 21; Students 298.
Catechesis/Religious Program—Students 217.

8—ST. HEDWIG (1912), (Polish), Closed. For inquiries for parish records contact the chancery.

9—ST. HILARY (1958) Revs. Steven K. Brunovsky; Gordon A. Yahner, Pastor Emeritus (Retired); Francis J. Basa, Senior Assoc.; Sr. Marlene LoGrasso, O.S.U., Pastoral Assoc.
Res.: 615 Moorfield Rd., Fairlawn, 44333-4236. Tel: 330-867-1055; Fax: 330-869-2312.
Church: 2750 W. Market St., Fairlawn, 44333-4236.
School—645 Moorfield Rd., Fairlawn, 44333. Tel: 330-867-8720; Fax: 330-867-5081. Mrs. Tracy Arnone, Prin. Religious 1; Lay Teachers 36; Students 622.
Catechesis/Religious Program—Students 316.

10—IMMACULATE CONCEPTION (1923) Rev. Michael B. Smith; Melissa Keegan, Pastoral Assoc. In Res., Rev. Samuel R. Ciccolini.
Res.: 2101 17th St., S.W., 44314-2315. Tel: 330-753-8429; Fax: 330-753-7440.
Church: 2100 16th St., S.W., 44314.
Catechesis/Religious Program—Students 12.

11—ST. JOHN THE BAPTIST (1907), (Slovak), Closed. For inquiries for parish records contact Visitation of Mary, Akron.

12—ST. MARTHA (1919) Closed. For inquiries for parish records contact Blessed Trinity, Akron.

13—ST. MARY (1887), For information call the Chancery.
Res.: 750 S. Main St., 44311-1094. Tel: 330-762-9247; Fax: 330-252-1768.
School—Tel: 330-253-1233; Fax: 330-253-1472. Mr. David M. Csank, Prin. Lay Teachers 13; Students 197.
Catechesis/Religious Program—Students 12.

14—ST. MATTHEW (1943) Revs. G. Michael Williamson; Thomas A. McGovern, Pastor Emeritus (Retired). In Res., Revs. Dismas Byarugala, A.J.; Milton Kiocha, A.J.
Res.: 2603 Benton Ave., 44312-1694. Tel: 330-733-9944; Fax: 330-733-9424.
Church: Berne & Woolf St., 44312.
School—2580 Benton Ave., 44312. Tel: 330-784-1711; Fax: 330-733-1004. Diane Kee, Prin. Lay Teachers 16; Students 272.
Catechesis/Religious Program—Students 193.

15—NATIVITY OF THE LORD JESUS (1977) Rev. David J. Halaiko; Deacon Dennis L. Smith.
Res.: 2425 Myersville Rd., 44312-4951. Tel: 330-699-5086; Fax: 330-699-4299.
Catechesis/Religious Program—Students 87.

16—ST. PAUL (1919) Revs. Ralph W. Thomas; John M. Jenkins, Pastor Emeritus (Retired); Therese Nesline, Pastoral Assoc.
Res.: 433 Mission Dr., 44301-2798. Tel: 330-724-1263; Fax: 330-724-7680.
School—1580 Brown St., 44301-2798. Tel: 330-724-1253; Fax: 330-724-1127. Mr. Robert Brodbeck, Prin. Lay Teachers 15; Students 198.
Catechesis/Religious Program—Students 91.

17—ST. PETER (1917) Closed. For inquiries for parish records contact St. Mary Parish, Akron.

18—SACRED HEART OF JESUS (1915), (Hungarian), Closed. For inquiries for parish records contact the Archives of the Diocese of Cleveland.

19—ST. SEBASTIAN (1928) Revs. John A. Valencheck; William D. Karg, Pastor Emeritus (Retired); John T. McDonough, Pastor Emeritus (Retired); Matthew E. Pfeiffer, Parochial Vicar; Deacon Terry W. Peacock. In Res., Rev. Thaddeus M. Swirski (Retired).
Res.: 476 Mull Ave., 44320-1299. Tel: 330-836-2233; Fax: 330-836-2235.
School—500 Mull Ave., 44320. Tel: 330-836-9107; Fax: 330-836-7690. Mr. Gregory Garey, Prin. Lay Teachers 27; Students 475.
Catechesis/Religious Program—Students 187.

20—ST. VINCENT (1837) [CEM] Rev. Joseph H. Kraker. In Res., Revs. Gordon A. Yahner (Retired); David L. McCafferty (Retired).
Res.: 164 W. Market St., 44303-2373. Tel: 330-535-3135; Fax: 330-535-4160.
Church: W. Market St. & Maple St., 44303.
School—17 S. Maple St., 44303. Tel: 330-762-5912; Fax: 330-535-2515. James Tawney, Prin. Lay Teachers 22; Students 225.
Catechesis/Religious Program—Students 66.

21—VISITATION OF MARY (2009) Rev. A. Jonathan Zingales; Diana Herhold, Pastoral Min.
87 Broad St., 44305. Tel: 330-535-4141; Fax: 330-475-0054.
Catechesis/Religious Program—Students 20.

AMHERST, LORAIN CO., ST. JOSEPH (1864) [CEM] Revs. Lawrence N. Martello; Michael J. Denk; Maria Maldonado, Pastoral Assoc.; Deacons Daniel Hancock; Paul Heise. In Res., Rev. Denis L. St. Marie (Retired).
Res.: 200 St. Joseph Dr., 44001-1663. Tel: 440-988-2848; 440-988-2849; Fax: 440-984-2301.
School—175 St. Joseph Dr., 44001. Tel: 440-988-4244; Fax: 440-988-5249. Mrs. Karen Casper-Linn, Prin. Lay Teachers 15; Students 244.
Catechesis/Religious Program—Students 392.
Convent—151 St. Joseph Dr., 44001. Tel: 440-988-2621.

ASHLAND, ASHLAND CO., ST. EDWARD (1853) [JC] Revs. James M. Cassidy, Pastor Emeritus (Retired); Rodney A. Kreidler; Deacons James A. Kaniecki; Joseph R. Dietz.
Res. & Administration Center: 501 Cottage St., 44805-2167. Tel: 419-289-7224; Fax: 419-289-0515.
School—433 Cottage St., 44805. Tel: 419-289-7456; Fax: 419-289-9474. Suellen Valentine, Prin. Lay Teachers 16; Students 143.
Catechesis/Religious Program—Students 43.

AVON, LORAIN CO.

1—HOLY TRINITY (1833) [CEM] Revs. John A. Misenko; John J. Gorski, Pastor Emeritus (Retired).
Res.: 33601 Detroit Rd., 44011-1999. Tel: 440-937-5363; Fax: 440-937-5128.
School—2610 Nagel Rd., 44011. Tel: 440-937-6420; Fax: 440-937-1029. Mary Marunowski, Prin. Lay Teachers 22; Students 534.
Catechesis/Religious Program—Students 650.
Convent—2620 Nagel Rd., 44011. Tel: 440-937-5005.

2—ST. MARY OF THE IMMACULATE CONCEPTION (1841) [CEM] Revs. C. Thomas Cleaton; Arthur B. Egan, Pastor Emeritus (Retired).
Res.: 2640 Stoney Ridge Rd., 44011-1899. Tel: 440-934-4212; Fax: 440-934-0507.
School—2680 Stoney Ridge Rd., 44011-1899. Tel: 440-934-6246; Fax: 440-934-6250. John Stipek, Prin. Lay Teachers 14; Students 198.
Catechesis/Religious Program—Students 252.
Convent—2680 Stoney Ridge Rd., 44011. Tel: 440-934-5173.

AVON LAKE, LORAIN CO.

1—HOLY SPIRIT (1965) Rev. James H. Beatty; Patricia A. Kassay, Pastoral Assoc.; Deacon Robert K. Walling.
Res.: 410 Lear Rd., 44012-2004. Tel: 440-933-3777; 440-871-8157 (Cleveland Line); Fax: 440-871-8157.
Catechesis/Religious Program—Tel: 440-933-8818. Students 527.

2—ST. JOSEPH (1949) Rev. Timothy J. O'Connor.
Res.: 32929 Lake Rd., 44012-1497. Tel: 440-933-3152; 440-933-4022; Fax: 440-933-8919.
School—Tel: 440-933-6233; Fax: 440-933-2463. Mrs. Patricia Vaccaro, Prin. Lay Teachers 24; Students 338.
Catechesis/Religious Program—Students 270.
Convent—32911 Lake Rd., 44012. Tel: 216-933-5769.

BARBERTON, SUMMIT CO.

1—ST. AUGUSTINE (1898) Revs. David J. Majikas; William A. Smith; Deacons Robin Adair; Harold R. Krause.
Res.: 204 Sixth St., N.W., 44203-2198. Tel: 330-745-0011; Fax: 330-745-0012.
Church: Corner of Sixth St., N.W. & Lake Ave., 44203.
School—195 Seventh St., N.W., 44203. Tel: 330-753-6435; Fax: 330-753-4095. Elaine Faessel, Prin. Lay Teachers 17; Students 210.
Catechesis/Religious Program—Students 129.

2—SS. CYRIL AND METHODIUS (1906), (Slovak), Closed. For inquiries for parish records contact the chancery.

3—HOLY TRINITY (1911), (Magyar), Closed. For inquiries for parish records contact the chancery.

4—ST. MARY'S (1912), (Polish), Closed. For inquiries for parish records contact the chancery.

5—SACRED HEART (1916), (Slovenian), Closed. For inquiries for parish records contact the chancery.

BAY VILLAGE, CUYAHOGA CO., ST. RAPHAEL (1946) Revs. Timothy W. Gareau; Nelson J. Callahan, Pastor Emeritus (Retired); Steven H. Breck, Parochial Vicar; Deacon Larry D. Gregg; Terri Telepak, Pastoral Assoc. In Res., Rev. Albert A. Krupp.
Res.: 525 Dover Center Rd., 44140-2366. Tel: 440-871-1100; Fax: 440-899-2911.
School—Tel: 440-871-6760; Fax: 440-871-1358. Ann Miller, Prin. Lay Teachers 36; Students 782.
Catechesis/Religious Program—Students 757.

BEDFORD, CUYAHOGA CO.

1—ST. MARY (1910) Closed. For inquiries for parish records contact Our Lady of Hope, Bedford.

2—OUR LADY OF HOPE (2009) Rev. John J. Wright; Deacon Daniel C. Terrion; Mrs. Louise Martin, Pastoral Assoc.
400 Center Rd., 44146-2296. Tel: 400-232-8166; Fax: 440-786-9929.
School—*Holy Spirit Academy*, 370 Center Rd., 44146. Tel: 440-232-1531; Fax: 440-232-1534. Email: holyspirit@leeca.org. Web: www.hsabedford.org. Mrs. Sharon Vejdovec, Prin.; Mrs. Debbie Sigmund, Sec.; Mrs. Jean Oulton, Librarian. Lay Teachers 10.
Catechesis/Religious Program—Mrs. Carolyn Zaranec, D.R.E. Students 25.

3—ST. PIUS X (1952) Closed. For inquiries for parish records contact Our Lady of Hope, Bedford.

BEDFORD HEIGHTS, CUYAHOGA CO., HOLY TRINITY (1965) Closed. For inquiries for parish records contact Holy Trinity, Bedford Heights.

BEREA, CUYAHOGA CO.

1—ST. ADALBERT (1873), (Polish), [CEM] Revs. Barry T. Gearing; Gerald J. Keller, Pastor Emeritus (Retired); Deacon Edmund A. Gardias.
Res.: 66 Adalbert St., 44017-1799. Tel: 440-234-6830; Fax: 440-234-2588.
School—*Academy of St. Adalbert*, 56 Adalbert St.,

44017. Tel: 440-234-5529; Fax: 440-234-2881. Mrs. Martha K. Jacobs, Prin. Lay Teachers 12; Students 183.
Catechesis/Religious Program—Students 165.
Convent—24 Adalbert St., 44017. Tel: 440-234-1096.
2—ST. MARY (1852) [CEM] Revs. George A. Vrabel; Christopher H. Weber, Parochial Vicar; Deacon Thomas Grasson.
Res.: 250 Kraft St., 44017-1449. Tel: 440-243-3877; 440-243-3878; Fax: 440-891-9417.
School—265 Baker St., 44017-1515. Tel: 440-243-4555; Fax: 440-243-6214. Andrew Carner, Prin. Lay Teachers 27; Students 412.
Catechesis/Religious Program—Students 222.
BRECKSVILLE, CUYAHOGA CO., ST. BASIL THE GREAT (1960) Revs. Walter H. Jenne; David D. Liberatore, Parochial Vicar; Deacon Louis M. Primozic; Sr. Judith Wood, S.S.J.-T.O.S.F., Pastoral Assoc.; Mrs. Robin Youngs, Pastoral Assoc.
Res.: 8700 Brecksville Rd., 44141-1999. Tel: 440-526-1686; 440-526-1687; Fax: 440-526-2373.
Catechesis/Religious Program—Tel: 440-526-3520; 440-526-3587. Mrs. Mary Ann Webb, D.R.E. Students 899.
Convent—6901 Mill Rd., 44141. Tel: 440-526-2850.
BROADVIEW HEIGHTS, CUYAHOGA CO., ASSUMPTION (1857) Rev. Justin Drywal, O.S.B.; Deacon David A. Streeter.
Res.: 9183 Broadview Rd., 44147-2596. Tel: 440-526-1177; 440-526-1178; Fax: 440-526-2838.
School—Tel: 440-526-4877; Fax: 440-526-3752. Donna Sejba, Prin. Sisters of Incarnate Word 1; Lay Teachers 18; Students 345.
Catechesis/Religious Program—Students 320.
Convent—9139 Broadview Rd., 44147. Tel: 216-526-4069.
BROOK PARK, CUYAHOGA CO.
1—ASSUMPTION OF MARY (1860) [CEM] Closed. For inquiries for parish records contact Mary Queen of the Apostles Parish, Brook Park.
2—MARY QUEEN OF THE APOSTLES PARISH (2010) Revs. James R. Stenger; Gregory J. Olszewski; Deacons John R. Zdolshek; Francis B. Wilson.
6455 Engle Rd., Brookpark, 44142-3503. Tel: 216-433-1440; Fax: 216-433-1434.
Catechesis/Religious Program—Patricia Solon, D.R.E. Students 257.
3—ST. PETER THE APOSTLE (1968) Closed. For inquiries for parish records contact Mary Queen of the Apostles Parish, Brook Park.
BROOKLYN, CUYAHOGA CO., ST. THOMAS MORE (1946) Revs. William G. Bouhall; James J. Vesely, Pastor Emeritus (Retired); Sr. Elaine Theresa Burrows, S.I.W., Pastoral Assoc.; Deacons Martin A. Thiel; Charles W. Zawadzki; Rudolph Jarosh Jr. In Res., Rev. Arthur Snedeker.
Res.: 4170 N. Amber Dr., 44144-1399. Tel: 216-749-0414; 216-749-0415; Fax: 216-749-1001.
School—4180 N. Amber Dr., 44144. Tel: 216-749-1660; Fax: 216-398-4265. Mrs. Jennifer Francis, Prin. Lay Teachers 16; Students 258.
Catechesis/Religious Program—Students 98.
BRUNSWICK, MEDINA CO.
1—ST. AMBROSE (1957) Revs. Robert G. Stec; Dennis McNeil, Parochial Vicar; Robert Wenz, Parochial Vicar; Deacons Clement J. Belter; Thomas J. Sheridan; Gary R. Tomazic.
Res.: 929 Pearl Rd., 44212-2597. Tel: 330-225-3116; Fax: 330-220-1748.
School—923 Pearl Rd., 44212. Tel: 330-225-2116; Fax: 330-225-5425. Christine Bopp, Prin. Lay Teachers 22; Students 536.
Catechesis/Religious Program—Students 825.
2—ST. COLETTE (1977) Revs. William R. Krizner; Thomas G. Montavon, Pastor Emeritus (Retired); Arthur A. Bacher, Senior Priest (Retired).
Res.: 330 W. 130th St., 44212-2309. Tel: 330-273-5500; Fax: 330-225-7909.
Catechesis/Religious Program—Students 303.
CHAGRIN FALLS, CUYAHOGA CO.
1—HOLY ANGELS (1977) Revs. Daniel F. Schlegel; Clyde K. Foster, Parochial Vicar; Sr. Susan Javorek, S.N.D., Pastoral Assoc.; Deacons Stephen L. Yates; Vincent L. Belsito.
Res.: 8390 Stoney Brook Dr., 44023-4879. Fax: 440-708-0787.
Church: 18205 Chillicothe Rd., 44023-4879. Tel: 440-708-0000.
Catechesis/Religious Program—Tel: 440-708-0808. Students 1,002.
2—ST. JOAN OF ARC (1948) Revs. David J. Walkowiak; John J. Kinkopf, Pastor Emeritus (Retired); John R. Olsavsky, Pastor Emeritus (Retired); Gary J. Malin; Sr. Ann Marie Kanusek, S.N.D., Pastoral Assoc.; Deacons Jeffrey Dunlop; Dennis A. Guritza.
Res.: 496 E. Washington St., 44022-2999. Tel: 440-247-7183; Fax: 440-247-2327.
School—498 E. Washington St., 44022-2998. Tel: 440-247-6530; Fax: 440-247-2045. Shelley DiBacco, Prin. Lay Teachers 16; Students 184.
Catechesis/Religious Program—Tel: 440-247-3606. Sr. Judith Bucco, D.R.E. Students 365.
Convent—456 E. Washington St., 44022. Tel: 440-247-4419.
CHARDON, GEAUGA CO., ST. MARY (1909) Revs. Daniel P. Redmond; Timothy D. Kalista; Carol Burtnett, Pastoral Assoc.; Deacons Lawrence Boehnlein; Thomas J. Peshek.
Res.: 401 North St., 44024-1087. Tel: 440-285-7051; Fax: 440-286-3886.
School—Tel: 440-286-3590; Fax: 440-285-2818. Sr. Mary Sandra Nativio, S.N.D., Prin. Sisters of Notre Dame 1; Lay Teachers 20; Students 318.
Catechesis/Religious Program—Students 527.
Convent—315 North St., 44024. Tel: 440-286-5641.
CHESTERLAND, GEAUGA CO., ST. ANSELM (1961) Rev. Thomas M. Sweany; Deacons Donald E. Sill; Robert Kovach; Jean Fitzgerald, Pastoral Assoc.
Church & Res.: 12969 Chillicothe Rd., 44026-3115. Tel: 440-729-9575; Fax: 440-729-9103.
School—Tel: 440-729-7806; Fax: 440-729-3524. Miss Joan Agresta, Prin. Lay Teachers 19; Students 268.
Catechesis/Religious Program—Students 470.
Convent—13055 Chillicothe Rd., 44026. Tel: 440-729-0292.
CLEVELAND HEIGHTS, CUYAHOGA CO.
1—ST. ANN (1915) Closed. For inquiries for parish records contact Communion of Saints Parish, Cleveland Heights.
2—COMMUNION OF SAINTS PARISH (2010) Revs. John P. McNulty; Daniel Begin, Parochial Vicar; Patrick S. Anderson, Parochial Vicar; Ms. Renee Barber, Pastoral Min.; Deacons Richard E. Woods; Raymond L. Daull.
Res.: 2175 Coventry Rd., 44118-2898. Tel: 216-321-0024; Fax: 216-321-7702.
Worship Site of Communion of Saints Parish at St. Philomena Church— (2010) 13824 Euclid Ave., East Cleveland, 44112.
School—2160 Stillman Rd., 44118. Tel: 216-932-4177; Fax: 216-932-7439. Meg Cosgriff, Prin. Lay Teachers 17; Students 267.
Catechesis/Religious Program—Students 58.
3—ST. LOUIS (1947) Closed. For inquiries for parish records contact Communion of Saints Parish, Cleveland Heights.
CLINTON, SUMMIT CO., ST. GEORGE (1908) Closed. For inquiries for parish records, contact SS. Peter & Paul Parish, Doylestown, OH.
COLUMBIA STATION, LORAIN CO., ST. ELIZABETH ANN SETON (1976) Rev. Charles J. Ryba.
Mailing Address: 25777 Royalton Rd., P.O. Box 968, 44028-0968.
Res.: 25777 Royalton Rd., 44028-0968. Tel: 440-236-5095; Fax: 440-236-5804.
Church: 25801 Royalton Rd., 44028.
Catechesis/Religious Program—Tel: 440-236-3711. Students 134.
CONCORD TWP., LAKE CO., ST. GABRIEL (1966) Revs. Frederick F. Pausche; Christopher J. Zerucha; Robert J. Kropac; Deacons Ronald Adkins; Daniel P. Clavin; Robert H. Grgic; Maureen Dowd, Pastoral Assoc.; Paul Kelly, Pastoral Assoc.
Res.: 9925 Johnnycake Ridge Rd., 44060-6294. Tel: 440-352-8282; 440-953-3867 (Cleveland); Fax: 440-354-7558.
School—9935 Johnnycake Ridge Rd., 44060. Tel: 440-352-6169; Fax: 440-639-0143. Donna Lee Saladino, Prin. Lay Teachers 35; Students 942.
Catechesis/Religious Program—Students 494.
Convent—9918 Johnnycake Ridge Rd., 44060. Tel: 440-354-7553.
COPLEY, SUMMIT CO., GUARDIAN ANGELS (1964) Rev. James F. Kramer; Rev. Msgr. Robert C. Wolff, Pastor Emeritus (Retired).
Church & Res.: 1686 Cleveland-Massillon Rd., 44321-1976. Tel: 330-666-1373; Fax: 330-666-8189.
Catechesis/Religious Program—Students 166.
CUYAHOGA FALLS, SUMMIT CO.
1—ST. EUGENE (1963) Rev. Neil A. Crosby.
Res.: 1821 Munroe Falls Ave., 44221-3699. Tel: 330-923-5244; Fax: 330-923-8436.
Catechesis/Religious Program—Students 130.
2—IMMACULATE HEART OF MARY (1952) Revs. Thomas W. McCann, Pastor Emeritus (Retired); John R. Rathfon, Pastor Emeritus (Retired); James E. Singler; Deacons Gregory Hoefler; William J. Yoho Jr. In Res., Revs. Robert E. Pahler (Retired); Joseph C. Weigand (Retired).
Res.: 1905 Portage Tr., 44223-1792. Tel: 330-929-8361; 330-929-8362; 330-929-8399; Fax: 330-929-8496.
School—2859 Lillis Dr., 44223. Tel: 330-923-1220; Fax: 330-929-4373. Robert Hardesty, Prin. Lay Teachers 24; Students 378.
Catechesis/Religious Program—Students 104.
3—ST. JOSEPH (1831) Rev. James J. Marsick; Deacon Robert Kochanski. In Res., Rev. David J. McCarthy (Retired).
Res.: 215 Falls Ave., 44221-3999. Tel: 330-928-2173; Fax: 330-928-3082.
Church: 1761 Second St., 44221.
School—1909 Third St., 44221-3894. Tel: 330-928-2151; Fax: 330-928-3139. Dr. Patricia Nugent, Prin. Lay Teachers 24; Students 342.
Catechesis/Religious Program—Students 31.
DOYLESTOWN, WAYNE CO., SS. PETER AND PAUL (1827) [CEM] [JC] Revs. Robert E. Stein; David J. McCarthy, Pastor Emeritus (Retired); Deacon Dale A. Youngblood.
Res.: 161 W. Clinton St., 44230-1297. Tel: 330-658-2145.
School—169 W. Clinton St., 44230. Tel: 330-658-2804; Fax: 330-658-2287. Susan Demeter, Prin. Lay Teachers 13; Students 151.
Catechesis/Religious Program—Students 150.
EAST CLEVELAND, CUYAHOGA CO.
1—CHRIST THE KING (1928) Closed. For inquiries for parish records contact Communion of Saints Parish, Cleveland Heights.
2—ST. PHILOMENA (1902) Closed. For inquiries for parish records contact Communion of Saints Parish, Cleveland Heights.
EASTLAKE, LAKE CO., ST. JUSTIN MARTYR (1962) Rev. Kevin M. Liebhardt.
Mailing Address: 35781 Stevens Blvd., 44095-5095. Tel: 440-946-1177; Fax: 440-946-9126. In Res., Rev. Joseph Hilinski.
Administration Center—Tel: 440-946-1177.
Res.: 35701 Stevens Blvd., 44095.
See St. Mary Magdalene-St. Justin Martyr under Elementary Schools Parochial & Diocesan located in the Institution section.
Catechesis/Religious Program—Students 190.
Convent—35711 Stevens Blvd., 44095. Tel: 440-946-1013.
ELYRIA, LORAIN CO.
1—ST. AGNES (1914) Rev. Albert Veigas; Deacon Bruce H. Tennant; Sr. Jennifer Kramer, S.N.D., Pastoral Assoc.
611 Lake Ave., 44035-3541. Tel: 440-322-5622; Fax: 440-322-0231.
Catechesis/Religious Program—Tel: 440-366-5999. Students 77.
2—HOLY CROSS (1922), (Polish), Closed. For inquiries for parish records contact the chancery.
3—ST. JUDE (1943) Revs. Frank P. Kosem; John G. Vrana, Senior Assoc.; Deacon Patrick J. Humphrey.
Res.: 590 Poplar St., 44035-3999. Tel: 440-366-5711; Fax: 440-366-1916.
School—594 Poplar St., 44035. Tel: 440-366-1681; Fax: 440-366-5238. Suzanne Lester, Prin. Lay Teachers 22; Students 385.
Catechesis/Religious Program—Students 165.
Convent—342 Longford, 44035. Tel: 440-366-1551.
4—ST. MARY (1845) [CEM] Revs. Charles T. Diedrick; Joseph C. Weigand, Pastor Emeritus (Retired); Sr. Mary Dorothy Tecca, C.S.A., Pastoral Assoc.; Deacons Frank A. Humphrey III; Edward R. Dillon.
Res.: 12531 State Rte. 301, Lagrange, 44050. Tel: 440-897-6972.
School—237 Fourth St., 44035. Tel: 440-322-2808; Fax: 440-322-1423. Sharon Brunkow, Prin. Lay Teachers 16; Students 190.
Catechesis/Religious Program—Tel: 440-322-3054. Students 119.
Convent—235 Fourth St., 44035-5796. Tel: 440-322-1423.
5—SACRED HEART OF JESUS (1922), (Hungarian), Closed. For inquiries for parish records contact the chancery.
ELYRIA TOWNSHIP, LORAIN CO., ST. VINCENT DE PAUL (1949) Revs. James R. Ols; William J. Kitt, Pastor Emeritus (Retired); Deacons John K. Slatcoff; Edgar Gonzalez.
Res.: 41295 N. Ridge Rd., 44035-1098. Tel: 440-324-4212; 440-277-5285; Fax: 440-324-2892.
Catechesis/Religious Program—Students 141.
EUCLID, CUYAHOGA CO.
1—ST. CHRISTINE (1925) Closed. For inquiries for parish records contact Our Lady of the Lake Parish, Euclid.
2—ST. FELICITAS (1950) Closed. For inquiries for parish records contact St. John of the Cross, Euclid.
3—HOLY CROSS (1924) Closed. For inquiries for parish records contact Our Lady of the Lake Parish, Euclid.
4—ST. JOHN OF THE CROSS (2009) Rev. Salvatore M. Ruggeri; Deacon Charles Doerpers; Lisa Radey, Pastoral Min.
140 Richmond Rd., 44143-1299. Tel: 216-289-0770; Fax: 216-289-0740.
School—St. John of the Cross School, Tel: 216-261-1240; Fax: 216-261-5843. Martha Dodd, Prin. Lay Teachers 20; Students 342.
Catechesis/Religious Program—Mrs. Rosalie A. Lewis, D.R.E. Students 33.
5—OUR LADY OF THE LAKE PARISH (2010) Rev. Joseph J. Fortuna; Mr. Shawn Witmer, Pastoral Assoc.; Mrs. Dana Heil, Pastoral Min.
19951 Lake Shore Blvd., 44123. Tel: 216-486-0850;

Fax: 216-486-0851.
School—Our Lady of the Lake Elementary School, 175 E. 200th St., 44119. Tel: 216-481-9841; Fax: 216-481-9841. Sr. Laura Bregar, O.S.U., Prin. Religious 1; Lay Teachers 21; Students 322.
Catechesis/Religious Program—Students 107.
6—ST. PAUL (1860) [CEM] Closed. For inquiries for parish records contact St. John of the Cross, Euclid.
7—SS. ROBERT & WILLIAM (2010) Revs. John D. Betters; David A. Novak, Parochial Vicar; Sr. Irene Charette, O.S.U., Pastoral Min.; Mrs. Gail Monroe, Pastoral Assoc.
367 E. 260th St., 44132-1495. Tel: 216-731-1515; Fax: 216-731-0300. In Res., Rev. Joseph A. Goebel (Retired).
School—SS. Robert & William, 351 E. 260 St., 44132. Tel: 216-731-3060. Miss Susan Pohly, Prin. Lay Teachers 23; Students 387.
Catechesis/Religious Program—Students 77.
8—ST. ROBERT BELLARMINE (1950) Closed. For inquiries for parish records contact SS. Robert & William, Euclid.
9—ST. WILLIAM (1946) Closed. For inquiries for parish records contact SS. Robert & William, Euclid.
FAIRPORT HARBOR, LAKE CO., ST. ANTHONY OF PADUA (1887) Rev. Peter M. Mihalic; Shanon Sterringer, Pastoral Assoc.; Deacon John T. Wenzel.
Res.: 316 Fifth St., 44077-5696. Tel: 440-354-4525; Fax: 440-354-8313.
Catechesis/Religious Program—Students 180.
FAIRVIEW PARK, CUYAHOGA CO., ST. ANGELA MERICI (1923) Revs. Michael J. Lanning; Gregory F. Schaut, Parochial Vicar; Joseph R. Spolny, Parochial Vicar; Deacons James L. Agrippe, (Retired); Erick Lupson.
Res.: 20970 Lorain Rd., 44126-2096. Tel: 440-333-2133; Fax: 440-333-8061.
School—20830 Lorain Rd., 44126. Tel: 440-333-2126; Fax: 440-333-8480. Denise Modic Urban, Prin. Lay Teachers 23; Students 520.
Catechesis/Religious Program—Tel: 216-333-2133. Students 277.
GARFIELD HEIGHTS, CUYAHOGA CO.
1—HOLY SPIRIT PARISH (2008) Rev. Philip J. Bernier, O.F.M.Cap.; Sr. Kathleen McCafferty, S.N.D., Pastoral Assoc.; Deacons Shelby Friend; Ronald R. James.
4341 E. 131st St., 44105-5563. Tel: 216-581-0981; Fax: 216-581-8222.
See Archbishop James P. Lyke Elementary School, Cleveland under Elementary Schools, Parochial and Diocesan located in the Institution section.
Catechesis/Religious Program—Students 131.
2—ST. MONICA (1952) Rev. Thomas A. Haren; Deacon Ralph W. Netzband, (Retired). In Res., Revs. Thomas G. Montavon (Retired); Jerome A. Lukachinsky (Retired).
Res.: 13623 Rockside Rd., 44125-5197. Tel: 216-662-8685; 216-662-8686; 216-662-8687; Fax: 216-662-1245.
School—13633 Rockside Rd., 44125. Tel: 216-662-9380; Fax: 216-662-3137. Ruth Downey, Prin. Lay Teachers 20; Students 303.
Catechesis/Religious Program—Students 46.
Convent—Tel: 216-581-0810.
3—SS. PETER AND PAUL (1927), (Polish), Rev. Michael A. Matusz; Deacon William R. Starkey. In Res., Rev. Donald P. Oleksiak.
Res.: 4750 Turney Rd., 44125-1448. Tel: 216-429-1515; 216-429-1516; Fax: 216-429-1889.
See John Paul II Academy, Garfield Heights under Elementary Schools, Parochial and Diocesan in the Institution Section.
Catechesis/Religious Program—Students 46.
Convent—Tel: 216-429-2666.
4—ST. THERESE (1927) Revs. Daniel R. Fickes; Norman A. Gajdzinski, Pastor Emeritus (Retired); Deacon Robert J. Bugaj.
Res.: 5276 E. 105th St., 44125-2698. Tel: 216-581-2852; 216-581-2853; Fax: 216-581-5091. In Res., Rev. Thomas V. O'Donnell (Retired).
See John Paul II Academy, Garfield Heights under Elementary Schools, Parochial and Diocesan in the Institution Section.
Catechesis/Religious Program—Sr. DeAnne Zawadzki, S.S.J.T.O.S.F., D.R.E. Students 93.
5—ST. TIMOTHY (1923) Closed. For inquiries for parish records, contact the Archives, Diocese of Cleveland.
GATES MILLS, CUYAHOGA CO., ST. FRANCIS OF ASSISI (1943) Revs. James L. Caddy; Franz C. Dool; Deacons Leo F. McNulty; William T. Elwood; Martha Stewart, Pastoral Assoc.
Res.: 6850 Mayfield Rd., 44040-9635. Tel: 440-461-0066; Fax: 440-461-9053.
School—Tel: 440-442-7450; Fax: 440-446-1132. Adrienne Publicover, Prin. Religious 1; Lay Teachers 26; Students 446.
Catechesis/Religious Program—Students 237.
GRAFTON, LORAIN CO.
1—ASSUMPTION (1894), (Polish), Closed. For inquiries for parish records contact the chancery.
2—IMMACULATE CONCEPTION (1835) [CEM] Closed. For inquiries for parish records contact the chancery.
3—OUR LADY QUEEN OF PEACE PARISH Rev. John P. Seabold.
708 Erie St., 44044. Tel: 440-926-2364; Fax: 440-926-3783.
Catechesis/Religious Program—Nancy Johnson, D.R.E. Students 168.
HIGHLAND HEIGHTS, CUYAHOGA CO., ST. PASCHAL BAYLON (1953) Revs. John Thomas Lane, S.S.S.; William Fickel, S.S.S., Parochial Vicar; Paul Bernier, S.S.S.; Roger Bourgeois, S.S.S.; Deacons Robert J. Bowers; Joseph Bourgeois.
Res.: 5384 Wilson Mills Rd., 44143-3092. Tel: 440-442-3410; Fax: 440-442-2001.
School—5360 Wilson Mills Rd., 44143. Tel: 440-442-6766; Fax: 440-446-9037. Mr. John V. Bednar, Prin. Lay Teachers 28; Students 473.
Catechesis/Religious Program—Students 258.
HINCKLEY, MEDINA CO., OUR LADY OF GRACE (1965) Revs. Joseph S. Mecir; William P. O'Neill, Pastor Emeritus (Retired). In Res., Rev. John T. McDonough (Retired).
Res.: 1088 Ridge Rd., 44233-9602. Tel: 330-278-4121; Fax: 330-278-2849.
Catechesis/Religious Program—Students 292.
HUDSON, SUMMIT CO., ST. MARY (1860) [CEM] Revs. Edward J. Kordas; Kevin P. Elbert, Parochial Vicar; Sr. Barbara Einloth, S.C., Pastoral Assoc.; Deacon Carl H. Winterich; Rose Gordyan, Pastoral Assoc.
Res.: 340 N. Main St., 44236-2242. Tel: 330-653-8118; Fax: 330-463-5759.
Church: 340 N. Main St., 44236.
Catechesis/Religious Program—Students 929.
INDEPENDENCE, CUYAHOGA CO., ST. MICHAEL (1851) [CEM] Revs. Peter Colletti; Carl L. D'Agostino, Pastor Emeritus (Retired); Janice M. Wisnieski, Pastoral Assoc.; Deacons James Vincent; Neal J. Novak.
Res.: 6912 Chestnut Rd., 44131-3399. Tel: 216-524-1394; 216-524-1395; Fax: 216-328-8537.
Church: 6540 Brecksville Rd., 44131.
School—6906 Chestnut Rd., 44131. Tel: 216-524-6405; Fax: 216-524-7538. Margaret Campisi, Prin. Lay Teachers 22; Students 434.
Catechesis/Religious Program—Tel: 216-447-4406. Students 353.
Convent—6800 Chestnut Rd., 44131-3399. Tel: 216-447-4406.
KIRTLAND, LAKE CO., DIVINE WORD (1977) Rev. David G. Woost; Deacon Carl M. Varga.
Res.: 8100 Eagle Rd., 44094-9714. Tel: 440-256-1412; 440-256-1413; 440-256-1417; Fax: 440-256-4929.
Peaceful Children Montessori—Tel: 440-256-1976; Fax: 440-256-4370. Jennifer Massiello, Prin. Lay Teachers 7; Students 72.
Catechesis/Religious Program—Students 148.
LAKEWOOD, CUYAHOGA CO.
1—ST. CLEMENT (1922) Revs. Joseph G. Workman; Alfred H. Winters, Pastor Emeritus (Retired).
Res.: 2022 Lincoln Ave., 44107-6099. Tel: 216-226-5116; Fax: 216-226-5117.
Church: Madison & Lincoln Aves., 44107.
See Lakewood Catholic Academy, Lakewood under Elementary Schools Parochial and Diocesan in the Institution Section.
Catechesis/Religious Program—Students 76.
Convent—14505 Madison Ave., 44107.
2—SS. CYRIL AND METHODIUS (1902), (Slovak), Closed. For inquiries for parish records contact the chancery.
3—ST. HEDWIG (1905), (Polish), Closed. For inquiries for parish records contact the Archives of the Diocese of Cleveland.
4—ST. JAMES (1908), For information call the Chancery.
Res.: 17514 Detroit Ave., 44107-3498. Tel: 216-221-0233; Fax: 216-221-2431.
Church: Detroit & Granger Ave., 44107.
Catechesis/Religious Program—Students 126.
5—ST. LUKE (1922) Rev. Francis P. Walsh; Marilyn Streeter, Pastoral Assoc.; Deacon John D. Henderson.
Res.: 1212 Bunts Rd., 44107-2699. Tel: 216-521-0184; 216-521-0185; 216-521-0186; Fax: 216-521-9360.
See Lakewood Catholic Academy, Lakewood under the Elementary Schools, Parochial and Diocesan in the Institution Section.
Catechesis/Religious Program—Students 184.
6—TRANSFIGURATION Rev. William J. Rooney, O.F.M. 12608 Madison Ave., 44107. Tel: 216-521-7288; Fax: 216-521-7005.
LITCHFIELD, MEDINA CO., OUR LADY HELP OF CHRISTIANS PARISH (1976) Rev. Ronald J. Bryda, Coord. Pastoral Team; Deacon Michael F. Jervis Sr.; Rev. Edward F. Weist, Pastoral Team; Sandra J. Lynn, Pastoral Team. In Res., Rev. James M. Cassidy (Retired).
Administration Center—9608 Norwalk Rd., 44253-9598. Tel: 330-722-1180; 330-273-1500 (Cleveland); Fax: 330-723-5891.
Catechesis/Religious Program—Students 137.
Convent—9608 Norwalk Rd., 44253.
Worship Sites:—
Our Lady Help of Christians in Litchfield—, Medina Co.
Our Lady Help of Christians in Nova—356 N. Main St., Nova-Savannah, Medina Co.
Our Lady Help of Christians in Seville—60 High St., Seville-Creston, Medina Co.
Our Lady Help of Christians in Lodi—Lodi, Medina Co.
LORAIN, LORAIN CO.
1—ST. ANTHONY OF PADUA (1923) Rev. Richard E. Hudak; Deacon James Stewart.
Res.: 1305 E. Erie Ave., 44052-2226. Tel: 440-288-0106; 440-288-0107; Fax: 440-288-0143.
School—1339 E. Erie Ave., 44052. Tel: 440-288-2155; Fax: 440-288-2159. Thomas McFadden, Prin. Lay Teachers 14; Students 260.
Catechesis/Religious Program—Students 82.
2—SS. CYRIL AND METHODIUS (1905), (Slovenian), Closed. For inquiries for parish records contact St. John, Lorain.
3—ST. FRANCES XAVIER CABRINI PARISH (2010) Rev. John Retar.
2143 Homewood Dr., 44055-2799. Tel: 440-277-7266.
Catechesis/Religious Program—Students 21.
4—HOLY TRINITY (1906), (Slovak), Closed. For inquiries for parish records contact Mary Mother of God, Lorain.
5—ST. JOHN THE BAPTIST (1900) Closed. For inquiries for parish records contact the chancery.
6—ST. JOSEPH (1896), (German), Closed. For inquiries for parish records contact the chancery.
7—ST. LADISLAUS (1890), (Hungarian), Closed. For inquiries for parish records contact the chancery.
8—ST. MARY (1873) Closed. For inquiries for parish records contact Mary Mother of God, Lorain.
9—MARY MOTHER OF GOD (2009) Rev. Daniel O. Divis; Deacon Luiz Moldonado; Mrs. Patricia Shullick, Pastoral Min.
309 Seventh St., 44052-1879. Tel: 440-245-5283; Fax: 440-246-0804.
Catechesis/Religious Program—Jane Bouman, D.R.E. Students 33.
10—NATIVITY OF THE BLESSED VIRGIN MARY (1898), (Polish), Rev. Robert J. Glepko; Deacon Robert J. Dybo.
Res.: 418 W. 15th St., 44052-3597. Tel: 440-244-9090; Fax: 440-244-0421.
Church: 1454 Lexington Ave., 44052.
Catechesis/Religious Program—Students 44.
11—ST. PETER (1909) Revs. Craig M. Hovanec; Kenneth J. Wolnowski, Pastor Emeritus (Retired); Eric Orzech; Deacon Jay R. Ogan.
Res.: 3655 Oberlin Ave., 44053-2759. Tel: 440-282-9103; Fax: 440-282-9490.
School—3601 Oberlin Ave., 44053. Tel: 440-282-9909. Ms. Emily Fabanich, Prin. Lay Teachers 22; Students 415.
Catechesis/Religious Program—Students 196.
Convent—3651 Oberlin Ave., 44053. Tel: 440-282-2378.
12—SACRED HEART CHAPEL (1952), (Hispanic), Rev. William A. Thaden; Sr. Catherine McConnell, H.M., Pastoral Assoc.; Deacons Jose A. Flores; Jose A. DeGracia; Juan Ortiz.
Mailing Address: 4301 Pearl Ave., 44055-2634.
Res.: 3921 Seneca Ave., 44055. Tel: 440-277-7379.
Church: 4301 Pearl Ave., 44055. Tel: 440-277-7231; Fax: 440-277-4886.
Catechesis/Religious Program—Students 166.
13—ST. STANISLAUS (1908), (Polish), Closed. For inquiries for parish records contact the chancery.
14—ST. VITUS (1922), (Croatian), Closed. For inquiries for parish records contact the chancery.
LOUDONVILLE, ASHLAND CO., ST. PETER (1870) [CEM] Rev. Vincent J. Hawk.
Res.: 132 N. Wood St., 44842-1235. Tel: 419-994-4396; Fax: 419-994-5263.
Catechesis/Religious Program—Students 18.
LYNDHURST, CUYAHOGA CO., ST. CLARE (1944) Revs. Stanley J. Klasinski; Thomas L. Weber, Parochial Vicar; Mrs. Lori Mascia, Pastoral Assoc.; Deacon Ross C. DeJohn Sr. In Res., Rev. Robert M. Wendelken (Retired).
Res.: 5659 Mayfield Rd., 44124-2981. Tel: 440-449-4242; Fax: 440-646-9648.
School—5655 Mayfield Rd., 44124. Fax: 440-449-1497. Frank Przybojewski, Prin. Lay Teachers 16; Students 249.
Catechesis/Religious Program—Students 272.
MACEDONIA, SUMMIT CO., OUR LADY OF GUADALUPE (1967) Rev. David R. Trask; Deacon David Govern; Mrs. Nancy Freibott, Pastoral Assoc.
Res.: 32820 Baldwin Rd., Solon, 44139. Tel:

440-447-0407.
Catechesis/Religious Program—Students 204.
MADISON, LAKE CO., IMMACULATE CONCEPTION (1863) Rev. Sean J. Donnelly; Deacons Thomas G. Hupertz; Michael C. Meade; Richard F. Kuhlman.
Res.: 2846 Hubbard Rd., 44057-2934. Tel: 440-428-5164; 440-428-3988; Fax: 440-428-3075.
Catechesis/Religious Program—Students 219.
MAPLE HEIGHTS, CUYAHOGA CO.
1—ST. MARTIN OF TOURS (1960) [CEM] Rev. Luigi C. Miola; Deacon Thaddeus C. Bizon Jr.
Res.: 14600 Turney Rd., 44137-4788. Tel: 216-475-4300; 216-475-4301; Fax: 216-475-8242.
School—Tel: 216-475-3633; Fax: 216-475-2484. Mrs. Kathy Krupar, Prin. Lay Teachers 10; Students 113.
Catechesis/Religious Program—Students 112.
2—ST. WENCESLAS (1923) Closed. For inquiries for parish records contact the chancery.
MEDINA, MEDINA CO.
1—ST. FRANCIS XAVIER (1860) [CEM] Revs. Anthony F. Sejba; Thomas E. Stock; John Sungwoong Lee; Deacons Joseph E. Loutzenhiser; Paul Kipfstuhl.
Res.: 606 E. Washington St., 44256-2183. Tel: 330-725-4968; Fax: 330-723-6234.
Church: 600 E. Washington St., 44256.
School—612 E. Washington St., 44256. Tel: 330-725-3345; Fax: 330-721-8626. Sandra Bevec, Prin. Lay Teachers 26; Students 502.
Catechesis/Religious Program—Tel: 330-722-7700; Fax: 330-723-6234. Students 543.
2—HOLY MARTYRS (1980) Revs. Stephen J. Dohner; Robert F. Pfeiffer, Pastor Emeritus (Retired); Deacon Alfred J. Koch; Robin Hawkins, Pastoral Assoc.; Janet Payton, Pastoral Assoc.
Res.: 3100 S. Weymouth Rd., 44256-9207. Tel: 330-722-6633; 330-273-1188 (Cleveland); Fax: 330-725-2193.
Catechesis/Religious Program—Students 765.
MENTOR, LAKE CO.
1—ST. BEDE THE VENERABLE (1964) Rev. Timothy J. Plavac; Mrs. Karen J. Roman, Pastoral Assoc.; Deacons Robert P. Ulman, Pastoral Assoc.; Kenneth Knight, Pastoral Assoc.
Res.: 9114 Lake Shore Blvd., 44060-1697. Tel: 440-257-5544; 440-257-5545; Fax: 440-257-2318.
Catechesis/Religious Program—Tel: 440-257-6988. Students 384.
2—ST. JOHN VIANNEY (1969) Revs. Thomas W. Johns; Jared P. Orndorff; Russell G. Rauscher; Deacons Gregory A. Leisure; Wayne W. Snyder; Mary Kovach, Pastoral Assoc.
7575 Bellflower Rd., 44060-3948. Tel: 440-943-3445 (Cleveland); 440-255-0600; Fax: 440-255-6482.
See All Saints of St. John Vianney School, Wickliffe under Elementary Schools, Parochial and Diocesan located in the Institution section.
Catechesis/Religious Program—Students 594.
3—ST. MARY OF THE ASSUMPTION (1857) Revs. Thomas G. Elsasser; Wilfred T. Smith, Pastor Emeritus (Retired); Deacon William A. Brys.
Res.: 8560 Mentor Ave., 44060-5853. Tel: 440-255-3404; 440-255-3405; 440-942-1774 (Cleveland); Fax: 440-255-4194.
School—8540 Mentor Ave., 44060. Tel: 440-255-9781; Fax: 440-974-8107. Mrs. Candice Konicki, Prin. Lay Teachers 30; Students 535.
Catechesis/Religious Program—Students 236.
MIDDLEBURG HEIGHTS, CUYAHOGA CO., ST. BARTHOLOMEW (1956) Revs. Leonard M. Bacik; William M. Jerse, Parochial Vicar; Deacon Robert G. Sabol.
Res.: 14865 E. Bagley Rd., 44130-5502. Tel: 440-842-5400; Fax: 440-842-2691.
School—Academy of St. Bartholomew, 14875 E. Bagley Rd., 44130-5502. Tel: 440-845-6660; Fax: 440-845-6672. Elizabeth Palascak, Prin. Sisters 1; Lay Teachers 23; Students 390.
Catechesis/Religious Program—Students 267.
MIDDLEFIELD, GEAUGA CO., ST. LUCY (1958) Revs. John T. Burkley; Harry S. Winca, Pastor Emeritus (Retired); Deacon Gregory C. Frania.
P.O. Box 709, Parkman, 44080.
Church & Mailing Address: 16280 Kinsman Rd., 44062-9405. Tel: 440-548-3812; Fax: 440-548-2221.
Catechesis/Religious Program—Students 58.
NEWBURY, GEAUGA CO., ST. HELEN (1949) Rev. James G. McPhillips; Deacons Willard Payne; Lawrence Somrack; Mary Weber, Pastoral Assoc.
Res.: 12060 Kinsman Rd., 44065-9678. Tel: 440-564-5805; 440-338-3358 (Cleveland); Fax: 440-564-7367.
School—Tel: 440-564-7125. Sr. Christin Alfieri, S.N.D., Prin. Sisters of Notre Dame 1; Lay Teachers 15; Students 243.
Catechesis/Religious Program—Students 343.
NORTH OLMSTED, CUYAHOGA CO.
1—ST. BRENDAN (1964) Revs. Thomas G. Woost; Cornelius J. Murray, Pastor Emeritus (Retired); Joseph Pednekar, Parochial Vicar; Deacon Stanley J. Fulton; Sr. Judy Friedel, Pastoral Assoc. In Res., Rev. William H. Severt.
Church & Mailing Address: 4242 Brendan Ln., 44070-2999.
Res.: 3920 Brendan Ln., 44070. Tel: 440-777-7222; Fax: 440-779-7997.
School—Tel: 440-777-8433; Fax: 440-779-7997. Miss Julie Onacila, Prin. Religious 1; Lay Teachers 14; Students 161.
Catechesis/Religious Program—Mary Madden, D.R.E. Students 144.
2—ST. CLARENCE (1978) Revs. Neil P. Kookoothe, Admin.; Neil Walters, Parochial Vicar; Deacon Wayne A. Bosau. In Res., Rev. Thomas A. Flynn, Pastor Emeritus (Retired).
Res.: 30106 Lorain Rd., 44070-3986. Tel: 440-734-2414; Fax: 440-734-4255.
Catechesis/Religious Program—Students 361.
Convent—30072 Lorain Rd., 44070. Tel: 440-777-5258.
3—ST. RICHARD (1950) Rev. Charles J. Stollenwerk; Deacon Gregory F. Noveske; Sr. M. Jerome Fitzgerald, S.I.W., Pastoral Assoc.; Mrs. Mary Ogan, Pastoral Assoc.; Mrs. Kathleen Huber, Pastoral Assoc.
Res.: 26855 Lorain Rd., 44070-3260. Tel: 440-777-5050; 440-777-5051; 440-777-5052; Fax: 440-777-3577.
School—Tel: 440-777-2922; Fax: 440-777-7374. Mr. Michael Cappabianca, Prin. Lay Teachers 22; Students 278.
Catechesis/Religious Program—Students 111.
Convent—5053 Whitethorn Ave., 44070. Tel: 440-777-2168.
NORTH RIDGEVILLE, LORAIN CO.
1—ST. JULIE BILLIART (1978) [JC] Rev. Richard A. Gonser; Deacons John M. Rivera; Kenneth A. DeLuca. In Res., Rev. Thomas Kowatch.
Res.: 5545 Opal Dr., 44039-2025. Tel: 440-327-1978; 440-327-1979; Fax: 440-327-1994.
Church: 5500 Lear Nagle Rd., 44039.
Catechesis/Religious Program—Students 208.
2—ST. PETER (1875) [CEM] Revs. Robert J. Franco; Robert J. Sanson, Parochial Vicar; Deacon Donald M. Jankowski.
Res.: 35777 Center Ridge Rd., 44039-3097. Tel: 440-327-2201; Fax: 440-327-2204.
School—35749 Center Ridge Rd., 44039. Tel: 440-327-3212; Fax: 440-327-6843. Sr. Mary Patricia Vovk, S.N.D., Prin. Sisters of Notre Dame 2; Lay Teachers 15; Students 321.
Catechesis/Religious Program—Students 316.
Convent—7209 Wil-Lou Ln. Tel: 440-327-8713.
NORTH ROYALTON, CUYAHOGA CO., ST. ALBERT THE GREAT (1959) Revs. Edward T. Estok Jr.; John L. Viall, Pastor Emeritus (Retired); Thomas J. Pajk; Charles M. Butkowski; Laura Kuhn, Pastoral Assoc.
Res.: 6667 Wallings Rd., 44133-3067. Tel: 440-237-6760; 440-237-6761; Fax: 440-237-5945.
School—Tel: 440-237-1032; Fax: 440-237-3308. Mr. Thomas Brownfield, Prin. Lay Teachers 35; Students 720.
Catechesis/Religious Program—Sr. Kathryn Mary O'Brien, O.S.U., D.R.E. Students 812.
NORTHFIELD, SUMMIT CO., ST. BARNABAS (1956) Revs. Ralph E. Wiatrowski; John M. Pfeifer; Edward J. Janoch, Parochial Vicar; Deacon Thomas J. Waken.
Res.: 9451 Brandywine Rd., 44067-2484. Tel: 330-467-7959; 330-467-6424; Fax: 330-467-6424.
School—9200 Olde Eight Rd., 44067. Tel: 330-467-7921; Fax: 330-468-1926. Mrs. Kimberly A. Browning, Prin. Lay Teachers 35; Students 723.
Catechesis/Religious Program—Students 637.
NORTON, SUMMIT CO.
1—ST. ANDREW THE APOSTLE (1951) Rev. James G. Maloney; Deacon Gregory A. Wunderle.
Res. & Church: 4022 Johnson Rd., 44203-5998. Tel: 330-825-2617; Fax: 330-825-5309.
Catechesis/Religious Program—Tel: 330-825-8264. Students 109.
2—PRINCE OF PEACE Revs. Robert H. Jackson; Albert A. Kunkel, Pastor Emeritus; Deacon Robert A. Youngblood; Lawrence G. Lauter, Pastoral Assoc.
Res.: 1263 Shannon Ave., 44203-6792. Tel: 330-825-9543; Fax: 330-706-1437.
Catechesis/Religious Program—Students 260.
OBERLIN, LORAIN CO., SACRED HEART (1880) Revs. Robert J. Cole, Admin.; William B. Padavick, Pastor Emeritus (Retired); Deacon Thomas B. Daw.
Res.: 410 W. Lorain St., 44074-1002. Tel: 440-774-6791; 440-774-1337; Fax: 440-775-1306.
Catechesis/Religious Program—Students 43.
OLMSTED FALLS, CUYAHOGA CO., ST. MARY OF THE FALLS (1854) [CEM] Revs. Walter J. Hyclak; Sean P. Ralph; Deacon Richard Mueller.
Res.: 25615 Bagley Rd., 44138-1915. Tel: 440-235-2222; 440-235-2223; Fax: 440-235-2937.
School—8262 Columbia Rd., 44138-2242. Tel: 440-235-4580; Fax: 440-235-6833. Sandra Isabella, Prin. Lay Teachers 15; Students 265.
Catechesis/Religious Program—Tel: 440-235-2808. Students 538.
ORANGE VILLAGE, CUYAHOGA CO., ST. MARGARET OF HUNGARY (1921), (Hungarian), Closed. For inquiries for parish records contact the chancery.
ORRVILLE, WAYNE CO., ST. AGNES (1879) Rev. Ronald J. Turek, Admin.; Deacon Steven K. Knox.
Res.: 541 Spring St., 44667-2414. Tel: 330-682-3606; 330-682-2611.
Church: E. Oak St. & Lake St., 44667.
Catechesis/Religious Program—Students 87.
PAINESVILLE, LAKE CO., ST. MARY (1848) [CEM] Revs. R. Stephen Vellenga; Mark R. Riley, Parochial Vicar; Deacon Thomas B. deHaas Jr. In Res., Rev. John M. Jenkins (Retired).
Res.: 242 N. State St., 44077-4095. Tel: 440-354-6200; 440-354-4381; 440-354-4382; Fax: 440-354-9174.
Catechesis/Religious Program—Students 422.
Convent—339 E. Erie St., 44077-4095. Tel: 440-354-3762.
PARKMAN, GEAUGA CO., ST. EDWARD (1928) Revs. John T. Burkley; Harry S. Winca, Pastor Emeritus (Retired); Deacon Gregory C. Frania.
P.O. Box 709, 44080-0709. Tel: 440-548-3812; Fax: 440-548-2221.
Res.: 16150 Center St., 44080-0709.
Church: 16150 Center St., 44080.
Catechesis/Religious Program—Students 60.
PARMA, CUYAHOGA CO.
1—ST. ANTHONY OF PADUA (1959) Revs. Dale W. Staysniak; Robert A. Lorkowski. In Res., Rev. Douglas T. Makowski (Retired).
Res.: 6750 State Rd., 44134-4518. Tel: 440-842-2666; 440-842-2667; 440-842-2668; Fax: 440-845-9549.
School—6800 State Rd., 44134-4632. Tel: 440-845-3444; Fax: 440-884-4548. Sr. Roberta Goebel, O.S.U., Prin. Religious 2; Lay Teachers 16; Students 270.
Catechesis/Religious Program—William R. Harris, D.R.E. Students 322.
Convent—6834 State Rd., 44134. Tel: 440-842-2211.
2—ST. BRIDGET OF KILDARE (1956) Revs. Robert W. Wisniewski; Lawrence J. Bayer, Pastor Emeritus (Retired); Deacon James J. Armstrong; Steven Malec, Pastoral Assoc.; Mr. Michael Schwark, Pastoral Assoc.
Res.: 5620 Hauserman Rd., 44130-1698. Tel: 440-886-4434; Fax: 440-886-4431.
School—Tel: 440-886-1468; Fax: 440-886-5121. Thomas Norton, Prin. Lay Teachers 13; Students 282.
Catechesis/Religious Program—Students 71.
Convent—
3—ST. CHARLES BORROMEO (1923) Revs. John T. Carlin; James T. Klein, Parochial Vicar; Edwin M. Leonard; Deacons John A. Talerico; Daniel M. Galla; Sr. Denise Marie Vlna, O.S.U., Pastoral Assoc.
Res.: 5891 Ridge Rd., 44129-3642. Tel: 440-884-3030; 440-884-3031; 440-884-8338; Fax: 440-884-5326.
School—7107 Wilber Ave., 44129-3445. Tel: 440-886-5546; Fax: 440-886-1163. Mrs. Eileen Updegrove, Prin. Ursuline Nuns of Cleveland 1; Lay Teachers 25; Students 558.
Catechesis/Religious Program—Students 308.
Convent—6818 Charles Ave., 44129. Tel: 440-886-0390.
4—ST. COLUMBKILLE (1956) Revs. Neil D. O'Connor; William E. Browne, Parochial Vicar; Kevin E. Estabrook; James F. Mazanec; Deacons Edward A. Telepak; Paul C. Kutolowski.
Res.: 6740 Broadview Rd., 44134-4898. Tel: 216-524-1987; 216-524-1988; Fax: 216-524-9146.
School—6740 Broadview Rd., 44134-4899. Tel: 216-524-4816; Fax: 216-524-4153. Miss Rita Klement, Prin. Lay Teachers 26; Students 440.
Catechesis/Religious Program—Students 328.
5—ST. FRANCIS DE SALES (1931) Rev. Mark J. Peyton; Deacon Robert J. Piskach. In Res., Rev. John G. Crawford (Retired).
Res.: 3434 George Ave., 44134-2904. Tel: 440-884-2319; 440-884-2320; 440-884-2321; Fax: 440-884-1661.
Church: State & Snow Rd., 44134.
School—3421 Snow Rd., 44134-2596. Tel: 440-884-2340; Fax: 440-884-8211. Michelle Nowakowski, Prin. Lay Teachers 12; Students 159.
Catechesis/Religious Program—Students 109.
Convent—3425 Snow Rd., 44134. Tel: 440-884-7242.
6—HOLY FAMILY (1872) [CEM] Revs. Richard A. Evans; Joseph R. Brankatelli; John J. Schneider; Deacons Joseph P. Litke; Charles E. Tweddell.
Res.: 7367 York Rd., 44130-5162. Tel: 440-842-5533; Fax: 440-842-3090.
School—Tel: 440-842-7785; Fax: 440-842-3634. Mrs. Mary Ann Murnyack, Prin. Lay Teachers 15; Students 218.
Catechesis/Religious Program—Students 217.
7—ST. JOHN BOSCO (1963) Rev. Lawrence Jurcak; Deacon Roger Polefko. In Res., Rev. Thomas C.

Gilles (Retired).
Res.: 6480 Pearl Rd., Parma Heights, 44130-2997. Tel: 440-886-3500; Fax: 440-886-0966.
Catechesis/Religious Program—Mrs. Carol Polefko, D.R.E. Students 113.

8—ST. MATTHIAS (1980) Rev. Raymond A. Sutter; Deacons Kenneth A. Golonka; Lindley W. Pennypacker; Mrs. Elaine Fechko, Pastoral Assoc.; Dianne Laheta, Pastoral Assoc.
Res.: 1200 W. Sprague Rd., 44134-6801. Tel: 440-888-8220; 440-888-8221; Fax: 440-888-8146.
Catechesis/Religious Program—Students 107.

PENINSULA, SUMMIT CO., MOTHER OF SORROWS (1882) Rev. John D. Terzano.
Res.: 6034 S. Locust St., 44264-9726. Tel: 330-657-2631; 330-657-2075; Fax: 330-657-2423.
Catechesis/Religious Program—Students 100.

PERRY, LAKE CO., ST. CYPRIAN (1968) Revs. Jerzy Kusy, Admin.; James J. Patton, Pastor Emeritus (Retired); Deacons Andrew Novak; James F. Daley Jr.; George P. Malec.
Res.: 4223 Middle Ridge Rd., 44081-9794. Tel: 440-259-2344; Fax: 440-259-2255.
Catechesis/Religious Program—Students 321.

RICHFIELD, SUMMIT CO., ST. VICTOR (1964) Revs. Allen F. Corrigan; Arthur A. Bacher, Pastor Emeritus (Retired).
Church & Res.: 3435 Everett Rd., 44286-0461. Tel: 330-659-6591; Fax: 330-659-3618.
Catechesis/Religious Program—Students 343.

RITTMAN, WAYNE CO., ST. ANNE (1855) [CEM] Revs. Phillip P. Pritt, Pastor Emeritus (Retired); Stephen P. Moran, Presbyteral Moderator; Sr. Joan Rader, O.P., Parish Life Coord.
Res.: 139 S. First St., 44270-1492. Tel: 330-927-2941; Fax: 330-927-3002.
Church: E. Ohio & S. First St., 44270.
Catechesis/Religious Program—

ROCKY RIVER, CUYAHOGA CO., ST. CHRISTOPHER (1922) Revs. John C. Chlebo; Timothy M. Daw; Deacon Thomas Long; Mrs. Marianne Betters, Pastoral Assoc.; Ms. Gayle Cilimburg, Pastoral Assoc.; Laura Peltz, Pastoral Assoc.
Res.: 20141 Detroit Rd., 44116-2420. Tel: 440-331-4255; 440-331-4256; Fax: 440-331-3885.
School—1610 Lakeview Ave., 44116-2409. Tel: 440-331-3075; Fax: 440-331-0674. Joyce M. Needham, Prin. Lay Teachers 24; Students 469.
Catechesis/Religious Program—Tel: 440-331-6226. Students 624.

SHAKER HEIGHTS, CUYAHOGA CO., ST. DOMINIC (1945) Rev. Thomas G. Fanta; Bonnie Stein, Pastoral Assoc.; Nick Borchers, Pastoral Assoc.; Russell Petrus, Pastoral Assoc.
Res.: 3450 Norwood Rd., 44122-4967. Tel: 216-991-1444; 216-991-1445; Fax: 216-491-0190.
Church: 19000 Van Aken Blvd., 44122.
School—3455 Norwood Rd., 44122-4901. Tel: 216-561-4400; Fax: 216-561-1573. Sue Biggs, Prin. Lay Teachers 18; Students 174.
Catechesis/Religious Program—Students 335.

SHEFFIELD, LORAIN CO., ST. TERESA OF AVILA (1845) [CEM] Revs. Edward J. Smith; Edward J. Luca, Pastor Emeritus (Retired).
Church: 1878 Abbe Rd., 44054-2322. Tel: 440-934-4227; Fax: 440-934-4500.
Catechesis/Religious Program—Students 44.

SHEFFIELD LAKE, LORAIN CO., ST. THOMAS THE APOSTLE (1962) Rev. Stephen L. Shields.
Res.: 521 Harris Rd., 44054-1409. Tel: 440-949-7744; Fax: 440-949-8611.
Catechesis/Religious Program—Students 69.
Convent—37954 French Creek Rd., 44054. Tel: 440-934-6964.

SOLON, CUYAHOGA CO.

1—RESURRECTION OF OUR LORD (1971) Rev. J. Mark Hobson, Coord., Pastoral Team; Ms. Elisabeth Frey, Pastoral Team; Theresa Battaglia, Pastoral Team.
Res. & Church: 32001 Cannon Rd., 44139-1699. Tel: 440-248-0980; 440-248-0981; Fax: 440-248-0992.
Catechesis/Religious Program—Students 257.

2—ST. RITA (1929) Revs. Richard Burchell; Robert M. Wendelken, Pastor Emeritus (Retired); Stephen A. Flynn; Deacon Robert Anderson; Mr. Albert E. Leko, Pastoral Assoc.
Res.: 32820 Baldwin Rd., 44139-4098. Tel: 440-248-1350; Fax: 440-248-2094.
School—33200 Baldwin Rd., 44139. Fax: 440-248-9442. Mary Petelin, Prin. Lay Teachers 25; Students 442.
Catechesis/Religious Program—Students 329.

SOUTH AMHERST, LORAIN CO., NATIVITY OF BLESSED VIRGIN MARY (1933) Revs. Lawrence N. Martello, Admin.; Denis L. St. Marie, Pastor Emeritus (Retired). In Res., Rev. John M. Tezie (Retired).
Res.: 333 S. Lake St., 44001-2013. Tel: 440-986-7011; Fax: 440-986-7012.
Catechesis/Religious Program—Students 26.

SOUTH EUCLID, CUYAHOGA CO.

1—ST. GREGORY THE GREAT (1922) Closed. For inquiries for parish records contact the chancery.

2—ST. MARGARET MARY (1948), For information call the Chancery.
Res.: 4217 Bluestone Rd., 44121-3427. Tel: 216-382-4114; 216-382-4115; Fax: 216-381-8730.
Catechesis/Religious Program—Tel: 216-382-4272. Students 10.
Convent—4215 Bluestone Rd., 44121. Tel: 216-381-8787.

3—SACRED HEART OF JESUS PARISH (2010) Revs. Dave R. Ireland; Thomas J. Winkel, Parochial Vicar; Deacon David N. Chordas.
1545 S. Green Rd., 44121-4085. Tel: 216-382-7601; Fax: 216-382-4992.
School—*Sacred Heart of Jesus Academy*, 4478 Rushton Rd., 44121. Tel: 216-381-0363; Fax: 216-381-7561. Mr. William DiBacco, Prin. Religious 1; Lay Teachers 25; Students 326.
Catechesis/Religious Program—Students 63.

STOW, SUMMIT CO., HOLY FAMILY (1946) Revs. Paul J. Rosing; Edward T. Holland; Deacons Louis C. Dobos; Philip P. Kamlowsky; John D. Green; Joan Skalak, Pastoral Assoc. In Res., Rev. Patrick J. Shields (Retired).
Res.: 3450 Sycamore Dr., 44224-3999. Tel: 330-688-6411; Fax: 330-689-0186.
Church: 3179 Kent Rd., 44224. Tel: 330-688-6412.
School—3163 Kent Rd., 44224. Tel: 330-688-3816; Fax: 330-688-3474. Mrs. Sharon Fournier, Prin. Lay Teachers 28; Students 529.
Catechesis/Religious Program—Students 301.

STRONGSVILLE, CUYAHOGA CO.

1—ST. JOHN NEUMANN (1977) Revs. Robert J. Kraig; Dennis J. Kristancic; Andrew B. Turner; Sr. Patricia Sylvester, S.N.D., Pastoral Assoc.; Deacon Kenneth J. Piechowski; Mrs. Sandy Zorn, Pastoral Assoc.
Res.: 16271 Pearl Rd., 44136-6095. Tel: 440-238-1770; 440-238-1771; Fax: 440-238-2030.
See SS. Joseph & John Interparochial, Strongsville under St. Joseph, Strongsville.
Catechesis/Religious Program—Students 704.

2—ST. JOSEPH (1946) Revs. Joseph R. Mamich; Kevin C. Shemuga, Parochial Vicar; Deacons Pete Moore; Robert Lester.
Res.: 12700 Pearl Rd., 44136-3484. Tel: 440-238-5555; 440-238-5556; 440-238-1038; Fax: 440-238-1059.
School—*SS. Joseph and John Interparochial*, 12580 Pearl Rd., 44136-3422. Tel: 440-238-4877; Fax: 440-238-8745. Mrs. Darlene Thomas, Prin. Lay Teachers 34; Students 721.
Catechesis/Religious Program—Tel: 440-238-5231. Students 480.
Convent—12600 Pearl Rd., 44136. Tel: 440-238-6352.

TALLMADGE, SUMMIT CO., OUR LADY OF VICTORY (1944) Rev. John R. Hengle; Diane Hardick, Pastoral Assoc.
Mailing Address: *Administration Center*, 73 North Ave., 44278-1996. Tel: 330-633-3637; 330-633-3672; Fax: 330-633-6978.
Rectory—55 North Ave., 44278.
Church: 105 North Ave., 44278.
Catechesis/Religious Program—Students 329.

THOMPSON, GEAUGA CO., ST. PATRICK (1854) [CEM] Rev. Paul F. Smith; Deacons Phillip P. Kraynik; James T. Martin; Robert F. Schwartz; Debra S. McCready, Pastoral Assoc.
Res.: 16550 Rock Creek Rd., 44086-8753. Tel: 440-298-1327; Fax: 440-298-1846.
Catechesis/Religious Program—Students 61.

TWINSBURG, SUMMIT CO., SS. COSMAS AND DAMIAN (1963) Revs. John P. Singler; Robert E. Friedel, Pastor Emeritus (Retired); Deacon Edward J. Chernick; Mrs. Darlene Bednarz, Pastoral Assoc.; Joni Smith, Pastoral Assoc.
Res.: 10419 Ravenna Rd., 44087-1726. Tel: 330-425-8141; 330-425-8142; Fax: 330-405-2947.
Church: 10439 Ravenna Rd., 44087-1726.
Catechesis/Religious Program—Students 342.

UNIONTOWN, SUMMIT CO., QUEEN OF HEAVEN (1964) Revs. David R. Durkee; Robert E. Pahler, Pastor Emeritus (Retired); Joseph P. O'Donnell, Parochial Vicar; Deacon Robert Bender.
Res.: 1800 Steese Rd., 44685-9555. Tel: 330-896-2345; Fax: 330-896-8882.
Catechesis/Religious Program—Students 562.

UNIVERSITY HEIGHTS, CUYAHOGA CO., GESU (1926) Revs. Lorn J. Snow, S.J.; Michael A. Vincent, S.J.; Deacon James K. O'Donnell; Sr. Kathleen Flannery, O.S.U., Pastoral Assoc.
Res.: 2470 Miramar Blvd., 44118-3896. Tel: 216-932-0616; 216-932-0617; 216-932-0618; Fax: 216-932-0731.
Church: 2490 Miramar Blvd., 44118.
School—2450 Miramar Blvd., 44118. Tel: 216-932-0620; Fax: 216-932-8326. Sr. Linda Martin, O.S.U., Prin. Ursuline Sisters 1; Lay Teachers 38; Students 745.
Catechesis/Religious Program—Sr. Karen Kirby, C.S.J., D.R.E. Students 211.
Convent—4070 Meadowbrook Blvd., 44118. Tel: 216-932-1660.

VALLEY CITY, MEDINA CO., ST. MARTIN OF TOURS (1840) [CEM] Rev. Thomas R. Dunphy; Mary Takacs, Pastoral Assoc.
Res.: 1824 Station Rd., 44280-9522. Tel: 330-483-3808; Fax: 330-483-3848.
Catechesis/Religious Program—Tel: 330-483-5925. Students 265.

WADSWORTH, MEDINA CO., SACRED HEART OF JESUS (1886) [JC] Revs. Joseph L. Labak; Michael D. Ausperk, Parochial Vicar; Deacons Roger N. Klaas; Richard Michney.
Res.: 260 Broad St., 44281-2113. Tel: 330-336-3049; Fax: 330-319-6340.
School—110 Humbolt Ave., 44281. Tel: 330-334-6272; Fax: 330-334-3236. Mr. William Adams, Prin. Lay Teachers 19; Students 232.
Catechesis/Religious Program—Students 240.

WARRENSVILLE HEIGHTS, CUYAHOGA CO., ST. JUDE (1945) Closed. For inquiries for parish records contact the chancery.

WELLINGTON, LORAIN CO., ST. PATRICK (1851) Rev. James J. Reymann.
Res.: 512 N. Main St., 44090-1198. Tel: 440-647-4375; Fax: 440-647-4675.
Catechesis/Religious Program—Students 198.

WEST SALEM, WAYNE CO., ST. STEPHEN (1952) Revs. James P. Schmitz; Carl A. Uhler, Pastor Emeritus (Retired); Deacon Peter J. Foradori.
Res.: 44 Britton St., 44287-9318. Tel: 419-853-4946; Fax: 419-853-7037.
Catechesis/Religious Program—Students 99.

WESTLAKE, CUYAHOGA, CO.

1—ST. BERNADETTE (1950) Revs. Philip Racco; Joseph Seebauer; Sr. Margaret O'Brien, O.S.U., Pastoral Assoc.
Res.: 2256 Clague Rd., 44145-4328. Tel: 440-734-1300; 440-734-1301; 440-734-1302; Fax: 440-734-1584.
School—2300 Clague Rd., 44145. Tel: 440-734-7717; Fax: 440-734-9198. John Stipek, Prin. Lay Teachers 22; Students 280.
Catechesis/Religious Program—Students 272.

2—ST. LADISLAS (1973) Rev. Donald E. Snyder; Sr. Johnica D'amico, Pastoral Assoc.; Mary Ellen Downs, Pastoral Assoc.; Mr. Robert Hertl, Pastoral Assoc. In Res., Most Rev. A. James Quinn (Retired).
Res. & Church Address: 2345 Bassett Rd., 44145-2999. Tel: 440-835-2300; Fax: 440-835-5895.
Catechesis/Religious Program—Students 504.

WICKLIFFE, LAKE CO., OUR LADY OF MOUNT CARMEL (1921) Revs. Thomas J. Behrend; David L. McCafferty, Pastor Emeritus (Retired); Deogratias M. Ruwaainenyi, Parochial Vicar; John J. Sullivan, Parochial Vicar; Deacon John W. Strmac. In Res., Revs. David G. Baugh (Retired); Stephen J. Kaminski.
Res.: 1730 Mount Carmel Dr., 44092-1835. Tel: 440-585-0700; Fax: 440-585-0870.
Church: 29850 Euclid Ave., 44092.
See Mater Dei Academy under Elementary Schools, Parochial & Diocesan located in the institution section
Catechesis/Religious Program—Students 200.

WILLOUGHBY, LAKE CO., IMMACULATE CONCEPTION (1866) Revs. Michael J. Troha; Francis D. Curran, Pastor Emeritus (Retired); Deacon Paul J. Hlabse Sr.; Mrs. Diana Lipfird, Pastoral Assoc.; William Christopher Hoag, Pastoral Assoc.
Res.: 37940 Euclid Ave., 44094-5899. Tel: 440-942-4500; Fax: 440-942-1540.
See Mater Dei Academy under Elementary Schools, Parochial & Diocesan located in the institution section
Catechesis/Religious Program—Students 169.

WILLOUGHBY HILLS, LAKE CO., ST. NOEL (1980) Rev. George Smiga; Deacon David T. Nethery; Alice M. Hinkel, Pastoral Assoc.
Res.: 35200 Chardon Rd., 44094-9193. Tel: 440-946-0887; Fax: 440-946-4331.
Catechesis/Religious Program—Mrs. Marianne Slattery, D.R.E. Students 93.

WILLOWICK, LAKE CO., ST. MARY MAGDALENE (1949) Revs. Ronald Wearsch, Pastoral Team; Theodore Lucas, Coord. Pastoral Team; Deacon Carl Toomey, Pastoral Team.
Res.: 32114 Vine St., 44095-3581. Tel: 440-943-2133; Fax: 440-943-3780.
Church: 32114 Vine St., 44095.
See St. Mary Magdalene-St. Justin Martyr Elementary School, Inc. under Elementary Schools Parochial and Diocesan in the Institution Section.
Catechesis/Religious Program—Tel: 440-944-2523. Students 189.

WOOSTER, WAYNE CO., ST. MARY OF THE IMMACULATE CONCEPTION (1846) [CEM] Revs. Stephen P. Moran; John J. Mueller, Pastor Emeritus (Retired); Christopher J. Trenta; Deacon Bernard E. Hosfeld; Ms. Judith Arzuaga, Pastoral Assoc.

Res.: 527 Beall Ave., P.O. Box 109, 44691-0109. Tel: 330-264-8824; 330-264-8822; Fax: 330-262-4633. Church: 527 Beall Ave., 44691.
School—515 E. Bowman St., 44691. Tel: 330-262-8671; Fax: 330-262-0967. Richard Carestia, Prin. Lay Teachers 14; Students 149.
Catechesis/Religious Program—Students 220.

Cleveland Diocesan Mission

EL SALVADOR, C.A. *Casa Parroquial Inmaculada Concepcion*. Rev. Paul E. Schindler. La Libertad Dept. La Libertad El Salvador, Central America.
Casa Parroquial San Pedro Teotepeque. Revs. John T. Ostrowski, Michael J. Stalla. La Libertad El Salvador, Central America.
Casa Parroquial Santo Domingo. Sr. Rose Elizabeth Terrell, O.S.U. Chiltiupan, La Libertad El Salvador, Central America.
Cathedral Square Plaza, 1404 E. 9th St., 44114. Tel: 216-696-6525, Ext. 4240. Rev. R. Stephen Vellenga, Dir. Society Propagation Faith.

Chaplains of Public Institutions

CLEVELAND. *Cleveland Clinic Foundation*. Revs. William T. Young, S.S.S. Tel: 440-442-6311, Cirilo A. Nacorda. Tel: 216-361-1444.
Cuyahoga County Detention Home. Rev. James P. O'Donnell. Tel: 216-566-9953.
Cuyahoga County Jail. Rev. Neil Walters. Tel: 440-238-1770.
Cuyahoga Hills Boys School. Vacant.
Euclid Hospital. Rev. Joseph Fortuna.
Fairview General Hospital. Rev. Edward N. Schwet.
Health Hill Hospital for Children. Attended from St. Andrew Abbey, Tel: 216-721-5300.
Hillcrest Hospital. Attended from St. Francis of Assisi, Tel: 216-461-0066.
Lakewood Hospital. Rev. Kenneth F. Wallace. Tel: 216-521-0184.
Lutheran Medical Center. Rev. Paul J. Pietrzyk, O.de.M. Tel: 216-961-8331.
Metro Health Medical Center & Rehabilitation Center. Rev. Justin Freeman, O.de.M., Chap. Tel: 216-778-6000. (Hospital)
Northcoast Behavioral Healthcare System North Campus. Rev. Gary Chmura. Tel: 216-421-4211.
Northeast Pre Release Center. Rev. James P. O'Donnell. Tel: 216-566-9953.
Parma Community Hospital. Rev. James R. Semonin. Tel: 440-886-4434.
Rainbow Hospital. (See University Hospitals)
Richmond Heights Hospital. Rev. Salvatore M. Ruggeri. Attended from St. John of the Cross, Tel: 216-288-0770.
South Pointe Hospital. Attended from Pastoral Care Office, Tel: 216-491-7924.
SouthWest General Hospital. Rev. Caroli B. Shayo, A.J. Tel: 440-938-8241.
University Hospitals. Rev. William H. Severt. Tel: 440-716-8591.
University Hospitals Bedford Medical Center. Rev. John J. Wright. Tel: 440-232-8166.
Veterans Administration Hospitals, Brecksville V.A., 1000 Brecksville Rd., 44141. Tel: 440-526-3030, Ext. 6268. Rev. Maurice D'Souza, C.S.C. Tel: 216-712-6506.
Cleveland V.A., 10701 East Blvd., 44106. Tel: 216-791-3800, Ext. 305. Rev. Lowell G. Neuzil.

AKRON. *Akron City Hospital*. Rev. Dismas Byarugala, A.J. Tel: 330-375-3000.
Akron General Hospital. Rev. Milton Kiocha, A.J. Tel: 330-733-9944.
Summit County Jail. Deacon Daniel Matusicky. Tel: 330-724-8043.

ASHLAND. *Ashland County Jail*. Attended from St. Edward, Tel: 419-289-7224.
Samaritan Hospital. Rev. Rodney A. Kreidler. Attended from St. Edward, Tel: 419-289-7224.

BARBERTON. *Barberton Citizens Hospitals*. Rev. David J. Majikas. Attended from St. Augustine, Tel: 330-745-0011.

CHAGRIN FALLS. *Windsor Hospital*. Attended from St. Joan of Arc, Tel: 440-247-7183.

CHARDON. *Geauga Community Hospital*. Rev. James G. McPhillips. Attended from St. Helen, Newbury, Tel: 440-564-5805.
Geauga County Jail. Deacon Frederick Giel. Tel: 440-834-8055.

CONCORD. *Tri Point Medical Center*. Rev. Stephen J. Kaminski. Tel: 440-585-0700. A Lake Health Hospital.

CUYAHOGA FALLS. *Fallsview Mental Health Center*. Rev. Neil A. Crosby. Attended from St. Eugene, Tel: 330-923-5244.
General Hospital. Rev. James J. Marsick. Attended from St. Joseph, Tel: 330-928-2173.

ELYRIA. *Elyria Memorial Hospital*. Sr. Joan Tomchey, O.S.U., Chap., Pastoral Care. Tel: 440-329-7680.

GRAFTON. *Grafton Correctional Institution*. Revs. Charles J. Ryba. Tel: 440-236-5095, John P. Seabold. Tel: 440-926-2364, Deacon John Rivera. Tel: 440-327-4426.

LODI. *Lodi Hospital*. Attended from Our Lady Help of Christians, Tel: 330-722-1180; 330-273-1500 (Cleveland).

LORAIN. *Lorain Correctional Institution*. Rev. Charles J. Ryba. Tel: 440-236-5095.

LOUDONVILLE. *Kettering-Mohican Area Medical Center*. Rev. Vincent J. Hawk. Attended from St. Peter, Tel: 419-994-4396.

MEDINA. *Medina Community Hospital*. Attended from St. Francis Xavier, Tel: 330-725-4968.
Medina County Jail. Deacon Daniel Norris. Tel: 330-725-4968.

NORTHFIELD. *Northcoast Behavioral Healthcare System South* 44067. Rev. Gary Chmura. Tel: 216-421-4211.

OBERLIN. *Mercy Allen Hospital*. Rev. Robert J. Cole. Attended from Sacred Heart, Tel: 330-774-6791.

ORRVILLE. *Dunlap Community Hospital*. Rev. Ronald J. Turek. Attended from St. Agnes, Tel: 330-682-3606.

SMITHVILLE. *Boys Village of Ohio*. Attended from St. Mary, Wooster, Tel: 330-264-8824.

WADSWORTH. *Wadsworth-Rittman Hospital*. Attended from Sacred Heart of Jesus, Tel: 330-336-3049.

WILLOUGHBY. *Lake Health Hospital, Willoughby Campus*. Rev. Stephen J. Kaminski. Tel: 440-585-0700.

WOOSTER. *Wayne County Jail*. Attended from St. Mary of the Immaculate Conception, Tel: 330-264-8824.
Wooster Community Hospital. Attended from St. Mary, Tel: 330-264-8824.

Released from Diocesan Assignment:
Revs.—
Conroy, Kevin M., Maryknoll Fathers & Brothers, Maryknoll, NY 10545.
Dickenson, William R.
Obloy, Leonard G.
Patrick, William J. (Retired)

Military Chaplains:
Revs.—
Glaros, Matthew J.
Kondik, Curtis L.

Absent on Leave:
Revs.—
Cornelius, Jeffrey L.
Marrone, Robert J.
Proehl, Douglas
Zamborsky, Leonard J.

Absent on Sick Leave:
Revs.—
Lajack, Edward F.
Ocilka, John A.
Snedeker, Arthur
Spisak, Stephen M.

Administrative Leave:
Revs.—
Banner, Russell
Brodnick, Joseph
Ischay, Matthew A.
Lieberth, Joseph
McBride, Daniel (Retired)
Pritt, Phillip P. (Retired)
Rebol, Anthony
Seminatore, Joseph
Viall, James A.
Weber, David

Life of Prayer and Penance:
Revs.—
Bruening, Allen
Lang, Joseph
Rupp, Edward F.

Retired:
Most Revs.—
Pevec, A. Edward, Ph.D. , Center for Pastoral Leadership, 28700 Euclid Ave., Wickliffe, 44092.
Pilla, Anthony M., D.D., M.A., Center for Pastoral Leadership, 28700 Euclid Ave., Wickliffe, 44092.
Quinn, A. James, J.C.D., J.D., V.G., 2345 Bassett Rd., Westlake, 44145.
Rev. Msgrs.—
Elliot, William, Ph.D.
Telesz, Leo, 5713 Frances Ave., 44127-1233.
Wolff, Robert C., 4516 Rex Lake Dr., Akron, 44319.
Revs.—
Bacher, Arthur A., 5269 Mill Creek Blvd., Brunswick Hills, 44212.
Baugh, David G., 1730 Mt. Carmel Dr., Wickliffe, 44092.
Bayer, Lawrence J., 13372 Olympus Way, Strongsville, 44149.
Becherer, James R., 4963 E. Lake Rd., Sheffield Lake, 44054.
Berardi, James J., 366 Aquaduct St., Akron, 44303-1958.
Bodziony, Ralph A., 5159 Everett Rd., Richfield, 44286.
Bryk, John J., 351 Falling Leaf, Seven Hills, 44131.
Burge, Robert
Callahan, Nelson J., 12550 Lake Rd., Apt. 1309, Lakewood, 44107.
Cappelletti, Joseph, 7054 Austin Point Dr., Concord, 44077.
Cassidy, James M., 9608 Norwalk Rd., Ashland, 44805.
Colletta, Ralph V., P.O. Box 605, Bath, 44210-0605.
Cozzens, Donald, 2650 University Blvd., Apt. 104, Shaker Heights, 44118.
Crawford, John G., 3434 George Ave., Parma, 44134.
Cregan, John J., 1967 Buckingham, Avon, 44011.
Cudnik, Chester C., 886 Eastlawn Dr., Highland Heights, 44143.
Curran, Francis D., 3553 Tuttle Ave., 44111.
D'Agostino, Carl L., 15712 Kipling Ave., 44110-3104.
Egan, Arthur B., 800 Brick Mill Run, #519, Westlake, 44145.
Flynn, Thomas A., St. Clarence, 30106 Lorain Rd., North Olmsted, 44070-3986.
Friedel, Robert E., 2943 Country Club Ln., Twinsburg, 44087.
Gajdzinski, Norman A., 20341 Brookstone Tr., Middleburg Heights, 44130.
Gallagher, Thomas J., Village of St. Edward, 3125 Smith Rd., Apt. 403, Fairlawn, 44333.
Gilles, Thomas C.
Goebel, Joseph A., SS. Robert & William, 367 E. 260th St., Euclid, 44132.
Gorski, John J., 615 N.E. 12th Ave., Apt. 207, Fort Lauderdale, FL 33304-2841. (May-June): 2820 N. Bay Dr., Apt. P-9, Westlake, 44145-6020.
Hagedorn, Thomas J., 312 4th St., Elyria, 44035.
Hayes, John J., 4129 Superior Ave., 44103.
Hepner, Ernest C., 101 Single Tree Ln., Aiken, SC 29803.
Horley, Ray J., 4291 Richmond Rd., Warrensville Heights, 44122.
Hritz, Paul J., 10210 Granger Rd., #381, Garfield Heights, 44125.
Jenkins, John M., 242 N. State St., Painesville, 44077.
Juhas, John J., 8100 Eagle Rd., Kirtland, 44094-9714.
Karg, William D., 7337 Trailside Dr., Unit B, Northfield, 44067.
Keller, Gerald J., 33896 Maple Ridge Rd., Avon, 44011.
Kinkopf, John J., Divine Word, 8100 Eagle Rd., Kirtland, 44094.
Kitt, William J., Grattan Park, Mountbellow, County Galway, Ireland.
Kline, John J., 33803 Electric Blvd., Apt. E-6, Avon Lake, 44012.
Krajnik, Paul A., 39 N. Portage Path, Rm. 448, Akron, 44303.
Kunkle, Albert A., 39 N. Portage Path, Akron, 44303.
Labella, Robert, 1255 Richmond Rd., Lyndhurst, 44124.
Lajack, Jerome M., 1485 Hollow Wood, Avon, 44011.
Laubenthal, Allan R., S.T.D., Center for Pastoral Leadership, 28700 Euclid Ave., Wickliffe, 44092.
Luca, Edward J., J.C.D., 1532 Elmwood Ave., Lakewood, 44107.
Lukachinsky, Jerome A., 13623 Rockside Rd., Garfield Heights, 44125.
Lusoski, Thomas J., 21108 Franklin Rd., Maple Heights, 44137.
Mackert, Albert J., 13719 Tartan Dr., Sun City West, AZ 85375. Winter Months, 3644 Rocky River Dr., 44111.
Mahoney, Thomas D., 15555 Hillard Rd., #805, Lakewood, 44107.
Makowski, Douglas T., 6750 State Rd., Parma, 44134.
Marquard, Elmer E., 3400 E. Shad Dr., Mansfield, 44903.
McCafferty, David L., 164 W. Market St., Akron, 44303-2395.
McCann, Thomas W.
McCarthy, David J., 215 Falls Ave., Cuyahoga Falls, 44221.
McDonough, John T., 1088 Ridge Rd., Hinckley, 44233.
McGovern, Thomas A., 1986 Village Pkwy., Tallmadge, 44278-3036.
Montavon, Thomas G., 13623 Rockside Rd., Garfield Heights, 44125-5197.
Mueller, John J., 533 1/2 Berlin Rd., Apt. 8, Huron, 44839-1920.
Mulvanity, Francis C., 37934 Brown Ave.,

Willoughby, 44094-5835.
Murphy, John F., 28700 Euclid Ave., Wickliffe, 44092-2585.
Murray, Cornelius J., 1742 Wagar Rd., Apt. 211, Rocky River, 44116-2367.
Nekic, Simon J., 1559 Roseland Way, Westlake, 44145.
O'Donnell, Thomas V.
O'Grady, Dennis R., 7096 Pearl Rd., Parma Heights, 44130.
O'Neill, William P., J.C.L., 3114 Scranton Rd., 44109.
Olsavsky, John R., J.C.L., 215 Village Dr., Seven Hills, 44131-5713.
Ondreyka, Richard J., M.S., P.O. Box 1132, Norton, 44203.
Padavick, William B., 7948 E. Bay Shore Rd., #34, Marblehead, 43440.
Pahler, Robert E., 1905 Portage Tr., Cuyahoga Falls, 44223-1792.
Patton, James J., 6421 Lake Rd. W., Madison, 44051.
Pfeiffer, Robert F., J.C.L., 2114 Industry Rd., Atwater, 44201-9354.
Piskura, Joseph, 29050 Detroit Rd., Apt. 329, Westlake, 44145.
Pizmoht, Louis A., 8276 Deepwood Blvd., Unit 1, Mentor, 44060.
Pritt, Phillip P., St. Matthias, 1200 W. Sprague Rd., Parma, 44134-6801.
Rath, Thomas V., 5171 Riverstyx Rd., Medina, 44256.
Rathfon, John R., 3428 E. Prescott Cir., Cuyahoga Falls, 44223-1792.
Rosko, Ladislaus
Schorr, James D., 3275 5th Ave., #304, San Diego, CA 92103-5729.
Sciarrotta, Paul J., 13000 Auburn Rd., Chardon, 44024-9331.
Sheehan, Thomas W.
Sheil, James E.
Shields, Patrick J., 3450 Sycamore Dr., Stow, 44224.
Smith, Wilfred T., 2846 Hubbard Rd., Madison, 44057-2998.
St. Marie, Denis L., 200 St. Joseph Dr., Amherst, 44001-1663.
Swirski, Thaddeus M., 476 Mull Ave., Akron, 44320.
Szudarek, Ronald J., 4880 E. 96th St., Garfield Heights, 44125.
Tesek, Albert J., 14277 State Rd., North Royalton, 44133.
Tezie, John M., 333 S. Lake St., South Amherst, 44001. (Dec.-June): 4550 Pinebrook Cr., Apt. 105, Bradenton, FL 34209.
Tomicky, Ronald
Uhler, Carl A., 12300 McCracken Rd., Garfield Heights, 44125.
Valley, John, P.O. Box 5302, Willowick, 44095-5302.
Van Bergen, Francis G., 111 E. 291st St., Wickliffe, 44092.
Vesely, James J., 4940 Broadview Rd., 44109-5799.
Viall, John L., 12195 Pheasant Run, North Royalton, 44133.
Weigand, John J., 12195 Pheasant Run, North Royalton, 44133.
Weigand, Joseph C., 1905 Portage Tr., Cuyahoga Falls, 44223.
Wendelken, Robert M., D.Min., St. Clare, 5659 Mayfield Rd., Lyndhurst, 44124-2915.
Wessel, John F., 2451 Crimson Dr., Westlake, 44145.
Winca, Harry S., 1620 Windrow La., Broadview Heights, 44147.
Winters, Alfred H., 12550 Lake Ave., #1403, Lakewood, 44107.
Wolnowski, Kenneth J., 3850 Galt Ocean Dr., Unit 504, Fort Lauderdale, FL 33308.
Wysocki, Paul, 8274 Kellogesville/Stanhope Rd., Williamsfield, 44093.
Yahner, Gordon A., 164 W. Market St., Akron, 44303.

Permanent Deacons:
Adair, Robin, St. Augustine, Barberton
Adkins, Ronald M., St. Gabriel, Concord Township
Agrippe, James L., (Retired)
Anderson, Robert C., St. Rita, Solon
Armstrong, James J., St. Bridget, Parma Heights
Bacik, Dale A., Apollo Beach, FL
Badillo, Tomas, (Retired)
Battista, Bruce J., Holy Rosary, Cleveland
Beercheck, Richard C., Blessed Trinity, Cleveland
Belsito, Vincent L., Holy Angels, Chagrin Falls
Belter, Clement J., St. Ambrose, Brunswick
Bender, Robert C., Queen of Heaven, Green
Berigan, Patrick F., Mary Queen of Peace, Cleveland
Bizon, Thaddeus C., Jr., St. Martin of Tours, Maple Heights
Boehnlein, Lawrence A., St. Mary, Chardon
Bosau, Wayne A., St. Clarence, North Olmsted
Bowers, Robert J., St. Paschal Baylon, Highland Heights
Broering, J. Harry, Jr., (Retired)
Bryan, Daniel L., St. Clement, Lakewood
Brys, William A., St. Mary of the Assumption, Mentor
Bubnick, Robert C., Sr., (Retired)
Buda, John M., (Retired)
Bugaj, Robert J., St. Therese, Garfield Heights
Burke, John Jr., (Retired), Commerce, GA
Butkovic, Donald P., (Retired)
Butz, Richard C., (Retired)
Cermak, Lawrence, (Leave of Absence)
Chernick, Edward J., SS. Cosmas & Damian, Twinsburg
Chordas, David N., Sacred Heart of Jesus, South Euclid
Clavin, Daniel P., St. Gabriel, Concord
Colon, Victor R., Sagrada Familia, Cleveland
Corrigan, William H., St. Colman, Cleveland
Croniger, James D., (Retired)
Cruz, Moises, St. Stephen, Cleveland
Daley, James F., Jr., St. Cyprian, Perry
Daull, Raymond L., Communion of Saints, Cleveland Heights
Daw, Thomas B., Diocesan Tribunal; Sacred Heart, Oberlin
DeGracia, Jose A., Sacred Heart Chapel, Lorain
DeHaas, Thomas B., Jr., St. Mary, Painesville
DeJohn, Ross C., Sr., St. Clare, Lyndhurst
DeLuca, Kenneth A., St. Julie Billiart, North Ridgeville
Di Mascio, Ramon J., St. Bernard-St. Mary, Akron
Dietz, Joseph R., St. Edward, Ashland
Dillon, Edward R., (Retired)
Dirk, William E., Our Lady of Peace, Cleveland
Dobos, Louis C., Holy Family, Stow
Doerpers, Charles B., St. John of the Cross, Euclid
Donlin, William A., (Retired)
Dunlop, Jeffrey F., St. Joan of Arc, Chagrin Falls
Dybo, Robert J., Nativity of the Blessed Virgin Mary, Lorain
Elwood, William T., St. Francis of Assisi, Gates Mills; Youth & Family Ministry, Eastern Region
Feldkamp, Edward J., (Retired)
Figueroa, Miguel A., St. Michael, Cleveland
Flores, Jose A., Sacred Heart Chapel, Lorain
Foradori, Peter J., St. Stephen, West Salem
Frania, Gregory C., St. Lucy Mission, Middlefield; St. Edward, Parkman
Friend, Shelby, Holy Spirit, Garfield Heights
Fulton, Stanley J., St. Brendan, North Olmstead
Galla, Daniel M., St. Charles Borromeo, Parma
Gardias, Edmund A., St. Adalbert, Berea
Giel, Frederick F., (Retired), The Villages, FL
Golonka, Kenneth A., St. Matthias, Parma
Gonzalez, Edgar, St. Vincent de Paul, Elyria
Gorman, William, (Retired)
Govern, David, Our Lady of Guadalupe, Macedonia
Grasson, Thomas J., St. Mary, Berea
Gregg, Larry D., St. Raphael, Bay Village
Grgic, Robert H., St. Gabriel, Concord Township
Guritza, Dennis A., St. Joan of Arc, Chagrin Falls
Hancock, Daniel J., St. Joseph, Amherst
Heise, Paul R., St. Joseph, Amherst
Herrick, Raymond S., St. Francis de Sales, Akron
Hill, Kenneth J., St. Vincent de Paul, Cleveland
Hinderscheid, Lee F., (Retired), Brooksville, FL
Hlabse, Paul J., Immaculate Conception, Willoughby
Hoefler, Gregory, Immaculate Heart of Mary, Cuyahoga Falls
Hosfeld, Bernard E., St. Mary of the Immaculate Conception, Wooster
Humphrey, Frank A., III, St. Mary, Elyria
Humphrey, Patrick J., St. Jude, Elyria
Hupertz, Thomas G., Immaculate Conception, Madison
James, Ronald R., Holy Spirit, Garfield Heights
Jankowski, Donald M., Dir. Pastoral Care, St. Mary of the Woods, Avon; St. Peter, North Ridgeville
Jarosh, Rudolph, Jr., (Retired)
Jervis, Michael F., Our Lady Help of Christians, Litchfield
Johnson, Joseph W., (Retired)
Kamlowsky, Philip P., Holy Family, Stow
Kaniecki, James A., (Leave of Absence)
Kipfstuhl, Paul J., St. Francis Xavier, Medina; Assoc. Dir., Office of Continuing Education for Ministers
Klaas, Roger N., Sacred Heart, Wadsworth
Knight, Kenneth, St. Bede the Venerable, Mentor
Knox, Steven K., St. Agnes, Orrville
Koch, Alfred J., Holy Martyrs, Medina
Koch, John A., Blessed Trinity, Cleveland
Kochanski, Robert M., St. Joseph, Cuyahoga Falls
Kovach, Robert C., St. Anselm, Chesterland
Kovitch, Joseph R., (Retired)
Kraynik, Phillip P., St. Patrick, Thompson
Krupp, Ralph J., (Retired)
Kuhlman, Richard F., Immaculate Conception, Madison
Kushner, David S., St. Mary, Cleveland
Kutolowski, Paul C., St. Columbkille, Parma
Leisure, Gregory A., St. John Vianney, Mentor
Lester, Robert J., St. Joseph, Strongville
Litke, Joseph P., Holy Family, Parma
Lobdell, Donald W., (Retired)
LoCascio, Phillip A., (Retired), Scottsdale, AZ
Long, Thomas T., St. Christopher, Rocky River
Lonteen, Francis R., (Retired)
Lopez, Gonzalo, St. Michael the Archangel, Cleveland
Loutzenhiser, Joseph E., St. Francis Xavier, Medina
Lozada, Frank, Our Lady of Lourdes, Cleveland
Lundeen, David J., St. Mark, Cleveland
Lupson, Erick N., St. Angela Merici, Fairview Park
Malcolm, Billy J., (Retired), Randleman, NC
Maldonado, Louis, Mary Mother of God, Lorain
Malec, George P., St. Cyprian, Perry
Martin, Hardin M., St. Agnes-Our Lady of Fatima, Cleveland
Martin, James T., St. Patrick, Thompson
Martin, P. Robert, (Retired)
Masony, Howard J., St. Mark, Cleveland
Matoney, Robert, Jr., St. Dominic, Shaker Heights
Matusicky, Daniel J., (Retired)
McCarthy, Edward J., Jr., (Retired), Naples, FL
McGraw, Joseph E.
McKenna, J. Kevin, Cathedral of St. John the Evangelist
McNulty, Leo F., St. Francis of Assisi, Gates Mills
Meade, Kenneth C., Immaculate Conception, Madison
Medina, Ceferino, Sagrada Familia, Cleveland
Merriman, William C., St. Patrick, Cleveland
Michney, Richard, Sacred Heart of Jesus, Wadsworth
Miranda, Ignacio, Sagrada Familia, Cleveland
Mueller, Richard A., St. Mary of the Falls, Olmstead Falls
Nethery, David T., St. Noel, Willoughby
Netzband, Ralph W., (Retired)
Norris, Daniel F., St. Francis Xavier, Medina.
Novak, Andrew J., St. Cyprian, Perry
Novak, Neal J., St. Michael, Independence
Noveske, Gregory F., St. Richard, North Olmsted
O'Connell, Frank J., St. Jude, Elyria
O'Donnell, James K., Gesu, University Heights
Ogan, Jay R., St. Peter, Lorain
Ortiz, Juan, Sacred Heart Chapel, Lorain
Paul, James, Jr., St. Aloysius-St. Agatha, Cleveland
Payne, Willard C., St. Helen, Newbury
Peacock, Terry W., St. Sebastian, Akron
Pecek, Louis G., Ph.D., (Retired)
Pecot, David E., (Retired)
Pennypacker, Lindley W., St. Matthias, Parma
Perkowski, Gregory A., (On Leave of Absence)
Peshek, Thomas J., St. Mary, Chardon
Piechowski, Kenneth J., St. John Neumann, Strongsville
Piskach, Robert J., St. Francis de Sales, Parma
Polefko, Roger F., St. John Bosco, Parma Heights
Primozic, Louis M., St. Basil the Great, Brecksville
Quiles, Rafael, (Retired)
Ramos, Jose L., (On Leave of Absence)
Reiland, George J., Jr., (Retired)
Rivera, Carlos, (Retired)
Rivera, John M., St. Augustine, Cleveland; St. Julie Billiart, North Ridgeville
Sabol, Robert G., St. Bartholomew, Middleburg Heights
Sanchez, Reinaldo, St. Michael the Archangel, Cleveland
Schill, William E., (Retired)
Schwartz, Robert F., St. Patrick, Thompson
Seal, J. David, (Retired)
Senn, Thomas J., Our Lady of Angels, Cleveland
Sferry, John P., Sr., Cathedral of St. John the Evangelist, Cleveland
Sheridan, Thomas, St. Ambrose, Brunswick
Sherman, Homer L., (Retired)
Shin, Charles C., St. Andrew Kim Pastoral Center, Cleveland
Sill, Donald E., (Retired)
Simon, Frederick F., Sagrada Familia, Cleveland
Slatcoff, John K., St. Vincent De Paul, Elyria Township
Smith, Dennis L., Nativity of the Lord Jesus, Akron
Snyder, Wayne W., (Retired)
Somrack, Lawrence A., St. Helen, Newbury
Staab, William M., Blessed Trinity, Cleveland
Starkey, William R., SS. Peter and Paul, Garfield Heights
Stewart, James, (Retired)
Stokes, Troy F., (Retired)
Streeter, David A., Assumption, Broadview Heights; Representative, Deacon Clergy Personnel Bd.

Strmac, John W., Our Lady of Mount Carmel, Wickliffe
Talerico, John A., St. Charles Borromeo, Parma
Tatulinski, Frank E., (On Leave of Absence)
Telepak, Edward A., St. Columbkille, Parma
Tennant, Bruce H., St. Agnes, Elyria
Terrion, Daniel C., Our Lady of Hope, Bedford
Thiel, Martin A., St. Thomas More, Brooklyn
Tomazic, Gary R., St. Ambrose, Brunswick
Toomey, Carl M., St. Mary Magdalene, Willowick
Torres, Epifanio, Sagrada Familia, Cleveland
Travalik, Peter M., St. Jerome, Cleveland
Travis, D. John, St. Ladislas, Westlake
Tweddell, Charles E., Holy Family, Parma
Ulman, Robert P., St. Bede the Venerable, Mentor
Varga, Carl M., Divine Word, Kirtland
Vincent, James C., St. Michael, Independence
Volek, Ronald J., Seiverville, TN
Vrabel, Jerome B., (Leave of Absence)
Waken, Thomas J., St. Barnabas, Northfield
Walling, Robert K., Holy Spirit, Avon
Weglicki, Frank L., Jr., St. Ambrose, Brunswick
Wenzel, John T., St. Anthony of Padua, Fairport Harbor
Wilson, Francis B., Mary Queen of the Apostles, Brook Park
Winterich, Carl H., St. Mary, Hudson
Woods, Richard E., Communion of Saints, Cleveland Heights
Woyton, Louis M., St. Augustine, Cleveland
Wunderle, Gregory A., St. Andrew the Apostle, Norton
Yates, Stephen L., Holy Angels, Bainbridge
Yoho, William J., Jr., Immaculate Heart of Mary, Cuyahoga Falls
Youngblood, Dale A., S.S. Peter and Paul, Doylestown
Youngblood, Robert A., Prince of Peace, Norton; Representative, Deacon Clergy Personnel Bd.
Zawadzki, Charles W., St. Thomas More, Cleveland
Zdolshek, John R., Mary Queen of the Apostles, Brook Park

INSTITUTIONS LOCATED IN THE DIOCESE

[A] SEMINARIES, DIOCESAN

WICKLIFFE. *Borromeo Seminary* (1954) 28700 Euclid Ave., 44092-2585. Tel: 440-943-7600; Fax: 440-943-7577. Email: tmd@dioceseofcleveland.org. Web: www.borromeoseminary.org. Very Rev. Thomas M. Dragga, D.Min., Pres. & Rector; Revs. Michael G. Woost, S.T.L., Liturgy Dir.; Michael Joyce, O.F.M.Cap., Pastoral Formation; John F. Loya, M.Div., M.A., Spiritual Dir.; Bro. Charles McElroy, O.F.M.Cap., Rel. Studies; Mr. Philip J. Guban, B.A., Treas.; Revs. Donald Dunson, Formation Advisor; Lester Knoll, O.F.M.Cap., Formation Advisor; John F. Murphy, Formation Advisor (Retired); Damian J. Ference, M.A., Ph.L., Teacher, Philosophy; Most Rev. Anthony M. Pilla, D.D., M.A., Religious Studies; Dr. Chad A. Engelland, Ph.D., Lay Teacher- Philosophy; Dr. Ed Kaczuk, M.M., Music Dir.; Mr. Alan K. Rome, M.L.S., Librarian. Priests 9; Brothers 1; Lay Teachers 2; Seminarians 29.

St. Mary Seminary and Graduate School of Theology (1948) (Our Lady of the Lake) , 28700 Euclid Ave., 44092-2585. Tel: 440-943-7600; Fax: 440-943-7577. Email: twt@dioceseofcleveland.org. Web: stmarysem.edu. Revs. Thomas W. Tifft, Ph.D., Pres./Rector; Mark A. Latcovich, Ph.D., Vice Pres.-Vice Rector, Academic Dean; Sr. Brendon Zajac, S.N.D., D.Min., Registrar; Revs. Gerald J. Bednar, Ph.D.; Donald Dunson; Very Rev. Thomas M. Dragga, D.Min.; Revs. Mark L. Hollis, M.Div., Spiritual Dir.; Joseph M. Koopman, S.T.D.; Michael G. Woost, S.T.L.; Lorenzo Tosco, S.S.D., S.S.L.; Sr. Mary McCormick, O.S.U., Ph.D.; Dr. Edward J. Kaczuk, M.M.; Mr. Alan K. Rome, M.L.S., Librarian; Mr. Philip J. Guban, B.A., Treas. Priests 9; Sisters 1; Adjunct Faculty 15; Students for Priesthood, Diocesan 32; Religious 3; Permanent Diaconate 15; Other 105.

[B] COLLEGES AND UNIVERSITIES

CLEVELAND. *Notre Dame College* (1922) 4545 College Rd., South Euclid, 44121. Tel: 216-381-1680; Fax: 216-381-3802. Email: bjohnston@ndc.edu. Web: www.notredamecollege.edu. Andrew P. Roth, Ph.D., Pres.; Deborah Sheren, Chief Information Officer; Karen Zoller, Dir. Clara Fritzsche Library. Priests 1; Sisters of Notre Dame 6; Lay Teachers 61; Total Staff 223; Students 2,156.

Ursuline College (1871) 2550 Lander Rd., Pepper Pike, 44124. Tel: 440-449-4200; Fax: 440-646-8102. Web: www.ursuline.edu. Sr. Diana Stano, O.S.U., Ph.D., Pres.; JoAnne Podis, Ph.D., Vice Pres. Academic Affairs; David Steiner, Vice Pres. & CFO; Deanne Hurley, Vice Pres. Student Affairs; Sr. Anna Margaret Gilbride, O.S.U., Ph.D., Asst. to the Pres.; Thandabantu Maceo, Vice Pres. Enrollment Mgmt.; June Gracyk, Vice Pres. Facilities Mgmt.; Kevin Gladstone, Vice. Pres. Inst. Advancement; Betsey Belkin, Dir., Library. Ursuline Sisters of Cleveland 9; Lay Professors 75; Students 1,488; Total Staff 222.

UNIVERSITY HEIGHTS. *John Carroll Jesuit Community* (1886) 2520 Miramar Blvd., 44118-3821. Tel: 216-397-1886; Fax: 216-397-4228. Email: jesuits@jcu.edu. Web: www.jcu.edu. Revs. Robert J. Niehoff, S.J., Pres.; William M. Bichl, S.J.; Casimir R. Bukala, S.J.; John E. Dister, S.J.; Harry J. Gensler, S.J.; Paul D. Panaretos, S.J.; Francis X. Ryan, S.J.; Gerald J. Sabo, S.J., Rector & Librarian; Thomas L. Schubeck, S.J.; Lorn J. Snow, S.J.; Bro. Denis Weber, S.J.; Revs. W. Jared Wicks, S.J.; James C. Ackerman, S.J.; Bernard F. McAniff, S.J. Jesuit Priests 13; Jesuit Brothers 1; Total Enrollment 3,800.

John Carroll University (1886) 20700 N. Park Blvd., 44118. Tel: 216-397-1886; Fax: 216-397-4256. Web: www.jcu.edu. Rev. Robert J. Niehoff, S.J., Pres.; Jonathan Smith, Vice Pres. & Exec. Asst. to Pres.; Mark D. McCarthy, Vice Pres. Student Affairs; Ms. Doreen Riley, Vice Pres., Univ. Advancement; Mr. Richard F. Mausser, Vice Pres. Finance; Dr. John T. Day, Academic Vice Pres. & Provost; Dr. James H. Krukones, Assoc. Academic Vice Pres.; Dr. Lauren Bowen, Assoc. Academic Vice Pres. Programs & Diversity; Steven P. Vitatoe, Exec. Dir. Enrollment; Mr. Brian Williams, Vice Pres. for Enrollment; Mr. Thomas Fanning, Dir. Recruitment & Admission; Dr. Karen Schuele, Dean, Boler School of Business; Dr. Jeanne Colleran, Dean College of Arts & Sciences; Dr. Sherri Crahen, Dean of Students; Dr. Peter Kvidera, Assoc. Dean College of Arts & Sciences; Dr. James Martin, Assoc. Dean Prog. & Curriculum, Boler School of Business; Dr. Lindsay Calkins, Assoc. Dean Faculty & Students, Boler School of Business; Dr. Mark Storz, Assoc. Dean Graduate Studies; Dr. Jeanne M. Somers, Dir., Grasselli Library. Priests 5; Lay Faculty 199; Students 3,709; Total Staff 555.

[C] HIGH SCHOOLS, DIOCESAN

CLEVELAND. *Cleveland Central Catholic High School* (1968) 6550 Baxter Ave., 44105. Tel: 216-441-4700; Fax: 216-441-8353. Email: agusdanovic@centralcatholichs.org. Web: www.centralcatholichs.org. Sr. Allison Marie Gusdanovic, S.N.D., Prin.; Mrs. Martha Croll, Librarian. Sisters of Notre Dame 8; Lay Teachers 38; Students 541.

**St. Martin de Porres High School* (2003) 6111 Lausche Ave., 44103. Tel: 216-881-1689; Fax: 216-881-8303. Email: rclark@stmdphs.org. Mary Ann Vogel, Prin.; Richard Clark, Contact Person. Sisters 1; Lay Teachers 25.

Villa Angela-St. Joseph High School (1990) 18491 Lakeshore Blvd., 44119. Tel: 216-481-8414; Fax: 216-486-1035. Email: dcsank@vasj.com. Web: www.VASJ.com. Richard J. Osborne, Pres.; Mr. David M. Csank, Prin.; Rev. H. James Bartlett, S.M., Chap.; Susan R. Skehan, Librarian. Marianist Priest 1; Ursuline Nuns 1; Lay Teachers 22; Students 274.

BEDFORD. *St. Peter Chanel High School*, 480 Northfield Rd., 44146. Tel: 440-232-5900; Fax: 440-232-9283. Email: mberlec@stpeterchanel.com. Web: www.stpeterchanel.com. Sr. Maria Berlec, O.S.U., Pres. & Prin.; Victoria Karakasis, Librarian. Sisters 1; Lay Teachers 21; Students 250.

ELYRIA. *Elyria Catholic High School* (1948) (Coed), 725 Gulf Rd., 44035. Tel: 440-365-1821; Fax: 440-365-7536. Web: www.elyriacatholic.com. Mr. Andrew G. Krakowaik, M.A., Pres.; Mrs. Amy Butler, Prin.; Ms. Kristen Frey, Librarian. Serving Elyria, Avon, Sheffield, North Ridgeville, Grafton, Oberlin, Amherst, Lorain, Avon Lake, Columbia Station, LaGrandge, Litchfield, Medina, N. Olmsted, New London, Olmsted Falls, Valley City, Vermilion, Wakeman, Wellington and Westlake. Deacons 1; Lay Teachers 25; Students 433.

MENTOR. *Lake Catholic High* (1970) 6733 Reynolds Rd., 44060. Tel: 440-578-1020; Fax: 440-974-9087. Web: www.lakecatholic.org. Rick Koenig, Prin.; Mr. Sal Miroglotta, Pres.; Sarah Goodman, Librarian. Ursuline Sisters of Cleveland (O.S.U.) 2; Lay Teachers 53; Students 837.

PARMA HEIGHTS. *Holy Name High School* (Coed), 6000 Queens Hwy., 44130. Tel: 440-886-0300; Fax: 440-886-1267. Email: benfarmer@holynamehs.com. Web: www.holynamehs.com. Benjamin B. Farmer, Pres. & Prin.; Sr. Paula Greggila, Librarian. Sisters 2; Lay Teachers 44; Administration 3; Students 657.

[D] HIGH SCHOOLS, PRIVATE

CLEVELAND. *Benedictine High School*, 2900 Martin Luther King Dr., 44104-4898. Tel: 216-421-2080; Fax: 216-421-1100; 216-421-0107. Email: cbhs@cbhs.net. Web: www.cbhs.net. Rt. Rev. Christopher Schwartz, O.S.B., Chancellor; Mr. Joseph Gressock, Prin.; Rev. Gerard Gonda, O.S.B., Pres.; Mr. Thomas Erzen, Asst. Prin.; Mr. Anthony Russ, Athletic Dir.; Revs. Michael Brunovsky, O.S.B., Academic Dean; Timothy Buyansky, O.S.B., Librarian; Very Rev. Gary Hoover, O.S.B., Dir. Spiritual Life; Rev. Bede Kotlinski, O.S.B.; Bro. Patrick Ryan, O.S.B.; Ms. Terri Haven, Dir. Business Operations; Rev. Finbar Ramsak, O.S.B. Priests 7; Brothers 1; Lay Teachers 29; Students 340.

St. Edward High School (Boys), 13500 Detroit Ave., Lakewood, 44107. Tel: 216-221-3776; Fax: 216-221-4609. Email: jkubacki@sehs.net. Web: www.sehs.net. James P. Kubacki, Pres.; Dr. Gregg Good, Exec. Vice Pres. Priests 1; Brothers 5; Lay Teachers 62; Students 863; Total Staff 100.

St. Ignatius High School (1886) 2926 Carroll Ave., 44113. Tel: 216-281-5392; Fax: 216-281-5393. 1911 W. 30th St., 44113. Tel: 216-651-0222; Fax: 216-651-6313. Web: www.ignatius.edu. Rev. John F. Libens, S.J., Dean of Teachers & Supr.; Peter H. Corrigan Jr., Prin.; Revs. Carl Bonk, S.J.; Francis E. Canfield, S.J., Counselor; William Murphy, S.J., Pres.; Lawrence M. Ober, S.J. (On Sabbatical); Bernard J. Streicher, S.J.; Kenneth A. Styles, S.J.; Robert J. Welsh, S.J.; Bros. Michael L. Nusbaum, S.J., Min. & Asst. to Rector; Ralph Cordero, S.J.; Mr. Patrick J. Gilday, S.J.; Milena Streen, Librarian. Priests 8; Lay Teachers 100; Students 1,462.

St. Joseph Academy (1890) 3430 Rocky River Dr., 44111. Tel: 216-251-6788; Fax: 216-251-5809. Web: www.sja1890.org. Mary Ann Corrigan-Davis, Pres.; Blake Prewitt, Prin.; Rebecca Synk, Librarian. Lay Teachers 57; Students 669; Total Staff 91.

Magnificat High School (Girls), 20770 Hilliard Blvd., 44116. Tel: 440-331-1572; Fax: 440-331-7257. Email: scasmith@magnificaths.org. Web: www.magnificaths.org. Sr. Carol Anne Smith, H.M., Pres. Sisters 2; Lay Teachers 53; Students 776.

**St. Martin de Porres High School Work Study Program* (2004) 6111 Lausche Ave., 44103. Tel: 216-881-1689; Fax: 216-881-8303. Email: tbennett@stmdphs.org. Thomas M. Bennett Jr., Pres.

AKRON. *Archbishop Hoban High School* (Coed), One Holy Cross Blvd., 44306. Tel: 330-773-6658; Fax: 330-773-9100. Email: beitingm@hoban.org. Web: www.hoban.org. Bro. Kenneth Haders, C.S.C., Pres.; Dr. Mary Anne Beiting, Prin.; Mrs. Tina Braman, Librarian. Brothers of Holy Cross. Brothers 7; Lay Teachers 60; Students 849.

Our Lady of the Elms School, (Grades 7-12), 1375 W. Exchange St., 44313-7697. Tel: 330-867-0880; Fax: 330-864-6488. Web: www.theelms.org. Lisa Massello, Prin.; Tim DeFrange, Librarian. Please see complete listing under Secondary Schools. Sisters 1; Deacons 1; Lay Teachers 26; Students 200.

St. Vincent-St. Mary High School, 15 N. Maple St., 44303. Tel: 330-253-9113; Fax: 330-996-0020. Email: webmaster@stvm.com. Web: www.stvm.com. David V. Rathz, Headmaster; Joanne Wiseman, Dir. of Admissions; Stella Weigand, Controller; Burke Stephens, Dean of Students; Ken McDonald, Campus Min.; Pamela Godshalk, Librarian. Lay Teachers 43; Students 703.

CHARDON. *Notre Dame-Cathedral Latin School*, 13000 Auburn Rd., 44024. Tel: 440-286-6226; 888-214-8108 (toll free); Fax: 440-286-7199. Email: ndcl@ndcl.org. Web: www.ndcl.org. Sr. Jacquelyn Gusdane, S.N.D., Pres.; Mr. Joseph A. Waler, M.A., M.Ed., Prin. Sisters of Notre Dame. Sisters 7; Lay Teachers 63; Students 746.

CLEVELAND HEIGHTS. *Beaumont School*, 3301 N. Park Blvd., 44118. Tel: 216-321-2954; Fax: 216-321-3947. Email: Info@beaumontschool.org. Web: www.beaumontschool.org. Sr. Gretchen Rodenfels, O.S.U., Pres.; Mrs. Mary Whelan, Prin.; Mrs. Marie Engstrom, Librarian. Ursuline Sisters. Sisters 8; Lay Teachers 47; Students 410.

CUYAHOGA FALLS. *Walsh Jesuit High School*, 4550 Wyoga Lake Rd., 44224. Tel: 330-929-4205; 800-686-4694 (Cleveland); Fax: 330-929-9749. Web: www.walshjesuit.org. Mark Hassman, Prin.; Karl Ertle, Pres.; Revs. Mark George, S.J.; Emmett P. Holmes, S.J.; James J. King, S.J.; Donald J. Petkash, S.J., Religious Supr.; John V. White, S.J.; Nancy Heil, Librarian. Priests 5; Lay

Teachers 69; Students 1,017.

GARFIELD HEIGHTS. *Trinity High School*, 12425 Granger, 44125. Tel: 216-581-1644; Fax: 216-581-9348. Email: bachol@ths.org. Web: www.ths.org. Sr. Shawn Lee, S.S.J.-T.O.S.F., Pres.; Thomas M. Maher, Ph.D., Spec. Asst. to Pres.; Mr. Daniel J. Thomeier, Business Mgr.; Ms. Carla E. Fritsch, Spec. Asst. to Pres.; Mrs. Linda Bacho, Prin.; Mr. William Svoboda, Asst. Prin. Sisters of St. Joseph of the Third Order of St. Francis. Sisters of St. Joseph 7; Lay Teachers 35; Students 350.

GATES MILLS. *Gilmour Academy*, (Grades PreK-12), Private., 34001 Cedar Rd., 44040-9356. Tel: 440-442-1104; Fax: 440-473-8010. Email: laveller@gilmour.org. Web: www.gilmour.org. Mr. Murlan J. Murphy Jr., Chm., Bd. of Trustees; Bro. Robert Lavelle, C.S.C., Headmaster; Todd R. Sweda, Asst. Headmaster; J. Brian Horgan, Dir. of Upper School; Yvonne Saunders, Dir. Middle School & Asst. Dir. Upper School; Diane Kingsley, Dir. of Lower School; Rev. John Blazek, C.S.C., Campus Min.; Lynn Hammond, Library Mgr. Congregation of Holy Cross., Day and Resident College Preparatory School. Priests 1; Brothers 6; Sisters 2; Lay Teachers 65; Students 693; Residents 56.

PARMA. *Padua Franciscan High School* (1961) 6740 State Rd., 44134. Tel: 440-845-2444; Fax: 440-845-5710. Email: padua@paduafranciscan.com. Web: www.paduafranciscan.com. Rev. Theodore Haag, O.F.M., Pres.; Gerald R. Jindra, Vice Pres. for Inst. Advancement; David G. Stec, Prin.; Robert Grgic, Campus Minister; Bro. Tom Carroll, O.F.M., Academic Dean; Linda George, Librarian. Priests 1; Sisters 1; Brothers 2; Lay Teachers 61; Students 837.

[E] ELEMENTARY SCHOOLS

CLEVELAND. *Villa Montessori Center* (1995) 5620 Broadway Ave., 44127. Tel: 216-641-4770; Fax: 216-641-4771. Email: villageecc@aol.com. Web: www.villamontessoricenter.org. Sr. Marie Veres, H.M., Pres. & Prin. Sisters 3; Lay Teachers 6.

AKRON. *North Akron Catholic School* (2003) 1570 Creighton Ave., 44310. Tel: 330-633-1383; Fax: 330-633-4512. Email: northakron@leeca.org. Web: www.nacs.k12.oh.us. Miss Christine Lackney, Prin. Lay Teachers 8.

Business Office: 300 E. Tallmadge Ave., 44310. Tel: 330-376-5144; Fax: 330-376-5311.

Our Lady of the Elms School, (Grades PreK-6), 1290 W. Market St., 44313-7108. Tel: 330-864-7210; Fax: 330-867-1262. Email: mreichart@theelms.org. Web: www.theelms.org. Marie Reichart, Prin. Lay Teachers 18; Students 155.

CHARDON. *Notre Dame Elementary School* (1957) 13000 Auburn Rd., 44024. Tel: 440-279-1127; Fax: 440-286-1235. Email: bdoering@ndec.org. Web: www.notredameelementary.org. Barbara Doering, Prin.; Mrs. Sabrina Mysyk, Librarian; Mrs. Kathryn Mullinger, Librarian. Sisters of Notre Dame 7; Lay Teachers 24; Students 410.

Notre Dame PreSchool (2000) 13000 Auburn Rd., 44024. Tel: 440-286-7101, Ext. 5920; Fax: 440-286-9364. Email: flelko@ndec.org. Alfreda Lelko, Dir.; Barbara Doering, Prin. Sisters of Notre Dame 1; Lay Teachers 3; Aides 2; Students 50.

HUDSON. *Seton Catholic School* (1997) 6923 Stow Rd., 44236. Tel: 330-342-4200; Fax: 330-342-4276. Web: www.setoncatholicschool.org. Mrs. Karen Alestock, Prin.; Michael Ritenour, Chm., Bd. Directors; Evelyn Kremyar, Librarian. Sisters 1; Lay Teachers 28; Students 433.

KIRTLAND. *Peaceful Children Montessori School* (1994) 8100 Eagle Rd., 44094. Tel: 440-256-1976; Fax: 440-256-4370. Email: pcmschool@roadrunner.com. Web: peacefulchildrenmontessori.org. Jennifer Massiello, Prin. Lay Teachers 10; Total Enrollment 74; Total Staff 18.

PARMA HEIGHTS. *Incarnate Word Academy* (1930) 6620 Pearl Rd., 44130. Tel: 440-842-6818; Fax: 440-888-1377. Email: jcicerchi@incarnatewordacademy.org. Web: incarnatewordacademy.org. Mrs. Janette Cicerchi, Prin. Sisters 3; Lay Teachers 24; Students 467.

[F] ELEMENTARY SCHOOLS, PAROCHIAL AND DIOCESAN

CLEVELAND. *Archbishop James P. Lyke Elementary School* St. Henry, St. Timothy, and Our Lady of Peace schools consolidated to form Archbishop James P. Lyke School., 18230 Harvard Ave., 44128. Tel: 216-991-9644; Fax: 216-991-9470. Email: lykesthenry@leeca.org. Web: www.archbishoplykeschool.org. Sr. Brigetta Waldron, O.S.U., Dir.; Mrs. Sandra Fletcher, Pres. Sisters 1; Lay Teachers 23; Students 356.

Archbishop Lyke School (Grades K-4), 18230 Harvard Ave., 44128. Tel: 216-991-9644; Fax: 216-991-9470. Email: lykesthenry@leeca.org. Web: www.archbishoplykeschool.org. Ms. Mary Pat Hable, Prin. Students 211.

Archbishop Lyke Middle School (Grades 6-8), 4351 E. 131st St., Garfield Heights, 44105. Tel: 216-581-3517; Fax: 216-581-6204. Email: lykesttimothy@leeca.org. Web: www.archbishoplykeschool.org. Mrs. Margarete W. Smith, Prin. Students 145.

St. Francis School, 7206 Myron Ave., 44103. Tel: 216-361-4858; Fax: 216-361-1673. Sr. Karen Somerville, S.N.D., Prin. Sisters of Notre Dame 4; Lay Teachers 12; Students 190.

Metro Catholic School (1988) Tel: 216-281-4044; Fax: 216-634-2853. Email: metro@leeca.org. Web: www.metrocatholic.org. Sr. Anne Maline, S.N.D., Dir.; Colleen Gutta, Librarian Aide. Sisters of Notre Dame 16; Ursuline Nuns 1; Humility of Mary Nuns 1; Lay Teachers 30; Students (K-8) 523; Preschool 42.

St. Stephen Bldg. (Grade 5-8), 1910 W. 54th St., 44102. Tel: 216-281-4044; Fax: 216-634-2853. Email: metro@leeca.org. Web: www.metrocatholic.org. Robert Finkovich, Prin.

St. Michael Bldg. (Grades 2-4), 1910 W. 54th St., 44102. Tel: 216-281-4044; Fax: 216-634-2853. Email: metro@leeca.org. Web: www.metrocatholic.org. Sr. Karen Bohan, O.S.U., Prin.

St. Boniface Bldg. (PreK-1), 3555 W. 54th St., 44102. Tel: 216-631-5733; Fax: 216-634-2853. Email: metro@leeca.org. Web: www.metrocatholic.org. Patricia Scholl, Prin.; Rose Cummings, Librarian.

St. Thomas Aquinas School (2010) 9101 Superior Ave., 44106. Tel: 216-421-4668; Fax: 216-721-8444. Mrs. Nancy Lynch, Prin. Notre Dame Nun 1; Lay Teachers 15; Students 218.

Urban Community School, 4909 Lorain Ave., 44102. Tel: 216-939-8441; Fax: 216-939-8198. Email: mdoyle2401@aol.com. Sr. Maureen Doyle, O.S.U., Dir.; Pam Delly, Prin.; Elizabeth Allard, Librarian. Ursuline Nuns of Cleveland 3; Lay Teachers 25; Students 450.

West Park Catholic Academy, (Grades PreSchool-8), 17720 Puritas Ave., 44135. Tel: 216-671-7900; Fax: 216-671-5277. Email: westpark@leeca.org. Annemarie Rajnicek, Prin. Lay Teachers 22.

EASTLAKE. *St. Mary Magdalene-St. Justin Martyr School, Inc.*, 35741 Stevens Blvd., 44095. Tel: 440-946-5414; Fax: 440-946-2074. Web: www.smmsjmschool.org; www.smmwillowick.org. Rev. Kevin M. Liebhardt, Pres.; Sr. Mary Quinlan, S.N.D., Prin.; Barbara Taraska, Librarian. Lay Teachers 15; Enrollment (K-8) 190; Preschool 34.

GARFIELD HEIGHTS. *John Paul II Academy*, (Grades PreK-8), 10608 Penfield Ave., 44125. Tel: 216-581-3080; Fax: 216-581-3031. Miss Christine Lackney, Prin.; Mrs. Linda Borowy, Librarian. Lay Teachers 16; Students 247.

LAKEWOOD. *Lakewood Catholic Academy* (includes Holy Family Learning Center), 14808 Lake Ave., 44107. Tel: 216-521-0559; Fax: 216-521-0515. Email: info@lakewoodcatholicacademy.com. Web: www.lakewoodcatholicacademy.com. Maureen Arbeznik, Prin.; Marilyn Wangler, Librarian. Lay Teachers 32.

WICKLIFFE. *All Saints of St. John Vianney School* (1977) (Grades PreSchool-8), 28702 Euclid Ave., 44092. Tel: 216-943-1395; Fax: 216-943-4468. Email: allsaints@oh.rr.com. Web: www.allsaintssjv.org. Mrs. Rosemary Wilson, Prin.; Mrs. Paula Kirchner, Librarian. Sisters 1; Lay Teachers 16; Students 285.

Mater Dei Academy (2010) Merger of Immaculate Conception School, Willoughby, OH; Our Lady of Mt. Carmel School, Wickliffe, OH, 29840 Euclid Ave., 44092. Tel: 440-585-0800; Fax: 440-585-9391. Loretta Pilla, Prin. Lay Teachers 22; Students 411.

[G] SPECIAL SCHOOLS AND CENTERS
For Exceptional Children

CLEVELAND

Julie Billiart School (1954) 4982 Clubside Rd., Lyndhurst, 44124-2596. Tel: 216-381-1191; Fax: 216-381-2216. Email: aloporto@jbschool.org. Web: www.juliebilliartschool.org. Sr. Agnesmarie, S.N.D., Pres. Non-graded school for children having learning problems. Sisters 5; Lay Teachers 22; Students 115.

[H] PRESCHOOL AND DAY CARE CENTERS

CLEVELAND. *Catholic Charities Community Services/ Head Start* (1964) 7911 Detroit Ave., 44102. Tel: 216-334-2942; Fax: 216-334-2948. Email: mcurry@clevelandcatholiccharities.org. Michelle Curry, Dir. Lay Teachers 48; Children 795.

GARFIELD HEIGHTS. *Marymount Child Care Center* (1991) 12215 Granger Rd., 44125. Tel: 216-581-3540; Fax: 216-518-2188. Email: marymountcare@aol.com. Sr. Dorothy Ann Krolikowski, S.S.J.-T.O.S.F., Dir. Sisters 1; Total Staff 15; Total Assisted Annually 120.

LAKEWOOD. *Holy Family Learning Center*, 14808 Lake Ave., 44107. Tel: 216-521-4352; Fax: 216-521-0515. Email: hflcsko@yahoo.com. Web: www.lakewoodcatholicacademy.com/holyfamily. Sr. Kathleen Ogrin, O.S.U., Dir. Total Assisted 106.

[I] GENERAL HOSPITALS
(For information on other Catholic related hospitals please contact the Chancery Office.)

CLEVELAND

St. John Hospital, 2475 E. 22nd St., 44115. Tel: 216-696-5560; Fax: 216-696-2204. Web: www.sistersofcharityhealth.org. Sr. Judith Ann Karam, C.S.A., Pres. & CEO.

**St. John Medical Center*, 2351 E. 22nd St., 44115. Tel: 888-223-1816; Fax: 216-696-2204. Web: www-.sistersofcharityhealth.org. Sr. Judith Ann Karam, C.S.A., Pres. & CEO.

Marymount Hospital, Inc., 12300 McCracken Rd., Garfield Heights, 44125. Tel: 216-587-8080; Fax: 216-587-8212. Email: dkilarski@marymount.org. Web: www.marymount.org. Mr. William Keckan, Interim Pres. & CEO; Rev. Dennis Mrosso; Sisters Betty Gulick, S.S.J.-T.O.S.F., Dir. Pastoral Care; Jo Ann Poplar, S.S.J.-T.O.S.F., Staff Chap.; Ms. Janet Elaine McDonald, Staff Chap. Sisters of St. Joseph of the Third Order of St. Francis 4; Bed Capacity 322; Patients Assisted Annually 136,725; Total Staff 1,358.

St. Vincent Charity Medical Center, 2351 E. 22nd St., 44115. Tel: 888-223-1816; Fax: 216-696-2204. Web: www.sistersofcharityhealth.org. Sr. Judith Ann Karam, C.S.A., Pres. & CEO.

LORAIN

Mercy Regional Medical Center, 3700 Kolbe Rd., 44053. Tel: 440-960-4000.

OBERLIN

**Mercy Allen Hospital* (1892) 200 W. Lorain St., 44074. Tel: 440-775-1211; Fax: 440-775-9147. Web: www.community-health-partners.com. Susan Bowers, Pres. Bed Capacity 25; Patients Assisted Annually 12,000; Total Staff 200.

[J] TRAINING SCHOOLS FOR NURSES

CLEVELAND. *Marymount School of Practical Nursing* (1952) 12300 McCracken Rd., Garfield Heights, 44125. Tel: 216-587-8160; Fax: 216-587-8632. Email: acarlucci@marymount.org. Web: www.marymount.org. Students 35.

[K] SPECIAL HOSPITALS

EUCLID. *Rose Mary, The Johanna Grasselli Rehabilitation and Education Center*, 19350 Euclid Ave., 44117. Tel: 216-481-4823; Fax: 216-481-4154. Web: rose-marycenter.com. Ms. Patricia A. Colombo, Exec. Dir. Children 42; Residents 93; Bed Capacity 93; Total Assisted Annually 180; Total Staff 270.

PARMA. *Holy Family Home and Hospice* (1956) 6707 State Rd., 44134. Tel: 440-888-7722; Fax: 440-866-6040. Email: info@holyfamilyhome.com. Web: www.holyfamilyhome.com. Rev. Simon Kimaryo, Chap.

Holy Family Home, Inpatient and community-based hospice care. Sisters 5; Total Staff 95; Bed Capacity 30; Patients Assisted Annually 423.

[L] PROTECTIVE INSTITUTIONS

CLEVELAND. *Catholic Charities Early Learning Center at the Quadrangle*, 2302 Community College Ave., 44115. Tel: 216-589-9750; Fax: 216-589-9702. Janet Lucha, Day Care Admin. Day Care program sponsored by Catholic Charities Services Corp. Funded by United Way Catholic Charities & County Vouchers. Students 85; Total Assisted Annually 150; Total Staff 15.

PARMA. *CCSC/Parmadale* (1925) 6753 State Rd., 44134. Tel: 440-845-7700; Fax: 440-845-5910. Email: pdale@clevelandcatholiccharities.org. Web: www.clevelandcatholiccharities.org. Jeffrey S. Jeney, Dir. Specialized Residential Services; Intensive Treatment Services; Chemical Dependency Treatment; Community-Based Family Services; Specialized Foster Care; Outpatient Services; Training and Consultation Services; and Volunteer Program; Adoption Services; Head Start. Capacity 80; Children in Foster Care 50; Total Assisted Annually 1,750; Total Staff 186.

[M] HOMES FOR AGED

CLEVELAND. *St. Augustine Manor*, 7801 Detroit Ave., 44102. Tel: 216-634-7400; Fax: 216-634-7483. Web: www.staugustinemanor.org. Edward Hack, Chm., Bd. of Trustees; Andrew Koha, Pres. & CEO. Affiliated with Catholic Charities. Provider of rehabilitation services, subacute care, skilled nursing, assisted living, hospice care, child day care and home health care. Bed Capacity 358; Patients Assisted Annually 755; Total in Residence 340; Total Staff 520.

Coterie of St. Augustine Manor, The, 7801 Detroit

Ave., 44102. Tel: 216-634-7400; Fax: 216-634-7483. Mrs. Margaret Lynch, Pres. (Operates the Coterie Boutique)

Jennings Center for Older Adults (1942) 10204 Granger Rd., 44125. Tel: 216-581-2900; Fax: 216-581-4505. Email: martha.kutik@jenningscenter.org. Web: www.jenningscenter.org. Mrs. Martha M. Kutik, Pres. & CEO; Rev. Kestutis Zemaitis (Lithuania), Chap. Tel: 216-581-2900. Continuum of Services Campus for older adults, including long term care facility, independent and assisted living apartments, an adult day center, short-term rehabilitation and intergenerational child day care center for 75 children. Under the sponsorship of the Sisters of the Holy Spirit. Sisters 7; Residents 394; Total Assisted Annually 884; Total Staff 320.

Jennings Assisted Living Tel: 216-581-2900; Fax: 216-581-4505. Email: welcome@jenningscenter.org. Web: www.jenningscenter.org. Two-bedroom Suites 52; One-bedroom Suites 2.

Jennings Hall Skilled Nursing Facility Tel: 216-581-2900; Fax: 216-581-4505. Email: welcome@jenningscenter.org. Web: www.jenningscenter.org. Skilled Nursing Facility Bed Capacity 174.

Jennings Manor Housing Corporation (1998) Tel: 216-581-2900; Fax: 216-581-4505. Email: welcome@jenningscenter.org. Web: www.jenningscenter.org. Apartment Bldg.-HUD 202 Supportive Housing for Older Adults Apartments 61; HUD 202.

Holy Spirit Villas (1998) Tel: 216-581-2900; Fax: 216-581-4505. Email: welcome@jenningscenter.org. Web: www.jenningscenter.org. Independent Housing Units 10.

St. Agnes Terrace Apartments Independent Housing, Tel: 216-581-2900; Fax: 216-581-4505. Email: welcome@jenningscenter.org. Web: www.jenningscenter.org. Apartments 42.

St. Rita Apartments Independent Housing Tel: 216-581-2900; Fax: 216-581-4505. Email: welcome@jenningscenter. Web: www.jenningscenter-.org. Apartments 63.

Eva L. Bruening Adult Day Center (2003) Tel: 216-581-2900; Fax: 216-581-4505. Email: welcome@jenningscenter.org. Web: www.jenningscenter.org. Clients Per Day Capacity 50.

The Learning Circle Child Day Care Center (1999) Tel: 216-581-2900. Email: marketing@jenningscenter.org. Web: www.jenningscenter.org. Infant to before and after school care. Capacity 75.

Little Sisters of the Poor dba Sts. Mary and Joseph Home for the Aged 4291 Richmond Rd., 44122-6199. Tel: 216-464-1222; Fax: 216-464-4794. Email: mscleveland@littlesistersofthepoor.org. Web: www.littlesistersofthepoorcleveland.org. Sr. Mary Michael. Little Sisters of the Poor. Sisters 10; Association Members 40; Nursing 62; Independent Living 21; Bed Capacity 94; Residential Care Beds 32; Total Assisted Annually 140; Total Staff 150. In Res. Rev. Ray J. Horley, Chap. (Retired).

Mount St. Joseph, 21800 Chardon Rd., 44117. Tel: 216-531-7426; Fax: 216-531-4033. Sr. M. Raphael Gregg, NHA. Conducted by Sisters of St. Joseph of St. Mark - Mount St. Joseph. Sisters 7; Bed Capacity 100; Residents 100; Total Assisted Annually 201; Total Staff 147.

AKRON. *Francesca Residence*, 39 N. Portage Path, 44303. Tel: 330-867-6334; Fax: 330-867-6334. Email: martinovich00@hotmail.com. Sr. M. Martin Green, F.D.C., Admin.; Rev. Albert A. Kunkel, Chap. Daughters of Divine Charity 6; Total Assisted Annually 30; Total in Residence 24; Total Staff 6.

BEDFORD. *Light of Hearts Villa, Inc.*, 283 Union St., 44146. Tel: 440-232-1991; Fax: 440-735-3429. Email: information@lightofheartsvilla.org. Web: www.lightofheartsvilla.org. Arlene C. Jaroscak, Exec. Dir. Bed Capacity 109; Total in Residence 90; Total Assisted 62; Total Staff 100.

FAIRLAWN. *St. Edward Home dba The Village at St. Edward Nursing Care and Assisted Living* (1964) 3131 Smith Rd., 44333. Tel: 330-666-1183. Web: www.vased.org. John J. Hennelly, Pres. & CEO; Rev. James F. Flood, Chap. Sisters 2; Nursing Care Residents 81; Assisted Living Residents 90; Total Staff 163.

St. Edward Home dba The Village at St. Edward Independent Living (1990) 3125 Smith Rd., 44333. Tel: 330-668-2828. Web: www.vased.org. John J. Hennelly, Pres. & CEO; Rev. James F. Flood, Chap. Total in Residence 77; Total Staff 40.

GARFIELD HEIGHTS. *Village at Marymount*, 5200 Marymount Village Dr., 44125. Tel: 216-332-1100; Fax: 216-332-1619. Email: jmyers@marymount.org. Web: www.villageatmarymount.org. Mr. Jeffry Myers, Pres.; Sr. Mary Alice Jarosz, S.S.F.-T.O.S.F., Dir. Mission Svcs.; Rev. George Jaskulski, O.F.M., Priest Chap. Village at Marymount provides comprehensive health care services in response to the needs of the local community by leasing and operating health care facilities and services, including Marymount Place, a 104-unit Senior Living Community for the Well-Elderly/Assisted Living and Villa St. Joseph, a 142-bed long-term facility (under an Operating Agreement with Marymount Health Care Systems within the philosophy and objectives of the Sisters of St. Joseph of the Third Order of St. Francis.) Bed Capacity 246; Total Assisted Annually 1,339; Total Staff 300.

PARMA. *Mount Alverna Village*, 6765 State Rd., 44134. Tel: 440-843-7800; Fax: 440-843-7107. Web: www.franciscancommunities.com/facilities/mtalverna. Patrick M. Welsh, Exec. Dir. Capacity 183; Residents 153; Total Assisted 183; Total Staff 253; Assisted Living 30.

RICHFIELD. *Regina Health Center* (1992) 5232 Broadview Rd., 44286-9608. Tel: 330-659-4161; Fax: 330-659-5113. Email: bflannery@reginahealthcenter.org. Sr. Miriam Erb, C.S.A., Congregational Leader; Brian J. Flannery, Admin. Sponsored by Sisters of Charity of St. Augustine. Nursing Home Beds 101; Assisted Living Units 54; Total in Residence 130; Total Assisted 38; Total Staff 192.

[N] MONASTERIES AND RESIDENCES OF PRIESTS AND BROTHERS

CLEVELAND. *Benedictine Order of Cleveland*, St. Andrew Abbey, 10510 Buckeye Rd., 44104-3728. Tel: 216-721-5300; Fax: 216-721-1253. Email: abbotchristopher@cbhs.net. Web: www.bocohio.org. Most Rev. Roger W. Gries, O.S.B., D.D., M.Ed., Auxiliary Bishop of Cleveland. Priests 18; Brothers 13. 1230 Ansel Rd., 44108. Tel: 216-721-0676; Fax: 216-721-0903. Rt. Rev. Clement Zeleznik, O.S.B., Chap., Loyola Retreat House (Retired); Rev. Bede Kotlinski, O.S.B.; Very Rev. Albert Marflak, O.S.B., Subprior; Revs. Joachim Pastirik, O.S.B.; Gerard Gonda, O.S.B., Pres. Benedictine High School; Timothy Buyansky, O.S.B.; Dominic Mondzelewski, O.S.B.; Placid Pientek, O.S.B.; Very Rev. Gary Hoover, O.S.B., Prior; Revs. Paschal Petcavage, O.S.B., Assoc. Pastor of Assumption; Justin Dyrwal, O.S.B., Pastor of Assumption. Assumption Church: 9183 Broadview Rd., Broadview Heights, 44147. Tel: 440-526-1177; Fax: 440-526-2838.

Other Assignments: Rev. Anthony J. Ozimek, O.S.B., St. Vincent Hospital, Billings, MT 59107-5200. Tel: 406-657-7000; Rt. Rev. Christopher Schwartz, O.S.B., Abbot, Incarnate Word Academy, 6634 Pearl Rd., 44130-3898. Tel: 440-886-6996; Revs. Michael Brunovsky, O.S.B., Novice Master, St. Andrew, 5135 Superior Ave., 44130. Tel: 216-431-2057; Dismas Boeff, O.S.B., Chap., Southwest General Hospital, St. Peter, 6455 Engle Rd., 44142. Tel: 216-433-1440; Fax: 216-433-1434; Kenneth J. Katricak, O.S.B., Assoc. Pastor, Assumption, St. Andrew Abbey, 2900 M.L. King Dr., 44104. Tel: 216-721-5300; Anselm Zupka, O.S.B.

Congregation of the Blessed Sacrament, 5384 Wilson Mills Rd., 44143-3092. Tel: 440-442-3410; Fax: 440-442-2001. Web: blessedsacrament.com. Very Rev. Norman B. Pelletier, S.S.S., Prov. Supr.; Revs. John Thomas Lane, S.S.S., Pastor; William Fickel, S.S.S., Supr.; Roger Bourgeois, S.S.S.; Michael Noreika, S.S.S.; William T. Young, S.S.S.; Paul Bernier, S.S.S.; Francisco Mendoza, S.S.S.; Deacon Joseph Bourgeois; Bros. Gerard Hickey, S.S.S.; Gary L. Laverdiere, S.S.S.; Allen Boeckman, S.S.S. Priests 8; Deacons 1; Brothers 3. *Regina Health Center*, 5232 Broadview Rd., Richfield, 44286-9608. Tel: 330-659-4161. Revs. George Evans, S.S.S.; Julian Rousseau, S.S.S.; Bros. Eugene Blee, S.S.S.; Thomas F. Flanagan, S.S.S.; David Phelan, S.S.S. Priests 2; Brothers 3.

Congregation of the Blessed Sacrament Provincial House, 5384 Wilson Mills Rd., Highland Heights, 44143-3092. Tel: 440-442-6311; Fax: 440-442-4752. Web: www.blessedsacrament.com. Very Rev. Norman B. Pelletier, S.S.S., Prov. Supr. Province of St. Ann.

Priests Serving Outside Country: Rev. Ralph Roberts, S.S.S., Parrocchia S. Marco Evangelista, Via Del Modiano 1/1, Trieste 34148 Italy. Tel: 011-39-040-941218; Fax: 011-39-040-938-1987.

Priests attached to Provincialate: Revs. Andrew Beaudoin, S.S.S., 11487 Kerridale Ave., Spring Hill, FL 34608-3111. Tel: 352-686-8078; John Kamas, S.S.S., St. Francis DeSales, 135 E. 96th St., New York, NY 10128-3503. Tel: 212-289-1742; Dennis Ruane, S.S.S., Congregation of the Blessed Sacrament, P.O. Box 16289, Salt Lake City, UT 84116-0289. Tel: 801-495-3691; Joseph Thai Minh Tran, S.S.S., St. Charles Borromeo Church, 1818 Coal Pl. S.E., Albuquerque, NM 87106-4025; George Evans, S.S.S., Regina Health Center, 5232 Broadview Rd., Richfield, 44286-9608. Tel: 330-659-4161; Anthony J. Marshall, S.S.S.; John Christman, S.S.S.

Marianist Community, 18340 Marcella Rd., 44119-2622. Tel: 216-481-1007; Fax: 216-486-1035. Email: willhall1966@yahoo.com. Rev. H. James Bartlett, S.M.; Bros. William G. Halloway, S.M., Dir.; David F. Murphy, S.M.; Joseph A. Scheible, S.M. Priests 1; Brothers 3.

Maryknoll Fathers & Brothers (1911) 10309 Edgewater Dr., 44102. Tel: 216-651-2121; Fax: 216-651-8242. Email: mklcleve@aol.com. Web: www.maryknoll.org. Rev. James H. Huvane, M.M., Dir. Total in Residence 1; Total Staff 1.

Mercedarians (1218) 6928 Detroit Ave., 44102-3093. Tel: 216-651-5043; Fax: 216-651-6641. Email: mtcarmel@megsinet.net. Web: www.massintransit.com; www.olmccleveland.com; orderofmercy.org. Order of the B.V.M. of Mercy. Priests 4; Mercedarian Sisters (H.M.S.S.) 4; Total Staff 35. In Res. Revs. Richard S. Rasch, O.de.M., Vicar Provincial & Pastor; Jerome P. Laubacker, O.de.M.; Anthony M. Fortunato, O.de.M., Rectory Supr. & Asst. Pastor; Michael Donovan, O.de.M., Teacher.

St. Paul Friary, 4120 Euclid Ave., 44103. Tel: 216-431-8854; Fax: 216-361-1951. Email: Stpaulshrine@sbcglobal.net. Web: www.saintpaulshrine.com. Revs. Philip J. Bernier, O.F.M.Cap.; Samuel Driscoll, O.F.M.Cap.; Robert Marva, O.F.M.Cap.; William Wiethorn, O.F.M.Cap.; Bro. Walter Robb, O.F.M.Cap. Priests 4; Brothers 1.

St. Agnes-Our Lady of Fatima, 6800 Lexington Ave., 44103. Tel: 216-391-1655; Fax: 216-391-7919. Rev. Robert Marva, O.F.M.Cap.; Deacon Hardin M. Martin. Capuchin Franciscan Friars

St. Stanislaus Friary (1906) 3649 E. 65th St., 44105-1293. Tel: 216-341-9091; Fax: 216-341-2688. Email: ststans@ameritech.net. Web: www.ststanislaus.org. Revs. Michael Surufka, O.F.M.; Leonard Stunek, O.F.M., Guardian; Placyd Kon, O.F.M. The Franciscan Friars, Province of the Assumption of the Blessed Virgin., (Please see St. Stanislaus, Cleveland in the parish section for additional information.) *Marymount Convent*, Garfield Heights, 44125. Tel: 216-587-8376. Rev. George Jaskulski, O.F.M., Chap.

AVON. *Congregation of St. Joseph* (1873) 4076 Case Rd., 44011. Tel: 440-934-6270; Fax: 440-934-6270. Email: avon@murialdo.org. Web: www.murialdo.org. Revs. Lawrence Tosco, C.S.J., Formation Dir. & Local Supr.; Gaetano Menegatto, C.S.J. Fathers and Brothers of St. Joseph. Priests 2; Candidates 2; Temporary Professed 3.

BROOKLYN. *St. Anthony of Padua Friary* (1960) 4185 Brookway Ln., 44144. Tel: 216-661-7138; Fax: 216-845-5710. Revs. Walter Dolan, O.F.M.; Tan Peter Duc Do, O.F.M., Vicar; Theodore Haag, O.F.M.; James Kelly, O.F.M.; James McManamon, O.F.M.; William J. Rooney, O.F.M.; Bros. Thomas Carroll, O.F.M., Guardian; Day Hoang, O.F.M.; Patrick T. Shea, O.F.M. Priests 6; Brothers 3.

[O] CONVENTS AND RESIDENCES FOR SISTERS

CLEVELAND. *Carmel of the Holy Family* (1923) 3176 Fairmount Blvd., 44118-4199. Tel: 216-321-6568; Fax: 216-321-1904. Email: sisters@clevelandcarmel.org. Web: www.clevelandcarmel.org. Sr. Barbara Losh, O.C.D., Prioress. Discalced Carmelite Nuns. Professed Nuns 12.

Congregation of the Sisters of St. Joseph, Inc. dba Congregation of St. Joseph Cleveland Center, 3430 Rocky River Dr., 44111-2997. Tel: 216-252-0440; Fax: 216-941-3430. Web: www.csjoseph.org. Sr. Marcella Clancy, Center Admin. Sisters 717.

Monastery of the Poor Clares (1877) Poor Clare Nuns (Colettine), 3501 Rocky River Dr., 44111-2998. Tel: 216-941-2821; Fax: 216-941-9298. Web: www.poorclarecolettines-cleveland.org. Observing the Primitive Rule of St. Clare (strictly cloistered, solemn vows). Perpetual exposition of the Blessed Sacrament. Cloistered Nuns 16; Extern Sisters 2.

Motherhouse and Novitiate of the Sisters of the Holy Spirit (1932) 10102 Granger Rd., 44125. Tel: 216-581-2941; Fax: 216-581-1207. Email: sister.mary.assumpta@jenningscenter.org. Sr. Patricia Raelene Peters, C.S.Sp., Supr. Gen. Professed Sisters 8.

Motherhouse and Novitiate of the Ursuline Sisters (1850) 2600 Lander Rd., 44124. Tel: 440-449-1200; Fax: 440-449-3588. Email: mgrady@ursulinesisters.org. Web: www.ursulinesisters.org. Sr. Maureen Grady, O.S.U., Pres.

The Ursuline Academy of Cleveland Professed Nuns 185.

Poor Clares of Perpetual Adoration, 4108 Euclid Ave., 44103. Tel: 216-361-0783; Fax: 216-361-0979. Email: angelspcpa@sbcglobal.net. Web: thepoorclares.com. Sr. Mary Thomas, P.C.P.A., Supr. Monastery adjoins Conversion of St. Paul Shrine, where they maintain Perpetual Adoration. Cloistered Sisters 17.

Provincial House of Sisters of the Most Holy Trinity, 21281 Chardon Rd., 44117. Tel: 216-481-8232; Fax: 216-481-6577. Email: osst@srstrinity.com. Web: www.srstrinity.com. Sr. M. Rochelle Guental, O.S.S.T., Regl. Delegate. Attended from Center for Pastoral Leadership. Sisters 22; Total in Residence 14.

Sisters of St. Joseph of St. Mark General Motherhouse and Novitiate of Sisters of St. Joseph of St. Mark-Generalate, Diocese of Cleveland, 21800 Chardon Rd., 44117-2199. Tel: 216-531-7426; Fax: 216-383-0511. Email: sr_mpaschal_msj@yahoo.com. Sr. M. Raphael Gregg, Gen. Supr. Sisters 7.

AKRON. *Dominican Sisters of Peace* (1929) Our Lady of the Elms Convent, 1230 W. Market St., 44313-7108. Tel: 330-836-4908; Fax: 330-836-5913. Web: www.oppeace.org. Sr. Arleen Kisiel, O.P., Motherhouse & Mission Group Coord. Sisters in Congregation 638; Sisters in Diocese 61.

Provincial Motherhouse and Novitiate of the Daughters of Divine Charity (1950) 39 N. Portage Path, 44303-1183. Tel: 330-867-4960; Fax: 330-867-6334. Email: smcoffeltl@hotmail.com. Sr. Mary Coffelt, F.D.C., Prov. Supr.; Rev. Albert A. Kunkel, Chap. Tel: 330-867-2618. Sisters 15.

CHARDON. *Provincial House of the Sisters of Notre Dame, Juniorate, Novitiate* (1874) Notre Dame Education Center, 13000 Auburn Rd., 44024. Tel: 440-286-7101; Fax: 440-286-3377. Email: cliberatore@ndec.org. Web: www.sndchardon.org. Rev. Paul J. Sciarrotta, Chap. (Retired). Sisters 343.

GARFIELD HEIGHTS. *Marymount Congregational Home* (1926) 12215 Granger Rd., 44125. Tel: 216-581-3535; Fax: 216-518-2187. Email: sisterjoyce@marymount-ch.org. Web: www.ssj-tosf.org. Sr. Joyce Hollkamp, S.S.J.-T.O.S.F., Business & Facilities Coord.; Rev. George Jaskulski, O.F.M., Chap. & Contact Person. Residence of the Sisters of St. Joseph, Third Order of St. Francis. Sisters 30; Priests 1; Lay Staff 3.

PARMA HEIGHTS. *Sisters of the Incarnate Word and Blessed Sacrament* (1625) 6618 Pearl Rd., 44130-3808. Tel: 440-886-6440; Fax: 440-842-6391. Email: smrksiw@yahoo.com. Sr. Mary Rose Kocab, S.I.W., Congregational Leader.

Sisters of the Incarnate Word and Blessed Sacrament Final Professed Sisters 25. 6634 Pearl Rd., 44130-3808. Tel: 440-886-6996.

RICHFIELD. *Mount Augustine, Motherhouse of the Sisters of Charity of St. Augustine* (1851) 5232 Broadview Rd., 44286-9608. Tel: 330-659-5100; Fax: 330-659-3899. Email: sme@srsofcharity.org. Web: www.srsofcharity.org. Sr. Miriam Erb, C.S.A., Congregational Leader. Final Professed Sisters 51.

Regina Health Center (1993) Tel: 330-659-4161; Fax: 330-659-5113. Religious Congregations 22; Total Assisted Care 54; Skilled Nursing Beds 101.

[P] SECULAR INSTITUTES

CLEVELAND HEIGHTS. *Society of Our Lady of the Way* (1936) c/o Mary Ann Tady, 1064 Oxford Rd., 44121. Tel: 216-381-5502. Email: matslow@aol.com. Web: www.secularinstitutes.org; www.saecimds.com. Secular Institute for Single Women.

[Q] HOMES FOR WOMEN

AKRON. *Leonora Hall* (1946) 39 N. Portage Path, 44303. Tel: 330-867-1752; Fax: 330-867-6334. Sr. M. Antoinette, F.D.C., Exec. Dir. Leonora Hall Residence "is a Home Away From Home" for Women who are working, going to school or unable to live independently. Semi-independent/ supported living services are also provided for women with mild/moderate developmental disabilities in collaboration with Summit County Board of Developmental Disabilities Daughters of Divine Charity 2; Residents 10; Personnel 4.

[R] LAY ASSOCIATIONS

CLEVELAND. *Community of Little Brothers and Sisters of the Eucharist, Inc.* (1977) 2186 E. 35th St., 44115-3039. Tel: 216-566-0531; 216-566-9953; Fax: 216-566-0531. Email: littlesismaggie@gmail.com. Rev. James P. O'Donnell, Dir.

Society of St. Vincent de Paul, Diocesan Council, Cathedral Square Plaza, 1404 E. 9th St., 3rd Fl., 44114. Tel: 216-696-6525, Ext. 3150; Fax: 216-861-3200. Frank J. Fearon, Pres.; Lawrence Lauter, A.C.S.W, L.I.S.W., M.Div., Exec. Dir.

Akron District Council, 127 Marwyck Dr., Northfield, 44067. Tel: 330-476-5762. Cathie Perusek, Pres.

Cuyahoga West District Council, 6538 Marianna Dr., Parma Heights, 44130. Tel: 440-888-4355. George Getz, Pres.

Cuyahoga East District Council, 384 Kenyon Ave., Bedford, 44146. Tel: 440-786-9971. Michael Birskovich, Pres.

Lake/Geauga District Council, 10589 Ridgewater Dr., Concord, 44077. Tel: 440-392-0971. Marilyne Brandoni, Pres.

[S] RETREAT HOUSES

CLEVELAND. *Jesuit Retreat House* (1898) 5629 State Rd., 44134. Tel: 440-884-9300; Fax: 440-885-1055. Email: jrhcleve@att.net. Web: www.jrh-cleveland.org. Sr. Mary Ann Flannery, S.C., Dir.

AVON. *St. Leonard Youth Retreat Center* (1998) 4076 Case Rd., 44011. Tel: 440-934-6735; Fax: 440-934-6270. Web: www.stleonardyrc.com. Molly Smith, Dir.

[T] SOCIAL SERVICE AGENCIES AND INSTITUTIONS

For information call Catholic Information and Referral Services (CIRS) Tel: 216-696-HELP (4357).

CLEVELAND

Bishop William M. Cosgrove Center (1994) 1736 Superior Ave., 44114. Tel: 216-781-8262; Fax: 216-566-9161. Email: nxevans@clevelandcatholiccharities.org. Nicole Evans, Prog. Dir. Total Assisted 120,000; Total Staff 6.

Catholic Charities Community Services Corporation, 7911 Detroit Ave., 44102. Tel: 216-334-2931; Fax: 216-334-2907. Email: bwashington@clevelandcatholiccharities.org. Web: www.clevelandcatholiccharities.org. Bernadette Washington, Exec. Dir.

Catholic Charities Community Services of Medina County, 740 E. Washington St., Medina, 44256. Tel: 330-723-9615 (Medina); Fax: 330-764-8795 (Medina). Web: www.clevelandcatholiccharities.org. Timothy Putka, Dir.

Catholic Charities Community Services of Geauga County, 10771 Mayfield Rd., 44024-9323. Tel: 800-242-9755; Fax: 440-285-4909. Web: www.clevelandcatholiccharities.org. James Clements, Dir.

Catholic Charities Community Services of Lake County, 8 N. State St., Suite 455, Painesville, 44077-3954. Tel: 440-946-7264; Fax: 440-953-1608. Web: www.clevelandcatholiccharities.org. James Clements, Dir.

Catholic Charities Community Services of Lorain County, 628 Poplar St., Elyria, 44035. Tel: 440-366-1106; Fax: 440-366-5645. Christine Horne, Dir.

St. Phillip Neri Family Center, 799 E. 82nd St., 44103. Tel: 216-391-4415. Armetta Landrum, Dir.

Employment & Training Services - Midtown Professional Center, 3135 Euclid Ave., Room 101, 44115-2507. Tel: 216-426-9870; Fax: 216-426-9932. Autumn Winfield, Dir.

Fatima Family Center, 6600 Lexington Ave., 44103. Tel: 216-391-0505; Fax: 216-391-1118. LaJean Ray, Dir.

Head Start, 7911 Detroit Ave., 44102-2815. Tel: 216-334-2942; Fax: 216-334-2948. Michelle Curry, Dir.

Hispanic Senior Center, 7800 Detroit Ave., 44102. Tel: 216-939-3714; Fax: 216-631-3654. Evelyn Santos, Prog. Dir.

St. Martin de Porres Family Center, 1264 E. 123rd St., 44108-4042. Tel: 216-268-3909; Fax: 216-268-0207. Kevin Hodges, Dir.

Catholic Charities Community Services Early Learning Centers

Arbor Park, 3750 Fleming Ave., 44115. Tel: 216-431-4818; Fax: 216-431-4255. Janet Lucha, Center Admin.

Fatima Early Learning Center, 6600 Lexington Ave., 44103. Tel: 216-391-5375; Fax: 216-391-1118. Robin Sumlin, Center Admin.

Early Learning Center at the Quadrangle, 2302 Community College, 44115. Tel: 216-589-9750; Fax: 216-589-9702. Karnese McKenzie, Center Admin.

Catholic Charities Community Services of Ashland County, 1260 S. Center St., Ashland, 44805-2000. Tel: 419-289-1903; Fax: 419-281-8342. Bob Hurdle, Dir.

Catholic Charities Community Services of Wayne County, 521 Beall Ave., Wooster, 44691-3523. Tel: 330-262-7836; Fax: 330-262-2867. Bob Hurdle, Dir.

Catholic Charities Community Services Corporation, 7911 Detroit Ave., 44102. Tel: 216-334-2931; Fax: 216-334-2907. Bernadette Washington, Exec. Dir.

Catholic Charities Community Services of Geauga County, 10771 Mayfield Rd., Chardon, 44024. Tel: 440-285-3537; 800-242-9755; Fax: 440-285-4909. James Clements, Dir. Outpatient counseling for families and individuals. Substance abuse counseling. Parenting programs. Services for the elderly. Services to strengthen and enrich the valued relationships of families and individuals for effective and healthy living. Employment programs for youth, young adults and adults.

Catholic Charities Community Services of Medina County, 740 E. Washington St., Medina, 44256-2136. Tel: 330-723-9615; Fax: 330-764-8795. Email: medina@clevelandcatholiccharities.org. Timothy J. Putka, M.S., Dir. Provides counseling, casework, and family life education in Medina County.
Medina. Tel: 330-723-9615; Fax: 330-764-8795.
Brunswick-Cleveland. Tel: 330-225-7100.
Wadsworth-Akron. Tel: 330-336-6657.

Catholic Charities Corporation (1919) 7911 Detroit Ave., 44102. Tel: 216-334-2959; 216-334-2900; Fax: 216-334-2983. Email: JPKlee@clevelandcatholiccharities.org. Web: www-.ClevelandCatholicCharities.org. John P. Klee, Exec. Dir.

Catholic Charities Health and Human Services, 7911 Detroit Ave., 44102. Tel: 216-334-2900; Fax: 216-334-2907. Web: www.clevelandcatholiccharities.org. Mr. Patrick Gareau, Pres. & CEO; Wayne Peel, CFO; Lisa Black, Gen. Counsel; Patricia Holian, Exec. Vice Pres.

Catholic Charities Services Corporation, 6753 State Rd., 44134. Tel: 440-843-5501; Fax: 440-843-1627. Email: medee@clevelandcatholiccharities.org. Web: www.clevelandcatholiccharities.org. Maureen Dee, Exec. Dir. Email: medee@clevelandcatholiccharities.org. Catholic Charities Services Corporation is part of the health and human services delivery system of the Diocese. Utilizing a holistic approach to healing, the system focuses on meeting the behavioral health needs of children and families in Cuyahoga County.

Chemical Dependency Services - Midtown Professional Center, 3135 Euclid Ave., Room 202, 44115-2507. Tel: 216-391-2030; Fax: 216-391-8946. Maureen Dee, Exec. Dir., Chemical Dependency Svcs.

Catholic Charities Services of Cuyahoga County, 6753 State Rd., Parma, 44134. Tel: 440-843-5501; Fax: 440-843-1627. Email: medee@clevelandcatholiccharities.org. Web: www-.clevelandcatholiccharities.org. Maureen Dee, Exec. Dir. A multi-function social service agency which offers social service programs. Individual, family, and group counseling; marital counseling, psychiatric consultations; and outpatient psychiatric services for children, youth, and adults. Chemical dependency assessments and outpatient counseling for youth and families having alcohol and other drug-related problems. Bilingual services for Hispanic youth and families.

LaProvidencia Family Center, 2012 W. 25th St., 5th Fl., 44113. Tel: 216-696-2197; Fax: 216-696-2088. Ramonita Johnson, Dir.

Matt Talbot Inn, 2270 Professor Ave., 44113-4489. Tel: 216-781-0288; Fax: 216-781-6270. Terry Morris, Dir.

Matt Talbot for Women, 7901 Detroit Ave., 44115. Tel: 216-634-7500; Fax: 216-939-7720. Colleen McKenna, Dir.

Diocese of Cleveland Facilities Services Corp., 1404 E. 9th St., 44114. Tel: 216-696-6525, Ext. 1501. Email: lxmurtaugh@clevelandcatholiccharities.org. Mr. Lawrence E. Murtaugh, Exec. Dir.

St. Malachi Center, Inc., 2416 Superior Viaduct, 44113. Tel: 216-771-3036; Fax: 216-771-3659. Email: anita@stmalachicenter.org. Web: www.stmalachicenter.org. Total Assisted 100 per day (Center); 20 per Monday (Health Services) 120; Total Staff 10.

Malachi House, Inc., 2810 Clinton Ave., 44113. Tel: 216-621-8831; Fax: 216-621-8841. Email: secretary@malachihouse.org. Web: www.malachihouse.org. Malachi House provides unskilled, family-like care to the dying poor without cost. Serves individuals who need an available caregiver, who have limited or no financial resources and are in need of special home care in the final stages of life. A trained staff and volunteers provide spiritual, emotional and physical support with the assistance of a hospice team. Acceptable only if care is manageable in a home setting. Handicapped access. Total Assisted Annually 110; Total Staff 25.

AKRON

Catholic Charities Services/Summit County (1920) 640 N. Main St., 44310-3098. Tel: 330-762-7481; Fax: 330-762-7484. Email: sglucas@clevelandcatholiccharities.org. Web: www.csssc.org. Donald P. Finn, Exec. Dir. Service sites throughout Summit County. Total Assisted 24,488; Total Staff 28.

Catholic Charities Services/Summit County (1936) 812 Biruta St., 44307-1104. Tel: 330-762-2961; Fax: 330-762-2001. Web: www.akroncyo.org.
CYO Adult Day Services:
812 Biruta St., 44307. Tel: 330-762-2961; Fax: 330-762-2001. Email:

dpfinn@clevelandcatholiccharities.org. Donald P. Finn, Exec. Dir. Total Assisted Annually (Adult Day Services) 206; Total Staff (Adult Day Services) 19.

Interval Brotherhood Home Alcohol-Drug Rehabilitation Center (1970) 3445 S. Main St., 44319. Tel: 330-644-4095; Fax: 330-645-2031. Email: dpfinn@ibh.org. Web: www.ibh.org. Donald P. Finn, Dir. Bed Capacity 62; Total in Residential Treatment 390; Total Assisted Annually 390; Total Staff 80.

**St. Patrick Manor, Inc. c/o Humility of Mary Housing, Inc.*, 3250 W. Market St., Ste. 204, 44333. Tel: 330-384-1555; Fax: 330-384-2144. Email: kradigan@hmhousing.org. Web: www.hmhousing.org. Richard Donahue, Chm. Units (Independent Living) 50; Total Staff 2.

ELYRIA

Catholic Charities Community Services of Lorain County, 628 Poplar St., 44035. Tel: 440-366-1106; Fax: 440-366-5645. Christine Horne, Dir.

Catholic Charities Family Center, 203 Eighth St., Lorain, 44052. Tel: 440-244-9915; Fax: 440-245-1057. David Boyce, Dir.

NORTHFIELD

St. Barnabas Villa, Inc. (1985) 9234 Olde Eight Rd., 44067. Tel: 330-467-3758; Fax: 330-908-1186. Natalie Priest, Mgr.; Mary Anne Cody, Asst. Mgr. A shared living facility for 11 people over 60 years of age. Bed Capacity 11; Total in Residence 9; Total Staff 15.

PAINESVILLE

Catholic Charities Community Services of Lake County, Mailing Address: 8 N. State St., Ste. 455, 44077. Tel: 440-946-7264; Fax: 440-953-1608. James Clements, Dir. Mental Health Services.

[U] SHRINES

CLEVELAND. *Our Lady of Lourdes Shrine* , Euclid, (U.S. Rtes. 20 & 6). Administered by the Sisters of the Most Holy Trinity., 21281 Chardon Rd., 44117. Tel: 216-481-8232; Fax: 216-481-6577. Email: osst@srstrinity.com. Web: www.srstrinity.com. Sr. M. Rochelle Guertal, O.SS.T., Regnl. Supr. Total in Residence 14.

St. Paul Shrine 4120 Euclid Ave., 44103. Tel: 216-431-8854. Rev. William Wiethorn, O.F.M.Cap.

GARFIELD HEIGHTS. *Our Lady of Czestochowa Shrine* , (Ohio Rte. 17). Administered by the Sisters of St. Joseph Third Order of St. Francis (S.S.J.-T.O.S.F.), 12215 Granger Rd., 44125. Tel: 216-581-3535; Fax: 216-518-2187. Sr. Joyce Hollkamp, S.S.J.-T.O.S.F., Business & Facilities Coord.

PARMA HEIGHTS. *Queen of the Holy Rosary Shrine* , (U.S. Rte. 42). Administered by the Sisters of the Incarnate Word and Blessed Sacrament (S.I.W.), 6618 Pearl Rd., 44130-3808. Tel: 440-886-6440; Fax: 440-842-6391. Email: smrksiw@yahoo.com. Sr. Mary Rose Kocab, S.I.W., Congregational Leader.

[V] MINISTRY TO THE SPANISH SPEAKING

CLEVELAND. *Office of Hispanic Ministry*, Diocese of Cleveland, 1404 E. 9th St., 44114. Tel: 216-696-6525, Ext. 2530; Fax: 216-861-3200. Email: mmayorga@dioceseofcleveland.org. Web: www.dioceseofcleveland.org/hispanicministry. Misael Mayorga, Dir.

Hispanic Parishes: Iglesia La Sagrada Familia, 7719 Detroit Ave., 44102. Tel: 216-631-6817; Fax: 216-631-3305. Rev. Robert J. Reidy.

Sacred Heart Chapel 4301 Pearl Ave., Lorain, 44055. Tel: 440-277-7231; 440-277-7232; Fax: 440-277-4886. Email: sacredheartchapel@yahoo.com. Rev. William A. Thaden, Admin.

Parishes with Ministry to Spanish Speaking: St. Bernard - St. Mary, 44 University Ave., Akron, 44308. Tel: 330-253-5161; Fax: 330-253-6949. Rev. Daniel J. Reed.

St. Michael, 3114 Scranton Rd., 44109. Tel: 216-861-6297; Fax: 216-696-9351. Rev. James H. McCreight.

St. Mary's - Painesville, 242 N. State St., Painesville, 44077. Tel: 440-354-4381; Fax: 440-354-9174. Rev. R. Stephen Vellenga.

Our Lady of Lourdes, 3395 E. 53rd St., 44127. Tel: 216-641-2829 (Rectory & Office); Fax: 216-641-0043. Email: info@ourladyoflourdes-cle.org. Web: www.ourladyoflourdes-cle.org. Rev. Joseph Callahan.

St. Mary of the Immaculate Conception, 527 Beall Ave., P.O. Box 109, Wooster, 44691. Tel: 330-264-8824; 330-264-8822; Fax: 330-262-4633. Email: stmarywoost@embarqmail.com. Revs. Stephen P. Moran; Christopher J. Trenta; Judith Caraballo-Arzuaga, Dir. Latino Ministry (Wayne, Ashland & Medina Districts).

[W] NEWMAN CENTERS

CLEVELAND. *Office of Newman Catholic Campus Ministry* 1404 E. 9th St., 44114. Tel: 216-696-6525, Ext. 2880; Fax: 216-696-6206. Web: www.oce-ocs.org/ocs. Mr. William B. Miller, Sec. Catechetical Svcs. Total Staff 9; Newman Centers 7.

Case-Western Reserve University Tel: 216-421-9614, Ext. 302; Fax: 216-791-2228. Tony Vento, Campus Min., 11205 Euclid Ave., 44106. Tel: 216-421-9614, Ext. 302; Fax: 216-791-2228.

University of Akron Newman Center, 44 University Ave., Akron, 44308. Tel: 330-376-3585; 216-696-6525, Ext. 3000; Fax: 216-696-8646. John Szarwark, Campus Min. (Akron)

Baldwin-Wallace College Newman Center 170 E. Center St., Berea, 44017. Tel: 216-243-4955; Fax: 216-243-0354. Mindy Kushlak, Campus Min.; Kirsten Vilinsky, Campus Min. (Berea)

Oberlin College Office of Religious & Spiritual Life, 135 W. Lorain St., Oberlin, 44074. Tel: 440-775-5190; Fax: 440-775-6896. Greg Stevens. (Oberlin)

The College of Wooster 1473 Beall Ave., Wooster, 44691. Tel: 330-287-3718; Fax: 330-263-2534. Email: khahn@dioceseofcleveland.org. Web: www.dioceseofcleveland.org. Karen Hahn, Campus Min. (Wooster)

University of Ashland 132 N. Wood St., Loudonville, 44842. Tel: 419-994-4396. Rev. Vincent J. Hawk, Campus Min.

Cleveland State University 2230 Euclid Ave., 44115. Tel: 216-771-3630, Ext. 7145. Debbie Dacone, Campus Min.

[X] ENDOWMENT TRUSTS

CLEVELAND. *The Benedictine High School Endowment Trust* (2001) 2900 Martin Luther King Jr. Dr., 44104. Tel: 216-721-5300, Ext. 207; Fax: 216-721-1253. Email: abbotchristopher@cbhs.net. Web: www.cbhs.net. Rt. Rev. Christopher Schwartz, O.S.B., Bd. Chm.

St. John Cathedral Endowment Trust, 1007 Superior Ave. E., 44114-2582. Tel: 216-771-6666; Fax: 216-781-5646. Email: stjohns@dioceseofcleveland.org. Web: www.saintjohncathedral.com. Revs. Theodore Marszal, S.T.D.; Rodel Angeles, Parochial Vicar; Deacon John P. Sferry Sr., Pastoral Assoc.

Sisters of Saint Joseph Community Support Charitable Trust, 3430 Rocky River Dr., 44111-2997. Tel: 216-252-0440; Fax: 216-941-3430. Email: jcmolik@csjoseph.org. Web: www.csjoseph.org. Sr. Jeanne Cmolik, C.S.J., Pres.

The Thomas C. and Sandra S. Sullivan Foundation, 1404 E. 9th St., 8th Fl., 44114. Tel: 216-696-6525, Ext. 4200; Fax: 216-348-0740. Email: lgannon@catholiccommunity.org. Web: www.catholiccommunity.org. Mr. Patrick J. Grace, Exec. Dir.; Mrs. Terri Preskar, Relationship Mgr.

Villa Angela-St. Joseph High School Education Endowment Trust (1990) 18491 Lake Shore Blvd., 44119. Tel: 216-481-8414; Fax: 216-486-1035. Email: rosborne@vasj.com. Web: www.vasj.com. Richard J. Osborne, Pres.; Mr. David M. Csank, Prin.; Megan Scheider, Asst. Prin.; Rev. H. James Bartlett, S.M., Chap.

AKRON. *The Daughters of Divine Charity, St. Mary Province, Charitable Trust*, 39 N. Portage Path, 44303-1183. Tel: 330-867-4960; Fax: 330-867-6334. Email: martinovich00@hotmail.com.

HMH Foundation, 3250 W. Market St., #204, 44333. Tel: 234-525-6402. Laurie Miller, Contact Person.

St. Vincent-St. Mary High School Endowment Trust (1983) 15 N. Maple St., 44303. Tel: 330-253-9113; Fax: 330-996-0000. Web: www.stvm.com. David V. Rathz, Headmaster.

CHARDON. *The Sisters of Notre Dame Charitable Trust*, 13000 Auburn Rd., 44024. Tel: 440-286-7101; Fax: 440-286-3377. Email: mgorman@ndec.org. Web: www.snd1.org; www.sndchardon.org. Sr. Margaret Mary Gorman, S.N.D., Chm.

FAIRLAWN. **St. Hilary Parish Foundation*, 2750 W. Market St., 44333. Tel: 330-867-1055; Fax: 330-869-2312. Mr. Edward F. Carter, Pres.

MENTOR. *St. Mary of the Assumption Parish Endowment Trust* (1857) 8560 Mentor Ave., 44060-5853. Tel: 440-255-3404; Fax: 440-255-4194. Email: tgelsass@ameritech.net. Web: www.stmarysmentor.org. Priests 1.

PARMA HEIGHTS. *Incarnate Word Academy Student and Faculty Advancement Endowment (IWA Endowment)* (2002) 6620 Pearl Rd., 44130. Tel: 440-842-6818, Ext. 3110; Fax: 440-888-1377. Email: info@incarnatewordacademy.org. Web: www.incarnatewordacademy.com. M. Elizabeth Davis.

Incarnate Word Endowment Trust (1986) 6618 Pearl Rd., 44130-3808. Tel: 440-886-6440; Fax: 440-842-6391. Email: smrksiw@yahoo.com. Sr. Mary Rose Kocab, S.I.W., Congregational Leader.

ROCKY RIVER. *Friends of the Poor Clares Foundation*, 22701 Lake Rd., #312B, 44116. Tel: 216-214-1679. Thomas J. Kelley, Pres. & Treas.

Poor Clares Perpetual Adoration Foundation of Cleveland, Ohio, 22701 Lake Rd., #312B, 44116. Tel: 216-214-1679.

SEVEN HILLS. *Sisters Servants of Mary Immaculate Endowment Fund in Memory of Sr. Amelia Kuska* (2000) 285 Panorama Dr., 44131. Tel: 216-441-5402; Fax: 216-441-4510. Email: ccsambor@hotmail.com. Web: www.ssmiendowment.org. Sr. Cecilia A. Sambor, S.S.M.I., Pres.

SHAKER HEIGHTS. *St. Dominic Endowment Fund* (2003) 3450 Norwood Rd., 44122. Tel: 216-991-1444; Fax: 216-491-0190. Email: kmqua@yahoo.com. Web: www.stdominicchurch.net. Rev. Thomas G. Fanta, Pres.

WELLINGTON. *St. Patrick Church Endowment Trust* (1990) 512 N. Main St., 44090. Tel: 440-647-4375; Fax: 440-647-4675. Email: stpatrickwellington@glwb.net.

WOOSTER. *St. Mary of the Immaculate Conception Elementary Day School Endowment Trust* (1990) 527 Beall Ave., P.O. Box 109, 44691. Tel: 330-264-8824; Fax: 330-262-4633. Email: stmarychurch@embarqmail.com. Web: stmarywooster.org.

[Y] MISCELLANEOUS

CLEVELAND. **St. Augustine Services Corporation*, 7801 Detroit Ave., 44102. Tel: 216-634-7400; Fax: 216-634-7483. Email: akoha@st-aug.org. Andrew Koha, Pres. Total Staff 15.

Catholic Charities Housing Corporation (CCHC), 7911 Detroit Ave., 44102. Tel: 216-696-6525, Ext. 1506. Email: lxmurtaugh@dioceseofcleveland.org. Mr. Lawrence E. Murtaugh, Exec. Dir.

Catholic Community Connection, 2475 E. 22nd St., 4th Fl., 44115. Tel: 216-875-4613; Fax: 216-696-2204. Email: lcalabrese@sistersofcharityhealth.org. Leonard M. Calabrese, Pres.

Cleveland Slovenian Community Center, 15519 Holmes Ave., 44110-2497. Tel: 216-761-7740; Fax: 216-761-6673. Email: johnkumse@yahoo.com. Rev. John M. Kumse.

Congregation of the Sisters of St. Joseph Ministries, Inc., 3430 Rocky River Rd., 44111-2997.

CSA Health Network, 2475 East 22nd St., 44115. Tel: 216-659-5560; Fax: 216-696-2204. Web: www.sistersofcharityhealth.org. Sr. Judith Ann Karam, C.S.A., Pres. & CEO. Serves as the general partner to the joint venture ownership of Catholic healthcare providers.

First Friday Club of Cleveland, Inc., 1404 E. Ninth St., Ste. 100, 44114. Tel: 440-390-0172. Email: ffcofccleveland@sbcglobal.net. Steve Suding, Pres.; Sue Gaughan, Sec.

L'Arche, Cleveland (1975) P.O. Box 20450, 44120. Tel: 216-721-2614; Fax: 216-229-2311. Email: office@larchecleveland.org. Web: www.larchecleveland.org. An ecumenical community providing homes for adults with developmental disabilities. Residents 14; Total Staff 31.

Mercedarian Apartments, Inc., c/o 7911 Detroit Ave., 44102.

Ninth Street CDC, 1404 E. Ninth St., 8th Fl., 44114-1722. Tel: 216-696-6525; Fax: 216-696-8084. James Gulick, Pres.

Pulaski Franciscan Community Development Corp. (2001) 3649 E. 65th St., 44105. Tel: 216-341-9091; Fax: 216-341-2688. Email: pfcdc@sbcglobal.net. Rev. Michael Surufka, O.F.M., Pres.

River's Edge A Place for Reflection and Action, 3430 Rocky River Dr., 44111. Tel: 216-688-1111. Email: rita@riversedgecleveland.com. Web: www.riversedgecleveland.com. Sr. Rita Petruziello, C.S.J., Exec. Dir.

Sisters of Charity Foundation of Cleveland (1996) 1228 Euclid Ave., Ste. 330, 44115. Tel: 216-241-9300; Fax: 216-241-9345. Web: www.socfcleveland.org. Susanna H. Krey, Pres.

Sisters of Charity of St. Augustine Health System, 2475 E. 22nd St., 44115. Tel: 216-696-5560; Fax: 216-696-2204. Web: www.sistersofcharityhealth.org. Sr. Judith Ann Karam, C.S.A., Pres. & CEO. Serves as the Member of St. Vincent Charity Medical Center and foundations and health and human service corporations sponsored by Sisters of Charity Health System Ministries, a public juridic person of ponitifcal right. Serves as one of two members of the joint venture corporation operating St. John Medical Center.

Sisters of St. Joseph, 3430 Rocky River Dr., 44111-2997. Tel: 216-252-0440; Fax: 216-941-3430.

St. Vincent Charity Medical Center Foundation, 2475 E. 22nd St., 44115.

**St. Vitus Development Corporation* (2000) 6019 Lausche Ave., 44103. Tel: 216-361-1444; Fax: 216-361-1445. Email: skuhar@hotmail.com. Stane Kuhar, Sec. & Contact Person; Rev. Joseph P. Boznar, Pres.; Joseph V. Hocevar, Treas.

AKRON. *First Friday Club of Greater Akron* (2000) 795 Russell Ave., 44307. Tel: 330-535-7668; Fax: 330-535-9040. Email: ffcofga@neo.rr.com. Web: www.firstfridayclubofgreaterakron.org. Linda Tucci Teodosio, Pres.

H M Housing Development Corporation, 3250 W. Market St., Ste. 204, 44333. Tel: 330-384-1555; Fax: 330-384-2144. Email: kradigan@hmhousing.org. Web: www.hmhousing.org. Dana Murphy, Prog. Dir.

H.M. Life Opportunity Services (1987) 1815 W. Market St., #301, 44313. Tel: 330-376-5600; Fax: 330-376-2277. Email: hmlife@hmlife.org.

Central Office - Humility of Mary Housing, Inc., 3250 W. Market St., #204, 44333. Tel: 330-384-1555; Fax: 330-384-2144. Web: www.hmhousing.org.

Humility of Mary Housing, Inc., 3250 W. Market St., Ste. 204, 44333. Tel: 330-384-1555; Fax: 330-384-2144. Email: kradigan@hmhousing.org. Web: www.hmhousing.org. Kenneth W. Radigan, Pres. Affordable housing and housing related services for low and moderate income individuals. Total Assisted 450; Total Staff 11.

BATH. **Crown Point Ecology Center*, 3220 Ira Rd., P.O. Box 484, 44210.

CHARDON. *Christ Child Society-Geauga Chapter*, P.O. Box 1133, 44024. Tel: 440-286-9426. Barbara Matejka, Pres.

CHIPPEWA LAKE. **The Community of Jesus, The Living Mercy*, P.O. Box 223, 44215-0235.

COPLEY. *Faith and Light U.S.A., Inc., Loyola Retreat House*, 700 Killinger Rd., Clinton, 44216-9653. Tel: 800-827-1416. Becki Haller, Diocesan Rep.

ELYRIA. *First Friday Forum of Lorain County*, 320 Middle Ave., 44035. Tel: 440-244-0643. Email: ffflorain@gmail.com. Sharon Kleppel, Pres.

GARFIELD HEIGHTS. *Jennings Manor Housing Corporation* (1996) 10204 Granger Rd., 44125. Tel: 216-581-2900; Fax: 216-581-4505. Email: marketing@jenningscenter.org. Web: www.jenningscenter.org. Mrs. Martha M. Kutik, Pres. & CEO; Allison Salopeck, Admin. & COO; Jim Patena, Assoc. Admin. 61 unit apartment building - HUD 202 Supportive Housing for Older Adults.

Marymount Health Care Systems, 12300 McCracken Rd., 44125. Tel: 216-587-8080; Fax: 216-587-8212. Mr. William D. Keckan, Pres. Provides comprehensive health and human services in response to the needs of the local community by owning, leasing and operating health care facilities and services consistent with the philosophy and objectives of the Roman Catholic religious congregation known as the Sisters of St. Joseph of the Third Order of St. Francis.

MHCS Real Estate Holding Company, 12300 McCracken Rd., 44125-2975. Tel: 216-587-8080; Fax: 216-587-8212. Mr. William D. Keckan, Pres. To assist in the provision of comprehensive health care services by acquiring, holding, owning, and leasing real estate (and interests therein) and health care facilities, including but not limited to leasing such as real estate and facilities to Marymount Hospital, consistent with the philosophy and objectives of the Roman Catholic Church as promulgated by the National Conference of Catholic Bishops and the local Ordinary. Holds the Title to Marymount Hospital as a part of the Marymount Health Care Systems Special Member responsibility.

HUDSON. **Laurel Lake Retirement Community, Inc.* (1989) 200 Laurel Lake Dr., 44236. Tel: 330-650-0681; Fax: 330-655-1700. Email: info@laurellake.org. Web: www.laurellake.org. David Oster, Exec. Dir. Independent Living Residents 350; Assisted Living Residents 60; Skilled Nursing Residents 75; Total Staff 250.

KIRTLAND. *St. Philip Neri/Divine Word Church in the City Partnership Inc.* (1914) 8100 Eagle Rd., 44094. Tel: 440-256-1412; Fax: 440-256-4929. Email: frdave@divinewordkirtland.org. Rev. David G. Woost, Pastor, Divine Word, Kirtland. (Partnership 1993) Total Staff 8.

LORAIN. *Mercy Regional Health System*, 3700 Kolbe Rd., 44053. Tel: 440-960-3295; Fax: 440-960-4630. Email: ed.oley@health-partners.org. Edwin Oley, Pres. Total Assisted 240,164.

PAINESVILLE. *Christ Child Society of the Western Reserve*, 1535-R Mentor Ave., 44077. Tel: 440-350-9836. Kay Leonard, Pres.

**Retrouvaille of Cleveland, Inc.*, 575 Southington Blvd., 44077-2858. Tel: 440-357-6580. Web: retrouvailleofcleveland.catholicweb.com.

PARMA. **Christ Child Society of Cleveland* (1916) 6753 State Rd., 44134. Tel: 440-843-1632; Fax: 440-843-1632 (call first). Email: christchildcleveland@yahoo.com. Web: www.christchildsocietycleveland.org. Mrs. Marybeth Baucco, Pres. & Contact.

Society of St. Joseph the Worker (1979) 7033 State Rd., 44134-4952. Tel: 440-888-4872; Fax: 440-888-6825. Email: bsjw@msn.com. Web: www.bsjw.org. Lawrence R. Verbiar, Dir.

PEPPER PIKE. *Ursuline Ministry Services Corp., Ursuline Educational Center*, 2600 Lander Rd., 44124. Tel: 440-449-1200, Ext. 280. Email: uil@ursulinesisters.org. Sisters 15.

SOLON. *The O'Neill Brothers Foundation*, 30000 Aurora Rd., Suite 250, 44139. Tel: 440-248-2027; Fax: 440-248-2153. Email: lstopar@aol.com. Mr. Robert K. Healey Jr., Pres.

STRONGSVILLE. *Healing Prayer Institute, St. John Neumann*, 16271 Pearl Rd., 44136. Tel: 440-238-1770. Email: info@healingprayerinstitute.com.

WESTLAKE. *The Center for Learning* (1970) Editorial/Administrative Office, 29313 Clemens Rd., Ste. 2E, 44145. Tel: 440-250-9341; Fax: 440-250-9715. Web: www.centerforlearning.org; www.clfreligion.org. Melanie Wall, Pres. & CEO. Educational Publisher of values-based curriculum and online professional development; Religion for Catholic schools and parishes; English/Language Arts, Social Studies, and Novel/Drama Curriculum Units for all schools.; Owned and operated by the Sisters of Humility of Mary. Directed by an Ecumenical Lay Board.

Customer Service Office, 590 E. Western Reserve Rd., Unit 10-H, P.O. Box 910, Youngstown, 44514. Tel: 800-767-9090; 724-964-8083; Fax: 888-767-8080. Web: www.centerforlearning.org; www.clfreligion.org.

**UHHS/CSAHS - Cuyahoga, Inc.* (1999) 29000 Center Ridge Rd., 44145. Tel: 440-835-8000; Fax: 440-827-5015.

WICKLIFFE. *Center for Pastoral Leadership Services, Inc.* (1991) 28700 Euclid Ave., 44092-2585. Tel: 440-943-7600; Fax: 440-943-7577. Email: pguban@dioceseofcleveland.org. Very Rev. Thomas M. Dragga, D.Min., CEO; Mr. Philip J. Guban, B.A., COO.

COAR Peace Mission, Inc. (1980) 28700 Euclid Ave., 44092. Tel: 440-943-7615; Fax: 440-943-7618. Email: coarpm@gmail.com. Web: www.coarpeacemission.org. Mary Stevenson, Exec. Dir. Total Staff 100; Total Assisted 900.

COAR Children's Village Tel: 011-2-314-0824. Sr. Martha Calderon. (Zaragoza, El Salvador, C.A.); Comunidad Oscar Arnulfo Romero (COAR) provides housing, education and health care for orphaned, abandoned and street children in Zaragoza, El Salvador, Central America. The Children's Village can house up to 120 children under the supervision and guidance of a housemother in fifteen home-like cottages. The COAR school provides a kindergarten to grade twelve school education to about 800 children from Zaragoza and neighboring villages. State approved vocational training is offered to high school students. The Santa Teresita Clinic, a quality medical clinic in an area with little other access to health care, serves the health and dental needs of up to 25-50 patients (adults and children) weekly. The Archdiocese of San Salvador through its Caritas ministries administers COAR Children's Village. The COAR Peace Mission in Cleveland, OH is the support and development office for the Children's Village in El Salvador. COAR was founded in August 1980 by Rev. Ken Myers, a priest of the Cleveland Diocese.

RELIGIOUS INSTITUTES OF MEN REPRESENTED IN THE DIOCESE

For further details refer to the corresponding bracketed number in the Religious Institutes of Men or Women section.

[]—*Apostles of Jesus* (Karen, Kenya)—A.J.

[0200]—*Benedictine Monks* (St. Andrew Abbey)—O.S.B.

[0600]—*Brothers of the Congregation of Holy Cross* (Midwest Prov.)—C.S.C.

[0470]—*The Capuchin Friars*—O.F.M.Cap.

[1150]—*Congregation of St. Joseph*—C.S.J.

[0220]—*Congregation of the Blessed Sacrament*—S.S.S.

[0520]—*Franciscan Friars* (Provs. of Our Lady of Consolation & Assumption)—O.F.M.

[0690]—*Jesuit Fathers and Brothers (Society of Mary)* (Detroit Prov.)—S.J.

[0800]—*Maryknoll*—M.M.

[]—*Missionaries of St. Francis de Sales*—M.S.F.S.

[0970]—*Order of Our Lady of Mercy*—O.de.M.

[0610]—*Priests of the Congregation of the Holy Cross* (Indiana Prov.)—C.S.C.

[0760]—*Society of Mary-Marianists* (Dayton, OH)—S.M.

[1060]—*Society of the Precious Blood* (Cincinnati Prov.)—C.PP.S.

RELIGIOUS INSTITUTES OF WOMEN REPRESENTED IN THE DIOCESE

[0230]—*Benedictine Sisters of Pontifical Jurisdiction* (Erie, PA)—O.S.B.

[3832]—*Congregation of the Sisters of St. Joseph*—C.S.J.

[1710]—*Congregation of the Third Order of St. Francis of Mary Immaculate, Joliet, IL*—O.S.F.

[0790]—*Daughters of Divine Charity*—F.D.C.

[0420]—*Discalced Carmelite Nuns*—O.C.D.

[1070-14]—*Dominican Sisters* (Adrian, MI)—O.P.

[1115]—*Dominican Sisters of Peace*—O.P.

[1210]—*Franciscan Sisters of Chicago*—O.S.F.

[2340]—*Little Sisters of the Poor*—P.S.D.P.

[]—*Mercedarian Sisters of the Blessed Sacrament*—H.M.S.S.

[3760]—*Order of St. Clare-Poor Clare Colettine Nuns*—P.C.C.

[3210]—*Poor Clares of Perpetual Adoration*—P.C.P.A.

[3420]—*Religious of the Eucharist*—R.E.

[3430]—*Religious Teachers Filippini*—M.P.F.

[0440]—*Sisters of Charity of Cincinnati, Ohio*—S.C.

[0570]—*Sisters of Charity of Seton Hill*—S.C.

[0580]—*Sisters of Charity of St. Augustine*—C.S.A.

[0990]—*Sisters of Divine Providence*—C.D.P.

[2580]—*Sisters of Mercy of the Americas* (South Central)—R.S.M.

[2990]—*Sisters of Notre Dame* (Cleveland)—S.N.D.

[]—*Sisters of Notre Dame* (Toledo)—S.N.D.

[3360]—*Sisters of Providence*—S.P.

[1530]—*Sisters of St. Francis* (Sylvania)—O.S.F.

[]—*Sisters of St. Francis of Neuman Community*—O.S.F.

[3910]—*Sisters of St. Joseph of St. Mark* (Cleveland)—S.J.S.M.

[]—*Sisters of St. Joseph of St. Mark* (Louisville)—S.J.S.M.

[3930]—*Sisters of St. Joseph of the Third Order of St. Francis*—S.S.J.-T.O.S.F.

[]—*Sisters of the Good Shepherd* (St. Louis)—O.S.U.

[1970]—*Sisters of the Holy Family of Nazareth*—C.S.F.N.

[2030]—*Sisters of the Holy Spirit*—C.S.Sp.

[2110]—*Sisters of the Humility of Mary*—H.M.

[2210]—*Sisters of the Incarnate Word and Blessed Sacrament*—S.I.W.

[2350]—*Sisters of the Living Word*—S.L.W.

[2060]—*Sisters of the Most Holy Trinity*—O.SS.T.

[3260]—*Sisters of the Precious Blood* (Dayton, Ohio)—C.PP.S.

[3620]—*Sisters, Servants of Mary Immaculate*—S.S.M.I.

[2150]—*Sisters, Servants of the Immaculate Heart of Mary*—I.H.M.

[]—*Social Mission Sisters*—S.M.

[4120-04]—*Ursuline Nuns of the Congregation of Paris* (Cleveland)—O.S.U.

[4120-07]—*Ursuline Nuns of the Congregation of Paris* (Youngstown)—O.S.U.

DIOCESAN CEMETERIES

CLEVELAND. *Assumption of Mary Cemetery*, Mailing Address: *Calvary Cemetery*, 10000 Miles Ave., 44105.

Calvary Cemetery, 10000 Miles Ave., 44105.

St. John Cemetery, Mailing Address: *Calvary Cemetery*, 10000 Miles Ave., 44105.

St. Joseph Cemetery, Mailing Address: 10000 Miles Ave., 44105. 7916 Woodland Ave, 44104.

St. Mary Cemetery, Mailing Address: 10000 Miles Ave., 44105.

Holy Cross Cemetery, Mailing Address: 10000 Miles Ave., 44105.

Elmhurst Park Cemetery, Mailing Address: 10000 Miles Ave., 44105. (Non-Sectarian)

St. Mary of the Falls Cemetery, Mailing Address: 10000 Miles Ave., 44105.

Holy Trinity Cemetery, Mailing Address: 10000 Miles Ave., 44105.

Holy Trinity Cemetery, Mailing Address: 10000 Miles Ave., 44105.

St. Joseph Cemetery, Mailing Address: 10000 Miles Ave., 44105.

Holy Cross Cemetery, Mailing Address: 10000 Miles Ave., 44105.

St. Mary Cemetery, Mailing Address: 10000 Miles Ave., 44105.

St. Mary Cemetery, Mailing Address: 10000 Miles Ave., 44105.

Calvary Cemetery, Mailing Address: 10000 Miles Ave., 44105.

All Saints Cemetery, Mailing Address: 10000 Miles Ave., 44105.

Resurrection Cemetery, Mailing Address: 10000 Miles Ave., 44105.

CHARDON. *All Souls Cemetery*, Mailing Address: 10000 Miles Ave., 44105.

NECROLOGY

† Boymer, Lloyd J., (Retired)—Died March 29, 2011
† Cimperman, Victor J., (Retired)—Died Nov. 15, 2011
† Ciprian, Carl A., (Retired)—Died Nov. 21, 2011
† Kline, Robert W., (Retired)—Died June 24, 2011
† McShane, Patrick E., (Retired)—Died Jan. 11, 2011

An asterisk (*) denotes an organization that has established tax-exempt status directly with the IRS and is not covered by the USCCB Group Ruling.

Diocese of Colorado Springs

Most Reverend

MICHAEL J. SHERIDAN, S.TH.D.

Bishop of Colorado Springs; ordained May 29, 1971; appointed Titular Bishop of Tibiuca and Auxiliary Bishop of Saint Louis July 9, 1997; ordained September 3, 1997; appointed Coadjutor Bishop of Colorado Springs December 4, 2001; succeeded to the See January 30, 2003.

Most Reverend

RICHARD C. HANIFEN, D.D., J.C.L.

Bishop Emeritus of Colorado Springs; ordained June 6, 1959; appointed Titular Bishop of Abercorn and Auxiliary of Denver July 6, 1974; consecrated September 20, 1974; appointed First Bishop of Colorado Springs November 10, 1983; installed January 30, 1984; retired January 30, 2003. *Office: 228 N. Cascade Ave., Colorado Springs, CO 80903-1498.*

VIRTUS IN INFIRMITATE PERFICITUR

Diocesan Offices: 228 N. Cascade Ave., Colorado Springs, CO 80903-1498. Tel: 719-636-2345; Fax: 719-636-1216.

ESTABLISHED AND CREATED A DIOCESE JANUARY 30, 1984.

Square Miles 15,493.

Comprising the Counties of Chaffee, Cheyenne, Douglas, Elbert, El Paso, Kit Carson, Lake, Lincoln, Park and Teller.

For legal titles of parishes and diocesan institutions, consult the Diocesan Offices.

STATISTICAL OVERVIEW

Personnel	
Bishop	1
Retired Bishops	1
Priests: Diocesan Active in Diocese	28
Priests: Diocesan Active Outside Diocese	3
Priests: Retired, Sick or Absent	8
Number of Diocesan Priests	39
Religious Priests in Diocese	14
Total Priests in Diocese	53
Extern Priests in Diocese	17
Ordinations:	
Diocesan Priests	4
Permanent Deacons	16
Permanent Deacons in Diocese	55
Total Brothers	1
Total Sisters	93
Parishes	
Parishes	41
With Resident Pastor:	
Resident Diocesan Priests	33
Resident Religious Priests	6
Without Resident Pastor:	
Administered by Priests	8
Administered by Deacons	1
Administered by Lay People	1
Pastoral Centers	2
Professional Ministry Personnel:	
Sisters	3
Lay Ministers	77
Welfare	
Catholic Hospitals	2
Total Assisted	277,379
Health Care Centers	3
Total Assisted	147
Homes for the Aged	3
Total Assisted	147
Special Centers for Social Services	1
Total Assisted	219,998
Educational	
Diocesan Students in Other Seminaries	12
Seminaries, Religious	1
Students Religious	9
Total Seminarians	21
High Schools, Private	1
Total Students	333
Elementary Schools, Diocesan and Parish	5
Total Students	1,367
Catechesis/Religious Education:	
High School Students	2,182
Elementary Students	7,181
Total Students under Catholic Instruction	11,084
Teachers in the Diocese:	
Sisters	1
Lay Teachers	165
Vital Statistics	
Receptions into the Church:	
Infant Baptism Totals	1,008
Minor Baptism Totals	134
Adult Baptism Totals	100
Received into Full Communion	158
First Communions	1,504
Confirmations	1,638
Marriages:	
Catholic	153
Interfaith	50
Total Marriages	203
Deaths	438
Total Catholic Population	161,770
Total Population	1,011,062

Former Bishops—Most Rev. RICHARD C. HANIFEN, D.D., J.C.L. (Retired), ord. June 6, 1959; appt. Titular Bishop of Abercorn and Auxiliary of Denver July 6, 1974; cons. Sept. 20, 1974; appt. first Bishop of Colorado Springs Nov. 10, 1983; installed Jan. 30, 1984; retired Jan. 30, 2003.

Diocesan Offices—228 N. Cascade Ave., Colorado Springs, 80903-1498. Tel: 719-636-2345; Fax: 719-636-1216. Office Hours: Mon.-Fri. 8-5.

Vicar General—Rev. Msgr. ROBERT E. JAEGER, V.G.

Vicar for Clergy—Rev. Msgr. ROBERT E. JAEGER, V.G.

Vicar for Hispanic Ministry—Rev. FRANCISCO J. QUEZADA.

Vicar for Religious—Rev. Msgr. RICARDO CORONADO-ARRASCUE, J.C.D.

Judicial Vicar and Chancellor—Rev. Msgr. RICARDO CORONADO-ARRASCUE, J.C.D.

Vice Chancellor—Rev. JAMES M. WILLIAMS.

Presbyteral Council—Rev. Msgrs. ROBERT E. JAEGER, V.G.; RICARDO CORONADO-ARRASCUE, J.C.D.; Revs. DONALD P. BROWNSTEIN, V.F.; ROBERT L. EPPING, C.S.C., V.F.; BRIAN QUINN MOHAN; STEPHEN J. PARLET, V.F.; KIRK SLATTERY; ANDRZEJ SZCZESNOWICZ.

College of Consultors—Rev. Msgrs. ROBERT E. JAEGER, V.G.; RICARDO CORONADO-ARRASCUE, J.C.D.; Revs. ROBERT L. EPPING, C.S.C., V.F.; GEORGE V. FAGAN, J.C.L., V.F.; ROBERT NEWBURY; KENNETH E. PRZYBYLA; FRANCISCO J. QUEZADA; MARK ZACKER.

Vicars Forane—Revs. ROBERT L. EPPING, C.S.C., V.F.; GEORGE V. FAGAN, J.C.L., V.F.; PAUL F. WICKER, V.F.; BRADFORD NOONAN, V.F.; STEPHEN J. PARLET, V.F.

Deaneries—Metro-North Deanery (Colorado Springs): Rev. PAUL F. WICKER, V.F., Vicar. Metro-South Deanery (Colorado Springs): Rev. ROBERT L. EPPING, C.S.C., V.F., Vicar. Eastern Deanery: Rev. GEORGE V. FAGAN, J.C.L., V.F., Vicar. Northern Deanery: Rev. BRADFORD NOONAN, V.F., Vicar. Western Deanery: Rev. STEPHEN J. PARLET, V.F., Vicar.

Diocesan Tribunal

Diocesan Tribunal—228 N. Cascade Ave., Colorado Springs, 80903. Tel: 719-636-2345.

Judicial Vicar—Rev. Msgr. RICARDO CORONADO-ARRASCUE, J.C.D.

Defender of the Bond—Rev. GEORGE V. FAGAN, J.C.L., V.F.

Judicial Auditor and Assessor—ANTHONY ST. LOUIS-SANCHEZ. Email: anthony@diocs.org.

Tribunal Secretary and Assistant to the Judicial Vicar and Ecclesiastical Notary—MARIA MAGALONG. Tel: 719-636-2345. Email: mmagalong@diocs.org.

Judicial Auditor and Ecclesiastical Notary—RAYMOND P. KELLEY. Tel: 719-636-2345. Email: rkelley@diocs.org.

Advocates— Appointed individually for particular cases

Diocese of Colorado Springs, a Colorado Corporation Sole

Diocesan Offices and Ministries

Unless otherwise indicated offices and ministries are located in the Pastoral Center, 228 N. Cascade Ave., Colorado Springs, CO 80903. Tel. 719-636-2345. Web: www.diocs.org

Office of the Bishop—

Bishop—Most Rev. MICHAEL J. SHERIDAN, S.Th.D. Tel: 719-636-2345.

Vicar General—Rev. Msgr. ROBERT E. JAEGER, V.G. Tel: 719-636-2345.

General Counsel and Chief of Staff—Deacon DOUGLAS M. FLINN, Esq. Tel: 719-636-2345. Email: dflinn@diocs.org.

Executive Assistant to the Bishop and Director of the Propagation of the Faith—ESPERANZA A. GRIFFITH. Tel: 719-636-2345. Email: egriffith@diocs.org.

Diocesan Senior Staff—

Vicar General—Rev. Msgr. ROBERT E. JAEGER, V.G. Tel: 719-636-2345.

Judicial Vicar and Chancellor—Rev. Msgr. RICARDO CORONADO-ARRASCUE, J.C.D. Tel: 719-636-2345.

Finance Officer—ROBERT G. DOERFLER JR. Tel: 719-636-2345. Email: rgdoerfler@diocs.org.

General Counsel and Chief of Staff—Deacon DOUGLAS M. FLINN, Esq. Tel: 719-636-2345. Email: dflinn@diocs.org.

President and CEO of Catholic Charities of Central Colorado—MARK C. ROHLENA ESQ., Esq. Tel:

719-636-2345. Email: mrohlena@ccharitiescc.org.

Diocesan Offices and Ministries—

Catholic Charismatic Renewal Services—Deacon CHARLES MATZKER, Liaison. Tel: 719-597-4249; Fax: 719-591-1816. Email: freshfire@q.com; deaconchuck@holyapostlescc.org; CCRS c/o Holy Apostles Catholic Church, 4925 N. Carefree Cir., Colorado Springs, 80917.

Chancellor—

Chancellor and Judicial Vicar—Rev. Msgr. RICARDO CORONADO-ARRASCUE, J.C.D. Tel: 719-636-2345. *Vice Chancellor*, Rev. JAMES M. WILLIAMS. Tel: 719-636-2345. Email: vocations@diocs.org. *Assistant to the Chancellor and Ecclesiastical Archivist*, RAYMOND P. KELLEY. Tel: 719-636-2345. Email: rkelley@diocs.org.

The Colorado Catholic Herald—WILLIAM HOWARD, Editor. Email: editor@diocs.org; VERONICA AMBUUL, Asst. Editor. Email: veronica@coloradocatholicherald.com.

Colorado Springs Council of Black Catholics—JULIA HYPOLITE, Pres. Tel: 719-574-8420. Email: anjuli_007@yahoo.com.

Office of Continuing Formation of Clergy—Rev. LAWRENCE C. BRENNAN, S.Th.D., Dir. Tel: 719-636-2345. Email: lbrennan@diocs.org.

Office of Permanent Diaconate—Deacon ROBERT BROUSSARD, Dir. Email: rbroussard@diocs.org; Rev. LAWRENCE C. BRENNAN, S.Th.D., Dir. Diaconate Formation. Tel: 719-636-2345. Email: lbrennan@diocs.org.

Finance Office—ROBERT G. DOERFLER JR., Dir. Tel: 719-636-2345. Email: rgdoerfler@diocs.org.

Director of Accounting—JERI THEIME. Tel: 719-636-2345. Email: jthieme@diocs.org.

Director of Properties and Construction—JANIS BALENTINE. Tel: 719-636-2345. Email: janisbalentine@diocs.org.

Benefits Administrator—KAREN SALAMON. Tel: 719-636-2345. Email: ksalamon@diocs.org.

Hispanic Ministry—Revs. FRANCISCO J. QUEZADA, Vicar. Tel: 719-636-2345. Email: fjquezada@diocs.org; JOHN TOEPFER, O.F.M.Cap. Tel: 719-473-4633. Email: fjtoepfer@diocs.org.

Human Resources—NANCY STROMER, Human Resources Admin. Tel: 719-636-2345. Email: nstromer@diocs.org.

Jail Ministry—Deacon PATRICK J. BIDON, Dir. Tel: 719-636-2345. Email: pat@diocs.org.

Mission Effectiveness—EDWARD GAFFNEY, Dir. Tel: 719-636-2345. Email: edgaffney@diocs.org.

Stewardship and Development—ROBERT C. FAUGHNAN, Dir. Tel: 719-636-2345. Email: rob@diocs.org.

Director of Employment Relations—TERRI SORTOR, Dir. Tel: 719-636-2345. Email: tsortor@diocs.org.

Director of Parish Legacy Initiative—PEGGY CUSICK, Dir. Tel: 719-636-2345. Email: pcusick@diocs.org.

Office of Marriage and Family Life Coordinators—CHRISTIAN MEERT; CHRISTINE MEERT. Tel: 719-471-9702. Email: christian@cmeert.com.

Total Catholic Education—

Superintendent of Catholic Education—HOLLY GOODWIN. Tel: 719-636-2345. Email: hgoodwin@diocs.org. *College Campus and Young Adult Ministry Coordinator*, VALERIE VELA. Tel: 719-636-2345. Email: valerie@diocs.org.

Catechesis, Youth Ministry, and Evangelization—MICHELLE MAHER, Dir. Tel: 719-636-2345. Email: michelle@diocs.org.

Traumatic Brain Injury Ministry—Deacon PATRICK JONES, Coord. Email: lamontglen@mac.com.

Victim Assistance—BARBARA MAHONEY, Coord. Tel: 719-633-8182.

Vocations—Most Rev. MICHAEL J. SHERIDAN, S.Th.D. Team: Rev. Msgr. RICARDO CORONADO-ARRASCUE, J.C.D. Tel: 719-636-2345; Revs. LAWRENCE C. BRENNAN, S.Th.D.; JAMES M. WILLIAMS. Email: vocations@diocs.org.

CLERGY, PARISHES, MISSIONS AND PAROCHIAL SCHOOLS

CITY OF COLORADO SPRINGS

(COUNTY OF EL PASO)

1—ST. MARY CATHEDRAL (1887) Revs. Francisco J. Quezada; John Toepfer, O.F.M.Cap.; Deacons Mark Griffith; Frank J. Ricotta Jr.
Mailing Address: 22 W. Kiowa St., 80903.
Office: 15 W. Bijou St., 80903. Tel: 719-473-4633; Fax: 719-473-5248. Email: staff@stmaryscathedral.org. Web: www.stmaryscathedral.org.
Catechesis/Religious Program—Kerry Susser, D.R.E.; Terrie Hernandez, C.R.E. Students 249.

2—ST. ANDREW KIM QUASI PARISH (1984), (Korean), Rev. Dong-Ho Chae.
Office: 4515 E. Pikes Peak Ave., 80916. Tel: 719-638-0100; 719-638-0105 (Rectory); Fax: 719-638-0101.
Catechesis/Religious Program—Helen Hwang, D.R.E. Students 31.

3—CORPUS CHRISTI (1916) Rev. Mark Zacker; Deacons Benedict Cruise, (Retired); Edward DeMattee.
Res.: 2313 N. Wood Ave., 80907. Tel: 719-633-1457; Fax: 719-473-7567. Email: parish@corpuschristicos.org. Web: corpuschristicos.org.
School—2410 N. Cascade Ave., 80907. Tel: 719-632-5092; Fax: 719-578-9124. Kimberly Schindler, Prin. Lay Teachers 23; Students 235.
Catechesis/Religious Program—Tel: 719-633-1457, Ext. 15. Gary Niemerg, D.R.E. Students 60.

4—DIVINE REDEEMER (1950) [JC] Revs. James J. Klein; Brian Roeseler; Deacons David Bull; Ray Milberg.
Parish Office—926 Farragut Ave., 80909. Tel: 719-633-5559; Fax: 719-234-0358. Email: jklein@divineredeemer.net. Web: www.divineredeemer.net.
School—901 N. Logan, 80909. Tel: 719-471-7771; Fax: 719-234-0300. Email: mweldele@divineredeemer.net. Web: www.divineredeemer.net/school. Marjie Weldele, Prin. Lay Teachers 20; Students 231.
Catechesis/Religious Program—Tel: 719-234-0342. Email: btittle@divineredeemer.net. Bernadette Tittle, D.R.E. Students 126.

5—ST. FRANCIS OF ASSISI (1981) Rev. Kenneth E. Przybyla; Deacons Patrick J. Bidon; Dave Camous; Michael Ciletti; Richard Harden.
Office: 2650 Parish View, 80919. Tel: 719-599-5031; Fax: 719-599-3360. Email: parish@stfrancis.org.
Catechesis/Religious Program—Terri Kowalczyk, D.R.E. Students 187.

6—ST. GABRIEL THE ARCHANGEL (1998) Revs. C. Robert Manning (STL); Rafael Torres-Rico, Parochial Vicar; Deacons Kenneth Huard; Christopher Phelps; Patrick O'Connor; Marc Lanning, Business Mgr.
Office: 8755 Scarborough, 80920. Tel: 719-528-8407; Fax: 719-598-1696. Email: office@saintgabriel.net. Web: www.saintgabriel.net.
Catechesis/Religious Program—Nico Mass, Youth Min. Students 479.

7—HOLY APOSTLES (1973) Revs. Paul F. Wicker; Michael Butler, Sacramental Min.; Deacons Michael Leverington; Charles Matzker; David Geislinger.
Res.: 4925 N. Carefree Cir., 80917. Tel: 719-597-4249; Fax: 719-591-1816. Email: haccoffice@holyapostlescc.org. Web: www.holyapostlescc.org.
Preschool—4925 N. Carefree Cir., 80917. Tel: 719-591-1566; Fax: 719-591-1816. Email: leslie@holyapostlescc.org. Web: www.holyapostle-spreschool.com. Leslie Versace, Dir. Lay Teachers 12; Students 118.
Catechesis/Religious Program—Tel: 719-597-4249. Email: msuperata@holyapostlescc.org. Mary Superata, D.R.E. Students 166.

8—HOLY TRINITY (1959) Rev. James M. Williams; Deacon Gerald Lachiewicz.
Office: 3122 Poinsetta Dr., 80907. Tel: 719-633-2132; Fax: 719-633-0975. Email: holytrinitycatholicparish@comcast.net. Web: www.holytrinitycs.com.
Catechesis/Religious Program—Students 89.

9—ST. JOSEPH'S (Southgate) (1968) Revs. Gregory Golyzniak; Francis Maher (Retired); Deacon Michael Bowen.
Res.: 1830 S. Corona Ave., 80905. Tel: 719-632-9903; Fax: 719-632-9170.
Catechesis/Religious Program—Tel: 719-635-3166. Randall Brungardt, D.R.E. & Liturgy. Students 432.

10—OUR LADY OF GUADALUPE (1948), (Hispanic), Rev. Alfredo Garcia (COL); Deacon Ernesto Romero.
Res.: 2715 E. Pikes Peak, 80909. Tel: 719-633-7204; Fax: 719-630-3184. Email: olgassist@olgcos.org.
Catechesis/Religious Program—Students 9.

11—OUR LADY OF THE PINES-BLACK FOREST (1965) Rev. Andrzej Szczesnowicz; Deacons Rick Bauer; Gene Eastham; David Evanitz.
Res.: 80908. Tel: 719-495-2351; Fax: 719-495-9062. Email: olp_blackforest@qwestoffice.net. Web: www.ourladyofthepines.org.
Catechesis/Religious Program—Vickie Welsh, D.R.E. Students 475.

12—ST. PATRICK (1981) Revs. Lawrence T. Solan; Michael Butler, Sacramental Min.; Deacons Richard Antinora; James Bachta; Richard Brown; Mathias J. Kasper; Becky Gaughan, Dir. Liturgy & Music; Scarlet Tubridy, Bus. Admin.
Office: 6455 Brook Park Dr., 80918. Tel: 719-598-3595; Fax: 719-599-5741. Email: stpatscs@stpatscs.org. Web: www.stpatscs.org.
Catechesis/Religious Program—Eric Siverts, Dir. Adult Faith Formation; Donna Gaffney, Coord. Children's Faith Formation; Nate Rose, Coord. Youth & Young Adult Min. Students 476.

13—SAINT PAUL (1925) Rev. Msgr. Robert E. Jaeger; Rev. David Ramsey Price; Deacons Richard J. Bowles; Gregory Papineau.
Office: 9 El Pomar Rd., 80906. Tel: 719-471-9700; Fax: 719-471-3009. Email: stpaul@stpaulcos.org. Web: stpaulcos.org.
School—*Pauline Memorial Catholic School*, Tel: 719-632-1846; Fax: 719-632-0495. Sandy Rivera, Prin. Lay Teachers 15; Students 168.
Catechesis/Religious Program—Students 10.

14—SACRED HEART (1891) Revs. Robert L. Epping, C.S.C.; Vincent A. Kuna, C.S.C.; Deacon Francisco Carpio.
Office: 2021 W. Pikes Peak Ave., 80904. Tel: 719-633-8711; Fax: 719-633-1859. Email: office@tricommunityorg. Web: tricommunity.org.
Catechesis/Religious Program—Sr. Mary Link, D.R.E.; Sue Gerlach, Liturgy Dir.; Rob Plush, Dir. Youth Ministry. Students 198.
Mission—*Our Lady of Perpetual Help* 218 Ruxton Ave., Manitou Springs, El Paso Co. 80829.
Mission—*Holy Rosary* 4435 Holiday Tr., Cascade, El Paso Co. 80809.

15—THE VIETNAMESE HOLY MARTYRS PARISH (1993), (Vietnamese), [CEM] Rev. Joseph P. Minh Vu.
Church: 1133 N. Wahsatch Ave., 80903. Tel: 719-635-0679.
Catechesis/Religious Program—Students 36.

OUTSIDE THE CITY OF COLORADO SPRINGS

BAILEY, PARK CO., ST. MARY OF THE ROCKIES (1990) Rev. Kizito Osudibia.
Res.: 224 Buggy Whip Rd., P.O. Box 319, 80421-8319. Tel: 303-838-2375; Fax: 303-816-9245. Email: stmaryrockies@evcohs.com. Web: www.stmaryrockies.org.
Catechesis/Religious Program—Students 16.

BUENA VISTA, CHAFFEE CO., ST. ROSE OF LIMA (1880) Rev. Stephen J. Parlet; Deacon Richard Willburn.
Res.: 118 S. Gunnison, P.O. Box 458, 81211. Tel: 719-395-8424; Fax: 719-395-8424. Email: stroseoffice@rockmountains.net.
Catechesis/Religious Program—Students 50.
Mission—*St. Joseph* 455 Castello Ave., Fairplay, Park Co. 80440. Tel: 719-395-8424. (Send all correspondence to Buena Vista address.)

BURLINGTON, KIT CARSON CO., ST. CATHERINE OF SIENA (1916) Rev. Robert Newbury.
Res. & Mailing Address: P.O. Box 266, Stratton, 80836. Tel: 719-348-5336; Fax: 719-348-4601.
Church: 450 3rd St., P.O. Box 38, 80807. Tel: 719-346-7156; Fax: 719-346-7172. Email: strattonstcharles@yahoo.com.
Catechesis/Religious Program—Students 122.

CALHAN, EL PASO CO., ST. MICHAEL'S (1905) Rev. Paul F. Wicker; Tony Rawe, Admin. & Contact Person.
Res.: 574 8th St., Box 199, 80808. Tel: 719-347-2290; Fax: 719-347-2848.
Catechesis/Religious Program—Students 33.

CASTLE ROCK, DOUGLAS CO., ST. FRANCIS OF ASSISI (1888) Rev. Bradford Noonan; Deacons Carlos Gallardo; Thomas F. Liotta; Charles J. Moss III.
Res.: 2746 Fifth St., 80104. Tel: 303-688-3025; Fax: 303-688-4016. Web: www.stfrancisc r.org.
Catechesis/Religious Program—Students 1,015.

CHEYENNE WELLS, CHEYENNE CO., SACRED HEART (1912) Rev. Kirk Slattery.
Res.: 105 W. 5th N., 80810. Tel: 719-767-5272.
Mission—*St. Augustine* (1918) P.O. Box 82, Kit Carson, Cheyenne Co. 80825. Tel: 719-962-3552.
Catechesis/Religious Program—Students 36.

ELIZABETH, ELBERT CO., OUR LADY OF THE VISITATION Rev. Marek Krol.
34201 County Rd. 33, P.O. Box 1689, 80107. Tel: 303-646-4964; Fax: 303-646-9811. Email: olvoffice@olv.cc. Web: www.ourladyofthevisitation.org.
Catechesis/Religious Program—Students 163.

FALCON, EL PASO CO., ST. BENEDICT QUASI-PARISH (2005) Deacon Lynn Sherman.
11625 Falcon Hwy., 80831. Tel: 719-495-1426. Email: stbeninfo@qwestoffice.net. Web: stbenedictfalcon.org.
Catechesis/Religious Program—Harriet Bauer, D.R.E. Students 82.

FOUNTAIN, EL PASO CO., ST. JOSEPH (1936) Merged with Holy Family, Security to form St. Dominic, Security.

HIGHLANDS RANCH, DOUGLAS CO.

1—ST. MARK CATHOLIC CHURCH (2000) Rev. John Auer; Deacons Garrett Christnacht; Bruce Sago.
Mailing Address: 9905 Foothills Canyon Blvd., 80129. Tel: 720-348-9700; Fax: 720-344-6847. Web: www.stmarkhighlandsranch.org.
Catechesis/Religious Program—Students 420.

2—PAX CHRISTI CATHOLIC CHURCH (1988) Rev. Brian

Quinn Mohan.
Office: 5761 McArthur Ranch Rd., Littleton, 80124. Tel: 303-799-1036; Fax: 303-799-1072. Email: frbrian@paxchristi.org. Web: www.paxchristi.org.
Catechesis/Religious Program—Sue Giudici, D.R.E. Students 1,224.

LEADVILLE, LAKE CO., HOLY FAMILY PARISH (1878) [CEM] [JC] Rev. Jesse Perez.
Office: 609 Poplar St., 80461. Tel: 719-486-1382; Fax: 719-486-3930. Email: himtnchurch@hotmail.com.
Res.: 424 W. 2nd, 80461.
Catechesis/Religious Program—Students 120.

LIMON, LINCOLN CO., OUR LADY OF VICTORY (1925) Rev. George V. Fagan.
Res.: 425 H Ave., P.O. Box 790, 80828. Tel: 719-775-2118.
Catechesis/Religious Program—Limon & Missions, Fax: 719-775-9406. Students 52.
Mission—St. Anthony of Padua 133 Fifth St., P.O. Box 275, Hugo, Lincoln Co. 80821. (Send all correspondence to Limon address.)
Mission—St. Mary [CEM] Flagler, Kit Carson Co. 80815. (Send all correspondence to Limon address.)

MONUMENT, EL PASO CO., ST. PETER (1911) Rev. Donald P. Brownstein; Deacons Michael Balchus; Douglas Flinn.
Mailing Address: P.O. Box 827, 80132. Tel: 719-481-3511. Web: www.petertherock.org. In Res., Rev. Lawrence C. Brennan.
Res.: 17440 Muzzleloader Way, 80132. Tel: 719-203-5723.
School—(Grades PreSchool-6) Tel: 719-481-1855; Fax: 719-955-0509. Mary Hoffmann, Prin.; Terri Mahon, Librarian. Teachers & Aides 21; Students 128.
Catechesis/Religious Program—Donna Hessel, Catechetical Leader. Students 465.

PARKER, DOUGLAS CO., AVE MARIA (1983) Revs. August Stewart; C. Joseph Dygert; Deacon Peter McCann.
Res.: 9056 E. Parker Rd., 80138-7209. Tel: 303-841-3750; Fax: 303-841-2412. Web: www.avemariaonline.org.
School—(2000)Tel: 720-842-5400; Fax: 720-842-5402. Web: www.aveangels.org. Mrs. Theresa Loiselle, Prin. Lay Teachers 27; Students 421.
Catechesis/Religious Program—Lynne K. Lane, D.R.E.; Angelle Schott, C.R.E. Students 1,015.

SALIDA, CHAFFEE CO., ST. JOSEPH (1907) Rev. Bogdan Siewiera (Poland).
Res.: 320 E. 5th St., P.O. Box 847, 81201. Tel: 719-539-6419; Fax: 719-539-7127. Email: stjosephsalida@q.com.
Catechesis/Religious Program—Students 50.

SECURITY, EL PASO CO.
1—ST. DOMINIC (2008) Rev. Lawrence W. Carmody; Deacons Albert E. Kimminau; Robert (Bob) Cole; Cathy Jane King, Pastoral Assoc.
Mailing Address: 331 Main St., 80911.
Office: 331 Main St, 80911.
Rectory—565 Marquette Dr., 80911. Tel: 719-392-7653; Fax: 719-392-1651. Email: st.dominic@pcisys.net. Web: www.coloradostdominic.org.
Church: 5354 S. Hwy. 85/87, 80911.
Catechesis/Religious Program—Sherry Staatz, D.R.E. Students 342.
2—HOLY FAMILY (1957) Merged with St. Joseph, Fountain to form St. Dominic, Security.
3—IMMACULATE CONCEPTION PARISH (2008) Rev. Stephane Dupre, F.S.S.P.
626 Aspen Dr., 80911. Mailing Address: P.O. Box 5211, 80931-5211. Tel: 719-382-0121.
Catechesis/Religious Program—

STRATTON, KIT CARSON CO., ST. CHARLES BORROMEO (1910) Rev. Robert G. Newbury Jr.
Res.: 513 Colorado Ave., P.O. Box 266, 80836. Tel: 719-348-4601; Fax: 719-348-4601. Email: strattonstcharles@yahoo.com.
Church: P.O. Box 266, 80836. Tel: 719-348-5336.
Catechesis/Religious Program—Students 56.

WOODLAND PARK, TELLER CO., TELLER COUNTY CATHOLIC COMMUNITY (1954), (Our Lady of the Woods) Rev. Timothy L. Corbley, I.V. Dei; Deacon Anthony McKee.
Office: 116 S. West St., P.O. Box 5590, 80866-5590. Tel: 719-687-9345; Fax: 719-687-0893.
Catechesis/Religious Program—Students 101.
Mission—St. Peter's 3rd & Golden, Cripple Creek, Teller Co. 80813. (Send all correspondence to Woodland Park address.)
Mission—St. Victor's 2nd & Portland, Victor, Teller Co. 80860. (Send all correspondence to Woodland Park address.)

On Duty Outside Diocese:
Revs.—
Baron, James, Pontifical North American College, Rome
Grabrian, Dennis, 7172 Regional St., PMB 434, Dublin, CA 94568.
Ponce, James, Graduate Degree Canon Law; Pontifical North American College, Rome (Casa Santa Maria)

Retired:
Most Rev.—
Hanifen, Richard C., D.D., J.C.L., 228 N. Cascade Ave., 80903.
Rev. Msgrs.—
Dunn, Donald F., 411 Lakewood Cir., # A-8-7, 80910.
Slattery, John F., 7665 Assisi Heights, 80919-3836.
Revs.—
Battiato, Patrick, P.O. Box 5402, 80931.
Bond, Ernest W., P.O. Box 307, Terry, MT 59349.
Halloran, James F., Medallion, 1719 E. Bijou St., #601, 80909.
Halloran, Joseph H., Fountain Terrace Apartments, 3211 E. Fountain Blvd., #103, 80910.
Krenzke, John W., 2626 Osceola St., Apt. 912 W., Denver, 80212.
Vollmer, William C., 35 Tilly Ln., Castle Rock, 80104.

Permanent Deacons:
Antinora, Richard, St. Patrick, Colorado Springs
Archunde, Gregory
Bachta, James, St. Patrick, Colorado Springs
Balchus, Michael, St. Peter Parish, Monument
Bauer, Richard, Our Lady of the Pines, Colorado Springs
Bidon, Patrick J., Dir., Office of Diaconate; St. Francis of Assisi, Colorado Springs
Bowen, Michael, M.D., St. Joseph, Colorado Springs
Bowles, Richard, St. Paul, Colorado Springs; Fort Carson, Colorado Springs
Broussard, Robert, Holy Apostles, Colorado Springs
Brown, Richard, St. Patrick, Colorado Springs
Bull, David, Divine Redeemer, Colorado Springs
Camous, Dave, Our Lady of the Pines, Colorado Springs; Pres. St. Mary's High School
Carpio, Francisco, Sacred Heart, Colorado Springs
Christnacht, Garrett, St. Mark, Highlands Ranch
Ciletti, Michael, Natl. Chap., Faith and Light USA; St. Francis of Assisi, Colorado Springs
Cole, Robert (Bob), St. Dominic, Security
Cruise, Benedict, (Retired), Colorado Springs
DeMattee, Edward, Corpus Christi, Colorado Springs
Eastham, Eugene S., Our Lady of the Pines, Colorado Springs
Estey, Russell
Evanitz, David, Our Lady of the Pines, Colorado Springs
Flinn, Douglas, St. Peter, Monument
Geislinger, David, Holy Apostles, Colorado Springs
Griffith, Mark, St. Mary's Cathedral, Colorado Springs
Harden, Richard, AFA Community Chapel, Colorado Springs
Huard, Kenneth, St. Gabriel the Archangel, Colorado Springs
Jones, Patrick, St. Dominic, Woodland Park; Coord. Traumatic Brain Injury Ministry
Kasper, Mathias J., St. Patrick, Colorado Springs
Kimminau, Albert E., St. Dominic, Security
Lachiewicz, Gerald, Holy Trinity, Colorado Springs
Leverington, Michael, Holy Apostles, Colorado Springs
Linehan, George D., Jr., (Retired), Parker
Liotta, Thomas F., St. Francis of Assisi, Castle Rock
Matzker, Charles, Contact Person for Catholic Charismatic Renewal Svcs., Holy Apostles Church, Colorado Springs
McCann, Peter, Ave Maria, Parker
McKee, Anthony, Our Lady of the Woods, Woodland Park
McLean, Arthur J., (Retired), Colorado Springs
Milberg, Raymond, Divine Redeemer, Colorado Springs
Moss, Charles J., III, St. Francis of Assisi, Castle Rock
O'Connor, Patrick, St. Gabriel, Colorado Springs
Ohnmacht, Norbert, St. Charles, Stratton
Osgood, Gregory, Corpus Christi, Colorado Springs
Papineau, Gregory, St. Paul, Colorado Springs
Phelps, Christopher, St. Gabriel, Colorado Springs
Ricotta, Frank J., Jr., St. Mary's Cathedral, Colorado Springs
Rohan, Peter, Corpus Christi, Colorado Springs
Romero, Ernesto, (Leave of Absence)
Ross, David, St. Francis of Assisi, Colorado Springs
Sago, Bruce, St. Mark, Highlands Ranch
Sherman, Lynn, Parish Dir., St. Benedict's, Falcon
Sherpa, Lee, (Retired), Colorado Springs
Specht, Charles W., (Retired), Colorado Springs
Toner, James, (Serving in South Carolina)
Waller, Robert L., (Serving Archdiocese Military Services, USA)
Walsh, Timothy (Tim), Ave Maria, Parker
Werckman, Anthony, Holy Family, Leadville
Willburn, Richard, St. Rose of Lima, Buena Vista

INSTITUTIONS LOCATED IN THE DIOCESE

[A] HIGH SCHOOLS

COLORADO SPRINGS. **St. Mary's High School*, 2501 E. Yampa, 80909. Tel: 719-635-7540; Fax: 719-471-7623. Email: rcross@smhscs.org. Web: www.smhscs.org. Ms. Karen Levi, Contact Person; Ky McCarty, Pres.; J. Michael Biondini, Prin.; Robyn Cross, Admissions. Full Time Lay Teachers 28; Students 355.

[B] GENERAL HOSPITALS

COLORADO SPRINGS. *St. Francis Health Center* (1968) 825 E. Pikes Peak Ave., 80903. Tel: 719-634-2156; Fax: 303-804-8198. Email: krisordelheide@centura.org. Kris Ordelheide, Contact Person. An operating unit of Catholic Health Initiatives Colorado (an affiliate of Catholic Health Initiatives)

Penrose-St. Francis Health Services, 2222 N. Nevada, P.O. Box 7021, 80907. Tel: 719-776-5007; Fax: 719-776-2770. Email: margaretsabin@centura.org. Web: www.centura.org. Mr. Larry Seidl, Vice Pres. Mission Integration. An operating unit of Catholic Health Initiatives Colorado (an affiliate of Catholic Health Initiatives) Bed Capacity 468; Total Staff 2,800; Patients Assisted Annually 350,528.

Penrose Hospital An operating unit of Catholic Health Initiatives Colorado (an affiliate of Catholic Health Initiatives), 2222 N. Nevada, 80907. Tel: 719-776-5000; Fax: 719-776-2770. Rev. Dan Ayers, Sacramental Min.; Theresa Gregoire, Catholic Chap.; Rosemary Partridge, Catholic Chap. Sponsored by Catholic Health Initiatives., An operating unit of Catholic Health Initiatives Colorado (an affiliate of Catholic Health Initiatives) Priests 2.

St. Francis Medical Center An operating unit of Catholic Health Initiatives Colorado (an affiliate of Catholic Health Initiatives), 6001 E. Woodmen Rd., 80923. Tel: 719-571-1000. An operating unit of Catholic Health Initiatives Colorado (an affiliate of Catholic Health Initiatives)

[C] NURSING HOMES

COLORADO SPRINGS. **St. Francis Nursing Center*, 7550 Assisi Heights, 80919. Tel: 719-598-1336; Fax: 719-598-6472. Rev. Stephen Akujobi, Spiritual Svcs. Dir.; Vivian Booker, Admin. Sisters of St. Francis of Perpetual Adoration. Total Staff 165; Beds 102; Total Assisted Annually 82.

[D] SPECIAL CARE FACILITIES

COLORADO SPRINGS. *Catholic Health Initiatives Colorado Foundation*, 6385 Corporate Dr., Ste. 301, 80919. Tel: 719-548-7057; Fax: 719-634-4925. Email: karlaprentiss@centura.org. Douglas A. Dillon, Pres.

Medalion Foundation An affiliate division of Catholic Health Initiatives Colorado Foundation (an affiliate of Catholic Health Initiatives)

Namaste Alzheimer Foundation An affiliate division of Catholic Health Initiatives Colorado Foundation (an affiliate of Catholic Health Initiatives)

Penrose-St. Francis Health Foundation An affiliate division of Catholic Health Initiatives Colorado Foundation (an affiliate of Catholic Health Initiatives)

Medalion Retirement Community, 1719 E. Bijou St., 80909. Tel: 719-381-1000; Fax: 719-381-4978. Dave Campbell, Chap. An operating unit of Catholic Health Initiatives Colorado. An affiliate of Catholic Health Initiatives. Skilled Nursing Beds 60; Assisted Living Beds 44; Independent Living Apartments 60; Bed Capacity 60; Total Assisted Annually 100; Total Staff 110.

Namaste Alzheimer Center, 2 Penrose Blvd., 80906. Tel: 719-776-6300; Fax: 719-520-9709. Marga Callender, Chap. An operating unit of Catholic Health Initiatives Colorado. An affiliate of Catholic Health Initiatives; Programs for seniors with Alzheimer's or dementia. Skilled Nursing/Alzheimer Beds 64.

[E] RESIDENCES FOR MEN RELIGIOUS

COLORADO SPRINGS. *Solanus Casey Friary*, 15 W. View Pl., 80903. Tel: 719-632-7584; Fax: 719-632-7718. Revs. John P. Cousins, O.F.M.Cap., Guardian; Cyrus Gallagher, O.F.M.Cap.; James E. Moster,

O.F.M. Cap., Vicar; John Toepfer, O.F.M.Cap., Bursar.

CASCADE. *Holy Cross Novitiate*, 7872 W. Hwy. 24, Box 749, 80809. Tel: 719-684-9277. Revs. Kevin Russeau, C.S.C., Dir. of Novices & Supr.; Donald W. Dilg, C.S.C., Asst. Dir. & Steward. Congregation of Holy Cross. Priests 2; Novices 10.

SEDALIA. *Sacred Heart Jesuit Community*, Box 185, 80135-0185. Tel: 303-688-5198; Fax: 303-688-9633. Email: information@sacredheartretreat.org. Web: www.sacredheartretreat.org. Revs. Vincent E. Hovley, S.J., Supr.; Edward Kinerk, S.J., Dir.; Richard W. Dunphy, S.J.; E. Eugene Arthur, S.J.; Bro. Richard P. May, S.J.

[F] RESIDENCES FOR WOMEN RELIGIOUS

COLORADO SPRINGS. **Benet Hill Monastery*, 3190 Benet Ln., 80921-1509. Tel: 719-633-0655; Fax: 719-471-0403. Email: info@benethillmonastery.org. Web: www.benethillmonastery.org. Sisters Clare Carr, O.S.B., Prioress; Joseph Marie Jacobsen, O.S.B., Community Archivist. Motherhouse of the Benedictine Sisters (1963).; Properties owned: Benet Hill Monastery and Benedictine Spirituality Center in the Pines Professed Sisters 31.

Sisters of St. Francis of Perpetual Adoration, 7665 Assisi Hts., 80919-3837. Tel: 719-598-5486; Fax: 719-598-1578. Email: nadine@stfrancis.org. Web: www.stfrancis.org. Sr. Nadine Heimann, O.S.F., Prov.; Rev. Msgr. John F. Slattery, Chap. (Retired). Provincial House. Sisters of St. Francis of Perpetual Adoration, Province of St. Joseph (The Sisters of St. Francis of Colorado Springs). Professed Sisters 56.

[G] RETREAT CENTERS

COLORADO SPRINGS. **Benedictine Spirituality Center in the Pines*, 3190 Benet Ln., 80921-1509. Tel: 719-633-0655, Ext. 132; Fax: 719-471-0403. Email: bpinescs@benethillmonastery.org. Web: www.benethillmonastery.org. Sr. Mary John Thomas, O.S.B., Center Dir. Total Staff 3.

Franciscan Retreat Center, Inc., 7740 Deer Hill Grove, 80919-3836. Tel: 719-955-7025; Fax: 719-260-8044. Email: frc@stfrancis.org. Web: www.franciscanretreatcenter.org. Sr. Joanne Moeller, F.S.P.A., Dir. Total Guests 11,000; Total Staff 8.

SEDALIA. *Sacred Heart Jesuit Retreat House*, Box 185, 80135-0185. Tel: 303-688-4198; Fax: 303-688-9633. Email: information@sacredheartretreat.org. Web: www.sacredheartretreat.org. Revs. Edward Kinerk, S.J.; Richard W. Dunphy, S.J.; E. Eugene Arthur, S.J.; Vincent E. Hovley, S.J.; Bro. Richard P. May, S.J.; Sr. Eileen Currie, M.S.C. Total in Residence 5.

[H] MISCELLANEOUS LISTINGS

COLORADO SPRINGS. *All for the Glory of God Ministry*, 5885 Del Paz Dr., 80918. Tel: 719-593-2120; Fax: 719-593-2120.

Ave Maria Catholic School Corporation, 228 N. Cascade Ave., 80903. Tel: 719-636-2345; Fax: 719-636-1216. Holly Goodwin, Supt. Catholic Educ.

Catholic Center at the Citadel, 750 Citadel Dr. E., Ste. 3056, 80909. Tel: 719-573-7364. Web: www.catholicchapelmall.org. Revs. James E. Moster, O.F.M. Cap., Dir.; Cyrus Gallagher, O.F.M. Cap.; John P. Cousins, O.F.M.Cap.

Catholic Charities of Central Colorado, Inc., 228 N. Cascade Ave., 80903. Tel: 719-636-2345; Fax: 719-636-1216. Email: info@ccharitiescc.org. Web: www.ccharitiescc.org. Mark C. Rohlena Esq., Esq., Interim Pres. & CEO.

The Catholic Foundation of the Diocese of Colorado Springs, Inc., 228 N. Cascade Ave., 80903. Tel: 719-636-2345; Fax: 719-636-1216. Web: www.diocs.org. Robert G. Doerfler Jr., Pres. & Exec. Dir.

Catholic Housing Corporation of Colorado Springs, 2445 Wimbleton Ct., 80920. Tel: 719-599-8758.

Colorado Springs Cursillo Movement, P.O. Box 25655, 80936.

Douglas County Catholic School Corporation, 228 N. Cascade Ave., 80903. Tel: 719-636-2345; Fax: 719-636-1216. Holly Goodwin, Supt., Catholic Educ.

Fostering Hope Foundation, 3055 Sunnybrook Ln., 80904. Tel: 719-635-6756.

Franciscan Community Counseling, Inc., 7665 Assisi Heights, 80919. Tel: 719-955-7008; Fax: 719-598-0346. Email: sharon@stfrancis.org. Web: www.franciscancommunitycounseling.org. Sharon Compono, Exec. Dir. Email: sharon@stfrancis.org. Total Assisted Annually 450; Total Staff 11.

The Franciscan Foundation of Colorado Springs, 7665 Assisi Hts., 80919-3836. Tel: 719-598-5486; Fax: 719-532-0567. Email: nadine@stfrancis.org. Sr. Nadine Heimann, O.S.F., Pres. & Prov.

**St. Mary's Catholic Education Foundation*, 2501 Yampa St., 80809. Tel: 719-635-7540. William G. Carter, Pres.

**Partners in Housing, Inc.*, 455 Gold Pass Heights, 80906. Tel: 719-473-8890; Fax: 719-635-9360. Email: office@partnersinhousing.org. Web: www.partnersinhousing.org. Frank Stampf, Exec. Dir.; Barbara Blumer, Dir. of Support Svcs. Total Staff 22; Total Assisted Annually (Adults 142); (Children 206); (Families 134) 472.

**S.E.T. of Colorado Springs dba S.E.T Family Medical Clinic* 825 E. Pikes Peak Ave., Bldg. 29, 80903. Tel: 719-776-8950; Fax: 719-776-8855. Email: Zelnajoseph@centura.org; info@setofcs.org. Web: www.setofcs.org. Zelna Joseph, Pres. & CEO.

**St. Thomas Aquinas Society*, P.O. Box 62908, 80962-2908. Tel: 719-448-0020; Fax: 877-207-3707. Web: www.StThomasAquinasSociety.org.

**Villa San Jose, Inc.*, 1810 S. Corona Ave., 80905. Tel: 719-632-7444; Fax: 719-520-9345. Web: www.archhousing.com. Total in Residence 50; Total Staff 9.

**Villa Santa Maria, Inc.*, 405 E. St. Elmo Ave., 80905. Tel: 719-520-9344; Fax: 719-520-9345. Web: www.archhousing.com. Total Staff 10; Total in Residence 50.

Women Partnering, 10 S. Institute, 80903. Tel: 719-577-9404; Fax: 719-577-9407. Email: womenpar@comcast.net. Web: stfrancis.org. Sr. Jeannette Kneifel, O.S.F., Pres. & CEO.

NECROLOGY

† Bruggeman, Gerald H., (Retired)—Died April 27, 2011

An asterisk (*) denotes an organization that has established tax-exempt status directly with the IRS and is not covered by the USCCB Group Ruling.

Diocese of Columbus

(Dioecesis Columbensis)

Most Reverend

FREDERICK F. CAMPBELL, Ph.D., D.D.

Bishop of Columbus; ordained May 31, 1980; appointed Titular Bishop of Afufenia and Auxiliary Bishop of St. Paul and Minneapolis March 2, 1999; consecrated May 14, 1999; appointed Eleventh Bishop of Columbus October 14, 2004; installed January 13, 2005. *Res.: 198 E. Broad St., Columbus, OH 43215.* Tel: 614-224-2251.

Most Reverend

JAMES A. GRIFFIN, J.D., J.C.L.

Retired Bishop of Columbus; ordained May 28, 1960; consecrated Titular Bishop of Holar and Auxiliary to the Bishop of Cleveland August 1, 1979; appointed Tenth Bishop of Columbus February 7, 1983; installed April 25, 1983; retired October 14, 2004; named Diocesan Administrator October 18, 2004 to January 12, 2005. *Mailing Address: 198 E. Broad St., Columbus, OH 43215.*

(Diocesan Seal)

Established 1868.

Square Miles 11,310.

Comprises the following 23 Counties in the State of Ohio: Hardin, Marion, Morrow, Knox, Holmes, Tuscarawas, Union, Delaware, Licking, Coshocton, Madison, Franklin, Muskingum, Fayette, Pickaway, Fairfield, Perry, Ross, Hocking, Pike, Jackson, Vinton and Scioto.

For legal titles of parishes and diocesan institutions, consult the Chancery Office.

Chancery Office: 198 E. Broad St., Columbus, OH 43215. Tel: 614-224-2251; Fax: 614-224-6306.

STATISTICAL OVERVIEW

Personnel	
Bishop	1
Retired Bishops	1
Priests: Diocesan Active in Diocese	106
Priests: Diocesan Active Outside Diocese	5
Priests: Retired, Sick or Absent	42
Number of Diocesan Priests	153
Religious Priests in Diocese	30
Total Priests in Diocese	183
Extern Priests in Diocese	17
Ordinations:	
Diocesan Priests	2
Permanent Deacons in Diocese	96
Total Sisters	233
Parishes	
Parishes	106
With Resident Pastor:	
Resident Diocesan Priests	82
Resident Religious Priests	4
Without Resident Pastor:	
Administered by Priests	18
Administered by Deacons	2
Missions	3
Professional Ministry Personnel:	
Sisters	20
Lay Ministers	32
Welfare	
Catholic Hospitals	6
Total Assisted	809,751
Homes for the Aged	19
Total Assisted	1,730
Residential Care of Children	1
Total Assisted	1,802
Specialized Homes	7
Total Assisted	10,182
Special Centers for Social Services	8
Total Assisted	520,732
Educational	
Seminaries, Diocesan	1
Students from This Diocese	30
Students from Other Diocese	180
Diocesan Students in Other Seminaries	3
Total Seminarians	33
Colleges and Universities	2
Total Students	4,017
High Schools, Diocesan and Parish	11
Total Students	4,688
Elementary Schools, Diocesan and Parish	42
Total Students	11,410
Elementary Schools, Private	2
Total Students	232
Catechesis/Religious Education:	
High School Students	1,241
Elementary Students	13,415
Total Students under Catholic Instruction	35,036
Teachers in the Diocese:	
Priests	19
Sisters	5
Lay Teachers	1,146
Vital Statistics	
Receptions into the Church:	
Infant Baptism Totals	3,189
Minor Baptism Totals	231
Adult Baptism Totals	358
Received into Full Communion	432
First Communions	3,681
Confirmations	3,666
Marriages:	
Catholic	559
Interfaith	385
Total Marriages	944
Deaths	1,426
Total Catholic Population	264,425
Total Population	2,580,134

Former Bishops—Rt. Revs. SYLVESTER HORTON ROSECRANS, D.D., ord. June 5, 1852; cons. Titular Bishop of Pompeiopolis and Auxiliary to the Bishop of Cincinnati, March 25, 1862; transferred to Columbus, March 3, 1868; died Oct. 21, 1878; JOHN AMBROSE WATTERSON, D.D., ord. Aug. 9, 1868; cons. Aug. 8, 1880; died April 17, 1899; Most Revs. HENRY MOELLER, D.D., cons. Bishop of Columbus, Aug. 25, 1900; promoted to the Archiepiscopal See of Areopolis and made Coadjutor to the Archbishop of Cincinnati, with the right of succession, April 27, 1903; succeeded to the See of Cincinnati, Oct. 31, 1904; died Jan. 5, 1925; JAMES JOSEPH HARTLEY, D.D., cons. Feb. 25, 1904; died Jan. 12, 1944; MICHAEL JOSEPH READY, D.D., cons. Dec. 14, 1944; died May 2, 1957; CLARENCE GEORGE ISSENMANN, S.T.D., cons. Titular Bishop of Phytea and Auxiliary Bishop of Cincinnati May 25, 1954; appt. Bishop of Columbus Dec. 5, 1957; transferred to Cleveland as Apostolic Administrator. "cum jure successionis," Oct. 7, 1964; died July 27, 1982; His Eminence JOHN CARDINAL CARBERRY, D.D., S.T.D., J.C.D., Ph.D., appt. Titular Bishop of Elis and Coadjutor of Lafayette in Indiana "cum jure successionis," May 3, 1956; cons. July 25, 1956; succeeded to See Nov. 20, 1957; transferred to Columbus Jan. 20, 1965; transferred to the Archdiocese of St. Louis, March 24, 1968; created Cardinal April 28, 1969; Most Revs. CLARENCE E. ELWELL, D.D., cons. Dec. 21, 1962; appt. to Columbus May 29, 1968; died Feb. 16, 1973; EDWARD J. HERRMANN, D.D., appt. Auxiliary Bishop of Washington and Titular Bishop of Lamzella, March 4, 1966; cons. April 26, 1966; appt. Ninth Bishop of Columbus, June 26, 1973; installed Aug. 21, 1973; retired Sept. 18, 1982; named Apostolic Administrator Sept. 1982 to April 1983; died Dec. 22, 1999; JAMES A. GRIFFIN, J.D., J.C.L., ord. May 28, 1960; cons. Titular Bishop of Holar and Auxiliary to the Bishop of Cleveland Aug. 1, 1979; appt. Tenth Bishop of Columbus Feb. 7, 1983; installed April 25, 1983; resigned Oct. 14, 2004.

Vicar General—Rev. Msgr. STEPHAN J. MOLONEY, M.A., M.Div., J.C.L.

Episcopal Moderator for Administration—Mr. DOMINIC PRUNTE.

Episcopal Moderator for Charities and Social Concerns—MARK H. HUDDY, J.D.

Episcopal Moderator for Education—LUCIA D. MCQUAIDE, M.S.Ed., M.Rel.Ed.

Episcopal Moderator for Spiritual Life and Parish Ministry—Deacon THOMAS M. BERG JR., B.A., M.J., M.P.S.

Chancery Office—198 E. Broad St., Columbus, 43215. Tel: 614-224-2251; Fax: 614-224-6306. Office Hours: Mon.-Fri. 8-4:30

Chancellor—Very Rev. SHAWN D. CORCORAN, M.Div., J.C.L.

Vice Chancellor—Deacon THOMAS M. BERG JR., B.A., M.J., M.P.S.

College of Consultors—Most Rev. FREDERICK F. CAMPBELL, D.D., Ph.D.; Rev. Msgr. STEPHAN J. MOLONEY, M.A., M.Div., J.C.L.; Very Rev. SHAWN D. CORCORAN, M.Div., J.C.L.; Rev. KEVIN J. KAVANAGH, S.T.L., M.Div.; Rev. Msgrs. GEORGE J. SCHLEGEL, B.A. (Retired); WILLIAM A. DUNN; Revs. JOHN E. STATTMILLER (Retired); MATTHEW N. HOOVER; Rev. Msgr. FRANK J. MEAGHER (Retired).

Parochial Examiners—Rev. JAMES A. WALTER; Rev. Msgr. STEPHAN J. MOLONEY, M.A., M.Div., J.C.L.; Revs. CHARLES F. KLINGER, M.A., M.Div., Ph.D.; JAMES C. CSASZAR; LEO L. CONNOLLY, M.Div.; TIMOTHY M. HAYES, S.T.L.; THEODORE F. MACHNIK; WILLIAM L. ARNOLD, M.E., M.Ed.; MARK J. HAMMOND, J.C.L., S.T.L.; DENIS KIGOZI; DAVID A. POLIAFICO; JOSEPH T. YOKUM.

Deaneries—Deanery 1: Center-South Columbus: Rev. DENIS S. KIGOZI, M.Div., St. Thomas the Apostle, 2692 E. Fifth Ave., Columbus, 43219-2752. Deanery 2: Northwest: Rev. TIMOTHY M. HAYES, S.T.L., St. Timothy Church, 1088 Thomas Ln., Columbus, 43220-5047. Deanery 3: North High: Rev. STANLEY L. (STASH) DAILEY, St. Michael Church, 5750 N. High St., Worthington, 43085-3986. Deanery 4: Northland: Rev. CHARLES F. KLINGER, M.A., M.Div., Ph.D., St. Paul, 313 N. State St., Westerville, 43082-8825. Deanery 5: West: Rev. LEO L. CONNOLLY, M.Div., St. Cecilia

Church, 434 Norton Rd., Columbus, 43228-7602. Deanery 6: East: Rev. WILLIAM L. ARNOLD, M.E., M.Ed., Holy Spirit, 4383 E. Broad St., Columbus, 43213-1357. Deanery 7: Marion: Rev. DAVID A. POLIAFICO, Our Lady of Lourdes Church, 1033 W. Fifth St., Marysville, 43040-8667. Deanery 8: Muskingum-Perry: Rev. JAMES C. CSASZAR, St. Rose Church, 309 N. Main St., New Lexington, 43764-1204. Deanery 9: Knox Licking: Rev. MARK J. HAMMOND, J.C.L., S.T.L., St. Vincent de Paul, 303 E. High St., Mount Vernon, 43050-3419. Deanery 10: Tuscarawas-Holmes-Coshocton: Rev. JAMES H. HATFIELD III, St. Joseph Church, 613 N. Tuscarawas Ave., Dover, 44622-2837. Deanery 11: Lancaster: Rev. JAMES A. WALTER, Mailing Address: St. Joseph Church, P.O. Box 209, Sugar Grove, 43155-0209. Deanery 12: Chillicothe: Rev. THEODORE F. MACHNIK, St. Joseph Church, P.O. Box 40, Circleville, 43113-0040. Deanery 13: Scioto County: Rev. JOSEPH T. YOKUM, St. Peter in Chains Church, 2167 Lick Run Lyra Rd., Wheelersburg, 45694-8882.

Presbyteral Council—Most Rev. FREDERICK F. CAMPBELL, D.D., Ph.D., Pres.; Revs. MARK J. HAMMOND, J.C.L., S.T.L., Chm.; WILLIAM L. ARNOLD, M.E., M.Ed., Vice Chm.; JOSEPH T. YOKUM, Sec.; CHARLES F. KLINGER, M.A., M.Div., Ph.D.; MARK J. HAMMOND, J.C.L., S.T.L.; TIMOTHY M. HAYES, S.T.L.; JAMES C. CSASZAR; LEO L. CONNOLLY, M.Div.; STANLEY L. (STASH) DAILEY; THEODORE F. MACHNIK; WILLIAM L. ARNOLD, M.E., M.Ed.; DAVID A. POLIAFICO; JOSEPH T. YOKUM; Rev. Msgr. STEPHAN J. MOLONEY, M.A., M.Div., J.C.L., Ex Officio; Rev. SHAWN D. CORCORAN.

Diocesan Pastoral Council—Most Rev. FREDERICK F. CAMPBELL, D.D., Ph.D., Pres.; LEW CAMPBELL, Chm.; ELLEN WEILBACHER, Exec. Sec., 197 E. Gay St., Columbus, 43215. Tel: 614-241-2550, Ext. 336.

Bishop's Council—Rev. Msgr. STEPHAN J. MOLONEY, M.A., M.Div., J.C.L., Vicar Gen.; Very Rev. SHAWN D. CORCORAN, M.Div., J.C.L., Chancellor; Deacon THOMAS M. BERG JR., B.A., M.J., M.P.S., Vice Chancellor & Episcopal Moderator for Spiritual Life and Parish Ministry; Ms. LUCIA D. MCQUAIDE, Episcopal Moderator for Educ.; Mr. MARK H. HUDDY, Episcopal Moderator for Catholic Charities & Social Concerns; Mr. RICK H. JERIC, Dir. Devel. & Planning; Mr. WILLIAM S. DAVIS, Dir. Finance; Mr. DOMINIC PRUNTE, Dir. Personnel & Episcopal Moderator for Admin.

Diocesan Board of Review for the Protection of Children—Rev. Msgr. STEPHAN J. MOLONEY, M.A., M.Div., J.C.L., Victims Asst. Coord.; Mr. MITCHELL J. BROWN; Mr. DOMINIC J. CAVELLO; Dr. PAULA COMPTON; Dr. KATHLEEN WODARCYK; Mr. JOHN J. KULEWICZ, Chm.; Mrs. MARY GINN RYAN; Rev. PAUL A. NOBLE, M.A., Ph.D.; Mrs. LINDA DAY-MACKESSY; Dr. JUANITA MURAWSKI, 198 E. Broad St., Columbus, 43215. Tel: 614-224-2251.

Diocesan Commission for Ecumenical and Interreligious Affairs—Rev. WILLIAM J. FERGUSON, Chm. Tel: 740-928-3266.

Diocesan Finance Council—Most Rev. FREDERICK F. CAMPBELL, D.D., Ph.D.; Rev. Msgr. STEPHAN J. MOLONEY, M.A., M.Div., J.C.L.; Very Rev. SHAWN D. CORCORAN, M.Div., J.C.L.; Mr. WILLIAM S. DAVIS; FRANK BETTENDORF, Chm.; THOMAS MCAULIFFE; HUGH DORRIAN; TIMOTHY BOTTS; MIKE DEASCENTIS; CHRISTOPHER FIDLER; ROBERT HETTERSCHEIDT; ED WALSH; Rev. MICHAEL B. WATSON, M.Div., B.S.

Tribunal—Ste. 500, 197 E. Gay St., Columbus, 43215-3290. Tel: 614-241-2500; Fax: 614-241-2522.

Judicial Vicar—Rev. Msgr. JAMES L.T. RUEF, M.A., J.C.L., M.Div., J.D. (Retired).

Adjutant Judicial Vicar—Rev. Msgr. JOHN K. CODY, B.A., M.Div., J.C.L.

Moderator of the Tribunal Chancery—Deacon JOHN R. CRERAND, M.A., J.C.L.

Presiding Judges of First Instance—Rev. Msgrs. JOHN K. CODY, B.A., M.Div., J.C.L.; JOHN G. JOHNSON, J.C.D.; Revs. DENNIS E. STEVENSON, M.A., M.Div., J.C.L.; JOSEPH N. BAY, M.A., M.Div., J.C.L.

Presiding Judge in Second Instance—Rev. Msgr. JAMES L.T. RUEF, M.A., J.C.L., M.Div., J.D. (Retired).

Promoter of Justice—Rev. Msgr. STEPHAN J. MOLONEY, M.A., M.Div., J.C.L.

Defenders of the Bond—Rev. MARK J. HAMMOND, J.C.L., S.T.L.; DANIEL M. SHAKAL, M.Div., M.C.L., J.C.L.; Deacon JOHN R. CRERAND, M.A., J.C.L.

Medical Experts—Rev. STEPHEN G. VIRGINIA, Ph.D.; Dr. FRANK J. OROSZ, Ph.D.

Diocesan Judges—Revs. WILLIAM L. ARNOLD, M.E., M.Ed.; LEO L. CONNOLLY, M.Div.; Rev. Msgrs. JOHN J. DREESE, S.S.L., S.T.L. (Retired); JAMES A. GEIGER, M.A., Ph.D. (Retired); Very Rev. G. MICHAEL GRIBBLE, M.Div.; Revs. TIMOTHY M. HAYES, S.T.L.; KEVIN J. KAVANAGH, S.T.L., M.Div.; CHARLES F. KLINGER, M.A., M.Div., Ph.D.; Rev. Msgr. FRANK P. LANE, Ph.D. (Retired); Revs. WILLIAM A. METZGER, B.A.; DANIEL J. MILLISOR, M.Div.; PAUL A. NOBLE, M.A., Ph.D.

Tribunal Staff—Sr. RAYMUNDA BROOKS, O.P., M.A.; Mrs. SUE ULMER; Ms. MARY BETH KRECSMAR; Ms. PATRICIA SMITH.

Procurator Advocates—Deacons THOMAS M. BERG JR., B.A., M.J., M.P.S.; CHRISTOPHER CAMPBELL; STEVEN DEMERS; JEFFREY D. FORTKAMP; DANIEL W. HANN; FRANK A. IANNARINO; ROBERT A. JOSEPH; JAMES W. KELLY; PETER C. LABITA; ROGER MINNER; JAMES MORRIS; DEAN W. RACINE; JAMES A. ROUSE, A.E., M.S., P.E.; MARK A. SCARPITTI; CRAIG SMITH; MARION E. SMITHBERGER; FRANK K. SULLIVAN; PATRICK WILSON.

Catholic Conference of Ohio

Catholic Conference of Ohio—CAROLYN JURKOWITZ, Dir., 9 E. Long St., Ste. 201, Columbus, 43215. Tel: 614-224-7147; Fax: 614-224-7150. Email: general@ohiocathconf.org. Web: ohiocathconf.org.

Diocesan Offices and Departments

Department of Administration

Black Catholic Ministries of Columbus—RACHELLE MARTIN, Chm., 197 E. Gay St., Columbus, 43215-5232. Tel: 614-228-0024; Fax: 614-221-1787. Email: blackcatholicministr@colsdioc.org.

Building Commission—Deacon JAMES A. ROUSE, A.E., M.S., P.E., Chm.; Mr. PAT DAVIS, Co Chm.

Catholic Center—PATRICK DAVIS, Supt. Bldgs., Diocesan Office Building, 197 E. Gay St., Columbus, 43215. Tel: 614-228-2453.

Catholic Latino Ministry Office—ANGELA JOHNSTON, Dir., 197 E. Gay St., Columbus, 43215. Tel: 614-262-7992. Email: ajohnston@colsdioc.org.

Catholic Record Society—DONALD SCHLEGEL, Vice Chm.; HAROLD WAGNER, Chm. Research Com.; RICK JACKSON, Sec., 197 E. Gay St., Columbus, 43215. Tel: 614-241-2571.

The Catholic Times, Inc.—DAVID A. GARICK, Editor; Deacon STEVEN DEMERS, Business Mgr., 197 E. Gay St., Columbus, 43215. Tel: 614-224-5195.

Cemeteries—RICHARD FINN, Dir., 6440 S. High St., Lockbourne, 43137. Tel: 614-491-2751; Fax: 614-491-4264. Email: ccocrfinn@aol.com.

Censor of Books—Rev. Msgr. JOHN V. WOLF, S.T.D. (Retired); Revs. WILLIAM THOMAS KESSLER; THOMAS J. BUFFER, S.T.D.

Central Purchasing Service—STEVE DEEDRICK, Dir., 197 E. Gay St., Columbus, 43215. Tel: 614-262-0010; 800-842-8319; Fax: 614-262-0013.

Communications Office—Deacon THOMAS M. BERG JR., B.A., M.J., M.P.S., Dir.; GEORGE A. JONES, B.S., Assoc. Dir., 197 E. Gay St., Columbus, 43215. Tel: 614-241-2555; Fax: 614-241-2557.

Deaf Apostolate—Rev. STANLEY BENECKI, St. Mary Magdalene, 473 S. Roys Ave., Columbus, 43204-2598. Tel: 614-274-1121 (Voice); 614-358-7323 (TDD); Fax: 614-274-1122.

Development and Planning Office—Mr. RICK H. JERIC, Exec. Dir., 197 E. Gay St., Columbus, 43215. Tel: 614-241-2550; Fax: 614-241-2567.

Diocesan Charities Membership Corporation—MARK H. HUDDY, J.D., Trustee & Sec., 198 E. Broad St., Columbus, 43215. Tel: 614-224-2251.

Diocesan Finance Office—Mr. WILLIAM S. DAVIS, Dir. Finance, 198 E. Broad St., Columbus, 43215. Tel: 614-224-1221; Fax: 614-241-2573.

Haitian Catholic Coalition of Ohio—NEDY MELIDOR, Founder & Counselor; Rev. FRITZNER VALCIN, Counselor, 1582 Ferris Rd., Columbus, 43224. Tel: 614-778-0459.

Information Technology Office—JAMES RATHBURN, Dir., 197 E. Gay St., Columbus, 43215. Tel: 614-221-1182.

Legion of Mary—Rev. JOSHUA J. WAGNER, Spiritual Dir. Tel: 614-252-5926.

Personnel Office—Mr. DOMINIC PRUNTE, Dir., 197 E. Gay St., Columbus, 43215. Tel: 614-241-2590.

Real Estate—Diocesan Finance Office, 198 E. Broad St., Columbus, 43215. Tel: 614-224-1221.

Retreats—MARY E. MURPHY, Dir., St. Therese's Retreat Center, 5277 E. Broad St., Columbus, 43213-1389. Tel: 614-866-1611; ROBERT OVERMAN, Dir., Ss. Peter and Paul Retreat Center, 2734 Seminary Rd., S.E., Newark, 43056-9339. Tel: 740-928-6400; Fax: 740-928-1512.

Insurance Office—Mr. DOMINIC PRUNTE, Dir. Insurance Office, 198 E. Broad St., Columbus, 43215. Tel: 614-224-1221.

Victim Assistance Coordinator—Rev. Msgr. STEPHAN J. MOLONEY, M.A., M.Div., J.C.L. Tel: 614-224-2251; 866-448-0217 (Toll Free). Email: helpisavailable@colsdioc.org.

Office of Clergy Personnel

Health Affairs Department (Hospitals)—Rev. MARK J. HAMMOND, J.C.L., S.T.L., Coord., 197 E. Gay St., Columbus, 43215. Tel: 740-392-4711.

Office of the Diaconate—Deacon FRANK A. IANNARINO, Dir., Office, 197 E. Gay St., Columbus, 43215. Tel: 614-241-2545. Email: fiannarino@colsdioc.org; School, 7625 N. High St., Columbus, 43235. Tel: 614-885-5585.

Office of Vocations—Rev. PAUL A. NOBLE, M.A., Ph.D., Dir., 197 E. Gay St., Columbus, 43215. Tel: 614-221-5565.

Priests Continuing Education—Very Rev. G. MICHAEL GRIBBLE, M.Div., St. Joseph Cathedral, 212 E. Broad St., Columbus, 43215. Tel: 614-224-1295.

Priests Personnel Board—Rev. Msgr. JOHN K. CODY, B.A., M.Div., J.C.L., Chm., St. Christopher, 1420 Grandview Ave., Columbus, 43212. Tel: 614-486-0457.

Department for Catholic Charities and Social Concerns

Catholic Charities and Social Concerns—MARK H. HUDDY, J.D., Episcopal Moderator, 197 E. Gay St., Columbus, 43215. Tel: 614-241-2540; Fax: 614-228-7302.

Catholic Campaign for Human Development—ERIN CORDLE, Dir., 197 E. Gay St., Columbus, 43215-3229. Tel: 614-241-2540; Fax: 614-228-7302. Email: ecordle@colsdioc.org.

Catholic Relief Services—ERIN CORDLE, Dir., Office for Social Concerns, 197 E. Gay St., Columbus, 43215. Tel: 614-241-2540; Fax: 614-228-7302. Email: ecordle@colsdioc.org.

J.O.I.N. (Joint Organization for Inner-City Needs)—Mrs. RUTH BECKMAN, Dir., 578 E. Main St., Columbus, 43215. Tel: 614-241-2530.

Office for Social Concerns—MARK H. HUDDY, J.D., Dir., 197 E. Gay St., Columbus, 43215. Tel: 614-241-2540; Fax: 614-228-7302.

Rural Life Apostolate—JERALD FREEWALT, Dir., 197 E. Gay St., Columbus, 43215. Tel: 614-241-2540; Fax: 614-228-7302.

Department for Education

Department for Education—LUCIA D. MCQUAIDE, M.S.Ed., M.Rel.Ed., Episcopal Moderator - Supt., 197 E. Gay St., Columbus, 43215. Tel: 614-221-5829.

Office of Religious Education & Catechesis—BARBARA ROMANELLO-WICHTMAN, Ph.D., Dir., 197 E. Gay St., Columbus, 43215. Tel: 614-221-4633.

Office of Youth and Young Adult Ministry—Mr. MIKE HALL, Dir.; REGINA E. QUINN, Safe Environment Consultant; Mr. SEAN ROBINSON, Prog. Coord., 197 E. Gay St., Columbus, 43215. Tel: 614-241-2565.

Scout Chaplain—Tel: 614-241-2565.

Council for Religious—198 E. Broad St., Columbus, 43215. Tel: 614-224-2251. Sisters MAUREEN ANNE SHEPARD, O.S.F., Pres.; EILEEN FITZSIMMONS, O.Carm., Vice Pres.; MARIE LOUISE POHLMAN, O.S.F., Sec.; Revs. SCOTT KRAMER, C.PP.S.; RAMON OWERA, C.F.I.C.; Sisters MARIA ELENA GARCIA-RAMIREZ, H.M.S.P.; ANNE KEENAN, O.P.; JEAN WELLING, S.C.

Department for Spiritual Life and Parish Ministry

Marriage and Family Life Office—STEPHANIE JENEMANN, Dir., 197 E. Gay St., Columbus, 43215. Tel: 614-241-2560. Email: flomailbox@colsdioc.org.

Liturgical Commission—Deacon MARTIN H. DAVIES, Dir., 197 E. Gay St., Columbus, 43215. Tel: 614-221-4640.

Office of Liturgy—Deacon MARTIN H. DAVIES, Dir., 197 E. Gay St., Columbus, 43215. Tel: 614-221-4640.

Pontifical Mission Societies— The Society for the Propagation of the Faith, Holy Childhood Association, The Society of St. Peter Apostle, Missionary Union of Priests & Religious Mr. LEANDRO M. TAPAY, M.A., Dir., 197 E. Gay St., Columbus, 43215. Tel: 614-228-8603. Email: mismailbox@colsdioc.org.

St. Francis Evangelization Center—LISA KEITA, Dir., 108 W. Mill St., McArthur, 45651-1229. Tel: 740-596-4316; Fax: 740-596-4316.

Diocesan Sponsored Catholic Social Agencies

Catholic Social Services—DONALD S. WISLER, Pres., 197 E. Gay St., Columbus, 43215. Tel: 614-221-5891.

St. Stephen's Community House—Ms. MICHELLE MILLS, Dir., 1500 E. 17th Ave., Columbus, 43219. Tel: 614-294-6347; Fax: 614-294-0258.

St. Vincent Family Center—Mr. SHAWN HOLT, Pres. & CEO, 1490 E. Main St., Columbus, 43205. Tel: 614-252-0731; 614-252-2069 (TDD & TTY); Fax: 614-252-8468.

Affiliate of National Organizations

Diocesan Council of Catholic Women—KAREN KITCHELL, Pres., 197 E. Gay St., Columbus, 43215. Tel: 614-228-8601.

CLERGY, PARISHES, MISSIONS AND PAROCHIAL SCHOOLS

CITY OF COLUMBUS

(FRANKLIN COUNTY)

1—ST. JOSEPH CATHEDRAL (1878) Very Rev. G. Michael Gribble, Rector; Deacons Thomas Johnston; James Gorski. In Res., Very Rev. Shawn D. Corcoran; Rev. Paul A. Noble.
Res.: 212 E. Broad St., 43215. Tel: 614-224-1295; Fax: 614-224-1176. Email: cathedral@columbus.rr.com. Web: www.saintjosephcathedral.org.
Church: E. Broad St. & N. Fifth St., 43215.
Catechesis/Religious Program—Students 25.

2—ST. AGATHA (Upper Arlington) (1940) Rev. Daniel L. Ochs; Gene Susi McClain, Pastoral Min.; Deacon Maurice N. Milne III.
Res.: 1860 Northam Rd., 43221. Tel: 614-488-6149; Fax: 614-488-6596. Email: stagatha@st-agatha.org. Web: www.st-agatha.org.
School—1880 Northam Rd., 43221. Tel: 614-488-9000; Fax: 614-488-5783. Web: www.cdeducation.org/schools/ag. Mrs. Joan Mastell, Prin. Lay Teachers 22; Students 312.
Catechesis/Religious Program—Tel: 614-488-4975. Mrs. Jeanne Altiero, D.R.E. Students 262.

3—ST. AGNES (1954) Rev. Homer D. Blubaugh, Priest Moderator; Deacon James Gorski, Parish Admin.
Res.: 2364 W. Mound St., 43204-2903. Tel: 614-276-5413; Fax: 614-276-5413. Email: st-agnes@sbcglobal.net.
Catechesis/Religious Program—4031 Clime Rd., 43228. Tel: 614-274-5589; Fax: 614-272-5200. Students 8.

4—ST. ALOYSIUS (1906) Deacon James Gorski, Parish Admin.; Rev. Homer D. Blubaugh, Priest Moderator. In Res., Rev. Dennis E. Stevenson.
Res.: 32 Clarendon Ave., 43223. Tel: 614-276-6587; Fax: 614-276-1793.
Catechesis/Religious Program—4031 Clime Rd., 43228. Tel: 614-272-5205; Fax: 614-272-5200. Email: stals32@yahoo.com. Students 6.

5—ST. ANDREW (1955) Revs. Michael B. Watson; Tyron J. Tomson, Parochial Vicar; Deacon Thomas M. Berg Jr.
Res.: 1899 McCoy Rd., 43220. Tel: 614-451-4290; Fax: 614-451-8300. Web: www.standrewparish.cc.
School—4081 Reed Rd., 43220. Tel: 614-451-1626; Fax: 614-451-0272. Web: www.standrewschool.com. Joel Wichtman, Prin. Lay Teachers 26; Students 482.
Catechesis/Religious Program—Tel: 614-451-2855; Fax: 614-451-8300. Kris Pellissier, Coord.; Suzanne Emsweller, D.R.E. Students 255.

6—ST. ANDREW KIM TAEGON KOREAN CATHOLIC COMMUNITY formerly Korean Catholic Community (1978), (Asian), [CEM] Rev. Jinseok Tae.
Mailing Address: 221 Hanford St., 43206-3656. Tel: 614-732-0714.
Catechesis/Religious Program—

7—SAINT ANTHONY (1963) Rev. Thomas G. Petry; Deacon Craig Smith.
Rectory—4913 Atwater Dr., 43229. Tel: 614-885-4857. Email: st.anthony@sbcglobal.net. Web: www.stanthonyparishcolumbus.org.
Church: 1300 Urban Dr., 43229.
School—(Grades K-8), 1300 Urban Dr., 43229. Tel: 614-888-4268; Fax: 614-888-4435. Web: stanthony-columbus.org. Chris Iaconis, Prin. Lay Teachers 9; Students 200.
Catechesis/Religious Program—Tel: 614-888-8190. Judy McElwee, D.R.E. Students 60.

8—STS. AUGUSTINE AND GABRIEL (1984) Rev. Joseph N. Bay.
Office: 1567 Loretta Ave., Ste. 111, 43211-1677. Tel: 614-268-3123; Fax: 614-268-8130. Email: contact@staugustinegabriel.com. Web: www.staugustinegabriel.com.
Church: 1550 E. Hudson St., 43211.
Catechesis/Religious Program—Students 11.

9—ST. CATHARINE (1931) Rev. Michael J. Lumpe; Deacon Martin Davies.
Res.: 500 S. Gould Rd., 43209. Tel: 614-231-4509; Fax: 614-231-8366. Email: sburr@stcatharine.com. Web: www.stcatharine.com.
School—2865 Fair Ave., 43209. Tel: 614-235-1396; Fax: 614-235-9708. Mrs. Janet Weisner, Prin. Lay Teachers 19; Students 276.
Catechesis/Religious Program—Tel: 614-231-4500. Mrs. Chris Schleicher, D.R.E. Students 232.

10—ST. CECILIA (1882) Revs. Leo L. Connolly; Thomas J. Brosmer.
Res.: 434 Norton Rd., 43228. Tel: 614-878-5353; Fax: 614-878-0459. Email: email@saintceciliachurch.org. Web: www.saintceciliachurch.org.
School—440 Norton Rd., 43228. Tel: 614-878-3555; Fax: 614-878-6852. Email: stcecilia@cdeducation.org. Web: www.cdeducation.org/schools/ce. Marge Moretti, Prin. Lay Teachers 17; Students 214.
Catechesis/Religious Program—Tel: 614-878-0133. Kathy Maggied, D.R.E. Students 239.

11—CHRIST THE KING (1946) Rev. David A. Schalk; Deacon Peter C. Labita. In Res., Revs. Sylvester Onyeachonam; Joshua J. Wagner.
Res.: 2770 Dover Rd., 43209. Tel: 614-237-0401; Fax: 614-237-4689.
Church: 2777 E. Livingston Ave., 43209.
School—All Saints Academy, (Grades PreSchool-8), 2855 E. Livingston Ave., 43209. Tel: 614-231-3391; Fax: 614-338-2170. Laura Miller, Prin. St. Thomas, St. Phillip & Christ the King. Lay Teachers 12; Students 250.
Catechesis/Religious Program—Students 45.

12—ST. CHRISTOPHER (1947) Rev. Msgr. John K. Cody; Deacon Carl A. Calcara Jr.
Res.: 1420 Grandview Ave., 43212. Tel: 614-486-0457; Fax: 614-486-0433. Web: stchristopherscc.com.
School—Trinity, 1440 Grandview Ave., 43212. Tel: 614-488-7650; Fax: 614-488-4687. Web: www.cdeducation.org/schools/tr/. James Silcott, Prin. Lay Teachers 18; Students 172.
Catechesis/Religious Program—Chris Ross, Catechetical Leader. Students 87.

13—COLUMBUS VIETNAMESE CATHOLIC COMMUNITY (1994) Rev. Joseph N. Bay, Chap.
1567 Loretta Ave., Ste. 111, 43211-1677. Tel: 614-268-3123; Fax: 614-268-8130. Email: josephbay@att.net.

14—COMMUNITY OF HOLY ROSARY AND ST. JOHN (1979), (African American), Rev. Joshua J. Wagner.
Res.: 648 S. Ohio Ave., 43205. Tel: 614-252-5926; Fax: 614-252-5933. Web: www.hrsj.org.
Catechesis/Religious Program—Tel: 614-252-5926, Ext. 226. Students 37.

15—CORPUS CHRISTI (1925) Revs. Donald E. Franks; Rodney M. Damico, Parochial Vicar; Deacon Jerry J. Butts.
Administrative Offices: 277 Reeb Ave., 43207. Email: csauer1004@att.net.
Church: 1111 E. Stewart Ave., 43206. Tel: 614-444-9871; Fax: 614-444-1018.
Catechesis/Religious Program—Tel: 614-443-2828; Fax: 614-444-0523. Clustered with St. Ladislas, Columbus. Students 16.

16—ST. DOMINIC (1889), (African American), Rev. Joshua J. Wagner; Deacon Robert A. Neely.
Mailing Address & Res.: 453 N. 20th St., P.O. Box 83572, 43203-0572. Tel: 614-252-4913; Fax: 614-252-1655. Email: stdominic@stdominic-church.org. Web: www.stdominic-church.org.
Catechesis/Religious Program—Students 48.

17—ST. ELIZABETH (1967) Rev. Charles E. Cotton; Deacon Dean W. Racine; Rich Krehnovi, Music Min.
Church: 6077 Sharon Woods Blvd., 43229. Tel: 614-891-0150; Fax: 614-891-3243. Email: stelizabethoffice@sbcglobal.net. Web: www.stelizabethchurch.org.
Res.: 1682 Lynnhurst Rd., 43229. Tel: 614-882-1782.
Catechesis/Religious Program—Email: stelizabethreled@sbcglobal.net. Dave Gruber, D.R.E. & RCIA Coord. Students 98.

18—ST. FRANCIS OF ASSISI (1892) Rev. Ronald J. Atwood. In Res., Rev. Fritzner Valcin (Haiti).
Res.: 386 Buttles Ave., 43215. Tel: 614-299-5781; Fax: 614-299-1987. Email: office@sfacolumbus.org. Web: www.sfacolumbus.org.

19—ST. GABRIEL, Merged with St. Augustine. See separate listing.

20—HOLY CROSS (1833), (German), Rev. Jerome D. Stluka; Sr. Anne Keenan, O.P., Pastoral Assoc. In Res., Revs. Jose Souru Manickathan, C.F.I.C.; Ramon Owera, C.F.I.C.
Res.: 204 S. Fifth St., 43215. Tel: 614-224-3416; Fax: 614-224-9916. Email: admmike@columbus.rr.com. Web: www.holycrosscatholic.com.
Catechesis/Religious Program—

21—HOLY FAMILY (1877) Rev. Kevin F. Lutz; Deacons W. Earl McCurry; Frank A. Paniccia.
Res.: 584 W. Broad St., 43215-2710. Tel: 614-221-4323; Fax: 614-221-9818. Email: hchurchl@columbus.rr.com. Web: www.holyfamilycolumbus.org.
Catechesis/Religious Program—Students 85.
**The Jubilee Museum*, The Diocesan Museum of Sacred Catholic Art., 57 S. Grubb St., 43215-2747. Tel: 614-461-6204; Fax: 614-461-1737.

22—HOLY NAME OF JESUS (1905) Rev. Antonio Carvalho, Admin. Pro Tem.
Res.: 154 E. Patterson Ave., 43202. Tel: 614-262-0390; Fax: 614-262-0390. Email: holynamechurch@columbus.rr.info. Web: www.holynamercc.com.
Catechesis/Religious Program—

23—HOLY SPIRIT (Whitehall) (1947) Rev. William L. Arnold; Sr. Joan Popovits, O.P., Pastoral Min.; Deacon George A. Zimmermann Jr.
Res.: 4383 E. Broad St., 43213. Tel: 614-861-1521; Fax: 614-861-3746. Email: frarnold@holyspiritcolumbus.org. Web: www.holyspiritcolumbus.org.
School—4382 Duchene Ln., 43213. Tel: 614-861-0475; Fax: 614-861-8608. Web: www.holy-spirit-school.org. Linda Saelzler, Prin. Lay Teachers 14; Students 255.
Catechesis/Religious Program—Delores Bukowski, C.R.E. Students 55.

24—IMMACULATE CONCEPTION (1917) Rev. Msgr. Stephan J. Moloney; Sr. Ruth Hamel, O.P., Pastoral Min.; Deacon Christopher Campbell.
Res.: 414 E. North Broadway, 43214. Tel: 614-267-9241; Fax: 614-267-7720.
School—366 E. North Broadway, 43214. Tel: 614-267-6579. Lori Thayer, Prin. Lay Teachers 21; Students 500.
Catechesis/Religious Program—440 E. North Broadway, 43214. Tel: 614-267-0279. John Hoffman, D.R.E. Students 68.

25—ST. JAMES-THE-LESS (1947) Revs. Scott Kramer, C.PP.S.; Patrick Patterson, C.PP.S.; Joseph Hinders, C.PP.S.; Sr. Patricia Dual, O.P., Pastoral Assoc.; Deacons Joseph P. Checca; Kasuma J. Santos Jr.; Tim Feeney, Business Mgr.
Res.: 1652 Oakland Park Ave., 43224. Tel: 614-262-1179; 614-262-1170; Fax: 614-262-6798. Email: sjamesless@yahoo.com. Web: www.stjames-cpps.org.
School—1628 Oakland Park Ave., 43224. Tel: 614-268-3311; Fax: 614-268-1808. Web: www.saintjames-theless.com. Yvonne Schwab, Prin. Lay Teachers 18; Students 400.
Catechesis/Religious Program—Sr. Pat Dual, O.P., D.R.E. Students 90.

26—ST. JOHN THE BAPTIST (1896), (Italian), Rev. William A. Metzger.
Res.: 720 Hamlet St., 43215-1534. Tel: 614-294-5319; Fax: 614-294-4303. Email: sbaptist@columbus.rr.com.

27—ST. LADISLAS (1908) Revs. Donald E. Franks; Rodney M. Damico, Parochial Vicar.
Administrative Offices: 277 Reeb Ave., 43207. Tel: 614-443-2828; Fax: 614-444-0523. Email: csauer1004@att.net.
Catechesis/Religious Program— (Clustered with Corpus Christi.) Students 88.

28—ST. LEO (1903), (German), Closed. For inquiries for parish records please see St. Mary, Columbus.

29—ST. MARGARET OF CORTONA (1921) Rev. Jeffrey J. Rimelspach; Deacon Andrew W. Naporano.
Res.: 1600 Hague Ave., 43204-1606. Tel: 614-279-1690; Fax: 614-279-2386. Email: stmargaretcol@yahoo.com. Web: www.stmargaretcolumbus.org.
Catechesis/Religious Program—Tel: 614-272-1127; 614-274-1922 (Trinity Pre School). Email: stmargaretpsr@yahoo.com. Ruth Ann Wolansky, Dir. Students 168.
Catechesis/Religious Program—Catechesis of the Good Shepherd Lisa LaTorre, Dir. Students 37.

30—ST. MARY CHURCH (1865), (German), Revs. Donald E. Franks; Rodney M. Damico; Deacon Roger Minner.
Office: 672 S. Third St., 43206. Tel: 614-445-9668; Fax: 614-444-1688. Email: info@stmarygv.com. Web: www.stmarygv.com.
School—700 S. Third St., 43206. Tel: 614-444-8994; Fax: 614-445-2853. Web: www.stmaryschoolgv.com. Mrs. Luna Alsharaiha, Prin. Lay Teachers 10; Students 220.
Catechesis/Religious Program—(with St. Ladislas, Columbus.) Students 4.

31—ST. MARY MAGDALENE (1928) Rev. Stanley Benecki.
Res.: 473 S. Roys Ave., 43204. Tel: 614-274-1121; Fax: 614-274-1122. Web: www.saintmarymag.org.
School—2940 Parkside Rd., 43204. Tel: 614-279-9935; Fax: 614-279-9575. Rocco Fumi, Prin. Lay Teachers 10; Students 225.
Catechesis/Religious Program—Tel: 614-279-9291. Students 20.

32—ST. MATTHIAS (1956) Rev. James T. Smith; Sr. Marie Shields, S.N.D.deN., Pastoral Assoc.
Res.: 1582 Ferris Rd., 43224. Tel: 614-267-3406. Email: stmatthiascolumbus@sbcglobal.net.
School—1566 Ferris Rd., 43224. Tel: 614-268-3030; Fax: 614-268-4681. Mr. Daniel Kinley, Prin. Sisters 1; Lay Teachers 12; Students 280.
Catechesis/Religious Program—Michelle Mead, D.R.E. Students 70.

33—OUR LADY OF PEACE (1946) Rev. Kevin J. Kavanagh; Deacon Jeffrey D. Fortkamp; Sisters Martha Langstaff, O.P., Pastoral Min.; Barbara Kolesar, O.P., Pastoral Min.
Res.: 20 E. Dominion Blvd., 43214. Tel: 614-263-8824; Fax: 614-263-3383. Email: olp@rrohio.com.
School—40 Dominion Blvd., 43214. Tel: 614-267-4535; Fax: 614-267-2333. Email: olp@cdeducation.org. Web: www.olpcolumbus.org.

Carol Folian, Prin. Lay Teachers 14; Students 257.
Catechesis/Religious Program—Students 83.
Convent—60 E. Dominion Blvd., 43214. Tel: 614-268-1980.

34—OUR LADY OF THE MIRACULOUS MEDAL (1967) Rev. James Coleman; Deacon Stephen A. Venturini, Pastoral Assoc.
Church & Office: 5225 Refugee Rd., 43232-5398. Tel: 614-861-1242; Fax: 614-861-1499. Email: cool5225@sbcglobal.net. Web: www.churchofourladycolumbus.org.
Catechesis/Religious Program—Tel: 614-868-1414. Students 57.

35—OUR LADY OF VICTORY (1922) [CEM] Rev. Msgr. Romano Ciotola; Deacon Rob Joseph.
Res.: 1559 Roxbury Rd., 43212. Tel: 614-488-2428; Fax: 614-488-0507. Email: olvc@sbcglobal.net. Web: www.olvonline.org.
See Trinity, Columbus under St. Christopher, Columbus for details.
Catechesis/Religious Program—Tel: 614-486-7678; Fax: 614-488-0507. Lisa Schechter, D.R.E. (Grades K-8). Students 347.

36—ST. PATRICK (1852), (Irish), Revs. Michael Dosch, O.P.; Thomas Blau, O.P.; Gregory Schnakenberg, O.P. In Res., Rev. J. Jordan Lenaghan, O.P.
Res.: 280 N. Grant Ave., 43215. Tel: 614-224-9522; Fax: 614-240-5928. Email: stpatrickcolumbus@sbcglobal.net. Web: www.stpatrickcolumbus.catholicweb.net.
Catechesis/Religious Program—Tel: 614-240-5925; Fax: 614-240-5928. Students 254.

37—ST. PETER (1970) Rev. Justin J. Reis; Deacons Joseph E. Schermer; Philip M. Paulucci. In Res., Rev. Stephen G. Virginia.
Res.: 6899 Smoky Row Rd., 43235-1998. Tel: 614-889-2221; Fax: 614-889-6612. Web: www.stpetercolumbus.com.
Catechesis/Religious Program—Tel: 614-889-1407. Students 481.

38—ST. PHILIP THE APOSTLE (1956) Rev. Patrick W. Rogers.
Res.: 1573 Elaine Rd., 43227. Tel: 614-237-1671; Fax: 614-231-8416. Email: stphilip@rrohio.com. Web: www.stphilipcolumbus.org.
Catechesis/Religious Program—Bradley E. Walters, D.R.E. Students 25.

39—SACRED HEART (1875) Rev. William A. Metzger, Admin. In Res., Revs. Joseph C. Klee; John Thomas.
Res.: 893 Hamlet St., 43201. Tel: 614-299-4191.

40—SANTA CRUZ PARISH (1993), (Spanish), Rev. Jose Perez (Venezuela).
Mailing Address: P.O. Box 82205, 43202.
Church: 143-155 E. Patterson Ave., 43202. Tel: 614-784-9732; Fax: 614-784-9732.
Catechesis/Religious Program—Celia Palma, D.R.E. Students 69.

41—SHRINE OF BLESSED MARGARET OF CASTELLO (1957) Mailing Address: *c/o St. Patrick*, 280 N. Grant Ave., 43215. Tel: 614-240-5915; Fax: 614-240-5928. Shrine dedicated to promoting the sanctity of life, and the cause of canonization of Blessed Margaret of Castello, O.P.

42—SAINT STEPHEN THE MARTYR (1963) Rev. Thomas J. Buffer.
Res.: 4131 Clime Rd., 43228. Tel: 614-272-5206; Fax: 614-272-5200.
Catechesis/Religious Program—Tel: 614-279-9291. Students 350.

43—ST. THOMAS THE APOSTLE (1900) Rev. Denis S. Kigozi. In Res., Rev. Dean Mathewson, part-time Chap., Riverside Hospital.
Res.: 2692 E. Fifth Ave., 43219. Tel: 614-252-0976; Fax: 614-252-7519. Web: www.saintthomasapostle.com.
Catechesis/Religious Program—Students 117.

44—ST. TIMOTHY (1961) Rev. Timothy M. Hayes; Deacon Marion E. Smithberger. In Res., Rev. William J. Faustner.
Res.: 1088 Thomas Ln., 43220. Tel: 614-451-2671; Fax: 614-451-4181.
School—1070 Thomas Ln., 43220. Tel: 614-451-0739; Fax: 614-451-3108. George Mosholder, Prin. Lay Teachers 13; Students 270.
Catechesis/Religious Program—Tel: 614-451-3867; Fax: 614-451-3108. Rita Feige, D.R.E. Students 75.

OUTSIDE THE CITY OF COLUMBUS

ADA, HARDIN CO., OUR LADY OF LOURDES (1874) Rev. David J. Young; Deacon J. Michael Hood; Deb Driscolli, Admin. Asst.
Res.: 222 E. Highland Ave., 45810. Tel: 419-634-2626; Fax: 419-634-6555. Email: oll@wcoil.com. Web: www.oll-ada.com.
Catechesis/Religious Program—Tel: 419-634-2445. Students 85.

BREMEN, FAIRFIELD CO., ST. MARY (1917) [CEM] Revs. William Thomas Kessler; John M. Reade.
Mailing Address: P.O. Box 85, 43107.
Res.: 602 Marietta St., 43107. Tel: 740-569-7929. Email: bremenstmary1@frontier.com.
Catechesis/Religious Program—Tel: 740-862-8839. Jim Barlow, D.R.E. Students 30.

BUCKEYE LAKE, LICKING CO., OUR LADY OF MT. CARMEL (1929) Rev. William J. Ferguson; Deacon Richard B. Busic, Pastoral Assoc.
Res.: 5133 Walnut Rd., S.E., P.O. Box 45, 43008. Tel: 740-928-3266; Fax: 740-928-3266. Email: olmc@avolve.net. Web: www.olmcbuckeyelake.org.
Catechesis/Religious Program—Tel: 740-928-3264. Silvia Zaboroski, D.R.E. Students 67.

CANAL WINCHESTER, FAIRFIELD CO., POPE JOHN XXIII (2000) Rev. Msgr. A. Anthony Frecker; Deacons Roger Pry; Charles J. Miller.
Office: 5170 Winchester Southern Rd., N.W., 43110. Tel: 614-920-1563; Fax: 614-920-1564. Email: popejohn@pjxxiiiparish.org. Web: www.popejohnxxiiiparish.com.
Res.: 7820 White Ash Ct., 43110. Tel: 614-920-1562.
Catechesis/Religious Program—Students 291.

CARDINGTON, MORROW CO., SACRED HEARTS (1868) Rev. John L. Bakle, S.M., Admin.
Res.: 4680 U.S. Rte. 42, 43315. Tel: 419-946-3611. Email: sacredhearts@embargmail.com. Web: www.sacredheartschurch.org.
Catechesis/Religious Program—Students 5.

CHILLICOTHE, ROSS CO.

1—ST. MARY (1837) [CEM] [JC] Rev. Lawrence L. Hummer.
Res.: 61 S. Paint St., 45601. Tel: 740-772-2061; Fax: 740-772-2061. Email: saintmary@roadrunner.com. Web: www.stmarychillicothe.com.
School—Bishop Flaget Elementary, (Grades PreSchool-8), 570 Parsons Ave., 45601. Tel: 740-774-2970; Fax: 740-774-2998. Web: www.bishopflaget.org. Laura Corcoran, Prin. Lay Teachers 14; Students 142.
Catechesis/Religious Program—Email: saintmary@roadrunner.com. Students 18.

2—ST. PETER (1845), (German), [CEM] [JC] Rev. William P. Hahn. In Res., Rev. Charles R. Griffin (Retired).
Office: 126 Church St., 45601. Email: secretary@stpeterchillicothe.com. Web: www.stpeterchillicothe.com.
Res.: 122 Church St., 45601. Tel: 740-774-1407.
School—Bishop Flaget Elementary, (Grades PreK-8), 570 Parsons Ave., 45601. Tel: 740-774-2970; Fax: 740-774-2889. Web: www.bishopflaget.org. Laura Corcoran, Prin. Lay Teachers 14; Students 159.
Catechesis/Religious Program—Tel: 740-773-3455. Students 58.

CIRCLEVILLE, PICKAWAY CO., ST. JOSEPH (1840) [CEM] Rev. Theodore F. Machnik.
Res.: 134 W. Mound St., P.O. Box 40, 43113. Tel: 740-477-2549; Fax: 740-477-1453. Email: church@hocking.net. Web: saintjosephcircleville.org.
Catechesis/Religious Program—Theresa Jenkins, D.R.E. Students 245.

CORNING, PERRY CO., ST. BERNARD (1882) Revs. James C. Csaszar; Victor R. Wesolowski, Parochial Vicar.
Res.: 425 Adams St., 43730. Tel: 740-347-4700. Web: www.strosepcc.org.
Catechesis/Religious Program—Students 20.

COSHOCTON, COSHOCTON CO., SACRED HEART (1856) [CEM] Rev. William A. Hritsko; Deacons Frank A. Duda; Douglas Mould.
Res.: 805 Main St., 43812. Tel: 740-622-8817. Email: shrectory@sbcglobal.net. Web: www.sacredheartcoshocton.org.
School—39 Burt Ave., 43812. Tel: 740-622-3728; Fax: 740-622-9151. Mary Stenner, Prin. Lay Teachers 7; Students (K-6) 60; Students (PreK) 25.
Catechesis/Religious Program—Tel: 740-622-8817. Deacon Douglas Mould, D.R.E. Students 54.

CROOKSVILLE, PERRY CO., CHURCH OF THE ATONEMENT (1896) [CEM] Revs. James C. Csaszar; Victor R. Wesolowski, Parochial Vicar.
Mailing Address: 309 N. Main St., New Lexington, 43764-1204. Tel: 740-342-1348; Fax: 740-342-1340. Web: www.strosepcc.org. 320 Winter St., 43731.
Catechesis/Religious Program—Tel: 740-982-2386. Students 40.

DANVILLE, KNOX CO., ST. LUKE (1820) [CEM] Rev. F. Richard Snoke.
Mailing Address: 307 S. Market St., P.O. Box P, 43014. Email: stluke@ecr.net.
Res.: 305 S. Market St., P.O. Box P, 43014. Tel: 740-599-6362.
Catechesis/Religious Program—St. Luke Community Center, 7 W. Rambo, P.O. Box P, 43014-0616. Tel: 740-599-7367. Thomas Harrmann, D.R.E. Students 157.

DELAWARE, DELAWARE CO., ST. MARY (1835) [CEM] Rev. James P. Black; Deacon Felix Azzola. In Res., Rev. Balonwu Augustine Okpe.
Res.: 82 E. William St., 43015. Tel: 740-363-4641; 740-369-9644; Fax: 740-363-9915. Email: stmary@delawarestmary.org. Web: www.delawarestmary.org.
School—66 E. William St., 43015. Tel: 740-362-8961; Fax: 740-362-3733. Web: www.stmarydelaware.org. Ryan Schwieterman, Prin. (Grades K-8). Lay Teachers 16; Students 362.
Catechesis/Religious Program—Tel: 740-369-8228. Ann Manning, D.R.E. Students 453.

DENNISON, TUSCARAWAS CO., IMMACULATE CONCEPTION (1871) [CEM] Rev. Anthony P. Lonzo.
Res.: 206 N. First St., 44621. Tel: 740-922-3533; Fax: 740-922-2486. Email: icdennison@sbcglobal.net.
School—100 Sherman St., 44621. Tel: 740-922-3539; Fax: 740-922-2486. Anthony L. Amicone, Prin. Lay Teachers 7; Students 80.
Catechesis/Religious Program—Cyndy Host, D.R.E. Students 20.

DOVER, TUSCARAWAS CO., ST. JOSEPH (1849), (German—Italian), [CEM 2] Revs. Matthew N. Hoover; James H. Hatfield III, Parochial Vicar.
Res.: 613 N. Tuscarawas Ave., 44622. Tel: 330-364-6661; Fax: 330-602-7488. Email: stjosephchurch@roadrunner.com.
School—Tuscarawas Central Catholic Elementary, (Grades PreK-6), 600 N. Tuscarawas Ave., 44622. Tel: 330-343-9134; Fax: 330-364-6509. Theresa Layton, Prin. Lay Teachers 12; Students 220.
Catechesis/Religious Program—Tel: 330-364-8257. Ms. Cindy Teynor, D.R.E. Students 121.

DRESDEN, MUSKINGUM CO., ST. ANN'S (1889) Rev. Jack G. Maynard.
Res.: 405 Chestnut St., Box 107, 43821. Tel: 740-754-2221. Email: saintann@columbus.rr.com.
Catechesis/Religious Program—Students 35.
Mission—St. Mary [CEM] 6280 St. Mary's Rd., Nashport, Muskingum Co. 43830.

DUBLIN, FRANKLIN CO., ST. BRIGID OF KILDARE (1987) Rev. Msgr. Joseph M. Hendricks; Rev. Mark S. Summers, Parochial Vicar; Deacons Frank A. Iannarino; Donald Poirier; Sisters Patricia McMahon, O.S.F., Pastoral Care/Bereavement; Joan M. Harper, C.D.P., Pastoral Assoc.; Joseph Burger, Business Mgr.
Res.: 7179 Avery Rd., P.O. Box 3130, 43016-0062. Tel: 614-761-3734; Fax: 614-889-6638. Email: kcremeans@midohio.twcbc.com. Web: www.stbrigidofkildare.org.
School—7175 Avery Rd., 43017. Tel: 614-718-5825; Fax: 614-718-5831. Ms. Kathleen O'Reilly, Prin. Lay Teachers 32; Students 567.
Catechesis/Religious Program—Tel: 614-761-1176; Fax: 614-718-5831. Mary Fran Cassidy, D.R.E. Students 1,334.

GAHANNA, FRANKLIN CO., ST. MATTHEW (1959) Revs. Theodore K. Sill; Ryan M. Schmit, Parochial Vicar.
Res.: 811 Havens Corners Rd., 43230. Tel: 614-471-0212; Fax: 614-471-0247. Web: www.stmatthew.net.
School—795 Havens Corners Rd., 43230. Tel: 614-471-4930; Fax: 614-471-1673. Web: www.cdeducation.org/schools/mat. Daniel P. Rotella, Prin. Lay Teachers 27; Students 600.
Catechesis/Religious Program—Tel: 614-471-2067; Fax: 614-471-1693. Karen Buford, D.R.E./RCIA Dir. Students 515.

GRANVILLE, LICKING CO., ST. EDWARD THE CONFESSOR (1946) Rev. Msgr. Paul P. Enke, Pastor; Michael Millisor, Pastoral Assoc.
Res.: 785 Newark Rd., 43023-1450. Tel: 740-587-3254; Fax: 740-587-0149. Email: church@saintedwards.org. Web: www.saintedwards.org.
Catechesis/Religious Program—Tel: 740-587-4160. Email: reled@saintedwards.org. Students 458.

GROVE CITY, FRANKLIN CO., OUR LADY OF PERPETUAL HELP (1954) Rev. Daniel J. Millisor.
Church & Mailing Address: 3730 Broadway, 43123. Tel: 614-875-3322; Fax: 614-875-6033. Email: bweber@ourladyofperpetualhelp.net. Web: www.ourladyofperpetualhelp.net.
School—3752 N. Broadway, 43123. Tel: 614-875-6779; Fax: 614-539-5719. Web: www.olphsaints.org. Susan Donovan, Prin. Lay Teachers 23; Students 450.
Catechesis/Religious Program—Tel: 614-875-9345. Mrs. Camille Kopczewski, D.R.E. Students 350.

GROVEPORT, FRANKLIN CO., ST. MARY (1871) Rev. Richard L. Metzger.
Res.: 5684 Groveport Rd., 43125. Tel: 614-497-1324; Fax: 614-497-2706. Email: stmarygroveport@hotmail.com. Web: www.stmarygroveport.org.
Catechesis/Religious Program—Tel: 614-497-1437. Email: stmarypsrgroveport@msn.com. Alice Doran, D.R.E. Students 85.

HEATH, LICKING CO., ST. LEONARD (1962) Rev. Michael J. Reis; Deacon Larry Wilson. In Res., Rev. Ronald Boccali, P.I.M.E. (Retired).
Res.: 57 Dorsey Mill Rd., 43056. Tel: 740-522-5270; Fax: 740-522-5261. Web: www.stleonard-heath.com.
Catechesis/Religious Program—Email: sdoyle@nextek.net. Students 65.

HILLIARD, FRANKLIN CO., ST. BRENDAN (1957) Rev. Msgr. John G. Johnson, Admin. ProTem; Deacons

Patrick J. Wiggins; Gilbert L. Plummer; James Morris. In Res., Rev. Saulius P. Laurinaitis (Retired).
Res.: 4475 Dublin Rd., 43026. Tel: 614-876-1272; Fax: 614-876-1482. Email: info@stbrendans.net. Web: www.stbrendans.net.
School—(Grades K-8) Tel: 614-876-6132; Fax: 614-529-8929. Mary Lang, Prin. Lay Teachers 22; Students 475.
Catechesis/Religious Program—Tel: 614-876-9533. S. Joanne Fogarty, D.R.E. Students 473.

JACKSON, JACKSON CO., HOLY TRINITY (1875) [CEM] Rev. Joseph J. Trapp II.
Res.: 215 Columbia St., 45640. Tel: 740-286-1428.
Catechesis/Religious Program—Students 38.

JOHNSTOWN, LICKING CO., CHURCH OF THE ASCENSION (1912) [CEM] Rev. J. Lawrence Reichert; Deacon William J. Andrews.
Res.: 555 S. Main St., 43031-1231. Tel: 740-967-7871 (Office); Fax: 740-967-0321 (Office). Email: ascensionjohnstown@gmail.com. Web: www.johnstownascension.org.
Catechesis/Religious Program—Tel: 740-967-1338. Kelly Pertee, D.R.E. Students 80.

JUNCTION CITY, PERRY CO., ST. PATRICK (1820) [CEM] Revs. James C. Csaszar; Victor R. Wesolowski, Parochial Vicar.
Mailing Address: c/o 309 N. Main St., New Lexington, 43764-1204. 1170 S.R. 668S, 43748. Tel: 740-342-1348; Fax: 740-342-1340.
Catechesis/Religious Program—Students 25.

KENTON, HARDIN CO., IMMACULATE CONCEPTION (1836) [CEM] Rev. Anthony A. Dinovo Jr.; Deacon J. Michael Hood.
Res.: 215 E. North St., 43326. Tel: 419-675-1162. Email: iccatholic@windstream.net. Web: www.immaculateconceptionkenton.org.
Parish Center—220 E. North St., 44326. Tel: 419-675-9461.
Catechesis/Religious Program—Tel: 419-675-1162. Jean M. Bruner, D.R.E. Students 30.

LA RUE, MARION CO., ST. JOSEPH'S (1864) Closed. For inquiries for parish records contact the Chancery.

LANCASTER, FAIRFIELD CO.

1—ST. BERNADETTE (1963) Revs. William Thomas Kessler; John M. Reade; Deacons Paul Deshaies; Mark A. Scarpitti.
Church & Office: 1343 Wheeling Rd., 43130-8701. Tel: 740-654-1893; Fax: 740-687-5926. Email: saintb@stbparish.org. Web: www.stbparish.org.
School—(Grades PreSchool-5), 1325 Wheeling Rd., 43130. Tel: 740-654-3137; Fax: 740-654-1602. Email: saintb@greenapple.com. Web: www.stbernadette-school.com. Pam Eltringham, Prin. Lay Teachers 8; Students 140.
Catechesis/Religious Program—Students 44.

2—ST. MARK (1960) [JC] Rev. Peter M. Gideon; Deacon Henry Gundrum.
Res.: 324 Gay St., 43130. Tel: 740-653-1229; Fax: 740-653-8329. Web: www.stmarklancaster.parishesonline.com.
Catechesis/Religious Program—331 Gay St., 43130. Tel: 740-654-7154. Kim Kirchgessner, D.R.E. Students 63.

3—ST. MARY (1818) [CEM] Rev. Craig R. Eilerman; Deacon Frank K. Sullivan, Pastoral Assoc.
Res.: 132 S. High St., 43130. Tel: 740-653-0997; Fax: 740-653-0337. Web: www.stmarylancaster.org.
School—309 E. Chestnut St., 43130. Tel: 740-654-1632; Fax: 740-654-0877. Web: www.greenapple.com/~stmarylab. Carlton B. Rider, Prin. Lay Teachers 14; Students 300.
Catechesis/Religious Program—Tel: 740-653-5054; Fax: 740-653-0337. Students 167.
Convent—229 E. Chestnut St., 43130. Tel: 740-653-2837.

LOGAN, HOCKING CO., ST. JOHN (1841) [CEM] Rev. Msgr. William A. Dunn; Deacon Donald Robers.
Res.: 351 N. Market St., 43138. Tel: 740-385-2549; Fax: 740-380-2837. Email: info@stjohnlogan.com. Web: www.stjohnlogan.com.
School—321 N. Market St., 43138. Tel: 740-385-2767; Fax: 740-385-9727. Email: eschorna@cdeducation.org. Web: www.stjohn.cdeducation.org. Erin Schornack, Prin. Lay Teachers 4; Students 72.
Catechesis/Religious Program—Cathy Kerns, D.R.E. Students 46.

LONDON, MADISON CO., ST. PATRICK (1865), (German—Irish), [CEM] Rev. Mark V. Ghiloni; Deacon Daniel W. Hann.
Res.: 61 S. Union St., 43140. Tel: 740-852-0942; Fax: 740-852-5008. Web: www.stpatricklondon.org.
School—(Grades K-8), 226 Elm St., 43140. Tel: 740-852-0161; Fax: 740-852-0602. Dr. Jacob Froning, Prin. Lay Teachers 11; Students 155.
Catechesis/Religious Program—Bernardine J. Hess, D.R.E. Students 58.

MARION, MARION CO., ST. MARY (1864) [CEM] Rev. Michael Nimocks, Pastor; Sr. Joan Brodman, O.S.F., Pastoral Min.
Res.: 251 N. Main St., 43302. Tel: 740-382-2118; Fax: 740-382-2110. Email: stmaryinfo@marionstmary.org. Web: www.marionstmary.org.
School—274 N. Prospect St., 44302. Tel: 740-382-1607. Web: www.marioncatholicschools.org. Bob Rush, Prin. Lay Teachers 10; Students 136.
High School—Marion Catholic Jr/Sr High School, (Grades 7-12), 1001 Mt. Vernon Ave., 43302. Tel: 740-389-2381; Fax: 740-389-5243. Web: www.marioncatholicschools.org. Al Seitter, Prin. Lay Teachers 17; Students 72.
Catechesis/Religious Program—Tel: 740-382-2262. Students 430.

MARYSVILLE, UNION CO., OUR LADY OF LOURDES (1866) [CEM] Rev. David A. Poliafico; Deacon Gordon T. Kunkler; Amy Rohyans, Pastoral Assoc.; Paul Cordell, Business Mgr.
Res.: 1033 W. Fifth St., 43040. Tel: 937-644-6020; Fax: 937-644-3297. Email: olol.marysville@rrohio.com.
Catechesis/Religious Program—Tel: 937-644-6030; Fax: 937-644-3297. Andrea Hawley, D.R.E. Students 325.
Mission—Haiti Parish Twinning Program (Saint Thomas d' Aquin) Aquin.

MILLERSBURG, HOLMES CO., ST. PETER (1877) [CEM] [JC] Rev. Stephen L. Krile.
Res.: 379 S. Crawford St., 44654-1463. Tel: 330-674-1671. Web: www.holmescountycatholic.org.
Catechesis/Religious Program—Fax: 330-674-1673. Email: ron@valkyrie.net. Bonnie Lee, D.R.E. Students 47.
Mission—SS. Peter and Paul (1857)Tel: 330-674-1671.
Catechesis/Religious Program—Students 9.

MINERAL CITY, TUSCARAWAS CO., SAINT PATRICK, Closed. For sacramental records contact Holy Trinity, Bolivar.

MT. VERNON, KNOX CO., ST. VINCENT DE PAUL (1842) [CEM] Rev. Mark J. Hammond; Greg Henkel, Pastoral Asst.
Res.: 303 E. High St., 43050. Tel: 740-392-4711; Fax: 740-392-4714. Web: www.stvincentmountvernon.org.
School—(Grades PreSchool-8), 206 E. Chestnut St., 43050. Tel: 740-393-3611; Fax: 740-393-0236. Martha Downs, Prin. Lay Teachers 9; Students 190.
Catechesis/Religious Program—Shirley Lower, C.R.E. Students 155.

MURRAY CITY, HOCKING CO., ST. PHILIP NERI, Closed. For inquiries for sacramental records contact St. John, Logan.

NEW ALBANY, FRANKLIN CO., CHURCH OF THE RESURRECTION (1983) Rev. Jerome P. Rodenfels; Deacon Byron Phillips.
Church: 6300 E. Dublin-Granville Rd., 43054. Tel: 614-855-1400; Fax: 614-855-0779. Email: info@churchoftheresurrection.com. Web: www.churchoftheresurrection.com.
Res.: 5575 Morgan Rd., 43054. Tel: 614-855-0476 (Rectory).
Catechesis/Religious Program—Tel: 614-939-1794; Fax: 614-855-0779. Ms. Joan Lucius, D.R.E. Students 760.

NEW BOSTON, SCIOTO CO., ST. MONICA (1915) [CEM] Rev. Joseph T. Yokum; Deacon James M. Sturgeon.
Res.: 4252 Pine St., 45662. Tel: 740-456-5154; Fax: 740-456-5154. Email: stmonica45662@yahoo.com.
Catechesis/Religious Program—Students 39.

NEW LEXINGTON, PERRY CO., ST. ROSE OF LIMA (1867) [JC] Revs. James C. Csaszar; Victor R. Wesolowski.
Res.: 309 N. Main St., 43764. Tel: 740-342-1348.
School—119 W. Water St., 43764. Tel: 740-342-3043; Fax: 740-342-1082. Roxanne Demeter, Prin. Lay Teachers 9; Students 137.
Catechesis/Religious Program—Tel: 740-987-2691; 740-342-3043. Students 69.

NEW PHILADELPHIA, TUSCARAWAS CO., SACRED HEART (1895) [CEM 2] Rev. Jeffrey J. Coning.
Res.: 139 3rd St., N.E., 44663-3900. Tel: 330-343-6976; Fax: 330-343-1406. Email: shchurch@neohio.twcbc.com. Web: sacredheartnpohio.catholicweb.com.
School—Tuscarawas Central Catholic Elementary, (Grades PreK-6), 600 N. Tuscarawas Ave., Dover, 44622. Tel: 330-343-9134; Fax: 330-364-6509. Theresa Layton, Prin. Lay Teachers 12; Students 220.
Catechesis/Religious Program—Students 85.

NEWARK, LICKING CO.

1—CHURCH OF THE BLESSED SACRAMENT (1904) [JC] Rev. Jonathan F. Wilson; Deacon Patrick Wilson.
Mailing Address: 394 E. Main St., 43055. Email: blsac43055@midohio.twcbc.com. Web: www.blsac.net.
Res.: 378 E. Main St., 43055. Tel: 740-345-4290; Fax: 740-345-3890.
School— Tel: 740-345-4125; Fax: 740-345-6168. Email: svanhorn@cdeducation.org. Mary Packham, Prin. Lay Teachers 10; Students 180.
Catechesis/Religious Program—Tel: 740-763-4304. Students 50.

2—ST. FRANCIS DE SALES (1842) [CEM 2] Rev. Robert Penhallurick; Deacon Steven DeMers.
Res.: 66 Granville St., 43055. Tel: 740-345-9874; Fax: 740-345-1585. Web: www.stfrancisparish.net.
School—38 Granville St., 43055. Tel: 740-345-4049; Fax: 740-345-9768. Web: www.cdeducation.org/schools/dse. Mary Walsh, Prin. Lay Teachers 21; Students 420.
Catechesis/Religious Program—Tel: 740-345-9874, Ext. 222; Fax: 740-345-1585. Lori Mazone, D.R.E. Tel: 740-345-9874, Ext. 222; Theresa DeMers, Pastoral Min. Tel: 740-345-9874, Ext. 224. Students 183.

NEWCOMERSTOWN, TUSCARAWAS CO., ST. FRANCIS DE SALES (1918) [JC] Rev. Matthew N. Hoover, Admin. Pro Tem.
Res.: 440 River St., 43832. Tel: 740-498-7368. Email: stfran10@att.net.
Catechesis/Religious Program—Laura Bridges, C.R.E. Students 15.

OTWAY, SCIOTO CO., OUR LADY OF LOURDES (1917) [CEM] Rev. David E. Young.
Res.: 2215 Galena Pike, West Portsmouth, 45663. Tel: 740-858-4600; Fax: 740-858-4600. Email: olosc@zoomnet.net.
Catechesis/Religious Program—Students 19.
Otway Community Service Center—P.O. Box 8, 45657. Tel: 740-372-2202.

PICKERINGTON, FAIRFIELD CO., SETON PARISH (1978) Rev. James A. Klima; Deacon Hector Raymond, Pastoral Min.
Res.: 600 Hill Rd., 43147. Tel: 614-833-0482; Fax: 614-833-4154. Email: bstory@setonparish.com. Web: www.setonparish.com.
Catechesis/Religious Program—Tel: 614-833-0485. Mary Jane Sobczyk, D.R.E.; Barbara Serrano, Youth Min. Students 875.

PLAIN CITY, UNION CO., ST. JOSEPH (1864) Rev. Patrick A. Toner; Deacon Anthony Bonacci; Sarah Reinhard, Admin.; Sue York, Volunteer & Prog. Coord.
Res.: 670 W. Main St., 43064. Tel: 614-873-8850; Fax: 614-873-0735. Email: office@saintjosephplaincity.com. Web: www.saintjosephplaincity.com.
Catechesis/Religious Program—Students 139.
Oratory—Sacred Heart Milford Center, Union Co.

PORTSMOUTH, SCIOTO CO.

1—HOLY REDEEMER (1852), (Irish), [CEM] [JC] Rev. Dwayne A. McNew; Mrs. Ann Kempf, Pastoral Min.
Office, Activities Center & Res.: 1325 Gallia St., 45662. Tel: 740-354-2716; Fax: 740-354-8692. Email: holyredeemer1325@yahoo.com.
School—Notre Dame Elementary, (Grades PreK-6), 1401 Gallia St., 45662. Tel: 740-353-8610; Fax: 740-353-6769. Web: www.nddev.com. Mrs. Ann Kempf, Prin. Serving all 7 parishes in Scioto County. Lay Teachers 12; Students 285.
Catechesis/Religious Program—Students 18.

2—ST. MARY (1841), (German), [CEM] Rev. Adam A. Streitenberger; Deacon Christopher Varacalli.
Res.: 524 Sixth St., 45662. Tel: 740-354-4551; Fax: 740-354-5797. Email: office@stmaryportsmouth.org. Web: www.stmaryportsmouth.org.
Catechesis/Religious Program—Students 15.

POWELL, DELAWARE CO., ST. JOAN OF ARC (1987) Revs. Raymond Larussa; Jeffrey E. Tigyer; Deacons Thomas M. Berg Sr.; James A. Rouse, (Retired).
Res.: 10700 Liberty Rd. S., 43065-9303. Tel: 614-761-0905; Fax: 614-761-0850. Email: office-staff@rrohio.com. Web: www.stjoanofarcpowell.org.
Catechesis/Religious Program—Tel: 614-761-0903. Email: psr-office@rrohio.com. Emily Winner, D.R.E. Students 1,527.

REYNOLDSBURG, FRANKLIN CO., ST. PIUS X (1958) Rev. Msgr. David R. Funk; Deacons John Vellani; John L. DuPrey; James W. Kelly; Charles Miller, Business Mgr.
Res.: 1051 Waggoner Rd., 43068. Tel: 614-866-2859; 614-367-1392; Fax: 614-866-1499. Email: st_piusx@ameritech.net. Web: www.spxreynoldsburg.com.
School—1061 Waggoner Rd., 43068. Tel: 614-866-6050; Fax: 614-866-6187. Web: www.coeducation.org/schools/px/index.html. Jonathan Cuniak, Prin. Lay Teachers 18; Students 530.
Catechesis/Religious Program—Tel: 614-864-3505. Judy Cafmeyer, D.R.E.; Judie Bryant, Dir. Youth Ministry. Students 255.

ROSWELL, TUSCARAWAS CO., ST. ELIZABETH, Closed. For sacramental records contact Sacred Heart Parish, New Philadelphia.

SHAWNEE, PERRY CO., ST. MARY & ST. AUGUSTINE, Closed. For sacramental records contact St. Rose of Lima Parish, New Lexington.

SOMERSET, PERRY CO.

1—HOLY TRINITY (1827) [CEM] Rev. Stephen F. Carmody, O.P.; Deacon Eugene C. Dawson.
Mailing Address: P.O. Box 190, 43783. Tel:

740-743-1317 (Office). Email: stjoe-holytrinity@columbus.rr.com.
Rectory—St. Joseph Rectory, St. Rte. 383, 43783. Tel: 740-743-1399.
*School—*S. Columbus St., 43783. Tel: 740-743-1324; Fax: 740-743-1324. Joan Miller, Prin. Lay Teachers 8; Students 140.
*Catechesis/Religious Program—*Tel: 740-743-1855. Students 67.

2—ST. JOSEPH'S (1818) [CEM] Rev. Stephen F. Carmody, O.P.; Deacon Eugene C. Dawson.
Rectory—St. Joseph Rectory, State Rte. 383, N.E., P.O. Box 190, 43783. Tel: 740-743-1399; 740-743-1317 (Office). Email: stjoe-holytrinity@columbus.rr.com.
*Catechesis/Religious Program—*Tel: 740-743-1855. Students 9.

STRASBURG, TUSCARAWAS CO., ST. ALOYSIUS (1911) Closed. For sacramental records contact Holy Trinity, Bolivar.

SUGAR GROVE, FAIRFIELD CO., ST. JOSEPH (1853) [CEM] [JC] Rev. James A. Walter; Frederick J. Krile, Pastoral Assoc.
Res.: 306 Elm St., P.O. Box 209, 43155-0209. Tel: 740-746-8302; Fax: 740-746-8805.
*Catechesis/Religious Program—*Tel: 740-746-8302. Students 50.

SUNBURY, DELAWARE CO., ST. JOHN NEUMANN (1983) Rev. David W. Sizemore; Deacon Carl A. Calcara Jr.
Res. & Mailing Address: 801 W. Cherry St., Ste. 120, 43074. Tel: 740-965-1358; Fax: 740-965-1377. Email: saintjohnneumann@stjohnsunbury.org. Web: www.saintjohnsunbury.org.
Church: 9633 E. State Rte. 37, 43074-9593. Tel: 740-965-1358.
*Social Hall—*Tel: 740-965-1358.
Catechesis/Religious Program— Robert M. Steinbauer, D.R.E. Students 377.

UTICA, LICKING CO., CHURCH OF THE NATIVITY (1909) Rev. Stephen A. Metzger.
Res.: 271 Jefferson St., P.O. Box 506, 43080. Tel: 740-892-2321.
*Catechesis/Religious Program—*Rose Gorius, D.R.E. Students 44.

WAINWRIGHT, TUSCARAWAS CO., PARISH COMMUNITY OF ST. THERESE AND ST. PAUL, Closed. For St. Therese's sacramental records contact Immaculate Conception, Dennison. For St. Paul's sacramental records contact Sacred Heart, New Philadelphia.

WASHINGTON COURT HOUSE, FAYETTE CO., ST. COLMAN (1885) [CEM] Rev. Jan C. P. Sullivan.
Office: 219 S. North St., 43160. Tel: 740-335-5000; Fax: 740-335-5066.
Res.: 223 E. East St., 43160. Tel: 740-335-3457.
*Catechesis/Religious Program—*Tel: 740-335-5005. Tracie Rush, D.R.E. (Grades PreK-12). Students 119.

WAVERLY, PIKE CO., ST. MARY, QUEEN OF THE MISSIONS (1878) [JC] Rev. William P. Hahn.
Res.: 407 S. Market St., 45690. Tel: 740-947-2436. Email: stmary_qm@frontier.com.
*Catechesis/Religious Program—*Students 23.

WELLSTON, JACKSON CO., SS. PETER AND PAUL (1881) [CEM] Rev. Donald M. Maroon.
Res.: 227 S. New York Ave., 45692. Tel: 740-384-2359; Fax: 740-384-2945.
*School—*229 S. New York Ave., 45692. Tel: 740-384-6354. Christine Unger, Prin. Lay Teachers 9; Students 98.
*Catechesis/Religious Program—*Students 90.

WEST JEFFERSON, MADISON CO., SS. SIMON AND JUDE (1866), (German—Irish), [CEM] Rev. Robert J. Kitsmiller.
9350 High Free Pike, 43162. Web: stsimonjude.org.
Res.: 311 Darbyview Dr., 43162. Tel: 614-879-8562; Fax: 614-879-7373.
*Catechesis/Religious Program—*Tel: 614-879-8579. Students 104.

WEST PORTSMOUTH, SCIOTO CO., OUR LADY OF SORROWS (1944) [CEM] Rev. David E. Young.
Res.: 2215 Galena Pike, 45663. Tel: 740-858-4600; Fax: 740-858-4600. Email: olosc@zoomnet.net.
*New To You Service Center—*Tel: 740-858-3176. Mary Horn, Dir.
*Catechesis/Religious Program—*P.O. Box 31, Otway, 45657. Tel: 740-372-7115; Fax: 740-372-7115. Students 10.
Mission—Holy Trinity 2215 Galena Pike, Pond Creek, Scioto Co. 45663.

WESTERVILLE, DELAWARE CO., ST. PAUL THE APOSTLE (1913) Revs. Charles F. Klinger; David E. Gwinner, Parochial Vicar; Daniel J. Dury, Parochial Vicar; Deacons Thomas Barford; Mickey B. Hawkins; Susan Bellotti, Pastoral Assoc.; Mary Reichley, Pastoral Assoc.
Res.: 313 N. State St., 43082. Tel: 614-882-7537. Email: stpaulchurch@stpacc.org. Web: www.stpaulcatholicchurch.org.
*School—*61 Moss Rd., 43082. Tel: 614-882-2710; Fax: 614-882-5998. Kathleen Norris, Prin.; Sharon Gillivan, Asst. Prin. Lay Teachers 39; Students 846.
*Catechesis/Religious Program—*Tel: 614-882-5045. Janet Brewer, D.R.E.; Linda Hall, Youth Min. Students 1,028.

WHEELERSBURG, SCIOTO CO., ST. PETER (1855) [CEM] Rev. Joseph T. Yokum; Deacon James M. Sturgeon.
Res.: 2167 Lick Run Lyra Rd., 45694. Tel: 740-574-5486; Fax: 740-574-6641 (Call before sending). Email: stpeterinchains@midohio.twcbc.com.
*Catechesis/Religious Program—*Cindy Gannon, C.R.E. Students 50.

WILLS CREEK, COSHOCTON CO., OUR LADY OF LOURDES, Closed. For sacramental records contact Sacred Heart, Coshocton.

WORTHINGTON, FRANKLIN CO., ST. MICHAEL (1946) Revs. Richard J. Pendolphi; Stanley L. (Stash) Dailey; Deacons John R. Crerand; Klaus Fricke; William F. Demidovich Jr. In Res., Rev. Carmen J. Arcuri (Retired).
Res.: 5750 N. High St., 43085. Tel: 614-885-7814; Fax: 614-885-3446. Email: saintmichael@ameritech.net. Web: www.saintmichael-cd.org.
*School—*64 E. Selby Blvd., 43085-3986. Tel: 614-885-3149; Fax: 614-885-1249. Web: www.cdeducation.org/schools/mi. Sr. Mary Michael Carlton, O.P., Prin. Lay Teachers 25; Students 585.
*Catechesis/Religious Program—*Tel: 614-888-5384. James Hahn, D.R.E. Students 286.

ZALESKI, VINTON CO., ST. SYLVESTER (1862), (Irish), [CEM] Rev. Joseph J. Trapp II. In Res., Rev. Richard F. Engle (Retired).
Res.: 119 N. Second St., P.O. Box 264, 45698-0264. Tel: 740-596-5474.
*Catechesis/Religious Program—*Students 11.

ZANESVILLE, MUSKINGUM CO.

1—ST. NICHOLAS (1842), (German), [CEM] Rev. Martin J. Ralko; Deacons Burdette N. (Pete) Peterson Jr., Pastoral Assoc.; Robert E. Staker, Pastoral Assoc.
Res.: 925 E. Main St., 43701. Tel: 740-453-0597; Fax: 740-453-0590. Web: www.stnickparish.org.
School—Bishop Fenwick Middle School, 1030 E. Main St., 43701. Tel: 740-453-2637; Fax: 740-454-0653. Kelly Sagan, Prin. (Preschool, Kindergarten & 6-8) Lay Teachers 22; Students 285.
*Catechesis/Religious Program—*Tel: 740-450-7461. Kevin Dooley, C.R.E. Students 98.

2—ST. THOMAS AQUINAS (1820) [CEM 2] Revs. Steven Jordan Turano, O.P.; Louis Luke Turon, O.P.; Stephen Dominic Hayes, O.P.; Sr. Maureen Mahon, O.S.F., Pastoral Assoc.
Res.: 130 N. Fifth St., 43701. Tel: 740-453-3301; Fax: 740-453-0333.
School—Bishop Fenwick Elementary School, (Grades 1-5), 139 N. Fifth St., 43701. Tel: 740-454-9731; Fax: 740-454-8775. Kelly Sagan, Prin. Lay Teachers 12; Students 301.
*Catechesis/Religious Program—*Tel: 740-453-3301, Ext. 15. Melanie Von Gunten, D.R.E.; Carol A. Luby, Business Mgr. Students 75.

ZOAR, TUSCARAWAS CO., CHURCH OF THE HOLY TRINITY (1995) [CEM 4] Rev. Ronald J. Aubry; Deacon Lyn Houze.
Mailing Address: 1835 Dover Zoar Rd., N.E., Bolivar, 44612.
Res.: 1841 Dover Zoar Rd., N.E., Bolivar, 44612. Tel: 330-874-4716 (Office & Church).
*Catechesis/Religious Program—*Students 72.

Chaplains of Public Institutions

COLUMBUS. *Children's Hospital*. Rev. Sylvester Onyeachonam.
Corrections Medical Center. Mrs. Rose Hamilton.
OSU Hospital East. Vacant.
OSU Medical Center. Vacant.

CHILLICOTHE. *Chillicothe Correctional Institution*, P.O. Box 5500, 45601. Tel: 740-773-2616, Ext. 248. Rev. Lawrence L. Hummer.
Ross Correctional Institution, P.O. Box 7010, 45601. Tel: 740-774-4182, Ext. 2519. Rev. Charles R. Griffin (Retired).
Res.: 122 Church St., 45601. Tel: 740-773-4391.
Veteran's Affairs Medical Center, 17273 S.R. 104, 45601. Tel: 740-773-1141, Ext. 7203. Rev. Vio O. Joseph, S.A.C.

LANCASTER. *Southeastern Correctional Institution*, Tel: 740-653-4324. Deacon Paul Deshais.

LONDON. *London Correctional Institution*. Rev. Homer D. Blubaugh. Tel: 740-852-2454, Ext. 451.
Madison Correctional Institution. Deacon Gordon T. Kunkler.

LUCASVILLE. *Southern Ohio Correctional Facility*, Tel: 740-259-5544. Deacons James M. Sturgeon, Christopher Varacalli.

MARION. *Marion Correctional Institution*. Vacant.

MARYSVILLE. *Ohio Reformatory for Women*. Rev. Patrick A. Toner. Tel: 614-873-8850.

MOUNT VERNON. *Mount Vernon Developmental Center*, St. Vincent de Paul Parish, 303 E. High St., 43050. Tel: 740-392-4711.

ORIENT. *Corrections Reception Center*. Rev. Joseph J. Trapp II, Sacramental Min.
Pickaway Correctional Institution, Tel: 614-877-4362. Deacon Donald Robers.

On Duty Outside the Diocese:
Revs.—
Ascencio, Joseph A., Chap., Federal Prison System, Florence, CO 81226.
Everett, Willis E.
Klein, Terrance W., Olean, NY
Naughton, Patrick J., St. David, Davie, FL.

Military Services:
Rev.—
Subler, Carl A.

Hospital Ministry:
Revs.—
Cruz, Ramon Macoy, C.F.I.C.
Manikathan, Jose Souru, C.F.I.C.

Retired:
Rev. Msgrs.—
Bender, Thomas G., The Villas at St. Therese Assisted Living, 25 Noe Bixby Rd., 43213.
Borrelli, Anthony, J.C.L., 3140 El Greco Dr., 43204.
Clagett, Carl P., Villas at St. Therese Assisted Living, 25 Noe Bixby Rd., 43213.
Dreese, John J., S.S.L., S.T.L., P.O. Box 39, New Straitsville, 43766.
Fairchild, Edward, 3306 Beachworth Dr., 43232.
Geiger, James A., M.A., Ph.D., Villas at St. Therese Assisted Living, 25 Noe Bixby Rd., 43213.
Huntzinger, Ralph J., Mohun Health Care Center, 2340 Airport Dr., 43219.
Lane, Frank P., Ph.D., Mt. St. Mary's Seminary, 6616 Beechmont Ave., Cincinnati, 45230-2006.
Meagher, Frank J., The Villas at St. Therese, 5253 E. Broad St., Apt. 207, 43213.
Metzger, Robert E., P.O. Box 277, Junction City, 43748.
Missimi, Anthony N., 1374 Lakeshore Dr., Apt. B, 43204.
Noon, Robert L., The Villas at St. Therese, 5253 E. Broad St. #127, 43213.
Ruef, James L.T., M.A., J.C.L., M.Div., J.D.
Schlegel, George J., B.A., 7592 Pickett Ln., 43235-1948.
Schneider, Robert E., The Villas at St. Therese, 5253 E. Broad St., # 108, 43213.
Schweitzer, Francis X., Columbus Rehab & Subacute, 44 S. Souder Ave., 43222.
Serraglio, Mario, P.O. Box 703, Canal Winchester, 43110.
Sorohan, David V., M.A., S.T.L., Ph.D., 925 Vernon Rd., Bexley, 43209.
Wolf, John V., S.T.D., 104 N. Mulberry St., Fredericktown, 43019-1051.
Revs.—
Arcuri, Carmen J., St. Michael Church, 5750 N. High St., Worthington, 43085.
Arter, Ronald L., 202 Elm St., Box 135, Sugar Grove, 43155.
Byrne, Patrick J., 4468 Beachwood Lake Dr., Naples, FL 34112.
DeVille, William H., 196 S. Grant Ave., Unit 304, 43215-8365.
Ehwald, Joseph A., 1308 Erickson Ave., 43227-2059.
Engle, Richard F., St. Sylvester Church, P.O. Box 264, Zaleski, 45698.
Gately, Robert E., 702 Valley Forge Blvd., Sun City, FL 33573.
Griffin, Charles R., 122 Church St., Chillicothe, 45601.
Keck, Edward
Laurinaitis, Saulius P., P.O. Box 1417, Hilliard, 43026.
Lavelle, Raymond E., Mohun Health Care Center, 2340 Airport Dr., 43219.
Losh, Joseph F., Villas at St. Therese, 25 Noe Bixby Rd., 43215.
McClory, Bernard J., P.O. Box 3103, Westerville, 43086.
Metzger, John L., P.O. Box 55, New Lexington, 43764.
Metzger, William J., 3941 Karl Rd., #235, 43224-5205.
Schilder, David M., 192 Grand Ave., Chillicothe, 45601.
Schneider, Harold E., 913 Hartney Dr., Gahanna, 43230.
Shonebarger, Thomas, Mohun Health Care Center, 2340 Airport Dr., 43219.
Smith, Paul O., 198 E. Broad St., 43215.
Stanton, Francis M., Villas at St. Therese, Independent Living, 5253 E. Broad St., # 124, 43213-3834.
Stattmiller, John E., P.O. Box 31, Otway, 45657.
Swickard, John L.

Permanent Deacons:
Allison, Mark D., (Leave of Absence)
Andrews, William J., Church of the Ascension, Johnstown
Azzola, Feliz F., St. Mary, Delaware
Ball, Frank X., (Retired)
Barford, Thomas M., St. Paul, Westerville
Baumann, Richard L., (Retired)
Berg, Thomas M., Sr., St. Joan of Arc, Powell
Berg, Thomas M., Jr., B.A., M.J., M.P.S., St. Andrew, Columbus; Vice Chancellor, Diocese of Columbus
Bonacci, Anthony C., St. Joseph, Plain City
Busic, Richard B., Our Lady of Mt. Carmel, Buckeye Lake
Butts, Jerome J., Corpus Christi, Columbus
Cain, Albert E., (Retired)
Calcara, Carl A., Jr., St. John Neumann, Sunbury; Business Mgr., St. Christopher, Columbus
Campbell, Christopher, Immaculate Conception, Columbus
Checca, Joseph P., St. James the Less, Columbus
Crerand, John R., M.A., J.C.L., St. Michael, Worthington; Defender of the Bond, Diocesan Tribunal
Davies, Martin H., Office of Liturgy, Dir.; St. Catharine of Siena, Columbus
Davis, James R., (Retired)
Davis, William J.F., (Retired)
Dawson, Eugene C., Holy Trinity, Somerset
DeMers, Steven, St. Francis DeSales, Newark; Business Mgr., Catholic Times
Demidovich, William F., Jr., St. Michael, Worthington
Deshaies, Paul, St. Bernadette, Lancaster; Chap., Pickaway Correctional
Drummer, Kenneth I., (Leave of Absence)
Duda, Frank A., Sacred Heart, Coshocton
DuPrey, John L., St. Pius X, Reynoldsburg
Eiden, Gregory L., Kairos Prison Ministry
Elam, Jack W., (Retired)
Fondriest, Ronald H., (Retired)
Fortkamp, Jeffrey D., Our Lady of Peace, Columbus
Fricke, Klaus, St. Michael, Worthington
Ghiloni, Robert W., (Retired)
Gorman, William J., (Retired)
Gorski, James, Deacon Parish Admin.; St. Aloysius & St. Agnes; Diaconal Ministry, St. Joseph Cathedral, Columbus
Gundrum, Henry, St. Mark, Lancaster
Hann, Daniel W., St. Patrick, London
Hawkins, Mickey, St. Paul, Westerville; Business Mgr.; St. Mary, Columbus
Hood, J. Michael, Our Lady of Lourdes, Ada; Immaculate Conception, Kenton
Houze, Lester, Holy Trinity, Zoar
Iannarino, Francis A., Dir. Diaconate Office, St. Brigid of Kildare, Dublin; Chap., Bishop Watterson High School, Columbus
Johnston, Thomas V., St. Joseph Cathedral, Columbus
Joseph, Robert A., Our Lady of Victory, Columbus
Kelly, James W., St. Pius X, Reynoldsburg
Killoren, Robert, Chap.; Diocesan Office of Scouting
Knight, Charles, (Retired)
Koebel, Lawrence F., (Retired)
Krick, Richard T., (Retired)
Kunkler, Gordon T., Our Lady of Lourdes, Marysville; Chap., Madison Correctional Institution
Labita, Peter C., Christ the King, Columbus
Lampe, Elmer L., (Retired)
Larcomb, Dwight T., (Retired)
McCurry, William E., Holy Family, Columbus
McDevitt, Francis X., (Retired)
Miller, Charles J., Pope John XXIII, Canal Winchester; Business Mgr.; St. Pius X, Reynoldsburg
Milne, Maurice N., III, St. Agatha, Columbus
Minner, Roger, St. Mary, Columbus
Morris, James, St. Brendan, Hilliard
Mould, Douglas, Sacred Heart, Coshocton
Mueller, Martin, (Unassigned)
Naporano, Andrew W., St. Margaret of Cortona, Columbus
Neely, Robert A., St. Dominic, Columbus
Paniccia, Frank A., (Retired)
Parsons, Ralph L., (Retired)
Paulucci, Philip M., St. Peter, Columbus
Peterson, Burdette N., St. Nicholas, Zanesville
Phillips, Byron, Church of the Resurrection, New Albany; Dir. Pastoral Formation, Pontifical College Josephinum
Plummer, Gil L., Sr., St. Brendan, Hilliard
Poirier, Donald, St. Brigid of Kildare, Dublin
Poland, Joseph D., (Retired)
Pry, Roger F., Pope John XXIII, Canal Winchester
Racine, Dean W., St. Elizabeth, Columbus
Rankin, John, (Retired)
Raymond, Hector, Seton Parish, Pickerington
Robers, Donald, St. John, Logan; Chaplain, Pickaway Correctional
Rouse, James A., A.E., M.S., P.E., (Retired), part time Diocesan Tribunal
Rzewnicki, Phil E., (Leave of Absence)
Santos, Kasuma J., Jr., St. James the Less, Columbus; Latino Commission; Diaconal Ministry Consultant
Scarpitti, Mark A., St. Bernadette, Lancaster
Schermer, Joseph E., St. Peter, Columbus
Smith, Craig, St. Anthony, Columbus
Smithberger, Marion E., St. Timothy, Columbus
Spina, Philip V., Jr., (Leave of Absence)
Staker, Eugene R., St. Nicholas, Zanesville
Sturgeon, James M., St. Peter in Chains, Wheelersburg; St. Monica, New Boston
Sullivan, Frank, St. Mary, Lancaster; Chap., Bishop Hartley High School
Supino, Bart, (Retired)
Turner, Harry, St. Matthew, Gahanna
Varacalli, Christopher, St. Mary, Portsmouth
Vellani, Albert J., St. Pius X, Reynoldsburg
Venturini, Stephen A., Our Lady of the Miraculous Medal, Columbus
Wiggins, Patrick J., St. Brendan, Hilliard
Wilson, Larry, St. Leonard, Heath
Wilson, Patrick, Blessed Sacrament, Newark
Zimmermann, George A., Jr., Holy Spirit, Columbus

INSTITUTIONS LOCATED IN THE DIOCESE

[A] SEMINARIES, PONTIFICAL COLLEGES

COLUMBUS. *Pontifical College Josephinum* (1888) 7625 N. High St., 43235-1498. Tel: 614-885-5585; Fax: 614-885-2307. Web: www.pcj.edu. Faculty 34; Total Enrollment 185.

Chancellor & Vice Chancellor: Most Revs. Carlo Maria Vigano, Apostolic Nuncio to the United States, Chancellor; Frederick F. Campbell, D.D., Ph.D., Vice Chancellor & Bishop of Columbus.

General Administration: Very Rev. James A. Wehner, S.T.D., Rector, Pres. & Prof.; Rev. Msgr. Christopher Schreck, Ph.D., S.T.D., Vice Pres. & Prof.; Deacon Michael Ross, Ph.D., Academic Dean; David J. DeLeonardis, Ph.D., Asst. Academic Dean; Revs. Walter R. Oxley, S.T.D., Vice Rector, School, Theology & Dir., Pastoral Formation; John F. Heisler (ARL), Vice Rector, College Liberal Arts; Michael Ciccone, O.P., S.T.L., Ph.D., Dir. Spiritual Formation, School of Theology; Paul Hrezo, S.T.L., Dir. Spiritual Formation, College; John Erwin, M.B.A., C.P.A., Treas.; Rev. Msgrs. Eugene C. Morris, S.T.L., Dir. Liturgy, Prof.; Michael A. Osborne, J.C.D., Dean of Men, School of Theology & Prof.; Deacon Byron Phillips, Dir. Pastoral Formation; Revs. Louis V. Iasiello, O.F.M., Ph.D., Dir. Human Formation & Prof.; W. Becket Soule, O.P., J.C.D., Bishop Griffin Chair, Canon Law & Spiritual Dir.; John M. Rozembajgier, S.T.L., J.C.D., Dean, Men, College Liberal Arts; Raymond N. Enzweiler, Ph.D., Be.L., Formation Advisor & Prof.; Jay Harrington, Ph.D., S.T.D., Formation Advisor & Prof.; David Monaco, C.P., Ph.D., S.S.L., Formation Advisor & Prof.

Administrative Officers: Danielle Andrews, Registrar; John Heise, Dir. Plant Opers.; Mr. Peter G. Veracka, M.S.L.S., Dir. Library; Mr. Doald Frye, Dir., Information Technology.

School of Theology full-time faculty: Perry J. Cahall, Ph.D.; Revs. Michael Ciccone, O.P., S.T.L., Ph.D.; Joseph A. Murphy, S.J., S.T.D.; William F. Murphy, S.T.D.; Rev. Msgrs. Christopher Schreck, Ph.D., S.T.D.; Kevin T. McMahon, S.T.D.; Eugene C. Morris, S.T.L.; Michael A. Osborn, S.T.D.; Revs. James A. Wehner, S.T.D.; R. John Boettcher, S.T.D.; Jay M. Harrington, O.P., Ph.D., S.T.D., C.I.I.; David Monaco, C.P., Ph.D., S.S.L.; W. Becket Soule, O.P., J.C.D.; Louis V. Iasiello, O.F.M., Ph.D.; Walter R. Oxley, S.T.D.

Other full-time faculty: Deacon Michael Ross, Ph.D.; Mr. Peter G. Veracka, M.S.L.S.

College of Liberal Arts-full-time faculty: Rev. John Heisler; Jason Keefer, Ph.D.; Alma Amell, Ph.D.; David J. De Leonardis, Ph.D.; Beverly Lane, M.L.S.; Loyann W. Brush, M.A.; Douglas C. Fortner, Ph.D.; Rev. Paul Hrezo, S.T.L.; Eric S. Graff, Ph.D.; Bradley G. Potter, Ph.D.; Patricia Pintado, Ph.D.; Patricia Polko, M.A.; Revs. Raymond N. Enzweiler, Ph.D., Be.L.; John M. Rozembajgier, S.T.L., J.C.D.; Caitlin Gilson, Ph.D.; Joseph T. Papa, Ph.D.

[B] COLLEGES AND UNIVERSITIES

COLUMBUS. *Ohio Dominican University*, 1216 Sunbury Rd., 43219. Tel: 614-253-2741; Fax: 614-252-0776. Email: admissions@ohiodominican.edu. Web: www.ohiodominican.edu. Dr. Peter Cimbolic, Pres.; Dr. Alison Benders, Vice Pres. Academic Affairs; David Kosanovic, Interim Vice Pres., Fin. & Admin.; Jamie Caridi, Vice Pres. Student Devel.; Sr. Catherine Colby, O.P., Ed.D., Vice Pres., Mission & Identity. Dominican Sisters of the Third Order of St. Dominic of Dominical Sisters of Peace. Sisters 3; Lay Teachers 73; Students 3,051.

[C] HIGH SCHOOLS, DIOCESAN OR INTERPAROCHIAL

COLUMBUS. *Bishop Hartley High School*, 1285 Zettler Rd., 43227. Tel: 614-237-5421; Fax: 614-237-3809. Email: hartley@cdeducation.org. Web: www.bishop-hartley.org. Mike Winters, Prin.; Barbara Recchie, Asst. Prin.; Dave Thompson, Athletic Dir. Lay Teachers 58; Students 720.

Bishop Ready High School (1961) 707 Salisbury Rd., 43204. Tel: 614-276-5263; Fax: 614-276-5116. Email: cseamen@cdeducation.org. Web: www.brhs.org. Celene A. Seamen, Prin.; Jeri Rod, Asst. Prin.; Patricia Moore, Librarian. Priests 1; Sisters 1; Administrators 2; Lay Teachers 30; Students 450.

Bishop Watterson High School (1954) 99 E. Cooke Rd., 43214. Tel: 614-268-8671; Fax: 614-268-0551. Web: www.cd.education.org/schools/bw. Mrs. Marian Hutson, Prin.; Virginia O'Connor, Asst. Prin.; Bill Weisner, Asst. Prin.; Deacon Frank A. Iannarino, Chap. Deacons 3; Sisters 1; Lay Teachers 87; Students 1,020.

Development Office, 99 E. Cooke Rd., 43214. Tel: 614-268-8671, Ext. 239; Fax: 614-268-4309. Web: www.bishopwatterson.com/.

St. Charles Preparatory School, 2010 E. Broad St., 43209. Tel: 614-252-6714; Fax: 614-251-6800. Email: dcavello@cdeducation.org. Web: www.stcharlesprep.org. Mr. Dominic J. Cavello, Prin.; Scott M. Pharion, Asst. Prin.; James Lower, Asst. Prin. Sisters 1; Lay Teachers 35; Students 640.

Cristo Rey Columbus High School, 840 W. State St., 43222-1422. Tel: 614-205-3958. Web: cristoreycolumbus.org. Jim Foley, Pres.; Barbara A. Brown, Prog. Coord.

St. Francis de Sales High School, 4212 Karl Rd., 43224. Tel: 614-267-7808; Fax: 614-265-3375. Email: dgarrick@cdeducation.org. Web: www.cdeducation.org/school/ds. Mr. Dan Garrick, Prin.; Jim Jones, Asst. Prin. Lay Teachers 65; Students 820.

LANCASTER. *William V. Fisher Catholic High School*, 1803 Granville Pike, 43130. Tel: 740-654-1231; Fax: 740-654-1233. Email: jsilcott@cdeducation.org. Web: fishercatholic.org. Mr. Sean P. Kenney, Pres.; Tiffany Wade, Prin.; Rev. John M. Reade, Chap. Lay Teachers 16; Students 240.

MARION. *Marion Catholic High School*, (Grades 7-12), (Junior/Senior High School), 1001 Mt. Vernon Ave., 43302. Tel: 740-389-2381; Fax: 740-389-5243. Email: fvoll@cdeducatoin.org. Web: www.marioncatholic.org. Al Seitter, Prin. Lay Teachers 12; Students 75.

NEW PHILADELPHIA. *Tuscarawas Central Catholic Junior/Senior High School*, (Grades 7-12), 777 Third St., N.E., 44663. Tel: 330-343-3302; Fax: 330-343-6388. Web: www.tccsaints.com. Scott Power, Prin. Lay Teachers 15; Students 188.

NEWARK. *Newark Catholic High School* (1958) 1 Green Wave Dr., 43055. Tel: 740-344-3594; Fax: 740-344-0421. Email: bhill@cdeducation.org. Web: www.newarkcatholic.org/. Beth Hill, Prin.; Rev. Robert Penhallurick, Chap. Lay Teachers 22; Students 268.

PORTSMOUTH. *Notre Dame High School* (1953) (Grades 7-12), (Junior/Senior High School), 2220 Sunrise Ave., 45662. Tel: 740-353-0719; Fax: 740-353-2526. Email: kmilliga@cdeducation.org. Kathleen Milligan, Prin. Lay Teachers 16; Students 156.

ZANESVILLE. *Bishop Rosecrans High School* (1950) 1040 E. Main St., 43701. Tel: 740-452-7504; Fax: 740-455-5080. Email: jmallett@cdeducation.org. Web: www.rosecrans.cdeducation.org. Rev. Martin J. Ralko; Jennifer Mallett, Prin. Priests 1; Lay Teachers 14; Students 152.

[D] MONTESSORI SCHOOLS

COLUMBUS. *St. Joseph Montessori School* (1968) 933 Hamlet St., 43201-3595. Tel: 614-291-8601; Fax: 614-291-7411. Email: sjmsoffice@cdeducation.org; sjmsdev@cdeducation.org. Web: www.sjms.net. Elma Pundavela, Head of School; Ernestine Jackson, Devel. Dir. Lay Teachers 30; Students 275.

[E] PRIVATE SCHOOLS

COLUMBUS. *Our Lady of Bethlehem School and Childcare*, 4567 Olentangy River Rd., 43214. Tel: 614-459-8285; Fax: 614-451-3706. Email: ldulin@cdeducation.org. Web: www.ourladyofbethlehem.org. Lori Dulin, Dir.; Janelle Obergfell, Librarian. Totally Terrific Twos; Preschool; Pre-Kindergarten; Full & Half Day Kindergarten; Full & Part Time Childcare; Summer Program. Total Staff 11; Children 91.

[F] GENERAL HOSPITALS

COLUMBUS. *Mohun Health Care Center* (1956) 2340 Airport Dr., 43219. Tel: 614-416-6132; Fax: 614-251-0338. Jeffrey Urban, Admin. Total Staff 118; Bed Capacity 72; Patients Assisted Annually 101.

Mount Carmel Health System, 6150 E. Broad St., 43213. Tel: 614-546-4533; Fax: 614-546-4573. Web: mountcarmelhealth.com. Claus von Zychlin, Pres. & CEO. Bed Capacity 1,350; Total Staff 8,587; Patients Assisted Annually 1,046,597.

Legal Holdings:

Mount Carmel Health System Tel: 614-546-4531; Fax: 614-546-4573.

Mount Carmel West (General Hospital) Tel: 614-234-5000; Fax: 614-234-5756. Bed Capacity 514; Total Staff 2,577; Inpatient Admits 16,271.

Mount Carmel East (General Hospital) Tel: 614-234-6000; Fax: 614-234-6408. Bed Capacity 438; Total Staff 3,569; Inpatient Admits 22,084.

Mount Carmel Care Continuum Businesses Tel: 614-234-0224; Fax: 614-234-5756. Web: www.mountcarmelhealth.com.

Mount Carmel College of Nursing Tel: 614-234-5800; Fax: 614-234-2875.

Mount Carmel St. Ann's (General Hospital), Westerville. Tel: 614-898-4000; Fax: 614-898-8668. Web: www.mountcarmelhealth.com. Bed Capacity 338; Total Staff 2,140; Inpatient Admits 19,516.

Mount Carmel New Albany Surgical Hospital, New Albany, 43054. Tel: 614-775-6610. Bed Capacity 60; Total Staff 301; Inpatient Admits 4,851.

Mount Carmel Health System Foundation Tel: 614-546-4500; Fax: 614-546-4501. Web: www.mountcarmelfoundation.org.

DENNISON. *Trinity Hospital Twin City*, 819 N. First St., 44621. Tel: 419-882-8373; Fax: 419-882-7360. James W. Pope, FACHE, Pres. Bed Capacity 25; Total Assisted Annually 162,958; Total Staff 210.

ZANESVILLE. *Genesis HealthCare System*, 2951 Maple Ave, 43701. Tel: 740-454-4633; Fax: 740-455-4914. Mr. Matthew Perry, CEO & Pres. Franciscan Sisters of Christian Charity 3; Bed Capacity 433; Total Staff 3,539.

[G] HOMES FOR AGED AND HOUSING FOR ELDERLY

COLUMBUS. *Mother Angeline McCrory Manor, Inc.* (2005) 5199 E. Broad St., 43213. Tel: 614-751-5700; Fax: 614-751-8311. Web: www.mangelinemanor.org. Sr. Pauline Ross, O.Carm., Admin.

Nazareth Towers (1967) 300 E. Rich St., 43215. Tel: 614-464-4780; Fax: 614-464-1733. Doug Decker, Admin. Total in Residence 152; Total Staff 5.

Seton Coshocton, Inc., 377 Clow Ln., Coshocton, 43812. Tel: 740-622-7664; 740-622-7664 (Coshocton No.); Fax: 740-622-4635. Email: setoncoshocton@midohio.twcbc.com. Roxana Wilson, Property Mgr.; Wayne Patterson, Maintenance; Cindy Smith, Svc. Coord. Apartments 40; Total in Residence 40; Total Staff 3.

Seton South Columbus, Inc. (1995) 155 Highview Blvd., 43207. Tel: 614-492-9944; Fax: 614-492-9955. Suzanne Ambrose, Mgr. Total in Residence 60; Total Staff 2.

Seton Square Dover, II, Inc., 139 Filmore Ave., Dover, 44622. Tel: 330-343-3611; Fax: 330-364-3147. Email: setonsquare@wifi7.com. Bob Campitelli, Mgr.; Mary Campitelli, Asst. Total in Residence 40; Total Staff 3.

Seton Square North, 1776 Drew Ave., 43235. Tel: 614-451-1995; Fax: 614-451-3793. Email: ssnaline@ameritech.net. Aline Taylor, Mgr. Total in Residence 242; Total Staff 5.

Seton Square, West, 3999 Clime Rd., 43228. Tel: 614-274-8550; Fax: 614-308-1550. Dionna Richardson, Mgr. Staff 3; Total in Residence 48.

**The Villas at St. Therese Assisted Living, Inc.*, 25 Noe-Bixby Rd., 43213-1411. Tel: 614-864-3576; Fax: 614-864-3577. Sr. Diane Mack, O.Carm., Admin.; Rev. Msgr. Joseph M. Hendricks, Contact Person.

**The Villas at St. Therese Independent Living, Inc.*, 5253 E. Broad St., 43213. Tel: 614-856-9951; Fax: 614-856-9654. Email: villasindependent@sbcglobal.net. Rev. Msgr. Joseph M. Hendricks, Contact Person.

DOVER. *Seton Development, Inc.*, 501 S. James St., 44622. Tel: 330-343-3611; Fax: 330-364-3147. Email: setonsquare@wifi7.com. Bob Campitelli, Mgr.; Mary Campitelli, Asst. Total in Residence 50; Total Staff 3.

KENTON. *Seton Kenton, Inc.*, 699 Morningside Dr., 43326. Tel: 419-673-7202; Fax: 419-673-7202. Kim Manns, Mgr. Total in Residence 50; In Residence 48; Total Staff 2.

LANCASTER. *Seton Lancaster, Inc.*, 232 Gay St., 43130. Tel: 740-681-1403; Fax: 740-681-9178. Roxanne Bailey, Mgr. Total in Residence 34; Total Staff 2.

LONDON. *Seton London, Inc.*, 350 Cambridge Dr., 43140. Tel: 740-852-4233. Kitty Binion, Mgr. Total in Residence 50; Total Staff 3.

MARION. *Seton Square Marion, Inc.*, 255 Richland Rd., 43302. Tel: 740-389-4746; Fax: 740-389-9780. Email: Seton504@yahoo.com. Debra J. Erwin, Mgr. Total in Residence 110; Total Staff 3.

REYNOLDSBURG. *Seton Square East, Inc.*, 1235 Briarcliff Rd., 43068. Tel: 614-861-4860; Fax: 614-861-8022. Gene Tolliver, Mgr. Total in Residence 106; Total Staff 3.

WASHINGTON COURT HOUSE. *Seton Washington Court House*, 400 N. Glenn Ave., 43160. Tel: 740-335-2292; Fax: 740-335-2291. Email: setonwch@sbcglobal.net. Rita Boggs, Mgr. Total in Residence 40; Total Staff 3.

WELLSTON. *Seton Square Wellston, Inc.* (1980) 570 W. First St., 45692. Tel: 740-384-6174; Fax: 740-384-1514. Email: setonrockets@yahoo.com. Tamra Jolly, Property Mgr. Total in Residence 48; Total Staff 2.

ZANESVILLE. *Seton Housing, Inc.*, 516 Sheridan St., 43701. Tel: 740-453-4422; Fax: 740-453-4950. David Sears, Mgr. Total in Residence 44; Total Staff 1.

[H] CONVENTS AND RESIDENCES FOR SISTERS

COLUMBUS. *Congregation of the Sisters of the Holy Cross, Mount Carmel East Convent*, 266 McNaughton Rd., 43213-2139. Tel: 614-866-9397. *Sisters of the Holy Cross, Inc.* Sisters 2.

Dominican Sisters of Peace, Inc., 2320 Airport Dr., 43219-2098. Tel: 614-416-1900; Fax: 614-252-7435. Email: srpeace@oppeace.org. Web: www.oppeace.org. Sisters in Columbus Diocese 153; Total in Congregation 587.

Leadership Team: Sisters Margaret Ormond, O.P., Prioress; Joan Scanlon, O.P., Gen. Councilor; Gene Poore, O.P., Gen. Councilor; Therese Leckert, O.P., Gen. Councilor, Sec.-General; Gemma Doll, O.P., Gen. Councilor.

Sisters' Residence:

St. Mary of the Springs Motherhouse, 2320 Airport Dr., 43219-2098. Tel: 614-416-1092; Fax: 614-416-1379. Sr. Teresa Tuite, O.P., Mission Group Coord.

Mohun Health Care Center, 2340 Airport Dr., 43219-2602. Tel: 614-416-6132; Fax: 614-251-0338. Email: smcintyre@oppeace.org. Sr. Sheila Marie McIntyre, Mission Group Coord.; Jeffrey Urban, Admin.; Rev. Stephen Fitzhenry, O.P., Chap.

Mother Angeline McCrory Manor Convent, 5199 E. Broad St., 43213. Tel: 614-751-5700. Email: srfcasey@sbcglobal.net. Carmelite Sisters operate the Villas at St. Therese, Assisted Living; Carmelite Sisters for the Aged and Infirm.

Sisters of the Good Shepherd (1865) 2440 Dawnlight Ave., 43211-1934. Tel: 614-416-8747; Fax: 614-428-7995. Email: srrose3@gmail.com. Web: www.handcraftingjustice.org. Handcrafting Justice buys from Good Shepherd Missions in the developing world for resale. Proceeds are sent back to the missions to better the lives of women in the developing world. Sisters of the Good Shepherd 3.

[I] NEWMAN CENTERS

COLUMBUS. *Campus Ministry St. Thomas More Newman Center at The Ohio State Univ.*, 64 W. Lane Ave., 43201. Tel: 614-291-4674; Fax: 614-291-2065. Email: mailbox@buckeyecatholic.com. Web: www.buckeyecatholic.com. Revs. Joe Ciccone, C.S.P., Dir.; Vincent W. McKiernan, C.S.P.; Charles Cunniff, C.S.P. Priests 4; Members 2,588; Staff 19. In Res. Rev. David W. O'Brien, C.S.P. (Retired).

[J] FOUNDATIONS

COLUMBUS. **The Foundation of the Catholic Diocese of Columbus dba The Catholic Foundation* 257 E. Broad St., 43215. Tel: 614-443-8893; Fax: 614-443-8894. Loren P. Brown, Pres. & CEO.

Legacy of Catholic Learning Endowment Program, 198 E. Broad St., 43215. Tel: 614-224-1221.

LANCASTER. **William V. Fisher Catholic High School Endowment Fund*, 1803 Granville Pike, 43130. Tel: 740-654-1231; Fax: 740-654-1233. Email: jsilcott@cdeducation.org. Web: fishercatholic.org.

MARION. *Marion Catholic High School Endowment Fund*, 1001 Mount Vernon Ave., 43302. Tel: 740-389-2381; Fax: 740-389-5243. Email: fvoll@cdeducation.org. Web: www.marioncatholic.org.

NEW PHILADELPHIA. *Tuscarawas Central Catholic High School Endowment Fund*, 777 Third St. N.E., 44663. Tel: 330-343-3302; Fax: 330-343-6388. Email: spower@cdeducation.org.

NEWARK. **Newark Catholic High School Foundation*, One Green Wave Dr., 43055. Tel: 740-344-5671; Fax: 740-344-0421. Email: kdellner@laca.org.

ZANESVILLE. *Bishop Rosecrans High School Foundation* (1986) 1040 E. Main St., 43701. Tel: 740-450-7993; Fax: 740-455-5080. Email: jod@brhsfoundation.org. Web: www.rosecrans.cdeducation.org.

[K] MISCELLANEOUS

COLUMBUS. *Blessed Margaret Guild, Inc. c/o St. Patrick Church*, 262 N. Grant Ave., 43215. Tel: 614-240-5915; Fax: 614-240-5928. Total Staff 1.

Catholic Alumni Club, P.O. Box 695, 43216. Tel: 614-575-0518; Fax: 614-575-0518. Email: peg42@att.net; dwdoell@yahoo.com. Web: www.angelfire.com/oh/CatholicAlumniClub. Peggy Schano, Contact Person. Tel: 614-575-0518; Dan Doell, Contact Person. Tel: 614-846-7489.

Catholic Men's Ministry, 1511 Teeway Dr., 43220. Tel: 614-235-0608. Web: cmmohio.org. Chuck Wilson, Dir.

The Christ Child Society of Columbus, Inc., P.O. Box 340091, 43234-0091. Tel: 614-294-6347, Ext. 305. Email: ccsofcolumbus@yahoo.com. Web: www.rc.net/columbus/christchild. Judy Walton, Pres.

Cristo Rey Columbus High School Work Study Program, 840 W. State St., 43222-1422. Tel: 614-205-3958. Web: cristoreycolumbus.org. Jim Foley, Pres.; Barbara A. Brown, Prog. Coord.

Diocesan Charities Membership Corporation, 198 E. Broad St., 43215.

Diocesan Retirement Community Corp., 198 E. Broad St., 43215. Tel: 614-224-2251; Fax: 614-224-6306. Rev. Msgr. Joseph M. Hendricks, Pres. & CEO.

Haitian Catholic Coalition of Ohio, 1582 Ferris Rd., 43224. Tel: 614-778-0459. Nedy Melidor, Founder & Counselor; Rev. Fritzner Valcin (Haiti), Counselor.

St. Stephen's Community House, 1500 E. 17th Ave., 43219. Tel: 614-294-6347; Fax: 614-294-0258. Email: brightenlives@saintstephensch.org. Web: www.saintstephensch.org. Ms. Michelle Mills, Pres. & CEO. Total Assisted 22,000; Total Staff 131.

LANCASTER. **St. Mary of the Assumption Foundation*, 132 S. High St., 43130. Tel: 740-653-0997; Fax: 740-653-0337.

ZANESVILLE. *St. Nicholas Foundation* (1842) 955 E. Main St., 43701. Tel: 740-453-0597; Fax: 740-453-0590. Web: www.stnickparish.org. Rev. Martin J. Ralko, Pres.

RELIGIOUS INSTITUTES OF MEN REPRESENTED IN THE DIOCESE

For further details refer to the corresponding bracketed number in the Religious Institutes of Men or Women section.

[0350]—*Cistercians Order of the Strict Observance-Trappists*—O.C.S.O.

[1000]—*Congregation of the Passion*

[]—*Congregation of the Sons of the Immaculate Conception*—C.F.I.C.

[0520]—*Franciscan Friars*—O.F.M.

[0690]—*Jesuit Fathers and Brothers* (Detroit and Maryland Provs.)—S.J.

[0430]—*Order of Preachers-Dominicans* (Prov. of St. Joseph)—O.P.

[1030]—*Paulist Fathers*—C.S.P.

[1050]—*Pontifical Institute for Foreign Missions*—P.I.M.E.

[0760]—*Society of Mary*—S.M.

[0990]—*Society of the Catholic Apostolate*—S.A.C.

[1060]—*Society of the Precious Blood* (Cincinnati Prov.)—C.PP.S.

RELIGIOUS INSTITUTES OF WOMEN REPRESENTED IN THE DIOCESE

[0330]—*Carmelite Sisters for the Aged and Infirm*—O.Carm.

[1070-25]—*Congregation of the Dominican Sisters of St. Catherine of Sienna of Kenosha*

[3710]—*Congregation of the Sisters of St. Agnes*—C.S.A.

[1920]—*Congregation of the Sisters of the Holy Cross*—C.S.C.

[1730]—*Congregation of the Sisters of the Third Order of St. Francis, Oldenburg, IN*—O.S.F.

[1710]—*Congregation of the Third Order of St. Francis of Mary Immaculate, Joliet, IL*—O.S.F.

[1070-13]—*Dominican Sisters* (Adrian, MI)—O.P.

[]—*Dominican Sisters of Mary, Mother of the*

Eucharist (Ann Arbor, MI)—O.P.
[1115]—*Dominican Sisters of Peace, Inc.*—O.P.
[1230]—*Franciscan Sisters of Christian Charity* (Manitowoc, WI)—O.S.F.
[]—*Missionary Servants of the World (Hermanas Misioneras Servidores de la Palabra)*—H.M.S.P.
[3210]—*Poor Clares of Perpetual Adoration*—P.C.P.A.
[0440]—*Sisters of Charity of Cincinnati, Ohio*—S.C.
[0500]—*Sisters of Charity of Nazareth, Kentucky*—S.C.N.
[0990]—*Sisters of Divine Providence*—C.D.P.
[3000]—*Sisters of Notre Dame de Namur*—S.N.D.deN.
[1630]—*Sisters of St. Francis of Penance and Christian Charity* (Stella Niagara, NY)—O.S.F.
[1830]—*Sisters of the Good Shepherd*—R.G.S.
[3220]—*Sisters of the Poor Child Jesus*—P.C.J.
[3260]—*Sisters of the Precious Blood* (Dayton, OH)—C.PP.S.
[3320]—*Sisters of the Presentation of the B.V.M.*—P.B.V.M.
[1760]—*Sisters of the Third Order of St. Francis of Penance and of Charity* (Tiffin, OH)—O.S.F.
[1720]—*Sisters of the Third Order Regular of St. Francis of the Congregation of Our Lady of Lourdes*—O.S.F.

DIOCESAN CEMETERIES

COLUMBUS. *Mount Calvary*, Mailing Address: 6440 S. High St., Lockbourne, 43137-9208. Tel: 614-491-2751; Fax: 614-491-4264. 581 Mt. Calvary Ave., 43223-2217. Tel: 614-491-2751; Fax: 614-491-4264. Rich Finn, Dir. & Gen. Mgr.

LEWIS CENTER. *Resurrection Cemetery*, 9571 N. High St., 43035-9413. Tel: 614-888-1805; Fax: 614-888-1810. Rich Finn, Dir. & Gen. Mgr.

LOCKBOURNE. *St. Joseph*, 6440 S. High St., 43137-9208. Tel: 614-491-2751; Fax: 614-491-4264. Rich Finn, Dir. & Gen. Mgr.

PATASKALA. *Holy Cross Cemetery*, 11539 National Rd., S.W., 43062-8304. Tel: 740-927-4442; Fax: 740-927-4645. Rich Finn, Dir. & Gen. Mgr.

NECROLOGY

† Carroll, Rev. Msgr. James J., (Retired)—Died May 10, 2011
† Grimes, Rev. Msgr. Kevin, (Retired)—Died Oct. 15, 2011
† McFarland, Rev. Msgr. Edward J., (Retired)—Died Jan. 8, 2011
† Schulz, Rev. Msgr. Donald C., (Retired)—Died May 28, 2011
† DiPietro, Rodric J., Hilliard, OH St. Brendan the Navigator.—Died Aug. 13, 2011
† Thomas, Charles T., Columbus, OH St. Mary Church.—Died April 24, 2011
† Totten, Raymond F., (Retired)—Died 2011

An asterisk (*) denotes an organization that has established tax-exempt status directly with the IRS and is not covered by the USCCB Group Ruling.

Diocese of Corpus Christi

(Dioecesis Corporis Christi)

Most Reverend

EDMOND CARMODY, D.D.

Bishop Emeritus of Corpus Christi; ordained June 8, 1957; appointed Auxiliary Bishop of the Archdiocese of San Antonio November 8, 1988; consecrated December 15, 1988; appointed Bishop of the Diocese of Tyler March 24, 1992; installed May 25, 1992; appointed Bishop of the Diocese of Corpus Christi February 3, 2000; installed March 17, 2000; retired Jan. 18, 2010. *Mailing Address: P.O. Box 2620, Corpus Christi, TX 78403-2620.* Tel: 361-882-6191; Fax: 361-654-1270.

Most Reverend

WM. MICHAEL MULVEY, S.T.L., D.D.

Eighth Bishop of Corpus Christi; ordained June 29, 1975; appointed Bishop of Corpus Christi January 18, 2010; ordained March 25, 2010. *Mailing Address: P.O. Box 2620, Corpus Christi, TX 78403-2620.* Tel: 361-882-6191; Fax: 361-882-1018.

SENTENTIA IN CHRISTO VOBIS

The Chancery Office: 620 Lipan St., P.O. Box 2620, Corpus Christi, TX 78403-2620. Tel: 361-882-6191; Fax: 361-882-1018; 361-883-8850; 361-654-1270.

Web: www.diocesecc.org

Email: chancery@diocesecc.org

Most Reverend

RENE H. GRACIDA, D.D.

Bishop Emeritus of Corpus Christi; ordained May 23, 1959; appointed Titular Bishop of Masuccaba and Auxiliary of Miami December 6, 1971; consecrated January 25, 1972; appointed Bishop of Pensacola-Tallahassee October 1, 1975; transferred to Corpus Christi May 19, 1983; installed July 11, 1983; retired April 1, 1997. *Res.: 4126 Ocean Dr., Corpus Christi, TX 78411-1224. Office: 620 Lipan St., P.O. Box 2620, Corpus Christi, TX 78403-2620.* Tel: 361-882-6191.

Square Miles 10,951.

Erected a Vicariate Apostolic in 1874; elevated to a Diocese March 23, 1912.

The territory embraced by the Diocese of Corpus Christi comprises the Counties of Aransas, Bee, Brooks, Duval, Jim Wells, Kleberg, Kenedy, Live Oak, Nueces, Refugio, San Patricio, and parts of McMullen in the State of Texas.

For legal titles of parishes and diocesan institutions, consult the Chancery Office.

STATISTICAL OVERVIEW

Personnel	
Bishop	1
Retired Bishops	2
Priests: Diocesan Active in Diocese	101
Priests: Diocesan Active Outside Diocese	6
Priests: Retired, Sick or Absent	25
Number of Diocesan Priests	132
Religious Priests in Diocese	26
Total Priests in Diocese	158
Extern Priests in Diocese	21
Ordinations:	
Diocesan Priests	3
Permanent Deacons in Diocese	79
Total Brothers	3
Total Sisters	142
Parishes	
Parishes	69
With Resident Pastor:	
Resident Diocesan Priests	41
Resident Religious Priests	5
Without Resident Pastor:	
Administered by Priests	23
Missions	32
Professional Ministry Personnel:	
Brothers	1
Sisters	11
Lay Ministers	56
Welfare	
Catholic Hospitals	6
Total Assisted	486,633
Health Care Centers	8
Total Assisted	77,751
Homes for the Aged	1
Total Assisted	54
Day Care Centers	1
Total Assisted	56
Specialized Homes	1
Total Assisted	231
Special Centers for Social Services	1
Total Assisted	195,090
Educational	
Diocesan Students in Other Seminaries	12
Total Seminarians	12
High Schools, Diocesan and Parish	1
Total Students	424
High Schools, Private	1
Total Students	318
Elementary Schools, Diocesan and Parish	14
Total Students	2,384
Elementary Schools, Private	2
Total Students	489
Catechesis/Religious Education:	
High School Students	3,719
Elementary Students	9,329
Total Students under Catholic Instruction	16,675
Teachers in the Diocese:	
Priests	3
Sisters	23
Lay Teachers	291
Vital Statistics	
Receptions into the Church:	
Infant Baptism Totals	2,050
Minor Baptism Totals	542
Adult Baptism Totals	172
Received into Full Communion	317
First Communions	2,723
Confirmations	1,604
Marriages:	
Catholic	533
Interfaith	91
Total Marriages	624
Deaths	1,832
Total Catholic Population	397,449
Total Population	571,987

Former Bishops—Rt. Revs. DOMINIC MANUCY, ord. Aug. 15, 1850; cons. Dec. 8, 1874; transferred to Mobile March 9, 1884; reappointed to Vicariate Apostolic of Brownsville Feb. 1, 1885; died Dec. 4, 1885, before taking possession; PETER VERDAGUER, ord. Dec. 12, 1862; cons. Nov. 9, 1890; died Oct. 26, 1911; PAUL JOSEPH NUSSBAUM, C.P., D.D., ord. May 30, 1894; cons. May 20, 1913; resigned March 26, 1920; Bishop of Marquette; appt. Nov. 14, 1922; died June 24, 1935; Most Revs. EMMANUEL B. LEDVINA, D.D., LL.D., appt. April 30, 1921; cons. June 14, 1921; Assistant at Pontifical Throne May 30, 1931; resigned March 15, 1949; died Dec. 15, 1952; MARIANO S. GARRIGA, D.D., LL.D., Coadjutor cum jure successionis,; appt. June 20, 1936; cons. Sept. 21, 1936; succeeded to See March 15, 1949; assistant at Pontifical Throne April 14, 1951; died Feb. 21, 1965; THOMAS J. DRURY, D.D., LL.D., Fourth Bishop of Corpus Christi; Bishop of San Angelo; appt. Oct. 16, 1961; cons. Jan. 24, 1962; fourth Bishop of Corpus Christi; appt. July 19, 1965; installed Sept. 1, 1965; retired Bishop of Corpus Christi; appt. May 19, 1983; died July 22, 1992; RENE H. GRACIDA, D.D. (Retired), Bishop Emeritus; Fifth Bishop of Corpus Christi; appt. Titular Bishop of Masuccaba and Auxiliary of Miami Dec. 6, 1971; cons. Jan. 25, 1972; appt. Bishop of Pensacola-Tallahassee Oct. 1, 1975; transferred to Corpus Christi May 19, 1983; installed July 11, 1983; retired April 1, 1997; ROBERTO O. GONZALEZ, O.F.M., Sixth Bishop of Corpus Christi; appt. Titular Bishop of Ursona and Auxiliary Bishop of Boston July 19, 1988; ord. Oct. 3, 1988; appt. Coadjutor Bishop of Corpus Christi May 16, 1995; transferred to Corpus Christi June 26, 1995; succeeded to See April 1, 1997; appt. Apostolic Administrator to Corpus Christi and Archbishop of San Juan, March 26, 1999; installed Archbishop of San Juan, Puerto Rico May 8, 1999; EDMOND CARMODY, D.D., ord. June 8, 1957; appt. Auxiliary Bishop of the Archdiocese of San Antonio Nov. 8, 1988; cons. Dec. 15, 1988; appt. Bishop of the Diocese of Tyler March 24, 1992; installed May 25, 1992; appt. Bishop of the Diocese of Corpus Christi Feb. 3, 2000; installed March 17, 2000; retired Jan. 18, 2010.

Diocesan Curia—620 Lipan St., P.O. Box 2620, Corpus Christi, 78403-2620.

Office of the Bishop—Most Rev. WM. MICHAEL MULVEY, S.T.L., D.D.; Rev. Msgr. LOUIS F. KIHNEMAN III, V.G., Vicar Gen.; Very Rev. JOSEPH A. LOPEZ, J.C.L., Chancellor; MARCO CRAWFORD, Vice Chancellor/In-House Legal Counsel; Rev. Msgr. THOMAS P. FEENEY, J.C.L., Judicial Vicar.

Bishop's Office—620 Lipan St., P.O. Box 2620, Corpus Christi, 78403-2620. Tel: 361-882-6191; Fax: 361-693-6726. Sr. ANNETTE WAGNER, I.W.B.S., Dir. Consecrated Life; Deacon MICHAEL MANTZ, Dir. Deacons; Very Revs. EMILIO B. JIMENEZ, Vicar for Priests; JOSEPH A. LOPEZ, J.C.L., Dir. Vocations.

Office of the Bishop Emeritus—Most Revs. EDMOND CARMODY, D.D. (Retired); RENE H. GRACIDA, D.D. (Retired).

Consultative Bodies—620 Lipan St., P.O. Box 2620, Corpus Christi, 78403-2620.

Council of Religious—Sr. ANNETTE WAGNER, I.W.B.S.

Deans—Rev. Msgr. LEONARD PIVONKA, J.C.D., Alice Deanery; Rev. LUKOSE THIRUNELLIPARAMABIL, Beeville Deanery; Rev. Msgrs. MARK CHAMBERLIN, Corpus Christi Central Deanery; LAWRENCE E. WHITE, Corpus Christi Westside Deanery; MORGAN J. ROWSOME, Fivepoints Deanery; TOM MCGETTRICK, Southside Deanery; Revs. JOHN C. OUELLETTE, Kingsville Deanery; PHILIP PANACKAL, Refugio Deanery.

College of Consultors—Rev. Msgr. Mark Chamberlin; Rev. Lukose Thirunelliparamabil; Very Rev. Joseph A. Lopez, J.C.L., Chancellor; Rev. Msgrs. Morgan J. Rowsome; Tom McGettrick; Rev. Philip Panackal; Rev. Msgrs. Leonard Pivonka, J.C.D.; Louis F. Kihneman III, V.G.; Lawrence E. White.

Diaconate Formation Screening Committee—Rev. Msgrs. Thomas P. Feeney, J.C.L.; Louis F. Kihneman III, V.G.; Elva Mantz, Recording Sec.; Deacons Paul Moore, Assoc. Dir. Deacons; Art Provencio, Assoc. Dir. Formation; Michael Mantz, Dir. Deacons; John R. Joiner, Dir. Formation; Bill Boastrom; Rick Gonzalez.

Finance Council—Most Rev. Wm. Michael Mulvey, S.T.L., D.D.; Rev. Msgrs. Louis F. Kihneman III, V.G.; Morgan J. Rowsome; Very Rev. Joseph A. Lopez, J.C.L., Chancellor; Deacon Adelfino Palacios Jr.; Mrs. Robin Perrone, CPA; Mr. Mike McLellan; Mr. Tom Carlisle. Consultants: Mr. Greg Seagrave; Mr. Gary A. Ramirez; Mr. Paul A. Damerow, CPA; Marco Crawford, Vice Chancellor.

Building Commission—Most Rev. Wm. Michael Mulvey, S.T.L., D.D.; Rev. Msgr. Louis F. Kihneman III, V.G.; Mr. Greg Seagrave, Chm.; Mr. Bud Colwell, P.E.; Mr. James Rome, ARCH. (Retired); Mr. Mike Lippincott; Mr. Ted Stephens; Jimmy Earnest; Leo Farias. Consultant: Mr. Jeff Kisel.

Personnel Board - Priests—Most Rev. Wm. Michael Mulvey, S.T.L., D.D.; Rev. Msgrs. Louis F. Kihneman III, V.G., Chm.; Michael Heras; Very Rev. Emilio B. Jimenez, Vice Chm.; Revs. Bob Dunn; Philip Panackal.

Presbyteral Council—Rev. Msgrs. Roger R. Smith; Mark Chamberlin; Rev. Lukose Thirunelliparamabil; Rev. Msgr. Michael Howell; Very Rev. Joseph A. Lopez, J.C.L., Chancellor; Rev. Peter Stanley, Sec.; Rev. Msgr. Louis F. Kihneman III, V.G.; Rev. John C. Ouellette; Rev. Msgr. Marcos Martinez; Revs. Raynaldo Yrlas Jr.; Peter G. Martinez, Chm.; Rev. Msgrs. Thomas P. Feeney, J.C.L.; Tom McGettrick; Revs. Patrick K. Donohoe, Vice Chm.; Philip Panackal; Rev. Msgrs. Leonard Pivonka, J.C.D.; Lawrence E. White; Morgan J. Rowsome; Very Rev. Emilio B. Jimenez, Vicar for Priests.

Tribunal—Rev. Msgr. Thomas P. Feeney, J.C.L., Judicial Vicar, 620 Lipan St., P.O. Box 2620, Corpus Christi, 78403-2620. Tel: 361-882-6191; Fax: 361-693-6782.

Judges—Rev. Msgrs. Thomas P. Feeney, J.C.L.; Leonard Pivonka, J.C.D.; Rev. James Hamilton (Retired); Very Rev. Joseph A. Lopez, J.C.L.; Rev. Msgrs. Michael Howell; Roger R. Smith; Mark Chamberlin.

Defenders of the Bond—Rev. Msgr. Richard Shirley, P.A., V.E.; Rev. Angel Montano, J.C.L.

Notaries-Secretaries—Belinda Harris; Olga Rodriguez.

Instructor—Vacant.

Administrative Offices

The Chancery Office—620 Lipan St., P.O. Box 2620, Corpus Christi, 78403-2620. Tel: 361-882-6191; Fax: 361-882-1018 (Admin.); 361-693-6753 (Fiscal Office); 361-693-6726 (Bishop's Office). Email: chancery@diocesecc.org. Web: www.diocesecc.org. Office Hours: Mon.-Fri. 8:30-5. Closed holy days and holidays.

Office of the Bishop—Most Rev. Wm. Michael Mulvey, S.T.L., D.D.

Office of the Bishop Emeritus—Most Revs. Edmond Carmody, D.D. (Retired); Rene H. Gracida, D.D. (Retired).

Canonical Affairs—Rev. Msgr. Thomas P. Feeney, J.C.L.

Executive Administrative Assistant to the Bishop—Martina Davila.

Priest Secretary to the Bishop—Very Rev. Joseph A. Lopez, J.C.L.

Vicar General—Rev. Msgr. Louis F. Kihneman III, V.G.

Executive Administrative Assistant to Vice General & Chancellor—Nancy Aleman.

Judicial Vicar—Rev. Msgr. Thomas P. Feeney, J.C.L.

Director Human Resources and Personnel—Marco Crawford.

Office for Permanent Diaconate—Deacons Michael Mantz, 1200 Lantana St., Kolbe Center, Corpus Christi, 78407-2454. Tel: 361-289-2343; Fax: 361-289-2454; Paul Moore, Assoc. Dir. Diaconate.

Vicar for Priests—Very Rev. Emilio B. Jimenez.

Chancellor—Very Rev. Joseph A. Lopez, J.C.L.

Family Life Office—Deacon Stephen Nolte.

Fiscal Officer—Mr. Greg Seagrave.

Controller—Mr. Paul A. Damerow, CPA.

Office of Parish Stewardship and Development—Cande De Leon, Dir.

Information Technology Services—Lee Alvarado, MIS Technical Dir.

Web Development Office—Alfredo Cardenas.

Real Property Office—Cy Richards, Mgr.

Propagation of the Faith Office—Rev. Raynaldo Yrlas Jr.

Seminary Formation & Vocations—Very Rev. Joseph A. Lopez, J.C.L., Dir. Vocations.

Archives—Cy Richards, Archivist, 1200 Lantana St., Corpus Christi, 78407. Tel: 361-855-2345 Mon.-Thurs. 9-2.

Catholic Schools Office—Mr. Rene Gonzalez, Supt.

Catholic Cemeteries—Mr. Greg Seagrave.

Office for Child and Youth Protection (OCYP)—Stephanie Bonilla.

Office of Communications—Marty Wind, Dir. Communications, 1200 Lantana, Corpus Christi, 78407. Tel: 361-289-6437; Fax: 361-289-1420.

Newspaper "The South Texas Catholic"—Most Rev. Wm. Michael Mulvey, S.T.L., D.D., Publisher; Alfredo Cardenas, Editor; Very Rev. Joseph A. Lopez, J.C.L., Theological Consultant.

Office for Persons with Disabilities—Managers: Celia Mendez; Aurora Martinez, 1322 Comanche, Corpus Christi, 78401. Tel: 361-814-2181; Fax: 361-654-2020.

Department of Catechesis and Religious Education—Margaret Alarilla, Dir.

Office of Young Adult and Campus Ministry—Adam Koll, Dir.

Office of Youth Ministry—Jaime Reyna, Dir.

Diocese of Corpus Christi Perpetual Benefit Endowment Fund, Inc.—Mailing Address: P.O. Box 2620, Corpus Christi, 78403-2620. Tel: 361-882-6191.

Diocese of Corpus Christi Deposit and Loan Fund, Inc.—Mailing Address: P.O. Box 2620, Corpus Christi, 78403-2620. Tel: 361-882-6191.

Office of Worship—Rev. Pedro T. Elizardo Jr., Dir.

Jail and Prison Ministry—Deacon Cristobal E. Luna Jr., Coord., Mailing Address: P.O. Box 2620, Corpus Christi, 78403-2620. Tel: 361-449-8876.

Other Offices and Organizations

Alhambra—Mike Caspar, Grand Commander, 5280 CR 3865, Taft, 78390. Tel: 361-854-4638; Sharron Odle, Grand Sultana, 309 Palmetto Dr., Corpus Christi, 78412. Tel: 361-991-7656.

Blue Army (World Apostolate of Fatima)—Mrs. Martha Majek, Pres., 12126 Up River Rd., Corpus Christi, 78410. Tel: 361-242-1533.

Campus Ministries—Texas A&M University-Kingsville, St. Thomas Aquinas University Catholic Center, 1119 Santa Gertrudis, Kingsville, 78363. Tel: 361-592-7831; Fax: 362-592-8617. *Del Mar College, St. Thomas More, 2045 18th St., Corpus Christi, 78404.* Tel: 361-883-9308. *The Cardinal John Henry Newman Catholic Student Center, at Texas A&M Univ.-Corpus Christi, 7002 Ocean Dr., Corpus Christi, 78412.* Tel: 361-993-5898.

Catholic Daughters of the Americas—Mary E. Gonzalez, Dist. 16, Corpus Christi. Tel: 361-854-0688; Diana Garcia, Dist. 36, Odem. Tel: 361-368-3521; Alicia Rodrigues, Dist. 47, Taft. Tel: 361-528-2683; Frances Salazar, Dist. 41, Corpus Christi. Tel: 361-993-6654; Eve Trevino, State Treas., Corpus Christi. Tel: 361-994-8553. Email: evetrevino@yahoo.com; Elva Pena, Dist. 48, Corpus Christi. Tel: 361-986-9679.

Catholic Charities—Mrs. Linda McKamie, Dir., 1322 Comanche, Corpus Christi, 78401. Tel: 361-884-0651; Fax: 361-884-3956.

The Catholic Charismatic Renewal Movement—Vacant.

Cursillo Movement—Irma Padilla, Pres. Secretariat. Tel: 361-688-2064.

English Cursillo—Dan Serrato, Dir. School. Tel: 361-815-6896.

Spanish Cursillo—Ofelia Garza, Dir. School. Tel: 361-756-1757.

Diocesan Council of Catholic Women—Rose Hickey, Pres., 1205 Palma St., Kingsville, 78364. Tel: 361-595-7663. Email: roseannahickey@yahoo.com; Rev. James Stembler, Spiritual Dir.

Diocesan Telecommunications Corporation—Marty Wind, Exec. Vice Pres. & Gen. Mgr., 1200 Lantana, Corpus Christi, 78407. Tel: 361-289-6437; Fax: 361-289-1420.

Disaster Relief—Mrs. Linda McKamie, Dir., 1322 Comanche St., Corpus Christi, 78401. Tel: 361-884-0651.

Emergency Aid—Sylvia Ortiz, Mgr., 1322 Comanche, Corpus Christi, 78401. Tel: 361-884-0651.

Family Counseling—Ms. Gloria Garcia, Mgr., 1322 Comanche St., Corpus Christi, 78401. Tel: 361-884-0651.

Housing Counseling—Doreya Dean, Mgr., 1322 Comanche St., Corpus Christi, 78401. Tel: 361-884-0651.

Catholic Singles in Christ—Deacon Stephen Nolte, Dir. Tel: 361-882-6191.

Representative Payee—Elsa Ortiz, Mgr., 1322 Comanche St., Corpus Christi, 78401. Tel: 361-884-0651.

Catholic Engaged Encounter—Deacon Stephen Nolte, Dir. Tel: 361-882-6191.

Immigration Services—Carolyn Thompson, Mgr. & Attorney, 1322 Comanche, Corpus Christi, 78401. Tel: 361-884-0651.

Knights of Columbus—Tom Garcia, Diocesan Deputy, 132 Whistlers Cove Dr., Rockport, 78382. Tel: 361-727-9814.

Legion of Mary—Viann Hermann, Pres., 610 Wilshire Pl., Corpus Christi, 78411. Tel: 361-855-8321; Deacon Solomon Willis, Spiritual Dir.

Marriage Encounter—Deacon Stephen Nolte, Dir. Contact Persons: Rolando R. Garza; Nelda Garza, Corpus Christi, 78407. Tel: 361-851-8306.

Radio Stations - KLUX FM—Russel Wayne Martin, Dir. Broadcast Oper., 1200 Lantana St., Corpus Christi, 78407. Tel: 361-289-2487.

Serra International—Mr. Wilburn H. Fischer, District Governor, Dist. 126, 4902 Elmhurst, Corpus Christi, 78413. Tel: 361-993-4881; Mr. Cliff Zarsky, Pres., 5202 Woolridge, Corpus Christi, 78407. Tel: 361-991-7465.

Theresians—Mrs. Helen Patrem, Team Leader, 625 Gregory #14, Corpus Christi, 78412. Tel: 361-980-8818.

Victim Assistance Coordinator—Kristi Skrobarczyk. Tel: 361-882-6191; Fax: 361-882-1018. Email: kskrobarczyk@diocesecc.org.

CLERGY, PARISHES, MISSIONS AND PAROCHIAL SCHOOLS

CITY OF CORPUS CHRISTI

(Nueces County)

1—Corpus Christi Cathedral (1853) [CEM] Revs. Pedro (Pete) T. Elizardo Jr., Rector; Gabriel P. Coelho (India); Deacons Michael Mantz; Adelfino Palacios Jr. In Res., Rev. Msgr. Louis F. Kihneman III.
Res.: 505 N. Upper Broadway, 78401. Tel: 361-883-4213; Fax: 361-883-1918. Email: info@cccathedral.com. Web: www.cccathedral.com.
Catechesis/Religious Program—Tel: 361-883-4213. Email: religioused@ccathedral.com. Students 221.
Chapel—Emmanuel, (Crypt)
Chapel—Blessed Sacrament

2—Saint Andrew By the Sea Parish (1986) Rev. Msgr. Tom McGettrick.
Res.: 14238 Encantada Ave., 78418-6432. Tel: 361-949-7193; Fax: 361-949-0717. Email: standrewcc@stx.rr.com.
Catechesis/Religious Program—Tel: 361-949-8834. Students 123.

3—St. Anselm Anglican Use Community (1992) Rev. Jean F. Hart, S.O.L.T.
Church: 1200 Lantana St., 78407-1112. Tel: 361-289-0807; Fax: 361-289-1402. Email: frjeanhart@hotmail.com.

4—Christ the King (1946) Revs. Glen F. Mullan; Kuriakose Ouseph (India); Deacon Israel Blanco.
Res.: 3423 Rojo, 78415. Tel: 361-883-2821; Fax: 361-888-7048.
Catechesis/Religious Program—Tel: 361-883-2821. Natasha Rios, D.R.E. Students 45.
Convent—

5—SS. Cyril and Methodius (1947), (Hispanic), Rev. Msgr. Lawrence E. White, Pastor; Rev. Peter Stanley, Vicar; Deacon Ron Dubuque.
Rectory—Rectory & Office: 3210 S. Padre Island Dr., 78415. Tel: 361-853-7371; Fax: 361-851-1438.
Catechesis/Religious Program—Tel: 361-852-1651. Mona Lucido, D.R.E. Students 481.

6—Holy Cross (1914), (African American), Rev. Arularasu Mathias (India), Admin.
Res.: 1109 N. Staples St., 78401. Tel: 361-888-4012; Fax: 361-883-2670. Email: holycrosscorchr@sbcglobal.net.
Catechesis/Religious Program—Students 27.

7—Holy Family (1946), (Hispanic), Revs. Patrick K. Donohoe; Joseph Nirmal Kumar (India), Vicar; Juan Fernando Gomez (Colombia).
Office: 2509 Nogales St., 78416. Tel: 361-882-3245; Fax: 361-882-4968. Email: holyfamilycatholicchurch@bizstx.rr.com. Web: www.holyfamilycc.net.
Priest's Res.: 2530 Presa, 78416.
Catechesis/Religious Program—Tel: 361-882-3245, Ext. 21. Email: Ianes@bizstx.rr.com. Students 299.

8—Saint John the Baptist (2001) Rev. Rodolfo D.

Vasquez, Admin.; Deacon Loni G. Lugo.
Mailing Address: 7522 Everhart Rd., 78413. Tel: 361-991-4400; Fax: 361-991-4401. Email: churchoffice@sjbcctx.org. Web: www.sjbcctx.org.
Rectory—4809 Lake Nocona, 78413. Tel: 361-993-7079.
Catechesis/Religious Program—Students 300.

9—ST. JOSEPH (1950), (Hispanic), Revs. Angel Montana; Joseph Lawless, M.S.F., Vicar; Deacons Reynaldo Rojas; Carlos Alvarado.
710 S. 19th St., P.O. Box 5196, 78465-5196.
Catechesis/Religious Program—Michelle Padilla, D.R.E. Students 156.

10—ST. MICHAEL THE ARCHANGEL LATIN MASS COMMUNITY (1995) Rev. Donald Downey, J.C.L.
Church, Res. & Mailing Address: 4130 S. Alameda, 78411. Tel: 361-446-1967 (Res.).
Catechesis/Religious Program—

11—MOST PRECIOUS BLOOD (1966) Revs. Bob Dunn; Kris Bauta, Vicar; Deacons Ken Bockholt; Sebastian Landagan; Frank N. Newchurch; Erick Simeus.
Res.: 3502 Saratoga Blvd., 78415. Tel: 361-854-3800; Fax: 361-854-9253. Email: mpb@mpbchurch.org. Web: www.mpbchurch.org.
Catechesis/Religious Program—Tel: 361-854-9219. Students 676.

12—NUESTRA SENORA DE SAN JUAN DE LOS LAGOS, MADRE DE LA IGLESIA (2010) Rev. Henry Artunduaga (Colombia), Admin.; Deacon Manuel Maldonado.
Mailing Address: 1755 Frio St., 78417. Tel: 361-852-0249; Fax: 361-852-8463.
Catechesis/Religious Program—Students 125.

13—OUR LADY OF GUADALUPE (1969) Rev. Salvatore James Farfaglia.
Res.: 540 Hiawatha, 78405. Tel: 361-882-1951; Fax: 361-888-5813.
Catechesis/Religious Program—Emma Botello, D.R.E. Students 227.

14—OUR LADY OF MOUNT CARMEL (1969) Rev. Sebastian Pasupalety (India), Admin.
Church: 1080 S. Clarkwood Rd., 78406. Tel: 361-265-0610; Fax: 361-265-0757. Email: pasupalety@gmail.com.
Catechesis/Religious Program—Students 58.
Mission—St. Vivian 3516 FM 665 W., Robstown, 78380. Tel: 361-767-5557; Fax: 361-767-5557.

15—OUR LADY OF PERPETUAL HELP (1954) Rev. Msgr. Michael Heras.
Mailing Address: 5830 Williams Dr., 78412. Tel: 361-991-7891; Fax: 361-993-1211. Email: msgrmh@olphcc.net. Web: www.olphcctex.org. In Res., Very Rev. Joseph A. Lopez, Chancellor & Vocation Dir.; Rev. Joseph Olikkara, M.S.T. (India).
Catechesis/Religious Program—Students 190.

16—OUR LADY OF PILAR (1964), (Hispanic), Rev. Msgr. Marcos Martinez; Deacon Armando M. Bolanos.
Res.: 1101 Bloomington St., 78416. Tel: 361-852-6327; Fax: 361-852-6843. Email: pillarchurch@stx.rr.com.
Catechesis/Religious Program—Students 327.

17—OUR LADY OF THE ROSARY (1967) Rev. Varghese Antony (India), Admin.
Res.: 1123 Main Dr., 78409. Tel: 361-241-2004; 361-242-9571; Fax: 361-242-1099. Email: olrosary@awesomenet.net.
Catechesis/Religious Program—Students 16.

18—OUR LADY STAR OF THE SEA (1950) Rev. Eulalio (Yul) P. Ibay, Admin.
Office: 3110 E. Causeway Blvd., P.O. Box 1899, 78403. Tel: 361-883-4507; Fax: 361-888-6411.
Catechesis/Religious Program—Students 25.

19—ST. PATRICK (1944) Rev. Msgr. Roger R. Smith; Rev. Patrick G. Higgins (Ireland), Vicar; Deacon Eleazar (Larry) Rodriguez.
Res.: 3350 S. Alameda St., 78411. Tel: 361-855-7391; Fax: 361-853-4790. Email: stpatrickschurch@bizstx.rr.com.
Catechesis/Religious Program—Tel: 361-855-7567. Students 560.

20—ST. PAUL THE APOSTLE (1967) Rev. Peter G. Martinez; Deacons Edward Nartowicz; Michael T. Noble.
Res.: 2233 Waldron Rd., 78418. Tel: 361-937-3864; Fax: 361-939-7774.
Catechesis/Religious Program—Tel: 361-937-6908. Sr. Victoria Cambronero, O.P., D.R.E. Students 240.

21—ST. PETER PRINCE OF APOSTLES (1967) Rev. Msgr. Morgan J. Rowsome.
Rectory & Office: 3901 Violet Rd., 78410-2924. Tel: 361-241-3249; Fax: 361-241-0533. Email: camolin@swbell.net. Web: www.stpeterprince.net.
Catechesis/Religious Program—Tel: 361-241-3372. Priscilla Chapa, D.R.E. Students 641.
Mission—St. Mary 4849 Cynthia, Nueces Co. 78410. Tel: 361-241-3432.

22—ST. PHILIP THE APOSTLE (1982) Rev. Hanh Van Pham; Deacons Paul Moore; Bob Allen.
Res.: 3513 Cimarron Rd., 78414. Tel: 361-815-0505. Web: www.stphilipcc.com.
Church: 3513 Cimarron Rd., 78414. Tel: 361-991-5146; Fax: 361-991-9135.
Catechesis/Religious Program—Tel: 361-993-1710. Katie Tipton, D.R.E. Students 520.

23—ST. PIUS X (1963) Revs. Paul A. Hesse; Joseph T. Nguyen, Vicar; Deacon Salvador Alvarado.
Res.: 5620 Gollihar Rd., 78412. Tel: 361-993-4053; Fax: 361-992-0352. Email: wtoledo@stpiusxcc.org. Web: stpiusxcc.org.
Catechesis/Religious Program—Tel: 361-993-9024. Students 330.

24—SACRED HEART (1916), (Hispanic), [CEM] Rev. Jairo Motta (Colombia).
Res.: 422 N. Alameda St., 78401-2604. Tel: 361-883-6082; Fax: 361-883-6248. Email: sacredheartchurch001@stx.rr.com.
Catechesis/Religious Program—Tel: 361-882-1472. Students 85.
Station—Nueces County Jail, Tel: 361-887-2300.
Station—Navarro Place, Tel: 361-882-4924.

25—SAINT HELENA OF THE TRUE CROSS OF JESUS (2001) Rev. William Marquis.
Mailing Address: P.O. Box 81210, 78468-1210.
Res. & Office: 7634 Wooldridge Rd., 78414. Tel: 361-994-8783; Fax: 361-994-7918. Email: truecross@sbcglobal.net. Web: www.StHelenacctx.org.
Catechesis/Religious Program—Tel: 361-994-8783, Ext. 21. Email: arsegovia15@gmail.com. Ada Segovia, D.R.E. Students 78.

26—ST. THERESA (1947) Rev. Randy N. Cain.
Res.: 1302 Lantana St., 78407. Tel: 361-289-2759; Fax: 361-299-2018.
Catechesis/Religious Program—Tel: 361-289-2238. Mrs. Josie Martinez, D.R.E. Students 73.

27—ST. THOMAS MORE PARISH (1990) Rev. Tomasz Kozub (Poland).
Church: 2045 18th St., 78404-3862. Tel: 361-888-9308; Fax: 361-888-6119.
Catechesis/Religious Program—Students 110.

OUTSIDE THE CITY OF CORPUS CHRISTI

AGUA DULCE, NUECES CO., ST. FRANCES OF ROME (1934), (Czech—Hispanic), Rev. Jacob John Valayath (India).
Mailing Address: P.O. Box 598, 78330. Tel: 361-998-2216; Fax: 361-236-4187. 410 Simmons St., 78330.
Catechesis/Religious Program—Students 105.

ALICE, JIM WELLS CO.

1—ST. ELIZABETH OF HUNGARY (1918) Rev. Msgr. Leonard Pivonka; Deacon James A. Carlisle.
Office: 603 E. 5th St., 78332. Tel: 361-664-6481; Fax: 361-664-7243. Email: steliz@stx.rr.com.
Res.: 518 N. Almond St., P.O. Box 1009, 78333.
School—615 E. 5th St., 78332. Tel: 361-664-6271; Fax: 361-668-4250. Email: smgarcia@myctsonline.com. Web: www.stelizabeth-.tx.schoolwebpages.com. Faculty 23; Students 183.
Catechesis/Religious Program—Tel: 361-664-7719. Students 152.

2—ST. JOSEPH (1911) Rev. Richard A. Libby.
Res. & Office: 801 S. Reynolds St., 78332. Tel: 361-664-7551; Fax: 361-664-2388. Email: sj-church@sbcglobal.net.
School—Students 204.
Catechesis/Religious Program—311 Dewey St. & 801 S. Reynolds, 78332. Students 176.
Chapel—Perpetual Eucharistic Adoration

3—OUR LADY OF GUADALUPE (1969), (Hispanic), Rev. Encarnacion J. Cabrera, Admin.
Res.: 1318 Guerra St., P.O. Box 411, 78333. Tel: 361-664-2953; Fax: 361-664-4001 (Church Office).
Catechesis/Religious Program—Tel: 361-664-0437. Sr. Claudia X. Ongpin, O.P., D.R.E. Students 515.
Mission—Santo Nino De Atocha P.O. Box 411, Jim Wells Co. 78333.

ARANSAS PASS, SAN PATRICIO CO., ST. MARY, STAR OF THE SEA (1948) Rev. Roy Jacob Kalayil (India), Admin.
Res.: 342 S. Rife St., 78336. Tel: 361-758-2662; Fax: 361-758-3964.
Catechesis/Religious Program—Sonya Gomez. Students 145.

BANQUETE, NUECES CO., SAINT MICHAEL THE ARCHANGEL (1857) [JC] Rev. J. Patrick Serna.
Mailing Address: 4325 Fourth St., P.O. Box 9, 78339. Tel: 361-387-8371; Fax: 361-387-7607. Email: archangelbanquete@yahoo.com. Web: www.stmichaelbanquete.com.
Catechesis/Religious Program—

BEEVILLE, BEE CO.

1—ST. JAMES (Alta Vista) (1966), (Hispanic), Rev. Balaswamy Pasala (India); Deacon Juan Vasquez.
Res.: 605 S. Alta Vista, 78102. Tel: 361-358-4825; Fax: 361-354-5757. Email: st.james2002@sbcglobal.net.
Catechesis/Religious Program—Juanita L. Martinez, D.R.E. Students 80.

2—ST. JOSEPH (1895) [CEM] Rev. Richard Gonzales; Deacons Russell W. Duggins; Paul Matula; Luis Trevino; Rolando R. Salazar.
Res.: 609 E. Gramman St., 78102. Tel: 361-358-3239; Fax: 361-358-4270. Email: staff@stjosephbeeville.org. Web: www.stjosephbeeville.org.
Catechesis/Religious Program—Santos R. Jones III, Dir. Faith Formation-High School; Debra Olivares, Dir. Faith Formation-Elementary. Students 270.

3—OUR LADY OF VICTORY (1908) [CEM 2] Rev. Lukose Thirunelliparamabil (India).
Mailing Address: 707 North Ave. E., 78102. Tel: 361-358-0088; Fax: 361-358-2028. Email: churcholv@yahoo.com.
Rectory—403 W. Carter St., 78102. Tel: 361-364-7172; Fax: 361-358-2028.
Catechesis/Religious Program—Email: iantha432@yahoo.com. Mary Jane Keller, D.R.E. Students 138.

BENAVIDES, DUVAL CO., SANTA ROSA DE LIMA (1941), (Hispanic), Rev. Johnson J. Machado (India), Admin.
Res.: 203 Santa Rosa de Lima St., P.O. Drawer W, 78341. Tel: 361-256-3427; Fax: 361-355-4762.
Catechesis/Religious Program—Tel: 361-256-3319. Marleigh Martinez, D.R.E. Students 100.
Mission—St. Joseph P.O. Box W, San Jose Ranch, Duval Co. 78341.
Mission—Sacred Heart P.O. Box W, Realitos, Duval Co. 78376.

BEN BOLT, JIM WELLS, CO., ST. PETER MISSION (1927) Rev. Cyriac John (India), Admin.
Mailing Address: 221 Salazar Ave., P.O. Box 678, 78342. Tel: 361-664-1688; Fax: 361-664-1688. Email: benboltparish@yahoo.com. Web: www.stpeterparishofbenbolt.com.
Catechesis/Religious Program—Students 65.

BISHOP, NUECES CO., ST. JAMES (1938) [CEM] Rev. Ryszard Andrzej Koziol (Poland), Admin.
Res.: 601 W. 3rd St., P.O. Box 843, 78343. Tel: 361-584-3250; Fax: 361-584-1046. Email: ryszardkoziol@poczta.onet.pl.
Catechesis/Religious Program—Students 131.
Mission—St. James 310 W. Ave. B, Driscoll, Nueces Co. 78351. Fax: 361-584-1046.

EDROY, SAN PATRICIO CO., OUR LADY OF GUADALUPE MISSION (1934) Rev. Varghese Kolencheril (India), Admin.
Mailing Address: P.O. Box 127, 78352. Tel: 361-368-3097; Fax: 361-368-2934. Email: edroyolg@gmail.com.
Catechesis/Religious Program—Students 36.

FALFURRIAS, BROOKS CO., SACRED HEART (1914), (Hispanic), [CEM] Rev. Matthew J. Stephan; Deacon Ricardo E. Costley.
Res.: 304 S. Caldwell St., 78355. Tel: 361-325-3455; Fax: 361-325-2486.
Catechesis/Religious Program— Joan Bostwick, D.R.E. Students 300.
Mission—St. Ann c/o Sacred Heart Parish, Encino, Brooks Co. 78355.

FREER, DUVAL CO., ST. MARY (1968) Rev. Carlos Alberto Bolivar (Colombia), Admin.; Deacons Eluterio Bitoni; Pete Trevino Jr.; Mary Alice Casas, Sec.; Violet Loney, Bookkeeper.
Res.: 1500 Duval St., P.O. Drawer B, 78357. Tel: 361-394-6832; Fax: 361-394-6568.
Catechesis/Religious Program—Students 186.

GEORGE WEST, LIVE OAK CO., ST. GEORGE (1924) Rev. George Johnson (India), Admin.
Oratory— [CEM] [JC] 304 Crockett St., P.O. Box 580, Live Oak Co. 78022. Tel: 361-449-1893; Fax: 361-449-1886.
Catechesis/Religious Program— Evangelina Alaniz, D.R.E.; Cris Luna, D.R.E. Students 133.
Mission—St. Joseph [CEM] [JC] Gussetville, Live Oak Co. Fax: 361-449-1886.

GREGORY, SAN PATRICIO CO., IMMACULATE CONCEPTION (1926), (Hispanic), Revs. Raju Thottankara (India); Jose Ortiz, Vicar; Deacon Juan Gomez.
Res.: 107 Church St., P.O. Box 108, 78359-0108. Tel: 361-643-8327; Fax: 361-643-1509.
Catechesis/Religious Program—Email: iccgregory@yahoo.com. Web: www.iccgregory.org. Students 422.

INGLESIDE, SAN PATRICIO CO., OUR LADY OF THE ASSUMPTION (1970) Rev. Thomas Wellar; Deacon Art Provenecio. In Res., Rev. Thomas L. Goodwin.
Res.: 2414 Main, 78362. Tel: 361-776-2446; Fax: 361-776-3963.
Catechesis/Religious Program—Students 262.

KINGSVILLE, KLEBERG CO.

1—ST. GERTRUDE (1908) Revs. James Stembler; John Chavarria; Deacons John R. Joiner; Edwin N. Rowley.
Res. & Office: 1120 S. 8th St., 78363. Tel: 361-592-7351; Fax: 361-592-0028.
School—Tel: 361-592-6522; Fax: 361-592-0100. Students 93.
Catechesis/Religious Program—Tel: 361-592-2443. Sr. Colette Brehony, I.W.B.S., D.R.E. Students 160.

2—ST. JOSEPH (1973), (Hispanic), Rev. Romeo Salinas; Deacons Ricardo Gonzalez; Ricardo B. Morin.

1400 Brookshire, P.O. Box 1602, 78364-1602.
Catechesis/Religious Program—Fax: 361-516-1397. Sylvia Molina, D.R.E. Students 216.
3—ST. MARTIN (1914), (Hispanic), Revs. Jose Naul Ordonez (Colombia); P. R. Victor, Parochial Vicar; Deacons Tiburcio Garcia; Raul G. Rosales.
Res.: 715 N. Eighth St., 78363. Tel: 361-592-4602; Fax: 361-592-0881. Email: stmartincatholic@sbcglobal.net.
Catechesis/Religious Program—Tel: 361-592-0881. Gloria DeLeon, D.R.E. Students 120.
Convent—919 N. Ninth St., 78363. Tel: 361-595-1087. Sisters 10.
Mission—Christ the King King Ranch, Kleberg Co.
4—OUR LADY OF GOOD COUNSEL (1954) [CEM 3] [JC] Rev. Peter Thenan (India), Admin.
Res.: 1102 E. Kleberg, 78363. Tel: 361-592-3489; Fax: 361-592-6370. Email: ourlady78363@gmail.com.
Catechesis/Religious Program—Mary A. Pena, D.R.E. Students 184.
5—ST. THOMAS AQUINAS, CATHOLIC CENTER (TEXAS A&M UNIVERSITY KINGSVILLE) Revs. James Stembler; John Chavarria; Deacon John R. Joiner.
Mailing Address: P.O. Box 2193, 78363.
Res.: 1120 S. 8th St., 78363. Tel: 361-592-5781.
Church: 1119 W. Santa Gertrudis, P.O. Box 2193, 78363.
MATHIS, SAN PATRICIO CO.
1—SAINT PATRICK MISSION (1829) [CEM] Rev. George Thomas (India), Admin.
Res.: 20742 Magnolia, 78368. Tel: 361-547-5748; Fax: 361-547-8004.
Catechesis/Religious Program—Students 26.
2—ST. PIUS X MISSION - SANDIA (1955) Rev. George Thomas (India), Admin.
20742 Magnolia, 78368-4456. Tel: 361-547-5748; Fax: 361-547-8004. Email: stpatrick@gtek.biz.
Catechesis/Religious Program—Students 50.
3—SACRED HEART (1942) [JC] Revs. James Putenparambil (India), Admin.; Juan Fernando Gomez (Colombia), Vicar.
Office & Res.: 217 W. San Patricio Ave., 78368-2259. Tel: 361-547-9181; Fax: 361-547-6111.
Catechesis/Religious Program—Jean McLerran, D.R.E. Students 414.
ODEM, SAN PATRICIO CO., SACRED HEART (1934) Rev. Isaias Estepa (Colombia), Admin.
Res.: 401 W. Willis St., P.O. Box 276, 78370. Tel: 361-368-9156; Fax: 361-368-2746. Email: sacredheartodem@yahoo.com.
Catechesis/Religious Program—Tel: 361-368-2746. Anita Lunoff, D.R.E. Students 316.
ORANGE GROVE, JIM WELLS CO., ST. JOHN OF THE CROSS (1925) [CEM] Rev. Prince Kuruvila (India).
Mailing Address: 200 S. Metz St., P.O. Box 329, 78372. Tel: 361-384-2795; Fax: 361-384-0056. Email: saintjohn0003@aol.com.
Catechesis/Religious Program—Tel: 361-384-0056. Students 225.
Mission—St. Francis of Assisi Mission Mailing Address: 303 FM 534, Sandia, Jim Wells Co. 78383. Tel: 361-547-2510; Fax: 361-547-2442. 303 FM 534 at County Rd. 185, Lagarto, 78371.
PETTUS, BEE CO., SACRED HEART MISSION (1916), (Independent) Rev. Joseph Varghese Vakayil, Admin.; Deacon Manuel G. Carranco.
Mailing Address: 104 N. Bee St., P.O. Box 414, 78146-0414. Tel: 361-375-2512. Email: vakayilachan@yahoo.com.
PORT ARANSAS, NUECES CO., ST. JOSEPH (1860) [JC] Rev. John Xaviour Amepparambil (India), Admin.
Mailing Address: 412 Lantana St., 78373. Tel: 361-749-5825; Fax: 361-749-5509. Email: saintjosephchurch@centurytel.net.
Catechesis/Religious Program—Students 32.
PORTLAND, SAN PATRICIO CO., OUR LADY OF MOUNT CARMEL (1961) Rev. Msgr. Mark Chamberlin; Rev. Jerome G. Zurovetz, Vicar.
Res.: 1008 Austin St., 78374. Tel: 361-643-7533; Fax: 361-643-5544. Email: olmc61@ainternet.biz.
Catechesis/Religious Program—Tel: 361-643-3548. Mrs. Melanee Warner, D.R.E. Students 366.
PREMONT, JIM WELLS CO., ST. THERESA OF THE INFANT JESUS (1958) Rev. John C. Ouellette; Deacon Javier Gonzalez.
Res.: 235 S.W. 4th St., P.O. Box 569, 78375. Tel: 361-348-2202; Fax: 361-348-3533. Email: st-theresas@stx.rr.com. Web: www.st-theresas.com.
Catechesis/Religious Program—Students 90.
Mission—Immaculate Conception Concepcion, Duval Co.
Mission—St. Francis of Assisi Rios, Duval Co.
Mission—Our Lady of Guadalupe Ramirez, Duval Co.
REFUGIO, REFUGIO CO.
1—ST. JAMES THE APOSTLE (1886) [CEM] [JC] Rev. John McKenzie.
Mailing Address: 202 E. Santiago St., 78377.
Catechesis/Religious Program—Tel: 361-526-4454; Fax: 361-526-2714. Students 97.
Mission—St. Catherine Mission Hwy. 2441.
2—OUR LADY OF REFUGE (1795) [CEM] [JC] Rev. Philip Panackal (India).
Res. & Office: 1008 S. Alamo St., 78377. Tel: 361-526-2083; Fax: 361-526-5653. Email: olrefuge@yahoo.com.
Catechesis/Religious Program—106 W. Roca, 78377. Tel: 361-526-2053. Students 81.
RIVIERA, KLEBER CO., OUR LADY OF CONSOLATION (1914), (German), [CEM] [JC] Rev. Peter Antony (India), Admin.
Res. & Office: 204 Palm Ave., 78379. Tel: 361-297-5255; Fax: 361-297-5155.
Catechesis/Religious Program—Students 69.
Mission—Our Lady of Guadalupe 111 S. Second St., Kleberg Co. 78379.
Mission—Sacred Heart W. County Rd. 2160, Ricardo, Kleberg Co. 78363.
ROBSTOWN, NUECES CO.
1—ST. ANTHONY (1914), (Hispanic), [CEM] Revs. Anthony Blount, S.O.L.T.; Michael Edward Crump, S.O.L.T., Parochial Vicar; George Nedeff, S.O.L.T., Parochial Vicar; Miguel A. Noyola, S.O.L.T. (Guatemala), Parochial Vicar; Deacon Wayne Lickteig, S.O.L.T.
Res.: 204 Dunne St., P.O. Box 792, 78380-0792. Tel: 361-767-1705; 361-387-2774; Fax: 361-387-5114.
Catechesis/Religious Program—Tel: 361-387-9874. Eva Hernandez, D.R.E. Students 175.
Mission—St. Mary, Nueces Co. Fax: 361-387-5114.
2—ST. JOHN NEPOMUCENE (1924), (Czech), [JC] Rev. Thomas Showalter, S.O.L.T.
Res.: 603 N. First St., 78380. Tel: 361-387-3705; Fax: 361-387-3681. Email: frtomshowalter@gmail.com.
Catechesis/Religious Program—Felipe Salazar, D.R.E. Students 50.
3—ST. THOMAS THE APOSTLE (1980) Rev. Msgr. Michael Howell; Deacon Bill Cleavelin.
Office: 16602 FM 624, 78380. Tel: 361-387-1312; Fax: 512-387-9311. Web: www.christon624.com.
Catechesis/Religious Program—Michele Hoelscher, D.R.E. Students 264.
ROCKPORT, ARANSAS CO.
1—ST. PETER'S PARISH (1989), (Vietnamese), [JC 2] Rev. Peter Nghi Duc Pham, S.O.L.T.
Mailing Address: P.O. Box 1060, 78382. Tel: 361-729-3008.
Catechesis/Religious Program—2761 FM 1781, 78381-1060. Tel: 361-549-7850. Students 17.
2—SACRED HEART (1838) Revs. Raynaldo Yrlas Jr.; Alejandro Saenz; Deacons Jerre H. Ledbetter; George Joe Wiest.
Res.: 704 E. Cornwall St., 78382. Tel: 361-729-2174; Fax: 361-729-1989. Email: shrockport@charter.net. Web: www.sacredheartchurchrockport.org.
Catechesis/Religious Program—Tel: 361-729-8283 (Rel. Educ. Office); 361-727-1333 (Youth Ministry Office); 361-729-9135 (Adult Ed Office); Fax: 361-729-1989. Email: reled@charter.net. Students 339.
Convent—114 N. Church St., 78382. Tel: 361-729-5311.
Mission—Tel: 361-729-9135. Aransas Co.
3—STELLA MARIS CHAPEL (1858) Rev. Ralph O. Jones, Admin.
P.O. Box 1980, Fulton, 78358.
SAN DIEGO, DUVAL CO., ST. FRANCIS DE PAULA (1866) Revs. Benito Retortillo, O.P.; Epifanio Rodriguez, O.P., Vicar; Deacons Abelardo Garza; Carlos Tamayo.
Res.: 401 S. Victoria St., P.O. Box 279, 78384. Tel: 361-279-3596; Fax: 361-279-8288.
Catechesis/Religious Program—411 S. Victoria St., 78384. Tel: 361-279-3586. Students 390.
Mission—St. Joseph Palito Blanco, Jim Wells Co. 78384.
SARITA, KENEDY CO., OUR LADY OF GUADALUPE (1935) Rev. James Foelker, O.M.I., Admin.
Mailing Address: P.O. Box 6, 78385. Tel: 361-294-5350; Fax: 361-294-5406.
Catechesis/Religious Program—Students 14.
Mission—Santa Elena Norias Ranch, Kenedy Co.
SINTON, SAN PATRICIO CO.
1—OUR LADY OF GUADALUPE (1954), (Hispanic), [CEM] [JC] Rev. Shaji Varghese (India), Admin.
Res.: 725 Sodville Ave., 78387. Tel: 361-364-2210; Fax: 361-364-5204.
Catechesis/Religious Program—Tel: 361-364-4007. Students 317.
2—SACRED HEART (1916) Rev. Paul Rajareegam (India).
Res. & Office: 906 E. Sinton St., P.O. Box 266, 78387. Tel: 361-364-1768; Fax: 361-364-5325. Email: shsinton@yahoo.com.
Catechesis/Religious Program—Mary Connors, D.R.E.; Deacon Solomon T. Willis III, C.R.E. Students 233.
Mission—St. Paul P.O. Box 266, St. Paul, San Patricio Co. 78387.
SKIDMORE, BEE CO., IMMACULATE CONCEPTION (1915) [JC] Rev. Sebastian Vettath Thomas (India), Admin.
Res.: 600 First St., P.O. Box 189, 78389. Tel: 361-287-3256; Fax: 361-287-3696.
Catechesis/Religious Program—Students 43.
Mission—St. Francis Xavier Frio St., Tynan, Bee Co. 78384.
TAFT, SAN PATRICIO CO.
1—HOLY FAMILY (1957) [JC] Rev. Dennis P. Zerr, Admin.
Mailing Address: P.O. Box 173, 78390. Tel: 361-528-3132; Fax: 361-528-3209.
Office: 701 Fetick, 78390.
Res.: 646 McIntyre Ave., 78390. Tel: 361-528-3075.
Catechesis/Religious Program—Students 120.
2—IMMACULATE CONCEPTION (1928) Rev. Jesus Francisco Lopez.
Res. & Mailing Address: 120 E. Escobedo, P.O. Box 868, 78390. Tel: 361-528-2626; Fax: 361-528-3907.
Catechesis/Religious Program—Students 177.
THREE RIVERS, LIVE OAK CO., SACRED HEART (1948) Rev. Ryszard Zielinski (Poland).
303 E. Alexander, P.O. Box 729, 78071-0729. Tel: 361-786-3398; Fax: 361-786-1010.
Catechesis/Religious Program—Students 56.
Mission—Our Lady of Guadalupe P.O. Box 729, Pawnee, Bee Co. 78071.
TIVOLI, REFUGIO CO., OUR LADY OF GUADALUPE (1936) Rev. Gabriel P. Coelho (India).
Mailing Address: P.O. Drawer I, 77990-0001. Tel: 361-286-3349; Fax: 361-286-3665.
Catechesis/Religious Program—Students 5.
Mission—St. Anthony of Padua Austwell, Refugio Co.
Mission—St. Dennis O'Connor Ranch, Refugio Co.
VIOLET, NUECES CO., ST. ANTHONY (1910) [CEM] Rev. Msgr. William C. Murray; Yvette Cavazos, Sec. & Bookkeeper.
Res.: 3894 Country Rd. 61, Robstown, 78380-5737. Tel: 361-387-4434; Fax: 361-767-3881. Email: stanthonyviolet@yahoo.com.
Catechesis/Religious Program—Jeannie Galufka, D.R.E. Students 11.
WOODSBORO, REFUGIO CO., ST. THERESE, THE LITTLE FLOWER (1915), (Hispanic), [CEM] Rev. Andrew Hejdak (Poland).
Res.: 315 Pugh St., P.O. Box 1076, 78393. Tel: 361-543-4166; Fax: 361-543-5922. Email: sttherese1076@gmail.com.
Catechesis/Religious Program—Students 107.
Mission—St. Mary Bayside, Refugio Co.

On Special Assignment:
Revs.—
Goodwin, Thomas L., Communications
Gutirerrez, Jose, Chap.
Martinez, Francisco Xavier, S.T.L., Chap.
Nwachukwu, Thomas Kizito, Chap.
Onuoha, Silas, Chap.

On Duty Outside the Diocese:
Revs.—
McGerity, Francis X., 2 Rosemere Ct., #3, Roslindale, MA 02131.
Salazar, Jose, St. Mary's Seminary, 9845 Memorial Dr., Houston, 77024-3498.
Serna, J. Patrick
Taurasi, David, 15 Waldemar Ave., Boston, MA 02128.
Vasquez, James, Holy Trinity Seminary, Irving, TX

Military Chaplains:
Revs.—
Gajda, Piotr J., Green Beret Chap., 5395 Wolfe Dr., Oklahoma City, OK 73145.
Shuley, Keith, C.C., Command Chap., U.S. Merchant Marine Academy, 300 Steamboat Rd., Kings Point, NY 11024.

Retired:
Most Revs.—
Carmody, Edmond, D.D., 4109-A Ocean Dr., 78411.
Gracida, Rene H., D.D., 4126 Ocean Dr., 78411.
Rev. Msgrs.—
Chilen, Michael D., 1905 CR 648, Hanceville, AL 35077.
McGowan, Seamus, 292 Long Point Rd., Portland, 78374.
Thompson, William P.A., 4809 Fern Forest, 78413.
Revs.—
Ashe, Michael B., Ireland.
Bergin, Paschal, 411 St. Mary St., Kenedy, 78119.
Burke, Michael, Mt Carmel Home, 4130 S. Alameda, 78411.
De Llano, Domingo, 6106 Vance Jackson, #5, San Antonio, 78230.
Dean, Gregory, 15 Charlotte, Rockport, 78382.
Doherty, Charles, 127 Lakeview Rd., Rockport, 78382.
Feminelli, John, Villa Maria, 3146 Saratoga, 78415.
Fidalgo, Federico, 8315 N. Vandiver, #34, San Antonio, 78209.

Garcia, Eduardo H., St. Joseph Parish, 609 E. Gramman St., Beeville, 78102.
Hamilton, James, P.O. Box 1541, Aransas Pass, 78335.
Heese, Henry, 132 E. Front St., Rockport, 78382.
Hernandez, Manuel, Jr., 118 W. Olive, Laredo, 78041.
Killeen, John P., Ireland
Linehan, Michael, P.O. Box 690415, San Antonio, 78261.
Mikolajczyk, Bruno, 120 S. Elizabeth St., Kingsville, 78363.
Ngyen, Joseph Liep Van, Mt. Carmel Home, 4130 S. Alameda, 78411.
O'Donovan, Thomas P., Villa Marie Apts., 3146 Saratoga # 46, 78415.
Walsh, Arthur, 140 Bourne Ave., Rumford, RI 02916.

Permanent Deacons:
Ahlers, Ray, (Retired)
Allen, Bob, Philip the Apostle, Corpus Christi
Alvarado, Salvador, St. Pius X, Corpus Christi
Barbour, Antonio, Our Lady of Good Counsel, Kingsville
Benys, Victor, Our Lady of Perpetual Help, Corpus Christi
Bitoni, Eluterio, St. Mary Parish, Freer
Blanco, Israel, Christ the King, Corpus Christi
Bockholt, Ken, Most Precious Blood, Corpus Christi
Bolanos, Armando M., Our Lady of Pillar, Corpus Christi
Borse, Alan T., St. Elizabeth, Alice
Botello, Armando, St. Joseph, Corpus Christi
Breland, Walter N., (Retired)
Carlisle, James A., St. Elizabeth, Alice
Carranco, Manuel G., Chap., Sacred Heart Mission, Pettus
Carrizales, Alejandro, (Retired)
Cavada, Armando, Our Lady of Guadalupe, Alice
Cicora, Allen, St. Peter Prince of the Apostles, Corpus Christi
Cleavelin, William, St. Thomas the Apostle, Calallen
Costley, Ricardo E., Sacred Heart, Falfurrias
Dubuque, Roland, SS. Cyril & Methodius Parish, Corpus Christi
Duggins, Russell W., St. Joseph, Beeville
Farias, Eluterio, St. Peter Prince of the Apostles, Corpus Christi
Flores, Arturo, (Retired)
Frazier, Garland, (Retired)
Garcia, Tiburcio, St. Martin, Kingsville
Garza, Abelardo, St. Francis de Paula, San Diego
Gomez, Juan, Immaculate Conception, Gregory
Gonzalez, Javier, St. Teresa of the Infant Jesus, Premont
Gonzalez, Pilar M., St. Michael the Archangel, Banquete
Gonzalez, Ricardo, St. Joseph, Kingsville
Grassedonio, Roy M.
Hinojosa, Raul, (Retired)
Horseman, M.M. Peter, (Retired)
Joiner, John R., Dir., St. Gertrude, Kingsville
Kaizen, Joseph, (Retired)
Landagan, Sebastian, Most Precious Blood, Corpus Christi
Lara, Antonio S., St. Francis Xavier Mission, Tynan
Ledbetter, Jerre H., Sacred Heart, Rockport
Lewinski, Richard R., St. Peter Prince of the Apostles, Corpus Christi
Lickteig, Wayne, S.O.L.T., Dir., Lay Council of Society, St. Anthony, Robstown
Lugo, Loni, St. John the Baptist, Corpus Christi
Luna, Cristobal E., Jr., Coord. Office of Prison Ministry, St. George, George West
Maldonado, Manuel, Mary, Mother of the Church, Corpus Christi
Mantz, Michael, Dir. Deacons, Corpus Christi Cathedral, Corpus Christi
Martinez, Homer, St. Anthony, Robstown
Martinez, Rodolfo R., Our Lady of Perpetual Help, Corpus Christi
Matula, Paul, St. Joseph, Beeville
Millsap, Stanley, (Retired)
Moore, Paul, Assoc. Dir. Deacons, St. Philip the Apostle, Corpus Christi
Morin, Ricardo B., St. Joseph, Kingsville
Nartowicz, Edward, St. Paul the Apostle, Our Lady of Guadalupe Chapel, N.A.S., Corpus Christi
Newchurch, Frank N., Most Precious Blood, Corpus Christi
Noble, Michael T., St. Paul the Apostle & St. Anselm, Corpus Christi
Nolte, Stephen, Holy Family, Corpus Christi
Oliver, Willard F., (Retired)
Ouellette, Roland, (Retired)
Palacios, Adelfino, Jr., Corpus Christi Cathedral, Corpus Christi
Phillips, George, St. Pius X, Corpus Christi
Postert, Anthony K., Sacred Heart, Three Rivers
Provencio, Arthur, Our Lady of the Assumption, Ingleside
Ramirez, Rudy, Ss. Cyril & Methodius, Corpus Christi
Rauen, Mike, Office for Persons with Disabilities, Corpus Christi
Rivera, Gonzalo, (Retired)
Rodriguez, Alonzo, (Retired)
Rodriguez, Eleazar (Larry), St. Patrick, Corpus Christi
Rodriguez, Reynaldo, Jr., (Retired)
Rojas, Reynaldo, St. Joseph, Corpus Christi
Rosales, Raul G., St. Martin, Kingsville
Rosenbaum, Rogelio, Our Lady of Victory, Beeville
Rowley, Edwin N., St. Gertrude, Kingsville
Salazar, Rolando R., St. Joseph, Beeville
Simeus, Erick, Most Precious Blood, Corpus Christi
Sullivan, Kevin, Saints Cyril & Methodius, Corpus Christi
Tamayo, Carlos, St. Francis de Paula, San Diego
Trevino, Luis, St. Joseph, Beeville
Trevino, Pedro R., Jr., St. Mary, Freer
Vasquez, Jesus, St. James, Beeville
Vasquez, Lupe, Sacred Heart, Corpus Christi
Wiest, George Joe, Sacred Heart, Rockport; Chap., Prision Ministry
Willis, Solomon T., III, Spiritual Dir. for Legion of Mary, Corpus Christi; Sacred Heart, Sinton
Ybarra, Pedro M., (Retired)

INSTITUTIONS LOCATED IN THE DIOCESE

[A] HIGH SCHOOLS

CORPUS CHRISTI. *Incarnate Word Academy High School* (1871) (Private), 2910 S. Alameda, 78404. Tel: 361-883-0857; Fax: 361-881-8742. Web: www.iwacc.org. Mr. Jose Torres, Prin.; Lisa York, Librarian. Sisters 6; Lay Teachers 26; Staff 7; Students 318.

John Paul II High School (2006) 3036 Saratoga Blvd., 78415. Tel: 361-855-5744; Fax: 361-855-1343. Web: www.jpiihighschool.org. Perry LeGrange, Prin. Bishops 1; Lay Teachers 41; Students 424.

[B] JUNIOR HIGH AND ELEMENTARY SCHOOLS

CORPUS CHRISTI. *Bishop Garriga Middle Preparatory School* (1987) (Grades 6-8), (Diocesan), 3114 Saratoga Blvd., 78415. Tel: 361-851-0853; Fax: 361-853-5145. Web: www.bgmps.org. Mario Vasquez, Prin. Lay Teachers 15; Students 167.

Central Catholic Elementary (1911) (Parochial), Mailing Address: P.O. Box 2997, 78403. 1218 Comanche St., 78401. Tel: 361-883-3873; Fax: 361-883-5879. Email: sisteranne@centralcatholic.us. Web: www.centralcatholic.us. Sr. Anne Brigid Schlegel, I.W.B.S., Prin. Sisters 2; Lay Teachers 8; Students 135.

Christ the King School (Parochial), 1625 Arlington Dr., 78415. Tel: 361-883-5391; Fax: 361-888-9207. Email: schooloffice@ctk-cc.org. Rich Barncord, Prin. Priests 2; Sisters 1; Lay Teachers 8; Students 79.

SS. Cyril and Methodius School (1957) (Parochial), 5002 Kostoryz Rd., 78415. Tel: 361-853-9392; Fax: 361-853-0282. Web: www.mahpro.com/sscm.html. Anna Peterson, Prin.; Carol Sanchez, Librarian. Lay Teachers 9; Students 120.

Holy Family Catholic School (1946) (Parochial), 2526 Soledad St., 78416. Tel: 361-884-9142; Fax: 361-884-1750. Sr. Patricia Rodriguez, H.M.S.S., Prin.; Very Rev. Emilio B. Jimenez; Nancy Davila, Librarian. Sisters 5; Lay Teachers 9; Students 261.

Incarnate Word Academy Elementary Level (1950) (Private), 450 Chamberlain, 78404. Tel: 361-883-0857; Fax: 361-881-9519. Email: sherlihy@iwacc.org. Web: www.iwacc.org. Sr. Camelia Herlihy, Prin.; Mrs. Rhonda Mumme, Librarian. Sisters 3; Lay Teachers 23; Students 265.

Incarnate Word Academy Middle School, (Grades 6-8), (Private), 2917 Austin St., 78404. Tel: 361-883-0857, Ext. 113; Fax: 361-882-9193. Email: agarza@iwacc.org. Web: www.iwacc.org. Mr. Adolfo Garza, Prin.; Lisa York, Librarian. Lay Teachers 29; Students 224.

Most Precious Blood School (Parochial), 3502 Saratoga Blvd., 78415. Tel: 361-852-4800; Fax: 361-855-8707. Web: www.mpbcs.org. Email: principal@mpbcs.org. Nelda Bazan, Prin.; Josie Kaufmann, Librarian. Lay Teachers 14; Students 202.

Our Lady of Perpetual Help Academy (1955) (Parochial), 5814 Williams Dr., 78412. Tel: 361-991-3305; 361-992-5951; Fax: 361-994-1806. Email: lindaecantu@hotmail.com. Web: www.olphacademy.org. Ms. Linda Cantu, Prin.; Iliana Ortiz, Librarian. Sisters 1; Lay Teachers 17; Students 211.

St. Patrick School (1949-1950) (Parochial), 3340 S. Alameda St., 78411. Tel: 361-852-1211; Fax: 361-852-4855. Email: sps@stpatrickschoolcc.org. Web: www.stpatrickschoolcc.org. Dr. Patricia Stegall, Prin.; Mrs. Constance Burkart, Librarian. Sisters 1; Lay Teachers 22; Students 308.

St. Pius X Catholic School (1965) (Parochial), 737 St. Pius Dr., 78412. Tel: 361-992-1343; Fax: 361-992-0329. Email: spxs@stpiusxschoolcc.org. Web: www.stpiusxschoolcc.org. Kathy Clark, Prin.; Carter Wooster, Librarian. Lay Teachers 15; Students 175.

ALICE. *St. Elizabeth School* (1949) (Parochial), 615 E. Fifth, 78332. Tel: 361-664-6271; Fax: 361-668-4250. Email: selinamgarcia@msn.com. Selina M. Garcia, Prin.; Lorina Gaytan, Librarian. Lay Teachers 11; Students 183.

St. Joseph School (Parochial), 311 Dewey, 78332. Tel: 361-664-4642; Fax: 361-664-4642. Email: sjsaints@awesomenet.net. Mrs. Mary Sandoval, Prin. & Librarian; Rosa Anna Gonzales, Librarian. Lay Teachers 13; Students 188.

KINGSVILLE. *St. Gertrude School* (Parochial), 400 E. Caesar St., 78363. Tel: 361-592-6522; Fax: 361-592-0100. Email: stgschool@stgertrudeparish.org. Web: www.stgertrudeparish.org. Beverly Lanmon, Prin.; Lisa Tucker, Librarian Mgr. Lay Teachers 7; Students 99.

ROBSTOWN. *St. Anthony School* (1916) (Grades K-8), (Parochial), 203 Dunne Ave., 78380. Tel: 361-387-3814; Fax: 361-387-3814. Sr. Maria Paz Aribon, O.P., Prin.; Elva Ybarra, Librarian; Norma Hernandez, Sec. Sisters 5; Lay Teachers 11; Students 130.

ROCKPORT. *Sacred Heart School* (Parochial), 111 N. Church St., 78382. Tel: 361-729-2672; Fax: 361-729-9382. Email: shsprin@shsrockport.org. Web: www.shsrockport.org. Katherine K. Barnes, Prin.; Randall E. Barnes, Librarian. Sisters 2; Lay Teachers 8; Students 144.

[C] DAY NURSERY, PRE-KINDER, KINDER

CORPUS CHRISTI. *Our Lady of the Rosary Catholic School* (1992) 2237 Waldron Rd., 78418. Tel: 361-939-9847; Fax: 361-937-0890. Email: rosary1512@yahoo.com. Sr. Begona Divinagracia, Dir. & Prin. Sisters 6; Lay Staff 2; Students 56.

ROBSTOWN. *St. Joseph's Dream*, 3660 Jack Dr., 78380. Tel: 361-387-9598. Email: paxsolt@aol.com. Sisters 2; Total Assisted 5; Total Staff 2.

[D] GENERAL HOSPITALS

CORPUS CHRISTI. *CHRISTUS Medical Group Dr. Hector P. Garcia Family Medicine Center - Residency Program*, 2601 Hospital Blvd., Ste. 117& 112, 78405. Tel: 361-902-4470. Mailing Address: 1702 Santa Fe, 78404. Jose R. Hinojosa, Prog. Dir.; William L. Pardue, Corp. Sec. Sisters of Charity of the Incarnate Word (San Antonio, TX). Total Assisted Annually 14,000; Total Staff 34.

CHRISTUS Spohn Family Health Center - Northside, 1406 Martin Luther King, 78401. Tel: 361-887-8811; Fax: 361-887-8874. Mailing Address: 1702 Sante Fe, 78404. Crystal Campos, M.D., Medical Dir.; William L. Pardue, Corp. Sec. Sisters of Charity of the Incarnate Word (San Antonio, TX). Total Assisted Annually 10,740; Total Staff 9.

CHRISTUS Spohn Family Health Center - Padre Island, 140202 S. Padre Island Dr., 78418. Tel: 361-949-7660; Fax: 361-949-9372. Mailing Address: 1702 Santa Fe, 78404. Crystal Campos, M.D., Medical Dir.; William L. Pardue, Corp. Sec. Sisters of Charity of the Incarnate Word (San Antonio, TX). Total Assisted Annually 9,830; Total Staff 8.

CHRISTUS Spohn Family Health Center - Robstown, 1038 Texas Yes Blvd., Robstown, 78380. Tel: 361-767-1200; Fax: 361-767-1208. Mailing Address: 1702 Santa Fe, 78404. Crystal Campos, M.D., Medical Dir.; William L. Pardue, Corp. Sec. Sisters of Charity of the Incarnate Word (San Antonio, TX). Total Assisted Annually 9,783; Total Staff 10.

CHRISTUS Spohn Family Health Center - Westside, 4617 Greenwood Dr., 78416. Tel: 361-857-2872; Fax: 361-857-2946. Mailing Address: 1702 Santa Fe, 78404. Crystal Campos, M.D., Medical Dir.; William L. Pardue, Corp. Sec. Sisters of Charity of the Incarnate Word (San Antonio, TX). Total Assisted Annually 14,071; Total Staff 12.

CHRISTUS Spohn Health System, 1702 Santa Fe, 78404. Tel: 361-881-3400; Fax: 361-885-0566. Email: larry.pardue@christushealth.org. Pamela

Robertson, Pres. & CEO; Brian Smith, Vice Pres., Mission Integration; William L. Pardue, Corp. Sec. Sisters of Charity of the Incarnate Word (San Antonio, TX). Bed Capacity 1,360; Total Staff 4,582; Total Assisted Annually 527,654.

CHRISTUS Spohn Hospital Corpus Christi - Memorial, 1702 Santa Fe, 78404. Tel: 361-881-3400; Fax: 361-885-0566. Email: larry.pardue@christushealth.org. Sisters of Charity of the Incarnate Word (San Antonio, TX). Bed Capacity 211; Total Assisted Annually 183,446; Total Staff 1,344.

2606 Hospital Blvd., 78405. Tel: 361-902-4103; Fax: 361-902-4949. Email: estela.chapa@christushealth.org. Paul Gaden, Vice Pres. & COO; William L. Pardue, Corp. Sec.

Pastoral Staff: Lynne Blackler, Chap.; Rev. Thomas Kizito Nwachukwu, Chap.; Rev. Mirjam Berger, Mgr. Clinical Pastoral Educ.; Revs. Silas Onuoha, Chap.; Efren Cruzada, Assoc. Chap.

CHRISTUS Spohn Hospital Corpus Christi - Shoreline, 1702 Santa Fe, 78404. Tel: 361-881-3141; Fax: 361-885-0566. Email: larry.pardue@christushealth.org. Sisters of Charity of the Incarnate Word (San Antonio, TX).

600 Elizabeth St., 78404. Tel: 361-881-3148; Fax: 361-881-3149. Email: paul.gaden@christushealth.org. Paul Gaden, Vice Pres. & COO; William L. Pardue, Corp. Sec. Bed Capacity 422; Total Assisted Annually 109,570; Total Staff 1,576.

Pastoral Staff: Revs. Frank Martinez, Mgr. Spiritual Care; Cuthbert Machamire, Chap.; Charlie Hornes, Chap.; Dr. Linda Frost, Chap.; Revs. Francis Sebastian, M.S.T., Chap.; Joseph Olikkara, M.S.T. (India), Chap.; Ray Claverla, Assoc. Chap.; Michael Doanne, System Dir.

CHRISTUS Spohn Hospital Corpus Christi - South, 1702 Santa Fe, 78404. Email: larry.pardue@christushealth.org. Sisters of Charity of the Incarnate Word (San Antonio, TX).

5950 Saratoga Blvd., 78414. Tel: 361-985-5000; Fax: 361-985-5109. Mark Casanova, COO & Vice Pres.; Revs. David Saenz, Mgr. Spiritual Care; Jose Gutierrez, Chap.; William L. Pardue, Corp. Sec. Bed Capacity 153; Patients Assisted Annually 62,654; Total Staff 615.

CHRISTUS Spohn Memorial - Specialty Clinic, 2606 Hospital Blvd., 7 West, 78405. Tel: 361-902-4765. Mailing Address: 1702 Santa Fe, 78404. David Foster, M.D., Medical Dir.; William L. Pardue, Corp. Sec. Sisters of Charity of the Incarnate Word (San Antonio, TX). Total Assisted Annually 12,647; Total Staff 9.

ALICE. *CHRISTUS Spohn Hospital Alice*, 1702 Santa Fe, 78404. Tel: 361-881-3400; Fax: 361-885-0566. Email: larry.pardue@christushealth.org. Web: www.christusspohn.org. Sisters of Charity of the Incarnate Word (San Antonio, TX). Bed Capacity 148.

2500 E. Main St, 78332. Tel: 361-661-8016; Fax: 361-661-8073. Steven Daniel, COO & Vice Pres.; Sr. Carmen Avila, Chap.; William L. Pardue, Corp. Sec. Bed Capacity 135; Patients Assisted Annually 55,407; Total Staff 384.

BEEVILLE. *CHRISTUS Spohn Hospital Beeville*, 1702 Santa Fe, 78404. Tel: 361-881-3400; Fax: 361-885-0566. Email: larry.pardue@christushealth.org. Web: www.christusspohn.org. Sisters of Charity of the Incarnate Word (San Antonio, TX). Bed Capacity 69.

1500 E. Houston Hwy., 78102. Tel: 361-354-2125; Fax: 361-358-9322. Raymond Ramos, COO & Vice Pres.; William L. Pardue, Corp. Sec.; Rev. Robert Styers, Assoc. Chap. Bed Capacity 68; Patients Assisted Annually 39,845; Total Staff 232.

CHRISTUS Spohn Women's Clinic, 301 S. Hillside Dr., Ste. 4, 78102. Tel: 361-358-6024. Email: larry.pardue@christushealth.org. Web: www.christusspohn.org. Sisters of Charity of the Incarnate Word (San Antonio, TX). Total Staff 3; Total Assisted Annually 2,400.

FREER. *CHRISTUS Spohn - Freer Clinic*, 123 S. Main, 78357. Tel: 361-394-7311. Email: larry.pardue@christushealth.org. Web: www.christusspohn.org. Sisters of Charity of the Incarnate Word (San Antonio, TX). Total Staff 3; Total Assisted Annually 4,280.

KINGSVILLE. *CHRISTUS Spohn Hospital Kleberg*, Mailing Address: 1702 Santa Fe, 78404. Tel: 361-881-3400; Fax: 361-885-0566. Web: christusspohn.org. Sponsorship: Sisters of Charity of the Incarnate Word (San Antonio, TX). Bed Capacity 100.

1311 General Cavazos Blvd., 78363. Norman L. McBride, Vice Pres. & COO; Sr. Elizabeth Smith, Chap. Bed Capacity 100; Patients Assisted Annually 35,711; Total Staff 351.

[E] HOMES FOR THE AGED

CORPUS CHRISTI. *Mount Carmel Home* (1954) 4130 S. Alameda St., 78411. Tel: 361-855-6243; Fax: 361-854-8513. Email: mtcarmelhome@yahoo.com. Sr. M. Michelle Carmel, D.C.J., Admin.; Rev. Msgr. Arnold Anders, Chap. Priests 6; Sisters 9; Bed Capacity 60; Total Assisted Annually 25; Total Staff 19.

Villa Maria, Inc., 3146 Saratoga Blvd., 78415. Tel: 361-857-6171; Fax: 361-857-6173. Email: villamaria@stx.rr.com. Apartment complex for senior adults. Total Staff 4; Total in Residence 57.

[F] RETREAT HOUSES

CORPUS CHRISTI. *Queen of Peace Retreat Center*, 1200 Lantana, Bldg. C, 78407. Tel: 361-289-9095, Ext. 13; Fax: 361-289-0087. Rev. Dan Estes, S.O.L.T., Dir.

SARITA. *Lebh Shomea House of Prayer* (1973) *Missionary Oblates of Mary Immaculate*, P.O. Box 9, 78385-0009. Tel: 361-294-5369; Fax: 361-294-5791. Email: admin@lebhshomea.org; nemeck@rivnet.com. Web: www.lebhshomea.org. Rev. Francis Kelly Nemeck, O.M.I., Co-Dir. & Treas. Priests 1; Total in Residence 3; Total Staff 10.

[G] MONASTERIES AND RESIDENCES OF PRIESTS AND BROTHERS

HEBBRONVILLE. *Catholic Solitudes* (1994) *Rancho Maria*, 11053 N. Hwy. 16, P.O. Box 748, 78361. Tel: 361-527-4636; Fax: 361-527-4482. Email: catholic.solitudes@gmail.com. Web: www.littlebrothersoftheeucharist.org. Rev. Patrick Meaney, Moderator. Special Apostolate: A fraternal community stressing eremitical contemplative prayer, welcoming eremitical vocations and spiritual formational retreats for young people under directives of Diocesan Bishop. Priests 4; Total in Residence 6; Total Assisted Annually 430; Total Staff 3.

ROBSTOWN. *Society of Our Lady of the Most Holy Trinity*, P.O. Box 152, 78380-0152. Tel: 361-387-2754; Fax: 361-387-3818. Email: dahliasolt@hotmail.com. Web: www.societyofourlady.com. 3816 CR 61, 78380. Revs. Terencio Ayo, S.O.L.T.; Anthony Blount, S.O.L.T., Gen. Second Asst.; Scott Braathan, S.O.L.T., Novice Servant; Dale Craig, S.O.L.T., Gen. Lay Servant; Jerry Drolshagen, S.O.L.T., Gen. Sec.; Michael Edward Crump, S.O.L.T.; Dan Estes, S.O.L.T., First Asst. to Reg. Priest Servant; Jean F. Hart, S.O.L.T., Gen. Procurator; Paul Johnston, S.O.L.T.; Michael Jordan, S.O.L.T., Second Asst. to Regl. Priest Servant; James R. Kelleher, S.O.L.T.; Benjamin Martin, S.O.L.T.; George Nedeff, S.O.L.T.; Miguel A. Noyola, S.O.L.T (Guatemala); John H. Patterson, S.O.L.T.; Peter Pham, S.O.L.T.; Rogel Rosalinas, S.O.L.T., Gen. Priest Servant; Robert Shaldone, S.O.L.T.; Zachary Shallow, S.O.L.T., Gen. Lay Servant; Gerard J. Sheehan, S.O.L.T., Regl. Priest Servant; Thomas Showalter, S.O.L.T., First Asst. to Regl. Priest Servant; Glenn Whewell, S.O.L.T., Vocations Dir. & Vicar Servant; Deacons Wayne Lickteig, S.O.L.T.; Francis Quan Ngoc Le, S.O.L.T.; Bernard Vessa, S.O.L.T.

SAN DIEGO. *Vicariate of Holy Rosary, St. Francis de Paul Church*, P.O. Box 279, 78384. Tel: 361-279-3596; Fax: 361-279-8288. Email: berem@vsta.com. Revs. Benito Retortillo, O.P., Local Supr.; Epifanio Rodriguez, O.P. Order of Preachers, U.S. Foundation of the Province of Spain.

[H] CONVENTS AND RESIDENCES FOR SISTERS

CORPUS CHRISTI. *Bethany Convent* Incarnate Word Residence, 3002 Austin St., 78404-2413. Tel: 361-887-6308; Fax: 361-880-4152. Web: iwbscc.org. Sisters of the Incarnate Word and Blessed Sacrament 2.

Blessed Sacrament Chapel (1970) 4105 Ocean Dr., 78411-1223. Tel: 361-852-6212; Fax: 361-852-8815. Email: bsccc@grandecom.net. Web: www.mountgraceconvent.org. Sr. Mary Margaret Friedl, S.Sp.S. de A.P., Supr. Sister-Servants of the Holy Spirit of Perpetual Adoration (Motherhouse, Steyl, Holland) 9.

Casa de Matel Residence, 2930 S. Alameda St., 78404-2798. Tel: 361-356-6998; Fax: 361-880-4152. Email: smigonzalez@iwbscc.org. Sr. Rosa Ortiz, I.W.B.S., Contact Person. Sisters of the Incarnate Word and Blessed Sacrament. Sisters 3.

Dominicas de Santo Tomas de Aquino (1913) 12217 Hearn Rd., 78410. Tel: 361-242-8829; Fax: 361-242-8829. Sr. Maria P. Vega, Local Supr. Sisters 4.

Incarnate Word Convent (1871) 2930 S. Alameda, 78404. Tel: 361-882-5413; Fax: 361-880-4152. Email: smmkuntscher@iwbscc.org. Web: www.iwbscc.org. Sr. Christina Bradley, I.W.B.S., Local Sr. in Charge.

Convent Academy of the Incarnate Word. Sisters of the Incarnate Word and Blessed Sacrament. Sisters 35; Total in Residence 35; Total Staff 15.

Mercedarian Sisters of the Blessed Sacrament (1910) 1723 Frio St., 78417. Tel: 361-854-2370; 361-854-2257. Sr. Dolores Castellanos, H.M.S.S., Local Supr. Sisters 7.

Mount Carmel Home Convent (1954) 4130 S. Alameda St., 78411. Tel: 361-855-6243; Fax: 361-854-8513. Email: mtcarmelhome@yahoo.com. Priests 6; Carmelite Sisters of the Divine Heart of Jesus 9; Total Staff 25.

Mount Tabor Convent, 12940 Leopard St., 78410. Tel: 361-241-1955; Fax: 361-241-2271. Email: mmbitoni@gmail.com. Sisters Maria Margarita Bitoni, M.J.M.J., Delegation Supr.; Milagros Tormo, M.J.M.J., Local Supr. Central Regional House of the Missionary Sisters of Jesus, Mary, and Joseph. Sisters 6.

The Ark Assessment Center & Emergency Shelter for Youth (1994) 12960 Leopard St., 78410. Tel: 361-241-6566; Fax: 361-241-5279.

Pax Christi Institute (1969) 4601 Calallen Dr., 78410. Tel: 361-241-2833; Fax: 361-241-5479. Email: paxchristisisters@gmail.com. Sr. Maria Elva Reyes, P.C.I., Supr. Gen. Sisters 9; Total Staff 9; Total Assisted 3,200.

Religious Missionaries of St. Dominic, Inc. (1986) 2237 Waldron Rd., 78418. Tel: 361-937-5978 (Community). Email: crmsdsis@swbell.net. Sisters 8.

Sisters of Adoration of Blessed Sacrament, Saint Alphonsa Convent, 454 Haroldson Dr., 78412. Tel: 361-288-7353. Sr. Elsamma Joseph, S.A.B.S., Contact Person.

Sisters of Adoration of the Blessed Sacrament, 1601 Ocean Dr., Apt. 5, 78404-1223. Tel: 361-884-7136. Email: sabs2000@sbcglobal.net. Sr. Roalia Aricatt, Supr. Sisters 3.

KINGSVILLE. *Missionary Daughters of the Most Pure Virgin Mary* (1916) 919 N. Ninth St., 78363. Tel: 361-595-1087; Fax: 361-221-9763. Sr. Consuelo Ramirez, M.D.P.V.M., Supr. Sisters 10.

ROBSTOWN. *Incarnate Word Ranch - Bluntzer*, 5939 FM 666, 78380. Tel: 361-882-5413; Fax: 361-880-4152. Email: socardona@iwbscc.org. Mailing Address: 2930 S. Alameda, 78404. Tel: 361-387-7397; Fax: 361-880-4152. Sisters of the Incarnate Word and Blessed Sacrament 3.

Sisters of the Society of Our Lady of the Most Holy Trinity, Regl. Headquarters - Casa Santo Tomas, P.O. Box 152, 78380. Tel: 361-387-8090; Fax: 361-387-3818. Email: srmhelensolt@yahoo.com. Web: www.soltsisters.org. Sr. Anne M. Walsh, S.O.L.T., Gen. Sister Servant.

Society of Our Lady of the Most Holy Trinity, Holy Family Ecclesial Team Formation Center, 700 W. Ave. D, P.O. Box 152, 78380. Tel: 361-767-9417. Sr. Margaret Mary Loehr, S.O.L.T., Contact Person. Sisters in Residence 4.

ROCKPORT. *Schoenstatt Sisters of Mary* (1926) 130 Front St., 78382-7800. Tel: 361-729-1868; Fax: 361-729-1685. Email: schsisterstx@cobridge.tv. Sr. M. Gabriella Maschita, Prov. Supr. Secular Institute of the Schoenstatt Sisters of Mary. Sisters 33; Total in Residence 18.

SARITA. *Lebh Shomea House of Prayer, Hermits*, P.O. Box 9, 78385-0009. Tel: 361-294-5369; Fax: 361-294-5791. Email: admin@lebhshomea.org. Web: www.lebhshomea.org. Sisters 2; Total Staff 10; Total in Residence 4.

[I] MISCELLANEOUS

CORPUS CHRISTI. *The Cathedral Concert Series* (1985) *Diocese of Corpus Christi*, P.O. Box 2620, 78403. Tel: 361-888-6520; 361-888-7444 (Information); Fax: 361-883-1918. Email: lgwozdz@diocesecc.org. Web: www.goccn.org/diocese/ccs/. Mr. Lee Gwozdz, Exec. Dir.

Fannie Bluntzer Nason Renewal Center, Inc. (2000) 2930 S. Alameda St., 78404. Tel: 361-882-5413; Fax: 361-880-4152. Email: smmkuntscher@iwbscc.org.

Hope, Faith & Love, Inc., 658 Robinson St., 78404. Tel: 361-939-9537. 630 Robinson St., 78404. Tel: 361-852-2273. Dr. Francette Meaney, Pres. Tel: 361-855-3534; Raymond Reeves, Sec.

Incarnate Word Academy Foundation (1989) 2930 S. Alameda, 78404. Tel: 361-882-5413; Fax: 361-880-4152. Email: smmkuntscher@iwbscc.org. Web: www.iwacc.org. Sr. Michelle Marie Kuntscher, I.W.B.S., Pres.

Journey to Damascus, Inc., P.O. Box 948, 78403. Tel: 888-546-7382. Email: j2damascus@yahoo.com. Web: www.journeytodamascus.org. Rev. Msgr. Richard Shirley, P.A., V.E., Spiritual Dir.; Rev. Thomas L. Goodwin, Spiritual Dir. Assisted 250 men and women in 2010, including approximately 60 on partial or full scholarship.

Mother Teresa Shelter, Inc. (2003) 513 Sam Rankin, 78401. Tel: 361-883-7372. Email: mteresashelter@diocesecc.org. Web: goccn.org. Sr. Rose Paul Madassery, S.A.B.S., Opers. Supvr. A day shelter used as a homeless gathering facility; providing bath, laundry, limited eating facilities and counseling services. Total Assisted Annually 33,500; Staff 6.

Secular Institute of the Schoenstatt Fathers aka Schoenstatt Fathers 4343 Gaines St., 78412-2541. Tel: 361-992-9841; Fax: 361-992-9842. Email: schtx@sbcglobal.net. Rev. Hector R. Vega, I.Sch., Supr. & Contact Person.

RELIGIOUS INSTITUTES OF MEN REPRESENTED IN THE DIOCESE

For further details refer to the corresponding bracketed number in the Religious Institutes of Men or Women section.

[]—*Catholic Solitudes (Hermits)*
[0630]—*Congregation of the Missionaries of the Holy Family*—M.S.F.
[]—*Congregation of the Rosarians (Society of Apostolic Life)*—C.R.
[0430]—*Dominican, Order of Preachers* (Spain)—O.P.
[]—*Missionary Society of St. Thomas the Apostle (Society of Apostolic Life)* (India)
[0910]—*Oblates of Mary Immaculate*—O.M.I.
[1190]—*Salesians of St. John Bosco*—S.D.B.
[]—*Schoenstatt Fathers (Secular Institute)*—I.Sch.
[]—*Secular Institute*
[0975]—*Society of Our Lady of the Most Holy Trinity, Society of Apostolic Life*—S.O.L.T.

RELIGIOUS INSTITUTES OF WOMEN REPRESENTED IN THE DIOCESE

[0360]—*Carmelite Sisters of the Divine Heart of Jesus*—Carmel D.C.J.
[0470]—*Congregation of Sisters of Charity of the Incarnate Word* (Houston, TX)—C.C.V.I.
[]—*Congregation of Sisters of St. Joseph of 'St. Marc'*—S.J.S.M.
[0460]—*Congregation of the Sisters of Charity of the Incarnate Word* (San Antonio, TX)—C.C.V.I.
[]—*Daughters of Divine Love*—D.D.L.
[]—*Daughters of St. Thomas Congregation*—D.S.T.
[1070-19]—*Dominican Sisters* (Houston, TX)—O.P.
[]—*Dominican Sisters of St. Thomas Aquinas*—O.P.
[2590]—*Mercedarian Sisters of the Blessed Sacrament*—H.M.S.S.
[2690]—*Missionary Catechists of Divine Providence* (San Antonio, TX)—M.C.D.P.
[]—*Missionary Daughters of the Most Pure Virgin Mary* (U.S. Foundation-Mexico)—M.D.P.V.M.
[2770]—*Missionary Sisters of Jesus, Mary, and Joseph*—M.J.M.J.
[]—*Missionary Sisters of the Rosary of Fatima*—H.M.R.F.
[]—*Pax Christi Institute*—P.C.I.
[]—*Religious Missionaries of St. Dominic* (Spanish Prov.)—O.P.
[]—*Schoenstatt Sisters of Mary (Secular Institute)*—I.S.S.M.
[3540]—*Sister Servants of the Holy Spirit of Perpetual Adoration*—S.Sp.S.deA.P.
[]—*Sisters for Christian Community*—S.F.C.C.
[]—*Sisters of Adoration of the Blessed Sacrament* (India)—S.A.B.S.
[3360]—*Sisters of Providence of Saint Mary-of-the-Woods, IN*—S.P.
[3718]—*Sisters of St. Anne*—S.S.A.
[2200]—*Sisters of the Incarnate Word & Blessed Sacrament* (Victoria)—I.W.B.S.
[2205]—*Sisters of the Incarnate Word and Blessed Sacrament* (Corpus Christi)—I.W.B.S.
[]—*Sisters of the Society of Our Lady of the Most Holy Trinity (Society of Apostolic Life)*—S.O.L.T.

NECROLOGY

† Bradley, Robert, (Retired)—Died March 22, 2011

An asterisk (*) denotes an organization that has established tax-exempt status directly with the IRS and is not covered by the USCCB Group Ruling.

Diocese of Covington

(Dioecesis Covingtonensis)

Most Reverend

ROGER J. FOYS, D.D.

Bishop of Covington; ordained May 16, 1973; appointed Bishop of Covington May 31, 2002; consecrated and installed July 15, 2002. *Mailing Address: P.O. Box 15550, Covington, KY 41015-0550.* Tel: 859-392-1512; Fax: 859-392-1508.

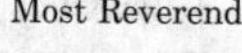

Most Reverend

WILLIAM A. HUGHES

Retired Bishop of Covington; ordained April 6, 1946; appointed Titular Bishop of Inis Cathaig and Auxiliary of Youngstown July 23, 1974; consecrated September 12, 1974; appointed Bishop of Covington April 13, 1979; transferred to Covington May 8, 1979; retired July 4, 1995. *Res.: Carmel Manor, 100 Carmel Manor Rd., Fort Thomas, KY 41075-2395.*

P.O. Box 15550, Covington, KY 41015-0550. Tel: 859-392-1515; Fax: 859-392-1508.

Web: www.covingtondiocese.org

Email: swagner@covingtondiocese.org

ESTABLISHED JULY 29, 1853.

Square Miles 3,359.

Comprises 14 Counties of the Commonwealth of Kentucky in the north and east of the Commonwealth, including Bracken, Boone, Campbell, Carroll, Fleming, Gallatin, Grant, Harrison, Kenton, Lewis, Mason, Owen, Pendleton and Robertson Counties.

For legal titles of parishes and diocesan institutions, consult the Chancery Office.

STATISTICAL OVERVIEW

Personnel	
Bishop	1
Retired Bishops	1
Priests: Diocesan Active in Diocese	50
Priests: Diocesan Active Outside Diocese	2
Priests: Retired, Sick or Absent	30
Number of Diocesan Priests	82
Religious Priests in Diocese	16
Total Priests in Diocese	98
Extern Priests in Diocese	4
Ordinations:	
Diocesan Priests	1
Transitional Deacons	1
Permanent Deacons in Diocese	35
Total Brothers	6
Total Sisters	292
Parishes	
Parishes	47
With Resident Pastor:	
Resident Diocesan Priests	42
Without Resident Pastor:	
Administered by Priests	3
Administered by Religious Women	1
Administered by Lay People	1
Missions	6
Professional Ministry Personnel:	
Sisters	5
Lay Ministers	24
Welfare	
Catholic Hospitals	5
Total Assisted	849,588
Homes for the Aged	3
Total Assisted	937
Residential Care of Children	2
Total Assisted	209
Day Care Centers	1
Total Assisted	75
Special Centers for Social Services	4
Total Assisted	107,344
Other Institutions	2
Total Assisted	6,975
Educational	
Diocesan Students in Other Seminaries	26
Total Seminarians	26
Colleges and Universities	1
Total Students	1,886
High Schools, Diocesan and Parish	7
Total Students	2,446
High Schools, Private	2
Total Students	804
Elementary Schools, Diocesan and Parish	27
Total Students	6,333
Elementary Schools, Private	2
Total Students	494
Catechesis/Religious Education:	
High School Students	276
Elementary Students	3,867
Total Students under Catholic Instruction	16,132
Teachers in the Diocese:	
Priests	1
Brothers	1
Sisters	19
Lay Teachers	720
Vital Statistics	
Receptions into the Church:	
Infant Baptism Totals	1,017
Minor Baptism Totals	234
Adult Baptism Totals	135
Received into Full Communion	95
First Communions	1,406
Confirmations	1,457
Marriages:	
Catholic	287
Interfaith	120
Total Marriages	407
Deaths	817
Total Catholic Population	92,042
Total Population	513,971

Former Bishops—Rt. Revs. GEORGE ALOYSIUS CARRELL, S.J., D.D., ord. Dec. 20, 1827; cons. Nov. 1, 1853; died Sept. 25, 1868; AUGUSTUS MARIA TOEBBE, D.D., ord. Sept. 14, 1854; cons. Jan. 9, 1870; died May 2, 1884; CAMILLUS PAUL MAES, D.D., ord. Dec. 19, 1868; cons. Jan. 25, 1885; died May 11, 1915; FERDINAND BROSSART, D.D., ord. Sept. 1, 1872; cons. Jan. 25, 1916; retired March 14, 1923; died Aug. 6, 1930; Most Revs. FRANCIS WILLIAM HOWARD, D.D., ord. June 16, 1891; cons. July 15, 1923; died Jan. 18, 1944; WILLIAM THEODORE MULLOY, D.D., LL.D., ord. June 7, 1916; cons. Jan. 10, 1945; died June 1, 1959; RICHARD HENRY ACKERMAN, C.S.Sp., D.D., cons. May 22, 1956; transferred to Covington April 6, 1960; retired Nov. 28, 1978; died Nov. 18, 1992; WILLIAM ANTHONY HUGHES, D.D., ord. April 6, 1946; cons. Sept. 12, 1974; appt. April 13, 1979; retired July 4, 1995; ROBERT W. MUENCH, D.D., ord. May 18, 1968; cons. June 29, 1990; appt. Bishop of Covington, Jan. 5, 1996; installed March 19, 1996; transferred to Baton Rouge, Dec. 15, 2001; installed Bishop of Baton Rouge March 14, 2002.

Vicar General—Rev. Msgr. J. MICHAEL DUE, V.G.

Chancellor—Ms. MARGARET M. SCHACK.

Diocesan Tribunal—Very Rev. MICHAEL D. BARTH, J.C.L., Judicial Vicar. Adjutant Judicial Vicars: Ms. KAREN GUIDUGLI, Case Promoter & Notary; Sr. MARY SHANNON KRIEGE, S.N.D., Sec. & Notary.

Judges—Revs. BARRY M. WINDHOLTZ; JAMES M. RYAN; Rev. Msgr. DONALD F. HELLMANN, P.A. (Retired); Very Rev. MICHAEL D. BARTH, J.C.L.; Sr. MARY CATHERINE WENSTRUP, O.S.B., J.C.L.

Defenders of the Bond—Revs. GREGORY E. OSBURG; GERALD E. TWADDELL, V.F.

Promoter of Justice—Rev. Msgr. WILLIAM B. NEUHAUS, V.F., J.C.L.

Diocesan Consultors—Rev. Msgrs. WILLIAM B. NEUHAUS, V.F., J.C.L.; J. MICHAEL DUE, V.G.; DONALD F. HELLMANN, P.A. (Retired); Very Rev. MICHAEL E. COMER; Rev. RYAN L. MAHER; Very Rev. GERALD L. REINERSMAN; Rev. DANIEL LYDEN SCHOMAKER.

Deans—Rev. Msgr. WILLIAM B. NEUHAUS, V.F., J.C.L., Covington; Very Revs. MARK A. KEENE, V.F., Northern Kenton County; MICHAEL E. COMER, Southwest; GERALD L. REINERSMAN, Campbell County; DOUGLAS J. LAUER, V.F., South East.

Deanery Pastoral Council—Rev. RYAN L. MAHER.

Presbyteral Council—Ms. MARGARET M. SCHACK, Chancery Contact.

Due Process Board of Administrative Review—Mr. STEPHEN KOPLYAY, Sec.

Diocesan Offices and Directors

401 E. 20th St., Third Fl., P.O. Box 15550, Covington, 41015-0550. Tel: 859-392-1510; Fax: 859-392-1508. Email: swagner@covingtondiocese.org. Office Hours: Mon.-Fri. 8:30-4:30.

Archives—Mr. THOMAS S. WARD, Archivist.

Board of Total Catholic Education—Mr. MICHAEL T. CLINES.

Campus Ministry-Newman Center—Rev. LAWRENCE A. SCHAEPER, Northern Kentucky Univ., 19 Clearview Dr., Highland Heights, 41076-1403. Tel: 859-261-5340. Email: newmanclub@nku.edu.

Cathedral Foundation, Inc.—VACANT, 1140 Madison Ave., Covington, 41011-3116. Tel: 859-431-2060; Fax: 859-431-8444. Email: foundation@covcathedral.com.

Catholic Charities—Mr. WILLIAM R. JONES, M.S.W., M.Div., B.A.E., Dir., 3629 Church St., Covington, 41015-1499. Tel: 859-581-8974; Fax: 859-581-9595.

Catholic Scouting—Mr. ISAAK A. ISAAK. Tel: 859-392-1533.

Cemeteries—Mr. DONALD KNOCHELMANN, Dir.

Censor Librorum—Rev. JAMES E. QUILL, S.T.D. (Retired).

Charismatic Renewal—Contact Persons: Mr. MICHAEL SCHEPER. Tel: 513-235-7635; Ms. CAROL HODGE. Tel: 859-341-5932.

Communication—Mr. TIMOTHY L. FITZGERALD, Dir.

Continuing Education of Priests—Very Rev. GERALD L. REINERSMAN.

Corpus Central Purchasing—Ms. SANDRA NARE, Gen. Mgr. Buyers: MIKE FREUDENBERG; BOB MOELLMAN, 845 Isabella St., Newport, 41071-1338. Tel: 859-491-8100; 800-955-2541; Fax: 859-491-6587. Email: sandien@corpuscentral.com. Web: www.corpuscentral.com.

Cursillo Movement—Mrs. CAROLYN BOSCH, Lay Dir.

Disabilities Committee—Mr. STEPHEN KOPLYAY, Chm.

Ecumenism—Rev. RONALD M. KETTELER, Thomas More College, 333 Thomas More Pkwy., Crestview Hills, 41017-3428. Tel: 859-344-3393.

Initiation—Rev. RYAN L. MAHER. Chancery

Family Ministry—Mr. ISAAK A. ISAAK. Tel: 859-392-1529.

Finance—Mr. DALE HENSON, Dir.

Hispanic Ministry—Rev. JOHN W. CAHILL, Cristo Rey Parish, P.O. Box 18400, Erlanger, 41018-0400. Tel: 859-538-1175; Fax: 859-538-1181.

Legion of Mary—Rev. MARIO J. TIZZIANI.

Vicar for Retired Priests—Rev. JOHN H. KROGER (Retired).

Ministry Development Program for Deacons—Rev. Msgr. WILLIAM B. NEUHAUS, V.F., J.C.L.

Mission Services— See Stewardship and Missions.

Missions Among Black and Native Americans—Sr. JANET BUCHER, C.D.P. Tel: 859-491-5872; Fax: 859-431-8444.

Mustard Seed Community—Contact Persons: Mr. MICHAEL SCHEPER. Tel: 513-235-7635; Ms. CAROL HODGE. Tel: 859-341-5932; Mr. HARRY HUMPERT.

Newspaper "Messenger"—Mr. TIMOTHY L. FITZGERALD, Editor & Gen. Mgr.

Deaf Ministry—Mother of God Parish, 119 W. Sixth St., Covington, 41011-1409. Tel: 859-392-1511; 859-291-2289 (TDD).

Permanent Diaconate Formation—Rev. Msgr. WILLIAM B. NEUHAUS, V.F., J.C.L.

Priest Personnel—Rev. Msgr. DONALD F. HELLMANN, P.A., Dir. (Retired).

Priests' Retirement Committee—Very Rev. MARK A. KEENE, V.F., Chm.

Pro Life—Ms. FAYE ROCH, Dir.

Religious—Rev. Msgr. J. MICHAEL DUE, V.G., Dir.

Religious Education—Mr. ISAAK A. ISAAK, Dir.

Serra Club of Diocese of Covington—Mr. JIM SUETHOLZ, Pres.; Rev. LAWRENCE A. SCHAEPER.

St. Vincent de Paul Community Pharmacy, Inc.— aka Faith Community Pharmacy. ROSANA AYDT, Dir.

Stewardship and Missions—Mr. MICHAEL MURRAY, Dir., Includes Pontifical Aid Societies, Campaign for Human Development, Catholic Relief Fund, Holy Childhood Assoc., Inner City Missions.

Catholic Schools—Mr. MICHAEL T. CLINES, Supt.

Vocations Office—Rev. GREGORY J. BACH, Recruiter.

Office of Worship—Rev. RYAN L. MAHER.

Office of Youth and Young Adult Ministry—Mr. ISAAK A. ISAAK.

Victim Assistance Coordinator—Ms. MARGARET M. SCHACK. Tel: 859-392-1515. Email: mschack@covingtondiocese.org.

CLERGY, PARISHES, MISSIONS AND PAROCHIAL SCHOOLS

CITY OF COVINGTON

(KENTON COUNTY)

1—CATHEDRAL, BASILICA OF THE ASSUMPTION (1837) Rev. Msgr. William B. Neuhaus, Rector; Rev. Gregory J. Bach; Deacon Gerald R. Franzen.
Res.: 1140 Madison Ave., 41011-3116. Tel: 859-431-2060; Fax: 859-431-8444. Web: www.covcathedral.com.
Catechesis/Religious Program—Students 15.

2—ST. AGNES (1930) Very Rev. Mark A. Keene; Revs. Brian K. Wigger; James E. Quill (Retired); Deacons Joseph Cleves; Robert Stoeckle.
Res.: 1680 Dixie Hwy., Fort Wright, 41011-2779. Tel: 859-431-1802; Fax: 859-291-7017.
School—(Grades K-8) Tel: 859-261-0543; Fax: 859-261-9778. Linda Groh, Prin. Lay Teachers 31; Students 401.
Catechesis/Religious Program—Students 89.

3—ST. AUGUSTINE (1870) Rev. Leo C. Schmidt. In Res., Rev. Robert J. Reinke (Retired).
Res.: 1839 Euclid Ave., 41014-1162. Tel: 859-431-3943; Fax: 859-431-4036. Web: www.staugustines.net.
School—(Grades K-8), 1840 Jefferson Ave., 41014-1165. Tel: 859-261-5564; Fax: 859-261-5402. Sr. Maria Therese Schappert, S.N.D., Prin.; Mrs. Toni Ash, Librarian. Sisters of Notre Dame 2; Lay Teachers 12; Students 138.
Catechesis/Religious Program—Students 6.
St. Augustine Outreach Center—Tel: 859-491-4584. Sr. Ellen Eckerle, C.D.P., Dir.

4—ST. BENEDICT (1885) Rev. Ryan L. Maher; Deacon Phillip J. Racine.
Res.: 338 E. 17th St., 41014-1315. Tel: 859-431-5607; Fax: 859-431-5847.

5—CHURCH OF OUR SAVIOR (1943), (African American), Sr. Janet Marie Bucher, C.D.P., Parish Life Collaborator.
Res.: 246 E. 10th St., 41011-3026. Tel: 859-491-5872; Fax: 859-431-8444. Email: jbucher@fuse.net.
Catechesis/Religious Program—Students 2.

6—HOLY CROSS (1890) Rev. Thomas C. Barnes; Sr. Helen Charles Wilke, C.D.P., Pastoral Assoc.; Mrs. Bernie Whittle, Pastoral Assoc. In Res., Rev. Msgr. Donald A. Enzweiler.
Res.: 3612 Church St., 41015-1431. Tel: 859-431-0636; Fax: 859-431-6917.
School—(Grades K-8) Tel: 859-581-6599; Fax: 859-392-3992. Mary Ellen Matts, Prin. Lay Teachers 12; Students 164.
Catechesis/Religious Program—Students 26.

7—ST. JOHN (1854) Rev. G. Michael Greer; Deacon Joseph L. Baker.
Res.: 627 Pike St., 41011-2148. Tel: 859-431-5314; Fax: 859-431-8397.
Catechesis/Religious Program—Students 20.
Mission—St. Ann (1860) 1274 Parkway, Kenton Co. 41011-1060. Tel: 859-261-9548.

8—MOTHER OF GOD (1841) Rev. Raymond S. Hartman; Deacon Steven I. Durkee.
Res.: 119 W. 6th St., 41011-1409. Tel: 859-291-2288; Fax: 859-291-2065. Email: motherofgod@insightbb.com.
Catechesis/Religious Program—Students 14.

OUTSIDE THE CITY OF COVINGTON

ALEXANDRIA, CAMPBELL CO., ST. MARY OF THE ASSUMPTION (1860) [CEM] Very Rev. James B. Egbers; Rev. Jose Kavungal; Deacon Timothy A. Britt.
Res.: 8246 E. Main St., 41001. Tel: 859-635-4188; Fax: 859-635-4189. Email: stmaryalex@fuse.net. Web: saintmaryparish.com.
School—(Grades PreSchool-8), 9 S. Jefferson St., 41001-1394. Tel: 859-635-9539; Fax: 859-448-4824. Matt Grosser, Prin. Lay Teachers 18; Students 316.
Catechesis/Religious Program—Students 201.

AUGUSTA, BRACKEN CO., ST. AUGUSTINE (1859) [JC] Rev. Edward J. Brodnick; Deacon Frank Estill.
Res.: 215 E. Fourth St., 41002-1117. Tel: 606-756-2377; Fax: 606-756-2377. Web: www.staugustine-augusta.org.
School—(Grades PreSchool-8) Tel: 606-756-3229; Fax: 606-756-2377. Ms. Janet Cropper, Prin. Sisters of Notre Dame 1; Lay Teachers 5; Students 89.
Catechesis/Religious Program—Students 9.

BELLEVUE, CAMPBELL CO.

1—ST. ANTHONY (1889) Merged with Sacred Heart, Bellevue to form Divine Mercy, Bellevue.

2—DIVINE MERCY (2003) Rev. Damian J. Hils; Deacons Charles J. Dietz; David W. Klingenberg. In Res., Rev. John H. Kroger (Retired).
Res.: 320 Poplar St., 41073-1198. Tel: 859-491-4735; Fax: 859-261-0016. Web: divinemercyparish.org.
Catechesis/Religious Program—Students 115.

3—SACRED HEART (1874) Merged with St. Anthony, Bellevue to form Divine Mercy, Bellevue.

BROOKSVILLE, BRACKEN CO., ST. JAMES (1868) [CEM] Rev. Edward J. Brodnick; Deborah Bartlett, Pastoral Assoc.
Res.: 122 Garrett Ave., 41004-0027. Tel: 606-735-2271; Fax: 606-735-2271.
Catechesis/Religious Program—Students 45.

BURLINGTON, BOONE CO., IMMACULATE HEART OF MARY (1954) Very Rev. Michael E. Comer; Rev. Andrews Athappilly, C.M.I.; Deacon Gregory L. Meier.
Church: 5876 Veterans Way, 41005-8824. Tel: 859-689-5010; Fax: 859-689-5636.
School—(Grades PreSchool-8) Tel: 859-689-4303; Fax: 859-689-5636. Michael Jacks, Prin. Sisters of Divine Providence of Kentucky 1; Lay Teachers 40; Students 706.
Catechesis/Religious Program—Students 334.

CALIFORNIA, CAMPBELL CO., STS. PETER AND PAUL (1854) [CEM 2] Rev. Martin John Pitstick.
Res.: 2162 California Crossroads, 41007-9713. Tel: 859-635-2924.
School—Tel: 859-635-4382; Fax: 859-635-0294. Harry Luebbers, Prin. Lay Teachers 17; Students 179.
Catechesis/Religious Program—Students 39.
Mission—Immaculate Conception Stepstone, Pendleton Co.

CAMP SPRINGS, CAMPBELL CO., ST. JOSEPH (1845) [CEM] Rev. Gerald E. Twaddell.
Mailing Address: 6833 Four Mile Rd., 41059-9746. Tel: 859-635-2491; Fax: 859-635-7336. Email: stjoschurchcamp@juno.com. Web: www.josephcampsprings.catholicweb.com.
School—Tel: 859-635-5652; Fax: 859-635-7336. Mr. Ronald Christensen, Headmaster. Lay Teachers 4; Students 52.
Catechesis/Religious Program—Students 12.

CARROLLTON, CARROLL CO., ST. JOHN THE EVANGELIST (1853) [CEM] Rev. Kavungal Lonappan Davy, C.M.I.; Sr. Paula Gohs, C.D.P., Pastoral Assoc.
Res.: 503 Fifth St., 41008-1203. Tel: 502-732-5776; Fax: 502-732-9062. Email: davykavu@yahoo.com. Web: www.home.catholicweb.com/stjohntransfiguration/ index.cfm.
Catechesis/Religious Program—Students 150.
Mission—Transfiguration Perry Park, Owen Co.

COLD SPRING, CAMPBELL CO., ST. JOSEPH (1870) [CEM] Very Rev. Gerald L. Reinersman; Rev. Joshua L. Lange, Parochial Vicar. In Res., Deacon Timothy B. Schabell.
Res.: 4011 Alexandria Pk., 41076-1895. Tel: 859-441-1604; Fax: 859-441-7681. Email: stjoseph@stjoeschool.net. Web: www.stjosephcoldspring.com.
School—(Grades K-8) Tel: 859-441-2025; Fax: 859-441-2057. Mrs. Melissa Holzmacher, Prin.; Jean Listerman, Librarian. Lay Teachers 30; Students 473.
Catechesis/Religious Program—Students 61.

CRESCENT SPRINGS, KENTON CO., ST. JOSEPH (1916) Rev. Phillip W. DeVous; Rev. Msgr. Dominic K. A. Fosu, Parochial Vicar; Deacon Joseph L. Baker.
Res.: 2470 Lorraine Ct., 41017-1406. Tel: 859-341-6609; Fax: 859-578-2741.
School—(Grades K-8) Tel: 859-578-2742; Fax: 859-578-2754. Cathy Stover, Prin.; Susan Barth, Librarian. Lay Teachers 26; Students 345.
Catechesis/Religious Program—Students 107.

CYNTHIANA, HARRISON CO., ST. EDWARD (1864) [CEM] Very Rev. Douglas J. Lauer.
Res.: 107 N. Walnut St., 41031-1225. Tel: 859-234-5444; Fax: 859-234-9823. Email: churchoffice@stedwardky.org. Web: www.stedwardky.org.
School—(Grades PreSchool-5) Tel: 859-234-2731; Fax: 859-234-9823. Email: schooloffice@stedwardky.org. Mrs. Debbie Henson, Prin. Lay Teachers 5; Students 34.
Catechesis/Religious Program—Students 63.

DAYTON, CAMPBELL CO., ST. BERNARD (1853) Rev. Damian J. Hils; Deacons Charles J. Dietz; David W. Klingenberg.
Church: 401 Berry St., 41074-1196. Tel: 859-261-8506; Fax: 859-581-7260. Email: frhils@gmail.com. Res.: 318 Division St., Bellevue, 41073-1198. Tel: 859-261-6172.
Catechesis/Religious Program—Students 14.

EDGEWOOD, KENTON CO., ST. PIUS X (1958) [CEM] Revs. Thomas P. Robbins; Baiju Kidaagen, V.C., Parochial Vicar; Deacon Lawrence L. Kleisinger. In Res., Rev. John J. Riesenberg (Retired).
Res.: 340 Dudley Rd., 41017-2609. Tel: 859-341-4900, Ext. 2; Fax: 859-578-8597. Web: stpiusx.com.
School—(Grades K-8) Tel: 859-341-4900; Fax: 859-578-8597. Judith Gerwe, Prin. Lay Teachers 36; Students 531.
Catechesis/Religious Program—Students 163.

ELSMERE, KENTON CO., ST. HENRY (1890) Revs. James M. Ryan; Niby Kannai, C.M.I.; Deacon Jack Alexander, Pastoral Assoc.; Sharon Brown, Youth Min.; Barbara Barczak, Music Min.
Res.: 3813 Dixie Hwy., 41018-1809. Tel: 859-342-2540; Fax: 859-342-2542. Web: sthenryel.com.
School—(Grades K-8) Tel: 859-342-2551; Fax: 859-342-2554. Mrs. Sue Greis, Prin.; Martha Bohman, Librarian. Religious 1; Lay Teachers 25; Students 300.
Catechesis/Religious Program—Students 90.

ERLANGER, BOONE CO.

1—CRISTO REY Rev. John W. Cahill.
947 Donaldson Rd., P.O. Box 18400, 41018. Tel: 859-538-1175; Fax: 859-538-1181. Email: cristorey@nkymail.net.
Catechesis/Religious Program—Students 175.
Centro de Amistad—Tel: 859-538-1177. Email: jmendez@nkymail.net. Sr. Juana Mendez, Dir.

2—MARY, QUEEN OF HEAVEN (1955) Revs. Kevin

James Kahmann; Nicholas E. C. Rottman, Parochial Vicar; Deacon Thomas Dushney.
Res.: 1150 Donaldson Hwy., 41018-1048. Tel: 859-525-6909; Fax: 859-525-7067. Web: www.mqhparish.com.
School—(Grades K-8) Tel: 859-371-8100; Fax: 859-371-3362. Ms. Lynn Mowery, Prin.; Cheryl Foltz, Librarian. Lay Teachers 18; Students 227.
Catechesis/Religious Program—Students 55.

ERLANGER, KENTON CO., ST. BARBARA (1967) Rev. John J. Sterling; Deacons Bernard J. Kaiser; Charles J. Melville.
Res.: 4042 Turkeyfoot Rd., 41018-2921. Tel: 859-371-3100; Fax: 859-371-5054.
Catechesis/Religious Program—Students 193.

FALMOUTH, PENDLETON CO., ST. FRANCIS XAVIER (1880) [CEM] Rev. Joseph Edakkulathoor, C.M.I., Parochial Admin.
Res.: 202 W. Second St., 41040-1118. Tel: 859-654-8241; Fax: 859-654-5203. Email: stxoffice@gmail.com. Web: www.fxfalmouth.org.
Catechesis/Religious Program—Students 53.

FLEMINGSBURG, FLEMING CO., ST. CHARLES (1859) Rev. Verne F. Hogan.
Res.: 211 Mt. Carmel Ave., 41041-1315. Tel: 606-845-4601; Fax: 606-845-4601.
Catechesis/Religious Program—Students 13.

FLORENCE, BOONE CO., ST. PAUL (1872) Rev. Msgr. Thomas B. Sacksteder; Rev. David B. Gamm; Deacon Nicholas J. Schwartz. In Res., Rev. Msgr. Donald F. Hellmann (Retired).
Res.: 7301 Dixie Hwy., 41042-2126. Tel: 859-371-8051; Fax: 859-647-4073. Email: stpaul2@saint-paul-school.org. Web: saintpaulflorence.com.
School—(Grades K-8) Tel: 859-647-4070; Fax: 859-647-0644. David Maher, Prin.; Shannon Bosley, Librarian. Lay Teachers 23; Students 402.
Catechesis/Religious Program—Students 153.

FORT MITCHELL, KENTON CO., BLESSED SACRAMENT (1920) Revs. Daniel J. Vogelpohl; Jose Pereppadan, C.M.I., Parochial Vicar; Deacons James J. Bayne; Hudson L. Henry. In Res., Rev. Thomas W. Franxman, S.J.
Res.: 2415 Dixie Hwy., 41017-2993. Tel: 859-331-4302; Fax: 859-578-4752. Email: parish@bscky.org. Web: www.bscky.org.
School—(Grades K-8) Tel: 859-331-3062; Fax: 859-344-7323. Mrs. Maureen Hannon, Prin.; Virginia Schneider, Librarian. Sisters of Divine Providence 1; Lay Teachers 35; Students 620.
Catechesis/Religious Program—Students 134.

FORT THOMAS, CAMPBELL CO.

1—ST. CATHERINE OF SIENA (1930) Rev. Stephen M. Bankemper.
Mailing Address: 1803 N. Ft. Thomas Ave., 41075-1170. Tel: 859-441-1352; Fax: 859-572-2686. Email: church@stcatherineofsiena.org. Web: stcatherineofsiena.org.
School—(Grades K-8) Tel: 859-572-2680; Fax: 859-572-2699. Douglas P. Lonneman, Prin.; Sue Perkins, Librarian. Lay Teachers 16; Students 162.
Catechesis/Religious Program—Students 163.

2—ST. THOMAS (1902) Rev. Msgr. Roger P. Cooney; Rev. Johnson L. Thekkudan, C.M.I., Parochial Vicar.
Mailing Address: 26 E. Villa Pl., 41075-2223. Tel: 859-441-1282; Fax: 859-572-4640. Web: www.saintthoschurch.org. In Res., Rev. Albert E. Ruschman (Retired); Deacon Charles J. Hardebeck.
School—(Grades PreSchool-8) Tel: 859-572-4641; Fax: 859-572-4644. Web: sttschool.org. Ms. Sharon Bresler, Prin.; Mrs. Judy Bailey, Librarian. Lay Teachers 18; Students 234.
Catechesis/Religious Program—Students 109.

INDEPENDENCE, KENTON CO., ST. CECILIA (1880) [CEM] Revs. Mario J. Tizziani; Matthias M. Wamala, Parochial Vicar; Deacon Michael J. Keller.
Res.: 5313 Madison Pk., 41051-0186. Tel: 859-363-4311; Fax: 859-363-4312. Email: bweller@stcindependence.org. Web: stcindependence.org.
School—(Grades K-8) Tel: 859-363-4314; Fax: 859-363-4315. Mrs. Kendra McGuire, Prin.; Celia Deters, Librarian. Lay Teachers 17; Students 295.
Catechesis/Religious Program—Students 130.

KENTON, KENTON CO., ST. MATTHEW (1909) [CEM] Very Rev. Michael D. Barth.
Res.: 13782 Decoursey Pk., Morning View, 41063. Tel: 859-356-6530; Fax: 859-356-1695. Email: stmatthew@zoomtown.com.
Catechesis/Religious Program—Students 9.
Mission—Assumption of the Blessed Virgin 3711 St. Mary Rd., Morning View, Kenton Co. 41063.

LUDLOW, KENTON CO., STS. BONIFACE AND JAMES (1872) Rev. Lawrence A. Schaeper; Deacon James C. Auton.
Res.: 304 Oak St., 41016-1417. Tel: 859-261-5340; Fax: 859-261-0939. Email: stbonjames@fuse.net.
Catechesis/Religious Program—Students 20.

MAY'S LICK, MASON CO., ST. ROSE OF LIMA (1864) Rev. Verne F. Hogan.
Church: 5011 Raymond Rd., P.O. Box 100, 41055-8821. Tel: 606-845-4601.

MAYSVILLE, MASON CO., ST. PATRICK (1847) [CEM] Revs. Ivan Kalamuzi, Parochial Admin.; Matthew A. Cushing, Parochial Vicar.
Res.: 110 E. Third St., P.O. Box 248, 41056-0248. Tel: 606-564-9015; Fax: 606-564-6108. Email: klamzey@yahoo.com.
School—(Grades PreK-12) Tel: 606-564-5949; Fax: 606-564-8795. Web: www.stpatschool.com. Ms. Anne Poe, Prin. Lay Teachers 9; Students 143.
High School—(Grades 1-12) Ms. Anne Poe, Prin. Lay Teachers 11; Students 92.
Catechesis/Religious Program—Students 42.
Mission—St. James Kentucky Rd. 435, Minerva, Mason Co. 41062. Tel: 606-735-2271.

MELBOURNE, CAMPBELL CO., ST. PHILIP (1910) Rev. Robert A. Rottgers.
Res.: 1402 Mary Ingles Hwy., 41059-9701. Tel: 859-441-8949; Fax: 859-442-0290. Email: rrottgers@stphilipky.org. Web: www.stphilipky.org.
School—(Grades K-8) Tel: 859-441-3423; Fax: 859-441-2611. Sr. Dolores Ann Gohs, C.D.P., Prin. Sisters of Divine Providence of Kentucky 3; Lay Teachers 6; Students 75.
Catechesis/Religious Program—Students 24.

NEWPORT, CAMPBELL CO.

1—ST. FRANCIS DE SALES, Closed. For sacramental records contact Holy Spirit, Newport.

2—HOLY SPIRIT (1997) Rev. Msgr. William F. Cleves; Deacon Joseph E. McGraw.
Res.: 825 Washington Ave., 41071-1999. Tel: 859-431-2533; Fax: 859-431-3247. Email: holyspirit@fuse.net. Web: holyspiritnewport.com.
Catechesis/Religious Program—Students 20.

3—ST. STEPHEN, Closed. For sacramental records contact Holy Spirit, Newport.

4—ST. VINCENT DE PAUL, Closed. For sacramental records contact Holy Spirit, Newport.

SOUTHGATE, CAMPBELL CO., ST. THERESE OF THE INFANT JESUS (1927) Rev. Clarence J. Heitzman. In Res., Rev. Paul L. Berschied; Deacon William R. Theis.
Res.: 11 Temple Pl., 41071-3133. Tel: 859-441-1654; Fax: 859-441-2395. Web: www.sainttherese.ws.
School—(Grades K-8), 2516 Alexandria Pike, 41071. Tel: 859-441-0449; Fax: 859-441-0449. Dot O'Leary, Prin.; Diana Green, Librarian. Lay Teachers 22; Students 337.
Catechesis/Religious Program—Students 65.

TAYLOR MILL, KENTON CO.

1—ST. ANTHONY (1878) Rev. Joseph A. Gallenstein.
Res.: 485 Grand Ave., 41015-0219. Tel: 859-431-1773; Fax: 859-431-0768. Email: saintanthonychurch@fuse.net. Web: saintanthonytaylormill.org.
School—(Grades K-8) Tel: 859-431-5987; Fax: 859-431-7353. Ms. Veronica Schweitzer, Prin.; Carole Talbert, Librarian. Lay Teachers 4; Students 52.
Catechesis/Religious Program—Students 38.

2—ST. PATRICK (1966) Rev. Jeffrey D. Von Lehmen; Deacon Carl A. Ledbetter.
Mailing Address: 3285 Mills Rd., 41015-2480. Tel: 859-356-5151; Fax: 859-344-7042. Email: parishpastor@fuse.net. Web: www.stpatrickchurch.us.
Catechesis/Religious Program—Students 230.

UNION, BOONE CO., ST. TIMOTHY (1989) Revs. Richard G. Bolte; Jacob Varghese, V.C.; Deacons Thomas L. Nolan; Steven E. Alley.
Res.: 10272 Hwy. 42, P.O. Box 120, 41091-0120. Tel: 859-384-1100; Fax: 859-384-1709. Web: www.saint-timothy.org.
Catechesis/Religious Program—Students 595.

VANCEBURG, LEWIS CO., HOLY REDEEMER (1965) Mrs. Michele Bertot, Parish Life Collaborator; Rev. Bruce Brylinski, G.H.M.
Mailing Address: P.O. Box 8, 41179-0008. Tel: 606-796-3052; Fax: 606-262-4741.
Catechesis/Religious Program—Students 6.

WALTON, BOONE CO., ALL SAINTS (1951) [CEM 2] Rev. Msgr. John R. Schulte; Deacon Paul V. Yancey.
Res.: 62 Needmore St., 41094-1029. Tel: 859-485-4476; Fax: 859-485-6476. Email: allsaints@fuse.net. Web: allsaintswalton.com.
Catechesis/Religious Program—Students 201.

WARSAW, GALLATIN CO., ST. JOSEPH (1864) [CEM] Rev. B. Gerald Witzemann, Parochial Admin. (Retired).
Mailing Address: P.O. Box 495, 41095-0495.
Res.: 602 Sparta Pike, P.O. Box 495, 41095-0495. Tel: 859-567-2425; Fax: 859-567-2425.
Catechesis/Religious Program—Students 30.
Mission—St. Edward (1958) 1335 Hwy. 22 E., R.R. 4, Owenton, Owen Co. 40359-9003.

WILDER, CAMPBELL CO., ST. JOHN THE BAPTIST (1847) Rev. Gregory E. Osburg.
Res.: 1307 John's Hill Rd., 41076-9762. Tel: 859-781-2117; Fax: 859-781-2117. Email: info@sjtbchurch.com. Web: sjtbchurch.com.

WILLIAMSTOWN, GRANT CO., ST. WILLIAM (1912) [CEM 2] Rev. William H. Hinds; Deacon Michael T. Lyman.
Res.: 6 Church St., 41097-9454. Tel: 859-824-5381; Fax: 859-824-0048. Email: william.hinds@gmail.com.
Catechesis/Religious Program—Students 80.
Mission—St. John's (1956) 834 Center Ridge Rd. (Hwy. 3184), De Mossville, 41033.

Chaplains of Public Institutions

FORT THOMAS. *Veterans Hospital*. Rev. Alexander A. Okoro (Nigeria), Chap., Archdiocese for Military Services.

Leave of Absence:
Revs.—
Witte, Mark G.
Wurth, Richard W.

Administrative Leave:
Rev.—
Broering, Raymond L. (Retired)

Retired:
Most Rev.—
Hughes, William A., Carmel Manor, 100 Carmel Manor Rd., 41075-2395.
Rev. Msgrs.—
Hellmann, Donald F., P.A., St. Paul Rectory, 7301 Dixie Hwy., Florence, 41042-2126.
Meier, Allen J., P.A., St. Charles Lodge, 600 Farrell Dr., Rm. 122, 41011-2798.
Rutz, Gilbert J., J.D., M.A., M.Ed., M.Div., Mt. Claret Retreat Center, 4633 N. 54th St., Phoenix, AZ 85018.
Revs.—
Broering, Raymond L., Atria Evergreen Woods, 7030 Evergreen Woods Tr., Spring Hill, FL 34608.
Delange, Maurice, P.O. Box 83, Milford, OH 45150.
Dickmann, Louis H., 6660 Licking Pike, Cold Spring, 41076-8807.
Gerrety, James P., 626 Laurel St., Ludlow, 41016-1341.
Henderson, Robert J., 202 Thornbush Ct., Cold Spring, 41076-1939.
Jasper, Louis H., Atria Evergreen Crossing, 400 Farrell Dr., Ft Wright, 41011-3785.
Krebs, Paul F., Carmel Manor, 100 Carmel Manor Rd., 41075-2395.
Kroger, John H., 320 Poplar St., Bellevue, 41073-1109.
McHugh, James L., 209 E. Second St., Maysville, 41056-1307.
Quill, James E., S.T.D., St. Agnes Rectory, 1680 Dixie Hwy., Park Hills, 41011.
Reinke, Robert J., St. Augustine Rectory, 1839 Euclid Ave., 41014-1162.
Riesenberg, John J., St. Pius X Rectory, 340 Dudley Rd., Edgewood, 41017-2609.
Robotnik, Lawrence R., Passionist Monastery, 1149 Donaldson Rd., Erlanger, 41018-1000.
Rooks, Charles W., St. Charles Lodge, 600 Farrell Dr., Apt. 224, 41011-5165.
Rosing, Robert C., St. Joseph Heights, 1601 Dixie Hwy., Park Hills, 41011-2798.
Ruschman, Albert E., St. Thomas Rectory, 26 E. Villa Pl., 41075-2223.
Seiler, John A., 17 Montvale Ct., Apt. 2, 41075-1820.
Smith, R. Leroy, Country Village, 10501 Becoming Dr., Hudson, FL 34667.
Tenhundfeld, Paul F., Madonna Manor, 2344 Amsterdam Rd., Villa Hills, 41017-3712.
Urlage, Robert J., 2327 Rolling Hills Dr., Crestview Hills, 41017-5136.
Vater, Robert L., Carmel Manor, 100 Carmel Manor Dr., 41075-2395.
Witzemann, B. Gerald, P.O. Box 495, Warsaw, 41095-0495.

Permanent Deacons:
Alexander, John N., St. Henry, Elsmere
Alley, Steven E., St. Timothy, Union
Auton, James C., Sts. Boniface & James, Ludlow
Baker, Joseph L., St. John, Covington
Bayne, James L., Blessed Sacrament, Ft. Mitchell
Britt, Timothy A., St. Mary, Alexandria
Cleves, Joseph A., St. Agnes, Park Hills
Dietz, Charles J., St. Bernard, Dayton & Divine Mercy, Bellevue
Durkee, Steven I., Mother of God, Covington
Dushney, Thomas M., Mary, Queen of Heaven, Erlanger
Estill, Andrew (Frank), St. Augustine, Augusta
Flynn, David J.
Franzen, Gerald R., Cathedral, Covington
Hardebeck, Charles J., St. Thomas, Fort Thomas
Henry, Hudson L., Blessed Sacrament, Ft. Mitchell
Hermann, Robert J., (Retired)
Hillenmeyer, Ernest B., (Retired)
Holstein, Marvin B., St. Elizabeth Healthcare
Kaiser, Bernard, St. Barbara, Erlanger

Keller, Michael J., St. Cecilia, Independence
Kleisinger, Lawrence L., St. Pius, Edgewood
Klingenberg, David W., Divine Mercy, Bellevue and St. Bernard, Dayton
Ledbetter, Carl A., Chaplain, St. Elizabeth Hospice; St. Patrick, Taylor Mill
Lyman, Michael T., St. William, Williamstown
McGraw, Joseph E., Holy Spirit, Newport
Meier, Gregory L., Immaculate Heart of Mary, Burlington
Melville, Charles J., St. Barbara, Erlanger
Nolan, Thomas L., St. Timothy, Union
Norris, Eugene F., (Retired)
Racine, Phillip J., St. Benedict, Covington
Schabell, Timothy B., St. Joseph, Cold Spring
Schwartz, Nicholas J., St. Paul, Florence
Stoeckle, Robert A., St. Agnes, Fort Wright
Sweigart, James H., (Retired)
Theis, William R., St. Therese, Southgate
Yancey, Paul V., Marydale Retreat Center and All Saints, Walton

PILGRIMAGE SHRINES

COVINGTON. *Shrine of St. Ann.* Attached to St. Ann Mission.

SOUTHGATE. *Shrine of the Little Flower.* Attached to St. Therese Church.

INSTITUTIONS LOCATED IN THE DIOCESE

[A] COLLEGES AND UNIVERSITIES

CRESTVIEW HILLS. *Thomas More College* (Coed), 333 Thomas More Pkwy., 41017. Tel: 859-341-5800; Fax: 859-344-3649. Web: www.thomasmore.edu. Sr. Margaret Stallmeyer, C.D.P., J.C.L., Pres.; Ms. Cathy Silvers, Vice Pres. Inst. Advancement; Dr. Bradley A. Bielski, Vice Pres. Academic Affairs; Mr. Peter Aamodt, Vice Pres. Finance & Admin.; Sr. Patricia Dorobek, S.N.D., Dir. Campus Ministry; Mr. James McKellogg, Dir. Library; Ms. Kelly Goyette, Registrar; Ms. Mary Givhan, Dir. Fin. Aid; Mr. Tom Foltz, Dir. Student Support Svcs.; Ms. Genie Wambaugh, Dir. Institute Planning & Effectiveness; Mr. Matthew Webster, Vice Pres. Student Svcs.; Ms. Stacey Rogers, Dir. Communications & Media Rels. Priests 2; Sisters 5; Lay Teachers 73; Administration: Lay People 15; Students 1,832.

[B] HIGH SCHOOLS, DIOCESAN

COVINGTON. *Covington Catholic High School*, 1600 Dixie Hwy., 41011-2797. Tel: 859-491-2247; Fax: 859-448-2242. Email: browe@covcath.org. Web: www.covcath.org. Mr. Robert J. Rowe, Prin.; Mr. Michael Guidugli, Asst. Prin.; Mr. Anthony Zechella, Asst. Prin.; Rev. Joseph A. Gallenstein, Chap. Lay Teachers 39; Boys 501.

Covington Latin School (1923) (Grades 8-12), 21 E. 11th St., 41011-3196. Tel: 859-291-7044; Fax: 859-291-1939. Email: headmaster@covingtonlatin.org. Web: www.covingtonlatin.org. Mr. Andrew J. Barczak, Headmaster; Mr. Brad Dunlevy, Dean; Rev. Gregory J. Bach, Chap.; Mrs. Rhonda Vrabel, Librarian. Lay Teachers 28; Boys 132; Girls 132.

Holy Cross High School, 3617 Church St., 41015-1498. Tel: 859-431-1335; Fax: 859-655-2184. Email: clay.eifert@hchscov.com. Web: hchscov.com. Mr. Clay Eifert, Prin.; Rev. Thomas P. Robbins, Chap. Priests 2; Religious 1; Lay Teachers 38; Students 430.

ALEXANDRIA. *Bishop Brossart High School* (1950) 4 Grove St., 41001-1295. Tel: 859-635-2108; Fax: 859-635-2135. Email: brossart@insightbb.com; rstewart@bishopbrossart.org. Web: www.bishopbrossart.org. Mr. Richard L. Stewart, Prin.; Rev. Martin John Pitstick, Chap. Sisters of Notre Dame 1; Lay Teachers 28; Students 362.

ERLANGER. *St. Henry District High School*, 3755 Scheben Dr., 41018-3597. Tel: 859-525-0255; Fax: 859-525-5855. Email: dmotte@SHDHS.org. Web: www.SHDHS.org. Mr. David M. Otte, Prin.; Rev. Nicholas E. C. Rottman, Chap.; Ms. Terri Manning, Librarian. Lay Teachers 39; Students 510.

MAYSVILLE. *St. Patrick High School*, 318 Limestone St., 41056-1248. Tel: 606-564-5949; Fax: 606-564-8795. Email: apoe@stpatschool.com. Rev. Matthew A. Cushing, Chap.; Ms. Anne Poe, Prin.; Mr. William Hauke, Academic Dean. Lay Teachers 12; Students 93.

NEWPORT. *Newport Central Catholic High School*, 13 Carothers Rd., 41071-2497. Tel: 859-292-0001; Fax: 859-292-0656. Web: www.ncchs.com. Mr. Robert Noll, Prin.; Revs. Robert A. Rottgers, Chap.; Stephen M. Bankemper, Pastoral Admin.; Ms. Joanne Loechel, Admin. Team; Mrs. Jenny Mertle, Admin. Team; Ms. Amy Gurley, Librarian. Sisters 1; Lay Teachers 39; Students 395.

[C] HIGH SCHOOLS, PRIVATE

COVINGTON. *Villa Madonna Academy High School*, 2500 Amsterdam Rd., Villa Hills, 41017-3798. Tel: 859-331-6333; Fax: 859-331-8615. Email: pmcqueen@villamadonna.net. Web: www.villamadonna.net. Ms. Pamela McQueen, Prin.; Rev. Baiju Kidaagen, V.C., Chap.; Ms. Debbie Young, Librarian. Sisters 3; Lay Teachers 21; Students 188.

PARK HILLS. *Notre Dame Academy, Inc.*, 1699 Hilton Dr., 41011-2769. Tel: 859-261-4300; Fax: 859-292-7722. Email: nda@ndapandas.org. Web: www.ndapandas.org. Dr. Laura Koehl, Prin.; Rev. Brian K. Wigger, Chap.; Barb Benkert, M.S., Librarian. Sisters of Notre Dame. Sisters 5; Lay Teachers 44; Girls 606.

[D] ELEMENTARY SCHOOLS, INTERPAROCHIAL

COVINGTON. *Holy Family Catholic School* (1988) (Grades K-8), 338 E. 16th St., 41014-1398. Tel: 859-581-0290; Fax: 859-581-0624. Email: holyfamilyschoolcov@insightbb.com. Diane Russell, Prin.; Sylvia Wilson, Librarian. Lay Teachers 5; Students 66.

Prince of Peace School, (Grades K-8), 625 Pike St., 41011-2798. Tel: 859-431-5153; Fax: 859-291-8632. Email: srose@popcov.com. Web: www.popcov.com. Sisters M. Suzanne Rose, S.N.D., Prin.; Mary Ellen Strunk, S.N.D., Librarian. Sisters of Notre Dame 3; Lay Teachers 9; Students 106.

BELLEVUE. *Holy Trinity Elementary School*, (Grades K-5), 235 Division St., 41073-1101. Tel: 859-291-6937; Fax: 859-291-6970. Email: jfinke@holytrinity-school.org. Web: holytrinity-school.org. Mr. Jeffrey Finke, Prin.; Ms. Liz Enzweiler, Librarian. Sisters 1; Lay Teachers 5; Students 75.

NEWPORT. *Holy Trinity Junior High School and Child Development Center*, 840 Washington Ave., 41071-2485. Tel: 859-292-0487; Fax: 859-431-8745. Email: jfinke@holytrinity-school.org. Web: holytrinity-school.org. Mr. Jeffrey Finke, Prin.; Mrs. Pat Lauer, Librarian. Lay Teachers 4; Students 44.

[E] ELEMENTARY SCHOOLS, DIOCESAN

FORT MITCHELL. *Guardian Angel* (1966) (Grades K-8), Orphanage Rd., P.O. Box 17007, 41017-0007. Tel: 859-331-2040; Fax: 859-344-5022. Email: sommer.alpiger@beechwood.kyschools.us. Ms. Sommer Alpiger, Educ. Prog. Dir. School for the Emotional Behavioral Disabled. Lay Teachers 4; Students 30.

[F] ELEMENTARY SCHOOLS, PRIVATE

COVINGTON. *Villa Madonna Academy*, (Grades K-8), 2500 Amsterdam Rd., Villa Hills, 41017-3798. Tel: 859-331-6333; Fax: 859-331-8615. Web: www.villamadonna.net. Mrs. Soshana Bosley, Prin.; Ms. Wilanne Stangel, Librarian. Lay Teachers 32; Students 335.

WALTON. *St. Joseph Academy* (1976) (Grades PreK-8), 48 Needmore St., 41094-1028. Tel: 859-485-6444; Fax: 859-485-4262. Email: principal@saintjosephacademy.net. Web: www.saintjosephacademy.net. Sr. Elizabeth Ann Barkett, Prin.; Mrs. Michelle Jones, Librarian. Sisters of St. Joseph the Worker. Sisters 4; Lay Teachers 10; Students 190.

[G] MONTESSORI SCHOOLS (PRESCHOOL)

VILLA HILLS. *Villa Madonna Montessori*, 2402 Amsterdam Rd., 41017-5316. Tel: 859-341-5145; Fax: 859-331-2136. Stacey R. Brosky, Admin. Sisters of Divine Providence 1; Lay Teachers 4; Students 48.

[H] PRESCHOOLS

COVINGTON. *Julie Learning Center, Inc.*, 1601 Dixie Hwy., 41011-2701. Tel: 859-392-8231; Fax: 859-291-1774. Email: smpatrycia@aol.com. Sr. M. Patrycia Sweeney, S.N.D., Dir. Daycare with educational emphasis for ages 4-6. Lay Teachers 6; Students 60.

[I] GENERAL HOSPITALS

COVINGTON. *St. Elizabeth, Covington*, 1500 James Simpson Jr. Way, 41011-0800. Tel: 859-655-8800. *St. Elizabeth Medical Center, Inc.* Patients Assisted Annually 122,222.

EDGEWOOD. *St. Elizabeth Edgewood*, 1 Medical Village Dr., 41017-3441. Tel: 859-301-2000; Fax: 859-301-5412. Email: jbozzell@stelizabeth.com. Web: www.stelizabeth.com. Mr. John Dubis, Pres. & CEO; Mr. Garren Colvin, Exec. Vice Pres. & COO; Mr. Joseph Bozzelli, Dir. Pastoral Care; Revs. John H. Kroger (Retired); Robert J. Henderson (Retired); James E. Quill, S.T.D. (Retired); Robert C. Rosing (Retired); John A. Seiler (Retired). Beds 480; Assisted 572,178.

FLORENCE. *St. Elizabeth, Florence*, 4900 Houston Rd., 41042-4824. Tel: 859-212-5200; Fax: 859-212-4050. Bed Capacity 161; Patients Assisted Annually 138,092.

FORT THOMAS. *St. Elizabeth, Fort Thomas*, 85 N. Grand Ave., 41075-1793. Tel: 859-572-3100; Fax: 859-572-2349. Bed Capacity 251; Patients Assisted Annually 103,230.

WILLIAMSTOWN. *St. Elizabeth, Grant County*, 238 Barnes Rd., 41097-9482. Tel: 859-824-8240; Fax: 859-824-8118. Bed Capacity 25; Patients Assisted Annually 52,529.

[J] NURSING HOMES

COVINGTON. *St. Charles Care Center, Inc.* (1960) 500 Farrell Dr., 41011-3798. Tel: 859-331-3224; Fax: 859-578-2065. Email: smluann@zoomtown.com. Web: www.stcharlescare.org. Sr. Mary Luann Bender, S.N.D., Admin. Adult Day Health Program; Licensed In and Outpatient Occupational Speech and Physical Therapy Department; and Private Duty Nursing; In home care, skilled nursing facility and Senior Living Accommodations. Sisters of Notre Dame 3; Nursing Bed Capacity 50; Senior Living Apartments 72; Cottages 44; Total Assisted Annually 700; Employees 174.

Madonna Manor (1966) 2344 Amsterdam Rd., Villa Hills, 41017-3712. Tel: 859-426-3981; Fax: 859-578-7475. Email: madelevak@madonnamanor.org. Web: www.madonnamanor.org. Rev. John J. Riesenberg, Chap. (Retired); Greg Nijak, Exec. Dir. Patients Assisted Annually 60; Bed Capacity 60; Staff 75.

[K] PROTECTIVE INSTITUTIONS

COVINGTON. *Diocesan Catholic Children's Home* (1961) Orphanage Rd., P.O. Box 17007, Fort Mitchell, 41017-2730. Tel: 859-331-2040; Fax: 859-344-5022. Email: jhoffman@dcchome.org. Web: www.dcchome.org. Sr. Jean Marie Hoffman, S.N.D., Exec. Dir.; Ms. Sommer Alpiger, Educ. Treatment Dir. Sisters of Notre Dame 2; Lay Staff 67; Children in Residence 34; Students 34.

COLD SPRING. *Campbell Lodge Boys Home*, 5161 Skyline Dr., 41076. Tel: 859-781-1214; Fax: 859-442-3473. Email: bjones@clbh.org. Web: www.clbh.org. Mr. Barry Jones, M.S.W., LLSW, Exec. Dir. Total Staff 32; Boys 25.

Campbell Lodge Boys' Home Foundation, 5161 Skyline Dr., 41076. Tel: 859-781-1214; Fax: 859-442-3473. Sr. Margaret Stallmeyer, C.D.P., J.C.L., Pres.

[L] HOMES FOR AGED

FORT THOMAS. *Carmel Manor*, 100 Carmel Manor Rd., 41075-2395. Tel: 859-781-5111; Fax: 859-781-2337. Email: carmelmanor@fuse.net. Web: carmelmanor.com. Sr. Teresa Kennedy, O.Carm., Admin. Carmelite Sisters for the Aged and Infirm. Total Staff 150; Residents 145; Bed Capacity 145; Total Assisted Annually 125.

[M] MONASTERIES AND RESIDENCES OF PRIESTS AND BROTHERS

COVINGTON. *Brothers of the Poor of St. Francis* (International Office), Holy Family Friary, 239 W. Robbins St., 41011-3078. Tel: 859-291-2938. Email: bjcphelan@fuse.net. In Res. Bros. William Anuszkiewicz; Blaise Betley, C.F.P.; John Conlin; Rock Larsen, C.F.P.; James Phelan, C.F.P.; Eric Lauer, C.F.P.

[N] CONVENTS AND RESIDENCES FOR SISTERS

COVINGTON. *The Franciscan Daughters of Mary (F.D.M.)* (Public Association of the Faithful), *St. Benedict Convent*, 336 E. 16th St., 41014-1303. Tel: 859-491-3899; Fax: 859-491-4900. Web: www.fdofmary.org. P.O. Box 122070, 41012-2070. Sisters 5.

St. Walburg Monastery, 2500 Amsterdam Rd., 41017-5316. Tel: 859-331-6324; Fax: 859-331-2136. Web: www.stwalburg.org. Sr. Mary Catherine Wenstrup, O.S.B., Prioress. Benedictine Sisters. Professed Sisters 65.

ERLANGER. *Monastery of the Sacred Passion*, 1151 Donaldson Hwy., 41018-1000. Tel: 859-371-8568; Fax: 859-371-8568. Sr. Margaret Mary, C.P., Supr.; Rev. Lawrence R. Robotnik, Chap. (Retired). Passionist Nuns. Professed 8.

FORT THOMAS. *Sisters of the Good Shepherd*, Pelletier Hall, 930 Highland Ave., 41075-1707. Tel: 859-441-5531; Fax: 859-441-7340. Email: srelise@fuse.net. Web: goodshepherdsisters.org. Sr. Mary Elise Kramer, Admin.; Rev. John A. Seiler, Chap. (Retired). Sisters of the Good Shepherd 20.

MELBOURNE. *St. Anne Convent*, 1000 St. Anne Dr., 41059-9603. Tel: 859-441-0679; Fax: 859-441-1510. Email: mhoffman@cdpkentucky.org. Web: www.cdpkentucky.org. Sr. Frances Moore, C.D.P., Prov. Supr.; Rev. Elmer Nadicksbernd, S.V.D., Chap. (Retired). Provincial House and Novitiate of the Sisters of Divine Providence of Kentucky. Sisters in Community 130; Sisters in Provincial House 11.

Holy Family Home, Rte. 8, 2000 St. Anne Dr., 41059-9604. Tel: 859-781-0712; Fax: 859-781-8854. Email: sisterluke@juno.com. Sr. Marilyn Hoffman, C.D.P., Admin. Sisters in Residence 52.

PARK HILLS. *Provincial House of the Sisters of Notre Dame* Juniorate, Novitiate (1924), 1601 Dixie Hwy., 41011-2701. Tel: 859-291-2040; Fax: 859-291-1774. Email: smcarol@sndky.org. Web: www.sndky.org. Sr. Marla Monahan, S.N.D., Prov. Supr.; Rev. Robert C. Rosing, Chap. (Retired). Sisters in Community 125; Sisters in Prov. House 64.

WALTON. *St. William Convent*, One St. Joseph Ln., 41094-1026. Tel: 859-485-4914; 859-485-4256; Fax: 859-485-4914. Email: motherchristina@ssjw.org. Sr. Christina Murray, S.J.W., Supr. Sisters of St. Joseph the Worker. Sisters in Community 13; Sisters in Motherhouse 7.

[O] SOCIAL SERVICES

COVINGTON. *Catholic Charities*, 3629 Church St., 41015-1499. Tel: 859-581-8974; Fax: 859-581-9595. Email: bjones@covingtoncharities.org. Web: www.covingtoncharities.org. Mr. William R. Jones, M.S.W., M.Div., B.A.E., Exec. Dir. Total Assisted Annually 11,000; Total Staff 38.

Parish Kitchen (1974) Pike St. & Russell St., P.O. Box 1234, 41012-1234. Tel: 859-581-7745. Email: parishkitchen@fuse.net. Web: parishkitchen.org. Mr. William R. Jones, M.S.W., M.Div., B.A.E., Dir. Total Assisted Annually 73,000.

Rose Garden Home Mission, 2040 Madison Ave., P.O. Box 122070, 41012-2070. Tel: 859-491-7673. Web: www.fdofmary.org. Sr. Seraphina Quinlan, F.D.M., Dir.

[P] DIOCESAN RETREAT HOUSES

ERLANGER. *Marydale Retreat Center*, 945 Donaldson Hwy., 41018-1093. Tel: 859-371-4224; Fax: 859-371-4604. Email: marydale@marydaleretreat.com. Web: marydaleretreat.com. Deacon Paul V. Yancey, Dir. Total Assisted Annually 3,954; Total Staff 16.

[Q] NEWMAN CLUBS

HIGHLAND HEIGHTS. *Catholic Newman Club - Northern Kentucky University* 19 Clearview Dr., 41076-1449. Tel: 859-957-9988. Rev. Lawrence A. Schaeper, Chap.

[R] MISCELLANEOUS

COVINGTON. *Notre Dame Urban Education Center, Inc.*, 14 E. 8th St., 41011. Tel: 859-261-4487; Fax: 859-261-4437. Sr. M. Lynette Shelton, S.N.D., Dir.

FORT MITCHELL. *Mission Share*, P.O. Box 176356, 41017-6356. Tel: 859-824-5381; 859-341-8405. Rev. William H. Hinds, Pres. Purpose: A mission society whose principal activity is to construct Catholic churches, priest houses, parish centers and other buildings of church work, for the advancement of the Catholic faith among the poorest of the poor, especially focused in Colombia, South America and Mexico.

RELIGIOUS INSTITUTES OF MEN REPRESENTED IN THE DIOCESE

For further details refer to the corresponding bracketed number in the Religious Institutes of Men or Women section.

[0460]—*Brothers of the Poor of St. Francis* (Aachen, Germany)—C.F.P.

[0275]—*Carmelites of Mary Immaculate* (Devamatha, India Province)—C.M.I.

[0820]—*Congregation of the Fathers of Mercy* (Auburn, Kentucky)—C.F.M.

[0570]—*Glenmary Home Missioners* (Cincinnati, Ohio)—G.H.M.

[0690]—*Jesuit Fathers and Brothers* (Chicago Prov.)—S.J.

[0730]—*Legionaries of Christ* (Thornwood, New York)—L.C.

[0420]—*Society of the Divine Word* (Chicago Prov.)—S.V.D.

[1335]—*Vincentian Congregation* (Padra, Rewa, India)—V.C.

RELIGIOUS INSTITUTES OF WOMEN REPRESENTED IN THE DIOCESE

[0230]—*Benedictine Sisters of Pontifical Jurisdiction* (Covington, Kentucky)—O.S.B.

[0330]—*Carmelite Sisters for the Aged and Infirm* (Germantown, NY)—O.Carm.

[3180]—*Congregation of the Passion of Jesus Christ* (Covington, Kentucky)—C.P.

[0440]—*Sisters of Charity of Cincinnati, Ohio*—S.C.

[1000]—*Sisters of Divine Providence of Kentucky* (Covington, Kentucky)—C.D.P.

[2990]—*Sisters of Notre Dame* (Covington, Kentucky)—S.N.D.

[1530]—*Sisters of St. Francis of the Congregation of Our Lady of Lourdes* (Sylvania, Ohio)—O.S.F.

[3920]—*Sisters of St. Joseph the Worker* (Covington, Kentucky)—S.J.W.

[1830]—*Sisters of the Good Shepherd* (St. Louis, Missouri)—R.G.S.

DIOCESAN CEMETERIES

COLD SPRING. *St. Joseph*

FORT MITCHELL. *St. John*

St. Mary

FORT THOMAS. *St. Stephen*

WILDER. *St. Joseph*

NECROLOGY

† Brink, Joseph C., (Retired)—Died Feb. 6, 2011

† Toner, Edward R., (Retired)—Died July 28, 2011

† Werner, John P., (Retired)—Died Sept. 26, 2011

An asterisk (*) denotes an organization that has established tax-exempt status directly with the IRS and is not covered by the USCCB Group Ruling.

Diocese of Crookston

(Dioecesis Crookstoniensis)

Most Reverend

MICHAEL J. HOEPPNER, D.D., J.C.L.

Bishop of Crookston; ordained June 29, 1975; appointed seventh Bishop of Crookston September 28, 2007; Episcopal ordination November 30, 2007. *1200 Memorial Dr., Crookston, MN 56716.* Tel: 218-281-4533. Email: mhoeppner@crookston.org.

Chancery Office: 1200 Memorial Dr., P.O. Box 610, Crookston, MN 56716. Tel: 218-281-4533; Fax: 218-281-3328.

Web: www.crookston.org

Email: dbaumgartner@crookston.org

Most Reverend

VICTOR H. BALKE, D.D., PH.D.

Bishop Emeritus of Crookston; ordained May 24, 1958; appointed July 7, 1976; Episcopal ordination September 2, 1976; retired September 28, 2007. *Res.: 1417 Belsly Blvd., Moorhead, MN 56560.* Tel: 218-287-2828. Email: vhbalke@crookston.org.

ESTABLISHED BY HIS HOLINESS PIUS X, DECEMBER 31, 1909.

Square Miles 17,210.

Comprises the Counties of Becker, Beltrami, Clay, Clearwater, Hubbard, Kittson, Lake of the Woods, Marshall, Mahnomen, Norman, Pennington, Polk, Red Lake and Roseau in the State of Minnesota.

Patroness of the Diocese: The Immaculate Conception.

Legal Title: Diocese of Crookston.
For legal titles of parishes and diocesan institutions, consult the Chancery Office.

STATISTICAL OVERVIEW

Personnel	
Bishop	1
Retired Bishops	1
Priests: Diocesan Active in Diocese	30
Priests: Diocesan Active Outside Diocese	4
Priests: Retired, Sick or Absent	12
Number of Diocesan Priests	46
Religious Priests in Diocese	2
Total Priests in Diocese	48
Extern Priests in Diocese	2
Permanent Deacons in Diocese	18
Total Brothers	1
Total Sisters	74
Parishes	
Parishes	66
With Resident Pastor:	
Resident Diocesan Priests	25
Resident Religious Priests	2
Without Resident Pastor:	
Administered by Priests	39
Professional Ministry Personnel:	
Brothers	1
Sisters	6
Lay Ministers	27
Welfare	
Catholic Hospitals	3
Total Assisted	127,751
Homes for the Aged	3
Total Assisted	624
Day Care Centers	1
Total Assisted	49
Educational	
Diocesan Students in Other Seminaries	7
Total Seminarians	7
High Schools, Diocesan and Parish	1
Total Students	143
Elementary Schools, Diocesan and Parish	8
Total Students	1,193
Catechesis/Religious Education:	
High School Students	1,747
Elementary Students	2,308
Total Students under Catholic Instruction	5,398
Teachers in the Diocese:	
Lay Teachers	104
Vital Statistics	
Receptions into the Church:	
Infant Baptism Totals	554
Adult Baptism Totals	20
Received into Full Communion	104
First Communions	496
Confirmations	399
Marriages:	
Catholic	85
Interfaith	84
Total Marriages	169
Deaths	449
Total Catholic Population	34,410
Total Population	260,616

Former Bishops—Most Revs. TIMOTHY CORBETT, D.D., ord. June 12, 1886; ord. May 19, 1910; resigned See Aug. 6, 1938; appt. Titular Bishop of Vita; died July 20, 1939; JOHN H. PESCHGES, D.D., ord. April 15, 1905; ord. Nov. 9, 1938; died Oct. 30, 1944; FRANCIS J. SCHENK, D.D., ord. June 13, 1926; ord. May 24, 1945; transferred to Duluth Jan. 27, 1960; died Oct. 28, 1969; LAURENCE A. GLENN, D.D., ord. June 11, 1927; ord. Sept. 12, 1956; appt. Bishop of Crookston Feb. 3, 1960; retired July 28, 1970; died Jan. 26, 1985; KENNETH J. POVISH, D.D., ord. June 3, 1950; appt. Bishop of Crookston July 28, 1970; ord. Sept. 29, 1970; transferred to Lansing Oct. 21, 1975; died Sept. 5, 2003; VICTOR H. BALKE, D.D. (Retired), ord. May 24, 1958; appt. July 7, 1976; Episcopal ord. Sept. 2, 1976; retired Sept. 28, 2007.

Vicar General & Moderator of the Curia—Very Rev. Msgr. DAVID BAUMGARTNER, V.G., J.C.L., 1200 Memorial Dr., P.O. Box 610, Crookston, 56716. Tel: 218-281-4533. Email: dbaumgartner@crookston.org.

Chancery Office—1200 Memorial Dr., P.O. Box 610, Crookston, 56716. Tel: 218-281-4533; Fax: 218-281-3328. Web: www.crookston.org. Most Rev. MICHAEL J. HOEPPNER, D.D., Bishop. Fax: 218-281-5991 (Bishop's Office); Very Rev. Msgr. DAVID BAUMGARTNER, V.G., J.C.L., 1200 Memorial Dr., P.O. Box 610, Crookston, 56716. Tel: 218-281-4533 (office); Fax: 218-281-3328. Email: dbaumgartner@crookston.org; Rev. Msgr. ROGER L. GRUNDHAUS, J.C.L., Tribunal (Retired), 620 Summit Ave., Crookston, 56716. Tel: 218-281-5951 (office & home). Email: rgrundhaus@crookston.org; Most Rev. VICTOR H. BALKE, D.D. (Retired), 1417 Belsly Blvd., Moorhead, 56560. Email: vhbalke@crookston.org. Office Hours Mon.-Fri. 8am-noon & 1-5. All official business should be directed to this office.

Chancellor—Very Rev. ROBERT SCHREINER, 702 Summit Ave., Crookston, 56716. Tel: 218-281-1735.

Information Officer—Very Rev. Msgr. DAVID BAUMGARTNER, V.G., J.C.L. Email: dbaumgartner@crookston.org.

Finance Officer—Mr. DAN JAMES. Tel: 218-281-4533, Ext. 429. Email: djames@crookston.org.

Diocesan Tribunal—Ms. REATHEL GIANNONATTI, 1200 Memorial Dr., P.O. Box 610, Crookston, 56716-0610. Tel: 218-281-4533, Ext. 420; 218-281-4050. Email: tribunal@crookston.com.

Judicial Vicar—Rev. Msgr. ROGER L. GRUNDHAUS, J.C.L. (Retired).

Adjutant Judicial Vicar—Rev. Msgr. MICHAEL H. FOLTZ, J.C.L.

Defenders of the Bond—Very Rev. Msgr. DAVID BAUMGARTNER, V.G., J.C.L.; JOANNE TOLLEFSON; Rev. VIRGIL HELMIN, J.C.L.

Promoter of Justice—Very Rev. Msgr. DAVID BAUMGARTNER, V.G., J.C.L.

Notaries—BONNIE SULLIVAN; MAUREEN WATELAND.

Psychological Consultant—GERALDINE CARIVEAU, M.S.L.P.C.C.

Diocesan Offices And Directors

Diocesan Consultors—Very Rev. Msgr. DAVID BAUMGARTNER, V.G., J.C.L.; Rev. Msgr. MICHAEL H. FOLTZ, J.C.L.; Very Rev. JERRY ROGERS; Rev. Msgrs. TIMOTHY H. MCGEE; JERRY NOESEN; Rev. TODD ARENDS.

Finance Council—Most Rev. MICHAEL J. HOEPPNER, D.D.; Very Rev. Msgr. DAVID BAUMGARTNER, V.G., J.C.L., Vicar Gen.; Rev. Msgrs. MICHAEL H. FOLTZ, J.C.L.; TIMOTHY H. MCGEE; Rev. GARY LAMOINE; Very Rev. ROBERT SCHREINER; KAY MACK; MARGEE KELLER; DAN RUST; GAYLE GUNNERSON; PETER ZAVORAL.

Adoption Referral/Post Adoption Search—Very Rev. Msgr. DAVID BAUMGARTNER, V.G., J.C.L., Mailing Address: P.O. Box 610, Crookston, 56716. Tel: 218-281-4533. Email: dbaumgartner@crookston.org.

Boy Scouts—DON VOTAVA, 32077 State Hwy. #1 N.W., Warren, 56762. Tel: 218-745-5423; Rev. THOMAS FRIEDL.

Catholic Campaign for Human Development—Very Rev. Msgr. DAVID BAUMGARTNER, V.G., J.C.L., Mailing Address: P.O. Box 610, Crookston, 56716. Tel: 218-281-4533, Ext. 419. Email:

dbaumgartner@crookston.org.

Catholic Charities—Very Rev. Msgr. DAVID BAUMGARTNER, V.G., J.C.L., Dir. Tel: 218-281-4533, Ext. 419. Email: dbaumgartner@crookston.org.

Catholic Relief Services—Very Rev. Msgr. DAVID BAUMGARTNER, V.G., J.C.L., Dir., Mailing Address: P.O. Box 610, Crookston, 56716. Tel: 218-281-4533, Ext. 419. Email: dbaumgartner@crookston.org.

Commission on Building and Planning—Revs. RICHARD D. LAMBERT; AUGUST GOTHMAN; RICHARD RUDE; ROGER WINTER.

Commission on Hispanic Affairs—VACANT.

Commission on Liturgy, Sacred Music and Art—Rev. AUGUST GOTHMAN; Sr. MARGUERITE STREIFEL; JULIE MAREK; BONNIE LEE; JULIE HARDMEYER; JANET WEAVER; SHERRY KNOTT; JIM DOTTENWHY.

Cursillo—ROSE E. WEBER, Lay Dir., Rte. 3, P.O. Box 116, Crookston, 56716. Tel: 218-281-6679.

Deans—Revs. WILLIAM DECRANS, Northwest; CHUCK HUCK, Northeast; JOSEPH DECRANS, Southwest; Rev. Msgr. TIMOTHY H. MCGEE, South-Central; Very Rev. DAVID J. SUPER, Southeast.

Diaconate Office—Rev. Msgr. MICHAEL PATNODE, 601-15th Ave. N., Moorhead, 56560. Tel: 218-233-4780. Email: frmike@stfrancismhd.org.

Diocesan Board of Conciliation and Arbitration—Rev. Msgr. WILLIAM MEHRKENS, Bemidji (Retired); ARTHUR DRENKHAHN, Warren (Attorney); Sr. DOREEN CHAREST, C.S.J., Moorhead.

Director of Schools—ALAN FOLEY. Tel: 218-444-4262.

School Board, Diocesan—Ex Officio Member: Most Rev. MICHAEL J. HOEPPNER, D.D. Members: Rev. Msgr. TIMOTHY H. MCGEE; JENNIFER LEISENHEIMER; MISTY MEHRKENS; BRIAN DINGMANN; JENNIFER LEMIRE; THOMAS HOUDEK; SCOTT OLSON; SUE LAGARE; DAVID STEFFL.

Hispanic Ministry—Rev. MARIO PRADA, Coord., Mailing Address: 120 W. Jefferson Ave., Mahnomen, 56557. Tel: 218-935-2503. Email: frmprada@gra.midco.net.

Holy Childhood Association—Very Rev. Msgr. DAVID BAUMGARTNER, V.G., J.C.L., Dir., Mailing Address: 1200 Memorial Dr., P.O. Box 610, Crookston, 56716-0610. Tel: 218-281-4533. Email: dbaumgartner@crookston.org.

Native American Indian Commission—KEN PERRAULT, Mailing Address: P.O. Box 965, Cass Lake, 56633-0965. Tel: 218-244-6393.

Natural Family Planning—Very Rev. Msgr. DAVID BAUMGARTNER, V.G., J.C.L., Mailing Address: 1200 Memorial Dr., P.O. Box 610, Crookston, 56716-0610. Tel: 218-281-4533. Email: dbaumgartner@crookston.org.

Newspaper, "Our Northland Diocese"—CHARMAINE BARRANCO, Editor, Diocese of Crookston, 1200 Memorial Dr., P.O. Box 610, Crookston, 56716-0610. Tel: 218-281-4533. Email: cbarranco@crookston.org.

Pastoral Office of Administration—Mr. DAN JAMES, 1200 Memorial Dr., P.O. Box 610, Crookston, 56716-0610. Tel: 218-281-4533, Ext. 429.

Pastoral Office of Worship/RCIA—Rev. AUGUST GOTHMAN, Dir.; BONNIE LEE, Coord., 1200 Memorial Dr., P.O. Box 610, Crookston, 56716-0610. Tel: 218-281-4533.

Priests' Council—Most Rev. MICHAEL J. HOEPPNER, D.D., Pres.; Very Rev. Msgr. DAVID BAUMGARTNER, V.G., J.C.L.; Rev. Msgr. JERRY NOESEN; Revs. RAUL PEREZ-COBO; EMMANUEL SYLVESTER; THOMAS FRIEDL; Very Rev. ROBERT SCHREINER; Revs. RICHARD D. LAMBERT; GARY LAMOINE, Chm.; XAVIER ILANGO; Rev. Msgr. ROGER L. GRUNDHAUS, J.C.L. (Retired); Rev. DUANE PRIBULA, Mailing Address: P.O. Box 610, Crookston, 56716. Tel: 218-281-4533.

Priests' Personnel Board—Most Rev. MICHAEL J. HOEPPNER, D.D.; Very Rev. Msgr. DAVID BAUMGARTNER, V.G., J.C.L., Ex Officio Member; Rev. Msgr. MICHAEL H. FOLTZ, J.C.L.; Revs. CHUCK HUCK; LARRY DELANEY; JOHN KLEINWACHTER.

Priests Retirement Board of Trustees—Revs. JOSEPH DECRANS; GARY LAMOINE; Rev. Msgr. JERRY NOESEN.

Propagation of the Faith—Very Rev. Msgr. DAVID BAUMGARTNER, V.G., J.C.L., Dir., Mailing Address: 1200 Memorial Dr., P.O. Box 610, Crookston, 56716-0610. Tel: 218-281-4533. Email: dbaumgartner@crookston.org.

Director of Faith Formation—VACANT, 1200 Memorial Dr., P.O. Box 610, Crookston, 56716-0610. Tel: 218-281-4533. Email: dbaumgartner@crookston.org.

Pastoral Leadership Program Board—Most Rev. MICHAEL J. HOEPPNER, D.D., Ex Officio; GERMAINE RIEGERT; MIGUEL BALDERAS; Rev. THOMAS FRIEDL; MICKY HULST; KRIS JENSEN; LOREE BRUGGEMAN; KATHLEEN SHILSON; Deacon DANIEL HANNIG, Dir.

TEC (Teens Encounter Christ)—JANE SIMS, 121 Mill St., Crookston, 56716. Tel: 218-281-7073.

Vocations—Revs. VINCENT MILLER, Dir.; XAVIER ILANGO, Assoc. Dir., Mailing Address: P.O. Box 610, Crookston, 56716. Tel: 218-281-4533.

Youth Ministry—VACANT, Mailing Address: 1200 Memorial Dr., P.O. Box 610, Crookston, 56716-0610. Tel: 218-281-4533.

Diocesan Board of Review for the Protection of Young Children—Very Rev. Msgr. DAVID BAUMGARTNER, V.G., J.C.L.; JOHN JEFFREY; Very Rev. DAVID J. SUPER; CINDY HULST; BRENDA ANDERSON; PAUL BIERMAIER, Chm.

Victim Assistance Coordinator—LOUANN MCGLYNN, Mailing Address: P.O. Box 610, Crookston, 56716. Tel: 218-281-7895. Email: lmcglynn@crookston.org.

Safe Environment Director—JAMES CLAUSON, Mailing Address: P.O. Box 610, Crookston, 56716. Tel: 218-281-4224. Email: jclauson@crookston.org.

CLERGY, PARISHES, MISSIONS AND PAROCHIAL SCHOOLS

CITY OF CROOKSTON

(POLK COUNTY)

1—CATHEDRAL OF THE IMMACULATE CONCEPTION Very Rev. Robert Schreiner, Rector; Deacons Dennis Bivens; Daniel Hannig.
Church: 702 Summit Ave., 56716-2736. Tel: 218-281-1735; Fax: 218-281-1747. Email: dpeterson.cathedral@midconetwork.com. Web: www.crookstoncathedral.org.
School—The Cathedral School, (Grades K-6) Tel: 218-281-1835; Fax: 218-281-1747. Email: cschool.cathedral@midconetwork.com (Office). Web: www.cathedralschool.org. Lay Teachers 9; Students 68.
Catechesis/Religious Program—Tel: 218-281-1735. Email: cathedral@midconetwork.com. Mark Hollcraft, D.R.E. (Grades 7-12). Students 243.
Mission—St. Peter Gentilly, Polk Co.

2—ST. ANNE'S, Closed. For inquiries for parish records contact the Cathedral of the Immaculate Conception, Crookston.

OUTSIDE THE CITY OF CROOKSTON

ADA, NORMAN CO., ST. JOSEPH'S (1895) [JC] Rev. Joseph DeCrans.
Res.: 405 E. Thorpe Ave., 56510. Tel: 218-784-4131.
Catechesis/Religious Program—(Grades K-12) Terry Steen, D.R.E. Students 101.
Mission—Holy Family Halstad, Norman Co.
Mission—St. William Twin Valley, Norman Co.

AKELEY, HUBBARD CO., ST. JOHN, Merged with Immaculate Conception, Nevis to form Our Lady of the Pines, Akeley/Nevis Community.

ALMA, MARSHALL CO., ST. JOHN THE BAPTIST, Closed. For inquiries for parish records contact St. Stephen, Stephen. Tel: 218-478-2231.

ARGYLE, MARSHALL CO., ST. ROSE OF LIMA, [CEM], Served by St. Stephen, Stephen. Rev. Bob Stone. P.O. Box 277, 56713. Tel: 218-437-6341. Email: stroser@wiktel.com.
Catechesis/Religious Program—Fax: 218-437-6341. Denise St. Germain, D.R.E. Students 95.

BADGER, ROSEAU CO., ST. MARY'S (1899), Served by Sacred Heart, Roseau. Tel: 218-463-2441, Fax: 218-463-2443., Mailing Address: 504 N. Main St., 56714.
Catechesis/Religious Program—Joni Burkel, D.R.E. Students 21.

BAGLEY, CLEARWATER CO., ST. JOSEPH (1912) Very Rev. David J. Super.
Mailing Address: P.O. Box 67, 56621. Tel: 218-694-6416; Fax: 218-694-6416. Email: stjoseph@gvtel.com.
Res.: 16 Red Lake Ave., 56621.
Catechesis/Religious Program—Clarissa Dowhower, D.R.E. Students 64.

BARNESVILLE, CLAY CO., ASSUMPTION (1883) [CEM] Rev. Gary LaMoine.
Res.: 307 Front St. N., P.O. Box 339, 56514. Tel: 218-354-7320; Fax: 218-354-7659.
Catechesis/Religious Program—Phyllis Peppel, D.R.E. Students 155.
Mission—St. Cecilia Sabin, Clay Co.

BAUDETTE, LAKE OF THE WOODS CO., SACRED HEART (1908), Served by St. Mary's, Warroad. Deacon James Lukenbill, Pastoral Assoc.
Res.: 104 1st St., S.W., P.O. Box 738, 56623. Tel: 218-634-2689. Email: ourlady@mncable.net.
Catechesis/Religious Program—Students 52.
Mission—St. Joseph [CEM] Williams, Lake of the Woods Co.

BEAULIEU, MAHNOMEN CO., ST. JOSEPH PARISH (1895) [CEM], Served by St. Michael, Mahnomen. Tel: 218-935-2503; Fax. 218-935-2503., Mailing Address: 120 W. Jefferson, Mahnomen, 56557.
Catechesis/Religious Program—Vickie Anderson, D.R.E.

BEJOU, MAHNOMEN CO., IMMACULATE CONCEPTION, Closed. For inquiries for parish records contact St. Michael's, Mahnomen.

BEMIDJI, BELTRAMI CO., ST. PHILIP'S, [CEM] Revs. Donald Braukmann; Craig J. Vasek.
Res. & Mailing Address: 702 Beltrami Ave., N.W., 56601-3046. Tel: 218-444-4262; Fax: 218-281-1381. Email: rector@stphilipsbemidji.org. Web: stphilipsbemidji.org.
School—(Grades PreK-8) Tel: 218-444-4938; Fax: 218-444-1379. Mrs. Carol Rettinger, Prin. Lay Teachers 21; Students 272.
Catechesis/Religious Program—620 Beltrami Ave., N.W., 56601. Tel: 218-444-5849; Fax: 218-444-1381. Kris Jensen, D.R.E., (Grades PreK-8). Students 334.
Mission—St. Charles Pennington, Beltrami Co.
Mission—Holy Spirit Newman Center, Beltrami Co.

BENWOOD, ROSEAU CO., ST. JOSEPH THE WORKER, Closed. For inquiries for parish records please contact Sacred Heart, Roseau.

BIG ELBOW LAKE, BECKER CO., ST. FRANCES CABRINI, Served by St. Ann, Waubun. Tel: 218-473-2101 Fax: 218-473-2101 Rev. Dwight Hoeberechts, O.M.I. Mailing Address: 1112 3rd St., Waubun, 56589. Email: 1112sta@arvig.net.

BLACKDUCK, BELTRAMI CO., ST. ANN'S (1905), Served by St. Patrick's, Kelliher. Tel: 218-647-8392., Mailing Address: P.O. Box 187, Kelliher, 56650.
Catechesis/Religious Program—Marie Kovar, D.R.E. Students 11.

BROOKS, RED LAKE CO., ST. JOSEPH (CHURCH OF BROOKS) (1916) [CEM], Mailing Address: P.O. Box 400, Red Lake Falls, 56750-0400. Email: frchuck@stjosephsrlf.org. Web: www.stjosephsrlf.org. Served by St. Joseph's, Red Lake Falls. Tel: 218-253-2685; Fax. 218-253-2195.
Catechesis/Religious Program—Students 36.

CALLAWAY, BECKER CO., ASSUMPTION (1912) [CEM], Served by Sacred Heart, Frazee Rev. Xavier Ilango. Res.: 206 Dakota St., P.O. Box 67, 56521. Tel: 218-375-3571.
Catechesis/Religious Program—Students 27.

DETROIT LAKES, BECKER CO.

1—HOLY ROSARY, [CEM] Rev. Msgr. Timothy H. McGee; Deacons James Thomas; Ole "Red" Elton; Gary Hager.
Office: 1043 Lake Ave., 56501-3499. Tel: 218-847-1393; Fax: 218-847-6367. Email: parish@holyrosarycc.org. Web: www.holyrosarycc.org.
School—(Grades PreK-8) Tel: 218-847-5306; Fax: 218-847-6367. Michael Connell, Prin.; Donna Kennedy, Librarian. Lay Teachers 14; Students 135.
Catechesis/Religious Program— Jean Olson, D.R.E. (PreK); JoAnne Knuttila, D.R.E. (Grades 1-6); Barbara Schmidt, D.R.E. (Grades 7-12). Students 315.

2—ST. MARY OF THE LAKES Rev. Bob J. LaPlante.
Res.: 20996 County Hwy. 20, 56501. Tel: 218-439-3938. Email: stmaryofthelakes@loretel.net. Web: stmaryofthelakes.cc.
Catechesis/Religious Program—Sue Livermore, D.R.E. Students 15.
Mission—St. Francis Xavier Lake Park, Becker Co.

DILWORTH, CLAY CO., ST. ELIZABETH (1910) Rev. Patrick A. Sullivan; Deacon Stephen Nemeth.
Mailing Address: P.O. Box 307, 56529-0307. Tel: 218-287-2705. Web: www.stlizdilworth.org.
Catechesis/Religious Program—Julie Knodel, D.R.E. Students 195.
Mission—St. Andrew Hawley, Clay Co. 56549. Tel: 218-483-4262.

DOROTHY, RED LAKE CO., ST. DOROTHY, Closed. For inquiries for parish records contact St. Joseph's, Red Lake Falls.

EAST GRAND FORKS, POLK CO., SACRED HEART, [CEM] Revs. Larry Delaney; Carlos Velez.
Church: 200 Third St., N.W., 56721-1806. Tel: 218-773-0877; Fax: 218-773-8312. Web: www.sacredheartegf.net.
School—(Grades PreK-6) Tel: 218-773-1579; Fax: 218-773-0318. Mr. David Andrys, Prin. Lay Teachers 15; Students 208.
High School—(Grades 7-12) Tel: 218-773-0230; Fax: 218-773-7042. Mr. Phillip E. Meyer, Prin. Lay Teachers 18; Students 143.
Catechesis/Religious Program—Tel: 218-773-0531; Fax: 218-773-8312. Najla Neuman, D.R.E. (Grades PreK-11). Students 254.
Mission—St. Francis Fisher, Polk Co.
Mission—Holy Trinity Tabor, Polk Co.

EUCLID, POLK CO., ST. MARY, Served by Sts. Peter &

Paul, Warren. Tel: 218-281-5422., Mailing Address: P.O. Box 213, 56722.
Catechesis/Religious Program—Janelle Dahlin, D.R.E. Students 6.

FALUN, ROSEAU CO., ST. PHILIP (1910), Served by Sacred Heart, Roseau., Mailing Address: 403 Main Ave. N., Roseau, 56751.
Catechesis/Religious Program—Patty Bennett, D.R.E. Students 15.

FELTON, CLAY CO., ST. LAWRENCE, Closed. For inquiries for parish records contact St. Joseph's, Ada.

FERTILE, POLK CO., ST. JOSEPH, [CEM] Rev. Joseph Richards; Sr. Mary Jean Gust, O.S.B., Pastoral Assoc.
Mailing Address: 205 S.E. Elm St., 56540. Tel: 218-945-6649. Web: www.stjosephsfertile.com.
Catechesis/Religious Program—Students 59.

FISHER, POLK CO., ST. FRANCIS OF ASSISI (1881) [CEM], (Fisher). Served by Sacred Heart, East Grand Forks. Tel: 218-773-0877., Mailing Address: 302 Park Ave., 56723. Tel: 218-891-2249.
Catechesis/Religious Program—Students 16.

FLORIAN, MARSHALL CO., ASSUMPTION - CHURCH OF FLORIAN (1881) [CEM], Served by St. Stephen, Stephen. Rev. Bob Stone; Deacon Courtney Abel, Pastoral Assoc.
Mailing Address: 26932 390th St. N.W., Strandquist, 56758. Tel: 218-478-3578; Fax: 218-478-3578. Web: www.wiktel.net/assumption.
Catechesis/Religious Program—Beth Budziszewski, D.R.E. Students 19.

FOSSTON, POLK CO., ST. MARY'S (1901) [CEM 2] Very Rev. David J. Super; Sr. Debra Berry, S.M.P., Pastoral Assoc.
Mailing Address: 725 6th St., N.E., 56542. Tel: 218-435-6484.
Catechesis/Religious Program—Email: stmarys@gvtel.com. Students 40.

FRAZEE, BECKER CO., SACRED HEART (1892) [CEM] Rev. Xavier Ilango.
Mailing Address: 202 W. Maple Ave., 56544. Tel: 218-334-4221.
Res.: 306 W. Walnut Ave., 56544. Tel: 218-850-0187.
Catechesis/Religious Program—Students 160.
Mission—Assumption Callaway, Becker Co. 56521.

GENTILLY, POLK CO., ST. PETER'S, [CEM], Mailing Address: 25723-185th Ave., S.W., 56716. Email: dbivens.cathedral@midconetwork.com. Served by Cathedral of the Immaculate Conception, Crookston. Tel: 218-281-1735.
Catechesis/Religious Program—Students 28.

GEORGETOWN, CLAY CO., ST. JOHN (1885), Served by St. Francis de Sales, Moorhead. Tel: 218-233-4780. Rev. Msgr. Michael Patnode.
Mailing Address: P.O. Box 248, 56546.
Catechesis/Religious Program—Students 18.

GOODRIDGE, PENNINGTON CO., ST. ANNE (GOODRIDGE), Served by St. Bernard's, Thief River Falls. Tel: 218-681-3571.
Catechesis/Religious Program—Students 17.

GREENBUSH, ROSEAU CO., BLESSED SACRAMENT, [CEM] Rev. Luis Segundo Buitron.
Res.: P.O. Box A, 56726. Tel: 218-782-2467; Fax: 218-782-4467. Email: blessedsacrament@wiktel.com.
Catechesis/Religious Program—Tel: 218-782-2263. Michelle Peppel, Coord., Faith Formation. Students 142.
Mission—St. Joseph Middle River, Marshall Co.
Mission—St. Edward Karlstad, Marshall Co.

GRYGLA, MARSHALL CO., ST. CLEMENT (GRYGLA), Served by St. Bernards, Thief River Falls. Tel: 218-681-3571
Catechesis/Religious Program—Students 29.

HALLOCK, KITTSON CO., ST. PATRICK'S Rev. William DeCrans.
Res.: 170 S. 5th St., P.O. Box 596, 56728-0596. Tel: 218-843-2323.
Catechesis/Religious Program—Students 28.
Mission—Holy Rosary Lancaster, Kittson Co.

HALSTAD, NORMAN CO., HOLY FAMILY (HALSTAD) (1984), Served by St. Joseph, Ada. Tel: 218-784-4131. [JC], Mailing Address: *Pastoral Administrative Office*, 405 E. Thorpe Ave., Ada, 56510. Email: holyfamily@rrv.net. Web: rrv.net/holyfamily.
Catechesis/Religious Program—Bonnie Lee, D.R.E. Students 19.

HAWLEY, CLAY CO., ST. ANDREW, [JC], Served by St. Elizabeth, Dilworth. Tel: 218-287-2705. Rev. Patrick A. Sullivan; Deacon Tom Jirik.
Mailing Address: 1418 Main St., P.O. Box 129, 56549. Tel: 218-483-4264.
Catechesis/Religious Program—Students 129.

KARLSTAD, KITTSON CO., ST. EDWARD THE CONFESSOR, Served by Blessed Sacrament, Greenbush. Tel: 218-782-2467.
Catechesis/Religious Program—Michelle Peppel, Coord., Faith Formation. Students 23.

KELLIHER, BELTRAMI CO., ST. PATRICK (1909) [JC] Rev. Raul Perez-Cobo.
165 5th St. N.E., P.O. Box 187, 56650. Tel: 218-647-8392.
Catechesis/Religious Program—Sissy Neft, D.R.E. Students 65.
Mission—St. Ann Blackduck, Beltrami Co.
Mission—St. John Nebish, Beltrami Co.

LAKE ITASCA, CLEARWATER CO., ST. CATHERINE, Closed. For inquiries for parish records contact St. Peter's, Park Rapids.

LAKE PARK, BECKER CO., ST. FRANCIS XAVIER'S, [CEM], Served by St. Mary of the Lakes, Detroit Lakes. Rev. Bob J. LaPlante.
Res.: 2066 Second St., 56554-4402. Tel: 218-238-6639; Fax: 218-238-6028. Email: sfxchurch@loretel.net. Web: www.sfxchurch.cc.
Catechesis/Religious Program—Rich Veit, D.R.E. (Grades 7-12); Toni Grabinger, D.R.E. (Grades K-6).

LANCASTER, KITTSON CO., HOLY ROSARY, Mailing Address: *St. Patrick's*, P.O. Box 596, Hallock, 56728. Served by St. Patrick, Hallock. Tel: 218-843-2323.
Catechesis/Religious Program—Students 11.

LAPORTE, HUBBARD CO., ST. THEODORE OF TARSUS - LAPORTE (1988) [CEM 2], Served by Our Lady of the Pines, Nevis Community. Tel: 218-652-4005. Rev. Duane Pribula.
Mailing Address: 205 Main St., W., P.O. Box 378, Nevis, 56467. Fax: 218-652-4022.
Catechesis/Religious Program—Students 6.

LEO, ROSEAU CO., ST. ALOYSIUS, Closed. For inquiries for parish records contact Blessed Sacrament, Greenbush.

MAHNOMEN, MAHNOMEN CO., ST. MICHAEL'S PARISH (1908) [CEM] Rev. Antony Fernando.
Res.: 120 W. Jefferson Ave., 56557. Tel: 218-935-2503; Fax: 218-935-2503. Web: stmichaelmahnomen.org.
School—(Grades PreK-6) Tel: 218-935-5222; Fax: 218-935-5222. Email: stmike@arvig.net. Lay Teachers 7; Students 69.
Catechesis/Religious Program—Kathy Haider, D.R.E., (PreK-6); Jolynn Pribula, D.R.E., (7-12). Students 162.
Mission—St. Joseph [CEM] Beaulieu, Mahnomen Co.

MENTOR, POLK CO., ST. LAWRENCE (1920) [CEM] Rev. Joseph Richards.
Church & Mailing Address: P.O. Box 51, 56736. Tel: 218-637-8178. Email: stlawrence@gvtel.com.
Catechesis/Religious Program—Jack Sullivan, D.R.E. Students 45.

MIDDLE RIVER, MARSHALL CO., ST. JOSEPH, HUSBAND OF MARY, [CEM], Served by Blessed Sacrament, Greenbush., Mailing Address: P.O. Box A, Greenbush, 56726. Tel: 218-782-2467.
Catechesis/Religious Program—Michelle Peppel, Coord., Faith Formation. Students 12.

MOORHEAD, CLAY CO.

1—ST. FRANCIS DE SALES (1948) [JC] Rev. Msgr. Michael Patnode.
601 15th Ave. N., 56560. Tel: 218-233-4780; Fax: 218-233-0270.
Catechesis/Religious Program—Lisa Eggert, D.R.E. & Youth Min. Students 170.
Mission—St. John Georgetown, Clay Co. 56546.

2—ST. JOSEPH'S, [JC] Rev. Msgr. Michael H. Foltz; Rev. Todd Arends; Deacons Tom Cerar; Allen Kukert.
Office: 218 10th St. S., 56560. Tel: 218-236-5066; 218-236-9503 (Res.); Fax: 218-233-0717. Email: stjoes@stjoesmhd.com. Web: www.stjoesmhd.com.
School—(Grades PreK-8) Tel: 218-233-0553. Web: www.stjoesmhdschool.com. Toby Biebl, Prin.; Cathy Bjorkland, Librarian. Lay Teachers 21; Students 248.
Catechesis/Religious Program—Email: stjoesmhd@stjoesmhd.com. Joann Koble, D.R.E. (Elem-8); John Bell, D.R.E. (9-12). Students 394.
Mission—St. Thomas Aquinas Newman Center

NAYTAHWAUSH, MAHNOMEN CO., ST. ANNE (1917), (Naytahwaush). Served by St. Ann's, Waubun. Tel: 218-473-2101. Rev. Dwight Hoeberechts, O.M.I.
Mailing Address: 1112-3rd St., Waubun, 56589. Tel: 218-473-2101; Fax: 218-473-2101. Email: 1112sta@arvig.net.
Catechesis/Religious Program—Ann LaVoy, D.R.E. Students 13.

NEBISH, BELTRAMI CO., ST. JOHN, Served by St. Patrick, Kelliher. Tel: 218-647-8392, Mailing Address: P.O. Box 187, Kelliher, 56650. Tel: 218-647-8392.
Catechesis/Religious Program—Students 27.

NEVIS, HUBBARD CO.

1—IMMACULATE CONCEPTION, Closed. Merged with St. John's, Akeley to form Our Lady of the Pines, Nevis.

2—OUR LADY OF THE PINES (2003) [CEM 2] Rev. Duane Pribula.
Mailing Address: 205 Main St. W., P.O. Box 378, 56467. Tel: 218-652-4005 (Office); 218-652-2785 (Rectory); Fax: 218-652-4022. Email: maryolp@unitelc.com. Web: www.olpparish.org.
Catechesis/Religious Program—Students 54.
Mission—St. Theodore Laporte, Hubbard Co. 56461.

OGEMA, BECKER CO., MOST HOLY REDEEMER, [CEM] Rev. Walter Butor, O.M.I.
Res.: P.O. Box 57, 56569-0057. Tel: 218-983-3261; Fax: 218-983-3808. Email: owep@tvutel.com. Web: whiteearthcatholiccommunity.com.
Catechesis/Religious Program—Darlene Ballard, D.R.E. Students 25.
Mission—St. Benedict White Earth, Becker Co. 56591.
Mission—St. Theodore Ponsford, Becker Co. 56575.

OKLEE, RED LAKE CO., ST. FRANCIS XAVIER'S (1881) [CEM], Served by St. Joseph, Red Lake Falls. Tel: 218-253-2188
301 Governor St., P.O. Box 160, 56742. Tel: 218-796-5844. Email: okstfran@gvtel.com.
Catechesis/Religious Program—Students 23.

OSLO, MARSHALL CO., ST. JOSEPH, [CEM], Served by SS. Peter and Paul, Warren. Tel: 218-745-4511.
Res.: 515 Main St., P.O. Box 97, 56744. Tel: 218-695-2641. Email: stjoseph@wiktel.com.
Catechesis/Religious Program—Susan Heinz, D.R.E.; Terri Reed, D.R.E. Students 21.

PARK RAPIDS, HUBBARD CO., ST. PETER THE APOSTLE (1887) [CEM] Rev. Thomas Friedl.
Res.: 506 7th St. W., P.O. Box 353, 56470-0353. Tel: 218-732-5142 (Office); 218-237-5881 (Res.); Fax: 218-237-6919.
Catechesis/Religious Program—Email: mrss@unitelc.com. Kathleen Shilson, D.R.E. (PreK-12). Students 136.
Mission—St. Mary, Two Inlets, Becker Co., MN.

PENNINGTON, BELTRAMI CO., ST. CHARLES CATHOLIC CHURCH OF PENNINGTON, Served by St. Philip's, Bemidji. Tel: 218-444-4262, Mailing Address: *St. Philip's*, 702 Beltrami Ave., N.W., Bemidji, 56601-3046.
Catechesis/Religious Program—

PLUMMER, RED LAKE CO., ST. VINCENT DE PAUL, Closed. For inquiries for parish records contact St. Francis Xavier, Oklee.

PONSFORD, BECKER CO., ST. THEODORE OF PONSFORD, Served by Most Holy Redeemer, Ogema. Tel: 218-936-3261., Mailing Address: *Most Holy Redeemer*, P.O. Box 57, Ogema, 56569-0057. Email: owep@tvutel.com. Web: whiteearthcatholiccommunity.com.
Catechesis/Religious Program—Students 4.

RED LAKE, BELTRAMI CO., ST. MARY'S MISSION CHURCH (1858) [CEM] Very Rev. Jerry Rogers.
Res.: Hwy. 1, P.O. Box 189, 56671-0189. Tel: 218-679-3614; Fax: 218-679-2212.
School—(Grades PreK-6) Tel: 218-679-3388. Email: mission@paulbunyan.net. Lay Teachers 8; Students 94.
Catechesis/Religious Program—
Mission—Sacred Heart Wilton, Beltrami Co.

RED LAKE FALLS, RED LAKE CO., ST. JOSEPH'S (1879) [CEM] Rev. Chuck Huck.
Office & Res.: P.O. Box 400, 56750-0400. Tel: 218-253-2004 (Res.); 218-253-2188 (Office); Fax: 218-253-2195. Email: frchuck@rllccatholic.org. Web: www.rllccatholic.org.
Catechesis/Religious Program—Students 116.
Mission—St. Francis Xavier Oklee, Red Lake Co. 56742.
Mission—St. Joseph [CEM] Brooks, Red Lake Co. 56715.

ROSEAU, ROSEAU CO., SACRED HEART, [CEM] Rev. John Kleinwachter.
Office: 403 Main Ave. N., 56751. Tel: 218-463-2441; Fax: 218-463-2443.
Catechesis/Religious Program—Rebecca Erdmann, D.R.E. Students 117.
Mission—St. Philip Falun, Roseau Co.
Mission—St. Mary's [CEM] Badger, Roseau Co.

SABIN, CLAY CO., ST. CECILIA (OF SABIN) (1910), Served by Assumption, Barnesville. Tel: 218-354-7320., Mailing Address: *Assumption*, P.O. Box 339, Barnesville, 56514-0339.
Catechesis/Religious Program—Students 47.

SHEVLIN, CLEARWATER CO., OUR LADY OF VICTORY, Closed. For inquiries for parish records contact St. Joseph's, Bagley.

STEPHEN, MARSHALL CO., ST. STEPHEN'S, [CEM] Rev. Bob Stone.
Res.: 515 5th St., P.O. Box 507, 56757. Tel: 218-478-2231; Fax: 218-478-2231.
Catechesis/Religious Program—Students 34.
Mission—Assumption Church of Florian Florian, Marshall Co. Tel: 218-478-3578.
Mission—St. Rose of Lima Argyle, Marshall Co. 56713. Tel: 218-437-6341.

TABOR, POLK CO., HOLY TRINITY CATHOLIC (OF TABOR), Served by Sacred Heart, East Grand Forks. Tel: 218-773-0877., Mailing Address: 37639 140th St., N.W., Angus, 56762-8929. Tel: 218-745-5853. Web: www.rc.net/crookston/holytrinity.
Catechesis/Religious Program—Students 23.

TERREBONNE, RED LAKE CO., ST. ANTHONY, Closed. For inquiries for parish records contact St. Joseph's, Red Lake Falls.

THIEF RIVER FALLS, PENNINGTON CO., ST. BERNARDS (1896) [CEM] Revs. Richard D. Lambert; John Suvakeen; Deacon John Eisbrenner.
Res.: 105 Knight Ave. N., 56701. Tel: 218-681-3571; Fax: 218-681-3560. Web: www.stbernardstrf.org.
School—(Grades PreK-5) Tel: 218-681-1539; Fax: 218-681-2261. Email: srkathy@mncable.net. Sr. Kathy Kuchar, O.S.B., Prin. Lay Teachers 9; Students 123.
Catechesis/Religious Program—Email: margerasmussen@mncable.net; rdplambert@hotmail.com. Web: www.stbernardstrf.org. Margaret Rasmussen, D.R.E.; Jayne Miller, Youth Min. Students 255.
Mission—St. Anne Goodridge, Pennington Co. 56725.
Mission—St. Clement Grygla, Marshall Co. 56727.

TWIN VALLEY, NORMAN CO., ST. WILLIAM (OF TWIN VALLEY), Served by St. Joseph Pastoral Administrative Office, Ada. Tel: 218-784-4131. Deacon Nick Revier.
Catechesis/Religious Program—Jodi Douville, C.R.E. Students 36.

TWO INLETS, BECKER CO., ST. MARY'S, [CEM] Deacon John Muller.
Mailing Address: 55744 Cty. Hwy. 44, Park Rapids, 56470. Tel: 218-732-4046; Fax: 218-732-4046. Email: sm2inlets@hughes.net. Served by St. Peter, Park Rapids.
Catechesis/Religious Program—Margaret Sharp, D.R.E. Students 16.

WARREN, MARSHALL CO., SS. PETER AND PAUL (1909) [CEM] Rev. Emmanuel Sylvester.
Res.: 208 N. Seventh St., 56762. Tel: 218-745-4511; Fax: 218-745-5484.
Catechesis/Religious Program—Students 64.
Mission—St. Joseph P.O. Box 97, Oslo, Marshall Co. 56744. Tel: 218-695-2641.
Mission—St. Mary Euclid, Polk Co. 56722.

WARROAD, ROSEAU CO., ST. MARY'S, [CEM] Rev. August Gothman.
Res.: P.O. Box 33, 56763. Tel: 218-386-1178.
Catechesis/Religious Program—Sue Ripplinger, D.R.E. Students 150.

WAUBUN, MAHNOMEN CO., ST. ANN (1912) [CEM] Rev. Dwight Hoeberechts, O.M.I.
Res.: 1112 3rd St., 56589-9402. Tel: 218-473-2101; Fax: 218-473-2101. Email: 1112sta@arvig.net.
Catechesis/Religious Program—Students 33.
Mission—St. Anne 204 County Rd. #4, P.O. Box 157, Naytahwaush, Mahnomen Co. 56566.
Mission—St. Frances Cabrini Big Elbow Lake, Becker Co.

WHITE EARTH, BECKER CO., ST. BENEDICT (OF WHITE EARTH), [CEM], Served by Most Holy Redeemer, Ogema. Tel: 218-936-3261. Bro. William Lundberg, O.M.I., Pastoral Assoc.
Mailing Address: P.O. Box 57, Ogema, 56569-0057. Tel: 218-983-3519; Fax: 218-983-3808. Email: owep@tvutel.com. Web: whiteearthcatholiccommunity.com.
Catechesis/Religious Program—Students 27.

WILLIAMS, LAKE OF THE WOODS CO., ST. JOSEPH (OF WILLIAMS), Served by Sacred Heart, Baudette. Tel: 218-634-2689., Mailing Address: P.O. Box 738, Baudette, 56623.

WILTON, BELTRAMI CO., SACRED HEART (WILTON), Served by St. Mary's Mission, Red Lake. Tel: 218-679-3614., Mailing Address: *St. Mary's Mission*, P.O. Box 1897, Bemidji, 56619-1897.
Catechesis/Religious Program—Students 30.

On Duty Outside the Diocese:
Revs.—
Bushy, Timothy F.
Silva, Luis
Wieland, Dennis J.

Retired:
Most Rev.—
Balke, Victor H., D.D., 1417 Belsly Blvd., Moorhead, 56560. Tel: 218-287-2828
Rev. Msgrs.—
Grundhaus, Roger L., J.C.L., 620 Summit Ave., 56716. Tel: 218-281-5951
Krebs, Donald H., 3344-38th St., S., Moorhead, 56560. Tel: 218-236-6644. Email: dkrebs@gomoorhead.com
Mehrkens, William, Goldpine Home, Rm. 115, 1700-30th St. N.W., Bemidji, 56601. Tel: 218-444-4346
Noesen, Gerald, 1602 Summerfield Dr., #23, 56716. Tel: 218-281-3060. Email: glnoesen@webtv.net
Revs.—
Bernauer, James, P.O. Box 7, Dent, 56528. Tel: 218-758-3377
Kieselbach, Joseph, P.O. Box 161, Barnesville, 56514. Tel: 218-354-7258
Kulhawik, Frank, 516 Walsh St., 56716. Tel: 218-784-2247
Noah, Timothy T., Villa Maria, 3102 S. University Dr., Fargo, ND 58103.
Palcisko, Raymond, 2769-28th St., N.W., Baudette, 56623. Tel: 651-276-0205. Email: raypal@ymail.com
Pryor, G. Robert, 286 Grantwood Dr., Henderson, NV 89014. Tel: 702-454-1440. Email: grpryor@embarqmail.com. U.S.A.F
Wesely, Eugene L., 209 Oak St. Apt. 113, Detroit Lakes, 56501. Tel: 218-844-8206
Wieseler, Larry, 15 Cassidy Hill Rd., Coventry, CT 06238-1386.

Permanent Deacons:
Abel, Courtney, Assumption, Florian
Bivens, Dennis, Cathedral of the Immaculate Conception, Crookston; St. Peter's, Gentilly
Bruggeman, John A., St. Joseph's, Red Lake Falls
Cerar, Tom, St. Joseph, Moorhead
Eisbrenner, John, (Retired), Trail, MN; St. Bernard, Thief River Falls
Elton, Ole "Red", Holy Rosary, Detroit Lakes
Hager, Gary, Holy Rosary, Detroit Lakes
Hannig, Daniel, Cathedral of the Immaculate Conception, Crookston
Jirik, Tom, St. Andrew, Hawley
Klick, Don, (On Duty Outside the Diocese)
Kukert, Allen, St. Joseph's, Moorhead
Lukenbill, James, Sacred Heart, Baudette
Muller, John, St. Mary's, Two Inlets
Revier, Nick, St. William, Twin Valley
Thomas, James, Holy Rosary, Detroit Lakes
Thomas, Steve, Sacred Heart, East Grand Forks
Vande Kamp, James, (On Duty Outside the Diocese)

INSTITUTIONS LOCATED IN THE DIOCESE

[A] GENERAL HOSPITALS

BAUDETTE. *LakeWood Health Center*, 600 Main Ave. S., 56623. Tel: 218-634-2120; Fax: 218-634-3416. Email: lakewood@catholichealth.net. Web: www.lakewoodhealthcenter.org. Jason J. Breuer, Admin. Affiliate of Catholic Health Initiatives. Bed Capacity: Acute 15; Long Term Care 44; Staff 154; Patients Assisted Annually 32,314.
LakeWood Care Center, 600 Main Ave. S., 56623. Tel: 218-634-3488; Fax: 218-634-3489. Affiliate of Catholic Health Initiatives. Bed Capacity 44; Residents Assisted Annually 44.

DETROIT LAKES. **St. Mary's Regional Health Center*, 1027 Washington Ave., 56501. Tel: 218-847-5611; Fax: 218-847-7674. Web: www.trustedcareforlife.org. Thomas R. Thompson, CEO; Tim Cook, Chap.; Lanny Sweeney, Chap.
St. Mary's EMS, 1240 Washington Ave., P.O. Box 1410, 56501. Tel: 218-847-0817; Fax: 218-847-0842. Thomas R. Thompson, CEO. (Sub. of St. Mary's Regional Health Center) Senior Nursing 153; Staff 725; Beds Acute 87; Long Term Care 96; Patients Assisted Annually 100,000.

PARK RAPIDS. *St. Joseph Area Health Services*, 600 Pleasant Ave., 56470. Tel: 218-732-3311; Fax: 218-732-1368. Email: kathydickinson@catholichealth.net. Mr. Ben Koppelman, Pres. & CEO. Affiliate of Catholic Health Initiatives. Sisters 3; Bed Capacity 50; Patients Assisted Annually 35,966.

[B] HOMES FOR THE AGED

CROOKSTON. *Villa St. Vincent*, 516 Walsh St., 56716. Tel: 218-281-3424; Fax: 218-281-4755. Ms. Judith Hulst, Admin. Sisters of St. Benedict 2; Assisted Living Apts. 71; Skilled Nursing Beds 80; Alzheimer's Beds 24; Residents 170; Staff 245.

ADA. *Bridges Care Center dba Bridges Care Community* Subs. of Benedictine Health System., 201 9th St. W., Ste. 2, 56510. Tel: 218-784-5500; Fax: 218-784-5245. Email: katie.redig@bhshealth.org. Ms. Katie Redig, Admin. Sponsored by the Benedictine Sisters Benevolent Association, Duluth. Staff 91; Skilled Nursing Beds 49; Residents 73.

DETROIT LAKES. *St. Mary's Nursing Center*, 1027 Washington Ave., 56501. Tel: 218-844-0776; Fax: 218-544-0780. Christy Brinkman, Admin., Sr. Housing. Attended by Staff of St. Mary's Regional Health Center. Assisted Living 30; Independent Living 58; Transitional Care 23; Long Term Care 73.

[C] CONVENTS AND RESIDENCES FOR SISTERS

CROOKSTON. *Mount St. Benedict Monastery*, 620 Summit Ave. E., 56716-2799. Tel: 218-281-3441; Fax: 218-281-6966. Web: www.msb.net. Sr. Jennifer Kehrwald, O.S.B., Admin. Motherhouse of the Order of the Sisters of St. Benedict of Pontifical Jurisdiction-The Federation of St. Gertrude. Sisters in Community 74.
Sisters of St. Benedict Initial Formation Tel: 218-281-3441; Fax: 218-281-6966. Sr. Lois Spors, O.S.B., Dir. of Novices.
Sunrise Center for Children and Families Tel: 218-281-6540; Fax: 218-281-6966. Sr. Judith Moen, O.S.B., Dir.

[D] NEWMAN CENTERS

CROOKSTON. *Cathedral Campus Ministry*, 702 Summit Ave., 56716. Tel: 218-281-1735. Mark Hollcraft, Campus Min.
University of Minnesota Cooperative Campus Ministry 56716. Tel: 218-281-8516; Fax: 218-281-8504. Email: cboike@mail.crk.umn.edu. Web: www.crk.umn.edu. Chris Boike, Dir. Coop. Campus Ministry.

BEMIDJI. *Holy Spirit Newman Center* 1701 Birch Ln., N.E., 56601-2607. Tel: 218-444-4762; Fax: 218-444-7244. Email: ncenter@paulbunyan.net. Web: www.newmancenterbsu.org. Rev. Donald Braukmann.

MOORHEAD. *St. Thomas Aquinas Newman Center* 218 S. 10th St., 56560. Tel: 218-236-9596. Email: stjoes@stjoesmhd.com. Web: www.mnstate.edu/newman. Rev. Todd Arends, Dir.

[E] MISCELLANEOUS

CROOKSTON. **The Diocese of Crookston Catholic Community Foundation*, 1200 Memorial Dr., 56716. Tel: 218-281-4533; Fax: 218-281-3328. Email: ccf@crookston.org. Web: www.crookston.org/ccf.
**Mount Saint Benedict Foundation*, 620 Summit Ave., 56716-2799. Tel: 218-281-3441; Fax: 218-281-6966.

RELIGIOUS INSTITUTES OF MEN REPRESENTED IN THE DIOCESE

For further details refer to the corresponding bracketed number in the Religious Institutes of Men or Women section.

[0910]—*Oblates of Mary Immaculate*—O.M.I.

RELIGIOUS INSTITUTES OF WOMEN REPRESENTED IN THE DIOCESE

[0230]—*Benedictine Sisters of Pontifical Jurisdiction* (Congregation of St. Gertrude)—O.S.B.

[0230]—*Benedictine Sisters of Pontifical Jurisdiction (Federation of St. Benedict)*—O.S.B.

[3832]—*Congregation of the Sisters of St. Joseph*—C.S.J.

[]—*Congregation of the Sisters of the Third Order of St. Francis*—O.S.F.

[]—*Franciscan Sisters*—O.S.F.

[2450]—*Sisters of Mary of the Presentation* (Valley City, ND)—S.M.P.

[]—*Sisters of St. Joseph of Concordia* (KS)—C.S.J.

NECROLOGY

† Felion, Jerome, (Retired)—Died May 10, 2011

An asterisk (*) denotes an organization that has established tax-exempt status directly with the IRS and is not covered by the USCCB Group Ruling.

Diocese of Dallas

(Dioecesis Dallasensis)

Most Reverend

KEVIN J. FARRELL

Bishop of Dallas; ordained December 24, 1978; appointed Auxiliary Bishop of Washington and Titular Bishop of Rusuccuru December 28, 2001; ordained February 11, 2002; appointed Bishop of Dallas March 6, 2007; installed May 1, 2007.

Diocesan Pastoral Center: *3725 Blackburn, P.O. Box 190507, Dallas, TX 75219*. Tel: 214-528-2240; Fax: 214-526-1743.

Web: www.cathdal.org

Most Reverend

CHARLES V. GRAHMANN, D.D.

Retired Bishop of Dallas; ordained March 17, 1956; appointed Titular Bishop of Equilio and Auxiliary of San Antonio June 30, 1981; consecrated August 29, 1981; appointed First Bishop of Victoria April 14, 1982; installed May 29, 1982; appointed Coadjutor of Dallas December 18, 1989; Reception as Coadjutor of Dallas February 21, 1990; appointed Bishop of Dallas July 14, 1990; retired March 6, 2007.

Most Reverend

MARK J. SEITZ

Auxiliary Bishop of Dallas; ordained priest May 17, 1980; appointed Auxiliary Bishop of Dallas and Titular Bishop of Cozyla March 11, 2010; Episcopal ordination April 27, 2010.

Most Reverend

J. DOUGLAS DESHOTEL

Auxiliary Bishop of Dallas; ordained priest May 13, 1978; appointed Auxiliary Bishop of Dallas and Titular Bishop of Cova March 11, 2010; Episcopal ordination April 27, 2010.

ESTABLISHED DIOCESE OF DALLAS ON JULY 15, 1890.

Square Miles 7,523.

Redesignated Diocese of Dallas-Fort Worth on October 20, 1953.

Redesignated Diocese of Dallas on August 27, 1969.

Comprises the following nine Counties in the State of Texas: Collin, Dallas, Ellis, Fannin, Grayson, Hunt, Kaufman, Navarro and Rockwall.

For legal titles of parishes and diocesan institutions, consult the Diocesan Pastoral Center.

STATISTICAL OVERVIEW

Personnel	
Bishop	1
Auxiliary Bishops	2
Retired Bishops	2
Abbots	1
Priests: Diocesan Active in Diocese	62
Priests: Diocesan Active Outside Diocese	5
Priests: Retired, Sick or Absent	33
Number of Diocesan Priests	100
Religious Priests in Diocese	75
Total Priests in Diocese	175
Extern Priests in Diocese	34
Ordinations:	
Diocesan Priests	3
Religious Priests	3
Transitional Deacons	8
Permanent Deacons	29
Permanent Deacons in Diocese	152
Total Brothers	8
Total Sisters	118
Parishes	
Parishes	69
With Resident Pastor:	
Resident Diocesan Priests	43
Resident Religious Priests	12
Without Resident Pastor:	
Administered by Priests	10
Administered by Deacons	4
Quasi Parishes	5
Pastoral Centers	3
Professional Ministry Personnel:	
Sisters	13
Lay Ministers	227
Welfare	
Homes for the Aged	2
Total Assisted	252
Day Care Centers	1
Total Assisted	163
Special Centers for Social Services	4
Total Assisted	59,579
Other Institutions	2
Total Assisted	6,330
Educational	
Seminaries, Diocesan	2
Students from This Diocese	38
Students from Other Diocese	49
Diocesan Students in Other Seminaries	32
Seminaries, Religious	1
Students Religious	13
Total Seminarians	83
Colleges and Universities	1
Total Students	2,861
High Schools, Diocesan and Parish	3
Total Students	2,850
High Schools, Private	4
Total Students	2,391
Elementary Schools, Diocesan and Parish	28
Total Students	9,737
Elementary Schools, Private	2
Total Students	487
Non-residential Schools for the Disabled	1
Total Students	150
Catechesis/Religious Education:	
High School Students	6,700
Elementary Students	40,919
Total Students under Catholic Instruction	66,178
Teachers in the Diocese:	
Priests	15
Scholastics	3
Brothers	4
Sisters	13
Lay Teachers	1,238
Vital Statistics	
Receptions into the Church:	
Infant Baptism Totals	15,390
Adult Baptism Totals	986
Received into Full Communion	529
First Communions	11,620
Confirmations	8,151
Marriages:	
Catholic	1,514
Interfaith	393
Total Marriages	1,907
Deaths	1,328
Total Catholic Population	1,165,415
Total Population	3,770,433

Former Bishops—Rt. Revs. THOMAS F. BRENNAN, D.D., cons. April 5, 1891; resigned Nov. 17, 1892; died March 21, 1916; EDWARD JOSEPH DUNNE, D.D., cons. Nov. 30. 1893; died Aug. 5, 1910; Most Revs. JOSEPH PATRICK LYNCH, D.D., LL.D., appt. June 8, 1911; cons. July 12, 1911; Assistant at Pontifical Throne, May 13, 1936; died Aug. 19, 1954; THOMAS K. GORMAN, D.D., D.Sc.Hist., ord. June 23, 1917; Bishop of Reno; appt. April 24, 1931; cons. July 22, 1931; Assistant at the Pontifical Throne, May 4, 1942; appt. Titular Bishop of Rhasus and Coadjutor to the Bishop of Dallas, Feb. 8, 1952; succeeded to Aug. 19, 1954; resigned and appointed Titular Bishop of Pinhel, Aug. 27, 1969. (Title rescinded); died Aug. 16, 1980; THOMAS TSCHOEPE, D.D., ord. May 30, 1943; appt. Bishop of San Angelo, Jan. 12, 1966; cons. March 9, 1966; appt. Bishop of Dallas, Aug. 27, 1969; installed Oct. 29, 1969; retired July 14, 1990; died Jan. 24, 2009; CHARLES V. GRAHMANN, ord. March 17, 1956; appt. Titular Bishop of Equilio and Auxiliary of San Antonio June 30, 1981; cons. Aug. 29, 1981; appt. First Bishop of Victoria April 14, 1982; installed May 29, 1982; appt. Coadjutor of Dallas Dec. 18, 1989; Reception as Coadjutor of Dallas Feb. 21, 1990; appt. Bishop of Dallas July 14, 1990; retired March 6, 2007.

Vicars General—Most Revs. J. DOUGLAS DESHOTEL, V.G.; MARK J. SEITZ, V.G.

Diocesan Pastoral Center—*3725 Blackburn, P.O. Box 190507, Dallas, 75219*. Tel: 214-528-2240; Fax: 214-526-1743. Office Hours: 9-5.

Episcopal Vicar—Rev. Msgr. MILAM J. JOSEPH.

Vicar for Clergy—Rev. GREGORY KELLY.

Chancellor—MARY EDLUND, J.C.L.

Diocesan Tribunal—*Mailing Address: P.O. Box 190507, Dallas, 75219*. Tel: 214-379-2840; Fax: 214-523-2437.

Judicial Vicar—Rev. Msgr. JOHN P. BELL, J.C.L.

Director of the Tribunal—WILLIAM C. HARE III, J.C.L.

Assessor—MARGARET GILLETT.

Defensor Vinculi—JOHN P. GARGAN, J.C.D., J.D.; Rev. Msgrs. RONNY E. JENKINS, J.C.D.; LEON DUESMAN, J.C.B.; MARY EDLUND, J.C.L.

Adjutant Judicial Vicars—Rev. Msgr. GLENN D. GARDNER, V.F., J.C.D.; Very Rev. JOHN LIBONE, V.F., J.C.L.

Promoter of Justice—MARY EDLUND, J.C.L.

Auditors and Notaries—MARIA LONGORIA-CHAVEZ; CAROL PHILLIPS; BRENDA M. SMITH; NORA D. SMITH; ELSA BUENDIA; DENISE SNIDER.

Diocesan Judges—WILLIAM C. HARE III, J.C.L.; LYNDA ROBITAILLE, J.C.D.; DIANE L. BARR, J.C.D., J.D.; Sr. MARIE BREITENBECK, O.P., J.C.D.; Rev. Msgr. MILAM J. JOSEPH; Deacon RAYMOND H. SMITH.

Procurator-Advocates—LARRIE W. ARNOLD, M.D.; SUSAN C. BOYD; BEBE CANTU; JUDY CLARK; DIANE DANIELS; THERESA ETCHEVERRY; ANTHONY R. FLEO; Deacon DON FORBRICH; JEANNE MARIE GIRSCH; SANDRA WARNE GIST; Deacon WALTER GOVE; MARY CATHERINE HARE; LANAY N. HARTMANN; Sr. MARY PAUL HAASE, C.S.F.N.; JOAN HEITING; LEO HEITING; MARY L. IZAK; CECILIA LYNNE JONES; Deacon JOHN PAUL KELLY; ANNE C. KEOUGH; BARBARA LANDREGAN; DONALD LENZ; PRISCILLA MAHAFFEY; MARGIE MEDLIN; Rev. JOSEPH A. MEHAN JR.; LINDA MOSES; YOLANDA ORTIZ; DENISE G. PHILLIPS; Deacons KENNETH REISOR; PAUL W. REITTINGER; MARY KAY RITCHIE; MARY ROBINSON; Deacon ROBERT

SANCHEZ; MONICA SPARKMAN; Deacons CARL H. THELIN; GARY M. VOGEL.

Pastors Consultors—Rev. Msgr. ROBERT M. COERVER, V.F.; Very Rev. T. MICHAEL DUGAN, V.F.; Rev. GREGORY KELLY, Vicar for Clergy Ex Officio; Rev. Msgrs. HENRY V. PETTER; LAWRENCE PICHARD.

College of Consultors—Rev. GREGORY KELLY; Rev. Msgr. HENRY V. PETTER; Most Rev. J. DOUGLAS DESHOTEL, V.G., Ex Officio; Very Rev. ROBERT WILLIAMS, V.F.; Rev. Msgr. GLENN D. GARDNER, V.F., J.C.D.; Rev. J. EDUARDO GONZALEZ; Most Rev. MARK J. SEITZ, V.G., Ex Officio; Rev. Msgr. MILAM J. JOSEPH; Very Rev. JOHN LIBONE, V.F., J.C.L.

Presbyteral Council—Appointed Members: Very Rev. ANDREW V. SEMLER, V.F.; Rev. Msgr. HENRY V. PETTER; Revs. VINCENT C. ANYAMA; J. EDUARDO GONZALEZ.

Deans—Very Rev. T. MICHAEL DUGAN, V.F., Southwest; Rev. Msgr. GLENN D. GARDNER, V.F., J.C.D., Eastern; Very Revs. ROBERT WILLIAMS, V.F., Southeast; DONALD ZEILER, V.F., Northern; JOHN LIBONE, V.F., J.C.L., Central; MICHAEL GUADAGNOLI, V.F., Northeast Deanery; Rev. Msgr. ROBERT M. COERVER, V.F., North Central.

At Large Members—Revs. BRUCE BRADLEY; EDMUNDO B. PAREDES, V.F.; Rev. Msgr. DONALD F. ZIMMERMAN; Revs. MICHAEL D. FORGE; J. EDUARDO GONZALEZ; SALVADOR GUZMAN.

Ex Officio Members—Most Revs. J. DOUGLAS DESHOTEL, V.G.; MARK J. SEITZ, V.G.; Rev. GREGORY KELLY, Vicar for Clergy; Rev. Msgr. MILAM J. JOSEPH.

Censor Librorum—Rev. Msgrs. GLENN D. GARDNER, V.F., J.C.D.; ROBERT M. COERVER, V.F.

Diocesan Pastoral Council—Most Rev. KEVIN J. FARRELL, D.D.; GLORIA ABANAKA; KAY YATES; JACK GUILLORY; TERRI DALKE; RENE DE LA FUENTE; BETTY BRUCE; RAUL PAREDES; GAIL HARTIN, Ph.D.; RICHARD KELLY; FELICITAS ALFARO; HUGO PONS; ESTELLA M. CASTILLO; ALEX EDOBOR; MARY EDLUND, J.C.L., Chancellor.

Diocesan Boards

Finance Council—Most Rev. KEVIN J. FARRELL, D.D.; EUGENE VILFORDI; MIKE CORBOY; MICHAEL T. WEIS; Most Rev. J. DOUGLAS DESHOTEL, V.G.; ROGER ENRICO; FRANK HUBACH; HARRY J. LONGWELL; JAMES MORONEY III; KATHY MULDOON; LYDIA NOVAKOV; JACK PRATT; ED SCHAFFLER; DENIS SIMON.

Building Commission—Rev. Msgr. JEROME P. DUESMAN; Deacon BRIAN MITCHELL; JOSEPH SCOLARO; MICHAEL T. WEIS; STEVE MALONE.

Personnel Board—Most Revs. J. DOUGLAS DESHOTEL, V.G.; KEVIN J. FARRELL, D.D.; MARK J. SEITZ, V.G.; Revs. GREGORY KELLY; THOMAS CLOHERTY; STEPHEN W. BIERSCHENK; EDMUNDO B. PAREDES, V.F.; Rev. Msgr. HENRY V. PETTER; Very Rev. MICHAEL GUADAGNOLI, V.F.

Accreditation Board—Revs. BRUCE BRADLEY; GREGORY KELLY; Sr. THERESA KHIRALLAH, S.S.N.D.; Deacon JESSE OLIVAREZ; MARY EDLUND, J.C.L., Chancellor.

Diocesan Offices and Directors

Judicial Vicar—Rev. Msgr. JOHN P. BELL, J.C.L.

Tribunal—

Episcopal Vicar—Rev. Msgr. MILAM J. JOSEPH.

Vicars General—Most Revs. J. DOUGLAS DESHOTEL; MARK J. SEITZ, V.G.

I. Vicar for Clergy—Rev. GREGORY KELLY, Dir.

Priest Personnel—Rev. GREGORY KELLY, Mailing Address: P.O. Box 190507, Dallas, 75219. Tel: 214-379-2848.

Vocations—Revs. RODOLFO GARCÍA, Dir.; ANTHONY F. LACKLAND, Assoc. Dir.

Diaconate—Deacon ARNOLD PICON, Dir., 901 S. Madison Ave., Dallas, 75208. Mailing Address: P.O. Box 190507, Dallas, 75219. Tel: 214-943-6585.

II. Catholic Schools Office—Sr. GLORIA CAIN, S.S.N.D., Supt., Mailing Address: P.O. Box 190507, Dallas, 75219. Tel: 214-379-2831.

III. Director of Ministries—Sr. THERESA KHIRALLAH, S.S.N.D., Mailing Address: P.O. Box 190507, Dallas, 75219. Tel: 214-379-2897.

Catechetical Services—LOURDES MAYER, Dir., Mailing Address: P.O. Box 190507, Dallas, 75219. Tel: 214-379-2848.

Youth and Young Adult Ministries—SUSAN DORFMEISTER, Dir., Mailing Address: P.O. Box 190507, Dallas, 75219. Tel: 214-379-2843.

Pastoral Services—Deacon CHARLES STUMP JR., Dir. Tel: 214-379-2882.

Substance Addictions Ministry—PHIL PASCHKE, Co-ord. Tel: 214-960-2166.

Ministries to People with Disabilities and Their Caregivers and to the Deaf—JOHN AUST, Coord. Tel: 214-379-2866.

Hospital Ministry—Deacon CHARLES STUMP JR., Dir. Tel: 214-379-2882.

Prison Ministry—Deacon JOSE TREVINO, Coord. Tel: 214-379-2883.

Liturgy Office—Dr. PATRICIA HUGHES, Dir. Worship. Tel: 214-379-2860.

Sacramental Ministries—

Sacrament of Marriage—DIANE DANIELS, Dir. Tel: 214-379-2881.

IV. Chief Financial Officer—

Business Office—MICHAEL T. WEIS, Dir. Tel: 214-379-2807.

Retreat/Conference Center— Catholic Conference and Formation Center Deacon JESSE OLIVAREZ, Dir., 901 S. Madison Ave., Dallas, 75208. Mailing Address: P.O. Box 190507, Dallas, 75219. Tel: 214-943-6585.

V. Director of Construction and Real Estate—STEVE MALONE.

VI. Director of Human Resources—JAY SALEM.

VII. Diocesan Risk Management—JOHN A. SMITH, Dir.

VIII. Director of Parish & School Financial Reporting—FRED VILLELA.

IX. Director of Catholic Charities—V. JOSEPH BROGDON, Interim Dir. Tel: 214-520-6590.

X. Director of Communications—ANNETTE GONZALES TAYLOR, Dir., Mailing Address: P.O. Box 190507, Dallas, 75219. Tel: 214-379-2873.

The Texas Catholic and La Revista Catolica—Official Catholic Newspapers of the Diocese of Dallas Tel: 214-528-8792; Fax: 214-528-3411. Web: www.texascatholic.com. Most Rev. KEVIN JOSEPH FARRELL, D.D., Publisher; DAVID SEDENO, Editor; ERIK RODRIGUEZ, Mng. Editor The Texas Catholic; CONSTANZA MORALES, Mng. Editor La Revista Cato Lica; ANTONIO RAMIREZ JR., Business Mgr. Tel: 214-379-2891; Fax: 214-528-3411.

XI. Director of Development—JIM URBANUS.

The Bishops Annual Appeal for Catholic Ministries—PAUL VITANZA, C.F.R.E., Dir. Tel: 214-379-2862.

Chancellor—MARY EDLUND, J.C.L., Mailing Address: P.O. Box 190507, Dallas, 75219. Tel: 214-379-2819.

Archives—STEVE LANDREGAN, Archivist. Tel: 214-379-2871.

Pastoral Planning and Research—LYNN ROSSOL, Dir. Tel: 214-379-2854.

Safe Environment Office—BARBARA LANDREGAN, Dir., Mailing Address: P.O. Box 190507, Dallas, 75219. Tel: 214-379-2812.

Victim Assistance Coordinator—MARY EDLUND, J.C.L. Tel: 214-379-2819.

CLERGY, PARISHES, MISSIONS AND PAROCHIAL SCHOOLS

CITY OF DALLAS

(DALLAS COUNTY)

1—CATHEDRAL-SANTUARIO DE GUADALUPE (1869) Revs. J. Eduardo Gonzalez; Henry Erazo Herrea; Deacons Benito Garcia; Charles Stump Jr.; Larry Harmon; Jose Luis Hernandez; Benigno Arana.
Mailing Address: 2215 Ross Ave., 75201. Fax: 214-954-1557.
Res.: 2102 Allen, 75204. Tel: 214-871-1362.
Catechesis/Religious Program—Imelda Ramirez, D.R.E. Students 879.

2—ALL SAINTS (1976) Most Rev. Mark J. Seitz; Revs. Paul Nguyen; Peter Chinnappan; Deacons Denis Simon; John R. Costello.
Res.: 5231 Meadowcreek, 75248. Tel: 972-661-9282; Fax: 972-233-5401.
School—(Grades K-8), 7777 Osage Plaza Pkwy., 75252. Tel: 214-217-3300; Fax: 214-217-3339. Denise Thompson, Prin.; Chris Sanders, Vice Prin. Students 396.
Catechesis/Religious Program—Students 591.

3—ST. ANDREW KIM (1977), (Korean), Rev. Dominic Kim, Pastoral Admin.
Res.: 7915 Enclave Way, 75258. Tel: 972-620-9150; Fax: 972-484-4628. Email: office@dallaskoreancatholic.org. Web: www.dallaskoreancatholic.org.
Catechesis/Religious Program—Nina Kang, D.R.E. Sisters 2; Students 233.

4—ST. ANTHONY (1938), (African American), Deacon Denis D. Corbin, Pastoral Admin.
Res.: 2711 Romine St., 75215. Tel: 214-428-6926.

5—ST. AUGUSTINE CATHOLIC CHURCH (1937) Revs. Anibal Adorno; Luis Fermin Sierra; Deacons Robert Sanchez; Jose Muniz; Sergio Carranza.
Res.: 1047 N. St. Augustine Dr., 75217. Tel: 214-792-9200; Fax: 214-398-2580. Email: churchoffice@stadallas.com.
School—(Grades K-8), 1054 N. St. Augustine Dr., Bldg B., 75217. Tel: 214-391-1381; Fax: 214-391-8781. Email: office@stadallas.com. Marian Davis, Prin. Lay Teachers 16; Students 145.
Catechesis/Religious Program—Arabelia Martinez, P.C.L. Students 672.

6—ST. BERNARD OF CLAIRVAUX (1947), (Hispanic), Revs. Walter Mallo, I.V.E.; Gaston Giacinti, I.V.E.
Res.: 1404 Old Gate Ln., 75218. Tel: 214-321-0454; Fax: 214-320-0119. Web: www.sbchurchdallas.com.
School—(Grades PreK-8), 1420 Old Gate Ln., 75218. Tel: 214-321-2897; Fax: 214-321-4060. Rosemary Kolbo, Librarian. Lay Teachers 16; Students 191.
Catechesis/Religious Program—Sandra Godina, P.C.L. Students 746.

7—BLESSED SACRAMENT (1901) Revs. Jose I. Figueroa; Agustin Fuertes; Deacon Salvador Pina.
Res.: 231 N. Marsalis Ave., 75203. Tel: 214-948-6535; Fax: 214-948-1660. Web: www.bsdallas.org.
Catechesis/Religious Program—Students 841.

8—ST. CECILIA (1933), (Hispanic), Revs. Edmundo B. Paredes; Antonio Salvador Rodriguez, Parochial Vicar; Deacons Gonzalo Gonzales; Onesimo Martinez.
Res.: 1809 W. Davis St., 75208. Tel: 214-941-5821; Fax: 214-946-4466. Email: stceciliachurch@sbcglobal.net.
School—(Grades K-8), 635 Marycliff Rd., 75208. Tel: 214-948-8628; Fax: 214-948-4956. Guadalupe Moreno, Librarian. Sisters of St. Mary of Namur 1; Lay Teachers 19; Students 236.
Catechesis/Religious Program—Students 571.

9—CHRIST THE KING (1941) Rev. Msgr. Donald F. Zimmerman; Mary Catherine Hare, Pastoral Assoc.; William C. Hare III, Pastoral Assoc.; Deacon Tim Muldoon. In Res., Rev. Anthony F. Lackland.
Res.: 8017 Preston Rd., 75225. Tel: 214-365-1200; Fax: 214-365-1205.
School—(Grades K-8), 4100 Colgate St., 75225. Tel: 214-365-1234; Fax: 214-365-1236. Lay Teachers 47; Students 425.
Catechesis/Religious Program—Students 520.

10—ST. EDWARD (1903) Revs. Edison Vela; Miguel Angel Bravo.
Res.: 4014 Simpson St., 75246. Tel: 214-823-1291; Fax: 214-823-7535. Web: stedwardparish.org.
Catechesis/Religious Program—Rita Lopez, D.R.E. Students 1,076.

11—ST. ELIZABETH OF HUNGARY (1956) Very Rev. T. Michael Dugan; Rev. Benjamin Molina; Deacons Denis Simon; Frank Kozarevich; Douglas Boyd. In Res., Rev. Alex Buitrago.
Res.: 4015 S. Hampton Rd., 75224. Tel: 214-331-4328; Fax: 214-331-2464. Web: stelizabethofh.org/parish.htm.
School—(Grades K-8), 4019 S. Hampton Rd., 75224. Tel: 214-331-5139; Fax: 214-467-4346. Web: www.stelizabethofh.org. Christina Clem, Prin.; Monica Connelly, Librarian. Lay Teachers 23; Students 285.
Catechesis/Religious Program—Kathy Price, P.C.L. Students 248.

12—HOLY CROSS (1956) Rev. Timothy A. Gollob; Deacon Antonio D. Trevino. In Res., Rev. James George McKenna (Retired).
Res.: 2926 E. Ledbetter Dr., 75216. Tel: 214-374-7952; Fax: 214-375-7457.
Catechesis/Religious Program—Students 212.

13—HOLY TRINITY (1907) Revs. Juan Antonio Ruiz, C.M.; Nhan Tran, C.M.; Donald J. Ours, C.M.; Deacons Don Forbrich; John Kelly; Michael Bolesta.
Mailing Address: 3826 Gilbert Ave., 75219. Web: www.htccd.org.
Res.: 3811 Oak Lawn Ave., 75219. Tel: 214-526-8555; Fax: 214-526-3477.
School—(Grades K-8), 3815 Oak Lawn Ave., 75219. Tel: 214-526-5113. Web: www.htcsdallas.org. Lay Ministers 8; Lay Teachers 16; Students 184.
Catechesis/Religious Program—Students 325.

14—ST. JAMES (1934) Rev. Jimwell Goyo; Rev. Msgr. Mario Magbanua; Deacon Vincent F. Jimenez.
Mailing Address: P.O. Box 763338, 75376.
Res.: 1002 E. Saner Ave., 75216. Tel: 214-371-9209; Fax: 214-371-0226. Email: stjamesdallas@sbcglobal.net.
Catechesis/Religious Program—Students 505.

15—ST. JUDE CHAPEL (Downtown Dallas) (1968) Rev. Jonathan Austin.
Res.: 1521 Main St., 75201. Tel: 214-742-2508; Fax: 214-748-5282. Web: stjudechapel.net.

16—MARY IMMACULATE (1956) Rev. Michael D. Forge; Rev. Msgr. Andrés Sagra; Deacons Patrick Hayes; Philip E. Webb; Martin Armendariz.
Res. & Mailing Address: 2800 Valwood Pkwy., 75234. Tel: 972-243-7104; Fax: 972-406-1254. Email: anny@maryimmaculatechurch.org. Web: maryimmaculatechurch.org.
School—(Grades K-8) Tel: 972-243-7105; Fax: 972-241-7678. Matthew Krause, Prin.; Karen Saldana, Librarian. Lay Teachers 32; Students 485.
Catechesis/Religious Program—Sr. Beatriz Ortega, O.C.D., P.C.L. Students 1,315.

17—ST. MARY OF CARMEL (1944) Revs. Jenaro de la Cruz, O.C.D.; John Michael Payne, O.C.D.
Res.: 2900 Vilbig Rd., 75212. Tel: 214-747-1433.
School—(Grades K-8), 1716 Singleton Blvd., 75212. Tel: 214-748-2934; Fax: 214-760-9052. Thomas Suhy, Prin. Sisters of the Holy Spirit 1; Lay Teachers 13; Students 184.
Catechesis/Religious Program—Students 290.

18—ST. MONICA (1954) Rev. Stephen W. Bierschenk; Rev. Msgr. John F. Meyers, Pastor Emeritus (Retired); Deacons Michael Weston; Larry Lucido; Bob Marrinan; Brian Mitchell; Abel Cortes. In Res., Rev. Alfonse Nazzaro, L.C.
Res.: 9933 Midway Rd., 75220. Tel: 214-358-1453; Fax: 214-351-1887. Web: stmonicachurch.org.
School—(Grades PreK-8), 4140 Walnut Hill Ln., 75229. Tel: 214-351-5688; Fax: 214-352-2608. Patricia Dulac, Prin. Lay Teachers 60; Students 861.
Catechesis/Religious Program—Marianela Byrne, Dir. Faith Formation. Students 1,189.

19—NUESTRA SENORA DEL PILAR (2001), (Hispanic), Rev. Wilmer de Jesus Daza. In Res., Most Rev. José A. Valbuena.
4455 W. Illinois Ave., 75211. Tel: 214-467-9116; Fax: 214-339-7249. Email: pilar.church@sbcglobal.net.
Catechesis/Religious Program—Students 701.

20—OUR LADY OF LOURDES (1954) Revs. Mario Garcia, O.F.M.Cap. (Spain); Roberto Viveros, O.F.M.-Cap. (Mexico); Deacon Pete Rodriguez.
Res.: 5605 Bernal Dr., 75212. Tel: 214-637-6673; Fax: 214-637-2454.
Catechesis/Religious Program—Amy Rodriguez, P.C.L. Students 714.

21—OUR LADY OF PERPETUAL HELP (1942), (Hispanic), Rev. Cruz Calderon; Deacons Albert Montes; Leopoldo Cortinas III; Felicito Laguna.
Res.: 7617 Cortland Ave., 75235. Tel: 214-352-6012; Fax: 214-351-9883. Email: secretary@olphdallas.org. Web: olphdallas.com.
School—(Grades PreK-8), 7625 Cortland Ave., 75235. Tel: 214-351-3396; Fax: 214-351-9889. Web: www.olphdallas.org. Colleen Walker, Librarian. Lay Teachers 12; Students 206.
Catechesis/Religious Program—Students 448.
Convent—Daughters of the Sacred Heart Sisters 4.

22—ST. PATRICK (1963) Revs. Josef Vollmer-Konig; Alan Paul McDonald; Deacon John C. Nordick.
Res.: 9643 Ferndale Rd., 75238. Tel: 214-348-7380; Fax: 214-340-5956.
School—(Grades PreK-8), 9635 Ferndale Rd., 75238. Tel: 214-348-8070; Fax: 214-503-7230. Web: www.stpatrickschool.org. Frances Thompson, Prin.; Ginger Loshelder, Librarian. Sisters of the Incarnate Word and Blessed Sacrament 2; Lay Teachers 33; Students 543.
Catechesis/Religious Program—Mrs. Martha Noel, P.C.L. Students 732.

23—ST. PETER (1905) Rev. Stanislaw Poszwa, S.Ch.
Res.: 2907 Woodall Rodgers Fwy., 75204. Tel: 214-855-1384; Fax: 214-855-1309. Web: www.stpeterdal.com.
Catechesis/Religious Program—Marcella Savala-Hamilton, P.C.L. Students 61.

24—ST. PETER VIETNAMESE (1996) Rev. Pham M. Joseph, C.M.; Deacon Uong Hung.
10123 Garland Rd., 75218. Tel: 214-321-9493; Fax: 214-320-2219. Web: www.giaoxuthanhphero.org.
Catechesis/Religious Program—Students 76.

25—ST. PHILIP (1954) Deacon David T. Obergfell, Pastoral Admin.; Rev. Eric Hernandez, M.N.M., Parochial Vicar.
Res.: 8131 Military Pkwy., 75227. Tel: 214-388-5464; Fax: 214-381-0466.
School—(Grades K-8), 8151 Military Pkwy., 75227. Tel: 214-381-4973. Linda Garrett, Librarian. Sisters of the Holy Spirit 1; Lay Teachers 13; Students 159.
Catechesis/Religious Program—Ginna Curts, P.C.L. Students 466.

26—ST. PIUS X (1954) Very Rev. Michael Guadagnoli; Rev. Lauro Gonzalez, M.N.M.; Deacons David Leerssen; Michael Shaw; John A. Schell; Paul Powers; Roberto Palomeque.
Res.: 3030 Gus Thomasson Rd., 75228. Tel: 972-279-6155; Fax: 972-686-7510.
School—(Grades K-8) Tel: 972-279-2339; Fax: 972-613-2059. Cynthia Elwood, Prin. Lay Teachers 25; Students 305.
Catechesis/Religious Program—Tel: 972-279-2558. Maria Elena Quiroz, P.C.L. Students 956.

27—QUASI-PARISH OF OUR LADY OF SAN JUAN DE LOS LAGOS - ST. THERESA (1928) Deacon Hugo A. Salinas.
Res.: 2601 Singleton Blvd., 75212. Tel: 214-631-9627; Fax: 214-631-9627.
Catechesis/Religious Program—Tel: 214-688-0942. Students 233.

28—ST. RITA (1961) Rev. Msgr. Robert M. Coerver; Rev. Jacinto Garcia; Deacons William J. Schuster; Charles T. Sylvester; Bill Fobes; Moses Chung.
Office: 12521 Inwood Rd., 75244. Tel: 972-934-8388; Fax: 972-934-8965.
Res.: 12626 Planters Glen, 75244. Tel: 972-239-5205.
School—(Grades K-8), 12525 Inwood Rd., 75244. Tel: 972-239-3203; Fax: 972-934-3657. Dr. Elena Hines, Prin. Lay Teachers 53; Students 672.
Catechesis/Religious Program—Susan Sheetz, Interim Coord., Children's Faith Formation. Students 507.

29—SAN JUAN DIEGO PARISH (2006) Rev. Jesus Belmontes, Admin.
10150 Monroe Dr., 75229. Tel: 214-271-4691; Fax: 214-271-4696.
Catechesis/Religious Program—Lupita Frausto, P.C.L. Students 1,432.

30—SANTA CLARA (1993), (Hispanic), Very Rev. Robert Williams; Rev. Jorge Arturo Carvajol.
Res.: 321 Calumet Ave., 75211. Tel: 214-337-3936; Fax: 214-333-9148. Web: www.santaclaracatholicchurch.net.
School—Santa Clara of Assisi Catholic Academy, (Grades PreK-8) Tel: 214-333-9423; Fax: 214-333-2556. Email: smatous@santaclaraacademy.org. Web: santaclaraacademy.org. Stephanie Matous, Prin. Lay Teachers 11; Students 150.
Catechesis/Religious Program—Students 947.

31—ST. THOMAS AQUINAS (1952) Very Rev. John Libone; Rev. Victor Bartolotta; Deacons Kenneth Reisor; Richard Harrington; Edward Leyden.
Res.: 6306 Kenwood Ave., 75214. Tel: 214-821-3360; Fax: 214-821-5395.
School—(Grades 3-8), Upper School, 3741 Abrams Rd., 75214. Tel: 214-826-0566; Fax: 214-826-0251. Patrick Magee, Prin. Lay Teachers 83; Students 876.
School—(Grades K-2), Lower School, 6255 E. Mockingbird, 75214. Tel: 469-341-0911.
Catechesis/Religious Program—Victor Bartolotta, Youth Min. (5-12). Students 524.

OUTSIDE THE CITY OF DALLAS

ALLEN, COLLIN CO.

1—ST. JUDE (1981) Revs. Timothy A. Church, Admin.; Eugene Okoli; Deacon Ronald Fejeran.
Res.: 1515 N. Greenville Ave., 75002. Tel: 972-727-1177; Fax: 972-727-1401. Web: www.stjudeparish.com.
Catechesis/Religious Program— Julie Buchanan, P.C.L. Students 2,079.

2—OUR LADY OF ANGELS (2000) Rev. Msgr. John P. Bell; Deacons Mike Picard; John O'Leary.
Church: 1914 Ridgeview Dr., 75013. Tel: 469-467-9669; Fax: 469-467-0114. Web: www.ourladyofangels.com.
Catechesis/Religious Program—Elizabeth Adams, C.R.E. (Grade School); Sheila Tullier, C.R.E. (Middle School); Matthew Decker, C.R.E. (High School). Students 859.

BONHAM, FANNIN CO., ST. ELIZABETH Rev. Manuel Sabando; Deacon Joseph Culling.
Res.: 916 Maple St., 75418. Tel: 903-583-7734; Fax: 903-583-7359. Email: stebonham@verizon.net. Web: www.se-bonham.com.
Catechesis/Religious Program—Students 108.

CARROLLTON, DALLAS CO., SACRED HEART OF JESUS CHRIST (1999) Rev. Joseph Son Van Nguyen.
2121 N. Denton, 75006. Tel: 972-446-3461; Fax: 972-446-9551.
Catechesis/Religious Program—Theresa Thee Hong Tran, P.C.L. Students 466.

COMMERCE, HUNT CO., ST. JOSEPH (1895) Rev. Marcus Chidozie; Deacon James Starr.
Rectory—1508 Cooper St., 75428. Tel: 903-886-7135; Fax: 903-886-8034. Web: www.stjoetx.net.
Church: P.O. Box 832, 75429-0832.

COPPELL, DALLAS CO., ST. ANN (1985) Rev. Msgr. Henry V. Petter; Revs. Patrick Olaleye; Orlando Cardozo; Deacons Ed Scarbrough; Pete Markwald; Kory Killgo.
Res.: 180 Samuel Blvd., 75019.
Church: Tel: 972-393-5544; Fax: 972-462-1617.
Catechesis/Religious Program—Debbie Matalone, D.R.E. Students 2,471.

CORSICANA, NAVARRO CO., IMMACULATE CONCEPTION (1871) Rev. Jason Cargo; Deacon Lewis J. Palos.
Res.: 3000 Hwy. 22 W., P.O. Box 798, 75151. Tel: 903-874-4473; Fax: 903-874-2619.
School—James L. Collins Catholic School, (Grades K-8) Tel: 903-872-1751. Lay Teachers 13; Students 175.
Catechesis/Religious Program—Gerardo Alvarado, P.C.L. Students 397.

DENISON, GRAYSON CO., ST. PATRICK (1872) Rev. Stephen J. Mocio.
Res.: 314 N. Rusk Ave., 75020. Tel: 903-463-3275; Fax: 903-463-3447. Web: www.saintpats.net.
Catechesis/Religious Program—Stephen Thompson, Youth Dir. Students 140.

DUNCANVILLE, DALLAS CO., HOLY SPIRIT (1974) Revs. Joseph C. Lee; Peter Tuan Le; Deacons Al Evans; Paul Wood.
Res.: 1111 W. Danieldale Rd., 75137-3719. Tel: 972-298-4971; Fax: 972-709-1443. Web: holyspiritcatholic.com.
Catechesis/Religious Program—Anne C. Keough, P.C.L. Students 684.

ENNIS, ELLIS CO., ST. JOHN NEPOMUCENE (1902) [CEM] Revs. John Dick; Antonio Liberman-Ormaza; Deacon Don Griffith.
401 E. Lampasas St., 75119. Tel: 972-878-2834; Fax: 972-875-2452. Web: stjohncc.net.
Rectory & Res.: 505 E. Lampasas, 75119.
Catechesis/Religious Program—Students 908.

FERRIS, ELLIS CO., CORPUS CHRISTI (1977), (Hispanic), Deacon Frutos Vega.
Res.: 111 N. Wood, 75125. Tel: 972-544-2161; Fax: 972-325-2168.
Catechesis/Religious Program—Antonio Duenas, P.C.L. Students 300.

FORNEY, KAUFMAN CO., ST. MARTIN OF TOURS (1891) Rev. Msgr. Glenn D. Gardner.
Res.: 9470 C.R. 213, 75126. Tel: 972-564-9114; Fax: 972-564-9138. Email: stmchurchoff@aol.com.
Catechesis/Religious Program—Email: stmreleducation@aol.com. Beth Wright, P.C.L. Students 220.

FRISCO, COLLIN CO., ST. FRANCIS OF ASSISI (1966) Rev. Msgr. Lawrence Pichard; Rev. Vincent C. Anyama; Deacons Frank Reyna; Carl Macero; Greg Kahrs.
Res.: 8000 El Dorado Pkwy., 75033. Tel: 972-712-2645; Fax: 972-712-1087. Email: office@stfoafrisco.org. Web: www.stfoafrisco.org.
Catechesis/Religious Program—Students 2,090.

GARLAND, DALLAS CO.

1—GOOD SHEPHERD (1944) Revs. Jose Luis Esparza, F.N.; Manuel Gutierrez, F.N.; Americo Lozaro; Deacons Jim Harris; Jose E. Lopez.
Res.: 201 S. 13th St., 75040. Tel: 972-276-8587; Fax: 972-494-3653.
School—(Grades K-8), 214 S. Garland Ave., 75040. Tel: 972-272-6533; Fax: 972-272-0512. Web: www-.goodshepherdcatholicschool.org. Gail R. Bassett, Prin. Brothers 1; Lay Teachers 20; Students 220.
Catechesis/Religious Program—Blanca Alanis, P.C.L. Students 1,664.

2—ST. MARY MALANKARA (1996) Rev. Joseph Nedumankuzhiyil.
2650 E. Scyene Rd., Mesquite, 75181. Tel: 972-352-1257.
Res.: *c/o Good Shepherd Church*, 201 S. 13th St., 75040. Tel: 516-216-4106.
Catechesis/Religious Program—Students 15.

3—ST. MICHAEL THE ARCHANGEL (1980) Rev. Joseph A. Mehan Jr.; Deacon Joe Perez.
Res.: 950 Trails Pkwy., 75043. Tel: 972-279-6581; Fax: 972-279-6647.
Catechesis/Religious Program—Students 662.

4—MOTHER OF PERPETUAL HELP (1992), (Vietnamese), Revs. Tuan Bui, C.Ss.R.; Thomas Ho, C.Ss.R.
Res.: 2121 W. Apollo Rd., 75044. Tel: 972-414-7073. Web: www.dmhcg.org.
Catechesis/Religious Program—Students 1,000.

GRAND PRAIRIE, DALLAS CO.

1—IMMACULATE CONCEPTION (1916) Rev. Douglas A. Zavala, Pastoral Admin.; Deacon David Maida.
Res.: 610 N.E. 17th St., 75050. Tel: 972-262-5137; Fax: 972-264-7657. Web: www.icgrandprairie.org.
School—(Grades PreK-8), 400 N.E. 17th St., 75050. Tel: 972-264-8777; Fax: 972-264-7742. Web: school.icgrandprairie.org. Linda Santos, Prin.; Sr. Catherine Marie Kawa, C.S.F.N., Librarian. Sisters of the Holy Family of Nazareth 4; Lay Teachers 10; Students 124.
Catechesis/Religious Program—Patricia T. Hidalgo, P.C.L.; Diana M. Hernandez, P.C.L. Students 604.

2—ST. JOSEPH VIETNAMESE PARISH (1993) Rev. Ansgar Pham, S.D.D.
Res.: 1902 S. Beltline Rd., 75051. Tel: 972-642-6747; Fax: 972-642-6746.
Catechesis/Religious Program—Students 280.

3—ST. MICHAEL THE ARCHANGEL (1985) Rev. Joseph Hoa Duc Trinh; Deacon J. Robert Miller.
2910 Corn Valley, 75052. Web: www.stmichaelgptx.org.
Res.: 2925 Lake Park Dr., 75052. Tel: 972-262-0552; Fax: 972-642-5429.
Catechesis/Religious Program—Tel: 972-262-6590. Email: 2910smgptx@sbcglobal.net. Students 411.

GREENVILLE, HUNT CO., ST. WILLIAM (1892) Rev. Paul L. Weinberger; Deacon Lee B. Davis.
Res.: 4300 Stuart St., 75401. Tel: 903-450-1177; Fax: 903-455-7134. Email: stwilliam@sbcglobal.net. Web: www.saintwilliamtheconfessor.com.
Catechesis/Religious Program—Tel: 903-455-8201. Students 222.

IRVING, DALLAS CO.

1—CHURCH OF THE INCARNATION (1973) Rev. Donald Dvorak, O.P.; Denise Phillips, Dir. Campus Ministry; Carol Norris, Dir. Music Ministry.
University of Dallas: 1845 E. Northgate Dr., 75062. Tel: 972-721-5375; Fax: 972-721-5351.

2—HOLY FAMILY OF NAZARETH (1964) Rev. Msgr. Jerome P. Duesman; Deacons Kenneth Hale; Ron Morgan.

Res.: 2330 Cheyenne St., 75062. Tel: 972-252-5521; Fax: 972-252-5523. Web: www.holyfamilychurch.net.
School—(Grades K-8), 2323 Cheyenne St., 75062. Tel: 972-255-0205; Fax: 972-252-4167. Web: www.h-fns.com. Mr. Dennis R. Poyant, Prin. Lay Teachers 16; Students 195.
Catechesis/Religious Program—Linda Moses, P.C.L. Students 401.

3—ST. LUKE (1902) Revs. Clair Orso, C.S.; Francesco D'Agostino, C.S.; Deacons Jose Trevino; Daniel D. Segovia; Roger Gette.
Res.: 1015 Schulze Dr., 75060. Tel: 972-259-3222; Fax: 972-259-3339. Web: www.stlukeirving.org.
School—(Grades K-8), 1023 Schulze Dr., 75060. Tel: 972-253-8285; Fax: 972-253-5535. Kathryn Carruth, Prin.; Lucy Sawezyn, Librarian. Lay Teachers 12; Students 116.
Catechesis/Religious Program—Deacon Daniel D. Segovia, P.C.L. Students 1,631.

4—MATER DEI PERSONAL PARISH Rev. Thomas Longua, F.S.S.P.
2030 E. Hwy. 356, 75060. Web: www.materdeiparish.com.
Catechesis/Religious Program—Joanne Dreyer, P.C.L. Students 44.

ITALY, ELLIS CO., EPIPHANY (QUASI PARISH) Revs. Antonio Liberman-Ormaza; John Dick.
434 S. Ward, 76651. Mailing: 401 E. Lampasas St., Ennis, 75119.
Catechesis/Religious Program—Paula Guerrero, P.C.L. Students 31.

KAUFMAN, KAUFMAN CO., ST. ANN (1935) Rev. Anthony M. Densmore; Deacons James Burkel; Sergio Morales.
Res.: 806 N. Washington St., 75142. Tel: 972-962-3247; Fax: 972-932-4003.
Catechesis/Religious Program—Gail Moore, P.C.L. Students 487.

LANCASTER, DALLAS CO., ST. FRANCIS OF ASSISI (1973) Rev. Albert B. Becher; Deacon Victor Carpio.
Res.: 1537 Rogers Ave., 75134. Tel: 972-227-4124; Fax: 972-227-2882. Email: stfran@swbell.net. Web: www.stfrancislancaster.org.
Catechesis/Religious Program—Tel: 972-227-0770. Sherry Granello, P.C.L. Students 402.

MCKINNEY, COLLIN CO.

1—ST. GABRIEL THE ARCHANGEL (1996) Very Rev. Donald Zeiler; Rev. Jose Pazheveettil, M.S.T.; Deacons Ray Smith; Robert Boduch; Victor M. Machiano.
Mailing Address: 110 St. Gabriel Way, 75071. Tel: 972-542-7170; Fax: 972-542-7756. Web: www.stgabriel.org.
Catechesis/Religious Program—Students 963.

2—ST. MICHAEL (1892) Revs. Salvador Gúzman; Arthur Unachukwu; Deacons George Polcer; Federico Marquez.
Res.: 411 Paula Rd., 75069. Tel: 972-542-4667; Fax: 972-542-4641.
Catechesis/Religious Program—Sr. Yolanda Perez, P.C.L. Students 830.

MESQUITE, DALLAS CO., DIVINE MERCY OF OUR LORD (2002) Revs. Ernesto Torres; Gil Mediana; Deacons Al Lopez; Mario Sanchez.
1585 E. Cartwright Rd., 75149. Tel: 972-591-5294; Fax: 972-289-7445. Email: carmen@divinemercytx.org. Web: www.divinemercyofourlord.org.
Rectory—510 Elderwood Loop, 75181. Tel: 972-222-0436.
Catechesis/Religious Program—Email: faithformation@divinemercytx.org. Ana L. Dávila, D.R.E. & P.C.L. Students 566.

PLANO, COLLIN CO.

1—ST. ELIZABETH ANN SETON (1976) Revs. Bruce Bradley; John Szatkowski; Deacons Michael Seibold; Thomas Roche; Bill Flynn; Jack Gulino.
Res.: 2701 W. Piedra Dr., 75023. Tel: 972-596-5505; Fax: 972-985-7573. Web: www.setonparish.org.
Catechesis/Religious Program—3100 W. Spring Creek Pkwy., 75023. Fax: 972-985-0431. Bruce Baumann, P.C.L. Students 1,573.

2—ST. MARK THE EVANGELIST (1966) Revs. Clifford G. Smith; Marco Rangel; John Hopka; Deacons Arnold Picon; Sid Little; Edward Putonti; Juan Jorge Hernandez.
Res.: 1100 W. 15th St., 75075. Tel: 972-423-5600; Fax: 972-423-5024. Web: www.stmarkplano.org.
School—1201 Alma Dr., 75075. Tel: 972-578-0610; Fax: 972-423-3299. Web: www.stmarkcatholicschool.com. Ann Hollenbeck, Librarian. Lay Teachers 48; Students 643.
Catechesis/Religious Program—Students 2,449.

3—PRINCE OF PEACE (1991) Rev. Thomas Cloherty; Rev. Msgr. R. James Balint, Pastor Emeritus (Retired); Rev. Dominic Colangelo, O.P.; Deacons Louis L. Munoz; Eugene T. Kowalski; David E. Tompsett.
Res.: 5100 W. Plano Pkwy., 75093. Tel: 972-380-2100; Fax: 972-380-5162. Web: www.popplano.org.
School—(Grades K-8) Tel: 972-380-5505; Fax: 972-380-2570. Kathy Bailey, Librarian. Lay Teachers 62; Students 848.
Catechesis/Religious Program—Students 412.

4—SACRED HEART OF JESUS (1993), (Chinese), Rev. Vincent Lin Yu Ming.
Church: 4201 14th St., 75074. Tel: 972-516-8500; Fax: 972-516-8500. Web: www.chinese-catholic.org.
Catechesis/Religious Program—Lisa Schutz, P.C.L. Students 51.

QUINLAN, HUNT CO., OUR LADY OF FATIMA Rev. Paul L. Weinberger.
1579 E. Quinlan Pkwy., 75474. Mailing Address: 4300 Stuart St., Greenville, 75401.
Catechesis/Religious Program—

RICHARDSON, DALLAS CO.

1—ST. JOSEPH (1976) Most Rev. J. Douglas Deshotel; Revs. Timothy Heines; Jacob Dankosa; Deacon Randall L. Engel.
Res.: 600 S. Jupiter Rd., 75081. Tel: 972-231-2951; Fax: 972-231-2875. Email: church@stjosephcc.net. Web: www.stjosephcc.net.
School—(Grades K-8) Tel: 972-234-4679; Fax: 972-692-4594. Phil R. Riley, Prin.; Sue Heflin, Librarian. Students 363.
Catechesis/Religious Program—Tel: 972-690-5588; Fax: 972-692-4575. Students 826.

2—ST. PAUL THE APOSTLE (1956) Very Rev. David J. Flori; Deacons Carl H. Thelin; Paul W. Reittinger; Jesse Olivarez; Ricardo Moreno. In Res., Rev. Benito Tamez.
Church: 720 S. Floyd Rd., 75080.
Res.: 709 James Dr., 75080. Tel: 972-235-6105; Fax: 972-480-8528. Web: www.saintpaulchurch.org.
School—(Grades PreK-8) Tel: 972-235-3263; Fax: 972-690-1542. Web: saintpaulschool.org. Lay Teachers 28; Students 330.
Catechesis/Religious Program—Tel: 972-235-2598; Fax: 972-664-9993. Becky Soto, P.C.L. Students 496.

ROCKWALL, ROCKWALL CO., OUR LADY OF THE LAKE (1978) Rev. George P. Monaghan; Deacons Hector Rodriguez; Paul Husting; Jim Daniels.
Res.: 1305 Damascus Rd., 75087. Tel: 972-771-6671 (Office); Fax: 972-771-7283. Web: www.ourladyrockwall.org.
Catechesis/Religious Program—Tel: 972-771-6671, Ext. 114. Carolyn Kribs, P.C.L. Students 707.

ROWLETT, DALLAS CO., SACRED HEART (1899) Deacons Kenneth Melston; Jack Hopkins; Jose Perez.
3905 Hickox Rd., 75030-1650.
Res.: 3502 Andrea, 75088. Tel: 972-475-2473; Fax: 972-675-6658. Web: www.sacredheartrowlett.org.
Catechesis/Religious Program—Esther Garcia, P.C.L. Students 473.

SHERMAN, GRAYSON CO., ST. MARY (1872) Revs. Jeremy Myers; Antonio Aureus; Deacons John Le Blanc; Tomas Avila; Albert Miller.
Res.: 727 S. Travis, 75090. Tel: 903-893-5148; Fax: 903-813-5489. Email: info@stmarych.org. Web: www.stmarych.org.
School—(Grades PreK-8), 713 Travis St., 75090. Tel: 903-893-2127; Fax: 903-892-3233. Karen Martin, Sec.; Kim Butterfield, Librarian. Lay Teachers 12; Students 152.
Catechesis/Religious Program—Annie Kremer, P.C.L. & D.R.E. Students 475.

TERRELL, KAUFMAN CO., ST. JOHN (1876) Rev. James P. Orosco; Deacon Ismael Reyes.
Res.: 702 N. Frances St., 75160. Tel: 972-563-3643; Fax: 972-563-9718. Web: www.stjohnterrell.org.
Catechesis/Religious Program—Susan Warner, D.R.E. Students 419.

VAN ALSTYNE, GRAYSON CO., HOLY FAMILY (1980) Rev. Salvador Gúzman.
P.O. Box 482, 75495.
Catechesis/Religious Program—Lydia Ford, P.C.L. Students 203.

WAXAHACHIE, ELLIS CO., ST. JOSEPH (1875) Rev. Martin Moreno; Deacon Hugo Monsanto.
Office: 512 E. Marvin St., 75165. Fax: 972-923-3501.
Res.: 504 E. Marvin St., 75165. Tel: 972-938-1953.
School—St. Joseph Catholic School, (Grades K-8), 506 E. Marvin St., 75165. Tel: 972-937-0956; Fax: 972-937-1742. Mary Kay Volker, Prin.; Pat Tidwell, Librarian. Lay Teachers 14; Students 168.
Catechesis/Religious Program—James Speelman, P.C.L. Students 425.

WHITESBORO, GRAYSON CO., ST. FRANCIS OF ASSISI (QUASI PARISH) Rev. Jeremy Myers.
Mailing Address: 727 Travis St., Sherman, 75090.
Church: 807 N. Union, 76273.
Catechesis/Religious Program—Hanna Ferguson. Students 48.

WYLIE, COLLIN CO., ST. ANTHONY (1858) [CEM] Deacons Walter Gove; Marco Antonio Cruz.
Res.: 404 N. Ballard, 75098. Tel: 972-442-2765; Fax: 972-429-9215. Web: www.saintanthony.com.
Catechesis/Religious Program—Students 779.

Chaplains of Public Institutions

DALLAS. *Baylor University Medical Center*, 3500 Gaston Ave., 75246. Tel: 214-820-2558. Deacon Hugo A. Salinas, Rev. Benito Tamez.
Childrens Medical Center of Dallas, 1935 Motor St., 75235. Tel: 214-456-2822. Ryan Campbell, Chap., Mrs. Shannon Burk, Chap.
Dallas/Fort Worth Airport Catholic Chaplain, 180 Samuel Blvd., Coppell, 75019. Tel: 972-393-5544. Deacon Ed Scarbrough, Rev. Joseph P. O'Neill.
Doctors Hospital, Tel: 214-321-0454. Rev. Walter Mallo, I.V.E.
Medical City Dallas Hospital, 7777 Forest Ln., 75230. Tel: 972-530-3004. Deacon Carl H. Thelin.
Methodist Charlton Medical Center, 3500 W. Wheatland Rd., 75237. Tel: 214-947-2470. Rev. Daniel Clayton.
Methodist Dallas Medical Center, 1441 N. Beckley Ave., 75265. Tel: 214-947-2470. Rev. Daniel Clayton.
Parkland Health & Hospital System, 5201 Harry Hines Blvd., 75235. Tel: 214-590-8512. Rev. Luis Buitrago, Luz Maria de la Paz Austin, Chap.
Texas Health Presbyterian Hospital - Dallas, 8200 Walnut Hill Ln., 75231. Tel: 214-345-7158. Deacon Paul Husting.
UT Southwestern University Medical Center, 5909 Harry Hines Blvd., 75390. Tel: 214-645-1155. Phyllis Carr.
VA - North Texas Health Care System, 2926 E. Ledbetter Dr., 75216. Tel: 214-374-7952. Rev. Timothy A. Gollob.

BONHAM. *Sam Rayburn Memorial Veterans Center*, 1201 E. 9th St., 75418. Tel: 214-682-6458. Rev. Manuel Sabando.

PLANO. *Children's Medical Center - Legacy*, 7609 Preston Rd., 75024. Tel: 469-303-2822. Mr. Witek Nowosiad, Chap.

SEAGOVILLE. *Federal Correctional Institution*, 2113 N. Hwy. 75, 75159. Tel: 972-287-2911. Rev. Anthony M. Densmore, Deacon Ismael A. Guerra.

TERRELL. *State Hospital*, 701 N. Frances St., 75160. Tel: 972-563-3643. Rev. James P. Orosco.

On Duty Outside the Diocese:
Revs.—
Brown, Richard
Martin, Sean, Aquinas Institute of Theology, 23 S. Spring Ave., St. Louis, MO 63108.
Phan, Cho Dink Peter
Riemer, Lawrence H., 1803 Laurel Oak Dr., Valrico, FL 33596.
Yamauchi, James, North American College, Rome, Italy.

On Leave of Absence:
Revs.—
Alphonso, John
Alvarez, Ramon
Crisp, Robert R.
Pratt, Dean (Retired)
Speiser, Thomas M.

Retired:
Rev. Msgrs.—
Balint, R. James, 4613 Yorkshire Tr., Plano, 75093.
Cuschieri, Albert, V.F., 218 Sisters St., Tarxien TNX2046 Malta.
Fischer, Don L., 10754 Wyatt Cir., 75218.
Johnson, Robert, 14 Greccio Ct., Crowley, 76036.
Meyers, John F., 6211 W. Northwest Hwy., Ste. 2205, 75225.
Rehkemper, Robert C., 1111 E. Sandy Lake Rd., Coppell, 75019.
Weinzapfel, Thomas, 321 Crooked Creek, Garland, 75043.
Revs.—
Caldwell, Fred, 2508 Dewberry Ct., Melissa, 75454.
Corcoran, Stanley D., 1115 E. Sandy Lake Rd., Coppell, 75019.
Diez, Oscar
Drozd, Henry J., P.O. Box 42063, Savannah, GA 31409-0001.
Fernandez, Edward P., 1147 E. Sandy Lake Rd., Coppell, 75019.
Fowler, John W., 1444 Rodando, Garland, 75042. Tel: 972-205-9307
Haugh, John, 1139 E. Sandy Lake Rd., Coppell, 75019.
Jayasuriya, Jerome, 305 Blake Ln., Midlothian, 76065.
McKenna, James George, P.O. Box 190507, 75219.
Morris, Loyd, 7406 Summit View Ln., Sachse, 75048.
Ortega, Efren
Pratt, Dean, 906 Lake Paint Cir., Mc Kinney, 75070.
Scott, Raymond, Walnut Pl. Rm. 281, 5515 Glen Lakes Dr., 75231.
Sharp, James, 5621 Cornerstone Dr., Garland,

75043. Tel: 973-681-8915
Slovacek, Emil C., 1815 Hamlet, 75203.
Villaroya, Ernesto
Weaver, Richard, 15736 Golden Creek Rd., 75248.
White, Gale, 16 St. Louis, Crowley, 76036. Tel: 214-357-4312

Permanent Deacons:
Alt, Les, (Retired)
Alvarez, Fidel
Andrade, Rafael
Arana, Benigno
Argumaniz, Fernando L., (Retired)
Armendariz, Martin
Ashley, Frank B., (On Duty Outside the Diocese)
Avila, Tomas
Berens, LeRoy J., (On Duty Outside the Diocese)
Boduch, Robert, (Retired)
Bolesta, Michael
Bourland, Fred, (On Duty Outside the Diocese)
Boyd, Douglas
Bryant, Dennis Phillip
Burkel, James, (On Duty Outside the Diocese)
Carpio, Victor
Carranza, Sergio
Carrell, Michael A., (Retired)
Castillo, Jorge
Catsoris, John A., (Retired)
Cerrato, Jesus, Jr., (Retired)
Chung, Hoan Moses
Coffey, Thomas, (On Duty Outside the Diocese)
Corbin, Denis D.
Cortes, Abel
Cortinas, Leopoldo, III
Costello, John R.
Crawley, Denver, (On Duty Outside the Diocese)
Cruz, Marco Antonio
Culling, Joseph
Daniels, James
Davis, Lee B.
Delin, Fred O., (Retired)
Dorsey, Timothy, (On Duty Outside the Diocese)
Ellerbrock, Michael, (On Duty Outside the Diocese)
Engel, Randall L.
Escalona, Eliecer
Evans, Al
Fejeran, Ronald
Flynn, Bill
Fobes, Bill
Forbrich, Don
Franklin, Sam, (Retired)
French, Shawn Patrick, (On Duty Outside the Diocese)
Friedman, William L., (On Duty Outside the Diocese)
Garcia, Benito
Garza, Gerardo
Garzon, Luis
Gette, Roger
Gonzales, Gonzalo
Gonzalez, Ronald, (On Duty Outside the Diocese)
Gove, Walter
Griffith, Don
Guerra, Ismael A.
Gulino, Jack
Gutting, Justin, (Retired Outside the Diocese)
Gutting, Paul, (On Duty Outside the Diocese)
Hale, Kenneth
Hancock, John, (On Duty Outside the Diocese)
Harmon, Larry
Harrington, Richard
Harris, Jim
Hayes, Patrick
Hernandez, Jose Luis
Hernandez, Juan Jorge
Hopkins, Jack
Husting, Paul
Ibarra, Juan, (On Duty Outside the Diocese)
Jimenez, Vincent F.
Jones, Edward S., (On Duty Outside the Diocese)
Kahrs, Greg
Kelly, John Paul
Killgo, Kory
Kowalski, Eugene T.
Kozarevich, Frank
Laguna, Felicito
LeBlanc, John D.
Leerssen, David
Leicht, Robert R., Jr., (On Duty Outside the Diocese)
Leyden, Edward
Little, Sid
Loera, Roberto
Lopez, Al
Lopez, Jose E.
Lucido, Larry
Macero, Carl, Sr.
Machiano, Victor M.
Maida, David
Markwald, Pete
Marquez, Federico
Marrinan, Robert, Sr.
Martinez, Onesimo
McAllister, Jerome, (Retired)
Melston, Kenneth
Miller, Albert
Miller, Carl V., (On Duty Outside the Diocese)
Miller, J. Robert
Milliken, Frank M., (Retired)
Miranda, Oscar
Mitchell, Brian
Monsanto, Hugo
Montes, Jesus Alberto
Morales, Sergio
Moreno, Ricardo
Morgan, Ron
Muldoon, Tim
Muniz, Jose
Munoz, Louis L.
Nordick, John C.
O'Leary, John
Obergfell, David T.
Olivarez, Jesse
Olvera, Isidro, (On Duty Outside the Diocese)
Orozco, Adolph, Jr., (Retired)
Osborne, Charles
Palms, Howard
Palomeque, Roberto
Palos, Lewis J.
Perez, Joe R.
Perez, Jose
Perras, Gonzolo
Picard, Michael
Picon, Arnold
Pina, Salvador
Polcer, George
Powers, Paul
Putonti, Edward
Rasins, Michael R., Sr., (Outside the Diocese)
Reisor, Kenneth
Reittinger, Paul W.
Rener, Bonnie Leo
Reyes, Ismael
Reyna, Frank, (Retired)
Ricard, Robert, (Retired)
Riojas, Ricardo
Roche, Thomas
Rodriguez, Hector
Rodriguez, Pete
Salinas, Hugo A.
Sanchez, Mario
Sanchez, Robert
Scarbrough, Ed
Schell, John A.
Schnurr, Don, (Retired)
Schuster, William J.
Segovia, Daniel D.
Seibold, Michael
Shaw, Michael, (Retired)
Shine, Mark
Simon, Denis
Smith, Raymond H.
Starr, James
Stieber, Lee, (Retired Outside the Diocese)
Stump, Charles, Jr.
Sykora, Richard, (On Duty Outside the Diocese)
Sylvester, Charles T.
Thelin, Carl H.
Tompsett, David E.
Tran, Anthony, (Retired)
Trevino, Antonio D.
Trevino, Jose
Vasquez, Gustavo
Vega, Frutos
Veyna, Manuel, (Retired)
Vogel, Gary M.
Washington, Warner, (Retired)
Webb, Philip E.
Weston, Michael
Wong, Peter
Wood, Paul

INSTITUTIONS LOCATED IN THE DIOCESE

[A] SEMINARIES, DIOCESAN

DALLAS. *The Redemptoris Mater House of Formation*, P.O. Box 211669, 75211. Tel: 214-467-2255; Fax: 214-467-5440. Email: rector@rmdallas.org. 419 N. Cockrell Hill Rd., 75211. Very Rev. Fernando Carranza, Rector & Contact Person; Rev. Eduardo Gonzalez-Martinez, Spiritual Dir. Students 25.

IRVING. *Holy Trinity Seminary* Diocesan College and Pre-Theology Seminary., P.O. Box 140309, 75014-0309. Tel: 972-438-2212; Fax: 972-438-6530. Email: molson@holytrinityseminary.com. Web: www.holytrinityseminary.com. Rev. Msgr. Michael F. Olson, Rector; Revs. Keith Koehl, Vice Rector; James P. Oberle, S.S., Dir. Spiritual & Liturgical Formation; Ronald Ramson, C.M., Spiritual Dir.; Juan Rendon, Dir. Field Educ.; Dr. William Brownsberger, Dir. Intellectual Formation; Dr. Gregory Hamilton, Music Dir.; Rev. James Vasquez. Priests 5; Seminarians 66; Lay Faculty 3; Total Staff 2.

[B] COLLEGES AND UNIVERSITIES

IRVING. *University of Dallas*, President's Office, 1845 E. Northgate, 75062. Tel: 972-721-5203; Fax: 972-721-4040. Students 2,860.
Administrative Officers: Dr. William Berry, Provost; Most Rev. Kevin J. Farrell, D.D., Chancellor; Mr. Robert Galecke, Exec. Vice Pres.; Thomas W. Keefe, J.D., Pres.
Cistercian Priests: Revs. David Balas, O.Cist., Ph.D., S.T.D.; Ralph March, O.Cist., Ph.D.; Roch Keresz Ty; James Lehrberger, O.Cist., Ph.D.; Robert Maguire, O.Cist., Ph.D.

[C] HIGH SCHOOLS, DIOCESAN

DALLAS. *Bishop Dunne Catholic School, Inc.*, (Grades 6-12), (Coed), 3900 Rugged Dr., 75224. Tel: 214-339-6561; Fax: 214-339-1438. Email: kdailey@bdhs.org. Web: www.bdhs.org. Mr. Patrick O'Sullivan, Prin.; Kate Collins Dailey, Pres.; Lydia Torres, Dir. Devel. & Alumni; Melanie Gibson, Librarian. Sisters (S.S.N.D.) 1; Lay Teachers 51; Administrators 11; Students 605.

Bishop Lynch High School, Inc., 9750 Ferguson Rd., 75228. Tel: 214-324-3607; Fax: 214-324-3600. Email: edleyden@bishoplynch.org. Web: www.bishoplynch.org. Deacon Edward Leyden, Pres.; Evelyn Grubbs, Prin.; Rev. Victor Bartolotta, Chap.; Gerry Cantalope, Librarian. Priests 1; Sisters 1; Deacons 2; Lay Teachers 85; Total Staff 115; Students 1,097.

PLANO. *John Paul II High School, Inc.*, 900 Coit Rd., 75075. Tel: 972-867-0005; Fax: 972-867-7555. Web: www.johnpauliihs.org. Mr. Brian McPheeters, Vice Pres. Finance & Admin.; Steve Minninger, Prin.; Gracelyn Shea, Librarian. Lay Teachers 50.

[D] HIGH SCHOOLS, PRIVATE

DALLAS. *Jesuit College Preparatory School* (Boys), 12345 Inwood Rd., 75244. Tel: 972-387-8700; Fax: 972-661-9349. Web: www.jesuitcp.org. Mr. Michael A. Earsing, Pres.; Mr. Thomas Garrison, Prin.; Revs. John H. Edwards, S.J.; Francis W. Huete, S.J.; Charles A. Leininger, S.J.; Bro. Gerald J. Landry, S.J.; Mr. Kevin Cormier, S.J.; Mr. John Nugent, S.J.; Mr. Stephen Pitts, S.J.; Rev. Anthony Weick, S.J.; Mr. Sam Wilson, S.J.; Mark Wester, Librarian. Society of Jesus. Priests 4; Brothers 1; Scholastics 4; Lay Teachers 109; Students 1,072; Total Staff 114.

Ursuline Academy (Girls), 4900 Walnut Hill Ln., 75229. Tel: 469-232-1800; Fax: 469-232-1836. Email: srmoser@ursulinedallas.org. Web: www.ursulinedallas.org. Sr. Margaret Ann Moser, O.S.U., Pres.; Elizabeth C. Bourgeois, Prin.; Christy L. Frazer, Dir. Inst. Advancement; Renee Chevallier, Librarian. Religious Sisters 3; Faculty 80; Students 828.

IRVING. *Cistercian Preparatory School*, (Grades 5-12), 3660 Cistercian Rd., 75039-4500. Tel: 469-499-5400; Fax: 469-499-5440. Email: admissions@cistercian.org. Web: www.cistercian.org. Rev. Peter Verhalen, O.Cist., M.A., M.Th., Headmaster; Jacqulyn Dudasko, Librarian. Cistercian Fathers of Our Lady of Dallas Abbey., (Boys) Priests 12; Brothers 2; Lay Teachers 36; Students 355.

The Highlands School, (Grades PreK-12), 1451 E. Northgate Dr., 75062. Tel: 972-554-1980; Fax: 972-721-1691. Email: highlands@thehighlandsschool.org. Web: www.TheHighlandsSchool.org. Dr. Richard VonWeber, Prin.; Michelle Reiff, Dir., Consecrated Women; Revs. Daniel Ray, L.C.; Bruno Montekio, L.C.; Eamonn Shelly, L.C.; Bros. Juan Disraely, L.C.; Jose M. Reyes, L.C.; Cherie L. Hoherty, M.L.S., Librarian. Priests 3; Consecrated Women 4; Lay Teachers 48; High School 136; Middle & Elementary 307; Students 443.

[E] ELEMENTARY SCHOOLS, PRIVATE

DALLAS. **Catholic Charismatic Services of Dallas Texas, Inc. dba Mount St. Michael Catholic School* (Grades PreK-8), 4500 W. Davis St., 75211. Tel: 214-337-0244; Fax: 214-339-1702. Email: gmontgomery@msmcatholic.org. Web: www.msmcatholic.org. Mailing Address: P.O. Box 225159, 75222-5159. Gretchen Montgomery, Prin.; Mary Krieg, M.S., Librarian. Priests 2; Lay Teachers 20; Students 189; Total Staff 33.

[F] SPECIAL SCHOOLS, PRIVATE

DALLAS. *Notre Dame of Dallas Schools, Inc.*, 2018 Allen St., 75204. Tel: 214-720-3911; Fax: 214-720-3913. Email: tfrancis@notredameschool.org. Web:

www.notredameschool.org. Ms. Theresa Francis, Prin. Day School: Provides instructional education for children with developmental disabilities, ages 6-15.; Vocational Center: Provides vocational training for young adults, ages 16-21. Sisters 1; Lay Staff 37; Teachers 17; Assistants 13; Students 150.

[G] CATHOLIC CHARITIES

DALLAS. *Catholic Charities of Dallas, Inc.*, 9461 LBJ Fwy., Ste. 128, 75243. Tel: 214-520-6590; Fax: 214-520-6595. Web: www.CatholicCharitiesDallas.org. V. Joseph Brogdon, Exec. Dir.

Children and Adoption Services and Community Outreach, 9461 LBJ Fwy., Ste. 110, 75243. Tel: 214-526-2772; Fax: 214-526-2941. Barbara Tenbroek, Div. Dir.

Maternity and Adoption Program Tel: 214-526-2772; (800) BABY-DUE; Fax: 214-526-2941.

Mary R. Saner Child Development Center, 2827 Lapsley St., 75212. Tel: 214-638-1635; Fax: 214-905-0822. Web: www.catholiccharitiesdallas.org.

Elderly and Family Services, 9461 LBJ Fwy., Ste 128, 75243. Tel: 214-826-8330; Fax: 214-826-8579. Web: www.catholiccharitiesdallas.org. Multiple locations offer bilingual social services.

Immigration and Legal Services, 9461 LBJ Fwy., Ste. 100, 75243. Tel: 214-634-7182; Fax: 214-634-2531. Email: vanna@ccicsdallas.org. Web: www.catholiccharitiesdallas.org. Vanna Slaughter, L.C.S.W., Div. Dir.

St. Martin Family Service Center, Inc., 9461 LBJ Freeway, Ste. 128, 75243. Tel: 214-520-6590; Fax: 214-520-6595. Web: www.catholiccharitiesdallas.org. Purpose: To operate facilities in which social services are provided to assist the poor and indigent families of Dallas to become self-reliant.

Refugee and Empowerment Services, V. Joseph Brogdon, Interim Exec. Dir.: 9461 LBJ Fwy., Ste. 128, 75243. Tel: 214-553-9909; Fax: 214-553-8116. Email: mrs@catholiccharitiesdallas.org. Web: www.catholiccharitiesdallas.org. Dionne Davis, Div. Dir.

[H] EDUCATION CENTERS

DALLAS. *Mount Carmel Center*, 4600 W. Davis St., 75211-3498. Tel: 214-331-6224; Fax: 214-330-0844. Web: www.mountcarmelcenter.org. Revs. Stephen Sanchez, O.C.D., Supr. & Prog. Dir.; Jerome Earley, O.C.D. Discalced Carmelite Fathers of the Southwestern Province., Adult Center for Catholic Spirituality

Mount St. Michael Spiritual Life Center, 4500 W. Davis St., 75211. Tel: 214-331-1754; Fax: 214-333-1659. Sr. Yolanda Martinez, O.L.C., Supr. Adult Center for Catholic Spirituality Sisters of Our Lady of Charity of Refuge 8.

[I] PERSONAL PRELATURES

IRVING. *Opus Dei* Prelature of the Holy Cross and Opus Dei, 3610 Wingren, 75062. Tel: 972-650-0064; Fax: 972-717-3580. Email: info@opusdei.org. Web: www.opusdei.org. Revs. Derrick Esclanda; John E. Solarski.

[J] MONASTERIES AND RESIDENCES OF PRIESTS

DALLAS. *Capuchin Franciscan Friars, Vice Province of Texas*, 5605 Bernal Dr., 75212. Tel: 214-500-8595; Fax: 214-637-2454. Email: mtellitu@yahoo.com. Revs. Mario Garcia, O.F.M.Cap. (Spain), Vice Prov.; Roberto Viveros, O.F.M.Cap. (Mexico); Bros. Marco A. Hernandez; Lucas A. Olivera. Priests 3; Brothers 2.

Congregation of the Mission, Western Province, 3826 Gilbert Ave., 75219. Tel: 214-526-0234; Fax: 214-526-2421. Email: cmstlouis@vincentian.org. Web: www.vincentian.org. Revs. Juan Antonio Ruiz, C.M.; Ronald Ramson, C.M.; Paul Sauerbier, C.M.; Nhan Tran, C.M.; F. Patrick Hanser, C.M.; Donald J. Ours, C.M.; Minh J. Pham, C.M. Priests 5.

St. John Neumann Formation House, 3912 S. Ledbetter Dr., 75236. Tel: 972-296-6735; Fax: 972-296-6765. Web: www.dccthaingrai.com. Revs. Domininc Hai Dinh, C.Ss.R., Formation Dir. & Contact Person; Joseph Hung Le, C.Ss.R.

Mt. Carmel Center, 4600 W. Davis St., 75211. Tel: 214-331-6224; Fax: 214-330-0844. Web: www.mountcarmelcenter.org. Revs. Stephen Sanchez, O.C.D., Supr.; Jerome Earley, O.C.D.

IRVING. *Cistercian Abbey of Our Lady of Dallas*, 3550 Cistercian Rd., 75039. Tel: 972-438-2044; Fax: 972-579-7637. Email: DMFDenis@aol.com. Web: www.cistercian.org. Rt. Rev. Denis M. Farkasfalvy, O.Cist., S.S.L., M.S., S.T.D., Abbot, Vicar of the Abbot Pres. of Zirc; Revs. Peter Verhalen, O.Cist., M.A., M.Th., Prior; Ralph March, O.Cist., Ph.D.; Bernard Marton, O.Cist., S.T.D., Subprior; Benedict Monostori, O.Cist., Ph.D.; Bede Lackner, O.Cist., Ph.D.; Pascal Kis-Horvath, O.Cist.; David Balas, O.Cist., Ph.D., S.T.D.; Matthew Kovacs, O.Cist., M.A.; Melchior Chladek, O.Cist., M.A.; Roch Kereszty, O.Cist., S.T.D.; Augustine Hoelke, O.Cist., M.T.H.; Philip Neri Lastimosa, O.Cist., B.A., M.T.H.; Julius Leloczky, O.Cist., S.T.D.; James Lehrberger, O.Cist., Ph.D.; Robert Maguire, O.Cist., Ph.D.; Gregory Schweers, O.Cist., M.A.; Mark Ripperger, O.Cist., M.A.; Paul McCormick, O.Cist., M.A., S.T.L.; Joseph Van House, O.Cist., S.T.L.; Bros. John Bayer, O.Cist., B.A.; Anthony Bigney, O.Cist., B.A.; Revs. Thomas Esposito, O.Cist., B.A., S.T.B., S.S.L.; Ignatius Peacher, O.Cist., B.A.; Ambrose Strong, O.Cist., B.A., M.Th., S.T.L.; Bros. Stephen Gregg, O.Cist., B.A.; Lawrence Brophy, O.Cist., M.S., B.A., S.T.B.; Justin McNamara, O.Cist., B.A. Priests 21; Brothers 8.

Dominican Priory of St. Albert the Great and Novitiate, 3150 Vince Hagan Dr., 75062-4701. Tel: 972-438-1626; Fax: 972-438-6948. Revs. Orlando Cardozo; Donald Dvorak, O.P.; Scott O'Brien, O.P., Novice Master; Edward M. Robinson, O.P.; Andrew Kolzow, O.P. Priests 5.

Legionaries of Christ, 3813 Cabeza de Vaca Cir., 75062. Tel: 972-890-3892; Fax: 972-281-5243. Email: dallas@legionaries.org. Web: www.thehighlandsschool.org. Revs. Peter Hopkins, L.C., Supr., Contact Person; Daniel Ray, L.C.; Michael Sullivan, L.C.; Bruno Montekio, L.C.; Eamonn Shelly, L.C.; Gregory Usselmann, L.C.; Bros. Lucio Boccacci, L.C.; Juan Disraely, L.C.; Manuel Reyes, L.C. Priests 3; Brothers 2.

KERENS. **Benedictine Monastery of Thien Tam*, 13055 S.E. CR 4271, 75144. Tel: 903-396-3201. Rev. Dominic Hanh Nguyen, O.S.B., Prior.

[K] CONVENTS AND RESIDENCES FOR SISTERS

DALLAS. *Bethany House*, 3017 Mallory, 75216. Tel: 214-371-4867. Email: patricia.ridgley@gmail.com. Web: www.ssmnwestern.com. Sr. Patricia Ann Ridgley, S.S.M.N., Contact Person. Sisters of St. Mary of Namur. Sisters 3.

Carmelites Nuns of Dallas, 600 Flowers Ave., 75211. Tel: 214-330-7440; Fax: 214-623-1885. Sr. Juanita Marie Horan, O.C.D., Prioress. Professed Sisters 12.

Daughters of the Sacred Heart, 7621 Cortland Ave., 75235. Tel: 214-351-4338. Sisters 3.

Missionaries of Charity, 2704 Harlandale, 75216. Tel: 214-374-3351. Sr. M. Celian, M.C, Supr. Sisters 4.

Missionary Catechist of the Poor, 950 N. Montclair Ave., 75208. Tel: 214-942-2799; Fax: 214-942-2799. Email: gucadi@yahoo.com. Sr. Sylvia Dominguez, M.C.P., Supr. Sisters 6.

School Sisters of Notre Dame, P.O. Box 227275, 75222. Tel: 214-330-9152; Fax: 214-330-9197. Web: www.ssnd.org. Sr. Mary Anne Owens, S.S.N.D., Provincial. Sisters 16.

Ursuline Sisters, 9905 Inwood Rd., 75220. Tel: 214-358-3922. Web: www.osucentral.org. Sisters 8.

GARLAND. *Dominican Sisters of Tam Hiep Community*, 2934 Landershine Ln., 75044. Tel: 972-530-5068.

GRAND PRAIRIE. *Sisters of the Holy Family of Nazareth* (Holy Family Province), 1814 Egyptian Way, 75053. Tel: 972-641-4496; Fax: 972-641-1668. Web: www.nazarethcsfn.org. Sr. Edyta Krayczyk, C.S.F.N., Prov. Counselor. Sisters 35.

IRVING. *Congregation of Mary, Queen-American Region (CMR)*, 723 Sunset Dr., 75061. Tel: 469-417-0123. Email: cmrvocation@yahoo.com. Web: www.trinhvuong.org. Sisters Teresita Au, C.M.R., Teacher; Gwen Do, C.M.R., Teacher; Leslie Dao, C.M.R., Social Worker; Jacinta Tran, C.M.R., Contact Person & P.C.L.; Janine Tran, C.M.R., Vocation Dir. Perpetually Professed Religious 5.

[L] CAMPUS MINISTRY

DALLAS. *Southern Methodist University-Catholic Campus Ministry* Neuhoff Catholic Student Ctr., 3057 University Blvd., 75205. Tel: 214-987-0044; Fax: 214-987-3731. Email: lackland@smu.edu. Sammy Argumaniz, Campus Min.; Christian Bryant, Campus Min.; Cindy Dixon, Business Mgr.

IRVING. *University of Dallas-Campus Ministry* 1845 E. Northgate Dr., 75062. Tel: 972-721-5375; Fax: 972-721-5351. Rev. Donald Dvorak, O.P.; Denise G. Phillips, Dir. Campus Ministry.

[M] MISCELLANEOUS LISTINGS

DALLAS. *Bishop Dunne Catholic School Building and Endowment Fund*, 3900 Rugged Dr., 75224. Tel: 214-339-6561; Fax: 214-339-1438. Web: www.bdhs.org. Kate Dailey, Pres.

Bishop Lynch High School Building and Endowment Trust, 9750 Ferguson Rd., 75228. Tel: 214-324-3607; Fax: 214-327-8242. Email: jayniepoff@bishoplynch.org. Deacon Edward Leyden, Pres.

Carmelite Nuns Foundation, 600 Flowers Ave., 75211. Tel: 214-373-2739; Fax: 214-373-2788. Sr. Juanita Marie Horan, O.C.D., Prioress.

**Catholic Charismatic Services of Dallas Texas, Inc. dba Christian Community of God's Delight* 4500 W. Davis-Michael Hall, 75211. Tel: 214-333-2337; Fax: 214-333-2595. Email: catfed@juno.com. P.O. Box 225008, 75222.

Catholic Charities Endowment Trust, 9461 LBJ Fwy., Ste. 128, 75243. Tel: 214-520-6590; Fax: 214-520-6595. Web: www.catholiccharitiesdallas.org. V. Joseph Brogdon, Interim Exec. Dir.

Catholic Community Appeal, Inc. dba Bishop's Annual Appeal for Catholic Ministries 3725 Blackburn St., P.O. Box 190507, 75219. Tel: 214-528-2240; Fax: 214-526-1743. Email: pvitanza@cathdal.org. Web: www.cathdal.org. Paul Vitanza, C.F.R.E., Dir.

Catholic Community Educational Services of Dallas, Inc., P.O. Box 190507, 75219. Tel: 214-379-2873; Fax: 214-520-3247. Email: agtaylor@cathdal.org. Annette G. Taylor, Pres.

The Catholic Pro-Life Committee of North Texas, Inc., P.O. Box 59852, 75229. Tel: 972-267-LIFE; Fax: 972-385-3851. Email: cplc@prolifedallas.org. Web: www.prolifedallas.org. Karen Garnett, Exec. Dir.

Commission on Ecumenism, P.O. Box 190507, 75219. Tel: 214-528-2240; Fax: 214-523-2429. Lynn Rossol, Contact Person; Very Rev. Robert Williams, V.F., Chm.

Dallas Cursillo Center, 5605 Bernal Dr., 75212. Tel: 214-631-7775. Rev. Roberto Viveros, O.F.M.Cap. (Mexico), Spiritual Dir.

Dallas Deanery Council of Catholic Women, 11236 Drummond Dr., 75228. Olga Sandoval, Pres.

Dallas Diocesan Council of Catholic Women, 7907 Thistletree Ln., Frisco, 75033. Tel: 214-794-5621.

Dallas Vocation Guild, P.O. Box 12153, 75225. Tel: 214-693-9978. Email: cmansour@catholicfoundation.com.

Diocesan Seminary Burse Endowment Fund Trust, P.O. Box 190507, 75219. Tel: 214-379-2800; Fax: 214-523-2422. Most Rev. Kevin J. Farrell, D.D., Trustee; Michael T. Weis, Contact Person. Trust Fund for education of seminarians for Diocese of Dallas.

Elementary Principals Association of the Diocese of Dallas, Inc. dba Dallas Parochial League P.O. Box 190507, 75219. Tel: 214-379-2800; Fax: 214-523-2422. Michael T. Weis, Contact Person.

Eocolare Movement-Women's Branch (Texas) (Work of Mary), 9517 Lyngrove Dr., 75238.

James L. Collins Catholic School Education Trust, P.O. Box 190507, 75219. Tel: 214-528-2240; Fax: 214-523-2422. Michael T. Weis, Contact Person.

St. Joseph Residence, Inc., 330 W. Pembroke, 75208. Tel: 214-948-3597; Fax: 214-948-1209. Sr. Adelaide Bocanegra, Bethl., Admin. For elderly ladies, gentlemen, and couples. Conducted by Daughters of the Sacred Heart of Jesus (Bethlemitas). Sisters 6; Residents 49.

Ladies of Charity of Dallas, P.O. Box 595666, 75359-0666. Tel: 214-821-5713. Email: ladiesofcharitydallas@sbcglobal.net. Web: www.ladiesofcharity.com. Sue Ann Gilman, Pres.

Lieutenancy, Equestrian Order of the Holy Sepulchre of Jerusalem formerly Southwestern Lieutenancy, Equestrian Order of the Holy Sepulchre of Jerusalem 4015 S. Hampton, 75224. Tel: 214-331-4328; Fax: 214-331-2464.

Mary Benavidez Education Fund, P.O. Box 190507, 75219. Tel: 214-379-2800; Fax: 214-523-2422. Most Rev. Kevin J. Farrell, D.D., Trustee; Michael T. Weis, Contact Person. Trust Fund for the education of Hispanics.

St. Mary of Carmel Building Trust, 2900 Vilbig Rd., 75212. Tel: 214-747-1433.

**New Evangelization of America*, 414 Ridgewood Dr., Richardson, 75080. Tel: 469-867-9650. Email: neamail@msn.com. Web: neawebsite.org. Gracie Stanford, Sec.

Nuestra Senora del Pilar Land & Development Trust, 4455W. Illinois Ave., 75211. Tel: 214-467-9116; Fax: 214-339-7249. Email: pilar.church@sbcglobal.net. Rev. Wilmer de Jesus Daza.

Santa Clara Endowment Fund Trust, P.O. Box 190507, 75219. Tel: 214-379-2800; Fax: 214-523-2422. Most Rev. Kevin J. Farrell, D.D., Trustee; Michael T. Weis, Contact Person. Trust Fund to support Santa Clara School.

School Sisters of Notre Dame of Dallas Charitable Trust, 4500 W. Davis, 75211. Tel: 214-330-9152; Fax: 214-330-9197. Web: www.ssnd.org. P.O. Box 227275, 75222-7275.

Texas Catholic Publishing Company, P.O. Box

190347, 75219.

The Timon Trust, 3826 Gilbert Ave., 75219.

Ursuline Academy of Dallas Foundation, Inc., 4900 Walnut Hill, 75229. Tel: 469-232-3584; Fax: 469-232-3593. Email: cfrazer@ursulinedallas.org. Web: www.ursulinedallas.org. Sr. Margaret Ann Moser, O.S.U., Pres.; Christy L. Frazer, Dir. Inst. Advancement.

ADDISON. *St. Thomas More Society of Diocese of Dallas, Texas*, 11520 N. Central Expwy., Ste. 130, 75243. Tel: 214-696-4771.

ALLEN. *St. Jude Parish Building Trust*, 1515 N. Greenville Ave., 75002. Tel: 972-727-1177; Fax: 972-727-1401. Web: www.stjudeparish.com. Sue Hawthorne, Contact Person.

Our Lady of Angels Building Trust, Mailing Address: 1914 Ridgeview Dr., 75013. Tel: 469-467-9669; Fax: 469-467-0114. Web: www.ourladyofangels.com. Fernando Santos, Contact Person.

GRAND PRAIRIE. *One America International, Inc.*, 3702 Iris Dr., 75052. Tel: 972-642-7841. Web: www.oneamericainternational.org. Thomas Matasso, Pres.

IRVING. *CHRISTUS Health*, 6363 N. Hwy. 161, Ste. 450, 75038. Tel: 877-980-0100; Fax: 214-492-8540. Web: www.Christushealth.org. Ernie W. Sadau, M.B.A., Pres. & CEO; William Pardue, Corp. Sec.

CHRISTUS St. Joseph Village, 1201 E. Sandy Lake Rd., Coppell, 75019. Tel: 972-304-0300; Fax: 972-462-1099. Email: kim.bomgardner@christushealth.org. Kim Bomgardner, Exec. Dir.

CHRISTUS Health Foundation, 6363 Hwy. 161 N., Ste. 450, 75038. Tel: 281-936-3184; Fax: 281-936-7802. Email: larry.pardue@christushealth.org.

Holy Trinity Seminary Scholarship Trust, P.O. Box 140309, 75014. Tel: 979-438-2212; Fax: 972-438-6530.

PLANO. *St. Elizabeth Ann Seton Parish Building Trust*, 2701 Piedra Dr., 75023. Tel: 972-596-5505; Fax: 972-985-7573. Email: twooliscroft@eseton.org. Web: www.setonparish.org. Terry Wooliscroft, Dir. Finance & Admin.

John Paul II High School Building and Endowment Fund, 900 Coit Rd., 75075. Tel: 469-229-5112; Fax: 972-867-7555. Email: brianmcpheeters@johnpauliihs.org. Web: www.johnpauliihs.org. Mr. Brian McPheeters, Vice Pres. Finance & Admin.

RICHARDSON. *Pastors Professional Development Endowment Trust*, 923 Creekdale Dr., 75080. Tel: 972-238-9382; Fax: 972-238-9276.

St. Paul Parish Endowment Trust Fund, 709 James Dr., 75080. Tel: 972-235-6105; Fax: 972-480-8528.

RELIGIOUS INSTITUTES OF MEN REPRESENTED IN THE DIOCESE

For further details refer to the corresponding bracketed number in the Religious Institutes of Men or Women section.

[0200]—*Benedictine Monks*—O.S.B.

[0470]—*The Capuchin Friars*—O.F.M.Cap.

[0340]—*Cistercian Fathers*—O.Cist.

[0260]—*Discalced Carmelite Friars* (Oklahoma Prov.)—O.C.D.

[]—*Fuego Nuevo*—F.N.

[]—*Institute of Incarnate Word*—I.V.E.

[0690]—*Jesuit Fathers and Brothers* (New Orleans Prov.)—S.J.

[0730]—*Legionaries of Christ*—L.C.

[]—*Misioneros de la Natividad de Maria*—M.N.M.

[1210]—*Missionaries of St. Charles-Scalabrinians*—C.S.

[]—*Missionaries of St. Thomas the Apostle*—M.S.T.

[0430]—*Order of Preachers (Dominicans)* (Southern Dominican Prov.)—O.P.

[1065]—*Priestly Fraternity of St Peter*—F.S.S.P.

[1070]—*Redemptorists, Congregation of Most Holy Redeemer*—C.SS.R.

[1260]—*Society of Christ*—S.Ch.

[]—*Society of Domus Dei*—S.D.D.

[1290]—*Society of the Priests of St. Sulpice*—S.S.

[1330]—*Vincentian Fathers* (Southern Prov.)—C.M.

RELIGIOUS INSTITUTES OF WOMEN REPRESENTED IN THE DIOCESE

[0910]—*Bethlemita, Daughters of the Sacred Heart of Jesus*—Bethl.

[0370]—*Carmelite Sisters of the Sacred Heart*—O.C.D.

[]—*Congregation of Mary Queen*—C.M.R.

[]—*Daughters of the Sacred Heart*—D.S.H.

[0420]—*Discalced Carmelite Nuns*—O.C.D.

[1070-03]—*Dominican Sisters*—O.P.

[]—*Dominican Sisters of Tam Hiep*

[2710]—*Missionaries of Charity*—M.C.

[2690]—*Missionary Catechists of Divine Providence*—M.C.D.P.

[]—*Missionary Catechists of the Poor* (Mexico)—M.C.P.

[2970]—*School Sisters of Notre Dame*—S.S.N.D.

[]—*Sisters of Blessed Korean Martyrs*

[3071]—*Sisters of Our Lady of Charity*—O.L.C.

[3950]—*Sisters of Saint Mary of Namur* (Western Prov.)—S.S.M.N.

[1970]—*Sisters of the Holy Family of Nazareth* (Sacred Heart Vice Prov.)—C.S.F.N.

[2050]—*Sisters of the Holy Spirit and Mary Immaculate*—S.H.Sp.

[4110]—*Ursuline Nuns (Roman Union)* (Central Prov.)—O.S.U.

DIOCESAN CEMETERIES

DALLAS. *Calvary Hill Cemetery*, Mailing Address: 3235 Lombardy Ln., 75220. Tel: 214-357-5754; Fax: 214-357-1271. Web: www.calvaryhillcemetery.com. A corporation that owns and operates Diocesan cemeteries

Old Cavalry Hill formerly Calvary Hill Cemetery and Old Cavalry Hill 2500 N. Hall St., 75201. Tel: 214-357-5754; Fax: 214-357-1271. *c/o Calvary Hill Cemetery*, 3235 Lombardy Ln., 75220. Tel: 214-357-5754; Fax: 214-357-1271.

Holy Redeemer Cemetery, Desoto, 75115. *c/o Calvary Hill Cemetery*, 3235 Lombardy Ln., 75220.

Sacred Heart Cemetery, 3900 Rowlett Rd., Rowlett, 75088. Tel: 214-357-5754. *c/o Calvary Hill Cemetery*, 3235 Lombardy Ln., 75220. Tel: 214-357-5754.

PARISH COLUMBARIA

FARMERS BRANCH. *Mary Immaculate Church*, 2800 Valwood Pkwy., 75234. Tel: 972-243-7104.

GARLAND. *Mother of Perpetual Help Church*, 2121 W. Apollo Rd., 75044. Tel: 972-414-7073.

PLANO. *Prince of Peace Church*, 5100 Plano Pkwy., 75093.

St. Mark the Evangelist Parish Columbarium

RICHARDSON. *St. Joseph Church*, 600 S. Jupiter Rd., 75081.

PARISH CEMETERIES

ENNIS. *St. Joseph Cemetery, St. John Nepomucene Parish*, 401 E. Lampasas, 75119. Tel: 972-878-2834; Fax: 972-875-2452.

WYLIE. *St. Paul Cemetery, St. Anthony Parish*, 404 N. Ballard Ave., 75098. Tel: 972-442-2765; Fax: 972-429-9215.

NECROLOGY

(No Deaths)

An asterisk (*) denotes an organization that has established tax-exempt status directly with the IRS and is not covered by the USCCB Group Ruling.

Diocese of Davenport

(Dioecesis Davenportensis)

Most Reverend

MARTIN J. AMOS

Bishop of Davenport; ordained May 25, 1968; appointed Titular Bishop of Meta and Auxiliary Bishop of Cleveland April 3, 2001; ordained June 7, 2001; appointed Bishop of Davenport October 12, 2006; installed November 20, 2006. *Office: Diocesan Pastoral Center, 780 W. Central Park Ave., Davenport, IA 52804-1901.* Tel: 563-324-1911.

Most Reverend

WILLIAM E. FRANKLIN, D.D.

Bishop Emeritus of Davenport; Retired October 12, 2006. *Office: Diocesan Pastoral Center, 780 W. Central Park Ave., Davenport, IA 52804-1901.* Tel: 563-324-1911.

Chancery: Diocesan Pastoral Center, 780 W. Central Park Ave., Davenport, IA 52804-1901. Tel: 563-324-1911; Fax: 563-324-5842.

Web: *www.davenportdiocese.org*

ERECTED MAY 8, 1881.

Square Miles 11,438.

Comprises that part of the State of Iowa bounded on the east by the Mississippi River; on the west by the western boundaries of the counties of Jasper, Marion, Monroe and Appanoose; on the south by the State of Missouri; on the north by the northern boundaries of the Counties of Jasper, Poweshiek, Iowa, Johnson, Cedar and Clinton.

For legal titles of parishes and diocesan institutions, consult the Chancery.

STATISTICAL OVERVIEW

Personnel	
Bishop	1
Retired Bishops	1
Priests: Diocesan Active in Diocese	66
Priests: Diocesan Active Outside Diocese	6
Priests: Retired, Sick or Absent	27
Number of Diocesan Priests	99
Religious Priests in Diocese	2
Total Priests in Diocese	101
Extern Priests in Diocese	5
Ordinations:	
Transitional Deacons	2
Permanent Deacons in Diocese	42
Total Brothers	1
Total Sisters	153
Parishes	
Parishes	80
With Resident Pastor:	
Resident Diocesan Priests	52
Resident Religious Priests	2
Without Resident Pastor:	
Administered by Priests	22
Administered by Deacons	2
Administered by Lay People	2
Welfare	
Catholic Hospitals	3
Total Assisted	421,719
Homes for the Aged	2
Total Assisted	397
Educational	
Diocesan Students in Other Seminaries	12
Total Seminarians	12
Colleges and Universities	1
Total Students	3,567
High Schools, Diocesan and Parish	5
Total Students	1,248
Elementary Schools, Diocesan and Parish	13
Total Students	3,620
Catechesis/Religious Education:	
High School Students	2,302
Elementary Students	8,553
Total Students under Catholic Instruction	19,302
Teachers in the Diocese:	
Priests	1
Sisters	3
Lay Teachers	407
Vital Statistics	
Receptions into the Church:	
Infant Baptism Totals	1,297
Minor Baptism Totals	35
Adult Baptism Totals	143
Received into Full Communion	144
First Communions	1,616
Confirmations	1,589
Marriages:	
Catholic	251
Interfaith	207
Total Marriages	458
Deaths	867
Total Catholic Population	97,332
Total Population	763,849

Former Bishops—Rt. Revs. JOHN MCMULLEN, D.D., ord. June 20, 1858; cons. July 25, 1881; died July 4, 1883; HENRY COSGROVE, D.D., ord. Aug. 27, 1857; cons. Sept. 14, 1884; died Dec. 22, 1906; JAMES DAVIS, D.D., ord. June 21, 1878; cons. Nov. 30, 1904; died Dec. 2, 1926; Most Revs. HENRY P. ROHLMAN, D.D., ord. Dec. 21, 1901; cons. July 26, 1927; appt. Coadjutor-Archbishop of Dubuque and Titular Archbishop of Macra in Rhodope, June 15, 1944; Archbishop of Dubuque, Nov. 21, 1946; appt. Titular Archbishop of Cotrada, Dec. 2, 1954; died Sept. 13, 1957; RALPH LEO HAYES, D.D., ord. Sept. 18, 1909; appt. Bishop of Helena June 23, 1933; cons. Sept. 21, 1933; appt. Rector of North American College in Rome in Sept. 1935; transferred to Titular See of Hierapolis Oct. 26, 1935; transferred to Davenport Nov. 16, 1944; appt. Assistant at the Pontifical Throne April 30, 1958; transferred to Titular See of Naraggara; retired Oct. 20, 1966; died July 4, 1970; GERALD FRANCIS O'KEEFE, D.D., ord. Jan. 29, 1944; appt. Auxiliary Bishop of St. Paul and Titular Bishop of Candyba May 5, 1961; cons. July 2, 1961; transferred to Davenport Oct. 20, 1966; installed Jan 4, 1967; retired Nov. 12, 1993; died April 12, 2000; WILLIAM E. FRANKLIN, ord. Feb. 4, 1956; appt. Titular Bishop of Surista and Auxiliary Bishop of Dubuque Jan. 29, 1987; ord. April 1, 1987; appt. Bishop of Davenport Nov. 12, 1993; installed Jan. 20, 1994; retired Oct. 12, 2006.

Pastoral Center—*780 W. Central Park Ave., Davenport, 52804-1901.* Tel: 563-324-1911; Fax: 563-324-5842. Email: communication@davenportdiocese.org. Web: www.davenportdiocese.org.

Vicar General and Moderator of the Curia—Rev. Msgr. JOHN M. HYLAND, V.G.

Chancellor—Rev. GEORGE W. MCDANIEL, Ph.D., Send marriage matters to Tribunal.

Vice-Chancellors—CHARLENE MAASKE, CPA, M.B.A.; Very Rev. JOSEPH M. WOLF, J.C.L.

Executive Secretary to the Bishop—MARY FRICK.

Diocesan Tribunal—*Pastoral Center, 780 W. Central Park Ave., Davenport, 52804-1901.* Tel: 563-324-1911.

Judicial Vicar—Very Rev. JOSEPH M. WOLF, J.C.L.

Adjutant Judicial Vicar—Rev. Msgr. MICHAEL J. MORRISSEY, M.A., J.C.L. (Retired).

Tribunal Auditor—THERESA M. DORAN.

Promoters of Justice—Rev. Msgr. FRANCIS C. HENRICKSEN, E.V. (Retired); Very Rev. Msgr. JAMES F. PARIZEK, J.C.L., V.F.

Defenders of the Bond—Revs. JOHN P. GALLAGHER, J.C.L. (Retired); WILLIAM E. REYNOLDS, J.C.L.

Notaries—Rev. GEORGE W. MCDANIEL, Ph.D.; Rev. Msgr. JOHN M. HYLAND, V.G.; Very Rev. JOSEPH M. WOLF, J.C.L.; CHARLENE MAASKE, CPA, M.B.A.; BETH BLOUGH; THERESA M. DORAN; MARY FRICK.

Judges—Revs. ROBERT J. BUSHER; EDWARD J. FITZPATRICK; Very Rev. RUDOLPH T. JUAREZ, J.C.L., E.V.; Revs. ROBERT T. MCALEER; GEORGE W. MCDANIEL, Ph.D.; Rev. Msgr. MICHAEL J. MORRISSEY, M.A., J.C.L. (Retired); Very Rev. JOSEPH M. WOLF, J.C.L.

Diocesan Consultors—Rev. Msgr. MICHAEL J. MORRISSEY, M.A., J.C.L. (Retired); Very Rev. NICHOLAS J. ADAM, V.F.; Rev. Msgr. JOHN M. HYLAND, V.G.; Rev. PAUL CONNOLLY; Very Revs. KENNETH E. KUNTZ, V.F.; RUDOLPH T. JUAREZ, J.C.L., E.V.; Rev. DAVID G. STEINLE.

Deans—Very Rev. Msgr. JAMES F. PARIZEK, J.C.L., V.F., Davenport; Very Revs. ANTHONY J. HEROLD, V.F., Keokuk; JAMES J. VRBA, V.F., Iowa City; KENNETH E. KUNTZ, V.F., Clinton; PATRICK J. HILGENDORF, V.F., Ottumwa; NICHOLAS J. ADAM, V.F., Grinnell.

Diocesan Corporate Board—Most Rev. MARTIN J. AMOS, D.D.; Rev. Msgr. JOHN M. HYLAND, V.G.; Rev. GEORGE W. MCDANIEL, Ph.D.; TIMOTHY L. MCMAHON, J.D.; ANNE MCATEE, J.D.

Finance Officer—CHARLENE MAASKE, CPA, M.B.A.

Finance Council—Most Rev. MARTIN J. AMOS, D.D.; Rev. Msgr. JOHN M. HYLAND, V.G.; Rev. GEORGE W. MCDANIEL, Ph.D.; TERRENCE KILBURG, CPA; JOEL DIECKMANN, CPA; TIMOTHY L. MCMAHON, J.D.; ANNE MCATEE, J.D.; MICHAEL POSTER, CPA; ROGER J. REILLY; JENNIFER WALKER.

Diocesan Offices

Pastoral Center—780 W. Central Park Ave., Davenport, 52804-1901. Tel: 563-324-1911.

Finance and Administration—CHARLENE MAASKE, CPA, M.B.A.

Accountant—SHERYL LACKEY.

Accounting Coordinator—NANCY KARN.

Receptionist—VACANT.

Database Coordinator—LYNNETTE SOWELLS.

Director of Development—SR. LAURA GOEDKEN, O.P.

Director of Stewardship and Parish Planning—DAN R. EBENER, D.B.A.

Communication Department—

Director of Communication—Deacon DAVID MONTGOMERY.

Director of Technology—ROBERT BUTTERWORTH.

Staff Support—LAURIE HOEFLING.

Archivist—Rev. GEORGE W. MCDANIEL, Ph.D.; ARNOLD WIESER, Archives Asst.

Pastoral Services—Rev. Msgr. JOHN M. HYLAND, V.G.

Director of Faith Formation—MARY M. WIESER.

Superintendent of Schools—LEE MORRISON, Ph.D.

Adult & Family Formation/Lay Ministry Coordinator—ILAMAE HANISCH.

Youth Ministry Coordinator—PAT FINAN.

Faith Formation Coordinator—PAT FINAN.

Director of Social Action—KENT E. FERRIS.

Immigration Program Counselors—GRICELDA GARNICA; KARINA GARNICA.

Director of Liturgy—Deacon FRANCIS L. AGNOLI.

Director of Catholic Charities—KENT E. FERRIS.

Scouting—Rev. JEFFRY W. BELGER, Mailing Address: P.O. Box 144, Pella, 50219-0144.

Catholic Relief Services—KENT E. FERRIS, Dir.

Cemetery Committee—ROBERT MCCABE, Sec., 614 Main St., Davenport, 52801. Tel: 563-322-4438.

Campaign for Human Development—LOXI HOPKINS.

Liturgical Commission—Deacon FRANCIS L. AGNOLI.

D.C.C.W.—Mrs. CAROL KAALBERG, Dir., Mailing Address: St. Mary Catholic Church, P.O. Box B, Nichols, 52766-0190. Tel: 319-723-4566.

Holy Childhood, Pontifical Association—LEE MORRISON, Ph.D.

Newspaper— "The Catholic Messenger" BARB ARLAND-FYE, Mng. Editor, 780 W. Central Park Ave., Davenport, 52804-1901. Tel: 563-323-9959; Fax: 563-324-5811. Email: messenger@davenportdiocese.org.

Pastoral Council—Most Rev. MARTIN J. AMOS, D.D., Pastoral Center, 780 W. Central Park Ave., Davenport, 52804-1901. Tel: 563-324-1911.

Permanent Diaconate—Deacon DAVID MONTGOMERY, Pastoral Center, 780 W. Central Park Ave., Davenport, 52804-1901. Tel: 563-324-1911.

Deacon Formation—Deacon FRANCIS L. AGNOLI, Pastoral Center, 780 W. Central Park Ave., Davenport, 52804-1901. Tel: 563-324-1911.

Personnel Board—Very Rev. ANTHONY J. HEROLD, V.F., Chm., 700 Division St., Burlington, 52601-5415.

Presbyteral Council—Rev. THOMAS JOSEPH HENNEN, 780 W. Central Park Ave., Davenport, 52804-1901. Tel: 563-324-1911.

Priests' Aid Society—Rev. GEORGE W. MCDANIEL, Ph.D., St. Ambrose University, 518 W. Locust St., Davenport, 52803-2898. Tel: 563-333-6299; ANN RATLIFF, Contact, Mailing Address: P.O. Box 1478, Newton, 50208-1478.

Priests Eucharistic League—Rev. MICHAEL T. PHILLIPS, Dir., St. Wenceslaus, 623 Fairchild St., Iowa City, 52245-2829. Tel: 319-337-4975; Fax: 319-337-5822. Email: phillipsm@diodav.org.

Propagation of the Faith—Rev. GEORGE W. MCDANIEL, Ph.D., Dir., Pastoral Center, 780 W. Central Park Ave., Davenport, 52804-1901. Tel: 563-324-1911.

Social Action Commission—KENT E. FERRIS, Pastoral Center, 780 W. Central Park Ave., Davenport, 52804-1901. Tel: 563-324-1911.

Serra Club—CHARLES MISSEL, 908 Grand Ct., Davenport, 52803. Tel: 563-324-7224.

Sisters Consortium—Sisters LAURA GOEDKEN, O.P., Pastoral Center, 780 W. Central Park Ave., Davenport, 52804-1901. Tel: 563-324-1911; RACHEL BEESON, C.H.M.; MICHELLE SCHIFFGENS, C.H.M.; ANNE MARTIN PHELAN, O.S.F.; MARY PAUL HUMMER, O.S.F.; JUDY HEROLD, S.S.N.D.; JANET KREBER, O.S.F.; JOAN MCCORKELL, O.C.D.

Vicar for Clergy—Rev. Msgr. FRANCIS C. HENRICKSEN, E.V. (Retired), 1113 First St., Tipton, 52772-9289. Tel: 563-886-6285.

Vicar for Religious—Rev. Msgr. FRANCIS C. HENRICKSEN, E.V. (Retired), 1113 First St., Tipton, 52772-9289. Tel: 563-886-6285.

Vicar for Hispanics—Very Rev. RUDOLPH T. JUAREZ, J.C.L., E.V., 4330 St. Patrick Dr., Iowa City, 52240-4733.

Vicar for Vietnamese—Very Rev. HAI D. DINH, E.V., 422 E. 10th St., Davenport, 52803-5499.

Victim Assistance Coordinator—ALICIA OWENS, Mailing Address: P.O. Box 232, Bettendorf, 52722-0004. Tel: 563-349-5002. Email: vacdav@attglobal.net.

Vocations—Rev. THOMAS JOSEPH HENNEN, Pastoral Center, 780 W. Central Park Ave., Davenport, 52804-1901. Tel: 563-324-1911; Fax: 563-324-5842.

CLERGY, PARISHES, MISSIONS AND PAROCHIAL SCHOOLS

CITY OF DAVENPORT

(SCOTT COUNTY)

1—SACRED HEART CATHEDRAL (1856) [JC] Revs. Richard A. Adam; Hai Duc Dinh; Deacons Robert McCoy; Francis L. Agnoli; Susan L. Stanforth, Pastoral Assoc.
Church: 422 E. 10th St., 52803-5499. Tel: 563-324-3257; Fax: 563-326-6014.
See All Saints Catholic School, Davenport under Elementary Schools, Interparochial located in the Institution Section.
Catechesis/Religious Program—Students 105.

2—ST. ALPHONSUS (1903) Rev. Thomas L. Parlette.
Res.: 2618 Boies Ave., 52802. Tel: 563-322-0987; Fax: 563-323-1458.
See All Saints Catholic School, Davenport under Elementary Schools, Interparochial located in the Institution Section.
Catechesis/Religious Program—Mary Ann Hagemann, D.R.E. Students 49.

3—ST. ANTHONY'S (1837) Rev. Apo T. Mpanda; Sr. Judy Herold, S.S.N.D., Pastoral Min.; Steve Vanderlinden, Business Mgr.
Office: 417 N. Main St., 52801. Tel: 563-322-3303; Fax: 563-326-5136.
Catechesis/Religious Program—Sr. Roberta Birch, C.H.M., C.R.E. Students 130.

4—HOLY FAMILY (1897) Revs. H. Robert Harness; George W. McDaniel; Deacon Joseph Rosenthal.
Office: 1315 W. Pleasant St., 52804. Tel: 563-322-0901 (Office); 563-322-0902 (Rectory); Fax: 563-884-4965.
See All Saints Catholic School, Davenport under Elementary Schools, Interparochial located in the Institution Section.
Catechesis/Religious Program—Roberta Pegorick, D.R.E., (Grades K-8); Thomas Perdan, Youth Min. Students 120.

5—ST. JOSEPH'S (1855) Closed. For inquiries for parish records contact Pastoral Center.

6—ST. MARY'S (1867), (Irish), Rev. Edward A. O'Melia; Deacon George D. Strader.
Res.: 516 Fillmore St., 52802. Tel: 563-322-3383; Fax: 563-322-3383.
Catechesis/Religious Program—Students 157.

7—OUR LADY OF VICTORY (1962) Very Rev. Msgr. James F. Parizek; Deacons Paul Hittner; Marcel Mosse; Al Boboth. In Res., Rev. William O. Meyer (Retired).
Res.: 4105 N. Division, 52806. Tel: 563-391-4245; Fax: 563-445-1003. Email: olvdav@qwestoffice.net. Web: www.olvjfk.com.
School—John F. Kennedy Catholic, (Grades K-8), 1627 W. 42nd St., 52806. Tel: 563-391-3030; Fax: 563-388-5206. Chad Steimle, Prin.; Janet Thomas, Librarian. Lay Teachers 30; Students 361.
Catechesis/Religious Program—Tel: 563-391-8384. Tommy Fallon, Youth Min.; Patricia Gallagher, D.R.E. Students 143.

8—ST. PAUL THE APOSTLE (1909) Revs. Michael J. Spiekermeier; Timothy J. Regan; Deacons Robert McCoy; Richard J. Rasmussen.
Res.: 916 E. Rusholme St., 52803. Tel: 563-322-7994; Fax: 563-322-7995.
School—1007 E. Rusholme, 52803. Tel: 563-322-2923; Fax: 563-322-9359. Mrs. Julie Delaney, Prin. Sisters of Charity of the Blessed Virgin Mary 1; Lay Teachers 29; Students 529.
Catechesis/Religious Program—Tel: 319-322-3768. Rosie Megraw, D.R.E. Students 128.

OUTSIDE THE CITY OF DAVENPORT

ALBIA, MONROE CO., ST. MARY'S (1874) [CEM] Rev. Michael Volkmer, C.PP.S.
Res.: 730 Benton Ave., W., P.O. Box 365, 52531. Tel: 641-932-5130; Fax: 641-932-5130.
Catechesis/Religious Program—Tel: 641-932-5589. Jackie Maddy, D.R.E. Students 209.

ARDON, MUSCATINE CO., ST. MALACHY, Closed. For sacramental records, inquiries should be addressed to St. Joseph Parish, Columbus Junction.

AUGUSTA, DES MOINES CO., ST. MARY'S (1881) Closed. For inquiries for parish records contact Pastoral Center.

BAUER, MARION CO., ST. JOSEPH ORATORY, [CEM], For inquiries for parish records contact Pastoral Center.

BETTENDORF, SCOTT CO.

1—ST. JOHN VIANNEY (1967) [JC] Rev. Robert T. McAleer; Deacons William Donnelly, (Retired); Daryl Fortin.
Office: 4097 18th St., 52722-2120. Tel: 563-332-7910; Fax: 563-332-0833.
School—(Grades PreSchool) Tel: 563-332-5308. Christy Barnum, Dir. Students 46.
Catechesis/Religious Program—Tel: 563-332-7564. Nicky Stevenson, D.R.E.; Anne Kurth, D.R.E.; Jan Stevenson, Youth Min. Students 1,004.

2—OUR LADY OF LOURDES (1903) Rev. Timothy J. Sheedy; Deacons Dennis Duff; Charles Metzger; John D. Weber.
Res.: 1506 Brown St., 52722. Tel: 563-359-0345; Fax: 563-344-6017.
School—(Grades PreSchool-8), 1453 Mississippi Blvd., 52722. Tel: 563-359-3466; Fax: 563-823-1595. Mrs. Katie Selden, Prin.; Jacqueline Rouse, Librarian. Lay Teachers 28; Students 360.
Catechesis/Religious Program—Tel: 563-359-1869. Students 171.

BLOOMFIELD, DAVIS CO., ST. MARY MAGDALEN (1953) Attended by St. Patrick's, Ottumwa.

BLUE GRASS, SCOTT CO., ST. ANDREW (1976) [JC] Revs. Apo T. Mpanda; Robert L. Grant (DM); Deacon Donald Frericks, Parish Life Admin.
Res.: 333 W. Lotte St., 52726. Tel: 563-381-1363; Fax: 563-381-4066.
Catechesis/Religious Program—Janet Friederichs, D.R.E. Students 135.

BROOKLYN, POWESHIEK CO., ST. PATRICK, [CEM] Rev. Brian J. Shepley.
Mailing Address: P.O. Box 512, 52211-0512. Tel: 641-522-4323. In Res., Rev. Philip V. Ryan (Retired).
Catechesis/Religious Program—Students 87.

BRYANT, CLINTON CO., ST. MARY, Consolidated with St. Joseph, Sugar Creek to form Sts. Mary and Joseph, Sugar Creek.

BUFFALO, SCOTT CO., ST. PETER'S (1912) [CEM] Attended by St. Alphonsus, Davenport. Rev. Thomas L. Parlette; Deacon Larry Dankert.
Mailing Address: 406 Fourth St., P.O. Box 488, 52728. Tel: 563-381-2865; 563-322-0987; Fax: 563-323-1458.
Catechesis/Religious Program—Students 38.

BURLINGTON, DES MOINES CO.

1—SS. JOHN & PAUL (1842) [JC] Very Rev. Anthony J. Herold; Rev. Bruce A. DeRammelaere; Sr. Kathy Braun, S.S.N.D., Pastoral Assoc.; Ruth Skeens, Pastoral Assoc.
Res.: 700 Division St., 52601-5415. Tel: 319-752-6733; Fax: 319-753-5211.
Catechesis/Religious Program—702 S. Roosevelt Ave., 52601. Tel: 319-753-0277. Mary Edwards, D.R.E. Students 108.

2—ST. JOHN'S (1855) Merged with St. Paul's, Burlington, to form SS. John & Paul, Burlington.

3—ST. PATRICK'S (1870) Merged with St. Mary, West Burlington to form SS. Mary and Patrick, West Burlington.

CAMANCHE, CLINTON CO., CHURCH OF THE VISITATION (1966) Rev. Richard U. Okumu.
1028 Middle Rd., 52730-1032. Tel: 563-259-1188; Fax: 563-259-4462.
Catechesis/Religious Program—Tel: 563-259-8966; 563-522-2654. Pam Drury, D.R.E.; Gail Grim, D.R.E. Students 53.

CENTERVILLE, APPANOOSE CO., ST. MARY'S (1870) Rev. Dennis Schaab, C.PP.S.
Res.: 828 S. 18th St., 52544. Tel: 641-437-1984.
Catechesis/Religious Program—Students 92.

CHARLOTTE, CLINTON CO., ASSUMPTION AND ST. PATRICK'S (1993) [CEM 2] Rev. Scott Lemaster.
Res.: 147 Broadway St., 52731. Tel: 563-677-2758.
Catechesis/Religious Program—Students 66.

CLEAR CREEK, KEOKUK CO., SS. PETER & PAUL, See separate listing. See Holy Trinity, Keota.

CLINTON, CLINTON CO., JESUS CHRIST, PRINCE OF PEACE (1990) [CEM 2] Very Rev. Kenneth E. Kuntz; Rev. Joseph T. Nguyen; Deacons Jeffrey Schuetzle; Ramon Hilgendorf; David Schnier, Business Mgr.
Parish Office—1105 LaMetta Wynn Dr., 52732. Tel: 563-242-3311; Fax: 563-242-3323.
St. Mary's—, Closed. See Jesus Christ, Prince of Peace, Clinton.
St. Boniface—, Closed. See Jesus Christ, Prince of Peace, Clinton.
St. Irenaeus—, Closed. See Jesus Christ, Prince of Peace, Clinton.
St. Patrick's—, Closed. See Jesus Christ, Prince of Peace, Clinton.
School—312 S. Fourth St., 52732. Tel: 563-242-1663; Fax: 563-243-8272. Mrs. Nancy Peart, Prin. Students 296.
Catechesis/Religious Program—Tel: 563-243-8269.

Brenda Bertram, D.R.E. & Youth Min. Students 195.
Chapel—Sacred Heart
COLFAX, JASPER CO., IMMACULATE CONCEPTION (1898) Revs. Jeffry W. Belger, Canonical Pastor; William E. Reynolds, Sacramental Min.; Deacon Joe Dvorak, Parish Life Admin.
Mailing Address: 305 E. Howard, 50054-1025. Tel: 515-674-3711.
Catechesis/Religious Program—Students 95.
COLUMBUS JUNCTION, LOUISA CO., ST. JOSEPH (1853) Revs. Jason Crossen, Admin.; Joseph M. Sia.
Mailing Address: 815 Second St., 52738. Tel: 319-728-8210.
Catechesis/Religious Program—Students 85.
CORALVILLE, JOHNSON CO., ST. THOMAS MORE (1944) [JC] Rev. Walter Helms.
Office: 3000 12th Ave., 52241. Tel: 319-337-2173; Fax: 319-337-2174.
Catechesis/Religious Program—Tel: 319-337-4231. Deacon Ed Goldsmith, D.R.E. Students 322.
COSGROVE, JOHNSON CO., ST. PETER'S (1878) Attended by St. Mary, Oxford. Rev. Edmond J. Dunn (Retired); Deacon David Montgomery.
4022 Cosgrove Rd., S.W., Oxford, 52322. Tel: 319-828-4180; 319-545-2077.
Catechesis/Religious Program—
DEWITT, CLINTON CO., ST. JOSEPH'S (1880) [CEM] Rev. Paul Connolly; Sr. Theresa Ann Spitz, R.S.M., Pastoral Assoc.
Mailing Address: 417 Sixth Ave., 52742.
Res.: 425 9th Ave., 52742. Tel: 563-659-3514; Fax: 563-659-2599.
School—Tel: 563-659-3812. Sharon Roling, Prin. Sisters of Mercy 1; Lay Teachers 14; Students 181.
Catechesis/Religious Program—Pat Sheil, D.R.E. Students 217.
DELMAR, CLINTON CO., ST. PATRICK'S (1882) [CEM] Rev. David L. Brownfield.
Res.: P.O. Box 293, 52037-0293. Tel: 563-674-4240.
Catechesis/Religious Program—Students 24.
DODGEVILLE, DES MOINES CO., ST. MARY'S (1850) [CEM] Rev. David G. Steinle; Deacon Clifford Beckman.
Mailing Address: P.O. Box 415, West Burlington, 52655-0415. Tel: 319-752-8771. Email: stmdodge@interl.net.
Catechesis/Religious Program—Tel: 319-394-9379. Jennifer Meller, D.R.E. Students 60.
EAST PLEASANT PLAIN, JEFFERSON CO., ST. JOSEPH'S (1902) [CEM] Merged with St. Frances Xavier Cabrini, Richland to form Ss. Joseph and Cabrini, Richland.
EDDYVILLE, MAHASKA CO., ST. MARY'S, Closed. For inquiries for parish records contact the Pastoral Center.
ELDON, WAPELLO CO., ST. ALOYSIUS, Closed. For inquiries for parish records contact the Pastoral Center.
FAIRFIELD, JEFFERSON CO., ST. MARY'S (1864) Rev. Stephen C. Page.
Office: 3100 W. Madison, 52556-2466. Tel: 641-472-3179; Fax: 641-472-6137.
Catechesis/Religious Program—Tel: 641-472-5996. Students 100.
FARMINGTON, VAN BUREN CO., ST. BONIFACE (1862) [CEM] Rev. Dennis L. Hoffman.
Church: 609 Washington St., P.O. Box 247, 52626. Tel: 319-837-6808.
Res.: 311 Ave. C, P.O. Box 68, West Point, 52656.
Catechesis/Religious Program—Tel: 319-837-8905; Fax: 319-837-6808. Students 31.
FORT MADISON, LEE CO.
1—HOLY FAMILY (2009) [CEM] Very Rev. David F. Wilkening; Rev. Mark P. Spring; Sr. Peggy Duffy, S.S.N.D., Pastoral Assoc.; Deacons Ronald Stein; Robert Gengengbacher.
Res.: 1013 Ave. E., 52627. Tel: 319-372-2127; Fax: 319-372-2083.
Catechesis/Religious Program—Students 81.
2—ST. JOSEPH'S, Consolidated with St. Mary's to form SS. Mary & Joseph Parish.
3—SS. MARY & JOSEPH (1871) Merged with Sacred Heart, Fort Madison to form Holy Family, Madison.
4—ST. MARY'S, Consolidated with St. Joseph's to form SS. Mary & Joseph Parish.
5—SACRED HEART (1893) Merged with SS. Mary & Joseph, Fort Madison to form Holy Family, Fort Madison.
GEORGETOWN, MONROE CO., ST. PATRICK'S (1851) [CEM] Attended by St. Peter's, Lovilia Rev. Patrick L. Lumsden; Sharon Crall, Pastoral Assoc.
Mailing Address: P.O. Box 183, Albia, 52531. Tel: 641-726-3529.
Catechesis/Religious Program—Clustered with St. Mary, Albia., Tel: 641-932-5589. Students 17.
GRAND MOUND, CLINTON CO., CHURCH OF ST. PHILIP AND JAMES (1876) [CEM] Rev. David L. Brownfield; Deacon Michael D. Sheil.
Res.: 606 Fulton St., P.O. Box 7, 52751-0007. Tel: 563-847-2271.
Catechesis/Religious Program—Students 52.
GRINNELL, POWESHIEK CO., ST. MARY'S (1924) [CEM] Very Rev. Nicholas J. Adam; Deacons William D. Olson; Stephen J. Witt.
Res.: 1018 Broad St., P.O. Box 623, 50112. Tel: 641-236-7486 (Church Office); Fax: 641-236-7488.
Catechesis/Religious Program—Tel: 641-236-8838. Students 148.
HARPER, KEOKUK CO., ST. ELIZABETH'S, See separate listing. See Holy Trinity, Keota.
HILLS, JOHNSON CO., ST. JOSEPH'S (1902) Rev. William C. Kneemiller.
Res.: 208 Iowa St., 52235. Tel: 319-679-2271.
Catechesis/Religious Program—Students 23.
HOLBROOK, IOWA CO., ST. MICHAEL, Closed. For inquiries for parish records contact the Pastoral Center.
HOUGHTON, LEE CO., ST. JOHN'S (1895) [CEM] Rev. Gary L. Beckman.
Res.: Box 100, 52631. Tel: 319-469-2001; Fax: 319-469-2001.
Catechesis/Religious Program—Tel: 319-837-8905; Fax: 319-837-6808. Dixie Booten, D.R.E. Students 16.
IOWA CITY, JOHNSON CO.
1—ST. MARY (1840) [CEM 2] [JC] Revs. John D. Spiegel; Richard J. Beyer; Sr. Mary Agnes Giblin, B.V.M., Pastoral Assoc.
Office: 302 E. Jefferson St., 52245-2137. Tel: 319-337-4314; Fax: 319-337-8551.
Catechesis/Religious Program—Regina Inter-Parish Catholic Education Center, Tel: 319-351-7638; Fax: 319-337-4109. Students 256.
2—ST. PATRICK'S (1872), (Irish), Very Rev. Rudolph T. Juarez.
Office: 4330 St. Patrick Dr., 52240. Tel: 319-337-2856; Fax: 319-354-5590.
Catechesis/Religious Program—2150 Rochester Ave., 52245. Tel: 319-351-7638; Fax: 319-337-4109. Sr. Mary Frances Michalec, D.R.E. Students 41.
3—ST. WENCESLAUS (1893) [JC] Rev. Michael T. Phillips.
Res.: 623 Fairchild St., 52245. Tel: 319-337-4957; Fax: 319-337-5822.
KEOKUK, LEE CO., ALL SAINTS (1982) Rev. Robert Lathrop.
Res.: 310 S. Ninth St., 52632. Tel: 319-524-8334; Fax: 319-524-8358.
Catechesis/Religious Program—Students 67.
KEOTA, KEOKUK CO.
1—HOLY TRINITY (1992) [CEM 3] Rev. Charles J. Fladung.
Res.: 109 N. Lincoln St., 52248-9757. Tel: 641-636-3883; Fax: 641-636-3198.
Catechesis/Religious Program—Tel: 641-636-3731. Becky Becker, D.R.E. Students 134.
2—ST. MARY'S, See separate listing. See Holy Trinity, Keota.
KESWICK, KEOKUK CO., OUR LADY OF LOURDES (1914), (Irish—German), Closed. For inquiries for parish records please see St. Mary's, Sigourney.
KINROSS, KEOKUK CO., SACRED HEART, Closed. For inquiries for parish records contact the Pastoral Center.
KNOXVILLE, MARION CO., ST. ANTHONY'S (1870) [CEM] Rev. Stephen P. Ebel.
Res.: 1202 Woodland St., 50138. Tel: 641-828-7050; Fax: 641-842-2338.
Catechesis/Religious Program—1602 & 1604 N. Lincoln St., 50138. Tel: 641-828-6332. Laura Hollinrake, Dir. Faith Formation. Students 90.
LE CLAIRE, SCOTT CO., OUR LADY OF THE RIVER (1969) Very Rev. Joseph M. Wolf.
Res.: 28200 226th St. Pl., P.O. Box 32, LeClaire, 52753. Tel: 563-289-5736.
Catechesis/Religious Program—Roberta Pegorick, D.R.E. Students 120.
LONE TREE, JOHNSON CO., ST. MARY'S (1853) [CEM] [JC] Rev. William C. Kneemiller; Mrs. Carol Kaalberg, Admin.
Mailing Address: 214 W. Jayne St., Box 416, 52755.
Res.: 214 W. Jayne St., 52755. Tel: 319-629-4225; Fax: 319-629-4944.
Catechesis/Religious Program—Students 63.
LONG GROVE, SCOTT CO., ST. ANN'S (1853) [CEM] Rev. Msgr. Drake R. Shafer.
Res.: 16550 290th St., 52756. Tel: 563-285-4596; Fax: 563-285-4897.
Catechesis/Religious Program—Joyce Kloft, D.R.E.; Julia Jones, D.R.E. & Youth Min. Students 303.
LOST NATION, CLINTON CO., SACRED HEART (1895) [CEM] Rev. Gregory A. Steckel.
Mailing Address: P.O. Box 127, 52254.
Res.: 309 Church St., Oxford Junction, 52323. Tel: 563-678-2200.
Catechesis/Religious Program—Dena Jensen, D.R.E. Students 11.
LOVILIA, MONROE CO., ST. PETER'S (1904) [CEM] Rev. Patrick L. Lumsden.
Res.: 603 W. 6th St., P.O. Box 8, 50150. Tel: 641-946-8298.
Catechesis/Religious Program—Clustered with St. Mary, Albia and St. Patrick, Georgetown., Tel: 641-932-5589. Students 11.
MARENGO, IOWA CO., ST. PATRICK'S (1878) [CEM] Rev. Joseph F. Roost.
Mailing Address: P.O. Box 183, 52301. Tel: 319-642-5438; Fax: 319-642-5648.
Catechesis/Religious Program—1526 Howard Ave., 52301. Tel: 319-642-3177. Angie Carney, D.R.E. Students 53.
MECHANICSVILLE, CEDAR CO., ST. MARY'S (1872) Rev. Andrew E. Kelly.
Res.: P.O. Box 457, 52306-0457. Tel: 563-432-6236.
Catechesis/Religious Program—Tel: 563-432-6678. Lori Crock, D.R.E. Students 60.
MELCHER, MARION CO., SACRED HEART (1912) [CEM] [JC] Rev. Stephen P. Ebel.
Res.: 204 S.W. D. St., P.O. Box 277, 50163. Tel: 641-947-4981.
Catechesis/Religious Program—Merrie Putz, Faith Formation Coord. Students 39.
MELROSE, MONROE CO., ST. PATRICK'S (1870) [CEM] Rev. Patrick L. Lumsden.
Res.: 200 Trinity St., P.O. Box 154, 52569-0154.
Catechesis/Religious Program—Jane Kamerick, D.R.E. Students 37.
MONTROSE, LEE CO., ST. JOSEPH'S (1860) [JC] Very Rev. David F. Wilkening; Rev. Mark P. Spring.
Mailing Address: 1111 Ave. E., Fort Madison, 52627.
Res.: 503 Spruce St., 52639. Tel: 319-463-5443.
Catechesis/Religious Program—Tel: 319-463-5571. Students 9.
MOUNT PLEASANT, HENRY CO., ST. ALPHONSUS (1862) [CEM] Rev. Joseph P. V. Phung.
Res.: 607 S. Jackson St., 52641-2696. Tel: 319-385-8410; Fax: 319-385-0545.
Catechesis/Religious Program—Tel: 319-385-4937. Margi Mountz, D.R.E. (Grades PreK-8); Margi Mountz, Adult Faith Formation. Students 155.
MUSCATINE, MUSCATINE CO.
1—SS. MARY AND MATHIAS OF MUSCATINE, [CEM] Revs. Jason Crossen; Joseph M. Sia; Deacon James Becker.
Res.: 215 W. Eighth St., 52761. Tel: 563-263-1878; 563-263-1416 (Parish Office); Fax: 563-263-2782.
Catechesis/Religious Program—2407 Cedar St., 52761. Tel: 563-263-3264; 563-363-3848; Fax: 563-263-6700. Sr. Mary Cheryl Demmer, P.B.V.M., D.R.E. Students 489.
2—ST. MARY'S (1876) Merged with St. Mathias to form SS. Mary and Mathias of Muscatine.
3—ST. MATHIAS (1842) Merged with St. Mathias to form SS. Mary and Mathias of Muscatine.
4—OUR LADY OF GUADALUPE CATHOLIC MISSION (1976), (Hispanic), Closed. For inquiries for parish records please see SS. Mary and Mathias of Muscatine, Muscatine.
MYSTIC, APPANOOSE CO., ST. FRANCIS, Closed. For inquiries for parish records contact the Pastoral Center.
NEWPORT, JOHNSON CO., ST. MARY, Closed. For inquiries for parish records contact the Pastoral Center.
NEWTON, JASPER CO., SACRED HEART (1867) [CEM] Rev. William E. Reynolds; Tammy Norcross, Pastoral Min.
Mailing Address: P.O. Box 1478, 50208-1478. Tel: 641-792-4625 (Rectory); Fax: 641-792-8639.
McCann Center—1115 S. Eighth Ave. E., P.O. Box 1478, 50208. Tel: 641-792-2050. (Parish Office and Religious Education Center)
Catechesis/Religious Program—Mary Beth Lawson, C.R.E. (Grades K-6). Students 144.
NICHOLS, MUSCATINE CO., ST. MARY'S (1874) [CEM] [JC] Rev. William C. Kneemiller; Mrs. Carol Kaalberg, Parish Life Admin.
201 Short St., Box B, 52766. Tel: 319-723-4566; Fax: 319-629-4944.
Catechesis/Religious Program—Students 15.
NOLAN SETTLEMENT, JOHNSON CO., ST. BRIDGET'S, Closed. For inquiries for parish records contact the Pastoral Center.
NORTH ENGLISH, IOWA CO., ST. JOSEPH'S (1896) [JC] Rev. Joseph F. Roost.
Res.: 221 N. Knoll Ridge St., P.O. Box 219, 52316. Tel: 319-664-3325.
Catechesis/Religious Program—Tel: 319-639-2550. Students 50.
OSKALOOSA, MAHASKA CO., ST. MARY'S (1871) [CEM] Revs. Jeffry W. Belger; Ronald E. Hodges.
Office: 301 High Ave. E., 52577-2823. Tel: 641-673-6680; Fax: 641-676-1766.
Res.: 464 N. 10th St., 52577. Tel: 641-676-4293.
Catechesis/Religious Program—Tel: 641-673-0659. Students 218.
OTTUMWA, WAPELLO CO.
1—ST. MARY OF THE VISITATION (1851) Rev. Bernard E. Weir; Deacon James J. Vonderhaar.
Res.: 216 N. Court St., 52501-2586. Tel: 641-682-4559; Fax: 641-682-4433.

Catechesis/Religious Program—Tel: 641-682-4496. Mary Ryan, D.R.E. Students 200.

2—St. Patrick's (1880) Very Rev. Patrick J. Hilgendorf.
Res.: 222 N. Ward St., 52501. Tel: 641-682-4212; Fax: 641-682-7915.
Catechesis/Religious Program—Ottumwa Regional Catholic Religious Education, Tel: 641-682-0320. Gail Bates, D.R.E.; Mary Ryan, D.R.E. Students 73.

3—Sacred Heart, Merged with St. Mary of the Visitation, Ottumwa.

Oxford, Johnson Co., St. Mary's (1860) [CEM] Rev. Edmond J. Dunn (Retired); Deacon David Montgomery.
Mailing Address: Box 80, 52322-0080. Tel: 319-828-4180; Fax: 319-828-4180.
Catechesis/Religious Program—Tel: 319-828-8190. Students 193.

Parnell, Iowa Co., St. Joseph's (1880) [CEM] Closed. For inquiries for parish records, contact the Pastoral Center.

Pella, Marion Co., St. Mary's (1869) [CEM] Revs. Jeffry W. Belger; Ronald E. Hodges; Deacon Don Efinger.
726 218th Pl., P.O. Box 144, 50219-0144. Tel: 641-628-3078; Fax: 641-628-3165.
Res.: 1104 Peace St., P.O. Box 144, 50219-0144. Tel: 641-628-4262.
Catechesis/Religious Program—Tel: 641-628-3078. Students 213.

Petersville, Clinton Co., Immaculate Conception (1853) [CEM] Rev. Scott Lemaster.
Church: 147 Broadway St., Charlotte, 52731. Tel: 563-677-2758.
Catechesis/Religious Program—Tel: 563-652-6971. Students 7.

Rathbun, Appanoose Co., St. Anthony (1895) Closed. For inquiries for parish records contact the chancery.

Richland, Keokuk Co.

1—St. Frances Xavier Cabrini (1946), (German), Merged with St. Joseph's, East Pleasant Plain to form Ss. Joseph and Cabrini, Richland.

2—Ss. Joseph and Cabrini (2008) Rev. Robert M. Striegel, Canonical Pastor & Sacramental Min.; Shirley Van Dee, Parish Life Admin.
Res.: 308 W. Main St., P.O. Box 130, 52585-0130. Tel: 319-456-3161; Fax: 319-456-6408.
Catechesis/Religious Program—Students 55.

Richmond, Washington Co., Holy Trinity (1854) [CEM] Rev. Martin G. Goetz.
Res.: 571 Howard St., Kalona, 52247-9558. Tel: 319-656-2802. Pastor's Res.: 51 St. Mary's St., Riverside, 52327-0482.
Catechesis/Religious Program—Tel: 319-656-5218. Students 94.

Riverside, Washington Co., St. Mary of the Assumption (1877) [CEM] Rev. Martin G. Goetz.
Mailing Address: 51 St. Mary's St., P.O. Box C, 52327-0482.
Res.: 360 Washburn St., P.O. Box C, 52327-0482. Tel: 319-648-2331; Fax: 319-648-5024.
Catechesis/Religious Program—Students 133.

St. Paul, Lee Co., St. James (1838) [CEM] Attended by St. John, Houghton. Rev. Gary L. Beckman.
Mailing Address: P.O. Box 100, Houghton, 52631-0100. Tel: 319-469-2001.
Catechesis/Religious Program—Tel: 319-837-8905; Fax: 319-837-8905. Dixie Booten, D.R.E. Students 24.

Sigourney, Keokuk Co., St. Mary's (1873) [CEM] [JC] Rev. Charles J. Fladung; Deacon James Striegel.
Res.: 415 E. Pleasant Valley St., 52591. Tel: 641-622-2316 (Rectory & Business); Fax: 641-622-2389.
Catechesis/Religious Program— Jenny Thompson, D.R.E. Students 70.

Solon, Johnson Co.

1—St. Mary's (1858) [CEM] Very Rev. James J. Vrba.
Mailing Address: 1749 Racine Ave., 52333-0069.
Res.: 313 E. 1st St., 52333-9728. Tel: 319-624-3455; Fax: 319-624-3564.
Catechesis/Religious Program—Julie Agne, D.R.E. Students 405.

2—SS. Peter & Paul, Closed. For inquiries for parish records contact the chancery.

String Prairie, Lee Co., St. Mary, Closed. For inquiries for parish records contact the Parish Center.

Sugar Creek, Clinton Co.

1—St. Joseph's, Consolidated with St. Mary, Bryant, to form Sts. Mary and Joseph, Sugar Creek.

2—Ss. Mary and Joseph (1993) [CEM 2] Rev. Scott Lemaster.
Res.: 147 Broadway St., Charlotte, 52731-9686. Tel: 563-677-2758.
Catechesis/Religious Program—Students 12.

Tipton, Cedar Co., St. Mary's (1856) [CEM] Rev. David Hitch; Deacon Robert Snavely, (Retired).
Res.: 208 Meridian St., P.O. Box 309, 52772-0309. Tel: 563-886-2506; Fax: 563-886-6326.
Catechesis/Religious Program—Tel: 563-886-2545. Mary Barnum, D.R.E. Students 166.

Toronto, Clinton Co., St. James (1855) [CEM] Attended by Sacred Heart, Lost Nation. Rev. Gregory A. Steckel.
Mailing Address: P.O. Box 127, Lost Nation, 52254. Tel: 563-678-2200.
Catechesis/Religious Program—Students 7.

Valeria, Jasper Co., Sacred Heart (1892) Closed. For inquiries for parish records contact the Pastoral Center.

Victor, Iowa Co., St. Bridget (1886) [CEM] [JC] Rev. Brian J. Shepley.
Res.: 104 Third St., 52347. Tel: 319-647-2220; Fax: 319-647-3231.
Catechesis/Religious Program—Tel: 319-647-2221. Students 58.

Villa Nova, Clinton Co., St. Patrick, Consolidated with Assumption of the Blessed Virgin Mary, Charlotte, to form Assumption and St. Patrick's, Charlotte.

Wapello, Louisa Co., St. Mary's (1867) Closed. For inquiries for parish records contact the Pastoral Center.

Washington, Washington Co., St. James (1860) [JC] Rev. Troy A. Richmond.
Office: 602 W. 2nd St., 52353-1994. Tel: 319-653-4504; Fax: 319-653-4019.
Res.: 540 W. 3rd St., 52353-1994. Tel: 319-653-5704.
School—Tel: 319-653-3631. Mrs. Teresa Beenblossom, Prin. Lay Teachers 12; Students 126.
Catechesis/Religious Program— Janis Vittetoe, C.R.E.; Linda Gent, Youth Min. Coord.

Weller, Monroe Co., St. Mary, Closed. For inquiries for parish records contact the Pastoral Center.

Wellman, Washington Co., St. Joseph (1969) [CEM] Rev. Martin G. Goetz.
Mailing Address: 235 11th St., P.O. Box C, Riverside, 52327-0482. Tel: 319-648-2331; Fax: 319-648-5024.
Catechesis/Religious Program—Tel: 319-646-2933. Cindy Duwa, D.R.E. Students 52.

Welton, Clinton Co., St. Anne (1910) Attended by St. Patrick, Delmar. Rev. David L. Brownfield.
Mailing Address: P.O. Box 293, Delmar, 52037-0293. Tel: 563-674-4240.
Catechesis/Religious Program—Students 1.

West Branch, Cedar Co., St. Bernadette (1960) Attended by St. Joseph, West Liberty. Rev. Dennis C. Martin.
Church & Mailing Address: 507 E. Orange, Box 103, 52358-0103. Tel: 319-643-2095; 319-627-2229 (Pastor Only).
Catechesis/Religious Program—1720 Madison St., Tipton, 52772. Tel: 319-946-2162. Martha Freeman, D.R.E. Students 87.

West Burlington, Des Moines Co., SS. Mary and Patrick (1870) [CEM] Rev. David G. Steinle.
Res.: 520 W. Mt. Pleasant St., P.O. Box 415, 52655-0415. Tel: 319-752-8771.
Catechesis/Religious Program—700 S. Roosevelt, Burlington, 52601. Tel: 319-754-8431. Mary Edwards, D.R.E. Students 58.

West Liberty, Muscatine Co., St. Joseph's (1892) [CEM] Rev. Dennis C. Martin.
Res.: 107 W. Sixth St., 52776-1246. Tel: 319-627-2229.
Catechesis/Religious Program—Students 96.

West Point, Lee Co., St. Mary of the Assumption, [CEM] Rev. Dennis L. Hoffman.
Res.: 311 Ave. C, P.O. Box 68, 52656. Tel: 319-837-6808; Fax: 319-837-6808.
Catechesis/Religious Program—Students 25.

What Cheer, Keokuk Co., St. Joseph's, Closed. For inquiries for parish records contact the Pastoral Center.

Williamsburg, Iowa Co., St. Mary's (1891) [CEM] Rev. Joseph F. Roost.
Res.: 102 E. Penn, Box 119, 52361. Tel: 319-668-1397; Fax: 319-668-2487.
Catechesis/Religious Program—Tel: 319-668-2757. Students 160.

Wilton, Muscatine Co., St. Mary's (1857) [CEM] Rev. Robert J. Busher.
Res.: 701 E. 3rd St., 52778. Tel: 563-732-2271; Fax: 563-732-2269.
Catechesis/Religious Program—Tel: 563-785-6266. Students 75.

Chaplains of Public Institutions

Iowa City. *State University of Iowa Hospital*. Revs. Vitolds Valainis, E. William Kaska.
Veteran's Administration Hospital. Rev. Robert M. Striegel.

On Duty Outside the Diocese:
Revs.—
Burnett, James E., 8505 Hemlock Ln., Darien, IL 60561.
Stecher, John E., 2701 Spring St., Fort Wayne, IN 46808.

Military Chaplains:
Rev. Msgr.—
Spiegel, Robert H., CMR 409, Box 616, Apo, AE 09053.

Retired:
Rev. Msgrs.—
Henricksen, Francis C., E.V., 1113 First St., Tipton, 52772.
Morrissey, Michael J., M.A., J.C.L., Pastoral Center, 780 W. Central Park Ave., 52804-1901.
Mottet, Marvin A., Pastoral Center, 780 W. Central Park Ave., 52804-1901.
Schmidt, Robert, Ph.D., 5510 Woodland Ave., 52807.
Walter, Robert J., Pastoral Center, 780 W. Central Park Ave., 52804-1901.
Revs.—
Bevenour, Richard F., 622 W. Escalon St., Fresno, CA 93704.
Borger, Theodore R., 6 Windy Ct., Verona, WI 53593-7904.
Braida, Ernest E., 1009 W. Marion St., Knoxville, 50138-2844.
Brothersen, Maynard J., Pastoral Center, 780 W. Central Park Ave., 52804-1901.
Dawson, William F., Ph.D., 518 W. Locust St., 52803.
Doyle, Thomas R., 925 Applewood Ct. #4, Coralville, 52241.
Gallagher, John P., J.C.L., 104 E.Gleneagles Rd. Apt. B, Ocala, FL 34472-8476.
Hoening, Gerald, 1432 Ave. E, Fort Madison, 52627-2629.
Hynes, John F., 3051 Holiday Ct., Bettendorf, 52722-3463.
Khan, Joseph Nguyen, 10421 Orangewood Ave., Garden Grove, CA 92840.
Leonhardt, Louis J., P.O. Box 454, Lone Tree, 52755.
Mannhardt, Daniel C., 1360 Kimberly Ridge Rd., Bettendorf, 52722.
Meyer, William O., Our Lady of Victory, 4105 N. Division St., 52806.
Mohr, Thomas H., 2122 E. Elm St., 52803.
Reilman, Thomas J., 2301 Agency St., #59, Burlington, 52601.
Rogers, Joseph, Kahl Home, 1101 W. Ninth St., 52804.
Ruppenkamp, Raymond, 4233 180th St., Clinton, 52732-8818.
Ryan, Philip V., St. Patrick Rectory, 215 S. Jackson St., P.O. Box 512, Brooklyn, 52211.
Shortall, Robert, 7100 Chase Oaks, Apt. 2313, Plano, TX 75025.
Spiegel, Thomas J., 2021 Edmundson Dr., Oskaloosa, 52577.
Stratman, Thomas F., Pastoral Center, 780 W. Central Park Ave., 52804-1901.
Whalen, John J., 2610 Newbury Cir. Apt. F, Burlington, 52601-1885.
Wiegand, William R., 216 Broadway, Pella, 50219.

Permanent Deacons:
Becker, James L., Muscatine
Beckman, Clifford C., Sperry
Boboth, Albert G., Davenport
Cadena, Juan J., Muscatine
Cosgrove, William T., Keokuk
Dankert, Larry F., Davenport
Donart, Arthur C., Thomson, IL
Donnelly, William G., Bettendorf
Duff, Dennis L., Bettendorf
Dvorak, Joseph F., Colfax
Frericks, Donald E., Blue Grass
Gengenbacher, Robert, Fort Madison
Gutierrez, Julian, Davenport
Hilgendorf, Ramon C., Clinton
Hittner, Paul F., East Moline, IL
Lennon, Patrick, Clinton
McCoy, Robert C., Davenport
Metzger, Charles A., Bettendorf
Miller, Jerome A., Iowa City
Montgomery, David, Oxford
Mosse, Marcel G., Davenport
O'Connor, Arthur, Olatha, KS
Olson, William D., Grinnell
Rasmussen, Richard J., Bettendorf
Reha, David, Wellman
Rosenthal, Joseph I., Davenport
Schmitt, John H., Low Moor
Schroeder, William E., Carroll
Schuetzle, Jeffrey C., Clinton
Sheil, Michael D., DeWitt

Snavely, Robert E., Tipton
Stein, Ronald K., Donnellson
Strader, George D., Davenport
Striegel, James L., Delta
Tometich, Anton I., Muscatine
Vonderhaar, James J., West Point
Weber, John R., Bettendorf
Witt, Stephen J., Grinnell

INSTITUTIONS LOCATED IN THE DIOCESE

[A] COLLEGES AND UNIVERSITIES

DAVENPORT. *St. Ambrose University*, 518 W. Locust St., 52803-2898. Tel: 563-333-6300; Fax: 563-333-6243. Email: admit@sau.edu. Web: www.sau.edu. Dr. Joan Lescinski, C.S.J., Pres.; Dr. Paul Koch, Vice Pres. Academic Affairs; Michael Poster, CPA, Vice Pres. Finance; Jeanne Kobuszewski, Vice Pres. Advancement; John Cooper, Vice Pres. Enrollment Mgmt.; Rev. Charles A. Adam, Campus Chap.; Charles Brock, Dir. Music Ministry & Spirituality; Rev. Charles A. Adam, Dir. Service Learning & Justice Ministry; Sheila Deluhery, Assoc. Dir. Campus Min.; Mary Heinzman, Librarian Dir. Priests 4; Sisters 1; Total Faculty & Staff 664; Students 3,567.
Priest Faculty: Revs. Charles A. Adam; William F. Dawson, Ph.D. (Retired); Joseph De Francisco, S.T.D. (BEA); Edmond J. Dunn, Ph.D. (Retired); Robert L. Grant, Ph.D. (DM); George W. McDaniel, Ph.D.; Brian Miclot, Ph.D.

[B] HIGH SCHOOLS, INTERPAROCHIAL

DAVENPORT. *Assumption High School*, 1020 W. Central Park Ave., 52804-1899. Tel: 563-326-5313; Fax: 563-326-3510. Email: craiga@mail.assumption.pvt.k12.ia.us. Web: www.assumptionhigh.org. Mr. Chuck Elbert, Prin.; Mr. Andrew Craig, Pres.; Eric Ries, Dean of Students. Lay Teachers 27; Students 437.

BURLINGTON. *Notre Dame High School*, 702 S. Roosevelt Ave., 52601-1602. Tel: 319-754-8431; Fax: 319-752-8690. Email: ron.glasgow@gpdea.k12.ia.us. Ron Glasgow, Prin. Lay Teachers 16; Students 187.

[C] EDUCATION CENTERS

CLINTON. *Prince of Peace Catholic School*, (Grades K-12), 312 S. 4th St., 52732-4499. Tel: 563-242-1663; Fax: 563-243-8272. Email: npeart@prince.pvt.k12.ia.us. Web: www.prince.pvt.k12.ia.us. Mrs. Nancy Peart, Prin.; Kay Schwendinger, Business Mgr. Lay Teachers 25; Students 223.

Prince of Peace Catholic High School, 312 S. 4th St., 52732. Tel: 563-242-1663; Fax: 563-243-8272. Email: npeart@prince.pvt.k12.ia.us. Web: www.princepvt.k12.ia.us.

Prince of Peace Catholic Elementary, 312 S. 4th St., 52732. Tel: 563-242-1663; Fax: 563-243-8272. Email: npeart@prince.pvt.k12.ia.us. Web: www.prince.pvt.k12.ia.us. Mrs. Nancy Peart, Prin.; Kay Schwendinger, Business Mgr.

Prince of Peace Catholic Preschool-Childcare, 245 26th Ave., N., 52732. Tel: 563-242-9258. Mrs. Mary Jensen, Dir.; Mrs. Nancy Peart, Prin. Students 73.

FORT MADISON. *Holy Trinity Schools*, 2600 Ave. A, 52627. Tel: 319-372-2486; Fax: 319-372-6310. Email: rick.facciolo@gpaea.k12.ia.us. Web: www.holytrinityschools.org. Dr. Richard A. Facciolo, Chief Admin. of Holy Trinity Schools, Inc. Lay Teachers 42; Students 322.

IOWA CITY. *The Regina Inter-Parish Catholic Education Center*, 2140 Rochester Ave., 52245. Tel: 319-337-2580; Fax: 319-337-4109. Web: www.icregina.com.

Regina Junior Senior High School, 2150 Rochester Ave., 52245. Tel: 319-338-5436; Fax: 319-887-3817. Email: david.krummel@icregina.com. David Krummel, Prin. Lay Teachers 31; Students 400.

Regina Elementary School, 2120 Rochester Ave., 52245-3527. Tel: 319-337-5739; Fax: 319-337-4109. Email: celeste.vincent@icregina.com. Ms. Celeste Vincent, Prin. Lay Teachers 31; Students 445.

Regina Religious Education, 2140 Rochester Ave., 52245. Tel: 319-351-7638; Fax: 319-337-4109. Sr. Mary Frances Michalec.

Regina Special Events Office, 2140 Rochester Ave., 52245. Tel: 319-358-2455; Fax: 319-337-4109.

Regina Preschool-Daycare, 2140 Rochester Ave., 52245. Tel: 319-337-6198; Fax: 319-337-4109. Ms. Mary Pechous.

KEOKUK. *Keokuk Catholic Schools, Inc.*, 2981 Plank Rd., 52632-2399. Tel: 319-524-5450; Fax: 319-524-7725. Laura Marsot, Chief Admin. & Prin.

St. Vincent's Extended Day Care Program, 2981 Plank Rd., 52632-5452. Tel: 319-524-5450. Lay Teachers 10; Students 71.

[D] ELEMENTARY SCHOOLS, INTERPAROCHIAL

DAVENPORT. *All Saints Catholic School*, (Grades K-8), 1926 N. Marquette St., 52804-2199. Tel: 563-324-3205; Fax: 563-324-9331. Jeanne Von Feldt, Prin.; David Sowells, Librarian. Lay Teachers 27; Students 400.

BURLINGTON. *Burlington Notre Dame Schools, Inc.*, (Grades PreK-5), Notre Dame Elementary School, 700 S. Roosevelt Ave., 52601-1602. Tel: 319-752-3776; 319-754-4417; Fax: 319-752-8690. Robert Carr, Prin.; Connie Siefken, Librarian. Lay Teachers 14; Students 253.

MUSCATINE. *Saints Mary and Mathias Catholic School*, 2407 Cedar St., 52761-2696. Tel: 563-263-3264; Fax: 563-263-6700. Email: ann-gomez@ssmarymathiascatholicschool.org. Web: www.bishophayescatholicschool.com. Ann Gomez, Prin.; Carla Meeke, Librarian. Lay Teachers 15; Students 214.

OTTUMWA. *Seton Catholic School*, 117 E. Fourth St., 52501-2992. Tel: 641-682-8826; Fax: 641-682-6202. Duane Siepker, Prin.; Connie Shaw, Librarian. Lay Teachers 10; Students 111.

[E] CATHOLIC STUDENT CENTERS

IOWA CITY. *Newman Catholic Student Center* 104 E. Jefferson St., 52245. Tel: 319-337-3106; Fax: 319-337-6858. Email: newman-center@uiowa.edu. Web: www.newman-ic.org. Revs. Edward J. Fitzpatrick, Dir.; Richard J. Beyer.

[F] RESIDENTIAL ADOLESCENT CARE CENTERS

CLINTON. *Arch, Inc.*, Box 0278, 52733-0278. Tel: 563-243-9035; Fax: 563-243-7796. Email: bettyk1983@hotmail.com. Keith Kalaukoa, Exec. Dir. Total Assisted 18; Total Staff 27.

Arch I, 402 S. Fourth St., 52732. Tel: 563-243-3980.

Arch II, 734 Fifth Ave. S., 52732. Tel: 563-242-5082.

Arch III, 505 7th Ave. S., 52732. Tel: 563-242-8740; Fax: 563-242-8740.

[G] GENERAL HOSPITALS

CENTERVILLE. *Mercy Medical Center - Centerville*, One St. Joseph's Dr., 52544. Tel: 641-437-4111; Fax: 641-437-3304. Web: www.mercycenterville.org. Clint Christianson, Pres. Owned by Mercy Medical Center, Des Moines.; Attended from St. Mary's, Centerville. Bed Capacity 25; Patients Assisted Annually 150,000; Total Staff 270.

Legacies, The Foundation of Mercy Medical Center Tel: 614-437-3434; Fax: 641-437-3304. Ann Young, Pres.

CLINTON. *Mercy Medical Center - Clinton* A subsidiary of Trinity Health., 1410 N. Fourth St., 52732. Tel: 563-244-5555; Fax: 563-244-5592. Web: www.mercyclinton.com. Sean J. Williams, Pres. & CEO; Rev. John J. Stack. Bed Capacity 175; Staff 900; Total Assisted Annually 170,000.

Mercy Living Center - South, 638 S. Bluff Blvd., 52732. Tel: 563-244-3704; Fax: 563-244-3756. Bed Capacity 97.

Mercy Living Center - North, 600 14th Ave. N., 52732. Tel: 563-244-3884; Fax: 563-244-3882. Bed Capacity 86.

IOWA CITY. *Mercy Hospital*, 500 E. Market St., 52245-2633. Tel: 319-339-0300. Web: www.mercyiowacity.org. Ronald R. Reed, Pres. & CEO; Tim Bernemann, Dir., Pastoral Care; Rev. Mary Johnston, Ph.D., Chap.; Sr. Theresa Kruml, O.S.U., Chap.; David Oakland, Chap. Sisters 1.

[H] SOCIAL ACTION DEPARTMENTS

DAVENPORT. *Project Renewal of Davenport, Inc.*, Nazarath House, 906 W. Fifth St., 52802. Tel: 563-324-0800. Email: projectrenewal@revealed.net. Ann Schwickerath, (In Res.); Carl Callaway, (In Res.).

**Thomas Merton House, Inc.*, P.O. Box 3375, 52808. Tel: 563-324-4472. Email: jtiedje@qcbt.com. James R. Tiedje, Contact Person.

[I] HOMES FOR AGED

DAVENPORT. *Kahl Home for the Aged and Infirm*, 1101 W. Ninth St., 52804. Tel: 563-324-1621; Fax: 563-324-1723. Sr. M. Lois Baniewicz, O.Carm., Asst. Admin. & Prioress; Rev. Joseph Rogers, Chap. (Retired). Carmelite Sisters for the Aged and Infirm. Sisters 5; Bed Capacity 130; Total Assisted 221; Total Staff 207.

CLINTON. *The Alverno Health Care Facility* 52732. Tel: 563-242-1521; Fax: 563-243-3016. Email: lgoodman@thealverno.com. Web: www.thealverno.com. Libby Goodman, Admin. Sisters of St. Francis, Clinton, IA 2; Bed Capacity 132; Total Assisted 331; Total Staff 198.

[J] MONASTERIES AND RESIDENCES FOR PRIESTS AND BROTHERS

DAVENPORT. *St. Vincent Center*, 780 W. Central Park Ave., 52804-1901. Tel: 563-324-1911; Fax: 563-324-5842. Email: maaske@davenportdiocese.org. Web: www.davenportdiocese.org. Most Rev. William E. Franklin, D.D., Bishop Emeritus; Rev. Msgrs. John M. Hyland, V.G.; Michael J. Morrissey, M.A., J.C.L. (Retired); Marvin A. Mottet (Retired); Robert J. Walter (Retired); Revs. Maynard J. Brothersen (Retired); Thomas Joseph Hennen; Thomas F. Stratman (Retired).

IOWA CITY. *O'Keefe Hall*, 104 E. Jefferson St., 52245. Tel: 319-337-3106; Fax: 319-337-6858. Email: newman-center@uiowa.edu. Web: www.newman-ic.org. Rev. Edward J. Fitzpatrick, Dir. In Res. Revs. E. William Kaska; Mansuetus Setonga; Vitolds Valainis.

WEVER. *Generalate of the Brothers of the Poor of Saint Francis*, 3405 190th St., 52658. Tel: 319-372-9543; Fax: 319-372-9543. Email: markgastel@hughes.net. Web: www.brothersofthepoorofstfrancis.org.

[K] CONVENTS AND RESIDENCES FOR SISTERS

DAVENPORT. *Franciscan Sisters of Christ the Divine Teacher*, 2605 Boies Ave., 52802. Tel: 563-323-1502. Sr. Susan Rueve, O.S.F., Supr. Sisters 3.

Humility of Mary Center - Motherhouse of the Congregation of the Humility of Mary, 820 W. Central Park Ave., 52804. Tel: 563-323-9466; Fax: 563-323-5209. Email: sisters@chmiowa.org. Web: chmiowa.org. Sr. Mary Rehmann, C.H.M., Pres. Total in Residence 38; Total Staff 34.

CLINTON. *The Canticle*, 841 13th Ave. N., 52732-5162. Tel: 563-242-7903; Fax: 563-242-8024. Sr. Janice Cebula, O.S.F., Pres. Residence of the Sisters of St. Francis, Clinton, Iowa. Total in Residence 31.

Sisters of St. Francis, Clinton, Iowa, Administrative Center, 843 13th Ave. N., 52732-5115. Tel: 563-242-7611; Fax: 563-243-0007. Email: sisters@clintonfranciscans.com. Web: www.clintonfranciscans.com. Sr. Janice I. Cebula, O.S.F., Pres. Sisters 66.

ELDRIDGE. *Carmel of the Queen of Heaven Discalced Carmelite Nuns*, 17937 250th St., 52748. Tel: 563-285-8387; Fax: 563-285-7467. Email: solitude@netins.net. Web: www.carmelitesofeldridge.org. Sr. Lynne Elwinger, O.C.D., Prioress. Professed Sisters 9.

[L] RETREAT PROGRAMS-CENTERS

WHEATLAND. **New Horizons of Faith: Our Lady of the Prairie Retreat*, 2664 145th Ave., 52777. Tel: 563-323-9466; Fax: 563-323-5209. Email: mrehmann@chmiowa.org. Mailing Address: 820 W. Central Park Ave., 52804.

[M] MISCELLANEOUS

DAVENPORT. **Assumption Foundation for K-12 Schools*, 1020 W. Central Park Ave., 52804. Tel: 563-326-5313; Fax: 563-326-3510. Email: craiga@mail.assumption.pvt.k12.ia.us. Web: www.assumptionhigh.org.

Catholic Foundation for the Diocese of Davenport, 780 W. Central Park Ave., 52804-1901. Tel: 563-324-1911; Fax: 563-324-5842. Web: www.davenportdiocese.org. Most Rev. Martin J. Amos, D.D., Contact Person.

Catholic Service Board, 230 W. 35th St., 52806.

Congregation of the Humility of Mary Charitable Trust, 820 W. Central Park Ave., 52804. Tel: 563-323-9466; Fax: 563-323-5209. Email: sisters@chmiowa.org. Web: www.chmiowa.org. Sr. Mary Rehmann, C.H.M., Contact Person.

Eagles' Wings Incorporated, P.O. Box 4804, 52808.

**Humility of Mary Housing, Inc.*, 820 W. Central Park Ave., 52804. Tel: 563-326-1330; Fax: 563-326-0756. Email: hmhiowa@netexpress.net. Web: www.humilityofmaryhousing.com. Sr. Mary Rehmann, C.H.M., Pres. Total Assisted 225; Total Staff 17; Total in Residence 150.

**Humility of Mary Shelter, Inc.*, 1016 W. 5th St., 52802-3404. Tel: 563-326-1330; Fax: 563-326-0756. Sr. Mary Rehmann, C.H.M., Contact Person.

Kingdom Co., 780 W. Central Park Ave., 52804-1901. Tel: 563-324-1911; Fax: 563-324-5842. Email: maaske@davenportdiocese.org. Web: www.davenportdiocese.org. Charlene Maaske, CPA, M.B.A., Contact Person.

St. Paul the Apostle Foundation, 916 E. Rusholme St., 52803. Tel: 563-322-7994. Email: davstpaul@diodav.org. Rev. Michael J. Spiekermeier, Contact Person.

Quad Cities Catholic Deaf Ministry, 4105 N. Division St., 52806-4741. Tel: 563-391-4245; Fax: 563-445-1003. Email: parizekj@diodav.org. Very Rev. Msgr. James F. Parizek, J.C.L., V.F., Contact Person.

School Tuition Organization of Southeast Iowa, 1860 E. 54th St., 52807. Tel: 563-391-1845. Web: stoseiowa.org. Steven M. Roling, Exec. Dir.

Scott County Catholic Education Services, Inc. dba All Saints Catholic School 1926 Marquette St., 52804. Tel: 563-324-3205; Fax: 530-324-9331. Web: www.saints.pvt.k12.ia.us. Jeanne Von Feldt, Prin. & Contact Person.

Spirit, Inc., 2214 Harrison St., 52803. Tel: 563-324-1776; 563-323-5499. Email: spiritinc.davenport.iowa@gmail.com. Paul Roe, Contact.

Vietnamese Catholic Community of Our Lady of Mong Trieu, 422 E. 10th St., 52803. Tel: 563-326-6279; Fax: 563-326-6014. Rev. Hai Duc Dinh.

St. Vincent Home Corporation, 780 W. Central Park Ave., 52804-1901. Tel: 563-324-1911; Fax: 563-324-5842. Email: ferris@davenportdiocese.org. Web: www.davenportdiocese.org. Kent E. Ferris, Contact Person.

BETTENDORF. *Catholic Endowment of Bettendorf, Iowa, Inc.*, 2898 Villa Ct., 52722. Tel: 563-332-4271. Gregory P. Adamson, Vice Pres. & Contact Person.

BROOKLYN. *St. Patrick Parish Foundation*, 215 Jackson St., 52211-0512. Tel: 641-522-7714. Glen J. Kriegel, Pres.

BURLINGTON. *Burlington Notre Dame Foundation*, 702 S. Roosevelt Ave., 52601. Tel: 319-752-8690; Fax: 319-752-8690. Val Giannettino, Devel. Dir.

St. Vincent De Paul Society, St. John the Baptist Church Conference, 700 Division St., 52601. Tel: 319-752-9332. Jim Wade, Contact Person.

CENTERVILLE. *St. Mary's Foundation of Centerville*, 828 S. 18th St., 52544. Tel: 641-437-1984.

CLINTON. *Mercy Home Care and Hospice*, 638 S. Bluff, 52732. Tel: 563-244-3766; Fax: 563-244-3719. Email: meistesk@mercyhealth.com. Web: www.mercyclinton.com. Sharon Meister, M.S., Dir.; Sean Williams, CEO.

Mount St. Clare Speech & Hearing Center, Inc., 562 N. Bluff Blvd., 52732. Tel: 563-242-4070; Fax: 563-242-2426. Email: marcella.narlock@mscspeechandhearingcenter.org. Web: www.clintonfranciscans.com. Sr. Marcella Marie Narlock, O.S.F., Dir. Sisters of St. Francis.

Mount St. Clare Education Foundation, 843 13th Ave. N., 52732-5115. Tel: 563-242-7611; Fax: 563-243-0007. Email: president@clintonfranciscans.com.

Sisters of St. Francis, Clinton, Iowa, Charitable Trust, 843 13th Ave. N., 52732. Tel: 563-242-7611; Fax: 563-243-0007. Email: sisters@clintonfranciscans.com. Web: www.clintonfranciscans.com. Sr. Janice Cebula, O.S.F., Pres.

CORALVILLE. *St. Thomas More New Season Charitable Trust*, 3000 12th Ave., 52241. Tel: 319-337-2173. Web: www.stthomasmoreic.com. Rev. Walter Helms, Contact Person.

GRINNELL. *St. Mary's Parish Foundation, Grinnell, Iowa*, 1022 Broad St., P.O. Box 655, 50112. Tel: 641-236-4545; Fax: 641-236-8770. Mr. William D. Olson, Contact Person.

HOUGHTON. *Marquette Foundation*, 309 2nd St., P.O. Box 24, 52631. Gale Thompson, Pres.

IOWA CITY. **John Paul II Stem Cell Research Institute*, 540 E. Jefferson St., 52245. Ms. Kim Lehman, Devel. Dir.

Mercy Hospital Foundation, 500 E. Market St., 52245-2689. Tel: 319-339-3657; Fax: 319-358-2624. Margaret N. Reese, Pres.

Mercy Hospital Guild of Iowa City, Iowa, 500 E. Market St., 52245. Tel: 319-339-3659. Carol Ebinger, Volunteer Coord.

Mercy Outreach Iowa City, Inc., 500 E. Market St., 52245. Tel: 319-339-3540. Ronald Reed, CEO.

Mercy Hospital, Iowa City, Iowa, 500 E. Market St., 52245. Tel: 319-339-3540. Ronald Reed, CEO.

Regina Foundation, 2140 Rochester Ave., P.O. Box 1581, 52244. Tel: 319-354-5866; Fax: 319-354-1911. Email: info@icreginafoundation.com. April E. Rouner, Exec. Dir.

Roman Catholic Ministries of Iowa City, Iowa (2002) 104 E. Jefferson, 52245. Tel: 319-337-3106; Fax: 319-337-6858.

KEOKUK. *Ladies of Charity of Keokuk*, 1524 High St., 52632. Madonna Kirchner, Pres.

OSKALOOSA. *Share Iowa, Inc.*, 1102 S. 7th St., P.O. Box 328, 52577. Tel: 641-673-4000; Fax: 641-673-6042. Rebecca S. Newman, Exec. Dir.

OTTUMWA. *The Center for International Resources, Inc. Mexico*, 205 Hill Ave., 52501. Tel: 641-682-4264; Fax: 641-684-4690. Kathryn Bissell, Ph.D., M.A., Chm. & Exec. Dir.

RELIGIOUS INSTITUTES OF MEN REPRESENTED IN THE DIOCESE

For further details refer to the corresponding bracketed number in the Religious Institutes of Men or Women section.

[0460]—*Brothers of the Poor of St. Francis*—C.F.P.

[]—*Claretian Missionaries* (Western Prov.)

[1060]—*Society of the Precious Blood*—C.PP.S.

RELIGIOUS INSTITUTES OF WOMEN REPRESENTED IN THE DIOCESE

[0330]—*Carmelite Sisters for the Aged and Infirm*—O.Carm.

[2100]—*Congregation of Humility of Mary*—C.H.M.

[1780]—*Congregation of the Sisters of the Third Order of St. Francis of Perpetual Adoration*—F.S.P.A.

[0420]—*Discalced Carmelite Nuns*—O.C.D.

[1070-03]—*Dominican Sisters* (Sinsinawa, WI)—O.P.

[1115]—*Dominican Sisters of Peace*—O.P.

[]—*Franciscan Sisters of Christ the Divine Teacher*—O.S.F.

[]—*Notre Dame Sisters*—N.D.

[2970]—*School Sisters of Notre Dame, Central Pacific*—S.S.N.D.

[]—*School Sisters of St. Francis of Milwaukee*—S.S.S.F.

[]—*Sisters for Christian Community*—S.F.C.C.

[0430]—*Sisters of Charity of Blessed Virgin Mary*—B.V.M.

[]—*Sisters of Mercy West Midwest Community*—R.S.M.

[1540]—*Sisters of Saint Francis, Clinton, Iowa*—O.S.F.

[1570]—*Sisters of St. Francis of the Holy Family*—O.S.F.

[3840]—*Sisters of St. Joseph of Carondelet*—C.S.J.

[3320]—*Sisters of the Presentation of the B.V.M.*—P.B.V.M.

[4120-03]—*Ursuline of Louisville, KY*—O.S.U.

NECROLOGY

† Manning, Martin B., (Retired)—Died May 24, 2011

† Young, Ronald E., (On Duty Outside Diocese)—Died Jan. 11, 2011

An asterisk (*) denotes an organization that has established tax-exempt status directly with the IRS and is not covered by the USCCB Group Ruling.

Archdiocese of Denver

Archidioecesis Denveriensis

Most Reverend

JAMES D. CONLEY, D.D., S.T.L.

Apostolic Administrator and Auxiliary Bishop of Denver; ordained May 18, 1985; appointed Auxiliary Bishop of Denver and Titular Bishop of Cissa April 10, 2008; ordained May 30, 2008; named Apostolic Administrator of Denver September 8, 2011.

(VACANT SEE)

Pastoral Center: 1300 S. Steele St., Denver, CO 80210. Tel: 303-722-4687.

Web: www.archden.org/archden

Email: info@archden.org

ESTABLISHED A VICARIATE-APOSTOLIC IN 1868.

Square Miles 40,154.

Erected a Diocese August 16, 1887; created an Archdiocese November 15, 1941.

Comprises the northern part of the State of Colorado, including the 25 Counties of Adams, Arapahoe, Boulder, Broomfield, Clear Creek, Denver, Eagle, Garfield, Gilpin, Grand, Jackson, Jefferson, Larimer, Logan, Moffat, Morgan, Phillips, Pitkin, Rio Blanco, Routt, Sedgwick, Summit, Washington, Weld and Yuma.

For legal titles of parishes and archdiocesan institutions, consult the Chancery.

STATISTICAL OVERVIEW

Personnel	
Auxiliary Bishops	1
Abbots	1
Priests: Diocesan Active in Diocese	120
Priests: Diocesan Active Outside Diocese	12
Priests: Diocesan in Foreign Missions	1
Priests: Retired, Sick or Absent	57
Number of Diocesan Priests	190
Religious Priests in Diocese	103
Total Priests in Diocese	293
Extern Priests in Diocese	24
Ordinations:	
Diocesan Priests	8
Religious Priests	2
Transitional Deacons	4
Permanent Deacons	8
Permanent Deacons in Diocese	196
Total Brothers	15
Total Sisters	238
Parishes	
Parishes	123
With Resident Pastor:	
Resident Diocesan Priests	101
Resident Religious Priests	17
Missions	20
New Parishes Created	4
Professional Ministry Personnel:	
Brothers	15
Sisters	238
Welfare	
Catholic Hospitals	4
Total Assisted	394,185
Health Care Centers	8
Total Assisted	27,753
Homes for the Aged	7
Total Assisted	1,017
Day Care Centers	9
Total Assisted	704
Specialized Homes	2
Total Assisted	1,158
Special Centers for Social Services	12
Total Assisted	74,815
Residential Care of Disabled	2
Total Assisted	52
Other Institutions	26
Total Assisted	265
Educational	
Seminaries, Diocesan	2
Students from This Diocese	66
Students from Other Diocese	64
Diocesan Students in Other Seminaries	14
Total Seminarians	80
Colleges and Universities	2
Total Students	14,971
High Schools, Diocesan and Parish	2
Total Students	933
High Schools, Private	5
Total Students	2,988
Elementary Schools, Diocesan and Parish	36
Total Students	8,683
Elementary Schools, Private	2
Total Students	543
Non-residential Schools for the Disabled	1
Total Students	85
Catechesis/Religious Education:	
High School Students	7,030
Elementary Students	20,908
Total Students under Catholic Instruction	56,221
Teachers in the Diocese:	
Priests	5
Brothers	3
Sisters	14
Lay Teachers	955
Vital Statistics	
Receptions into the Church:	
Infant Baptism Totals	9,244
Minor Baptism Totals	575
Adult Baptism Totals	471
Received into Full Communion	599
First Communions	8,406
Confirmations	6,180
Marriages:	
Catholic	1,291
Interfaith	248
Total Marriages	1,539
Deaths	2,566
Total Catholic Population	557,049
Total Population	3,352,228

Former Bishops—Most Revs. JOSEPH PROJECTUS MACHEBEUF, D.D., cons. Titular Bishop of Epiphania and Vicar Apostolic of Colorado and Utah, Aug. 16, 1868; first Bishop of Denver in 1887; died July 10, 1889; NICHOLAS CHRYSOSTOM MATZ, D.D., cons. Titular Bishop of Telmessa and Coadjutor of Denver cum jure successionis, Oct. 28, 1887; succeeded to the See of Denver, July 10, 1889; died Aug. 9, 1917; J. HENRY TIHEN, D.D., ord. April 26, 1886; cons. Bishop of Lincoln, July 6, 1911; transferred to the See of Denver, Sept. 21, 1917; resigned Jan. 6, 1931; Apostolic Admin. until July 16, 1931; died Jan. 14, 1940.

Former Archbishops—Most Revs. URBAN J. VEHR, D.D., ord. May 29, 1915; Bishop of Denver; appt. April 17, 1931; cons. June 10, 1931; installed July 16, 1931; elevated to Archiepiscopal dignity, Nov. 15, 1941; appt. Jan. 6, 1942; installed as Archbishop of Denver; resigned Feb. 22, 1967; died Sept. 19, 1973; JAMES V. CASEY, D.D., J.C.D., ord. Dec. 8, 1939; Titular Bishop of Citium and Auxiliary of Lincoln; appt. Auxiliary Bishop April 5, 1957; cons. April 24, 1957; appt. Bishop of Lincoln June 14, 1957; promoted to Archbishop of Denver, Feb. 22, 1967; died March 14, 1986; J. FRANCIS CARDINAL STAFFORD, D.D., ord. Dec. 15, 1957; cons. Auxiliary Bishop of Baltimore, Feb. 29, 1976; installed Bishop of Memphis Jan. 18, 1983; appt. Nov. 16, 1982; installed Archbishop of Denver July 31, 1986; appt. June 3, 1986; appt. President of the Pontifical Council for the Laity in Rome, Aug. 1996; elevated to Cardinal Feb. 21, 1998; CHARLES J. CHAPUT, O.F.M.Cap., D.D., ord. Aug. 29, 1970; Episcopal ordination July 26, 1988; appt. Bishop of Rapid City April 11, 1988; appt. Archbishop of Denver Feb. 18, 1997; appt. Archbishop of Philadelphia July 19, 2011.

The Pastoral Center—1300 S. Steele St., Denver, 80210-2599. Tel: 303-722-4687.

Executive Assistant to the Archbishop—VACANT. Tel: 303-715-3129.

Vicar General—VACANT.

Moderator of the Curia—Rev. Msgr. THOMAS S. FRYAR.

Vicar for Clergy—Rev. Msgr. BERNARD A. SCHMITZ. Tel: 303-715-3197. Email: father.schmitz@archden.org.

Vicar for Hispanic Ministry—Rev. Msgr. JORGE DE LOS SANTOS.

Chancellor—JAMES DANIEL FLYNN, J.C.L.

Archivist—KARYL KLEIN.

Chief Financial Officer—DAVID A. HOLDEN.

Presbyteral Council— (awaiting appointment of a new archbishop)

College of Consultors—VACANT, Archbishop; Most Rev. JAMES D. CONLEY, D.D., S.T.L.; Very Rev. STEPHEN E. ADAMS, V.F.; Rev. Msgrs. EDWARD BUELT, J.C.L.; THOMAS S. FRYAR; MICHAEL G. GLENN, S.T.L.; ROBERT J. KINKEL; BERNARD A. SCHMITZ; Rev. FRANK MARONEY; Rev. Msgr. JORGE DE LOS SANTOS.

Archdiocesan Finance Council—VACANT, Archbishop; Most Rev. JAMES D. CONLEY, D.D., S.T.L.; Rev. Msgr. THOMAS S. FRYAR; MICHAEL L. O'DONNELL; DAVID A. HOLDEN; WILLIAM E. KEEFE, Chm.; REID GODBOLT, Esq.; JAMES S. HARRINGTON; BROOKE B. LEER; STEVE MARKEL; WENDY DOMINGUEZ; JOHN A. IKARD; LOWELL A. HARE; KATHY LUTITO; JEFF SCHMITZ; WILLIAM G. TRAINOR; DAVID RUNBERG.

Deaneries—Very Rev. JAMES E. FOX, V.F., East Denver; Rev. KENNETH KOEHLER, North Denver; Very Rev. JAMES K. GOGGINS, V.F., West Denver; Rev. Msgr. PETER QUANG NGUYEN, V.F., Southeast Denver; Very Revs. MICHAEL PAVLAKOVICH, V.F., Southwest Denver; STEPHEN E. ADAMS, V.F., Aurora; REINHOLD WEISSBECK, V.F., Boulder; GREGORY CIOCH, V.F., Fort Collins; JASON M. THUERAUF, V.F., Eastern Plains; JAMES SPAHN, V.F., Greeley; RANDY DOLLINS, V.F., Western Slope; JEROME M. ROHR, V.F., West Central Denver.

Metropolitan Tribunal

Metropolitan Tribunal—1535 Logan St., Denver, 80203. Tel: 303-894-8994.

Judicial Vicar—Very Rev. JAMES S. MORENO, J.C.D.

Chancellor and Executive Director—JAMES DANIEL FLYNN, J.C.L.

Metropolitan Judges—Very Revs. JAMES S. MORENO, J.C.D.; ROBERT P. HUNDT, J.C.L.; JAMES DANIEL FLYNN, J.C.L.; CARLOS VENEGAS, J.C.L.

Defenders of the Bond—Sr. MARY PIERRE JEAN WILSON, R.S.M., J.C.D.; ROBERT FLUMMERFELT.

Judicial Auditors and Assessors—Deacon ANTHONY PIERSON; CHRISTOPHER SCROGGIN; HEATHER AKERS.

Advocates— Advocates appointed individually for particular cases.

Ecclesiastical Notaries—RONDA WHITEHURST; ANN SANCHEZ; ELIZABETH DELINE.

Coordinator of Second Instance—RONDA WHITEHURST.

The Archdiocese of Denver, a Colorado Corporation Sole

Archdiocesan Offices and Ministries

Unless otherwise indicated, offices and ministries are located in the Pastoral Center on the campus of The John Paul II Center for the New Evangelization, 1300 S. Steele St., Denver, Colorado 80210. Tel: 303-722-4687. Web: www.archden.org.

Office of Archbishop—

Archbishop—VACANT.

Executive Assistant—MARLENE MURILLO. Tel: 303-715-3129. Email: marlene.murillo@archden.org.

Secretary—HATTY ARENIVER, Sec. Tel: 303-715-3185. Email: hatty.areniver@archden.org.

Events Coordinator—TESS STONE. Tel: 303-715-3207. Email: tess.stone@archden.org.

Apostolic Administrator/Auxiliary Bishop—Most Rev. JAMES D. CONLEY, D.D., S.T.L. Tel: 303-715-3100. Email: bishop.conley@archden.org.

Executive Assistant—SHARON DOERFLINGER. Tel: 303-715-3100. Email: sharon.doerflinger@archden.org.

Moderator of the Curia—Rev. Msgr. THOMAS S. FRYAR. Tel: 303-715-3263. Email: msgr.fryar@archden.org.

Administrative Assistant—CARRIE SIGMAN. Tel: 303-715-3263. Email: carrie.sigman@archden.org.

Vicar for Clergy—Rev. Msgr. BERNARD A. SCHMITZ. Tel: 303-715-3197. Email: father.schmitz@archden.org.

Administrative Assistant—MARIE SAILAS. Tel: 303-715-3197. Email: marie.sailas@archden.org.

Vicar for Hispanic Ministry—Rev. Msgr. JORGE DE LOS SANTOS. Tel: 303-715-3169. Email: father.santos@archden.org.

Executive Assistant—MARIA INES RAMIREZ. Tel: 303-715-3247. Email: maria.ramirez@archden.org.

Chancellor—JAMES DANIEL FLYNN, J.C.L. Tel: 303-894-8994. Email: james.flynn@archden.org.

Ecumenical and Interreligious Affairs—PHIL WEB. Tel: 303-715-3160. Email: phil.webb@archden.org.

Imprimaturs—VACANT, Dir.

Masters of Ceremonies—Deacon CHARLES W. PARKER JR. Tel: 303-715-3156. Email: deacon.parker@archden.org.

Pastoral Health Care—Most Rev. JAMES D. CONLEY, D.D., S.T.L. Tel: 303-715-3100. Email: bishop.conley@archden.org; Rev. Msgr. BERNARD A. SCHMITZ. Tel: 303-715-3197. Email: msgr.schmitz@archden.org.

Annual Giving—

Director—TODD J. SMITH. Tel: 303-715-3116. Email: todd.smith@archden.org.

Executive Assistant—JOANN BACA. Tel: 303-715-3111. Email: joann.baca@archden.org.

Archives—

Archivist—KARYL KLEIN. Tel: 303-520-9986. Email: archives@archden.org.

Black Catholics—

Director—MARY LEISRING. Tel: 303-715-3165. Email: mary.leisring@archden.org.

Catholic Schools—

Superintendent—RICHARD L. THOMPSON. Tel: 303-715-3132. Email: richard.thompson@archden.org.

Associate Superintendents—Sr. ELIZABETH YOUNGS, S.C.L. Tel: 303-715-3189. Email: sister.youngs@archden.org; MARY COHEN. Tel: 303-715-3155. Email: mary.cohen@archden.org.

Special Programs Director and Assistant to the Superintendent—BARBARA ANGLADA. Tel: 303-715-3132. Email: barbara.anglada@archden.org.

Cemeteries and Mortuary—

Director—MICHAEL J. WRIGHT (See also Section S, Archdiocesan Cemeteries).Tel: 303-424-7785. Email: michael.wright@archden.org.

Child and Youth Protection—

Director—CHRISTOPHER POND, O.C.D.S. Tel: 303-715-3226. Email: chris.pond@archden.org.

Safe Environment Coordinator and Assistant to Director—CHRISTI SULLIVAN. Tel: 303-715-3241. Email: christi.sullivan@archden.org.

Colorado Catholic Conference—1535 Logan St., Denver, 80203. Tel: 303-894-8808. Web: cocatholicconference.org. Email: ccc@cocatholicconference.org.

Executive Director—JENNIFER KRASKA.

Coordinator—DIANE CHAVEZ.

Communications and Periodicals—

Director—JEANETTE DEMELO. Tel: 303-715-3230. Email: info@archden.org.

Denver Catholic Register—ROXANNE KING, Editor. Tel: 303-715-3215. Email: editor@archden.org.

El Pueblo Catolico—ROSSANA GONI, Editor. Tel: 303-715-3219. Email: elpueblo@archden.org.

Diaconate—

Director of Deacon Personnel—Deacon JOSEPH H. DONOHOE. Tel: 303-715-3198. Email: deacon.donohoe@archden.org.

Diaconate Coordinator—MARY BORDA. Tel: 303-715-3198. Email: mary.borda@archden.org.

Diaconate Formation— (See section A, Seminaries, Religious or Scholasticates: Saint John Vianney Theological Seminary).

Evangelization and Catechesis—

Metro Area Parishes—JAMES CAVANAGH, Dir. Tel: 303-715-3107. Email: james.cavanagh@archden.org.

Coordinator—URSULA JIMENEZ. Tel: 303-715-3260. Email: ursula.jimenez@archden.org.

Northern, Eastern Plains and Western Slope Parishes—DONALD SCHNEIDER, Dir., Mailing Address: P.O. Box 124, Longmont, 80501. Tel: 303-678-0900. Email: archden-northern@msn.com.

Finance, Administration and Planning—

CFO and Executive Director—DAVID A. HOLDEN. Tel: 303-715-3258. Email: david.holden@archden.org.

Executive Assistant—CAROLINE ROSE. Tel: 303-715-3258. Email: caroline.rose@archden.org.

Hispanic Ministry—

Director—LUIS SOTO. Tel: 303-715-3117. Email: luis.soto@archden.org.

Executive Assistant—MARIA RAMIREZ. Tel: 303-715-3247. Email: maria.ramirez@archden.org.

Centro San Juan Diego—2830 Lawrence St., Denver, 80205. Tel: 303-295-9470. Web: www.centrosanjuandiego.org.

Lay Formation— (See section A, Seminaries, Religious or Scholasticates: Saint John Vianney Theological Seminary).

Liturgy—

Director—Deacon CHARLES PARKER JR. Tel: 303-715-3156. Email: deacon.parker@archden.org.

Associate Director—JOHN MILLER. Tel: 303-715-3156. Email: liturgy.office@archden.org.

Marriage and Family Life—

Director—PHIL WEBB. Tel: 303-715-3160. Email: phil.webb@archden.org.

Coordinator—WENDY CURLEY. Tel: 303-715-3259. Email: wendy.curley@archden.org.

Priestly Vocations—

Director—Rev. JAMES H. CRISMAN. Tel: 303-282-3429. Email: vocation@archden.org.

Administrative Assistant—NATALIA SCHUMANN. Tel: 303-282-3429. Email: natalia.schumann@archden.org.

Consecrated Life—

Director—Sr. SHARON FORD, R.S.M. Tel: 303-343-2095.

Seminaries— (See section A, Seminaries, Religious or Scholasticates).

Saint John Vianney Theological Seminary—Rev. Msgr. MICHAEL G. GLENN, S.T.L., Rector.

The Redemptoris Mater House of Formation—Very Rev. FLORIAN MARTIN-CALAMA, S.T.L., Rector.

Social Ministry—

Executive Director—JONATHAN REYES. Tel: 720-377-1398. Email: jonathan.reyes@archden.org.

Gabriel House—MIMI ECKSTEIN, Dir., 1341 S. Oneida St., Denver, 80220. Tel: 303-377-1577. Web: www.gabrielhousedenver.org. Email: mimi.eckstein@archden.org.

Respect Life Office—LYNN GRANDON, Dir. Tel: 303-715-3205. Web: www.archden.org/respectlife. Email: lynn.grandon@archden.org.

Social Ministry Office—AL HOOPER, Dir. Tel: 303-715-3220. Email: al.hooper@archden.org.

Program Associate—BETSY BUETTGENBACH. Tel: 303-715-3171. Email: betsy.buettgenbach@archden.org.

Youth, Young Adult and Campus Ministry—

Director—CHRIS STEFANICK. Tel: 303-715-3203. Email: chris.stefanick@archden.org.

Associate Director—MICHELLE PETERS. Tel: 303-715-3245. Email: michelle.peters@archden.org.

The Archdiocese of Denver Management Corporation—

President—DAVID A. HOLDEN. Tel: 303-715-3258. Email: david.holden@archden.org.

Executive Assistant—CAROLINE ROSE. Tel: 303-715-3258. Email: caroline.rose@archden.org.

Construction and Planning—PHILLIP J. CRISTE, Dir. Tel: 303-715-3251. Email: deacon.criste@archden.org.

Controller—JOYCE TALBURT, CPA, Dir. Tel: 303-715-3181. Email: joyce.talburt@archden.org.

Human Resources—BARBARA BUCHANAN, Dir. Tel: 303-715-3193. Email: barbara.buchanan@archden.org.

Information Systems—MICHAEL MCKEE, Dir. Tel: 303-715-3299. Email: michael.mckee@archden.org.

Insurance and Risk Management—PETER CRONAN, Dir. Tel: 303-715-3150. Email: peter.cronan@archden.org.

Legal Department—REBECCA N. WELBORN, Esq., Dir. Tel: 303-715-3273. Email: rebecca.welborn@archden.org.

Parish Finance—ERNEST W. ARMSTRONG, CPA, Dir. Tel: 303-715-3120. Email: ernie.armstrong@archden.org.

Parish Review and Advisory Services—MAC BRYANT, CPA, Dir. Tel: 303-715-3174. Email: mac.bryant@archden.org.

Real Estate—LINDA BISHOP ESQ., Dir. Tel: 303-715-3194. Email: lou.bishop@archden.org.

CLERGY, PARISHES, MISSIONS AND PAROCHIAL SCHOOLS

CITY OF DENVER

(COUNTY OF DENVER)

1—CATHEDRAL BASILICA OF THE IMMACULATE CONCEPTION (1860) Rev. Msgr. Thomas S. Fryar; Rev. Michael Bodzioch; Deacons Robert E. Finan; Robert Rinne. In Res., Rev. Andreas Hoeck.
Mailing Address & Office: 1530 Logan St., 80203. Tel: 303-831-7010; Fax: 303-831-9514. Email: info@denvercathedral.org. Web: www.denvercathedral.org.

2—ALL SAINTS (1950) Rev. James R. Purfield; Deacon Arthur A. Vigil.
Mailing Address & Office: 2560 S. Grove St., 80219. Tel: 303-922-3758; Fax: 303-922-3750. Email: churchofallsaint@qwestoffice.net.
Church: 2559 S. Federal Blvd., 80219.

3—ANNUNCIATION (1883) Rev. Francisco Ramirez, O.F.M.Cap.; Deacon James W. Blume.
Mailing Address & Office: 1408 E. 36th Ave., 80205. Tel: 303-296-1024; Fax: 303-296-1026. Web: www.lukeone26.org.
Church: 3601 Humboldt St., 80205.
School—(Grades K-8), 3536 Lafayette St., 80205. Tel: 303-295-2515; Fax: 303-295-2516. Deborah Roberts, Prin.

4—ST. ANTHONY OF PADUA (1947) Revs. Mark S. Kovacik, Admin.; Alvaro Panqueva (Colombia), Parochial Vicar.
Mailing Address & Office: 3801 W. Ohio Ave., 80219. Tel: 303-935-2431; Fax: 303-935-8969. Email: anthonyofpadua@comcast.net.

5—ASSUMPTION OF THE BLESSED VIRGIN MARY (1912) Rev. Msgr. Jorge De Los Santos, Admin.; Deacon Harold Del Real.
Mailing Address & Office: 2361 E. 78th Ave., 80229. Tel: 303-288-2442; Fax: 303-289-2713.
School—(Grades K-8), 2341 E. 78th Ave., 80229. Tel: 303-288-2159; Fax: 303-288-4716. Thomas Hamilton, Prin.

6—BLESSED SACRAMENT (1912) Rev. Christopher Hellstrom.
Mailing Address & Office: 1912 Eudora St., 80220. Tel: 303-355-7361; Fax: 303-355-0894. Email: parishoffice@blessedsacrament.net. Web: www.blessedsacrament.net.
Church: 4900 Montview Blvd., 80220.
School—(Grades PreSchool-8), 1973 Elm St., 80220. Tel: 303-377-8835; Fax: 303-321-7765. Email: parishschool@blessedsacrament.net. Greg Kruthaupt, Prin.

7—ST. CAJETAN (1922), (Hispanic), Rev. Tomas Fraile, C.R.; Deacon Henry Concha.
Mailing Address & Office: 299 S. Stuart St., 80219. Tel: 303-922-6306; 303-922-6307; Fax: 303-936-8285.
Church: 299 S. Raleigh St., 80219. Tel: 303-935-4483.

8—ST. CATHERINE OF SIENA (1912) Revs. Gregoire Vidal; Nathanael Pujos (France), Parochial Vicar.
Mailing Address & Office: 4200 Federal Blvd., 80211. Tel: 303-455-9090; Fax: 303-455-6651. Web: saintcatherine.us.
School—(Grades PreSchool-8) Tel: 303-477-8035; Fax: 303-477-0110. Suzanne Scheck, Prin.

9—CHRIST THE KING (1947) In Res., Very Rev. Daniel Leonard; Deacon Jack Sutton.
Mailing Address & Office: 830 Elm St., 80220-4313.

Tel: 303-388-1643; Fax: 303-355-0141. Email: churchoffice@christthekingdenver.com. Web: christthekingdenver.org.
School—(Grades PreSchool-8), 860 Elm St., 80220. Tel: 303-321-2123; Fax: 303-321-2191. Alison Higgins, Prin.

10—CHURCH OF THE ASCENSION (1972) Revs. Gerardo Puga, C.C.R.; Jorge Aguera, D.C.J.M. (Spain), Parochial Vicar.
Mailing Address & Office: 14050 Maxwell Pl., 80239. Tel: 303-373-4950; Fax: 303-373-4954. Web: www.mcpascension.org.

11—CHURCH OF THE RISEN CHRIST (1967) Revs. Lawrence Christensen, C.M., Admin.; Douglas Grandon, Parochial Vicar; Deacon Joe Babish.
Mailing Address & Office: 3060 S. Monaco Pkwy., 80222. Tel: 303-758-8826; Fax: 303-782-9667. Web: risenchristchurch.org.

12—CURE D'ARS (1952) Rev. Simon Kalonga (Congo); Deacon Clarence G. McDavid.
Mailing Address & Office: 4701 Martin Luther King Blvd., 80207-1862. Tel: 303-322-1119; Fax: 303-322-9335. Email: curedarsoffice@yahoo.com. Web: curedarschurch.org.
Church: 3201 Dahlia St., 80207.

13—ST. DOMINIC (1889) Rev. Clinton P. Honkomp, O.P.; Deacons Pablo Salas; Franklin Fricke III. In Res., Revs. Thomas P. Lynch, O.P.; John G. McGreevy, O.P.; Robert Keller, O.P., Novice Master; Robert F. Staes, O.P.; Very Rev. Gerald L. Stookey, O.P., Prior; Bro. Jordan Coonen, O.P.; Rev. Patrick Reardon, O.P.
Mailing Address & Office: 3053 W. 29th Ave., 80211. Tel: 303-455-3613. Web: www.stdominicdenver.org.

14—ST. ELIZABETH OF HUNGARY (1878), (Roman Catholic & Sts. Cyril and Methodius Russian Byzantine Catholic Community) Rev. Chrysostom Frank; Deacon Walter Sweeney.
Mailing Address & Office: 1060 St. Francis Way, 80204. Tel: 303-534-4014; Fax: 303-534-4140. Email: saintelizabeth@qwestoffice.net.

15—ST. FRANCIS DE SALES (1892) Rev. Kenneth J. Liuzzi, Admin. Pro Tem.
Mailing Address & Office: 301 S. Sherman St., 80209. Tel: 303-744-7211; Fax: 303-777-0305. Web: www.sfdsdenver.com.
Church: 300 S. Sherman St., 80209.
School—(Grades PreK-8), 235 S. Sherman St., 80209. Tel: 303-744-7231; Fax: 303-744-1028. Sr. Eleanor O'Hearn, C.S.J., Prin.

16—GOOD SHEPHERD (1981) Very Rev. James E. Fox; Rev. Faustinus Anyamele, Parochial Vicar; Deacon Patrick Whaley.
Mailing Address & Office: 2626 E. Seventh Ave. Pkwy., 80206. Tel: 303-322-7706; Fax: 303-399-1382. Email: goodshep@aol.com. Web: goodshepherdchurchdenver.org.
School—(Grades PreSchool-8), 620 Elizabeth St., 80206. Tel: 303-321-6231; Fax: 303-261-1059. Mary Bartek, Prin.

17—GUARDIAN ANGELS (1954) Rev. Lawrence B. Kaiser; Deacon Henry Sandoval.
Mailing Address & Office: 1843 W. 52nd Ave., 80221. Tel: 303-433-8361; Fax: 303-477-2066.
School—Tel: 303-480-9005. Mary Gold, Prin.

18—HOLY FAMILY (1889) Very Rev. James S. Moreno.
Mailing Address & Office: 4377 Utica St., 80212. Tel: 303-455-1664; Fax: 303-455-7732. Email: holyfamilychurch4377@comcast.net.
Church: 4380 Utica St., 80212.

19—HOLY GHOST (1905) Revs. Christopher W. Uhl, O.M.V.; Michael Warren, O.M.V., Parochial Vicar; Deacon Vernon L. Rompot.
2161 Tremont Pl., 80205.
Mailing Address & Office: 1900 California St., 80202. Tel: 303-292-1556; Fax: 303-292-5378. Email: info@holyghostchurch.info. Web: www.holyghostchurch.info.

20—HOLY ROSARY (1918) Rev. Noe Carreon, Admin. Pro Tem.
Mailing Address & Office: 4688 Pearl St., 80216. Tel: 303-297-1962; Fax: 303-297-1682.

21—ST. IGNATIUS LOYOLA (1923) Rev. Tom Cwik, S.J., Parochial Vicar; Deacon Philip Harrington. In Res., Revs. Joseph Tuoc Nguyen, S.J.; Leo F. Weber, S.J.; Stephen T. Yavorsky, S.J.
Mailing Address & Office: 2309 Gaylord St., 80205. Tel: 303-322-8042; Fax: 303-322-2927. Web: loyoladenver.com.
Church: 2301 York St., 80205.

22—ST. JAMES (1904) Rev. Felix P. Medina-Algaba; Deacon Dennis Morales.
Mailing Address & Office: 1314 Newport St., 80220. Tel: 303-322-7449; Fax: 303-399-2850. Email: parish.office@stjamesdenver.org. Web: www.stjamesdenver.org.
Church: 1311 Oneida St., 80220.
School—(Grades PreK-8), 1250 Newport St., 80220. Tel: 303-333-8275; Fax: 303-780-0137. Carol Hovell-Genth, Prin.

23—ST. JOSEPH (1882) Rev. Mario Ramirez, S.T.B.
Mailing Address & Office: 623 Fox St., 80204. Tel: 303-534-4408; Fax: 303-534-0177. Email: office@stjosephc.com. Web: www.stjosephc.org.
Church: 605 W. 6th Ave., 80204.

24—ST. JOSEPH POLISH (1902) Rev. Marek Ciesla.
Mailing Address & Office: 517 E. 46th Ave., 80216. Tel: 303-296-3217; Fax: 303-296-3217.

25—ST. MARY MAGDALENE (1907) Rev. Henri Tshibambe; Deacons Richard Vieira, Pastoral Admin.; Dominic DeProfio; Wilfred G. Sanchez. In Res., Rev. Luis Ecandon.
Mailing Address & Office: 2771 Zenobia St., 80212. Tel: 303-477-4533; Fax: 303-477-2049.

26—MOST PRECIOUS BLOOD (1952) Rev. Patrick Dolan.
Mailing Address & Office: 2250 S. Harrison, 80210. Tel: 303-756-3083; Fax: 303-756-5628. Email: parish@mpbdenver.org. Web: www.mpbdenver.org.
Church: 2200 S. Harrison St., 80210.
School—(Grades K-8), 3959 E. Iliff, 80210. Tel: 303-757-1279; Fax: 303-757-1270. Colleen McManamon, Prin.

27—MOTHER OF GOD (1949) Rev. Msgr. Bernard A. Schmitz. In Res., Most Rev. James D. Conley.
Mailing Address & Office: 475 Logan St., 80203. Tel: 303-744-1715; Fax: 303-744-1716.

28—NOTRE DAME (1957) Rev. Michael W. Gass; Deacons Charles W. Parker Jr.; Kevin Leiner.
Mailing Address & Office: 5100 W. Evans Ave., 80219. Tel: 303-935-3900; Fax: 303-937-6699. Web: denvernotredame.org.
Church: 2190 S. Sheridan Blvd., 80219.
School—(Grades PreK-8), 2165 S. Zenobia St., 80219. Tel: 303-935-3549; Fax: 303-937-4868. Email: cmolis@notredamedenver.org. Web: www.notredamedenver.org. Charlene Molis, Prin.

29—OUR LADY OF GRACE (1951) Rev. Noe Carreon, Admin.
Mailing Address & Office: 2645 E. 48th Ave., 80216. Tel: 303-297-3440; Fax: 303-296-3486.

30—OUR LADY OF GUADALUPE (1936) Revs. Benito A. Hernandez, C.R.; Miguel Guzman, C.R., Parochial Vicar; Deacons William Martinez; Jesus Ramirez.
Mailing Address & Office: 1209 W. 36th Ave., 80211. Tel: 303-477-1402; Fax: 303-477-4013.

31—OUR LADY OF LOURDES (1947) Rev. Msgr. Peter Quang Nguyen; Deacon John Driesbach; Sr. Marilyn Skluzacek, O.P., Pastoral Assoc. In Res., Rev. Jason Wallace.
Mailing Address & Office: 2200 S. Logan St., 80210. Tel: 303-722-6861; Fax: 303-722-4810. Web: ololdenver.com.
Church: 2298 S. Logan St., 80210.
School—(Grades PreK-8), 2256 S. Logan St., 80210. Tel: 303-722-7525; Fax: 303-765-5305. Rosemary Anderson, Prin.

32—OUR LADY OF MOUNT CARMEL (1894) Rev. Hugh M. Guentner, O.S.M. In Res., Revs. Mark Franceschini, O.S.M.; Gabriel M. Ramacciotti, O.S.M.; Gabriel M. Weber, O.S.M.
Mailing Address & Office: 3549 Navajo St., 80211-3040. Tel: 303-455-0447; Fax: 303-455-5487. Email: omcchurch@qwestoffice.net. Web: www.ourladymountcarmel.com.

33—PRESENTATION OF OUR LADY (1913) Rev. Edward J. Poehlmann; Deacon Eugeno Torrez.
Mailing Address & Office: 665 Irving St., 80204. Tel: 303-534-4882; Fax: 303-893-5056.
Church: 695 Julian St., 80204.
School—(Grades PreK-8), 660 Julian St., 80204. Tel: 303-629-6562; Fax: 303-573-3993. Sandra Howard, Prin.

34—ST. ROSE OF LIMA (1924) Very Rev. Jerome M. Rohr.
Mailing Address & Office: 1320 W. Nevada Pl., 80223. Tel: 303-778-7673; Fax: 303-778-6601. Email: jerryohr@gmail.com.
Church: 355 S. Navajo St., 80223.
School—1345 W. Dakota Ave., 80223. Tel: 303-733-5806; Fax: 303-733-0125. Email: stroseschools@netscape.net. Web: www.strosedenver.org. Tracy Alarcon, Prin.

35—SACRED HEART (1879) Rev. Gene Emrisek, O.F.M.Cap.
Mailing Address & Office: 2760 Larimer St., 80205. Tel: 303-294-9830; Fax: 303-296-0171.

36—ST. VINCENT DE PAUL (1926) Rev. Daniel Zimmerschied; Deacons Sam Lopez; George C. Morin.
Mailing Address & Office: 2375 E. Arizona Ave., 80210. Tel: 303-744-6119; Fax: 303-744-6124. Email: parish@saint-vincents.org. Web: www.svdponline.net.
School—1164 S. Josephine St., 80210. Tel: 303-777-3812; Fax: 303-773-9528. Sr. Maria Ivana Begovic, O.P., Prin.

OUTSIDE THE CITY OF DENVER

AKRON, WASHINGTON CO., ST. JOSEPH (1917) [CEM] Rev. Timothy Hjelstrom.
Mailing Address & Office: 551 W. 6th St., 80720. Tel: 970-345-6996; Fax: 970-345-6504.

ARVADA, JEFFERSON CO.

1—ST. JOAN OF ARC (1967) Rev. Joseph T. Cao; Deacons Joseph Gerber; Rex Pilger; Matt Archer.
Mailing Address & Office: 12735 W. 58th Ave., 80002. Tel: 303-420-1232; Fax: 303-420-0126. Email: office@saintjoancatholic.org. Web: www.saintjoancatholic.org.

2—SHRINE OF ST. ANNE (1920) [CEM] Rev. Piotr Mozdyniewicz; Deacons Rodger Creel; Terry Schmader; Ken Hawkins, (Retired).
Office: 7555 Grant Pl., 80002. Tel: 303-420-1280; Fax: 303-420-1341. Web: www.shrineofstanne.org.
School—(Grades K-8), 7320 Grant Pl., 80002. Tel: 303-422-1800; Fax: 303-422-1011. Email: info@stannescatholic.org. Web: www.stannescatholic.com. Kathie Kuehl, Prin.

3—SPIRIT OF CHRIST (1974) Revs. David Bluejacket; Shaji (Jacob) Thomas, V.C., Parochial Vicar; Deacons Richard Baker; Ross Casados; Mel Corley; Charles Hahn; Steven Hinkle; Don St. Louis; Earl Webster.
Mailing Address & Office: 7400 W. 80th Ave., 80003. Tel: 303-422-9173; Fax: 303-422-8251. Email: staff@spiritofchrist.org. Web: www.spiritofchrist.org.

ASPEN, PITKIN CO., ST. MARY (1882) Rev. John L. Hilton.
Mailing Address & Office: 533 E. Main St., 81611. Tel: 970-925-7339; Fax: 970-925-1889. Email: stmary@sopris.net. Web: www.stmaryaspen.4lpi.com.

AULT, WELD CO., ST. MARY (1953) Mailing Address: P.O. Box 1373, 80610. Tel: 970-834-1609; Fax: 970-686-9169. Administered by Our Lady of the Valley, Windsor.
Church: 267 E. 4th St., 80610.

AURORA, ARAPAHOE CO.

1—ST. LAWRENCE KOREAN CATHOLIC CHURCH (1981) Rev. Eun Keun Shin.
Mailing Address & Office: 4310 S. Pitkin St., 80015-1974. Tel: 303-617-7400; Fax: 303-617-8265.

2—ST. MICHAEL THE ARCHANGEL (1978) Rev. Terrence Kissell; Deacons Willie Liwanag; Anthony Pierson; Craig Fucci.
Mailing Address & Office: 19099 E. Floyd Ave., 80013. Tel: 303-690-6797; Fax: 303-690-6932. Email: stmtac@aol.com. Web: www.st.michael-aurora.com.

3—ST. PIUS X (1954) Very Rev. Stephen E. Adams; Rev. Armando Marsal, D.C.J.M. (Spain), Parochial Vicar.
Mailing Address & Office: 13670 E. 13th Pl., 80011. Tel: 303-364-7435; Fax: 303-340-0122. Web: stpiusxparish.org.
School—(Grades PreK-8), 13680 E. 14th Pl., 80011. Tel: 303-364-6515; Fax: 303-364-1822. Web: stpiusxschool.net. Mr. Mark Strawbridge, Prin.

4—QUEEN OF PEACE (1968) Revs. Martin Lally; Mauricio Bermudez-Hernandez; Deacons John Thunblom; Bill Senger; Ruben Duran.
Mailing Address & Office: 13120 E. Kentucky Ave., 80012. Tel: 303-364-1056; Fax: 303-364-3944. Email: info@queenofpeace.net. Web: www.queenofpeace.net.

5—ST. THERESE (1926) Revs. Elbert Chilson; Miguel Enriquez; Deacons Geraldo Martinez; Edgar Vale. In Res., Rev. Thomas McCormick (Retired).
Mailing Address & Office: 1243 Kingston St., 80010. Tel: 303-344-0132; Fax: 303-344-0133. Web: sttheresechurch.org.
School—(Grades PreK-8), 1200 Kenton St., 80010. Tel: 303-364-7494; Fax: 303-364-1340. Laura Dement, Prin.

BASALT, EAGLE CO., ST. VINCENT (1970) Rev. José Saenz.
Mailing Address & Office: 397 White Hill Rd., Carbondale, 81623. Tel: 970-704-0820; Fax: 970-704-0830.
Church: 250 Midland Ave., 81621. Email: annmariew@stmv.org.

BOULDER, BOULDER CO.

1—ST. MARTIN DE PORRES (1968) Rev. Hermanagild Jayachandra; Deacon Karl T. Matz.
Mailing Address & Office: 3300 Table Mesa Dr., 80305. Tel: 303-499-7744; Fax: 303-494-8754. Email: parishoffice@stmartindeporreschurch.org. Web: www.stmartindeporreschurch.org.

2—SACRED HEART OF JESUS (1875) [JC] Rev. William E. Breslin; Deacon David Luksch.
Mailing Address & Office: 2312 14th St., 80304. Tel: 303-442-6158; Fax: 303-442-7905. Web: www.shjboulder.org.
Church: 1318 Mapleton Ave., 80304.
School—(Grades PreK-8) Tel: 303-447-2362; Fax: 303-443-2466. Web: www.shjboulder.org/school. Mary Bartsch, Prin.
Chapel—Chapel of Ease Nederland, Boulder Co. 80466.

3—SACRED HEART OF MARY (1873) [CEM] Rev. Marcus Mallick.
Mailing Address & Office: 6739 S. Boulder Rd., 80303. Tel: 303-494-7572; Fax: 303-494-7371. Web: sacredheartofmary.org.

4—ST. THOMAS AQUINAS UNIVERSITY PARISH (1950), (Campus Ministry), University of Colorado. Revs. Peter Mussett; John Nepil, Parochial Vicar.
Mailing Address & Office: 904 14th St., 80302. Tel: 303-443-8383; Fax: 303-443-8399.
Church: 898 14th St., 80302.

BRECKENRIDGE, SUMMIT CO., ST. MARY (1875) Very Rev. Randy Dollins; Rev. Dennis K. Ryan (Retired); Deacons Charles Lamar, Admin.; James Doyle.
Mailing Address: P.O. Box 2670, Frisco, 80443.
Office & Church: 109 S. French St., 80424. Tel: 970-668-3141; Fax: 970-668-3213. Web: www.summitcatholic.org.
Mission—Our Lady of Peace Dillon, Summit Co. 80435.

BRIGHTON, ADAMS CO., ST. AUGUSTINE (1887) Rev. Humberto Marquez; Deacons Bill Jordan; Modesto Garcia.
Mailing Address & Office: 675 E. Egbert St., 80601. Tel: 303-659-1410; Fax: 303-659-6449. Web: www.staugustinebrighton.com.

BROOMFIELD, BOULDER CO., NATIVITY OF OUR LORD (1958) Revs. Michael Carvill, F.S.C.B.; Gabriele Azzalin, F.S.C.B.; Deacons Richard Medenwaldt; Leonard "Buz" Onesky; Diego Garcia. In Res., Rev. Accursio Ciaccio, F.S.C.B.
Mailing Address & Office: 900 W. Midway Blvd., 80020. Tel: 303-469-5171; Fax: 303-469-5172. Web: nool.us.
School—(Grades K-8) Tel: 303-466-4177. Kathy Shadel, Prin.

BRUSH, MORGAN CO., ST. MARY (1911) Rev. Frank A. Lomica.
Mailing Address & Office: 340 Stanford St., 80723. Tel: 970-842-2216; Fax: 970-842-4461.
Mission—St. John Stoneham, Weld Co. 80754.

BYERS, ARAPAHOE CO., OUR LADY OF THE PLAINS (1972) Rev. Jeffrey Wilborn.
Mailing Address & Office: 186 N. McDonnell St., 80103. Tel: 303-822-5880; Fax: 303-822-5780. Email: ourladyoftheplains@gmail.com. Web: www.ourladyoftheplains.org.

CARBONDALE, GARFIELD, CO., ST. MARY 1980 Rev. Daniel J. Norick, Admin.
Mailing & Office: 397 White Hill Rd., 81623. Tel: 970-704-0820; Fax: 970-704-0830.

CENTENNIAL, ARAPAHOE CO., ST. THOMAS MORE (1971) Revs. Andrew Kemberling; Marlon Rodrigues, O.C.D.; John Green, Parochial Vicar; Israel Gonsalves, O.C.D.; Deacons Gary Rogge; John Neal; Alan Rastrelli; Steven Stemper; Timothy Kenny; Robert Cropp; Robert Gregorius; Dick Rapp, Business Mgr.; Mila Glodava, Dir. Communication & Stewardship.
Mailing Address & Office: 8035 S. Quebec St., 80112. Tel: 303-770-1155; Fax: 303-770-1160. Email: parishoffice@stthomasmore.org. Web: www.stthomasmore.org.
School—(Grades K-8), 7071 E. Otero Ave., 80112. Tel: 303-770-0441; Fax: 303-267-1899. Web: www.stmk8.com. Jan Altevogt, Prin.

CENTRAL CITY, GILPIN CO., ST. MARY OF THE ASSUMPTION (1865), Administered by St. Paul, Idaho Springs., Mailing Address: P.O. Box 848, Idaho Springs, 80452.

COMMERCE CITY, ADAMS CO., OUR LADY MOTHER OF THE CHURCH (1954) Rev. Tomasz Wikarski.
Mailing Address & Office: 6690 E. 72nd Ave., 80022. Tel: 303-289-6489; Fax: 303-289-6480. Email: olmcparish@gmail.com.

CONIFER, JEFFERSON CO., OUR LADY OF THE PINES (1979) Rev. James Baird; Deacon Gerald F. Kotas.
Mailing Address & Office: 9444 Eagle Cliff Rd., 80433. Tel: 303-838-0338; Fax: 303-838-1663. Email: olpines@hotmail.com.
Mission—St. Elizabeth Buffalo Creek, Jefferson Co. 80425.

CRAIG, MOFFAT CO., SAINT MICHAEL (1920) Revs. James R. Fox; Michael Rapp, Parochial Vicar.
Mailing Address & Office: 678 School St., 81625. Tel: 970-824-5330; Fax: 970-824-7870. Email: smhfsi@qwestoffice.net.

CROOK, LOGAN CO., ST. PETER (1924), Administered by St. Anthony of Padua, Julesburg., Mailing Address: 606 W. 3rd St., Julesburg, 80737.
Church: 612 E. 3rd Ave., 80726.

EDWARDS, EAGLE CO., ST. CLARE OF ASSISI (1993) Rev. Msgr. Robert J. Kinkel; Rev. Jesus Garcia.
Mailing Address: P.O. Box 1390, 81632.
Church: 31622 U.S. Hwy. 6, 81632. Tel: 970-569-3093; Fax: 970-926-1089. Email: stclare@vail.net. Web: www.stclareparish.com.
School—(Grades K-8), P.O. Box 667, 81632. Tel: 970-926-8980. Sr. Mary Rita Rae Schneider, Prin.
Mission—St. Mary Eagle, Eagle Co. 81631.

ENGLEWOOD, ARAPAHOE CO.

1—ALL SOULS (1954) Rev. Robert D. Fisher; Deacons Kevin R. Brath; Martin A. Wager; Alex P. Rohr, Business Mgr.; Brian Mulheran, Music Min.
Mailing Address & Office: 4950 S. Logan St., 80113-6847. Tel: 303-789-0007; Fax: 720-833-2777. Email: recept@allsouls55.org. Web: allsoulscatholicchurch.org.
School—(Grades PreK-8), 4951 S. Pennsylvania, 80113. Tel: 303-789-2155; Fax: 303-833-2778. Web: allsoulsschool.com. William T. Moore, Prin.

2—HOLY NAME (1894) Rev. Daniel Cardo, S.C.V.; Deacon Donald Schaefer.
Mailing Address & Office: 3290 W. Milan Ave., 80110. Tel: 303-781-6093; Fax: 303-781-6398. Email: office@holynamedenver.org.

3—ST. LOUIS KING OF FRANCE (1911) Rev. Robert J. Reycraft.
Mailing Address & Office: 3310 S. Sherman St., 80113. Tel: 303-761-3940; Fax: 303-806-5394. Email: stlouischurch@frii.com.
School—(Grades K-8), 3301 S. Sherman St., 80113. Tel: 303-762-8307; Fax: 303-762-0156. Web: www.stlouiscatholicschool.org. Pattie Hagen, Prin.

ERIE, WELD CO., ST. SCHOLASTICA (1899) Attended by St. Theresa, Frederick., Mailing Address: P.O. Box 418, Frederick, 80530.
Church: 615 Main St., 80516.

ESTES PARK, LARIMER CO., OUR LADY OF THE MOUNTAINS (1915) Rev. Joseph A. Hartmann.
Mailing Address: P.O. Box 1706, 80517. Tel: 970-586-8111; Fax: 970-586-8112. Web: www.olmestes.org.
Church: 920 Big Thompson Ave., 80517.

EVERGREEN, JEFFERSON CO., CHRIST THE KING (1932) Revs. Christopher A. Renner; Dennis Garrou, Parochial Vicar; Deacons Brian Kerby; Ronald Roderick; Timothy Kelly.
Mailing Address & Office: 4291 Evergreen Pkwy., 80439-7723. Tel: 303-674-3155; Fax: 303-674-3285.

FORT COLLINS, LARIMER CO.

1—BLESSED JOHN XXIII (1967) Revs. Rocco S. Porter; Tadeusz Kopczynski, Parochial Vicar.
Mailing Address & Office: 1220 University Ave., 80521.

2—ST. ELIZABETH ANN SETON (1981) Very Rev. Gregory Cioch; Rev. Joseph Toledo, Parochial Vicar; Deacons William Trewartha; Donald Weiss.
Mailing Address & Office: 5450 S. Lemay Ave., 80525. Tel: 970-226-1303. Email: seas@seas-parish.org. Web: www.seas-parish.org.

3—HOLY FAMILY (1924) Rev. Antonio Flores, C.R.
Mailing Address & Office: 326 N. Whitcomb St., 80521. Tel: 970-482-6599; Fax: 970-482-8045. Email: holyfamilychurc1@qwestoffice.net.
Church: 328 N. Whitcomb St., 80521.

4—ST. JOSEPH (1879) Revs. Steven Voss; Grzegorz Wojcik, Parochial Vicar; Deacon Warren G. Lybarger.
Mailing Address & Office: 101 N. Howes St., 80521.
Church: 300 W. Mountain Ave., 80521. Email: sjchurch@stjosephchurchfc.org. Web: www.stjosephchurchfc.org.
School—(Grades PreK-8), 127 N. Howes St., 80521. Tel: 970-484-1171; Fax: 970-221-0635. Barbara Bullock, Prin.

FORT LUPTON, WELD CO., ST. WILLIAM (1909) Rev. Gregorio L. Mirto; Deacon Louis Arambula.
Mailing Address & Office: 1025 Fulton Ave., 80621. Tel: 303-857-6642; Fax: 303-857-6643.
Mission—Our Lady of Grace Wattenburg, Weld Co. 80621.

FORT MORGAN, MORGAN CO., ST. HELENA (1910) Very Rev. Jason M. Thuerauf; Rev. Martin E. Hernandoz Baeza, Parochial Vicar; Deacons Mario Martha-Pro; Richard Wilson.
Mailing Address & Office: 917 W. 7th Ave., 80701. Tel: 970-867-2885.
Mission—St. Francis of Assisi Warren St., Weldona, Morgan Co. 80653.

FOXFIELD, ARAPAHOE CO., OUR LADY OF LORETO (1998) Rev. Msgr. Edward Buelt; Rev. Gregg Pedersen, Parochial Vicar; Deacons Michael Magee; Richard Miller.
Mailing Address & Office: 18000 E. Arapahoe Rd., 80016. Tel: 303-766-3800; Fax: 303-766-3700. Email: mail@ourladyofloreto.org. Web: ourladyofloreto.org.

FREDERICK, WELD CO., ST. THERESA (1923) Rev. Hernan Florez.
Mailing Address: P.O. Box 418, 80530. Tel: 303-833-2966; Fax: 303-833-3000. Email: sttheresafred@earthlink.net. Web: www.sttheresafred.org.
Church: 502 Walnut, 80530.

GLENWOOD SPRINGS, GARFIELD CO., ST. STEPHEN (1885) Revs. Cliff J. McMillan; William Smith, Parochial Vicar; Deacons Victor Kimminau; Charles Sprick, (Retired).
515 W. 12th St., 81601.
Mailing Address & Office: 1885 Blake Ave., 81601. Tel: 970-945-6673; Fax: 970-945-6677.
School—414 S. Hyland Park Dr., 81601. Tel: 970-945-7746; Fax: 970-945-1208. Dr. Tom Alby, Prin.

GOLDEN, JEFFERSON CO., ST. JOSEPH (1859) Rev. Joseph E. Monahan; Deacons Dennis J. Langdon; Edward Clements.
Mailing Address & Office: 969 Ulysses St., 80401. Tel: 303-279-4464; Fax: 303-273-9811. Email: terrih@stjoegold.org. Web: www.stjoegold.org.

GRAND LAKE, GRAND CO., ST. ANNE (1944) Rev. Michael Freihofer; Deacon James R. Moat.
Mailing Address: P.O. Box 2029, Granby, 80446.
Church: 219 Hancock St., 80447. Tel: 970-887-0032; Fax: 970-887-9662. Email: admin@grandcatholic.com. Web: www.grandcatholic.com.
Mission—Our Lady of the Snow Granby, Grand Co. 80446.
Mission—St. Bernard of Montjoux Winter Park, Grand Co. 80482.

GREELEY, WELD CO.

1—ST. MARY (1965) Rev. Pawel Zborowski; Susan Benke, Business Mgr.; Deacons Joseph H. Meilinger, Liturgy Dir.; Andrew Sanchez; Frederick L. Torrez.
Mailing Address & Office: 2222 23rd Ave., 80634. Tel: 970-352-1724; Fax: 970-352-1729.
School—2351 22nd Ave., 80631. Tel: 970-353-8100; Fax: 970-353-8102. Mary Reese, Prin.

2—OUR LADY OF PEACE (1948) Rev. Stephen A. Siebert.
Mailing Address & Office: 1311 3rd St., 80631. Tel: 970-353-1747; Fax: 970-353-4830. Email: ourladyofpeacegreeley@msn.com.

3—ST. PETER (1903) Rev. Matthew Hartley.
Mailing Address & Office: 915 12th St., 80631. Tel: 970-352-1060; Fax: 970-352-1062. Web: www.stpetergreeley.org.

HOLYOKE, PHILLIPS CO., ST. PATRICK (1893) Rev. William Jungmann.
Mailing Address & Office: 519 S. Interocean, 80734. Tel: 970-854-2762; 970-854-2866.
Church: 541 S. Interocean Ave., 80734.
Mission—Christ the King Haxtun, Phillips Co. 80731. Tel: 970-774-7640.
Mission—St. Peter the Apostle [CEM] Fleming, Logan Co. 80728. Tel: 970-265-2792.

IDAHO SPRINGS, CLEAR CREEK CO., ST. PAUL (1881) Rev. Michael F. Kerrigan.
Mailing Address: P.O. Box 848, 80452.
Church: 1632 Colorado Blvd., 80452. Tel: 303-567-4662; Fax: 303-567-4662.
Mission—Our Lady of Lourdes [CEM] Georgetown, Clear Creek Co. 80452.

ILIFF, LOGAN CO., ST. CATHERINE OF SIENA (1927), Administered by St. Anthony, Sterling., Mailing Address: 326 S. 3rd St., Sterling, 80751.
Church: 111 S. Fifth St., 80736. Tel: 970-522-6422; Fax: 970-522-6442.

JOHNSTOWN, WELD CO., ST. JOHN THE BAPTIST (1937) Rev. Emilio Franchomme; Mary Raker, Business Mgr.
Mailing Address & Office: 809 Charlotte St., 80534. Tel: 970-587-2879; Fax: 970-587-2881. Email: johnstownsjb@earthlink.net. Web: www.saintjohnsjohnstown.org.

JULESBURG, SEDGWICK CO., ST. ANTHONY (1907) Rev. Joseph Tran.
Mailing Address & Office: 606 W. 3rd St., 80737. Tel: 970-474-2655; Fax: 970-474-2655.

KREMMLING, GRAND CO., ST. PETER (1944), Administered by St. Mary, Breckenridge., Mailing Address: P.O. Box 428, 80459.
Church: 106 S. 5th St., 80459. Tel: 970-724-3428.
Mission—St. Ignatius Walden, Jackson Co. 80459.

LAFAYETTE, BOULDER CO., IMMACULATE CONCEPTION (1907) Rev. Msgr. Robert L. Amundsen; Rev. Thomas P. Lynch, O.P., Parochial Vicar.
Mailing Address & Office: 715 Cabrini Dr., 80026-2676. Tel: 303-665-5103; Fax: 303-604-9077. Email: parishoffice@lafayettecatholic.org. Web: www.lafayettecatholic.org.

LAKEWOOD, JEFFERSON CO.

1—ST. BERNADETTE (1947) Very Rev. James K. Goggins; Deacon Phil Criste.
Mailing Address & Office: 7240 W. 12th Ave., 80214. Tel: 303-233-1523; Fax: 303-233-7285.
Church: W. 12th Ave. & Teller St., 80214.
School—(Grades PreK-8), 1100 Upham St., 80214. Tel: 303-237-0401; Fax: 303-237-0608. Mr. James Feldewerth II, Prin.

2—CHRIST ON THE MOUNTAIN PARISH (1975) Rev. John Grabrian; Deacon Mickey Webre.
Mailing Address & Office: 13922 W. Utah Ave., 80228-4110. Tel: 303-988-2222; Fax: 303-986-6956. Email: office@christonthemountain.org. Web: www.christonthemountain.org.

3—ST. JUDE (1967) Rev. J. Darrell Schaffer; Deacons Michael L. Bunch; Jay Garland; Alan C. Spears.
Mailing Address & Office: 9405 W. Florida Ave., 80232-5111. Tel: 303-988-6435; Fax: 303-988-6438. Web: www.saintjudelakewood.org.

4—OUR LADY OF FATIMA (1958) Rev. Henri Tshibambe; Deacons Joseph W. Hawley; Rich Boyd. In Res., Rev. James H. Crisman.
Mailing Address & Office: 1985 Miller St., 80215. Tel: 303-233-6236; Fax: 303-237-6097.
School—(Grades PreK-8), 10530 W. 20th Ave.,

80215. Tel: 303-233-2500. Miss Lisa Taylor, Prin.
LITTLETON, ARAPAHOE CO.
1—ST. MARY (1901) [JC] Revs. Alvaro Montero, D.C.J.M. (Spain); Javier Nieva, D.C.J.M. (Spain), Parochial Vicar; Deacons Timothy M. Kilbarger; Anthony Dudzic; Greg Frank; William Ward; Jack Sutton. In Res., Rev. Armando Marsal, D.C.J.M. (Spain).
Mailing Address & Office: 6853 S. Prince, 80120. Tel: 303-798-8506; Fax: 303-347-2270. Web: www.stmarylittleton.org.
School—(Grades PreK-8), 6833 S. Prince St., 80120. Tel: 303-798-2375; Fax: 720-283-4756. Greg Caudle, Prin.
2—OUR LADY OF MOUNT CARMEL (1997) [CEM] Revs. James Jackson, F.S.S.P.; Joseph Hearty, F.S.S.P., Parochial Vicar.
Mailing Address & Office: 5620 S. Hickory Cir., 80120. Tel: 303-703-8538; Fax: 303-795-5411.
Church: 5612 S. Hickory St., 80120.
LITTLETON, JEFFERSON CO.
1—ST. FRANCES CABRINI (1972) Revs. Sean J. McGrath; Braden Wagner, Parochial Vicar. In Res., Deacons Chet Ubowski; Russ Barrows.
Mailing Address & Office: 6673 W. Chatfield Ave., 80128. Tel: 303-979-7688; Fax: 303-972-8566.
2—LIGHT OF THE WORLD PARISH (1979) Very Rev. Michael Pavlakovich; Deacons Eugene Mooneyham; Joseph H. Donohoe; Rick Montagne.
Mailing Address & Office: 10316 W. Bowles Ave., 80127. Tel: 303-973-3969; Fax: 303-973-2122. Web: www.lotw.org.
LONGMONT, BOULDER CO.
1—ST. FRANCIS OF ASSISI (1982) [JC] Rev. Frank Maroney.
Mailing Address & Office: 2410 B Trade Centre Ave., 80503. Tel: 303-772-6322; Fax: 303-772-9415. Email: parish@saintfrancislongmont.org. Web: www.saintfrancislongmont.org.
2—ST. JOHN THE BAPTIST (1882) [JC] Revs. Reinhold Weissbeck; Geronimo Gonzalez, Parochial Vicar; Deacons Bob Howard; Mike Berens.
Mailing Address & Office: 323 Collyer St., 80501. Tel: 303-776-0737; Fax: 303-772-5636. Web: www.johnthebaptist.org.
School—(Grades PreK-8), 350 Emery St., 80501. Tel: 303-776-8760. Mrs. Julie Rossi, Prin.
LOUISVILLE, BOULDER CO., ST. LOUIS (1884) Rev. G. Timothy Gaines; Deacons Steven J. Vallero; Ronald Darschewski. In Res., Rev. Daniel J. Flaherty (Retired).
Mailing Address & Office: 902 Grant Ave., 80027. Tel: 303-666-6401; Fax: 303-666-0826. Email: stlouis.office@stlouisoflsv.org. Web: www.stlouisoflsv.org.
School—(Grades K-8), 925 Grant Ave., 80027. Tel: 303-666-6220; Fax: 303-666-5244. Web: www.stlouisschool-co.com. Karen Herlihy, Prin.
LOVELAND, LARIMER CO., ST. JOHN THE EVANGELIST (1902) Revs. Francisco J. Garcia; Jose Maria Quera, Parochial Vicar; Deacon Edward Armijo.
Mailing Address & Office: 1515 Hilltop Dr., 80537. Tel: 970-635-5800; Fax: 970-669-5743. Web: www.saintjohns.net.
Church: 1730 W. 12th St., 80537.
School—(Grades K-8) Tel: 970-635-5830; Fax: 970-667-9298. Lois Schmitt, Prin.
MEAD, WELD CO.
1—GUARDIANS ANGELS (1911), (Administered by Immaculate Heart of Mary, Northglenn), Mailing Address: P.O. Box 444, 80542. Tel: 970-535-0721; Fax: 970-535-0721.
Church: 15179 County Rd., 80542.
MEEKER, RIO BLANCO CO., HOLY FAMILY (1905) Rev. James R. Fox.
Mailing Address: P.O. Box 866, 81641.
Church: 889 Park Ave., 81641. Tel: 970-878-3300; Fax: 970-878-3300. Email: smhfsi@qwestoffice.net.
MINTURN, EAGLE CO., ST. PATRICK (1913) Rev. Roger L. Lascelle.
Mailing Address: P.O. Box, 81645-0219. Tel: 970-477-0378; Fax: 970-476-3347. Email: st_patricks@comcast.net. Web: www.stpatricksminturn.com.
Church: 476 Pine St., 81645. Tel: 970-827-9559.
Mission—Our Lady of Mt. Carmel Red Cliff, Eagle Co. 81649.
NORTHGLENN, ADAMS CO., IMMACULATE HEART OF MARY (1967) Very Rev. Gregory Ames; Rev. Brian Larkin, Parochial Vicar; Deacons Taylor Elder; Jerome Durnford.
Mailing Address & Office: 11385 Grant Dr., 80233. Tel: 303-452-2041; Fax: 303-452-7546. Email: admin@ihmco.org. Web: ihmco.org.
PEETZ, LOGAN CO., SACRED HEART (1914) [CEM], Administered by St. Anthony, Sterling., Mailing Address & Office: 326 S. 3rd St., Sterling, 80751.
Church: 621 Logan, 80747. Tel: 970-522-6422; Fax: 970-522-6442.
PLATTEVILLE, WELD CO., ST. NICHOLAS (1889), Administered by St. John the Baptist, Johnston. Mary Raker, Business Mgr.
Mailing Address: P.O. Box 576, 80651.
Church: 514 Marion Ave., 80651. Tel: 970-785-2143; Fax: 970-785-2143. Email: stnickschurch@qwestoffice.net.
RANGELY, RIO BLANCO CO., ST. IGNATIUS OF ANTIOCH (1931), Administered by St. Michael, Craig., Mailing Address: 678 School St., Craig, 81625.
Church: 109 S. Stanolind Ave., 81648. Tel: 970-675-8935; Fax: 970-675-8935. Email: smhfsi@qwestoffice.net.
RIFLE, GARFIELD CO., ST. MARY (1910) Rev. Robert E. Hehn.
Mailing Address: P.O. Box 191, 81650. In Res., Rev. Jude Geilenkirchen (Retired).
Church: 761 Birch Ave., 81650. Tel: 970-625-2547; Fax: 970-625-9025.
Mission—Sacred Heart Silt, Garfield Co. 81652.
Mission—St. Brendan Parachute, Garfield Co. 81650.
ROGGEN, WELD CO., SACRED HEART (1924) Rev. Hector Chiapa-Villarreal.
Mailing Address & Office: 38044 Weld County Rd. 16, 80652. Tel: 303-849-5313; Fax: 303-849-5674.
Mission—Holy Family Keenesburg, Weld Co. 80643.
Mission—Our Lady of Lourdes Wiggins, Morgan Co. 80654.
STEAMBOAT SPRINGS, ROUTT CO., HOLY NAME (1907) Rev. Ernest Bayer; Deacon John Franklin. In Res., Rev. Msgr. Thomas Dentici (Retired).
Mailing Address & Office: P.O. Box 774198, 80477-4198. Tel: 970-879-0671; Fax: 970-879-7406. Email: holyname@catholicsteamboat.org. Web: catholicsteamboat.org.
504 Oak St., 80477-4198.
Mission—St. Martin of Tours Oak Creek, Routt Co. 80467.
STERLING, LOGAN CO., ST. ANTHONY (1888) Rev. Robert L. Wedow.
Mailing Address & Office: 326 S. 3rd St., 80751. Tel: 970-522-6422; Fax: 970-522-6442.
School—(Grades PreK-8), 324 S. 3rd St., 80751. Tel: 970-522-7567. Joseph Skerjanec, Prin.
THORNTON, ADAMS CO., HOLY CROSS (1957) Rev. Thomas Coyte; Deacons Russell Halpine; Joe Benedetto; Nehemias Ruiz.
Mailing Address & Office: 9371 Wigham St., 80229. Tel: 303-289-2258 (Voice VP); Fax: 303-289-2259. Email: holy.cross@comcast.net. Web: www.holycrossthornton.com.
WESTMINSTER, ADAMS CO.
1—HOLY TRINITY (1956) Revs. John Paul Leyba; Richard Nakvasil, Parochial Vicar; Deacon Lloyd Quintana.
Mailing Address & Office: 7595 N. Federal Blvd., 80030. Tel: 303-428-3594; Fax: 303-427-4125. Web: www.htcatholic.org.
School—3050 W. 76th Ave., 80030. Tel: 303-427-5632. Sharon Rubin, Interim Prin.
Mission—Our Lady of Visitation
2—ST. MARK (1973) Rev. Kenneth Koehler; Deacons Gordon D. Hudec; Sydney Atencio.
Mailing Address & Office: 3141 W. 96th Ave., 80031. Tel: 303-466-8720; Fax: 303-466-0998.
WHEAT RIDGE, JEFFERSON CO.
1—STS. PETER AND PAUL (1949) Revs. Reuben Payo; Walter Watson, S.J., Parochial Vicar; Deacon John Pontillo.
Mailing Address & Office: 3900 Pierce St., 80033. Tel: 303-424-3706; Fax: 303-424-0819. Email: dianam@peterandpaulcatholic.org. Web: peterandpaulcatholic.org.
School—3920 Pierce St., 80033. Tel: 303-420-0402; Fax: 303-456-1888. Email: pglassmeyer@sppscatholic.com. Kathy Byrnes, Prin.
Convent—Carmel of the Holy Name of Jesus Convent, 4040 Pierce St., 80033. Tel: 303-422-6419.
2—QUEEN OF VIETNAMESE MARTYRS (1976) Revs. Joseph M. Vu Kim Ngan, C.M.C.; Gregory Tran, C.M.C.; Deacons Joseph Le Van Tam; Peter Hung Phi Dang; Lawrence Tong Ngo.
Mailing Address & Office: 4655 Harlan St., 80033. Tel: 303-431-0382; Fax: 303-431-1876. Email: queenvietnam@gmail.com. Web: www.giaoxudenver.org.
WINDSOR, WELD CO., OUR LADY OF THE VALLEY (1969) Very Rev. James Spahn; Deacons Harold Kimble; John Riviera.
Mailing Address & Office: 1250 7th St., 80550. Tel: 970-686-5084; Fax: 970-686-9169. Email: ella@ourladyofthevalley.net. Web: www.ourladyofthevalley.net.
WRAY, YUMA CO., ST. ANDREW THE APOSTLE (1888) Rev. Jonathan Dellinger.
Mailing Address & Office: 412 Dexter St., 80758. Tel: 970-332-5858; Fax: 970-332-4604. Email: standrewapostle@centurytel.net.
YUMA, YUMA CO., ST. JOHN THE EVANGELIST (1888) Rev. Jonathan Dellinger.
Mailing Address & Office: 508 S. Ash St., 80759. Tel: 970-848-5973; Fax: 970-848-2817.

On Duty Outside the Archdiocese:
Rev. Msgr.—
McDaid, J. Anthony, Congregation for the Clergy, 00120, Vatican City State.
Revs.—
Book, Matthew, Pontificia Accademia Ecclestiastica, Piazza della Minerva, Rome 74-00186 Italy.
Denig, Philip P., Chap. (Capt.), 9 B Ardsley Ave., Whiting, NJ 08759.
Murphy, John J., St. Gabriel the Archangel, 203 E. Arnold Ave., Port Allegany, PA 16743.
Romero, Donald, PSC2 Box 8352, Apo, AE 09012.
Simko, James, Sts. Peter & Paul the Apostles, 2850 75th St. W., Bradenton, FL 34209.

Graduate Studies:
Very Rev.—
Augustyn, Kevin, V.F.
Revs.—
Capucci, Giovanni
Morrow, Brian
Perez, Angel
Phung, Vincent

Retired:
Rev. Msgrs.—
Croak, David P., 13952 E. Marina Dr., #603, Aurora, 80014.
Dentici, Thomas, St. Mary of the Crown, 397 White Hill Rd., Carbondale, 81623.
Horrigan, Leo R., 795 S. Alton Way, #4-C, 80247.
Jones, Raymond N., V.G., P.A., 700 S. Yarrow St., Lakewood, 80226.
Jones, William H., Mullen Home, 3629 W. 29th Ave., 80211.
Madden, Edward T., 565 Mohawk Dr., #B1, Boulder, 80303.
Rasby, James W., 460 S. Marion Pkwy., #1206-C, 80209.
Schroeder, George, St. Patrick Parish, 10815 N. 84th St., Scottsdale, AZ 85260.
Revs.—
Banigan, Herbert, 606 Sundance Dr., Loveland, 80538.
Blach, Leo M., Gardens St. Elizabeth, 2835 W. 32nd Ave., #12, 80211.
Blanco, Joseph, 6340 W. 38th Ave., #405, Wheat Ridge, 80033.
Bradtke, Thomas, 142 Country Rd. 156, Glenwood Springs, 81601.
Brock, William, P.O. Box 948, Cheyenne, WY 82003.
Canjar, John A., 6780 E. Cedar Ave., Apt. 706A, Denver 80224.
Cuneo, James J., 6991 Nile Ct., Arvada, 80007.
Deml, Francis S., 625 S. Alton Way, #7C, 80231.
Flaherty, Daniel J., 902 Grant St., Louisville, 80027.
Gabel, Emanuel, 8983 W. Jewell, Apt. #304, Lakewood, 80232.
Geilenkirchen, Jude, P.O. Box 191, Rifle, 81650.
Gibbons, John M., Mullen Home, 3629 W. 29th Ave., 80211.
Kane, James E., 2397 S. Xanadu Way, Bldg. 9, #402, Aurora, 80014.
Kennedy, Patrick J., 9360 E. Center Ave., #3D, 80247.
Kleiner, James, P.O. Box 300545, 80203-0545.
McCormick, Thomas, V.F., c/o St. Therese, 1243 Kingston St., Aurora, 80010.
Medrano, Marcus, 2576 104th Cir., Westminster, 80234.
Meznar, Joseph A., P.O. Box 211067, 80221.
Mucha, Jan, Mullen Home, 3629 W. 29th Ave., 80211.
Ossino, Angelo, 13800 E. Marina Dr., #312, Aurora, 80014.
Ryan, Dennis K., P.O. Box 131, Frisco, 80443.
Smith, Vincent Leo, P.O. Box 82, Fairplay, 80440.
Stahl, David A., 460-C Autumn Ridge Cir., Colorado Springs, 80906.
Thompson, Melvin F., 8035 S. Quebec St., Centennial, 80112.
Urban, Peter, 110 W. Simpson St., Lafayette, 80026.
Walsh, Michael, 1893 E. Lake Dr., Centennial, 80121.
Willette, Donald, P.O. Box 16, Masonville, 80541.
Woerth, Thomas, 700 Washington St., #40, 80203.

Permanent Deacons:
Allison, Glenn, Our Lady of Fatima, Lakewood
Anderson, Ernest J., (Retired)
Ansay, Ronald J., (Retired)
Arambula, Louis, St. Williams, Fort Lupton
Archer, Matthew, St. Joan of Arc, Aruada
Armijo, Edward, St. John the Evangelist, Loveland
Atencio, Sidney, St. Mark, Westminster
Babish, Joseph, Risen Christ, Denver
Baez, David, Queen of Peace, Aurora

Baker, Richard L., (Retired)
Ball, James, (Away)
Barrows, Russell D., St. Frances Cabrini, Littleton
Beabout, Norman, (Retired)
Benedetto, Joseph, Holy Cross, Thornton
Benjamin, Joseph G., St. Joseph, Akron
Benzel, Leonard, (Retired)
Berens, Michael, St. John the Baptist, Longmont
Blume, James W., Office of Diaconate
Borda, Richard S., Buckley Air Force Base Chapel
Boyd, Richard M., Our Lady of Fatima, Lakewood
Brath, Kelvin All Souls, Englewood
Brown, George, Blessed Sacrament, Denver
Bunch, Michael L., St. Jude, Lakewood
Casados, Ross, Spirit of Christ, Arvada
Clements, Edward R., St. Joseph, Golden
Coleman, Colins, St. Catherine of Siena, Denver
Concha, Henry, St. Cajetan, Denver
Corley, Melvin G., Spirit of Christ, Arvada
Coursey, Nathan D., (Retired)
Creel, Rodger L., Shrine of St. Anne, Arvada
Criste, Philip, St. Bernadette, Lakewood
Cropp, Robert, St. Thomas More, Centennial
Dang, Peter Hung Phi, Queen of Vietnamese Martyrs, Wheat Ridge
Darschewski, Ronald, St. Louis, Louisville
Del Real, Harold, Assumption Parish, Denver
DelVillar, Oscar, Immaculate Conception, Lafayette
DeProfio, Dominic, St. Mary Magdalene, Denver
DiPentino, John L., Our Lady of Mount Carmel, Denver
Donohoe, Joseph H., Office of Diaconate, Dir. of Deacon Personnel
Dorwart, Jason, (Retired)
Downey, Hugh, Missionary in Africa
Doyle, James, Our Lady of Peace, Dillon
Dreiling, L. Kenneth, (Retired)
Driesbach, John, (Retired)
Dudzic, Anthony, St. Mary, Littleton
Duran, Ruben, Queen of Peace, Aurora
Durnford, Jerome, Immaculate Heart of Mary, Northglenn
Elder, R. Taylor, Immaculate Heart of Mary, Northglenn
Enderle, Frank, Office of Diaconate
Engel, Witold, (Retired)
Ertmer, William, Holy Family Parish, Meeker
Estrada, Ruben, Sacred Heart, Denver
Finan, Robert E., Cathedral Basilica of the Immaculate Conception, Denver
Fitterer, George, (Retired)
Fletcher, Michael, Christ on the Mountain, Lakewood
Fortunato, George R., St. Ignatius of Antioch, Rangely
Fox, Thomas, (Away)
Frank, Gregory L., St. Mary, Littleton
Franklin, John, (Retired)
Fricke, Franklin, III, St. Dominic, Denver
Frisinger, Howard, (Retired)
Fucci, Craig, St. Michael the Archangel, Aurora
Gallagher, Michael, St. Patrick, Minturn
Garcia, Modesto, St. Augustine, Brighton
Garland, Jay, St. Jude, Lakewood
Gerber, Joseph, St. Joan of Arc, Arvada
Gollhofer, James D., Nativity of Our Lord Parish, Broomfield
Gregorius, Robert, St. Thomas More, Centennial
Grimler, Richard, (Retired)
Grimm, R. Paul, St. Frances Cabrini, Littleton
Hahn, Charles, Spirit of Christ, Arvada
Haigh, Robert, (Retired)
Halpine, Russell, Holy Cross, Thornton
Harrington, Philip, St. Ignatius of Loyola, Denver
Hastings, William O., St. Peter, Greeley
Hawkins, Kenneth I., Jr., (Retired)
Hawley, Joseph W., (Retired)
Hegarty, Marvin A., (Retired)
Hetzel, Martin, St. Thomas Aquinas, Boulder
Hinkle, Steven, Spirit of Christ, Arvada
Howard, Michael J., (Retired)
Howard, Robert J., St. John the Baptist, Longmont
Hudec, Gordon D., St. Mark, Westminster
Jordan, Bill, St. Augustine, Brighton
Kelly, Timothy M., St. Thomas More, Centennial
Kerby, Brian J., Christ the King, Evergreen
Kilbarger, Timothy M., St. Mary, Littleton
Kimble, Harold, Our Lady of the Valley, Windsor
Kimminau, Victor H., (Retired)
Kotas, Gerald F., Our Lady of the Pines, Conifer
Kraft, Jerome, St. Joseph, Ft. Collins
Lamar, Charles, St. Joseph, Golden
Langdon, Dennis J., St. Mary, Breckenridge
Le, Joseph Tam Van, (Retired)
Leiner, Kevin, Notre Dame, Denver
Liwanag, Wilfredo B., St. Michael the Archangel, Aurora
Lopez, Samuel, St. Vincent de Paul, Denver
Loushin, Albert J., St. Vincent, Basalt
Luksch, David, Sacred Heart of Jesus, Boulder
Lybarger, Warren G., (Retired)
Magee, Michael, Our Lady of Loreto, Foxfield
Martha-Pro, Mario, St. Helena, Ft. Morgan
Marthe, Daniel M., (Retired)
Martin, Gregory "Dusty", St. Pius X, Aurora
Martin, Richard, (Away)
Martinez, Gerardo, St. Therese, Aurora
Martinez, William, Our Lady of Guadalupe, Denver
Matz, Karl T., (Retired)
McClellan, William, St. John XXIII, Ft. Collins
McDavid, Clarence G., Cure D'Ars, Denver
McKeown, John, (Retired)
Medenwaldt, Richard A., Nativity of Our Lord, Broomfield
Meilinger, Joseph H., St. Mary, Greeley
Menogan, Guffie E., (Retired)
Michieli, Ronald, St. Anthony, Sterling
Miller, Gary E., St. Mary Magdalene, Denver
Miller, Richard, Our Lady of Loreto, Foxfield
Moat, James, St. Anne, Grand Lake
Montagne, Eric, Light of the World, Littleton
Mooneyham, E. Gene, (Retired)
Morales, Dennis, St. James Parish, Denver
Morin, George C., St. Vincent de Paul, Denver
Neal, John R., St. Thomas More, Centennial
Ngo, Lawrence Tong, Queen of Vietnamese Marytrs, Wheat Ridge
Nusse, John, (Away)
Oehrle, Leo A., (Retired)
Onesky, Leonard "Buz", Nativity of Our Lord, Broomfield
Padilla, Carlos L., (Retired)
Parker, Charles W., Jr., Notre Dame Parish, Denver
Patino, Hugo, (Away)
Paulson, Joel, (Sabbatical)
Pelis, Richard F., (Retired)
Perez, Cesar, Our Lady of Peace, Greeley
Peverley, David, St. Peter, Greeley
Pierson, Anthony, St. Michael the Archangel, Aurora
Pilger, Rex H., Jr., St. Joan of Arc, Arvada
Pomrening, Christopher, St. Michael the Archangel, Aurora
Pontillo, John E., Sts. Peter & Paul, Wheat Ridge
Quinlan, Thomas, (Retired)
Quintana, Lloyd, (Retired)
Ramirez, Manuel de Jesus, Our Lady of Guadalupe, Denver
Rastrelli, Alan, M.D., St. Thomas More, Centennial
Reinert, George J., (Retired)
Rinne, Robert, Cathedral Basilica of Immaculate Conception, Denver
Ritz, Michael P., (Retired)
Riveria, John J., Lady of the Valley, Windsor
Roderick, Ronald, II, Christ the King, Evergreen
Rogge, Gary, St. Thomas More, Centennial
Rompot, Vernon L., K.H.S., Holy Ghost, Denver
Rouco, Anthony F., (Retired)
Ruiz, Nehemias, Holy Cross, Thornton
Salas, Pablo, St. Dominic, Denver
Salvato, Mark, Office of Diaconate
Sanchez, Alfredo, (Retired)
Sanchez, Andrew, St. Mary, Greeley
Sanchez, Maclovio, (Retired)
Sanchez, Wilfred G., (Retired)
Sandoval, Alfonso M., St. Pius X, Aurora
Sandoval, Antonio A., Our Lady Mother of the Church, Commerce City
Sandoval, Henry, Guardian Angels, Denver
Schaefer, Donald, Holy Name, Englewood
Schmader, Terry, Shrine of St. Anne, Arvada
Senger, William, Jr., Queen of Peace, Aurora
Smith, John L., Office of Diaconate
Sorber, William M., (Retired)
Spears, Alan C., St. Jude, Lakewood
Spellman, William, (Retired)
Sprick, Charles B., (Retired)
St. Louis, Donald, Spirit of Christ, Arvada
Stemper, Steven, St. Thomas More, Centennial
Stow, William J., Kateri Catholic Comm., Lakewood
Sutton, Jack, Christ the King, Denver
Sweeney, Walter, St. Elizabeth of Hungary, Denver
Thunblom, John, Queen of Peace, Aurora
Torrez, Eugeno, Presentation of Our Lady, Denver
Torrez, Frederick L., St. Mary, Greeley
Trewartha, William, St. Elizabeth Ann Seton, Fort Collins
Trujillo, Samuel R., (Retired)
Ubowski, Chester W., St. Frances Cabrini, Littleton
Usera, Joseph, Office of Diaconate
Valle, Edgar, St. Therese, Aurora
Vallero, Steven J., St. Louis, Louisville
Vieria, Richard, St. Mary Magdalene, Denver
Vigil, Arthur A., (Retired)
Volk, John, St. John the Baptist, Johnstown; St. Nicholas of Antioch, Platteville
Wager, Martin A., All Souls, Englewood
Wall, James R., SS. Peter and Paul, Wheat Ridge
Ward, William, (Retired)
Webre, Milton G., Christ on the Mountain, Lakewood
Webster, Earl, Spirit of Christ, Arvada
Wehrman, John J., St. Peter, Greeley
Weiss, Donald, St. Elizabeth Ann Seton, Fort Collins
Whaley, Patrick, Church of the Good Shepherd, Denver
Wilhelm, Martin A., (Retired)
Wilson, Richard, Immaculate Conception, Lafayette
Wolfe, James, Immaculate Conception, Lafayette
Zajac, Paul M., St. Anthony of Padua, Denver

INSTITUTIONS LOCATED IN THE ARCHDIOCESE

[A] SEMINARIES, RELIGIOUS OR SCHOLASTICATES

DENVER. *Saint John Vianney Theological Seminary*, 1300 S. Steele St., 80210. Tel: 303-282-3427; Fax: 303-282-3453. Rev. Msgr. Michael G. Glenn, S.T.L., Rector; Rev. Jorge Rodriguez, Vice Rector.

Redemptoris Mater House of Formation, 3434 E. Arizona Ave., 80210. Tel: 303-733-2220; Fax: 303-733-2223. Email: redemptoris.mater@archden.org. Very Rev. Florian Martin-Calama, S.T.L., Rector for Redemptoris Mater Archdiocesan Missionary Seminary; Revs. Federico Colautti, S.T.D., Vice Rector; Jose Maria Fuenmayor, Spiritual Dir.

[B] COLLEGES AND UNIVERSITIES

DENVER. **Augustine Institute, Inc.*, 3001 S. Federal Blvd., Box 1126, 80236. Tel: 303-937-4420; Fax: 303-468-2933. Email: info@augustineinstitute.org. Web: www.augustineinstitute.org. Dr. Tim Gray, Pres. Faculty 7; Adjunct 3; Students 265.

Regis University (1877) 3333 Regis Blvd., 80221-1099. Tel: 303-458-4100; Fax: 303-458-4921. Web: www.regis.edu. Mr. Richard C. Kelly, Chm. Bd. of Trustees; Revs. Michael J. Sheeran, S.J., Pres.; David M. Clarke, S.J., Chancellor; Ms. Diane McSheehy, Dean of Students; Dr. Patricia A. Ladewig, Vice Pres. Academic Affairs; Ms. Karen Webber, Vice Pres. Admin.; Dr. Thomas E. Reynolds, Vice Pres. Mission; Ms. Julie Crockett, Vice Pres. Univ. Rels.; Dr. Paul Ewald, Dean Regis College; Dr. William J. Husson, Vice Pres. Professional Studies & Strategic Alliances; Dr. Janet Houser, Academic Dean, Rueckert-Hartman College for Health Professions; Dr. Ivan Gaetz, Dean Libraries; Mr. Peter Rogers, Dir. University Min.; Dr. Roxanne Gonzales, Academic Dean, College of Professional Studies; Dr. Soon Beng Yeap, Chief Mktg. Officer; Mr. Charles Dahlman, CFO; Ms. Sandra Mitchell, Asst. Provost for Diversity. A university conducted under the auspices of the Society of Jesus. Jesuits 2; (full time) 249; (part time) 1,973; Students 14,706.

[C] INTER-PAROCHIAL HIGH SCHOOLS

DENVER. *Bishop Machebeuf High School*, 458 Uinta Way, 80230-6934. Tel: 303-344-0082; Fax: 303-344-1582. Web: www.machebeuf.org. Jessie Skipwith, Prin.; Stephanie Chaney, Librarian. Brothers 2; Sisters 2; Lay Teachers 29; Students 365.

BROOMFIELD. *Holy Family High School*, 5195 W. 144th Ave., 80023. Tel: 303-410-1411; Fax: 303-466-1935. Email: tim.gallic@holyfamilyhs.com. Web: www.holyfamilyhs.com. Mr. Timothy Gallic, Prin.; Stephanie Brown, Librarian. Sisters 3; Lay Teachers 46; Students 575.

[D] HIGH SCHOOLS, PRIVATE

DENVER. *Arrupe Jesuit High School* (2003) 4343 Utica St., 80212. Tel: 303-455-7449; Fax: 303-455-7453. Web: www.arrupejesuit.com. Rev. Timothy M. McMahon, S.J., Pres.; Michael O'Hagan, Prin. Priests 4; Religious 2; Lay Teachers 18; Volunteers 4; Administrators 28; Students 330.

J K Mullen High School (1931) 3601 S. Lowell Blvd., 80236. Tel: 303-761-1764; Fax: 303-761-0502. Web: www.mullenhigh.com. James Gmelich, Prin.; Bro. Charles Miller, F.S.C., Librarian.

The Christian Brothers of J.K. Mullen High School Brothers of the Christian Schools, Coed High School Brothers 3; Sisters 1; Lay Teachers 55; Students 825.

AURORA. *Regis Jesuit High School Corporation* (1877) Co-Institutional, *Boys Div.*, 6400 S. Lewiston Way, 80016. Tel: 303-269-8000 (Boys Div.); Fax: 303-766-2240 (Boys Div.). Web: www.regisjesuit.com. *Girls Div. & Central Admin.*, 6300 S. Lewiston Way, 80016. Tel: 303-269-8100 (Girls Div.); Fax: 303-221-4772 (Girls Div.). Revs.

Philip G. Steele, S.J., Pres. Boys & Girls Div.; David A. Wayne, S.J., Facilities Mgr. Emeritus; Robert L. Sullivan, S.J., Faculty Chap.; Jeffrey D. Harrison, S.J., Supr. of Community & Girls Div. Chap. & Teacher; Kevin B. Dyer, S.J., Boys Div. Chap. & Teacher; Jeffrey M. Howard, Prin., Boys Div.; Ms. Gretchen Kessler, Prin. Girls Div.; Bruce Raymond, Librarian Boys Div.; Carol Ann Sass, Librarian Girls Div. Day School for Boys.; Day School for Girls. Priests 4; Seminarians 1; Lay Staff 195; Students - Boys Division 908; Students - Girls Division 698.

ENGLEWOOD. *St. Mary's Academy High School* (1864) 4545 S. University Blvd., 80113. Tel: 303-762-8300; Fax: 303-783-6201. Web: www.smanet.org. Deirdre V. Cryor, Pres.; Kathryn McNamee, Prin.; Kristen Ferguson, Librarian. Sisters of Loretto at the Foot of the Cross. Lay Teachers 24; Students 248.

[E] ELEMENTARY SCHOOLS, PRIVATE

DENVER. *Escuela De Guadalupe Elementary School*, (Grades K-5), 3401 Pecos St., 80211. Tel: 303-964-8456; Fax: 303-964-0755. Email: david_card@escuelaguadalupe.org. Web: www.escuelaguadalupe.org. Ms. Mariella Robledo, Prin.; David A. Card, Pres. Lay Teachers 14; Students 119.

ENGLEWOOD. *St. Mary's Academy Lower School* (1864) (Grades K-5), 4545 S. University Blvd., 80113. Tel: 303-762-8300; Fax: 303-783-6201. Web: www.smanet.org. Deirdre V. Cryor, Pres.; Mary Jane Frederick, Prin.; Margaret Gross, Librarian. Sisters of Loretto at the Foot of the Cross. Lay Teachers 21; Students 220.

St. Mary's Academy Middle School (1864) (Grades 6-8), 4545 S. University Blvd., 80113. Tel: 303-762-8300; Fax: 303-783-6201. Web: www.smanet.org. Martha Ashley, Prin.; Deirdre V. Cryor, Pres.; Alexandra Bronston, Librarian. Lay Teachers 19; Students 209.

[F] THERAPEUTIC CHILD CARE FACILITIES/SPECIAL EDUCATION

DENVER. *Mount St. Vincent Home, Inc.* (1883) (Grades PreSchool-8), (Special Education), 4159 Lowell Blvd., 80211. Tel: 303-458-7220; Fax: 303-477-7559. Web: www.msvhome.org. Sr. Amy Willcott, S.C.L., Exec. Dir.; Kay McDowell, Dir. Donor Devel. Therapeutic Residential Child Care Facility. Mount Saint Vincent Sisters 3; Mental Health Workers 66; Crisis Team 9; Residential Staff 45; Residents 44.

LITTLETON. **Havern Center, Inc. dba Havern School* (1966) (Grades K-8), 4000 S. Wadsworth Blvd., 80123. Tel: 303-986-4587; Fax: 303-986-0590. Email: cathyp@havernschool.org. Web: www.haverncenter.org. Cathleen M. Pasquariello, Head of School & Exec. Dir.; Sally Dalton, Librarian. Sisters 2; Faculty & Staff 32; Students 85.

[G] MINISTRY TO THE HANDICAPPED

DENVER. *The Bridge Community, Inc.*, 3101 W. Hillside Pl., 80219. Tel: 303-935-4740; Fax: 303-935-7795. Email: rishabridge@comcast.net. Risha Dimas, Contact Person & Dir. Sisters 1; Priests 1; Lay Staff 6; Bed Group Home 8.

Special Religious Education-Pastoral Care of Developmentally Disabled Persons (1976) (An office of the Archdiocese of Denver), 3101 W. Hillside Pl., 80219. Tel: 303-934-1999; Fax: 303-935-7795. Rev. Roland P. Freeman, Dir. Special Educ. & Chap.; Sr. Mary Catherine Widger, S.L., Assoc. Dir. Spec. Educ. Religious education of mentally retarded children and adults. Priests 1; Total Assisted Annually 400.

[H] GENERAL HOSPITALS

DENVER. *Saint Joseph Hospital*, 1835 Franklin St., 80218. Tel: 303-837-7111; Fax: 303-837-7123. Bain Farris, CEO; Revs. John J. Waters, S.J., Chap.; Gabriel Okafor, Chap.; Deacon Dominic DeProfio, Chap. Bed Capacity 565; Inpatients Assisted Annually 19,800; Outpatients Assisted Annually 217,000.

FRISCO. *St. Anthony Summit Medical Center* (1968)Mailing Address: 188 Inverness Dr., W., Ste. 500, Englewood, 80112. 340 Peak One Dr., P.O. Box 738, 80443. Tel: 303-804-8103; Fax: 303-804-8198. Email: krisordelheide@centura.org. Kris Ordelheide, Contact Person. An operating unit of Catholic Health Initiatives Colorado (an affiliate of Catholic Health Initiatives). Bed Capacity 35; Total Assisted Annually 18,481; Total Staff 263.

LAKEWOOD. *St. Anthony Hospital*, Mailing Address: 188 Inverness Dr., W., Ste. 500, Englewood, 80112. 11650 W. 2nd Ave., 80228. Tel: 720-321-0000; Fax: 720-321-0011. Email: krisordelheide@centura.org. Jeff Brickman, CEO; Kris Ordelheide, Contact & Gen. Counsel. An operating unit of Catholic Health Initiatives Colorado (an affiliate of Catholic Health Initiatives). Bed Capacity 222; Total Assisted Annually 73,800; Total Staff 1,142.

WESTMINSTER. *St. Anthony North Hospital*, Mailing Address: 188 Inverness Dr., W., Ste. 500, Englewood, 80112. 2551 W. 84th Ave., 80030. Tel: 303-804-8103; Fax: 303-804-8198. Email: krisordleheide@centura.org. Kris Ordelheide, Contact Person. An operating unit of Catholic Health Initiatives Colorado (an affiliate of Catholic Health Initiatives). Bed Capacity 196; Total Assisted Annually 64,744; Total Staff 780.

[I] HOSPICE AND HOMEBOUND SERVICE

DENVER. *St. Anthony Hospice* (1968) Mailing Address: 188 Inverness Dr., W., Ste. 500, Englewood, 80112. 1391 Speer Blvd., Ste. 600, 80204. Tel: 303-804-8103; Fax: 303-804-8198. Email: krisordelheide@centura.org. Kris Ordelheide, Gen. Counsel & Contact. An operating unit of Catholic Health Initiatives Colorado (an Affiliate of Catholic Health Initiatives). Total Assisted Annually 276; Total Staff 16.

Dominican Sisters Home Health Agency of Denver, Inc., 2501 Gaylord St., 80205. Tel: 303-322-1413; Fax: 303-322-2702. Krisandra Panting, R.N., B.S.N., M.B.A., Exec. Dir. Serves more than 1500 poor, sick and elderly patients annually with over 20,000 in-home nursing visits, durable medical equipment loans and wellness clinics throughout metro Denver. Total Assisted Annually 1,500.

**Health S.E.T.* (1988)Mailing Address: 188 Inverness Dr., W., Ste. 500, Englewood, 80112. Raleigh Bldg., 4200 W. Conejos, #436, 80204-1312. Tel: 303-595-6633; Fax: 303-595-6645. Web: www.healthset.org. An Operating Unit of Catholic Health Initiatives Colorado (an affiliate of Catholic Health Initiatives); Services for Home-Bound Seniors. Total Staff 6; Total Volunteers 164; Total Assisted 800.

The Villas at Sunny Acres (1968) Mailing Address: 188 Inverness Dr., W., Ste. 500, Englewood, 80112. 2501 E. 104th Ave., Thornton, 80233. Tel: 303-452-4181; Fax: 303-457-9885. Web: www.centura.org. An operating unit of Catholic Health Initiatives Colorado (an affiliate of Catholic Health Initiatives).; Independent, Assisted & Nursing Home. Total Apartments 295; Bed Capacity 160; Assisted Living 35; Independent Living 295; Total Assisted 490.

[J] INDEPENDENT AND ASSISTED LIVING

DENVER. *Dayspring Villa, Inc.* (1993) 3777 W. 26th Ave., 80211. Tel: 303-455-5066; Fax: 303-455-8966. Susan M. Dillberg, Chairperson. Total Assisted 70; Total Staff 34.

Gardens at St. Elizabeth (1968) Mailing Address: 188 Inverness Dr., W., Ste. 500, Englewood, 80112. 2835 W. 32nd Ave., 80211. Tel: 303-804-8103; Fax: 303-804-8198. Email: krisordelheide@centura.org. Web: www.centura.org. Beth Breen, Admin.; Sr. Jacqueline Leech, Chap.; Kris Ordelheide, Contact Person. Sisters of St. Francis of Colorado Springs (O.S.F.).Catholic Health Care Federation, (Men and Women); An operating unit of Catholic Health Initiatives Colorado (an affiliate of Catholic Health Initiatives). Sisters 4; Independent Living 144; Assisted Living 145; Total Staff 92.

Little Sisters of the Poor (1918) 3629 W. 29th Ave., 80211. Tel: 303-433-7221; Fax: 303-455-9184. Email: msdenver@littlesistersofthepoor.org. Sr. Mary Thomas D'Mello, L.S.P., Mother Supr.; Rev. Timothy M. Kremen, O.S.M. Total Staff 94; Bed Capacity 48; Total Assisted 48.

AURORA. *St. Anna's Home (Congregation of Sisters of Charity of St. Vincent de Paul, Colorado Chapter Inc.)*, 13901 E. Quincy Ave., 80015. Tel: 303-627-2986; Fax: 303-627-2986. Email: st.annashome@hotmail.com. Sisters Elizabeth Kim, Dir.; Lydia Lee, Dir.; Vincent Chung, Contact Person. Tel: 303-324-7783. Total Assisted Annually 6; Total Staff 3.

WESTMINSTER. *Clare of Assisi Homes - Westminster, Inc* (1995) 2451 W. 82 Pl., 80031-4099. Tel: 303-412-5771; 303-462-9271 (Corporate). Housing and services for elderly and disabled. Total Apartments 62; Total Staff 5.

Villa Maria, Inc. (1996) 2461 W. 82nd Pl., 80031-4099. Tel: 303-427-4406; Fax: 303-412-5771. Housing and services for elderly and disabled. Total Assisted 40; Total Staff 5.

[K] SPECIAL TRANSITIONAL HOUSING

DENVER. *Decatur Place*, Mailing Address: 1999 Broadway, #1000, 80202. 1155 Decatur St., 80204. Tel: 303-830-3300; Fax: 303-830-3301. Web: www.mercyhousing.org. Brian Shuman, Pres.; Patricia O'Roark, Contact. Two year single parent transitional housing program. Total Assisted Annually 500.

Sacred Heart House of Denver (1980) 2844 Lawrence St., 80205. Tel: 303-296-6686; Fax: 303-296-2903. Web: sacredhearthouse.org. Ms. Janet L. Morris, Exec. Dir. Housing and services for homeless mothers and children and for single women. Homeless Women and Children served annually 1,150; Staff 8.

[L] AFFORDABLE HOUSING AND SERVICES FOR SENIORS, FAMILIES, AND THE DISABLED

DENVER. *Archdiocesan Housing, Inc.* (1968) 4045 Pecos St., Ste. A, 80211. Tel: 303-830-0215; Fax: 303-830-2885. Email: jrussell@archdiocesanhousing.org. Web: www.archdiocesanhousing.com. Total Assisted Annually 2,500.

Archdiocesan Family Housing, Inc. (1968) 4045 Pecos St., Ste. A, 80211. Tel: 303-830-0215; Fax: 303-830-2885. Housing for Low-Income Families.

Cathedral Plaza Inc. (1980) 4045 Pecos St., Ste. A, 80211. Tel: 303-830-0215; Fax: 303-830-2885. Web: www.archdiocesanhousing.org.

Holy Family Plaza, Inc. (1981) 4045 Pecos St., Ste. A, 80211. Tel: 303-830-0215; Fax: 303-830-2885. Web: www.archdiocesanhousing.org.

Marian Plaza, Inc. (1983) 4045 Pecos St., Ste. A, 80211. Tel: 303-830-0215; Fax: 303-830-2885. Web: www.archdiocesanhousing.org.

Higgins Plaza, Inc. (1990) 4045 Pecos St., Ste. A, 80211. Tel: 303-830-0215; Fax: 303-830-2885. Web: www.archdiocesanhousing.org.

Madonna Plaza, Inc. (1989) 4045 Pecos St., Ste. A, 80211. Tel: 303-830-0215; Fax: 303-830-2885. Web: www.archdiocesanhousing.org.

St. Martin Plaza, Inc. (1988) 4045 Pecos St., Ste. A, 80211. Tel: 303-830-0215; Fax: 303-830-2885. Web: www.archdiocesanhousing.org.

Colorado Affordable Catholic Housing Corp. (1991) 4045 Pecos St., Ste. A, 80211. Tel: 303-830-0215; Fax: 303-830-2885. Web: www.archdiocesanhousing.org.

Housing Management Services, Inc. (1986) 4045 Pecos St., Ste. A, 80211. Tel: 303-830-0215; Fax: 303-830-2885. Web: www.archdiocesanhousing.org.

Clare Gardens, Inc. (1972) 2626 Osceola St., 80212. Tel: 303-433-6268; Fax: 303-455-5359. Web: www.fm-inc.org. Franciscan Sisters, Daughters of the Sacred Hearts of Jesus and Mary (Wheaton, IL)., Housing Ministry, low-income family units. Housing Units 128; Residents 488; Total Staff 14.

Francis Heights, Inc. (1970) 2626 Osceola St., 80212. Tel: 303-433-6268; Fax: 303-455-5359. Web: www.fm-inc.org. Franciscan Sisters, Daughters of the Sacred Hearts of Jesus and Mary, (Wheaton, IL)., Housing Ministry and Senior Citizens. Housing Units 383; Total Staff 30; Residents 414.

Holy Cross Village, Inc., 4045 Pecos St., Ste. A, 80211. Tel: 303-715-3194. Web: www.archdiocesanhousing.org. Josh Russell, Exec. Dir., Archdiocesan Housing.

Homes for Greeley (1996) 1999 Broadway, Ste. 1000, 80202. Tel: 303-830-3300; Fax: 303-830-3301. Patricia O'Roark, Contact. Affordable housing for singles and families. Units 16; Residents 45; Total Staff 2; Total Assisted Annually 55.

Machebeuf Apartments, Inc., 4045 Pecos St., Ste. A, 80211. Tel: 303-830-0215. Email: jrussell@archdiocesanhousing.org. Web: www.archdiocesanhousing.org. Josh Russell, Exec. Dir. Low income housing for families located in Glenwood Springs, CO.

Mercy Holly Park East, 1999 Broadway, Ste. 1000, 80202. Tel: 303-830-3300; Fax: 303-830-3301. Affordable housing for singles and families. Units 72; Residents 145; Total Staff 3; Total Assisted Annually 200.

Prairie Rose Plaza, 4045 Pecos St., Ste. A, 80211. Josh Russell, Exec.

The Sacred Heart of Jesus Housing Foundation (1999) 1300 S. Steele St., 80210. Tel: 303-715-3194; Fax: 303-715-2041. Independent Living 16.

Villa Sierra Madre, Inc., 4045 Pecos St. Ste. A, 80211. Tel: 303-715-3194. Web: www.archdiocesanhousing.org. Josh Russell, Exec. Dir., Archdiocesan Housing.

Willow Street Apartments (1996) 1999 Broadway, Ste. 1000, 80202. Tel: 303-830-3300; Fax: 303-830-3301. Affordable housing for persons with chronic mental illness. Total Assisted Annually 15.

CARBONDALE. *Villas de Santa Lucia, Inc.*, Mailing Address: 4045 Pecos St., Ste. A, 80211. 302 Meadowood Dr. #K, 81623. Low income housing for families.

[M] CATHOLIC CHARITIES & COMMUNITY SERVICES

DENVER. *Catholic Charities and Community Services of the Archdiocese of Denver, Inc.*, 4045 Pecos St., 80211. Tel: 303-742-0828; Fax: 303-742-0774. Email: info@ccdenver.org. Web: www.ccdenver.org. Jonathan Reyes, Pres., CEO & Admin. Shelters for the Homeless, Emergency Assistance Services, Individual & Family Counseling Services, Adoption Services, Pregnancy Counseling, Senior Services, Child Care, Foster Care, Immigration Services Day Care Centers 6; Total Assisted 390; Special Centers for Social Services 10; Total Assisted 43,415.

Catholic Charities Samaritan House, 2301 Lawrence St., 80205. Tel: 303-294-0241; Fax: 303-294-9523. Homeless Shelter

Catholic Charities Fr. Ed Judy House, 4024 S. Newton St., 80236. Tel: 303-866-7641; Fax: 303-866-7643. Homeless Shelter

Catholic Charities Margery Reed Mayo Day Nursery, 1128 28th St., 80205. Tel: 303-308-1420; Fax: 303-308-1421. Child Care, Colorado Preschool & Kindergarten Program, Head Start & Early Head Start.

Catholic Charities Child Development Center, 1155 Decatur St., 80204. Tel: 303-629-5466; Fax: 303-629-6710. Child Care, Colorado Preschool & Kindergarten Program, Head Start & Early Head Start.

Catholic Charities Head Start Services, 4045 Pecos St., 80211. Tel: 303-742-0828; Fax: 303-742-4410.

Catholic Charities Family Services, 4045 Pecos St., 80211. Tel: 303-742-0828; Fax: 303-742-4373. Counseling, Adoption, Foster Care, Senior Services.

Catholic Charities Immigration Services, 4045 Pecos St., 80211. Tel: 303-742-0828; Fax: 303-742-4410.

Catholic Charities Larimer Regional Office, 460 Linden Center Dr., Fort Collins, 80524. Tel: 970-484-5010; Fax: 970-484-0259. The Mission Shelter for Homeless, Emergency Assistance, Senior Services, Immigration Services.

Catholic Charities Guadalupe Community Center, 1442 N. 11th Ave., Greeley, 80631. Tel: 970-353-6433; Fax: 970-353-3861. Emergency Assistance, Senior Services, Case Management, Immigration Services.

Catholic Charities Western Slope Office, 1004 Grand Ave., Glenwood Springs, 81601. Tel: 970-384-2060; Fax: 970-945-2089. Immigration Services, Emergency Assistance, Transitional Housing.

Catholic Charities St. Veronica Outreach, 4045 Pecos St., 80211. Tel: 303-742-0828; Fax: 303-455-9008. Serving Adams, Arapahoe, Denver & Jefferson Counties.

Catholic Charities Mulroy Senior Center, 3550 W. 13th Ave., 80204. Tel: 303-892-1540.

Catholic Charities St. Joseph's Group Home, 4626 Pennsylvania St., 80216. Tel: 303-292-2591; Fax: 303-292-1860.

Catholic Charities Farm Labor Housing Corporation, 2501 Ash Ave. #36, Greeley, 80631. Tel: 970-378-1171; Fax: 970-378-1176. Email: info@ccdenver.org. Web: www.ccdenver.org.

Catholic Charities Plaza Del Milagro, 2500 1st Ave., #CB, Greeley, 80631. Tel: 970-346-2888; Fax: 970-378-1176. Migrant & Seasonal Housing.

Catholic Charities Plaza Del Sol, 2501 Ash Ave., #36, Greeley, 80631. Tel: 970-378-1171; Fax: 970-378-1176. Migrant & Seasonal Housing.

[N] MONASTERIES AND RESIDENCES OF PRIESTS AND BROTHERS

DENVER. *Capuchin Province of Mid-America, Inc.* (1977) 3613 Wyandot St., 80211-2950. Tel: 303-477-5436; Fax: 303-477-6925. Web: www.midamcaps.org. Revs. Charles Polifka, O.F.M.Cap., Provincial Min.; John Lager, O.F.M.Cap., Vocation Dir.; David Songy, O.F.M.Cap., Treas.; Blaine Burkey, O.F.M.Cap., Communications Dir. & Archivist. *St. Francis of Assisi Friary*, 3553 Wyandot St., 80211-2948. Tel: 303-477-5542; Fax: 303-477-1676. (Order of Friars Minor Capuchin) Total in Residence 8; Total Staff 3. In Res. Revs. Charles Polifka, O.F.M.Cap., Provincial Min. & Guardian; Blaine Burkey, O.F.M.Cap., Vicar; Julian Haas, O.F.M.Cap.; John Lager, O.F.M.Cap.; Matthew Gross, O.F.M.Cap.; David Gottschalk, O.F.M.Cap.; Simeon Gallagher, O.F.M.Cap.; Regis Scanlon, O.F.M.Cap. *San Antonio Friary*, 3554 Humboldt St., 80205-3940. Tel: 303-292-5110; Fax: 303-292-5148. In Res. Revs. Gene Emrisek, O.F.M.Cap., Guardian; Francisco Ramirez, O.F.M.Cap., Vicar; Benignus Scarry, O.F.M.Cap.; Bro. Joseph Mary Elder, O.F.M.Cap. *St. Anthony of Padua Friary*, 3805 W. Walsh Pl., 80219-3241. Tel: 303-936-6242; Fax: 303-936-6255. Revs. Gilmary Tallman, O.F.M.Cap., Vicar; David Songy, O.F.M.Cap., Guardian & Dir., Postulants; Michael Suchnicki, O.F.M.Cap. Postulants 3. *San Damiano Friary*, 605 W. 6th St., 80204. Tel: 303-893-6770. In Res. Revs. Christopher Popravak, O.F.M.Cap., Guardian & Formation Dir.; William Kraus, O.F.M.Cap., Vicar; Bros. Christopher Gama, O.F.M.Cap.; Anthony Monahan, O.F.M.Cap.; Augustine Rhode, O.F.M.Cap.; Ryan Tidball, O.F.M.Cap.

Congregation of the Mission Western Province: De Paul House, 2340 S. University Blvd., 80210. Tel: 303-715-9123. Revs. Lawrence Christensen, C.M., Supr.; Paul L. Golden, C.M.; Richard R. Ryan, C.M.; Thomas J. Nelson, C.M.; Bro. F. Joseph Hess, C.M.

Dominican Friars, 3005 W. 29th Ave., 80211-3701. Tel: 303-455-3614; Fax: 303-455-3087. Very Rev. Gerald L. Stookey, O.P., Prior; Bro. Jordan Coonen, O.P.; Revs. Robert F. Staes, O.P.; Robert Keller, O.P., Novice Master; Clinton P. Honkomp, O.P., Pastor; Thomas P. Lynch, O.P.; Patrick Reardon, O.P.; John G. McGreevy, O.P. St. Dominic Priory & Dominican Novitiate; Province of St. Albert the Great. Priests 7; Brothers 1; Novices 5.

Maryknoll Fathers and Brothers, Mailing Address: *St. Therese*, 1243 Kingston St., Aurora, 80010. Web: www.maryknoll.org. Rev. Thomas McCormick, V.F., Mission Promoter (Retired).

The Redemptorists/Denver Province (1996) 1230 S. Parker Rd., 80231. Tel: 303-370-0035; 303-565-5450 (Mission Advancement Ministry); Fax: 303-370-0036. Email: info@redemptoristsdenver.org; development@redemptoristsdenver.org. Web: www.redemptoristsdenver.org. Revs. Harry Grile, C.Ss.R., Prov. Supr.; Robert Halter, C.Ss.R., Prov. Vicar; John Schmidt, C.Ss.R., Prov. Consultor; Allan Weinert, C.Ss.R., Office Fin. Svcs., Treas.; Bro. Steven E. Fruge, C.Ss.R. Priests 166; Deacons 2; Brothers 24.

Serving abroad: Most Rev. Joseph W. Tobin, C.Ss.R., Sec., Congregation for Institutes of Consecrated Life & Societies for Apostolic Life, Casa Sant'Alfonso, C.P. 2458, 00100 Rome, Italy. Tel: 39-06-49490-1; Fax: 39-06-44660-12; Revs. Daniel Andree, C.Ss.R.; Matthew Bonk, C.Ss.R.; Joseph Dorcey, C.Ss.R.; Gilbert Enderle, C.Ss.R.; Stephen Rehrauer, C.Ss.R.; John Vargas, C.Ss.R.; Gary Ziuraitis, C.Ss.R.

Serving elsewhere, not listed: Revs. John Steingraeber, C.Ss.R., Assoc. Dir. CMSM; John Cody, C.Ss.R.; Thomas Fransiscus, C.Ss.R.; Mathew Kessler, C.Ss.R.; Gary Lauenstein, C.Ss.R.; Kingsley Onyekuru, C.Ss.R.; Luong Uong, C.Ss.R.; Dr. William Green, C.Ss.R., P.O. Box 1209, Coeur D Alene, ID 83816. Tel: 208-765-1894; Fax: 208-666-1598.

Regis High Jesuit Community, 16810 E. Caley Ave., Centennial, 80016-1005. Tel: 303-690-4782; Fax: 303-680-7662. Revs. Jeffrey D. Harrison, S.J., Supr.; Kevin B. Dyer, S.J.; David A. Wayne, S.J.; Philip G. Steele, S.J., Pres. Regis Jesuit High School; Robert L. Sullivan, S.J.

Regis Jesuit Community (The Jesuits at Regis University), Jesuit House M12, 3333 Regis Blvd., 80221-1099. Tel: 303-458-4100; Fax: 303-964-5525. Revs. Barton T. Geger, S.J., Rector; David M. Clarke, S.J., Chancellor, Regis Univ.; James B. Guyer, S.J.; Andrew R. Kirschman, S.J.; Timothy M. McMahon, S.J.; Gerard E. Menard, S.J.; Hanh Pham, S.J.; Michael J. Sheeran, S.J.; Charles M. Shelton, S.J.

Society of Jesus - St. Ignatius Loyola Jesuit Community (1944) 2309 Gaylord St., 80205-5627. Tel: 303-322-8042; Fax: 303-322-2927. Email: loyoladenver@yahoo.com. Web: www.loyoladenver.com. Revs. Eustace Sequeira, S.J., Supr.; Leo F. Weber, S.J.; Joseph Tuoc Nguyen, S.J.; Stephen T. Yavorsky, S.J.; Tom Cwik, S.J.

The Theatine Fathers (1923) 1050 S. Birch St., 80246. Tel: 303-757-4280. Rev. Antonio Flores, C.R., Prov. Theatine Fathers. Priests 1.

Xavier Jesuit Center (1993) 3450 W. 53rd, 80221-6568. Tel: 303-480-3900; Fax: 303-480-3913. Revs. C. Thomas Jost, S.J., Supr. & Contact for Xavier Center; Richard S. Anthonysamy, S.J.; David E. Barry, S.J.; Joseph F. Bona, S.J.; John R. Daly, S.J.; Robert R. DeRouen, S.J.; Edward F. Flaherty, S.J.; Harry E. Hoewischer, S.J.; William T. Miller, S.J.; John J. Waters, S.J.; Walter Watson, S.J.; William W. Williams, S.J., Min.; Bro. Alois H. Dorsey, S.J. (Society of Jesus)

BROOMFIELD. *Priestly Fraternity of St. Charles Borromeo (F.S.C.B.)*, 1154 Ridgeview Cir., 80020. Tel: 301-983-4624. Web: www.fraternityofsaintcharles.org. Revs. Michael Carvill, F.S.C.B.; Gabriele Azzalin, F.S.C.B.; Accursio Ciaccio, F.S.C.B.

LITTLETON. *Disciples of the Hearts of Jesus and Mary, St. Mary Parish*, 6853 S. Prince St., 80120. Tel: 303-798-8506. Revs. Alvaro Montero, D.C.J.M. (Spain), Local Supr.; Javier O'Connor, D.C.J.M. (Spain), Parochial Vicar; Javier Nieva, D.C.J.M. (Spain), Parochial Vicar In Res. Revs. Jorge Aguera, D.C.J.M. (Spain); Armando Marsal, D.C.J.M. (Spain).

SNOWMASS. *St. Benedict's Monastery* (1956) 1012 Monastery Rd., 81654. Tel: 970-920-5990; Fax: 970-927-3399. Email: retreat@rof.net. Web: www.snowmass.org. Rt. Rev. Joseph Boyle, O.C.S.O.; Revs. Thomas Keating, O.C.S.O.; William Meninger, O.C.S.O.; Charles Albanese, O.C.S.O.; Micah Schonberger, O.C.S.O. The Order of Cistercians of the Strict Observance (Trappists). Professed Monks 10.

[O] CONVENTS AND RESIDENCES FOR SISTERS

DENVER. *Missionaries of Charity*, 633 Fox St., 80204. Tel: 303-860-8040. Sr. Rosalie, M.C., Supr. & Contact. Shelter for Homeless Women (8 Beds)

Monastery of Our Lady of Light (Capuchin Poor Clares) (1989) 3325 Pecos, 80211. Tel: 303-458-6339; Fax: 303-477-6925. Web: www.capuchinpoorclares.org/denver/index.html. Sr. Maria de Cristo Palafox, O.S.C.Cap., Abbess. *Capuchin Poor Clares of Denver, Inc.* Sisters 9.

Our Lady of Mercy Convent, 1300 S. Steele St., 80210. Tel: 303-765-4592; Fax: 303-765-4595. Email: denver@rsmofalma.org. Web: rsmofalma.org. Sr. Mary Prudence Allen, R.S.M., Local Supr. Religious Sisters of Mercy (Alma, Michigan). Sisters 6.

Sisters of St. Francis of Penance and Christian Charity (1939) 5314 N. Columbine Rd., 80221-1277. Tel: 303-458-6270; Fax: 303-477-4105. Web: www.franciscanway.org. Sisters Rita Cammack, Prov. Min.; Patricia Podhaisky, O.S.F., First Councilor.

Sisters of St. Francis, Denver, CO Sisters in Province 46.

Marycrest Convent (1958) (Campus for sisters' ministries), 2851 W. 52nd Ave., 80221.

Casa Chiara (Provincial offices, sisters' residences & ministries), 5312-5326 N. Columbine Rd., 80221. Tel: 303-458-6270. Sisters 8.

GOLDEN. *Mother Cabrini Shrine*, 20189 Cabrini Blvd., 80401. Tel: 303-526-0758; Fax: 303-526-9795. Web: www.mothercabrinishrine.org. Jeff Lewis, Admin. Missionary Sisters of the Sacred Heart of Jesus (M.S.C.) 3.

LITTLETON. *Carmel of Holy Spirit* (1947) 6138 S. Gallup St., 80120-2702. Tel: 303-798-4176. Sr. Gemma Marie of the Passion of Jesus Hughes, O.C.D., Prioress.

Corporate Name: The Discalced Carmelite Nuns of Colorado Discalced Carmelites (O.C.D.). Sisters 11.

Loretto Center (1964) 4000 S. Wadsworth Blvd., 80123-1309. Tel: 303-986-1541; Fax: 303-986-8453. Sr. Marlene Spero, S.L., Co-Coord. (Sisters of Loretto) Sisters 12.

Sisters of Benedict of Colorado, Inc., 4264 W. Ponds View Dr., 80123. Tel: 303-795-2378. Email: seanosb@aol.com. Sr. Judith Elms, O.S.B., Supr.

VIRGINIA DALE. *Abbey of St. Walburga* (1935) 1029 Benedictine Way, 80536-7633. Tel: 970-472-0612; Fax: 970-484-4342. Email: abbey@walburga.org. Web: www.walburga.org. Sr. Maria-Michael Newe, O.S.B., Abbess.

Corporate Name: Abbey of St. Walburga, Incorporated Benedictine Nuns 22; Novices 1; Claustral Oblate 1.

WHEAT RIDGE. *Carmelite Sisters of the Most Sacred Heart of Los Angeles (California), Carmel of the Holy Name of Jesus Convent*, 4040 Pierce St., 80033. Tel: 303-422-6419.

[P] RETREAT CENTERS

ALLENSPARK. *Retreat, Conference and Spirituality Center - Camp St. Malo*, 10758 Hwy. 7, 80510. Web: www.saintmalo.org. Mailing Address: 1300 S. Steele St., 80210.

LITTLETON. *Jesus Our Hope Hermitage*, 10519 S. Deer Creek Rd., 80127. Tel: 303-697-7539; Fax: 303-697-7539. Web: www.jesus-our-hope.org. Deacon Joseph H. Donohoe, Dir.; Theresa B. Donohoe, Dir.

[Q] CAMPUS MINISTRY

DENVER. *Youth, Young Adult and Campus Ministry Office* 1300 S. Steele St., 80210. Tel: 303-715-3203; Fax: 303-715-2042. Email: chris.stefanick@archden.org. Web: www.archden.org. Chris Stefanick, Dir. Please contact this office directly for a complete listing of campus ministry offices in Northern Colorado.

FORT COLLINS. *Theologian in Residence Program, Inc.* 1220 University Ave., 80521. Tel: 970-493-8984.

NORTHGLENN. **Fellowship of Catholic University Students (FOCUS)* (1999) 603 Park Point Dr. #200, Golden, 80402. Tel: 303-962-5750; Fax: 303-565-5738. Email: info@focusonline.org. Web:

www.focusonline.org. Mailing Address: P.O. Box 33656, 80233. Katherine LeBlanc, CFO.

[R] ASSOCIATIONS OF CONSECRATED LIFE

DENVER. *The Catholic Community of the Beatitudes*, 2924 W. 43rd Ave., 80211. Tel: 720-855-9412; Fax: 303-455-6651. Email: beatitudes.denver@gmail.com. Web: www.beatitudes.us. Rev. Nathanael Pujos (France), Shepherd.

Companions of Christ, 1050 Pennsylvania St., 80203. Email: denver.companions@gmail.com. Web: www.denvercompanionsofchrist.org. Rev. John Nepil, Mod.

Marian Community of Reconciliation (1991) 1060 St. Francis Way, 80204. Tel: 303-629-0500. Email: rgoni@fraternas.org. Web: www.fraternasusa.org/colorado. Rossana Goni, Supr.

ALLENSPARK. *Sodalitium Christianae Vitae*, 10758 Hwy. 7, 80510. Tel: 303-747-0201, Ext. 321; Fax: 303-747-2892. Email: contact@sodalitium.com. Web: www.sodalitium.com.

[S] MISCELLANEOUS LISTINGS

DENVER. *St. Anthony Health Foundation*, Mailing Address: 188 Inverness Dr., W., Ste. 500, Englewood, 80112. 4231 W. 16th Ave., 80204. Tel: 303-629-4446; Fax: 303-629-4241. Leslie Strate, Pres. & Chief Devel. Officer. An operating unit of Catholic Health Initiatives Colorado Foundation.

Archbishops Guild, 2191 E. 97th Ave., 80229. Rita Niblack, Spiritual Advisor.

The Archdiocese of Denver Cemeteries Perpetual Care Trust, 1300 S. Steele St., 80210.

The Archdiocese of Denver Irrevocable Revolving Trust, 1300 S. Steele St., 80210. Tel: 303-715-3258; Fax: 303-715-2046.

The Archdiocese of Denver Management Corporation, 1300 S. Steele St., 80210. Tel: 303-715-3258.

The Archdiocese of Denver Risk Management Property/Casualty Insurance Trust, 1300 S. Steele St., 80210.

The Archdiocese of Denver Welfare Benefits Trust, 1300 S. Steele St., 80210.

Arrupe Corporate Work-Study Program (2003) 4343 Utica St., 80212. Tel: 303-455-7449, Ext. 237; Fax: 303-455-7453. Email: tmallary@arrupejesuit.com. Web: www.arrupejesuit.com. Thomas C. Mallary, Dir.

Blessed Sacrament Catholic Education Foundation (1989) 4930 Montview Blvd., 80207. Tel: 303-355-7361; Fax: 303-355-0894.

Catholic Education Capital Corporation (2010) 1535 Logan St., 80203-7939. Tel: 303-894-8808; Fax: 303-894-7939. Jennifer Kraska, Exec. Dir.

**The Catholic Foundation for the Roman Catholic Church in Northern Colorado*, 3801 E. Florida Ave., Ste. 725, 80210. Tel: 303-468-9885; Fax: 303-468-9889. Email: info@thecatholicfoundation.com. Web: www.thecatholicfoundation.com.

**Christian Life Movement, Inc.* (1985) 1060 11th St., 80204. Tel: 303-629-5100; Fax: 303-629-5100. Email: denverclm@clmusa.org. Web: www.clmusa.org.

Colorado Catholic Education Conference, 1535 Logan St., 80203-7939. Tel: 303-894-8808; Fax: 303-894-7939. Jennifer Kraska, Exec. Dir.

**Colorado Vincentian Volunteers* (1994) 1732 Pearl St., 80203. Tel: 303-863-8141; Fax: 303-863-8141 (Call office first). Email: cvv@covivo.org. Web: www.covivo.org. Bill Jaster, Co-Dir.

**Endow*, 1300 S. Steele St., 80210. Tel: 303-715-3224; Fax: 303-715-2040. Email: terry.polakovic@archden.org. Web: endowgroups.org. Mrs. Therese A. Polakovic, Exec. Dir.; Kate E. Sweeney, Assoc. Dir.

Franciscan Sisters Charitable Fund of Colorado, Inc., 2626 Osceola St., 80212. Tel: 303-433-6268; Fax: 303-455-5359. Email: theresalan@aol.com. Sr. Theresa Langfield, O.S.F., Pres. & Admin. Franciscan Sisters, Daughters of the Sacred Heart of Jesus and Mary, (Wheaton, IL).

John Paul II Center for the New Evangelization, 1300 St. Steele St., 80210.

**Saint Joseph Hospital Foundation* (1977) 1835 Franklin St., 80218. Tel: 303-837-7043; Fax: 303-837-7115. Email: unreinc@exempla.org. Web: www.sjhfdenver.org. Carl Unrein, Pres. & CEO.

Mercy Housing Management Group (1983) 1999 Broadway, Ste. 1000, 80202. Tel: 303-830-3300; Fax: 303-830-3301. Cheryll O'Bryan, Pres.

Mercy Commercial Finance Properties (1990) Patricia O'Roark, Contact.

Mercy Housing Properties (1994) Patricia O'Roark, Contact.

**Mercy Properties, Inc.* (1991) Patricia O'Roark, Contact.

**Mercy Housing Mountain Plains*, 1999 Broadway, Ste. 1000, 80202. Tel: 303-830-3300; Fax: 303-830-3301. Web: www.mercyhousing.org. Jennifer Erixon, Pres.

**Mercy Housing, Inc.* (1981) 1999 Broadway, Ste. 1000, 80202. Tel: 303-830-3300; Fax: 303-830-3301. Email: mail@mercyhousing.org. Web: www.mercyhousing.org. Sr. Lillian Murphy, CEO. Affordable Housing Properties. Units 835; Total Served 2,040; Day Care Centers 3; Total Served 334.

**Mercy Portfolio Services*, 1999 Broadway, Ste. 1000, 80202.

**Queen of the Apostles Mission Association, Inc.* (1992) c/o St. Hungary of Elizabeth Church, 1060 St. Francis Way, 80204. Tel: 720-234-7223. Email: qama@aol.com. Web: www.qama.org. Matt Werner, Pres. Supporting Catholic missionary priests and religious in the former Soviet Union with spiritual and financial support. More than $2 Million given since 1994.

Redemptorist Fathers (1914) c/o The Redemptorists/Denver Province, 1230 S. Parker Rd., 80231. Tel: 303-370-0035; Fax: 303-370-0036.

The Redemptorist of Greeley, Colorado, Inc. (1983) c/o The Redemptorists/Denver Province, 1230 S. Parker Rd., 80231. Tel: 303-370-0035; Fax: 303-370-0036.

Redemptorist Society of Alaska (1964) c/o The Redemptorists/Denver Province, 1230 S. Parker Rd., 80231. Tel: 303-370-0035; Fax: 303-370-0036.

Redemptorist Society of Iowa (1908) c/o The Redemptorist/Denver Province, 1230 S. Parker Rd., 80231. Tel: 303-370-0035; Fax: 303-370-0036.

Redemptorist Society of Oregon (1906) c/o The Redemptorists/Denver Province, 1230 S. Parker Rd., 80231. Tel: 303-370-0035; Fax: 303-370-0036.

The Redemptorists of Denver, Colorado (1981) 1230 S. Parker Rd., 80231. Tel: 303-370-0035; Fax: 303-370-0036.

Seeds of Hope Charitable Trust (1996) 1300 S. Steele St., 80210. Tel: 303-715-3127; Fax: 303-715-2042. Email: betsyb@seedsofhopetrust.org. Web: www.seedsofhopetrust.org. Sasha Hutchings, Prog. & Finance Dir.

St. Vincent de Paul Stores, Inc., Store Location: 6260 E. Colfax Ave., 80205. Tel: 303-388-3315.

BOULDER. **John Paul II Adventure Institute*, 876 14th St., 80302. Web: jp2adventures.com. Sandra Harem, Pres.

Sacred Heart School Foundation, Mailing Address: 2242 Juniper Ct., 80304. Tel: 303-442-2520, Ext. 224; Fax: 303-442-0930. 2312 14th St., 80304. Tel: 303-444-3478. Mr. James Mullen, Contact.

CENTENNIAL. *LC Pastoral Services Inc.*, 8077 S. Quince Cir., 80112. Tel: 303-689-9932; Fax: 303-721-9492. Rev. Jon Budke, L.C., Dir.

ENGLEWOOD. *Association for Catholic Information* (2003) 3392 S. Broadway, 80113. Tel: 303-747-2684; Fax: 303-484-2824. Email: jluna@catholicna.com. Web: www.catholicnewsagency.com. Bro. Jorge S. Luna Diaz del Olmo.

Catholic Health Initiatives (2004) 198 Inverness Dr. W., 80112. Tel: 303-298-9100; Fax: 303-383-6295. Email: peggymartin@catholichealth.net. Web: www.catholichealthinit.org. Kevin Lofton, Pres. & CEO; Sr. Peggy Ann Martin, O.P., J.C.L., Contact.

Catholic Health Initiatives Colorado (1968) 188 Inverness Dr. W, Ste. 500, 80112. Tel: 303-290-6500; Fax: 303-804-8198. Mr. Gary S. Campbell, Pres. & CEO; Kris Ordelheide, Contact. An affiliate of Catholic Health Initiatives.

**Centura Health* (1996) 188 Inverness Dr. W, Ste. 500, 80112. Tel: 303-804-8103; Fax: 303-804-8198. Email: krisordelheide@centura.org. Web: www.centura.org. Kris Ordelheide, Contact Person; Mr. Gary S. Campbell, Pres. & CEO. An operating unit of Colorado Health Initiatives Colorado. (An affiliate of Catholic Health Initiatives.)

CHI National Home Care, 198 Inverness Dr. W., 80112. Tel: 303-383-2746. Web: www.catholichealthinit.org. Sr. Peggy Ann Martin, O.P., J.C.L., SVP Sponsorship & Governance.

CHI National Services, 198 Inverness Dr. W., 80112. Tel: 303-383-2746. Web: www.catholichealthinit.org. Sr. Peggy Ann Martin, O.P., J.C.L., SVP Sponsorship & Governance.

Family of Nazareth, Inc., 3151 S. Bannock St., 80110. Tel: 303-758-1280; Fax: 303-758-1380. Email: stevewaymel@actioncoach.com. Donald McLeod, Pres.

ESTES PARK. **Our Lady of Tenderness, Poustinia* (1983) Box 4311, 80517. Tel: 970-577-1383. Web: www.ourladyoftenderness.org. Lucille Dupuis, Dir.

FORT COLLINS. *West African Development Support Organization, c/o Blessed John XXIII*, 1220 University Ave., 80521-4555. Tel: 970-484-3356. Web: www.wadso.org. Rev. Rocco Porter, V.F.; John Nystrom, PR & Event Coord.; Steve Henry, Contact Person.

GREELEY. *St. Mary's Catholic Education Foundation Greeley*, 2222 23rd Ave., 80634. Tel: 970-352-1724; Fax: 970-352-1729. Email: benke99714@yahoo.com. Susan Benke, Contact.

LITTLETON. *Sisters of Loretto: Administrative Offices*, 4000 S. Wadsworth Blvd., 80123. Tel: 303-783-0450; Fax: 303-783-0611. Web: www.lorettocommunity.org. Sr. Catherine Mueller, S.L., Pres.

LONGMONT. **From Mission To Mission*, 303 Atwood St., 80501. Tel: 720-494-7211; Fax: 720-494-7211. Email: missiontomission@hotmail.com. Web: www.missiontomission.org. Julie Lupien, Exec. Dir.

RELIGIOUS INSTITUTES OF MEN REPRESENTED IN THE ARCHDIOCESE

For further details refer to the corresponding bracketed number in the Religious Institutes of Men or Women section.

[0330]—*Brothers of the Christian Schools* (Christian Brothers)—F.S.C.

[0470]—*Capuchin Friars*—O.F.M.Cap.

[0350]—*Cistercian Order of the Strict Observance* (Trappists)—O.C.S.O.

[0650]—*Congregation of the Holy Spirit* (Spiritans)—C.S.Sp.

[1330]—*Congregation of the Mission* (Vincentians)—C.M.

[]—*Congregation of the Mother Coredemptrix*—C.M.C.

[]—*Disciples of the Hearts of Jesus and Mary*—D.C.J.M.

[0690]—*Jesuit Fathers and Brothers*—S.J.

[0730]—*Legionaires of Christ*—L.C.

[0800]—*Maryknoll*—M.M.

[0940]—*Oblates of the Virgin Mary*—O.M.V.

[0430]—*Order of Preachers* (Dominicans)—O.P.

[1030]—*Paulist Fathers* (Sacred Heart of Jesus)—C.S.P.

[1065]—*Priestly Fraternity of St. Peter*—F.S.S.P.

[1205]—*Priestly Fraternity of the Missionaries of St. Charles Borromeo*—F.S.C.B.

[1070]—*Redemptorist Fathers*—C.Ss.R.

[1240]—*Servites*—O.S.M.

[]—*Sociedad de Cruzados de Cristo Rey*—C.C.R.

[1260]—*Society of Christ*—S.Ch.

[1300]—*Theatine Fathers*—C.R.

[1335]—*Vincentian Congregation*—V.C.

RELIGIOUS INSTITUTES OF WOMEN REPRESENTED IN THE ARCHDIOCESE

[0190]—*Benedictine Nuns*—O.S.B.

[0230]—*Benedictine Sisters of Pontifical Jurisdiction*—O.S.B.

[3765]—*Capuchin Poor Clares*—O.S.C.Cap.

[0370]—*Carmelite Sisters of the Most Sacred Heart of Los Angeles*—O.C.D.

[3110]—*Congregation of Our Lady of the Cenacle*—R.C.

[0420]—*Discalced Carmelite Nuns*—O.C.D.

[1070-14]—*Dominican Sisters* (Grand Rapids, MI)—O.P.

[1070-03]—*Dominican Sisters* (Sinsinawa)—O.P.

[1105]—*Dominican Sisters of Hope*—O.P.

[1115]—*Dominican Sisters of Peace*—O.P.

[1070-07]—*Dominican Sisters of the Congregation of St. Cecilia* (Nashville)—O.P.

[1240]—*Franciscan Sisters, Daughters of the Sacred Hearts of Jesus and Mary* (Wheaton, IL)—O.S.F.

[1845]—*Guadalupan Missionaries of the Holy Spirit*—M.G.Sp.S.

[2340]—*Little Sisters of the Poor*—L.S.P.

[2710]—*Missionaries of Charity*—M.C.

[]—*Missionaries of Charity of Mary Immaculate*—M.C.M.I.

[2860]—*Missionary Sisters of the Sacred Heart of Jesus*—M.S.C.

[2960]—*Notre Dame Sisters*—N.D.

[3130]—*Our Lady of Victory Missionary Sisters*—O.L.V.M.

[2519]—*Religious Sisters of Mercy of Alma, Michigan*—R.S.M.

[2970]—*School Sisters of Notre Dame*—S.S.N.D.

[0440]—*Sisters of Charity of Cincinnati, Ohio*—S.C.

[0480]—*Sisters of Charity of Leavenworth, Kansas*—S.C.L.

[0655]—*The Sisters of Charity of St. Vincent De Paul of Suwon*—S.C.V.

[0430]—*Sisters of Charity of the Blessed Virgin Mary*—B.V.M.

[2360]—*Sisters of Loretto at the Foot of the Cross* (Nerinx, KY)—S.L.

[2575]—*Sisters of Mercy of the Americas*—R.S.M.

[1705]—*Sisters of St. Francis of Assisi* (Milwaukee, WI)—O.S.F.

[1630]—*Sisters of St. Francis of Penance and Christian Charity*—O.S.F.

[3840]—*Sisters of St. Joseph of Carondelet*—C.S.J.

[3260]—*Sisters of the Precious Blood* (Dayton, OH)—C.PP.S.

ARCHDIOCESAN CEMETERIES

AURORA. *St. Simeon Cemetery Association* (2003) 22001 E. State Hwy. 30, 80018. Tel: 720-859-9785; Fax: 720-859-9788. Email: lloyd.swint@archden.org. Web: www.stsimeondenver.org.

WHEAT RIDGE. *Archdiocese of Denver Mortuary at Mount Olivet, Inc.* (1981) 12801 W. 44th Ave., 80033. Tel: 303-425-9511; Fax: 303-425-0242.

The Mount Olivet Cemetery Association, 12801 W. 44th Ave., 80033. Tel: 303-424-7785; Fax: 303-424-5263.

NECROLOGY

† Meznar, Robert P., (Retired)—Died July 30, 2011
† O'Malley, Joseph M., (Retired)—Died Feb. 12, 2011

An asterisk (*) denotes an organization that has established tax-exempt status directly with the IRS and is not covered by the USCCB Group Ruling.

Diocese of Des Moines

(Dioecesis Desmoinensis)

Most Reverend

RICHARD E. PATES

Bishop of Des Moines; ordained December 20, 1968; appointed Titular Bishop of Suacia and Auxiliary Bishop of Saint Paul and Minneapolis December 22, 2000; ordained March 26, 2001; appointed Bishop of Des Moines April 10, 2008; installed May 29, 2008. *Office: 601 Grand Ave., Des Moines, IA 50309.*

Most Reverend

JOSEPH L. CHARRON, C.PP.S., S.T.D.

Retired Bishop of Des Moines; ordained June 3, 1967; appointed Titular Bishop of Bencenna and Auxiliary Bishop of Saint Paul and Minneapolis November 6, 1989; consecrated January 25, 1990; appointed Bishop of Des Moines November 12, 1993; installed January 21, 1994; retired April 10, 2007.

Chancery: 601 Grand Ave., Des Moines, IA 50309. Tel: 515-243-7653; Fax: 515-237-5070.

Web: www.dmdiocese.org

Email: bishop@dmdiocese.org

ERECTED BY POPE ST. PIUS X, AUGUST 12, 1911.

Square Miles 12,446.

Comprises that part of the State of Iowa which is bounded on the east by the eastern boundaries of the Counties of Polk, Warren, Lucas and Wayne; on the south by the State of Missouri; on the west by the Missouri River; and on the north by the northern boundaries of the Counties of Harrison, Shelby, Audubon, Guthrie, Dallas and Polk.

Patrons of the Diocese: I. Blessed Virgin Mary Queen; II. Pope Saint Pius X. Diocese solemnly consecrated to the Immaculate Heart of Mary on May 16, 1948.

Legal Title: "The Roman Catholic Diocese of Des Moines."
For legal titles of parishes and diocesan institutions, consult the Chancery Office.

STATISTICAL OVERVIEW

Personnel	
Bishop	1
Retired Bishops	1
Priests: Diocesan Active in Diocese	55
Priests: Diocesan Active Outside Diocese	2
Priests: Retired, Sick or Absent	28
Number of Diocesan Priests	85
Religious Priests in Diocese	10
Total Priests in Diocese	95
Extern Priests in Diocese	6
Ordinations:	
Diocesan Priests	1
Permanent Deacons in Diocese	87
Total Sisters	57
Parishes	
Parishes	81
With Resident Pastor:	
Resident Diocesan Priests	50
Resident Religious Priests	3
Without Resident Pastor:	
Administered by Priests	28
New Parishes Created	1
Closed Parishes	2
Professional Ministry Personnel:	
Sisters	11
Lay Ministers	50
Welfare	
Catholic Hospitals	3
Total Assisted	1,429,332
Homes for the Aged	1
Total Assisted	425
Specialized Homes	1
Total Assisted	5,102
Special Centers for Social Services	5
Total Assisted	25,000
Educational	
Diocesan Students in Other Seminaries	15
Total Seminarians	15
Colleges and Universities	1
Total Students	832
High Schools, Diocesan and Parish	2
Total Students	1,622
Elementary Schools, Diocesan and Parish	15
Total Students	4,854
Catechesis/Religious Education:	
High School Students	2,657
Elementary Students	11,088
Total Students under Catholic Instruction	21,068
Teachers in the Diocese:	
Priests	1
Sisters	3
Lay Teachers	287
Vital Statistics	
Receptions into the Church:	
Infant Baptism Totals	1,667
Minor Baptism Totals	83
Adult Baptism Totals	77
Received into Full Communion	210
First Communions	1,958
Confirmations	1,517
Marriages:	
Catholic	273
Interfaith	189
Total Marriages	462
Deaths	658
Total Catholic Population	94,052
Total Population	816,196

Former Bishops—Most Revs. AUSTIN DOWLING, D.D., first Bishop of Des Moines; ord. June 24, 1891; appt. Bishop Jan. 31, 1912; cons. April 25, 1912; promoted to the See of St. Paul, Jan. 1919; THOMAS W. DRUMM, D.D., Bishop of Des Moines; ord. Dec. 21, 1901; cons. May 21, 1919; died Oct. 24, 1933; GERALD T. BERGAN, D.D., ord. Oct. 28, 1915; appt. March 24, 1934; cons. June 13, 1934; Enthroned June 21, 1934; elevated to Archiepiscopal dignity and promoted to Omaha Feb. 9, 1948; EDWARD C. DALY, O.P., S.T.M., Bishop of Des Moines; ord. June 12, 1921; appt. March 13, 1948; cons. May 13, 1948; named Asst. at Papal Throne, May 23, 1958; died Nov. 23, 1964; GEORGE J. BISKUP, D.D., ord. March 19, 1937; appt. Auxiliary Bishop of Dubuque, March 9, 1957; cons. April 24, 1957; appt. Bishop of Des Moines, Feb. 3, 1965; appt. Coadjutor Archbishop of Indianapolis, July 26, 1967; succeeded to See Jan. 14, 1970; MAURICE J. DINGMAN, D.D., Bishop of Des Moines; ord. Dec. 8, 1939; appt. Bishop of Des Moines April 2, 1968; cons. June 19, 1968; installed July 7, 1968; retired Oct. 14, 1986; died Feb. 1, 1992; WILLIAM H. BULLOCK, ord. June 7, 1952; appt. Auxiliary Bishop of St. Paul and Minneapolis and Titular Bishop of Natchez June 3, 1980; cons. Aug. 12, 1980; appt. Bishop of Des Moines Feb. 10, 1987; installed April 2, 1987; appt. to Diocese of Madison April 13, 1993; died April 3, 2011.; JOSEPH L. CHARRON, C.PP.S. (Retired), ord. June 3, 1967; appt. Titular Bishop of Bencenna and Auxiliary Bishop of Saint Paul and Minneapolis Nov. 6, 1989; cons. Jan. 25, 1990; appt. Bishop of Des Moines Nov. 12, 1993; installed Jan. 21, 1994; retired April 10, 2007.

Vicar General—Rev. CHRISTOPHER HARTSHORN.

Chancery—601 Grand Ave., Des Moines, 50309. Tel: 515-243-7653; Fax: 515-237-5070. Office Hours: Mon.-Fri. 8:30-4:30.

Chancellor—Sr. JUDE FITZPATRICK, C.H.M., Chm., All Matrimonial Correspondence to Tribunal.

Vice Chancellors—Deacon MICHAEL E. RILEY, J.C.L.; Mr. JASON KURTH.

Executive Assistant to the Bishop—ANGIE HEMMINGSEN, 601 Grand Ave., Des Moines, 50309. Tel: 515-237-5039; Fax: 515-237-5071.

Finance Officer—PAUL CARLSON, 601 Grand Ave., Des Moines, 50309. Tel: 515-237-5008.

Vicar for Finance—Rev. Msgr. EDWARD HURLEY. Tel: 515-223-4577.

Judicial Vicar—Rev. CHRISTOPHER PISUT.

Director of Tribunal—Deacon MICHAEL E. RILEY, J.C.L.

Defenders of the Bond—Revs. MICHAEL AMADEO; LAWRENCE R. HOFFMANN; DAVID J. POLICH; Deacon ROBERT L. HOWE.

Judges—Rev. Msgr. LAWRENCE A. BEESON, J.C.D. (Retired); Revs. CHRISTOPHER PISUT; DANIEL F. KRETTEK; Deacon MICHAEL E. RILEY, J.C.L.; Rev. Msgrs. STEPHEN L. ORR; EDWARD B. PFEFFER, J.C.L. (Retired).

Notary—DORIS KLANG.

Advocates—Revs. EUGENE R. KOCH (Retired); JOHN P. LUDWIG; JOHN DORTON; HOWARD E. FITZGERALD; Mrs. PHYLLIS CACCIATORE; Mrs. SARAH LUFT; Mrs. JOYCE RILEY; Deacon DENNIS LUFT.

Diocesan Consultors—Revs. DAVID FLEMING; CHRISTOPHER HARTSHORN; LAWRENCE R. HOFFMANN; PAUL MONAHAN (Retired); JOSEPH PINS; RAYMOND HIGGINS.

Diocesan Corporation Board—Most Rev. RICHARD PATES; Rev. CHRISTOPHER HARTSHORN; Sr. JUDE FITZPATRICK, C.H.M.; SARA EIDE; MATT MADSEN; PAUL CARLSON.

Diocesan Offices and Directors

Campus Ministry—Rev. JOEL MCNEIL, Dir.

Catholic Council for Social Concern aka Catholic Charities—NANCY GALEAZZI, Exec. Dir., 601 Grand

Ave., Des Moines, 50309. Tel: 515-237-5055.

Charismatic Renewal Liaison—Rev. DANIEL F. KRETTEK, 1521 Center St., Des Moines, 50314. Tel: 515-282-4839.

Communications, Office of—ANNE MARIE COX, Dir., 601 Grand Ave., Des Moines, 50309. Tel: 515-237-5057; Fax: 515-237-5070.

Continuing Education for Clergy—Rev. RAYMOND MCHENRY.

Deaf-Handicapped, Office of—PEGGY CHICOINE, Coord. Tel: 515-289-1311. Email: dpchicoine@msn.com.

Development Office—JOAN BINDEL, Dir. Devel. Tel: 515-237-5079. 601 Grand Ave., Des Moines, 50309.

Diocesan Council of Catholic Women—CAROLYN SMITH, Pres., 55386 Forrester Valley Ln., Glenwood, 51534. Tel: 712-527-4206. Email: csmith55386@mchsi.com.

Diaconate (Permanent)—Deacon MICHAEL E. RILEY, J.C.L., Dir., 601 Grand Ave., Des Moines, 50309.

Diaconate Formation—Directors: Deacon RON MYERS; TAMMY MYERS, 601 Grand Ave., Des Moines, 50309. Tel: 515-237-5037.

Holy Childhood, Pontifical Association—Dr. LUVERN GUBBELS, 601 Grand Ave., Des Moines, 50309. Tel: 515-237-5013.

Legislative Activities, Office of—VACANT.

Newspaper— "The Catholic Mirror" ANNE MARIE COX, Editor, 601 Grand Ave., Des Moines, 50309. Tel: 515-237-5057.

Priests' Pension Fund Society—Rev. JOHN P. LUDWIG; Rev. Msgr. EDWARD HURLEY; Revs. CHRISTOPHER HARTSHORN; ROBERT L. SCHOEMANN (Retired); Rev. Msgr. MICHAEL HESS.

Propagation of the Faith—Sr. JUDE FITZPATRICK, C.H.M.

Office of Catechetical Services—JOHN GAFFNEY, Dir., 601 Grand Ave., Des Moines, 50309. Tel: 515-237-5026.

St. Vincent de Paul Society—Deacon TROY THOMPSON, Spiritual Dir., 3210 74th St., Urbandale, 50322. Tel: 515-278-2957.

Schools—Dr. LUVERN GUBBELS, Supt. & Dir. Educ.; DENISE MULCAHY, Dir. Teaching & Learning. Tel: 515-237-5035; JULIE MELCHER, Dir. Educational Svcs., 601 Grand Ave., Des Moines, 50309. Tel: 515-237-5015; DARCIE TALLMAN, Mktg. Specialist, 601 Grand Ave., Des Moines, 50309. Tel: 515-237-5088.

Seminarians—Rev. DANIEL J. KIRBY, Dir.

Vocations—Rev. DAVID MUENCHRATH, Dir., 601 Grand Ave., Des Moines, 50309. Tel: 515-237-5014; Mr. JASON KURTH, Vocations Specialist. Tel: 515-237-5061.

Office of Worship (Liturgy, Music, Art and Architecture)—Mr. KYLE LECHTENBERG, Dir., 601 Grand Ave., Des Moines, 50309. Tel: 515-237-5046.

Youth Ministry, Office of—VACANT, Dir., St. Thomas More Center, 6177 Panorama Rd., Panora, 50216. Tel: 515-755-3164.

Office of Evangelization and Adult Faith Formation—Dr. CHERYL FOURNIER, Dir., 601 Grand Ave., Des Moines, 50309. Tel: 515-237-5006.

Office of Lay Ecclesial Ministry Formation—Dr. CHERYL FOURNIER, Dir., 601 Grand Ave., Des Moines, 50309. Tel: 515-237-5006.

Office of Marriage Ministry—Mr. ADAM STOREY, 601 Grand Ave., Des Moines, 50309. Tel: 515-237-5056.

Victim Assistance Coordinator—MARY MCCOY. Tel: 515-286-2024. Email: advocate@dmdiocese.org.

CLERGY, PARISHES, MISSIONS AND PAROCHIAL SCHOOLS

CITY OF DES MOINES

(POLK COUNTY)

1—ST. AMBROSE CATHEDRAL (1856) [JC] Rev. John Bertogli, Rector; Sr. Patricia Scherer, Pastoral Min.; Deacons Michael E. Riley; Francis Chan; Lee Pao Yang; Michael McCarthy; Debbie S. Rohrer, Liturgy Coord.
Res.: 607 High St., 50309. Tel: 515-288-7411; Fax: 515-288-3969. Web: www.saintambrosecathedral.org.
Catechesis/Religious Program—Dorothy Miller, D.R.E. Students 158.

2—ALL SAINTS (1914) [JC] Rev. Robert Harris; William Connet, Liturgy Coord.; Sue A. Christensen, Accountant & Bookkeeper.
Mailing Address: 650 N.E. 52nd Ave., 50313. Tel: 515-265-5001; Fax: 515-265-5636. Web: www.dmallsaints.org.
Catechesis/Religious Program—Amanda DeVries, Catechetical Leader; Julie Burdt, Youth Min. Students 231.
Nick R. and Carole P. Zagar Endowment Scholarship Fund—

3—ST. ANTHONY'S (1905) Rev. Msgr. Frank Chiodo; Revs. Thomas V. Dooley, Parochial Vicar; Guthrie Dolan, Parochial Vicar; Juan Antonio Hernandez Lozano, Hispanic Chap.; Deacons Thomas Starbuck; David Wadle.
Res.: 15 Indianola Rd., 50315. Tel: 515-244-4709; Fax: 515-280-6959. Email: comphelp@ecity.net. Web: www.stanthonydsm.org.
School—(Grades PreK-8), 16 Columbus Ave., 50315. Tel: 515-243-1874; Fax: 515-243-4467. Dr. Joseph F. Cordaro, Prin. Sisters 1; Lay Teachers 16; Students 337.
Catechesis/Religious Program—Tel: 515-244-1119. Susan Ort, D.R.E. (K-6). Students 371.

4—ST. AUGUSTIN'S (1920) Revs. Zachary Kautzky, Parochial Vicar; James Livingston, Senior Assoc.; Deacons Kevin Heim; Michael Manno; Joe Coan; Mrs. Patricia Neal, Music Min.; C. Andy Ball, Business Finance Officer.
Church: 545 42nd St., 50312. Tel: 515-255-1175; Fax: 515-255-7969. Email: info@staugustin.org. Web: www.staugustin.org.
School—(Grades PreK-8), 4320 Grand Ave., 50312. Tel: 515-279-5947; Fax: 515-279-8049. Dr. Nancy Dowdle, Prin. Lay Teachers 19; Students 285.
Catechesis/Religious Program—Christen Cota, Catechetical Leader. Students 79.
St. Augustin Foundation—

5—BASILICA OF SAINT JOHN (1905) Revs. Aquinas Nichols, O.S.B.; Juan Antonio Hernandez Lozano, Hispanic Chap.; Deacons Frank Lopez; Luke Tieskoetter.
Church: 1915 University Ave., 50314. Tel: 515-244-3101; Fax: 515-244-3165. Email: basilicadm@msn.com. Web: www.basilicaofstjohn.org.
Catechesis/Religious Program—Jennifer Parsons, Catechetical Leader. Students 150.
Basilica of St. John Foundation—

6—ST. CATHERINE OF SIENA CATHOLIC STUDENT CENTER (1969), (Non-Territorial University Parish) Rev. Joel McNeil (AUS).
Church: 1150-128th St., 50311-4142. Tel: 515-271-4747; Fax: 515-271-1918. Web: www.stcatherinedrake.org.
Catechesis/Religious Program—Barb James, Catechetical Leader. Students 34.
St. Catherine of Siena Foundation—

7—CHRIST THE KING (1939) Rev. Msgr. Frank E. Bognanno; Rev. Juan Antonio Hernandez Lozano, Hispanic Chap.; Deacons Larry Kehoe; Patrick Kirkman; Charles Putbrese; Deanna Magnee, Accountant/Bookkeeper; Christopher Aldinger, Business Mgr.
Res. & Office: 5711 S.W. 9th St., 50315. Tel: 515-285-2888; Fax: 515-285-8182. Email: msgr@dmchristtheking.com. Web: www.christthekingparish.org.
School—(Grades PreK-8), 701 Wall St., 50315. Tel: 515-285-3349; Fax: 515-285-0381. Becky Johnson, Prin. Sisters 1; Lay Teachers 15; Students 248.
Catechesis/Religious Program—Susan Kehoe, Catechetical Leader. Students 273.
Christ the King Housing Services—
Christ the King Foundation—

8—CHURCH OF ST. PETER VIETNAMESE CATHOLIC COMMUNITY Rev. Joseph Ly Quy Chu; Deacons Gene Jager; Quan Tong; Mrs. Kelly Truong Tong, Accountant/Bookkeeper.
Mailing Address: 1746 Des Moines St., 50316.
Church: 618 E. 18th St., 50316.
Catechesis/Religious Program—Beth Drazhozal, Catechetical Leader. Students 117.

9—HOLY TRINITY (1920) Rev. Michael Amadeo; Deacons Thomas Bradley; James Obradovich; Helen Roberts, Pastoral Assoc.; Regina Montgomery, Business Mgr.; Diane Tellis, Accountant/Bookkeeper.
Res.: 2926 Beaver Ave., 50310-4040. Tel: 515-255-3162; Fax: 515-255-1381. Email: parishoffice@holytrinitydm.org. Web: www.holytrinitydm.org.
School—(Grades PreK-8) Audra Meyer, Prin. Lay Teachers 30; Students 509.
Catechesis/Religious Program—Paulette Chapman, D.R.E. Students 799.
Holy Trinity Foundation—

10—ST. JOSEPH'S (1924) Rev. Msgr. Edward Hurley; Deacons Marvin Brewer; William Hare; Bill Konnath, Business Mgr.; Debbie Muse, Accountant/Bookkeeper.
Res.: 3300 Easton Blvd., 50317. Tel: 515-266-2226; Fax: 515-266-8348. Email: stjoseph@stjosephdsm.org. Web: www.dmdiocese.org/mass.htm.
School—(Grades PreK-8), 2107 E. 33rd St., 50317. Tel: 515-266-3433; Fax: 515-266-2860. Phyllis Konchar, Prin. Lay Teachers 17; Students 259.
Catechesis/Religious Program—Tel: 515-266-2449. Melanie Stoner, Catechetical Leader. Students 259.
St. Joseph Foundation—
St. Joseph School Foundation—

11—ST. MARY OF NAZARETH (1964) Rev. Gregory Leach; Deacons Steven Reed; Terry Schleisman; John Robert Hanna, Youth Min.; Rhonda Brown, Business Mgr.
Res.: 4600 Meredith Dr., P.O. Box 13170, 50310. Tel: 515-276-4042; Fax: 515-252-1995. Email: stmarydsm@aol.com. Web: www.dmdiocese.org/mass.htm.
Catechesis/Religious Program— Deb Richards, Catechetical Leader. Students 432.

12—OUR LADY OF THE AMERICAS (1882) Revs. Christopher Reising; Jose Reynaldo Hernandez, Parochial Vicar; Deacon Gene Jager.
Mailing Address: 1271 E. 9th St., 50316. Tel: 515-266-6695; Fax: 515-266-9803. Email: oloa@dwx.com.
Catechesis/Religious Program—Irma Jaime-Cruz, D.R.E. Students 428.
Worship Center—
Visitation: 1271 E. 9th St., 50316. Tel: 515-266-6695; Fax: 515-266-9803.

13—ST. PETER'S (1915) Merged with Visitation, Des Moines to form Our Lady of the Americas, Des Moines.

14—ST. THERESA OF THE CHILD JESUS (1951) [JC] Revs. Lawrence R. Hoffmann; Mark Neal, Parochial Vicar; Deacons Joe Cortese II; Earl Weisenhorn; Sr. Joyce Blum, Pastoral Min.; Anne Dols, Pastoral Min.; Mary Gisler, Business Mgr.; Maggie Schopp, Youth Min.
Res.: 1230 Merle Hay Rd., 50311-2098. Tel: 515-279-4654; Fax: 515-277-0838. Email: parishoffice@yahoo.com. Web: www.sainttheresaiowa.org.
School—54810 Cara Carpenter, 50311. Tel: 515-277-0178; Fax: 515-255-2415. Ellen Stemler, Prin. Lay Teachers 26; Students 302.
Catechesis/Religious Program—Kathy Wipf, Catechetical Leader; Barbara Woods, Catechetical Leader. Students 217.
St. Theresa of the Child Jesus Foundation—

15—VISITATION (1882) Merged with St. Peter's, Des Moines to form Our Lady of the Americas, Des Moines.

OUTSIDE THE CITY OF DES MOINES

ADAIR, ADAIR CO., ST. JOHN (1879) Attended by All Saints, Stuart Rev. Raymond Higgins; Deacon Fred Cornwell; Rita Rilea, Accountant Bookkeeper.
Mailing Address: *c/o All Saints*, 216 All Saints Dr., P.O. Box 605, Stuart, 50250. Tel: 515-523-1943; Fax: 515-523-1954.
Church: 501 Adair St., 50002. Tel: 712-762-3773 (Office); Fax: 712-762-3484.
Catechesis/Religious Program—Included with All Saints Parish in Stuart, Tel: 712-762-3484. Julie Plowman, Catechetical Leader. Students 19.

ADEL, DALLAS CO., ST. JOHN (1917) Rev. Wayne Gubbels; Tonia Pals, Youth Min.; Lori Glanz, Business Mgr.
Mailing Address: 24043 302nd Pl., P.O. Box 185, 50003-0185. Tel: 515-993-4482; Fax: 515-993-3973. Email: saintjc3@aol.com. Web: www.dmdiocese.org/mass.htm.
Catechesis/Religious Program—Tel: 515-993-4590; Fax: 515-993-3973. Majorie Livermore, D.R.E. Students 188.

AFTON, UNION CO., ST. EDWARD (1878) Attended by Paul VI Pastoral Ministry from Creston. Rev. Joseph Pins; Sheila Brown, Liturgy Coord.
Mailing Address: 406 W. Clark, Creston, 50801. Tel: 641-782-5278; Fax: 515-782-7628. Email: holyspiritst.edward@iowatelecom.net. Web: www.geocities.com/spirit_edwards/.
Church: 104 W. Union, 50830. Tel: 641-347-8452.
Catechesis/Religious Program—Kathy Simmerman, D.R.E./Youth Min. Students 21.

ALTOONA, POLK CO., SS. JOHN AND PAUL (1983) Rev. Timothy Fitzgerald; Deacon Dennis Luft; Sr. Virginia Jennings, Pastoral Min.; David Ortega, Business Mgr.; Patty Hormann, Liturgy Coord. & Music Min.
Mailing Address: 1401 1st Ave. S., 50009. Tel: 515-967-3796; Fax: 515-967-7197. Email: ssjohnpaul@ssjohnpaul.org. Web: www.ssjohnpaul.org.
Catechesis/Religious Program—Tel: 515-967-8047. Patsy Carlson, D.R.E.; Mr. Terry Lee Clark, Youth Min. Students 258.

ANITA, CASS CO., ST. MARY (1924) Attended by parishioners from SS. Peter & Paul, Atlantic. Rev. Daniel Siepker.
Mailing Address: 106 W. 6th St., Atlantic, 50022.

Church: 302 Chestnut St., P.O. Box 277, 50020. Tel: 712-762-3773. Web: www.dmdiocese.org/mass.htm.
Catechesis/Religious Program—

ANKENY, POLK CO.
1—OUR LADY'S IMMACULATE HEART (1961) Rev. Msgr. Stephen L. Orr; Deacons Jeffrey Boehlert; Steven Udelhofen; Becky J. Robovsky, Business Mgr.
Res.: 510 E. First St., 50021. Tel: 515-964-3038; Fax: 515-964-5997. Email: elaine@olih.org. Web: www.olih.org.
Catechesis/Religious Program—Tel: 515-964-3545. Joyce Clawson, D.R.E. (Grades Pre-K-3); Diane Thierer, Catechetical Leader (Grades 4&5, 8-12); Abby Henderson, Catechetical Leader (Grades 6-7); Randy Henderson, Youth Min. Students 1,189.
Our Lady's Immaculate Heart Charitable Foundation—
2—ST. LUKE THE EVANGELIST CHURCH, P.O. Box 1087, 50021.

ATLANTIC, CASS CO., SS. PETER AND PAUL (1871) Rev. Daniel Siepker; Nathan Renz, Business Mgr.; Rose Rueb, Accountant Bookkeeper.
Res.: 106 W. 6th St., 50022. Tel: 712-243-4721; Fax: 712-243-2064. Email: petepaul@metc.net. Web: www.metc.net/petepaul/index.htm.
Catechesis/Religious Program—Tel: 712-243-2144. Julie Williamson, D.R.E.; Nathan Renz, Youth Min. Students 138.

AUDUBON, AUDUBON CO., ST. PATRICK (1918) [CEM] Rev. Emmanuel S. Agwuoke, C.S.Sp., Admin.
Res.: 116 E. Division St., 50025. Tel: 712-563-2283; Fax: 712-563-3238. Email: sph@iowatelecom.net. Web: www.dmdiocese.org/mass.htm.
Catechesis/Religious Program—Candy Chambers, D.R.E. Students 104.

AVOCA, POTTAWATTAMIE CO., ST. MARY, MEDIATRIX OF ALL GRACES (1882) Rev. Thomas V. Dooley; Pamela Paulson, Liturgy Coord.; Gayle Prokupek, Liturgy Coord.; Jane True, Accountant Bookkeeper.
Res.: 109 N. Maple St., P.O. Box 38, 51521-0038. Tel: 712-343-6948. Email: smpavoca@walnutel.net. Web: stmaryavoca.tripod.com.
Catechesis/Religious Program—Mary Beth Roskins, Catechetical Leader; Gwen Blum, Catechetical Leader; Carmella Pigneri, Youth Min. Students 86.

BAYARD, GUTHRIE CO., ST. PATRICK (1882) Rev. Michael G. Peters.
Mailing Address: *St. Mary*, 603 Main St., Guthrie Center, 50115. Email: stmstc@netins.net. Web: showcase.netins.net/web/pgcatholic.
Res.: 214 Prairie St., 50029. Tel: 641-747-2569.
Catechesis/Religious Program—Students 35.

BEDFORD, TAYLOR CO., SACRED HEART, Attended by St. Clare, Clarinda. Rev. Joy Vincent Thaiparambil; Glenda Stockwell, Accountant/Bookkeeper.
Mailing Address: 300 E. Lincoln Blvd., Clarinda, 51632. Tel: 712-542-2030. Email: stclare@clarinda.heartland.net. Web: www.dmdiocese.org/mass.htm.
Church: 707 Main St., 50833.
Catechesis/Religious Program—Dee Rankin, D.R.E. Students 18.

CARLISLE, WARREN CO., ST. ELIZABETH SETON (1979) Rev. Jim Kirby.
Mailing Address: 2566 Scotch Ridge Rd., P.O. Box 35, 50047. Tel: 515-989-0659; Fax: 515-989-4525. Email: steliz256@aol.com.
Catechesis/Religious Program—Christine Stickley, D.R.E.; Stacie Henkelman, D.R.E. Students 84.

CARTER LAKE, POTTAWATTAMIE CO., OUR LADY OF CARTER LAKE (1970) Merged with Our Lady Queen of the Apostles, Council Bluffs and Holy Family, Council Bluffs to form Corpus Christi, Council Bluffs.

CASEY, GUTHRIE CO., ST. JOSEPH (1898) Closed. For inquiries for parish records contact the chancery.

CHARITON, LUCAS CO., SACRED HEART (1869) Rev. Christopher Pisut.
Res.: 407 N. Main, 50049. Tel: 641-774-4978; Fax: 641-774-2517. Web: www.dmdiocese.org.
Catechesis/Religious Program—Sheila Adams, Catechetical Leader. Students 103.

CHURCHVILLE, WARREN CO., ASSUMPTION (1855) Rev. John P. Ludwig; Connie Brommel, Business Mgr.
Mailing Address: 101 Saint James St., Saint Marys, 50241. Tel: 515-981-4855. Web: www.dmdiocese.org.
Res.: 897 South St., Norwalk, 50211.
Catechesis/Religious Program—Lola Hill, Adult Faith Formation Coord.; Josh Hart, Youth Min.; Jessica Hart, Youth Min. Students 22.

CLARINDA, PAGE CO., ST. CLARE (1942) Rev. Joy Vincent Thaiparambil.
Res.: 300 E. Lincoln Blvd., 51632. Tel: 712-542-2030. Email: stclare@clarinda.heartland.net.
Catechesis/Religious Program—Mark Baldwin, D.R.E. Students 48.

CORNING, ADAMS CO., ST. PATRICK'S (1869) [CEM] Rev. Lazarus Kirigia; Beth Waddle, Liturgy Coord.; Beth Waddle, Business Mgr., Accountant/Bookkeeper.
Res.: 504 Grove Ave., 50841. Tel: 515-322-3363. Email: pat_corning@yahoo.com. Web: www.dmdiocese.org/mass.htm.
Catechesis/Religious Program—Jane Rychnoysky, D.R.E. Students 37.

CORYDON, WAYNE CO., ST. FRANCIS (1969) Attended by Chariton of the South Central Catholic Ministry Team. Rev. Christopher Pisut; Mary Rita Van Valkenburg, Business Mgr.
Mailing Address: 407 N. Main St., Chariton, 50049. Web: www.dmdiocese.org/mass.htm.
Church: *c/o United Methodist Church of Corydon*, 213 W. Jackson St., 50060. Tel: 641-774-4978; Fax: 641-774-4978.
Catechesis/Religious Program—Tel: 712-328-7272. Classes held at Methodist Church.

COUNCIL BLUFFS, POTTAWATTAMIE CO.
1—CORPUS CHRISTI Revs. Daniel J. Kirby; Kenneth Halbur, Parochial Vicar; Thomas Coenen, Parochial Vicar; Deacons Darwin Kruse; Monty Montagne; Jean Plourde; Wilma Ernesti, Accountant/Bookkeeper.
Res.: 3304 4th Ave., 51501. Tel: 712-323-2916; Fax: 712-323-4716. Email: corpuschristi@cox.net. Web: www.corpuschristiparishiowa.org.
Worship Sites—
Our Lady, Queen of Apostles—3304 4th Ave., 51501.
Holy Family—2217 Ave. B, 51501.
Our Lady of Carter Lake—3501 N. 9th St., Carter Lake, 51510.
Catechesis/Religious Program—Jill Faust, Catechetical Leader; Catherine Jayjack, Catechetical Leader. Students 178.
2—HOLY FAMILY (1908) Merged with Our Lady, Queen of Apostles, Council Bluffs and Our Lady of Carter Lake, Carter Lake to form Corpus Christi, Council Bluffs.
3—OUR LADY, QUEEN OF APOSTLES (1957) Merged with Holy Family, Council Bluffs and Our Lady of Carter Lake, Carter Lake to form Corpus Christi, Council Bluffs.
4—ST. PATRICK (1924) Rev. David Fleming; Deacons Charles Hannan; James Mason; Emmet Tinley.
Res.: 223 Harmony St., 51503. Tel: 712-323-1484; Fax: 712-328-7595. Web: www.saintpatschurch.org.
Catechesis/Religious Program—LuAnn Baumker, D.R.E. Students 141.
Saint Patrick Church of Council Bluffs Iowa Foundation—
5—ST. PETER (1887), (German), Rev. Charles Kottas; Deacons Stephen Rallis; Dennis Kirlin; Dolores Kral, Business Mgr.
Res.: One Bluff St., 51503. Tel: 712-322-8889; Fax: 712-323-8267. Email: ckottas@aol.com. Web: www.dmdiocese.org/mass.htm.
Catechesis/Religious Program—Jennifer Hundtofte, D.R.E.; Jean Thomas, Youth Min. Students 138.
St. Francis Worship Center—238 6th St., 51501. Tel: 712-328-7272.

CRESTON, UNION CO., HOLY SPIRIT (1975) Rev. Joseph Pins.
Res. & Mailing Address: 406 W. Clark St., 50801. Tel: 641-782-5278; Fax: 641-782-7628. Email: holyspiritst.edward@iowatelecom.net.
Church: 107 W. Howard St., 50801. Also serving the parish of St. Edward, Afton.
School—St. Malachy, (Grades PreK-8), 403 W. Clark, 50801. Fax: 641-782-7125; 641-782-5924. John Walsh, Prin. Lay Teachers 15; Students 184.
Catechesis/Religious Program—Barb Hudson, D.R.E.; June Huewe, Liturgy Coord. Students 57.
St. Malachy School Foundation—

CUMBERLAND, CASS CO., ST. TIMOTHY (Reno) (1883) Rev. Robert J. Dufford, S.J.
Mailing Address: 106 W. 6th St., Atlantic, 50022.
Church: 69488 Wichita Rd., 50843. Tel: 712-243-4721. Email: pacm@netins.net. Web: www.dmdiocese.org/mass.htm.
Catechesis/Religious Program—Bonnie Boswell, Catechetical Leader. Students 16.

DEFIANCE, SHELBY CO., ST. PETER (1882), Served from Earling. Rev. Chris Fontanini; Nancy Schaben, Business Mgr.
Res.: 501 Fifth St., P.O. Box 127, 51527. Tel: 712-748-3501; Fax: 712-748-3500. Email: stpeters@netins.net. Web: www.dmdiocese.org.
Catechesis/Religious Program—Tel: 712-748-3602. Emily Sonderman, Catechetical Leader; Diane Mulligan, Liturgy Coord. Students 39.

DUNLAP, HARRISON CO., ST. PATRICK Rev. Felix A. Onuora, C.S.Sp.; Deacons Marvin Klein; Gail Stressman; Marilyn Grote, Liturgy Coord.
Res.: 509 S. 3rd St., 51529. Tel: 712-643-5808. Email: dwchurch@iowatelecom.net. Web: www.dmdiocese.org.
Catechesis/Religious Program—2005 Beech Rd., 51529. Tel: 712-643-2222. Betty J. Kimmen, Catechetical Leader. Students 88.

EARLING, SHELBY CO., ST. JOSEPH (1882), (German), Rev. Chris Fontanini; Elaine Kramer, Business Mgr.
Res.: 212 2nd St., P.O. Box 225, 51530-0225. Tel: 712-747-2091; Fax: 712-747-9501. Email: stjoseph@fmctc.com. Web: www.dmdiocese.org/mass.htm.
See Shelby County Board of Catholic Education, Panama under Education Centers located in the Institution section.
Catechesis/Religious Program—Joanie Erlbacher, Catechetical Leader. Students 49.

ELKHART, POLK CO., ST. MARY/HOLY CROSS (1885) Rev. Daniel F. Krettek; Deacon Jerry Barnwell; Peter Relyea, Accountant/Bookkeeper.
St. Mary—Res.: 214 N. Washington Ave., P.O. Box 110, 50073. Tel: 515-367-2685; Fax: 515-367-2685.
Holy Cross—Church: 12704 N.E. 98th St., Maxwell, 50161.
Catechesis/Religious Program—Melissa Kahler, Youth Min.; Angelina Willard, Catechetical Leader. Students 211.

EXIRA, AUDUBON CO., HOLY TRINITY, Attended by St. Patrick. Rev. Emmanuel S. Agwuoke, C.S.Sp., Admin.; Larry Beckendorf, Accountant/Bookkeeper.
Mailing Address: 116 E. Division St., Audubon, 50025.
Church & Res.: 208 Kilworth St. N., 50076. Tel: 712-563-2283; Fax: 712-268-3238. Email: spht@metc.net. Web: www.holytrinityexira.parishesonline.com.
Catechesis/Religious Program—Judy Bintner, Catechetical Leader. Students 10.

GLENWOOD, MILLS CO., OUR LADY OF THE HOLY ROSARY (1955) Rev. Howard E. Fitzgerald; Deacon Ronald Kohn; Jane Buckley, Accountant/Bookkeeper.
Res.: 24116 Marian Ave., 51534-5291. Tel: 712-527-5211; Fax: 712-527-3829. Email: holyrosary@aol.com. Web: www.ourladyoftheholyrosaryglenwood.parishesonline.com.
Catechesis/Religious Program—Fax: 712-527-3829. Theresa Romens, D.R.E. Students 243.

GRAND RIVER, DECATUR CO., ST. PATRICK, Served from St. Bernard, Osceola Rev. Glen Wilwerding; Mary Rita Van Valkenburg, Business Mgr.
Mailing Address: 222 E. Pearl St., Osceola, 50213. Tel: 641-342-2850. Web: www.dmdiocese.org.
Res.: 460 Wabonsy St., 50108. Tel: 641-342-2850. Web: www.dmdiocese.org.
Catechesis/Religious Program— Twinned with St. Bernard, Osceola.

GRANGER, DALLAS CO., ASSUMPTION OF THE BLESSED VIRGIN MARY (1871) Rev. Remigius C. Okere, C.S.Sp.; Deacons Daniel McGuire, Pastoral Min.; Gregg Erickson; Cathy Moellenbeck, Music Min.; Vacant, Business Mgr., Accountant/Bookkeeper.
1906 Sycamore, P.O. Box 159, 50109. Tel: 515-999-2239; Fax: 515-999-2208. Email: assumptionp@mchsi.com. Web: www.parishesonline.com/assumption.
School—(Grades PreK-8), 1904 Sycamore, P.O. Box 100, 50109. Tel: 515-999-2211. Herb Hartman, Prin. Lay Teachers 11; Students 71.
Catechesis/Religious Program—Cathy Davidson, D.R.E. Students 280.

GREENFIELD, ADAIR CO., ST. JOHN (1907) Rev. Kenneth A. Gross; Deacon Eugene Krawczyk.
Res.: 303 N.E. Elm St., 50849. Tel: 515-343-7065. Web: www.dmdiocese.org.
Catechesis/Religious Program—Tel: 515-343-7065. Renee Schwartz, D.R.E. Students 88.

GRISWOLD, CASS CO., OUR LADY OF GRACE (1911) Rev. Robert J. Dufford, S.J.
Mailing Address: 106 W. 6th St., Atlantic, 50022. Tel: 712-243-4721. Email: jennifer.renz@yahoo.com; rdufford@creighton.edu. Web: www.dmdiocese.org/mass.htm.
Res.: 203 Adair, 51535.
Catechesis/Religious Program—

GUTHRIE CENTER, GUTHRIE CO., ST. MARY (1906) [JC] Rev. Michael G. Peters; Deacons Richard Ziller; Hans Seeman.
Res.: 603 Main St., 50115. Tel: 515-747-2569; Fax: 641-747-3843. Email: stmstc@netins.net. Web: www.showcase.netins.net/web/pgcatholic.
Catechesis/Religious Program—Cynthia Ahrens, D.R.E. Students 48.

HAMBURG, FREMONT CO., ST. MARY (1874) Attended by St. Mary, Shenandoah. Rev. Vernon Smith; Anne Hendrickson, Accountant/Bookkeeper.
1306 Washington St., 51640. Tel: 712-382-2871. Web: www.stmaryparishhamburg.pa. Mailing Address: P.O. Box 67, 51640.
Catechesis/Religious Program—Monica Whitehead, D.R.E. Students 48.

HARLAN, SHELBY CO., ST. MICHAEL (1888) Rev. John M. Frost; Deacons Patrick Davitt; James DeBlauw; John Rosman, Liturgy Coord.
Mailing Address: 1912 18th St., 51537.
Church & Res.: 2001 College Pl., 51537. Tel: 712-755-5244. Web: www.stmichaelparish.com/.
School—(Grades PreK-8), 2005 College Pl., 51537. Tel: 712-755-5634. Mrs. Ann Anderson, Prin. Lay

Teachers 14; Students 156.
See Shelby County Board of Catholic Education, Panama under Education Centers located in the Institution section.
Catechesis/Religious Program—Tel: 712-755-5366. Charlotte Willenborg, D.R.E. Students 288.
St. Michael Parish Foundation—

IMOGENE, FREMONT CO., ST. PATRICK (1880), (Irish), Rev. Thomas Kunnel, T.O.R.; Annie Van Houten, Liturgy Coord.
Res. & Mailing Address: 304 Third St., 51645. Tel: 712-386-2277. Web: www.rc.net/desmoines/stpatrick.
Catechesis/Religious Program—Tel: 712-386-2239. Vicki Kelly, Catechetical Leader. Students 76.

INDIANOLA, WARREN CO., ST. THOMAS AQUINAS (1958) Rev. Raymond McHenry; Steph Binter, Business Mgr.; Connie Brommel, Accountant/Bookkeeper.
Res.: 1202 W. Iowa Ave., 50125. Tel: 515-961-3026; Fax: 515-961-3458. Web: www.stthomasindianola.com.
Catechesis/Religious Program—Tel: 515-961-3458. Heidi Klodd, Catechetical Leader. Students 279.

IRISH SETTLEMENT, MADISON CO., ST. PATRICK (1852) Rev. Christopher Hartshorn.
Mailing Address: 1026 N. 8th St., Winterset, 50273. Tel: 515-462-1083. Web: www.dmdiocese.org.
Church: 3396 155th St., Cumming, 50061.
Catechesis/Religious Program—3183 155th St., Cumming, 50061. Tel: 515-981-4686. Virginia Darr, D.R.E.; Drew Dinsmore, Youth Min.

JAMAICA, GUTHRIE CO., ST. JOSEPH (1903) Closed. For inquiries for parish records contact the chancery.

LACONA, WARREN CO., HOLY TRINITY CHURCH OF SOUTHEAST WARREN COUNTY (1978) Rev. Dean Nimerichter; Connie Brommel, Bookkeeper/ Accountant.
Mailing Address: 101 Saint James St., 50139-0145.
Res.: 304 N. Washington Ave., P.O. Box 145, 50139-0145. Tel: 641-534-4691; Fax: 641-534-4691. Email: immacula@netins.net. Web: www.dmdiocese.org/mass.htm.
Worship Centers—
St. Mary of the Assumption Church: 50139. Tel: 641-534-4691.
St. Augustine Church: Milo, 50166.
Catechesis/Religious Program—Amy Welch, Catechetical Leader. Students 24.

LENOX, TAYLOR CO., ST. PATRICK (1872) Attended by St. Patrick, Corning. Rev. Lazarus Kirigia, Admin.
Church: 600 W. Michigan, 50851. Tel: 641-336-2893. Web: www.dmdiocese.org/mass.htm.
Catechesis/Religious Program—1041 130th St., Diagonal, 50845. Tel: 641-336-2893. Kathy Ecklin, Catechetical Leader. Students 35.

LEON, DECATUR CO., ST. BRENDAN (1856), (Irish), Rev. Christopher Pisut; Deacon Reinhold Kunze.
Res.: 1001 N.W. Church St., 50144. Tel: 515-446-4789; Fax: 641-446-8110. Email: southch3@grm.net. Web: www.dmdiocese.org.
Catechesis/Religious Program—Sara Lefleur, Youth Min. Students 51.

LOGAN, HARRISON CO., ST. ANNE (1920) Rev. Michael Berner; Deacon Dennis Lovell; Judy Pinkel, Accountant/Bookkeeper; Kathy Lovell, Liturgy Coord.
Res.: 112 W. 3rd St., 51546. Tel: 712-644-2535; Fax: 712-644-2535. Email: stanne@iowatelecom.net. Web: www.dmdiocese.org.
Catechesis/Religious Program—Joe Esser, D.R.E.; Becky Loftus, Youth Min. Students 82.

MALOY, RINGGOLD CO., IMMACULATE CONCEPTION (1874) [CEM] Closed. For inquiries for parish records contact the chancery.

MASSENA, CASS CO., ST. PATRICK (1888), Served from Greenfield. Rev. Kenneth A. Gross; Deacon Eugene Krawczyk; Julie Symonds, Liturgy Coord.; Peg Hemsley, Account/bookkeeper.
Res.: 503 Main St., 50853. Tel: 712-779-3397; Fax: 712-779-3397. Email: stjohns@iowatele.com.net.
Catechesis/Religious Program—Theresa Hensley, Catechetical Leader. Students 39.

MISSOURI VALLEY, HARRISON CO., ST. PATRICK (1877) Rev. Michael Berner; Deacon Mike Woltanski; Beverly Kragskrow, Accountant/Bookkeeper.
Res.: 215 N. Seventh St., 51555. Tel: 712-642-2611; Fax: 712-642-2518. Email: stpatsch@loganet.net. Web: www.dmdiocese.org.
Catechesis/Religious Program—Annette Lorenzen, D.R.E. Students 77.

MONDAMIN, HARRISON CO., HOLY FAMILY (1970) Attended by St. Patrick. Rev. Felix A. Onuora, C.S.Sp.; Deacon James Herman; Loene Herman, Liturgy Coord.; JoAnn Hodgson, Music Coord.; Susan Maule, Accountant/Bookkeeper.
Mailing Address: 509 S. 3rd St., Dunlap, 51529.
Church: 307 Mulberry, 51557. Tel: 712-644-2535. Email: pesser@iowatelecom.net. Web: www.dmdiocese.org/mass.htm.
Catechesis/Religious Program—*St. Anne*, 104 W. 3rd St., Logan, 51546. Tel: 712-644-2520. Christine Hussing, D.R.E.

MT. AYR, RINGGOLD CO., ST. JOSEPH (1913) Attended by St. Bernard, Osceola Rev. Glen Wilwerding; Mary Rita Van Valkenburg, Business Mgr.
Mailing Address: 222 E. Pearl St., Osceola, 50213.
Church: 100 N. Polk, 50854. Tel: 515-446-4789; Fax: 641-446-8110. Web: www.dmdiocese.org.
Catechesis/Religious Program—Marcia Showalter, Catechetical Leader.

NEOLA, POTTAWATTAMIE CO., ST. PATRICK (1882) Rev. Raphael Masabakhwa; Sr. Rosie Restelli, C.H.M, Pastoral Min.; RaeShelle Jensen, Business Mgr.
Res.: 308 4th St., P.O. Box 127, 51559. Tel: 712-485-2124; Fax: 712-485-2124. Email: stpats@novia.net. Web: www.dmdiocese.org/mass.htm.
Catechesis/Religious Program—Amy Ausdemore, Catechetical Leader; Bernadette Koch, Catechetical Leader. Students 235.
Saint Patrick Foundation—

NORWALK, WARREN CO., ST. JOHN THE APOSTLE CHURCH (1892) Rev. John P. Ludwig; Deacon David Miller; Michele Miller, Music Coord.; Timothy Mineart, Business Mgr.; Kathleen Ballard, Accountant/Bookkeeper.
Res.: 720 Orchard St., 50211. Tel: 515-981-4855; Fax: 515-981-9475. Email: stjohns@stjohnsnorwalk.org. Web: www.stjohnsnorwalk.org.
Catechesis/Religious Program—Sharon Ewell, D.R.E. Students 136.

ORIENT, ADAIR CO., ST. MARK, Closed. For inquiries for parish records contact the chancery.

OSCEOLA, CLARKE CO., ST. BERNARD (1885) Rev. Glen Wilwerding.
Res.: 222 E. Pearl, 50213. Tel: 641-342-2850; Fax: 641-342-2850. Email: stbernar@pionet.net. Web: www.dmdiocese.org.
Catechesis/Religious Program—530 N. Fillmore, 50213. Nicki Smith, D.R.E. Students 93.

PANAMA, SHELBY CO., ST. MARY OF THE ASSUMPTION (1899) Rev. John Dorton.
Res.: 104 N. 2nd St., 51562.
See Shelby County Board of Catholic Education, Panama under Education Centers located in the Institution section.
Catechesis/Religious Program—P.O. Box 209, 51562. Tel: 712-489-2504. Eileen Schwery, Catechetical Leader; Keith Schwery, Catechetical Leader. Students 40.
St. Mary Parish Religious Education Foundation—

PANORA, GUTHRIE CO., ST. CECILIA (1907) [JC] Attended by St. Mary, Guthrie Center Tel: 515-747-2569. Rev. Michael G. Peters; Deacon Richard Ziller; Marsha Richter, Accountant/Bookkeeper.
Mailing Address: 603 Main St., Guthrie Center, 50115. Tel: 641-747-2569; Fax: 641-747-3843. Email: stmstc@netins.net. Web: www.showcase.netins.net/web/pages.
Church: 221 N. First St., 50216.
Catechesis/Religious Program—Students 77.

PERRY, DALLAS CO., ST. PATRICK (1881) Rev. David J. Polich; Robin Smith, Business Mgr.
Res.: 1312 3rd St., 50220. Tel: 515-465-4387; Fax: 515-465-4387. Email: stpatsperry@iowatelecom.net. Web: www.dmdiocese.org.
School—(Grades PreSchool-8), 1302 5th St., 50220. Tel: 515-465-4186; Fax: 515-465-9808. Tonya Eaton, Prin. Lay Teachers 14; Students 131.
Catechesis/Religious Program—Barbara Wolter, D.R.E.; Aaron Weddle, Youth Min. Students 162.

PORTSMOUTH, SHELBY CO., ST. MARY (1885) Rev. John Dorton.
Res.: 412 Fourth St., P.O. Box 98, 51565. Tel: 712-743-2625; Fax: 712-743-2625. Email: hankhu@iowatelecom.net. Web: www.dmdiocese.org.
Catechesis/Religious Program—Henrietta (Hank) Hughes, Catechetical Leader. Students 69.

RED OAK, MONTGOMERY CO., ST. MARY (1902) Rev. Thomas Kunnel, T.O.R.
Res.: 1510 Highland Ave., 51566. Tel: 712-623-2744. Email: stmarysredoak@msn.com. Web: www.stmaryredoak.parishesonline.com.
Catechesis/Religious Program—Cindee Hays, Catechetical Leader, Youth Min. Students 123.

ST. MARYS, WARREN CO., IMMACULATE CONCEPTION (1871) Rev. Raymond McHenry; Suzanne Stills, Liturgy Coord.; Connie Brommel, Business Mgr.
Res.: 101 St. James, P.O. Box 88, 50241. Tel: 641-297-2267. Email: immacula@netins.net. Web: www.dmdiocese.org.
Catechesis/Religious Program—220 Iowa St., P.O. Box 113, Saint Marys, 50241. Michelle Fick, Catechetical Leader. Students 105.

SHENANDOAH, PAGE CO., ST. MARY Rev. Vernon Smith; Bruce Baldwin, Accountant & Bookkeeper; Jane Emge, Music Min.; Tara Menke, Business Mgr.
Mailing Address: 512 W. Thomas Ave., 51601. Tel: 712-246-1718; Fax: 712-246-1776. Email: stmarys@heartland.net. Web: www.dmdiocese.org.
Catechesis/Religious Program—Lynda Marshall, Catechetical Leader. Students 64.

STUART, GUTHRIE CO., ALL SAINTS (1876) Rev. Raymond Higgins; Rita Rilea, Accountant/Bookkeeper.
Res.: 216 All Saints Dr., P.O. Box 605, 50250. Tel: 515-523-1943; Fax: 515-523-1954. Email: stuartsaints@netins.net.
Catechesis/Religious Program—Tel: 515-523-1943. Ginger Peterson, Catechetical Leader. Students 110.

URBANDALE, POLK CO., ST. PIUS X (1955) Rev. Msgr. Joseph McDonnell; Rev. John Harmon, Parochial Vicar; Deacons Dave Bartemes; Rick Condon; James Houston; Eric Webster, Music Coord., Liturgy Coord.; William Duff, Business Mgr.
Mailing Address: 3663 66th St., 50322. Tel: 515-276-2059; Fax: 515-276-8351. Email: vferin@dowling.pvt.k12.ia.us. Web: www.stpiusx-urbandale.e-paluch.com.
School—(Grades PreK-8), 3601 66th St., 50322. Tel: 515-276-1061; Fax: 515-276-0350. Lawrence Zahm, Prin. Lay Teachers 31; Students 370.
Catechesis/Religious Program—Tel: 515-278-5684. Mary Heinrich, D.R.E.; Sherri Hunt, D.R.E.; Barb Mease, Youth Min.; Suzanne Crowley, Catechetical Leader. Students 371.
St. Pius X Parish Foundation—

VILLISCA, MONTGOMERY CO., ST. JOSEPH (1947) Attended by St. Clare, Clarinda. Rev. Joy Vincent Thaiparambil.
Mailing Address: 300 E. Lincoln Blvd., Clarinda, 51632. Tel: 712-542-2030. Web: www.dmdiocese.org/mass.htm.
Church: 131 W. High St., 50864.
Catechesis/Religious Program—

WALNUT, POTTAWATTAMIE CO., ST. PATRICK (1882) Attended by St. Mary, Mediatrix of All Graces, Avoca. Rev. Thomas V. Dooley; Donna Muell, Liturgy Coord.; Ellen Holtz, Liturgy Coord.; Barb Butcher, Accountant/Bookkeeper.
Mailing Address: c/o 109 N. Maple St., P.O. Box 38, Avoca, 51521-0038. Tel: 712-343-6948. Email: smpavoca@walnutel.net. Web: www.stmaryavoca.tripod.com.
Church & Res.: 718 Antique City Dr., 51577.
Catechesis/Religious Program—Gwen Blum, Catechetical Leader; Julie Gross, Youth Min.

WAUKEE, DALLAS CO., ST. BONIFACE (1880) Rev. Vince G. Rosonke; Linda Henson, Business Mgr., Accountant & Bookkeeper; Deb Purcell, Business Mgr.; Donna Dressel, Pastoral Min.
Res.: 1200 Warrior Ln., 50263-9587. Tel: 515-987-4597; Fax: 515-987-5272. Email: office@saintbonifacechurch.org. Web: www.dmdiocese.org.
Catechesis/Religious Program—Sue Peterson, D.R.E.; Steve Dressel, Adult Faith Formation, Catechetical Leader & Music Min.; T. J. Irvin, Youth Min.; Gloria Day-Dally, Youth Min. Students 922.

WEST DES MOINES, POLK CO.

1—ST. FRANCIS OF ASSISI (1991) Revs. Robert Hoefler; George Komo, Parochial Vicar; Deacons David O'Brien; William Richer; Lori Lyons, Accountant & Bookkeeper; Thomas Nolan, Business Mgr.
Mailing Address: 7075 Ashworth Rd., 50266. Tel: 515-223-4577; Fax: 515-223-4768. Email: info@saintfrancischurch.org. Web: www.saintfrancischurch.org.
School—Tel: 515-457-7167. Mrs. Misty Hade, Prin. Sisters 1; Lay Teachers 44; Students 669.
Catechesis/Religious Program—Mary Green, D.R.E.; Deb Ryan, D.R.E.; Jade Wadding, D.R.E.; Jeanne Mullenbach, Youth Min. Students 840.

2—SACRED HEART (1892) Revs. Michael N. Hess; Paul Cuong Hung Nguyen, S.V.D., Parochial Vicar; Deacons Ron Myers; Randy Horn; Sheila Hancock, Music Coord.; Barbara Harkin, Business Mgr.; Josie O'Halloran, Accountant/Bookkeeper.
Mailing Address: 1627 Grand Ave., 50265. Tel: 515-225-6414; Fax: 515-225-0286. Email: pbaliff@dowling.pvt.k12.ia.us. Web: www.sacredheartwdm.org/.
School—(Grades PreK-8), 1601 Grand Ave., 50265. Tel: 515-223-1284; Fax: 515-223-9413. Frank Vito, Prin.; Tiffany Bayless, Librarian. Lay Teachers 30; Students 491.
Catechesis/Religious Program—Tel: 515-225-1641. Kayla Richer, D.R.E.; Deb Chalik, D.R.E., Coord.; Rebra Lane, Youth Min. Students 530.
Sacred Heart School Foundation—

WESTON, POTTAWATTAMIE CO., ST. COLUMBANUS (1883) Attended by St. Patrick, Neola. Rev. Raphael Masabakhwa; RaeShelle Jensen, Business Mgr.; Jan Reineke, Accountant/Bookkeeper.
Mailing Address: P.O. Box 127, Neola, 51559. Tel: 712-485-2124. Web: www.dmdiocese.org.

Church: 22720 Weston Ave., Underwood, 51576.
Catechesis/Religious Program—23232 Magnolia Rd., Underwood, 51576. Tel: 712-566-2603. Bernadette Koch, D.R.E. Students 28.

WESTPHALIA, SHELBY CO., ST. BONIFACE (1873) Rev. John Dorton; Joan Schneider, Liturgy Coord.; Lorene Kaufmann, Business Mgr. & Music Coord. Church & Res.: 207 Duren Strasse, 51578. Tel: 712-627-4151; Fax: 712-627-4151. Email: stboniface@fmctc.com. Web: www.dmdiocese.org.
Catechesis/Religious Program—Cynthia Schechinger, Catechetical Leader; Jan Hastert, Catechetical Leader. Students 31.

WINTERSET, MADISON CO., ST. JOSEPH (1893) Rev. Christopher Hartshorn; Deacon Sam Sullivan; Victoria Williams, Accountant/Bookkeeper.
Res.: 607 W. Green St., 50273. Tel: 515-462-1083; Fax: 515-462-2378. Email: office@saintjosephchurch.net. Web: www.saintjosephchurch.net.
Catechesis/Religious Program—Teresa Hoffelmeyer, D.R.E.; Gerene Farrell, Youth Min.; Tiffany Bond, Youth Min. Students 195.

WOODBINE, HARRISON CO., SACRED HEART (1902) Attended by St. Patrick's, Dunlap. Rev. Felix A. Onuora, C.S.Sp.; Deacons Marvin Klein; Gail Stressman; Mary Weis, Liturgy Coord.; John Davie, Accountant/Bookkeeper; Christie Kenkel, Accountant/Bookkeeper.
Mailing Address: 509 S. 3rd St., Dunlap, 51529. Tel: 712-643-5115. Email: dwchurch@iowatelecom.net. Web: www.dmdiocese.org.
Church: 33 - 7th St., 51579.
Catechesis/Religious Program—710 Weare St., 51579. Tel: 712-647-3057. Andrea Harper, Youth Min. Students 79.

WOODWARD, DALLAS CO., ST. ANN (1934) Closed. For inquiries for parish records contact Assumption Church, Granger.

Chaplains of Public Institutions

DES MOINES. *Des Moines City Chaplaincy Program*, c/o P.O. Box 371, Dexter, 50070. Rev. Michael R. McLaughlin.
United States Veterans Hospital, 3600 30th St., 50310. Rev. Adolfo A. Aban, Chap.

CLARINDA. *State Hospital*. Served from St. Clare Church, Clarinda.

COUNCIL BLUFFS. *Iowa School for the Deaf*, 411 E. Broadway, 51503. Tel: 712-322-2449. Vacant.

GLENWOOD. *Glenwood State School*. Vacant.

MITCHELLVILLE. *Iowa Correctional Institution for Women*. Kay Kopatich, Chap. & Coord., Svcs. to Catholic Residents.

On Special Assignment:
Revs.—
Hutchins, Michael, S.V.D., Divine Word Farm, Weldon, IA
Kirby, Daniel J., Diocesan Dir. Seminarians
McLaughlin, Michael R., Des Moines City Chaplaincy
McNeil, Joel (AUS), Diocesan Dir. Campus Ministry

On Duty Outside the Diocese:
Revs.—
Chevalier, Martin, St. Joseph Medical Center, Kansas City, MO
Grant, Robert, St. Ambrose University, Davenport, 52803.

Retired:
Rev. Msgrs.—
Beeson, Lawrence A., J.C.D., 1390 Buffalo Rd., West Des Moines, 50265.
Chamberlain, Robert J., 3105 67th St., Urbandale, 50322.
Pfeffer, Edward B., J.C.L., 1390 Buffalo Rd., West Des Moines, 50265.
Stessman, Gerald, 1390 Buffalo Rd., West Des Moines, 50265.
Revs.—
Acrea, John, 2115 Summit Ave., Saint Paul, MN 55105.
Aiello, Anthony
Aubrey, Robert J., 3429 Belmar Dr., 50317.
Bergman, Richard, 1390 Buffalo Rd., West Des Moines, 50265.
Bruck, Donald, 1110 Elm St., Harlan, 51537.
Culver, Garry, 746 N. Waterway, Venice, FL 34285.
Fenelon, David, 934 Lincoln St., Waterloo, 50703.
Freeman, James, 207 N. Wilmont Rd., #429, Tucson, AZ 85711.
Gittons, Gordon, 5815 Winwood Dr., Johnston, 50131.
Kenkel, Benedict J., Elmcrest Retirement Community, 2108-12th St., Apt. 151, Harlan, 51537.
Kenkel, Leonard A., 1390 Buffalo Rd, West Des Moines, 50265.
Kiernan, James W., 1390 Buffalo Rd., West Des Moines, 50265.
Kleffman, James, 4624 Navajo St., #17, Council Bluffs, 51501.
Koch, Eugene R., 1390 Buffalo Rd., West Des Moines, 50265.
Koch, Paul M., 238 S. 6th St., Council Bluffs, 51501.
Laurenzo, James, 1205 Lewis, 50315.
Leto, Nelo A., 710 Davis, 50315.
Lorenz, John F., 1390 Buffalo Rd., West Des Moines, 50265.
Maier, John, 507 Spencer Pl., Leavenworth, KS 66048.
McCann, Arthur L., 1654 S.E. Holiday Crest Cir., Waukee, 50263.
Monahan, Paul, 238 S. 6th St., Council Bluffs, 51501.
Palmer, Frank S., 4460 - 88th St., Urbandale, 50322.
Reischl, Fred P., 3121 MacIneery Dr., Council Bluffs, 51501.
Schoemann, Robert L., 1390 Buffalo Rd., West Des Moines, 50265.
Sherbo, Albert, 811 - 3rd St., P.O. Box 508, Anita, 50020.

Permanent Deacons:
Ayers, John
Barnwell, Jerry, (Retired)
Bartemes, David
Blankenship, Joseph, (Retired)
Boehlert, Jeffrey
Bradley, Thomas
Bray, Robert, (Retired)
Brewer, Marvin
Chan, Francis
Coan, Joseph II, (Retired)
Condon, Rick
Cornwell, Fred
Cortese, Joseph
Davitt, Patrick, (Retired)
DeBlauw, James
Doyle, James, (Retired)
Erickson, Gregg
Garza, David, (Retired)
Gaul, Leo, (Retired)
Hannan, Charles
Hare, William
Heim, Kevin
Herman, James
Horn, Randy
Houston, James
Howe, Robert, (Retired)
Huynh, Joseph, (Retired)
Inman, Jack, (Retired)
Jacobi, Donald, (Retired)
Jager, Gene
Kehoe, Laurence
Kirkman, Patrick, (Retired)
Kirlin, Dennis, (Retired)
Klein, Marvin
Knotek, Lawrence, (Retired)
Kohn, Ronald
Krawczyk, Gene, (Retired)
Kruse, Darwin
Kunze, Reinhold
Lopez, Frank
Lovell, David, (Retired)
Lovell, Dennis
Luft, Dennis M.
Maiers, Richard, (Retired)
Maly, Thomas, (Retired)
Manno, Michael
Mason, James
McCarthy, Michael
McClellan, Robert
McGuire, Dan
Miller, Dave
Montagne, Monty
Myers, Ron
O'Brien, David
Obradovich, James
Pantaloni, Ed, (Retired)
Pins, Fred
Plourde, Jean
Putbrese, Charles
Rallis, Stephen
Reed, Steven
Richardson, Alan, (Retired)
Richer, William
Riley, Mike
Rohwer, Chris, (Retired)
Romeo, Tony, (Retired)
Schenk, Thomas
Schleisman, Terry
Scurlock, Joseph, (Retired)
Seeman, Hans
Starbuck, Tom
Stessman, Gail
Stessman, John, (Retired)
Sullivan, Robert, (Retired)
Sullivan, Sam
Thompson, Troy
Tieskoetter, Luke
Tinley, Emmet
Tong, Quan
Udelhofen, Steven
Wadle, David
Webering, James, (Retired)
Weisenhorn, Earl
Wolford, Charles
Woltanski, Mike
Yang, LyPao
Ziller, Richard

INSTITUTIONS LOCATED IN THE DIOCESE

[A] EDUCATION CENTERS

DES MOINES. *Holy Family School*, (Grades PreK-8), 1265 E. 9th St., 50316. Tel: 515-262-8025; Fax: 515-262-9665. Email: mflaherty@hfsdm.org. Web: hfsdm.org. Martin P. Flaherty, Prin.; Janet Holmes, Asst. Prin.; Traci Rogo, Librarian. Participating parishes: Our Lady of the Americas, Des Moines; Basilica of St. John, Des Moines; St. Ambrose Cathedral, Des Moines; All Saints, Des Moines; St. Peter, Des Moines. Lay Teachers 16; Students 242.

COUNCIL BLUFFS. *Council Bluffs Area Catholic Education Systems, Inc.*, 400 Gleason Ave., 51503. Tel: 712-329-9000; Fax: 712-328-0228. Web: www.saintalbertschools.org. Jonna Andersen, Prin. Priests 1; Lay Teachers 60; Total Staff 136; Total Enrollment (PreK-12) 701.
St. Albert Jr/Sr High School, 400 Gleason Ave., 51503. Tel: 712-328-2316; Fax: 712-328-8316. Jonna Andersen, Prin.; Donella Pauli, Librarian. Priests 1; Lay Teachers 30; Total Staff 39; Students 320.
St. Albert Elementary School (Grades PreK-6), 400 Gleason Ave., 51503. Tel: 712-323-3703; Fax: 712-323-6132. Anne Jensen, Prin.; Donella Pauli, Librarian. Lay Teachers 24; Students 456.

HARLAN. *Elementary School: Shelby County Catholic School*, (Grades PreK-8), 2005 College Pl., 51537. Tel: 712-755-5634; Fax: 712-755-3332. Email: aandersen@shelcocath.pvt.k12.ia.us. Web: www.shelcocath.pvt.k12.ia.us. Rev. John M. Frost, Canonical Admin.; Ann Andersen, Prin.; Marilyn Fox, Librarian. Lay Teachers 14; Total Staff 25; Students 156.

WEST DES MOINES. *St. Joseph Educational Center*, 1400 Buffalo Rd., 50265. Tel: 515-225-3000; Fax: 515-222-1056. Web: stjosepheducationalcenter.org. Dr. Thomas Neal, Dir.
Religious Education Tel: 515-222-1084.

[B] COLLEGES AND UNIVERSITIES

DES MOINES. *Mercy College of Health Sciences* (1995) 928-6th Ave., 50309-1239. Tel: 515-643-3180; Fax: 515-643-6698. Email: admissions@mchs.edu. Web: www.mchs.edu. Barbara Q. Decker, Pres.; Brian Tingleff, B.A., Vice Pres. External Affairs; Eileen Hansen, M.A., Dir., Librarian & Media Svcs.; Shirley Beaver, Dean of Nursing; Jeannine Matz, Assoc. Dean of Liberal Arts & Sciences; Theresa Smith, Assoc. Dean of Allied Health; Joan McCleish, Dean of Research, Assessment & Grants; Steven Langdon, Interim Vice Pres. Academic Affairs; Thomas Leahy, Vice Pres. Business & Regulatory Affairs. Member of Mercy Health Network; Sponsored by Catholic Health Initiatives. Lay Teachers 52; Total Staff 106; Students 832.

[C] HIGH SCHOOLS, INTERPAROCHIAL

COUNCIL BLUFFS. *Saint Albert Catholic Schools*, 400 Gleason Ave., 51503. Tel: 712-329-9000; Fax: 712-328-0228. Email: rousej@saintalbertschools.org. Web: www.saintalbertschools.org. Jonna Andersen, Prin. (7-12); Anne Jensen, Prin. (PreK-6); James W. Rouse, Pres.; Revs. George Komo; Kenneth Halbur, Chap. Serving all parishes in Council Bluffs; St. Patrick, Missouri Valley; St. Patrick, Neola; Holy Rosary, Glenwood; St. Columbanus, Weston. Priests 1; Lay Teachers 60; Total Staff 136; Students 701.

WEST DES MOINES. *Dowling Catholic High School*, 1400 Buffalo Rd., 50265. Tel: 515-225-3000; Fax: 515-222-1056. Email: Jdeegan@dowlingcatholic.org. Web: www.dowlingcatholic.org. Dr. Jerry Deegan, Pres.; Dr. James Dowdle, Prin.; Carol Aina, Registrar;

Rev. Zachary Kautzky, Chap. Serving all parishes in Des Moines; Sacred Heart, West Des Moines; St. Francis of Assisi, West Des Moines; St. Boniface, Waukee; Assumption, Granger; St. John, Cumming; St. Mary, Elkhart; Holy Cross, Elkhart; SS. John and Paul, Altoona; Immaculate Heart, Ankeny. Priests 1; Lay Teachers 90; Students 1,450.

[D] GENERAL HOSPITALS

DES MOINES. *Mercy Medical Center*, 1111 Sixth Ave., 50314-2611. Tel: 515-247-3121; Fax: 515-247-4259. Web: www.mercydesmoines.org. Dave Vellinga, Pres. & CEO; Rev. Anthony Adibe, C.S.Sp. Catholic Health Initiatives Denver, CO. Patients Assisted Annually 1,371,978; Bed Capacity 802; Total Staff 6,600.

Mercy Clinics, Inc.
Mercy Court
Mercy College of Health Sciences
Mercy Foundation
Mercy Foundation of Des Moines dba Mercy Foundation, Bishop Drumm Retirement Center, Mercy Hospice-Johnston
Mercy Hospice and Home Care
Mercy Park Apartments
Mercy Professional Practice Associates
Clark Street House of Mercy
Graduate Medical Education

CORNING. *Alegent Health Mercy Hospital*, 603 Rosary Dr., 50841. Tel: 641-322-3121; Fax: 651-322-4872. Debra Goldsmith, Admin.; Rev. Lazarus Kirigia, Chap. Inpatients 309; Outpatients 27,178; Bed Capacity 22; Staff 142.

COUNCIL BLUFFS. *Alegent Health: Mercy Hospital*, 800 Mercy Dr., 51503. Tel: 712-328-5000; Fax: 712-325-2432. Web: www.alegent.org. Dorothy Lawson, Chap. Bed Capacity 284; Patients Assisted Annually 30,176.

[E] HOMES FOR AGED

JOHNSTON. *Bishop Drumm Retirement Center* (1939) 5837 Winwood Dr., 50131-1651. Tel: 515-270-1100; Fax: 515-276-1714. Mr. Brian E. Farrell, Pres. & CEO; Mrs. Heather Rehmer, Admin. (Affiliate of Catholic Health Initiatives, Mercy Health Network & Mercy Medical Center-Des Moines). Sisters of Mercy of the Americas (Omaha Province) 1; Congregation of the Humility of Mary Sisters 14; Care Center Residents 150; Bed Capacity 289; Total Staff 425; Total Assisted Annually 235. In Res. Rev. Thomas M. DeCarlo, Resident Chap.

McAuley Terrace Apts. (1981) 5921 Winwood Dr., 50131-1670. Tel: 515-270-6640; Fax: 515-331-8875. Sandra Dzankovic, Mgr. Apartment Residents 75.

Martina Place Assisted Living Residence (1997) 5815 Winwood Dr., 50131-1666. Tel: 515-251-7999; Fax: 515-331-8860. Mrs. Sharon Brown, Mgr. Assisted Living Residents 64.

[F] SPECIAL CARE FACILITIES

DES MOINES. *House of Mercy*, 1409 Clark St., 50314-1964. Tel: 515-643-6500; Fax: 515-643-6598. Email: tbeveridge@mercydesmoines.org. Web: houseofmercydesmoines.org. Mr. Todd Beveridge, Dir.

[G] SECULAR INSTITUTES

DES MOINES. *Institute of the Heart of Jesus* (1791) P.O. Box 4634, 50305-4634. Tel: 515-222-1089; Fax: 515-222-1056. Email: fatherjfl1@aol.com. Web: www.secularinstitutes.org. Rev. John F. Lorenz (Retired). Secular Priests and Lay People.

[H] SPIRITUAL MINISTRY TO THE DIOCESE

DES MOINES. *Emmaus House*, 1521 Center St., 50314. Tel: 515-282-4839. Email: emmaus_house@yahoo.com. Rev. Daniel F. Krettek, Co-Dir.; Sr. Joyanne Mueller, O.S.F., Co-Dir.

[I] NEWMAN CENTERS

DES MOINES. *St. Catherine of Siena Catholic Student Center* , (Drake Newman Community), 1150-28th St., 50311-4142. Tel: 515-271-4747; Fax: 515-271-1918. Email: saint.catherine@drake.edu. Rev. Joel McNeil (AUS). Students 360; Non-Students 90.

[J] MISCELLANEOUS LISTINGS

DES MOINES. *Bishop's Endowment Fund Foundation*, 601 Grand Ave., 50309.

Catholic Tuition Organization, Diocese of Des Moines, 601 Grand Ave., 50309. Tel: 515-237-5010; Fax: 515-237-5070. Email: jwells@dmdiocese.org. Jeanne Wells, Exec. Dir.

Dowling-St. Joseph Alumni Association Investment Co. L.L.C., 1400 Buffalo Rd., West Des Moines, 50265. Tel: 515-225-3000; Fax: 515-222-1056. Email: jdeegan@dowlingcatholic.org. Web: www.dowlingcatholic.org. Dr. Jerry Deegan, Mgr.

Dowling-St. Joseph Alumni Foundation, 1400 Buffalo Rd., West Des Moines, 50265. Tel: 515-225-3000; Fax: 515-222-1056. Email: jdeegan@dowlingcatholic.org. Web: www.dowlingcatholic.org. John Campbell, Pres.; Dr. Jerry Deegan, Sec.

Endowment for Educational Excellence, 601 Grand Ave., 50309. Most Rev. Richard Pates; Rev. Christopher Hartshorn, Dir.; Sr. Jude Fitzpatrick, C.H.M., Dir.

Holy Family School Inner-City Youth Foundation, P.O. Box 8437, 50301. Tel: 515-262-7466; Fax: 515-263-8172. Email: hfsfoundation@qwest.net. Web: www.hfsdm.org. Suzanne Farley, Foundation Admin.

Iowa Catholic Conference, 530-42nd St., 50312-2707. Tel: 515-243-6256; Fax: 515-243-6257. Email: info@iowacatholicconference.org. Thomas Chapman, Exec. Dir.

Larry Breheny Endowment Fund, 601 Grand Ave., 50309. Most Rev. Richard Pates; Sr. Jude Fitzpatrick, C.H.M., Chancellor; Nancy Galeazzi, Dir.

Life in the Spirit Community, Inc., 5419 S.E. 32nd St., 50320. Tel: 515-287-4480. Eric Zingler, Contact Person.

Mercy Child Development Center, 6th & University, 50314. Tel: 515-243-6232. Diane Engelking, Dir.

Mercy Foundation of Des Moines - Affiliate of Catholic Health Initiatives, 1111 6th Ave., 50314. Tel: 515-247-3248. Shannon Duval, Pres.

National Catholic Rural Life Conference (1923) 4625 Beaver Ave., 50310-2145. Tel: 515-270-2634; Fax: 515-270-9447. Email: info@ncrlc.com. Web: www.ncrlc.com. Most Rev. Frank J. Dewane (VEN), Pres., (Bishop of Venice, FL); James F. Ennis, Dir.

Roman Catholic Pastoral Center Foundation, 601 Grand Ave., 50309. Tel: 515-237-5044; Fax: 515-237-5070. Email: finance@dmdiocese.org. Web: www.dmdiocese.org. Most Rev. Richard Pates; Rev. Christopher Hartshorn, Vicar Gen.

Roman Catholic Priests' Medical Fund Foundation, 601 Grand Ave., 50309.

Roman Catholic Seminary Fund Foundation, 601 Grand Ave., 50309. Most Rev. Richard Pates, Contact Person.

Society of Saint Vincent de Paul, 1426 6th Ave., 50314. Tel: 515-282-8327. Tom Varilek, Pres.

COUNCIL BLUFFS. *St. Albert Educational Foundation*, 400 Gleason Ave., 51503. Tel: 712-329-9000, Ext. 339; Fax: 712-328-0228. Email: kochj@saintalbertschools.org. Web: www.saintalbertschools.org.

Alegent Health Foundation - Mercy Hospital, 800 Mercy Dr., 51503. Tel: 712-328-5372; Fax: 712-325-2425. Matthew Gronstal, Pres.

St. Joseph Catholic Cemetery Association, 17510 Sunnydale Rd., 51503. Tel: 712-322-7963. John E. O'Connor, Mgr.

GRISWOLD. *Creighton University Retreat Center* (1967) 16493 Contrail Ave., 51535. Tel: 712-778-2466; Fax: 712-778-2467. Email: curc@netins.net. Web: www.creighton.edu/CURC/. Revs. David L. Smith, S.J., Dir. & Contact Person; William F. Gerut, S.J., Retreat/Pastoral Ministry.

HARLAN. *Shelby County Catholic Education Foundation*, 2005 College Pl., 51537. Tel: 712-755-5634; Fax: 712-755-3332. Email: aanderse@shelcocath.pvt.k12.ia.us. Web: shelcocath.pvt.k12.ia.us. Mrs. Ann Anderson, Admin.

JOHNSTON. *Bishop Drumm Development Office*, 5921 Winwood Dr., Ste. 1, 50131. Tel: 515-331-8890; Fax: 515-331-8875. Email: afletcher@mercydesmoines.org. Amanda Fletcher. A division of Mercy Foundation - Affiliate of Catholic Health Initiatives and Mercy Health Network.

PANORA. *St. Thomas More Center*, 6177 Panorama Rd., 50216. Tel: 515-309-1936; Fax: 515-309-1885. Email: office@stmcenter.com. Web: www.stmcenter.com. Rev. David Muenchrath.

WEST DES MOINES. *City Hospital Chaplaincy Service*, 1390 Buffalo Rd., 50265. Tel: 515-681-1746. Email: DMMH11688408@live.com. Rev. Michael R. McLaughlin. Serving all non-Catholic hospitals in Des Moines.

St. Francis of Assisi Roman Catholic School Foundation, 7075 Ashworth Rd., 50266. Tel: 515-223-4577; Fax: 515-223-4768. Email: info@saintfrancischurch.org. Web: www.saintfrancischurch.org. Rev. Robert Hoefler, Sec.

RELIGIOUS INSTITUTES OF MEN REPRESENTED IN THE DIOCESE

For further details refer to the corresponding bracketed number in the Religious Institutes of Men or Women section.

[0600]—*Brothers of the Congregation of the Holy Cross*—C.S.C.

[]—*Congregation of the Holy Ghost* (Nigeria)

[0690]—*Jesuit Fathers and Brothers* (Wisconsin Prov.)—S.J.

[0430]—*Order of Preachers-Dominicans*—O.P.

[0200]—*Order of St. Benedict* (Conception, MO)—O.S.B.

RELIGIOUS INSTITUTES OF WOMEN REPRESENTED IN THE DIOCESE

[0230]—*Benedictine Sisters of Pontifical Jurisdiction*—O.S.B.

[2100]—*Congregation of the Holy Humility of Mary*—C.H.M.

[1920]—*Congregation of the Sisters of the Holy Cross*—C.S.C.

[1070-14]—*Dominican Sisters*—O.P.

[1070-03]—*Dominican Sisters*—O.P.

[1070-13]—*Dominican Sisters*—O.P.

[1120]—*Dominican Sisters of the Roman Congregation*—O.P.

[1310]—*The Franciscan Sisters of Little Falls, MN*—F.S.M.

[2575]—*Institute of the Sisters of Mercy of the Americas* (Cedar Rapids, IA; Omaha, NE; Chicago, IL)—R.S.M.

[2960]—*Notre Dame Sisters* (Omaha, NE)—N.D.

[1680]—*School Sisters of St. Francis*—O.S.F.

[3580]—*Servants of Mary*—O.S.M.

[0480]—*Sisters of Charity of Leavenworth, Kansas*—S.C.L.

[0430]—*Sisters of Charity of the Blessed Virgin Mary*—B.V.M.

[2630]—*Sisters of Mercy of the Holy Cross*—S.C.S.C.

[3000]—*Sisters of Notre Dame de Namur*—S.N.D.de.N

[3320]—*Sisters of Presentation of the Blessed Virgin Mary*—P.B.V.M.

[1540]—*Sisters of Saint Francis, Clinton, Iowa*—O.S.F.

[1705]—*The Sisters of St. Francis of Assisi*—O.S.F.

[1570]—*Sisters of St. Francis of the Holy Family*—O.S.F.

[1930]—*Sisters of the Holy Cross*—F.D.N.S.C.

NECROLOGY

† Ryan, Rev. Msgr. Gerald E., (Retired)—Died March 20, 2011

† Polich, James C., Des Moines, IA St. Augustin Church.—Died Nov. 20, 2011

Archdiocese of Detroit

(Archidioecesis Detroitensis)

His Eminence

EDMUND CARDINAL SZOKA, J.C.L., D.D.

Archbishop Emeritus of Detroit; ordained June 5, 1954; appointed Bishop of Gaylord June 15, 1971; consecrated and installed July 20, 1971; promoted to See of Detroit March 28, 1981; installed May 17, 1981; created Cardinal June 28, 1988; appointed President, Prefacture for Economic Affairs of the Holy See June 25, 1990; President, Pontifical Commission for Vatican City State October 14, 1997; President emeritus of the Pontifical Commission for Vatican City State; President of the government of Vatican City State February 22, 2001; retired September 15, 2006.

His Eminence

ADAM CARDINAL MAIDA, J.C.L., J.D., S.T.L.

Archbishop Emeritus of Detroit; ordained May 26, 1956; appointed to Green Bay November 8, 1983; consecrated January 25, 1984; installed as Archbishop of Detroit June 12, 1990; created Cardinal on November 26, 1994; retired January 5, 2009.

Most Reverend

THOMAS J. GUMBLETON, D.D.

Retired Auxiliary Bishop of Detroit; ordained June 2, 1956; appointed Auxiliary Bishop of Detroit and Titular Bishop of Ululi March 8, 1968; consecrated May 1, 1968; retired February 2, 2006. *Office: 1234 Washington Blvd., Detroit, MI 48226.*

Most Reverend

MOSES B. ANDERSON, S.S.E., D.D.

Retired Auxiliary Bishop of Detroit; ordained May 30, 1958; appointed Auxiliary Bishop of Detroit and Titular Bishop of Vatarba December 3, 1982; consecrated January 27, 1983; retired October 24, 2003. *Office: 1234 Washington Blvd., Detroit, MI 48226.*

Most Reverend

ALLEN H. VIGNERON, D.D.

Archbishop of Detroit; ordained July 27, 1975; appointed Auxiliary Bishop of Detroit and Titular Bishop of Sault Ste. Marie June 12, 1996; consecrated July 9, 1996; appointed Coadjutor Bishop of Oakland January 10, 2003; installed February 26, 2003; succeeded to See October 1, 2003; appointed Archbishop of Detroit January 5, 2009; installed January 28, 2009.

Archbishop's Office: 1234 Washington Blvd., Detroit, MI 48226. Tel: 313-237-5816; Fax: 313-237-4642.

Most Reverend

MICHAEL JUDE BYRNES

Auxiliary Bishop of Detroit; ordained May 25, 1996; appointed Auxiliary Bishop of Detroit and Titular Bishop of Eguga March 22, 2011; consecrated May 5, 2011. *Office: 1234 Washington Blvd., Detroit, MI 48226.*

Most Reverend

DONALD FRANCIS HANCHON

Auxiliary Bishop of Detroit; ordained October 19, 1974; appointed Auxiliary Bishop of Detroit and Titular Bishop of Horreomargum March 22, 2011; consecrated May 5, 2011. *Office: 1234 Washington Blvd., Detroit, MI 48226.*

Most Reverend

FRANCIS R. REISS, D.D.

Auxiliary Bishop of Detroit; ordained June 4, 1966; appointed Auxiliary Bishop of Detroit and Titular Bishop of Remesiana July 7, 2003; consecrated August 12, 2003. *Office: 1234 Washington Blvd., Detroit, MI 48226.*

Most Reverend

JOSE ARTURO CEPEDA ESCOBEDO

Auxiliary Bishop of Detroit; ordained June 1, 1996; appointed Auxiliary Bishop of Detroit and Titular Bishop of Tagase April 18, 2011; consecrated May 5, 2011. *Office: 1234 Washington Blvd., Detroit, MI 48226.*

Square Miles 3,901.

Established March 8, 1833; Created An Archbishopric August 3, 1937.

Comprises the Counties of Lapeer, Macomb, Monroe, Oakland, St. Clair and Wayne.

For legal titles of parishes and archdiocesan institutions, consult the Cardinal's Office.

STATISTICAL OVERVIEW

Personnel	
Retired Cardinals	2
Archbishops	1
Auxiliary Bishops	4
Retired Bishops	2
Priests: Diocesan Active in Diocese	243
Priests: Diocesan Active Outside Diocese	6
Priests: Retired, Sick or Absent	132
Number of Diocesan Priests	381
Religious Priests in Diocese	196
Total Priests in Diocese	577
Extern Priests in Diocese	45
Ordinations:	
Diocesan Priests	3
Transitional Deacons	3
Permanent Deacons	11
Permanent Deacons in Diocese	198
Total Brothers	89
Total Sisters	1,023
Parishes	
Parishes	268
With Resident Pastor:	
Resident Diocesan Priests	199
Resident Religious Priests	28
Without Resident Pastor:	
Administered by Priests	41
Missions	1
Closed Parishes	3
Professional Ministry Personnel:	
Brothers	1
Sisters	47
Lay Ministers	468
Welfare	
Catholic Hospitals	10
Total Assisted	1,074,882
Homes for the Aged	21
Total Assisted	12,890
Specialized Homes	14
Total Assisted	2,548
Special Centers for Social Services	42
Total Assisted	67,200
Other Institutions	6
Total Assisted	200
Educational	
Seminaries, Diocesan	2
Students from This Diocese	41
Students from Other Diocese	84
Diocesan Students in Other Seminaries	4
Seminaries, Religious	2
Students Religious	19
Total Seminarians	64
Colleges and Universities	3
Total Students	13,027
High Schools, Diocesan and Parish	10
Total Students	3,872
High Schools, Private	14
Total Students	6,455
Elementary Schools, Diocesan and Parish	70
Total Students	21,868
Elementary Schools, Private	1
Total Students	287
Catechesis/Religious Education:	
High School Students	6,021
Elementary Students	50,114
Total Students under Catholic Instruction	101,708
Teachers in the Diocese:	
Priests	28
Brothers	13
Sisters	15
Lay Teachers	2,129
Vital Statistics	
Receptions into the Church:	
Infant Baptism Totals	8,784
Minor Baptism Totals	392
Adult Baptism Totals	636
Received into Full Communion	1,040
First Communions	10,820
Confirmations	9,980
Marriages:	
Catholic	1,924
Interfaith	686
Total Marriages	2,610
Deaths	8,764
Total Catholic Population	1,378,979
Total Population	4,267,293

Former Bishops—Rt. Revs. FREDERIC RESE, D.D., cons. Oct. 6, 1833; resigned Aug. 19, 1840; died Dec. 30, 1871; PETER PAUL LEFEVERE, D.D., cons. Nov. 22, 1841; Bishop of Zela, coadjutor and admin. of Detroit; died March 4, 1869; CASPAR HENRY BORGESS, D.D., cons. April 24, 1870; Bishop of Calydon, coadjutor and admin. of Detroit; became Bishop of Detroit Dec. 30, 1871; resigned April 16, 1887; died May 3, 1890; JOHN SAMUEL FOLEY, D.D., cons. Nov. 4, 1888; died Jan. 5, 1918; Most Rev. MICHAEL JAMES GALLAGHER, D.D., cons. Sept. 8, 1915; Bishop of Tipasa, coadjutor of Grand Rapids; became Bishop of Grand Rapids Dec. 26, 1916; transferred to Detroit July 18, 1918; died Jan. 20, 1937; His Eminence EDWARD CARDINAL MOONEY, D.D., appt. Apostolic Delegate in India Jan. 8, 1926; appt. Titular Archbishop of Irenopolis Jan. 18, 1926; cons. Jan. 31, 1926; appt. Apostolic Delegate in Japan Feb. 25, 1931; transferred to the Diocese of Rochester Aug. 28, 1933; transferred to the Archdiocese of Detroit Aug. 3, 1937; created Cardinal Priest of the title of S. Susanna Feb. 18, 1946; died Oct. 25, 1958; JOHN CARDINAL DEARDEN, D.D., S.T.D., ord. Dec. 8, 1932; cons. Titular Bishop of Sarepta and Coadjutor Bishop of Pittsburgh Dec. 22, 1950; installed Archbishop of Detroit Jan. 29, 1959; created Cardinal April 28, 1969; resigned as Archbishop July 15, 1980; died Aug. 1, 1988; EDMUND CARDINAL SZOKA, J.C.L., D.D. (Retired), Archbishop Emeritus of Detroit; ord. June 5, 1954; appt. Bishop of Gaylord June 15, 1971; cons. July 20, 1971; installed July 20, 1971; promoted to See of Detroit March 28, 1981; installed May 17, 1981; created Cardinal June 28, 1988; appt. Pres., Prefacture for Economic Affairs of the Holy See June 25, 1990; Pres., Pontifical Commission for Vatican City State Oct. 14, 1997; Pres. emeritus of the Pontifical Commission for

Vatican City State; Pres. of the government of Vatican City State Feb. 22, 2001; resigned Sept. 15, 2006; ADAM CARDINAL MAIDA, J.C.L., J.D., S.T.L., ord. May 26, 1956; appt. to Green Bay Nov. 8, 1983; cons. Jan. 25, 1984; installed as Archbishop of Detroit June 12, 1990; created Cardinal on Nov. 26, 1994; retired Jan. 5, 2009.

College of Consultors—Rev. Msgr. RICARDO E. BASS; Revs. THOMAS JOHNSON; GERALD A. MCENHILL; Rev. Msgr. JAMES A. MOLONEY, P.A.; Revs. THEODORE K. PARKER; WILLIAM TINDALL; Rev. Msgr. ANTHONY M. TOCCO; Rev. STANLEY A. ULMAN; Rev. Msgr. JOHN P. ZENZ.

Presbyteral Council—Revs. DONALD ARCHAMBAULT; PAUL K. BALLIEN; RICHARD BARTOSZEK; Rev. Msgr. RICARDO E. BASS; Revs. DAVID J. BLAZEK; DAVID A. BUERSMEYER; STEPHEN BURR, Sec.; Rev. Msgr. G. MICHAEL BUGARIN; Revs. PATRICK P. CASEY; MICHAEL N. COONEY, Chm.; BERNARDO CRUZ; DAVID CYBULSKI; Rev. Msgr. WILLIAM H. EASTON; Revs. MARC A. GAWRONSKI; MARIE-ELIE HABY; JOHN F. HALL (Retired); TIMOTHY D. HOGAN; JOSEPH R. HORN, Vice Chm.; THOMAS JOHNSON; Rev. Msgr. MICHAEL C. LEFEVRE, J.C.L.; Rev. JOSEPH MALLIA; Rev. Msgr. ROBERT MCCLORY; Rev. GERALD A. MCENHILL; Rev. Msgr. ROBERT V. MONTICELLO (Retired); Revs. MICHAEL C. NKACHUKWU; ROMAN PASIECZNY; ROBERT J. SCULLIN, S.J.; RICHARD L. TREML; STANLEY A. ULMAN; CLARENCE E. WILLIAMS, C.PP.S., Ph.D.

Archdiocesan Vicars—Revs. DONALD ARCHAMBAULT, Trinity; PAUL K. BALLIEN, West Wayne; DAVID J. BLAZEK, Lakes; DAVID A. BUERSMEYER, North Macomb; Rev. Msgr. G. MICHAEL BUGARIN, SERF; Revs. PATRICK P. CASEY, Northwest Wayne; MICHAEL N. COONEY, Central Macomb; Rev. Msgr. WILLIAM H. EASTON; Revs. MARC A. GAWRONSKI, Monroe; MARIE-ELIE HABY, Southwest; JOSEPH R. HORN, Blue Water; Rev. Msgr. MICHAEL C. LEFEVRE, J.C.L., Genesis; Revs. JOSEPH MALLIA, Downriver; MICHAEL C. NKACHUKWU, Renaissance; RICHARD L. TREML, Thumb; STANLEY A. ULMAN, Pontiac Area.

Archdiocesan Pastoral Council—Mr. AARON ADAMKIEWICZ; Ms. HERMENIA ADAMS; Mr. JOHN ANTILLA; Mr. KEVIN ATKINSON; Mr. BENNY CRUZ; Ms. VICTORIA FIGUEROA; Mr. MARIO GIACONA; Ms. RHONDA GILBERT; Mr. JIM GISMONDI; Ms. BARBARA GLINSKI; Mr. LOUIS JOSEPH; Mr. NORBERT KIDD; Mr. DICK LAJINESS; Ms. MARY LAMBRIX; Mrs. LAURA LAUER; Mr. STEPHEN LAWLESS; Mr. RICHARD LEWNAU; Mr. ROBERT MCBRAYER; Mr. CHIP MILLER, Chm.; Mr. JERRY RAUCH; Ms. JEANNE ROBINSON; Mr. BRIAN SADOWSKI; Rev. WILLIAM TINDALL; Deacon HUBERT SANDERS; Sr. BARBARA RUND, O.P. Contact: Mr. MICHAEL R. TRUEMAN, J.C.L., Chancellor. Tel: 313-237-5847.

Archdiocesan Departments and Offices

General Information and Reference—Tel: 313-237-5800.

Office of the Archbishop— All official mail should be directed to this office. *1234 Washington Blvd., Detroit, 48226.* Tel: 313-237-5816; Fax: 313-237-4642. Rev. CHARLES D. FOX, Personal Sec. to Archbishop.

Moderator of the Curia—Rev. Msgr. ROBERT J. MCCLORY. Tel: 313-237-5783; Fax: 313-237-4642; Mrs. KRISTA BAJOKA, Adjunct to Moderator of the Curia. Tel: 313-596-7147; Fax: 313-237-4642.

Office of the Chancellor—Mr. MICHAEL R. TRUEMAN, J.C.L., Chancellor. Tel: 313-237-5847; Fax: 313-237-4643; 313-237-4642.

Archives—Ms. HEIDI CHRISTEIN, Archivist. Tel: 313-237-5864; Fax: 313-596-7199.

Marriage Permissions/Dispensations—Rev. RONALD RICHARDS, J.C.L. Tel: 313-237-5848; Fax: 313-237-4642.

The Metropolitan Tribunal—305 Michigan Ave., Detroit, 48226. Tel: 313-237-5865; Fax: 313-237-5872. Office Hours: Mon.-Fri. 8:30-4:30.

Judicial Vicar—Most Rev. FRANCIS R. REISS, J.C.L., D.D.

Adjutant Judicial Vicar—Rev. ROBERT HAYES WILLIAMS, J.C.L.

Administrative Director—Mr. TIMOTHY FERGUSON, J.C.L.

Judges—Revs. TIMOTHY F. BABCOCK; JAMES L. BJORUM, J.C.L.; Mr. TIMOTHY FERGUSON, J.C.L.; Rev. RONALD J. JOZWIAK, J.C.L.; Rev. Msgr. GEORGE P. MILLER, J.C.L.; Revs. JOVITA OKOLI, J.C.L.; JEROME SLOWINSKI, J.C.L.

Defenders of Bond—Rev. MICHAEL LOYSON; Ms. PATRICIA MKRTUMIAN; Revs. NORMAN D. NAWROCKI, J.C.L.; RONALD RICHARDS, J.C.L.

Advocates—Rev. MICHAEL N. COONEY; EDWARD PETERS, J.C.D.; Mr. ROBERT CADOTTE, Other priests, deacons and certified lay advocates (ad actum).

Notaries—Mr. ADAM DWORNICK; Ms. JACQUELINE L. LOVE; Ms. DOLORES PAULL; Ms. FRANCINE VANDENBROECK.

Coordinator of Administrative Support Staff—Ms. JACQUELINE L. LOVE.

Office for Clergy and Consecrated Life—Rev. TIMOTHY D. HOGAN, Dir., 1234 Washington Blvd., Detroit, 48226. Tel: 313-596-7155; Fax: 313-237-4643.

Permanent Diaconate Program—Deacon MICHAEL J. MCKALE, Assoc. Dir. Tel: 313-596-7142; Fax: 313-237-4643.

Delegate for Consecrated Life—Sr. KELLEY CONNORS, P.M., 1234 Washington Blvd., Detroit, 48226. Tel: 313-596-7152; Fax: 313-237-4643.

Immigration Legal Services for Clergy, Consecrated Life and Schools—Ms. VIVIANA LANDE, Esq., Immigration Lawyer, 1234 Washington Blvd., Detroit, 48226. Tel: 313-596-7148.

Office of Priestly Vocations—Rev. TIMOTHY P. BIRNEY, Dir., 2701 Chicago Blvd., Detroit, 48206. Tel: 313-237-5875; Fax: 313-883-6070; Mrs. JAN DEFOUR, Coord. Fax: 313-237-5839.

Department of Communications—Mr. NED MCGRATH, Dir., 305 Michigan Ave., Detroit, 48226. Tel: 313-237-5943; Fax: 313-237-4644.

Office of Public Relations—Mr. JOSEPH KOHN, Assoc. Dir. Tel: 313-237-5802; Fax: 313-237-4644.

Office of Digital Media—Ms. PATRICIA MOLDONADO, Assoc. Dir. Tel: 313-237-5938; Fax: 313-237-5928; Rev. Msgr. THOMAS G. RICE, The Michigan Catholic Newspaper, Editor & Assoc. Publisher. Tel: 313-224-8000; Mrs. CASSANDRA ZAKENS, Web Mgr. Tel: 313-237-5973.

Office of Printing and Publications—Mr. DENNIS MILLIGAN, Dir. Tel: 313-237-5967; Fax: 313-965-8471.

Department of Development and Stewardship—Mr. DAVID KELLEY, Dir., 2701 Chicago Blvd., Detroit, 48206. Tel: 313-883-8657; 800-986-3925; Fax: 313-883-8681.

Planned Giving—Mr. THOMAS P. SCHOLLER, Assoc. Dir. Tel: 313-883-8657; Ms. DIANA MENDIOLA, Scholarship Prog. Coord. Tel: 313-883-8532.

Special Services—Mr. DAVID P. CASNOVSKY, Assoc. Dir. Tel: 313-883-8684.

Marketing—Ms. KATHRYN BUA, Dir. Mktg. Tel: 313-883-8533; Mr. DANIEL GALLIO, Editor. Tel: 313-883-8773.

Charitable Gift Planning—Mr. DARREN HOGAN, Assoc. Dir. Tel: 313-883-8748.

Major Gifts—Ms. MARIA JEROME, Assoc. Dir. Major Gifts. Tel: 313-883-8559.

Annual Giving—Ms. JAN STUART CHMIELARCZYK, Assoc. Dir. Tel: 313-883-8567.

Catholic Services Appeal—Ms. THERESA J. KACH, Assoc. Dir. Tel: 313-883-8656.

Development Services—Ms. JESSICA I. ORZECHOWSKI, Coord. Tel: 313-883-8629.

Department of Evangelization, Catechesis and Schools—Dr. MARGIE CROOKS, Dir., 305 Michigan Ave., Detroit, 48226. Tel: 313-596-7305; Fax: 313-237-5867.

Office of Catholic Schools—Ms. BERNADETTE SUGRUE, Supt. Tel: 313-237-5775. Regional Associate Superintendents: Ms. SUSAN LESLIE. Tel: 313-237-5772; Mrs. GEORGENE WOJCIECHOWSKI. Tel: 313-237-4654; Ms. MARY SWINKEY. Tel: 313-237-4658; Ms. KIMBERLY YOUNG-RIPPEY. Tel: 313-237-5776.

Health, Athletics and Physical Safety—Mr. VICTOR MICHAELS, Admin. Tel: 313-237-5960; Mr. MICHAEL EVOY, Assoc. Admin. Tel: 313-237-5960.

Office of Evangelization and Catechesis—Ms. JUDITH MATEN, Assoc. Dir. Tel: 313-237-4664; Fax: 313-237-5867. Coordinators, Catechetical Programming & Formation: Sr. KATHLEEN MATZ, C.D.P.; Ms. ANITA HOUGHTON. Tel: 313-237-4667.

RCIA Coordinator—VACANT. Tel: 313-237-5956.

Sacramental Preparation Coordinator—Ms. PATRICIA CHASE. Tel: 313-237-5758.

Adult Evangelization Coordinators—Rev. SEAN A. WENGER, C.C. Tel: 313-237-5909; Mr. ERIK COULES. Tel: 810-689-8560; Ms. JUDITH MATEN. Tel: 313-237-4664.

Marriage and Family Life—Mr. DAVID P. GROBBEL, Assoc. Dir. Tel: 313-237-5894; Ms. SOCORRO TRUCHAN, Coord. Tel: 313-237-4691; Mrs. DOROTHY STAPEL, Natural Family Planning. Tel: 313-237-4679.

Cultural Ministries—Mr. JOHN THORNE, Coord. Black Catholic Ministries. Tel: 313-596-7103.

Youth, Young Adults and Campus Ministries—Rev. SIMON C. LOBO, C.C. Tel: 313-237-4687.

Department of Finance and Administration—Mr. RICHARD AUSTIN, Dir., 1234 Washington Blvd., Detroit, 48226. Tel: 313-237-5834; Fax: 313-237-5868; Mr. FREDERICK BARTEL, Treas. Tel: 313-596-7132.

Office of Financial Services—Mrs. FRANCES ASHE, Dir. Tel: 313-237-5903.

Accounting Services—Ms. ROSEMARY WATKINS, Controller. Tel: 313-237-5825.

Parish Support Services—Ms. KIM SHEPARD, Assoc. Dir. Tel: 313-596-7163.

Audit—Mrs. LORI RAFFERTY, Assoc. Dir. Tel: 313-237-5841.

Office of Facilities Services—Mr. JOHN DUNCAN, Dir. Tel: 313-883-8599; Fax: 313-883-8699.

Sacred Heart Major Seminary/Cathedral Campus Building Administration—Deacon LAZARUS DER-GHAZARIAN, Assoc. Dir. Tel: 313-883-8506.

Archdiocesan Properties—Mr. MICHAEL MORAN, Assoc. Dir. Tel: 313-237-5830; Fax: 313-237-5791.

Buildings—Mr. FRANK MACDONELL, Contractor, PMNet. Tel: 313-237-5829; Fax: 313-596-7187.

Office of Computing and Network Services—Mr. CHRISTOPHER SNYDER, Dir. Tel: 313-237-5797; Fax: 313-237-5979.

Department of Human Resources—Ms. PAMELA BEECH, Dir., 1234 Washington Blvd., Detroit, 48226. Tel: 313-237-5948; Fax: 313-596-7194.

Benefits and School Personnel—Ms. ERIN TAFT, Coord. Tel: 313-596-7156.

Safe Environments—Ms. SHARON GORMAN, Coord. Tel: 313-596-5826; Fax: 313-596-7197.

Department of Parish Life—Mrs. LORY MCGLINNEN, Dir., 305 Michigan Ave., Detroit, 48226. Tel: 313-237-5798; Fax: 313-237-5869.

Office of Pastoral Planning and Leadership Services—Mr. ANTHONY LATARSKI, Assoc. Dir. & Regl. Coord. Tel: 313-237-5765; Fax: 313-237-5869; Mr. MICHAEL MCCALLION, Regl. Coord. - Research. Tel: 313-237-5760; Deacon WILLIAM KOLARIK, Regl. Coord. - Pastoral Staffs. Tel: 313-596-7317; Mr. ALTON M. JAMES, Regl. Coord. - Leadership Svcs. Tel: 313-596-7327; Ms. JANET SHAY, Statistics Coord. Tel: 313-596-7314; Ms. MEGAN LAMONT, Mapping and Surveys Coord. Tel: 313-237-8011.

Office of Christian Worship—Mr. DANIEL MCAFEE, Dir. Tel: 313-237-4697; Fax: 313-237-5869; Sr. GEORGETTE ZALESKA, Coord. Tel: 313-237-6064; Mr. JOSEPH BALISTRERI, Coord. Worship & Music. Tel: 313-237-5782; Ms. STACEY MASON, Coord. Music Ministries - St. John Ctr. Tel: 734-414-1161; Fax: 734-414-1150.

Office of Catholic Charities—Mr. MICHAEL HARNING, Dir. Tel: 313-237-5978; Fax: 313-237-5869.

Christian Service and Health Care Ministries—Ms. JOYCE HYTTINEN, Assoc. Dir. Tel: 313-237-5905; Fax: 313-237-5869.

Ecumenical/Interfaith Relations—Rev. JEFFREY DAY, Archbishop's Ecumenical/Interfaith Advisor, St. Sebastian, 20710 Colgate, Dearborn Heights, 48125. Tel: 313-562-5356; Fax: 313-562-0058; Mr. MICHAEL HOVEY, Coord. Tel: 313-237-4678; Fax: 313-237-5869.

Victim Assistance Coordinator—Ms. MARGARET A. HUGGARD, M.S.W. Tel: 866-343-8055.

Promoter of Ministerial Standards—Ms. INA GRANT. Tel: 313-237-4813; Fax: 313-237-5844.

Propagation of the Faith (Missions)—Rev. Msgr. JAMES A. MOLONEY, P.A., 1230 Washington Blvd., Detroit, 48226. Tel: 313-237-5807.

Association of the Holy Childhood—1230 Washington Blvd., Detroit, 48226. Tel: 313-237-5807.

Catholic Youth Organization—Ms. SUZANNE HEATH, Dir., 305 Michigan Ave., Detroit, 48226. Tel: 313-963-7172; Fax: 313-963-7179.

Archdiocesan Theological Commission—Rev. Msgr. ROBERT J. MCCLORY. Tel: 313-237-5783.

Priests Conference for Polish Affairs of the Archdiocese of Detroit—Rev. Msgr. STANLEY E. MILEWSKI, Pres. (Retired).

CLERGY, PARISHES, MISSIONS AND PAROCHIAL SCHOOLS

CITY OF DETROIT

(WAYNE COUNTY)

1—CATHEDRAL, CHURCH OF THE MOST BLESSED SACRAMENT Rev. Msgrs. Michael C. LeFevre, Rector; James P. Robinson, S.S.E., Rector Emeritus.
Res.: 9844 Woodward Ave., 48202. Tel: 313-865-6300; Fax: 313-867-4613.
Catechesis/Religious Program—Students 14.

2—ALL SAINTS Rev. Guy Christopher Snyder, P.I.M.E.; Deacon Norbert Motowski.
Res.: 7824 W. Fort St., 48209. Tel: 313-841-1428; Fax: 313-841-3009.
All Saints Soup Kitchen and Food Pantry—Denise Balogh, Outreach Dir.
Catechesis/Religious Program—Students 133.

3—ST. ALOYSIUS Rev. Tod Laverty, O.F.M.; Bros. Al Mascia, O.F.M., Pastoral Assoc.; Michael Radomski, O.F.M. In Res., Rev. Alexander Kratz, O.F.M.

Chancery Bldg.—1234 Washington Blvd., 48226. Tel: 313-237-5810; Fax: 313-963-9076.
Catechesis/Religious Program—Sr. Grace Keane, O.S.F., D.R.E. Students 25.

4—St. Andrew, (Polish), Merged into Our Lady Queen of Angels, Detroit.

5—SS. Andrew and Benedict Rev. Edward F. Zaorski.
Res.: 2430 S. Beatrice St., 48217. Tel: 313-381-1184; Fax: 313-381-0416.
Catechesis/Religious Program—Mary Ann Wallace, D.R.E. Students 18.

6—St. Anthony, Merged with Our Lady of Sorrows, Detroit to form Good Shepherd, Detroit.

7—St. Anthony, (Lithuanian), Rev. Gintaras Jonikas.
Res.: 1750 25th St., 48216. Tel: 313-554-1284.

8—Assumption Grotto, [CEM] Revs. Eduard Perrone; John Christopher Bustamante.
Res.: 13770 Gratiot Ave., 48205. Tel: 313-372-0762; Fax: 313-372-2064.
Catechesis/Religious Program—Students 25.

9—St. Augustine and St. Monica Rev. Daniel J. Trapp.
Res.: 4151 Seminole St., 48214. Tel: 313-921-4107; Fax: 313-921-1115.
Catechesis/Religious Program—Students 11.

10—St. Bartholomew, Merged with St. Rita, Detroit to form St. Bartholomew/St. Rita, Detroit.

11—St. Bartholomew/St. Rita Rev. Ronald Borg, C.S.B.
Res.: 2291 E. Outer Dr., 48234. Tel: 313-892-1446; Fax: 313-892-1149.
School—20001 Wexford, 48234. Tel: 313-366-3640; Fax: 313-366-0257. Ms. Sharon Perko, Prin. Lay Teachers 9; Students 73.

12—St. Brendan, Closed. For inquiries for parish records contact the chancery.

13—St. Catherine of Siena, Closed. For inquiries for parish records contact the chancery.

14—St. Cecilia Rev. Theodore K. Parker.
Res.: 10400 Stoepel Ave., 48204. Tel: 313-933-6788; Fax: 313-933-1439.
Church: Livernois at Stearns, 48204.
Catechesis/Religious Program—Students 55.

15—St. Charles Borromeo Rev. Raymond Stadmeyer, O.F.M.Cap.
Res.: 1491 Baldwin Ave., 48214. Tel: 313-331-0253; Fax: 313-331-4834.
Catechesis/Religious Program—Students 32.

16—Christ the King Rev. Victor Clore; Sr. Fiorentina D'Amore, H.V.M., Pastoral Assoc. & D.R.E.
Res.: 16805 Pierson, 48219. Tel: 313-532-1211; Fax: 313-532-1216.
Church: 20800 Grand River & Burt Rd., 48219.
School—16800 Trinity, 48219. Tel: 313-532-1213; Fax: 313-532-1050. Mrs. Rosanne Jodway, Prin. Lay Teachers 16; Students 151.
St. Christine Christian Services—22261 Fenkell, 48223. Office: 15317 Dacosta, 48223. Tel: 313-535-7272.
Catechesis/Religious Program—Students 85.

17—St. Christine, Closed. For inquiries for parish records contact the chancery.

18—St. Christopher Rev. Charles M. Morris.
Res.: 7800 Woodmont Ave., 48228. Tel: 313-584-7460; Fax: 313-584-6361.
Convent—7800 Woodmont Ave., 48228. Tel: 313-584-7579.
Catechesis/Religious Program—Theresa Zaleski, D.R.E. Students 5.

19—Church of the Madonna Rev. Msgr. Michael C. LeFevre; Rev. Timothy J. Kane.
Res.: 1125 Oakman Blvd., 48238. Tel: 313-868-4308; Fax: 313-868-9771.
Catechesis/Religious Program—Students 10.

20—Corpus Christi (2006) Rev. Donald Archambault; Sr. Stephanie Holub, R.S.M., Pastoral Assoc.; Deacon Paul Mueller; Beryl Harriott, Pastoral Assoc.
Res.: 19800 Pembroke Ave., 48219-2145. Tel: 313-537-5770; Fax: 313-537-5773.
Catechesis/Religious Program—Sr. Therese MacKinnon, D.C., D.R.E. Students 54.

21—St. Cunegunda Rev. Zbigniew Grankowski.
Res.: 5900 St. Lawrence Ave., 48210. Tel: 313-843-4717; Fax: 313-841-4255.
Catechesis/Religious Program—Michael Peck, D.R.E. Students 60.

22—St. Elizabeth Rev. Norman P. Thomas, Admin.
Res.: 3138 E. Canfield Ave., 48207. Tel: 313-921-9225; Fax: 313-921-9475. Email: npt@sacredheartdetroit.com.
Catechesis/Religious Program—Velma Coleman, D.R.E. Students 30.

23—St. Francis D'Assisi Very Rev. Kenneth Mazur, P.I.M.E.; Rev. Ravi Thanaiah Marneni.
Res.: 4500 Wesson St., 48210. Tel: 313-897-7229; Fax: 313-897-7485.
Catechesis/Religious Program—Leonard Meir, D.R.E.

24—St. Francis de Sales, Merged with Precious Blood, Detroit to form St. Peter Claver, Detroit.

25—St. Gabriel Rev. Jaime Hinojos.
Res.: 8118 W. Vernor Hwy., 48209-1524. Tel: 313-841-0753; Fax: 313-841-0916.
Catechesis/Religious Program—Tel: 313-841-0753, Ext. 11. Students 495.

26—St. Gemma Galgani, Closed. For inquiries for parish records contact the chancery.

27—St. Gerard, Merged with Immaculate Heart of Mary, Detroit to form Corpus Christi, Detroit.

28—Gesu Rev. Robert J. Scullin, S.J.
Office: 17180 Oak Dr., 48221. Tel: 313-862-4400; Fax: 313-862-1083.
School—17139 Oak Dr., 48221. Tel: 313-863-4677; Fax: 313-862-4395. Mr. John Champion, Prin. Lay Teachers 10; Students 212.
Catechesis/Religious Program—Laura Silveri, D.R.E. Students 56.

29—Good Shepherd (2006) Rev. Michael C. Nkachukwu; Mr. Alton M. James, Pastoral Assoc.
Res.: 1265 Parkview Ave., 48214. Tel: 313-822-1262; Fax: 313-822-8988.
Catechesis/Religious Program—Ms. Gayle Koyton, D.R.E. Students 16.

30—St. Gregory the Great Rev. Msgr. Michael C. LeFevre, Admin.; Rev. Timothy J. Kane.
Res.: 15031 Dexter Ave., 48238. Tel: 313-865-6300; Fax: 313-867-4613.
Catechesis/Religious Program—Students 18.

31—Guardian Angels, Closed. For inquiries for parish records contact the chancery.

32—St. Hedwig Very Rev. Kenneth Mazur, P.I.M.E.; Rev. Ravi Thanaiah Marneni; Deacon Rafael Jimenez.
Res.: 3245 Junction Ave., 48210. Tel: 313-894-5409; Fax: 313-894-4730.
Catechesis/Religious Program—

33—Holy Cross, (Hungarian), Revs. Barnabas G. Kiss, O.F.M.; Angelus Ligeti, O.F.M.
Res.: 8423 South St., 48209. Tel: 313-842-1133; Fax: 313-842-2773. Email: sztkereszt@comcast.net.
Catechesis/Religious Program—Emma T. Mahar, D.R.E. Students 10.

34—Holy Family, (Italian), Rev. Giuseppe Licciardi (Italy), Admin.
Res.: 641 Walter P. Chrysler Expwy., 48226. Tel: 313-963-2046; Fax: 313-963-0646.

35—Holy Redeemer Revs. Dennis Walsh, S.O.L.T.; Richard Klepac, S.O.L.T.; Brady Williams, S.O.L.T.; Deacon Ronald L. McIntyre.
Res.: 1721 Junction Ave., 48209. Tel: 313-842-3450; Fax: 313-849-0539.
School—Tel: 313-841-5230; Fax: 313-841-3640. John Kiley, Prin. Sisters Servants of the Immaculate Heart of Mary 1; Sisters of St. Joseph 1; Sisters of Mercy 1; Lay Teachers 9; Students 137.
Catechesis/Religious Program—Marcela Solis, D.R.E. Students 580.

36—St. Hyacinth, (Polish), Rev. Janusz Iwan.
Res.: 3151 Farnsworth Ave., 48211. Tel: 313-922-1507; Fax: 313-922-2459. Email: st.hyacinth@att.net.

37—Immaculate Heart of Mary, Merged with St. Gerard, Detroit to form Corpus Christi, Detroit.

38—St. John Cantius, (Polish), Closed. For inquiries for parish records contact the chancery.

39—St. Josaphat, (Polish), Rev. Darrell Roman, Admin.; Deacon Bill Stimpson.
Office: 4440 Russell St., 48202.
Church: 691 E. Canfield Ave., 48201. Tel: 313-831-6659; Fax: 313-831-8522.

40—St. Joseph Rev. Darrell Roman, Admin.; Deacon Bill Stimpson.
Office: c/o 4440 Russell St., 48202.
Church: 1828 Jay St., 48207. Tel: 313-831-6659; Fax: 313-891-8522.

41—St. Jude Rev. Jovita Okoli, Admin.
Mailing Address: 15889 E. Seven Mile Rd., 48205.
Res.: 20955 Bournemouth St., Harper Woods, 48225. Tel: 313-527-0380; Fax: 313-527-3511.
Catechesis/Religious Program—Students 14.

42—St. Ladislaus, (Polish), Rev. Andrew Wesley.
Res.: 5830 Simon K., 48212. Tel: 313-891-1310; Fax: 313-872-5906.

43—St. Leo Rev. Theodore K. Parker; Angela Thomas-Weldon, Pastoral Assoc.
Church & Res.: 4860 15th St., 48208. Tel: 313-894-1176; Fax: 313-894-1176 (call first).
Catechesis/Religious Program—Sandra Hill, D.R.E. Students 20.

44—St. Louis the King Rev. Boleslaus Krol.
Res.: 18891 St. Louis Ave., 48234. Tel: 313-891-1766; Fax: 313-891-7959.

45—St. Luke Rev. Tyrone Robinson, Admin.; Sr. Marie Roy, S.S.J., Pastoral Assoc.
Res.: 8017 Ohio Ave., 48204. Tel: 313-935-6161; Fax: 313-935-0788.
Catechesis/Religious Program—Students 16.

46—Martyrs of Uganda, Closed. For inquiries for parish records contact the chancery.

47—St. Mary Revs. Simon Lobon, C.S.Sp.; Edward J. Vilkauskas, C.S.Sp.
Res.: 646 Monroe Ave., 48226. Tel: 313-961-8711; Fax: 313-961-4994.
Catechesis/Religious Program—Students 6.

48—St. Mary's of Redford Rev. Tyrone Robinson, Admin.
Mailing Address: 14750 St. Mary's, 48227. Tel: 313-273-1100; Fax: 313-273-2002.
Catechesis/Religious Program—Ada Taylor, D.R.E. Students 42.

49—St. Matthew Rev. Duane R. Novelly.
Res.: 6021 Whittier Ave., 48224. Tel: 313-884-4470; Fax: 313-884-4276.
Catechesis/Religious Program—

50—Most Holy Trinity Rev. Russell E. Kohler.
Res.: 1050 Porter St., 48226. Tel: 313-965-4450; Fax: 313-965-4453.
School—1229 Labrosse, 48226. Tel: 313-961-8855; Fax: 313-961-5797. Ms. Kathleen McBride, Prin. Lay Teachers 9; Students (K-8) 136; Preschool 20.
Catechesis/Religious Program—Students 136.

51—Nativity of Our Lord Rev. Jerome C. Singer.
Res.: 5900 McClellan Ave., 48213. Tel: 313-922-0033; Fax: 313-922-8553.
Catechesis/Religious Program—Sr. Jolene Van Handel, O.P., D.R.E. Students 43.

52—Our Lady Gate of Heaven, Closed. For inquiries for parish records please see St. Suzanne/Our Lady Gate of Heaven, Detroit.

53—Our Lady Help of Christians, (Polish), Merged with Transfiguration, Detroit to form Transfiguration-Our Lady Help of Christians, Detroit.

54—Our Lady of Good Counsel, Merged with St. Raymond, Detroit June 2011.

55—Our Lady of Mt. Carmel, Closed. For inquiries for parish records contact the chancery.

56—Our Lady of the Rosary Rev. Robert Morand.
Res.: 5930 Woodward Ave., 48202. Tel: 313-875-6011; Fax: 313-872-0758.
Catechesis/Religious Program—Students 31.

57—Our Lady Queen of Angels Rev. Marie-Elie Haby.
Res.: 4311 Central Ave., 48210. Tel: 313-897-8160; Fax: 313-897-8126.
Catechesis/Religious Program—Students 322.

58—Our Lady Queen of Heaven Revs. Robert J. Kotlarz; Thomas Puzio.
Res.: 8200 Rolyat Ave., 48234. Tel: 313-891-4553; Fax: 313-891-5782.
Catechesis/Religious Program—

59—St. Patrick Rev. Tod Laverty, O.F.M.; Floria Ellison, Pastoral Assoc.
Church: 58 Parsons, 48201. Tel: 313-833-0857; Fax: 313-831-1619.

60—SS. Peter and Paul (West Side) Revs. Jaroslaw Pilus, Admin.; Mark Borkowski.
Res.: 7685 Grandville Ave., 48228. Tel: 313-846-2222; Fax: 313-584-1484.
Catechesis/Religious Program—Lawrence Kowalski, D.R.E. Students 29.

61—SS. Peter and Paul Jesuit Rev. Robert J. Scullin, S.J.; Bro. Denis Weber, S.J., Parish Coord.
Res.: 438 St. Antoine St., 48226. Tel: 313-961-8077; Fax: 313-963-5134.

62—St. Peter Claver Rev. James E. O'Reilly, S.J.
13305 Grove Ave., 48235. Tel: 313-342-5292; Fax: 313-342-3513.
Catechesis/Religious Program—Mary Caroline Jonah, D.R.E. Students 33.

63—St. Philomena Rev. Peter S. Lentine.
Res.: 4281 Marseilles Ave., 48224. Tel: 313-882-4300; Fax: 313-882-1661.
Catechesis/Religious Program—4351 Marseilles, 48224. Kelly Woolums, D.R.E. Tel: 313-884-2422. Students 77.

64—Precious Blood, Merged with St. Francis de Sales, Detroit to form St. Peter Claver, Detroit.

65—Presentation/Our Lady of Victory Rev. Msgr. Robert J. McClory; Deacon Hubert Sanders, Pastoral Admin.
Res.: 19760 Meyers Rd., 48235. Tel: 313-342-1333; Fax: 313-342-4182.
Catechesis/Religious Program—Students 10.

66—St. Raymond-Our Lady of Good Counsel Revs. Robert J. Kotlarz; Thomas Puzio.
Res.: 20103 Joann Ave., 48205. Tel: 313-527-0525; Fax: 313-527-9776.
Community Center—20055 Joann Ave., 48205. Tel: 313-372-0437.
Catechesis/Religious Program—Sr. Rosemarie Abate, H.V.M., Evangelization Coord.; Mrs. My Xiong, D.R.E. Students 95.

67—St. Rita, Merged with St. Bartholomew, Detroit to form St. Bartholomew/St. Rita, Detroit.

68—Sacred Heart of Jesus Rev. Norman P. Thomas, Admin.
Res.: 1000 Eliot St., 48207. Tel: 313-831-1356; Fax: 313-831-8603.
Catechesis/Religious Program—Barbara Hunt, D.R.E. Students 165.

69—St. Scholastica Revs. Marc P. Syrenne, C.C.; Sean A. Wenger, C.C.; Simon C. Lobo, C.C.

Res.: 17320 Rosemont Rd., 48219. Tel: 313-531-0140; Fax: 313-531-0739.
Church: Southfield Rd. & W. Outer Dr., 48219.
School—Tel: 313-532-1916; Fax: 313-532-0140. Faye Vaughn, Elementary Prin. Lay Teachers 6; Students 85.
Catechesis/Religious Program—Bro. Gregory David Jones, O.S.B., D.R.E. Students 7.
Convent—17305 Ashton, 48219.

70—STE. ANNE DE DETROIT Rev. Thomas W. Sepulveda, C.S.B. In Res., Revs. José Jaime DelToro, C.S.B.; A. Leo Reilly, C.S.B.; Manuel J. Chircop, C.S.B.
Res.: 1000 Ste. Anne St., 48216-2027. Tel: 313-496-1701; Fax: 313-496-0429.
Catechesis/Religious Program—Students 160.

71—ST. STEPHEN-MARY MOTHER OF THE CHURCH Rev. Marie-Elie Haby, Admin.
Res.: 4311 Central Ave., 48210. Tel: 313-841-0783; Fax: 313-841-4868.
Catechesis/Religious Program—4200 Martin St., 48210. Tel: 313-897-8160; Fax: 313-897-8126. Mariateresita Rodriguez, D.R.E. Students 260.

72—ST. SUZANNE/OUR LADY GATE OF HEAVEN Rev. Jaroslaw Pilus; Deacon Alex Jones Jr.
Res.: 9357 Westwood Ave., 48228. Tel: 313-838-6780; Fax: 313-838-1063.
Catechesis/Religious Program—Students 15.

73—SWEETEST HEART OF MARY, (Polish), [CEM] Rev. Darrell Roman; Deacon Bill Stimpson.
Res.: 4440 Russell St., 48207. Tel: 313-831-6659; Fax: 313-831-8522.

74—ST. THOMAS AQUINAS Rev. Charles K. Altermatt; Catherine Odom Prowse, Music Min.
Parish Center—5780 Evergreen Rd., 48228. Tel: 313-271-3266; Fax: 313-271-8773.
Catechesis/Religious Program—Tel: 313-271-0813. Armando Bravo, D.R.E. Students 50.

75—TRANSFIGURATION-OUR LADY HELP OF CHRISTIANS Rev. Andrew Wesley.
Res.: 5830 Simon K. St., 48212. Tel: 313-892-1310; Fax: 313-893-2478.
Convent—5821 Rupert, 48212. Tel: 313-891-9273.
Catechesis/Religious Program—Sr. Angelica Zajkowski, D.R.E. Students 8.

OUTSIDE THE CITY OF DETROIT

ALGONAC, ST. CLAIR CO., ST. CATHERINE OF ALEXANDRIA, [CEM] Merged with Holy Cross, Marine City & St. Mark, Harsens Island to form Our Lady on the River, Marine City.

ALLEN PARK, WAYNE CO., ST. FRANCES CABRINI Rev. Joseph Mallia.
Res.: 9000 Laurence Ave., 48101. Tel: 313-381-5601; Fax: 313-381-7837.
School—St. Frances Cabrini Elementary, 13500 Wick Rd., 48101. Tel: 313-928-6610; Fax: 313-928-8502. Patricia Pollick, Prin. Lay Teachers 30; Students 536.
High School—Cabrini High School, Tel: 313-388-0110; Fax: 313-388-1876. James J. Wasukanis, Pres. & Prin. Lay Teachers 34; Students 509.
Catechesis/Religious Program—Peggy Durocher, Pastoral Min.; Christine Brennan, D.R.E. Students 261.

ALLENTON, ST. CLAIR CO., ST. JOHN THE EVANGELIST Revs. Wayne G. Ureel; John Ortman.
Res.: 872 Capac Rd., 48002. Tel: 810-395-7074; Fax: 810-395-7718.
Catechesis/Religious Program—883A Capac Rd., 48002. Tel: 810-395-2301. Students 160.

ARMADA, MACOMB CO., ST. MARY MYSTICAL ROSE Rev. Siaosi E. Patau.
Res.: 24040 Armada Ridge, 48005. Tel: 586-784-5966; Fax: 586-784-9330.
Catechesis/Religious Program—Students 201.

AUBURN HILLS, OAKLAND CO.

1—ST. JOHN FISHER CHAPEL UNIVERSITY PARISH Rev. Jerome A. Brzezinski; Sr. Mary Van Gilder, Pastoral Assoc.; Mrs. Lisa Brown, Pastoral Assoc.; Mr. Paul Borucki, Pastoral Assoc.; Mrs. Susan Buratto, Pastoral Assoc.; Mrs. Nancy Mason Bordley, Pastoral Assoc.
Res.: 3665 Walton Blvd., 48326. Tel: 248-373-6457; Fax: 248-373-5479. Web: www.stjohnfisherparish.org.
Catechesis/Religious Program—Tel: 248-373-3130. Michelle Pittel, D.R.E. Students 345.

2—SACRED HEART Rev. Richard Cavellier.
Res.: 3400 Adams Rd., 48326. Tel: 248-852-4170; Fax: 248-852-5745.
Catechesis/Religious Program—Tel: 248-852-3620. Students 150.

BELLEVILLE, WAYNE CO., ST. ANTHONY Rev. Thomas H. Cusick; Edward Haggerty, Parish Admin.; Deacon Peter Cornell.
Res.: 409 W. Columbia Ave., 48111. Tel: 734-697-1211; Fax: 734-697-6217.
Catechesis/Religious Program—Tel: 734-699-3373. Students 189.
Convent—371 W. Columbia Ave., 48111. Tel: 734-697-6661.

BERKLEY, OAKLAND CO., OUR LADY OF LA SALETTE Rev. Patrick J. Connell; Deacons Daniel M. Darga, Pastoral Assoc.; Brian Carroll, Pastoral Assoc.
Res.: 2600 Harvard Rd., 48072. Tel: 248-541-3762; Fax: 248-541-4250.
School—(Grades PreK-8), 2219 Coolidge Hwy., 48072. Fax: 248-541-6559. Mr. Dan Terbrack, Prin.; Ann Jaski, Librarian. Lay Teachers 10; Students 110.
Catechesis/Religious Program—Students 152.

BEVERLY HILLS, OAKLAND CO., OUR LADY QUEEN OF MARTYRS Revs. Scott A. Thibodeau; Gerard W. Buttersby, Weekend Asst.; Sr. Michael Clare Mauntel, S.C., Pastoral Min.
32340 Pierce Ave., 48025. Tel: 248-644-8620; Fax: 248-644-8623.
School—(Grades PreK-8), 32460 Pierce Ave., 48025. Tel: 248-642-2616; Fax: 248-642-3671. Joseph Vincler, Prin. Lay Teachers 21; Students 248.
Catechesis/Religious Program—Tel: 248-647-6068. Sarah Hogan, D.R.E. Students 325.

BIRMINGHAM, OAKLAND CO.

1—ST. COLUMBAN Rev. Donald L. Demmer; Robert Mervak, Music Min.
Church: 1775 E. Melton, 48009. Tel: 248-646-5224; Fax: 248-642-7889. Email: stcbhm@aol.com. Web: www.saintalan-saintcolumban.com.
Catechesis/Religious Program—Tel: 248-646-5224, Ext. 104. Betty Sheehan, D.R.E. Students 55.

2—HOLY NAME Rev. Msgr. John P. Zenz; Deacon Michael J. McKale; Deborah Shinder, Pastoral Assoc.
Parish Office—630 Harmon St., 48009. Tel: 248-646-2244; Fax: 248-646-2286.
School—(Grades PreK-8) Tel: 248-644-2722; Fax: 248-644-1191. Mary Ann Grady, Prin.; Sue Lambert, Librarian. Lay Teachers 25; Students 366.
Catechesis/Religious Program—Tel: 248-642-4130. Mary Morian, Dir. Faith Formation. Students 425.

BLOOMFIELD HILLS

1—ST. HUGO OF THE HILLS Rev. Msgr. Anthony M. Tocco; Rev. Michael Wilkes; Deacon Oscar A. Brown; Sr. Barbara Rund, O.P., Pastoral Assoc.; Deacon Michael T. Smith.
Res.: 2215 Opdyke Rd., 48304. Tel: 248-644-5460; Fax: 248-644-1758. Web: www.sthugo.org.
School—380 E. Hickory Grove, 48304. Tel: 248-642-6131; Fax: 248-642-4457. Sr. Margaret Van Velzen, I.H.M., Prin. Sisters, Servants of the Immaculate Heart of Mary 3; Lay Teachers 41; Students 653.
Catechesis/Religious Program—Tel: 248-642-6062. Margaret Bucchi, C.R.E. Students 270.

2—ST. OWEN Rev. James F. Cronk; Karen Heuer, Christian Svc.; Mary Mills, Youth Min.; Sharon Dreisig, Youth Min.
Res.: 6869 Franklin Rd., 48301. Tel: 248-626-0840; Fax: 248-626-0345. Web: www.stowen.org.
Catechesis/Religious Program—6855 Franklin Rd., 48301. Tel: 248-626-3200; Fax: 248-626-1415. Jarrod Dillon, D.R.E.; Patricia Watanabe, Music Min. Students 353.

3—ST. REGIS Rev. Msgr. Charles G. Kosanke.
Res.: 3695 Lincoln Rd., 48301. Tel: 248-646-2686; Fax: 248-646-4643.
School—3691 Lincoln Rd., 48301-4055. Tel: 248-646-2686, Ext. 300; Fax: 248-644-0944. Chris Ciagne, Prin. Lay Teachers 30; Students 488.
Catechesis/Religious Program—Students 176.

CANTON, WAYNE CO.

1—SAINT JOHN NEUMANN Revs. Ronald Richards; Mark P. Prill; Eugene Kijek, Pastoral Assoc.
Res.: 44745 Windmill Dr., 48187. Tel: 734-453-9434.
Catechesis/Religious Program—Donna Franke, D.R.E. Students 333.

2—RESURRECTION Rev. Kenneth M. Chase.
48755 Warren Rd., 48187-1216. Tel: 734-451-0444; Fax: 734-451-0454.
Catechesis/Religious Program—Students 203.

3—ST. THOMAS A'BECKET Revs. Patrick P. Casey; James Fredrick Arwady.
Res.: 555 S. Lilley Rd., 48188. Tel: 734-981-1333; Fax: 734-981-1481.
Catechesis/Religious Program—Tel: 734-981-6680. Students 950.

CAPAC, ST. CLAIR CO., ST. NICHOLAS Revs. Wayne G. Ureel; John Ortman.
Church: 4331 Capac Rd., Box 129, 48014. Tel: 810-395-7572; Fax: 810-395-7830.
Catechesis/Religious Program—Julie Laeder, D.R.E. Students 91.

CARLETON, MONROE CO., ST. PATRICK, [CEM 3] Rev. Robert A. Bauer.
Res.: 2996 W. Labo Rd., 48117. Tel: 734-654-2500; Fax: 734-654-6594.
School—Tel: 734-654-2522; Fax: 734-654-8120. Ms. Ruth Meiring, Prin. Lay Teachers 9; Students 109.
Catechesis/Religious Program—Tel: 734-654-6444. Jan Doederlien, D.R.E. Students 155.

CENTER LINE, MACOMB CO., ST. CLEMENT, [CEM] Rev. Michael R. Gawlowski.
Res.: 12255 Frazho Rd., Warren, 48089. Tel: 586-757-3306; Fax: 586-757-5390.
Catechesis/Religious Program—Tel: 586-427-2761. Alice Baron, D.R.E.; Donna VanGheluwe, D.R.E. Religious education now held at St. Teresa of Avila.
Mission—St. Joseph Malankara

CLARKSTON, OAKLAND CO., ST. DANIEL Rev. Christopher P. Maus; Deacon Stephen Marks.
Res.: 7010 Valley Park Dr., 48346. Tel: 248-625-4580; Fax: 248-620-9839.
Catechesis/Religious Program—Betty Haran, D.R.E. Students 733.

CLAWSON, OAKLAND CO., GUARDIAN ANGELS Revs. Gerard LeBoeuf; Craig Anthony Giera; Deacon Robert Schwartz.
Res.: 581 E. 14 Mile Rd., 48017. Tel: 248-588-1222; Fax: 248-588-8767.
School—Tel: 248-588-5545; Fax: 248-589-7356. Ms. Sharon Hammerschmidt, Prin. Lay Teachers 20; Students 315.
Catechesis/Religious Program—John David Kuhar, D.R.E. Students 217.

CLINTON TWP., MACOMB CO.

1—ST. CLAUDE, Merged with St. Thecla, Clinton Twp.

2—ST. LOUIS Rev. Lawrence A. Pettke.
Res.: 24415 Crocker Blvd., Clinton Township, 48036. Tel: 586-468-8734; Fax: 586-468-9647.
Catechesis/Religious Program—39140 Ormsby St., Clinton Township, 48036. Tel: 586-468-8734, Ext. 104. Sr. Kathy Onderbeke, I.H.M., D.R.E. Students 167.

3—ST. PAUL OF TARSUS Rev. Ronald Essman; Deacon Thomas Carter.
Res.: 41300 Romeo Plank Rd., Clinton Township, 48038. Tel: 586-228-1210; Fax: 586-228-8935. Email: parishoffice@stpauloftarsus.com. Web: www.stpauloftarsus.com.
Catechesis/Religious Program—Claudia Dombrowski, D.R.E. Students 521.

4—ST. RONALD Rev. Msgr. George P. Miller; Diane McDonald, Pastoral Assoc.
Res.: 17701 15 Mile Rd., Clinton Township, 48035-2401. Tel: 586-792-1190; Fax: 586-792-0765.
Catechesis/Religious Program—Tel: 586-792-1276. Students 288.

5—SAN FRANCESCO COMMUNITY Rev. Giulio Schiavi, PIME.
Res.: 22870 S. Nunneley Rd., Clinton Township, 48035. Tel: 586-792-5346; Fax: 586-792-5119.
Catechesis/Religious Program—Students 130.

6—ST. THECLA, Merged with St. Claude, Clinton Twp. Rev. Douglas Bignall.
Res.: 20740 S. Nunneley Rd., Clinton Township, 48035-1628. Tel: 586-791-3930; Fax: 586-791-3890. Email: info2@stthecla.com.
School—20762 S. Nunneley Rd., Clinton Township, 48035. Tel: 586-791-2170; Fax: 586-791-2356. Sr. Mary Kathleen White, C.S.S.F., Prin. Felician Sisters 1; Lay Teachers 26; Students 450.
Catechesis/Religious Program—Tel: 586-792-0550. Students 200.

7—ST. VALERIE OF RAVENNA, Merged into St. Louis, Clinton Township.

COLUMBUS, ST. CLAIR CO., ST. PHILIP NERI, [CEM] Merged with All Saints, Memphis & Holy Rosary Mission, Smiths Creek to form Holy Family, Memphis.

DAVISBURG, OAKLAND CO., DIVINE MERCY Rev. Msgr. John G. Budde.
4055 Parker, 48350-2321. Tel: 248-634-7015; Fax: 248-634-7029.
Catechesis/Religious Program—Students 84.

DEARBORN, WAYNE CO.

1—ST. ALPHONSUS Rev. David Lesniak.
Res.: 7455 Calhoun Ave., 48126. Tel: 313-581-5218; Fax: 313-584-9560.
Catechesis/Religious Program—Tel: 313-581-5218. Students 7.

2—ST. BARBARA Rev. Zbigniew Grankowski.
Res.: 13534 Colson Ave., 48126. Tel: 313-582-8383; Fax: 313-582-1581.
Catechesis/Religious Program—Michael Peck, D.R.E. Students 60.

3—ST. CLEMENT Rev. Charles S. Fontana; Sr. Mary Downey, I.H.M., Pastoral Assoc.; Deacon Robert Rowland.
Res.: 5275 Kenilworth St., 48126. Tel: 313-581-7495; Fax: 313-581-4233.
Catechesis/Religious Program—Tel: 313-846-2443. Maurine Dailey, D.R.E. Students 24.

4—DIVINE CHILD Revs. James D. Bilot; David Bechill; Deacons Roger O'Donnell; James Thibodeau.
Res.: 25001 Hollander, 48128. Tel: 313-277-3110; Fax: 313-277-3211.
School—Tel: 313-562-1090; Fax: 313-562-9306. Sr. Cecilia Bondy, Elementary Prin. Bernardine Sisters 4; Lay Teachers 32; Students 611.
High School—1001 N. Silvery Ln., 48128. Tel: 313-562-1990; Fax: 313-562-9361. Margaret Knuth, High School Prin. Lay Teachers 59; Students 844.
Catechesis/Religious Program—Karen Mitchell, D.R.E. & Youth Min. Students 148.

Convent—1045 N. Silvery Ln., 48128. Tel: 313-561-5455.

5—ST. JOSEPH, Clustered with St. Martha, Dearborn. Rev. Terrence D. Kerner.
Res.: 16101 Rotunda Dr., 48120. Tel: 313-336-3227; Fax: 313-441-6769.

6—ST. MARTHA, Clustered with St. Joseph, Dearborn. Rev. Terrence D. Kerner.
Mailing Address: 18200 Oakwood Blvd., 48124. Tel: 313-336-4090; Fax: 313-336-3318.
Res.: 16101 Rotunda, 48120. Tel: 313-336-3227; Fax: 313-441-6769.
Catechesis/Religious Program—Erin Holmes, D.R.E. Students 50.

7—SACRED HEART, [CEM] Rev. Peter Petroske; Fran Helner, Pastoral Assoc.; Rev. John F. Child, Weekend Assoc. (Retired).
Res.: 22430 W. Michigan Ave., 48124. Tel: 313-278-5555; Fax: 313-278-8582.
School—22513 Garrison, 48124. Tel: 313-561-9192; Fax: 313-561-1598. Mrs. Melissa Lambrecht, Prin. Lay Teachers 12; Students 205.
Catechesis/Religious Program—Julie Wieleba-Milkie, Youth Min. Students 200.

8—ST. SEBASTIAN Rev. Aaron DePeyster; Deacons Lawrence Girard; Stephen Bussa.
Res.: 3844 Merrick St., 48124. Tel: 313-562-5356; Fax: 313-562-0058.
School—3997 Merrick, Dearborn Heights, 48125. Tel: 313-563-6640; Fax: 313-563-6641. Sr. Geraldine Kaczynski, F.S.S.J., Prin. Franciscan Sisters of St. Joseph 2; Lay Teachers 11; Students 220.
Catechesis/Religious Program—Tel: 313-563-0960; Fax: 313-562-0058. Susan Campbell, D.R.E. Students 180.
Convent—20700 Colgate Ave., Dearborn Heights, 48125. Tel: 313-562-7733.

DEARBORN HEIGHTS, WAYNE CO.

1—ST. ALBERT THE GREAT Rev. Daniel Zaleski; Sr. Barbara Ennis, S.S.J.-T.O.S.F., Pastoral Assoc.; Deacon Ray Gabel.
Res.: 4855 Parker, 48125. Tel: 313-292-0430; Fax: 313-292-8565.
Catechesis/Religious Program—Tel: 313-292-9370. Students 51.

2—ST. ANSELM Rev. Msgr. James A. Moloney, Pastor & Dir., Society for The Propagation of The Faith.
Res.: 17650 W. Outer Dr., 48127. Tel: 313-565-4808; Fax: 313-565-7514.
School—Tel: 313-563-3430; Fax: 313-563-2435. Mrs. Katie Brydges, Prin. Lay Teachers 11; Students 147.
Catechesis/Religious Program—Tel: 313-561-0512. Maryanne Walkuski, D.R.E. Students 69.

3—ST. JOHN THE BAPTIST Rev. Edwin W. Balazy.
Res.: 26123 McDonald Ave., 48125. Tel: 313-292-9693; Fax: 313-292-1755.

4—ST. LINUS Rev. Paul K. Ballien; Deacon Jerry Schiffer.
Parish Office—6466 Evangeline, 48127-2086. Tel: 313-274-4500; Fax: 313-562-2821.
School—Tel: 313-274-5320. Christine Lee, Prin. Lay Teachers 11; Students 218.
Catechesis/Religious Program—Tel: 313-274-5778. Students 166.

5—ST. MEL Rev. Thomas J. Kramer.
Church: 7506 Inkster Rd., 48127. Tel: 313-274-0684; Fax: 313-274-4248.
Catechesis/Religious Program—Tel: 313-274-3977. Donna Trudell, D.R.E. Students 35.

6—OUR LADY OF GRACE Rev. Donald L. Walker, Admin. (Retired); Deacon Robert DeWitt, Pastoral Min.
Res.: 8679 Riverview, 48127. Tel: 313-561-6373; Fax: 313-359-2727.
Church: 23700 Joy Rd., 48127.

7—ST. SABINA Rev. Raymond H. Bucon.
Res.: 25605 Ann Arbor Tr., 48127. Tel: 313-561-1977; Fax: 313-561-1315.
Catechesis/Religious Program—Tel: 313-274-5635. Students 60.

DRYDEN, LAPEER CO., ST. CORNELIUS Revs. Wayne G. Ureel; John Ortman.
Res.: 3834 Mill St., P.O. Box 208, 48428. Tel: 810-796-2926; Fax: 810-796-9713.
Catechesis/Religious Program—Donna Sandoffsky, D.R.E. Students 203.

DUNDEE, MONROE CO., ST. IRENE Rev. Michael A. Woroniewicz.
Res.: 576 Main St., 48131. Tel: 734-529-2160; Fax: 734-529-3463.
Catechesis/Religious Program—Mary Mead, D.R.E. Students 71.

EASTPOINTE, MACOMB CO.

1—ST. BARNABAS, Merged with Holy Innocents, Roseville to form Holy Innocents-St. Barnabas, Roseville.

2—ST. BASIL Rev. Anthony P. Sulkowski.
Parish Center—22851 Lexington Ave., 48021. Tel: 586-777-5610; Fax: 586-779-3341.
Catechesis/Religious Program—Tel: 586-772-5434. Students 33.

3—OUR LADY OF GRACE VIETNAMESE PARISH (1999) Rev. Vincent Nguyen An Ninh.
Church & Res.: 26256 Ryan Rd., Warren, 48091. Tel: 586-755-1313; Fax: 586-393-6623.
Catechesis/Religious Program—Phil Long Nguyen, D.R.E. Students 95.

4—ST. VERONICA Revs. Stanley L. Pachla Jr.; Kulandaisamy Arokiasamy (India).
Res.: 21440 Universal Dr., 48021-2998. Tel: 586-777-0331; Fax: 586-777-0615.
Catechesis/Religious Program—Tel: 586-777-5810. Mary Fortunate, D.R.E. Students 62.
Convent—21357 Redmond, 48021. Tel: 586-777-0321.

ECORSE, WAYNE CO., ST. FRANCIS XAVIER, [CEM] Rev. James F. Wieging (Retired).
Res.: 4250 W. Jefferson Ave., 48229. Tel: 313-383-8514; Fax: 313-383-7508.
Catechesis/Religious Program—Genevieve Beaudrie, D.R.E. Students 94.

EMMETT, ST. CLAIR CO., OUR LADY OF MOUNT CARMEL Rev. Thomas Kuehnemund; Deacon William Kolarik.
Rectory—10828 Brandon Rd., 48022. Tel: 810-384-1338; Fax: 810-384-8708.
Catechesis/Religious Program—10817 Brandon Rd., 48022. Students 100.

ERIE, MONROE CO., ST. JOSEPH, [CEM] Rev. Frederik Kalaj.
Res.: 2214 Manhattan Ave., 48133. Tel: 734-848-6125; Fax: 734-848-2784.
School—2238 Manhattan St., 48133. Tel: 734-848-6985. Mrs. Janet Hardy, Prin. Sisters 2; Lay Teachers 10; Students 113.
Catechesis/Religious Program—Students 68.
Convent—2238 Manhattan Ave., 48133.

FARMINGTON, OAKLAND CO.

1—ST. COLMAN Rev. Norbert V. Kendzierski.
Res.: 32500 Middlebelt Rd., Farmington Hills, 48334. Tel: 248-626-0285; Fax: 248-626-5420. Email: colmancloyne@att.net.
Catechesis/Religious Program—Tel: 248-626-0287. Students 63.

2—ST. GERALD Rev. Festus N. Ejimadu.
Res.: 21300 Farmington Rd., 48336. Tel: 248-477-7470; Fax: 248-477-3878.
Catechesis/Religious Program—Tel: 248-476-7677; Fax: 248-381-5803. Mary Taylor, D.R.E. Students 160.

3—OUR LADY OF SORROWS Revs. Mark S. Brauer; David Cybulski; Deacons Clement Stankiewicz; Donald Quigley; Michael Von Ende; Mrs. Patricia Ernst, Pastoral Assoc.
Res.: 23815 Power Rd., 48336. Tel: 248-474-5720; Fax: 248-474-1340.
School—(Grades PreK-8), 24040 Raphael, 48336-2465. Tel: 248-476-0977; Fax: 248-615-5567. Ann Whitfield, Prin.; Tracy Vlahos, Media Specialist; Andrea Lencione, Asst. Librarian. Lay Teachers 39; Students 756.
Catechesis/Religious Program—Tel: 248-474-6480. Students 249.

FARMINGTON HILLS, OAKLAND CO.

1—ST. ALEXANDER Rev. Robert McGrath; Deacon Mark Springer.
Res.: 27835 Shiawassee, 48336. Tel: 248-474-5748; Fax: 248-427-0883.
Catechesis/Religious Program—Tel: 248-474-8126. Students 156.

2—ST. CLARE OF ASSISI Rev. Gregory Tokarski.
Res.: 29200 W. Ten Mile, 48336. Tel: 248-919-1931; Fax: 248-477-4785.
Catechesis/Religious Program—Students 30.

3—ST. FABIAN Rev. Jeffrey Day; Celia St. Charles, Pastoral Assoc.; Deacon Jene Baughman.
Church & Office: 32200 W. 12 Mile Rd., 48334. Tel: 248-553-4610; Fax: 248-553-6296.
School—Tel: 248-553-2750; Fax: 248-848-3035. Dena Jayson, Prin. Lay Teachers 25; Students 378.
Catechesis/Religious Program—Tel: 248-553-4860; Fax: 248-553-2041. Nancy Pawlukiewicz, D.R.E.; Andy Karl, Youth Min.; Lara Druffner, Middle School Coord. Students 434.

FERNDALE, OAKLAND CO., ST. JAMES Rev. Steven A. Wertanen.
Res.: 241 Pearson St., 48220-1824. Tel: 248-542-8835; Fax: 248-542-0267.
Catechesis/Religious Program—Beth LeAnnais, D.R.E. Students 59.

FLAT ROCK, WAYNE CO., ST. ROCH Rev. Richard A. Hartmann.
Res.: 25022 Gibraltar Rd., 48134. Tel: 734-782-4471; Fax: 734-782-5450.
Catechesis/Religious Program—MaryAnn Dobbs, M.S.E., D.R.E. Students 325.

FRASER, MACOMB CO., OUR LADY QUEEN OF ALL SAINTS Rev. Ronald J. Babich; Sr. Nancy Zajac, O.P., Pastoral Assoc.
Res.: 31740 Cyril Ave., 48026. Tel: 586-293-4050; Fax: 586-293-1041.
Catechesis/Religious Program—Tel: 586-293-4050, Ext. 5. Sr. Nancy Zajac, O.P., D.R.E. Students 122.

GARDEN CITY, WAYNE CO.

1—ST. DUNSTAN Rev. Don A. LaCuesta; Deacon Ziggy Kucharek.
Res.: 1646 Belton Ave., 48135. Tel: 734-425-6721.
Church: 1526 Belton Ave., 48135. Tel: 734-425-6720; Fax: 734-425-8411.
Catechesis/Religious Program—Randy Husaynu, C.R.E./Youth Ministry Coord. Students 93.

2—ST. RAPHAEL THE ARCHANGEL Rev. Raymond H. Lewandowski; Deacon Frederick Burrell; Cindy Briody, Pastoral Min.
Parish Center—31530 Beechwood, 48135. Tel: 734-427-1533; Fax: 734-744-2148.
School—(Grades K-8) Tel: 734-425-9771; Fax: 734-427-8895. DeAnn Brzezinski, Prin. Lay Teachers 12; Students 207.
Catechesis/Religious Program—Tel: 734-425-5550; Fax: 734-744-2148. Carol Bregand, D.R.E. Students 245.

GIBRALTAR, WAYNE CO., ST. VICTOR Revs. James R. Rafferty, Admin.; John Britto Chinnapa, M.S.F.S.
Res.: 14100 Navarre, 48173. Tel: 734-675-0100; Fax: 734-675-6952. Email: stvictor@comcast.net.
Catechesis/Religious Program—Rel. Educ. held at St. Mary, Rockwood

GROSSE ILE, WAYNE CO., SACRED HEART, [CEM] Rev. Michael Molnar.
Parish Center—21599 Parke Ln., 48138. Tel: 734-676-1378; Fax: 734-676-3623.
Catechesis/Religious Program—Students 313.

GROSSE POINTE, WAYNE CO., OUR LADY STAR OF THE SEA Rev. Gary T. Smetanka; Deacon William E. Jamieson.
Church: 467 Fairford, 48236. Tel: 313-884-5554; Fax: 313-885-5591.
School—Tel: 313-884-1070; Fax: 313-884-0406. Julie Aemisegger, Prin. Religious 1; Lay Teachers 29; Students 361.
Catechesis/Religious Program—Tel: 313-884-7407. Michael King, D.R.E. Students 367.
Convent—19950 Morningside Dr., 48236. Tel: 313-884-4074.

GROSSE POINTE FARMS, WAYNE CO., ST. PAUL CATHOLIC CHURCH, [CEM] Rev. Msgr. Patrick F. Halfpenny; Revs. John Wynnycky; Raymond Arwady; Deacon Richard Shubik, Pastoral Assoc.
Res.: 157 Lake Shore Rd., 48236. Tel: 313-885-8855; Fax: 313-886-6467.
School—170 Grosse Pointe Blvd., 48236. Tel: 313-885-3430; Fax: 313-885-9357. Mary Miller, Prin. Lay Teachers 34; Students 506.
Catechesis/Religious Program—Tel: 313-885-7022; Fax: 313-885-9316. Mrs. Judith Jones, D.R.E. Students 495.

GROSSE POINTE PARK, WAYNE CO.

1—ST. AMBROSE Rev. Timothy R. Pelc; Deacon Michael H. Cummins; Mr. Charles J. Dropiewski, Pastoral Assoc.
Res.: 15020 Hampton, 48230. Tel: 313-822-2814; Fax: 313-822-9838.
Catechesis/Religious Program—Elizabeth Haley, D.R.E. Students 268.

2—ST. CLARE OF MONTEFALCO Rev. David L. Brecht, O.S.A.; Janet Guensche, Pastoral Assoc. In Res., Rev. Thomas E. Griffin, O.S.A.
Res.: 1401 Whittier Rd., 48230. Tel: 313-647-5000; Fax: 313-647-5005.
School—16231 Charlevoix, 48230. Tel: 313-647-5100; Fax: 313-647-5105. Sr. Kathleen Jo Avery, O.S.M., Prin. Sisters 2; Lay Teachers 14; Students 161.
Catechesis/Religious Program—Tel: 313-647-5050; Fax: 313-647-5055. Michelle C. Brock, D.R.E.; David Troiano, Music Min. Students 176.

HAMTRAMCK, WAYNE CO.

1—ST. FLORIAN Revs. Miroslaw Frankowski, S.Ch.; Hubert Zasada, S.Ch.
Res. & Church: 2626 Poland Ave., 48212. Tel: 313-871-2778; Fax: 313-871-5947.
Catechesis/Religious Program—Students 103.

2—OUR LADY QUEEN OF APOSTLES, (Polish), Rev. Bogdan Milosz.
Res.: 3851 Prescott Ave., 48212-3115. Tel: 313-891-1520; 313-891-1521; Fax: 313-891-3552.
Catechesis/Religious Program—Debbie Warren, D.R.E. Students 51.

HARPER WOODS, WAYNE CO.

1—OUR LADY QUEEN OF PEACE Rev. William J. Herman.
Res.: 20955 Bournemouth Ave., 48225. Tel: 313-881-5212; Fax: 313-881-7813.
Catechesis/Religious Program—Tel: 313-884-8744. Students 38.

2—ST. PETER THE APOSTLE Rev. Robert J. Keller.
Res.: 19851 Anita St., 48225. Tel: 313-886-1770; Fax: 313-886-1489.
Catechesis/Religious Program—Michaline Chmielewski, D.R.E. Students 31.

HARRISON TWP., MACOMB CO., ST. HUBERT Rev. Msgr.

Ricardo E. Bass.
Res.: 38775 Prentiss, Harrison Township, 48045. Tel: 586-463-5877; Fax: 586-463-1734.
Catechesis/Religious Program—Tel: 586-463-5875; Fax: 586-463-4520. Mrs. Sandra Tapp, C.R.E. Students 244.

HARSENS ISLAND, ST. CLAIR CO., ST. MARK, Merged with Holy Cross, Marine City & St. Catherine of Alexandria, Algonac to form Our Lady on the River, Marine City.

HAZEL PARK, OAKLAND CO.

1—ST. JUSTIN Rev. Robert Hayes Williams.
Res.: 1631 E. Elza St., 48030. Tel: 248-542-2129; Fax: 248-542-2715.
Catechesis/Religious Program—Connie M. Giden, D.R.E. Students 20.

2—ST. MARY MAGDALEN Rev. Bede Louzon, O.F.M.Cap.
Res.: 50 E. Annabelle, 48030. Tel: 248-542-8060; Fax: 248-542-4563.
Catechesis/Religious Program—Tel: 248-547-0323. David Troiano, D.R.E. Students 70.

HIGHLAND, OAKLAND CO., CHURCH OF THE HOLY SPIRIT Rev. Leo T. Lulko; Deacon Michael Somervell.
Church: 3700 Harvey Lake Rd., 48356. Tel: 248-887-5364; Fax: 248-889-1374.
Catechesis/Religious Program—Tel: 248-887-1634. Jillian Peck, D.R.E. Students 445.

HIGHLAND PARK, WAYNE CO., ST. BENEDICT Rev. Msgr. Michael C. LeFevre; Rev. Timothy J. Kane.
Res. & Mailing Address: 9844 Woodward Ave., 48202. Tel: 313-865-6300; Fax: 313-867-4613.
Church: 60 Church Ave., 48203. Tel: 313-868-3876; Fax: 313-868-0110.
Catechesis/Religious Program—Students 14.

HOLLY, OAKLAND CO., ST. RITA Rev. David J. Blazek.
Res.: 309 E. Maple, 48442. Tel: 248-634-4841; Fax: 248-634-4858.
Catechesis/Religious Program—Tel: 248-634-1658; Fax: 248-634-4863. Email: stritasym@sbcglobal.net. Shelly Rau, D.R.E. Students 185.

IDA, MONROE CO., ST. JOSEPH, [CEM] Rev. Michael A. Woroniewicz.
Res.: 8295 Van Akin St., 48140. Tel: 734-269-3895.
Catechesis/Religious Program—Tel: 734-269-3414; Fax: 734-269-2153. Linda Wilson, D.R.E. Students 184.

IMLAY CITY, LAPEER CO., SACRED HEART, [CEM] Rev. Paul Ward.
Res.: 700 Maple Vista, 48444. Tel: 810-724-1135; Fax: 810-724-0870.
Catechesis/Religious Program—Tel: 810-724-1145. Students 87.

INKSTER, WAYNE CO., HOLY FAMILY PARISH Revs. David G. Burgard, Admin.; Gary Morelli.
Res.: 27800 Annapolis Rd., 48141. Tel: 313-563-8242; Fax: 313-563-0696.
Catechesis/Religious Program—Rutha Burney, D.R.E. Students 17.

IRA TOWNSHIP, ST. CLAIR CO., IMMACULATE CONCEPTION, [CEM] Rev. Tomek Maka; Deacon Kenneth Nowicki.
Mailing Address: 9764 Dixie Hwy., 48023. Tel: 586-725-3051; Fax: 586-725-2474.
School—7043 Church Rd., 48023. Tel: 586-725-0078; Fax: 586-725-8240. Kathleen Steele, Prin. Lay Teachers 12; Students 214.
Catechesis/Religious Program—Jane Petitpren, D.R.E. Tel: 586-725-1762. Students 370.

LAKE ORION, OAKLAND CO., ST. JOSEPH Revs. C. Michael Verschaeve; Stephen Pullis; Deacons Steven Mitchell; John Santeramo; Mary Martin, Pastoral Assoc.; Kathy Hasty, Pastoral Assoc.; Leszek Bartkiewicz, Music Min.
Res.: 715 N. Lapeer Rd., 48362. Tel: 248-693-0440; Fax: 248-693-3724.
School—Tel: 248-693-6215; Fax: 248-693-0958. Sr. Theresa Darga, O.S.F., Prin. Lay Teachers 23; Students 385.
Catechesis/Religious Program—Kim Myers, D.R.E. Students 970.

LAKEPORT, ST. CLAIR CO., ST. EDWARD'S ON THE LAKE, [CEM] Rev. Joseph M. Esper.
Res.: 6945 Lakeshore Rd., 48059. Tel: 810-385-4340; Fax: 810-385-6972.
School—(Grades K-5) Tel: 810-385-4461; Fax: 810-385-6070. Sr. Patricia Magee, O.P., Prin. For grades 6-8 please refer to St. Mary/McCormick Catholic Academy, Port Huron, under Elementary Schools, Inter-Parochial in the Institutions Located in the Archdiocese section. Sisters 1; Lay Teachers 6; Students 80.
Catechesis/Religious Program—Paula McCarthy, D.R.E. Students 92.
Convent—6995 Lakeshore Rd., 48059.

LAPEER, LAPEER CO., IMMACULATE CONCEPTION OF THE BLESSED VIRGIN MARY, [CEM] Revs. Douglas J. Terrien; Clement Suhy, O.S.B.; Deacon Gerald DeShaw.
Res.: 814 W. Nepessing, 48446. Tel: 810-664-8594; Fax: 810-664-4564. Email: office@lapeercatholic.org. Web: www.lapeercatholic.org.
School—*Bishop Kelley School*, 926 W. Nepessing St., 48446. Tel: 810-664-5011; Fax: 810-664-5606. Lay Teachers 14; Students 229.
Catechesis/Religious Program—Mrs. Kenlin Botello, D.R.E. Students 230.

LINCOLN PARK, WAYNE CO.

1—CHRIST THE GOOD SHEPHERD Rev. Anthony Charles Richter.
Res.: 1540 Riverbank Ave., 48146. Tel: 313-928-1324; Fax: 313-928-1326.
School—*John Paul II Catholic School*, 1590 Riverbank St., 48146. Tel: 313-386-0633. Mrs. Mariann Lupinacci, Prin. Sponsored by Christ the Good Shepherd, Our Lady of Mount Carmel, St. Joseph and St. Patrick Parishes. Lay Teachers 17; Students 210.
Catechesis/Religious Program—Students 150.

2—ST. HENRY Rev. Gerard J. Cupple.
Res.: 1358 Council Ave., 48146. Tel: 313-381-0711; 313-381-0712; Fax: 313-381-6746.
Catechesis/Religious Program—Anna Hankins, C.R.E. Students 55.

LIVONIA, WAYNE CO.

1—ST. AIDAN Rev. Kevin Thomas.
Res.: 17500 Farmington Rd., 48152. Tel: 734-425-5950; Fax: 734-425-3687.
Catechesis/Religious Program—Tel: 734-425-9333. David Conrad, D.R.E. Students 338.

2—ST. COLETTE Rev. Gary Michalik; Deacons Alfred J. Morad; Gary Pardo.
Res.: 17600 Newburgh, 48152-2699. Tel: 734-464-4433; Fax: 734-464-1694.
Catechesis/Religious Program—Tel: 734-464-4435. Theresa Lisiecki, D.R.E. Students 426.

3—ST. EDITH Rev. James McNulty; Deacon Richard Misiak.
Res.: 15089 Newburgh, 48154. Tel: 734-464-1222; Fax: 734-464-7582.
School—Tel: 734-464-1250; Fax: 734-464-6765. Sr. Margaret Kijek, C.S.S.F., Prin. Felician Sisters 1; Lay Teachers 9; Students 237.
Catechesis/Religious Program—Tel: 734-464-2020. Colleen Misiak, Dir. Faith Formation. Students 443.

4—ST. GENEVIEVE Rev. Howard L. Vogan; Deacon Kevin Breen, Pastoral Assoc.
Res.: 29015 Jamison St., 48154-4021. Tel: 734-427-5220; Fax: 734-422-1763.
School—28933 Jamison St., 48154-4019. Tel: 734-425-4420; Fax: 734-458-3915. Ann Tonissen, Prin. Lay Teachers 10; Students 220.
Catechesis/Religious Program—Tel: 734-261-5920. Sheryl Nordstrom, D.R.E.; Diane Montes, Dir. Youth Ministry. Students 195.

5—ST. MAURICE Rev. Howard L. Vogan; Mr. David A. Carignan, Pastoral Assoc.
Church: 32765 Lyndon Ave., 48154. Tel: 734-522-1616; Fax: 734-522-5092.
Res.: 29015 Jamison, 48154-4021. Tel: 734-427-5220; Fax: 734-427-1763.
Catechesis/Religious Program—Tel: 734-421-5240. Religious education now held at St. Genevieve Parish, Livonia.

6—ST. MICHAEL Revs. William Tindall; Hendrico Rebello.
Res.: 11441 Hubbard Ave., 48150. Tel: 734-261-1455; Fax: 734-522-1123.
School—11311 Hubbard, 48150. Tel: 734-421-7360; Fax: 734-466-9713. Sr. M. Carolyn Ratkowski, C.S.S.F., Prin. Lay Teachers 29; Students 801.
Catechesis/Religious Program—Tel: 734-261-1790. Students 134.
Convent—11400 Fairfield, 48154. Tel: 734-421-7522.

7—ST. PRISCILLA Rev. Theodore D'Cunha, S.A.C.; Deacon Robert C. Fitzgerald.
19120 Purling Brook Rd., 48152. Tel: 248-476-4700; Fax: 248-476-7831. Web: www.saintpriscilla.org.
Catechesis/Religious Program—Tel: 248-476-4702. Students 146.

MACOMB, MACOMB CO.

1—ST. ISIDORE Revs. Michael Hrydziuszko; John Gerald Dumas.
Res.: 18201 Twenty-Three Mile Rd., 48042. Tel: 586-286-1700; Fax: 586-286-8753.
Catechesis/Religious Program—Tel: 586-286-4433. Diane Bucko, D.R.E. Students 1,141.

2—ST. MAXIMILIAN KOLBE, Merged with St. Francis of Assisi, Ray Township to form St. Francis of Assisi-St. Maximilian Kolbe, Ray Township.

MADISON HEIGHTS, OAKLAND CO., ST. VINCENT FERRER Rev. John C. Esper; Deacon Andrew Fairbanks.
Res.: 1087 E. Gardenia Ave., 48071. Tel: 248-542-8720; Fax: 248-542-8721.
Catechesis/Religious Program—Mrs. Sue Gordon, D.R.E. Students 100.

MARINE CITY, ST. CLAIR CO.

1—HOLY CROSS, [CEM] Merged with St. Catherine of Alexandria, Algonac & St. Mark, Harsens Island to form Our Lady on the River, Marine City.

2—OUR LADY ON THE RIVER Rev. Robert C. Schuster; Sr. Mary Ann Ankoviak, C.S.J., Pastoral Assoc.
610 S. Water St., 48039-1557. Tel: 810-765-3568; Fax: 810-765-2974. Web: www.ourladyontheriver.net.
School—(Grades PreK-8), 618 S. Water St., 48039. Tel: 810-765-3591; Fax: 810-765-9074. Mrs. Marilyn Pavlov, Prin.; Mrs. Margaret Smith, Librarian. Lay Teachers 9; Students 85.
Catechesis/Religious Program—Mrs. Margaret Smith, D.R.E. Students 285.

MARYSVILLE, ST. CLAIR CO., ST. CHRISTOPHER Rev. Arthur R. Baranowski.
Res.: 1000 Michigan Ave., 48040. Tel: 810-364-4100; Fax: 810-364-5947.
Catechesis/Religious Program—Tel: 810-364-7080. Theresa Doyle, D.R.E. Students 206.

MAYBEE, MONROE CO., ST. JOSEPH, [CEM] Revs. Robert A. Bauer; Richard Luberti, C.Ss.R.
Res.: 9207 Joseph St., Box 125, 48159. Tel: 734-587-8835; Fax: 734-587-3490.
Catechesis/Religious Program—Patricia Eisenhauer, D.R.E. Students 85.
Convent—9147 Joseph St., Box 118, 48159. Tel: 734-587-8785.

MELVINDALE, WAYNE CO.

1—ST. CONRAD, Merged into St. Mary Magdalen, Melvindale.

2—ST. MARY MAGDALEN Rev. Edward F. Zaorski.
Res.: 19624 Wood St., 48122. Tel: 313-381-8566; Fax: 313-381-1319.
Catechesis/Religious Program—Tel: 313-381-8566, Ext. 104. Cheryl Reynolds, D.R.E. Students 90.

MEMPHIS, MACOMB CO.

1—ALL SAINTS, Merged with St. Philip Neri, Columbus & Holy Rosary Mission, Smiths Creek to form Holy Family, Memphis.

2—HOLY FAMILY Revs. Joseph R. Horn; Janusz Marzynski.
Church: 79780 Main St., 48041. Tel: 810-392-2056; Fax: 810-392-2043.
Catechesis/Religious Program—Susan Finley, D.R.E. Students 336.

MILFORD, OAKLAND CO., ST. MARY, OUR LADY OF THE SNOWS, [CEM] Rev. Ronald Anderson; Valerie Thompson, Pastoral Assoc.
Res.: 1955 E. Commerce, 48381. Tel: 248-685-1482; Fax: 248-684-5642.
Catechesis/Religious Program—Tel: 248-685-2702. Anita Daroczy, D.R.E. Students 1,010.

MONROE, MONROE CO.

1—ST. ANNE Revs. William F. Fisher, O.S.F.S.; Robert C. Mossett, O.S.F.S.
Res.: 2420 N. Dixie Hwy., 48162. Tel: 734-289-2910; Fax: 734-289-1098.
Catechesis/Religious Program—Barbara Rumschlag, D.R.E. Students 65.

2—ST. JOHN THE BAPTIST Rev. James A. Smalarz.
Res.: 511 S. Monroe St., 48161. Tel: 734-241-8910; Fax: 734-241-1943.
School—521 S. Monroe St., 48161. Tel: 734-241-1670; Fax: 734-241-8782. Jacqueline Mojeske, Prin. Lay Teachers 10; Students 231.
Catechesis/Religious Program—Yvonne Davison, D.R.E. Students 102.

3—ST. JOSEPH, [JC] Rev. William F. Fisher, O.S.F.S.
Res.: 924 E. Second St., 48161. Tel: 734-241-9590; Fax: 734-241-5296.
Catechesis/Religious Program—Mrs. Joan Allor, D.R.E. Students 120.

4—ST. MARY, [JC] Rev. Marc A. Gawronski. In Res. May-November, Rev. Robert K. Singelyn (Retired).
Res.: 127 N. Monroe St., 48162. Tel: 734-241-1644; Fax: 734-241-3077.
School—151 N. Monroe St., 48162. Tel: 734-241-3377; Fax: 734-241-0497. Mrs. Melody M. Curtis, Exec. Prin. Lay Teachers 15; Students 317.
Catechesis/Religious Program—Tel: 734-241-6097. Lorie Bronson, D.R.E. & Pastoral Minister. Students 146.

5—ST. MICHAEL THE ARCHANGEL, [JC] Rev. Stephen L. Vileo.
Res.: 502 W. Front St., 48161. Tel: 734-241-8645; Fax: 734-241-6132.
School—510 W. Front St., 48161. Tel: 734-241-3923; Fax: 734-241-7314. Michelle Sontag, Prin. Lay Teachers 10; Students 191.
Catechesis/Religious Program—Tel: 734-241-8663. Mrs. Kathleen Dubay, D.R.E. Students 109.

MOUNT CLEMENS, MACOMB CO., ST. PETER, [CEM] Rev. Michael N. Cooney; Sheila Roy, Pastoral Min.; Moira Shaum, Admin.
Admin. Bldg.—110 New St., 48043. Tel: 586-468-4578; Fax: 586-468-3199. Web: www.saintpeterchurch.us.
School—*St. Mary*, 105 Market St., 48043. Tel: 586-468-4570; Fax: 586-468-6454. Maureen Miscavich, Prin. Lay Teachers 25; Students 462.
Catechesis/Religious Program—Judy Coll, D.R.E. Students 603.

NEW BALTIMORE, MACOMB CO., ST. MARY QUEEN OF CREATION, [CEM] Revs. Nicholas Zukowski; Saji

George Mukkoot; Richi Taylor, Parish Nurse Co-ord.; Deacons Anthony Lewandoski, (Retired); William Schmitz.
Res.: 51041 Maria St., 48047. Tel: 586-725-2441; Fax: 586-725-3647.
Catechesis/Religious Program—36254 Main, 48047. Tel: 586-725-7579. Angela Laesch, D.R.E. Students 698.

NEW BOSTON, WAYNE CO., ST. STEPHEN, [CEM] Rev. John P. Hedges; Deacon Kenneth Trabbic.
Res.: 18858 Huron River Dr., 48164-9272. Tel: 734-753-5268; Fax: 734-753-5828.
School—Tel: 734-753-4175; Fax: 734-753-4579. Mr. Joseph Monte, Prin. Lay Teachers 9; Students 153.
Catechesis/Religious Program—Students 122.
Convent—Tel: 734-753-9937.

NEWPORT, MONROE CO., ST. CHARLES BORROMEO, [CEM] Rev. Victor Roman.
Res.: 8109 Swan Creek Rd., 48166. Tel: 734-586-2531; Fax: 734-586-3900.
School—8125 Swan Creek Rd., 48166. Tel: 734-586-2531, Ext. 3. Mrs. Karen Johnson, Prin. Lay Teachers 9; Students 186.
Catechesis/Religious Program—Tel: 734-586-2531, Ext. 4. Gina Baker, D.R.E. Students 316.

NORTH BRANCH, LAPEER CO.

1—ST. MARY'S BURNSIDE, [CEM] Rev. Richard L. Treml.
Res.: 5622 Summers Rd., P.O. Box 268, 48461. Tel: 810-688-3648; Fax: 810-688-9068.
Catechesis/Religious Program—Lisa Verellen, D.R.E. Twinned with SS. Peter and Paul, North Branch.

2—SS. PETER AND PAUL, [CEM] Rev. Richard L. Treml.
Res.: 6645 Washington, Box 208, 48461. Tel: 810-688-3797; Fax: 810-688-2969.
Catechesis/Religious Program—Tel: 810-688-8343. Lisa Verellen, D.R.E. Twinned with St. Mary's Burnside, North Branch. Students 158.
Chapel—St. Patrick's Clifford, Lapeer Co.

NORTHVILLE, WAYNE CO.

1—ST. ANDREW KIM KOREAN CATHOLIC CHURCH Rev. Dong Hyuk Jeon.
Res.: 21155 Halsted Rd., 48167. Tel: 248-442-9026; Fax: 248-442-9020.

2—OUR LADY OF VICTORY Rev. Denis B. Theroux; Deacon Kenneth Fry; Kathryn Ling, Pastoral Assoc.
Church & Res.: 133 Orchard Dr., 48167. Tel: 248-349-2621; Fax: 248-349-7329.
School—132 Orchard Dr., 48167. Tel: 248-349-3610; Fax: 248-380-7247. Karen Sanford, Prin. Lay Teachers 26; Students 444.
Catechesis/Religious Program—Tel: 248-349-2559. Mary Ellen Skene, Dir. Faith Formation. Students 466.

NOVI, OAKLAND CO.

1—HOLY FAMILY Revs. Robert A. LaCroix; Michael Christopher Zuelch; Deacons William L. Waldmann; Timothy Pilon; Robert Ervin.
Res.: 41445 Fawn Tr., 48375. Tel: 248-349-8847; Fax: 248-349-3711.
Catechesis/Religious Program—Tel: 248-349-8837. Maria Koncius, Pastoral Min. Students 488.

2—ST. JAMES Rev. George Charnley.
Church: 46325 Ten Mile Road, 48374-3007. Tel: 248-347-7778; Fax: 248-347-9625.
Catechesis/Religious Program—Sylvia Shorter, D.R.E. Students 960.

OAK PARK, OAKLAND CO., OUR LADY OF FATIMA Rev. Paul F. Chateau. In Res., Rev. John T. Nowlan (Retired).
Res.: 13500 Oak Park Blvd., 48237. Tel: 248-545-2310; Fax: 248-545-2312.
Catechesis/Religious Program—Natalie LaCroix, D.R.E. Students 54.

ORCHARD LAKE, OAKLAND CO., OUR LADY OF REFUGE Rev. Gerald A. McEnhill.
Parish Office: 3725 Erie Dr., 48324.
Res.: 3663 Erie Dr., 48324. Tel: 248-682-0933.
School—3750 Commerce Rd., 48324. Tel: 248-682-3422; Fax: 248-683-2265. Mr. Robert Pyles, Prin. Lay Teachers 26; Students 284.
Catechesis/Religious Program—Tel: 248-682-6381. Marianne Boesch, C.R.E. Students 290.

ORION TOWNSHIP, OAKLAND CO., CHRIST THE REDEEMER Rev. Joseph E. Dailey.
Res.: 2700 Waldon Rd., Lake Orion, 48360. Tel: 248-391-1621; Fax: 248-391-3412.
Catechesis/Religious Program—Tel: 248-391-4074. Nancy Clancy, D.R.E. Students 764.

ORTONVILLE, OAKLAND CO., ST. ANNE Rev. Gerard Frawley, S.A.C.
Res.: 825 S. Ortonville Rd., 48462. Tel: 248-627-3965; Fax: 248-627-5153.
Catechesis/Religious Program—Gloria Boesch, D.R.E. Students 203.

PLYMOUTH, WAYNE CO.

1—ST. KENNETH Rev. Thomas A. Belczak.
Res.: 14951 N. Haggerty Rd., 48170. Tel: 734-420-0288; Fax: 734-420-2921. Web: www.stkenneth.org.
Catechesis/Religious Program—Tel: 734-420-3031. Mrs. Gretchen Hennen, D.R.E. Students 625.

2—OUR LADY OF GOOD COUNSEL Revs. John Riccardo; Stanislaw Obloj; Charles White IV; Deacon Vincent Small.
Office: 1062 Penniman Ave., 48170.
Res.: 1160 Penniman Ave., 48170. Tel: 734-453-0326; Fax: 734-416-9257.
School—1151 William St., 48170. Tel: 734-453-3053; Fax: 734-357-5331. Kay Reilly, Prin. Lay Teachers 30; Students 625.
Catechesis/Religious Program—Mary DelPup, D.R.E. Students 935.

PONTIAC, OAKLAND CO.

1—ST. DAMIEN OF MOLOKAI PARISH (2009) [CEM] Revs. James F. Kean; Bernardo Cruz-Ramirez; Deacon Brian S. White.
Rectory—46408 Woodward Ave., 48342. Tel: 248-332-0283; Fax: 248-332-7041.
Catechesis/Religious Program—Ms. Maria Charria, D.R.E. Students 376.

2—ST. JOSEPH, Merged with St. Vincent de Paul, Pontiac & St. Michael, Pontiac, to form St. Damien of Molokai, Pontiac.

3—ST. MICHAEL, Merged with St. Vincent de Paul, Pontiac & St. Joseph, Pontiac to form St. Damien of Molokai, Pontiac.

4—ST. VINCENT DE PAUL, Merged with St. Michael, Pontiac & St. Joseph, Pontiac to form St. Damien of Molokai, Pontiac.

PORT HURON, ST. CLAIR CO.

1—HOLY TRINITY, [CEM] Rev. Brian K. Cokonougher. 325 32nd St., 48060. Tel: 810-984-2689; Fax: 810-984-8559.
Catechesis/Religious Program—Karen Clor, D.R.E. Students 208.
Mission—Our Lady of Guadalupe Mission 3110 Goulden St., St. Clair Co. 48060. Tel: 810-985-5212; Fax: 810-985-5314.

2—ST. JOSEPH, [JC] Merged with St. Stephen, Port Huron & Our Lady of Guadalupe Mission, Port Huron to form Holy Trinity, Port Huron.

3—ST. MARY Rev. Zbigniew Zomerfeld.
Res.: 1505 Ballentine St., 48060. Tel: 810-982-7906; Fax: 810-987-8255.
School—Ms. Rachael Becker, Prin. Lay Teachers 16; Students 168.
Catechesis/Religious Program—Patricia Isaacson, D.R.E. Students 219.

4—OUR LADY OF GUADALUPE MISSION, Merged with St. Joseph, Port Huron & St. Stephen, Port Huron to form Holy Trinity, Port Huron.

5—ST. STEPHEN, Merged with St. Joseph, Port Huron & Our Lady of Guadalupe Mission, Port Huron to form Holy Trinity, Port Huron.

RAY TOWNSHIP, MACOMB CO.

1—ST. FRANCIS OF ASSISI, Merged with St. Maximilian Kolbe, Macomb Township to form St. Francis of Assisi-St. Maximilian Kolbe, Ray Township.

2—ST. FRANCIS OF ASSISI-ST. MAXIMILIAN KOLBE Rev. Christopher Talbot.
Church: 62811 New Haven Rd., Ray Twp., 48096. Tel: 586-598-3314; Fax: 586-749-6021.
Catechesis/Religious Program—Jane Van Belle, D.R.E. Students 132.

REDFORD, WAYNE CO.

1—ST. AGATHA, Closed. For inquiries for parish records contact the chancery.

2—ST. HILARY Rev. Donald L. Walker, Admin. (Retired); Sr. Marie Miller, I.H.M.
Res.: 23901 Elmira, 48239. Tel: 313-533-1560; Fax: 313-533-1735.
Catechesis/Religious Program—Christine Laing, D.R.E. Students 5.

3—ST. JOHN BOSCO Rev. Richard A. Osebold.
Res.: 12100 Beech-Daly Rd., 48239. Tel: 313-937-9690; Fax: 313-937-2927.
Catechesis/Religious Program—Sr. Helen Gazarek, D.R.E. Students 38.

4—OUR LADY OF LORETTO Rev. Socorro Fernandes, S.A.C.; Sr. Margretta Wojcik, O.S.F., Pastoral Assoc.
Res.: 17116 Olympia Ave., 48240. Tel: 313-534-9000; Fax: 313-534-6744.
Catechesis/Religious Program—Tel: 313-532-3707. Donna Kohn, D.R.E. Students 62.

5—ST. ROBERT BELLARMINE Rev. Richard M. Leliaert; Laura Scanlan, Pastor Emeritus.
Res.: 27101 W. Chicago, 48239. Tel: 313-937-1500; Fax: 313-937-1185. Web: www.strobertbellarmine.com.
School—27201 W. Chicago, 48239. Tel: 313-937-1655; Fax: 313-937-9795. Nancy Kuszczak, Prin. Lay Teachers 10; Students 150; Preschool 20.
Catechesis/Religious Program—Tel: 313-937-1531. Mrs. Dawn Dwyer, Faith Formation Coord. Students 94.

6—ST. VALENTINE Rev. Suresh Rajaian, S.A.C.; Deacon Lawrence Toth.
Res.: 25881 Dow, 48239. Tel: 313-532-4394; Fax: 313-537-2237.
School—(Grades PreK-8), 25875 Hope St., 48239. Tel: 313-533-7149; Fax: 313-533-3060. Rachel Damuth, Prin.; Maureen Kelly, Librarian. Lay Teachers 12; Students 198.
Catechesis/Religious Program—Tel: 313-538-9161. Lynne O'Brien, D.R.E. Students 86.

RICHMOND, MACOMB CO., ST. AUGUSTINE, [CEM] Revs. Joseph A. Plawecki; John Nedumcheril.
Church: 68035 Main St., 48062. Tel: 586-727-5215; Fax: 586-727-3760. Email: stjosepherie@yahoo.com.
Res.: 36341 Franklin St., 48062. Tel: 586-727-6469.
School—67901 Howard, 48062. Tel: 586-727-9365. Mr. Gerald Bagierek, Prin. Lay Teachers 18; Students 183.
Catechesis/Religious Program—Tel: 586-727-9290. Students 148.

RIVER ROUGE, WAYNE CO., OUR LADY OF LOURDES Rev. James F. Wieging (Retired); Dr. Paul D. Bodrie, Pastoral Assoc.
Res.: 1440 Coolidge Highway, 48218. Tel: 313-842-3320; 313-842-3321; Fax: 313-842-4507.
Catechesis/Religious Program—Genevieve Beaudrie, D.R.E. Students 87.

RIVERVIEW, WAYNE CO., ST. CYPRIAN Rev. William J. Promesso.
Res.: 13249 Pennsylvania, 48193. Tel: 734-283-1366; Fax: 734-283-2809.
Catechesis/Religious Program—Tel: 734-283-1366, Ext. 118. Mrs. Stacey Sutowski-Shurtz, D.R.E. Students 228.

ROCHESTER, OAKLAND CO., ST. ANDREW Rev. Thomas F. Slowinski; Deacon Marc Gemellaro; Sr. Rebecca Hodge, O.P., Pastoral Assoc.
Res.: 1400 Inglewood, 48307. Tel: 248-651-7486; Fax: 248-651-3950.
Catechesis/Religious Program—Tel: 248-651-6401; Fax: 248-651-2844. Students 1,785.

ROCHESTER HILLS, OAKLAND CO.

1—ST. IRENAEUS Rev. Brian J. Chabala.
Res.: 771 Old Perch Rd., 48309. Tel: 248-651-9595; Fax: 248-651-1504.
Catechesis/Religious Program—Tel: 248-651-2443; Fax: 248-651-8767. Patricia Egan-Myers, D.R.E. Students 453.

2—ST. MARY OF THE HILLS Rev. Stanley A. Ulman.
Church: 2675 John R., 48307-4652. Tel: 248-853-5390; Fax: 248-853-7989.
Catechesis/Religious Program—Tel: 248-844-8662. Peggy Casing, D.R.E. Students 429.

3—ST. PAUL ALBANIAN CATHOLIC COMMUNITY Rev. Frane Kolaj.
Office: 525 Auburn Rd., 48307. Tel: 248-844-8201; Fax: 248-844-8092.
Catechesis/Religious Program—Kanto Dushaj, D.R.E. Students 150.

ROCKWOOD, WAYNE CO., ST. MARY, [CEM] Rev. James R. Rafferty.
Res.: 32477 Church, 48173. Tel: 734-379-9248; Fax: 734-379-6548.
School—Tel: 734-379-9285; Fax: 734-379-9088. Kevin DuFresne, Prin. Lay Teachers 10; Students 171.
Catechesis/Religious Program—Kimberley Amos, Catechism Coord. Students 143.

ROMEO, MACOMB CO., ST. CLEMENT OF ROME Rev. Stephen C. Reckker.
Res.: 343 S. Main St., 48065. Tel: 586-752-9611; Fax: 586-752-1601.
Catechesis/Religious Program—Tel: 586-752-6951; Fax: 586-752-7093. Deborah Knoblock, D.R.E. Students 683.

ROMULUS, WAYNE CO., ST. ALOYSIUS Rev. John M. Currin.
Res.: 11280 Ozga St., 48174. Tel: 734-941-5056; Fax: 734-941-6018.
Church: 37200 Neville St., 48174.
Catechesis/Religious Program—Maxine Smith, D.R.E. Students 40.

ROSEVILLE, MACOMB CO.

1—ST. ANGELA Rev. Paul Czarnota. In Res., Rev. Dennis J. Nowinski.
Res.: 25001 Chippendale, 48066.
Church: Ten Mile Rd. and Chippendale, 48066. Tel: 586-445-6360; Fax: 586-445-6366.
Catechesis/Religious Program—Tel: 586-775-4650. Elizabeth Haley, D.R.E. Students 13.

2—ST. ATHANASIUS Rev. Ronald J. Victor; Deacon Michael O'Keefe.
Res.: 18720 Thirteen Mile Rd., 48066. Tel: 586-772-1170; Fax: 586-776-2945.
Catechesis/Religious Program—Carol Buboi, D.R.E. Students 185.

3—ST. DONALD Rev. Michael A. Donovan.
Res.: 16330 Twelve Mile Rd., 48066. Tel: 586-773-3440; Fax: 586-773-1235.
Catechesis/Religious Program—Students 14.

4—HOLY INNOCENTS-ST. BARNABAS Rev. Clarence E. Williams, C.PP.S.
Res. & Mailing Address: 26100 Ridgemont, 48066. Tel: 586-777-7543; Fax: 586-777-1536.
Catechesis/Religious Program—24800 Phlox,

Eastpointe, 48021. Tel: 586-775-4650; Fax: 586-775-6933. Elizabeth Haley, Dir., Faith Formation. Students 87.
5—HOLY INNOCENTS, Merged with St. Barnabas, Eastpointe to form Holy Innocents-St. Barnabas, Roseville.
6—SACRED HEART Rev. Eugene Katcher; Deacons Lawrence Sullivan; Paul Lippard.
Res.: 18430 Utica Rd., 48066. Tel: 586-777-9116; Fax: 586-777-7958.
Catechesis/Religious Program—Tel: 810-777-8150; Fax: 586-777-3288. Paula Davis, D.R.E. Students 48.
ROYAL OAK, OAKLAND CO.
1—ST. DENNIS Revs. John P. Christ, O.S.C.; Tony Ong; Deacon Francis X. Chau Ngoc Doan.
Res.: 2200 E. 12 Mile Rd., 48067-1504. Tel: 248-544-2181; Fax: 248-544-9443.
Catechesis/Religious Program—Tel: 248-545-1926. Stacie Sniezek, D.R.E. Students 113.
2—ST. MARY, [CEM] Rev. Steven A. Wertanen; Deacon Christopher Stark; Christine Wagberg, Pastoral Assoc.
Res.: 730 Lafayette Ave. S., 48067. Tel: 248-547-1818; Fax: 248-547-4577.
School—628 Lafayette Ave. S., 48067. Tel: 248-545-2140; Fax: 248-545-2303. Gabriela Bala, Prin. Lay Teachers 11; Part-Time Teachers 13; Students 207.
Catechesis/Religious Program—Tel: 248-547-1810. Mrs. Joanne Jones, D.R.E. Students 194.
3—NATIONAL SHRINE OF THE LITTLE FLOWER Rev. Msgr. William H. Easton; Revs. Anthony E. Camilleri; Adalberto Espinoza; Joseph Lang; Deacon Thomas Avery.
Res. & Church: 2100 W. 12 Mile Rd., 48073-3973. Tel: 248-541-4122 (Office); Fax: 248-541-2838.
School—1621 Linwood, 48067. Tel: 248-541-4622; Fax: 248-541-6969. Sharon Dixon, Prin.; Kelly Neighbors, Asst. Prin. Lay Teachers 29; Students 525.
School—Academy, 3500 W. Thirteen Mile Rd., 48073. Tel: 248-549-2928; Fax: 248-546-2953. Ms. Gabrielle Erken, Prin. Lay Teachers 15; Students 129.
High School—Tel: 248-549-2925; Fax: 248-549-2953. Lay Teachers 26; Students 282.
Catechesis/Religious Program—Tel: 248-541-5133. Students 423.
ST. CLAIR, ST. CLAIR CO., ST. MARY, [CEM] Rev. Gregory J. Deters.
Res.: 415 N. 6th St., 48079. Tel: 810-329-2255; Fax: 810-329-5997.
School—Tel: 810-329-4150; Fax: 810-329-5705. Mr. Gary Tomlin, Prin. Lay Teachers 10; Students 112.
Catechesis/Religious Program—Tel: 810-329-7801. Mrs. Mary Beth Blum, D.R.E. Students 355.
Community Center—811 Orchard St., 48079. Tel: 810-329-2400.
ST. CLAIR SHORES, MACOMB CO.
1—ST. GERMAINE, Merged with St. Gertrude, St. Clair Shores to form Our Lady of Hope, St. Clair Shores.
2—ST. GERTRUDE, [CEM] Merged with St. Germaine, St. Clair Shores to form Our Lady of Hope, St. Clair Shores.
3—ST. ISAAC JOGUES Rev. James F. Lopez.
Parish Center—21120 Benjamin Dr., 48081. Tel: 586-778-5100; Fax: 586-778-4458.
School—21100 Madison St., Saint Clair Shores, 48081. Tel: 586-771-3525; Fax: 586-778-8183. Ann E. Kolley, Prin. Lay Teachers 20; Students 360.
Catechesis/Religious Program—Jean Hartman, Faith Formation. Students 234.
4—ST. JOAN OF ARC Rev. Msgr. G. Michael Bugarin; Revs. Hoang Chi Lam; Lee E. Acervo; Sr. Carol Juhasz, I.H.M., Pastoral Min. & Coord.
Parish Center—22412 Overlake, 48080. Tel: 586-777-3670; Fax: 586-774-5528.
School—22415 Overlake, 48080. Tel: 586-777-8370; Fax: 586-447-3574. Mr. Don Ancypa, Prin. Lay Teachers 31; Students 503.
Catechesis/Religious Program—Tel: 586-772-1282. Suzanne Cornelius, D.R.E. Students 380.
5—ST. LUCY Rev. James E. Commyn; Deacon Robert Herta. In Res., Rev. Michael Loyson.
Res.: 23401 Jefferson, 48080. Tel: 586-771-8300; Fax: 586-447-4220.
Catechesis/Religious Program—Tel: 586-447-4223. Students 44.
6—ST. MARGARET OF SCOTLAND Rev. Ronald DeHondt; Deacon Ronald Channell.
Church: 21201 Thirteen Mile Rd., 48082. Tel: 586-293-2240; Fax: 586-293-0116.
Res.: 21101 Thirteen Mile Rd., Saint Clair Shores, 48082. Tel: 586-296-3190.
Catechesis/Religious Program—Tel: 586-293-3280. Students 300.
7—OUR LADY OF HOPE Rev. James L. Bjorum.
Office: 28301 Little Mack, 48081. Tel: 586-771-1750; Fax: 586-771-7634.
School—Tel: 586-771-0890; Fax: 586-779-3667. Mrs. Julie DeGrez, Prin. Lay Teachers 13; Students 265.
Catechesis/Religious Program—28839 Jefferson, Saint Clair Shores, 48081. Tel: 586-775-5820; Fax: 586-447-4729. Kathleen Thompson, D.R.E. Students 247.
SHELBY TWP.
1—ST. JOHN VIANNEY CHURCH Rev. Timothy P. Mazur; Fritzi Bohlmann, Pastoral Assoc.; Barbara Bakotich, Youth Min.
Res.: 54045 Schoenherr Rd., 48315. Tel: 586-781-6525; Fax: 586-781-6527.
Catechesis/Religious Program—Tel: 586-781-2627. Mary Lundgaard, D.R.E. Students 1,714.
2—ST. KIERAN Rev. H. Thomas Johnson; Patricia Radacsy, Pastoral Assoc.
Res.: 53600 Mound Rd., 48316. Tel: 586-781-4901; Fax: 586-781-6516.
Catechesis/Religious Program—Tel: 586-781-6515. Students 1,012.
3—ST. THERESE OF LISIEUX Revs. Lawrence Zurawski; Matthew Ellis; Deacon Donald Sandstrom.
Church: 48115 Schoenherr Rd., 48315-4225. Tel: 586-254-4433; Fax: 586-254-5463.
Catechesis/Religious Program—Students 927.
SOUTH LYON, OAKLAND CO., ST. JOSEPH Revs. Stan Tokarski; Grzegorz Rozborski; Deacon Chris Booms.
Church & Res.: 830 S. Lafayette, 48178. Tel: 248-446-8700; Fax: 248-446-8746. Email: office@saintjosephsouthlyon.org. Web: www.saintjosephsouthlyon.org.
Catechesis/Religious Program—Laura Quinn Rector, D.R.E. Students 870.
SOUTHFIELD, OAKLAND CO.
1—ST. BEATRICE, Merged with St. Bede, Southfield, St. Ives, Southfield & St. Michael, Southfield to form Church of the Transfiguration, Southfield.
2—ST. BEDE, Merged with St. Beatrice, Southfield, St. Ives, Southfield & St. Michael, Southfield to form Church of the Transfiguration, Southfield.
3—CHURCH OF THE TRANSFIGURATION Rev. William Ollendick, O.F.M.
25225 Code Rd., 48034-5807. Tel: 248-356-8787; Fax: 248-356-1240.
Catechesis/Religious Program—Diane Klucka, D.R.E. Students 40.
4—DIVINE PROVIDENCE, (Lithuanian), Rev. Gintaras Jonikas.
Res.: 25335 W. 9 Mile Rd., 48033-3933. Tel: 248-354-3429; Fax: 248-354-1773.
5—ST. IVES, Merged with St. Beatrice, Southfield, St. Bede, Southfield & St. Michael, Southfield to form Church of the Transfiguration, Southfield.
6—ST. MICHAEL, Merged with St. Beatrice, Southfield, St. Bede, Southfield & St. Ives, Southfield to form Church of the Transfiguration, Southfield.
7—OUR LADY OF ALBANIANS Rev. Nue Gjergji, Admin.
29350 Lahser Rd., 48034. Tel: 248-353-3410; Fax: 248-353-5412.
Catechesis/Religious Program—Dr. Gjecka Gjelaj, D.R.E. Students 130.
SOUTHGATE, WAYNE CO.
1—ST. HUGH, Merged into St. Francis Cabrini Parish, Allen Park.
2—ST. PIUS X Rev. Robert J. McCabe.
Office: 14101 Superior Ave., 48195. Tel: 734-285-1100; Fax: 734-285-5310.
Res.: 14160 Longtin Ave., 48195.
School—14141 Pearl St., 48195. Tel: 734-284-6500; Fax: 734-285-6525. Michelle E. Seward, Elementary Prin. Lay Teachers 18; Students 302.
Catechesis/Religious Program—Philippa Monteleon, D.R.E. Students 156.
STERLING HEIGHTS, MACOMB CO.
1—ST. BLASE Rev. Randall Phillips; Dr. Mary Dumm, Pastoral Assoc.
Res.: 12151 E. 15 Mile Rd., 48312-5120. Tel: 586-268-2244; Fax: 586-268-1174.
Catechesis/Religious Program—Students 320.
2—SS. CYRIL AND METHODIUS Rev. Benjamin Kosnac (Slovakia), Admin.; Deacons Gerald Smigell; James Gennette.
Res.: 41233 Ryan Rd., 48314. Tel: 586-726-6911; Fax: 586-685-1070.
Catechesis/Religious Program—Paul Schuller, D.R.E.; Carroll Schuller, D.R.E. Students 380.
3—ST. EPHREM Rev. Ronald Milligan; Deacon Edwin McLeod.
Res.: 38900 Dodge Rd., 48312. Tel: 586-264-1230; Fax: 586-264-2757.
Catechesis/Religious Program—Tel: 586-264-2777; Fax: 586-264-2783. Students 122.
4—ST. JANE FRANCES DE CHANTAL Rev. Jerome Slowinski.
Res.: 38750 Ryan Rd., 48310. Tel: 586-977-8080; Fax: 586-977-9305.
Catechesis/Religious Program—Tel: 586-977-0310. Students 238.
5—ST. MALACHY Rev. Joseph J. Gembala.
Res.: 14115 14 Mile Rd., 48312-6506. Tel: 586-264-1220; Fax: 586-264-1656.
Catechesis/Religious Program—Tel: 586-268-4430. Ms. Patricia Whelan, D.R.E. Students 320.
6—ST. MATTHIAS Rev. Francisco Restrepo.
Res.: 12509 Nineteen Mile Rd., 48313. Tel: 586-731-1300; Fax: 586-731-2576.
Catechesis/Religious Program—Tel: 586-731-0650. Donna Latimer, D.R.E. Students 118.
7—ST. MICHAEL Revs. Michael W. Quaine; Artemio Galos; Deacon Lawrence Healy.
Church: 40501 Hayes Rd., 48313. Tel: 586-247-0020; Fax: 586-247-4081.
Res.: 39443 Heatherheath, Clinton Township, 48038. Tel: 313-268-6379.
Catechesis/Religious Program—Tel: 586-247-0098. Cathy McInerney, D.R.E. Students 460.
8—OUR LADY OF CZESTOCHOWA Revs. Slawomir Murawka, S.Ch.; Jozef Siedlarz, S.Ch. In Res., Revs. Konrad Urbanowski, S.Ch.; Stanislaw Drzal, S.Ch.
Res.: 3100 18 Mile Rd., 48314-3810. Tel: 586-977-7267; Fax: 586-977-2074. Web: www.parafiasterlinghts.org.
Catechesis/Religious Program—Sr. Malgorzota Tomalka, D.R.E. Students 323.
9—ST. RENE GOUPIL Rev. Steven C. Koehler; Deacon David Fleming.
Mailing Address: 35955 Ryan Rd., 48310.
Res.: 35670 Ryan Rd., 48310. Tel: 586-939-7500; Fax: 586-939-7839. Email: mmay@strene.org.
Catechesis/Religious Program—Michael Novak, D.R.E. Students 190.
TAYLOR, WAYNE CO.
1—ST. ALFRED Rev. Maurice Henry Sands.
Res.: 9500 Banner, 48180. Tel: 313-291-6464; Fax: 313-291-2733.
Catechesis/Religious Program—Tel: 313-291-6464, Ext. 104; Fax: 313-291-2700. Annah Rogal, D.R.E. Students 291.
2—ST. CONSTANCE Rev. Leo F. Sabourin; Deacon Joseph Mouro.
Res.: 21555 Kinyon Rd., 48180. Tel: 313-291-4050; Fax: 313-291-5655.
Catechesis/Religious Program—Bernadine Shook, D.R.E. Students 130.
3—ST. CYRIL OF JERUSALEM, Merged with St. Paschal, Taylor to form Our Lady of the Angels, Taylor.
4—OUR LADY OF THE ANGELS Rev. Dariusz Strzalkowski; Deacons Daniel J. Hurley; William A. Thome.
Church: 6442 Pelham Rd., 48180. Tel: 313-381-3000; Fax: 313-381-5528.
Catechesis/Religious Program—Michael Grube, D.R.E. Students 170.
5—ST. PASCHAL, Merged with St. Cyril of Jerusalem, Taylor to form Our Lady of the Angels, Taylor.
TEMPERANCE, MONROE CO.
1—ST. ANTHONY, [CEM] Rev. Brian K. Hurley.
Res.: 4605 St. Anthony Rd., 48182. Tel: 734-854-1143; Fax: 734-854-4622.
Catechesis/Religious Program—Students 74.
2—OUR LADY OF MT. CARMEL Revs. Stephen Rooney; Sama F. Muma.
Res.: 8330 Lewis Ave., 48182. Tel: 734-847-2805; Fax: 734-847-8970.
Catechesis/Religious Program—Tel: 734-847-1725. Students 450.
TRENTON, WAYNE CO.
1—ST. JOSEPH, [JC] Rev. Bradley Forintos; Deacon Mark Redwine; Donald Scott Anastasia, Pastoral Assoc.
Parish Center—2565 Third St., 48183. Tel: 734-676-9082; Fax: 734-676-6255.
School—2675 Third St., 48183. Tel: 734-676-2565; Fax: 734-676-9744. Wanda Rovenskie, Prin. Lay Teachers 9; Students 217.
Catechesis/Religious Program—Tel: 734-676-7115; Fax: 734-676-9082. Thomas J. Clark, D.R.E. Students 283.
2—ST. TIMOTHY Rev. Robert J. Shafer.
Parish Office—2901 Manning Dr., 48183. Tel: 734-676-5115; Fax: 734-676-6863. Email: st.timothy@att.net.
Catechesis/Religious Program—Tel: 734-676-5616. Dennae Petrlich, D.R.E.; Theresa Kramer, D.R.E. Students 70.
TROY, OAKLAND CO.
1—ST. ALAN Rev. Donald L. Demmer, Admin.; Sr. Mary Choiniere, S.S.J., Pastoral Assoc.
Res.: 2345 Coolidge Rd., 48084. Tel: 248-649-5511.
Church: 3077 Glouchester, 48084. Tel: 248-649-5510; Fax: 248-649-6729.
Catechesis/Religious Program—Betty Sheehan, D.R.E. Students 59.
2—ST. ANASTASIA Revs. John J. Mech; Eric Fedewa; Deacons Ronald W. Cook, Pastoral Assoc.; Donald Baross, Pastoral Assoc.
Res.: 4571 John R. Rd., 48085. Tel: 248-689-8380; Fax: 248-689-7489.
Catechesis/Religious Program—Marian Bart, D.R.E. Students 922.
3—ST. ELIZABETH ANN SETON Rev. Norman D.

Nawrocki; Deacon Gregory Formanczyk.
Res.: 301 Tara, 48085. Tel: 248-879-1086.
Church: 280 E. Square Lake Rd., 48085. Tel: 248-879-1310; Fax: 248-879-2886.
Catechesis/Religious Program—Tel: 248-879-1314. Students 193.

4—ST. LUCY, (Croatian), Rev. Philip Pavich, O.F.M.
Res.: 200 E. Wattles Rd., 48085. Tel: 248-619-9910; Fax: 248-619-9912. Email: stlucy@sbcglobal.net. Ms. Anica Letica, D.R.E.

5—ST. THOMAS MORE Rev. Edward A. Belczak; Deacon John Vanneste.
Res.: 4580 Adams Rd., 48098. Tel: 248-647-2222; Fax: 248-647-8192.
Catechesis/Religious Program—Tel: 248-647-4680. Students 687.

UTICA, MACOMB CO., ST. LAWRENCE Revs. Robert J. Fisher; Philip Ching; Sr. Janet Sullivan, I.H.M., Pastoral Assoc.
Church: 44633 Utica Rd., 48317. Tel: 586-731-5347; Fax: 586-731-5393.
Res.: 44657 Utica Rd., 48317.
School—(Grades PreK-8), 44429 Utica Rd., 48317. Tel: 586-731-0135. Cathy Ciolino, Prin.; Nancy Krantz, Librarian. Lay Teachers 33; Students 813.
Catechesis/Religious Program—Tel: 586-731-5072. Lisa Rajnicek, D.R.E. Students 664.

WALLED LAKE, OAKLAND CO., ST. WILLIAM Rev. Michael G. Savickas; Deacons Charles R. Dreyer; John Liddle.
Res.: 531 Common St., 48390-3417. Tel: 248-624-1421; Fax: 248-624-5273.
School—135 O'Flaherty, 48390. Tel: 248-669-4440; Fax: 248-669-2245. Linda Jackson, Prin. Lay Teachers 20; Students 194.
Catechesis/Religious Program—Tel: 248-624-1371. Jeanne Martin, D.R.E. Students 352.

WARREN, MACOMB CO.

1—ST. ANNE Rev. Alberto P. Bondy.
Res.: 32000 Mound Rd., 48092. Tel: 586-264-0713; Fax: 586-264-0718.
School—Tel: 586-264-2911; Fax: 586-264-4533. Anthony Sahadi, Prin. Lay Teachers 25; Students 601.
Catechesis/Religious Program—Students 100.

2—ASCENSION, Merged into St. Clement, Center Line.

3—ST. CLETUS, Closed. For inquiries for parish records contact the chancery.

4—ST. DOROTHY, Merged with St. Leonard of Port Maurice, Warren to form St. Teresa of Avila, Warren.

5—ST. EDMUND Rev. Robert J. Witkowski.
Res.: 14025 Twelve Mile Rd., 48088. Tel: 586-772-2720; Fax: 586-772-5576.
Catechesis/Religious Program—Tel: 586-773-9220; Fax: 586-772-5021. Students 241.

6—ST. LEONARD OF PORT MAURICE, [CEM] Merged with St. Dorothy, Warren to form St. Teresa of Avila, Warren.

7—ST. LOUISE Rev. Msgr. Thomas G. Rice; Deacons Wilhelm Kessler; Art Majewski.
Res.: 2500 Twelve Mile Rd., 48092. Tel: 586-751-3340; Fax: 586-751-0603.
Catechesis/Religious Program—Tel: 586-751-3486. Peggy DeClercq, D.R.E. Students 187.

8—ST. MARK Rev. Thomas E. Urban; Deacons George R. Posavetz; Paul Lippard.
Res.: 4401 Bart, 48091. Tel: 586-759-3020; Fax: 586-759-3024.
Catechesis/Religious Program—

9—ST. MARTIN DE PORRES Rev. Roman Pasieczny.
Res.: 31555 Hoover Rd., 48093. Tel: 586-264-7515; Fax: 586-264-4013.
Catechesis/Religious Program—Tel: 586-264-7970. Mrs. Christine Cabe, D.R.E. Students 410.

10—ST. SYLVESTER Rev. Gary W. Schulte; Deacon John L. Skladanowski, Pastoral Assoc.
Res.: 11200 Twelve Mile Rd., 48093. Tel: 586-751-3636; Fax: 586-751-1766.
Catechesis/Religious Program—Tel: 586-751-3510; Fax: 586-751-3512. Students 95.

11—ST. TERESA OF AVILA Rev. Michael R. Gawlowski.
12255 Frazho Rd., 48089-1200. Tel: 586-757-3306; Fax: 586-757-5390.
Catechesis/Religious Program—Alice Baron, D.R.E. Students 205.

WASHINGTON, MACOMB CO., SS. JOHN AND PAUL Rev. David A. Buersmeyer; Deacon John Wright.
Res.: 61847 Glenwood Trail, 48094.
Church: 7777 W. 28 Mile Rd., 48094. Tel: 586-781-9010; Fax: 586-781-7061.
Catechesis/Religious Program—Tel: 586-781-9488. Students 227.

WATERFORD, OAKLAND CO.

1—ST. BENEDICT Rev. Paul Larry Siroskey.
Parish Office—80 S. Lynn, 48328. Tel: 248-681-1534; Fax: 248-681-4501.
Catechesis/Religious Program—Students 160.

2—OUR LADY OF THE LAKES Revs. Lawrence Delonnay; Krzysztof Nowak.
Mailing Address: 5481 Dixie Hwy., 48329. Tel: 248-623-0274; Fax: 248-623-2723.
School—5501 Dixie Hwy., 48329. Tel: 248-623-0250; Fax: 248-623-2274. Lauri Hoffman, Elementary Prin. Lay Teachers 16; Students 374.
High School—5495 Dixie Hwy., 48329. Tel: 248-623-0340. Carl Uberti, Pres. Sisters 1; Lay Teachers 13; Students 175.
Catechesis/Religious Program—Tel: 248-623-0291; Fax: 248-623-1280. Artha Horowitz, D.R.E. Students 325.

3—ST. PERPETUA Rev. Jack H. Baker.
Res.: 134 Airport Rd., 48327. Tel: 248-682-6431; Fax: 248-682-7088.
Catechesis/Religious Program—Pauline Zorza, D.R.E. Students 203.

WAYNE, WAYNE CO., ST. MARY, [CEM] Rev. David G. Burgard.
34530 W. Michigan Ave., 48184-1748. Tel: 734-721-8745; Fax: 734-721-0260. Email: parishoffice@stmarywayne.org. Web: www.stmarywayne.org.
School—34516 Michigan Ave., 48184-1748. Tel: 734-721-1240; Fax: 734-467-7381. Mr. Donald Lipinski, Prin. Lay Teachers 15; Students 247.
Catechesis/Religious Program—Tel: 734-721-8745, Ext. 42. Students 131.

WEST BLOOMFIELD, OAKLAND CO., PRINCE OF PEACE Rev. Ronald J. Jozwiak.
Res.: 4300 Walnut Lake Rd., 48323. Tel: 248-681-9424; Fax: 248-681-5543.
Catechesis/Religious Program—Tel: 248-681-5070. Carol Kania, D.R.E. Students 200.

WESTLAND, WAYNE CO.

1—ST. BERNARDINE, Closed. For inquiries for parish records contact the chancery.

2—CHURCH OF THE DIVINE SAVIOR Rev. Alexander A. Kuras; Deacon Paul F. Pelchat.
Church: 39375 Joy Rd., 48185. Tel: 734-455-3620; Fax: 734-455-7998.
Res.: 9249 Caprice, Plymouth, 48170. Tel: 734-664-1592.
Catechesis/Religious Program—Sr. Gemma Legel, O.S.F., D.R.E. Students 54.

3—ST. DAMIAN Rev. Salvino P. Briffa (Retired).
Res.: 30055 Joy Rd., 48185-1728. Tel: 734-421-6130; Fax: 734-513-4916.
School—29891 Joy Rd., 48185. Tel: 734-427-1680; Fax: 734-427-1272. Mary Stempin, Prin. Lay Teachers 10; Students 155.
Catechesis/Religious Program—Tel: 734-522-5383. Students 90.

4—ST. RICHARD Rev. Terence Treppa.
Res.: 35637 Cherry Hill, 48186. Tel: 734-729-2240; Fax: 734-729-3132.
Church Office: 35637 Cherry Hill Rd., 48186.
Catechesis/Religious Program—Tel: 734-729-4411; Fax: 734-727-0466. Judy Gorman, D.R.E. Students 64.

5—SS. SIMON AND JUDE Rev. Gerard V. Bechard.
Office: 32500 Palmer Rd., 48186. Tel: 734-722-1343; Fax: 734-326-5466.
Catechesis/Religious Program—Mary Ann Kocsis, D.R.E.; Margaret Reyez, D.R.E. Students 90.

6—ST. THEODORE OF CANTERBURY Revs. Salvino P. Briffa, Admin. (Retired); John J. O'Keefe.
Res.: 8200 Wayne Rd., 48185. Tel: 734-425-4421; Fax: 734-425-0650.
Catechesis/Religious Program—Denette Plant, D.R.E. Students 71.

WHITE LAKE, OAKLAND CO., ST. PATRICK Revs. Thomas L. Meagher; John Peter Arulanandam, M.S.F.S.; Deacon Michael Chesley.
Res.: 9086 Hutchins Rd., 48386. Tel: 248-698-3100; Fax: 248-698-2350.
School—9040 Hutchins Rd., 48386. Tel: 248-698-3240; Fax: 248-698-4339. Carol Budchuk, Prin. Lay Teachers 28; Students 438.
Catechesis/Religious Program—Students 805.

WOODHAVEN, WAYNE CO., OUR LADY OF THE WOODS Rev. Andrew Czarnecki.
Res.: 21892 Gudith Rd., 48183. Tel: 734-671-5101; Fax: 734-671-2901.
Catechesis/Religious Program—Tel: 734-671-0525. Jeanette Russell, D.R.E. Students 771.

WYANDOTTE, WAYNE CO.

1—ST. ELIZABETH, [JC] Rev. Michael Cremin, S.A.C.
Mailing Address: 138 Goodell St., 48192. Tel: 734-284-7727; Fax: 734-284-7891.
Res.: 334 Elm St., 48192. Tel: 734-285-9840; Fax: 734-285-1623.
Catechesis/Religious Program—Julie Dzanbazoff, D.R.E. Students 11.

2—ST. HELENA, Closed. For inquiries for parish records contact the chancery.

3—ST. JOSEPH Rev. Michael Cremin, S.A.C.
Res.: 334 Elm St., 48192. Tel: 734-285-9840; Fax: 734-285-9745.
See Pope John Paul II Regional School at Christ the Good Shepherd, Lincoln Park.
Catechesis/Religious Program—Tel: 734-285-9840, Ext. 2. Julie Dzanbazoff, D.R.E. Students 141.

4—OUR LADY OF MT. CARMEL, (Polish), [CEM] Rev. Walter J. Ptak; Deacon Richard Bloomfield. (High school closed on June 30, 2011. Contact Parish for records)
Res.: 976 Pope John Paul II Ave., 48192. Tel: 734-284-9135; Fax: 734-284-1367.
See Pope John Paul II Regional School at Christ the Good Shepherd, Lincoln Park.
Catechesis/Religious Program—Tel: 734-284-6145. Mrs. Karen Cameron, D.R.E. Students 155.
Convent—2609 Tenth St., 48192. Tel: 734-284-7253.

5—ST. PATRICK, [JC] Revs. Michael Cremin, S.A.C.; Linus Kinyua.
Office: 135 Superior Blvd., 48192. Tel: 734-285-9470; Fax: 734-285-1623. Email: stpatrick1857@gmail.com.
Res.: 105 Superior Blvd., 48192. Tel: 734-285-9472.
See Pope John Paul II Regional School at Christ the Good Shepherd, Lincoln Park.
Catechesis/Religious Program—Julie Dzanbazoff, D.R.E. Students 61.

6—ST. STANISLAUS KOSTKA, (Polish), Rev. Walter J. Ptak.
Church & Mailing Address: 266 Antoine St., 48192-3496.
Res.: 976 Pope John Paul Ave., 48192. Tel: 734-285-9509; Fax: 734-285-0124.
Catechesis/Religious Program—Program held at Our Lady of Mt. Carmel, Wyandotte Students 42.

YALE, ST. CLAIR CO., SACRED HEART, [CEM] Rev. Thomas Kuehnemund; Deacon William Kolarik.
Res.: 310 N. Main St., 48097-2845. Tel: 810-387-9800; Fax: 810-387-0538.
Catechesis/Religious Program—Brenda Heilig, D.R.E. Students 114.
Mission— P.O. Box 479, Brown City, Sanilac Co. 48416. Tel: 810-346-3036; Fax: 810-346-3036. Email: sacredheart@greatlakes.net.

Chaplains of Public Institutions

DETROIT. *Children's Hospital*, Tel: 313-745-5917. Sr. Beverly Hindson, I.H.M.
Cottage Hospital, Tel: 810-785-8855. Vacant. Attended from St. Paul on the Lake Parish, Grosse Pointe Farms, MI
Detroit Osteopathic Hospital, Tel: 313-865-6300. Attended from Cathedral of the Most Blessed Sacrament, Detroit.
Detroit Receiving Hospital 48226. Tel: 313-745-3000. Vacant.
DMC Sinai-Grace Hospital, Tel: 313-966-3300. Vacant.
Harper University Hospital, Tel: 313-745-6000. Vacant.
Henry Ford Hospital, Tel: 800-436-7936. Sr. Ellen Burke, O.S.F.
Hutzel Hospital, Tel: 313-831-3139. Vacant.
John D. Dingell Veterans Administration Medical Center, Tel: 313-576-1000.
St. John Hospital, 22101 Moross Rd., 48236. Tel: 313-343-7850. Rev. Janusz Marzynski, Sr. Jane Dutkiewicz.
Karmanos Cancer Institute, Tel: 800-527-6266. Vacant.
Mound Correctional Facility, 17601 Mound Rd., 48212. Mr. Anthony Latarski.
Ryan Correctional Facility, 17600 Ryan Rd., 48212. Mr. Anthony Latarski.
Wayne County Jail, 1231 St. Antoine, 48226. Mr. Anthony Latarski.
Wayne County Juvenile Detention Facility, 1326 St. Antoine, 48226. Ida Johns. Tel: 313-237-6056.

DEARBORN. *Oakwood Hospital*, Tel: 313-593-7000. Rev. Luke Iwuji.

FARMINGTON HILLS. *Botsford Hospital*, Tel: 248-471-8000. Rev. Paschal Igwe.

GARDEN CITY. *Garden City Hospital*, Tel: 734-421-3300. Rev. Bernard Pilarski.

GROSSE POINTE. *Beaumont Hospital*, Tel: 313-343-1000. Rev. Richard Bartoszek.

LAPEER. *Lapeer County Jail*, 3231 John Conley Dr., 48446. Mr. Anthony Latarski.
Thumb Correctional Facility, 3225 John Conley Dr., 48446. Mr. Anthony Latarski.

MONROE. *Monroe County (juveniles), HCCS, Moreau Center*, 3500 Comboni Way, 48162. Ida Johns. Tel: 313-237-6056. (fka Boysville)
Monroe County Jail, 100 E. Second St., 48161. Mr. Anthony Latarski.

MOUNT CLEMENS. *Macomb County Jail*, 43565 Elizabeth Rd., 48043. Tel: 586-307-9326. Jo Kudela.
Macomb County Juvenile Justice Center, 400 N. Rose Rd., 48043. Ida Johns. Tel: 313-237-6056. Attended from St. Peter's, Mount Clemens.
Mount Clemens General Hospital, Tel: 586-493-8500. Vacant.

NEW HAVEN. *Macomb Correctional Facility*, 26 Mile Rd, 48048. Mr. Anthony Latarski.

PONTIAC. *St. Clair County Jail*, 1170 Michigan Rd., Port Huron, 48060. Mr. Anthony Latarski.
Doctors' Hospital of Michigan, 461 W. Huron, 48341. Tel: 248-857-7200. Vacant.
Oakland County Children's Village, 1200 N. Telegraph Rd., 48341. Tel: 313-237-6056. Ida Johns, Coord. of Min. to Youth in Detention, Carleen Ward, Chap. Tel: 248-858-1183.
Oakland County Jail, 1201 N. Telegraph, 48341. Tel: 248-338-9310; Fax: 248-338-2695. Sr. Margaret Devaney.
Pontiac Osteopathic Hospital, Tel: 248-338-5000. Vacant.
PORT HURON. *St. Clair County Juvenile Intervention Center*, 1170 Michigan, 48060. Tel: 313-237-6056. Ida Johns, Coord. of Min to Youth in Detention, Kevin Totty, Chap. Tel: 810-966-4106.
Port Huron Hospital, Tel: 810-985-7750. Attended from Holy Trinity Parish, Port Huron.
PLYMOUTH. *Robert Scott Correctional Facility*, 47500 Five Mile Rd., 48170. Mr. Anthony Latarski.
ROCHESTER. *Crittendon Hospital*, Tel: 248-652-5000. Rev. Joy Chakian.
ROYAL OAK. *Beaumont Hospital*, Tel: 248-898-5000. Rev. Christopher Welsh.
TRENTON. *Oakwood Southshore Medical Center*, Tel: 734-671-7779. Beverly Beltramo.
TROY. *Beaumont Hospital*, Tel: 248-964-5000. Rev. Joy Chakian.
WARREN. *Henry Ford Macomb Hospital*, Tel: 586-759-7300. Rev. Luke Krotkiewicz.
WAYNE. *Oakwood Annapolis Hospital*, Tel: 734-467-4000. Rev. Bernard Pilarski.
WHITE LAKE. *Camp White Lake*, 8110 E. White Lake, 48386. Mr. Anthony Latarski.
WYANDOTTE. *Henry Ford Wyandotte Hospital*, Tel: 734-246-6000. Rev. Gary Morelli, Karen Gorski.
YALE. *Yale Community Hospital*, Tel: 810-387-2998. Attended from Sacred Heart Parish, Yale, MI.

Special Assignment:
Rev. Msgrs.—
Bugarin, G. Michael, Archbishop's Delegate to the Archdiocesan Review Board
Kasza, John C., Dean of Studies, SS. Cyril and Methodius Seminary
Revs.—
Babcock, Timothy F., Coord. Acculturation Services & Coord. Mentors
Banazak, Gregory, Faculty SS. Cyril and Methodius Seminary
Cassidy, Richard, Faculty, S.H.M.S.
Jones, Daniel J., Faculty, S.H.M.S.
Kiselica, John J., Faculty St. Mary's Preparatory

Graduate Studies:
Revs.—
Laboe, Timothy A., Pontifical North American College, Rome
McDonell, Clint W., Catholic Universtiy of America

On Duty Outside the Archdiocese:
Rev. Msgr.—
Sable, Robert M., Prelate Auditor of the Roman Rota, Vatican
Revs.—
Browne, Ronald T., J.C.L., Moderator of the Curia, Diocese of Marquette.
Kaul, John L., Archdiocese for Military Svcs.
Walsh, Jerome, Faculty Univ. of Dallas, TX

Absent on Leave:
Revs.—
Bloomfield, Andrew
Brady, Reginald
Brewczynski, Jacek M.
Fraser, Bernard
Gawlowski, Michael R.
Hogan, Richard
Kaczmarczyk, Pawel
Kaucheck, Kenneth R., J.C.D.
Liberty, Robert S.
Livingston, James
Mistor, Todd C.
Mondragon, Ezequiel
Prince, Michael J.
Quinlan, Jack
Schulte, Gary W.
Slowinski, Thomas F.
Sopiak, Donald A.
Stochmal, Marek
Tomasko, Andrew J.

Retired:
Rev. Msgrs.—
Baldwin, Edward J., Sacred Heart Major Seminary, 2701 Chicago Blvd., 48206.
Browne, George T., 165 S. Water St., Apt. 204, Marine City, 48039.
Edyk, Eugene, 45000 Geddes Rd., Canton, 48188.
Flanigan, Gerald A., 14469 Levan Rd., Apt. B, Livonia, 48154-5094.
Harrity, Dennis, 1401 S. 33rd Ave., Hollywood, FL 33021.
Humitz, Robert S., 6160 Brockway, Commerce Township, 48382.
Milewski, Stanley E., SS. Cyril & Methodius Seminary, 3535 Indian Trail, Orchard Lake, 48324.
Monticello, Robert V., 14469 Levan Rd., Apt. C, Livonia, 48154-5094.
Schweder, John F., 900 N. 70th Ave., Hollywood, FL 33024.
Villerot, Thomas H., 14453 Levan Rd., Apt. A, Livonia, 48154-5090.
Ziemba, Walter J., SS. Cyril & Methodius Seminary, 3535 Indian Trail, Orchard Lake, 48324.
Revs.—
Alder, Ronald J., St. Francis Cabrini Parish, 9000 Laurence, Allen Park, 48101-1598.
Anifer, Jeffrey R., 4600 Allen Rd., #401, Allen Park, 48101.
Babonas, Alphonse, 22525 Fairway Dr., Southfield, 48033.
Bauer, Erwin J., St. Philip Neri Rectory, 9735 Dolan Rd., Columbus, 48063-1105.
Blaska, John A., 875 W. Avon Rd., Apt. 128 C., Rochester Hills, 48307-2757.
Blondell, Robert H., 53256 Pineridge Dr., Chesterfield, 48051.
Bodde, Frederick A., 6116 River Rd., East China, 48054-4731.
Bonnici, William C., 2189 Cat Lake Hills, Mayville, 48744.
Briffa, Salvino P., 30055 Joy Rd., Westland, 48185-1728.
Brock, David F., 41464 White Tail Ln., Canton, 48188-2073.
Broderick, Leo P., 407 S. Parkway, Algonac, 48001.
Canavan, John D., 11395 Oakwood Dr., Jerome, 49249-9516.
Child, John F., Sacred Heart Parish, 22430 Michigan Ave., Dearborn, 48124.
Chmura, Julian, 41842 Lindsay Dr., Plymouth, 48170.
Complo, Daniel C., 38 E. Willow, Apt. C, Monroe, 48162-2644.
Cyr, Richard E., 5971 Fordham Dr., Shelby Twp, 48316-2528.
D'Achille, Arnold V., 7518 Hazleton, Dearborn Heights, 48127-1544.
Dacey, Donald, Fairlane Meadows, 5148 Heather Dr., #116, Dearborn, 48126-2884.
Dunn, John F., Lourdes Nursing Home, 2300 Watkins Lake Rd., Waterford, 48328-1439.
Eckert, Sidney J., 26256 Ryan Rd., Warren, 48091.
Esper, Thomas, 164 Shoreline Dr. E., Port Sanilac, 48469.
Fabian, John V., P.O. Box 320, Paradise, 49768.
Fares, Lawrence T., 31980 Mark Adam Lange, Warren, 48093.
Flynn, Thomas P., 22034 Sunnyside, St. Clair Shores, 48080.
Gagala, John, J.C.L., 22750 Ten Mile Rd., Southfield, 48033.
Gagnon, Joseph A., 1000 St. Joseph Ln., Marysville, 48040-1596.
Gattari, Valentine A., 15894 Nineteen Mile Rd., Clinton Twp, 48038.
Grandpre, Louis, 555 Brush St. #3108, 48226.
Hall, John F., Sacred Heart Major Seminary, 2701 Chicago Blvd., 48206.
Jackson, Lawrence J., 24348 Eastwood Village Ct., Apt. 106, Clinton Twp., 48035.
Jacobi, Arthur, 49726 Alpine Dr., Apt. 147, Macomb, 48044-6125.
Jagielski, James J.
Janiga, Joseph, 873 W. Avon Rd., Rochester Hills, 48307-2705.
Kaiser, Lawrence H., 14465 Levan Rd., Apt. B., Livonia, 48154-5092.
Klettner, Frederick J., 2208 Bowman Rd., Franklin, TN 37064.
Konopka, Edward F., 7950 N. McNab, Bldg. 10, Apt. 210, Tamarac, FL 33321-8436.
Kosicki, Bohdan W., 5630 Klettner, St. Clair, 48079-1918.
Kowalczyk, Sigismund C., 879 N. Channel Dr., Harsens Island, 48028.
Kowalski, George, 12765 Walnut St., Southgate, 48195.
Kuntz, Donald B., 9245 North River Rd., Algonac, 48001-4007.
Kurzawa, Ronald, 38694 L'Anse Creuse, Harrison Township, 48045.
Maciejewski, Norbert F.
MacLennan, Donald B., 30105 Avenida Alvera, Cathedral City, CA 92234-2869.
Mayworm, James A., 48726 Alpine Dr., Macomb, 48044-6125.
Meyer, James, 4600 Woodward Ave., Ste. 308, 48201-1894.
Mikus, Elemir, 90863 Oreske 5, Skalica, Slovakia.
Misiolek, Frederick, 21663 Thornbush Dr., Woodhaven, 48183.
Mitchell, Edward J., 14467 Levan Rd., Apt. C, Livonia, 48154-5093.
Muir, Edmund D., 14465 Levan Rd., Apt. C, Livonia, 48154.
Murphy, Daniel J., 14455 Levan Rd., Apt A, Livonia, 48154-5091.
Murphy, William J., 14455 Levan Rd., Apt. D, Livonia, 48154-5091.
Nowlan, John T., Our Lady of Fatima Parish, 13500 Oak Park Blvd., Oak Park, 48237-2099.
O'Dea, Loren F., Our Lady of Sorrows Parish, 23815 Power, Farmington, 48336-2461.
O'Leary, James J., American House East I, 17255 Common Rd., Apt. 126C, Roseville, 48066.
O'Sullivan, Daniel, 3941 Crooks Rd., Troy, 48084.
Page, Leon J., 12109 Avondale, Warren, 48089-3922.
Perfetto, Richard A., 37610 Barkridge, Westland, 48185.
Petron, William G., 15745 Charleston Dr., Clinton Township, 48038-1016.
Phalen, John L., 9314 Top Flight Dr., Lakeland, FL 33810.
Pollie, A. Frank, 3304 Grove Ln., Auburn Hills, 48326.
Profota, James H., 34594 Maple Ln., Sterling Heights, 48312-5213.
Prus, Edward J., St. James Parish, 241 Pearson, Ferndale, 48220-1896.
Rakoczy, Richard S., 999 Stratton Dr., Waterford, 48328.
Reckinger, Robert A., 14455 Levan Rd., Apt. C, Livonia, 48154-5091.
Redwanski, Dale H., O.S.C., 22212 Ardmore Park Dr., Saint Clair Shores, 48081.
Reyesmedina, Carlos, Our Lady of Mt. Thabor Monastery, 1295 Bald Eagle Lake, Ortonville, 48462-9096.
Romano, Joseph L., 14453 Levan Rd., Apt. B, Livonia, 48154-5090.
Roodbeen, Henry W., 4663 Norfold Dr., Northville, 48167.
Ruedisueli, Robert A., 6306 Custer Rd., Port Sanilac, 48469.
Ruskowski, Clifford F., 8200 E. Jefferson, Apt. 409, 48214.
Rutkowski, George A., 15171 Granada Plaza, Warren, 48088.
Ryder, Joseph F., 3015 Moon Lake Dr., West Bloomfield, 48323-1844.
Sayers, Raymond J., 408 Fox Hills Dr., Apt. 2, Bloomfield Hills, 48304-1346.
Sayes, Ronald E., Andover Heights, 8401 Eighteen Mile Rd., #217, Sterling Heights, 48313-3064.
Scheick, James C., 14469 Levan Rd., Apt. D, Livonia, 48154-5094.
Scheuerman, Edward L., 14453 Levan Rd., Apt. D, Livonia, 48154-5090.
Schmidberger, Richard, 4171 Fourth St., P.O. Box 535, Brown City, 48416.
Siebert, William P., 16041 Vergi Ct., Clinton Township, 48038.
Sinatra, William D., 43225 Polo Cir., Apt. 3, Sterling Heights, 48313-2064.
Singelyn, Robert K., St. Mary Parish, 127 N. Monroe St., Monroe, 48162-2686.
Slominski, Fabian B., 5405 Christi Dr., Warren, 48091-4196.
Stanievich, J. Walter, Marquette House, 36000 Campus Dr., #423, Westland, 48185.
Strain, Eugene R., 320 Elm, Rochester, 48307.
Sullivan, John J., St. Frances Cabrini Parish, 9000 Laurence, Allen Park, 48101-1598.
Sutherland, Thomas J., 49230 Arlington Ct., Shelby Township, 48315-3903.
Taube, Sylvester, 9008A Bissonette, Oscoda, 48750.
Tierney, Gary M., J.C.L., 5568 N. Adams Way, Bloomfield Hills, 48302-4000.
Villerot, Henry E., American House East I, 17255 Common Rd., Apt. B-200, Roseville, 48066-1954.
Walker, Donald L., 26900 Van Buren, Dearborn Heights, 48127.
Weingartz, Francis A., 19737 Colman, Clinton Township, 48035.
Welsh, Richard C., 26560 Burg Rd., Bldg. B, Apt. 324, Warren, 48089-3503.
Wieging, James F., 1440 Coolidge Hwy, River Rouge, 48218.
Wojcicki, Wojciech, 14453 Levan Rd., Apt. C, Livonia, 48154-5090.
Wojtewicz, Eugene E., 14467 Levan Rd., Apt. D, Livonia, 48154-5093.
Worthy, Donald L., St. Philomena Parish, 4281 Marseilles, 48224.
Wurm, Robert L., 66 Lakeshore Ln., Grosse Pointe Shores, 48236.
Zielinski, Francis A., 2477 Yordy Rd., Mio, 48647.

Permanent Deacons:
- Abler, Donald, Senior Status
- Alex, Frank, Sr. Status.
- Avery, Stanley, St. Teresa of Avila, Warren
- Avery, Thomas, National Shrine of the Little Flower, Royal Oak
- Ball, John H., Senior Status
- Barbera, John, St. Louis, Clinton Twp.; Macomb Correctional Facility, New Haven
- Bark, Kenneth, St. Patrick, White Lake
- Baross, Donald, Anastasia, Troy
- Barthel, Michael, St. Joan of Arc; St. Clair Shores
- Baughman, Jene, St. Fabian, Farmington Hills
- Berch, James, St. Isaac Jogues, St. Clair Shores
- Bloomfield, Richard, Senior Status
- Booms, Chris, St. Joseph, South Lyon
- Bousamra, Thomas, (Serving in the Gaylord Diocese)
- Bovitz, Robert, Senior Status
- Breen, Kevin, St. Genevieve, Livonia
- Brown, Oscar A., St. Hugo of the Hills, Bloomfield Hills
- Bruen, Patrick T., Senior Status
- Bujold, Francis, Holy Name, Birmingham
- Burke, John, St. Theodore of Canterbury, Westland
- Burrell, Frederick, St. Raphael, Garden City
- Busch, Robert F., Senior Status
- Bussa, Stephen, Senior Status
- Butler, Lenard, Our Lady of Hope, St. Clair Shores
- Buyle, Valere, St. Hubert, Harrison Twp.
- Campernel, Jerome, St. John Vianney, Shelby Twp.
- Carroll, Brian, Our Lady of La Salette, Berkley
- Carter, Thomas, St. Paul of Tarsus, Clinton Twp.
- Channell, Ronald, St. Margaret of Scotland, St. Clair Shores
- Chesley, Michael, St. Patrick, White Lake
- Conlen, Patrick, St. John Neumann, Canton
- Conlin, Richard R., Senior Status
- Connors, John J., Holy Trinity, Port Huron
- Cook, Ronald W., St. Anastasia, Troy
- Cornell, Peter, St. Anthony, Belleville
- Cousino, George, St. Joseph, Maybee; St. Patrick, Carleton
- Cousino, Wesley, Senior Status
- Cox, Donald J., Sr. Status
- Darga, Daniel M., Our Lady of La Salette, Berkley
- Delbeke, Robert G., Senior Status
- DeShaw, Gerald, Senior Status
- Desjarlais, Eugene B., Senior Status
- DeWitt, Robert, Our Lady of Grace, Dearborn Heights
- Doan, Francis X. Chau Ngoc, St. Dennis, Royal Oak
- Donnelly, Thomas, (Serving in the Pensacola-Tallahasse Diocese)
- Dreyer, Charles R., St. William, Walled Lake; St. Patrick, White Lake
- Ervin, Robert, Holy Family, Novi
- Fairbanks, Andrew, St. Vincent Ferrer, Madison Heights
- Feliciano, Raul, Senior Status
- Fitzgerald, Robert C., St. Priscilla, Livonia
- Fleming, David, St. Rene Goupil, Sterling Hts.
- Flores, Luis A., St. Frances Cabrini, Allen Park
- Formanczyk, Gregory, St. Elizabeth Ann Seton, Troy
- Fosmire, Charles, Senior Status
- Friend, Harry, (Serving in the Gaylord Diocese)
- Fry, Kenneth, Our Lady of Victory, Northville
- Gabel, Raymond, Senior Status
- Gajda, Robert, St. Perpetua, Waterford
- Gardner, Jack Jr., St. Linus, Dearboru Heights
- Gemellaro, Marc, St. Andrew, Rochester
- Gennette, James, Senior Status
- Gergosian, Edward, (Serving in the Phoenix Diocese)
- Girard, Lawrence, Senior Status
- Godfryd, Kurt, St. Clement of Rome, Romeo
- Goetz, Robert, (Serving in the Gaylord Diocese)
- Gonos, Daniel, St. Regis, Bloomfield Hills
- Goodhue, Harold, (Serving in the Gaylord Diocese)
- Grenda, Ronald, St. Gerald, Farmington
- Gwozdz, Alan, Holy Family, Memphis
- Hammond, Michael, Charles Borromeo, Newport
- Healy, Lawrence, St. Michael, Sterling Heights
- Hensel, James L., Senior Status
- Herta, Robert, Senior Status
- Hoffer, Franz, St. Ronald, Clinton Twp.
- Hogrebe, Alfons, Senior Status
- Houle, Thomas, St. Thecla, Clinton Township
- Hulan, Richard, Senior Status
- Hulway, Joseph A., SS Cyril; Methodius, Sterling Heights
- Hurley, Daniel J., Our Lady of the Angels, Taylor
- Igoe, James, Sr. Status
- Ingels, Michael M., St. Richard, Wetland
- Iskra, Joseph, SS. Augustine & Monica, Detroit
- Jablonowski, Alexander, St. Kieran, Shelby Township
- Jackson, Douglas, St. Cecilia, Detroit
- Jamieson, William E., Our Lady Star of the Sea, Grosse Pointe Woods
- Jimenez, Rafael, Senior Status
- Jones, Alex, Jr., St. Suzanne/Our Lady Gate of Heaven, Detroit; SS. Peter & Paul, Detroit
- Junak, Donald C., Senior Status
- Jurewicz, Marion, St. Martin de Porres, Warren
- Karle, Joseph, III, St. Mary of the Hills, Rochester Hills
- Kendzierski, Anthony, St. Isidore, Macomb
- Kessler, Wilhelm, St. Louise de Marillac, Warren
- Kibit, Henry J., St. Albert the Great, Dearborn Hills
- Kolarik, William, Our Lady of Mt. Carmel, Emmett
- Krueger, Gary R., Senior Status
- Krzeminski, Eugene, (Serving in the Las Vegas Diocese)
- Kucharek, Zigment, St. Dunstan, Garden City
- Kunik, Raymond L., (Serving in the Lansing Diocese)
- LaForest, Scott, Our Lady of the Woods, Woodhaven
- Lalone, Norman, Senior Status (Diocese of Venice, Florida)
- Lang, Michael, Sr., Holy Innocents & St. Barnabas, Roseville
- Leach, Donald, St. Aloysius & St. Patrick, Detroit
- Lennon, Joseph, St. Clare of Assisi, Farmington Hills
- Lewandoski, Anthony, Senior Status
- Liddle, John, St. William, Walled Lake
- Lippard, Paul, St. Mark, Warren
- Loffreda, Dennis, St. Francis of Assisi-St. Maximilian Kolbe, Ray
- Luddecke, Ralph, St. Mary, Wayne
- Majkowski, Arthur, St. Louise de Marillac, Warren
- Malloy, John, Jr., St. Roch, Flat Rock
- Marks, Stephen, St. Daniel, Clarkston
- Marku, John, Senior Status
- McGowan, Gerard, Christ the Good Shepard, Lincoln Park
- McIntyre, Ronald L., Senior Status
- McKale, Michael J., Holy Name, Birmingham; Assoc. Dir. for Deacons
- McLeod, Edwin, St. Ephrem, Sterling Heights
- McLeod, Robert E., Senior Status
- Meahan, William, Sr. Status
- Meerschaert, Gary, (Unassigned)
- Melenyk, Glenn, St. James, Novi
- Meyer, Edward, Sr. Status
- Misiak, Richard, St. Edith, Livonia
- Mitchell, Steven, St. Joseph, Lake Orion
- Modes, Robert, St. John Bosco, Redford
- Morad, Alfred J., Senior Status
- Morello, Steven, (Unassigned)
- Morici, Anthony, St. Lawrence, Utica
- Motowski, Norbert, All Saints, Detroit
- Mouro, Joseph, Senior Status
- Mueller, Paul, Corpus Christi, Detroit
- Murphy, Thomas P., Sr. Status
- Nelson, Joseph, (Serving in the Gaylord Diocese)
- Noon, Archie J., Senior Status
- Nowicki, Kenneth, Immaculate Conception, Ira Twp.
- O'Donnell, C. Roger, Divine Child, Dearborn; Chaplain, Angela Hospice
- O'Keefe, Michael, St. Athanasius, Roseville
- Oldani, Michael, Our Lady on the River, Marine City
- Ovies, Robert, Senior Status
- Pardo, Gary, St. Colette, Livonia
- Parent, John, Sacred Heart, Auburn Hills
- Pelchat, Paul F., Senior Status
- Pilon, Timothy, Holy Family, Novi
- Piro, Rudolph P., Senior Status
- Posavetz, George R., Senior Status
- Quigley, Donald, Our Lady of Victory, Northville
- Rabault, Christopher, St. Augustine & St. Monica, Detroit
- Redwine, Mark, St. Joseph, Trenton
- Riopelle, Ernest, Senior Status
- Rivera, Rafael, Senior Status
- Rodriguez, Brigido, Senior Status
- Rohlman, Ronald E., Senior Status, St. Joseph Mercy Hospital, Pontiac
- Root, Joseph, (Retired in the Phoenix Diocese)
- Rowland, Robert, St. Clement, Dearborn
- Ruehlen, Lawrence, St. Isaac Jogues; St. Clair Shores
- Sanders, Hubert, Presentation/Our Lady of Victory, Detroit
- Sandstrom, Donald, St. Therese of Lisieux, Shelby Twp.
- Santeramo, John, St. Joseph, Lake Orion
- Schiffer, Gerald, St. Linus, Dearborn Hts.
- Schlesser, Peter, (Serving in the Miami Diocese)
- Schmitz, William, St. Mary Queen of Creation, New Baltimore
- Schulte, John, Our Lady of the Lakes, Waterford
- Schwartz, Robert, Guardian Angels, Clawson
- Shubik, Richard, St. Paul, Grosse Pointe Farms
- Skladanowski, John L., St. Sylvester, Warren
- Skubick, Charles G., Senior Status
- Small, Vincent, Our Lady of Good Counsel, Plymouth
- Smigell, Gerald, Senior Status
- Smith, Lee, Sr. Status
- Smith, Michael T., Senior Status
- Smith, Richard T., (Serving in the Phoenix Diocese)
- Sobolewski, Don, (Serving in the Lansing Diocese)
- Somervell, Michael, Holy Spirit, Highland
- Sorensen, Eric, (Unassigned)
- Springer, Mark, St. Alexander, Farmington Hills
- Stach, Michael, Sacred Heart, Auburn Hills
- Stankiewicz, Clement, Our Lady of Sorrows, Farmington
- Stark, Christopher, St. Mary & St. James, Royal Oak
- Stevens, Paul, St. Ladislaus, Hamtramck; Transfiguration/Our Lady Help of Christians, Detroit
- Stewart, Michael, St. John the Baptist, Monroe
- Stimpson, Bill, Sweetest Heart of Mary; St. Josaphat; St Joseph, Detroit
- Strasz, Thomas, St. Joan of Arc, St. Clair Shores
- Sullivan, Lawrence, Sacred Heart, Roseville
- Swartz, Edward, Senior Status
- Talbot, Stephen, Our Lady of the Lakes, Waterford
- Thibodeau, James, St. Sebastian, Dearborn Hts.
- Thomas, Thomas, Senior Status
- Thome, William A., Our Lady of the Angels, Taylor
- Thompson, John, St. Basil, Eastpointe
- Tombler, Eugene, Senior Status
- Toth, Lawrence, St. Valentine, Redford
- Trabbic, Kenneth, St. Stephen, New Boston
- Tremmel, Robert, Senior Status
- Urbiel, Joseph, Christ the King, Detroit
- Vader, Ronald, Our Lady of Loretto, Redford
- Valade, Ronald, St. Irenaeus, Rochester Hills
- Van Brook, Arthur, Sr. Status
- Vanneste, John, St. Thomas More, Troy
- Vasquez, Jesus, Senior Status
- Von Ende, Michael, Prince of Peace, West Bloomfield
- Waldmann, William L., Senior Status
- Wallace, John, (Serving in the Gaylord Diocese)
- Ward, James, St. Thomas A'Becket, Canton
- Weiss, Kenneth, (Unassigned)
- White, Brian S., St. Damian of Molokai, Pontiac
- Wilder, James, Assumption Grotto, Detroit
- Wilson, Edward C., Jr., Senior Status
- Wright, John, SS. John & Paul, Washington Twp.
- Yezak, Thomas, Senior Status

INSTITUTIONS LOCATED IN THE DIOCESE

[A] SEMINARIES, ARCHDIOCESAN

DETROIT. *Sacred Heart Major Seminary, Inc.*, 2701 Chicago Blvd., 48206. Tel: 313-883-8500; Fax: 313-868-8685. Email: information@shms.org. Web: www.shms.edu. Rev. Msgr. Jeffrey M. Monforton, Rector & Pres.; Revs. Gerard Battersby, Vice Rector & Dean, Seminarian Formation; Todd Lajiness, Dean of Studies; Ms. Astrid Caicedo, Asst. Dean; Ms. Ann Marie Connolly, Dir. Finance & Treas.; Mr. John D. Meldrum, Registrar; Mr. David Kelley, Dir. Devel.; Mr. Chad Hughes, Dir. Educational Technology; Tamara Fromm, Dir. Admissions & Enrollment.

The College of Liberal Arts Revs. Stephen Burr, Dir. Undergraduate Seminarians; Robert Spezia, Spiritual Dir. Undergraduate Seminarians; Mr. Christopher Spilker, Dir. Libraries; Dr. Ronald Prowse, Dir. Music.

The School of Theology Revs. Daniel J. Trapp, Spiritual Dir. Grads.; Douglas Bignall, Dir. Graduate Pastoral Formation; Daniel J. Jones, Dir., Graduate Seminaries.

The Institute for Pastoral Ministry Mrs. Janet Diaz, Dean Institute for Ministry. Priests 17; Sisters 2; Lay Faculty 16; Students 466.

ORCHARD LAKE. *SS. Cyril and Methodius Seminary*, 3535 Indian Tr., 48324. Tel: 248-683-0311; Fax: 248-738-6735. Web: www.sscms.edu. Very Rev. Thomas C. Machalski, Rector/Pres.; Sr. Karen Shirilla, S.J., Dir. Lay Ministry Programs; Rev. Msgr. Francis Koper, Dean Pastoral Formation; Rev. Robert Marczewski, Dean of Spiritual Formation; Timothy Bailey, Comptroller; Rev. Pawel Lis, Dean, Discipline & Prefect; Rev. Msgr. John C. Kasza, Dean of Studies; Ms. Caryn Noel, Librarian; Rev. Peter S. Glabik, Dean, Human Formation. Students 85.

[B] SEMINARIES, RELIGIOUS OR SCHOLASTICATES

OXFORD. *St. Benedict Monastery*, 2711 E. Drahner Rd., 48370. Tel: 248-628-2249; Fax: 248-628-0014. Web: www.benedictinemonks.com. Revs. Michael R.

Green, O.S.B., Conventual Prior; Damien Gjonaj, O.S.B., Subprior; John Martin Shimkus, O.S.B., Oblate Dir. Headquarters Novitiate House of Sylvestrine Benedictine Monks in the United States. Priests 3; Brothers 6; Chapels 2.

[C] COLLEGES AND UNIVERSITIES

DETROIT. *Marygrove College* (Coed); Incorporated, 8425 W. McNichols Rd., 48221. Tel: 313-927-1200; Fax: 313-927-1345. Email: info@marygrove.edu. Web: www.marygrove.edu. Dr. David J. Fike, Pres.; Ms. Jane Hammang-Buhl, Vice Pres. Academic Affairs; Mr. William Johnson, Vice Pres. Finance & Admin.; Mr. Kenneth Malecke, Vice Pres. Institutional Advancement; Ms. JoAnn Cusmano, Vice Pres. Strategic Initiatives; Juliana Mosley, Vice Pres., Student Affairs & Enrollment Mgmt.; Ms. Gladys Smith, Registrar; Ms. Linnea M. Dudley, Librarian, Head of Reference. Sisters, Servants of the Immaculate Heart of Mary. I.H.M. 5; Lay Staff 367; Students 2,692.

University of Detroit Mercy, McNichols Campus, 4001 W. McNichols Rd. at Livernois, 48221-3038. Tel: 313-993-1000; Fax: 313-993-3317. Web: www.udmercy.edu. Priests 12; Sisters 7; Lay Staff 547; Faculty 312; Total Enrollment 5,534.

Law School, 851 E. Jefferson, 48226. Tel: 313-596-0210; Fax: 313-596-0280. Web: www.law.udmercy.edu.

Dental School, 2700 Martin Luther King Blvd., 48208-2576. Tel: 313-494-6621; Fax: 313-494-6627. Web: www.dental.udmercy.edu. Dr. Antoine M. Garibaldi, Pres.; Ms. Pamela Zarkowski, Vice Pres. Academic Affairs; Mr. Vincent Abatemarco, Vice Pres. Business & Finance; Mr. Gregory Cascione, Vice Pres. Univ. Advancement; Ms. Denise Williams Mallett, Vice Pres. Enrollment Mgmt. & Student Affairs; Rev. John M. Staudenmaier, S.J., Asst. to the Pres. for Mission & Identity; Ms. Monica Barbour, Sr. Attorney & Sec. to the University; Margaret Auer, Dean, Libraries.

LIVONIA. *Madonna University*, 36600 Schoolcraft Rd., 48150. Tel: 734-432-5300; 800-852-4951; Fax: 734-432-5393. Web: www.madonna.edu. Sr. Rose Marie Kujawa, C.S.S.F., Pres.; Ms. Andrea R. Nodge, Vice Pres. Univ. Advancement; Dr. Ernest Nolan, Provost & Vice Pres. Academic Affairs; Dr. Connie Tingson-Gatuz, Vice Pres. Student Affairs; Ms. Dina Dubuis, Registrar; Mr. Leonard Wilhelm, Vice Pres. Finance; Dr. Michael Kenney, Vice Pres. Planning & Enrollment Mgmt.; Sr. Serafina Dixon, C.S.S.F., Dir. Information Systems; Mr. Chris Ziegler, Dir. Fin. Aid; Sr. Anita M. Taddonio, C.S.S.F., Dir. Campus Ministry; Ms. Joanne Lumetta, Librarian. Coeducational, resident & non-resident.; Conducted by the Felician Sisters. Priests 4; Sisters 10; Lay Staff 617; Students 4,300.

Madonna Outreach Centers:

Madonna University Orchard Lake Center, 3535 Indian Tr., Orchard Lake, 48324. Tel: 248-683-1757; Fax: 248-683-1756. James Novak, Ph.D., Dean, Outreach & Distance Learning. Lay Staff 2; Students 57.

SWEEP Center, 2051 Rosa Parks Blvd., 48216. Tel: 734-432-5733. Lay Staff 2; Students 46.

Macomb University Center, 44575 Garfield Rd., Clinton Township, 48038-1139. Tel: 586-263-6330. Email: lmcintyre@madonna.edu. Linda McIntyre, Coord. Lay Staff 1.

[D] HIGH SCHOOLS, INTER-PAROCHIAL

MADISON HEIGHTS. *Bishop Foley Catholic High School*, 32000 Campbell Rd., 48071. Tel: 248-585-1210; Fax: 248-585-3667. Email: domagala@bishopfoley.org. Web: www.bishopfoley.org. Rev. Gerard LeBoeuf, Pres.; Ms. Patricia A. Domagala, Prin.; Mr. Gary Rushton, Pres., Bd. of Ed.; Mr. Timothy Scanlon, Dean, Academic Affairs; Ms. Heather Shiveley, Librarian. Priests 1; Lay Teachers 21; Students 311.

Bishop Foley Venture Fund, 32000 Campbell Rd., 48071. Tel: 248-585-1210; Fax: 248-585-3667. Email: moore@bishopfoley.org.

MARINE CITY. *Cardinal Mooney Catholic School*, 660 S. Water St., 48039. Tel: 810-765-8825; Fax: 810-765-7164. Web: www.cardinalmooney.org. Ms. Celeste Conflitti, Prin.; Ms. Mary Patrick, Librarian. Lay Teachers 16; Students 182.

MONROE. *St. Mary Catholic Central High School* (Coed), 108 W. Elm Ave., 48162. Tel: 734-241-7622; Fax: 734-241-9042. Web: www.smccmonroe.com. Mrs. Jenny Biler, Prin.; Mr. Sean Jorgensen, Pres.; Mr. Jack Giarmo, COO; Ms. Diane Tuller, Dean & Athletic Dir.; Mr. Timothy Magg, Campus Minister. Priests 1; Lay Teachers 28; Students 446.

PONTIAC. *Notre Dame Preparatory School and Marist Academy* (Consists of three schools), 1300 Giddings Rd., 48340-2108. Tel: 248-373-5300; Fax: 248-373-8024. Email: ndp@ndpma.org. Web: www.ndpma.org. Revs. Leon M. Olszamowski, S.M., Pres.; Joseph C. Hindelang, S.M., Upper School Prin.; James Strasz, S.M.; Ms. Jill Mistretta, Middle School Prin.; Ms. Diana C. Atkins, Lower School Prin.; Ms. Marna Nemon, Upper & Middle School Librarian; Ms. Suzanne Braverman, Lower School Librarian. Priests 3; Brothers 1; Sisters 1; Lay Teachers 87; Students 1,023.

RIVERVIEW. *Gabriel Richard Catholic High School*, 15325 Pennsylvania Rd., 48193. Tel: 734-284-1875; Fax: 734-284-9304. Email: admin@grriverview.org. Web: www.grriverview.org. Mr. Joseph Whalen, Prin.; Mrs. Elizabeth Conroy, Counselor. Lay Teachers 29; Students 335.

ROYAL OAK. *Shrine Catholic High School & Academy*, 3500 W. 13 Mile Rd., 48073. Tel: 248-549-2925; Fax: 248-549-2953. Email: erken@shrineschools.com. Web: www.shrineschools.com. Rev. Msgr. William H. Easton, Pres.; Ms. Gabrielle Erken, Prin.; Ms. Barbara Myler, Librarian. Lay Teachers 41; Students 411.

[E] HIGH SCHOOLS, PRIVATE

DETROIT. *Detroit Cristo Rey High School, Inc.*, 5679 Vernor Hwy., 48209. Tel: 313-843-2747; Fax: 313-843-2750. Email: info@detroitcristorey.org. Web: www.detroitcristorey.org. Michael J. Khoury, Pres.; Ms. Susan A. Rowe, Prin.; Mr. Robert S. Quinn, Dir. Devel.; Mr. Bruce A. Brinson, Dir. Admin.; Shanina Draughn, Dir. Admissions; Mr. David K. McIntyre, Dir. CWSP; Mr. Leon Dixon, Dean Students. Priests 1; Sisters 1; Lay Teachers 12; Students 233.

Detroit Cristo Rey High School Corporate Work Study Program, Inc., 5679 W. Vernor Hwy., 48209. Tel: 313-843-2747; Fax: 313-843-2750. Mr. David K. McIntyre, CWSP Dir.; Pamela Jackson, CWSP Coord.

Loyola High School, 15325 Pinehurst, 48238-1633. Tel: 313-861-2407; Fax: 313-861-4718. Email: dmastrangelo@loyolahsdetroit.org. Web: www.loyolahsdetroit.org. Revs. David F. Mastrangelo, S.J., Pres.; James E. O'Reilly, S.J., Chap.; Mrs. DeLisa Jones, Prin. Priests 1; Lay Teachers 14; Students 170. In Res. Rev. Justin J. Kelly, S.J.

Loyola Work Experience Program, Inc., 15325 Pinehurst, 48238. Tel: 313-861-2407; Fax: 313-861-4718. Web: www.loyolahsdetroit.org. Rev. David F. Mastrangelo, S.J., Pres.; Mrs. DeLisa Jones, Prin.

**University of Detroit Jesuit High School and Academy*, (Grades 7-12), 8400 S. Cambridge, 48221. Tel: 313-862-5400; Fax: 313-862-3299. Web: www.uofdjesuit.org. Revs. Karl Kiser, S.J., Pres.; Patrick F. Peppard, S.J.; Brian J. Lehane, S.J., Supr.; Jerome K. Odbert, S.J., Min.; Bros. James J. Boynton, S.J., History Teacher; Michael O'Grady, S.J., Grounds Care & Retreat Dir., Manresa Retreat House; Denis Weber, S.J., Admin., SS. Peter & Paul Warming Ctr.; Mr. Ryan Duns, S.J., Jesuit Regent, Seminarian & Theology Teacher; Mr. Richard J. Fichtinger, S.J., Jesuit Regent, Seminarian, Counselor & Theology Teacher; Mr. Cyril N. Penchak, S.J., Jesuit Regent, Seminarian & English Teacher; Mr. Anthony Trudel, Prin.; Mrs. Vondra Abbott, Librarian. Priests 4; Brothers 3; (Regents) 3; Lay Teachers 64; Students 847; Chapels 1.

BLOOMFIELD HILLS. *Academy of the Sacred Heart*, 1250 Kensington Rd., 48304-3029. Tel: 248-646-8900; Fax: 248-646-4143. Web: www.ashmi.org. Sr. Bridget Bearss, R.S.C.J., Head of School. Religious of the Sacred Heart. Lay Teachers 24; Students 127.

Brother Rice Endowment Fund (The "Foundation"), 7101 Lahser Rd., 48301-4045. Tel: 248-647-2526; Fax: 248-647-2532. Web: www.brrice.edu. Mr. John Birney, Pres.; Mr. Edward Shaffer, Dir. Advancement & Contact Person; Mr. Mike Tyranski, Bd. Pres.; Mr. Neal Kuehn, Dir. Fin.; Bro. Michael S. Segvich, C.F.C., Prin.; Ms. Cathy Treboldi, Librarian.

Brother Rice High School, 7101 Lahser Rd., 48301-4045. Tel: 248-647-2526; Fax: 248-647-8170. Mr. John Birney, Pres.; Bro. Michael S. Segvich, C.F.C.; Ms. Cathy Treboldi, Librarian. Congregation of Christian Brothers. Brothers 5; Sisters 3; Lay Teachers 44; Students 670.

Marian High School for Young Women, 7225 Lahser Rd., 48301. Tel: 248-644-1750; Fax: 248-644-6107. Web: www.marian-hs.org. Sr. Lenore Pochelski, I.H.M., Pres. & Prin.; Mr. Richard Copland, Asst. Prin. & Dean; Mrs. Vivian Christy, Academic Dean; Mrs. Stefanie Hughes, Librarian & Media Specialist. Sisters 2; Lay Teachers 38; Students 526.

FARMINGTON HILLS. *Mercy High School for Girls*, 29300 Eleven Mile Rd., 48336. Tel: 248-476-8020; Fax: 248-476-3691. Email: mhs@mhsmi.org. Web: www.mhsmi.org. Mrs. Carolyn R. Witte, Prin.; Mrs. Katy Koskela, Librarian. Sisters of Mercy. Sisters 1; Lay Teachers 45; Faculty 46; Students 749.

LIVONIA. *Ladywood High School*, 14680 Newburgh Rd., 48154. Tel: 734-591-1544; Fax: 734-591-4214. Web: www.ladywood.org. Mrs. Joan Fitzgerald, Pres. & Prin.; Mrs. Linda Ferenczi, Asst. Prin.; Mrs. Molly Stewart, Librarian. (Private School for Girls) Priests 1; Sisters 1; Lay Teachers 30; Students 316.

NOVI. *Catholic Central High School*, 27225 Wixom Rd., 48374. Tel: 248-596-3810; Fax: 248-596-3811. Email: jhuber@catholiccentral.net. Web: www.catholiccentral.net. Revs. Richard A. Ranalletti, C.S.B., Pres.; Richard J. Elmer, C.S.B.; Raymond Paramo, C.S.B.; Edwin J. Kline, C.S.B.; Robert W. Moslosky, C.S.B.; James M. O'Neill, C.S.B.; Jefferson M. Thompson, C.S.B.; Dennis Kauffman, C.S.B.; John B. Huber, C.S.B., Prin.; Roy Kronsbein, Librarian. Basilian Fathers. Priests 9; Lay Teachers 65; Students 1,043.

ORCHARD LAKE. *St. Mary's Preparatory*, 3535 Indian Tr., 48324. Tel: 248-683-0530; Fax: 248-683-1740. Email: lkosco@stmarysprep.com. Web: www.stmarysprep.com. Mr. James Glowacki, Headmaster; Rev. Timothy Whalen, Chancellor; Mr. Richard Rychcik, Vice Headmaster; Mr. Tony Koterba, Dir. Admissions; Candice Knight, Asst. Dir. Admissions. Priests 2; Lay Teachers 37; Students 474.

RAY TOWNSHIP. *Austin Catholic Academy*, 24125 26 Mile Rd., 48096. Tel: 586-749-7900; Fax: 586-749-5217. Mr. Leonard J. Brillati, Pres.; Rev. David L. Brecht, O.S.A., Headmaster. Priests 1; Lay Teachers 4; Students 10.

WARREN. *De La Salle Collegiate*, 14600 Common Rd., 48088-3387. Tel: 586-778-2207; Fax: 586-778-6016. Web: www.delasallehs.com. Bros. Thomas Lackey, Pres.; Robert Carnaghi, F.S.C., Pres. Emeritus; Mr. Patrick Adams, Prin.; Mrs. Nanette Maltz, Librarian. High School Brothers of the Christian Schools. Brothers 5; Sisters 2; Lay Teachers 46; Students 781.

Regina High School for Girls, 13900 Masonic Blvd., 48088. Tel: 586-585-0500; Fax: 586-585-0507. Web: www.reginahs.com. Sisters Mary Leanne, S.S.J.-T.O.S.F., Prin.; Mary Hyacinth, S.S.J.-T.O.S.F., Asst. Prin.; Mrs. Karen Forys, Asst. Prin.; Donald Kalpin, Business Mgr.; Ms. Julie Mann, Librarian. Sisters of St. Joseph of the Third Order of St. Francis 2; Dominican Sisters 1; I.H.M. Sisters 1; Lay Teachers 31; Students 460.

WIXOM. *St. Catherine of Siena Academy* A private Catholic high school for girls., 28200 Napier Rd., 48393. Tel: 248-946-4848; Fax: 248-438-1679. Email: info@saintcatherineacademy.org. Web: www.saintcatherineacademy.org. Kathy Tarnacki, Prin. Faculty 8; Campus Minister 1; Chaplain 1; Total Enrollment 49.

[F] ELEMENTARY SCHOOLS, INTER-PAROCHIAL

CANTON. *All Saints Catholic School*, (Grades PreSchool-8), 48735 Warren Rd., 48187-1233. Tel: 734-459-2490; Fax: 734-459-0981. Email: ascs9@hotmail.com. Web: www.allsaintscs.com. Ms. Kristen Strausbaugh, Prin. Lay Teachers 31; Total Enrollment 535.

CLARKSTON. *Everest Academy*, 5935 Clarkston Rd., 48348. Tel: 248-620-3390; Fax: 248-620-3942. Email: mnalepa@everestacademy.org. Web: www.everestacademy.org. Rev. John Connor, Pres.; Greg Reichert, Prin.; Ms. Susan Ender, Asst. Prin.; Ms. Christine Cataldi, Asst. Prin. & Academic Coord.; Lisa Murawa, Librarian. Priests 3; Consecrated Women 3; Lay Teachers 42; Students 480.

PORT HURON. *St. Mary/McCormick Catholic Academy*, (Grades PreK-8), 1429 Ballentine St., 48060. Tel: 810-982-7906; Fax: 810-987-8255. Email: stmaryacademy@hotmail.com. Web: www.stmarypthuron.org. Mrs. Deborah A. Krueger, Prin.; Ms. Candice Mendoza, Librarian. (2 schools merged) Lay Teachers 16; Students 168.

ROCHESTER. *Holy Family Regional School - South Campus*, (Grades 4-8), 2633 John R. Rd., Rochester Hills, 48307. Tel: 248-299-3798; Fax: 248-299-3843. Mr. Jon R. Myers, Prin. Sisters 2; Lay Teachers 54; Students 1,032.

[G] ELEMENTARY, PRIVATE

BLOOMFIELD HILLS. *Academy of the Sacred Heart*, (Grades PreK-8), 1250 Kensington Rd., 48304-3029. Tel: 248-646-8900; Fax: 248-646-4143. Web: www.ashmi.org. Sr. Bridget Bearss, R.S.C.J., Head of School. Religious of the Sacred Heart. Lay Teachers 47; Students 287.

[H] GENERAL HOSPITALS

DETROIT. *St. John Hospital and Medical Center* (a unit of St. John Health System), 22101 Moross Rd., 48236. Tel: 313-343-4000; Fax: 313-343-7533. Ms. Diane Radloff, Pres. Ascension Health 12; Bed Capacity 804; Total Staff 4,941; Patients Assisted Annually 179,596; Outpatients 109,071.

BRIGHTON. *Brighton Hospital* (a unit of St. John Health), 12851 Grand River Rd., 48116. Tel: 877-967-2371. Web: www.brightonhospital.org. Ken Van Elslander, Dir. Bed Capacity 99; Total Staff 223; Patients Assisted Annually 6,077.

EAST CHINA. *St. John River District Hospital* (a unit of St. John Health), 4100 River Rd., 48054. Tel: 810-329-7111; Fax: 810-329-8920. Web: www.stjohn.org/riverdistrict. Frank Poma, Pres. Bed Capacity 68; Total Staff 400; Inpatient 2,000; ER Patients 9,000.

LIVONIA. *St. Mary Mercy Hospital*, 36475 W. Five Mile Rd., 48154. Tel: 734-655-4800; Fax: 734-655-1620. Web: www.stmarymercy.org. Mr. David Spivey, Pres. & CEO; Revs. Luke Iwuji; Peter Ben Opara. (A Division of Trinity Health-Michigan) Sisters 4; Bed Capacity 304; Patients Assisted Annually 248,471; RN's 550; LPN's 5; Total Inpatient Days 77,149; Total Staff 1,670.

MADISON HEIGHTS. *St. John Macomb-Oakland Hospital, Oakland Center* (a unit of St. John Health), 27351 Dequindre, 48071. Tel: 248-967-7000. Web: www.stjohn.org/macomb-oakland. Mr. Michael Beaubien, COO; Mr. Joseph Tasse, Pres. Bed Capacity 180; Total Staff 1,077; Patients Assisted Annually 88,804.

NOVI. *Providence Park Hospital* (a unit of St. John Health), 47601 Grand River Ave., 48374. Tel: 248-465-4100; Fax: 248-465-4501. Jean Meyer, Pres.; Michael Wiemann, M.D., Exec. V.P. Bed Capacity 200; Staff 1,500.

PONTIAC. *St. Joseph Mercy Oakland* (Div. of Trinity Health-Michigan), 44405 Woodward Ave., 48341-2985. Tel: 248-858-3000; Fax: 248-858-3299. Web: www.stjoesoakland.com. Mr. Jack Weiner, Pres. & CEO; Dr. Ann Suziedelis, Vice Pres. Mission & Ethics; Ms. Alice Murphy, Chap.; Deacon Ronald E. Rohlman, Chap.; Ms. Linda Thompson, Chap. Bed Capacity 438; Total Staff 3,000; Total Assisted Annually 21,050.

PORT HURON. *St. Joseph Mercy Port Huron* (Div. of Trinity Health-Michigan), 2601 Electric, 48060-6518. Tel: 810-985-1510; Fax: 810-985-1579. Mr. Peter Karadjoff, Pres. & CEO. Bed Capacity 119; Patients Assisted Annually 154,019; Total Staff 775.

SOUTHFIELD. *Providence Hospital* (A unit of St. John Health), 16001 W. Nine Mile Rd., 48037. Tel: 248-849-3000; Fax: 248-849-3035. Michael Wiemann, M.D., Pres.; Lisa Ann Roth, Dir. Mission Integration; Rev. Felix S. Alsola (Philippines), Chap. Daughters of Charity of St. Vincent de Paul 6; Bed Capacity 365; Bassinets 65; Lay Staff 3,160; Patients Assisted Annually 23,794; Total Staff 3,282.

WARREN. *St. John Macomb-Oakland Hospital, Macomb Center* (a unit of St. John Health), 11800 E. 12 Mile Rd., 48093. Tel: 586-573-5000. Web: www.stjohn.org/macombFax: 586-573-5541. Ms. Diane Radloff, Pres.; Sr. Diane Rondeau, R.S.M., Chap.; Ms. Deborah A. Condino, Site Admin. Bed Capacity 376; Total Staff 3,400; Patients Assisted Annually 233,000.

[I] SPECIAL HOSPITALS AND SANATORIA FOR INVALIDS

FRASER. *Sanctuary at Fraser Villa* (a unit of Trinity Senior Living Communities), 33300 Utica Rd., 48026. Tel: 586-293-3300. Email: sliwinsg@trinity-health.org. Web: www.trinityseniorsanctuary.org. Ms. Gail Sliwinski, Admin.

LAKE ORION. *Guest House, Inc.*, 1601 Joslyn Rd., P.O. Box 420, 48360. Tel: 248-391-4445; Fax: 248-391-0210. Web: www.guesthouse.org. Denise Bertin-Epp, Pres. & COO. Management Services Offices; State licensed, CARF-accredited residential treatment centers for priests, brothers, deacons, seminarians, sisters and women in formation. Bed Capacity 37.

Guest House for Women Religious, 1720 W. Scripps Rd., 48360. Tel: 248-391-3100; Fax: 248-393-0186. Web: www.guesthouse.org. Sr. MaryEllen Merrick, I.H.M., Exec.Dir., Women's Program. A state-licensed and CARF accredited endorsed residential treatment center for Catholic sisters and women in formation.; Central Admissions Office, from U.S. & Canada call: 800-626-6910. Bed Capacity 16.

Guest House Recovery Residence, 444 Nakomis Rd., 48362. Tel: 248-693-8973; Fax: 248-693-8973. Bro. Richard D. Hittle, S.J., Residential Mgr.

Guest House Institute, 1601 Joslyn Rd., 48360. Tel: 248-391-4445; Fax: 248-391-0210. Web: www.guest-houseinstitute.org. The Institute promotes health and wellness of Catholics by providing educational services regarding alcoholism and other addictions and by promoting and providing research in alcoholism and other addictions affecting the Catholic Church.

National Catholic Council on Addictions, 1601 Joslyn Rd., 48360. Tel: 248-391-4445; Fax: 248-391-0210. Email: ncca@guesthouse.org. Web: nccatoday.org. NCCA is committed to assisting its members to a greater awareness and acceptance of alcoholism, other chemical addictions and prevention issues.

LIVONIA. *Marycrest Manor*, 15475 Middlebelt Rd., 48154. Tel: 734-427-9175; Fax: 734-427-5044. Mr. James Butler, Admin. Served by Marianhill Fathers., Ownership: Franciscan Sisters of St. Joseph. Sisters 3; Residents 55; Bed Capacity 55; Total Staff 85; Total Assisted Annually 172.

Marywood Nursing Care Center, 36975 W. Five Mile Rd., 48154. Tel: 734-464-0600; Fax: 734-464-4846. Mr. John Mimnaugh, N.H.A., Admin. Skilled Nursing Facility. Sisters 4; Capacity 103; Total Staff 180.

MEMPHIS. *Sacred Heart Rehabilitation Center, Inc.*, 400 Stoddard Rd., Box 41038, 48041-1038. Tel: 810-392-2167; Fax: 810-392-3385. Mr. John Sass Jr., Pres. Treatment for alcoholism and drug dependency to adult men and women. Detox and residential services. Bed Capacity 112.

ROCHESTER HILLS. *Sanctuary at Bellbrook* (A unit of Trinity Senior Living Communities), 873 W. Avon Rd., 48307. Tel: 248-656-6300; Fax: 248-656-8160. Email: lundb@trinity-health.org. Web: www.trinityseniorsanctuary.org. Becky Lund, Exec. Dir. Total Staff 220; Skilled Nursing 66; Assisted Living 64; Independent Apartments 125; Memory Loss 30.

ROYAL OAK. *Sanctuary at Alexander* (A unit of Trinity Senior Living Communities), 718 W. Fourth St., 48067. Tel: 248-545-0571; Fax: 248-545-9819. Email: goynesb@trinity-health.org. Web: www.trinityseniorsanctuary.org. Birdie Goynes, Admin. Bed Capacity 79; Total Staff 100.

WARREN. *Sanctuary at the Abbey* (a unit of Trinity Senior Living Communities), 12250 E. Twelve Mile Rd., 48093. Tel: 586-751-6200. Email: loriusl@trinity-health.org. Web: www.trinityseniorsanctuary.org. Lisa Lorius, Admin. Bed Capacity 182; Total Staff 215.

WATERFORD. *Lourdes Alzheimers Special Care Center*, 2400 Watkins Lake Rd., 48328. Tel: 248-674-4732; Fax: 248-618-6269. Web: www.lourdescampus.com. Sr. Maureen Comer, O.P., CEO. Bed Capacity 20; Total Assisted Annually 28; Total Staff 26.

Lourdes Nursing Home, 2300 Watkins Lake Rd., 48328. Tel: 248-674-2241; Fax: 248-674-1211. Web: www.lourdes-sc.org. Sr. Maureen Comer, O.P., CEO. Skilled & basic nursing facility for men and women rehabilitation and 24 hour nursing care. Residents 108; Bed Capacity 108; Total Assisted Annually 179; Total Staff 182.

[J] HOUSING AND/OR COMMUNITY FACILITIES FOR THE AGING

BLOOMFIELD HILLS. *St. Elizabeth Briarbank Home for the Aged*, 39315 Woodward Ave., 48304. Tel: 248-644-1011; Fax: 248-644-1596. Daughters of Divine Charity. Sisters 5; Aged Residents 38; Bed Capacity 38; Total Assisted Annually 25; Total Staff 17.

CLINTON TOWNSHIP. *A Friend's House Adult Day Services*, 15945 Canal, 48038. Tel: 586-412-8494; Fax: 586-416-2311. Web: www.csmacomb.org. 26238 Ryan, Warren, 48091. Tel: 586-759-8700; Fax: 586-759-8789. Mary Toupin, Prog. Dir. Daytime care for older adults. Support services for caregiving families. A service of Catholic Services of Macomb. Total Staff 11; Total Assisted Annually 200.

Sanctuary at Clinton Villa, 17825 Fifteen Mile Rd., 48035. Tel: 586-792-0358; Fax: 586-792-4409. Email: nelsonsh@trinity-health.org. Web: www.trinityseniorsactuary.org. Ms. Dianne Wettergren, Admin. A unit of Trinity Senior Living Communities. Total Staff 15; Units 78; Total Assisted Annually 1,032.

FARMINGTON HILLS. *Sanctuary at Marian Oakland*, 29250 W. Ten Mile Rd., 48336. Tel: 248-474-7204; Fax: 248-474-8662. Web: www.sanctuaryatmarianoakland.org. Mr. Joseph Theisen, Housing Mgr. A unit of Trinity Senior Living Communities. Total Staff 12; Units 81; Total Assisted Annually 1,080.

FORT GRATIOT. *Sanctuary at Mercy Village* (A member of Trinity Senior Living Communities), 4170 24th Ave., 48059. Tel: 810-989-7440; Fax: 810-989-7449. Email: koppelmj@trinity-health.org. Web: www.sanctuaryatmercyvillage.org. Maura Koppel, Admin. Bed Capacity 134; Total Assisted Annually 134; Total Staff 63.

IMLAY CITY. *Sanctuary at Maple Vista*, 600 Maple Vista, 48444. Tel: 810-724-6300; Fax: 810-724-3840. Email: campagnc@trinity-health.org. Web: www.sanctuaryatmaplevista.org. Ms. Crystal Campagne, Housing Mgr. A unit of Senior Living Communities. Total Staff 15; Units 69; Total Assisted Annually 1,080.

LIVONIA. *Sanctuary at Villa Marie*, 15131 Newburgh, 48154. Tel: 734-464-9494; Fax: 734-464-4010. Web: www.sanctuaryatvillamarie.org. Ms. Sharon Powell, Housing Mgr. A unit of Trinity Senior Living Communities. Total Staff 10; Units 69; Total Assisted Annually 1,080.

Trinity Continuing Care Services dba Trinity Senior Living Communities 17410 College Pkwy., Ste. 200, 48152-2363. Tel: 734-542-8349; Fax: 248-488-9169. Email: robbinsk@trinity-health.org. Web: www.trinityccs.org. Ken Robbins, Pres. & CEO. Bed Capacity 3,506; Total Assisted Annually 6,000; Total Staff 2,300.

MONROE. *Sanctuary at Marian Place*, 408 W. Front St., 48161. Tel: 734-241-2414. Email: morrink@trinity-health.org. Web: www.mercymarianplace.org. Ms. Karen Morrin, Housing Mgr. A unit of Trinity Senior Living Communities. Total Staff 9; Units 52; Total Assisted Annually 636.

PORT HURON. *Sanctuary at Marydale*, 3147 Tenth Ave., 48060. Tel: 810-985-9683. Email: hungerr@trinity-health.org. Web: www.trinityseniorsanctuary.org. Maura Koppel, Admin. A unit of Trinity Senior Living Communities. Total Staff 13; Units 51; Total Assisted Annually 612.

SOUTHGATE. *Sanctuary at Maryhaven*, 11350 Reeck Rd., 48195. Tel: 734-287-2111; Fax: 734-287-6905. Web: www.trinityseniorsanctuary.org. Joe Rzepka, Housing Mgr. A unit of Trinity Senior Living Communities. Total Staff 12; Units 85; Total Assisted Annually 76; Bed Capacity 76.

WATERFORD. *Fox Manor, Inc.*, 2350 Watkins Lake Rd., 48328. Tel: 248-674-9590; Fax: 248-674-3463. Web: www.lourdes-sc.org. Sr. Maureen Comer, O.P., CEO. Dominican Sisters., Residential facility for independent senior citizens of moderate or limited means. Bed Capacity 57; Total Staff 21; Total Assisted Annually 64.

Lourdes Assisted Living Corporation, 2450 Watkins Lake Rd., 48328. Tel: 248-618-6362; Fax: 248-618-6361. Web: www.lourdes-sc.org. Sr. Maureen Comer, O.P., CEO; Ms. Cori Sharrard, Dir. Bed Capacity 80; Total Assisted Annually 117; Total Staff 55.

[K] MONASTERIES AND RESIDENCES OF PRIESTS AND BROTHERS

DETROIT. *St. Bonaventure Friary*, 1740 Mt. Elliott Ave., 48207-3496. Tel: 313-579-2100; Fax: 313-579-5388.

Province of St. Joseph of the Capuchin Order, Inc. Provincialate, 1820 Mt. Elliott Ave., 48207. Tel: 313-579-2100; Fax: 313-579-2275. Very Rev. John Celichowski, O.F.M.Cap., Prov. Min.; Bros. Mark Joseph Costello, O.F.M.Cap., Prov. Vicar; Larry LaCross, O.F.M.Cap., Dir., Devel.; Rev. Patrick McSherry, O.F.M.Cap., Archivist.

Priests of the Province Assigned Outside the U.S.: Revs. Carmel Flora, O.F.M.Cap., St. Lawrence Community, 545 Tingal Rd., Wynnum, Qld. 4178, Australia. Fax: 011-61-73348-5141; Glenn Gessner, O.F.M.Cap.; Walter Kasuboski, O.F.M.Cap.; Paul Koenig, O.F.M.Cap.; Benjamin Markwell, O.F.M-.Cap.; Andre Weller, O.F.M.Cap.; Paul Craig, O.F.M-.Cap.; Kevin Heagerty, O.F.M.Cap.; Bro. Jozef Timmers, O.F.M.Cap.

Assigned to St. Bonaventure Friary: Very Rev. John Celichowski, O.F.M.Cap.; Bro. Larry LaCross, O.F.M-.Cap.; Revs. Philip Naessens, O.F.M.Cap.; Joseph Maloney, O.F.M.Cap.; Albert Sandor, O.F.M.Cap.; Patrick McSherry, O.F.M.Cap.; Bros. Mark Carrico, O.F.M.Cap., Local Min.; Michael Drobnicki, O.F.M-.Cap.; Paul Hanisko, O.F.M.Cap.; Thomas Kroll, O.F.M.Cap.; Richard Merling, O.F.M.Cap., Vicar; Leo Wollenweber, O.F.M.Cap.

Detroit Province of the Society of Jesus-Provincial Office, 2050 N. Clark St., Chicago, IL 60614-4788. Tel: 773-975-6888; Fax: 733-975-0230. Email: provincial@jesuits-chgdet.org. Web: www.jesuits-chgdet.org. Very Rev. Timothy P. Kesicki, S.J., Prov. Superior; Revs. Walter C. Deye, S.J., Exec. Asst. Prov.; Theodore G. Munz, S.J., Treas.; Jane Glynn-Nass, R.N., B.S.N., Asst., Health Care; Rev. James S. Prehn, S.J., Asst. Secondary Educ.; Ms. Jenene Francis, Asst. Pastoral Ministry; Rev. Raymond P. Guiao, S.J., Asst. for Formation; David K. McNulty, Vice Pres., Advancement; Revs. James F. Riley, S.J., Asst., Special Projects; Patrick A. Fairbanks, S.J., Asst., Vocations; Mr. Jeremy W. Langford, Asst., Communications; Bro. John P. Moriconi, S.J., Provincial Sec.; Mr. John Sealey, Asst., Social & International Ministries.

Priests 110; Brothers 14; Scholastics 18. Treasurer: 7303 W. Seven Mile Rd., 48221-2121. Tel: 313-861-7500; Fax: 313-861-4230.

Priests assigned outside the U.S.: Revs. Martin T. Connell, S.J.; Theodore W. Walters, S.J., St. Augustine University of Tanzania, P.O. Box 307, Mwanza, Tanzania. Tel: 255-0744-617396; Fax: 255-28-2550167; Kevin L. Flannery, S.J., Pontifica Universita Gregoriana, Piazza Della Pilotta 4, Rome 00187 Italy. Tel: 39-6-6701-5213; Fax: 39-6-6701-5413; Joseph E. Mulligan, S.J., Colegio Centroamericano, Apdo. 2419, Managua, Nicaragua. Tel: 505-278-6965; Joseph P. Daoust, S.J., Borgo S. Spirito, 4, Rome 00193 Italy; J. Thomas McClain, S.J.; John M. McManamon, S.J.

Members in the U.S. not listed elsewhere: Revs. Thomas S. Acker, S.J., 200 Main St., Beckley, WV 25801; Donald Vettese, S.J.

Jesuit Community at the University of Detroit Mercy, Lansing-Reilly Hall, 4001 W. McNichols Rd., 48221-3038. Tel: 313-993-1000; Fax: 313-993-1653. Revs. R. Gerard Albright, S.J.; Frederick J. Benda, S.J.; Gerald F. Cavanagh, S.J.; Thomas W. Florek, S.J.; Simon J. Hendry, S.J.; J. Timothy Hipskind, S.J.; Jean Ngeyeye Ikanga, S.V.D.; John A. Saliba, S.J.; Robert J. Scullin, S.J.; James K. Serrick, S.J.; Raphael Shen, S.J. (China); John M. Staudenmaier, S.J.; Gilbert Sunghera, S.J.; David E. Watson, S.J.; Gary R. Wright, S.J.; Bro. Richard D. Hittle, S.J. (Corporate Title: The Jesuit Community Corporation at the University of Detroit).

St. Mary's Friary, 1057 Parker, 48214-2612. Tel: 313-821-5883; Fax: 313-922-0404; 313-579-5365. Email: jhast@thecapuchins.org. Web: www.thecapuchins.org. Revs. Lawrence E. Webber, O.F.M.Cap.; James C. Hast, O.F.M.Cap.; Bros. Michael Gaffney, O.F.M.Cap.; Joseph Monachino, O.F.M.Cap.

P.I.M.E. Missionaries (Pontifical Institute for Foreign Missions), 17330 Quincy, 48221. Tel: 313-342-4066; Fax: 313-342-6816. Email: info@pimeusa.org. Web: www.pimeusa.org. Very Rev. Kenneth Mazur, P.I.M.E., North American Regional Supr.; Revs. Dino Vanin, P.I.M.E., Treas.; George Berendt, P.I.M.E.; Noel Cornelio, P.I.M.E.; Giorgio Ferrara, P.I.M.E., Mission Outreach Dir.; Ravi Thanaiah Marneni; Guy Christopher Snyder, P.I.M.E.; Giancarlo Ghezzi, Rector.

St. Paul of the Cross Community, Congregation of the Passion, 23335 Schoolcraft, 48223. Tel: 313-531-0562; Fax: 313-535-8468. Revs. Randal Joyce, C.P.; Ronald Corl, C.P.; Enno Dango, C.P.; Philip Paxton, C.P., Rev. Supr.; Bros. William Baalman, C.P.; Raymond Sanchez, C.P. A center for the Passionist Fathers & Brothers in mid-western & north central United States. Members of this community conduct parish missions, renewals & retreats for laity, clergy & religious, Forty Hours Devotion & other ministries. Priests 5; Brothers 1.

St. Sylvester Monastery, 17320 Rosemont Rd., 48219. Tel: 313-532-6064; Fax: 313-531-0739. Rev. Michael R. Green, O.S.B., Prior; Bro. Gregory David Jones, O.S.B., Rel. Dir. St. Scholastica School.

BLOOMFIELD HILLS. *Congregation of Christian Brothers, Mater Dei Community*, 7350 Parkstone Ln., 48301. Tel: 248-258-1186; Fax: 248-647-8170. Email: macintyre@brrice.edu. Bros. David A. MacIntyre, C.F.C.; Arthur M. Arndt, C.F.C.; Benjamin L. Favero, C.F.C.; Michael S. Segvich, C.F.C.; Ross E. Wielatz, C.F.C. Brothers 4.

CLARKSTON. *Colombiere Center*, 9075 Big Lake Rd., 48346-1015. Tel: 248-625-5611; Fax: 248-625-3526. Revs. Richard H. Twohig, S.J., Supr. & Dir.; Thomas F. Ankenbrandt, S.J.; Raymond C. Baumhart, S.J.; Robert E. Beckman, S.J.; Joseph H. Boel, S.J.; Joseph T. Brennan, S.J.; R. Michael Brophy, S.J.; Francis X. Budovic, S.J.; William T. Burke, S.J.; James E. Chambers, S.J.; John P. Coakley, S.J.; Paul F. Conen, S.J.; Matthew E. Creighton, S.J.; J. Peter Deane, S.J.; John T. Dillon, S.J.; Robert C. Dressman, S.J.; Raymond A. Dunne, S.J.; Eugene F. Dwyer, S.J.; Edward A. Flint, S.J.; Vincent A. Hagarman, S.J.; W. Henry Kennedy, S.J.; John H. Kleinhenz, S.J.; John A. Knapek, S.J.; James V. Lewis, S.J.; Daniel P. Liderbach, S.J.; Lewis J. Lipps, S.J.; Mark J. Link, S.J.; Richard M. Mackowski, S.J.; Edward J. Mattimoe, S.J.; Harold R. Meirose, S.J.; Benjamin R. Morin, S.J.; Edward M. Nemeth, S.J.; Lothar Nurnberger, S.J.; John D. O'Neill, S.J.; Frank M. Oppenheim, S.J.; John F. Pennington, S.J.; Cletus H. Pfab, S.J.; Herbert J. Raterman, S.J.; John E. Reilly, S.J.; L. Harold Sanford, S.J.; Timothy J. Shepard, S.J.; Francis J. Smith, S.J.; Harold J. Sommer, S.J.; Ralph H. Talkin, S.J.; Theodore C. Thepe, S.J.; Jerome F. Treacy, S.J.; Gerald C. Walling, S.J.; Earl A. Weiss, S.J.; Glenn Williams, S.J.; Bros. John F. Buchman, S.J.; Robert G. Cardosi, S.J.; Richard C. Conroy, S.J.; William R. Haas, S.J.; David L. Henderson, S.J.; Anthony R. Kreutzjans, S.J.; Henry C. Kuhn, S.J.; Daniel J. McCullough, S.J.; Bernard L. Polinak, S.J.; Jerome Pryor, S.J.; John J. Sebian, S.J. Jesuit Health Care Community for the Chicago-Detroit Province.

DEARBORN. *Society of St. Paul*, 7050 Pinehurst, 48126. Tel: 313-582-2033. Email: sspdearborn@comcast.net. Rev. Arthur Palisada, S.S.P.; Bro. Aloysius Milella, S.S.P. Priests 1; Brothers 1.

DEARBORN HEIGHTS. *All Saints Friary*, 23755 Military Rd., 48127. Tel: 313-278-5129; Fax: 313-278-5828. Email: mariebernardo101@hotmail.com. Web: www.franciscancommunity.com. Bro. James O'Brien, O.F.M.Conv., Guardian; Revs. Justin Kusibab, O.F.M.Conv.; Anthony Fox, O.F.M.Conv., Vicar All Saints Friary. (This is a subsidiary of St. Bonaventure, Chicago, IL.) Priests 2; Brothers 1; Deacons 1.

Our Lady of Grace Monastery, Mariannhill Mission Society, 23715 Ann Arbor Tr., 48127. Tel: 313-561-7140; 313-561-8888; Fax: 313-561-9486. Email: cmm-usa@juno.com. Web: www.mariannhill.us. *Vocation Office* Tel: 313-561-7140, Ext. 25; Fax: 313-561-9486. Email: vocation@mariannhill.us. Web: www.mariannhill.us. Revs. Raymond Lucasinsky, C.M.M., Supr. of House; Timothy Mock, C.M.M., Asst. Prov. Treas.; Thomas Szura, C.M.M., Prov. Treas.; Thomas Heier, C.M.M., Editor of LEAVES & District Supr.; Vergil Heier, C.M.M., Vocation Dir.; Michael Sheehy, C.M.M., Mission Procurator. Priests 6; Brothers 3. In Res. Bros. Francis Berridge, C.M.M.; Jamie Miller, C.M.M.; Otto Waldmueller, C.M.M.

GROSSE POINTE. *Order of Canons Regular of the Holy Cross*, 576 Neff Rd., 48230. Tel: 313-884-1121; Fax: 313-882-1763. Email: frwolfgang@opusangelorum.org. Web: www.cruzios.org. Revs. Wolfgang Seitz, O.R.C.; Michael Hincks, O.R.C.

LIVONIA. *Marist Fathers & Brothers Community*, 32509 Scone St., 48154-4165. Tel: 734-266-1475; Fax: 734-266-0197. Revs. Ronald G. DesRosiers, S.M., Local Supr., Asst. Prof. & Madonna Univ.; Frank Grispino, S.M., Adj. Prof., Madonna Univ.; John Sajdak, S.M., Chm., Rel. Studies Dept., Asst. Prof., Madonna University.

NORTHVILLE. *Miles Christi*, P.O. Box 701200, Plymouth, 48170. Tel: 248-596-9677; Fax: 248-596-9678. Email: infousa@mileschristi.org. Web: www.mileschristi.org. Revs. Caesar Bertolacci, M.C., Supr. Gen, Delegate., U.S.A.; John Ezratty, M.C., Supr.

REDFORD. *Society of the Catholic Apostolate-Indian Province of the State of Michigan*, 17116 Olympia, 48240. Tel: 313-534-9000; Fax: 313-534-6744. Rev. Paul Coutinha, S.A.C., Local Rector; Deacon Robert Bovitz, Contact Person.

WYANDOTTE. *Society of the Catholic Apostolate (Pallottine Fathers)* (Irish Province), 3352 Fourth St., 48192. Tel: 734-285-2966; Fax: 734-285-1059. Rev. Noel O'Connor, S.C.A., Pres., Rector & Mission Promotion Dir.; Bro. Faustino Paez, S.C.A., Mission Promotion Assoc. *Pallottine Missionary Center (Irish Province)*, 424 Orange St., 48192. Tel: 734-282-3019; Fax: 734-285-1059. Revs. Denny Murphy, S.C.A., Prov.; John Kelly, S.C.A., Prov. Bursar, Treas.; Noel O'Connor, S.C.A., Pres. *Pallottine Peer Ministry*, P.O. Box 66, 48192. Tel: 734-770-8262; Fax: 734-752-6545. Rev. Brendan Walsh, S.C.A., Chap.

[L] CONVENTS AND RESIDENCES FOR SISTERS

DETROIT. *Missionaries of Charity*, 1917 Cabot St., 48209. Tel: 313-841-1394. Sr. M. Davis, M.C., Supr.

Sisters, Home Visitors of Mary Convent, 121 E. Boston, 48202. Tel: 313-869-2160. Email: homevisitors@att.net. Sr. Rosemarie Abate, H.V.M., Admin. Sisters 21.

ALLEN PARK. *Little Sisters of the Poor*, P.O. Box 610, 48101-0610. Tel: 419-698-4331; Fax: 419-698-1109. Email: msoregon@littlesistersofthepoor.org. Web: www.littlesistersofthepoor.org. Sr. Anne Joseph, L.S.P., Pres. & Contact Person.

BLOOMFIELD HILLS. *Daughters of Divine Charity - Holy Trinity Province* (1972) Holy Trinity Provincialate, 39315 N. Woodward Ave., 48304. Tel: 248-644-1011; Fax: 248-644-1596. Sr. Hyacinth Vamos, F.D.C., Prov. Supr. Sisters in Community 11.

CLINTON TWP. *Monastery of St. Therese of the Child Jesus*, 35750 Moravian Dr., Clinton Township, 48035-2138. Tel: 586-790-7255; Fax: 586-790-7271. Email: carmelctwp@sbcglobal.net. Web: www.rc.net/detroit/carmelite. Sr. Mary Elizabeth, O.C.D., Prioress. Discalced Carmelite Nuns. Professed Nuns 8; Extern Sisters 1.

DEARBORN HEIGHTS. *Sisters of the Good Shepherd (RGS)*, 20651 W. Warren Ave., 48127-2698. Tel: 313-271-3050, Ext. 270; Fax: 313-271-6250.

EASTPOINTE. *Marist Sisters, Inc.*, 16057 Hauss, 48021. Tel: 586-772-2577; Fax: 586-772-8302. Email: maristsep@yahoo.com. Sisters Linda Sevcik, S.M., Regl. Leader; Constance Dodd, S.M., Sec. & Treas.

FARMINGTON HILLS. *Bernardine Franciscan Sisters of Michigan*, Our Lady of the Rosary Convent, 27405 W. 10 Mile Rd., 48336-2201. Tel: 248-476-4111; Fax: 248-476-6950. Web: www.bfranciscan.org. Sr. Marilisa da Silva, O.S.F., Congregational Min. Bernardine Sisters of the Third Order of St. Francis. Sisters in Area 23.

Monastery of the Blessed Sacrament, 29575 Middlebelt Rd., 48334-2311. Tel: 248-626-8253; Fax: 248-626-8724. Email: opnunsfh@sbcglobal.net. Web: www.opnuns-fh.org. Sr. Mary Thomas, O.P., Prioress; Rev. David J. Santoro, O.P, Chap. Nuns of the Order of Preachers (Cloistered Dominican Nuns, Perpetual Adoration). Cloistered Sisters 33; Extern Sisters 3.

Sisters of Mercy of the Americas West Midwest Community, Inc., 29000 Eleven Mile Rd., 48336. Tel: 248-476-8000; Fax: 248-476-4222. Email: info@mercywmw.org. Web: www.mercywestmidwest.org. Sisters Judith Frikker, R.S.M., Pres.; Sheila Megley, R.S.M., Treas.; Judith Cannon, R.S.M., Sec.; Kathy Thornton, R.S.M., Leadership Team; Michelle Gorman, R.S.M., Leadership Team; Kim Kinsel, Community Oper. Officer; Carol Kelley, Community Fin. Officer; Sandy Goetzinger-Comer, Dir. Communications. Sisters 740; Associates 536.

West Midwest FIDES, Inc., 29000 Eleven Mile Rd., 48336. Tel: 248-476-8000; Fax: 248-476-4222. Email: info@mercywmw.org. Web: www.mercywestmidwest.org. Sisters Sheila Megley, R.S.M., Pres.; Sheila Browne, R.S.M., Vice Pres.; Judith Frikker, R.S.M., Sec. & Treas.; Helen Amos, R.S.M., Governing Bd. Member; Katherine Graber, R.S.M., Governing Bd. Member.

LIVONIA. *Presentation of the BVM Central Convent*, 36800 Schoolcraft Rd., 48150. Tel: 734-591-1730; Fax: 734-591-1710. Email: sconniet@feliciansisters.org. Web: www.feliciansna.org. Sr. Mary Christopher Moore, C.S.S.F., Prov. Min.

Provincial House and Novitiate of the Congregation of the Sisters of St. Felix, C.S.S.F., Felician Sisters Professed Sisters in Michigan 139; Professed Sisters in North America, Our Lady of Hope Prov. 774; Novices 1.

MONROE. *Sisters, Servants of the Immaculate Heart of Mary, Leadership Council*, 610 W. Elm Ave., 48162-7909. Tel: 734-240-9700; Fax: 734-240-9784. Web: www.ihmsisters.org. Sisters Joan Mumaw, I.H.M., Interim Pres. & Mission Councilor; Helen Ingles, I.H.M., CFO; Carol Quigley, I.H.M., Leadership Council & Mission Councilor; Margaret Sweeney, I.H.M., Leadership Council & Mission Councilor; Janet Ryan, I.H.M., Leadership Council & Mission Councilor.

Institute for Communal Contemplation and Dialogue, 8531 W. McNichols, 48221. Tel: 313-971-3668; Fax: 313-342-7421. Email: circles@engagingimpasse.org. Web: engagingimpasse.org. Sr. Nancy Sylvester, I.H.M., Exec. Dir.

Intercultural Consultation Services, 8531 W. McNichols Rd., 48221-2500. Tel: 313-341-4841; Fax: 313-342-7421. Sr. Kathryn Pierce, I.H.M., Pres. & Exec. Dir.

SSIHM Charitable Trust (Retired and Infirm Sisters), 610 W. Elm Ave., 48162-7909. Tel: 734-240-9700; Fax: 734-240-9784. Sr. Helen Ingles, I.H.M., Trustee.

ORTONVILLE. *Our Lady of Mt. Thabor Monastery*, 1295 Bald Eagle Lake Rd., 48462. Tel: 248-627-4355. Email: mtthabor@aol.com. Web: www.mtthabornunsop.com. Sr. Anne Mary, O.P., Prioress. Dominican Nuns of Mt. Thabor.

OXFORD. *Dominican Sisters of Peace* (2009) *Oxford Motherhouse*, 775 W. Drahner Rd., 48371-4866. Tel: 248-628-2872; Fax: 248-628-1725. Email: srpeace@oppeace.org. Web: www.oppeace.org. Sr. Teresita Lipar, O.P., Mission Group Coord. Sisters in Congregation 610; Sisters in Diocese 24.

RIVERVIEW. *Sisters of Mary Reparatrix*, 17320 Grange Rd., 48193. Tel: 734-285-4510; Fax: 734-285-8147. Sisters 10.

Mary Reparatrix Retreat House, 17380 Grange Rd., 48193. Tel: 734-324-0901; Fax: 734-324-0903. Email: mrretreats@comcast.net. Web: www.mrretreats.org. Ms. Denise LaPorte, Dir.

[M] HOMES FOR MEN AND WOMEN

DETROIT. *St. Mary's Residence Adult Foster Care*, 2120 Orleans St., 48207. Tel: 313-259-6874; 313-259-0459; Fax: 313-259-2001. Sr. M. Hyacinthe, F.D.C., Admin. Daughters of Divine Charity., A residence for women desiring home-like surroundings. Sisters 4; Lay Associate 1;

Residents 25.

[N] CATHOLIC SOCIAL SERVICE AGENCIES

DETROIT. *Catholic Charities of Southeast Michigan*, 305 Michigan Ave., 10th Fl., 48226. Mr. Thomas Reed, Acting Exec. Dir.; Rev. Msgr. Charles Kosanke, Chm. Bd.

Catholic Social Services of Wayne County, 9851 Hamilton Ave., 48202. Tel: 313-883-2339; Fax: 313-883-3957. Email: csswc@csswayne.org. Web: www.csswayne.org. Mr. Patrick J. Heron, Pres. & CEO. Educational programs; Adoption services; Services to unwed mothers; Substance abuse counseling and prevention; foster family care and services to youth and older persons including Foster Grandparent, Senior Companion and Retired Senior Volunteer Programs; Domestic Violence counseling and services to parolees and probationers; literacy project; residential program for homeless teen moms and children.

Branches:

20382 Van Born Rd., Dearborn Heights, 48125. Tel: 313-792-9286; Fax: 313-792-0444. Email: csswc@csswayne.org. Web: www.csswayne.org.

15200 E. Jefferson, Ste. 105, Grosse Pointe Park, 48230. Tel: 313-821-2590; Fax: 313-821-1046. Email: csswc@csswayne.org. Web: www.csswayne.org.

Teen, Infant, Parent Services (TIPS), 1600 Blaine, 48206. Tel: 313-873-0117; Fax: 313-873-0136.

CLINTON TOWNSHIP. *Catholic Services of Macomb*, 15945 Canal Rd., 48038. Tel: 586-416-2300; Fax: 586-416-2311. Web: www.csmacomb.org. Mr. Thomas Reed, Pres. & CEO.

Branch Offices:

18720 Thirteen Mile Rd., Roseville, 48066. Tel: 586-416-2300; Fax: 586-416-2311.

347 S. Main, Romeo, 48065. Tel: 586-336-6844; Fax: 586-336-6843.

26238 Ryan Rd., Warren, 48091. Tel: 586-759-8700; Fax: 586-759-8789.

Christian Family Services of Lapeer County, Inc., 15945 Canal Rd., 48038. Tel: 586-416-2300; Fax: 586-416-2311.

MONROE. *Catholic Charities of Monroe County*, 14930 LaPlaisance Rd., Ste. 123, 48161. Tel: 734-240-3850; Fax: 734-240-3863. Web: www.ccmonroe.org. Greg Schafer, Dir. Bd.

Carleton Head Start Program, 1735 Ash St., Carleton, 48117. Tel: 734-654-2866; Fax: 734-654-2886.

Harwood 1 and 2 Head Start, 14930 LaPlaisance Rd., Ste. 121 & 122, 48161. Tel: 734-242-0165; 734-242-0190 (Family Advocates).

Harwood Head Start 3, 14930 LaPlaisance Rd., 48161. Tel: 734-240-2606.

Ida Elementary Head Start, 7900 Ida St., Ida, 48140.

Monroe Townsite 1, 2, 3, 4, & 5 Head Start, 15488 Eastwood St., 48161. Tel: 734-265-5000; Fax: 734-265-5001.

South Monroe Townsite Head Start, 15488 Eastwood St., 48161.

Summerfield Head Start, 232 E. Elm St., Summerfield, 49270. Tel: 734-249-5254.

Temperance Head Start Program, 9144 Lewis Ave., Temperance, 48182. Tel: 734-847-3460; Fax: 734-847-3460.

PORT HURON. *Catholic Social Services of St. Clair County, Inc.*, 2601 Thirteenth St., 48060. Tel: 810-987-9100; Fax: 810-987-9105. Patrick L. Cogley, M.A., Pres.

ROYAL OAK. *Catholic Social Services of Oakland County*, 1424 E. Eleven Mile Rd., 48067. Tel: 248-548-4044; Fax: 248-548-9239. Web: www.cssoc.org. Ms. Margaret A. Huggard, M.S.W., Pres.

Branches:

53 Franklin Blvd., Pontiac, 48341. Tel: 248-334-3595; Fax: 248-334-3781.

6637 Highland Rd., Waterford, 48327. Tel: 248-666-8870; Fax: 248-666-5023.

1424 E. Eleven Mile Rd., 48067. Tel: 248-548-4044; Fax: 248-548-9239.

3300 S. Adams Rd., Auburn Hills, 48326. Tel: 248-537-3300; Fax: 248-537-3306.

715 N. Lapeer Rd., Lake Orion, 48362. Tel: 248-693-7526; Fax: 248-693-2426.

Child Welfare Services, 17500 W. Eight Mile Rd., Southfield, 48075. Tel: 248-552-0750; Fax: 248-552-9019.

Older Adult Services, 18310 W. 12 Mile Rd., Southfield, 48076. Tel: 248-557-7373; Fax: 248-559-1140.

Hispanic Outreach, 76 Williams St., Pontiac, 48341. Tel: 248-338-4250; Fax: 248-335-8130.

[O] SPECIALIZED CHILD CARE FACILITIES AND SCHOOLS

DETROIT. *Christ Child House*, 15751 Joy Rd., 48228. Tel: 313-584-6077; Fax: 313-584-1148. Email: jyablonky@christchildhouse.org. Web: www.christchildhouse.org. Mr. John Yablonky, A.C.S.W, M.S.W., L.M.S.W., Exec. Dir. Educational Specialist 1; Educational Coordinator 1; Volunteer Tutors 12.

Don Bosco Hall, Inc., 2340 Calvert, 48206. Tel: 313-869-2200; Fax: 313-869-8220. Email: csmall@donboscohall.org. Web: www.donboscohall.org. Mr. Charles Small, Pres. & CEO. Residential treatment center for boys, ages 12-17, in need of care, guidance and therapy. Lay Staff 125; Residents 140; Transitional Services 180; Mentoring Program 155.

Holy Cross Children's Services, 5555 Conner, 48213. Tel: 517-423-7556; Fax: 517-423-5442. Email: lbrown@hccsnet.org; fboylan@hccsnet.org. Web: www.hccsnet.org. Bro. Francis Boylan, C.S.C., Exec. Dir.; Valerie Duffin, Regl. Dir. Residential and community based treatment programs for troubled youth and families with facilities located throughout the state of Michigan under the auspices of the Brothers of Holy Cross at Notre Dame.

Bowman House/Holy Cross Children's Services, 17200 Rowe St., 48205. Tel: 517-423-7556; Fax: 517-423-5442. Email: fboylan@hccsnet.org. Web: www.hccsnet.org.

Holy Cross Family & Community Support Program, 23915 Elmira, Redford, 48239. Tel: 517-423-7556; Fax: 517-423-5442. Email: fboylan@hccsnet.org. Web: www.hccsnet.org. Bro. Francis Boylan, C.S.C., Exec. Dir.; Valerie Duffin, Regl. Dir. Includes specialized foster care, supervised independent living, in-home family treatment.

Holy Cross Center/Holy Cross Children's Services, 5690 Cecil, 48210. Tel: 313-895-2200; Fax: 313-895-4010. Email: fboylan@hccsnet.org. Web: www.hccsnet.org. Day treatment, education, recreation program for Detroit region.

King House/Holy Cross Children's Services, 24455 Crocker Blvd., Clinton Twp, 48036. Tel: 586-463-7130; Fax: 586-463-7131. Email: fboylan@hccsnet.org. Web: www.hccsnet.org.

St. Vincent and Sarah Fisher Center, 16800 Trinity, 48219. Tel: 313-535-9200; Fax: 313-535-7804. Email: diane.renaud@svsfcenter.org. Diane Renaud, Exec. Dir. & CEO. (Educational) Staff 9.

DEARBORN HEIGHTS. *Vista Maria*, 20651 W. Warren Ave., 48127. Tel: 313-271-3050; Fax: 313-271-6250. Web: www.vistamaria.org. Angela Aufdemberge, Pres. & CEO. Residential treatment programs for adolescent girls, and community-based programs, e.g. foster care for boys and girls all involved in The Juvenile Justice & Child Welfare Systems. Sponsored by the Sisters of the Good Shepherd. Sisters 1; Girls Residential 162; Lay Staff 274; Foster Care 86; Youth Assistance Program 13.

[P] RETREAT HOUSES

DETROIT. *St. Paul of the Cross Passionist Retreat* Conducted by the Passionist Community., 23333 Schoolcraft Rd., 48223-2499. Tel: 313-535-9563; Fax: 313-535-9207. Email: stpauls@passionist.org. Web: www.passionist.org/stpauls. Revs. Philip Paxton, C.P., Retreat Dir.; Ronald Corl, C.P., Staff Member; Sr. Joanne Peters, O.P., Team Member; Mrs. Cathy Anthony, Team Member; Ms. Bernadette Beach, Exec. Dir.

BLOOMFIELD HILLS. *Visitation North Spirituality Center*, 7227 Lahser Rd., 48301. Tel: 248-433-0950; Fax: 248-433-0952. Email: visitationnorth@ihmsisters.org. Web: www.visitationnorth.org. Sisters 5.

Manresa Jesuit Retreat House, 1390 Quarton Rd., 48304-3554. Tel: 248-644-4933; Fax: 248-644-8291. Email: office@manresa-sj.org. Web: www.manresa-sj.org. Revs. Gregory J. Hyde, S.J., Exec. Dir. & Supr.; Walter L. Farrell, S.J., Retreat Dir. & Spiritual Dir.; Leo P. Cachat, S.J., Retreat Dir. & Spiritual Dir.; Peter J. Fennessy, S.J., Retreat Dir.; Bernard J. Owens, S.J., Dir. Internship in Ignatian Spirituality; Reynaldo A. Garcia, S.J., Spiritual Dir. Priests 6.

MONROE. *River House - IHM Spirituality Center*, 805 W. Elm Ave., 48162. Tel: 734-240-5494; Fax: 734-240-5495. Email: riverhouse@ihmsisters.org. Web: www.ihmsisters.org. Sponsorship of I.H.M. Congregation. Sisters 4.

OXFORD. *Queen of the Family Retreat Center*, 751 W. Drahner Rd., 48371. Tel: 248-628-5560; Fax: 248-628-4898. Email: karol.murray@queenofthefamily.org. Web: www.queenofthefamily.org. Rev. Lorenzo Gomez, L.C., Dir.

PLYMOUTH. *The Retreat Center at St. John's*, 44011 Five Mile Rd., 48170-2555. Tel: 734-414-1111; Fax: 734-414-1150.

WASHINGTON. *Capuchin Retreat*, 62460 Mt. Vernon Rd., P.O. Box 396, 48094. Tel: 248-651-4826; Fax: 248-650-4910. Revs. Kenneth Reinhart, O.F.M.Cap., Dir.; Gerald Kessel, O.F.M.Cap.; John Guimond, O.F.M. Cap.; James Andres, O.F.M.Cap.; Bro. Joseph Howe, O.F.M.Cap.

[Q] SPECIAL SERVICES

DETROIT. *Capuchin Soup Kitchen*, 1820 Mt. Elliott, 48207. Tel: 313-579-2100; Fax: 313-571-1822. Jerry Smith, O.F.M.Cap., Exec. Dir.; Bob Malloy, O.F.M.Cap., Pastoral Dir.; Ray Stadmeyer, O.F.M.Cap., Site Dir.

On the Rise Bakery, 6110 McClellan, 48213. Tel: 313-922-8510.

Conner Kitchen, 4390 Conner, 48215. Tel: 313-822-8606. Mike Breen, Site Dir.; Nancyann Turner, O.P., Mgr. Children & Youth Program. Tel: 313-822-8606, Ext. 21.

Capuchin Services, 6333 Medbury, 48211. Tel: 313-925-1730, Ext. 100. George Gaerig, Opers. Mgr.

Meldrum Kitchen, 1264 Meldrum, 48207. Tel: 313-579-2100. Alison Costello, Site Dir.; Ed Conlin, S.W., Chap.

Jefferson House, 8311 E. Jefferson, 48214. Tel: 313-331-8900; Fax: 313-331-2322. Joe Monachino, O.F.M.Cap., Site Dir. Transitional alcohol-drug residence.

Catholic Community Services of the Archdiocese of Detroit, Inc., 1234 Washington Blvd., 48226. Tel: 313-237-5885; Fax: 313-237-4642. Most Rev. Allen J. Vigneron, D.D., Pres.; Rev. Msgr. Robert J. McClory, Sec.; Mr. Daniel Oliver, Treas.

Manna Community Meal (Soup Kitchen), 1050 Porter St., 48226. Tel: 313-963-8708.

St. Patrick Senior Center, Inc., 58 Parsons, 48201. Tel: 313-833-7080; Fax: 313-833-0128. Web: www.stpatseniorcenter.com. Mrs. Satrice Coleman-Betts, Exec. Dir. Lay Staff 10; Patients Assisted Annually 1,600.

Pope John XXIII Hospitality House, 3977 2nd Ave., 48201. Tel: 313-965-4450; Fax: 313-965-4453. Rev. Russell E. Kohler. Cancer outpatient-residents, Transportation for Area Pediatric Cancer Patients.

Society of St. Vincent de Paul, 3000 Gratiot Ave., 48207. Tel: 313-393-2930; Fax: 313-393-2934. Email: bbrazier@svdpdet.org. Web: www.moreforthepoor.org. Mr. William D. Brazier, Exec. Dir.

HARRISVILLE. *The Oratory*, 407 N. Lake St., 48740. Tel: 313-965-4450; Fax: 313-965-4453. Email: corktown99@sbcglobal.net. Rev. Russell E. Kohler, Dir.

ONSTED. *St. Patrick's Retreat*, 11528 Killarney Hwy., 49265. Tel: 313-965-4450; Fax: 313-965-4453. Email: corktown99@sbcglobal.net. Rev. Russell E. Kohler, Dir. Tel: 313-832-4357. Retreats for Family with cancer outpatient; small groups of handicapped-developmentally disabled; small parish team meetings; hospice & chaplain's meetings and offers assistance for patient visits to world shrines.

St. Patrick's Chapel, Tipton, Michigan 4345 US12, Tipton, 49287. Tel: 313-965-4450; Fax: 313-965-4453. Email: corktown99@sbcglobal.net. 14-acre site for children's chapel and nature sanctuary to memorialize victims of childhood cancer and programs of aftercare for bereaved family members.

TROY. *Gabriel Richard Institute*, 3641 Estates Dr., 48084. Tel: 248-643-8887; 248-229-6877; Fax: 248-643-8887. Ms. Dolores Ammar, Exec. Dir. Adult and youth Christopher Leadership training for Catholic laymen, women, clergy & religious.

WARREN. *St. John's Deaf Center*, 14057 E. Nine Mile Rd., 48089. Tel: 586-758-0710 (TDD); 866-281-7108 (VP); 586-774-8476 (Voice); Fax: 586-774-8476. Revs. Richard J. Yost, O.S.F.S.; Michael Depcik, Dir.; Diane Chrenko.

[R] CAMPS AND COMMUNITY CENTERS

DETROIT. *C.Y.O. Boys Camp*, 305 Michigan Ave., 48226. Tel: 313-963-7172; Fax: 313-963-7179. Email: sheath@cyodetroit.org. Web: www.cyocamps.org.

C.Y.O. Girls Camp, 305 Michigan Ave., 48226. Tel: 313-963-7172; Fax: 313-963-7179. Email: sheath@cyodetroit.org. Web: www.cyocamps.org.

Camp Ozanam, 3000 Gratiot Ave., 48207. Tel: 313-393-2930; Fax: 313-393-2934. Web: www.moreforthepoor.org. Mr. William D. Brazier, Exec. Dir. A free week-long Christian camping experience for boys 8-12. Recruitment through Parish Conferences of the Society of St. Vincent de Paul.

Camp Stapleton, 3000 Gratiot Ave., 48207. Tel: 313-393-2930; Fax: 313-393-2934. Web: www.moreforthepoor.org. Mr. William D. Brazier, Exec. Dir. A free week long Christian camping experience for girls 8-12. Recruitment through Parish Conferences of the Society of St. Vincent de Paul.

[S] CAMPUS MINISTRIES

DETROIT. *Center for Creative Studies Campus Ministry* 5221 Gullen Mall, #761, 48202. Tel: 313-577-3462. Email: faithformation@aod.org.

Marygrove College Campus Ministry 8425 W. McNichols Rd., 48221. Tel: 313-927-1404; Fax: 313-927-1345. Sr. Barbara Beesley, Campus Ministry & Svc. Learning Coord.

University of Detroit Mercy University Ministry University Ministry UC106, 4001 W. McNichols Rd., 48221-3038. Tel: 313-993-1560. Web: www.udmercy.edu/ministry.

McNichols Campus Tel: 313-993-1560. David E. Nantais, Dir.; Sisters Beth Ann Finster, S.S.J., Asst. Dir.; Katherine Hill, R.S.M., Campus Min.; Drew Peters, Campus Min.

Wayne County Community College 305 Michigan Ave., 48226. Tel: 313-237-4687.

Wayne State Medical School 5221 Gullen Mall, #761, 48202. Tel: 313-577-3462.

Wayne State University, Newman Center 5221 Gullen Mall, #761, 48202. Tel: 313-577-3462; Fax: 313-577-8580.

DEARBORN. *Archdiocesan Catholic Campus Ministry Association, Gabriel Richard Campus Ministry Center, University of Michigan-Dearborn, Gabriel Richard Campus Ministry Center*, 5001 Evergreen, 48128. Tel: 313-271-6000. Email: grcministry@yahoo.com. Ms. Jennifer Horn, Campus Min.; Rev. Brendan Walsh, S.C.A., Campus Min.

University of Michigan-Dearborn, Henry Ford Community College Newman Center 5001 Evergreen Rd., 48128. Tel: 313-271-6000. Ms. Jennifer Horn, Campus Min.; Rev. Brendan Walsh, S.C.A., Campus Min. Gabriel Richard Campus Ministry Center.

FARMINGTON HILLS. *Oakland Community College* 305 Michigan Ave., 48226. Tel: 313-237-4687.

LIVONIA. *Madonna University Campus Ministry* 36600 Schoolcraft, 48150. Tel: 734-432-5419; Fax: 734-432-5393. Sr. Anita M. Taddonio, C.S.S.F., Dir. & Campus Min.

Schoolcraft College 305 Michigan Ave., 48226. Tel: 313-237-4687.

MONROE. *Monroe Community College* 305 Michigan Ave., 48226. Tel: 313-237-4687.

PORT HURON. *Blue Water/Thumb Regional Campus Ministry* 305 Michigan Ave., 48226. Tel: 313-237-4687. (Baker College and St. Clair Community College)

ROCHESTER. *St. John Fisher Campus Ministry-Oakland University, Rochester* 3665 Walton Blvd., Auburn Hills, 48326. Tel: 248-370-2189. Web: www.oucampusministry.com. Mrs. Lisa Brown, Pastoral Assoc.

SOUTHFIELD. *Lawrence Technological University* Mailing Address: 305 Michigan Ave., 48226. Tel: 313-237-4687.

WARREN. *Macomb Community College Campus Ministry* 305 Michigan Ave, 48226. Tel: 313-237-4687.

[T] MISCELLANEOUS LISTINGS

DETROIT. *Annunciation Institute*, 2701 Chicago Blvd., 48206. Tel: 313-980-0622.

St. Catherine of Siena Academy Foundation, 500 Woodward Ave., Ste. 3500, 48226-3435. Tel: 313-965-8293; Fax: 313-965-8252.

Christ Child Society, 15751 Joy Rd., 48228. Tel: 313-584-6077. Rev. Msgr. John P. Zenz, Spiritual Dir.; Shondell Patterson, Pres.

Clergy Health Plan, Chancery Building, 1234 Washington Blvd., 48226.

Detroit Catholic Charismatic Renewal Center, 5780 Evergreen Ave., 48228-3912. Tel: 313-982-3811; Fax: 313-982-3812. Email: dccrcenter@aol.com. Web: www.bobandmaryann.com. Rev. John C. Esper, Liaison; Arlene Apone, Assoc. Liaison.

Dominican Center for Religious Development, 23333 Schoolcraft, 48223. Tel: 313-387-9574; Fax: 313-535-9207. Email: info@dominicancenter.org. Web: www.dominicancenter.org. Sr. Joanne Podlucky, O.P., Dir.; Faith Offman, Staff & Spiritual Dir.; Rev. Victor Clore; Sr. Charlotte Hoefer, O.P., Staff & Spiritual Dir.

Dominican Literacy Center, 11148 Harper, 48213. Tel: 313-267-1000. Sr. Janice Brown, O.P., Exec. Dir.

Gabriel Richard Historical Society, 1000 Ste. Anne St., 48216. Tel: 313-963-1888; Fax: 313-496-0429. Rev. Thomas W. Sepulveda, C.S.B., Contact Person.

Institute for Communal Contemplation and Dialogue, 8531 W. McNichols, 48221. Tel: 313-971-3668; Fax: 313-342-7421. Email: circles@engagingimpasse.org. Web: www.engagingimpasse.org. Sr. Nancy Sylvester, I.H.M., Exec. Dir.

Jesuit Volunteer Corps. Midwest, Inc., 7333 W. Seven Mile Rd., 48221. Tel: 313-345-3480; Fax: 313-345-5410. Email: jvcmw@jesuitvolunteers.org. Web: www.jesuitvolunteers.org. P.O. Box 21936, 48221-0936. Angela Moloney, Exec. Dir.

Latino Cultural Pastoral Center, 4329 Central, 48210. Tel: 248-398-4565.

**Mercy Education Project*, 1450 Howard St., 48216. Tel: 313-963-5881; Fax: 313-963-0209. Email: mep@mercyed.net. Web: www.mercyed.net. Sr. Maureen Mulcrone, R.S.M., Dir. Devel. & Mktg.

Missionary Medical Relief, 17330 Quincy St., 48221. Tel: 313-342-4066; Fax: 313-342-6816. Email: mmr@pimeusa.org. Web: www.pimeusa.org. Ms. Barbara J. Rubaie, Dir. An agency of the P.I.M.E. Missionaries.

PIME Foster Parents-Adoptions at a Distance, 17330 Quincy Ave., 48221. Tel: 313-342-4066; Fax: 313-342-6816. Rev. Giorgio Ferrara, P.I.M.E., Mission Outreach Dir.; Ms. Maria Biernacki, Dir. An agency of the PIME Missionaries.

Pontiac Vision 2000 Schools, Inc., 1234 Washington Blvd., 48226. Tel: 313-237-5803. Mr. Daniel Oliver, Sec. & Treas.

Pope John Paul II Cultural Foundation, Inc. His Eminence Adam Cardinal Maida, J.C.L., J.D., S.T.L., Contact Person (Retired).

Foundation Office, 1234 Washington Blvd., 48226. Tel: 313-237-5816; Fax: 313-237-4642. Web: www.jp2cc.org.

Operations Office, Pope John Paul II Cultural Center, 3900 Harewood Rd., N.E., Washington, DC 20017-1555. Tel: 202-635-5400; Fax: 202-635-5411. His Eminence Adam Cardinal Maida, J.C.L., J.D., S.T.L., Pres.; Most Rev. John J. Myers, D.D., J.C.D., First Vice Pres.; His Eminence Donald Cardinal Wuerl, S.T.D., Vice Pres.; Most Rev. Bernard J. Harrington, D.D., Sec.; Mr. Daniel Oliver, Treas.; Rev. Steven C. Boguslawski, O.P., M.A., M.Div., S.T.M., S.T.L., Ph.D., Acting Exec. Dir.; Dr. Hugh Dempsey, K.M.O.B., Deputy Dir. & Dir. Devel.

Siena Literacy Center, 16888 Trinity St., 48219. Tel: 313-532-8404; Fax: 313-532-8409. Email: info@sienaliteracy.org. Web: www.sienaliteracy.org. Donna J. Nesbitt, Dir.

Solanus Casey Center, 1780 Mt. Elliott, 48207-3596. Tel: 313-579-2100, Ext. 130; Fax: 313-579-5365. Web: www.solanuscaseycenter.org. Revs. Lawrence E. Webber, O.F.M.Cap., Dir.; James C. Hast, O.F.M.Cap., Asst. Dir., Pastoral Care.

BLOOMFIELD HILLS. **Christus Medicus Foundation*, 3707 W. Maple Rd., 48301. Tel: 248-980-8456; Fax: 248-822-4001. Mr. Michael J. O'Dea, Exec. Dir.

Logos, Inc. (Michigan), 2460 Opdyke Rd., 48304. Tel: 248-644-2954; Fax: 248-642-4668. Revs. Lorenzo Gomez, L.C., Rector; Daniel Pajerski, L.C.

Mercy Homecare - Oakland, 281 Enterprise Dr., Ste. 200, 48302. Tel: 248-858-7735; Fax: 248-858-8323. Web: www.trinity-health.org. Ms. Mary Ann Rayrat, Exec. Dir.

**Mercy Hospice*, 281 Enterprise Ct., Ste. 200, 48302. Tel: 800-832-1155; Fax: 248-858-8323. Ms. Mary Ann Rayrat, Exec. Dir.

Opdyke, Inc., 2460 Opdyke Rd., 48304. Tel: 248-644-2954; Fax: 248-642-4668. Rev. Jose Felix Ortega, L.C., Contact.

WCVA, Inc. - Michigan Catholic Radio, P.O. Box 1090, 48303-1090. Tel: 248-642-6226; Fax: 248-642-6027. Web: www.catholicradio.org. Mr. John F.X. Browne, Pres.

CLARKSTON. *Clarkston Pastoral Center, Inc.*, 5935 Clarkson Rd., 48348. Tel: 248-241-9043; Fax: 248-922-2084. Revs. Lorenzo Gomez, L.C.; Daniel Pajerski, L.C., Everest Academy Boys School Dir.

DEARBORN. *Council of Catholic Women/AD*, P.O. Box 5097, 48128. Tel: 313-563-1734. Lorraine McFee, Pres.

Leo XIII Society, 1840 N. Melborn, 48128. Tel: 313-359-1499; Fax: 313-359-1767. P.O. Box 666, Elmore, OH 43416. Ernie Scarano, Pres.

EASTPOINTE. *Servants of Jesus of The Divine Mercy*, 16103 Chesterfield, 48021-1106. Tel: 586-777-8591; Fax: 586-777-7989. Email: sdivine2013@wowway.com. Web: www.sjdivinemercy.org. Mrs. Catherine M. Lanni, Spiritual Moderator/Pres.

FARMINGTON HILLS. *Living Faith - Fine Arts Apostolate*, 36703 Kenmore Dr., 48335. Tel: 248-444-1034. Web: www.livingstations.org. Kelly Nieto, Pres. & Contact Person.

Trinity Health International, 34605 Twelve Mile Rd., 48331. Tel: 248-489-6100; Fax: 248-488-9220. Mr. Joseph Swedish, Bd. Chm.; Mr. Jim Cotelingam, Pres.

GROSSE POINTE. *John Paul II Foundation of Michigan, Inc.*, 1 Elmsleigh Ln., 48230. Tel: 313-882-2140; Fax: 313-882-1292. Conducts religious, cultural, educational, humanitarian and fund raising activities in Michigan in liaison with the John Paul Foundation in Rome. Regular, supporting and life memberships.

LIVONIA. **Angela Hospice Home Care, Inc.*, 14100 Newburgh Rd., 48154-5010. Tel: 734-464-7810; Fax: 734-779-4601. Email: ahospice@aol.com. Web: www.angelahospice.org. Bed Capacity 32; Total Assisted Annually (with home care) 1,750; Total Staff 219.

Felician Sisters of Livonia Foundation, 36800 Schoolcraft, 48150. Tel: 734-591-1730; Fax: 734-591-1710. Email: sconniet@feliciansisters.org. Web: www.feliciansna.org. Sr. Mary Christopher Moore, C.S.S.F., Pres.

Marian Village Corporation aka Marywood Nursing Care Center 36975 Five Mile Rd., 48154. Tel: 734-464-0600; Fax: 734-464-4846. Email: sconniet@feliciansisters.org. Web: www.feliciansna.org. Sr. Mary Renetta Rumpz, C.S.S.F., Pres.

Mercy Services for Aging, Non-profit Housing Corporation Wholly owned subsidiary of Trinity Continuing Care Services, 17410 College Pkwy., Ste. 200, 48152-2363. Tel: 734-542-8349; Fax: 248-488-9169. Email: robbinsk@trinity-health.org. Web: www.trinityccs.org. Ken Robbins, Pres. & CEO.

Trinity Continuing Care Services - Indiana, Inc., 17410 College Pkwy., Ste. 200, 48152-2363. Tel: 734-542-8349; Fax: 248-488-9169. Email: robbinsk@trinity-health.org. Web: www.trinityccs.org. Ken Robbins, Pres. & CEO.

**Trinity Home Health Services, Inc.*, 17410 College Pkwy., Ste. 150, 48152. Tel: 734-542-8200; Fax: 734-542-8285. Email: samynm@trinity-health.org. Web: www.trinityhomehealth.org. Ms. Grace C. McCauley, CEO.

MARYSVILLE. *National Alliance of Parishes Restructuring into Communities (NAPRC)*, 1000 Michigan Ave., 48040. Tel: 810-364-3228; Fax: 810-364-5947. Email: naprcoffice@ameritech.net. Rev. Arthur R. Baranowski, Dir.

MONROE. *SSIHM Charitable Trust (Retired and Infirm Sisters)*, 610 W. Elm Ave., 48162-7909. Tel: 734-240-9700; Fax: 734-240-9784. Sr. Helen Ingles, I.H.M., Trustee.

NOVI. *Trinity Health Corporation*, 27870 Cabot Dr., 48377-2920. Tel: 248-489-6000; Fax: 248-489-6775. Email: neumannp@trinity-health.org. Web: www.trinity-health.org. Mr. Joseph Swedish, Pres. & CEO.

Trinity Health-Michigan, 27870 Cabot Dr., 48377-2920. Tel: 248-489-6000; Fax: 248-489-6775. Web: www.trinity-health.org. Mr. Joseph Swedish, Pres. Organization owns & operates 6 hospital divisions in Michigan. In addition to acute care facilities, Trinity Health - Michigan operates other related health care programs and facilities. Trinity Health - Michigan is part of Trinity Health, a multi-state health care organization.

ORCHARD LAKE. *American Friends of the Vatican Library*, 3535 Indian Tr., 48324. Tel: 248-683-0311; Fax: 248-738-6735. Rev. Msgr. Charles G. Kosanke, Pres.

PONTIAC. *Mt. Hope Catholic Cemetery Association*, 46408 Woodward Ave., 48342. Tel: 248-332-1079. Rev. James F. Kean; Joseph E. Alessi, Supt.

PORT HURON. *Port Huron Mercy Family Care*, 2601 Electric Ave., P.O. Box 610669, 48061-0669. Tel: 810-985-1868. Ms. Nancy Mason, Dir. (A unit of Trinity Health).

REDFORD. *Catholic Biblical School of Michigan, Ltd.*, 26234 Graham Rd., 48239. Tel: 313-570-8105; Fax: 586-774-4040.

ROMEO. **BVM Foundation*, 11070 W. Gates, 48065. Tel: 586-752-6744; Fax: 888-950-3329. Email: phl2004@mac.com. Mr. Brian Palmer, Pres.

SHELBY TWP. *Holy Trinity Apostolate*, 53565 Sherwood Ln., 48315. Tel: 586-781-6051; Fax: 568-781-6099. Barbara Middleton, Pres.

ST. CLAIR SHORES. *Catholic Kolping Society of America, Detroit Branch, Inc.*, 24409 Jefferson, 48080. Tel: 586-775-9159. Mrs. Rosalinda Seubert, Pres.; Ms. Thekla Abels, Contact Person. Tel: 313-885-1189; Rev. Lawrence E. Webber, O.F.M.Cap.

**Celebrate Life Ministries*, P.O. Box 537, Roseville, 48066. Tel: 313-882-9639. Sr. Loretta Mellon, O.P., Exec. Dir.

TROY. **Mary's Mantle*, 1977 E. Wattles Rd., 48085. Tel: 248-376-5338. Email: info@marysmantle.net. Beth Collison, Contact Person.

WARREN. *St. John Health System* Holding Company sponsored by Sisters of St. Joseph, the Daughters of Charity of St. Vincent de Paul and Sisters of St. Joseph of Carondelet which operates: St. John Hospital & Medical Center; Medical Resources Group; Affiliated Health Services, Inc.; Eastwood Community Clinics; St. John River District Hospital; St. John Macomb-Oakland Hospital; St. John Home Care; Providence Hospital and Medical Centers, Inc.; Seton Health Corporation of Southeast Michigan; St. John Community Health Investment Corporation; St. John Hospital Foundation; St. John Macomb Foundation., 28000 Dequindre Rd., 48092. Tel: 586-753-0911; Fax: 586-753-1228. Patricia Maryland, Pres. & CEO.

WATERFORD. *Dominican Health Care Corporation*, 2300 Walkins Lake Rd., 48328. Tel: 248-674-2241; Fax: 248-674-1211. Web: www.lourdes-sc.org. Sr. Maureen Comer, O.P., CEO.

Lourdes Campus Fund, 2300 Watkins Lake Rd., 48328. Tel: 248-674-2241; Fax: 248-674-1211. Web: www.lourdes-sc.org. Sr. Maureen Comer, O.P., CEO.

WESTLAND. *Chinese Catholic Society of Michigan, Inc.*, 39375 Joy Rd., 48185. Tel: 248-855-4517; Fax: 248-647-7736. Mr. Francis G. King, Pres.; Mr. Thomas McGuire, Spiritual Dir.

[U] ARCHDIOCESAN CEMETERIES

DETROIT. *Holy Cross*, 8850 Dix Ave., 48209. Tel: 313-841-0545; Fax: 313-841-2313. (owned by the Archdiocese of Detroit)

Mt. Elliott, 1701 Mt. Elliott Ave., 48207. Tel: 313-567-0048. (owned & operated by the Mt. Elliott Cemetery Assoc.)

Mt. Olivet, 17100 Van Dyke, 48234. Tel: 313-365-5650. (owned & operated by the Mt. Elliott Cemetery Assoc.)

BROWNSTOWN. *Our Lady of Hope*, 18303 Allen Rd., 48193. Tel: 734-285-2155; Fax: 734-285-6510. (owned & operated by the Archdiocese of Detroit)

CLINTON TOWNSHIP. *Resurrection*, 18201 Clinton River Rd., 48038. Tel: 586-286-9020; Fax: 586-286-2441. (owned & operated by the Mt. Elliott Cemetery Assoc.)

DEARBORN HEIGHTS. *St. Hedwig Cemetery*, 23755 Military, 48127. Tel: 313-562-1900; Fax: 313-562-8238. (owned & operated by the Conventual Franciscan Friars)

MONROE. *St. Joseph Cemetery*, 909 N. Monroe St., 48162. Tel: 734-241-1411; Fax: 734-241-1422. James DuBay, Gen. Mgr.

ROCHESTER. *Guardian Angel*, 4701 Rochester Rd., 48306. Tel: 800-275-9574; Fax: 248-601-1711. (owned & operated by the Mt. Elliott Cemetery Assoc.)

SOUTHFIELD. *Holy Sepulchre*, 25800 W. Ten Mile Rd., P.O. Box 68, 48037. Tel: 248-350-1900. Sr. Mary V. Korb, R.S.M., Dir. Archdiocesan Cemeteries. (owned & operated by the Archdiocese of Detroit)

WATERFORD. *All Saints*, 4401 Nelsey Rd., 48329. Tel: 248-623-9633. (owned & operated by the Mt. Elliott Cemetery Assoc.)

[V] CLOSED INSTITUTIONS

DETROIT. *Archdiocesan Archives* The following institutional sacramental records can be found at the following address unless otherwise indicated., 1234 Washington Blvd., 48226. Tel: 313-237-5846; Fax: 313-596-7199.

St. Agnes
St. Albertus
Anawim Community
St. Andrew Records at Our Lady Queen of Angels, Detroit.
Annunciation Records at Good Shepherd, Detroit.
Annunciation/Our Lady of Sorrows Records at Good Shepherd, Detroit.
St. Anthony Records at Good Shepherd, Detroit.
Assumption of the Blessed Virgin Mary
St. Augustine
St. Bartholomew Records at St. Bartholomew-St. Rita, Detroit.
St. Benedict the Moor
St. Bernadette Chapel
St. Bernard
St. Boniface
St. Brendan
St. Brigid
St. Camillus
Cardinal Leger Community
St. Casimir
St. Catherine
St. Catherine of Siena
St. Christine
Corpus Christi
St. David
St. Dominic
St. Edward
Emmaus Community
Epiphany
Episcopal Residence
St. Eugene
St. Francis de Sales Records at St. Peter Claver, Detroit.
St. Francis Hospital
St. Gemma
St. George (Lithuanian)
St. Gerard Records at Corpus Christi, Detroit.
Grace Hospital
Guardian Angels
Henry Ford Hospital
Holy Ghost
Holy Name of Jesus
St. Ignatius of Antioch
Immaculate Conception
Immaculate Heart of Mary Records at Corpus Christi, Detroit.
St. Jerome Records at St. Lucy Croatian, Troy
St. Joachim
St. John Berchmans
St. John Berchmans/St. Juliana
St. John Cantius
St. John the Evangelist
St. John Nepomucene
St. Joseph Mercy Hospital, St. Clemens
St. Juliana
St. Lawrence
St. Margaret Mary
St. Martin of Tours
Martyrs of Uganda
St. Mary Hospital - Detroit Memorial Hospital
Mercy Hospital/St. Joseph Hospital
St. Monica
Mother of Consolation Mission
Mother of Our Savior
Mount Carmel Mercy Hospital
Our Lady Gate of Heaven Records at St. Suzanne/Our Lady Gate of Heaven, Detroit
Our Lady of Guadalupe
Our Lady of Help
Our Lady Help of Christians Records at Transfiguration-Our Lady Help of Christians, Detroit.
Our Lady of Mt. Carmel
Our Lady Queen of Hope
Our Lady of Sorrows Records at Good Shepherd, Detroit.
St. Paul Maltese
Patronage of St. Joseph
St. Peter Claver Records at Sacred Heart, Detroit
St. Peter (Lithuanian)
St. Philip Neri
Precious Blood Records at St. Peter Claver, Detroit.
Resurrection
St. Rita Records at St. Bartholomew-St. Rita, Detroit.
St. Rose of Lima
St. Stanislaus Bishop and Martyr
St. Suzanne Records at St. Suzanne/Our Lady Gate of Heaven, Detroit
St. Theresa
St. Thomas the Apostle
Transfiguration Records at Transfiguration-Our Lady Help of Christians, Detroit.
St. Vincent de Paul
Santa Maria
Visitation
St. Wenceslaus

ALGONAC. *St. Catherine of Alexandria* Records at Our Lady on the River, Marine City.

CLINTON TOWNSHIP. *St. Claude* Records at St. Thecla, Clinton Twp.
St. Valerie of Ravenna Records at St. Louis, Clinton Twp.

COLUMBUS. *Holy Rosary Mission* Records at Holy Family Parish - All Saints Church, Memphis.
St. Philip Neri Records at Holy Family Parish - All Saints Church, Memphis.

DEARBORN. *St. Bernadette*
St. Joseph Retreat House

EASTPOINTE. *St. Barnabas* Records at Holy Innocents-St. Barnabas, Roseville.

HARSENS ISLAND. *St. Mark* Records at Our Lady of the River, Marine City.

HIGHLAND PARK. *St. John Vianney*

INKSTER. *St. Kevin*
SS. Kevin & Norbert
St. Norbert

MACOMB. *St. Maximilian Kolbe* Records at St. Francis of Assisi-St. Maximilian Kolbe, Ray.

MARINE CITY. *Holy Cross* Records at Our Lady on the River, Marine City.

MELVINDALE. *St. Conrad* Records at St. Mary Magdalen, Melvindale.

MEMPHIS. *All Saints* Records at Holy Family, Memphis.

NORTH BRANCH. *St. Patrick Mission* Records at SS. Peter & Paul, North Branch.

PONTIAC. *St. Joseph* Records at St. Damien of Molokai, Pontiac.
St. Michael Records at St. Damien of Molokai, Pontiac.
St. Vincent de Paul Records at St. Damien of Molokai, Pontiac.

PORT HURON. *St. Joseph* Records at Holy Trinity, Port Huron.
Our Lady of Guadalupe Mission Records at Holy Trinity, Port Huron.
St. Stephen Records at Holy Trinity, Port Huron.

RAY. *St. Francis of Assisi* Records at St. Francis of Assisi-St. Maximilian Kolbe, Ray.

REDFORD. *St. Agatha*

ROSEVILLE. *Holy Innocents* Records at Holy Innocents-St. Barnabas, Roseville.

ST. CLAIR SHORES. *St. Germaine* Records at Our Lady of Hope, St. Clair Shores.
St. Gertrude Records at Our Lady of Hope, St. Clair Shores.

SOUTHFIELD. *St. Beatrice* Records at Church of the Transfiguration, Southfield.
St. Bede Records at Church of the Transfiguration, Southfield.
St. Ives Records at Church of the Transfiguration, Southfield.
St. Michael Records at Church of the Transfiguration, Southfield.

SOUTHGATE. *St. Hugh* Records at St. Frances Cabrini, Allen Park.

TAYLOR. *St. Cyril of Jerusalem* Records at Our Lady of the Angels, Taylor.
St. Paschal Baylon Records at Our Lady of the Angels, Taylor.

TROY. *Our Lady of the Hills*

UTICA. *Vida Nueva Community*

WARREN. *Ascension* Records at St. Clement, Center Line.
St. Cletus Records at Our Lady of Grace Vietnamese, Warren.
St. Dorothy Records at St. Teresa of Avila, Warren.
St. Leonard of Port Maurice Records at St. Teresa of Avila Parish.

WESTLAND. *St. Bernardine of Siena* Records at St. Damian, Westland.

WYANDOTTE. *St. Helena*

RELIGIOUS INSTITUTES OF MEN REPRESENTED IN THE ARCHDIOCESE

For further details refer to the corresponding bracketed number in the Religious Institutes of Men or Women section.

[0140]—*The Augustinians* (Chicago)—O.S.A.
[0170]—*Basilian Fathers* (Toronto, Ont.)—C.S.B.
[0200]—*Benedictine Monks* (Detroit Prov.)—O.S.B.
[0330]—*Brothers of the Christian Schools* (District of Eastern North America)—F.S.C.
[0600]—*Brothers of the Congregation of Holy Cross* (Midwest Prov.)—C.S.C.
[]—*Canons Regular of the Holy Cross*—O.R.C.
[0470]—*The Capuchin Friars* (St. Joseph Prov.)—O.F.M.Cap.
[0310]—*Congregation of Christian Brothers* (American Prov.)—C.F.C.
[0750]—*Congregation of Marianhill Missionaries*—C.M.M.
[]—*Congregation of the Holy Spirit*—C.S.Sp.
[1000]—*Congregation of the Passion* (Western Prov.)—C.P.
[1140]—*Congregation of the Sacred Hearts of Jesus and Mary*—SS.CC.
[0480]—*Conventual Franciscans*—O.F.M.Conv
[0520]—*Franciscan Friars (Custody of the Holy Family/Croatian)* (Prov. of St. John the Baptist; Prov. of St. Stephen, King of Hungary)—O.F.M.
[0690]—*Jesuit Fathers and Brothers* (Detroit, Chicago, New Orleans, New York, Maryland Provinces)—S.J.
[0730]—*Legionaries of Christ*—L.C.
[]—*Little Brothers of Jesus*
[0780]—*Marist Fathers* (Northeastern Prov.)—S.M.
[]—*Miles Christi Institute*—M.C.
[]—*Missionaries of St. Francis de Sales* Visakhapatnam Province, India—M.S.F.S.
[]—*Missionary Society of St. Paul*—M.S.S.P.
[0920]—*Oblates of St. Francis De Sales*—O.S.F.S.
[0430]—*Order of Preachers-Dominicans* (Prov. of St. Albert the Great)—O.P.
[1020]—*Pious Society of St. Paul*—S.S.P.
[1050]—*Pontifical Institute for Foreign Missions*—P.I.M.E.
[1070]—*Redemptorist Fathers* (Denver Prov.)—C.SS.R.
[]—*Salesians of Don Bosco*—S.D.B.
[1260]—*Society of Christ* (American-Canadian Prov.)—S.Ch.
[0440]—*Society of Saint Edmund*—S.S.E.
[]—*Society of St. Paul*—S.S.P.
[0990]—*Society of the Catholic Apostolate*—S.A.C.
[]—*Voluntas Dei Institute, I.V. Dei*

RELIGIOUS INSTITUTES OF WOMEN REPRESENTED IN THE ARCHDIOCESE

[1810]—*Bernardine Sisters of the Third Order of St. Francis*—O.S.F.
[3810]—*Catholic Mission Sisters of St. Francis Xavier*—X.S.
[]—*Congregation of Sisters of Bon Secours*—C.B.S.
[]—*Congregation of the Sisters of Divine Providence*—C.D.P.
[3832]—*Congregation of the Sisters of St. Joseph*—C.S.J.
[0760]—*Daughters of Charity of St. Vincent de Paul*—D.C.

[0790]—*Daughters of Divine Charity*—F.D.C.
[]—*Daughters of Mary* (India)—D.M.
[]—*Daughters of Mary Immaculate (Chaldean)*—D.M.I.
[]—*Daughters of Mary, Mother of Mercy*—D.M.M.M.
[]—*Daughters of the Heart of Mary*—D.H.M.
[0420]—*Discalced Carmelite Nuns*—O.C.D.
[1050]—*Dominican Contemplative Nuns*—O.P.
[1070-13]—*Dominican Sisters (Adrian, MI)*—O.P.
[1070-14]—*Dominican Sisters (Grand Rapids, MI)*—O.P.
[]—*Dominican Sisters of Mt. Thabor*—O.P.
[1115]—*Dominican Sisters of Peace*—O.P.
[1170]—*Felician Sisters*—C.S.S.F.
[]—*Franciscan Missionaries of Jesus Crucified*—F.M.J.C.
[]—*Franciscan Sisters of St. Joseph*—F.S.S.J.
[]—*Franciscan Sisters of the Atonement*—S.A.
[1440]—*Franciscan Sisters of the Poor*—S.F.P.
[]—*Holy Name of Jesus and Mary*—S.N.J.M.
[2430]—*Marist Sisters Congregation of Mary*—S.M.
[]—*Mission Helpers of the Sacred Heart*—M.H.S.H.
[2710]—*Missionaries of Charity*—M.C.
[]—*Missionaries of the Kingship of Christ*—S.I.M.
[M.Chr.]—*Missionary Sisters of Christ the King for Polonia*
[]—*Order of St. Basil the Great*—O.S.B.M.
[2970]—*School Sisters of Notre Dame*—S.S.N.D.
[3560]—*Servants of Jesus*—S.J.
[3590]—*Servants of Mary (Servite Sisters)*—O.S.M.
[0440]—*Sisters of Charity of Cincinnati, Ohio*—S.C.
[0520]—*Sisters of Charity of Our Lady, Mother of Mercy*—S.C.M.M.
[2245]—*Sisters of Jesus the Savior*—S.J.S.
[2575]—*Sisters of Mercy of the Americas* (Mid-Atlantic Community; West Midwest Community)—R.S.M
[2990]—*Sisters of Notre Dame*—S.N.D.
[]—*Sisters of St. Francis* Oldenburg
[1530]—*Sisters of St. Francis of the Congregation of Our Lady of Lourdes* (Sylvania, OH & Tiffin, OH)—O.S.F.
[3930]—*Sisters of St. Joseph of the Third Order of St. Francis*—S.S.J.-T.O.S.F.
[1830]—*Sisters of the Good Shepherd*—R.G.S.
[]—*Sisters of the Holy Cross*
[1970]—*Sisters of the Holy Family of Nazareth*—C.S.F.N.
[]—*Sisters of the Imitation of Christ* (India)—S.I.C.
[2350]—*Sisters of the Living Word*—S.L.W.
[]—*Sisters of the Precious Blood*—C.P.P.S.
[2090]—*Sisters, Home Visitors of Mary*—H.V.M.
[2150]—*Sisters, Servants of the Immaculate Heart of Mary*—I.H.M.
[2460]—*Society of Mary Reparatrix*—S.M.R.
[4070]—*Society of the Sacred Heart*—R.S.C.J.
[]—*Vestiarski Sisters of Jesus*—V.S.

NECROLOGY

† Cusmano, John C., (Retired)—Died Oct. 29, 2011
† Kirwan, Thomas P., (Retired)—Died May 30, 2011
† LaCasse, John P., (Retired)—Died Sept. 29, 2011
† Lunnon, William, (Special Assignment)—Died May 28, 2011
† McGoldrick, William J., (Retired)—Died Jan. 8, 2011
† Partensky, Leonard J., (Retired)—Died April 14, 2011
† Trent, James F., (Retired)—Died April 28, 2011
† Vu, Joseph Duc, Detroit, MI John D. Dingell Veterans Admin. Medical Center—Died March 23, 2011
† Wojciechowski, Robert J.—Died April 8, 2011
† Wytrwal, Alexander J., (Retired)—Died March 11, 2011
† Xuereb, Paul D., (Retired)—Died April 27, 2011

An asterisk (*) denotes an organization that has established tax-exempt status directly with the IRS and is not covered by the USCCB Group Ruling.

Diocese of Dodge City

(Dioecesis Dodgepolis)

Most Reverend

JOHN B. BRUNGARDT

Bishop of Dodge City; ordained May 23, 1998; appointed Bishop of Dodge City December 15, 2010; installed February 2, 2011. *Office: 910 Central Ave., P.O. Box 137, Dodge City, KS 67801-0137.*

Most Reverend

RONALD M. GILMORE, S.T.L., D.D.

Bishop Emeritus of Dodge City; ordained June 7, 1969; appointed Bishop of Dodge City May 12, 1998; installed July 16, 1998; retired December 15, 2010. *Office: 910 Central Ave., P.O. Box 137, Dodge City, KS 67801.*

Most Reverend

STANLEY G. SCHLARMAN, D.D.

Bishop Emeritus of Dodge City; ordained July 13, 1958; appointed to the Titular See of Capri and Auxiliary Bishop of Belleville, March 13, 1979; consecrated May 14, 1979; appointed Bishop of Dodge City March 1, 1983; installed May 4, 1983; retired May 12, 1998. *Res.: 2620 Lebanon Ave., Belleville, IL 62221.*

ESTABLISHED MAY 19, 1951.

Square Miles 23,000.

Comprises the following Counties in the State of Kansas: Barton, Stafford, Pratt, Barber, Rush, Ness, Lane, Scott, Wichita, Greeley, Hamilton, Kearny, Finney, Hodgeman, Pawnee, Edwards, Ford, Gray, Haskell, Grant, Stanton, Morton, Stevens, Seward, Meade, Clark, Kiowa and Comanche.

Principal Patron: Our Lady of Guadalupe.

Secondary Patron: St. John the Baptist.

For legal titles of parishes and diocesan institutions, consult the Chancery Office.

Catholic Church Offices: 910 Central Ave., P.O. Box 137, Dodge City, KS 67801-0137. Tel: 620-227-1500; Fax: 620-227-1545.

Web: www.dcdiocese.org

Email: dcdiocese@dcdiocese.org

STATISTICAL OVERVIEW

Personnel	
Bishop	1
Retired Bishops	1
Priests: Diocesan Active in Diocese	18
Priests: Diocesan Active Outside Diocese	1
Priests: Retired, Sick or Absent	13
Number of Diocesan Priests	32
Religious Priests in Diocese	4
Total Priests in Diocese	36
Extern Priests in Diocese	8
Ordinations:	
Diocesan Priests	1
Permanent Deacons in Diocese	8
Total Sisters	72
Parishes	
Parishes	48
With Resident Pastor:	
Resident Diocesan Priests	14
Resident Religious Priests	2
Without Resident Pastor:	
Administered by Priests	25
Administered by Religious Women	3
Administered by Lay People	1
Completely Vacant	4
Quasi Parish	1
Professional Ministry Personnel:	
Sisters	16
Lay Ministers	14
Welfare	
Catholic Hospitals	2
Total Assisted	132,135
Health Care Centers	1
Special Centers for Social Services	4
Total Assisted	7,656
Educational	
Diocesan Students in Other Seminaries	3
Total Seminarians	3
Elementary Schools, Diocesan and Parish	7
Total Students	989
Catechesis/Religious Education:	
High School Students	1,421
Elementary Students	3,645
Total Students under Catholic Instruction	6,058
Teachers in the Diocese:	
Lay Teachers	88
Vital Statistics	
Receptions into the Church:	
Infant Baptism Totals	961
Minor Baptism Totals	82
Adult Baptism Totals	40
Received into Full Communion	136
First Communions	1,120
Confirmations	845
Marriages:	
Catholic	147
Interfaith	55
Total Marriages	202
Deaths	369
Total Catholic Population	45,457
Total Population	215,895

Former Bishops—Most Revs. JOHN BAPTIST FRANZ, D.D., cons. Aug. 29, 1951; transferred to the See of Peoria Aug. 8, 1959; retired June 1, 1971; died July 3, 1992.; MARION F. FORST, D.D., cons. March 24, 1960; transferred to See of Kansas City, KS as Auxiliary Oct. 16, 1976; retired as Auxiliary Bishop Dec. 23, 1986; died June 2, 2007; EUGENE J. GERBER, D.D., cons. Dec. 14, 1976; transferred to See of Wichita, KS Nov. 23, 1982; STANLEY G. SCHLARMAN, D.D. (Retired), cons. May 14, 1979; appt. Bishop of Dodge City March 1, 1983; installed May 4, 1983; retired May 12, 1998; RONALD M. GILMORE, ord. June 7, 1969; appt. Bishop of Dodge City May 12, 1998; installed July 16, 1998; retired Dec. 15, 2010.

Chancery Office and Administration— Unless otherwise noted, the mailing address is: *P.O. Box 137, Dodge City, 67801-0137.* Tel: 620-227-1500; Fax: 620-227-1545. Office Hours: Mon.-Fri. 9-4:30.

Vicar General and Moderator of the Curia—Rev. ROBERT A. SCHREMMER, V.G. Tel: 620-227-1555. Email: rschremmer@dcdiocese.org.

Chancellor—Sr. JANICE GROCHOWSKY, C.S.J., J.C.L. Tel: 620-227-1527. Email: jgrochowsky@dcdiocese.org.

Diocesan Archivist—Mr. TIMOTHY F. WENZL. Tel: 620-227-1556. Email: twenzl@dcdiocese.org.

Finance Officer—Mr. DANIEL M. STREMEL, CPA. Tel: 620-227-1517. Email: dmstremel@dcdiocese.org.

Office of Priestly Vocations—Rev. WESLEY W. SCHAWE, Dir. Tel: 620-227-1533. Email: wschawe@dcdiocese.org; vocations@dcdiocese.org; Mrs. BECKY HESSMAN, Coord. Tel: 620-227-1530; Fax: 620-227-1545. Email: bhessman@dcdiocese.org.

Administrative Assistant to Bishop—Mrs. GEORGINA PAZ. Tel: 620-227-1531; Fax: 620-227-1545. Email: gpaz@dcdiocese.org.

Executive Secretary—Mrs. AMY SEACHRIS. Tel: 620-227-1525. Email: aseachris@dcdiocese.org; Mrs. PEGGY SCHULTE, Asst. Tel: 620-227-1500; Fax: 620-227-1545. Email: pschulte@dcdiocese.org.

Safe Environment—

Coordinator—Sr. JANICE GROCHOWSKY, C.S.J., J.C.L. Tel: 620-227-1527. Email: jgrochowsky@dcdiocese.org.

Diocesan Fitness Review Administrator—Mr. DAVID H. SNAPP. Tel: 620-225-5051 (office); 620-225-2412 (home).

Assistance Minister—Mrs. DONNA STAAB, M.S.N., R.N., B.C. Tel: 620-792-2098; 620-786-5785. Email: donna@cpcis.net.

Office of Stewardship—Mr. ERIC HASELHORST, Dir. Tel: 620-227-1537. Email: ehaselhorst@dcdiocese.org.

Office of Finance—Mr. DANIEL M. STREMEL, CPA, Dir. Tel: 620-227-1517. Email: dmstremel@dcdiocese.org.

Development and Accounting Services—Mr. JOHN ACKERMAN. Tel: 620-227-1534; Fax: 620-227-1545. Email: jackerman@dcdiocese.org.

Employee Benefits Specialist—Mrs. AMY SEACHRIS. Tel: 620-227-1525. Email: aseachris@dcdiocese.org.

Tribunal—

Judicial Vicar—Rev. JOHN V. HOTZE (WCH).

Defender of the Bond—Rev. DAVID H. KRAUS, J.C.L. (Retired).

Judge—Rev. JAMES E. BAKER, J.C.L. (Retired).

Notary—Sr. JANICE GROCHOWSKY, C.S.J., J.C.L.

Promoter of Justice—Rev. DAVID H. KRAUS, J.C.L. (Retired).

All matrimonial correspondence may be sent to the attention of Sr. Janice Grochowsky, C.S.J., J.C.L. Tel: 620-227-1527; Fax: 620-227-1545. Email: jgrochowsky@dcdiocese.org.

Catholic Education and Formation—

Catholic Elementary Schools—Mr. RANDALL STEINLE, Supt. Tel: 620-227-1535; Fax: 620-227-1545. Email: rksteinle@gmail.com; KATHRYN WERNER, Sec. Email: kwerner@dcdiocese.org.

Diocesan School Council—Mr. RANDALL STEINLE, Supt. Schools, 910 Central Ave., Dodge City, 67801. Tel: 620-227-1535; COURTNEY RANKIN, Sacred Heart School, 905 Central, Dodge City, 67801. Tel: 620-225-6532; MARLA STUCKY, Sacred Heart School, 330 N. Oak, Pratt, 67124. Tel: 620-672-3687; MONTE DOLL, St. Joseph School, 111 W. Third, Ellinwood, 67526. Tel: 620-564-2721; LISA CURRIE, St. Mary School, 503 St. John St.,

Garden City, 67846. Tel: 620-275-2241; ELOISE DORAN, Holy Family School, 4200 Broadway, Great Bend, 67530. Tel: 620-793-3265; ALAN ROTHS, Sacred Heart School, 510 S. School St., Ness City, 67560. Tel: 785-798-3530; LYNN DUNFORD, St. Dominic School, 617 JC St., Garden City, 67846. Tel: 620-276-8981.

Pastoral Ministry Formation—Mrs. COLEEN STEIN, Coord. Tel: 620-227-1538; Fax: 620-227-1545. Email: cstein@dcdiocese.org.

Youth/Family Ministry and Religious Formation—Mr. STEVEN D. POLLEY, Dir. Tel: 620-227-1540; Fax: 620-227-1545. Email: spolley@dcdiocese.org; Rev. TED D. STOECKLEIN, Assoc. Dir. Young Adult Ministry, P.O. Box 187, Spearville, 67876-0187. Tel: 620-385-2212; Fax: 620-385-2396. Email: frstoecklein@hotmail.com.

Catechist Formation—Mrs. COLEEN STEIN, Coord., English. Tel: 620-227-1538; Fax: 620-227-1545. Email: cstein@dcdiocese.org.

Catholic Social Service: Catholic Charities for Southwest Kansas—Web: www.catholicsocialservice.org. DEBBIE SNAPP, Exec. Dir., 906 Central, Dodge City, 67801. Tel: 620-227-1588; Fax: 620-227-1572. Email: dsnapp@catholicsocialservice.org; Mailing Address: P.O. Box 137, Dodge City, 67801-0137.

Satellite Offices—Garden City: 603 N. 8th, Garden City, 67846. Great Bend: 2201 16th St., Great Bend, 67530. Family Crisis Center, 1924 Broadway, P.O. Box 1543, Great Bend, 67530. Tel: 620-793-9941; 620-792-1885 (Crisis Line); Fax: 620-793-9943. *Sommerset Place, 5830 16th Ter., Great Bend, 67530.* Tel: 620-793-8075; Fax: 620-793-7417.

Respect Life Activities—Rev. WESLEY W. SCHAWE, Coord.; Sr. CATHERINE THERESE PAULIE, C.S.J., Assoc. Coord.

Hispanic Ministry—Sr. ANGELA EREVIA, M.C.D.P., Dir. Tel: 620-227-1542. Email: aerevia@dcdiocese.org.

Vietnamese Ministry—Rev. TRONG BINH TRAN, Chap., Mailing Address: 804 N. Colorado, Ulysses, 67880-1734. Tel: 620-356-1532; Fax: 620-424-1065.

Mission Outreach and Propagation of the Faith—Mr. JOHN ACKERMAN, Dir. Tel: 620-227-1534; Fax: 620-227-1545. Email: jackerman@dcdiocese.org.

Migration and Refugee Services—Ms. LEVITA ROHLMAN, Exec. Dir., 1510 Taylor Plaza E., Garden City, 67846. Tel: 620-276-7610; Fax: 620-276-9228.

Media and Communications—

Diocesan Newspaper— semi-monthly, "Southwest Kansas Register" Mr. DAVID MYERS, Editor. Tel: 620-227-1519; Fax: 620-227-1545. Email: skregister@dcdiocese.org.

Interactive Television Network—Mrs. COLEEN STEIN, Coord. Tel: 620-227-1538; Fax: 620-227-1545. Email: cstein@dcdiocese.org.

Media/Press Liaison—Mr. TIMOTHY F. WENZL. Tel: 620-227-1556; Fax: 620-227-1545. Email: twenzl@dcdiocese.org.

Scouting—

Catholic Committee on Scouting—Mr. DAVE GEIST. Tel: 620-225-8230; 620-225-0161. Email: dave.geist@swkaging.org.

Legal Services—

Diocesan Attorney—Foulston Siefkin, L.L.P., 9 Corporate Woods, 9200 Indian Creek Pkwy., Ste. 450, Overland Park, 66210. Tel: 913-498-2100; Fax: 913-498-2101. TAMARA L. DAVIS, P.A., 107 Layton, Ste. A, Dodge City, 67801. Tel: 620-225-1674; Fax: 620-227-2770.

Consultative Bodies—

Presbyteral Council—Most Rev. JOHN B. BRUNGARDT; Revs. ROBERT A. SCHREMMER, V.G.; HENRY F. HILDEBRANDT; FLOYD E. MCKINNEY; BERNARD H. FELIX; WESLEY W. SCHAWE; RENE LABRADOR; DAVID H. KRAUS, J.C.L. (Retired).

College of Consultors—Rev. Msgr. BRIAN R. MOORE (Retired); Revs. TED A. SKALSKY, V.F.; ROBERT A. SCHREMMER, V.G.; TED D. STOECKLEIN; JOHN R. STRASSER; JOHN J. MAES (Retired).

Diocesan Finance Council—Most Rev. JOHN B. BRUNGARDT, Ex Officio; Mr. DANIEL M. STREMEL, CPA, Ex Officio, Sec. & Treas.; Mr. JOHN ACKERMAN, Ex Officio; Revs. JOHN R. STRASSER; JOHN J. MAES (Retired); Sr. JUDITH LINDELL, O.P.; STEVE RICE, CPA; RICHARD GLEASON; JOHN ALIG.

Diocesan Review Board—Mr. DAVID H. SNAPP, Chm.; Mrs. DEBBIE SCHARTZ-ROBINSON; Dr. PATRICK STANG, M.D.; Mrs. HATTIE STEIN; Rev. JOHN R. STRASSER; Mr. MIKE MARTINEZ.

Deans—Revs. CHARLES MAZOUCH, V.F., Great Bend; TED A. SKALSKY, V.F., Dodge City; JAMES P. DIEKER, V.F., Garden City.

Priest Continuing Formation Commission—Rev. Msgr. BRIAN R. MOORE (Retired); Revs. REGINALD A. URBAN; WESLEY W. SCHAWE.

CLERGY, PARISHES, MISSIONS AND PAROCHIAL SCHOOLS

CITY OF DODGE CITY

(FORD COUNTY)

1—CATHEDRAL OF OUR LADY OF GUADALUPE CATHOLIC CHURCH OF DODGE CITY, KANSAS (2001) [JC] Revs. Ted A. Skalsky; Ted D. Stoecklein, Parochial Vicar; Donald E. Bedore; Sisters Rose Mary Stein, O.P., Pastoral Min./Coord.; Maria Virginia Alfaro-Osorio, C.F.P., Hispanic Pastoral Min.; Enedina Lulo, C.F.P., Hispanic Pastoral Min.; Cleotilda Orunda, C.F.P., Hispanic Pastoral Min.; Jodi D. Lix, Dir. Administration & Stewardship; Deanna Jones, Pastoral Min.
Mailing Address: 3231 N. 14th St., P.O. Box 670, 67801. Tel: 620-225-4802; 620-227-3442; Fax: 620-338-8268. Email: info@dodgecitycathedral.com. Web: www.dodgecitycathedral.com.
Church: 3231 N. 14th St., 67801.
School—905 Central Ave., 67801. Tel: 620-227-6532; Fax: 620-227-3221. Email: shcs@dodgecitycathedral.com. Chad Meitner, Prin. (19 full time & 2 part-time) 21; Students 229.
Catechesis/Religious Program—Email: nalvarez@dodgecitycathedral.com. Norma Alvarez, D.R.E.; Anne Shaughnessy, D.R.E.; Deborah Sotomayor, Dir. Youth & Young Adult Min. Students 649.

2—CHURCH OF THE SACRED HEART, Closed. For inquiries for sacramental records, please contact The Cathedral of Our Lady of Guadalupe, Dodge City.

OUTSIDE THE CITY OF DODGE CITY

ASHLAND, CLARK CO., ST. JOSEPH CATHOLIC CHURCH OF ASHLAND, KANSAS (1886) [JC] Rev. Maurice H. Cummings, O.Carm.
512 Cedar St., P.O. Box 577, 67831-0577.
Res.: 514 Main St., P.O. Box 577, 67831-0577. Tel: 620-635-2338; 620-635-2240 (office).
Catechesis/Religious Program—Tel: 620-635-2679. Becky Luerman, D.R.E. Students 1.

BEAVER, BARTON CO., ST. JOSEPH, Closed. Sacramental records can be found at St. John, Hoisington.

BELPRE, EDWARDS CO., ST. BERNARD CATHOLIC CHURCH OF BELPRE, KANSAS (1901) Rev. Warren L. Stecklein; Sr. Catherine Therese Paulie, C.S.J., Pastoral Min.
Res.: 203 Hudson St., P.O. Box 188, 67519-0188. Tel: 620-995-4305.
Catechesis/Religious Program—Tel: 620-324-5472. Denise Wheaton, D.R.E. Students 39.

BUCKLIN, FORD CO., ST. GEORGE, Closed. Sacramental records can be found at Our Lady of Guadalupe, Dodge City.

BURDETT, PAWNEE CO., HOLY ROSARY, Closed. Sacramental records can be found at Sacred Heart, Larned.

CLAFLIN, BARTON CO., IMMACULATE CONCEPTION CATHOLIC CHURCH OF CLAFLIN, KANSAS (1904) [JC] Rev. Charles Mazouch.
Mailing Address: P.O. Box 197, 67525. Tel: 620-587-3628; Fax: 620-588-3628.
Catechesis/Religious Program—Sr. Andre Kravec, O.P., D.R.E. (includes Odin students) 85.

COLDWATER, COMANCHE CO., HOLY SPIRIT, Quasi-parish. Sacramental records can be found at St. Joseph, Ashland.

DEERFIELD, KEARNEY CO., CHRIST THE KING CATHOLIC CHURCH OF DEERFIELD, KANSAS (1937) Rev. Michael L. Helms.
Mailing Address: P.O. Box 455, 67838. Tel: 620-355-6405.
Catechesis/Religious Program—Tel: 620-277-0309. Twinned with St. Anthony, Lakin.

DIGHTON, LANE CO., ST. THERESA CATHOLIC CHURCH OF DIGHTON, KANSAS (1927) [JC] Rev. Bernard H. Felix.
Res.: 322 S. First St., P.O. Box 787, 67839. Tel: 620-397-5357.
Catechesis/Religious Program—Rene Roberts, D.R.E. Students 49.

DUBUQUE, BARTON CO., ST. CATHERINE, Closed. Sacramental records can be found at St. John the Evangelist, Hoisington.

ELKHART, MORTON CO., ST. JOAN OF ARC CATHOLIC CHURCH OF ELKHART, KANSAS (1921) [JC] Rev. Francis Khoi Nguyen.
Res.: 723 S. Baca Ave., P.O. Box 570, 67950-0570. Tel: 620-697-4622. Email: stjoan@elkhart.com.
Catechesis/Religious Program—Tel: 620-697-4587. Traci O'Hanlon, D.R.E. Students 50.

ELLINWOOD, BARTON CO., ST. JOSEPH CATHOLIC CHURCH OF ELLINWOOD, KANSAS (1876) [JC] Rev. Charles Mazouch.
Res.: 214 N. Main St., 67526. Tel: 620-564-2534; Fax: 620-564-2613. Web: www.stjosephellinwood.com.
School—111 W. Third, 67526. Tel: 620-564-2721; Fax: 620-564-2714. Marlene Clayton, Headmaster. Lay Teachers 6; Students 63.
Catechesis/Religious Program—Students 31.

FOWLER, MEADE CO., ST. ANTHONY CATHOLIC CHURCH OF FOWLER, KANSAS (1910) [JC] Rev. Louis Trung Dinh Hoang, Parochial Admin.; Judy Dewell, Pastoral Asst.; Steve Dewell, Pastoral Asst.
Mailing Address: 411 Fourth St., P.O. Box 80, 67844.
Res.: 412 W. Carthage St., Box 1207, Meade, 67864. Tel: 620-873-2003.
Catechesis/Religious Program—Sarah Weber, D.R.E. Students 36.

GARDEN CITY, FINNEY CO.

1—ST. DOMINIC CATHOLIC CHURCH OF GARDEN CITY, KANSAS (1965) Revs. Rene Labrador; Peter Fernandez Jr., Parochial Vicar; Lola Wilson, Dir. Adult Formation; Alissa Bell, Dir. Admin. & Stewardship; Veronica Aguiniga, Sec.
Office: 615 J. C. St., 67846. Tel: 620-276-2024; Fax: 620-276-2086. Email: stdomoffice@st-dominic.org. Web: www.st-dominic.org.
School—617 J. C. St., 67846. Tel: 620-276-8981. Email: ldrevnick@st-dominic.org. Web: www.st-dominic.org/school/. LeaAnn Drevnick, School Sec.; Trina Delgado, Prin. Lay Teachers 13; Students (Preschool to 6th) 189.
Catechesis/Religious Program—Tel: 620-276-3500. Email: rformation@st-dominic.org. Sr. Myra Arney, O.P., D.R.E. & Dir. Youth Formation. Students 195.

2—ST. MARY CATHOLIC CHURCH OF GARDEN CITY, KANSAS (1898) [CEM 2] [JC 2] Revs. Charles F. Seiwert (WCH); Matthew Kumi, Parochial Vicar; Sr. Marie Elena Martinez-SiFuentes, M.C.M.I., Pastoral Min./Coord. Tel: 620-275-4204.
Res.: 509 St. John St., 67846. Fax: 620-272-9971.
School—503 St. John St., 67846. Tel: 620-276-2241; Fax: 620-276-7067. Trina Delgado, Prin. Lay Teachers 11; Students 125.
Catechesis/Religious Program—Tel: 620-276-2716. Hector Rivera, D.R.E. Students 576.

GREAT BEND, BARTON CO.

1—ST. PATRICK (1960) [JC] Merged with St. Rose to form Prince of Peace, Great Bend.

2—PRINCE OF PEACE CATHOLIC CHURCH OF GREAT BEND, KANSAS (2006) Revs. Reginald A. Urban; Donald E. Bedore, Parochial Vicar.
Mailing Address: 4100 Broadway, P.O. Box 87, 67530-0087.
Res. & Mailing Address: 1423 Holland, P.O. Box 87, 67530-0087. Tel: 620-792-1396; Fax: 620-792-3642. Church: 4100 Broadway, 67530-0087. Email: bookkeeper@gbpeace.kscoxmail.com.
School—Holy Family School, (Grades PreK-6), 4200 Broadway, 67530. Tel: 620-793-3265; Fax: 620-792-2798. Email: office@gbholyfamily.org. Mrs. Karen Moeder, Prin. Total Staff 22; Students 222.
Catechesis/Religious Program—Email: dre@greatbendcatholic.com. Cheryl Alexander, D.R.E.; Pam Vainer, D.R.E. Merged with St. Rose of Lima, Great Bend. Students 406.

3—ST. ROSE OF LIMA (1878) [JC] Merged with St. Patrick, Great Bend to form Prince of Peace, Great Bend.

GREENSBURG, KIOWA CO., ST. JOSEPH CATHOLIC CHURCH OF GREENSBURG, KANSAS (1952) Ellen Peters, Parish Life Coord.; Rev. Robert A. Schremmer, Priest Supvr. & Sacramental Min.; Katie Vigness, Sec.
820 Walnut, 67054. Cell: 620-255-3636. Email: st.joe.greensburg@att.net.
Catechesis/Religious Program—Tel: 620-723-3474. Students 13.

HANSTON, HODGEMAN CO., ST. ANTHONY CATHOLIC CHURCH OF HANSTON, KANSAS (1908) [CEM] Rev. Benjamin Dande, M.S.F.S., Parochial Admin.
Mailing Address: *c/o St. Lawrence Church*, P.O. Box 278, Jetmore, 67854. Tel: 620-357-8791.
Catechesis/Religious Program—Jaimi Burke, D.R.E. Students 23.

HOISINGTON, BARTON CO., ST. JOHN THE EVANGELIST CATHOLIC CHURCH OF HOISINGTON, KANSAS (1892) [CEM] Rev. Francis Oroffa, M.S.P., Parochial Admin.
Office: 122 E. 5th St., 67544. Tel: 620-653-2963. Email: stjohnevangel@dc.kscoxmail.com.
Rectory—108 E. 5th St., 67544. Tel: 620-653-2695.
Catechesis/Religious Program— Pam Willis, D.R.E. Students 140.

HUGOTON, STEVENS CO., ST. HELEN CATHOLIC CHURCH OF HUGOTON, KANSAS (1948) Rev. Francis Khoi Nguyen.
Parish Office—1011 S. Jefferson St., 67951-2823. Tel: 620-544-2551.
Catechesis/Religious Program—Tel: 316-544-7544. Amanda Mangels, D.R.E. Students 116.

INGALLS, GRAY CO., ST. STANISLAUS CATHOLIC CHURCH

OF INGALLS, KANSAS (1909) [JC] Revs. Rene Labrador; Peter Fernandez Jr., Parochial Vicar; Francis G. Jordan (Retired); Theresa Andersen, Admin.
Mailing Address: 200 N. Rush, P.O. Box 175, 67853. Tel: 620-335-5202; Fax: 620-335-5865.
Church Address: 200 N. Rush St., 67853. Fax: 620-335-5865.
Catechesis/Religious Program—Mandy Pfeifer, D.R.E. Students 111.

JETMORE, HODGEMAN CO., ST. LAWRENCE CATHOLIC CHURCH OF JETMORE, KANSAS (1923) Rev. Benjamin Dande, M.S.F.S., Parochial Admin.
Mailing Address: P.O. Box 278, 67854. Tel: 620-357-8791.
Catechesis/Religious Program—P.O. Box 278, 67854. Greta Chaar, D.R.E. Students 39.

JOHNSON, STANTON CO., ST. BERNADETTE CATHOLIC CHURCH OF JOHNSON, KANSAS (1949) Rev. Trong Binh Tran.
Mailing Address: *c/o Mary, Queen of Peace Church*, 804 Colorado, Ulysses, 67880. Tel: 620-356-1532; Fax: 620-424-1065.
Catechesis/Religious Program—105 N. Chestnut, 67855. Tel: 620-492-1554. Jana Brady, D.R.E. Students 95.

KINSLEY, EDWARDS CO., ST. NICHOLAS CATHOLIC CHURCH OF KINSLEY, KANSAS (1883) Rev. John R. Strasser.
Res.: 706 E. Sixth St., 67547. Tel: 620-659-2692; Fax: 620-659-2049.
Catechesis/Religious Program— Beth Frame, D.R.E. Twinned with St. Joseph, Offerle. Students 90.

KIOWA, BARBER CO., ST. JOHN THE APOSTLE CATHOLIC CHURCH OF KIOWA, KANSAS (1885) [JC] Rev. Firmin Kyaw, Parochial Admin.; Ms. Terry Deokaran, Pastoral Min.
Church: 920 E. Main St., 67070. Tel: 620-825-4361; 620-886-3596. Email: ccbc@sctelcom.net.
Res.: 350 Curry Ln., Medicine Lodge, 67104.
Catechesis/Religious Program—Tel: 620-825-4836. Lori Schrock, D.R.E. Students 28.

LACROSSE, RUSH CO., ST. MICHAEL CATHOLIC CHURCH OF LACROSSE, KANSAS (1911) [JC] Rev. Pascal L. Klein.
Res.: 918 Lincoln St., P.O. Box 309, 67548. Tel: 785-222-2561; Fax: 785-222-3292. Email: church@gbta.net.
Catechesis/Religious Program—Tel: 913-222-2869. Email: rbbaalmann@gbta.net. Ruth Baalmann, D.R.E. Students 65.

LAKIN, KEARNY CO., ST. ANTHONY OF PADUA CATHOLIC CHURCH OF LAKIN, KANSAS (1909) [JC] Rev. Michael L. Helms.
Res.: 600 Soderberg St., P.O. Box 983, 67860. Tel: 620-355-6405; Fax: 620-355-6406.
Catechesis/Religious Program—Tel: 620-355-6663. Julie Rains, D.R.E. Students 153.

LARNED, PAWNEE CO., SACRED HEART OF JESUS CATHOLIC CHURCH OF LARNED, KANSAS (1912) [CEM] [JC] Rev. Warren L. Stecklein.
Res.: 1111 State St., 67550. Tel: 620-285-2035; Fax: 620-285-3025.
Catechesis/Religious Program— Brenda Johnson, D.R.E. Students 124.

LEOTI, WICHITA CO., ST. ANTHONY OF PADUA CATHOLIC CHURCH OF LEOTI, KANSAS (1887) [JC] Rev. Benjamin Martin.
Res.: P.O. Box D, Marienthal, 67863. Tel: 620-379-4431; Fax: 620-379-4428.
Catechesis/Religious Program—Tel: 620-379-4427. Students 26.

LIBERAL, SEWARD CO., ST. ANTHONY OF PADUA CATHOLIC CHURCH OF LIBERAL, KANSAS (1916) Revs. James P. Dieker; J. Hector de la Vega, Parochial Vicar; Deacons Victor Mencos; Ruben Sigala; Oscar Rodriguez; Hector Rios; Araceli LaPoint, Office Mgr.; Jana Widener, Bookkeeper.
Office: 1510 N. Calhoun, 67901. Tel: 620-624-4135; Fax: 620-624-3553.
Rectory—1230 N. Pershing, 67901. Tel: 620-624-7846.
Catechesis/Religious Program—Tel: 620-624-1552. Sisters Arlene Vasquez, M.C.D.P., D.R.E.; Rocio Maldonado, M.C.M.I., D.R.E. Hispanic Ministry. Students 535.

LIEBENTHAL, RUSH CO., ST. JOSEPH CATHOLIC CHURCH OF LIEBENTHAL, KANSAS (1876) [CEM] Rev. Pascal L. Klein.
Mailing Address: P.O. Box 98, 67553. Tel: 785-222-3160.
Catechesis/Religious Program—Tel: 785-222-2561. (attending St. Michael's Program at LaCrosse, KS)

LORETTO, ST. MARY, HELP OF CHRISTIANS, Closed. Sacramental records can be found at St. Joseph, Liebenthal.

MARIENTHAL, WICHITA CO., ST. MARY CATHOLIC CHURCH OF MARIENTHAL, KANSAS (1886) [CEM] Rev. Benjamin Martin.
Mailing Address: 208 N. Second St., 67863. Tel: 620-379-4427; Fax: 620-379-4428.
Catechesis/Religious Program— Jenni Winter, D.R.E. Students 29.

MCCRACKEN, RUSH CO., ST. MARY (1886) Closed. For inquiries for sacramental records please contact St. Michael, La Crosse.

MEADE, MEADE CO., ST. JOHN THE BAPTIST CATHOLIC CHURCH OF MEADE, KANSAS (1889) [JC] Rev. Louis Trung Dinh Hoang, Parochial Admin.
Res.: 412 W. Carthage St., P.O. Box 1207, 67864. Tel: 620-873-2003.
Catechesis/Religious Program—Tel: 620-873-2654. Audrey Flowers, D.R.E. Students 43.

MEDICINE LODGE, BARBER CO., HOLY ROSARY CATHOLIC CHURCH OF MEDICINE LODGE, KANSAS (1952) [JC] Rev. Firmin Kyaw, Parochial Admin.; Ms. Terry Deokaran, Pastoral Min.
Res.: 300 Curry Ln., 67104. Tel: 620-886-3596. Email: ccbc@sctelcom.net.
Catechesis/Religious Program—Tel: 620-294-5526. Students 44.

NESS CITY, NESS CO., SACRED HEART CATHOLIC CHURCH OF NESS CITY, KANSAS (1912) [CEM] Rev. Henry F. Hildebrandt.
Res.: 510 S. School St., 67560. Tel: 785-798-3195.
School—(Grades PreK-8), 510 S. School St., 67560. Tel: 785-798-3530; Fax: 785-798-3004. Don Ruda, Prin. Lay Teachers 8; Students 75.
Catechesis/Religious Program—Students 49.

NORTH ELLINWOOD, BARTON CO., STS. PETER & PAUL, Closed. Sacramental records can be found at St. Joseph, Ellinwood.

NORTH KINSLEY, EDWARDS CO., SS. PETER AND PAUL, Closed. Sacramental records can be found at St. Nicholas, Kinsley.

ODIN, BARTON CO., HOLY FAMILY CATHOLIC CHURCH OF ODIN, KANSAS (1879) [CEM] Sr. Andre Kravec, O.P., Parish Life Coord.; Rev. Charles Mazouch, Priest Supvr.
Mailing Address: *c/o Immaculate Conception Parish*, P.O. Box 197, Claflin, 67525. Tel: 620-587-3628; Fax: 620-588-3628.
Catechesis/Religious Program—Students 32.

OFFERLE, EDWARDS CO., ST. JOSEPH CATHOLIC CHURCH OF OFFERLE, KANSAS (1876) [CEM 2] Rev. John R. Strasser.
Res.: c/o 706 E. Sixth St., Kinsley, 67547. Tel: 620-659-2692.
Catechesis/Religious Program—Twinned with St. Nicholas, Kinsley. Students 8.

OLMITZ, BARTON CO., ST. ANN CATHOLIC CHURCH OF OLMITZ, KANSAS (1889) [CEM] Rev. Ultan P. Murphy, Admin.
Res.: 115 Cleveland St., P.O. Box 8, 67564. Tel: 620-586-3306; Cell: 620-923-5766. Email: lisabahr15@hotmail.com.
Catechesis/Religious Program—Tel: 620-923-4225; Cell: 620-923-3228. Lisa Starr, D.R.E. Students 45.

PLAINS, MEADE CO., ST. PATRICK CATHOLIC CHURCH OF PLAINS, KANSAS (1916) [JC] Rev. Louis Trung Dinh Hoang, Parochial Admin.
Mailing Address: P.O. Box 247, 67869. Tel: 620-563-7663.
Res.: 412 W. Carthage St., Meade, 67864. Tel: 620-873-2003.
Catechesis/Religious Program—P.O. Box 247, 67869. Tel: 620-563-7780 (Home). Traci Eakes, D.R.E. Students 104.

PRATT, PRATT CO., SACRED HEART CATHOLIC CHURCH OF PRATT, KANSAS (1887) Rev. Floyd E. McKinney (WCH).
Res.: 332 N. Oak St., 67124. Tel: 620-672-6352; Fax: 620-672-3748.
School—(Grades PreK-5), 330 N. Oak St., 67124. Tel: 620-672-3687. Email: school1@sacredheartpratt.com. Web: www.sacredheartpratt.com. Linda Conkle, Headmaster. Lay Teachers 7; Students 77.
Catechesis/Religious Program— Erin Crouch, D.R.E. Students 115.

RANSOM, NESS CO., ST. ALOYSIUS CATHOLIC CHURCH OF RANSOM, KANSAS (1903) [CEM] Rev. Henry F. Hildebrandt.
Mailing Address: *c/o Sacred Heart*, 510 S. School St., Ness City, 67560. Tel: 785-731-2497.
Catechesis/Religious Program—

ST. JOHN, STAFFORD CO., ST. JOHN THE APOSTLE CATHOLIC CHURCH OF ST. JOHN, KANSAS (1949) Sr. Catherine Therese Paulie, C.S.J., Parish Life Coord.; Rev. Floyd E. McKinney (WCH), Priest Supvr. & Sacramental Min.
Res., Church & Office: 609 E. Fourth St., Box 475, 67576. Fax: 620-549-3538.
Catechesis/Religious Program—Tel: 620-549-3847. Johnna Stanford, D.R.E.; Janice Nusser, D.R.E. Students 78.

ST. MARY, HODGEMAN CO., ST. MARY, Closed. Sacramental records can be found at St. John the Baptist, Spearville.

SATANTA, HASKELL CO., ST. ALPHONSUS CATHOLIC CHURCH OF SATANTA, KANSAS (1946) Sr. Matilde Monterrosso, M.C.M.I., Parish Life Coord.; Rev. James P. Dieker, Priest Supvr.
Res.: 603 Tecumseh, Box 65, 67870. Tel: 620-649-2692; Fax: 620-649-2550. Email: catholic@pld.com.
Church: 601 Tecumseh, 67870.
Catechesis/Religious Program—P.O. Box 452, 67870. Tel: 620-649-2200, Ext. 508; Fax: 620-649-2776. Email: c_folk3@hotmail.com. Martha Bencomo, D.R.E. Students 111.

SCOTT CITY, SCOTT CO., ST. JOSEPH CATHOLIC CHURCH OF SCOTT CITY, KANSAS (1911) [JC] Rev. Bernard H. Felix.
Mailing Address: 1006 S. Main, P.O. Box 228, 67871-0228.
Res.: 606 W. 10th, P.O. Box 228, 67871-0228. Tel: 620-872-7388; 620-872-3644 (Sec.); Fax: 620-872-3644. Email: sjscsecretary@att.net.
Catechesis/Religious Program—Tel: 620-874-1560. Denise Strecker, D.R.E. Students 125.

SEWARD, STAFFORD CO., ST. FRANCIS XAVIER CATHOLIC CHURCH OF SEWARD, KANSAS (1886) Rev. Rene Guesnier, O.S.B.
Mailing Address: 504 Main St., 67576. Tel: 620-458-5691. Email: ccsc@ruraltel.net.
Catechesis/Religious Program— Attended at St. John Students 6.

SHARON, BARBER CO., ST. BONIFACE CATHOLIC CHURCH OF SHARON, KANSAS (1904) [CEM] Rev. Firmin Kyaw, Parochial Admin.
Res.: 300 Curry Ln., Medicine Lodge, 67104. Tel: 620-886-3596. Email: ccbc@sctelcom.net.
Church: 410 N. Main St., P.O. Box 118, 67138. Tel: 620-294-5526.
Catechesis/Religious Program—Ms. Terry Deokaran, D.R.E. & Pastoral Min. Students 54.

SPEARVILLE, FORD CO., ST. JOHN THE BAPTIST CATHOLIC CHURCH OF SPEARVILLE, KANSAS (1904) [CEM] [JC 2] Rev. Ted D. Stoecklein.
Res.: 100 S. Main St., P.O. Box 187, 67876. Tel: 620-385-2212.
Catechesis/Religious Program—Tel: 620-385-2881. Judy Gleason, D.R.E. Students 123.

SYRACUSE, HAMILTON CO., ST. RAPHAEL CATHOLIC CHURCH OF SYRACUSE, KANSAS (1906) [CEM] [JC] Rev. Michael L. Helms.
Mailing Address: P.O. Box 731, 67878. Tel: 620-384-7357; Fax: 620-384-5946. Email: church@straphaelsyracuse.org.
Catechesis/Religious Program—Tel: 620-384-5582. Email: gama@wbsnet.org. Mary Ann Fair, D.R.E. Students 68.

TIMKEN, RUSH CO., HOLY TRINITY CATHOLIC CHURCH OF TIMKEN, KANSAS (1904) [CEM] [JC] Rev. Pascal L. Klein.
Mailing Address: *c/o St. Michael Church*, P.O. Box 309, LaCrosse, 67548. Tel: 785-222-2561.
Catechesis/Religious Program—Tel: 785-623-1917. JoAnn Tomecek, D.R.E. Students 19.

TRIBUNE, GREELEY CO., ST. JOSEPH THE WORKER CATHOLIC CHURCH OF TRIBUNE, KANSAS (1950) [JC] Rev. Benjamin Martin.
Mailing Address: Box 67, 67879. Tel: 620-376-2292.
Catechesis/Religious Program—Tel: 620-376-2490. Teressa Ricke, D.R.E. Students 26.

ULYSSES, GRANT CO., MARY, QUEEN OF PEACE CATHOLIC CHURCH OF ULYSSES, KANSAS (1948) Rev. Trong Binh Tran; Deacon Apolonio Rodriguez.
Res.: 804 N. Colorado, 67880. Tel: 620-356-1532; 620-356-3994 (Parish Hall); Fax: 620-424-1065. Email: mqop@pld.com. Web: www.mqopp.org.
Catechesis/Religious Program—Tel: 620-356-1532; Fax: 620-424-4397. Email: mqopdre@pld.com. Toney Hernandez, D.R.E. Students 306.

WINDTHORST, FORD CO., IMMACULATE HEART OF MARY, Closed. Sacramental records can be found at St. John the Baptist, Spearville.

WRIGHT, FORD CO., ST. ANDREW CATHOLIC CHURCH OF WRIGHT, KANSAS (1909) [CEM] Rev. Robert A. Schremmer.
Mailing Address: 10893 St. Andrew Rd., P.O. Box 125, 67882. Tel: 620-227-3363; Fax: 620-227-9979.
Parish Center—11792 Jewel Rd., 67882. Tel: 620-225-7345.
Catechesis/Religious Program—Tel: 620-225-1299. Regina Lix, D.R.E. Students 26.

On Special Diocesan Assignment:
Rev.—
Tran, Trong Binh, Diocesan Chap. Vietnamese Community

Retired:
Revs.—
Baker, James E., J.C.L., 1707 Belmont, Garden City, 67846.
Fiedler, Donald J.
Herrman, Gilbert P., 6900 E. 45th St. N., Apt. D4, Bel Aire, 67226.
Jordan, Francis G., P.O. Box 175, Ingalls, 67853.
Kenny, Eugene, 6900 E. 45th St. N., Apt. E-4, Wichita, 67226.

Kraus, David H., J.C.L., 104 N. Rhode Island Ave., Ransom, 67572.
Maes, John J., 6900 E. 45th St. N., Apt. F2, Bel Aire, 67226.
Pottorff, Lisle J., 6900 E. 45th St. N., Apt. D2, Bel Aire, 67226.
Suellentrop, Anthony J., P.O. Box 982, Ulysses, 67880.
Tighe, Dermot F., 1420 Wilson, Great Bend, 67530.

Permanent Deacons:
Hermocillo, Martin, Diaconate Convenor
Lampe, Dwaine, (Retired)
Mencos, Victor A., St. Anthony, Liberal
Rael, Gilbert E., Larned State Hospital/Larned Mental Health Correctional Facility, Larned
Rios, Hector, St. Anthony, Liberal
Rodriguez, Apolonio, Mary Queen of Peace, Ulysses
Rodriguez, Erasmo, (Retired)
Rodriguez, Oscar, St. Anthony, Liberal
Rondeau, Richard, (Retired)
Sigala, Ruben, St. Anthony, Liberal

INSTITUTIONS LOCATED IN THE DIOCESE

[A] GENERAL HOSPITALS

GARDEN CITY. *St. Catherine Hospital*, 401 E. Spruce, 67846-5679. Tel: 620-272-2222; Fax: 620-272-2566. Web: www.stcath-hosp.org. Scott Taylor, Pres. & CEO; John E. Yox, Senior Vice Pres.; Carol Schmekel, Vice Pres., Patient Svcs.; Amanda Vaughan, CFO; Victor Hawkins, Exec. Dir. & Mktg.; Kathy Morrison, Exec. Dir. Human Resources; Doug Williams, Chap.; Remigius Ekweariri, Chap.; Edward Smink, Exec. Dir., Mission & Ministry. Affiliated with Catholic Health Initiatives. Bed Capacity 132; Patients Assisted Annually 107,123; Total Staff 623.

GREAT BEND. *Central Kansas Medical Center dba St. Rose Ambulatory & Surgery Center* (1902) 3515 Broadway, 67530. Tel: 620-792-2511; Fax: 620-786-6298. Email: ckmc@greatbend.com. Web: www.ckmc.org. Scott Taylor, Pres. & CEO; Leanne Irsik, Senior Vice Pres. & Site Admin.; Mary Klinge, Dir. Mission. Dominican Sisters of Peace., Member-Catholic Health Initiatives. Sisters 1; Bed Capacity 62; Total Staff 307; Patients Assisted Annually 25,012.

[B] RETREAT CENTERS

GREAT BEND. *Heartland Center for Spirituality* (1985) 3600 Broadway, 67530-3692. Tel: 620-792-1232; Fax: 620-792-1746. Email: office@heartlandspirituality.org. Web: www.heartlandspirituality.org. Sr. Renee Dreiling, O.P., Dir. Retreat Center. Total Staff 7.

PAWNEE ROCK. *Heartland Farm* (1988) 1049 County Rd. 390, 67567-7002. Tel: 620-923-4585. Email: hfarm@gbta.net. Sr. Mary Terence Wasinger, O.P., Contact Person. A Ministry of the Dominican Sisters of Peace., Organic sustainable agriculture, body massage, retreat opportunities in rural setting. Total Membership 6.

[C] EDUCATIONAL ENDOWMENT FUNDS

DODGE CITY. *Sacred Heart Cathedral School Endowment Fund*, 3231 N. 14th St., P.O. Box 670, 67801. Tel: 620-225-4802; Fax: 620-338-8268. Email: colg@starrtech.net.

ELLINWOOD. *St. Joseph School Education Endowment Fund*, 109 W. 3rd, 67526. Tel: 620-564-2534; Fax: 620-564-2613. Rev. Charles Mazouch, V.F., 109 W. 3rd, 67526. Tel: 620-564-2290.

GARDEN CITY. *St. Dominic Grade School Endowment Fund*, 615 J.C. St., 67846. Tel: 620-276-2024; Fax: 620-276-2086.

St. Mary Catholic Education Endowment Fund, 509 St. John St., 67846. Tel: 620-275-4204; Fax: 620-272-9971.

GREAT BEND. *The Holy Family Grade School Education Endowment Fund*, 4200 Broadway, 67530. Tel: 620-792-1396; Fax: 620-792-3642. Email: bookkeeper@gbpeace.kscoxmail.com.

KINSLEY. *St. Nicholas School Endowment*, 401 E. 9th St., 67547. Tel: 620-659-2692; Fax: 620-659-2049.

LARNED. *The Sacred Heart Grade School of Larned Educational Endowment Fund*, 1111 State St., 67550. Tel: 620-285-2035; Fax: 620-285-3025.

LIBERAL. *St. Anthony School Endowment Fund*, 1510 N. Calhoun St., 67901. Tel: 620-624-4135; Fax: 620-624-3553.

NESS CITY. *The Sacred Heart School Endowment Fund*, 510 S. School St., 67560. Tel: 785-798-3530; Fax: 785-798-3004.

PRATT. *The Sacred Heart School Education Endowment, Inc.*, 332 N. Oak St., 67124. Tel: 620-672-6352; Fax: 620-672-3748.

[D] CONVENTS AND RESIDENCES FOR SISTERS

GREAT BEND. *Dominican Sisters of Peace*, 3600 Broadway, 67530-3692. Tel: 620-792-1232; Fax: 620-792-1746. Email: srpeace@oppeace.org; sisters@ksdom.org. Web: www.oppeace.org. Sr. Charlotte Brungardt, Mission Group Coord.

Dominican Sisters of Peace, Inc. Dominican Sisters of Peace. Perpetually Professed Sisters in Diocese 58; Lay Associates in Diocese 26; Partners in Mission in Diocese 1; Total Sisters in Congregation 616; Temporary Professed 1.

[E] SERVICES FOR THE ELDERLY

GREAT BEND. *Cedar Park Place, Inc.*, 3910 Cedar Park Pl., 67530-3692. Tel: 620-793-8115; Fax: 620-793-6702. Email: jmurray@mercyhousing.org. Low and Middle Income Housing for Elderly and Disabled. Bed Capacity 66; Total Assisted Annually 63; Total Staff 2.

[F] MISCELLANEOUS

DODGE CITY. *Catholic Social Service Endowment Fund* (1989) 906 Central Ave., 67801. Tel: 620-227-1562; Fax: 620-227-1572. Email: mlegleiter@dcdiocese.org.

Dechant Foundation, 910 Central, P.O. Box 137, 67801.

The Diocese of Dodge City Priest Retirement Fund, Inc., 2210 1st Ave., 67801. Rev. Msgr. Brian R. Moore (Retired); Revs. Ted D. Stoecklein; Charles Mazouch, V.F., Sec./Treas,; John R. Strasser, Chairperson; Dermot F. Tighe (Retired); Warren L. Stecklein.

Manna House, 1012 First Ave., 67801. Tel: 620-227-6707. Laura Koehn, Exec. Dir.; David Orellona, Chm.; Louise Jambor, Vice Chm., 1707 Ave. A, 67801. Tel: 620-227-6767; Marsha Morrison, 925 Club View, 67801. Tel: 620-227-6767; Maria Musick; Ronald Schneweis, Treas. Short-term housing and food distribution need. Total Staff 3; Total Assisted 3,595.

Newman University, 236 San Jose #26, 67801. Tel: 620-227-9616; Fax: 620-227-9688. Email: greenb@newmanu.edu. Web: www.newmanu.edu/. Bonita Green, Dir.

GARDEN CITY. *St. Catherine Hospital Development Foundation*, 401 E. Spruce, 67846. Tel: 620-272-2567; Fax: 620-272-2180. Email: victorhawkins@catholichealth.net. Web: www.schdf.org. Victor Hawkins, Exec. Dir. & Contact Person.

GREAT BEND. *Heartland Center for Wholistic Health* (1988) 1005 Williams, 67530. Tel: 620-793-9067; Fax: 620-793-5817. Email: anita@hcwh.net. Web: www.hcwh.net. Sr. Anita Schugart, O.P., Dir., Contact Person. A Ministry of the Dominican Sisters of Peace., Body massage, herbals, chiropractic, natural remedies. Total Staff 5.

St. Rose - Dominican Nurses Alumnae Association, 3600 Broadway, 67530. Tel: 620-792-1232; Fax: 620-792-1746. Email: terrywasinger40@gmail.com. Sr. Mary Terence Wasinger, O.P., Sec. & Contact Person.

RELIGIOUS INSTITUTES OF MEN REPRESENTED IN THE DIOCESE

For further details refer to the corresponding bracketed number in the Religious Institutes of Men or Women section.

[0200]—*Benedictine Monks*—O.S.B.

[]—*Missionaries of St. Francis de Sales*—M.S.F.S.

[]—*Missionaries of St. Paul*—M.S.P.

[0270]—*Order of Carmelites*—O.Carm.

RELIGIOUS INSTITUTES OF WOMEN REPRESENTED IN THE DIOCESE

[3832]—*Congregation of St. Joseph*—C.S.J.

[1115]—*Dominican Sisters of Peace*—O.P.

[]—*Mexican Passionist Sisters*—C.F.P.

[]—*Missionaries of the Charity of Mary Immaculate*—M.C.M.I.

[2690]—*Missionary Catechists of Divine Providence*—M.C.D.P.

NECROLOGY

(No Deaths)

An asterisk (*) denotes an organization that has established tax-exempt status directly with the IRS and is not covered by the USCCB Group Ruling.

Archdiocese of Dubuque

(Archidioecesis Dubuquensis)

Most Reverend

JEROME HANUS, O.S.B., D.D.

Archbishop of Dubuque; ordained July 30, 1966; appointed Bishop of St. Cloud July 6, 1987; ordained and installed August 24, 1987; appointed Coadjutor Archbishop of Dubuque August 23, 1994; welcomed October 27, 1994; succeeded to the See October 16, 1995.

Most Reverend

DANIEL W. KUCERA, O.S.B., PH.D., D.D.

Retired Archbishop of Dubuque; ordained May 26, 1949; appointed Titular Bishop of Natchez and Auxiliary Bishop of Joliet June 6, 1977; ordained Bishop July 21, 1977; appointed Bishop of Salina March 11, 1980; installed May 7, 1980; appointed Archbishop of Dubuque December 20, 1983; installed February 23, 1984; retired October 16, 1995. *Villa Raphael, 1155 Mt. Loretta Ave., Dubuque, IA 52003.*

Chancery-Archdiocesan Center: P.O. Box 479, Dubuque, IA 52004-0479. Tel: 563-556-2580; Fax: 563-556-5464.

Web: www.arch.pvt.k12.ia.us

Email: dbqcco@arch.pvt.k12.ia.us

Square Miles 17,403.

Established July 28, 1837; Created an Archdiocese June 15, 1893.

Patrons of the Archdiocese: Primary: St. Raphael, the Archangel; Secondary: St. John Mary Vianney, Cure of Ars.

Corporate Title: The Archdiocese of Dubuque.

Comprises 30 Counties, that part of the State of Iowa north of the Counties of Polk, Jasper, Poweshiek, Iowa, Johnson, Cedar and Clinton and east of the Counties of Kossuth, Humboldt, Webster and Boone.

For legal titles of parishes and archdiocesan institutions, consult the Chancery.

STATISTICAL OVERVIEW

Personnel	
Archbishops	1
Retired Archbishops	1
Abbots	1
Retired Abbots	1
Priests: Diocesan Active in Diocese	97
Priests: Diocesan Active Outside Diocese	1
Priests: Retired, Sick or Absent	88
Number of Diocesan Priests	186
Religious Priests in Diocese	32
Total Priests in Diocese	218
Extern Priests in Diocese	4
Ordinations:	
Diocesan Priests	2
Transitional Deacons	1
Permanent Deacons	7
Permanent Deacons in Diocese	105
Total Brothers	23
Total Sisters	677
Parishes	
Parishes	168
With Resident Pastor:	
Resident Diocesan Priests	74
Resident Religious Priests	1
Without Resident Pastor:	
Administered by Priests	87
Administered by Religious Women	4
Administered by Lay People	2
Pastoral Centers	1
New Parishes Created	1
Closed Parishes	8
Professional Ministry Personnel:	
Sisters	20
Lay Ministers	425
Welfare	
Catholic Hospitals	7
Total Assisted	1,167,697
Health Care Centers	2
Total Assisted	256
Homes for the Aged	4
Total Assisted	692
Special Centers for Social Services	3
Total Assisted	480
Educational	
Seminaries, Diocesan	1
Students from This Diocese	13
Students from Other Diocese	3
Diocesan Students in Other Seminaries	7
Seminaries, Religious	1
Students Religious	125
Total Seminarians	145
Colleges and Universities	3
Total Students	4,639
High Schools, Diocesan and Parish	7
Total Students	2,329
Elementary Schools, Diocesan and Parish	44
Total Students	9,489
Catechesis/Religious Education:	
High School Students	4,771
Elementary Students	12,719
Total Students under Catholic Instruction	34,092
Teachers in the Diocese:	
Priests	1
Sisters	9
Lay Teachers	901
Vital Statistics	
Receptions into the Church:	
Infant Baptism Totals	2,456
Minor Baptism Totals	92
Adult Baptism Totals	102
Received into Full Communion	291
First Communions	2,631
Confirmations	2,308
Marriages:	
Catholic	538
Interfaith	330
Total Marriages	868
Deaths	2,153
Total Catholic Population	202,601
Total Population	995,357

Former Bishops—Most Revs. MATHIAS LORAS, D.D., cons. Dec. 10, 1837; died Feb. 19, 1858; CLEMENT SMYTH, O.C.S.O., D.D., named Coadjutor Bishop of Dubuque Jan. 9, 1857; cons. May 3, 1857; Succeeded Feb. 19, 1858; died Sept. 22, 1865; JOHN HENNESSY, D.D., First Archbishop; named Bishop of Dubuque April 24, 1866; cons. Sept. 30, 1866; raised to the Archiepiscopal Dignity, June 16, 1893; died March 4, 1900; JOHN J. KEANE, D.D., cons. Bishop of Richmond, Aug. 25, 1878; transferred to the Titular See of Jasso, Aug. 12, 1888; elevated to the Archiepiscopal Dignity with the title of Archbishop of Damascus, Jan. 29, 1897; transferred to the See of Dubuque, July 24, 1900; resigned April 3, 1911; appt. Titular Archbishop of Cios, April 28, 1911; died June 22, 1918; JAMES JOHN KEANE, D.D., ord. Dec. 23, 1882; cons. Bishop of Cheyenne, Oct. 28, 1902; elevated to the Archiepiscopal Dignity and transferred to Dubuque, Aug. 11, 1911; died Aug. 2, 1929; FRANCIS J. L. BECKMAN, S.T.D., Titular Archbishop of Phulli; ord. June 20, 1902; appt. Bishop of Lincoln, Dec. 23, 1923; cons. Bishop of Lincoln, May 1, 1924; Apostolic Administrator of Omaha, June 1, 1926 to July 4, 1928; elevated to Archiepiscopal Dignity and transferred to Dubuque, Jan. 17, 1930; appt. Assistant at the Pontifical Throne, April 21, 1928; resigned Nov. 11, 1946; died Oct. 17, 1948; HENRY P. ROHLMAN, D.D., appt. Bishop of Davenport, May 20, 1927; cons. July 25, 1927; appt. Coadjutor Archbishop of Dubuque "cum jure successionis" and Apostolic Administrator, June 15, 1944; installed Sept. 12, 1944; succeeded Nov. 11, 1946; named Assistant at Pontifical Throne, Sept. 2, 1950; resigned and named Titular Archbishop of Cotrada, Dec. 2, 1954; died Sept. 13, 1957; LEO BINZ, D.D., ord. March 15, 1924; appt. Titular Bishop of Pinara, Coadjutor Bishop and Apostolic Administrator of Winona, Nov. 21, 1942; cons. Dec. 21, 1942; named Titular Archbishop of Silyum and Coadjutor to the Archbishop of Dubuque "cum jure successionis," Oct. 15, 1949; named Assistant at the Pontifical Throne, June 11, 1954; Archbishop of Dubuque, Dec. 2, 1954; Pallium conferred, June 12, 1958; appt. Archbishop of St. Paul, Dec. 16, 1961; retired July, 1975; died Oct. 9, 1979; JAMES J. BYRNE, S.T.D., appt. Titular Bishop of Etenna and Auxiliary Bishop of St. Paul, May 10, 1947; ord. Bishop, July 2, 1947; transferred to Boise, ID, June 16, 1956; appt. Archbishop of Dubuque, March 19, 1962; retired Aug. 23, 1983; named Apostolic Administrator; died Aug. 2, 1996; DANIEL W. KUCERA, O.S.B., Ph.D., D.D. (Retired), ord. May 26, 1949; appt. Titular Bishop of Natchez and Auxiliary Bishop of Joliet, June 6, 1977; ord. Bishop, July 21, 1977; appt. Bishop of Salina, KS, March 11, 1980; installed May 7, 1980; named Archbishop of Dubuque, Dec. 20, 1983; installed Feb. 23, 1984; retired Oct. 16, 1995.

Archbishop—Most Rev. JEROME HANUS, O.S.B., D.D., Archdiocesan Center, 1229 Mt. Loretta Ave., P.O. Box 479, Dubuque, 52004-0479. Tel: 563-556-2580.

Vicar General and Episcopal Vicar for Dubuque Region—Rev. Msgr. THOMAS E. TOALE, Ph.D., Archdiocesan Center, 1229 Mt. Loretta Ave., P.O. Box 479, Dubuque, 52004-0479. Tel: 563-556-2580; Fax: 563-556-5464.

Episcopal Vicar for Cedar Rapids Region—Rev. THOMAS R. ZINKULA, J.D., J.C.L., 120 Fifth St., N.W., Cedar Rapids, 52405. Tel: 319-366-1647;

Fax: 319-366-0426.

Episcopal Vicar for Waterloo Region—Rev. Msgr. LYLE L. WILGENBUSCH, 320 Mulberry St., Waterloo, 50703. Tel: 319-236-0241; Fax: 319-232-1118.

Vicar for Hispanic Ministry—Rev. JAMES L. MILLER, St. Mary, 9 W. Linn St., Marshalltown, 50158. Tel: 641-753-6278.

Judicial Vicar—Rev. SCOTT E. BULLOCK, J.C.L., Archdiocesan Center, 1229 Mt. Loretta Ave., P.O. Box 479, Dubuque, 52004-0479. Tel: 563-556-2580.

Chancellor—Sr. MAUREEN MCPARTLAND, O.P., J.C.L., Archdiocesan Center, 1229 Mt. Loretta Ave., P.O. Box 479, Dubuque, 52004-0479. Tel: 563-556-2580.

Director of the Pastoral Center—LYNN OSTERHAUS, Archdiocesan Center, 1229 Mt. Loretta Ave., P.O. Box 479, Dubuque, 52004-0479. Tel: 563-556-2580.

Finance Officer—RICHARD L. RUNDE, Archdiocesan Center, 1229 Mt. Loretta Ave., P.O. Box 479, Dubuque, 52004-0479. Tel: 563-556-2580.

Archbishop's Cabinet—Most Rev. JEROME HANUS, O.S.B., D.D.; Rev. THOMAS R. ZINKULA, J.D., J.C.L.; LYNN OSTERHAUS; DAN ROHNER; RICHARD L. RUNDE; Sr. MAUREEN MCPARTLAND, O.P., J.C.L.; Rev. Msgrs. THOMAS E. TOALE, Ph.D.; LYLE L. WILGENBUSCH; Sr. LYNN FANGMAN, P.B.V.M.

College of Consultors—Most Rev. JEROME HANUS, O.S.B.; Rev. Msgrs. RUSSELL M. BLEICH, S.T.L.; JAMES O. BARTA, Ph.D. (Retired); LYLE L. WILGENBUSCH; THOMAS E. TOALE, Ph.D.; Revs. RICHARD G. GAUL; PHILIP E. THOMPSON; Rev. Msgrs. RALPH P. SIMINGTON (Retired); WALTER L. BRUNKAN.

Deans—Very Revs. JOHN A. GOSSMAN, Cedar Rapids; MARVIN C. SALZ, Decorah; DWAYNE J. THOMAN, Dubuque; PHILLIP F. KRUSE, Dyersville; PAUL R. PETERS, Elkader; JOHN R. KREMER, Independence; MICHAEL J. MESCHER, Marshalltown; KENNETH B. GEHLING, Mason City; CARL A. RIES, New Hampton; JERRY F. KOPACEK, Waterloo; BERNARD C. GRADY, Webster City.

Archdiocesan Central Offices

Archdiocesan Pastoral Center—1229 Mt. Loretta Ave., Dubuque, 52003-7826. Tel: 563-556-2580; Fax: 563-556-5464. *Mailing Address: P.O. Box 479, Dubuque, 52004-0479.* Most Rev. JEROME HANUS, O.S.B., D.D.; Rev. Msgr. THOMAS E. TOALE, Ph.D., Vicar Gen.; Rev. THOMAS R. ZINKULA, J.D., J.C.L., Episcopal Vicar - Cedar Rapids Region; Rev. Msgr. LYLE L. WILGENBUSCH, Episcopal Vicar - Waterloo Region; Sr. MAUREEN MCPARTLAND, O.P., J.C.L., Chancellor. Office Hours: Mon.-Fri. 8:30-4:30. Secretaries: SARAH OTTING, M.A.P.S.; JULIE KAPSCH, Cedar Rapids Region.

Adult Faith Formation—VACANT, Dir.; PATRICIA NEISES, Sec., Archdiocesan Center, 1229 Mt. Loretta Ave., Dubuque, 52003-7286. Tel: 563-556-2580.

Archives—VACANT, Dir.

Campaign for Human Development—TRACY MORRISON, M.S., L.M.H.C., N.C.C., Dir., 1229 Mt. Loretta Ave., P.O. Box 1309, Dubuque, 52004-1309. Tel: 563-556-2580.

Catholic Cemeteries of the Archdiocese of Dubuque—RICHARD L. RUNDE, Dir., Finance Office, 1229 Mt. Loretta Ave., Dubuque, 52003-7826. Tel: 563-556-2580.

Catholic Charities—

Administrative Offices—Business Office: 1229 Mt. Loretta Ave., P.O. Box 1309, Dubuque, 52004-1309. Tel: 563-588-0558; Fax: 563-557-3140. TRACY MORRISON, M.S., L.M.H.C., N.C.C., Exec. Dir.; DEBRA JASPER, Exec. Asst.; ZOE HOULIHAN, Community Outreach Dir.; Sr. JANICE HANCOCK, P.B.V.M., Admin. Asst.; CHERYL WOOD, Administrative Asst. Counselors: AMY MAHONEY; ANGELLA LINK; JOANN WEITZ; Deacon WILLIAM HICKSON, Jail & Prison Min. Coord.

Branch Offices—

Ames—MARY JO PFEIFER-WULF, Counselor & Clinical Dir.; LISA TURNER, Counselor, 2210 Lincoln Way, Ames, 50014. Tel: 515-296-2759.

Cedar Rapids—420 Sixth St., S.E., Ste. 220, Cedar Rapids, 52401. Tel: 319-364-7121. STEPHEN SCHMITZ, Prog. Dir.; LORI WIDHALM, Prog. Svcs. Specialist; TERRI REYNOLDS, Immigration Outreach Coord.; TERINA HEIDELBERG, Pathway Partners Team Leader. Counselors: BLAIR A'HEARN; MARIA CAHALAN.

Decorah—LORI EASTWOOD, 307 W. Main St., Decorah, 52101. Tel: 563-382-9631.

Mason City—Will F. Muse Center, 600 First St., N.W., Ste. 105, Mason City, 50401. Tel: 641-424-9683. Rev. MICHAEL G. SCHUELLER, Counselor.

Waterloo—KELLEY DICKEY-CUDDY, Regl. Mgr. & Counselor; Rev. KENNETH C. STECHER, Kimball Ridge Center, 2101 Kimball Ave., LL 11, Waterloo, 50702. Tel: 319-272-2080.

Special Programs—

Barnabas Uplift—MARY KLAUKE ABBAS.

Community Outreach Programs—Programs Director, STEPHEN SCHMITZ. *Disaster Services*, LORI WIDHALM. *Immigration Outreach Services*, TERRI REYNOLDS. *Jail and Prison Ministry*, Deacon WILLIAM HICKSON, Coord. *Pathway Partners*, LORI WIDHALM, Pathway Partners. *Refugee Resettlement and Immigration*, STEPHEN SCHMITZ.

Post Adoption Services—ANGELLA LINK, Post Adoption Search; CHERYL WOOD, Post Adoption Asst.

Catholic Charities Housing—TRACY MORRISON, M.S., L.M.H.C., N.C.C., Dir., Mailing Address: P.O. Box 1309, Dubuque, 52004. Tel: 563-556-2580; STEVE JACOBS, Housing Admin. Tel: 563-556-5125; PAT HUSEMAN, Maintenance Supvr.; DANIEL MEYER, L.B.S.W., Svc. Coord.

Housing Projects—Kennedy Manor, 2671 Owen Court, Dubuque, 52002. BETH WEDEWER, Office Mgr.; SCOTT PUCCIO, Maintenance. *Ecumenical Tower, 250 W. Sixth St., Dubuque, 52001.* MATTHEW RODDY, Housing Svcs. Specialist; AARON WENZEL, Maintenance. *Carter Plaza, 2520 Carter Rd., Dubuque, 52001. Alabar Plaza, 1110 Doreen Ct., Waterloo, 50701.*

Catholic Committee on Scouting—AARON RANDOLPH JR., Chm., 3805 Monarch Ave., Marion, 52302. Tel: 319-377-0497; Deacon MICHAEL KLAPPHOLZ, Chap., Mailing Address: All Saints Parish, 720 29th St., S.E., Cedar Rapids, 52403. Tel: 319-363-6130.

Continuing Formation of Priests—Rev. Msgrs. JAMES O. BARTA, Ph.D., Dir., Sabbaticals & Priests' Graduate Studies (Retired); LYLE L. WILGENBUSCH, Dir. Continuing Educ. & Priests' Convocation; SARAH OTTING, M.A.P.S., Sec., Mailing Address: Archdiocesan Center, 1229 Mt. Loretta Ave., Dubuque, 52003-7826. Tel: 563-556-2580.

Council of Catholic Women—Rev. Msgr. W. DEAN WALZ, J.C.D., Moderator (Retired); ROSE ANN JERO, 1909 Edgebrook Dr., Marshalltown, 50158. Tel: 641-752-2165.

Faith Formation Division—

Office of Faith Formation & Education—JAMES OSTERBERGER, Dir.; ITZA HEIM, Sec.

Catholic Schools—JEFF HENDERSON, Supt. Schools; DEB FLECKENSTEIN, Special Projects Coord.; ALICE CONLON, Dir. Pre K-12 Prog.; JULIE KAPSCH, Sec. Cedar Rapids Office.

Catechetical Services—JOANNE POHLAND, Dir.; JULIE JOHNSON, Assoc. Dir.; JULIE SANDERS, Sec.

Adolescent & Young Adult Faith Formation—KEVIN FEYEN, M.T.S., Dir.; JUDY ARLEN, Sec.

Family Life Office—Ms. LINDA MANTERNACH, Dir.; DIANE KONSHAK, Sec., Archdiocesan Center, 1229 Mt. Loretta Ave., Dubuque, 52003-7826. Tel: 563-556-2580.

Beginning Experience—SARA JOHNSON, Contact. Tel: 563-556-6501.

Christian Family Movement—Contact: Deacon GARY AITCHISON; KAY AITCHISON, 3312 Ross Rd., Ames, 50014. Tel: 515-296-2966.

Courage—Very Rev. JERRY F. KOPACEK, Contact, St. Edward Parish, 1423 Kimball Ave., Waterloo, 50702. Tel: 319-233-8060.

Engaged Encounter—Rev. PHILLIP E. SCHMITT, Spiritual Advisor (Retired), 212 1/2 7th St., S.E., Mt. Vernon, 52314-1518. Tel: 319-895-0404.

For Registration—Family Life Office, 1229 Mt. Loretta Ave., Dubuque, 52003-7826. Tel: 563-556-2580.

Marriage Encounter— (contact Family Life Office).

National Marriage Encounter—Rev. PHILLIP E. SCHMITT (Retired). Tel: 319-895-0404.

Worldwide Marriage Encounter—Contact: ROGER LUENSMAN; MARSHA LUENSMAN. Tel: 563-927-4352; JOHN FINK; SUE FINK. Tel: 641-753-6953.

Marriage Retorno—Rev. MELVIN D. HEMANN, Dir. (Retired). Tel: 319-266-3889. Contact: RICK GIARUSSO; DEB GIARUSSO. Tel: 319-277-8170.

Marrying & Trusting Together (M.A.T.T.) Remarriage Preparation Program—Contact: Family Life Office, 1229 Mt. Loretta Ave., Dubuque, 52003-7826. Tel: 563-556-2580.

Ministry of Mothers Sharing (M.O.M.S.)—Contact: Family Life Office, 1229 Mt. Loretta Ave., Dubuque, 52003-7826. Tel: 563-556-2580.

Natural Family Planning and Fertility Care—Contact: Family Life Office, 1229 Mt. Loretta Ave., Dubuque, 52003-7826. Tel: 563-556-2580.

Parish Nurses and Healthcare Ministry— (contact Family Life Office).

Pre-Cana—Family Life Office, 1229 Mt. Loretta Ave., Dubuque, 52003-7826. Tel: 563-556-2580. Dubuque Area: SANDY ERNSDORFF, Contact, 2085 Hale St., Dubuque, 52001. Tel: 563-556-2859; TOM DANNER, Co Dir.; MARY JO DANNER, Co Dir., 16247 Country Club Dr., Peosta, 52068. Tel: 563-590-7082. Dyersville Area Contacts: MARK FALLON; LAURIE FALLON, 1029 1st St., S.W., Dyersville, 52040. Tel: 563-875-2276. Independence & Waterloo Areas: LISA GEISLER, St. Stephen the Witness Student Center, 1019 W. 23rd St., Cedar Falls, 50613. Tel: 319-266-9863. Cedar Rapids Area: MARY BETH NEAL, Co Dir.; TIM NEAL, Co Dir., 3505 Prairie Creek Rd., S.W., Cedar Rapids, 52404. Tel: 319-390-3933. Ames, Marshalltown & Webster City Areas - Contact: TOM LYNCH; SHELLY LYNCH, St. Thomas Aquinas, 2210 Lincoln Way, Ames, 50010. Tel: 515-292-8696. Mason City Area, Directors: Deacon DENNIS POPOWSKI; CHAR POPOWSKI, 560 Center Ave., Garner, 50438. Tel: 641-923-6045. North/Northeast Iowa Area: JOHN O'NEILL, Lansing; MARY O'NEILL, Lansing. Tel: 563-586-2380; Deacon VICTOR J. DESLOOVER, New Hampton; NANCY DESLOOVER, New Hampton. Tel: 563-429-2773; JOE KREINER, Ossian; KRISTIN KREINER, Ossian. Tel: 563-532-7065.

Sponsor Couple— (contact local parish for more information).

Finance Office—RICHARD L. RUNDE, Finance Officer; PENNY MINNIHAN, Auditor; PAULA MONTAG, Controller; KEN RAHE, Business Mgr.; JANICE TUEGEL, Accounting Clerk; CAROL CALLAHAN, Accounting Asst.; ELAINE HILDEBRAND, Bookkeeper/Sec., Mailing Address: P.O. Box 479, Dubuque, 52004-0479. Tel: 563-556-2580.

Director of Educational Development Emeritus—PAUL J. FROMMELT.

Health Care Ethics & Life Issues—JANINE MARIE IDZIAK, Ph.D., Consultant, Mailing Address: P.O. Box 479, Dubuque, 52004-0479. Tel: 563-556-2580; NANCY EISBACH, Sec.

Hispanic Ministry Office—

Vicar for Hispanic Ministry—Rev. JAMES L. MILLER.

Director—GISELLA AITKEN-SHADLE.

Human Resources—LYNN OSTERHAUS, Dir.; BARB GLEASON, Sec., 1229 Mt. Loretta Ave., Dubuque, 52003-7826. Tel: 563-556-2580.

Information Technology—JOHN NIGG, Dir.; ROB AESCHLIMAN, Email Admin.; DENISE AIRD, Sec.

Design & Printing Services—JOHN ROBBINS, Mgr.; ROBERT GOLDTHORPE, Print Shop.

Insurance: Property and Liability (Dubuque Archdiocesan Protection Program)—RICH EARLES, Claims Risk Mgr., Archdiocesan Center, 1229 Mt. Loretta Ave., Dubuque, 52003-8787. Tel: 563-556-2580; PATRICIA NEISES, Sec.

Lay Formation—VACANT, Dir.; DIANE KONSHAK, Sec., Archdiocesan Center, 1229 Mt. Loretta Ave., P.O. Box 479, Dubuque, 52004-0479. Tel: 563-556-2580.

Leadership Development and Pastoral Planning—DAN ROHNER, Dir.; ED HABERKORN, Sec., Mailing Address: P.O. Box 479, Dubuque, 52004-0479. Tel: 563-556-2580.

Maintenance—BOB RUNDE, Dir.; JIM FOUST, Assoc. Dir.

Media Services—KIM FELDMAN, Dir.; Sr. CAROL HOVERMAN, O.S.F., Dir. Communications; TRICIA TRANEL, Resource Center Specialist, 1229 Mt. Loretta Ave., Dubuque, 52003-7826. Tel: 563-556-2580.

Metropolitan Tribunal—Mailing Address: P.O. Box 479, Dubuque, 52004-0479. Tel: 563-556-2580. (Please send all dispensation requests to the Tribunal).

Director—Sr. MAUREEN MCPARTLAND, O.P., J.C.L.

Judicial Vicar—Rev. SCOTT E. BULLOCK, J.C.L.

Defenders of the Bond—Rev. Msgrs. JAMES O. BARTA, Ph.D. (Retired); RICHARD P. FUNKE, J.C.L. (Retired); Rev. DONALD J. PLAMONDON, J.C.L.

Judges—Revs. SCOTT E. BULLOCK, J.C.L.; JOSEPH L. HAUER, J.C.D.; Deacon GERALD T. JORGENSEN, Ph.D., J.C.L.; Revs. DOUGLAS J. LOECKE, J.C.L.; MARK R. NEMMERS (Retired); MICHAEL J. PODHAJSKY, J.C.L.; Sr. FRANCINE QUILLIN, P.B.V.M., J.C.L.; Rev. Msgr. W. DEAN WALZ, J.C.D. (Retired); Rev. THOMAS R. ZINKULA, J.D., J.C.L.

Promoter of Justice—Deacon GERALD T. JORGENSEN, Ph.D., J.C.L.

Office Secretaries—MADONNA WHITAKER, Notary; ED HABERKORN.

Recently Ordained Program—Rev. KENNETH J. GLASER, Dir.; LISA GIESLER, Sec., 1229 Mt. Loretta Ave., Dubuque, 52003-7826. Tel: 563-556-2580.

Newspaper "The Witness"—Sr. CAROL HOVERMAN, O.S.F., Editor, Archdiocesan Center, 1229 Mt. Loretta Ave., P.O. Box 917, Dubuque, 52004-0917. Tel: 563-588-0556; Fax: 563-588-0557. Staff: BRET FEAR, Production, Design & Advertising; CATHY WHITE, Circulation & Sec.; STEVE MCMAHON, Staff Writer & Copy Editor; DAN RUSSO, Reporter & Design.

Permanent Diaconate Program—Deacon TOM LANG, Dir., 1229 Mt. Loretta Ave., P.O. Box 479, Dubuque, 52004-0479. Tel: 563-556-2580. Assistant Directors: Deacons RICHARD WALLACE; GERALD T. JORGENSEN, Ph.D., J.C.L.; RAYMOND LARSEN.

Persons With Disabilities—MINDY HART, Dir.; PATRICIA NEISES, Sec.; MARY KOETZ, Coord. Retreats/ Renewal Days.

Pontifical Missions/Mission Awareness—Rev. Msgr. JOHN R. MCCLEAN, Dir. (Retired), Archdiocesan Center, 1229 Mt. Loretta Ave., Dubuque, 52003-7826. Tel: 563-556-2580; NANCY EISBACH, Sec.

Protection of Children and Young People—CAROL GEBHART, M.A., Dir.

Respect Life—JANINE MARIE IDZIAK, Ph.D., Dir.; NANCY EISBACH, Sec.

School Tuition Organization (STO)—1229 Mt. Loretta Ave., P.O. Box 479, Dubuque, 52004-0479. Tel: 563-556-2580.

Seminarians—Revs. SCOTT E. BULLOCK, J.C.L., Dir.; G. ROBERT GROSS, Asst. Dir.; BARB GLEASON, Sec., 1229 Mt. Loretta Ave., Dubuque, 52003-7826. Tel: 563-556-2580.

Stewardship—Sr. LYNN FANGMAN, P.B.V.M., Dir.

Vocation Awareness—Rev. DAVID A. SCHATZ, M.A., Dir. Associate Directors: Revs. KENNETH J. GLASER; JON M. SEDA; DUSTIN L. VU; BARB GLEASON, Sec., Archdiocesan Center, 1229 Mt. Loretta Ave., Dubuque, 52003-7826. Tel: 563-556-2580.

Worship Office—PEGGY LOVRIEN, M.A., Dir.; Rev. JOHN S. HAUGEN, Assoc. Dir.; SUSAN BLACK, Sec., 1229 Mt. Loretta Ave., P.O. Box 479, Dubuque, 52004-0479. Tel: 563-556-2580.

Archdiocesan Boards, Commissions and Councils

The Archdiocese of Dubuque Corporate Board—Most Rev. JEROME HANUS, O.S.B.; Rev. Msgr. THOMAS E. TOALE, Ph.D.; RICHARD L. RUNDE, Treas. (non-voting); SARAH OTTING, M.A.P.S., Recording Sec.; Sisters MAUREEN MCPARTLAND, O.P., J.C.L.; DOLORES MARIE MCHUGH, B.V.M.; MARK MOLO.

Archdiocese of Dubuque Deposit & Loan Fund Board—Most Rev. JEROME HANUS, O.S.B., D.D.; Rev. Msgr. THOMAS E. TOALE, Ph.D.; Sr. DOLORES MARIE MCHUGH, B.V.M.; MARK MOLO; Sr. MAUREEN MCPARTLAND, O.P., J.C.L.; RICHARD L. RUNDE, Treas. (non-voting); SARAH OTTING, M.A.P.S., Recording Sec.

Archdiocese of Dubuque Education Fund Board—Most Rev. JEROME HANUS, O.S.B., D.D., Pres.; PAUL J. FROMMELT, Vice Pres.; VACANT, Sec.; RICHARD L. RUNDE, Treas. (non-voting); MATTHEW BRANDES; EDWARD J. GALLAGHER JR.; C. RICHARD STARK; Rev. Msgr. THOMAS E. TOALE, Ph.D.

Archdiocese of Dubuque Perpetual Care Fund Board—Most Rev. JEROME HANUS, O.S.B., D.D.; Rev. Msgr. THOMAS E. TOALE, Ph.D.; ARNOLD HONKAMP; Sisters HELEN HUEWE, O.S.F.; MAUREEN MCPARTLAND, O.P., J.C.L.; RICHARD L. RUNDE, Treas. (non-voting); SARAH OTTING, M.A.P.S., Recording Sec.

Archdiocese of Dubuque Seminarian Education Fund Board—Most Rev. JEROME HANUS, O.S.B., D.D.; Rev. Msgr. THOMAS E. TOALE, Ph.D.; Sr. DOLORES MARIE MCHUGH, B.V.M.; MARK MOLO; Sr. MAUREEN MCPARTLAND, O.P., J.C.L.; RICHARD L. RUNDE, Treas. (non-voting); SARAH OTTING, M.A.P.S., Recording Sec.

American Martyrs Retreat House Advisory Board—Sr. M. JEANINE KUHN, P.B.V.M, Dir.; ROGER KUETER, Chm.; Deacon GREG LIEVENS, Chm.; MARY FOY; TOM HOAG; Rev. LOUIS M. JAEGER; ANASTASIA NICKLAUS SCHMELZER; DALE ROETHLER; Rev. Msgr. LYLE L. WILGENBUSCH, Ex Officio.

Audit Committee—DENISE DOLAN, Chm.; Sr. MARGARET MARY COSGROVE, B.V.M.; STEPHEN J. SCHMALL; RICHARD L. RUNDE, Staff (non-voting).

Archdiocesan Faith Formation Commission—Ex-Officio: Most Rev. JEROME HANUS, O.S.B. Represented by: Rev. Msgr. Thomas E. Toale; THERESA BREITBACH; DAVE CUSHING; MICHAEL ERICKSON; SHIRLEY FORD; CORRINE HEIMER BREITSPRECKER; KIM HERMSEN; Deacon MICHAEL KLAPPHOLZ; LEON KEUHNER; SUSAN KEUNE; Rev. NICHOLAS B. MARCH; KATHY OBERREUTER; RUTH PALMER; Deacon JIM PATERA; JOSEPH SCHMALL; ERIC STROMBERG; SUE VERNON; SARAH WHITE. Executive Officer: JAMES OSTERBERGER.

Archdiocesan Catholic School Board—Ex-Officio: JAMES OSTERBERGER; JEFF HENDERSON, Executive Officer; CORRINE HEIMER BREITSPRECKER; TIM KNEELAND; JACKIE LUECHT; WILLIAM MCCARTAN; MARY NICHOLS; KATHY OBERREUTER; Deacon JIM PATERA; MARTHA REAL; Rev. PHILIP E. THOMPSON.

Building Commission—Rev. Msgr. RUSSELL M. BLEICH, S.T.L., Chair; MILT DAKOVICH; Deacon LAVERNE FLAGEL; Rev. Msgr. STANLEY J. HAYEK (Retired); JAMES HYNES; Deacon RAY LARSEN; PEGGY LOVRIEN, M.A.; Rev. NEIL J. MANTERNACH; JEFF MORROW; JOHN J. NEGRO; JAMES OSTERBERGER; KEN RAHE, Recording Sec.; RICHARD L. RUNDE, Exec. Sec.; Rev. Msgr. CARL L. SCHMITT (Retired); ED WINEINGER.

Catholic Charities Board of Directors—Most Rev. JEROME HANUS, O.S.B., Pres.; Rev. Msgr. THOMAS E. TOALE, Ph.D., Vice Pres.; TRACY MORRISON, M.S., L.M.H.C., N.C.C., (Staff Non-Voting); Sr. MARGARET MARY COSGROVE, B.V.M.; NANCY ZACHAR FETT; JEFFREY FITZPATRICK; JAMES JACKSON; TOM JOHNSON; MARY JO RATER; STEPHANIE SAVAGE; RICHARD SCHRAD; PAUL SIGWARTH; Deacon TOM SINK, Diaconate Representative.

Catholic Charities Foundation—Most Rev. JEROME HANUS, O.S.B., D.D., Pres.; Rev. Msgr. THOMAS E. TOALE, Ph.D., Vice Pres.; GREG BURBACH; Sr. MARGARET MARY COSGROVE, B.V.M.; MICHAEL COYLE; STEPHANIE SAVAGE; NICHOLAS SCHRUP III; TRACY MORRISON, M.S., L.M.H.C., N.C.C., (Staff Non-Voting).

CEW Advisory Board—BARBARA BRUMM; MIKE DUDLEY; PAUL HANSON; STEVE KAMMEYER; Rev. GEORGE W. KARNIK (Retired); DEBBIE LANDUYT; BOB RAHE; CATHY ROBERTSON; BECKY SEYMOUR; PAM WASHINGTON; LORAS WEBER; CAROLYN WEBER.

Christian Initiation Advisory Committee—KAREN BYRNE; Rev. KENNETH J. GLASER, Chm.; JAMES HAWKINS; Sr. CONNIE HOWE, R.S.M.; JO MEISTER, Vice Chm.; Sisters FRANCINE QUILLIN, P.B.V.M., J.C.L.; JEANNE TRANEL, O.P.

Church Design/Renovation Commission—Revs. JOHN S. HAUGEN; DAVID G. KUCERA; PEGGY LOVRIEN, M.A., Exec. Sec.; PAM JOHNSTON, Vice Chm.; Rev. NEIL J. MANTERNACH, Chm.; Sr. RUTH JACKSON, S.V.M.; Rev. DENNIS D. JUHL; RAE REILLY.

Diaconal Community Council—Most Rev. JEROME HANUS, O.S.B., Pres.; Deacon TOM LANG, Exec. Sec.

Ames Region—LOIS POLT; Deacon RON SMITH.

Cedar Rapids Region—Deacons MICHAEL KLAPPHOLZ; RICHARD WALLACE.

Dubuque Region—Deacons JAMES STEGER; JAMES THILL.

Northeast Region—Deacons NICK FRANCOIS; MICHAEL WARD.

Mason City Region—JEAN CASEY; KAREN BYRNE.

Waterloo Region—Deacons JIM PATERA; TIM POST.

Appointed By The Archbishop—Deacons HORACIO QUILES; TIMOTHY LOBIANCO; SEAN SMITH, APC Liaison; Rev. JAMES P. BROKMAN, Archbishop's Delegate.

Social Concern Committee Liaison—Deacon TOM SINK.

Due Process Board—Rev. GABRIEL C. ANDERSON; Sr. JEAN GORDON, B.V.M.; DAVID HEIAR; JULIE NIEMEYER, Chm.; Deacon STEVEN W. STRANG; KAREN A. VOLZ; JOHN WALDMEIR; LYNN OSTERHAUS, Staff (non-voting).

Family Life & Marriage Advisory Committee—Deacon GARY AITCHISON; KAY AITCHISON; KAREN BONFIG; JENNIFER CLANCY; MIKE ERIKSON; JANICE LOECKE, L.P.N., B.S.; Ms. LINDA MANTERNACH; Rev. PHILLIP E. SCHMITT (Retired); AMY SHANNON; BECKY SHAFFER; ERIK STROMBERG; DIANE WALSTON.

Finance Council—Most Rev. JEROME HANUS, O.S.B., Chm.; RICHARD L. RUNDE, Exec. Sec.; PAULA MONTAG, Recording Sec.; Rev. Msgr. JAMES O. BARTA, Ph.D. (Retired); DONALD BERGAN; Deacon MATTHEW F. BERRY; Sr. MARGARET MARY COSGROVE, B.V.M.; THOMAS W. HANLEY; Rev. JOSEPH L. HAUER, J.C.D.; ROBERT KUCHARSKI; JASON MCDERMOTT; KAREN STURM; Rev. Msgr. THOMAS E. TOALE, Ph.D.; STEVE WEISS.

Human Resources Advisory Committee—LYNN OSTERHAUS, Chm.; Sr. JEAN GORDON, B.V.M.; KATHY KRUSIE; JULIE NIEMEYER.

Investment Committee—ROBERT KUCHARSKI, Chm.; Rev. Msgr. JAMES O. BARTA, Ph.D. (Retired); DON FLYNN; PAUL J. FROMMELT; EDWARD J. GALLAGHER JR.; GREG GRECO; Rev. DOUGLAS J. LOECKE, J.C.L.; Deacon PAUL PECKOSH; RICHARD L. RUNDE.

Lay Formation Advisory Board—PATRICIA BRUSH; DREW CONRAD; ROGER KUETER; Rev. LOUIS M. JAEGER; DEAN MANTERNACH; JERRY MANTERNACH; KATHY OBERREUTER; Rev. Msgr. THOMAS E. TOALE, Ph.D.; MAUREEN UTTER.

Medical-Moral Commission—JANINE MARIE IDZIAK, Ph.D., Chm.; Rev. WILLIAM M. JOENSEN, Ph.D.; JANICE LOECKE, L.P.N., B.S.; Rev. STEPHEN A. LUNDGREN; Sr. SUSAN O'CONNOR, R.S.M., M.S.W., M.A.; CAROL SCHMIDT, R.N.C., M.S.H.; MARK VALLIERE, M.D., M.M.M.; RICHARD WHITTY, J.D.

PAMAD (Pastoral Associates/Ministers of the Archdiocese of Dubuque)—TODD FLOWERDAY, Pres.; KAREN BONFIG, Vice Pres.; KAREN BYRNE, Sec.; RODNEY BLUML, Treas.

Pastoral Council—Most Rev. JEROME HANUS, O.S.B., Pres.; DANIEL HAYES, Chm.; PEGGY O'NEILL, Vice Chair; Deacon SEAN SMITH, Sec.; DAN ROHNER, Exec. Sec.; Rev. Msgrs. THOMAS E. TOALE, Ph.D.; RUSSELL M. BLEICH, S.T.L.; JIM BAILEY; Sr. LINDA BECHEN, R.S.M.; PATRICK BYRNE; PETER GONZALEZ; Sr. VIRGINIA HELDORFER, O.S.F.; NATHAN KOCH; NORMA LEIBOLD; MIKE MANTERNACH; PAT MCPHERSON; DAVID MITCHELL; Sr. SUSAN O'CONNOR, R.S.M., M.S.W., M.A., Sec.; ALEX PFIFFNER; Sr. JOELLEN PRICE, P.B.V.M.; NANCY RIGEL; MARCI ROE; RICHARD SCHRAD; PAULA TEIG; Rev. Msgr. LYLE L. WILGENBUSCH; MALINDA WELTON.

Permanent Diaconate Formation Board—Deacon TOM LANG, Chm.; JOAN M. HEAD; Deacons DANIEL HOEGER; GERALD T. JORGENSEN, Ph.D., J.C.L.; JOANN KOOPMANN; Deacon RAY LARSEN; Revs. JAMES L. MILLER; DAVID H. O'CONNOR; Deacon MICHAEL WHITTERS.

Personnel Advisory Board—Revs. PHILIP E. THOMPSON, Age Group II; NEIL J. MANTERNACH, At Large; DONALD L. KLEIN, Age Group I (Retired); THOMAS J. MCDERMOTT, Age Group III; DENNIS J. QUINT, Age Group IV, Chair.

Persons with Disabilities Advisory Committee—MARTHA HANLEY; ANDY HASLEY; D. J. JAEGER; NORMA LEIBOLD; Deacon STEPHEN MACDONALD; HAZEL MARTIN; RUTH PALMER; JEAN TRAINOR.

Priests' Council—Most Rev. JEROME HANUS, O.S.B., Pres.; Revs. MARK J. REASONER, Chm.; PHILLIP G. GIBBS, Vice Chm.; DENNIS W. MILLER, Sec. Ex Officio Members: Rev. Msgrs. RUSSELL M. BLEICH, S.T.L.; LYLE L. WILGENBUSCH; THOMAS E. TOALE, Ph.D.

Retired Priests' Representatives—Rev. DONALD L. KLEIN (Retired); Rev. Msgr. CARL L. SCHMITT (Retired).

Religious Priests Representative—Rev. JONAH WHARF, O.C.S.O.

Deanery Representatives—Revs. ANTHONY J. KRUSE, Cedar Rapids Deanery; PHILLIP G. GIBBS, Decorah Deanery; G. ROBERT GROSS, Dubuque Deanery; RAYMOND A. BURKLE, Dyersville Deanery; STEPHEN A. LUNDGREN, Elkader Deanery; ARDEL H. BARTA, Independence Deanery (Retired); JAMES L. MILLER, Marshalltown Deanery; DENNIS W. MILLER, Mason City Deanery; Rev. Msgr. WALTER L. BRUNKAN, New Hampton Deanery; Revs. KENNETH C. STECHER, Waterloo Deanery; NILS HERNANDEZ, Webster City Deanery.

Priestly Life and Ministry Committee— (Standing Committee of the Priests' Council) Revs. RODNEY M. ALLERS; JOHN R. FLAHERTY; PHILLIP G. GIBBS; KENNETH J. GLASER; LOUIS M. JAEGER; Rev. Msgr. LYLE L. WILGENBUSCH.

Review Board for the Protection of Minors—JOHN E. BECKMAN, Waterloo; CHERIE CASEY, Dyersville; ELIZABETH CORKEN DEEGAN, Cedar Rapids; Pastor DARREL GERRIETTS, Waverly; Sr. CORITA HEID, R.S.M., Mason City; Deacon MICHAEL KLAPPHOLZ, Cedar Rapids; Very Rev. JERRY F. KOPACEK, Waterloo; Judge RANDAL NIGG, Dubuque; PAM WHITTERS; Deacon GERALD T. JORGENSEN, Ph.D., J.C.L., Promoter of Justice; Dr. BARBARA SULLIVAN WOODWARD, Chm., Dubuque.

Saint Raphael Priest Fund Society—

Board of Directors/Priest Pension Plan Board of Trustees—Most Rev. JEROME HANUS, O.S.B., Pres.; Rev. Msgrs. THOMAS E. TOALE, Ph.D., Vice Pres.; JAMES O. BARTA, Ph.D., Sec. & Treas. (Retired); RICHARD L. RUNDE, Plan Admin.; PAULA MONTAG, Recording Sec. Directors: Rev. Msgrs. JAMES O. BARTA, Ph.D. (Retired); WALTER L. BRUNKAN; Rev. DENNIS J. COLTER (Retired); Rev. Msgr. STANLEY J. HAYEK (Retired); Rev. DOUGLAS J. LOECKE, J.C.L.; Rev. Msgr. JOHN R. MCCLEAN (Retired); Rev. THOMAS J. MCDERMOTT; Very Rev. MICHAEL J. MESCHER; Rev. MARK J. REASONER; Rev. Msgrs. CARL L. SCHMITT (Retired); RALPH P. SIMINGTON (Retired); Rev. THOMAS R. ZINKULA, J.D., J.C.L.

Seminary Admissions and Advisory Board—Revs. SCOTT E. BULLOCK, J.C.L., Chm.; G. ROBERT GROSS; THOMAS J. MCDERMOTT; MARY JO PFEIFER-WULF; Revs. NEIL J. MANTERNACH; DUSTIN L. VU.

School Tuition Organization Board of Directors—Rev. Msgr. THOMAS E. TOALE, Ph.D., Pres.; JAMES OSTERBERGER, Vice Pres.; JEFF HENDERSON, Sec.; MAE BECKER; JEFF ENGEL; JULIE HERMANN; JUDY RUDMAN; JOSEPH SCHMALL.

Stewardship Committee—SUE BAHLS, (Elkader Deanery); MIKE O'BRIEN, (Webster City Deanery); ROBERT BREITFELDER, (Dyersville Deanery); SHIRLEY FORD, (Marshalltown Deanery); Deacon JIM FREET, (Waterloo Deanery); Very Rev. BERNARD C. GRADY, (Priest Representative); JAMES HAWKINS, (Decorah Deanery); JOANNE KOOPMAN, (Dyersville Deanery), Chair; VACANT, (Dubuque Deanery); SUSAN MARTINEK, (Cedar Rapids Deanery); JODY DOYLE, (Independence Deanery); VACANT, (Mason City Deanery); CONNIE WAGNER, (New Hampton Deanery); Rev. Msgr. LYLE L. WILGENBUSCH, Regl. Vicar; Sr. LYNN FANGMAN, P.B.V.M., Staff.

Victim Assistance Coordinators—Dr. THOMAS ANDEREGG. Tel: 563-556-1225; JOAN HOFFMANN. Tel: 866-319-4636.

Vocation Awareness Advisory Committee—Rev. HENRY P. HUBER; Very Revs. PHILLIP F. KRUSE; MARVIN C. SALZ.

Witness Advisory Committee—Sr. CAROL HOVERMAN, O.S.F., Chm.; LORI BAHL; MARILYN GORUN; AL GRIVETTI; DALE KUETER; PAULA MONTAG; Sr. MIRA MOSLE, B.V.M.; Deacon SEAN SMITH.

Witness Corporate Board—Most Rev. JEROME HANUS, O.S.B.; Rev. Msgr. THOMAS E. TOALE, Ph.D.; Sisters MAUREEN MCPARTLAND, O.P., J.C.L.; CAROL HOVERMAN, O.S.F. Treasurer: RICHARD L. RUNDE.

Worship Commission—CHRISTINE CARRIER, Chm.; PEGGY LOVRIEN, M.A., Exec. Sec.; VACANT, Vice Chm.; Revs. GREG E. BAHL; SCOTT E. BULLOCK, J.C.L.; Sisters LINDA BECHEN, R.S.M.; KATHLEEN GRACE, O.S.F.; BOB HAUSER; Revs. NILS HERNANDEZ; DANIEL J. KNEPPER; JOANN KOOPMANN; Rev. DENNIS J. QUINT; ANASTASIA NICKLAUS SCHMELZER; Deacon ROBERT STIRM.

CLERGY, PARISHES, MISSIONS AND PAROCHIAL SCHOOLS

CITY OF DUBUQUE

(DUBUQUE COUNTY)

1—ST. RAPHAEL CATHEDRAL (1833) [JC] Rev. Daniel J. Knepper; Deacons Paul Peckosh; Horacio Quiles; Jim Luksetich; Barbara Gatch, Pastoral Assoc.; James Mandralla, Music Dir. & Liturgist.
Church, Res. & Office: 231 Bluff St., 52001-6918. Tel: 563-582-7646; Fax: 563-556-6796.
See Holy Family Catholic Schools under Consolidated K-12 Systems located in the Institution section
Catechesis/Religious Program—Jean Leute, D.R.E. Linked with St. Patrick, Dubuque Students 133.

2—ST. ANTHONY (1867) [JC] Rev. Steven J. Rosonke; Deacons William Mauss; William Hickson; Sr. Margaret Anne Kramer, P.B.V.M., Pastoral Assoc.
Res. & Office: 1870 St. Ambrose St., 52001-4196. Tel: 563-588-0571; Fax: 563-588-0572.
Church: 1880 St. Ambrose St., 52001.
See Holy Family Catholic Schools under Consolidated K-12 Systems located in the Institution Section.
Catechesis/Religious Program—Carol A. Witry, Dir. Faith Formation. Students 187.

3—CHURCH OF THE NATIVITY (1923) [JC] Revs. Scott E. Bullock; G. Robert Gross; Deacon David McGhee, Pastoral Assoc.
Church & Office: 1225 Alta Vista St., 52001. Tel: 563-582-1839; Fax: 563-582-1830.
Res.: 1075 University, 52001. Tel: 563-582-0703.
See Holy Family Catholic Schools under Consolidated K-12 Systems located in the Institution section
Catechesis/Religious Program—Judith Calcari, Dir. Faith Formation. Students 81.

4—CHURCH OF THE RESURRECTION (1857) [CEM] Revs. Joseph L. Hauer; Gary A. Mayer; Deacons Gerald T. Jorgensen; Timothy LoBianco, Pastoral Assoc.; Sr. Francine Quillin, P.B.V.M., Pastoral Assoc.
Church & Office: 4300 Asbury Rd., 52002. Tel: 563-556-7511; Fax: 563-556-7419.
Res.: 2525 St. Anne Dr., 52001. Tel: 563-582-5634.
See Holy Family Catholic Schools under Consolidated K-12 Systems located in the Institution Section.
Catechesis/Religious Program—Sr. Francine Quillin, P.B.V.M., Dir. Faith Formation. Students 448.

5—ST. COLUMBKILLE (1887) [JC] Rev. Gabriel C. Anderson; Deacon William Biver; Alice Noethe, Pastoral Assoc.
Church, Res. & Office: 1240 Rush St., 52003-7598. Tel: 563-583-9117; Fax: 563-583-5909.
See Holy Family Catholic Schools under Consolidated K-12 Systems located in the Institution Section.
Catechesis/Religious Program—Alice Noethe, Dir. Faith Formation. Students 53.

6—HOLY GHOST (1896) [JC] Merged with Holy Trinity and Sacred Heart, Dubuque to form Holy Spirit, Dubuque. For sacramental records contact Holy Spirit, Dubuque.

7—HOLY SPIRIT Very Rev. Dwayne J. Thoman; Rev. Steven M. Garner; Deacons Dave Brinkmoeller; Stephen MacDonald; James J. Thill; John Stierman.
2215 Windsor Ave., 52001.
Worship Sites—
Holy Ghost Church—2921 Central Ave., 52001.
Holy Trinity Church—1701 Rhomberg Ave., 52001.
Sacred Heart Church—2215 Windsor Ave., 52001.
Catechesis/Religious Program—Victoria Wadle, Dir. Faith Formation. Students 182.

8—HOLY TRINITY (1910) [JC] Merged with Holy Ghost and Sacred Heart, Dubuque to form Holy Spirit, Dubuque. For sacramental records contact Holy Spirit, Dubuque.

9—ST. JOSEPH THE WORKER (1949) [JC] Rev. Mark A. Ressler.
Res.: 90 S. Algona St., 52001-5605. Tel: 563-588-2934.
Office: 60 S. Algona, 52001-5605. Tel: 563-588-1433; Fax: 563-588-4108.
Church: 2001 St. Joseph St., 52001.
See Holy Family Catholic Schools under Consolidated K-12 Systems located in the Institution Section.
Catechesis/Religious Program—Cindy Pfiffner, Dir. Faith Formation. Students 169.

10—ST. MARY (1850) [JC] Closed. For sacramental records contact Cathedral of St. Raphael, Dubuque.

11—ST. PATRICK (1862) [JC] Rev. Daniel J. Knepper; Deacons Horacio Quiles; Paul Peckosh; Jim Luksetich; Barbara Gatch, Pastoral Assoc.; Gisella Aitken-Shadle, Hispanic Min. Coord.
Parish Office—1425 Iowa St., 52001-4890. Tel: 563-583-9749.
Church: 15th & Iowa St., 52001.
See Holy Family Catholic Schools under Consolidated K-12 Systems located in the Institution Section
Catechesis/Religious Program—Susan Dazey, Dir. Faith Formation. Linked with Cathedral of St. Raphael, Dubuque. Students 53.

12—SACRED HEART (1879) [JC] Merged with Holy Ghost and Holy Trinity, Dubuque to form Holy Spirit, Dubuque. For sacramental records contact Holy Spirit, Dubuque.

OUTSIDE THE CITY OF DUBUQUE

ACKLEY, FRANKLIN CO., ST. MARY (1891) [CEM] Very Rev. Bernard C. Grady; Deacon David Jones.
Mailing Address: 1405 N. Federal, Hampton, 50441-1005.
Office & Church: 611 Sherman Ave., P.O. Box 2, 50601. Tel: 641-847-2329.
Res.: 2 19th Ave., N.E., Hampton, 50441. Tel: 641-456-3406.
Catechesis/Religious Program—Jolene Harms, D.R.E. Students 67.

ALLISON, BUTLER CO., IMMACULATE CONCEPTION, Closed. For sacramental records, contact St. Mary, Greene.

ALTA VISTA, CHICKASAW CO., ST. BERNARD (1897) [CEM] Rev. Ray E. Atwood.
Office: 203 Seventh St., Elma, 50628. Tel: 641-393-2520; Fax: 641-393-2069.
Church: 116 E. Washington, 50603.
Catechesis/Religious Program—Sheila Kobliska, D.R.E. Students 25.

AMES, STORY CO.

1—ST. CECILIA (1899) Rev. James L. Secora; Deacons John McCully, Hispanic Min. Coord.; Ron Smith; Alan Christy; Joann Dalhoff, Pastoral Assoc.
Res.: 1642 Reagan Dr., 50010. Tel: 515-233-9477.
Church & Office: 2900 Hoover Ave., 50010-4498. Tel: 515-233-3092; Fax: 515-233-6423.
School—(Grades PreSchool-5) Tel: 515-232-5290. Brandt Snakenberg, Prin. Lay Teachers 15; Students 250.
Catechesis/Religious Program—Tel: 515-232-3514. Tom Primmer, Dir. Faith Formation. Students 329.

2—ST. THOMAS AQUINAS CHURCH (AND CATHOLIC STUDENT CENTER) (1947) Revs. Jon M. Seda; James W. Dubert; Sr. Lorraine Schmaltz, P.B.V.M., Pastoral Assoc.
Church & Office: 2210 Lincoln Ave., 50014-7184. Tel: 515-292-3810; Fax: 515-292-3841.
Res.: 2801 Bristol Dr., 50010.
Res.: 1504 Little Bluestem Ct., 50014.
Catechesis/Religious Program—Kathy White, Dir. Faith Formation. Students 198.

ANAMOSA, JONES CO., ST. PATRICK (1861) [CEM] Sr. Susan Dunnwald, R.S.M., Parish Life Coord.; Very Rev. John A. Gossman, Priest Supvr.; Rev. Wayne J. Droessler, Sacramental Priest.
Res. & Office: 215 N. Garnavillo St., 52205-1121. Tel: 319-462-2141.
Church: 217 N. Garnavillo St., 52205.
School—(Grades PreSchool-6), 216 N. Garnavillo St., 52205-1122. Tel: 319-462-2688; Fax: 319-462-3239. Chris Frimml, Prin. Lay Teachers 8; Students 70.
Catechesis/Religious Program—Chris Frimml, D.R.E. Students 84.

ANDREW, JACKSON CO., ST. JOHN (1914) [CEM] Closed. For sacramental records, please contact Sacred Heart Parish, Maquoketa.

BALDWIN, JACKSON CO., HOLY TRINITY, [CEM] Closed. For sacramental records, contact Sacred Heart, Maquoketa.

BALLTOWN, DUBUQUE CO., ST. FRANCIS OF ASSISI (1891) [CEM] Rev. Raymond A. Burkle.
Parish Office & Mailing Address: 875 Church St., P.O. Box 398, Holy Cross, 52053. Tel: 563-870-4041.
Res.: 103 S. Andres St., P.O. Box 140, Luxemburg, 52056. Tel: 563-853-3369.
Church: 468 Balltown Rd., Sherrill, 52073.
See LaSalle Elementary Schools, Holy Cross under Elementary School Systems located in the Institution section.
Catechesis/Religious Program—Brian Niles, C.R.E. Students 31.

BANKSTON, DUBUQUE CO., ST. CLEMENT (1859) [CEM] Rev. Dennis R. Cain; Deacons James Kean; Gerald Koopmann; Betty Pins, Pastoral Assoc.
Office: 104 First St., S.E., P.O. Box 286, Epworth, 52045-0286. Tel: 563-876-5540.
Res.: 22511 E. Pleasant Grove Rd., Epworth, 52045. Tel: 563-876-5501.
Church: 24287 New Vienna Rd., Epworth, 52045-9732.
See Seton Catholic Schools, Farley under Elementary School Systems located in the Institution section.
Catechesis/Religious Program—Betty Pins, C.R.E. Students 59.

BARCLAY, BLACKHAWK CO., ST. FRANCIS (1862) [CEM] Rev. Kenneth C. Stecher.
Office: 7837 E. Airline Hwy., Dunkerton, 50626. Tel: 319-822-7477.
Res.: 634 Stevens St., P.O. Box 316, Jesup, 50648. Tel: 319-827-3003.
Church: 7830 E. Airline Hwy., Dunkerton, 50626.
Catechesis/Religious Program—Arlene Widdel, Dir. Faith Formation. Students 39.

BELLE PLAINE, BENTON CO., ST. MICHAEL (1885) Very Rev. Michael J. Mescher; Deacon Joseph Behounek, Pastoral Assoc.; Laura Galvez, Hispanic Min.Coord.
Church & Mailing Address: 1304 Ninth Ave., 52208-1614. Tel: 319-444-3106; Fax: 319-444-3737.
Catechesis/Religious Program—Jackie Toennies, D.R.E. Students 60.

BELLEVUE, JACKSON CO., ST. JOSEPH (1841) [CEM] Very Rev. Phillip F. Kruse; Andrew Lang, Pastoral Assoc.
Church, Res., & Office: 405 Franklin St., 52031-1596. Tel: 563-872-3234.
See Bellevue, Marquette High School under Consolidated K-12 Systems located in the Institution section.
Catechesis/Religious Program—Andrew Lang, Dir. Faith Formation. Students 93.

BELMOND, WRIGHT CO., ST. FRANCIS XAVIER (1870) [CEM] Rev. Nils Hernandez; Deacons Michael Whitters; Pedro Garcia; Jerry Temeyer; Beatriz Garcia, Hispanic Min.Coord.
Church, Parish Office & Mailing Address: 1207 Third St. N.E., 50421-1608. Tel: 641-444-3249; Fax: 641-444-4499.
Catechesis/Religious Program—Gloria Kisor, C.R.E. Students 78.

BLAIRSTOWN, BENTON CO., ST. JOHN (1948) Rev. Brian M. Dellaert; Deacon Robert F. Hurych.
Office & Mailing Address: 405 4th Ave., P.O. Box 250, Van Horne, 52346-0250. Tel: 319-228-8131; Fax: 319-228-8800.
Res.: 512 Evergreen St., P.O. Box 89, Norway, 52318-0089.
Church: 105 West St. N.W., 52209-0170.
Catechesis/Religious Program—Students 23.

BLESSING, BLACKHAWK CO., IMMACULATE CONCEPTION (1875) [CEM] Closed. For sacramental records, contact St. Mary of Mt. Carmel, Eagle Center.

BLUFFTON, WINNESHIEK CO., ST. BRIDGET ORATORY (1858) [CEM] Closed. For sacramental records, contact Notre Dame, Cresco.
Church: 3094 253rd Ave., Ridgeway, 52165.

BRITT, HANCOCK CO., ST. PATRICK (1880) [CEM] Revs. Dennis W. Miller; Paul E. Lippstock, Sacramental Priest; Deacon Dennis Popowski.
Office & Mailing Address: 139 Third St. S.E., 50423-1726. Tel: 641-843-3215; Fax: 641-843-3557.
Res.: 660 Bush Ave., Garner, 50438. Tel: 641-923-2329.
Church: 335 First Ave. S.E., 50423.
Catechesis/Religious Program—Sheryl Chiezek, D.R.E. Students 111.

BUFFALO CENTER, WINNEBAGO CO., ST. PATRICK (1899) Revs. Dennis W. Miller; Paul E. Lippstock, Sacramental Priest; Deacon Dennis Popowski.
Office & Mailing Address: 906 W. O St., Forest City, 50436. Tel: 641-585-4856.
Pastor's Res.: 660 Bush Ave., Garner, 50438-1513.
Church: 115 5th Ave. N.W., 50424.
Catechesis/Religious Program—Melissa Dave, Dir. Faith Formation. Students 21.

CALMAR, WINNESHIEK CO., ST. ALOYSIUS (1875) [CEM] Rev. Donald J. Hawes.
Church, Res. & Mailing Address: 304 S. Maryville, P.O. Box 819, 52132-0819. Tel: 563-562-3603; Fax: 563-562-3292.
See Calmar-Festina-Spillville Catholic School, Calmar under Elementary School Systems located in the Institution section.

Catechesis/Religious Program—Patty Frana, D.R.E. Students 72.

CARROLL TOWNSHIP, CARROLL CO., ST. WENCESLAUS ORATORY, Closed. For sacramental Records, contact St. Paul, Traer.

CARTERSVILLE, CERRO GORDO CO., ST. JOHN, Closed. For sacramental Records, contact Sacred Heart, Rockwell.

CASCADE, DUBUQUE CO.

1—ST. MARTIN (1848) Closed. Merged with St. Mary, Cascade to form St. Matthias, Cascade. For sacramental records, contact St. Matthias, Cascade.

2—ST. MARY (1857) Closed. Merged with St. Martin, Cascade to form St. Matthias, Cascade. For sacramental records, contact St. Matthias, Cascade.

3—ST. MATTHIAS (1995) [CEM] Rev. Douglas J. Loecke; Deacons Steven W. Strang; Marvin Recker; Ray Noonan; Joe Schockemoehl; Jean Conrad, Pastoral Assoc.
Mailing & Parish Office Address: 408 Third Ave., N.W., P.O. Box 699, 52033. Tel: 563-852-3524.
Church: 410 3rd Ave., NW, 52033.
See Aquin Educational System, Cascade under Consolidated K-12 Systems located in the Institution section.
Catechesis/Religious Program—Students 12.

CASTLE GROVE, JONES CO., IMMACULATE CONCEPTION (1877) [CEM] Closed. For sacramental records contact Sacred Heart, Monticello.

CEDAR FALLS, BLACKHAWK CO., ST. PATRICK (1855) Rev. Dennis J. Colter, Parochial Admin. (Retired); Deacons Tom Sink, Pastoral Assoc.; Peter Loving, Pastoral Assoc.
Mailing & Parish Office Address: 705 Main St., 50613-2950. Tel: 319-266-3523; Fax: 319-266-2179.
Church: 8th & Washington St., 50613.
School—(Grades Day Care-8), 615 Washington St., 50613. Tel: 319-277-6781; Fax: 319-266-5806. Sr. Marilou Irons, P.B.V.M., Prin. Sisters 1; Lay Teachers 18; Students 239.
Catechesis/Religious Program—Amy Hoyer, Dir. Faith Formation. Students 402.

CEDAR RAPIDS, LINN CO.

1—ALL SAINTS (1947) [JC] Rev. David H. O'Connor; Deacon Michael Klappholz; Linda Stavropoulos, Pastoral Assoc.
Church, Parish Office & Mailing Address: 720 29th St., S.E., 52403-3099. Tel: 319-363-6130; Fax: 319-861-2240.
Res.: 830 Beaver Ridge Ct. S.E., 52403. Tel: 319-362-1691.
School—(Grades Day Care-5), 720 29th St., SE, 52403. Tel: 319-363-4110; Fax: 319-363-9547. Marlene Bartlett, Prin. Lay Teachers 16; Students 242.
Catechesis/Religious Program—Deanna Gerber, Dir. Faith Formation. Students 146.

2—BLESSED JOHN XXIII, [CEM] Rev. Dustin L. Vu; Ann Petrzelka, Pastoral Assoc.
8100 Roncalli Dr., S.W., 52404-9178. Tel: 319-846-3139; Fax: 319-846-3159.
Pastor's Res.: 3108 80th St. S.W., 52404.
Catechesis/Religious Program—Sherry Manchester, C.R.E. Students 263.

3—IMMACULATE CONCEPTION (1858) [JC] Rev. Christopher R. Podhajsky; Deacon Diego Ramirez; Naida Garza, Pastoral Assoc. & Hispanic Min. Coord.; Marion Moreland, Pastoral Assoc.; Sr. Brian Kelly, R.S.M., Pastoral Min.
Mailing Address: P.O. Box 1247, 52406-1247.
Church, Office & Res.: 857 Third Ave. S.E., 52403. Tel: 319-362-7181; Fax: 319-369-9528.
Catechesis/Religious Program—Mary Ann McEniry, Dir. Faith Formation. Students 136.

4—JOHN XXIII (2000) [JC] Merged with John XXII, Cedar Rapids and St. Patrick, Fairfax to form Blessed John XXIII, Cedar Rapids.

5—ST. JUDE (1962) [JC] Rev. Mark J. Reasoner; Sr. Linda Bechen, R.S.M., Pastoral Assoc.
Res.: 3601 First Ave. S.W., 52404. Tel: 319-396-8827.
Church & Office: 50 Edgewood Rd., N.W., 52405. Tel: 319-390-3520; Fax: 319-390-3457.
See Holy Family School, Cedar Rapids under Elementary School Systems located in the Institution section.
Catechesis/Religious Program—June Speltz, C.R.E.; Erin Hughes, C.R.E. Students 188.

6—ST. LUDMILA (1922) [JC] Rev. Dennis D. Juhl; Deacons Richard Manning; Paul "Jim" Berger; Sr. Mary L. Lechtenberg, O.S.F., Pastoral Assoc.
Office & Res.: 2107 J St., S.W., 52404-3615. Tel: 319-362-7282; Fax: 319-398-0352.
Church: 211 21st Ave., S.W., 52404.
See Holy Family School, Cedar Rapids under Elementary School Systems located in the Institution section.
Catechesis/Religious Program—Sue Berger, D.R.E. Students 308.

7—ST. MATTHEW (1922) [JC] Rev. David M. Beckman; Deacons Phil Saunders; Richard Wallace; Becky Shaffer, Pastoral Assoc.
Church, Res. & Office: 2310 First Ave. N.E., 52402-4999. Tel: 319-363-8269; Fax: 319-363-8260.
School—(Grades Day Care-5), 125 24th St., NE, 52402. Tel: 319-362-3021; Fax: 319-362-7946. Joe Wolf, Prin. Sisters 1; Lay Teachers 20; Students 280.
Catechesis/Religious Program—Betsy Schmuck, Dir. Faith Formation; Sarah White, C.R.E. Students 208.

8—ST. PATRICK (1886) [JC] Rev. Ivan R. Nienhaus; Deacon Daniel Hoeger.
Parish Office & Mailing Address: 120 5th Ave N.W., 52405. Tel: 319-362-7966; Fax: 319-366-7260.
Church: 500 First Ave. N.W., 52405.
Catechesis/Religious Program—Penny Ackerman, Dir. Faith Formation. Students 76.

9—ST. PIUS X (1959) [JC] Revs. Philip E. Thompson; David J. Ambrosy, Sacramental Priest; Deacons Paul Zimmerman; Lanny Peterson; Anne Johnson, Pastoral Assoc.; Sr. Joellen Price, P.B.V.M., Pastoral Assoc.
Church and Office: 4949 Council St. N.E., 52402-2492. Tel: 319-393-4445; Fax: 319-393-9424.
Res.: 1500 48th St. N.E., 52402. Tel: 319-395-0452.
See St. Pius and St. Elizabeth Ann Seton Schools under Elementary School Systems located in the Institution section.
Catechesis/Religious Program—Linda Van Etten, D.R.E. Students 275.

10—ST. WENCESLAUS (1874) [JC] Rev. Christopher R. Podhajsky; Deacon Diego Ramirez.
Parish Office & Mailing Address: 510 16th Ave. S.E., 52401.
Res.: 857 Third Ave., S.E., P.O. Box 1247, 52406-1247. Tel: 319-362-7181; Fax: 319-369-9528.
Church: 1224 Fifth St. S.E., 52401.
Catechesis/Religious Program—Mary McEniry, D.R.E. Students 14.

CENTRAL CITY, LINN CO., ST. STEPHEN (1932) Rev. Wayne J. Droessler; Sr. Anne Kisting, O.S.F., Pastoral Min.
Res. & Mailing Address: 410 Terrace Dr., P.O. Box 496, 52214-0496. Tel: 319-438-6625.
Parish Office Address—211 3rd St. N., P.O. Box 47, Coggon, 52218-0047. Tel: 319-435-2236.
Church: 4700 Valley Farm Rd., 52214.
Catechesis/Religious Program—Marci Luedeman, C.R.E. Students 23.

CHARLES CITY, FLOYD CO., IMMACULATE CONCEPTION (1857) [CEM] Very Rev. Carl A. Ries; Sr. M. Diana Blong, P.B.V.M., Pastoral Assoc.
Church, Res. & Office: 106 Chapel Ln., 50616-2810. Tel: 641-228-1071; Fax: 641-228-1072.
School—(Grades PreSchool-6), 1203 Clark St., 50616. Tel: 641-228-1225; Fax: 641-228-7692. Mindy Hart, Prin. Lay Teachers 15; Students 198.
Catechesis/Religious Program—Wendy Wandro, Dir. Faith Formation. Students 135.

CHELSEA, TAMA CO., ST. JOSEPH (1867) [CEM] Very Rev. Michael J. Mescher; Deacon Joseph Behounek, Pastoral Assoc.; Laura Galvez, Hispanic Min. Co-ord.
Mailing Address: 900 Park St., Tama, 52339. Tel: 641-484-3039; Fax: 641-484-8039.
Church: 307 Station St., 52215.
Catechesis/Religious Program—Jackie Toennies, D.R.E. Students 22.

CHERRY MOUND, ALLAMAKEE CO., ST. PIUS ORATORY (1863) [CEM] Closed. Rev. Daniel J. Knipper (Retired).
Mailing Address: 1416 Great River Rd., Lansing, 52151. Tel: 563-586-2150. For sacramental records contact Immaculate Conception, Lansing.
Church: 699 State Forest Rd., Harpers Ferry, 52146.
Catechesis/Religious Program—Shari Curran, Dir. Faith Formation. Students 10.

CHESTER, HOWARD CO., ST. STEPHEN (1916) Closed. For sacramental records, contact Immaculate Conception, Elma.

CLARION, WRIGHT CO., ST. JOHN (1883) [CEM] Rev. Nils Hernandez; Deacons Michael Whitters; Pedro Garcia; Jerry Temeyer; Jo Ann Kramer, Pastoral Assoc.; Beatriz Garcia, Hispanic Ministry Coord.
Church and Mailing Address: 608 Second Ave., N.E., 50525. Tel: 515-532-3586; Fax: 515-532-2478.
Catechesis/Religious Program—Gloria Kisor, C.R.E. Students 134.

CLEAR LAKE, CERRO GORDO CO., ST. PATRICK (1901) Rev. John R. Tilp.
Church, Res. & Office: 1001 Ninth Ave. S., 50428-2615. Tel: 641-357-3214; Fax: 641-357-3210.
Catechesis/Religious Program—Ann Kunst, C.R.E. Students 128.

CLERMONT, FAYETTE CO., ST. PETER (1855) [CEM] Revs. James P. Brokman; Dale J. Rausch, Sacramental Priest.
Res.: 413 W. First St., Sumner, 50674-1313. Tel: 563-578-5366.
Church and Mailing Address: 608 Larrabee, P.O. Box 25, 52135-0025.
Catechesis/Religious Program—Mary Olson, D.R.E. Students 71.

CLUTIER, TAMA CO., IMMACULATE CONCEPTION ORATORY (1900) Closed. For sacramental records, contact St. Paul, Traer.

COGGON, LINN CO., ST. JOHN THE EVANGELIST (1912) [CEM] Rev. Wayne J. Droessler; Sr. Anne Kisting, O.S.F., Pastoral Assoc.
Mailing Address: 211 Third St. N., P.O. Box 47, 52218-0047. Tel: 319-435-2236; Fax: 319-435-2236.
Church: 211 Third St. N., 52218.
Catechesis/Religious Program—Pamela Klima, C.R.E. Students 53.

COLESBURG, DELAWARE CO., ST. PATRICK (1862) [CEM] Rev. Stephen A. Lundgren.
Mailing Address: 203 S. Locust, P.O. Box 365, Edgewood, 52042-0365. Tel: 563-928-7200.
Res.: 207 S. Locust, P.O. Box 365, Edgewood, 52042-0365. Tel: 563-928-6938.
Church: Delaware St., 52035.
Catechesis/Religious Program—Deanne Wulfekuhle, Dir. Faith Formation. Students 51.

COLO, STORY CO., ST. MARY, [CEM] Rev. Rick D. Dagit; Deacon Steven Van Kerckvoorde.
Res. & Mailing Address: 410 Bailey, P.O. Box 236, 50056-0236. Tel: 641-377-2710.
Church: 422 Fourth St., 50056.
Catechesis/Religious Program—Tracy Birchmier, C.R.E. Students 18.

CORWITH, HANCOCK CO., ST. MARY (1912) [CEM] Closed. For sacramental records, please contact St. Patrick, Britt.

CRESCO, HOWARD CO.

1—ASSUMPTION OF THE BLESSED VIRGIN MARY (1858) Closed. Merged with St. Joseph's, Cresco to form Notre Dame, Cresco. For sacramental records, please contact Notre Dame, Cresco.

2—ST. JOSEPH (1870) Closed. Merged with Assumption of the Blessed Virgin Mary, Cresco to form Notre Dame, Cresco. For sacramental records, please contact Notre Dame, Cresco.

3—NOTRE DAME (1999) [JC] Rev. Dennis H. Cahill; LeRoy Webb, Pastoral Min.
Mailing Address & Parish Office: 116 Third St. E., 52136. Tel: 563-547-3565; Fax: 563-547-3835.
Res.: 131 Third St. E., 52136. Tel: 563-547-5826.
Church: 223 2nd Ave. E., 52136.
School—(Grades PreSchool-6), 221 Second Ave. E., 52136. Tel: 563-547-4513. Wendy Schatz, Prin. Teachers 14; Students 172.
Catechesis/Religious Program—Pam Daley, C.R.E. Students 203.

DECORAH, WINNESHIEK CO., ST. BENEDICT (1864) [CEM] Rev. Phillip G. Gibbs; Deacon Nick Francois.
Church, Res. & Office: 307 W. Main St., 52101-1778. Tel: 563-382-9631; Fax: 563-382-6436.
School—(Grades PreSchool-8), 402 Rural Ave., 52101. Tel: 563-382-4668; Fax: 563-382-3193. Dana Holkesvik, Prin. Lay Teachers 14; Students 163.
Catechesis/Religious Program—June Francois, Dir. Faith Formation. Students 230.

DELHI, DELAWARE CO., ST. JOHN (1872) [CEM] Very Rev. John R. Kremer.
Office, Pastor's Res. & Mailing Address: 307 South St., P.O. Box 187, 52223-0187. Tel: 563-922-2251.
Church: 303 South St., 52223.
Catechesis/Religious Program—Linda Jay, D.R.E. Students 120.

DIKE, GRUNDY CO., ST. MARY (1880) Closed. Merged with Sacred Heart, Grundy Center; St. Patrick, Parkersburg; Queen of Heaven, Reinbeck to form Holy Family, Reinbeck. For sacramental records, contact Holy Family, Reinbeck.

DORCHESTER, ALLAMAKEE CO., ST. MARY (1865) [CEM] Rev. Joseph M. Schneider; Deacons Michael Ward, Pastoral Assoc.; Jeff Molitor.
Mailing Address: 109 2nd St., S.W., P.O. Box 146, Waukon, 52172. Tel: 563-568-3671; Fax: 563-568-4432.
Church: 590 Waterloo Creek Rd., 52140.
Catechesis/Religious Program—Michael Erickson, D.R.E. Students 29.

DOUGHERTY, CERRO GORDO CO., ST. PATRICK (1870) [CEM] Rev. Rodney M. Allers.
Res.: 305 Elm St., P.O. Box 30, Rockwell, 50469-0030. Tel: 641-822-4957.
Church, Parish Office & Mailing Address: 420 E. Patrick St., 50433. Tel: 641-794-3416.
Catechesis/Religious Program—Kim Staudt, C.R.E. Students 7.

DUMONT, BUTLER CO., ST. FRANCIS (1890) Closed. For sacramental records please contact St. Patrick, Hampton.

DUNCAN, HANCOCK CO., ST. WENCESLAUS (1900) [CEM] Revs. Dennis W. Miller; Paul E. Lippstock, Sacramental Priest; Deacon Dennis Popowski.
Mailing Address: 660 Bush Ave., Garner, 50438-1513. Tel: 641-923-2329; Fax: 641-923-2480.
Church: 2343 Navy Ave., Britt, 50423.
Catechesis/Religious Program—Rebecca Rolling, Dir. Faith Formation. Students 26.

DYERSVILLE, DUBUQUE CO., BASILICA OF ST. FRANCIS XAVIER (1859) [CEM] Revs. Dennis J. Quint; Noah J. Diehm; Deacons Fredrick J. Pins; James Steger; Cookie Scherrman, Pastoral Min.
Res. & Mailing Address: 104 Third St. S.W., 52040-1696. Tel: 563-875-7325; Fax: 563-875-8716.
Church: Second St. S.W., 52040.
Catechesis/Religious Program—Students 143.

DYSART, TAMA CO., ST. JOSEPH (1878) [CEM] Closed. For sacramental records, please contact St. Paul, Traer.

EAGLE CENTER, BLACKHAWK CO., ST. MARY OF MT. CARMEL (1859) [CEM] Rev. Jerry W. Blake.
Church & Mailing Address: 1435 E. Eagle Rd., Waterloo, 50701-9545. Tel: 319-342-3491; Fax: 319-342-3491.
Catechesis/Religious Program—Jeffrey Lumpa, D.R.E. Students 93.

EAGLE GROVE, WRIGHT CO., SACRED HEART (1882) [CEM] Rev. Nils Hernandez; Deacons Michael Whitters; Pedro Garcia; Jerry Temeyer, Pastoral Min.; Joann Kramer, Pastoral Assoc.; Beatriz Garcia, Hispanic Min. Coord.
Parish Office & Mailing Address: 221 S. Jackson Ave., 50533-2311. Tel: 515-603-4765; Fax: 515-603-6131.
Res.: 608 2nd Ave., N.E., Clarion, 50525.
Church: 201 S. Jackson Ave., 50533.
Catechesis/Religious Program—Michele Choquette, C.R.E. Students 88.

EARLVILLE, DELAWARE CO., ST. JOSEPH (1887) [CEM] Revs. Dennis J. Quint; Noah J. Diehm; Deacons James Steger; Fredrick J. Pins.
Mailing Address: 307 Mary St., 52041. Tel: 563-923-3135; Fax: 563-923-2096.
Church: 303 Mary St., 52041.
Res.: 104 3rd St. S.W., Dyersville, 52040-1696. Tel: 563-875-7325.
Catechesis/Religious Program—Joan Steger, Dir. Faith Formation. Students 98.

EDGEWOOD, DELAWARE CO., ST. MARK (1916) [CEM] Rev. Stephen A. Lundgren.
Church & Office: 203 S. Locust St., P.O. Box 365, 52042. Tel: 563-928-7200.
Res.: 207 S. Locust, P.O. Box 365, 52042. Tel: 563-928-6938.
Catechesis/Religious Program—Jody Kerns, Dir. Faith Formation. Students 157.

ELDORA, HARDIN CO., ST. MARY (1868) [CEM] Rev. Paul C. Baldwin; Sr. Connie Howe, R.S.M., Pastoral Assoc.
Church & Parish Office: 614 Washington, 50627-1257. Tel: 641-939-5545.
Res.: 415 Main St., P.O. Box 368, Iowa Falls, 50126-0368. Tel: 641-648-9547; Fax: 641-648-9562.
Catechesis/Religious Program—Gary Cashatt, D.R.E. Students 37.

ELKADER, CLAYTON CO., ST. JOSEPH (1844) [CEM] Very Rev. Paul R. Peters.
Church & Office: 330 First St., S.W., P.O. Box 626, 52043-0626. Tel: 563-245-2548; Fax: 563-245-2937.
Res.: Tel: 563-245-1325.
Catechesis/Religious Program—Jamie Wingert, C.R.E. Students 103.

ELMA, HOWARD CO., IMMACULATE CONCEPTION (1887) [CEM] Rev. Ray E. Atwood.
Parish Office, Pastor's Res. & Mailing Address: 203 Seventh St., 50628. Tel: 641-393-2520; Fax: 641-393-2069.
Church: 207 Seventh St., 50628.
Catechesis/Religious Program—Sheila Kobliska, D.R.E. Students 39.

EPWORTH, DUBUQUE CO., ST. PATRICK (1879) [CEM] Rev. Dennis R. Cain; Deacons James Kean; Gerald Koopmann; Joann Koopmann, Pastoral Assoc.
Parish Office & Mailing Address: 104 First St., S.E., P.O. Box 286, 52045-0286. Tel: 563-876-5540; Fax: 563-876-9062.
Res.: 22511 E. Pleasant Grove Rd., 52045. Tel: 563-876-5501.
Church: 102 1st St. S.E., 52045.
See Seton Catholic Schools, Farley under Elementary School Systems located in the Institution section.
Catechesis/Religious Program—Marilyn Connor Ryan, C.R.E. Students 144.

EVANSDALE, BLACKHAWK CO., ST. NICHOLAS (1951) Closed. Merged with St. Mary, St. John & St. Joseph, Waterloo to form Queen of Peace, Waterloo. For sacramental records, please contact Queen of Peace, Waterloo.

FAIRBANK, BUCHANAN CO., IMMACULATE CONCEPTION (1858) [CEM] Rev. Harry H. Koelker; Deacon Jim Patera.
Church, Office and Mailing Address: 302 W. Main St., P.O. Box 505, 50629. Tel: 319-635-2211.
Res.: 628 S. Frederick Ave., Oelwein, 50662. Tel: 319-283-9577.
Catechesis/Religious Program—Dan Cutsforth, D.R.E. Students 123.

FAIRFAX, LINN CO., ST. PATRICK ORATORY (1875) [CEM] Merged with John XXIII, Cedar Rapids to form Blessed John XXIII, Cedar Rapids. For sacramental records, contact Blessed John XXIII, Cedar Rapids.

FARLEY, DUBUQUE CO., ST. JOSEPH (1914) [CEM] Rev. Dennis R. Cain; Deacons James Kean; Gerald Koopmann; Sr. Sharon Kelchen, P.V.B.M., Pastoral Assoc.
Mailing Address: P.O. Box 67, 52046.
Office: 104 First St., S.E., P.O. Box 286, Epworth, 52045. Tel: 563-876-5540; Fax: 563-876-9062.
Res.: 22511 E. Pleasant Grove Rd., Epworth, 52045. Tel: 563-876-5501.
Church: 202 2nd Ave., S.E., 52046.
See Seton Catholic Schools, Farley under Elementary School Systems located in the Institution section.
Catechesis/Religious Program—Joann Koopmann, Dir. Faith Formation; Marian Bourek, C.R.E. Students 134.

FAYETTE, FAYETTE CO., ST. FRANCIS OF ASSISI (1879) [CEM] Revs. James P. Brokman; Dale J. Rausch, Sacramental Priest.
Mailing Address: P.O. Box 276, 52142-0276.
Office & Pastor's Res.: 413 W. First St., Sumner, 50674. Tel: 563-578-5366; Fax: 563-578-3286.
Church: 205 Lovers Ln., 52142.
Catechesis/Religious Program—Holly Streeter, D.R.E. Students 45.

FESTINA, WINNESHIEK CO., OUR LADY OF SEVEN DOLORS (1843) [CEM] Rev. Msgr. Cletus J. Hawes.
Mailing Address: 418 E. Main St., Ossian, 52161. Tel: 563-532-9366; Fax: 563-532-9353.
Church: 2348 County Rd. B 32, 52144-7701.
See Calmar-Festina-Spillville Catholic School, Calmar under Elementary School Systems located in the Institution section.
Catechesis/Religious Program—Patty Frana, C.R.E. Students 11.

FILLMORE, DUBUQUE CO., SACRED HEART (1890) [CEM] Rev. Douglas J. Loecke; Deacons Marvin Recker; Steven W. Strang; Ray Noonan; Joe Schockemoehl.
Parish Office: 408 Third Ave. N.W., Cascade, 52033. Tel: 563-852-3524.
Res.: 401 3rd Ave., N.W., P.O. Box 699, Cascade, 52033-0699. Tel: 563-852-7805.
Church: 19661 Sacred Heart Ln., Bernard, 52032.
See Aquin Educational System, Cascade under Consolidated K-12 Systems located in the Institution section.
Catechesis/Religious Program—Students 12.

FOREST CITY, WINNEBAGO CO., ST. JAMES (1870) [CEM] Revs. Dennis W. Miller; Paul E. Lippstock, Sacramental Priest; Deacon Dennis Popowski.
Church, Mailing & Parish Office Address: 906 W. O St., 50436. Tel: 641-585-4856; Fax: 641-585-3336.
Catechesis/Religious Program—Rita Kleemeier, Dir. Faith Formation. Students 77.

FORT ATKINSON, WINNESHIEK CO., ST. JOHN NEPOMUCENE (1875) [CEM] Rev. Nicholas B. March; Very Rev. Marvin C. Salz, Sacramental Priest; Tyler Wheeler, Pastoral Min.; Lynette Wheeler, Pastoral Min.
Office & Mailing Address: 110 Commercial Ave., P.O. Box 205, Protivin, 52163. Tel: 563-569-8259.
Church: 201 Oak St., 52144.
See Trinity Catholic School, Protovin under Elementary School Systems located in the Institution section.
Catechesis/Religious Program—Martin Ahrndt, Dir. Faith Formation. Students 41.

GARBER, CLAYTON CO., ST. MICHAEL (1917) [CEM] Closed. For sacramental records, please contact St. Joseph, Garnavillo.

GARNAVILLO, CLAYTON CO., ST. JOSEPH (1846) [CEM] Rev. Marvin J. Bries; Deacon James Pfaffly.
Mailing Address, Parish Office & Res.: 520 2nd St., P.O. Box 847, Guttenberg, 52052. Tel: 563-252-1247.
Church: 204 W. Oak St., 52049.
Catechesis/Religious Program—Lisa Robinson, D.R.E. Students 55.

GARNER, HANCOCK CO., ST. BONIFACE (1883) [CEM] Revs. Dennis W. Miller; Paul E. Lippstock, Sacramental Priest; Deacon Dennis Popowski.
Office & Res.: 660 Bush Ave., 50438-1513. Tel: 641-923-2329; Fax: 641-923-2480.
Church: 600 Bush Ave., 50438.
Catechesis/Religious Program—Rebecca Rolling, Dir. Faith Formation. Students 101.

GARRYOWEN, JACKSON CO., ST. PATRICK (1840) [CEM] Rev. Douglas J. Loecke; Deacons Steven W. Strang; Marvin Recker; Ray Noonan; Joe Schockemoehl; Jean Conrad, Pastoral Assoc.
Parish Office & Mailing Address: 408 3rd Ave., N.W., P.O. Box 699, Cascade, 52033-0699. Tel: 563-852-3524.
Church: 28914 46th Ave., Bernard, 52032-9289. Tel: 563-879-3303.
Res.: 401 3rd Ave., N.W., P.O. Box 699, Cascade, 52033-0699. Tel: 563-852-7805.
See Aquin Educational System, Cascade under Consolidated K-12 Systems located in the Institution section.
Catechesis/Religious Program—Rebecca Smith, D.R.E. Students 25.

GARWIN, TAMA CO., ST. BONIFACE (1884) Closed. For sacramental records, please contact St. Patrick Parish, Tama.

GENEVA, FRANKLIN CO., ST. PAUL, [CEM] Closed. For sacramental records, contact St. Mary, Ackley.

GILBERT, STORY CO., SS. PETER AND PAUL (1882) [CEM] Revs. Jon M. Seda; James W. Dubert.
Mailing Address: P.O. Box 327, 50105. Tel: 515-292-3810.
Res.: 2821 Bristol Dr., Ames, 50010. Tel: 515-292-1192.
Res.: 1504 Little Bluestem Ct., Ames, 50014-7830. Tel: 515-450-5598.
Church: 14238 500th Ave., 50105.
Catechesis/Religious Program—Tony Gustafson, Dir. Faith Formation. Students 80.

GILBERTVILLE, BLACKHAWK CO., IMMACULATE CONCEPTION (1875) [CEM] Rev. Henry P. Huber.
Office & Res.: 311 15th Ave., P.O. Box 136, 50634. Tel: 319-296-1092; Fax: 319-296-2087.
Church: 325 15th Ave., 50634-0136.
See Gilbertville-Raymond, Don Bosco High School, Gilbertville-Raymond Elementary under Consolidated K-12 Systems located in the Institution section.
Catechesis/Religious Program—Students 5.

GREELEY, DELAWARE CO., ST. JOSEPH (1870) [CEM] Closed. For sacramental records, contact St. Mary, Manchester.

GREEN ISLAND, JACKSON CO., SACRED HEART, Closed. For sacramental records, please contact St. Peter, Sabula.

GREENE, BUTLER CO., ST. MARY (1872) [CEM] Rev. Msgr. Walter L. Brunkan.
Church & Res.: 105 N. Main, P.O. Box 480, 50636-0480. Tel: 641-823-4146.
Catechesis/Religious Program—Sherilyn Backer, D.R.E. Students 90.

GRUNDY CENTER, GRUNDY CO., SACRED HEART (1885) Closed. Merged with St. Mary, Dike, St. Patrick, Parkersburg & Queen of Heaven, Reinbeck to form Holy Family, Reinbeck. For sacramental records, contact Holy Family, Reinbeck.

GUTTENBERG, CLAYTON CO., ST. MARY (1851) [CEM] Rev. Marvin J. Bries; Deacon James Pfaffly.
Res. & Office: 520 S. Second St., P.O. Box 847, 52052-0847. Tel: 563-252-1247; Fax: 563-252-1363.
Church: 520 S. 2nd St., 52052.
See St. Mary and Immaculate Conception School System, Guttenberg under Elementary School Systems located in the Institution section.
Catechesis/Religious Program—Becky Pfaffly, D.R.E. Students 80.

HAMPTON, FRANKLIN CO., ST. PATRICK (1870) Very Rev. Bernard C. Grady.
Res.: 2 19th Ave. N.E., 50441. Tel: 641-456-3406.
Church & Parish Office: 1405 N. Federal, 50441-1005. Tel: 641-456-4857.
Catechesis/Religious Program—Jolene Harms, Dir. Faith Formation. Students 120.

HANOVER, ALLAMAKEE CO., ST. MARY (1875) [CEM] Rev. Joseph M. Schneider; Deacons Michael Ward; Jeff Molitor.
Mailing Address: *c/o St. Patrick Parish*, 109 Second St. S.W., P.O. Box 146, Waukon, 52172-0146. Tel: 563-568-3671; Fax: 563-568-4432.
Church: 2096 Hwy. 76, Waukon, 52172.
Catechesis/Religious Program—Jackie Johnson, Dir. Faith Formation. Students 13.

HARPERS FERRY, ALLAMAKEE CO., ST. ANN-ST. JOSEPH (1855) [CEM] Rev. John A. Moser.
Res. & Mailing Address: Immaculate Conception (Wexford), 1416 Great River Rd., Lansing, 52151-7519. Tel: 563-586-2150.
Church: 307 W. Orange, Harper's Ferry, 52146.
Catechesis/Religious Program—Shari Curran, Dir. Faith Formation. Students 34.

HAVERHILL, MARSHALL CO., IMMACULATE CONCEPTION ORATORY (1877) Closed. For sacramental records, contact St. Henry, Marshalltown.

HAWKEYE, FAYETTE CO., ST. FRANCIS XAVIER (1891) Closed. For sacramental records, contact Immaculate Conception, Sumner.

HAZLETON, BUCHANAN CO., ST. MARY (1881) [CEM] Closed. For sacramental records, contact Sacred Heart, Oelwein.

HIAWATHA, LINN CO., ST. ELIZABETH ANN SETON PARISH (1989) [JC] Rev. Neil J. Manternach; Deacon Dennis Mulherin; Sr. Annette Kestel, P.B.V.M., Pastoral Assoc.; Tricia Lokmer, Pastoral Assoc.
Church & Office: 1350 Lyndhurst Dr., 52233. Tel: 319-393-3778; Fax: 319-393-7165.
Res.: 1385 Lyndhurst Dr., 52233. Tel: 319-393-2646.
See St. Pius and St. Elizabeth Ann Seton Schools under Elementary School Systems located in the Institution section.

Catechesis/Religious Program—Tricia Lokmer, Dir. Faith Formation. Students 469.

HOLY CROSS, DUBUQUE CO., HOLY CROSS (1845) [CEM] Rev. Raymond A. Burkle.
Church & Office: 875 Church St., P.O. Box 398, 52053. Tel: 563-870-4041.
Res.: 103 S. Andres St., P.O. Box 140, Luxemburg, 52056. Tel: 563-853-3369.
See LaSalle Elementary Schools, Holy Cross under Elementary School Systems located in the Institution section.
Catechesis/Religious Program—Brian Nilles, C.R.E. Students 23.

HOPKINTON, DELAWARE CO., ST. LUKE (1922) Very Rev. John R. Kremer.
Office & Mailing Address: 206 First St., S.E., P.O. Box 159, 52237-0159. Tel: 563-926-2613.
Res.: 307 South St., P.O. Box 187, Delhi, 52223. Tel: 563-922-2251.
Church: 206 First St. S.E., 52237.
Catechesis/Religious Program—Patricia Hucker, D.R.E. Students 61.

INDEPENDENCE, BUCHANAN CO., ST. JOHN THE EVANGELIST (1856) [CEM] Rev. Donald J. Plamondon; Deacon Tim Post; Sharon Bainbridge, Pastoral Assoc.
Church, Res. & Office: 209 Fifth Ave. N.E., 50644-1998. Tel: 319-334-7191; Fax: 319-334-7192.
School—(Grades PreSchool-8), 314 Third St., NE, 50644. Tel: 319-334-7173; Fax: 319-334-9088. Justin Nosbisch, Prin. Lay Teachers 12; Students 193.
Catechesis/Religious Program—Sharon Bainbridge, C.R.E. Students 213.

IONIA, CHICKASAW CO., ST. BONIFACE (1899) [CEM] Rev. Mark Osterhaus; Deacon Victor J. DeSloover; Sr. Jeanne Tranel, O.P., Pastoral Assoc. & Hispanic Min. Coord.; Christine Carrier, Pastoral Assoc.
Parish Office & Mailing Address: 313 W. Ct. St., New Hampton, 50659.
Pastor's Res.: 202 N. Broadway, New Hampton, 50659. Tel: 641-394-2105.
Church: 204 E. Prairie, 50645.
Catechesis/Religious Program—Christine Carrier, D.R.E.; Karen Bonfig, C.R.E. Students 22.

IOWA FALLS, HARDIN CO., ST. MARK (1855) [CEM] Rev. Paul C. Baldwin; Sr. Connie Howe, R.S.M., Pastoral Assoc.
Church, Res. & Office: 415 Main St., P.O. Box 368, 50126-0368. Tel: 641-648-9547; Fax: 641-648-9562.
Catechesis/Religious Program—Brenda Koppes, C.R.E. Students 53.

JESUP, BUCHANAN CO., ST. ATHANASIUS (1880) [CEM] Rev. Kenneth C. Stecher; Sr. Donna Burke, O.S.F., Pastoral Assoc.
Res. & Mailing Address: 635 Stevens St., P.O. Box 316, 50648-0316. Tel: 319-827-3003; Fax: 319-827-1124.
Church: 623 Stevens St., 50648.
School—(Grades K-8), 641 Stevens St., P.O. Box 288, 50648-0288. Tel: 319-827-1314. Ray Pechous, Prin. Lay Teachers 10; Students 63.
Catechesis/Religious Program—Carla Even, C.R.E. Students 98.

JEWELL, HAMILTON CO., GOOD SHEPHERD (1915) Closed. For sacramental records, contact St. Cecelia, Ames.

KEY WEST, DUBUQUE CO., ST. JOSEPH (1872) Rev. Donald V. Bakewell; Deacon Tom Lang.
Office & Res.: 10204 Key West Dr., 52003-8936. Tel: 563-582-7392; Fax: 563-582-7392.
Church: 10270 Key West Dr., 52003.
See Holy Family Catholic Schools under Consolidated K-12 Systems located in the Institution Section.
Catechesis/Religious Program—Linda Frommelt, D.R.E. Students 163.

LA MOTTE, JACKSON CO., HOLY ROSARY (1893) [CEM] Closed. For sacramental records please contact Sacred Heart, Maquoketa.

LA PORTE CITY, BLACKHAWK CO., SACRED HEART (1887) Rev. Jerry W. Blake.
Mailing Address, Church & Parish Office: 1021 Poplar St., 50651. Tel: 319-342-2991.
Res.: 1102 Walnut St., Traer, 50675. Tel: 319-478-2222.
Catechesis/Religious Program—Jeffrey Lumpa, D.R.E. Students 107.

LAKE MILLS, WINNEBAGO CO., ST. PATRICK (1870) [CEM] Revs. Dennis W. Miller; Paul E. Lippstock, Sacramental Priest; Deacon Dennis Popowski.
Mailing Address: 906 W O St., Forest City, 50436-1131. Tel: 641-585-4856; Fax: 641-585-3336.
Church: 406 S. Grant St., 50450.
Catechesis/Religious Program—Carla Langfald, Dir. Faith Formation. Students 29.

LAMONT, BUCHANAN CO., ST. MARY (1894) [CEM] Closed. For sacramental records, contact St. Mary, Strawberry Point.

LANSING, ALLAMAKEE CO., IMMACULATE CONCEPTION (1855) [CEM] Rev. John A. Moser; Karen Weber, Pastoral Min.
Church, Res. & Office: 648 Main St., 52151. Tel: 563-538-4171.
Catechesis/Religious Program—Rita Mooney, Dir. Faith Formation. Students 65.

LATTNERVILLE, DUBUQUE CO., ANNUNCIATION ORATORY, Closed. Parish closed. For sacramental records, contact St. John the Baptist, Peosta.

LAWLER, CHICKASAW CO., OUR LADY OF MT. CARMEL (1869) [CEM] Rev. Nicholas B. March; Very Rev. Marvin C. Salz, Sacramental Priest; Tyler Wheeler, Pastoral Min.; Lynette Wheeler, Pastoral Min.
Church, Mailing Address & Parish Office: 3040 Iowa Hwy. 24, P.O. Box 119, 52154. Tel: 563-238-3444.
Res.: 110 Commercial Ave., P.O. Box 205, Protivin, 52163-0205. Tel: 563-569-8259.
Catechesis/Religious Program—Martin Ahrndt, Dir. Faith Formation. Students 44.

LITTLE TURKEY, CHICKASAW CO., ASSUMPTION OF THE B.V.M. (1902) [CEM] Rev. Nicholas B. March; Very Rev. Marvin C. Salz, Sacramental Priest; Tyler Wheeler, Pastoral Min.; Lynette Wheeler, Pastoral Min.
Office, Res. & Mailing Address: 110 Commercial Ave., P.O. Box 205, Protivin, 52163. Tel: 563-569-8259.
Church: 3303 160th St., Lawler, 52154.
Catechesis/Religious Program—Martin Ahrndt, Dir. Faith Formation. Students 34.

LITTLEPORT, CLAYTON CO., SACRED HEART, [CEM] Closed. For sacramental records, please contact St. Joseph, Garnavillo.

LOURDES, HOWARD CO., OUR LADY OF LOURDES (1875) [CEM] Rev. Ray E. Atwood.
Office, Res. & Mailing Address: 203 7th St., Elma, 50628. Tel: 641-393-2520; Fax: 641-393-2069.
Church: 14068 175th St., Elma, 50628.
Catechesis/Religious Program—Sheila Kobliska, D.R.E. Students 29.

LUXEMBURG, DUBUQUE CO., HOLY TRINITY (1865) [CEM] Rev. Raymond A. Burkle.
Office & Mailing Address: 875 Church St., P.O. Box 398, Holy Cross, 52053. Tel: 563-870-4041.
Church & Rectory: 103 S. Andres St., 52056. Tel: 563-853-3369.
See LaSalle Elementary Schools, Holy Cross under Elementary School Systems located in the Institution section.
Catechesis/Religious Program—Brian Nilles, C.R.E. Students 17.

LYCURGUS, ALLAMAKEE CO., ST. MARY ORATORY (1859) Closed. For sacramental records please contact St. Patrick, Waukon.

MANCHESTER, DELAWARE CO., ST. MARY (1872) [CEM] Revs. John R. Flaherty; Richard G. Gaul, Sacramental Priest; Deacon Dave Loecke.
Church, Res. & Office: 119 W. Fayette St., 52057-1596. Tel: 563-927-4710; Fax: 563-927-9949.
School—(Grades K-6), 132 W. Butler, 52057-1502. Tel: 563-927-3689; Fax: 563-927-1437. Vicki Palmer, Prin. Sisters 1; Lay Teachers 13; Students 161.
Catechesis/Religious Program—Kathy Oberrueter, Dir. Faith Formation. Students 298.

MANLY, WORTH CO., SACRED HEART (1883) [CEM] Rev. Michael G. Schueller; Deacons Matthew F. Berry; Charles Cooper; Michael Romig, Pastoral Min.
Res. & Office: 120 E. North, P.O. Box 160, 50456-0160. Tel: 641-454-2586.
Church: 412 N. Broadway, 50456.
Catechesis/Religious Program—Kelley O'Keefe, C.R.E. Students 48.

MAQUOKETA, JACKSON CO., SACRED HEART (1873) [CEM] Rev. Donald A. Hertges; Deacon Robert Head; Phyllis Koschmeder, Pastoral Assoc.; Sr. Helen Stejskal, S.S.N.D., Pastoral Min.
Church, Res. & Office: 200 S. Vermont St., 52060-0635. Tel: 563-652-6931; Fax: 563-652-6931.
School—(Grades PreK-6), 806 Eddy St., 52060. Tel: 563-652-3743; Fax: 563-652-2698. Angela Ruley, Prin. Lay Teachers 10; Students 110.
Catechesis/Religious Program—Sr. Helen Stejskal, S.S.N.D., D.R.E. Students 107.

MARION, LINN CO., ST. JOSEPH (1890) [JC] Very Rev. John A. Gossman; Rev. Anthony J. Kruse; Rodney Bluml, Pastoral Assoc.; Mary Hauschildt, Pastoral Min.
Res.: 1483 14th St., 52302. Tel: 319-377-2605.
Church & Office: 1790 14th St., 52302-2267. Tel: 319-377-4869; Fax: 319-377-9043.
School—(Grades PreSchool-8), 1430 14th St., 52302-2499. Tel: 319-377-6348; Fax: 319-377-9358. Cathy Walz, Prin. Lay Teachers 15; Students 152.
Catechesis/Religious Program—Rodney Bluml, Dir. Faith Formation; Elizabeth Lockhart, D.R.E. Students 575.

MARSHALLTOWN, MARSHALL CO.
1—ST. HENRY (1959) Rev. Donald J. Czapla; Deacons Roger Polt; Gary Pusillo; Karen Mroz, Pastoral Min.
Church & Parish Office: 221 W. Olive St., 50158-4248. Tel: 641-753-7374; Fax: 641-753-1499.
Res.: 1610 Crestview Dr., 50158. Tel: 641-752-2043.
See Marshalltown Area Catholic Schools, Marshalltown under Elementary School Systems located in the Institution section.
Catechesis/Religious Program—Patty Cook, Dir. Faith Formation. Students 146.
2—ST. MARY (1869) Rev. James L. Miller; Deacons Jeff Harris; Felix Hernandez; Tom Renze; Sr. Christine Feagan, O.P., Coord. Hispanic Ministry.
Office & Res.: 9 W. Linn St., 50158. Tel: 641-753-6278; Fax: 641-753-1279.
Church: 11 W. Linn St., 50158.
See Marshalltown Area Catholic Schools, Marshalltown under Elementary School Systems located in the Institution section.
Catechesis/Religious Program—Jeannine Grady, D.R.E. Students 230.

MASON CITY, CERRO GORDO CO.
1—HOLY FAMILY (1908) Rev. Michael G. Schueller; Deacons Matthew F. Berry; Charles Cooper; Lisa Paloma, Pastoral Min.
Church: 716 N. Adams St., 50401.
Res. & Office: 714 N. Adams St., 50401-2199. Tel: 641-423-7301; Fax: 641-423-7663.
See Newman Catholic School System, Mason City under Consolidated K-12 Systems located in the Institution section.
Catechesis/Religious Program—Jennifer Clancy, D.R.E. Students 64.
2—ST. JOSEPH (1873) Rev. Craig E. Steimel; Deacon Michael G. Byrne; Karen Byrne, Pastoral Assoc.; Patricia Dixon, Pastoral Min.
Res.: 507 4th St., S.E., 50401. Tel: 641-424-3940.
Church & Parish Office: 302 Fifth St. S.E., 50401-4005. Tel: 641-423-5001; Fax: 641-423-8553.
See Newman Catholic School System, Mason City under Consolidated K-12 Systems located in the Institution section.
Catechesis/Religious Program—Jennifer Clancy, Dir. Faith Formation. Students 144.

MASONVILLE, DELAWARE CO., IMMACULATE CONCEPTION (1883) [CEM] Revs. John R. Flaherty; Richard G. Gaul, Sacramental Priest; Deacon Dave Loecke.
Mailing Address & Office: 119 W. Fayette St., Manchester, 52057. Tel: 563-927-4710; Fax: 563-927-9949.
Church: 606 Bernhart St., 50654.
Catechesis/Religious Program—Kathy Oberrueter, Dir. Faith Formation. Students 28.

MCGREGOR, CLAYTON CO., ST. MARY (1873) [CEM] Rev. Greg E. Bahl; Deacon Patrick J. Malanaphy.
Office: 405 S. East St., P.O. Box U, Monona, 52159. Tel: 563-539-4442; Fax: 563-539-4383.
Church: 311 Seventh St., 52157.
Catechesis/Religious Program—Nancy Hammes, C.R.E. Students 58.

MCINTIRE, MITCHELL CO., ST. MEL, Closed. For sacramental records, please contact Sacred Heart, Osage.

MEYER, MITCHELL CO., SACRED HEART ORATORY (1900) [CEM] Closed. Parish closed. For sacramental records, please contact, Sacred Heart, Osage.

MONONA, CLAYTON CO., ST. PATRICK (1856) [CEM] Rev. Greg E. Bahl; Deacon Patrick J. Malanaphy, Pastoral Admin.
Office & Mailing Address: 405 East St. S., P.O. Box U, 52159-0557. Tel: 563-539-4442; Fax: 563-539-4383.
Church: 405 S. East St., 52159.
Catechesis/Religious Program—Carla Pester, D.R.E. Students 90.

MONTI, BUCHANAN CO., ST. PATRICK ORATORY (1855) [CEM] Closed. For sacramental records, contact, St. John the Evangelist, Independence.

MONTICELLO, JONES CO., SACRED HEART (1868) [CEM] Rev. Keith L. Birch; Antoinette Muller, Pastoral Min.
Office: 210 E. Third St., 52310-1535. Tel: 319-465-5944; Fax: 319-465-7065.
Res.: 410 N. Maple St., Unit #301, 52310. Tel: 319-465-3034.
Church: 312 N. Sycamore, 52310.
School—(Grades PreSchool-6), 234 N. Sycamore, 52310-1515. Tel: 319-465-4605; Fax: 319-465-6183. Jim Zimmerman, Prin. Lay Teachers 10; Students 161.
Catechesis/Religious Program—Leanna Manternach, C.R.E. Students 184.

MOUNT VERNON, LINN CO., ST. JOHN THE BAPTIST (1843) [CEM] Susan M. Schettler, Parish Life Coord.; Very Rev. John A. Gossman, Priest Supvr. In Res., Rev. Phillip E. Schmitt (Retired).
Church & Office: 212 7th St. S.E., P.O. Box 169, 52314-0169. Tel: 319-895-6246; Fax: 319-895-0973.
Catechesis/Religious Program—Linda Hamsmeier, Dir. Faith Formation. Students 235.

NASHUA, CHICKASAW CO., ST. MICHAEL (1870) [CEM] Very Rev. Carl A. Ries; Dick Baldwin, Parish Coord.; Sue Baldwin, Parish Coord.
Mailing Address & Parish Office: 612 Cedar St., P.O. Box 308, 50658-0308. Tel: 641-435-2070.

Res.: 106 Chapel Ln., Charles City, 50616. Tel: 641-228-1071.
Church: 602 Cedar St., 50658.
Catechesis/Religious Program—Jessica Huck, C.R.E. Students 46.

NEVADA, STORY CO., ST. PATRICK (1870) [CEM] Rev. Rick D. Dagit; Deacon Steven Van Kerckvoorde.
Parish Office: 1110 11th St., 50201. Tel: 515-382-2974.
Res. and Mailing Address: 410 Bailey St., P.O. Box 236, Colo, 50056-0236. Tel: 641-377-2710.
Church: 1127 Tenth St., 50201.
Catechesis/Religious Program—Barb Kuebler, Dir. Faith Formation. Students 177.

NEW ALBIN, ALLAMAKEE CO., ST. JOSEPH (1910) [CEM] Rev. John A. Moser; Karen Weber, Pastoral Min.
Parish Office, Res. & Mailing Address: 648 Main St., Lansing, 52151. Tel: 563-538-4171.
Church: 154 Third St. N.E., Lansing, 52151.
Catechesis/Religious Program—Rita Mooney, Dir. Faith Formation. Students 31.

NEW HAMPTON, CHICKASAW CO.

1—HOLY FAMILY (2002) [CEM] Rev. Mark Osterhaus; Deacon Victor J. DeSloover; Christine Carrier, Pastoral Assoc.; Sr. Jeanne Tranel, O.P., Pastoral Assoc. & Hispanic Min. Coord.
Parish Office & Mailing Address: 313 W. Ct. St., 50659. Tel: 641-394-2105; Fax: 641-394-5154.
Churches:—St. Joseph, 202 N. Broadway, 50659.
St. Mary, 239 S. Walnut Ave., 50659.
School—(Grades PreSchool-8), 216 N. Broadway, 50659. Tel: 641-394-2865. Beth Wright, Prin. Lay Teachers 15; Students 179.
Catechesis/Religious Program—Karen Bonfig, C.R.E. Students 193.

2—ST. JOSEPH (1870) Closed. Merged with St. Mary, New Hampton to form Holy Family, New Hampton. For sacramental records, contact Holy Family, New Hampton.

3—ST. MARY (1894) Closed. Merged with St. Joseph, New Hampton to form Holy Family, New Hampton.; Sacramental records are located at Holy Family, New Hampton.

NEW HARTFORD, BUTLER CO., ST. JOSEPH, Closed. For sacramental records, contact Holy Family, Reinbeck.

NEW HAVEN, MITCHELL CO., ST. PETER (1876) [CEM] Rev. Ray E. Atwood.
Mailing Address, Res. & Office: 203 7th St., Elma, 50628. Tel: 641-393-2520; Fax: 641-393-2069.
Church: 2985 360th St., Osage, 50461.
Catechesis/Religious Program—Meg Schutjer, Dir. Faith Formation. Students 62.

NEW MELLERAY, DUBUQUE CO., HOLY FAMILY (1850) [CEM] Rev. Michael J. Podhajsky.
Office & Mailing Address: 10204 Key W. Dr., Apt B, 52003. Tel: 563-845-0600.
Church: 16500 Holy Family Ln., Peosta, 52068.
Catechesis/Religious Program—Kay Goedken, Dir. Faith Formation. Students 108.

NEW VIENNA, DUBUQUE CO, ST. BONIFACE (1845) [CEM] Revs. John J. O'Connor; Noah J. Diehm; Deacons Fredrick J. Pins; James Steger.
Parish Office, Church, Res. & Mailing Address: 7401 Columbus St., P.O. Box 215, 52065. Tel: 563-921-2465; Fax: 563-921-3003.
See Archbishop Hennessy Catholic School, New Vienna under Elementary School Systems located in the Institution section.
Catechesis/Religious Program—Michelle Klas, Dir. Faith Formation. Students 10.

NEWHALL, BENTON CO., ST. PAUL (1914) Rev. Brian M. Dellaert; Deacon Robert F. Hurych.
Office & Mailing Address: 405 Fourth Ave., P.O. Box 250, Van Horne, 52346-0250. Tel: 319-228-8131; Fax: 319-228-8800.
Res.: 512 Evergreen St., P.O. Box 89, Norway, 52318-0089. Tel: 319-227-7169.
Church: 303 Third St. E., 52315.
Catechesis/Religious Program—Students 58.

NORTH BUENA VISTA, CLAYTON CO., IMMACULATE CONCEPTION (1898) [CEM] Rev. Marvin J. Bries; Deacon James Pfaffly.
Mailing Address & Office: 520 S. 2nd St., P.O. Box 847, Guttenberg, 52052-0847. Tel: 563-252-1247.
Church: 218 Main St., 52066.
See St. Mary & Immaculate Conception School System, Guttenberg under Elementary School Systems located in the Institution Section
Catechesis/Religious Program—Students 9.

NORTH WASHINGTON, CHICKASAW CO., IMMACULATE CONCEPTION (1868) [CEM] Rev. Mark Osterhaus; Deacon Victor J. DeSloover; Sr. Jeanne Tranel, O.P., Pastoral Assoc. & Hispanic Min. Coord.; Christine Carrier, Pastoral Assoc.
Mailing & Office Address: 313 W. Court St., New Hampton, 50659. Tel: 641-394-2105; Fax: 641-394-5154.
Church: 114 N. Wapsie St., 50661.
Catechesis/Religious Program—Karen Bonfig, C.R.E. Students 34.

NORWAY, BENTON CO., ST. MICHAEL (1867) [CEM] Rev. Brian M. Dellaert; Deacon Robert F. Hurych.
Office, & Mailing Address: 405 Fourth Ave., P.O. Box 250, Van Horne, 52346-0250. Tel: 319-228-8131; Fax: 319-228-8800.
Church & Pastor's Res.: 512 Evergreen, 52318. Tel: 319-227-7169.
Catechesis/Religious Program—Students 82.

OELWEIN, FAYETTE CO., SACRED HEART (1876) [CEM] Rev. Harry H. Koelker; Deacon Jim Patera; Carol Hamilton, Pastoral Assoc.
Res.: 628 S. Frederick Ave., 50662. Tel: 319-283-9577.
Parish Office & Mailing Address: 600 1st Ave. S.W., 50662. Tel: 319-283-3743.
School—(Grades PreSchool-6), 601 First Ave., S.W., 50662. Tel: 319-283-1366; Fax: 319-283-5279. Deacon Jim Patera, Prin. Deacons 1; Lay Teachers 9; Students 141.
Catechesis/Religious Program—Craig Sanger, Dir. Faith Formation. Students 126.

OSAGE, MITCHELL CO., SACRED HEART (1878) [CEM] Rev. Jack H. McClure, C.PP.S.; Sr. Millie Leuenberger, O.S.F., Pastoral Assoc.
Office: 1209 State St., 50461. Tel: 641-732-4342; Fax: 641-832-2447.
Res.: 506 S. Randolph, Stacyville, 50476. Tel: 641-732-4509.
Church: 1204 State St., 50461.
School—(Grades PreSchool-6), 218 S. 12th St., 50461-1725. Tel: 641-732-5221; Fax: 641-732-3248. Kim Weigle, Headmistress. Lay Teachers 7; Students 67.
Catechesis/Religious Program—Barbara Brumm, D.R.E. Students 146.

OSSIAN, WINNESHIEK CO., ST. FRANCIS DE SALES (1876) [CEM] Rev. Msgr. Cletus J. Hawes.
Res. & Office: 418 E. Main St., 52161-9998. Tel: 563-532-9366.
Church: 420 E. Main St., 52161.
School—(Grades Day Care-8), 414 E. Main St., 52161. Tel: 563-532-9352; Fax: 563-532-9353. Mae Becker, Prin. Lay Teachers 10; Students 106.
Catechesis/Religious Program—Patricia Frana, C.R.E. Students 67.

OTTER CREEK, JACKSON CO., ST. LAWRENCE (1854) [CEM] Rev. Donald A. Hertges; Deacon Robert Head. In Res., Rev. Richard J. Ament.
Parish Office, Res. & Mailing Address: 200 S. Vermont, Maquoketa, 52060. Tel: 563-652-6931.
Church: 17434 Bellevue-Cascade Rd., Zwingle, 52079.
Catechesis/Religious Program—Sr. Helen Stejskal, S.S.N.D., C.R.E. Students 5.

OXFORD JUNCTION, JONES CO., SACRED HEART (1890) Rev. Gregory A. Steckel (DAV), Parochial Admin.
Office, Res. & Mailing Address: P.O. Box 178, 52323. Tel: 563-826-2611.
Church: 301 Church St., 52323.
Catechesis/Religious Program—Dena Jensen, D.R.E. Students 24.

PARKERSBURG, BUTLER CO., ST. PATRICK, Closed. Merged with St. Mary, Dike, Sacred Heart, Grundy Center & Queen of Heaven, Reinbeck to form Holy Family, Reinbeck. For sacramental records, contact Holy Family, Reinbeck.

PEOSTA, DUBUQUE CO., ST. JOHN THE BAPTIST CHURCH OF PEOSTA, IOWA (1874) [CEM] Rev. Richard W. Kuhn; Sr. Mary Kent Pearson, O.P., Pastoral Assoc.
Mailing Address & Office: 241 Peosta St., 52068-9507. Tel: 563-582-4217; Fax: 563-582-4217.
Res.: 476 Lezlie Dr., Apt. 1, 52068. Tel: 563-582-2821.
Church: 235 Peosta St., 52068.
See Seton Catholic Schools, Farley under Elementary School Systems located in the Institution section.
Catechesis/Religious Program—Marybeth Wagner, D.R.E. Students 218.

PETERSBURG, SS. PETER AND PAUL (1867) [CEM] Revs. John J. O'Connor; Noah J. Diehm; Deacons Frederick J. Pins; James Steger.
Res.: 7401 Columbus St., P.O. Box 215, New Vienna, 52065. Tel: 563-921-2465.
Church & Mailing Address: 1625 300th Ave., Dyersville, 52040. Tel: 563-875-7992.
See Archbishop Hennessy Catholic School, New Vienna under Elementary School Systems located in the Institution section.
Catechesis/Religious Program—Students 5.

PINHOOK, ST. BRIDGET ORATORY, [CEM] Closed. For sacramental Records, contact Immaculate Conception, Sumner.

PLACID, DUBUQUE CO., ST. JOHN (1874) [CEM] Rev. Dennis R. Cain; Deacons Gerald Koopmann; James Kean; Joann Koopmann, Pastoral Assoc.
Office: 104 First St., S.E., P.O. Box 286, Epworth, 52045. Tel: 563-876-5540; Fax: 563-876-9062.
Church & Res.: 22511 E. Pleasant Grove Rd., Epworth, 52045. Tel: 563-876-5501.
See Seton Catholic Schools, Farley under Elementary School Systems located in the Institution section.
Catechesis/Religious Program—Marilyn Connor Ryan, D.R.E. Students 22.

PLYMOUTH ROCK, WINNESHIEK CO., ST. AGNES ORATORY (1857) [CEM] Closed. For sacramental records, contact Notre Dame, Cresco.

PLYMOUTH, CERRO GORDO CO., ST. MICHAEL, Closed. For sacramental records, contact Sacred Heart, Manly.

POSTVILLE, ALLAMAKEE CO., ST. BRIDGET (1872) Rev. Greg E. Bahl; Deacon Patrick J. Malanaphy.
405 S. East St., P.O. Box U, Monona, 52159-0557.
Parish Office: 135 W. Williams St., P.O. Box 369, 52162-0369. Tel: 563-864-3138; Fax: 563-864-7000.
Church: 141 W. Williams St., 52162.
Catechesis/Religious Program—Barbara Drahos, C.R.E. Students 59.

PRAIRIE, DUBUQUE CO., ST. JOSEPH, [CEM] Closed. For parish records, contact St. John the Baptist, Peosta.

PRAIRIEBURG, LINN CO., ST. JOSEPH (1874) [CEM] Rev. Wayne J. Droessler; Sr. Anne Kisting, O.S.F., Pastoral Min.
Parish Office & Mailing Address: 211 3rd St. N., P.O. Box 47, Coggon, 52218-0047. Tel: 319-435-2236; Fax: 319-435-2236.
Res.: 410 Terrace Dr., P.O. Box 496, Central City, 52214-0496. Tel: 319-438-6625.
Church: 300 West Ave., 52219.
Catechesis/Religious Program—Marci Luedeman, C.R.E. Students 20.

PRESTON, JACKSON CO., ST. JOSEPH (1881) [CEM] Rev. Donald A. Hertges; Deacon Robert Head; Phyllis Koschmeder, Pastoral Assoc.
Church, Res. & Mailing Address: 250 S. Faith St., P.O. Box 309, 52069-0309. Tel: 563-689-5161.
Catechesis/Religious Program—Irene Entsminger, D.R.E.; Rosemary Sievers, C.R.E. Students 175.

PROTIVIN, HOWARD CO., HOLY TRINITY (1878) [CEM] Rev. Nicholas B. March; Very Rev. Marvin C. Salz, Sacramental Priest; Tyler Wheeler, Pastoral Min.; Lynette Wheeler, Pastoral Min.
Res. & Mailing Address: 110 Commercial Ave., P.O. Box 205, 52163-0205. Tel: 563-569-8259.
Church: 124 N. Main St., 52163.
See Trinity Catholic School, Protovin under Elementary School Systems located in the Institution Section.
Catechesis/Religious Program—Martin Ahrndt, Dir. Faith Formation. Students 31.

RAYMOND, BLACKHAWK CO., ST. JOSEPH (1905) [CEM] Rev. Henry P. Huber.
Res., Office & Mailing Address: 311 15th Ave., P.O. Box 136, Gilbertville, 50634. Tel: 319-296-1092; Fax: 319-296-2087.
Church: 313 E. Central St., 50667.
See Gilbertville-Raymond, Don Bosco High School, Gilbertville-Raymond Elementary under Consolidated K-12 Systems located in the Institution section.
Catechesis/Religious Program—Students 3.

REILLY SETTLEMENT, CHICKASAW CO., SACRED HEART, [CEM] Closed. For sacramental records, please contact Holy Trinity, Protivin.

REINBECK, GRUNDY CO.

1—HOLY FAMILY CHURCH, REINBECK, IOWA (2004) Rev. David G. Kucera; Deacons Greg Lievens; John Schwennen.
Office & Mailing Address: 21275 U Ave., 50669. Tel: 319-345-2006; Fax: 319-345-2006.
Res.: 702 Grant St., Parkersburg, 50665.
Worship Sites—
St. Patrick—304 Second St., Parkersburg, 50665.
St. Gabriel Church—21275 U Ave., 50669.
Catechesis/Religious Program—Alyssa Sealman, C.R.E. Students 164.

2—QUEEN OF HEAVEN (1958) Closed. Merged with St. Mary, Dike, Sacred Heart, Grundy Center & St. Patrick, Parkersburg to form Holy Family, Reinbeck. For sacramental records, contact Holy Family, Reinbeck.

RHODES, MARSHALL CO., ST. JOSEPH, [CEM] Closed. For sacramental records, please contact St. Joseph, State Center.

RICEVILLE, HOWARD CO., IMMACULATE CONCEPTION (1879) [CEM] Rev. Ray E. Atwood.
Res. and Mailing Address: 203 7th St., Elma, 50628. Tel: 641-393-2520; Fax: 641-393-2069.
Church: 211 Main St., 50466.
Catechesis/Religious Program—Deborah Oulman, C.R.E. Students 61.

RICKARDSVILLE, DUBUQUE CO., ST. JOSEPH (1840) [CEM] Rev. Raymond A. Burkle.
Office: 875 Church St., P.O. Box 398, Holy Cross, 52053. Tel: 563-870-4041.
Res.: 103 S. Andres St., Luxemburg, 52056. Tel: 563-853-3369.
Church: 20249 St. Joseph Dr., 52039-9757.
See LaSalle Elementary Schools, Holy Cross under Elementary School Systems located in the Institution section.

Catechesis/Religious Program—Brian Nilles, C.R.E. Students 16.

ROCKFORD, FLOYD CO., HOLY NAME (1910) Rev. Rodney M. Allers.
Church & Parish Office: 507 First Ave. N.W., 50468. Tel: 641-756-3569.
Res.: 305 Elm St. E., Rockwell, 50469. Tel: 641-822-4957.
Catechesis/Religious Program—Donna Jones, Dir. Faith Formation. Students 60.

ROCKWELL, CERRO GORDO CO., SACRED HEART (1878) [CEM] Rev. Rodney M. Allers.
Church, Res. & Mailing Address: 305 Elm St. E., P.O. Box 30, 50469. Tel: 641-822-4957.
Catechesis/Religious Program—Julie Novotney, Dir. Faith Formation. Students 51.

ROSEVILLE, FLOYD CO., ST. MARY (1867) [CEM] Rev. Msgr. Walter L. Brunkan.
Office & Mailing Address: 105 N. Main, P.O. Box 480, Greene, 50636-0480. Tel: 641-823-4146.
Church: 2397 Hwy. 14, Marble Rock, 50653.
Catechesis/Religious Program—Janet Willert, Dir. Faith Formation. Students 59.

ROWLEY, BUCHANAN CO., ALL SAINTS (1896) Closed. For sacramental records, contact St. John the Evangelist, Independence.

RYAN, DELAWARE CO., ST. PATRICK (1882) [CEM] Revs. John R. Flaherty; Richard G. Gaul, Sacramental Priest; Deacon Dave Loecke.
Office & Mailing Address: 615 Howard St., P.O. Box 219, 52330-0219. Tel: 563-932-2151.
Res.: 119 W. Fayette St., Manchester, 52057. Tel: 563-927-4710.
Church: 606 Franklin St., 52330.
Catechesis/Religious Program—Kathy Oberrueter, Dir. Faith Formation. Students 60.

ST. ANSGAR, MITCHELL CO., ST. ANSGAR (1951) Closed. For sacramental records, contact Sacred Heart, Osage.

ST. ANTHONY, MARSHALL CO., SACRED HEART (1878) [CEM] Closed. For sacramental records contact St. Mary, Colo.

ST. CATHERINE, DUBUQUE CO., ST. CATHERINE (1887) [CEM] Very Rev. Phillip F. Kruse; Rev. Scott E. Bullock; Deacon Sean Smith; Andrew Lang, Pastoral Assoc.
Office & Mailing Address: 405 Franklin St., P.O. Box 6, Bellevue, 52031. Tel: 563-872-3234.
Church: 5189 St. Catherine Rd., 52003.
See Marquette High School Bellevue under Consolidated K-12 Systems located in the Institution section.
Catechesis/Religious Program—Andrew Lang, Dir. Faith Formation. Students 26.

ST. CECILIA, HOWARD CO., ST. PATRICK, [CEM] Closed. For sacramental records, contact Immaculate Conception, Elma.

ST. DONATUS, JACKSON CO., ST. DONATUS (1853) [CEM] Very Rev. Phillip F. Kruse; Rev. Scott E. Bullock; Deacon Sean Smith; Andrew Lang, Pastoral Assoc.
Office & Mailing Address: 405 Franklin St., P.O. Box 6, Bellevue, 52031. Tel: 563-872-3234.
Church: 97 E. First St., 52071.
See Marquette High School, Bellevue under Consolidated K-12 Systems located in the Institution section.
Catechesis/Religious Program—Andrew Lang, Dir. Faith Formation. Students 14.

ST. LUCAS, FAYETTE CO., ST. LUKE (1855) [CEM] Rev. Nicholas B. March; Very Rev. Marvin C. Salz, Sacramental Priest; Tyler Wheeler, Pastoral Min.; Lynette Wheeler, Pastoral Min.
Res. & Mailing Address: 110 Commercial Ave., P.O. Box 205, Protivin, 52163-0205.
Church: 207 E. Main St., 52166.
See Trinity Catholic School, Protovin under Elementary School Systems located in the Institution section.
Catechesis/Religious Program—Martin Ahrndt, Dir. Faith Formation. Students 46.

ST. THERESA, JACKSON CO., ST. THERESA (1853) [CEM] Closed. For sacramental records, contact Sacred Heart, Maquoketa.

SABULA, JACKSON CO., ST. PETER (1840) [CEM] Closed. For sacramental records, please contact St. Joseph, Preston.

SAND SPRINGS, DELAWARE CO., IMMACULATE CONCEPTION, Closed. For sacramental records, please contact St. Luke, Hopkinton.

SCHLEY, HOWARD CO., HOLY CROSS, [CEM] Closed. For sacramental records, contact Holy Trinity, Protivin.

SHELL ROCK, BUTLER CO., HOLY NAME, Closed. For sacramental records, contact St. Mary, Waverly.

SHERRILL, DUBUQUE CO., SS. PETER AND PAUL (1852) [CEM] Rev. Raymond A. Burkle.
Office & Mailing Address: 875 Church St., P.O. Box 398, Holy Cross, 52053. Tel: 563-870-4041.
Res.: 103 S. Andres St., Luxemburg, 52056. Tel: 563-853-3369.
Church: 5131 Sherrill Rd., 52073-9612.
See LaSalle Elementary Schools, Holy Cross under Elementary School Systems located in the Institution section.
Catechesis/Religious Program—Brian Nilles, C.R.E. Students 64.

SOUTH GARRYOWEN, JACKSON CO., ST. ALOYSIUS, [CEM] Closed. For sacramental records, contact St. Patrick, Garryowen.

SPILLVILLE, WINNESHIEK CO., ST. WENCESLAUS (1860) [CEM] Rev. Donald J. Hawes.
Church & Parish Office: 207 Church St., P.O. Box 128, 52168-0128. Tel: 563-562-3637.
Res.: 304 S. Maryville, P.O. Box 819, Calmar, 52132. Tel: 563-562-3603.
See Calmar-Festina-Spillville Catholic School, Calmar under Elementary School Systems located in the Institution section.
Catechesis/Religious Program—Helen Pinter, C.R.E. Students 56.

SPRINGBROOK, JACKSON CO., SS. PETER AND PAUL (1864) [CEM] Very Rev. Phillip F. Kruse; Deacon Sean Smith.
Mailing Address: P.O. Box 97, 52075. Tel: 563-872-3875.
Church: 107 E. Main St., 52075.
See Marquette High School, Bellevue under Consolidated K-12 Systems located in the Institution section.
Catechesis/Religious Program—Students 25.

SPRINGVILLE, LINN CO., ST. ISIDORE (1961) Susan M. Schettler, Parish Life Coord.; Very Rev. John A. Gossman, Priest Supvr.
Office & Mailing Address: 603 6th St., P.O. Box 318, 52336. Tel: 319-854-6141; Fax: 319-854-7161.
Church: 603 6th St. S., 52336.
Catechesis/Religious Program—Michele Loehr, D.R.E. Students 54.

STACYVILLE, MITCHELL CO., CHURCH OF THE VISITATION (1894) [CEM] Rev. Jack H. McClure, C.PP.S.; Sr. Millie Leuenberger, O.S.F., Pastoral Assoc.
Parish Office & Mailing Address: 1209 State St., Osage, 50461. Tel: 641-732-4342; Fax: 641-832-2447.
Res.: 506 S. Randolph, 50476. Tel: 641-732-4509.
Church: 604 N. Broad St., 50476.
Catechesis/Religious Program—Barb Brumm, C.R.E. Students 97.

STATE CENTER, MARSHALL CO., ST. JOSEPH (1870) [CEM] Rev. Rick D. Dagit; Deacon Steven Van Kerckvoorde.
Office: 1110 11th St., Nevada, 50201. Tel: 515-382-2974; Fax: 515-382-2974.
Res. & Mailing Address: 410 Bailey St., P.O. Box 236, Colo, 50056. Tel: 641-377-2710.
Church: 610 Third St. S.W., 50247.
Catechesis/Religious Program—Julie Anne Bovenmyer, Dir. Faith Formation. Students 68.

STONE CITY, JONES CO., ST. JOSEPH ORATORY, Closed. For sacramental records, contact St. Patrick, Anamosa.

STRAWBERRY POINT, CLAYTON CO., ST. MARY (1876) [CEM] Very Rev. Paul R. Peters; Sr. Carla Popes, P.B.V.M., Pastoral Assoc.
Mailing Address: 314 W. Mission St., 52076-9432. Tel: 563-933-6166.
Res.: 330 1st St. S.W., P.O. Box 626, Elkader, 52043. Tel: 563-245-2548.
Church: 320 W. Mission St., 52076.
Catechesis/Religious Program—Patty Hilton, D.R.E.; Jennifer Palmersheim, C.R.E. Students 135.

SUMNER, BREMER CO., IMMACULATE CONCEPTION (1894) [CEM] Revs. James P. Brokman; Dale J. Rausch, Sacramental Priest.
Church, Res. & Office: 413 W. First St., 50674-1313. Tel: 563-578-5366.
Catechesis/Religious Program—Jill Le, C.R.E. Students 76.

SWALEDALE, CERRO GORDO CO., ST. LAWRENCE, Closed. For sacramental records, contact Sacred Heart, Rockwell.

SYLVIA, DUBUQUE CO., ASSUMPTION (1896) [CEM] Closed. For sacramental records, please contact Sacred Heart, Maquoketa.

TAMA, TAMA CO., ST. PATRICK (1864) [CEM] Very Rev. Michael J. Mescher; Deacon Joe Behounek, Pastoral Assoc.; Laura Galvez, Hispanic Min. Coord.
Church, Pastor's Res. & Parish Office: 900 Park St., 52339. Tel: 641-484-3039; 641-484-4242; Fax: 641-484-8039.
Catechesis/Religious Program—Jackie Toennies, D.R.E. Students 145.

TEMPLE HILL, JONES CO., ST. PETER (1852) [CEM] Rev. Douglas J. Loecke; Deacons Marvin Recker; Steven W. Strang; Ray Noonan; Joe Schockemoehl; Jean Conrad, Pastoral Assoc.
Mailing Address & Parish Office: 408 Third Ave. N.W., P.O. Box 699, Cascade, 52033-0699. Tel: 563-852-3524; Fax: 563-852-5269.
Church: 20123 Temple Hill Rd., Cascade, 52033.
See Aquin Educational System, Cascade under Consolidated K-12 Systems located in the Institution section.
Catechesis/Religious Program—Students 14.

TRAER, TAMA CO., ST. PAUL (1912) [CEM] Rev. Jerry W. Blake.
Church, Res. & Office: 1102 Walnut St., 50675-1440. Tel: 319-478-2222; Fax: 319-478-2222.
Catechesis/Religious Program—Jeffrey Lumpa, D.R.E. Students 83.

URBANA, BENTON CO., ST. MARY (1872) [JC] Sr. Mary Hargrafen, O.S.F., Parish Life Coord.; Rev. Msgr. Russell M. Bleich, Priest Supvr.; Rev. Ardel H. Barta, Sacramental Priest (Retired).
Mailing Address: 516 Rowley St., P.O. Box 116, Walker, 52352-0116. Tel: 319-448-4241; Fax: 319-448-4241.
Church: 402 Ash Ave., 52345.
Catechesis/Religious Program—Diane Walston, D.R.E.; Melissa Holthaus, C.R.E. Students 153.

VAN HORNE, BENTON CO., IMMACULATE CONCEPTION (1869) [CEM] Rev. Brian M. Dellaert; Deacon Robert F. Hurych.
Church & Parish Office: 405 Fourth Ave., P.O. Box 250, 52346-0250. Tel: 319-228-8131; Fax: 319-228-8800.
Res.: 512 Evergreen St., P.O. Box 89, Norway, 52318-0089. Tel: 319-227-9169.
Catechesis/Religious Program—Students 53.

VINING, TAMA CO., ST. MARY ORATORY (1874) [CEM] Closed. For sacramental records, contact St. Paul, Traer.

VINTON, BENTON CO., ST. MARY (1878) [CEM] Sr. Mary Hargrafen, O.S.F., Paris Life Coord.; Rev. Msgr. Russell M. Bleich, Priest Supvr.; Rev. Ardel H. Barta, Sacramental Priest (Retired).
Church, Res. & Office: 2200 Second Ave., 52349. Tel: 319-472-3368; Fax: 319-472-3042.
Catechesis/Religious Program—Diane Walston, D.R.E. Students 142.

VOLGA, CLAYTON CO., SACRED HEART (1889) [CEM] Very Rev. Paul R. Peters; Sr. Carla Popes, P.B.V.M., Pastoral Assoc.
Mailing Address: P.O. Box 135, 52077-0135.
Parish Office & Rectory: 330 1st St., S.W., P.O. Box 626, Elkader, 52043-0626. Tel: 563-245-2548.
Church: 306 White St., 52077.
Catechesis/Religious Program—Sr. Carla Popes, P.B.V.M., D.R.E. Students 28.

WADENA, FAYETTE CO., ST. JOSEPH, [CEM] Closed. Parish closed. For sacramental records, contact St. Joseph, Elkader.

WALFORD, LINN CO., HOLY TRINITY (1890) Closed. For sacramental records, contact John XXIII, Cedar Rapids.

WALKER, LINN CO., SACRED HEART (1885) [CEM] Sr. Mary Hargrafen, O.S.F., Parish Life Coord.; Rev. Msgr. Russell M. Bleich, Priest Supvr. In Res., Rev. Ardel H. Barta, Sacramental Priest (Retired).
Mailing & Parish Office: 516 Rowley St., P.O. Box 116, 52352-0116. Tel: 319-448-4241; Fax: 319-448-4241.
Church: 518 Rowley St., 52352.
Catechesis/Religious Program—Diane Walston, Dir. Faith Formation; Melissa Holthaus, C.R.E. Students 137.

WATERLOO, BLACKHAWK CO.

1—BLESSED SACRAMENT (1947) [JC] Rev. Thomas J. McDermott; Deacons John Herman; James Freet; Norman Schauls; Robert Stirm, Pastoral Assoc.; Sr. Madonna M. Friedman, O.S.F., Pastoral Min.
Church, Res. & Office: 650 Stephan Ave., 50701. Tel: 319-233-6179; Fax: 319-233-6051.
See Cedar Valley Catholic Schools under Consolidated K-12 Systems located in the Institution Section.
Catechesis/Religious Program—Barbara Duggan, Dir. Faith Formation; Lori Zabler, C.R.E. Students 104.

2—ST. EDWARD (1945) [JC] Very Rev. Jerry F. Kopacek; Deacons John Baker; Raymond Larsen; Richard Lynch; Karol Rae Hoth, Pastoral Assoc.
Church, Res. & Office: 1423 Kimball Ave., 50702. Tel: 319-233-8060; Fax: 319-233-3808.
See Cedar Valley Catholic Schools under Consolidated K-12 Systems located in the Institution Section.
Catechesis/Religious Program—Hazel Martin, Dir. Faith Formation. Students 76.

3—ST. JOHN (1923) Closed. Merged with St. Mary & St. Joseph, Waterloo and St. Nicholas, Evansdale to form Queen of Peace, Waterloo. For sacramental records, contact Queen of Peace, Waterloo.

4—ST. JOSEPH, Closed. Merged with St. Mary & St. John, Waterloo and St. Nicholas, Evansdale to form Queen of Peace, Waterloo. For sacramental records, contact Queen of Peace, Waterloo.

5—ST. MARY (1898) Closed. Merged with St. John & St. Joseph, Waterloo and St. Nicholas, Evansdale to form Queen of Peace, Waterloo. For sacramental records contact Queen of Peace, Waterloo.

6—QUEEN OF PEACE (2002) [JC] Rev. Jose Luis

Comparan; Deacons Ed Weber; Rigoberto Real, Hispanic Min. Coord.
Mailing, Parish Office & Church Address: 320 Mulberry St., 50703. Tel: 319-226-3655; Fax: 319-232-1118.
Res.: 327 Alta Vista Ave., 50703.
See Cedar Valley Catholic Schools under Consolidated K-12 Systems located in the Institution Section
Catechesis/Religious Program—Bev Byford, D.R.E. Students 47.

7—SACRED HEART (1909) [JC] Rev. Louis M. Jaeger; Deacon Alan Weber; Nancy Rigel, Pastoral Assoc.; Sr. Kathleen Grace, O.S.F., Pastoral Assoc. & Hispanic Min. Coord.
Office: 627 W. Fourth St., 50702. Tel: 319-234-4996; Fax: 319-233-0531.
Res.: 3711 Loralin Dr., 50701. Tel: 319-236-6530.
Church: 623 W. Fourth St., 50702.
See Cedar Valley Catholic Schools under Consolidated K-12 Systems located in the Institution Section.
Catechesis/Religious Program—Pam Johnston, Dir. Faith Formation; Cathy Mills, C.R.E. Students 105.

WATKINS, BENTON CO., ST. PATRICK (1880) [CEM] Rev. Brian M. Dellaert; Deacon Robert F. Hurych.
Parish Office & Mailing Address: 405 Fourth Ave., P.O. Box 250, Van Horne, 52346. Tel: 319-228-8131; Fax: 319-228-8800.
Church: 109 2nd St., 52354.
Res.: 512 Evergreen St., P.O. Box 89, Norway, 52318-0089. Tel: 319-227-7169.
Catechesis/Religious Program—Students 6.

WAUCOMA, FAYETTE CO., ST. MARY (1898) [CEM] Rev. Nicholas B. March; Very Rev. Marvin C. Salz, Sacramental Priest; Tyler Wheeler, Pastoral Min.; Lynette Wheeler, Pastoral Min.
Mailing Address & Church: 218 3rd St., N.W., P.O. Box 215, 52171. Tel: 563-776-6364.
Res.: 110 Commercial Ave., P.O. Box 205, Protivin, 52163-0205. Tel: 563-569-8259.
Catechesis/Religious Program—Martin Ahrndt, Dir. Faith Formation. Students 30.

WAUKON, ALLAMAKEE CO., ST. PATRICK (1851) [CEM] Rev. Joseph M. Schneider; Deacons Michael Ward, Pastoral Assoc.; Jeff Molitor.
Res., Office & Mailing Address: 109 Second St., S.W., Box 146, 52172. Tel: 563-568-3671; Fax: 563-568-4432.
Church: 101 2nd St., S.W., 52172.
School—(Grades PreSchool-6), 200 Second St., S.W., 52172. Tel: 563-568-2415; Fax: 563-568-2170. Richard Wede, Prin. Lay Teachers 11; Students 125.
Catechesis/Religious Program—Michael Erickson, D.R.E. Students 201.

WAVERLY, BREMER CO., ST. MARY (1856) [CEM] Rev. Michael L. Tauke; Deacon Phil Paladino; Theresa Buss, Pastoral Min.
Parish Office, Church & Mailing Address: 2700 Horton Rd., 50677. Tel: 319-352-2493; Fax: 319-352-3122.
Res.: 313 Third Ave., N.E., 50677. Tel: 319-483-9009.
Catechesis/Religious Program—Eric Stromberg, Dir. Faith Formation. Students 266.

WEBSTER CITY, HAMILTON CO., ST. THOMAS AQUINAS (1870) [CEM] Rev. Stephen L. Meyer; Amy Shannon, Pastoral Assoc.
Mailing & Office: 1000 Des Moines St., 50595-2147. Tel: 515-832-1190; Fax: 515-832-3757.
Church: 1008 Des Moines St., 50595.
Res.: 2209 Summit Dr., 50595.
School—(Grades PreSchool-6), 624 Dubuque St., 50595-2245. Tel: 515-832-1346; Fax: 515-832-1212. Michael Pavik, Prin. Lay Teachers 10; Students 85.
Catechesis/Religious Program—Lynn Houdeshell, D.R.E. Students 106.

WEST RIDGE, ALLAMAKEE CO., ST. JOHN THE BAPTIST, [CEM] Closed. Parish closed. For sacramental records, contact St. Patrick, Waukon.

WEST UNION, FAYETTE CO., HOLY NAME (1870) [CEM] Revs. James P. Brokman; Dale J. Rausch, Sacramental Priest.
Office, Pastor's Res. & Church: 128 N. Walnut St., 52175. Tel: 563-422-3184.
Catechesis/Religious Program—Marion Broghammer, C.R.E.; Sue McDonough, C.R.E. Students 122.

WEXFORD, ALLAMAKEE CO., IMMACULATE CONCEPTION (1851) [CEM] Rev. John A. Moser.
Res., Parish Office & Mailing Address: 648 Main St., Lansing, 52151. Tel: 563-538-4171.
Church: 1416 Great River Rd., Lansing, 52151.
Catechesis/Religious Program—Shari Curran, C.R.E. Students 15.

WILLIAMS, HAMILTON CO., ST. MARY (1875) [CEM] Rev. Stephen L. Meyer.
Parish Office & Mailing Address: 1000 Des Moines St., Webster City, 50595. Tel: 515-832-1190; Fax: 515-832-3757.
Res.: 2209 Summit Dr., Webster City, 50595.
Church: 404 Fourth St., 50271.
Catechesis/Religious Program—Lynn Houdeshell, C.R.E. Students 5.

WINTHROP, BUCHANAN CO., ST. PATRICK (1894) [CEM] Rev. Donald J. Plamondon; Deacon Tim Post; Sharon Bainbridge, Pastoral Assoc.; Mary Ann Fangman, Pastoral Min.
Office, Res. & Mailing Address: 209 5th Ave. N.E., Independence, 50644-1998. Tel: 319-334-7191; Fax: 319-334-7192.
Church: 555 First St. S., 50682.
Catechesis/Religious Program—Connie Fawcett, C.R.E. Students 139.

WODEN, HANCOCK CO., SACRED HEART (1900) Closed. For sacramental records, please contact St. Patrick, Britt.

WORTHINGTON, DUBUQUE CO., ST. PAUL (1875) [CEM] Revs. Dennis J. Quint; Noah J. Diehm; Deacons Fredrick J. Pins; James Steger.
Parish Office & Mailing Address: 309 Third Ave., S.W., P.O. Box 38, 52078.
Church: 301 S. 2nd Ave. S.W., 52078.
School—(Grades PreSchool-6), 309 Third Ave., S.W., P.O. Box 68, 52078-0068. Tel: 563-855-2125; Fax: 563-855-2022. Jayne Intlekofer, Prin. Lay Teachers 5; Students 47.
Catechesis/Religious Program—Deacon Fredrick J. Pins, Dir. Faith Formation. Students 26.

ZEARING, STORY CO., ST. GABRIEL (1904) Rev. Rick D. Dagit; Deacon Steven Van Kerckvoorde.
Mailing Address: 410 Bailey St., P.O. Box 236, Colo, 50056-0236.
Office: 1110 11th St., Nevada, 50201. Tel: 515-382-2974; Fax: 515-382-5966.
Church: 302 N. Center, 50278.
Catechesis/Religious Program—Rex Gogerty, Dir. Faith Formation. Students 12.

On Special or Other Archdiocesan Assignment:
Rev. Msgrs.—
Bleich, Russell M., S.T.L., Episcopal Vicar, Cedar Rapids Region
Toale, Thomas E., Ph.D., Vicar General & Episcopal Vicar Dubuque Region
Wilgenbusch, Lyle L., Episcopal Vicar, Waterloo Region
Revs.—
Boone, Scott F., Assoc. Chap., Loras College, 830 Loras Blvd., 52001. Tel: 563-588-7108
Bullock, Scott E., J.C.L., Dir. Seminarians, Vianney House, 1235 Mt. Loretta Ave., 52003. Tel: 563-556-2580
Glaser, Kenneth J., Dir. Campus Ministry, St. Stephen the Witness Student Center, 1019 W. 23rd, Cedar Falls, 50613. Tel: 319-266-9863
Haugen, John S., Assoc. Dir., Worship, Visitation Convent, 2950 Kaufmann Ave., 52001. Tel: 563-556-2580
Miller, James L., Vicar for Hispanic Min.
Schatz, David A., M.A., Dir. Vocation Awareness, Vianney House, 1235 Mt. Loretta Ave., 52003. Tel: 563-556-2580
Wild, Alexander, P. O. Box 479, 52004-0479.
Zinkula, Thomas R., J.D., J.C.L., Sabbatical, Rome

Military Chaplains:
Revs.—
Lawrence, Andrew Ch. (MAJ) 2ID/HHSC, DSTB, Unit 15041, Box 1015, Apo, AP 96258.
Lippstock, Paul E., Iowa Army National Guard

On Leave of Absence (Not Authorized for Priestly Ministry):
Revs.—
McDermott, John J.
O'Brien, Steven G.
Rastrelli, Thomas P.

Retired:
Rev. Msgrs.—
Barta, James O., Ph.D., Villa Raphael, 1155 Mt. Loretta Ave., 52003. Tel: 563-583-2321
Dalton, John W., 1301 Rhodes, Naperville, IL 60540. Tel: 630-355-2664
Friedl, Francis P., Villa Raphael, 1155 Mt. Loretta Ave., 52003. Tel: 563-588-8018
Funke, Richard P., J.C.L., 7974 Sailboat Key Blvd., Box 602, South Pasadena, FL 33707. Tel: 727-363-1754
Glovik, Karl L., Villa Raphael, 1155 Mt. Loretta Ave., 52003. Tel: 563-556-4378
Hayek, Stanley J., 307 Meadow Ln., Charles City, 50616. Tel: 641-228-1664
Heineman, Donald P., 108 3rd St., S.E., P.O. Box 187, Fort Atkinson, 52144-0187. Tel: 563-534-3052
Hemann, John W., 481 N. Shore Dr., Apt. #301, Clear Lake, 50428-1368. Tel: 641-357-4539
Lang, Charles E., Ph.D., 8727 W. Bryn Mawr, #409, Chicago, IL 60631. Tel: 773-391-2888
Laughlin, Martin T., P.O. Box 258, Ave Maria, FL 34142.
Lechtenberg, Edward W., 321 Diagonal St., Lansing, 52151. Tel: 563-538-4773
McClean, John R., 1539 Bies Dr., 52002. Tel: 563-556-1922
O'Brien, Joseph, Villa Raphael, 1155 Mt. Loretta Ave., 52003. Tel: 563-556-4326
Ralph, Thomas J., 400 Woodland Ridge, 52003. Tel: 563-587-1977
Ressler, Wayne A., St. Joseph the Worker Rectory, 90 S. Algona St., 52001. Tel: 563-588-2934
Schmitt, Carl L., 619 Rural St., New Hampton, 50659. Tel: 641-394-2744
Simington, Ralph P., 931 E. Ridgeway Ave., Waterloo, 50702. Tel: 319-236-6638
Slepicka, Joseph J., 313 N. 13th St., Clear Lake, 50428. Tel: 641-357-2448
Steimel, Paul T., 3709 W. 9th St., Apt. 8, Waterloo, 50702. Tel: 319-233-5287
Vogl, Robert R., Villa Raphael, 1155 Mt. Loretta Ave, 52003. Tel: 563-556-4997
Walz, W. Dean, J.C.D., 24701 207th Ave., P.O. Box 182, Delhi, 52223-0182. Tel: 563-927-6672
Revs.—
Barnes, John G., 114 S. Sheakley #8, New Hampton, 50659. Tel: 641-394-2394
Barta, Ardel H., Sacred Heart Rectory, 516 Rowley St., P.O. Box 116, Walker, 52352-0116. Tel: 563-581-2760
Beck, Robert L., 1220 N. Booth, 52001. Tel: 563-583-4230
Blocklinger, James L., 1331 Oak Park Pl., Unit 361, 52002. Tel: 563-585-4988
Bodensteiner, Peter C., 108 W. Spring St., Apt. A-1, Lawler, 52154. Tel: 563-238-8751
Braak, Thomas E., 205 W. Ingledue St., Marshalltown, 50158. Tel: 641-752-3846
Bruggeman, Donald R., 411 Burdette Dr., S.W., Apt. 1022, Cedar Rapids, 52404. Tel: 319-396-0504
Burke, Clement J., 3720 23rd Ave. S., Rm. #108-2, Minneapolis, MN 55407. Tel: 612-238-5189
Carpender, John W., 720 Duggan Dr., #1, 52003-0250. Tel: 563-582-6993
Chappell, James T., 1910 Madison St., 52001. Tel: 563-590-0280
Colter, Dennis J., 813 Wildwood Rd., Waterloo, 50702. Tel: 319-404-4754
Condon, Gerald A., 130 Thompson Dr., S.E., #120, Cedar Rapids, 52403. Tel: 319-366-1287
Devine, William P., 2302 Rick Collins Way, Apt. 6, Eldora, 50627-8357. Tel: 641-858-2222
Drexler, Harold J., Villa Raphael, 1155 Mt. Loretta Ave., 52003. Tel: 563-556-7197
Engler, Ernest J., 14300 W. Bell Rd., #210, Surprise, AZ 85374. Tel: 623-975-1965
Fangmann, Frederick C., Villa Raphael, 1155 Mount Loretta Ave., 52003. Tel: 563-557-3717
Flanagan, James W., 1723 Vickers Cir., Decatur, GA 30030-1033. Tel: 404-378-0366
Friedell, John C., 1381 Oak Park Pl., Unit #221, 52002. Tel: 563-556-9176
Friedell, Ronald G., 1001 Assisi Dr., #301, 52001. Tel: 563-556-1285
Geary, Patrick G., 2817 Roxboro Dr., Ames, 50014. Tel: 515-451-2732
Heimerman, Francis D., 151 Main St., P.O. Box 623, Nashua, 50658. Tel: 641-435-2261
Hemann, Everett, St. Patrick Rectory, 115 W. 8th St., Cedar Falls, 50613.
Hemann, Melvin D., 127 Kaspend Pl., Cedar Falls, 50613-1683. Tel: 319-266-3889
Herzog, John M., 1004 Mesa Verde Pl., Ames, 50014. Tel: 515-292-0558
Karnik, George W., 750 River Forest Rd., #35, Evansdale, 50707. Tel: 319-226-5412
Katz, Roger L., 400 17th St. W., Clear Lake, 50428. Tel: 641-357-2003
Kissling, John M., 419 3rd St., P.O. Box 356, Chetek, WI 54728-0356. Tel: 715-924-3514
Klein, Donald L., 3492 Laurel Ln., Marion, 52302-8000. Tel: 319-377-1530
Kleinfehn, Walter J., 4850 16th Ave., S.W., Apt. 103, Cedar Rapids, 52404. Tel: 319-390-0643
Knipper, Daniel J., 502 Valley Dr., #24, Decorah, 52101. Tel: 563-568-7913
Krapfl, Gary F., 1960 Great River Rd., Lansing, 52151. Tel: 563-380-0994
Kurt, Allan J., P.O. Box 479, 52004-0479.
Kutsch, Eugene C., 2622 New Haven St., 52001. Tel: 563-583-1638
Levenhagen, Robert J., 6158 Forest Hills Dr., Asbury, 52002. Tel: 563-582-5041
Maichen, Richard F., 1009 New St., Manchester, 52057. Tel: 563-927-8137
Manternach, Carl J., 1001 Assisi Dr., Apt. 110, 52001. Tel: 563-583-6727
McAndrew, Thomas F., 14258 Sagewood Dr., 52002.

Tel: 563-588-3389
McDonald, Paul F., Villa Raphael, 1155 Mt. Loretta Ave., 52003. Tel: 563-583-5105 U.S.A.F.
McGovern, Mark J., 2961 6th St., S.W., Unit 3, Cedar Rapids, 52404. Tel: 563-543-5178
McGuire, Joseph E., Mercy Medical Center-Hallmar, 701 Tenth St., S.E., Cedar Rapids, 52403.
McManus, Paul C., 419 3rd St., N.W., Independence, 50644. Tel: 319-332-0411
Nemmers, Mark R., 801 Davis St., #212, 52001. Tel: 563-557-5094
O'Brien, William D., Villa Raphael, 1155 Mt. Loretta Ave., 52003. Tel: 563-582-9933
Otting, Loras C., Villa Raphael, 1155 Mt. Loretta Ave., 52003. Tel: 563-583-3866
Otting, Paul J., Villa Raphael, 1155 Mt. Loretta Ave., 52003. Tel: 563-582-2709
Ouderkirk, Lloyd Paul, Academy Apartments, 511 County Road Z, Hazel Green, WI 53811. Tel: 608-748-5341
Paisley, John C., 816 Euclid St., 52001-8123. Tel: 563-583-9242
Pepper, J. David, 102 W. Spring, Box 120, Lawler, 52154. Tel: 563-238-2701
Perry, Francis J., Stonehill Care Center, 3485 Windsor Ave., 52001.
Ptacek, John P., 206 7th St. S.E., Farley, 52046. Tel: 563-744-9105
Purtell, John J., 105 Union St., Apt. 10, Sumner, 50674. Tel: 563-578-3234
Rasing, Linus E., 615 W. Prospect St., New Hampton, 50659. Tel: 641-394-4504
Recker, Philip F., 1849 Doral Park Rd., S.E., Rio Rancho, NM 87124-7118. Tel: 505-896-9449
Remy, David P., CDR, CHC, USN, 3101 Marcus Pointe Blvd., Pensacola, FL 32505. Tel: 850-473-9426
Reuter, Lloyd E., 1905 5th St., P.O. Box 114, Gilbertville, 50634. Tel: 319-296-0848
Rhomberg, Thomas W., Villa Raphael, 1155 Mt. Loretta Ave., 52003. Tel: 563-582-3545
Rogers, Daniel J., 7678 Moonlight Ln., Bellevue, 52031. Tel: 563-582-6605
Schmidt, Florian J., 2249 Del Monaco Dr., 52002. Tel: 563-582-4066
Schmitt, Phillip E., 212-1/2 7th St., S.E., Mt. Vernon, 52314-1518. Tel: 319-895-0404
Schueller, La Verne L., CH (COL), 622 Cottage Grove Ave., P.O. Box 1983, Cedar Rapids, 52406. Tel: 319-365-0500
Tegeler, Herbert L., River Bend Retirement Community, 813 Tyler St., Cascade, 52033.
Trzil, Louis J., Thornton Manor Nursing Center, 1329 Main St., P.O. Box 700, Lansing, 52151.
Vorwald, Aloysius J., 203 3rd St., S.W. #2, Dyersville, 52040. Tel: 563-875-2627
Walsh, John J., Villa Raphael, 1155 Mt. Loretta Ave., 52003. Tel: 563-556-4897
Wilkie, William E., Ph.D., 660 W. 17th St., 52001.
Zee, Louis C., Ascension Catholic Church, 4605 Jetty Lane, Houston, TX 77072. Tel: 281-575-8855

Permanent Deacons:
Aitchison, Gary, (Retired), Ames
Baker, John, St. Edward, Waterloo
Baltes, Robert, (Retired), New Hampton
Behounek, Joseph, St. Joseph, Chelsea; St. Michael, Belle Plaine; St. Patrick, Tama
Berger, Paul "Jim", St. Ludmila, Cedar Rapids
Berry, Matthew F., Holy Family, Mason City; Sacred Heart Parish, Manly
Biver, William, St. Columbkille, Dubuque
Blouin, Michael, Naples, FL
Brinkmoeller, Dave, Holy Spirit, Dubuque
Brustkern, Leo J., (Retired), La Porte City
Byrne, Michael G., St. Joseph, Mason City
Cashatt, Wayne, (Retired), Eldora
Christy, Alan, St. Cecilia, Ames
Cisler, William J., (Retired), Cedar Rapids
Cooper, Charles, Holy Family, Mason City; Sacred Heart, Manly
DeSloover, Vic, Holy Family, New Hampton; St. Boniface, Ionia; Immaculate Conception, North Washington
Dunn, Frank, (Retired), Dubuque
Flagel, LaVerne, (Retired), Marion
Francois, Nick, St. Benedict, Decorah
Freet, James, Blessed Sacrament, Waterloo
Froyen, Leonard, Ph.D., (Retired), Cedar Falls
Garcia, Pedro, St. Francis Xavier, Belmond; St. John, Clarion; Sacred Heart, Eagle Grove
Gehrke, Richard, (Retired), Oelwein
Gram, Clarence, II, (Retired), Waterloo
Harris, Jeff, St. Mary, Marshalltown
Head, Robert, Sacred Heart, Maquoketa; St. Lawrence, Otter Creek; St. Joseph, Preston
Herman, John, Blessed Sacrament, Waterloo
Hernandez, Felix, St. Mary, Marshalltown
Hickson, William, St. Anthony, Dubuque
Hoeger, Daniel, St. Patrick, Cedar Rapids
Hurych, Robert F., St. John, Blairstown; St. Paul, Newhall; St. Michael, Norway; Immaculate Conception, Van Horne; St. Patrick, Watkins
Jones, David, St. Mary, Ackley; St. Patrick, Hampton
Jorgensen, Gerald T., Ph.D., J.C.L., Resurrection, Dubuque
Kean, James, St. Patrick, Epworth; St. John, Placid; St. Clement, Bankston; St. Joseph, Farley
Klappholz, Mike, All Saints, Cedar Rapids
Koopmann, Gerald, St. John, Placid; St. Patrick, Epworth; St. Clement, Bankston; St. Joseph, Farley
Lang, Tom, St. Joseph, Key West
Larsen, Raymond, St. Edward, Waterloo
Lievens, Greg, Holy Family Parish, Reinbeck
LoBianco, Timothy, Resurrection, Dubuque
Loecke, Dave, St. Mary, Manchester; Immaculate Conception, Masonville; St. Patrick, Ryan
Loving, Peter, St. Patrick, Cedar Falls
Luksetich, Jim, Cathedral of St. Raphael & St. Patrick Parish, Dubuque
Lynch, Richard, St. Edward, Waterloo
MacDonald, Stephen, Holy Spirit, Dubuque
Malanaphy, Patrick J., St. Mary, McGregor; St. Patrick, Monona & St. Bridget, Postville
Malone, John, (Retired), Cedar Rapids
Manning, Richard, St. Ludmila, Cedar Rapids
Mauss, William, St. Anthony, Dubuque
McCully, John, (Retired), Ames
McGhee, David, Nativity, Dubuque
Mead, Edward J., (Retired), Marshalltown
Molitor, Jeff, St. Mary Parish, Dorchester; St. Mary Parish, Hanover; St. Patrick Parish, Waukon
Mulherin, Dennis, St. Elizabeth Ann Seton, Hiawatha
Noonan, Ray, St. Matthias, Cascade; Sacred Heart, Fillmore; St. Patrick, Garryowen; St. Peter, Temple Hill
Paladino, Phil, St. Mary Parish, Waverly
Pantaloni, Ed, (Retired Outside the Archdiocese) Grimes
Patera, Jim, Sacred Heart, Oelwein; Immaculate Conception, Fairbank
Peckosh, Paul, St. Raphael Cathedral & St. Patrick, Dubuque
Peterson, Lanny, St. Pius X, Cedar Rapids
Pfaffly, James, St. Mary, Guttenberg; Immaculate Conception, North Buena Vista; St. Joseph, Garnavillo
Pienze, Tom, St. Mary Parish, Marshalltown
Pins, Fredrick J., St. Francis Xavier, Dyersville; St. Paul, Worthington; St. Joseph, Earlville; St. Boniface, New Vienna; SS. Peter & Paul, Petersburg
Polt, Roger, St. Henry, Marshalltown
Popowski, Dennis, St. Patrick, Britt; St. Patrick, Buffalo Center; St. Wenceslaus, Duncan; St. James, Forest City, St. Boniface, Garner; St. Patrick, Lake Mills
Post, Tim, St. John the Evangelist, Independence; St. Patrick, Winthrop
Pusillo, Gary, St. Henry, Marshalltown
Quiles, Horacio, St. Patrick, Dubuque; Cathedral of St. Raphael, Dubuque
Ramirez, Diego, Immaculate Conception, Cedar Rapids; St. Wenceslaus, Cedar Rapids
Real, Rigoberto, Queen of Peace, Waterloo
Recker, Marvin, St. Matthias, Cascade; Sacred Heart, Fillmore; St. Patrick, Garryowen; St. Peter, Temple Hill
Saunders, Phil, St. Matthew, Cedar Rapids
Scharosch, Albert, (Retired), Cedar Rapids
Schauls, Norman, Blessed Sacrament, Waterloo
Schmit, Nick, (Retired), Belmond
Schockemoehl, Joe, St. Matthias Parish, Cascade Sacred Heart Parish, Fillmore; St. Patrick Parish, Garryowen; St. Peter Parish, Temple Hill
Schwennen, John, Holy Family Parish, Reinbeck
Sink, Tom, St. Patrick, Cedar Falls
Smith, Ron, St. Cecilia, Ames
Smith, Sean, St. Joseph, Bellevue; St. Catherine, St. Catherine; St. Donatus, St. Donatus; SS. Peter & Paul, Springbrook
Steger, James, St. Joseph, Earlville; St. Francis Xavier, Dyersville; St. Boniface, New Vienna; SS. Peter & Paul, Petersburg; St. Paul, Worthington
Stierman, John, Holy Spirit, Dubuque
Stirm, Bob, Blessed Sacrament, Waterloo
Strang, Steven W., St. Matthias, Cascade; Sacred Heart, Fillmore & St. Patrick, Garryowen; St. Peter, Temple Hill
Temeyer, Jerry, St. Francis Xavier, Belmond; St. John, Clarion; Sacred Heart, Eagle Grove
Thill, James J., Holy Spirit, Dubuque
Tondra, Richard, (Retired), Ames
Van Kerckvoorde, Steven, St. Mary, Colo; St. Patrick, Nevada; St. Joseph, State Center; St. Gabriel, Zearing
Vaske, Irvin, (Retired), Marshalltown
Wallace, Richard, St. Matthew, Cedar Rapids
Walsh, Tom, (Retired), Springville
Ward, Mike, St. Patrick, Waukon; St. Mary, Dorchester; St. Mary, Hanover
Weber, Alan, Sacred Heart, Waterloo
Weber, Ed, Queen of Peace, Waterloo
Whitters, Michael, St. Francis Xavier, Belmond; St. John, Clarion; Sacred Heart, Eagle Grove
Wilson, James, (Retired), Waterloo
Zimmerman, Paul, St. Pius X, Cedar Rapids

Deacons Active Outside the Archdiocese:
Deacons—
Brock, Cary, Irrigon, OR
Brown, Paul, Auburn, AL
DiPietre, Dennis, Columbia, MO
Fortin, Daryl, LeClaire
Jenney, William, Brooklyn, MN
Moetsch, Michael, LeClaire, Iowa

INSTITUTIONS LOCATED IN THE DIOCESE

[A] SEMINARIES, ARCHDIOCESAN

DUBUQUE. *Seminary of St. Pius X, Loras College*, 1450 Alta Vista St., P.O. Box 178, 52004-0178. Tel: 563-588-7662. Revs. Scott E. Bullock, J.C.L., Rector; G. Robert Gross, Vice Rector; David A. Schatz, M.A., Vice Rector; William M. Joensen, Ph.D., Spiritual Dir. Priests 4; Students for Archdiocese of Dubuque 14; Other Diocesan Students 2.

[B] SEMINARIES, RELIGIOUS OR SCHOLASTICATES

EPWORTH. *Divine Word College*, 102 Jacoby Dr., S.W., P.O. Box 380, 52045-0380. Tel: 563-876-3353; Fax: 563-876-3407. Email: tlenchak@dwci.edu. Web: www.dwci.edu. Revs. William Shea, S.V.D.; Kenneth Anich, S.V.D.; Khien Luu, S.V.D., Vice Pres. Formation & Dean of Students; Joseph McDermott, S.V.D.; James Bergin, S.V.D., Rector SVD Community; Walter Bunofsky, S.V.D.; James Heiar, S.V.D.; Paul LaForge, S.V.D.; Timothy Lenchak, S.V.D., Pres.; Adam MacDonald, S.V.D.; Cuong (Paul) Hung Nguyen, S.V.D.; Joseph Chau Nguyen, S.V.D.; Nick Hien Nguyen, S.V.D.; Stephen Kha Nguyen, S.V.D.; Thang Hoang, S.V.D.; Trung Thanh Mai, S.V.D.; Linh Pham, S.V.D.; Cong Bang Tran, S.V.D.; Nhan Van Tran, S.V.D.; Bros. Kevin Diederich, S.V.D.; Tony Kreinus, S.V.D.; Wayne Till, S.V.D.; Rev. Khoa Nguyen, S.V.D. Society of the Divine Word (S.V.D.). Priests 20; Brothers 3; Sisters 1; Lay Teachers 19; Students 125.

[C] COLLEGES AND UNIVERSITIES

DUBUQUE. *Clarke University of Dubuque, Iowa*, 1550 Clarke Dr., 52001. Tel: 563-588-6300; Fax: 563-588-6789. Email: clarke-info@clarke.edu. Web: www.clarke.edu. Sr. Joanne M. Burrows, S.C., Ph.D., Pres.; Kristi Bagstad, Registrar; Sr. Joan Lingen, B.V.M., Ph.D., Vice Pres. Academic Affairs & Provost; Graciela Canerio-Livingston, Ph.D., Academic Dean & Provost; Kate Zanger, Vice Pres. Student Life; Deanna McCormick, Vice Pres. Business & Finance; Beth Triplett, Ph.D., Vice Pres., Enrollment Mgmt. Liberal Arts College. (Coed); Conducted by Sisters of Charity, B.V.M. Sisters 6; Lay Teachers 151; Students 1,255.

Loras College, 1450 Alta Vista St., P.O. Box 178, 52004-0178. Tel: 563-588-7100; Fax: 563-588-7964. Email: jim.collins@loras.edu. Web: www.loras.edu. Mr. Jim Collins, Pres.; Stephen J. Schmall, C.P.A., Vice Pres. Finance & Admin. Svcs.; Cheryl Jacobsen, Ph.D., Provost/Academic Dean; Arthur Sunleaf, Asst. Vice Pres. Student Devel./Dean of Students; Joyce A. Meldrem, Dir. Academic Resource Ctr.; Rev. Msgr. Charles E. Lang, Ph.D. (Retired); Revs. William M. Joensen, Ph.D., Dean of Campus Spiritual Life; Scott F. Boone, Assoc. Chap. (Accredited by the North Central Assoc. of Colleges and Secondary Schools) Priests 3; Students 1,560.

College Faculty: Revs. Douglas O. Wathier, S.T.D.; William M. Joensen, Ph.D.

CEDAR RAPIDS. *Mount Mercy University*, 1330 Elmhurst Dr., N.E., 52402-4797. Tel: 319-363-8213; Fax: 319-368-5270. Email: admission@mtmercy.edu. Web: www.mtmercy.edu. Christopher R. L. Blake, Ph.D., Pres.; Dr. Sue Oatey, Ph.D., Vice Pres. for Enrollment & Student Life; Barb Pooley, C.P.A., C.M.A., Vice Pres. Finance & Business Operations; Melody A. Graham, Ph.D., Provost & Vice Pres. Academic Affairs; Lori Heying, Dir. Inst. Research; Duff Ridgeway, Vice Pres. Inst. Advancement; Rev. Dustin L. Vu, Chap. Priests 1; 80 full-time; 68

part-time 148; Students 1,824.

[D] HIGH SCHOOLS, INTERPAROCHIAL

CEDAR RAPIDS. *Metropolitan Office of Catholic Education, Cedar Rapids Metro Office*, 120 5th St., N.W., 52405. Tel: 319-366-2517; Fax: 319-366-0426. Email: dbqasup@arch.pvt.k12.ia.us. Web: www.cr-cath.pvt.k12.ia.us. Jeff Henderson, Supt. Schools. Priests 1; Lay Teachers 210.

Xavier High School (Coed), 6300 42nd St., N.E., 52411. Tel: 319-294-6635; Fax: 319-294-6712. Email: DBQH02@arch-pvt.k12.ia.us. Rev. Philip E. Thompson, Pastoral Coord.; Tom Keating, Prin. & Contact Person; Angela Olson, Asst. Prin.; Dee Davis, Librarian. Serving Blessed John XXIII; St. Jude, St. Ludmila, St. Patrick, Immaculate Conception, St. Wenceslaus, St. Matthew, All Saints, St. Pius X, Cedar Rapids; St. Joseph, Marion; St. Elizabeth Ann Seton, Hiawatha. Lay Teachers 56; Students 751.

Xavier High School Foundation, 6300 42nd St., N.E., P.O. Box 10956, 52410-0956. Tel: 319-378-4571; Fax: 319-378-2953. Email: jruff@xavierfoundation.org. Jody Ruff, Dir. & Contact Person; Rev. Philip E. Thompson, Pastoral Coord.

DYERSVILLE. *Beckman High School*, (Grades 7-12), (Coed), 1325 Ninth St. S.E., 52040. Tel: 563-875-7188; Fax: 563-875-7242. Email: dbqh05@arch.pvt.k12.ia.us. Pat Meade, Prin.; Pat Lehmann, Asst. Prin.; Rev. Dennis J. Quint, Pastoral Coord.; Emmy Brehm, Librarian; Bernard Knepper, Librarian. Serving the following parishes: St. Francis Xavier, Dyersville; St. Joseph, Earlville; St. Boniface, New Vienna; Ss. Peter and Paul, Petersburg; St. Paul, Worthington. Lay Teachers 33; Students 455.

[E] SCHOOLS OF RELIGION

CALMAR. *Christian Family School of Religion* Serving: St. Aloysius, Calmar; Our Lady of Seven Dolors, Festina; St. Francis de Sales, Ossian; St. Wenceslaus, Spillville, 107 E. South St., P.O. Box 821, 52312. Tel: 563-562-3045; Fax: 563-562-3292. Email: cfsrstaff@mchsi.com. Rev. Msgr. Cletus J. Hawes, Pastoral Coord.; Patty Frana, D.R.E. Priests 1; Lay Teachers 1; Students 133.

MANCHESTER. *St. Paul School of Religion*, (Grades 7-12), Serving: St. Mary, Manchester; Immaculate Conception, Masonville; St. Patrick, Ryan, Mailing Address: 119 W. Fayette St., 52057. Tel: 563-927-4710; Fax: 563-927-9949. 408 Clara Ave., 52057. Tel: 563-927-2900; Fax: 563-927-6506. Email: stpaulsor@iowatelecom.net. Rev. John R. Flaherty, Pastoral Coord.; Kathy Oberrueter, Dir. of Catechetical Programming. Lay Teachers 1; Students 234.

NEW HAMPTON. *St. John School of Religion* Serving: St. Bernard, Alta Vista; St. Boniface, Ionia; Our Lady of Lourdes, Lourdes; Holy Family, New Hampton; Immaculate Conception, North Washington, 313 W. Court St., 50659. Tel: 641-394-3171. Email: dbqrt4@arch.pvt.k12.ia.us. Rev. Mark Osterhaus, Pastoral Coord.; Marjorie Zipse, Dir. Priests 1; Lay Teachers 3; Students 131.

[F] ELEMENTARY SCHOOL SYSTEMS

CALMAR. *Calmar-Festina-Spillville Catholic School*, (Grades PreSchool-8), 302 S. Maryville, Box 815, 52132. Tel: 563-562-3291; Fax: 563-562-3292. Email: dbqe05@arch.pvt.k12.ia.us. Katie Schmitt, Prin.; Rev. Donald J. Hawes, Pastoral Coord. Consolidation of the following parishes: Our Lady of Seven Dolors (St. Mary), Festina; St. Wenceslaus, Spillville; St. Aloysius, Calmar; St. Wenceslaus (Grades K-3); St. Aloysius (Grades 4-8). Lay Teachers 12; Students 128.

CEDAR RAPIDS. *Holy Family Consolidated School*, (Grades Day Care-8) Rick Louk, Prin.; Rev. Mark J. Reasoner, Pastoral Coord. Parishes Served: Blessed John XXIII, St. Jude, St. Ludmila and St. Patrick, Cedar Rapids. Lay Teachers 37; Students 444.

LaSalle Middle School (Grades 5-8), 3700 First Ave. N.W., 52405. Tel: 319-396-7792; Fax: 319-390-6527. Email: dbqe12@arch.pvt.k12.ia.us. Rick Louk, Prin.; Rev. Mark J. Reasoner, Pastoral Coord.

St. Ludmila Center (Grades Day Care-4), 215 21st Ave. S.W., 52404. Tel: 319-362-1943; Fax: 319-364-4149. Email: dbqe10@arch.pvt.k12.ia.us. Janet Whitney, Assoc. Admin.

St. Jude Elementary (Grades Day Care-2), 3700 First Ave. N.W., 52405. Tel: 319-396-7818; Fax: 319-390-0952. Email: dbqe09@arch.pvt.k12.ia.us. Ronda Krystofiak, Assoc. Admin.

St. Pius and St. Elizabeth Ann Seton Schools, (Grades PreSchool-5), 4901 Council St. N.E., 52402-2402. Tel: 319-393-4507; Fax: 319-393-0216. Email: dbqe13@arch.pvt.k12.ia.us. Candace Hurley, Prin.; Marilyn Olson, Librarian. Lay Teachers 27; Students 395.

Regis Middle School, (Grades 6-8), Parishes Served: All Saints, Immaculate Conception, St. Matthew, St. Pius X, Cedar Rapids; St. Elizabeth Ann Seton, Hiawatha, 735 Prairie Dr. N.E., 52402. Tel: 319-363-1968; Fax: 319-247-6099. Email: dbqmM02@arch.pvt.k12.ia.us. Rev. Neil J. Manternach, Pastoral Coord.; Elizabeth Globokar, Prin.; Cindy Glynn, Asst. Prin.; Mary Bryan, Librarian. Lay Teachers 28; Students 453.

DYERSVILLE. *St. Francis Xavier School, Dyersville, Iowa*, (Grades PreSchool-6), 203 Second St., S.W., 52040. Tel: 563-875-7376; Fax: 563-875-7037. Peter Smith, Prin. Lay Teachers 28; Students 404.

FARLEY. *Seton Catholic Schools*, (Grades PreK-8), St. Joseph Center: 210 Second St. S.E., 52046. Tel: 563-744-3290; Fax: 563-744-3450. Email: dbqe28@arch.pvt.k12.ia.us. St. Patrick Center: 106 First St., S.E., Epworth, 52045. Tel: 563-876-5586; Fax: 563-876-3055. St. John Center: 10801 Sundown Rd., Peosta, 52068. Tel: 563-556-5967; Fax: 563-556-7579. Mary Smock, Prin.; Melissa O'Brien, Asst. Prin.; Rev. Richard W. Kuhn, Pastoral Coord. Consolidation of the following parishes: St. Patrick, Epworth; St. John, Peosta; St. John, Placid; St. Joseph, Farley; St. Clement, Bankston. Lay Teachers 27; Students 353.

GUTTENBERG. *St. Mary and Immaculate Conception School System*, (Grades K-8), 510 S. Second St., P.O. Box 100, 52052. Tel: 563-252-1577; Fax: 563-252-1363. Email: dbqe32@arch.pvt.k12.ia.us. Steven Cornelius, Prin.; Rev. Marvin J. Bries, Pastoral Coord.; Michelle Fassbinder, Librarian. Consolidation of the following parishes: St. Mary, Guttenberg; Immaculate Conception, North Buena Vista. Lay Teachers 10; Students 94.

HOLY CROSS. *LaSalle Elementary Schools*, (Grades PreSchool-8), Holy Cross Center: 835 Church St., P.O. Box 368, 52053-0368. Tel: 563-870-2405; Fax: 563-870-4101. Email: dbqe34@arch.pvt.k12.ia.us. Holy Trinity Center: 100 W. Main St., P.O. Box 139, Luxemburg, 52056. Tel: 563-853-2325; Fax: 563-870-4101. Steven Cornelius, Prin.; Rev. Raymond A. Burkle, Pastoral Coord. Consolidation of the following parishes: St. Joseph, Rickardsville; Holy Cross, Holy Cross; Holy Trinity, Luxemburg (Grades K-3); SS. Peter and Paul, Sherrill; St. Francis of Assisi, Balltown. Lay Teachers 12; Students 105.

MARSHALLTOWN. *Marshalltown Area Catholic Schools*, (Grades Day Care-6), St. Mary Center: 10 W. Linn St., 50158. Tel: 641-753-7977; Fax: 641-753-0337. Email: dbqe40@arch.pvt.k12.ia.us. St. Henry Center: 310 Columbus Dr., 50158. Tel: 641-753-8744. James Wessling, Prin.; Rev. James L. Miller, Pastoral Coord.; Carol Johnson, Librarian. Serving the following parishes: St. Mary, Marshalltown (Grades 3-6); St. Henry, Marshalltown (Grades K-2). Lay Teachers 18; Students 162.

NEW VIENNA. *Archbishop Hennessy Catholic School*, (Grades PreK-6), St. Boniface Center: 7420 Columbus, P.O. Box 170, 52065. Tel: 563-921-2635; Fax: 563-921-3003. Email: dbqe33@arch.pvt.k12.ia.us. SS. Peter & Paul Center: 1623 300th Ave., Dyersville, 52040. Tel: 563-875-7572. Dianne Makovec, Prin.; Rev. John J. O'Connor, Pastoral Coord. Consolidation of the following parishes: St. Boniface Center (Grades K-3), New Vienna; SS. Peter & Paul Center (Grades PreK, 4-6), Petersburg. Sisters 2; Lay Teachers 9; Students 68.

PROTIVIN. *Trinity Catholic School*, (Grades K-6), 116 N. Main St., P.O. Box 246, 52163-0246. Tel: 563-569-8556; Fax: 563-569-8477. Email: dbqe47@arch.pvt.k12.ia.us. Jim Zajicek, Prin.; Rev. Nicholas B. March, Pastoral Coord.; Colleen Stika, Librarian. Consolidation of the following parishes: Holy Trinity, Protivin; St. Luke, St. Lucas; St. John, Fort Atkinson. Lay Teachers 7; Students 54.

[G] CONSOLIDATED K-12 SYSTEMS

DUBUQUE. *Holy Family Catholic Schools*, (Grades Day Care-12), 2005 Kane St., 52001. Tel: 563-582-5456; Fax: 563-583-3885. Carol Trueg, Chief Admin.; Todd Wessels, Curriculum Dir.; Rev. Joseph L. Hauer, J.C.D., Pastoral Coord. Serving the parishes of Dubuque and Key West. Sisters 3; Lay Teachers 140; K-12 1,827.

St. Joseph the Worker Early Childcare Center, 2105 Saint Joseph St., 52001. Tel: 563-582-1246; Fax: 563-588-3960.

Holy Ghost School & Childcare Center (Grades PreSchool-5), 2981 Central Ave., 52001. Tel: 563-556-1511; Fax: 563-556-4768. Email: dbqe17@arch.pvt.k12.ia.us. Denise Grant, Prin.

Resurrection School (Grades Day Care-5), 4320 Asbury Rd., 52002. Tel: 563-583-9488; Fax: 563-557-7995. Email: dbqe20@arch.pvt.k12.ia.us. Dave Gross, Prin.

St. Anthony School (Grades Day Care-5), 2175 Rosedale, 52001. Tel: 563-556-2820; Fax: 563-556-2131. Email: dbqe17@arch.pvt.k12.ia.us. Lori Apel, Prin.

St. Columbkille School (Grades Day Care-5), 1198 Rush St., 52003. Tel: 563-582-3532; Fax: 563-583-4884. Email: dbqe22@arch.pvt.k12.ia.us. Barb Roling, Prin.

Mazzuchelli Catholic Middle School (Grades 6-8), 2005 Kane St., 52001. Tel: 563-582-1198; Fax: 563-582-5428. Email: dbqm03@arch.pvt.k12.ia.us. Kim Hermsen, Prin.; Doug Varley, Asst. Prin.

Wahlert High School, 2005 Kane St., 52001. Tel: 563-583-9771; Fax: 563-583-9775. Email: dbqh04@arch.pvt.k12.ia.us. Ronald Meyers, Prin.; Cindy Wagner, Asst. Admin.; Mark Huettner, Librarian. Parishes Served: The Parishes in Dubuque; Holy Family, New Melleray; St. Joseph's, Key West.

BELLEVUE. *Marquette High School*, 502 Franklin St., 52031. Tel: 563-872-3356; Fax: 563-872-3285. Email: dbqe04@arch.pvt.k12.ia.us. Jim Squiers, Prin.; Randy Rubel, Curriculum Dir. & Business Mgr.; Very Rev. Phillip F. Kruse, Pastoral Coord. Parishes Served: St. Joseph, Bellevue; St. Catherine, St. Catherine; St. Donatus, St. Donatus; SS. Peter and Paul, Springbrook. Lay Teachers 18; Students 254.

Bellevue Area Elementary School (Grades Day Care-8), 403 Park St., 52031. Tel: 563-872-3284; Fax: 563-872-3285. Jim Squiers, Prin.; Randy Rubel, Curriculum Dir. & Business Mgr.; Very Rev. Phillip F. Kruse, Pastoral Coord. Parishes Served: St. Joseph, Bellevue; SS. Peter & Paul, Springbrook; St. Donatus, St. Donatus.

CASCADE. *Aquin Educational System*, (Grades Day Care-12), Serving: St. Matthais, Cascade; Sacred Heart, Fillmore; St. Patrick, Garryowen; St. Peter, Temple Hill, 608 Third Ave., N.W., P.O. Box 460, 52033-0460. Tel: 563-852-7875; Fax: 563-852-5269. Email: dbqcdir@arch.pvt.k12.ia.us. Deacon Ray Noonan, Pastoral Coord.; Rebecca Smith, D.R.E. Lay Teachers 20; PK-8 258.

Little Angels (Grades Day Care), 608 Third Ave., N.W., P.O. Box 460, 52033-0460. Tel: 563-852-7020.

Aquin Elementary School (Grades PreSchool-8), 608 Third Ave., N.W., P.O. Box 460, 52033-0460. Tel: 563-852-3331; Fax: 563-852-5269. Email: dbqe06@arch.pvt.k12.ia.us. Mary Yamoah, Prin.

Aquin School of Religion (Grades 9-12), 608 Third Ave., N.W., P.O. Box 460, 52033-0460. Tel: 563-852-7875; Fax: 563-852-5269. Email: dbq023re@arch.pvt.k12.ia.us. Rebecca Smith, D.R.E.

GILBERTVILLE. *Don Bosco High School*, (Grades K-12), 405 16th Ave., 50634. Tel: 319-296-1692; Fax: 319-296-1693. Email: dbqH06@arch.pvt.k12.ia.us. Eric Eckerman, Prin.; Rev. Henry P. Huber, Spiritual Dir. Parishes Served: St. Francis, Barclay; St. Mary of Mt. Carmel, Eagle Center; Immaculate Conception, Gilbertville; St. Athanasius, Jesup; Sacred Heart, LaPorte City; St. Joseph, Raymond. Lay Teachers 34; Students 354.

Gilbertville-Raymond Consolidation (Grades K-8), *Immaculate Conception Center*, 311 16th Ave., 50634. Tel: 319-296-1089; Fax: 319-296-3847. *St. Joseph Center*, 6916 Layafette Rd., P.O. Box 158, Raymond, 50667. Tel: 319-233-5980. Email: dbqe31@arch.pvt.k12.ia.us. Sharon Mayer, Prin.; Rev. Kenneth C. Stecher, Pastoral Coord. Parishes served: Immaculate Conception, Gilbertville & St. Joseph, Raymond

MASON CITY. *Newman Catholic School System*, (Grades Day Care-12), Parishes served: Holy Family, St. Joseph, Mason City. Sisters 1; Lay Teachers 43; K-12 Students 622.

Newman Child Care formerly Newman Catholic Child Care 2050 S. McKinley Ave., 50401. Tel: 641-423-0168; Fax: 641-423-3521. Kathy Lloyd, Early Childhood Dir.

Newman Elementary School (Grades K-8), 2000 S. McKinley Ave., 50401. Tel: 641-423-3101; Fax: 641-422-1181. Email: dbqe41@arch.pvt.k12.ia.us. Jan Avery, Admin.; Rev. Michael G. Schueller, Pastoral Coord.

Newman High School, 2445 19th St. S.W., 50401. Tel: 641-423-6939; Fax: 641-423-6653. Email: dbqh07@arch.pvt.k12.ia.us. Tony Adams, Prin.; Rev. Michael G. Schueller, Pastoral Coord. Parishes Served: St. Patrick, Clear Lake; Sacred Heart, Manly; Holy Family, St. Joseph, Mason City; Sacred Heart, Rockwell.

WATERLOO. *Cedar Valley Catholic Schools*, (Grades Day Care-12), 3231 W. 9th St., 50702. Tel: 319-232-1422; Fax: 319-232-3977. Jeff Frost, Dir. Educ.; Rev. Louis M. Jaeger, Pastoral Coord. Lay Teachers 93; Students (K-12) 962.

Blessed Sacrament School (Grades Day Care-8), 600 Stephan Ave., 50701. Tel: 319-233-7863; Fax: 319-233-8237. Email: dbqe49@arch.pvt.k12.ia.us. Nancy Stirm, Prin.

Sacred Heart School (Grades Day Care-8), 620 W. 5th St., 50702. Tel: 319-234-6593; Fax: 319-235-7987. Email: dbqe50@arch.pvt.k12.ia.us. Julie

Niemeyer, Prin.

St. Edward School (Grades Day Care-8), 139 E. Mitchell, 50702. Tel: 319-233-6202; Fax: 319-235-2898. Email: dbqe51@arch.pvt.k12.ia.us. Pam Schowalter, Prin.

Blessed Maria Assunta Pallotta Middle School, 3231 W. 9th St., 50702. Tel: 319-233-3358. Amy Sandvold, Prin.

Columbus High School, 3231 W. 9th St., 50702. Tel: 319-233-3358; Fax: 319-235-0733. Email: dbqh08@arch.pvt.k12.ia.us. Mr. Tom Ulses, Prin.; Rev. Louis M. Jaeger, Pastoral Coord. Parishes Served: St. Patrick's, Cedar Falls; Blessed Sacrament, Queen of Peace, Sacred Heart and St. Edward, Waterloo.

[H] GENERAL HOSPITALS

DUBUQUE. *Mercy Medical Center-Dubuque* (A Division of Mercy Health Services-Iowa), 250 Mercy Dr., 52001. Tel: 563-589-8000; Fax: 563-589-8073. Web: www.mercydubuque.com. Russell Knight, Pres.; Patrick Conlon, Dir. Pastoral Care Dept.; Sr. Maureen Fury, B.V.M., Chap.; Maryann Dunn, Chap.; Rev. Richard L. Schaefer, Chap.; Deacon William Biver, Chap.; Cindy Serpliss, Chap. Bed Capacity 263; Total Staff 1,177; Patients Assisted Annually 48,290.

CEDAR FALLS. *Sartori Memorial Hospital, Inc.* (Formerly known as S.F.H., Inc.), 515 College St., 50613. Tel: 319-268-3000; Fax: 319-268-3270. Email: jack.dusenbery@wfhc.org. Jack Dusenbery, Contact Person. Bed Capacity 101; Patients Assisted Annually 43,148; Total Staff 200.

CEDAR RAPIDS. *Mercy Medical Center, Endowment Foundation, Inc., Cedar Rapids, IA*, 701 Tenth St. S.E., 52403. Tel: 319-398-6206. Sue Hawn, Pres.; Sr. James Marie Donahue, R.S.M., Ph.D., Chairwoman of the Bd.

Mercy Medical Center-Cedar Rapids (Sisters of Mercy-Regional Community of Cedar Rapids), 701 Tenth St. S.E., 52403. Tel: 319-398-6011. Email: kcrist@mercycare.org. Web: www.mercycare.org. Tim Charles, Pres. & CEO; Revs. David J. Ambrosy, Resident Priest Chap.; Ken Glandorf, Chap.; Mark McDermott, Dir. Pastoral Care Office; Mark Eccles, Chap.; Deacon Daniel Hoeger, Chap.; Sr. Margaret Murphy, R.S.M., Chap. Sponsored by the Sisters of Mercy, West Midwest Community. Total Staff 2,283; Bed Capacity Acute 369; Skilled Nursing 21; Patients Assisted Annually 243,000.

Mercycare Service Corporation (Parent Corp.), 701 10th St. S.E., 52403. Tel: 319-398-6011. Tim Charles, CEO & Pres. Sponsored by the Sisters of Mercy, West Midwest Community.

DYERSVILLE. *Mercy Medical Center-Dubuque (Dyersville)* (A Division of Mercy Health Services Iowa), 1111 Third St. S.W., 52040. Tel: 563-875-7101; Fax: 563-875-2957. Web: www.mercydubuque.com. Russell Knight, Pres. Bed Capacity 25; Total Staff 71; Patients Assisted Annually 4,322.

MASON CITY. *Mercy Medical Center-North Iowa* (Member of Mercy Health Network), 1000 4th St. S.W., 50401. Tel: 641-428-7000; Fax: 641-428-7827. James G. Fitzpatrick, Pres. & CEO; Very Rev. Kenneth B. Gehling, Chap.; Rev. Barbara McCaulley, Vice Pres., Mission & Ethics (Episcopal); Susan Kennedy, Chap. (Evangelical). Bed Capacity 346; Total Staff 2,427; Patients Assisted Annually 554,066.

NEW HAMPTON. *Mercy Medical Center-New Hampton* (Member of Mercy Health Network), 308 N. Maple Ave., 50659. Tel: 641-394-4121; Fax: 641-394-1669. Web: www.mercynewhampton.com. Bruce Roesler, Pres. & CEO; Richard Kriener, Bd. Chm., Member Organization Board. Bed Capacity 17; Patients Assisted Annually 31,378; Total Staff 127.

OELWEIN. *Mercy Hospital of Franciscan Sisters, Inc.* formerly Mercy Hospital of Franciscan Sisters , 201 8th Ave. S.E., 50662. Tel: 319-283-6000; Fax: 319-283-6004. Jack Dusenbery, Contact Person, Pres. & CEO. Franciscan Sisters. Daughters of the Sacred Hearts of Jesus and Mary, Wheaton, IL. Bed Capacity 64; Patients Assisted Annually 25,430; Total Staff 123.

WATERLOO. *Covenant Medical Center, Inc.*, 3421 W. Ninth St., 50702. Tel: 319-272-8000; Fax: 319-272-7313. Email: jack.dusenbery@wfhc.org. Web: www.covhealth.com. Jack Dusenbery, Pres. & Contact Person. Franciscan Sisters. Daughters of the Sacred Hearts of Jesus and Mary, Wheaton, IL. Total Staff 1,138; Bed Capacity 346; Patients Assisted Annually 218,063.

[I] SPECIAL HEALTH CENTERS

DUBUQUE. *Clare House*, 3340 Windsor Ave., 52001-1300. Tel: 563-583-9786; Fax: 563-583-6080. Email: info@osfdbq.org. Web: www.osfdbq.org. Rev. Ronald G. Friedell, Chap. (Retired); Sisters Margaret Burkle, O.S.F., Pre-Retirement Dir.; Nancy Schreck, O.S.F., Pres. Sisters of St. Francis, Dubuque. Bed Capacity 76; Professed Sisters 69; Total Staff 100; Patients Assisted Annually 90.

Marian Hall Infirmary, 1050 Carmel Dr., 52003. Tel: 563-556-5474; Fax: 563-588-1975. Email: bvmcenter@bvmcong.org. Web: www.bvmcong.org. Rev. Msgr. James O. Barta, Ph.D., Chap. (Retired); Joyce Cravens, Admin. Professed Sisters 96; Bed Capacity 105; Total Staff 162.

Caritas Center, 1130 Carmel Dr., 52003-7911. Tel: 563-556-3240. Email: bvmcenter@bvmcong.org. Web: www.bvmcong.org. Joyce Cravens, Admin. Professed Sisters 37; Bed Capacity 53; Total Staff 79.

[J] HOMES FOR AGED

DUBUQUE. *Stonehill Franciscan Services, Inc.*, 3485 Windsor Ave., 52001-1312. Tel: 563-557-7180; Fax: 563-584-9282. Email: ethomas@stonehilldbq.com. Web: www.stonehilldbq.com. Nancy Dunkel, Svcs. Bd. Chm.; Eric L. Thomas, Pres. & CEO. Bed Capacity 290; Total Staff 335; Total Assisted Annually 530; Apartments & Villas 52; Residents 65.

Stonehill Benevolent Foundation Tel: 563-557-7180; Fax: 563-584-9282. John Gonner, Chair, Stonehill Benevolent Foundation Board. Sponsored by Sisters of St. Francis of the Holy Family.

Villa Raphael, 1155 Mt. Loretta Ave., 52003. Tel: 563-588-2049. Email: dbqvilla@arch.pvt.k12.ia.us. Patricia Flores, Dir. Administered by the Archdiocese of Dubuque.; Accommodations for 16 priests. Total in Residence 16; Total Staff 5.

CEDAR RAPIDS. *Hallmar-Mercy Medical Center*, 701 Tenth St. S.E., 52403. Tel: 319-398-6241. Tim Charles, CEO/Pres. Sisters of Mercy, West Midwest Community., Cedar Rapids Regional, owned and operated by Mercy Medical Center. Total Assisted 50; Residents 55; Total Staff 50.

DYERSVILLE. *Ellen Kennedy Living Center*, 1177 7th St., S.W., 52040. Tel: 563-875-6323; Fax: 563-875-6268. Kari A. Wittmeyer, Dir. & Contact Person. Sponsor: Mercy Medical Center.; Purpose: to provide funds to assure persons of limited resources will be able to access programs and services at the Ellen Kennedy Living Center. Assisted Living 32; Independent Living 26; Total Staff 29.

Mercy Medical Center-Dubuque-Dyersville-Oakcrest Manor (A Division of Mercy Health Services - Iowa), 1111 Third St. S.W., 52040. Tel: 563-875-7101; Fax: 563-875-2957. Web: www.mercydubuque.com. Russell Knight, Pres. Bed Capacity 40; Patients Assisted Annually 49; Total Staff 39.

[K] MONASTERIES AND RESIDENCES OF PRIESTS AND BROTHERS

PEOSTA. *New Melleray Abbey, Order of Cistercians of the Strict Observance*, 6632 Melleray Cir., 52068. Tel: 563-588-2319; Fax: 563-588-4117. Email: monks@newmelleray.org. Web: www.newmelleray.org. Rt. Rev. David R. Bock, O.C.S.O., Retired Abbot (Retired); Revs. Bernard J. Cullen, O.C.S.O.; Xavier L. Dieter, O.C.S.O.; Alberic R. Farbolin, O.C.S.O.; Rt. Rev. Brendan J. Freeman, O.C.S.O., Abbot; Revs. James B. Henderson, O.C.S.O.; Thaddeus J. Kennedy, O.C.S.O.; Daniel F. Lenihan, O.C.S.O.; Thomas A. MacMaster, O.C.S.O.; James E. O'Connor, O.C.S.O.; Neil Paquette, O.C.S.O., Prior; Kenneth F. Tietjen, O.C.S.O.; Stephen Verbest, O.C.S.O., Novice & Vocation Dir.; Jonah Wharff, O.C.S.O.; Bros. Albert Bracket, O.C.S.O.; Gilbert B. Cardillo, O.C.S.O.; Juan Diego, O.C.S.O.; Michael Gajarski, O.C.S.O.; Cyprian Griffith, O.C.S.O.; Paul Halaburt, O.C.S.O.; Kevin Knox, O.C.S.O.; Nicholas Koenig, O.C.S.O.; Joseph Kronebusch, O.C.S.O.; Felix Leja, O.C.S.O.; John O'Driscoll, O.C.S.O.; Ephrem Poppish, O.C.S.O.; Walter Schoenberg, O.C.S.O.; Tobias Shanahan, O.C.S.O.; Robert Simon, O.C.S.O.; Paul Andrew Tanner, O.C.S.O.; Dennis Vavra, O.C.S.O.; Placid Zilka, O.C.S.O.; Rt. Rev. David Wechter, O.C.S.O., Retired Abbot (Retired).

Corporation of New Melleray Total in Residence 33; Priests 14; Brothers 19; Absent on Medical Leave 3; Chaplains 1.

[L] CONVENTS AND RESIDENCES FOR SISTERS

DUBUQUE. *St. Joseph's Convent, Mount Carmel*, 1150 Carmel Dr., 52003. Tel: 563-556-3240. Email: bvmcenter@bvmcong.org. Web: www.bvmcong.org. Joyce Cravens, Admin.; Rev. Msgr. Thomas E. Toale, Ph.D., Chap.; Christine Olsem, Contact Person. Motherhouse of the Sisters of Charity of the Blessed Virgin Mary. Professed Sisters 70; Total Staff 10; Bed Capacity 78.

Mt. Loretto Convent, 2360 Carter Rd., 52001-2997. Tel: 563-588-2008; Fax: 563-588-4463. Email: jennifer@dubuquepresentations.org. Web: www.dubuquepresentations.org. Sr. Jennifer Rausch, P.B.V.M., Pres.; Jean Lange, House Coord.; Rev. Douglas O. Wathier, S.T.D., Chap. Motherhouse and Novitiate of the Sisters of the Presentation of the B.V.M. Professed Sisters 62.

International Presentation Association Tel: 212-370-0075; Fax: 212-370-0075. Email: ipanetworker@pbvm.org.au. Web: ipa.ozehosting-.com.

Mt. St. Francis, 3390 Windsor Ave., 52001-1311. Tel: 563-583-9786; Fax: 563-583-3250. Email: info@osfdbq.org. Web: www.osfdbq.org. Sisters Marie Cigrand, O.S.F., Contact Person; Nancy Schreck, O.S.F., Pres.; Pat R. Farrell, O.S.F., Vice Pres.; Rev. Robert R. Beck, Chap. (Retired). Sisters of St. Francis of the Holy Family Charitable Trust., Motherhouse and Novitiate of the Sisters of St. Francis of the Holy Family. Professed Sisters 91.

Our Lady of the Mississippi Abbey, 8400 Abbey Hill Ln., 52003. Tel: 563-582-2595; Fax: 563-582-5511. Email: sisters@olmabbey.org. Web: www.mississippiabbey.org. Sr. Nettie Gamble, O.C.S.O., Abbess. The Cistercian Nuns of the Strict Observance., (Monastery of Trappistine Nuns). Professed Nuns 20; Novices 2.

Sisters of Charity of the Blessed Virgin Mary, BVM Center, Mount Carmel, 1100 Carmel Dr., 52003-7991. Tel: 563-588-2351; Fax: 563-588-4832. Email: bvmcenter@bvmcong.org. Web: www.bvmcong.org. Sisters Mary Ann Zollmann, B.V.M., Pres. Congregation; Mira Mosle, B.V.M., 1st Vice Pres.; Teri Hadro, B.V.M., 2nd Vice Pres.; Deanna Marie Carr, B.V.M., Archivist. Total Staff 32.

Sisters of the Visitation, 2950 Kaufmann Ave., 52001-1631. Tel: 563-556-2440. Email: dbqsvm@arch.pvt.k12.ia.us. Sr. Patricia Clark, S.V.M., Pres. & Contact Person. Sisters of the Visitation of the Immaculate Heart of Mary. Professed Sisters 5.

CEDAR RAPIDS. *Sisters of Mercy of the Americas West Midwest Community, Inc. Sacred Heart Convent*, 1125 Prairie Dr., N.E., 52402-4737. Tel: 319-364-5196; Fax: 319-364-7383. Email: info@mercywmw.org. Web: www.mercywestmidwest.org. Theresa Baldus-Kokontis, Admin.; Sisters Judith Frikker, R.S.M., Pres.; Sheila Megley, R.S.M., Treas.; Judith Cannon, R.S.M., Sec.; Kathy Thornton, R.S.M., Leadership Team; Michelle Gorman, R.S.M., Leadership Team; Kim Kinsel, Community Oper. Officer; Carol Kelley, Community Fin. Officer; Sandy Goetzinger-Comer, Dir. Communications; Rev. David J. Ambrosy, Chap. Motherhouse of the Sisters of Mercy of the Americas - West Midwest Community.; (As of July 1, 2008 the Sisters of Mercy of the Americas Regional Communities of Auburn, CA; Burlingame, CA; Cedar Rapids, IA; Chicago, IL; Detroit, MI; and Omaha, NE merged to create Sisters of Mercy of the Americas West Midwest Community, Inc.) Sisters 810; Associates 565.

Sisters of Mercy Charitable Trust Tel: 319-364-5196; Fax: 319-364-7383.

Catherine McAuley Center, Cedar Rapids Tel: 319-363-4993; Fax: 319-363-8332.

Mount Mercy College, Cedar Rapids Tel: 319-363-8213; Fax: 319-363-5270. Web: www.mtmercy.edu.

Mercy Medical Center, Cedar Rapids Tel: 319-398-6011; Fax: 319-398-6912.

[M] RETREAT HOUSES

DUBUQUE. *New Melleray Guest House*, 6632 Melleray Cir., Peosta, 52068. Tel: 563-588-2319; Fax: 563-588-4117. Email: monks@newmelleray.org. Web: www.newmelleray.org.

Shalom Retreat Center, 1001 Davis St., 52001-1398. Tel: 563-582-3592; Fax: 563-582-5872. Email: info@shalomretreats.org. Web: www.shalomretreats.org. Sr. Marci Blum, O.S.F., Dir. Retreatants 8,000; Total Staff 9.

CEDAR FALLS. *American Martyrs Retreat House*, 2209 North Union Rd., 50613-9441. Tel: 319-266-3543; Fax: 319-266-3543. Email: dbqamrh@arch.pvt.k12.ia.us. Web: americanmartyrs.tripod.com. Sr. Jeanine Kuhn, P.B.V.M., Dir. Total Staff 18.

HIAWATHA. *Prairiewoods Franciscan Spirituality Center*, 120 E. Boyson Rd., 52233-1277. Tel: 319-395-6700; Fax: 319-395-6703. Email: ecospirit@prairiewoods.org. Web: www.prairiewoods.org. Bro. Barry Donaghue, C.F.C., Dir. & Contact Person.

[N] NEWMAN CENTERS

AMES. *St. Thomas Aquinas Church and Catholic Student Center (Iowa State University)* 2210 Lincoln Way, 50014-7184. Tel: 515-292-3810; Fax: 515-292-3841. Email: dbq004@arch.pvt.k12.ia.us. Web: www.staparish.net. Revs. Jon M. Seda;

James W. Dubert, Campus Min. & Assoc. Pastor; Shari Reilly, Dir. Campus Ministry & Social Justice Coord.; Todd Flowerday, Dir. Liturgy & Music; Robert LeBlanc, Church Business Mgr. & Contact Person; Misty Prater, Campus Min.; Kathy White, D.R.E.; Cynthia Sneller, Youth Min.

CEDAR FALLS. *St. Stephen the Witness Catholic Student Center, University of Northern Iowa* 1019 W. 23rd St., 50613-3550. Tel: 319-266-9863; Fax: 319-266-3706. Email: kjglaser@ststephenuni.org. Web: www.ststephenuni.org. Rev. Kenneth J. Glaser, Dir. Campus Ministry; Deacon Leonard Froyen, Ph.D.; Shannon Duffy, Campus Min.; Anastasia Nicklaus Schmelzer, Dir. of Liturgy & Music; Mary Beckey Kelly, Devel. Coord.; Lisa Geisler, Office Mgr.; Don Walsh, Business Mgr. Total Staff 7.

FAYETTE. *Upper Iowa University* 605 Washington St., P.O. Box 1857, 52142. Tel: 563-425-5200; Fax: 563-425-5323.

[O] MISCELLANEOUS

DUBUQUE. *Archdiocese of Dubuque Deposit and Loan Fund*, 1229 Mt. Loretta, 52003-8787. Tel: 563-556-2580; Fax: 563-556-5464. Email: DBQCFO@arch.pvt.k12.ia.us. Richard L. Runde, Finance Officer.

Archdiocese of Dubuque Education Fund, 1229 Mt. Loretta, 52003-8787. Tel: 563-556-2580; Fax: 563-556-5464. Email: DBQCFO@arch.pvt.12.ia.us. Richard L. Runde, Finance Officer.

Archdiocese of Dubuque Perpetual Care Fund, 1229 Mt. Loretta, 52003-8787. Tel: 563-556-2580; Fax: 563-556-5464. Email: DBQCFO@arch.pvt.k12.ia.us. Richard L. Runde, Finance Officer.

Archdiocese of Dubuque Seminarian Education Fund, 1229 Mt. Loretta, 52003-8787. Tel: 563-556-2580; Fax: 563-556-5464. Email: DBQCFO@arch.pvt.k12.ia.us. Richard L. Runde, Finance Officer.

Cistercian Studies Quarterly, Inc., Mississippi Abbey, 8400 Abbey Hill, 52003. Tel: 563-582-2595, Ext. 153; Fax: 563-582-5511. Email: csq@mississippiabbey.org. Web: www.cistercian-studies-quarterly.org. Evelyn Redling, Admin. & Contact Person. Sponsor: Cistercian Order of the Strict Observance of the USA Region.

Declaration of Trust of the Paul & Janet Auterman Charitable Educational Trust, 4300 Asbury Rd., 52002. Tel: 563-556-7511; Fax: 563-556-7419. Julie Hermann, Co-Trustee & Contact Person. Archdiocese of Dubuque, Resurrection Parish, Purpose: To establish a fund to assist students in attending Catholic schools, Pre-K through grade 12, and for such related purposes as allowed by Internal Revenue code Section 501(c)(3) of the 1986 Internal Revenue Code, as amended, or any successor section.

Heartland Housing Initiative, 90 Main St., 52001. Tel: 563-583-9653; Fax: 563-583-6490. Email: jschmidt@mercyhousing.org. Julie Schmidt, Contact Person & Property Mgr., Sponsored by the Wheaton Franciscan Sisters, Wheaton, IL and a corporation of Wheaton Franciscan System. (A member of the Mercy Housing System, Mercy Housing Corp.) Total Staff 2; Total Assisted 92.

Hennessy Charitable Trust, 2360 Carter Rd., 52001-2997. Tel: 563-588-2008; Fax: 563-588-4463. Email: lynn@dubuquepresentations.org. Web: www.dubuquepresentations.org. Sisters Jennifer Rausch, P.B.V.M., Pres.; Lynn Fangman, P.B.V.M., Contact Person. Sponsored by the Sisters of the Presentation.

Opening Doors, 1561 Jackson St., 52001. Tel: 563-582-7480; Fax: 563-582-7467. Email: mbrown@openingdoorsdbq.org. Web: www.openingdoorsdbq.org. Art Roche, Bd. Pres.; Michelle Brown, Exec. Dir. & Contact Person. Sponsors: Sinsinawa Dominicans, Sisters of the Presentation, Sisters of Charity, B.V.M, Sisters of the Visitation and Dubuque Franciscan Sisters., Purpose: Maria House provides transitional housing and related support services for women and children at 1561 Jackson Street. Teresa Shelter provides emergency shelter for women and children at 1111 Bluff Street. Total Assisted Annually 320.

Maria House, 1561 Jackson St., 52001.

Teresa Shelter, 1111 Bluff St., 52001. Tel: 563-690-0086.

Our Faith, Our Children, Our Future, School Tuition Organization formerly Our Faith, Our Children, Our Future School Tuition Organization, Inc. 1229 Mt. Loretta Ave., 52003-7800. Tel: 563-556-2580; Fax: 563-556-5464. Richard L. Runde, Contact Person. Purpose: to provide tuition assistance to students enrolled in accredited non-public schools located within the Archdiocese of Dubuque in conformance with the Iowa law.

Presentation Lantern, 1584 White St., 52001. Tel: 563-557-7134; Fax: 563-557-7466. Email: lanterncenter@aol.com. Sr. Corine Murray, P.B.V.M., Exec. Dir. & Contact Person.

Second Chances, 2600 Dodge St., 52003. Tel: 563-583-5474. Paula Evers, Contact Person. Sponsored by the Archdiocese of Dubuque., Purpose: providing financial assistance for the operation of Wahlert High School and Holy Family Catholic Schools of Dubuque.

Society of St. Vincent de Paul Particular Council of the City of Dubuque, Iowa Gary Anglin, National Trustee & Contact Person.

Dubuque Council, 4990 Radford Rd., 52002. Tel: 563-584-2226; Fax: 563-690-1581. Gary Anglin, Natl. Trustee & Contact Person.

CEDAR FALLS. **Sartori Health Care Foundation, Inc.*, 515 College St., 50613. Tel: 319-268-3161; Fax: 319-268-3270. Heather Bremer-Miller, Devel. Dir.

CEDAR RAPIDS. *Sisters of Mercy of the Americas. Regional Community of Cedar Rapids, Iowa Charitable Trust*, 1125 Prairie Dr., N.E., 52402-4737. Tel: 319-364-5196; Fax: 319-364-7383. Sr. Laura Reicks, R.S.M., Chm.; Theresa Baldus-Kokontis, Admin. Sisters of Mercy of the Americas, West Midwest Community.

St. Vincent de Paul Particular Counsel of Cedar Rapids, Iowa, 928 7th St., S.E., 52401. Tel: 319-365-5091. Robert Crawford, Pres.

WATERLOO. *Covenant Foundation, Inc.*, 3421 W. Ninth St., 50702. Tel: 319-272-7676; Fax: 319-272-5093. Email: heather.bremermiller@wfhc.org. Heather Bremer-Miller, Exec. Dir.

Ridgeway Place, Inc., 155 E. Ridgeway Ave., 50702. Tel: 319-272-2622; Fax: 319-272-2633. Web: www.fm-inc.org. Susan Dillberg, Chm. & Contact Person. Assisted Living Housing Units 96; Residents 85; Total Staff 32.

Society of St. Vincent de Paul District Council of Waterloo, Iowa, 320 Broadway St., 50703. Tel: 319-232-3366; Fax: 319-232-5114. Patrick A. Russo, Exec. Dir.; Richard Kerns, Pres.

Wheaton Franciscan Healthcare-Iowa, Inc., 3421 W. Ninth St., 50702. Tel: 319-272-8000; Fax: 319-272-7313. Jack Dusenbery, Pres. & Contact Person.

WEBSTER CITY. *St. Thomas Aquinas Foundation*, 1000 Des Moines St., 50595-2147. Tel: 515-832-1190; Fax: 515-832-3757. Web: www.stthomaswc.org. Rev. Stephen L. Meyer, Contact Person. St. Thomas Aquinas Parish.

RELIGIOUS INSTITUTES OF MEN REPRESENTED IN THE ARCHDIOCESE

For further details refer to the corresponding bracketed number in the Religious Institutes of Men or Women section.

[1180]—*Brothers of Saint Pius X*—C.S.P.X.

[0330]—*Brothers of the Christian Schools* (Midwest Prov.)—F.S.C.

[0350]—*Order of Cistercians of the Strict Observance-Trappists* (Our Lady of New Melleray)—O.C.S.O.

[0420]—*Society of the Divine Word* (Northern Prov.)—S.V.D.

[1060]—*Society of the Precious Blood* (Kansas City Province)—C.PP.S.

RELIGIOUS INSTITUTES OF WOMEN REPRESENTED IN THE ARCHDIOCESE

[0670]—*Cistercian Nuns of the Strict Observance*—O.C.S.O.

[2100]—*Congregation of the Humility of Mary* (Davenport, IA)—C.H.M.

[1780]—*Congregation of the Sisters of the Third Order of St. Francis of Perpetual Adoration*—F.S.P.A.

[1070-03]—*Dominican Sisters Congregation of the Most Holy Rosary* (Sinsinawa, WI)—O.P.

[3530]—*Missionary Sisters Servants of the Holy Spirit*—S.Sp.S.

[2960]—*Notre Dame Sisters* (Omaha, NE)—N.D.

[3130]—*Our Lady of Victory Missionary Sisters*—O.L.V.M.

[2970]—*School Sisters of Notre Dame* (Mankato, MN)—S.S.N.D.

[1680]—*School Sisters of St. Francis* (Milwaukee, WI)—O.S.F.

[0440]—*Sisters of Charity of Cincinnati, Ohio*

[0430]—*Sisters of Charity of the Blessed Virgin Mary*—B.V.M.

[2575]—*Sisters of Mercy of the Americas* (West Midwest Community)—R.S.M.

[1540]—*Sisters of St. Francis* (Clinton, IA)—O.S.F.

[1705]—*Sisters of St. Francis* (St. Francis, WI)

[1570]—*Sisters of St. Francis of the Holy Family*—O.S.F.

[3320]—*Sisters of the Presentation of the B.V.M.* (Dubuque, IA; Fargo, SD)—P.B.V.M.

[4200]—*Sisters of the Visitation of the Immaculate Heart of Mary* (Dubuque, IA)—S.V.M.

CEMETERIES

DUBUQUE. *Catholic Cemeteries of Dubuque, Inc.*, P.O. Box 479, 52004-0479. Tel: 563-556-2580; Fax: 563-556-5464. Email: dbqcfo@arch.pvt.k12.ia.us.

Mount Calvary

Mount Olivet

CEDAR RAPIDS. *St. John*

St. Joseph

Mount Calvary

MCINTIRE. *St. Patrick*

WATERLOO. *Catholic Cemeteries, Inc.*

NECROLOGY

† Connolly, Rev. Msgr. Leon L., (Retired)—Died Sept. 27, 2011

† Heuring, Rev. Msgr. Alvan P., (Retired)—Died Dec. 8, 2010

† Manternach, Rev. Msgr. Albert V., (Retired)—Died Jan. 3, 2011

† Auer, Robert F., (Retired)—Died May 23, 2011

† Carpender, Thomas J., (Retired)—Died Jan. 15, 2011

† Charipar, Henry W., (Retired)—Died Oct. 14, 2011

† Krapfl, Daniel A., (Retired)—Died Sept. 12, 2011

† Purtell, Thomas W., (Retired)—Died Aug. 19, 2011

An asterisk (*) denotes an organization that has established tax-exempt status directly with the IRS and is not covered by the USCCB Group Ruling.

Diocese of Duluth

(Dioecesis Duluthensis)

Most Reverend

PAUL D. SIRBA

Bishop of Duluth; ordained May 31, 1986; appointed Bishop of Duluth October 15, 2009; ordained December 14, 2009. *Pastoral Center: 2830 E. Fourth St., Duluth, MN 55812.*

Pastoral Center: 2830 E. Fourth St., Duluth, MN 55812.
Tel: 218-724-9111; Fax: 218-724-1056.

Web: www.dioceseduluth.org

Email: duluth@dioceseduluth.org

ESTABLISHED OCTOBER 3, 1889.

Square Miles 22,354.

Corporate Title: Diocese of Duluth.

Comprises the counties of Aitkin, Carlton, Cass, Cook, Crow Wing, Itasca, Koochiching, Lake, Pine and St. Louis in the State of Minnesota.

For legal titles of parishes and diocesan institutions, consult the Chancery Office.

STATISTICAL OVERVIEW

Personnel	
Bishop	1
Priests: Diocesan Active in Diocese	45
Priests: Diocesan Active Outside Diocese	3
Priests: Retired, Sick or Absent	24
Number of Diocesan Priests	72
Religious Priests in Diocese	8
Total Priests in Diocese	80
Extern Priests in Diocese	5
Ordinations:	
Diocesan Priests	1
Transitional Deacons	6
Permanent Deacons in Diocese	45
Total Sisters	97
Parishes	
Parishes	93
With Resident Pastor:	
Resident Diocesan Priests	38
Resident Religious Priests	6
Without Resident Pastor:	
Administered by Priests	48
Administered by Deacons	1
Professional Ministry Personnel:	
Sisters	4
Lay Ministers	27
Welfare	
Catholic Hospitals	2
Total Assisted	301,963
Homes for the Aged	5
Total Assisted	646
Day Care Centers	1
Total Assisted	110
Educational	
Diocesan Students in Other Seminaries	16
Seminaries, Religious	2
Students Religious	1
Total Seminarians	17
Colleges and Universities	1
Total Students	4,014
Elementary Schools, Diocesan and Parish	12
Total Students	1,659
Catechesis/Religious Education:	
High School Students	2,734
Elementary Students	3,129
Total Students under Catholic Instruction	11,553
Teachers in the Diocese:	
Priests	1
Sisters	5
Lay Teachers	314
Vital Statistics	
Receptions into the Church:	
Infant Baptism Totals	643
Minor Baptism Totals	34
Adult Baptism Totals	34
Received into Full Communion	87
First Communions	644
Confirmations	650
Marriages:	
Catholic	145
Interfaith	130
Total Marriages	275
Deaths	903
Total Catholic Population	56,925
Total Population	447,042

Former Bishops—Rt. Revs. JAMES MCGOLRICK, D.D., cons. Dec. 27, 1889; died Jan. 23, 1918; JOHN T. MCNICHOLAS, O.P., S.T.D., cons. Sept. 8, 1918; appt. Archbishop of Cincinnati July 8, 1925; died April 22, 1950; Most Revs. THOMAS A. WELCH, D.D., cons. Feb. 3, 1926; died Sept. 9, 1959; FRANCIS J. SCHENK, D.D., cons. May 24, 1945; appt. to Duluth Jan. 19, 1960; resigned April 30, 1969; died Oct. 28, 1969; PAUL F. ANDERSON, D.D., appt. Titular Bishop of Polignando and Coadjutor Bishop with right of succession July 19, 1968; cons. Oct. 17, 1968; succeeded to See April 10, 1969; resigned Aug. 7, 1982; appt. Apostolic Administrator Aug. 7, 1982; appt. Auxiliary Bishop of Sioux Falls, SD March 25, 1983; died Jan. 4, 1987; ROBERT H. BROM, D.D., cons. May 23, 1983; appt. Coadjutor Bishop of San Diego, CA, May 9, 1989; ROGER L. SCHWIETZ, O.M.I., D.D., ord. Dec. 20, 1967; appt. Bishop of Duluth Dec. 12, 1989; cons. Feb. 2, 1990; appt. Coadjutor Archbishop of Anchorage, Jan. 18, 2000; installed March 24, 2000; succeeded to See March 3, 2001; DENNIS M. SCHNURR, ord. July 20, 1974; appt. Bishop of Duluth Jan. 18, 2001; ord. April 2, 2001; appt. Coadjutor Archbishop of Cincinnati Oct. 17, 2008.

Pastoral Center—2830 E. Fourth St., Duluth, 55812. Tel: 218-724-9111; Fax: 218-724-1056. Office Hours: Mon.-Thurs. 8-12 & 12:30-4:30, Fri. 8-1.

Vicar General—Rev. JAMES B. BISSONETTE, J.C.L.

Finance Officer—Mr. FRANZ HOEFFERLE.

Moderator of the Curia—VACANT.

Safe Environment—Rev. DALE NAU, J.C.L.

Chancellor—Rev. DALE NAU, J.C.L.

Vice Chancellor—Rev. ERIC F. HASTINGS, J.C.L.

Diocesan Tribunal—2830 E. Fourth St., Duluth, 55812. Tel: 218-724-9111.

Judicial Vicar—Rev. ERIC F. HASTINGS, J.C.L.

Defender of the Bond—Rev. DALE NAU, J.C.L.

Promoter of Justice—Rev. JAMES B. BISSONETTE, J.C.L.

Advocate—Ms. ELIZABETH DAMBERG.

Auditor—Rev. RICHARD KUNST.

Notary—Mrs. ROSE MARIE EICHMUELLER.

College of Consultors—Revs. JAMES B. BISSONETTE, J.C.L.; FREDRICK METHOD; JOHN O'DONNELL; JUSTIN FISH; JEROME P. WEISS; ANTHONY WROBLEWSKI.

Diocesan Deans—Revs. PAUL FRUTH; CORNELIUS KELLEHER; THOMAS RADAICH; FREDRICK METHOD; JOHN O'DONNELL.

Diocesan Corporate Board—Most Rev. PAUL D. SIRBA; Revs. JAMES B. BISSONETTE, J.C.L.; DALE NAU, J.C.L.; Mrs. MARILYN GRATTO; Mr. DOUGLAS HILDENBRAND.

Diocesan Finance Council Chair—Mr. FRANZ HOEFFERLE.

Diocesan Offices and Departments

Archivist (Historical)—Mrs. CHRISTINE SKALKO, 2830 E. Fourth St., Duluth, 55812. Tel: 218-724-9111.

Boy Scouts—Rev. LLOYD MUDRAK (Retired), Mailing Address: P.O. Box 290, Coleraine, 55722. Tel: 218-245-1684.

Campus Ministry—Rev. MICHAEL SCHMITZ, 421 St. Marie St., Duluth, 55811. Tel: 218-728-3757.

Cemeteries—Rev. JAMES B. BISSONETTE, J.C.L., 2830 E. Fourth St., Duluth, 55812. Tel: 218-724-9111.

Censor of Books—Rev. ERIC F. HASTINGS, J.C.L.

Council of Catholic Women—Rev. PAUL FRUTH, Moderator, Mailing Address: P.O. Box 156, McGregor, 55760. Tel: 218-768-2702.

Cursillo Movement—Rev. STEVEN DAIGLE, Spiritual Advisor, 16 W. 5th Ave. N., Aurora, 55705-1359. Tel: 218-229-3210; RICHARD SCHMIDT, Lay Dir., 16598 Simpson Blvd., Pengilly, 55775.

Department of Catechesis, RCIA, and Lay Apostolate—Ms. LIZ HOEFFERLE, 2830 E. Fourth St., Duluth, 55812. Tel: 218-724-9111.

Department of Catholic Schools—Ms. CYNTHIA ZOOK, 2830 E. Fourth St., Duluth, 55812. Tel: 218-724-9111.

Department of Communications—Mr. KYLE ELLER, 2830 E. Fourth St., Duluth, 55812. Tel: 218-724-9111.

Department of Continuing Formation of Clergy—Rev. DALE NAU, J.C.L., 2830 E. Fourth St., Duluth, 55812. Tel: 218-724-9111.

Department of Development—Mr. MIKE BILDEN, 2830 E. Fourth St., Duluth, 55812. Tel: 218-724-9111.

Department of Indian Ministry—Sr. MARIE ROSE MESSINGSCHLAGER, C.D.P., 2830 E. Fourth St., Duluth, 55812. Tel: 218-724-9111.

Department of Liturgy—Rev. JOEL HASTINGS, 2830 E. Fourth St., Duluth, 55812. Tel: 218-724-9111.

Department of Marriage and Family Life—Ms. GRACE ROMANEK, Contact Person, 2830 E. Fourth St., Duluth, 55812. Tel: 218-724-9111.

Department of Vocations and Priestly Formation—Rev. RICHARD KUNST; Deacon MICHAEL KNUTH, 2830 E. Fourth St., Duluth, 55812. Tel: 218-724-9111.

Department of Permanent Diaconate—Deacon DAVID CRAIG, 2830 E. Fourth St., Duluth, 55812. Tel: 218-724-9111.

Department of Protection of Children & Young People—Mr. ERNIE STAUFFENECKER, 2830 E. Fourth St., Duluth, 55812. Tel: 218-724-9111.

Victim Assistance Coordinators—Mrs. ESTHER REAGAN. Tel: 218-820-9220; Mr. TAB

BAUMGARTNER. Tel: 218-249-5495; Mrs. DAYLE PETERSON. Tel: 218-724-5310.

Department of Social Apostolate and CHD—Ms. PATRICE CRITCHLEY-MENOR, 2830 E. Fourth St., Duluth, 55812. Tel: 218-724-9111.

Department of Youth and Young Adult Ministry—Rev. MICHAEL SCHMITZ, 2830 E. Fourth St., Duluth, 55812. Tel: 218-724-9111.

Mission Outreach and Propagation of the Faith—Rev. PETER MUHICH, 2830 E. Fourth St., Duluth, 55812. Tel: 218-724-9111.

Diocesan Newspaper "The Northern Cross"—Mr. KYLE ELLER, Editor, 2830 E. Fourth St., Duluth, 55812. Tel: 218-724-9111.

CLERGY, PARISHES, MISSIONS AND PAROCHIAL SCHOOLS

CITY OF DULUTH

(ST. LOUIS COUNTY)

1—CATHEDRAL OF OUR LADY OF THE ROSARY (1919) Rev. Peter Muhich, Rector; Deacon Rodger Brannan.
Office: 2801 E. 4th St., 55812. Tel: 218-728-3646; Fax: 218-728-3647. Email: duluthcathedral@gmail.com.
School—Holy Rosary, (Grades K-8) Tel: 218-724-8565. Jesse Murray, Prin. Lay Teachers 24; Students 295.
Catechesis/Religious Program—Tel: 218-728-6985. Amy Kane, D.R.E. Students 145.

2—ST. ANTHONY, Closed. For inquiries for parish records contact St. Benedict Church, Duluth.

3—ST. BENEDICT (1950) Rev. Eric F. Hastings; Deacons Dennis Anderson; John Weiske; Scott Peters.
Parish Office—1419 St. Benedict St., 55811. Tel: 218-724-4828; Fax: 218-728-2683. Web: www.stbensduluth.org.
Res.: 1419 Arrowhead Rd., 55811.
Catechesis/Religious Program—Colleen McDonald, D.R.E.; Jenny Boran, Youth Min. Students 180.

4—SS. CLEMENT AND JEAN, Closed. For inquiries for parish records contact Holy Family Church, Duluth.

5—ST. ELIZABETH (1913) Rev. Jon Anthony Wild.
Office: 610 99th Ave. W., 55808. Tel: 218-626-2283.
Catechesis/Religious Program—Mrs. Ann Menart, D.R.E. Students 21.

6—GOOD SHEPHERD, Closed. For inquiries for parish records contact St. James Church, Duluth.

7—HOLY FAMILY Rev. Terence Figel, O.M.I.; Deacon Timothy Kittelson. In Res., Rev. James Datko, O.M.I.
Parish Office—2430 W. 3rd St., 55806-1801. Tel: 218-722-4445; Fax: 218-722-8979. Email: info@holyfamilyduluth.org. Web: www.holyfamilyduluth.org.
Res.: 202 N. 25th Ave W., 55806. Tel: 218-722-0730.
Catechesis/Religious Program—Desiree Taylor, D.R.E. Students 49.

8—ST. JAMES (1888) Rev. James B. Bissonette.
Office: 721 N. 57th Ave. W., 55807. Tel: 218-624-0125; Fax: 218-624-3435.
School—St. James, (Grades PreSchool-8) Tel: 218-624-1511. Web: www.stjamesduluth.org. Mr. William VanLoh, Prin. Lay Teachers 15; Students 128.
Catechesis/Religious Program—Mary Ann Rotondi, D.R.E. Students 54.

9—ST. JOHN (Woodland) (1915) Rev. Richard Kunst; Deacon Walt Beier.
Office: 4230 St. John's Ave., 55803. Tel: 218-724-6332; Fax: 218-724-4605.
Church: 3 W. Chisholm St., 55803. Tel: 218-724-3464.
School—St. John, (Grades PreSchool-6), 1 W. Chisholm St., 55803. Tel: 218-724-9392; Fax: 218-724-9368. Peggy Frederickson, Prin. Lay Teachers 11; Students 140.
Catechesis/Religious Program—Students 97.

10—ST. JOSEPH (1921) Rev. William Fider; Deacon Chico Anderson.
Office: 2410 Morris Thomas Rd., 55811. Tel: 218-722-2259; Fax: 218-733-0414. Email: stlawrencechurch@msn.com. Web: www.stjosephchurchduluth.org.
Catechesis/Religious Program—Coordinated with St. Lawrence, Duluth. Karen Ball, D.R.E. Students 8.

11—ST. LAWRENCE (1959) Rev. William Fider; Deacon Chico Anderson.
Office: 2410 Morris Thomas Rd., 55811. Tel: 218-722-1900; 218-722-2259; Fax: 218-733-0414. Email: stlawrencechurch@msn.com.
Catechesis/Religious Program—Tel: 218-722-6965. Karen Ball, D.R.E. (PreK-8); Julie Stauber, D.R.E. (9-12). Students 315.

12—ST. MARGARET MARY (1917), (Morgan Park) Rev. Jon Wild.
Office: 1467 88th Ave. W., 55808. Tel: 218-626-2379.
Catechesis/Religious Program—Students 36.

13—ST. MARY STAR OF THE SEA (1883) Rev. John C. Petrich.
Office: 325 E. Third St., 55805. Tel: 218-722-3078; Fax: 218-279-5070. Email: stmarys@cpinternet.com.
Catechesis/Religious Program—Tel: 218-722-3078. Shirley Baker, D.R.E. Students 52.

14—ST. MICHAEL (1914) Revs. Thomas Radaich; Noel Stretton (Retired). Email: noels@stmichaelsduluth.org.
Office: 4901 E. Superior St., 55804. Tel: 218-525-1902; Fax: 218-525-1904.
School—St. Michael Lakeside School, (Grades PreSchool-5), 4628 Pitt St., 55804. Tel: 218-525-1931; Fax: 218-525-0296. Web: www.smlsduluth.org. Amy Flaig, Prin. Teachers 6; Students 76.
Catechesis/Religious Program—Students 135.

15—OUR LADY OF MERCY 1922 Rev. John C. Petrich.
Mailing Address: 325 E. Third St., 55805. Tel: 218-722-3078; Fax: 218-279-5070.
Church: 2002 Minnesota Ave., 55802.

16—ST. PETER, Closed. For sacramental records, contact St. Mary Star of the Sea.

17—SS. PETER AND PAUL, Closed. For inquiries for parish records contact Holy Family Church, Duluth.

18—ST. RAPHAEL (1959) Rev. Dale Nau.
Parish Office—5779 Seville Rd., 55811. Tel: 218-729-7537 (Office); 218-729-5546 (Rectory); Fax: 218-729-8122. Email: raphaelchurch@yahoo.com.
Catechesis/Religious Program—Tel: 218-729-7537. Rebecca Kroll, D.R.E. Students 135.

OUTSIDE THE CITY OF DULUTH

AITKIN, AITKIN CO., ST. JAMES (1881) [CEM] Rev. David Forsman; Deacons William Stein; Luverne Anderson.
Office: 299 Red Oak Dr., 56431. Tel: 218-927-6581. Email: aggie.stiago@embarqmail.com.
Catechesis/Religious Program—Matthew Bugnacki, D.R.E. Students 105.

AURORA, ST. LOUIS CO., HOLY ROSARY (1908) Rev. Steven Daigle.
Office: 16 W. Fifth Ave. N., 55705. Tel: 218-229-3210; Fax: 218-229-3434. Email: ercpmn@yahoo.com.
Catechesis/Religious Program—Tel: 218-229-3434. Students 32.

BABBITT, ST. LOUIS CO., ST. PIUS X (1957) Rev. William Skarich; Deacon Gregory Hutar, Parish Coord.
Parish Office—15 Ash Blvd., 55706. Tel: 218-827-2291.
Res.: 231 E. Camp St., Ely, 55731. Tel: 218-365-4017.
Catechesis/Religious Program—Students 21.

BALL CLUB, ITASCA CO., ST. JOSEPH, [CEM] Rev. Stephen Solors.
Office: 51061 Wolf Dr., Deer River, 56636. Tel: 218-246-8105.
Catechesis/Religious Program—Students 17.

BAXTER, CROW WING CO., ALL SAINTS (2007) Rev. Anthony Wroblewski; Deacon Michael Knuth.
Parish Office—P.O. Box 464, Brainerd, 56401-0464. Tel: 218-828-7738.
Catechesis/Religious Program—Students 26.

BENA, CASS CO., ST. ANNE, [CEM] Closed. For inquiries for parish records contact St. Joseph, Ball Club.

BEROUN, PINE CO., ST. JOSEPH (1896) [CEM] Rev. Cornelius Kelleher.
Parish Office: P.O. Box 490, Hinckley, 55037. Tel: 320-384-6313 (Office); Fax: 320-384-6357. Email: frcon@live.com.
Church: 19390 Praha Ave., 55063.

BIGFORK, ITASCA CO., OUR LADY OF THE SNOWS (1960) Rev. Thomas Galarneault.
Mailing Address: P.O. Box 11, 56628.
Parish Office—320 Golf Course Ln., 56628. Tel: 218-743-3255; Fax: 218-743-3257. Email: olschurch@bigfork.net. Web: www.olschurch.net.
Catechesis/Religious Program—Students 34.

BIWABIK, ST. LOUIS CO., ST. JOHN 1893 Rev. Steven Daigle.
Parish Office: Box 569, 55708. Tel: 218-865-6774. Email: ercpmn@yahoo.com.
Res.: 16 W. 5th Ave. N., Aurora, 55705. Tel: 218-229-3210.
Catechesis/Religious Program—Students 20.

BRAINERD, CROW WING CO.

1—ST. ANDREW Revs. Anthony Wroblewski; Steven Laflamme; Keith Bertram; Deacons Roger Marks; Mike Koecheler; David Brown; Keith Grow.
1108 Willow St., 56401. Tel: 218-822-4040; Fax: 218-829-1340. Email: baccoffice@lakescatholic.org. Web: www.lakescatholic.org.
Catechesis/Religious Program—Kim Holmes, D.R.E.; Celeste Badger, D.R.E. Students 185.

2—ST. FRANCIS, [CEM] Revs. Anthony Wroblewski; Steven Laflamme; Keith Bertram; Deacons Roger Marks; Michael Koecheler; David Brown; Keith Grow.
Office: 1108 Willow St., 56401. Web: www.lakescatholic.org.
Res.: 1205 S. Ninth St., 56401. Tel: 218-828-1192.
Church: 404 9th St., N., 56401. Tel: 218-822-4040; Fax: 218-829-1340.
School—St. Francis of the Lakes, (Grades PreK-8), 817 Juniper St., 56401. Tel: 218-829-2344; Fax: 218-828-4157. Email: info@stfranciscatholicschool.org. Web: www.stfranciscatholicschool.org. Debra Euteneuer, Prin. Lay Teachers 18; Students 233.
Catechesis/Religious Program—Celeste Badger, D.R.E. (Elementary); Kim Holmes, D.R.E. (High School). Students 257.

BRUNO, PINE CO., SACRED HEART 1952 [CEM] Rev. Lourdusamy Kanagarajan.
Office: Box 644, Sandstone, 55072. Tel: 320-245-5175.

BUHL, ST. LOUIS CO., OUR LADY OF THE SACRED HEART (1905) Rev. Fredrick Method.
Parish Office—P.O. Box 27, 55713-0027. Tel: 218-254-5703; Fax: 218-254-3636. Email: stjoes@cpinternet.com.
Pastor Res.: 113 4th St. S.W., Chisholm, 55719-2017. Tel: 218-254-5703; Fax: 218-254-3636.
Catechesis/Religious Program—Deanne Hildenbrand, D.R.E. Students 1.

CARLTON, CARLTON CO., ST. FRANCIS (1928) [CEM] Rev. David Tushar.
Parish Office: 509 Sunrise Dr., 55718. Tel: 218-384-4563.
Catechesis/Religious Program—Students 98.

CASS LAKE, CASS CO., ST. CHARLES Rev. Kuriakose Nediakala, M.C.B.S.
Office: 308 Central Ave., P.O. Box 368, 56633. Tel: 218-335-2359; Fax: 218-335-2618.
Catechesis/Religious Program—

CHISHOLM, ST. LOUIS CO., ST. JOSEPH (1905) [CEM] Rev. Fredrick Method.
Office: 113 Fourth St. S.W., 55719. Tel: 218-254-5703; Fax: 218-254-3636. Email: stjoes@cpinternet.com.
Catechesis/Religious Program—Students 130.

CLOQUET, CARLTON CO.

1—HOLY FAMILY (1889) [CEM] Rev. Justin Fish; Deacon Terry Twomey.
Office: 102 4th St., 55720. Tel: 218-879-6793.
Church: 280 Reservation Rd., 55720. Tel: 218-879-9669.
Catechesis/Religious Program—Students 12.

2—QUEEN OF PEACE (1881) [CEM 2] Rev. Justin Fish; Deacon Terry Twomey.
Office: 102 4th St., 55720. Tel: 218-879-6793. Email: qop@qwestoffice.net.
Church: 102 4th St., 55720. Tel: 218-879-6793; Fax: 218-879-8930.
School—Queen of Peace, (Grades K-6) Tel: 218-879-8516. Sr. Therese Gutting, Prin. Lay Teachers 9; Students 98.
Catechesis/Religious Program—Irene McKay, D.R.E. Students 320.

COHASSET, ITASCA CO., ST. AUGUSTINE (1908) Rev. Paul Larson.
Office: P.O. Box 98, Deer River, 56636. Tel: 218-246-8582; Fax: 218-246-4017. Email: stmary@paulbunyan.net.
Catechesis/Religious Program—Liann Norris, D.R.E. Students 25.

COLERAINE, ITASCA CO., MARY IMMACULATE (1964) Rev. Dennis H. Hoffman.
Office: c/o 326 Second St., Nashwauk, 55769-1239. Tel: 218-885-1126.
Catechesis/Religious Program—Students 67.

COOK, ST. LOUIS CO., ST. MARY (1906) [CEM] Unassigned.
Office: Box 609, 55723. Tel: 218-666-5334.
Catechesis/Religious Program—Students 13.

CROMWELL, CARLTON CO., IMMACULATE CONCEPTION, [CEM] Rev. Peter S. Lambert.
Office: Box 378, Floodwood, 55736. Tel: 218-476-1617. Email: churchstlouis@gmail.com.
Church: Tel: 218-476-2367.
Catechesis/Religious Program—Tanya Davis, D.R.E.

CROSBY, CROW WING CO., ST. JOSEPH Rev. Timothy Deutsch; Deacons Philip Mayer; John Reed.
Office: 617 Poplar St., 56441. Tel: 218-546-6559; Fax: 218-545-1548.
Catechesis/Religious Program— (Combined with Deerwood) Students 103.

CROSSLAKE, CROW WING CO., IMMACULATE HEART (1955) Rev. Ryan John Moravitz; Deacons James Kirzeder; Barry Olson.
Mailing Address: P.O. Box 155, 56442. Tel: 218-692-3731 (Office); Fax: 218-692-3732.
Res.: 35162 County Rd. 37, 56442. Tel: 218-692-2233. Email: ihc@crosslake.net. Web: www.ihmstemilys.org.
Catechesis/Religious Program—Students 92.
Chapel—Our Lady of Snows

DEER RIVER, ITASCA CO., ST. MARY (1908) Rev. Paul

Larson.
Office: P.O. Box 98, 56636. Tel: 218-246-8582; Fax: 218-246-4017. Email: stmarys@paulbunyan.net.
Catechesis/Religious Program—Liann Norris, D.R.E. Students 59.

DEERWOOD, CROW WING CO., ST. JOSEPH Rev. Timothy Deutsch; Deacons Philip Mayer; John Reed.
Office: 617 Poplar St., Crosby, 56441. Tel: 218-546-6559; 218-534-3182 (Church).

ELY, ST. LOUIS CO., ST. ANTHONY (1888) Rev. William Skarich; Deacon Gregory Hutar.
Office: 231 E. Camp St., 55731. Tel: 218-365-4017; Fax: 218-365-3296. Email: stefaniessaintant@frontiernet.net.
Catechesis/Religious Program—Alisoun Forsmark, D.R.E. Students 68.

EMILY, CROW WING CO., ST. EMILY Rev. Ryan John Moravitz; Deacons Barry Olson; Jim Kirzeder.
Office: Box 25, 56447. Tel: 218-763-2101; 218-763-2301 (Res.).
Catechesis/Religious Program—Students 6.

EVELETH, ST. LOUIS CO., RESURRECTION (1909) Rev. Charles P. Flynn.
Mailing Address: P.O. Box 586, 55734.
Office: 301 Adams Ave., 55734. Tel: 218-744-3277; Fax: 218-744-1723. Email: vickie@joeres.org.
Catechesis/Religious Program—Tel: 218-744-3305. Pam Rapacz, D.R.E., (Grades K-11). Students 187.

FEDERAL DAM, CASS CO., SACRED HEART Rev. Stephen Solors.
Office: 51061 Wolf Dr., Deer River, 56636. Tel: 218-246-8105. Email: joemiss@paulbunyan.net.
Catechesis/Religious Program—

FINLAYSON, PINE CO., ST. JOSEPH (1909) [CEM] Rev. Lourdusamy Kanagarajan.
Office: Box 644, Sandstone, 55702. Tel: 320-245-5175.

FLOODWOOD, ST. LOUIS CO., ST. LOUIS, [CEM] Rev. Peter S. Lambert.
Office: Box 378, 55736. Tel: 218-476-2367; 218-476-1617 (Rectory); Fax: 218-476-2376. Email: churchstlouis@gmail.com.
Catechesis/Religious Program—Students 50.

FORT RIPLEY, CROW WING CO., ST. MATHIAS, [CEM] Revs. Anthony Wroblewski; Steven Laflamme; Keith Bertram. In Res., Rev. Richard G. Oberstar, M.S.F. (Retired).
Office: 1108 Willow St., S.E., Brainerd, 56401. Tel: 218-822-4040; Fax: 218-829-1340.
Church: 4529 County Rd. 121, 56449. Tel: 218-822-4041 (Res.). Web: www.lakescatholic.org.
Catechesis/Religious Program—Students 103.
Station—Crow Wing State Park St. Mathias.

GARRISON, CROW WING CO., OUR LADY OF FATIMA (1954) Rev. David Forsman.
Office: c/o 299 Red Oak Dr., Aitkin, 56431. Tel: 218-927-6581.
Church: 27332 Central St., 56450. Tel: 320-692-4466.
Catechesis/Religious Program—Students 6.

GILBERT, ST. LOUIS CO., ST. JOSEPH (1909) Rev. Charles P. Flynn.
Mailing Address: Box 788, 55741.
Office & Res: 515 Summit St., S., 55741. Tel: 218-741-9551; Fax: 218-744-1723. Email: shirley@joeres.org.
Catechesis/Religious Program—Students 45.

GNESEN, ST. LOUIS CO., ST. JOSEPH (1896) [CEM] Rev. Richard Kunst; Deacon Walt Beier.
Office: 4230 St. John's Ave., 55803. Tel: 218-724-6332.
Catechesis/Religious Program—Students 32.

GRAND MARAIS, COOK CO., ST. JOHN (1933) [CEM] Rev. Seamus Walsh; Deacon Peter Mueller.
Office: 10 E. 5th St., Box 549, 55604. Tel: 218-387-1409. Email: stjohns@boreal.org. Web: www.stjohns-holyrosary.org.
Catechesis/Religious Program—Students 52.

GRAND PORTAGE, COOK CO., HOLY ROSARY, [CEM] Rev. Seamus Walsh; Deacon Peter Mueller.
P.O. Box 549, Grand Marais, 55604.
Office: 10 E. St., P.O. Box 549, Grand Marais, 55604. Tel: 218-387-1409.
Catechesis/Religious Program—Students 4.

GRAND RAPIDS, ITASCA CO., ST. JOSEPH Rev. Jerome P. Weiss; Deacon Jerome Sura.
Parish Office—P.O. Box 110, 55744. Tel: 218-326-2843; 218-326-3959; Fax: 218-326-1663.
School—(Grades PreSchool-6) Tel: 218-326-6232; Fax: 218-326-6034. Teresa Matetich, Prin. Lay Teachers 13; Students 200.
Catechesis/Religious Program—Tel: 218-326-3720. Kitty Pollock, D.R.E., (Grades 6-12); Holli Busching, D.R.E., (Grades K-5). Students 383.

HACKENSACK, CASS CO., SACRED HEART Rev. Francis Kabiru.
Office: Box 874, Walker, 56484. Tel: 218-547-1054. Email: stagnes@arvig.net. Web: www.stagnescatholic.org.
Catechesis/Religious Program—

HIBBING, ST. LOUIS CO.

1—BLESSED SACRAMENT Revs. Gabriel Waweru; Anthony John Craig; Deacons James Griffiths; Ray Sampson.
Office: 2310 7th Ave. E., 55746. Tel: 218-262-5541; Fax: 218-263-3682. Email: parish@blsachibbing.org. Web: www.blsachibbing.org.
Res.: 2328 Seventh Ave. E., 55746. Tel: 218-263-3681.
School—(Grades PreSchool-6) Tel: 218-263-3054; Fax: 218-263-5058. Email: assump@mchsi.com. Susan Scipioni, Prin.; Stacey Okerberg, Librarian. Lay Teachers 12; Students 165.
Catechesis/Religious Program—Jeff Austin, D.R.E. Students 300.
Chapel—Side Lake, Blessed Sacrament Chapel

2—IMMACULATE CONCEPTION, Consolidated with Blessed Sacrament, Hibbing.

3—ST. LEO, Consolidated with Blessed Sacrament, Hibbing.

HILL CITY, AITKIN CO., ST. JOHN Rev. Jerome P. Weiss.
Office: c/o St. Joseph's Church, P.O. Box 110, Grand Rapids, 55744. Tel: 218-326-2843.
Church: 55748. Tel: 218-697-2465.
Catechesis/Religious Program—

HILLMAN, CROW WING CO., HOLY FAMILY (1925) [CEM] Rev. David Forsman.
Office: 299 Red Oak Dr., Aitkin, 56431. Tel: 218-927-6581.
Church: 1182 County Rd. 8, 56338. Tel: 320-277-3386.
Catechesis/Religious Program—Matthew Bugnacki, D.R.E. Students 15.

HINCKLEY, PINE CO., ST. PATRICK (1875) [CEM] Rev. Cornelius Kelleher.
Office: 203 Lawler Ave. S., Box 490, 55037-0490. Tel: 320-384-6313; Fax: 320-384-6357.
Church: 203 Lawler Ave. S., 55037.
Catechesis/Religious Program—Students 98.

HOYT LAKES, ST. LOUIS CO., QUEEN OF PEACE (1955) Rev. Steven Daigle.
Office: P.O. Box 211, 55750. Tel: 218-225-2867.
Catechesis/Religious Program—Tel: 218-229-3434. Students 31.

INTERNATIONAL FALLS, KOOCHICHING CO., ST. THOMAS AQUINAS, [CEM] Rev. Kristoffer McKusky; Deacon Francis Zaren.
Office: 810 Fifth St., 56649. Tel: 218-283-3293; Fax: 218-283-3553.
School—St. Thomas Aquinas, (Grades PreSchool-8) Tel: 218-283-3430. Mike Gerard, Prin. Lay Teachers 7; Students 45.
Catechesis/Religious Program—Mary Morrisseau, D.R.E. Students 160.

KEEWATIN, ITASCA CO., ST. MARY (1912) Rev. Dennis H. Hoffman.
Office: 326 2nd St., Nashwauk, 55769. Tel: 218-885-1126. Email: stcekema@hotmail.com.
Church: Box 219, 55753. Tel: 218-778-6379.
Catechesis/Religious Program—Students 16.

LITTLEFORK, KOOCHICHING CO., ST. COLUMBAN Rev. Kristoffer McKusky.
Office: 810 5th St., International Falls, 56649. Tel: 218-283-3293; Fax: 218-283-3553.
Church: Box 44, 56653. Tel: 218-278-6638.
Catechesis/Religious Program—Students 8.

LONGVILLE, CASS CO., ST. EDWARD (1917) Rev. Joseph A. Sirba.
Office: P.O. Box 38, 56655-0038. Tel: 218-363-2799.
Catechesis/Religious Program—Students 10.

MARBLE, ITASCA CO., ST. MARY (1937) Rev. Dennis H. Hoffman.
Office & Church: Box 411, 55764. Tel: 218-245-1684.

MCGRATH, AITKIN CO., OUR LADY OF FATIMA (1910) [CEM] Rev. Paul Fruth; Deacon Michael Barta.
Office: Box 156, McGregor, 55760. Tel: 218-768-2702.

MCGREGOR, AITKIN CO., HOLY FAMILY Rev. Paul Fruth; Deacon Michael Barta.
Office: Box 156, 55760. Tel: 218-768-2702; Fax: 218-768-2131.
Catechesis/Religious Program—Students 28.

MEADOWLANDS, ST. LOUIS CO., ST. MARY, [CEM] Rev. Peter S. Lambert.
Office: Box 378, Floodwood, 55736. Tel: 218-476-1617.
Church: 55765. Tel: 218-427-2626.
Catechesis/Religious Program—Students 20.

MOOSE LAKE, CARLTON CO., HOLY ANGELS (1926) [CEM] Rev. Eamonn Boland.
Office: P.O. Box 487, 55767. Tel: 218-485-4909. Email: holyangelschurch@hotmail.com.
Church: 60 Hartman Dr., 55767.
Catechesis/Religious Program—Tel: 218-485-8214. Kari Janz, D.R.E.; Kathy Burke, D.R.E. Students 116.

MOUNTAIN IRON, ST. LOUIS CO., SACRED HEART (1925) Revs. John O'Donnell; John Doyle (Retired); Deacon Daniel Schultz.
Church: 8861 Main St., 55768. Tel: 218-735-8248.
Catechesis/Religious Program—Students 25.

NASHWAUK, ITASCA CO., ST. CECILIA'S (1905) Rev. Dennis H. Hoffman; Deacon Richard Johnston.
Office: 326 Second St., 55769. Tel: 218-885-1126; Fax: 218-885-1145. Email: stcekema@hotmail.com.
Catechesis/Religious Program—Julie Dasovich, D.R.E.; Deanne Faulkner, D.R.E. Students 65.

NISSWA, CROW WING CO., ST. CHRISTOPHER (1949) Rev. George Zeck.
Office: P.O. Box 759, Pequot Lakes, 56472. Tel: 218-568-4760.
Church: 25574 Church St., P.O. Box 12, 56468. Tel: 218-963-2766; 218-963-1119 (Liturgy Office); Fax: 218-568-6707. Email: stchris_judy@msn.com. Web: www.lakecountryparishes.4lpi.com.
Catechesis/Religious Program—Students 204.

NORTHOME, KOOCHICHING CO., ST. MICHAEL (1906) Rev. Thomas Galarneault; Deacon James Vande Kamp.
Office: *c/o Our Lady of the Snows*, 320 Golf Course Ln., P.O. Box 11, Bigfork, 56628. Tel: 218-743-3255; Fax: 218-743-3257.
Church: 12026 Lake St., P.O. Box 52, 56661. Tel: 218-897-5628.
Catechesis/Religious Program—Students 25.

ORR, ST. LOUIS CO., HOLY CROSS (1958) Unassigned.
Office: P.O. Box 218, 55771. Tel: 218-757-3273.
Church: 10696 Shady Grove Ln. S., Box 218, 55771. Tel: 218-757-3273.
Catechesis/Religious Program—
Chapel—Buyck, St. Joseph's

PENGILLY, ITASCA CO., ST. KEVIN (1947) Rev. Dennis H. Hoffman; Deacon Richard Johnston.
Office: 326 2nd St., Nashwauk, 55769. Tel: 218-885-1126; Fax: 218-885-1145. Email: stcekema@hotmail.com.
Catechesis/Religious Program—Students 4.

PEQUOT LAKES, CROW WING CO., ST. ALICE Rev. George Zeck; Deacons David Craig; Richard Paine.
Office: Box 759, 56472. Tel: 218-568-4760; Fax: 218-568-6707. Email: stalice@uslink.net. Web: www.lakecountryparishes.4lpi.com.
Catechesis/Religious Program—Students 239.

PINE BEACH, CROW WING CO., ST. THOMAS, [CEM] Rev. Anthony Wroblewski.
Parish Office: P.O. Box 464, Brainerd, 56401. Tel: 218-828-7738; Fax: 218-828-4548.

PINE CITY, PINE CO., IMMACULATE CONCEPTION (1910) [CEM] Rev. Msgr. Aleksander Suchan; Deacons Eugene Biever; Mark Pulkrabek.
Office: 535 8th St. S.W., 55063. Tel: 320-629-2935; Fax: 320-629-1438.
School—St. Mary, (Grades PreK-6), 815 Sixth Ave., S.W., 55063. Tel: 320-629-3953. Deacon Eugene Biever, Co-Prin.; Deanna Jahnz, Co-Prin. Lay Teachers 6; Students 68.
Catechesis/Religious Program—Tel: 320-629-3911. Students 136.

PINE RIVER, CASS CO., OUR LADY OF LOURDES (1917) Rev. George Zeck. In Res., Rev. Bruce Engen (Retired).
Office: Box 44, 56474. Tel: 218-587-4163; Fax: 218-568-6707. Email: stalice@uslink.net. Web: www.lakecountryparishes.4lpi.com.
Catechesis/Religious Program—Tel: 218-587-4203. Students 41.

PROCTOR, ST. LOUIS CO., ST. ROSE Rev. Joel Hastings.
Office: 3 Sixth Ave., 55810. Tel: 218-624-0007; Fax: 218-628-1462. Email: saintroseproctor@qwestoffice.net. Web: www.stroseproctor.org.
School—(Grades PreK-6) Tel: 218-624-0818; Fax: 218-624-0984. Nicole M. Paulson, Prin. Lay Teachers 7; Students 91.
Catechesis/Religious Program—Tel: 218-624-9580. Becky Kubat, D.R.E. Students 56.

REMER, CASS CO., ST. PAUL Rev. Joseph A. Sirba.
Office: P.O. Box 38, Longville, 56655. Tel: 218-363-2799.
Catechesis/Religious Program—Students 25.

SAGINAW, ST. LOUIS CO., ST. PHILIP NERI Rev. Joel Hastings.
Office: c/o 3 Sixth Ave., Proctor, 55810. Tel: 218-624-0007; Fax: 218-628-1462.
Church: 4904 Independence Rd., 55779.
Catechesis/Religious Program—Students 12.

SANDSTONE, PINE CO., ST. LUKE, [CEM] Rev. Lourdusamy Kanagarajan.
Office: 122 Commercial Ave. N., Box 644, 55072. Tel: 320-245-5175; Fax: 320-591-9190. Email: saintlukes@scicable.com.
Catechesis/Religious Program—Geneve Vaughn, D.R.E. Students 15.

SAWYER, CARLTON CO., SS. MARY & JOSEPH (1859) Rev. David Tushar.
Office: 509 Sunrise Dr., Carlton, 55718. Tel: 218-384-4563.
Church: 1225 Mission Rd., 55780.
Catechesis/Religious Program—Students 40.

SILVER BAY, LAKE CO., ST. MARY (1955) Revs. Michael J. Lyons; Francis Paquette (Retired); Deacons Fred Wright; Jack Ferris.
Office: 57 Horn Blvd., 55614. Tel: 218-226-3100; Fax: 218-226-3116. Email: stmary@mchsi.com.
Catechesis/Religious Program—Students 28.

SQUAW LAKE, ITASCA CO., ST. CATHERINE (1942) Rev. Thomas Galarneault.
Office: *c/o Our Lady of the Snows*, 320 Golf Course Ln., P.O. Box 11, Bigfork, 56628-0011. Tel: 218-743-3255; Fax: 218-743-3257.
Church: 52265 State Hwy 46, P.O. Box 379, 56681. Tel: 218-659-4353.
Catechesis/Religious Program—

STURGEON LAKE, PINE CO., ST. ISIDORE (1887) [CEM] Rev. Sunny Thomas, M.C.B.S. (India).
Office: *c/o St. Mary Church*, 8118 Lake St., Willow River, 55795. Tel: 218-372-3284.
Church: 9010 Main St., 55783. Tel: 218-372-3208.
Catechesis/Religious Program—Sr. Janet Marie, D.R.E. Students 18.

TACONITE, ITASCA CO., ST. JOSEPH (1965) Rev. Dennis H. Hoffman.
Office: Box 290, Coleraine, 55722. Tel: 218-245-1684.

TOWER, ST. LOUIS CO., ST. MARTIN (1884) Rev. Joseph Valliyamthadathil, M.C.B.S.
Office: Box 757, 55790. Tel: 218-753-4310.
Catechesis/Religious Program—Pam Moraski, D.R.E. Students 24.

TWO HARBORS, LAKE CO., HOLY SPIRIT, [CEM] Rev. Michael J. Lyons.
Office: 227 Third St., 55616. Tel: 218-834-4313. Email: hspirit@mchsi.com.
Catechesis/Religious Program—Students 100.

VIRGINIA, ST. LOUIS CO.
1—HOLY SPIRIT Revs. John O'Donnell; John Doyle (Retired); Deacon Daniel Schultz.
Office: 306 S. Second St., 55792. Tel: 218-741-6344; Fax: 218-741-6345. Email: holyspirit@q.com. Web: www.catholic-parishes.org.
See Marquette Catholic School under Elementary Schools, Interparochial located in the Institution section
Catechesis/Religious Program—Tel: 218-741-6344. Students 165.
2—SACRED HEART (1950) Revs. John O'Donnell; John Doyle (Retired); Deacon Daniel Schultz.
Office: 306 S. Second St., 55792.
Church: 603 12th St. N., 55792. Tel: 218-741-2322.

WALKER, CASS CO., ST. AGNES Rev. Francis Kabiru.
Office: Box 874, 56484. Tel: 218-547-1054. Email: stagnes@arvig.net. Web: www.stagnescatholic.org.
Catechesis/Religious Program—Students 100.

WARBA, ITASCA CO., ST. PAUL Rev. Jerome P. Weiss.
Office: c/o St. Joseph Church, P.O. Box 110, Grand Rapids, 55744. Tel: 218-326-2843.
Church: Hwy. 2, 55793. Tel: 218-697-2465.

WILLOW RIVER, PINE CO., ST. MARY (1907) [CEM] Rev. Sunny Thomas, M.C.B.S. (India).
Office: 8118 Lake St., 55795. Tel: 218-372-3284; Fax: 218-372-3284. Email: st.mary.church@frontiernet.net.
Catechesis/Religious Program—Students 17.

INDIAN MISSIONS

DULUTH, ST. LOUIS CO., INDIAN MISSIONS Sr. Marie Rose Messingschlager, C.D.P.

c/o Chancery Office, 2830 E. Fourth St., 55812. Tel: 218-724-9111; Fax: 218-724-1056.

Chaplains of Public Institutions
Hospitals

DULUTH. *St. Luke's Hospital*, Tel: 218-726-5555. Rev. John C. Petrich, Chap., 325 E. Third St., 55805. Tel: 218-726-5555.
Miller Dwan Hospital. Mrs. Jan Rohweder, Dir. of Chaplains. Tel: 218-727-1089.

MOOSE LAKE. *Moose Lake State Hospital*. Rev. Eamonn Boland, Chap., 60 Hartman Dr., 55767. Tel: 218-485-4909.

Correctional Institutions

DULUTH. *Duluth Federal Prison*. Rev. Noel Stretton (Retired), 4926 Pitt St., 55804.

SAGINAW. *Northeast Regional Correctional Institution*. Rev. John C. Petrich, Chap. Tel: 218-626-4724.

WILLOW RIVER. *Youth Conservation Camp*. Rev. Sunny Thomas, M.C.B.S. (India), Chap. Tel: 218-372-3284.

On Duty Outside the Diocese:
Revs.—
Fournier, William, Sacred Heart Church, 1201 Bogard Rd., Wasilla, AK 99654.
Johnson, Lawrence P., 1820 Froude St., San Diego, CA 92107.
Kaster, Alfred D., 6716 Woodland Dr., Paradise, CA 95969.
Patullo, Michael, St. Anthony of Padua Friary, 3805 W. Walsh Pl., Denver, CO 80219.

Retired:
Rev. Msgr.—
O'Shea, Lawrence, 935 Kenwood Ave., Apt. 353, 55811.
Revs.—
Antus, Roland, 221 Boulder Dr., Cloquet, 55720. Tel: 218-393-7900
Arimond, Vincent, 4000 London Rd., Apt. 219, 55804.
Bouchard, Thomas, 20 6th St., S.W., Chisholm, 55712. Tel: 218-254-4529
Cossette, Raymond, 12788 County Rd. 8, S.E., Brainerd, 56401. Tel: 218-764-2941
Doyle, John, P.O. Box 475, Mountain Iron, 55768. Tel: 218-735-8248
Engen, Bruce, P.O. Box 44, Pine River, 56474. Tel: 218-587-4163
Foster, Edward, 3 Cliftonville, Crosshaven, Co. Cork Ireland.
Gagne, Ronald, 6894 Paulson Rd., Cotton, 55724. Tel: 218-482-3415
Golden, James, 204 4th Ave., Keewatin, 55753. Tel: 218-778-6949
Kosciesza, Bogumil, 2301 Douglas Ct., Silver Spring, MD 20902. Tel: 301-933-1896
La Patka, Gerald, 4202 E. Broadway Rd., #75, Mesa, AZ 85206. Tel: 480-325-5103
Lyttle, Eugene, 925 Kenwood Ave., Apt. 3132, 55811.
Moran, Patrick, Strokestown Rd., Ballyleague, Lanesboro, Co. Longford Ireland.
Mudrak, Lloyd, 10 Corey Ave., Coleraine, 55722.
Paquette, Francis, 57 Horn Blvd., Silver Bay, 55614. Tel: 218-220-0122
Partika, Richard, 925 Kenwood Ave., #1157, 55811. Tel: 218-728-3498
Perkovich, Frank, 12 1/2 S.W. 2nd. St., Chisholm, 55719. Tel: 218-254-5444
Schultz, Brian, 5624 West Pl., 55811. Tel: 218-786-0458
Stretton, Noel, 4926 Pitt St., 55804. Tel: 218-464-1292
Sustarsic, John, 935 Kenwood Ave., 55811.
Thevarkunnel, Anselm (India)
White, Stephen, 122 Ridge Rd, New London, 56273. Tel: 320-354-3397

Permanent Deacons:
Anderson, Dennis, St. Benedict, Duluth
Anderson, H. L., St. Lawrence, Duluth
Anderson, Luverne, St. James, Aitkin
Barta, Michael, Holy Family, McGregor
Bassa, Bryan, SS, Mary & Joseph, Sawyer
Beier, Walter, St. John, Duluth
Biever, Eugene, Immaculate Conception, Pine City
Brannan, Rodger, Cathedral of Our Lady of the Rosary, Duluth
Brown, David, Brainerd Area Catholic Churches
Craig, David, St. Alice, Pequot Lakes
Ferris, Jack, (Retired)
Griffiths, James, Blessed Sacrament, Hibbing
Grow, Keith, Brainerd Area Catholic Churches
Hedlund, Steven, St. Francis, Carlton
Hutar, Gregory, St. Anthony, Ely
Johnson, Lyle, St. James, Duluth
Johnston, Richard, Nashwauk, Keewatin, Pengilly
Kirzeder, James, Immaculate Heart, Crosslake
Kittelson, Timothy, Holy Family, Duluth
Knuth, Michael, All Saints, Baxter
Koecheler, Michael, Brainerd Area Catholic Churches
Kubat, Thomas, St. Rose, Proctor
Laumeyer, Richard, St. Mary Star of the Sea, Duluth
Marks, Roger, Brainerd Area Churches, Brainerd
Mayer, Philip, St. Joseph, Crosby
Moravitz, Richard, St. Anthony, Ely
Mueller, Peter, St. John, Grand Marais
Olson, Barry, St. Emily, Emily
Paine, Richard, St. Alice, Pequot Lakes
Peters, Scott, St. Benedicts, Duluth
Pulkrabek, Mark, Immaculate Conception, Pine City
Ramsey, Herbert, St. Agnes, Walker
Reed, John, St. Joseph, Crosby
Riley, Herbert, (Retired)
Sampson, Ray, Blessed Sacrament, Hibbing
Schultz, Daniel, Holy Spirit, Virginia
Skala, Mark, (On Duty Outside the Diocese)
Stein, William, St. James, Aitkin
Sura, Jerome, (Retired)
Twomey, Terence, (Retired)
Vande Kamp, James, St. Michael's, Northome
Weiske, John, St. Benedict, Duluth
Windus, Theodore, Sr., St. Mary of the Sea, Duluth
Wright, Fred, St. Mary, Silver Bay
Zaren, Francis, St. Thomas, International Falls

INSTITUTIONS LOCATED IN THE DIOCESE

[A] COLLEGES AND UNIVERSITIES

DULUTH. *College of St. Scholastica*, 1200 Kenwood Ave., 55811. Tel: 218-723-6000; Fax: 218-723-6290. Web: www.css.edu. Dr. Larry Goodwin, Pres.; Steve Lyons, Vice Pres. for Student Affairs & Dean of Students; Kevin McGrew, Dir., Library; Rev. William C. Graham, Instructor. A coed Benedictine college for resident, day and evening students. Priests 1; Sisters 3; Lay Faculty 176; Students 4,014.

[B] ELEMENTARY SCHOOLS, INTERPAROCHIAL

DULUTH. *Duluth Area Catholic Schools System*, (Grades PreK-8), 2830 E. Fourth St., 55812-1501. Mary Ann Rotondi, Area Coord. Tel: 218-724-9111; Fax: 218-724-1056. Holy Rosary School, Duluth, Tel: 218-724-8565; St. James Catholic School, Duluth, Tel: 218-624-1511; St. John the Evangelist School, Duluth, Tel: 218-724-9392; St. Michael's Lakeside School, Duluth, Tel: 218-525-1931; St. Rose School, Proctor, Tel: 218-624-0818. Sisters 2; Lay Teachers 53; Principals 5; Librarians 1.

VIRGINIA. *Marquette Catholic School*, (Grades PreSchool-6), 311 Third St. S., 55792. Tel: 218-741-6811; Fax: 218-741-2158. Email: marquette@qwestoffice.net. Georgia Brown Epp, Prin.; Claudia Zupancic, Librarian. Serving the parishes of Holy Spirit & Sacred Heart. Lay Teachers 11; Students 120.

[C] GENERAL HOSPITALS

DULUTH. *St. Mary's Medical Center*, 407 E. Third St., 55805. Tel: 218-786-4000; Fax: 218-786-4888. Email: kathleen.hofer@essentiahealth.org. Web: www.stmarysduluth.org. Sr. Kathleen Hofer, O.S.B., Pres.; John Gibbs, M.Div., Dir. of Chap. Svcs.; Rev. Thomas J. Foster, Chap. Sisters 3; Nurses 879; Patients Assisted Annually 148,954; Bed Capacity 313; Bassinets 45; Total Staff 2,690.

BRAINERD. *St. Joseph's Medical Center*, 523 N. Third St., 56401. Tel: 218-829-2861; Fax: 218-828-3103. Email: info@essentiahealth.org. Web: www.essentiahealth.org. Jani M. Wiebolt, Admin.; Karen DuBord, Dir. Spiritual Care. Nurses 413; Patients Assisted Annually 153,009; Bed Capacity 162; Total Staff 1,328.

[D] HOMES FOR AGED

DULUTH. *St. Ann's Senior Residence*, 330 E. Third St., 55805. Tel: 218-727-8831; Fax: 218-727-8833. Web: www.stanns.com. Sisters of St. Benedict 1; Residents 176.
Benedictine Health Center (Sub. of Benedictine Health System), 935 Kenwood Ave., 55811. Tel: 218-723-6408; Fax: 218-723-6449. Mark Broman, Admin. & CEO. Senior Housing Apartments 45; Assisted Living Apartments 35; Skilled Nursing Beds 90; Short Term Stay/Rehabilitative Beds 30; Day Care (Adults) 25; Children 85; Westwood Terrace Memory Care 21.
St. Eligius Health Center (Sub. of Benedictine Health System); A Benedictine Care Center, 7700 Grand Ave., 55807. Tel: 218-628-2341; Fax: 218-628-0395. Steve Baukner, Admin. Skilled Nursing Beds 99.

EVELETH. *Arrowhead Senior Living Community dba St. Raphael's Health and Rehab Center* 601 Grant Ave., 55734. Tel: 218-744-9800; Fax: 218-744-9829. Dawn Chiabotti, Admin. Assisted Units 14; Skilled Beds 76.

VIRGINIA. *Arrowhead Senior Living Community dba St. Michael's Health and Rehabilitation Center* 1201 8th St., S., 55792. Tel: 218-748-7800; Fax: 218-748-7890. Cheri High, Admin. Skilled Beds 96; Residents 250.

[E] CONVENTS AND RESIDENCES FOR SISTERS

DULUTH. *Motherhouse and Novitiate of the Sisters of Saint Benedict*, St. Scholastica Monastery, 1001 Kenwood Ave., 55811. Tel: 218-723-6555; Fax: 218-723-5902. Email: lois@duluthosb.org. Web: www.duluthbenedictines.org. Sr. Margaret Clarke, O.S.B., Archivist. Professed Sisters 90.

[F] NEWMAN CENTERS

DULUTH. *Newman Catholic Campus Ministry* 421 W. Marie St., 55811. Tel: 218-728-3757. Heather Serena, Coord.; Rev. Michael Schmitz, Dir.

[G] MISCELLANEOUS LISTINGS

DULUTH. *Benedictine Sisters Benevolent Association*

(Parent Co.), 1001 Kenwood Ave., 55811-2300. Tel: 218-723-6539; Fax: 218-723-5902. Email: lois@duluthosb.org. Web: www.duluthbenedictines.org. Sr. Lois Eckes, O.S.B., Pres.

Benedictine Health System, 503 E. Third St., Ste. 400, 55805. Tel: 218-786-2370; Fax: 218-786-2373. Web: www.bhshealth.org. Dale M. Thompson, Pres. & CEO. Sponsored by Benedictine Sisters Benevolent Association., Benedictine Health System Subsidiaries and Sponsored Entities Not Located In The Diocese: Benedictine Care Centers; (St. Brigid's at Hi-Park & The Villa at Hi-Park, Red Wing, MN; St. Isidore Health Center of Greenwood Prairie & Green Prairie Place, Plainview, MN; Benedictine Health Center at Innsbruck, New Brighton, MN; St. Eligius Health Center, Duluth, MN); Benedictine Health Dimensions, Inc. Benedictine Living Communities, Inc. (Benedictine Living Center of Garrison, Garrison, ND; Prince of Peace Care Center and Evergreen Place, Ellendale, ND; St. Benedict's Health Center and Benedict Court, Dickinson, ND; St. Catherine's Living Center, Wahpeton, ND; Benedictine Living Communities-Bismarck, Inc. dba St. Gabriel's Community, Bismarck, ND; St. Rose Care Center and Rosewood Court, LaMoure, ND; Benedictine Living Communities Foundation, Bismarck, ND); Benedictine Living Community of St. Peter, St. Peter, MN; Bridges Care Center dba Bridges Care Community, Ada, MN; Madonna Towers of Rochester, Inc., Rochester, MN; Saint Anne of Winona, Winona, MN; St. Gertrude's Health and Rehabilitation Center, Shakopee, MN; Tekakwitha Living Center, Inc., Sisseton, SD; Villa St. Benedict, Lisle, IL; Villa St. Vincent, Crookston, MN; Benedictine Health Center of Minneapolis, MN; Madonna Meadows of Rochester, Rochester, MN; Living Community of St. Joseph, St. Joseph, MO; Benedictine Senior Living at Steeple Pointe, Osseo, MN; Benedictine Living Community of Spooner, Spooner, WI; Benedictine Senior Living Community of New London dba GlenOaks Senior Living Campus, New London, MN; Benedictine Senior Living Community of Mora dba Villa Health Care Center, Mora, MN; Benedictine Senior Living Community of Winsted dba St. Mary's Care Center, Winsted, MN.

Benedictine Health System Foundation, Inc., 503 E. Third St., Ste. 400, 55805. Tel: 218-786-2370; Fax: 218-786-2373. Lowell Larson, Pres. (Sub. of Benedictine Health System) Comprised of the following Associated Foundations: Benedictine Health Center Foundation, Duluth, MN; Benedictine Health Center of Minneapolis Foundation, Minneapolis, MN; Benedictine Living Communities Foundation, Bismarck, ND (serving Benedictine Living Center of Garrison, Prince of Peace Care Center, St. Benedict's Health Center, St. Catherine's Living Center, St. Gabriel's Commuinity and St. Rose Care Center); Benedictine Living Community of St. Peter Foundation, St. Peter, MN; Bridges Care Community Foundation, Ada, MN; Cerenity Foundation, St. Paul, MN (serving Cerenity Care Center-Bethesda of South St. Paul, Cerenity Care Center on Humboldt and Cerenity Care Center on Dellwood Place); Cerenity-Marian of St. Paul Foundation; Cerenity-White Bear Lake Foundation; Hi-Park Foundation, Red Wing, MN; Innsbruck Foundation, New Brighton, MN; Koda Living Community Foundation, Owatonna, MN; Living Community of St. Joseph Foundation, St. Joseph, MO; Madonna Living Community Foundation of Rochester, Rochester, MN; Nazareth Living Center Foundation, St. Louis, MO; Saint Anne Foundation, Winona, MN; St. Mary's of Winsted Foundation, Winsted, MN; Saints Healthcare Foundation, Shakopee, MN; St. Eligius Foundation, Duluth MN; St. Isidore Health Center of Greenwood Prairie Foundation, Plainview, MN; St. Michael's Foundation, Virginia, MN; St. Raphael's Foundation, Eveleth, MN; Tekakwitha Living Center Foundation, Sisseton, SD; Villa St. Benedict Foundation, Lisle, IL; Villa St. Vincent/The Summit Foundation, Crookston, MN.

Benedictine Health Center (Sub. of Benedictine Health System), 935 Kenwood Ave., 55811. Tel: 218-723-6408; Fax: 218-723-6449. Mark Broman, Admin. & CEO.

Benedictine Living Communities Inc., 503 E. Third St., Ste. 400, 55805. Tel: 218-786-2370; Fax: 218-786-2373. Kevin Greff, Vice Pres. Opers. (Sub. of Benedictine Health System)

502 E. Second St., 55805. Tel: 218-786-8376. Web: www.essentiahealth.org. Peter Person, M.D., CEO. Sponsored by Benedictine Sisters Benevolent Association, (Affiliated with Essentia Health). Entities not located in the Diocese: St. Francis Regional Medical Center, Shakopee, MN; St. Mary's Hospital & Clinics, Cottonwood, ID; Clearwater Valley Hospital & Clinics, Orifino, ID; St. Mary's Regional Health Center, Detroit Lakes, MN. Holy Trinity Hospital, Graceville Health Center Clinic, Grace Home, Grace Village, all in Graceville, MN.

St. Mary's Medical Center, 407 E. Third St., 55805. Tel: 218-786-4000; Fax: 218-786-4383. Sr. Kathleen Hofer, O.S.B., Sr. Vice Pres., Benedictine Sponsorship of Essentia Health & Chm. Bd., Essentia Health; Thomas Patnoe, M.N., Pres., Essentia Health East Region; Ruth Strom McCutcheon, COO; Rev. Thomas J. Foster, Chap. Affiliate: St. Mary's Hospital of Superior, WI

St. Joseph's Medical Center, Brainerd Affiliated with Essentia Health, 523 N. Third St., Brainerd, 56401. Tel: 218-829-2861; Fax: 218-828-3103. Jani M. Weibolt, Pres. & CEO.

Polinsky Medical Rehabilitation Center, 530 E. Second St., 55805. Tel: 218-786-5360; Fax: 218-786-5340. Barb Wessberg, Dir. (Sub. of St. Mary's Medical Center)

The Blessed Nuno Society, P.O. Box 3484, 55803. Tel: 218-310-5110. Email: director@blessednuno.org. Web: www.blessednuno.org. Tim Heinan, Dir.

Holy Rosary Parish Endowment Fund, 2801 E. Fourth St., 55812. Tel: 218-728-3646.

The Human Life and Development Fund of the Diocese of Duluth, 2830 E. Fourth St., 55812. Tel: 218-724-9111; Fax: 218-724-1056.

The Seminary Endowment Fund of the Diocese of Duluth, 2830 E. 4th St., 55812. Tel: 218-724-9111; Fax: 218-724-1056. Mr. Franz Hoefferle, Dir., Fin.

The Catholic Religious Education Endowment Fund of the Diocese of Duluth, 2830 E. 4th St., 55812. Tel: 218-724-9111; Fax: 218-724-1056. Mr. Franz Hoefferle, Fin. Dir.

CLOQUET. *Educational Endowment Trust, Queen of Peace Church*, 102 4th St., 55720. Tel: 218-879-6793. Rev. Justin Fish.

DEER RIVER. **Our Lady of the Holy Trinity Magnificat Chapter*, 33350 State Hwy. 46, 56636. (Subchapter of S.W. Deanery Chapter of the Magnificat-Our Lady of the Lakes)

HACKENSACK. *S.W. Deanery Chapter of Magnificat of the Diocese of Duluth*, 3989 Bayview Dr., N.W., 56452. Tel: 218-675-6180. Email: garoutte@tds.net.

HIBBING. *Hibbing Catholic Schools Endowment Fund*, 2310 7th Ave., E., 55746. Tel: 218-262-5541; Fax: 218-263-3682. Rev. Gabriel Waweru, Contact Person.

**Sister Thea Bowman Black Catholic Educational Foundation*, 627 E. 39 St., 55746. Tel: 216-263-4865. Email: maryloujll@aol.com. Mrs. Mary Lou Jennings, Exec. Dir.

TWO HARBORS. *Saint Raphaels Guild A Chartered Guild of the Catholic Medical Association*, 398 Scenic Dr., 55616. Timothy J. Egan, M.D., Pres.

RELIGIOUS INSTITUTES OF MEN REPRESENTED IN THE DIOCESE

For further details refer to the corresponding bracketed number in the Religious Institutes of Men or Women section.

[]—*Missionary Congregation of the Blessed Sacrament*—M.C.B.S.

[0910]—*Oblates of Mary Immaculate*—O.M.I.

RELIGIOUS INSTITUTES OF WOMEN REPRESENTED IN THE DIOCESE

[0230]—*Benedictine Sisters of Pontifical Jurisdiction* (St. Joseph, MN; Watertown, SD; St. Paul, MN; Duluth, MN)—O.S.B.

[1000]—*Congregation of Divine Providence of Kentucky*—C.D.P.

[1250]—*The Institute of the Franciscan Sisters of the Eucharist* (Meriden, CT)—F.S.E.

[3840]—*Sisters of St. Joseph of Carondelet*—C.S.J.

[2150]—*Sisters Servants of the Immaculate Heart of Mary*—I.H.M.

DIOCESAN CEMETERIES

DULUTH. *Calvary Cemetery*, 4820 Howard Gnesen Rd., 55803. Tel: 218-724-3376; Fax: 218-724-9700. Mr. Tim Stresow, Supt.

NECROLOGY

† Popesh, Rev. Msgr. Bernard, (Retired)—Died Feb. 26, 2011

† Crossman, James, (Retired)—Died Nov. 3, 2011

† Golobich, John, (Retired)—Died June 5, 2011

† Spors, Roman, (Retired)—Died March 25, 2011

An asterisk (*) denotes an organization that has established tax-exempt status directly with the IRS and is not covered by the USCCB Group Ruling.

Diocese of El Paso

(Dioecesis Elpasensis)

(VACANT SEE)

ERECTED MARCH 3, 1914.

Square Miles 26,686.

Comprises in Texas, the Counties of El Paso, Brewster, Culberson, Hudspeth, Jeff Davis, Loving, Presidio, Reeves, Ward and Winkler.

For legal titles of parishes and diocesan institutions, consult the Chancery Office.

Chancery Office: 499 St. Matthews St., El Paso, TX 79907. Tel: 915-872-8407; Fax: 915-872-8413.

Web: www.elpasodiocese.org

STATISTICAL OVERVIEW

Personnel	
Priests: Diocesan Active in Diocese	43
Priests: Diocesan Active Outside Diocese	5
Priests: Retired, Sick or Absent	31
Number of Diocesan Priests	79
Religious Priests in Diocese	40
Total Priests in Diocese	119
Extern Priests in Diocese	5
Ordinations:	
Diocesan Priests	2
Permanent Deacons in Diocese	25
Total Brothers	13
Total Sisters	121
Parishes	
Parishes	57
With Resident Pastor:	
Resident Diocesan Priests	34
Resident Religious Priests	11
Without Resident Pastor:	
Administered by Priests	7
Administered by Deacons	3
Administered by Religious Women	1
Administered by Lay People	1
Missions	19
Professional Ministry Personnel:	
Sisters	1
Lay Ministers	1
Welfare	
Health Care Centers	2
Total Assisted	56,919
Homes for the Aged	1
Total Assisted	230
Special Centers for Social Services	3
Total Assisted	34,065
Educational	
Seminaries, Diocesan	1
Students from This Diocese	2
Diocesan Students in Other Seminaries	10
Seminaries, Religious	1
Students Religious	13
Total Seminarians	25
High Schools, Private	3
Total Students	1,145
Elementary Schools, Diocesan and Parish	8
Total Students	2,487
Elementary Schools, Private	2
Total Students	446
Catechesis/Religious Education:	
High School Students	7,407
Elementary Students	11,657
Total Students under Catholic Instruction	23,167
Teachers in the Diocese:	
Brothers	7
Sisters	9
Lay Teachers	268
Vital Statistics	
Receptions into the Church:	
Infant Baptism Totals	4,908
Minor Baptism Totals	463
Adult Baptism Totals	112
Received into Full Communion	218
First Communions	5,218
Confirmations	4,282
Marriages:	
Catholic	710
Interfaith	69
Total Marriages	779
Deaths	2,166
Total Catholic Population	686,037
Total Population	858,546

Former Bishops—Most Revs. JOHN J. BROWN, S.J., preconized Bishop of El Paso, Jan. 22, 1915; resigned June 16, 1915; ANTHONY J. SCHULER, S.J., D.D., cons. Oct. 28, 1915; died June 3, 1944; SIDNEY M. METZGER, S.T.D., J.C.D., cons. April 10, 1940; succeeded to See, Nov. 29, 1942; retired May 29, 1978; died April 12, 1986; PATRICK F. FLORES, D.D., cons. May 5, 1970; installed Bishop of El Paso, May 29, 1978; appt. Archbishop of San Antonio, Aug. 28, 1979; RAYMUNDO J. PENA, D.D., cons. Dec. 13, 1976; appt. Bishop of El Paso, April 29, 1980; appt. Bishop of Brownsville, May 23, 1995; ARMANDO X. OCHOA, D.D., ord. May 23, 1970; appt. Titular Bishop of Sitifi and Auxiliary of the Archdiocese of Los Angeles Dec. 29, 1986; ord. Bishop Feb. 23, 1987; appt. Bishop of El Paso April 1, 1996; installed June 26, 1996; appt. Bishop of Fresno Dec. 1, 2011.

Vicars General—Rev. Msgr. FRANCIS J. SMITH, P.A., V.G.; Rev. ANTHONY C. CELINO, J.C.L., V.G.

Vicar for Clergy—Rev. Msgr. DAVID G. FIERRO.

Moderator of the Curia—Rev. ANTHONY C. CELINO, J.C.L., V.G.

Chancellor—Deacon CARLOS E. RUBIO.

Liaison for Women Religious—Sr. ISABEL FIERRO, D.C., 499 St. Matthews St., El Paso, 79907. Tel: 915-872-8407.

Diocesan Pastoral Center—499 St. Matthews St., El Paso, 79907. Tel: 915-872-8400; Fax: 915-872-8423. Refer all official business to this address.

Presbyteral Council—Revs. FRANCISCO HERRERA (Retired); PABLO MATTA; ANTONIO MENA; EMANUEL ALCAZAR; EDWARD PAUL RODEN-LUCERO, J.C.L.; ROLANDO FONSECA; MARK N.P. SALAS. Ex Officio Members: Rev. Msgrs. FRANCIS J. SMITH, P.A., V.G.; DAVID G. FIERRO; Revs. ANTHONY C. CELINO, J.C.L., V.G., Mod. of the Curia; WILSON CUEVAS; ANTONIO LASHERAS, O.A.R.; FRANK LOPEZ; JOHN LUCIDO; JOE MOLINA; Very Rev. RICHARD A. MATTY.

Diocesan Tribunal—499 St. Matthews St., El Paso, 79907. Tel: 915-872-8402. Rev. ANTHONY C. CELINO, J.C.L., V.G., Mod. of the Curia & Judicial Vicar. Adjutant Vicars: Revs. STEPHEN PETERS; ROBERT S. KOBE.

Judges—Revs. ANTHONY C. CELINO, J.C.L., V.G.; STEPHEN PETERS; ROBERT S. KOBE; Bro. JAMES WORCHUCK, O.F.M.Conv., J.C.L.; Revs. JAMES W. HALL; GILES CARIE, O.F.M.Conv.

Defenders of the Bond—Rev. Msgr. DAVID G. FIERRO; Revs. TRINIDAD FUENTEZ; VIDAL ROBLES JR., J.D., J.C.L.; Sr. DIANE MASSON, C.S.S.F., J.C.L.

Advocates—Rev. Msgr. FRANCIS J. SMITH, P.A., V.G.; Revs. ROLANDO FONSECA; EDWARD C. CARPENTER; SAUL PACHECO, J.C.L. (Cand.); Deacon JOSE LUIS SANCHEZ, J.D.

Lay Advocates—Ms. CARMEN RODRIGUEZ; Judge SUE KURITA, J.D.; Ms. CARMEN HAGEMANN, J.D.

Tribunal Ecclesiastical Notary—Ms. YOLANDA RUIZ.

Peritus—VACANT.

Promoter of Justice—Rev. VIDAL ROBLES JR., J.D., J.C.L.

Vicars-Vicariates—St. Peter: Very Rev. RICHARD A. MATTY, St. Patrick Cathedral, 1118 N. Mesa, El Paso, 79902. Tel: 915-533-4451. St. Paul: Rev. ANTONIO LASHERAS, O.A.R., Little Flower Parish, 171 Polo Inn Rd., El Paso, 79915. Tel: 915-772-1285. St. John: Rev. JOE MOLINA, Most Holy Trinity, 10000 Pheasant Rd., El Paso, 79924. Tel: 915-751-6416. St. Mark and St. Luke: Rev. JOHN LUCIDO, St. John the Apostle Parish, 5th & S. Ike St., Monahans, 79756. Tel: 432-943-5114. St. Matthew: Rev. WILSON CUEVAS, Corpus Christi Parish, 9205 N. Loop Dr., El Paso, 79907. Tel: 915-858-0488. Our Lady of Guadalupe: Rev. FRANK LOPEZ, St. Frances Xavier Cabrini Parish, 12200 Vista del Sol, El Paso, 79936. Tel: 915-857-1263.

Diocesan Master of Ceremonies—Rev. MARCUS MCFADIN.

Peace & Justice Office—Mr. MARCO RAPOSO, Dir., 499 St. Matthews, El Paso, 79907. Tel: 915-872-8422.

Finance Council—Rev. Msgrs. FRANCIS J. SMITH, P.A., V.G.; DAVID G. FIERRO; Rev. ANTHONY C. CELINO, J.C.L., V.G., Vicar Gen. & Mod. of the Curia; Mr. E. H. BAEZA; Deacon CARLOS E. RUBIO; Ms. MARIA ELENA FLOOD; Mr. PHILLIP MULLIN; Mr. JOSE VILLA, CPA; Ms. CAROLYN MORA, CPA.

Diocesan Building Committee—Mr. CRUZ GARCIA; Mr. JORGE VERGEN; Mr. ALLAN SIMPSON; Revs. MARCUS MCFADIN; FRANK LOPEZ; Mr. THOMAS EYEINGTON, R.A.; Ms. IRENE RAMIREZ; Mrs. IRAZEMA SOLIS-ROJAS.

Priests' Personnel Advisory Committee—Rev. Msgr. FRANCIS J. SMITH, P.A., V.G.; Very Rev. RICHARD A. MATTY; Revs. ANTONIO LASHERAS, O.A.R.; FRANK LOPEZ; JOHN LUCIDO; WILSON CUEVAS; JOE MOLINA; ANTHONY C. CELINO, J.C.L., V.G., Mod. of the Curia; Rev. Msgr. DAVID G. FIERRO.

Diocesan Review Board—Ms. JULIETA CASTANEDA, R.N.; MAUREEN DE LA ROSA, M.S.; Mr. ENRIQUE MORENO, J.D.; Very Rev. RICHARD A. MATTY; Sr. ELIZABETH ANNE SWARTZ, S.S.N.D.; Mr. JOSE CASTRELLON, L.C.S.W.; Mr. WALTER DEINES, L.C.S.W.; Mrs. SUSAN MARTINEZ, L.C.S.W.; Dr. ROBERT RANKIN, Ph.D.

Youth and Young Adult Ministry—NORMA VALDEZ, Dir., 499 St. Matthews St., El Paso, 79907. Tel:

915-872-8438; Sr. JANET GILDEA, S.C., M.D., Dir. Young Adult.

Catholic Communications Ministry—Rev. RAUL TRIGUEROS, 499 St. Matthews St., El Paso, 79907. Tel: 915-872-8414.

Diocesan Newspaper— "Rio Grande Catholic" ANDY SPARKE, Editor, 499 St. Matthews St., El Paso, 79907. Tel: 915-872-8414.

Campaign for Human Development—Mr. MARCO RAPOSO, 499 St. Matthews St., El Paso, 79907. Tel: 915-872-8422.

Office of Marriage and Family Life—Mrs. DIANA BULKO, 499 St. Matthews St., El Paso, 79907. Tel: 915-872-8401.

Permanent Diaconate Office—Rev. ROBERT DUEWEKE, O.S.A., 499 St. Matthews, El Paso, 79907. Tel: 915-872-8420.

Priests' Retirement and Disability Plan—Rev. Msgrs. JOHN PETERS (Retired); FRANCIS J. SMITH, P.A., V.G., Pres.; Revs. EDILBERTO LOPEZ; LEONIDES RIVERO; ANTHONY C. CELINO, J.C.L., V.G., Mod. of the Curia; Ms. CAROLYN MORA, CPA.

Missions Office/Propagation of the Faith/Catholic Relief Services—Rev. ANTHONY C. CELINO, J.C.L., V.G., 499 St. Matthews St., El Paso, 79907. Tel: 915-872-8407.

Office of Education—Sr. ELIZABETH ANNE SWARTZ, S.S.N.D., Supt., 499 St. Matthews St., El Paso, 79907. Tel: 915-872-8426.

Tepeyac Institute—Rev. ROBERT DUEWEKE, O.S.A., Dir.

Reverence for Life Ministry—VACANT, 499 St. Matthews St., El Paso, 79907. Tel: 915-872-8401.

Vocations & Seminarians—Rev. MIGUEL ANGEL SANCHEZ, Dir. & Rector, 499 St. Matthews, El Paso, 79907. Tel: 915-872-8403. 8330 Park Haven, El Paso, 79907. Tel: 915-872-8460.

Religious Formation—Dr. VERONICA RAYAS, Dir., 499 St. Matthews, El Paso, 79907. Tel: 915-872-8432.

Native American (Tigua) Ministry—MIKE LARA, 131 S. Zaragosa, El Paso, 79907. Tel: 915-859-9848.

Victim Assistance Coordinator—Mrs. SUSAN MARTINEZ, L.C.S.W. Tel: 915-872-8465. Email: smartinez@elpasodiocese.org.

Catholic Campus Ministry—2230 N. Oregon, El Paso, 79902. Tel: 915-838-0300. Rev. HENRY BECK, O.F.M., Dir.

Finance Office—Mr. LAWRENCE MARTINEZ. Tel: 915-872-8404.

Human Resources—Ms. PATRICIA FIERRO, Dir. Tel: 915-872-8421.

Office of Worship—Rev. MARCUS MCFADIN.

Office of Safe Environment—Ms. ELENA BEJARANO, Coord. Tel: 915-872-8427.

CLERGY, PARISHES, MISSIONS AND PAROCHIAL SCHOOLS

CITY OF EL PASO

(EL PASO COUNTY)

1—ST. PATRICK CATHEDRAL Very Rev. Richard A. Matty, Rector; Rev. Mariano H. Lopez; Deacons Jose Luis Sanchez; Ernesto Rodriguez.
Res.: 1118 N. Mesa St., 79902. Tel: 915-533-4451; Fax: 915-532-8761.
School—(Grades K-8), 1111 N. Stanton St., 79902. Tel: 915-532-4142. Email: stpat1111@netzero.net. Liliana Esparza, Prin. Lay Teachers 16; Students 333.
Catechesis/Religious Program—Rosa M. Thorpe, P.C.L. Students 450.

2—ALL SAINTS (1967) Rev. Kennon Y. Ducre.
Res.: 1415 Dakota St., 79930. Tel: 915-566-9711; Fax: 915-566-9737. Email: allsaintselptx@aol.com.
Catechesis/Religious Program—Students 37.

3—BLESSED SACRAMENT Rev. Benjamin Flores.
Res.: 9025 Diana Dr., 79904. Tel: 915-755-7658.
Catechesis/Religious Program—Tel: 915-755-7658, Ext. 15; Fax: 915-757-6310. Rosenda Rodriguez-Ramirez, P.C.L. Students 569.

4—CHRIST THE SAVIOR (1982) Rev. Robert S. Kobe.
Res.: 5301 Wadsworth Ave., 79924. Tel: 915-821-3766; Fax: 915-821-3020.
Catechesis/Religious Program—Mrs. Irma Mejia, P.C.L. Students 402.

5—CORPUS CHRISTI Rev. Wilson Cuevas.
Res.: 9205 N. Loop Dr., 79907. Tel: 915-858-0488; Fax: 915-858-0812. Email: corpuschristiadmin@gmail.com.
Catechesis/Religious Program—Juan Rios, P.C.L. Students 751.

6—CRISTO REY CHURCH Mr. Jose Manny Barrios Jr., Parish Life Coord.; Rev. Benjamin Mones, Sacramental Min.; Deacon Ignacio M. Bustillos.
Res.: 8011 Williamette, 79907. Tel: 915-591-0688; Fax: 915-593-0470. Email: cristorey8011@sbcglobal.net.
Catechesis/Religious Program—Gloria Ibarra, P.C.L. Students 265.

7—EL BUEN PASTOR MISSION, Unassigned.
Church: 311 Peyton, 79928. Tel: 915-852-4010.
Mission—La Resurreccion Mission 1140 Timothy, El Paso Co. 79928.
Catechesis/Religious Program—Maria Teresa Gonzalez, P.C.L. Students 134.

8—ST. FRANCES XAVIER CABRINI PARISH (1993) Rev. Frank Lopez.
Church: 12200 Vista del Sol, 79936. Tel: 915-857-1263; Fax: 915-921-1709. Email: mothercabrini@sbcglobal.net. Web: www.stfrancesxcabrini.com.
Catechesis/Religious Program—Ms. Rosie Torres, P.C.L. Students 484.

9—ST. FRANCIS OF ASSISI MISSION Rev. Maximino J. Rangel, O.F.M.
Mailing Address: P.O. Box 220034, 79932. Tel: 915-584-7130.
Church & Res.: 5750 Doniphan, 79932. Tel: 915-584-7130; Fax: 915-584-4167.
Catechesis/Religious Program—Lorena Villeia, P.C.L. Students 217.

10—ST. FRANCIS XAVIER (1932) Rev. Esteban Sescon.
Res.: 519 S. Latta St., 79905. Tel: 915-532-2761; Fax: 915-544-5103.
Catechesis/Religious Program—Gloria Serna, P.C.L. Students 129.

11—GUARDIAN ANGEL (1908) Revs. Jesus Maria Mena, O.A.R.; Jose Luis Duenas, O.A.R.
Res.: 3021 Frutas Ave., 79905. Tel: 915-533-2077; Fax: 915-533-3649.
Catechesis/Religious Program—Salvador Vargas, P.C.L. Students 204.

12—HOLY FAMILY (1916), (Hispanic), Deacon Frederick C. Rotchford, Parish Life Coord.; Rev. Roberto Alvarado, Sacramental Min.
Rectory & Mailing Address: 104 Fewel St., 79902. Tel: 915-532-8462; Fax: 915-577-0236. Email: holyfamily@elp.rr.com.
Catechesis/Religious Program—Angie Escarciga, P.C.L. Students 65.

13—ST. IGNATIUS OF LOYOLA Revs. Angel M. Maldonado, O.S.M.; Jorge M. Palacio, O.S.M.; Deacon Aurelio Melucci.
Res.: 408 Park St., 79901. Tel: 915-532-9534; Fax: 915-532-9534.
Catechesis/Religious Program—Robert Hernandez, P.C.L. Students 214.

14—IMMACULATE CONCEPTION Rev. Msgr. William H. Ryan, Pastor Emeritus (Retired).
Res.: 118 N. Campbell St., 79901-2404. Tel: 915-533-3427; Fax: 915-533-3228. Email: immaculatec499@yahoo.com.

15—ST. JOSEPH'S Rev. Edward C. Carpenter.
Res.: 1315 Travis St., 79903. Tel: 915-566-9396; Fax: 915-566-5606. Email: stjoseph@elp.rr.com.
School—(Grades K-8), 1300 Lamar, 79903. Tel: 915-566-1661; Fax: 915-566-2006. Email: stjosephs@aol.com. Bro. Edwin Gallagher, Prin.; Cristina Gomez Landero, Librarian. Brothers 3; Lay Teachers 27; Students 518.
Catechesis/Religious Program— Rose Lowe, P.C.L. Students 105.

16—LA PURISIMA (1863) Deacon William Reyes, Parish Life Coord.
Res.: 328 S. Nevarez St., Socorro, 79927. Tel: 915-859-7718; Fax: 915-859-9452. Email: lapurisima@earthlink.net.
Catechesis/Religious Program—Eloy Carmona, P.C.L. Students 92.

17—ST. LUKE (1992) Rev. Edilberto Lopez.
Res.: 930 E. Redd Rd., 79912. Tel: 915-585-0255; Fax: 915-585-6355.
Catechesis/Religious Program—Mary L. Hernandez, P.C.L. Students 1,148.

18—ST. MARK (1992) Revs. Raul Trigueros; Jose A. Morales; Deacon Jesus A. Cardenas.
Church: 11700 Pebble Hills, 79936. Tel: 915-857-2955; Fax: 915-857-7133. Email: stmarkcatholic@sbcglobal.net. Web: home.catholicweb.com/StMarkCatholic/.
Catechesis/Religious Program—Yolanda Valdez, P.C.L. Students 1,641.

19—ST. MATTHEW Rev. Msgr. David G. Fierro.
Res.: 400 W. Sunset Rd., 79922. Tel: 915-584-3461; Fax: 915-584-2107. Email: stmatthewcatholic@sbcglobal.net.
School—(Grades PreK-8) Tel: 915-581-8801; Fax: 915-581-8816. Email: smcschool@stmatthewelpaso.org. Olga Macias, Prin.; Estela Loy, Librarian. Lay Teachers 11; Students 205.
Catechesis/Religious Program—Tel: 915-587-1524. Mrs. Jane Fuller, P.C.L. Students 650.

20—MOST HOLY TRINITY (1967) Revs. Joe Molina; Mark N.P. Salas; Sharon Johnston-Vass, Librarian.
Res.: 10000 Pheasant Rd., 79924. Tel: 915-751-6416; Fax: 915-751-5440. Email: mostholytrinity@gmail.com.
School—(Grades K-8) Tel: 915-751-2566; Fax: 915-751-2596. Email: holytrinityschoolep@yahoo.com. James Horan, Prin. Lay Teachers 10; Students 106.
Catechesis/Religious Program—Students 413.

21—OUR LADY OF ASSUMPTION Revs. Wallace Blake Fry; John Canu.
Res.: 4800 Byron St., 79930. Tel: 915-566-4040; Fax: 915-566-1104.
School—(Grades PreK-8) Tel: 915-565-3411; Fax: 915-564-5724. Email: olacs@elp.rr.com. Karen Biddle, Prin.; Nikki Duran, Library Mgr. Lay Teachers 11; Students 133.
Catechesis/Religious Program—Daniel Hernandez, P.C.L. Students 275.

22—OUR LADY OF GUADALUPE (1929) Revs. J. Santos Perez, O.F.M.; Erasmo Rodriguez Vega, Vicar; Mauro Munoz, O.F.M.
Res.: 2709 Alabama St., 79930. Tel: 915-562-4304; Fax: 915-562-3509.
Catechesis/Religious Program—Fax: 915-566-3307. Students 509.

23—OUR LADY OF MT. CARMEL Revs. Miguel Briseno, O.F.M.Conv.; John W. Curran, O.F.M.Conv. In Res., Rev. Maurice C. Hayes, O.F.M.Conv.; Bro. James Worchuck, O.F.M.Conv.
Res.: 131 S. Zaragoza, 79907. Tel: 915-859-9848; Fax: 915-860-9340. Email: olmcsecretary@sbcglobal.net. Web: www.ysletamission.org.
Catechesis/Religious Program—Mike Lara, P.C.L. Students 296.

24—OUR LADY OF SORROWS Revs. Arturo M. Gonzalez, O.S.M.; Tomas M. Xotta, O.S.M.; Federico M. Franco, O.S.M.
Res.: 7712 Rosedale St., 79915. Tel: 915-772-4834; Fax: 915-772-9078. Email: olsorrows@netzero.net.
Catechesis/Religious Program—Gloria Moreno, P.C.L. Students 220.

25—OUR LADY OF THE LIGHT Rev. Chris Angelo Otuibe, O.P.
Res.: 4700 Delta Dr., 79905. Tel: 915-532-1757; Fax: 915-351-2129. Email: olol4700@yahoo.com.
Catechesis/Religious Program—Cookie Valdiviez, P.C.L. Students 445.

26—OUR LADY OF THE VALLEY (1945) Rev. Maurice C. Hayes, O.F.M.Conv.; Deacon Carlos E. Rubio.
Res.: 8600 Winchester, 79907. Tel: 915-859-7939; Fax: 915-859-7576. Email: olvchurch@elp.rr.com.
School—(Grades PreK-8) Tel: 915-859-6448; Fax: 915-859-3908. Email: olvschool@msn.com. Sr. Caroline Vasquez, O.S.F., Prin.; Janice Cook, Librarian. Lay Teachers 15; Students 257.
Catechesis/Religious Program—David Perez, P.C.L. Students 212.

27—ST. PAUL THE APOSTLE (1963) Rev. Emanuel Alcazar; Deacon Vicente Aguirre.
Res.: 7424 Mimosa Ave., 79915. Tel: 915-778-5304; Fax: 915-778-5398. Email: stplap@netzero.net.
Catechesis/Religious Program—Concepcion Pantoja, P.C.L. Students 103.

28—STS. PETER AND PAUL Rev. Saul de Jesus Uribe.
Res.: 673 Old Hueco Tanks Rd., 79927. Tel: 915-859-3758; Fax: 915-858-1501. Email: stspeterandpaulelp@yahoo.com.
Catechesis/Religious Program—Hector Manuel Decanini, P.C.L. Students 597.

29—ST. PIUS X Rev. Msgr. Arturo Banuelas; Deacons Jim Szostek; Juan M. Alvarez; Rolando Lujan.
Res.: 1050 N. Clark Rd., 79905. Tel: 915-772-3226; Fax: 915-771-6665. Email: stpiusxparish@sbcglobal.net. Web: groups.yahoo.com/group/stpiusxchurch_elpaso.
School—(Grades PreK-8) Tel: 915-772-6598; Fax: 915-225-0010. Web: www.stpiusxschelpaso.org. Jesse Armendariz, Prin.; Lucy Loveridge, Librarian. Sisters 2; Lay Teachers 21; Students 413.
Catechesis/Religious Program—Tel: 915-772-0224. Email: formation.stpiusx@sbcglobal.net. Eva Rodriguez, P.C.L. Students 660.

30—QUEEN OF PEACE Rev. Trinidad Fuentez.
Res.: 1551 Belvidere, 79912. Tel: 915-584-5817; Fax: 915-584-7761.
Catechesis/Religious Program—Elizabeth Mata, P.C.L. Students 706.

31—ST. RAPHAEL (1967) Rev. Msgr. Francis J. Smith; Rev. Phil Briganti.
Res.: 2301 Zanzibar Rd., 79925. Tel: 915-598-3431; 915-598-3432; Fax: 915-598-0944.
School—(Grades PreK-8), 2310 Woodside, 79925. Tel: 915-598-2241; Fax: 915-598-3002. Email: st_raphael_principal@hotmail.com. Catherine S. Pynes, Prin.; Rachel Banales, Librarian. Lay Teachers 31; Students 518.
Catechesis/Religious Program—Eva Morales-Casas, P.C.L. Students 842.

32—SACRED HEART Revs. Edwin L. Gros, S.J.; Louis Lambert, S.J.; Frank Renfroe, S.J.; Johnathan L. Brown, S.J. In Res., Revs. Samuel Rosales, S.J.; John L. Vessels, S.J.
Res.: 602 S. Oregon St., 79901. Tel: 915-532-5447;

Fax: 915-533-0013. Web: www.sacredheartelpaso.org. *Catechesis / Religious Program*—Sr. Maria de la Luz Oseguera, O.P., P.C.L. Students 86.

33—SAN ANTONIO (1917), (Mexican—American), Rev. Leonides Rivero.
Mailing Address: 503 Hunter Dr., 79915. Tel: 915-598-1457; Fax: 915-590-1312. Web: www.paduaofelpaso.org.
Res.: 7420 North Loop, 79915. Tel: 915-598-1457; Fax: 915-590-1312.
Catechesis / Religious Program—Zulema Frausto, P.C.L. Students 458.

34—SAN JOSE Rev. Jose Alcocer.
Res.: 8100 San Jose Rd., 79907. Tel: 915-598-6285.
Catechesis / Religious Program—Rosa Aguon, P.C.L. Students 66.

35—SAN JUAN BAUTISTA Rev. Msgr. Arturo Banuelas, Admin.
Res.: 5649 Dailey Ave., 79905. Tel: 915-779-1583.
Catechesis / Religious Program—Mrs. Martha Drake, P.C.L. Students 26.

36—SAN JUAN DIEGO PARISH (1992) Rev. Edward Paul Roden-Lucero.
Res.: 14520 E. Montana, 79938. Tel: 915-855-2217; Fax: 915-855-7716. Email: jubileejuan@aol.com.
Catechesis / Religious Program—Mr. Christopher Romero, P.C.L. Students 284.

37—SAN JUDAS TADEO (1982) Rev. Pablo Matta; Deacon Francisco Segura.
Res.: 4006 Hidden Way, 79922. Tel: 915-584-1095. Email: pmatta@elp.rr.com. Web: www.santuariosanjudastadeo.com.
Catechesis / Religious Program—Rudy Gonzales, P.C.L. Students 606.
Mission—Santa Teresita 3400 Zapal St., El Paso Co. 79922.

38—SANTA LUCIA Rev. Anthony C. Celino, Admin.
Res.: 518 Gallagher St., 79915. Tel: 915-592-5245; Fax: 915-592-5336. Email: santaluciachurch@sbcglobal.net.
Catechesis / Religious Program—Ralph Aguilera, P.C.L. Students 115.

39—SANTO NINO DE ATOCHA Deacon Roberto E. Saucedo, Parish Life Coord.
Res.: 210 S. Clark, 79905. Tel: 915-779-3164; Fax: 915-779-1811. Email: secretarysantonino@sbcglobal.net.
Catechesis / Religious Program—Laura Lopez, P.C.L.; Lucy Herrera, Confirmation Coord. Students 143.

40—ST. STEPHEN, DEACON AND MARTYR Rev. Marcus McFadin; Deacons Gus J. Rodriguez Sr.; Hector E. Grijalva.
Church: 1700 George Dieter, 79936. Tel: 915-855-1661; Fax: 915-857-5800.
Catechesis / Religious Program—Deborah Montoya, P.C.L. Students 548.

41—SAINT THERESE OF THE LITTLE FLOWER PARISH Rev. Antonio Lasheras, O.A.R.
Church: 171 Polo Inn, 79915. Tel: 915-772-1285. Email: littleflower@elp.rr.com.
Catechesis / Religious Program—Catalina Chacon, P.C.L. Students 78.

42—ST. THOMAS AQUINAS (1981) Rev. James W. Hall; Deacons Jose E. Soto; Ignacio J. Torres.
Church: 10970 Bywood, 79936. Tel: 915-592-1313; Fax: 915-592-9733. Email: saintthomasa@aol.com.
Catechesis / Religious Program—Betty Vigil, P.C.L. Students 407.

OUTSIDE THE CITY OF EL PASO

ALPINE, BREWSTER CO., OUR LADY OF PEACE, [CEM] Rev. Miguel Alcuino, Admin.; Deacon Paul A. Lister.
Mailing Address: 406 S. Sixth, 79830. Tel: 432-837-3304; Fax: 432-837-1752.
Mission—St. Mary P.O. Box 268, Marathon, Brewster Co. 79842.
Catechesis / Religious Program—Barbara Tucker, P.C.L.; David Sanchez, P.C.L.; Cathy Lammons, P.C.L. Students 167.

BALMORHEA, REEVES CO., CHRIST THE KING, Under pastoral care of Santa Rosa, Pecos., Mailing Address: P.O. Box 686, Pecos, 79772.
Res.: Rte. 1, Box 3, 79718. Tel: 432-375-2347.
Catechesis / Religious Program—Samuel Anchondo, P.C.L. Students 34.
Mission—Our Lady of Guadalupe Saragosa, Reeves Co. Tel: 432-375-2636.

CANUTILLO, EL PASO CO., ST. PATRICK (1912) [CEM] Rev. Pablo Matta, Admin.
Mailing Address: P.O. Box 10, 79835.
Res.: 7065 Second St., 79835. Tel: 915-877-3997.
Catechesis / Religious Program— Maria Teresa C. Rivera, P.C.L. Students 210.
Mission—Immaculate Heart of Mary 8701 Joplin Rd., Westway, El Paso Co. 79835. Tel: 915-886-3539.
Catechesis / Religious Program—Students 146.

CLINT, EL PASO CO., SAN LORENZO (1914) Revs. Jose Delacruz Longoria, M.N.M.; Francisco Lopez, M.N.M.
Mailing Address: P.O. Box 215, 79836.
Res.: 13021 Center Way, 79836. Tel: 915-851-2255; Fax: 915-851-5251. Email: sanlorenzo1914@sbcglobal.net.
Catechesis / Religious Program—Minnie Montoya, P.C.L. Students 115.

FABENS, EL PASO CO., OUR LADY OF GUADALUPE, [CEM] Rev. Antonio Mena.
Mailing Address: P.O. Box 356, 79838.
Res.: 127 W. Main St., 79838. Tel: 915-764-3942.
Catechesis / Religious Program—Terry Avila, P.C.L. Students 415.
Mission—San Jose Cuadrilla, El Paso Co.
Mission—Santa Rita Tornillo, El Paso Co.
Mission—San Luis La Isla, El Paso Co.

FORT DAVIS, JEFF DAVIS CO., ST. JOSEPH, [CEM] Rev. Miguel Alcuino, Admin.
Res.: P.O. Box 787, 79734. Tel: 432-426-3284.
Catechesis / Religious Program—Alfonso Gonzales, P.C.L.; Janie Gonzales, P.C.L. Students 29.

FORT HANCOCK, HUDSPETH CO., SANTA TERESA (1920) Sr. Silvia Chacon, A.S.C., Pastoral Life Coord.
Mailing Address: P.O. Box 215, 79839. Tel: 915-769-3771; Fax: 915-769-3771. Email: santa_teresa215@netscape.com.
Res.: 1042 N. Knox, 79839.
Catechesis / Religious Program—Students 42.

HORIZON CITY, EL PASO CO., HOLY SPIRIT, (Independent Mission) Rev. Ralph Solis Jr., Admin.
Res.: 14132 McMahon, 79928. Tel: 915-852-3582; Fax: 915-852-0585. Email: holyspiritchurch@sbcglobal.com. Web: www.holyspiritcommunity.org.
Church: 14100 Horizon Blvd., 79928.
Catechesis / Religious Program—Cindy Hernandez, P.C.L.; Nora Obregon, P.C.L. Students 346.

KERMIT, WINKLER CO.

1—ST. JOSEPH THE WORKER, Consolidated with St. Thomas in 1990.

2—ST. THOMAS & ST. JOSEPH Revs. John Lucido; Richard Waiwood (Retired).
Res.: 838 Bellaire Rd., 79745. Tel: 432-586-3922.
Catechesis / Religious Program—Lorina Lujan, P.C.L. Students 220.

MARFA, PRESIDIO CO., ST. MARY'S, [CEM] Rev. Rolando Fonseca, Admin.
Mailing Address: Box 356, 79843. Tel: 432-729-4694. Email: churchmarfa@gmail.com.
Catechesis / Religious Program—Students 60.

MONAHANS, WARD CO., ST. JOHN THE APOSTLE AND EVANGELIST, [JC] Revs. John Lucido; Richard Waiwood (Retired).
Mailing Address: 5th & S. Ike St., 79756.
Res.: 500 S. Ike St., 79756. Tel: 432-943-5114.
Catechesis / Religious Program—Renee French, P.C.L.; Eloiza Collazo, P.C.L. Students 205.
Mission—St. Gertrude P.O. Box 181, Grandfalls, Ward Co. 79742. Tel: 432-547-2484.

PECOS, REEVES CO.

1—ST. CATHERINE Rev. Fabian Marquez; Deacon George Vasquez.
Mailing Address: P.O. Box 686, 79772.
Res.: 1201 S. Plum, 79772. Tel: 432-447-9231.
Mission—St. Emily Toyah, Reeves Co.

2—SANTA ROSA DE LIMA, [CEM] Rev. Fabian Marquez; Deacon George Vasquez.
Mailing Address: P.O. Box 686, 79772.
Res.: 620 E. 4th St., 79772. Tel: 432-445-2309; Fax: 432-445-2977. Email: wtcc@classicnet.net.
Catechesis / Religious Program—Samuel Anchondo, P.C.L. Students 300.
Mission—Our Lady of Refuge Barstow, Ward Co.

PRESIDIO, PRESIDIO CO., SANTA TERESA DE JESUS, [CEM] Revs. Jose Alfredo Hinojosa, Admin.; Michael Rodriguez.
Mailing Address: P.O. Box 2049, 79845.
Res.: 1101 W. O'Reilly, 79845. Tel: 432-229-3235; Fax: 432-229-3953.
Catechesis / Religious Program—Students 111.
Mission—Sgdo. Corazon de Jesus Shafter, Presidio Co. Tel: 432-229-4679.
Mission—San Jose Redford, Presidio Co.
Mission—Our Lady of Peace Candelaria, Presidio Co.
Mission—Lajitas Mission Lajitas, Brewster Co.

SAN ELIZARIO, EL PASO CO.

1—SAN ELCEARIO, [JC] Rev. Juan Martinez, M.N.M.; Deacon Pilar Grijalva Jr.
Res.: P.O. Box 910, 79849. Tel: 915-851-2333; Fax: 915-851-3511.
Catechesis / Religious Program—Students 211.

2—SAN FELIPE DE JESUS Rev. Celimo Osorio.
Mailing Address: P.O. Box 1070, 79849.
Res.: 401 Passmore, 79849. Tel: 915-851-3039.
Catechesis / Religious Program—David Solis, P.C.L. Students 370.

VAN HORN, CULBERSON CO., OUR LADY OF FATIMA Rev. Rodolfo Lacerna, Admin.
Mailing Address: P.O. Box 398, 79855.
Res.: 308 Almond St., 79855. Tel: 432-283-2042.
Catechesis / Religious Program—Corina Flores, P.C.L. Students 107.
Mission—Our Lady of Miracles P.O. Box 144, Sierra Blanca, Hudspeth Co. 79851.
Mission—San Isidro P.O. Box 65, Dell City, Hudspeth Co. Tel: 915-964-2601.
Mission—Sacred Heart General Delivery, Valentine, Jeff Davis Co. 79854.

Chaplains of Public Institutions

EL PASO. *El Paso County Jail*. Vacant.
El Paso Juvenile Detention Center. Vacant.

ANTHONY. *La Tuna Federal*. Rev. Vidal Robles Jr., J.D., J.C.L.
7045 Second St., P.O. Box 10, Canutillo, 79835.

On Duty Outside of Diocese:
Revs.—
Aguilera, Salvador, U.S. Naval Academy, Annapolis, MD 21402. U.S. Navy
Kim, Nam Joseph (Society of St. Sulpice)
Rowland, Thomas, Madonna House, Combermere ON K0J 1L0 Canada.
Zamorano, Richard (Diocese of Tucson)

Absent on Leave:
Revs.—
Bengert, Tony
Knopp, John
Lopez, Richard
Maraya, Felipe
Marin, Miguel
Munoz, Manuel
Narez, Juan
Olivas, J. Alfredo
Ponce, Demetrio
Ramirez, Jose Nieves
Ruiz, Rick

Retired:
Rev. Msgrs.—
Calles, Robert S.
Frias, Carlos
Peters, John
Ryan, William H.
Revs.—
Burkus, John
Calderon, Vicente, Jr.
Cervantes, Fidel
Herrera, Francisco
Lafrenz, James
Lucero, Lorenzo
Meneses, Miguel
Rini, John
Rizzo, Mark
Stegman, Leonard F.
Weiss, Richard

Permanent Deacons:
Aguirre, Vicente G., St. Paul, El Paso
Alvarez, Juan M., St. Pius X, El Paso
Andrade, Paul, Jr., Blessed Sacrament, El Paso
Bustillos, Ignacio M., Cristo Rey, El Paso
Cardenas, Jesus A., St. Mark, El Paso
Grijalva, Hector E., St. Stephen, El Paso
Grijalva, Pilar, Jr., San Elceario, San Elizario
Lister, Paul A., Our Lady of Peace, Alpine
Lujan, Rolando, St. Pius X, El Paso
Melucci, Aurelio, St. Ignatius, El Paso
Reyes, William, La Purisima, El Paso
Rodriguez, Ernesto, St. Patrick Cathedral, El Paso
Rodriguez, Gus J., Sr., St. Stephen, El Paso
Rotchford, Frederick C., Holy Family, El Paso
Rubio, Carlos E., Our Lady of the Valley, El Paso
Sanchez, Jose L., St. Patrick Cathedral, El Paso
Saucedo, Roberto E., Santo Nino, Jesus de Atucha, El Paso
Segura, Francisco R., San Judas Tadeo, El Paso
Solis, Ralph, (Retired)
Soto, Jose E., St. Thomas Aquinas, El Paso
Szostek, James T., St. Pius X, El Paso
Torres, Ignacio J., St. Thomas Aquinas, El Paso
Vasquez, George, (Retired)
Wauson, Thomas J., (Retired)

INSTITUTIONS LOCATED IN THE DIOCESE

[A] SEMINARIES, DIOCESAN

EL PASO. *St. Charles Seminary* (1961) 8330 Park Haven, 79907. Tel: 915-872-8460; Fax: 915-872-8468. Rev. Miguel Angel Sanchez, Rector; Sr. Darlene Stoecklein, A.S.C., Librarian/Formation Staff; Rev. Stephen Peters, Spiritual Dir. Seminarians 3.

[B] SEMINARIES, RELIGIOUS OR SCHOLASTICATES

EL PASO. *St. Anthony's School of Theology* (1935) 4601 Hastings Dr., 79903. Tel: 915-566-2261; Fax: 915-566-8851. Email: sas1936@hotmail.com. Revs. Maximino J. Rangel, O.F.M., Rector & Prof.; Alfredo Villagran, O.F.M., Guardian & Prof.; Gerardo Francisco Salgado, O.F.M., Student Master & Prof.; Jorge Frausto, O.F.M., Prof.; Jose Alfredo Ramirez, O.F.M., Prof.; Bro. Hermenegildo Resendiz. Franciscan Fathers of St. Peter and St. Paul Province, Michoacan, Mexico. Priests 5; Scholastics 13; Brothers 1; Sisters 3.

Roger Bacon College (1940) 2400 Marr St., 79903. Tel: 915-565-2921; Fax: 915-562-4756. Revs. Jose Arturo Bustamante, O.F.M., Rector; Jose Vera-Perez, O.F.M. Minor Seminary of the Franciscan Fathers, Province of the Holy Gospel. Priests 2; Brothers 1.

[C] HIGH SCHOOLS, PRIVATE

EL PASO. *Cathedral High School, Inc.* (Boys), 1309 N. Stanton St., 79902. Tel: 915-532-3238; Fax: 915-533-8248. Email: ngonzalez80@cathedral-elpaso.org. Web: cathedral-elpaso.org. Bro. Nick Gonzalez, F.S.C., Prin.; Peter Salas, Librarian. Brothers 3; Lay Teachers 34; Students 480.

Father Yermo Schools, (Grades PreK-12), High School/Elementary/Learning Center., 220 Washington St., 79905. Tel: 915-532-6875; Fax: 915-532-2827. Email: srmariafys@hotmail.com. Web: fatheryermoschools.com. Sisters Maria Jesus Munguia, S.S.H.J.P., Pres. & Admin.; Karina Tapia, S.S.H.J.P., High School Prin.; Angelica Omana, S.S.H.J.P., Elem. Prin.; Alice Escamilla, S.S.H.J.P., Librarian. Servants of the Sacred Heart of Jesus and of the Poor. Sisters 7; Lay Teachers 43; Students 488.

Loretto Academy, (Grades PreK-12), 1300 Hardaway, 79903. Tel: 915-566-8400; Fax: 915-566-0636. Email: bboesen@loretto.org. Web: www.loretto.org. Sr. Mary E. Boesen, S.L., Pres.; Mr. Abe Ramirez, Middle/High School Prin.; Ms. Jane German, Elementary Prin.; Ms. Margie Niemira, Librarian; Ms. Connie Hartley, Librarian. Sisters of Loretto at the Foot of the Cross. Sisters 2; Lay Teachers 50; Students 659.

Northeast El Paso Catholic Schools Consortium (2009) 499 St. Matthews St., 79907. Tel: 915-872-8464; Fax: 915-872-8464. Sr. Elizabeth Anne Swartz, S.S.N.D., Pres.

[D] CLINICS

EL PASO. *Centro San Vicente* (1988) 8061 Alameda, 79915. Tel: 915-859-7545; Fax: 915-859-9862. Email: csv@csv.tachc.org. Web: www.sanvicente.org. Donald M. Tufts, CEO. *Centro San Vicente* Total Assisted 56,919; Total Staff 167.

La Clinica Guadalupana, Inc. (1995) 901 Ascencion, 79928. Tel: 915-852-3328; Fax: 915-852-4246. Email: dbenedict@umcelpaso.org. Deborah Benedict, Exec. Dir. Total Assisted Annually 1,540.

[E] MULTIPURPOSE CENTER

EL PASO. *St. Joseph of the Valley* (Multi-purpose Center), 7681 Barton, 79915. Tel: 915-778-3407; Fax: 915-778-3407. Sr. Rachel Vallarta, M.J.M.J., Dir. Sisters 1; Total Assisted Annually 50.

[F] HOMES FOR AGED

EL PASO. *Nazareth Hall Nursing Center*, 4614 Trowbridge, 79903. Tel: 915-565-4677; Fax: 915-565-5118. Email: jmartinez@nazarethhall.org. Web: nazarethhall.org. Total Staff 123; Bed Capacity 101; Total Assisted Annually 150.

[G] MONASTERIES & RESIDENCES FOR PRIESTS & BROTHERS

EL PASO. *Christian Brothers*, 1204 N. Mesa, 79902-4012. Tel: 915-532-9314.

[H] CONVENTS AND RESIDENCES FOR WOMEN

EL PASO. *Adorers of the Blood of Christ (A.S.C.)* (1834) 199 Pendale Rd., 79907. Tel: 915-566-5855. Email: micasa2chante@msn.com. Sr. Darlene Stoecklein, A.S.C., Contact Person. Sisters 2.

Daughters of Charity of St. Vincent De Paul (D.C.), 3014 Taylor St., 79930. Tel: 915-564-5921; Fax: 915-859-9862. Email: dctaylorelpaso@gmail.com. Sisters 4.

11540 Montana, D1, 79936. Tel: 915-855-6451. Email: dcredsails@aol.com. Sisters 3.

Hermanas Contemplativas del Buen Pastor (H.C.B.P.) (1835) (Cloistered), *Good Shepherd Convent*, 8824 Old County Rd., P.O. Box 17254, 79917. Tel: 915-859-3683; Fax: 915-872-0698. Sr. Ernestina Estrada, Supr. Sisters 4.

Hermanas del Servicio Social (1945) 6372 Saint Lo Dr., 79925-1807. Tel: 915-771-0780; Fax: 915-771-0780. Email: hsscarmena@yahoo.com.

Hermanas Dominicas de la Doctrinia Cristiana (O.P.) (1948) *San Alberto Provincial Magno Convent*, 634 Hampton Rd., 79907. Tel: 915-590-3107; Fax: 915-590-6169. Sisters Ana Christina Soto, O.P., Prov. Supr.; Maria de la Luz Oseguera, O.P., Local Supr.; Margarita Cortez, O.P., Provincial Vicar. Sisters 8.

Missionary Sisters of Jesus, Mary & Joseph (M.J.M.J.), 7681 Barton Dr., 79915. Tel: 915-778-3407; 915-779-6943. Email: menobye@hotmail.com. Sr. Julia Donez, Supr. Sisters 4.

Servants of the Sacred Heart of Jesus and of the Poor (S.S.H.J.P.), Father Yermo Convent, 237 Tobin Pl., 79905. Tel: 915-533-3338; Fax: 915-532-7511. Sr. Maria Angelica Omana, S.S.H.J.P., Supr. Sisters 10.

Queen of Peace Convent, 3119 Pera Ave., 79905. Tel: 915-533-0590; Fax: 915-838-9640. Sr. Elia Lucia Hernandez, S.S.H.J.P., Supr. Sisters 7.

Sisters of Loretto at the Foot of the Cross (S.L.), 1300 Hardaway St., 79903. Tel: 915-566-8400; Fax: 915-566-0636. Web: www.lorettocommunity.org. Sisters 10.

Sisters of Our Lady of Charity (1931) 415 N. Glenwood Dr., 79905. Tel: 915-772-0737; Fax: 915-779-2664. Email: mescobar1125@hotmail.com. Web: nauolc.org. Sr. Martha Escobar, Supr. Sisters 10.

Sisters of Our Lady of Charity of the Good Shepherd (R.G.S.) (1835) *Good Shepherd Convent*, 8824 Old County Rd., P.O. Box 17635, 79917. Tel: 915-858-0692. Sr. Maria del Rocio Hernandez, Supr. Sisters 3.

Sisters of Perpetual Adoration (A.P.) (1937) Corpus Christi Monastery, 451 Mockingbird Ln., 79907. Tel: 915-591-5662; Fax: 915-598-6203. Email: ccmonast@aol.com. Sr. Maria Sagrario Perez, A.P., Supr. (Cloistered) Sisters 8.

Sisters of Perpetual Adoration (A.P.) (1979) *Cristo Rey Monastery*, 145 Cotton St., 79901. Tel: 915-533-5323. Sr. Maria Rocio de la Eucaristia, Supr. Sisters 13.

MARFA. *Missionary Sisters of Jesus, Mary & Joseph*, P.O. Box 1118, 79843. Tel: 432-729-3385. Sisters 2.

[I] NEWMAN CENTERS

EL PASO. *Catholic Campus Ministry at University of Texas at El Paso* 2230 N. Oregon, 79902. Tel: 915-838-0300; Fax: 915-838-0300. Email: campusministry@elpasodiocese.org. Rev. Henry Beck, O.F.M., Campus Minister.

ALPINE. *Sul Ross State University Newman Center* P.O. Box C 78, 79832. Tel: 432-837-8790; Fax: 915-837-8714. Email: joecal3ramirez@sbcglobal.net.

[J] MISCELLANEOUS LISTINGS

EL PASO. *Adoracion Nocturna (Nocturnal Adoration)*, c/o 499 St. Matthews St., 79907.

Annunciation House (1978) 1003 E. San Antonio, 79901. Tel: 915-533-4675; Fax: 915-351-1343. Email: rubengarcia@annunciationhouse.org. Web: www.annunciationhouse.org. Mr. Ruben Garcia, Dir.

Apostolado de la Cruz (Apostolate of the Cross), c/o 499 St. Matthews St., 79907.

Blue Army, c/o 499 St. Matthews St., 79907. Rev. Benjamin Mones.

Casa Vides (Shelter for displaced families), 325 Leon St., 79901. Mr. Ruben Garcia, Dir.

Catholic Counseling Services, Inc., 499 St. Matthews St., 79907. Tel: 915-872-8424; Fax: 915-872-8425. Email: jcastrellon@elpasodiocese.org. Mr. Jose Castrellon, L.C.S.W., Exec. Dir.

Catholic Daughters of America, c/o 499 St. Matthews St., 79907.

Catholic Knights of America, c/o 499 St. Matthews St., 79907.

Catholic Legal Immigration Network, Inc. (CLINIC) Subsidiary of the USCCB Southwest Regional Office., 2400-A E. Yandell, 79903. Tel: 915-532-3975; Fax: 915-532-4071. Email: clinictx@aol.com. Services: National immigration support network to the Catholic Dioceses throughout the U.S. Southwest regional CLINIC office provides technical assistance, basic organizational program services, management assessments, and immigration law training for its diocesan affiliates. CLINIC assists dioceses in applying for agency recognition and staff accreditation before the Immigration Board of Appeals. CLINIC assists dioceses and religious congregations in obtaining legal status for foreign clergy as non-immigrant and legal permanent residents.

Catholic Properties of El Paso, Inc., 499 St. Matthews St., 79907. Tel: 915-872-8406. Mr. Jorge Vergen, Exec. Dir.

Christ Child Society, 10560 Lakewood, 79925. Tel: 915-241-5440; 915-591-7266.

Cursillos de Cristianidad, c/o 499 St. Matthews St., 79907. Rev. Pablo Matta, Diocesan Dir.

Diocesan Migrant and Refugee Services, Inc. (1987) 2400-A E. Yandell, 79903. Tel: 915-532-3975; Fax: 915-532-4071. Web: www.dmrs-ep.org. Mrs. Iliana Holguin, J.D., Exec. Dir.

Diocese of El Paso Charity Trust, 499 St. Matthews St., 79907. Tel: 915-872-8400.

Diocese of El Paso Clergy Continuing Education Trust, 499 St. Matthews St., 79907.

Diocese of El Paso Education Assistance Fund, Inc., c/o 499 St. Matthews, 79907. Tel: 915-872-8426; Fax: 915-872-8464. Email: elpasocs@elpasodiocese.org.

Diocese of El Paso Historic Missions Restoration Trust, 499 St. Matthews St., 79907.

Diocese of El Paso Insurance Trust, 499 St. Matthews St., 79907.

Diocese of El Paso Investment Trust, 499 St. Matthews St., 79907.

Diocese of El Paso Seminarian Education Trust, 499 St. Matthews St., 79907.

El Paso Villa Maria, 920 S. Oregon, 79901. Tel: 915-544-5500; Fax: 915-544-5502. Email: villamaria_elp@sbcglobal.net. Sisters Helen Santamaria, S.L., Exec. Dir.; Mary Margaret Murphy, S.L., Case Mgr.

Foundation for the Diocese of El Paso (2001) 499 St. Matthews, 79907. Tel: 915-872-8412; Fax: 915-872-8411. Email: tyellen@elpasodiocese.org. Web: www.elpasodiocesefoundation.org. Ms. Tracy Yellen, COO. Tel: 915-872-8412, Ext. 170; Fax: 915-872-8411.

Franciscans, Secular Order of Franciscans, c/o 499 St. Matthews St., 79907. Rev. John Stowe, O.F.M.Conv., V.G., Spiritual Asst.

Historic Missions Restoration, Inc., 499 St. Matthews St., 79907.

Knights of Columbus, c/o 499 St. Matthews St., 79907. Rev. Msgr. Francis J. Smith, P.A., V.G.

Knights of St. Gregory, c/o 499 St. Matthews St., 79907.

Knights of the Holy Sepulchre, c/o 499 St. Matthews St., 79907. Rev. Msgr. Francis J. Smith, P.A., V.G.

Ladies of the Holy Sepulchre, c/o 499 St. Matthews St., 79907. Rev. Msgr. Francis J. Smith, P.A., V.G.

Legion of Mary, c/o 499 St. Matthews St., 79907.

Mount Carmel Cemetery Perpetual Care Trust, 499 St. Matthews St., 79907. Tel: 915-872-8400.

Open Arms Community, Centro Santa Fe (1972) 8210 N. Loop Dr., 79907. Tel: 915-595-0589; Fax: 915-851-2251. Email: contactus@hsrctr.org. Web: openarmscommunity.org. Joanne D. Ivey, Dir.

Our Lady's Youth Center (1953) 501 E. Paisano, P.O. Box 1371, 79948. Tel: 915-533-9122; Fax: 575-233-3829. Email: olyc77@gmail.com. Rev. John L. Vessels, S.J., Dir. The Lord's Ranch & The Lord's Food Bank.

Serra Club, c/o 499 St. Matthews St., 79907. Elizabeth Rios Carl, Contact Person.

St. Vincent de Paul Society, c/o 499 St. Matthews St., 79907. Arturo Moreno, Contact Person.

Zaragosa, Texas Catholic Relief Trust, 499 St. Matthews St., 79907. Tel: 915-872-8407.

RELIGIOUS INSTITUTES OF MEN REPRESENTED IN THE DIOCESE

For further details refer to the corresponding bracketed number in the Religious Institutes of Men or Women section.

[0330]—*Brothers of the Christian Schools* (New Orleans and Santa Fe Provs.)—F.S.C.

[0460]—*Brothers of the Poor of St. Francis*—C.F.P.

[]—*Catholic Foreign Mission Society of America, Inc.*—M.M.

[0480]—*Conventual Franciscan Friars* (Province of Our Lady of Consolation)—O.F.M.Conv

[0520]—*Franciscan Friars* (Holy Gospel Prov. and St. Peter & Paul Prov.)—O.F.M.

[0520]—*Franciscan Friars* (Prov. of Saint John the Baptist.)—O.F.M.

[0690]—*Jesuit Fathers and Brothers* (Prov. of New Orleans)—S.J.

[]—*Misioneros de la Natividad de Maria*—M.N.M.

[0370]—*Missionary Society of Saint Columban*—S.S.C.

[]—*Order of Augustinian* (Province of Our Mother of Good Counsel)—O.S.A.

[]—*Order of Preachers* (Province of St. Joseph the Worker Nigeria & Ghana)—O.P.

[0150]—*Order of the Augustinian Recollects* (Prov. of San Nicolas of Tolentino, Italy)—O.A.R.

[1240]—*Servites* (Province of Mexico)—O.S.M.

RELIGIOUS INSTITUTES OF WOMEN REPRESENTED IN THE DIOCESE

[3190]—*Adoratrices del Santisimo Sacramento*—A.P.

[0100]—*Adorers of the Blood of Christ*—A.S.C.

[]—*Adrian Dominican Sisters*—O.P.

[3832]—*Congregation of the Sisters of St. Joseph*—C.S.J.
[0760]—*Daughters of Charity of St. Vincent de Paul*—D.C.
[1370]—*Franciscan Missionaries of Mary*—F.M.M.
[1430]—*Franciscan Sisters of Our Lady of Perpetual Help*—O.S.F.
[]—*Franciscan Sisters of Perpetual Adoration*—F.S.P.A.
[]—*Hermanas Contemplativas del Buen Pastor*—H.C.B.P.
[]—*Hermanas de San Jose de Lyon* (Prov. Mex.)
[]—*Hermanas del Servico Social*—H.S.S.
[]—*Hermanas Dominicas de la Doctrina Cristiana*—O.P.
[]—*Hermanas Franciscanas de San Jose*—H.F.S.J.
[2770]—*Missionary Sisters of Jesus, Mary and Joseph*—M.J.M.J.
[2970]—*School Sisters of Notre Dame*—S.S.N.D.
[1680]—*School Sisters of St. Francis*—S.S.S.F.
[3660]—*Servants of the Sacred Heart of Jesus and of the Poor*—S.S.H.J.P.
[]—*Sisters of Charity of Cincinnati*—S.C.
[]—*Sisters of Charity of New Jersey*—S.C.
[0460]—*Sisters of Charity of the Incarnate Word*—C.C.V.I.
[2360]—*Sisters of Loretto at the Foot of the Cross*—S.L.
[]—*Sisters of Mercy*—R.S.M.
[]—*Sisters of Our Lady of Charity*—O.L.C.
[]—*Sisters of Our Lady of Charity of the Good Shepherd*—R.G.S.
[1630]—*Sisters of St. Francis of Penance and Christian Charity*—O.S.F.
[]—*Sisters of St. Joseph of Concordia, Kansas*—C.S.J.
[]—*Sisters of the Living Word*—S.L.W.

DIOCESAN CEMETERY

EL PASO. *Mount Carmel*, Box 17655, 79917. Tel: 915-860-0606.

NECROLOGY

† Acevedo, Luis H., (Retired)—Died July 3, 2011
† Guerrero, Jose, (Retired)—Died Jan. 28, 2011

An asterisk (*) denotes an organization that has established tax-exempt status directly with the IRS and is not covered by the USCCB Group Ruling.

Diocese of Erie

(Dioecesis Eriensis)

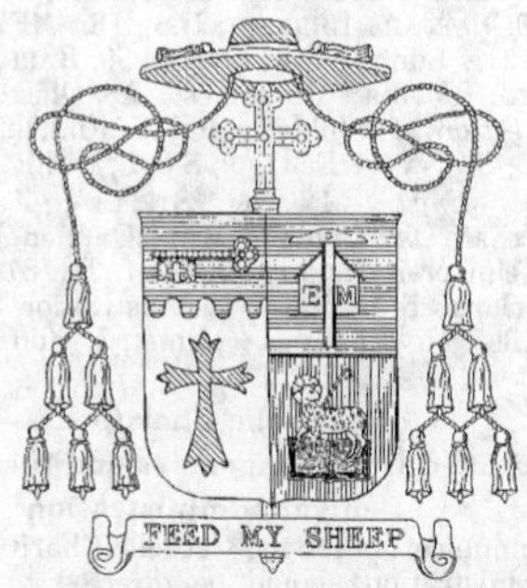

Most Reverend

DONALD W. TRAUTMAN, S.T.D., S.S.L.

Bishop of Erie; ordained April 7, 1962; appointed Titular Bishop of Sassura and Auxiliary Bishop of Buffalo February 27, 1985; consecrated April 16, 1985; appointed to Erie June 12, 1990; installed July 16, 1990. *Res.: 205 West 9th St., Erie, PA 16501.* Tel: 814-824-1120; Fax: 814-824-1124.

Chancery: St. Mark Catholic Center, P.O. Box 10397, Erie, PA 16514. Tel: 814-824-1111; Fax: 814-824-1128.

Web: www.eriercd.org

ESTABLISHED 1853.

Square Miles 10,167.

Comprises the following Counties in Northwestern Pennsylvania: Erie, Crawford, Mercer, Venango, Forest, Clarion, Jefferson, Clearfield, Cameron, Elk, McKean, Potter and Warren.

For legal titles of parishes and diocesan institutions, consult the Chancery.

STATISTICAL OVERVIEW

Personnel	
Bishop	1
Priests: Diocesan Active in Diocese	130
Priests: Diocesan Active Outside Diocese	6
Priests: Retired, Sick or Absent	51
Number of Diocesan Priests	187
Religious Priests in Diocese	7
Total Priests in Diocese	194
Extern Priests in Diocese	5
Ordinations:	
Diocesan Priests	1
Transitional Deacons	1
Permanent Deacons in Diocese	62
Total Sisters	321
Parishes	
Parishes	117
With Resident Pastor:	
Resident Diocesan Priests	95
Resident Religious Priests	2
Without Resident Pastor:	
Administered by Priests	20
Missions	21
Professional Ministry Personnel:	
Lay Ministers	11
Welfare	
Catholic Hospitals	1
Total Assisted	440,600
Homes for the Aged	4
Total Assisted	1,596
Day Care Centers	1
Total Assisted	216
Specialized Homes	3
Total Assisted	220
Special Centers for Social Services	24
Total Assisted	56,046
Educational	
Seminaries, Diocesan	1
Students from This Diocese	14
Students from Other Diocese	8
Diocesan Students in Other Seminaries	4
Total Seminarians	18
Colleges and Universities	2
Total Students	8,741
High Schools, Diocesan and Parish	6
Total Students	1,646
High Schools, Private	1
Total Students	630
Elementary Schools, Diocesan and Parish	32
Total Students	4,852
Elementary Schools, Private	1
Total Students	221
Catechesis/Religious Education:	
High School Students	4,768
Elementary Students	7,148
Total Students under Catholic Instruction	28,024
Teachers in the Diocese:	
Priests	7
Sisters	10
Lay Teachers	568
Vital Statistics	
Receptions into the Church:	
Infant Baptism Totals	1,530
Minor Baptism Totals	70
Adult Baptism Totals	130
Received into Full Communion	65
First Communions	1,800
Confirmations	1,700
Marriages:	
Catholic	370
Interfaith	240
Total Marriages	610
Deaths	2,400
Total Catholic Population	221,550
Total Population	855,252

Former Bishops—Most Revs. MICHAEL O'CONNOR, D.D., ord. June 1, 1833; appt. Bishop of Pittsburgh Aug. 11, 1843; cons. Aug. 15, 1843; appt. Bishop of Erie July 29, 1853; reappt. Bishop of Pittsburgh Dec. 20, 1853; cons. Feb. 18, 1854; resigned May 20, 1860; entered Society of Jesus Dec. 22, 1860; died Oct. 18, 1872.; JOSUE M. YOUNG, D.D., ord. April 1, 1838; appt. Bishop of Erie Dec. 20, 1853; cons. April 23, 1854; died Sept. 18, 1866; TOBIAS MULLEN, D.D., ord. Sept. 1, 1844; appt. Bishop of Erie March 3, 1868; cons. Aug. 2, 1868; resigned Aug. 10, 1899; appt. Titular See of Germanicopolis; died April 22, 1900; JOHN E. FITZMAURICE, D.D., ord. Dec. 21, 1862; appt. Coadjutor Bishop of Erie Dec. 14, 1897; cons. Feb. 24, 1898; succeeded to See Sept. 15, 1899; died June 18, 1920; EDWARD P. MCMANAMAN, S.T.D., Titular Bishop of Floriana and Auxiliary Bishop of Erie; cons. Oct. 28, 1948; died July 18, 1964; JOHN MARK GANNON, D.D., Archbishop-Bishop of Erie; ord. Dec. 21, 1901; appt. Titular Bishop of Nilopolis, Nov. 13, 1917; cons. Feb. 6, 1920; appt. Bishop of Erie, Aug. 16, 1920; installed Dec. 16, 1920; appt. Assistant at the Pontifical Throne Nov. 4, 1944; appt. Archbishop "ad personam" Nov. 25, 1953; resigned Sept. 21, 1966 and transferred to Titular See of Tacarata, Dec. 14, 1966; died Sept. 5, 1968; JOHN F. WHEALON, S.T.L., S.S.L., appt. Titular Bishop of Andrapa and Auxiliary Bishop of Cleveland, June 2, 1961; cons. July 6, 1961; appt. Bishop of Erie Nov. 30, 1966; appt. Archbishop of Hartford Dec. 28, 1968; died Aug. 2, 1991; ALFRED M. WATSON, D.D., Bishop of Erie; ord. May 10, 1934; Titular Bishop of Nationa and Auxiliary Bishop of Erie; appt. May 17, 1965; cons. June 29, 1965; succeeded to See, March 19, 1969; retired July 16, 1982; died Jan. 4, 1990; MICHAEL J. MURPHY, D.D., S.T.L., Titular Bishop of Arindola and Auxiliary Bishop of Cleveland; appt. April 20, 1976; cons. June 11, 1976; Coadjutor Bishop of Erie; appt. Nov. 28, 1978; succeeded to See, July 16, 1982; retired July 1, 1990; died April 2, 2007.

Vicars General—Rev. Msgrs. ROBERT J. SMITH, J.C.L., V.G., Mailing Address: St. Mark Catholic Center, P.O. Box 10397, Erie, 16514-0397. Tel: 814-824-1130; Fax: 814-824-1124; CHARLES A. KAZA, V.G., E.V., 1135 Hewett St., Brockway, 15824. Tel: 814-265-1374.

Office of the Bishop—ROBERTA PALMISANO, Sec. to the Bishop, Mailing Address: St. Mark Catholic Center, P.O. Box 10397, Erie, 16514. Tel: 814-824-1120; Fax: 814-824-1124.

Chancery—Mailing Address: St. Mark Catholic Center, P.O. Box 10397, Erie, 16514. Tel: 814-824-1135; Fax: 814-824-1124.

Chancellor—Rev. CHRISTOPHER J. SINGER, J.C.L.

Vice Chancellor—Sr. CATHERINE MANNING, S.S.J.

Diocesan Archivist—Rev. JUSTIN P. PINO, St. Mark Catholic Center, P.O. Box 10397, Erie, 16514. Tel: 814-824-1135.

Episcopal Vicars—

Northern Vicariate—Rev. Msgr. ROBERT J. SMITH, J.C.L., V.G., Mailing Address: St. Mark Catholic Center, P.O. Box 10397, Erie, 16514. Tel: 814-824-1130.

Eastern Vicariate—Rev. Msgr. CHARLES A. KAZA, V.G., E.V., 1135 Hewett St., Brockway, 15824. Tel: 814-265-1374.

Western Vicariate—Rev. Msgr. ROBERT M. MALENE, E.V., Mailing Address: P.O. Box 226, West Middlesex, 16159. Tel: 724-528-3539.

Director of the Office for Religious—Sr. NANCY FISCHER, S.S.J., Mailing Address: St. Mark Catholic Center, P.O. Box 10397, Erie, 16514-0397. Tel: 814-824-1125.

Office for the Protection of Children and Youth—KAREN STREETT, Coord., Mailing Address: St. Mark Catholic Center, P.O. Box 10397, Erie, 16514-0397. Tel: 814-824-1222.

Advisory To Bishop

Administrative Cabinet—Rev. Msgrs. ROBERT J. SMITH, J.C.L., V.G.; CHARLES A. KAZA, V.G., E.V.; Sr. NANCY FISCHER, S.S.J.; Rev. NICHOLAS J. ROUCH, S.T.D.; MARY C. MAXWELL, M.A.; DAVID J. MURPHY; Rev. CHRISTOPHER J. SINGER, J.C.L.; Rev. Msgr. ROBERT M. MALENE, E.V.; ANNE-MARIE WELSH; Dr. EMMA LEE MCCLOSKEY, Ed.D., C.F.R.E., Consultant.

College of Consultors—Rev. CHRISTOPHER J. SINGER, J.C.L.; Rev. Msgrs. CHARLES A. KAZA, V.G., E.V.; ROBERT J. SMITH, J.C.L., V.G.; DANIEL E. MAGRAW; ROBERT M. MALENE, E.V.; H. DESMOND MCGEE JR., V.F.; Very Rev. MATTHEW J. RUYECHAN, V.F.

Finance Council—Most Rev. DONALD W. TRAUTMAN, S.T.D., S.S.L.; Rev. Msgr. JOHN W. SWOGER, E.V. (Retired); THOMAS C. GUELCHER; JOSEPH M. HILBERT; Ms. MAUREEN BARBER-CAREY, Ed.D.; JAMES E. MARTIN; Ms. C. ANGELA BONTEMPO, F.A.C.H.E.; AL LANDER, Esq.; Rev. Msgrs. ROBERT L. BRUGGER; CHARLES A. KAZA, V.G., E.V. Ex Officios: Rev. Msgr. ROBERT J. SMITH, J.C.L., V.G.; DAVID J. MURPHY.

Deans—Very Revs. JAMES G. GUTTING, V.F., Erie East; JOHN J. DETISCH, V.F., Erie West; JOSEPH C. GREGOREK, V.F., Ph.D., Gannon University; JEFFERY J. NOBLE, V.F., Sharon; MATTHEW J. RUYECHAN, V.F., Oil City; PHILLIP A. PINCZEWSKI, V.F., Bradford; Rev. Msgr. H. DESMOND MCGEE

JR., V.F., Clearfield; Very Rev. MARK O'HERN, V.F., Meadville; Rev. Msgr. JOSEPH J. RICCARDO, V.F., DuBois; Rev. THOMAS L. TYLER, V.F., St. Marys; Very Rev. RICHARD J. TOOHEY, V.F., Warren.

Presbyteral Council—Most Rev. DONALD W. TRAUTMAN, S.T.D., S.S.L., Pres.; Rev. Msgrs. CHARLES A. KAZA, V.G., E.V.; DANIEL E. MAGRAW; ROBERT M. MALENE, E.V.; H. DESMOND MCGEE JR., V.F.; ROBERT J. SMITH, J.C.L., V.G.; L. THOMAS SNYDERWINE; Revs. MICHAEL P. ALLISON; SCOTT P. DETISCH, Ph.D.; JOSEPH V. DOUGHERTY; Very Rev. JAMES G. GUTTING, V.F.; Revs. MEINRAD LAWSON, O.S.B.; CHRISTOPHER J. SINGER, J.C.L.; Very Rev. MARK O'HERN, V.F.; Revs. WALTER E. PACKARD; NICHOLAS J. ROUCH, S.T.D.; Very Rev. MATTHEW J. RUYECHAN, V.F.; Revs. STEPHEN J. SCHREIBER; GLENN R. WHITMAN; THOMAS J. WHITMAN.

Priest Personnel Board—Most Rev. DONALD W. TRAUTMAN, S.T.D., S.S.L.; Rev. Msgrs. ROBERT J. SMITH, J.C.L., V.G., Chm.; H. DESMOND MCGEE JR., V.F.; Very Rev. JAMES G. GUTTING, V.F.; Revs. JOHNATHAN P. SCHMOLT; GEORGE E. STROHMEYER, M.A., Sec.; GLENN R. WHITMAN; JOHN P. MALTHANER.

Priest Retirement Board—Most Rev. DONALD W. TRAUTMAN, S.T.D., S.S.L., Chm. Members: THOMAS C. GUELCHER; Rev. Msgrs. ERNEST J. DALEY (Retired); JOHN B. HAGERTY (Retired); ROBERT J. SMITH, J.C.L., V.G.; Rev. CHRISTOPHER J. SINGER, J.C.L.; Deacon WILLIAM SABORSKY; SAMUEL ZAFFUTO; Rev. Msgr. DANIEL E. MAGRAW. Staff: DAVID J. MURPHY, CFO.

Episcopal Delegate for Retired Priests—Rev. Msgrs. ERNEST J. DALEY (Retired); JOHN B. HAGERTY (Retired).

Pennsylvania Catholic Conference—Rev. NICHOLAS J. ROUCH, S.T.D., Personal Rep. of the Bishop, Mailing Address: St. Mark Catholic Center, P.O. Box 10397, Erie, 16514. Tel: 814-824-1140.

The Bishop's Theological Advisory Committee—Revs. NICHOLAS J. ROUCH, S.T.D.; EDWARD KRAUSE, C.S.C., Ph.D.; CASIMIR WOZNIAK, Ph.D.; Very Rev. MICHAEL T. KESICKI; Mr. PATRICK O'CONNELL, Ph.D.; Sr. MICHELE HEALY, S.S.J., M.A.; Rev. SCOTT P. DETISCH, Ph.D.

Matrimonial Concerns

All requests for marriage dispensations, permissions, and rogatory commissions should be sent to this office.

Diocesan Tribunal—Mailing Address: St. Mark Catholic Center, P.O. Box 10397, Erie, 16514. Tel: 814-824-1140; Fax: 814-824-1149.

Judicial Vicar—Rev. Msgr. ROBERT J. SMITH, J.C.L., V.G.

Adjutant Judicial Vicar—Rev. CHRISTOPHER J. SINGER, J.C.L.

Director of the Office of Matrimonial Concerns and Tribunal—BARBARA A. BETTWY, J.C.L.

Promoter of Justice—Rev. CHRISTOPHER J. SINGER, J.C.L.

Defenders of the Bond—Ms. ANNE BRYANT, J.C.L., 1511 Blackburn Dr., Pasadena, TX 77502. Email: abryant@archgh.org; Ms. ANNA MARIE CHAMBLIS, 6013 Pegy Dr., Fort Worth, TX 76133. Email: amchamblee@sbeglobal.net; Ms. CHERRY CLARK, J.C.L., 5004 Wetheredsville Rd., Gwynn Oak, MD 21207. Email: clark.cherry@g.mail.com; Ms. DANIELA KNEPPER, J.C.L., W126 S6480 Chesterton Ct., Muskego, WI 53150. Email: d.knepper@earthlink.net; Ms. HEIDI KRUPP, J.C.L., 12109 W. Dodge Rd., Montrose, MI 48457. Email: heidiraj@gmail.com; Ms. JEANNINE MARINO, J.C.L., 6803 Chillum Manor Rd., Hyattsville, MD 20783. Email: jeanninemarino@gmail.com.

Matrimonial Judges—Rev. Msgr. ROBERT J. SMITH, J.C.L., V.G.; Rev. JOHN P. BEAL, J.C.D.; Deacon RICHARD D. SHEWMAN, D.Min., J.C.L.; BARBARA A. BETTWY, J.C.L.

Auditors—Sisters JEAN BAPTISTE DILUZIO, S.S.J.; SYLVIA BURNETT, O.S.B.M.; JULIANNE PERTZ, J.D.

Secretaries/Notaries—PATRICIA WIERBINSKI; CINDY MANGIARACINA.

Catholic Education

Unless otherwise indicated, all correspondence for Catholic Education should be directed to St. Mark Catholic Center, P.O. Box 10397, Erie, PA 16514-0397.

Vicar for Catholic Education—Rev. NICHOLAS J. ROUCH, S.T.D. Tel: 814-824-1220.

Special Assistant to the Vicar—Deacon RONALD FRONZAGLIA. Tel: 814-824-1220.

Elementary Curriculum and Teacher Personnel—KIMBERLY LYTLE, Dir. Tel: 814-824-1248.

Government Programs—ROBERTA BUCCI, Dir. Govt. Programs. Tel: 814-824-1238.

Director of Catholic Schools and Principal Personnel—Ms. PATRICIA MCLAUGHLIN. Tel: 814-824-1247.

Elementary Athletic Programs—DOUGLAS CHUZIE, Dir. Athletics. Tel: 814-824-1245.

Diocesan Director of Athletics—DOUGLAS CHUZIE. Tel: 814-824-1245.

Religious Education—Mr. JOSEPH STREETT, D.R.E. Tel: 814-824-1210; Sr. NANCY FISCHER, S.S.J., Dir. Community Formation & Lay Ministry Training. Tel: 814-824-1210; Rev. STEPHEN J. SCHREIBER, Dir. Office of Youth & Young Adults. Tel: 814-824-1210; BARBARA BURKETT, B.S., Dir. NFP & Coord. Chastity Educ. Tel: 814-824-1259; KAREN STREETT, Coord. Media Resources & Office for the Protection of Children and Youth. Tel: 814-824-1222; Sr. NANCY FISCHER, S.S.J., Dir. RCIA.

Campus Ministry—Deacon STEPHEN J. WASHEK, Diocesan Dir. Campus Min., Gannon University, 109 University Sq., Erie, 16541. Tel: 814-871-7435 See Separate listing in the Institution Section for details on Campus Ministry and Newman Centers.

Catholic Charities

Affiliated Offices, Agencies and Institutions

Central Administration

All communication for the Catholic Charities Central Administration should be directed to St. Mark Catholic Center, P.O. Box 10397, Erie, PA 16514-0397. Tel: 814-824-1251.

Office of Catholic Charities—MARY C. MAXWELL, M.A., Exec. Dir.

Catholic Charities of the Diocese of Erie, Inc.—MARY C. MAXWELL, M.A., Charities program and fiscal development corporation.

Director of Development—Dr. EMMA LEE MCCLOSKEY, Ed.D., C.F.R.E., Dir.

Pastoral Social Services

Unless otherwise indicated, all communication for Catholic Charities Pastoral Social Services should be directed to St. Mark Catholic Center, P.O. Box 10397, Erie, PA 16514-0397. Tel: 814-824-1251.

Family Life—ANN BADACH, M.A., Dir., Office includes Marriage Preparation and Enrichment Programs, Family Ministry, Retrouvaille.

Parish Social Ministry/Respect Life—ERIN LANDINI-GROGAN, M.S., N.C.C., L.P.C., Dir., Consultant for Parish Care and Concern and Social Justice & Respect Life Programs.

Refugee Ministry—JOSEPH J. HAAS, L.P.C., Dir. Tel: 800-673-2535. Email: jhaas@cccas.org.

Catholic Rural Ministry - Bradford Deanery—Co Directors: Sisters PHYLLIS SCHLEICHER, O.S.B.; MARY WILLIAM HOFFMAN, O.S.B., 472 Sartwell Creek Rd., Port Allegany, 16743. Tel: 814-544-8017.

Catholic Rural Ministry - Oil City Deanery—Sr. MARIAN WEHLER, O.S.B., Dir., Mailing Address: 7 Pulaski St., Oil City, 16301. Tel: 814-677-2032.

Rainbows—ERIN LANDINI-GROGAN, M.S., N.C.C., L.P.C.

Office of Diocesan and International Mission Activities—PAT MARSHALL, B.A., Supvr.

Office of Disabilities/Deaf Ministry/Healing Ministries—JACKLYN JOHNSON, R.N., Dir.

Victim Assistance Coordinator—Dr. ROBERT NELSEN. Tel: 814-871-7723. Email: nelsen001@gannon.edu.

Community Counseling Services

Catholic Charities Counseling and Adoption Services—JOSEPH J. HAAS, L.P.C., Agency Dir. Tel: 814-456-2091.

Northern Vicariate - Erie Office—KRISTEN HUEMMERICH, L.C.S.W., Area Supvr., 329 W. Tenth St., Erie, 16502. Tel: 814-456-2091.

Western Vicariate - Sharon Office—CONNIE MASIAN, L.S.W., Area Supvr., 995 Linden St., Sharon, 16146. Tel: 412-346-4142.

Eastern Vicariate - DuBois Office—NANCI MATTISON, M.A., Area Supvr., 90 Beaver Dr., Ste. 119 D, Box 2, DuBois, 15801. Tel: 814-371-4717.

Residential Services for Older Persons

John XXIII Home—KIRK HAWTHORNE, Admin., 2250 Shenango Fwy., Hermitage, 16148. Tel: 814-981-3200.

Christ the King Manor—SAMUEL ZAFFUTO, Admin., 1100 W. Long Ave., Du Bois, 15801. Tel: 814-371-3180.

Community Social Services

**St. Martin Center*CHERYL KOBEL, M.A., Dir., 1701 Parade St., Erie, 16503. Tel: 814-452-6113.

Harborcreek Youth Services—Mr. JOHN D. PETULLA, A.C.S.W., M.S.W., 5712 Iroquois Ave., Harborcreek, 16421. Tel: 814-899-7664.

Prince of Peace Center—JOSEPH FLECHER, B.S., Dir., 502 Darr Ave., Box 89, Farrell, 16121. Tel: 412-346-5777.

Better Housing for Erie—JENNIFER MERLINO, Site Mgr., 515 State St., Erie, 16501. Tel: 814-456-0510.

Good Samaritan Center—Deacon ANTHONY INDELICATO, Dir., 1 E. Locust St., Clearfield, 16830. Tel: 814-768-7229.

St. Elizabeth Center—Deacon JOHN WREN, 311 Emerald St., Oil City, 16301. Tel: 814-677-0203.

Parish Services

Unless otherwise noted, all communication for Parish Services should be directed to St. Mark Catholic Center, P.O. Box 10397, Erie, PA 16514-0397. Tel: 814-824-1274.

Office of Worship—MATTHEW CLARK, Admin.

Office of Communications—ANNE-MARIE WELSH, Dir.

Faith Magazine— The Magazine of the Catholic Diocese of Erie ANNE-MARIE WELSH, Exec. Editor, 429 E. Grandview Blvd., Erie, 16504. Tel: 814-824-1167; Fax: 814-824-1128. Email: faith@eriercd.org.

Financial Services

Unless otherwise noted, all communication for Financial Services should be directed to St. Mark Catholic Center, P.O. Box 10397, Erie, PA 16514-0397. Tel: 814-824-1180.

Chief Financial Officer—DAVID J. MURPHY.

Financial Services Office—DAVID J. MURPHY, Dir.; JAMES L. BOGNIAK, Dir. Accounting; THOMAS E. BURIK, CPA, Dir. Parish Financial Svcs.; Deacon WILLIAM SABORSKY, Consultant, Human Resources; CHARLES BANDUCCI, Dir. School Financial Svcs.

Stewardship and Annual Appeals Office—WILLIAM GRANT II, C.F.R.E.

Diocesan Attorney—FRANK L. KROTO JR., Esq., Quinn, Buseck, Leemhuis, Toohey & Kroto, Inc., 2222 W. Grandview Blvd., Erie, 16506. Tel: 814-833-2222.

Erie Diocesan Cemeteries—Directors: Most Rev. DONALD W. TRAUTMAN, S.T.D., S.S.L.; Rev. Msgr. ROBERT J. SMITH, J.C.L., V.G.; Revs. CHRISTOPHER J. SINGER, J.C.L.; THOMAS M. FIALKOWSKI, Bishop's Liaison (Retired); DAVID J. MURPHY; JOHN HROMYAK, Dir., 3325 West Lake Rd., Erie, 16505. Tel: 814-838-7724.

Clergy Formation

Clergy Personnel—Rev. Msgr. ROBERT J. SMITH, J.C.L., V.G., Dir., Mailing Address: St. Mark Catholic Center, P.O. Box 10397, Erie, 16514-0397. Tel: 814-824-1130; Fax: 814-824-1124.

Permanent Diaconate Program—Rev. MARK A. NOWAK, Dir.; Deacon RICHARD D. SHEWMAN, D.Min., J.C.L., Assoc. Dir.

Clergy Continuing Education and Formation—Rev. Msgr. RICHARD R. SIEFER, Coord., St. Catherine Parish, 116 S. State St., DuBois, 15801. Tel: 814-371-8556. Mailing Address: St. Mark Catholic Center, P.O. Box 10397, Erie, 16514-0397. Tel: 814-824-1195.

Vocation Office—Revs. STEPHEN J. SCHREIBER, Dir.; WILLIAM R. BARRON, Assoc. Dir., Mailing Address: St. Mark Catholic Center, P.O. Box 10397, Erie, 16514-0397. Tel: 814-824-1200.

St. Mark Seminary—Very Rev. MICHAEL T. KESICKI, Rector & Dir. Seminarians; Revs. NICHOLAS J. ROUCH, S.T.D., Vice Rector & Assoc. Dir. Seminarians; STEPHEN J. SCHREIBER, Resident Spiritual Dir.; Sr. MARY ANDREW HIMES, R.S.M., Dir. Liturgical Music, Mailing Address: St. Mark Catholic Center, P.O. Box 10397, Erie, 16514-0397. Tel: 814-824-1200.

Special Apostolates

Hispanic Apostolate—Rev. AMILCAR MATIAS ROSADO SOSA, 1237 W. 21st St., Erie, 16502. Tel: 814-459-0543.

Apostleship of the Sea and Chaplain to the Port of Erie—Rev. Msgr. L. THOMAS SNYDERWINE, Dir., c/o St. Luke Church, 421 E. 38th St., Erie, 16504-1699. Tel: 814-825-6920.

World Apostolate of Fatima (Blue Army)—Rev. DAVID L. POULSON, Dir., 502 Peach St., Erie, 16501-1104. Tel: 814-454-6494.

Cursillo Movement—Co Directors: Rev. Msgrs. DANIEL K. ARNOLD; WILLIAM E. SUTHERLAND, Mailing Address: St. Mark Catholic Center, P.O. Box 10397, Erie, 16514. Tel: 814-824-1111.

Legion of Mary—Rev. JAMES T. O'HARA, Spiritual Dir., 913 Fulton St., Erie, 16503. Tel: 814-452-4832.

Charismatic Movement—MICHAEL VEHEC, Diocesan Liaison, Mailing Address: St. Mark Catholic Center, P.O. Box 10397, Erie, 16514-0397.

Bread of Life Community—Rev. LAWRENCE R. RICHARDS, Moderator, St. Joseph Parish, 147 W. 24th St., Erie, 16502-2897. Tel: 814-452-2982.

Word of Life Charismatic Renewal—St. Mark Catholic Center, 429 E. Grandview Blvd., P.O. Box 10397, Erie, 16514-0397. Tel: 814-824-1286.

Inner-City Outreach—Very Rev. JAMES G. GUTTING, V.F., St. Mary of the Immaculate Conception Parish, 315 E. 9th St., Erie, 16503. Tel: 814-452-2410; Sr. ROSEMARY O'BRIEN, S.S.J.; Deacon ROBERT L. WALKER.

Ecumenism

Pennsylvania Conference on Inter-Church Cooperation—Rev. CHRISTOPHER J. SINGER, J.C.L.

Ecumenical Officers—

Eastern Vicariate—Very Rev. PHILLIP A. PINCZEWSKI, V.F., St. Callistus Church, 342 Chase St., Kane, 16735. Tel: 814-837-6694.

Western Vicariate—Rev. STEPHEN A. ANDERSON, Mailing Address: Our Lady Queen of the Americas, P.O. Box 110, Conneaut Lake, 16316. Tel: 814-382-7252.

Northern Vicariate—Rev. Msgr. WILLIAM E. BIEBEL, V.F., St. Peter Cathedral, 230 W. 10th St., Erie, 16501. Tel: 814-453-6677.

CLERGY, PARISHES, MISSIONS AND PAROCHIAL SCHOOLS

CITY OF ERIE

(ERIE COUNTY)

1—ST. PETER CATHEDRAL (1893) Rev. Msgr. William E. Biebel, Rector; Rev. John L. Miller, Parochial Vicar. In Res., Rev. Msgr. Robert G. Barcio, Archivist (Retired).
Res.: 230 W. 10th St., 16501. Tel: 814-453-6677; Fax: 814-456-1351.
Church: 10th St. & Sassafras St., 16501.
School—(Grades K-8), 160 W. 11th St., 16501. Tel: 814-452-4276; Fax: 814-452-0479. Kathleen Lane, Prin. Lay Teachers 23; Students 258; Preschool 27.
Catechesis/Religious Program—Karen Hund, D.R.E. Students 10.

2—ST. ANDREW (1871) Rev. Msgr. Richard J. Sullivan; Deacon Ralph DeCecco.
Res.: 1116 W. Seventh St., 16502. Tel: 814-454-2486; Fax: 814-456-4443.
Catechesis/Religious Program—Carol Hoffman, D.R.E. Students 85.

3—ST. ANN (1887) Merged with St. Casimir and Holy Family to create Our Mother of Sorrows.

4—BLESSED SACRAMENT (1938) Rev. Msgr. Daniel E. Magraw; Deacon Kevin Kunik. In Res., Rev. Msgrs. John B. Hagerty (Retired); Richard J. Stack (Retired); Richard G. Mayer (Retired).
Res.: 1626 W. 26th St., 16508. Tel: 814-454-0171; Fax: 814-459-6832.
School—(Grades K-8) Tel: 814-455-1387; Fax: 814-461-0247. Sheri Kurczewski, Prin.; Liz Hokaj, Librarian. Lay Teachers 23; Students 305; Religious 1; Clergy 1; Preschool 94.
Catechesis/Religious Program—Tracey Kunik, D.R.E. Students 142.

5—ST. BONIFACE (1857) [CEM] Rev. John M. Schultz; Deacon Timothy Good.
Res.: 9367 Wattsburg Rd., 16509. Tel: 814-825-4439; Fax: 814-825-2819.
School—(Grades K-8) Tel: 814-825-4238; Fax: 814-825-4274. Barbara Portenier, Prin. Lay Teachers 8; Students 69; Preschool 20; Religious 2.
Catechesis/Religious Program—Tel: 814-825-4439, Ext. 230. Sr. Rose Kuzma, O.S.F., D.R.E. Students 190.

6—ST. CASIMIR (1914), (Polish), Merged with St. Ann and Holy Family to create Our Mother of Sorrows.

7—ST. GEORGE (1922) Rev. Msgr. Robert L. Brugger; Rev. Johnathan P. Schmolt, Parochial Vicar; Sr. Josephine Vuodi, F.S.O., Pastoral Min.; Deacons Robert Ball; Stephen Washek.
Res.: 5145 Peach St., 16509. Tel: 814-864-0622; Fax: 814-866-7532.
School—(Grades K-8) Tel: 814-864-4821; Fax: 814-866-8297. Lawrence Neubauer, Prin.; Tara Carrera, Librarian. Lay Teachers 29; Students 436; Preschool 81.
Catechesis/Religious Program—Tel: 814-864-0622, Ext. 281; 814-864-0622, Ext. 225. Mary Lou Pacoe, D.R.E.; Kris Rudy, D.R.E. Students 359.

8—ST. HEDWIG (1910) Rev. Msgr. Henry A. Kriegel.
Res.: 521 E. 3rd St., 16507.
Catechesis/Religious Program—Tel: 814-454-6232; Fax: 814-454-8096 (Call first). Sr. Marie Stephen Kebort, S.S.J., D.R.E.

9—HOLY FAMILY/ST. ANN/ST. CASIMIR (1902), (Slovak), Merged with St. Ann and St. Casimir to create Our Mother of Sorrows.

10—HOLY ROSARY (1927) Rev. John B. Jacquel; Deacon Fred Keck. In Res., Rev. Christopher J. Singer.
Res.: 2701 East Ave., 16504. Tel: 814-456-4254; Fax: 814-459-8082.
Catechesis/Religious Program—Tel: 814-454-6322. Kathleen Kutz, D.R.E., Eastside Faith Formation. Students 63.

11—HOLY TRINITY (1903), (Polish), Rev. Msgr. Thomas J. McSweeney.
Res.: 2220 Reed St., 16503. Tel: 814-456-0671; Fax: 814-461-1150.

12—IMMACULATE CONCEPTION (1946), (African American), Closed. For inquiries for parish records contact the chancery.

13—ST. JAMES (1921) Revs. James McCormick; Scott W. Jabo; Deacon Charles Adamczyk; Sr. Susan Freitag, O.S.B., Sec.
Res.: 2602 Buffalo Rd., 16510. Tel: 814-899-6178; Fax: 814-899-7681.
School—(Grades K-8) Tel: 814-899-3429; Fax: 814-898-8285. Sr. Collette Hilow, C.D.S., Prin.; Mrs. Sandra Benek, Librarian. Sisters of the Congregation of the Divine Spirit 4; Lay Teachers 12; Students 219; Preschool 22.
Catechesis/Religious Program—Sr. Collette Hilow, C.D.S., D.R.E. Students 110.

14—ST. JOHN THE BAPTIST (1870) Rev. John B. Jacquel; Deacon Denis Coan.
Res.: 2701 East Ave., 16504. Tel: 814-456-4254.
School—St. John-Holy Rosary Eastside Catholic School, (Grades K-8), St. John merged with Holy Rosary to form St. John-Holy Rosary Eastside Catholic School., 504 E. 27th St., 16504. Tel: 814-452-6874; Fax: 814-455-0358. Susan Clarke-Bhagwandien, Prin. Lay Teachers 12; Students 108; Preschool 15.
Catechesis/Religious Program—Kathleen Kutz, D.R.E.

15—ST. JOSEPH (1867) Rev. Lawrence R. Richards. In Res., Rev. Gerald Wright, O.M.V.; Deacons Andrew Froberg; Douglas Konzel.
Res.: 147 W. 24th St., 16502. Tel: 814-452-2982; Fax: 814-452-4400.
Catechesis/Religious Program—Margie Frezza, D.R.E. Students 134.

16—ST. JUDE THE APOSTLE (1955) Revs. Mark A. Hoffman; J. Thomas Dugan, Senior Priest; Matthew J. Strickenberger, Parochial Vicar; Deacons David Pratt; James B. McGuinness; Richard Brogdon.
Res.: 2801 W. 6th St., 16505. Tel: 814-833-0927.
School—Our Lady's Christian, (Grades K-8) Tel: 814-838-7676. Rebecca Carey, Prin. School is sponsored by the following Parishes: St. Jude the Apostle; St. Julia; St. Andrew. Lay Teachers 26; Students 314; Preschool 51.
Catechesis/Religious Program—Anne Osborn, D.R.E. Students 286.

17—ST. JULIA (1938) Rev. Msgr. Bruce R. Allison.
Res.: 638 Roslyn Ave., 16505. Tel: 814-833-4347; Fax: 814-833-4596.
See Our Lady's Christian, Erie under St. Jude the Apostle, Erie for details.
Catechesis/Religious Program—Cheryl Ann Morrison, D.R.E. Students 153.

18—ST. LUKE (1954) Rev. Msgr. L. Thomas Snyderwine; Deacons Richard Shewman; Glenn Kuzma; Jerome Sobrowski.
Res.: 421 E. 38th St., 16504. Tel: 814-825-6920; Fax: 814-825-6905.
School—(Grades K-8) Tel: 814-825-7105; Fax: 814-825-7169. Karen Beer, Prin.; Paula Mielnik, Librarian. Lay Teachers 24; Students 310; Preschool 45.
Catechesis/Religious Program—Mary Tirak, C.R.E. Students 169.

19—ST. MARK THE EVANGELIST (Lawrence Park) (1938) Rev. Msgr. Daniel K. Arnold; Deacons Frederick Weaver, (Retired); James Kaschalk.
Res.: 4306 Morse St., 16511. Tel: 814-899-3000; Fax: 814-899-5212.
Catechesis/Religious Program—Pat Marshall, D.R.E. (6-12); Geri Hadlock, D.R.E. (K-5) & Youth Min. Students 187.

20—ST. MARY OF THE IMMACULATE CONCEPTION (2009) Very Rev. James G. Gutting; Sr. Rosemary O'Brien, S.S.J., Pastoral Assoc.; Deacon Robert L. Walker, Dir. Facilities.
Res.: 315 E. 9th St., 16503. Tel: 814-452-2410; Fax: 814-455-7992.
Catechesis/Religious Program—Kathleen Kutz, D.R.E. Eastside Faith Formation, Twinned with Holy Rosary.

21—ST. MATTHEW IN THE WOODS (1966) Merged to become All Saints, Waterford.

22—MOUNT CALVARY (1951) Rev. Michael G. DeMartinis, Admin.
Res.: 2022 E. Lake Rd., 16511. Tel: 814-454-0061; Fax: 814-454-7177.
Catechesis/Religious Program—Don McClallen, D.R.E. Twinned with St. Mark the Evangelist, Erie.

23—OUR LADY OF MERCY (1946) Rev. Msgr. Gerald T. Ritchie; Sr. Mary Rose Romeo, S.J., Liturgical Min.; Deacon John Brophy; Donna Clark, Pastoral Min.
Res.: 837 Bartlett Rd., Harborcreek, 16421. Tel: 814-899-5342; Fax: 814-898-3306.
Catechesis/Religious Program—Irene Lucas, D.R.E. Students 232.

24—OUR LADY OF MT. CARMEL (1960) Rev. Raymond W. Hahn; Deacon Frank Pregler.
Res.: 1553 E. Grandview Blvd., 16510. Tel: 814-825-7313; Fax: 814-825-4190.
School—(Grades K-8) Tel: 814-825-2822; Fax: 814-824-5063. Veronica Antoske, Prin.; Patty Drabina, Librarian. Lay Teachers 15; Students 118; Preschool 35.
Catechesis/Religious Program—Sue Berois, D.R.E. Students 117.

25—OUR LADY OF PEACE (1955) Revs. Theodore B. Marconi; William R. Barron, Parochial Vicar; Jason R. Feigh, Parochial Vicar; Deacons Anthony Alleruzzo; John Mang.
Res.: 2401 W. 38th St., 16506. Tel: 814-833-7701; Fax: 814-833-7702.
School—(Grades K-8) Tel: 814-838-3548; Fax: 814-838-9133. Jeffrey Lipiec, Prin. Lay Teachers 20; Students 356; Preschool 68.
Catechesis/Religious Program—Tammie Mang, D.R.E. Students 558.

26—OUR MOTHER OF SORROWS (2009) Rev. James T. O'Hara.
913 Fulton St., 16503. Tel: 814-452-4832; Fax: 814-453-2275. In Res., Rev. Msgr. Gerald J. Koos (Retired); Revs. Ronald E. Gmerek; Jerry S. Priscaro.
St. Ann Church—921 East Ave., 16503.
St. Casimir Church—629 Hess Ave., 16503.
Holy Family Church—913 Fulton St., 16503.
School—Holy Family, (Grades PreSchool-8) Tel: 814-452-4720. Sr. M. Kevin Berdis, O.S.F., Prin.; Mrs. Charlotte Newcamp, Librarian. Religious 1; Lay Teachers 7; Students 78; Preschool students 2.
Catechesis/Religious Program—Patricia Devore, D.R.E. Students 13.

27—ST. PATRICK (1834) Rev. Msgr. Henry A. Kriegel. In Res., Rev. Msgr. Joseph V. Wardanski; Rev. Daniel J. Prez.
Res.: 130 E. 4th St., 16507. Tel: 814-454-8085; Fax: 814-459-8685.
Catechesis/Religious Program—Eastside Faith Formation, 2701 East Ave., 16504. Tel: 814-454-6322; Fax: 814-459-8082. Sr. Marie Stephen Kebort, S.S.J., D.R.E. Students 14.

28—ST. PAUL (1891), (Italian), Rev. Alexander D. Amico.
Res.: 1617 Walnut St., 16502. Tel: 814-459-3173; Fax: 814-456-0105.

29—SACRED HEART (1894) Very Rev. John J. Detisch. In Res., Rev. Jerome S. Simmons.
Res.: 816 W. 26th St., 16508. Tel: 814-456-6256; Fax: 814-459-9533.
Catechesis/Religious Program—Tony Del Rio, D.R.E. Students 94.

30—ST. STANISLAUS (1885), (Polish), Rev. Msgr. Bernard J. Urbaniak.
Res.: 516 E. 13th St., 16503. Tel: 814-452-6606; Fax: 814-459-0939.
Catechesis/Religious Program—Michelle Inter, D.R.E. Students 20.

31—ST. STEPHEN (1917), (Hungarian—Hispanic), Rev. Amilcar Matias Rosado Sosa; Deacon Miguel Alvarez.
Res.: 1237 W. 21 St., 16502. Tel: 814-459-0543.
Catechesis/Religious Program—Sr. Severiana Morales, O.L.C., D.R.E. Students 47.

OUTSIDE THE CITY OF ERIE

ALBION, ERIE CO., ST. LAWRENCE (1914) Rev. Philip M. Oriole.
Res.: 180 E. State St., 16401. Tel: 814-756-3623; Fax: 814-756-5918.
St. Lawrence Catechetical Center—129 E. Pearl St., 16401. Tel: 814-756-4840.
Catechesis/Religious Program—Cheryl Niedermeyer, D.R.E. Students 101.

ANITA, JEFFERSON CO., ST. JOSEPH, HUSBAND OF MARY, (Mission of SS. Cosmas & Damian, Punxsutawney, PA.) Rev. Msgr. Joseph J. Riccardo.
Res.: 616 Mahoning St., Punxsutawney, 15767. Tel: 814-938-6540; Fax: 814-938-7439.

BRADFORD, MCKEAN CO.

1—ST. BERNARD (1880) [CEM] Rev. Raymond C. Gramata; Deacon Gerald Beeman.
Res.: 95 E. Corydon St., 16701-5394. Tel: 814-362-6825; Fax: 814-362-1479.
School—(Grades K-8), 450 W. Washington St., 16701. Tel: 814-368-5302; Fax: 814-368-1464. Kimberly Mooney, Prin.; Lisa Webster, Librarian. Lay Teachers 20; Students 136; Preschool 34.
Catechesis/Religious Program—Students 61.

2—ST. FRANCIS OF ASSISI (1946) [JC] Rev. Stephen L. Collins (Retired).
15 St. Francis Dr., 16701.
Res.: *Our Mother of Perpetual Help*, 31 Lafayette Ave., Lewis Run, 16738. Tel: 814-368-6959; Fax: 814-368-6959.
Catechesis/Religious Program—Students 39.

BRANDY CAMP, ELK CO., HOLY CROSS (1908), (Italian), [CEM] Rev. Msgr. Charles A. Kaza, Admin.
Mailing Address: 1135 Hewett St., Brockway, 15824. Tel: 814-268-3655; Fax: 814-268-1147.

BROCKWAY, JEFFERSON CO., ST. TOBIAS (1898) [CEM] Rev. Msgr. Charles A. Kaza; Deacon Robert P.

DeNoon.
Res.: 1135 Hewett St., 15824. Tel: 814-268-3655; Fax: 814-268-1147.
Catechesis/Religious Program—Kathryn Matson, C.R.E.; Tara Starr, D.R.E. Students 186.

BROOKVILLE, JEFFERSON CO., IMMACULATE CONCEPTION (1852) [CEM] Rev. William M. Laska.
Res.: 129 Graham Ave., 15825. Tel: 814-849-8697; Fax: 814-849-5265.
Catechesis/Religious Program—Penny Rakovan, D.R.E. Students 105.
Mission—St. Dominic [CEM] Sigel, Jefferson Co.

CAMBRIDGE SPRINGS, CRAWFORD CO., ST. ANTHONY (1894) Rev. David L. Poulson.
Res.: 165 Beach Ave., P.O. Box 214, 16403. Tel: 814-398-4234; Fax: 814-398-1531.
Catechesis/Religious Program—Sue Parkin, C.R.E. Students 86.

CLARION, CLARION CO., IMMACULATE CONCEPTION (1855) [CEM] Rev. Monty Sayers.
Res.: 720 Liberty St., 16214. Tel: 814-226-8433; Fax: 814-226-1092.
School—(Grades K-8) Fax: 814-226-4998. Donna Gaydash, Prin. Lay Teachers 13; Students 78; Preschool 26.
Catechesis/Religious Program—Dawn Kidney, D.R.E.; Ann Enderle Liska, D.R.E. Students 288.

CLEARFIELD, CLEARFIELD CO., ST. FRANCIS (1830) [CEM] Rev. Msgr. H. Desmond McGee Jr. In Res., Rev. Msgr. Henry L. Krebs; Deacon Eugene Miller Jr.
Res.: 212 S. Front St., 16830. Tel: 814-765-9671; Fax: 814-765-9489.
School—(Grades K-8) Tel: 814-765-2618; Fax: 814-765-6704. Dr. Michael Spencer, Prin.; Sheila Clancy, Librarian. Lay Teachers 12; Students 160; Preschool 32.
Catechesis/Religious Program—Rita McConnell, D.R.E. Students 108.

COALPORT, CLEARFIELD CO., ST. BASIL THE GREAT (1887) [CEM] Rev. Zab Amar.
Res.: 183 Locust St., 16627. Tel: 814-672-3561; Fax: 814-672-5954.
Catechesis/Religious Program—Ann Smith, D.R.E. Students 83.

CONNEAUT LAKE, CRAWFORD CO., OUR LADY QUEEN OF THE AMERICAS (1958) [CEM] Rev. Stephen A. Anderson.
Res.: 155 S. 9th St., 16316. Tel: 814-382-7252; Fax: 814-382-9575.
Catechesis/Religious Program—Tel: 814-382-7256. Pam Davis, C.R.E. Students 129.

CONNEAUTVILLE, CRAWFORD CO., ST. PETER (1853), (Irish), [CEM] In Res., Rev. John A. Walsh.
Res.: 501 Washington St., P.O. Box F, 16406. Tel: 814-587-3435; Fax: 814-587-6436.
Catechesis/Religious Program—Debbie Monnie, D.R.E. Tel: 814-587-0071. Students 28.

CORRY, ERIE CO.
1—ST. ELIZABETH (1876) [CEM] Rev. Msgr. Casimir A. Bogniak, Admin. (Retired); Deacons William Saborsky; William Sproveri.
Res.: 26 W. Pleasant St., 16407. Tel: 814-664-7105; Fax: 814-663-0505.
Catechesis/Religious Program—Vickie Stull, D.R.E. Twinned with St. Thomas the Apostle, Corry. Students 60.
2—ST. THOMAS THE APOSTLE (1856) [CEM] Rev. Msgr. Casimir A. Bogniak, Admin. (Retired); Deacons William Saborsky; William Sproveri.
Res.: 26 W. Pleasant St., 16407. Tel: 814-663-3041; Fax: 814-663-0505.
Church: 203 W. Washington St., 16407.
School—(Grades PreK-6) Tel: 814-665-7375; Fax: 814-664-4025. Kathy Bowes, Prin. Lay Teachers 7; Students 65.
Catechesis/Religious Program—Vickie Stull, D.R.E. Students 60.

COUDERSPORT, POTTER CO., ST. EULALIA (1891) [CEM] Rev. James C. Campbell.
Res.: 6 E. Maple St., 16915. Tel: 814-274-8646; Fax: 814-642-7990.
Catechesis/Religious Program—Tel: 814-274-8552. Andrea Streich, D.R.E. Students 98.

CROSSINGSVILLE, CRAWFORD CO., ST. PHILIP (1840) [CEM] Rev. Thaddeus T. Kondzielski.
Res.: 25797 State Hwy. 98, Edinboro, 16412. Tel: 814-734-7395.
Catechesis/Religious Program—Alyssa Leone, D.R.E. Students 24.

CROWN, CLARION CO., ST. MARY (1848) [CEM 2] Rev. Gregory P. Passauer.
Res.: 117 Lencer Dr., P.O. Box 41, 16220. Tel: 814-744-9919; Fax: 814-744-8624.
Catechesis/Religious Program—Lynn Tarr, C.R.E. Students 52.
Mission—St. Ann Marienville, Forest Co.

CURWENSVILLE, CLEARFIELD CO., ST. TIMOTHY (1915) [CEM] Rev. Mark J. Mastrian; Deacon Anthony Indelicato.
Res.: 306 Walnut St., 16833. Tel: 814-236-1845; Fax: 814-236-1196.
Catechesis/Religious Program—Terri A. Clarkson, D.R.E. Students 55.

DAGUSCAHONDA, ELK CO., ST. BENEDICT, Closed. Effective April 30, 1995, St. Benedict in Daguscahonda became a Public Oratory (Cannon 1223).

DU BOIS, CLEARFIELD CO.
1—ST. CATHERINE (1877) [CEM] Rev. Msgr. Richard R. Siefer; Rev. Thomas S. Hoderny. In Res., Rev. Matias M. Quimno.
Res.: 116 S. State St., 15801. Tel: 814-371-8556; Fax: 814-371-0592.
Catechesis/Religious Program—Pat McAllister, D.R.E. Students 145.
2—ST. JOSEPH (1893), (Lithuanian), [CEM] Rev. V. David Foradori.
Res.: 25 Robinson St., 15801. Tel: 814-371-5773; Fax: 814-371-5028.
Catechesis/Religious Program—Students 59.
3—ST. MICHAEL (1912), (Polish), [CEM] Rev. V. David Foradori.
Res.: 15 Robinson St., 15801. Tel: 814-371-5773; Fax: 814-371-5028.
Catechesis/Religious Program—Kathleen Clement, C.R.E. Students 149.

EAST BRADY, CLARION CO., ST. EUSEBIUS (1877) [CEM] Rev. William M. Kuba, Admin.
Res.: 301 E. 2nd St., 16028. Tel: 724-526-3366; Fax: 724-526-3294.
Catechesis/Religious Program—
Mission—St. Richard Rimersburg, Clarion Co.

EDINBORO, ERIE CO., OUR LADY OF THE LAKE (1950) Rev. William E. Sutherland.
Res.: 128 Sunset Dr., Box 838, 16412. Tel: 814-734-3113; Fax: 814-734-3085.
Catechesis/Religious Program—Mary Rose Shinsky, D.R.E. Students 210.

ELDRED, MCKEAN CO., ST. RAPHAEL (1847) [CEM 2] Very Rev. Thomas E. Brown.
Res.: 16 First St., Box 252, 16731. Tel: 814-225-4231; Fax: 814-225-3172.
Catechesis/Religious Program—Students 25.
Mission—St. Mary [CEM] Sartwell, McKean Co.

EMLENTON, VENANGO CO., ST. MICHAEL (1867) [CEM] Rev. Msgr. Jan C. Olowin.
Res.: 811 Chestnut St., P.O. Box 177, 16373. Tel: 724-867-2422; Fax: 724-867-6815.
Catechesis/Religious Program—Pam Gent, D.R.E. Students 36.

EMPORIUM, CAMERON CO., ST. MARK (1888) [CEM] Rev. Paul S. Siebert.
Res.: 235 E. 4th St., 15834. Tel: 814-486-0569; Fax: 814-486-3298.
Catechesis/Religious Program—Jennifer Abriatis, D.R.E. Students 108.
Mission—St. James Driftwood, Cameron Co.

FAIRVIEW, ERIE CO., HOLY CROSS (1963) Rev. Scott P. Detisch. In Res., Rev. Paul D. Panaretos Jr., S.J.
Res.: 7125 Old Ridge Rd., P.O. Box 10, 16415. Tel: 814-474-2605; Fax: 814-474-1256.
Catechesis/Religious Program—Sylvia Smith, D.R.E. Students 230.

FALLS CREEK, JEFFERSON CO., ST. BERNARD (1952) Very Rev. Richard C. Tomasone.
Res.: 205 Taylor Ave., 15840. Tel: 814-371-7419.
Catechesis/Religious Program—Tel: 814-449-3624. Students 32.

FARRELL, MERCER CO.
1—ST. ADALBERT (1913), (Polish), [CEM] Rev. Daniel J. Kresinski.
1035 Fruit Ave., 16121.
Res.: 804 Idaho St., Sharon, 16146. Tel: 724-342-7391; Fax: 724-342-3349.
Catechesis/Religious Program—Mary Lou Nogay, C.R.E.; Cyndi Serafin, C.R.E. Students 27.
2—ST. ANN (1904), (Slovak), [CEM] Closed. For inquiries for parish records contact the chancery.
3—HOLY TRINITY (1915), (Hungarian), [CEM] Closed. For inquiries for parish records contact the chancery.
4—OUR LADY OF FATIMA-ST. ANN (1952) [CEM 3] Rev. Donald E. Berdis.
Res.: 601 Roemer Blvd., 16121. Tel: 724-346-3359; Fax: 724-346-2326.
School—Monsignor Geno Monti School, (Grades K-8), 1225 Union St., 16121. Tel: 724-347-1440; Fax: 724-347-1440. Alice Connelly, Prin. Lay Teachers 9; Students 69; Clergy 1.
Catechesis/Religious Program—Deacon Joseph Messina, D.R.E.

FORCE, ELK CO., ST. JOSEPH (1906) [CEM] Rev. Thomas L. Tyler.
Res.: 17735 Bennetts Valley Hwy., P.O. Box 124, 15841. Tel: 814-787-4151; Fax: 814-787-4478.
Catechesis/Religious Program—Mary Stoker, Coord. Faith Formation. Students 71.

FRANKLIN, VENANGO CO., ST. PATRICK (1867) [CEM] Rev. Msgr. John J. Herbein; Deacons Walter Jones; Richard Reed; Richard O'Polka.
Res.: 949 Liberty St., 16323. Tel: 814-437-5763; Fax: 814-437-6326.
School—(Grades K-8), 952 Buffalo St., 16323. Tel: 814-432-8689; Fax: 814-437-6538. Carol Long, Prin. Lay Teachers 10; Students 65; Preschool 16.
Catechesis/Religious Program—Therese Marshall, C.R.E. Students 132.

FRENCHTOWN, CRAWFORD CO., ST. HIPPOLYTE (1838) [CEM] Rev. Dennis J. Veltri.
Res.: 25997 Hwy. 27, Guys Mills, 16327. Tel: 814-789-2022; Fax: 814-789-2025.
Catechesis/Religious Program—Joyce Tarr, D.R.E. Students 90.
Mission—Our Lady of Lourdes Cochranton, Crawford Co.
Chapel— Sts. Peter & Paul, Pettis. (Devotional Chapel)

FRENCHVILLE, CLEARFIELD CO., ST. MARY OF THE ASSUMPTION (1840) [CEM] Rev. David A. Perry; Deacons Joseph Lyncha; Robert Hoover.
Res.: P.O. Box 159, 16836. Tel: 814-263-4354; Fax: 814-263-4219.
Catechesis/Religious Program—Ann Butler, D.R.E. (Elementary); Tina Hicks, D.R.E. (High School); Shelly Cowder, D.R.E. (Elementary & High School). Students 33.
Mission—SS. Peter & Paul [CEM] Grassflat, Clearfield Co. 16839.
Mission—St. Severin [CEM] Drifting, Clearfield Co.
Catechesis/Religious Program— Twinned with Mission - SS. Peter & Paul. Students 43.

FRYBURG, CLARION CO., ST. MICHAEL (1846) [CEM] Rev. D.G. "Skip" Davis III.
Res.: 18765 Rt. 208, P.O. Box 27, 16326. Tel: 814-354-2467; Fax: 814-354-6375.
Catechesis/Religious Program—Bernice Strauser, D.R.E. Students 144.

GALETON, POTTER CO., ST. BIBIANA (1888), (Italian), [CEM] Rev. Joseph V. Dougherty.
Res.: 111 Germania, 16922. Tel: 814-435-2303; Fax: 814-435-3453.
Catechesis/Religious Program—Students 20.
Mission—St. Augustine [CEM] Austin, Potter Co.
Mission—Sacred Heart Genesee, Potter Co.
Chapel— St. Germain, Germania. (Devotional Chapel)

GIRARD, ERIE CO., ST. JOHN THE EVANGELIST (1853) [CEM] Rev. William J. O'Brien; Sr. Geraldine Kasper, O.S.F., D.R.E.; Deacon Joseph Cicero.
Res.: 101 Olin Ave., Box 336, 16417. Tel: 814-774-4108; Fax: 814-774-2097.
Catechesis/Religious Program—Tel: 814-774-4061. Sr. Geraldine Kasper, O.S.F., D.R.E. Students 164.

GRAMPIAN, CLEARFIELD CO., ST. BONAVENTURE (1833) [CEM] Rev. Mark J. Mastrian; Deacon Anthony Indelicato Sr.
Res.: 461 Main St., P.O. Box F, 16838. Tel: 814-236-0364; Fax: 814-236-0733.
Catechesis/Religious Program—Terri A. Clarkson, D.R.E. Students 56.

GREENVILLE, MERCER CO., ST. MICHAEL (1850) [CEM] Revs. Christopher M. Hamlett; Christopher M. Barnes, Parochial Vicar; Sr. Mary Gertrude McElhinny, S.C., Pastoral Min.; Deacon William Brown. In Res., Rev. Paul A. Schill (Retired).
Office: Tel: 412-588-9800; Fax: 412-588-7053.
Res.: 81 N. 2nd St., 16125.
Church: 85 N. High St., 16125.
School—(Grades K-8), 80 N. High St., 16125. Tel: 724-588-7050; Fax: 724-588-7056. Mary Jo Lipani, Prin. Lay Teachers 12; Students 111; Preschool 29.
Catechesis/Religious Program—Elaine Shearer, D.R.E. Students 248.
Mission—St. Margaret 701 Denver St., Jamestown, Mercer Co. Tel: 724-932-5959.

GROVE CITY, MERCER CO., BELOVED DISCIPLE (1925) [CEM] Rev. Michael P. Allison.
1310 S. Center St. Ext., 16127.
Office: Tel: 724-748-6700.
Res.: 321 N. Broad St., 16127.
Catechesis/Religious Program—Angie Felicetty, D.R.E. Students 220.

HERMITAGE, MERCER CO., CHURCH OF NOTRE DAME (1960) Very Rev. Jeffery J. Noble; Rev. Msgr. Edward J. Zeitler (Retired); Deacons W. Jack Tupper; Owen Wagner.
Res.: 2325 Highland Rd., 16148. Tel: 724-981-5566; Fax: 724-981-3215.
Catechesis/Religious Program—Pat Polesnak, D.R.E.; Joe Ranelli, Youth Min. Students 333.

HOUTZDALE, CLEARFIELD CO., CHRIST THE KING (1970) [CEM] Rev. Stanley J. Swacha.
Res.: 123 Good St., 16651. Tel: 814-378-7653; Fax: 814-378-8333.
Catechesis/Religious Program—Tel: 814-378-7109. Nancy Yarger, D.R.E. Students 136.
Mission—Immaculate Conception Madera, Clearfield Co.

JOHNSONBURG, ELK CO., HOLY ROSARY (1896) [CEM] Rev. David Wilson.
Res.: 606 Penn St., 15845. Tel: 814-965-2819; Fax: 814-965-3482.

Catechesis/Religious Program—Tel: 814-965-2812. Margaret Griffin, D.R.E. Students 194.

KANE, MCKEAN CO., ST. CALLISTUS (1866) [CEM] Very Rev. Phillip A. Pinczewski.
Res.: 342 Chase St., 16735. Tel: 814-837-6694; Fax: 814-837-4304.
Catechesis/Religious Program—Sr. Francis Therese Matia, S.S.J., D.R.E. Students 169.
Chapel— Sts. John & Stephen, James City, 16734. (Devotional Chapel)

KERSEY, ELK CO., ST. BONIFACE (1832) [CEM] Rev. James G. Falusczak.
Res.: 355 Main St., 15846. Tel: 814-885-8941; Fax: 814-885-8931.
School—(Grades K-5) Tel: 814-885-8093; Fax: 814-885-8611. Marie Giazzoni, Prin. Lay Teachers 10; Students 69; Preschool 48.
Catechesis/Religious Program—Tel: 814-885-6195. Leslie Gahr, D.R.E. Students 154.

LEWIS RUN, MCKEAN CO., OUR MOTHER OF PERPETUAL HELP (1946) Rev. Stephen L. Collins (Retired).
Res.: 31 Lafayette, 16738. Tel: 814-368-6355.
Catechesis/Religious Program—Students 17.

LINESVILLE, CRAWFORD CO., ST. PHILIP (1959) [CEM] Rev. John A. Walsh.
Res.: 401 S. Mercer St., 16424. Tel: 814-683-5313; Fax: 814-683-5824.
Catechesis/Religious Program—Maria Pilarcik, C.R.E. Students 12.

LUCINDA, CLARION CO., ST. JOSEPH (1840) [CEM] Rev. William C. Miller.
Rectory—112 Rectory Ln., P.O. Box 9, 16235. Tel: 814-226-7288; Fax: 814-226-5538.
School—(Grades PreSchool-6), 72 Rectory Ln., 16235. Tel: 814-226-8018; Fax: 814-223-9620. Sr. Monica Steiner, O.S.B., Prin.; Susie Beary, Librarian. Sisters 1; Lay Teachers 11; Students 76; Preschool 29.
Catechesis/Religious Program—Mr. Norm Wolbert, D.R.E.; Mrs. Judy Wolbert, D.R.E. Students 58.

MCKEAN, ERIE CO., ST. FRANCIS XAVIER (1838) [CEM] Rev. Mark A. Nowak.
Res.: 8880 Main St., P.O. Box 317, 16426-0317. Tel: 814-476-7657; Fax: 814-476-0160.
Catechesis/Religious Program—Cynthia Zemcik, C.R.E. Students 167.

MEADVILLE, CRAWFORD CO.
1—ST. AGATHA (1849) [CEM] Rev. Matthew J. Kujawinski; Deacon Harvey McQueen.
Res.: 353 Pine St., 16335. Tel: 814-336-1112; Fax: 814-724-4051.
School—Seton School, (Grades K-8) Tel: 814-336-2320; Fax: 814-336-2328. Julia Strzalka, Prin.; Joshua Sherretts, Librarian. Lay Teachers 15; Students 148; Preschool 30.
Catechesis/Religious Program—Tel: 814-336-1112. Eileen O'Day, D.R.E. Students 100.
Mission—St. Bernadette 222 Renner Ln., Saegertown, Crawford Co. 16433. Tel: 814-763-2831.
2—ST. BRIGID (1865), (Irish), [CEM] Very Rev. Mark O'Hern.
Res.: 967 Chancery Ln., 16335. Tel: 814-336-4459; Fax: 814-724-2996.
Catechesis/Religious Program—Shari Bronson, D.R.E. Students 104.
3—ST. MARY OF GRACE (1909), (Italian), Rev. Marc J. Solomon.
Res.: 1085 Water St., 16335. Tel: 814-333-6161; Fax: 814-336-3145.
Catechesis/Religious Program—Tel: 814-333-6161, Ext. 5. Kathleen Allen, D.R.E. Students 56.

MERCER, MERCER CO., IMMACULATE HEART (1838) [CEM] Rev. James J. Kennelley.
Res.: 100 Penn Ave., 16137. Tel: 724-662-2999; Fax: 724-662-5094.
Catechesis/Religious Program—Barb Kehlbeck, C.R.E.
Chapel— St. Hermenegild, Pardoe. (Devotional Chapel)

MORRISDALE, CLEARFIELD CO., ST. AGNES (1891) [CEM] Rev. Robert Horgas; Deacon Dennis Socash.
Res.: 16858. Tel: 814-342-2583; Fax: 814-342-6377.
Catechesis/Religious Program—Tel: 814-342-2583. Students 72.
Mission—SS. Peter & Paul [CEM] Hawk Run, Clearfield Co.

MOUNT JEWETT, MCKEAN CO., ST. JOSEPH (1898) Rev. Vincent P. Cieslewicz.
Res.: 20 Division St., P.O. Box 520, 16740. Tel: 814-778-5520; Fax: 814-887-5271.
Catechesis/Religious Program—Carol Walker, D.R.E. Students 17.

NEW BETHLEHEM, CLARION CO., ST. CHARLES CHURCH (1872) [CEM] Rev. Samuel Bungo.
Res.: 201 Washington St., 16242. Tel: 814-275-3446; Fax: 814-275-7550.
Catechesis/Religious Program—Amy Toth, D.R.E.
Mission—St. Nicholas [CEM] Crates, Clarion Co.

NORTH EAST, ERIE CO., ST. GREGORY THAUMATURGUS (1875) [CEM] Rev. Thomas M. Brooks.
Res.: 136 W. Main St., 16428. Tel: 814-725-9691; Fax: 814-725-1225.
School—(Grades PreSchool-8), 140 W. Main St., 16428. Tel: 814-725-4571; Fax: 814-725-4572. Nancy Pierce, Prin. Lay Teachers 12; Students 61; Preschool 24.
Catechesis/Religious Program—Loraine Fetzer, D.R.E. Students 218.

OIL CITY, VENANGO CO.
1—ASSUMPTION OF THE BLESSED VIRGIN MARY (1899), (Polish), Rev. Justin P. Pino.
7 Pulaski St., 16301.
Rectory—35 Pearl St., 16301. Tel: 814-677-4004; Fax: 814-677-5977.
Catechesis/Religious Program—Twinned with St. Joseph, Oil City.
2—ST. JOSEPH (1865) [CEM 2] Rev. Justin P. Pino.
Res.: 35 Pearl Ave., 16301. Tel: 814-677-4004; Fax: 814-677-5977.
Catechesis/Religious Program—Oil City Catholic Community Dianne Phillips, C.R.E. Students 43.
3—OUR LADY HELP OF CHRISTIANS (1914) Rev. John P. Mathaner, Admin.
Res.: 69 Willow St., 16301. Tel: 814-677-3078; Fax: 814-677-3078.
Catechesis/Religious Program— Twinned with St. Stephen.
4—ST. STEPHEN (1898) Very Rev. Matthew J. Ruyechan; Rev. Msgr. William C. Karg.
Res.: 210 Reed St., 16301. Tel: 814-677-3020; Fax: 814-678-8841.
School—(Grades K-8) Tel: 814-677-3035; Fax: 814-677-2053. Marge Hajduk, Prin. Lay Teachers 14; Students 133; Preschool 16.
Catechesis/Religious Program—Dianne Phillips, D.R.E. Students 90.

PORT ALLEGANY, MCKEAN CO., ST. GABRIEL THE ARCHANGEL (1876) [CEM] Rev. James C. Campbell.
Res.: 203 E. Arnold Ave., 16743. Tel: 814-642-2847; Fax: 814-642-7990.
Catechesis/Religious Program—Andrea Streich, D.R.E. Students 44.

PUNXSUTAWNEY, JEFFERSON CO., SS. COSMAS AND DAMIAN (1885) [CEM] Rev. Msgr. Joseph J. Riccardo.
Res.: 616 W. Mahoning St., 15767. Tel: 814-938-6540; Fax: 814-938-7439.
School—(Grades PreSchool-8), 205 N. Chestnut St., 15767. Tel: 814-938-4224; Fax: 814-939-3759. Jessica Newcome, Prin. Lay Teachers 9; Students 78; Preschool 23.
Catechesis/Religious Program—Sue Dahrouge, C.R.E. Students 146.
Mission—St. Anthony of Padua Walston, Jefferson Co. 15781.
Mission—St. Joseph Anita, Jefferson Co. 15711.
Mission—St. Adrian De Lancey, 15733.

RAMEY, CLEARFIELD CO., HOLY TRINITY (1937) [CEM] Rev. Zab Amar.
Mailing Address: Box 196, 16671. Tel: 814-378-7193; Fax: 814-378-4855.
Res.: 183 Locust St., Coalport, 16627. Tel: 814-672-3561; Fax: 814-672-5954.
Catechesis/Religious Program—

REYNOLDSVILLE, JEFFERSON CO., ST. MARY (1872) [CEM] Rev. Richard J. Allen.
Res.: 607 E. Main St., 15851. Tel: 814-653-8586; Fax: 814-653-2769.
Catechesis/Religious Program—Barb Murray, D.R.E. Students 72.

RIDGWAY, ELK CO., ST. LEO THE GREAT (1874) [CEM] Rev. Brian E. Vossler. In Res., Rev. Ross R. Miceli.
Res.: 111 Depot St., 15853. Tel: 814-772-3135; Fax: 814-772-6627.
School—(Grades K-8) Tel: 814-772-9775; Fax: 814-772-9295. Mary Detwiler, Prin. Lay Teachers 12; Students 96; Preschool 33.
Catechesis/Religious Program—Marjorie Gausman, D.R.E. Students 224.

ROUSEVILLE, VENANGO CO., ST. VENANTIUS (1872) Very Rev. Matthew J. Ruyechan, Admin.
Res.: 210 Reed St., Oil City, 16301. Tel: 814-677-3020; Fax: 814-678-8841.
Church & Mailing Address: 403 Main St., 16344.
Catechesis/Religious Program— Twinned with St. Stephen Catholic Community. Students 8.

ST. MARYS, ELK CO.
1—ST. MARY (1842), (German), [CEM] Revs. Meinrad Lawson, O.S.B.; Daniel C. Wolfel, O.S.B., Senior Priest.
315 Church St., 15857.
Res.: 144 Church St., 15857-7594. Tel: 814-781-7594; Fax: 814-834-6795.
2—QUEEN OF THE WORLD (1954) Revs. Michael P. Ferrick; Daniel C. Wolfel, O.S.B.
Res.: 134 Queens Rd., 15857. Tel: 814-834-4701; Fax: 814-834-3422.
Catechesis/Religious Program—Tel: 814-834-9077. Georgia Wagner, D.R.E. Students 420.
3—SACRED HEART CHURCH (1876) [JC] Rev. Eric T. Vogt, O.S.B.; Deacon William Gibson.
337 Center St., 15857.
Res.: 144 Church St., 15857. Tel: 814-834-7861; Fax: 814-834-1376.
Catechesis/Religious Program—Georgia Wagner, Dir. Faith Formation; Melissa Singh, Coord. Youth & Young Adult Ministry. Teachers 497.

SHARON, MERCER CO.
1—ST. ANTHONY (1924), (Croatian), [CEM] Rev. Daniel J. Kresinski; Deacon Richard Rueberger.
Res.: 804 Idaho St., 16146. Tel: 724-342-7391; Fax: 724-342-3349.
Catechesis/Religious Program—Mary Lou Nogay, C.R.E.; Cyndi Serafin, C.R.E. Students 15.
2—ST. JOSEPH (1860) [CEM] [JC] Rev. Glenn R. Whitman. In Res., Rev. Joseph C. Campbell.
Res.: 79 Case Ave., 16146. Tel: 724-981-3232; Fax: 724-981-4174.
Catechesis/Religious Program—Sr. Sandy Pedone, H.M., D.R.E.; Mary Beth Jones, Asst. High School Dir. Students 181.
3—SACRED HEART (1864) [CEM] Rev. Henry C. Andrae.
Res.: 40 S. Irvine Ave., 16146. Tel: 724-346-3567; Fax: 724-346-4464.
Catechesis/Religious Program—Students 5.
4—ST. STANISLAUS KOSTKA-HOLY TRINITY (1931), (Polish—Hungarian), [CEM 2] Rev. Jeffrey Lucas.
Res.: 370 Spruce Ave., 16146. Tel: 724-347-7526; Fax: 724-347-1760.
Catechesis/Religious Program—Nancy Radachy, C.R.E. Students 27.

SHARPSVILLE, MERCER CO., ST. BARTHOLOMEW (1874) Rev. Marc Stockton.
Res.: 311 W. Ridge Ave., 16150. Tel: 724-962-7130; Fax: 724-962-1771.
Catechesis/Religious Program—Students 164.

SHEFFIELD, WARREN CO., ST. ANTHONY (1878) Very Rev. Thomas M. Aleksa.
7222 Rte. 6, 16347.
Res.: 106 Four Mile Rd., P.O. Box 518, 16347. Tel: 814-968-5915; Fax: 814-968-4214.
Catechesis/Religious Program—Sara Korchak, C.R.E. Students 29.

SHINGLEHOUSE, POTTER CO., ST. THERESA (1901) [CEM] Very Rev. Thomas E. Brown.
Mailing Address: P.O. Box 277, 16748. Tel: 814-225-4231; Fax: 814-225-3172.
Res.: P.O. Box 252, Eldred, 16731.
Catechesis/Religious Program—Gail McGee, D.R.E. Students 11.

SMETHPORT, MCKEAN CO., ST. ELIZABETH (1875) [CEM] Rev. Vincent P. Cieslewicz.
Res.: 307 Franklin St., 16749. Tel: 814-887-9254; Fax: 814-887-5271.
Catechesis/Religious Program—Amy Sage, D.R.E. Students 65.

STONEBORO, MERCER CO., ST. COLUMBKILLE (1860) [CEM] Rev. Robert A. Manning, Admin.
Res.: 70 Franklin St., P.O. Box 206, 16153. Tel: 724-376-3393; Fax: 724-376-2292.
Catechesis/Religious Program—Students 11.

SYKESVILLE, JEFFERSON CO., ASSUMPTION OF BLESSED VIRGIN MARY (1923) [CEM] Rev. Richard J. Allen.
Res.: 20 Shaffer St., P.O. Box J, 15865. Tel: 814-894-2772; Fax: 814-894-2445.
Catechesis/Religious Program—Elaine Fike, D.R.E. Students 34.

TIDIOUTE, WARREN CO., ST. JOHN (1866) [CEM] Rev. Joseph R. Czarkowski.
Res.: 25 First St., 16351. Tel: 814-484-7747; Fax: 814-484-0275.
Catechesis/Religious Program—Melissa Sabella, D.R.E. Students 48.
Mission—St. Anthony Tionesta, Forest Co.
Catechesis/Religious Program—James Knauff, D.R.E.; Mary Alyce Knauff, D.R.E.

TITUSVILLE, CRAWFORD CO.
1—ST. TITUS (1962) [CEM] [JC] Rev. Walter E. Packard.
Res.: 513 W. Main St., 16354. Tel: 814-827-4636; Fax: 814-827-3958.
Catechesis/Religious Program—Frances Schneider, D.R.E. Students 82.
Mission—Immaculate Conception Mageetown, Crawford Co. Tel: 814-827-2075.
2—ST. WALBURGA (1872), (German), [CEM] Rev. Walter E. Packard.
Mailing Address: 513 W. Main St., 16354. Tel: 814-827-4636; Fax: 814-827-3958.
Res.: 120 Brook St., 16354.
Catechesis/Religious Program—Frances Schneider, D.R.E. Twinned with St. Titus, Titusville

UNION CITY, ERIE CO., ST. TERESA OF AVILA (1906) [CEM] Rev. F. Thomas Suppa.
Res.: 9 Third Ave., 16438. Tel: 814-438-2000; Fax: 814-438-2073.
Catechesis/Religious Program—Tel: 814-438-3408. Cheryl Godak-Nothum, D.R.E. Students 138.
Mission—Our Lady of Fatima Canadohta Lake, Crawford Co.

WALSTON, JEFFERSON CO., ST. ANTHONY OF PADUA (1898), Became a mission of SS. Cosmas & Damian,

Punxsutawney. Rev. Msgr. Joseph J. Riccardo.
Res.: *SS Cosmas & Damian*, 616 W. Mahoning St., Punxsutawney, 15767. Tel: 814-938-9687; Fax: 814-938-1257.
Catechesis/Religious Program—Mary Butler, D.R.E.
Mission—St. Adrian, Named a mission of SS. Cosmas & Damian, Punxsutawney., Delancey.

WARREN, WARREN CO.
1—HOLY REDEEMER (1912) Rev. Msgr. John J. Lucas; Deacons Joseph Lucia Jr.; Raymond Wiehagen.
Res.: 11 Russell St., 16365. Tel: 814-726-3360; Fax: 814-726-3361.
Catechesis/Religious Program—Diana Lillard, D.R.E. Students 185.
2—ST. JOSEPH (1858) [CEM] [JC] Very Rev. Richard J. Toohey; Rev. Michael C. Polinek, Parochial Vicar.
Res.: 600 Penna Ave., W., 16365. Tel: 814-723-2090; Fax: 814-723-6042.
School—(Grades K-4) Tel: 814-723-2030; Fax: 814-723-6042. Dr. Howard Ferguson, Prin. Lay Teachers 6; Students 60.
Catechesis/Religious Program—Jennifer Wortman, D.R.E. Students 161.

WATERFORD, ERIE CO.
1—ALL SAINTS (2005) Rev. Thomas J. Whitman; Deacon William C. Spinks.
11264 Rte. 97, 16441. Tel: 814-796-3023; Fax: 814-796-3025.
Catechesis/Religious Program—Lia Ghering, D.R.E. Students 176.
2—ST. CYPRIAN (1878) Closed. For inquiries for parish records contact the chancery.

WEST MIDDLESEX, MERCER CO., GOOD SHEPHERD (1955) [JC] Rev. Msgr. Robert M. Malene.
Mailing Address: P.O. Box 226, 16159.
Res.: 3613 Sharon Rd., 16159. Tel: 724-528-3539; Fax: 724-528-2928.
Catechesis/Religious Program—Rose DeMarco, F.R.E. Students 145.

WILCOX, ELK CO., ST. ANNE (1890) [JC] Rev. David Wilson.
Mailing Address: P.O. Box 65, 15870. In Res., Rev. John G. Barwin (Retired).
Res.: Clarion St., P.O. Box 65, 15870. Tel: 814-965-2819; Fax: 814-965-3482.
Catechesis/Religious Program—Margaret Griffin, D.R.E. Through Holy Rosary, Johnsonburg, PA

YOUNGSVILLE, WARREN CO., ST. LUKE (1957) Rev. John Neff; Deacon Philip Skerda.
Res.: 420 N. Main St., 16371. Tel: 814-563-4432; Fax: 814-563-9686.
Catechesis/Religious Program—Dolores Stec, D.R.E. Students 28.

Chaplains of Public Institutions

ERIE. *Erie County Prison* (1961). Rev. Gerald Wright, O.M.V.
Hamot Medical Center, 201 State St., 16550. Rev. John J. Murphy.
Pleasant Ridge Manor East. Rev. Msgr. Gerald L. Orbanek, M.A. (Retired).
Pleasant Ridge Manor West. Rev. Daniel J. Prez.
Soldiers and Sailors Home. Rev. Jerry S. Priscaro, Deacon James B. McGuinness.
Veterans Administration Hospital. Rev. Gerald Wright, O.M.V., Chap.
St. Vincent's Health Center, 232 W. 25th St., 16544. Rev. Dennis A. Martin, Chap.

ALBION. *Albion State Correctional Facility*. Deacon Ralph DeCecco, Staff Chaplain, Diocesan Coordinator of Prison Ministry.

BRADFORD. *Federal Correction Institution*, P.O. Box 5000, 16701-0950. Rev. Vincent P. Cieslewicz.

CAMBRIDGE SPRINGS. *Cambridge Springs Correction Institution*. Rev. Daniel J. Prez.

DU BOIS. *Du Bois Regional Hospital*, 100 Hospital Ave., 15801. Rev. Matias M. Quimno, Deacon Robert P. DeNoon, Chap.

MEADVILLE

MERCER

POLK. *Polk Center*, Box 94, 16342. Sr. Claire Hudert, O.S.B., M.A.

WARREN. *Warren State Hospital*. Rev. Thomas M. Aleska.

On Duty Outside Diocese:
Revs.—
Beal, John P., J.C.D., Washington, DC
Gula, Richard, S.S.
Hoffman, Daniel R.
Kalinowski, Joseph J., CHC
Lohse, Edward M., J.C.L.
Witherup, Ronald, S.S.

On Leave of Absence:
Rev.—
Hadberg, Dennis C.

Retired:
Rev. Msgrs.—
Adams, George
Barcio, Robert G., Ph.D.
Bobal, Joseph K., V.F.
Carter, John T.
Daley, Ernest J.
DeWalt, Homer C.
Hagerty, John B.
Koos, Gerald J.
Mayer, Richard G.
McGuire, Richard J.
Mitchell, Salvatore P.
Murcko, Charles S.
Orbanek, Gerald L., M.A.
Peterson, James W.
Reilly, Robert J.
Sanner, James E.
Schauerman, Henry J.
Snyder, John R.
Spiece, Lawrence T.
Stack, Richard J., J.C.L.
Swoger, John W., E.V.
Revs.—
Andersen, Emil
Barwin, John G.
Bauer, John F.
Burke, John R.
Buzga, John P.
Cooper, Donald J.
Dipre, Gilio L., Ph.D.
Fedor, Robert P.
Fialkowski, Thomas M.
Fischer, John M.
Jeselnick, Stephen E., Col.
King, Howard J.
Levis, Robert J., Ph.D.
Lynch, John S.
Maloney, William J.
Maryland, Joseph A.
Matuszak, Edward S.
Meenihan, Regis J.
Powers, Richard E.
Rice, William A.
Santor, John E.
Schill, Paul A.
Schmitt, Charles R.
Skinner, Charles D.
Somers, Eldon K.
Staszewski, Joseph P., V.F.
Susa, Robert P., M.A.
Tito, Rocco A.

INSTITUTIONS LOCATED IN THE DIOCESE

[A] SEMINARIES, DIOCESAN

ERIE. *St. Mark's Seminary*, 429 E. Grandview Blvd., P.O. Box 10397, 16514. Tel: 814-824-1200. Very Rev. Michael T. Kesicki, Rector; Revs. Nicholas J. Rouch, S.T.D., Vice Rector; Stephen J. Schreiber, Res. Spiritual Dir.

[B] COLLEGES AND UNIVERSITIES

ERIE. *Gannon University*, University Square, 16541. Tel: 814-871-7000; Fax: 814-871-5372. Web: www.gannon.edu. Keith Taylor, Ph.D., Pres.; Very Rev. Joseph C. Gregorek, V.F., Ph.D.; Revs. Gilio L. Dipre, Ph.D. (Retired); Edward Krause, C.S.C., Ph.D.; Casimir Wozniak, Ph.D.; Very Rev. Michael T. Kesicki; Revs. George E. Strohmeyer, M.A.; Jason A. Glover, S.T.L.; Ken Brundage, Librarian & Dir. Priests 7; Sisters 3; Lay Teachers 192; Students 4,076.
Mercyhurst College, 501 E. 38th St., 16546. Tel: 814-824-2000; Fax: 814-824-3333. Web: www.mercyhurst.edu. Thomas J. Gamble, Ph.D., Pres.; Rev. James Piszker, Chap.; Sue Johnson, Asst. to the Pres., Dir. Admin. Svcs.; Darcy Jones, Librarian; Rev. Msgr. David A. Rubino, Interim Dir., Walker School of Business. Priests 2; Sisters 3; Lay Teachers 148; Students 3,192.

[C] HIGH SCHOOLS, DIOCESAN

ERIE. *Erie Catholic Preparatory School*, 225 W. 9th St., 16501. Tel: 814-453-7737; Fax: 814-459-6188. Rev. Scott W. Jabo, Pres.
Cathedral Preparatory School, 225 W. 9th St., 16501. Tel: 814-453-7737; Fax: 814-459-6188. Rev. Scott W. Jabo, Pres.; Richard J. Fessler, Prin.; Gail Dragich, Librarian. Priests 4; Sisters 1; Laymen 28; Laywomen 12; Students 550.
Faculty: Revs. Michael G. DeMartinis; James McCormick; John L. Miller; William R. Barron; Sr. James Francis Mulligan.
Villa Maria Academy, 2403 W. 8th St., 16505. Tel: 814-838-2061; Fax: 814-836-0881. Email: villa@villamaria.com. Web: www.villamaria.com. Rev. Scott W. Jabo, Pres.; Sr. Mary Drexler, S.S.J., Prin.; Sue Dobson, Librarian. Priests 1; Sisters 2; Laymen 8; Laywomen 21; Students 301.
Faculty: Rev. T. Shane Mathew.

DU BOIS. *DuBois Area Catholic School*, (Grades PreK-12), P.O. Box 567, 15801. Tel: 814-371-3060; Fax: 814-371-3215. Email: rtomasone@duboiscatholic.com. Very Rev. Richard C. Tomasone, V.F., Pres.; Rev. Edward J. Walk, Asst. Headmaster. Priests 2; Lay Teachers 44; Students 500.
Du Bois Area Catholic School dba Central Catholic High School Tel: 814-371-3060; Fax: 814-371-3215.
Du Bois Area Catholic School dba Central Catholic Middle School (Grades 6-8) Tel: 814-371-3060; Fax: 814-371-3215.
DuBois Area Catholic School dba DuBois Central Catholic Elementary School (Grades PreK-5), P.O. Box 567, 15801-1698. Tel: 814-371-2570; Fax: 814-371-1551. Mrs. Rita Wray, Prin.

OIL CITY. *Venango Catholic High School*, 1505 W. 1st St., 16301-3298. Tel: 814-677-3098; Fax: 814-676-4453. Email: jpsm5.vchs@choiceonemail.com. Rev. John P. Malthaner, Headmaster & Prin.; Barbara Reszkowski, Librarian. Priests 1; Lay Teachers 12; Students 97.

[D] HIGH SCHOOLS, PRIVATE

ERIE. *Mercyhurst Preparatory School*, 538 E. Grandview Blvd., 16504. Tel: 814-824-2210; Fax: 814-824-2116. Email: maste@mpslakers.com. Sr. Mary Ann Bader, R.S.M., Pres.; Mrs. Deborah Laughlin, Prin.; Marcia DiTullio, Contact Person; Ms. Deborah Servey, Librarian. Priests 1; Sisters 1; Lay Teachers 50; Students 625.

[E] ELEMENTARY SCHOOLS, PRIVATE

ERIE. *Villa Maria Elementary School*, (Grades PreK-8), 2551 W. 8th St., 16505. Tel: 814-838-5451; Fax: 814-833-6132. Mr. Damon Finazzo, Prin. Sisters of St. Joseph 1; Lay Teachers 29; Students 355.

[F] SCHOOLS, DIOCESAN

HERMITAGE. *Shenango Valley Catholic School System, Inc.*, 2120 Shenango Valley Freeway, 16148-3011. Tel: 724-346-5531; Fax: 724-346-3011. Email: kchs@kennedy-catholic.org. Rev. Marc Stockton, Pres.
Kennedy Catholic High School, 2120 Shenango Valley Freeway, 16148-2563. Email: kchs@kennedy-catholic.org. Rev. Marc Stockton, Pres.; Mr. Peter P. Iacino, Headmaster & Dir. Finance; Mrs. Heidi Patterson, Prin. Priests 2; Sisters 1; Lay Teachers 20; Students 260.
Kennedy Catholic Middle School (Grades 6-8), 2120 Shenango Valley Freeway, 16148-2563. Email: vwagner.kcms@gmail.com. Rev. Marc Stockton, Pres.; Mrs. Victoria Wagner, Prin. Lay Teachers 10; Students 111.
Blessed John Paul II Elementary School (Grades PreK-5), 2335 Highland Rd., 16148-2820. Tel: 724-342-2205; Fax: 724-704-7397. Email: mesmith7@verizon.net. Rev. Marc Stockton, Pres.; Mrs. Marian Smith, Prin. Lay Teachers 15; Students 194.

SAINT MARYS. *Elk County Catholic School System, Inc.*, 600 Maurus St., 15857. Tel: 814-834-7800; Fax: 814-781-3441. Email: fathermichael@eccss.org.
Elk County Catholic High School, 600 Maurus St., St. Marys, 15857. Email: florigs@eccs.org. Rev. Michael P. Ferrick, Pres.; Mrs. Sandy Florig, Prin.; Rev. Ross R. Miceli, Campus Min.; Mrs. Jen Meyer, Campus Min.; Mrs. Dana Gebauer, Librarian. Priests 1; Lay Teachers 25; Students 275.
St. Marys Catholic Middle School, 325 Church St., 15857. Tel: 814-834-2665; Fax: 814-834-5339. Email: schneiderj@eccss.org. Rev. Michael P. Ferrick, Pres.; Mr. John Schneider, Prin.; Miss Mary Ann Rettger, Campus Min.; Mrs. Susan Bon, Librarian. Lay Teachers 14; Students 142.
St. Marys Catholic Elementary School, 114 Queens Rd., 15857. Tel: 814-834-4169; Fax: 814-834-7830. Email: schautm@eccss.org. Rev. Michael P. Ferrick, Pres.; Mrs. Mary Beth Schaut, Prin.; Mrs. Patricia Cotter, Campus Min. & Librarian. Lay Teachers 19; Students 217.

[G] SPECIAL MINISTRIES

ERIE. *St. Benedict Child Development Center*, 345 E. 9th St., 16503. Tel: 814-454-4514; Fax: 814-452-1905. Email: admin@stbenedictctr.com. Sr. Diane Rabe, O.S.B., Admin. Students 50; Sisters 3; Lay Staff 20.
St. Benedict Education Center, 330 E. 10th St., 16503. Tel: 814-452-4072, Ext. 299; Fax: 814-454-2686. Sr. Christine Vladimiroff, O.S.B. Students 2,900; Personnel 71.
Erie East Coast Migrant Program, 345 E. 9th St.,

16503. Tel: 814-454-4514; Fax: 814-452-1905. Email: admin@stbenedictctr.com. Sr. Diane Rabe, O.S.B., Dir. Benedictine Sisters of Erie. Students 55.

Inner-City Neighborhood Art House, 201 E. 10th St., 16503. Tel: 814-455-5508; Fax: 814-480-8942. Sr. Annette Marshall, O.S.B., Exec. Dir.

L'Arche Erie, 3745 W. 12th St., 16505. Tel: 814-452-2065; Fax: 814-452-4188. Email: office@larcheerie.org.

Mercy Center of the Arts, 444 E. Grandview Blvd., 16504. Tel: 814-824-2519; Fax: 814-824-2127. Email: catherine_ed@yahoo.com.

Word of Life Catholic Charismatic Renewal, St. Mark Catholic Center, 429 E. Grandview Blvd., P.O. Box 10397, 16514-0397. Tel: 814-824-1286; Fax: 814-824-1128. Email: wolccrc@aol.com. Web: www.wordoflifeccrc.org.

FAIRVIEW. *Camp Notre Dame*, 400 Eaton Rd., P.O. Box 74, 16415. Tel: 814-474-5001; Fax: 814-474-4818. Email: office@campnotredame.com. Web: www.campnotredame.com. Rev. Mark A. Nowak, Pres.; Paula Mielnik, Vice Pres.; John Yonko, Exec. Dir.

[H] GENERAL HOSPITALS

ERIE. **Saint Vincent Health Center*, 232 W. 25th St., 16544. Tel: 814-452-5000; Fax: 814-452-7611. Web: www.saintvincenthealth.com. Scott A. Whalen, Ph.D., Pres. & CEO; Rev. Dennis A. Martin, Chap.; Julie M. DeMarco, Dir. Tel: 814-452-7611.

Saint Vincent Health System Scott A. Whalen, Ph.D., Pres. & CEO.

[I] PROTECTIVE INSTITUTIONS

ERIE. *Gannondale, Inc.*, 4635 E. Lake Rd., 16511. Tel: 814-899-7659; Fax: 814-898-4266. Email: gdale@gannondale.org. Web: www.gannondale.org. Sr. Carol Pregno, O.L.C., Pres.; Nancy Sabol, Exec. Dir. North American Union of Sisters of Our Lady of Charity-Erie. Residents 47; Staff 75.

HARBORCREEK. *Harborcreek Youth Services*, 5712 Iroquois Ave., 16421. Tel: 814-899-7664; Fax: 814-899-3075. Email: jpetulla@hys-erie.org. Mr. John D. Petulla, A.C.S.W., M.S.W., C.E.O. Children 78; Staff 145.

[J] APARTMENTS FOR SENIOR CITIZENS

ERIE. *Mercy Terrace Apartments*, 430 E. Grandview Blvd., 16504. Tel: 814-825-6791; Fax: 814-824-2127. Email: mta430@verizon.net. Sr. M. Felice Duska, R.S.M., Exec. Dir. Sponsored by Sisters of Mercy of the Americas - New York, Pennsylvania, Pacific West Community.

HARBORCREEK. **Benetwood Apartments for Persons Elderly and Disabled*, 641 Troupe Rd., 16421-1048. Tel: 814-899-0088; Fax: 814-898-2513. Email: benetwood@neohio.twcbc.com. Sr. Patricia Hause, O.S.B., Admin. Benedictine Sisters of Erie. Residents 80.

[K] RESIDENCES FOR RETIRED PRIESTS

ERIE. *Bishop Michael J. Murphy Residence for Retired Priests*, 400 E. Gore Rd., 16509. Tel: 814-825-0680; Fax: 814-825-9761. Rev. Msgr. Robert J. Smith, J.C.L., V.G., Dir.

[L] NURSING HOMES

ERIE. *Saint Mary's Home of Erie*, Mailing Address: 607 E. 26th St., 16504. Tel: 814-459-0621; Fax: 814-454-0909. Email: pmccracken@stmaryshome.org. Web: www.stmaryshome.org. Sr. Phyllis McCracken, S.S.J., M.S., R.N., N.H.A., Pres., CEO & Contact Person.

Saint Mary's Home of Erie dba Saint Mary's East 607 E. 26th St., 16504. Tel: 814-459-0621; Fax: 814-454-0909. Sisters Phyllis McCracken, S.S.J., M.S., R.N., N.H.A., Pres., CEO & Contact Person; Mary Fromknecht, S.S.J., Admin.; Rev. Msgr. Joseph V. Wardanski, Chap. Sisters 8; Residents 131; Adult Day Services 49; Patients in Nursing Home 139.

Saint Mary's Home of Erie dba Saint Mary's at Asbury Ridge 4855 W. Ridge Rd., 16506. Tel: 814-836-5300; Fax: 814-836-5326. Sr. Phyllis McCracken, S.S.J., M.S., R.N., N.H.A., Pres., CEO & Contact Person; Audrey Urban, Admin.; Rev. G. William Fischer, O.S.F.S., Chap. Sisters 3; Residents 164; Patients in Nursing Home 80; Carriage Homes Independent Living 26.

Saint Mary's Home of Erie dba Carleton Court 2710 Carleton Ct., 16506. Tel: 814-833-2787. Apartments (Independent Living) 60; Total Assisted Annually 91.

DU BOIS. *Christ the King Manor, Inc.*, 1100 W. Long Ave., 15801. Tel: 814-371-3180; Fax: 814-371-4101. Email: ctkm@penn.com. Web: www.christthekingmanor.org. Rev. Matias M. Quimno. Residents 220.

HERMITAGE. *John XXIII Home*, 2250 Shenango Fwy., 16148. Tel: 724-981-3200; Fax: 724-981-1677. Email: klhawthorne@johnxxIIIhome.org. Web: www.johnXXIIIhome.org. Rev. Msgr. Charles S. Murcko (Retired); Kirk L. Hawthorne, Admin. Residents 198.

[M] SHELTERS FOR MEN AND WOMEN

ERIE. *Maria House Projects*, P.O. Box 10682, 16514. Tel: 814-454-0891. Rev. Msgr. James W. Peterson, Dir. (Retired).

St. Patrick Haven, Inc., 147 E. 12th St., 16501. Tel: 814-454-7219; 814-836-4134; Fax: 814-836-4278. Peggy Rusnak, Dir.

MEADVILLE. *St. James Haven*, 169 Walnut St., 16335.

[N] CONVENTS AND RESIDENCES FOR SISTERS

ERIE. *Congregation of the Divine Spirit*, 444 E. Grandview Blvd., 16504. Tel: 814-825-2724; Fax: 814-825-7108. Email: AdSum409@verizon.net. Sr. Michele Beauseigneur, C.D.S., Supr. Gen. Members 27.

Holy Family Monastery, 510 E. Gore Rd., 16509-3799. Tel: 814-825-0846; Fax: 814-825-0865. Sr. Emmanuel of the Mother of God, O.C.D., Prioress; Very Rev. Michael T. Kesicki, Chap.; Rev. Nicholas J. Rouch, S.T.D., Chap. Discalced Carmelites 5.

Julia House, 608 Walnut St., 16502. Tel: 814-871-5756. Sr. Kathleen Dietz, F.S.O., Supr. The Spiritual Family the Work Members 2.

Mount Saint Benedict Monastery, 6101 E. Lake Rd., 16511. Tel: 814-899-0614; Fax: 814-898-4004. Email: prioress@mtstbenedict.org. Web: www.eriebenedictines.org. Sisters Anne Wambach, O.S.B., Prioress; Susan Doubet, O.S.B., Sub-Prioress. Benedictine Sisters of Erie. Professed Sisters in Community 100.

Benedicta Riepp Priory, 3904 Tuttle Ave., 16504. Tel: 814-825-2767. Benedictine Sisters of Erie 2.

Benet Priory, 330 E. 10th St., 16503. Tel: 814-459-5103. Benedictine Sisters of Erie 2.

Bethany House, 218 E. 11th St., 16503. Tel: 814-455-4574. Benedictine Sisters of Erie 3.

Kraus House Priory, 436 E. 9th St., 16503. Tel: 814-454-4846. Benedictine Sisters of Erie. Sisters 2.

Pax Priory, 345 E. Ninth St., 16503. Tel: 814-452-6318; Fax: 814-459-8066. Email: PAXPRIORY@peoplepc.com. Web: www.eriebenedictines.org. Benedictine Sisters of Erie 4.

Peace House, 103 E. 35th St., 16504. Tel: 814-455-6066. Email: mmashank@stben.org. Benedictine Sisters of Erie 2.

Saint Benedict Community Center, 320 E. 10th St., 16503. Tel: 814-459-2406. Email: iluv2kayak@hotmail.com. Sr. Dianne Sabol, O.S.B., Dir.

St. Scholastica Priory, 355 E. 9th St., 16503. Tel: 814-454-4052; Fax: 814-459-8066. Email: scholpriory@benetvision.org. Web: eriebenedictines.org. Benedictine Sisters of Erie 4.

St. Walburga Priory, 302 E. 10th St., 16503. Tel: 814-454-3706. Email: walburga@peoplepc.com. Web: www.eriebenedictines.org. Benedictine Sisters of Erie 2.

Sisters of Mercy of the Americas - New York, Pennsylvania, Pacific West Community, 444 E. Grandview Blvd., 16504. Tel: 814-824-2516; Fax: 814-824-2127. Web: www.sistersofmercy.org. Sr. Nancy Hoff, R.S.M., Pres. (Erie Diocese) 45; Total in Community 463.

Sisters of Saint Joseph of Northwestern Pennsylvania, 5031 W. Ridge Rd., 16506-1249. Tel: 814-836-4100; Fax: 814-836-4278. Web: www.ssjerie.org. Sr. Mary Ellen Dwyer, S.S.J., Pres.; Rev. Jerome S. Simmons, Chap. The Sisters of St. Joseph of Northwestern PA. Professed Sisters in Community 116.

Union of Our Lady of Charity/United States Province, 4635 E. Lake Rd., 16511. Tel: 814-899-1052. Email: srcgentile@hotmail.com. Sisters Catherine Gentile, Local Supr.; Carol Pregno, O.L.C., Provincial. Sisters 4.

ST. MARYS. *Benedictine Sisters of Elk County St. Joseph Monastery*, 303 Church St., 15857. Tel: 814-834-2267; Fax: 814-834-3270. Email: srjacintaconklin@yahoo.com. Sr. Anne Stedman, O.S.B., Prioress. Professed Sisters 17.

[O] SOCIOLOGICAL

ERIE. *Emmaus Ministries, Inc.*, 345 E. 9th St., 16503. Tel: 814-459-8349; Fax: 814-459-8066. Sr. Mary Miller, O.S.B., Dir.

ERIE DAWN, 2549 W. 8th St., 16505-4430. Tel: 814-453-5921; Fax: 814-453-5831. Email: maureen@eriedawn.org. Web: www.eriedawn.org. Maureen Dunn, Admin.

Mercy Center for Women, 1039 E. 27th St., 16504. Tel: 814-455-4577; Fax: 814-459-7012. Email: ctombaugh@mcwerie.org. Web: www.mcwerie.org. Christine Tombaugh, Exec. Dir.

Mercy Hilltop Center, Inc., 444 E. Grandview Blvd., 16504-2604. Tel: 814-824-2214; Fax: 814-824-2127. Web: mercycenteronaging.com. Sr. Mary Dolores Jablonski, R.S.M., Exec. Dir.

Partnership of Women Religious, 6101 E. Lake Rd., 16511. Tel: 814-899-0614.

Sisters of St. Joseph Neighborhood Network, Inc., 425 W. 18th St., 16502. Tel: 814-454-7814; Fax: 814-454-7915. Web: ssjnn.org. Rose Graham, Exec. Dir.

[P] RETREAT & RENEWAL CENTERS

ERIE. *Ecclesia Ministry*, 1626 W. 26th St., 16508. Tel: 814-454-0810. Email: ecclesia@adelphia.net. Web: www.ecclesiacenter.org. Rev. Jerome S. Simmons; Sr. Marilyn Zimmerman, S.S.J., Contact Person.

Glinodo Center, 6270 E. Lake Rd., 16511. Tel: 814-899-0614; Fax: 814-898-4004. Email: physical@mstbenedict.org. Web: www.eriebenedictines.org. Sr. Charles Marie Holze, O.S.B., Dir. Benedictine Sisters of Erie.

FRENCHVILLE. *Young People Who Care Inc.*, 1031 Germania Rd., P.O. Box 129, 16836. Tel: 814-263-4855; Fax: 814-263-7106. Email: bethanyyouth@pennswoods.net. Web: www.ypwcministries.org. Sr. Therese Dush, C.A., Dir.

UNION CITY. *Avila Retreat Center*, 61 E. High St., 16438. Tel: 814-438-7020. Richard Raid, Contact Person.

[Q] CAMPUS MINISTRY

ERIE. *Newman Centers and Campus Ministry* Gannon Univ., 109 University Sq., 16541. Tel: 814-871-7435. Deacon Stephen J. Washek.

Allegheny College 520 N. Main St., P.O. Box 14, Meadville, 16335. Tel: 814-332-2800; Fax: 814-332-2340. Rev. Marc J. Solomon.

University of Pittsburgh - Bradford Campus St. Bernard Parish, P.O. Box 2394, Bradford, 16701. Tel: 814-362-6825; Fax: 814-362-1497.

Clarion University of Pennsylvania P.O. Box 177, Emlenton, 16373. Tel: 724-867-2422; Fax: 724-867-6815. Rev. Msgr. Jan C. Olowin.

Lockhaven University - Clearfield Campus 212 S. Front St., Clearfield, 16830. Tel: 814-765-9671; Fax: 814-226-1090.

Penn State University - Du Bois Campus 116 State St., DuBois, 15801. Tel: 814-371-8556.

Edinboro University of PA Newman Center, 128 Sunset Dr., P.O. Box 820, Edinboro, 16412. Tel: 814-734-1651; Fax: 814-734-3085. Rev. William E. Sutherland.

Gannon University University Sq., 16541. Tel: 814-871-7435. Deacon Stephen J. Washek, Campus Min.; Rev. George E. Strohmeyer, M.A., Chap.

Grove City College Beloved Disciple Parish, 321 N. Broad St., Grove City, 16127. Tel: 412-458-7145.

Mercyhurst College 501 E. 38th St., 16546. Tel: 814-456-6189. Greg Baker, Campus Min.; Rev. James Piszker, Chap. & Dir. Tel: 814-824-2467; Paul Mocosko, Campus Min. Tel: 814-456-6189.

Mercyhurst College, North East 204 W. 6th St., 16507. Tel: 814-456-6189.

Clarion State University of PA - Venango Campus St. Stephen Parish, 210 Reed St., Oil City, 16301. Tel: 814-677-3020.

Penn State Erie, The Behrend College 5091 Station Rd., 16563-0901. Tel: 814-898-6245; Fax: 814-898-6608.

Indiana University of PA - Punxsutawney Campus Ss. Cosmas & Damian Parish, 616 W. Mahoning St., Punxsutawney, 15767. Tel: 814-938-6540.

Penn State University - Shenango Valley Campus St. Joseph Parish, 74 Case Ave., Sharon, 16146. Tel: 412-981-3232.

Thiel College, St. Michael Parish, 85 N. High St., Greenville, 16125. Tel: 724-588-9800.

University of Pittsburgh - Titusville Campus St. Titus Parish, 513 W. Main St., Titusville, 16354. Tel: 814-827-4636.

[R] MISCELLANEOUS

ERIE. *Alliance for International Monasticism (AIM)-USA Secretariat (AIM-USA)*, 345 E. 9th St., 16503-1107. Tel: 814-453-4724; Fax: 814-459-8066. Email: aim@aim-usa.org. Web: www.aim-usa.org. Sr. Stephanie Schmidt, O.S.B., Exec. Dir. AIM is an organization founded to assist Benedictine and Cistercian monasteries in Africa, Asia and Latin America.

St. Martin's Center Culinary Lab, 1701 Parade St., 16503. Tel: 814-452-6113, Ext. 232; Fax: 814-452-6124.

Star Foundation, c/o St. Mark Catholic Center, 429 E. Grandview Blvd., P.O. Box 10397, 16514-0397. Tel: 814-824-1188; Fax: 814-824-1181. Email: cbanducci@eriercd.org. Charles Banducci, Coord.

The Catholic Foundation of the Roman Catholic Diocese of Erie, Inc., Mailing Address: *St. Mark Catholic Center*, P.O. Box 10397, 16514-0397. Tel:

814-824-1236; Fax: 814-824-1264. Email: thecatholicfoundation@eriercd.org. 429 E. Grandview Blvd., 16504.

St. Thomas More Society, P.O. Box 10397, 16514-0397. Tel: 814-824-1140; Fax: 814-824-1149.

FRENCHVILLE. *Anawim Community of Frenchville*, 1031 Germania Rd., P.O. Box 129, 16836. Tel: 814-263-4855; Fax: 814-263-7106. Email: anawimco@pennswoods.net. Web: www.anawimcommunity.org. Sr. Therese Dush, C.A., Dir.

ST. MARYS. *Opportunity for Parochial Education Network (OPEN)*, 575 Charles St., 15857. Tel: 814-834-6181. Richard J. Reuscher, Trustee.

RELIGIOUS INSTITUTES OF MEN REPRESENTED IN THE DIOCESE

For further details refer to the corresponding bracketed number in the Religious Institutes of Men or Women section.

[0200]—*Benedictine Monks* (St. Vincent's Archabbey)—O.S.B.

[0290]—*Oblates of St. Francis de Sales*—O.S.F.S.

[0940]—*Oblates of the Virgin Mary*—O.M.V.

[0610]—*Priests of the Congregation of Holy Cross*—C.S.C.

[]—*Society of Jesus*—S.J.

RELIGIOUS INSTITUTES OF WOMEN REPRESENTED IN THE DIOCESE

[0230]—*Benedictine Sisters of Elk Co.*—O.S.B.

[0160]—*Benedictine Sisters of Erie*—O.S.B.

[]—*Congregation of Divine Providence* (Pittsburgh)—C.D.P.

[]—*Congregation of the Divine Spirit*—C.D.S.

[]—*Congregation of the Sisters of St. Joseph* Pittsburgh—C.S.J.

[0420]—*Discalced Carmelite Nuns*—O.C.D.

[]—*Franciscan Missionary Sister of Assisi* (Italy)—S.F.M.A.

[]—*Handmaids of the Holy Child Jesus*—H.H.C.J.

[]—*Mission Helpers of the Sacred Heart*—M.H.S.H.

[2820]—*Missionary Sisters of Our Lady of Africa*—M.S.O.L.A.

[3070]—*North American Union of Sisters of Our Lady of Charity*—N.A.U.-O.L.C.

[]—*Private Association of the Christian Faithful* (Anawim Community)—A.C.

[1690]—*School Sisters of the Third Order of St. Francis*—O.S.F.

[0507]—*Sisters of Charity of Seton Hill, Greensburg, PA*—S.C.

[2570]—*Sisters of Mercy of the Americas* (New York, PA, Pacific West Community)—R.S.M.

[]—*Sisters of St. Basil the Great*—O.S.B.M.

[3830]—*Sisters of St. Joseph of Northwestern Pennsylvania, S.S.J.*—S.S.J.

[]—*Sisters of the Holy Family*—S.H.F.

[2110]—*Sisters of the Humility of Mary*—H.M.

[]—*Spiritual Family the Work*—F.S.O.

DIOCESAN CEMETERIES

ERIE. *Queen of Peace*

Trinity, Calvary & Gate of Heaven

NECROLOGY

† Daniszewski, Rev. Msgr. John D., (Retired)—Died Aug. 31, 2011

† Speice, Rev. Msgr. Lawrence T., (Retired)—Died Jan. 16, 2011

† Kirsch, Gregory A., Houtzdale, PA Christ the King—Died April 28, 2011

† Wolf, Norbert G., (Retired)—Died May 10, 2011

An asterisk (*) denotes an organization that has established tax-exempt status directly with the IRS and is not covered by the USCCB Group Ruling.

Diocese of Evansville

(Dioecesis Evansvicensis)

Most Reverend

CHARLES C. THOMPSON

Bishop of Evansville; ordained May 30, 1987; appointed Bishop of Evansville April 26, 2011; ordained June 29, 2011. *Mailing Address: Catholic Center, 4200 N. Kentucky Ave., P.O. Box 4169, Evansville, IN 47724-0169. Res.: 3980 Woodcastle, Evansville, IN 47711.*

Most Reverend

GERALD ANDREW GETTELFINGER

Bishop Emeritus of Evansville; ordained May 7, 1961; appointed Fourth Bishop of Evansville March 11, 1989; ordained and installed April 11, 1989; retired April 26, 2011. *Res.: 12222 St. Wendel Rd., Evansville, IN 47720.*

Catholic Center: 4200 N. Kentucky Ave., P.O. Box 4169, Evansville, IN 47724-0169. Tel: 812-424-5536; Fax: 812-421-1334.

Web: www.evansville-diocese.org

ESTABLISHED NOVEMBER 11, 1944.

Square Miles 5,010.

Comprises twelve Counties in the Southwestern part of Indiana: Daviess, Dubois, Gibson, Greene, Knox, Martin, Pike, Posey, Spencer (except township of Harrison), Sullivan, Vanderburgh, Warrick.

The Diocese of Evansville was established by decree of Pope Pius XII, November 11, 1944, and the See was fixed at Evansville.

For legal titles of parishes and diocesan institutions, consult the Chancery.

STATISTICAL OVERVIEW

Personnel	
Bishop	1
Retired Bishops	1
Priests: Diocesan Active in Diocese	45
Priests: Diocesan Active Outside Diocese	1
Priests: Retired, Sick or Absent	25
Number of Diocesan Priests	71
Religious Priests in Diocese	5
Total Priests in Diocese	76
Ordinations:	
Transitional Deacons	2
Permanent Deacons in Diocese	49
Total Sisters	242
Parishes	
Parishes	69
With Resident Pastor:	
Resident Diocesan Priests	37
Resident Religious Priests	3
Without Resident Pastor:	
Administered by Priests	23
Administered by Deacons	5
Administered by Religious Women	1
Pastoral Centers	8
Professional Ministry Personnel:	
Sisters	8
Lay Ministers	43
Welfare	
Catholic Hospitals	2
Total Assisted	570,103
Health Care Centers	1
Total Assisted	58
Homes for the Aged	3
Total Assisted	128
Day Care Centers	1
Total Assisted	211
Special Centers for Social Services	10
Total Assisted	175,380
Educational	
Diocesan Students in Other Seminaries	10
Total Seminarians	10
High Schools, Diocesan and Parish	4
Total Students	1,465
High Schools, Private	1
Total Students	16
Elementary Schools, Diocesan and Parish	24
Total Students	5,797
Catechesis/Religious Education:	
High School Students	1,917
Elementary Students	4,641
Total Students under Catholic Instruction	13,846
Teachers in the Diocese:	
Sisters	10
Lay Teachers	441
Vital Statistics	
Receptions into the Church:	
Infant Baptism Totals	1,153
Adult Baptism Totals	87
Received into Full Communion	162
First Communions	1,142
Confirmations	1,057
Marriages:	
Catholic	245
Interfaith	151
Total Marriages	396
Deaths	884
Total Catholic Population	83,329
Total Population	509,553

Former Bishops—Most Revs. HENRY JOSEPH GRIMMELSMAN, D.D., appt. Nov. 11, 1944; cons. Dec. 21, 1944; retired and named Titular Bishop of Tabla Oct. 20, 1965; died June 26, 1972; PAUL F. LEIBOLD, D.D., J.C.D., appt. Titular Bishop of Trebenna and Auxiliary of Cincinnati April 10, 1958; cons. June 17, 1958; appt. to Evansville April 6, 1966; translated to Archbishop of Cincinnati July 23, 1969; died June 1, 1972; FRANCIS R. SHEA, appt. Dec. 10, 1969; retired April 11, 1989; died Aug. 18, 1994; GERALD A. GETTELFINGER, ord. May 7, 1961; appt. Fourth Bishop of Evansville March 11, 1989; ord. and installed April 11, 1989; retired April 26, 2011.

Catholic Center—4200 N. Kentucky Ave., P.O. Box 4169, Evansville, 47724-0169. Tel: 812-424-5536; Fax: 812-421-1334. Office Hours: Mon.-Thurs. 8-5, Fri. 8-4:30.

Vicar General—Very Rev. BERNARD T. ETIENNE.

Chief Operating Officer—TIMOTHY J. MCGUIRE.

Chancellor—JUDITH A. NEFF.

Secretary to the Bishop—LYNDA D. PROVENCE.

Treasurer—ROBERT J. COX, CPA.

Associate Treasurer—SCOTT BRITT.

Assistant Treasurer—PHYLLIS HIGGINS.

Diocesan Tribunal—Mailing Address: P.O. Box 4169, Evansville, 47724-0169.

Judicial Vicar—Rev. J. KENNETH WALKER, B.A., M.Div., M.C.L., J.C.L.; MARY GEN BLITTSCHAU, M.A., M.C.L., J.C.L., Asst. to Judicial Vicar & Judge.

Defender of the Bond—Rev. JOSEPH F. ERBACHER.

Judges—Revs. RAYMOND L. KUPER (Retired); DAVID G. FLECK; STEPHEN P. LINTZENICH.

Advocates—Revs. JOHN H. SCHIPP; MICHAEL MADDEN.

Secretaries and Notaries—CHARLEEN KAELIN; GAYLE SPALDING.

Archivist—JUDITH A. NEFF.

Diocesan Consultors—Rev. J. KENNETH WALKER, B.A., M.Div., M.C.L., J.C.L.; Very Rev. BERNARD T. ETIENNE; Revs. GARY EDWARD KAISER; JAMES KORESSEL; STEPHEN P. LINTZENICH; BERNARD A. LUTZ (Retired); MICHAEL MADDEN; DAVID G. FLECK.

Diocesan Council of Priests—Revs. J. KENNETH WALKER, B.A., M.Div., M.C.L., J.C.L.; PHILIP KREILEIN; RONALD KREILEIN; MARK O'KEEFE, O.S.B.; DAVID G. FLECK; JOHN BROSMER; STEPHEN P. LINTZENICH; JOSEPH F. ERBACHER; MICHAEL MADDEN; ANTHONY ERNST; Very Rev. BERNARD T. ETIENNE; Revs. BERNARD A. LUTZ (Retired); EUGENE SCHMITT.

Clergy Personnel Board—Rev. STEPHEN P. LINTZENICH, Dir.; Deacon DAVID RICE, Asst. Dir.; Revs. RONALD S. ZGUNDA; RALPH SCHIPP (Retired); JAMES KORESSEL; JACK J. DURCHHOLZ; GARY EDWARD KAISER; Rev. Msgr. KENNETH R. KNAPP, A.C.S.W., M.S.

Deans—Very Rev. BERNARD T. ETIENNE, Evansville, East; Revs. DAVID H. NUNNING, Evansville, West; RAYMOND BRENNER, Jasper; JOSEPH ZILIAK, S.T.L., Newburgh; RONALD S. ZGUNDA, Princeton; DAVID G. FLECK, Vincennes; JAMES KORESSEL, Washington.

Censors of Books—Revs. J. KENNETH WALKER, B.A., M.Div., M.C.L., J.C.L.; JOSEPH ZILIAK, S.T.L.

Diocesan Offices And Directors

Boy Scouts—Deacon CHARLES KORESSEL, Chap.

Campus Ministry—CHRISTINE HOEHN, Coord.

Catholic Charities—GAYLE UEBELHOR, Interim Exec. Dir., Court Bldg., Ste. 603, 123 N.W. Fourth St., Evansville, 47708. Tel: 812-423-5456.

Catholic Diocese of Evansville, Inc.—Most Rev. CHARLES C. THOMPSON.

Catholic Education Endowment, Inc. (Washington)—JAMES WERNE, Pres.

Catholic Education Foundation, Inc. (Evansville)—MARGARET ANGERMEIER, Exec. Dir.

The Catholic Foundation of Southwestern Indiana, Inc.—LINDA COX, Exec. Dir., Mailing Address: P.O. Box 4169, Evansville, 47724-0169.

Holy Family Catholic School Foundation, Inc.—WILFRED WEINZAPFEL, Pres., 950 Church Ave.,

Jasper, 47546.

Catholic Education, Office of—DARYL HAGAN, Supt. Assistant Superintendents: DONNA HALVERSON; MICHELLE PRIAR; RHONDA WEISSMANN, Sec.

Catholic Communication Office—PAUL LEINGANG, Dir., Mailing Address: P.O. Box 4169, Evansville, 47724-0169.

Catholic Hospitals, Diocesan Representative—VACANT.

Catholic Relief Services—JUDITH A. NEFF, 4200 N. Kentucky Ave., Evansville, 47711. Tel: 812-424-5536.

Cemeteries—Rev. EUGENE A. SCHROEDER, Dir., 6202 W. St. Joseph Rd., Evansville, 47720. Tel: 812-963-3273.

Christian Educational Foundation of Vincennes, Inc.—MIKE RUSCH, Pres.

Continuing Education of Clergy—VACANT, Mailing Address: 4200 N. Kentucky Ave., Evansville, 47711.

Cursillos in Christianity—NICK WOLF, Lay Dir.

Deaf Ministry—Rev. HENRY KUYKENDALL, 3635 Pollack, Evansville, 47714. Tel: 812-491-3173.

Diocesan Finance Council—Ex Officio: Most Rev. CHARLES C. THOMPSON; Very Rev. BERNARD T. ETIENNE; TIMOTHY J. MCGUIRE; ROBERT COX; GARY BECKMAN; ALAN HOFFMAN; JAMES MUEHLBAUER; STEVE WITTING; JAMES ROACH; DEAN HAPPE; WILLIAM KAISER; MARGARET CONWAY.

Diocese of Evansville Retirement Trust Agreement and Plan for Priests—Office of the Bishop: 4200 N. Kentucky Ave., P.O. Box 4169, Evansville, 47724-0169. Tel: 812-424-5536.

Ecumenism—4200 N. Kentucky Ave., P.O. Box 4169, Evansville, 47724-0169. Tel: 812-424-5536.

Evangelization, Office of—4200 N. Kentucky Ave., P.O. Box 4169, Evansville, 47724-0169. Tel: 812-424-5536.

Girl Scouts—Deacon CHARLES KORESSEL, Chap.

Spanish Speaking Ministry—Sr. KAREN DURLIAT, O.S.B., Dir.; Rev. EUGENE HEERDINK, Sacramental Min. (Retired), Guadalupe Center, 511 E. 4th St., Ste. 1, Huntingburg, 47542. Tel: 812-683-5212.

Propagation of the Faith and Holy Childhood Association—CATHY CROWDUS, 4200 N. Kentucky Ave., P.O. Box 4169, Evansville, 47724-0169. Tel: 812-424-5536.

Justice and Peace— (Please refer to Catholic Charities for further information).

Legion of Mary—VACANT, Evansville; Deacon DONALD HAAG, Washington.

Message, The— Catholic Press of Evansville; Publisher, Most Rev. CHARLES C. THOMPSON; PAUL LEINGANG, Editor.

Permanent Diaconate Program—Deacons DAVID SEIBERT, Interim Dir., 600 Herndon Dr., Evansville, 47711; THOMAS EVANS, Assoc. Dir.

Office of Catechesis—VACANT, Dir.; DONNA GISH, Asst. Dir.

Rural Life Conference—Rev. JOHN BOEGLIN, Dir., Holy Family Church, 950 E. Church Ave., Jasper, 47546-3797.

Sarto Retreat House—MARGIE NORD, Coord.; GEORGE FLEMING, Dir. Maintenance.

Secretariat for Charismatic Renewal—JOHN BENNETT.

Stewardship / Development, Office of—VACANT, Mailing Address: P.O. Box 4169, Evansville, 47724-0169. Tel: 812-424-5536.

Victim Assistance Coordinator—REBECCA LUZIO, Ph.D. Tel: 812-490-9565 (local); 866-200-3004 (long distance). Email: rluzio@luzioassociates.com.

Vocation Office—Rev. ALEX ZENTHOEFER, Vocation Dir. Associate Directors: Rev. JASON GRIES; Sr. MICHELLE SINKHORN, O.S.B., Mailing Address: P.O. Box 4169, Evansville, 47724-0169. Tel: 812-424-5536.

Worship—MATT J. MILLER, 4200 N. Kentucky, P.O. Box 4169, Evansville, 47724-0169. Tel: 812-424-5536.

Youth and Young Adult Ministry—STEVEN DABROWSKI JR., Dir., 4200 N. Kentucky, P.O. Box 4169, Evansville, 47724-0169. Tel: 812-424-5536.

CLERGY, PARISHES, MISSIONS AND PAROCHIAL SCHOOLS

CITY OF EVANSVILLE

(VANDERBURGH COUNTY)

1—ST. BENEDICT CATHEDRAL Rev. Gregory Chamberlin, O.S.B.; Sr. Patricia McGuire, O.S.B., Pastoral Assoc.; Deacons David Cook; James Flynn; Kevin Bach.
Parish Center—1328 Lincoln Ave., 47714-1598. Tel: 812-425-3369; Fax: 812-425-3378.
Res.: 1312 Lincoln Ave., 47714.
School—(Grades PreK-8), 530 S. Harlan Ave., 47714-1598. Tel: 812-425-4596. Sr. Karlene Sensmeier, O.S.B., Prin.; Jeanne McGinnis, Librarian. Sisters of St. Benedict 2; Lay Teachers 23; Students 457.
Catechesis / Religious Program—Marty Horning, D.R.E. Students 84.

2—ST. AGNES, [CEM] Rev. David H. Nunning; Deacon Thomas Kempf.
Res.: 1600 Glendale Ave., 47712. Tel: 812-425-9140; Fax: 812-423-4240.
School—Westside Catholic Consolidated, (Grades K-4) Tracey Unfried, Prin.; Doriene Markin, Librarian. Lay Teachers 7; Students 89.
Catechesis / Religious Program—Jenny Mayer, D.R.E. Students 9.

3—ST. ANTHONY Rev. John Davidson; Sr. Jackie Kissel, O.S.B., Pastoral Assoc.; Lisa Foster, Pastoral Assoc.
Res.: 704 First Ave., 47710. Tel: 812-423-5209; Fax: 812-424-5498.
Catechesis / Religious Program—Sr. Jackie Kissel, O.S.B., D.R.E. Students 111.

4—ASSUMPTION CATHEDRAL, Closed. For inquiries for parish records contact Holy Trinity.

5—ST. BONIFACE Rev. Kenneth H. Herr; Deacons Richard Preske; David Franklin.
Res.: 418 N. Wabash Ave., 47712. Tel: 812-425-8375; Fax: 812-401-7690.
School—(Grades 5-8) Tracey Unfried, Prin.; Doriene Markin, Librarian. Lay Teachers 8; Students 84.
Catechesis / Religious Program—Jenny Mayer, D.R.E. Students 13.

6—CHRIST THE KING Rev. Msgr. Kenneth R. Knapp; Rev. Ryan Paul Hilderbrand; Deacons Francis Hillenbrand; Vincent Bernardin, Pastoral Assoc.
Office: 3010 E. Chandler Ave., 47714-2602. Tel: 812-476-3061; Fax: 812-476-3062.
School—(Grades PreK-8) Gwen Godsey, Prin. Lay Teachers 15; Students 187.
Catechesis / Religious Program—Students 76.

7—CORPUS CHRISTI Rev. James Blessinger; Deacon Tom Goebel.
Res.: 5528 Hogue Rd., 47712-3218. Tel: 812-422-2027; Fax: 812-421-8316.
School—(Grades PreK-8) Martha Craig, Prin.; Donna Martin, Librarian. Lay Teachers 17; Students 252.
Catechesis / Religious Program—Kathryn Curtis, D.R.E. Students 23.

8—GOOD SHEPHERD Rev. Zachary J. Etienne; Deacon Cyril Will.
Res.: 2301 N. Stockwell, 47715. Tel: 812-477-5405; Fax: 812-469-2907.
School—(Grades K-8) Judy Van Hoosier, Prin.; Lucy Ashley, Librarian. Lay Teachers 25; Students 333.
Catechesis / Religious Program—Karen Robertson, D.R.E. Students 34.

9—HOLY REDEEMER Rev. Paul Anthony Ferguson; Deacons Robert Hayden; David Mayer.
Office: 918-A W. Mill Rd., 47710. Tel: 812-424-8344; Fax: 812-424-7166.
School—(Grades PreK-8) Marianne Webster, Prin. Lay Teachers 20; Students 216.
Catechesis / Religious Program—Doug Rasler, D.R.E. Students 124.

10—HOLY ROSARY Very Rev. Bernard T. Etienne; Rev. Alex Zenthoefer; Sr. Mary Mundy, S.P., Pastoral Assoc.; Deacon Christian Borowiecki.
Office: 1301 S. Green River Rd., 47715. Tel: 812-477-8923; Fax: 812-471-7226.
School—(Grades PreK-8) Joan Fredrich, Prin.; Sally Pfafflin, Librarian. Lay Teachers 36; Students 438.
Catechesis / Religious Program—Carol Ann Gaddis, D.R.E. Students 54.

11—HOLY SPIRIT Rev. Claude Thomas Burns.
Church: 1800 S. Lodge Ave., 47714. Tel: 812-477-1738; Fax: 812-469-6633.
School—(Grades PreK-8) David Memmer, Prin. Lay Teachers 17; Students 193.

12—HOLY TRINITY Rev. Eugene Schroeder, Temporary Admin.; Deacon Charles Koressel.
219 N.W. Third St., 47708-1233. Tel: 812-422-5150.
Catechesis / Religious Program—Gail Shetler, D.R.E. Students 63.

13—ST. JOHN THE APOSTLE Sr. Jane Nesmith, S.B.S., Pastoral Life Coord.; Rev. Stephen P. Lintzenich, Pastoral Moderator.
Church: 617 Bellemeade Ave., 47713-1707. Tel: 812-424-9261; Fax: 812-424-5933.
Catechesis / Religious Program—Mary Ann Joyce, D.R.E. Students 18.

14—ST. JOHN THE EVANGELIST, [CEM] Rev. David Martin; Deacon David Rice.
Church: 5301 Daylight Dr., 47725-7636. Tel: 812-867-3718.
Catechesis / Religious Program—Leah Haley, D.R.E. Students 119.

15—ST. JOSEPH Rev. Stephen P. Lintzenich, Moderator; Deacons Richard Grannan, Parish Life Coord.; Emil Altmeyer.
Office: 607 E. Iowa, 47711. Tel: 812-422-5668; Fax: 812-425-2730.
Catechesis / Religious Program—

16—ST. JOSEPH, [CEM] Rev. Eugene A. Schroeder.
Res.: 6202 W. St. Joseph Rd., 47720. Tel: 812-963-3273; Fax: 812-963-6254.
School—(Grades PreK-8) Melba Wilderman, Prin.; Donna Hiestand, Librarian. Sisters 1; Lay Teachers 12; Students 214.
Catechesis / Religious Program—Sharon Vogler, D.R.E. Students 35.

17—ST. MARY Rev. Stephen P. Lintzenich; Lisa Covington, Dir. Pastoral Formation; Deacon Dennis Russell.
Parish Office—613 Cherry St., 47713.
Res.: 609 Cherry St., 47713. Tel: 812-425-1577; Fax: 812-426-1416.
Catechesis / Religious Program—Students 103.

18—NATIVITY Rev. Henry Kuykendall; Sr. Sharon Haskins, D.C., Pastoral Assoc.; Deacon John McMullen.
Res.: 3635 Pollack, 47714. Tel: 812-476-7186; Fax: 812-476-7956.
Catholic Ministry of the Deaf Office—Tel: 812-491-3173.
Catechesis / Religious Program—Abraham Brown, D.R.E. Students 135.

19—RESURRECTION Rev. Philip Kreilein.
Res.: 5301 New Harmony Rd., 47720-1774. Tel: 812-963-3121; Fax: 812-963-1141.
School—(Grades PreK-8) Theresa Berendes, Prin. Sisters of St. Benedict 1; Lay Teachers 22; Students 344.
Catechesis / Religious Program—Karen Muensterman, D.R.E. Students 66.

20—SACRED HEART Rev. David H. Nunning; Deacon Tom Lehman.
Office: 2701 W. Franklin St., 47712. Tel: 812-425-5505; Fax: 812-425-8443.
School—Westside Catholic Consolidated, (Grades PreK) Tracey Unfried, Prin. Lay Teachers 5; Students 60.
Catechesis / Religious Program—Jenny Mayer, D.R.E. Students 5.

21—ST. THERESA Rev. Msgr. Kenneth R. Knapp, Moderator; Rev. John Breidenbach, Sacramental Min.; Deacons David Seibert, Pastoral Life Coord.; Donald Yochum.
Mailing Address: 600 Herndon Dr., 47711-3830.
Res.: Tel: 812-422-8211; Fax: 812-422-5345.
School—(Grades PreK-8) Nancy Mills, Prin.; Peggy Epley, Librarian. Lay Teachers 14; Students 111.
Catechesis / Religious Program—Deacon David Seibert, D.R.E. Students 10.
Convent—Sisters of St. Benedict Sisters 5.

22—ST. WENDEL, [CEM] Rev. Edward Schnur; Deacon Mark McDonald.
Parish Office—10542 W. Boonville-New Harmony Rd., 47720-7901. Tel: 812-963-3733; Fax: 812-963-3835.
School—(Grades PreK-8) Ron Pittman, Prin. Lay Teachers 16; Students 162.
Catechesis / Religious Program—Twinned with St. Francis, Poseyville Sherie Cooley, D.R.E. Students 156.

OUTSIDE CITY OF EVANSVILLE

BICKNELL, KNOX CO., ST. PHILIP NERI Rev. Jason Gries.
Res.: 605 W. Fourth St., 47512. Tel: 812-735-4069.
Catechesis / Religious Program—Elaine Pepmeier, D.R.E.; Marcia Yochum, D.R.E. Students 39.

BLOOMFIELD, GREENE CO., HOLY NAME, [CEM] Rev. Michael Madden.
Res.: 700 Lincoln Dr., 47424-0124. Tel: 812-384-8415.
Catechesis / Religious Program—Lora Burris, D.R.E. Students 14.

BOONVILLE, WARRICK CO., ST. CLEMENT Rev. Lowell Will; Deacon Tom Lambert.
Res.: 422 E. Sycamore, 47601. Tel: 812-897-4653; Fax: 812-897-4653.
Catechesis / Religious Program—Deborah Findley, D.R.E. Students 70.

CANNELBURG, DAVIESS CO., ALL SAINTS, Attended by St. Peter, Montgomery. Rev. James Koressel; Deacon Michael Jones.
Tel: 812-486-3149.
Catechesis / Religious Program—Twinned with St. Peter Montgomery Donna Bradley, D.R.E.; Karen Kane, D.R.E. Students 90.

CELESTINE, DUBOIS CO., ST. PETER CELESTINE, [CEM] Rev. Eugene Schmitt; Deacon Michael Seibert.
Res.: 6864 E. State Rd. 164, P.O. Box 1, 47521-0001. Tel: 812-634-1875; Fax: 812-634-1875.
Catechesis / Religious Program—Glenda Prechtel,

D.R.E. Students 227.

CHRISNEY, SPENCER CO., ST. MARTIN, [CEM] Rev. Christopher A. Forler, Admin.; Deacon Michael Waninger.
Office:—58 S. Church St., 47611-0147. Tel: 812-362-7313; Fax: 812-362-7390.
Catechesis/Religious Program—Deacon Michael Waninger, D.R.E. Students 35.

DALE, SPENCER CO., ST. JOSEPH, [CEM] Rev. John Brosmer; Deacon James Woebkenberg.
Res.: 8 E. Maple St., R.R. 1, Box 684, 47523. Tel: 812-937-2200; Fax: 812-937-4349.
Catechesis/Religious Program—Emily Herr, D.R.E. Students 70.

DUBOIS, DUBOIS CO., ST. RAPHAEL, [CEM] Rev. Eugene Schmitt; Deacon Michael Seibert.
Res.: 5564 E. St. Raphael St., 47527. Tel: 812-678-2011; Fax: 812-678-5096.
Catechesis/Religious Program—Lavone Mangin, D.R.E. Students 195.

FERDINAND, DUBOIS CO.
1—ST. FERDINAND, [CEM] Rev. Jack J. Durchholz; Deacon James King.
Res.: 840 Maryland, P.O. Box 156, 47532. Tel: 812-367-1212; Fax: 812-367-1066.
Spiritual Life Center—Tel: 812-367-1092.
Catechesis/Religious Program—Mickie Paulin, D.R.E. Students 441.
2—ST. HENRY, [CEM] Rev. Damian Schmelz, O.S.B.
Res.: 1311 W. 1100 S., 47532-9710. Tel: 812-367-2731.
Catechesis/Religious Program—Laura McAninch, D.R.E. Students 104.

FORT BRANCH, GIBSON CO.
1—ST. BERNARD, [CEM] Rev. Anthony Ernst; Deacon Steve Hall.
Res.: 5342 E. State Rd., 47648-9632. Tel: 812-753-4568.
Catechesis/Religious Program—Rose Obert, D.R.E.; Jeanne Vieke, D.R.E. Students 60.
2—HOLY CROSS, [CEM] Rev. Anthony Ernst; Deacon Steve Hall.
Office: 305 E. Walnut St., 47648. Tel: 812-753-3548.
School—(Grades PreK-5) John Hollis, Prin.; Mary Jane Buehner, Librarian. Lay Teachers 11; Students 150.
Catechesis/Religious Program—Laura Goedde, D.R.E. Students 84.

HAUBSTADT, GIBSON CO.
1—ST. JAMES, [CEM] Rev. Kenneth Betz.
Res.: 12300 S. 50 W., 47639-9752. Tel: 812-867-5175; Fax: 812-867-5589.
School—(Grades PreK-8) Angie Johnson, Prin. Sisters 1; Lay Teachers 11; Students 171.
Catechesis/Religious Program—Connie Baehl, D.R.E. Students 52.
2—SS. PETER AND PAUL, [CEM] Rev. Anthony Ernst; Deacon William Brandle.
Res.: 211 N. Vine St., 47639. Tel: 812-768-6457; Fax: 812-768-6521.
School—(Grades PreK-5) Kalyn Herrmann, Prin. Lay Teachers 13; Students 166.
Catechesis/Religious Program—Laura Goedde, D.R.E. Students 196.

HUNTINGBURG, DUBOIS CO., VISITATION OF THE BLESSED VIRGIN MARY, [CEM] Rev. Mark O'Keefe, O.S.B.
Res.: 313 Washington St., 47542. Tel: 812-683-4903; Fax: 812-683-2747.
Catechesis/Religious Program—Michelle Fischer, D.R.E. Students 366.

IRELAND, DUBOIS CO., ANNUNCIATION OF THE BLESSED VIRGIN MARY, [CEM], (St. Mary's) Rev. Ronald Kreilein.
Res.: P.O. Box 67, 47545. Tel: 812-482-7041; Fax: 812-482-3699.
Catechesis/Religious Program—Martha Schmitt, D.R.E. Students 545.

JASONVILLE, GREENE CO., ST. JOAN OF ARC, Attended by St. Mary, Sullivan, Tel: 812-268-4088. Rev. Frank G. Renner.

JASPER, DUBOIS CO.
1—HOLY FAMILY, [JC] Rev. John Boeglin; Deacons Michael Helfter; David McDaniel.
Res.: 950 E. Church Ave., 47546-3797. Tel: 812-482-3076; Fax: 812-634-6998.
School—(Grades PreK-8) Sally Sternberg, Prin.; Judy Linette, Librarian. Sisters 1; Lay Teachers 18; Students 214.
Catechesis/Religious Program—Mary Altman, D.R.E. Students 56.
2—ST. JOSEPH, [JC] Revs. Raymond Brenner; William Traylor; Deacon Levi Schnellenberger.
Res.: 1020 Kundek St., 47546. Tel: 812-482-1805; Fax: 812-482-1814.
Catechesis/Religious Program—Pam Freyberger, D.R.E. Students 433.
3—PRECIOUS BLOOD, [JC] Rev. Gary Edward Kaiser; Sr. Betty Koressel, S.P., Pastoral Assoc.; Deacon Gerald Gagne.
Res.: 1517 Gregory Ln., 47546.
Church: 1385 W. Sixth St., 47546. Tel: 812-482-3589; Fax: 812-482-3589.
School—(Grades PreK-5) Joseph Brake, Prin.; Judy Buechlein, Librarian. Lay Teachers 16; Students 257.
Catechesis/Religious Program—Bonnie Meadows, D.R.E. Students 167.

LINTON, GREENE CO., ST. PETER, [CEM] Rev. Michael Madden.
Res.: 489 E St. N.E., 47441. Tel: 812-847-7821; Fax: 812-847-8892.
Catechesis/Religious Program—Marcia Waters, D.R.E. Students 48.

LOOGOOTEE, MARTIN CO.
1—ST. JOHN, [CEM] Rev. Joseph F. Erbacher.
Office: 408 Church St., 47553. Tel: 812-295-2225; Fax: 812-295-2031.
Catechesis/Religious Program—Julie Sutton, C.R.E. Students 249.
2—ST. MARTIN, [CEM] Rev. Joseph F. Erbacher.
Mailing Address: 408 Church St., 47553. Tel: 812-295-2225; Fax: 812-295-3445.
Catechesis/Religious Program—Roberta Burch, C.R.E. Students 28.

MARIAH HILL, SPENCER CO., MARY, HELP OF CHRISTIANS, [CEM] Deacon James Woebkenberg, Parish Life Coord.
Church: P.O. Box 170, 47556. Tel: 812-937-4326.
Catechesis/Religious Program—Twinned with St. John Chrysostom. Marilyn Satkamp, D.R.E. Students 96.

MONTGOMERY, DAVIESS CO., ST. PETER, [CEM] Rev. James Koressel; Deacon Michael Jones.
Res.: P.O. Box 10, 47558. Tel: 812-486-3149; Fax: 812-486-2571.
Catechesis/Religious Program—Twinned with All Saints Cannelburg Donna Bradley, D.R.E.; Karen Kane, D.R.E. Students 90.
Chapel—Corning, St. Patrick's

MOUNT VERNON, POSEY CO.
1—ST. MATTHEW, [CEM] Revs. Thomas Kessler; James Sauer; Deacon Thomas Evans.
Res.: 421 Mulberry St., 47620. Tel: 812-838-2535; Fax: 812-838-0237.
School—(Grades PreK-5) Vickie Wannemuehler, Prin. Lay Teachers 12; Students 84.
Catechesis/Religious Program—Michelle Gondi, C.R.E. Students 42.
2—ST. PHILIP, [CEM] Rev. Thomas Kessler; Deacon Thomas Evans.
Res.: 3500 St. Philip Rd. S., 47620. Tel: 812-985-2275; Fax: 812-985-2590.
School—(Grades PreK-8) Andrea Lodato Dickel, Prin.; Joan Frazer, Librarian. Sisters 1; Lay Teachers 15; Students 227.
Catechesis/Religious Program—Students 27.

NEW BOSTON, SPENCER CO., ST. JOHN CHRYSOSTOM, [CEM] Deacon Michael Waninger, Parish Life Coord.
Mailing Address: c/o P.O. Box 178, Chrisney, 47611.

NEW HARMONY, POSEY CO., HOLY ANGELS Revs. Thomas Kessler; James Sauer; Deacon Thomas Evans.
Mailing Address: 423 South St., P.O. Box 795, 47631. Tel: 812-682-4224.
Catechesis/Religious Program—Jackie Maier, C.R.E. Students 17.

NEWBURGH, WARRICK CO., ST. JOHN THE BAPTIST, [CEM] Rev. Joseph Ziliak; Deacons Vincent Bernardin, Pastoral Assoc.; Joseph Seibert; Anthony Schapker.
Res.: 625 Frame Rd., 47630. Tel: 812-490-1000; Fax: 812-490-1010.
School—(Grades PreK-8) Dr. Charlotte Bennett, Prin.; Dawn Durcholz, Librarian. Lay Teachers 24; Students 374.
Catechesis/Religious Program—Connie Schnapf, D.R.E.; Cindy Shoulders, D.R.E. Students 410.

OAKLAND CITY, GIBSON CO., BLESSED SACRAMENT Rev. Ronald S. Zgunda; Deacon Mark Wade.
Res.: 11092 E. Lincoln Hts. Rd., 47660. Tel: 812-749-4474.
Catechesis/Religious Program—Susan Williams, D.R.E. Students 21.

PETERSBURG, PIKE CO., SS. PETER AND PAUL Rev. David G. Fleck; Deacon Donald Haag.
Res.: 711 Walnut St., 47567. Tel: 812-354-6942.
Catechesis/Religious Program—Stacy Mosby, D.R.E. Students 29.

POSEYVILLE, POSEY CO., ST. FRANCIS XAVIER, [CEM] Rev. Edward Schnur; Deacon Mark McDonald.
Res.: 10 N. St. Francis Ave., 47633. Tel: 812-874-2258; Fax: 812-874-2639.
Catechesis/Religious Program—Twinned with St. Wendel Sherie Cooley, D.R.E. Students 156.
Convent—Sisters of St. Benedict 3.

PRINCETON, GIBSON CO., ST. JOSEPH, [CEM] Rev. Ronald S. Zgunda; Deacon Mark Wade.
Res.: 410 S. Race St., 47670. Tel: 812-385-2617; Fax: 812-385-2603.
School—(Grades PreK-8) Dan Gilbert, Prin.; Lucy Parnell, Librarian. Lay Teachers 10; Students 162.
Catechesis/Religious Program—Susan Williams, D.R.E. Students 75.

RED BRUSH, WARRICK CO., ST. RUPERT, [CEM] Rev. Lowell Will.
Church: 1244 Red Brush Rd., Newburgh, 47630. Tel: 812-853-3040.
Catechesis/Religious Program—Students 14.

ROCKPORT, SPENCER CO., ST. BERNARD, [CEM] Rev. Christopher A. Forler, Admin.; Deacon Michael Waninger.
Res.: 547 Elm St., 47635. Tel: 812-649-4811; Fax: 812-649-4176.
School—(Grades PreK-8) Sara Guth, Prin. Sisters 1; Lay Teachers 16; Students 167.
Catechesis/Religious Program—Carolyn Thorpe, D.R.E. Students 70.

ST. ANTHONY, DUBOIS CO., ST. ANTHONY, [CEM] Rev. Timothy Tenbarge; Deacon Ken Johanning.
Res.: 4444 S. Ohio St., P.O. Box 98, 47575-0098. Tel: 812-326-2777; Fax: 812-326-9028.
Catechesis/Religious Program—Janie Kempf, D.R.E. Students 204.

ST. JOSEPH, MARTIN CO., ST. JOSEPH, [CEM] Rev. Joseph F. Erbacher.
Mailing Address: 408 Church St., Loogootee, 47553. Tel: 812-295-2225.
Catechesis/Religious Program—Kathy Wittmer, C.R.E.; Peggy Padgett, C.R.E. Students 25.
Chapel—Barr Township, St. Mary

SANTA CLAUS, SPENCER CO., ST. NICHOLAS Rev. John Brosmer; Deacon James Woebkenberg.
Res.: 181 Balthazar, P.O. Box 351, 47579. Tel: 812-937-2380; Fax: 812-937-2385.
Catechesis/Religious Program—Students 156.

SCHNELLVILLE, DUBOIS CO., SACRED HEART, [CEM] Rev. Timothy Tenbarge; Deacon Ken Johanning.
Res.: 2504 Walnut St., 47580. Tel: 812-389-2535.
Catechesis/Religious Program—Mary Jane Durcholz, C.R.E. Students 113.

SHOALS, MARTIN CO., ST. MARY'S, [CEM] Attended by St. John, Loogootee, Tel: 812-295-2225. Rev. Joseph F. Erbacher.
Catechesis/Religious Program—Alice Boyd, C.R.E. Students 17.

SULLIVAN, SULLIVAN CO., ST. MARY Rev. Frank G. Renner.
Res.: 105 E. Jackson St., P.O. Box 506, 47882. Tel: 812-268-4088.
Catechesis/Religious Program—Colleen Ataras, D.R.E. Students 37.

VINCENNES, KNOX CO.
1—BASILICA OF ST. FRANCIS XAVIER, [JC] Rev. John H. Schipp.
Res.: 205 Church St., 47591. Tel: 812-882-5638; Fax: 812-882-4042.
See Vincennes Schools Consolidated, Vincennes under St. John the Baptist, Vincennes for details.
Catechesis/Religious Program—Patricia Earley, D.R.E. Students 30.
2—ST. JOHN THE BAPTIST, [JC] Rev. David G. Fleck; Ron Shafer, Pastoral Assoc.
Res.: 803 Main St., 47591. Tel: 812-882-1762; Fax: 812-886-9151.
Parish Center—828 Vigo St., 47591.
School—Vincennes Schools Consolidated, (Grades PreK-5) Lori Wissel, Prin.; Mary Nowaskie, Librarian. Lay Teachers 15; Students 239.
Catechesis/Religious Program—Sr. Regina Baker, D.R.E. Students 70.
3—SACRED HEART, [JC] Rev. Jason Gries.
Res.: 2004 N. Second St., 47591. Tel: 812-882-8382; Fax: 812-886-4676.
See Vincennes Schools Consolidated, Vincennes under St. John the Baptist, Vincennes for details.
Catechesis/Religious Program—Max Pawlowski, D.R.E. Students 118.
4—ST. THOMAS THE APOSTLE, [CEM] Rev. John H. Schipp, Mod.; Deacon Earl Ruppel, Parish Life Coord.
Office: 6268 S. St. Thomas Rd., 47591. Tel: 812-882-2478.
Catechesis/Religious Program—Students 39.
5—ST. VINCENT DE PAUL, [CEM] Rev. David G. Fleck.
Office: 1837 S. Hart St. Rd., 47591. Tel: 812-882-8968.
Catechesis/Religious Program—Candi Williams, D.R.E. Students 27.

WASHINGTON, DAVIESS CO.
1—IMMACULATE CONCEPTION, [JC] Closed. For inquiries for parish records, contact Our Lady of Hope, Washington
2—OUR LADY OF HOPE, [JC] Rev. Gordon Mann; Deacon Dennis Hilderbrand; Yvonne Evans, Pastoral Assoc.
Office: 315 N.E. Third St., 47501. Tel: 812-254-2883; Fax: 812-254-2884.
School—(Grades PreK-5), 310 N.E. Second St., 47501. Jeanne Heltzel, Prin. Washington Catholic Interparochial Schools Elementary. Lay Teachers 13; Students 314.
See High Schools, Diocesan under Institutions Located in the Diocese for details.

Catechesis/Religious Program—Gayle Ostby, D.R.E. Students 93.

Special Assignment:
Very Rev.—
Etienne, Bernard T., Vicar Gen., P.O. Box 4169, 47724-0169.
Revs.—
Gries, Jason, 918 W. Mill Rd., 47710-3956.
Lintzenich, Stephen P., 613 Cherry St., 47713.
Nemergut, Robert S., P.O. Box 432, Carlisle, 47838.
Walker, J. Kenneth, B.A., M.Div., M.C.L., J.C.L., Judicial Vicar, P.O. Box 4169, 47724-0169.
Zenthoefer, Alex, 1301 S. Green River Rd., 47715.

On Duty Outside the Diocese:
Rev.—
Kissel, Anthony, 14235 21st St., Dade City, FL 33523.

On Leave:
Revs.—
Frohlich, Attila
Silva, John

Absent on Medical Leave:
Rev.—
Steckler, Kenneth

Retired:
Rev. Msgr.—
Hirsch, Clinton F., J.C.L., Mount Vernon Nursing Home, 1415 Country Club Rd., Mount Vernon, 47620.
Revs.—
Ackerman, Donald K., 310 W. 4th, Jasper, 47546.
Busch, August, 5221 New Harmony Rd., 47720.
Deig, Robert A., St. John's Home, 1236 Lincoln Ave., 47714.
Dietsch, William, 2562 E. County Rd. 8505, Fort Branch, 47648.
Dilger, Donald, 6621 Smith Diamond Rd., 47712.
Egloff, Adolph, 2017 N. Second St., Vincennes, 47591.
Endress, James, S.T.L., M.S., M.A., 600 Cullen Ave., Apt. 510.
Graehler, Kenneth, 104 Southside Ave., 47501.
Heerdink, Eugene, 212 W. 13th St., Jasper, 47546.
Hut, Clemens, Friendship Village, 2525 E. Southern Ave., Tempe, AZ 85282.
Kane, Joseph, 8427 Gannon, Saint Louis, MO 63132-4906.
Kiesel, Leo C., 315 Doyle Ave., Loogootee, 47553.
Kuper, Raymond L., 1404 Timberlake Ln., 47710.
Lutz, Bernard A., 5044 E. 750 S., Fort Branch, 47648-9607.
Rogers, James, 801 N. Shortridge Rd., Apt. F4, Indianapolis, 46219.
Rohleder, Earl, 2540 Calle Rincon Bonito, Santa Fe, NM 87505.
Schipp, Ralph, 278 S. Tinsel Cir. E., Santa Claus, 47579.
Spaulding, Donald E., 603 E. National Hwy. 50, 47501.
Tempel, Theodore, 1236 Lincoln Ave., 47714.
Vogler, Jean, P.O. Box 4169, 47724-0169.
Wargel, William, 3130 N. Chigger Ridge Rd., Birdseye, 47513.

Permanent Deacons:
Altmeyer, Emil, St. Joseph Church, Evansville
Bach, Kevin, St. Benedict Cathedral; Catholic Center
Bernardin, Vincent, St. John the Baptist, Newburgh
Borowiecki, Christian, Holy Rosary, Evansville
Brandle, William, Sts. Peter & Paul, Haubstadt
Cook, David, St. Benedict Cathedral, Evansville
Dow, Lancaster, Jr., (Unassigned)
Evans, Thomas, St. Matthew, Mt. Vernon; Holy Angels, New Harmony; St. Philip, Mt. Vernon; Asst. Dir., Deacons
Flynn, James, St. Benedict Cathedral, Evansville
Franklin, David, St. Boniface
Gagne, Gerald, Precious Blood, Jasper
Goebel, Thomas, Corpus Christi, Evansville
Grannan, Richard, St. Joseph Parish, Evansville
Haag, Donald, SS. Peter & Paul Parish, Petersburg
Hall, Steve, St. Bernard Parish & Holy Cross, Fort Branch
Hayden, Robert, Holy Redeemer, Evansville
Helfter, Michael, Holy Family Parish, Jasper
Hilderbrand, Dennis, Our Lady of Hope, Washington
Hillenbrand, Francis, Christ the King, Evansville
Holsworth, Thomas, Master of Ceremony
Johanning, Kenneth, St. Anthony, Indiana; Sacred Heart, Schnellville
Jones, Michael R., St. Peter, Montgomery; All Saints, Cannelburg
Kempf, Thomas, St. Agnes, Evansville
King, James, St. Ferdinand, Ferdinand
Koressel, Charles, Holy Trinity, Evansville
Lambert, Thomas, St. Clement, Boonville
Lehman, Thomas, Sacred Heart, Evansville
Mayer, David, Holy Redeemer, Evansville
McDaniel, David, Holy Family, Jasper
McDonald, Mark, St. Wendel, St. Wendel; St. Francis Xavier, Poseyville
McMullen, John, Nativity, Evansville; Chap., Evansville State Hospital
Morris, Michael, Prison Ministry
Pierpont, Philip, (Unassigned)
Preske, Richard, (Retired)
Rice, David, Assoc. Clergy Personnel Dir., St. John, Daylight
Ruppel, Earl, St. Thomas, Vincennes
Russell, Dennis, St. Mary, Evansville
Schapker, Anthony, St. Theresa, Evansville; Interim Dir., Permanent Diaconate
Schnellenberger, Levi, St. Joseph, Jasper
Seibert, David, St. Theresa, Evansville; Interim Dir., Permanent Diaconate
Seibert, Joseph S., St. John the Baptist, Newburgh
Seibert, Michael, St. Peter, Celestine; St. Raphael, Dubois
Stofleth, Joseph, (Retired)
Sturgis, Joseph V., (Retired)
Wade, Mark, St. Joseph, Princeton; Blessed Sacrament, Oakland City
Waninger, Michael, St. Martin, Chrisney, St. Bernard, Rockport & St. John Chrysostom, New Boston
Wilkerson, Edward, (Unassigned)
Will, Cyril, Good Shephard, Evansville
Woebkenberg, James, Mary, Help of Christians, Mariah Hall, St. Joseph, Dale & St. Nicholas, Santa Claus
Yochum, Donald, St. Theresa, Evansville

INSTITUTIONS LOCATED IN THE DIOCESE

[A] HIGH SCHOOLS, DIOCESAN

EVANSVILLE. *Mater Dei High School*, 1300 Harmony Way, 47712. Tel: 812-426-2258; Fax: 812-421-5717. Web: www.materdeiwildcats.com. Timothy Dickel, Exec. Dir.; Chris Tanner, Prin. Sisters 2; Lay Teachers 42; Students 501.

Reitz Memorial High School, 1500 Lincoln Ave., 47714. Tel: 812-476-4973; Fax: 812-474-2942. Web: www.memorial.evansville.net. Cynthia Schneider, Prin.; Mr. Rick Wilgus, Asst. Prin., Student Svcs.; Rev. Alex Zenthoefer, Chap.; Mrs. Lisa Popham, Asst. Prin., Curriculum & Instruction. Lay Teachers 56; Students 781.

VINCENNES. *Jean Francois Rivet High School*, (Grades 6-12), (Vincennes Area), 210 Barnett St., 47591. Tel: 812-882-6215; Fax: 812-886-1939. Web: www.vincennescatholicschools.org. Janice Jones, Prin. Lay Teachers 14; Students 186.

WASHINGTON. *Washington Catholic Interparochial Schools*, (Grades 6-12), 201 N.E. Second St., 47501. Tel: 812-254-2050; Fax: 812-254-2050. Karie Craney, Prin.; Roberta Collison, Librarian. Sisters 1; Lay Teachers 15; Students 129.

[B] DAY CARE CENTERS

EVANSVILLE. *St. Vincent Center for Children and Families*, 730 W. Delaware, 47710. Tel: 812-424-4780; Fax: 812-425-2502. Web: stvincentsdaycarecenter.com. Sr. Brenda Fritz, Exec. Dir. Daughters of Charity of St. Vincent de Paul 1; Children 211.

[C] GENERAL HOSPITALS

EVANSVILLE. *St. Mary's Medical Center of Evansville, Inc.*, 3700 Washington Ave., 47750. Tel: 812-485-4000; Fax: 812-485-4927. Web: www.stmarys.org. Tim Flesch, Pres. & CEO St. Mary's Health System Services; Sr. Jane Burger, D.C., Sr. Vice Pres., Mission Integration. (Includes St. Mary, Warrick County) Daughters of Charity of St. Vincent de Paul 7; Bed Capacity 455; Patients Assisted Annually 350,103.

JASPER. *Memorial Hospital and Health Care Center, Little Company of Mary Hospital of Indiana, Inc.*, 800 W. Ninth St., 47546. Tel: 812-996-2345; Fax: 812-996-0302. Ray Snowden, Pres. & CEO; Sr. M. Adrian Davis, L.C.M., Bd. Chairperson; Deacon Michael Jones, Chap. Sisters of the Little Company of Mary 2; Bed Capacity 144; Patients Assisted Annually 220,000; Palliative Care Patients 60.

Memorial Hospital Foundation, Inc., 800 W. 9th St., 47546. Tel: 812-996-8426; Fax: 812-996-8427. William A. Rubino, Chair Person; Michael A. Jones, Exec. Dir.

[D] HOMES FOR AGED

EVANSVILLE. *St. John's Home for the Aged*, 1236 Lincoln Ave., 47714. Tel: 812-464-3607; Fax: 812-464-2141. Sr. Mary Sylvia Karl, L.S.P., Pres.; Rev. Theodore Tempel, Chap. (Retired). Little Sisters of the Poor 8; Residents 47; Apartments 22.

Seton Residence, 9200 New Harmony Rd., 47720-8918. Tel: 812-963-7600; Fax: 812-963-7654. Sr. Theresa Peck, D.C., Admin. Home for the Senior Sisters of the Daughters of Charity of St. Vincent de Paul.

FERDINAND. *Hildegard Health Center, Inc.*, 802 E. 10th St., 47532-9239. Tel: 812-367-2022; Fax: 812-367-1309. Web: www.thedome.org. Sr. Kathy Bilskie, O.S.B. Sisters on Staff 4; Sisters in Residence 17.

JASPER. *Providence Home, Nursing Home for the Needy*, 520 W. Ninth St., 47546. Tel: 812-482-6603; Fax: 812-481-1778. Michael O'Brien, Admin.; Rev. Angelo Quadrini, Supr. Conducted by the Sons of Divine Providence. Residents 58; Staff 75.

[E] RETREAT HOUSES

EVANSVILLE. *Sarto Retreat House*, 4200 N. Kentucky Ave., P.O. Box 4169, 47724-0169. Tel: 812-424-5536; Fax: 812-421-1334. Margie Nord, Coord.

FERDINAND. *Kordes Center*, 841 E. 14th St., 47532-9216. Tel: 812-367-1411; Fax: 812-367-2313. Email: kordes@thedome.org. Web: www.thedome.org/kordes. Sr. Marilyn Schroering, O.S.B., Dir.

[F] CONVENTS AND RESIDENCES FOR SISTERS

EVANSVILLE. *Daughters of Charity of St. Vincent de Paul - Mater Dei House*, 9400 New Harmony Rd., 47720. Tel: 812-963-3341; Fax: 812-963-7589. Web: www.daughtersofcharity.org. Sr. Theresa Peck, D.C., Admin.; Rev. John Clark, C.M., Chap. Sisters in Residence 12.

Monastery of St. Clare, 6825 Nurrenbern Rd., 47712. Tel: 812-425-4396; Fax: 812-425-0089. Sisters Jeanne Maffet, O.S.C., Abbess; Catherine K. Janeway, O.S.C., Vicaress. Franciscan Poor Clare Nuns. Solemnly Professed Cloistered Nuns 8.

FERDINAND. *Sisters of St. Benedict of Ferdinand, IN, Inc., Monastery Immaculate Conception*, 802 E. Tenth St., 47532. Tel: 812-367-1411; Fax: 812-367-2313. Web: www.thedome.org. Sr. Kristine Harpenau, O.S.B., Prioress; Rev. Pius Klein, O.S.B., Chap., St. Meinrad Chaplain Team Coord. Sisters of St. Benedict. Professed Sisters in Community 154; Temporary Commitment 3; Postulants 2; Novices 1.

[G] NEWMAN CENTERS & CAMPUS MINISTRY

EVANSVILLE. *Newman Center for the University of Evansville* 1901 Lincoln Ave., 47714. Tel: 812-477-6446.

University of Southern Indiana Newman Center 8113-A O'Daniel Ln., 47712. Tel: 812-465-7095. Christine Hoehn, Dir.

OAKLAND CITY. *Oakland City College Newman Center* R.R. 1, Box 72-A, 47660. Tel: 812-749-4474.

VINCENNES. *Vincennes University-Newman Center c/o St. John Parish*, 803 Main St., 47591. Tel: 812-882-1762.

[H] MISCELLANEOUS

EVANSVILLE. *Catholic Education Foundation, Inc.*, 520 S. Bennighof, 47714. Tel: 812-402-6700, Ext. 302. Margaret Angermeier, Dir.

Evansville Catholic Interparochial High Schools, 4200 N. Kentucky Ave., 47711. Tel: 812-424-5536.

Marian Educational Outreach, 520 S. Benninghof, 47714. Tel: 812-402-6700, Ext. 312; Fax: 812-474-2949. Bev Williamson, Dir.

Mission and Ministry, Inc., 9404 New Harmony Rd., 47720. Tel: 812-963-7580; Fax: 812-963-7526. Mary Wildeman, Exec. Dir.

Seton Health Corporation of Southern Indiana, 3700 Washington Ave., 47750. Tel: 812-485-1502; Fax: 812-485-7800. Gwen Sandefur, Senior Vice Pres., Strategic Devel. & Regl. Opers.

HUNTINGBURG. *Guadalupe Center*, 511 E. 4th St., Ste. 1, 47542.

JASPER. **Regional Catholic School Corporation*, 218 W. 13th St., 47546. Lay Teachers 8; Students 16.

LOOGOOTEE. *American-Innsbruck Alumni Association*, P.O. Box 4169, 47724-0169. Tel: 812-295-3214. Rev. Michael Scheible, Contact Person (Retired).

VINCENNES. *Old Cathedral Library & Museum, Inc.*, 205 Church St., 47591. Tel: 812-882-7016. Web: www.evansville-diocese.org/chancellor/oldcath.htm.

Rev. John H. Schipp, Registered Agent.

RELIGIOUS INSTITUTES OF MEN REPRESENTED IN THE DIOCESE

For further details refer to the corresponding bracketed number in the Religious Institutes of Men or Women section.

[0200]—*Benedictine Monks*—O.S.B.

[1330]—*Congregation of the Mission Western Province*—C.M.

RELIGIOUS INSTITUTES OF WOMEN REPRESENTED IN THE DIOCESE

[0230]—*Benedictine Sisters of Pontifical Jurisdiction*—O.S.B.

[1000]—*Congregation of Divine Providence*

[1730]—*Congregation of the Third Order of St. Francis*—O.S.F.

[0760]—*Daughters of Charity of St. Vincent de Paul*—D.C.

[2340]—*Little Sisters of the Poor*—L.S.P.

[3760]—*Order of St. Clare*—O.S.C.

[]—*Sisters for Christian Community*—S.F.C.C.

[3360]—*Sisters of Providence of Saint Mary-of-the-Woods, Indiana*—S.P.

[0260]—*Sisters of the Blessed Sacrament*—S.B.S.

[2270]—*Sisters of the Little Company of Mary*—L.C.M.

JOINT CEMETERIES

EVANSVILLE. *St. Joseph*, 2500 Mesker Park Dr., 47712.

JASPER. *Fairview*, 1215 Newton St., 47546.

VINCENNES. *Calvary*, P.O. Box 4, 47591.

WASHINGTON. *St. John*, 101 N. Meridian St., 47501-2931.

NECROLOGY

† Koch, Rev. Msgr. Charles J., (Retired)—Died Feb. 12, 2011

† Wannemuehler, Robert J., (Retired)—Died Jan. 26, 2011

An asterisk (*) denotes an organization that has established tax-exempt status directly with the IRS and is not covered by the USCCB Group Ruling.

Diocese of Fairbanks

Most Reverend

DONALD J. KETTLER

Bishop of Fairbanks; ordained May 29, 1970; appointed Bishop of Fairbanks June 7, 2002; installed August 22, 2002. *Office: 1316 Peger Rd., Fairbanks, AK 99709.*

Chancery Office: 1316 Peger Rd., Fairbanks, AK 99709. Tel: 907-374-9500; Fax: 907-374-9580.

Web: www.cbna.info

Email: info@cbna.org

Square Miles 409,849.

Corporate Title: "Catholic Bishop of Northern Alaska."

Established as the Prefecture Apostolic of Alaska, July 27, 1894.

Erected into the Vicariate of Alaska, Dec. 22, 1916; elevated to a Diocese, Aug. 8, 1962.

Comprises all of the State of Alaska, north of the old Territorial Third Judicial Division whose boundary extended in a northwesterly direction from the Canadian Border along the crest of the Alaska range to Mount McKinley, thence southwesterly to Cape Newenham and west along the 58 parallel north of the Pribilof Islands.

For legal titles of parishes and diocesan institutions, consult the Chancery Office.

STATISTICAL OVERVIEW

Personnel	
Bishop	1
Priests: Diocesan Active in Diocese	11
Priests: Diocesan Active Outside Diocese	2
Priests: Retired, Sick or Absent	2
Number of Diocesan Priests	15
Religious Priests in Diocese	7
Total Priests in Diocese	22
Extern Priests in Diocese	4
Ordinations:	
Diocesan Priests	1
Permanent Deacons	1
Permanent Deacons in Diocese	25
Total Brothers	2
Total Sisters	12
Parishes	
Parishes	46
With Resident Pastor:	
Resident Diocesan Priests	10
Resident Religious Priests	2
Without Resident Pastor:	
Administered by Priests	4
Administered by Deacons	2
Administered by Professed Religious Men	4
Administered by Lay People	15
Administered by Pastoral Teams, etc.	9
Pastoral Centers	2
Professional Ministry Personnel:	
Brothers	2
Sisters	12
Welfare	
Special Centers for Social Services	1
Total Assisted	2,000
Educational	
High Schools, Diocesan and Parish	1
Total Students	204
Elementary Schools, Diocesan and Parish	1
Total Students	292
Catechesis/Religious Education:	
High School Students	240
Elementary Students	755
Total Students under Catholic Instruction	1,491
Teachers in the Diocese:	
Lay Teachers	51
Vital Statistics	
Receptions into the Church:	
Infant Baptism Totals	323
Minor Baptism Totals	21
Adult Baptism Totals	31
Received into Full Communion	52
First Communions	219
Confirmations	134
Marriages:	
Catholic	31
Interfaith	14
Total Marriages	45
Deaths	165
Total Catholic Population	13,496
Total Population	162,941

Former Bishops—Most Revs. JOSEPH RAPHAEL CRIMONT, S.J., D.D., Vicar-Apostolic of Alaska; ord. Aug. 26, 1888; appt. Prefect-Apostolic March 28, 1904; appt. Vicar-Apostolic of Alaska Feb. 15, 1917; preconized Titular Bishop of Ammaedera, March 22, 1917; cons. July 25, 1917; died May 20, 1945; WALTER J. FITZGERALD, S.J., D.D., Vicar-Apostolic of Alaska; ord. May 16, 1918; appt. Coadjutor Vicar-Apostolic of Alaska cum jure successionis, Dec. 14, 1938; cons. Titular Bishop of Tymbrias, Feb. 24, 1939; succeeded to as Vicar-Apostolic of Alaska, May 20, 1945; died July 19, 1947; GEORGE T. BOILEAU, S.J., D.D., appt. Coadjutor Bishop cum jure successionis, April 21, 1964; cons. Titular Bishop of Ausuccura, July 31, 1964; died Feb. 25, 1965; FRANCIS D. GLEESON, S.J., D.D., ord. July 29, 1926; appt. Titular Bishop of Cotenna and Vicar-Apostolic of Alaska Jan. 8, 1948; cons. April 5, 1948; appt. First Bishop of Fairbanks Aug. 8, 1962; retired Nov. 30, 1968; transferred to Titular See of Cuicul in Numidia and Assistant at the Pontifical Throne by Pope Paul VI, Feb. 3, 1969; died April 30, 1983; ROBERT LOUIS WHELAN, S.J., D.D., retired Bishop of Fairbanks; ord. June 17, 1944; appt. Titular Bishop of Sicilibba and Coadjutor Bishop of Fairbanks, cum jure successionis Dec. 6, 1967; cons. Feb. 22, 1968; succeeded to Nov. 30, 1968; retired July 28, 1985; died Sept. 15, 2001; MICHAEL J. KANIECKI, S.J., D.D., ord. June 5, 1965; appt. Coadjutor Bishop cumjure successionis, March 8, 1984; cons. May 1, 1984; succeeded to July 28, 1985; died Aug. 6, 2000.

Vicar General—Rev. PATRICK D. BERGQUIST, V.G.

Superior Regular—Rev. GREGG D. WOOD, S.J., Pastoral Ministry, Mailing Address: Bro. Joe Prince House, P.O. Box 3064, Bethel, 99559.

Chancery Office—1316 Peger Rd., Fairbanks, 99709. Tel: 907-374-9500; Fax: 907-374-9580.

Chancellor and Special Assistant—ROBERT HANNON, 1316 Peger Rd., Fairbanks, 99709. Tel: 907-374-9510.

Secretary to Bishop—GERALDINE JAUHOLA.

Treasurer—Deacon GEORGE W. BOWDER.

Diocesan Tribunal—

Tribunal Administrator—BARBARA THIEME TOLLIVER.

Judicial Vicar—Rev. PATRICK TRAVERS, J.C.L., J.D.

Defenders of the Bond—Revs. SCOTT GARRETT, J.C.L.; TOM BRUNDAGE, J.C.L.

Promoter of Justice—Sr. CAROLYN A. ROEBER, O.P.

Auditor—BARBARA THIEME TOLLIVER.

Notaries—Tribunal: BARBARA THIEME TOLLIVER; GERALDINE JAUHOLA.

Presbyteral Council—Revs. GREGG D. WOOD, S.J.; GERALD ORNOWSKI, M.I.C.; PATRICK D. BERGQUIST, V.G.; JOHN MARTINEK; JOSEPH HEMMER, O.F.M.; ROBERT FATH; ROSS TOZZI; STANISLAW JASZEK; CHARLES J. PETERSON, S.J.

Consultors—Revs. CHARLES J. PETERSON, S.J.; GREGG D. WOOD, S.J.; JOHN MARTINEK; JOSEPH HEMMER, O.F.M.; ROSS TOZZI; GERALD ORNOWSKI, M.I.C.; STANISLAW JASZEK.

Diocesan Archivist—VACANT, Archivist; DAVID SCHIENLE, Archives Clerk.

Diocesan Offices and Directors

Alaskan Shepherd Office—Mrs. PATTY WALTER, Editor & Dir. Direct Mail Fundraising. Tel: 907-374-9536; LIN CRAIG, Office Mgr., 1312 Peger Rd., Fairbanks, 99709. Tel: 907-374-9532.

Catholic Campaign for Human Development—Deacon GEORGE BOWDER.

Campus Ministry—MARY PAT BOGER, 514 Copper Ln. - UAF, P.O. Box 750166, Fairbanks, 99775-0166. Tel: 907-474-6776.

Communications, Radio and TV—NORMAN "RIC" E. SCHMIDT, Gen. Mgr.; KELLY BRABEC, Prog. Dir., Mailing Address: P.O. Box 988, Nome, 99762. Tel: 907-443-5221.

The Children and Family Life Center—VACANT.

Construction Committee—JAMES WALTER; Deacons PAUL PERREAULT, Chm.; GEORGE W. BOWDER.

Engaged Encounter—Deacon ROBERT P. BARNARD.

Fairbanks Counseling and Adoption—CAMILLE CONNELLY-TERHUNE, Exec. Dir., 912 Barnette, P.O. Box 71544, Fairbanks, 99707. Tel: 907-456-4729.

Finance Advisory Board—CYNTHIA KLEPASKI; SUSAN MURPHY; Rev. PATRICK D. BERGQUIST, V.G.; JEFFREY JOHNSON; HAROLD ESMAILKA; JOSEPH PASKVAN; Sr. KATHLEEN RADICH, O.S.F.; Deacon ROBERT FROEHLE; JEFFREY BROOKS; CLAIRE WINGFIELD.

Hispanic Ministry—Rev. FREDERICK C. BAYLER.

Human Resources—RONNIE ROSENBERG, Dir.

Native Alaskan Ministries Coordinators—Sr. KATHLEEN RADICH, O.S.F., Mailing Address: St. Mary's Conf. Ctr., P.O. Box 29, St. Marys, 99658; Bro. ROBERT J. RUZICKA, O.F.M., Mailing Address: Our Lady of the Snows, P.O. Box 89, Nulato, 99765.

Ministry of Sick, Aged and Imprisoned—ANN NICKERSON, Dir. Stephen Ministry. Tel: 907-374-9553.

Office of Child Protection—BARBARA THIEME TOLLIVER, Dir. Tel: 907-374-9516.

Office of Religious Education—Sr. DOROTHY GILOLEY, S.S.J., Dir. Tel: 907-374-9572.

Office of Native Permanent Diaconate—Rev. THEODORE E. KESTLER, S.J., Mailing Address: P.O. Box 29, St. Marys, 99658. Tel: 907-438-2336; Fax: 907-438-2536.

Office of Urban Permanent Diaconate—Rev. GERALD ORNOWSKI, M.I.C.

Office of Worship—Sr. JOSEPHINE ALORALREA, O.S.U., Liturgy Coord.

Pontifical Association of the Holy Childhood—Chancery Office.

Pontifical Society for Propagation of the Faith—Deacon GEORGE W. BOWDER, Chancery Office.

Schools—NANCY HANSON, Acting Exec. Dir., 615 Monroe St., Fairbanks, 99701. Tel: 907-456-7970.

Victim Assistance Coordinator—BARBARA THIEME TOLLIVER.

Vocation Director—Rev. ROSS TOZZI, Mailing Address: P.O. Box 1010, Nome, 99762. Tel: 907-443-5527.

Urban Native Ministry Liaison—Sr. JOSEPHINE ALORALREA, O.S.U. Tel: 907-374-9573.

Retrouvaille—Deacon GEORGE W. BOWDER; WANDA BOWDER.

Youth Ministry—VACANT.

Catholic Relief Services—Deacon GEORGE BOWDER.

Catholic Trust of Northern Alaska—Deacon GEORGE BOWDER, Exec. Officer.

CLERGY, PARISHES, MISSIONS AND PAROCHIAL SCHOOLS

CITY OF FAIRBANKS

NORTH STAR BOROUGH

1—SACRED HEART CATHEDRAL CATHOLIC CHURCH FAIRBANKS (1966) Most Rev. Donald J. Kettler; Rev. Clint Landry, Parochial Vicar; Dr. Charles Geist, Pastoral Admin.
Res.: 2890 N. Kobuk Ave., 99709. Tel: 907-374-9938.
Church: 2501 Airport Way, 99709. Tel: 907-474-9032; Fax: 907-479-3327. Email: shc@mosquitonet.com. Web: www.sacredheartak.org.
Catechesis/Religious Program—Gigi Martinez, D.R.E. Students 124.

2—IMMACULATE CONCEPTION CATHOLIC CHURCH FAIRBANKS (1904) [JC] Rev. Frederick C. Bayler; Deacons Robert Mantei; Sean Stack.
Res.: 115 N. Cushman St., 99701. Tel: 907-452-3533; Fax: 907-456-3336.
Catechesis/Religious Program—Deacon Robert P. Barnard, D.R.E. Students 39.

3—ST. MARK UNIVERSITY CATHOLIC PARISH FAIRBANKS (1977) Mary Pat Boger, Parish Admin.
Mailing Address: P.O. Box 750166, 99775-0166.
Res.: 514 Copper Ln.-UAF, P.O. Box 750166, 99775-0166. Tel: 907-474-6776.

4—ST. RAPHAEL CATHOLIC CHURCH FAIRBANKS (1991) Rev. Kasparaj Mallavarapu, Sacramental Min.; Lisa Brose, Pastoral Admin.
Res.: 1125 Old Steese Hwy. N., 99710. Tel: 907-457-6603; Fax: 907-457-4461.
Catechesis/Religious Program—Students 49.

OUTSIDE CITY OF FAIRBANKS

ALAKANUK, ST. IGNATIUS CATHOLIC CHURCH ALAKANUK (1954), (Yup'ik), [CEM] [JC] Mary Ayunerak, Parish Admin.; Deacons Denis Shelden, Pastoral Coord.; Joseph Phillip, (Retired); Emmanuel Stanislaus; John Ayunerak.
Res.: P.O. Box 53, 99554. Tel: 907-238-3914.
Mission—St. Peter Catholic Church Nunam Iqua P.O. Box 45, Nunam Iqua, 99666. Tel: 907-498-4246.

ANIAK, ST. THERESA CATHOLIC CHURCH ANIAK (1935), (Yup'ik), [CEM] Edith Morgan, Acting Pastoral Coord.
Res.: P.O. Box 308, 99557. Tel: 907-675-4448.
Catechesis/Religious Program—Students 9.

BARROW, NORTH SLOPE BOROUGH, ST. PATRICK CATHOLIC CHURCH BARROW (1954) [JC], (Served out of Fairbanks) Sue Bowen, Parish Admin.
Mailing Address: P.O. Box 389, 99723. Tel: 907-852-3515. Email: stpatrickschurch@barrow.com.
Catechesis/Religious Program—Students 3.

BETHEL, IMMACULATE CONCEPTION CATHOLIC CHURCH BETHEL (1942) Rev. Charles J. Peterson, S.J.; Susan Murphy, Parish Admin.; Deacons Louie Andrew; Brian McCaffery; Al Wasuli; Ryan O'Connell, Youth Min.
Res.: 775 2nd Ave., P.O. Box 429, 99559. Tel: 907-543-2464; Fax: 907-543-3142.
Catechesis/Religious Program—Students 85.

CHEFORNAK, ST. CATHERINE OF SIENA CATHOLIC CHURCH CHEFORNAK (1937), (Yup'ik), [CEM] Agnes Kairaiuak, Acting Parish Admin.; Deacons David Panruk; Joe Avugiak.
Res.: P.O. Box 90, 99561. Tel: 907-867-8702.
Catechesis/Religious Program—Students 150.

CHEVAK, SACRED HEART CATHOLIC CHURCH CHEVAK (1952), (Cup'ik), [CEM] Clotilda Tikium, Acting Parish Admin.; Deacons Stephan F. Smart Sr.; David Boyscout, (Retired); Peter Boyscout.
Res.: P.O. Box 249, 99563. Tel: 907-858-7826.
Catechesis/Religious Program—Charlene Tuluk, D.R.E. Students 37.

DELTA JUNCTION, OUR LADY OF SORROWS CATHOLIC CHURCH DELTA JUNCTION (1959) Rev. John Martinek.
Res.: 2565 Deborah St., Box 446, 99737. Tel: 907-895-5232. Email: olsdelta@wildak.net.
Catechesis/Religious Program—Students 34.
Mission— Eagle.

EMMONAK, SACRED HEART CATHOLIC CHURCH EMMONAK (1953), (Yup'ik), [JC] Larry Yupanik, Acting Parish Admin.; Deacon Raymond Waska.
P.O. Box 69, 99581.
Res.: P.O. Box 190, 99581. Tel: 907-949-1012.
Catechesis/Religious Program—Matrona Kozevenikoff, D.R.E.; Patrick Tam, Dir. Adult Faith Formation.

GALENA, ST. JOHN BERCHMANS CATHOLIC CHURCH GALENA (1923), (Athabascan), Agnes Sweetsir, Admin.; Bro. R Justin Huber, O.F.M., Pastoral Min.
Res.: P.O. Box 131, 99741. Tel: 907-656-1240.
Catechesis/Religious Program—Students 20.

HEALY, DENALI BOROUGH, HOLY MARY OF GUADALUPE CATHOLIC CHURCH HEALY (1984) Rev. Patrick D. Bergquist; Barbara Walters, Pastoral Min.
P.O. Box 10508, 99743.
Church & Mailing Address: P.O. Box 32, 99743. Tel: 907-683-2535; 907-683-1007 (Rectory). Web: www.holymaryofguadalupe.org.
Catechesis/Religious Program—Students 29.
Mission— [JC] Denali National Park, 99755. Tel: 907-768-2768. *Clear Air Force Base*, Clear, 99704.

HOLY CROSS, HOLY FAMILY CATHOLIC CHURCH HOLY CROSS (1888) Connie Werba, Acting Parish Admin.
Res.: P.O. Box 101, 99602. Tel: 907-476-7144; Fax: 907-476-7144.
Catechesis/Religious Program—

HOOPER BAY, LITTLE FLOWER OF JESUS CATHOLIC CHURCH HOOPER BAY (1928), (Yup'ik), [JC] Unassigned.
Res.: P.O. Box 9, 99604. Tel: 907-758-4620.
Catechesis/Religious Program—

HUSLIA, ST. FRANCIS REGIS CATHOLIC CHURCH HUSLIA Bro. R Justin Huber, O.F.M., Parish Admin.
P.O. Box 89, 99746-0089. Tel: 907-656-1240.

KALSKAG, IMMACULATE CONCEPTION CATHOLIC CHURCH KALSKAG, Unassigned. P.O. Box 11, Bethel Census Area 99607. Tel: 907-471-2298.
Catechesis/Religious Program—Julia Durous, D.R.E.; Marous Dammeyer, D.R.E.

KALTAG, ST. TERESA CATHOLIC CHURCH, (Athabascan), [JC] Rev. Joseph Hemmer, O.F.M.
P.O. Box 69, 99748.
Res.: P.O. Box 69, 99748. Tel: 907-534-2218.
Catechesis/Religious Program—Students 8.

KOTLIK, ST. JOSEPH CATHOLIC CHURCH KOTLIK (1949), (Yup'ik), Rev. Mariusz Wirkowski; Pius Akran, Parish Admin.; Delle Hunt, Acting Pastoral Coord.
Church: P.O. Box 20228, 99620. Tel: 907-899-4715.
Catechesis/Religious Program—

KOTZEBUE, NORTHWEST ARCTIC BOROUGH, ST. FRANCIS XAVIER CATHOLIC CHURCH KOTZEBUE (1929) [CEM] [JC], (Served out of Nome) Winifred Reeve, Parish Admin.; Rev. Ross Tozzi.
342 Second St., 99752.
Res.: Box 358, 99752. Tel: 907-442-3239.
Catechesis/Religious Program—Students 12.

KOYUKUK, ST. PATRICK CATHOLIC CHURCH GALENA, (Athabascan), (Served out of Galena) Eliza Jones, Acting Parish Admin.; Bro. Bob Ruzicka, O.F.M.
Res.: P.O. Box 10, 99754. Tel: 907-927-2240.
Catechesis/Religious Program—Elizabeth Jones, D.R.E. Students 3.

MARSHALL, IMMACULATE HEART OF MARY CATHOLIC CHURCH MARSHALL (1930) Ms. Clara Shorty, Parish Admin.
Mailing Address: P.O. Box 69, 99585. Tel: 907-679-6639; Fax: 907-679-6639.
Catechesis/Religious Program—Students 14.
Mission—Our Lady of Guadalupe Catholic Church Russian Mission P.O. Box 56, Russian Mission, Wade Hampton Co. 99657. Tel: 907-584-5173.

MCGRATH, ST. MICHAEL CATHOLIC CHURCH MCGRATH (1960) Sharon Strick, Parish Admin.; Roger Seavoy, Co-Parish Admin.; Izabelle Harrington, Co-Parish Admin.
Res.: P.O. Box 141, 99627. Tel: 907-524-3928.

MOUNTAIN VILLAGE, ST. LAWRENCE CATHOLIC CHURCH MOUNTAIN VILLAGE Deacon Elmer Beans.
Res. & Mailing Address: P.O. Box 32205, 99632. Tel: 907-591-2348; Fax: 907-591-2348 (Prior Arrangement).
Catechesis/Religious Program—

NENANA, ST. THERESA CATHOLIC CHURCH NENANA (1922) [JC 2], Served out of Healy, AK. Penelope A. Forness, Acting Admin.
Mailing Address: P.O. Box 312, 99760. Tel: 907-832-5617.
Catechesis/Religious Program—Students 5.

NEWTOK, HOLY FAMILY CATHOLIC CHURCH NEWTOK (1950), (Yup'ik), [CEM] Ignatius Tommy, Acting Parish Admin.; Deacons Mark Tom, (Retired); John F. Andy.
Res.: P.O. Box 5569, 99559. Tel: 907-237-2427.
Catechesis/Religious Program—Freida Carl, D.R.E.

NIGHTMUTE, OUR LADY OF PERPETUAL HELP CATHOLIC CHURCH NIGHTMUTE (1950), (Yup'ik), [CEM] Jane Tulik, Acting Parish Admin.; Deacons Thomas Jumbo, (Retired); Camillus Tulik, (Retired); Ignatius Matthias; Christopher Tulik.
Res.: 99690. Tel: 907-647-6428.
Catechesis/Religious Program—Students 21.

NOME, ST. JOSEPH CATHOLIC CHURCH NOME (1901) Rev. Ross Tozzi; Maureen Koezuna, Parish Admin & Pastoral Facilitator; Deacon Robert Froehle.
Rectory—100 W. King Pl., P.O. Box 1010, 99762. Tel: 907-443-5527.
Church: 409 Steadman, 99762.
Catechesis/Religious Program—Students 25.
Mission—St. Jude Catholic Church Little Diomede P.O. Box 7999, Little Diomede, Nome Census Area 99762-7999.

NORTH POLE, FAIRBANKS, NORTH STAR BOROUGH, ST. NICHOLAS CATHOLIC CHURCH NORTH POLE (1975) Rev. Robert Fath; Anne Armour, Pastoral Coord.; Deacon Walt Gelinas.
Res.: 707 St. Nicholas Dr., 99705. Tel: 907-488-2595; Fax: 907-488-9625. Email: stnicks@acsalaska.net. Web: www.saintnicholasnorthpole.parishesonline.com.
Catechesis/Religious Program—Eileen Wehner, C.R.E.; Lisa Sagers, Youth Min. Students 119.

NULATO, OUR LADY OF SNOWS CATHOLIC CHURCH NULATO (1877), (Served out of Galena) Bro. Robert J. Ruzicka, O.F.M., Pastoral Admin.
Res.: P.O. Box 89, 99765. Tel: 907-898-2242.
Catechesis/Religious Program—Students 5.

PILOT STATION, ST. CHARLES SPINOLA CATHOLIC CHURCH PILOT STATION (1914), (Yup'ik), [JC] Rev. Stanislaw Jaszek, Ministerial Residence; Abraham Kelly, Acting Parish Admin.; Annie Greene, Acting Pastoral Coord.
Mailing Address: P.O. Box 5120, 99650. Tel: 907-549-3231; Fax: 907-549-3231.
Catechesis/Religious Program—

RUBY, ST. PETER-IN-CHAINS CATHOLIC CHURCH GALENA (1912) [JC] Unassigned. (Served out of Kaltag)
Res.: P.O. Box 207, 99768. Tel: 907-468-4413.
Catechesis/Religious Program—Students 6.

ST. MARYS, CHURCH OF THE NATIVITY CATHOLIC CHURCH ST. MARYS (1970) Rev. Theodore E. Kestler, S.J.
Mailing Address: P.O. Box 109, 99658.
Res.: P.O. Box 49, 99658. Tel: 907-438-2536.
Catechesis/Religious Program—

ST. MICHAEL, ST. MICHAEL CATHOLIC CHURCH ST. MICHAEL (1895) [JC] Rita Oyoumick, Acting Parish Admin.
Res.: P.O. Box 29, 99659. Tel: 907-923-3151.
Catechesis/Religious Program—

SCAMMON BAY, BLESSED SACRAMENT CATHOLIC CHURCH SCAMMON BAY (1968) [JC] Evelyn Ulak, Acting Parish Admin.
Res.: P.O. Box 170, 99662. Tel: 907-558-5229.
Catechesis/Religious Program—Elizabeth Kasayuli, D.R.E.

STEBBINS, ST. BERNARD CATHOLIC CHURCH STEBBINS (1908) [JC] Francis Pete, Acting Parish Admin.
Res.: P.O. Box 71102, 99671. Tel: 907-934-3151.
Catechesis/Religious Program—Students 8.

TANANA, ST. ALOYSIUS CATHOLIC CHURCH GALENA (1887) [JC], (Served out of Fairbanks) Lois Huntington, Parish Admin.
Res.: P.O. Box 6, 99777. Tel: 907-366-7238.

TELLER, ST. ANN CATHOLIC CHURCH TELLER (1909) Unassigned. (Served out of Nome), General Delivery, 99778.
Res.: 100 W. King Pl., Nome, 99762. Tel: 907-443-5527.

TOK, HOLY ROSARY CATHOLIC CHURCH TOK (1949), (Served out of Delta Junction) Sr. Margaret Butler, S.S.J., Parish Admin.
Res.: P.O. Box 369, 99780. Tel: 907-883-4111. Email: hrtok@aptalaska.net.
Catechesis/Religious Program—Students 12.

TOKSOOK BAY, ST. PETER THE FISHERMAN CATHOLIC CHURCH TOKSOOK BAY (1964) [CEM] Maggie John, Parish Admin./Pastoral Coord.; Deacons James Charlie; Nick Therchik Sr.; Joe Asuluk.
Mailing Address: P.O. Box 37046, 99637. Tel: 907-427-7813; Fax: 907-427-7813. Email: stpeter@gci.net.
Catechesis/Religious Program—Tel: 907-427-7826; Fax: 907-427-7820. Students 189.

TUNUNAK, ST. JOSEPH CATHOLIC CHURCH TUNUNAK (1889), (Yup'ik), [CEM] Iris Angaiak, Acting Parish Admin.; Sophie Oscar, Acting Pastoral Coord.; Deacon Dick Lincoln, (Retired).
Res.: P.O. Box 9, 99681. Tel: 907-652-6214.
Catechesis/Religious Program—

UNALAKLEET, CHURCH OF THE HOLY ANGELS CATHOLIC CHURCH UNALAKLEET (1952) Anne Ivanoff, Parish Admin.
Res.: P.O. Box 152, 99684. Tel: 907-624-3711.

Chaplains of Public Institutions:
Revs.—
Mallavarapu, Kasparaj, Fairbanks Memorial Hospital
Thomson, Sean P., Fairbanks Correctional Center

Leave of Absence:
Revs.—
de Verteuil, Jack
Wallner, Gerhard

Retired:
Rev.—
Hinsvark, John (Retired), 200 W. 34th Ave., #545, Anchorage, 99503.

Permanent Deacons:
Andrew, Louie, Immaculate Conception, Bethel
Andy, John F., Holy Family, Newtok
Asuluk, Joe, St. Peter Fisherman, Toksook Bay
Avugiak, Joe, St. Catherine, Chefornak
Ayunerak, John, St. Ignatius, Alakanuk
Barnard, Robert P., Immaculate Conception, Fairbanks
Beans, Elmer, Mountain Village
Bowder, George, St. Raphael, Fairbanks
Boyscout, David, (Retired), Sacred Heart Church, Chevak
Boyscout, Peter, Sacred Heart, Chevak
Charlie, James, St. Peter the Fisherman, Toksook Bay
Froehle, Robert, St. Joesph Catholic Church, Nome
Gelinas, Walt, St. Nicholas, North Pole
Jumbo, Thomas, (Retired), Our Lady of Perpetual Help, Nightmute
Lincoln, Dick, (Retired), St. Joseph's, Tununak
Mantei, Robert, Immaculate Conception, Fairbanks
Matthias, Ignatius, Our Lady of Perpetual Help, Nightmute
McCaffrey, Brian, Immaculate Conception, Bethel
Panruk, David, St. Catherine, Chefornak
Perreault, Paul, Fairbanks
Phillip, Joseph, (Retired), St. Ignatius, Alakanuk
Shelden, Denis, St. Ignatius, Alakanuk
Smart, Stephan F., Sr., Sacred Heart Church, Chevak
Stack, Sean, Immaculate Conception, Fairbanks
Stanislaus, Emmanuel, St. Ignatius, Alakanuk
Therchik, Nick, St. Peter the Fisherman, Toksook Bay
Tom, Mark, (Retired), Holy Family, Newtok
Tulik, Camillus, (Retired), Our Lady of Perpetual Help, Nightmute
Tulik, Christopher, Our Lady of Perpetual Help, Nightmute
Waska, Ray, Sacred Heart, Emmonak
Wasuli, Aloysius, Immaculate Conception, Bethel

INSTITUTIONS LOCATED IN THE DIOCESE

[A] HIGH SCHOOLS, DIOCESAN

FAIRBANKS. *Monroe Catholic Junior-Senior High School*, (Grades 7-12), 615 Monroe St., 99701. Tel: 907-452-2044; Fax: 907-452-5978. Email: monroeprincipal@catholic-schools.org. Web: www.catholic-schools.org. Vincent Fantazzi, Prin. Lay Teachers 28; Students 204.

[B] GRADE SCHOOLS, DIOCESAN

FAIRBANKS. *Immaculate Conception Grade School*, (Grades PreK-6), 615 Monroe St., 99701. Tel: 907-456-4574; Fax: 907-452-5978. Email: icsprincipal@catholic-schools.org. Web: www.catholic-schools.org. Helen Clark, Prin. Lay Teachers 23; Students 292.

[C] RESIDENCES FOR PRIESTS AND BROTHERS

FAIRBANKS. *Kobuk Center*, 2890 Kobuk Ave., 99709. Most Rev. Donald J. Kettler; Revs. Mark Szczur; Clint Landry; Gerald Ornowski, M.I.C.

Peger Road House, 1318 Peger Rd., 99709. Revs. Frederick C. Bayler; Sean P. Thomson.

[D] CONVENTS AND RESIDENCES OF SISTERS

NOME. *Little Sisters of Jesus*, Box 845, 99762. Tel: 907-443-2094. Sisters 3.

[E] MISCELLANEOUS LISTINGS

FAIRBANKS. *Catholic Trust of Northern Alaska*, 1320 Peger Rd., 99709. Tel: 907-374-9530. Email: finance@cbna.org. Deacon George Bowder, Exec. Officer.

House of Prayer, 1310 Peger Rd., 99709. Tel: 907-474-9379. Geraldine Jauhola, Coord.

**Monroe Foundation, Inc.*, 718 Betty St., 99707. Tel: 907-456-7970; Fax: 907-456-7481. Email: director@catholic-schools.org. Web: www.catholic-schools.org. Nancy Hanson, Pres.

Voice in the Wilderness Prayer Community, 4028 Birch Ln., 99709. Tel: 907-479-8512. Email: spiritfilled@gci.net. Gail Riedman, Dir.

GALENA. *Kateri Tekakwitha Center*, 1316 Peger Rd., 99709. Email: robert@cbna.org. Robert Hannon.

NOME. **KNOM Radio Mission, Inc.*, 107 W. Third Ave., Box 988, 99762. Tel: 907-443-5221; Fax: 907-443-5757. Email: business@knom.org. Web: www.knom.org. Norman "Ric" E. Schmidt, Gen. Mgr.; Kelly Brabec, Prog. Dir. Total Staff 12; Total in Residence 4.

ST. MARYS. *Brother Joe Prince Jesuit Community*, P.O. Box 3064, Bethel, 99559. Tel: 907-438-2536. Email: gwood@nwjesuits.org. Revs. Gregg D. Wood, S.J., Supr., Pastoral Ministry, Hooper Bay, Scammon Bay, Chevak, AK; Theodore E. Kestler, S.J., Asst. in Native Ministry Training Prog. & Deacon Prog. Pastoral Ministry, St. Mary's, Chefornak; Thomas G. Provinsal, S.J. Pastoral Ministry, Villages of Nelson Island & SW Coast; Charles J. Peterson, S.J. Pastoral Ministry, Bethel, AK. Priests 4; Total Assisted 6,000.

Native Ministry Training Program, P.O. Box 29, 99658-0029. Tel: 907-438-2832; Fax: 907-438-2823. Email: nmtp@juno.com. Sr. Ellen Callaghan, O.S.F., Dir.; Rev. Theodore E. Kestler, S.J., Scripture/Theology Resource Staff; Sr. Kathleen Radich, O.S.F. Staff 2; Total in Residence 2.

RELIGIOUS INSTITUTES OF MEN REPRESENTED IN THE DIOCESE

For further details refer to the corresponding bracketed number in the Religious Institutes of Men or Women section.

[0200]—*Benedictine Monks*—O.S.B.

[0520]—*Franciscan Friars and Brothers*—O.F.M.

[0690]—*Jesuit Fathers and Brothers*—S.J.

[0740]—*Marian Fathers*—M.I.C.

RELIGIOUS INSTITUTES OF WOMEN REPRESENTED IN THE DIOCESE

[2330]—*Little Sisters of Jesus*—L.S.J.

[0590]—*Sisters of Charity of Saint Elizabeth, Convent Station* (Northern Prov.)—S.C.

[1650]—*The Sisters of St. Francis of Philadelphia*—O.S.F.

[3830-12]—*Sisters of St. Joseph* (Philadelphia, PA)—S.S.J.

[4110]—*Ursuline Nuns*—O.S.U.

NECROLOGY

(No Deaths)

An asterisk (*) denotes an organization that has established tax-exempt status directly with the IRS and is not covered by the USCCB Group Ruling.

Diocese of Fall River

(Dioecesis Riverormensis)

Most Reverend

GEORGE W. COLEMAN

Bishop of Fall River; ordained December 16, 1964; appointed Bishop of Fall River April 30, 2003; consecrated July 22, 2003. *Office: P.O. Box 2577, Fall River, MA 02722.*

The Chancery: P.O. Box 2577, Fall River, MA 02722. Tel: 508-675-1311; Fax: 508-730-2447.

Email: chancery@dioc-fr.org

ESTABLISHED MARCH 12, 1904.

Square Miles 1,194.

Comprises Bristol, Barnstable, Dukes and Nantucket Counties, and the Towns of Marion, Mattapoisett and Wareham in Plymouth County, Massachusetts.

For legal titles of parishes and diocesan institutions, consult the Chancery Office.

STATISTICAL OVERVIEW

Personnel	
Bishop	1
Priests: Diocesan Active in Diocese	94
Priests: Diocesan Active Outside Diocese	8
Priests: Diocesan in Foreign Missions	1
Priests: Retired, Sick or Absent	47
Number of Diocesan Priests	150
Religious Priests in Diocese	89
Total Priests in Diocese	239
Extern Priests in Diocese	5
Ordinations:	
Diocesan Priests	1
Permanent Deacons in Diocese	84
Total Brothers	16
Total Sisters	179
Parishes	
Parishes	90
With Resident Pastor:	
Resident Diocesan Priests	73
Resident Religious Priests	10
Without Resident Pastor:	
Administered by Priests	7
Missions	11
Professional Ministry Personnel:	
Sisters	9
Lay Ministers	66
Welfare	
Homes for the Aged	5
Total Assisted	1,141
Residential Care of Children	1
Total Assisted	200
Day Care Centers	1
Total Assisted	45
Specialized Homes	2
Total Assisted	55
Special Centers for Social Services	4
Total Assisted	45,252
Residential Care of Disabled	2
Total Assisted	450
Other Institutions	142
Total Assisted	12,450
Educational	
Diocesan Students in Other Seminaries	6
Total Seminarians	6
Colleges and Universities	1
Total Students	2,520
High Schools, Diocesan and Parish	5
Total Students	2,856
Elementary Schools, Diocesan and Parish	21
Total Students	4,569
Catechesis/Religious Education:	
High School Students	3,932
Elementary Students	21,399
Total Students under Catholic Instruction	35,282
Teachers in the Diocese:	
Priests	7
Brothers	3
Sisters	10
Lay Teachers	718
Vital Statistics	
Receptions into the Church:	
Infant Baptism Totals	2,883
Minor Baptism Totals	96
Adult Baptism Totals	75
Received into Full Communion	223
First Communions	3,536
Confirmations	3,355
Marriages:	
Catholic	771
Interfaith	163
Total Marriages	934
Deaths	3,646
Total Catholic Population	313,115
Total Population	823,654

Former Bishops—Most Revs. WILLIAM STANG, D.D., ord. June 15, 1878; appt. March 12, 1904; cons. May 1, 1904; died Feb. 2, 1907; DANIEL F. FEEHAN, D.D., ord. Dec. 20, 1879; appt. July 2, 1907; cons. Sept. 19, 1907; died July 19, 1934; JAMES E. CASSIDY, D.D., ord. Sept. 8, 1898; appt. Titular Bishop of Ibora and Auxiliary, March 21, 1930; cons. May 27, 1930; succeeded to the See, July 28, 1934; died May 17, 1951; JAMES L. CONNOLLY, D.D., D.Sc.H., ord. Dec. 21, 1923; appt. Titular Bishop of Mylasa and Coadjutor "cum jure successionis," April 18, 1945; cons. May 24, 1945; succeeded to See, May 17, 1951; retired Oct. 30, 1970; died Sept. 12, 1986; DANIEL A. CRONIN, D.D., S.T.D., ord. Dec. 20, 1952; appt. Titular Bishop of Egnatia and Auxiliary Bishop of Boston, June 10, 1968; cons. Sept. 12, 1968; transferred to Fall River, Oct. 30, 1970; installed Dec. 16, 1970; transferred to Hartford, Dec. 9, 1991; His Eminence SEAN CARDINAL O'MALLEY, O.F.M.Cap., Ph.D., ord. Aug. 29, 1970; appt. Coadjutor Bishop of St. Thomas, Virgin Islands May 30, 1984; ord. Aug. 2, 1984; succeeded to See Oct. 16, 1985; appt. Bishop of Fall River June 16, 1992; installed Aug. 11, 1992; transferred to Palm Beach Sept. 3, 2002; installed Oct. 19, 2002; transferred to Boston July 1, 2003; installed July 30, 2003; Named Cardinal Priest with the title of Santa Maria della Vittoria, in the consistory of March 24, 2006; installed October 1, 2006.

Vicar General—Rev. Msgr. JOHN A. PERRY, V.G., Mailing Address: P.O. Box 2577, Fall River, 02722.

The Chancery—450 Highland Ave., Fall River, 02720. Mailing Address: P.O. Box 2577, Fall River, 02722-2577. Tel: 508-675-1311; Fax: 508-730-2447.

Chancellor—Rev. MICHAEL K. MCMANUS.

Secretary to the Bishop—Rev. KARL C. BISSINGER, 47 Underwood St., Fall River, 02720.

Diocesan Tribunal—887 Highland Ave., Fall River, 02720. Tel: 508-675-7150; Fax: 508-675-7295.

Judicial Vicar—Rev. PAUL F. ROBINSON, O.Carm., J.C.D.

Promotor Justitiae—Rev. JEFFREY CABRAL, J.C.L.

Judges—Revs. PAUL F. ROBINSON, O.Carm., J.C.D.; THOMAS L. RITA; RODNEY E. THIBAULT, J.C.L.; JAY T. MADDOCK, J.C.L.; JEFFREY CABRAL, J.C.L.

Defenders of the Bond—Rev. Msgrs. THOMAS J. HARRINGTON, J.C.L. (Retired); DANIEL F. HOYE, J.C.L.; Rev. GERARD A. HEBERT, J.C.L.

Procurator-Advocates—Revs. MARC H. BERGERON; BRUCE M. NEYLON.

Auditors—Revs. DANIEL W. LACROIX; JOHN J. PERRY; HENRY J. DAHL (Retired); MARK R. HESSION, J.C.L.; Deacon ROBERT L. SURPRENANT.

Office Manager—Mrs. DENISE D. BERUBE.

Notaries—Mrs. DENISE D. BERUBE; Mrs. HELENE P. BEAUDOIN.

Diocesan Consultors—Rev. Msgrs. STEPHEN J. AVILA, V.F.; EDMUND J. FITZGERALD, V.F.; Revs. GREGORY A. MATHIAS; MICHAEL K. MCMANUS; JOHN J. OLIVEIRA; Rev. Msgr. JOHN A. PERRY, V.G.; Rev. BARRY W. WALL (Retired).

Deans—Fall River Deanery: Rev. Msgr. EDMUND J. FITZGERALD, V.F., St. Thomas More Rectory, 386 Luther Ave., Somerset, 02726. Taunton Deanery: Very Rev. TIMOTHY P. REIS, V.F., St. Andrew the Apostle Rectory, 19 Kilmer Ave., Taunton, 02780. Attleboro Deanery: Rev. Msgr. STEPHEN J. AVILA, V.F., St. Mary's Rectory, 330 Pratt St., Mansfield, 02048. Cape Cod Deanery: Very Rev. GEORGE C. BELLENOIT, V.F., St. Pius Tenth Rectory, 5 Barbara St., South Yarmouth, 02664. New Bedford Deanery: Very Rev. RICHARD D. WILSON, J.C.L., V.F., Our Lady of Guadalupe Rectory, 233 County St., New Bedford, 02740.

Diocesan Offices and Directors

Apostolate for Persons with Disabilities—MATTHEW DANSEREAU, Coord., 1600 Bay St., Fall River, 02724. Tel: 508-997-7337; 508-679-8373.

Campus Ministry—

Director—Rev. MICHAEL A. CIRYAK.

Bristol Community College—Rev. MICHAEL A. CIRYAK, Interim, 777 Elsbree St., Fall River, 02720. Tel: 508-678-2811, Ext. 301.

University of Massachusetts Dartmouth—Rev. DAVID C. FREDERICI; Sr. MADELEINE TACY, O.P., 285 Old Westport Rd., North Dartmouth, 02747. Tel: 508-999-8872.

Wheaton College—Rev. JAMES R. LACKENMIER, C.S.C., Norton.

Massachusetts Maritime Academy—VACANT.

Cape Cod Campus Ministry—Rev. DAVID C. FREDERICI, 494 Slocum Rd., North Dartmouth, 02747. Tel: 508-993-2351; Fax: 508-993-2437.

Catholic Youth Organization—Rev. JAY T. MADDOCK, J.C.L., Dir., 403 Anawan St., Fall River, 02720.

Catholic Charities Appeal—VACANT.

Diocesan Apostolate to Hispanics—Very Rev. RICHARD D. WILSON, J.C.L., V.F., Diocesan Dir., Mailing Address: 233 County St., New Bedford, 02740. Tel: 508-996-5862; Fax: 508-990-0575. Area Offices: Fall River: Rev. GERMAN CORREA AGUDELO, Dir., Saint Mary's Cathedral, 327 Second St., Fall River, 02721. Tel: 508-672-9303. Attleboro: Rev. JOHN M. MURRAY, Dir., Saint Joseph's Church, 208 S. Main St., Attleboro, 02702. Tel: 508-222-1730. Taunton: Revs. JAMES J. DOHERTY, C.S.C, Dir. Tel: 508-822-7116; Fax: 508-822-7117; MARC F. FALLON, C.S.C., St. Mary's Church, 14 St.

Mary's Square, Taunton, 02780. Tel: 508-880-0410. New Bedford: Very Rev. RICHARD D. WILSON, J.C.L., V.F., Dir., Our Lady of Guadalupe Parish, 233 County St., New Bedford, 02740. Tel: 508-996-5862; Fax: 508-990-0575; Rev. HUGO G. CARDENAS, I.V.E., Dir., Mailing Address: St. Kilian's Church, 306 Ashley Blvd., New Bedford, 02746. Tel: 508-992-7587; Fax: 508-994-0281. Nantucket: Revs. MARCEL H. BOUCHARD, V.F., Pastor; CARLOS ALBERTO PATINO VILLA, Dir., Mailing Address: St. Mary/Our Lady of the Isle, P.O. Box 1168, Nantucket, 02554-1168; NOE PINEDA, Contact Person, Mailing Address: P.O. Box 2067, Nantucket, 02584. Tel: 508-843-5873; Fax: 508-325-7991. Cape Cod: Rev. CARLOS ALBERTO PATINO VILLA, Dir., 246 Main St., P.O. Box 428, West Harwich, 02671. Tel: 774-238-0714; Fax: 508-771-5940.

Director of Portuguese Ministry—Rev. JOHN J. OLIVEIRA, 230 Bonney St., New Bedford, 02744.

Diocesan Archives—Rev. BARRY W. WALL (Retired), Mailing Address: P.O. Box 2577, Fall River, 02722.

Diocesan Office of Communications—JOHN E. KEARNS JR., Dir., 887 Highland Ave., Fall River, 02720. Tel: 508-675-0211; Fax: 508-675-5204. Mailing Address: P.O. Box 7, Fall River, 02722.

Diocesan Director of Cemeteries—Rev. JOHN J. PERRY, 249 Whittenton St., Taunton, 02780.

Diocesan Education Center—Dr. MICHAEL S. GRIFFIN, Supt. Schools; Dr. DONNA BOYLE, Asst. Supt. Curriculum; KATHLEEN A. SIMPSON, Asst. Supt. Personnel; CLAIRE M. MCMANUS, S.T.L., Dir. Faith Formation; Deacon BRUCE J. BONNEAU, Asst. Dir. Faith Formation; FRANCES THOMAS, R.S.M., Asst. Dir. Catechesis & Faith Formation; ROSEMARY SARAIVA, Events Coord. & Bereavement Min.; CRYSTAL-LYNN MEDEIROS, Asst. Dir. Youth & Young Adult Ministries, Catholic Education Center, 423 Highland Ave., Fall River, 02720. Tel: 508-678-2828; Fax: 508-674-4218.

Diocesan Department of Pastoral Care for the Sick—Rev. MAREK S. TUPTYNSKI, Dir., Office: 306 South St., Somerset, 02726. Tel: 508-672-1523; Fax: 508-675-5787.

St. Anne's Hospital—795 Middle St., Fall River, 02721. Sr. CAROLE V.M. MELLO, O.P.; Deacon DAVID B. PEPIN; Sisters MARIE THERESE DYER, F.C.J.; GLORINA JUGO, O.P.; Mr. CHARLES FOLEY; Mr. DANIEL SULLIVAN; Mrs. MEREKA HULL.

Charlton Memorial Hospital—Highland Ave. at New Boston Rd., Fall River, 02720. Rev. ANDREW JOHNSON; Sisters ROBERTA O'CONNELL, F.C.J.; LUCILLE SOCCIARELLI, R.S.M.; Mrs. JANICE M. HART.

Sturdy Memorial Hospital—211 Park St., P.O. Box 649, Attleboro, 02703. Rev. MICHEL G. CORRIVEAU, C.P.M.; Deacon PAUL M. FOURNIER; Sr. ANNETTE LANGLOIS, S.A.S.V.

Cape Cod Hospital—27 Park St., Hyannis, 02601. Revs. THOMAS E. COSTA; PETER J. FOURNIER; Deacon GREGORY J. BECKEL; Mrs. KATHERINE SULLIVAN.

St. Luke's Hospital—101 Page St., New Bedford, 02741. Revs. RODNEY E. THIBAULT, J.C.L.; DAVID C. FREDERICI; Deacon ROBERT G. LORENZO; Sr. JUDITH COSTA, S.S.D., M.Div.; DENISE BENJAMIN.

Morton Hospital—Taunton, 02780. Rev. EDWARD A. MURPHY; Deacon PHILIP E. BEDARD.

Tobey Hospital—43 High St., Wareham, 02571. Revs. JOHN M. SULLIVAN; RONNIE PAUL FLOYD.

Rehabilitation Hospital of the Cape and Islands—311 Service Rd., East Sandwich, 02537. Ms. JUDI GRASSI; Deacon C. MICHAEL HICKEY.

Falmouth Hospital—100 Ter Heun Dr., Falmouth, 02540. Rev. JOSEPH H. MAURITZEN.

Diocesan Department of Catholic Social Services—ARLENE A. MCNAMEE, L.C.S.W., Exec. Dir., Office, 1600 Bay St., Box M, S. Station, Fall River, 02724. Tel: 508-674-4681; Fax: 508-675-2224.

Diocesan Finance Council—Members: Rev. Msgr. JOHN A. PERRY, V.G.; Mr. PAUL KAWA; FREDERIC J. TORPHY, Esq.; Mr. WILLIAM N. WHELAN; Rev. MICHAEL K. MCMANUS, Finance Officer; Deacon ALAN J. THADEU, Asst. Finance Officer, Mailing Address: P.O. Box 2577, Fall River, 02722. Tel: 508-675-1311.

Diocesan Guild for the Blind—Rev. BRUCE M. NEYLON, 36 Rockland St., P.O. Box 111, Fall River, 02724. Tel: 508-672-0423.

Diocesan Health Facilities—Rev. Msgr. EDMUND J. FITZGERALD, V.F., Dir., Office, 368 N. Main St., Fall River, 02720. Tel: 508-679-8154; Fax: 508-679-1422.

Diocesan Insurance Department—JOSEPH A. FIGLOCK, Benefits Mgr. & Insurance Coord.; SHAUN P. KERRIGAN, Asst. Benefits Mgr., Mailing Address: P.O. Box 2577, Fall River, 02722. Tel: 508-675-1311; Fax: 508-672-3802.

Diocesan Newspaper— "The Anchor" Rev. ROGER J. LANDRY, Exec. Editor; Mr. DAVID B. JOLIVET, Editor, Office, 887 Highland Ave., Fall River, 02722. Tel: 508-675-7151. Mailing Address: P.O. Box 7, Fall River, 02722.

Ecumenical Officer—Rev. MARC H. BERGERON, 818 Middle St., Fall River, 02721. Tel: 508-674-5651.

Episcopal Representative for Religious—Sr. CATHERINE DONOVAN, R.S.M., 47 Underwood St., P.O. Box 2577, Fall River, 02722-2577. Tel: 508-675-1311; Fax: 508-679-9220.

Family Ministry—CLAIRE M. MCMANUS, S.T.L., Dir.; Rev. GREGORY A. MATHIAS, Priest Coord., 423 Highland Ave., Fall River, 02720. Tel: 508-678-2828; Fax: 508-675-3864.

Holy Childhood Association, The—Rev. Msgr. JOHN J. OLIVEIRA, P.A., Dir., 106 Illinois St., New Bedford, 02745. Tel: 508-995-3593.

Missionary Cooperative Plan—Rev. Msgr. JOHN J. OLIVEIRA, P.A., Dir., 106 Illinois St., New Bedford, 02745. Tel: 508-995-3593.

Office for Divine Worship—Rev. Msgr. STEPHEN J. AVILA, V.F., St. Mary's Rectory, 330 Pratt St., Mansfield, 02048. Tel: 508-339-2981; Fax: 508-339-0612.

Office of Pastoral Planning—DOUGLAS RODRIGUES, Dir.; DIANE RINKACS, Assoc. Dir., Mailing Address: P.O. Box 2577, Fall River, 02722. Tel: 508-675-1311; Fax: 866-515-2933.

Permanent Diaconate Program—Rev. Msgr. JOHN J. OLIVEIRA, P.A., Dir.

Pro-Life Apostolate—Mrs. MARIAN DESROSIERS, Dir., 450 Highland Ave., P.O. Box 2577, Fall River, 02722. Tel: 508-675-1311; Fax: 508-730-2887.

Propagation of the Faith—Rev. Msgr. JOHN J. OLIVEIRA, P.A., Dir., Office, 106 Illinois St., New Bedford, 02745. Tel: 508-995-3593; Fax: 508-995-2453.

St. Vincent De Paul Society—VACANT.

Television Apostolate—Rev. Msgr. STEPHEN J. AVILA, V.F., Coord., St. Mary's Rectory, 330 Pratt St., Mansfield, 02048. Tel: 508-339-2981; Fax: 508-339-0612.

Victim Assistance Coordinator—ARLENE A. MCNAMEE, L.C.S.W. Tel: 508-674-4681. Email: aam@cssdioc.org.

Vocations—Revs. KARL C. BISSINGER, Dir.; KEVIN A. COOK, Assoc. Dir. for Recruitment; JAY MELLO, Asst. Dir. for Recruitment, 47 Underwood St., Fall River, 02720. Tel: 508-675-1311; Fax: 508-679-9220.

Commissions and Councils

Campaign for Human Development—ARLENE A. MCNAMEE, L.C.S.W., Mailing Address: S. Station, P.O. Box M, Fall River, 02724. Tel: 508-674-4681; Fax: 508-675-2224.

Catholic Scouting Program—Rev. DAVID C. FREDERICI, Dir., 494 Slocum Rd., North Dartmouth, 02747. Tel: 508-993-2351; Fax: 508-993-2437.

Continuing Education of the Clergy—Rev. MARK R. HESSION, J.C.L., Dir., 230 S. Main St., Centerville, 02632. Tel: 508-775-5744; Fax: 508-771-0170.

Diocesan Council of Catholic Nurses—Rev. MARK R. HESSION, J.C.L., Moderator, 230 S. Main St., Centerville, 02632. Tel: 508-775-5744; Fax: 508-771-0170.

Diocesan Council of Catholic Women—Sr. EUGENIA BRADY, S.J.C., Moderator, Cluny Convent, 90 Brenton Rd., Newport, RI 02840. Tel: 401-924-0953.

Diocesan Liaison with Charismatic Groups—Rev. EDWARD A. MURPHY, Dir., 249 Whittenton St., Taunton, 02780. Tel: 508-824-7794; Fax: 508-880-3865.

Diocesan Liaison with Portuguese Charismatic Groups—Rev. HENRY S. ARRUDA, St. Anthony's Rectory, 126 School St., Taunton, 02780. Tel: 508-822-0714.

Diocesan Pastoral Council—Rev. Msgr. JOHN A. PERRY, V.G., Mailing Address: P.O. Box 2577, Fall River, 02722.

Legion of Mary—Rev. BARRY W. WALL (Retired), 450 Highland Ave., P.O. Box 2577, Fall River, 02722. Tel: 508-675-1311.

CLERGY, PARISHES, MISSIONS AND PAROCHIAL SCHOOLS

CITY OF FALL RIVER

(BRISTOL COUNTY)

1—CATHEDRAL OF ST. MARY OF THE ASSUMPTION (1838) Rev. Paul Bernier, Rector; Deacon Peter R. Cote. In Res., Revs. Paulo Barbosa, Dir. Brazilian Apostolate; German Correa Agudelo, Spanish Apostolate.
Res.: 327 Second St., 02721. Tel: 508-673-2833; Fax: 508-672-0667. Web: www.cathedralfallriver.com.
Catechesis/Religious Program—467 Spring St., 02721. Tel: 508-672-5531. Ms. Alizabeth Camara, C.R.E. Students 64.

2—ST. ANNE'S (1869), (French), Revs. Marc H. Bergeron; Christopher Stanibula, Parochial Vicar. In Res., Rev. Roger J. Levesque (Retired).
420 Bradford Ave., 02721. Tel: 508-674-5651; Fax: 508-672-0939. Email: marcbergeron@comcast.net. Web: www.stanneshrine.com/.
Catechesis/Religious Program—Tel: 508-678-1510. Susan Chapdelaine, Catechetical Leader. Students 348.

3—ST. ANTHONY OF PADUA (1911), (Portuguese), Rev. Brian E. Albino.
Res.: 48 Sixteenth St., 02723. Tel: 508-673-2402; Fax: 508-730-2519.
Catechesis/Religious Program—Tel: 508-674-1986. Students 194.

4—BLESSED SACRAMENT (1902), (French), Merged with Our Lady of the Angels and St. Patrick's, Fall River to form the Parish of the Good Shepherd, Fall River.

5—ST. ELIZABETH'S (1915) Merged with St. Jean Baptiste and St. William to form Holy Trinity.

6—ESPIRITO SANTO (1904), (Portuguese), Rev. James Ferry; Deacon Thomas J. Souza.
Res.: 311 Alden St., 02723. Tel: 508-672-3352; Fax: 508-646-1787. Email: esfallriver@yahoo.com.
School—(Grades PreSchool-8), 143 Everett St., 02723. Tel: 508-672-2229; Fax: 509-672-7724. Mrs. Louise Kane, Prin. - Elementary. Lay Teachers 16; Students 206.
Catechesis/Religious Program—Students 205.

7—HOLY CROSS (1916), (Polish), Merged with SS. Peter & Paul, Fall River.

8—HOLY NAME (1923) Rev. Jay T. Maddock. In Res., Rev. John A. Raposo.
Res.: 709 Hanover St., 02720. Tel: 508-679-6732; Fax: 508-675-4755. Email: office@holynamefr.com. Web: www.holynamefr.com.
School—(Grades PreK-8), 850 Pearce St., 02720. Tel: 508-674-9131; Fax: 508-679-0571. Email: pwardell@holynamefr-school.com. Web: www.holynamefr-school.com. Dr. Patricia M. Wardell, Prin. - Elementary. Religious Sisters of Mercy 1; Lay Teachers 18; Students 234.
Catechesis/Religious Program—Tel: 508-678-7532. Email: faithformation@holynamefr.com. Ms. Diane Baron, Catechetical Leader. Students 158.

9—HOLY TRINITY (2000) Rev. David M. Andrade; Deacon John F. Branco.
Res.: 951 Stafford Rd., 02721. Tel: 508-672-3200; Fax: 508-673-5518. Email: holytrinityparish@comcast.net. Web: www.holytrinityfallriver.com.
School—(Grades PreK-8), 64 Lamphor St., 02721. Tel: 508-673-6772; Fax: 508-730-1864. Email: htfr@comcast.net. Mrs. Brenda Gagnon, Prin. - Elementary. Lay Teachers 15; Students 230.
Catechesis/Religious Program—Tel: 508-673-1284; Fax: 508-730-1864. Ms. Patricia Pasternak, Catechetical Leader. Students 135.

10—ST. JEAN BAPTISTE (1901) Merged with St. Elizabeth and St. William to form Holy Trinity Parish.

11—ST. JOSEPH'S (1873) Rev. Edward E. Correia.
Res.: 1335 N. Main St., 02720. Tel: 508-673-1123; Fax: 508-673-7230. Email: stjosfr@juno.com. Web: www.stjosephachurchfr.com.
Catechesis/Religious Program—Students 138.

12—ST. LOUIS (1885) Closed. Sacramental records can be found at St. Mary's Cathedral.

13—ST. MICHAEL (1902), (Portuguese), Rev. Edward E. Correia; Deacon Jose Medeiros.
Res.: 189 Essex St., 02720. Tel: 508-672-6713; Fax: 508-679-1841. Email: smfr929@comcast.net. Web: www.smpfr.org/.
School—(Grades PreK-8), 209 Essex St., 02720. Tel: 508-678-0266; Fax: 508-324-4433. Email: stmfr@comcast.net. Web: www.smfr.org. Sr. Marie Baldi, S.U.S.C., Prin. - Elementary. Religious of the Holy Union of the Sacred Hearts 1; Lay Teachers 15; Students 205.
Catechesis/Religious Program—Students 195.

14—NOTRE DAME DE LOURDES (1874), (French), Rev. Richard L. Chretien. In Res., Rev. Kenneth R. Gumbert, O.P.
Res.: 529 Eastern Ave., 02723. Tel: 508-679-1991; Fax: 508-676-5276. Email: chreechie@aol.com.
Catechesis/Religious Program—Tel: 508-679-1991; Fax: 508-676-5276. Ms. Colleen Laliberte, Catechetical Leader. Students 72.

15—OUR LADY OF HEALTH (1924), (Portuguese), Closed. For inquiries for parish records, please see Espirito Santo Parish, Fall River.

16—OUR LADY OF THE ANGELS (1915), (Portuguese), Merged with Blessed Sacrament and St. Patrick's, Fall River to form the Parish of the Good Shepherd, Fall River.

17—OUR LADY OF THE HOLY ROSARY (1904), (Italian), Closed. For inquiries for parish records contact Cathedral of St. Mary of the Assumption, Fall River.

18—OUR LADY OF THE IMMACULATE CONCEPTION (1882) Rev. Richard L. Chretien.
Res.: 15 Thomas St., P.O. Box 4127, 02723. Tel: 508-673-2122; Fax: 508-730-1694.
Catechesis/Religious Program—Tel: 508-679-1991. Ms. Colleen Laliberte, Catechetical Leader. Students 66.

19—PARISH OF THE GOOD SHEPHERD (2002) Rev. Fred Babiczuk; Deacon John F. Branco.
Res.: 1598 S. Main St., 02724-2586. Tel: 508-678-7412; Fax: 815-366-8198. Email: goodshepherdfallriver@yahoo.com. Web: gsfallriver.com.
Catechesis/Religious Program—Tel: 774-955-0656. Students 190.

20—ST. PATRICK'S (1873) Merged with Blessed Sacrament and Our Lady of the Angels, Fall River to form the Parish of the Good Shepherd, Fall River.

21—SS. PETER AND PAUL (1882) Rev. Stephen B. Salvador.
Res.: 250 Snell St., 02721. Tel: 508-676-8463; Fax: 508-678-8070. Email: ssppchurch@aol.com. Web: www.saintspeterandpaulparish.org.
School—(Grades PreK-8), 240 Dover St., 02721. Tel: 508-672-7258; Fax: 508-674-6042. Ms. Kathleen A. Burt, Prin. (Elementary). Lay Teachers 11; Students 171.
Catechesis/Religious Program—Tel: 508-672-3720. Ms. Kathleen A. Burt, Catechetical Leader. Students 109.

22—SACRED HEART (1872) Rev. Raymond Cambra.
Res.: 160 Seabury St., 02720. Tel: 508-673-0852; Fax: 508-563-3112. Email: sacredheartchurch1872@gmail.com. Web: www.sacredheartchurch-1872.org.
Catechesis/Religious Program—Tel: 508-730-1481. Students 58.

23—SANTO CHRISTO (1892), (Portuguese), Revs. Gastao A. Oliveira; Thomas M. Kocik, Parochial Vicar.
Res.: 185 Canal St., 02721. Tel: 508-676-1184; Fax: 508-676-9701. Email: scp1892@yahoo.com. Web: www.santochristo.com.
Catechesis/Religious Program—Tel: 508-675-3007. Mr. Osvaldo Pacheco, Catechetical Leader. Students 335.

24—ST. STANISLAUS (1898), (Polish), Rev. Bruce M. Neylon.
Res.: 36 Rockland St., P.O. Box 300, 02724. Tel: 508-672-0423; Fax: 508-677-1378. Web: www.saintstanislaus.com.
School—(Grades PreK-8), 37 Rockland St., P.O. Box 300, 02724. Tel: 508-674-6771; Fax: 508-677-1622. Miss Jean Willis, Prin. (Elementary). Lay Teachers 16; Students 190.
Catechesis/Religious Program—Students 43.

25—ST. WILLIAM'S (1905) Merged with St. Elizabeth and St. Jean Baptiste to form Holy Trinity Parish.

OUTSIDE THE CITY OF FALL RIVER

ACUSHNET, BRISTOL CO., ST. FRANCIS XAVIER'S (1915) Rev. Msgr. Gerard P. O'Conner; Deacon David B. Pepin; Mr. Steve Guillotte, Pastoral Assoc.
Res.: 125 Main St., 02743. Tel: 508-995-7600; Fax: 508-995-1794. Email: stfrancisx@comcast.net. Web: www.sfxacushnet.org/churchhome.htm.
School—(Grades PreK-8), 223 Main St., 02743. Tel: 508-995-4313; Fax: 508-995-0456. Email: dpelletier@sfxacushnet.org. Web: sss.sfxacushnet.org. Donald A. Pelletier, Prin. (Elementary). Sisters of Saint Joseph 1; Lay Teachers 11; Students 241.
Catechesis/Religious Program—Tel: 508-998-7445. Email: stfrancisxreled@aol.com. Janine Hammarquist, Catechetical Leader. Students 149.

ASSONET, BRISTOL CO., ST. BERNARD'S (1938) Rev. Michael S. Racine.
Res.: 32 S. Main St., P.O. Box 370, 02702. Tel: 508-644-5585; Fax: 508-644-2136. Email: stbernardassonet@aol.com. Web: www.stbernardassonet.org.
Catechesis/Religious Program—Tel: 508-644-2032. Students 509.

ATTLEBORO, BRISTOL CO.

1—HOLY GHOST (1921) Rev. John M. Murray; Deacon Paul M. Fournier.
Res.: 71 Linden St., 02703. Tel: 508-222-3266; Fax: 888-239-9322. Email: hgchurch@verizon.net.
Catechesis/Religious Program—Tel: 508-222-6756. Students 56.

2—ST. JOHN THE EVANGELIST (1883) Rev. Richard M. Roy; Deacon Adelbert F. Malloy.
Res.: One St. John Pl., 02703-2249. Tel: 508-222-1206; Fax: 508-226-6461. Email: sjparish@naiimail.net. Web: www.stjohns-attleboro.org.
School—(Grades K-8), 13 Hodges St., 02703. Tel: 508-222-5062; Fax: 508-223-1737. Web: www.sjeschool.com. Sr. Mary Holden, C.P., Prin. (Elementary). Sisters 3; Lay Teachers 14; Students 260.
Catechesis/Religious Program—Tel: 508-222-0707; Fax: 508-222-0701. Email: mkennan@sjescvhool.com. Margaret Keenan, Catechetical Leader. Students 735.

3—ST. JOSEPH'S (1905) Rev. John M. Murray; Deacon Paul M. Fournier; Sr. Ana Maria Corona, O.P., Pastoral Assoc.
Res.: 208 S. Main St., 02703. Tel: 508-226-1115; Fax: 888-239-9322. Email: stjosephattleboro@gmail.com.
Catechesis/Religious Program—10 Maple St. Tel: 508-222-6756. Students 80.

4—ST. STEPHEN'S (1875) [CEM] Closed. For inquiries for parish records contact Our Lady Queen of Martyrs Parish, Seekonk.

5—ST. THERESA OF THE CHILD JESUS (1925) Rev. Jon-Paul Gallant.
Res.: 18 Baltic St., 02703. Tel: 508-761-8111; Fax: 508-761-5475. Email: sttcj@aol.com.
Catechesis/Religious Program—Tel: 508-761-5367. Ms. Wendy Smith, D.R.E. Students 346.

ATTLEBORO FALLS, BRISTOL CO., ST. MARK'S (1967) Rev. Thomas A. Frechette; Deacon Richard J. Gundlach.
Res.: 105 Stanley St., P.O. Box 1240, 02763-0240. Tel: 508-699-7566; Fax: 508-643-0103. Email: stmarkoffice@comcast.net. Web: www.stmarks-attleborofalls.org.
Catechesis/Religious Program—Tel: 508-695-7773. Mrs. Elaine Corvese, Catechetical Leader. Students 619.

BREWSTER, BARNSTABLE CO., OUR LADY OF THE CAPE (1961) Revs. Bernard Baris, M.S.; John R. Dolan, M.S., Parochial Vicar; Deacon R. Donald Biron; Mr. Becket Senchur, Music Dir. In Res., Rev. Paul N. Belhumeur, M.S.
Res.: 468 Stony Brook Rd., P.O. Box 1799, 02631-7799. Tel: 508-385-3252; Fax: 508-385-6864. Email: ourladyofthecapebrewster@gmail.com. Web: www.ourladyofthecape.org.
Catechesis/Religious Program—Tel: 508-385-2115. Sr. Elizabeth Doyle, R.S.M., Catechetical Leader; Mrs. Priscilla Silva, Catechetical Leader. Students 258.
Mission—Immaculate Conception 2580 Main St., Rte. 6A, Barnstable Co. 02631.

BUZZARDS BAY, BARNSTABLE CO., ST. MARGARET (1915) [JC] Revs. Thomas Washburn, O.F.M.; Giles Barreda, O.F.M., Parochial Vicar; Deacon Ernest J. Gendron.
Res.: 141 Main St., 02532. Tel: 508-759-7777; Fax: 508-759-3920. Email: stmargarets.rectory@verizon.net. Web: www.stmargaretbbay.com.
School—St. Margaret Regional School, (Grades K-8), 143 Main St., 02532. Tel: 508-759-2213; Fax: 508-759-8776. Email: lplante@saintmargaretregional.com. Web: www.saintmargaretregional.org. Mrs. Laurie L. Plante, Prin. Elementary. Lay Teachers 14; Students 196.
Catechesis/Religious Program—Tel: 508-743-4604. Students 245.
Mission—St. Mary Star of the Sea Onset Bay Ln., Onset, Plymouth Co. 02558.

CENTERVILLE, BARNSTABLE CO., OUR LADY OF VICTORY (1957) Revs. Mark R. Hession; Thomas E. McGlynn, Parochial Vicar; Deacons James M. Barrett; Theodore E. Lukac.
Res.: 230 S. Main St., 02632. Tel: 508-775-5744; Fax: 508-771-0170. Email: office@olvparish.org. Web: www.olvparish.org.
Catechesis/Religious Program—Tel: 508-771-1614. William Bussiere, Catechetical Leader; Helen L. Curran, Catechetical Leader. Students 671.
Mission—Our Lady of Hope Rte. 6A, West Barnstable, Barnstable Co. 02668.

CHATHAM, BARNSTABLE CO., HOLY REDEEMER (1955) [JC] Rev. George Scales; Deacons Richard S. Stenberg; Joseph F. Mador.
Res.: 57 Highland Ave., Box 687, 02633. Tel: 508-945-0677; Fax: 508-945-3186. Email: parish@holyredeemerchatham.org.
Catechesis/Religious Program—Ms. Bethel Norcross, Catechetical Leader. Students 90.
Mission—Our Lady of Grace Rte. 28, 02633.
Chapel—Our Lady of Grace Chapel 60 Meetinghouse Rd. (Rte. 137), South Chatham, 02659.

DIGHTON, BRISTOL CO., ST. PETER'S (1904) Closed. For inquiries for parish records contact St. Nicholas of Myra Parish, North Dighton.

EAST FALMOUTH, BARNSTABLE CO., ST. ANTHONY'S (1923) [CEM] Rev. Gerard A. Hebert.
Res.: 167 E. Falmouth Hwy., 02536. Tel: 508-548-0108; Fax: 508-457-1723. Email: stanthonyschurch@cape.com. Web: www.stanthonyscapecod.org.
Catechesis/Religious Program—Tel: 508-548-3515; Fax: 508-548-3515. Email: stanthonyfaithformation@comcast.net. Patricia Friel, Catechetical Leader. Students 377.

EAST FREETOWN, BRISTOL CO., ST. JOHN NEUMANN (1984) Rev. Richard E. Degagne. In Res., Rev. Rodney E. Thibault.
Res.: 157 Middleboro Rd., Box 718, 02717. Tel: 508-763-2240; Fax: 508-763-3040. Email: contact@sjnfreetown.org. Web: www.sjn.freetown.org.
Catechesis/Religious Program—Tel: 508-763-8122. Ms. Suzanne Medeiros, Catechetical Leader. Students 508.

EAST SANDWICH, BARNSTABLE CO., CORPUS CHRISTI (1830) [CEM] Revs. George E. Harrison; Michael J. Fitzpatrick, Parochial Vicar; Deacons David Boucher; Arthur LaChance; Dennis O'Connell; Mr. George J. Campeau Jr., Music Dir.
Res. & Parish Center: 324 Quaker Meetinghouse Rd., 02537-1327. Tel: 508-888-0209; Fax: 508-888-8961. Email: frgharrison@corpuschristiparish.org. Web: www.corpuschristiparish.org.
Catechesis/Religious Program—Email: dmboucher@corpuschristiparish.org. Ms. Deborah M. Boucher, Catechetical Leader; Mr. Richard V. Fish Jr., Catechetical Leader. Students 821.
Mission—St. Theresa Sagamore, Barnstable Co.

EAST TAUNTON, BRISTOL CO., HOLY FAMILY (1900) Rev. Kevin A. Cook; Deacon John J. Fitzpatrick. In Res., Rev. Jeffrey Cabral.
Res.: 370 Middleboro Ave., P.O. Box 619, 02718. Tel: 508-824-5707; Fax: 508-824-5665. Email: secretary@holyfamilytaunton.org. Web: www.hfparish.net.
Catechesis/Religious Program—Ms. Karen Coughlin, Catechetical Leader. Students 409.

EDGARTOWN, DUKES CO., ST. ELIZABETH (1925) Closed. For inquiries for parish records contact Good Shepherd Parish, Oak Bluffs.

FAIRHAVEN, BRISTOL CO.

1—ST. JOSEPH'S (1905) Rev. Thomas McElroy, SS.CC.; Deacons Robert Lorenzo; Douglas Medeiros; Mr. John Jannis, Music Dir.
Res.: 74 Spring St., 02719. Tel: 508-994-9714; Fax: 508-979-4659. Email: stjosephparish@comcast.net.
School—(Grades PreK-8), 100 Spring St., 02719. Tel: 508-996-1983; Fax: 508-996-1998. Ms. Julie Vareika, Prin. Elementary. Lay Teachers 11; Students 222.
Catechesis/Religious Program—Tel: 508-245-8724. Ms. Margie Copeland, Catechetical Leader. Students 211.

2—ST. MARY'S (1933) Rev. Patrick Killilea, SS.CC.; Deacon Bruce Bonneau.
Res.: 41 Harding Rd., 02719. Tel: 508-992-7300; Fax: 508-992-0685. Email: stmarysfairhaven@comcast.com. Web: www.sscc.org/stmaryfhvn.
Catechesis/Religious Program—Tel: 508-992-8721. Sr. Eleanor Marie Cyr, SS.CC., Catechetical Leader. Students 209.

FALMOUTH, BARNSTABLE CO., ST. PATRICK'S (1928) [CEM] Rev. Msgr. John A. Perry; Rev. Jay Mello, Parochial Vicar; Deacons Patrick J. Mahoney; John E. Simonis. In Res., Rev. Messias Alburquerque.
Res.: 511 Main St., P.O. Box 569, 02541. Tel: 508-548-1065; Fax: 508-495-0875. Email: stpatrick80@gmail.com. Web: www.stpatricksonline.org.
Catechesis/Religious Program—Tel: 508-548-2306. Students 172.
Chapel—St. Thomas Falmouth Heights Rd., 02540.

HYANNIS, BARNSTABLE CO., ST. FRANCIS XAVIER'S (1904) [CEM 2] Revs. Daniel W. Lacroix; Peter J. Fournier, Parochial Vicar; Deacons Richard M. Dresser; Richard J. Murphy; Mr. Daniel Nunes, Pastoral Assoc.
Res.: 21 Cross St., 02601. Tel: 508-775-0818; Fax: 508-771-5940. Email: stfrancis@stfrancishyannis.org. Web: http://stfrancishyannis.homestead.com/sfx1.htm.
Church: 347 South St., 02601.
School—St. Francis Xavier Preparatory School, (Grades 5-8), 33 Cross St., 02601. Tel: 508-771-7200; Fax: 508-771-7233. Email: moffiler@sfxp.org. Web: http://www.sfxp.org. Mr. Robert H. Deburro, Prin. Elementary. Lay Teachers 23; Students 236.
Catechesis/Religious Program—Tel: 508-775-6200; Fax: 508-771-7233. Students 106.
Mission—Sacred Heart Chapel 32 Summer St., Yarmouth Port, Barnstable Co. 02675.

MANSFIELD, BRISTOL CO., ST. MARY'S (1894) [CEM] Rev. Msgr. Stephen J. Avila; Rev. William M. Sylvia, Parochial Vicar; Sr. Ann William Publicover, M.S.B.T., Pastoral Assoc.; Jeffrey T. Cahill, Pastoral Assoc.; Deacon Thomas P. Palanza; Mr. Daniel Davey, Music Dir.
Res.: 330 Pratt St., 02048-1581. Tel: 508-339-2981; Fax: 508-339-0612. Email: office@stmarymans.org. Web: www.stmarymans.org.
School—(Grades K-8) Tel: 508-339-4800; Fax: 508-337-2063. Email: info@stmarymansschool.org. Web: www.stmarymansschool.org. Mrs. Joanne N. Riley, Prin. Elementary. Lay Teachers 10; Students 217.

Catechesis/Religious Program—Tel: 508-339-4621; 508-339-2064 Confirmation. Mr. Matthew Bensman, Catechetical Leader. Students 1,691.

MARION, PLYMOUTH CO., ST. RITA'S (1972) Rev. Paul A. Caron.
Res.: 113 Front St., P.O. Box 902, 02738. Tel: 508-748-1497; Fax: 508-748-0604. Email: stritamarion@comcast.net.
Catechesis/Religious Program—Tel: 508-748-2072. Email: stritamarion@comcast.net. Theresa Fitzpatrick, Catechetical Leader. Students 182.

MASHPEE, BARNSTABLE CO., CHRIST THE KING (1984) Rev. Msgr. Daniel F. Hoye; Deacons Gregory J. Beckel; Frank D. Fantasia.
5 Jobs Fishing Rd., P.O. Box 1800, 02649. Tel: 508-477-7700; Fax: 508-477-8158. Email: ctk@cape.com. Web: www.christthekingparish.com.
Catechesis/Religious Program—Tel: 508-477-7700, Ext. 21. Sisters Claire Sinotte, O.P., Catechetical Leader; Shirley Agnew, R.S.M., Catechetical Leader. Students 391.

MATTAPOISETT, PLYMOUTH CO., ST. ANTHONY'S (1908) [CEM] Rev. Paul A. Caron.
Mailing Address: 22 Barstow St., P.O. Box 501, 02739.
Res.: 22 Barstow St., 02739. Tel: 508-758-3719; Fax: 508-758-3019. Email: st.anthony@verizon.net. Web: www.mystanthonys.org.
Catechesis/Religious Program—Tel: 508-758-3735. Ms. Mary Chaplain, Catechetical Leader. Students 295.

NANTUCKET, NANTUCKET CO., ST. MARY'S, OUR LADY OF THE ISLE (1903) [CEM] Rev. Marcel H. Bouchard; Deacon Donald L. Battiston.
Res.: 3 Federal St., P.O. Box 1168, 02554. Tel: 508-228-0100; Fax: 508-325-7991. Email: stmarys@stmarysnantucket.org. Web: www.stmarysnantucket.org.
Catechesis/Religious Program—Tel: 508-228-4852. Ms. Elaine Boehm, Catechetical Leader. Students 198.

NEW BEDFORD, BRISTOL CO.

1—ST. ANNE (1908), (French), Closed. For inquiries for parish records contact Our Lady of Guadalupe Parish, New Bedford.

2—ST. ANTHONY OF PADUA'S (1895), (French), Rev. Roger J. Landry.
Res.: 1359 Acushnet Ave., 02746. Tel: 508-993-1691; Fax: 508-999-4775. Email: fatherlandry@saintanthonynewbedford.com. Web: www.saintanthonynewbedford.com/.
Catechesis/Religious Program—Mr. Philip Martin, Catechetical Leader. Students 91.

3—ST. CASIMIR (1927), (Polish), Closed. For inquiries for parish records, please see Our Lady of Perpetual Help, New Bedford.

4—ST. FRANCIS OF ASSISI (1928), (Italian), Rev. Kevin J. Harrington.
Res.: 247 North St., 02740. Tel: 508-997-7732; Fax: 508-991-6630. Email: jbelli72@comcast.net.
Catechesis/Religious Program—Students 40.

5—ST. HEDWIG, Closed. For inquiries for Parish records, please contact Our Lady of Guadalupe, New Bedford.

6—HOLY NAME, Merged with Sacred Heart, New Bedford to form Holy Name of the Sacred Heart of Jesus, New Bedford.

7—HOLY NAME OF THE SACRED HEART OF JESUS (1999) Rev. Robert A. Oliveira; Deacon Eugene E. Sasseville.
Res.: 121 Mt. Pleasant St., 02740. Tel: 508-992-3184; Fax: 508-984-3406. Email: holynamesacredheartparish@comcast.net.
Catechesis/Religious Program—Tel: 508-996-8654. Students 170.

8—ST. JAMES (1888) Closed. For inquiries for parish records contact Our Lady of Guadalupe Parish, New Bedford.

9—ST. JOHN THE BAPTIST (1871), (Portuguese), [CEM] Revs. John J. Oliveira; Michael M. Camara, Parochial Vicar; William M. Rodrigues, Parochial Vicar; Deacon Paul J. Macedo.
Res.: 344 County St., 02740. Tel: 508-992-7727; Fax: 508-997-1462. Email: sjb1871@comcast.net.
School—St. James-St. John School, (Grades PreK-8), 180 Orchard St., 02740. Tel: 508-996-0534; Fax: 508-717-6969. Email: principal@sjsjschool.com. Web: www.sjsjschool.com. Mrs. Cristina Raposo, Prin. - Elementary. Lay Teachers 10; Students 262.
Catechesis/Religious Program—Tel: 508-996-3087. Ms. Marge Ferreira, Catechetical Leader. Students 103.

10—ST. JOSEPH (1910) Merged with St. Theresa, New Bedford to form St. Joseph-St. Therese, New Bedford.

11—ST. JOSEPH-ST. THERESE (1999) Rev. Philip N. Hamel.
Office: 51 Duncan St., 02745-6108. Tel: 508-995-5235; Fax: 508-995-7266. Email: stjossttherese@aol.com.
Catechesis/Religious Program—Fax: 508-995-7266. Students 136.

12—ST. KILIAN (1896) Rev. Hugo G. Cardenas, I.V.E.
Res.: 306 Ashley Blvd., 02746. Tel: 508-992-7587; Fax: 508-994-0281.
Catechesis/Religious Program—Students 81.

13—ST. LAWRENCE MARTYR (1821) Rev. Marek Chmurski.
Res.: 110 Summer St., 02740. Tel: 508-992-4251; Fax: 508-984-4136. Email: stloffice@saintlawrencemartyr.com. Web: saintlawrencemartyr.com.
School—Holy Name of the Sacred Heart of Jesus, (Grades PreK-8), 91 Summer St., 02740. Tel: 508-993-3547; Fax: 508-993-8277. Web: www.hfh-n.org. Ms. Cecilia M. Felix, Prin. - Elementary. Sisters 1; Lay Teachers 11; Students 296.
Catechesis/Religious Program—Tel: 508-993-3547. Ms. Teresa Ouellette, Catechetical Leader; Ms. Cecilia M. Felix, Catechetical Leader. Students 296.

14—ST. MARY'S (1927) Rev. Msgr. John J. Oliveira.
Res.: 106 Illinois St., 02745. Tel: 508-995-3593. Email: stmarysnb@gmail.com. Web: www.stmarysnb.com.
Church: 343 Tarkiln Hill Rd., 02745.
School—All Saints Catholic School, (Grades PreK-8), 115 Illinois St., 02745. Tel: 508-995-3696; Fax: 508-995-0840. Web: www.ascsnb.org. Mrs. Sherri Swainamer, Prin. - Elementary. Lay Teachers 13; Students 250.
Catechesis/Religious Program—Tel: 508-995-3693. Mrs. Cathy Lacroix, Catechetical Leader. Students 184.

15—NUESTRA SENORA DE GUADALUPE (1993), (Hispanic), Closed. For inquiries for parish records contact Our Lady of Guadalupe Parish, New Bedford.

16—OUR LADY OF FATIMA (1966) Rev. John C. Ozug.
Res.: 4256 Acushnet Ave., 02745. Tel: 508-995-7351; Fax: 508-995-4401. Email: olofnb@comcast.net. Web: www.fatimanewbedford.org.
Catechesis/Religious Program—Tel: 508-995-6685. Students 157.

17—OUR LADY OF GUADALUPE (2004) Very Rev. Richard D. Wilson; Deacon Lawrence A. St. Onge.
Res.: 233 County St., 02740-4717. Tel: 508-992-9408; Fax: 508-990-0575. Email: rdwilson1@comcast.net. Web: http://www.saintjames-nb.org.
School—St. James-St. John, (Grades PreK-8), 180 Orchard St., 02740. Tel: 508-996-0534. Mrs. Cristina Raposo, Prin. Lay Teachers 11; Students 258.
Catechesis/Religious Program—Mr. Timothy Mitchell, Catechetical Leader. Students 176.

18—OUR LADY OF MT. CARMEL (1902), (Portuguese), Revs. John J. Oliveira; Michael M. Camara, Parochial Vicar; William M. Rodrigues, Parochial Vicar; Deacon Abilio Pires.
Res.: 230 Bonney St., 02744. Tel: 508-993-4704; Fax: 508-991-5536. Email: olmcnb@comcast.net. Web: http://www.mtcarmelschool.com/parish.htm.
Catechesis/Religious Program—Ms. Nancy Morin, C.R.E. Students 403.

19—OUR LADY OF PERPETUAL HELP (1905), (Polish), Rev. Conrad Salach, O.F.M.Conv.
Res.: 235 N. Front St., 02746. Tel: 508-992-9378; Fax: 508-993-4881. Email: olphrectory@comcast.net. Web: www.olphchurchnb.org.
Catechesis/Religious Program—Students 18.

20—OUR LADY OF THE ASSUMPTION (1905), (Cape Verdean), Rev. Christopher Santangelo, SS.CC.
Mailing Address: 47 S. 6th St., 02740. Tel: 508-994-7602 Parish Center; Fax: 508-994-9461. Email: oloaoffice@verizon.net.
Res. & Parish Center: 54 S. 6th St., 02740. Tel: 508-994-0106.
Catechesis/Religious Program—Students 125.

21—OUR LADY OF THE IMMACULATE CONCEPTION (1909), (Portuguese), Rev. Daniel O. Reis; Deacon Albertino F. Pires.
Res.: 136 Earle St., 02746. Tel: 508-992-9892; Fax: 508-992-9907. Email: i.conception@comcast.net.
Catechesis/Religious Program—Tel: 508-990-0249. Students 298.

22—SACRED HEART (1874), (French), Merged With Holy Name, New Bedford to form Holy Name of the Sacred Heart of Jesus, New Bedford.

23—ST. THERESA (1926), (French), Merged with St. Joseph's, New Bedford to form St. Joseph-St. Therese, New Bedford.

NORTH ATTLEBORO, BRISTOL CO.

1—ST. MARY'S (1890) [CEM] Rev. David A. Costa; Sr. Kathleen Corrigan, S.U.S.C., Pastoral Assoc.
Res.: 14 Park St., 02760. Tel: 508-695-6161; Fax: 508-695-5248. Email: stmary@noozi.com. Web: www.saintmaryna.com.
See St. Mary's-Sacred Heart Consolidated School, North Attleboro under Sacred Heart, North Attleboro details.
Catechesis/Religious Program—Tel: 508-695-3823. Email: michelecre@comcast.net. Mrs. Michele Dillon, Catechetical Leader. Students 402.

2—SACRED HEART (1904) Rev. David A. Costa; Deacon Joseph E. Regali; Sr. Kathleen Corrigan, S.U.S.C., Pastoral Assoc.
Res.: 58 Church St., 02760. Tel: 508-699-8383; Fax: 508-699-7016. Email: shna@comcast.net. Web: www.shna.org.
School—St. Mary-Sacred Heart School, (Grades K-8), 57 Richards Ave., 02760. Tel: 508-695-3072; Fax: 508-695-9074. Email: smsh@comcast.net. Web: www.smshna.com. Mrs. Denise M. Peixoto, Prin. - Elementary. Lay Teachers 16; Students 264.
Catechesis/Religious Program—Tel: 508-643-9009. Mrs. Kate Leighton, Catechetical Leader. Students 276.

NORTH DARTMOUTH, BRISTOL CO., ST. JULIE BILLIART (1969) Rev. Gregory A. Mathias; Deacon Maurice A. Ouellette. In Res., Rev. David C. Frederici.
Res.: 494 Slocum Rd., 02747. Tel: 508-993-2351; Fax: 508-993-2437. Email: stjuliebilliart@gmail.com. Web: www.saintjulies.org.
Catechesis/Religious Program—Tel: 508-990-0287. Mr. Peter Healy, Catechetical Leader; Ms. Paula Raposo, Catechetical Leader. Students 513.

NORTH DIGHTON, BRISTOL CO.

1—ST. JOSEPH'S (1913) [JC 2] Closed. For inquiries for parish records contact St. Nicholas of Myra Parish, North Dighton.

2—ST. NICHOLAS OF MYRA PARISH (2008) Rev. Timothy J. Goldrick; Sr. Mauricia A. Burke, O.P., Pastoral Assoc.
Mailing Address: 499 Spring St., P.O. Box 564, 02764. Tel: 508-822-1425; Fax: 508-822-3886. Email: st.nicholasofmyra@comcast.net. Web: saintnicholasofmyra.org.
Res.: 2039 County St., Dighton, 02715. Tel: 508-669-6743.
Catechesis/Religious Program—Mr. Gregory Bettencourt, Catechetical Leader. Students 438.

NORTH EASTON, BRISTOL CO., IMMACULATE CONCEPTION (1871) [CEM] Rev. Paul C. Fedak, Parochial Admin.
Res.: 193 Main St., 02356. Tel: 508-238-3232; Fax: 508-238-7849. Email: rectory@icceaston.org. Web: www.icceaston.org.
Catechesis/Religious Program—Tel: 508-238-3230; Fax: 508-238-7849. Email: religiousED@icceaston.org. Ms. Elide Rodrigues, Catechetical Leader. Students 529.

NORTH FALMOUTH, BARNSTABLE CO., ST. ELIZABETH SETON (1977) Revs. Arnold R. Medeiros; John P. Kelleher, O.S.B., Parochial Vicar; Deacons William A. Martin; Peter M. Guresh; David E. Pierce.
Res.: 481 Quaker Rd., P.O. Box 861, 02556. Tel: 508-563-7774; Fax: 508-563-7794. Email: saintelizabethseton@comcast.net. Web: www.stelizabethseton.org.
Catechesis/Religious Program—Mr. Jack Goulet, Catechetical Leader. Students 217.

NORTON, BRISTOL CO., ST. MARY'S (1925) Rev. Marc P. Tremblay; Deacon Michael T. Zonghetti.
Mailing Address: 1 Power St., 02766-0430.
Res.: 133 S. Worcester St., 02766-0430. Tel: 508-285-4462; Fax: 508-285-5589. Email: stmarysnorton@verizon.net. Web: www.stmarysnorton.com.
Catechesis/Religious Program—Tel: 508-285-3237. Ms. Laura Vergow, Catechetical Leader. Students 818.

OAK BLUFFS, DUKES CO.

1—GOOD SHEPHERD (2004) [JC] Rev. Michael R. Nagle; Deacons Fred Lapiana; Karl G. Buder.
Mailing Address: P.O. Box 1058, Vineyard Haven, 02568. Tel: 508-693-0342. In Res., Rev. Messias Alburquerque.
Office: 55 School St., 02557. Fax: 508-693-8517. Email: frnagle@goodshepherdmv.com. Web: www.goodshepherdmv.com.
Worship Sites—
Our Lady Star of the Sea—22 Massasoit Ave., 02557.
St. Elizabeth's Church—86 Main St., Edgartown, 02539.
St. Augustine's Church—56 Franklin St., Vineyard Haven, 02568.
Catechesis/Religious Program—Ms. Susan Pagliccia, Catechetical Leader. Students 191.

2—SACRED HEART (1880) [CEM] Closed. For inquiries for parish records contact Good Shepherd Parish, Oak Bluffs.

ORLEANS, BARNSTABLE CO., ST. JOAN OF ARC (1947) Rev. Robert J. Powell; Deacons Donald Joslin; John Twerago; Norman McEnaney.
Res.: 61 Canal Rd., 02653. Tel: 508-255-0170; Fax: 508-240-6741. Email: joanarc@c4.net. Web: http://joanarc.org/.
Catechesis/Religious Program—Tel: 508-255-1257. Email: religed@c4.net. Ms. Judy Burt-Walker, Catechetical Leader. Students 153.

OSTERVILLE, BARNSTABLE CO., OUR LADY OF THE ASSUMPTION (1928) Rev. Philip A. Davignon; Deacon Paul K. Roma.

Res.: 76 Wianno Ave., P.O. Box E., 02655. Tel: 508-428-2011; Fax: 508-428-2891. Web: http://www.assumption-capecod.org/.
Church: 86 Wianno Ave., P.O. Box E, 02655.
Catechesis/Religious Program—Students 82.

POCASSET, BARNSTABLE CO., ST. JOHN THE EVANGELIST (1969) Revs. Arnold R. Medeiros; John P. Kelleher, O.S.B., Parochial Vicar; Deacons David E. Pierce; Peter M. Guresh; Leonard C. Dexter Jr.; William A. Martin.
Mailing Address: 841 Shore Dr., P.O. Box 1558, 02559.
Res.: 15 Virginia Rd., P.O. Box 1558, 02559. Tel: 508-563-5887; Fax: 508-563-7794. Email: stjohn.rectory@verizon.net. Web: stjohnspocasset.org.
Catechesis/Religious Program—Students 245.

PROVINCETOWN, BARNSTABLE CO., ST. PETER THE APOSTLE (1874) [CEM] Rev. Hugh J. McCullough; Deacon Steven M. Minninger.
Res.: 11 Prince St., 02657. Tel: 508-487-0095; Fax: 508-487-2564. Email: stpetersptown@aol.com. Web: www.stpeters-provincetown.4lpi.com.
Catechesis/Religious Program—Students 49.

RAYNHAM CENTER, BRISTOL CO., ST. ANN (1960) Rev. Michael K. McManus; Deacon Joseph A. McGinley.
Res.: 660 N. Main St., P.O. Box 247, 02768. Tel: 508-823-9833; Fax: 508-823-8935. Email: office@stannsraynham.org. Web: www.stannsraynham.org.
Catechesis/Religious Program—725 N. Main St., Box 247, 02768. Tel: 508-824-9021; Fax: 508-824-1090. Ms. Lisa Donahue, Catechetical Leader; Kristin Kreckler, Catechetical Leader. Students 960.

SEEKONK, BRISTOL CO.
1—ST. MARY'S (1906) Closed. For inquiries for parish records contact Our Lady Queen of Martyrs Parish, Seekonk.
2—OUR LADY OF MT. CARMEL (1922) Rev. William M. Costello; Deacon Richard G. Lemay.
Res.: 984 Taunton Ave., P.O. Box 519, 02771. Tel: 508-336-5549; Fax: 508-336-9010. Email: mountcarmel1@verizon.net. Web: www.mountcarmel1.com.
Catechesis/Religious Program—1040 Taunton Ave., 02771. Tel: 508-336-8608 (Grades 1-6). Students 637.
3—OUR LADY QUEEN OF MARTYRS, [JC] Rev. Thomas L. Rita.
385 Central Ave., 02771. Tel: 508-399-8440; Fax: 508-399-7398. Email: olqmseekonk@comcast.net. Web: www.olqmseekonk.org.
Catechesis/Religious Program—Students 432.

SOMERSET, BRISTOL CO.
1—ST. JOHN OF GOD (1928), (Portuguese), [CEM] Rev. Raul M. Lagoa; Deacon Robert A. Faria. In Res., Rev. Luciano J. de M Pereira (Retired).
Res.: 996 Brayton Ave., Box 113, 02726. Tel: 508-678-5513; Fax: 508-678-6458. Web: stjohnofgodsomerset.org.
Catechesis/Religious Program—1036 Brayton Ave., 02726. Tel: 508-678-5139; Fax: 508-678-5513. Students 254.
2—ST. PATRICK'S (1883) [CEM] Rev. Marek S. Tuptynski; Deacon Edward Hussey; Mrs. Anne Marie Bouchard, Pastoral Assoc.
Res.: 306 South St., 02726-5617. Tel: 508-672-1523; Fax: 508-675-5787. Email: stpatparish@comcast.net. Web: www.stpatricksomerset.com.
Catechesis/Religious Program—Ms. Janet Rausch, Catechetical Leader. Students 276.
3—ST. THOMAS MORE (1949) Rev. Msgr. Edmund J. Fitzgerald; Mr. Thomas A. Roussell Jr., Music Dir.
Res.: 386 Luther Ave., 02726. Tel: 508-673-7831; Fax: 508-567-5177. Email: office@stthomasmoresomerset.org. Web: http://www.stthomasmoresomerset.org.
Catechesis/Religious Program—Tel: 508-679-1236. Ms. Janis Johnson, Catechetical Leader. Students 175.

SOUTH DARTMOUTH, BRISTOL CO., ST. MARY'S (1930) Revs. John A. Gomes; Francis J. Moy, S.J., Parochial Vicar.
Res.: 783 Dartmouth St., 02748. Tel: 508-992-7163; Fax: 508-992-5209. Email: info@stmarysdartmouth.org. Web: www.stmarysdartmouth.org.
Catechesis/Religious Program—789 Dartmouth St., 02748. Tel: 508-992-7505. Mr. Peter Carvalho, Catechetical Leader; Ms. Beni Costa-Reedy, Catechetical Leader; Mr. Ken Sylvia, Catechetical Leader. Students 412.

SOUTH EASTON, BRISTOL CO., HOLY CROSS (1967) Revs. James E. Fenstermaker, C.S.C.; Lawrence A. Jerge, C.S.C., Parochial Vicar; Deacon George Zarella.
225 Purchase St., 02375. Tel: 508-238-2235; Fax: 508-238-0500. Email: info@holycrosseaston.org. Web: http://www.holycrosseaston.org.
Catechesis/Religious Program—Ms. Anne Tarallo, C.R.E. Students 725.

SOUTH YARMOUTH, BARNSTABLE CO., ST. PIUS TENTH (1954) Very Rev. George C. Bellenoit; Rev. David C. Deston Jr., Parochial Vicar; Deacons C. Michael Hickey; William Gallerizzo; Thomas Bailey; David Akin; Richard C. Zeich.
Res.: 5 Barbara St., 02664. Tel: 508-398-2248; Fax: 508-398-7233. Email: stpiusxoffice@comcast.net. Web: http://www.stpiusxsy.com.
School—(Grades PreK-8), 321 Wood Rd., 02664. Tel: 508-398-6112; Fax: 508-398-6113. Web: www.spxschool.org. Mrs. Anne Dailey, Prin. - Elementary. Lay Teachers 31; Students 213.
Catechesis/Religious Program—Station Ave., 02664. Tel: 508-394-0709; 508-394-0708. Email: stpiusxreled@comcast.net. Students 322.
Chapel—Our Lady of the Highway Rte. 28, 02664.

SWANSEA, BRISTOL CO.
1—ST. DOMINIC'S (1911) Rev. Joseph F. Viveiros.
Res.: 1277 Grand Army Hwy., P.O. Box 205, 02777. Tel: 508-675-7206; Fax: 508-675-4626.
Catechesis/Religious Program—Tel: 508-675-7002. Students 265.
2—SAINT FRANCIS OF ASSISI (1922) Rev. Michael A. Ciryak.
Res.: 270 Ocean Grove Ave., 02777. Tel: 508-673-2808; Fax: 508-672-6241. Email: stfrancisswansea@comcast.net. Web: www.stfrancisswansea.com.
Church: 530 Gardner Neck Rd., 02777.
Catechesis/Religious Program—Tel: 508-674-0024. Students 236.
3—ST. LOUIS DE FRANCE (1928), (French), Rev. Richard R. Gendreau; Deacon Robert G. Normandin.
Res.: 56 Buffington St., 02777. Tel: 508-674-1103; Fax: 508-672-8889. Email: sldfo@comcast.net. Web: http://stlouisdefrance.net.
Catechesis/Religious Program—Tel: 508-672-0615. Ms. Paulette J. Normandin, Catechetical Leader. Students 386.
4—ST. MICHAEL'S, Closed. For inquiries for parish records please see Saint Francis of Assisi, Swansea.
5—OUR LADY OF FATIMA (1958) Closed. For inquiries for parish records, please see Saint Francis of Assisi, Swansea.

TAUNTON, BRISTOL CO.
1—SAINT ANDREW THE APOSTLE PARISH (2008) Very Rev. Timothy P. Reis; Deacon Alan J. Thadeu.
Res.: 19 Kilmer Ave., 02780. Tel: 508-824-5577; Fax: 508-822-1401. Email: standrewtaunton@comcast.net. Web: http://www.standrewtaunton.org.
Catechesis/Religious Program—Tel: 508-822-9672. Students 456.
2—ANNUNCIATION OF THE LORD (2001) Rev. Timothy Paul Driscoll.
Res.: 31 First St., 02780. Tel: 508-823-2521; Fax: 508-823-2522. Email: annol325@comcast.net. Web: www.annunciationtaunton.com.
School—Our Lady of Lourdes, 52 First St., 02780. Tel: 508-822-3746; Fax: 508-822-1450. Email: olol@tmlp.com. Web: www.ololtaunton.com. Dr. Lincoln A. De Moura, Prin. -Elementary. Sisters 2; Lay Teachers 5; Students 132.
Catechesis/Religious Program—Tel: 508-824-6791. Ms. Susan Finney, Catechetical Leader. Students 71.
Convent—49 First St., 02780. Tel: 508-822-0357.
3—ST. ANTHONY'S (1903), (Portuguese), Rev. Henry S. Arruda; Deacon Jose H. Medina.
Res.: 126 School St., 02780. Tel: 508-822-0714; Fax: 508-828-5844. Email: hsarruda@comcast.net. Web: www.stanthonytaunton.com.
Catechesis/Religious Program—Tel: 508-824-6241. Students 265.
4—ST. JAMES (1904), (French), Closed. For inquiries for parish records contact St. Jude the Apostle Parish, Taunton.
5—ST. JOSEPH'S (1896) Closed. For inquiries for parish records contact St. Andrew the Apostle Parish, Taunton.
6—ST. JUDE THE APOSTLE (2007) Rev. John J. Perry; Deacon Philip E. Bedard.
Mailing Address: 249 Whittenton St., 02780. Tel: 508-824-3330; Fax: 508-880-3865. Email: whittenton@verizon.net. In Res., Rev. Edward A. Murphy.
Catechesis/Religious Program—468 Bay St., 02780. Tel: 508-824-4545. Miss Elizabeth Hoye, Catechetical Leader. Students 202.
Convent—279 Whittenton St., 02780. Tel: 508-824-8946.
7—ST. MARY'S (1828) Rev. James J. Doherty, C.S.C. In Res., Revs. David S. Marcham; John P. Phalen, C.S.C.
Res.: 14 St. Mary's Square, 02780. Tel: 508-822-7116; Fax: 508-822-7117. Email: stmarystaunton@verizon.net. Web: www.saintmarystaunton.com.
School—St. Mary Primary School, (Grades PreK-5), 106 Washington St., 02780. Tel: 508-822-9480; Fax: 508-822-7164. Web: www.stmarystaunton-.com. Mr. Brian M. Cote, Prin. - Elementary. Lay Teachers 34; Students 266.
Catechesis/Religious Program—Tel: 508-822-7116; Fax: 508-822-7117. Ms. Judith Silvia, Catechetical Leader. Students 136.
Dolan Parish Center—
8—OUR LADY OF LOURDES (1905), (Portuguese), Merged with Sacred Heart, Taunton to form Annunciation of the Lord, Taunton.
9—OUR LADY OF THE HOLY ROSARY (1909), (Polish), [JC] Rev. David M. Stopyra, O.F.M.Conv.
Res.: 80 Bay St., 02780. Tel: 508-823-3046; Fax: 508-823-0585. Email: myholyrosary@comcast.net. Web: www.holyrosarytaunton.org.
Catechesis/Religious Program—Students 80.
10—OUR LADY OF THE IMMACULATE CONCEPTION (1883) Closed. For inquiries for parish records contact St. Jude the Apostle Parish, Taunton.
11—ST. PAUL'S (1904) Closed. For inquiries for parish records contact St. Andrew the Apostle Parish, Taunton.
12—SACRED HEART (1873) Merged with Our Lady of Lourdes, Taunton to form Annunciation of the Lord, Taunton.

VINEYARD HAVEN, DUKES CO., ST. AUGUSTINE (1962) Closed. For inquiries for parish records contact Good Shepherd Parish, Oak Bluffs.

WAREHAM, PLYMOUTH CO., ST. PATRICK'S (1911) [CEM] Revs. John M. Sullivan; Ronnie Paul Floyd, Parochial Vicar; Deacons Henry A. Gardyna; Daniel M. Donovan.
Res.: 82 High St., 02571-0271. Tel: 508-295-2411; Fax: 508-295-2417. Email: info@stpatrickswareham.org.
Catechesis/Religious Program—Tel: 508-295-0780; Fax: 508-295-2417. Email: stpatricksre@yahoo.com. Ms. Paula Wilk, Catechetical Leader. Students 354.
Mission—St. Anthony Gault Rd., Plymouth Co. 02571.

WELLFLEET, BARNSTABLE CO., OUR LADY OF LOURDES (1911) [CEM 2] Rev. Hugh J. McCullough; Deacon Steven M. Minninger.
Res.: 2282 Rt. 6, P.O. Box 1414, 02667-1414. Tel: 508-349-2222; Fax: 508-349-9612. Email: webmaster@ololwellfleet.org. Web: http://www.ololwellfleet.org.
Catechesis/Religious Program—Students 26.
Mission—Visitation Church 930 Massasoit Rd., North Eastham, Barnstable Co. 02651. Fax: 508-349-9612.

WEST HARWICH, BARNSTABLE CO., HOLY TRINITY (1918) [CEM] Rev. Edward J. Healey; Deacons John W. Foley; Ralph F. Cox; Vincent P. Walsh. In Res., Rev. Carlos Patino.
Res.: 246 Main St., P.O. Box 428, 02671. Tel: 508-432-4000; Fax: 508-432-3494. Email: htchurch@comcast.net. Web: http://www.htchurch.4lpi.com.
School—Holy Trinity Regional School, (Grades PreSchool-5), Holy Trinity; Our Lady of Victory; Corpus Christi; St. Patrick's; St. Francis Xavier; St. Pius X; Our Lady of the Cape; St. Joan of Arc., 245 Main St., 02671. Tel: 508-432-8216; Fax: 508-432-9349. Email: dlalumiere@holytrinityelementary.org. Web: www.holytrinityelementary.org. Mrs. Linda Mattson, Prin. -Elementary. Lay Teachers 10; Students 67.
Catechesis/Religious Program—Tel: 508-432-2898. Mrs. Barbara-Anne Foley, Catechetical Leader. Students 157.
Mission—Our Lady of the Annunciation [CEM] 187 Upper County Rd., Dennis Port, 02639.

WESTPORT, BRISTOL CO.
1—ST. GEORGE'S (1914) Rev. Maurice O. Gauvin.
Res.: 12 Highland Ave., 02790. Tel: 508-636-4965; Fax: 508-636-4188.
Catechesis/Religious Program—Students 108.
2—ST. JOHN THE BAPTIST (1930) Rev. Leonard P. Hindsley; Mr. Alex P. M. Naglowsky, Pastoral Assoc.
Res.: 945 Main Rd., Box 3328, 02790. Tel: 508-636-2251; Fax: 508-636-8306. Email: stjb@sprintout.net. Web: stjohnthebaptistwestport.org.
Catechesis/Religious Program—Tel: 508-636-5506. Ms. Susan Orzeck, Catechetical Leader. Students 292.
3—OUR LADY OF GRACE (1954) Rev. Horace J. Travassos.
Res.: 569 Sanford Rd., 02790. Tel: 508-674-6271; Fax: 508-675-4128. Email: ologwestportma@aol.com.
Catechesis/Religious Program—Tel: 508-675-5857. Jane Callahan, Rel. Coord. Students 218.

WOODS HOLE, BARNSTABLE CO., ST. JOSEPH'S (1882) Rev. Joseph H. Mauritzen.
Mailing Address: 33 Millfield St., P.O. Box 3, 02543.
Church: 33 Millfield St., 02543. Tel: 508-548-0990; Fax: 508-457-7849. Email: stjosephchurch@verizon.net.
Catechesis/Religious Program—

Chaplains of Public Institutions

BARNSTABLE. *Barnstable County House of Correction*. 82 High St., P.O. Box 271, Wareham, 02571. Deacon Daniel M. Donovan, Coord.

NEW BEDFORD. *Bristol Co. House of Correction & Eastern Massachusetts Correctional Alcohol Center*.
824 Tucker Rd., North Dartmouth, 02747. Tel: 508-996-2413. Vacant.

Awaiting Assignment:
Revs.—
Blyskosz, Joseph J.
Harrington, John P.
Kozanko, Andrzej J.
Swiercz, Pawel A.

Special Assignment:
Rev.—
Pregana, Craig A., St. Rose of Lima & St. Francis of Assisi, Casa Cural, Guaimaca, Honduras.

Graduate Studies:
Revs.—
Kalinowski, Dariusz, 3015 4th St. N.E., Washington, DC 20017.
Williams, Riley J., Pontifical North American College 00120 Vatican City State.

On Duty Outside the Diocese:
Revs.—
Dominguez, Ramon, McLean, VA
Kuhn, Michael F., McLean, VA
Magee, Patrick, St. Theresa Parish, 80 13th Ave., Paterson, NJ 07544.
Pacholczyk, Tadeusz, The National Catholic Bioethics Center, 6399 Drexel Rd., Philadelphia, PA 19151.
Pignato, David A., S.T.L., St. John's Seminary, 127 Lake St., Brighton, 02135.
Sharland, David, McLean, VA

Absent on Sick Leave:
Rev.—
Fitzpatrick, James M.

Retired:
Rev. Msgrs.—
Harrington, Thomas J., J.C.L., 375 Elsbree St., 02720.
Moore, John F., P.O. Box 2114, Cotuit, 02635.
Munroe, Henry T., P.A., 375 Elsbree St., 02720.
Regan, John J., P.O. Box 1094, North Falmouth, 02556.
Smith, John J., 375 Elsbree St., 02720.
Tosti, Ronald A., P.O. Box 814, Cotuit, 02635-0814.
Revs.—
Almeida, George F., 375 Elsbree St., 02720.
Andrews, John F.
Barnwell, Gerald P., 430 Eastern Ave., 02723.
Blottman, William P., 375 Elsbree St., 02720.
Buckley, James F., 209 Union St., Yarmouthport, 02675.
Buote, Martin L., 54 Salisbury St., 02744.
Burns, Edward J., 4234 N. Main St., Apt. 301, 02720.
Byington, Edward J., P.O. Box 571, Taunton, 02780.
Campbell, William G., 16 White Pine Ave., W., West Wareham, 02576.
Canuel, Paul E., 375 Elsbree St., 02720.
Dahl, Henry J.
Delano, Kenneth J., 22 Ingell St., Taunton, 02780.
Donovan, Robert C., 2446-2474 Highland Ave., 02720.
dos Santos, Jose A.F., 375 Elsbree St., 02720.
Driscoll, John P., 375 Elsbree St., 02720.
Fahey, James W.
Ferreira, Manuel P., 375 Elsbree St., 02720.
Freitas, Daniel L., P.O. Box 411154, Melbourne, FL 32941-1154.
Graziano, Peter N., S.T.L., M.A., M.S.W., 185 Woodside Ave., Winthrop, 02152.
Harrington, Brian J.
Kirby, Robert F., 50 Otis Trailer Village, Buzzards Bay, 02542-1302.
Kropiwnicki, Henry, 19 Rutland St., 02745-5830.
Lamb, Paul T., 15 Toby Cir., Hyannis, 02601.
LeDuc, Roger D., P.O. Box 2538, Tehachapi, CA 93581-2538.
Levesque, Roger J., 818 Middle St., 02721-1734.
Lopes, Thomas C., 375 Elsbree St., 02720.
McLellan, James R., 375 Elsbree St., 02720.
Morse, James H., 385 Central Ave., Seekonk, 02771.
Mullaney, Leonard M., 2446-2474 Highland Ave., 02720.
Pereira, Luciano J., P.O. Box 113, Somerset, 02726.
Ryan, Albert J., 375 Elsbree St., 02720.
Shovelton, Gerald T., 419 Chula Vista Ave., Lady Lake, FL 32159.
Shovelton, William J., 419 Chula Vista Ave., Lady Lake, FL 32159.
Wall, Barry W., 375 Elsbree St., 02720.
Wallace, Francis X., P.O. Box 3737, Pocasset, 02559.
Wingate, Arthur K., 375 Elsbree St., 02720.

Permanent Deacons:
Akin, David P., St. Pius X, South Yarmouth
Alence, Robert, (Retired), Corpus Christi, East Sandwich
Bailey, Thomas C., (Retired), St. Pius Tenth, South Yarmouth
Barrett, James M., Our Lady of Victory, Centerville
Battiston, Donald L., St. Mary, Our Lady of the Isle, Nantucket
Beckel, Gregory J., Christ the King, Mashpee
Bedard, Philip E., St. Jude the Apostle, Taunton
Biron, Donald R., Our Lady of the Cape, Brewster
Bonneau, Bruce J., St. Mary, Fairhaven
Boucher, David R., Corpus Christi, Sandwich
Bousquet, Louis A., (Unassigned)
Branco, John F., Good Shepherd & Holy Trinity, Fall River
Buder, Karl G., Good Shepherd, Martha's Vineyard
Camacho, Francis, Florida
Cipriano, A. Anthony, Fall River
Coates, Vincent, Jr., (Retired), St. Elizabeth Seton, North Falmouth
Connor, John, (Retired), St. Mary, Norton; Boston, MA
Cook, Chester O., (Retired), St. Peter the Apostle, Provincetown
Cote, Peter R., St. Mary's Cathedral, Fall River
Cox, Ralph F., (Retired), Holy Trinity, West Harwich
Dexter, Leonard C., Jr., St. John the Evangelist, Pocasset
Donovan, Daniel M., St. Patrick, Wareham
Dresser, Richard M., (Retired), St. Francis Xavier, Hyannis
Emmert, John J., (Unassigned)
Fantasia, Frank D., Christ the King, Mashpee
Faria, Robert A., St. John of God, Somerset
Fitzpatrick, John J., Holy Family, East Taunton
Foley, John W., Holy Trinity, West Harwich
Fournier, Paul M., St. Joseph & Holy Ghost, Attleboro
Gallerizzo, William, St. Pius X, South Yarmouth; Washington
Gardyna, Henry A., (Retired), St. Patrick, Wareham; Boston, MA
Gendron, Ernest J., St. Margaret, Buzzards Bay
Grant, John D., (Unassigned)
Gundlach, Richard J., St. Mark, Attleboro Falls
Guresh, Peter M., St. Elizabeth Seton, North Falmouth
Guy, Michael P., New Hampshire
Haddad, Victor, (Retired), St. Thomas More, Somerset
Hickey, C. Michael, St. Pius X, South Yarmouth; Boston, MA
Hill, Robert J., (Retired)
Hussey, Edward J., St. Patrick, Somerset
Joslin, Donald, St. Joan of Arc, Orleans; Syracuse, NY
Kane, Joseph K., Hartford
LaChance, Arthur L., Jr., Corpus Christi, Sandwich
LaPiana, Fred G., III, Good Shepherd, Martha's Vineyard
Leavitt, James P., (Retired), Our Lady of the Cape, Brewster
Lemay, Richard G., Our Lady of Mt. Carmel, Seekonk
Lemay, Robert D., Christ the King, Mashpee
Liegey, Gabriel J., (Retired), Vermont
Lorenzo, Robert G., St. Joseph, Fairhaven; Camden, NJ
Lukac, Theodore E., Our Lady of Victory, Centerville
Macedo, Paul J., St. John the Baptist & Our Lady of Mt. Carmel, New Bedford
Mador, Joseph F., Holy Redeemer, Chatham
Mahoney, Patrick J., (Retired), St. Patrick, Falmouth
Malloy, Adelbert F., St. John the Evangelist, Attleboro
Martin, William A., (Retired), St. Elizabeth Seton, North Falmouth
Massoud, Donald P., St. Anthony of the Desert, Fall River
Mattar, Jean E., Our Lady of Purgatory, New Bedford
McCarthy, Dana G., Florida
McEnaney, Norman F., St. Joan of Arc, Orleans
McGinley, Joseph A., St. Ann, Raynham
Medeiros, Douglas R., St. Joseph, Fairhaven
Medeiros, Joseph P., St. Michael, Fall River
Medina, Jose H., St. Anthony, Taunton
Metilly, Paul, Florida
Minninger, Steven M.
Moniz, John de A., Florida
Morency, Marcel G., (Retired), Our Lady of Fatima, New Bedford
Murphy, Richard J., St. Francis Xavier, Hyannis
Nasser, Andre P., (Retired) St. Anthony of the Desert, Fall River
Nogueira, Benjamin, Diocese of Worcester
Normandin, Robert G., St. Louis de France, Swansea
Norton, Victor K., Texas
O'Connell, Dennis G., Corpus Christi, Sandwich
Ouellette, Maurice A., St. Julie Billiart, No. Dartmouth
Pacheco, Eduardo M., (Retired), Our Lady of the Assumption, New Bedford
Palanza, Thomas P., St. Mary, Mansfield
Pelland, Robert W., (Retired), Rhode Island
Pepin, David B., St. Francis Xavier, Acushnet
Pierce, David E., St. John the Evangelist, Pocasset
Pires, Abilio dos A., Our Lady of Mt. Carmel & St. John the Baptist, New Bedford
Pires, Albertino F., Our Lady of the Immaculate Conception, New Bedford
Racine, Leo W., (Retired), St. Joseph-St. Therese, New Bedford
Regali, Joseph E., Sacred Heart, North Attleboro
Roma, Paul K., Our Lady of the Assumption, Osterville
Sasseville, Eugene E., Holy Name of the Sacred Heart of Jesus, New Bedford
Simonis, John E., St. Patrick, Falmouth
Souza, Thomas J., Espirito Santo, Fall River
St. Onge, Lawrence A., Our Lady of Guadalupe at St. James Church, New Bedford
Stenberg, Richard S., Holy Redeemer, Chatham; Bridgeport CT
Surprenant, Robert L., (Retired), St. John Neumann, East Freetown
Thadeu, Alan J., St. Andrew the Apostle, Taunton
Thomas, Walter D., Florida
Twerago, John P., St. Joan of Arc, Orleans
Wallace, Forrest, Cincinnati, Ohio
Walsh, Vincent, (Retired), Holy Trinity, West Harwich
Welch, John, (Retired), St. Ann, Raynham
Zarella, George H., Holy Cross, South Easton
Zeich, Richard C., St. Pius X, South Yarmouth
Zonghetti, Michael T., St. Mary, Norton

INSTITUTIONS LOCATED IN THE DIOCESE

[A] COLLEGES AND UNIVERSITIES

NORTH EASTON. *Holy Cross Fathers Religious*, 480 Washington St., 02356. Tel: 508-238-5942; Fax: 508-238-1297. Email: jlack@hcep.com. Web: www.holycrosscsc.org. Revs. James R. Lackenmier, C.S.C., Supr.; Richard E. Gribble, C.S.C.; David J. Arthur, C.S.C.; Foster J. Burbank; Joseph F. Callahan, C.S.C.; Thomas L. Campbell; Rudolph V. Carchidi, C.S.C.; James W. Chichetto, C.S.C.; Hugh Cleary, C.S.C.; Mark T. Cregan, C.S.C.; John F. Denning, C.S.C.; Marc F. Fallon, C.S.C.; Thomas P. Gariepy, C.S.C., Asst. Supr.; Thomas M. Halkovic, C.S.C.; Robert J. Kruse, C.S.C.; Pinto Paul, C.S.C.; James H. Phalan, C.S.C.; George Piggford, C.S.C.; Leo Polselli, C.S.C., Asst. Supr.; Kevin J. Sandberg, C.S.C.; Richard J. Segreve, C.S.C.; Patrick J. Sullivan, C.S.C.; Francis M. Walsh, C.S.C.; Stephen S. Wilbricht, C.S.C.; Robert A. Wiseman, C.S.C.; Bro. Subal Rosario, C.S.C. (Bangladesh).

Stonehill College (1948) 320 Washington St., 02357. Tel: 508-565-1301; Fax: 508-565-1432. Email: mcregan@stonehill.edu. Web: www.stonehill.edu. Revs. Mark T. Cregan, C.S.C., Pres.; Rudolph V. Carchidi, C.S.C.; James W. Chichetto, C.S.C.; Hugh Cleary, C.S.C., Dir., Campus Min.; John F. Denning, C.S.C.; Thomas P. Gariepy, C.S.C.; Richard E. Gribble, C.S.C.; Thomas M. Halkovic, C.S.C.; Robert A. Wiseman, C.S.C.; Pinto Paul, C.S.C., Campus Min.; George Piggford, C.S.C.; Bro. Subal Rosario, C.S.C. (Bangladesh); Revs. Kevin P. Spicer, C.S.C.; Stephen S. Wilbricht, C.S.C. Priests 7; Lay Teachers 148; Students 2,520.

[B] HIGH SCHOOLS, DIOCESAN

FALL RIVER. *Bishop Connolly High School*, 373 Elsbree St., 02720. Tel: 508-676-1071; Fax: 508-676-8594. Email: bchs@bishopconnolly.com. Web: www.bishopconnolly.com. E. Christopher Myron, Prin.; Rev. David M. Andrade, Chap. Brothers 3; Lay Teachers 19; Students 276.

ATTLEBORO. *Bishop Feehan High School*, 70 Holcott Dr., 02703. Tel: 508-226-6223; Fax: 508-226-7696. Email: webmaster@bishopfeehan.com. Web: www.bishopfeehan.com. Mr. Christopher E. Servant, Pres.; William Runey, Prin.; Rev. David A. Costa, Chap. Sisters 1; Lay Teachers 112; Students 1,059.

HYANNIS. *Pope John Paul II High School*, 120 High School Rd., 02601. Tel: 508-862-6336; Fax: 508-862-6339. Email: ckeavy@pjp2hs.org. Web: www.pjp2hs.org. Christopher W. Keavy, Prin. Lay Teachers 22; Students 230.

NORTH DARTMOUTH. *Bishop Stang High School*, 500 Slocum Rd., 02747-2999. Tel: 508-996-5602; Fax: 508-994-6756. Email: office@bishopstang.com. Web: www.bishopstang.com. Theresa E. Dougall, Pres.; Peter Shaughnessy, Prin.; Michael P. O'Brien, Asst. Prin. Students; Rev. Gregory A. Mathias, Chap.; Kathleen Ruginis, Asst. Prin. Academics; George Wrobel, Dir. Guidance; Jennifer Thomas, Librarian. Priests 1; Lay Teachers 57; Support Staff 19; Students 714.

TAUNTON. *Coyle and Cassidy High School* (1971) (Grades 9-12), 2 Hamilton St., 02780. Tel: 508-823-6164; Fax: 508-823-2530. Email: gchaves@coylecassidy.com. Web: www.coylecassidy.com. Dr. Mary Patricia Tranter, Ph.D., Pres.; Robert Gay, Prin.; Rev. David M. Stopyra, O.F.M.Conv., Chap.; Rosemary Gately, Librarian. Priests 1; Lay Teachers 41; Students 577.

[C] ELEMENTARY SCHOOLS, DIOCESAN

TAUNTON. *Taunton Catholic Middle School* (1971) (Grades 5-8), 61 Summer St., 02780. Tel: 508-822-0491; Fax: 508-824-0469. Email: tcms@catholicmiddle.com. Web: www.catholicmiddle.com. Dr. Corinne R. Merritt, Prin. Lay Teachers 15; Students 211.

[D] RESIDENTIAL CHILD CARE FACILITIES

FALL RIVER. *St. Vincent's Home Corp.*, 2425 Highland Ave., 02720. Tel: 508-679-8511; Fax: 508-672-2558. Web: www.stvincentshome.org. Mr. John T. Weldon, Exec. Dir.; Sheila Wilkins, M.Ed., Spec. Educ. Admin. Sisters 4; Lay Teachers 5; Total Staff 240; Children & Families 200.

[E] HOMES FOR AGED

FALL RIVER. *Catholic Memorial Home Inc.*, 2446 Highland Ave., 02720-4599. Tel: 508-679-0011; Fax: 508-672-5858. Email: thealy@dhfo.org. Thomas F. Healy, Supr. & Admin.; Rev. John A. Raposo. Total Assisted Annually 450; Total Staff 416; Bed Capacity 290.

FAIRHAVEN. *Our Lady's Haven of Fairhaven Inc.*, 71 Center St., 02719. Tel: 508-999-4561; Fax: 508-997-0254. Email: mmedeiros@dhfo.org. Web: www.dhfo.org. Michael Medeiros, Admin.; Rev. Michael Shanahan, SS.CC., Chap. Bed Capacity 117; Residents 117; Total Staff 160; Total Assisted Annually 178.

NEW BEDFORD. *Sacred Heart Home*, 359 Summer St., 02740. Tel: 508-996-6751; Fax: 508-992-3145. Web: www.dhfo.org. Manuel Benevides, M.S., Admin.; Rev. Michael Annunziato, SS.CC., Chap. (Retired). Total Staff 275; Residents 197; Bed Capacity 217; Total Assisted Annually 197.

NORTH ATTLEBORO. *Madonna Manor Inc.* (1966) 85 N. Washington St., 02760. Tel: 508-699-2740; Fax: 508-699-0481. Email: mmurpy@dhfo.org. Web: www.dhfo.org. Mary-Ellen Murphy, R.N., B.S.N., M.S., Admin.; Sr. Mary Duffy, S.S.J., Dir. of Pastoral Care. Bed Capacity 129; Total Assisted Annually 225; Total Staff 208.

TAUNTON. *Bethany House Adult Day Care*, 72 Church Green, 02780. Tel: 508-822-9200. Raymond A. McAndrews, Admin. Bed Capacity 30; Total Assisted 45; Total Staff 6.

Marian Manor Inc., 33 Summer St., 02780. Tel: 508-822-4885; Fax: 508-880-3386. Email: rmcandrews@dhfo.org. Raymond A. McAndrews, Admin.; Rev. Bernard Vanasse, Chap.; Sr. Paulina Cardenas, O.P., Dir. Pastoral Care. Dominican Sisters of Charity of the Presentation of the Blessed Virgin Mary 1; Total Staff 165; Bed Capacity 116; Patients Assisted Annually 116.

[F] MONASTERIES AND RESIDENCES OF PRIESTS AND BROTHERS

FALL RIVER. *Brothers of Christian Instruction*, 555 Eastern Ave., 02723. Tel: 508-672-5763; Fax: 508-676-8594. Email: fallriverfic@comcast.net. Web: ficbrothers.org. Bros. Daniel Caron, F.I.C., Local Supr.; Roger Millette, F.I.C.; Walter Zwierchowski, F.I.C. Brothers 3; Faculty of Bishop Connolly High 3.

Cardinal Medeiros Residence-Retirement Facility for Priests, 375 Elsbree St., 02720-7211. Tel: 508-675-1050; Fax: 508-675-2181.

Priests' Hostel, 2402 Highland Ave., 02720. Tel: 508-672-1632; Fax: 508-679-1422. In Res. Revs. Joseph J. Blyskosz; Andrzej J. Kozanko; Michael J. O'Hearn; Pawel A. Swiercz; Bernard Vanasse.

ATTLEBORO. *La Salette Missionary Association*, 947 Park St., P.O. Box 2965, 02703. Tel: 508-222-0027; Fax: 508-222-2504. Email: lsmajp@aol.com. Web: www.lasalettemissionary.org. Very Rev. Joseph G. Bachand, M.S., Provincial; Rev. Bernard Baris, M.S., Dir.

Missionaries of La Salette (MA), Inc.

La Salette Shrine, 947 Park St., 02703. Tel: 508-222-5410; Fax: 508-222-6770. Email: programsoffice@lasalette-shrine.org. Web: www.lasalette-shrine.org. Revs. Nicodemus Aung Than Aye, M.S.; Gerard J. Boulanger, M.S., Supr.; Ronald A. Beauchemin, M.S.; Bro. Robert W. Russell, M.S., Dir. Shrine. Priests 13; Brothers 7. In Res. Revs. Henry C. Brodeur, M.S.; Fernand Cassista, M.S.; Victor Chaupetta, M.S.; Ronald G. Gagne, M.S., Prov. Communications Dir.; Cyriac Mattathilanickal, M.S., Dir. Retreat House; Donald Paradis, M.S. (Retired); Tom Puthusseril, M.S.; John P. Sullivan, M.S.; John A. Welch, M.S., Vocation Dir.; Bros. Paul Boucher, M.S.; Lucien Brodeur, M.S.; Roger Moreau, M.S.; Rev. Manuel C. Pereira, M.S.; Bro. Roger St. Germain, M.S., (Retired); Rev. John P. Sullivan, M.S.; Bro. Ronald Taylor, M.S.; Rev. Raymond Vaillancourt, M.S. (Retired). *La Salette Communications Office*, 947 Park St., 02703. Email: rongagne@aol.com. Revs. Manuel C. Pereira, M.S.; Raymond Vaillancourt, M.S. (Retired); Bro. David Eubank, M.S.

FAIRHAVEN. *Sacred Hearts Provincial House*, 77 Adams St., P.O. Box 111, 02719-0111. Tel: 508-993-2442; Fax: 508-996-5499. Web: www.sscc.org. Revs. Thomas McElroy, SS.CC., Vicar Provincial; William F. Petrie, SS.CC., Prov.; Bro. Paul R. Alves, SS.CC., Treas., Prov. Councilor. Congregation of the Sacred Hearts of Jesus and Mary. Fathers 1. *National Center of the Enthronement*, P.O. Box 111, 02719-0111. Tel: 508-999-2680; Fax: 508-993-8233. Email: necenter@juno.com. Web: www.sscc.org. Congregation of the Sacred Hearts of Jesus and Mary. Total Staff 2. *Damien Residence*, 73 Adams St., P.O. Box 111, 02719-0111. Tel: 508-999-0500; Fax: 508-990-7173. Revs. Matthias Shanley, SS.CC., Dir.; Michael Annunziato, SS.CC., Asst. Dir. (Retired); William Heffron, SS.CC.; Albert Dagnoli, SS.CC.; John Fee, SS.CC.; Benedict Folger, SS.CC.; Owen F. Goodwin, SS.CC. (Retired); Gabriel Healy, SS.CC. (Retired); Michael Kelly, SS.CC.; Leo King, SS.CC. (Retired); Brian Marggraf, SS.CC. (Retired); Austin Nagle, SS.CC.; Michael Shanahan, SS.CC. Fathers 12; Brothers 1.

In Nassau, Bahamas: Revs. Martin Gomes, SS.CC.; Patrick F. Fanning, SS.CC.

In India: Revs. Alexis Nayak, SS.CC.; Subal Nayak, SS.CC.; Sudhir Nayak, SS.CC.; Sudhir Cristo Das Nayak, SS.CC.; Roche Iruthayaraj Thiruchiluvai, SS.CC.; Joseph Anthony Raja, SS.CC.; Stephen Joseph Sarto, SS.CC.; Ajith Kumar Dass, SS.CC.; Tony Biswas, SS.CC.

In Rome, Italy: Rev. Richard McNally, SS.CC., Vicar Gen.

NEW BEDFORD. *Marian Friary of Our Lady, Queen of the Seraphic Order*, 600 Pleasant St., 02740-6299. Tel: 508-996-8274. Email: ffi@marymediatrix.com. Web: www.marymediatrix.com. P.O. Box 3003, 02741-3003. Revs. Raphael M. Magee, F.I., Vicar; Louis Maximilian M. Smith, F.I., Father Guardian; Joshua M. Delos Santos, F.I.; Maximilian M. Warnisher, F.I. Priests 4; Brothers 2.

NORTH DARTMOUTH. *Holy Cross Residence* (1934) 824 Tucker Rd., 02747-3531. Tel: 508-993-2238; Fax: 508-984-4339. Revs. James T. Preskenis, C.S.C., Supr.; William G. Condon, C.S.C. (Retired); Albert A. Croce, C.S.C. (Retired); John F. Dias, C.S.C. (Retired); J. Robert Rioux, C.S.C. (Retired); Charles L. Wallen, C.S.C. (Retired); Patrick C. Walsh, C.S.C.; Bros. Harold Hathaway, C.S.C., Asst. Supr. & Steward; Robert Vozzo, C.S.C., (Retired).

St. Joseph's Hall, 800 Tucker Rd., 02747-3599. Tel: 508-996-2413; Fax: 508-984-4339. Email: cscda@aol.com. Revs. James T. Preskenis, C.S.C., Supr.; J. Robert Rioux, C.S.C., Dir. (Retired); John F. Dias, C.S.C. (Retired); William G. Condon, C.S.C. (Retired); Bros. Robert Vozzo, C.S.C., (Retired); Harold Hathaway, C.S.C., Financial Admin.

ONSET. *St. Joseph Friary-Franciscan Friars*, 46 Robinwood Rd., P.O. Box 63, 02558. Tel: 508-759-7280; Fax: 508-743-9551. Email: gjsilverio17@hotmail.com. Revs. Gilbert J. Silverio, O.F.M., M.Ed., Guard.; Brennan Egan, O.F.M., Ph.D. Total Staff 2; Total in Residence 2.

[G] CONVENTS AND RESIDENCES FOR SISTERS

FALL RIVER. *Bishop's Residence Convent*, 394 Highland Ave., 02720. Tel: 508-675-1311. Sisters of St. Jeanne d'Arc.

DIGHTON. *Dominican Sisters of Charity of the Presentation of the Blessed Virgin*, 3012 Elm St., 02715. Tel: 508-669-5425; 508-669-5023 (Novitiate); Fax: 508-669-6521. Email: domsrs@presentation-op-usa-org. Web: www.presentation-op-usa-.org. Sr. Vimala Vadakumpadan, O.P., Major Supr. Provincial House-Residence, Residence for Aged Sisters, Novitiate. Sisters 37.

FAIRHAVEN. *Sisters of the Sacred Hearts, Community Headquarters*, 35 Huttleston Ave., 02719-3154. Tel: 508-994-9341. Email: srmuriellebeau@cs.com. Sisters Eleanor Marie Cyr, SS.CC., Supr.; Claire Bouchard, SS.CC.; Muriel Ann Lebeau, SS.CC.

Sisters of the Sacred Hearts of Jesus and Mary and of Perpetual Adoration, SS.CC. Sisters in Community 3.

HARWICHPORT. *Sisters of the Good Shepherd Contemplative Community* (1831) 88 Bank St., 02646. Tel: 508-432-5582; Fax: 508-432-6293. Email: aureenbehrend@verizon.net.

NEW BEDFORD. *Franciscan Sisters of the Immaculate*, 106 Bullard St., 02746. Tel: 508-990-0335. Email: fsiusa@verizon.net. Web: www.marymediatrix.com; www.franciscansoftheimmaculate.com. Sr. Maria Simona Pia, F.I., Local Supr. Professed Sisters 5; Postulants 4.

SOUTH DARTMOUTH. *Dominican Sisters of Hope* (1995) *Bethany Community*, 21 Thatcher St., 02748. Tel: 508-996-1305. Web: www.ophope.org. Sisters 2.

TAUNTON. *Villa Fatima* (1934) 90 County St., 02780. Tel: 508-822-6282; Fax: 508-823-0825. Email: sr.dot@att.net; srdot@fctuplus.net. Web: www.ssdmission.org; www.sistersofsaintdorothy.org. Sr. Rosalie Patrello, S.S.D., Local Coord. Sisters of St. Dorothy. Professed Sisters 4.

WAREHAM. *St. Patrick's Missionary Cenacle*, 86 High St., 02571. Tel: 508-295-0799. Email: srcathl@verizon.net. Outreach to the homebound.

[H] RETREAT HOUSES

ATTLEBORO. *La Salette Retreat Center*, 947 Park St., 02703-0965. Tel: 508-222-8530; Fax: 508-236-9089. Email: office@lasaletteretreatcenter.com. Web: www.lasaletteretreatcenter.com. Revs. Cyriac Mattathilanickal, M.S., Dir.; Fernand Cassista, M.S.; Tom Puthusseril, M.S., Retreat Facilitator; Bro. Roger A. Moreau, M.S.; Dorothy J. Levesque, Retreat Leader; Mrs. Karen Laroche, M.A., Youth Leader; Lauren Murphy, La Salette Youth Min.Web: lasaletteyouthministry.org. Priests 3; Total Staff 11; Total Assisted 4,200.

EAST FREETOWN. *Cathedral Camp and Retreat Center* (1919) 167 Middleboro Rd., P.O. Box 428, 02717-0428. Tel: 508-763-8874; Fax: 508-763-2230. Email: rena@cathedralcamp.net. Web: www.cathedralcamp.net. Rena Lemieux, Asst. Dir. Total Staff 60.

Cathedral Camp Retreat Center, 167 Middleboro Rd., P.O. Box 428, 02717-0428. Tel: 508-763-8874; Fax: 508-763-2230. Email: rena@cathedralcamp.net. Web: www.cathedralcamp.net. Total Staff 6.

NORTH EASTON. *Holy Cross Retreat House*, 490 Washington St., 02356-1294. Tel: 508-238-2051; Fax: 508-238-0164. Email: jfcal44@hotmail.com. Web: www.retreathouse.org. Rev. Joseph F. Callahan, C.S.C., Spiritual Dir. Priests 1.

WAREHAM. *Sacred Hearts Retreat Center*, 226 Great Neck Rd., 02571. Tel: 508-295-0100; Fax: 508-291-2624. Email: retreats@sscc.org. Web: www.sscc.org/wareham. Rev. Stanley Kolasa, SS.CC., Dir.; Sr. Claire Bouchard, SS.CC., Admin.; Rev. David Lupo, SS.CC., Retreat Staff. Congregation of the Sacred Hearts of Jesus and Mary and of the Perpetual Adoration of the Most Blessed Sacrament. Priests 2; Sisters 1; Total Staff 6.

[I] DEPARTMENT OF CATHOLIC SOCIAL SERVICES AND SPECIAL APOSTOLATES

FALL RIVER. *Campaign For Human Development Apostolate*, 1600 Bay St., P.O. Box M, South Station, 02724. Tel: 508-674-4681; Fax: 508-675-2224. Email: aam@cssdioc.org. Arlene A. McNamee, L.C.S.W., Coord.

Catholic Social Services of Fall River, 1600 Bay St., P.O. Box M, S. Station, 02724. Tel: 508-674-4681; Fax: 508-675-2224. Email: aam@cssdioc.org. Arlene A. McNamee, L.C.S.W., Exec. Dir.

Program Directors: Debora Jones, Office Child Protectivity; Elaine Abdow, Pregnancy & Adoption Svcs.; Maria A. Pereira, L.I.C.S.W., COO; Matt Dausereau, Office for Persons with Disabilities;

Carol Hernandez, Coord. Basic Needs & Housing Counseling; Aaron McNamee, Coord. Supportive Housing Programs.

Catholic Social Services of New Bedford, 238 Bonney St., New Bedford, 02744. Tel: 508-997-7337; Fax: 508-984-1667.

Catholic Social Services of Cape Cod, 261 South St., Hyannis, 02601. Tel: 508-771-6771; Fax: 508-771-4711.

Catholic Social Services of Taunton, 78 Broadway, Taunton, 02780. Tel: 508-824-3264; Fax: 508-880-1903.

Adoption By Choice, 311 Hooper St., Tiverton, RI 02878. Tel: 401-624-9270; Fax: 508-675-2224.

HYANNIS. *St. Clare's Residence for Women* 02601. Bed Capacity 5; Total Staff 2; Total Assisted Annually 19.

[J] CAMPS AND COMMUNITY CENTERS

FALL RIVER. *Diocesan Catholic Youth Organization*, 709 Hanover St., 02720. Tel: 508-679-6732; Fax: 508-675-4755. Rev. Jay T. Maddock, J.C.L., Diocesan Dir.

Fall River Area Catholic Youth Organization, Sullivan-McCarrick CYO Center, 403 Anawan St., 02720. Tel: 508-672-9644; Fax: 508-675-4755.

New Bedford Area Catholic Youth Organization, Kennedy Youth Center, 377 County St., New Bedford, 02740. Tel: 508-996-0536; Fax: 508-675-4755. Mr. Nelson Macedo, Area Dir.

Taunton Area Catholic Youth Organization, 61 Summer St., Taunton, 02780. Tel: 508-822-5218; Fax: 508-675-4755. Mr. Donald Morrison, Area Dir.

[K] NEWMAN CENTERS AND CAMPUS MINISTRY

FALL RIVER. *Bristol Community College Newman Center* 777 Elsbree St., 02720-7395. Tel: 508-678-2811, Ext. 2247; Fax: 508-730-3286. Web: www.bristol.mass.edu/students/counseling/min_cath.html. Rev. Michael A. Ciryak, Campus Minister. Total Staff 1.

Diocesan Education Center 423 Highland Ave., 02720. Tel: 508-678-2828; Fax: 508-674-4218. Email: mgriffin@dfrcec.com. Web: www.dfrcec.com. Dr. Michael S. Griffin, Supt. of Schools; Dr. Donna Boyle, Asst. Supt. Curriculum; Kathleen A. Simpson, Asst. Supt. Personnel; Claire M. McManus, S.T.L., Dir. Faith Formation.

NORTH DARTMOUTH. *UMass Dartmouth Campus Ministry* 285 Old Westport Rd., 02747-2300. Tel: 508-999-8872. Email: dfrederici@umassd.edu. Rev. David C. Frederici, Chap.; Sr. Madeleine Tacy, O.P., Campus Min. Total Staff 2.

NORTH EASTON. *Wheaton College Newman Center* 480 Washington St., 02356. Tel: 508-238-5942. Web: catholiccampusministry.com. Rev. James R. Lackenmier, C.S.C.

NORTH FALMOUTH. *Cape Cod Campus Ministry* P.O. Box 182, Centerville, 02632. Tel: 508-744-3561; Fax: 508-444-3674. Email: dfrederici@umass.edu. Rev. David C. Frederici, Chap.

[L] MISCELLANEOUS LISTINGS

FALL RIVER. *Assisi Housing Corporation*, 1600 Bay St., 02724.

Carmelite Convent of Dartmouth, Inc., P.O. Box 2577, 02722.

Community Action for Better Housing, Inc., 1600 Bay St., P.O. Box M, S. Station, 02724. Tel: 508-674-4681; Fax: 508-675-2224. Email: AAM@cssdioc.org. Ed Allard, Prog. Coord.

Diocesan Facilities Self-Insurance Group, Inc., P.O. Box 1110, 02722.

Saint Mary's Education Fund, Inc., P.O. Box 2577, 02722. Tel: 508-675-1311.

St. Dominic's Apartments, Inc., 1600 Bay St., 02724. Tel: 508-674-4681; Fax: 508-675-2224. Arlene A. McNamee, L.C.S.W., Dir.

FAIRHAVEN. *Congregation of the Sacred Hearts - United States Province*, 77 Adams St., P.O. Box 111, 02719. Tel: 508-993-2442; Fax: 508-996-5499. Web: www.sscc.org. Alfred M. Gauthier, Fin. Mgr.

NEW BEDFORD. *The Institute of the Incarnate Word, Inc.*, 306 Ashley Blvd., 02746. Tel: 508-992-7587; Fax: 508-994-0281. Rev. Hugo G. Cardenas, I.V.E. Priests 1; Brothers 1; Total Staff 4; Total Assisted 150.

St. Mary's Home of New Bedford, Inc., P.O. Box 2577, 02722. Tel: 508-675-1311.

Missionaries of Charity, 556 County St., 02740. Tel: 508-997-7347. Shelter for homeless women. Total in Residence 4; Total Assisted 203.

NORTH EASTON. *Holy Cross Family Ministries* (1942) 518 Washington St., 02356-1200. Tel: 508-238-4095; Fax: 508-238-3953. Email: mission@HCFM.org. Web: www.hcfm.org. Robert Alzapiedi, Chief Admin. Officer; Revs. John P. Phalen, C.S.C., Pres.; James H. Phalan, C.S.C., Intl. Dir. Family Rosary; Wilfred Raymond, C.S.C., Natl. Dir. of Family Theater Productions; Beth Mahoney, Mission Dir. Corporate Name: The Family Rosary, Inc.; Sponsored by Congregation of Holy Cross (US Province).

RELIGIOUS INSTITUTES OF MEN REPRESENTED IN THE DIOCESE

For further details refer to the corresponding bracketed number in the Religious Institutes of Men or Women section.

[0200]—*Benedictine Monks*—O.S.B.

[0320]—*Brothers of Christian Instruction*—F.I.C.

[0600]—*Brothers of the Congregation of Holy Cross*—C.S.C.

[0270]—*Carmelite Fathers*—O.Carm.

[0802]—*Congregation of the Fathers of Mercy*—C.P.M.

[1140]—*Congregation of the Sacred Hearts of Jesus and Mary*—SS.CC.

[0480]—*Conventual Franciscans* (Buffalo, NY)—O.F.M.Conv.

[0520]—*Franciscan Friars* (Immaculate Conception Prov.)—O.F.M.

[0533]—*Franciscan Friars of the Immaculate*—F.F.I.

[]—*Institute of the Incarnate Word*—I.V.E.

[0690]—*Jesuit Fathers and Brothers*—S.J.

[0720]—*Missionaries of Our Lady of La Salette*—M.S.

[0430]—*Order of Preachers (Dominicans)*—O.P.

[0610]—*Priests of the Congregation of Holy Cross* (Eastern Prov.)—C.S.C.

RELIGIOUS INSTITUTES OF WOMEN REPRESENTED IN THE DIOCESE

[1810]—*Bernadine Franciscan Sisters*—O.S.F.

[3815]—*Congregation of the Sisters of St. Joan of Arc*—S.J.A.

[0750]—*Daughters of the Charity of the Sacred Heart of Jesus* (Sacred Heart Prov.)—F.C.S.C.J.

[1100]—*Dominican Sisters of Charity of the Presentation of the Blessed Virgin*—O.P.

[1105]—*Dominican Sisters of Hope*—O.P.

[]—*Franciscan Sisters of the Immaculate*—F.I.

[3790]—*Institute of the Sisters of St. Dorothy*—S.S.D.

[2710]—*Missionaries of Charity*—M.C.

[2790]—*Missionary Servants of the Most Blessed Trinity*—M.S.B.T.

[3450]—*Religious of Jesus and Mary*—R.J.M.

[2070]—*Religious of the Holy Union of the Sacred Hearts* (Immaculate Heart and Sacred Heart Provs.)—S.U.S.C.

[0640]—*Sisters of Charity of St. Vincent de Paul (Halifax)*—S.C.

[2575]—*Sisters of Mercy of the Americas*—R.S.M.

[]—*Sisters of Our Lady of LaSalette*—S.N.D.S.

[3720]—*Sisters of Saint Anne*—S.S.A.

[3830-16]—*Sisters of St. Joseph* (Springfield, MA)—S.S.J.

[0150]—*Sisters of the Assumption*—S.A.S.V.

[3180]—*Sisters of the Cross and Passion*—C.P.

[1830]—*Sisters of the Good Shepherd (Contemplative/Religious)*—C.G.S./R.G.S.

[3320]—*Sisters of the Presentation of the Blessed Virgin Mary*—P.B.V.M.

[3690]—*Sisters of the Sacred Hearts of Perpetual Adoration*—SS.CC.

[4048]—*Society of the Sisters, Faithful Companions of Jesus*—F.C.J.

DIOCESAN CEMETERIES

FALL RIVER. *St. John*
St. Mary
New Bedford Catholic Cemeteries, 1540 Stafford Rd., 02721.
Notre Dame
St. Patrick

ATTLEBORO. *St. John*
St. Stephen

EAST FALMOUTH. *St. Anthony*

HYANNIS. *St. Francis*

MANSFIELD. *St. Mary*

MATTAPOISETT. *St. Anthony*

NANTUCKET. *St. Mary*

NEW BEDFORD. *St. John*
St. Mary
Sacred Heart

NORTH ATTLEBORO. *St. Mary*

NORTH EASTON. *Immaculate Conception*

OAK BLUFFS. *Sacred Heart*

PROVINCETOWN. *St. Peter*

SANDWICH. *St. Peter*

SOMERSET. *St. Patrick*

TAUNTON. *St. Francis*
St. James
St. Joseph
St. Mary

TRURO. *Sacred Heart*

WAREHAM. *St. Patrick*

WELLFLEET. *Our Lady of Lourdes*

WEST HARWICH. *Holy Trinity*

NECROLOGY

† Levesque, Rev. Msgr. Edmond R., (Retired)—Died June 5, 2011

† Cardoso, Luis A., (Retired)—Died June 3, 2011

An asterisk (*) denotes an organization that has established tax-exempt status directly with the IRS and is not covered by the USCCB Group Ruling.

Diocese of Fargo

(Dioecesis Fargensis)

Most Reverend

SAMUEL J. AQUILA, D.D.

Bishop of Fargo; ordained June 5, 1976; appointed Coadjutor Bishop of Fargo June 12, 2001; ordained August 24, 2001; appointed Bishop of Fargo March 18, 2002. *Mailing Address: 5201 Bishops Blvd., Ste. A, Fargo, ND 58104-7605.*

Chancery Office: 5201 Bishops Blvd., Ste. A, Fargo, ND 58104-7605. Tel: 701-356-7900; Fax: 701-356-7999.

Web: www.fargodiocese.org

Email: webadmin2007@fargodiocese.org

Square Miles 35,786.

Corporate Title: The Diocese of Fargo.

Formerly Diocese of Jamestown.

Established November 12, 1889; Transferred to Fargo, April 6, 1897.

Comprises the Counties of Barnes, Benson, Bottineau, Cass, Cavalier, Dickey, Eddy, Foster, Grand Forks, Griggs, Kidder, LaMoure, Logan, McHenry, McIntosh, Nelson, Pembina, Pierce, Ramsey, Ransom, Richland, Rolette, Sargent, Sheridan, Steele, Stutsman, Towner, Traill, Walsh and Wells in the State of North Dakota.

For legal titles of parishes and diocesan institutions, consult the Chancery Office.

STATISTICAL OVERVIEW

Personnel	
Bishop	1
Priests: Diocesan Active in Diocese	76
Priests: Diocesan Active Outside Diocese	8
Priests: Retired, Sick or Absent	48
Number of Diocesan Priests	132
Religious Priests in Diocese	9
Total Priests in Diocese	141
Extern Priests in Diocese	8
Ordinations:	
Diocesan Priests	2
Transitional Deacons	4
Permanent Deacons	2
Permanent Deacons in Diocese	45
Total Sisters	114
Parishes	
Parishes	132
With Resident Pastor:	
Resident Diocesan Priests	64
Resident Religious Priests	4
Without Resident Pastor:	
Administered by Priests	64
Professional Ministry Personnel:	
Sisters	4
Lay Ministers	67
Welfare	
Catholic Hospitals	8
Total Assisted	141,077
Homes for the Aged	12
Total Assisted	1,400
Specialized Homes	1
Total Assisted	44
Special Centers for Social Services	3
Total Assisted	3,197
Residential Care of Disabled	1
Total Assisted	283
Educational	
Diocesan Students in Other Seminaries	18
Total Seminarians	18
Colleges and Universities	1
Total Students	300
High Schools, Diocesan and Parish	1
Total Students	325
Elementary Schools, Diocesan and Parish	12
Total Students	1,598
Catechesis/Religious Education:	
High School Students	2,128
Elementary Students	5,234
Total Students under Catholic Instruction	9,603
Teachers in the Diocese:	
Priests	1
Sisters	3
Lay Teachers	192
Vital Statistics	
Receptions into the Church:	
Infant Baptism Totals	1,124
Minor Baptism Totals	46
Adult Baptism Totals	36
Received into Full Communion	260
First Communions	1,049
Confirmations	1,142
Marriages:	
Catholic	212
Interfaith	142
Total Marriages	354
Deaths	920
Total Catholic Population	72,219
Total Population	390,972

Former Bishops—Rt. Rev. JOHN SHANLEY, D.D., ord. 1874; cons. Dec. 27, 1889; died July 16, 1909; Most Rev. JAMES O'REILLY, D.D., ord. June 24, 1880; cons. May 19, 1910; installed June 1, 1910; died Dec. 19, 1934; His Eminence ALOISIUS CARDINAL MUENCH, ord. June 8, 1913; appt. Bishop of Fargo, Aug. 10, 1935; cons. Oct. 15, 1935; installed Nov. 6, 1935; appt. Apostolic Visitator for Germany, July 8, 1946; granted personal title of Archbishop, Nov. 1, 1950; appt. Papal Nuncio to Germany, March 10, 1951; created Cardinal Priest and elevated to the Roman Curia, Dec. 14, 1959; died Feb. 15, 1962; Most Revs. LEO F. DWORSCHAK, D.D., ord. May 29, 1926; appt. Coadjutor Bishop of Rapid City, June 23, 1946; cons. Aug. 22, 1946; appt. Auxiliary Bishop of Fargo, April 10, 1947; succeeded to See, May 10, 1960; retired Sept. 8, 1970; died Nov. 5, 1976; JUSTIN A. DRISCOLL, D.D., ord. July 28, 1945; appt. Bishop of Fargo, Sept. 8, 1970; cons. and installed Oct. 28, 1970; died Nov. 19, 1984; JAMES S. SULLIVAN, ord. June 4, 1955; cons. Auxiliary Bishop of Lansing Sept. 21, 1972; appt. Bishop of Fargo April 2, 1985; installed May 30, 1985; retired March 18, 2002; died June 12, 2006.

Chancery Office—5201 Bishops Blvd., Fargo, 58104. Tel: 701-356-7900; Fax: 701-356-7999.

Moderator of the Curia—Rev. Msgr. JOSEPH P. GOERING, V.G.

Vicar General—Rev. Msgr. JOSEPH P. GOERING, V.G.

Chancellor and Secretary to the Bishop—Very Rev. LUKE D. MEYER.

Vicar for Clergy—Rev. Msgr. JOSEPH P. GOERING, V.G.

Vice Chancellor—Rev. Msgr. JEFFREY WALD.

Archivist—Very Rev. LUKE D. MEYER.

Chief Financial Officer—Mr. SCOTT A. HOSELTON, CPA.

Diocesan Tribunal—5201 Bishops Blvd., Fargo, 58104. Tel: 701-356-7940.

Judicial Vicar—Very Rev. K. S. KOPACZ, J.C.L.

Promotor Justitiae—VACANT.

Defensor Vinculi—Rev. Msgr. DANIEL J. PILON, J.C.L.

Presiding Judge—Very Rev. K. S. KOPACZ, J.C.L.

Judges—Rev. Msgr. WENDELYN VETTER, V.F. (Retired); Revs. JARED KADLEC, J.C.L.; JAMES GOODWIN, J.C.L.

Advocates—Rev. Msgr. WENDELYN VETTER, V.F. (Retired); Rev. ROBERT IRWIN; JONI TOLLEFSON; Ms. ELLEN O'CONNOR; Ms. JOAN HOUDEK.

Auditor—Rev. ROBERT IRWIN.

Notaries—Very Rev. LUKE D. MEYER, Chancellor; Rev. Msgr. GREGORY J. SCHLESSELMANN; Mr. SCOTT A. HOSELTON, CPA; Ms. JOLETTE KRABBENHOFT.

Diocesan College of Consultors—Revs. RICHARD FINEO; ANDREW JASINSKI; Rev. Msgrs. JOSEPH P. GOERING, V.G.; DENNIS A. SKONSENG; Very Rev. ROSS LAFRAMBOISE; Revs. GARY LUITEN; JAMES A. MEYER.

Deans—Deanery 1: Very Rev. DALE LAGODINSKI, Wahpeton. Deanery 2: Very Rev. JAMES MEYER, Fargo. Deanery 3: Very Rev. PHILLIP ACKERMAN, Grand Forks. Deanery 4: Very Rev. JOHN KLEINSCHMIDT, Minto. Deanery 5: Very Rev. DALE H. KINZLER, Devils Lake. Deanery 6: Very Rev. FRANKLIN MILLER, Harvey. Deanery 7: Very Rev. AL M. BITZ, Jamestown. Deanery 8: Very Rev. ROSS LAFRAMBOISE, Napoleon.

Diocesan Offices and Directors

Corporate Board—Most Rev. SAMUEL J. AQUILA, D.D.; Rev. Msgr. JOSEPH P. GOERING, V.G.; Very Rev. LUKE D. MEYER; Mr. BOB WILMOT; Mr. SCOTT A. HOSELTON, CPA; Mr. TERRY W. KNOEPFLE ESQ.

Apostleship of Prayer—Very Rev. CHAD F. WILHELM, Dir.

Diocesan Finance Council—Most Rev. SAMUEL J. AQUILA, D.D.; Rev. Msgr. JOSEPH P. GOERING, V.G.; Very Rev. LUKE D. MEYER; Mr. GRANT SHAFT; Ms. SHARON FROLEK; Ms. KAREN LESTER; Mr. STEVEN SCHONS; Mr. SCOTT A. HOSELTON, CPA; Ms. TERRI CLARK; Mr. LARRY EXNER; Ms. JULIE FLATEN; Mr. BRIAN SCHANILEC; Mr. BOB WILMOT; Mr. RICK SIMONSON.

Catholic Church Deposit & Loan Fund of Eastern North Dakota— Same as corporate board.

Pension Plan—Mr. SCOTT A. HOSELTON, CPA.

Censor Librorum—Rev. Msgr. ROBERT LALIBERTE, Ph.D. (Retired).

Office of Worship and Sacraments—Very Rev. LUKE D. MEYER.

Continuing Education of Priests—Rev. RAYMOND P. COURTRIGHT.

Arbitration & Conciliation Board—JENNIFER HASELBERGER; Sr. MARLYSS DIONNE, S.M.P.; MICHAEL MOE; PAUL RICHARD; Rev. Msgr. JOSEPH P. GOERING, V.G.; BARB AUGDAHL.

Ecumenical Commission—Rev. JASON ASSELIN.

Director of Stewardship and Development—Mr. STEVEN SCHONS.

Holy Childhood Association—Very Rev. LUKE D. MEYER.

Communications—Ms. TANYA WATTERUD.

The "New Earth" (Diocesan Newspaper)—Ms. TANYA WATTERUD, Editor.

North Dakota Catholic Conference—Mr. CHRISTOPHER

DODSON, 103 S. 3rd St., Ste. 10, Bismarck, 58501-3800.

Permanent Diaconate—Rev. Msgr. GREGORY J. SCHLESSELMANN, Dir.; Rev. KURTIS L. GUNWALL, Sec. Diaconate; Deacons DAVID EBLEN, Dir. Formation; STUART LONGTIN, Dir. Life & Ministries; EDWARD DIDIER, Asst. Dir. Formation.

Presbyteral Council—Rev. JAMES GOODWIN, J.C.L., Chm.

Propagation of the Faith—Very Rev. LUKE D. MEYER.

Rural Life—Rev. THOMAS GRANER, Dir., Mailing Address: 218 3rd St., S.E., Rugby, 58368. Tel: 701-776-6388.

Technology/Computer Office—Ms. JOCELYN SLOAN.

Catholic Education and Formation—Rev. ANDREW JASINSKI, Dir.

Evangelization/Catechesis—Ms. KATIE DUBAS.

Healthcare Director—Very Rev. DALE H. KINZLER.

Youth/Young Adults—Ms. KATHY LONEY.

Catholic Schools—Deacon DAVID HANEY.

Respect Life Office—Ms. RACHELLE L. SAUVAGEAU.

Vocation Director—Rev. KURTIS L. GUNWALL.

Catholic Cemeteries—Mr. SCOTT A. HOSELTON, CPA.

Hispanic Ministry—Rev. TIMOTHY SCHROEDER, Mailing Address: St. John the Evangelist, P.O. Box 636, Grafton, 58237-0636.

Native American Ministries—Rev. EDWARD SHERMAN, Chap. at Large (Retired).

Apostolate for Native Americans—Rev. GERALD A. MCCARTHY (Retired).

Prison Apostolate—Rev. PAUL R. SCHUSTER; Deacon STUART LONGTIN.

Liaison with Charismatic Movement—Very Rev. LUKE D. MEYER.

CLERGY, PARISHES, MISSIONS AND PAROCHIAL SCHOOLS

CITY OF FARGO

(CASS COUNTY)

1—ST. MARY'S CATHEDRAL OF FARGO (1880) [JC] Very Rev. Chad F. Wilhelm, Rector; Rev. Anthony Hession; Deacon George Loegering. In Res., Rev. Charles Fischer.
Office: 619 7th St. N., 58102. Tel: 701-235-4289; 701-235-4280; Fax: 701-235-2986. Email: geralyn@cathedralofstmary.com. Web: www.cathedralofstmary.com.
Res.: 679 6th Ave. N., 58102. Tel: 701-235-4280.
Catechesis/Religious Program—Students 154.

2—STS. ANNE & JOACHIM CHURCH OF FARGO (1995) [JC] Revs. Paul C. Duchschere; Peter Sharpe; Deacons David Eblen; Michael Dodge.
5202 25th St. S., 58104. Tel: 701-235-5757; Fax: 701-235-0764. Email: stsaaj@stsaaj.org. Web: www.stsaaj.org. In Res., Revs. Duaine Cote (Retired); Charles LaCroix.
Res.: 5202 25th St. S., 58104. Tel: 701-235-1514.
Catechesis/Religious Program—Students 464.

3—ST. ANTHONY OF PADUA'S CHURCH OF FARGO (1917) [JC] Rev. Raymond P. Courtright; Deacons Stuart Longtin; Donald Bunce. In Res., Rev. Msgr. Gregory J. Schlesselmann; Rev. Peter Hughes, C.S.Sp.
Church: 710 S. 10th St., 58103. Tel: 701-237-6063; Fax: 701-237-6064.
Catechesis/Religious Program—Tel: 701-232-3995. Students 59.

4—HOLY SPIRIT CHURCH OF FARGO (1951) [JC] Rev. Msgr. Jeffrey Wald. In Res., Rev. Msgr. Val Gross (Retired).
Church: 1420 N. 7th St., 58102. Tel: 701-232-5900; Fax: 701-232-5902. Web: holyspirit-church.org.
School—(Grades PreSchool-5), 1441 8th St. N., 58102. Tel: 701-232-4087; Fax: 701-232-8240. Jason Kotrba, Prin.; Jan Nowatski, Librarian. Lay Teachers 16; Students 165.
Catechesis/Religious Program—Students 225.

5—NATIVITY CHURCH OF FARGO (1960) [JC] Revs. Kevin Boucher; Thomas M. Feltman; Duane Koble, Admin.
Church: 1825 11th St. S., 58103. Tel: 701-232-2414; Fax: 701-232-4491. Email: duanek@nativitycatholicchurch.net. Web: www.nativitycatholicchurch.net.
School—(Grades K-5) Tel: 701-232-7461; Fax: 701-298-8981. Web: www.fcsn.k12nd.us/index2ntm. Cindy Hutchins, Prin.; Jan Nowatzki, Librarian. Lay Teachers 26; Students 339.
Catechesis/Religious Program—Students 170.

6—ST. PAUL'S NEWMAN CHURCH OF FARGO (1957) [JC] Rev. James Cheney.
Church: 1141 N. University Dr., 58102. Tel: 701-235-0142; Fax: 701-298-6431. Email: ndsunewmanctr@yahoo.com. Web: www.ndsunewman.org.
Catechesis/Religious Program—Students 25.

OUTSIDE THE CITY OF FARGO

ALICE, CASS CO., ST. HENRY (1902) Closed. For inquiries for parish records contact the Chancellor's Office. Sacramental records are at St. Patrick in Enderlin.

ANAMOOSE, MCHENRY CO., ST. FRANCIS XAVIER CHURCH OF ANAMOOSE (1899) [CEM], Also serving Drake. Rev. Robert Wapenski.
Mailing Address: P.O. Box 49, 58710-0049.
Church: 605 1st St. W., 58710. Tel: 701-465-3780; Fax: 773-496-3780. Email: stfx@gondtc.com.

ANETA, NELSON CO., SACRED HEART CHURCH OF ANETA (1907), Served from Cooperstown. Rev. Richard Fineo.
Mailing Address: *c/o St. George*, P.O. Box 217, Cooperstown, 58425. Tel: 701-797-2624.
Catechesis/Religious Program—Students 12.

ARDOCH, WALSH CO., ST. JOHN THE BAPTIST (1883) [CEM] Closed. For inquiries for parish records contact the chancery. Sacramental records are at Sacred Heart, Minto.

ARGUSVILLE, CASS CO., ST. WILLIAM (1942) [JC], Served from Hillsboro. Rev. Leo Kinney.
Mailing Address: P.O. Box 1, Harwood, 58042-0001.
Church: 107 Drake Ave., 58005.
Catechesis/Religious Program—Tel: 701-484-5211. Students 62.

ASHLEY, MCINTOSH CO., ST. DAVID (1920), Served from Wishek. Rev. Wenceslaus Katanga.
Mailing Address: *c/o St. Patrick*, P.O. Box 293, Wishek, 58495. Tel: 701-423-5494.
Catechesis/Religious Program—Students 16.

BALFOUR, MCHENRY CO., ST. JOSEPH (1906) Closed. For inquiries for parish records please contact the Chancellor's office. Sacramental records are at St. Margaret Mary, Drake.

BALTA, PIERCE CO., OUR LADY OF MT. CARMEL CHURCH OF BALTA (1902) [CEM], Served from Esmond. Rev. Brian Bachmeier.
Mailing Address: *c/o St. Boniface*, P.O. Box 37, Esmond, 58332-0037.
Church: 301 Main St. N., 58313.

BATHGATE, PEMBINA CO., ST. ANTHONY (1883) Closed. For inquiries for parish records contact the Chancellor's Office. Sacramental records are at St. Brigid, Cavalier.

BECHYNE, STS. PETER & PAUL CHURCH OF BECHYNE (1886) [CEM], Served from Pisek. Rev. Samuel Ezeibekwe.
Mailing Address: P.O. Box 27, Pisek, 58273. Tel: 701-284-6060.
Catechesis/Religious Program—Students 15.

BELCOURT, ROLETTE CO.

1—ST. ANN (1885) [CEM], Also serving St. Anthony. Revs. Mark Ropel, S.O.L.T.; Robert J. Cronin, S.O.L.T.; Shane Mckee, S.O.L.T.; David Mumba, S.O.L.T.; Deacon Francis Davis.
Church: Box 2000, 58316. Tel: 701-477-5601; Fax: 701-477-0602.
School—*St. Ann*, (Grades K-6), P.O. Box 2020, 58316-2020. Tel: 701-477-2667. Betty Laducer, Prin. Sisters 1; Lay Teachers 6; Students 39.
Catechesis/Religious Program—Students 132.

2—ST. ANTHONY (1885) [CEM], Served from Belcourt. Rev. Mark Ropel, S.O.L.T.
Mailing Address: *c/o St. Ann*, P.O. Box 2000, 58316. Tel: 701-477-5601.
Catechesis/Religious Program—Students 10.

3—ST. BENEDICT'S CHURCH OF BELCOURT (1940), Served from St. John. Rev. Fred Alexander, S.O.L.T.
Mailing Address: P.O. Box 170, St. John, 58369-0170. Tel: 701-477-3081; Fax: 701-477-0256.

BISBEE, TOWNER CO., HOLY ROSARY (1889) [CEM], Served from Rolette. Rev. Philip Chacko.
Mailing Address: P.O. Box 155, 58317.
Church: 304 3rd Ave. W., 58317. Tel: 701-246-3449; Fax: 701-246-3449.

BOTTINEAU, BOTTINEAU CO., ST. MARK'S CHURCH OF BOTTINEAU (1901) [CEM], Also serving Westhope. Rev. Paul R. Schuster.
322 Sinclair St., 58318-1024. Tel: 701-228-3164.
Catechesis/Religious Program—Students 107.

BREMEN, WELLS CO., ST. JOSEPH (1896) [CEM] Closed. For inquiries for parish records contact the chancery. Sacramental records located at St. John, New Rockford.

BROCKET, RAMSEY CO., ST. JOSEPH (1910) Closed. For inquiries for parish records contact the Chancellor's Office. Sacramental records are at St. Mary, Lakota.

BUCHANAN, STUTSMAN CO., ST. MARGARET ALACOQUE (1924) [CEM], Served from Jamestown. Very Rev. Al M. Bitz.
Mailing Address: *c/o St. James Basilica*, 622 1st Ave. S., Jamestown, 58401-4648. Tel: 701-252-0119; Fax: 701-952-6992. Email: parish@csicable.net.
Catechesis/Religious Program—Twinned with St. Michael in Pingree. Students 10.

BUFFALO, CASS CO., ST. THOMAS (1900) [JC], Served from Casselton. Rev. James Ermer.
Mailing Address: *c/o St. Leo*, P.O. Box 340, Casselton, 58012. Tel: 701-347-4609.
Church: 401 3rd St. N., 58011. Tel: 701-633-5150.
Catechesis/Religious Program—Students 15.

BURNSTAD, LOGAN CO., ST. CLARE OF ASSISI (1915) Closed. For inquiries for parish records contact the chancery. Sacramental records are at St. Philip Meri, Napoleon.

CANDO, TOWNER CO., SACRED HEART CHURCH OF CANDO (1893) [CEM], Also serving Leeds. Rev. Joseph D'Aco.
Mailing Address: P.O. Box 399, 58324.
Church: 310 3rd Ave., 58324. Email: shparish@dvl.midco.net.
Catechesis/Religious Program—Tel: 701-968-3830. Students 38.

CARRINGTON, FOSTER CO., SACRED HEART CHURCH OF CARRINGTON (1887) [CEM], Also serving Sykeston. Rev. David Syverson.
Mailing Address: P.O. Box 420, 58421. Tel: 701-652-2519.
Church: 663 1st St. S., 58421. Fax: 701-652-2518.
Catechesis/Religious Program—Tel: 701-652-2072. Students 145.

CASSELTON, CASS CO., ST. LEO'S CHURCH OF CASSELTON (1880) [CEM], Also serving Buffalo. Rev. James Ermer.
Mailing Address: P.O. Box 340, 58012.
Church: 211 Langer Ave., 58012. Tel: 701-347-4609; Fax: 701-347-4611. Email: stleo@casselton.net.
Catechesis/Religious Program—Students 153.

CAVALIER, PEMBINA CO., ST. BRIGID OF IRELAND CHURCH OF CAVALIER (1883) [CEM], Also serving Crystal. Rev. Robert Pecotte.
Mailing Address: P.O. Box 280, 58220-0280. Tel: 701-265-8877; Fax: 701-265-8848.
Church: 201 W. 1st Ave. S., 58220.
Catechesis/Religious Program—Students 37.

CAYUGA, SARGENT CO., STS. PETER & PAUL CHURCH OF CAYUGA (1916), Served from Lidgerwood. Rev. Robert Smith.
Mailing Address: *c/o St. Boniface*, P.O. Box 449, Lidgerwood, 58053-0449. Tel: 701-538-4604; Fax: 701-538-4600.
Church: 229 Franklin Ave. W., 58032.
Catechesis/Religious Program—Students 2.

COGSWELL, SARGENT CO., OUR LADY OF MERCY (1903) [CEM] Closed. For inquiries for parish records contact the chancery. Sacramental records are at St. Mary, Forman.

CONWAY, WALSH CO., ST. MARK (1884) Closed. For inquiries for parish records contact the Chancellor's Office. Sacramental records are at St. John, Pisek.

COOPERSTOWN, GRIGGS CO., ST. GEORGE (1939) [CEM], Also serving Aneta, Jessie, Finley. Rev. Richard Fineo.
Mailing Address: P.O. Box 217, 58425.
Church: 804 Foster Ave. N.W., 58425. Tel: 701-797-2624; Fax: 701-797-2632.
Catechesis/Religious Program—Students 11.

COURTENAY, STUTSMAN CO., ST. MARY, [CEM] Closed. For inquiries for parish records contact the chancery. Sacramental records are at St. Boniface, Wimbledon.

CRARY, RAMSEY CO., ST. BENEDICT (1910) [CEM] Closed. For inquiries for parish records contact the chancery. Sacramental records are at St. Joseph, Devil Lake.

CROW HILL, BENSON CO., ST. JEROME'S CHURCH OF CROW HILL (1892), (Native American), [CEM], Served from Fort Totten. Rev. Charles J. Leute, O.P.
Mailing Address: Box 299, Fort Totten, 58335. Tel: 701-766-4314.
Catechesis/Religious Program—Students 12.

CRYSTAL, PEMBINA CO., ST. PATRICK'S CHURCH OF CRYSTAL (1892) [CEM], Served from Cavalier. Rev. Robert Pecotte.
Mailing Address: P.O. Box 280, Cavalier, 58220. Tel: 701-265-8877; Fax: 701-265-8848.
Catechesis/Religious Program—Students 17.

DAZEY, BARNES CO., ST. MARY'S CHURCH OF DAZEY (1899) [CEM], Served from Wimbledon. Rev. Steven J. Meyer.
Mailing Address: P.O. Box 9, Wimbledon, 58492.
Church: 1606 16th St., S.E., 58429. Tel: 701-435-2310.
Catechesis/Religious Program—Students 24.

DEVILS LAKE, RAMSEY CO., ST. JOSEPH'S CHURCH OF DEVILS LAKE (1884) Very Rev. Dale H. Kinzler; Rev. Jason Asselin.
Mailing Address & Church: 501 4th St., N.E., Box 898, 58301. Tel: 701-662-7558; Fax: 701-662-7559. Email: stjosephschurch@dvl.midco.net.

School—(Grades PreK-6), 824 10th Ave., N.E., 58301. Tel: 701-662-5016; Fax: 701-662-5017. Tom Burckhard, Prin.; Linda Schwab, Librarian. Lay Teachers 15; Students 126.
Catechesis/Religious Program—Students 229.

DICKEY, LAMOURE CO., ASSUMPTION OF MARY (1909) [CEM], Served from LaMoure. Rev. Jerome Okafor.
Mailing Address: *c/o Holy Rosary*, P.O. Box 217, Lamoure, 58458. Tel: 701-883-5987; Fax: 701-883-4359.
Church: 106 Main St., 58431.

DRAKE, MCHENRY CO., ST. MARGARET MARY (1910) [CEM], Served by Anamoose. Rev. Robert Wapenski.
Res.: 605 Main St., P.O. Box 197, 58736. Tel: 701-465-3284; Fax: 773-496-3780.
Catechesis/Religious Program—Students 35.

DRAYTON, PEMBINA CO., ST. EDWARD'S CHURCH OF DRAYTON (1889) [CEM], Also serving Pembina. Rev. Joseph Okogba.
Mailing Address: P.O. Box 215, 58225. Tel: 701-454-6171; Fax: 701-454-6171. Email: stedward@polarcomm.com.
Church: 211 N. Main St., 58225.
Catechesis/Religious Program—Students 12.

DUNSEITH, ROLETTE CO.
1—IMMACULATE HEART OF MARY (1948) [CEM] Closed. For inquiries for parish records please see St. Michael's Church, Dunseith.
2—ST. LOUIS KING OF FRANCE (1882) [CEM] Closed. For inquiries for parish records please St. Michael's Church, Dunseith.
3—ST. MICHAEL THE ARCHANGEL DUNSEITH (2007) Rev. Scott Brossart, S.O.L.T., Admin.
Mailing Address: P.O. Box 160, 58329. Tel: 701-244-5738.
Res.: 112 First St., N.W., 58329.
Catechesis/Religious Program—Students 33.

EDGELEY, LAMOURE CO., TRANSFIGURATION CHURCH OF EDGELEY (1889) [CEM], Also serving Nortonville. Rev. Thaines Arulandu.
Mailing Address: 205 Second St., P.O. Box 347, 58433. Tel: 701-493-2387; Fax: 701-493-2823.
Catechesis/Religious Program—Students 79.

ELLENDALE, DICKEY CO., ST. HELENA'S CHURCH OF ELLENDALE (1888) [CEM], Also serving Fullerton. Rev. John Fisher Kizito.
Mailing Address: P.O. Box 796, 58436. Tel: 701-349-3297; Fax: 701-349-3297.
Church: 421 N. 2nd St., 58436.
Catechesis/Religious Program—Tel: 701-349-4128. Students 75.

ENDERLIN, RANSOM CO., ST. PATRICK'S CHURCH OF ENDERLIN (1901) [CEM], Also serving Sheldon and Fingal. Rev. Msgr. Daniel J. Pilon.
Mailing Address: 302 Bluff St., 58027. Tel: 701-437-2791; Fax: 262-437-2791. Email: stpatrick@mlgc.com. Web: www.fargodiocese.org/parish/enderlin.
Catechesis/Religious Program—Students 14.

ESMOND, BENSON CO., ST. BONIFACE (1909) [CEM], Also serving Maddock and Balta. Rev. Brian Bachmeier.
Mailing Address: P.O. Box 37, 58332-0037. Tel: 701-249-8360; Fax: 701-249-3459.
Church: 108 Alta Ave. N., 58332.
Catechesis/Religious Program—Students 17.

FAIRMOUNT, RICHLAND CO., ST. ANTHONY'S CHURCH OF FAIRMOUNT (1909) [CEM], Served from Hankinson. Rev. Scott Sautner.
Mailing Address: Box 292, 58030. Tel: 701-474-5518.
Church: 204 2nd St. N., 58030.
Catechesis/Religious Program—Students 18.

FESSENDEN, WELLS CO., ST. AUGUSTINE'S CHURCH OF FESSENDEN (1896), Also serving Hurdsfield and McClusky. Rev. Thomas J. Krupich.
105 7th Ave. S., 58438-7404. Tel: 701-547-3430.
Catechesis/Religious Program—Students 6.

FINGAL, BARNES CO., HOLY TRINITY CHURCH OF FINGAL (1889) [CEM 2], Served by Enderlin. Rev. Msgr. Daniel J. Pilon.
Mailing Address: 302 Bluff St., Enderlin, 58027. Tel: 701-437-2791; Fax: 701-437-2791. Web: www.fargodiocese.org/parish/fingal.
Catechesis/Religious Program—Students 13.

FINLEY, STEELE CO., ST. OLAF (1948) [JC], Served from Cooperstown. Rev. Richard Fineo.
Mailing Address: P.O. Box 217, Cooperstown, 58425. Tel: 701-797-2624.
Church: 100 Taft St., 58230.
Catechesis/Religious Program—Tel: 701-524-1101. Students 10.

FORMAN, SARGENT CO., ST. MARY (1913) [CEM], Served from Oakes. Rev. William Peter Gerlach.
Mailing Address: 484 4th St., S.W., 58032. Tel: 701-724-3319; Fax: 701-724-3310. Email: 4steeples@drtel.net.
Catechesis/Religious Program—Tel: 701-724-3440. Students 15.

FORT TOTTEN, BENSON CO., SEVEN DOLORS (1875), (Native American), [CEM], Also serving Crow Hill, Tokio. Rev. Charles J. Leute, O.P.; Deacon Anthony McDonald.
Mailing Address: P.O. Box 299, 58335. Tel: 701-766-4314; Fax: 701-766-1842.
Catechesis/Religious Program—Tel: 701-766-4314. Students 12.

FRIED, STUTSMAN CO., SACRED HEART (1888) Closed. For inquiries for parish records contact the Chancellor's Office. Sacramental records are at Basilica St. James, Jamestown.

FULDA, MCHENRY CO., ST. ANSELM (1901) [CEM] Closed. For inquiries for parish records contact the chancery. Sacramental records are at St. Therese, Rugby.

FULLERTON, DICKEY CO., ST. PATRICK (1921) [CEM], Served from Ellendale. Rev. John Fisher Kizito.
Mailing Address: *c/o St. Helena*, P.O. Box 796, Ellendale, 58436. Tel: 701-349-3297.
Church: 207 Monroe St. N., 58441.
Catechesis/Religious Program—Students 7.

GACKLE, LOGAN CO., ST. ANNE (1951) Closed. For inquiries for parish records contact the chancery. Sacramental records are at St. Philip Neri, Napoleon.

GENESEO, SARGENT CO., ST. MARTIN'S CHURCH OF GENESEO (1907) [CEM], Served from Lidgerwood. Rev. Robert Smith.
413 Main St., 58053. Tel: 701-538-4604.
Catechesis/Religious Program—Students 17.

GRAFTON, WALSH CO., ST. JOHN THE EVANGELIST'S CHURCH OF GRAFTON (1881) [CEM] Rev. Timothy Schroeder; Deacon Michael Grzadzielewski.
Church: 344 15th St. W., 58237. Tel: 701-352-1648; Fax: 701-352-1608.
St. John's Catechetical Center— 58237. Brent Hermans, D.R.E.; Rose Marie Kerner, D.R.E.; Brian Herding, Pastoral Assoc. Students 252.
Catechesis/Religious Program—Students 271.

GRAND FORKS, GRAND FORKS CO.
1—HOLY FAMILY CHURCH OF GRAND FORKS (1960) [JC] Very Rev. Phillip Ackerman; Rev. Richard LaCorte.
1018 18th Ave. S., 58201-6828. Tel: 701-746-1454; Fax: 701-746-1456. Web: holyfamilygrandforks.parishesonline.com.
School—(Grades K-5) Tel: 701-775-9886; Fax: 701-775-0221. Mr. Charles Scherr, Prin.; Yvonne Hanley, Librarian. Lay Teachers 6; Students 71.
Catechesis/Religious Program—Fax: 701-746-1456. Students 321.
2—ST. MARY (1915) [JC] Rev. Daniel Mrnarevic.
216 Belmont Rd., 58201. Tel: 701-775-9318; Fax: 701-775-7568. Email: stmarysgfnd@yahoo.com.
Catechesis/Religious Program—Tel: 701-775-2842. Students 105.
3—ST. MICHAEL'S CHURCH OF GRAND FORKS (1872) [JC] Revs. H. Gerard Braun; Neil J. Pfeifer.
520 N. Sixth St., 58203. Tel: 701-772-2624. Email: gfstmichaels@yahoo.com. Web: www.stmichaelsgf.com.
School—(Grades PreK-5), 504 5th Ave. N., 58203. Tel: 701-772-1822; Fax: 701-772-0211. Stephanie Schuster, Prin.; Katherine Schuh, Librarian. Lay Teachers 13; Students 119.
Catechesis/Religious Program—Tel: 701-772-2282; Fax: 701-772-2282. Students 252.
4—ST. THOMAS AQUINAS NEWMAN CHURCH OF GRAND FORKS (1951) [JC] Rev. Jason Lefor; Deacon Samuel Pupino.
410 Cambridge St., 58203. Tel: 701-777-6850; Fax: 701-777-6851. Web: www.und.nodak.edu/dept/newman.
Catechesis/Religious Program—Students 16.

GRANVILLE, MCHENRY CO., OUR LADY OF PERPETUAL HELP (1933) Closed. For inquiries for parish records contact the chancery. Sacramental records are at St. Cecilia, Towner.

GWINNER, SARGENT CO., ST. VINCENT'S CHURCH OF GWINNER (1984) [CEM], Served from Lisbon. Rev. Jerald L.C. Finnestad.
Mailing Address: *c/o St. Aloysius*, 701 Oak St., Lisbon, 58054. Tel: 701-683-4620; Fax: 701-683-5703.
Church: 302 Hwy. 13 E., 58040. Tel: 701-683-4620.
Catechesis/Religious Program—Tel: 701-678-2364. Students 37.

HANKINSON, RICHLAND CO., ST. PHILIP'S CHURCH OF HANKINSON (1889) [CEM] Rev. Scott Sautner.
612 S. Main, P.O. Box 419, 58041. Tel: 701-242-7327; Fax: 701-242-7773.
Catechesis/Religious Program—Students 95.

HANSBORO, TOWNER CO., SACRED HEART, Closed. For inquiries for parish records please contact the Chancellor's Office. Sacramental records are at St. Joachim, Rolla.

HARVEY, WELLS CO., ST. CECILIA'S CHURCH OF HARVEY (1895) [CEM], Also serving Selz. Very Rev. Franklin Miller; Deacon Jeffrey M. Faul.
413 E. Brewster St., 58341. Tel: 701-324-2144; Fax: 701-324-2637.
Catechesis/Religious Program—Tel: 701-324-2637. Students 87.

HILLSBORO, TRAILL CO., ST. ROSE OF LIMA'S CHURCH OF HILLSBORO (1892) [CEM], Also serves Argusville. Rev. Leo Kinney.
Mailing Address: P.O. Box 459, 58045-0459. Tel: 701-636-4541.
Church: 503 3rd St. S.E., 58045.
Catechesis/Religious Program—Students 101.

HOPE, STEELE CO., ST. AGATHA'S CHURCH OF HOPE (1907), Served from Oriska. Rev. Timothy Johnson.
Mailing Address: *c/o St. Bernard's Church of Oriska*, 606 5th St., Oriska, 58063. Tel: 701-845-3713; Fax: 701-845-0172. Email: oriska_tri_parish@yahoo.com.
Church: 819 Steele Ave., 58046.
Catechesis/Religious Program—Students 14.

HUNTER, CASS CO., ST. AGNES (1898) Unassigned. Served by Mayville., Mailing Address: c/o Our Lady of Peace, 846 5th St. S.E., Mayville, 58257. Tel: 701-788-3234.
Church: 102 1st St. E., 58048.
Catechesis/Religious Program—Tel: 701-967-8970. Students 21.

HURDSFIELD, WELLS CO., ST. PATRICK'S CHURCH OF HURDSFIELD (1907), Served from Fessenden. Rev. Thomas J. Krupich.
Mailing Address: *c/o St. Augustine*, 105 7th Ave S., Fessenden, 58438. Tel: 701-547-3430; Fax: 701-547-3766.
Church: 12 3rd St. W., 58451.
Catechesis/Religious Program—Students 13.

JAMESTOWN, STUTSMAN CO., ST. JAMES BASILICA OF JAMESTOWN (1881) [CEM], Also Serving Buchanan, Windsor and Pingree. Very Rev. Al M. Bitz; Revs. Joseph Barrett; Arogyaiah Godagotti; Sr. Michaeleen Jantzer, O.S.B., Pastoral Min.; Deacons Thomas Geffre; Geary McCleery.
Mailing Address: 622 1st Ave. S., 58401-4648. Tel: 701-252-0119; Fax: 701-952-6992. Email: basilica@stjamesbasilica.org. Web: www.stjamesbasilica.org.
Church: 622 1st Ave. S., 58401.
School—St. John Academy, (Grades PreK-6), 215 5th St., S.E., 58401. Tel: 701-252-3397; Fax: 701-952-2434. Email: mark.g.wiest.2@sendit.nodak.edu. Web: www.stjamesbasilica.org/stjohn. Mark Wiest, Prin. Lay Teachers 18; Students 248.
St. James Faith Formation—214 4th St., S.E., 58401. Tel: 701-252-0478; Fax: 701-252-0478. Email: faithformation@csicable.net. Shirley Wallace, D.R.E. Lay Teachers 40.
Catechesis/Religious Program—Students 137.

JESSIE, GRIGGS CO., ST. LAWRENCE (1888) [CEM], Served from Cooperstown. Rev. Richard Fineo.
Mailing Address: *c/o St. George*, P.O. Box 217, Cooperstown, 58425. Tel: 701-797-2624.
Church: 105 Dewey St., 58452.
Catechesis/Religious Program—Students 9.

KARLSRUHE, MCHENRY CO., STS. PETER & PAUL CHURCH OF KARLSRUHE (1905) [CEM], Served from Velva. Rev. James Gross.
Mailing Address: *c/o St. Cecilia*, P.O. Box K, Velva, 58790-0496. Tel: 701-338-2663; Fax: 701-338-2883.
Church: 401 N. Main, 58744.
Catechesis/Religious Program—Students 14.

KENSAL, STUTSMAN CO., ST. JOHN'S CHURCH OF KENSAL (1917) [CEM], Served from Wimbledon. Rev. Steven J. Meyer.
Mailing Address: *c/o St. Boniface*, P.O. Box 9, Wimbledon, 58492. Tel: 701-435-2310.
Church: 407 Pleasant Ave., 58455.

KINDRED, CASS CO., ST. MAURICE (1965), Served from Wild Rice. Rev. Jared Kadlec; Deacon Clarence Vetter.
Mailing Address & Church: 5313 165th Ave., S.E., P.O. Box 272, 58051. Tel: 701-428-3094; Fax: 701-428-3094. Web: www.fargodiocese.org/parish/kindred.
Catechesis/Religious Program—Tel: 701-428-3094. Students 65.

KINTYRE, LOGAN CO., ST. BONIFACE (1905) [CEM] Closed. For inquiries for parish records contact the chancery. Sacramental records are at St. Philip Neri, Napoleon.

KNOX, BENSON CO., ST. MARY'S CHURCH OF KNOX (1936) [CEM], Served from Rugby. Rev. Thomas Graner.
c/o St. Therese, 218 3rd St., S.E., Rugby, 58368-1814. Tel: 701-776-5327.
Church: 129 Morgan, 58343.
Catechesis/Religious Program—Students 8.

LA MOURE, LA MOURE CO., HOLY ROSARY CHURCH OF LA MOURE (1890) [CEM], Also serving Dickey and Verona. Rev. Jerome Okafor.
Mailing Address: P.O. Box 217, 58458.
Church: 209 1 St., S.E., 58458. Tel: 701-883-5987; Fax: 701-883-4359.
Catechesis/Religious Program—Students 64.

LAKE WILLIAMS, KIDDER CO., OUR LADY OF THE LAKE (1946) Closed. For inquiries for parish records contact the Chancellor's Office. Sacramental records are at St. Francis de Sales, Steele.

LAKOTA, NELSON CO., ST. MARY'S CHURCH OF LAKOTA

(1902), Also serving Tolna and Michigan. Rev. John F. Aerts.
Mailing Address: P.O. Box 509, 58344. Tel: 701-247-2594. Email: smcc@polarcomm.com.
Church: 109 East Ave. E., 58344.
Catechesis/Religious Program—Tel: 701-247-2584. Students 20.

LANGDON, CAVALIER CO., ST. ALPHONSUS CHURCH OF LANGDON (1888) [CEM], Also serving Nekoma and Wales. Rev. William McDermott.
Mailing Address: 1010 3rd St., 58249. Tel: 701-256-5966; Fax: 701-256-2358.
School—(Grades K-8), 209 10th Ave., 58249. Tel: 701-256-2354. Mr. Andrew DelaBarre, Prin. Lay Teachers 12; Students 76.
Catechesis/Religious Program—Students 59.

LANKIN, WALSH CO., ST. JOSEPH'S CHURCH OF LANKIN (1906) [CEM], Served by Pisek. Rev. Samuel Ezeibekwe.
Mailing Address: *c/o St. John Nepomucene*, P.O. Box 27, Pisek, 58273.
Church: 506 4th St., 58250. Tel: 701-284-6060.
Catechesis/Religious Program—Students 5.

LANSFORD, BOTTINEAU CO., ST. JOHN'S CHURCH OF LANSFORD (1903) Rev. Gary Benz, Admin.
680 3rd St., 58750. Tel: 701-756-6601; Fax: 701-756-6901.

LARIMORE, GRAND FORKS CO., ST. STEPHEN'S CHURCH OF LARIMORE (1882) Rev. James Goodwin.
Mailing Address: P.O. Box 778, 58251. Tel: 701-343-2377; Fax: 701-343-2316. Email: ststlarimore@msn.com.
Church: 311 W. Front St., 58251.
Catechesis/Religious Program—Tel: 701-343-2747. Students 69.

LEEDS, BENSON CO., ST. VINCENT DE PAUL CHURCH OF LEEDS (1897) [CEM], Served from Cando. Rev. Joseph D'Aco.
Mailing Address: P.O. Box 399, Cando, 58324. Tel: 701-968-3462; Fax: 701-968-3830.
Church: 315 Central Ave., Cando, 58324.
Catechesis/Religious Program—Students 23.

LEROY, PEMBINA CO., ST. JOSEPH (1873) [CEM] Closed. For inquiries for parish records contact the chancery. Sacramental records are at St. Boniface, Walhalla.

LIDGERWOOD, RICHLAND CO., ST. BONIFACE CHURCH OF LIDGERWOOD (1887) [CEM], Also serving Geneseo and Cayuga. Rev. Robert Smith.
Mailing Address: P.O. Box 449, 58053.
Church: 230 1st St., N.W., 58053. Tel: 701-538-4600.
Catechesis/Religious Program—Tel: 701-538-4604. Students 57.

LISBON, RANSOM CO., ST. ALOYSIUS CHURCH OF LISBON (1884) [CEM], Also serving Gwinner. Rev. Jerald L.C. Finnestad.
Church & Mailing Address: 701 Oak St., 58054-4256. Tel: 701-683-4620; Fax: 701-683-5703.
Catechesis/Religious Program—Students 58.

LOMICE, WALSH CO., ST. CATHERINE (1936) [CEM] Closed. For inquiries for parish records contact the chancery. Sacramental records are at St. Mary, Lakota.

MADDOCK, BENSON CO., ST. WILLIAM (1954), Served from Esmond. Rev. Brian Bachmeier.
Mailing Address: *c/o St. Boniface*, P.O. Box 37, Esmond, 58332. Tel: 701-249-8360.
Catechesis/Religious Program—Students 25.

MANTADOR, RICHLAND CO., STS. PETER & PAUL CHURCH OF MANTADOR (1881) [CEM], Served from Mooreton. Rev. Peter J. Anderl.
Mailing Address: P.O. Box 39, 58058. Tel: 701-274-8259.
Church: 609 County Rd. 25, 58058.
Catechesis/Religious Program—Students 11.

MANVEL, GRAND FORKS CO., ST. TIMOTHY'S CHURCH OF MANVEL (1882) [CEM] Rev. Bernard Schneider.
Church: 1207 Oldham Ave., 58256-4335. Tel: 701-696-2219.
Catechesis/Religious Program—Students 55.

MARION, LA MOURE CO., ST. FRANCIS (1910) [CEM] Closed. For inquiries for parish records contact the chancery. Sacramental records are at Holy Rosary, La Moure.

MAYVILLE, TRAILL CO., OUR LADY OF PEACE CHURCH OF MAYVILLE (1945) Unassigned. Also serving Hunter.
Church: 846 5th St., S.E., 58257. Tel: 701-788-3234; Fax: 701-788-3234.
Catechesis/Religious Program—Students 49.

MCCLUSKY, SHERIDAN CO., HOLY FAMILY (1905), Served from Fessenden. Rev. Thomas J. Krupich.
Mailing Address: *c/o St. Augustine*, 105 7th Ave S., Fessenden, 58438. Tel: 701-547-3430; Fax: 701-547-3766.
Church: 409 Ave. B E., 58463.
Catechesis/Religious Program—Students 2.

MCHENRY, FOSTER CO., STS. PETER & PAUL CHURCH OF MCHENRY (1912) [CEM], Served from New Rockford. Rev. Bernard Pfau.
Mailing Address: *c/o St. John*, P.O. Box 389, New Rockford, 58356. Tel: 701-947-5325; Fax: 701-947-5325. Web: www.newrockford.com.
Church: 391 Conn St., 58464.
Catechesis/Religious Program—Students 6.

MEDINA, STUTSMAN CO., ST. MARY'S CHURCH OF MEDINA (1905) [CEM], Served from Steele. Rev. Jerome Hunkler.
Mailing Address: P.O Box 87, Steele, 58482-0087. Tel: 701-475-2333.
Church: 105 3rd Ave. S.E., 58467.
Catechesis/Religious Program—Students 19.

MICHIGAN, NELSON CO., ST. LAWRENCE O'TOOLE'S CHURCH OF MICHIGAN (1883), Served from Lakota. Rev. John F. Aerts.
Mailing Address: P.O. Box 509, Lakota, 58344. Tel: 701-247-2594.
Church: 214 Broadway St., 58259.
Catechesis/Religious Program—Students 4.

MILNOR, SARGENT CO., ST. ARNOLD'S CHURCH OF MILNOR (1905) [CEM], Served from Wyndmere. Rev. Leonard Loegering.
Mailing Address: P.O. Box 295, 58060.
Church: 107 3rd St., 58060. Tel: 701-427-9288.
Catechesis/Religious Program—Tel: 701-427-5327. Students 49.

MILTON, CAVALIER CO., ST. CLOTILDE (1893) Closed. For inquiries for parish records contact the Chancellor's Office. Sacramental records are at St. Alphonsus, Langdon.

MINNEWAUKAN, BENSON CO., ST. JAMES (1899) Closed. For inquiries for parish records, contact the Chancellor's Office. Sacramental records are at St. Joseph, Devil's Lake.

MINTO, WALSH CO., SACRED HEART CHURCH OF MINTO (1905) [CEM], Also serving Warsaw. Very Rev. John Kleinschmidt.
Mailing Address: P.O. Box 316, 58261. Tel: 701-248-3589; Fax: 701-248-3139.
Church: 621 3rd St., 58261.
Catechesis/Religious Program—Students 57.

MOORETON, RICHLAND CO., ST. ANTHONY'S (1884) [CEM], Also serving Mantador. Rev. Peter J. Anderl.
204 Mooreton Ave. N., 58061. Tel: 701-274-8259.
Catechesis/Religious Program—Students 42.

MOUNT CARMEL, CAVALIER CO., OUR LADY OF MOUNT CARMEL (1888) [CEM] Closed. For inquiries for parish records contact the chancery. Sacramental records located at St. Alphonsus, Langdon.

MUNICH, CAVALIER CO., ST. MARY (1916) [CEM 3], Also serving Starkweather. Rev. Mathew V. Pamplaniyil.
Mailing Address: P.O. Box 159, 58352-0159. Tel: 701-682-5178; Fax: 701-682-5124.
Church: 607 Main, 58352.
Catechesis/Religious Program—Tel: 701-682-5124. Students 21.

NAPOLEON, LOGAN CO., ST. PHILIP'S CHURCH OF NAPOLEON (1906) [CEM] Very Rev. Ross Laframboise; Deacons Allen Baumgartner; Gary Schumacher.
401 Broadway, 58561-7013. Tel: 701-754-2860.
Catechesis/Religious Program—Students 138.

NECHE, PEMBINA CO., STS. NEREUS & ACHILLEUS CHURCH OF NECHE (1887) [CEM], Served from Walhalla. Rev. Jude Okafor, Admin.
Mailing Address: *c/o St. Boniface*, P.O. Box 228, Walhalla, 58282-0228. Tel: 701-549-2729; Fax: 701-549-3256.
Church: 6th St., 58265.
Catechesis/Religious Program—Students 12.

NEKOMA, CAVALIER CO., ST. EDWARD (1907) [CEM], Served from Langdon. Rev. William McDermott.
Mailing Address: *c/o St. Alphonsus*, 1010 3rd St., Langdon, 58249. Tel: 701-256-5966; Fax: 701-256-2358.
Church: 323 Main, 58355.
Catechesis/Religious Program—Students 3.

NEW ROCKFORD, EDDY CO., ST. JOHN'S CHURCH OF NEW ROCKFORD (1904) [CEM], Also serving McHenry. Rev. Bernard Pfau.
Mailing Address: P.O. Box 389, 58356. Tel: 701-947-5325.
Church: 116 1st Ave. N., 58356.
Catechesis/Religious Program—Students 97.

NORTONVILLE, LAMOURE CO., HOLY SPIRIT CHURCH OF NORTONVILLE (1912) [JC], Served from Edgeley. Rev. Thaines Arulandu.
Mailing Address: *c/o Transfiguration*, P.O. Box 347, Edgeley, 58433. Tel: 701-493-2387; Fax: 701-493-2823.
Church: 705 1st St., 58454.
Catechesis/Religious Program—Students 23.

OAKES, DICKEY CO., ST. CHARLES CHURCH OF OAKES (1905) [CEM], Also serving Forman. Rev. William Peter Gerlach, Admin.
410 Seventh St. N., 58474. Tel: 701-742-2418; Fax: 701-742-2418.
Catechesis/Religious Program—Tel: 701-742-2911. Students 100.

OAKWOOD, WALSH CO., SACRED HEART CHURCH OF OAKWOOD (1881) [CEM], Also serving St. Thomas. Rev. James P. Lauerman.
7010 County Rd. 4, Grafton, 58237-8860. Tel: 701-352-1392.
Catechesis/Religious Program—Students 22.

OLGA, CAVALIER CO., OUR LADY OF THE SACRED HEART (1882) [CEM 2] Closed. For inquiries for parish records contact the chancery. Sacramental records are at St. Boniface, Walhalla.

ORISKA, BARNES CO., ST. BERNARD'S CHURCH OF ORISKA (1881) [CEM], Also serving Hope and Sanborn. Rev. Timothy Johnson; Deacon Jim McAllister.
606 Fifth St., 58063. Tel: 701-845-3713; Fax: 701-845-0172. Email: oriska_tri_parish@yahoo.com.
Catechesis/Religious Program—Students 12.

ORRIN, PIERCE CO., SACRED HEART (1903) [CEM] Closed. For inquiries for parish records contact the chancery. Sacramental records located at St. Therese, Rugby.

OSNABROCK, CAVALIER CO., ST. JOSEPH (1909) Closed. For inquiries for parish records contact the Chancellor's Office. Sacramental records are at St. Alphonsus, Langdon.

PAGE, CASS CO., ST. JAMES (1909) [CEM] Closed. For inquiries for parish records contact the chancery. Sacramental records are at St. Bernard, Oriska.

PARK RIVER, WALSH CO., ST. MARY (1888) [CEM], Also serving Veseleyville. Rev. Gary Luiten; Deacon Gerald F. Sobolik.
Mailing Address: P.O. Box 110, 58270-0110. Tel: 701-284-6165; Fax: 701-284-7789.
Church: 505 Park St. E., 58270.
Catechesis/Religious Program—Tel: 701-284-7789. Students 92.

PEMBINA, PEMBINA CO., ASSUMPTION CHURCH OF PEMBINA (1818) [CEM], Served from Drayton. Rev. Joseph Okogba.
Church: 143 Hayden St., 58271. Tel: 701-825-6266; Fax: 701-825-6266.
Catechesis/Religious Program—Students 20.

PENN, RAMSEY CO., IMMACULATE CONCEPTION (1986) Closed. For inquiries for parish records contact the Chancellor's Office. Sacramental records are at St. Vincent de Paul, Leeds.

PINGREE, STUTSMAN CO., ST. MICHAEL (1905) [CEM], Served from Jamestown. Very Rev. Al M. Bitz.
Mailing Address: *c/o St. James Basilica*, 622 1st. Ave. S., Jamestown, 58401-4648. Tel: 701-252-0119; Fax: 701-952-6992.
Catechesis/Religious Program—Students 3.

PISEK, WALSH CO., ST. JOHN NEPOMUCENE'S CHURCH OF PISEK (1886) [CEM], Also serving Lankin and Bechyne. Rev. Samuel Ezeibekwe.
Mailing Address: P.O. Box 27, 58273. Tel: 701-284-6060; Fax: 701-284-6692.
Church: 167 Newton Ave., 58273.
Catechesis/Religious Program—Students 7.

REYNOLDS, GRAND FORKS CO., OUR LADY OF PERPETUAL HELP CHURCH OF REYNOLDS (1895) [CEM], Serves Thompson. Rev. John Cavanaugh.
Mailing Address: Box 68, 58275. Tel: 701-847-3096.
Church: 424 5th St., 58275.
Catechesis/Religious Program—Students 42.

ROCK LAKE, TOWNER CO., IMMACULATE HEART OF MARY CHURCH OF ROCK LAKE (1949), Served from Rolla. Rev. Jake Miller.
Mailing Address: *c/o St. Joachim*, P.O. Box 788, Rolla, 58367. Tel: 701-477-3568.
Catechesis/Religious Program—Students 5.

ROLETTE, ROLETTE CO., SACRED HEART (1918) [CEM 3], Also serving Willow City and Bisbee. Rev. Philip Chacko.
Mailing Address: P.O. Box 127, 58366. Tel: 701-246-3449; Fax: 701-246-3449. Email: shrolette@fargodiocese.org.
Church: 505 Main, 58366.
Catechesis/Religious Program—Students 32.

ROLLA, ROLETTE CO., ST. JOACHIM'S CHURCH OF ROLLA (1894) [CEM], Also serving Rock Lake. Rev. Jake Miller.
Mailing Address: P.O. Box 788, 58367-0788. Tel: 701-477-3568. Email: stjhm@utma.com.
Church: 210 2nd St., 58367.
Catechesis/Religious Program—Students 60.

RUGBY, PIERCE CO., ST. THERESA, LITTLE FLOWER CHURCH OF RUGBY (1910) [CEM], Also serves Knox. Revs. Thomas Graner; John Ejike; Deacon Arlen Blessum.
218 Third St., S.E., 58368-1814. Tel: 701-776-6388; Fax: 701-776-5327. Email: lfparish@gondtc.com. Web: www.littleflowerrugby.org.
School—(Grades PreSchool-6), 306 Third Ave., S.E., 58368. Tel: 701-776-6258. Bruce Gannarelli, Prin.; Sr. Jean Louise Schafer, O.S.F., Librarian. Sisters of St. Francis of the Immaculate Heart of Mary (Hankinson, ND) 1; Lay Teachers 8; Students 68.
Catechesis/Religious Program—Students 168.

ST. JOHN, ROLETTE CO., ST. JOHN'S CHURCH OF ST. JOHN (1882) [CEM], Also serves St. Benedict,

Belcourt. Rev. Fred Alexander, S.O.L.T.
Mailing Address: P.O. Box 170, 58369. Tel: 701-477-3081.
Church: 107 St. Ann St., S.E., 58369.

ST. MICHAEL, BENSON CO., ST. MICHAEL'S CHURCH OF ST. MICHAEL (1874), (Native American), [CEM] Rev. Brian Moen.
Mailing Address: P.O. Box 42, 58370. Tel: 701-766-4151; Fax: 701-766-1085.
Catechesis/Religious Program—Students 40.

ST. THOMAS, PEMBINA CO., ST. THOMAS CHURCH OF ST. THOMAS (1882) [CEM], Served from Oakwood. Rev. James P. Lauerman.
Mailing Address: *c/o Sacred Heart*, 7010 Country Rd. 4, Grafton, 58237. Tel: 701-352-1392.
Church: 640 Main St., 58276.
Catechesis/Religious Program—Students 13.

SANBORN, BARNES CO., SACRED HEART CHURCH OF SANBORN (1904) [CEM], Served from Oriska. Rev. Timothy Johnson.
Mailing Address: *c/o St. Bernard's Church of Oriska*, 606 5th St., Oriska, 58063. Tel: 701-845-3713.
Church: 711-4th St., 58480.

SELZ, PIERCE CO., ST. ANTHONY (1916) [CEM], Served from Harvey. Very Rev. Franklin Miller.
Mailing Address: 29 Girard St., 58341. Tel: 701-324-4059.
Catechesis/Religious Program— Twinned with St. Cecilia, Harvey. Students 8.

SHELDON, RANSOM CO., OUR LADY OF THE SCAPULAR CHURCH OF SHELDON (1883) [CEM], Served from Enderlin. Rev. Msgr. Daniel J. Pilon.
Mailing Address: *c/o St. Patrick*, 302 Bluff St., Enderlin, 58027. Tel: 701-437-2791. Web: www.fargodiocese.org/parish/sheldon.
Church: 6 Crosswell St., 58068.
Catechesis/Religious Program—Students 32.

STARKWEATHER, RAMSEY CO., ASSUMPTION CHURCH OF STARKWEATHER (1905) [CEM], Served from Munich. Rev. Mathew V. Pamplaniyil.
Mailing Address: *c/o St. Mary*, P.O. Box 159, Munich, 58352-0159. Tel: 701-682-5178; Fax: 701-682-5124.
Church: 502 Main St., 58377.
Catechesis/Religious Program—Students 10.

STEELE, KIDDER CO., ST. FRANCIS DE SALES (1958) [CEM], Also serves Tappen and Medina. Rev. Jerome Hunkler.
Mailing Address: P.O. Box 87, 58482-0087. Tel: 701-475-2333; Fax: 701-475-2335.
Church: 318 2nd St., S.W., 58482-0087.
Catechesis/Religious Program—Students 58.

STIRUM, SARGENT CO., ST. VINCENT (1986) Closed. For inquiries for parish records contact the Chancellor's Office. Sacramental records are at St. Aloysius, Lisbon.

SYKESTON, WELLS CO., ST. ELIZABETH'S CHURCH OF SYKESTON (1906), (German), [CEM], Served from Carrington. Rev. David Syverson.
Mailing Address: P.O. Box 397, 58486. Tel: 701-984-2266.
Church: 130 Anson Ave., N.E., 58486.
Catechesis/Religious Program—

TAPPEN, KIDDER CO., ST. PAUL (1924), Served from Steele. Rev. Jerome Hunkler.
Mailing Address: *c/o St. Francis*, P.O. Box 87, Steele, 58482-0087. Tel: 701-475-2333; Fax: 701-475-2335.
Church: 218 1st St. , N.E., 58487.
Catechesis/Religious Program—Students 6.

THOMPSON, GRAND FORKS CO., ST. JUDE'S CHURCH OF THOMPSON (1895) [CEM], Served from Reynolds. Rev. John Cavanaugh; Deacon Jim West.
Mailing Address: P.O. Box 305, 58278. Tel: 701-599-2574.
Res.: 421 Sanborn St., Reynolds, 58275. Tel: 701-847-3096.
329 Broadway St., 58278.
Catechesis/Religious Program—Students 73.

TOKIO, BENSON CO., CHRIST THE KING CHURCH OF TOKIO (1938), (Native American), Served from Fort Totten. Rev. Charles J. Leute, O.P.
Mailing Address: *c/o Seven Dolors*, P.O. Box 299, Fort Totten, 58335. Tel: 701-766-4314; Fax: 701-766-1842.
Church: 134 2nd St., 58379.

TOLNA, NELSON CO., ST. JOSEPH (1911) [CEM], Served from Lakota. Rev. John F. Aerts.
Mailing Address: *c/o St. Mary*, P.O. Box 509, Lakota, 58344.
Church: 220 Main St., 58380.
Catechesis/Religious Program—

TOWNER, MCHENRY CO., ST. CECILIA'S CHURCH OF TOWNER (1903) [CEM] Rev. Michael Schommer.
Mailing Address: Box 267, 58788-0267. Tel: 701-537-5133. Email: stcs@srt.com.
Church: 503 1st St., S.W., 58788.
Catechesis/Religious Program—Students 39.

VALLEY CITY, BARNES CO., ST. CATHERINE'S CHURCH OF VALLEY CITY (1882) [CEM] Rev. Msgr. Dennis A. Skonseng; Deacons Arlie Braunberger; Raphael Grim; Edward Didier; Carl M. Orthman; Joseph Leitner; Eugene Klein.
540 Third Ave., N.E., 58072-2628. Tel: 701-845-0354; Fax: 701-845-0556.
School—(Grades K-6) Tel: 701-845-1453; Fax: 701-845-0556. Mr. Ralph Dyrness, Prin.; Carol Gulka, Librarian. Lay Teachers 6; Students 58.
St. Catherine's Parish Education Center—540 Third Ave., N.E., 58072. Mr. Ralph Dyrness, Parish Education Dir. Lay Teachers 20.
Catechesis/Religious Program—Students 127.

VELVA, MCHENRY CO., ST. CECILIA'S CHURCH OF VELVA (1905) [CEM], Also serving Karlsruhe. Rev. James Gross.
Mailing Address: P.O. Box K, 58790-0496. Tel: 701-338-2663; Fax: 701-338-2883. Email: velvakarls@srt.com.
Church: 201 2nd Ave. W., 58790.
Catechesis/Religious Program—Students 112.

VERONA, LAMOURE CO., ST. RAPHAEL'S CHURCH OF VERONA (1898) [CEM], Served from Lamoure. Rev. Jerome Okafor.
Mailing Address: *c/o Holy Rosary*, P.O. Box 217, Lamoure, 58458. Tel: 701-883-5987.
Church: 205 1st St., 58490.
Catechesis/Religious Program—

VESELEYVILLE, WALSH CO., ST. LUKE'S CHURCH OF VESELEYVILLE (1880) [CEM], Served from Park River. Rev. Gary Luiten.
Mailing Address: 14207 63rd St., N.E., Grafton, 58237.

WAHPETON, RICHLAND CO., ST. JOHN'S CHURCH OF WAHPETON (1876) [CEM] Very Rev. Dale Lagodinski; Rev. Terry Dodge; Deacon Douglas Campbell.
Office: 115 Second St. N., 58075. Tel: 701-642-6982; Fax: 701-642-2601. Web: www.stjohns-wahpeton.org.
Res.: 222 Dakota Ave., 58075. Tel: 701-642-4985.
School—(Grades PreK-6), 212 Dakota Ave., 58075. Tel: 701-642-6116; Fax: 701-642-9134. Renee Langenwalter, Prin. Lay Teachers 11; Students 135.
St. John Day Care Center—Tel: 701-642-4922. Chanda Hogness, Dir. Total Staff 26; Students 75.
Catechesis/Religious Program—Students 266.

WALES, CAVALIER CO., ST. MICHAEL'S (1889) [CEM], Served from Langdon. Rev. William McDermott.
Mailing Address: *c/o St. Alphonsus*, 1010 3rd St., Langdon, 58249-2415. Tel: 701-256-5966.
Church: 221 2nd Ave., 58281.

WALHALLA, PEMBINA CO., ST. BONIFACE CHURCH OF WALHALLA (1848) [CEM], Also serving Neche. Rev. Jude Okafor, Admin.; Deacon Stanley (Jim) Carpenter.
Mailing Address: P.O. Box 228, 58282. Tel: 701-549-2729; Fax: 701-549-3256. Email: boniface@utma.com.
Church: 801 Central Ave., 58282.
Catechesis/Religious Program—Tel: 701-549-2750. Students 66.

WARSAW, WALSH CO., ST. STANISLAUS CHURCH OF WARSAW (1882) [CEM], Served from Minto. Very Rev. John Kleinschmidt.
P.O. Box 316, Minto, 58261. Tel: 701-248-3589; Fax: 701-248-3139.
Catechesis/Religious Program—Students 53.

WEST FARGO, CASS CO.
1—BLESSED SACRAMENT CHURCH OF WEST FARGO (1936) [CEM] Rev. Bert Miller; Deacon James Hunt.
210 Fifth Ave. W., 58078-1747. Tel: 701-282-3321; Fax: 701-282-6503. Web: www.blessedsacramentwestfargo.org. In Res., Very Rev. KS Kopacz, J.C.L.
Catechesis/Religious Program—Tel: 701-282-4554. Students 145.
2—HOLY CROSS CHURCH OF WEST FARGO (1981) [CEM] Very Rev. James Meyer; Rev. Andrew Jasinski; Deacons James Eggl; David Haney.
1420 16th St. E., 58078-3411. Tel: 701-282-7217; Fax: 701-282-2753. Email: holycrosscc@ideaone.net. Web: www.holycrosscatholicchurch.com.
Catechesis/Religious Program—Students 414.

WESTHOPE, BOTTINEAU CO., ST. ANDREW'S CHURCH OF WESTHOPE (1904) [CEM], Served from Bottineau. Rev. Paul R. Schuster.
Mailing Address: *c/o St. Mark's*, 322 Sinclair St., Bottineau, 58318. Tel: 701-245-6171.
Church: 260 1st Ave. E., 58793.
Catechesis/Religious Program—Students 45.

WILD RICE, CASS CO., ST. BENEDICT'S CHURCH OF WILD RICE (1870) [CEM], Also serving Kindred. Rev. Jared Kadlec.
Mailing Address: 11743 38th St. S., Horace, 58047-9512. Tel: 701-588-4288; Fax: 701-588-9290. Email: office@stbensnd.org. Web: www.stbensnd.org.
Catechesis/Religious Program—Michelle Herrington, D.R.E. Students 86.

WILLOW CITY, BOTTINEAU CO., NOTRE DAME DE LA VICTOIRE CHURCH OF WILLOW CITY (1895) [CEM 2], Served by Rolette. Rev. Philip Chacko.
Mailing Address: P.O. Box 115, 58384. Tel: 701-246-3449; Fax: 701-246-3449.
Church: 215 1st St., 58384.
Catechesis/Religious Program—Students 14.

WIMBLEDON, BARNES CO., ST. BONIFACE CHURCH OF WIMBLEDON (1886) [CEM], Also serving Kensal and Dazey. Rev. Steven J. Meyer.
Mailing Address: P.O. Box 9, 58492. Tel: 701-435-2310.
Church: 301 1st Ave., 58492.
Catechesis/Religious Program—Students 34.

WINDSOR, STUTSMAN CO., ST. MATHIAS CHURCH OF WINDSOR (1910) [CEM], Served from Jamestown. Very Rev. Al M. Bitz.
c/o St. James Basilica, 622 1st Ave. S., Jamestown, 58401-4648. Tel: 701-252-0119; Fax: 701-952-6992. Email: parish@csicable.net.
Church: 207 Washington Ave., 58424.
Catechesis/Religious Program—Students 6.

WISHEK, MCINTOSH CO., ST. PATRICK (1925) [CEM], Also serving Zeeland and Ashley. Rev. Wenceslaus Katanga.
Mailing Address: P.O. Box 293, 58495-0293.
Church: 322 Centennial St. S., 58495. Tel: 701-452-2970.
Catechesis/Religious Program—Students 31.

WYNDMERE, RICHLAND CO., ST. JOHN THE BAPTIST (1912) [CEM], Also serving Milnor. Rev. Leonard Loegering.
630 Sixth St., 58081. Tel: 701-439-2200.
Catechesis/Religious Program—Students 86.

ZEELAND, MCINTOSH CO., ST. ANDREW'S CHURCH OF ZEELAND (1906) [CEM 2], Served from Wishek. Rev. Wenceslaus Katanga.
Mailing Address: *c/o St. Patrick*, P.O. Box 293, Wishek, 58495. Tel: 701-423-5494.
Church: 301 1st Ave., S.E., 58581.
Catechesis/Religious Program—Students 34.

INDIAN MISSIONS

FORT TOTTEN RESERVATION
MISSION—CHRIST THE KING - TOKIO (1938) *c/o Seven Dolors*, Box 299, Benson Co. 58335-0299. Tel: 701-766-4314. Rev. Charles J. Leute, O.P.
Mission—St. Jerome - Crow Hill (1892) *c/o Seven Dolors*, Box 299, Benson Co. 58334-0299. Tel: 701-766-4314.
Mission—Seven Dolors Indian Mission [CEM] Seven Sorrows Dr., Box 299, Benson Co. 58335. Tel: 701-766-4314. Rev. Charles J. Leute, O.P.; Deacon Anthony McDonald. Also serving Crow Hill, Tokio.

ST. MICHAEL
MISSION—ST. MICHAEL'S CHURCH OF ST. MICHAEL (1874) P.O. Box 42, 58370-0042. Tel: 701-766-4151; Fax: 701-766-1085. Rev. Brian Moen.

TURTLE MOUNTAIN RESERVATION
MISSION—ST. ANN Belcourt, Rolette Co. Revs. Mark Ropel, S.O.L.T.; Robert J. Cronin, S.O.L.T.; Shane Mckee, S.O.L.T.; Scott Brossart, S.O.L.T.; Deacon Francis Davis.
Mission—St. Anthony St. Anthony, Rolette Co. Served from Belcourt.
Mission—St. Benedict Belcourt, Rolette Co. Rev. Mark Wheelan, S.O.L.T. Served from Saint John.

Chaplains of Public Institutions

GRAND FORKS. *Altru Hospital*. Rev. Bernard Schneider, Chap., P.O. Box 6002, 58206-6002.
Grand Forks Air Force Base. Jane Hutzol, Contact Person. Tel: 701-747-3073.
Our Lady of the Snows, 319 ARW/HC Blvd., 58205-6335.

Special Assignment:
Very Revs.—
Kopacz, K. S., J.C.L., Judicial Vicar, 5201 Bishops Blvd., 58104.
Meyer, Luke D., Chancellor & Priest Sec. to the Bishop, 5201 Bishops Blvd., Ste. A, 58104-7605.
Revs.—
Brooks, Armand L., Chaplain Franciscan Sisters of Dillingen, Hankinson, 58041.
Christensen, Joseph, F.M.I., Franciscans of Mary Immaculate, Warsaw, ND
Fischer, Charles, Fargo, ND
Fitzpatrick, Vincent, Fargo, ND
Hughes, Peter, C.S.Sp., Chap., Fargo, ND
LaCroix, Charles, Chap., Shanley High School, 5600 25th St. S., 58104.
Seeberger, Claude, O.S.B., Chap., 11550 River Rd., Valley City, 58072.
Tiu, Jim, Chap., Carmelites, Wahpeton
Vos, Jude, Sheldon, ND

On Duty Outside the Diocese:
Revs.—
Evans, John, II, Chap., Mayo Clinic, Rochester, MN
Hickin, Michael, North American College
Mikes, Pavel, Zahradni 32/2 41002 Czech Republic.
Schill, Damien, Chap., VA, St. Paul, MN
Willis, Kevin, Broken Arrow, OK

Graduate Studies:
Rev.—
Markman, Christopher J.

Military Chaplains:
Rev. Msgr.—
Donahue, Brian G., Chap. (MAJ), West Point
Rev.—
Herron, Jack B., Chap. CMR, El Paso, TX

Absent on Leave:
Rev.—
Fallon, John P.

Retired:
Rev. Msgrs.—
Gross, Val, Fargo, ND
Huebsch, Joseph R., Hankinson, ND
Laliberte, Robert, Ph.D., Guild, NH
Nilles, Allan F., Fargo, ND
Senger, Joseph, Minot, ND
Vetter, Wendelyn, V.F., Grand Forks, ND
Revs.—
Bachmeier, A. Bernard, San Diego, CA
Billman, George, Traverse City, MI
Callery, William V., Grand Fork, ND
Campbell, Joseph, Bella Vista, AR
Cosentino, Jack, Venice, FL
Cote, Duaine, Fargo, ND
Davis, John E., Peru
Flisk, Louden-Hans W., Nortonville, ND
Goellen, Richard M., Trinidad, CO
Grady, Peter W., Fargo, ND
Gross, Richard J., Grand Forks, ND
Haas, Lawrence W., Carrington, ND
Hasey, Adam, Oakes, ND
Jeffrey, C. James, Belleville, IL
Kupisz, Julian, Poland
Leiphon, Donald A., Napoleon, ND
Lewandowski, John, Mountain View, AR
McCarthy, Gerald A., Fargo, ND
McGinnis, John Arthur, Conshohocken, PA
Myers, Gerald, Nogales, AZ
Ovsak, William, Chap., Fayetteville, NC
Parrotta, Michael, Wellington, FL
Potter, Gerald, Grand Forks, ND
Ruge, Paul, Washington, NJ
Sherman, Edward, Grand Forks, ND
Sherman, William C., Grand Forks, ND
Snell, Roger K., Edgeley, ND
Stelten, Leo F., Fargo, ND
Tuchscherer, Vincent, Fargo, ND
Unger, Robert P., Bradenton, FL

Permanent Deacons:
Baumgartner, Allen, St. Phillip Neri, Napoleon
Blessum, Arlen, St. Therese Little Flower, Rugby
Braunberger, Arlie, St. Catherine, Valley City
Bunce, Donald A., St. Anthonys, Fargo
Buresh, Leonard, (Retired)
Campbell, Douglas, Wahpeton
Carpenter, Stanley (Jim), St. Boniface, Walhalla
Davis, Francis R., St. Ann, Belcourt
Desjarlais, Raymond, St. Joachim, Rolla
Didier, Edward, St. Catherine, Valley City
Didier, Harry, Jr., (Retired)
Dodge, Michael, Sts. Anne & Joachim, Fargo
Eberle, Edward, (Retired)
Eblen, David, Sts. Anne, Joachim, Fargo
Eggl, James, Holy Cross, West Fargo
Ethier, George, (Retired)
Faul, Jeffrey, St. Cecilia, Harvey
Geffre, Thomas, St. James Basilica, Jamestown
Grim, Raphael, St. Catherine, Valley City
Grzadzielewski, Michael, St John the Evangelist, Grafton
Haney, David, Holy Cross, West Fargo; Catholic Schools
Hoefs, Gene, (Retired)
Hunt, James, Blessed Sacrament, West Fargo
Klein, Eugene, (Retired)
Leitner, Joseph, St. Catherine, Valley City
Loegering, George, St. Mary Cathedral, Fargo
Longtin, Stuart, St. Anthony, Fargo
Marcy, Timothy, Missions
McAllister, James, St. Bernard, Oriska
McCleery, Geary, Basilica St. James, Jamestown
McDonald, Anthony, Seven Dolors, Fort Totten
Mears, Emery, St. Joachim, Rolla
Mrozla, Julian, (Retired)
Opsahl, David, Surprise, AZ
Orthman, Carl M., St. Catherine, Valley City
Perius, James, (Retired)
Prom, Mathias, (Retired)
Pupino, Samuel, St. Thomas Aquinas Newman Center, Grand Forks
Schumacher, Gary, St. Philip Neri, Napoleon
Schuster, Conrad, (Retired)
Sobolick, Gerald, (Retired)
Tinguely, Donald, (Retired)
Uline, James, (Retired)
Vetter, Clarence, St. Maurice, Kindred
West, James, St. Jude, Thompson

INSTITUTIONS LOCATED IN THE DIOCESE

[A] HIGH SCHOOLS, DIOCESAN

FARGO. *Blessed John Paul II Catholic Schools Network*, (Grades PreK-12), 5600 25th St. S.W., 58104. Tel: 701-893-3200; Fax: 701-893-3277. Email: david.haney@fdjp2.k12.nd.us. Web: www.fdjp2.k12.nd.us. Most Rev. Samuel J. Aquila, D.D., Pres.; Deacon David Haney, Supt. Priests 1; Lay Teachers 68; Total Enrollment 1,054.

Shanley High School and Sullivan Middle School, (Grades 6-12), 5600 25th St. S.W., 58104. Tel: 701-893-3200; Fax: 701-893-3277. Email: sean.safranski@fdjp2.k12.nd.us. Web: www.fdjp2.k12.nd.us. Mr. Sean Safranski, Prin., Shanley Middle School/Shanley High School; Gail Ringey, Student Asst. Coord.; Rev. Charles LaCroix, Chap.; Pam Brusegaard, Librarian. Priests 1; Lay Teachers 35; Students 548.

[B] PROTECTIVE INSTITUTIONS

FARGO. *Villa Nazareth dba Friendship, Inc.* 801 Page Dr., 58103. Tel: 701-235-8217; Fax: 701-235-7538. Email: jeffpederson@catholichealth.net. Jeff Pederson, CEO. Presentation Sisters (P.B.V.M.). Catholic Health Initiatives., A community-based facility providing an array of residential, vocational, educational, social and clinical services for children and adults with mental retardation and other developmental disabilities. Total Assisted 250; Total Staff 350.

[C] GENERAL HOSPITALS

BOTTINEAU. *St. Andrew's Health Center*, 316 Ohmer St., 58318. Tel: 701-228-9300; Fax: 701-228-9384. Email: sahc@utma.com. Web: www.standrewshealth.com. Jodi Atkinson, C.E.O. Sisters of Mary of the Presentation 2; Bed Capacity 25; Total Staff 104; Patients Assisted Annually 11,047.

CARRINGTON. *Carrington Health Center* Catholic Health Initiatives., P.O. Box 461, 58421. Tel: 701-652-3141; Fax: 701-652-2884. Web: www.carringtonhealthcenter.org. Bed Capacity 25; Staff 173; Patients Assisted Annually 22,072.

DEVILS LAKE. *Mercy Hospital*, 1031 7th St., N.E., 58301-2798. Tel: 701-662-2131; Fax: 701-662-9651. Email: jamesmarshall@catholichealth.net. Web: www.mercyhospitaldl.com. James Marshall, Admin. Total Staff 211; Bed Capacity 25; Bassinets 7; Patients Assisted Annually 25,000.

HARVEY. *St. Aloisius Medical Center* (1938) 325 E. Brewster St., 58341. Tel: 701-324-4651; Fax: 701-324-4687. Email: rockyz@staloisius.com. Web: www.staloisius.com. Rockford Zastoupil, Admin. Sisters of Mary of the Presentation. Total Staff 316; Bed Capacity 25; Long Term Care 106; Patients Assisted Annually 48,891.

LISBON. *Lisbon Area Health Services, Catholic Health Initiatives*, 905 Main St., Box 353, 58054. Tel: 701-683-6400; Fax: 701-683-4345. Email: peggylarson@catholichealth.net. Bed Capacity 25; Total Staff 118; Total Assisted Annually 11,100.

OAKES. *Oakes Community Hospital*, 1200 N. 7th St., 58474-2502. Tel: 701-742-3291; Fax: 701-742-3639. Email: leeboyles@catholichealth.net. Sr. M. Dianna Hell, O.S.F., Supr.; Lee Boyles, Inst. Admin. Sisters of St. Francis of the Immaculate Heart of Mary (Hankinson, ND) 1; Total Staff 105; Bed Capacity 20; Patients Assisted Annually 8,328.

ROLLA. *Presentation Medical Center*, 213 Second Ave., N.E., P.O. Box 759, 58367-0759. Tel: 701-477-3161; Fax: 701-477-5564. Web: www.pmc-rolla.com. Michael Pfeifer, CEO. Total Staff 97; Acute Beds 25; Patients Assisted Annually 11,500.

VALLEY CITY. *Mercy Hospital* (1928) Catholic Health Initiatives., 570 Chautauqua Blvd., 58072. Tel: 701-845-6400; Fax: 701-845-6413. Email: keithheuser@catholichealth.net. Bed Capacity 25; Patients Assisted 15,834; Total Staff 140.

[D] HOMES FOR AGED

FARGO. *Riverview Place* (1987) 5300 12th St. S., 58104. Tel: 701-237-4700; Fax: 701-235-5738. Email: jeffpederson@catholichealth.net. Web: www.riverviewplace.org. Jeff Pederson, Admin. Residents 150; Total Staff 80; Total Assisted Annually 140.

Rosewood on Broadway, SMP Health System, 1351 Broadway, 58102. Tel: 701-277-7999; Fax: 701-277-7989. Email: meldinetang@smphs.org. Web: rosewoodonbroadway.com. Meldine Tang, Admin. Bed Capacity 111; Total Staff 194; Resident Days 39,891.

Villa Maria, SMP Health System, 3102 University Dr. S., 58103. Tel: 701-293-7750; Fax: 701-293-5845. Email: michael.pfeifer@smphs.org. Michael Pfeifer, CEO & Pres. Bed Capacity 140; Total Staff 210; Total Assisted 230; Resident Days 48,800.

EDGELEY. *Manor St. Joseph*, 404 Fourth Ave., P.O. Box 305, 58433. Tel: 701-493-2477; Fax: 701-493-2477. Email: stjoseph@drtel.net. Tammy Jangula, Admin. Sister Servants of Christ the King 1; Total Assisted Annually 26; Bed Capacity 40; Staff 33.

ELLENDALE. *Prince of Peace Care Center*, 201 8th St. N., 58436. Tel: 701-349-3312; Fax: 701-349-3944. Mr. Tony Hanson, Admin. Operated by Benedictine Living Communities, Inc. Bed Capacity 53; Total Staff 77; Total Assisted Annually 81.

ENDERLIN. *Maryhill Manor, SMP Health System*, 110 Hillcrest Dr., 58027. Tel: 701-437-3544; Fax: 701-437-3816. Email: nancy.farnham@smphs.org. Web: www.maryhillmanor.net. Nancy Farnham, Admin. Bed Capacity 54; Total Staff 86; Resident Days 19,057; Total Assisted Annually 85.

GRAND FORKS. *St. Anne's Guest Home*, 524 N. 17th St., 58203. Tel: 701-746-9401; Fax: 701-795-7825. Email: stannes@midconetwork.com. Sr. Rebecca Metzger, O.S.F., Admin. Sisters of St. Francis of the Immaculate Heart of Mary (Hankinson, ND) 4; Total Staff 36; Guests 84; Total Assisted Annually 155; Beds 84.

HANKINSON. *St. Gerard Community Nursing Home*, P.O. Box 448, 58041. Tel: 701-242-7891; Fax: 701-242-7896. Karen Gabbert, Admin.; Sr. Mary Louise, O.S.F., Asst. Admin. Sisters of St. Francis of the Immaculate Heart of Mary (Hankinson, ND) 3; Bed Capacity 37; Patients Assisted Annually 100; Independent Living Unit Beds 11; Children in Daycare 18; Total Staff 80.

JAMESTOWN. *Ave Maria Village, SMP Health System*, 501 19th St., N.E., 58401. Tel: 701-252-5660; Fax: 701-251-2643. Email: tim.burchill@smphs.org. Timothy N. Burchill, Admin. Bed Capacity 100; Total Staff 175; Resident Days 36,188; Total Assisted Annually 205.

LA MOURE. *St. Rose Care Center*, 315 1st St. S.E., 58458. Tel: 701-883-5363; Fax: 701-883-5711. Email: helen.wamstad@bhshealth.org. Ms. Helen Wamstad, Admin./CEO. Operated by Benedictine Living Communities, Inc. Bed Capacity 40; Total Staff 65.

VALLEY CITY. *Sheyenne Care Center, SMP Health System*, 979 N. Central Ave., 58072. Tel: 701-845-8222; Fax: 701-845-8270. Email: craig.christianson@smphs.org. Craig Christianson, CEO. Bed Capacity 170; Total Staff 290; Resident Days 60,041; Total Assisted Annually 210.

WAHPETON. *St. Catherine's Living Center*, 1307 N. Seventh St., 58075. Tel: 701-642-6667; Fax: 701-642-2485. Emmy Tretter, Admin. Operated by Benedictine Living Communities, Inc. Long Term Care Beds 100; Basic Care Beds 16; Total Staff 156.

[E] CATHOLIC CHARITIES

FARGO. *Catholic Charities North Dakota - Fargo* (1923) 5201 Bishops Blvd., Ste. B, 58104. Tel: 701-235-4457; Fax: 701-356-7993. Email: fargo@catholiccharitiesnd.org. Web: www.catholiccharitiesnd.org. Larry Bernhardt, Exec. Dir. Statewide social service agency providing adoption services, child welfare, guardianship services, pregnancy services, Adults Adopting Special Kids (AASK), and counseling services. Total Staff 49.

GRAND FORKS. *St. Joseph's Social Care and Thrift Store*, 620 8th Ave. S., 58201-4816. Tel: 701-795-8614; Fax: 701-746-6648. Email: joannbrundin@yahoo.com. Jo Ann Brundin, Dir. Total Assisted Annually 8,000.

MINTO. *Saint Gianna's Home Inc.* Residence for pregnant women and their children., 15605 Country Rd. 15, 58261. Tel: 701-248-3077. Email: saintgiannahome@hotmail.com. Web: www.saintgiannahome.com. Mary Pat Jahner, Dir.; Rev. Joseph Christensen, F.M.I., Spiritual Dir. Priests 1; Staff 5.

[F] CONVENTS AND RESIDENCES FOR SISTERS

FARGO. *Presentation Center-Sacred Heart Convent*, 1101 32nd Ave. S., 58103. Tel: 701-237-4857; Fax: 701-237-9822. Web:

www.presentationsistersfargo.com. Sr. Mary Margaret Mooney, P.B.V.M., Pres. Sisters 45.

HANKINSON. *Sisters of St. Francis of the Immaculate Heart of Mary*, P.O. Box 447, 58041-0447. Tel: 701-242-7195; Fax: 701-242-7198. Email: osfhank2009@rrt.net. Web: www.dillingenfranciscansusa.org. 102 6th St., S.E., 58041. Sr. Donna Welder, O.S.F., Prov. Supr. Sisters 31.

VALLEY CITY. *Sisters of Mary of the Presentation*, 11550 River Rd., 58072. Tel: 701-845-2864; Fax: 701-845-0805. Email: carol.kuntz@fargodiocese.org. Sr. Carol Jean Kuntz, S.M.P., Prov. Supr.; Rev. Claude Seeberger, O.S.B., Chap. Sisters 29.

WAHPETON. *Carmel of Mary* (1954) 17765 78th St., S.E., 58075. Tel: 701-642-2360. Sr. Joseph-Marie of the Child of Jesus, O.Carm., Prioress; Rev. Jim Tiu, Chap. Carmelite Nuns of the Ancient Observance. Solemn Professed Nuns 9.

[G] RETREAT HOUSES

FARGO. *St. Joseph's House of Retreat*, P.O. Box 1323, 58107.

Presentation Prayer Center (1981) 1101 32nd Ave., 58103. Tel: 701-237-4857; Fax: 701-237-9822. Email: presprayerctr@cableone.net. Web: www.presentationsistersfargo.com. Sr. Andrea Arendt, P.B.V.M., Dir. Sisters 2.

[H] NEWMAN FOUNDATIONS

FARGO. *St. Paul's Newman Church of Fargo* (1928) 1141 N. University Dr., 58102. Tel: 701-235-0142; Fax: 701-298-6431. Email: ndsunewmanctr@yahoo.com. Web: www.bisoncatholic.org. Rev. James Cheney, Dir. Campus Ministry. Total Staff 15; Catholic Students 450.

GRAND FORKS. *St. Thomas Aquinas Newman Church of Grand Forks* (1951) 410 Cambridge St., 58203. Tel: 701-777-6850; Fax: 701-777-6851. Web: www.und.edu/dept/newman. Rev. Jason Lefor. Total Staff 13; Catholic Students 3,000.

WAHPETON. *State College of Science Newman Student Parish* 701 N. Seventh St., 58075. Tel: 701-642-6982; Fax: 701-642-2601. Very Rev. Dale Lagodinski.

[I] MISCELLANEOUS LISTINGS

FARGO. *Calvary Cemetery Association*, 5201 Bishops Blvd., 58104-7605.

Cardinal Muench Seminary Closed. For inquiries contact the Finance Office., 5201 Bishops Blvd., 58104-7605. Tel: 701-356-7900.

Catholic Chaplains Association, Diocese of Fargo, Pastoral Center, 5201 Bishops Blvd., 58104. Tel: 701-356-7950. Email: luke.meyer@fargodiocese.org. Very Rev. Luke D. Meyer.

Catholic Development Foundation (1989) 5201 Bishops Blvd. S., Ste A, 58104-7605. Tel: 701-356-7930; Fax: 701-356-7998. Email: scott.hoselton@fargodiocese.org. Web: www.fargodiocese.org. A nonprofit foundation for religious charitable and educational purposes.

Cursillo Movement, 5202 25th St. S., 58104. Tel: 701-320-7402. Web: www.natl-cursillo.org. Rev. Duaine Cote, Spiritual Advisor (Retired).

Fargo Catholic Schools Network Foundation, c/o Todd Mickelson, 5600 25th St. S., 58104. Tel: 701-893-3200; Fax: 701-893-3277. Email: todd.mickelson@fdjp2.k12.nd.us. Web: www.fdjp2.k12.nd.us. A nonprofit foundation for religious charitable and educational purposes. The Foundation is organized to financially support, assist, promote, expand and strengthen religious educational institutions affiliated with and under the governance of the Blessed John Paul II Catholic Schools Network.

Fargo Guild of Catholic Physicians, 5201 Bishops Blvd., 58104.

Hughes, Inc., 1101 32nd Ave. S., 58103. Tel: 701-237-4857; Fax: 701-237-9822. Web: www.presentationsistersfargo.com. Sr. Mary Margaret Mooney, P.B.V.M., Pres. Assisting, providing and expanding low-cost housing (in part for senior citizens along with other groups).

Marriage Encounter, P.O. Box 898, Devils Lake, 58301. Tel: 701-662-7558; Fax: 701-662-7559. Very Rev. Dale H. Kinzler.

Prairieland Home Care, 1102 Page Dr., S.W., 58103. Tel: 701-235-5750; Fax: 701-232-0906. Email: lynn.elliot@smphs.org. Web: www.prairielandhomecare.org.

The Presentation Foundation, Sacred Heart Convent, 1101 32nd Ave. S., 58103. Tel: 701-237-4857; Fax: 701-237-9822. Email: foundation@presentationsistersfargo.com. Web: www.presentationsistersfargo.com. Sr. Stella Olson, P.B.V.M., Dir.

Presentation Partners in Housing, 1101 32nd Ave S., 58103. Tel: 701-235-6861; Fax: 701-237-9822. Email: skk1978@hotmail.com. Web: www.presentationsistersfargo.com.

BATHGATE. *Bethlehem Community*, 10194 Garfield St., S., 58216. Tel: 701-265-3717; Fax: 701-265-3716. Email: contact@bethlehembooks.com. Web: www.vmcenter.org. Lydia Reynolds, Contact Person.

GRAND FORKS. *Grand Forks Catholic Schools Association*, 1001 17th Ave. S., 58201. Tel: 701-775-9886; Fax: 701-775-0221. Mr. Charles Scherr, Contact Person. A nonprofit organization developing curriculum study, scholarship, transportation, personnel and fund raising.

JAMESTOWN. *Jamestown College*, 214 4th St. S.E., 58401. Tel: 701-252-0478; Fax: 701-252-0478. Email: swallace@jc.edu. Very Rev. Al M. Bitz; Shirley Wallace, Pastoral Min. & Campus Min. Catholic Students 214.

LANGDON. *St. Alphonsus School Foundation*, 908 3rd St., 58249. Tel: 701-256-3717; Fax: 701-256-3720. Cameron Sillers, Pres.

MANVEL. *Beginning Experience Apostolate, c/o St. Timothy's Catholic Church*, 1207 Oldham Ave., 58256-4335. Tel: 701-696-2219. Email: bernard.schneider@fargodiocese.org. Rev. Bernard Schneider.

VALLEY CITY. *Valley City State University*, c/o St. Catherine, 540 3rd Ave., N.E., 58072. Tel: 701-845-0354; Fax: 701-845-0556. Catholic Students 150.

RELIGIOUS INSTITUTES OF MEN REPRESENTED IN THE DIOCESE

For further details refer to the corresponding bracketed number in the Religious Institutes of Men or Women section.

[0200]—*Benedictine Monks* (Assumption Abbey, Richardton, ND)—O.S.B.

[0650]—*Holy Ghost Fathers*—C.S.Sp.

[0430]—*Order of Preachers-Dominicans*—O.P.

[0975]—*Society of Our Lady of the Most Holy Trinity*—S.O.L.T.

[]—*Third Order Franciscans of Mary Immaculate*

RELIGIOUS INSTITUTES OF WOMEN REPRESENTED IN THE DIOCESE

[0300]—*Calced Carmelites*—O.Carm.

[]—*Francisan Sisters of Dilligen*

[3510]—*Sister Servants of Christ the King*—S.S.C.K.

[2450]—*Sisters of Mary of the Presentation* (Valley City, ND)—S.M.P.

[3320]—*Sisters of the Presentation of the B.V.M.* (Fargo, ND)—P.B.V.M.

[]—*Sisters of the Society of Our Lady of the Most Holy Trinity*—S.O.L.T.

DIOCESAN CEMETERIES

Holy Cross Cemeteries of Fargo, 5201 Bishops Blvd., 58104-7605.

NECROLOGY

† Lanz, Mathias, (Retired)—Died April 15, 2011

An asterisk (*) denotes an organization that has established tax-exempt status directly with the IRS and is not covered by the USCCB Group Ruling.

Diocese of Fort Wayne - South Bend

(Dioecesis Wayne Castrensis-South Bendensis)

Most Reverend

KEVIN C. RHOADES

Bishop of Fort Wayne-South Bend; ordained July 9, 1983; appointed Bishop of Harrisburg October 14, 2004; consecrated December 9, 2004; appointed Bishop of Fort Wayne-South Bend November 14, 2009; installed Bishop of Fort Wayne-South Bend January 13, 2010. *Mailing Address: P.O. 390, Fort Wayne, IN 46801.*

Most Reverend

JOHN M. D'ARCY, D.D., M.D., S.T.D.

Retired Bishop of Fort Wayne-South Bend; ordained February 2, 1957; appointed Auxiliary Bishop of Boston and Titular Bishop of Mediana December 31, 1974; consecrated February 11, 1975; appointed Bishop of Fort Wayne-South Bend February 26, 1985; installed May 1, 1985; retired November 14, 2009. *Mailing Address: P.O. Box 390, Fort Wayne, IN 46801.*

Archbishop Noll Catholic Center: 915 S. Clinton St., P.O. Box 390, Fort Wayne, IN 46801. Tel: 260-422-4611; Fax: 260-969-9145.

Web: www.diocesefwsb.org

Email: bishopsoffice@diocesefwsb.org

ESTABLISHED SEPTEMBER 22, 1857.

Square Miles 5,792.

Redesignated Diocese of Fort Wayne-South Bend on July 22, 1960.

Comprises the Counties of Adams, Allen, Dekalb, Elkhart, Huntington, Kosciusko, La Grange, Marshall, Noble, St. Joseph, Steuben, Wabash, Wells, Whitley in the State of Indiana.

For legal titles of parishes and diocesan institutions, consult the Chancery Office.

STATISTICAL OVERVIEW

Personnel	
Bishop	1
Retired Bishops	1
Priests: Diocesan Active in Diocese	64
Priests: Retired, Sick or Absent	16
Number of Diocesan Priests	80
Religious Priests in Diocese	137
Total Priests in Diocese	217
Extern Priests in Diocese	18
Ordinations:	
Diocesan Priests	2
Religious Priests	2
Transitional Deacons	2
Permanent Deacons	11
Permanent Deacons in Diocese	21
Total Brothers	113
Total Sisters	458
Parishes	
Parishes	81
With Resident Pastor:	
Resident Diocesan Priests	64
Resident Religious Priests	17
Pastoral Centers	4
New Parishes Created	1
Professional Ministry Personnel:	
Sisters	10
Lay Ministers	102
Welfare	
Catholic Hospitals	2
Total Assisted	254,349
Health Care Centers	4
Total Assisted	57,795
Homes for the Aged	7
Total Assisted	2,257
Special Centers for Social Services	9
Total Assisted	271,359
Other Institutions	3
Total Assisted	10,238
Educational	
Diocesan Students in Other Seminaries	24
Seminaries, Religious	2
Students Religious	29
Total Seminarians	53
Colleges and Universities	5
Total Students	16,704
High Schools, Diocesan and Parish	4
Total Students	3,125
Elementary Schools, Diocesan and Parish	37
Total Students	10,783
Catechesis/Religious Education:	
High School Students	1,191
Elementary Students	9,375
Total Students under Catholic Instruction	41,231
Teachers in the Diocese:	
Sisters	6
Lay Teachers	720
Vital Statistics	
Receptions into the Church:	
Infant Baptism Totals	2,680
Minor Baptism Totals	182
Adult Baptism Totals	185
Received into Full Communion	465
First Communions	2,939
Confirmations	2,548
Marriages:	
Catholic	529
Interfaith	242
Total Marriages	771
Deaths	1,459
Total Catholic Population	159,888
Total Population	1,248,405

Former Bishops—Rt. Revs. JOHN HENRY LUERS, D.D., ord. Nov. 11, 1846; cons. Jan. 10, 1858; died June 29, 1871; JOSEPH DWENGER, C.PP.S., D.D., ord. Sept. 4, 1859; cons. April 14, 1872; died Jan. 27, 1893; JOSEPH RADEMACHER, D.D., ord. Aug. 2, 1863; cons. Bishop of Nashville, June 24, 1883; transferred to Fort Wayne, July 14, 1893; died Jan. 12, 1900; HERMAN JOSEPH ALERDING, D.D., cons. Nov. 30, 1900; died Dec. 6, 1924; Most Revs. JOHN FRANCIS NOLL, D.D., ord. June 4, 1898; cons. June 30, 1925; promoted to rank of Archbishop "ad personam," Sept. 2, 1953; died July 31, 1956; LEO A. PURSLEY, D.D., ord. June 11, 1927; cons. Sept. 19, 1950; retired Oct. 19, 1976; died Nov. 15, 1998; WILLIAM E. MCMANUS, D.D., ord. April 15, 1939; appt. Auxiliary Bishop of Chicago, June 21, 1967; appt. Bishop of Fort Wayne, Aug. 31, 1976; installed as 7th Bishop of Fort Wayne, Oct. 19, 1976; retired Feb. 25, 1985; died March 3, 1997; JOHN M. D'ARCY, M.D., S.T.D. (Retired), ord. Feb. 2, 1957; appt. Auxiliary Bishop of Boston and Titular Bishop of Mediana Dec. 31, 1974; cons. Feb. 11, 1975; appt. Bishop of Fort Wayne-South Bend Feb. 26, 1985; installed May 1, 1985; retired Nov. 14, 2009.

Chancery Office—Archbishop Noll Catholic Center, 915 S. Clinton St., Fort Wayne, 46802. Mailing Address: P.O. Box 390, Fort Wayne, 46801. Tel: 260-422-4611; Fax: 260-969-9145. *Blessed John Paul II Center, 1328 W. Dragoon Tr., Mishawaka, 46544.* Tel: 574-234-0687; Fax: 574-234-0687. Office Hours: Mon.-Fri. 8:30-4:30. Other times by appointment.

Diocese of Fort Wayne-South Bend, Inc.—(Incorporated Aug. 29, 1955). Board of Directors: Most Rev. KEVIN C. RHOADES, D.D., S.T.L., J.C.L., Pres.; Rev. Msgr. ROBERT C. SCHULTE, Vice Pres.; Mr. JOSEPH RYAN, Sec. & Treas.

Diocese of Fort Wayne-South Bend Officials

Vicar General-Chancellor—Rev. Msgr. ROBERT C. SCHULTE, Archbishop Noll Catholic Center, 915 S. Clinton St., Fort Wayne, 46802. Mailing Address: P.O. Box 390, Fort Wayne, 46801. Tel: 260-422-4611; Fax: 260-969-9145.

Vice Chancellor—Rev. JASON FREIBURGER, Archbishop Noll Catholic Center, 915 S. Clinton St., Fort Wayne, 46802. Mailing Address: P.O. Box 390, Fort Wayne, 46801. Tel: 260-422-4611; Fax: 260-969-9145.

Moderator of the Curia—Rev. Msgr. ROBERT C. SCHULTE, Archbishop Noll Catholic Center, 915 S. Clinton St., Fort Wayne, 46802. Mailing Address: P.O. Box 390, Fort Wayne, 46801. Tel: 260-422-4611; Fax: 260-969-9145.

Assistant to the Bishop-Fort Wayne—Rev. JASON FREIBURGER, Archbishop Noll Catholic Center, 915 S. Clinton St., Fort Wayne, 46802. Mailing Address: P.O. Box 390, Fort Wayne, 46801. Tel: 260-422-4611; Fax: 260-969-9145.

Assistant to the Bishop-South Bend—FRED EVERETT, Blessed John Paul II Center, 1328 W. Dragoon Tr., Mishawaka, 46544. Tel: 574-234-0687; Fax: 574-234-0687.

Judicial Vicar—Rev. MARK A. GURTNER, J.C.L., Archbishop Noll Catholic Center, 915 S. Clinton St., Fort Wayne, 46802. Mailing Address: P.O. Box 390, Fort Wayne, 46801. Tel: 260-422-4611; Fax: 260-969-9140.

Secretary for Administrative Services—Mr. JOSEPH RYAN, CFO, Archbishop Noll Catholic Center, 915 S. Clinton St., Fort Wayne, 46802. Mailing Address: P.O. Box 390, Fort Wayne, 46801. Tel: 260-422-4611; Fax: 260-423-3382.

Secretary for Catholic Education—MARK MYERS,

Ph.D., Archbishop Noll Catholic Center, 915 S. Clinton St., Fort Wayne, 46802. Mailing Address: P.O. Box 390, Fort Wayne, 46801. Tel: 260-422-4611; Fax: 260-426-3077.

Secretary for Evangelization and Special Ministries—MARY L. GLOWASKI, Archbishop Noll Catholic Center, 915 S. Clinton St., Fort Wayne, 46802. Mailing Address: P.O. Box 390, Fort Wayne, 46801. Tel: 260-422-4611; Fax: 260-483-1881.

Secretary for Stewardship and Development—HARRY W. VERHILEY, Archbishop Noll Catholic Center, 915 S. Clinton St., Fort Wayne, 46802. Mailing Address: P.O. Box 390, Fort Wayne, 46801. Tel: 260-422-4611; Fax: 260-969-9145. Blessed John Paul II Center, 1328 W. Dragoon Tr., Mishawaka, 46544. Tel: 574-234-0687; Fax: 574-256-2709.

Diocesan Offices, Commissions, Boards and Programs

Budget Committee—Rev. Msgr. BERNARD J. GALIC; Rev. MARK A. GURTNER, J.C.L.; Mr. JOSEPH RYAN; Rev. Msgr. ROBERT C. SCHULTE; Rev. THOMAS SHOEMAKER; Rev. Msgr. JOHN N. SUELZER.

Buildings and Improvements—Advisory Board: BILL ARNOLD; JOHN BERGHOFF; JIM BRECKLER; Rev. JOHN DELANEY; MIKE HAMILTON; MICHAEL KINDER; Mr. JOSEPH RYAN; Rev. Msgr. ROBERT C. SCHULTE; Rev. WILLIAM SULLIVAN.

Business Administration Office—Mr. JOSEPH RYAN, CFO, Archbishop Noll Catholic Center, 915 S. Clinton St., Fort Wayne, 46802. Mailing Address: P.O. Box 390, Fort Wayne, 46801. Tel: 260-422-4611; Fax: 260-423-3382.

Catechesis—Deacon JAMES TIGHE, Dir., Archbishop Noll Catholic Center, 915 S. Clinton St., Fort Wayne, 46802. Mailing Address: P.O. Box 390, Fort Wayne, 46801. Tel: 260-422-4611; Fax: 260-483-1881. Blessed Pope John Paul II Center, 1328 W. Dragoon Tr., Mishawaka, 46544. Tel: 574-259-9994; Fax: 574-258-6569.

Cathedral Books and Gifts—KARA SLOCUM, Coord., Archbishop Noll Catholic Center, 915 S. Clinton St., Fort Wayne, 46802. Mailing Address: P.O. Box 390, Fort Wayne, 46801. Tel: 260-422-4611; Fax: 260-969-1475.

Cathedral Museum—Rev. PHILLIP WIDMANN, Dir., Archbishop Noll Catholic Center, 915 S. Clinton St., Fort Wayne, 46802. Mailing Address: P.O. Box 390, Fort Wayne, 46801. Tel: 260-744-2765; Fax: 260-744-1972.

Catholic Campaign for Human Development—ANN HELMKE, Dir., 2827 Holton Ave., Fort Wayne, 46806. Tel: 260-456-4172; Fax: 260-456-4075.

Catholic Cemeteries—THOMAS E. ALTER, Dir., Catholic Cemetery Assoc., 3500 Lake Ave., Fort Wayne, 46805. Tel: 260-426-2044; Fax: 260-422-7418.

Catholic Communications Office—VINCE LABARBERA, Dir., Archbishop Noll Catholic Center, 915 S. Clinton St., Fort Wayne, 46802. Mailing Address: P.O. Box 390, Fort Wayne, 46801. Tel: 260-744-0012; Fax: 260-744-1473.

Catholic Schools—MARK MYERS, Ph.D., Supt.; Mrs. MARSHA A. JORDAN, Assoc. Supt., Archbishop Noll Catholic Center, 915 S. Clinton St., Fort Wayne, 46802. Mailing Adress: P.O. Box 390, Fort Wayne, 46801. Tel: 260-422-4611; Fax: 260-426-3077. Blessed John Paul II Center, 1328 W. Dragoon Tr., Mishawaka, 46544. Tel: 574-255-1387; Fax: 574-256-2709.

Catholic School Board—MARK MYERS, Ph.D., Supt.; Revs. JOHN M. DERISO, C.S.C.; JOSEPH GAUGHAN; JUAN GIRON; THOMAS GUINAN; JIM HOCH; LISA MATEJKA; ROBERTA POLOVIK; ANDY SCHNEIDER.

Catholic Schools Office Administration—

Ex Officio Member—Most Rev. KEVIN C. RHOADES, D.D., S.T.L., J.C.L.

Censor Librorum—Rev. Msgr. MICHAEL W. HEINTZ, Ph.D., 1701 Miami St., South Bend, 46613. Tel: 574-289-5539; Fax: 574-289-0227.

Clergy Retirement Board—Revs. ROBERT D'SOUZA; WILLIAM KUMMER; Rev. Msgrs. JOHN M. KUZMICH; ROBERT C. SCHULTE; Rev. JAMES F. SECULOFF; Rev. Msgr. JOHN N. SUELZER; Rev. PHILLIP A. WIDMANN.

Consultors—Rev. MARK A. GURTNER, J.C.L.; Rev. Msgrs. MICHAEL W. HEINTZ, Ph.D.; BRUCE PIECHOCKI, J.C.L.; Rev. DANIEL D. SCHEIDT; Rev. Msgr. ROBERT C. SCHULTE; Revs. JAMES SHAFER; THOMAS SHOEMAKER; DERRICK SNEYD; DAVID W. VOORS.

Continuing Formation of Priests and Deacons—Rev. Msgr. ROBERT C. SCHULTE, Archbishop Noll Catholic Center, 915 S. Clinton St., Fort Wayne, 46802. Mailing Address: P.O. Box 390, Fort Wayne, 46801. Tel: 260-422-4611; Fax: 260-969-9145.

Diocesan Archives—JANICE CANTRELL, Archivist, Archbishop Noll Catholic Center, 915 S. Clinton St., Fort Wayne, 46802. Mailing Address: P.O. Box 390, Fort Wayne, 46801. Tel: 260-422-4611; Fax: 260-420-6306. Email: jhackbush@diocesefwsb.org.

Diocesan Council of Catholic Women—Rev. RICHARD HIRE, Priest Mod.; GEORGETTA GUNTHORP, Pres. (Elkhart), 0240 N. 850 E., LaGrange, 46761. Tel: 260-367-2359.

Development—HARRY W. VERHILEY, Dir., Blessed John Paul II Center, 1328 W. Dragoon Tr., Mishawaka, 46544. Tel: 574-234-0687.

Diocesan Purchasing Agency—MARY LOU O'KEEFFE, Archbishop Noll Catholic Center, 915 S. Clinton St., Fort Wayne, 46802. Mailing Address: P.O. Box 390, Fort Wayne, 46801. Tel: 260-422-4611; 800-856-4611; Fax: 260-420-6306; JOHN KLEIN, Opers. Mgr.

Ecumenism—Rev. JASON FREIBURGER, Dir., Archbishop Noll Catholic Center, 915 S. Clinton St., Fort Wayne, 46802. Mailing Address: P.O. Box 390, Fort Wayne, 46801. Tel: 260-422-4611; Fax: 260-969-9145.

Evangelization and Spiritual Development—NATALIE KOHRMAN, Office Dir., Archbishop Noll Catholic Center, 915 S. Clinton St., Fort Wayne, 46802. Mailing Address: P.O. Box 390, Fort Wayne, 46801. Tel: 260-422-4611.

Family Life—Co Directors: FRED EVERETT; LISA EVERETT, Blessed Pope John Paul II Center, 1328 W. Dragoon Tr., Mishawaka, 46544. Tel: 574-234-0687; Fax: 574-232-8483.

Finance Council—Most Rev. KEVIN C. RHOADES, D.D., S.T.L., J.C.L.; Mr. JOSEPH RYAN, CFO; THOMAS BLEE; JOSEPH DAHM; ARTHUR DECIO; Deacon JAMES FITZPATRICK; ALBERT L. GUTIERREZ; Mr. JERRY HAMMES; MICHAEL HAMMES; JEROME KEARNS; Sr. JANE MARIE KLEIN, O.S.F.; ALICE KOPFER; SCOTT MALPASS; CHRISTOPHER MURPHY; Rev. Msgr. ROBERT C. SCHULTE; THOMAS SKIBA; VINCENT TIPPMANN; GEORGE WITWER.

Hispanic Ministry—ENID ROMAN-DEJESUS, Dir., Blessed John Paul II Center, 1328 W. Dragoon Trail, Mishawaka, 46544. Tel: 574-234-0687; Fax: 574-258-6569.

Angola—St. Anthony of Padua, 700 W. Maumee St., Angola, 46703. Tel: 260-665-2259. Rev. ANDREW MARTINEZ, O.F.M.Conv.

Bremen—St. Dominic, 803 W. Bike St., Bremen, 46506. Tel: 574-546-3601. Rev. BOB J. LENGERICH.

Elkhart—St. Vincent de Paul, 1108 S. Main St., Elkhart, 46516. Tel: 574-389-9634. Rev. GLENN KOHRMAN.

Fort Wayne—St. Patrick, 2120 Harrison St., Fort Wayne, 46802. Tel: 260-744-1450. Revs. ANDREW THU PHAM, S.V.D.; JESUS BRIONES, S.V.D.

Goshen—St. John the Evangelist, 109 W. Monroe St., Goshen, 46526-3957. Tel: 574-534-7554. Rev. FERNANDO JIMENEZ.

Kendallville—Immaculate Conception, 319 E. Diamond St., Kendallville, 46755. Tel: 260-347-4045. Rev. JOHN STEELE, C.S.C.

LaGrange—St. Joseph, P.O. Box 69, LaGrange, 46761. Tel: 260-463-3472. Rev. ANDREW MARTINEZ, O.F.M.Conv.

Ligonier—St. Patrick, 300 Ravine Dr., Ligonier, 46767. Tel: 260-894-4946. Rev. WILSON O. CORZO.

Plymouth—St. Michael, 612 N. Walnut St., Plymouth, 46563. Tel: 574-936-4935. Rev. ELOY JIMENEZ.

South Bend—St. Adalbert, 2505 W. Grace St., South Bend, 46619. Tel: 574-288-5708. *St. Casimir, 1308 W. Dunham St., South Bend, 46619.* Tel: 574-287-9551. Revs. PETER PACINI, C.S.C.; THOMAS LEMOS, C.S.C.

Our Lady of Hungary—829 W. Calvert St., South Bend, 46613. Tel: 574-287-1700. Rev. KEVIN M. BAUMAN.

Warsaw—Our Lady of Guadalupe, 225 Gillian Dr., Warsaw, 46580. Tel: 574-658-9384. Rev. CONSTANTINO ROCHA; Sr. JOAN HASTREITER, S.S.J.

Permanent Diaconate—Rev. Msgr. ROBERT C. SCHULTE, Dir. Deacon Personnel, Archbishop Noll Catholic Center, 915 S. Clinton St., Fort Wayne, 46802. Mailing Address: P.O. Box 390, Fort Wayne, 46801. Tel: 260-422-4611; Fax: 260-969-9145; MARY SZYMCZAK, Assoc. Dir., Blessed John Paul II Center, 1328 W. Dragoon Tr., Mishawaka, 46544. Tel: 574-234-0687; Fax: 574-232-8483.

Pontifical Mission Societies—Dr. KATHLEEN SCHNEIDER, Dir., Mailing Address: P.O. Box 390, Fort Wayne, 46801. Tel: 260-396-2552; Fax: 260-396-2048.

Presbyteral Council—Revs. WILSON CORZO; TERRY FISHER; JASON FREIBURGER; JOSEPH GAUGHAN; MARK A. GURTNER, J.C.L.; WILLIAM KUMMER; Rev. Msgr. JOHN M. KUZMICH; Rev. JOHN F. PFISTER; Rev. Msgr. BRUCE PIECHOCKI, J.C.L.; Rev. DAVID RUPPERT; Rev. Msgr. ROBERT C. SCHULTE; Revs. JAMES F. SECULOFF; JAMES SHAFER; THOMAS SHOEMAKER; WILLIAM SULLIVAN; NEIL F. WACK, C.S.C.

Pro-Life—Co Directors: FRED EVERETT; LISA EVERETT, Blessed Pope John Paul II Center, 1328 W. Dragoon Tr., Mishawaka, 46544. Tel: 574-234-0687; Fax: 574-232-8483.

Retired Clergy Committee—Rev. Msgr. ROBERT C. SCHULTE, Vicar for Retired Clergy; Revs. ROBERT D'SOUZA; WILLIAM KUMMER; Rev. Msgr. JOHN M. KUZMICH; Rev. JAMES F. SECULOFF; Rev. Msgr. JOHN SUELZER; Rev. PHILLIP WIDMANN.

Safe Environment Youth Protection—CATHIE CICCHIELLO, Coord., Archbishop Noll Catholic Center, 915 S. Clinton St., Fort Wayne, 46802. Mailing Address: P.O. Box 390, Fort Wayne, 46801. Tel: 260-672-1510; Fax: 260-969-1475.

Scouting—Rev. ANTHONY STEINACKER, Fort Wayne Chap., 4916 Trier Rd., Fort Wayne, 46815. Tel: 260-482-2186; VACANT, South Bend Chap.

Serra International—Fort Wayne Serra Club: DAVE STEFFEN, Pres., 4928 Indiana Ave., Fort Wayne, 46807. Tel: 260-745-9711. Chaplains: Revs. JASON FREIBURGER; ANTHONY STEINACKER. South Bend Serra Club: STEPHEN ELEK JR., Pres., 20087 Roosevelt Rd., South Bend, 46614-5026; Rev. PAUL MCCARTHY, Chap.

"Today's Catholic" Official Publication—TIMOTHY JOHNSON, Editor, Archbishop Noll Catholic Center, 915 S. Clinton St., Fort Wayne, 46802. Mailing Address: P.O. Box 390, Fort Wayne, 46801. Tel: 260-456-2824; Fax: 260-744-1473.

Tribunal—Rev. MARK A. GURTNER, J.C.L., Judicial Vicar, Archbishop Noll Catholic Center, 915 S. Clinton St., Fort Wayne, 46802. Mailing Address: P.O. Box 390, Fort Wayne, 46801. Tel: 260-422-4611; Fax: 260-969-9140.

Administrative Assistant and Notary—JANICE BRELL.

Advocates—ELLEN BECKER; VICKI FERRIER.

Auditor—PAULA SHOAF.

Defender of the Bond—DEBORAH PAINTER.

First Court of Judges—Revs. FRANCIS CHUKWUMA, J.C.L.; MARK A. GURTNER, J.C.L.

Appeal Court Judges—Revs. FRANCIS CHUKWUMA, J.C.L.; MARK A. GURTNER, J.C.L.; LAWRENCE KRAMER; Rev. Msgr. BRUCE PIECHOCKI, J.C.L., Blessed John Paul II Center, 1328 W. Dragoon Tr., Mishawaka, 46544. Tel: 574-287-6531; Fax: 574-287-9391.

Advocate—DEBRA HANSEN.

Defenders of the Bond—MONICA BAUTERS; Rev. Msgr. BRUCE PIECHOCKI, J.C.L.

Pro-Synodal Judges—Rev. MARK A. GURTNER, J.C.L.; Rev. Msgrs. MICHAEL W. HEINTZ, Ph.D.; BRUCE PIECHOCKI, J.C.L.; WILLIAM C. SCHOOLER; Revs. JAMES SHAFER; THOMAS SHOEMAKER.

Court Consultants—AURA DESCHAMPS, Psy.D. LLC; JEFFREY FEATHERGILL, Psy.D.; STEPHEN ROSS, Psyd., HSPP, ABPP; CHRISTINE SHESTAK, M.S., LMHC; GREGORY SOWLES, Ph.D., MSPP; PATRICK W. UTZ, Ph.D.; JUDITH WILLIAMS, Psy.D., HSPP.

Victim Assistance—MARY L. GLOWASKI, Coord., Archbishop Noll Catholic Center, 915 S. Clinton St., Fort Wayne, 46802. Mailing Address: P.O. Box 390, Fort Wayne, 46801. Tel: 260-399-1458. Email: mglowaski@diocesefwsb.org.

Vocation Office—Rev. Msgr. BERNARD J. GALIC, Dir.; Rev. JACOB RUNYON, Assoc. Dir.; MARY SZYMCZAK, Assoc., Blessed John Paul II Center, 1328 W. Dragoon Tr., Mishawaka, 46544. Tel: 574-234-0687; Fax: 574-232-8483.

Youth Organizations—

CYO—Mailing Address: P.O. Box 445, Monroeville, 46773. Tel: 260-623-6007; Fax: 260-623-6007. Ms. MARY SCHREIBER, Pres., 2021 Reckeweg Dr., Fort Wayne, 46804. Tel: 260-432-1921.

Inter City Catholic League—Rev. Msgr. MICHAEL W. HEINTZ, Ph.D., Mod., 1701 Miami St., South Bend, 46613. Tel: 574-289-5539; Fax: 574-289-0227; TONY VIOLI, Pres., 225 Omer Ave., Mishawaka, 46545. Tel: 574-259-1638; Fax: 574-259-0995.

Worldwide Marriage Encounter—RICK NILL; JULIE NILL, 10917 Otter Creek Ct., Fort Wayne, 46814. Tel: 260-436-8026.

Worship Office—BRIAN MACMICHAEL, Dir., Archbishop Noll Catholic Center, 915 S. Clinton St., Fort Wayne, 46802. Mailing Address: P.O. Box 390, Fort Wayne, 46801. Tel: 260-422-4611; Fax: 260-423-3382.

Liturgical Commission—Rev. Msgr. WILLIAM C. SCHOOLER, Chair; CINDY BLACK; Rev. MICHAEL DRISCOLL, Ph.D.; DAVID FAGERBERG, Ph.D.; Deacon JAMES FITZPATRICK; Rev. MARK A. GURTNER, J.C.L.; Rev. Msgr. MICHAEL W. HEINTZ, Ph.D.; JEREMY HOY; Rev. PETER D. ROCCA, C.S.C.; ENID ROMAN-DEJESUS.

Sacred Art and Architecture Committee—WILLIAM COLEMAN JR., A.I.A.; Rev. MARK A. GURTNER, J.C.L.; SAM JONES, A.I.A.; Bro. DENNIS MEYERS, C.S.C.; Rev. DANIEL D. SCHEIDT; CHRISTOPHER SCHENKEL; DUNCAN STROIK.

Youth, Young Adult & Campus Ministries—CINDY BLACK, Dir., Archbishop Noll Catholic Center, 915 S. Clinton St., Fort Wayne, 46802. Mailing Address: P.O. Box 390, Fort Wayne, 46801. Tel: 260-422-4611.

CLERGY, PARISHES, MISSIONS AND PAROCHIAL SCHOOLS

CITY OF FORT WAYNE

(ALLEN COUNTY)

1—CATHEDRAL OF THE IMMACULATE CONCEPTION (1836), (Calhoun, between Lewis and Jefferson Sts.). Rev. Msgr. Robert C. Schulte, Rector; Revs. Dale A. Bauman; Jason Freiburger.
Mailing Address: P.O. Box 10898, 46854. Web: cathedralfw.catholicweb.com.
Res.: Tel: 260-424-1485; Fax: 260-424-7625.
Catechesis/Religious Program—Fax: 260-424-7625. Sr. Marilyn Ellert, O.S.F., D.R.E./Pastoral Min. (PreK-8) 90.
Chapel—St. Mother Theodore Guerin Chapel 1139 S. Calhoun St., 46802.

2—ST. ANDREW (1910) Closed. Parish closed June 28, 2003. Sacramental records are located in the Diocesan Archives Office, P.O. Box 390, Fort Wayne, IN. Tel: 260-422-4611.

3—ST. CHARLES BORROMEO (1957) [CEM] Rev. Msgr. John N. Suelzer; Revs. Anthony Steinacker; James Kumbakkeel, O.S.B. (India); Casey Ryan, Dir. Adult Formation; Margaret Sorg, Business Admin.
Res.: 4916 Trier Rd., 46815. Tel: 260-482-2186; Fax: 260-471-2144. Web: stcfw.org.
School—(Grades K-8), 4910 Trier Rd., 46815. Tel: 260-484-3392; Fax: 260-482-2006. Robert Sordelet, Prin.; Barbara Fisher, Librarian. Franciscan Sisters of the Sacred Heart 1; Lay Teachers 44; Students 729.
Catechesis/Religious Program—Tel: 260-484-7322. Amy Johns, D.R.E. Students 116.

4—ST. ELIZABETH ANN SETON (1988) Revs. James Shafer; Lawrence Kramer; Deacon James Kitchens.
Office: 10700 Aboite Center Rd., 46804. Tel: 260-432-0268; Fax: 260-436-5851.
Catechesis/Religious Program—Students 1,344.

5—ST. HENRY (1956) Rev. Daniel Durkin.
Parish Office: 4643 Gaywood Dr., 46806. Tel: 260-744-2519; Fax: 260-387-5044. Email: sainthenry@frontier.com.
Res.: 2929 E. Paulding Rd., 46816. Tel: 260-447-4100; Fax: 260-447-4100.
Catechesis/Religious Program—Students 38.

6—ST. HYACINTH (1910) Closed. Parish closed November 4, 1995. Sacramental records are located in the Diocesan Archives Office, P.O. Box 390, Fort Wayne, IN. Tel: 260-422-4611.

7—ST. JOHN THE BAPTIST (1929) Rev. Cyril Fernandes; Mary L. Glowaski, Pastoral Assoc.
Res.: 4525 Arlington Ave., 46807. Tel: 260-744-4393; Fax: 260-456-3072. Web: www.stjohnsfw.org.
School—(Grades PreK-8), 4500 Fairfield Ave., 46807. Tel: 260-456-3321. Amanda Robinson, Prin.; Cindy Kinney, Librarian. Lay Teachers 20; Students 283.
Catechesis/Religious Program—Sr. Celeste Marie, D.R.E. Students 45.

8—ST. JOSEPH (1914), (Italian), Rev. Timothy A. Wrozek; Ken Jehle, Music Dir.
Office: 2213 Brooklyn Ave., 46802.
Res.: 1910 Hale Ave., 46802. Tel: 260-432-5113; Fax: 260-432-4711.
School—(Grades PreK-8), 2211 Brooklyn Ave., 46802. Tel: 260-432-4000; Fax: 260-432-8642. Ms. Lois Widner, Prin. Email: lwinder@stjstefwin.org; Kaylynn Isca, Librarian. Lay Teachers 33; Students 526.
Catechesis/Religious Program—Students 96.

9—ST. JOSEPH (1851) [CEM] Rev. Thomas Lombardi.
Res.: 11337 Old U.S. 27 S., 46816. Tel: 260-639-3748; Fax: 260-639-3331.
School—(Grades PreK-8), 11521 Old U.S. 27 S., 46816. Tel: 260-639-3580; Fax: 260-639-3675. Louise Schultheis, Prin.; Tammy Gladding, Librarian. Lay Teachers 13; Students 135.
Catechesis/Religious Program—Students 27.

10—ST. JUDE (1929) Revs. Thomas Shoemaker; Robert D'Souza; Mary Pohlman, Pastoral Assoc.
Res.: 2130 Pemberton Dr., 46805. Tel: 260-484-6609; Fax: 260-969-1607. Web: www.stjudefw.org.
School—(Grades PreK-8), 2110 Pemberton Dr., 46805. Tel: 260-484-4611; Fax: 260-969-1607. Web: www.stjudefw.org/school. Sr. Kathleen Marie Knueven, Prin.; Kathleen Houser, Librarian. Sisters of Notre Dame 3; Lay Teachers 36; Students 507.
Catechesis/Religious Program—Sue Sherburne, D.R.E. Students 156.

11—ST. MARY (1848), (German), [CEM] Rev. Phillip A. Widmann.
Mailing Address: P.O. Box 11383, 46857-1383. Tel: 260-424-8231; Fax: 260-426-2029. Email: stmarysfw@verizon.net.
Res.: 518 E. Dewald, 46803. Tel: 260-744-2765.
Catechesis/Religious Program—Students 24.

12—MOST PRECIOUS BLOOD (1897) Rev. Joseph Gaughan.
Res.: 1515 Barthold St., 46808. Tel: 260-424-5535; Fax: 260-426-7765.
School—(Grades PreK-8), 1529 Barthold St., 46808. Tel: 260-424-4832. Mrs. Alexandria Bergman, Prin. Lay Teachers 12; Students 192.
Catechesis/Religious Program—Students 29.

13—OUR LADY OF GOOD HOPE (1969) Revs. Mark A. Gurtner; Andrew Curry, Parochial Vicar; David Zehr, Pastoral Assoc.; Jeanne Kawiecki, Liturgy & Music Dir.; Donna Weldy, Business Admin. Asst.
Res.: 7215 St. Joe Rd., 46835. Tel: 260-485-9615; Fax: 260-485-4463.
Catechesis/Religious Program—Tel: 260-485-9615, Ext. 107. Email: olgh.info@gmail.com. Web: olghfw-.com. Kelly Ley, D.R.E.; Jackie Oberhausen, Youth Dir. (PreK-6); Nick Oberhausen, Youth Min. (7-12). Students 137.

14—ST. PATRICK (1889), (Multicultural), Revs. Thu Pham, S.V.D.; Jesus Briones, S.V.D.; Lloyd (Samuel) Cunningham, S.V.D. In Res., Rev. Jesus Briones, S.V.D.
Res.: 2120 S. Harrison St., 46802. Tel: 260-744-1450; Fax: 260-745-3643. Email: stpartrickfortwayne@yahoo.com.
Catechesis/Religious Program—Students 287.

15—ST. PAUL (1865) Closed. Parish closed June 28, 2003. Sacramental records are located at St. Patrick Catholic Church, 2120 Harrison St., Fort Wayne, IN 46802. Tel: 260-744-1450.

16—ST. PETER (1872), (German), Rev. Phillip A. Widmann.
Res.: 518 E. De Wald St., 46803. Tel: 260-744-2765; Fax: 260-744-1972. Web: www.stpeterscatholicfw.org.
Catechesis/Religious Program—

17—QUEEN OF ANGELS (1947) [CEM] Rev. Gary L. Sigler; Deacon John Hilger.
Res.: 1500 W. State Blvd., 46808. Tel: 260-482-9411; Fax: 260-471-0005.
School—(Grades PreK-8), 1600 W. State Blvd., 46808. Tel: 260-483-8214; Fax: 260-482-9412. Mrs. Anne Miller, Prin. Lay Teachers 15; Students 240.
Catechesis/Religious Program—Students 63.

18—SACRED HEART (1947) Revs. Daniel Durkin; George Gabet, F.S.S.P.
Church & Office: 4643 Gaywood Dr., 46806. Tel: 260-744-2519. Email: sacredheartcc@verizon.net.
Res.: 2929 E. Paulding Rd., 46816. Tel: 260-447-4100; Fax: 260-387-5044.
Catechesis/Religious Program—

19—ST. THERESE (1947) Rev. Lawrence Teteh, C.S.Sp. (Nigeria).
Res.: 2304 Lower Huntington Rd., 46819. Tel: 260-747-9139; Fax: 260-747-1494. Email: sttheresefw@sttheresefw.org. Web: www.sttheresefw.org.
School—(Grades PreK-8), 2222 Lower Huntington Rd., 46819. Tel: 260-747-2343; Fax: 260-747-4767. Charles Grimm, Prin. Lay Teachers 14; Students 190.
Catechesis/Religious Program—Students 48.

20—ST. VINCENT DE PAUL (1846) [CEM] Rev. Msgr. John M. Kuzmich; Revs. Andrew Budzinski; Polycarp Fernando, Parochial Vicar; Dorothy Schuerman, Pastoral Assoc.; Ms. Sherry Miller, Admin.; Julia Thill, Pastoral Assoc.
Res.: 1502 E. Wallen Rd., 46825. Tel: 260-489-3537; Fax: 260-497-9405. Email: stvincentchurch@hotmail.com. Web: www.saintv.org.
School—(Grades K-8), 1720 E. Wallen Rd., 46825. Tel: 260-489-3537, Ext. 213; Fax: 260-489-5318. Mrs. Sandra Guffey, Prin. Lay Teachers 42; Students 757.
Catechesis/Religious Program—Tel: 260-489-3537, Ext. 235. Beth Amick, D.R.E. Students 440.

CITY OF SOUTH BEND

(ST. JOSEPH COUNTY)

1—ST. ADALBERT (1910), (Polish), Revs. Peter Pacini, C.S.C.; Thomas Lemos, C.S.C.
Mailing Address: 2505 W. Grace St., 46619. Email: stadal139@diocesefwsb.org. In Res., Rev. Leonard J. Collins, C.S.C.
Res.: 2420 W. Huron St., 46619. Tel: 574-288-5708; Fax: 574-251-2786.
School—519 S. Olive St., 46619. Tel: 574-288-6645; Fax: 574-251-2788. Mary Ann Bachman, Prin. Lay Teachers 10; Students 217.
Catechesis/Religious Program—Students 247.

2—ST. ANTHONY DE PADUA (1949) Rev. David Ruppert; Deacon Brian L. Miller.
2120 E. Jefferson Blvd., 46617. Tel: 574-282-2308; Fax: 574-288-8877.
School—(Grades PreK-8), 2310 E. Jefferson Blvd., 46615. Tel: 574-233-7169; Fax: 574-233-7290. Chad Barwick, Prin.; Josie Goepfrich, Librarian. Lay Teachers 22; Religious Teachers 3; Students 389.
Catechesis/Religious Program—Students 20.

3—ST. AUGUSTINE (1928), (African American), Rev. Leonard J. Collins, C.S.C.; Deacon Melvin Tardy.
Mailing Address: P.O. Box 3198, 46619-0198. Tel: 574-234-7082; Fax: 574-251-2786.
Res.: 2420 Huron St., 46619. Tel: 574-288-5708.
Catechesis/Religious Program—

4—ST. CASIMIR (1899), (Polish), Revs. Peter Pacini, C.S.C.; Thomas Lemos, C.S.C.
Mailing Address: 2505 W. Grace St., 46619.
Res.: 2420 W. Huron, 46619. Tel: 574-288-5708.
Catechesis/Religious Program—

5—CHRIST THE KING (1933) Revs. Neil F. Wack, C.S.C.; Ronald Tripi, C.S.C.; John Santone, C.S.C.
Res.: 52473 Indiana State Rte. 933, 46637. Tel: 574-272-3113; Fax: 574-273-6702. Email: xtherex@aol.com. Web: christthekingonline.org.
School—(Grades PreK-8) Tel: 574-272-3922; Fax: 574-273-6707. Stephen Hoffmann, Prin. Lay Teachers 36; Students 474.
Catechesis/Religious Program—Students 50.

6—CORPUS CHRISTI (1961) Rev. Daryl Rybicki; Sr. M. Carmella Chojnacki, F.D.C., Pastoral Assoc.
Res.: 2822 Corpus Christi Dr., 46628. Tel: 574-272-9982; Fax: 574-272-2545. Email: corpuschristi2005@sbcglobal.net. Web: www.corpuschristisb.org.
School—(Grades PreK-8), 2817 Corpus Christi Dr., 46628. Tel: 574-272-9868; Fax: 574-272-9894. Web: www.corpuschristisb.org. Maggie Mackowiak, Prin.; Joan Kreskai, Librarian. Lay Teachers 17; Students 280.
Catechesis/Religious Program—Students 24.

7—ST. HEDWIG (1877), (Polish), Rev. Leonard F. Chrobot.
Res.: 331 S. Scott St., 46601. Tel: 574-287-8932; Fax: 574-232-9787.
Catechesis/Religious Program— Twinned with St. Patrick.

8—HOLY CROSS (1929) Revs. Michael C. Mathews, C.S.C.; Jeffrey A. Schneibel, C.S.C.
Res.: 1520 Vassar Ave., 46628. Tel: 574-233-2179; Fax: 574-237-6736. Web: www.hcssparish.org.
School—(Grades PreSchool-8), 1020 Wilber St., 46628. Tel: 574-234-3422; Fax: 574-237-6725. Web: www.holycrosscrusaders.org. Mrs. Angela Budzinski, Prin. Lay Teachers 22; Students 338.
Catechesis/Religious Program—Students 28.

9—HOLY FAMILY (1945) [JC] Revs. Charles A. Herman; Vincent Joseph, V.C., Parochial Vicar. In Res., Rev. Camillo Tirabassi (Retired).
Res.: 56405 Mayflower Rd., 46619. Tel: 574-282-2317; Fax: 574-282-2318. Web: www.holyfamilysouthbendcatholicweb.com.
School—(Grades PreK-8), 56407 Mayflower Rd., 46619. Tel: 574-289-7375; Fax: 574-289-7386. Sr. Joan Marie Shillinger, C.S.S.F., Prin. Felician Sisters (Livonia, MI) 2; Lay Teachers 21; Students 316.
Catechesis/Religious Program—Linda Lagodney, D.R.E. Students 104.

10—ST. JOHN THE BAPTIST (1956) Revs. Charles A. Herman; Vincent Joseph, V.C., Parochial Vicar.
Res.: 3526 St. Johns Way, 46628. Tel: 574-233-5414; Fax: 574-233-5414. Email: johnthebaptistcc@aol.com.
School—(Grades PreK-8), 3616 St. Johns Way, 46628. Tel: 574-232-9849; Fax: 574-232-9855. Janet Wroblewski, Prin. Lay Teachers 6; Students 110.
Catechesis/Religious Program—Students 15.

11—ST. JOSEPH (1853) Revs. John M. DeRiso, C.S.C.; John P. Riley, C.S.C.
Res.: 226 N. Hill St., 46617. Tel: 574-234-3135.
Parish Office—211 N. St. Louis Blvd., 46617. Tel: 574-234-3134; Fax: 574-234-2822. Web: www.stjoeparish.com.
School—(Grades K-8), 216 N. Hill St., 46617. Tel: 574-234-0451; Fax: 574-234-0524. Web: www.stjosephgradeschool.com. Mrs. Suzanne Wiwi, Prin. Lay Teachers 25; Students 446.
Catechesis/Religious Program—Students 42.

12—ST. JUDE CHURCH (1948) Revs. John Delaney; Charles Oyo, C.S.C.
Res.: 19704 Johnson Rd., 46614. Tel: 574-291-0570; Fax: 574-299-3051. Email: stjude@catherinesiena.org. Web: www.catherinesiena.org.
School—(Grades K-8), 19657 Hildebrand St., 46614. Tel: 574-291-3820; Fax: 574-299-3053. Email: principal@stjudeschool.net. Mr. Steve Donndelinger, Prin. Lay Teachers 14; Students 167.

Catechesis / Religious Program—Tel: 574-291-2797. Students 60.

13—ST. MARY OF THE ASSUMPTION (1882), (German), Closed. For inquiries for parish records see St. Jude, South Bend.

14—ST. MATTHEW CATHEDRAL (1921) Rev. Msgr. Michael W. Heintz, Rector; Rev. Jacob Runyon; Deacon Emilio Gizzi; David Laux, Business Mgr. Res.: 1701 Miami St., 46613. Tel: 574-289-5539; Fax: 574-289-0227. Email: info@stmatthewcathedral.org. Web: stmatthewcathedral.org.
School—(Grades PreK-8), 1015 E. Dayton, 46613. Tel: 574-289-4535; Fax: 574-289-5439. Mrs. Susan Clark, Prin.; Joanne Palmer, Librarian. Lay Teachers 23; Students 374.
Catechesis / Religious Program—1721 Miami St., 46613. Tel: 574-289-0940; Fax: 574-289-0940. Richard Becker, D.R.E.; Nancy Becker, D.R.E. Students 175.

15—OUR LADY OF HUNGARY (1921) [CEM] Rev. Kevin M. Bauman; Deacon Ervin Kuspa.
Res.: 829 W. Calvert St., 46613. Tel: 574-287-1700; Fax: 574-289-6704. Email: olhp@sbcglobal.net. Web: www.ourladyofhungary.com.
School—(Grades PreK-8), 735 W. Calvert St., 46613. Tel: 574-289-3272; Fax: 574-289-3272. Mrs. Melissa Wroblewski-Jay, Prin. Lay Teachers 12; Students 216.
Catechesis / Religious Program—Melissa Murawski, D.R.E. Students 120.

16—ST. PATRICK (1858) Rev. Leonard F. Chrobot.
Res. & Office: 331 S. Scott St., 46601. Tel: 574-287-8932; Fax: 574-232-9787. Email: stspatrick-hedwig@att.net.
Catechesis / Religious Program—Students 25.

17—SACRED HEART OF JESUS (LAKEVILLE) (1932) [JC] Revs. John Delaney; Charles Oyo, C.S.C.
Mailing Address: P.O. Box 2528, 46680-2528.
Res.: 63568 U.S. 31 S., 46614-9409. Tel: 574-291-2826; Fax: 574-291-3775. Email: sacredheart11@juno.com.
Catechesis / Religious Program—Twinned with St. Jude., Tel: 574-291-2826.

18—ST. STANISLAUS (1899), (Polish), Revs. Michael C. Matthews, C.S.C.; Jeffrey A. Schneibel, C.S.C.
Res.: 920 Wilber St., 46628. Tel: 574-233-2179; Fax: 574-237-6736. Web: www.hcssparish.org.

19—ST. STEPHEN (1909), (Hispanic—Hungarian), Closed. Parish closed May 31, 2003. Sacramental records are located at St. Adalbert Catholic Church, 2420 W. Huron St., South Bend, IN 46619. Tel: 574-288-5708.

20—ST. THERESE, LITTLE FLOWER (1937) Rev. Jeffery A. Largent; Deacon Gregory Gehred.
54191 Ironwood Rd., 46635. Tel: 574-272-7070; Fax: 574-243-3434. Email: littleflowerchurch@sbcglobal.net. Web: www.littleflowerchurch.org.
Catechesis / Religious Program—Tel: 574-243-3439. Students 110.

OUTSIDE THE CITIES OF FORT WAYNE AND SOUTH BEND

ALBION, NOBLE CO., BLESSED SACRAMENT (1875) [JC] Rev. Jan (John) Klimczyk.
Res.: 807 Rolling River Run, 46701. Tel: 260-239-4017; Fax: 260-236-2072.
Church: 2290 N. State Rd. 9 S., 46701-0102. Tel: 260-636-2072.
Catechesis / Religious Program—

ANGOLA, STEUBEN CO., ST. ANTHONY (1926) Revs. Fred Pasche, O.F.M.Conv.; Bernard Zajdel, O.F.M-.Conv.; Andrew Martinez, O.F.M.Conv., Hispanic Ministry. In Res., Rev. Philip Schneider, O.F.M.Conv.
Res.: 700 W. Maumee St., 46703. Tel: 260-665-2259; Fax: 260-665-2268.
Catechesis / Religious Program—Cathy Bryan, D.R.E.; Lisa Lysaght, Youth Min. Students 241.

ARCOLA, ALLEN CO., ST. PATRICK (1862) [CEM] Rev. Alexius Dodrai (India).
Res.: 12305 Arcola Rd., 46818. Tel: 260-625-4151; Fax: 260-625-3095. Email: stpatarcola@earthlink.net.
Catechesis / Religious Program—Tel: 260-625-4104. Students 148.

AUBURN, DE KALB CO., IMMACULATE CONCEPTION (1872) [CEM] Rev. Derrick Sneyd.
Mailing Address: 500 E. 7th St., 46706.
Res.: 204 N. McClellan St., 46706. Tel: 260-925-3930; Fax: 260-925-3186.
Catechesis / Religious Program—Tel: 260-925-1621, Ext. 5. Phyllis Gurtner, D.R.E.; Melody Rolston, D.R.E. Students 137.

AVILLA, NOBLE CO., ST. MARY OF THE ASSUMPTION (1853) [CEM] Rev. Edward Erpelding.
Res.: 228 N. Main St., Box 700, 46710-0700. Tel: 260-897-3261; Fax: 260-897-2284.
School—(Grades PreK-8), 232 N. Main St., 46710. Tel: 260-897-3481; Fax: 260-897-3706. Mr. Jeffrey Kieffer, Prin. Lay Teachers 10; Students 145.
Catechesis / Religious Program—Students 48.

BESANCON, ALLEN CO., ST. LOUIS (1846), (French), [CEM 2] Rev. Stephen E. Colchin.
Res.: 15535 Lincoln Hwy. E., New Haven, 46774. Tel: 260-749-4525.
School—(Grades K-8), 15529 Lincoln Hwy. E., New Haven, 46774. Tel: 260-749-5815; Fax: 260-748-2072. Mrs. Cheryl Klinker, Prin. Lay Teachers 5; Students 62.
Catechesis / Religious Program—Students 23.

BIG LONG LAKE, LAGRANGE CO., ST. MARY OF THE ANGELS (1937) Closed. Parish closed February 25, 2006. Sacramental records are located at St. Michael Catholic Church, 1098 County Rd. 39, Waterloo, IN. Tel: 260-837-7115.

BLUFFTON, WELLS CO., ST. JOSEPH (1875) Rev. Francis Chukwuma.
Res.: 1300 N. Main St., 46714-1127. Tel: 260-824-1380; Fax: 260-824-2792. Email: stjosephchurch@adamswell.com.
Catechesis / Religious Program—Students 125.

BREMEN, MARSHALL CO., ST. DOMINIC (1947) [JC] Rev. Bob J. Lengerich.
803 W. Bike St., 46506.
Church: 212 N. Maryland St., 46506. Tel: 574-546-3601; Fax: 574-546-3659.
Catechesis / Religious Program—803 W. Bike St., 46506. Students 295.

BRISTOL, ELKHART CO., ST. MARY OF THE ANNUNCIATION (1942) [JC] Rev. Robert Van Kempen.
Res.: 411 W. Vistula St., Box 245, 46507. Tel: 574-848-4305; Fax: 574-622-0159.
Rectory—Tel: 574-622-0039.
Catechesis / Religious Program—Students 332.

CHURUBUSCO, WHITLEY CO., ST. JOHN BOSCO (1971) Rev. Danny Pinto (Sri Lanka), Admin.
Res.: 216 N. Main St., 46723. Tel: 260-693-9578; Fax: 260-693-1608.
Catechesis / Religious Program—Tel: 260-693-3332. Students 76.

CLEAR LAKE, STEUBEN CO., ST. PAUL CHAPEL (1941) Rev. Philip Schneider, O.F.M.Conv., Admin.
Rectory—St. Anthony Rectory, 700 W. Maumee, Angola, 46703. Tel: 260-665-2259; Fax: 260-665-2268.
Church: 8780 E. 700 N., Fremont, 46737. Tel: 260-495-9913.
Catechesis / Religious Program—Tel: 260-238-2047. Margaret Carlson, D.R.E. Students 30.

COLUMBIA CITY, WHITLEY CO., ST. PAUL OF THE CROSS (1860) [CEM] [JC] Rev. Nicholas Nilema.
Mailing Address: 315 S. Line St., 46725. Email: saintpaulchurch@embargmail.com. Web: www.saintpaulofthecross.org.
Res.: 308 S. Chauncey St., 46725. Tel: 260-244-5723; Fax: 260-244-2833.
Catechesis / Religious Program—Tel: 260-244-2926. Students 181.

CULVER, MARSHALL CO., ST. MARY OF THE LAKE, [JC] Rev. Msgr. Thadeus Balinda (Uganda).
Office: 605 N. Plymouth St., 46511-1015. Email: stmarys@culcom.net. Web: www.culcom.net/~stmarys.
Res.: 124 College Ave., 46511. Tel: 574-842-2522; Fax: 574-842-5009.
Catechesis / Religious Program—Tel: 574-842-3667; Fax: 574-842-2549. Students 62.

DECATUR, ADAMS CO., ST. MARY OF THE ASSUMPTION (1840), (German), [CEM] Rev. David W. Voors; Jason Garrett, Pastoral Assoc.; Ron Gage, Music Dir.; Judith Converset, Business Mgr.; Deacon Jerry Kohrman.
Res.: 414 W. Madison St., 46733. Tel: 260-724-9159; Fax: 260-724-8948. Email: tdebolt@stmarysdecatur.org. Web: www.stmarysdecatur.org.
School—St. Joseph, (Grades PreK-8), 127 N. Fourth St., 46733. Tel: 260-724-2765; Fax: 260-724-4953. Web: www.stjosephdecatur.org. Karla Hormann, Prin.; Elizabeth Alberding, Librarian. Lay Teachers 21; Students 347.
Catechesis / Religious Program—Students 83.

EGE, NOBLE CO., IMMACULATE CONCEPTION (1876) [CEM] Rev. Danny Pinto (Sri Lanka), Admin.
216 N. Main St., Churubusco, 46723. Tel: 260-693-9578; Fax: 260-693-1608.
Catechesis / Religious Program—Students 73.

ELKHART, ELKHART CO.

1—ST. THOMAS THE APOSTLE (1949) [JC] Rev. William Sullivan.
Res.: 1405 N. Main St., 46514. Tel: 574-262-1505; Fax: 574-264-4186.
School—(Grades K-8), 1331 N. Main St., 46514. Tel: 574-264-4855; Fax: 574-262-8477. Lay Teachers 23; Students 375.
Catechesis / Religious Program—Tel: 574-264-0491. Students 118.

2—ST. VINCENT DE PAUL (1868) [CEM] Revs. Glenn Kohrman; Matthew M. Coonan, Parochial Vicar.
Res.: 1108 S. Main St., 46516. Tel: 574-293-8231; Fax: 574-293-1105.
School—(Grades PreK-6), 1114 S. Main St., 46516. Tel: 574-293-8451; Fax: 574-295-9702. Mr. Tom Gropp, Prin.; Debbie Chris, Librarian; Mrs. Vickie Bayer, Librarian. Lay Teachers 7; Students 163.
Catechesis / Religious Program—Tel: 574-293-8071. Patricia O'Connor, D.R.E. Students 571.

GARRETT, DE KALB CO., ST. JOSEPH (1876) [CEM] Rev. Andrew L. Nazareth (India).
Office: 300 W. Houston, 46738-1424. Tel: 260-357-3122; 260-357-3122.
Res.: 307 S. Ijams St., 46738. Tel: 260-357-0381.
School—(Grades PreK-7), 301 W. Houston, 46738. Tel: 260-357-5137; Fax: 260-357-5138. Kristine Call, Prin.; Julie Crager, Librarian. Lay Teachers 7; Students 109.
Catechesis / Religious Program—Students 65.

GENEVA, ADAMS CO., ST. MARY OF THE PRESENTATION (1883) [CEM] Rev. J. Bosco Perera (Sri Lanka).
Res.: 5790 E. 1100 S., 46740-9132. Tel: 260-997-6558.
Catechesis / Religious Program—Students 4.

GOSHEN, ELKHART CO., ST. JOHN THE EVANGELIST (1840) [CEM] Revs. Christopher L. Smith; Fernando Jimenez; Deacon David Elchert.
Res.: 109 W. Monroe St., 46526. Tel: 574-533-3385; Fax: 574-533-1814. Email: parishoffice@stjohncatholic.com. Web: stjohncatholic.com.
School—(Grades PreSchool-5), 117 W. Monroe, 46526. Tel: 574-533-9480. Amy Weidner, Prin.; Angela Hein, Librarian. Sisters 1; Lay Teachers 8; Students 151.
Catechesis / Religious Program—Darlene Leitz, D.R.E. Students 386.

GRANGER, ST. JOSEPH CO., ST. PIUS X (1955) Rev. Msgr. William C. Schooler.
Res.: 52553 Fir Rd., 46530. Tel: 574-272-8462; Fax: 574-272-8493. Web: www.stpius.net.
School—(Grades PreK-8) Tel: 574-272-4935; Fax: 574-533-1814. Elaine Holmes, Prin.; Chelle Erichsen, Librarian. Students 630.
Catechesis / Religious Program—Tel: 574-277-5760. Students 710.

HUNTINGTON, HUNTINGTON CO.

1—ST. MARY (1896) [JC] Rev. John F. Pfister.
Office & Res.: 903 N. Jefferson St., 46750. Tel: 260-356-4398; Fax: 260-356-3529. Email: stmary083@comcast.net.
School—Middle Building, (Grades PreK-8), 960 Warren St., 46750. Tel: 260-356-1926; Fax: 260-356-8419. Primary Building: 820 Cherry St., 46750. Tel: 260-356-2320. Jason Woolard, Prin. Faculty 16; Students 185.
Catechesis / Religious Program—Students 117.

2—SS. PETER AND PAUL (1843) [JC] Revs. Ronald Rieder, O.F.M.Cap.; Augustine Kochuparathanathu, V.C. (India).
Res.: 860 Cherry St., 46750. Tel: 260-356-4798; Fax: 260-356-7154.
See Huntington Catholic School, Huntington under St. Mary, Huntington for details.
Catechesis / Religious Program—Sr. Miriam Gill, S.S.N.D., D.R.E. Students 275.

KENDALLVILLE, NOBLE CO., IMMACULATE CONCEPTION (1867) [CEM] Rev. James Stoyle.
Res. & Mailing Address: 319 E. Diamond St., 46755. Tel: 260-347-2522 (Rectory).
Church: 301 E. Diamond St., 46755. Tel: 260-347-4045; Fax: 260-347-4045.
Catechesis / Religious Program—Students 66.

LAGRANGE, LAGRANGE CO., ST. JOSEPH (1930) [JC] Rev. Andrew Martinez, O.F.M.Conv.
Res.: 050 N. 100 E., 46761. Tel: 260-463-3472; Fax: 260-456-3472. Email: stjosephlagrange@embarq.com.
Catechesis / Religious Program—Students 220.

LAGRO, WABASH CO., ST. PATRICK (1838) Closed. Parish closed February 1, 1997. Sacramental records are located at St. Bernard Catholic Church, 207 North Cass St., Wabash, IN 46992-2441. Tel: 260-563-4750.

LIGONIER, NOBLE CO., ST. PATRICK (1860) [JC] Rev. Wilson O. Corzo (Colombia).
Res.: 300 Ravine Park Dr., 46767-1301. Tel: 260-894-4946; Fax: 260-894-4911.
Catechesis / Religious Program—Students 410.

MISHAWAKA, ST. JOSEPH CO.

1—ST. BAVO (1903) Rev. Barry C. England; Deacon Kevin M. Ranaghan.
Res.: 511 W. 7th St., 46544. Tel: 574-255-1437; Fax: 574-255-0404. Web: www.stbavochurch.com.
School—Mishawaka Catholic School, (Grades PreK-2), Consolidated with St. Joseph and St. Monica., 524 W. 8th St., 46544. Tel: 574-259-4214; Fax: 574-258-0403. Vikki Wojcik, Prin.
Catechesis / Religious Program—Students 125.

2—ST. JOSEPH (1848) [CEM] Rev. Terry Fisher; Deacon Robert Byrne.
Res.: 225 S. Mill St., 46544. Tel: 574-255-6134; Fax: 574-255-6387.
School—Mishawaka Catholic School, (Grades 3-5), Consolidated with St. Bavo and St. Monica., 230 S. Spring St., 46544. Tel: 574-255-5554; Fax: 574-255-6381. Vikki Wojcik, Prin.; Margaret Van der Heyden,

Librarian.
Catechesis/Religious Program—Consolidated with St. Bavo and St. Monica. Students 125.

3—ST. MONICA (1915) Rev. Msgr. Bruce Piechocki.
Res.: 222 W. Mishawaka Ave., 46545. Tel: 574-255-2247; Fax: 574-255-8375.
School—Mishawaka Catholic School, (Grades 6-8), Consolidated with St. Bavo and St. Joseph., 223 W. Grove St., 46545. Tel: 574-255-0709; Fax: 574-255-0311. Web: www.mishawakacatholic.org. Vikki Wojcik, Prin.; Victoria Zmirski, Librarian.
Catechesis/Religious Program—Consolidated with St. Bavo and St. Joseph. Students 125.

4—QUEEN OF PEACE (1957) Rev. Daniel D. Scheidt.
Res.: 4508 Vistula Rd., 46544. Tel: 574-255-9674; Fax: 574-255-9675. Web: www.queenofpeace.cc.
School—(Grades PreSchool-8) Tel: 574-255-0392; Fax: 574-255-1029. Email: schoolinfo@queenofpeace.cc. Web: www.queenofpeace.cc/school. Tina Dover, Prin.; Lynette Delahanty, Librarian. Lay Teachers 10; Students 219.
Catechesis/Religious Program—Carol Cone, D.R.E. Students 197.

MONROEVILLE, ALLEN CO., ST. ROSE OF LIMA (1868) [CEM] Rev. Lourdino Fernandes.
Res.: 206 Summit St., P.O. Box 406, 46773. Tel: 260-623-6437; Fax: 260-623-6437. Web: www.saintrosechurch.com.
School—St. Joseph, (Grades K-8), 209 Mulberry St., 46773. Tel: 260-623-3447; Fax: 260-623-3447. Mrs. Carolyn Kirkendall, Prin. Lay Teachers 5; Students 95.
Catechesis/Religious Program—

NAPANEE, ELKHART CO., ST. ISIDORE, Closed. Parish closed August 1, 1995. Sacramental records are located at St. Dominic, 803 W. Bike St., Bremen, IN. Tel: 574-546-3601.

NEW CARLISLE, ST. JOSEPH CO., ST. STANISLAUS KOSTKA (1884), (Polish), Rev. Paul McCarthy.
Res.: 55756 Tulip Rd., 46552. Tel: 574-654-3781; Fax: 574-654-3781.
Catechesis/Religious Program—Tel: 574-654-8132. Jacqueline Sheedy, D.R.E. Students 60.

NEW HAVEN, ALLEN CO., ST. JOHN THE BAPTIST (1859) [CEM] Rev. James F. Seculoff.
Res.: 943 Powers St., 46774. Tel: 260-493-4553; Fax: 260-749-6164.
School—(Grades PreK-8), 204 Rufus St., 46774. Tel: 260-749-9903; Fax: 260-749-6047. Janice Comito, Prin. Lay Teachers 16; Students 335.
Catechesis/Religious Program—Students 126.

NIX SETTLEMENT, WHITLEY CO., ST. CATHARINE (1850) [CEM] Rev. Kenneth J. Sarrazine.
Rectory—St. Joseph, 641 N. Main St., P.O. Box 250, Roanoke, 46783-0250. Tel: 260-672-2838; Fax: 260-672-3069.
Church: Ind. Hwy. 9 & Whitley Co. Rd., 1,000 S., Columbia City, 46725.
Catechesis/Religious Program—Dr. Kathleen Schneider, D.R.E. Students 30.

NORTH MANCHESTER, WABASH CO., ST. ROBERT BELLARMINE (1963) [JC] Rev. Thomas Kodakassery, O.S.B. (India).
Res.: 1203 State Rd., 114 E., 46962. Tel: 260-982-4404; Fax: 260-982-6979.
Catechesis/Religious Program—Students 21.

NOTRE DAME, ST. JOSEPH CO., SACRED HEART (1842) [CEM] [JC] Revs. Thomas J. Jones, C.S.C.; Timothy O'Connor, C.S.C.
Res.: 104 The Presbytery, 46556-5658. Tel: 574-631-7511; Fax: 574-631-8080.
Catechesis/Religious Program—Tel: 574-631-9436; Fax: 574-631-9687. Students 21.

PIERCETON, KOSCIUSKO CO., ST. FRANCIS XAVIER (1841) [CEM] Rev. Dale A. Bauman.
Mailing Address: P.O. Box 376, 46562.
Church: 408 W. Catholic St., 46562. Tel: 574-594-5750; Fax: 574-594-2347.
Catechesis/Religious Program—Tel: 574-594-5750, Ext. 12. Students 25.

PLYMOUTH, MARSHALL CO., ST. MICHAEL (1862) [CEM] Revs. William Kummer; Eloy Jimenez (Mexico).
Res., Office & Mailing Address: 612 N. Walnut St., 46563. Tel: 574-936-4935; Fax: 574-936-9293. Web: www.stmichaelchurchplymouth.com.
School—(Grades K-8), 612 N. Center St., 46563. Tel: 574-936-4329; Fax: 574-936-1151. Web: www-.saintmichaelschool.org. Miss Gertrude Nawara, Prin.; Mrs. Jennifer Matchett, Librarian. Lay Teachers 11; Students 156.
Catechesis/Religious Program—Gregory Lenburg, D.R.E. Students 180.

ROANOKE, HUNTINGTON CO., ST. JOSEPH (1867) [CEM] Rev. Kenneth J. Sarrazine.
Res.: 641 N. Main St., P.O. Box 250, 46783-0250. Tel: 260-672-2838; Fax: 260-672-3069.
Catechesis/Religious Program—Dr. Kathleen Schneider, D.R.E. Students 46.

ROME CITY, NOBLE CO., ST. GASPAR DEL BUFALO (1957) [CEM] Rev. Bernard Ramenaden, O.S.B. (Sri Lanka).
Res.: 10871 N. State Rd. 9, 46784. Tel: 260-854-3100; Fax: 260-854-4083. Email: stgasparchurch@embarqmail.com.
Catechesis/Religious Program—Students 28.

SYRACUSE, KOSCIUSKO CO., ST. MARTIN DE PORRES (1966) Rev. Richard Hire.
Res.: 6941 E. Waco Dr., 46567-9496. Tel: 574-457-8176; Fax: 574-457-3542.
Catechesis/Religious Program—Students 59.

WABASH, WABASH CO., ST. BERNARD (1864) Rev. Sextus Don (Sri Lanka).
Res.: 207 N. Cass St., 46992. Tel: 260-563-4750; Fax: 260-563-0313.
School—(Grades PreK-6), 191 N. Cass St., 46992. Tel: 260-563-5746; Fax: 260-563-4898. Theresa Carroll, Prin. Lay Teachers 6; Students 85.
Catechesis/Religious Program—Students 63.

WALKERTON, ST. JOSEPH CO., ST. PATRICK (1856) Rev. Pius N. Ilechukwu (Nigeria); Mrs. Anna Chaffee, Music Min.
Office: 807 Tyler St., 46574. Fax: 574-586-7152.
Res.: 801 Tyler St., 46574. Tel: 574-586-7404.
Letko Hall—811 Tyler St., 46574.
Catechesis/Religious Program—Barbara Blad, D.R.E. Students 75.

WARSAW, KOSCIUSKO CO.

1—OUR LADY OF GUADALUPE (1972), (Hispanic), [CEM] Rev. Constantino Rocha.
Mailing Address: P.O. Box 1136, 46581-1136.
Church: 225 Gilliam Dr., 46581. Tel: 574-267-5324.
Catechesis/Religious Program—Students 192.

2—SACRED HEART (1852) [JC] Rev. Philip DeVolder.
Res.: 125 N. Harrison St., 46580. Tel: 574-267-5842; Fax: 574-268-1030.
School—(Grades K-6), 135 N. Harrison, 46590. Tel: 574-267-5874; Fax: 574-267-5136. Mr. James L. Faroh Sr., Prin. Lay Teachers 13; Students 210.
Catechesis/Religious Program—Students 175.

WATERLOO, DEKALB CO., ST. MICHAEL THE ARCHANGEL (1880) [CEM] Rev. David Carkenord.
Res.: 1098 County Rd. 39, 46793-9779. Tel: 260-837-7115; Fax: 260-837-7727.
Catechesis/Religious Program—Students 131.
Oratory—St. Mary of the Angels 5725 S. 1025 E., Hudson, Steuben Co. 46747-9605. Tel: 260-837-5401.

YODER, ALLEN CO., ST. ALOYSIUS (1859) [CEM] Rev. Msgr. Bernard J. Galic.
Res.: 14623 Bluffton Rd., 46798-9741. Tel: 260-622-4491. Email: parish@stalyoder.org. Web: www.stalyoder.org.
School—(Grades PreK-8), 14607 Bluffton Rd., 46798-9741. Tel: 260-622-7151; Fax: 260-622-7961. Tina Voors, Prin. Lay Teachers 8; Students 85.
Catechesis/Religious Program—Students 37.

Chaplains of Public Institutions

FORT WAYNE. *St. Joseph Hospital*, 700 Broadway, 46802-1402. Tel: 260-425-3000. Rev. Daniel Chukwuleta, Chap.
Lutheran Hospital, Tel: 260-435-7001. Roseann Bloomfield. Tel: 260-435-7722.
Parkview Memorial Hospital, Tel: 260-484-6636, Ext. 26311. Rev. Robert D'Souza, Chap.
Veterans Administration Hospital. Rev. Daniel R. Leeuw, Chap. (Retired).

On Special Assignment:
Rev.—
Gurtner, Mark A., J.C.L., Officialis of Diocese, Chancery

Retired:
Revs.—
Balzer, Raymond, c/o Rev. Msgr. Robert Schulle, P.O. Box 390, 46801.
Bly, Walter J., 903 Cashew Cir., Barefoot Bay, FL 32976.
Doriot, Thomas E., 2724 Elvyra Way, Apt. 2, Sacramento, CA 95821. Tel: 916-484-6145
Gall, Jacob M., 51958 Fawn Meadow Dr., Elkhart, 46514. Tel: 574-264-1119
Leeuw, Daniel R., 1608 Tyler Ave., 46808. Tel: 260-424-0645
McNulty, Patrick J., 2888 Dafoe Rd., RR 2, Combermere ON KOJILO Canada.
Miller, Paul D., St. Anne Home, 1900 Randallia Dr., 46805. Tel: 260-748-4042
Peil, William, St. Anne Home, 1900 Randallia Dr., #1023, 46805. Tel: 260-339-3066
Rose, James, 536 Fallen Oaks Dr., Coldwater, MI 49036. Tel: 517-238-5522
Ruetz, Edward J., 621 Portage, 46616. Tel: 574-234-5652
Schmitt, Adam, St. Anne Home, 1900 Randallia Dr., #1022, 46805.
Sienkiewicz, Matthew, 19080 Three Oaks Rd., Three Oaks, MI 49128. Tel: 269-756-6316
Tippmann, Laurence, 1608 Reckeweg Rd., 46804. Tel: 260-432-3197
Tirabassi, Camillo, Holy Family Church, 56405 Mayflower Rd., 46619.
Traub, Robert, Saint Anne Home, 1900 Randallia Dr. #1020, 46805. Tel: 260-399-3305

Permanent Deacons:
Baumgartner, Paul E., (Retired), 417 Howard St., 46617.
Byrne, Robert, 1819 Colony Dr., 46635.
Dits, Paul, (Retired), 17433 Battles Rd., 46614.
Elchert, David, 813 Braxton Ct., Goshen, 46526.
Fitzpatrick, James, 202 Osprey Ct., Huntertown, 46748.
Fuchs, James, 54686 Sagewood Dr., Mishawaka, 46545.
Gallagher, William, 552 East Angela, 46617.
Gehred, Greg, M.D., 2613 Corby Blvd., 46615.
Gizzi, Emilio, 1136 E. Fairview Ave., 46614.
Hilger, John, 12903 Washington Center Rd., 46845.
Kitchens, James, 9404 Fireside Ct., 46804.
Kohrman, Jerry, 809 Perry Lake Rd., 46835.
Kuspa, Ervin, 434 S. Liberty, 46619.
LeMieux, Stanley, 67426 Kensington Dr., Goshen, 46526-7349.
Miller, Brian L., 2120 E. Jefferson, 46617.
Ranaghan, Kevin, 1003 St. Vincent, 46617.
Tardy, Melvin, 1732 Fawn Ct., 46628.
Tighe, James, 2120 Springfield Ave., 46850.
Tugman, John, 15932 Preswick Ln., Granger, 46530.
Walsh, James M., (Retired), 2212 Broadmoor Dr., Elkhart, 46514.

INSTITUTIONS LOCATED IN THE DIOCESE

[A] SEMINARIES, RELIGIOUS, OR SCHOLASTICATES

NOTRE DAME. *Moreau Seminary*, P.O. Box 668, 46556. Tel: 574-631-7735; Fax: 574-631-9233. This is a college level and Theological Seminary run by the Indiana Province of the Congregation of Holy Cross for Religious Priesthood and Brotherhood candidates. Priests 16; Brothers 2; Seminarians 38; Total Staff 8.
Formation Staff: Revs. Peter A. Jarret, C.S.C., Rector & Supr.; Francis T. Cafarelli, C.S.C.; Peter D. Rocca, C.S.C.; Stephen A. Lacroix, C.S.C., Dir. Undergraduate Prog.; Charles W. Kohlerman, C.S.C.; Stephen Kempinger, C.S.C., Asst. Supr. & Dir. Candidate Prog.; Bradley J. Metz, C.S.C.; Andrew Gawrych, C.S.C.; Bro. Edward C. Luther, C.S.C In Res. Revs. Francis T. Cafarelli, C.S.C.; Andrew Gawrych, C.S.C.; Stephen Kempinger, C.S.C.; Peter A. Jarret, C.S.C.; Charles W. Kohlerman, C.S.C.; Wilson D. Miscamble, C.S.C.; Bradley J. Metz, C.S.C.; Peter D. Rocca, C.S.C.; Douglas Smith, C.S.C.; John H. Pearson, C.S.C.; David Eliaona, C.S.C.; Thomas C. Bertone, C.S.C.; Robert H. Moss, C.S.C.; Bros. J. Rodney Struble, C.S.C.; John Platte, C.S.C.; Rev. Patrick Lynch, C.S.C.
Vocations Office: Revs. Peter M. McCormick, C.S.C.; James T. Gallagher, C.S.C.; Andrew Gawrych, C.S.C.; Tom Cashore, Librarian.

Old College, Box 638, 46556-0638. Tel: 574-631-0778; Fax: 574-631-0111. Email: slacroix@nd.edu. Web: oldcollege.nd.edu. Rev. Stephen A. Lacroix, C.S.C., Dir.; Bro. Edward C. Luther, C.S.C. College candidates study here for up to three years before entering Moreau Seminary. Priests 1; Brothers 1; Candidates for the Priesthood in the First Three Years of Undergraduate Formation 16; Total Staff 2.

[B] COLLEGES AND UNIVERSITIES

FORT WAYNE. *University of Saint Francis* (1890) 2701 Spring St., 46808-3994. Tel: 260-399-7700. Email: ekriss@sf.edu. Web: www.sf.edu. Sr. M. Elise Kriss, O.S.F., B.Ed., M.S., Ph.D., Pres.; Ms. Karla Alexander, Librarian. Conducted by Sisters of St. Francis of Perpetual Adoration. Priests 1; Sisters 9; Students 2,366; Lay Teachers 153; Total Staff 241.

DONALDSON. *Ancilla Domini College*, P.O. Box 1, 46513. Tel: 574-936-8898; Fax: 574-935-1773. Email: admissions@ancilla.edu. Web: www.ancilla.edu. Ronald L. May, Pres.; Sr. Carleen Wrasman, P.H.J.C., Coord. Pastoral Min. & Mission Integration Coord.; Michael Brown, Exec. Dir. Finance & Admin.; Joanna Blount, Dean, Academic & Student Svcs.; Todd Zeltwanger, Exec. Dir. Inst. Advancement; Cassaundra Bash, Head Librarian. Poor

Handmaids of Jesus Christ (Ancilla Domini Sisters). Sisters 1; Lay Teachers 42; Students 518.

NOTRE DAME. *Holy Cross College, Holy Cross College, Inc.* (1966) 54515 State Rd., 933 N., 46556-0308. Tel: 574-239-8400; Fax: 574-239-8323. Email: jpaige@hcc-nd.edu. Web: www.hcc-nd.edu. Bro. John R. Paige, Pres.; Robert Benjamin, Dir. Fin. Aid; Mark P. Mullaney, B.B.A., CFO; Mary Ellen Hegedus, Librarian; Richard J. Sullivan, B.B.A., M.B.A., Registrar; Marie E. Bensman, Dean Admissions & Enrollment Mgmt.; Robert Kloska, M.A., Vice Pres. Mission Advancement; Tina Holland, Ph.D., Sr. Vice Pres.; Daniel M. Haverty, B.B.A., M.B.A., Vice Pres. Opers., CBO. Tel: 574-239-8350; Daniel Cochran, B.S., M.S., Dean Students; Andrew Polaniecki, Dir. Campus Ministry; Bro. Chris Dreyer, C.S.C., B.A., M.S., B.S.W., Dir. Student Counseling Svcs.

Holy Cross College, Inc. Priests 1; Brothers 9; Lay Teachers 42; Students 451; Total Staff 52.

Saint Mary's College (1844) 46556. Tel: 574-284-4556; Fax: 574-284-4707. Email: jhersche@saintmarys.edu. Web: www.saintmarys.edu. Carol A. Mooney, J.D., Pres.; Janet Fore, Librarian. Sisters of the Holy Cross., An institution of higher education for women. Lay Professors 132; Total Enrollment 1,510.

**University of Notre Dame Du Lac* (1842) Provost Office, 300 Main Bldg., 46556. Tel: 574-631-5000; 574-631-6631 (Provost); Fax: 574-631-6897. Email: cleichty@nd.edu. Web: www.nd.edu. The Graduate School (25 departments). The Law School. The Undergraduate School (four colleges, 45 departments), 14 University Institutes, 6 College Institutes, and 20 College Centers. Priests 60; Sisters 6; Total Faculty 1,527; Staff 1,087; Total Enrollment 11,992.

President's Leadership Council Rev. John I. Jenkins, C.S.C., Pres.; Thomas G. Burish, Ph.D., Provost; John Affleck-Graves, Ph.D., Exec. Vice Pres.; Christine Maziar, Ph.D., Vice Pres. & Senior Assoc. Provost; Don Pope-Davis, Ph.D., Vice Pres. & Assoc. Provost; Daniel J. Myers, Ph.D., Vice Pres. & Assoc. Provost; Revs. James E. McDonald, C.S.C., Assoc. Vice Pres. & Counselor to the Pres.; Thomas P. Doyle, C.S.C., Vice Pres. Student Affairs; James B. King, C.S.C., Holy Cross Supr.; Frances Shavers, Ph.D., Chief of Staff & Asst. to Pres.; Robert Bernhard, Ph.D., Vice Pres. Research; Marianne Corr, J.D., Vice Pres. & General Counsel; Gregory E. Sterling, Ph.D., Dean, Graduate School; Scott C. Malpass, M.B.A., Vice Pres. & Chief Investment Officer; Louis M. Nanni, Vice Pres. Univ. Rels.; John A. Sejdinaj, Vice Pres. for Finance; J. Nicholas Entrikin, Vice Pres. & Assoc. for Internationalization; Erin Hoffmann Harding, Assoc. Vice Pres. Strategic Planning; Robert K. McQuade, Vice Pres. for Human Resources; Jack Swarbrick, Vice Pres. & Dir. Athletics; Ronald D. Kraemer, M.A., Vice Pres. & Chief Information Officer.

Administrative Group: Sr. Susan Dunn, O.P., Ph.D., Asst. Vice Pres. Student Affairs; Ann Firth, Assoc. Vice Pres. Student Affairs; Jannifer Crittendon, Dir. of Inst. Equity; Gilberto Cardenas, Dir. Institute for Latino Studies; Roger P. Mahoney, Chief Audit Exec.; Jennifer Monahan, Exec. Asst. to the Vice Pres. Student Affairs; David Moss, Asst. Vice Pres. Student Affairs; Iris Outlaw, Dir. Multicultural Student Programs & Svcs.; Donald Bishop, Assoc. Vice Pres. Undergraduate Enrollment.

Assistant Vice Presidents & Counsels: Lisa Anderson, Assoc. Dir., Career Svcs., Graduate School Career Prog.; Dolly Duffy, Exec. Dir. Alumni Assoc.; Drew Buscareno, Asst. Vice Pres. Univ. Rels.; Maureen Collins, Mgr. Data & Report, Graduate School; Micki Kidder, Asst. Vice Pres. Devel.; Susan Vissage, Business Mgr., Graduate School; Timothy J. Flanagan, Assoc. Vice Pres. & Counsel; David Harr, Assoc. Vice Pres. Auxiliary Svcs.; Lois C. Jackson, Asst. Vice Pres. & Counsel; Jean Gorman, Asst. Vice Pres. for Devel.; David Morrissey, Asst. Vice Pres. Univ. Rels.; Charles Hurley, Interim Registrar; Andrew M. Paluf, Asst. Vice Pres. Finance & Controller; Warren von Eschenbach, Senior Advisor to the Provost; Daniel G. Reagan, Assoc. Vice Pres. for Univ. Rels.; Joseph A. Russo, Dir. Student Finance Strategies, Fin. Aid; Dennis Brown, Asst. Vice Pres. Public Information & Communications.

C.S.C. Faculty & Personnel: Revs. Robert J. Austgen, C.S.C., Emeritus Faculty; Nicholas Ayo, C.S.C.; Leonard N. Banas, C.S.C.; Ernest J. Bartell, C.S.C.; Thomas E. Blantz, C.S.C.; James Bracke, C.S.C.; Richard S. Bullene, C.S.C.; Joseph H. Carey, C.S.C., Campus Min.; Austin I. Collins, C.S.C.; John E. Conley, C.S.C.; Michael Connors, C.S.C.; Joseph Corpora, C.S.C.; William R. Dailey, C.S.C.; Louis A. Delfra, C.S.C.; Robert A. Dowd, C.S.C.; Paul F. Doyle, C.S.C.; Thomas P. Doyle, C.S.C.; John S. Dunne, C.S.C.; Carl F. Ebey, C.S.C.; James F. Flanigan, C.S.C.; James K. Foster, C.S.C.; Patrick D. Gaffney, C.S.C.; James T. Gallagher, C.S.C.; Thomas E. Gaughan, C.S.C.; Eugene F. Gorski, C.S.C.; Gregory A. Green, C.S.C.; Daniel G. Groody, C.S.C.; Ralph L. Haag, C.S.C.; John I. Jenkins, C.S.C., Pres.; Thomas J. Jones, C.S.C.; James King, C.S.C., Holy Cross Supr.; Jerome E. Knoll, C.S.C.; Paul V. Kollman, C.S.C.; Stephen A. Lacroix, C.S.C.; Andre E. Leveille, C.S.C.; William M. Lies, C.S.C.; Robert L. Loughery, C.S.C.; Edward A. Malloy, C.S.C., Prof. Theology; Patrick H. Maloney, C.S.C.; Peter M. McCormick, C.S.C.; James E. McDonald, C.S.C., Senior Exec. Asst. & Counselor to the Pres.; Sean D. McGraw, C.S.C.; Donald McNeill, C.S.C.; Leon J. Mertensotto, C.S.C.; Bradley J. Metz, C.S.C.; Wilson D. Miscamble, C.S.C.; Martin Lam Nguyen, C.S.C.; Edwin H. Obermiller, C.S.C.; Edward D. O'Connor, C.S.C.; Leonard Olobo, C.S.C.; Robert S. Pelton, C.S.C.; Peter D. Rocca, C.S.C.; George A. Rozum, C.S.C.; Timothy R. Scully, C.S.C.; S. Douglas Smith, C.S.C.; Thomas G. Streit, C.S.C.; Michael B. Sullivan, C.S.C. (Eastern Prov.); Mark B. Thesing, C.S.C.; Joseph L. Walter, C.S.C.; Oliver F. Williams, C.S.C.; Bros. Louis Hurcik, C.S.C.; Edward C. Luther, C.S.C.; Jerome Meyer, C.S.C. (Midwestern Prov.); Thomas Tucker, C.S.C.

Non-C.S.C. Religious Faculty: Revs. Joseph P. Amar (SAM); Paul F. Bradshaw; William Buggert; Richard Clifford; John J. Coughlin, O.F.M.; Brian Daley, S.J.; Michael Driscoll, Ph.D.; Virgilio P. Elizondo; Michael Findikyan; Thomas Florek; Rev. Msgr. Michael W. Heintz, Ph.D.; Revs. Maxwell E. Johnson; J. Michael Joncas; James B. Lewis; Richard P. McBrien; Thomas McDade; Revs. John P. Meier; James Murphy-O'Connor; Ronald J. Nuzzi; Paulinus I. Odozor, C.S.Sp.; Abdul Omar; Revs. Hugh R. Page; Frederick W. Pfotenhauer; Robert E. Sullivan; Sisters Kathleen Cannon, O.P.; Mary Jane Herb, I.H.M.; Mary Catherine Hilkert, O.P.; Irene Martineau; Gail Mayotte; J. Keith Rigby; Sr. Mary Shaughnessy, S.C.N.; Gregory E. Sterling, Ph.D.

[C] HIGH SCHOOLS, DIOCESAN

FORT WAYNE. *Bishop Dwenger High School* (1963) 1300 E. Washington Center Rd., 46825. Tel: 260-496-4700; Fax: 260-496-4702. Email: bdhs@bishopdwenger.com. Web: www.bishopdwenger.com. Mr. Jason Schiffli, Prin.; Mr. Chris Svarczkopf, Asst. Prin.; Amy Johns, Asst. Prin.; Katie Burns, Devel. Dir.; Diane Stein, Librarian; Revs. Jason Freidburger; Anthony Steinacker. Priests 2; Lay Teachers 59; Students 1,023; Total Staff 94.

Bishop Luers High School (1959) 333 E. Paulding Rd., 46816. Tel: 260-456-1261; Fax: 260-456-1262. Email: mkeefer@bishopluers.org. Web: www.bishopluers.org. Mary Keefer, Prin.; Tiffany Albertson, Asst. Prin.; Jane Anderson, Librarian. Priests 3; Lay Teachers 34; Students 568.

SOUTH BEND. *Saint Joseph's High School* (1953) 1441 N. Michigan St., 46617. Tel: 574-233-6137; Fax: 574-232-3482. Email: sbdstjoehs@saintjoehigh.com. Web: www.saintjoehigh.com. Mrs. Susan Richter, Prin.; Mr. Marty Harshman, Asst. Prin.; Mrs. Marilyn Gibbs, Asst. Prin.; Revs. Walter J. Bly, Chap. (Retired); Camillo Tirabassi, Chap. (Retired); Terrence Coonan Jr., Chap.; Jane Goldsberry, Librarian. Priests 3; Sisters of the Holy Cross 1; Lay Teachers 64; Students 821.

MISHAWAKA. *Marian High School* (1964) 1311 S. Logan St., 46544. Tel: 574-259-5257; Fax: 574-258-7668. Email: secretary@marianhs.org. Web: www.marianhs.org. Mr. Carl Loesch, B.A., M.A., Prin.; Carol Miller, Pastoral Min.; Debbie Davisson, Librarian. Priests 1; Sisters 1; Lay Teachers 46; Students 720.

[D] GENERAL HOSPITALS

MISHAWAKA. *Saint Joseph Regional Medical Center*, 5215 Holy Cross Pkwy., 46545. Tel: 574-335-5000; Fax: 574-335-1002. Email: paintelm@sjrmc.com. Web: www.sjmed.com. Albert L. Gutierrez, CEO; Sr. Laureen M. Painter, O.S.F., Vice Pres., Mission Integration. Bed Capacity 254; Patients Assisted Annually 171,767; Total Staff 1,723.

PLYMOUTH. *Saint Joseph Regional Medical Center - Plymouth*, 1915 Lake Ave., P.O. Box 670, 46563. Tel: 574-936-3181; Fax: 574-935-2235. Email: pricel@sjrmc.com. Web: www.sjmed.com. Albert L. Gutierrez, CEO; Lori Price, Pres.; Sr. Laureen M. Painter, O.S.F., Vice Pres. Mission Integration. Total Staff 330; Bed Capacity 58; Patients Assisted Annually 82,582.

[E] SPECIAL HOSPITALS

NOTRE DAME. *University Health Services* 46556. Tel: 574-239-8013; Fax: 574-631-6047. Email: Ann.E.Kleva.4@nd.edu. Web: www.nd.edu/~uhs. Rev. Robert J. Austgen, C.S.C., Health Center Chap. Bed Capacity 8; Total Staff 36; Patients Assisted Annually 18,000.

[F] HOMES FOR THE AGED

FORT WAYNE. *Saint Anne Home & Retirement Community*, 1900 Randallia Dr., 46805. Tel: 260-484-5555; Fax: 260-482-8929. Email: skendrick@sah1900.com. Web: www.saintannehome.com. Rev. John Overmyer, Chap.; Mary E. Haverstick, Admin. A Service of the Fort Wayne-South Bend Diocese, Inc. Residents 256; Bed Capacity 334; Total Apartments 168; Total Assisted Annually 511; Total Staff 308. In Res. Rev. Robert Traub (Retired).

AVILLA. *Provena LaVerna Terrace*, 517 N. Main St., 46710. Tel: 260-897-2093; Fax: 260-897-2086. Email: laverna@drinc.com. Thomas F. Nehring, Vice Pres. & Mission Leadership Devel.; Rev. Daniel R. Leeuw (Retired); Polly Workman, Property Mgr.

LaVerna Terrace Housing Corp., Conducted by Franciscan Sisters Health Care Corp. whose sole member is Provena Health. Total Staff 2; Apartments 51.

Provena Sacred Heart Home, 515 N. Main St., 46710-9602. Tel: 260-897-2841; Fax: 260-897-3724. Email: craig.prokupek@provena.org. Web: www.provena.org/sacredheart. Craig Prokupek, Admin.; Sr. Theresa Renninger, O.S.F., Religious Leader; Tom Novy, Dir. Pastoral Care.

Provena Sacred Heart Home Bed Capacity 175; Residents 162; Total Assisted Annually 250; Total Staff 204.

[G] PERSONAL PRELATURES

SOUTH BEND. *Prelature of the Holy Cross and Opus Dei*, Windmoor Center, 1121 N. Notre Dame Ave., 46617. Tel: 574-232-0550; Fax: 574-287-4798. Web: www.opusdei.org. Rev. Charles Trullols. Total Staff 4; Total in Residence 14.

[H] MONASTERIES AND RESIDENCES OF PRIESTS AND BROTHERS

MISHAWAKA. *St. Francis of Assisi Novitiate*, 1316 W. Dragoon Tr., 46544. Tel: 574-259-7843; Fax: 574-259-7845. Rev. Giles Zakowicz, O.F.M.Conv., Novice Dir. Priests 2; Brothers 1; Novices 7. In Res. Rev. Camillus Gott, O.F.M.Conv.; Bro. Paschal Kolodziej, O.F.M.Conv.

NOTRE DAME. *Congregation of Holy Cross, Midwest Province, Provincial Admin.*, 54515 State Rd. 933 N., P.O. Box 460, 46556-0460. Tel: 574-631-4000; Fax: 574-631-2999. Email: cfreel@brothersofholycross.com. Web: www.brothersofholycross.com. Bros. Chester Freel, C.S.C., Prov. Supr.; Raymond Papenfuss, C.S.C., Asst. Prov. & Vicar; Kenneth Haders, C.S.C., Prov. Steward; Richard Gilman, C.S.C., Prov. Councilor; Thomas Minta, C.S.C., Prov. Sec.; Robert Lavelle, C.S.C., Prov. Councilor; Lewis Brazil, C.S.C., Prov. Councilor.

Brothers of Holy Cross, Inc. Holy Cross Village, P.O. Box 839, 46556. Tel: 574-251-2214; Fax: 574-631-2999. Rev. Kenneth E. Grabner, C.S.C., Chap.; Bro. Joseph Fox, C.S.C., Dir. of Religious. Religious 20; Laity 180. *Dujarie House, Infirmary*, P.O. Box 706, 46556-0706. Tel: 574-287-1838; Fax: 574-289-7277. Jack Mueller, Admin. Total in Residence 36; Laity 24. *Helen D. Schubert Villa, Assisted Living*, P.O. Box 706, 46556-1020. Tel: 574-287-1986; Fax: 574-289-7277. Jack Mueller, Admin. Total in Residence 36.

Columba Hall, P.O. Box 776, 46556. Tel: 574-631-6284; Fax: 574-631-9882. Bro. Walter Gluhm, C.S.C., Supr.; Rev. William G. Blum, C.S.C., Chap. Total in Residence 42.

Congregation of Holy Cross, United States Province of Priests & Brothers (1841) *Provincial Administration Center*, 54515 State Rd. 933 N., P.O. Box 1064, 46556-1064. Tel: 574-631-6196; Fax: 574-631-5655. Email: david.t.tyson.4@nd.edu. Revs. David T. Tyson, C.S.C., Prov. Supr.; Kenneth M. Molinaro, C.S.C., First Asst. Prov. & Vicar; Anthony V. Szakaly, C.S.C., Second Asst. Prov.; Edwin H. Obermiller, C.S.C., Third Asst. Prov.; Thomas Cooney, C.S.C., Fourth Asst. Prov.; E. William Beauchamp, C.S.C., Councilor; Thomas E. Blantz, C.S.C., Councilor; Charles W. Kohlerman, C.S.C., Councilor; William M. Lies, C.S.C., Councilor; Peter A. Jarret, C.S.C., Councilor; Francis J. Murphy, C.S.C., Councilor; Neil F. Wack, C.S.C., Councilor; Michael C. Mathews, C.S.C., Councilor; James E. McDonald, C.S.C., Councilor; Thomas C. Bertone, C.S.C., Councilor; James Lacfenmier, C.S.C., Councilor; John J. Ryan, C.S.C., Councilor.

Congregation of the Holy Cross, United States Province, Inc.

Holy Cross Priests Serving in Foreign Countries: Chile: Revs. Jose E. Ahumanda, C.S.C., Casa

Maoreau, St. George, Congregacion de Santa Cruz, Casilla 1271, Santiago 1, Chile. Tel: 56-2-673-3278; Fax: 56-2-206-9339; Gerald R. Barmasse, C.S.C., Congregacion de Santa Cruz, Casilla 1271, Santiago 1, Chile. Tel: 56-2-673-3278; Fax: 56-2-206-9339 Casa Santa Cruz, Santingo, Chile; Deacon Patricio Becerra; Revs. Jorge A. Canepa, C.S.C., Congregacion de Santa Cruz, Casilla 1271, Santiago 1, Chile. Tel: 56-2-673-3278; Fax: 56-2-206-9339 St. George's College, Chile; Christopher Cox, C.S.C.; Charles A. Delaney, C.S.C., Congregacion de Santa Cruz, Casilla 1271, Santiago 1, Chile. Tel: 56-2-673-3278; Fax: 56-2-206-9339 St. George College; Michael DeLaney, C.S.C.; Fermin J. Donoso, C.S.C., Parroquia Nuestra Senora de Andacollo, Congregacion de Santa Cruz, Casilla 1271, Santiago 1, Chile. Tel: 56-2-673-3278; Fax: 56-2-206-9339; Joseph A. Dorsey, C.S.C., Congregacion de Santa Cruz, Casilla 1271, Santiago 1, Chile. Tel: 56-2-673-3278; Fax: 56-2-206-9339 St. George's College, Chile; Erwin A. Fonseca, C.S.C., Exclausation, Congregacion de Santa Cruz, Casilla 1271, Santiago 1, Chile. Tel: 56-2-673-3278; Fax: 56-2-206-9339; Roberto M. Gilbo, C.S.C., Parroquia Nuestra Senora de la Merced, Congregacion de Santa Cruz, Casilla 1271, Santiago 1, Chile. Tel: 56-2-673-3278; Fax: 56-2-206-9339; Diego Irarrazaval, C.S.C.; Daniel Panchot, C.S.C.; Gerald T. Papen, C.S.C., Parroquia Nuestra Senora de Andacollo, Casilla 1271, Santiago 21, Chile. Tel: 56-2-673-3278; Fax: 56-2-206-9339; Pedro Parra, C.S.C., Congregacion de Santa Cruz, Casilla 1271, Santiago 1, Chile. Tel: 56-2-673-3278; Fax: 56-2-206-9339 Casa Andes, Chile; Bro. Joaquin R. Parada, C.S.C., Congregacion de Santa Cruz, Casilla 1271, Santiago 1, Chile. Tel: 56-2-673-3278; Fax: 56-2-206-9339 Parroquia Nuestra Senora De La Merced; Revs. Robert G. Simon, C.S.C., Congregacion de Santa Cruz, Casilla 1271, Santiago 1, Chile. Tel: 56-2-673-3278; Fax: 56-2-206-9339 Colegio Nuestra Senora de Andacollo; Joseph Tomei, C.S.C.; Deacon Rodrigo Valenzuela; Rev. Romulo E. Vera, C.S.C., St. George College, Congregacion de Santa Cruz, Casilla 1271, Santiago 1, Chile. Tel: 56-2-673-3278; Fax: 56-2-206-9339.

Lima Revs. Robert R. Baker, C.S.C.; Arthur J. Colgan, C.S.C.; Jose Tineo Coral, C.S.C.; David E. Farrell, C.S.C.; Jorge R. Izaguirre, C.S.C.; George J. Lucas, C.S.C.; Jorge M. Mallea, C.S.C.; Anibal Loarte Nino, C.S.C.

Peru: *Instituto de Estudios Aymaras*, Apartado 295, Puno, Peru. Fax: 011-51-54-351574. Rev. Philip T. Devlin, C.S.C., Apartado 313, Lima, Peru. Canto del Sol.

District of East Africa (Uganda): Revs. David Kashangaki, C.S.C., Our Lady of Fatima House, P.O. Box 929, 46556. Fort Portal, Uganda; Dandora Community; Russell K. McDougall, C.S.C., Holy Cross Bugembe, P.O. Box 1037, Jinja, Uganda. Tel: 011-256-43-120013; Fax: 011-256-43-121322 Congregazione di Santa Croce; Rome, Italy; Prosper Tesha, C.S.C., Holy Cross Bugembe, P.O. Box 1037, Jinja, Uganda. Tel: 011-256-43-120013; Fax: 011-256-43-121322 Holy Cross Parish; Jinja, Uganda; Leopold Temba, C.S.C., Bishop McCauley House, Kampala; Serapio Wamara, C.S.C., Holy Cross Bugembe, P.O. Box 1037, Jinja, Uganda. Tel: 011-256-43-120013; Fax: 011-256-43-121322 Holy Cross Parish-Bugembe Community; Jinja, Uganda; Lucius Atwine, C.S.C., Kyarusozi Parish Community, P.O. Box 46, Fort Portal, Uganda. Tel: 011-256-077-548-307 King's College; Holy Cross Parish-Bugembe Community; Jinja, Uganda; Andrew Massawe, C.S.C., Holy Cross Novitiate, Lake Saaka, P.O. Box 176, Fort Portal, Uganda. Tel: 011-256-77-609469 Dandora Community; Nairobi, Kenya; Pascal Mugabe, C.S.C., McCauley Formation House; Nairobi, Kenya; Francis J. Murphy, C.S.C., Holy Cross Novitiate, Lake Saaka, P.O. Box 176, Fort Portal, Uganda. Tel: 011-256-77-609469. University of Portland, 500 N. Willamette Blvd., Portland, OR 97203-5798. University of Portland; Richard L. Potthast, C.S.C., Holy Cross Novitiate, Lake Saaka, P.O. Box 176, Fort Portal, Uganda. Tel: 011-256-77-609469 Fort Portal Region; Richard E. Stout, C.S.C., Holy Cross Novitiate, Lake Saaka, P.O. Box 176, Fort Portal, Uganda. Tel: 011-256-77-609469 Holy Cross Novitiate; Fort Portal, Uganda; James Burasa, C.S.C., District Supr., Bishop McCauley House, P.O. Box 25827, Kampala, Uganda. Tel: 001-256-41-510662 Bishop McCauley House; Kampala, Uganda; Fulgentius Katende, C.S.C., Bishop McCauley House, P.O. Box 25827, Kampala, Uganda. Tel: 001-256-41-510662 Andre House; Jinja, Uganda; George Muganyizi, C.S.C., Bishop McCauley House, P.O. Box 25827, Kampala, Uganda. Tel: 001-256-41-510662 Fort Portal Region; Fort Portal, Uganda; Leonard Olobo, C.S.C., Bishop McCauley House, P.O. Box 25827, Kampala, Uganda. Tel: 001-256-41-510662 Holy Cross Mission Center; Notre Dame, IN; Fred Jenga, C.S.C., Bishop McCauley House; Kampala, Uganda.

District of East Africa (Kenya): Revs. Bernard Amani (KCK), Dandora Community; Nairobi, Kenya; Richard Kyazze, C.S.C., P.O. Box 58078-00200, Nairobi, Kenya. Tel: 011-254-20-791157; Fax: 001-254-20-780506 Jirika Community; Fort Portal, Uganda; Silvester Makwali, C.S.C., P.O. Box 58078-00200, Nairobi, Kenya. Tel: 011-254-20-791157; Fax: 001-254-20-780506. University of Portland, 500 N. Willamette Blvd., Portland, OR 97203-5798. Holy Cross Lake View School; Jinja, Uganda; Willy Frank Lukati, C.S.C., McCauley House of Formation, Box 355-00517, Uhuru Gardens, Nairobi, Kenya. Tel: 011-254-2-601014 Fort Portal Region, Uganda.

Tanzania: Revs. Aristides Massawe, C.S.C., St. Brendan, P.O. Box 39, Karatu, Arusha, Tanzania. Dandora Community; Nairobi, Kenya; Comfort Agele, C.S.C., St. Brendan, P.O. Box 39, Karatu, Arusha, Tanzania. St. Brendan Parish-Kitete; Karatu, Arusha, Tanzania.

On Leave for Higher Studies: Revs. William R. Dailey, C.S.C., Holy Trinity Parish, 213 W. 82nd St., New York, NY 10024. Tel: 212-787-0634 University of Notre Dame; John F. Denning, C.S.C., University of Massachusetts; Terrence P. Ehrman, C.S.C., 1201 Perry St., Washington, DC 20017. Tel: 202-635-8515 Catholic University of America; Kevin G. Grove, C.S.C., Trinity College at Cambridge; Gregory P. Haake, C.S.C.; Stephen M. Koeth, C.S.C., Catholic University of America; Washington, D.C.; Brent A. Kruger, C.S.C., 1201 Perry St., Washington, DC 20017. Tel: 202-635-8515 Catholic University of America; Washington, D.C.; Russell K. McDougall, C.S.C., Pontifical Biblical Institute; Aaron J. Michka, C.S.C., Studies, Oxford University, UK; Daniel J. Parrish, C.S.C., University of Michigan; Kevin J. Sandberg, C.S.C., Fordham University; Nathan D. Wills, C.S.C., University of Wisconsin; Michael B. Wurtz, C.S.C., Pontifical University San Anselmo.

Military Chaplains: Rev. William Dorwart, C.S.C.

Priests of the Province in Residences Not Listed Elsewhere: Revs. Milton Adamson, C.S.C., Casa Santa Cruz; Phoenix, AZ; Genaro P. Aguilar, C.S.C., King's College, Wilkes-Barre; Maurice E. Amen, C.S.C., Columba Hall, P.O. Box 47, 46556. Tel: 574-631-8440 Holy Cross House; Robert Antonelli, C.S.C., University of Portland; David J. Arthur, C.S.C.; Duane Balcerski, C.S.C., Casa Santa Cruz; Phoeniz, AZ; James T. Banas, C.S.C., Mathis House, P.O. Box 5, Motijhell, Dhaka 1000, Bangladesh. Tel: 011-88-02-710324 Mathis House; Dhaka, Bangladesh; R. Bradley R. Beaupre, C.S.C., St. John the Evangelist, Viera; Richard Berg, C.S.C., University of Portland; George Bernard, C.S.C., University of Portland; Thomas C. Bertone, C.S.C., Moreau Seminary, Notre Dame; Michael T. Belinsky, C.S.C., 3320 Toledo Pl., Apt. G, Hyattsville, MD 20782. Tel: 240-893-7273 Univ. of Portland; Thomas Bill, C.S.C., Holy Cross House, Notre Dame; William G. Blum, C.S.C., Holy Cross House, P.O. Box 1048, 46556-1064. Tel: 574-631-6196 Our Lady of Fatima, Notre Dame; Robert J. Brennan, C.S.C., Holy Cross House, Notre Dame; William Brinker, C.S.C., Holy Cross House, Notre Dame; John A. Britto, C.S.C., Sacred Heart St. Francis Parish, Bennington; Foster J. Burbank, C.S.C.; James Burtchaell, C.S.C., Holy Cross House, Notre Dame; Francis T. Cafarelli, C.S.C., Moreau Seminary, Notre Dame; Lawrence E. Calhoun, C.S.C., 13645 Riverside Dr., Sherman Oaks, CA 91423. Tel: 818-386-1931 Our Lady of Fatima House; Notre Dame, IN; Joseph F. Callahan, C.S.C.; Thomas L. Campbell, C.S.C.; Rudolph V. Carchidi, C.S.C.; Joseph H. Carey, C.S.C., University of Notre Dame; Thomas F. Carten, C.S.C.; Bruce Cecil, C.S.C., Holy Cross Ctr., Berkeley, CA; Gary S. Chamberland, C.S.C., University of Portland, 5000 N. Willamette Blvd., Portland, OR 97203-5798. University of Portland; Thomas E. Chambers, C.S.C., Ph.D., Sacred Heart of Jesus, 139 S. Lopez, New Orleans, LA 70119-5109. Tel: 504-827-1481 Willwoods Community; Metairie, LA; James W. Chichetto, C.S.C.; Hugh W. Cleary, C.S.C., Ministry, North Easton; LeRoy E. Clementich, C.S.C., Archdiocese of Anchorage, 225 Cordova St., Anchorage, AK 99501. Tel: 907-297-7734; Fax: 907-279-3885 Holy Cross House, Notre Dame; William G. Condon, C.S.C.; James Connelly, C.S.C., Holy Cross House, Notre Dame (Supr.); John Connor, C.S.C., Our Lady of Perpetual Help Parish, 82450 Bliss Ave., Indio, CA 92201-4110; Richard Conyers, C.S.C., Notre Dame College Prep; Niles, IL; Jeffrey Cooper, C.S.C., University of Portland; Vincent J. Coppola, C.S.C., St. Bridget Parish, West Rutland; Joseph Corpora, C.S.C., University of Notre Dame; Charles W. Corso, C.S.C., 43326 Mission Blvd., Fremont, CA 94539-5829. Tel: 510-659-9717 Saint Joseph's Oratory of Mt. Royal; Michael D. Couhig, C.S.C., St. Ignatius Martyr Parish; Austin, TX; Christopher Cox, C.S.C., Casa Santa Cruz; Santiago, Chile; Mark T. Cregan, C.S.C., Stonehill College, Easton; Albert A. Croce, C.S.C.; Harry C. Cronin, C.S.C., Holy Cross Center, 2597 Virginia St., Berkeley, CA 94709. Tel: 510-548-8515; Fax: 510-548-7903 Holy Cross Center; Berkeley, CA; Alfred F. D'Alonzo, C.S.C., Holy Cross House, Notre Dame; Anthony J. DeConcilliis, C.S.C., Our Lady of Holy Cross College, New Orleans; Michael DeLaney, C.S.C., St. George College, Chile; Robert E. DeLeon, C.S.C., St. Joseph Center, Valatie; John M. DeRiso, C.S.C., St. Joseph Parish; South Bend, IN (Pastor); James J. Denn, C.S.C., Holy Cross House, P.O. Box 1048, 46556. Holy Cross House, Notre Dame; John F. Denning, C.S.C.; John F. Dias, C.S.C.; Donald W. Dilg, C.S.C., Our Lady of the Woods Parish, P.O. Box 416, Woodland Park, CO 80866. Tel: 719-687-9345 Holy Cross Novitiate; Cascade, CO (Asst. Supr.); James J. Doherty, C.S.C., St. Mary's Parish, Taunton; William H. Donahue, C.S.C. (Retired), Holy Cross House, Notre Dame; John P. Donato, C.S.C., Holy Trinity Parish, 213 W. 82nd St., New York, NY 10024. Tel: 212-787-0634. Our Lady Help of Christians Parish, 573 Washington St., Newton, MA 02458. Tel: 617-527-7560, Ext. 25 University of Portland; John Dougherty, C.S.C., Holy Redeemer Parish; Portland, OR (Pastor); Paul J. Duff, C.S.C., Holy Cross House, Notre Dame; Bro. Thomas Dziekan, C.S.C., 1st Asst. & Vicar, Generalate; Rome, Italy; Revs. Thomas F. Elliott, C.S.C., School Sisters of Notre Dame, 345 Belden Hill Rd., Wilton, CT 06897. Tel: 203-762-3318 School Sisters of Notre Dame; Wilton, CT; William W. Faiella, C.S.C., Holy Cross Center, 2597 Virginia St., Berkeley, CA 94709. Tel: 510-548-8515; Fax: 510-548-7903 St. Bernard of Clairvaux Parish (Assoc. Pastor); Scottsdale, AZ; Marc F. Fallon, C.S.C., St. Mary's Parish, Taunton; James E. Fenstermaker, C.S.C., Holy Cross Parish, South Easton; Dennis J. Fleming, C.S.C., Christopher Lodge, Cocoa Beach; John T. Ford, C.S.C., M.A., S.T.D., Catholic University, Cardinal Station, 125.12 Caldwell Hall, Box 236, Washington, DC 20064. Tel: 202-319-6501; Fax: 202-319-5875; 202-319-4967 Hyattsville, MD; Catholic University of America; Washington, D.C.; James T. Gallagher, C.S.C., Holy Cross Office of Vocation (Dir.); Notre Dame, IN; Thomas P. Gariepy, C.S.C.; Stephen C. Gibson, C.S.C., Fr. Peyton Centre, Ireland; Charles Gordon, C.S.C., University of Portland; Anthony R. Grasso, C.S.C., King's College, Wilkes-Barre; Richard E. Gribble Jr., C.S.C., Stonehill College, 480 Washington St., North Easton, MA 02356. Tel: 508-238-4515; Donald F. Guertin, C.S.C., Our Lady of Fatima, Notre Dame; David L. Guffey, C.S.C., St. Monica Parish; Santa Monica, CA; Andrew Guljas, C.S.C., Our Lady of Fatima, Notre Dame; Michael W. Glockner, C.S.C., St. Paul's Retirement Community, 3602 S. Ironwood Dr., 46614. Tel: 574-231-8647; Fax: 574-291-0858 Sisters of Charity of Cincinnati; Mt. St. Joseph, OH; Mark R. Ghyselinck, C.S.C., Holy Cross College, P.O. Box 308, 46556. Tel: 574-631-9484; Fax: 219-631-9233 University of Portland; Kenneth E. Grabner, C.S.C., Holy Cross Village, Notre Dame; Gregory P. Haake, C.S.C., Resides at St. Raymond's; Stanford University; Thomas M. Halkovic, C.S.C.; W. Hannon, C.S.C., University of Portland; Donald J. Haycock, C.S.C., St. Lawrence Parish, Rochester; Lawrence J. Henry, C.S.C., 1406 Buffalo, Michigan City, 46360. Tel: 219-873-2410 Our Lady of Fatima, Notre Dame; John Herman, C.S.C., St. John Vianney Parish; Avondale, AZ; Alfred Z. Hernandez, C.S.C.; Richard C. Hockman, C.S.C.; Cajetan Holland, C.S.C., Holy Cross House, Notre Dame; Thomas Hosinski, C.S.C., University of Portland; William Hund, C.S.C., University of Portland; James W. Irwin, C.S.C., Calle Esmeralda, Holy Cross Center, 2597 Virginia St., Berkeley, CA 94709. Tel: 510-548-8515 Asilo San Vicente, Mexico; Daniel J. Issing, C.S.C.; Walter E. Jenkins, C.S.C.; Lawrence A. Jerge, C.S.C., Holy Cross Parish, South Easton; Thomas J. Jones, C.S.C., Sacred Heart Parish, Notre Dame; Edward J. Kaminski, C.S.C., 3220 W. Greenway Rd., Phoenix, AZ 85053. Tel: 602-993-1213 St. Raphael Parish (Pastor); Glendale, AZ; Our Lady of the Valley, Phoenix; Daniel R. Kayajan, C.S.C., St. Rita Parish, Dade City; John Keefe, C.S.C., Casa Santa Cruz; Phoenix, AZ; William H. Kelley, C.S.C., Sacred Heart St. Francis Parish, Bennington; Thomas King, C.S.C., St. Mark Parish (Pastor); Niles, MI; Jerome E. Knoll, C.S.C., University of Notre Dame; Charles J. Kociolek, C.S.C.; Edward C. Krause, C.S.C., Gannon University, Erie, PA 16541. Tel: 814-871-7702 Gannon University; Erie, PA; Robert J. Kruse, C.S.C., Stonehill College, Easton; Christopher Kuhn, C.S.C., Indiana Province Archives Center, Notre Dame (Dir.); Howard Kuhns, C.S.C., Holy Cross House; Vincent A. Kuna, C.S.C., Sacred Heart Parish; John Kurtzke, C.S.C.,

Holy Cross House; James Lackenmier, C.S.C.; Richard Laurick, C.S.C., Our Lady of Fatima House, Notre Dame; Charles J. Lavely, C.S.C., Holy Cross House (Asst. Supr.), Notre Dame; Thomas Lemos, C.S.C., St. Adalbert Parish & St. Casimir Parish; South Bend, IN; James M. Lies, C.S.C., 325 Prior Ave. S., Saint Paul, MN 55105. Tel: 651-696-5426 University of Portland; Joseph J. Long, C.S.C., Christopher Lodge, Cocoa Beach; Thomas P. Looney, C.S.C., Provincial Administration, Bridgeport; Robert L. Loughery, C.S.C., University of Notre Dame; Robert W. Lozinski, C.S.C., St. Michael Byzantine Church, Dunmore; Patrick Lynch, C.S.C., Moreau Seminary, Notre Dame; Bartley J. MacPhaidin, C.S.C., Holy Cross House, Notre Dame; James P. Madden, C.S.C., St. Joseph Center, Valatie; Patrick H. Maloney, C.S.C., University of Notre Dame; Louis A. Manzo, C.S.C., Christopher Lodge, Cocoa Beach; Jose M. Martelli, C.S.C., Valley Missionary Program, 52-565 Oasis Palms St., Coachella, CA 92236. Tel: 760-398-9277; Fax: 760-398-9281 Our Lady of Fatima House, Notre Dame; Michael A. Massaro, C.S.C., Holy Cross Parish, Vero Beach; Michael C. Mathews, C.S.C., St. Stanislaus Parish (Pastor); South Bend, IN; Holy Cross Parish, South Bend, IN; Jerome F. Matthews, C.S.C.; Peter M. McCormick, C.S.C., University of Notre Dame, Notre Dame, IN; Charles F. McCoy, C.S.C., University of Portland; James E. McDonald, C.S.C., Corby Hall, P.O. Box 514, 46556. Tel: 574-631-7325; Fax: 574-631-6715 University of Notre Dame; Sean D. McGraw, C.S.C., Our Lady Help of Christians Parish, 573 Washington St., Newton, MA 02458. Tel: 617-527-7560, Ext. 25 University of Notre Dame; Thomas McNally, C.S.C., Our Lady of Fatima House; Notre Dame, IN; Donald McNeill, C.S.C., St. Ann's Parish; Chicago, IL; Bradley J. Metz, C.S.C., University of Notre Dame, Notre Dame, IN; Bro. Dennis Meyers, C.S.C., St. Mark Parish; Niles, MI; Revs. James H. Miller, C.S.C., King's College, Wilkes-Barre; John M. Mulcahy, C.S.C., Morris Camp, Box 550, Atikokan ON Canada. Tel: 807-929-2341; Fax: 807-929-7181 Morris Camp; Ontario, Canada; George B. Mulligan, C.S.C., Christopher Lodge, Cocoa Beach; James F. Murphy, C.S.C., Christopher Lodge, Cocoa Beach; William Neidhart, C.S.C., Holy Cross House, Notre Dame; Stephen P. Newton, C.S.C., St. Cletus, 101 N. Horner Ln., Mount Prospect, IL 60056. Tel: 847-824-5049 St. Andre Bessette (Downtown Chapel); Portland, OR; Joseph O'Donnell, C.S.C., Casa Santa Cruz; Phoenix, AZ; Thomas J. O'Hara, C.S.C.; Laurence M. Olszewski, C.S.C., Christopher Lodge, Cocoa Beach; Peter Pacini, C.S.C., St. Adalbert Parish & St. Casimir Parish; South Bend, IN; William R. Persia, C.S.C., St. Rita Parish, Dade City; James H. Phalan, C.S.C.; John P. Phalen, C.S.C., St. Mary's Parish, Taunton; George Piggford, C.S.C.; Leo Polselli, C.S.C.; Claude Pomerleau, C.S.C., University of Portland; James T. Preskenis, C.S.C.; Chester Prusynski, C.S.C., Holy Cross House, Notre Dame; Ronald Raab, C.S.C., St. Andre Bessette, Portland, OR; Wilfred J. Raymond, C.S.C.; James L. Rebeta, C.S.C.; Randall C. Rentner, C.S.C., Benedictine High School, Richmond, VA; James Rigert, C.S.C., University of Portland; J. Robert Rioux, C.S.C.; Robert E. Roetzel, C.S.C., Benedictine High School; Richmond, VA; H. Rutherford, C.S.C., University of Portland; Cornelius Ryan, C.S.C., Our Lady of Fatime House, Notre Dame, IN; John J. Ryan, C.S.C., King's College, Wilkes-Barre; Batholomew C. Salter, C.S.C., St. Catherine By-The-Sea, Ventura; David Scheidler, C.S.C., Mexico Vocations Office; N.L., Mexico; Eric Schimmel, C.S.C., Andre House; Phoenix, AZ; David E. Schlaver, C.S.C., Holy Cross Mission Center, P.O. Box 543, 46556. Tel: 219-631-8884; 574-631-5477; Fax: 574-631-6813 (Sabbatical); Stephen J. Sedlock, C.S.C., Casa Santa Cruz; Phoenix, AZ; Richard J. Segreve, C.S.C., Holy Cross Residence, North Easton; Fred Serraino, C.S.C., Christopher Lodge, Cocoa Beach; Thomas J. Shea, C.S.C., Nativity Catholic Church, Brandon; Charles Sherrer, C.S.C., University of Portland; Joseph A. Sidera, C.S.C.; Kenneth J. Silvia, C.S.C., Christopher Lodge, Cocoa Beach; Norbert J. Sinski, C.S.C., 319 Ave. C, Apt. 2B, New York, NY 10009. Tel: 212-673-1101 Housing Works Inc.; New York, NY; S. Douglas Smith, C.S.C., University of Notre Dame; Thomas W. Smith, C.S.C., Holy Cross Mission Center, P.O. Box 543, 46556. Tel: 219-631-6814; 574-631-5477; Fax: 574-631-6813 St. Brendan Parish-Kitete; Karatu, Arusha, Tanzania; Kevin P. Spicer, C.S.C.; Bro. J. Rodney Struble, C.S.C., Mathis House, Norte Dame College, G.P.O. Box 5, Motijhell, Dhaka 1000, Bangladesh. Bangladesh; Revs. John A. Struzzo, C.S.C., St. Louise De Marillac, 1720 E. Covina Blvd., Covina, CA 91724-1640. Tel: 626-915-7873. St. Martha Catholic Church, Murrieta, CA 92563-5040; Michael B. Sullivan, C.S.C.; Patrick J. Sullivan, C.S.C.; Edmund J. Sylvia, C.S.C.; Joseph H. Tate, C.S.C., Holy Cross House, Notre Dame; James Thornton, C.S.C., Casa Santa Cruz; Phoenix, AZ; Fidel Arocutipa Ticona, C.S.C.; Ronald Tripi, C.S.C., Christ the King Parish (Assoc. Pastor); South Bend, IN; John V. VandenBossche, C.S.C., St. Francis High School, 1885 Miramonte Ave., Mountain View, CA 94040. Tel: 650-961-4276; Fax: 650-698-3241 Holy Cross House, Notre Dame; David H. Verhalen, C.S.C., Holy Cross Mission House, P.O. Box 929, 46556. Tel: 574-631-4757 Holy Cross House, Notre Dame; Robert A. Vozzo, C.S.C.; Neil F. Wack, C.S.C., Christ the King Parish (Pastor); South Bend, IN; William Wack, C.S.C., St. Ignatius Martyr Parish; Austin, TX; Charles L. Wallen, C.S.C.; Francis M. Walsh, C.S.C.; Patrick C. Walsh, C.S.C.; Peter J. Walsh, C.S.C., St. John The Evangelist Parish, Viera; Ronald Wasowski, C.S.C., University of Portland; James N. Watzke, C.S.C., 400 E. Randolph St., Apt. 3230, Chicago, IL 60601. Tel: 312-861-0651 Notre Dame Family Center; Oakbrook Terrace, IL; Ambrose Wheeler, C.S.C., Holy Cross House, Notre Dame; Arthur Wheeler, C.S.C., University of Portland; Bro. Ronald Whelan, C.S.C., Casa Santa Cruz; Phoenix, AZ; Revs. William Wickham, C.S.C., University of Portland; Stephen S. Wilbricht, C.S.C., Stonehill College, 320 Washington St., Easton, MA 02357; John Wironen, C.S.C., University of Portland; Robert A. Wiseman, C.S.C., Stonehill College, Easton; Herbert C. Yost, C.S.C., Holy Cross Association, P.O. Box K, 46556. Tel: 574-631-6022; Fax: 574-631-7291. Sanctuary at St. Paul's, 3602 S. Ironwood Dr., 46614-2453. Notre Dame; John L. Young, C.S.C.; Herman F. Zaccarelli, C.S.C., Christopher Lodge, Cocoa Beach; Richard P. Zang, C.S.C., Holy Cross Mission House, P.O. Box 929, 46556-0929. Tel: 574-631-5492 Casa Santa Cruz, Phoenix, AZ; Francis D. Zagorc, C.S.C., Holy Cross Mission House, P.O. Box 929, 46556-0929. Tel: 574-631-5492 Our Lady of Fatima House, Notre Dame; Francis T. Zlotkowski, C.S.C.; Thomas Zurcher, C.S.C., Casa de Formacion (Dir.); Guadalupe, N.L. *Holy Cross House, Casa de Formacion*, 5 de Febeno 124, Guadalupe, NL 6701 Mexico. Tel: 574-631-6337; Fax: 574-631-5172. Revs. David J. Porterfield, C.S.C., Supr. (Retired), Our Lady of Fatima House, Notre Dame; James F. Blaes, C.S.C. (Retired), Holy Cross House, Notre Dame; William G. Blum, C.S.C., Our Lady of Fatima House, Notre Dame; Theodore M. Hesburgh, C.S.C., Holy Cross House, Notre Dame; Robert M. Hoffman, C.S.C. (Retired), Holy Cross House, Notre Dame; George G. Kahle, C.S.C., Holy Cross House, Notre Dame; Bro. James Lakofka, C.S.C., Holy Cross House, Notre Dame; Revs. James McGrath, C.S.C., Holy Cross House, Notre Dame; William P. Melody, C.S.C., Holy Cross House, Notre Dame; Timothy O'Connor, C.S.C., Holy Cross House, Notre Dame; William O'Connor, C.S.C., Holy Cross House, Notre Dame; Louis W. Rink, C.S.C. (Retired), Holy Cross House, Notre Dame; Robert C. Steigmeyer, C.S.C. (Retired), Our Lady of Fatima House, Notre Dame; Richard Teall, C.S.C. (Retired), (Southern Prov.); Holy Cross House, Notre Dame; James R. Trepanier, C.S.C. (Retired), Holy Cross House, Notre Dame; Paul G. Wendel, C.S.C., Holy Cross House, Notre Dame; Bros. Clarence J. Breitenbach, C.S.C., Holy Cross House, Notre Dame; Thomas J. Combs, C.S.C., Holy Cross House, Notre Dame; Revs. James R. Blantz, C.S.C., Holy Cross Sisters, 1931 Poli St., Ventura, CA 93001. Tel: 805-648-7651 Casa Santa Cruz; Phoenix, AZ; John J. Blazek, C.S.C., Gilmour Academy, 34001 Cedar Rd., Gates Mills, OH 44040-9356. Tel: 440-473-3560; Fax: 440-473-8010 Holy Cross House at Gilmour Academy; Gates Mills, OH; Joseph P. Browne, C.S.C. (Retired), St. Birgitta Parish, 11820 N.W. St. Helens Rd., Portland, OR 97231-2319. Tel: 503-286-3929 Holy Cross House, Notre Dame; Michael J. Heppen, C.S.C., National Shrine of the Little Flower, 2123 Roseland Ave., Royal Oak, MI 48073. Tel: 248-541-4122 Our Lady of Fatima House, Notre Dame; Robert J. Nogosek, C.S.C., Our Lady of the Rosary Cathedral, 265 W. 25th St., San Bernardino, CA 92405. Tel: 909-648-1562 Our Lady of Fatima; Thomas E. Seidel, C.S.C., Sacred Heart, 201 S. Walnut St., Bangor, MI 49013. Tel: 269-427-7514; Fax: 269-427-5558 Our Lady of Fatima.

Congregation of Holy Cross, United States Province, Inc., 54515 State Rd. 933 N., P.O. Box 774, 46556. Tel: 574-631-9584; Fax: 574-631-3444. Rev. David T. Tyson, C.S.C., Pres.

Holy Cross Community, Corby Hall, University of Notre Dame 46556. Tel: 574-631-7325; Fax: 574-631-6715. Revs. Robert J. Austgen, C.S.C., Emeritus Faulty; Nicholas Ayo, C.S.C.; Leonard N. Banas, C.S.C.; Ernest J. Bartell, C.S.C.; Thomas E. Blantz, C.S.C.; James Bracke, C.S.C.; Richard S. Bullene, C.S.C.; Joseph H. Carey, C.S.C., Campus Min.; Austin I. Collins, C.S.C.; John E. Conley, C.S.C.; Michael Connors, C.S.C.; Joseph Corpora, C.S.C.; William R. Dailey, C.S.C.; Louis A. Delfra, C.S.C.; Robert A. Dowd, C.S.C.; Paul F. Doyle, C.S.C.; Thomas P. Doyle, C.S.C.; John S. Dunne, C.S.C.; Carl F. Ebey, C.S.C.; James F. Flanigan, C.S.C.; James K. Foster, C.S.C.; Patrick D. Gaffney, C.S.C.; James T. Gallagher, C.S.C.; Thomas E. Gaughan, C.S.C.; Eugene F. Gorski, C.S.C.; Gregory A. Green, C.S.C.; Daniel G. Groody, C.S.C.; Ralph L. Haag, C.S.C.; Bro. Louis F. Hurcik, C.S.C.; Revs. John I. Jenkins, C.S.C., Pres. of Univ. Notre Dame; Thomas J. Jones, C.S.C.; James B. King, C.S.C., Rel. Supr. Corby Hall; Jerome E. Knoll, C.S.C.; Paul V. Kollman, C.S.C.; Stephen A. Lacroix, C.S.C.; Andre E. Leveille, C.S.C.; William M. Lies, C.S.C.; Robert L. Loughery, C.S.C.; Bro. Edward C. Luther, C.S.C; Revs. Edward A. Malloy, C.S.C., Prof. Theology; Patrick H. Maloney, C.S.C.; Peter M. McCormick, C.S.C.; James E. McDonald, C.S.C., Senior Exec. & Counselor to Pres.; Sean D. McGraw, C.S.C.; Donald McNeill, C.S.C.; Leon J. Mertensotto, C.S.C.; Bradley J. Metz, C.S.C.; Bro. Jerome Meyer, C.S.C., (Midwest Prov.); Revs. Wilson D. Miscamble, C.S.C.; Martin Lam Nguyen, C.S.C.; Edwin H. Obermiller, C.S.C.; Edward D. O'Connor, C.S.C.; Leonard Olobo, C.S.C.; Robert S. Pelton, C.S.C.; Peter D. Rocca, C.S.C.; George A. Rozum, C.S.C.; Timothy R. Scully, C.S.C.; S. Douglas Smith, C.S.C.; Thomas G. Streit, C.S.C.; Michael B. Sullivan, C.S.C., (Eastern Prov.); Mark B. Thesing, C.S.C.; Bro. Thomas P. Tucker, C.S.C.; Revs. Joseph L. Walter, C.S.C.; Oliver F. Williams, C.S.C.

[I] CONVENTS AND RESIDENCES OF SISTERS

FORT WAYNE. *Marian Convent* (St. Joseph Hospital), 4138 S. Harrison, 46807. Tel: 260-745-4041. Web: www.poorhandmaids.org. Poor Handmaids of Jesus Christ 2; Candidate 1.

Sisters of St. Joseph of the Third Order of St. Francis Residences S.S.J.-T.O.S.F., 5327-3 Stone Hedge, 46835. Tel: 260-515-9927. Email: trueway@frontier.com.

Other Location:

Sisters of St. Joseph of the Third Order of St. Francis Residences S.S.J.-T.O.S.F., 2222 Abbey Dr., 46835. Tel: 260-485-4616.

SOUTH BEND. *Handmaids of the Most Holy Trinity Monastery-Hermitage* (1968) 23089 Adams Rd., 46628-9674. Tel: 574-272-9425. Sr. Mary Emmanuel Baggoo, H.T., Representative. Contemplative Community; Prayer Ministry; Prayer Witness which includes Retreats and Spiritual Direction.

Sarah House (1996) 1213 E. Bronson, 46615. Tel: 574-287-8342; Fax: 574-287-8342. Email: connie.ss@att.net. Owned by the Poor Handmaids of Jesus Christ. Sisters 2.

The Sisters of St. Joseph of the Third Order of St. Francis, S.S.J.-T.O.S.F. (1901) 1425 Clayton Dr., 46614. Tel: 574-287-5435; Fax: 574-291-1555. Email: Chiarahome@att.net. Sr. Gretchen Clark, S.S.J.-T.O.S.F., Contact Person. Sisters 1.

DONALDSON. *Convent Ancilla Domini* (1922) 9601 Union Rd., P.O. Box 1, 46513. Tel: 574-936-9936; Fax: 574-935-1785. Email: nhahn@poorhandmaids.org. Web: www.poorhandmaids.org. Sr. Nora Hahn, P.H.J.C., Prov. Provincialate, Poor Handmaids of Jesus Christ (The Ancilla Domini Sisters) Professed Sisters 31.

Catherine's Cottage, 9601 Union Rd., P.O. Box 1, 46513. Tel: 574-935-1703; Fax: 574-935-1785. Email: nhahn@poorhandmaids.org. Web: www.poorhandmaids.org. Professed Sisters 10.

Catherine Kasper Home, 46513. Tel: 574-935-1742. Nursing home for retired sisters & laity. Rooms 81.

Catherine Kasper Life Center, Inc. (1970) Tel: 574-935-1742; Fax: 574-935-1755. Retired Sisters 24.

Maria Center 46513. Tel: 574-935-1784; Fax: 574-935-1790. Senior Apartments (Efficiency and Singles) Apartments 27.

Poor Handmaids of Jesus Christ Community Support Trust Tel: 574-936-9936; Fax: 574-935-1785.

Ancilla College Tel: 574-936-8898; Fax: 574-935-1779. Email: admissions@ancilla.edu. Web: www.ancilla.edu.

Lindenwood, Retreat & Conference Center Tel: 574-935-1780; Fax: 574-935-1728. Email: lw@lindenwood.org. Web: www.lindenwood.org.

Moontree Community, P.O. Box 1, 46513. Tel: 574-935-1712. Email: moontree@poorhandmaids.org. Web: www.moontreecomunity.org.

St. Joseph Community Health Foundation Tel: 260-969-2001; Fax: 260-969-2004. Email: mdistler@sjchf.org. Web: sjchf.org.

**Catherine Kasper Place, Inc.*, 2826 S. Calhoun St., 46807. Tel: 260-456-8969; Fax: 260-969-2004. Email:

hchaille@sjchf.org. Web: catherinekasperplace.org. Holly Chaille, Dir. The Community Resource Center for Refugees serves foreign-born, new arrivals to the greater Fort Wayne area by offering educational, health, social and employment services designed to help individuals become self-sufficient and successfully integrate into their new community. The emphasis for service is to those refugees who no longer qualify for assistance through one of the local resettlement agencies and who have relocated in this community within the past five years.

Earthworks, Inc., 9815 Union Rd., Plymouth, 46563. Tel: 574-935-4164. Email: earthworks@fourway.net. Web: www.earthworksonline.org.

HUNTINGTON. *Victory Noll--Motherhouse of Our Lady of Victory Missionary Sisters* (1922) 1900 W. Park Dr., P.O. Box 109, 46750-0109. Tel: 260-356-0628; Fax: 260-358-1504. Email: victorynoll@olvm.org. Web: www.olvm.org. Rev. Thomas C. Fahey, Chap. (Retired). Legal Holding: Victory Noll Sisters Community Support Trust. Professed Sisters 103.

MISHAWAKA. *St. Francis Provincialate*, 1515 Dragoon Tr., P.O. Box 766, 46546-0766. Tel: 574-259-5427; Fax: 574-256-0822. Web: www.ssfpa.org. Sr. M. Angela Mellady, O.S.F., Prov. Supr.; Rev. Francis Affelt, O.F.M., Chap. Sisters of St. Francis of Perpetual Adoration, Inc., St. Francis Convent and Novitiate of Immaculate Heart of Mary Province. Sisters 113; Novices 6; Postulants 2.

Our Lady of the Angels Convent, 1515 Dragoon Tr., P.O. Box 766, 46546-0766. Tel: 574-259-5427; Fax: 574-256-0822. Web: www.ssfpa.org. Sr. M. Blanche Rausch, O.S.F., Supr.; Rev. James Kendzierski, O.F.M., Chap. Convent for retired and infirm sisters. Sisters 35.

NOTRE DAME. *Congregation of the Sisters of the Holy Cross*, Saint Mary's of the Immaculate Conception, 309 Bertrand Hall, 46556-5000. Tel: 574-284-5550; Fax: 574-284-5779. Web: www.cscsisters.org. Sisters Joan Marie Steadman, C.S.C., B.S., M.A., Pres.; Mary Louise Full, C.S.C., B.A., M.A., First Councilor; Geraldine Hoyler, C.S.C., B.S.B.A., M.S.B.A., C.P.A., Gen. Treas.; Philomena Quiah, C.S.C., B.A., B.Ed., M.Sc., M.Phil., Councilor; Sharlet Ann Wagner, C.S.C., B.J., J.D., Gen. Sec.

Sisters of the Holy Cross, Inc.; Sisters of the Holy Cross, Inc. dba CSC Consultation Services., Generalate, Candidate Program, Associate Program. Professed Sisters in Congregation 416; Temporarily Incorporated 27; Novices 15; Candidates 15.

Sisters of the Holy Cross Other Residences and Programs: *Rainbow House*, 2710 Trader Ct. W., 46628. Tel: 574-247-2512. Sisters 2. 52700 Shellbark Ave., 46628-4082. Tel: 574-273-9598. Sisters 2. 727 Forest Ave., 46616-1310. Tel: 574-246-0673; Fax: 574-246-0674. Sisters 2. 1023 Portage Ave., 46616. Tel: 574-234-3208. Sisters 2. 2121 W. Madison St., 46617. Tel: 574-287-6071. Sisters 1. *Immaculata Convent*, 200 Augusta Hall-Saint Mary's, 46556-5002. Tel: 574-284-5707. Sisters 3. *Moreau Convent*, 100 Lourdes Hall St. Mary's, 46556-5030. Tel: 574-284-5663. Sisters 5. *Rosary Convent*, 100 Rosary Convent, Saint Mary's, 46556-5013. Tel: 574-284-5841. Sisters 30. *House of Shalem*, 100 House of Shalem, Saint Mary's, 46556-5025. Tel: 574-284-5740. Sisters 2. *St. Bridget's Convent*, 100 Saint Bridget's Convent, Saint Mary's, 46556-5024. Tel: 574-284-5752. Sisters 2. *International Novitiate at St. John's*, 100 Solitude, Saint Mary's, 46556-5022. Tel: 574-284-5695. Sisters 3; Novices 6. *Bethany Convent*, 100 Bethany Convent, Saint Mary's, 46556-5038. Tel: 574-284-5674. Sisters 4. *Saint Mary's Convent*, 100 Saint Mary's Convent, 46556-5007. Tel: 574-284-5688; Fax: 574-284-5801. Sisters 76. *Loretto Convent*, 100 Loretto Convent, Saint Mary's, 46556-5039. Tel: 574-284-5667. Sisters 4. *Holy Spirit Convent*, 300 Augusta Hall Saint Mary's, 46556-5002. Tel: 574-284-5715. Sisters 3. *Kateri Convent*, 400 Augusta Hall Saint Mary's, 46556-5002. Tel: 574-284-5993. Sisters 3. *Madonna Convent*, 400 Augusta Hall St. Mary's, 46556-5002. Tel: 574-284-5890. Sisters 5. *Nazareth Convent*, 200 Augusta Hall St. Mary's, 46556-5002. Tel: 574-284-5822. Sisters 1. *Saint Ann's Convent*, 300 Augusta Hall St. Mary's, 46556-5002. Tel: 574-284-5713. Sisters 2. *Saint Claire Convent*, 400 Augusta Hall St. Mary's, 46556-5002. Tel: 574-284-5892. Sisters 2. *Visitation Convent*, 200 Augusta Hall St. Mary's, 46556-5002. Tel: 574-284-5820. Sisters 2. *Guadalupe Convent*, 300 Augusta Hall St. Mary's, 46556-5002. Tel: 574-284-5717. Sisters 2. *Andre House - East*, 100 Andre House-E., Saint Mary's, 46556-5015. Tel: 574-284-5644. Sisters 3. *Andre House - West*, 100 Andre House-W., Saint Mary's, 46556-5016. Tel: 574-284-5645. Sisters 3. *Marian Convent*, 300 Augusta Hall St. Mary's, 46556-5002. Tel: 574-284-5710. Sisters 5. *Novitiate at the Solitude, Saint Mary's*, 100 Saint Mary's Solitude, 46556-5002. Tel: 574-284-5120. Sisters 3; Novices 9. *Saint Theresa Convent*, 400 Augusta Hall - Saint Mary's, 46556-5002. Tel: 574-284-5995. Sisters 2. *Queen of Peace Convent*, 100 Lourdes Hall - St. Mary's, 46556-5014. Tel: 574-284-5579. Sisters 10.

All Saints Convent, 100 Lourdes Hall-St. Mary's, 46556-5014. Tel: 574-284-5660. Sisters 3.

Sisters of the Holy Cross, 701 Marquette Ave., 46617. Tel: 574-520-1447. Sisters 3.

Sisters of the Holy Cross

The Corporation of Saint Mary's College Sponsored Ministry.

[J] RETREAT HOUSES & EDUCATIONAL CENTERS

SOUTH BEND. *Forever Learning Institute, Inc.* (1974) 54191 Ironwood Rd., 46635. Tel: 574-282-1901; Fax: 574-282-1901. Email: jmloranger@comcast.net. Web: www.foreverlearninginstitute.org. Sr. Ellen Taylor, C.S.C., Pres. Bd. Directors; William Darden, Vice Pres. & Bd. Member; Joan Loranger, Exec. Dir. To promote and support the quality and dignity of older adults and to assist older adults in finding enrichment, joy and fellowship through educational and recreational activities.

DONALDSON. *Lindenwood Retreat & Conference Center* (1986) PHJC Ministry Center, 9601 Union Rd., P.O. Box 1, 46513-0001. Tel: 574-935-1706; Fax: 574-935-1728. Email: lpeters@poorhandmaids.org. Web: www.lindenwood.org. Sr. Loretta Peters, F.S., Dir. Overnight facilities for 100, Conference rooms for 250, Handicapped accessibility. Total Staff 6; Total in Residence 1.

[K] MISCELLANEOUS

FORT WAYNE. *Cathedral Museum* (1980) P.O. Box 390, 46801. Tel: 260-744-2765; Fax: 260-744-1972. 915 S. Clinton St., 46802. Tel: 260-422-4611, Ext. 3307. Rev. Phillip A. Widmann, Dir.

Catholic Charities of the Diocese of Ft. Wayne-South Bend, Inc. (1922) Tel: 260-422-5625; Fax: 260-422-5657. Email: ccoffice@ccfwsb.org. Web: www.ccfwsb.org.

Fort Wayne Community Service Center, 315 E. Washington Blvd., 46802. Debbie Schmidt, Exec. Dir. Total Staff 48; Total Assisted 19,783.

South Bend Community Service Center, 1817 Miami St., 46613. Tel: 574-234-3111; Fax: 574-289-1034. Total Staff 7.

Villa of the Woods-Catholic Charities Residential Living, 5610 Noll Ave., 48606. Tel: 260-745-7039; Fax: 260-744-4887. Cheryl Smith, Admin. Residential facilities for the elderly including housing, meals, laundry services and planned activities. Total Staff 11; Residents 15.

RSVP (Retired Senior Volunteer Program), 107 W. 5th St., Auburn, 46706. Tel: 260-925-0917; Fax: 260-925-1732. Total Staff 3; Volunteers Placed 601.

Refugee Resettlement Program Debra Schmidt, Dir., 315 E. Washington, 46802. Tel: 260-422-5625; 800-686-7459; Fax: 260-422-5657.

Catholic Community Foundation of Northeast Indiana, Inc., 915 S. Clinton St., P.O. Box 390, 46801. Tel: 260-422-4611; Fax: 260-423-3382. Email: rschulte@fw.diocesefwsb.org. Web: www.diocesefwsb.org. Most Rev. Kevin C. Rhoades, D.D., S.T.L., J.C.L., Contact Person.

**The Christ Child Society of Fort Wayne, Inc.* (1997) P.O. Box 12708, 46864. Web: www.christchildsocietyfw.org. Sherri Miller, Pres. Total Assisted Annually 5,000.

Crosier Fathers of Fort Wayne, 1721 Magnavox Way, 46802. Tel: 320-532-5225; Fax: 320-532-5222. Email: abecker@crosier.org. William G. Niezer, Registered Agent. Total Staff 1.

Diocese of Fort Wayne-South Bend Investment Trust, Inc., 915 S. Clinton St., P.O. Box 390, 46801. Tel: 260-422-4611; Fax: 260-423-3382. Most Rev. Kevin C. Rhoades, D.D., S.T.L., J.C.L., Admin.; Joseph Ryan, Contact Person & Chief Fin. Officer. To invest money received from qualified 501(c)(3) organizations that buy shares offered by the organization. All investments of share purchase proceeds shall be directed and conducted consistent with the investment policies and objectives established by the organization that are applicable to the type of share(s) sold to the participating 501 (c)(3) entities. All gains and any losses on investments, after administrative and money management fees, shall be reflected in share values.

**Fort Wayne Catholic Radio Group, Inc.* (Redeemer Radio, Catholic Radio AM 1450), 4618 E. State Blvd., Ste. 200, 46815. Tel: 260-436-9598; Fax: 260-432-6179. Web: www.redeemerradio.com. Dave Stevens, Exec. Dir.

The St. Joseph Community Health Foundation, Inc. (1998) 2826 S. Calhoun St., 46807. Tel: 260-969-2001; Fax: 260-969-2004. Email: mdistler@sjchf.org; jromelfanger@sjchf.org. Web: www.sjchf.org. Meg Distler, Exec. Dir.; Loaine Hagerty, Community Initiatives; Julie Romelfanger, Bookkeeper & Record Mgmt.; Marla Rust, Office & Prog. Asst. Total Staff 4.

Scholarship Granting Organization of Northeast Indiana, Inc., 915 S. Clinton St., P.O. Box 390, 46801. Tel: 260-422-4611; Fax: 260-426-3077. Email: mmyers@fw.diocesefwsb.org. Mark Myers, Ph.D., Supt.

SOUTH BEND. *Chiara Home, Inc.* (1993) 1425 Clayton Dr., 46614. Tel: 574-287-5435; Fax: 574-291-1555. Email: chiarahome@att.net. Web: www.chiarahomerespite.org. Sr. Gretchen Clark, S.S.J.-T.O.S.F., Pres. & Admin. Respite Care for people with special needs. Total Staff 2; Families Served 400.

Christ Child Society of South Bend, P.O. Box 1286, 46624. Tel: 574-288-6028; Fax: 574-288-4282. Web: www.christchildsb.org. Total Assisted 5,000.

The Foundation of Saint Joseph Regional Medical Center, 837 E. Cedar St., Ste. 350, 46617. Tel: 574-237-7377; Fax: 574-472-6800. Email: thefoundation@sjrmc.com. Web: www.sjmed.com. Ann Rathburn-Lacopo, Chief Devel. Officer.

The Foundation of Saint Joseph Regional Medical Center, Inc. Total Staff 4.

Jesuit Community, 1713 Burdette St., 46637. Tel: 574-243-0601. Revs. Brian Daley, S.J.; John S. Thiede, S.J.; Andrew N. Downing, S.J.; Edoth Mukasa, S.J.; Brian P. Dunkle, S.J. Priests 5.

HUNTINGTON. *Our Sunday Visitor, Inc.* (1912) 200 Noll Plaza, 46750. Tel: 260-356-8400; Fax: 260-359-0029. Email: osvinc@osv.com. Web: www.osv.com. Most Rev. Kevin C. Rhoades, D.D., S.T.L., J.C.L., Bd. Chm. Publishers of Catholic Periodicals, Books, Religious Education Materials, Offering Envelopes and Curriculum.

MISHAWAKA. *Franciscan Alliance, Inc.* (1974) P.O. Box 1290, 46546-1290. Tel: 574-256-3935; Fax: 574-257-8669. Web: www.franciscanalliance.org.

**Hills Insurance Company, Inc.*, P.O. Box 1290, 46544-4797. Sr. Jane Marie Klein, O.S.F., Chairperson of Bd.

Saint Joseph Regional Medical Center, Inc., 5215 Holy Cross Pkwy., 46545. Tel: 574-335-5000; Fax: 574-335-1002. Email: gutieral@sjrmc.com. Web: www.sjmed.com. Albert L. Gutierrez, CEO; Sr. Laureen M. Painter, O.S.F., Vice Pres. Mission Integration. Total Staff 506; Total Assisted 156,873.

Sisters of St. Francis of Perpetual Adoration, Inc., P.O. Box 766, 46546-0766. Tel: 574-259-5427; Fax: 574-256-0822. Web: www.ssfpa.org.

Sisters of St. Francis of Perpetual Adoration, Inc., Medical Benefits Trust Tel: 574-259-5427; Fax: 574-256-0822.

Sisters of St. Francis of Perpetual Adoration, Inc. Capital Improvements Trust, 1515 Dragoon Tr., P.O. Box 766, 46546-0766. Tel: 574-259-5427; Fax: 574-256-0822. Web: www.ssfpa.org.

Sisters of St. Francis Charitable Mission Trust Tel: 574-259-5427; Fax: 574-256-0822.

Sisters of St. Francis Retirement Fund Tel: 574-259-5427; Fax: 574-256-0822.

SSFPA Ministry Corporation, 1515 Dragoon Tr., P.O. Box 766, 46546. Tel: 574-259-5427; Fax: 574-256-0822. Web: www.ssfpa.org. Sr. M. Angela Mellady, O.S.F., Prov. Supr.

Yves R. Simon Institute (1988) 3921 Glenview Dr., 46628. Tel: 574-271-1187. Email: aos1936@comcast.net. Mr. Anthony O. Simon, Dir. & Contact Person. Catholic academic institute. Total Staff 2.

NOTRE DAME. *American Maritain Association, Jacques Maritain Center*, 430 Geddes Hall, 46556. Tel: 574-631-5825. Email: osberger.l@nd.edu. Web: www.jacquesmaritain.org. Alice Osberger, Admin.; John Tripani, Pres. & Dir. Purpose: For the purpose of perpetuating the wisdom, influence and inspiration of Jacques Maritain as a Catholic intellectual, saintly Christian and classical creative exponent of the philosophia perennis. To promote research, study and critical interpretations of the life and work of Jacques Maritain especially as that work continues and expands into a broader area of the tradition of the thought of Saint Thomas, to develop social and formative cultural movement based on the results of this research and study, cooperation with the Institute International "Jacques Maritain and its national and regional branches, and the promotion of publications, lecturers, study groups and similar activities."

Ave Maria Press, Inc. (1865) P.O. Box 428, 46556. Tel: 574-287-2831; Fax: 574-239-2904. Email: avemariapress.1@nd.edu. Web: www.avemariapress.com. Thomas Grady, Pres. & Publisher. Owned and operated by the

Congregation of Holy Cross, Indiana Province, Inc.

Blessed Basil Moreau Endowment Trust, 54515 State Road 933 N., P.O. Box 774, 46556. Tel: 574-631-9584; Fax: 574-631-3444. Rev. E. William Beauchamp, C.S.C., Pres.

Brothers of Holy Cross Life Development Trust, P.O. Box 460, 46556. Tel: 574-631-4000; Fax: 574-631-2999. Bro. Peter Graham, C.S.C., Trustee; J. Lynne Pawlick, Trustee; Fred G. Botek, Trustee; Bros. William Dygert, C.S.C., Trustee & Chairperson; Paul Kelly, C.S.C., Trustees; Robert Lavelle, C.S.C., Trustees; Lawrence Skitzki, C.S.C., Trustees.

Father Edward Sorin Trust, 54515 State Rd. 933 N., P.O. Box 774, 46556. Tel: 574-631-9584; Fax: 574-631-3444. Rev. Peter C. Jarret, C.S.C., Pres.

Holy Cross Village at Notre Dame, Inc. dba Dujarie House 54515 State Rd. 933 N., P.O. Box 303, 46556-0303. Tel: 574-251-3252; Fax: 574-232-7933. Email: jmueller@holycrossvillage.com. Web: www.holycrossvillage.com. Thomas Cassady Jr., Chm. Bd.; Bros. Joseph Fox, C.S.C., Dir. of Religious, Independent Brothers; Tom Cunningham, C.S.C., Dir., Religious, Brother in Assisted Living & Nursing Facility.

Saint Andre Bessette Continuing Care Trust, 54515 State Rd. 933 N., P.O. Box 774, 46556. Tel: 574-631-9584; Fax: 574-631-3444. Rev. Thomas C. Bertone, C.S.C., Pres.

PLYMOUTH. *Catherine Kasper Life Center, Inc.*, 9601 Union Rd., P.O. Box 1, Donaldson, 46513. Tel: 574-935-1742; Fax: 574-935-1760. Email: nhahn@poorhandmaids.org. Sisters Nora Hahn, P.H.J.C., Prov.; Judith Diltz, P.H.J.C., Vice Pres. & Sec.; Margaret Anne Henss, P.H.J.C., Treas. Sponsored by the Poor Handmaids of Jesus Christ. (The Ancilla Domini Sisters, Inc.), Purpose: To provide quality care and address the spiritual, emotional, and physical needs of the aged, sick and disabled. Total Assisted 208.

Earthworks, Inc., 9815 Union Rd., 46563. Tel: 574-935-4164. Email: earthworks@fourway.net. Web: www.earthworksonline.org. Sr. Suzanne Rogers, Dir. An environmental education center; a sponsored entity of the Poor Handmaids of Jesus Christ (P.H.J.C.) affiliated with Convent Ancilla Domini, Donaldson, IN.

RELIGIOUS INSTITUTES OF MEN REPRESENTED IN THE DIOCESE

For further details refer to the corresponding bracketed number in the Religious Institutes of Men or Women section.

[0600]—*Brothers of the Congregation of Holy Cross* (Midwest Province)—C.S.C.

[0470]—*The Capuchin Friars* (Prov. of St. Joseph)—O.F.M.Cap.

[0480]—*Conventual Franciscans* (Prov. of Our Lady of Consolation)—O.F.M.Conv

[0520]—*Franciscan Friars* (Prov. of St. John the Baptist)—O.F.M.

[0690]—*Jesuit Fathers and Brothers*—S.J.

[]—*Missionaries of the Holy Spirit*—M.Sp.S.

[]—*Priestly Fraternity of Saint Peter*—F.S.S.P.

[0610]—*Priests of the Congregation of Holy Cross* (Indiana Province)—C.S.C.

[]—*Society of the Divine Word*—S.V.D.

[1060]—*Society of the Precious Blood* (Cincinnati Province)—C.PP.S.

RELIGIOUS INSTITUTES OF WOMEN REPRESENTED IN THE DIOCESE

[3710]—*Congregation of the Sisters of Saint Agnes*—C.S.A.

[3832]—*Congregation of the Sisters of St. Joseph*—C.S.J.

[1920]—*Congregation of the Sisters of the Holy Cross*—C.S.C.

[1710]—*Congregation of the Third Order of St. Francis of Mary Immaculate* (Joliet, IL)—O.S.F.

[0790]—*Daughters of Divine Charity* (Holy Trinity Province)—F.D.C.

[]—*Daughters of Mary Mother of Mercy*—D.M.M.M.

[1070-03]—*Dominican Sisters* (Adrian Dominican Sisters)—O.P.

[1170]—*Felician Sisters* (Presentation of the B.V.M. Province)—C.S.S.F.

[1450]—*Franciscan Sisters of the Sacred Heart*—O.S.F.

[]—*Handmaids of the Most Holy Trinity*—H.T.

[3130]—*Our Lady of Victory Missionary Sisters*—O.L.V.M.

[3230]—*Poor Handmaids of Jesus Christ*—P.H.J.C.

[2970]—*School Sisters of Notre Dame*—S.S.N.D.

[]—*Sisters of Divine Providence*—C.D.P.

[2990]—*Sisters of Notre Dame* (Province of Toledo)—S.N.D.

[3360]—*Sisters of Providence of Saint Mary-of-the-Woods, Indiana*—S.P.

[]—*Sisters of Saint Agnes*—C.S.A.

[1640]—*Sisters of St. Francis of Perpetual Adoration* (Province of the Immaculate Heart of Mary)—O.S.F.

[3930]—*Sisters of St. Joseph of the Third Order of St. Francis*—S.S.J.-T.O.S.F.

DIOCESAN CEMETERY

FORT WAYNE. *Catholic Cemetery Association of Fort Wayne, Inc. dba Catholic Cemetery Association, Inc.* 3500 Lake Ave., 46805-5572. Tel: 260-426-2044; Fax: 260-422-7418. Web: www.catholic-cemetery.org. Thomas E. Alter, Diocesan Dir. Cemeteries/Supt. Catholic Cemetery.

NECROLOGY

† Hammond, Robert, (Retired)—Died May 8, 2011

† Yast, Robert A., (Retired)—Died Oct. 30, 2011

An asterisk (*) denotes an organization that has established tax-exempt status directly with the IRS and is not covered by the USCCB Group Ruling.

Diocese of Fort Worth

(Dioecesis Arcis-Vorthensis)

Most Reverend

KEVIN W. VANN

Bishop of Fort Worth; ordained May 30, 1981; appointed Coadjutor Bishop of Fort Worth May 17, 2005; succeeded July 12, 2005; ordained July 13, 2005. *Office: 800 West Loop 820 S., Fort Worth, TX 76108.*

The Catholic Center: 800 West Loop 820 S., Fort Worth, TX 76108. Tel: 817-560-3300; Fax: 817-244-8839.

Web: www.fwdioc.org

ESTABLISHED AUGUST 09, 1969.

Square Miles 23,950.

Comprises the following twenty-eight Counties in the State of Texas: Archer, Baylor, Bosque, Clay, Comanche, Cooke, Denton, Eastland, Erath, Foard, Hardeman, Hill, Hood, Jack, Johnson, Knox, Montague, Palo Pinto, Parker, Shackleford, Stephens, Somervell, Tarrant, Throckmorton, Wichita, Wilbarger, Wise and Young.

For legal titles of parishes and diocesan institutions, consult the Chancery Office.

STATISTICAL OVERVIEW

Personnel	
Priests: Diocesan Active in Diocese	49
Priests: Diocesan Active Outside Diocese	3
Priests: Diocesan in Foreign Missions	1
Priests: Retired, Sick or Absent	21
Number of Diocesan Priests	74
Religious Priests in Diocese	53
Total Priests in Diocese	127
Extern Priests in Diocese	10
Ordinations:	
Diocesan Priests	3
Transitional Deacons	2
Permanent Deacons in Diocese	109
Total Brothers	11
Total Sisters	81
Parishes	
Parishes	89
With Resident Pastor:	
Resident Diocesan Priests	35
Resident Religious Priests	23
Without Resident Pastor:	
Administered by Priests	22
Administered by Deacons	8
Completely Vacant	1
Missions	2
Professional Ministry Personnel:	
Brothers	11
Sisters	82
Lay Ministers	316
Welfare	
Homes for the Aged	4
Total Assisted	348
Special Centers for Social Services	19
Total Assisted	110,199
Educational	
Diocesan Students in Other Seminaries	27
Total Seminarians	27
Colleges and Universities	1
Total Students	8
High Schools, Diocesan and Parish	4
Total Students	1,319
Elementary Schools, Diocesan and Parish	16
Total Students	4,502
Elementary Schools, Private	1
Total Students	140
Catechesis/Religious Education:	
High School Students	8,028
Elementary Students	35,402
Total Students under Catholic Instruction	49,426
Teachers in the Diocese:	
Brothers	1
Sisters	18
Lay Teachers	486
Vital Statistics	
Receptions into the Church:	
Infant Baptism Totals	5,982
Adult Baptism Totals	342
First Communions	6,360
Confirmations	3,403
Marriages:	
Catholic	783
Interfaith	270
Total Marriages	1,053
Deaths	1,208
Total Catholic Population	710,000
Total Population	3,260,246

Former Bishops—Most Revs. JOHN J. CASSATA, D.D., ord. Dec. 8, 1932; Titular Bishop of Bida and Auxiliary of Dallas-Fort Worth; appt. March 20, 1968; cons. June 5, 1968; first Bishop, Fort Worth; appt. Aug. 22, 1969; retired Sept. 16, 1980; died Sept. 8, 1989; JOSEPH P. DELANEY, ord. Dec. 18, 1960; appt. Bishop of Fort Worth July 10, 1981; ord. Bishop Sept. 13, 1981; died July 12, 2005.

Vicar General and Moderator of the Curia—Rev. Msgr. STEPHEN J. BERG.

Chancellor—Very Rev. DANIEL KELLEY, Chancellor.

Vice Chancellor of Administrative Services—Mr. PETER M. FLYNN.

Vice Chancellor of Parish Services and Women Religious—Sr. YOLANDA CRUZ, S.S.M.N.

Vicar for Priests—Rev. Msgr. JUAN RIVERO.

Vicar for Special Projects—Rev. Msgr. E. JAMES HART.

Priest Secretary to the Bishop—Rev. ISAAC OROZCO.

Deans—Rev. Msgr. JOSEPH S. SCANTLIN, Arlington Area Deanery; Revs. ANH TRAN, Northeast Deanery; THOMAS STABILE, T.O.R., West Central Deanery; DAVID BRISTOW, East Central Deanery; JOHN MCKONE, Northwest Deanery; Rev. Msgr. RAYMUND A. MULLAN, Southwest Deanery; Rev. KEN ROBINSON, North Deanery; Rev. Msgr. JUAN RIVERO, South Deanery.

Diocesan Pastoral Council—Ms. BECKY LUCAS; Deacon POPO GONZALEZ; Mr. JOE FRANCIS; Dr. LOUIS GASPER; Mr. CHARLIE MARTINEZ; Mr. VINCENT KEIS; Ms. LISA KUPPER; Ms. KATHERINE LUBKE; Mr. JIM MCSORLEY; Mr. HECTOR SALDUA; Ms. ANDREA SCANLAND; Mr. MARK SHADOWENS; Mr. RONALD SUMCIZK; Mr. DICK SCHIEFELBEIN; MELANI SONNIER; Ms. PILAR FRASER; Ms. TERESA RAMOS; Ms. JANAE TINSLEY-PAGE; Mr. DUSTIN DURHAM; Rev. RICHARD ELDREDGE, T.O.R.; Rev. Msgr. STEPHEN J. BERG, Ex Officio; Most Rev. KEVIN W. VANN, J.C.D., D.D.; Rev. ISAAC OROZCO, Staff.

Consultors—Rev. MEL BESSELLIEU; Rev. Msgr. E. JAMES HART; Very Rev. DANIEL KELLEY; Rev. RICHARD ELDREDGE, T.O.R.; Rev. Msgr. MICHAEL OLSON; Revs. HECTOR MEDINA; HOA NGUYEN; D. TIMOTHY THOMPSON; Rev. Msgrs. JUAN RIVERO, Ex Officio; STEPHEN J. BERG, Ex Officio.

Presbyteral Council—Revs. DENNIS SMITH; JOHN SWISTOVICH; JOHN PACHECO; THOMAS KENNEDY; RICHARD ELDRIDGE, T.O.R.; RICHARD VILLA, S.M.; THOMAS CRAIG; Rev. Msgrs. JUAN RIVERO, Ex Officio; STEPHEN J. BERG, Ex Officio.

Diocesan Finance Council—Mr. CHUCK BARTUSH JR.; Mr. JOHN HERNANDEZ; Ms. BARBARA MAY; Ms. ELAINE PETRUS; Mr. EARLE SHIELDS JR.; Mr. PETER M. FLYNN, Staff; Rev. Msgr. STEPHEN J. BERG, Ex Officio.

Catholic Foundation of North Texas—Mr. PETER M. FLYNN, Exec. Dir.; Mr. CHUCK BARTUSH JR.; Mr. JOHN HERNANDEZ; Ms. BARBARA MAY; Mr. DAVID MORITZ; Ms. ELAINE PETRUS; Mr. DON CRAM; Mr. EARLE SHIELDS JR.; Rev. JOHN SWISTOVICH; Rev. Msgr. STEPHEN J. BERG, Ex Officio.

Catholic Schools' Trust—Mr. EARLE SHIELDS JR., Chm.; Ms. LAURA RICHARDS; Dr. JOAN MORAN; Mr. DONALD MILLER, Supt. Schools; Mr. PETER M. FLYNN, Exec. Officer.

Catholic Cemeteries Trust—Mr. KEVIN O'BRIEN.

St. Joseph's Health Care Trust—Most Rev. KEVIN W. VANN, J.C.D., D.D.; Mr. PETER M. FLYNN; Mr. CHUCK BARTUSH JR.; Mr. JOHN HERNANDEZ; Ms. BARBARA MAY; Mr. EARLE SHIELDS; Ms. ELAINE PETRUS.

North Texas San Benito, Inc.—Most Rev. KEVIN W. VANN, J.C.D., D.D.; Very Rev. DANIEL KELLEY; Mr. PETER M. FLYNN.

Boards and Associations

Building Commission—Mr. BEN HARRIS; Mr. W. J. DICKENS III; Mr. JACK DREWETT; Mr. GARY JONES; Mr. BRAD RUPAY; Mr. RICHARD FLORES; Mr. ROBERT BARHAM; Mr. GARY FRAGOSSO, Staff.

Diocesan Pastoral Finance Committee—Rev. Msgr. STEPHEN J. BERG, Chm.; Rev. JEFF POIROT; Mr. EDWARD DOSKOCIL; Mr. DON PHIFER; Revs. KARL SCHILKEN; RAY MCDANIEL; Mr. PETER M. FLYNN, Staff; Mr. KEVIN O'BRIEN, Staff.

Diocesan School Advisory Council—Mr. JOHN JOYCE; Mr. JOSEFS BERG; Mr. JEFF MARTINEZ; Mrs. LONIN CRANE; Mr. SCOTT KALLSEN; Rev. STEPHEN JASSO, T.O.R.; Mr. DONALD MILLER; Ms. LISA GRIFFITH.

Mission Council—Rev. THOMAS CRAIG; Mr. DARRYL CLEMENTS; Revs. STEPHEN JASSO, T.O.R.; MATHEW KAVIPURAYIDAM, T.O.R.; Ms. JUANITA CLEMENTS; Rev. DOMINGO ROMERO, O.F.M.Cap.; Deacon TOMAS A. BACA; Mr. PETER M. FLYNN; Ms. KIRSTIN KLOESEL; Ms. AMY ZEDER; Mr. STEVE ZEDER; Rev. THOMAS CRAIG; Mr. BOB EILENFELDT; Ms. COLLEEN CARGILE; Mr. WALTER WELBORN; Mr. JULIO CARRILLO; Rev. JOHN MCKONE; Ms. FELICIA GEHRIG; Mr. AL MIRABEL (representative from Maryknoll).

Priests' Personnel Board—Rev. Msgr. JUAN RIVERO.

Priests' Pension Plan Trustees—Rev. Msgr. JUAN RIVERO; Ms. BARBARA MAY; Mr. FRANKLIN MOORE; Revs. THOMAS CRAIG; D. TIMOTHY THOMPSON; Mr. PETER M. FLYNN, Staff; Mr. EARLE SHIELDS; Mr. MARK SIMEROTH, Staff.

Diocesan Programs

Vocations and Seminarians—Rev. KYLE WALTERSCHEID; Sr. YOLANDA CRUZ, S.S.M.N.

Deacons—Deacon DON WARNER.

Conduct Review Board—Rev. Msgr. STEPHEN J. BERG.

Victims' Assistance—Ms. JUDY LOCKE.

Tribunal—Rev. D. TIMOTHY THOMPSON, Judicial Vicar. Tel: 940-387-6223. Email: fr.tim@stmarkdenton.org; Ms. MEG HOGAN, Dir.; Rev.

FRANCIS OSEI; MS. ANNA MARIE CHAMBLEE, Case Coord.
Finance & Administrative Services Department—Mr. PETER M. FLYNN.
Financial Services—Mr. PETER M. FLYNN; Ms. CAROLYN JONES; Mr. KEVIN O'BRIEN; Mr. JORGE MONTENEGRO.
Property Management and Construction—Mr. GARY FRAGOSSO.
Claims and Risk Management - Catholic Mutual—Ms. CHRISTINA ABLORH.
Center City School Consortium—Ms. TRUDY MILLER.
Advancement Department—Mr. MICHAEL MISSANO; Ms. PATRICIA MILLER; Ms. LISA GRIFFITH.
Records Management & Archives Department—Ms. CLAIRE JENKINS.
Cemeteries—Mr. KEVIN O'BRIEN.
Catechetical Department—Mr. LUCAS POLLICE.
Adult Catechesis—Mr. LUCAS POLLICE.
Family Life—Mr. CHRIS VAUGHAN.
Natural Family Planning—Mr. ANTHONY ABADIE.
Children's Catechesis—Mr. MARLON DE LA TORRE.
Cursillo Center—Rev. FRANCIS X. FERNANDEZ, O.F.M.Cap. Tel: 817-624-9411; 817-624-8526. Email: cursillocntr@aol.com.
Pope John Paul II Institute for Lay Ministry—Rev. CARMEN MELE, O.P.
Respect Life—Ms. CHANACEE RUTH-KILLGORE, Dir.; Ms. DEBRA HERON, Gabriel Project; Ms. BETSY KOPER, Rachel Min.; Ms. SUE LAUX, Youth For Life.
Youth and Campus Ministry—Mr. KEVIN PREVOU; Rev. CHARLES CALABRESE, TCU Catholic Campus Ministry, P.O. Box 297310, Fort Worth, 76129. Tel: 817-257-7830; Ms. DEBRA NEELY, Catholic Campus Center, 3410 W. Louis Rodriguez Dr., Wichita Falls, 76308. Tel: 940-692-9778. Email: neelydeb@yahoo.com; Ms. LUISA MARTINI, University of North Texas/Texas Woman's University, 1303 Eagle Dr., Denton, 76201. Tel: 940-566-0004. UTA. Tel: 817-460-1155.
Young Adult Ministry—Mr. JEFF HEDGLEN.
Catholic Schools Department—Mr. DONALD MILLER.
Catholic Schools—Mr. DONALD MILLER, Supt. Schools; CHARLENE HYMEL, Assoc. Supt.
Marketing—Ms. LISA GRIFFITH.
School Nurses—Ms. NANCY EDER.
School Athletics—Ms. MICHELLE GUNTER.
Communications Department—Mr. PAT SVACINA.
Communications—Mr. PAT SVACINA.
Web Site—Mr. CHRIS KASTNER.
Newspaper— "North Texas Catholic" Mr. JEFF HENSLEY; Mr. TONY GUTIERREZ, Assoc. Editor.
Human Resources Department—Mr. MARK SIMEROTH.
Personnel—Mr. MARK SIMEROTH.
Benefits—Ms. SHARON FIELDER.
Office of Child & Youth Protection—Ms. JUDY LOCKE.
Liturgy and Chaplaincy Department—Deacon DON WARNER.
Justice and Peace—Deacon DON WARNER.
Deaf Ministry—Ms. CONNIE MARTIN.
Hospital Chaplaincy—Deacon BRUCE CORBETT; Rev. GEORGE THENNATTIL, T.O.R.
Prison Ministry—Deacons BRUCE CORBETT; RUSS DETWEILLER.
Mission Outreach—Rev. THOMAS CRAIG.
Delegate for Hispanic Ministry—Sr. INES DIAZ, S.S.M.N.
Society for the Propagation of the Faith—Rev. THOMAS CRAIG, Dir.
Scouting—Rev. ANH TRAN.
Clergy Personnel Services—Rev. Msgr. JUAN RIVERO.
Priests' Care Fund—Rev. Msgr. JUAN RIVERO.
Continuing Pastoral Formation—Rev. Msgr. JUAN RIVERO.
Catholic Women, Council of—Rev. IVOR KOCH.
Women Religious Services—Sr. YOLANDA CRUZ, S.S.M.N.
Campaign for Human Development—Mr. PETER M. FLYNN.
Ecumenism, Office of—Rev. JONATHAN WALLIS.
Holy Childhood Association—Rev. THOMAS CRAIG.

CLERGY, PARISHES, MISSIONS AND PAROCHIAL SCHOOLS

CITY OF FORT WORTH

(TARRANT COUNTY)

1—ST. PATRICK CATHEDRAL (1870) Very Rev. Joseph Pemberton; Rev. Joy Joseph, T.O.R.
1206 Throckmorton St., 76102. Tel: 817-332-4915; Fax: 817-338-1988. Email: stpatricktx@sbcglobal.net. In Res., Revs. Raphael Eagle, T.O.R.; Isaac Orozco; Kyle Walterscheid.
Catechesis/Religious Program—Tel: 817-338-4441. Students 340.

2—ALL SAINTS (1902) Revs. Stephen Jasso, T.O.R.; Angel Infante, T.O.R.
214 N.W. 20th St., 76104. Tel: 817-626-3055; Fax: 817-626-3050.
School—2006 N. Houston St., 76164. Tel: 817-624-2670; Fax: 817-624-1221. Christina Mendez, Prin. Lay Teachers 9; Students 101.
Catechesis/Religious Program—Tel: 817-740-9176. Students 780.

3—ST. ANDREW (1953) Revs. Thomas Stabile, T.O.R.; Gerald Gordon, T.O.R.; Luke Robertson, T.O.R.
Res.: 46 Chelsea Dr., 76134. Tel: 817-927-5383; Fax: 817-927-8507. Web: www.standrewcc.org.
Church: 3717 Stadium Dr., 76109.
School—*St. Andrew Catholic School*, 3304 Dryden Rd., 76109. Tel: 817-924-8917. Mr. Charles Llewellyn, Prin. Lay Teachers 42; Students 701.
Catechesis/Religious Program—Students 500.

4—ST. BARTHOLOMEW (1969) Rev. James Pemberton, Parochial Admin.; Deacons Gary Brooks; Reyes Tello.
Res.: 3601 Altamesa Blvd., 76133. Tel: 817-292-7703; Fax: 817-292-2568. Email: stbarts@stbartsfw.org. Web: www.stbartsfw.org.
Catechesis/Religious Program—Students 758.

5—CHRIST THE KING Revs. Louis Pham Ha, C.M.C.; Michael M. TracPham, C.M.C.
1112 Eagle Dr., 76111. Tel: 817-831-7200; Fax: 817-881-7200.

6—ST. GEORGE (1941) Revs. Thu Nguyen; Armando Flores Rodriguez; Deacon James Crites.
825 Karnes, 76111. Tel: 817-831-4404; Fax: 817-834-0121. In Res., Rev. Carmen Mele, O.P.
School—824 Hudgins Ave., 76111. Tel: 817-222-1221; Fax: 817-838-0424. Email: principalsg@charter.net. Ms. Mary Longoria, Prin. Lay Teachers 13; Students 213.
Catechesis/Religious Program—Tel: 817-831-4404. Students 500.

7—HOLY FAMILY (1942) Rev. Jeff Poirot; Deacon Michael Mocek.
6150 Pershing Ave., 76107. Tel: 817-737-6768; Fax: 817-737-6876. Email: pastoraloffice@holyfamilyfw.org. Web: www.holyfamilyfw.org. In Res., Rev. Msgr. Philip Johnson.
School—Tel: 817-737-4201. Mr. Albert Herrera, Prin. Lay Teachers 20; Students 232.
Catechesis/Religious Program—Students 235.

8—HOLY NAME OF JESUS (1952) Unassigned.2637 Avenue L., 76105. Tel: 817-536-9604.
Catechesis/Religious Program—Tel: 817-535-8495. Students 780.

9—IMMACULATE HEART OF MARY (1961) Revs. Jose Gilardo Alvarez Abonce, C.O.R.C.; Fernando Mendez, C.O.R.C.
Mailing Address: 108 E. Hammond St., 76115. Tel: 817-923-6323; Fax: 817-923-6325.
Catechesis/Religious Program—Tel: 817-923-8582. Students 1,287.

10—ST. JOHN THE APOSTLE (North Richland Hills) (1964) Revs. Karl Schilken; Alfredo Barba; John Hennessy, Parochial Vicar.
7341 Glenview Dr., 76180. Tel: 817-284-4811; Fax: 817-284-1729.
School—7421 Glenview Dr., 76180. Tel: 817-284-2228; Fax: 817-284-1800. Ms. Geraldine Syler, Prin. Lay Teachers 25; Students 311.
Catechesis/Religious Program—Students 641.

11—ST. MARY OF THE ASSUMPTION (1909) Rev. David Bristow; Deacon Hector Salva.
509 W. Magnolia Ave., 76104. Tel: 817-923-1911; Fax: 817-923-0769. Email: stmarysfw@catholicweb.com. Web: stmarysftw-.catholic.com. In Res., Revs. George Thennattil, T.O.R.; Robert Strittmatter.
Catechesis/Religious Program—Students 795.

12—OUR LADY OF FATIMA Rev. Jim Ngo Huang Khoi, C.M.C.
Mailing Address: 5109 E. Lancaster Ave., 76112. Tel: 817-446-4196. Email: ourladyoffatima@sbcglobal.net. Web: nhathofatima-.com.

13—OUR LADY OF GUADALUPE (1977), (Hispanic), Revs. Domingo Romero, O.F.M.Cap.; Francis Garces, O.F.M.Cap.; Pablo Jaramillo, O.F.M.Cap.
4100 Blue Mound Rd., 76106. Tel: 817-626-7421; Fax: 817-626-4461. Email: doromero@yahoo.com. In Res., Rev. Francis X. Fernandez, O.F.M.Cap.
Catechesis/Religious Program—Tel: 817-624-3240. Students 1,411.

14—OUR MOTHER OF MERCY (1929), (African American), Rev. Jerome G. LeDoux, S.V.D.
1001 E. Terrell Ave., 76104-3788. Tel: 817-335-1695.
School—(Grades K-12), 1003 E. Terrell Ave., 76104-3799. Tel: 817-923-0058; Fax: 817-338-3368. Dr. Carolyn Yusuf, Prin. Lay Teachers 8; Students 85.

15—ST. PAUL THE APOSTLE (1952) Rev. Ellsworth T. Wigginton; Deacons Ron Aziere; Pedro Garcia.
5508 Black Oak Ln., 76114. Tel: 817-738-9925; Fax: 817-735-8579.
Church: 5508-B Black Oak Ln., 76114.
Catechesis/Religious Program—Students 375.

16—ST. PETER THE APOSTLE (1952) Rev. Richard Flores; Deacons Esteban Cardenas; Wendell Geiger.
Office: 1201 S. Cherry Ln., 76108. Tel: 817-246-3622.
School—Tel: 817-246-2032; Fax: 817-246-3686. Dr. Cindy Cummins, Prin. Lay Teachers 11; Students 110.
Catechesis/Religious Program—Students 237.

17—ST. RITA (1910) Revs. Paul Kahan, S.V.D.; Anthony Anala, S.V.D., Parochial Vicar.
5550 E. Lancaster, 76112. Tel: 817-451-9395; Fax: 817-451-9421.
School—712 Weiler Blvd., 76112. Tel: 817-451-9383. Kathleen Krick, Prin. Lay Teachers 15; Students 211.
Catechesis/Religious Program—Students 397.

18—SAN MATEO (1939) Rev. Robert Strittmatter.
Mailing Address: c/o 1206 Throckmorton St., 76102.
Office: 2909 Photo Ave., 76107. Tel: 817-737-5470.
Catechesis/Religious Program—Students 184.

19—ST. THOMAS (1937) Rev. Antony Mathew, T.O.R.
2920 Azle Ave., 76106. Tel: 817-624-2184; Fax: 817-624-9688.
Catechesis/Religious Program—Students 423.
Mission—*Holy Trinity* 800 High Crest Dr., Azle, Tarrant Co. 76020. Tel: 817-444-3063; Fax: 817-444-2217. Email: holytrinity1@prodigy.net.

20—ST. THOMAS MORE, Closed. For inquiries for parish records contact the chancery.

OUTSIDE THE CITY OF FORT WORTH

ABBOTT, HILL CO., IMMACULATE HEART OF MARY (1946) [CEM] Rev. Ouseph I. Thekkumthala.
601 W. Houston St., 76621. Tel: 254-582-3092; Fax: 254-582-0613.
Catechesis/Religious Program—Students 83.

ALBANY, SHACKELFORD CO., JESUS OF NAZARETH (1970) Rev. Jerome Jayasuriya, Sacramental Min.
Catechesis/Religious Program—Students 8.

ALEDO, PARKER CO., HOLY REDEEMER PARISH Rev. Msgr. Publius Xuereb; Deacon Scott France.
Mailing Address: P.O. Box 550, 76008. Tel: 817-441-3500. Email: parishoffice@holyredeemeraledo.org. Web: www.holyredeemeraledo.org.
Catechesis/Religious Program—Students 288.

ARLINGTON, TARRANT CO.

1—CHURCH OF ST. MARY THE VIRGIN (1994) Rev. Allan R.G. Hawkins.
1408 N. Davis Dr., 76012. Tel: 817-460-2278; Fax: 817-277-9927. Email: stmaryarl@sbcglobal.net.
Catechesis/Religious Program—Students 65.

2—CHURCH OF THE VIETNAMESE MARTYRS (2000) Revs. Polycarp Nguyen, C.M.C.; Dominic M. Trung Nguyen, C.M.C.; Andrew M. Tuan Van Nguyen.
801 E. Mayfield Rd., 76014. Tel: 817-466-0800. Email: vpgxtd@yahoo.com. Web: www.cttdvn.com.

3—ST. JOSEPH'S (1988) Very Rev. Daniel Kelley; Rev. Philip Brembah.
Office: 1927 S.W. Green Oaks Blvd., 76017-2734. Tel: 817-472-5181; Fax: 817-467-9319. Email: frdkelley@stjoe88.org. Web: www.stjoe88.org.
Catechesis/Religious Program—Students 910.

4—ST. MARIA GORETTI (1941) Revs. James Gigliotti, T.O.R.; Michael Ciski, T.O.R.
Res.: 306 Cecile Ct., 76013. Tel: 817-274-0643; Fax: 817-277-4193.
School—Tel: 817-275-5081. Mary Ellen Doskocil, Prin. Lay Teachers 35; Students 456.
Catechesis/Religious Program—Tel: 817-274-0643, Ext. 226. Students 284.

5—ST. MATTHEW (1964) Revs. Hector Medina; Philip Petta; Alfredo Barba; Deacons Eduardo Garcia; Benito Serenil.
2021 New York Ave., 76010-6097. Tel: 817-860-0130; Fax: 817-277-7159.
Catechesis/Religious Program—Students 1,374.

6—MOST BLESSED SACRAMENT (1978) Rev. Msgr. Joseph S. Scantlin; Deacon Mike Krempp.
2100 N. Davis Dr., 76012. Tel: 817-460-2751; Fax: 817-460-2761. Web: mostblessedsacrament.org.
Catechesis/Religious Program—Students 450.

7—ST. VINCENT DE PAUL (1976) Rev. Thomas Craig; Deacons Charles Castleberry; Bruce Corbett.
5819 W. Pleasant Ridge Rd., 76016. Tel: 817-478-8206; Fax: 817-478-8513. Email: svdpcc@svdpcc.org.
Catechesis/Religious Program—Fax: 817-478-8513. Students 837.

BEDFORD, TARRANT CO., ST. MICHAEL (1977) Revs. John Swistovich; Fernando Preciado; Khiem Nguyen; Deacons Harold Heinz; Sangote Ulupano.
3713 Harwood, 76021-4097. Tel: 817-283-8746; Fax: 817-283-1908. Web: www.smcchurch.org.
Catechesis/Religious Program—Students 722.

BOWIE, MONTAGUE CO., ST. JEROME (1986) Attended by St. Mary, Henrietta. Rev. Richard Collins.
Mailing Address: 105 S. Barrett, Henrietta, 76365. Tel: 940-538-4214. Email: stmaryhenrietta@yahoo.com.
Catechesis/Religious Program—Students 60.

BRECKENRIDGE, STEPHENS CO., SACRED HEART (1920) Rev. Jerome Jayasuriya, Sacramental Min.
208 S. Miller St., 76424. Tel: 254-559-2860; Fax: 254-559-5289. Email: galilee@pgrb.com.
Catechesis/Religious Program—Students 182.

BRIDGEPORT, WISE CO., ST. JOHN THE BAPTIZER (1889) Rev. Jacob Alvares, S.A.C.
1801 Irvin, 76426. Tel: 940-683-2743; Fax: 940-683-5958. Email: stjohns76426@embarqmail.com. Web: jackandwisecatholics.org.
Catechesis/Religious Program—Students 222.

BURKBURNETT, WICHITA CO., ST. JUDE THADDEUS (1965) Rev. Joseph Meledom.
600 Davey Dr., 76354. Tel: 940-569-1222; Fax: 940-569-2714. Email: stjudeth@yahoo.com.
Catechesis/Religious Program—Students 59.

BURLESON, TARRANT CO., ST. ANN (1971) Rev. Mel Bessellieu.
100 S.W. Alsbury Blvd., 76028. Tel: 817-295-5621; Fax: 817-295-5482. Email: stannoffice@sbcglobal.net.
Catechesis/Religious Program—Tel: 817-426-1101; Fax: 817-426-1106. Email: stannccd@sbcglobal.net. Web: www.stanninburleson.com. Students 562.

CARROLLTON, DENTON CO., ST. CATHERINE OF SIENA (1981) Revs. Mathew Kavipurayidam, T.O.R.; Augustine J. Kohapural, T.O.R.; Deacon Walter Stone.
Mailing Address: 1705 Peters Colony, 75007-3704. Tel: 972-492-3237; Fax: 972-394-0676. Email: churchinfo@stcatherine.org. Web: www.stcatherine.org.
Catechesis/Religious Program—Students 533.

CISCO, EASTLAND CO., HOLY ROSARY (1920) Attended by St. Rita, Ranger. Rev. Kyle Walterscheid, Sacramental Min.; Deacon Ruben Castaneda, Pastoral Admin.
1109 Blackwell St., Ranger, 76470. Tel: 254-647-3167.
Catechesis/Religious Program—

CLEBURNE, JOHNSON CO., ST. JOSEPH (1888) Rev. Sergio Rizo.
Mailing Address: 807 N. Anglin St., 76031. Tel: 817-645-4478; Fax: 817-558-9938. Email: stjolv123@sbcglobal.net.
Catechesis/Religious Program—Tel: 817-645-8079. Students 395.

CLIFTON, BOSQUE CO., HOLY ANGELS (1954) Rev. Thomas Kennedy.
1915 W. Fifth St., 76634. Tel: 254-675-8877. Email: holyangels@embarqmail.com.
Catechesis/Religious Program—Tel: 254-874-5272. Students 107.

COLLEYVILLE, TARRANT CO., GOOD SHEPHERD (1992) Rev. Richard Eldredge, T.O.R.; Bro. Paul McMullen, T.O.R.; Deacon John Clark.
1000 Tinker Rd., 76034. Tel: 817-421-1387; Fax: 817-421-4709.
See Holy Trinity Catholic School, Grapevine under Elementary and Secondary Schools, Parochial located in the Institution section.
Catechesis/Religious Program—Students 1,451.

COMANCHE, COMANCHE CO., SACRED HEART (1964) Attended by St. Brendan, Stephenville. Rev. Philip McNamara, S.A.C.; Deacon Tomie Diaz.
Mailing Address: 1444 W. Washington Ave., Stephenville, 76401. Tel: 254-965-5693.
Catechesis/Religious Program—Tel: 325-356-2040. Students 93.

CROWELL, FOARD CO., ST. JOSEPH (1910) Attended by Holy Family, Vernon. Rev. John McKone.
Res. & Mailing Address: 2200 Roberts, Vernon, 76384. Tel: 940-552-2895; 940-552-9870 (Rel. Ed.); Fax: 940-552-6084.

DE LEON, COMANCHE CO., OUR LADY OF GUADALUPE (1975) Attended by St. Brendan, Stephenville. Rev. Philip McNamara, S.A.C.
1444 W. Washington, Stephenville, 76401. Tel: 254-965-5693.
Catechesis/Religious Program—Students 33.

DECATUR, WISE CO., ASSUMPTION OF THE BLESSED VIRGIN MARY (1938) Attended by St. John the Baptizer, Bridgeport. Rev. Jacob Alvares, S.A.C.
1305 Deer Park Rd., 76234-9701. Tel: 940-627-3307; Fax: 940-683-5958. Email: stjohns76426@embarqmail.com. Web: jackandwisecatholics.org.
Church Rectory: 1801 Irvin, Bridgeport, 76426.
Catechesis/Religious Program—Tel: 940-683-2743. Students 341.

DENTON, DENTON CO.

1—IMMACULATE CONCEPTION (1894) Revs. D. Timothy Thompson; Richard Kirkham; Deacons Popo Gonzalez; Barry Sweeden; Alfonso Ramirez.
Res.: 2237 Northway Dr., 76207. Tel: 940-565-1770; Fax: 940-382-7939.
Catechesis/Religious Program—Martha Tona, Dir. Faith Formation. Students 1,200.

2—ST. MARK (1995) Rev. George Pullambrayil.
2800 Pennsylvania, 76205. Tel: 940-387-6223; Fax: 940-382-1641. Email: cwalker@stmarkdenton.org. Web: www.stmarkdenton.org.
Catechesis/Religious Program—Students 465.

DUBLIN, ERATH CO., ST. MARY (1916) Attended by St. Brendan, Stephenville., 1444 W. Washington Ave., Stephenville, 76401. Tel: 254-965-5693.
Catechesis/Religious Program—Tel: 254-445-0237. Students 122.

EASTLAND, EASTLAND CO., ST. FRANCIS XAVIER (1920) Attended by St. Rita, Ranger. Rev. Kyle Walterscheid, Sacramental Min.; Deacon Ruben Castaneda, Pastoral Admin.
1109 Blackwell St., Ranger, 76470. Tel: 254-647-3167; Fax: 254-647-3167.

ELECTRA, WICHITA CO., ST. PAUL (1966) [JC] Attended by Christ the King, Iowa Park. Deacon Patrick Burke, Admin.
Office: 1008 First St., Iowa Park, 76367. Tel: 940-592-2802; Fax: 940-592-2802. Email: ctkip@sbcglobal.net.
Res.: 3422 Stirling St., Wichita Falls, 76310. Tel: 940-691-7893.
Church: 500 N. Bailey, 76360. Tel: 940-495-3464; 940-592-2802.

GAINESVILLE, COOKE CO., ST. MARY (1879) Revs. Victor Cruz; Philip Aju Prince, H.G.N.
Res.: 805 N. Weaver St., 76240. Tel: 940-665-5395, Ext. 2; Fax: 940-665-0957. Web: stmaryscatholic.com.
School—931 N. Weaver St., 76240. Tel: 940-665-5395; Fax: 940-668-1881. Ms. Karen Lee, Prin. Lay Teachers 15; Students 146.
Catechesis/Religious Program—Students 317.
Convent—825 N. Weaver St., 76240.

GLEN ROSE, SOMERVELL CO., ST. ROSE OF LIMA (1969) [JC] Attended by St. Frances Cabrini. Rev. Msgr. Juan Rivero; Deacon Franklin Eschbach.
P.O. Box 7324, 76048.
Catechesis/Religious Program—Students 117.

GRAFORD, PALO PINTO CO., ST. FRANCIS OF ASSISI (1949) Attended by Our Lady of Lourdes.
Res.: P.O. Box 404, 76449. Tel: 940-779-2023.

GRAHAM, YOUNG CO., ST. MARY (1922) [JC] Rev. Msgr. Raymund A. Mullan.
Res.: 1218 S. Rodgers Dr., Box 547, 76450. Tel: 940-549-4314; Fax: 940-549-2690. Email: stmarygm@sbcglobal.net. Web: www.stmarygraham.org.
Catechesis/Religious Program—Tel: 940-549-1058. Students 208.

GRANBURY, HOOD CO., ST. FRANCES CABRINI (1976) [JC] Rev. Msgr. Juan Rivero; Rev. Gonzalo Morales; Deacons Jim Bell; Richard Stojak; Craig McAlister.
2301 Acton Hwy., 76049. Tel: 817-326-2131; Fax: 817-326-3211.
Catechesis/Religious Program— 76048. Tel: 817-326-2131. Students 406.

GRAPEVINE, TARRANT CO., ST. FRANCIS OF ASSISI (1949) Rev. Anh Tran; Deacon M. C. Marquez.
Res.: 861 Wildwood, 76051-3398. Tel: 817-481-2685; Fax: 817-488-3169. Web: www.sfatx.org.
See Holy Trinity Catholic School, Grapevine under Elementary and Secondary Schools, Parochial located in the Institution section.
Catechesis/Religious Program—Students 1,165.

HENRIETTA, CLAY CO., ST. MARY (1879) [CEM] Rev. Richard Collins.
105 S. Barrett St., 76365. Tel: 940-538-4214; Fax: 940-538-6638. Email: stmaryhenrietta@yahoo.com.
Catechesis/Religious Program—Students 25.

HILLSBORO, HILL CO., OUR LADY OF MERCY (1887) Rev. Ouseph I. Thekkumthala; Deacon James Poole.
Mailing Address: Interstate 35, P.O. Box 567, 76645. 107 Crestridge, 76645. Tel: 254-582-5640; Fax: 254-582-0347. Email: olm@hillsboro.net.
Catechesis/Religious Program—Students 300.

HURST, TARRANT CO., KOREAN MARTYRS Rev. Augustine Park.
415 Brown Tr., 76053. Tel: 817-788-5530; Fax: 817-485-2460. Email: chrysantpaul@yahoo.com. Web: www.koreancatholic.us.

IOWA PARK, WICHITA CO., CHRIST THE KING (1980) Deacon Patrick Burke, Pastoral Admin.
Mailing Address: P.O. Box 239, 76367.
Office: 1008 First St., 76367. Tel: 940-592-2802; Fax: 940-592-2802. Email: ctkip@sbcglobal.net.
Res.: 3422 Stirling St., Wichita Falls, 76310. Tel: 940-691-7893.
Catechesis/Religious Program—Students 25.

JACKSBORO, JACK CO., ST. MARY (1911) Attended by St. John the Baptizer, 1801 Irvin St., Bridgeport, TX 76426. Tel: 940-683-2743; Fax: 940-683-5958; 940-683-2743 (Rel. Ed.). Rev. Jacob Alvares, S.A.C.

KELLER, TARRANT CO., ST. ELIZABETH ANN SETON (1985) Rev. Msgr. E. James Hart; Revs. Dennis Smith; James McGhee; Deacons Klaus Gutbier; Myles Miller; Robert Montini; Donald E. Warner; Jose Hernandez; Jerry Rustman.
Office: 2016 Willis Ln., 76248. Tel: 817-431-3857; Fax: 817-431-9568. Web: www.seascc.org.
School—(Grades PreK-8) Tel: 817-431-4845; Fax: 817-431-1865. Web: www.seascc.org. Kay Burrell, Prin.; Ms. Nancy Stone, Librarian. Students 710.
Catechesis/Religious Program—Tel: 817-431-6023; Fax: 817-431-3871. Students 1,550.

KNOX CITY, KNOX CO., SANTA ROSA (1948) [JC] Attended by St. Joseph, Rhineland. Rev. Jeremias Tigga, H.G.N.; Deacons Jim Novak, Pastoral Admin.; Ben Vasquez.
Mailing Address: P.O. Box 428, 79529. Tel: 940-658-5062.
Church: N. 3rd and Ave. G, 79529. Tel: 940-658-5062.

LEWISVILLE, DENTON CO., ST. PHILIP THE APOSTLE (1976) Rev. John Stasiowski; Deacons Raymond G. Lamarre; John Kerrigan; Ramiro Rodriguez.
Office: 1897 W. Main St., 75067. Tel: 972-436-9581; Fax: 972-436-5302. Email: connieg@stphilipcc.org. Web: www.stphilipcc.org.
Catechesis/Religious Program—Tel: 972-219-7448. Students 878.

LINDSAY, COOKE CO., ST. PETER (1892) [CEM] Rev. Ray McDaniel.
Res.: 424 Main St., P.O. Box 148, 76250. Tel: 940-668-7609; Fax: 940-668-7723. Email: stpeterchurch@ntin.net.
Catechesis/Religious Program—Tel: 940-665-6763. Students 267.

MANSFIELD, TARRANT CO., ST. JUDE (1898) [CEM] Revs. George Foley; Amado Vallejo; Deacons Rubén Curiel; Victor Norton; Jose Aragon.
500 E. Dallas St., 76063. Tel: 817-473-6709; Fax: 682-518-6508. Web: www.stjudecc.org.
Catechesis/Religious Program—Tel: 817-473-0768. Students 1,062.

MEGARGEL, ARCHER CO., ST. MARY (1909) [CEM] Attended by Sacred Heart, Seymour. Rev. Albert Francis Kanjirathumkal, H.G.N., Sacramental Min.; Deacon Jim Novak.
13th St. & St. Mary St., 76370. Tel: 940-889-5252; Fax: 940-889-2136. Email: shseymour@srcaccess.net.

MINERAL WELLS, PALO PINTO CO., OUR LADY OF LOURDES (1960) Rev. Balaji Boyalla.
Res.: 108 N.W. 4th Ave., 76067. Tel: 940-325-4789; Fax: 940-327-8170.
Catechesis/Religious Program—Students 255.

MONTAGUE, MONTAGUE CO., ST. WILLIAM (1899) [CEM] Attended by St. Mary. Rev. Richard Collins.
105 S. Barrett, Henrietta, 76365. Tel: 940-538-4214; Fax: 940-538-6638. Email: stmaryhenrietta@yahoo.com.
Catechesis/Religious Program—Students 100.

MORGAN, BOSQUE CO., OUR LADY OF GUADALUPE (1987) Rev. Thomas Kennedy.

MUENSTER, COOKE CO., SACRED HEART (1889) [CEM] Rev. Ken Robinson.
714 N. Main St., 76252. Tel: 940-759-2511; Fax: 940-759-4422. Email: sacredheart@ntin.net. Web: www.shmuenster.com.
Preschool—Lay Teachers 4; Students 33.
School—Dr. Rafael Rondon, Prin. Lay Teachers 9; Students 106.
High School—Lay Teachers 14; Students 81.
Catechesis/Religious Program—Tel: 940-759-2511, Ext. 16. Students 232.

NOCONA, MONTAGUE CO., ST. JOSEPH (1948) Attended by St. Mary. Rev. Richard Collins.
105 S. Barrett, Henrietta, 76365. Tel: 940-538-4214; Fax: 940-538-6638. Email: stmaryhenrietta@yahoo.com.
Catechesis/Religious Program—Students 40.

OLNEY, YOUNG CO., ST. THERESA OF THE INFANT JESUS (1935) [JC] Attended by St. Mary, Graham. Rev. Msgr. Raymund A. Mullan.
P.O. Box 547, Graham, 76450. Tel: 940-549-4314. Email: stmarygm@sbcglobal.net.
Church: Oak & Ave. E, 76374.

PENELOPE, HILL CO., NATIVITY OF THE BLESSED VIRGIN MARY (1909) [CEM 2] Attended by Immaculate Heart of Mary, Abbot. Rev. Ouseph I. Thekkumthala.
Mailing Address: P.O. Box 98, 76676. Tel: 254-582-3092; Fax: 254-582-3092.
Catechesis/Religious Program—Tel: 254-533-2486. Students 39.

PILOT POINT, DENTON CO., ST. THOMAS AQUINAS (1891) [CEM] Rev. James Flynn.
Res.: 400 St. Thomas Aquinas Ave., 76258. Tel: 940-686-2088; Fax: 360-925-2952. Email: office@stthomaspilotpoint.org. Web: www.stthomaspilotpoint.org.
Catechesis/Religious Program—400 E. Gibbons, 76258. Tel: 940-686-2360. Students 291.

QUANAH, HARDEMAN CO., ST. MARY (1914) [JC] Attended by Holy Family, Vernon. Rev. John McKone.
2200 Roberts, Vernon, 76384. Tel: 940-552-2895; Fax: 940-552-6084.

RANGER, EASTLAND CO., ST. RITA (1919) Rev. Kyle Walterscheid; Deacon Ruben Castaneda, Pastoral Admin.
Res.: 1109 Blackwell St., 76470. Tel: 254-647-3167; Fax: 254-647-3167.

RHINELAND, KNOX CO., ST. JOSEPH (1895) [CEM] Rev. Jeremias Tigga, H.G.N., Sacramental Min.; Deacons

Jim Novak, Pastoral Admin.; Ben Vasquez.
Res.: 10180 CR 6010, Munday, 76371. Tel: 940-422-4994; Fax: 940-422-4994.
Catechesis/Religious Program—Students 123.

SCOTLAND, ARCHER CO., ST. BONIFACE (1911) [CEM] Attended by St. Mary, Windthorst. Rev. David Kraeger, T.O.R.
Tel: 940-423-6687; Fax: 940-423-6657. Email: windscot@comcell.net. Web: www.st-boniface.org.

SEYMOUR, BAYLOR CO., SACRED HEART (1910) [CEM] Rev. Jeremias Tigga, H.G.N., Sacramental Min.; Deacon Jim Novak.
Sacred Heart Pastoral Center—206 N. Cedar St., 76380. Tel: 940-889-5252; Fax: 940-889-2136. Email: shseymour@srcaccess.net.
Catechesis/Religious Program—Students 70.

STEPHENVILLE, ERATH CO., ST. BRENDAN (1958) Rev. Philip McNamara, S.A.C.; Deacons William Bolf; Joe Stanridge.
Res.: 1444 W. Washington Ave., 76401. Tel: 254-965-5693.
Catechesis/Religious Program—Students 208.

STRAWN, PALO PINTO CO., ST. JOHN (1912) Attended by St. Rita. Rev. Kyle Walterscheid; Deacon Ruben Castaneda, Pastoral Admin.
Res.: 1109 Blackwell Rd., Ranger, 76470. Tel: 254-647-3167.

THE COLONY, DENTON CO., HOLY CROSS (1981) Rev. J. Michael Holmberg; Deacons Tomas A. Baca; Simon Torrez.
Mailing Address: P.O. Box 5365, Frisco, 75035. Tel: 972-625-5252; Fax: 972-370-5524. In Res., Rev. Emmanuel Lewis.
Church: 7000 Morning Star Dr., 75056.
Catechesis/Religious Program—Students 335.

VALLEY VIEW, COOKE CO., ST. JOHN (1946) [JC] Closed. For inquiries for parish records contact the chancery.

VERNON, WILBARGER CO., HOLY FAMILY (1891) Rev. John McKone.
2200 Roberts, 76384. Tel: 940-552-2895; Fax: 940-552-6084.
Catechesis/Religious Program—Tel: 940-553-1580. Students 100.

WEATHERFORD, PARKER CO., ST. STEPHEN (1882) Rev. John Casey, S.A.C.; Deacon Carlos Frias.
Office: 1802 Bethel Rd., 76086. Tel: 817-596-9585; Fax: 817-613-0808. Web: www.ss-cc.org.
Res.: 1904 Bethel Rd., 76086. Tel: 817-596-9586.
Catechesis/Religious Program—Students 643.

WICHITA FALLS, WICHITA CO.

1—IMMACULATE CONCEPTION OF MARY, [CEM] [JC] Rev. Mark M. Nguyen Thanh Huyn, C.M.C.
2901 Barnett Rd., 76310. Tel: 940-692-1825.

2—OUR LADY OF GUADALUPE (1927) [JC] Rev. John Pacheco; Deacon Anastasio Perez.
421 Marconi, 76301. Tel: 940-766-2735; Fax: 940-766-4052. Email: guadalupewf@sbcglobal.net. Web: www.guadalupewf.org.
Catechesis/Religious Program—Students 211.

3—OUR LADY QUEEN OF PEACE (1956) [JC] Rev. Sojan George, H.G.N.; Deacon Larry W. Bills.
4040 York Ave., 76309. Tel: 940-696-1253; Fax: 940-696-1216. Email: olqp@wf.net. Web: olqpwf.org.
Catechesis/Religious Program—Fax: 940-696-1253. Students 196.

4—SACRED HEART (1891) [JC] Revs. Hoa Nguyen; Albert Francis Kanjirathumkal, H.G.N.; Fernando Preciado; Deacons Roland Benoit; Russell Detwiller; Bill Archer.
Mailing Address: 1504 Tenth St., 76301. Tel: 940-723-5288; Fax: 940-767-0160. Email: sheart@sacredheartwf.org.
Catechesis/Religious Program—Students 251.

WINDTHORST, ARCHER CO., ST. MARY (1892) [CEM] Rev. David Kraeger, T.O.R.
Res.: P.O. Box 230, 76389. Tel: 940-423-6687; Fax: 940-423-6657. Email: windscot@comcell.net. Web: www.st-boniface.com.

Catechesis/Religious Program—Students 288.

Chaplains of Public Institutions

FORT WORTH. *Federal Medical Center* 76199.

DENTON. *State School*, 1215 E. Elm St., 76201. Tel: 817-387-1755. Deacon Emilio (Popo) Gonzalez.

GAINESVILLE. *Texas Youth Council Youth Facility*, 805 N. Weaver, 76240. Tel: 817-665-2413.

WICHITA FALLS. *State Hospital*, Tel: 817-723-4111.

On Duty Outside the Diocese:
Very Rev.—
Olson, Michael F., Dallas, TX.
Revs.—
Spong, William, Ogdensburg, NY.
Thames, Robert, Residencia de Arzobispado, Casilla 25, Santa Cruz, Bolivia.

Graduate Studies:
Revs.—
Skeldon, John Robert
Wallis, Jonathan

On Leave of Absence:
Revs.—
Gremmels, John
Sorrano, Rodrigo

Retired:
Rev. Msgr.—
Schumacher, Joseph A.
Revs.—
Beaumont, Richard, 6240 Horton Circle, Apt. D, 76133.
Cooney, Gerald, c/o 1824 Clark Rd., Crowley, 76036-9714.
Curtsinger, George, P.O. Box 101148, 76185.
Edwards, Dale
Geurtz, Gary
Miller, James, St. Francis Village, 134 St. Anthony Dr., Crowley, 76036.
Miranda, Luke, 3240 Daniels, Apt. 101, Dallas, 75205.
O'Toole, James, c/o The Catholic Center, 800 W. Loop 820 S., 76108.
Perez, Salvador, Calle 22 #678, N. con Avenida Guerrero, Torreon, Coah 27000 Mexico.

Permanent Deacons:
Aguirre, Ruben
Aragon, Jose
Archer, William
Baca, Tomas A.
Bates, Thomas
Beaton, William
Benoit, Roland
Berens, LeRoy
Bills, Larry
Bindel, James
Blake, Vincent
Bolf, William
Bowden, Edgar
Bressler, Patrick
Brooks, Gary
Burke, Patrick
Camargo, Moisés
Cardenas, Jesus Esteban
Carranza, Marcelino
Casias, Arturo
Castaneda, Ruben
Castellon, Damaso
Castleberry, Charles
Clark, John
Corbett, Bruce
Crites, James
Curiel, Ruben
Detwiler, Russell
Diaz, Tommy
Escamilla, Juan
Eschbach, Franklin
France, Scott
Frias, Carlos
Galbraith, James
Garcia, Eduardo
Garcia, Gelasio
Garcia, Martin
Garcia, Pedro
Garza, Dave
Geiger, Wendell
Germann, Joe
Giovannitti, Thomas
Gonzalez, Adolfo
Gonzalez, Emilio
Gray, Glen Eldon
Greene, Clifford
Griego, Richard
Gutbier, Klaus
Guzman, N. John
Harvey, James
Heinz, Harold
Hernandez, Mauricio
Hoang, Dominic T.
Hoang, Michael
Howard, Terrance
Huerta, Lauro
Jasso, Juan
Johnson, William
Kerrigan, John
Krempp, Michael
Kunath, Wolfgang
Lagunas, Matias
Lamarre, Raymond
Lavery, Patrick
Leyva, Rigoberto
Marquez, Mario
Maskow, Kurt
McAlister, Craig
McDermott, John
Miller, Myles
Milligan, Joseph
Mocek, Michael
Montini, Robert
Nguyen, John Ban
Norton, Victor
Novak, Jim
Onofre, Jose
Pereda, Manuel
Perez, Anastasio
Perez, Julio
Poole, James
Poth, Louis J.
Ramirez, Alfonso
Reyes, Juan
Rodriguez, Jose
Rustand, Gerald
Salva, Hector
Salvo, Joseph
Sanchez, Jose
Sanchez, Leonard
Sandoval, Larry
Serenil, Benito
Sowers, Lynn
Standridge, Joe
Stojak, Richard
Stone, Walter
Sweeden, Barry
Tello, Reyes, Jr.
Torrez, Simon
Ulupano, Sangote
Vasquez, Ben
Warner, Don
Weaver, Lonnie, Jr.
Wolf, George
Wuenchel, Douglas

INSTITUTIONS LOCATED IN THE DIOCESE

[A] COLLEGES & UNIVERSITIES

FORT WORTH. *The College of St. Thomas More*, 3020 Lubbock St., 76109. Tel: 817-923-8459; Fax: 817-394-2340. Email: mklump@cstm.edu. Web: www.cstm.edu. Michael G. King, Pres. Priests 1; Fellows 7; Lay Teachers 4; Students 8.

[B] HIGH SCHOOLS, DIOCESAN

FORT WORTH. *Cassata High School* (Coed Secondary)., 1400 Hemphill St., 76104-4796. Tel: 817-926-1745; Fax: 817-926-3132. Email: sflood@cassatahs.org. Web: www.cassatahs.org. Susan Flood, Pres.; Nancy F. Martin, Prin. Teachers 8; Students 283.
Nolan Catholic High School (Coed), 4501 Bridge St., 76103. Tel: 817-457-2920; Fax: 817-496-9775. Email: office@nolancatholichs.org. Web: www.nolancatholichs.org. Rev. Richard Villa, S.M., Pres.; Cathy Buckingham, Prin. Society of Mary. Priests 2; Sisters 1; Brothers 3; Lay Teachers 76; Students 1,000.
Nolan School Trust

WICHITA FALLS. *Notre Dame Middle-High School*, 2821 Lansing Blvd., 76309. Tel: 940-692-6041; Fax: 940-692-2811. Web: www.notredamecatholic.org. Mrs. Cindy Huckabee, Prin. Lay Teachers 17; Students 95.

[C] HIGH SCHOOLS, PAROCHIAL

MUENSTER. *Sacred Heart School*, (Grades PreK-12), 153 E. Sixth, Box 588, 76252. Tel: 940-759-2511; Fax: 940-759-4422. Email: principalshs@ntin.net. Web: www.sacredheartschoolmuenster.com. Dr. Rafael Rondon, Prin. Sisters 2; Lay Teachers 30; Students 258.
**Sacred Heart Teachers Trust Fund*

[D] ELEMENTARY AND SECONDARY SCHOOLS, PAROCHIAL

ARLINGTON. *Holy Rosary Catholic School*, (Grades PreK-8), 2015 S.W. Green Oaks Blvd., 76017. Tel: 817-419-6800; Fax: 817-419-7080. Email: holy_rosary@hotmail.com. Web: www.hrcstx.com. Mr. Chad Riley, Prin.; Cindy Bryant, Librarian. Sisters 2; Total Staff 39; Students 441.

DENTON. *Immaculate Conception Catholic School*, (Grades PreK-8), 2301 N. Bonnie Brae, 76207. Tel: 940-381-1155; Fax: 940-381-1837. Email: eschad@runbox.com. Web: www.catholicschooldenton.org. Mrs. Elaine Schad, Prin. Lay Teachers 22; Students 258.

GRAPEVINE. *Holy Trinity Catholic School*, (Grades PreK-8), 3750 William D. Tate Ave., 76051. Tel: 817-421-8000; Fax: 817-421-4468. Web: www.holytcs.org. Dr. Valerie Johnson, Prin.; Mrs. Andrea Volding, Asst. Prin. Lay Teachers 29; Students 390.

WICHITA FALLS. *Notre Dame Elementary School*, 4060 York Ave., 76309. Tel: 940-696-1011; Fax: 940-691-6913. Web: www.notredamecatholic.org. Mrs.

Cindy Huckabee, Prin. Sisters 1; Lay Teachers 11; Students 112.

[E] ELEMENTARY SCHOOLS, PRIVATE

FORT WORTH. *Our Lady of Victory Catholic School*, 3320 S. Hemphill St., 76110. Tel: 817-924-5123; Fax: 817-923-9621. Email: tmiller@olvfw.com. Web: www.olvfw.com. Ms. Tawilhua Mitchell, Prin. Sisters 1; Lay Teachers 16; Students 180.

[F] SOCIAL AGENCIES, CATHOLIC CHARITIES

FORT WORTH. *Catholic Charities Diocese of Fort Worth Endowment, Inc.*, 249 W. Thornhill Dr., 76115.

Catholic Charities, Diocese of Fort Worth, Inc., 249 W. Thornhill Dr., 76115. Tel: 817-534-0814; Fax: 817-536-1556. Email: infoccdofw@ccdofw.org. Web: www.catholiccharitiesfortworth.org. Heather Reynolds, Pres. & CEO. An Independent Corporation Founded by the Diocese of Fort Worth.

Office Sites:

Senior Disabled Housing, P.O. Box 15610, 76119. Tel: 817-534-0814; Fax: 817-535-8779. Administers residential programs for the elderly, and disabled.

Program Sites:

Nuestro Hogar, Inc., 709 Magnolia St., Arlington, 76012. Tel: 817-216-0608; Fax: 817-861-6178.

CASA, Inc., 3201 Sondra Dr., 76107. Tel: 817-332-7276; Fax: 817-877-0487.

CASA Brendan & CASA II, Inc., 1300 Hyman St., Stephenville, 76401. Tel: 817-965-6964; Fax: 817-968-3072. Monica Quiroz, Exec. Dir. Housing.

Program Sites: Immigration Counseling, Refugee Resource Center and Refugee Resettlement. Assistance in migration matters: family reunification, adjustment of status, naturalization, ESL, and employment services.; Coordinates the Emergency Assistance Association of Tarrant County, Social Concerns, Holiday Network, Disaster Relief, Public Relations.

Healthy Start, 249 W. Thornhill Dr., 76115. Tel: 817-534-0814; Fax: 817-536-4671.

Assessment Center of Tarrant, 249 W. Thornhill Dr., 76115. Tel: 817-534-0814; Fax: 817-531-2996. (Children's Shelter)

School Based Services, 249 W. Thornhill Dr., 76115. Tel: 817-534-0814; Fax: 817-536-1556.

Clinical Counseling Department, 249 W. Thornhill Dr., 76115. Tel: 817-534-0814; Fax: 817-536-1556.

Immigration & Refugee Services, 249 W. Thornhill Dr., 76115. Tel: 817-920-7733; Fax: 817-923-3415.

Enrollment Solutions, 249 W. Thornhill Dr., 76115. Tel: 817-920-7733; Fax: 817-923-3415.

Pharmaceutical Services, 249 W. Thornhill Dr., 76115. Tel: 817-920-7733; Fax: 817-923-3415.

Financial Stability, 249 W. Thornhill Dr., 76115. Tel: 817-922-0384; Fax: 817-923-6818.

School Based Services, 249 W. Thornhill Dr., 76115. Tel: 817-534-0814; Fax: 817-536-1556.

St. Joseph's Health Care Trust, 249 W. Thornhill Dr., 76115. Tel: 817-920-7733; Fax: 817-923-3415.

Disaster Response Service, 249 W. Thornhill Dr., 76115. Tel: 817-534-0834; Fax: 817-535-6280.

Translation and Interpreter Network (TIN), 249 W. Thornhill Dr., 76115. Tel: 817-920-7733; Fax: 817-923-3415.

Central Intake, 249 W. Thornhill Dr., 76115. Tel: 817-534-0815; Fax: 817-536-1556.

Housing Opportunity Model for Empowerment and Stability (HOMES), 249 W. Thornhill Dr., 76115. Tel: 817-534-0815; Fax: 817-536-1556.

Urban Manor, 249 W. Thornhill Dr., 76115.

[G] RETIREMENT & DISABILITY HOUSING

FORT WORTH. *Casa, Inc. Housing for the Elderly and Handicapped*, 3201 Sondra Dr., 76107. Tel: 817-332-7276; Fax: 817-877-0487. Email: infoccdofw@ccdofw.org. Web: www.catholiccharitiesfortworth.org. Monica Quiroz, Dir. Housing. Units 200; Total in Residence 196; Total Staff 17.

ARLINGTON. *Nuestro Hogar, Inc. Catholic Charities*, 709 Magnolia St., 76012. Tel: 817-261-0608. Email: infoccdofw@ccdofw.org. Web: www.catholiccharitiesfortworth.org. 65 unit apartment complex for the elderly and disabled. Total in Residence 65; Total Staff 10.

CROWLEY. *St. Francis Village, Inc.*, 4070 St. Francis Village Rd., 76036. Tel: 817-292-5786; Fax: 817-294-2989. Email: deanah@saintfrancisvillage.com. Web: www.saintfrancisvillage.com. Deana Harris, Executive Dir.; Rev. John Abts, O.F.M. Active Retirement village, on shores of Lake Benbrook near Fort Worth, for retirees and the elderly sponsored by Franciscan Tertiary Provinces Foundation & SFV, Inc. (Illinois). Residents 550. In Res. Rev. Msgr. W. Robert Johnson (Retired); Rev. James Miller (Retired).

Franciscan Tertiary Provinces Foundation, 4070 St. Francis Village Rd., 76036. Tel: 817-292-5786. Sponsor corporation of St. Francis Village (retirement village) in Crowley, TX. Total Staff 17.

San Damiano, Inc., 4070 St. Francis Village Rd., 76036. Tel: 817-292-5786; Fax: 817-294-2989. Email: deanah@saintfrancisvillage.com. Web: saintfrancisvillage.com.

STEPHENVILLE. *CASA Brendan & CASA II, Inc. Catholic Charities*, 1300 Hyman, 76401. Tel: 254-965-6964; Fax: 254-968-3072. Email: infoccdofw@ccdofw.org. Web: www.catholiccharitiesfortworth.org. 86 unit apartment complex for the elderly and handicapped. Total in Residence 88; Total Staff 9.

[H] MONASTERIES AND RESIDENCES OF PRIESTS AND BROTHERS

FORT WORTH. *Community of Franciscan Friars of the Renewal Sacred Heart of Jesus Friary*, 1003 E. Terrell, 76104. Tel: 817-332-2435; Fax: 817-334-7930. Revs. Pio Maria, C.F.R.; Juan Diego Sutherland, C.F.R.; Bro. Timothy Pio Sgoutas, C.F.R.

Society of Mary (Province of the USA), *Nolan Catholic High School*, 4501 Bridge St., 76103. Tel: 817-457-2920; Fax: 817-496-9775. Revs. Richard Villa, S.M.; Robert Hackel, S.M.; Bros. Al Kuntemeier, S.M.; Louis Ernst, S.M.; Hugh Charlson, S.M.

CARROLLTON. **Third Order Regular of St. Francis, Province of St. Thomas*, 2920 Azle Ave., 76106-4909.

CROWLEY. *St. Maximilian Kolbe Friary* (Fort Worth), One Marquard Cir., St. Francis Village, 76036. Tel: 817-370-9747; Fax: 817-361-9522. Revs. John J. Abts, O.F.M.; Richard Baranski, O.F.M.; Cal Giesen; Robert Leonhardt, O.F.M.; Lambert Leykam, O.F.M.; Luis Runde, O.F.M.; Bro. Lester Kocklin.

SEYMOUR. *Heralds of Good News Mother Theresa Province, Inc.* (2010) *Sacred Heart Catholic Church*, 206 N. Cedar St., 76380-2102. Tel: 940-889-5252; Fax: 940-889-2136. Web: www.heraldsofgoodnews.org. Rev. Albert Francis Kanjirathumkal, H.G.N., Pres.

[I] CONVENTS AND RESIDENCES FOR SISTERS

FORT WORTH. *Hermanas Catequistas Guadalupanas*, 1001 Altamont Dr., 76106. Tel: 817-386-4161. Sisters 3.

Provincialate, Our Lady of Victory Center, 909 W. Shaw St., 76110. Tel: 817-923-8393; Fax: 817-921-5064. Email: mary.merdian@charter.net. Web: www.ssmnwestern.com. Sr. Mary Merdian, S.S.M.N. Provincial House of the Western Province, Sisters of St. Mary of Namur.

Sisters of St. Mary Namur, 909 W. Shaw, 76110. Tel: 817-923-8393; Fax: 817-921-5064. Email: mary.merdian@charter.net. Web: www.ssmnwestern.com. Sr. Mary Merdian, S.S.M.N. Sisters of St. Mary of Namur.

ARLINGTON. *Monastery of the Most Holy Trinity, Discalced Carmelites*, 5801 Mt. Carmel Dr., 76017. Tel: 817-468-1781; Fax: 817-468-1782. Email: supcarmel@aol.com. Web: www.carmelnuns.com. Sr. Maria Brinkley, O.C.D., Prioress. Solemn Professed Nuns 10; Novices 1; Postulants 1.

WICHITA FALLS. *Mercy Convent*, 3000 Lansing Blvd., 76309. Tel: 940-692-9770; Fax: 940-689-0139. Email: mercycom@sbcglobal.net. Web: www.ssmnwestern.com. Sisters 4.

Notre Dame House of Prayer and Hospitality, 2820 Lansing Blvd., 76309. Tel: 940-692-2043. Email: sjstewart99@gmail.com. Sisters 2.

[J] RETREAT HOUSES

LAKE DALLAS. *Montserrat Jesuit Retreat House*, 600 N. Shady Shores Rd., P.O. Box 1390, 75065. Tel: 940-321-6020; 940-321-6030; Fax: 940-321-6040. Web: www.montserratretreat.org. Revs. Ronald J. Boudreaux, S.J.; Edmundo Rodriguez, S.J., Assoc. Dir.; Edward Salazar, S.J.

Montserrat Foundation, Inc. Tel: 940-321-6010; Fax: 940-321-6040.

Board Members & Directors: Revs. Ronald J. Boudreaux, S.J.; Edmundo Rodriguez, S.J.

[K] SOCIETY OF ST. VINCENT DE PAUL

FORT WORTH. *St. Vincent de Paul Diocesan Council of Fort Worth*, 1901 Layton, Haltom City, 76117. Tel: 817-975-3255. Email: fwcouncilPresident@gmail.com. Web: www.svdpfw.org. Ms. Bonnie Vredenburg, Pres.

WICHITA FALLS. *Particular Council of Wichita Falls, St. Vincent de Paul Society*, 4516 Lake Park Dr., 76302. Tel: 817-322-2920. Mr. Walter Brady.

[L] COLLEGE CAMPUS MINISTRIES

FORT WORTH. *Texas Christian University Catholic Community* TCU Box 297310, 76129-0001. Tel: 817-257-7830; Fax: 817-257-7304. Email: c.calabrese@tcu.edu. Web: www.catholic.tcu.edu. Rev. Charles Calabrese.

ARLINGTON. *UTA Catholic Campus Center* 1010 Benge Dr., 76013-2643. Tel: 817-460-1155. Email: smilligan@fwdioc.org. Web: utacatholics.org. Ms. Marion Cannon, Dir.

University of Texas at Arlington University Catholic Community

DENTON. *University of North Texas & Texas Womens University* 1303 Eagle Dr., 76201. Tel: 940-566-0004. Email: lmartini@fwdioc.org. Ms. Luisa Martini, Campus Min.

HILLSBORO. *Hill College (United Christian Fellowship)* 2006 Brandon Rd., Box 1628, 76645. Tel: 254-580-0022. Email: director@UCFHill.org. Web: UCFHill.org. Deacon Jim Poole, Campus Min.

WICHITA FALLS. *Catholic Campus Ministry* Midwestern State University, 3410 Louis Rodriguez Dr., 76308. Tel: 940-692-9778. Email: msuccc@yahoo.com. Ms. Debra Neely.

[M] MISCELLANEOUS

FORT WORTH. *Catholic Diocese of Fort Worth Advancement Corporation*, 800 W. Loop 820 S., 76108. Tel: 817-560-3300; Fax: 817-244-8839. Email: pflynn@fwdioc.org. Mr. Peter M. Flynn, Pres. Board of Directors Most Rev. Kevin W. Vann, J.C.D., D.D.; Rev. Msgr. Stephen J. Berg; Mr. Guadalupe Ayala; Mr. Peter M. Flynn; Mr. Robert Garrison; Mr. David Kimbell; Ms. Duff O'Dell.

**Catholic Divorce Ministry*, 800 W. Loop 820 S., 76108-2919. Tel: 855-727-2269; Fax: 855-729-8751. Email: office@nacsdc.org. Web: www.nacsdc.org. Bob Zulinski, Office Mgr.; Most Rev. Kevin W. Vann, J.C.D., D.D., Liaison.

The Catholic Renewal Center of North Texas, Inc., 4503 Bridge St., 76103. Tel: 817-429-2920 (Metro); Fax: 817-492-8668. Email: crcwomen@sbcglobal.net.

Beginning Experience

Special Days for Special People

National Marriage Encounter of North Texas

Engaged Encounter of North Texas

CRC Ministries Outreach Tel: 940-382-3594. Sisters Pat Miller, S.S.N.D., Contact Person; Kay Kolb, S.S.N.D., Contact Person.

Franciscan Renewal Ministries of Texas, Inc., 1003 E. Terrell Ave., 76104. Tel: 817-332-2435; Fax: 817-334-7930. Rev. Juan Diego Sutherland, C.F.R., Apostolate Dir.

Magnificat, Grapevine Chapter, 3212 Heartfield, Flower Mound, 75022. Gloria Salerno Keiderling, Coord.

GRAND PRAIRIE. *Focolare Movement Men's Branch*, 2816 Olympia Dr., 75052. Tel: 972-606-0886. Email: southwest.m@foclare.us. Web: www.focolare.us. Claudio Amato, Regional Dir.

RELIGIOUS INSTITUTES OF MEN REPRESENTED IN THE DIOCESE

For further details refer to the corresponding bracketed number in the Religious Institutes of Men or Women section.

[0470]—*The Capuchin Friars*—O.F.M.Cap.

[]—*Confraternity of Operarios del Reino de Christo*—C.O.R.C.

[]—*Dominicans*—O.P.

[0520]—*Franciscan Friars*—O.F.M.

[]—*Franciscan Friars of the Renewal*—C.F.R.

[0585]—*Heralds of Good News*—H.G.N.

[0690]—*Jesuit Fathers and Brothers*—S.J.

[]—*Priests and Brothers of the Congregation of Mother Coredemptrix*—C.M.C.

[0420]—*Saviors of the Divine Word*—S.V.D.

[0760]—*Society of Mary (Marianists)*—S.M.

[0990]—*Society of the Catholic Apostolate*—S.A.C.

[0560]—*Third Order Regular of Saint Francis*—T.O.R.

RELIGIOUS INSTITUTES OF WOMEN REPRESENTED IN THE DIOCESE

[0100]—*Adorers of the Blood of Christ*—A.S.C.

[]—*Carmelites of Our Lady (Carm. O.L.)*

[4060]—*Congregation of Sisters of Charity of the Incarnate Word*—C.C.V.I.

[0420]—*Discalced Carmelite Nuns*—O.C.D.

[]—*Franciscan Sisters of the Immaculate Conception*

[1900]—*Hermanas Catequistas Guadalupanas*—H.C.G.

[]—*Missionary Catechists of the Divine Providence*

[]—*Missionary Catechists of the Sacred Hearts of Jesus and Mary*

[]—*Missionary of the Sacred Heart Ad Gentes*

[]—*Olivetan Benedictine Sisters*—O.S.B.

[2970]—*School Sisters of Notre Dame*—S.S.N.D.

[3950]—*Sisters of Saint Mary of Namur*—S.S.M.N.
[1970]—*Sisters of the Holy Family of Nazareth*—C.S.F.N.
[2050]—*Sisters of the Holy Spirit and Mary Immaculate*—S.H.Sp.
[]—*Vietnamese Dominican Sisters*

NECROLOGY

† King, Rev. Msgr. Charles, Denton, TX Immaculate Conception—Died June 1, 2011

An asterisk (*) denotes an organization that has established tax-exempt status directly with the IRS and is not covered by the USCCB Group Ruling.

Diocese of Fresno

(Dioecesis Fresnensis)

Most Reverend

ARMANDO XAVIER OCHOA

Bishop of Fresno; ordained May 23, 1970; appointed Titular Bishop of Sitifi and Auxiliary of the Archdiocese of Los Angeles December 29, 1986; ordained Bishop February 23, 1987; appointed Bishop of El Paso April 1, 1996; installed June 26, 1996; appointed Bishop of Fresno December 1, 2011; installed February 2, 2012. *Chancery Office: 1550 N. Fresno St., Fresno, CA 93703.*

Chancery Office: 1550 N. Fresno St., Fresno, CA 93703-3788. Tel: 559-488-7400; Fax: 559-488-7464.

ESTABLISHED DECEMBER 15, 1967.

Square Miles 36,072.

Formerly Diocese of Monterey-Fresno.

Comprises the Counties of Fresno, Inyo, Kern, Kings, Madera, Mariposa, Merced and Tulare in the State of California.

Diocesan Patroness: St. Therese of the Child Jesus.

Legal titles of parishes and institutions, the Roman Catholic Bishop of Fresno, a Corporation Sole, Diocese of Fresno Education Corporation (for schools).

STATISTICAL OVERVIEW

Personnel	
Bishop	1
Priests: Diocesan Active in Diocese	85
Priests: Diocesan Active Outside Diocese	2
Priests: Retired, Sick or Absent	33
Number of Diocesan Priests	120
Religious Priests in Diocese	37
Total Priests in Diocese	157
Extern Priests in Diocese	19
Ordinations:	
Diocesan Priests	2
Transitional Deacons	3
Permanent Deacons	16
Permanent Deacons in Diocese	63
Total Brothers	1
Total Sisters	109
Parishes	
Parishes	89
With Resident Pastor:	
Resident Diocesan Priests	59
Resident Religious Priests	10
Without Resident Pastor:	
Administered by Priests	19
Administered by Deacons	1
Missions	44
Professional Ministry Personnel:	
Sisters	20
Lay Ministers	67
Welfare	
Catholic Hospitals	3
Total Assisted	630,745
Health Care Centers	2
Total Assisted	217
Special Centers for Social Services	2
Total Assisted	50,000
Educational	
Diocesan Students in Other Seminaries	18
Seminaries, Religious	1
Total Seminarians	18
High Schools, Private	2
Total Students	1,178
Elementary Schools, Diocesan and Parish	20
Total Students	5,242
Catechesis/Religious Education:	
High School Students	11,192
Elementary Students	26,315
Total Students under Catholic Instruction	43,945
Teachers in the Diocese:	
Priests	2
Sisters	18
Lay Teachers	295
Vital Statistics	
Receptions into the Church:	
Infant Baptism Totals	19,547
Minor Baptism Totals	873
Adult Baptism Totals	354
Received into Full Communion	524
First Communions	12,673
Confirmations	5,956
Marriages:	
Catholic	1,804
Interfaith	195
Total Marriages	1,999
Deaths	7,011
Total Catholic Population	1,074,901
Total Population	2,756,266

Former Prelates of Diocese of Monterey-Fresno—Most Revs. JOHN B. MACGINLEY, D.D., ord. June 8, 1895; cons. May 10, 1910; First Bishop of Monterey-Fresno, July 31, 1924; resigned Sept. 30, 1932; died Oct. 18, 1969; PHILIP G. SCHER, ord. June 6, 1903; appt. April 28, 1933; cons. June 29, 1933; died Jan. 3, 1953; ALOYSIUS J. WILLINGER, C.Ss.R., ord. July 2, 1911; cons. Bishop of Ponce, Puerto Rico, Oct. 28, 1929; Coadjutor Bishop of Monterey/Fresno "cum jure successionis," Dec. 12, 1946; succeeded to the See, Jan. 3, 1953; resigned Oct. 25, 1967; died July 25, 1973; HARRY ANSELM CLINCH, D.D., ord. June 6, 1936; cons. Feb. 27, 1957; appt. Auxiliary to the Bishop of Monterey-Fresno, Dec. 5, 1956; transferred to the See of Monterey, Dec. 14, 1967; retired Jan. 19, 1982; died March 8, 2003.

Former Bishops of the Diocese of Fresno—His Eminence TIMOTHY CARDINAL MANNING, D.D., J.C.D., ord. June 16, 1934; appt. Titular Bishop of Lesvi and Auxiliary of Los Angeles, Aug. 3, 1946; consecrated Oct. 15, 1946; installed as First Bishop of Fresno, Dec. 15, 1967; elevated to Coadjutor Archbishop of Los Angeles "cum jure successionis," May 26, 1969; succeeded to the See, Jan. 21, 1970; created Cardinal, March 5, 1973; died June 23, 1989; Most Rev. HUGH A. DONOHOE, D.D., Ph.D., ord. June 14, 1930; appt. Auxiliary in San Francisco, Aug. 2, 1947; consecrated Oct. 7, 1947; appt. Bishop of Stockton, Feb. 21, 1962; appt. Second Bishop of Fresno, Aug. 28, 1969; resigned July 1, 1980; died Oct. 26, 1987; His Eminence ROGER CARDINAL MAHONY, D.D., ord. May 1, 1962; appt. Auxiliary Bishop of Fresno, Jan. 7, 1975; ord. Bishop, March 19, 1975; transferred to Diocese of Stockton, Feb. 26, 1980; installed April 17, 1980; appt. Archbishop of Los Angeles, July 16, 1985; installed Sept. 5, 1985; created Cardinal, June 28, 1991; Most Revs. JOSEPH J. MADERA, M.Sp.S., D.D., ord. June 15, 1957; consecrated March 4, 1980; succeeded to the See on July 1, 1980; transferred to Archdiocese for the Military Services, Washington, DC May 28, 1991; retired 2004; JOHN T. STEINBOCK, ord. May 1, 1963; appt. Titular Bishop of Midila and Auxiliary Bishop of Orange May 29, 1984; cons. July 14, 1984; appt. Bishop of Santa Rosa Jan. 27, 1987; appt. Bishop of Fresno Oct. 15, 1991; died Dec. 5, 2010.

Diocesan Administrator—Rev. Msgr. MYRON J. COTTA appointed Dec. 7, 2010.

Chancellor—VACANT.

Vice Chancellor—Rev. Msgr. E. JAMES PETERSEN (Retired). Email: ejpetersen@dioceseoffresno.org.

Chancery Office—1550 N. Fresno St., Fresno, 93703-3788. Tel: 559-488-7400; Fax: 559-488-7464. Web: www.dioceseoffresno.org.

Diocesan Tribunal—1550 N. Fresno St., Fresno, 93703-3788. Tel: 559-488-7490; Fax: 559-488-7498. Email: tribunal@dioceseoffresno.org.

Judicial Vicar—Rev. MICHAEL A. BURCHFIELD, J.C.L.

Adjutant Judicial Vicar—Rev. JESUS DEL ANGEL, J.C.L.

Tribunal Director—NANCY S. STEVENS, J.C.L. Email: nstevens@dioceseoffresno.org.

Tribunal Judges—Revs. MICHAEL A. BURCHFIELD, J.C.L.; THOMAS FRANCISCUS, C.Ss.R., J.C.L.; NANCY S. STEVENS, J.C.L.

Assessor & Tribunal Bilingual Auditor—PATRICIA RUIZ. Tel: 559-488-7425. Email: pruiz@dioceseoffresno.org.

Tribunal Secretaries—ESTELA MANZANO. Email: estela@dioceseoffresno.org; HORTENSIA RUBIO. Email: hrubio@dioceseoffresno.org; ADELINA GAMEZ. Email: lina@dioceseoffresno.org.

Ecclesiastical Notaries—ADELINA GAMEZ; ESTELA MANZANO; HORTENSIA RUBIO; MARIA ALANIS FLORES.

Defenders of the Bond—Rev. Msgrs. MICHAEL BRAUN; PATRICK JOSEPH MCCORMICK, V.F.

Advocates—Rev. CARLOS ESQUIVEL, O.S.J.; Rev. Msgrs. PERRY J. KAVOOKJIAN; JOHN MORETON; RICHARD URIZALQUI; ROBERT D. WENZINGER.

Promoter of Justice—NANCY S. STEVENS, J.C.L.

Diocesan Consultors—Rev. Msgrs. JOHN ESQUIVEL, V.F.; RAYMOND C. DREILING, V.F.; CRAIG F. HARRISON, V.F.; PATRICK JOSEPH MCCORMICK, V.F.; MYRON J. COTTA, Diocesan Admin.; JAMES T. LOGAN (Retired); E. JAMES PETERSEN (Retired); Rev. ROBERT BORGES, V.U.

Vicar Urbanis—Rev. ROBERT BORGES, V.U.

Vicars Forane—Rev. Msgrs. CRAIG F. HARRISON, V.F.; RAYMOND C. DREILING, V.F.; JOHN ESQUIVEL, V.F.; PATRICK MCCORMICK, V.F.

Diocesan Offices and Directors

Catechetical Ministries—JOSIE CONTENTE, Coord.

Catholic Charities—KELLY LILLES, Agency Admin., 149 N. Fulton, Fresno, 93701. Tel: 559-237-0851; Fax: 559-237-7050.

Diocese of Fresno - KNXT - TV Channel 49/38—(streaming on KNXT.TV) COLIN DOUGHERTY, Gen. Mgr., 1550 N. Fresno St., Fresno, 93703-3788. Tel: 559-488-7400; Fax: 559-488-7444.

Cursillo Movement Spiritual Advisor—

English—Deacon LEONARD RODRIGUEZ, Mailing Address: 1742 N. 10th Ave., Hanford, 93230. Tel: 559-582-6471.

Development Director—GILBERT J. HARO. Tel: 559-488-7414. Email: baa@dioceseoffresno.org.

Diocese of Fresno Education Corporation—1550 N. Fresno St., Fresno, 93703-3788. Tel: 559-488-7414.

Diocesan Newspaper— "Central California Catholic Life" Rev. Msgr. E. JAMES PETERSEN, Exec. Editor (Retired). Co Editors: Sr. ROSALIE ROHRER, I.H.M.; Rev. JAMES RUDE, S.J., 1550 N. Fresno St., Fresno, 93703-3788. Tel: 559-488-7400; Fax: 559-488-7464. Email: cccl@dioceseoffresno.org.

Finance Committee—Rev. Msgrs. MYRON J. COTTA, Diocesan Admin., 1550 N. Fresno St., Fresno, 93703-3788. Tel: 559-488-7400; MICHAEL BRAUN; GARY BETHKE, CPA; GARY RENNER; GARY MARSELLA; JOSEPH ZIEMANN; ROSEMARY MCCAVE.

Deposit and Loan Fund—Rev. Msgrs. MYRON COTTA, Diocesan Admin., 1550 N. Fresno St., Fresno, 93703-3788. Tel: 559-488-7400; MICHAEL BRAUN; JOSEPH ZIEMANN; JAMES F. SWEENEY; ROSEMARY MCCAVE; GARY BETHKE, CPA.

Detention Ministry—CLAUDE A. MUNCEY, 1550 N. Fresno St., Fresno, 93703-3788. Tel: 559-488-7474; Fax: 559-493-2847.

Holy Childhood Association—Rev. Msgr. MYRON J. COTTA, Dir., 1550 N. Fresno St., Fresno, 93703-3788. Tel: 559-488-7400; Fax: 559-488-7464.

Italian Catholic Federation—NETTIE DESCALSO-DEL-NERO, Pres. Tel: 209-383-4819.

Legion of Mary—CARLOS DEL POZO, Pres., 5389 N. Valentine, Fresno, 93711. Tel: 559-270-6484; JESSIE MORENO, Vice Pres., 5294 E. Tulare Ave., Fresno, 93727. Tel: 559-252-8542; PATRICIA DEL POZO, Sec., 5389 N. Valentine, Fresno, 93711. Tel: 559-270-6484.

Federacion Mariana de Guadalupe—LUIS MAGOS, Pres., 1733 Adanac Ct., Madera, 93638-1726. Tel: 559-673-1463.

Newman Apostolate—Deacon JOHN SUPINO, Parish Life Coord., St. Paul Newman Center, 1572 E. Barstow Ave., Fresno, 93710. Tel: 559-436-3434.

Office of Catholic Education—RICHARD SEXTON, Supt., 1510 N. Fresno St., Fresno, 93703-3711. Tel: 559-488-7420; Fax: 559-488-7422; Sr. MARY JEAN WILLIAMS, O.P., Asst. Supt.

Diocesan Advisory Board of Education—DEBORAH LEARY, Pres., 1510 N. Fresno St., Fresno, 93703-3711. Tel: 559-488-7420; Fax: 559-488-7422.

Property/Construction Management—DOUGLAS DURIVAGE, 1550 N. Fresno St., Fresno, 93703-3788. Tel: 559-493-2872.

Office of Finances—GARY BETHKE, CPA, Fiscal Mgr., 1550 N. Fresno St., Fresno, 93703-3788. Tel: 559-488-7426; Fax: 559-488-7461.

Office of Human Resources—RALPH S. JIMENEZ, Dir. Human Resources, 1550 N. Fresno St., Fresno, 93703-3788. Tel: 559-488-7488.

Office of Ministries—PATRICIA JIMENEZ, Dir.; PAUL MENTLEWSKI, Admin. Asst., 1550 N. Fresno St., Fresno, 93703-3788. Tel: 559-488-7474.

Multicultural and Campesino Ministry (Spanish)—Rev. MICHAEL MCANDREW, C.SS.R.

Family Life Ministry—Sr. JOANNE BAUER, C.S.C., Coord.

School of Ministry—Mr. FELICIANO TAPIA, Coord., 1550 N. Fresno St., Fresno, 93703-3788. Tel: 559-488-7474.

Youth Ministry—ALEJANDRO BARRAZA, Coord.

Worship and Evangelization—Rev. JEAN-MICHAEL LASTIRI, Dir., 1550 N. Fresno St., Fresno, 93703-3788. Tel: 559-642-3452; Fax: 559-642-4655.

Ecumenical Affairs—Rev. GREGORY J. BEAUMONT, Mailing Address: P.O. Box 798, Kingsburg, 93631. Tel: 559-897-5953.

Master of Ceremonies—Rev. Msgr. PATRICK JOSEPH MCCORMICK, V.F., Mailing Address: 671 E. Yosemite, Merced, 95340. Tel: 209-383-9261; Fax: 209-383-6796.

St. Anthony Retreat Center—Rev. Msgr. JOHN GRIESBACH, Dir.; Sr. DANIELLE WITT, S.S.N.D., Co Dir. Retreats, Mailing Address: P.O. Box 249, Three Rivers, 93271. Tel: 559-561-4595. Web: www.stanthonyretreat.org.

Santa Teresita Youth Conference Center—VINCENT OLEA, Dir., Mailing Address: P.O. Box 249, Three Rivers, 93271. Tel: 559-561-4595.

Permanent Diaconate Office—Deacon JOHN SOUSA, Interim Dir., 1550 N. Fresno St., Fresno, 93703-3788. Tel: 559-493-2840.

Personnel Board—Rev. Msgrs. PERRY KAVOOKJIAN; ROBERT D. WENZINGER; RONALD SWETT; JOHN MORETON; MYRON J. COTTA, Diocesan Admin.; JOHN ESQUIVEL, V.F.; RAYMOND C. DREILING, V.F.; CRAIG F. HARRISON, V.F.; PATRICK JOSEPH MCCORMICK, V.F.; Rev. ROBERT BORGES, V.U.

The Society for the Propagation of the Faith/The Society of St. Peter Apostle—Rev. Msgr. MYRON J. COTTA, Dir., 1550 N. Fresno St., Fresno, 93703-3788. Tel: 559-488-7400.

Scouting—Rev. GREGORY J. BEAUMONT, Chap., Sequoia Council, Mailing Address: P.O. Box 798, Kingsburg, 93631. Tel: 559-897-5953.

Vicar for Priests—VACANT.

Continuing Formation of Priests—Rev. Msgr. MYRON J. COTTA, 1550 N. Fresno St., Fresno, 93703-3788. Tel: 559-488-7400; Fax: 559-488-7464.

Interim Vicar for Religious—Sr. MARY JEAN WILLIAMS, O.P., 1510 N. Fresno St., Fresno, 93703-3788. Tel: 559-488-7420; Fax: 559-488-7422.

Safe Environment/Victim Assistance—TERESA DOMINGUEZ, Mgr. Tel: 559-584-4349. Email: tadominguez@sbcglobal.net; CHERYL SARKISIAN, Office Asst., 1550 N. Fresno St., Fresno, 93703-3788. Tel: 559-250-9851; Fax: 559-584-4349. Email: sarkisian_cheryl@yahoo.com; Mailing Address: P.O. Box 1306, Hanford, 93232-1306.

Vocations—Rev. DANIEL AVILA, Dir.

CLERGY, PARISHES, MISSIONS AND PAROCHIAL SCHOOLS

CITY OF FRESNO

(FRESNO COUNTY)

1—ST. JOHN CATHEDRAL (1882) Revs. Salvador Gonzalez Jr., Rector; Hector Lopez, Parochial Vicar; Deacon Salvador de la Torre. In Res., Rev. Daniel Avila.
Res.: 2814 Mariposa St., 93721. Tel: 559-485-6210; Fax: 559-485-8409.
Catechesis/Religious Program—Tel: 559-485-0161. Students 880.

2—ST. ALPHONSUS (1908) Revs. Dominic Savio Rajappa; Jim Torrens, S.J.
351 E. Kearney Blvd., 93706. Tel: 559-233-8275; Fax: 559-233-9379. Email: stalphonsus_church@yahoo.com.
Catechesis/Religious Program—Email: stalphonsus_church@yahoo.com. Students 83.

3—ST. ANTHONY CLARET (Calwa Area) (1952) Revs. Gabriel Ruiz, C.M.F.; Albert Vazquez, C.M.F., Parochial Vicar; Ralph Berg, C.M.F., Parochial Vicar.
Res.: 2494 S. Chestnut Ave., 93725. Tel: 559-255-4260; Fax: 559-255-4264.
Catechesis/Religious Program—Tel: 559-255-0223. Students 576.
Mission—Christ the King 3565 Calvin St., Malaga, Fresno Co. 93725.

4—ST. ANTHONY OF PADUA (1953) Rev. Msgr. Robert D. Wenzinger; Revs. Loren Blessing; Ricardo Magdaleno, Parochial Vicar, Chap., Fresno Heart Hospital & Children's Hospital; Deacons Edward C. Valdez; Ricardo DeLeon.
Office: 5770 N. Maroa Ave., 93704-2038. Tel: 559-439-0124; Fax: 559-439-3050. Web: www.stanthonyfresno.org.
School—(Grades K-8), 5680 N. Maroa Ave., 93704-2038. Tel: 559-435-0700; Fax: 559-435-6749. Web: www.sasfresno.com. Mrs. Kim Cochran, Prin.; Thomas Neumeier, Vice Prin.; Mrs. Maryclaire Polacek, Librarian. Lay Teachers 24; Students 614.
Catechesis/Religious Program—Tel: 559-439-0124. Students 800.
Mission—St. Agnes 111 W. Birch, Pinedale, Fresno Co. 93650. Tel: 559-439-2100; Fax: 559-439-0248.

5—ST. GENEVIEVE (1941) [CEM] Rev. Victor T. Dinh.
Church: 1127 Tulare St., 93706. Tel: 559-486-2988; Fax: 559-442-4318.
Catechesis/Religious Program—Email: stgenevieve@yahoo.com. Students 15.

6—ST. HELEN (1955) Rev. Genaro C. Demecais.
Office: 4870 E. Belmont, 93727. Tel: 559-255-3871; Fax: 559-255-7625. Email: office.sthelens@sbcglobal.net.
School—(Grades K-8), 4888 E. Belmont, 93727. Tel: 559-251-5855; Fax: 559-251-5948. Mr. Robert Peerson, Prin. Lay Teachers 13; Students 295.
Junior Kindergarten— Monica Kay, Dir.
Catechesis/Religious Program—4875 E. Grant, 93727. Students 296.

7—HOLY SPIRIT (1981) Rev. Eric Swearingen; Linda Fierro, Business Mgr.
355 E. Champlain Dr., 93720-1273. Tel: 559-434-7701; Fax: 559-434-7734. Email: holyspirit@holyspiritfresno.org. Web: www.holyspiritfresno.org.
Catechesis/Religious Program—Tel: 559-434-3522. Email: tafolla4@hotmail.com. Tomas Tafolla, D.R.E. Students 657.
Life Teen—Tel: 559-434-7708. Email: holyspirityouthminister@yahoo.com. Web: www.holyspiritlifeteen.catholicweb.com. Martha Perry, Youth Min. Tel: 559-434-7708.
Station—Shaver Lake Comm. Chapel 41340 Tollhouse Rd., Shaver Lake, 93634.

8—ST. MARY QUEEN OF APOSTLES CATHOLIC CHURCH (1967) [CEM] Rev. Timothy N. Cardoza.
Res.: 4636 W. Dakota, 93722. Tel: 559-275-2022; Fax: 559-275-2040. Email: stmaryfresno@att.net.
Catechesis/Religious Program—Tel: 559-271-1459. Students 518.

9—OUR LADY OF LAVANG Rev. Joseph Nguyen, (Vietnamese Ministry).
1046 S. 9th St., 93702. Tel: 559-485-9467; Fax: 559-485-8548. Email: josephnguyen39@gmail.com.
Catechesis/Religious Program—Students 85.

10—OUR LADY OF MT. CARMEL (1955) Rev. Joaquin S. Arriaga.
Office: 816 Pottle Ave., 93706. Tel: 559-264-2587; Fax: 559-264-2539. Email: olmcfresno@gmail.com.
Catechesis/Religious Program—Students 266.

11—OUR LADY OF VICTORY (1950) Rev. Msgr. John Moreton; Deacon Nai Her.
Parish Center & Rectory: 2850 N. Crystal Ave., 93705. Tel: 559-226-1163; Fax: 559-226-2093.
Church: 2838 N. West Ave., 93705.
School—(Grades PreSchool-8), 1626 W. Princeton Ave., 93705. Tel: 559-229-0205; Fax: 559-229-3230. Email: olvoffice@fresnoolv.org. Web: www.fresnoolv.org. Mrs. Deborah Nettell, Prin. Lay Teachers 8; Students 150.
Catechesis/Religious Program—Students 327.

12—ST. PAUL NEWMAN CENTER (1964) Rev. David J. Norris, Sacramental Min.; Deacon John Supino, Parish Life Coord. & Admin.
1572 E. Barstow St., 93710. Tel: 559-436-3434; Fax: 559-436-3430. Web: www.csufnewman.com.
Catechesis/Religious Program—Students 233.

13—SACRED HEART (1947) Rev. Alejandro Ignacio.
Res.: 2140 N. Cedar Ave., 93703. Tel: 559-237-4121; Fax: 559-237-0122. Email: sacredheartfresno@att.net. Web: sacredheart.org.
School—(Grades PreSchool-8), 4460 E. Yale, 93703. Tel: 559-251-3171; Fax: 559-251-7778. Web: www.shsfresno.net. Sr. Kathleen Drilling, S.S.N.D., Prin. Lay Teachers 9; Students 117.
Catechesis/Religious Program—Fax: 559-237-4121. Students 243.

14—SHRINE OF ST. THERESE (1925) Revs. Michael A. Burchfield; Flordito Redulla, S.V.D. In Res., Rev. Jesus del Angel.
Mailing & Res.: 855 E. Floradora Ave., 93728. Tel: 559-268-6388; Fax: 559-268-0852.
Catechesis/Religious Program—Email: religioused@shrineofsttherese.com. Students 343.

OUTSIDE THE CITY OF FRESNO

ARVIN, KERN CO., ST. THOMAS THE APOSTLE (1941) Rev. Jorge de la Torre.
Res.: 350 E. Bear Mountain Blvd., 93203. Tel: 661-854-6150; Fax: 661-854-2564.
Catechesis/Religious Program—Students 390.

ATWATER, MERCED CO., ST. ANTHONY (1909) Rev. Thomas Timmings; Deacons Kelly Canelo; Tony Mendez; Albert Montejano.
Office: 1799 Winton Way, 95301. Tel: 209-358-5743; Fax: 209-358-2423.
Res.: 1999 Juniper Ave., 95301.
School—(Grades PreK-8), 1801 Winton Way, 95301. Tel: 209-358-3341. Tricia Espanola, Prin.; Dianne Silva, Librarian. Lay Teachers 8; Students 150.
Preschool—Tel: 209-358-3341. Mary Hernandez, Dir.
Catechesis/Religious Program—Tel: 209-357-3259. Gloria Torres, D.R.E. Students 710.
Mission—Immaculate Conception 1799 Winton Way, 95301.

AVENAL, KINGS CO., ST. JOSEPH (1941) Revs. Raul Silva; Juan Pineda Lira, M.S.C.
Res.: 428 E. Kern St., 93204. Tel: 559-386-9523; Fax: 559-386-1068. Email: st.josephsparish@yahoo.com.
Catechesis/Religious Program—Students 256.
Mission—St. Cecilia Milham & 8th St., Kettleman City, Kings Co. 93239.

BAKERSFIELD, KERN CO.

1—CHRIST THE KING (1952) Rev. Msgr. Stephen A. Frost; Rev. John P. Burns (Retired).
Res.: 1800 Bedford Way, 93308. Tel: 661-391-4640; Fax: 661-391-4649.
Catechesis/Religious Program—Tel: 661-399-1956. Students 236.

2—ST. ELIZABETH ANN SETON Rev. Msgr. Perry Kavookjian; Deacons David Rodriguez; Nicholas Amicone.
Church: 12803 Montbatten Pl., 93312-6799. Tel: 661-587-3626; Fax: 661-587-3844. Email: padre@setoncatholicchurch.org. Web: www.setoncatholicchurch.org.
Catechesis/Religious Program—Students 192.

3—ST. FRANCIS OF ASSISI (1881) Rev. Msgr. Craig F. Harrison; Revs. David Greskowiak, Parochial Vicar; Denis Ssekannyo, Parochial Vicar; Deacons Scotty Bourne; Richard Lambert; Frank Vargas.
Res.: 900 H St., 93304. Tel: 661-327-4734; Fax: 661-327-4930. Email: jjacobs@stfran.org. Web: stfran.org.
School—(Grades PreK-8), 2516 Palm St., 93304. Tel: 661-326-7955; Fax: 661-327-0395. Lay Teachers 33; Students 510.
Day Care/Preschool—Tel: 661-326-7958. Mary Johnson, Dir. Students 92.
Catechesis/Religious Program—2424 Palm St., 93304. Tel: 661-323-8800; Fax: 661-323-1445. Alice Fry, D.R.E. Students 982.

4—ST. JOSEPH (1907) Revs. Miguel Flores; John Okeke Agwu, S.M.M.M., Parochial Vicar.
Mailing Address: 1515 Baker St, 93305.
Res.: 2701 Panorama Dr., 93306. Tel: 661-327-2744; Fax: 661-327-0133.
Catechesis/Religious Program—Tel: 661-325-2581.

Students 941.

5—OUR LADY OF GUADALUPE (1925) Revs. Larry Toschi, O.S.J.; Chummar Chirayath, O.S.J.; Jacob Shaji Athipozhi, O.S.J., Parochial Vicar.
Res.: 601 E. California Ave., 93307. Tel: 661-323-3148; Fax: 661-323-6016.
School—(Grades PreK-8), 609 E. California Ave., 93307. Tel: 661-323-6059. Sr. Guadalupe Hernandez, S.J.S., Prin. Sisters 3; Lay Teachers 8; Students 137.
Catechesis/Religious Program—Tel: 661-323-7642. Rosemary Pizana, D.R.E. Students 1,217.
Mission—Holy Spirit 720 E. Belle Terrace, Kern Co. 93307.
Mission—St. Jude 825 Chapman, Kern Co. 93307.

6—OUR LADY OF PERPETUAL HELP (1948) Rev. Msgr. Michael Braun.
Res.: 124 Columbus St., 93305. Tel: 661-323-3108; Fax: 661-325-7067. Email: olphbaker@aol.com. Web: olphbakersfield.org.
School—(Grades PreSchool-8) Tel: 661-327-7741. Email: dsmith@olph1.com. Web: olph1.com. Donna Smith, Prin. Lay Teachers 20; Students 340.
Catechesis/Religious Program—Tel: 661-322-7200. Students 190.

7—ST. PHILIP THE APOSTLE (1968) Rev. Msgr. Ronald Swett; Rev. Ivan Hernandez, Parochial Vicar; Deacons John Monsma; Michael Richard.
Mailing Address: 7100 Stockdale Hwy., 93309-1399. Tel: 661-834-7483; Fax: 661-834-2214. Web: stphilipchurch.org.
Preschool—Mrs. Karen Cerri, Dir.
Catechesis/Religious Program—Diana Akroush, D.R.E. Students 1,095.

8—SACRED HEART (1952) Rev. Dan Coyle.
Res.: 9915 Ramos St., 93307. Tel: 661-831-8905; Fax: 661-837-8075. Web: sacredheartbfl.org.
Catechesis/Religious Program—Tel: 661-831-6223; Fax: 661-837-8073. Students 242.

9—SAN CLEMENTE MISSION PARISH Rev. Joachim Cheon.
1305 Water St., Kern Co. 93305. Tel: 661-871-9190; Fax: 661-873-7286.
Catechesis/Religious Program—Students 364.

BISHOP, INYO CO., OUR LADY OF PERPETUAL HELP (1947) Rev. John Gracey.
Res.: 849 N. Home St., 93514. Tel: 760-872-7231; Fax: 760-873-8862. Email: olph2@verizon.net. Web: olphbishop.com.
Catechesis/Religious Program—Tel: 760-873-8862. Email: davidbruce.olph@verizon.net. Students 109.
Mission—St. Stephen 461 S. Main St., Big Pine, Inyo Co. 93513. Tel: 760-872-7231.

BUTTONWILLOW, KERN CO., ST. MARY (1941) Rev. Msgr. Craig F. Harrison, Admin.; Rev. Lucas Azpericueta, Sacramental Priest (Retired).
Res.: 420 N. Main St., Box 875, 93206. Tel: 661-764-5486.
Catechesis/Religious Program—Students 79.

CALIFORNIA CITY, KERN CO., OUR LADY OF LOURDES (1982) Rev. Kris Sorenson, Admin.
Catechesis/Religious Program—Students 60.
Mission—St. Joseph (1969) P.O. Box 2060, Kern Co. 93504.

CHOWCHILLA, MADERA CO., ST. COLUMBA (1921) [JC] Rev. Angel Sotelo.
Res.: 213 Orange Ave., 93610. Tel: 559-665-3376.
Catechesis/Religious Program—Tel: 559-665-5104. Students 310.
Mission—St. George El Nido, 95317.

CLOVIS, FRESNO CO., OUR LADY OF PERPETUAL HELP (1929) Revs. Robert Borges; Adrian Kim, C.P., Parochial Vicar; Craig Plunkett, Parochial Vicar; Deacon Gary Stevens.
Res.: 929 Harvard Ave., 93612. Tel: 559-299-4270; Fax: 559-299-7126. Web: olphclovis.org.
Church: Ninth & DeWitt, 93612.
School—(Grades K-8), 886 DeWitt, 93612. Tel: 559-299-7504; Fax: 559-299-4627. Web: olphschool-.net. Patrick Dodd, Prin. Immaculate Conception Sisters 3; Lay Teachers 8; Students 187.
Catechesis/Religious Program—(Grades K-8) Students 1,079.
Mission—Infant Jesus of Prague 32054 Whispering Spring Rd., Tollhouse, Fresno Co. 93667. Tel: 559-855-4659; Fax: 559-855-4659. Mailing Address: P.O. Box 357, Prather, 93651.

COALINGA, FRESNO CO., ST. PAUL THE APOSTLE (1907) [JC] Rev. Viktor Perez, O.F.M.Conv.; Bro. Andres Amador, O.F.M.Conv.
Res.: 637 Sunset St., P.O. Box 812, 93210. Tel: 559-935-1872; Fax: 559-935-3763.
Catechesis/Religious Program—Students 52.

CORCORAN, KINGS CO., OUR LADY OF LOURDES (1939) Rev. Alfredo Arias.
Res.: 1404 Hanna, 93212. Tel: 559-992-4414; Fax: 559-992-2512. Email: ourladyoflourdescorcoran@comcast.net.
Catechesis/Religious Program—Tel: 559-992-4698. Students 470.
Mission—Sacred Heart 3860 Ave. 54, Alpaugh, Tulare Co. 93201. Tel: 559-949-8352.

CUTLER, TULARE CO., ST. MARY (1953) Rev. Israel Avila.
Res.: 12588 Avenue 407, 93615. Tel: 559-528-3566.
Catechesis/Religious Program—Tel: 559-528-3077; Fax: 559-528-3535. Students 400.

DEL REY, FRESNO CO., ST. KATHERINE (1956), (Quasi-parish included with St. Mary, Sanger). Revs. Jupeter Quinto, R.C.J.; Philip Puntrello, R.C.J., Parochial Vicar; Renato Panlasigui, R.C.J.; Deacon John Biedermann.
Res.: 828 "O" St., P.O. Box 335, Sanger, 93657. Tel: 559-888-2889; 559-875-2025; Fax: 559-875-2618. Email: stmarysanger@msn.com.
Catechesis/Religious Program—Students 134.

DELANO, KERN CO.

1—ST. MARY OF THE MIRACULOUS MEDAL (1920) Rev. Rick Fierros.
Res.: 916 Lexington St., 93215. Tel: 661-725-8456; Fax: 661-725-8485.
Catechesis/Religious Program—Tel: 661-725-9041. Students 615.
Mission—St. Vincent 1732 11th Ave., Richgrove, Tulare Co. 93215.

2—OUR LADY OF GUADALUPE (1954) Revs. Javier Alvarez, O.F.M.; Ervan Beers, O.F.M.
Res.: 1015 Clinton St., 93215. Tel: 661-725-9087; 661-725-9115; Fax: 661-725-7129.
Catechesis/Religious Program—Tel: 661-725-2777. Students 616.

DINUBA, TULARE CO., ST. CATHERINE OF SIENA (1948) Rev. Raul Diaz.
Res.: 356 N. Villa Ave., 93618. Tel: 559-591-0931; Fax: 559-591-2965.
Catechesis/Religious Program—Tel: 559-591-2988. Laura Rico, D.R.E. Students 619.

DOS PALOS, MERCED CO., SACRED HEART (1924) Rev. Robert R. Vanoncini; Deacon David Mumby.
Res.: 1650 Lucerne, 93620-2623. Tel: 209-392-2724; Fax: 209-392-1037. Email: sacredheartchurch1655@comcast.net.
Church: 1655 Lucerne Ave., 93620-2623.
Catechesis/Religious Program—Students 400.

EARLIMART, TULARE CO., ST. JUDE THADDEUS (1968) Rev. Pastor Hermosillo Lomeli, M.S.C.
Mailing Address: 1270 E. Washington Ave., P.O. Box 12187, 93219. Tel: 661-849-3170; Fax: 661-849-0704.
Res.: 964 Dove St., 93219. Tel: 661-849-2858.
Catechesis/Religious Program—Students 95.

EASTON , FRESNO CO., THE CATHOLIC COMMUNITY OF ST. JUDE AND OUR LADY OF THE ASSUMPTION (1967) Rev. Jerry Amerando.
208 W. Jefferson, 93706. Tel: 559-485-3870; Fax: 559-485-3880. Email: stjudechurch@attitude.com.
Catechesis/Religious Program—Students 213.
Mission—Our Lady of the Assumption 13540 S. Henderson Ave., Caruthers, Fresno Co. 93609. Tel: 559-864-8224; Fax: 559-864-3656. P.O. Box 388, Caruthers, 93609-0388.

EXETER, TULARE CO., SACRED HEART (1950) Rev. Juan Manuel Flores.
Res.: 417 North E St., 93221. Tel: 559-592-2465; Fax: 559-592-6075.
Catechesis/Religious Program—Tel: 559-592-1020. Students 714.
Mission—St. Anthony of Egypt 521 W. Visalia Rd., Farmersville, Tulare Co. 93223. Tel: 559-747-0234 (Religious Educ. Office).

FIREBAUGH, FRESNO CO., ST. JOSEPH (1950) Rev. Guillermo Preciado, Admin.
Res.: 1900 Saipan, 93622.
Church: 1558 12th St., 93622. Tel: 559-659-2225; Fax: 559-659-0408.
Catechesis/Religious Program—Tel: 559-659-2943. Students 180.

FOWLER, FRESNO CO., ST. LUCY 1st Church (1943); 2nd Church (1965) Rev. John Theophane, Admin.
Res.: 512 S. 5th, 93625. Tel: 559-834-2624; Fax: 559-834-6814. Email: stlucyparish@hotmail.com.
Catechesis/Religious Program—Students 206.

FRAZIER PARK, KERN CO., OUR LADY OF THE SNOWS MISSION (1968), (Quasi-parish) Rev. Thomas O'Neill.
7115 Lakewood Dr. Lake of the Woods, 93225. Tel: 661-245-3741; Fax: 661-245-1680.
Catechesis/Religious Program—Students 37.

GOSHEN, TULARE CO., ST. THOMAS THE APOSTLE (1963) [CEM] Rev. Msgr. Raymond C. Dreiling; Revs. Rod L. Craig; Carlos Serrano; John Bosco Prasit Kruesuwan; Jose Luis Varo (Retired); Rev. Msgr. Anthony Janelli (Retired); Deacons Julian Ponce; Paul Hernandez; James Rooney, (Retired).
Mailing Address: 506 N. Garden St., Visalia, 93291.
6735 Ave. 308, 93227. Tel: 559-734-9522; Fax: 559-734-3435.
Catechesis/Religious Program—Tel: 559-553-2450. Students 137.

GUSTINE, MERCED CO., SHRINE OF OUR LADY OF MIRACLES (1919) Rev. Leonard J. Trindade.
Res.: 370 Linden Ave., 95322. Tel: 209-854-6692; Fax: 209-854-1344.
School—(Grades PreK-8) Tel: 209-854-3180; Fax: 209-854-3961. Adrienne Lopes, Admin. Lay Teachers 8; Students 114.
Preschool—Tel: 209-854-3180. Terri Amarante, Dir. Students 29.
Catechesis/Religious Program—Tel: 209-854-2834. Nancy Corgiat, D.R.E. Students 324.

HANFORD, KINGS CO.

1—ST. BRIGID (1886) [CEM] Rev. Michael Moore; Deacons Anthony Silveira; John Sousa.
Office & Mailing Address: 200 E. Florinda, 93230. Tel: 559-582-2533; Fax: 559-582-9193. Email: stbrigid@sierratel.com.
School—St. Rose-McCarthy Memorial School, (Grades K-8), 1000 N. Harris St., 93230. Tel: 559-584-5218; Fax: 559-584-0899. Web: www-.strosemccarthy.org. Michael Mendoza, Prin. Religious Teachers 1; Lay Teachers 10; Students 167.
Catechesis/Religious Program—Tel: 559-583-6563; Fax: 559-582-9193. Students 405.

2—IMMACULATE HEART OF MARY (1948) Rev. Stephen M. Devine.
Res.: 10355 Hanford Armona Rd., 93230. Tel: 559-584-8576; Fax: 559-584-0436.
Catechesis/Religious Program—Tel: 559-582-5688. Students 444.

HILMAR, MERCED CO., HOLY ROSARY (1948) Rev. Hilary Silva.
Res.: 8471 Cypress, P.O. Box 429, 95324. Tel: 209-667-8961; Fax: 209-667-5239.
Catechesis/Religious Program—Tel: 209-632-7163. Students 280.
Mission—St. Mary 2809 Railroad, Stevinson, Merced Co. 95374.

HURON, FRESNO CO., ST. FRANCES CABRINI (1961) Revs. Juan Pineda Lira, M.S.C.; Raul Silva Arredondo.
Res.: 36986 Los Angeles St., P.O. Box 939, 93234. Tel: 559-945-2507; Fax: 559-945-2630. Email: s.cabrini@att.net.
Catechesis/Religious Program—Students 160.

KERMAN, FRESNO CO., ST. PATRICK (1953) Revs. David Reed; Marcelinus Okenedo, S.M.M.M.
Mailing Address: 567 S. 6th St., P.O. Box 375, 93630. Tel: 559-846-8190; Fax: 559-846-7705.
Res.: 567 S. Sixth St., 93630.
Catechesis/Religious Program—Students 460.

KINGSBURG, FRESNO CO., HOLY FAMILY (1950) [JC] Rev. Gregory J. Beaumont.
Res.: 1301 Smith St., P.O. Box 798, 93631-0798. Tel: 559-897-5953; Fax: 559-897-8599.
Church: 1700 Lewis St., 93631.
Catechesis/Religious Program—Students 423.
Mission—Santa Cruz 5626 Ave. 378, London, Tulare Co. 93631.
Mission—St. John the Baptist Educational Center 4204 Merritt Dr., Traver, Tulare Co. 93673.

LAMONT, KERN CO., ST. AUGUSTINE (1962) Rev. John Schmoll, O.S.B. oblate.
Res.: 10601 Myrtle Ave., 93241-2111. Tel: 661-845-0003; Fax: 661-845-0259.
Catechesis/Religious Program—Tel: 661-845-3622. Students 877.

LATON, FRESNO CO., SHRINE OF OUR LADY OF FATIMA (1953) Rev. Richard Smith; Deacon Jesus Hernandez.
Res.: P.O. Box 119, 93242. Tel: 559-923-4935; Fax: 559-923-2284.
Catechesis/Religious Program—Tel: 559-923-3715. Students 208.

LEMOORE, KINGS CO., ST. PETER PRINCE OF APOSTLES (1912) Rev. Msgr. John Coelho-Harguindeguy; Rev. Isaque Meneses, Parochial Vicar; Deacon Joseph Biangone.
870 N. Lemoore Ave., 93245. Tel: 559-924-2562; Fax: 559-924-5727. Email: stpeters@lemoorenet.net.
Res.: 951 Murphy Dr., 93245.
School—(Grades K-8), 884 N. Lemoore Ave., 93245. Tel: 559-924-3424; Fax: 559-924-7848. Email: miqprince@lemoorenet.com. Web: miqschool.com. Sr. Beena Joseph, C.S.S.T., Prin. Carmelite Sisters of St. Teresa 7; Lay Teachers 6; Students 183.
Catechesis/Religious Program—Tel: 559-924-2826. Shirley Roberts, D.R.E. Students 495.
Mission—St. Joseph 19300 Empire St., Stratford, 93266. Tel: 559-924-2562.
Mission—Santa Rosa [CEM] 16111 Alkaki, Tache Indian Reservation, Kings Co. 93245.

LINDSAY, TULARE CO., SACRED HEART (1925) Rev. Kenneth Bozzo.
Res.: 217 Lindero Ave., 93247-2623. Tel: 559-562-4008; Fax: 559-562-5511. Email: shlindsay@clear.net.
Catechesis/Religious Program—Students 460.
Mission—St. Anthony Church 21631 Brooks Ave., Tonyville, Tulare Co. 93247.
Mission—St. James Catholic Church 19752 Guthrie Rd., P.O. Box 4010, Strathmore, Tulare Co. 93267. Tel: 559-568-0435.
Station—Plainview, Santa Cruz Plainview.

LIVINGSTON, MERCED CO., ST. JUDE THADDEUS (1937) Rev. Msgr. Harvey Fonseca.
Office: 330 Franci St., 95334. Tel: 209-394-7512;

Fax: 209-394-3089.
Catechesis/Religious Program—Tel: 209-394-7516. Rosa Maria Mercado, D.R.E. Students 711.
Mission—Blessed Teresa of Calcutta P.O. Box 86, Delhi, Merced Co. 95315.

LONE PINE, INYO CO., SANTA ROSA (1919) Rev. Douglas Walker.
Res.: P.O. Box 246, 93545. Tel: 760-876-4350.
Catechesis/Religious Program—Students 12.
Mission—St. John the Baptist Shoshone-Tecopa.
Mission—St. Vivian Independence, Inyo Co.
Station— Death Valley.
Station— Olancha.

LOS BANOS, MERCED CO., ST. JOSEPH (1905) Revs. Robert E. Gamel; Guadalupe Rios, Parochial Vicar; Deacon Leon Miller.
Res.: 1516 Center Ave., 93635. Tel: 209-826-4246; Fax: 209-827-3457. Email: stjosephlb@sbcglobal.net.
School—Our Lady of Fatima, (Grades PreK-8), 1625 Center Ave., 93635. Tel: 209-826-2709; Fax: 209-826-7320. Email: jsuter@olfdof.org. Web: olfdof.org. Jeanette Suter, Prin. Lay Teachers 16; Students 196.
Catechesis/Religious Program—Tel: 209-826-1512. Students 624.

MADERA, MADERA CO., ST. JOACHIM (1881) Revs. Carlos Esquivel, O.S.J.; Gustavo Lopez, O.S.J.; George Paliyathara, O.S.J., Parochial Vicar.
Res.: 401 W. Fifth St., 93637. Tel: 559-673-3290; Fax: 559-673-6471. Email: church@sjoachim.org. Web: sjoachim.org.
School—(Grades K-8), 310 N. I St., 93637. Tel: 559-674-7628; Fax: 559-674-8770. Email: school@sjoachim.org. Thomas Spencer, Prin. Immaculate Conception Sisters 2; Lay Teachers 10; Students 284.
Catechesis/Religious Program—Tel: 559-674-5871. Students 1,500.
Convent—310 N. "J" St., 93637. Tel: 559-674-4085. Sisters of the Immaculate Conception (RCM)
Mission—St. Agnes 7308 Hwy. 145, Madera Co. 93637.
Mission—St. Anne Raymond-Knowles, Raymond, Madera Co. 93653.

MARIPOSA, MARIPOSA CO., ST. JOSEPH (1863) [CEM 3] Rev. Stephen C. Bulfer.
Mailing Address: P.O. Box 215, 95338-0215. Tel: 209-966-2522; Fax: 209-966-2522. Email: sjccoff@yahoo.com.
Res.: 4985 Bullion St., 95338.
Catechesis/Religious Program—Students 17.
Mission—St. Catherine of Siena Hornitos, Mariposa Co.

MCFARLAND, KERN CO., ST. ELIZABETH (1966) Rev. Antero Sanchez, M.S.C.
Res.: 835 E. Perkins, 93250. Tel: 661-792-3225; Fax: 661-792-5645.
Catechesis/Religious Program—Tel: 661-792-3429. Esperanza Melendez, D.R.E. Students 461.

MENDOTA, FRESNO CO., OUR LADY OF GUADALUPE (1953) Rev. Gaspar Bautista.
Res.: P.O. Box 248, 93640. Tel: 559-655-3631; 559-655-4237; Fax: 559-655-3785. Email: padregaspar@yahoo.com.
Catechesis/Religious Program—Students 235.
Mission—Our Lady of Lourdes 161015 S. Derrick, Three Rocks, Fresno Co. 93608. Tel: 559-829-3358.

MERCED, MERCED CO.

1—OUR LADY OF MERCY/ST. PATRICK'S (1868) [JC] Rev. Msgr. Patrick Joseph McCormick; Revs. Leocadio Morales, Parochial Vicar; Michael Cox, Parochial Vicar; Deacons Joseph Smith; Charles Reyburn; Jose Morales; Rich Brown.
(1968) St. Patrick Church & Mailing Address: 671 E. Yosemite, 95340. Tel: 209-383-3924; 209-383-3930 (Mass recording); Fax: 209-723-6510. Email: info@olmstpatrick.org. Web: olmstpatrick.org.
(1867) Our Lady of Mercy: 459 W. 21st St., 95340.
Res.: 3700 Ithaca Ct., 95340.
School—Our Lady of Mercy Elementary, (Grades PreSchool-8), 1400 E. 27th St., 95340. Tel: 209-722-7496; Fax: 209-722-7532. Email: info@olmlancers.com. Web: www.olmlancers.com. Mrs. Judy Blackburn, Prin. Lay Teachers 13; K-8 274; Pre-School 96.
Preschool—Tel: 209-722-6657. Jill Serpa, Vice Prin.
Catechesis/Religious Program—Tel: 209-723-8888; Fax: 209-723-8888. Debbie Rosa, D.R.E. Students 601.

2—SACRED HEART (1945) Rev. Jose de Jesus Reynaga.
Res.: 519 W. 12th St., 95340. Tel: 209-383-6604; Fax: 209-383-6608. Email: sacredheart1merced@sbcglobal.net. Web: jeaf.com/shc.
Catechesis/Religious Program—Tel: 209-383-1528; Fax: 209-383-0187. Ms. Rocio Maciel, D.R.E. Students 596.

OAKHURST, MADERA CO., OUR LADY OF THE SIERRA (1999) Rev. Jean-Michael Lastiri; Deacon Ernie Molloy.
P.O. Box 2499, 93644.
Res.: 49552 Pierce Dr., 93644. Tel: 559-642-3452; Fax: 559-642-4655. Email: olsparish@sti.net. Web: olscatholic.org.
Catechesis/Religious Program—Students 77.
Mission—St. Joseph the Worker 56522 Rd. 200, North Fork, Madera Co. 93643.
Mission—St. Dominic Savio (1961) 40077 Rd. 222, Bass Lake, Madera Co. 93604.

ORANGE COVE, FRESNO CO., ST. ISIDORE THE FARMER (1978) Rev. David Enriquez.
Mailing Address & Res.: 480 Adams Ave., 93646. Tel: 559-626-4943; Fax: 559-626-4648. Email: stisidore3802@sbcglobal.net.
Catechesis/Religious Program—Tel: 559-626-2420. Students 195.
Mission—St. Rita 30673 George Smith Rd., Squaw Valley, Fresno Co. 93675.

PARLIER, FRESNO CO., OUR LADY OF SORROWS (1965) Rev. Jose Luis Rico.
Res.: 830 Tulare St., 93648. Tel: 559-646-2161; Fax: 559-646-9511.
Catechesis/Religious Program—Students 262.

PLANADA, MERCED CO., SACRED HEART (1966) [JC] Rev. Msgr. Patrick Joseph McCormick, Admin.; Revs. Leocadio Morales, Parochial Vicar; Michael Cox, Parochial Vicar; Deacons Javier Higareda; Higinio Yanez.
Res.: 9360 E. Amistad St., P.O. Box 278, 95365. Tel: 209-382-0459; Fax: 209-382-0814. Email: sacredheartplanada@sbcglobal.net.
Catechesis/Religious Program—9317 Amistad St., P.O. Box 278, 95365. Students 142.
Mission—Our Lady of Lourdes 13145 Le Grand Rd., LeGrand, Merced Co. 95333.

PORTERVILLE, TULARE CO., ST. ANNE (1896) Rev. Msgrs. Scott Daugherty; Ronald Royer (Retired); Rev. David Bustamante; Deacon James Dieterle.
Res.: 378 N. F St., 93257. Tel: 559-784-2800; Fax: 559-784-4338. Email: stannes@ocsnet.net. Web: stannesparish.com.
School—(Grades PreK-8), 385 N. F St., 93257. Tel: 559-784-4096. Sr. Carmen Fernandez, R.A.D., Prin. Sisters of the Love of God 3; Lay Teachers 7; Students 179.
Preschool—331 F St., 93257. Tel: 559-781-8614. Rhonda Dotters, Dir.
Catechesis/Religious Program—Students 1,301.
Mission—Mater Dolorosa Tule Indian Reservation, Tulare Co. Tel: 559-784-2800.
Mission—Blessed Miguel Agustin Pro 9120 Rd. 236, Terra Bella, Tulare Co. 93270.
Station—Springville, Community Church 35725 Hwy. 190, Springville, 93265.

REEDLEY, FRESNO CO., ST. ANTHONY OF PADUA (1906) Rev. Msgr. John Esquivel; Rev. Raul Sanchez.
Res.: 1060 F. St., 93654. Tel: 559-638-2012; Fax: 559-638-8211. Email: stanthonychurch_reedley@comcast.net.
LaSalle Preschool/Child Care Center—Tel: 559-638-2621; Fax: 559-638-5542. Email: hannibalmarylucy@yahoo.com. Web: www.stlasalle-.com. Sr. Lucy Cassarino, F.D.Z., Prin., Preschool & School.
School—St. La Salle Grammar School, (Grades PreK-8), 404 E. Manning Ave., 93654. Tel: 559-638-2621; Fax: 559-638-5542. Sr. Lucy Cassarino, F.D.Z., Prin. Sisters 3; Lay Teachers 11; Students 303.
Catechesis/Religious Program—Tel: 559-638-5608. Students 613.

RIDGECREST, KERN CO., ST. ANN (1965) [JC] Rev. Paul Kado.
Res.: 446 W. Church St., P.O. Box 127, 93556. Tel: 760-375-2110; Fax: 760-375-8899. Web: parishofsaintann.org.
School—(Grades K-8) Tel: 760-375-4713. Email: school@parishofsaintann.org. Mary Little, Prin. Lay Teachers 11; Students 170.
Catechesis/Religious Program—Students 205.
Mission—Santa Barbara 72 Lexington Ave., Randsburg, Kern Co. 93554.

RIVERDALE, FRESNO CO., ST. ANN (1928) [JC] Rev. Victor Piansay.
Res.: 3047 W. Mt. Whitney, P.O. Box 335, 93656. Tel: 559-867-3035.
Catechesis/Religious Program—Students 104.
Mission—Holy Family Chapel c/o St. Ann, Riverdale Ca. 93656, Diener Ranch At Five Points, Fresno Co.

ROSAMOND, KERN CO., ST. MARY OF THE DESERT (1999) Rev. Patrick Geo, Admin.
Mailing Address: 3100 Fifteenth St. W., 93560. Tel: 661-256-4505; Fax: 661-256-7127. Email: st.mary3100@att.net.
Catechesis/Religious Program—Students 186.
Mission—St. Francis of Assisi Church 15382 Meyer Rd., Mojave, 93501.

SANGER, FRESNO CO., ST. MARY (1922) [JC] Revs. Jupeter Quinto, R.C.J.; Philip Puntrello, R.C.J.; Deacon John Biedermann. In Res., Revs. Salvatore Ciranni, R.C.J. (Retired); Renato Panlasigui, R.C.J.
Res.: 828 O St., P.O. Box 335, 93657. Tel: 559-875-2025; Fax: 559-875-1281. Email: stmarysanger@verizon.net.
Catechesis/Religious Program—2590 North Ave., 93657. Tel: 559-875-6340; Fax: 559-875-6340. Students 526.

SELMA, FRESNO CO., ST. JOSEPH (1913) Rev. Efrain Martinez; Deacon Ed Harmon III.
Res.: 2441 Dockery Ave., 93662. Tel: 559-896-1052; Fax: 559-896-3975.
Catechesis/Religious Program—Tel: 559-896-2620. Students 501.

SHAFTER, KERN CO., ST. THERESE (1952) Rev. Pedro Umana, O.F.M.
Res.: 300 W. Lerdo, P.O. Box 1448, 93263. Tel: 661-746-4471; Fax: 661-746-0945.
Catechesis/Religious Program—Students 170.

TAFT, KERN CO., ST. MARY (1918), Under the administration of St. Francis of Assisi, Bakersfield. Rev. Msgr. Craig F. Harrison, Admin.
Res.: 110 E. Woodrow St., 93268. Tel: 661-765-4292.
Catechesis/Religious Program—Students 110.

TEHACHAPI, KERN CO., ST. MALACHY (1887) Rev. Joel Davadilla.
Res.: 407 W. "E" St., 93561-1642. Tel: 661-822-3060; Fax: 661-822-3159.
Catechesis/Religious Program—Tel: 661-822-6327. Students 400.

TIPTON, TULARE CO., ST. JOHN THE EVANGELIST (1945) Rev. Miguel Campos.
Res.: 232 S. Adam Rd., 93272. Tel: 559-752-4544; Fax: 559-752-4313. Email: st.john93272@parishworld.net.
Catechesis/Religious Program—Tel: 559-752-4313. Students 338.
Mission—St. Francis of Assisi 16410 Ave. 168, Woodville, Tulare Co. 93258. Tel: 559-688-8412.
Station—Our Lady of the Assumption Pixley.

TRANQUILLITY, FRESNO CO., ST. PAUL (1924) Revs. David Reed; Marcelinus Okenedo, S.M.M.M., Parochial Vicar.
Res.: 25592 Doughty St., 93668. Tel: 559-698-7429; Fax: 559-698-1059.
Catechesis/Religious Program—Tel: 559-693-4320. Students 220.
Mission—St. Vincent de Paul San Joaquin, Fresno Co.

TULARE, TULARE CO.

1—ST. ALOYSIUS (1905) Rev. Msgrs. Richard Urizalqui; Raul Marta.
Res.: 125 E. Pleasant Ave., 93274. Tel: 559-688-1796; 559-688-1797; Fax: 559-688-0948.
School—(Grades K-8) Tel: 559-686-6250; Fax: 559-686-0479. Joel Nunes, Prin. Lay Teachers 11; Students 195.
Catechesis/Religious Program—Tel: 559-688-8644. Students 441.

2—ST. RITA (1967) Rev. Ignacio Villafan.
Res.: 954 S. O St., 93274. Tel: 559-686-3847; Fax: 559-686-9672.
Catechesis/Religious Program—Tel: 559-686-0802. Students 609.

VISALIA, TULARE CO.

1—HOLY FAMILY (1950) Rev. Msgr. Raymond C. Dreiling; Revs. Rod L. Craig; Carlos Serrano; John Bosco Prasit Kruesuwan; Jose Luis Varo (Retired); Rev. Msgr. Anthony Janelli (Retired); Deacons Paul Hernandez; Julian Ponce; James Rooney, (Retired); Henry Medina.
506 N. Garden St., 93291. Res.: 1908 N. Court St., 93291. Tel: 559-734-9522; Fax: 559-734-3435. Email: rparlier@ccov.org.
Catechesis/Religious Program—Tel: 559-732-9651. Irma Gaitan, C.R.E. Students 702.

2—ST. MARY (1861) Rev. Msgr. Raymond C. Dreiling; Revs. Rod L. Craig; Carlos Serrano; John Bosco Prasit Kruesuwan; Jose Luis Varo (Retired); Rev. Msgr. Anthony Janelli (Retired); Deacons Ken Ramage; Rick Miller; Doug Pingel; Charles Culbreth, Dir., Music.
Res.: 506 N. Garden St., 93291. Tel: 559-734-9522; Fax: 559-734-3435. Web: tccov.org.
School—George McCann Memorial School, (Grades PreK-8), 200 E. Race St., 93291. Tel: 559-732-5831; Fax: 559-741-1562. Web: gmccatholicschool.org. Sheila Rast, Prin. Lay Teachers 10; Students 230.
Catechesis/Religious Program—Tel: 559-733-3929; Fax: 559-733-1255. Mrs. Joan Bell, D.R.E.; Ruben Cabatic, Youth Min. Students 901.
Bethlehem Center— (1968) 1638 N. Dinuba Blvd., 93291. Tel: 559-734-1572; Fax: 559-734-4921.

WASCO, KERN CO., ST. JOHN THE EVANGELIST (1913) Rev. John P. Fluetsch.
Res.: 1300 Ninth Pl., 93280. Tel: 661-758-6688; Fax: 661-758-7751.

Catechesis/Religious Program—(Family Catechesis) Students 292.
Mission—Nuestra Senora de la Paz Lost Hills. 14846 Hwy. 33, Blackwell's Corner, Kern Co. 93249.

WOFFORD HEIGHTS, KERN CO., ST. JUDE (1969) Rev. Anthony Iromenu, Admin.; Deacon James Dewey. Mailing Address: P.O. Box 1190, 93285.
Res.: 86 Nellie Dent Dr., 93285. Tel: 760-376-2416; Fax: 760-376-2253.
Catechesis/Religious Program—Students 28.
Station—

WOODLAKE, TULARE CO., ST. FRANCES CABRINI (1963) Rev. Jesse C. Venzor.
Res.: 599 N. Valencia Blvd., P.O. Box 459, 93286. Tel: 559-564-2647; Fax: 559-564-2647.
Catechesis/Religious Program—Students 365.
Mission—St. Clair Alta Acres Dr., Three Rivers, Tulare Co. 93271.
Mission—San Felipe de Jesus 32809 Rd. 159, Ivanhoe, Tulare Co. 93235.

YOSEMITE NATIONAL PARK, MARIPOSA CO., OUR LADY OF THE SNOWS (1963), Under the administration of Our Lady of the Sierra, Oakhurst.
Catechesis/Religious Program—

Chaplains of Public Institutions

FRESNO. *Children's Hospital Central California*, Tel: 559-353-5308. Rev. Ricardo Magdaleno, Chap.
Community Medical Center, Clovis, Tel: 559-324-4000. Rev. Adrian Kim, C.P., Chap.
Community Regional Medical Center, Tel: 559-459-6490; 559-459-6000. Revs. Dominic Savio Rajappa, Chap., (Part-time), Victor T. Dinh, Chap.
Kaiser Permanente Medical Center. Tel: 559-448-4500. Rev. Ricardo Magdaleno, Chap.
Veterans Administration Medical Center, 3636 N. First St., 93726. Tel: 559-225-6100, Ext. 5351. Revs. Dominic Savio Rajappa, Chap., (Part-time), Victor T. Dinh, Chap.

AVENAL. *Avenal State Prison*, Tel: 559-386-0587, Ext. 6384. Rodney Ornellas, Chap.

BAKERSFIELD. *Bakersfield Memorial Hospital & San Joaquin Community Hospital*, Tel: 661-237-4734.

CHOWCHILLA. *Department of Corrections, Central California Women's Facility*, P.O. Box 1501, 93610-1501. Tel: 559-665-5531, Ext. 7232. Sr. Mary Anne DiVicenzo, C.S.J., Chap.
Valley State Prison for Women, P.O. Box 92, 93610-0092. Tel: 559-665-6100, Ext. 6060. Danilo Grajales, Chap.

COALINGA. *Coalinga State Hospital*, Tel: 559-935-4300. Bro. Andres Amador, O.F.M.Conv.
Pleasant Valley State Prison, P.O. Box 8500, 93210-8500. Tel: 559-935-4900, Ext. 6777. Vacant, Chap.

CORCORAN. *California State Prison*, P.O. Box 8800, 93212. Tel: 559-992-8800, Ext. 6412.
California Substance Abuse Treatment Facility & State Prison - Corcoran, P.O. Box 7100, 93212-7100. Tel: 559-992-7100, Ext. 7037. Rosa Maria Guembe, Chap., Jose Ojeda, Chap.

DELANO. *Kern Valley State Prison*, P.O. Box 6000, 93216-6000. Tel: 661-721-6300. Rev. Francisco Diaz, Chap.
North Kern State Prison, P.O. Box 567, 93216-0567. Tel: 661-721-2345, Ext. 6861. Vacant, Chap.

PORTERVILLE. *Developmental Center*, P.O. Box 2000, 93258-2000. Tel: 559-782-2402, Ext. 2401. Sr. Marion Morua, M.C.D.P. Tel: 559-782-2401.

TEHACHAPI. *California Correctional Institution*, P.O. Box 1031, 93581-1031. Tel: 661-822-4402, Ext. 4387. Deacon Clyde Davis, Chap.

WASCO. *State Prison*, P.O. Box 8800, 93280-8800. Tel: 661-758-8400, Ext. 5649. Rev. Daniel Bringas, Chap.

On Special Assignment:
Rev. Msgrs.—
Cotta, Myron J., Diocesan Admin., 1550 N. Fresno St., 93703-3788.
Griesbach, John, St. Anthony Retreat Center, Dir.
Petersen, E. James, Vice Chancellor (Retired)
Revs.—
Avila, Dan, Vocation Dir.
Burchfield, Michael A., J.C.L., Asst. Tribunal Dir.
del Angel, Jesus, J.C.L., Adjutant Judicial Vicar
Norris, David J., D.Min., Coord. Hospital & Chaplaincy Ministry

On Duty Outside the Diocese:
Revs.—
Congdon, John, Military Chap.
Okorie, Onyema, Military Chap.

Absent on Sick Leave:
Revs.—
Baca, Joseph
Bray, Kevin
Madera, Juan

Retired:
Rev. Msgrs.—
Bezunartea, Herman O.
Cleary, Kevin
Herrero, Nicolas
Janelli, Anthony
Logan, James T.
Lopez, Daniel
Meyer, Gilbert
Minhoto, Walter F.
O'Friel, John
Petersen, E. James
Pointek, Francis J.
Poschen, Ed
Revs.—
Alvernaz, Dennis
Azpericueta, Lucas
Burns, John P.
Casale, Charles B.
Duffy, Raymond
Flickinger, Don D.
Gonzalez, Angel
Gonzalez, Antonio
Heffernan, Joseph A.
Kudilil, James
Montiel, Jose
Pascual, Manuel
Persinger, Patrick
Raffel, Godfrey
Shenoy, Leslie
Simeone, Francis
Varo, Jose Luis
Vega, Jose Luis

INSTITUTIONS LOCATED IN THE DIOCESE

[A] HIGH SCHOOLS, DIOCESAN

FRESNO. *San Joaquin Memorial High School* (1945) 1406 N. Fresno St., 93703-3789. Tel: 559-268-9251; Fax: 559-268-1351. Web: www.sjmhs.org. Edward R. Borges, Prin.; Rev. David J. Norris, D.Min., Rector. Lay Teachers 35; Students 555.

BAKERSFIELD. *Garces Memorial High School* (1947) 2800 Loma Linda Dr., 93305. Tel: 661-327-2578; Fax: 661-327-5427. Email: kbears@garces.org. Web: www.garces.org. Kathleen Bears, Prin.; Susan Rizo, Dir. Campus Ministry; Rev. James LaCasse, S.J., Chap.; Rev. Msgr. Michael Braun, Rector; Kim Harper, Librarian. Priests 1; Lay Teachers 45; Students 622.

[B] GENERAL HOSPITALS

FRESNO. *Saint Agnes Medical Center* (1929) 1303 E. Herndon, 93720. Tel: 559-450-3000; Fax: 559-450-2143. Email: nancy.hollingsworth@samc.com. Web: www.samc.com. James N. Leonard, CEO; Craig Saladino, Chm., Bd. of Trustees. Trinity Health. Sisters 5; Nurses 908; Bed Capacity 436; Patients Assisted Annually 328,279; Total Staff 2,764.
Professional Office Corporation, Saint Agnes Medical Center, 1303 E. Herndon Ave., 93720. Tel: 559-449-3000; Fax: 559-449-2143. Nancy Hollingsworth, CEO; Craig Saladino, Chm. P.O.C. Bd.

BAKERSFIELD. *Mercy Hospital dba Catholic Healthcare West* (1910) Mercy Southwest is a campus of Mercy Hospital., 2215 Truxtun Ave., 93301. Tel: 661-632-5000; Fax: 661-327-2592. Web: www.mercybakersfield.org. Russell V. Judd, Pres. Sponsored by Sisters of Mercy of the Americas West Midwest Community Patients Assisted Annually 150,023; Bed Capacity 222; Sisters 4; Total Staff 1,512.
Mercy Southwest Hospital dba Catholic Healthcare West 400 Old River Rd., 93311. Tel: 661-663-6000; Fax: 661-663-6570. Web: mercybakersfield.org.
Mercy Foundation, Bakersfield dba Friends of Mercy Foundation 2215 Truxtun Ave., 93302. Tel: 661-663-6700; Fax: 661-663-6755. Web: mercybakersfield.org. Stephanie Weber, Vice Pres., Fund Devel.

MERCED. *Mercy Medical Center dba Catholic Healthcare West* (1923) 333 Mercy Ave., 95340. Tel: 209-564-5000; Fax: 209-564-5096. Web: mercymercedcares.org. David Dunham, Pres. Sponsored by the Dominican Sisters of St. Catherine of Siena of Kenosha, Wisconsin. Bed Capacity 186; Staff 1,361; Patients Assisted Annually 152,443.

[C] HOMES FOR INVALID AND AGED

FRESNO. *Nazareth House*, 2121 N. First St., 93703. Tel: 559-237-2257; Fax: 559-237-1958. Email: Rosemary@nazarethfresno.org. Rosemary O'Neill, Admin. Sisters of Nazareth of Fresno Inc. 3; Residential Care/Assisted Living 100; Total Staff 73.

LOS BANOS. *New Bethany Residential Care and Skilled Nursing Community*, 1441 Berkeley Dr., 93635. Tel: 209-827-8933; Fax: 209-827-8989. Email: jdf2003@yahoo.com. Web: www.newbethanyfhic.org. Sisters Helen Petrovich, F.H.I.C., Dir. Nurses; Julia Fonseca, F.H.I.C., Pres.; Lucinda Fonseca, F.H.I.C., Skilled Nursing Admin.; Rev. Barry Brunsman, O.F.M., Chap. Franciscan Hospitaller Sisters of the Immaculate Conception 10; Residential Care 55; Skilled Nursing 62; Total Staff 100; Capacity 111.

[D] CATHOLIC CHARITIES

FRESNO. *Catholic Charities of the Diocese of Fresno*, 149 N. Fulton St., 93701. Tel: 559-237-0851; Fax: 559-237-7050. Email: klilles@ccdof.org. Kelly Lilles, Agency Admin. Total Staff 26; Total Assisted in all 3 Locations 200,000.
Catholic Charities Thrift Store, 149 N. Fulton St., 93701-1607. Tel: 559-237-0851; Fax: 559-237-7050. Email: jhudson@ccdof.org. Jody Hudson, Retail & Food Distribution Center. Total Staff 1.
Senior Companion Program, 149 N. Fulton St., 93701. Tel: 559-498-6377; Fax: 559-485-1591. Email: alopes@ccdof.org. Alan Lopes, Sr. Companion Prog. Total Staff 4; Total Assisted 350.

BAKERSFIELD. *Catholic Charities, Diocese of Fresno, Kern and Inyo County Resource Center*, 825 Chester Ave., 93301. Tel: 661-281-2130; Fax: 661-281-2139. Rev. Msgr. Craig F. Harrison, V.F., Dir. Total Staff 7; Total Assisted Annually 38,000.

MERCED. *Catholic Charities*, 366 W. Main #1, 95340. Tel: 209-383-2494; 209-383-5220; Fax: 209-383-3975. Email: sleonalfaro@ccdof.org. Total Staff 3.
Catholic Charities Social Services, 366 W. Main, #1, 95340. Tel: 209-383-2494; Fax: 209-383-3975.

[E] CONVENTS AND RESIDENCES FOR SISTERS

FRESNO. *St. Agnes Medical Center Convent* (1975) 1261 E. Los Altos Ave., 93710. Tel: 559-431-3376. Congregation of the Sisters of the Holy Cross. Sisters of the Holy Cross 5.
Congregation of the Sisters of Nazareth, 2121 N. First St., 93703. Tel: 559-237-2257; Fax: 559-237-2323. Email: mbrody@gmail.com. Sr. Margaret Brody, C.S.N., Supr. Sisters 4.
Pious Disciples of the Divine Master, 3700 N. Cornelia Ave., 93722. Tel: 559-275-1656; Fax: 559-275-2725. Sr. M. Peter Mendes, P.D.D.M., Supr. Sisters 14.

BAKERSFIELD. *Sister Servants of the Blessed Sacrament (SJS)*, 1100 S. Kern St., 93307. Tel: 661-869-1086 (Convent); Fax: 661-323-6058. Email: lbakersfielsjs@yahoo.com. Sisters 5.

CLOVIS. *Sisters of the Immaculate Conception (RCM)* (1892) 859 Harvard Ave., 93612. Tel: 559-299-8407; Fax: 559-299-4627. Email: clovisrcm@yahoo.com. Sisters 4.

LEMOORE. *Carmelite Sisters of St. Teresa (CSST)*, 884 N. Lemoore Ave., 93245. Tel: 559-924-2347; Fax: 559-924-7848. Email: tessypius@hotmail.com. Sisters 5.

LOS BANOS. *Franciscan Hospitallers of the Immaculate Conception (FHIC)*, 1441 Berkeley Dr., 93635-9599. Tel: 209-827-8933; Fax: 209-827-8989. Email: confhic@sbcglobal.net. Web: www.fhiccalp.org. Sisters 10.

REEDLEY. *Daughters of Divine Zeal (FDZ)* (1897) 379 E. Manning Ave., 93654. Tel: 559-638-1916; Fax: 559-638-5542. Email: hannibalmarylucy@yahoo.com. Web: www.figliedivinozelo.it. Sisters 3.

TEHACHAPI. *Norbertine Sisters of the Bethlehem Priory of St. Joseph*, 17831-A Water Canyon Rd., 93561. Tel: 661-823-1066; Fax: 661-823-1066. Email: mothermarya@aol.com.

[F] RETREAT HOUSES

THREE RIVERS. *St. Anthony's Retreat Center*, P.O. Box 249, 93271. Tel: 559-561-4595; Fax: 559-561-4493. Email: fatherjohn@stanthonyretreat.org. Web: stanthonyretreat.org. Rev. Msgr. John Griesbach, Dir.; Sr. Danielle Witt, S.S.N.D., Co-Dir. Priests 1; Religious 1.
Santa Teresita Youth Center, P.O. Box 249, 93271. Tel: 559-561-4595. Vincent Olea, Dir.

[G] NEWMAN CENTERS

FRESNO. *St. Paul Newman Center* (1964) 1572 E. Barstow Ave., 93710. Tel: 559-436-3434; Fax: 559-436-3430. Web: csufnewman.com. Deacon John Supino, Parish Life Coord.
California State University at Fresno & Fresno City College 93740. Tel: 559-436-3434; Fax: 559-436-3430. Web: csufnewman.com. Karey Spach, Campus Min.

[H] MISCELLANEOUS & AGENCIES

FRESNO. *Catholic Professional and Business Club of Fresno*, c/o 1550 N. Fresno St., 93703-3788. Tel: 559-434-2722. Email: president@cpbcfresno.org.

Our Faith, Our Family, Our Future Foundation, Inc., 1550 N. Fresno St., 93703. Tel: 559-488-7426; Fax: 559-488-7461.

The Sisters of Nazareth of Fresno Real Estate Holdings, Inc., 2121 N. First St., 93703. Tel: 559-237-2257; Fax: 559-237-1958. Sr. Margaret Brody, C.S.N., Pres.

MERCED. **Apostoles de la Palabra of California*, 168 Cone Ave., 95341. Tel: 209-385-0795. Associates 5.

Catholic Professional & Business Club of the Fresno Diocese, 593 Elmwood, Livingston, 95334. Fernando Palomino, Pres.

SANGER. *Fr. Hannibal House Social Service Center*, 1401 14th St., P.O. Box 37, 93657. Tel: 559-875-0564; Fax: 559-875-1281. Email: hanibalhouse@aol.com. Linda Rodriguez, Exec. Dir. Total Assisted: Food Distribution 30,000.

RELIGIOUS INSTITUTES OF MEN REPRESENTED IN THE DIOCESE

For further details refer to the corresponding bracketed number in the Religious Institutes of Men or Women section.

[0360]—*Claretian Missionaries* (Western Prov.)—C.M.F.

[]—*Community of Discalced Carmelites* (Manjummel Prov., India)—O.C.D.

[]—*Congregation of the Passionists* (Korea)—C.P.

[0480]—*Conventual Franciscans* (St. Joseph Cupertino Prov.)—O.F.M.Conv.

[0520]—*Franciscan Friars* (St. Barbara Prov.)—O.F.M.

[0690]—*Jesuit Fathers* (Los Gatos, CA)—S.J.

[]—*Missionaries of St. Paul*—M.S.P.

[]—*Missioneros del Sagrado Corazon y Santa Maria de Guadalupe*—M.S.C.

[0930]—*Oblates of St. Joseph* (Asti, Italy)—O.S.J.

[]—*Redemptorists*—C.Ss.R.

[1090]—*Rogationist Fathers*—R.C.J.

[0420]—*Society of the Divine Word* (Philippines)—S.V.D.

[]—*Sons of Mary Mother of Mercy* (Umvahia, Nigeria)—S.M.M.M.

RELIGIOUS INSTITUTES OF WOMEN REPRESENTED IN THE DIOCESE

[]—*Carmelite Sisters of St. Teresa* (Gidellahalli, Bangalore-India)—C.S.S.T.

[0795]—*Daughters of Divine Zeal* (Rome, Italy)—F.D.Z.

[1070-20]—*Dominican Sisters* (Congregation of St. Thomas Aquinas, Tacoma, WA)—O.P.

[1070-25]—*Dominican Sisters* (Congregation of of St. Catherine of Siena)—O.P.

[1070-13]—*Dominican Sisters* (Congregation of the Most Holy Rosary, Adrian, MI)—O.P.

[1270]—*Franciscan Hospitaller Sisters of the Immaculate Conception* (San Jose, CA)—F.H.I.C.

[1190]—*Franciscan Sisters of the Atonement* (Garrison, NY)—S.A.

[]—*Hijas del Sagrado Corazon de Jesus y Santa Maria* (Mexico)—H.S.C.M.G.

[2180]—*Immaculate Heart Community* (Los Angeles, CA)—I.H.M.

[]—*Instituto Misionero Apostoles de la Palabra*—I.M.A.P.

[]—*Misioneras Carmelitas de Santa Teresa del Nino Jesus* (Puebla, Puebla Mexico)—M.C.S.T.N.J.

[]—*Misioneras Eucaristicas de Maria Inmaculada* (Colima, Mexico)—M.E.M.I.

[]—*Missionary Catechists of Divine Providence*—M.C.D.P.

[]—*Norbertine Sisters of the Bethlehem Priory of St. Joseph*

[0980]—*Pious Disciples of the Divine Master* (Staten Island, NY)—P.D.D.M.

[2970]—*School Sisters of Notre Dame* (St. Louis, MO)—S.S.N.D.

[3499]—*Servants of the Blessed Sacrament* (El Segundo, CA)—S.J.S.

[0430]—*Sisters of Charity of Blessed Virgin Mary* (Dubuque, IA)—B.V.M.

[2570]—*Sisters of Mercy of the Americas* (Silver Spring, MD)—R.S.M.

[3242]—*Sisters of Nazareth* (Los Angeles, CA)—S.N.

[]—*Sisters of Our Lady of Nazareth* (Fiji)—S.O.L.N.

[3830-13]—*Sisters of St. Joseph* (Baden, PA)—C.S.J.

[3840]—*Sisters of St. Joseph of Carondelet* (Los Angeles, CA)—C.S.J.

[1920]—*Sisters of the Holy Cross* (Notre Dame, IN)—C.S.C.

[1960]—*Sisters of the Holy Family* (Mission San Jose, CA)—S.H.F.

[2130]—*Sisters of the Immaculate Conception* (San Francisco, CA & Spain)—R.C.M.

[]—*Sisters of the Love of God* (La Puente, CA & Spain)—R.A.D.

[3320]—*Sisters of the Presentation of the Blessed Virgin Mary* (San Francisco, CA)—P.B.V.M.

DIOCESAN CEMETERIES

FRESNO. *Fresno Catholic Cemeteries*, 264 N. Blythe, 93706. Tel: 559-488-7449; Fax: 559-488-7485. Staff 7.

NECROLOGY

† Belluomini, Rev. Msgr. Ralph, Chap., Bakersfield, CA Bakersfield Memorial Hospital & San Joaquin Community Hospital.—Died June 17, 2011

† Byrne, Rev. Msgr. Laserian, (Retired)—Died May 20, 2011

† Marth, Rev. Msgr. Loydell J., (Retired)—Died April 5, 2011

† Riccomini, Rev. Msgr. Dino, (Retired)—Died Sept. 1, 2011

An asterisk (*) denotes an organization that has established tax-exempt status directly with the IRS and is not covered by the USCCB Group Ruling.

Diocese of Gallup

(Dioecesis Gallupiensis)

Most Reverend

JAMES S. WALL

Bishop of Gallup; ordained June 6, 1998; appointed Bishop of Gallup February 5, 2009; ordained and installed April 23, 2009. *Office: 711 S. Puerco Dr., P.O. Box 1338, Gallup, NM 87305.*

Chancery: 711 S. Puerco Dr., P.O. Box 1338, Gallup, NM 87305. Tel: 505-863-4406; Fax: 505-722-9131.

ESTABLISHED DECEMBER 16, 1939.

Square Miles 55,468.

Comprises Apache, Navajo and those parts of the Navajo and Hopi Reservations in Coconino Counties in the State of Arizona; San Juan, McKinley, Catron, Cibola and those parts of Rio Arriba, Sandoval, Bernalillo and Valencia Counties lying west of 106, 52', 41" meridian in the State of New Mexico.

Legal Title: New Mexico: Roman Catholic Church of the Diocese of Gallup. Arizona: Bishop of the Roman Catholic Church of the Diocese of Gallup.

For legal titles of parishes and diocesan institutions, consult the Chancery Office.

STATISTICAL OVERVIEW

Personnel	
Bishop	1
Priests: Diocesan Active in Diocese	26
Priests: Diocesan Active Outside Diocese	6
Priests: Retired, Sick or Absent	17
Number of Diocesan Priests	49
Religious Priests in Diocese	21
Total Priests in Diocese	70
Permanent Deacons in Diocese	26
Total Brothers	8
Total Sisters	100
Parishes	
Parishes	52
With Resident Pastor:	
Resident Diocesan Priests	21
Resident Religious Priests	14
Without Resident Pastor:	
Administered by Priests	12
Administered by Professed Religious Men	1
Administered by Religious Women	2
Completely Vacant	2
Missions	22
Professional Ministry Personnel:	
Brothers	6
Sisters	51
Lay Ministers	55
Welfare	
Homes for the Aged	1
Total Assisted	50
Specialized Homes	1
Total Assisted	25
Special Centers for Social Services	12
Total Assisted	75,000
Educational	
Diocesan Students in Other Seminaries	3
Total Seminarians	3
High Schools, Diocesan and Parish	1
Total Students	43
High Schools, Private	1
Total Students	130
Elementary Schools, Diocesan and Parish	11
Total Students	1,000
Elementary Schools, Private	1
Total Students	216
Catechesis/Religious Education:	
High School Students	759
Elementary Students	2,513
Total Students under Catholic Instruction	4,664
Teachers in the Diocese:	
Sisters	12
Lay Teachers	135
Vital Statistics	
Receptions into the Church:	
Infant Baptism Totals	639
Minor Baptism Totals	100
Adult Baptism Totals	77
Received into Full Communion	80
First Communions	754
Confirmations	466
Marriages:	
Catholic	95
Interfaith	27
Total Marriages	122
Deaths	714
Total Catholic Population	61,990
Total Population	495,000

Former Bishop—Most Revs. BERNARD T. ESPELAGE, O.F.M., D.D., ord. May 16, 1918; appt. Bishop of Gallup, July 20, 1940; cons. Oct. 9, 1940; resigned Sept. 3, 1969; died Feb. 19, 1971; JEROME J. HASTRICH, D.D., ord. Feb. 9, 1941; cons. Auxiliary Bishop of Madison and Titular Bishop of Gurza, July 31, 1963; transferred to the See of Gallup, Sept. 3, 1969; installed Dec. 3, 1969; retired March 20, 1990; died May 12, 1995; DONALD E. PELOTTE, S.S.S., D.D., Ph.D., ord. Sept. 2, 1972; appt. Coadjutor Bishop of Gallup Feb. 24, 1986; cons. May 6, 1986; succeeded to See, March 20, 1990; retired April 30, 2008; died Jan. 7, 2010.

Vicar General—Very Rev. JAMES E. WALKER, Ph.D., V.G.

Judicial Vicar—Very Rev. MICHAEL A. VIGIL, J.C.L., J.V.

Office of the Bishop—711 S. Puerco Dr., P.O. Box 1338, Gallup, 87305. Tel: 505-863-4406.

Chancery—711 S. Puerco Dr., P.O. Box 1338, Gallup, 87305. Tel: 505-863-4406; Fax: 505-722-9131. Office Hours: Mon.-Fri. 8:30-12 & 1-4:30.

Chancellor—Very Rev. KEVIN H. FINNEGAN, J.C.L., Chancellor; Mrs. VERA PLACENCIO, Exec. Asst. to the Bishop.

Chief Financial Officer—Deacon JAMES P. HOY.

Diocesan Tribunal (First Instance)—711 S. Puerco Dr., P.O. Box 1338, Gallup, 87305. Tel: 505-863-4406; Fax: 505-722-9324.

Adjutant Judicial Vicar—Very Rev. LAWRENCE J. O'KEEFE, J.C.D.

Judges—Very Revs. LAWRENCE J. O'KEEFE, J.C.D.; MICHAEL A. VIGIL, J.C.L., J.V.; Deacon JAMES P. HOY.

Defenders of the Bond—Rev. THOMAS R. MAIKOWSKI, Ph.D., Ed.D.; Very Rev. KEVIN H. FINNEGAN, J.C.L.; Rev. RAYMOND MAHLMANN.

Notary—MARGIE MARES.

Promoter of Justice—Very Rev. KEVIN H. FINNEGAN, J.C.L.

Vicars Forane—Very Revs. KEVIN H. FINNEGAN, J.C.L., McKinley Vicariate; GILBERT SCHNEIDER, O.F.M., Apache Vicariate; CLAY KILBURN, C.M., Navajo Vicariate; JOHN SAUTER, Lower Arizona Vicariate; VACANT, San Juan Vicariate; Very Rev. ALBERTO AVELLA, Cibola Vicariate.

Bishop's Delegate for Religious—Sr. RENE BACKE, C.S.A.

Presbyteral Council—Most Rev. JAMES S. WALL; Very Revs. JAMES E. WALKER, Ph.D., V.G.; FRANK CHACON; KEVIN H. FINNEGAN, J.C.L.; JOACHIM BLONSKI, Moderator; ALBERTO AVELLA, Vice Moderator; EDUARDO ESPINOSA, O.F.M.; LAWRENCE J. O'KEEFE, J.C.D.; CLAY KILBURN, C.M.; JOHN SAUTER; GILBERT SCHNEIDER, O.F.M.; MICHAEL A. VIGIL, J.C.L., J.V.; Mrs. VERA PLACENCIO, Sec., Mailing Address: P.O. Box 1338, Gallup, 87305.

Diocesan Consultors—Very Revs. JAMES E. WALKER, Ph.D., V.G.; LAWRENCE J. O'KEEFE, J.C.D.; JOACHIM BLONSKI; EDUARDO ESPINOSA, O.F.M.; GILBERT SCHNEIDER, O.F.M.; FRANK CHACON.

Diocesan Offices and Directors

Archivist—VACANT.

Catholic Committee on Scouting—Rev. JEFFREY KING, Mailing Address: P.O. Box 489, Reserve, 87830-0489. Tel: 575-533-6719.

Chief Financial Officer—Deacon JAMES P. HOY, Dir.

Catholic Charities—STEVEN N. PEARSON, Exec. Dir., Main Office, Gallup: P.O. Box 3146, Gallup, 87305. Tel: 505-722-4407. Chinle: P.O. Box 417, Chinle, AZ 86053. Tel: 928-674-3238. Grants-Milan: 2595 W. Hwy. 66, Grants, 87020. Tel: 505-285-5451. Farmington: 119 W. Broadway, Farmington, 87401. Tel: 505-325-3734. Holbrook: P.O. Box 41, Holbrook, AZ 86025. Tel: 928-524-9720. White Mountain: P.O. Box 552, McNary, AZ 85930. Tel: 928-334-2244.

Cursillos—THERESA BROPHY, Lay Dir., Mailing Address: P.O. Box 202, Gallup, 87305. Tel: 505-409-7315; Rev. ROBERT E. MATHIEU, Spiritual Dir., 307 N. Church St., Bloomfield, 87413. Tel: 505-632-2014.

Diocesan Superintendent of Catholic Schools—Rev. RAVI KIRAN.

Ecumenical Affairs in Arizona, Arizona Ecumenical Council—Rev. DANIEL P. DALEY.

Ecumenical Affairs in New Mexico—Rev. RAYMOND MAHLMANN, 2100 E. 20th, Farmington, 87401.

Newspaper— "Voice of the Southwest" CHARLES L. LAMB, Editor in Chief, Mailing Address: P.O. Box 1338, Gallup, 87305. Tel: 505-863-4406.

Diocesan Director of Religious Education—Sr. EVE MARIE KORZYM, O.S.F., Mailing Address: P.O. Box 1338, Gallup, 87305. Tel: 505-863-4406, Ext. 32.

Priests' Retirement Board—Revs. JOACHIM BLONSKI, Chm.; DONALD RICHARDSON (Retired); Very Rev. ALBERTO AVELLA; Revs. MATTHEW A. KELLER; TIMOTHY W. FARRELL.

Propagation of the Faith—Rev. MATTHEW A. KELLER, Dir., Mailing Address: P.O. Box 1338, Gallup, 87305.

Radio—LEE LAMB; Rev. CORMAC ANTRAM, O.F.M., Mailing Address: P.O. Box 668, Saint Michaels, AZ 86511.

Search—TED GOMEZ, Dir., Mailing Address: P.O. Box 5243, Farmington, 87499-5243.

Life, Peace, Justice and Creation Stewardship—Sr. ROSE MARIE CECCHINI, M.M., Mailing Address: P.O. Box 3146, Gallup, 87305. Tel: 505-722-4407, Ext. 103.

Vocations— For Priesthood: Rev. MATTHEW A. KELLER, Mailing Address: P.O. Box 1338, Gallup, 87305. Tel: 505-863-4406, Ext. 14. Deacon Vocations: Deacon FRANK T. CHAVEZ, Mailing Address: 3023 E. 22nd St., Farmington, 87401. Tel: 505-793-5735. Bishop's Delegate for Religious: Sr. RENE BACKE, C.S.A., Mailing Address: P.O. Box 1338, Gallup, 87305.

Gallup. Cure of Ars House of Discernment— (2009)

300 Mount Carmel Ave., Gallup, 87301. Tel: 505-863-4406; Fax: 505-722-9131. Email: gallupvocationsoffice@gmail.com. Web: dioceseofgallup.org. Rev. MATTHEW A. KELLER, Dir. Vocations.

Youth Ministry—CHRISTINE RAYNER, Coord., Mailing Address: P.O. Box 972, Saint Michaels, AZ 86511. Tel: 928-871-3567.

Ministry Formation Program—Mailing Address: P.O. Box 1338, Gallup, 87305. Tel: 505-863-4406, Ext. 24. Rev. BLANE GREIN, O.F.M., Builders of the New Earth & Native American Formation; Deacon FRANK T. CHAVEZ, Dir. Diaconate Life & Ministry. Email: ftchavez@mac.comTel: 505-793-5735; Sisters ROSE MARIE CECCHINI, M.M., Lay Spirituality; RENE BACKE, C.S.A., Academics, Diaconate Candidates: 4; Lay Ministry Candidates: 2.

Diocesan Review Board for Sexual Abuse & Misconduct by Clergy, Religious and Other Church Personnel—Mailing Address: P.O. Box 3932, Gallup, 87305.

Victim Assistance Coordinator—Mailing Address: P.O. Box 3932, Gallup, 87305. DIANE DIPAOLO.

CLERGY, PARISHES, MISSIONS AND PAROCHIAL SCHOOLS

CITY OF GALLUP

(MCKINLEY COUNTY)

1—CATHEDRAL OF THE SACRED HEART (1939), (Dedicated June 19, 1955) Very Rev. Lawrence J. O'Keefe, Rector; Deacons Randolf Copeland; James P. Hoy; Michael Sullivan.
Res. & Mailing Address: 415 E. Green Ave., 87301. Tel: 505-722-6644; Fax: 505-722-6645. Email: sacredheartcathedralgallup@dioceseofgallup.org.
Catechesis/Religious Program—Tel: 505-722-5485. Debbie Trujillo, D.R.E. Students 170.

2—ST. FRANCIS OF ASSISI (1943), (Hispanic), Revs. Lawrence Bernard, O.F.M.; Joseph Gonsalves, O.F.M., Parochial Vicar; Deacon Paul Endter.
Res.: 411 N. Second, 87301. Tel: 505-863-3033; Fax: 505-863-6887.
Catechesis/Religious Program—Tel: 505-979-3407. Cynthia Rangel, D.R.E. Students 160.

3—ST. JEROME, Closed. For inquiries for parish records contact Sacred Heart Cathedral.

4—ST. JOHN VIANNEY (1973) Very Rev. James E. Walker.
Res.: 3408 Zia Dr., 87301. Tel: 505-722-3361; Fax: 505-722-3361. Email: stjohnvianeygallup@dioceseofgallup.org.
Catechesis/Religious Program—Tel: 505-722-5085. JoNell Becenti, D.R.E. Students 35.

OUTSIDE THE CITY OF GALLUP, NEW MEXICO

ACOMA, CIBOLA CO., SAN ESTEBAN, ACOMA CATHOLIC INDIAN MISSION (1629), (Native American), [CEM 3] Revs. Wayne Gibbeaut, O.F.M.; Don Billiard, O.F.M.; Deacon Larry Valdo.
Res.: P.O. Box 448, Pueblo of Acoma, 87034-0448. Tel: 505-552-6403; Fax: 505-522-6221. Email: sanestebanacoma@dioceseofgallup.org.
Catechesis/Religious Program—Miriam Salvador, D.R.E. Students 19.
Mission—St. Anne Pueblo of Acoma, P.O. Box 448, Acomita, Cibola Co. 87034.
Mission—Santa Maria de Acoma McCartys, Cibola Co. 87034.

ARAGON, CATRON CO., SANTO NINO (1910), (Hispanic), Rev. Jeffrey King; Deacon Juan Aragon.
Res.: P.O. Box 489, Reserve, 87830-0489. Tel: 575-533-6240 (Parish); 575-533-6719 (Office). Email: santoninoaragon@dioceseofgallup.org.
Catechesis/Religious Program—Students 11.
Mission—Nativity of the Blessed Virgin Mary Datil, Catron Co.
Mission—San Isidro Lower San Francisco, Catron Co.
Mission—St. Francis Reserve, Catron Co.
Mission—St. Anne Horse Springs, Catron Co.
Station— Apache Creek.

AZTEC, SAN JUAN CO., ST. JOSEPH (1946), (Hispanic), Revs. Robert E. Mathieu, Canonical Pastor; Thomas Pudota; Deacon Steve Moffett.
Res.: 500 N. Mesa Verde St., 87410. Tel: 505-334-6535; Fax: 505-334-5902. Email: stjosephaztec@dioceseofgallup.org.
Catechesis/Religious Program—Tel: 505-334-3542. Sr. Sara Marie Gomez, O.S.U., D.R.E. Students 167.

BLANCO, SAN JUAN CO., ST. ROSE OF LIMA (1900) [CEM] Rev. Robert E. Mathieu, Canonical Pastor; Deacons Roger Garcia; Patrick R. Valdez.
Res.: 307 N. Church St., Bloomfield, 87413. Tel: 505-632-2014; Fax: 505-634-0312.
Catechesis/Religious Program—Abby Florez, D.R.E. Students 49.
Mission—Our Lady of Guadalupe Los Martinez, San Juan Co.

BLOOMFIELD, SAN JUAN CO., ST. MARY (1960) [CEM] Rev. Robert E. Mathieu; Deacons Roger Garcia; Patrick R. Valdez.
Res.: 307 N. Church St., 87413. Tel: 505-632-2014; Fax: 505-634-0312. Email: stmarybloomfield@dioceseofgallup.org.
Catechesis/Religious Program—Kristi Lucero, D.R.E. Students 225.

CHICHILTAH, MCKINLEY CO., ST. PATRICK (1965), (Native American), Rev. Eugene Bowski. (Navajo Mission)
Res.: P.O. Box 267, Vanderwagen, 87326. Tel: 505-778-5410. Email: stpatrickchichiltah@dioceseofgallup.org.
Catechesis/Religious Program—Sr. M. Cristena, M.C., D.R.E. Students 34.
Mission—Good Shepherd Catholic Mission
Catechesis/Religious Program—Students 12.

CHURCH ROCK, MCKINLEY CO., ST. PHILIP BENIZI, Closed. For inquiries for parish records please see Sacred Heart Cathedral, Gallup.
Station— Pindale.

CROWNPOINT, MCKINLEY CO., ST. PAUL (1961), (Native American), [JC] Very Revs. Lawrence J. O'Keefe, Canonical Pastor; Kevin H. Finnegan, Sacramental Min.; Sr. Maureen Farrar, A.S.C., Pastoral Admin.; Deacon Sherman Manuelito, Pastoral Admin.
Res.: P.O. Box 268, 87313. Tel: 505-786-5376; Fax: 505-786-5376. Email: stpaulcrownpoint@dioceseofgallup.org.
Catechesis/Religious Program—Christine Smith, D.R.E. Students 14.
Mission—Risen Savior Thoreau. H.C. 62, Box 5095, Bluewater, McKinley Co. 87323-9517.
Station— Lake Valley.
Station—St. Bonaventure Thoreau.

CUBA, SANDOVAL CO., IMMACULATE CONCEPTION (Nacimiento) (1914) [CEM 4] Unassigned.
Res.: P.O. Box 40, 87013. Tel: 505-289-3803. Email: immaculateconceptioncuba@dioceseofgallup.org.
Catechesis/Religious Program—Students 89.
Mission—Santo Nino La Jara, Sandoval Co.
Mission—Saint Aloysius Gonzaga San Luis, Sandoval Co.
Mission—San Jose Cabezon, Sandoval Co.

FARMINGTON, SAN JUAN CO.

1—ST. MARY'S (1976), (Hispanic), Very Rev. Michael A. Vigil; Rev. Raymond Mahlmann; Deacon Frank T. Chavez, Pastoral Assoc.
Res.: 2100 E. 20th, 87401. Tel: 505-325-0287; Fax: 505-564-8515. Email: stmaryfarmington@dioceseofgallup.org.
Catechesis/Religious Program—Tel: 505-325-0287, Ext. 115; 505-325-0287, Ext. 122. Teresa Garcia, D.R.E. Students 246.

2—SACRED HEART (1929) Rev. Timothy W. Farrell.
Res.: 414 N. Allen Ave., 87401. Tel: 505-325-9743; Fax: 505-325-8860. Email: sacredheartfarmington@dioceseofgallup.org.
Catechesis/Religious Program—Tel: 505-564-8164. Anne Weigel, D.R.E. Students 471.

FLORA VISTA, SAN JUAN CO., HOLY TRINITY (1986), (Hispanic), Revs. Robert E. Mathieu, Canonical Pastor; Thomas Pudota.
Res.: 500 N. Mesa Verde Ave., Aztec, 87410. Tel: 505-334-6535; Fax: 505-334-5902. Email: holytrinityfloravista@dioceseofgallup.org.
Catechesis/Religious Program—Sr. Sara Marie Gomez, O.S.U., D.R.E. Students 15.

FORT WINGATE, MCKINLEY CO., ST. ELEANOR, Closed. For inquiries for parish records contact Sacred Heart Cathedral.
Station— Iyanbito.

GRANTS, CIBOLA CO., ST. TERESA OF AVILA (1942) Very Rev. Alberto Avella; Revs. Edwin Bryan Diesen; Joseph (Jo Joppa) Madanu, M.F. (India); Deacons Timoteo Lujan; Rogelio Fernandez-Rojo; Larry Chavez.
Res.: 213 Smith St., P.O. Box 668, 87020. Tel: 505-285-6645; Fax: 505-285-6646. Email: stteresagrants@dioceseofgallup.org.
Catechesis/Religious Program—Tel: 505-287-3549. Velma Dees, D.R.E. Students 16.

LAGUNA, CIBOLA CO., ST. JOSEPH (Laguna Indian Pueblo) (1699) Revs. Wayne Gibbeaut, O.F.M.; Don Billiard, O.F.M.; Deacon Larry Valdo, Pastoral Assoc.
Res.: P.O. Box 1000, 87026. Tel: 505-552-9330. Email: stjosephlaguna@dioceseofgallup.org.
Catechesis/Religious Program—Tel: 505-552-7464; Fax: 505-552-9330. Angela Riley, Coord.; Virginia Siow, D.R.E. Students 76.
Mission—Nativity of the Blessed Virgin Mary Encinal, Valencia Co.
Mission—Sacred Heart Mesita, Valencia Co.
Mission—St. Elizabeth of Hungary Paguate, Valencia Co.
Mission—St. Margaret Mary Paraje, Valencia Co.
Mission—St. Anne Seama, Valencia Co.

LUMBERTON, RIO ARRIBA CO., ST. FRANCIS OF ASSISI (1910), (Hispanic—Native American), Rev. Mohana Rao Bathineni, Pastoral Admin.
Res.: P.O. Box 1147, Dulce, 87528. Tel: 505-759-1307. Email: stfrancislumberton@dioceseofgallup.org.
Catechesis/Religious Program—Valerie Gomez, D.R.E. Students 18.
Mission—St. Anthony 3760 Sandhill, Dulce, Rio Arriba Co. 87528.

MILAN, CIBOLA CO., ST. VIVIAN (1969) Very Rev. Alberto Avella; Revs. Edwin Bryan Diesen; Joseph (Jo Joppa) Madanu, M.F. (India); Deacons Larry Chavez; Timoteo Lujan; Rogelio Fernandez-Rojo.
Res.: P.O. Box 2938, 87201-2938. Tel: 505-287-9327. Email: stvivianmilan@dioceseofgallup.org.
Catechesis/Religious Program—Combined with St. Teresa, Grants, NM. Students 16.

NAVAJO, MCKINLEY CO., ST. BERARD (1963), (Native American), [JC] Very Rev. Gilbert Schneider, O.F.M.; Bro. Michael Haag, O.F.M.; Sisters Magdalena Studer, S.C., Pastoral Assoc.; Zoe Brenner, S.B.S., Pastoral Assoc.; Deacon Wilson Gorman.
Res.: P.O. Box 1284, 87328. Tel: 505-777-2251. Email: stberardnavajo@dioceseofgallup.org.
Catechesis/Religious Program—Tel: 505-777-2490. Students 80.
Mission—St. Francis Mission P.O. Box 41, Sawmill, Apache Co., AZ 86549. Tel: 602-729-5224.
Station— Crystal.

PINEHAVEN, MCKINLEY CO., GOOD SHEPHERD CATHOLIC MISSION (1972), (Native American), [CEM] Rev. Eugene Bowski.
Res.: P.O. Box 2170, 87305. Tel: 505-778-5658. Email: goodshepherdpinehaven@dioceseofgallup.org.
Catechesis/Religious Program—Combined with St. Patrick, Chichiltah. Students 16.
Convent—Missionaries of Charity, Box 267, Vanderwagen, 87326. Tel: 505-778-5740. Sisters 4.

QUEMADO, CATRON CO., SACRED HEART (1881), (Hispanic), [CEM] Rev. Daniel P. Daley, Canonical Pastor.
Res.: P.O. Box 339, 87829. Tel: 575-773-4631. Email: sacredheartquemado@dioceseofgallup.org.
Catechesis/Religious Program—

SAN FIDEL, CIBOLA CO., ST. JOSEPH MISSION (1920), (Hispanic), [CEM] Attended by Acoma, NM. Sr. Ellen Corcoran, S.C.S.J.A., Admin.
Res.: P.O. Box 370, 87049. Tel: 505-552-6257; Fax: 505-552-6382.

SAN MATEO, CIBOLA AND MCKINLEY COS., SAN MATEO Very Rev. Alberto Avella; Revs. Edwin Bryan Diesen; Joseph (Jo Joppa) Madanu, M.F. (India); Deacons Larry Chavez; Timoteo Lujan; Rogelio Fernandez-Rojo.
Mailing Address: P.O. Box 2938, Milan, 87021. Tel: 505-287-9327.
Catechesis/Religious Program—Combined with St. Teresa, Grants, NM.

SAN RAFAEL, CIBOLA CO., SAN RAFAEL Very Rev. Alberto Avella; Revs. Edwin Bryan Diesen; Joseph (Jo Joppa) Madanu, M.F. (India); Deacons Larry Chavez; Timoteo Lujan; Rogelio Fernandez-Rojo.
Mailing Address: P.O. Box 2938, Milan, 87201. Email: sanrafaelsanrafael@dioceseofgallup.org.
Catechesis/Religious Program—Combined with St. Teresa, Grants, NM.

SEBOYETA, CIBOLA CO., OUR LADY OF SORROWS (1774), (Hispanic), [CEM] Very Rev. Alberto Avella, Canonical Pastor; Sr. Ellen Corcoran, S.C.S.J.A., Admin.
Res.: H.C. 77, P.O. Box 13, 87014. Tel: 505-552-6301. Email: olscebolleta@dioceseofgallup.org.
Catechesis/Religious Program—Students 4.
Mission—Our Lady of Light P.O. Box 8098, Cubero, Cibola Co. 87014.
Mission—Our Lady of Loretto Bibo, Cibola Co.
Mission—Santa Rosalia Moquino, Valencia Co.
Station— Marquez.

SHIPROCK, SAN JUAN CO., CHRIST THE KING (1924), (Native American), [JC] Rev. Benjamin Onwumelu Onyema.
Res.: P.O. Box 610, 87420. Tel: 505-368-4532. Email: christthekingshiprock@dioceseofgallup.org.
Catechesis/Religious Program—Tel: 505-368-5845. Jerome Herbert, D.R.E. Students 4.

THOREAU, MCKINLEY CO., ST. BONAVENTURE, Unassigned.Mailing Address: P.O. Box 268, Crownpoint, 87313. Tel: 505-786-7110.

TINAJA, CIBOLA CO., SAN LORENZO (1981), (Hispanic—Native American), Attended by St. Teresa, Grants, NM. Rev. Eugene Bowski.
Res.: State Rte. 2, Box 47, Ramah, 87321. Tel: 505-783-4301. Email: sanlorenzotinaja@dioceseofgallup.org.
Catechesis/Religious Program—
Mission—El Morro Fence Lake, Valencia Co.

TOHATCHI, MCKINLEY CO., ST. MARY CHURCH (1920), (Native American), [CEM] Revs. Pio O'Connor,

O.F.M.; Robert Ross, S.J., Sacramental Min.; Bro. Maynard Shurley, O.F.M.; Deacon Marcellino Morris Jr.
Res.: Box 39, 87325. Tel: 505-733-2243; Fax: 505-733-2657. Email: stmarytohatchi@dioceseofgallup.org.
Catechesis/Religious Program—Tel: 505-733-2382. Sisters Marlene Kochert, O.S.F., D.R.E.; Pat Bietsch, O.S.F., D.R.E. Students 27.
Mission—St. Anthony Naschitti, San Juan Co. Tel: 505-733-2468.
Station— Mexican Springs.
Station— Twin Lakes.
Station— Sheep Springs.
Station— Chuska.

WATERFLOW, SAN JUAN CO., SACRED HEART (1917) [CEM] Rev. Benjamin Onwumelu Onyema; Deacon Joseph Didde.
Res.: 9 Rd. 6820, 87421. Tel: 505-598-5454. Email: sacredheartwaterflow@dioceseofgallup.org.
Catechesis/Religious Program—Tel: 505-598-9856. Sr. Ann Regis Barret, M.S.B.T., D.R.E. Students 42.
Mission—San Juan Catholic Center P.O. Box 857, Kirtland, San Juan Co. 87417. Tel: 505-598-6799.
Mission—Sacred Heart Missionary Cenacle Fruitland. P.O. Box 1037, Ojo Armarillo, San Juan Co. 87416. Tel: 505-598-9856. Sr. Ann Regis Barrett, M.S.B.T., Dir.

ZUNI, MCKINLEY CO., ST. ANTHONY, OUR LADY OF GUADALUPE (Zuni Indian Pueblo) (1923) Rev. Ravi Kiran.
Res.: P.O. Box 486, 87327. Tel: 505-782-2888; Fax: 505-782-2888. Email: stanthonyzuni@dioceseofgallup.org.
Catechesis/Religious Program—Tel: 505-782-2527. Sr. Jean Glach, O.P., D.R.E. Students 10.

ARIZONA

ALPINE, APACHE CO., ST. HELENA (1971) Very Rev. John Sauter.
Res.: P.O. Box 229, AZ 85920. Tel: 928-339-4363. Email: sthelenaalpine@dioceseofgallup.org.
Catechesis/Religious Program—
Mission—Santo Nino Glenwood, Catron Co.

CHINLE, APACHE CO., OUR LADY OF FATIMA (1905), (Native American), Rev. Blane Grein, O.F.M.
Res.: P.O. Box 2119, AZ 86503. Tel: 928-674-5413; Fax: 928-674-5813. Email: olfchinle@dioceseofgallup.org.
Mission—St. Anthony P.O. Box 578, Many Farms, Apache Co., AZ 86538. Tel: 928-781-6350.
Catechesis/Religious Program—Sr. Michael Clare Wilson, O.P., D.R.E. Students 20.
Mission—St. Mary of the Rosary P.O. Box 432, Pinon, Navajo Co., AZ 86510. Tel: 928-725-3365.
Catechesis/Religious Program—Students 7.

CIBECUE, NAVAJO CO., ST. CATHERINE (1929), (Native American), Rev. Edward Fronske, O.F.M.
Mailing Address: P.O. Box 80156, AZ 85911.
Res.: P.O. Box 679, Whiteriver, AZ 85941. Tel: 928-338-4432; Fax: 928-338-1568. Email: stcatherinecibecue@dioceseofgallup.org.
Mission—St. Anthony Cedar Creek, Gila Co., AZ. (TUC)

CONCHO, APACHE CO., SAN RAFAEL (1977) Rev. Timothy Conlon, C.M.; Deacon Filomeno Ulibarri.
Church: P.O. Box 309, St. Johns, AZ 85936-0309. Tel: 928-337-4390. Email: sanrafaelconcho@dioceseofgallup.org.
Catechesis/Religious Program—Combined with St. John the Baptist, St. Johns, AZ. Sr. Angeline Chauez, O.S.F., D.R.E. Students 12.

FORT DEFIANCE, APACHE CO., OUR LADY OF BLESSED SACRAMENT (1915), (Native American), [JC] Very Rev. Gilbert Schneider, O.F.M.; Bro. Michael Haag, O.F.M.
Res.: P.O. Box 70, AZ 86504-0070. Tel: 928-729-5068; Fax: 928-729-5069. Email: olbsftdefiance@dioceseofgallup.org.
Catechesis/Religious Program—Sisters Mary Hottenroth, S.B.S., D.R.E.; Zoe Brenner, S.B.S., D.R.E. Students 87.

GANADO, APACHE CO., ALL SAINTS (1968), (Native American), Rev. Flann O'Neil, O.F.M.
Res.: P.O. Box 119, AZ 86505. Tel: 928-755-3401. Email: allsaintsganado@dioceseofgallup.org.
Catechesis/Religious Program—Tel: 928-652-3236; Fax: 928-652-3236. Sr. Monica Dubois, O.P., D.R.E. Students 10.
Mission—St. Anne Klagetoh, AZ. #50, HC 58, P.O. Box 90, Apache Co., AZ 86505. Tel: 928-652-3264. Sr. Monica Dubois, O.P.
Mission—Our Lady of the Rosary #161, HC 58, Box 70, Greasewood, Navajo Co., AZ 86505. Tel: 928-654-3236. Bro. Paul O'Brien, O.F.M.
Station— Cornfields, AZ.
Station— Wide Ruins, AZ.

HOLBROOK, NAVAJO CO., OUR LADY OF GUADALUPE (1923) Rev. Anthony O. Dike, Pastoral Admin.; Deacon Michael Ashenfelder.
Res.: 212 E. Arizona St., P.O. Box 849, AZ 86025. Tel: 928-524-3261; Fax: 928-524-1507. Email: ologholbrook@dioceseofgallup.org.
Catechesis/Religious Program—Tel: 928-288-3565. Students 70.

HOUCK, APACHE CO., ST. JOHN THE EVANGELIST (Tekakwitha Mission) (1927), (Native American), Unassigned.
Res.: P.O. Box 48, AZ 86506. Tel: 928-688-2921; Fax: 928-688-2921. Email: stjohnhouck@dioceseofgallup.org.
Catechesis/Religious Program—Students 20.
Mission—St. Rose Pine Springs, Apache Co., AZ.

KAYENTA, NAVAJO CO., OUR LADY OF GUADALUPE (1967) Rev. Stephen Gallegos, C.M.
Res.: P.O. Box 517, AZ 86033. Tel: 928-697-3429; Fax: 928-697-3429. Email: ologkayenta@dioceseofgallup.org.
Catechesis/Religious Program—Students 1.

KEAMS CANYON, NAVAJO CO., ST. JOSEPH'S INDIAN MISSION (1920), (Hopi-Navajo), Very Rev. Clay Kilburn, C.M.
Res.: P.O. Box 128, AZ 86034. Tel: 928-738-2325; Fax: 928-738-2325. Email: stjosephkeamscanyon@dioceseofgallup.org.
Catechesis/Religious Program—Students 15.
Station— Toyei, AZ.

LUKACHUKAI, APACHE CO., ST. ISABEL (1910), (Native American), Rev. Blane Grein, O.F.M.
P.O. Box 128, AZ 86507. Tel: 928-787-2322. Email: stisabelukachukai@dioceseofgallup.org.
Catechesis/Religious Program—Anna Sandoval, D.R.E.; Sr. Rose Beck, S.S.N.D., D.R.E. Students 15.
Mission—Our Lady of Guadalupe Round Rock, Apache Co., AZ.
Mission—St. Ann Tsaile, Apache Co., AZ.
Mission—Our Lady of the Lake Wheatfields, Apache Co., AZ.

MCNARY, APACHE CO., ST. ANTHONY (1922) Rev. Robert Hyman.
Res.: SAC 628, AZ 85930-0628. Tel: 928-334-2394. Email: stanthonymcnary@dioceseofgallup.org.
Catechesis/Religious Program—

OVERGAARD, NAVAJO CO., OUR LADY OF ASSUMPTION (1982) Very Rev. John Sauter.
P.O. Box 628, AZ 85933. Tel: 928-535-5329; Fax: 928-535-6602.
Res.: 3048 Hwy. 277, Page, AZ 86040. Email: olaovergaard@dioceseofgallup.org.
Catechesis/Religious Program—Irene Onstott, D.R.E. Students 16.

PAGE, COCONINO CO., IMMACULATE HEART OF MARY (1958) Rev. Thomas Maikowski, Admin.; Deacons Jerry Lindsay; Gerald Kocjan.
Res.: 455 S. Lake Powell Blvd., P.O. Box 1387, AZ 86040. Tel: 928-645-2301; Fax: 928-645-1261. Email: immaculateheartofmarypage@dioceseofgallup.org.
Catechesis/Religious Program—Tel: 928-645-3124. Carla Corn, C.R.E. Students 120.

PINETOP, NAVAJO CO., ST. MARY OF THE ANGELS (1974) Rev. Daniel P. Daley.
Res.: 1915 S. Penrod Ln., Box 819, AZ 85935. Tel: 928-367-2080; Fax: 928-367-2085. Email: stmaryoftheangelspinetop@dioceseofgallup.org. Web: www.stmaryoftheangels.us.
Catechesis/Religious Program—Fax: 928-367-2085. Beverly Cloud, D.R.E. Students 145.

PINON, NAVAJO CO., ST. MARY OF THE ROSARY (1937), (Native American), Attended by Chinle, AZ.
Res.: P.O. Box 432, AZ 86510. Tel: 928-725-3365.
Catechesis/Religious Program—Students 6.
Station— Tachee, AZ.
Station— Blue Gap, AZ.
Station— Forest Lake, AZ.
Station— Whippoorwill Spring, AZ.
Station— Hardrock, AZ.
Station— Kits'iiLi, AZ.

ST. JOHNS, APACHE CO., ST. JOHN THE BAPTIST (1890) Very Rev. Joachim Blonski, Canonical Pastor; Rev. Timothy Conlon, C.M., Admin.; Deacon Filomeno Ulibarri.
Res.: P.O. Box 309, AZ 85936. Tel: 928-337-4390. Email: stjohnstjohn@dioceseofgallup.org.
Catechesis/Religious Program—Tel: 928-337-4461. Sr. Angelina Chavez, O.S.F., D.R.E. Students 120.

ST. MICHAELS, APACHE CO., ST. MICHAEL (1898), (Native American), [JC] Revs. Florecito Pobalao, O.F.M., Parochial Vicar; Abel Olivas, O.F.M. In Res., Very Rev. Eduardo Espinosa, O.F.M.; Revs. Cormac Antram, O.F.M.; Flann O'Neil, O.F.M.
Res.: P.O. Box 680, AZ 86511-0680. Tel: 928-871-4171; Fax: 928-871-4186. Email: stmichaelsstmichaels@dioceseofgallup.org.
Catechesis/Religious Program—Tel: 928-871-4173. Christine Rayner, Youth Min.; Sisters Josephine Goebel, C.S.A., D.R.E.; Zoe Brenner, S.B.S., D.R.E. Students 37.
Mission—St. Michael's Mission for Navajo Indians, Apache Co., AZ.

SHOW LOW, NAVAJO CO., ST. RITA (1962) Very Rev. Joachim Blonski; Deacon John Heal.
Res.: 1400 E. Owens St., P.O. Box 1449, AZ 85901. Tel: 928-537-2543; Fax: 928-532-8441. Email: stritashowlow@dioceseofgallup.org.
Catechesis/Religious Program—Rebecca Quintana, D.R.E. Students 149.

SNOWFLAKE, NAVAJO CO., OUR LADY OF THE SNOWS (1963) Rev. William J. Welch; Deacon Raymond Melcher.
Res.: 1655 S. Main St., AZ 85937. Tel: 928-536-4559; Fax: 928-536-5852. Email: olssnowflake@dioceseofgallup.org.
Catechesis/Religious Program—Tel: 928-243-8264; Fax: 928-536-5052. Pearl Poritt, D.R.E. Students 64.

SPRINGERVILLE, APACHE CO., ST. PETER (1880), (Hispanic), Revs. Daniel P. Daley, Canonical Pastor; Kingsley George-Obilonu, Admin.; Deacon Jorge Campos, Pastoral Admin.
Mailing Address: P.O. Box 1566, AZ 85938.
Res.: 145 N. Papago St., P.O. Box 1566, AZ 85938. Tel: 928-333-2112; Fax: 928-333-0448. Email: stpeterspringerville@dioceseofgallup.org.
Catechesis/Religious Program—Tel: 928-333-4423. Lora Harrison, D.R.E. Students 94.

TUBA CITY, COCONINO CO., ST. JUDE (1956) Rev. Stephen Gallegos, C.M., Sacramental Min.; Sr. Mary Rogers, D.C., Admin.
Res.: P.O. Box 248, AZ 86045. Tel: 928-283-5391. Email: stjudetubacity@dioceseofgallup.org.
Catechesis/Religious Program—Camille Denetclaw, D.R.E. Students 64.

WHITERIVER, NAVAJO CO., ST. FRANCIS (1921), (Native American), Rev. Edward Fronske, O.F.M.
Res.: 9 W. Elm St., P.O. Box 679, AZ 85941. Tel: 928-338-4432. Email: stfranciswhiteriver@dioceseofgallup.org.
Catechesis/Religious Program—Fax: 928-338-1568. Mary Lou Areno, D.R.E. Students 20.

WINSLOW, NAVAJO CO.
1—ST. JOSEPH'S (1896) Very Rev. Frank Chacon.
Res.: 300 W. Hillview St., AZ 86047. Tel: 928-289-2350; Fax: 928-289-9226. Email: stjosephwinslow@dioceseofgallup.org.
Catechesis/Religious Program—Sr. Joanna Duran, D.R.E.; David Sanchez, D.R.E. Students 201.
2—MADRE DE DIOS (1950), (Hispanic), Very Rev. Frank Chacon.
Res.: 300 W. Hillview St., AZ 86047. Tel: 928-289-2350; Fax: 928-289-9226.
Catechesis/Religious Program—Sr. Joanna Duran, D.R.E.; David Sanchez, D.R.E. Twinned with St. Joseph's, Winslow. Students 237.

Chaplains of Public Institutions

GALLUP. *Gallup Area Hospitals & Nursing Homes*, Tel: 505-722-0999. Vacant.

FARMINGTON. *Farmington Area Hospitals*, 414 N. Allen Ave., 87401. Tel: 505-325-9743. Vacant.

On Duty Outside of Diocese:
Revs.—
Curran, Oliver, 1 Elkspoint Rd., P.O. Box 115, Zephyr Cove, NV 89448.
Hussey, Daniel C., Chap. (Maj.), St. Joseph Church, 1035 C St., Elko, NV 89801.
Juric, Jakov, Gospinica 18, 21000 Split, Croatia.
Kassis, Daniel F., 1000 E. Maple Ave., Mundelein, IL 60060.
Kugler, Michael, 5852 N. Sherman Blvd., Milwaukee, WI 53208.
Wedeking, Patrick, 4844 Woodview Dr., Del City, OK 73115.

On Leave of Absence:
Revs.—
Mangampo, Gil
McConvey, Michael
Obersteiner, Ernest
Sanchez, Raul N., Ch. Lt. Col.

Retired:
Rev. Msgrs.—
Gomez, Leo, V.G., 100098 Bridgepointe N.E., Albuquerque, 87111.
MacDonald, Arthur F., P.O. Box 222, Glenwood, AZ 88039.
Revs.—
Boland, John
Day, William F., 2828 Park Cir., Unit 3, Pinetop, AZ 85935.
Downie, Arley T., #15 Rd. 6015, 87401.
Mesley, Jerome T., P.O. Box 1947, 87305.
Morello, Peter, P.O. Box 234, Hammondsport, NY 14840.
O'Neill, Hugh, 1900 Mark Ave., 87301.
Richardson, Donald
Smith, Norman, Mullen Home, 3629 W. 29th Ave., Denver, CO 80211.
Stanfield, Francis E., 5300 W. 61 Pl., 308 N., Mission, KS 66205.

Tachias, Alfred A., J.C.L., 1900 Mark Ave., 87301.
Universal, Patrick J. (BO), 24 Clark St., Boston, MA 02109.

Permanent Deacons:
Aragon, Juan, HC62, Box 637, Aragon, 87820.
Ashenfelder, Michael, P.O. Box 584, Joseph City, AZ 86032-0584.
Beaton, William P., (Retired), 1815 Wrsteria St., Denton, TX 76205.
Campos, Jorge, 639 South Ave., Springerville, AZ 85938.
Chavez, Frank T., 3023 E. 22nd St., 87401.
Chavez, Larry, P.O. Box 1883, Grants, 87020.
Conn, Richard, (Retired), P.O. Box 6449, Mesa, AZ 85216.
Copeland, Randolf, M.D., 1609 Red Rock Dr., 87301.
Didde, Joseph, 12 CR 6427, Kirtland, 87417.
Endter, Paul, 3071 Red Bluff Ct., 87301.
Fernandez-Rojo, Rogelio, 80011 Lobo Canyon Rd., Grants, 87020.
Garcia, Roger, 14 CR 4989, Bloomfield, 87413.
Gorman, Wilson C., P.O. Box 218, Fort Defiance, AZ 86504-0218.
Heal, John, P.O. Box 2845, Snowflake, AZ 85937.
Hoy, James, 411 East Logan, 87301.
Kelley, Timothy, 416 Valentine Dr., 87301. (On Leave of Absence)
Kocjan, Gerald, P.O. Box 3748, Page, AZ 86040.
Lente, Michael, 133 Camino del Pueblo, Bernalillo, 87004.
Lindsay, Jerry, P.O. Box 3607, Page, AZ 86040-3607.
Lucero, Levy, 414 San Andreas, Alamogordo, 88310.
Lujan, Timoteo, P.O. Box 2612, Milan, 87021-2612.
Manuelito, Sherman, P.O. Box 538, Crownpoint, 87313.
Martin, Daniel Nez, P.O. Box 724, Window Rock, AZ 86515.
Melcher, Raymond, P.O. Box 1266, Snowflake, AZ 85937-1226.
Moffett, Stephen, P.O. Box 1892, Aztec, 87410.
Morris, Marcelino, P.O. Box 768, Fort Defiance, AZ 86505.
Peterson, Charles, 30 Rd. 3011, Aztec, 87410.
Racicot, Robert, P.O. Box 697, Ruidoso, 88355.
Rogers, William, P.O. Box 217, Taylor, AZ 85939-0217.
Scott, James, 3509 Kayenta Dr., 87402.
Stando, Matthew, 2446 Harlem Rd., Cheektowaga, NY 14225.
Stringfellow, Roy, 379 W. Strawberry Dr., Pueblo West, CO 81007.
Sullivan, Michael, P.O. Box 3327, 87305.
Ulibarri, Fiomeno, P.O. Box 453, Concho, AZ 85924.
Valdez, Patrick R., P.O. Box 526, Blanco, 87412.
Valdo, Larry, P.O. Box 352, Pueblo Of Acoma, 87034.
Valencia, Ernest, P.O. Box 461, Blanco, 87412. (On Leave of Absence)
Wilson, Ronald, P.O. Box 574, Overgaard, AZ 85933.

INSTITUTIONS LOCATED IN THE DIOCESE

[A] HIGH SCHOOLS

GALLUP. *Gallup Catholic High School*, 515 Park Ave., 87301. Tel: 505-722-6089; Fax: 505-726-8142. Email: gallupcatholicschool@dioceseofgallup.org. Web: www.gcschool.pvt.k12.nm.us. Barbara Kozeliski, Prin. Lay Teachers 7; Students 43.

ST. MICHAELS, AZ. *St. Michael High School*, P.O. Box 650, AZ 86511. Tel: 928-871-4443; Fax: 928-871-3191. Email: stmichaelhighschool@dioceseofgallup.org. James M. Anderson, Prin.; Melissa Coles, Librarian. Sisters 2; Lay Teachers 15; Students 130.

[B] ELEMENTARY SCHOOLS

GALLUP. *St. Francis of Assisi School*, (Grades PreK-5), 215 W. Wilson, 87305. Tel: 505-863-3145; Fax: 505-863-7452. Email: stfrancisschoolgallup@dioceseofgallup.org. Don Joseph Frank, Prin. Sisters 6; Lay Teachers 14; Students 110.

Gallup Catholic School, (Grades PreK-8), 515 Park Ave., 87301. Tel: 505-863-6652; Fax: 505-726-8142. Email: gallupcatholicschool@dioceseofgallup.org. Barbara Kozeliski, Prin.; Ann Sloan, Librarian. Lay Teachers 9; Students 101.

CUBA. *Immaculate Conception School*, (Grades PreK-8), P.O. Box 218, 87013. Tel: 575-289-3749; Fax: 575-289-0031. Richard Barncord, Prin. Lay Teachers 3; Students 20.

FARMINGTON. *Sacred Heart School*, (Grades PreK-7), 404 N. Allen Ave., 87401. Tel: 505-325-7152; Fax: 505-325-6157. Email: olybrook@shcsfarmington.com. Web: www.shcsfarmington.org. Jeffrey J. Raichel, Prin.; Ronscilla Pipkens, Librarian. Lay Teachers 15; Students 116.

GRANTS. *St. Teresa of Avila School*, (Grades PreK-8), 402 E. High St., 87020. Tel: 505-287-2261; Fax: 505-285-4350. Email: stteresaschool@dioceseofgallup.org. Maria Mirabal, Prin. Lay Teachers 12; Students 90.

LUMBERTON. *St. Francis School*, (Grades K-8), HC 71, Rte. 356, Box 26, 87528. Tel: 505-759-3252; Fax: 505-759-3844. Email: stfrancisschoollumberton@dioceseofgallup.org. Leonard Meyer, Prin. Lay Teachers 10; Students 80.

ST. MICHAELS, AZ. *St. Michael Elementary School*, (Grades K-8), P.O. Box 650, AZ 86511. Tel: 928-871-4636; Fax: 928-871-3027. Email: stmichaelelementaryschool@dioceseofgallup.org. Web: www.smis1902.org. Tracie Lee, Prin. Sisters 3; Lay Teachers 10; Students 216.

SAN FIDEL. *St. Joseph School*, (Grades K-7), P.O. Box 370, 87049. Tel: 505-552-6362; Fax: 505-552-0168. Maria Mirabal, Prin.; Antonio Trujillo, Admin. Lay Teachers 4; Students 44.

SHOW LOW. *Our Lady of Perpetual Help dba St. Anthony Catholic School* (Grades PreK-6), P.O. Box 789, AZ 85902. 1400 E. Owens, AZ 85901. Jose I. Garcia, Ph.D., Prin. Lay Teachers 14; Students 131.

THOREAU. *St. Bonaventure School*, (Grades PreK-8), 25 Navarre Blvd. W., P.O. Box 909, 87323. Tel: 505-862-7465; Fax: 505-862-7790. Web: www.sbms.k12.nm.us. Sr. Natalie Bussiere, S.N.D.deN., Prin. Sisters 5; Lay Teachers 12; Students 226.

ZUNI. *St. Anthony Indian School*, (Grades PreK-8), P.O. Box 486, 87327. Tel: 505-782-4596; Fax: 505-782-2013. Deborah Goering, Prin. Sisters 3; Lay Teachers 12; Students 72.

[C] CONVENTS AND RESIDENCES FOR SISTERS

GALLUP. *Casa Reina*, 217 E. Black Diamond Canyon Rd., 87301. Tel: 505-722-5511; Fax: 505-863-0075. Email: casareina@questoffice.net. Sr. Magda Garcia, H.N.S.G., Supr. Sisters of Guadalupe and St. Joseph., Perpetual Adoration Chapel. Immigration and Naturalization Services, Hispanic Ministry. Sisters 9.

GOBERNADOR. *Monastery of Our Lady of the Desert*, P.O. Box 556, Blanco, 87412. 10258 Hwy 64, 87412. Tel: 505-419-2938. Email: benedcta@aol.com. Sisters Benedicta Serna, O.S.B., Prioress; Elizabeth Tran, O.S.B., Subprioress. Benedictine Nuns Subiaco Congregation Sisters 6; Final Professed Nuns 6.

[D] HOMES FOR THE AGED

GALLUP. *Villa Guadalupe Home for the Aged*, 1900 Mark Ave., 87301. Tel: 505-863-6894; Fax: 505-722-4121. Email: adgallup@littlesistersofthepoor.org. Sr. Andrea Munarriz, L.S.P.; Rev. Alfred A. Tachias, J.C.L., Chap. (Retired). Little Sisters of the Poor 7; Total Assisted 50; Total Staff 50.

[E] MISCELLANEOUS LISTINGS

GALLUP. *Blue Army* (Fatima Apostolate), 217 E. Black Diamond Canyon Rd., 87301. Tel: 505-722-5511; Fax: 505-863-0075. Email: casareina@questoffice.net. Sisters Magda Leticia Garcia, H.N.S.G., Spiritual Dir.; Rosa M. Zuniga, H.N.S.G., Contact Person.

Catholic Charities of Gallup, Inc., 506 W. Hwy. 66, P.O. Box 3146, 87301. Tel: 505-722-4407; Fax: 505-722-7512. Email: director@catholiccharitiesgallup.com. Web: www.catholiccharitiesgallup.com. Steven N. Pearson, Exec. Dir.

Catholic Peoples' Foundation, Inc., P.O. Box 369, 87305. Tel: 505-726-8295; Fax: 505-863-3309. Web: www.catholicpeoplesfoundation.com. Mary Alice Salaz, Interim Dir.

Gallup Catholic School Foundation, Inc., 515 Park Ave., 87301. Tel: 505-863-6652; Fax: 505-726-8142. Email: gc.school@hotmail.com.

St. Joseph's Shelter and Soup Kitchen, Mailing Address: 207 E. Wilson St., 87301. Tel: 505-722-5261. 207 E. Black Diamond Canyon Dr., 87301. Tel: 505-722-5156. Sr. M. Alinda, M.C., Supr. & Contact Person. Missionaries of Charity., Soup Kitchen & Shelter for Native American Clients. Missionaries of Charity 6; Total Assisted 49,800.

Sacred Heart Retreat, P.O. Box 1338, 87305. Tel: 505-722-6755; Fax: 505-863-9852. Email: shrc@cnetco.com. Web: www.dioceseofgallup.org. Sr. Rene Backe, C.S.A., Program Dir.

Southwest Indian Foundation, 100 W. Coal Ave., P.O. Box 307, 87305. Tel: 505-863-2837; Fax: 505-863-2760. Email: swif@cia-g.com. Web: www.southwestindian.com. Mr. William McCarthy, CEO.
Board of Directors: Most Rev. James S. Wall; Mr. James Mason, Pres.; Mr. John Dowling, Vice Pres.; Mrs. Mary Constant, Sec.; Very Rev. Gilbert Schneider, O.F.M.; Hon. Judge Marie Nezwood; Phillip G. Garcia; Cathy Gasparich; Angelo Di Paolo.

CHINLE, AZ. *Talbot House-Catholic Charities*, P.O. Box 417, AZ 86503. Tel: 928-674-3238; Fax: 928-674-5813. Web: www.catholiccharitiesgallup.com. Steven N. Pearson, Dir. Total Assisted 2,600; Total Staff 3.

GRANTS-MILAN. *Casa San Jose*, 2595 W. Hwy. 66, 87020-9626. Tel: 505-285-5451; Fax: 505-285-6436. Email: casa@7cities.net. Web: www.cnetco/~Catholiccharities.com. Sr. Francine Schuster, A.S.C., Admin. Residence of pregnant & parenting teenagers. Operated by Catholic Charities. Sisters Adorers of the Blood of Christ 1; Sinsinawa Dominicans of the Most Holy Rosary 1; Total Staff 10; Total Assisted 24.

PINETOP, AZ. *St. Vincent DePaul Society* (1990) P.O. Box 376, AZ 85935. Tel: 928-367-2029 (Thrift Shop); 928-367-3057 (Emergency Aid Office). Mary Alcon Young, Pres.; Lucy Wallace, Asst. Officer. Thrift Shop & Emergency Aid Office. Total Assisted 1,080; Total Staff 3.

THOREAU. *St. Bonaventure Indian Mission & School*, 25 Navarre Blvd. W., P.O. Box 610, 87323. Tel: 505-862-7847; Fax: 505-862-7029. Email: chaltar@stbonaventuremission.org. Web: www.stbonaventuremission.org.

TUBA CITY. *Life Sharing Center, Inc., St. Jude Food Bank*, 100 Aspen Dr., AZ 86045. Tel: 928-283-6886; Fax: 928-283-6614. Email: stjudefoodbank@frontiernet.net. P.O. Box 1277, AZ 86045.

WINSLOW, AZ. *La Casa de Nuestra Senora (Madonna House)* (1957) 213 Jefferson St., AZ 86047. Tel: 928-289-9284. Email: madonnahouse@cableone.net. Web: www.madonnahouse.org. Kathy McVady, Dir. Mission of Madonna House Apostolate Combermere, Ontario, Canada; Prayer and Community Service Center; Catechesis of the Good Shepherd Program for 3 - 5 yr. olds. Total in Residence 6.

RELIGIOUS INSTITUTES OF MEN REPRESENTED IN THE DIOCESE

For further details refer to the corresponding bracketed number in the Religious Institutes of Men or Women section.

[1100]—*Brothers of the Sacred Heart*—S.C.
[1330]—*Congregation of the Mission* (Western Prov.)—C.M.
[0490]—*Franciscan Brothers of Brooklyn, NY*—O.S.F.
[0520]—*Franciscan Friars* (Provs. of Our Lady of Guadalupe; St. John the Baptist & Santa Barbara)—O.F.M.
[]—*Heralds of the Good News Society of Jesus*
[]—*Missionaries of Faith*—M.F.

RELIGIOUS INSTITUTES OF WOMEN REPRESENTED IN THE DIOCESE

[0100]—*Adorers of the Blood of Christ*—A.S.C.
[]—*Benedictine Sisters*—O.S.B.
[3710]—*Congregation of the Sisters of Saint Agnes*—C.S.A.
[0760]—*Daughters of Charity of St. Vincent de Paul*—D.C.
[]—*Discalced Carmelite Nuns*
[1070-13]—*Dominican Sisters (Adrian, MI)*—O.P.
[1115]—*Dominican Sisters of Peace*—O.P.
[]—*Dominican Sisters of Roman Congregation*
[1070-09]—*Dominican Sisters (Racine, WI)*—O.P.
[1350]—*Franciscan Missionary Sisters of the Immaculate Conception*—O.S.F.
[1180]—*Franciscan Sisters of Allegany* (New York)—O.S.F.
[1780]—*Franciscan Sisters of Perpetual Adoration*—F.S.P.A.
[2340]—*Little Sisters of the Poor*—L.S.P.
[2470]—*Maryknoll Sisters of St. Dominic*—M.M.
[2490]—*Medical Mission Sisters*—M.M.S.
[]—*Mission Servants of the Most Blessed Trinity*—M.S.B.T.
[2710]—*Missionaries of Charity*—M.C.
[2790]—*Missionary Servants of the Most Blessed Trinity*—M.S.B.T.
[2760]—*Missionary Sisters of the Immaculate Conception of the Mother of God*—S.M.I.C.
[]—*Religious of the Good Shepherd*
[0480]—*Sisters of Charity Levenworth*—S.C.L.
[0600]—*Sisters of Charity of St. Joan Antide*—S.C.S.J.A.
[2360]—*Sisters of Loretto*—S.L.
[3000]—*Sisters of Notre Dame de Namur*—S.N.D.deN.

[0590]—*Sisters of St. Elizabeth* (Convent Station)—S.C.

[1510]—*Sisters of St. Francis*—O.S.F.

[1730]—*Sisters of St. Francis of Oldenburg*—O.S.F.

[]—*Sisters of St. Francis of the Congregation of Our Lady of Lourdes*

[]—*Sisters of St. Francis of the Newman Communities*

[0260]—*Sisters of the Blessed Sacrament for Indians and Colored People*—S.B.S.

[1830]—*The Sisters of the Good Shepherd*—R.G.S.

[]—*Sisters of the Immaculate Heart of Mary* Nigeria

[4120-05]—*Ursuline Nuns of Mount St. Joseph*—O.S.U.

NECROLOGY

(No Deaths)

An asterisk (*) denotes an organization that has established tax-exempt status directly with the IRS and is not covered by the USCCB Group Ruling.

Archdiocese of Galveston-Houston

(Archidioecesis Galvestoniensis Houstoniensis)

His Eminence

DANIEL CARDINAL DiNARDO

Archbishop of Galveston-Houston; ordained July 16, 1977; appointed Coadjutor Bishop of Sioux City August 19, 1997; consecrated October 7, 1997; appointed Bishop of Sioux City November 28, 1998; appointed Coadjutor Bishop of Galveston-Houston January 16, 2004; installed March 26, 2004; appointed Coadjutor Archbishop December 29, 2004; succeeded to the See February 28, 2006; elevated to Cardinal November 24, 2007. *Mailing Address: P.O. Box 907, Houston, TX 77001-0907.* Tel: 713-659-5461.

Most Reverend

JOSEPH A. FIORENZA, D.D.

Retired Archbishop of Galveston-Houston; ordained May 29, 1954; appointed Bishop of San Angelo September 4, 1979; consecrated and installed October 25, 1979; appointed Bishop of Galveston-Houston December 18, 1984; installed February 18, 1985; appointed Archbishop December 29, 2004; retired February 28, 2006. *Mailing Address: P.O. Box 907, Houston, TX 77001-0907.* Tel: 713-659-5461.

Most Reverend

GEORGE A. SHELTZ

Auxiliary Bishop of Galveston-Houston; ordained May 15, 1971; appointed Auxiliary Bishop of Galveston-Houston February 21, 2012; ordained May 2, 2012. *Mailing Address: P.O. Box 907, Houston, TX 77001-0907.* Tel: 713-659-5461.

Chancery Office: P.O. Box 907, Houston, TX 77001-0907. Tel: 713-659-5461; Fax: 713-759-9151.

Most Reverend

VINCENT M. RIZZOTTO, J.C.L.

Retired Auxiliary Bishop of Galveston-Houston; ordained May 26, 1956; appointed Auxiliary Bishop of Galveston-Houston June 22, 2001; ordained July 31, 2001; retired November 6, 2006.

ESTABLISHED IN 1847.

Square Miles 8,880.

Redesignated Diocese of Galveston-Houston on July 25, 1959; created Archdiocese December 29, 2004.

Comprises the Counties of Austin, Brazoria, Fort Bend, Galveston, Grimes, Harris, Montgomery, San Jacinto, Walker and Waller in the State of Texas.

For legal titles of parishes and archdiocesan institutions, consult the Chancery Office.

STATISTICAL OVERVIEW

Personnel	
Cardinals	1
Retired Archbishops	1
Auxiliary Bishops	1
Retired Bishops	1
Priests: Diocesan Active in Diocese	139
Priests: Diocesan Active Outside Diocese	4
Priests: Retired, Sick or Absent	55
Number of Diocesan Priests	198
Religious Priests in Diocese	224
Total Priests in Diocese	422
Extern Priests in Diocese	43
Ordinations:	
Diocesan Priests	4
Transitional Deacons	7
Permanent Deacons	35
Permanent Deacons in Diocese	402
Total Brothers	12
Total Sisters	449
Parishes	
Parishes	146
With Resident Pastor:	
Resident Diocesan Priests	103
Resident Religious Priests	39
Without Resident Pastor:	
Administered by Priests	4
Missions	7
Pastoral Centers	18
Welfare	
Catholic Hospitals	4
Total Assisted	234,274
Health Care Centers	8
Total Assisted	102,000
Homes for the Aged	4
Total Assisted	855
Residential Care of Children	4
Total Assisted	958
Day Care Centers	36
Total Assisted	3,498
Specialized Homes	5
Total Assisted	9,861
Special Centers for Social Services	10
Total Assisted	770,911
Educational	
Seminaries, Diocesan	1
Students from This Diocese	18
Students from Other Diocese	63
Diocesan Students in Other Seminaries	29
Students Religious	10
Total Seminarians	57
Colleges and Universities	1
Total Students	3,754
High Schools, Private	9
Total Students	4,419
Elementary Schools, Diocesan and Parish	44
Total Students	11,584
Elementary Schools, Private	6
Total Students	2,107
Catechesis/Religious Education:	
High School Students	17,801
Elementary Students	68,029
Total Students under Catholic Instruction	107,751
Teachers in the Diocese:	
Priests	7
Scholastics	4
Sisters	27
Lay Teachers	1,377
Vital Statistics	
Receptions into the Church:	
Infant Baptism Totals	10,071
Minor Baptism Totals	13,378
Adult Baptism Totals	1,894
Received into Full Communion	854
First Communions	20,719
Confirmations	11,093
Marriages:	
Catholic	2,558
Interfaith	702
Total Marriages	3,260
Deaths	3,843
Total Catholic Population	1,170,403
Total Population	6,099,524

Former Bishops—Rt. Revs. J. M. ODIN, C.M., D.D., ordained May 4, 1823; cons. Bishop of Claudiopolis and Vicar-Apostolic of Texas, March 6, 1842; transferred to Galveston 1847; promoted to New Orleans in 1861; died in Ambierle, France, May 25, 1870; C. M. DUBUIS, D.D., ordained June 1, 1844; cons. Nov. 23, 1862; resigned 1881; remained Titular Bishop of Galveston till 1892, when he was promoted to an Archbishopric i.p.i.; died May 21, 1895; at Vernaison, France; P. DUFAL, C.S.C., D.D., ordained Sept. 29, 1852; cons. Nov. 25, 1860; Bishop of Delcon, and Vicar-Apostolic of Eastern Bengal; transferred to Galveston; as Coadjutor of Rt. Rev. C. M. Dubuis, cum jure successionis, May 14, 1878; resigned 1880; died in Paris 1898; NICHOLAS A. GALLAGHER, D.D., ordained Dec. 25, 1868; consecrated Titular Bishop of Canopus, April 30, 1882; succeeded to Galveston, Dec. 16, 1892; died Jan. 21, 1918; Most Revs. CHRISTOPHER E. BYRNE, D.D., appt. July 18, 1918; cons. Nov. 10, 1918; made Assistant at the Pontifical Throne, May 8, 1941; died April 1, 1950; WENDELIN J. NOLD, S.T.D., appt. Nov. 29, 1947; consecrated Feb. 25, 1948; died Oct. 1, 1981; JOHN L. MORKOVSKY, S.T.D., ord. Dec. 5, 1933; Titular Bishop of Hieron and Auxiliary Bishop of Amarillo; appt. Dec. 22, 1955; cons. Feb. 22, 1956; succeeded to See Aug. 18, 1958; transferred to Galveston-Houston as Titular Bishop of Tigava and Coadjutor and Apostolic Administrator "cum jure successionis"April 1963; installed June 11, 1963; succeeded to the See of Galveston-Houston, April 22, 1975; retired Aug. 16, 1984; died March 24, 1990; JOSEPH A. FIORENZA, ord. May 29, 1954; appt. Bishop of San Angelo Sept. 4, 1979; cons. and installed Oct. 25, 1979; appt. Bishop of Galveston-Houston Dec. 18, 1984; installed Feb. 18, 1985; appt. Archbishop Dec. 29, 2004; retired Feb. 28, 2006.

Chancery Office—1700 San Jacinto St., Houston, 77002-8291. Mailing Address: P.O. Box 907, Houston, 77001-0907. Tel: 713-659-5461; Fax: 713-759-9151. Office Hours: Mon.-Fri. 8:30-4:30.

Chancellor and Moderator of the Curia—Rev. Msgr. GEORGE A. SHELTZ, 1700 San Jacinto St., Houston, 77002-8291. Tel: 713-659-5461.

Vice Chancellor and Associate General Counsel—Ms. CHRISTINA DEAJON, 1700 San Jacinto St., Houston, 77002-8291. Tel: 713-659-5461.

Vicars General—Rev. Msgrs. GEORGE A. SHELTZ; FRANK H. ROSSI, S.T.L.

Ethnic Vicars—Deacon LEONARD P. LOCKETT, Vicar of African American Catholics; VACANT, Vicar of Hispanic Catholics; Rev. JOSEPH THANH VU, Vicar of Vietnamese Catholics; Rev. Msgr. SETH F. HERMOSO, Vicar of Filipino Catholics.

Vicar for Religious—Sr. HELOISE CRUZAT, O.P., 2403 Holcombe, Houston, 77021. Tel: 713-741-8733.

Deans and Vicariates—

Central Vicariate—Revs. ALBERT ZANATTA, C.R.S., Episcopal Vicar. Tel: 281-447-6381; SALVATORE DEGEORGE, O.M.I., Central Dean. Tel: 713-695-0631; MIGUEL A. SOLORZANO, Northeast Dean; OSCAR M. CASTRO, Southeast Dean. Tel: 713-645-6614.

Northern Vicariate—Revs. JOSEPH A. GIETL, Episcopal Vicar. Tel: 713-942-3447; STEPHEN J. PAYNE, Northern Dean. Tel: 936-756-8186;

DWIGHT M. CANIZARES, Eastern Dean; FRED W. VALONE, San Jacinto Dean. Tel: 281-351-8106.

Southern Vicariate—Rev. Msgr. LEO WLECZYK, Episcopal Vicar. Tel: 979-297-3041; Revs. PAUL G. FELIX, V.F., Galveston-Mainland Dean; ROBERT BARRAS, V.F., Bay Area Dean. Tel: 281-485-2421; MAURICE L. RESTIVO, S.T.D., Southern Dean. Tel: 979-849-2421.

Western Vicariate—Rev. Msgr. DANIEL L. SCHEEL, Episcopal Vicar. Tel: 713-468-9555; Rev. STEPHEN B. REYNOLDS, Western Dean. Tel: 979-793-4477; Rev. Msgr. BILL YOUNG, V.F., Southwest Dean. Tel: 713-729-0221; Revs. CLINT C. RESSLER, Northwest Dean. Tel: 713-692-9123; ERIC J. PITRE, M.Div., Bluebonnet Dean. Tel: 979-885-3868.

Secretariat Directors—

Secretariat For Administration—Rev. Msgr. GEORGE A. SHELTZ, 1700 San Jacinto St., Houston, 77002-8291. Tel: 713-659-5461.

Secretariat For Clergy Formation and Chaplaincy Services—Rev. BRENDAN CAHILL, 1700 San Jacinto St., Houston, 77002-8291. Tel: 713-659-5461.

Secretariat For Communication—Mrs. JENNY FABER, 1700 San Jacinto St., Houston, 77002-8291. Tel: 713-659-5461.

Secretariat For Finance—Mr. DAVID HESSEL, 1700 San Jacinto St., Houston, 77002-8291. Tel: 713-659-5461.

Secretariat For Pastoral and Educational Ministries—Mr. JIM BARRETTE, Dir., 2403 Holcombe, Houston, 77021-2099. Tel: 713-741-8786.

Secretariat for Catholic Schools—Sr. KEVINA KEATING, C.C.V.I., 2403 Holcombe Blvd., Houston, 77021.

Secretariat for Social Concerns—VACANT, Dir., 2403 Holcombe, Houston, 77021-2099. Tel: 713-741-8769.

Tribunal Judicial—

Metropolitan Tribunal—Very Rev. LAWRENCE W. JOZWIAK, J.C.L., Judicial Vicar, Mailing Address: P.O. Box 907, Houston, 77001-0907. Tel: 713-807-9286; Fax: 713-807-9296. Email: tribunal@archgh.org.

Adjutant Judicial Vicar—Rev. RICHARD A. WAHL, C.S.B., J.C.L., Mailing Address: P.O. Box 907, Houston, 77001-0907. Tel: 713-807-9286; Fax: 713-807-9296. Email: tribunal@archgh.org.

Director of the Tribunal—Ms. ANNE BRYANT, J.C.L.

Archdiocesan Judges—Rev. Msgr. PHILIPPE LE-XUAN THUONG, J.C.D.; Revs. TRUNG V. NGUYEN, J.C.L.; ERIC J. PITRE, M.Div.; THU NGOC NGUYEN.

Promoter of Justice—Rev. JOHN E. CAHOON, J.C.L.

Defenders of the Bond—Rev. Msgrs. DAVID KENNEDY, J.C.L. (Retired); WILLIAM M. PICKARD, J.C.D. (Retired); Rev. EDWIN A. COREAS, J.C.L.; Ms. ANNE BRYANT, J.C.L.

Censor Librorum—Rev. TERENCE P. BRINKMAN, S.T.D., St John the Evangelist, Baytown, 77522.

Archdiocesan Councils, Commissions and Committees

Archdiocesan Presbyteral Council—1700 San Jacinto St., Houston, 77002-8291.

Presbyteral Council—His Eminence DANIEL CARDINAL DINARDO, Pres. Ex Officio Members: Rev. Msgrs. FRANK H. ROSSI, S.T.L., Vicar Gen.; GEORGE A. SHELTZ, Vicar Gen. Appointees: Rev. Msgr. LEO WLECZYK; Rev. ALBERT ZANATTA, C.R.S.; Rev. Msgrs. DANIEL L. SCHEEL; CHESTER L. BORSKI; Rev. JOSEPH A. GIETL. Elected Members: Revs. DANIEL K. LAHART, S.J., Educational; BRENDAN CAHILL, Spiritual and Admin., Mailing Address: P.O. Box 907, Houston, 77001. Chaplains: Rev. PAGE E. POLK, O.F.M. International Priest Representative: Rev. MICHAEL A. BARROSA, D.S. Area Representatives: Revs. ERIC J. PITRE, M.Div., Northern, Western and Bluebonnet; PAUL G. FELIX, V.F., Galveston-Mainland and Southern; RIVERS PATOUT, Bay Area and Southeast; SEAN HORRIGAN, Southwest and Northwest; DWIGHT M. CANIZARES, Eastern and San Jacinto.

College of Consultors—Rev. Msgrs. DANIEL L. SCHEEL; LEO WLECZYK; FRANK H. ROSSI, S.T.L.; GEORGE A. SHELTZ; CHESTER L. BORSKI; Revs. JOSEPH A. GIETL; ALBERT ZANATTA, C.R.S.

Priests Personnel Committee—His Eminence DANIEL CARDINAL DINARDO; Rev. BRENDAN CAHILL, Chm., 1700 San Jacinto, Houston, 77002. Tel: 713-659-5461, Ext. 8241; Rev. Msgr. WILLIAM L. YOUNG; Rev. THU NGOC NGUYEN; Rev. Msgr. FRANK H. ROSSI, S.T.L. (16-24 yrs.); Revs. CHARLES J. SAMPERI; JAMES BURKART; ITALO DELL'ORO, C.R.S.

Building and Planning Commission—Rev. NORBERT J. MADUZIA JR., D.Min.; Rev. Msgr. GEORGE A. SHELTZ; Ms. CHRISTINA DEAJON; Deacons GERALD W. DUPONT; DON SENGER; Mr. STEVE FAUGHT, Chm., 1700 San Jacinto, Houston, 77002. Tel: 713-659-5461.

Archdiocesan School Council—ERNEST A. FORZANO. Tel: 713-241-1424.

Ecumenism and Interreligious Affairs Commission—Rev. REGINALD WAYNE SAMUELS, 1700 San Jacinto, Houston, 77002. Tel: 713-659-5461.

Liturgical Commission—Rev. JAMES M. BURKART, Chm., 11011 Hall Rd., Houston, 77089. Tel: 281-481-6816.

Secretariat for Administration—Rev. Msgr. GEORGE A. SHELTZ, 1700 San Jacinto St., Houston, 77002-8291. Tel: 713-659-5461.

Administrative Service Department—Deacon CHARLES DUCK, 1700 San Jacinto, Houston, 77002. Tel: 713-659-5461, Ext. 4484.

Archives and Current Records—Ms. LISA MAY, Dir., 1700 San Jacinto St., Houston, 77002-8291. Tel: 713-659-5461.

Catholic Cemeteries—Mr. GUS HOLLIS, Dir., Gulf Fwy. at Hughes Rd., P.O. Box 965, Dickinson, 77539. Tel: 281-337-1641; 409-948-1455.

Construction/Preventative Maintenance—Mr. STEVE FAUGHT, Dir.; Deacon DON SENGER, Preventive Maintenance, 1700 San Jacinto St., Houston, 77002-8291. Tel: 713-659-5461.

Information Services—Mr. ED HERRERA, 1700 San Jacinto St., Houston, 77002-8921. Tel: 713-659-5461.

Internal Auditor—Ms. MARGARET THOMPSON, 1700 San Jacinto St., Houston, 77002-8291. Tel: 713-659-5461.

Legal Services—Mr. FRANK RYND, Dir. Gen. Counsel, 1700 San Jacinto St., Houston, 77002-8291. Tel: 713-659-5461.

Real Estate—Mr. KEN SYKES, 1700 San Jacinto St., Houston, 77002-8291. Tel: 713-659-5461.

Human Resources—Mrs. MICHELE YANTA, Dir., 1700 San Jacinto St., Houston, 77002. Tel: 713-659-5461.

Secretariat for Clergy Formation and Chaplaincy Services—Rev. BRENDAN CAHILL, 1700 San Jacinto St., Houston, 77002-8291. Mailing Address: P.O. Box 907, Houston, 77001-0907. Tel: 713-659-5461.

Apostleship of the Sea (Port Ministry)—Rev. RIVERS PATOUT, Houston Dir. Tel: 713-923-5843. Mailing Address: Houston International Seaman's Center, P.O. Box 9506, Houston, 77261. Tel: 713-672-0511; Mrs. KAREN PARSONS, Galveston, P.O. Box 2742, League City, 77574. Tel: 409-762-0021; Fax: 409-762-1436.

Catholic Chaplain Corps (Hospital Chaplains)—Rev. PAGE E. POLK, O.F.M., 4206 MacGregor Way S., Houston, 77021-1598. Tel: 713-526-6438.

Catholic Relief Services—Mrs. HILDA OCHOA, Dir., 1700 San Jacinto St., Houston, 77002-8921. Tel: 713-659-5461.

Correctional Ministries (Jail Chaplains)—Rev. RONALD F. CLOUTIER, Dir. (Chaplain Office at Harris County Jail), Office and Mailing Address, 2403 E. Holcombe, Houston, 77021-2098. Tel: 713-741-8745; 713-755-5326 (Jail).

Director of Ministry to Priests—Rev. ITALO DELL'ORO, C.R.S., Somascan Formation House, 610 W. Melwood, Houston, 77009. Tel: 713-880-8243.

Diaconal Formation/Diaconal Ministry—Deacon GERALD W. DUPONT, Dir., 1700 San Jacinto St., Houston, 77002-8291. Tel: 713-659-5461.

Permanent Deacons—Deacon GERALD W. DUPONT, Dir., 1700 San Jacinto St., Houston, 77002-8291. Tel: 713-659-5461.

Mission Office—Ms. HILDA OCHOA, Dir., 1700 San Jacinto St., Houston, 77002-8291. Tel: 713-659-5461 Holy Childhood, Propagation of the Faith.

Seminarian Support—Rev. DAT HOANG, Dir., 1700 San Jacinto St., Houston, 77002-8291. Tel: 713-659-5461.

Vocations Office—Rev. DAT HOANG, Dir., 1700 San Jacinto St., Houston, 77002-8291. Tel: 713-659-5461.

Secretariat for Communication—Mrs. JENNY FABER, Dir., 1700 San Jacinto St., Houston, 77002-8291. Tel: 713-659-5461.

Radio—Mrs. MADELINE JOHNSON, 1700 San Jacinto St., Houston, 77002-8291. Tel: 713-659-5461.

Texas Catholic Herald—Mrs. JENNY FABER, Editor, 1700 San Jacinto St., Houston, 77002-8291. Tel: 713-659-5461; Fax: 713-659-3444.

Secretariat for Finance—Mr. DAVID HESSEL, Dir., 1700 San Jacinto St., Houston, 77002-8291. Tel: 713-659-5461.

Accounting Department—Ms. VICKI STROMAN, Controller, 1700 San Jacinto St., Houston, 77002-8291. Tel: 713-659-5461.

Development Office—Mrs. ROZ HILL, Dir., 1700 San Jacinto St., Houston, 77002-8291. Tel: 713-659-5461.

Insurance & Risk Manager—J. KIRK JENINGS, 1700 San Jacinto St., Houston, 77002-8291. Tel: 713-659-5461.

Claims Risk Manager—Mrs. CHRISTINA SANDOVAL, Dir., 2403 Holcombe, Houston, 77021-2099. Tel: 713-741-8758; 800-856-4040; Fax: 713-748-3205.

Parish Accounting Services (PAS)—Mrs. JANIE MORALES, Dir., 1700 San Jacinto St., Houston, 77002-8291. Tel: 713-659-5461.

Secretariat for Pastoral and Educational Ministries—Mr. JIM BARRETTE, Dir., 2403 Holcombe, Houston, 77021-2099. Tel: 713-741-8786.

Aging Ministry—Mrs. KATHY BINGHAM, Dir., 2403 Holcombe, Houston, 77021-2098. Tel: 713-741-8712.

Boy and Girl Scouts—Rev. PATRICK STUART GARRETT, 10330 Hillcroft, Houston, 77096. Tel: 713-729-0221.

Campus Ministry and Young Adults—Mr. ROBERTO NAVARRO, Dir., 2403 Holcombe, Houston, 77021-2098. Tel: 713-741-8786.

Continuing Christian Education—VACANT, Dir., 2403 Holcombe, Houston, 77021-2099. Tel: 713-741-8730.

Circle Lake Retreat Center—Mrs. GLORIA BUSTILLO, Dir., Mailing Address: P.O. Box 1410, Pinehurst, 77362-1410. Tel: 281-356-6764, Ext. 11; Fax: 281-356-6678. Email: circlelake@sbcglobal.net.

Deaf Apostolate—Rev. LEONARD BRONIAK, C.Ss.R., Dir., 2403 Holcombe Blvd., Houston, 77021-2099. Tel: 713-741-8721.

Family Life Ministry—Deacon ARTURO MONTERRUBIO, Dir., 2403 Holcombe, Houston, 77021-2099. Tel: 713-741-8710.

Resource Center—Mrs. DIANE O'CONNOR, 2403 E. Holcombe, Houston, 77021-2099. Tel: 713-741-8781.

Respect Life Office—Dr. MARCELLA COLBERT, Dir., 2403 Holcombe, Houston, 77021-2098. Tel: 713-741-8730 (Main Tel.).

Worship—Mr. DAVID WOOD, Dir., 2403 Holcombe, Houston, 77021-2099. Tel: 713-741-8760.

Youth Ministry—Mr. BRIAN JOHNSON, Dir., 2403 Holcombe, Houston, 77021-2099. Tel: 713-741-8723.

Special Youth Services (Juvenile Detention Ministry)—Ms. FRANCHELLE LEE, Dir., 2403 Holcombe, Houston, 77021-2099. Tel: 713-527-1894; 832-541-4718.

Secretariat for Catholic Schools—Sr. KEVINA KEATING, C.C.V.I., 2403 Holcombe Blvd., Houston, 77021. Tel: 713-741-8704.

Catholic School Office—Sr. KEVINA KEATING, C.C.V.I., Supt., 2403 Holcombe, Houston, 77021-2099. Tel: 713-741-8704.

School of Environmental Education - Camp Kappe—Sr. THOMAS ANN LA COUR, O.P., Prin., 7738 Camp Kappe Rd., Navasota, 77363. Tel: 936-894-2141.

Secretariat for Social Concerns—VACANT, Dir., 2403 Holcombe, Houston, 77021-2099. Tel: 713-741-8769.

Campaign for Human Development—Deacon SAM DUNNING, Dir., 2403 Holcombe, Houston, 77021-2098. Tel: 713-741-8731.

Catholic Charities—BONNA KOL, Pres. & CEO, 2900 Louisiana St., Houston, 77006. Tel: 713-526-4611; Fax: 713-526-1546. Mailing Address: P.O. Box 66508, Houston, 77266; VACANT, Exec. Vice Pres. Tel: 713-874-6740.

Program Services—VACANT.

Finance and Human Resources—KATHY FOUNTAIN, CPA. Tel: 713-874-6741.

Fund Development/Marketing—Tel: 713-526-4611. Ms. JOANIE WENTZ, Vice Pres. Tel: 713-874-6659.

Community Relations and Advocacy—Deacon JOE RUBIO, Vice Pres. Tel: 713-874-6657.

Technology and Facilities—MICHAEL GILLESPIE, Vice Pres. Tel: 713-874-6729.

Human Resources—GLENDA BATES. Tel: 713-874-6748.

Children & Family Services—VALERIE PERALES, L.M.S.W.-A.C.P., Admin. Tel: 713-874-6589.

Children Placement Services Adoption and Foster Care—SHARON JORGESON, L.M.S.W., Supvr. Tel: 713-874-6594.

Services to Pregnant and Parenting Adolescents—CAROL SHULSE, C.C.A. Supvr. Tel: 713-874-6593.

Post Adoption Services—LILLIAN SALINAS, L.M.S.W. Tel: 713-874-6575.

St. Jerome Emiliani's Home for Children—MICHELLE MITCHELL, M.S., N.C.C., S.W.A., Supvr. Tel: 713-874-6587.

Community Outreach Services—VACANT.

AIDS Ministry—VACANT, Supvr., 2900 Louisiana St., Houston, 77006. Tel: 713-874-6699.

Guadalupe Center—ANA RAUSH, Dir. Housing, 326 S. Jensen, Houston, 77003-1599. Family Assistance Program, Villa Guadalupe-Transitional Housing for Women.

Parish Social Ministry—CHRIS RUBIO. Tel: 713-526-4611.

Services to the Alone and Frail Elderly—VACANT, Supvr. Tel: 713-874-6670.

Family Counseling—VALERIE PERALES, L.M.S.W.-A.C.P., Dir. Admin.; Sr. CARMEN SANCHEZ. Tel: 713-874-6590 (Appointments); 713-874-6608 (Direct).

Immigration and Refugee Services—VACANT, Admin.

St. Frances Cabrini Center for Immigrant Legal Assistance—WAFA ABDIN, J.D., Supvr. Tel: 713-874-6570.

Refugee Resettlement Services—DANIELLE BOLKS, Supvr. Tel: 713-874-6527.

St. Michael's Home for Children—LETICIA HARMON, Supvr. Tel: 713-526-4611.

Serenity House—CONNIE HIDALGO. Tel: 713-874-6668.

Galveston County Center—ELIZABETH KINARD, Supvr., 4418 Ave. M, Galveston, 77550-3726. Tel: 409-762-2143; 409-949-9884 (Texas City Office); Fax: 409-762-2088.

Justice and Peace—Deacon SAM DUNNING, Dir., 2403 E. Holcombe, Houston, 77021-2099. Tel: 713-741-8730.

St. Vincent de Paul Society—Ms. ANN SCHORNO, Exec. Dir., 2403 Holcombe, Houston, 77021-2099. Tel: 713-741-8783.

Council of Catholic Women—Rev. Msgr. DANIEL L. SCHEEL, Archdiocesan Moderator, 8825 Kempwood Dr., Houston, 77080. Tel: 713-468-9555.

Cursillos in Christianity—Deacon HECTOR MORALES, Admin.; Rev. EUGENE CANAS, O.M.I., Spiritual Dir., St. Paul Cursillo Center, 4000 Belk St., Houston, 77087. Tel: 713-643-7682.

Disaster Relief—VACANT, 1700 San Jacinto, Houston, 77002. Tel: 713-659-5461.

Rural Life Bureau—VACANT, 1700 San Jacinto St., Houston, 77002-8291. Tel: 713-659-5461.

Victim Assistance Coordinator—Sr. MAUREEN O'CONNELL, O.P. Tel: 713-659-5461, Ext. 499; 713-654-5799. Email: moconnell@archgh.org.

CLERGY, PARISHES, MISSIONS AND PAROCHIAL SCHOOLS

CITY OF GALVESTON

(GALVESTON COUNTY)

1—ST. MARY'S CATHEDRAL BASILICA (1840), (Unattended)
Res., Church & Mailing Address: 2011 Church St., 77550-2091. Tel: 409-762-9611; Fax: 409-765-8585. Email: cathedralstmary@sbcglobal.net. Web: www.marycath.org.

2—HOLY FAMILY (2009) Revs. John Stein, O.F.M.; John Paul Flajole, O.F.M., Parochial Vicar; Maynard Tetreault, O.F.M., Parochial Vicar; John Kare Taosan, C.I.M., Parochial Vicar.
1010 35th St., 77550. In Res., Rev. Juan Arellano, C.P.
Catechesis/Religious Program—Tel: 409-762-9646; Fax: 409-765-7636. Email: jjefferies@holyfamilygb.org. Mrs. Jo Anita Jefferies, D.R.E. Students 497.

3—HOLY ROSARY (1888) Closed. For parish records contact the Archives of Galveston-Houston.

4—OUR LADY OF GUADALUPE, Closed. August 1992. Contact St Patrick, Galveston for further information.

5—ST. PATRICK (1870) Closed. For parish records contact the Archives of Galveston-Houston.

6—ST. PETER THE APOSTLE (1965) Closed. For parish records contact the Archives of Galveston-Houston.

7—SACRED HEART (1884) Closed. For parish records contact the Archives of Galveston-Houston.

CITY OF HOUSTON

(HARRIS COUNTY)

1—ST. ALBERT OF TRAPANI (1970) Rev. Vincent Tran; Deacons Carlito Buhay; Alvaro Casas Jr.; Larry T. Longley.
Church & Mailing Address: 11027 S. Gessner Dr., 77071-3599. Tel: 713-771-3596; Fax: 713-270-0441. Email: secretary@stalberthouston.org. Web: www.stalberthouston.org.
Catechesis/Religious Program— Peggy Popkey, D.R.E. Students 215.

2—ALL SAINTS (1908) Rev. Msgr. Adam S. McClosky; Deacons Gary Hilbig; Rodolfo Cerda. In Res., Rev. Ronald F. Cloutier.
Res., Church & Mailing Address: 215 E. 10th St., 77008-7025. Tel: 713-864-2653; Fax: 713-864-0761. Email: christine.reyes@allsaints.us.com. Web: www.allsaints.us.com.
Catechesis/Religious Program— Daniel Schwieterman, D.R.E. Students 472.

3—ST. ALPHONSUS (1966) Rev. Rivers Patout, Admin.
Res., Church & Mailing Address: 9217 E. Ave. L, 77012-2727. Tel: 713-923-5843; Fax: 713-923-5866. Email: stalphonsusch@aol.com.
Catechesis/Religious Program—Mrs. Mary Elizondo, C.R.E. Students 598.

4—ST. AMBROSE (1958) Revs. Benjamin Smaistrla; Miguel A. Alvizures, Parochial Vicar.
Res., Church & Mailing Address: 4213 Mangum Rd., 77092-5599. Tel: 713-686-3497; Fax: 713-686-6604. Web: www.stambrosehouston.org.
School—Tel: 713-686-6990; Fax: 713-686-6902. Email: info@sashornets.org. Web: www.sashornets.org. Judy A. Fritsch, Prin. Lay Teachers 29; Students 356.
Catechesis/Religious Program—Tel: 713-686-3857. Miguel Vences, D.R.E. Students 600.

5—ST. ANDREW KIM (1977), (Korean), Rev. Yong Huyk Lee.
Church & Mailing Address: 1706 Bingle Rd., 77055-2336. Tel: 713-465-2682; Fax: 713-465-5974. Email: standrewkimhouston@yahoo.com. Web: www.stakim.org.
Rectory—8557 Hiridge St., 77055. Tel: 713-465-2926.
Convent—Handmaids of the Sacred Heart of Jesus (H.S.H.), Tel: 713-465-1196; Fax: 713-465-2682. Email: sea4628@hotmail.com. Sisters 2.
Catechesis/Religious Program—Tel: 281-489-9952. Mr. Young Kim, C.R.E. Students 166.

6—ST. ANNE (1925) Revs. Alvin A. Sinasac, C.S.B.; Jay Francis Walsh, C.S.B.; William J. Frankenberger, C.S.B.; Deacons William Garrett; Jean-Paul Budinger. In Res., Rev. Thomas Bernard Mailloux, C.S.B. (Retired).
Res., Church & Mailing Address: 2140 Westheimer, 77098-1496. Tel: 713-526-3276; Fax: 713-525-4365. Email: church@saintanne.org. Web: www.saintanncommunity.org.
School—2120 Westheimer, 77098. Tel: 713-526-3279. Kathy Barnosky, Prin. Lay Teachers 34; Students 493.
Catechesis/Religious Program—Tel: 713-526-2936. Students 498.

7—ST. ANNE DE BEAUPRE (1948) Rev. Oliver O. Obele, M.S.P.
Res., Church & Mailing Address: 2810 Link Rd., 77009-1196. Tel: 713-869-1319; Fax: 713-869-4527. Email: stanne@prodigy.net.
Catechesis/Religious Program—Tel: 281-537-6825. Maria Brown, D.R.E. Students 40.

8—ANNUNCIATION (1869) Rev. Msgr. James L. Golasinski; Deacons Bart Hock; Robert George Alexander.
Mailing Address: P.O. Box 214, 77001-0214. Tel: 713-222-2289; Fax: 713-222-2280. Email: info@annunciationcc.org.
Church: 1618 Texas Ave., 77001-0214. Email: info@annunciationcc.org.
Catechesis/Religious Program—Herman Jadloski, S.T.L., D.R.E. Students 72.

9—ASCENSION CHINESE MISSION (1988), (Chinese), Rev. Louis C. Zee; Deacon Paul Kiang.
Office Mailing Address: P.O. Box 749, Alief, 77411-0749.
Church: 4605 Jetty Ln., 77411-0749. Tel: 281-575-8855; Fax: 281-575-6940. Email: zeeplace@juno.com. Web: www.ascensionchinesemission.org.
Catechesis/Religious Program—Tel: 281-495-9257. Rita Huang, D.R.E. Students 60.

10—ASSUMPTION (1948) Revs. Albert Zanatta, C.R.S.; Romualdo Lopez, C.R.S., Parochial Vicar; Deacon Mario Ortega.
Res., Church & Mailing Address: 901 Rose Ln., 77037-4699. Tel: 281-447-6381; Fax: 281-447-6382. Email: acchurch@comcast.net.
Catechesis/Religious Program—Tel: 281-931-1460. Mario Ortega, D.R.E. Students 1,044.

11—ST. AUGUSTINE (1955) Rev. Julian "Mike" Barrosa, D.S.; Deacons Benito Meza; Jose E. Fuentez.
Mailing Address: 5438 Laurel Creek Way, 77017-6746.
Church & Res.: 5560 Laurel Creek Way, 77017-6729. Tel: 713-946-8968; Fax: 713-946-0080. Email: sacc@staugustinecc.com. Web: www.staugustinecc.com.
School—5500 Laurel Creek Way, 77017. Tel: 713-946-9050; Fax: 713-943-3444. Lonnie Burgett, Prin. Lay Teachers 16; Students 201.
Catechesis/Religious Program—Teresa Fuentez, D.R.E. Students 352.

12—ST. BENEDICT THE ABBOT (1963) Revs. Joseph Huy Quang Dinh, C.S.Sp.; Andy H. Do, C.S.Sp.
Church & Mailing Address: 4025 Grapevine, 77045-6320. Tel: 713-433-9836; Fax: 713-433-3949. Email: stbenedictabbotcc@sbcglobal.net. Web: www.stbenedictchurchhouston.org.
Rectory—3931 Grapevine, 77045.
Catechesis/Religious Program—Tel: 713-433-2436. Adela Tijerina, D.R.E. Students 394.

13—ST. BERNADETTE SOUBIROUS (1977) Revs. Robert Barras; Matthew Thottiyil, M.S.F.S.; Ruben C. Nwankwor, Chap.; Deacon Bob Rumford.
Church & Mailing Address: 15500 El Camino Real, 77062-5793. Tel: 281-486-0337; Fax: 281-218-9440. Email: office@stbchurch.org. Web: www.stbchurch.org.
Rectory—959 El Dorado Blvd., 77062.
School— Pam Calandra, Prin. Lay Teachers 16; Students 130.
Catechesis/Religious Program—Tel: 281-486-0337, Ext. 112. Barbara Aubuchon, D.R.E. (K-5); Marianne Bartos, D.R.E. (6-8). Students 1,060.

14—BLESSED SACRAMENT (1910) Rev. Rudolfo Sanchez, Admin.
Res., Church & Mailing Address: 4015 Sherman, 77003-2695. Tel: 713-224-5291; Fax: 713-224-5292.
Catechesis/Religious Program—Students 360.

15—ST. CATHERINE OF SIENA (1975) Rev. Niall Nolan.
Church & Mailing Address: 10688 Shadow Wood Dr., 77043-2826. Tel: 713-467-8170; Fax: 713-467-7149. Email: stcat7433@sbcglobal.net. Web: www.stcat.net.
Rectory—1902 Stebbins Dr., 77043-2417.
Catechesis/Religious Program—Students 46.

16—ST. CECILIA (1956) Revs. John E. Cahoon; Victor Perez; Carlos V. de la Torre; Deacons Donald E. Bradley; Gregory Evans; Carlos Porras; Roberto Chavez; Robert J. Hesse; Sam Mancuso. In Res., Rev. Thao Lam.
Church & Mailing Address: 11720 Joan of Arc Dr., 77024-2602. Tel: 713-465-3414; Fax: 713-465-1305. Email: frcahoon@saintcecilia.org. Web: www.saintcecilia.org.
Rectory—11701 Joan of Arc Dr., 77024.
School—11740 Joan of Arc Dr., 77024. Tel: 713-468-9515; Fax: 713-468-4698. Dr. Carol Ann Everling, Prin. Lay Teachers 45; Students 584.
Catechesis/Religious Program— Rosemary Munoz, D.R.E. Students 1,642.

17—ST. CHARLES BORROMEO (1962) Revs. Miguel A. Solorzano; Eduardo Lopez, C.M.; Deacons Charles R. Conant; Rodrigo Lozano; Thomas Gandara.
Res., Church & Mailing Address: 501 Tidwell, 77022-2121. Tel: 713-692-6303; Fax: 713-692-6314. Email: miguel@solorzano.com.
Rectory—601 Cravens, 77076.
School—Tel: 713-692-4898; Fax: 713-692-1376.
Catechesis/Religious Program—Sr. Marcella I. Perez, D.J., D.R.E. Students 371.

18—CHRIST THE KING (1928) Revs. Giulio Veronesi, C.R.S.; Remo Zanatta, C.R.S., Parochial Vicar; Deacon Gerardo J. Garcia. In Res., Revs. Italo Dell'Oro, C.R.S.; Julian Gerosa, C.R.S.
Res., Church & Mailing Address: 4419 N. Main St., 77009-5199. Tel: 713-869-1449; Fax: 713-869-1491. Email: secretary@ctkcc.org. Web: www.ctkcc.org.
Catechesis/Religious Program—Tel: 713-869-3140. Deacon Gerry Garcia, D.R.E. Students 884.

19—CHRIST THE REDEEMER (1980) Revs. Sean Horrigan; Reginald Wayne Samuels; Deacons James H. Osterhaus; Ralph R. Gregory Jr.; Phillip Jackson; Lupe Trevino; Greg Hall; William Bradley. In Res., Rev. Ignatius C. Nwgnkwocha.
Church & Mailing Address: 11507 Huffmeister Rd., 77065-1051. Tel: 281-469-5533; Fax: 281-469-8441. Email: office@ctrcc.com. Web: www.ctrcc.com.
Catechesis/Religious Program—Tel: 281-469-5533. Mary Phillips, D.R.E. Students 2,471.

20—CHRIST, THE INCARNATE WORD (1997), (Vietnamese), Rev. Msgr. Philippe Le-Xuan Thuong; Rev. Joseph T.P. Bui; Deacon Joseph Si Nguyen Bach.
Res., Church & Mailing Address: 8503 S. Kirkwood Rd., 77099-4056. Tel: 281-495-8133; Fax: 281-495-4220.
Catechesis/Religious Program—Tel: 281-495-3741. Anthony Nguyen, C.R.E. Students 756.

21—ST. CHRISTOPHER (1924) Revs. Joseph Thu Le; Francisco F. Arboleda-Restrepo, M.X.Y., Parochial Vicar; Deacons Allan Fredericksen; Merce C. Leal Jr.; Benito Tristan Jr.
Res., Church & Mailing Address: 8150 Park Place Blvd., 77017-3033. Tel: 713-645-6614; Fax: 713-640-1640. Email: mary.avila@comcast.net. Web: www.stchristopherhouston.org.
School—8134 Park Place Blvd., 77017. Tel: 713-649-0009; Fax: 713-649-1104. Jo Ann Prater, Prin. Sisters 2; Lay Teachers 13; Students 239.
Catechesis/Religious Program—Tel: 713-645-6142. Maria Fernandez, D.R.E. Students 578.

22—ST. CLARE OF ASSISI (1990) Revs. Vincent Vuong Quoc Nguyen; Robert J. Matzinger, C.S.B.; Deacons John H. Dean; Jim Wright.
Res., Church & Mailing Address: 3131 El Dorado Blvd., 77059-5100. Tel: 281-286-7729; Fax: 281-286-1256. Email: carmen.dalberg@stclarehouston.org. Web: www.stclarehouston.org.
Rectory—15906 Laurelfield, 77059.
School—Tel: 281-286-3395. Al Varisco, Prin. Lay Teachers 30; Students 219.

Catechesis/Religious Program—Tel: 281-486-0874. Sandra Trevino, D.R.E. Students 398.

23—CO-CATHEDRAL OF THE SACRED HEART (1896) Very Rev. Lawrence W. Jozwiak; Revs. Thu Ngoc Nguyen; Jude Ezuma; Deacons Marvin R. Fikac; John Salinas; Leonard P. Lockett; Juan Parejo; John Carrara.
Res.: 1111 St. Joseph Pkwy., 77002-8127. Tel: 713-659-1561; Fax: 713-651-1365. Email: office@sacredhearthouston.org. Web: www.sacredhearthouston.org.
Catechesis/Religious Program— Teresa Albright, D.R.E. Students 315.

24—CORPUS CHRISTI (1956) Revs. Dana Pelotte, S.S.S.; Robert A. Chabot, S.S.S. In Res., Rev. Peter J. Dorairaj, S.S.S.; Bro. Anthony Ornelas.
Res., Church & Mailing Address: 9900 Stella Link Rd., 77025-4718. Tel: 713-667-0497; Fax: 713-668-4742. Email: danagsss@yahoo.com. Web: www.corpuschristichurchhouston.org.
School—4005 Cheena St., 77025. Tel: 713-664-3351; Fax: 713-664-6095. Email: cmueller@corpuschristihouston.org. Web: www.corpuschristihouston.org. Ms. Claire Mueller, Prin. Lay Teachers 16; Students 209.
Catechesis/Religious Program—Tel: 713-667-0497. Susie Way, D.R.E.; Leonor Castillo, D.R.E. Students 480.

25—ST. CYRIL OF ALEXANDRIA (1963) Rev. Mario J. Arroyo; Deacon Eduardo M. Dolpher.
Res., Church & Mailing Address: 10503 Westheimer Rd., 77042-3502. Tel: 713-789-1250; Fax: 713-780-0967. Email: marroyo@stcyrilhouston.org. Web: www.stcyrilhouston.org.
Catechesis/Religious Program—Tel: 713-789-1250. Aida Silva, D.R.E. Students 725.

26—ST. DOMINIC (1965) Rev. Roger O. Estorque.
Res., Church & Mailing Address: 8215 Reservoir St., 77049-1728. Tel: 281-458-2910; Fax: 281-458-7114. Email: stdominicchurch@comcast.net. Web: www.parishesonline.com.
Catechesis/Religious Program—Sr. Olga Rivera, D.R.E. Students 341.

27—ST. ELIZABETH ANN SETON (1977) Revs. Paul E. Lockey, Admin.; Philip M. Ba Son Lam; Gregorio Filipe Can-Vasquez; Deacons German Godoy, Pastoral Assoc.; Charles G. Pennell; Gilbert R. Johnson; Alfonso Sosa; Joe Zamora; Peter Hoang. In Res., Rev. Charles Van Vliet, F.S.S.P.
Church & Mailing Address: 6646 Addicks-Satsuma Rd., 77084-1599. Tel: 281-463-7878; Fax: 281-463-4822. Email: seasoffice@seascatholic.org. Web: www.seascatholic.org.
School—Tel: 281-463-1444; Fax: 281-463-8707. Jan Krametbauer, Prin. Lay Teachers 36; Students 543.
Catechesis/Religious Program—Tel: 281-463-7356. Students 2,215.

28—ST. FRANCES CABRINI (1962) Rev. Frank T. Fabj; Deacons Robert Gregory Stevens; Servando J. Rojas.
Church & Mailing Address: 10727 Hartsook St., 77034-3523. Tel: 713-946-5768; Fax: 713-946-3282. Email: cabrini@sfchoutx.org. Web: www.sfchoutx.org.
Rectory—10726 Bessemer St., 77034.
Catechesis/Religious Program— Mrs. Nancy Patyrak, D.R.E. Students 1,158.

29—ST. FRANCIS DE SALES (1962) Rev. Wayne W. Wilkerson; Deacon Antonio Flores. In Res., Rev. Enrique V. Salen.
Church & Mailing Address: 8200 Roos Rd., 77036-6399. Tel: 713-774-7475; Fax: 713-774-6591. Email: shirleyg@sfdshouston.org. Web: www.sfdshouston.org.
Res.: 8018 Roos Rd., 77036. Tel: 713-774-7475; Fax: 713-774-6591.
School—8100 Roos Rd., 77036. Tel: 713-774-4447; Fax: 713-271-6744. Diane Wooten, Prin. Lay Teachers 32; Students 445.
Catechesis/Religious Program—Mrs. Ann Cashiola, D.R.E. Students 515.

30—ST. FRANCIS OF ASSISI (1950) Rev. Edmund C. Nnadozie, M.S.P.; Deacons Ignatius Joseph; Michael St. Julian.
Res., Church & Mailing Address: 5102 Dabney St., 77026-3015. Tel: 713-672-7773; Fax: 713-673-1913. Email: stfrancisofhouston@yahoo.com. Web: www.sfahouston.org.
School—5100 Dabney St., 77026. Tel: 832-674-1966; Fax: 713-674-9901. Diane Fuccgrini, Prin. Priests 1; Sisters 3; Lay Teachers 12; Students 197.
Catechesis/Religious Program—Tel: 713-672-7773, Ext. 106. Sr. Anthonia Osueso, C.R.E. Students 197.

31—ST. FRANCIS XAVIER (1952) Revs. Peter Weiss, S.S.J.; Joseph C. Benjamin, S.S.J., Parochial Vicar; Deacons Michael V. Jenkins; Frank Laugerman.
Res., Church & Mailing Address: 4600 Reed Rd., 77051-2857. Tel: 713-738-2311; Fax: 713-738-3337. Email: stfrancishou@att.net. Web: www.josephite.com/parish/tx/sfx.
Catechesis/Religious Program—Tel: 281-753-8087. Judy Simon, D.R.E.; Kimberly Chandler, D.R.E. Students 121.

32—ST. GREGORY THE GREAT (1962) Revs. Francis Huan Ton Ngo; Puschal O. Ezeihuona (GA), Parochial Vicar; Deacons Julio M. Ramirez; Abner Brown Sr.
Res., Church & Mailing Address: 10500 Nold Dr., 77016-2921. Tel: 713-631-3681; Fax: 713-631-6114. Email: nuantngo@aol.com.
Catechesis/Religious Program—Tel: 713-631-0058. Sr. Ann Theresa Nguyen, C.R.E. Students 170.

33—HOLY CROSS CHAPEL (Downtown) (1982) Rev. Michael J. Barrett, S.T.D.
Chapel— 905 Main St., 77002-6408. Tel: 713-650-1323; Fax: 713-650-8836. Email: info@holycrosschapel.org. Web: www.holycrosschapel.org.

34—HOLY GHOST (1946) Revs. Jaime C. Arrambide, C.Ss.R.; Eugene Batungbacal; Peter H. Voelker, C.Ss.R.; Andrew Thompson, C.Ss.R.; Stephen Benden, C.Ss.R., Parochial Vicar. In Res., Revs. Leonard Broniak, C.Ss.R.; John E.P. Gouger, C.Ss.R.; Bro. John (Patrick) F. Concidine, C.Ss.R.; Deacon Robert T. Brueggerhoff.
Res., Church & Mailing Address: 6921 Chetwood Dr., 77081-5697. Tel: 713-668-0463; Fax: 713-661-4645. Email: hgc@holyghostchurch.net. Web: www.holyghostchurch.net.
School—6920 Chimney Rock Rd., 77081. Tel: 713-668-5327; Fax: 713-667-4410. Sr. Judy Scheffler, S.S.N.D., Prin. Lay Teachers 12; Students 112.
Catechesis/Religious Program—Tel: 713-668-8001. Ms. Marilynn Wilson, D.R.E. Students 646.

35—HOLY NAME (1920) Revs. Brendan Murphy, S.V.D.; Siprianus Ola Rotok, S.V.D.
Mailing Address: 1917 Cochran St., 77009-8497.
Church: 1920 Marion St., 77009. Tel: 713-222-1255; Fax: 713-222-1260. Web: holynamecatholic.org.
Catechesis/Religious Program—Students 341.

36—HOLY ROSARY (1913) Revs. Ian G. Bordenave, O.P.; Isidore V. Vicente, O.P.; Juan M. Torres, O.P. In Res., Revs. Joseph D. Konkel, O.P.; Art Kerwin, O.P., Parochial Vicar; Victor B. Brown, O.P.; Francois Pouliot, O.P.; Richard Williams, O.P.; Martin Iott, O.P.
Res. & Mailing Address: 3600 Travis St., 77002-9591. Tel: 713-529-4854; Fax: 713-522-3967. Email: office@holyrosaryparish.org. Web: www.holyrosaryparish.org.
Church: 3600 Milan St., 77002.
Catechesis/Religious Program—Tel: 713-526-4389. Janet Hafernik, D.R.E. Students 178.

37—IMMACULATE CONCEPTION (1911) Revs. Kevin A. Collins, O.M.I.; Henry B. Walker, O.M.I.
Res., Church & Mailing Address: 7250 Harrisburg Blvd., 77011-4791. Tel: 713-921-1261; Fax: 713-921-2304. Email: iccsec@comcast.net.
Catechesis/Religious Program— Teresa Martinez, C.R.E. Students 613.

38—IMMACULATE HEART OF MARY (1926) Revs. Ramiro Cortez, O.M.I.; Edward M. Ward, O.M.I. In Res., Rev. Eugene Canas, O.M.I.
Res., Church & Mailing Address: 7539 Ave. K, 77012-1033. Tel: 713-923-2394; Fax: 713-923-6497. Email: ihmhouston@hotmail.com.
Catechesis/Religious Program—Tel: 713-921-5431. Becky Arcizo, D.R.E. Students 331.

39—ST. JEROME (1960) Rev. Msgr. Daniel L. Scheel; Revs. Michael S. Van Cleve; Joseph A. Doran; Deacons Pedro Salas; Antonio Moya; Dan O'Dowd.
Church & Mailing Address: 8825 Kempwood, 77080-4199. Tel: 713-468-9555; Fax: 713-464-0325. Email: stjeromehou@msn.com. Web: www.stjeromechurch.org.
Rectory—9011 Friendship, 77080.
School—Tel: 713-468-7946. Sharon Makulski, Prin. Sisters 1; Lay Teachers 22; Students 305.
Catechesis/Religious Program—Tel: 713-464-5029. Ms. Gabriela Kavaszewski, D.R.E. Students 1,380.

40—ST. JOHN NEUMANN (1977) Rev. Msgr. Seth F. Hermoso; Rev. Linh N. Nguyen, Parochial Vicar.
Church & Mailing Address: 2730 Nelwood Dr., 77038-1025. Tel: 281-931-0684; Fax: 281-931-5363. Email: stjneumannparish@hotmail.com.
Rectory—2715 Nelwood Dr., 77038-1025.
Catechesis/Religious Program—Tel: 281-580-5415. Valerie Ponce, D.R.E. Students 667.

41—ST. JOHN VIANNEY (1966) Revs. R. Troy Gately; Charles J. Talar; Daniel L. Warden (Retired); Deacons Dale W. Steffes; Albert E. Vacek Jr.; Frederick Kossegi. In Res., Rev. Daniel L. Warden (Retired).
Res., Church & Mailing Address: 625 Nottingham Oaks Tr., 77079-6234. Tel: 281-497-1500; Fax: 281-584-2024. Email: sjv@stjohnvianney.org. Web: www.stjohnvianney.org.
Catechesis/Religious Program—Tel: 281-497-6665. Daniel Marcantel, D.R.E. Students 1,521.

42—ST. JOSEPH (1880) Rev. Alberto A. Rodriguez; Deacon Reynaldo S. Gil. In Res., Rev. Jan Kubisa.
Res., Church & Mailing Address: 1505 Kane St., 77007-7711. Tel: 713-222-6193; Fax: 713-222-1729. Email: stjosephoffice@stjosephcch.org. Web: www.stjosephcch.org.
Catechesis/Religious Program—Tel: 713-222-6579. Marina Ramirez, D.R.E. Students 190.

43—ST. JUSTIN MARTYR (1982) Revs. Paul R. Chovanec; Greg Viet Nguyen, I.C.M.; Deacons Garey Boyd; Cornelius C. Llorens; Louis Provenzano; Nhat Tran.
Church & Mailing Address: 13350 Ashford Point Dr., 77082-5100. Tel: 281-556-5116; Fax: 281-556-6932. Email: sjm@sjmtx.com. Web: www.sjmtx.org.
Rectory—3142 W. Hampton, 77082.
Catechesis/Religious Program— Debbie Lazarou, D.R.E. Students 830.

44—ST. LEO THE GREAT (1973) Revs. Rafael Becerra, C.S.; Leandro Fossa.
Res., Church & Mailing Address: 2131 Lauder Rd., 77039-3199. Tel: 281-449-2344; Fax: 281-442-3156. Email: stleohou@sbcglobal.net.
Catechesis/Religious Program— Sr. Concepcion, D.R.E. Students 1,233.

45—ST. LUKE THE EVANGELIST (1975) Revs. James M. Burkart; Thomas Joseph Puthusseril, O.S.H.; Deacons Tom Hawxhurst; Jesse Tollett; Alvin Birsinger; Charles Roessler Jr.; Adolfo Mejia.
Church & Mailing Address: 11011 Hall Rd., 77089-2999. Tel: 281-481-6816; Fax: 281-481-8780. Email: parishadministrator@stlukecatholic.com. Web: www.stlukecatholic.com.
Rectory: 8402 Kirkville, 77089.
Catechesis/Religious Program—Marilyn Kiel, D.R.E. Students 1,218.

46—ST. MARK THE EVANGELIST (1974) Rev. Hugh G. Cullen; Deacons John Benoit; Tony Alessi; Marcelino Villareal.
Church and Mailing Address: 5430 W. Ridgecreek Dr., 77053-3211. Email: mgosline@stmarkshouston.org.
Rectory—5302 Castlecreek Ln., 77053. Tel: 281-437-9114; 281-437-4828; Fax: 281-835-6303.
Catechesis/Religious Program—Tel: 281-416-0186. Zulema Perez, D.R.E. Students 250.

47—ST. MARY OF THE PURIFICATION (1929) Revs. Francis Borgia Aubespin, S.V.D.; Chien Dinh, S.V.D.; Deacon Andrew B. Malveaux Sr. In Res., Rev. Tan Viet Nguyen, SV.D.
Res., Church & Mailing Address: 3006 Rosedale, 77004-6128. Tel: 713-528-0571; Fax: 713-528-0572. Email: baubespin@stmaryshouston.org. Web: www.stmaryshouston.org.
School—3002 Rosedale, 77004. Tel: 713-522-9276; Fax: 713-522-1879. Mrs. Mazie McCoy, Prin. Sisters 2; Lay Teachers 14; Students 151.
Catechesis/Religious Program—Tel: 281-437-4110. Students 213.

48—ST. MATTHEW THE EVANGELIST (1974) Revs. Luis Evardoni; Arthur P. Alban; Deacon John W. Adams.
Res., Church & Mailing Address: 9915 Hollister Dr., 77040-1702. Tel: 713-466-4030; Fax: 713-896-7235. Email: admin@stmatthewhou.org. Web: www.stmatthewhou.org.
Catechesis/Religious Program—Tel: 713-466-0510. John Guzman, D.R.E. Students 332.

49—ST. MAXIMILIAN KOLBE (1983) Rev. John F. Ulm; Deacons Dennis Hayes; Stacy Millsap; Joseph Weir; Robert Henkel Sr. In Res., Rev. Msgr. Milam Kleas (Retired).
Church and Mailing Address: 10135 West Rd., 77064-5361. Tel: 281-955-7324; Fax: 281-955-7328. Email: stmaximilian@stmaximilian.org. Web: www.stmaximilian.org.
Rectory—10218 Great Plains, 77064.
Catechesis/Religious Program— Stephanie Slattery, D.R.E. Students 747.

50—ST. MICHAEL (1925) Rev. Msgr. Frank H. Rossi; Rev. Douglas Guthrie, Parochial Vicar; Deacons Thomas C. Newhouse; Henry Woods Martin; Jack Alexander; Leonard P. Lockett. In Res., Rev. Leon Strieder.
Res., Church & Mailing Address: 1801 Sage Rd., 77056-3502. Tel: 713-621-4370; Fax: 713-850-8341. Email: parishoffice@stmichaelchurch.net. Web: www.stmichaelchurch.net.
School—1833 Sage Rd., 77056-3502. Tel: 713-621-6847; Fax: 713-877-8812. Chris Skowronek, Prin. Sisters 1; Lay Teachers 33; Students 449.
Catechesis/Religious Program—Tel: 713-840-8213. Mrs. Mary Jo Wilt, D.R.E. Students 513.

51—ST. MONICA (1960) Rev. John M. Ayang, S.O.L.T.; Deacon John Lane.
Res., Church & Mailing Address: 8421 W. Montgomery Rd., 77088-7116. Tel: 281-447-5837; Fax: 281-447-8410. Email: stmonica@sbcglobal.net. Web: www.stmonicahouston.com.
Catechesis/Religious Program—Jennifer Sims, D.R.E. Students 104.

52—ST. NICHOLAS (1887) Rev. Desmond C. Ohankwere, M.S.P.
Res., Church & Mailing Address: 2508 Clay St., 77003-4406. Tel: 713-223-5210; Fax: 713-222-0424.

Catechesis/Religious Program— Mary Owens, D.R.E. Students 29.

53—NOTRE DAME (1969) Rev. Msgr. Rolando V. Diokno; Rev. Lukose Manuel, O.S.H.; Deacons F.L. Ostrowski; Ernesto Abadejos; Elie P. Calonge; Anthony Rudnicki.
Rectory—11226 Pompano Ln., 77072-3595.
Church & Mailing Address: 7720 Boone Rd., 77072-3595. Tel: 281-498-4653; Fax: 281-879-1527. Email: pastor@notredamechurch.org. Web: notredamechurch.org.
Catechesis/Religious Program—Tel: 281-495-1256. Farah Najjar, D.R.E. Students 704.

54—OUR LADY OF CZESTOCHOWA (1982), (Polish), Rev. Waldemar Matusiak, S.Ch.; Deacon Anthony Rudnicki.
Mailing Address: 1712 Oak Tree, 77080-7240. Tel: 713-973-1081; Fax: 713-984-9501.
Church: 1731 Blalock Rd., 77080. Tel: 713-973-1081; Fax: 713-984-9501. Email: parish@parafiahouston.com. Web: www.parafiahouston.com.
Catechesis/Religious Program—Students 50.

55—OUR LADY OF GUADALUPE (1912) [JC] Rev. Edward Kilianski, S.C.J.; Deacons Manuel A. Laurel; Gabriel Z. Quiroga. In Res., Revs. Joseph Thien Dinh, S.C.J.; Peter Mastrobuono, S.C.J.; Vien Nguyen, S.C.J.
Res., Church & Mailing Address: 2405 Navigation Blvd., 77003-1599. Tel: 713-222-0203; Fax: 713-357-6255. Email: parish@olghouston.org. Web: www.olghouston.org.
School—Tel: 713-224-6904; Fax: 713-225-2122. Katherine Costello, Prin. Lay Teachers 18; Students 242.
Catechesis/Religious Program— Sr. Anne Garcia, M.C.D.P., D.R.E. Students 665.

56—OUR LADY OF LAVANG CHURCH (1985), (Vietnamese), Revs. Joseph Chung Van Do, O.P., Admin.; John Baptist Minh Doan, O.P., Parochial Vicar; Deacon Michael Kim Khanh Nguyen.
Mailing Address: 12320 Old Foltin Rd., 77086-3514. Tel: 281-999-1672; Fax: 281-820-7095. Email: info@lavangchurch.org. Web: www.lavangchurch.org.
Church: 12311 Old Foltin Rd., 77086-3513. Email: lavangchurch@yahoo.com.
Catechesis/Religious Program—Tel: 281-955-9395. Deacon Michael Kim Khanh Nguyen, D.R.E. Students 748.

57—OUR LADY OF LOURDES (1994) Revs. Peter Thien Van Hoang, O.P.; J. B. Duc Minh Nguyen, O.P., Parochial Vicar.
Church & Mailing Address: 6550 Fairbanks N. Houston, 77040-4307. Tel: 713-939-1906; Fax: 713-939-0771. Email: lourdes@loduc.org. Web: www.loduc.org.
Catechesis/Religious Program— Rev. Peter Thien Van Hoang, O.P. Students 700.

58—OUR LADY OF MT. CARMEL (1952) Rev. J. Abelardo Cobos; Deacons Juan Aguilar; Frank Bernstsen.
Church: 6723 Whitefriars Dr., 77087. Tel: 713-645-6673; Fax: 713-645-6674. Email: olmcparish@olmchou.org. Web: www.mtcarmelalive.org.
School—6703 Whitefriars Dr., 77087. Tel: 713-643-0676; Fax: 713-649-1835. Mrs. Stephanie Murphy Couty, Prin. Sisters 3; Lay Teachers 8; Students 101.
Catechesis/Religious Program— Diana Zamora, C.R.E. Students 396.

59—OUR LADY OF SORROWS (1936) Rev. Norberto Conde.
Church & Mailing Address: 3006 Kashmere St., 77026-5999. Tel: 713-673-5600; Fax: 713-673-5667. Email: olosch@sbcglobal.net.
Catechesis/Religious Program—Tel: 713-695-3928. Mrs. Rosemary Cadena, Prin. Students 121.

60—OUR LADY OF ST. JOHN (1947) Rev. Edwin A. Coreas.
Church & Mailing Address: 7500 Hirsch Rd., 77016-6215. Tel: 713-631-0810; Fax: 713-631-0781. Email: virgendesanjuan@comcast.net. Web: www.ourladyofstjohns.org.
Catechesis/Religious Program— Sr. Antonia Nerio, D.R.E. Students 168.

61—OUR LADY OF WALSINGHAM (1984) Rev. James Ramsey; Deacons James Barnett; John Denson.
Church & Mailing Address: 7809 Shady Villa Ln., 77055-5011. Tel: 713-683-9407; Fax: 713-683-1518. Email: office@walsingham-church.org. Web: www.walsingham-church.org.
Rectory—1502 Shadyvilla Fern, 77055.
Catechesis/Religious Program—Tel: 281-961-8756. Mark Baker, D.R.E. Students 72.

62—OUR LADY STAR OF THE SEA (1950) Rev. Brian P. Fox, S.S.J.; Deacons Charles J. Allen Sr.; Irvin Johnson Jr.; Rick L. Simon.
Church & Mailing Address: 1401 Fidelity St., 77029-4624. Tel: 713-674-9206; Fax: 713-675-7842. Email: ourlady2@comcast.com. Web: www.ourladystarofthesea2.com.
Catechesis/Religious Program— Daisy Fields, D.R.E. Students 30.

63—OUR MOTHER OF MERCY (1930) Revs. Brian P. Fox, S.S.J.; Kenneth C. Ugwu, S.S.J., Parochial Vicar; Francis D. Ansomkase; Deacons Irvin Johnson Jr.; Rick L. Simon; Charles J. Allen Sr.
Mailing Address: P.O. Box 15640, 77220-5640. In Res., Rev. Kenneth J. Howard, S.S.J.
Res. & Church: 4000 Sumpter St., 77020-2497. Tel: 713-672-0026; Fax: 713-672-2031. Email: pastor@ourmotherofmercy.net. Web: www.ourmotherofmercy.net.
Catechesis/Religious Program—Tel: 713-672-2037. Students 164.

64—ST. PATRICK (1880) Revs. Salvatore DeGeorge, O.M.I.; J. Isidore Garcia, O.M.I.; Deacon Reynaldo Torres.
Church & Mailing Address: 4918 Cochran St., 77009-2117. Tel: 713-695-0631; Fax: 713-695-6255. Email: stpatric4918@sbcglobal.net. Web: www.stpatrickhouston.org.
Catechesis/Religious Program—Tel: 713-697-4325. Ms. Rita Ann Martinez, D.R.E. Students 755.

65—ST. PAUL (1964) Rev. Wencil C. Pavlovsky; Deacons Luis Lopez; Jerry Coenen; James A. Lockwood; Arturo Monterrubio. In Res., Rev. Frederico Ablog, S.S.S.
Church & Mailing Address: 18223 Point Lookout Dr., 77058-3594. Tel: 281-333-3891; Fax: 281-333-3815. Email: parishadministrator@stpaulcatholic.org. Web: www.stpaulcatholic.org.
Rectory—18326 Point Lookout Dr., 77058.
Catechesis/Religious Program—Heidi Clark, D.R.E. Students 604.

66—ST. PETER CLAVER (1964) Rev. Romanus O. Muoneke.
Church & Mailing Address: 6005 N. Wayside Dr., 77028-4494. Tel: 713-674-3338; Fax: 713-674-6524. Email: spclaver1@aol.com.
Catechesis/Religious Program— Martha Gardner, D.R.E. Students 29.

67—ST. PETER THE APOSTLE (1941) Revs. Emmanuel Esukpa, M.S.P.; Aloysius Nzekwe, M.S.P.; Deacon Dan Gilbert.
Res., Church & Mailing Address: 6220 La Salette Dr., 77021-1323. Tel: 713-747-7800; Fax: 713-747-9671. Email: stpetercc@sbcglobal.net.
School—Tel: 713-747-9484; Fax: 713-747-2621. Tandelyn Johnson, Prin. Lay Teachers 16; Students 97.
Catechesis/Religious Program—Tel: 713-842-1226. Stephanie Jackson, D.R.E. Students 59.

68—ST. PHILIP NERI (1961) Rev. Robert T. Kajoh, M.S.P.; Deacons Ronald Simon; James Brooks; Orrin D. Burroughs.
Mailing Address: P.O. Box 330190, 77233-0190. Tel: 713-734-0320; Fax: 713-734-0331. Email: st.philipneri@hotmail.com. Web: www.spnchurch.org.
Church: 10960 Martin Luther King Jr. Blvd., 77048.
School—10950 Martin Luther King Jr. Blvd., 77048. Tel: 713-733-2343. Mrs. Melina Harris, Prin. Priests 2; Sisters 1; Lay Teachers 8; Students 64.
Catechesis/Religious Program—Tel: 713-734-0320. Mary E. Freeman, D.R.E. Students 126.

69—ST. PHILIP OF JESUS (1958) Rev. Jesus E. Suarez; Deacon Roy Breaux.
Church & Mailing Address: 9700 Villita St., 77013-3851. Tel: 713-672-6141; Fax: 713-672-8675. Email: stphilipofjesus@gmail.com.
Catechesis/Religious Program— Marcela Gamez, D.R.E. Students 556.

70—PRINCE OF PEACE (1971) Revs. John T. Keller; Eurel Manzano; Alfonso Delgado, SS.CC.; Deacons Allen W. Prescott; Fred Dinges; Charles Butler; C.J. Mangano; Jeronimo R. Bazan; George Trosclair; Timothy Harnett; Kenneth Stanley; John Hagyari.
Church & Mailing Address: 19222 Tomball Pkwy., 77070-3510. Tel: 281-469-2686; Fax: 281-469-8418. Email: info@pophouston.org. Web: www.pophouston.org.
Catechesis/Religious Program— Jill McAboy, Dir. Faith Formation. Students 2,575.

71—QUEEN OF PEACE (1942) Revs. John A. Vandenakker, C.C.; David Bergeron, C.C., Parochial Vicar; John Paul Bolger, C.C., Parochial Vicar; Deacons Jose L. Liendo; Jose M. Galvan. In Res., Revs. Ed Wade, C.C.; Michael J. Minifie, C.C.; Michael Scherrey, C.C.; Francis A. Frankovich, C.C.
Res., Church & Mailing Address: 3011 Telephone Rd., 77023-5312. Tel: 713-921-6127; Fax: 713-921-6128. Email: queenofpeace.catholic@yahoo.com. Web: www.qophouston.com.
School—2320 Oakcliff St., 77023. Tel: 713-921-1558; Fax: 713-921-0855. Marie Malinsky, Prin. Sisters 1; Lay Teachers 13; Students 191.
Catechesis/Religious Program—Tel: 713-921-1917; Fax: 713-921-6127. Mrs. Tammy Juarez, D.R.E. Students 1,098.

72—ST. RAPHAEL THE ARCHANGEL (1961) Rev. Humberto Sanchez; Deacons Antonio Marquez; Juan De Dios Perez.
Mailing Address: P.O. Box 630787, 77263-0787. Tel: 713-781-9511; Fax: 713-278-9705.
Res. & Church Address: 3915 Ocee, 77063-5417. Email: straphaelcc@comcast.net.
Catechesis/Religious Program—Araceli Perez, D.R.E. Students 400.

73—RESURRECTION (1920) Revs. Christopher M. Plant, Admin.; Blas P. Herrador.
Res., Church & Mailing Address: 915 Zoe St., 77020-6898. Tel: 713-675-5333; Fax: 713-673-3605. Email: acobos@rcchouston.com. Web: www.resurrectioncc.org.
School—916 Majestic St., 77019. Tel: 713-674-2151; Fax: 713-678-4036. Danny Brogee, Prin. Lay Teachers 17; Students 142.
Catechesis/Religious Program—Tel: 713-673-1443. Gloria Hewitt, D.R.E. Students 410.
Station—*La Divina Providencia* Port Houston.

74—ST. ROSE OF LIMA (1947) Revs. Clint C. Ressler, Admin.; Phuong J. Nguyen; Deacons Julio Suriano; John T. Murrell; Larry Hernandez.
Church & Mailing Address: 3600 Brinkman St., 77018-6329. Tel: 713-692-9123; Fax: 713-692-5638. Email: parishmail@stroselima.org. Web: www.stroselima.org.
Rectory—802 Judiway, 77018-6329.
School—Tel: 713-691-0104; Fax: 713-692-8073. Cathy Stephen, Prin. Lay Teachers 14; Students 197.
Catechesis/Religious Program— Deacon John T. Murrell, D.R.E. Students 352.

75—ST. STEPHEN (1941) Rev. Oscar Hernandez, M.J., Admin.
Rectory—Rectory & Mailing Address: 1912 Center St., 77007-6106.
Church: 1912 Center St., 77007. Tel: 713-864-4075; Fax: 713-880-8611. Email: gc.ststephen@sbcglobal.net.
Catechesis/Religious Program—Tel: 281-827-4484. Ms. Maria Costillo, D.R.E. Students 168.

76—ST. THERESA (1946) Rev. Philip P. Lloyd; Deacons Larry A. Vaclavik; Antonio Moya; Rodolfo Cerda. In Res., Rev. Donald S. Nesti, C.S.Sp.
Church & Mailing Address: 6622 Haskell St., 77007-2097. Tel: 713-869-3783; Fax: 713-869-3784. Email: britishbulldog@sttheresa.cc. Web: www.sttheresa.cc.
School—Tel: 713-864-4536; Fax: 713-869-5184. Dr. Sandra Derby, Prin. Lay Teachers 24; Students 194.
Catechesis/Religious Program—Tel: 713-869-9725. Ginger Tamborello, D.R.E. Students 174.

77—ST. THOMAS MORE (1962) Revs. William A. Oliver; Lawrence Clifton Wilson, Parochial Vicar; Deacons Edwin F. Gosline; Edward T. Stoessel; Jorge Garcia. In Res., Revs. Don A. Neumann; Job Kalluvilayil.
Church & Mailing Address: 10330 Hillcroft, 77096-4795. Tel: 713-729-0221; Fax: 713-729-3294. Email: frbill@stmhouston.org. Web: www.stmhouston.org.
School—5927 Wigton, 77096. Tel: 713-729-3434. Mrs. Nadine Mouser, Prin. Lay Teachers 42; Students 548.
Catechesis/Religious Program—Tel: 713-729-3435. Marianne Strzelecki, D.R.E. Students 866.

78—VIETNAMESE MARTYRS (1986), (Vietnamese), Revs. Joseph Thanh Vu; John Hung Manh Nguyen; Deacons Joseph Pham Nguyen; Joseph Ro Van Le.
Mailing Address: 10612 Kingspoint Rd., 77075-4114.
Rectory—10614 Kingspoint Rd., 77075-4114. Tel: 713-941-0521.
Church: 10610 Kingspoint Rd., 77075-4114. Fax: 713-941-2464. Email: vnmartyrs@live.com.
Catechesis/Religious Program— Pham Nguyen, D.R.E. Students 420.

79—ST. VINCENT DE PAUL (1939) Rev. Msgr. William L. Young; Revs. Hoang H Bui; Joy James, O.S.H.; Deacons Daniel Pagnano; Gustavo Camacho del Rio.
Church & Mailing Address: 6800 Buffalo Speedway, 77025-1499. Tel: 713-667-9111; Fax: 713-667-3453. Web: www.stvincentcatholicchurch.org.
School—6802 Buffalo Speedway, 77025. Tel: 713-666-2345; Fax: 713-663-3562. Carolyn Sears, Prin. Lay Teachers 50; Students 515.
Catechesis/Religious Program—Tel: 713-663-3524. Sr. Jean Marie Goukas, C.V.I., D.R.E. Students 879.

OUTSIDE THE CITIES OF GALVESTON AND HOUSTON

ALVIN, BRAZORIA CO., ST. JOHN THE BAPTIST (1952) Revs. Charles J. Borski, O.M.I.; John Franko, O.M.I.; Deacons David Bowman; B. Edward Stoughton; Dale Hayden. In Res., Rev. Henry A. Laenen, O.M.I.
Res., Church & Mailing Address: 110 E. South St., 77511-3570. Tel: 281-331-3751; Fax: 281-331-5430.

Email: stjohns110@att.net.
Catechesis/Religious Program—Tel: 281-824-0877. Mrs. Mary Voight, C.R.E. Students 950.

ANDERSON, GRIMES CO., ST. STANISLAUS (1866) [CEM] Rev. Rodolfo L. Cal-Ortiz Jr., Admin.
Church: 1511 Hwy. 90 S., 77830. Tel: 936-873-2291; Fax: 936-873-3304. Email: ststan@embarqmail.com. Web: www.saintstans.org.
Catechesis/Religious Program— Dana Wagner, C.R.E. Students 102.

ANGLETON, BRAZORIA CO., MOST HOLY TRINITY (1960) Rev. Maurice L. Restivo; Deacons Robert Ward; Luis Hernandez; Cheryl Scott, Pastoral Assoc.
Church & Mailing Address: 1713 N. Tinsley St., 77515-3551. Tel: 979-849-2421; Fax: 979-849-2425. Email: ccang@mostholytrinitychurch.org. Web: www.mostholytrinitychurch.org.
Catechesis/Religious Program—Students 465.

BARRETT STATION, HARRIS CO., ST. MARTIN DE PORRES (1944) [JC] Rev. Alphonsus I. Enelichi, M.S.P.; Mrs. Vicki L. Forrest, Parish Admin. & Bus. Mgr.; Mrs. Constance Duhon, Parish Sec.
Church & Mailing Address: 12606 Crosby-Lynchburg Rd., 77532-8628. Tel: 281-328-4451; Fax: 281-328-7306. Email: smdpbarret@aol.com.
Catechesis/Religious Program—Tel: 281-328-1972. Mrs. Louise Salandy, D.R.E. Students 107.

BAYTOWN, HARRIS CO.

1—ST. JOHN THE EVANGELIST (1974) Rev. Terence P. Brinkman; Deacons Justin J. Wewer; John William Singer Jr.; Dan Foley; Robert Corbett, Pastoral Assoc.; Noreen Provins, Parish Sec.
Church & Mailing Address: 800 W. Baker Rd., 77521-2311. Tel: 281-837-8180; Fax: 281-837-8181. Email: stjohn1974@verizon.net. Web: www.stjohnbaytown.org.
Catechesis/Religious Program—Tel: 281-837-0532. Mrs. Cynthia Hill, D.R.E. Students 258.

2—ST. JOSEPH (1924) Rev. Dwight M. Canizares; Deacon John William Singer Jr.; Evelyn Kohles, Parish Sec.
Res., Church & Mailing Address: 1907 Carolina St., 77520-6098. Tel: 281-420-3588; Fax: 281-422-3044. Email: st_josephbaytown@yahoo.com.
School—1811 Carolina St., 77520-6099. Tel: 281-422-9749. Dr. Ann Mullins, Prin. Sisters 2; Lay Teachers 13; Students 162.
Catechesis/Religious Program—Tel: 281-427-5720. Mrs. Jude Arceneaux, D.R.E. Students 262.

3—OUR LADY OF GUADALUPE (1958) Rev. Jesus Lizalde; Deacons Fernando Gonzalez Bangs; Rudy Venegas; George Rincon.
Church & Mailing Address: 1124 Beech St., 77520-4143. Tel: 281-428-1507; Fax: 281-427-0595. Email: olguadalupe@verizon.net.
Catechesis/Religious Program—Tel: 281-427-0810. Maria Ramirez, D.R.E. Students 637.

BEASLEY, FT. BEND CO., ST. WENCESLAUS MISSION (1923) [CEM], (Independent Mission) Rev. William D. Bartniski.
Mailing Address: 1416 George St., Rosenberg, 77471-3198. Tel: 979-532-4747; Fax: 979-532-8713. Church: 407 S. 3rd St., 77417.
Catechesis/Religious Program—Angie Reid, D.R.E. Students 43.

BELLVILLE, AUSTIN CO., STS. PETER & PAUL (1860) Rev. Timothy P. Bucek; Deacon Gerald W. DuPont. Mailing Address: P.O. Box 808, 77418-0808. Tel: 979-865-2368; Fax: 979-865-9929.
Church: 936 S. Front St., 77418-0176. Email: stspandp@sbcglobal.net.
Catechesis/Religious Program—Tel: 979-865-0071. Whitney Malhmann, C.R.E. Students 158.
Mission—Immaculate Conception (1875) Industry, Austin Co.

BRAZORIA, BRAZORIA CO., ST. JOSEPH ON THE BRAZOS (1840) Rev. Tin Cosmas Kim Pham; Deacons Raul A. Castillo; Jimmy Smith.
Church & Mailing Address: 219 Country Rd. 762, 77422-7621. Tel: 979-798-2288; Fax: 979-798-2271. Email: stjoseph@brazoriainet.com.
Catechesis/Religious Program—Tel: 979-798-4702. Deacon Jimmy T. Smith, C.R.E. Students 149.

CHANNELVIEW, HARRIS CO., ST. ANDREW (1970) Rev. Christopher Shackelford; Deacon Javier Gomez.
Res., Church & Mailing Address: 827 Sheldon Rd., 77530-3511. Tel: 281-452-9865; Fax: 281-452-2157. Email: standrew7067@sbcglobal.net. Web: standrewcatholicchurch.net.
Catechesis/Religious Program—Maria del Rosario Guerrero, D.R.E. Students 871.

CLUTE, BRAZORIA CO., ST. JEROME (1969) Rev. James F. Lynes; Deacons Julio Garcia; Jaime Morales; Agustin Cruz.
Mailing Address: 201 N. Lazy Ln., 77531-4001. Tel: 979-265-5179; Fax: 979-265-4601. Email: jerome-clute@att.net.
Church: 107 N. Lazy Ln., 77531-4001.
Catechesis/Religious Program—Tel: 979-266-8634. Dina A. Tonche, D.R.E. Students 374.

CONROE, MONTGOMERY CO., SACRED HEART (1916) Revs. Philip A. Wilhite; Thomas W. Hopper, Parochial Vicar; Deacons Rick Garcia; Steve Miller.
Church & Mailing Address: 109 N. Frazier St., 77301-2802. Tel: 936-756-8186; Fax: 936-756-8105. Email: parishoffice@shconroe.org. Web: www.shconroe.org.
School—615 McDade St., 77301-2758. Tel: 936-756-3848. Gerard Kubelka, Prin. Lay Teachers 23; Students 320.
Catechesis/Religious Program—Tel: 936-756-8186. Becki Lipari, D.R.E. Students 1,139.

CROSBY, HARRIS CO., SACRED HEART (1935) Rev. Arnel B. Barrameda; Deacons Archie Benham; Pete Melancon. In Res., Rev. Msgr. Fred P. O'Connor (Retired).
Res., Church & Mailing Address: 915 Runneburg Rd., 77532-5826. Tel: 281-328-4871; Fax: 281-328-1075. Email: parishoffice@sacredheartcrosby.org. Web: www.sacredheartcrosby.org.
School—907 Runneberg Rd., 77532. Tel: 281-328-6561; Fax: 281-462-0072. Susan Harris, Prin. Sisters 2; Lay Teachers 13; Students 132.
Catechesis/Religious Program—Tel: 281-328-4871, Ext. 16. Mrs. Margaret Benham, D.R.E. Students 194.

DAMON, BRAZORIA CO., STS. CYRIL AND METHODIUS (1925) [CEM] Rev. Joseph Son Thanh Phan; Deacons Jerry J. Michalec; Danny Naranjo.
Mailing Address: P.O. Box 309, 77430-0309.
Rectory—P.O. Box 95, Needville, 77461.
Church: 603 Parrott Ave., 77430-0309. Tel: 979-742-3383; Fax: 979-742-3395. Email: patsystcyril@consolidated.net.
Catechesis/Religious Program—Tel: 832-715-5241. Mrs. Julia Mueck, D.R.E. Students 43.

DANBURY, BRAZORIA CO., ST. ANTHONY DE PADUA (1911) [CEM] Rev. Joseph Phiet The Nguyen; Deacon Gerald Peltier; Imelda Jez, Parish Sec.
Mailing Address: P.O. Box 299, 77534-0299.
Rectory—1603 Main St., 77534. Tel: 979-922-1253.
Church: 1523 Main St., 77534-0299. Tel: 979-922-1240; Fax: 979-922-8643. Email: st1523@sbcglobal.net. Web: www.saopdtx.org.
Catechesis/Religious Program—Tel: 409-922-1241. Mrs. Monica Sebesta, C.R.E. Students 134.

DEER PARK, HARRIS CO., ST. HYACINTH (1965) Revs. Antonio Castro; Sebastian Rama, M.S.F.S.
Church & Mailing Address: 2921 Center St., 77536-4997. Tel: 281-479-4298; Fax: 281-478-6123. Email: info@sthyacinthchurch.org. Web: www.sthyacinthchurch.org.
Catechesis/Religious Program—Tel: 281-479-8832. Mr. Tom Butler, D.R.E. Students 685.

DICKINSON, GALVESTON CO., SHRINE OF THE TRUE CROSS (1909) Revs. Paul G. Felix; Hipolitus I. Ezenwa, S.M.M.M.; Deacons Sam Ausmus III; Jose Duplan Jr.; Neil Lewis.
Mailing Address: P.O. Box 687, 77539-0687.
Res.: 3720 Spruce, 77539. Tel: 281-337-4112; Fax: 281-337-5779. Email: info@truecrosschurch.org. Web: www.truecrosschurch.org.
Church: 300 FM 517 E., 77539.
School—400 FM 517 E., 77539. Tel: 281-337-5212. Mike Sofia, Prin. Lay Teachers 16; Students 166.
Catechesis/Religious Program—Tel: 281-337-3130. Raquel Hinojosa, D.R.E. Students 638.

FREEPORT, BRAZORIA CO.

1—ST. HENRY (1932) Closed. For inquiries for parish records contact the chancery.

2—ST. MARY: STAR OF THE SEA (1926) Rev. Edmund P. Eduarte; Deacon Wallace Shaw.
Church, Rectory & Mailing Address: 1019 W. 6th St., 77541-5423. Tel: 979-233-5271; Fax: 979-233-4418. Email: stmarysos@sbcglobal.net. Web: www.stmarystarofthesea.org.
Catechesis/Religious Program—Tel: 979-233-2771. Marilyn Saccomanno, C.R.E. Students 332.

FRIENDSWOOD, GALVESTON CO., MARY, QUEEN (1965) Revs. Phil "Skip" M. Negley, M.S.; Benny Thadathilkunnel, M.S.; Deacons Paul Robinson; Darryl Moulton. In Res., Rev. John A. Zabelskas.
Church & Mailing: 606 Cedarwood Dr., 77546. Tel: 281-482-1391; Fax: 281-482-4886. Email: carlamartin@maryqueenchurch.org. Web: www.maryqueenchurch.org.
Rectory—608 Cedarwood Dr., 77546.
Catechesis/Religious Program—Students 1,143.

FRYDEK, AUSTIN CO., ST. MARY (1908) [CEM] Rev. Thuy Quang Nguyen, Admin.; Deacon Jerome D. Losack Jr.
Mailing Address: 10471 Grotto Rd., Sealy, 77474-9801. Tel: 979-885-3131; Fax: 979-885-4555. Email: st.mary@twlt.net.
Catechesis/Religious Program—Tel: 979-885-3178. Gloria Howard, D.R.E. Students 179.

GALENA PARK, HARRIS CO., OUR LADY OF FATIMA (1946) Rev. Angel Vincente Agila.
Res. & Church Address: 1705 Eighth St., 77547-2924. Tel: 713-675-0981; Fax: 713-675-0982. Email: ourladyoffatimacc@comcast.com.
School—1702 Ninth St., 77547. Tel: 713-674-5832; Fax: 713-674-3877. Frances Ramsey, Prin. Lay Teachers 12; Students 75.
Catechesis/Religious Program—Tel: 713-671-0717. Margarita Alaniz, D.R.E. Students 459.

HEMPSTEAD, WALLER CO.

1—ST. KATHERINE DREXEL (2001) Revs. David G. Harris; Juan G. Pineda (Colombia). In Res., Deacon John Pelletier.
Church & Rectory: 800 F.M. 1488 Rd., 77445-1700. Tel: 979-826-2275; Fax: 979-826-8057. Email: info@stkdrexel.org. Web: www.stkdrexel.org.
Catechesis/Religious Program— Lucille Pavlock, D.R.E. Students 534.

2—MARY, MOTHER OF GOD (1879) Merged with St. Martin de Porres, Prairie View to form St. Katherine Drexel, Hempstead.

HIGHLANDS, HARRIS CO., ST. JUDE THADDEUS (1946) Rev. Maynard V. Parangan.
Church & Mailing Address: 800 S. Main St., 77562-4236. Tel: 281-843-2422; Fax: 281-426-3671. Email: muap@gmail.com.
Catechesis/Religious Program—Tel: 281-426-6800. Mrs. Claudine Lewis, D.R.E. Students 74.

HITCHCOCK, GALVESTON CO., OUR LADY OF LOURDES (1953) Rev. John H. Kappe.
Church & Mailing Address: 10114 Hwy. 6, 77563-4515. Tel: 409-925-3579; Fax: 409-925-5094. Email: jgrassmuck@olochurch.org.
School—Tel: 409-925-3224. Mr. Mark Priest, Prin. Lay Teachers 8; Students 81.
Catechesis/Religious Program— Yvonne Routh, D.R.E. Students 171.

HUFFMAN, HARRIS CO., ST. PHILIP THE APOSTLE (1977) Rev. Richard E. Barker.
Mailing Address: P.O. Box 2363, 77336-2363.
Church: 2308 Third St., 77336. Tel: 281-324-1478; Fax: 281-324-2775. Email: stphiliphuffmantx@gmail.com. Web: www.stphiliphuffmantx.org.
Catechesis/Religious Program— Lisa Griffin, D.R.E. Students 187.

HUMBLE, HARRIS CO., ST. MARY MAGDALENE (1911) Revs. Michael J. Carmody; Wilfred A. Legal, O.S.B.; Deacons David W. Illingworth; James Meshell; James N. Caruso.
Church & Mailing Address: 527 S. Houston Ave., 77338-4763. Tel: 281-446-8211; Fax: 281-446-8213. Email: jlemoine@st-mm.com. Web: www.st-mm.com.
Rectory—525 S. Houston Ave., 77338-4763.
School—530 Ferguson, 77338. Tel: 281-446-8535; Fax: 281-446-8527. Lori Holmes, Prin. Sisters 1; Lay Teachers 20; Students 262.
Catechesis/Religious Program—Tel: 281-446-2933. Mike Smith, D.R.E. Students 1,408.

HUNTSVILLE, WALKER CO., ST. THOMAS THE APOSTLE (1963) Revs. Stephen J. Payne; Mark Czarnecki; Deacons Richard Lopez; Felix Ramos.
Church & Mailing Address: 1323 16th St., 77340-4431. Tel: 936-295-8159; Fax: 936-295-3543. Email: stthomashuntsville@sbcglobal.net.
Rectory—1608 Ave. M, 77340-4431.
Catechesis/Religious Program— Kathy Boscarino, D.R.E. Students 384.

KATY, HARRIS CO.

1—ST. BARTHOLOMEW THE APOSTLE (1965) Revs. John Kha Tran; Fernando Anaya-Maida; Desmond Daniels; Deacons William C. Wagner; Michael J. McGuire; Arthur Chin-Fatt; Rolando J. Garcia; Humberto Carrasco; Gordon Robertson.
Church & Mailing Address: 5356 11th St., 77493-1748. Tel: 281-391-4758; Fax: 281-391-3978. Email: contact@st-bart.org. Web: www.st-bart.org.
Rectory—5356-B 11th St., 77493-1748.
Catechesis/Religious Program—Tel: 281-391-0839. Mrs. Isabel Chandler, D.R.E. Students 1,271.

2—ST. EDITH STEIN (1999) Rev. Ryszard Kulma; Deacons Leonard J. Broussard; Timothy Borbas; Lawrence Biediger Jr.; Samuel Hull III; Gary Walsh PP; Edwin Tripp.
Church & Mailing Address: 3311 N. Fry Rd., 77449-6235. Tel: 281-492-7500; Fax: 281-492-0266. Email: pm@stedithstein.org. Web: www.stedithstein.org.
Rectory—2903 Sinton Ct., 77449.
Catechesis/Religious Program— Amy Auzenne, D.R.E. Students 465.

3—EPIPHANY OF THE LORD (1981) Rev. Msgr. Jack M. Dinkins; Deacons Don Kish; Jim Hite; John Evanoff.
Church & Mailing Address: 1530 Norwalk Dr., 77450-4918. Tel: 281-578-0707; Fax: 281-578-9161. Email: epiphany@epiphanycatholic.org. Web: www.epiphanycatholic.org.
Catechesis/Religious Program—Tel: 281-578-8271. Lou Ann Svoboda, Coord. Students 2,841.

KINGWOOD, HARRIS CO., ST. MARTHA (1979) Rev. Msgr. Chester L. Borski; Rev. Thomas Joseph T.J. Dolce; Deacons Alfred J. O'Brien; Robert MacFarlane; Ed. Kleinguetl; John Schuster; Alfredo Soto; Guy Puglia.
Mailing Address: 2302 Oak Shores Dr., 77339-1801. Tel: 281-358-6637; Fax: 281-358-7973. Email:

indianaf@stmartha.com. Web: www.stmartha.com. Church: 4301 Woodridge Pkwy., Porter, 77365-7709. *School*—2411 Oakshores Dr., 77339. Tel: 281-358-5523; Fax: 281-358-5526. Tina Lewis, Prin. Lay Teachers 30; Students 443.
Catechesis/Religious Program—Tel: 281-358-1959, Ext. 212. Linda Cussen, D.R.E. Students 1,769.

LA MARQUE, GALVESTON CO., QUEEN OF PEACE (1951) Rev. Chacko Puthumayil; Deacon Harold B. Eskew Jr.
Mailing Address: 1224 Cedar Dr., 77568-3932.
Church: 1200 Cedar Dr., 77568. Tel: 409-938-7000; Fax: 409-935-9791. Email: queenofpeaclm@sbcglobal.net.
Rectory—626 Laurel, 77568.
Catechesis/Religious Program—Tel: 409-935-3535. Martha Cantu, D.R.E. Students 132.

LA PORTE, HARRIS CO., ST. MARY (1954) Rev. Gary A. Rickles; Deacon Julio C. Matallana.
Church & Mailing Address: 816 Park Dr., 77571-5811. Tel: 281-471-2000; Fax: 281-471-9365. Email: stmaryslaportecc@sbcglobal.net. Web: www.stmaryslaporte.com.
Catechesis/Religious Program— Kristina Sommer, D.R.E. Students 444.

LAKE JACKSON, BRAZORIA CO., ST. MICHAEL (1966) Rev. Msgr. Leo Wleczyk; Rev. Marty Pham; Deacon David Mitchell.
Church & Mailing Address: 100 Oak Dr. S., 77566-5630. Tel: 979-297-3041; Fax: 979-297-7895. Email: lynne@smlj.org. Web: www.smlj.org.
Catechesis/Religious Program—Tel: 979-297-3043. Mrs. Debra Kyle, D.R.E. Students 554.

LEAGUE CITY, GALVESTON CO., ST. MARY (1910) Rev. Howard E. Drabek; Deacons George Blanford Jr.; Louis (Sam) Dell'Olio.
Church & Mailing Address: 1612 E. Walker St., 77573-4137. Tel: 281-338-0195; 281-332-7211 (Rectory); Fax: 281-332-8328.
School—Tel: 281-332-4014. Lydia Mondragon, Prin. Lay Teachers 22; Students 215.
Catechesis/Religious Program—Tel: 281-332-7459. Lisa Sabatier, D.R.E. Students 757.

MAGNOLIA, MONTGOMERY CO., ST. MATTHIAS THE APOSTLE (1978) Rev. Nicolas O. Pasadilla.
Church & Mailing Address: 302 S. Magnolia Blvd., 77355-8535. Tel: 281-356-2000; Fax: 832-446-0080. Email: stmatthias@st-matthias.net. Web: www.st-matthias.net.
Catechesis/Religious Program— Marlene Grauvogl, D.R.E. Students 503.

MANVEL, BRAZORIA CO., SACRED HEART OF JESUS (1945) Revs. David J. Zapalac, C.S.B.; Charles E. Lynch, C.S.B., Parochial Vicar; John S. Broussard, C.S.B.; Deacons Robert Reed Leicht Jr.; Brian Lambert; Hector J. Ibarra; Arturo Monterrubio.
Church & Mailing Address: 6502 County Rd. 48, 77578-4146. Tel: 281-489-8720; Fax: 281-489-8727. Email: admin@sacredheartmanvel.org. Web: www.sacredheartmanvel.org.
Catechesis/Religious Program—Tel: 281-489-7603. Connie Bowers, D.R.E. Students 976.

MCNAIR, HARRIS CO., HOLY FAMILY (1945) [JC] Rev. Rodney J. Armstrong, S.S.J.; Deacon Steve Arceneaux Jr.
Church & Mailing Address: 7122 Whiting Rock St., Baytown, 77521-1124. Tel: 281-426-8448; Fax: 281-426-8449. Email: hfrcc7122@comcast.net.
Catechesis/Religious Program—Tel: 281-421-7042. Mrs. Vivian Randell-Alfred, D.R.E. Students 50.

MISSOURI CITY, FT. BEND CO.

1—ST. ANGELA MERICI (2007) Rev. John Rooney; Deacon Kevin McCarthy.
Mailing Address: PMB 99, 6140 Hwy. 6, 77549-3802. Tel: 281-778-0400; Fax: 281-778-0401. Email: parishoffice@stamericigh.org. Web: www.stamericigh.org.
Church: 9009 Sienna Ranch Rd., 77459. Tel: 281-778-0400; Fax: 281-778-0401. Email: parishoffice@stamericigh.com. Web: www.stamericigh.com.
Rectory—3814 S. Barnett Way, 77459.
Catechesis/Religious Program—Karen Martin, D.R.E. Students 443.

2—HOLY FAMILY (1913) Revs. Sunny Joseph Plammoottil, O.S.H.; Ramon J. Arechua, Parochial Vicar; Deacons William E. Seifert Jr.; Jose Melendez; Lynn Carney.
Church & Mailing Address: 1510 Fifth St., 77489-1298. Tel: 281-499-9688; Fax: 281-499-9680. Email: gail.hutchins@holyfamilychurch.us. Web: www.holyfamilychurch.us.
Catechesis/Religious Program—Tel: 281-499-4612. Yolanda Pena, D.R.E. Students 735.

NAVASOTA, GRIMES CO., CHRIST OUR LIGHT (1869) Revs. Rodolfo L. Cal-Ortiz Jr., Admin.; Juan G. Pineda (Colombia); Deacons Grant E. Holt; Gregory N. Jelinek.
Mailing Address: 510 Manley St., 77868-3926. Tel: 936-825-3920; Fax: 936-825-7612. Email: info@christourlight.org.
Church: 9677 Hwy. 6, 77868.
Rectory—9685 Hwy. 6, 77868-3905.
Catechesis/Religious Program—Tel: 936-825-1869. Eva Rico, D.R.E. Students 221.

NEEDVILLE, FORT BEND CO., ST. MICHAEL (1913) [CEM] Rev. Joseph Son Thanh Phan; Deacons Jerry Michaelz; Danny Naranjo.
Mailing Address: P.O. Box 95, 77461-0095.
Church: 9214 Main St., 77461-0095. Tel: 979-793-4477; Fax: 979-793-7456. Email: stmichaelschurch@consolidated.net. Web: www.needvillecatholic.com.
Rectory—9202 Main St., 77461.
Catechesis/Religious Program—Tel: 281-232-5290. Jacki Mikel, D.R.E. Students 332.

NEW CANEY, MONTGOMERY CO., ST. JOHN OF THE CROSS (1989) Rev. Hai Duc Dang; Deacon Winfield S. Matz.
Church & Mailing Address: 20000 Loop 494, 77357-8213. Tel: 281-399-9008; 281-399-5541 (Rectory); Fax: 281-399-1500. Email: stjohn@argolink.net. Web: www.stjohnofthecross.com.
Catechesis/Religious Program— Debbie Davis, D.R.E. Students 471.

NEW WAVERLY, WALKER CO., ST. JOSEPH (1869) [CEM 2] Rev. Daokim Nguyen; Deacon Klaus Petereit.
Church & Mailing Address: 101 Elmore, 77358-4105. Tel: 936-344-6104; Fax: 936-344-2818. Email: stjosephnw@gmail.com. Web: www.stjosephnewwaverlytx.net.
Catechesis/Religious Program—Tel: 936-856-3713. Deacon Klaus Petereit, D.R.E. Students 176.
Mission—St. Stephen the Martyr 101 Stagecoach, Pointblank, San Jacinto Co. 77364. Deacon Melvin Mouton.

PASADENA, HARRIS CO.

1—ST. JUAN DIEGO (1954), (Hispanic), (Formerly Guardian Angel) Revs. Jose Romero, O.S.A.; J. Jesus Guerrero-Almanza, O.S.A.; Deacons Jose Jimenez; Adolfo Mejia-Parada; Servando J. Rojas.
Church & Mailing Address: 3301 Pasadena Blvd., 77503-3201. Tel: 713-477-6693; Fax: 713-477-0523. Email: padreromero@comcast.net. Web: www.sjdchurch.org.
Catechesis/Religious Program—Tel: 713-459-5699. Diego Monroy, D.R.E. Students 1,155.

2—ST. PIUS THE FIFTH (1941) Revs. Oscar M. Castro; J. Christopher C. Nguyen; Deacons Celestino M. Perez; Daniel Seiler.
Church & Mailing Address: 824 S. Main St., 77506-3532. Tel: 713-473-9484; Fax: 713-473-2731. Web: www.stpiusvchurch.com.
School—812 S. Main St., Pasaena, 77506. Tel: 713-472-5172. Sr. Krysia A. Pilon, M.C.D.P., Prin. Sisters 1; Lay Teachers 29; Students 225.
Catechesis/Religious Program— Alicia Alvarado, D.R.E. Students 1,161.

PATTISON/BROOKSHIRE, WALLER CO., SACRED HEART (1914) Rev. David J. DuBois.
Mailing Address: P.O. Box 300, 77466-0300.
Church: 4445 F.M. 359 N., 77466. Tel: 281-375-6799; Fax: 281-375-5799. Email: shpoffice@consolidated.net.
Catechesis/Religious Program—Tel: 281-375-6638. Mrs. Marie Pattison, D.R.E. Students 132.

PEARLAND, BRAZORIA CO., ST. HELEN (1952) Rev. Msgr. Reginald R. Nesvadba; Rev. Carl James Courville; Deacons Darvin A. Bordelon; J. Cruz Trujillo; Dale Almenario.
Res., Church & Mailing Address: 2209 Old Alvin Rd., 77581-4499. Tel: 281-485-2421; Fax: 281-485-6789. Email: shcc@sthelenchurch.org. Web: www.sthelenchurch.org.
School—2213 Old Alvin Rd., 77581. Tel: 281-485-2845; Fax: 281-485-7607. Elaina Satsky, Prin. Lay Teachers 18; Students 218.
Catechesis/Religious Program—Tel: 281-485-5457. Julie Martinez, D.R.E. Students 1,730.

PLANTERSVILLE, GRIMES CO., ST. MARY (1894) [CEM] Rev. Edward C. Kucera Jr.
Mailing Address: P.O. Box 388, 77363-0388. In Res., Rev. William T. Kelly (Retired).
Church: 8227 County Rd. 205, 77363. Tel: 936-894-2223; Fax: 936-894-3613. Email: info@smsj.org. Web: www.smsj.org.
Catechesis/Religious Program—Tel: 936-894-2223. Cheryl Schratwieser, D.R.E. Students 204.
Mission—St. Joseph Stoneham, Grimes Co11323 County Rd. 304, 77363-0388.

PORT BOLIVAR, GALVESTON CO., OUR MOTHER OF MERCY (1968) Closed. For parish records contact the Archives of Galveston-Houston.

PRAIRIE VIEW, WALLER CO., ST. MARTIN DE PORRES (1962) Merged with Mary, Mother of God, Hempstead to form St. Katherine Drexel, Hempstead.

RICHMOND, FORT BEND CO.

1—ST. JOHN FISHER (1952) Rev. Manuel LaRosa-Lopez; Deacons Ruben Torres; Hector R. Rodriguez.
Church & Mailing Address: 410 Clay St., 77469-1708. Tel: 281-342-5092; Fax: 281-633-9465. Email: info@stjfisher.com. Web: www.stjfisher.com.
Rectory—610 N. Fourth St., 77469.
Catechesis/Religious Program—Mrs. Helen Mata, D.R.E. Students 352.

2—SACRED HEART (1935) Rev. Josefino P. Templado. In Res., Deacons Donald G. Ries; Billy Guerrero Jr.; Don Murrile.
Church & Mailing Address: 507 S. Fourth St., 77469-3599. Tel: 281-342-3609; Fax: 281-342-9833. Email: info@sacredheartrichmond.com. Web: www.sacredheartrichmond.com.
Rectory—303 Houston, 77469.
Catechesis/Religious Program—Tel: 281-342-8371. Emily Kucherka, D.R.E. Students 1,144.

ROSENBERG, FORT BEND CO.

1—HOLY ROSARY (1911) Rev. William D. Bartniski; Deacon Brick Hodge.
Church & Mailing Address: 1416 George St., 77471-3198. Tel: 281-342-3089; Fax: 281-342-7688. Email: office@hrccr.com. Web: www.hrccr.com.
School—1408 James St., 77471. Tel: 281-342-5813; Fax: 281-344-1107. Mrs. Nancy Moore, Prin. Lay Teachers 21; Students 199.
Catechesis/Religious Program— Tina Hollopeter, D.R.E. Students 162.

2—OUR LADY OF GUADALUPE (1936) [CEM] Rev. Lee A. Flores; Deacons Enrique G. Avila; Albert Yanez.
Church: 514 Carlisle St., 77471-1822. Tel: 281-232-5113; Fax: 281-342-4008. Email: olgc1936@yahoo.com.
Catechesis/Religious Program—Tel: 281-232-4322. Pauline Cano, D.R.E. Students 441.

SEALY, AUSTIN CO., IMMACULATE CONCEPTION (1889) [CEM] Rev. Eric J. Pitre; Deacons Frank Laredo; Robert Kent; Ben Munguia.
Mailing Address: P.O. Box 337, 77474-0337.
Rectory—525 5th St., 77474. Tel: 979-885-3868; Fax: 979-885-2246. Email: iccsealy@aol.com. Web: www.iccsealy.com.
Church: 600 4th St., 77474-2607.
Catechesis/Religious Program— Carol Thormaehlen, D.R.E. Students 367.

SOUTH HOUSTON, HARRIS CO., OUR LADY OF GRACE (1971) Rev. Jesus M. Martinez-Irigoyen, Admin.
Mailing Address: P.O. Box 164, 77587-0164.
Church: 1211 Michigan St., 77587-0164. Tel: 713-946-6461; Fax: 713-378-9983. Email: ourladyofgrace587@sbcglobal.net.
Res.: 1204 Michigan St., 77587.
Catechesis/Religious Program—Tel: 281-461-9417. Rosa Nelly Garcia, D.R.E. Students 259.

SPRING, HARRIS CO.

1—CHRIST THE GOOD SHEPHERD (1978) Revs. John Upton; Hoang H Bui; Deacons Pat W. Camerino; Alberto J. Patetta; Pat Hancock; James Gallagher; Bill Hartman.
Church & Mailing Address: 18511 Klein Church Rd., 77379-4998. Tel: 281-376-6831; Fax: 281-376-8945. Email: center@cgsccdogh.org. Web: www.cgsccdogh.org.
Catechesis/Religious Program—Students 946.

2—ST. EDWARD (1969) Revs. Joseph A. Gietl; Patrick Stuart Garrett, Parochial Vicar; Deacons Nicholas Thompson; Dominic Romaguera; Kenneth Martin.
Church & Mailing Address: 2601 Spring Stuebner Rd., 77389-4824. Tel: 281-353-9774; Fax: 281-353-9786. Email: info@saintedward.com. Web: www.saintedward.com.
School—Tel: 281-353-4570; Fax: 281-353-8255. Nell Schell, Prin. Sisters 1; Lay Teachers 28; Students 303.
Catechesis/Religious Program—Students 677.

3—ST. IGNATIUS OF LOYOLA (1985) Revs. Norbert J. Maduzia Jr.; David W. Garnier; Deacons William Sheffield; Glen H. Cuiper; Michael E. Higgins; Larry Vines; Mike Baker; Greg Mouton; Martial Oya, (Seminarian Interim); Mary Blanton, Parish Sec.
Church & Mailing Address: 7810 Cypresswood Dr., 77379-7101. Tel: 281-370-3401; Fax: 281-370-9306. Email: ignatiusloyola@silcc.org. Web: www.ignatius-loyola.org; www.silcc.org.
Rectory—7802 King Arthur Ct., 77379.
Catechesis/Religious Program— Mary Wright, D.R.E. Students 1,115.

4—ST. JAMES THE APOSTLE (1976) Revs. Charles J. Samperi; Joseph Manappuram; Deacons Ray Oden; Arthur Zepeda; Alfonso Chicas; Kay Beasley, Parish Sec.; Lalura Lara, Parish Sec.
Church & Mailing Address: 22800 Aldine Westfield Rd., 77373-6565. Tel: 281-353-5053; Fax: 281-355-8847. Email: saintjta@swbell.net. Web: www.stjta.org.
Catechesis/Religious Program—Students 315.

SUGAR LAND, FORT BEND CO.

1—ST. LAURENCE (1985) Revs. William Andrew Wood; Santy M. Kurian, M.S.F.S.; Deacons Don Burns; Charles Plant; Albert G. Bothe; Renato Arellano; Tony Oltremari, Parish Admin. & Bus. Mgr.
Church & Mailing Address: 3100 Sweetwater Blvd., 77479-2630. Tel: 281-980-9812; Fax: 281-980-0686.

Email: contact@stlaurenceparish.com. Web: www.stlaurence.com.
School—2630 Austin Pkwy., 77479. Tel: 281-980-0500; Fax: 281-980-0026. Debra Haney, Prin. Sisters 1; Lay Teachers 52; Students 711.
Catechesis/Religious Program—Tel: 281-265-5774. Mrs. Laura Stephens, D.R.E. Students 1,286.

2—ST. THERESA (1924) Revs. Stephen B. Reynolds; Miguel Obregon-Vallejos, Parochial Vicar; Jose J. Tharayil; Deacons Glenn F. Haller; Frank P. Cromer; Joaquin Garcia; Don Senger; Diane Senger, Parish Admin. & Bus. Mgr.
Mailing Address: P.O. Box 968, 77487-0968. Church: 705 St. Theresa Blvd., 77498.
Res. & Church Address: 115 Seventh St., 77478. Tel: 281-494-1156; Fax: 281-242-1393. Email: fcromer@sttheresasugarland.org. Web: www.sttheresasugarland.org.
School—St. Theresa Academy, Tel: 281-494-1157. Jonathan M. Beeson, Headmaster. Lay Teachers 7; Students 90.
Catechesis/Religious Program—Students 1,176.

3—ST. THOMAS AQUINAS (1978) Rev. Joseph K. Kalladan; Deacons Sam Dunning; Robert Kirkpatrick. Church & Mailing Address: 12627 W. Bellfort Ave., 77478-1844. Tel: 281-240-6721; Fax: 281-240-6733. Email: contact@stthomasaquinas.info. Web: www.stthomasaquinas.info.
Rectory—10415 Huntington Wood Dr., 77099-3721.
Catechesis/Religious Program— Rebecca Gotting, D.R.E. Students 343.

SWEENY, BRAZORIA CO., OUR LADY OF PERPETUAL HELP (1954) Rev. Daniel S. Baguio.
Church & Mailing Address: 310 N. McKinney St., 77480-2899. Tel: 979-548-2020; Fax: 979-548-4253. Web: www.olphsja.org.
Catechesis/Religious Program—Tel: 979-798-8129. Mrs. Chris Kasper, D.R.E. Students 127.
Mission—St. John the Apostle 807 Loggins, West Columbia, Brazoria Co. 77486-3843.

TEXAS CITY, GALVESTON CO., ST. MARY (1911) Rev. Thomas V. Ponzini; Deacons Joseph A. Hensley; Miguel Hernandez; Stephen A. Mistretta; Sid Cammeresi; Sue Mistretta, Pastoral Assoc.
Mailing Address: 1620 Ninth Ave. N., 77590-5708. Church: 722 Third Ave. N., 77590. Tel: 409-948-8448; Fax: 409-945-8662. Email: st_marys@swbell.net. Web: www.stmarycctc.org.
School—Our Lady of Fatima, 1600 Ninth Ave. N., 77590. Tel: 409-945-3326; Fax: 409-945-3389. Sheryl Calton, Prin. Sisters 2; Lay Teachers 11; Students 128.
Catechesis/Religious Program—Tel: 409-948-1383. Deacon Joseph A. Hensley, D.R.E. Students 353.

THE WOODLANDS, MONTGOMERY CO.

1—ST. ANTHONY OF PADUA (1997) Revs. Thomas F. Rafferty; George Vattapara Devasia, M.S.F.S.; Deacons Joseph Mignogna; Michael Mims; Tom Vicknair; Charles Duck; Michael Mort.
Church & Mailing Address: 7801 Bay Branch Dr., 77382-5359. Tel: 281-296-2800; Fax: 281-296-7238. Email: frtom@staoptw.org. Web: www.staoptw.org.
Rectory—7979 Bay Branch Dr., 77382-5312.
School—7901 Bay Branch Dr., 77382. Tel: 281-296-0300. Renee Nunez, Prin. Lay Teachers 37; Students 492.
Catechesis/Religious Program— Julie Korniewicz, D.R.E. Students 1,934.

2—STS. SIMON AND JUDE (1979) Rev. Msgr. Charles C. Domec; Rev. Joseph Loc D. Phan; Deacons John E. Charnisky Jr.; Sid Sandiford; Michael Schmidt; Anthony G. Cantania; Joe Mignogna.
Res., Church & Mailing Address: 26777 Glen Loch Dr., 77381-2921. Tel: 281-367-9885; Fax: 281-367-9888. Email: reedc@ssjwoodlands.com. Web: www.ssjwoodlands.com.
Catechesis/Religious Program—Jean Stanley, D.R.E. Students 579.

TOMBALL, HARRIS CO., ST. ANNE (1964) Rev. Fred W. Valone; Deacons Ted F. Heap; Thomas Davis; Garry Janota.
Church & Mailing Address: 1111 S. Cherry St., 77375-6675. Tel: 281-351-8106; Fax: 281-351-8142. Email: fvalone@stanne-tomball.org. Web: www.stanne-tomball.org.
School—Tel: 281-351-0093. Margaret Morgan, Prin. Lay Teachers 26; Students 357.
Catechesis/Religious Program— Domenica Weir, D.R.E. Students 803.

WALLIS, AUSTIN CO., GUARDIAN ANGEL (1892) [CEM] Rev. Thuy Quang Nguyen, Admin.; Deacon Jerome D. Losack Jr.
Mailing Address: P.O. Box 487, 77485-0487. Tel: 979-478-6532.
Church & Res.: 5610 Demel St., 77485.
Catechesis/Religious Program—Tel: 979-478-6717. Barbara Litzmann, D.R.E. Students 152.

Chaplains of Public Institutions

GALVESTON. *Galveston County Jail*, 715 19th St., 77550. Tel: 409-766-2315. Deacon Javier Gomez.
John Sealy Hospital, 809 Harborside Dr., 77555. Tel: 409-762-1810. Deacon Javier Gomez. Prison Unit

HOUSTON. *Federal Correctional Center*, 1200 Texas Ave., 77002. Tel: 713-229-4172. Vacant.
George Bush Intercontinental Airport. Rev. Charles J. Samperi.
Harris County Jail. Rev. Ronald F. Cloutier. Tel: 713-755-5326, Deacon Eddie Stoughton. Tel: 713-741-8745.
Res.: 1200 Baker St., 77002. Tel: 713-755-5326.
701 San Jacinto Bldg., 77002. Tel: 713-755-8562.
INS Houston Process Center, 15850 Export Plaza Dr., 77032. Tel: 281-449-1481. Vacant.
Juvenile Detention Center. Ms. Franchelle Lee. Tel: 713-741-8779. Special Youth Svcs.
Kegan State Jail, 707 Top St., 77002. Tel: 713-224-6584.
William P. Hobby Airport.

ANGLETON. *Brazoria County Jail*, 3602 Co. Rd. 45, 77515. Tel: 979-849-2441. Vacant.
Pam Lychner State Jail. Vacant.
2350 Atoscocita Rd., Humble, 77396. Tel: 281-454-5036, Ext. 358.
Scott Unit. Vacant.
6999 Retrieve County Rd. 290, 77515. Tel: 979-849-9306.

CONROE. *Montgomery County Jail*, #1 Criminal Justice Dr., 77301. Tel: 936-760-5870. Vacant.

BRAZORIA. *Clemens Unit*. Vacant.
11034 Hwy. 36, 77422. Tel: 979-798-2188.

DICKINSON. *Young Unit/Young Medical Facility*, 5509 Attwater Ave., 77539. Tel: 409-948-0001.

HUNTSVILLE. *Byrd Unit*. Vacant.
21 FM 247, 77320. Tel: 936-295-5786.
Diagnostic Unit.
P.O. Box 100, 77340. Tel: 936-295-8459. Anthony Velasquez.
Ellis I Unit, 1697 FM 980, 77343. Tel: 936-295-5756, Ext. 217. Vacant.
Estelle Unit, 264 FM 3478, 77320. Tel: 936-291-4200, Ext. 2274. Vacant.
Goree Unit. Vacant.
7504 Hwy. 75 S., 77344. Tel: 936-295-6331.
Holliday Unit, 295 IH-45N, 77320. Tel: 936-437-1975. Vacant.
Huntsville Walls Unit, 815 12th St., 77340. Tel: 936-295-8159; 409-291-4200. Vacant.
Texas Department of Criminal Justice, 1060 State Hwy. 190 E., 77340. Tel: 936-294-6548 (Regl. Program Admin.). Deacon Richard Lopez.
Wynne Unit.
FM 2821, 77349. Tel: 936-295-9126. Linda Hill.

NAVASOTA. *Luther Unit*, 1800 Luther Dr., 77868. Tel: 936-825-7547.
Pack Unit, 2400 Wallispack Rd., 77869. Tel: 409-825-3728. Vacant.

RICHMOND. One Circle Dr., 77478. Tel: 281-491-2146.
Jester I, III, IV Unit/Vance Unit/Central Unit. Deacon Brent Larsen, Chap.
Rte. 2, 77469. Tel: 281-277-3700.

ROSHARON. *Darrington Unit*.
59 Darrington Rd., 77583. Tel: 281-595-3465, Ext. 275. Vacant.
Ramsey I Unit. Deacon Bob Leicht.
1100 FM 655, 77583. Tel: 281-595-3491.
Stringfellow Unit.
1200 FM 655, 77583. Tel: 281-595-3413. Vacant.
Terrell Unit. Vacant.
1300 FM 655, 77583. Tel: 281-595-3481.

On Duty Outside the Archdiocese:
Revs.—
McGinnis, Jack P., Chap., P.O. Box 2456, Idyllwild, CA 92549-2456.
Perez, Joseph, The Chancery, P.O. Box 907, 77001.

Retired:
Rev. Msgrs.—
Beck, Albert J., Pope John XXIII Residence, 2407 Holcombe Blvd., #B1, 77021-2023. Tel: 713-748-0644
Francis, Eugene, 6651 Camptown Cir., 77069-1214. Tel: 281-440-1303
Fruge, Donald J., 5000 Montrose, Apt. 7F, 77006-6560. Tel: 713-521-3267
Kennedy, David, J.C.L., 12121 Maverick Dr., Willis, 77378-4814. Tel: 936-228-5209
Kleas, Milam, St. Maximilan Kolbe, 10135 West Rd., 77064-5361.
O'Connor, Fred P., St. John the Evangelist Church, 800 W. Baker Rd., Baytown, 77521-2311. Tel: 281-837-8180
Pickard, William M., J.C.D., Pope John XXIII Residence, 2407 Holcombe Blvd., Apt. A-4, 77021-2023. Tel: 713-842-7770
Procella, Paul, 1101 Parthenon Pl., New Caney, 77357-3276. Tel: 281-785-0017
Randall, Edward, P.O. Box 444, Coldspring, 77331-0444. Tel: 936-767-8313
Wells, Patrick R., Land Fall Towers, 6403 Padre Blvd., Unit #85, South Padre Island, 78597-7708. Tel: 956-761-3953
Zientek, Boleslaus, Pope John XXIII Residence, 2407 Holcombe Blvd., 77021.

Revs.—
Abell, Edward, Cenacle Retreat House, 420 North Kirkwood, 77079-6807. Tel: 713-417-6272
Anton, Ronald J., S.J., Pope John XXIII Residence, 2407 Holcombe Blvd., 77021-2023. Tel: 713-748-1553
Asenjo, Jose Maria, P.O. Box 464, South Houston, 77587-0464. Tel: 832-428-8832
Carlson, Robert D., Maloney Hall Nursing Home, 2409 Holcombe Blvd., #304, 77021-2033. Tel: 713-741-8701
Cejudo, Serafin, 6618 Limestone St., 77092-5794. Tel: 713-703-8074
Chia, Luis P., St. Dominic Village-Maloney Hall Room 305, 2409 Holcombe Blvd., 77021-2023. Tel: 713-741-8700
Chu, Peter Ngoc Thanh, Pope John XXIII Residence, 2407 Holcombe Blvd., #B6, 77021-2023. Tel: 713-747-8774
Connelly, Laurence D., 7 Tourney Cove, Austin, 78738-1119. Tel: 512-261-8063
Corrigan, Michael T., Pope John XXIII Residence, 2407 Holcombe Blvd., #B4, 77021-2023. Tel: 832-578-6860
Doroin, Elias E., 2432 Sheridan St., 77030-1922. Tel: 713-922-1230
Ferguson, Peter A., P.O. Box 552, Ellenton, FL 34222-0552. Tel: 813-671-6967
Guenter, Frank
Heberlein, Kenneth, 7811 Rolling Brook Dr., 77071-1707. Tel: 713-988-2468
Hoang, John Minh Toan, Pope John XXIII Residence, 2407 Holcombe Blvd., #A1, 77021-2023. Tel: 713-747-7707
Kellick, John W., 6517 Burdock Dr., Santa Fe, 77510-9340. Tel: 409-925-6817
Kelly, William T., St. Mary Church, P.O. Box 388, Plantersville, 77363-0388. Tel: 936-894-2016
Mandry, Stephen, Pope John XXIII Residence, 2407 Holcombe Blvd., #B2, 77021-2023. Tel: 713-747-2593
Martin, Roosevelt, Jr., 1601 Pennsylvania St. N.E., Apt. U-8, Albuquerque, NM 87110-5546.
McGinnis, John P., 11734 Wilshire Blvd., #C 1103, Los Angeles, CA 90025-6450. Tel: 760-902-6925
Mikulik, Kenneth E., St. Dominic Village Assisted Living, 2401 Holcombe Blvd., Tower Rm. 507, 77021-2099. Tel: 713-741-3522
Moore, James T., 5478 County Rd. 113A, Iola, 77861-5378. Tel: 936-394-1940
Morfin, John N., 8429 Sands Point Dr., Bldg. #18, 77036-2769. Tel: 281-650-7629
Olsovsky, George J., P.O. Box 292, Huffman, 77336-0292. Tel: 281-324-2873
Rodriguez, Armando J., Pope John XXIII Residence, 2407 Holcombe Blvd., #A6, 77021-2023. Tel: 713-842-2053
Sanchez, Jose M., Pope John XXIII Residence, 2407 Holcombe Blvd., A3, 77021-2023. Tel: 713-440-6329
Schwarting, J. Donald, 679 Ashmore St., New Braunfels, 78130-4601. Tel: 830-214-7177
Sikorski, Louis S., Pope John XXIII Residence, 2407 Holcombe Blvd., #B8, 77021-2023. Tel: 936-870-5133
Simmons, Franklin, 2000 Westborough Dr., #1104, Katy, 77449-3291. Tel: 713-397-3057
Snock, Bernard C., 4044 Chew Rd., Sealy, 77474. Tel: 979-885-3930
Tenhundfeld, Carl Anthony, 11002 Hammerly #167, 77043. Tel: 713-932-8977
Walker, Anselm, 1815 Parker, 77093. Tel: 713-697-7109
Warden, Daniel L., V.F., 1815 Parker Rd., 77093-5221. Tel: 713-697-7109

Permanent Deacons:
Abadejos, Ernesto, Notre Dame, Houston
Abram, Alfred, Sr., (Unassigned)
Adame, David, St. Matthew, Houston
Adams, John W., St. Matthew the Evangelist, Houston
Addis, Daniel, Assumption, Houston
Aguilar, Juan, Our Lady of Mount Carmel, Houston
Alessi, Tony, St. Thomas More, Houston
Alexander, Jack, St. Michael, Houston
Alexander, Robert George, Annunciation and St. Paul, Houston
Allen, Charles J., Sr., Our Mother of Mercy, Houston
Almenario, Adelfo, St. Helen, Pearland
Arceneaux, Leon, St. Anthony, The Woodlands
Arceneaux, Steve, Jr., Holy Family, McNair
Arellano, Jose, Immaculate Heart of Mary, Houston
Arellano, Renato, St. Laurence, Sugar Land

Ausmus, Sam, III, Shrine of the True Cross, Dickinson
Avila, Enrique G., Our Lady of Guadalupe, Rosenberg
Baker, J. M., St. Ignatius, Spring
Barnett, James, Our Lady of Walsingham, Houston
Bart, James L., St. Pius V, Pasadena
Bazan, Jeronimo, Prince of Peace, Houston
Becker, Henry, Holy Family, Galveston
Benham, Archie, Sacred Heart, Crosby
Benoit, John, St. Mark the Evangelist, Houston
Berntsen, Frank, Our Lady of Mount Carmel, Houston
Biediger, Lawrence, Jr., Sr. Edith Stein, Katy
Birsinger, Alvin, St. Luke the Evangelist, Houston
Blanford, George, Jr., St. Mary, League City
Bobb, William J., (Retired), St. George Villa, Rosewell
Borbas, Timothy, St. Edith Stein, Katy
Bordelon, Darvin A., St. Helen, Pearland
Bothe, Albert G., St. Lawrence, Sugar Land
Bottjer, Albert, Assumption, Houston; Ben Taub Hospital; Jail Chap.
Bowman, David, St. John the Baptist, Alvin
Boyd, Gary, St. Justin Martyr, Houston
Bradley, Donald V., Jr., St. Cecilia, Houston
Bradley, William, Christ the Redeemer, Houston
Breaux, Roy, St. Phillip of Jesus, Houston
Brinkman, Fred H., TDC-Ramsey Units I, II, III/Drug Trustee Camp
Brooks, James, St. Philip Neri, Houston
Broussard, Leonard J., St. Edith Stein
Brown, Abner, Sr., St. Gregory the Great, Houston
Brueggerhoff, Robert T., Holy Ghost, Houston
Budinger, Jean-Paul, St. Anne, Houston
Buhay, Carlito, St. Albert, Houston
Burns, Don, St. Laurence, Sugar Land
Burroughs, Orrin D., St. Philip Neri, Houston
Busa, Walter, St. Mary, Plantersville
Butler, Charles, Prince of Peace, Houston
Cabler, Paul Stephen, Unassigned
Calonge, Elie P., Notre Dame, Houston
Calvillo, Pedro, St. Helen, Pearland
Camacho-del Rio, Gustavo, St. Vincent de Paul, Houston
Camerino, Pat W., Christ the Good Shepherd, Spring
Cammersi, Sammy, St. Mary, Houston
Camunez, Richard F., St. Hyacinth, Deer Park
Cantu, Hector, St. Mary, La Porte
Carnay, Lynn, Holy Family, Missouri City
Carranza, Joe, On Duty Outside the Archdiocese
Carrara, John, Sacred Heart, Co-Cathedral, Houston
Carrasco, Humberto, St. Bartholomew, Houston
Caruso, James N., St. Michael, Houston
Casas, Alvaro, Jr., St. Albert, Houston
Castaneda, Guillermo F., Jr., Diocese of Brownsville
Castillo, Raul A., St. Joseph, Brazoria
Catania, Anthony, SS. Simon & Jude, The Woodlands
Cerda, Rodolfo, All Saints, Houston
Charnisky, John E., Jr., St. Simon & St. Jude, The Woodlands
Chavez, Roberto, St. Cecilia, Houston
Chicas, Alfonso, St. James the Apostle, Spring
Chin-Fatt, Arthur, St. Bartholomew
Clough, Richard L., (Retired)
Coenen, Jerry, On Duty Outside the Archdiocese
Conant, Charles, St. Charles Borromeo, Houston
Contla, Juan M., St. John Neumann, Houston
Cooper, Leslie F., (Unassigned)
Cox, Ralph, Holy Trinity
Crawley, Denver, St. Maximilian Kolbe, Houston
Cromer, Frank P., St. Theresa, Sugarland
Cruz, Agustin, Parish Life Coord., St. Jerome, Clute
Cuiper, Glen H., St. Ignatius of Loyola, Spring
D'Agnolo, Louis, On Duty Outside the Archdiocese
Dalecki, Robert, St. Leo the Great, Centerville
Davies, Martin, On Duty of the Archdiocese
Davis, Thomas, St. Anne, Tomball
Dean, John H., St. Clare of Assisi, Houston
Dell-Olio, L. S., Holy Family, Galveston
Denson, John, Our Lady of Walsingham, Houston
Despania, Raymond L., Sr., St. Peter Claver, Houston
Dinges, Adrian F., Jr., Prince of Peace, Houston
Do, Joseph Chuong Nguyen, Our Lady of Lourdes, Houston
Doherty, James, St. Anthony of Padua, The Woodlands
Dolpher, Eduardo M., St. Cyril of Alexandria, Houston
Duck, Charles, St. Anthony, The Woodlands
Dunham, Bob, Unassigned
Dunning, Sam, St. Thomas Aquinas, Sugar Land
Duplan, Jose, Jr., Shrine of the True Cross, Dickenson
Dupont, Gerald W., SS. Peter & Paul, Bellville
Durden, Jonathon, On Duty Outside of Archdiocese
Ehrman, John W., Jr., Sacred Heart, Conroe
Eskew, Harold B., Jr., Queen of Peace, La Marque
Evanoff, John, Epiphany of the Lord, Katy
Evans, Gregory, St. Cecilia, Houston
Fikac, Marvin R., Sacred Heart Co-Cathedral, Houston
Finger, Eugene, (Retired)
Flores, Antonio, St. Francis de Sales, Houston
Floyd, Ivy C., St. Thomas the Apostle, Huntsville
Flynn, Robert E., Sr., Sts. Simon & Jude, The Woodlands
Foley, Dan, St. John the Evangelist, Baytown
Foreman, Boyce, (Retired)
Frederiksen, Allan, St. Christopher, Houston
Fuentes, Jose, St. Augustine, Houston
Gallagher, James, Christ the Good Sheperd, Spring
Galvan, Jose M., Queen of Peace, Houston
Gandara, Thomas, St. Charles Borromeo, Houston
Garcia, Gerardo J., Christ the King, Houston
Garcia, Joaquin, St. Theresa, Sugar Land
Garcia, Jorge, Catholic Charismatic Center, Houston
Garcia, Julio, St. Jerome, Clute
Garcia, Michael, Catholic Charismatic Center, Houston
Garcia, Rick, Sacred Heart, Conroe
Garcia, Rolando J., St. Bartholomew, Katy
Garrett, William, St. Anne, Houston
Garvis, David, St. Mary, Plantersville
Germann, Joseph, On Duty Outside of the Archdiocese
Gil, Reynaldo S., St. Joseph, Houston
Gilbert, Daniel W., St. Peter the Apostle, Houston
Godinez-Galvan, Jorge, On Duty Outside the Archdiocese
Godoy, German, St. Elizabeth Ann Seton, Houston
Gomez, Javier, St. Andrew, Channelview
Gonzales, Emiliano, On Duty Outside of Archdiocese
Gonzalez, Enrique, St. Charles Borromeo, Houston
Gonzalez, Guadalupe, St. Charles, Houston
Gonzalez, Miguel A., St. Mary Magdalene, Humble
Gonzalez Bangs, Fernando, Our Lady of Guadalupe, Baytown
Gosline, Edwin F., St. Thomas More, Houston
Graham, Michael G., Unassigned
Granado, Alfred E., Jr., Leave of Absence
Gregory, Ralph R., Jr., Christ the Redeemer, Houston
Griesmyer, Steven, Sr., Catholic Charismatic Center, Houston
Guajardo, Fredrico, Our Lady of Mt. Carmel, Houston
Guerra, Daniel, Sr., St. Cecilia, Houston
Guerrero, Billy, Jr., Sacred Heart, Richmond
Hagyari, John, Prince of Peace, Houston
Hall, Greg, Christ the Redeemer, Houston
Hall, Raymond J., Unassigned
Haller, Glenn F., St. Theresa, Sugar Land
Hamilton, L. William, St. Bartholomew, Katy
Hancock, James, Christ the Good Sheperd, Spring
Harnett, Timothy, Prince of Peace, Houston
Harper, Stephen Edwin, On Duty Outside of Archdiocese
Hartman, William, Christ the Good Shepherd, Spring
Hayden, Dale, St. John the Baptist, Alvin
Hayes, Dennis, St. Maximilian Kolbe, Houston
Heap, Theodore, Jr., St. Anne, Tomball
Henkel, Robert, Sr., Christ the Redeemer, Houston
Hennessy, Robert, St. John the Evangelist, Baytown
Hensley, Joseph, Jr., St. Mary of the Miraculous Medal, Texas City
Hernandez, Larry, St. Rose of Lima, Houston
Hernandez, Luis, Most Holy Trinity, Angleton
Hernandez, Miguel, St. Mary of the Miraculous Medal, Texas City
Herrera, Enrique, Holy Family, Galveston
Herrera, Rolando, Archdiocese of San Antonio
Hesse, Robert J., St. John Vianney, Houston
Hickey, Dennis, St. Hyacinth, Deer Park
Higgins, Michael E., St. Ignatius, Spring
Hilbig, Gerard, All Saints, Houston
Hill, Russell, On Duty Outside of the Archdiocese
Hite, James, Epiphany of the Lord, Katy
Hoang, Tuu, St. Elizabeth Ann Seton, Houston
Hock, Leslie Bart, Annunciation, Houston
Hodge, Brick, St. Rose, Houston
Holt, Grant E., Christ Our Light, Navasota
Horbowy, Thaddeus J., Chap. Fed. Bureau of Prisons and Medical Center, Lexington, KY
Horr, Louis, St. Catherine of Siena, Houston
Hull, Samuel, III, St. Edith Stein, Katy
Hunger, Willie, Assumption, Houston
Hunsucker, Paul, St. Thomas the Apostle, Canyon Lake
Ibarra, Hector J., Sacred Heart of Jesus, Manvel
Illingworth, David W., St. Mary Magdalene, Humble
Jackson, Clifford X., Unassigned
Jackson, Phillip, Christ the Redeemer, Houston
Janota, Garry, St. Anne, Tomball
Jelinek, Gregory N., M.D., Christ Our Light-Navasota; O.C. Luther TDC
Jenkins, Michael V., St. Francis Xavier, Houston
Jimenez, Jose, St. Juan Diego, Pasadena
Johnson, Gilbert R., St. Elizabeth Ann Seton, Houston
Johnson, Irvin, Jr., Our Mother of Mercy, Houston
Joseph, Ignatius, St. Francis of Assisi, Houston
Keller, Robert C., St. John of the Cross, Houston
Kelly, Joseph R., Sr., Our Lady of Lourdes, Hitchcock
Kent, Robert, Immaculate Conception, Sealy
Kiang, Paul, Ascension Chinese Mission, Houston
Kirkpatrick, Robert, St. Thomas Aquinas, Sugar Land
Kish, Don, Epiphany of the Lord, Katy
Kleinguetl, Edward, St. Martha, Kingwood
Koch, William E., Sr., Deaf Ministry Center
Kossegi, Frederick, St. John Vianney, Houston
Krupa, Joe, (Retired)
Kulhanek, Jerry Peter, Sr., Our Lady of Fatima, Galena Park
Labrecque, Richard, On Duty Outside of Archdiocese
Lambert, Bernard, Sacred Heart of Jesus, Manvel
Landry, Burke J., Unassigned
Lane, John, St. Monica, Houston
Lansch, John, St. Justin Martyr, Houston
Laredo, Frank, Immaculate Conception, Sealy
Laugermann, Frank J., Jr., St. Francis Xavier, Houston
Laurel, Manuel A., Our Lady of Guadalupe, Houston
Le, Ro, Vietnamese Martyrs, Houston
Leach, Bruce, On Duty Outside of the Archdiocese
Leal, Merce C., Jr., St. Christopher, Houston
Leicht, Robert Reed, Jr., Sacred Heart, Manvel
Leija, Valeriano, Blessed Juan Diego, Pasadena
Lerma, Pedro, Sr., Blessed Sacrament, Houston
Lewis, Edward Thomas, St. Mary, La Porte
Lewis, George, Shrine of the True Cross, Dickinson
Liendo, Jose L., Queen of Peace, Houston
Llorens, Cornelius C., St. Justin Martyr, Houston
Lockett, Leonard P., Sacred Heart Co-Cathedral, Houston
Lockwood, James A., Mary, Queen, Friendswood
Longley, Larry T., St. Albert of Trapani, Houston
Lopez, Luis, St. Paul, Houston
Lopez, Richard, St. Thomas the Apostle, Huntsville
Lorino, Joseph E., St. Vincent de Paul, Houston
Losack, Jerome D., Jr., Guardian Angel, Wallis
Lovelady, Alvin, Our Lady of Lourdes, Hitchcock
Loving, Peter, On Duty Outside of the Archdiocese
Lozano, Rodrigo, St. Charles Borromeo, Houston
Lugo, Loni G., Unassigned
MacFarlane, Robert, St. Martha, Kingwood
Malveaux, Andrew B., Sr., St. Mary of the Purification, Houston
Mancuso, Salvatore, St. Cecilia, Houston
Mangano, Collie J., Jr., Prince of Peace, Houston
Marquez, Antonio, St. Raphael, Houston
Martin, Henry Woods, St. Michael, Houston
Martin, Kenneth, St. Edward, Spring
Matallana, Julio C., St. Mary, La Porte
Matthews, Douglas W., Holy Family, Galveston
Matula, Francis L., All Saints, Houston
Matz, Winfield S., St. John of the Cross, New Caney
McAllister, Jerome, On Duty Outside the Archdiocese
McCarthy, Kevin, St. Angela Merici, Missouri City
McGuire, Michael J., St. Bartholomew the Apostle, Katy
Mejia Parada, Adolfo, St. Juan Diego, Pasadena
Melancon, Mervin, Sacred Heart, Crosby
Melendez, Jose, Holy Family, Missouri City
Meshell, James, St. Mary, Humble
Meza, Benito, St. Augustine, Houston
Michalec, Jerry J., St. Michael, Needville
Middleton, Carl L., On Duty Outside of the Archdiocese
Mignogna, Joseph, St. Anthony of Padua, The Woodlands
Miller, Arthur, Unassigned
Miller, Steve, Sacred Heart, Conroe
Millsap, Stacy, St. Maximillian Kolbe, Houston
Mims, Michael, St. Anthony of Padua, The Woodlands
Mistretta, Stephen A., St. Mary of the Miraculous Medal, Texas City
Mitchell, David D., St. Michael, Lake Jackson
Monterrubio, Arturo, Sacred Heart of Jesus, Manvel
Morales, Hector Hernando, Our Lady of Fatima, Galena Park
Morales, Jaime, St. Jerome, Clute
Moreno, Aurelio Frank, Jr., St. Frances Cabrini, Houston

Moreno, Leopold R., Catholic Charismatic Center, Houston
Mort, Michael, St. Anthony of Padua, The Woodlands
Motley, John M., Unassigned
Moulton, Darryl, Covenant House, Houston
Mouton, Gregory, St. Ignatius, Spring
Mouton, Melvin, St. Stephen the Martyr Mission, Point Blank
Moya, Antonio, St. Jerome, Houston
Mulcare, Terrance D., On Duty Outside the Archdiocese
Munguia, Ben, Immaculate Conception, Sealy
Murrell, John T., St. Rose of Lima, Houston
Murrile, Donald, Sacred Heart, Richmond
Naranjo, Danny, Our Lady of Guadalupe, Rosenberg
Navarro, Raul G., Immaculate Heart of Mary, Houston
Nelms, D. Cade, St. Cecilia, Houston
Newhouse, Thomas C., St. Michael, Houston
Nguyen, Dinh Van, Christ the Incarnate Word, Houston
Nguyen Kim Khanh, Michael, Our Lady of Lavang, Houston
Nguyen Pham, Joseph, Vietnamese Martyrs, Houston
Nguyen Si Bach, Joseph, Christ the Incarnate Word, Houston
O'Brien, Alfred J., St. Martha, Kingwood
O'Dowd, Daniel, St. Jerome, Houston
Oden, Edgar, St. James the Apostle, Spring
Olsovsky, Anthony, Notre Dame, Houston
Ortego, Frank P., St. Thomas the Apostle, Huntsville
Ortego, Mario, Assumption, Houston
Ospina, Alberto, Shrine of the True Cross, Dickinson
Osterhaus, James H., Christ the Redeemer, Houston
Ostrand, Gerard, St. Martha, Kingwood
Ostrowski, F. L., Notre Dame, Houston
Pagnano, Daniel, St. Vincent de Paul, Houston
Pareja, Juan Francisco, Holy Name, Houston
Parr, Kenneth, Catholic Charismatic Center, Houston
Patetta, Alberto J., Christ the Good Sheperd, Spring
Pelletier, John, St. Katherine Drexel, Hempstead
Peltier, Gerald, St. Anthony, Danbury
Pennell, Charles G., St. Elizabeth Ann Seton, Houston
Perez, Celestino M., St. Pius V, Pasadena
Perez, Juan de Dios, St. Raphael the Archangel, Houston
Petereit, Klaus, St. Joseph, New Waverly
Philpot, Clarence, (Retired)
Pistone, John Salvadore, Holy Family, Galveston
Plant, Charles, St. Laurence, Sugar Land
Porras, Carlos, St. Cecilia, Houston
Poth, Louis, On Duty Outside the Archdiocese
Prescott, Allen W., Prince of Peace, Houston
Provenzano, Luis, St. Justin Martyr, Houston
Puglia, Guy, St. Martha, Kingwood
Quiroga, Gabriel Z., Our Lady of Guadalupe, Houston
Ramirez, Fernando, St. Frances Cabrini, Houston
Ramirez, Julio M., St. Gregory the Great, Houston
Ramos, Felix, St. Joseph, New Waverly
Rangel, Francisco M., St. Joseph, Houston
Rapp, Donald, St. Albert of Trapini, Houston
Richards, Thomas, (Retired)
Ries, Donald G., Sacred Heart, Richmond
Rincon, George, Our Lady of Guadalupe, Baytown
Risk, Ralph F., On Duty Outside the Archdiocese
Robertson, Gordon, St. Bartholomew the Apostle, Katy
Robison, Paul L., Jr., Mary Queen, Friendwood
Rodriguez, Hector R., St. John Fisher, Richmond
Rodriguez, Luis, St. Albert of Trapani, Houston
Roessler, Charles F., Jr., St. Frances Cabrini, Houston
Rojas, Servando J., St. Juan Diego, Pasadena
Romaguera, Dominic, St. Edward, Spring
Romeu, Hector J., St. John Vianney, Houston
Rowan, Vincent A., (Retired)
Rubio, Jesus J., St. Bernadette, Houston
Rudnicki, Anthony, Our Lady of Czestochowa, Houston
Rumford, Robert, St. Bernadette
Salas, Pedro, St. Jerome, Houston
Salinas, Johnny, Sacred Heart Co-Cathedral, Houston
Saltzmann, Peter, Catholic Charismatic Center, Houston
Sanchez, Martin G., St. Joseph, Houston
Sandiford, Sid, Sts. Simon & Jude, The Woodlands
Satterwhite, Michael, (Unassigned)
Schmidt, Michael, SS. Simon & Jude, The Woodlands
Schuster, John, St. Martha, Kingwood
Seifert, William E., Jr., Holy Family, Missouri City
Seiler, Daniel, St. Pius V, Pasadena
Senger, Don, St. Theresa, Sugar Land
Shaw, Wallace, St. Mary Star of the Sea, Freeport
Sheffield, William L., St. Ignatius, Spring
Shefts, Andrew, Most Holy Trinity, Angleton
Simon, Rick L., Our Mother of Mercy, Houston
Simon, Ronald, St. Philip Neri, Houston
Singer, John William, Jr., St. Joseph, Baytown
Smaistrla, Denis J., St. Mary's Seminary, Houston
Smith, Jimmy, St. Joseph, Brazoria
Smith, Ronald, (Retired)
Sosa, Alfonso, St. Elizabeth Ann Seton, Houston
Soto, Alfredo, St. Martha, Kingwood
St. Aubin, Leo F., St. Anthony of Padua, The Woodlands
St. Julian, Michael, St. Francis of Assisi
Standridge, Robert, Holy Family, Galveston
Stanley, Kenneth, Prince of Peace, Houston
Stasiulis, Stan, (Retired)
Steffes, Dale W., St. John Vianney, Houston
Stevens, Robert Gregory, St. Francis Cabrini, Houston
Stoessel, Edward T., St. Thomas More, Houston
Stoughton, Bruce, St. John the Baptist, Alvin
Sullivan, John, On Duty Outside of Archdiocese
Suriano, Julio S., Sacred Heart Co-Cathedral
Thomson, Nicholas, St. Edwards, Spring
Tollett, Jesse, St. Luke, Houston
Tollett, Lee, St. Catherine of Siena, Houston
Torres, Reynaldo, St. Patrick, Houston
Torres, Ruben, St. John Fisher, Richmond
Tran, Nhat, St. Justin Martyr, Houston
Trevino, Jose, Christ the Redeemer, Houston
Tripp, Edwin, St. Edith Stein, Katy
Tristan, Benito, Jr., St. Christopher, Houston
Trosclair, George, Prince of Peace, Houston; St. Mary, Plantersville
Trujillo, J. Cruz, St. Helen, Pearland
Tse, Ming Fai, St. Theresa, Houston
Vacek, Albert E., Jr., St. John Vianney, Houston
Vaclavik, Larry A., St. Theresa, Houston
Vasquez, Miguel, (Unassigned)
Venegas, Rudy, Our Lady of Guadalupe, Baytown
Vicknair, Tom Jude, St. Anthony of Padua, The Woodlands
Vigil, Benjamin, On Duty Outside of the Archdiocese
Villareal, Marcelino, St. John Vianney, Houston
Vines, Larry, St. Ignatius, Spring
Vocelka, Frank Jay, Jr., Duty Outside of Archdiocese
Wagner, William C., St. Bartholomew, Katy
Walsh, Gary, PP, St. Edith Stein, Katy
Ward, Robert, Most Holy Trinity, Angleton
Waterman, John H., On Duty Outside of Archdiocese
Weaver, Lonnie, (Retired)
Weaver, William A., St. Elizabeth Ann Seton, Houston
Weir, Joseph, St. Maximillian Kolbe, Houston
Welsh, James, (Retired)
Wewer, Justin J., St. John the Evangelist, Baytown
Wiles, Philip Arlen, St. Dominic, Houston
Wright, Jim, St. Clare of Assisi
Yanez, Albert, Our Lady of Guadalupe, Rosenberg
Zamora, Joe, St. Elizabeth Ann Seton, Houston
Zbylut, Robert, On Duty Outside of the Archdiocese
Zepeda, Arthur, St. James the Apostle, Spring

INSTITUTIONS LOCATED IN THE ARCHDIOCESE

[A] SEMINARIES, ARCHDIOCESAN

HOUSTON. *St. Mary's Seminary* (1901) 9845 Memorial Dr., 77024-3498. Tel: 713-686-4345; Fax: 713-681-7550. Email: sms@smseminary.com. Revs. Trung V. Nguyen, J.C.L., Rector; Michael T. Grey, C.S.Sp, Vice Rector; John Telles (ELP), Spiritual Dir.; Giusepppe Barbieri, C.P., Spiritual Dir.; Jose Salazar (CC), Formation Dir.; James E. Robertson (AUS), Formation Dir.; Michael G. Earthman, Pastoral Formation; Sr. Rosalie Karstedt, C.D.P., Pastoral Formation; Revs. Rafael R. Davila, M.M.; Francis M. Macatangay, Formation Dir.; Sr. Patricia Regan, C.D.P., Business Mgr.; Sandra Magie, S.T.D., Dean School of Theology; Mrs. Laura Olejnik, Librarian; Rev. Msgr. James B. Anderson, Prof.; Mrs. Laura Olejnik, Librarian. Priests 9; Sisters 2; Lay Teachers 5; Diocesan Seminarians 81; Religious Seminarians 10; Total Enrollment 91.

[B] SEMINARIES, RELIGIOUS OR SCHOLASTICATES

HOUSTON. *Holy Ghost Fathers and Brothers, Spiritan Hall*, 4410 Yoakum Blvd., 77006-5820. Tel: 713-529-0405; Fax: 713-529-4236. Web: www.spiritans.org. Rev. Joseph Huy Quang Dinh, C.S.Sp., Dir. Priests 1.

SUGAR LAND. *Basilian Fathers of Sugarland* (2004) (St. Basil's Novitiate), 106 Fifth St., 77498. Tel: 281-491-1565. Email: vdulock@earthlink.net. Revs. Vincent Dulock, C.S.B., Rector, Supr. & Master of Novices; Jamie M. Abercrombie, C.S.B.; John L. Boscoe, C.S.B.; Robert J. Klem, C.S.B.; Robert J. Duggan, C.S.B. Priests 2.

Basilian Fathers Mission Center, 114 Main St., P.O. Box 708, 77498.

[C] COLLEGES AND UNIVERSITIES

HOUSTON. **University of St. Thomas* (1947) 3800 Montrose Blvd., 77006-4696. Tel: 713-522-7911; Fax: 713-525-2125. Email: president@stthom.edu. Web: www.stthom.edu. Dr. Robert Ivany, Pres.; Dr. Dominic A. Aquila, Vice Pres. Academic Affairs; Mr. James Piccininni, Dir., Doherty Library; Dr. Sandra C. Magie, Dean School of Theology; Dr. Bahman Mirshab, Dean Cameron School of Business; Nora Hutto, Dean, School Educ.; Ms. Lynda McKendree, Dean Scholarships & Fin. Aid; Ms. Kia Wissmiller, Dir. Major Constituents; Ms. Joanna Palasota, Dir. Admin. Computing Svcs.; Mr. James Booth, Vice Pres. Finance; Dr. John Palasota, Assoc. Vice Pres.; Dr. Ravi Srinivas, Dir., Master in Liberal Arts Prog. & Dean, Extended Programs; Dr. Rose Signorello, Exec. Dir. Counseling, Wellness, & Disability Svcs.; Dr. Mary Catherine Sommers, Dir. Center for Thomistic Studies; Mr. Gary McCormack, Vice Pres. Information Technology & Special Assistant to Pres.; Mr. H. Ken DeDominicis, Vice Pres. Inst. Advancement; Mr. Matthew Prasifka, Asst. Vice Pres. Campus Life; Mr. Daryl Bissett, Dir. Security; Mr. Howard Rose, Asst. Vice Pres. Facilities Opers.; Ms. Karen Burns, Controller; Ms. Susan Rose, Treas.; Rev. Donald S. Nesti, C.S.Sp., Dir. Center for Faith and Culture; Ms. Patricia McKinley, Vice Pres. Student Affairs; Ms. Vickie Alleman, Vice Pres. Mktg., Communications & Enrollment Mgmt.; Ms. Marionette Mitchell, Dir. Publications; Ms. Laura Dozier, Dir. Advancement Projects; Ms. Susan Bradford, Advancement Exec. Dir.; Mr. Tony Reyna, Dir. Network & Campus Computing; Ms. Christine Barry, Dir. Central Computing Svcs.; Mr. Mark Henderson, Dir., Technology Support Svcs.; Sr. Paula Jean Miller, FSE, Dir. Catholic Studies Prog.; Ms. Laura P. Olejnik, Dir. Cardinal Beran Library; Dr. Terry Hall, Dir. Honors Prog.; Dr. Connie Michalos, Dir. Tutorial Svcs.; Ms. Deborah Crofoot-Morley, Dir. Devel.; Ms. Roya Esfandi, Dir. Information Resources; Ms. Yolanda Norman, Dir. Residence Life; Ms. Diane Thornton, Dir. Planned Giving; Mr. John Meuser, Assoc. Vice Pres., Admin. Svcs.; Ms. Sara Laidlaw, Dir., Advising; Dr. Vleses Balderas, Dir. Study Abroad; Rev. Joseph E. Pilsner, C.S.B., Dean Arts & Sciences; Mr. Hank Emery, Dir. Alumni Rels. & Annual Giving; Ms. Lori Gallagher, Dir., Center for Irish Studies; William J. Flynn, Dir. Center for Irish Studies; Mr. Todd Smith, Dir. Athletics; Ms. Elsie Biron, Dir. Catholic Outreach; Rev. Michael A. Buentello, C.S.B., Univ. Chap. & Dir. Campus Ministry; Dr. Poldi Tschirsch, Dir., Nursing Programs Devel.; Mr. Philip Butcher, Dir. Veteran Svcs.; Mr. Lee Holm, Dir. Transfer Admissions & Opers.; Dr. John Burke, Dir. Catholic Social Justice Learning; Dr. Jean-Philippe Faletta, Dir. Svc. Learning; Sandra Soliz, Dir. Mktg. & Communications; Angie Montelongo, Dir. Student Activities; Lindsey McPherson, Dean, Students & Dir. Career Svcs. & Testing; Kimberly Sanders, Registrar, Dean Academic Progs.; Dr. Michele Simms, Dir. Center for Business Ethics & Center for Faculty Excellence; Dr. Hans Stockton, Dir. Center for Intl. Studies; Arthur Ortiz, Dir., Freshman Admissions; Dr. Ricardo Montelongo, Dir., Student Success; Fawziyia Alsarraj, Dir., Intl. Student & Scholar Svcs.; Dr. Jerome A. Kramer, Dir., Writing Prog.; Rick Young, Dir., Pre-Law Prog.; Jessica Domann, Dir., Recreational Sports. Founded in 1947, Graduate Division (Four Schools). Undergraduate Division (21 Departments). Center for Thomistic Studies. Center for International Studies. Center for Business Ethics.; Liberal Arts University. Priests 14; Sisters 5; Lay Professors 135; Total Enrollment 3,754; Total Staff 205.

[D] JUNIOR HIGH SCHOOLS, ARCHDIOCESAN

HOUSTON. *Assumption Catholic School*, 801 Roselane St., 77037-4696. Tel: 281-447-2132; Fax: 281-447-1825. Email: PWClark@houstonassumption.org. Web: www.houstonassumption.org. Mr. Patrick W. Clark, Prin.; Sr. Francis Marie Bordages, Librarian. Sisters 2; Lay Teachers 16; Students 241; Total Staff 31.

[E] HIGH SCHOOLS, PRIVATE

GALVESTON. *O'Connell College Preparatory School*, 1320 Tremont St., 77550-4513. Tel: 409-765-5534; Fax: 409-765-5536. Email: info@oconnellprep.com. Web: www.oconnellprep.com. Marc Martinez, Prin.; Barbara Alcala, Librarian. Priests 1; Lay Teachers 15; Total Staff 20; Students 97.

HOUSTON. *St. Agnes Academy* (1906) 9000 Bellaire Blvd., 77036-4683. Tel: 713-219-5400; Fax: 713-219-5499. Email: sjmeyer@st-agnes.org. Web: www.st-agnes.org. Sr. Jane Meyer, O.P., Head of School. Tel: 713-219-5400; Fax: 713-219-5499; Deborah Whalen, Prin.; Herman Sutter, Librarian. Dominican Sisters 2; Lay Teachers 57; Full time faculty 74; Girls 871.

Duchesne Academy of the Sacred Heart (1960) (Girls), 10202 Memorial Dr., 77024-3299. Tel: 713-468-8211; Fax: 713-465-9809. Email: administration@duchesne.org. Web: www.duchesne.org. Sr. Jan Dunn, R.S.C.J., Headmistress; Dr. Rae Flory, Prin. (Upper School); Ms. Julie Meyer, Prin. (Middle School); Ms. Debra Johnson, Prin. (Lower School); Jean Pfluger, Librarian (Upper School); Laura Leib, Librarian (Middle School); Katie Turner, Librarian (Lower School); Megan Woods, Librarian (Lower School). Religious of the Sacred Heart. Sisters 1; Lay Teachers 89; Students (9-12) 240; Total Enrollment (PreK-12) 683.

Incarnate Word Academy (1873) 609 Crawford St., 77002-3668. Tel: 713-227-3637; Fax: 713-227-1014. Email: mgetschow@incarnateword.org. Web: www.incarnateword.org. Sr. Lauren Beck, C.V.I., Pres.; Mary Getschow, Prin.; Rebecca Shields, Librarian. Sisters of the Incarnate Word and Blessed Sacrament. Lay Teachers 25; Girls 280.

Jesuit Cristo Rey High School of Houston, Inc. dba Cristo Rey Jesuit College Preparatory School of Houston, Inc. 6700 Mt. Carmel St., 77087. Tel: 281-501-1298. Web: www.cristoreyjesuit.org. Rev. Antonio Martinez, S.J., Pres.; Katherine Cater, Prin. Priests 1; Lay Teachers 15.

St. Pius X High School, Inc. (1956) 811 W. Donovan, 77091-5699. Tel: 713-692-3581; Fax: 713-692-5725. Email: pollardd@stpiusx.org. Web: www.stpiusx.org. Sr. Donna M. Pollard, O.P., B.S., M.A., M.Ed., Head of School; Diane Larsen, Academic Dean; Jeff Donaruma, Dean of Students; Susie Kramer, Dir. Admissions; Deborah Mosichuk, Librarian. Dominican Sisters 1; Lay Teachers 60; Students 661; Total Staff 85.

Strake Jesuit College Preparatory Inc., 8900 Bellaire Blvd., 77036-4699. Tel: 713-774-7651; Fax: 713-774-6427. Email: sjcom@strakejesuit.org. Web: www.strakejesuit.org. Mr. Ken lojo, Prin.; Revs. Christopher A. Billac, S.J., Faculty; Flavio Bravo, S.J., Pastoral Ministry; John N. Folzenlogen, S.J., Faculty; Daniel K. Lahart, S.J., Pres.; Bro. Castenzio A. Ferlita, S.J., Asst. to Prin.; Ms. Susan Penny, Librarian. Priests 4; Brothers 2; Scholastics 4; Lay Teachers 80; Boys 900.

St. Thomas High School (1900) 4500 Memorial Dr., 77007-7332. Tel: 713-864-6348 (School); 713-868-9209 (Residence); Fax: 713-864-5750. Web: www.sths.org. Revs. Jack H. Hanna, C.S.B., Treas.; Patrick W. Fulton, C.S.B., Prin.; Ronald G. Schwenzer, C.S.B., Pres.; Albert R. Gaelens, C.S.B.; Richard A. Wahl, C.S.B., J.C.L.; Kevin J. Storey, C.S.B.; Robert H. Glass, C.S.B., Supr.; Les F. Schaefer, C.S.B.; James F. Blocher, C.S.B.; James F. Murphy. Basilian Residence, Basilian Fathers. Priests 7; Lay Teachers 65; Total Staff 100; Total Enrollment 740.

KATY. *Pope John XXIII High School, Inc.* (2004) 1800 W. Grand Pkwy., 77449. Tel: 281-693-1000; Fax: 281-693-1001. Email: tpetersen@pj23.org. Web: www.pj23.org. Tim Petersen, Prin.; Candace Brawner, Admissions; Keith Myers, Advancement; Ms. Theresa Bramanti, Bd. Pres.; Tim Peterson, Prin.; Jenelle Drymalla, Librarian. Teachers 36; Total Staff 48; Total Enrollment 360.

[F] ELEMENTARY SCHOOLS, PRIVATE

HOUSTON. *St. Catherine's Montessori* (1966) 9821 Timberside, 77025. Tel: 713-665-2195; Fax: 713-665-1478. Email: stracy@stcathmont.org. Susan Tracy, Prin.; Sarah Case, Librarian. Lay Teachers 17; Students 231; Total Staff 42.

John Paul II Catholic School (1988) 1400 Parkway Plaza Dr., 77077-1503. Tel: 281-496-1500; Fax: 281-496-2943. Email: principal@jp2.org. Web: www.jp2.org. Janie Hengst, Prin.; Rebecca Bogard, Asst. Prin.; Dan Courtney, Asst. Prin.; Sherry Lamb, Librarian. Lay Teachers 44; Students 717; Total Staff 73.

The Regis School, 7330 Westview Dr., 77055-5122. Tel: 713-682-8383; Fax: 713-682-8388. Email: ntaylor@theregisschool.org. Web: www.theREGISschool.org. Dr. Nancy O. Taylor, Headmistress; Laura Luong, Librarian; Mrs. pilar Lopez, Middle School Division Head. Catholic School for Boys. Lay Teachers 41; Students 254; Total Staff 57.

[G] ELEMENTARY SCHOOLS, CONSOLIDATED

GALVESTON. *Galveston Catholic School* (1986) (Consolidation) 2601 Ursuline Ave., 77550-4398. Tel: 409-765-6607; Fax: 409-765-5154. Email: pdiaz@hfcsgalv.org. Web: hfcsgalv.org. Paul Diaz, Prin.; Dawn Cromie, Librarian & Mgr. Sisters 1; Lay Teachers 13; Students 114; Total Staff 24.

GALVESTON/HOUSTON. *School of Environmental Education - Camp Kappe* (1982) (Grades 5), 7738 Camp Kappe Rd., Plantersville, 77363. Tel: 936-894-2141; Fax: 936-894-2198. Email: stalsee@aol.com. Sr. Thomas Ann LaCour, O.P., Prin. Sisters 1; Lay Teachers 3; Total Staff 4; Total Enrollment 1,400.

RICHWOOD. *Our Lady Queen of Peace*, 1600 Hwy. 2004, 77531. Tel: 979-265-3909; Fax: 979-265-9780. Email: marianne@olqpschool.org. Web: www.olqpschool.org. Mr. Michael C. Duran, Prin. Serving the parishes of Holy Trinity, Angleton; St. Jerome, Clute; St. Anthony, Danbury; St. Mary Star of the Sea, Freeport; Lady of Perpetual Help, Sweeny; St. John the Apostle Mission, West Columbia; St. Joseph's, Brazoria, TX; St. Michaels, Lake Jackson. Lay Teachers 20; Students 241.

[H] SOCIAL AGENCIES CATHOLIC CHARITIES

HOUSTON. *Catholic Charities of the Archdiocese of Galveston-Houston* (1943) 2900 Louisiana St., P.O. Box 66508, 77006. Tel: 713-526-4611; Fax: 713-526-1546. Email: info@catholiccharities.org. Web: www.catholiccharities.org. Bonna Kol, Pres.

AIDS Ministry Tel: 713-227-9981; Fax: 713-225-1242.

Galveston County Basic Needs, Galveston County Basic Needs, Texas City. Tel: 409-948-0405; Fax: 409-942-1068.

Noran Health Center, 2615 Fannin, 77002. (Basic needs counseling Cabrini)

Guadalupe Center Tel: 713-227-9981; Fax: 713-225-1242. (Family Assistance)

Children's and Family Services Tel: 713-526-4611; Fax: 713-526-1546. (Adoption, Foster Care and Post-Adoption)

Disaster Recovery Tel: 713-526-4611; Fax: 713-526-1546.

Services to Pregnant and Parenting Adolescents Tel: 713-526-4611; Fax: 713-526-1546.

Family Counseling Tel: 713-526-4611; Fax: 713-526-1546.

St. Frances Cabrini Center for Immigrant Legal Assistance Tel: 713-874-6570; Fax: 713-874-6792.

St. Jerome Emiliani's Home for Children Tel: 713-526-4611; Fax: 713-526-1546.

Refugee Resettlement Program Tel: 713-526-4611; Fax: 713-526-1546.

St. Michael's Home for Children Tel: 713-526-4611; Fax: 713-526-1546.

Senior Services Tel: 713-526-4611; Fax: 713-526-1546.

Parish Social Ministry Tel: 713-526-4611; Fax: 713-526-1546.

Villa Guadalupe Tel: 713-227-9981; Fax: 713-225-1242. Transitional Housing

Mamie George Community Center All services in Ft. Bend County., Tel: 281-202-6200.

The Oaks at Rio Bend (Children services in Ft. Bend County)

[I] HEALTH AND HOSPITALS

HOUSTON. *CHRISTUS Health Gulf Coast*, 1700 W. Loop S., #1200, 77027. Tel: 713-277-2775; Fax: 713-277-2778. Email: diana.smith@christushealth.org. Web: www.christushealth.org. Ellen Jones, Pres. & CEO. Total Staff 1,153; Total Assisted Annually 200,254; Bed Capacity 232.

Christus Literacy Center, 2420 Winnie, 77550. Tel: 409-621-1337. Personnel 2.

CHRISTUS Our Daily Bread (1985) Tel: 409-765-6971; Fax: 409-765-8547. Staff 7.

KATY. *CHRISTUS St. Catherine Hospital*, 701 S. Fry Rd., 77450. Tel: 281-599-5700; Fax: 281-398-2265. Bed Capacity 102; Patients Assisted Annually 91,373; Total Staff 681.

NASSAU BAY. *CHRISTUS St. John Hospital*, 18300 St. John Dr., 77058. Tel: 281-333-5503 (Hospital); Fax: 281-333-8891. Email: tom.permetti@christushealth.org. Web: www.christusstjohn.org. Tom Permetti, Admin. Tel: 281-333-8898. Bed Capacity 178.

[J] CLINICS

HOUSTON. *San Jose Clinic* (1922) 2615 Fannin, 77002. Tel: 713-490-2602; Fax: 713-228-2612. Email: leeannkroon@sanjoseclinic.org. Web: www.sanjoseclinic.org. Paule Anne Lewis, Exec. Dir.; Lee Ann Kroon, CFO & COO. Patients Assisted Annually 5,000; Lay Staff 50.

[K] PROTECTIVE INSTITUTIONS

HOUSTON. *Casa de Esperanza De Los Ninos, Inc.* (1982) P.O. Box 66581, 77266-6581. Tel: 713-529-0639; Fax: 713-529-9179. Email: casa@casahope.org. Web: www.casahope.org. Kathleen Foster, Dir.; Mr. William Jones, Assoc. Dir. Homes for children in crisis situations, foster care, adoption. Sisters 1; Served 3,500; Total Assisted 400; Total Staff 54; Bed Capacity 50.

Casa Juan Diego (1980) P.O. Box 70113, 77270. Tel: 713-869-7376; Fax: 713-864-7295. Email: info@cjd.org. Web: www.cjd.org. 4818 Rose, 77007. Mr. Mark Zwick, Dir.; Mrs. Louise Zwick, Dir. Houses 8; People Served Annually 62,660; Personnel 14.

Casa Maria de Guadalupe Medical Clinic and Social Service Center, 6101 Edgemoor, 77081. Tel: 713-869-7376; Fax: 713-864-7295. Email: info@cjd.org. Web: www.cjd.org. (Catholic Worker) Patients Assisted Annually 9,500; Total Staff 4.

Covenant House Texas, 1111 Lovett Blvd., 77006. Tel: 713-523-2231; Fax: 713-523-6904. Email: Rgrobinson@covenanthouse.org. Web: www.covenanthousetx.org. Kevin M. Ryan, Pres.; Ronda G. Robinson, Exec. Dir. & CEO; Martin Galicia, Pastoral Min.; John Lampson, Dir. Finance. Bed Capacity 114; Total Assisted Annually 5,367; Total Staff 87.

Magnificat Houses Inc. (1968) P.O. Box 25415, 77265. Tel: 713-520-0461; Fax: 713-520-0461. Email: magnificathouseinc@sbcglobal.net. Web: www.mhihouston.org. Rose Mary Badami, Founder, Pres. & Exec. Dir. Bed Capacity 170; Staff 16; Resident Staff 42; Contract Staff 2; Total Assisted Annually (Houses) 615; Meals Served Annually (Houses) 158,950; Meals Served Annually (Soup Kitchen) 102,846.

Santa Maria Hostel, 2605 Parker Rd., 77093. Tel: 713-691-0900; 713-957-2413; Fax: 713-691-0910. Email: kaustin@santamariahostel.org. Web: www.santamariahostel.org. 2005 Jacquelyn Rd., 77055. Tel: 713-957-2413; Fax: 713-400-1119. Kay Austin, CEO. Intensive and supportive residential treatment; housing, shelter and outpatient services (substance abuse) for women ages 18 and above and women with their children. Treatment for co-occurring disorders is also provided. Residents 136; Patients Assisted Annually 1,662; Total Staff 109; Bed Capacity 231.

[L] HOMES FOR THE AGED

HOUSTON. *St. Dominic Village* (1998) 2409 Holcombe Blvd., 77021. Tel: 713-741-8701; Fax: 713-741-9811. Email: sreiter@stdominicvillage.org. Web: www.stdominicvillage.org. Steven B. Reiter, CEO. Bed Capacity 331; Total Staff 185.

Pope John Paul XXIII Priests' Residence (1981) 2407 Holcombe Blvd., 77021-2023. Tel: 713-748-4608; Fax: 713-748-4608. Revs. Gabre-Tinsaye Adhana (Retired). Tel: 713-748-4425; Peter Ngoc Thanh Chu (Retired). Tel: 713-747-8774; Armando J. Rodriguez (Retired). Tel: 713-842-2053; Hoang Toan (Retired); Jose M. Sanchez (Retired). Total in Residence 16; Total Staff 2.

St. Dominic Nursing Home (1981) 2409 Holcombe Blvd., 77021. Tel: 713-741-8701; Fax: 713-741-9811. Web: www.stdominicvillage.org. Email: rstanley@stdominicvillage.org. Ruth Stanley, Admin. & COO. Aged Residents 342; Total Staff 140.

St. Dominic Residence Hall (1975) 2401A Holcombe Blvd., 77021. Tel: 713-741-8700; Fax: 713-748-8305. Ruth Stanley, Admin. & COO. Total in Residence 166; Total Staff 20.

[M] RESIDENTIAL TREATMENT AND RENEWAL CENTERS

SPLENDORA. *Shalom Center, Inc.* (1980) 13516 Morgan Dr., 77372-3121. Tel: 281-399-0520; Fax: 281-399-3366. Email: info@shalomcenterinc.org. Web: www.shalomcenterinc.org. Daniel A. Kidd, Exec. Dir. A residential treatment center for priests, brothers and sisters. Bed Capacity 16; Total Assisted Annually 376; Total Staff 14.

[N] PERSONAL PRELATURES

HOUSTON. *Opus Dei*, 5505 Chaucer Dr., 77005-2631. Tel: 713-528-4081; Fax: 713-523-6829. Web: www.opusdei.org. Very Rev. Paul D. Kais, B.A., M.A., Ph.D., Vicar Opus Dei in Texas; Revs. Francisco Vera; Michael Barrett; Michael J. Manz. Prelature of the Holy Cross and Opus Dei.

[O] MONASTERIES AND RESIDENCES OF PRIESTS AND BROTHERS

HOUSTON. *Companions of the Cross (Texas), Companions of the Cross (Texas)*, 1949 Cullen Blvd., 77023. Tel: 713-644-8400. Email: companionstx@gmail.com. Web: www.companionscross.org. Rev. John A.

Vandenakker, C.C., Local Supr.

Congregation of the Holy Spirit, Province of the United States (1964) 1700 W. Alabama St., 77098-2808. Tel: 713-522-2882; Fax: 713-522-8063. Email: spiritans@aol.com. Web: www.spiritans.org. Rev. Thomas J. Byrne, C.S.Sp. Total in Residence 1.

Congregation of the Passion, Holy Name Passionist Community and Retreat Center, 430 Bunker Hill Rd., 77024. Tel: 713-464-4932; Fax: 713-932-7303. Email: kennetho'malleycp@gmail.com. Web: www.passionist.org. Very Rev. Kenneth O'Malley, C.P., Local Supr. & Formation Dir.; Revs. Joseph Moons, C.P., Retreat Center Dir.; Peter Berendt, C.P.; Simon Herbers, C.P.; Cedric Pisegna, C.P.; Robert Bovenzi, C.P.; Alfredo Ocampo, C.P.; Bro. Carl Hund, C.P., Retreat Center Team.

Dillon House, 1302 Kipling, 77006-4297. Tel: 713-529-3994; Fax: 713-942-7623. Revs. Philip Anthony Acquaro, C.S.B., Supr. (Retired); Wilfred S. Canning, C.S.B. (Retired); Donald E. Kuder, C.S.B. (Retired); Robert G. Ritz, C.S.B. (Retired); Joseph Charles Mitrano, C.S.B. (Retired); Carl L. Belisch, C.S.B. (Retired); Edward Arthur Roberts, C.S.B. (Retired). Basilian Fathers.

Disciples of Hope (Texas) (1995) 15403 Palmway St., 77071. Tel: 713-721-2894; Fax: 713-721-2894. Web: www.disciplesofhope.org. Rev. Eugene E. Cagoco, D.S., Local Coord. *St. Matthew the Evangelist*, 9915 Hollister Dr., 77040-1702. Tel: 713-466-4030; Fax: 713-896-7235. Email: minorstar0817@yahoo.com. Web: www.discipli-spei.org. Revs. Luis Paolo Agostino V. Evardoni, D.S.; Eugene E. Cagoco, D.S.

Dominican Friars, St. Mark Priory, Inc., 10430 Hunington Point Dr., 77099. Tel: 281-879-5239; Fax: 281-879-5355. Revs. Richard Martin Patrick, O.P.; Anthony Hung N. Tran, O.P., Prior.

Maryknoll Fathers and Brothers, 2360 Rice Blvd., 77005-2652. Tel: 713-529-1912; Fax: 713-529-0372. Email: mklhouston@maryknoll.org. Web: www.maryknoll.org. Rev. Gerald E. Kelly, M.M., Dir.

Priests Residing Elsewhere: Revs. Rafael R. Davila, M.M., St. Mary Seminary, 9845 Memorial Dr., 77024-3498. Tel: 713-686-4345; Fax: 713-681-7550; Richard E. Paulissen, M.M., P.O. Box 9592, 77261. Tel: 713-921-2736.

Residence of the Basilian Fathers of the University of St. Thomas (1947) 4019 Yoakum Blvd., 77006-4833. Tel: 713-525-3515; Fax: 713-529-0844. Revs. Robert W. Crooker, C.S.B.; Edward J. Baenziger, C.S.B.; Patrick O. Braden, C.S.B.; Michael A. Buentello, C.S.B.; Anthony E. Giampietro, C.S.B.; George H. Hosko, C.S.B.; Janusz Ihnatowicz (Poland); James J. Keon, C.S.B.; Joseph E. Pilsner, C.S.B.; T. Patrick Warden, C.S.B.; John R. Whitley, C.S.B.

Vietnamese Dominican Vicariate of St. Vincent Liem, 12314 Old Foltin Rd., 77086. Tel: 281-999-4928; Fax: 281-820-7095. Very Rev. Liem Trung Tran, O.P., Reg. Supr.

MISSOURI CITY. *The Society of the Oblates of Sacred Heart*, 1510 Fifth St., 77489-1298. Tel: 281-798-8579; Fax: 281-499-9680. Email: sunny.joseph@holyfamilychurch.us. Web: www.oshcongregation.org. Revs. Sunny Joseph Plammoottil, O.S.H., Supr.; Thomas Joseph Puthusseril, O.S.H.; Joy James, O.S.H.; Lukose Manuel, O.S.H.

NEW CANEY. *Congregation of the Mother Coredemptrix* (1985) 23404 Oak Shadows Pl., 77357-8516. Tel: 281-354-4764. Rev. Joseph Doan Huy Chuong, Admin. (Retired). Total in Residence 1.

SUGAR LAND. *Basilian Mission Center* (1936) 414 Main St., P.O. Box 708, 77487-0708. Tel: 281-240-8714; Fax: 281-240-8713. Email: basmissions@earthlink.net. Web: www.basilianfathersmissions.org. Revs. John L. Boscoe, C.S.B., Mission Procurator, Treas.; Robert J. Klem, C.S.B. Associates 7; Scholastics 4.

Priests Serving in Foreign Missions: Revs. Jamie M. Abercrombie, C.S.B.; Francis A. Amico, C.S.B.; Thomas P. Dugan, C.S.B.; Alberto A. Ferrara, C.S.B.; Rafael I. Lopera, C.S.B., (Supr. of Colombia); Pedro M. Mora, C.S.B.; Bernard C. Owens, C.S.B.; Philip Wallace Platt, C.S.B.; Juan Carlos Rojas, C.S.B.; Roberto P. Rojas, C.S.B.; Alejandro Romero, C.S.B., (Supr. of Mexico); Robert J. Seguin, C.S.B.; Charles Daniel Porter, C.S.B.; Oscar Fernando Gomez Soto, C.S.B.

Franciscan Missionary Brothers, St. Francis Friary, 11710 Cobblestone Point Dr., 77498. Tel: 281-495-1558; Fax: 281-561-8659. Email: brothersfriary@yahoo.com. Web: www.cmsf-brothers.org. Bro. Rogi Ignatius Devakulam, C.M.S.F.

[P] CONVENTS AND RESIDENCES FOR SISTERS

HOUSTON. *Carmelite Sisters of the Sacred Heart (C.S.H.)* (1904) 22 Farrell, 77022-2609. Tel: 713-697-6020; Fax: 713-697-6020. Email: Carmelitas200@hotmail.com. Sisters Antonia Albarran, Supr.; Rosa Maria Garcia, Sec. Total Staff 4.

Casa Providencia, 3907 Rotman, 77003. Tel: 713-227-2555; Fax: 713-923-5866.

Congregation of Divine Providence (1762) (France) *Providence House*, 1339 Friarcreek Ln., 77055. Tel: 713-984-8041; Fax: 713-956-1891. Email: pjregancdp@att.net. Sisters 3.

Congregation of Our Lady of the Retreat in the Cenacle (R.C.), Cenacle Retreat House, 420 N. Kirkwood, 77079. Tel: 281-497-3131; Fax: 281-497-7632. Email: ministry@cenacleretreathouse.org. Web: www.cenacleretreathouse.org. Sisters 6.

Cenacle Novitiate, 14103 Heatherfield Dr., 77079. Tel: 281-597-0944. Sisters 2.

Congregation of the Incarnate Word & Blessed Sacrament (C.V.I.) (Houston) (1873) Incarnate Word Convent, 3400 Bradford Pl., 77025-1398. Tel: 713-668-0423; Fax: 713-668-1857. Email: lbeck@incarnateword.org. Web: www.incarnatewordsistershouston.org. Sisters 29. *Casa Pacis Convent*, 3428 Bradford Pl., 77025. Tel: 713-661-3785. Sisters 2. *Incarnate Word Academy Convent*, 609 Crawford St., 77002-3668. Tel: 713-223-4143. Sisters 3. *St. Christopher Convent*, 8711 Glen Loch, 77061. Tel: 713-649-4700. Sisters 2. *Visitation Convent*, 3418A Bradford Pl., 77025-1328. Tel: 713-664-8370. Sisters 3. *St. Michael Convent*, 4225 Mangum Rd., Apt. 14, 77092-5522. Tel: 713-682-2242. Sisters 1.

Marian Convent, Marian Convent, 3719 Glen Haven, 77025-1204. Tel: 713-667-2238. Sisters 2.

Congregation of the Sisters of Charity of the Incarnate Word, Houston, Texas (CCVI) (1866) 6510 Lawndale St., P.O. Box 230969, 77223-0969. Tel: 713-928-6053; Fax: 713-928-8148. Email: lhealy@ccvi-vdm.org. Web: www.sistersofcharity.org. Sr. M. Rose Scanlan, Contact Person. Total Sisters in Congregation (Professed) 161. *St. Anne Community* Tel: 713-928-6053; Fax: 713-921-1070. Sisters 7. *Annunciation Community* Tel: 713-928-6053; Fax: 713-928-9962. Sisters 6.

Bernice Place Community Tel: 713-928-6053; Fax: 713-928-9962.

Casa de la Paz Community, 6641 Wildwood Way, 77023. Tel: 713-928-6053; Fax: 713-928-8148. Sisters 3. *De Matel Community* Tel: 713-928-6053; Fax: 713-928-8148. Sisters 7. *Edith Stein Community*, 6405 Pinehurst, 77023-3329. Tel: 713-926-6024; Fax: 713-926-6024. Sisters 2.

Incarnate Word Charitable Trust Tel: 713-928-6053; Fax: 713-926-3085. Sr. Elizabeth Ann Hayes, CCVI, Chairperson. *St. Jeanne Community* Tel: 713-928-6053. Sisters 2. *Marian Community* Tel: 713-928-6053; Fax: 713-928-8148. Sisters 19.

Dubuis Community Tel: 713-928-6053; Fax: 713-218-7339. Sisters 2.

Placidus Place Community Tel: 713-928-6053. Sisters 8. *St. Placidus Community* Tel: 713-928-6053; Fax: 713-928-8148. Sisters 29.

Shalom Community Tel: 713-921-5305.

St. Veronica Community Tel: 713-928-6053. Sisters 5. *St. John Community*, 1623 Antigua Ln., Nassau Bay, 77058-4126. Tel: 281-333-9363. Sisters 2.

Discipulas de Jesus, 9601 McGallion Rd., 77076. Tel: 713-691-3960; Fax: 713-691-3960. Email: discipulasdejesushouston@yahoo.com. Web: www.discipulasdejesus.org. Sr. Maria Rosalinda Navarro, D.J., Local Supr.

Dominican Sisters of Houston (1882) Motherhouse Complex & Administrative Offices: 6501 Almeda Rd., 77021-2095. Tel: 713-747-3310; Fax: 713-747-4707. Email: houstonop@domhou.org. Web: www.domhou.org. Sr. Carol Mayes, O.P., Prioress. *Dominican Sisters of Houston, Texas Inc. (O.P.)*, The Sacred Heart Convent Retirement Trust.; St. Agnes Academy, Inc.; St. Agnes Academy Foundation, Inc.; St. Pius X High School, Inc.; St. Pius X High School Foundation, Inc.; The Sacred Heart Convent Retirement Trust.

Dominican Sisters of Mary Immaculate Province (1978) Provincial House, 5250 Gasmer Dr., 77035. Tel: 713-723-8250; Fax: 713-723-8229. Web: www.nutudaminh.org. Professed in Province 90. *Dominican Sisters of Mary Immaculate Province (St. Catherine Convent), Provincial House*, 5250 Gasmer Dr., 77035. Tel: 713-723-4815; 713-723-8250; Fax: 713-723-8229. Sisters 45. *Mary Immaculate Convent*, 5900 Chippewa Blvd., 77086. Tel: 281-445-9574; 281-591-6081; Fax: 281-445-6716. Sisters 15. *Our Lady of the Holy Rosary Convent (Novitiate)*, 1602 Adams St., Missouri City, 77489. Tel: 281-403-9300; Fax: 281-403-9300. Sisters 21.

Sacred Heart Convent, 911 Runneburg, Crosby, 77532. Tel: 281-328-4073; Fax: 281-328-4073. Sisters 4.

Marian Convent, 3719 Glenhaven Blvd., 77025-1204. Tel: 713-667-2238. Sisters Lauren Beck, C.V.I., Pres., Incarnate Word Academy; Carmel O'Malley, C.V.I.

Maryknoll Sisters of St. Dominic (M.M.), 7490 Brompton, No. 265, 77025. Tel: 713-666-5245; Fax: 713-666-5245. Email: joyagnes000@sbcglobal.net.

Missionary Carmelites of St. Teresa (C.M.S.T.) (1903) Holy Family Provincial House, 9548 Deer Trail Dr., 77038. Tel: 281-445-5520; Fax: 281-445-5748. Email: hfamprovcmst@yahoo.com. Sisters 6.

Infant Jesus of Prague Convent, 9600 Deer Trail Dr., 77038. Tel: 281-445-8830. Sisters 11.

St. Joseph Convent, 9815 Marek Rd., 77038. Tel: 281-445-0056. Sisters 10. *St. Therese Novitiate*, 9819 Marek Rd., 77038. Tel: 281-820-3732. Sisters 4.

St. Teresa Postulancy, 9608 Deer Trail Dr., 77038. Tel: 281-999-4435. Sisters 6.

Missionary Sisters of the Eucharist, 3301 San Jacinto St., 77004. Tel: 713-523-8831. Sr. Maria Chali, M.S.E., Contact Person. Sisters 4.

Religious of the Sacred Heart (R.S.C.J.) (1960) Duchesne Community, 10204 Memorial Dr., 77024. Tel: 713-467-5312; Fax: 713-465-9809. Email: acaire@rscj.org. Web: www.rscj.org. Sisters 4. 2020 Harvard St., 77008. Tel: 713-868-9607. Sisters 2.

Sisters for Christian Community (S.F.C.C.) Tel: 936-756-3051; Fax: 936-756-8105. *SFCC Community*, 109 N. Frazier, Conroe, 77301. Tel: 409-756-3051; Fax: 409-756-8105. *Sacred Heart Convent*, 105 N. Frazier St., Conroe, 77301. Tel: 936-756-8288; Fax: 936-756-8105.

Sisters of the Holy Spirit and Mary Immaculate (S.H.Sp.), St. Charles Borromeo Convent, 9601 McGallion, 77076-5122. Tel: 713-694-4264 (Convent); 281-447-2132 (School); Fax: 713-692-1376. Sr. Miriam Mitchell, S.H.Sp., Gen. Supr. Tel: 210-533-5149; 210-533-5522; Fax: 210-533-3434.

Sisters of the Incarnate Word and Blessed Sacrament (C.V.I.), Marian Convent, 3719 Glen Haven, 77025-1204. Tel: 713-667-2738.

Sisters of the Sacred Heart (S.S.C.J.) (1816) Sacred Heart Convent, 1707 Chapman St., 77009-8715. Tel: 713-236-9294. Email: maryssscj@hotmail.com. Sisters 4.

NEW CANEY. *Discalced Carmelite Nuns of New Caney, Texas* (1958) 1100 Parthenon Pl., 77357-3276. Tel: 281-399-0270, Ext. 4; Fax: 281-689-3615. Email: carmelnewcaney@gmail.com. Web: www.icansurf.net/ocdnewcaney. Sisters 8.

PEARLAND. *Handmaids of the Holy Child Jesus* (1931) 3614 Englewood Dr., 77584. Tel: 281-692-0098; Fax: 281-692-0049; 713-995-6706. Email: handmaidsusa@handmaidsisters.org. Web: www.hhcjsisters.org. P.O. Box 740099, 77274. Tel: 281-914-4664. Sisters Felicia Agibi, H.H.C.J., Dir. Devel.; Leonie-Martha Okaraga, H.H.C.J., Supr. Gen., Generalate H.H.C.J., P.O. Box 155, Ifuho-Ikot Ekpene, Akwa Ibom Nigeria. Sisters 805.

Mission Development Office, Office: P.O. Box 740099, 77274. Tel: 281-914-4664. Email: missiondev@hhcjsisters.org. Web: www.hhcjsisters.org. Sr. Caroline Onyeoziri, Supr.

ROSENBURG. *Missionary Catechists of the Sacred Hearts of Jesus and Mary (M.C.S.H.)* (1918) Our Lady of Guadalupe Convent: 504 Carlisle St., Rosenberg, 77471. Tel: 281-232-9881; Fax: 281-342-4008. Sisters Antonieta Salazar, Coord.; Enriqueta Salgado. Sisters 3.

STAFFORD. *Missionary Sisters of Mary Immaculate*, 630 Easy Jet Dr., 77477-6358. Tel: 281-499-0030; Fax: 281-499-0030. Email: msmisisters@hotmail.com. Sisters Betsy Ulahannan; Agnes Maria, M.S.M.I., Supr. & Contact Person.

Schoenstatt Sisters of Mary (I.S.S.M.), 550 Stafford Run, #707, 77477. Tel: 281-499-2616. Sr. M. Carmen Rodriguez, Tri-City Center Site Mgr.

[Q] RETREAT HOUSES

HOUSTON. *Cenacle Retreat House*, 420 N. Kirkwood Rd., 77079. Tel: 281-497-3131; Fax: 281-497-7632. Email: ministry@cenacleretreathouse.org. Web: www.cenacleretreathouse.org. Sisters Dorothy Briscoe, r.c.; Pat Burke, r.c., Treas.; Lois Dideon, r.c.; Mary Dennison, r.c., Sabbatical (Houston Area); Roselle Haas, r.c.; Ann Goggin, r.c.; Mary Guido, r.c., Local Leader; Sue Ellen Ruggles, Exec. Dir. Congregation of Our Lady of the Retreat in the Cenacle. Sisters 6.

Holy Name Retreat Center, 430 Bunker Hill Rd., 77024-6399. Tel: 713-464-0211; Fax: 713-464-0671. Email: holyname@passionist.org. Web:

passionist.org/holyname. Bro. Carl Hund, C.P., Assoc. Dir.; Revs. Joseph Moons, C.P., Dir.; Peter Berendt, C.P. Total in Residence 1; Total Staff 2.

DICKINSON. *Christian Renewal Center*, 1515 Hughes Rd., P.O. Box 699, 77539-0699. Tel: 281-337-1312 (Center); Fax: 281-337-2615. Email: deaconjim@retreatcentercrc.org. Web: www.retreatcentercrc.org. Deacon Jim Wright, Exec. Dir.; Christy Wright, Ministry & Marketing Coord. Total in Residence 2; Total Staff 16.

[R] NEWMAN CENTERS

GALVESTON. *Galveston Newman Center* 602 Seawolf Pkwy., Ste. B, Pelican Island #5, 77550. Tel: 409-740-3797; Fax: 409-740-3798. Email: gal.newmancenterum@gmail.com. Carl Erickson, Dir. Texas A & M University at Galveston; University of Texas Medical Branch; Galveston College; College of the Mainland.

HOUSTON. *Catholic Newman Association at the University of Houston Central Campus* (1968) Catholic Center, 4805 Calhoun Rd., 77004. Tel: 713-748-2529; Fax: 713-748-8412. Email: catholic@uh.edu. Web: www.uhcatholic.org. Rev. Joseph Lam Nguyen, C.S.Sp., Dir. Priests 1; Total Assisted 10,000; Total Staff 3.

Satellite Office (1964) 203 AD Bruce Religion Center, 77204-3050. Tel: 713-748-2529; Fax: 713-748-8412. Rev. Joseph Lam Nguyen, C.S.Sp., Campus Min. & Dir.; Dolores Perez, Sec.; Giovan Cuchapin, Campus Min.

Rice University/Texas Medical Center Schools; Catholic Student Center 1703 Bolsover Rd., 77005. Tel: 713-526-3809; Fax: 713-526-6010. Email: cathcen@rice.edu. Web: www.rice.edu/catholic. Sr. Antoinette "Kitty" Carter, O.P., Dir.; Rev. Binh T. Ta, C.Ss.R., Chap.; Rita M. Seng, Sec. & Ministry Asst. Total Staff 3.

Texas Southern University Catholic Newman Hall 3535 Wheeler Ave., 77004. Tel: 713-747-7595; Fax: 713-747-3198. Email: jlane21132@comcast.com. Deacon John Lane, Dir. Total Assisted 300; Total Staff 2.

University of St. Thomas Campus Ministry 3800 Montrose Blvd., 77006. Tel: 713-525-3589; Fax: 713-525-3524. Email: campusministry@stthom.edu. Web: www.stthom.edu. Rev. Michael A. Buentello, C.S.B., Dir. & Chap.

HUNTSVILLE. *Catholic Student Center, S.H.S.U.* 1310 17th St., 77340-4415. Tel: 936-291-2620; Fax: 936-291-2620. Email: org_cath@shsu.edu. Web: www.shsu-catholic.org. Joseph Magee, Ph.D., Dir. Total Assisted 350; Total Staff 3.

PRAIRIE VIEW. *Prairie View A & M University Catholic Center* P.O. Box 2876, 77446. Tel: 832-372-8056. Deacon Irvin Johnson Jr., Campus Min. Total Staff 1.

[S] MISCELLANEOUS

GALVESTON. *The Bishop's Palace* (1886) 1402 Broadway, 77550. Tel: 409-762-2475; Fax: 409-762-1801. Rev. Msgr. George A. Sheltz, Chancellor.

HOUSTON. *Angela House*, 425 Shane, #18, 77037. Tel: 281-445-9696. Email: moconnell@angelahouse.org. Web: www.angelahouse.orgFax: 281-445-8891. Sr. Maureen O'Connell, O.P., Exec. Dir./Contact Person.

The Catholic Chaplain Corps (1967) 4206 S. MacGregor Way, 77021. Tel: 713-747-8445; Fax: 713-747-3642. Revs. Joseph Bang-Doan; Patrick J. Cummings; Don A. Neumann; Page E. Polk, O.F.M.; Teodoro Tim Y. Prado; Enrique V. Salen. Cell: 713-922-0700; Michael S. Van Cleve; Eugene E. Cagoco, D.S.; Peter J. Dorairaj, S.S.S. Houston Hospitals: St. Luke's Episcopal, Texas Children's Hospital, Methodist, M. D. Anderson Cancer Center, The Institute of Rehabilitation and Research, Ben Taub General Hospital, Kindred Hospital, LBJ General Hospital, Memorial Hermann Medical Center, Memorial Hermann Southwest, Memorial Hermann Memorial City.

Catholic Charismatic Center (1972) 1949 Cullen, P.O. Box 230287, 77023-0287. Tel: 713-236-9977; Fax: 713-236-0073. Email: ccc@catholiccharismaticcenter.org. Web: www.catholiccharismaticcenter.org. Revs. Mark J. Goring, Dir.; Francis A. Frankovich, C.C., Assoc. Dir.; Michael J. Minifie, C.C., Assoc. Dir.

The Catholic Endowment Foundation of Galveston-Houston, P.O. Box 907, 77001-0907. Tel: 713-654-1133; Fax: 713-654-1188. Boone Schwartzel, Sec.

Charity Guild of Catholic Women (1922) 1203 Lovett Blvd., 77006-3857. Tel: 713-529-0995; Fax: 713-529-9263. Web: www.charityguildshop.org.

Charity Guild of St. Joseph (1988) 4218 Markham, 77027. Tel: 713-623-2935; Fax: 713-623-2935. Catherine Cash, Pres.

CHRISTUS Health (1999) 2707 N. Loop W., 77008. Tel: 281-936-3184; Fax: 281-936-7802. Email: larry.pardue@christushealth.org. Web: www.christushealth.org. Ernie W. Sadau, M.B.A., Pres. & CEO; William L. Pardue, B.A., M.A., Corp. Sec.; Mary D. Silva, Deputy Corp. Sec.

CHRISTUS Health Liability Retention Trust Tel: 281-936-3184; Fax: 281-936-7802.

CHRISTUS Health Cash Balance Plan Trust Tel: 281-936-3184; Fax: 281-936-7802.

CHRISTUS Health Matched Savings Plan Tel: 281-936-3184; Fax: 281-936-7802.

CHRISTUS Tax-Deferred Annuity Plans

CHRISTUS Health Rabbi Trust

St. Dominic Center, Inc., 2401 E. Holcombe, 77021. Tel: 713-741-8743; Fax: 713-741-8705. Email: wknight@archgh.org. Wayne Knight, Diocesan Facility Admin.

Equestrian Order of the Holy Sepulchre of Jerusalem, Southwestern USA Lieutenancy, 2001 Kirby Dr., Ste. 902, 77019-1402. Tel: 713-524-5444; Fax: 713-524-5333. Email: Lieutenant@EOHSsouthwest.com. Web: eohssouthwest.com. Mr. Dennis M. Malloy, KGCHS, Lieutenant.

St. Francis de Sales School Foundation, 8100 Roos, 77036. Tel: 713-774-4447; Fax: 713-271-6744. Email: webmaster@st-francis-de-sales.org. Web: www.sfdshouston.org. Tom Overbeck, Pres.; Mike Masera, Treas.; Thomas Norman, Advisor & Finance Council.

Martha's Kitchen Food Services (1992) 322 S. Jensen Dr., 77003. Tel: 713-224-2522; Fax: 713-224-7814. 4301 Woodridge Pkwy., Porter, 77365. Tel: 281-358-6637. Rev. Msgr. Chester L. Borski. Sisters 2.

St. Mary's Children's Relief Fund, Chancery Bldg., 1700 San Jacinto, P.O. Box 907, 77001-0907. Tel: 713-659-5461; Fax: 713-759-9151. His Eminence Daniel Cardinal DiNardo, Pres.

St. Pius X High School Foundation, Inc., 811 W. Donovan, 77091-5699. Tel: 713-692-3581; Fax: 713-692-5725. Email: pollardd@stpiusx.org. Web: www.stpiusx.org. James Black, Pres.; Sisters Donna M. Pollard, O.P., B.S., M.A., M.Ed., Head of School; Lavergne Schwender, O.P., Sec.; Patrick Svrcek, Treas.

Sociedad San Martin de Porres, 931 Euclid, 77009. Tel: 713-869-0999; 713-860-6431. Email: ccampbell@abhr.com.

Strake Jesuit Retreat and Leadership Center, Inc., 8900 Bellaire Blvd., 77036. Tel: 713-490-8102; Fax: 713-271-3407. Rev. Daniel K. Lahart, S.J., Pres.

The Society of the Holy Spirit, 1700 W. Alabama, 77098-2808. Tel: 713-522-2882; Fax: 713-522-8064. Email: nesti@stthom.edu. Web: www.spiritans.org. Rev. Donald S. Nesti, C.S.Sp., Contact Person.

The St. Thomas More Parish School Endowment Foundation, 10330 Hillcroft, 77096. Tel: 713-729-0221; Fax: 713-729-3294. Web: www.stmhouston.org. Rev. William A. Oliver, Contact Person & Pastor.

UST Chapelle, 3034 Quenby Ave., 77005. Tel: 713-349-0921; Fax: 832-201-7556. Web: ustchapelle.org. Alain Maury, Contact Person.

MISSOURI CITY. *Catholic Clerical Student Fund* (1933) 2722 Glen Echo Ln., 77459. Cell: 832-283-3902; Tel: 281-437-8188. His Eminence Daniel Cardinal DiNardo, Chm.; Carole E. Updyke, Pres. Higher learning for the priesthood.

RELIGIOUS INSTITUTES OF MEN REPRESENTED IN THE ARCHDIOCESE

For further details refer to the corresponding bracketed number in the Religious Institutes of Men or Women section.

[0140]—*The Augustinians*—O.S.A.
[0170]—*Basilian Fathers* (Toronto, Canada)—C.S.B.
[]—*Benedictine Monks*—O.S.B.
[0275]—*Carmelites of Mary Immaculate*—C.M.I.
[]—*Companions of the Cross* (Ottowa, Canada)—C.C.
[0220]—*Congregation of the Blessed Sacrament*—S.S.S.
[]—*Congregation of the Holy Spirit (Spiritans)*—C.S.Sp.
[]—*Congregation of the Mother Coredemptrix*—C.M.C.
[1130]—*Congregation of the Priests of the Sacred Heart*—S.C.J.
[]—*Disciples of Hope* Careres, Philippines—D.S.
[]—*Divine Word Fathers*—S.V.D.
[0520]—*Franciscan Friars*—O.F.M.
[]—*Franciscan Missionary Brothers*—C.M.S.F.
[0650]—*Holy Ghost Fathers* (Western Prov.)—C.S.Sp.
[0690]—*Jesuit Fathers and Brothers* (New Orleans Prov.)—S.J.
[]—*Legionaries of Christ*—L.C.
[0800]—*Maryknoll*—M.M.
[0720]—*The Missionaries of Our Lady of La Salette* (Prov. of Mary Queen)—M.S.
[]—*Missionaries of St. Joseph* (Mexico)—M.J.
[]—*Missionaries of St. Paul*—M.S.P.
[1110]—*Missionaries of the Sacred Heart*—M.S.C.
[0910]—*Oblates of Mary Immaculate*—O.M.I.
[0920]—*Oblates of St. Francis de Sales*—O.S.F.S.
[0430]—*Order of Preachers-Dominicans* (Prov. of St. Albert the Great)—O.P.
[1070]—*Redemptorist Fathers* (New Orleans Vice Prov.)—C.SS.R.
[]—*Scalabrinians*—C.S.
[1260]—*Society of Christ*—S.Ch.
[0975]—*Society of Our Lady of the Most Holy Trinity*—S.O.L.T.
[0420]—*Society of the Divine Word*—S.V.D.
[]—*Society of the Precious Blood Sanguinist Fathers*—C.P.P.S.
[1250]—*Somascan Fathers*—C.R.S.

RELIGIOUS INSTITUTES OF WOMEN REPRESENTED IN THE ARCHDIOCESE

[0230]—*Benedictine Sisters of the Sacred Heart*—O.S.B.
[0390]—*Carmelite Missionaries of St. Teresa*—C.M.S.T.
[]—*Carmelite Sisters of the Sacred Heart*—C.S.C.
[]—*Communidad Apostolica de Maria Siempre Virgen*—C.A.M.S.V.
[]—*Community of the Holy Spirit (A Private Association of the Faithful)*—C.H.S.
[1010]—*Congregation of Divine Providence*—C.D.P.
[3110]—*Congregation of Our Lady of the Retreat in the Cenacle*—R.C.
[3830-01]—*Congregation of St. Joseph* (Boston, MA)—C.S.J.
[]—*Congregation of the Lovers of the Cross* (N. Vietnam)—H.C.L.
[0470]—*Congregation of the Sisters of Charity of the Incarnate Word* (Houston)—CCVI
[]—*Daughters of Divine Love* (Nigeria)—D.D.L.
[]—*Daughters of Mary Mother of Mercy*—D.M.M.M.
[0420]—*Discalced Carmelite Nuns of New Caney, Texas*—O.C.D.
[]—*Discipulas de Jesus*—D.J.
[1070-13]—*Dominican Sisters* (Adrian, MI)—O.P.
[1070-19]—*Dominican Sisters, Congregation of the Sacred Heart* (Houston)—O.P.
[]—*Eucharistic Missionaries of St. Theresa* (Mexico)—M.E.S.T.
[]—*Family of the Visitation of Mary*—F.M.V.
[]—*Franciscan Sisters of the Eucharist*—F.S.E.
[]—*Handmaids of the Holy Child Jesus* (Nigeria)—H.H.C.J.
[]—*La Salle Sisters*—L.S.S.
[2470]—*Maryknoll Sisters of St. Dominic*—M.M.
[]—*Missionaries of Charity*—M.C.
[2690]—*Missionary Catechists of Divine Providence*—M.C.D.P.
[2700]—*Missionary Catechists of the Sacred Hearts of Jesus and Mary*—M.C.S.H.
[]—*Missionary Sisters of Mary Immaculate*—M.S.M.I.
[2725]—*Missionary Sisters of the Eucharist*—M.S.E.
[4070]—*Religious of the Sacred Heart*—R.S.C.J.
[4110]—*Roman Union of the Order of St. Ursula*—O.S.U.
[]—*Schoenstatt Sisters of Mary*—I.S.S.M.
[2970]—*School Sisters of Notre Dame*—S.S.N.D.
[]—*Sisters for Christian Community*—S.F.C.C.
[]—*Sisters of Loretto*—S.L.
[]—*Sisters of St. Michael the Archangel*—S.S.M.A.
[2050]—*Sisters of the Holy Spirit and Mary Immaculate*—S.H.Sp.
[2150]—*Sisters of the Immaculate Heart of Mary*—I.H.M.
[]—*Sisters of the Immaculate Heart of Mary Mother of Christ* (Onitsha, Nigeria)—I.H.M.
[2183]—*Sisters of the Immaculate Heart of Mary Mother of Christ, Nigeria*—L.P.
[2190]—*Sisters of the Incarnate Word and Blessed Sacrament* (Houston)—C.V.I.
[3670]—*Sisters of the Sacred Heart of Jesus*—S.S.C.J.
[]—*Vietnamese Dominican Sisters*—O.P.

ARCHDIOCESAN CEMETERIES

GALVESTON. *Old Catholic, Calvary*

HOUSTON. *Holy Cross*

St. Vincent

DICKINSON. *Mount Olivet*

NECROLOGY

† Cargill, Rev. Msgr. Eugene, (Retired)—Died Jan. 17, 2011

† Crosthwait, Rev. Msgr. Joseph H., (Retired)—Died Feb. 13, 2011

† Jones, Frank W., (Retired)—Died July 29, 2011

† Noble, David H., Houston, TX Catholic Chaplain Corps.—Died Feb. 24, 2011

An asterisk (*) denotes an organization that has established tax-exempt status directly with the IRS and is not covered by the USCCB Group Ruling.

Diocese of Gary

(Dioecesis Gariensis)

Most Reverend

DALE J. MELCZEK, D.D.

Bishop of Gary; ordained June 6, 1964; appointed Auxiliary Bishop of Detroit and Titular Bishop of Trau December 3, 1982; consecrated January 27, 1983; appointed Apostolic Administrator of Gary August 19, 1992; appointed Coadjutor Bishop of Gary October 20, 1995; succeeded to the See of Gary June 1, 1996. *Office: 9292 Broadway, Merrillville, IN 46410.* Tel: 219-769-9292; Fax: 219-769-2066.

Chancery: 9292 Broadway, Merrillville, IN 46410. Tel: 219-769-9292; Fax: 219-738-9034.

Web: www.dcgary.org

ESTABLISHED DECEMBER 17, 1956.

Square Miles 1,807.

Comprises the Counties of Lake, LaPorte, Porter and Starke in the State of Indiana.

For legal titles of parishes and diocesan institutions, consult the Chancery.

STATISTICAL OVERVIEW

Personnel	
Bishop	1
Priests: Diocesan Active in Diocese	61
Priests: Diocesan Active Outside Diocese	4
Priests: Diocesan in Foreign Missions	1
Priests: Retired, Sick or Absent	35
Number of Diocesan Priests	101
Religious Priests in Diocese	37
Total Priests in Diocese	138
Extern Priests in Diocese	8
Ordinations:	
Transitional Deacons	2
Permanent Deacons	10
Permanent Deacons in Diocese	66
Total Brothers	10
Total Sisters	75
Parishes	
Parishes	68
With Resident Pastor:	
Resident Diocesan Priests	50
Resident Religious Priests	4
Without Resident Pastor:	
Administered by Priests	14
Missions	4
Pastoral Centers	6
Closed Parishes	1
Professional Ministry Personnel:	
Brothers	1
Sisters	6
Lay Ministers	68
Welfare	
Catholic Hospitals	6
Total Assisted	1,209,733
Homes for the Aged	2
Total Assisted	226
Residential Care of Children	2
Total Assisted	222
Day Care Centers	2
Total Assisted	500
Specialized Homes	2
Total Assisted	700
Special Centers for Social Services	7
Total Assisted	10,000
Educational	
Diocesan Students in Other Seminaries	11
Total Seminarians	11
Colleges and Universities	1
Total Students	1,275
High Schools, Diocesan and Parish	3
Total Students	1,218
High Schools, Private	1
Total Students	33
Elementary Schools, Diocesan and Parish	20
Total Students	5,371
Catechesis/Religious Education:	
High School Students	745
Elementary Students	8,694
Total Students under Catholic Instruction	17,347
Teachers in the Diocese:	
Sisters	5
Lay Teachers	424
Vital Statistics	
Receptions into the Church:	
Infant Baptism Totals	1,573
Minor Baptism Totals	121
Adult Baptism Totals	97
Received into Full Communion	173
First Communions	2,007
Confirmations	1,854
Marriages:	
Catholic	344
Interfaith	139
Total Marriages	483
Deaths	1,420
Total Catholic Population	185,300
Total Population	794,178

Former Bishops—Most Revs. ANDREW GREGORY GRUTKA, D.D., ord. Dec. 5, 1933; appt. Bishop of Gary Dec. 29, 1956; cons. Feb. 25, 1957; retired July 9, 1984; died Nov. 11, 1993; NORBERT F. GAUGHAN, D.D., Ph.D., ord. Nov. 4, 1945; appt. Auxiliary Bishop of Greensburg April 2, 1975; cons. June 26, 1975; appt. Bishop of Gary July 9, 1984; retired June 1, 1996; died Oct. 1, 1999.

Vicar General—Rev. JOSEPH M. PAWLOWSKI.

Deans—Revs. JON J. PLAVCAN, Gary-Hobart Deanery; RICHARD A. ORLINSKI, South Lake County Deanery; MICHAEL J. YADRON, South Lake County Deanery; JOSEPH M. PAWLOWSKI, Porter-Starke County Deanery; DAVID W. KIME, LaPorte County Deanery.

Chancery—9292 Broadway, Merrillville, 46410. Tel: 219-769-9292; Fax: 219-738-9034.

Administrative Assistant to the Bishop—Rev. JON J. PLAVCAN.

Bishop's Delegate for Sexual Misconduct Matters—KELLY VENEGAS, SPHR.

Director of Finance and Administration—KARL P. DYTRYCH.

Executive Secretary to the Bishop—VALERIE D. MCMANUS. Tel: 219-769-9181; Fax: 219-769-2066.

Diocesan Tribunal—9292 Broadway, Merrillville, 46410. Tel: 219-769-9292.

Judicial Vicar—Rev. BRIAN D. CHADWICK, J.C.L.

Director of the Tribunal—Sr. EVELYN OVALLES, S.P., J.C.L.

Judges—Rev. BRIAN D. CHADWICK, J.C.L.; Sr. EVELYN OVALLES, S.P., J.C.L.

Defender of the Bond—Rev. Msgr. JOHN J. SIEKIERSKI, J.C.L.

Second Instance—Judges: Rev. Msgrs. EDWARD F. LITOT (Retired); VINCENT L. LENGERICH (Retired); Rev. LOURDU PASALA, J.C.L. Defender of the Bond: Sr. EVELYN OVALLES, S.P., J.C.L.

Adjutant Defender of the Bond—Rev. TED J. MAUCH.

Auditors—Deacon SHERMAN BROWN; DONNA V. CALLAWAY.

Notaries—VALERIE MCMANUS; MARY ANN O'CONNELL; MILDRED VIRUS.

Bishop's Council of Priests—Revs. DAVID W. KIME; JON J. PLAVCAN; GERALD H. SCHWEITZER; KEVIN R. HUBER, D.Min.; JOSEPH M. PAWLOWSKI; CHARLES A. MOSLEY; MICHAEL J. YADRON; BRIAN D. CHADWICK, J.C.L.; WILLIAM F. O'TOOLE; RICHARD A. ORLINSKI; DAVID H. GOSNELL (Retired); EDWARD G. TLUCEK, O.F.M.; THEODORE J. MENS; KEITH MCCLELLAN; TED J. MAUCH; J. PATRICK GAZA; MARTIN J. DOBRZYNSKI; WALTER M. CIESLA; DOUGLAS J. MAYER; EDWARD J. MOSZUR.

Consultors—Revs. JOSEPH M. PAWLOWSKI; RICHARD A. ORLINSKI; MICHAEL J. YADRON; DAVID W. KIME; JON J. PLAVCAN.

Priests' Personnel Board—Revs. JOSEPH M. PAWLOWSKI; RICHARD A. ORLINSKI; JON J. PLAVCAN; ROY T. BEECHING; MICHAEL J. YADRON; DAVID W. KIME; MARTIN J. DOBRZYNSKI; EDWARD J. MOSZUR; DOUGLAS J. MAYER; WILLIAM F. O'TOOLE.

Diocesan Offices and Directors

African American Catholic Ministry—9292 Broadway, Merrillville, 46410. Tel: 219-769-9292; Fax: 219-738-9034.

Blue Army—Rev. WALTER M. CIESLA, Chap., Mailing Address: P.O. Box 3036, Munster, 46321. Tel: 219-836-8779.

Boy Scouts Liaison—Deacon RONALD L. PYLE, Chap., 1830 Govert Dr., Schererville, 46375; TOM CARR, Chm., 3360 N. 950 W., Michigan City, 46360.

Catholic Campaign for Human Development—Mrs. SANDRA MORGAN; Deacon DUANE W. DEDELOW, 940 Broadway, Gary, 46402. Tel: 219-886-3549; Fax: 219-886-2428.

Campus Ministry— St. Teresa of Avila Catholic Student Center (Valparaiso University) Rev. KEVIN P. MCCARTHY, Chap., 1511 LaPorte St., Valparaiso, 46383. Tel: 219-464-4042; Fax: 219-462-2711.

Catholic Relief Services— Operation Rice Bowl, annual Lenten collection, and disaster relief collections. *Catholic Charities, 940 Broadway, Gary, 46402.* Tel: 219-886-3549; Fax: 219-886-2428.

Global Solidarity Partnership Program—Deacons DUANE W. DEDELOW; DAVID J. KAPALA, 940 Broadway, Gary, 46402. Tel: 219-886-3549; Fax: 219-886-2428.

Catholic Foundation for the Diocese of Gary—DIANA MURRAY, Dir., 9292 Broadway, Merrillville, 46410. Tel: 219-769-9292; Fax: 219-738-9034.

Catholic Services Appeal—JOYCE ILLYES, 9292 Broadway, Merrillville, 46410. Tel: 219-769-9292; Fax: 219-738-9034.

Catholic Youth Organization (CYO) Office—PAUL WENGEL, 7725 Broadway, Ste. C, Merrillville, 46410. Tel: 219-736-8931; Fax: 219-736-9457.

Cemeteries—Rev. ROY T. BEECHING, Dir., 5885 Harrison St., Merrillville, 46410. Tel: 219-980-2693; MICHAEL P. WELSH, 1547 167th St., Hammond, 46324. Tel: 219-844-9475.

Charismatic Apostolate—Rev. BRIAN D. CHADWICK,

J.C.L., Dir., 801 W. 73rd Ave., Merrillville, 46410. Tel: 219-769-8534; BRITTA NEINAST, 204 Appletree Ln., Valparaiso, 46383. Tel: 219-531-4194.

Charities—940 Broadway, Gary, 46402. Tel: 219-886-3549; Fax: 219-886-2428. Deacon DUANE W. DEDELOW, Exec. Dir.

Communications Office—DEBBIE BOSAK, Dir., 9292 Broadway, Merrillville, 46410. Tel: 219-769-9292, Ext. 286.

Council of Catholic Women—Rev. ROY T. BEECHING, Diocesan Moderator, 5885 Harrison St., Merrillville, 46410. Tel: 219-980-2693.

Cursillos in Christianity—Revs. EDUARDO MALAGON, Chap. (Spanish), 2447 Putnam St., Lake Station, 46405. Tel: 219-962-8626; JAMES P. MCGROGAN (Retired), 638 N. Calumet Rd., Chesterton, 46304. Tel: 219-926-1282.

Diaconate—Deacons PHILLIP L. MUVICH, Dir. Diaconate Formation, 508 Timber Point Dr., Valparaiso, 46385. Tel: 219-364-8338; THOMAS GRYZBEK, Diaconate Dir. - Post Ordination, 1335 Capri Lane, Dyer, 46311. Tel: 219-865-2440.

Ecumenical Officer—JOAN CRIST, 7 Detroit St., Hammond, 46320. Tel: 219-932-2706.

Employee Benefits—KAREN WALSH, Coord., 9292 Broadway, Merrillville, 46410. Tel: 219-769-9292; Fax: 219-738-9034.

Family Life Ministry—176 S. West St., Crown Point, 46307. Tel: 219-663-8417.

Finance Council—DENNIS BIELFELDT; CALVIN E. BELLAMY; MITCH GAFFIGAN; KARL DYTRYCH; JOHN J. DIEDERICH; DONNA SMITH; Rev. JOSEPH M. PAWLOWSKI; ANA GRANDFIELD.

Girl Scout Liaison—Rev. THEODORE A. NORDQUIST; JACKIE KRILICH, Chm., 10621 State Line Rd., Dyer, 46311. Tel: 219-365-5217.

Holy Childhood Association— cf. Mission Office

Hispanic Diocesan Ministries—ADELINE TORRES, 3814 Grand Blvd., East Chicago, 46312. Tel: 219-397-2125; Fax: 219-397-2168.

Human Resources—KELLY VENEGAS, SPHR, Mgr., 9292 Broadway, Merrillville, 46410. Tel: 219-769-9292; Fax: 219-769-7597.

Indiana Catholic Conference—Deacons DUANE W. DEDELOW; DAVID J. KAPALA; ADELINE TORRES, 940 Broadway, Gary, 46402. Tel: 219-886-3549; Fax: 219-886-2428.

Lay Ministry Formation Office—Mrs. ANNE VERBEKE, Dir., 9292 Broadway, Merrillville, 46410. Tel: 219-769-9292; Fax: 219-738-9034.

Legal Counsel—ROBERT M. SCHWERD, 1158 Lincolnway, Ste. 2, Valparaiso, 46385. Tel: 219-841-5683.

Marriage Dispensations—Rev. GERALD H. SCHWEITZER, Mailing Address: P.O. Box 386, Wanatah, 46390. Tel: 219-733-2955.

Marriage Encounter—JIM MCCULLOUCH; KRIS MCCULLOUCH. Tel: 800-442-3553.

Ministry to Deaf—Rev. JOHN J. ZEMELKO, 356 W. Seven Mile Rd., Valparaiso, 46385. Tel: 219-759-2400.

Mission Office—Rev. JOHN J. ZEMELKO, Dir., 356 W. Seven Mile Rd., Valparaiso, 46385. Tel: 219-759-2400.

Newspaper— "Northwest Indiana Catholic" DEBBIE BOSAK, Editor; CAROL MACINGA, Circulation Mgr., 9292 Broadway, Merrillville, 46410. Tel: 219-769-9292; Fax: 219-738-9034.

Parish Pastoral Councils—Mrs. ANNE VERBEKE, Dir., 9292 Broadway, Merrillville, 46410. Tel: 219-769-9292; Fax: 219-738-9034.

Peace and Social Justice, Office of—Mrs. SANDRA MORGAN; Deacon DAVID J. KAPALA, 9292 Broadway, Merrillville, 46410. Tel: 219-769-9292; Fax: 219-738-9034.

Priestly Life—Rev. KEVIN R. HUBER, D.Min., Dir., 9292 Broadway, Merrillville, 46410. Tel: 219-769-9292; Fax: 219-738-9034.

Pro-Life Activities—Rev. THEODORE J. MENS, Dir., 525 N. Broad St., Griffith, 46319. Tel: 219-924-4163.

Propagation of the Faith and Holy Childhood Association— cf. Mission Office

Religious Education Office—FRANK J. ZOLVINSKI, Dir., 9292 Broadway, Merrillville, 46410. Tel: 219-769-9292; Fax: 219-738-9034.

Religious, Liaison for Women—Sr. M. CAROL ANN TERLICHER, S.S.C.M., 5959 Broadway, Merrillville, 46410. Tel: 219-887-5287.

Retirement Plan of the Diocese of Gary, Indiana—KELLY VENEGAS, SPHR, Plan Admin., 9292 Broadway, Merrillville, 46410. Tel: 219-769-9292; Fax: 219-769-7597.

Rural Life Conference—Rev. GERALD H. SCHWEITZER, Dir., Mailing Address: P.O. Box 386, Wanatah, 46390. Tel: 219-733-2955.

Safe Environment Program—KELLY VENEGAS, SPHR, Bishop's Delegate for Sexual Misconduct Cases, 9292 Broadway, Merrillville, 46410. Tel: 219-769-9292; Fax: 219-769-7597.

Victim Assistance Coordinator—STEVEN J. BUTERA, M.S., 12490 Marshall St., Crown Point, 46307. Tel: 219-662-7066, Ext. 25; Fax: 219-662-3478.

St. Vincent de Paul Society—DIANE MCKERN, Pres., 7132 Arizona Ave., Hammond, 46324. Tel: 219-845-7531.

Schools Office—BARBARA O'BLOCK, Ed.D., Supt. Schools, 9292 Broadway, Merrillville, 46410. Tel: 219-769-9292; Fax: 219-738-9034.

Spiritual Life/Seimetz Center—1441 Hoffman St., Hammond, 46327. Tel: 219-932-8321.

Stewardship—Mrs. ANNE VERBEKE, Dir., 9292 Broadway, Merrillville, 46410. Tel: 219-769-9292; Fax: 219-738-9034.

Vocations—Rev. MICHAEL J. KOPIL, Dir., 9292 Broadway, Merrillville, 46410. Tel: 219-769-9292; Fax: 219-738-9034.

Worship and Spirituality, Office of—Dr. KRISTOPHER SEAMAN, Dir., 9292 Broadway, Merrillville, 46410. Tel: 219-769-9292; Fax: 219-738-9034.

Youth and Young Adult Ministry—KEVIN DRISCOLL, Dir., 9292 Broadway, Merrillville, 46410. Tel: 219-769-9292; Fax: 219-738-9034.

CLERGY, PARISHES, MISSIONS AND PAROCHIAL SCHOOLS

CITY OF GARY

(LAKE COUNTY)

1—CATHEDRAL OF HOLY ANGELS (1906) Rev. Jon J. Plavcan, Rector; Deacon Robert Angelich.
Res.: 640 Tyler St., Gary, 46402-2299. Tel: 219-882-6079; Fax: 219-882-0133. Web: www.garycluster.org.
Catechesis/Religious Program—Students 3.

2—ST. ANN (1942) Rev. Theodore J. Mens, Admin.
Res.: 525 N. Broad St., Griffith, 46319. Tel: 219-924-4163; Fax: 219-922-2291.
Catechesis/Religious Program—Paula Hammersley, D.R.E. Students 32.

3—ST. ANTHONY (1918) Closed. For inquiries for parish records contact Cathedral of Holy Angels, Gary.

4—BLESSED SACRAMENT (1947) Closed. For inquiries for parish records, contact Ss. Peter and Paul, Merrillville.

5—ST. CASIMIR (1916), (Lithuanian), Closed. For inquiries for parish records contact Holy Angels Cathedral.

6—ST. EMERIC (1911) Closed. For inquiries for parish records contact Holy Trinity (Hungarian), East Chicago.

7—ST. HEDWIG MISSION (1908), (Polish), [JC] Attended by Salvatorian Fathers., 1746 Pennsylvania St., Gary, 46407. Tel: 219-882-2584; Fax: 219-981-9224.

8—HOLY FAMILY (1926), (Polish), Closed. For inquiries for parish records, contact St. Bridget, Hobart.

9—HOLY ROSARY (1931) Rev. Jon J. Plavcan.
Mailing Address: 719 Clark Rd., Gary, 46406.
Res.: 640 Tyler St., Gary, 46402. Tel: 219-882-6079; Fax: 219-949-7465. Email: hrosaryp@yahoo.com. Web: www.garycluster.org.
Catechesis/Religious Program—Students 22.

10—HOLY TRINITY (1911), (African American), Closed. For inquiries for parish records contact Cathedral of Holy Angels, Gary.

11—ST. JOSEPH THE WORKER (1912), (Croatian), Rev. Stephen Loncar, O.F.M.Conv.
Res.: 330 E. 45th Ave., Gary, 46409. Tel: 219-980-1846.

12—ST. LUKE (1917) See separate listing. See Sts. Monica-Luke, Gary.

13—ST. MARK (1921) Rev. J. Patrick Gaza.
Mailing Address: P.O. Box 2100, Gary, 46409-0100. Tel: 219-887-0514. Email: stmarkch@yahoo.com.
Res.: 6060 Miller Ave., Gary, 46403.
Church: 505 W. Ridge Rd., Gary, 46408. Tel: 219-887-0514.
Catechesis/Religious Program—Generations of Faith, Tel: 219-801-5722. Mrs. Ester Serrano, D.R.E. Students 200.
Convent—Missionaries of Charity (1999) 509 W. Ridge Rd., Gary, 46408. Tel: 219-884-2140. Missionaries of Charity 4.

14—ST. MARY OF THE LAKE (1929) Rev. Selvaraj Selladurai.
Res.: 6060 Miller Ave., Gary, 46403. Tel: 219-938-1373; Fax: 219-938-1316. Email: smlake1929@sbcglobal.net. Web: www.garycluster.org.
Catechesis/Religious Program—

15—SS. MONICA-ST. LUKE (1927; 1917) Rev. J. Patrick Gaza.
Mailing Address: 645 Rhode Island, Gary, 46402.
Res.: 6060 Miller Ave., Gary, 46403. Tel: 219-883-1861.
Catechesis/Religious Program—Students 14.

16—SACRED HEART (1918), (Polish), Closed. For inquiries for parish records contact Cathedral of Holy Angels, Gary.

OUTSIDE THE CITY OF GARY

BEVERLY SHORES, PORTER CO., ST. ANN (1950), (Lithuanian), Revs. John B. Barasinski; Antanas Grazulis, S.J., (Pastoral Care for the Lithuanian Community).
Res.: P.O. Box 727, 46301. Tel: 219-879-7565; Fax: 219-879-8893. Email: stannesdunnes@comcast.net. Web: www.st-ann-of-the-dunes.org.
Catechesis/Religious Program—Students 88.

CEDAR LAKE, LAKE CO., HOLY NAME (1859) [CEM] Rev. Edward G. Tlucek, O.F.M.
Res.: 11000 W. 133rd Ave., 46303. Tel: 219-374-7160; Fax: 219-374-7165. Email: holyname4884@att.net.
Parish Center—13209 Schneider St., 46303. Tel: 219-374-8798.
Catechesis/Religious Program—Generations of Faith, Tel: 219-374-8798. Students 160.

CHESTERTON, PORTER CO., ST. PATRICK (1858) [CEM] Rev. James W. Meade; Deacons Nicholas Juracevich; William Jones. In Res., Rev. James P. McGrogan (Retired).
Res.: 638 N. Calumet Rd., 46304. Tel: 219-926-1282; Fax: 219-926-1282. Email: churchoffice@stpatsparish.org. Web: www.stpatsparish.org.
Rectory—642 N. Calumet Rd., 46304. Tel: 219-926-9633.
School—640 N. Calumet Rd., 46304. Tel: 219-926-1707; Fax: 219-921-1922. Email: schooloffice@stpatsparish.org. Lee Ann Cosh, Prin. Lay Teachers 14; Students 271.
Catechesis/Religious Program—Students 376.

CROWN POINT, LAKE CO.

1—ST. MARY (1865), (German), [CEM] Rev. Patrick J. Kalich.
Res.: 321 E. Joliet St., 46307. Tel: 219-663-0044; Fax: 219-663-1027. Email: stmarycp2004@yahoo.com. Web: www.stmarycrownpoint.org.
School—405 E. Joliet St., 46307. Tel: 219-663-0676; Fax: 219-663-1347. L. Thomas Ruiz, Prin. Lay Teachers 25; Students 535.
Catechesis/Religious Program—Marian Weeks, D.R.E. Students 1,231.

2—ST. MATTHIAS (1967) Rev. James E. Wozniak; Deacon Gregory Fabian.
Res.: 101 W. Burrell Dr., 46307. Tel: 219-663-2201; Fax: 219-663-2567. Email: office@stmatthiasparish.net. Web: www.stmatthiasparish.net.
Catechesis/Religious Program—Tel: 219-663-4281. Email: stmatthiasff@sbcglobal.net. Students 275.

DYER, LAKE CO.

1—ST. JOSEPH (1867) [CEM] Rev. Terrence J. Steffens.
Res.: 440 Joliet St., 46311. Tel: 219-865-2271; Fax: 219-865-2350. Email: dyerstjoe@sbcglobal.net.
Catechesis/Religious Program—430 Joliet St., 46311. Tel: 219-865-2355. Email: yseweaver@yahoo.com. Students 165.

2—ST. MARIA GORETTI (1977) Rev. Charles W. Niblick.
Res.: 500 Northgate Dr., 46311. Tel: 219-865-8956; Fax: 219-322-1670. Email: goretti@stmariagorettichurch.org. Web: www.stmariagorettichurch.org.
Catechesis/Religious Program—Tel: 219-322-6124; Fax: 219-865-4677. Email: smg.religed@yahoo.com. Web: www.stmariagorettichurch.org. Bernadine Smierciak, D.R.E.; Kimberly Hoogeveen, D.R.E. Students 317.

EAST CHICAGO, LAKE CO.

1—ASSUMPTION (1915), (Slovak), Closed. For inquiries for parish records contact St. Patrick, East Chicago.

2—ST. FRANCIS (1913), (Lithuanian), Closed. For inquiries for parish records contact St. John Cantius, East Chicago.

3—HOLY TRINITY (1916), (Croatian), Rev. Msgr. John J. Siekierski, Admin.; Deacon James Haugh.
Res.: 4754 Carey St., 46312. Tel: 219-398-3061. Email: holytrinitycroatia@sbcglobal.net.
Catechesis/Religious Program—Mrs. Rose Dado, D.R.E.; Mrs. Pauline Dergo, D.R.E. Students 20.

4—HOLY TRINITY (1906), (Hungarian), Rev. Alphonse Skerl.
Res.: 4759 McCook Ave., 46312. Tel: 219-397-1907; Fax: 219-397-1907.

5—IMMACULATE CONCEPTION (1933), (Italian), Closed. For inquiries for parish records contact St. Stanislaus, East Chicago.

6—ST. JOHN CANTIUS (1905), (Polish), Closed. For inquiries for parish records, contact St. Stanislaus, East Chicago

7—ST. JOSEPH (1916), (Polish), Closed. For inquiries

for parish records contact St. John Cantius, East Chicago.
8—ST. JUDE (1933) Closed. For inquiries for parish records contact Our Lady of Guadalupe, East Chicago.
9—ST. MARY (1890) Rev. Stephen G. Gibson.
822 W. 144th St., 46312. Tel: 219-398-2409; Fax: 219-391-8999. Email: stmaryechicagoin@aol.com.
School—816 W. 144th St., 46312. Tel: 219-397-4404; Fax: 219-397-0924.
Catechesis/Religious Program—Students 482.
10—OUR LADY OF GUADALUPE (1927), (Hispanic), Revs. Juan Gonzalez, C.PP.S.; Carlos Martinez.
Res.: 3526 Deodar St., 46312. Tel: 219-398-0253; Fax: 219-398-0257. Email: olguadalupe@hotmail.com.
Catechesis/Religious Program—Marilyn A. Baron, D.R.E. Students 141.
11—ST. PATRICK (1902), (Hispanic), Rev. David G. Nowak, Part-Time Temp. Admin.; Deacon Raymond E. Helfen. In Res., Rev. David G. Nowak.
Res.: 3810 Grand Blvd., 46312. Tel: 219-398-1036; Fax: 219-397-6901. Email: co.spc@live.com. Web: www.st-pat-ec-in.org.
School—
Catechesis/Religious Program—3510 Deodar St., 46312. Tel: 219-398-0253; Fax: 219-398-0257. Students 20.
12—SACRED HEART (1926), (Slovak), Closed. For inquiries for parish records, contact St. Stanislaus, East Chicago.
13—ST. STANISLAUS (1900), (Polish), Rev. Msgr. John J. Siekierski.
Res.: 808 W. 150th St., 46312. Tel: 219-398-2341; Fax: 219-398-2388.
School—4930 Indianapolis Blvd., 46312. Tel: 219-398-1316; Fax: 219-398-9080. Kathleen A. Lowry, Prin. Lay Teachers 13; Students 272.
Catechesis/Religious Program—4914 Magoun Ave., 46312. Tel: 219-397-7059. Sr. Gloria Jean Kozlowski, D.R.E. Students 15.
Convent—4914 Magoun Ave., 46312. Tel: 219-397-7059.
FISH LAKE, LA PORTE CO., ST. ANTHONY OF PADUA (1948) Rev. Michael G. Heimer.
Res.: 7732 E. State Rd. 4, Walkerton, 46574. Tel: 219-369-1210; Fax: 219-369-9500. (Fish Lake)
Catechesis/Religious Program—Students 5.
GRIFFITH, LAKE CO., ST. MARY (1928) Rev. Theodore J. Mens.
Res.: 525 N. Broad St., 46319-2225. Tel: 219-924-4163; Fax: 219-922-2291.
School—(Grades PreK-8) Tel: 219-924-8633; Fax: 219-922-2279. Mrs. Rebecca Maskovich, Prin.; Mrs. Yvonne Tucker, Librarian. Sisters of St. Francis of Perpetual Adoration 1; Lay Teachers 13; Students 237.
Catechesis/Religious Program—Tel: 219-922-2277. Students 230.
Convent—508 N. Lafayette St., 46319. Tel: 219-922-2278.
HAMLET, STARKE CO., HOLY CROSS (1888) [CEM] Rev. Anthony L. Spanley.
Res.: 6 W. Pearl St., P.O. Box 230, 46532. Tel: 574-867-2461.
Catechesis/Religious Program—Students 7.
Mission—St. Dominic (1981)Tel: 574-867-2461.
HAMMOND, LAKE CO.
1—ALL SAINTS (1896) Rev. Stephen D. Kosinski.
Res.: 570 Sibley St., P.O. Box 836, 46325-0836. Tel: 219-932-0204; Fax: 219-932-4507. Email: allsaint@comcast.net.
Catechesis/Religious Program—Josephine Perez, D.R.E. Students 43.
2—ST. CASIMIR (1890), (Polish), [JC] Revs. William F. O'Toole; Nestor Lopez; Vladimir Janeczek, Senior Priest (Retired); Deacon Martin J. Brown.
Res.: 4340 Johnson St., 46327. Tel: 219-931-2589; Fax: 219-932-0467. Email: saintcasimirchurch@comcast.net. Web: www.stcasschool.org.
School—4329 Cameron St., 46327. Tel: 219-932-2686; Fax: 219-932-2686. Mr. Daniel McCabe, Prin. Lay Teachers 11; Students 284.
Catechesis/Religious Program—Tel: 219-931-2589, Ext. 16. Email: an-jo-lu@sbcglobal.net. Maria Marsh, D.R.E. Tel: 219-931-8130. Students 83.
3—ST. CATHERINE OF SIENA (1956) Rev. Larry J. Kew.
Res.: 6605 Kentucky Ave., 46323. Tel: 219-845-1939; Fax: 219-845-4772. Web: www.scos.catholicweb.com.
Catechesis/Religious Program—Mrs. Shirley Brown, D.R.E. Students 35.
4—ST. JOHN BOSCO (1934) Rev. Richard A. Orlinski.
Res.: 7113 Columbia Ave., 46324. Tel: 219-844-9027, Ext. 319; Fax: 219-844-6986. Email: sjboffice@comcast.net. Web: www.sjbhammond.org.
Pastoral Center—1247 171st Pl., 46324. Fax: 219-989-7947.
School—(Grades PreK-8), 1231 171st Pl., 46324. Tel: 219-845-6226; Fax: 219-989-7946. Email: sjbprincipalmk@gmail.com. Mark Kielbania, Prin.; Yvette Markovic, Librarian. Lay Teachers 13; Students 253.
Catechesis/Religious Program—Tel: 219-844-9027, Ext. 310. Mrs. Vickie Blackwood, D.R.E. Students 150.
5—ST. JOSEPH (1879) Rev. Richard A. Orlinski.
Res.: 5304 Hohman Ave., 46320-1808. Tel: 219-932-0702; Fax: 219-932-0059. Email: SaintJoe5304@SBCglobal.net.
Catechesis/Religious Program—Tel: 219-932-7294. Patricia A. Malinowski, D.R.E. Students 20.
6—ST. MARGARET MARY (1947) [CEM] Revs. Stephen G. Gibson; Erlin Yoan Garcia.
Res.: 1445 Hoffman St., 46327. Tel: 219-931-5229; Fax: 219-937-4357. Email: stmargaretmary@sbcglobal.net.
Catechesis/Religious Program—Students 195.
7—ST. MARY (1912) Closed. For inquiries for parish records, contact St. John Bosco, Hammond.
8—OUR LADY OF PERPETUAL HELP (1937) Rev. Charles A. Mosley.
Res.: 7132 Arizona St., 46323. Tel: 219-844-3438; Fax: 219-844-3580. Web: olphparish.net.
Catechesis/Religious Program—7128 Arizona St., 46323. Robert Meaney, D.R.E. Students 208.
HEBRON, PORTER CO., ST. HELEN (1946) Rev. Derrick F. Dudash.
Res.: 302 N. Madison St., 46341. Tel: 219-996-4611.
Catechesis/Religious Program—Tel: 219-996-4612. Karen Yankauskas, D.R.E. Students 56.
HIGHLAND, LAKE CO.
1—ST. JAMES THE LESS (1967) Rev. Keith M. Virus; Deacons Martin Denkhoff; Raymond Dec; Michael W. Halas; Michael L. Hogan.
Mailing Address: 9640 Kennedy Ave., 46322. Web: www.stjameshighland.org.
Res.: 2703 45th St., 46322. Tel: 219-924-4220; Fax: 219-924-4295.
Catechesis/Religious Program—Tel: 219-924-4222. Email: dre@stjameshighland.org. Cheryl Johnson, D.R.E. Students 341.
2—OUR LADY OF GRACE (1949) Rev. Edward J. Moszur.
Office: 3005 Condit St., 46322. Tel: 219-838-0395; Fax: 219-972-6372. Email: ourladygrace@sbcglobal.net. Web: olgcatholicchurchhighland.org.
School—3025 Highway Ave., 46322. Tel: 219-838-2901; Fax: 219-972-6389. Email: olgsecretary@yahoo.com. Web: www.olgrac-eschool.org. Mark Topp, Prin. Lay Teachers 13; Students 131.
Catechesis/Religious Program—Tel: 219-838-6790. Patricia Franz, D.R.E. Students 166.
HOBART, LAKE CO., ST. BRIDGET (1873) Rev. Dominic V. Bertino; Deacon Jamie D. Lewis.
Res.: 568 E. Second St., 46342. Tel: 219-942-6441; Fax: 219-942-4573. Email: churchsecretary@stbridgethobart.org. Web: www.stbridgethobart.org.
School—(Grades PreK-8), 107 Main St., 46342. Tel: 219-942-1894; Fax: 219-942-0939. Ruthie Pacheco, Librarian. Lay Teachers 8; Students 99.
Catechesis/Religious Program—Tel: 219-955-0186. Students 150.
KINGSFORD HEIGHTS, LA PORTE CO., IMMACULATE HEART OF MARY (1953) Closed. For inquiries for parish records contact St. Anthony, Fish Lake.
KNOX, STARKE CO., ST. THOMAS AQUINAS (1923) Rev. John V. Scott.
Res.: 406 E. Washington St., 46534. Tel: 574-772-4134.
Catechesis/Religious Program—Tel: 574-772-3237. Mrs. Linda Kelly, D.R.E. Students 52.
KOUTS, PORTER CO., ST. MARY (1884) [CEM] Rev. Thomas T. Tibbs; Deacon Jim F. Knopf.
Res.: P.O. Box 663, 46347. Tel: 219-766-3680. Email: stmarykouts@frontier.com.
Catechesis/Religious Program—Lynn Wichlinski, D.R.E.; Kari Balon, D.R.E. Students 85.
LA PORTE, LA PORTE CO.
1—ST. JOSEPH (1858) [CEM] Rev. David W. Kime; Deacon Robert Bucheit.
Res.: 109 C St., 46350. Tel: 219-362-9595; Fax: 219-325-9021. Email: stjosephch@frontier.com.
School—101 C St., 46350. Tel: 219-362-6472; Fax: 219-362-2707. Web: st-joe.net. Fonda Mauch, Prin. Sisters of St. Francis of Perpetual Adoration 2; Lay Teachers 5; Students 79.
Catechesis/Religious Program—Students 320.
Convent—102 B St., 46350. Tel: 219-362-2587.
2—ST. PETER (1853) Rev. Joseph A. Angotti.
Res.: 1104 Monroe St., 46350. Tel: 219-362-6186; Fax: 219-324-9277. Email: stpeterlaport@csinet.net. Web: members.csinet.net/stpeterschurch.
Catechesis/Religious Program—Tel: 219-362-2509; Fax: 219-362-2748. Sandra Ransom, D.R.E. & Pastoral Assoc. Students 74.
3—SACRED HEART (1912), (Polish), Rev. Ian J. Williams.
Res.: 130 Bach St., 46350. Tel: 219-362-2815; Fax: 219-362-4822. Email: office@sacredheartlp.org. Web: www.sacredheartlp.org.
Catechesis/Religious Program—Tel: 219-362-4822. Madelon Albert, D.R.E. Students 104.
LAKE STATION, LAKE CO., ST. FRANCIS XAVIER (1930) [CEM] Rev. Eduardo Malagon; Deacons Leonard Holland; Michael J. Green.
Res.: 2447 Putnam St., 46405. Tel: 219-962-8626; Fax: 219-962-8627. Email: st.francis@frontier.com.
Catechesis/Religious Program—Tel: 219-962-4507. LaVerne Papich, D.R.E. Students 115.
LOWELL, LAKE CO., ST. EDWARD (1870) [CEM] Rev. Theodore A. Nordquist; Deacons William Hathaway; Roberto Mendoza.
Res.: 216 S. Nichols St., 46356. Tel: 219-696-7307; Fax: 219-696-3525. Email: stedwardchurch@sbcglobal.net. Web: home.catholicweb.com/stedwardlowell.
School—(Grades PreSchool-8), 210 S. Nichols St., 46356. Tel: 219-696-9876; Fax: 219-696-2524. Lay Teachers 3; Students 46.
Catechesis/Religious Program—Tel: 219-696-4282; Fax: 219-696-3525. Students 237.
MERRILLVILLE, LAKE CO.
1—ST. ANDREW (1965) Rev. Brian D. Chadwick; Deacon Thomas Gryzbek.
Res.: 801 W. 73rd Ave., 46410. Tel: 219-769-8534; Fax: 219-769-8543. Email: standrew73rd@sbcglobal.net.
School—Tel: 219-769-2049. Bruce Schooler, Prin. Lay Teachers 9; Students 148.
Catechesis/Religious Program—Tel: 219-769-2049. Students 53.
2—ST. JOAN OF ARC (1968) Rev. Roy T. Beeching.
Mailing Address: 200 E. 78th Ave., 46410.
Res.: 5885 Harrison, 46410. Tel: 219-980-2693.
Catechesis/Religious Program—Fax: 219-769-9056. Candice Hanusin, D.R.E. Students 24.
St. Joan of Arc Center—Fax: 219-769-9056.
3—OUR LADY OF CONSOLATION (1947) Rev. Peter J. Muha; Deacon Robert E. Gill.
Res.: 8303 Taft St., 46410. Tel: 219-769-2785; Fax: 219-769-2177. Email: olcsec@sbcglobal.net. Web: www.olcweb.org.
Catechesis/Religious Program—Tel: 219-769-2295. Email: olcffp@live.com. Marilyn Huber, D.R.E. Students 146.
4—SS. PETER AND PAUL (1841) [CEM] Rev. Roy T. Beeching.
Res.: 5885 Harrison St., 46410. Tel: 219-980-2693; Fax: 219-980-2851.
Catechesis/Religious Program—Tel: 219-887-2940. Jennifer Rausei, D.R.E. Students 110.
5—ST. STEPHEN, MARTYR (1968) Rev. Michael L. Maginot.
Res.: 5920 Waite St., 46410. Tel: 219-980-9348; Fax: 219-980-9354.
Catechesis/Religious Program—5885 Harrison, 46410. Tel: 219-887-2940. Students 6.
MICHIGAN CITY, LA PORTE CO.
1—ST. MARY OF THE IMMACULATE CONCEPTION (1867) Rev. Walter J. Rakoczy.
Res.: 411 W. 11th St., 46360. Tel: 219-874-7231. Email: saintmary.school@comcast.net.
Catechesis/Religious Program—Students 12.
Mission—Sacred Heart 1001 W. Eighth St., 46360.
2—NOTRE DAME (1953) Rev. Keith J. McClellan.
Res.: 1010 Moore Rd., 46360. Tel: 219-872-4844; Fax: 219-872-2510. Email: fatherkeith@notredameparish.net. Web: notredameparish.net.
School—(Grades PreK-8) Tel: 219-872-6216; Fax: 219-872-6273. Mr. Benjamin Potts, Prin. Lay Teachers 20; Students 215.
3—QUEEN OF ALL SAINTS (1950) Revs. Kevin R. Huber, Admin.; Frank D. Torres.
Res.: 606 S. Woodland Ave., 46360. Tel: 219-872-9196; Fax: 219-872-9176.
School—1715 E. Barker Ave., 46360. Tel: 219-872-4420; Fax: 219-872-1943. Anita Peters, Prin. Lay Teachers 12; Students 206.
Catechesis/Religious Program—Tel: 219-878-9348. Kathy Moskovich, D.R.E. Students 140.
Convent—
4—SACRED HEART MISSION (1915), (Lebanese), Rev. Walter J. Rakoczy, Admin.
Res.: 411 W. 11th St., 46360. Tel: 219-874-7231; Fax: 219-873-1322.
Catechesis/Religious Program—
5—ST. STANISLAUS KOSTKA (1891), (Polish), Rev. Walter M. Ciesla; Deacon Daniel Bowmar.
Mailing Address: 1506 Washington St., 46360.
Res.: 109 Ann St., 46360. Tel: 219-879-9281; Fax: 219-872-2295. Email: ststanskostka@yahoo.com.
School—1506 Washington St., 46360. Tel: 219-872-2258; Fax: 219-872-2295. Lay Teachers 16; Students 145.
Catechesis/Religious Program—Cynthia McGuire, D.R.E. Students 30.
MUNSTER, LAKE CO., ST. THOMAS MORE (1945) Revs. Michael J. Yadron; Richard C. Holy; Deacons David

J. Kapala; Joseph Stodola; Napoleon Tabion; Daniel W. Zurawski.
Res.: 8501 Calumet Ave., 46321. Tel: 219-836-8610; Fax: 219-836-9185. Email: parish.office@stm-church.com. Web: www.stm-church.com.
School—8435 Calumet Ave., 46321. Tel: 219-836-9151; Fax: 219-836-0982. Web: www.stm-school.com. Chet A. Nordyke, Prin. Lay Teachers 30; Students 641.
Catechesis/Religious Program—Tel: 219-836-9152. Mrs. Sandra Morgan, D.R.E.; Angie Lorandos, Music Min. Students 465.

NEW CHICAGO, LAKE CO., ASSUMPTION OF THE BLESSED VIRGIN MARY (P.O. Hobart) (1917), (Polish), Rev. Lourdu Pasala.
Res.: 3530 Illinois St., Hobart, 46342. Tel: 219-962-1073; Fax: 219-962-1073.
Catechesis/Religious Program—Tel: 219-962-6678. Students 52.

NORTH JUDSON, STARKE CO., SS. CYRIL AND METHODIUS (1881) [CEM] Rev. Terrence W. Bennis, Admin.; Peggy Okeley, Pastoral Assoc.
Res.: 303 Keller Ave., 46366. Tel: 574-896-2195; Fax: 574-896-5131.
Catechesis/Religious Program—Email: sscyrilandmethodius@hotmail.com. Students 29.

OTIS, LA PORTE CO., ST. MARY (1873), (Polish), [CEM] Rev. Gerald H. Schweitzer; Deacon Dale Walsh.
P.O. Box 386, Wanatah, 46390.
Church: 199 W. Snyder Rd., Westville, 46391-9551.
Res.: 202 N. Ohio, Wanatah, 46390. Tel: 219-733-2955; Fax: 219-733-0001. Web: thecatholiccommunities.org.
Catechesis/Religious Program—Students 75.

PORTAGE, PORTER CO., NATIVITY OF OUR SAVIOR (1964) Rev. Andrew J. Corona; Deacons Robert J. Bonta; Richard Huber; Dennis M. Guernsey.
Res.: 2949 Willowcreek Rd., 46368. Tel: 219-762-4858; Fax: 219-762-6678. Email: nativity174@gmail.com.
School—2929 Willowcreek Rd., 46368. Tel: 219-763-2400; Fax: 219-764-3225. Kemberly Markham, Prin. Lay Teachers 9; Students 186.
Catechesis/Religious Program—Tel: 219-764-3143. Email: nativityfaithformation@yahoo.com. Doris Stanish, D.R.E. Students 490.

ROLLING PRAIRIE, LAPORTE CO., ST. JOHN KANTY (1888), (Polish), [CEM] Rev. Michael G. Heimer, Admin.
Res.: 7732 E. State Rd. 4, Walkerton, 46574. Tel: 219-369-1210; Fax: 219-369-9500.
Catechesis/Religious Program— Sharon DeGroote, D.R.E. Students 60.

ST. JOHN, LAKE CO., ST. JOHN THE EVANGELIST (1839) [CEM] Rev. Sammie L. Maletta.
Res. & Office: 11301 W. 93rd Ave., 46373. Tel: 219-365-5678; Fax: 219-365-2703. Web: www.stjohnparish.org.
School—9400 Wicker Ave., 46373. Tel: 219-365-5451; Fax: 219-365-6173. Web: www.stjohnparish.org/sjeschool. Sr. Gianna Marie Webber, Prin. Lay Teachers 23; Students 350.
Catechesis/Religious Program—Tel: 219-365-3709. Joan Backe, D.R.E. Students 268.

SAN PIERRE, STARKE CO., ALL SAINTS (1858) [CEM] Rev. Terrence W. Bennis.
Res.: 303 Keller Ave., North Judson, 46366. Tel: 219-828-4281.
Catechesis/Religious Program—Tel: 219-828-4111. Students 4.

SCHERERVILLE, LAKE CO., ST. MICHAEL (1874) [CEM] Revs. Martin J. Dobrzynski; Michael J. Kopil; Ted J. Mauch; Deacons Edwin Gatons; Jack Krol.
Res.: One Wilhelm St., 46375. Tel: 219-322-4505; Fax: 219-322-4508. Web: stmichaels-parish.org.
Preschool—Tel: 219-322-3077. (Good Shepherd Program) Students 30.
School—16 W. Wilhelm St., 46375. Tel: 219-322-4531; Fax: 219-322-1710. Web: saintmichaelscher-.org. Lay Teachers 27; Students 328.
Catechesis/Religious Program—Tel: 219-322-3077. Students 587.

SHELBY, LAKE CO., ST. THERESA (1939) Closed. Records kept at St. Edward, Lowell.

VALPARAISO, PORTER CO.
1—ST. ELIZABETH SETON (1978) Rev. Douglas J. Mayer; Deacons James J. Keough; Michael Prendergast; Brian Nosbusch.
Res.: 509 W. Division Rd., 46385. Tel: 219-464-1624; Fax: 219-465-7673. Email: ffseseton@comcast.net. Web: www.seton.com.
Catechesis/Religious Program—Tel: 219-462-2202. Students 257.
2—OUR LADY OF SORROWS (South Haven) (1967) Rev. John J. Zemelko; Deacon Sherman Brown.
Res.: 356 W. 700 N., 46385. Tel: 219-759-2400; Fax: 219-759-0054. Email: ols.parish@yahoo.com.
Catechesis/Religious Program—Tel: 219-759-2286. Students 103.
3—ST. PAUL (1858) [CEM] Revs. Joseph M. Pawlowski; Michael J. Hoffman; Frank D. Torres, Chap., Hispanic Ministry; Deacons John Roscoe; Michael Foster; James Caristi; David A. Bergstedt.
Mailing Address: P.O. Box 1475, 46384-1475.
Res.: 452 W. Chicago St., 46383. Tel: 219-465-3723.
Church: P.O. Box 1475, 46384-1475. Tel: 219-464-4831; Fax: 219-464-4833. Email: stpaulcathvalpo@netnitco.net.
School—1755 W. Harrison Blvd., 46385. Tel: 219-462-3374; Fax: 219-477-1763. Email: principal@stpaulvalpo.org. Web: www.stpaulvalpo.org. Jane Scupham, Prin. Full-time Lay Teachers 16; Part-time Lay Teachers 5; Students 361.
Catechesis/Religious Program—Tel: 219-464-8502; Fax: 219-531-6854. Joanne White, D.R.E.; Meghan Chargualaf, Youth Min. Students 459.
Tiny Tim's Child Development Center—1857 Harrison Blvd., 46385. Tel: 219-465-0882; Fax: 219-531-2047. Email: sptinytim@aol.com. Janet McCorkle, Dir.
St. Agnes Adult Day Service Center—1859 Harrison Blvd., 46385. Tel: 219-477-5433; Fax: 219-462-9553. Barbara Kubiszak, Dir.

WANATAH, LA PORTE CO., SACRED HEART (1887) [CEM] Rev. Gerald H. Schweitzer; Deacon Dale Walsh.
Res.: 202 N. Ohio St, P.O. Box 386, 46390. Tel: 219-733-2955; Fax: 219-733-0001. Web: thecatholiccommunities.org.
Catechesis/Religious Program—Tel: 219-733-2315. Email: shreligioused@thecatholiccommunities.org. Students 117.
Mission—St. Martin (1860) Lowell & Dominic Sts., LaCrosse, LaPorte Co. 46348.

WHITING, LAKE CO.
1—ST. ADALBERT (1902), (Polish), Revs. John E. Kalicky, C.PP.S.; Stanley J. Dominik, Admin. (Retired).
1340 121st St., 46394.
Res.: 1849 Lincoln Ave., 46394. Tel: 219-659-0733; Fax: 219-659-0195. Email: sheartwhiting@sbcglobal.net.
Catechesis/Religious Program—Sacred Heart Parish, 1723 LaPorte Ave., 46394. Tel: 219-473-7557; Fax: 219-473-7553. Diane Puplava, D.R.E.
2—IMMACULATE CONCEPTION (1922), (Slovak), Revs. John E. Kalicky, C.PP.S.; Stanley J. Dominik, Admin. (Retired).
Res.: 1731 LaPorte Ave., 46394. Tel: 219-659-0733; Fax: 219-659-0195. Email: sheartwhiting@sbcglobal.net.
Catechesis/Religious Program—1723 LaPorte Ave., 46394. Tel: 219-473-7557. Students 8.
3—ST. JOHN THE BAPTIST (1897) Revs. John E. Kalicky, C.PP.S.; Stanley J. Dominik, Senior Priest (Retired); Leon Flaherty, C.PP.S.; Deacon Joseph Manchak.
Res.: 1849 Lincoln Ave., P.O. Box 711, 46394. Tel: 219-659-0023; Fax: 219-473-7551. Email: churchparishoffice@yahoo.com. Web: sjbcatholicparish.org.
School—1844 Lincoln Ave., 46394. Tel: 219-659-3042; Fax: 219-473-7553. Marilyn Tomko, Prin. Lay Teachers 22; Students 363.
Catechesis/Religious Program—Tel: 219-473-7557; Fax: 219-473-7553. Diane Puplava, D.R.E. Students 134.
4—STS. PETER AND PAUL (1910) Closed. For inquiries of parish records, contact Sacred Heart, Whiting.
5—SACRED HEART (1889) Revs. John E. Kalicky, C.PP.S.; Stanley J. Dominik, Admin. (Retired).
Res.: 1731 Laporte Ave., 46394. Tel: 219-659-0733; Fax: 219-659-0195. Email: sheartwhiting@sbcglobal.net.
Catechesis/Religious Program—1723 LaPorte Ave., 46394. Tel: 219-473-7557; Fax: 219-473-7551. Students 58.

WINFIELD TOWNSHIP, LAKE CO., HOLY SPIRIT (1998) Rev. Thomas E. Mischler.
Res.: 7667 E. 109th Ave., Crown Point, 46307. Tel: 219-661-0644; Fax: 219-662-2611. Email: information@holy-spiritchurch.org. Web: www.holy-spiritchurch.org.
Catechesis/Religious Program—Students 273.

Chaplains of Public Institutions

MICHIGAN CITY. *Indiana State Prison*. Deacon Michael Prendergast.
123 Shorewood Dr., Valparaiso, 46385.

ROLLING PRAIRIE. *Sharing Meadows*. Rev. Dennis J. Blaney (Retired).
P.O. Box 400, 46371. Tel: 219-778-9130.

WESTVILLE. *Westville Correctional Center*. Deacon James Etter.
P.O. Box 473, 46391. Tel: 219-785-2511.

On Duty Outside the Diocese:
Revs.—
Coriden, James A., 6896 Laurel St., N.W., Washington, DC 20012.
Hand, Dennis M., Pje. 6, Poligno E-Casa #101, Col. San Luis, San Martin, Depto. de San Salvador, El Salvador.
Hendricks, Clare, 1428 Lyon St., Columbia, TN 38401.

Retired:
Rev. Msgrs.—
Charlebois, Robert L., 2474 S. Toledo Ave., Palm Springs, CA 92264.
Lengerich, Vincent L., 2860 U.S. Rte. 127, Carthagena, OH 45822.
Litot, Edward F., 317 Waverly Rd., La Porte, 46350.
Melevage, F. J., 3214 Milestone Creek Ct., Valparaiso, 46383.
Morales, John F., 333 N. Palm Dr., #305, Beverly Hills, CA 90210.
Semancik, Joseph F., 1919 Lake Ave, Whiting, 46394.
Urbonas, Ignatius L., 14911 127th St., Lemont, IL 60439.
Zollinger, Richard, 301 S. Main St., Knox, 46534.
Revs.—
Blaney, Dennis J., P.O. Box 400, Rolling Prairie, 46371.
Daniels, John W., 9389 W 1160 N., DeMotte, 46310.
de Cristobal, Fernando, 3810 Grand Blvd., East Chicago, 46312.
Dettmer, Alfred J., 1134 Bluebird Ln., Munster, 46321.
Dominik, Stanley J., 1731 LaPorte Ave., Whiting, 46394.
Doyle, Charles E., 105 Autumn Tr., Michigan City, 46360.
Evers, Robert B., P.O. Box 3546, Munster, 46321.
Gehring, Robert P., 419 Autumn Tr. S., Michigan City, 46360.
Gosnell, David H., 917 Beechnut Blvd., 46391.
Heeg, Lawrence M., 1159 N. 325 E, Chesterton, 46304.
Hogan, John A., 318 Garden Tr., Michigan City, 46360.
Janeczek, Vladimir, 211 Autumn Tr., Michigan City, 46360.
Kashmer, George B., P.O. Box 37, San Pierre, 46374.
Kish, Matthew J., 1501 Hoffman St., Hammond, 46327.
Kronkowski, Leonard J., 2440 Polish Lane Rd., Cheboygan, MI 49721.
Link, David T., 306 Outlook Cove Dr., La Porte, 46350.
McGrogan, James P., 638 N. Calumet Rd., Chesterton, 46304.
Minnich, John F., P.O. Box 537, Georgetown, 47122.
Nondorf, Aloysius J., 410 Autumn Tr., Michigan City, 46360.
Peil, L. William, 1841 N. Anthony Blvd., Fort Wayne, 46805.
Sroka, Gerald A., 209 Autumn Tr., Michigan City, 46360.
Strebig, John J., 135 Kingsbury Ave., La Porte, 46350.
Teles, Dennis J., 230 Lilac Dr., Walkerton, 46574.
Vamos, Joseph E., 10789 Pike St., Crown Point, 46307.

Permanent Deacons:
Angelich, Robert
Bacon, John
Bergstedt, David A.
Bodley, Edwin J.
Bonta, Robert J., Senior Deacon
Bowmar, Daniel L., Senior Deacon
Brown, Martin J.
Brown, Sherman, Senior Deacon
Bucheit, Robert J.
Caristi, James
Cichoracki, Eugene, Senior Deacon
Codespoti, Joseph
Dec, Raymond, Senior Deacon
Dedelow, Duane W.
Denkhoff, Martin J., Senior Deacon
Etter, James
Fabian, Gregory G.
Foster, Michael
Gatons, Edwin
Gill, Robert E.
Green, Michael J.
Gryzbek, Thomas
Guernsey, Dennis M.
Halas, Michael W.
Hathaway, William R.
Haugh, James
Hawkins, Christopher
Hawkins, Dennis, Senior Deacon
Helfen, Raymond E.
Hogan, Michael L.
Holland, Leonard D.
Huber, Richard

Janowski, Victor
Jones, William E., Jr.
Jurasevich, Nicholas J.
Kapala, David J.
Keough, James J., Senior Deacon
Knopf, Jim F.
Kozub, Edward, Senior Deacon
Kreidler, Thomas, Senior Deacon
Krilich, Paul M.
Krol, Jack
Kubik, Thomas R.
Lewis, Jamie D.
Litavecz, Robert J.
Lunsford, Malcolm
Maldonado, Felipe
Manchak, Joseph C.
Marben, Robert W.
Mendoza, Roberto
Muvich, Phillip L.
Newburn, Jeffery L.
Nosbusch, Brian
Plaiss, Mark
Prendergast, Michael
Pyle, Ronald L.
Roscoe, John, Senior Deacon
Sayre, William P.
Shultz, Edward J.
Stodola, Joseph
Tabion, Napoleon
Viviano, Robert L.
Walsh, Dale
Webdell, Dale P.
Zubel, Steven
Zurawski, Daniel W.

INSTITUTIONS LOCATED IN THE DIOCESE

[A] COLLEGES AND UNIVERSITIES

WHITING. *Calumet College of St. Joseph*, 2400 New York Ave., 46394. Tel: 219-473-7770; Fax: 219-473-4259. Web: www.ccsj.edu. Dr. Daniel Lowery, Pres.; Rev. Alphonse Spilly, C.PP.S., Chap. & Faculty; Bros. James Ballmann, C.PP.S., Computer Svcs.; Jerry Schwieterman, C.PP.S., Campus Ministry; Benjamin Basile, C.PP.S., Faculty; Sr. Michele Dvorak, Dir., Educ. Prog., Faculty; Mr. Charles Myers, Dir., Library. Priests 1; Brothers 3; Sisters 1; Lay Teachers 150; Total Staff 140; Total Enrollment 1,275.

[B] HIGH SCHOOLS, DIOCESAN

HAMMOND. *Bishop Noll Institute* (1921) 1519 Hoffman St., 46327. Tel: 219-932-9058; Fax: 219-853-1736. Email: cmccoycejka@bishopnoll.org. Web: www.bishopnoll.org. Colleen McCoy-Cejka, Prin.; Mary Lou Cowperthwaite, Librarian. Students 478; Lay Teachers 39; Total Staff 68; Total Enrollment 585.

MERRILLVILLE. *Andrean High School*, 5959 Broadway, 46410. Tel: 219-887-5281; Fax: 219-981-5072. Web: www.andreanhs.com. Rev. Paul E. Quanz, C.S.B., Prin. Basilian Fathers 1; Sisters of Sts. Cyril and Methodius 1; Lay Teachers 39; Total Staff 45; Students 585.

MICHIGAN CITY. *Marquette Catholic High School*, 306 W. Tenth St., 46360. Tel: 219-873-1325; Fax: 219-873-1327. Web: www.marquette-hs.org. James G. White, Prin. Email: jwhite1117@att.net. Lay Teachers 18; Total Staff 28; Students 187.

[C] ELEMENTARY SCHOOLS, INTERPAROCHIAL

ROLLING PRAIRIE. *Sacred Heart Apostolic School, Inc.*, 5901 N. 500 E., 46371. Tel: 219-778-4596; Fax: 219-778-9018. P.O. Box 7, 46371. Rev. Daren Weisbrod, L.C., Vice Pres., Rector & Prin. Priests 3; Brothers 4; Lay Teachers 7; Students 33.

[D] GENERAL HOSPITALS

CROWN POINT. *Franciscan St. Anthony Health - Crown Point* (1974) 1201 S. Main St., 46307-8483. Tel: 219-738-2100; Fax: 219-757-6242. Email: david.ruskowski@franciscanalliance.org. Web: www.stanthonymedicalcenter.com. David Ruskowski, Pres.; Revs. Anthony F. Janik, O.F.M., Dir.; Patrick Okoroh, Chap. Franciscan Alliance, Inc. Sisters of St. Francis of Perpetual Adoration 1; Franciscan Sisters of Chicago 2; Bed Capacity (Includes 30 bassinets) 268; Total Staff 1,555; Patients Assisted Annually 330,956.

DYER. *St. Margaret Mercy Healthcare Centers, South Campus*, 24 Joliet, 46311. Tel: 219-865-2141; Fax: 219-933-2585. Email: tom.gryzbek@ssfhs.org. Web: www.smmhc.com. Thomas Gryzbek, Pres.; Rev. Ignatius Ijere, Chap. Sisters of St. Francis Health Services, Inc. Sisters 2; Licensed 297; Total Staff 883; Patients Assisted Annually 172,850.

EAST CHICAGO. *St. Catherine Hospital* (1928) 4321 Fir St., 46312. Tel: 219-392-1700; Fax: 219-392-7002. Web: www.comhs.org. JoAnn Birdzell, Admin. & CEO; Craig Bolda, COO; Mary Ann Shacklett, Sr. Vice Pres., Finance & CFO; Sr. Mary Ellen Goeller, P.H.J.C., Regl. Dir. Mission Integration. Sisters 1; Bed Capacity 189; Bassinets 9; Total Staff 1,137; Patients Assisted Annually 123,286.

HAMMOND. *Franciscan St. Margaret Health - Hammond*, 5454 Hohman Ave., 46320. Tel: 219-932-2300; Fax: 219-933-2585. Email: Tom.Gryzbek@ssfhs.org. Web: www.smmhc.com. Thomas Gryzbek, Pres.; Rev. Gregory Holicky. Sisters of St. Francis Health Services, Inc. Sisters 5; Licensed 485; Licensed 46; Total Staff 1,196; Patients Assisted Annually 163,708.

HOBART. *St. Mary Medical Center*, 1500 S. Lake Park Ave., 46342. Tel: 219-942-0551; Fax: 219-947-6037. Web: www.stmary-hobart.com. Janice Ryba, Admin. & CEO; Sr. Mary Ellen Goeller, P.H.J.C., Regl. Dir., Mission Integration; Mary Sudicky, CFO. Sisters 2; Bed Capacity 190; Bassinets 18; Total Staff 1,352; Patients Assisted Annually 179,077.

MICHIGAN CITY. *Franciscan St. Anthony Health - Michigan City* (1904) 301 W. Homer St., 46360. Tel: 219-879-8511; Fax: 219-877-1409. Email: darla.ream@franciscanalliance.org. Web: www.saintanthonymemorial.org. James T. Callaghan III, M.D., M.B.A., Pres.; Rev. Jose Pottokaran, C.M.I., Chap. Franciscan Alliance, Inc. Sisters 3; Staffed Beds (plus 26 research beds) 172; Bassinets 20; Total Staff 974; Patients Assisted Annually 239,856.

[E] PROTECTIVE INSTITUTIONS

EAST CHICAGO. *Carmelite Home for Girls/Holy Innocents Shelter* (1913) 4840 Grasselli Ave., 46312. Tel: 219-397-1085; Fax: 219-392-3574. Email: srmariagiuseppe@me.com. Web: www.carmelitedcjnorth.org. Sr. Maria Giuseppe Moxley, Supr. & Admin. Carmelite Sisters of the Divine Heart of Jesus 8; Total Staff 70; (Tauscher Center: 2 Infants, 8 Toddlers) 10; Holy Innocents Children 16; Residential Girls 10; Total Assisted Annually 212.

[F] HOMES FOR THE AGED

CROWN POINT. *Franciscan Communities at St. Anthony Campus*, 203 Franciscan Dr., 46307-4824. Tel: 219-661-5100; Fax: 219-661-5102. Web: www.stanthonyhome.com. Linda O'Neill, Exec. Dir.; Rev. Myron Lowisz, O.F.M., Pastoral Care. Priests 1; Franciscan Sisters of Chicago 4; Deacons 2; Total Staff 476.

St. Anthony Home Tel: 219-661-5100; Fax: 219-661-5102. Web: www.stanthonyhome.com. Capacity 190.

St. Anthony Assisted Living Apartments Tel: 219-661-5150; Fax: 219-661-5205. Web: www.stanthonyhome.com. Capacity 60.

St. Anthony Hospice Tel: 219-661-5306; Fax: 219-661-5305. Web: www.stanthonyhome.com.

Franciscan Adult Day Services Tel: 219-661-5200. Web: www.stanthonyhome.com. Capacity 25.

Holy Family Child Care Tel: 219-661-5250. Children 175.

HAMMOND. *Albertine Home*, 1501 Hoffman St., 46327. Tel: 219-937-0575; Fax: 219-937-0575. Email: albertineusa@att.net. Sr. Loretta Soja, Dir. Albertine Sisters 9; Guests 36.

[G] PERSONAL PRELATURES

VALPARAISO. *Opus Dei*, 359 West 200 N., 46385. Tel: 219-462-6594; 219-462-0931; Fax: 219-465-6241. Email: shellbourne2@aol.com. Web: www.shellbourne.org. Prelature of the Holy Cross and Opus Dei, Shellbourne Conference Center.

[H] MONASTERIES AND RESIDENCES OF PRIESTS AND BROTHERS

CEDAR LAKE. *Our Lady of Lourdes Friary*, 12921 Parrish St., P.O. Box 156/500, 46303. Tel: 219-374-5931. Revs. Anthony F. Janik, O.F.M.; Francis Affelt, O.F.M.; Anthony Chojnacki, O.F.M.; James Kendzierski, O.F.M.; Myron Lowisz, O.F.M.; Bert Pepowski, O.F.M.; Edward G. Tlucek, O.F.M., Guardian; Bro. James Wisnewski, O.F.M.; Rev. Sergius Wroblewski, O.F.M.; Bros. Reynold Lesnar, O.F.M.; Andrew Martino, O.F.M. Franciscan Friars of the Assumption of the B.V.M. Province (Order of Friars Minor). Priests 8; Brothers 2; Deacons 1; Postulants 2.

MERRILLVILLE. *Basilian Fathers Residence* (1959) 5959 Broadway, 46410. Tel: 219-887-5284; Fax: 219-981-5072. Email: pquanz@andreanhs.com. Revs. John J. Fiore, C.S.B. (Retired); Paul E. Quanz, C.S.B., Rector. Priests 2.

Salvatorian Fathers (Society of the Divine Savior) (1954) 5755 Pennsylvania St., 46410. Tel: 219-884-0714; Fax: 219-981-9224. Email: info@salvatorianie.us. Web: www.salvatorianie.us. Revs. Lukasz Kleczka, S.D.S., Supr.; Rafal Ziajka, S.D.S., Treas. Email: ziajka@sds.org; Joseph R. Zuziak, S.D.S.: Walter M. Pawlik, S.D.S.; Adam Styc, S.D.S.; Bro. Piotr Bogaliski, S.D.S. Mission House for Polish Priests and Brothers. Priests 5; Brothers 1.

MUNSTER. *Discalced Carmelite Fathers Monastery*, 1628 Ridge Rd., 46321. Tel: 219-838-7111; Fax: 219-838-7214. Email: carmelmunster@yahoo.com. Revs. Jacek Palica, O.C.D.; Joseph Ivans, O.C.D.; Edward C. Spyrka, O.C.D.; Waclaw L. Lech, O.C.D.; Bronislaw F. Socha, O.C.D.; Bartlomiej Stanowski, O.C.D.; Jacek Chodzynski, O.C.D.; Franciszek Czaicki, O.C.D., Prior; Pawel Furdzik, O.C.D.; Lukasz Nowak, O.C.D.; Bros. Marian Leszewicz, O.C.D.; Tomasz S. Paczek, O.C.D. Priests 11; Brothers 2.

[I] CONVENTS AND RESIDENCES OF SISTERS

GARY. *Missionaries of Charity* (1999) 509 W. Ridge Rd., 46408. Tel: 219-884-2140. Sr. Maria Agnes, M.C., Supr. Sisters 5.

EAST CHICAGO. *St. Catherine Convent*, 4325 Elm St., 46312. Tel: 219-398-0403. Email: magdalenhellmann@yahoo.com. Web: www.poorhandmaids.org. Sisters Annemarie Kampwerth, P.H.J.C.; Pamela Thelkes, P.H.J.C. Poor Handmaids of Jesus Christ 5.

HAMMOND. *Albertine Sisters (Prov. of Krakow, Poland)*, 1501 Hoffman St., 46327. Tel: 219-937-0575; Fax: 219-937-0575. Email: albertineusa@att.net. Sr. Danuta Karwacka, Supr. Sisters 9.

MERRILLVILLE. *Andrean H.S. Sisters' Residence*, 5959 Broadway, 46410. Tel: 219-887-5287. Email: barbarasable@hotmail.com. Web: www.sscm.org. Sr. Joanne Marie Schutz, SS.C.M., Pastoral Assoc., St. Mary, Crown Point, IN. Sisters of SS. Cyril and Methodius Sisters 5.

[J] RETREAT HOUSES

EAST CHICAGO. *Bethany Retreat House* (1992) 2202 Lituanica Ave., 46312. Tel: 219-398-5047; Fax: 219-398-9329. Email: bethanyrh@sbcglobal.net. Web: www.bethanyretreathouse.org. Sr. Joyce Diltz, P.H.J.C., D.Min., M.Chr.Sp., Spiritual Dir. & Dir. Retreat House. Total Staff 2; Guests 400.

MICHIGAN CITY. *Angela House* (1994) Congregation of the Sisters of the Holy Cross, 412 W. 10th St., 46360. Tel: 219-873-1324. Email: prayercentermc@sbcglobal.net. Sisters Rita Bray, C.S.C., Co-Dir.; Julia Marie Jacomet, C.S.C., Co-Dir.

Sisters of the Holy Cross, Inc. Total Staff 2; Total in Residence 2.

[K] DIOCESAN CHARITIES

GARY. *Catholic Charities, Diocese of Gary, Inc.* (1937) 940 Broadway, 46402. Tel: 219-886-3549; Fax: 219-886-2428. Web: www.catholic-charities.org. Duane W. Dedelow Jr., Exec. Dir.

Catholic Charities, 940 Broadway, 46402. Tel: 219-886-3549; Fax: 219-886-2428.

176 S. West St., Crown Point, 46307. Tel: 219-663-8417; Fax: 219-663-8421.

3901 Fir St., East Chicago, 46312. Tel: 219-397-5803; Fax: 219-397-5804.

6919 Indianapolis Blvd., Hammond, 46324. Tel: 219-844-4883; Fax: 219-844-4885.

6350 Central Ave., Portage, 46368. Tel: 219-762-1177; Fax: 219-762-1827.

321 W. 11th St., Michigan City, 46360. Tel: 219-879-9312; Fax: 219-879-9073.

Family Life Ministry, Crown Point. Tel: 219-663-8417; Fax: 219-663-8421.

Family Life Ministry, Marriage Preparation & Anniversary Mass.

Services to the Aging, Retired & Senior Volunteer Program

LaPorte & Starke Co., 321 W. 11th St., Michigan City, 46360. Tel: 219-874-8195; Fax: 219-879-9073.

Senior Companion Program, 6919 Indianapolis Blvd., Hammond, 46324. Tel: 219-844-4883; Fax: 219-844-4885.

Foster Grandparent Program, 6919 Indianapolis Blvd., Hammond, 46324. Tel: 219-844-4883; Fax: 219-844-4885.

[L] NEWMAN APOSTOLATES

VALPARAISO. *Newman Apostolate-Valparaiso University* (1974) 1511 La Porte Ave., 46383-5818. Tel: 219-464-4042; Fax: 219-462-2711. Email: kevin.mccarthy@valpo.edu. Revs. Kevin P. McCarthy, Chap.; Ted J. Mauch. St. Teresa of Avila Catholic Student Center; Chapel and Center for Students attending Valparaiso University Students 836.

[M] MISCELLANEOUS

GARY. *Sojourner Truth House, Inc.*, 410 W. 13th Ave., 46407. Tel: 219-885-2282; Fax: 219-885-1984. Web: www.sojournertruthhouse.org. Sr. Peg Spindler, C.S.A., Exec. Dir.

CROWN POINT. *Franciscan Home Care Services, Inc.*, 203 Franciscan Dr., 46307. Tel: 219-661-5321; Fax: 219-661-5305. Email: cgrantner@franciscancommunities.com. Catherine Grantner-Coltun, Exec. Dir.

EAST CHICAGO. *Office of Hispanic Ministry* (1983) 3814 Grand Blvd., 46312. Tel: 219-397-2125; Fax: 219-397-2168. Email: atorres@dcgary.org. Web: www.dcgary.org. Adeline Torres, Coord. Total Staff 3.

HAMMOND. **Alverno Provena Hospital Laboratories, Inc.*, 2434 Interstate Plaza Dr., 46324. Tel: 219-989-3814; Fax: 219-989-3900. Email: sam.terese@franciscanalliance.org. Sam Terese, Pres.

HealthVisions Midwest, 3700 179th St., 46323. Tel: 219-844-2698; Fax: 219-844-2702. Email: akampwerth@hvusa.org. Web: www.hvusa.org. Mr. Donald G. Barnes, Pres. & CEO.

Spiritual Life/Seimetz Center, 1441 Hoffman St., 46327. Tel: 219-932-8321; Fax: 219-932-8321. Bed Capacity 35; Total Assisted Annually 500; Total Staff 1.

HOBART. *Ancilla Systems Incorporated* (1967) 1419 S. Lake Park Ave., 46342. Tel: 219-947-8570; Fax: 219-947-3708. Email: tmola@ancilla.org. Web: www.ancilla.org. Sr. Nora Hahn, P.H.J.C., Chairperson; Toni Mola, Admin.

Ancilla Domini Hospitals Self Insurance Trust Tel: 219-947-8570; Fax: 219-947-3708.

St. Joseph Medical Center of Fort Wayne, Inc. Tel: 219-947-8665; Fax: 219-947-3708.

Nazareth Home, East Chicago, 46312. Tel: 219-947-8570; Fax: 219-947-3708. Web: www.nazarethhome-.com. Toni Mola, Admin.

**Poor Handmaids of Jesus Christ Foundation, Inc.*, 1419 S. Lake Park Ave., 46342. Tel: 877-829-5500. Jacob A. McDonald, Contact Person.

VALPARAISO. *Camp Lawrence* Diocesan Spiritual Center and Youth Camp., 68 E. 700 N., 46383. Tel: 219-462-8243; 219-462-5261. Email: camplawrence@verizon.net; jplaucan@dcgary.org.

Catholic Youth Organization, 77725 Broadway, Ste. C, 46410. Tel: 219-736-8931; Fax: 219-736-9457.

RELIGIOUS INSTITUTES OF MEN REPRESENTED IN THE DIOCESE

For further details refer to the corresponding bracketed number in the Religious Institutes of Men or Women section.

[]—*Association of the Immaculate Conception*

[0170]—*Basilian Fathers* (Toronto)—C.S.B.

[0200]—*Benedictine Monks*—O.S.B.

[0600]—*Brothers of the Congregation of Holy Cross*—C.S.C.

[0275]—*Carmelites of Mary Immaculate*—C.M.I.

[1130]—*Congregation of the Priests of the Sacred Heart*—S.C.J.

[0480]—*Conventual Franciscans* (Croatia)—O.F.M.Conv.

[0260]—*Discalced Carmelite Friars* (Holy Ghost Prov., Poland)—O.C.D.

[0520]—*Franciscan Friars* (Prov. of Assumption of B.V.M.; Prov. of St. John the Baptist; Prov. of the Sacred Heart)—O.F.M.

[0610]—*Priests of the Congregation of Holy Cross*—C.S.C.

[1200]—*Society of the Divine Savior*—S.D.S.

[1060]—*Society of the Precious Blood*—C.PP.S.

RELIGIOUS INSTITUTES OF WOMEN REPRESENTED IN THE DIOCESE

[]—*Albertine Sisters* (Prov. of Krakow, Poland)—C.S.A.

[0230]—*Benedictine Sisters of the Pontifical Jurisdiction*—O.S.B.

[0360]—*Carmelite Sisters of the Divine Heart of Jesus*—Carmel D.C.

[3710]—*Congregation of the Sisters of Saint Agnes*—C.S.A.

[1920]—*Congregation of the Sisters of the Holy Cross*—C.S.C.

[1070-03]—*Dominican Sisters*—O.P.

[1070-13]—*Dominican Sisters*—O.P.

[1115]—*Dominican Sisters of Peace*—O.P.

[1210]—*Franciscan Sisters of Chicago*—O.S.F.

[1450]—*Franciscan Sisters of the Sacred Heart*—O.S.F.

[2710]—*Missionaries of Charity*—M.C.

[3130]—*Our Lady of Victory Missionary Sisters*—O.L.V.M.

[3230]—*Poor Handmaids of Jesus Christ*—P.H.J.C.

[2970]—*School Sisters of Notre Dame*—S.S.N.D.

[3340]—*Sisters of Providence*—S.P.

[3780]—*Sisters of Saints Cyril and Methodius*—SS.C.M.

[]—*Sisters of St. Anne of Bangalore*—S.A.B.

[1640]—*Sisters of St. Francis of Perpetual Adoration*—O.S.F.

[3930]—*Sisters of St. Joseph of the Third Order of St. Francis* (Immaculate Conception Prov.)—S.S.J.-T.O.S.F.

DIOCESAN CEMETERIES

HAMMOND. *Saint John-Saint Joseph*, 1547 167th St., 46320. Tel: 219-844-9475; Fax: 219-844-3770. Email: michaelpwelsh@sbcglobal.net. Rev. Roy T. Beeching, Dir. of Cemeteries; Michael P. Welsh, Cemetery Mgr. Employees 10.

MICHIGAN CITY. *Saint Stanislaus*, 1015 Greenwood Ave., P.O. Box 642, 46360. Tel: 219-874-4310.

NECROLOGY

(No Deaths)

An asterisk (*) denotes an organization that has established tax-exempt status directly with the IRS and is not covered by the USCCB Group Ruling.

Diocese of Gaylord

(Dioecesis Gaylordensis)

Most Reverend

BERNARD A. HEBDA, J.C.L., J.D.

Bishop of Gaylord; ordained July 1, 1989; appointed Bishop of Gaylord October 7, 2009; ordained December 1, 2009. *Diocesan Pastoral Center: 611 W. North St., Gaylord, MI 49735-8349.*

Diocesan Pastoral Center: 611 W. North St., Gaylord, MI 49735-8349. Tel: 989-732-5147; Fax: 989-705-3589.

Web: www.dioceseofgaylord.org

Email: vlooker@dioceseofgaylord.org

ESTABLISHED JULY 20, 1971.

Square Miles 11,171.

Comprises the following 21 Counties in the State of Michigan: Alcona, Alpena, Antrim, Benzie, Charlevoix, Cheboygan, Crawford, Emmet, Grand Traverse, Iosco, Kalkaska, Leelanau, Manistee, Missaukee, Montmorency, Ogemaw, Oscoda, Otsego, Presque Isle, Roscommon and Wexford.

For legal titles of parishes and diocesan institutions, consult the Chancery Office.

STATISTICAL OVERVIEW

Personnel	
Bishop	1
Priests: Diocesan Active in Diocese	36
Priests: Diocesan Active Outside Diocese	3
Priests: Retired, Sick or Absent	24
Number of Diocesan Priests	63
Religious Priests in Diocese	6
Total Priests in Diocese	69
Extern Priests in Diocese	16
Ordinations:	
Diocesan Priests	1
Transitional Deacons	2
Permanent Deacons in Diocese	23
Total Sisters	29
Parishes	
Parishes	80
With Resident Pastor:	
Resident Diocesan Priests	29
Resident Religious Priests	3
Without Resident Pastor:	
Administered by Priests	39
Administered by Religious Women	3
Administered by Lay People	2
Professional Ministry Personnel:	
Sisters	6
Lay Ministers	47
Welfare	
Catholic Hospitals	3
Total Assisted	375,000
Day Care Centers	11
Total Assisted	392
Special Centers for Social Services	22
Total Assisted	47,691
Educational	
Diocesan Students in Other Seminaries	12
Total Seminarians	12
High Schools, Diocesan and Parish	4
Total Students	477
Elementary Schools, Diocesan and Parish	16
Total Students	1,837
Catechesis/Religious Education:	
High School Students	858
Elementary Students	2,138
Total Students under Catholic Instruction	5,322
Teachers in the Diocese:	
Priests	1
Sisters	1
Lay Teachers	182
Vital Statistics	
Receptions into the Church:	
Infant Baptism Totals	610
Minor Baptism Totals	52
Adult Baptism Totals	70
Received into Full Communion	131
First Communions	721
Confirmations	816
Marriages:	
Catholic	149
Interfaith	93
Total Marriages	242
Deaths	866
Total Catholic Population	58,830
Total Population	504,530

Former Bishops—Most Revs. EDMUND C. SZOKA, J.C.L., D.D., First Bishop of Gaylord; ord. June 5, 1954; cons. July 20, 1971; installed July 20, 1971; appt. Archbishop of Detroit March 28, 1981; installed May 17, 1981; named Cardinal Priest May 29, 1988; elevated June 28, 1988; Assigned to the Vatican, 1990; ROBERT J. ROSE, S.T.L., D.D., ord. Dec. 21, 1955; appt. Bishop of Gaylord Oct. 13, 1981; installed Dec. 6, 1981; transferred to Diocese of Grand Rapids July 11, 1989; installed Aug. 30, 1989; PATRICK R. COONEY, S.T.B., S.T.L., ord. Dec. 20, 1959; appt. Titular Bishop of Hodelm and Auxiliary Bishop of Detroit Dec. 3, 1982; cons. Jan. 27, 1983; appt. Bishop of Gaylord Nov. 21, 1989; installed Jan. 28, 1990; retired Oct. 7, 2009.

Vicar General—Rev. FRANCIS J. MURPHY, St. Ann Parish, 800 W. 13th, Cadillac, 49601. Tel: 231-775-2471.

Diocesan Offices and Departments

Diocesan Pastoral Center—611 W. North St., Gaylord, 49735-8349. Tel: 989-732-5147; Fax: 989-705-3589. Office Hours: Mon.-Fri. 8-4:30; All business should be directed to this office.

Members of the College of Consultors—Revs. CHARLES G. DONAJKOWSKI; MICHAEL S. JANOWSKI; DONALD L. LIBBY; WILLIAM W. LIPSCOMB; T. PATRICK MAHER; JOHN E. MCCRACKEN, Ex Officio.

Administrative Services, Secretariat for—KIM SMITH, Dir., 611 W. North St., Gaylord, 49735. Tel: 989-732-5147.

Audiovisual Resource Center—CANDACE NEFF, 611 W. North St., Gaylord, 49735. Tel: 989-732-5147.

Archivist—Rev. JOSEPH A. BLASKO, 611 W. North St., Gaylord, 49735. Tel: 989-732-5147.

Communications, Secretariat for—CANDACE NEFF, Dir., 611 W. North St., Gaylord, 49735. Tel: 989-732-5147.

Council of Catholic Women, Diocesan—KATHLEEN MELVILLE-HALL, Pres., 342 S. 3rd, Alpena, 49707.

Cursillo—Rev. LAWRENCE J. SERGOTT, Mailing Address: P.O. Box 189, Mio, 48647-0189. Tel: 989-826-5509.

Ecumenical and Interreligious Affairs, Delegate for—Rev. JOSEPH P. GRAFF, 150 W. Main St., Harbor Springs, 49740.

Faith Development, Secretariat for—DANORA BRZEZINSKI, Dir., 611 W. North St., Gaylord, 49735-8349. Tel: 989-732-5147.

Finance Council, Diocesan—Most Rev. BERNARD A. HEBDA, J.C.L., J.D.; Rev. FRANCIS J. MURPHY; JAMES S. BERISH JR.; STAN DOMBROWSKI; LORI A. REICHARD; TODD STACHNIK.

Holy Childhood Pontifical Association—Rev. ROBERT H. BISSOT, 2188 Nicholson Hill Rd., Ossineke, 49766.

Native American Apostolate—Rev. ANDREW G. BUVALA, O.F.M., Coord., Blessed Kateri Tekakwitha Parish, P.O. Box 369, Suttons Bay, 49682. Tel: 231-271-6651.

Knights of Columbus—MICHAEL J. STANCHINA, Eastern Diocesan Prog. Dir., 937 Joyce Court, Mio, 48647. Tel: 989-848-5322; RUSSELL SCHOLTENS, Western Diocesan Prog. Dir., Mailing Address: P.O. Box 37, Suttons Bay, 49682. Tel: 231-271-6865.

Worship and Liturgical Formation, Secretariat for—Rev. DUANE A. WACHOWIAK JR., Dir., 611 W. North St., Gaylord, 49735. Tel: 989-732-5147.

Marriage Enrichment, Secretariat for—DANORA BRZEZINSKI, Dir., 611 W. North St., Gaylord, 49735. Tel: 517-732-5147.

Hispanic Apostolate—SILVIA CORTES-LOPEZ, 1026 Hannah, Ste. A, Traverse City, 49686. Tel: 231-929-4738.

Justice and Peace—Rev. WAYNE H. DZIEKAN, 611 W. North St., Gaylord, 49735. Tel: 989-732-5147.

Vicar for Clergy—Rev. JOHN E. MCCRACKEN, Delegate, 611 W. North St., Gaylord, 49735. Tel: 989-732-5147.

Priests' Retirement Fund Board—Most Rev. BERNARD A. HEBDA, J.C.L., J.D. Elected Members: Revs. ROBERT W. NALLEY (Retired); JAMES K. GARDINER; JAMES P. HAYDEN (Retired); JOHN E. MCCRACKEN; JOSEPH MUSZKIEWICZ. Appointed Member: DON BARTOSH, Chm.; ANITA LAWNICHAK.

Director of Vocations—Rev. DONALD R. GEYMAN, Diocese of Gaylord, 611 W. North St., Gaylord, 49735. Tel: 989-732-5147.

Propagation of the Faith—Rev. ROBERT H. BISSOT, Dir., 2188 Nicholson Hill Rd., Ossineke, 49766. Tel: 989-471-5121.

Spiritual Formation—MICHAEL FONSECA, Dir., 611 W. North St., Gaylord, 49735. Tel: 989-732-5147.

Tribunal Diocesan—Rev. ROBERT W. NALLEY, Judicial Vicar (Retired). Adjutant Judicial Vicar: Rev. PETER O. EKE. Defender of the Bond: Rev. BENEDETTO J. PARIS. Procurator-Advocate: MARY DICKERSON, Notary Inquiries may be made through the local pastors or directed to this office: 611 W. North St., Gaylord, 49735. Tel: 989-732-5147.

Victim Assistance Coordinator—THOMAS TENEROVICZ. Tel: 800-727-5147, Ext. 3525 (Toll Free); 989-705-3525. Email: ttenerovicz@dioceseofgaylord.org.

CLERGY, PARISHES, MISSIONS AND PAROCHIAL SCHOOLS

CITY OF GAYLORD

(OTSEGO COUNTY), ST. MARY CATHEDRAL, [CEM] Revs. James M. Bearss, Rector; Polycarp P. Mblarawa, Parochial Vicar; Sr. Cecilia Faber, O.P., Pastoral Min.
Res.: 606 N. Ohio Ave., 49735-1999. Tel: 989-732-5448; Fax: 989-705-3585.
Catechesis/Religious Program—Students 343.

OUTSIDE THE CITY OF GAYLORD

ACME, GRAND TRAVERSE CO., CHRIST THE KING Rev. Raymond C. Cotter.
Res. & Mailing: P.O. Box 95, 49610. Tel: 231-938-9214; Fax: 231-938-3266.
Church: 3801 Shore Rd., Williamsburg, 49690.
See Grand Traverse Area Catholic School, Traverse City, under Interparochial Parish Schools located in the Institution section.
Catechesis/Religious Program—Denise Elsenheimer, D.R.E. Students 133.

AFTON, CHEBOYGAN CO., ST. MONICA, [CEM] Rev. Peter O. Eke, Admin.
3856 Oak St., P.O. Box 130, Onaway, 49765. Tel: 989-733-6053; Fax: 989-733-6053.
Church: M-68, 49705.
Catechesis/Religious Program—Debra Nash, D.R.E. Students 2.

ALPENA, ALPENA CO.

1—ST. ANNE, [JC] Revs. Gregory P. McCallum; Gerald C. Okoli.
Res.: 203 S. Ninth Ave., 49707. Tel: 989-356-0622; Fax: 989-354-3918.
Church: 201 S. Ninth Ave., 49707.
Catechesis/Religious Program—All 4 Alpena parishes combined. Twinned with St. Bernard, Alpena; St. John the Baptist, Alpena; St. Mary, Alpena. Jackie Benson, D.R.E. Students 210.

2—ST. BERNARD, [JC] Revs. Gregory P. McCallum; Gerald C. Okoli.
Mailing Address: 322 W. Chisholm St., 49707. Tel: 989-354-2676; Fax: 989-354-5142. Email: sbc@stbernardchurch332.com.
Catechesis/Religious Program—Twinned with St. Anne, Alpena., Tel: 989-354-8655. Jackie Benson, D.R.E.

3—ST. JOHN THE BAPTIST Revs. Gregory P. McCallum; Gerald C. Okoli.
Res.: 2550 S. First Ave., 49707. Tel: 989-354-3019; Fax: 989-358-9079.
Catechesis/Religious Program—Twinned with St. Anne, Alpena. Jackie Benson, D.R.E.

4—ST. MARY, [JC] Revs. Gregory P. McCallum; Rolando Silva.
Church and Rectory: 120 E. Miller St., 49707. Tel: 989-354-2322 (Rectory); Fax: 989-354-2030 (Rectory).
Catechesis/Religious Program—Twinned with St. Anne, Alpena., Tel: 989-354-8655. Jackie Benson, D.R.E.

ALVERNO, CHEBOYGAN CO., ST. FRANCIS OF ASSISI, Closed. For sacramental records contact St. Mary-St. Charles Parish, Cheboygan.

ATLANTA, MONTMORENCY CO., JESUS THE GOOD SHEPHERD Rev. Rolando Silva.
Res. & Mailing: P.O. Box 216, Hillman, 49746. Tel: 989-742-4542; Fax: 989-742-8090.
Church: 4521 County Rd. 491, 49709. Email: staug.jtgs@src-milp.com.
Catechesis/Religious Program—Debra Banks, D.R.E.

BAY SHORE, EMMET CO., ST. FRANCIS SOLANUS, Closed. For inquiries for parish records contact the chancery.

BEAVER ISLAND, CHARLEVOIX CO., HOLY CROSS, [CEM] Rev. Joseph A. Blasko, Admin.
Res.: P.O. Box 145, 49782.
Office: Kings Hwy., 49782. Tel: 231-448-2230; Fax: 231-448-2230.
Catechesis/Religious Program—Students 19.

BELLAIRE, ANTRIM CO., ST. LUKE Rev. James K. Gardiner.
Res.: 3088 S. M-88, P.O. Box 799, 49615-0799. Tel: 231-533-8121; Fax: 231-533-9254. Email: stluke@torchlake.com. Web: www.stlukebellaire.com.
Catechesis/Religious Program—Debbie Balon, D.R.E. Students 40.

BLACK RIVER, ALCONA CO., ST. GABRIEL, [CEM] Rev. Robert H. Bissot.
Res.: 2188 W. Nicholson Hill Rd., Ossineke, 49766-9736. Tel: 989-471-2556; Fax: 989-471-2697.
Church: 5570 N. Lake Shore Dr., 48721. Tel: 989-471-5121.
Catechesis/Religious Program—Cathy MacFalda, D.R.E.

BOYNE CITY, CHARLEVOIX CO., ST. MATTHEW, [JC] Rev. Duane A. Wachowiak Jr.
Res.: 1303 Boyne Ave., 49712. Tel: 231-582-7718; Fax: 231-582-7490. Email: parishoffice@jamcc.org.
Catechesis/Religious Program—Patty Furtaw, D.R.E. & Pastoral Assoc. Students 90.

BOYNE FALLS, CHARLEVOIX CO., ST. AUGUSTINE, [CEM] Rev. Duane A. Wachowiak Jr.
Res.: 1303 Boyne Ave., Boyne City, 49712. Tel: 231-582-7718; Fax: 231-582-7490. Email: parishoffice@jamcc.org.
Church: Grove St., 49713. Tel: 231-549-2350.
Catechesis/Religious Program—Patty Furtaw, D.R.E. & Pastoral Assoc. Students 18.

BURT LAKE, CHEBOYGAN CO., ASSUMPTION OF ST. MARY
Res.: P.O. Box 122, Pellston, 49769. Tel: 231-539-8805; Fax: 231-539-8572.

CADILLAC, WEXFORD CO., ST. ANN, [CEM] Revs. Francis J. Murphy; Santiago Hoyumpa; Deacons James Barton, Pastoral Min.; James Siler, Pastoral Min.
Res.: 800 W. 13th St., 49601-9281. Tel: 231-775-2471; Fax: 231-775-0161. Email: ellenhovey@yahoo.com.
Catechesis/Religious Program—Therese Abee, D.R.E.; Geralyn Kohler, D.R.E. Students 45.

CEDAR, LEELANAU CO., HOLY ROSARY, [CEM] Rev. Donald L. Libby.
Church & Res.: 6982 S. Schomberg Rd., 49621. Tel: 231-228-5429 (Res.); Fax: 231-228-5529 (Res.). Email: holyrosarycedar@gmail.com.
Catechesis/Religious Program—Students 69.

CHARLEVOIX, CHARLEVOIX CO., ST. MARY Rev. Matthew Wigton.
Res.: 1003 Bridge St., 49720. Tel: 231-547-6652; Fax: 231-547-6658.
Catechesis/Religious Program—Students 57.

CHEBOYGAN, CHEBOYGAN CO., ST. MARY-ST. CHARLES, [JC] Revs. Paul Megge; Richard C. Schaeffer; Mrs. Patricia Watson, Pastoral Assoc.
Mailing Address: P.O. Box 40, 49721. Tel: 231-627-2105; Fax: 231-627-5362. Email: sts.marycharles@ymail.com.
Church: 120 N. D St., 49721.
Catechesis/Religious Program—Students 83.

COPEMISH, MANISTEE CO., ST. RAPHAEL, [CEM] Rev. Ruben D. Munoz.
Res.: P.O. Box 150, Onekama, 49675. Tel: 231-378-2984; Fax: 231-378-4953.
Church: M-115, 49625. Tel: 231-889-4254; Fax: 231-889-3706. Email: stjosephonekama@hotmail.com.
Catechesis/Religious Program—Carlina Breitner, D.R.E. Students 10.

CROSS VILLAGE, EMMET CO., HOLY CROSS, [CEM] Rev. Joseph P. Graff.
Mailing Address & Res.: 150 W. Main, Harbor Springs, 49740.
Church: 6624 N. Lake Shore Dr., 49723. Tel: 231-526-2017; Fax: 231-526-9299. Email: office@holychildhoodchurch.org.

EAST JORDAN, CHARLEVOIX CO., ST. JOSEPH, [CEM] Rev. James K. Gardiner.
Res.: P.O. Box 379, 49727. Tel: 231-536-2934; Fax: 231-536-2988.
Catechesis/Religious Program—Barbara Kowal, D.R.E. Students 38.

EAST TAWAS, IOSCO CO.

1—HOLY FAMILY Revs. Charles G. Donajkowski; Craig Haider.
Res.: P.O. Box 472, 48730.
Church: 516 W. Lincoln, 48730. Tel: 989-362-3162; Fax: 989-362-9077. Email: holyfamily3@hotmail.com.
Catechesis/Religious Program—Pattie Rioux, D.R.E. Students 75.

2—ST. JOSEPH, Merged with Immaculate Heart of Mary, Tawas City to form Holy Family, East Tawas.

ELK RAPIDS, ANTRIM CO., SACRED HEART, [CEM] Rev. Robert J. Zuchowski.
Res.: 143 Charles St., 49629. Tel: 231-264-8087; Fax: 231-264-6350. Email: sacredheart@sacredheartelkrapids.org.
Catechesis/Religious Program—Denise Elsenheimer, D.R.E. Students 66.

ELMIRA, ANTRIM CO., ST. THOMAS AQUINAS, [CEM] Revs. James M. Bearss; Polycarp P. Mblarawa, Parochial Vicar.
Res.: P.O. Box 128, 49730. Tel: 231-546-3326.
Church: 2567 Buell Rd., 49730.
Catechesis/Religious Program—Students 10.

EMPIRE, LEELANAU CO., ST. PHILIP NERI, [CEM] Revs. Zeljko J. Guberovic, Team. Min.; Mariano N. Dellagiovanna, Team. Min.
Mailing Address: P.O. Box 257, 49630.
Res. & Church: 11411 LaCore Ave., 49630. Tel: 231-326-5255; Fax: 231-326-5839. Email: stphilipneriempire@gmail.com.
Catechesis/Religious Program—Carolyn Ballmer, D.R.E. Students 25.

FIFE LAKE, GRAND TRAVERSE CO., ST. ALOYSIUS, [CEM] Rev. Norman Dickson, S.J., Admin. Email: ndsj@aol.com.
Res.: 0438 County Rd. 612, Kalkaska, 49646. Tel: 231-258-5021; Fax: 231-258-2842.
Church: 403 E. Merritt St., 49633. Tel: 231-258-2752.
Catechesis/Religious Program—Robert Bowersox, D.R.E. Students 7.

FRANKFORT, BENZIE CO., ST. ANN Rev. Msgr. John F. Porter, Admin. (Retired).
Res.: 508 Crystal Ave., P.O. Box 1168, 49635. Tel: 231-352-4421; Fax: 231-352-9940.
Catechesis/Religious Program—Students 28.

GILLS PIER, LEELANAU CO., ST. WENCESLAUS, [CEM] Rev. Andrew G. Buvala, O.F.M., Sacramental Min.; Martin Korson, Lay Admin.
Church & Res.: 8500 E. Kolarik Rd., Suttons Bay, 49682. Tel: 231-271-3574.

GLENNIE, ALCONA CO., ST. FRANCIS OF ASSISI, Closed. For inquiries for parish records contact the chancery.

GOOD HART, EMMET CO., ST. IGNATIUS, [CEM] Rev. Joseph P. Graff.
Mailing Address & Res.: 150 W. Main St., Harbor Springs, 49740. Tel: 231-526-2017; Fax: 231-526-9299.
Church: 101 Lamkin Rd., 49737.

GRAYLING, CRAWFORD CO., ST. MARY Revs. James M. Bearss; Polycarp P. Mblarawa.
Res.: 707 Spruce St., 49738-1259. Tel: 989-348-7657 (Office); Fax: 989-348-7658.
Catechesis/Religious Program—Students 66.

HALE, IOSCO CO., ST. PIUS X Rev. Charles G. Donajkowski, Temp. Admin.
Res.: P.O. Box 428, 48739. Tel: 989-728-2278; Fax: 989-728-7487.
Church: 3900 M-65, 48739. Email: spxhale@centurytel.net.
Catechesis/Religious Program—Tel: 989-728-2278; Fax: 989-728-7487. Karol Shellenbarger, D.R.E. Students 9.

HANNAH, GRAND TRAVERSE CO., ST. MARY, [CEM] Rev. Michael P. Conner.
Res.: 6955 Hannah Rd., Kingsley, 49649. Tel: 231-263-7300; Fax: 231-263-7489. Email: pstmaryhannah@inbox.com.
Catechesis/Religious Program—2912 W. M-113, Kingsley, 49649. Norm Schichtel, D.R.E. Students 45.

HARBOR SPRINGS, EMMET CO., HOLY CHILDHOOD OF JESUS, [CEM] Rev. Joseph P. Graff.
Res.: 150 W. Main St., 49740. Tel: 231-526-2017; Fax: 231-526-9299. Email: office@holychildhoodchurch.org. Web: www.holychildhoodchurch.org.
Catechesis/Religious Program—Tel: 231-526-9299; Fax: 231-526-7181. Students 115.

HARRIETTA, WEXFORD CO., ST. EDWARD Rev. Francis J. Murphy.
Res.: 800 W. 13th St., Cadillac, 49601-9281. Tel: 231-775-2471; Fax: 231-775-0161.
Church: 207 W. Gaston, 49638.

HARRISVILLE, ALCONA CO., ST. ANNE, [CEM] Rev. Robert H. Bissot.
Res.: P.O. Box 345, 48740. Tel: 989-724-6713; Fax: 989-724-5210.
Church: 110 State St., 48740. Email: stanne@charter.net.
Catechesis/Religious Program—Students 16.

HERRON, ALPENA CO., ST. ROSE OF LIMA Rev. Gregory P. McCallum; Theresa M. Zbytowski, Admin.
Church: 3433 Herron Rd., 49744. Tel: 989-379-4316; Fax: 989-379-3796. Email: strose@speedconnect.com.
Catechesis/Religious Program—Dianne Blissland, D.R.E. Students 22.

HIGGINS LAKE, ROSCOMMON CO., ST. HUBERT Revs. Joseph Muszkiewicz; Bernard L. Tyler, Admin. (Retired).
Res.: P.O. Box 75, 48627. Tel: 989-821-5591; Fax: 989-821-5895. Email: jambert@charter.net.
Church: 7612 W. Higgins Lake Dr., 48627.
Catechesis/Religious Program—

HILLMAN, MONTMORENCY CO., ST. AUGUSTINE, [CEM] Rev. Rolando Silva.
Res.: P.O. Box 216, 49746. Tel: 989-742-4542; Fax: 989-742-8090.
Church: 24140 Veterans Memorial Hwy., 49746. Email: staug.jtgs@src-milp.com.
Catechesis/Religious Program—Debra Banks, D.R.E. Students 30.

HOUGHTON LAKE, ROSCOMMON CO., ST. JAMES Revs. Joseph Muszkiewicz; Bernard L. Tyler, Admin. (Retired).
Res.: P.O. Box 75, Higgins Lake, 48627. Tel: 989-821-5591; Fax: 989-821-5895.
Church: 7878 E. Houghton Lake Dr., 48629. Tel: 989-422-3925.

INDIAN RIVER, CHEBOYGAN CO., CROSS IN THE WOODS CATHOLIC SHRINE, [CEM] Revs. Michael Haney, O.F.M.; Harry Speckman, O.F.M.; Thomas Vos, O.F.M.; Miro Wiese, O.F.M.
Res.: 7078 M-68, 49749. Tel: 231-238-8973; Fax: 231-238-7012.

Catechesis/Religious Program— 49749. Tel: 231-238-8542; Fax: 231-238-7012. Shirley Ronk, D.R.E. Students 42.

KALKASKA, KALKASKA CO., ST. MARY OF THE WOODS, [CEM] Rev. Norman Dickson, S.J., Admin.
Res.: 0438 County Rd. 612, 49646. Tel: 231-258-5021; Fax: 231-258-2842.
Catechesis/Religious Program—Robert Bowersox, D.R.E. Students 32.

KLACKING CREEK, HOLY FAMILY, [CEM] Rev. T. Patrick Maher.
Res.: 402 W. Peters Rd., West Branch, 48661. Tel: 989-345-3422. Email: holyfamily@ziggynet.com.
Catechesis/Religious Program—Mary Ann Kaniewski, D.R.E. Students 6.

LAKE CITY, MISSAUKEE CO., ST. STEPHEN Revs. Francis J. Murphy; Santiago Hoyumpa.
Res.: P.O. Box 379, 49651. Tel: 231-839-2121; Fax: 231-839-3755.
Church: 506 Union St., 49651.
Catechesis/Religious Program—Patricia Crane, Dir. Adult Ed.; Geralyn Kohler, D.R.E. Students 35.

LAKE LEELANAU, LEELANAU CO., ST. MARY, [CEM] Rev. Michael S. Janowski.
Mailing Address: P.O. Box 340, 49653. Tel: 231-256-9676; Fax: 231-256-7812.
Res.: 307 S. St. Mary St., 49653.
Church: 403 S. St. Mary St., 49653.
Catechesis/Religious Program—Michael Collins, D.R.E. Students 45.

LARKS LAKE, EMMET CO., ST. NICHOLAS, [CEM] Rev. Joseph P. Graff.
Mailing Address: P.O. Box 120, Cross Village, 49723.
Res.: 150 W. Main St., Harbor Springs, 49740. Tel: 231-526-9299.
Catechesis/Religious Program—Students 13.

LEWISTON, MONTMORENCY CO., ST. FRANCIS OF ASSISI, [CEM] Rev. Lawrence J. Sergott.
Res.: P.O. Box 182, 49756. Tel: 989-786-2235; Fax: 989-786-7685.
Church: 4086 Salling Ave., 49756. Email: stfrancisassisi@i2k.net.
Catechesis/Religious Program—Students 24.

MACKINAW CITY, EMMET CO., ST. ANTHONY OF PADUA, [CEM] Sr. Chris Herald, O.P., Pastoral Admin.
Res.: P.O. Box 460, 49701. Tel: 231-436-5561; 231-436-5601; Fax: 231-436-5699.
Church: 600 W. Central Ave., 49701.
Catechesis/Religious Program—Students 12.

MANCELONA, ANTRIM CO., ST. ANTHONY OF PADUA, [CEM] Rev. R. Dale Magoon.
Mailing Address: P.O. Box 677, 49659-0677.
Church: 209 Jefferson St., 49659. Tel: 231-587-8401; Fax: 231-587-5643. Email: st.anthony@torchlake.com.

MANISTEE, MANISTEE CO.

1—GUARDIAN ANGELS, [JC] Revs. John E. McCracken; Sylvestre L. Obwaka.
Res.: 254 Sixth St., 49660. Tel: 231-723-2619; Fax: 231-723-6827.
Convent—501 Michael St., 49660.
Catechesis/Religious Program—Twinned with St. Joseph, Manistee. Students 175.

2—ST. JOSEPH, [JC] Revs. John E. McCracken; Sylvestre L. Obwaka.
Res.: 254 Sixth St., 49660. Tel: 231-723-2619; Fax: 231-723-6827.
Catechesis/Religious Program—Tel: 231-723-2619, Ext. 26. Liz Hainstock, D.R.E. Combined for all three Manistee parishes. Students 182.

3—ST. MARY OF MT. CARMEL SHRINE, [JC] Revs. John E. McCracken; Sylvestre L. Obwaka.
Res.: 254 Sixth St., 49660. Tel: 231-723-2619; Fax: 231-723-6827.
Catechesis/Religious Program—Twinned with St. Joseph, Manistee. Liz Hainstock, D.R.E. Students 175.

MANTON, WEXFORD CO., ST. THERESA Revs. Francis J. Murphy; Santiago Hoyumpa.
Res.: P.O. Box 379, Lake City, 49651. Tel: 231-839-2121.
Church: 9475 14th & 1/4 Rd., 49663.

MAPLE CITY, LEELANAU CO., ST. RITA-ST. JOSEPH Rev. Donald L. Libby.
Mailing Address: P.O. Box 75, 49664-0075. Tel: 231-228-5823; Fax: 231-228-5823.
Church: 8707 Hill St., 49664. Tel: 231-228-5823.
Catechesis/Religious Program—(Combined with Holy Rosary, Cedar)

MAPLETON, GRAND TRAVERSE CO., ST. JOSEPH, [CEM] Rev. Edwin A. Thome (Retired).
Mailing Address: 13400 Center Rd., Traverse City, 49686. Tel: 231-223-7211. Email: stjoebus@pentel.net. Web: www.stjosephchurchtraversecity.org.
Catechesis/Religious Program—Howard Byrne III, D.R.E. Students 112.

MCBAIN, MISSAUKEE CO., ST. RITA, Closed. For inquiries for parish records contact the chancery.

METZ, PRESQUE ISLE CO., ST. DOMINIC, [CEM] Sr. Rita Epple, R.S.M., Pastoral Admin.
Res.: 9269 County Rd. 441, Posen, 49776. Tel: 989-766-2694; Fax: 989-766-8654.
Catechesis/Religious Program—Carolyn Haske, D.R.E. Students 19.

MIKADO, ALOCONA CO., ST. RAPHAEL, [CEM] Rev. Robert H. Bissot.
Res.: P.O. Box 345, Harrisville, 48740. Tel: 989-724-6713; Fax: 989-724-5210.
Church: 2531 E. Mikado Rd., 48745. Tel: 989-736-6071. Email: stanne@charter.net.
Catechesis/Religious Program—Ruth Johnson, D.R.E. Students 5.

MIO, OSCODA CO., ST. MARY Rev. Lawrence J. Sergott.
Res.: P.O. Box 189, 48647. Tel: 989-826-5509; Fax: 989-826-1333. Email: stmarymio@m33access.com.
Church: 100 Deyarmond St., 48647.
Ministry Office—
Catechesis/Religious Program—Students 23.

NORTHPORT, LEELANAU CO., ST. GERTRUDE Rev. James Doherty, Admin.
Res.: P.O. Box 9, Suttons Bay, 49682. Tel: 231-271-3744; Fax: 231-271-3733.
Church: 701 Warren, 49670. Tel: 231-386-5221.
Catechesis/Religious Program—(Combined with St. Michael, Suttons Bay), 315 Broadway, Suttons Bay, 49682. Email: stmichaelparish@juno.com. Mary Mills, D.R.E.

ONAWAY, PRESQUE ISLE CO., ST. PAUL, [CEM] Rev. Peter O. Eke.
Office, Res. & Church: 3856 Oak St., P.O. Box 130, 49765. Tel: 989-733-6053; Fax: 989-733-6053.
Catechesis/Religious Program—Students 33.

ONEKAMA, MANISTEE CO., ST. JOSEPH, [CEM] Rev. Ruben D. Munoz.
Res.: P.O. Box 150, 49675. Tel: 231-889-4254; Fax: 231-889-3706.
Church: 8380 Fifth St., 49675. Email: stjosephonekama@hotmail.com.
Catechesis/Religious Program—Students 19.

OSCODA, IOSCO CO., SACRED HEART, [CEM] Revs. Charles G. Donajkowski; Craig Haider, Parochial Vicar.
Res.: 5300 N. U.S.-23, 48750. Tel: 989-739-9511; Fax: 989-739-3010. Email: sacredheart@sacredheartoscoda.com.
Catechesis/Religious Program—Tel: 989-739-9062. Mrs. Jackie Welles, D.R.E. Students 17.

OSSINEKE, ALPENA CO., ST. CATHERINE, [CEM] Rev. Robert H. Bissot.
Res.: 2188 W. Nicholson Hill Rd., 49766-9736. Tel: 989-471-2556; Fax: 989-471-2697.
Catechesis/Religious Program—Tel: 989-471-5121. Cathy MacFalda, D.R.E. Students 36.

PELLSTON, EMMET CO., ST. CLEMENT, [CEM] Revs. Paul Megge; Richard C. Schaeffer.
Mailing Address: P.O. Box 122, 49769-0122.
Res.: 118 N. D St., Cheboygan, 49721. Tel: 231-627-5795.
Church: 202 Maple, 49769. Tel: 231-539-8805; Fax: 231-539-8572.
Catechesis/Religious Program—Larry Cassidy, D.R.E. Students 18.

PESHABESTOWN, LEELANAU CO., BLESSED KATERI TEKAKWITHA Rev. Andrew G. Buvala, O.F.M.
Res.: P.O. Box 369, Suttons Bay, 49682. Tel: 231-271-6651. Email: kateri369@aol.com.

PETOSKEY, EMMET CO., ST. FRANCIS XAVIER, [CEM] Rev. Dennis R. Stilwell.
Res.: 513 Howard St., 49770. Tel: 231-347-4133; Fax: 231-347-4134. Email: sfxpetoskey@hotmail.com. Web: www.petoskeystfrancis.org.
School—(Grades K-8), 414 Michigan St., 49770. Tel: 231-347-3651; Fax: 231-348-6475. Phyllis Daily, Prin. Students 215.
Catechesis/Religious Program—Tel: 231-347-2681. Students 80.

POSEN, PRESQUE ISLE CO., ST. CASIMIR, [CEM] Rev. Arthur F. Duchnowicz.
Res.: 10075 M-65 N., P.O. Box 217, 49776. Tel: 989-766-2660.
Church: 10075 M-65 N., 49776-0217. Web: stcasimirposen.catholicweb.com.
Catechesis/Religious Program—Joan Chappa, D.R.E. Students 82.

PRAGA, ANTRIM CO., ST. JOHN NEPOMUCENE, [CEM] Rev. Duane A. Wachowiak Jr.
Res.: 1303 Boyne Ave., Boyne City, 49712. Tel: 231-582-7718; Fax: 231-582-7490.
Catechesis/Religious Program—Students 5.

PRUDENVILLE, ROSCOMMON CO., OUR LADY OF THE LAKE Rev. Joseph Muszkiewicz.
Res.: 1037 W. Houghton Lake Dr., P.O. Box 800, 48651. Tel: 989-366-5533; Fax: 989-366-5988. Email: olotlparish@gmail.com.
Catechesis/Religious Program—Students 15.

RIGGSVILLE, CHEBOYGAN CO., SACRED HEART Revs. Paul Megge; Richard C. Schaeffer.
Mailing Address: P.O. Box 122, Pellston, 49769.
Church: 4989 Polish Line Rd., Cheboygan, 49721. Tel: 231-539-8805 (Parish); Fax: 231-539-8572.
Catechesis/Religious Program—Kim Socolovitch, D.R.E. Students 25.

ROGERS CITY, PRESQUE ISLE CO., ST. IGNATIUS, [CEM] Rev. Arthur F. Duchnowicz.
Business Office & Mailing Address: 585 S. Third St., 49779. Tel: 989-734-2753; Fax: 989-734-7671. Email: parishoffice@stignatiuscs.org.
Catechesis/Religious Program—Tel: 989-734-3443. Students 10.

ROSCOMMON, ROSCOMMON CO., ST. MICHAEL Rev. Joseph Muszkiewicz.
Res.: 104 N. 6th St., P.O. Box 8, 48653. Tel: 989-275-5212; Fax: 989-275-9020.
Catechesis/Religious Program—Tel: 989-275-5212. Deborah Harris, Dir. Faith Formation. Students 96.

ST. HELEN, ROSCOMMON CO., ST. HELEN Sr. Barbara Matievich, O.P., Parish Life Coord.
Mailing Address: P.O. Box 318, Saint Helen, 48656.
Res.: 737 N. St. Helen Rd., Saint Helen, 48656. Tel: 989-389-4959. Email: st.helen@sbcglobal.net.
Catechesis/Religious Program—

SKIDWAY LAKE, OGEMAW CO., ST. STEPHEN OF HUNGARY Rev. T. Patrick Maher.
Res.: 2811 E. Greenwood Rd., Prescott, 48756. Tel: 989-873-3340; Fax: 989-873-5209. Email: ststephenofhungary@frontier.com.
Catechesis/Religious Program—Wayne Winter, D.R.E. Students 10.

SUTTONS BAY, LEELANAU CO., ST. MICHAEL THE ARCHANGEL, [CEM] Rev. James Doherty.
Res.: 315 W. Broadway, P.O. Box 9, 49682. Tel: 231-271-3744; Fax: 231-271-3733.
Church: 104 S. Elm St., 49682.
Catechesis/Religious Program—Mary Mills, D.R.E. Students 32.

TAWAS CITY, IOSCO CO., IMMACULATE HEART OF MARY, Merged with St. Joseph, East Tawas to form Holy Family, East Tawas.

TRAVERSE CITY, GRAND TRAVERSE CO.

1—ST. FRANCIS OF ASSISI Rev. Kenneth R. Stachnik.
Res.: 1025 S. Union St., 49684. Tel: 231-947-4620; Fax: 231-947-4693. Email: ann@sfparish.org. Web: www.sfparish.org.
Catechesis/Religious Program—Beth Hicks, D.R.E. Students 225.

2—IMMACULATE CONCEPTION Revs. Anthony M. Citro; James P. Hayden (Retired); Deacon Jim Krupka.
Res.: 720 W. Second, 49684. Tel: 231-946-4211; Fax: 231-946-0567. Email: office@immaculatetc.org.
Catechesis/Religious Program—Tel: 231-946-2782. Fred Robb, D.R.E. Students 122.

3—ST. PATRICK Rev. Donald R. Geyman.
Res.: 630 W. Silver Lake Rd. S., 49685. Tel: 231-943-4633; Fax: 231-943-8886. Email: stpattc@stpatricktc.org. Web: www.stpatricktc.org.
Catechesis/Religious Program—Students 89.

VANDERBILT, OTSEGO CO., HOLY REDEEMER Revs. James M. Bearss; Polycarp P. Mblarawa.
Res. & Mailing: 606 N. Ohio Ave., 49735-1999. Tel: 989-732-5448; Fax: 989-705-3585.
Church: 8075 Lincoln St., 49795.
Catechesis/Religious Program—Students 20.

WEST BRANCH, OGEMAW CO., ST. JOSEPH, [CEM] Rev. T. Patrick Maher.
Mailing Address: 961 W. Houghton Ave., 48661. Tel: 989-345-0064; Fax: 989-345-8757. Email: stjoseph@m33access.com. Web: www.stjosephwestbranch.org.
Res.: 907 W. Houghton Ave., 48661. Tel: 989-343-9818.
School—(Grades K-8), 935 W. Houghton Ave., 48661. Tel: 989-345-0220; Fax: 989-345-3030. Katie Nimcheski, Prin. Students 159.
Catechesis/Religious Program—Tel: 989-345-0670. Students 35.

WHITTEMORE, IOSCO CO., ST. JAMES, [CEM] Rev. Charles G. Donajkowski, Temp. Admin.
Res.: P.O. Box 206, 48770. Tel: 989-756-2591; Fax: 989-756-3255.
Church: 202 E. Sherman, 48770.

Special Assignment:
Revs.—
Deka, Robbie, Diocese of Honolulu
Gallagher, Daniel B., Secretariat of State Office, Rome
Greene, John C.
Zielinski, Chad W., Military Service

Retired:
Revs.—
Bereda, Stanislaw J., 1180 Barepoint Rd., Alpena, 49707.
Boks, Lawrence E., 5853 Nancy Ct., Tawas City, 48763.
Brucksch, James L., 10208 Tennesse St., Oscoda, 48750.

Dominiak, Thomas M., 7150 Tuscarora Cir., Indian River, 49749.

Fox, Gabriel, 5020 Park Lake Dr., Pinellas Park, FL 33782.

Franczek, J. August, c/o 611 W. North St., 49735-8349.

Gietzen, Albin J., P.O. Box 311, Buckley, 49620.

Hannon, Richard T., 61 Augur Rd. Ext., Northford, CT 06472.

Hayden, James P., 13071 Beechwood Dr., Charlevoix, 49720.

Kelleher, Lawrence A., Senior Clergy Village, 14469-A Levan Rd., Livonia, 48154-5094.

Kosterman, Richard A., P.O. Box 613, Antigo, WI 54409.

Ladd, John O., 3069 E. Snover Rd., Mayville, 48744.

Mulka, Arthur C., 2388 Emmett, Alpena, 49707.

Mulka, Raymond C., 300 Washington, Alpena, 49707.

Nalley, Robert W., 2878 Wild Juniper Tr., Traverse City, 49686.

Partridge, Francis C., P.O. Box 84, Conway, 49722.

Reitz, Joseph A., 52 Marble Rd., Lowell, 49331.

Seifferly, Richard R., P.O. Box 422, West Branch, 48661-0422.

Sitar, Richard T., 12039 Leer Rd., Posen, 49776.

Suchocki, James A., 7525 N.W. Second Ave., Miami, FL 33150.

Thome, Edwin A., 6844 Deepwater Point Rd., Acme, 49610.

Permanent Deacons:

Ashmore, John

Barton, James, St. Ann, Cadillac

Bousamra, Thomas, (Retired)

Duggan, Dennis, St. Francis, Petoskey

Falicki, John, Christ the King, Acme

Fifer, Paul, St. Francis Xavier, Petoskey

Friend, Harry, St. Philip, Empire

Goetz, Robert, (Unassigned)

Goodhue, Harold

Hoenscheid, Rene, St. Patrick, Traverse City

Krupka, Jim, St. Joseph of Mapleton, Traverse City

LoVetere, Arthur, Jesus the Good Shepherd, Atlanta

Lyberg, Matthew, Christ the King, Acme

Moeggenberg, John, (Retired), (Outside of Diocese)

Nelson, Joseph B., (Retired)

Painter, Glen, Holy Family, Klacking Creek

Riley, Charles, St. Francis of Assisi, Traverse City

Trapp, Richard, (Retired)

Wallace, John, (Retired)

Wendell, Max, (Unassigned)

Wigton, Douglas, Holy Rosary, Cedar

INSTITUTIONS LOCATED IN THE DIOCESE

[A] INTERPAROCHIAL SCHOOLS

MANISTEE. *Manistee Catholic Central School*, (Grades PreK-12), 1200 U.S. 31 S., 49660. Tel: 231-723-2529; Fax: 231-723-0669. Web: www.manisteecatholiccentral.com. Jan Bigalke, Prin.; Ed Kolanowski, Asst. Prin. Lay Teachers 15; Students 233.

TRAVERSE CITY. *St. Elizabeth Ann Seton Middle School*, (Grades 6-8), 1601 Three Mile Rd. N., 49696. Tel: 231-932-4810; Fax: 231-932-4814. Web: www.gtacs.org. Lori Phillips, Prin.; Donna Grayson, Librarian. Lay Teachers 13; Students 256.

St. Francis High School, 123 E. 11th St., 49684. Tel: 231-946-8038; Fax: 231-946-1878. Email: echitt@gtacs.org. Web: www.gtacs.org. Erick Chittle, Prin.; Amy West, Librarian. Lay Teachers 20; Students 303.

Grand Traverse Area Catholic Schools, (Grades PreK-12), 123 E. 11th St., 49684. Tel: 231-946-8100; Fax: 231-946-1878. Web: www.gtacs.org. Michael R. Buell, Supt.; Erick Chittle, Prin.; Amy West, Librarian. Lay Teachers 62; Students 983.

Holy Angels Elementary, (Grades PreK-2), 130 E. 10th, 49684. Tel: 231-946-5961; Fax: 231-946-1878. Web: www.gtacs.org. Janet M. Troppman, Prin.; Shannon Robertson, Librarian; Donna Grayson, Librarian. Lay Teachers 12; Students 231.

Immaculate Conception Elementary School, (Grades 3-5), 218 Vine St., 49684. Tel: 231-947-1252; Fax: 231-947-2508. Web: www.gtacs.org. Matt Bauman, Prin.; Margaret Wilson, Librarian. Lay Teachers 15; Students 223.

[B] PAROCHIAL SCHOOLS

GAYLORD. *St. Mary Cathedral School*, (Grades PreSchool-12), 321 N. Otsego Ave., 49735. Tel: 989-732-5801; Fax: 989-732-2085. Cynthia Pineda, Prin. Lay Teachers 25; Students 319.

ALPENA. *All Saints Catholic School*, (Grades PreK-7), (Consolidation of St. Anne Elementary, Alpena and St. Mary Elementary, Alpena), 500 N. Second Ave., 49707. Tel: 989-354-4911; Fax: 989-354-3752. Email: nhatch@alpenaallsaints.org. Web: alpenaallsaints.org. Nicole M. Hatch, Prin. Lay Teachers 5; Students 84; PreK Students 18.

CADILLAC. *St. Ann Elementary*, (Grades PreK-7), 800 W. 13th, 49601. Tel: 231-775-1301; Fax: 231-775-5433. Web: www.stanncadillac.org. Robert Kellogg, Prin. Lay Teachers 9; Students 190; PreK Students 40.

CHARLEVOIX. *St. Mary Elementary*, (Grades PreK-6), 1005 Bridge St., 49720. Tel: 231-547-9441; Fax: 231-547-6658. Email: mjoy@stmaryschoolchx.com. Web: www.stmaryschoolcharlevoix.com. Nancy Philp, Prin. Lay Teachers 8; Students 68; PreK Students 16.

CHEBOYGAN. *Bishop Baraga Catholic School*, (Grades PreK-6), 623 W. Lincoln Ave., 49721. Tel: 231-627-5608; Fax: 231-627-6048. Email: klablance@bishopbaraga.com. Web: www.bishopbaraga.com. Kitty LaBlance, Prin. Lay Teachers 7; Students 145.

EAST TAWAS. *Holy Family Elementary School*, (Grades K-7), 411 N. Wilkinson, 48730. Tel: 989-362-5651; Fax: 989-362-6916. Email: principal@holyfamilyschool.biz. Linda Howe, Prin. Lay Teachers 6; Students 78.

KINGSLEY. *St. Mary - Hannah School*, (Grades PreK-6), 2912 M-113, 49649. Tel: 231-263-5288; Fax: 231-263-5288. Email: smh.school@inbox.com. Lisa Medina, Prin. Lay Teachers 4; Students 85.

LAKE LEELANAU. *St. Mary School*, (Grades PreK-12), 303 S. St. Mary St., 49653. Tel: 231-256-9636; Fax: 231-256-7239. Web: www.stmarysll.org. P.O. Box 340, 49653. Megan Glynn, Prin.; Donna Allington, Librarian. Lay Teachers 19; Students 192; PreK Students 21.

PETOSKEY. *St. Francis Xavier*, (Grades K-8), 414 Michigan, 49770. Tel: 231-347-3651; Fax: 231-348-6475. Web: www.petoskeystfrancis.com. Phyllis Daily, Prin.; Rebecca Wimmer, Librarian. Lay Teachers 16; Students 196.

PRUDENVILLE. *Our Lady of the Lake*, (Grades PreK-8), 1039 W. Houghton Lake Dr., P.O. Box 800, 48651. Tel: 989-366-5592; Fax: 989-366-1348. Email: olotlschool@gmail.com. Mary K. Murphy, Prin.; Mary Walker, Librarian. Lay Teachers 4; Students 45; PreK Students 43.

ROGERS CITY. *St. Ignatius*, (Grades 1-8), 545 S. Third, 49779. Tel: 989-734-3443; Fax: 989-734-3443. Web: www.stignatiusparishschool.com. Amy Rabeau, Prin.; Donna Dubbs, Librarian. Sisters 1; Lay Teachers 5; Students 74.

WEST BRANCH. *St. Joseph*, (Grades K-8), 935 W. Houghton Ave., 48661. Tel: 989-345-0220; Fax: 989-345-3030. Web: www.wbstjoseph.com. Katie Nimcheski, Prin.; Traci Hintz, Librarian. Lay Teachers 9; Students 163.

[C] GENERAL HOSPITALS

CADILLAC. *Mercy Hospital* Mercy Health Services North, Ministry Organization of Trinity Health, Novi, MI, 400 Hobart St., 49601. Tel: 231-876-7200; Fax: 231-876-7439. Email: mercycadillac@trinity-health.org. Web: www.mercycadillac.com. Mr. John L. MacLeod, CEO. Bed Capacity 97; Total Staff 611; Patients Assisted Annually 106,695.

GRAYLING. *Mercy Hospital*, 1100 E. Michigan Ave., 49738. Tel: 989-348-5461; Fax: 989-348-0477. Email: lking1@trinity-health.org. Stephanie J. Riemer-Matuzak, CEO; Lorelei King, Mission Leader. Member Organization of Trinity Health. Acute Care 90; Continued Care Nursing Unit 39; Total Staff 574; Patients Assisted Annually 140,320.

TAWAS CITY. *St. Joseph Health System*, 200 Hemlock, P.O. Box 659, 48764-0659. Tel: 989-362-3411; 989-362-4611; Fax: 989-362-7277. Email: shelleyburesh@sjhsys.org. Web: www.sjhsys.org. Ann M. Balfour, Pres.; Michael Sullivan, Chap. & Mgr. Spiritual Care. Associated with Ascension Health, St. Louis, MO. Congregation of St. Joseph (Nazareth, MI) 2; Bed Capacity 49; Total Staff 566; Patients Assisted Annually 200,000.

[D] CONVENTS AND RESIDENCES FOR SISTERS

CONWAY. *Sacramentine Monastery of Perpetual Adoration*, P.O. Box 86, 49722-0086. Tel: 231-347-0447. Sr. Mary Rosalie, O.S.S., Prioress. Sacamentine Sisters 2.

TRAVERSE CITY. *Infant Jesus of Prague Monastery*, 3501 Silver Lake Rd., 49684-8949. Tel: 231-946-4960; Fax: 231-947-7729. Web: www.carmelitenunsstjoseph.org. Sr. Mary of Jesus Markey, O.C.D. Carmelite Nuns 4; In Formation 2.

[E] RETREAT CENTERS AND CAMPS

GAYLORD. *Camp Sancta Maria*, P.O. Box 338, 49734. Tel: 231-546-3878; Fax: 866-875-1933. Email: office@campsanctamaria.org. Web: www.campsanctamaria.org. Michael Hickey, Exec. Dir.; Andrew Dawson, Contact Person. Total Staff 50; Campers 555.

CONWAY. *Augustine Center*, P.O. Box 84, 49722-0084. Tel: 231-347-3657; Fax: 231-347-9502. Email: augustinecenter@gmail.com. Sr. Barbara Hubeny, O.P., Dir.

[F] CATHOLIC SOCIAL SERVICE AGENCIES

GAYLORD. *Catholic Human Services*, 611 W. North St., 49735. Tel: 989-732-5147; Fax: 989-705-3589. Email: chstraverse@catholichumanservices.org. Web: www.catholichumanservices.org. Mr. David Martin, Pres. & CEO.

Area Offices:

154 S. Ripley Blvd., Alpena, 49707. Tel: 989-356-6385; Fax: 989-356-4909. Email: chsalpena@catholichumanservices.org. Web: www-.catholichumanservices.org. Joseph Garant, Admin.

421 S. Mitchell, Cadillac, 49601. Tel: 231-775-6581; Fax: 231-775-5421. Email: chscadillac@catholichumanservices.org. Web: www-.catholichumanservices.org. Mr. David Martin, Admin.

2090 W. M-32, 49735. Tel: 989-732-6761; Fax: 989-732-6763. Email: chsgaylord@catholichumanservices.org. Web: www-.catholichumanservices.org. Nancy Morgridge, Admin.

1000 Hastings St., Traverse City, 49686. Tel: 231-947-8110; Fax: 231-947-3522. Email: chstraverse@catholichumanservices.org. Web: www.catholichumanservices.org. Mr. David Martin, Admin.

[G] MISCELLANEOUS

GAYLORD. *Northern Michigan Catholic Foundation, Inc.*, 611 W. North St., 49735. Tel: 989-732-5147; Fax: 989-705-3589. Email: dparish@dioceseofgaylord.org. Joel Myler, Pres.; Brian Bartosh, Vice Pres.; Jean Stevenson, Sec.; Kim Smith, Treas.; Most Rev. Bernard A. Hebda, J.C.L., J.D.

ALPENA. *Madonna House Apostolate*, 309 Lockwood, 49707-2543. Tel: 989-354-4073. Rosemary Horan, Dir.

HARBOR SPRINGS. *Christ Child Society of Northern Michigan, Inc.*, P.O. Box 132, 49740-0132. Tel: 231-526-7271. Deborah L. Dicken, Pres.

INDIAN RIVER. **Baraga Broadcasting, Inc.*, 7119 W. M-68, P.O. Box 1109, 49749. Tel: 231-238-0811; Fax: 231-238-0803.

JOHANNESBURG. *Stella Maris Hermitage*, 19920 Black River Rd., 49751-9645. Tel: 989-732-9580. Email: rwkropf@stellamar.net. Web: www.stellamar.net. Rev. Richard Kropf.

TAWAS CITY. *House of the Holy Shroud*, 2922 W. M-55, 48763. Tel: 989-305-6236. Bro. Michael W. Whitman, Facilitator.

TRAVERSE CITY. *Respect Life of the Diocese of Gaylord, Michigan*, 1028 Hannah Dr., Ste. D, 49686. Tel: 231-946-7360; Fax: 231-929-4775. Web: www.respectlifegaylord.com. Doug Wigton, Registered Agent.

RELIGIOUS INSTITUTES OF MEN REPRESENTED IN THE DIOCESE

For further details refer to the corresponding bracketed number in the Religious Institutes of Men or Women section.

[0520]—*Franciscan Friars* (Assumption, Sacred Heart Provs.)—O.F.M.

[0690]—*Jesuit Fathers & Brothers* (Detroit Prov.)—S.J.

RELIGIOUS INSTITUTES OF WOMEN REPRESENTED IN THE DIOCESE

[3832]—*Congregation of the Sisters of St. Joseph*—C.S.J.

[0420]—*Discalced Carmelite Nuns*—O.C.D.

[1070]—*Dominican Sisters*—O.P.

[2580]—*Institute of the Sisters of Mercy of the Americas*—R.S.M.

[3490]—*Sacramentine Nuns*—O.S.S.

[3560]—*Servants of Jesus*—S.J.
[3590]—*Servants of Mary*—O.S.M.
[]—*Sisters for Christian Community*—S.F.C.C.
[3830]—*Sisters of St. Joseph*—S.S.J.
[]—*Sisters of St. Francis*—O.S.F

NECROLOGY

† Harnish, Lionel A., (Retired)—Died June 10, 2011

An asterisk (*) denotes an organization that has established tax-exempt status directly with the IRS and is not covered by the USCCB Group Ruling.

Diocese of Grand Island

(Dioecesis Insulae Grandis)

Most Reverend

WILLIAM J. DENDINGER, D.D., M.A.

Bishop of Grand Island; ordained May 29, 1965; appointed Bishop of Grand Island October 14, 2004; ordained December 13, 2004. *Mailing Address: P.O. Box 1531, Grand Island, NE 68802.* Tel: 308-382-6565; Fax: 308-382-6569.

Chancery Office: 2708 Old Fair Rd., P.O. Box 996, Grand Island, NE 68802. Tel: 308-382-6565; Fax: 308-382-6569.

Square Miles 40,000.

Erected at Kearney, March 8, 1912; See Transferred to Grand Island, April 11, 1917.

Comprises the Counties of Arthur, Banner, Blaine, Box Butte, Brown, Buffalo, Cherry, Cheyenne, Custer, Dawes, Deuel, Garden, Garfield, Grant, Greeley, Hooker, Howard Keyapaha, Kimball, Logan, Loup, McPherson, Morrill, Rock, Scotts Bluff, Sheridan, Sherman, Wheeler, Sioux, Thomas, Valley, and those portions of Dawson, Hall, Lincoln and Keith lying north of the South Platte River in the State of Nebraska.

For legal titles of parishes and diocesan institutions, consult the Chancery Office.

STATISTICAL OVERVIEW

Personnel	
Bishop	1
Priests: Diocesan Active in Diocese	36
Priests: Diocesan Active Outside Diocese	2
Priests: Retired, Sick or Absent	26
Number of Diocesan Priests	64
Total Priests in Diocese	64
Extern Priests in Diocese	8
Ordinations:	
Diocesan Priests	1
Permanent Deacons	1
Permanent Deacons in Diocese	6
Total Sisters	62
Parishes	
Parishes	36
With Resident Pastor:	
Resident Diocesan Priests	30
Resident Religious Priests	5
Without Resident Pastor:	
Administered by Priests	1
Missions	33
Professional Ministry Personnel:	
Sisters	14
Lay Ministers	28
Welfare	
Health Care Centers	2
Total Assisted	184,550
Homes for the Aged	1
Total Assisted	50
Educational	
Diocesan Students in Other Seminaries	6
Total Seminarians	6
High Schools, Diocesan and Parish	4
Total Students	505
Elementary Schools, Diocesan and Parish	6
Total Students	1,071
Catechesis/Religious Education:	
High School Students	2,046
Elementary Students	3,662
Total Students under Catholic Instruction	7,290
Teachers in the Diocese:	
Sisters	2
Lay Teachers	117
Vital Statistics	
Receptions into the Church:	
Infant Baptism Totals	835
Minor Baptism Totals	79
Adult Baptism Totals	71
Received into Full Communion	132
First Communions	851
Confirmations	665
Marriages:	
Catholic	173
Interfaith	102
Total Marriages	275
Deaths	508
Total Catholic Population	50,021
Total Population	307,587

Former Bishops—Most Revs. JAMES ALBERT DUFFY, D.D., cons. April 16, 1913; resigned See, May 7, 1931; appt. Titular Bishop of Silando; died Feb. 12, 1968; STANISLAUS V. BONA, D.D., appt. Bishop of Grand Island, Dec. 18, 1931; cons. Feb. 25, 1932; appt. Coadjutor Bishop of Green Bay and Titular Bishop of Mela, Dec. 2, 1944; succeeded to See, March 3, 1945; died Dec. 1, 1967; EDWARD J. HUNKELER, D.D., ord. June 14, 1919; appt. March 10, 1945; cons. May 1, 1945; transferred to Kansas City in Kansas, March 31, 1951; died Oct. 1, 1970; JOHN L. PASCHANG, D.D., Ph.D., J.C.D., ord. June 12, 1921; appt. July 28, 1951; cons. Oct. 9, 1951; resigned July 25, 1972; died March 21, 1999; JOHN J. SULLIVAN, D.D., ord. Sept. 23, 1944; appt. July 25, 1972; cons. Sept. 19, 1972; transferred to Kansas City-St. Joseph in Missouri, Aug. 17, 1977; died Feb. 11, 2001; LAWRENCE J. MCNAMARA, D.D., S.T.L., ord. May 30, 1953; appt. Jan. 10, 1978; cons. March 28, 1978; retired Oct. 14, 2004; died Dec. 17, 2004.

Vicar General—Very Rev. CHARLES L. TORPEY, S.T.L., J.C.L., St. Leo, 2410 S. Blaine, Grand Island, 68801. Tel: 308-382-4753.

Chancery Office—2708 Old Fair Rd., P.O. Box 996, Grand Island, 68802. Tel: 308-382-6565; Fax: 308-382-6569. Office Hours: 8-4:30.

Chancellor—KATHLEEN M. HAHN, J.C.L.

Vice Chancellor—Sr. MARGARET A. PROSKOVEC, N.D.

Diocesan Tribunal—Mailing Address: P.O. Box 5405, Grand Island, 68802. Tel: 308-382-6364.

Vicar-Judicial—Rev. MICHAEL F. MCDERMOTT, J.C.L.

Adjutant Vicars-Judicial—Rev. RICHARD L. PIONTKOWSKI JR., S.T.L., J.C.D.; Very Rev. CHARLES L. TORPEY, S.T.L., J.C.L.

Defender of the Bond—Rev. THOMAS A. RYAN.

Promoter Justitiae—Rev. PATRICK C. HARRISON, J.C.L.

Judges—Very Rev. CHARLES L. TORPEY, S.T.L., J.C.L.; Revs. RICHARD L. PIONTKOWSKI JR., S.T.L., J.C.D.; MICHAEL F. MCDERMOTT, J.C.L.

Procurator—Rev. JAMES M. HUNT.

Advocates—Rev. JAMES M. HUNT; CONNIE RUHLMAN; KATHLEEN M. HAHN, J.C.L.

Associate Director-Notary—MARIE RYAN.

Diocesan Consultors—Revs. DONALD A. BUHRMAN; LOUIS A. NOLLETTE; PAUL J. COLLING; JOSEPH A. HANNAPPEL; JAMES E. NOVAKOWSKI; RICHARD L. PIONTKOWSKI JR., S.T.L., J.C.D.; MICHAEL F. MCDERMOTT, J.C.L.; Very Rev. CHARLES L. TORPEY, S.T.L., J.C.L.; Rev. MARTIN L. EGGING.

Vicar for Religious Communities of Women—VACANT.

Diocesan Offices and Directors

Charismatic Renewal—Rev. HAROLD R. KURTENBACH, Dir. (Retired), 2647 Brennen Lane, Grand Island, 68803.

Charities—Rev. CHRISTOPHER KUBAT, Dir., Catholic Social Svcs., 515 W. 3rd St., Hastings, 68901. Tel: 402-463-2112.

Communications—Most Rev. WILLIAM J. DENDINGER, D.D., M.A., Dir.

Ongoing Formation for Clergy and Liturgy—Revs. JAMES R. GOLKA, Mailing Address: P.O. Box 399, North Platte, 69103. Tel: 308-532-0942; LOUIS A. NOLLETTE, 1104 Cheyenne Ave., Alliance, 69301. Tel: 308-762-2009.

Council of Catholic Women, Diocesan—Rev. STEPHEN F. DEAVER, Diocesan Moderator (Retired).

Hispanic Ministry—Rev. PAUL J. COLLING, Vicar, Mailing Address: P.O. Box 578, Lexington, 68850. Tel: 308-324-4647; Sr. M. VERONICA RIVAS, M.C.D.P., Dir., 1225 S. Poplar, North Platte, 69101. Tel: 308-532-2707.

Newspaper— "The West Nebraska Register" MARY PARLIN, Editor; COLLEEN GALLION, Assoc. Editor, Address all correspondence to: P.O. Box 608, Grand Island, 68802. Tel: 308-382-4660; Fax: 308-382-6569.

Personnel Board—Revs. DONALD A. BUHRMAN; MATTHEW J. KOPERSKI; JOSEPH A. HANNAPPEL; JAMES R. GOLKA; JAMES H. HEITHOFF; JAMES E. NOVAKOWSKI; BRYAN D. ERNEST.

Priests' Advisory Board (Presbyteral Council)—Revs. MICHAEL F. MCDERMOTT, J.C.L.; VINCENT L. PARSONS; BRYAN D. ERNEST; RAYMOND M. KOSMICKI; NEAL P. NOLLETTE; JAMES M. HUNT; PAUL J. COLLING; ANTONY THEKKEKARA; Very Rev. CHARLES L. TORPEY, S.T.L., J.C.L.

Catholic Relief Services—Most Rev. WILLIAM J. DENDINGER, D.D., M.A., Dir.

Priests' Pension and Welfare Board— Address all mail to: Rev. LAWRENCE W. COULTER (Retired), Mailing Address: 1301 S. "D" St., Broken Bow, 68822.

Propagation of the Faith—Rev. MICHAEL D. MCDONALD, Dir., 2407 56th St., Kearney, 68845. Tel: 308-236-9171.

Religious Education—DONALD KURRE, Dir., 1225 S. Poplar, North Platte, 69101. Tel: 308-532-2707.

Rural Life Conference—Rev. NEAL P. NOLLETTE, Dir., Mailing Address: P.O. Box 586, Chappell, 69129.

Schools—Rev. THOMAS A. RYAN, Diocesan Supt. of Schools, 2708 Old Fair Rd., P.O. Box 996, Grand Island, 68802. Tel: 308-682-6565; Fax: 308-382-6569.

Vocations—Rev. MATTHEW J. KOPERSKI, Dir., P.O. Box 1024, Kearney, 68848. Tel: 308-234-1539.

Youth & Young Adult—EMILY WYATT, Dir., 1225 S. Poplar, North Platte, 69101. Tel: 308-532-2707.

CEC (Catholics Encounter Christ)—Rev. PAUL J. COLLING, Spiritual Dir., Mailing Address: P.O. Box 578, Lexington, 68850.

Community Mental Health—Rev. MICHAEL F. MCDERMOTT, J.C.L., Mailing Address: P.O. Box 996, Grand Island, 68802.

Victim Assistance Coordinators—Grand Island: ELIZABETH HEIDT, Ph.D. Tel: 308-379-1949. Email: cpo@gidiocese.org; AILEEN D. GRUENDEL, Ph.D. Tel: 308-381-2233. Email: gruendel@hamilton.net. Ravenna: CHERYL ALBRIGHT, M.S. Tel: 308-440-7644. Email: calbright@gidiocese.org. Scottsbluff: MATTHEW HUTT, Ph.D. Tel: 308-632-8080; ANNE TALBOT, Ph.D. Tel: 308-632-8547; OLIVIA GONZALEZ, DAC. Tel: 308-635-3181.

Office of Child Protection—ELIZABETH HEIDT, Ph.D., Dir.; CHERYL ALBRIGHT, M.S., Outreach Coord., Mailing Address: P.O. Box 1531, Grand Island, 68802. Tel: 308-382-6565; Fax: 308-382-6569.

Email: cpo@gidiocese.org.

Office of Planning and Lay Ministry—MICHAEL S. DAVIS, Dir., 1225 S. Poplar #100, North Platte, 69101.

CLERGY, PARISHES, MISSIONS AND PAROCHIAL SCHOOLS

CITY OF GRAND ISLAND

(HALL COUNTY)

1—CATHEDRAL OF THE NATIVITY OF THE BLESSED VIRGIN MARY (1864) Revs. Richard L. Piontkowski Jr.; Jonathan D. Sorensen; Deacons John Farlee; Randy Lewandowski; Frank Moreno; Robert Puhalla.
Res.: 207 S. Elm St., 68801. Tel: 308-384-2523; Fax: 308-384-2527. Email: office@stmarysgi.com.
Catechesis / Religious Program—112 S. Cedar, 68801. Tel: 308-382-1198. Esther Gomez, D.R.E.; Sr. Isabel Sandino, O.Carm., Adult Formation. Students 394.

2—BLESSED SACRAMENT (1949) Revs. Todd K. Philipsen; Joseph K. Joseph; Deacon Charles Cantrell; Sr. Clarice Korger, O.S.B., Pastoral Min.
Res.: 1724 N. Walnut, 68801. Tel: 308-381-1361.
Church: 518 W. State St., 68801. Tel: 308-384-0532; Fax: 308-384-0424. Email: bscc_1@msn.com. Web: blsachurch.net.
Catechesis / Religious Program—518 W. State St., 68801. Tel: 308-395-8521. Ms. Debra Wetzel, D.R.E. Students 345.

3—ST. LEO (1972) Very Rev. Charles L. Torpey; Sr. Mary Margaret McGowen, Pastoral Min.
Church: 2410 S. Blaine, 68801. Tel: 308-382-4753.
Catechesis / Religious Program—Jodi Stauffer, D.R.E. Students 211.

4—RESURRECTION (1973) Rev. Michael F. McDermott.
Res.: 4110 Cannon Rd., 68803. Tel: 308-382-8644; Fax: 308-382-1845.
Catechesis / Religious Program—Tel: 308-382-0976. Therese Stump, D.R.E.; Michalene Iverson, Youth Dir. Students 235.

OUTSIDE THE CITY OF GRAND ISLAND

AINSWORTH, BROWN CO., ST. PIUS X (1955) Rev. James H. Heithoff.
Res.: P.O. Box 7, 69210. Tel: 402-387-1275. Email: stpiusxne@msn.com.
Catechesis / Religious Program—Tel: 402-387-2260. Jessica Pozehl, D.R.E. Students 95.
Mission—Holy Cross Bassett, Rock Co. Tel: 402-684-3640.

ALLIANCE, BOX BUTTE CO., HOLY ROSARY (1894) [CEM] Rev. Louis A. Nollette.
Parish Offices—1104 Cheyenne Ave., 69301. Tel: 308-762-2009; Fax: 308-762-7474.
Res.: 916 Cheyenne Ave., 69301. Tel: 308-762-1418.
School—St. Agnes Academy, (Grades PreSchool-8) Tel: 308-762-2315. Email: saasecretary@stagnesacademy.com. Web: www.stagnesacademy.com. Doyle Christensen, Prin. Lay Teachers 12; Students 132; Preschool 13.
Catechesis / Religious Program—Tel: 308-762-2830. Email: faithformation@bbc.net. Web: www.2bcatholic.org. Noreen Placek, D.R.E.; Ralph Yeager, Youth Min. Students 109.
Mission—St. Bridget (1888) 801 Niobrara Ave., P.O. Box 67, Hemingford, Box Butte Co. 69348. Tel: 308-487-3617; Fax: 308-487-3608. Email: stbridget@bbc.net. Sr. Sarah Manchester, O.S.F., Pastoral Min.
Catechesis / Religious Program—Students 53.

BRIDGEPORT, MORRILL CO., ALL SOULS (1919) [CEM] Rev. David L. Rykwalder.
Res.: 702 P St., P.O. Box 250, 69336-0250. Tel: 308-262-1332; Fax: 308-262-0709.
Catechesis / Religious Program— Colleen Cruise, D.R.E.; Mary Asmus, D.R.E.; Paula Contraras, D.R.E. Students 106.
Mission—St. Mary P.O. Box 346, Dalton, Cheyenne Co. 69131-0346. Tel: 308-377-2440.
Mission—Sacred Heart P.O. Box 190, Bayard, Morrill Co. 69334-0190. Tel: 308-586-1160.

BROKEN BOW, CUSTER CO., ST. JOSEPH'S (1888) [CEM] Rev. James M. Hunt.
Mailing Address: P.O. Box 405, 68822. Tel: 308-872-5809 (Office); Fax: 308-872-5809.
Res.: 1407 S. E St., 68822. Tel: 308-872-5716; Fax: 308-872-5809.
Catechesis / Religious Program— Rashelle Ryan, D.R.E. Students 117.
Mission—St. Anselm's [CEM 2] Anselmo, Custer Co.
Catechesis / Religious Program— Connie Chandler, D.R.E. (Grades P-12). Students 47.
Mission—Assumption of the Blessed Virgin Mary Sargent, Cluster Co.
Catechesis / Religious Program—Laura Kipp, D.R.E. Students 45.

CHADRON, DAWES CO., ST. PATRICK'S (1886) [CEM] Rev. Timothy L. Stoner.
Office: 340 Cedar St., P.O. Box 231, 69337. Tel: 308-432-2626; Fax: 308-432-4969. Email: stpats@chadronstpatricks.org.
Catechesis / Religious Program—Tel: 308-432-2161. Linda Yeradi, D.R.E.; Terri Connealy, Youth Min. Students 121.

CHAPPELL, DEUEL CO., ST. JOSEPH'S (1909) [CEM] Rev. Neal P. Nollette.
Res.: 1049 2nd St., P.O. Box 586, 69129. Tel: 308-874-3221. Email: joelizgal@embarqmail.com.
Catechesis / Religious Program—Students 26.
Mission—St. Elizabeth 300 W. 4th, P.O. Box 586, Oshkosh, Garden Co. 69154. Tel: 308-772-3221; Fax: 308-772-3221.
Catechesis / Religious Program—Tel: 308-722-3445. Students 16.
Mission—St. Gall 307 1st St., Lisco, Garden Co. 69148.

COZAD, DAWSON CO., CHRIST THE KING (1951), (Irish), Rev. Donald J. O'Brien.
Res.: 1220 Ave. M, 69130. Tel: 308-784-3959.
Catechesis / Religious Program—512 E. 19th. Tel: 308-784-2696. Donna Kolbo, D.R.E. Students 189.
Mission—Our Lady of Good Counsel 1915 Ave. J, Gothenburg, Dawson Co. 69138.

CRAWFORD, DAWES CO., ST. JOHN THE BAPTIST (1896), (German—Irish), [CEM 2] Rev. Bernard M. Berger.
Res.: 808 4th St., 69339. Tel: 308-665-1584. Email: stjohnscrawford@bbc.net.
Catechesis / Religious Program—Tel: 308-665-2240. Email: mhughes@bbc.net. Melany Hughes, D.R.E. Students 25.
Mission—Church of the Nativity of the Blessed Virgin Mary 426 Kate St., Harrison, Sioux Co. 69339.
Catechesis / Religious Program—Students 13.

ELM CREEK, BUFFALO CO., IMMACULATE CONCEPTION (1879) [CEM] Rev. Jose M. Chavez; Deacon William O'Donnell; Eileen Smith, Office Mgr.
Res.: 314 N. Church, 68836. Tel: 308-856-4375; Fax: 308-856-4017.
Church: P.O. Box 530, 68836.
Catechesis / Religious Program— Denise Ourada, D.R.E. Students 47.
Mission—Holy Rosary 503 D St., Overton, Dawson Co. 68863.
Catechesis / Religious Program—Sue Kizer, C.R.E. Students 37.
Mission—St. John Capistran 118 N. Ash, Amherst, Buffalo Co. 68812.
Catechesis / Religious Program—Angie Kenney, C.R.E. Students 44.

GERING, SCOTTS BLUFF CO., CHRIST THE KING (1958) Rev. Gerald J. Harr.
Res.: 1730 'N' St., P.O. Box 33, 69341. Tel: 308-436-4000; Fax: 308-436-2923.
Catechesis / Religious Program—P.O. Box 33, 69341. Tel: 308-436-2290. Micki Walker, D.R.E. & Dir. Youth Ministry. Students 240.

GORDON, SHERIDAN CO., ST. LEO'S (1887) [JC] Rev. James Joseph, S.D.B.
Res.: 228 N. Maverick, 69343. Tel: 308-282-0427.
Catechesis / Religious Program—Students 50.
Mission—Immaculate Conception 606 Church St., P.O. Box 279, Rushville, Sheridan Co. 69360. Tel: 308-327-2430.
Mission—St. Columbkille 545 N. Main, Hay Springs, Sheridan Co. 69347.

KEARNEY, BUFFALO CO.

1—ST. JAMES (1881) Revs. Joseph A. Hannappel; Joshua S. Brown; Mary Bowman, Adult Faith Formation.
Church Office: 3801 Ave. A, 68847. Tel: 308-234-5536.
Res.: 7 Sioux Ln., 68847. Tel: 308-233-5051.
High School—Kearney Catholic, (Grades 6-12), 110 E. 35th St. Tel: 308-234-2610; Fax: 308-234-4986. Mr. Terrence Torson, Admin.; Janet Anderson, Librarian. Lay Teachers 23; Students 301.
Catechesis / Religious Program—Tel: 308-234-9695; Fax: 308-234-9818. Deb Kratochvil, D.R.E.; Stephen Zimmer, Youth Min. Students 417.

2—PRINCE OF PEACE (1986) Rev. Michael D. McDonald; Sisters Mary Chamberlain, O.S.M., Pastoral Min.; Doris Durant, O.S.M., Pastoral Min.
Church: 2407 W. 56th St., 68845-4113. Tel: 308-236-9171. Email: popchurch@princeofpeacec.com.
Catechesis / Religious Program— Lynn Cooper, D.R.E. Students 355.

KIMBALL, KIMBALL CO., ST. JOSEPH'S (1921) Rev. Robert Karnish.
Mailing Address: P.O. Box 576, 69145.
Res.: 507 S. Howard, 69145. Tel: 308-235-2162.
Catechesis / Religious Program—Students 34.

LEXINGTON, DAWSON CO., ST. ANN'S (1883) [CEM] Revs. Paul J. Colling. Tel: 308-324-4648; Jorge Canela; Sr. Mary Ann Flax, C.S.J., Pastoral Min. Tel: 308-324-2450.
Res.: 303 E. 6th St., P.O. Box 578, 68850. Tel: 308-324-4648. Email: stanns@cozadtel.net.
Catechesis / Religious Program—St. Ann's Parish Center, 10th & Taft St., 68850. Tel: 308-324-4647; Fax: 308-324-5320. Linda Saiz, D.R.E. (Grades K-5); DeLinda Glaze, D.R.E. (Grades 6-12); Frances Peterson, Youth Dir. Students 500.

LOUP CITY, SHERMAN CO., ST. JOSAPHAT'S (1882), (Polish), Rev. Martin L. Egging.
Res.: 704 N. 9th St., P.O. Box 626, 68853. Tel: 308-745-0315. Email: josaphatsaint@yahoo.com.
Catechesis / Religious Program—Tel: 308-745-1235. Students 118.
Mission—St. Francis [CEM] Ashton, Sherman Co. 68817.
Catechesis / Religious Program—Loretta Halinsky, D.R.E. Students 38.
Mission—St. Gabriel Hazard, Sherman Co. 68844.
Catechesis / Religious Program—Heather Paitz, D.R.E. Students 31.

MITCHELL, SCOTTS BLUFF CO., ST. THERESA'S (1930) Revs. Anthony Madhichetti; Thomas Gudipalli.
Res.: 1715 17th St., 69357. Tel: 308-623-1745. Email: frsttheresa@embarqmail.com.
Catechesis / Religious Program—Tel: 308-623-2245. Students 75.
Mission—St. Ann Hwy. 26 & Walsh, Morrill, Scotts Bluff Co. 69358.
Mission—Sacred Heart 203 E. "O" St., Lyman, Scotts Bluff Co. 69352.

MULLEN, HOOKER CO., ST. MARY'S (1910) Rev. Joseph Kadaprayil, S.D.B.
Res.: 302 S. Blaine, P.O. Box 191, 69152. Tel: 308-546-2250.
Catechesis / Religious Program—Students 72.
Mission—All Saint's Hyannis, Grant Co. 69152.
Mission—St. Thomas of Canterbury Thedford, Thomas Co. 69152.

NORTH PLATTE, LINCOLN CO.

1—HOLY SPIRIT (1973) Revs. James E. Novakowski; Jerry P. Wetovick.
Res.: 2120 West C, P.O. Box 427, 69103. Tel: 308-534-4334; 308-534-6623 (Church).
Res.: 410 Poplar St., Sutherland, 69165.
Catechesis / Religious Program—Tel: 308-534-7906; Fax: 308-534-6525. Kathy Schroeder, D.R.E. Students 105.
Mission—Sacred Heart P.O. Box 398, Sutherland, Lincoln Co. 69165. Tel: 308-386-4300.
Catechesis / Religious Program—Kyleen Stokey, D.R.E. Students 94.

2—ST. PATRICK (1875) [CEM] Revs. James R. Golka; Mathew Thekkekara.
Res.: 415 N. Chestnut, P.O. Box 399, 69103. Tel: 308-532-0942; Fax: 308-532-0944. Email: office@st-pats-online.org. Web: www.st-pats-online.org.
School—McDaid Elementary, (Grades K-6), 1000 East E St., P.O. Box 970, 69101. Tel: 308-532-1874; Fax: 308-532-8015. Web: athena.esu16.org/~npcs/1npcsHome.html. Mr. Rick D. Elsasser, Prin.; Mary Ellis, Librarian. Lay Teachers 14; Students 218.
High School—(Grades 7-12), 500 S. Silber, 69101. Tel: 308-532-1874. *c/o North Platte Catholic Schools*, P.O. Box 970, 69103. Mark Skillstad, Prin.; Mr. Kevin Dodson, Supt. Lay Teachers 15; Students 214.
Catechesis / Religious Program—Tel: 308-532-6388, Ext. 203. Email: formation@st-pats-online.org; religioused@st-pats-online.org. Web: www.st-pats-online.org. Mary Wyatt, Dir. Faith Formation; Teresa Smith, C.R.E. Students 113.

OGALLALA, KEITH CO., ST. LUKE'S (1887) [JC] Rev. Bryan D. Ernest; Sr. Shirley Simmons, O.S.U., Pastoral Min. In Res., Rev. Loren G. Pohlmeier (Retired). Tel: 308-289-7885.
Res.: 417 E. Third, 69153. Tel: 308-284-3196; Fax: 308-284-3599. Email: stlukerectory@charter.net.
School—(Grades PreSchool-5), 406 E. 3rd St., 69153. Tel: 308-284-4841; Fax: 308-284-9839. Email: stlukesschool@charterinternet.com. Sr. Loretta Krajewski, O.S.U., Prin. Lay Teachers 4; Students 64.
St. Luke Catholic School Endowment—Office: 417 E. 3rd., 69153. Fax: 308-284-3599.
Catechesis / Religious Program—Tel: 308-520-4094. Lori Beckius, Faith Formation. Students 88.
Mission—St. Patrick's Church Paxton, Keith Co. 69155.

ORD, VALLEY CO., OUR LADY OF PERPETUAL HELP (1908) [CEM] Revs. Thomas A. Ryan; Mark Maresh.
Res.: 527 N. 19th St., P.O. Box 123, 68862. Tel: 308-728-3351; Fax: 308-728-3360.
School—(Grades K-8) Tel: 308-728-5389. Patricia Valasek, Prin., Head Teacher. Sisters 1; Lay Teachers 7; Students 52.
Catechesis / Religious Program—Sr. Lee Anne Danczak, S.J., D.R.E. Elem.; Julie Scott, D.R.E. High School. Students 114.
Mission—Sacred Heart Burwell, Garfield Co. 68823. Tel: 308-346-4190.

Catechesis/Religious Program—Betty Kovarik, D.R.E. Students 59.

RAVENNA, BUFFALO CO., OUR LADY OF LOURDES (1887), (German), Rev. Martin L. Egging; Sr. Paulette Kuta, Pastoral Min.
Res.: 515 Sicily Ave., Box 90, 68869. Tel: 308-452-3314; Fax: 308-452-9102. Email: ourladyoflourdes@nctc.net. Web: oll-Ravenna.com.
Catechesis/Religious Program—Joan Clifton, D.R.E. & Youth Min. Students 114.
Mission—St. Mary's [CEM] 406 Fair St., Rockville, Sherman Co. 68871.
Mission—St. Mary's (1909) [CEM] [JC] 504 N. Syracuse St., Box 134, Pleasanton, Buffalo Co. 68866. Tel: 308-388-2181.

ST. LIBORY, HOWARD CO., ST. LIBORY'S (1884) [CEM] Rev. Sidney B. Bruggeman.
Res.: 505 Spruce St., 68872. Tel: 308-687-6276; Fax: 308-687-6093.
Catechesis/Religious Program—Tel: 308-687-6273. Donna Placke, D.R.E. Students 86.

ST. PAUL, HOWARD CO., SS. PETER AND PAUL (1878) [JC] Rev. Raymond M. Kosmicki.
Res.: 1405 Custer St., 68873. Tel: 308-754-4649; Fax: 308-754-4002.
Catechesis/Religious Program—713 Elm St., 68873. Tel: 308-754-4002. Sandi Mudloff, Youth Min. Students 201.
Mission—St. Joseph 1803 Hwy. 11, Elba, Howard Co. 68838. Tel: 308-336-3323.
Catechesis/Religious Program—Cynthia Paczosa, D.R.E. Students 27.
Mission—St. Anthony of Padua (1877) [CEM 3] 103 Kearns Ave., Box 156, Farwell, Howard Co. 68838. Tel: 308-336-3323.
Catechesis/Religious Program—Tel: 308-754-3351. Kathy Gorecki, D.R.E. Tel: 308-336-3351; Shelly Wolinski, D.R.E. Tel: 308-863-2232. Students 37.

SCOTTSBLUFF, SCOTTS BLUFF CO.
1—ST. AGNES (1912) Rev. Vincent L. Parsons; Sr. Vera Meis, C.S.J., Pastoral Min.
Office: 2314 3rd Ave., P.O. Box 349, 69363. Tel: 308-632-2541; Fax: 308-632-2146. Email: office@st-agnes-church.com. Web: www.st-agnes-church.com.
Res.: 2201 2nd Ave., 69361.
School—(Grades K-5) Tel: 308-632-6918; Fax: 308-632-6943. Julie Brown, Prin. Lay Teachers 9; Students 113.
Catechesis/Religious Program—Email: dre@st-agnes-church.com. Terri Calvert, D.R.E. Students 205.
2—OUR LADY OF GUADALUPE (1955), (Hispanic), Rev. Phil Flott.
Res.: 1103 12th Ave., P.O. Box 2485, 69361. Tel: 308-632-2845; Fax: 308-632-7356. Email: olguadalupe@embarqmail.com.
Catechesis/Religious Program— Monica Longoria, D.R.E. (High School); Laura Lopez, D.R.E., Elementary; Paul Vostades, Asst. D.R.E. Students 137.

SIDNEY, CHEYENNE CO., ST. PATRICK'S (1878) [JC] Rev. Arthur A. Faesser; Sr. Marietta Spenner, O.S.F., Pastoral Assoc.
Res.: 1039 14th Ave., P.O. Box 99, 69162. Tel: 308-254-2828; Fax: 308-254-2830.
Catechesis/Religious Program— Sr. Marietta Spenner, O.S.F., D.R.E.; Pat Mertz, Youth Min. Students 170.

SPALDING, GREELEY CO., ST. MICHAEL'S (1887) [CEM 2] Rev. Donald A. Buhrman.
Res.: 150 E. Marguerite, P.O. Box 310, 68665. Tel: 308-497-2662.
School—Spalding Academy, (Grades K-12) Tel: 308-497-2103; Fax: 308-497-2105. Amy McKay, Prin. Lay Teachers 13; Students 90.
Catechesis/Religious Program—Maggie Smith, Dir. Faith Formation. Students 73.
Mission—St. Theresa of the Child Jesus Ericson, 68637.
Catechesis/Religious Program—Students 19.
Mission—Sacred Heart P.O. Box 99, Greeley, Greeley Co. 68842. Tel: 308-428-2855.
Catechesis/Religious Program—Students 78.

STAPLETON, LOGAN CO., ST. JOHN THE EVANGELIST (1913), (German), [CEM] Rev. Antony Thekkekara.
Res.: 304 H St., P.O. Box 309, 69163. Tel: 308-636-2421. Email: stjohnscatholic@hotmail.com.
Catechesis/Religious Program—Jane Haake, D.R.E. Students 41.
Mission—St. Agnes 503 N. Carroll, Arnold, Custer Co. 69163. Tel: 308-848-2442.
Catechesis/Religious Program—Aleta Ambler, D.R.E. Students 15.
Mission—St. Boniface 204 S. Morgan Ave., Callaway, Logan Co. 68825. Tel: 308-836-2606.
Catechesis/Religious Program—Marla Stallbaumer, D.R.E. Students 13.

VALENTINE, CHERRY CO., ST. NICHOLAS (1893) [JC] Rev. John Kakkuzhiyil, S.D.B.
Res.: P.O. Box 510, 69201. Tel: 402-376-1672. Email: stnicholas@shwisp.net.
Catechesis/Religious Program—Wanda Nielson, D.R.E.; Jessica McGinley, D.R.E. Students 108.
Mission—St. Mary [CEM] Nenzel, Cherry Co. 69201.

WOOD RIVER, HALL CO., ST. MARY'S (1884) [CEM] Rev. James J. Janovec.
Res.: P.O. Box 37, 68883. Tel: 308-583-2464. Email: stmary-sheart@hotmail.com.
Catechesis/Religious Program—Students 108.
Mission—Sacred Heart P.O. Box 190, Shelton, Buffalo Co. 68876. Tel: 308-647-5123.
Catechesis/Religious Program—Students 80.

Chaplains of Public Institutions

GRAND ISLAND. *Nebraska Veterans Home*. Vacant.
U.S. Veterans' Hospital. Rev. Sidney B. Bruggeman.

KEARNEY. *Youth Development Center*, W. Hwy. 30, 68847. Tel: 308-237-3181. Vacant.

Military Chaplains:
Rev.—
Borzych, Alexander J.

On Duty Outside the Diocese:
Rev.—
Hock, Neal J., Pontifical North American College Vatican City State.

Retired:
Revs.—
Bauer, Jacob F., 404 Woodland Dr., #208, 68801.
Chamberlain, Robert F., 1220 Estates Dr., Gering, 69341.
Coulter, Lawrence W., 1301 S. D St., Broken Bow, 68822.
Curran, Francis T., 4000 S. 56th St., Unit 105A, Lincoln, 68506.
Deaver, Stephen F., 615 W. 42nd St., Scottsbluff, 69361.
Dillon, Thomas J., 901 S. Bryan St., #A-8, North Platte, 69101.
Dowd, Thomas M., 6340 W. 38th Ave., #1002, Wheat Ridge, CO 80033.
Fenton, Lawrence E., 10351 Sprague St., Omaha, 68134.
Ferris, Carl A., 716 N. Main, Valentine, 69201.
Guevara, Miguel H., 333 Maple St., P.O. Box 307, Sutherland, 69165.
Krystosek, Robert H., Box 425, Clara City, MN 56222.
Kurtenbach, Harold R., 2647 Brennen Ln., 68803.
Larmore, Donald E., J.C.D., 4358 N. Rio Cancion #312, Tucson, AZ 85718.
Mullowney, Thomas E., 3915 Ave. H, 68847.
Murphy, James E., 82167 509th Ave., Spalding, 68665.
Nekoliczak, Ted A., 1516 E. 43rd St., 68848.
O'Kane, James D., 105 S. 9th St., #702, Omaha, 68102.
Pohlmeier, Loren G., 417 E. Third, Ogallala, 69153.
Pruss, Rodney Lee A., 15723 W. Amelia Dr., Goodyear, AZ 85338.
Rademacher, John R., 2497 Marston Hts., Colorado Springs, CO 80920.
Rooney, Robert B., 4419 Ave. P, 68847.
Schlaf, John E., 708 W. 7th St., Concordia, KS 66901.
Schmitt, James C., 23 Chantilly, 68803.
Snyder, Frederick, St. Mary's Convent, 2649-US20, Swanton, OH 43558.
Spanel, Hubert J., 745 N. 5th Ave., Broken Bow, 68822.
Warner, James P., 726 E. Carrol, Harlingen, TX 78552.

INSTITUTIONS LOCATED IN THE DIOCESE

[A] HIGH SCHOOLS, DIOCESAN

GRAND ISLAND. *Central Catholic Schools*, (Grades 6-12), 1200 Ruby Ave., 68803. Tel: 308-384-2440; Fax: 308-389-3274. Email: glogsdon@gicentralcatholic.org. Web: www.gicentralcatholic.org. John Golka, Prin.; Howard Schumann, Asst. Prin.; Greg Logsdon, Supt. Lay Teachers 32; Students 331.

[B] GENERAL HOSPITALS

GRAND ISLAND. *Saint Francis Medical Center, Affiliate of Catholic Health Initiatives*, 2620 W. Faidley Ave., P.O. Box 9804, 68802. Tel: 308-398-4600; Fax: 308-389-5589. Email: dsanders@sfmc-gi.org. Web: www.saintfrancisgi.org. Mr. Dan McElligott, Pres. & CEO. Catholic Health Initiatives. Bed Capacity 159; Bassinets 17; Patients Assisted Annually 107,798; Total Staff 1,100.

KEARNEY. *Good Samaritan Hospital, Affiliate of Catholic Health Initiatives*, 10 E. 31st St., P.O. Box 1990, 68848-1990. Tel: 308-865-7100. Email: robertsmoot@catholichealth.net. Web: www.gshs.org. Michael H. Schnieders, Pres. & CEO. Sisters 4; Total Staff 1,500; Bed Capacity 248.
Richard H. Young Hospital, 4600 17th Ave., 68847. Tel: 308-865-2000. Bed Capacity 80.

[C] HOMES FOR THE AGED

KEARNEY. *Mount Carmel Home-Keens' Memorial*, 412 W. 18th St., 68847. Tel: 308-338-1263; Fax: 308-236-9380. Email: brownun@yahoo.com. Web: www.corpuschristicarmelites.org. Sr. Dorothy Cavaness, O.Carm., Supr. Sisters (Carmelites) 9; Residents 50; Total Staff 120.

[D] NEWMAN CENTERS

CHADRON. *Chadron State College-Newman House* 907 Main St., 69337. Tel: 308-432-4286. Email: newmanhousecsc@yahoo.com. Total in Residence 1; Total Staff 1.

KEARNEY. *University of Nebraska at Kearney Newman Apostolate* 821 W. 27th St., 68845. Tel: 308-234-1539; Fax: 308-233-5718. Email: cathnewman@unk.edu. Web: http://newmancenter.unk.edu. Rev. Matthew J. Koperski, Chap.; Sr. Rosemarie Maly, O.S.B., Dir.; Dianne Keiter, Dir. Music Ministry; Pam Cinfel, Admin. Asst. Total in Residence 6; Total Staff 4.

[E] MISCELLANEOUS

KEARNEY. *Magnificat-Mary Full of Grace, Inc.*, 1516 First Ave., 68847. Tel: 308-234-3906.

RELIGIOUS INSTITUTES OF WOMEN REPRESENTED IN THE DIOCESE

For further details refer to the corresponding bracketed number in the Religious Institutes of Men or Women section.

[0230]—*Benedictine Convent of the Sacred Heart*
[0350]—*Carmelite Sisters (Corpus Christi)*—O.Carm.
[3832]—*Congregation of the Sisters of St. Joseph*—C.S.J.
[1115]—*Dominican Sisters of Peace*—O.P.
[2690]—*Missionary Catechists of Divine Providence*
[2960]—*Notre Dame Sisters*—N.D.
[]—*School Sisters of St. Francis, WI*
[3580]—*Servants of Mary* (Omaha, NE)—O.S.M.
[]—*Sinsinawa Sisters, WI*
[1630]—*Sisters of St. Francis of Penance and Christian Charity*—O.S.F.
[1640]—*Sisters of St. Francis of Perpetual Adoration*—O.S.F.
[3830-18]—*Sisters of St. Joseph*—C.S.J.
[3930]—*Sisters of St. Joseph of the Third Order of St. Francis P*—S.S.J.-T.O.S.F.
[2110]—*Sisters of the Humility of Mary*—H.M.
[4120-03]—*Ursuline Nuns of the Congregation of Paris* (Louisville, KY)—O.S.U.

NECROLOGY

† Hayden, Rev. Msgr. Carl T., (Retired)—Died Oct. 18, 2011
† Augustyn, Andrew M., (Retired)—Died Nov. 22, 2010
† Carlson, Gerald J., (Retired)—Died Sept. 8, 2011
† Cortney, Edward P., (Retired)—Died June 26, 2011
† Koprowski, Mitchell J., (Retired)—Died Dec. 14, 2010
† Phelan, Walter M., (Retired)—Died Dec. 8, 2010

An asterisk (*) denotes an organization that has established tax-exempt status directly with the IRS and is not covered by the USCCB Group Ruling.

Diocese of Grand Rapids

(Dioecesis Grandormensis)

Most Reverend

WALTER A. HURLEY

Bishop of Grand Rapids; ordained June 5, 1965; appointed Titular Bishop of Chunavia and Auxiliary Bishop of Detroit July 7, 2003; consecrated August 12, 2003; appointed Bishop of Grand Rapids June 21, 2005; installed August 4, 2005. *Office: Cathedral Square Center, 360 Division Ave., S., Grand Rapids, MI 49503-4539.* Tel: 616-243-0491.

Most Reverend

ROBERT J. ROSE, S.T.L., D.D.

Retired Bishop of Grand Rapids; ordained December 21, 1955; appointed Bishop of Gaylord October 13, 1981; consecrated December 6, 1981; appointed Bishop of Grand Rapids July 11, 1989; installed August 30, 1989; retired October 13, 2003. *Res.: 1200 104th, Apt. A, Byron Center, MI 49315.* Tel: 616-583-1260.

ESTABLISHED MAY 19, 1882.

Square Miles 6,795.

Comprises the following Counties of the Lower Peninsula of the State of Michigan: Ionia, Kent, Lake, Mason, Mecosta, Montcalm, Muskegon, Newaygo, Oceana, Osceola, Ottawa.

For legal titles of parishes and diocesan institutions, consult the Chancery Office.

Administrative Office of Diocese of Grand Rapids: Cathedral Square Center, 360 Division Ave., S., Grand Rapids, MI 49503-4539. Tel: 616-243-0491; Fax: 616-243-4910.

Web: www.dioceseofgrandrapids.org

STATISTICAL OVERVIEW

Personnel	
Bishop	1
Retired Bishops	1
Priests: Diocesan Active in Diocese	65
Priests: Diocesan Active Outside Diocese	1
Priests: Retired, Sick or Absent	38
Number of Diocesan Priests	104
Religious Priests in Diocese	16
Total Priests in Diocese	120
Extern Priests in Diocese	10
Ordinations:	
Diocesan Priests	1
Transitional Deacons	2
Permanent Deacons in Diocese	39
Total Brothers	1
Total Sisters	370
Parishes	
Parishes	89
With Resident Pastor:	
Resident Diocesan Priests	71
Resident Religious Priests	8
Without Resident Pastor:	
Administered by Priests	9
Administered by Deacons	1
Administered by Lay People	2
Missions	9
Pastoral Centers	1
Closed Parishes	2
Professional Ministry Personnel:	
Brothers	1
Welfare	
Catholic Hospitals	2
Total Assisted	935,560
Homes for the Aged	3
Total Assisted	900
Specialized Homes	16
Total Assisted	10,862
Special Centers for Social Services	12
Total Assisted	938,472
Residential Care of Disabled	69
Total Assisted	173
Other Institutions	1
Total Assisted	950
Educational	
Diocesan Students in Other Seminaries	17
Total Seminarians	17
Colleges and Universities	1
Total Students	2,141
High Schools, Diocesan and Parish	3
Total Students	1,284
High Schools, Private	1
Total Students	181
Elementary Schools, Diocesan and Parish	26
Total Students	4,844
Elementary Schools, Private	1
Total Students	283
Catechesis/Religious Education:	
High School Students	1,573
Elementary Students	9,531
Total Students under Catholic Instruction	19,854
Teachers in the Diocese:	
Sisters	2
Lay Teachers	385
Vital Statistics	
Receptions into the Church:	
Infant Baptism Totals	2,334
Minor Baptism Totals	156
Adult Baptism Totals	212
Received into Full Communion	894
First Communions	7,693
Confirmations	2,219
Marriages:	
Catholic	412
Interfaith	244
Total Marriages	656
Deaths	1,359
Total Catholic Population	178,000
Total Population	1,283,717

Former Bishops—Most Revs. HENRY JOSEPH RICHTER, D.D., cons. April 22, 1883; died Dec. 26, 1916; MICHAEL JAMES GALLAGHER, D.D., ord. March 19, 1893; appt. titular Bishop of Tipasa and Coadjutor Bishop of Grand Rapids July 5, 1915; cons. Sept. 8, 1915; succeeded to the Diocese of Grand Rapids, Dec. 26, 1916; transferred to the See of Detroit, July 18, 1918; died Jan. 20, 1937; EDWARD D. KELLY, ord. June 16, 1886; cons. Auxiliary Bishop of Detroit, Jan. 26, 1911; transferred to the See of Grand Rapids, Jan. 16, 1919; died March 26, 1926; JOSEPH G. PINTEN, D.D., ord. Nov. 1, 1890; cons. Bishop of Superior May 3, 1922; transferred to See of Grand Rapids June 25, 1926; resigned and appt. Titular Bishop of Sela Nov. 1, 1940; died Nov. 6, 1945; JOSEPH CASIMIR PLAGENS, ord. July 5, 1903; cons. Sept. 30, 1924, Auxiliary Bishop of Detroit and Titular Bishop of Rhodiopolis; transferred to See of Marquette Nov. 16, 1935; transferred to See of Grand Rapids Dec. 16, 1940; installed as Bishop of Grand Rapids Feb. 18, 1941; died March 31, 1943; FRANCIS J. HAAS, D.D., ord. June 11, 1913; appt. Sept. 26, 1943; cons. and installed as Bishop of Grand Rapids, Nov. 18, 1943; died Aug. 29, 1953; ALLEN J. BABCOCK, D.D., ord. March 7, 1925; appt. Titular Bishop of Irenopolis and Auxiliary of Detroit Feb. 15, 1947; cons. March 25, 1947; appt. to Grand Rapids March 23, 1954; died June 27, 1969; JOSEPH M. BREITENBECK, D.D., ord. May 30, 1942; appt. Titular Bishop of Tepelta and Auxiliary of Detroit Oct. 18, 1965; cons. Dec. 20, 1965; appt. Bishop of Grand Rapids Oct. 15, 1969; installed Dec. 2, 1969; retired Aug. 3, 1989; died March 12, 2005; ROBERT J. ROSE, D.D., S.T.L. (Retired), ord. Dec. 21, 1955; appt. Bishop of Gaylord Oct. 13, 1981; cons. Dec. 6, 1981; appt. Bishop of Grand Rapids July 11, 1989; installed Aug. 30, 1989; retired Oct. 13, 2003; KEVIN M. BRITT, ord. June 28, 1970; appt. Auxiliary Bishop of Detroit, Titular Bishop of Esco Nov. 23, 1993; cons. Jan. 6, 1994; appt. Coadjutor Bishop of Grand Rapids Dec. 10, 2002; Succeeded to See Oct. 13, 2003; died May 15, 2004.

Office of the Bishop

Office of the Bishop—Most Rev. WALTER ALLISON HURLEY, Cathedral Square Center, 360 Division Ave., S., Grand Rapids, 49503-4539. Tel: 616-243-0491.

Assistant to the Bishop—Bro. ERICJON THOMAS.

Administrative Assistant—Sr. SARAH DOSER, F.S.E.

Secretary to the Bishop—GAIL WELSH.

Vicar General/Moderator of the Curia—Rev. Msgr. WILLIAM H. DUNCAN, Cathedral Square Center, 360 Division Ave., S., Grand Rapids, 49503-4539. Tel: 616-243-9508.

Chancellor—Mr. T. EDWARD CAREY JR. Tel: 616-475-1247.

Vice Chancellor—VACANT.

Chief Financial Officer—Mr. T. EDWARD CAREY JR. Tel: 616-475-1247; Mr. JOHN S. CZACHORSKI, Comptroller. Tel: 616-475-1253; Mr. MARK MORROW, Dir. Stewardship & Devel., Cathedral Square Center, 360 Division Ave., S., Grand Rapids, 49503-4539. Tel: 616-475-1251.

Tribunal Office—Rev. EDWARD A. HANKIEWICZ, J.C.L.,

Officialis, Diocese of Grand Rapids: Cathedral Square Center, 360 Division Ave., S., Grand Rapids, 49503-4539. Tel: 616-551-5672.

Director of Planning—VACANT.

Director of Communications—MARY HAARMAN, Cathedral Square Center, 360 Division Ave., S., Grand Rapids, 49503-4539. Tel: 616-475-1240.

Victim Assistance Coordinator—MARYANNE L. KOWALSKI. Tel: 231-730-1060.

Clergy Fund—Rev. GEORGE E. DARLING. Tel: 616-361-7339.

Deans—Revs. JOSEPH J. FIX, Big Rapids, Mailing Address: P.O. Box 778, Evart, 49631. Tel: 231-734-3171; JOSEPH W. KENSHOL, Grand Rapids North, 1 Maple St., P.O. Box 140, Sand Lake, 49343. Tel: 616-636-5671; THEODORE KOZLOWSKI, Grand Rapids South, 101 Hall, S.E., Grand Rapids, 49507. Tel: 616-243-0222; Rev. Msgr. ERNEST SCHNEIDER, Grand Rapids East, 2750 Burton St., S.E., Grand Rapids, 49546. Tel: 616-949-4170; VACANT, Grand Rapids West; Revs. LARRY KING, Ionia, 140 Church St., Portland, 48875-1095. Tel: 517-647-6505; RONALD F. SCHNEIDER, Northwest Lake Shore Deanery, Mailing Address: St. Ann Parish, P.O. Box 729, Baldwin, 49304. Tel: 231-745-7997; WILLIAM F. ZINK, Grand Haven Deanery, 15164 Juniper Dr., Marne, 49435. Tel: 616-677-3934; THOMAS J. BROWN, Muskegon Deanery, 150 E. Summit Ave., Muskegon, 49444. Tel: 231-733-2440.

Presbyteral Council—Revs. RONALD F. SCHNEIDER, Exec. Coord.; JOSEPH W. KENSHOL, Asst. Exec. Coord.; MICHAEL CILIBRAISE; GODFREY C. ONYEKWERE, and the Deans of the Diocese.

College of Consultors—Rev. Msgrs. ERNEST SCHNEIDER; WILLIAM H. DUNCAN; Revs. THEODORE KOZLOWSKI; GODFREY C. ONYEKWERE; LARRY KING; WILLIAM F. ZINK.

Diocesan Finance Council Membership—Mr. THOMAS CZERNEY; Mr. JOHN NOWAK; Mr. WILLIAM J. MCCALL; Mrs. NANCY KENNEDY; MARY LEHMAN PANEK; JOSEPH PAWLANTA; Rev. LEONARD SUDLIK; Mr. GEORGE SHARPE JR.; Mr. RICHARD WENDT; Sr. AQUINAS WEBER, O.P.; Rev. Msgr. WILLIAM H. DUNCAN, Vicar Gen.; Mr. T. EDWARD CAREY JR., CFO; Mr. JOHN S. CZACHORSKI, Comptroller.

Finance Council—Most Rev. WALTER ALLISON HURLEY, Cathedral Square Center, 360 Division Ave., S., Grand Rapids, 49503-4539. Tel: 616-243-0491.

Finance—

Parish Review Services—Mr. THOMAS CZERNEY, Dir. Tel: 616-551-5670.

Delegate for Religious—Sr. SARAH DOSER, F.S.E.

Catholic Services Appeal—Cathedral Square Center, 360 Division Ave., S., Grand Rapids, 49503-4539. Tel: 616-243-0491. LISA DAVIS.

Vicar For Priests—Rev. DONALD E. WEBER (Retired), 7523 Pinegrove Dr., Jenison, 49428.

Associate Vicar for Priests—Rev. THOMAS P. PAGE.

Moderator of the Curia—Rev. Msgr. WILLIAM H. DUNCAN, Cathedral Square Center, 360 Division Ave., S., Grand Rapids, 49503-4539. Tel: 616-475-1250.

Pro-Life Ministry—Sr. COLLEEN ANN NAGLE, F.S.E., Dir., Cathedral Square Center, 360 Division Ave. S., Grand Rapids, 49503. Tel: 616-551-5633.

Inclusion/Diversity Initiatives—Rev. GODFREY C. ONYEKWERE, Office for Black Catholic Ministry; Mr. LUIS BETETA, Office for Hispanic Ministry.

Worship—Rev. CHRIS W. ROUECH, Dir., Cathedral Square Center, 360 Division Ave. S., Grand Rapids, 49503. Tel: 616-475-1241.

Catechesis—Sr. BARBARA CLINE, F.S.E. Tel: 616-551-4742.

Music—Mr. DENNIS RYBICKI. Tel: 616-243-5590.

Faith Formation—Sr. BARBARA CLINE, F.S.E. Tel: 616-551-4743.

Family and Youth—Mr. MARK MANN. Tel: 616-475-1243.

Evangelization—Catholic Information Center, 360 Division Ave., S. 2A, Grand Rapids, 49503. Tel: 616-459-7267. Revs. JOHN J. GEANEY, C.S.P.; MARCOS ZAMORA, C.S.P.; JOHN J. KENNY, C.S.P.; THOMAS TAVELLA, C.S.P.

Hispanic Ministry—Mr. LUIS BETETA. Tel: 616-246-0598.

Black Catholic Ministry—Rev. GODFREY C. ONYEKWERE, Dir., Cathedral Square Center, 360 Division Ave. S, Grand Rapids, 49503. Tel: 616-243-0491.

Native American Ministry—Ms. DEBRA GUTOWSKI. Tel: 616-514-6065.

Vietnamese Ministry—Rev. PETER NGHIEM, Our Lady of LaVang, 2420 Avon, S.W., Wyoming, 49519. Tel: 616-531-5213; Fax: 616-261-0232.

Campus Ministry—Rev. DONALD A. ANDRIE, C.S.P. Tel: 616-916-4290.

Health Ministry—VACANT.

Prison/Jail Ministry—Ms. JUDE GRANSTROM. Tel: 616-475-1255.

Diocesan Council of Catholic Women—HELEN WEISNECK, 4979 S. Ferris Ave., Newaygo, 49337. Tel: 231-924-4709; Rev. ANTHONY C. VAINAVICZ, Chap. (Retired).

Clergy and Religious Services Division

Director—VACANT.

Vicar for Clergy—Rev. DONALD E. WEBER (Retired), 7523 Pinegrove Dr., Jenison, 49428.

Associate Vicar for Clergy—Rev. THOMAS P. PAGE.

Vocations Office—Rev. RONALD D. HUTCHINSON. Tel: 616-475-1254; Fax: 616-243-4910.

Continuing Education for Clergy—Rev. MARK C. PRZYBYSZ, 1776 Acacia Dr., N.W., Grand Rapids, 49504. Tel: 616-453-8229; Fax: 616-453-8053.

Clergy Services—VACANT.

Permanent Diaconate—VACANT, Cathedral Square Center, 360 Division Ave., S., Grand Rapids, 49503-4539. Tel: 616-243-0491, Ext. 1551; Fax: 616-243-1442.

Ecumenical Affairs—VACANT, Cathedral Square Center, 360 Division Ave. S., Grand Rapids, 49503.

Pastoral Council Membership— (In formation)

Education Division

Superintendent of Catholic Schools—DAVID A. FABER, Cathedral Square Center, 360 Division Ave. S., Grand Rapids, 49503. Tel: 616-233-5975.

Catholic Secondary Schools Pastor—Rev. Msgr. R. LOUIS STASKER, Cathedral Square Center, 360 Division Ave., S., Grand Rapids, 49503-4539. Tel: 616-233-5979.

Catholic Secondary Schools President—THOMAS MAY, Prin., Cathedral Square Ctr., 360 Division Ave. S., Grand Rapids, 49503-4539. Tel: 616-233-5814.

Catholic Charities of West Michigan

Catholic Charities of West Michigan—Cathedral Square Center, 360 Division Ave., S., Grand Rapids, 49503-4539. DEBORAH NYKAMP, Pres. Tel: 616-243-9122; Mr. BRIAN PENEYCAD, CFO. Tel: 616-475-1252.

Bishops Overseas Appeal—

Catholic Relief Services—

Catholic Charities West Michigan, Grand Rapids—40 Jefferson Ave., S.E., Grand Rapids, 49506. Tel: 616-456-1443. *212 1/2 Maple St., Big Rapids, 49307.* Tel: 231-796-1583. *601 E. Washington St., Ste. A, Ionia, 48846.* Tel: 616-522-0836. *212 W. Main, Ste. B, Stanton, 48888.* Tel: 989-831-8306. *303 Division Ave., S., Grand Rapids, 49503.* Tel: 616-454-4110. *1935 Plainfield Ave., N.E., Grand Rapids, 49505.* Tel: 616-364-0845. *1195 E. Wilcox, White Cloud, 49349.* Tel: 231-689-6701.

Catholic Charities West Michigan, Lakeshore—1095 Third St., Ste. 125, Muskegon, 49441. Tel: 231-726-4735. *11 Washington, Hart, 49420.* Tel: 231-726-4735. *5816 W. US 10, Ludington, 49431.* Tel: 231-843-4899. *6660 Blair Ln., Holland, 49424.* Tel: 616-796-9595. *540 E. Hackley Ave., Muskegon Heights, 49444.* Tel: 231-725-7579.

Administration Division

Chief Financial Officer—Mr. T. EDWARD CAREY JR., Cathedral Square Center, 360 Division Ave., S., Grand Rapids, 49503-4539. Tel: 616-475-1247; Fax: 616-475-1247.

Catholic Services Appeal—Mr. MARK MORROW; JENNIFER HOLMES.

Accounting—Mr. JOHN S. CZACHORSKI, Comptroller.

Parish Audits—Mr. THOMAS CZERNEY. Tel: 616-551-5670.

Human Resources Management—LAURA PLOOF. Tel: 616-475-1242.

Facilities/Real Estate—Mr. T. EDWARD CAREY JR. Tel: 616-475-1247.

Technology—Ms. SUE SWANSON.

Cemeteries—Mr. ROBERT MENZEL, 4100 Clyde Park, S.W., Wyoming, 49509-0063. Tel: 616-531-9320; Fax: 616-531-9780 Resurrection Cemetery; Mt. Calvary Cemetery; St. Andrew Cemetery; Holy Cross Cemetery.

Deposit and Loan Program—Mr. JOHN S. CZACHORSKI, Comptroller.

Catholic Foundation of West Michigan—Mr. MARK MORROW, Dir. Tel: 616-475-1251.

Self-Insurance Program—Mr. T. EDWARD CAREY JR.

Building and Planning Committee—Mr. T. EDWARD CAREY JR., Cathedral Square Center, 360 Division Ave., S., Grand Rapids, 49503-4539. Tel: 616-475-1247.

Archivist—Rev. DENNIS W. MORROW, Cathedral Square Center, 360 Division Ave., S., Grand Rapids, 49503-4539. Tel: 616-246-0580.

CLERGY, PARISHES, MISSIONS AND PAROCHIAL SCHOOLS

CITY OF GRAND RAPIDS

(KENT COUNTY)

1—CATHEDRAL OF ST. ANDREW (1833) [CEM] Revs. John J. Geaney, C.S.P., Rector; Thomas Tavella, C.S.P., Parochial Vicar; Marcos Zamora, C.S.P.
Res.: 265 Sheldon S.E., 49503. Tel: 616-456-1454; Fax: 616-456-5110. Web: cathedralofsaintandrew.org.
Catechesis/Religious Program—Students 139.

2—ST. ALPHONSUS (1888) [JC] Revs. Patrick Grile, C.Ss.R.; Lamar Partin, C.Ss.R.; Bernard Carlin, C.Ss.R. In Res., Revs. Robert Balser, C.Ss.R.; Thomas Danielsen, C.Ss.R.
Res.: 224 Carrier St., N.E., 49505. Tel: 616-451-3043; Fax: 616-458-5667. Email: stalphonsusgr@catholicweb.com. Web: www.stalphonsusre.org.
See All Saints Academy under Diocesan Elementary Schools, located in the Institution section
Catechesis/Religious Program—Tel: 616-459-5472. Students 121.

3—ST. ANTHONY OF PADUA (1906) Rev. Mark C. Przybysz; Deacon Leo Ferguson.
Res.: 2510 Richmond St., N.W., 49504. Tel: 616-453-8229; Fax: 616-453-8053. Email: parishoffice@saparish.com. Web: www.saparish.com.
School—(Grades K-8) Julie Whalen, Prin. Lay Teachers 20; Students 379.
Catechesis/Religious Program— Lynne Haley, D.R.E. Students 355.

4—BASILICA OF ST. ADALBERT (1881), (Polish), [JC] Rev. Msgr. R. Louis Stasker; Deacon Stanley Lechtanski, Homebound Ministry.
Parish Office:—701 4th St., N.W., 49504-5199. Tel: 616-458-3065; Fax: 616-458-0563. Email: aoatley@basilicagr.org. Web: basilicagr.org.
Church: 4th and Davis, N.W., 49504.
Catechesis/Religious Program—Margaret Downer, C.R.E. Students 18.

5—BLESSED SACRAMENT (1946) [JC] Rev. George E. Darling.
Res.: 2275 Diamond Ave., N.E., 49505-4313. Tel: 616-361-7339; Fax: 616-361-1327. Email: church@bsacrament.net. Web: bsacrament.net.
See All Saints Academy under Diocesan Elementary Schools, located in the Institution section
Catechesis/Religious Program—Tel: 616-361-7738; Fax: 616-361-1327. Jody DeGraw, D.R.E. Students 123.

6—ST. DOMINIC (1974) Rev. Charles R. Dautremont.
Office: 50 Bellevue, S.W., 49548-3144. Tel: 616-531-1480; Fax: 616-531-0759. Email: chrisst.dominic@comcast.net.

7—HOLY NAME OF JESUS (1908) [JC] Rev. Stephen S. Dudek; Deacons Jeffrey Burns; Carlos Gutierrez.
Res.: 1630 Godfrey Ave., S.W., 49509. Tel: 616-241-6489; Fax: 616-241-6480. Email: holynameofjesus@comcast.net.
Catechesis/Religious Program—Tel: 616-245-3359. Students 132.

8—HOLY SPIRIT Rev. John F. Vallier; Daryl E. Nowicki, Business Mgr.
Res.: 2230 Lake Michigan Dr., N.W., 49504. Tel: 616-453-6369; Fax: 616-453-0244. Email: office@hsparish.com. Web: www.hsparish.com.
School—(Grades PreK-8), 2222 Lake Michigan Dr., N.W., 49504. Tel: 616-453-2772; Fax: 616-453-0018. Email: sgrant@hsparish.org. Web: www.holyspiritschoolgr.com. Sharon Grant, Prin. Lay Teachers 19; Students 338.
Catechesis/Religious Program—Tel: 616-453-1591. Students 182.

9—IMMACULATE HEART OF MARY Rev. Troy Nevins; Deacon Ken Baldwin.
Res.: 2101 Griggs St., S.E., 49506. Tel: 616-241-4477; Fax: 616-241-2832. Email: parish@ihmparish.com. Web: ihmparish.com.
School—(Grades K-8), 1953 Plymouth, S.E., 49506. Tel: 616-241-4633; Fax: 616-241-4418. Stacy Slomski, Prin.; Beth McDermott, Librarian. Lay Teachers 21; Students 344.
Catechesis/Religious Program—Tel: 616-241-4477, Ext. 101. Prisilla Baldwin, C.R.E. Students 200.

10—ST. ISIDORE (1897), (Polish), [JC] Rev. Donald E. Lomasiewicz.
Res.: 628 Diamond Ave., N.E., 49503. Tel: 616-459-4731; Fax: 616-454-5832. Email: pastor@saintisidorechurch.org.
See All Saints Academy under Diocesan Elementary Schools, located in the Institution section
Catechesis/Religious Program—Kathryn Mulderink, C.R.E. Students 110.

11—ST. JAMES (1870) Rev. Msgr. R. Louis Stasker; Deacon Robert McClintick.
Res.: 733 Bridge St., N.W., 49504. Tel: 616-458-3213; Fax: 616-458-9002. Email: stjamesgr@catholicweb.com. Web:

stjamesparish.catholicweb.com.
Catechesis/Religious Program—Students 7.

12—St. John Vianney, [JC] Revs. Michael Alber; Luis F. Garcia, Parochial Vicar; Jim Kulfan, Business Mgr.
Res.: 4101 Clyde Park, S.W., 49509. Tel: 616-534-5449; Fax: 616-530-8224. Email: parish@stjohnvianney.net. Web: www.stjohnvianney.net.
School—(Grades K-8) Tel: 616-532-7001; Fax: 616-532-1884. Mr. Tom Priest, Prin. Lay Teachers 20; Students 262.
Catechesis/Religious Program—Tel: 616-532-2397. Students 116.

13—St. Joseph The Worker Rev. Steven D. Cron; Deacons Martin Zapata, Pastoral Assoc.; Carlos Gutierrez, Pastoral Assoc.
Office: 3138 Birchwood, S.W., 49548. Tel: 616-456-7982; Fax: 616-301-1759.
Church: 225 32nd St., S.W., Wyoming, 49548.
Catechesis/Religious Program—Students 268.

14—St. Jude (1946) Rev. Thomas P. Page; Deacon Larry Hoogeboom.
Office: 1120 Four Mile, N.E., 49525. Tel: 616-363-6885; Fax: 616-363-1470. Web: www.stjudes.net.
See All Saints Academy under Diocesan Elementary Schools, located in the Institution section
Catechesis/Religious Program—1120 Four Mile, N.E., 49525. Tel: 616-363-6897; Fax: 616-363-1470. Students 147.

15—St. Mary Magdalen (1956) Rev. Godfrey C. Onyekwere; Deacons Michael Dordan; Michael L. Wood.
Res.: 1213 52nd St., S.E., 49508. Tel: 616-455-9310; Fax: 616-455-4139. Email: witness@stmmagdalen.org. Web: stmmagdalen.org.
Catechesis/Religious Program—Students 233.

16—St. Mary's (1857) Rev. Dick Host; Deacon Edward Harwood.
Res.: 423 First St., N.W., 49504. Tel: 616-459-7390; Fax: 616-459-9630. Email: parish@stmarygr.org. Web: www.stmarygr.org.
Catechesis/Religious Program—David Bulkowski, D.R.E. Students 105.

17—Our Lady of Sorrows (1908), (Italian), Rev. Theodore Kozlowski.
Office: 116 Green St., S.E., 49507.
Res.: 101 Hall St., S.E., 49507. Tel: 616-243-0222; Fax: 616-243-6612; 616-247-0545 (Rectory). Web: ourladyofsorrows-gr.org.
Catechesis/Religious Program—Students 61.

18—St. Paul the Apostle (1965) Rev. Msgr. Ernest Schneider; Deacon Richard Radecki; Sr. Rosanne Szocinski, O.P., Pastoral Assoc.
Mailing Address: 2750 Burton St., S.E., 49546. Tel: 616-949-4170; Fax: 616-949-5295. Web: www.stpaulapostle.com.
School—Tel: 616-949-1690; Fax: 616-949-0836. Web: www.stpaul-school.org. Lori Salva, Prin. Lay Teachers 11; Students 214.
Catechesis/Religious Program— Beth Kolenda, D.R.E. Students 263.

19—SS. Peter and Paul (1904), (Lithuanian), [CEM] Rev. Dennis W. Morrow; Deacon Manuel E. Herrera.
Res.: 520 Myrtle St., N.W., 49504-3277. Tel: 616-454-6000; Fax: 616-454-4532.
Catechesis/Religious Program—1433 Hamilton Ave. N.W., 49504. Tel: 616-454-5611. Students 57.

20—Sacred Heart of Jesus (1904) [JC] Rev. Aaron R. Ferris.
Res.: 156 Valley Ave., S.W., 49504. Tel: 616-459-8362; Fax: 616-458-0602. Email: fatherferris@aol.com.
School—(Grades K-8), 1200 Dayton S.W., 49504. Tel: 616-459-0948; Fax: 616-459-0899. Web: www.sacredheartgr.org. Dr. Bernard Stanko, Prin. Lay Teachers 10; Students 175.
Catechesis/Religious Program—Students 3.

21—Shrine of St. Francis Xavier and Our Lady of Guadalupe (1914) [JC] Rev. Jose Quintana.
Res.: 250 Brown St., S.E., 49507. Tel: 616-241-2485; Fax: 616-241-2079. Email: sfxolgoffice@sbcglobal.net. Web: www.sfxgr.org.
Catechesis/Religious Program—Students 259.

22—St. Stephen Catholic Church (1925) [JC] Rev. Paul Milanowski.
Res.: 760 Gladstone Ave., S.E., East Grand Rapids, 49506. Tel: 616-243-8998; Fax: 616-245-7360. Email: parishoffice@ststephenparish.com. Web: www.ststephenparish.com.
School—(Grades K-8), 740 Gladstone Dr., S.E., East Grand Rapids, 49506. Tel: 616-243-8998, Ext. 206; Fax: 616-243-0451. Web: ststephenschoolgr.com. Cindy Thomas, Prin.; J. Klein, Librarian; N. Mulvihill, Librarian. Lay Teachers 22; Students 283.
Catechesis/Religious Program—Sheila Murphy, Dir. Faith Formation. Students 254.

23—St. Thomas the Apostle (1924) [JC] Rev. James A. Chelich; Deacons James Thorndill; Dennis Williams.
Res.: 1449 Wilcox Park Dr., S.E., 49506. Tel: 616-459-4662; Fax: 616-458-4047. Web: www.stthomasgr.org.
School—(Grades PreK-8), 1429 Wilcox Park Dr., S.E., 49506. Tel: 616-458-4228; Fax: 616-458-4583. Web: www.stthomasapostle.catholicweb.com. Suzi Furtwangler, Prin.; Marni White, Librarian; Kelly Olive, Librarian. Lay Teachers 20; Students 350.
Catechesis/Religious Program—Students 280.

OUTSIDE THE CITY OF GRAND RAPIDS

Ada, Kent Co., St. Robert of Newminster (1951) Sr. Ann Michael Farnsworth, O.P., Pastoral Assoc.
Res.: 6477 Ada Dr., S.E., 49301. Tel: 616-676-9111; Fax: 616-676-0950. Email: parishmail@strobertchurch.org. Web: www.strobertchurch.org.
Catechesis/Religious Program—Tel: 616-676-1488. Mary Ann Snyder, D.R.E.; Anne Gruscinski. Students 1,019.

Allendale, Ottowa Co., St. Luke University Parish (2007) Revs. Bradford C. Schoeberle, C.S.P.; Donald A. Andrie, C.S.P., Parochial Vicar.
6163 Lake Michigan Dr., 49401-9244. Tel: 616-895-2247; Fax: 616-895-2249. Web: www.lukespot.com.
Catechesis/Religious Program—Ms. Beth Price, D.R.E. Email: bethprice@lukespot.com. Students 94.
Mission—Grand Valley State University - Catholic Campus Ministry

Alpine, Kent Co., Holy Trinity (1848) [CEM] Rev. Thomas G. Simons; Deacon Gerald Roersma.
Res.: 1200 Alpine Church Rd., N.W., 49321. Tel: 616-784-0677; Fax: 616-784-0678. Email: holytrinityalpine@gmail.com.
School—(Grades K-8), Comstock Park, 49321. Tel: 616-784-0696; Fax: 616-988-9415. Web: holytrinitycatholic.net. Kathy Rand, Prin.; Sherry Brown, Librarian. Lay Teachers 9; Students 145.
Catechesis/Religious Program—Tel: 616-784-3242. Rebecca Chicklon, D.R.E. Students 214.

Baldwin, Lake Co., St. Ann - St. Luther (1912) Rev. Ronald F. Schneider.
Res.: 740 Ninth St., P.O. Box 729, 49304. Tel: 231-745-7997; Fax: 231-745-9844. Email: annigna@triton.net.
Catechesis/Religious Program—Students 12.

Belding, Ionia Co., St. Joseph's (1894) [CEM] Rev. Philip A. Shangraw; Deacon Daniel Schneider.
Office: 409 S. Bridge St., 48809. Tel: 616-794-2145; Fax: 616-794-2145. Email: sjsmoffice@charterinternet.com. Web: joseph-mary.catholicweb.com.
Catechesis/Religious Program—Students 28.

Belmont, Kent Co., Assumption of the Blessed Virgin Mary (1913) [CEM] Rev. Peter G. Vu; Deacons Peter P. Conigliaro; Michael J. Mauer.
Res.: 6369 Belmont Ave., 49306. Tel: 616-361-5126; Fax: 616-361-5503. Email: officesecretary@assumptionbvm.com. Web: www.assumptionbvm.com.
School—(Grades K-8), 6393 Belmont Ave., 49306. Tel: 616-361-5483; Fax: 616-361-2553. Michael Micele, Prin.; Noreen Eshleman, Librarian. Lay Teachers 10; Students 157.
Catechesis/Religious Program—6391 Belmont Ave., 49306. Tel: 616-361-5126, Ext. 257. Email: religiouseddirector@assumptionbvm.com. Students 248.

Big Rapids, Mecosta Co.
1—St. Mary's (1873) [CEM] Revs. Lam T. Le; David C. Gross.
1009 Marion Ave., 49307. Tel: 231-796-5202; Fax: 231-796-9231.
School—(Grades K-8), 927 Marion Ave., 49307. Tel: 231-796-6731; Fax: 231-976-9293. Email: kbrejcha@stmarybr.org. Web: www.stmarybr.org. Barbara J. Borth, Prin. Lay Teachers 7; Students 128.
Catechesis/Religious Program—Students 16.
2—St. Paul's Campus Parish (1958) Revs. Lam T. Le; David C. Gross. Email: fatherdave@stmarybr.org.
Res.: 1009 Marion Ave., 49307. Tel: 231-796-7393; Fax: 231-796-3990. Email: stpauls1@charterinternet.com.
Catechesis/Religious Program—Students 41.

Brunswick, Newaygo Co., St. Michael (1886) [CEM] Rev. Roc Majalla, S.A.C.
Res.: 6382 S. Maple Island Rd., Fremont, 49412. Tel: 231-924-3389; Fax: 231-924-0402. Email: stmctke@ncats.net.
Catechesis/Religious Program—Students 57.
Mission—Christ the King Hesperia, Oceana Co.

Byron Center, Kent Co., St. Sebastian's (1852) [CEM] Rev. Msgr. William H. Duncan.
Res.: 9408 Wilson Ave., S.W., 49315. Tel: 616-878-1893. Web: www.sebastianmi.org.
Catechesis/Religious Program—Tel: 616-878-1619; Fax: 616-878-0715. Debbie Mayer, D.R.E.; Patrick Rossi, Youth Min. Students 234.

Caledonia, Kent Co., Holy Family (1970) [CEM 3] Rev. Dung Anton Tran.
Res.: 9669 Kraft Ave., S.E., 49316. Tel: 616-891-1160 (Rectory); 616-891-9259 (Office); Fax: 616-891-1346. Web: www.holyfamilycaledonia.org.
Catechesis/Religious Program—Tel: 616-891-8867. Christine Shafer, D.R.E. Students 483.

Carson City, Montcalm Co., St. Mary's (1896) [CEM] Nancy Woodcock, Pastoral Dir.
Office: 404 N. Division St., 48811. Tel: 989-584-6044 (office); 989-762-5320 (home); Fax: 989-584-6044. Email: smsjchurch@cmsinter.net.
Catechesis/Religious Program— Nancy Woodcock, D.R.E. Students 102.

Conklin, Ottawa Co., St. Francis Xavier (1892) [CEM] Rev. G. Fredrick Brucker.
Res.: 2044 Gooding Rd., 49403. Tel: 616-899-2471; Fax: 231-853-2191. Email: stfrancisconklin@gmail.com.
Catechesis/Religious Program—Students 38.

Coopersville, Ottawa Co., St. Michael's (1950) [CEM] [JC] Rev. Norman P. Droski, Admin. (Retired).
Res.: 17151 88th Ave., 49404. Tel: 616-837-8792; 616-837-8158 (Parish Office); Fax: 616-837-7893. Email: admin@saintmichaels.us. Web: www.saintmichaels.us.
School—(Grades K-8), 17150 88th Ave., 49404. Tel: 616-837-6346. Richard E. Kosla, Prin. Lay Teachers 2; Students 55.
Catechesis/Religious Program—Students 90.

Custer, Mason Co., St. Mary's (1933) [CEM] [JC] Rev. Edward Boucher, Admin.
85 S. Madison, P.O. Box 68, 49405.
Res.: 80 S. Monroe St., P.O. Box 68, 49405. Tel: 231-757-3709.
Catechesis/Religious Program—Combined with St. Jerome, Scottville., Tel: 231-757-9711. Kathy Papes, D.R.E. Students 48.

Edmore, Montcalm Co., St. Margaret Mary (1963) Rev. Dominic Tirkey.
Res.: 1051 E. Howard City Rd., 48829. Tel: 989-427-5645; Fax: 989-831-5707. Email: sbl.smm.church@frontier.com.
Catechesis/Religious Program—Students 20.

Evart, Osceola Co., Sacred Heart (1874) Rev. Joseph J. Fix.
Res.: 9878 E. US 10, P.O. Box 778, 49631. Tel: 231-734-3171; Fax: 231-734-6880. Email: sacred@netonecom.net.
Catechesis/Religious Program—Tel: 231-734-3165. Ann Johnson, D.R.E. Students 52.

Free Soil, Mason Co., St. John Cantius (1906) [CEM] Rev. Dennis O'Donnell.
Res.: 2845 E. Michigan, 49411-9691. Tel: 231-464-5672; Fax: 231-464-5859.
Catechesis/Religious Program—Tel: 231-464-5698. Students 7.

Fremont, Newaygo Co., All Saints, [CEM] Rev. Peter O. Omogo.
Res.: 500 Iroquois Dr., 49412. Tel: 231-924-7705; Fax: 231-924-7708. Email: peteromogo@yahoo.com. Web: www.rc.net/grandrapids/allsaints.
Catechesis/Religious Program—Tel: 231-924-7571. Students 97.

Grand Haven, Ottawa Co., St. Patrick - St. Anthony (1857) Rev. William A. Langlois; Deacons Richard Fett; Joseph Finnigan.
Res.: 920 Fulton St., 49417. Tel: 616-842-0001; Fax: 616-842-1174. Web: stpatsgh.org.
Catechesis/Religious Program—Tel: 616-842-8230. Jeff Andrini, D.R.E. Students 468.

Grandville, Kent Co., St. Pius X (1953) Rev. Chris W. Rouech.
Res.: 3937 Wilson Ave., S.W., 49418. Tel: 616-532-9344; Fax: 616-538-6340. Email: parishoffice@spxcatholic.org. Web: www.spxcatholic.org.
Catechesis/Religious Program—Tel: 616-538-2600. Students 453.

Greenville, Montcalm Co., St. Charles Borromeo (1849) [CEM] Rev. Michael Cilibraise.
Res.: 109 W. Oak St., 48838. Tel: 616-754-3512; Fax: 616-754-2357. Web: home.catholicweb.com/stcharles.
School—(Grades K-8), 502 S. Franklin St., 48838. Tel: 616-754-3416; Fax: 616-754-9262. Margaret Karpus, Prin.; Sr. David Therese Korson, O.P., Librarian. Lay Teachers 8; Students 143.
Catechesis/Religious Program—Tel: 616-754-3196. Dave Mendrea, Youth Min. Students 114.
Mission—St. Margaret [CEM] Cedar Springs. 10195 16 Mile Rd., Harvard, Kent Co. 49319. Tel: 616-696-3904. Web: www.vritsworks.com/church.

Hart, Oceana Co., St. Gregory's (1908) Rev. M. Thomas Bolster.
Res.: 316 Peach St., 49420. Tel: 231-873-2660; Fax: 616-551-5623. Email: parish@stgregoryathart.org.
Catechesis/Religious Program—Tel: 231-873-2578. Andrea Bosse, D.R.E. Students 221.
Mission—Kateri Tekawitha Native American Center & St. Joseph Center Elbridge, Oceana Co.

Holland, Ottawa Co.
1—St. Francis de Sales (1903) Rev. Charles D.

Brown; Deacon Juan Garcia.
Office: 195 W. 13th St., 49423. Tel: 616-396-7641; Fax: 616-392-2474. Email: cbrown@stfrancisholland.org. Web: www.stfrancisholland.org.
School—(Grades K-8), 12100 Quincy St., 49424. Tel: 616-994-9864; Fax: 616-994-9870. Corpus Christi Catholic School
Catechesis/Religious Program—195 W. 13th St., 49423. Tel: 616-392-6700. Marilyn Torborg, D.R.E.
2—OUR LADY OF THE LAKE (1979) Rev. Charles D. Hall; Sr. Brigid Clingman, Pastoral Assoc.
Office: 480 152nd Ave., 49424. Tel: 616-399-1062; Fax: 616-399-5766. Email: cdhall@oll.org. Web: www.oll.org.
School—(Grades K-8), 12100 Quincy St., 49424. Tel: 616-994-9864; Fax: 616-994-9870. Joanne Swan-Jones, Prin. Corpus Christi Catholic School Lay Teachers 16; Students 144.
Catechesis/Religious Program—Students 480.

HOWARD CITY, MONTCALM CO., CHRIST THE KING-ST. FRANCIS DE SALES (1975) [CEM] Rev. James B. Wyse; Deacon Richard Dubridge.
Res.: 9596 N. Reed Rd., 49329. Tel: 231-937-5757; Fax: 231-937-8211. Email: king-francis@ctknsf.org. Web: king-francis.catholicweb.com.
Catechesis/Religious Program— Sandy Weiks, D.R.E.; Pat Berry, D.R.E. Students 84.

HUBBARDSTON, IONIA CO., ST. JOHN THE BAPTIST (1853) [CEM] Nancy Woodcock, Pastoral Dir.
Res.: c/o 404 N. Division St., Carson City, 48811. Tel: 989-584-6044; 989-762-5320 (home); Fax: 989-584-6044. Email: nwoodcock@cmsinter.net.
Catechesis/Religious Program—Tel: 989-981-6668. Nancy Woodcock, D.R.E. Students 77.

IONIA, IONIA CO., SS. PETER AND PAUL (1861) [CEM] Rev. Thomas F. Boufford; Deacon Zenon Cardenas Sr.
Parish Office—434 High St., 48846. Tel: 616-527-3610; Fax: 616-527-3697. Web: www.ssppcatholic.com.
School—(Grades K-8), 317 Baldie St., 48846. Tel: 616-527-3561; Fax: 616-527-3562. Julie Palmer, Prin.; Patricia Zander, Librarian. Lay Teachers 8; Students 103.
Catechesis/Religious Program—Tel: 616-527-3575. Students 127.

IRONS, LAKE CO., ST. BERNARD'S Rev. Dennis O'Donnell.
Res.: One Oak St., P.O. Box 155, 49644. Tel: 231-266-5155; Fax: 231-266-8948.
Catechesis/Religious Program—

JENISON, OTTAWA CO., HOLY REDEEMER (1975) Rev. Ronald D. Hutchinson; Deacon Richard Pitt.
Res.: 2734 Baldwin Dr., 49428. Tel: 616-669-9220; Fax: 616-669-9360. Web: www.holyredeemerparish.org.
Catechesis/Religious Program—Tel: 616-669-0820. Bobby DeVries, D.R.E. Students 449.

LAKE ODESSA, IONIA CO., ST. EDWARD'S (1945) Rev. Victor Kynam.
Res.: 531 Jordan Lake St., 48849-6200. Tel: 616-374-7253; Fax: 616-374-1559. Email: stewards@cablespeed.com.
Catechesis/Religious Program—Tel: 616-374-8809. Gary Coates, D.R.E. Students 60.

LAKEVIEW, MONTCALM CO., ST. FRANCIS DE SALES (1943) Merged with Christ the King, Howard City to form Christ the King-St. Francis de Sales, Howard City.

LAKEWOOD CLUB, MUSKEGON CO., ST. MARY OF THE WOODS (1916) Rev. Donn Tufts.
Church: 150 Church St., Twin Lake, 49457. Tel: 231-893-3085; Fax: 231-894-9929. Email: parishoffice@stjamescatholicparish.org. Web: stjamescatholicparish.org.
Catechesis/Religious Program—

LOWELL, KENT CO., ST. MARY'S (1879) [CEM] Rev. Edward A. Hankiewicz.
Res.: 402 Amity St., 49331-1308. Tel: 616-897-9820; Fax: 616-897-9683. Email: stmarylowell@att.net. Web: stmarylowell.com.
Catechesis/Religious Program—300 Amity St., 49331. Tel: 616-897-7915; Fax: 616-897-7915. Preston (Pete) Wiggins, D.R.E. & Youth Min. Students 73.

LUDINGTON, MASON CO.
1—ST. SIMON'S, [CEM] Rev. Wayne B. Wheeler Jr.
Res.: 702 E. Bryant Rd., 49431. Tel: 231-843-8606; Fax: 231-843-2052. Email: stsimon@stsimonchurch.com. Web: www.stsimonchurch.com.
School—(Grades K-8) Tel: 231-843-3188. Collin Thompson, Prin. Lay Teachers 14; Students 150.
Catechesis/Religious Program—Tel: 231-843-3497. Students 164.
2—ST. STANISLAUS, [JC] Closed. For inquiries for parish records see St. Simon's Ludington.

MARION, OSCEOLA CO., ST. AGNES (1888) Rev. Joseph J. Fix.
Res.: P.O. Box 778, Evart, 49631. Tel: 231-734-3171. Church: Tel: 231-743-6401; Fax: 231-734-6880.
Catechesis/Religious Program—Tel: 231-825-2971; Fax: 231-825-0230. Lynne Nolan, D.R.E. Students 24.

MARNE, OTTAWA CO., ST. MARY'S, [CEM] Rev. William F. Zink.
Res.: 15164 Juniper Dr., 49435. Tel: 616-677-3934; Fax: 616-677-5866.
Catechesis/Religious Program—Tel: 616-677-5065. Students 155.

MIRIAM, IONIA CO., ST. MARY'S (1871) [CEM] Rev. Philip A. Shangraw; Deacon Daniel Schneider.
Office: 409 S. Bridge St., Belding, 48809. Tel: 616-794-2145; Fax: 616-794-2145. Email: sjsmoffice@sjbelding.com. Web: www.joseph-mary.catholicweb.com.
See St. Joseph-St. Mary under St. Joseph, Belding for details.
Catechesis/Religious Program—Twinned with St. Joseph, Belding. Students 68.

MONTAGUE, MUSKEGON CO., ST. JAMES (1876) [CEM] Rev. Donn Tufts; Deacon Gregory Anderson.
Res.: 5149 Dowling St., 49437. Tel: 231-893-3085; Fax: 231-894-9929. Email: parishoffice@stjamescatholicparish.org. Web: www.stjamescatholicparish.org.
Catechesis/Religious Program—Email: faithformation@stjamescatholicparish.org. Pat Jackson, Faith Formation Coord. Students 150.

MUSKEGON, MUSKEGON CO.
1—ST. FRANCIS DE SALES (1948) [JC] Rev. Philip J. Salmonowicz; Deacon William McCabe.
Res.: 2929 McCracken St., 49441. Tel: 231-755-1953; Fax: 231-759-7074. Email: parish@sfnortonshores.com. Web: www.sfnortonshores.com.
Catechesis/Religious Program—Tel: 231-755-1307. Students 180.
2—ST. JEAN BAPTISTE (1883) [JC] Rev. Matthew J. Barnum; Deacon William Cook.
Res.: 1292 Jefferson St., 49441. Tel: 231-722-2793; Fax: 231-726-5976. Email: stjeanbaptiste@frontier.com. Web: stjeanbaptiste.catholicweb.com.
Catechesis/Religious Program—Mary Yack, D.R.E. Students 116.
3—ST. JOSEPH'S, Closed. For inquiries for parish records please see Our Lady of Grace, 451 S. Getty St., Muskegon, MI 49442
4—ST. MARY'S (1856) [JC] Rev. Matthew J. Barnum.
Res.: 239 W. Clay Ave., 49440-1213. Tel: 231-722-2844; Fax: 231-726-5976. Email: stmaryschurch@frontier.com. Web: www.stmaryschurchmuskegon.org.
Catechesis/Religious Program—Students 46.
5—ST. MICHAEL'S (1909) [JC] Rev. Thomas J. Brown.
Res.: 1716 Sixth St., 49441. Tel: 231-722-3071; Fax: 231-722-3243. Email: stmichaelmusk@aol.com.
Catechesis/Religious Program— Sr. Agnes Mary Wojtkowiak, O.P., D.R.E.; Andrea Piotrowski, Dir. Youth Ministry. Students 34.
6—OUR LADY OF GRACE (1923) [JC] Rev. Antony Britto, S.A.C., Admin.
Res.: 451 S. Getty St., 49442. Tel: 231-722-2803; Fax: 231-722-3622. Email: ourladyofgracechurch@comcast.net.
Catechesis/Religious Program—Students 81.
7—ST. THOMAS THE APOSTLE (1948) Rev. Antony Britto, S.A.C., Admin.; Deacon David Kasprzyk.
Office: 3252 Apple Ave., 49442. Tel: 231-773-3160; Fax: 231-777-7866. Email: saint_thomas@frontier.com; stthomasmuskegon@frontier.com.
Catechesis/Religious Program—451 S. Getty, 49442. Students 38.

MUSKEGON HEIGHTS, MUSKEGON CO., SACRED HEART (1919) [JC] Rev. Thomas J. Brown.
Res.: 150 E. Summit Ave., 49444. Tel: 231-733-2440; Fax: 231-733-5128.
Catechesis/Religious Program—Tel: 231-733-2440. Students 40.

NEWAYGO, NEWAYGO CO., ST. BARTHOLOMEW'S (1885) [CEM] Rev. Peter Schafer; Jan Vile, Pastoral Assoc.
Res.: 599 W. Brooks St., 49337. Tel: 231-652-1286; Fax: 231-652-6669. Email: stbaresj@hotmail.com. Web: www.catholicweb.com/stbartourlady.
Catechesis/Religious Program—Jan Vile, D.R.E. Students 130.

NORTH MUSKEGON, MUSKEGON CO., PRINCE OF PEACE (1975) Rev. Anthony M. Pelak; Deacon James J. Schlitz.
Res.: 1110 Dykstra, 49445. Tel: 231-744-3321; Fax: 231-744-4859. Email: pofpeace.church@frontier.com. Web: www.princeofpeacemusk.org.
Catechesis/Religious Program—Tel: 231-744-5445. Walter Elliott, Youth Min.; Donna Phillips, D.R.E. Students 169.

PARNELL, KENT CO., ST. PATRICK'S (1844) [CEM] Rev. Mark E. Peacock.
Res.: 4351 Parnell, Ada, 49301. Tel: 616-691-8541; Fax: 616-691-6309. Email: secrepat@wmis.net. Web: stpatrickparnell.org.
School—(Grades K-8), 4333 Parnell Ave., N.E., Ada, 49301. Tel: 616-691-8833. Web: www.stpatrickparnell.org/school. Scott Czarnopys, Prin.; Deb Russo, Librarian. Lay Teachers 5; Students 76.
Catechesis/Religious Program—Email: rciaham@wmis.net. Students 209.

PEWAMO, IONIA CO., ST. JOSEPH'S (1903) [CEM] Rev. Charlon O. Mason.
Res.: 106 East St., 48873. Tel: 989-593-2913; Fax: 989-593-3184. Email: stjoseph@cablespeed.com. Web: www.stjosephpewamo.org.
School—(Grades 2-8), 160 East St., P.O. Box 38, 48873. Tel: 989-593-3400; Fax: 989-593-3400. Patricia O'Mara, Prin. Lay Teachers 6; Students 88.
Catechesis/Religious Program—126 East St., P.O. Box 37, 48873. Tel: 989-593-3384. Aaron Epkey. Students 94.

PORTLAND, IONIA CO., ST. PATRICK'S (1878) Rev. Larry King; Deacon Don F. Sobolewski, Pastoral Assoc.
Res.: 140 Church St., 48875. Tel: 517-647-6505; Fax: 517-647-7807. Email: parishoffice@portlandstpats.com. Web: www.portlandstpats.com.
School—(Grades K-8), 122 West St., 48875. Tel: 517-647-7551; Fax: 517-647-4545. Email: office@portlandstpats.org. Anne Bennett, Librarian. Lay Teachers 16; Students 251.
High School—Randy Hodge, Prin. Lay Teachers 8; Students 102.
Catechesis/Religious Program— Thomas Jandernoa, D.R.E. Students 239.

RAVENNA, MUSKEGON CO., ST. CATHERINE (1908) [CEM] Rev. G. Fredrick Brucker.
Res.: 12285 Hts. Ravenna Rd., P.O. Box 216, 49451. Tel: 231-853-6222; Fax: 231-853-2191. Email: stcatherinealex@aol.com.
School—(Grades K-6), 3375 Thomas St., 49451. Tel: 231-853-6743; Fax: 231-853-8673. Richard E. Kosla, Prin. Lay Teachers 2; Students 41.
Catechesis/Religious Program—Tel: 231-853-2191. Students 24.

REED CITY, OSCEOLA CO., ST. PHILIP NERI, [CEM] Rev. Loc Trinh.
Res.: 831 S. Chestnut, 49677. Tel: 231-832-5544; Fax: 231-832-5545.
Catechesis/Religious Program—Elizabeth Dake, Dir. Faith Formation. Students 49.
Mission—St. Anne 23949 22 Mile Rd., Paris, Mecosta Co. 49338.

REMUS, MECOSTA CO., ST. MICHAEL'S (1888) [CEM] Rev. Michael E. Burt; Deacon Robert Cathcart.
Res.: 5045 Nine Mile Rd., 49340. Tel: 989-967-3520; Fax: 989-967-8246. Email: stmichael@winntel.net. Web: stmichaelsremus.net.
School—(Grades K-6), 8944 50th Ave., 49340. Tel: 989-967-3681; Fax: 989-967-3061. Web: www.stmike-s.us. Mrs. Mary Schoner, Prin.; Amber Snow, Librarian. Lay Teachers 5; Students 79.
Catechesis/Religious Program—Students 45.

ROCKFORD, KENT CO., OUR LADY OF CONSOLATION (1972) Rev. Anthony S. Russo; Frank Siegel, Business Mgr.
Office: 4865 Eleven Mile Rd., 49341. Tel: 616-866-0931; Fax: 616-866-3668. Email: olcparish@olcparish.net. Web: www.olcparish.net.
School—(Grades PreK-8) Tel: 616-866-2427; Fax: 616-866-5475. Email: olcschool@olcparish.net. Kevin Varner, Prin.; Mandy McGregor, Librarian. Lay Teachers 11; Students 256.
Catechesis/Religious Program—Tel: 616-866-2577. Students 844.

ROTHBURY, OCEANA CO., OUR LADY OF THE ASSUMPTION (1923) [CEM], Twinned with Our Lady of Fatima, Rothbury Rev. Phillip J. Witkowski.
Res.: 1372 S. Oceana Dr., Shelby, 49455. Tel: 231-861-2620; Fax: 231-861-6878.
Church: 3000 Winston Rd., P.O. Box 8, 49452. Tel: 231-893-0905.

SAND LAKE, KENT CO., MARY QUEEN OF APOSTLES, [CEM 2] Rev. Joseph W. Kenshol.
Res.: 1 Maple St., P.O. Box 140, 49343-0140. Tel: 616-636-5671; Fax: 616-636-4570. Email: mqapostles@sbcglobal.net.
Catechesis/Religious Program—Tel: 616-636-5923. Students 93.
Mission—St. Clara 4584 N. Bailey Rd., Coral, Montcalm Co. 49322.

SARANAC, IONIA CO., ST. ANTHONY (1951) Rev. Victor Kynam.
6070 David Hwy., 48881.
Res.: 3927 Jackson Rd., 48881. Tel: 616-642-6119; Fax: 616-642-0390. Email: victorkynam@gmail.com.
Catechesis/Religious Program—Michele Westbrook, D.R.E. Students 45.

SCOTTVILLE, MASON CO., ST. JEROME (1912) [CEM] Rev. Edward Boucher.
Office: 203 W. State St., 49454. Tel: 231-757-2855; Fax: 231-757-2855. Email: stjeromesc@sbcglobal.net. 85 Madison Ave., Custer, 49405. Tel: 231-757-4709; Fax: 231-757-4709.

Catechesis/Religious Program—Barbara Burwell, D.R.E. Students 49.

SHELBY, OCEANA CO., OUR LADY OF FATIMA Rev. Phillip J. Witkowski.
Res.: 1372 S. Oceana Dr., 49455. Tel: 231-861-2620; Fax: 231-861-6878.
Catechesis/Religious Program—Students 73.
Mission—St John, Oceana Co.

SPARTA, KENT CO., HOLY FAMILY (1947) Rev. Msgr. Terrence L. Stewart.
Res.: 425 S. State St., 49345. Tel: 616-887-8222; Fax: 616-887-0681.
Catechesis/Religious Program—Tel: 616-887-8857. Students 178.

SPRING LAKE, OTTAWA CO., ST. MARY'S (1863) Rev. Daniel R. DePew; Deacon William Charron.
Res.: 406 E. Savidge, 49456. Tel: 616-842-1702; Fax: 616-842-3392.
Rectory—421 E. Exchange St., 49456. Tel: 616-842-1615.
School—(Grades PreSchool-8), 421 E. Exchange, 49456. Tel: 616-842-1282; Fax: 616-842-8048. Web: www.stmaryschoolspringlake.com. Mike Devitt, Prin. Lay Teachers 12; Students 185.
Catechesis/Religious Program—Tel: 616-842-2840. Jim Penrice, D.R.E. Students 284.

STANTON, MONTCALM CO., ST. BERNADETTE OF LOURDES (1963) Rev. Dominic Tirkey.
Res.: 1051 E. Howard City, Edmore, 48829. Tel: 989-427-5645; Fax: 989-831-5707. Email: sbl.smm.church@frontier.com.
Catechesis/Religious Program—Students 31.

WEARE TWP., OCEANA CO., ST. JOSEPH'S (1884) [CEM] Rev. Philip Sliwinski.
Office: 2380 W. Jackson Rd., Hart, 49420. Tel: 231-873-5776; Fax: 231-873-5327. Email: st.joseph@lakeshore.net.
Catechesis/Religious Program—Renee Dennert, D.R.E. Students 29.
Mission—St. Vincent 637 E. Sixth, Pentwater, Oceana Co. 49449. Tel: 231-869-2601.

WHITE CLOUD, NEWAYGO CO., ST. JOSEPH'S, [CEM] Rev. Peter O. Omogo.
Office: 500 Iroquois, Fremont, 49412.
Church: 965 Newell St., 49349. Tel: 231-924-7705; Fax: 231-924-7708. Email: allsinsfremont2@sbcglobal.net.
Catechesis/Religious Program—Students 35.

WRIGHT TOWNSHIP, OTTAWA CO., ST. JOSEPH'S (1853) [CEM] Rev. G. Fredrick Brucker.
Res.: 18784 Eighth Ave., Conklin, 49403. Tel: 616-899-2286; Fax: 616-899-2212. Email: stjosephwright@gmail.com.
School—(Grades PreK-8), 18768 Eighth Ave., Conklin, 49403. Tel: 616-899-5300; Fax: 616-899-5491. Web: www.stjoseph-school.org. Richard E. Kosla, Prin. Lay Teachers 3; Students 68.
Catechesis/Religious Program—Tel: 616-899-2384. Students 133.

WYOMING, CHISAGO CO., OUR LADY OF LAVANG (1999) [JC] Rev. Peter Nghiem; Deacon Thanh Van Nguyen. 2420 Avon S.W., 49519. Tel: 616-261-9422; Fax: 616-531-1948.
Catechesis/Religious Program—Students 249.

CHAPELS

GRAND RAPIDS
CHAPEL OF OUR LADY OF AGLONA, LATVIAN APOSTOLATE—Cathedral Square Center, 360 Division Ave., S., 49503-4539. Tel: 616-243-0491.
Michigan Veterans' Facility Catholic Chapel—3000 Monroe Ave., N.E., 49505. Tel: 616-364-5323.

On Special Assignment:
Rev. Msgrs.—
Duncan, William H., Vicar Gen. & Moderator of the Curia, 660 Burton, S.E., 49507. Tel: 616-243-0491
Stasker, R. Louis, Pastor & Pres., Catholic Secondary Schools. Tel: 616-233-5979

Revs.—
Brucker, G. Fredrick, Adjutant Judicial Vicar for the Tribunal. Tel: 616-794-2145
Dudek, Stephen S., Dir., Missions Office and the Society for the Propagation of Faith, Cathedral Square Center, 360 Division Ave., S., 49503. Tel: 616-459-4516; Fax: 616-243-4910
Hankiewicz, Edward A., J.C.L., Judicial Vicar, Tribunal Office. Tel: 616-551-5672
Hutchinson, Ronald D., Dir., Priestly Vocations. Tel: 616-475-1274
Morrow, Dennis W., Adjutant Judicial Vicar for the Tribunal; Diocesan Archivist; Chap. Grand Rapids Fire Dept. & Grand Rapids Police Dept.
Nghiem, Peter, Dir. Vietnamese Apostolate, 2420 Avon S.W., 49509. Tel: 616-531-5213 National service to community of Vietnamese Clergy and Religious; Serving Vietnamese Catholic Federation of USA.
Onyekwere, Godfrey C., Dir., Office of Black Catholic Ministry, Cathedral Square Center, 360 Division Ave., S., 49503. Tel: 616-243-0491
Page, Thomas P., Assoc. Vicar for Priests. Tel: 616-363-1093
Przybysz, Mark C., Dir. of Continuing Formation of Priests. Tel: 616-453-8229
Quintana, Jose, Liaison & Delegate, Cursillo Movement, 250 Brown St., S.E., 49507. Tel: 616-241-2485
Rouech, Chris W., Dir., Office of Worship, Cathedral Square Center, 360 Division Ave., S., 49503. Tel: 616-475-1241
Sliwinski, Philip, Archives and projects as assigned by Bishop
Weber, Donald E., Vicar for Priests (Retired). Tel: 616-457-1378

Personal Leave:
Rev.—
Nguyen, Phillip D.

Faculties Suspended:
Revs.—
Cook, Daniel
Harpe, David L.
Kurylowicz, Martin

Unassigned:
Rev.—
Badgerow, Rock J.

Retired:
Rev. Msgrs.—
Ancona, Gaspar F., 5920 W. Lyn Haven Dr., Kentwood, 49512.
Giammona, John J., 3803 Old Elm Dr., S.E., Kentwood, 49512.
Porter, John F., 7332 Chippewa Hwy., Kaleva, 49645.
Revs.—
Anderson, Louis, 4753 Rock Valley Dr., N.E., 49525.
Antekeier, Charles R.
Bernott, Ernest J., 1409 Quarry Ave., N.W., 49504.
Bozung, James M., 601 Spring Ave., N.E., 49503.
Bruck, Raymond E., 1200 104th, S.W., Byron Center, 49315.
Cawley, Patrick, c/o General Delivery, Vanderbilt, 49795.
Danner, Michael A.
DeYoung, Thomas J., 3543 Brook Tr., S.E., 49508.
Droski, Norman P., 2858 Oak Ct., Spring Lake, 49456. Tel: 231-865-6171
Fekete, George J., 628 Diamond, N.E., 49503.
Fox, Melvin E.
Garcia, Pedro, 13685 New Holland St., Holland, 49424.
Golas, Eugene S., 601 Spring Ave., N.E., 49503.
Hack, Thomas, 601 Spring Ave., N.E., 49503.
La Goe, John P., 3119 Scenic Dr., North Muskegon, 49445.
Leyrita, Norbert, 6253 E. Woodrow Rd., Hesperia, 49421.
Lowie, Richard J., 4223 Valleyside Dr., N.E., 49525.
McKinney, Thomas A., St. Ann's Home, 2161 Leonard, N.W., 49504.
Mitchell, Mark E., 601 Spring Ave., N.E., 49503.
Olson, Michael P.
Reginato, Julian, 17468 Dunewood Ct., D, Spring Lake, 49456.
Reitz, William J., 52 Marble Rd., Lowell, 49331.
Schichtel, Kenneth H., 17502 Meadow Wood, Spring Lake, 49456.
Schiller, Thomas A., 3816 Fountain R., Ludington, 49431.
Toolis, Martin, 317 N. Lavina St., Ludington, 49431.
Vainavicz, Anthony C., 11968 Reyburn Dr., Sparta, 49345.
VanLente, Richard
Vesbit, Thomas, 2608 Inverness Rd., S.E., 49546.
Weber, Donald E., 7523 Pinegrove Dr., Jenison, 49428.
Wisneski, John J., 2066 Ter Van Dr., 49505.

Permanent Deacons:
Anderson, Gregory, St. James, Montague
Baldwin, Kenneth, Immaculate Heart of Mary, Grand Rapids
Burns, Jeffrey, Holy Name of Jesus, Wyoming
Cardenas, Zenon, Sr., SS. Peter and Paul, Ionia; St. Patrick, Grand Haven
Carrero, Edwin, St. Francis deSales, Holland
Cathcart, Robert, St. Michael, Remus
Charron, William, St. Mary, Spring Lake
Conigliaro, Pietro, Assumption of the Blessed Virgin Mary, Belmont; Jail Ministry
Cook, William, St. Jean Baptiste & St. Mary, Muskegon
Dordan, Michael, St. Mary Magdalen, Kentwood
Dubridge, Richard, Christ the King, Howard City
Ferguson, Leo, St. Anthony of Padua, Grand Rapids
Fett, Richard, Jail Ministry, Ottawa Co.
Finnigan, Joseph, St. Patrick, Grand Haven
Garcia, Juan, St. Francis de Sales, Holland
Gutierrez, Carlos, Holy Name of Jesus, St. Joseph the Worker, Grand Rapids (& Bishop Liaison to Marriage Encounter for Spanish speaking)
Harwood, Edward, St. Mary, Grand Rapids
Herrera, Manuel E., SS. Peter and Paul, Grand Rapids
Hoogeboom, Larry, St. Jude, Grand Rapids
Jurek, Thomas
Kasprzyk, David, St. Thomas the Apostle, Muskegon
Lechtanski, Stanley, St. James, Grand Rapids
Mauer, Michael J., Assumption of BVM
McCabe, William, St. Francis de Sales, Muskegon
McClintic, Robert, St. James, Grand Rapids; Prison & Jail Ministry
Nguyen, Thanh Van, Our Lady of LaVang, Wyoming
Pitt, Richard, Holy Redeemer, Jenison
Radecki, Richard, (Retired), St. Paul the Apostle, Grand Rapids
Riksen, Norman, (Retired)
Roersma, Gerald, Holy Trinity, Comstock Park
Scheid, Howard, (Retired)
Schlitz, James, Prince of Peace, North Muskegon
Schneider, Daniel, St. Joseph & St. Mary's Parishes, Belding
Sobolewski, Donald F., St. Patrick, Portland
Thorndill, James, St. Thomas, Grand Rapids
VandeVoren, Lawrence
Williams, Dennis, St. Thomas, Grand Rapids
Wood, Michael, St. Mary Magdalen, Grand Rapids
Zapata, Martin, St. Joseph the Worker, Grand Rapids

INSTITUTIONS LOCATED IN THE DIOCESE

[A] COLLEGES AND UNIVERSITIES

GRAND RAPIDS. *Aquinas College*, 1607 Robinson Rd., S.E., 49506. Tel: 616-632-8900; Fax: 616-732-4589. Web: www.aquinas.edu. Juan Olivarez, Ph.D., Pres.; Charles Gunnoe, Ph.D., Provost; Michael C. Keller, M.S.A., Vice Pres. Planning & Research; Greg McAleenan, B.A., J.D., Vice Pres. Advancement; Paula Meehan, Vice Pres. Enrollment Mgmt.; Nanette Clatterbuck, M.Ed., Assoc. Provost; Thomas Mikowski, B.S., Dean of Admissions; Cecilia Mesler, B.A., Registrar; David J. Steffee, Dir. Financial Aid; Mary Clark-Kaiser, Dir. Campus Ministry; Terry Marshall, Liturgist; Eric Bridge, Service Learning Coord.; Francine Paolini, Co-Dir. Library; Shellie Jeffries, Co-Dir. Library; Patricia Chase, Ed.D., Dean Students; Terrence Bocian, M.A., Dir. Athletics; Stephen J. Wonch, C.P.A., M.B.A., Vice Pres. Finance. Sisters 5; Lay Teachers 86; Students 2,312.

[B] HIGH SCHOOLS, DIOCESAN

GRAND RAPIDS. *Catholic Central High School*, 319 Sheldon Ave., S.E., 49503. Tel: 616-233-5803; Fax: 616-459-0257. Email: gregdeja@grcss.org. Web: www.grcatholiccentral.com. Greg Deja, Prin.; Karen Harag, Librarian. Sisters of St. Dominic 1; Lay Teachers 44; Students 773.
West Catholic High School, 1801 Bristol, N.W., 49504. Tel: 616-233-5900; Fax: 616-453-4320. Web: grwestcatholic.org. Mrs. Cindy Kneibel, Interim Prin.; Karen Harag, Librarian. Lay Teachers 31; Students 506.

[C] HIGH SCHOOLS, PRIVATE

MUSKEGON. *Greater Muskegon Catholic Schools*, 1145 W. Laketon Ave., 49441. Tel: 231-755-2201; Fax: 231-755-2415. Robert Bridges, Supt.; Penny Johnson, Prin.; Margaret Alexander, Librarian. Lay Teachers 35; Students 494.

[D] INTERPAROCHIAL ELEMENTARY SCHOOLS

HOLLAND. *Corpus Christi School*, (Grades K-8), 12100 Quincy St., 49424. Tel: 616-994-9864; Fax: 616-994-9870. Web: www.corpuschristischool.us. Joanne Swan Jones, Prin. Lay Teachers 14; Students 136.

WYOMING. *San Juan Diego Academy*, 1650 Godfrey Ave., S.W., 49509.

[E] DIOCESAN ELEMENTARY SCHOOLS

GRAND RAPIDS. *All Saints Academy*, (Grades PreSchool-8), PS-4 Campus: 2233 Diamond Ave.,

N.E., 49505. Tel: 616-364-9453; Fax: 616-361-6991. 5-8 Campus: 1120 Four Mile N.E., 49525. Tel: 616-363-7725; Fax: 616-363-3086. Anne Harpold, Prin.; Michael Debri, Asst. Prin.; Linda Kozminski, Librarian. Lay Teachers 21.

[F] GRADE SCHOOLS, PRIVATE

MUSKEGON. *Muskegon Catholic Central Elementary School*, (Grades PreSchool-4), 2947 McCracken St., 49441. Tel: 231-755-1045; Fax: 231-759-7009. Web: www.gmcs.org. Penny Johnson, Prin. Lay Teachers 10; Students 191.

[G] GENERAL HOSPITALS

GRAND RAPIDS. *Saint Mary's Health Care*, 200 Jefferson, S.E., 49503. Tel: 616-685-6090; Fax: 616-685-6151. Web: www.smhc.org. Philip McCorkle, Pres. & CEO; Rev. Ayub Nasar, Chap.; Sr. Myra Bergman, R.S.M., Vice Pres. Mission Svcs. Sponsored by Catholic Health Ministries. Bed Capacity 344; Patients Assisted Annually 916,000; Total Staff 2,124.

MUSKEGON. *Mercy Health Partners*Roger Spoelman, Pres. & CEO; Rev. Bartholomew Okagbue, Chap. Sponsored by Trinity Health. Bed Capacity 458; Totally Assisted Annually Inpatient 19,560; Total Staff 3,800.

Mercy Health Partners, Mercy Campus, 1500 E. Sherman Blvd., 49444. Tel: 231-672-2000; Fax: 231-672-3074.

Mercy Health Partners, General Campus, 1700 Oak Ave., 49242. Tel: 231-672-2000. Priests 1; Sisters 1.

Mercy Health Partners, Hackley Campus, 1700 Clinton Ave., 49442. Tel: 231-672-2000.

Mercy Health Partners, Lakeshore Campus, 72 S. State St., Shelby, 49455. Tel: 231-861-2156.

[H] HOMES FOR THE AGED

GRAND RAPIDS. *St. Ann's Home* (1951) 2161 Leonard St., N.W., 49504. Tel: 616-453-7715; Fax: 616-453-7359. Email: sisterg@stannshome.com. Carmelite Sisters of the Divine Heart of Jesus. Priests 2; Sisters 6; Residents 150; Total Assisted 150; Total Staff 200.

[I] CONVENTS AND RESIDENCES FOR SISTERS

GRAND RAPIDS. *Dominican Center at Marywood*, 2025 E. Fulton St., 49503-3895. Tel: 616-454-1241; Fax: 616-454-2861. Web: www.dominicancenter.com. Mary Vaccaro, Prog. Dir.

Marywood Health Center, 111 Lakeside Dr., N.E., 49503-3811. Tel: 616-643-0272; Fax: 616-454-6105. Sisters 48; Bed Capacity 50.

Motherhouse of the Dominican Sisters, Marywood, 2025 E. Fulton St., 49503-3895. Tel: 616-459-2910; Fax: 616-454-6105. Web: www.grdominicans.org. Sisters Nathalie Meyer, O.P., Prioress; Janet Brown, O.P., Dir. Pastoral Life; Maureen Geary, O.P., Treas.

Sisters of St. Dominic of the Congregation of Our Lady of the Sacred Heart (The Religious Institute) Sisters of the Order of St. Dominic of Grand Rapids, Michigan (The Corporation)., Motherhouse and Novitiate for the Sisters of the Order of St. Dominic of the Congregation of Our Lady of the Sacred Heart. Sisters 245.

ADA. *Discalced Carmelite Nuns, Monastery of Our Lady of Guadalupe* (1916) (Parnell), 4300 Mount Carmel Dr., N.E., 49301-9784. Tel: 616-691-7625; Fax: 616-691-8538. Sr. Elizabeth Ann, O.C.D., Prioress. Professed Carmelite Nuns 10; Extern Sisters 2.

BELMONT. *Motherhouse of the Consolata Missionary Sisters* (1954) 6801 Belmont Rd., P.O. Box 371, 49306. Tel: 616-361-2072; Fax: 616-361-2072. Email: reusamc@consolatasisters.org. Web: www.consolatasisters.org. Sr. Zelita M. Bragagnolo, M.C., Supr. Consolata Sisters 10.

LOWELL. *Franciscan Sisters of the Eucharist*, 11600 Downes St., 49331-9489. Tel: 616-897-5590; Fax: 616-897-5088. Email: smaschmitz@fsecommunity.org. Sr. Rita Brunner, F.S.E., Supr. Sisters 14.

[J] RETREAT HOUSES

SPRING LAKE. *St. Lazare Retreat House*, 18600 W. Spring Lake Rd., 49456. Tel: 616-842-3370; Fax: 616-842-6815. Email: secretaryst@att.net. Web: www.stlazareretreat.org. Revs. Vincent J. O'Malley, C.M.; Francis W. Sacks, C.M.

[K] NEWMAN CENTERS

ALLENDALE. *St. Luke University Parish and Catholic Campus Ministry* Cook-Dewitt Center, GVSU, Rm. 120, 49401-9403. Tel: 616-331-3131. Email: frbrad@gvsucatholic.org. Revs. Bradford C. Schoeberle, C.S.P., Campus Min.; Donald A. Andrie, C.S.P., Campus Min.

BIG RAPIDS

St. Paul Campus Parish listed under Parishes Outside the City of Grand Rapids

[L] MISCELLANEOUS LISTINGS

GRAND RAPIDS. *Basilica of St. Adalbert Education Foundation* (1985) 701 4th St., N.W., 49504. Tel: 616-458-3065; Fax: 616-458-0563. Email: stasker@basilicagr.org. Web: basilicagr.org.

Bishops' Housing Corporation, Cathedral Square Center, 360 Division Ave., S., 49503-4539. Tel: 616-475-1247; Fax: 616-551-5635.

Cathedral Square, Inc., Cathedral Square Center, 360 Division Ave., S., 49503-4539. Tel: 616-475-1247; Fax: 616-551-5635.

Catholic Charities West Michigan, Catholic Charities West Michigan, 360 Division Ave., S., 49503-4539. Tel: 616-551-4747; Fax: 616-243-1442. Web: www.ccwestmi.org. Deborah Nykamp, Ph.D., L.M.S.W., Pres. & CEO.

The Catholic Foundation of West Michigan, 360 Division Ave. S., 49503. Tel: 616-243-0491; Fax: 616-243-4910. T. Edward Carey Jr.

Catholic Information Center, Cathedral Square Center, 360 Division Ave. S., Ste. 2A, 49503-4539. Tel: 616-459-7267; Fax: 616-459-4645. Rev. John Geaney, C.S.P., Dir.

Christopher House, Cathedral Square Center, 360 Division Ave., S., 49503-4539. Tel: 616-475-1247; Fax: 616-551-5635.

The Foundation for Catholic Secondary Education of Greater Grand Rapids, Inc., Cathedral Square Center, 360 Division Ave., S., 49503-4539. Tel: 616-514-6069; Fax: 616-458-7740.

Marywood Academy, 2025 E. Fulton St., 49503-3895. Tel: 616-454-2910; Fax: 616-454-6105.

Ministry Ventures, 2025 E. Fulton St., 49503-3895. Tel: 616-643-0133; Fax: 616-454-6105. Email: mgeary@grdominicans.org. Sr. Maureen Geary, O.P., Treas.; Jack Peltier, Dir. Finance.

St. Philip Neri House, 360 Division Ave. S., 49503.

Sisters of St. Dominic Charitable Trust, 2025 E. Fulton St., 49503-3895. Tel: 616-459-2910; Fax: 616-454-6105. Sr. Nathalie Meyer, O.P.

Sisters of St. Dominic of the Congregation of Our Lady of the Sacred Heart Charitable Trust (The Trust).

The Society of the Redemptorists of the City of Grand Rapids, 224 Carrier St., N.E., 49505. Tel: 616-451-3043; Fax: 616-458-5667. Email: stalphonsusgr@catholicweb.com. Web: stalphonsusgr.com. Revs. Patrick Grile, C.Ss.R.; Lamar Partin, C.Ss.R.; Robert Balser, C.Ss.R.; Bernard Carlin, C.Ss.R.; Thomas Danielson, C.Ss.R.; Bro. Andrew Patin, C.Ss.R. Represented in the Diocese.

Steepletown Neighborhood Services, Inc. (1994) 671 Davis, N.W., Steepletown Center, 49504. Tel: 616-451-4215; Fax: 616-451-0557. Email: dick@steepletowncenter.org. Neighborhood Center for Social Service and Assistance.

The Society For The Propagation Of The Faith, Cathedral Square Center, 360 Division Ave., S., 49503-4539. Tel: 616-459-4516; Fax: 616-243-4910. Rev. Stephen S. Dudek, Dir.

BELMONT. *Grand Rapids Catholic Committee on Scouting*, 6550 Belmont Ave., 49306. Tel: 616-780-9088; 616-364-9093. Email: scottharvey@prodigy.net. Web: www.grccscouting.org. Scott Harvey, Treas.

LOWELL. *Franciscan Life Process Center* (1999) 11650 Downes St., 49331-9489. Tel: 616-897-7842; Fax: 616-897-7054. Email: scanagle@lifeprocesscenter.org. Sr. Colleen Ann Nagle, F.S.E., Dir.

PORTLAND. *The Father Flohe Foundation*, 140 Church St., 48875. Tel: 517-647-6505; Fax: 517-647-7807.

VESTABURG. *Emmaus Monastery*, 10154 N. Pine Grove Rd., 48891. Tel: 989-268-5494. Email: emmaus.monastery@gmail.com. Web: www.emmausmonastery.org. Sr. Diane Stier, E.C., Prioress.

WYOMING. *Catholic Cemeteries Extended Care Fund*, 4100 Clyde Park, S.W., 49509-0063. Tel: 616-531-9320; Fax: 616-531-9780. Mr. Robert Menzel, Dir. & Mgr.

RELIGIOUS INSTITUTES OF MEN REPRESENTED IN THE DIOCESE

For further details refer to the corresponding bracketed number in the Religious Institutes of Men or Women section.

[1330]—*Congregation of the Mission*—C.M.
[1030]—*Paulist Fathers*—C.S.P.
[1070]—*Redemptorist Fathers* (Denver Prov.)—C.Ss.R.
[0990]—*Society of the Catholic Apostolate*—S.A.C.

RELIGIOUS INSTITUTES OF WOMEN REPRESENTED IN THE DIOCESE

[0360]—*Carmelite Sisters of the Divine Heart of Jesus Carmel*—C.D.C.J.
[3832]—*Congregation of the Sisters of St. Joseph*—C.S.J.
[0720]—*Consolata Missionary Sisters*—M.C.
[0420]—*Discalced Carmelite Nuns*—O.C.D.
[1070-14]—*Dominican Sisters*—O.P.
[]—*Emmaus Community*—E.C.
[2575]—*Institute of the Sisters of Mercy of the Americas*—R.S.M.
[]—*Mexican Passionist Sisters*—C.F.P.
[2970]—*School Sisters of Notre Dame*—S.S.N.D.
[3560]—*Servants of Jesus*—S.J.
[2990]—*Sisters of Notre Dame*—S.N.D.
[3980]—*Sisters of St. Paul De Chartres*—S.D.C.
[1250]—*The Institute for the Franciscan Sisters of the Eucharist*—F.S.E.

NECROLOGY

† Zerfas, Rev. Msgr. Herman H., (Retired)—Died Dec. 6, 2010
† Gillespie, Robert B., (Retired)—Died July 30, 2011
† Pettit, Joseph, (Retired)—Died July 22, 2011

An asterisk (*) denotes an organization that has established tax-exempt status directly with the IRS and is not covered by the USCCB Group Ruling.

Diocese of Great Falls - Billings

(Dioecesis Magnocataractensis-Billingensis)

Most Reverend

MICHAEL W. WARFEL

Bishop of Great Falls-Billings; ordained April 26, 1980; appointed Bishop of Juneau November 19, 1996; ordained December 17, 1996; appointed Apostolic Administrator of Fairbanks October 23, 2001; resigned June 7, 2002; appointed Bishop of Great Falls-Billings November 20, 2007; installed January 16, 2008. *Office: 121 23rd St. S., Great Falls, MT 59401-3939.* Tel: 406-727-6683.

ALWAYS TO WALK IN CHRIST

Pastoral Office: 121 23rd St. S., Great Falls, MT 59401-3939. Mailing Address: P.O. Box 1399, Great Falls, MT 59403-1399. Tel: 406-727-6683; 800-332-9998 (Toll Free); Fax: 406-454-3480.

Web: www.dioceseofgfb.org

Email: chancery@dioceseofgfb.org

Most Reverend

ANTHONY M. MILONE, D.D.

Bishop Emeritus of Great Falls-Billings; ordained December 15, 1957; appointed Titular Bishop Plestia and Auxiliary of Omaha November 10, 1981; Episcopal ordination January 6, 1982; appointed Bishop of Great Falls-Billings December 14, 1987; installed February 23, 1988; resigned July 12, 2006. *Res.: St. Bernadette, 7600 S. 42nd St., Bellevue, NE 68147-1702.* Tel: 402-933-8707. Email: bishopmilone@cox.net.

ERECTED MAY 18, 1904.

Square Miles 94,158.

Corporation Title: "Roman Catholic Bishop of Great Falls, Montana, a corporation sole."

Comprises the eastern part of the State of Montana and is made up of the following Counties: Big Horn, Blaine, Carbon, Carter, Cascade, Chouteau, Custer, Daniels, Dawson, Fallon, Fergus, Garfield, Golden Valley, Hill, Judith Basin, Liberty, McCone, Musselshell, Park, Petroleum, Phillips, Powder River, Prairie, Richland, Roosevelt, Rosebud, Sheridan, Stillwater, Sweet Grass, Treasure, Valley, Wibaux, Yellowstone and parts of Toole.

For legal titles of parishes and diocesan institutions, consult the Pastoral Office.

STATISTICAL OVERVIEW

Personnel	
Bishop	1
Retired Bishops	1
Priests: Diocesan Active in Diocese	31
Priests: Diocesan Active Outside Diocese	4
Priests: Retired, Sick or Absent	27
Number of Diocesan Priests	62
Religious Priests in Diocese	12
Total Priests in Diocese	74
Extern Priests in Diocese	4
Ordinations:	
Transitional Deacons	1
Permanent Deacons in Diocese	5
Total Sisters	49
Parishes	
Parishes	53
With Resident Pastor:	
Resident Diocesan Priests	28
Resident Religious Priests	10
Without Resident Pastor:	
Administered by Priests	9
Administered by Deacons	1
Administered by Religious Women	1
Administered by Lay People	3
Missions	52
New Parishes Created	1
Closed Parishes	2
Professional Ministry Personnel:	
Brothers	1
Sisters	16
Lay Ministers	45
Welfare	
Catholic Hospitals	2
Total Assisted	435,039
Homes for the Aged	1
Total Assisted	74
Day Care Centers	6
Total Assisted	448
Specialized Homes	1
Total Assisted	6
Educational	
Diocesan Students in Other Seminaries	7
Total Seminarians	7
Colleges and Universities	1
Total Students	1,075
High Schools, Diocesan and Parish	2
Total Students	426
High Schools, Private	1
Total Students	139
Elementary Schools, Diocesan and Parish	9
Total Students	1,384
Elementary Schools, Private	3
Total Students	543
Catechesis/Religious Education:	
High School Students	795
Elementary Students	2,446
Total Students under Catholic Instruction	6,815
Teachers in the Diocese:	
Priests	1
Brothers	3
Sisters	7
Lay Teachers	385
Vital Statistics	
Receptions into the Church:	
Infant Baptism Totals	616
Minor Baptism Totals	173
Adult Baptism Totals	63
Received into Full Communion	160
First Communions	728
Confirmations	785
Marriages:	
Catholic	71
Interfaith	73
Total Marriages	144
Deaths	711
Total Catholic Population	43,731
Total Population	402,523

Former Bishops—Most Revs. MATHIAS C. LENIHAN, D.D., ord. Dec. 20, 1879; cons. First Bishop of Great Falls, Sept. 21, 1904; resigned Jan. 18, 1930; created Titular Archbishop of Preslavo, Feb. 14, 1930; died Aug. 19, 1943; EDWIN V. O'HARA, D.D., ord. June 10, 1905; appt. Aug. 1, 1930; cons. Oct. 28, 1930; appt. Bishop of Kansas City April 15, 1939; made asst. at the Pontifical Throne Jan. 5, 1949; appt. Archbishop "Ad Personam" June 29, 1954; died Sept. 11, 1956, Milan, Italy; WILLIAM J. CONDON, D.D., ord. Oct. 14, 1917; appt. Aug. 5, 1939; cons. Oct. 18, 1939; asst. at the Pontifical Throne Dec. 9, 1964; died Aug. 17, 1967; ELDON BERNARD SCHUSTER, D.D., ord. May 27, 1937; appt. Titular Bishop of Amblada; cons. Dec. 21, 1961; appt. Bishop of Great Falls Dec. 2, 1967; resigned Dec. 27, 1977; died Sept. 4, 1998; THOMAS JOSEPH MURPHY, D.D., S.T.D., ord. April 12, 1958; appt. Bishop of Great Falls July 5, 1978; Episcopal ordination and installation Aug. 21, 1978; appt. Coadjutor Archbishop of Seattle May 26, 1987; died June 26, 1997; ANTHONY M. MILONE, D.D., ord. Dec. 15, 1957; appt. Titular Bishop Plestia and Auxiliary of Omaha Nov. 10, 1981; Episcopal ord. Jan. 6, 1982; appt. Bishop of Great Falls-Billings Dec. 14, 1987; installed Feb. 23, 1988; resigned July 12, 2006.

Vicar General—Very Rev. JAY H. PETERSON, V.G.. Email: vicargeneral@dioceseofgfb.org.

Pastoral Office—121 23rd St. S., P.O. Box 1399, Great Falls, 59403. Tel: 406-727-6683; 800-332-9998 (Toll Free Number); Fax: 406-454-3480. All applications for dispensations and official communications should be addressed to this office.

Chancellor—Sr. LYNN CASEY, S.C.L.. Email: chancellor@dioceseofgfb.org. Send all Marriage Correspondence to the Director of the Tribunal.

Moderator of the Curia—Very Rev. JAY H. PETERSON, V.G.

Business Manager/Fiscal Officer—JOSEPH LONCKI. Email: business@dioceseofgfb.org.

Diocesan Tribunal—121 23rd St. S., P.O. Box 1399, Great Falls, 59403. Tel: 406-727-6683; 800-332-9998 (Toll Free Number). Email: tribunal@dioceseofgfb.org.

Judicial Vicar—Rev. ROBERT D. GROSCH, J.C.L.

Promoter of Justice—Rev. JOHN W. ROBERTSON, J.C.L.

Defender of the Bond—Rev. MICHAEL SCHNEIDER, J.C.L. (Cand.).

Director of the Tribunal—TERRYAL ANN REAVLEY.

Notary—TERRYAL ANN REAVLEY.

Diocesan Consultors—Revs. JAMES O'NEILL; PETER E. GUTHNECK; GREGORY STAUDINGER; ROBERT SEWVELLO; TED F. SZUDERA; WILLIAM D'SOUZA; DANIEL WATHEN; ROBERT OSWALD; PATRICK ZABROCKI.

Personnel Board—Revs. JOSEPH DIEKHANS; BARTON K. STEVENS; RICHARD SCHLOSSER; ROBERT OSWALD; JAMES O'NEIL.

Vicars Forane—Revs. STEPHEN J. ZABROCKI, Billings; RICHARD SCHLOSSER, Great Falls; PETER E. GUTHNECK, Havre; ROBERT OSWALD, Miles City; FRANCIS SCHREIBER, Wolf Point.

Cemetery Board—Mount Olivet Cemetery (Great Falls): Most Rev. MICHAEL W. WARFEL; JOSEPH LONCKI; DEBRA WAGNER. Holy Cross Cemetery (Billings): Rev. ROBERT D. GROSCH, J.C.L.; JOHN GLEN, Chm.

Cum Christo/Cursillo—BOB MEYERS. Tel: 406-453-5304. Web: www.bigskycumchristo.org.

Vicar for Ministry to Native Americans—VACANT.

Diocesan Offices and Directors

Catholic Committee on Scouting—Rev. LEO G. MCDOWELL, Chap., Mailing Address: P.O. Box 849, Fort Benton, 59442. Tel: 406-622-3726. Email: frleo@frleo.org.

Catholic Campaign for Human Development—Sr. LYNN CASEY, S.C.L., Diocesan Dir., 121 23rd St. S., Great Falls, 59401. Mailing Address: P.O. Box 1399, Great Falls, 59403. Tel: 406-727-6683; Fax: 406-454-3480.

Catechesis—ANTHONY ALLEN, Office of Evangelization & Catechesis, Mailing Address: Pastoral Center, P.O. Box 1399, Great Falls, 59403. Tel: 406-727-6683. Email: 7treasures@dioceseofgfb.org.

Catholic Relief Services—Sr. LYNN CASEY, S.C.L.

Clerical Benefit Association—Most Rev. MICHAEL W. WARFEL; Revs. PATRICK ZABROCKI; DANIEL WATHEN; JAMES BIRKMAIER, Retired Priest Rep. (Retired); ROBERT D. GROSCH, J.C.L.; JAMES R. SIKORA; STEPHEN ZABROCKI; WAYNE M. PITTARD; JOSEPH LONCKI, Consultant.

Continuing Formation of Clergy—Rev. RICHARD SCHLOSSER.

Diocesan Pastoral Council—Sisters LYNN CASEY, S.C.L., Exec. Coord.; BERNADETTE HELFERT, S.C.L., Chm., Mailing Address: 121 23rd St. S., P.O. Box 1399, Great Falls, 59403-1399. Tel: 406-727-6683; Fax: 406-454-3480; MARY RONAN-WILLIAMS, Campus Min.; Rev. RYAN ERLENBUSH, Priest Council; CAROL ELLIOTT, Havre; STEPHEN GANNON, Great Falls; JENNIFER VAIRA, Wolf Point; Most Rev. MICHAEL W. WARFEL, Presider; Very Rev. JAY H. PETERSON, V.G., Ex Officio; DEBI RHINES, Havre.

Membership—JARED HARRIS, Billings; RICHARD HALL, Billings; ROGER SEILSTAD, Great Falls; JOHN LANE, Miles City; MIKE FISHER, Wolf Point; ANNE O'BRIEN, Wolf Point; Sr. CATHERINE KINSELLA, O.P., Sister Council.

D.C.C.W.—SHIRLEY WEISGERBER, Pres.; Rev. CORY D. STICHA, Mod.

Ecumenical Officer—Deacon WILLIAM MEDVED.

Education—PATRICK HAGGARTY, Ed.D., Supt. Catholic Schools, Mailing Address: P.O. Box 1399, Great Falls, 59403-1399. Tel: 406-727-6683; 800-332-9998; Fax: 406-454-3480. Email: superintendent@dioceseofgfb.org.

Finance Council—Most Rev. MICHAEL W. WARFEL; BILL BELINSKI; Rev. THOMAS TOBIN; Very Rev. JAY H. PETERSON, V.G., Vicar Gen. Ex Officio; FRANK FRENCH; STELLA ZIEGLER; Rev. PATRICK ZABROCKI; Sr. LYNN CASEY, S.C.L., Chancellor & Ex Officio; JOSEPH LONCKI, Consultant; MARILYN HARMON; JOHN NELSON; ALBERT MARTENS; MARILYN ROSE; ELLEN SOLEM; Rev. LEO G. MCDOWELL.

Office of Ministry Formation—Deacon MARK ZENNER. Email: layministry@dioceseofgfb.org; Very Rev. JAY H. PETERSON, V.G., Spiritual Dir.

Deacon Formation—Deacon MARK ZENNER, Dir.

Worship Commission—Very Rev. JAY H. PETERSON, V.G.; PAM ZERR; ROSALIE FOSTER; JOBY PARKER; Sr. MARGARET MARY O'DOHERTY, O.P.; Most Rev. MICHAEL W. WARFEL; RITA RAUSCHENDORFER; Revs. STEPHEN J. ZABROCKI; CORY D. STICHA.

Office of Worship—VACANT, Dir.

Newspaper— "The Harvest" Very Rev. JAY H. PETERSON, V.G., Editor.

Pastoral Outreach—Very Rev. JAY H. PETERSON, V.G., Coord.; ANTHONY ALLEN, Dir. Office of Evangelization & Catechesis; Deacon MARK ZENNER, Dir. Office of Min. Formation; Sr. LYNN CASEY, S.C.L., Chancellor, Diocesan Pastoral Council & Liaison for Planning; PATRICK HAGGARTY, Ed.D., Supt. of Catholic Schools; TERRYAL ANN REAVLEY, Dir. Tribunal; JUDY HELD, Dir. Stewardship & Devel.; DEBRA WAGNER, Asst. Business Mgr.; JOSEPH LONCKI, Fiscal Officer, Business Mgr.

Priests' Council—Most Rev. MICHAEL W. WARFEL; Revs. ROBERT SEWVELLO; TED F. SZUDERA; ROBERT OSWALD; WILLIAM D'SOUZA; DANIEL WATHEN; PATRICK ZABROCKI; GREGORY STAUDINGER; PETER E. GUTHNECK; JAMES O'NEILL; Very Rev. JAY H. PETERSON, V.G., Ex Officio.

Sister's Council—Sr. LYNN CASEY, S.C.L., Liaison.

Director of Vocations and Recruitment—Rev. LEO G. MCDOWELL, Mailing Address: Immaculate Conception Church, P.O. Box 849, Fort Benton, 59442. Tel: 406-622-3726. Email: frleo@frleo.org.

Director of Seminarian Formation—Very Rev. JAY H. PETERSON, V.G.. Email: vicargeneral@dioceseofgfb.org.

Inter-Diocesan Organizations

Montana Catholic Conference—MOE WOSEPKA, Exec. Dir., Mailing Address: P.O. Box 1708, Helena, 59624. Tel: 406-442-5761; Fax: 406-442-9047. Email: mccadmin@bresnan.net. Web: www.montanacc.org.

Catholic Social Services of Montana—ROSEMARY MILLER, Dir., 1301 11th Ave., Helena, 59601. Mailing Address: P.O. Box 907, Helena, 59624-0907. Tel: 406-442-4130; 800-222-9383; Fax: 406-442-4192. Web: www.cssmt.org. Email: rosemary@cssmt.org. Provides adoption and counseling services for families, children and infants.

Billings Office—Social Workers: BECKY HUBBERT; SAM HUBBERT; LINDA CLADIS, 1048 N. 30th St., Billings, 59101. Tel: 406-252-3399; Fax: 406-252-9173. Email: billings@cssmt.org.

Great Falls Office—KYLA WRIGHT; DELJEAN WADSWORTH, Mailing Address: 410 Central Ave., #601, Great Falls, 59401. Tel: 406-771-7805. Email: greatfalls@cssmt.org.

Helena Office—HELEN BEAUSOLEI, Mailing Address: P.O. Box 907, Helena, 59601. Tel: 406-442-4130; Fax: 406-442-4192.

Missoula Office—BETSY ROBEL, 420 W. Pine St., Missoula, 59802. Tel: 406-728-5429; Fax: 406-327-8537. Email: missoula@cssmt.org.

Montana Association of Churches—Rev. DAN KREBILL, Yellowstone Presbytery, P.O. Box 1150, Bozeman, 59771; PAM SHELDEN, Admin., 25 S. Ewing St., Ste. 408, Helena, 59601-6072. Tel: 406-449-6010; Fax: 406-449-6657. Web: www.montana-churches.net.

Victim Assistance Coordinator—Sr. KATHLEEN KANE, O.P. Tel: 406-378-2250. Email: asstcoord@dioceseofgfb.org.

Safe Environment Coordinator—SANDRA GUYNN.

CLERGY, PARISHES, MISSIONS AND PAROCHIAL SCHOOLS

CITY OF GREAT FALLS

(CASCADE COUNTY)

1—ST. ANN'S CATHEDRAL Rev. Oliver Doyle; Mary Katherine Toeckes, Pastoral Assoc.; Patty Jo Sheldon, Fin. Mgr.
Res.: 715 Third Ave. N., P.O. Box 1708, 59403. Tel: 406-761-5456; Fax: 406-761-5457. Email: stannscathedral@mt.net. Web: www.stannscathedral.org.
Catechesis/Religious Program—Georgia Miller, Youth Min. Students 72.

2—CORPUS CHRISTI (2012) Very Rev. Jay H. Peterson, Canonical Pastor; Deacon William Medved, Parish Life Coord.
Res.: 410 22nd Ave., N.E., 59404. Tel: 406-453-6546.
Chapel—St. Joseph (1912), Contact Corpus Christi for sacramental records.
Chapel—Most Blessed Sacrament 1325 Smelter Ave., Black Eagle, 59414.
Parish Center: 500-2nd Ave. S.W., 59404.
Catechesis/Religious Program—Gary Gaudreau, D.R.E. Students 112.

3—ST. GERARD MAJELLA, Closed. For inquiries for parish records contact the chancery.

4—HOLY FAMILY, Closed. See Holy Spirit.

5—HOLY SPIRIT (1998) Rev. Richard Schlosser; Sr. Catherine Kinsella, O.P., Pastoral Assoc.; Mark Meyer, Parish Admin.
Parish Office—201 44th St. S., 59405. Tel: 406-452-6491; Fax: 406-452-6495. Email: hsparish@holyspiritgf.org. Web: www.holyspiritgf.org.
Sts. Peter & Paul Education Center—200 44th St. S., 59405. Tel: 406-761-4805.
School—(Grades PreK-8), 2820 Central Ave., 59401. Tel: 406-761-5775; Fax: 406-761-5887. Email: robbins@holyspirits.org. Web: www.holyspiritcs.org. Roger Robbins, Prin. Lay Teachers 32; Students 203.
Catechesis/Religious Program—Students 203.
Chapel—Holy Family 2800 Central Ave., 59401.

6—ST. LUKE THE EVANGELIST (1967) Merged with St. Joseph and Most Blessed Sacrament to form Corpus Christi, Great Falls. Contact Corpus Christi for sacramental records.

7—OUR LADY OF LOURDES Rev. Lothar Krauth; Barbara Brown, Pastoral Assoc.
Res.: 409 13th St. S., 59405. Tel: 406-452-6464; Fax: 406-452-6464. Email: lourdes@bresnan.net. Web: www.angelfire.com/mt/ollgf.
School—(Grades PreK-8), 1305 Fifth Ave. S., 59405. Tel: 406-452-0551; Fax: 406-761-7180. Web: www.ollschool.info. Mrs. Sherri Schmitz, Prin. Lay Teachers 30; Students 225.
Catechesis/Religious Program—Roslyn Gallagher, D.R.E.; Mary Jo Bailly, Youth Min. Students 65.

8—STS. PETER & PAUL, Closed. See Holy Spirit.

CITY OF BILLINGS

(YELLOWSTONE COUNTY)

1—ST. BERNARD (1971) Rev. David Reichling, O.F.M.Cap.
Office: 226 Wicks Ln., 59105. Tel: 406-259-4350; Fax: 406-259-0433. Email: davidr@stbernardblgs.org. Web: www.stbernardblgs.org.
Catechesis/Religious Program—Brian Shea, D.R.E. (Youth Group); Ann Salisburg, D.R.E. (Elementary). Students 204.
Mission—Sts. Cyril & Methodius c/o St. Bernard's Church, 226 Wicks Ln., Yellowstone Co. 59105. Tel: 406-259-4350. Church: 16 S. Corner Rd., Ballantine, 59006.
Catechesis/Religious Program—Students 33.

2—HOLY ROSARY (1951) Revs. Stephen Zabrocki, Canonical Pastor; Barton K. Stevens, Parochial Vicar; Michael Mayott, Parish Life Coord.
521 Custer Ave., 59101.
Office: Tel: 406-259-7611; Fax: 406-248-8921. Email: info@billingscatholiccluster.org.
Catechesis/Religious Program— Debbie Murtagh, D.R.E. Students 74.

3—LITTLE FLOWER (1931) Revs. Stephen Zabrocki, Canonical Pastor; Barton K. Stevens, Parochial Vicar; Michael Mayott, Parish Life Coord.
Mailing Address: P.O. Box 20938, 59104.
Office: 521 Custer Ave., 59101. Tel: 406-259-7611; Fax: 406-248-8921.
Church: 209 S. 35th St., 59101.

4—OUR LADY OF GUADALUPE (1953) Revs. Stephen Zabrocki, Canonical Pastor; Barton K. Stevens, Parochial Vicar; Michael Mayott, Parish Life Coord.
Mailing Address: P.O. Box 20938, 59104.
Office: 521 Custer Ave., 59101. Tel: 406-259-7611; Fax: 406-248-8921.
Church: 523 S. 29th St., 59101. Tel: 406-245-4717.

5—ST. PATRICK CO-CATHEDRAL (1906) Rev. Robert D. Grosch.
Rectory—34 Yellowstone Ave., 59101. Tel: 406-371-5479.
Church: 215 N. 31st St., 59101. Tel: 406-259-3389; Fax: 406-248-1185. Email: stpatrickblgs@yahoo.com. Web: www.catholic-church.org/stpatricksbillings.
Catechesis/Religious Program— Brenda Estill, D.R.E. Students 101.

6—ST. PIUS X (1958) Rev. Msgr. John Steiner, Interim Parochial Admin.; Bob Bender, Admin. & Business Mgr.
Parish Center—717 18th St. W., 59102. Tel: 406-656-2522; Fax: 406-656-2584. Email: info@stpiusxblgs.org. Web: www.stpiusxblgs.org.
Catechesis/Religious Program— Jennifer Mack, D.R.E. Students 140.
Billings Catholic Campus Ministry Program—Tel: 406-850-4488. Email: billingsccm@gmail.com. Mary Ronan-Williams, Campus Ministry Dir.

7—ST. THOMAS THE APOSTLE (1965) Rev. Stephen J. Zabrocki; Deacon Tim Birkle.
Res.: 2101-24th St. W., 59102. Tel: 406-656-5578.
Church & Mailing Address: 2055 Woody Dr., 59102. Tel: 406-656-5800; Fax: 406-656-8260. Email: st_thomas@qwestoffice.net.
Catechesis/Religious Program—Joyce Hollowell, D.R.E.; Cathy Day, Youth Min. Students 173.

OUTSIDE THE CITIES OF GREAT FALLS AND BILLINGS

ASHLAND, ROSEBUD CO., ST. LABRE (1884) Rev. Paschal Siler, O.F.M.Cap.
Res.: P.O. Box 228, 59003. Tel: 406-784-4536. Email: psiler@stlabre.org.
Catechesis/Religious Program—Pam Kania, D.R.E. Students 8.

BAKER, FALLON CO., ST. JOHN THE EVANGELIST Rev. Thomas Tobin.
Res.: P.O. Box 1519, 59313. Tel: 406-778-2297.
Church: 210 W. Center Ave., 59313.
Catechesis/Religious Program—Joan Grammond, D.R.E.; Gail Brence, D.R.E. Students 68.
Mission—St. Joan of Arc Ekalaka, Carter CoChurch: 100 Church Ave., Ekalaka, 59324.
Mission—St. Anthony [CEM] Plevna, Fallon CoChurch: 201 W. Conser Ave., Plevna, 59344.

BELT, CASCADE CO., ST. MARK THE EVANGELIST Rev. Wm. Paul McKane, O.S.B., Parochial Admin.
Res.: P.O. Box 213, 59412. Tel: 406-277-3537.
Church: 132 Castner St., 59412.
Catechesis/Religious Program—Tel: 406-277-3366. Lisa Jasen, D.R.E. Students 74.
Mission—St. Clement Monarch, Cascade CoChurch:

62 Cascade Ave., Monarch, 59463.
Mission—St. Mary Raynesford, Judith Basin CoChurch: 100 Main St., Raynesford, 59469.
Mission—Holy Trinity Centerville, Cascade CoChurch: 692 Stockett Rd., Centerville.

BIG SANDY, CHOUTEAU CO., ST. MARGARET MARY (1910) Rev. Peter E. Guthneck; Sisters Margaret Mary O'Doherty, O.P., Pastoral Assoc. & D.R.E.; Kathleen Kane, O.P., Pastoral Assoc.
Res.: P.O. Box 3009, Box Elder, 59521. Tel: 406-395-4380.
Church: 365 Johannes, 59520.
St. Mary's Rocky Boy Indian Reservation: P.O. Box 3009, Box Elder, 59521. Tel: 406-395-4380.
Catechesis/Religious Program—Tel: 409-395-4870. Students 135.
Mission—St. Anthony Box Elder, Hill CoChurch: 235 E. Main, Box Elder, 59521.
Mission—St. Mary Rocky Boys Indian Reservation, Hill CoChurch: 88 Church Hill Rd., Box Elder, 59521.

BIG TIMBER, SWEET GRASS CO., ST. JOSEPH Rev. Wayne M. Pittard.
Res.: P.O. Box 871, 59011. Tel: 406-932-4728.
Church: 910 McLeod, 59011.
Catechesis/Religious Program—MaryAnn Finnan, D.R.E. Students 25.

BLACK EAGLE, CASCADE CO., MOST BLESSED SACRAMENT, Merged with St. Joseph, Great Falls and St. Luke the Evangelist, Great Falls to form Corpus Christi, Great Falls. Contact Corpus Christi for sacramental records.

BRIDGER, CARBON CO., SACRED HEART Sr. Nancy Malburg, O.P., Parish Life Coord.
Mailing Address: P.O. Box 309, 59014-0309.
Res.: 209 S. 4th St., 59014-0309. Tel: 406-662-3550. Email: trinity@brmt.net.
Catechesis/Religious Program—Students 60.
Mission—St. Joseph Fromberg, Carbon CoChurch: 202 N. Montana St., Fromberg, 59029.
Mission—St. John Joliet, Carbon CoChurch: 404 W. Central, Joliet, 59041.

BROADUS, POWDER RIVER CO., ST. DAVID (1931) Rev. William D'Souza.
Mailing Address: P.O. Box 52, 59317. 217 N. Wilbur, 59317. Tel: 406-436-2430.
Catechesis/Religious Program—Students 20.

CHESTER, LIBERTY CO., ST. MARY (1950) Rev. Joseph Diekhans; Natalie Ghekiere, Parish Coord.
Res.: 504 Main, P.O. Box 647, 59522. Tel: 406-759-5377; Fax: 406-759-5568.
Church: 11 W. Quincy Ave., 59522.
Catechesis/Religious Program—Tel: 406-759-5389. Natalie Ghekiere, D.R.E. Students 54.

CHINOOK, BLAINE CO., ST. GABRIEL (1896) Rev. Jose Valliparambil.
Res.: 404 Eighth St., P.O. Box 1089, 59523. Tel: 406-357-2073; Fax: 406-357-2173.
Catechesis/Religious Program—Mrs. Ellen Pyette, D.R.E., (Elementary); Mrs. Carol Elliot, D.R.E., (High School). Students 46.
Mission—St. Thomas the Apostle 210 1st Ave., S.E., Harlem, Blaine Co. 59526. P.O. Box 1125, Harlem, 59526.
Mission—St. Thomas Aquinas 10610 Wing Rd., Hogeland, Blaine Co. 59529. Mailing Address: *c/o Mary Ann Olszewski*, 1570 Poland Rd., Hogeland, Blaine Co. 59529. Tel: 406-379-2582; Fax: 406-379-2582.

CIRCLE, MCCONE CO., ST. FRANCIS XAVIER Revs. Joseph Ponessa; Alex Pulickaparambil, Parochial Vicar.
Res.: 1102 C Ave., P.O. Box 160, 59215-0160. Tel: 406-485-3520; Fax: 406-485-3520. Email: stx@midrivers.com.
Church: 1100 C Ave., 59215.
Catechesis/Religious Program—Janna Munson, D.R.E. Students 20.
Mission—St. Francis de Sales Richey, Dawson CoChurch: 301 S. Main St., Richey, 59259.

COLSTRIP, ROSEBUD CO., ST. MARGARET MARY (1924) Rev. Anthony J. Ozimek, O.S.B.
Res.: P.O. Box 1112, 59323. Tel: 406-748-3216. Email: stmargaretmary1@gmail.com. Web: bhwi.net/stmm.
Church: 320 Water Ave., 59323. Tel: 406-748-2234.
Catechesis/Religious Program—Students 35.

COLUMBUS, STILLWATER CO., ST. MARY (1916) Rev. Gregory Staudinger.
Mailing Address: P.O. Box 956, 59019. Tel: 406-322-5541. Email: secretary@stmarycolumbus.org. Web: stmarycolumbus.org.
Church: 240 N. 4th St., 59019.
Catechesis/Religious Program—Students 35.
Mission—St. Michael Absarokee, Stillwater CoChurch: 307 S. Woodard St., Absorokee.

CROW AGENCY, BIG HORN CO., ST. DENNIS (1892) Rev. Charles Robinson, O.F.M.Cap.; Sr. Loretta Sedlmayer, R.S.M., Pastoral Assoc.
Res.: P.O. Box 57, 59022. Tel: 406-638-2641.
Church: 8750 Magic Carpet Rd., 59022.
Catechesis/Religious Program—Students 70.
Mission—St. Francis Xavier P.O. Box 138, St. Xavier, Big Horn Co. 59075. Tel: 406-666-2380. Church: 5936 W. 18300 S., St. Xavier, 59075. Leah Big Hair, Pastoral Assoc.

CULBERTSON, ROOSEVELT CO., ST. ANTHONY, Now a mission of Our Lady of Lourdes, Poplar.

FORSYTH, ROSEBUD CO., IMMACULATE CONCEPTION Rev. Michael Schneider.
Res.: 591 N. 12th Ave. N., P.O. Box 166, 59327. Tel: 406-346-2101 (Rectory); 406-346-9239 (Parish Center).
Church: 509 N. 12th Ave., 59327.
Catechesis/Religious Program—Students 15.
Mission—St. Joseph 206 Orchard Ave., Hysham, Treasure Co.

FORT BENTON, CHOUTEAU CO., IMMACULATE CONCEPTION (1846) Rev. Leo G. McDowell.
Res.: P.O. Box 849, 59442. Tel: 406-622-3726.
Church: 1223-16th St., 59442. Email: icc@itstriangle.com.
Catechesis/Religious Program—Tel: 406-622-5288. Students 26.
Mission—St. Margaret P.O. Box 50, Geraldine, Chouteau Co. 59446-0050. Tel: 406-737-4573. Church: 700 Brewster St., Geraldine, 59446.

FORT SHAW, CASCADE CO., ST. ANN Rev. Marcel Vogel, Parochial Admin.
Res.: 13327 MT. Hwy 200, 59443. Tel: 406-264-5554.
Catechesis/Religious Program—Carla Blanchard, D.R.E., (St. Ann). Tel: 406-264-5495. Students 90.
Mission—Sacred Heart 22 2nd St., N.W., Cascade, Cascade Co. 59421.

GLASGOW, VALLEY CO., ST. RAPHAEL Rev. Robert Sewvello; Amanda Bell, Pastoral Assoc.
Office: 412 Third Ave. N., P.O. Box 471, 59230. Tel: 406-228-9800; Fax: 406-228-9717. Email: straphael@nemontel.net.
Church: 402 Third Ave. N., 59230.
Catechesis/Religious Program—Tel: 406-228-4651. Students 91.
Mission—Holy Family Glentana, Valley CoChurch: 102 1st Ave., N., Glentana, 59240.
Mission—St. Albert Hinsdale, Valley CoChurch: 304 Minnesota, Hinsdale, 59241.
Mission—Queen of the Angels Nashua, Valley CoChurch: 206 Hobart, Nashua, 59248.

GLENDIVE, DAWSON CO., SACRED HEART (1907) Revs. Joseph Ponessa; Alex Pulickaparambil, Parochial Vicar.
Res.: 316 W. Benham St., P.O. Box 36, 59330. Tel: 406-377-2585. Email: sacred@midrivers.com.
Catechesis/Religious Program—Tel: 406-377-4569. Bro. Aelred Reid, O.S.B., D.R.E. Students 182.
Mission—St. Peter P.O. Box 217, Wibaux, Wibaux Co. 59353. Tel: 406-796-2215. Church: 312 W. 1st Ave., S., Wibaux, 59353.
Mission—St. Philip P.O. Box 217, Wibaux, Wibaux Co. 59353. Tel: 406-796-8188. Church: 61 Lanesteer Rd., Wibaux, 59353.

HARDIN, BIG HORN CO., ST. JOSEPH Rev. Fabian Fehring, O.F.M.Cap.
Res.: 710 N. Custer, P.O. Box 510, 59034. Tel: 406-665-1432; Fax: 406-665-1432.
Catechesis/Religious Program—Students 40.
Mission—St. Mary Custer, Yellowstone Co.

HAVRE, HILL CO., ST. JUDE THADDEUS (1904) Rev. Daniel Wathen; Timothy Maroney, Pastoral Min.
Res.: 440 7th Ave., P.O. Box 407, 59501. Tel: 406-265-4261; Fax: 406-265-4408. Email: stjude@ttc-cmc.net. Web: www.stjudehavre.catholicweb.com.
School—(Grades PreK-8), 430 7th Ave., 59501. Tel: 406-265-4613; Fax: 406-265-1315. Email: stjude2@ttc-cmc.net. Web: stjudeschoolmt.org. Mrs. Carol Ortman, Prin. Lay Teachers 22; Students 131.
Catechesis/Religious Program—Students 85.
Chapel—St. John the Baptist Cottonwood.

HAYS, BLAINE CO., ST. PAUL'S INDIAN MISSION (1886) Revs. Joseph R. Retzel, S.J.; Robert L. Erickson, S.J.; Sr. Laura Fucito, O.P., Pastoral Assoc.
Res.: Mission Dr. #1, P.O. Box 40, 59527. Tel: 406-673-3300; Fax: 406-673-3403. Email: josephrr@mtintouch.net.
School—(Grades K-6) Tel: 406-673-3123. Sr. Helen Durso, O.P., Prin. Sisters 3; Lay Teachers 14; Students 99.
Catechesis/Religious Program—Students 46.
Mission—St. Joseph Zortman, Phillips CoChurch: 300 Azure Ave., Zortman, 59546.
Mission—St. Thomas HC63, Box 5240, Lodgepole, Blaine Co. 59524. Tel: 406-673-3677; Fax: 406-673-3454. Sr. Laura Fucito, O.P., Pastoral Assoc.
Mission—Sacred Heart, Fort Belknap 303 Chipewa Ln., P.O. Box 429, Harlem, Blaine Co. 59526. Tel: 406-353-2257; Fax: 406-353-2927. Mary Beth Talks Different, Pastoral Admin.

HINGHAM, HILL CO., OUR LADY OF RANSOM (1910) Rev. Joseph Diekhans.
Mailing Address: P.O. Box 647, Chester, 59522-0647. Church: 201-2nd. St., 59528. Tel: 406-759-5377; Fax: 406-759-5568.
Catechesis/Religious Program—Dianne Folk, D.R.E. Students 22.
Mission—Sacred Heart 630 Main, Inverness, Hill Co.
Church: 630 Main, Inverness, 59530.

LAME DEER, ROSEBUD CO., BLESSED SACRAMENT Deacon Joseph Kristufek, Pastoral Admin.; Rev. Paschal Siler, O.F.M.Cap., Sacramental Min.; Sr. LeAnn Probst, O.P., Pastoral Assoc.
Res.: P.O. Box 100, 59043. Tel: 406-477-6384; Fax: 406-477-6224.
Church: 630 Cheyenne Ave., 59043.
Catechesis/Religious Program—Students 20.
Mission—Christ the King P.O. Box 315, Busby, Big Horn Co. 59016. Tel: 406-592-3568. Church: 13268 S. 5th St., Busby, 59016.

LAUREL, YELLOWSTONE CO., ST. ANTHONY (1907) [CEM] Rev. Thomas C. Harney.
Res.: 317 W. 7th St., P.O. Box 955, 59044. Tel: 406-628-7182.
Church: 700 3rd Ave., 59044.
Catechesis/Religious Program—Tel: 406-628-7484. Barb Hoppel, D.R.E. Students 144.

LEWISTOWN, FERGUS CO., ST. LEO (1888) [CEM] Rev. Daniel O'Rourke.
Res.: P.O. Box 421, 59457. Tel: 406-538-9306; Fax: 406-538-7624. Email: stleos@midrivers.com.
Church: 102 W. Broadway, 59457.
Catechesis/Religious Program— Pam Zerr, D.R.E., (Grades K-6); Mari Krumwiede, Youth Min. Students 136.
Mission—Holy Family P.O. Box 421, 59457. Church: 530 Main St., Winifred, Fergus Co. 59489. Jody DeMars, Coord.

LIVINGSTON, PARK CO., ST. MARY, [CEM] Rev. Wayne M. Pittard; Joannie Lee, Pastoral Min. & D.R.E.
Res.: 511 S. F St., P.O. Box 646, 59047-0646. Tel: 406-222-1393; Fax: 406-222-1405.
School—(Grades PreK-8) Tel: 406-222-3303. Kimberly Taylor, Prin. Lay Teachers 19; Students 65.
Catechesis/Religious Program—Students 7.
Mission—St. Margaret 206 1st. Ave. N., Clyde Park, Park Co. 59018.
Mission—St. William 705 Scott St., W., Gardiner, Park Co. 59030.

LODGE GRASS, BIG HORN CO., OUR LADY OF LORETTO (1909) Rev. James Antoine, O.F.M.Cap.
Res.: P.O. Box 509, 59050. Tel: 406-639-2254; Fax: 406-639-2688. Email: jimanto@nemont.net.
Church: 219 S. Helen St., 59050.
Catechesis/Religious Program—Autumn D. White Clay, D.R.E. Students 20.
Mission—Blessed Kateri Tekakwitha Wyola, Big Horn CoChurch: 309 S. Mondel Ave., Wyola, 59089.

MALTA, PHILLIPS CO., ST. MARY Rev. Cory D. Sticha, Parochial Admin.
Res.: 27 S. Seventh St. W., P.O. Box 70, 59538. Tel: 406-654-1446; Fax: 406-654-1467. Email: smp1435@hotmail.com. Web: saintmarysmalta.org.
Catechesis/Religious Program—Tel: 406-654-1311. Carly Bishop, D.R.E. Students 60.
Mission—Sacred Heart Dodson, Phillips CoChurch: 225 2nd St., E., Dodson, 59524.
Mission—St. Francis of Assisi Saco, Phillips CoChurch: 500 Wilson Ave., Saco, 59261.
Chapel—St. John 230 1st Ave. E., Whitewater.

MILES CITY, CUSTER CO., SACRED HEART (1881) Revs. Robert Oswald; Ryan Erlenbush, Parochial Vicar; Michael Dorsey, Pastoral Assoc.
Mailing Address: P.O. Box 1016, 59301. Tel: 406-234-1691; Fax: 406-234-9233.
Res.: 110 N. Montana, 59301. Tel: 406-234-7585.
Church: 120 N. Montana Ave., 59301.
Parish Center—520 N. Montana Ave., 59301.
School—(Grades PreSchool-8), 519 N. Center Ave., 59301. Tel: 406-234-3850. Web: www.midrivers.com/~shschool. Bart Freese, Prin. Lay Teachers 9; Students 81.
Catechesis/Religious Program—Students 67.
Mission—Sacred Heart 302 S. McDonald Ave., Terry, Prairie Co. 59349. Tel: 406-635-5569.
Mission—St. John the Baptist Jordan, Garfield Co. Tel: 406-557-6135. Email: stjohn@midrivers.com. Church: 412 Leavitt Ave., Jordan, 59337.

PLENTYWOOD, SHERIDAN CO., ST. JOSEPH Rev. Patrick Zabrocki.
Res.: P.O. Box 167, 59254. Tel: 406-765-2250; Fax: 406-765-2345.
Church: 301 N. Main St., 59254.
Catechesis/Religious Program—Students 40.
Mission—St. Patrick Medicine Lake, Sheridan CoChurch: 401 Main St., Medicine Lake, 59247.

POPLAR, ROOSEVELT CO., OUR LADY OF LOURDES Rev. Francis Schreiber.
Res.: 105 F St. W., P.O. Box 187, 59255. Cell: 406-768-7488; Tel: 406-768-3305 (Office); Fax: 406-768-3305.
Catechesis/Religious Program—Students 20.
Mission—St. Anthony 413 3rd St., W., Culbertson, Roosevelt Co. 59218. Tel: 406-787-6666.

Mission—St. Thomas Church: 3022 BIA Rd. 173, Brockton, Roosevelt Co. 59213.
Mission—Sacred Heart Church: 314 Clinton St., Bainville, Roosevelt Co. 59212.
Chapel—Fort Kipp, St. Anthony

PRYOR, BIG HORN CO., ST. CHARLES BORROMEO CHURCH Rev. Randolph Graczyk, O.F.M.Cap.
Res.: P.O. Box 29, 59066. Tel: 406-259-9747; Fax: 406-259-7092.
Church: 21228 S. Pryor Gap Rd., 59066.
Catechesis/Religious Program—Students 116.

RED LODGE, CARBON CO., ST. AGNES (1889) Rev. Denis J. Keane.
Res.: P.O. Box 1067, 59068. Tel: 406-446-1237; Fax: 406-446-1237. Email: sachurch1003@qwestoffice.net.
Church: 1 N. Word Ave., 59068.
Catechesis/Religious Program—Students 36.

ROUNDUP, MUSSELSHELL CO., ST. BENEDICT (1908) Rev. Raymond J. Nyquist, Interim Pastor (Retired).
Res.: 503 Main St., 59072. Tel: 406-323-1019; Fax: 406-323-1054. Email: stbenedict@midrivers.com.
Catechesis/Religious Program—Students 32.
Mission—Our Lady of Mercy Church: 121 6th Ave., Melstone, Musselshell Co. 59054.
Mission—St. Aloysius Church: 112 W. Main St., Winnett, Petroleum Co. 59087.
Mission—St. Theresa the Little Flower Broadview, Yellowstone Co.
Mission—St Mathias Church: 305 Kemp St., Ryegate, Golden Valley Co. 59074.
Chapel—St. Honorata 22 3rd Ave., Musselshell, 59059.
Chapel—Our Lady of the Assumption Broadview, 59015.

SCOBEY, DANIELS CO., ST. PHILIP BONITUS Rev. Patrick Zabrocki.
Res.: P.O. Box 827, 59263. Tel: 406-487-5525; Fax: 406-487-5566.
Church: 404 Timmons St., 59263.
Catechesis/Religious Program—Matt Goettle, D.R.E. Students 33.

SIDNEY, RICHLAND CO., ST. MATTHEW Rev. Jim O'Neil; Linda Latka, Parish Admin.
Res.: 219 Seventh St., S.E., 59270. Tel: 406-433-1068.
Catechesis/Religious Program—Tel: 406-433-2510. Stacie Olson, D.R.E. Students 102.
Mission—St. Catherine P.O. Box 494, Fairview, Richland Co. 59221. Tel: 406-742-5293. Church: 317 7th St., W., Fairview, 59221.
Mission—St. Theresa P.O. Box 153, Lambert, Richland Co. 59243. Tel: 406-774-3360. Church: 212 N. Main St., Lambert, 59243.
Mission—St. Bernard 301 Rd. 148, Charley Creek, Richland Co. Tel: 406-774-3401. Mailing Address: 31789 CR148, Box 409, Brockton, 59213. Regina Murray, Pastoral Assoc.; Rita Rauschendorfer, Pastoral Assoc.

Mission—St. Michael P.O. Box 95, Savage, Richland Co. 59262. Church: 120 2nd Ave., Savage, 59262.

STANFORD, JUDITH BASIN CO., ST. ROSE OF LIMA (1908) Rev. Ted F. Szudera.
Mailing Address: P.O. Box 250, 59479. Tel: 406-566-2531.
Res.: 305 S. 2nd, 59479.
Church: 101 Fourth St. W., 59479.
Catechesis/Religious Program—Students 5.
Mission—St. Anthony P.O. Box 333, Denton, Fergus Co. 59430. Tel: 406-567-2438.
Church: 1100 Main Ave., Denton, 59430.
Mission—St. Cyril R.R. 1, Box 50A, Geyser, Judith Basin Co. 59447. Tel: 406-735-4388.
Church: 100 Hill Ave., Geyser, 59447.
Mission—St. Mathias P.O. Box 104, Moore, Fergus Co. 59464.
Church: 310-2nd St., N.E., Moore, 59464.
Mission—Sacred Heart P.O. Box 225, Hobson, Judith Basin Co. 59452.
Church: 100-2nd Ave. E., Hobson, 59452.

WOLF POINT, ROOSEVELT CO., IMMACULATE CONCEPTION, [CEM] Rev. Jolly Pathiyamoola Ouseph.
Res.: 500 Fifth Ave. S., P.O. Box 789, 59201. Tel: 406-653-2610.
Church: 513 Dawson St., 59201.
Catechesis/Religious Program—Ann Wienke, D.R.E. Students 77.
Mission—St. Joseph Church: 331 Moccasin, Frazer, Valley Co. 59225.
Mission—St. Ann Church: 102 Shell St., Vida, McCone Co. 59274. Tel: 406-525-3378.
Chapel—Sacred Heart 1022 Hwy. 201, Riverside.

Special Assignment:
Revs.—
Pathiyamoola Ouseph, Jolly, Immaculate Conception Church, P.O. Box 789, 59201-0789.
Pulickaparambil, Alex, Sacred Heart Church, P.O. Box 84, Glendive, 59330-0084.
Sikora, James R., University of Great Falls, 1301 20th St., S., 59405.

On Duty Outside of the Diocese:
Revs.—
Cawley, William M., St. Patrick Rectory, 231 S. Beaver St., York, PA 17403-5499.
Crowley, Cale J., S.S., Rector, St. Augustine's Major Seminary, P.O. Box 81011, Kabwe, Zimbabwe.
Kirkness, Michael D., 2801 Eucalyptus Ave., Long Beach, CA 90806.
Krier, John P., P.O. Box 125, Medical Lake, WA 99022-0125.

Retired:
Revs.—
Beggin, Thomas M., 1631-41st St. W., 59106-1742.
Birkmaier, James, 1701 26th St. S., #1, 59405-5173.
Bourke, Nathaniel J., 2003 Woody Dr., #2, 59102-2891.
Coady, John, P.O. Box 57128, Tucson, AZ 85732-7128.
Connolly, Jerry, P.O. Box 456, Joliet, 59041.
Fisher, Martin, 507 Parkhill Dr., 59102-3619.
Fox, Robert J., 1000-6th St. N., Apt. 16, 59201-1867.
Frazer, Edward J., S.S., St. Charles Villa, 603 Maiden Choice Ln., Baltimore, MD 21228-3697.
Gedvila, Izidorius, 1718 Haverhill Cir., Chipley, FL 32428-3179.
Gorman, Charles, 2351 Solomon Ave., Apt. 157, 59102.
Guinan, Michael, 1701 26th St. S., #4, 59405-5173.
Hoffman, Emmett G., Soaring Eagle Heritage Living Center, P.O. Box 687, Ashland, 59003-0687.
Hogan, William A., 1901 9th St. S, Apt. 116, 59405.
Hopkins, Richard J., Mother of Confidence Church, 3131 Governor Dr., San Diego, CA 92122-2229.
Houlihan, John J., 2003 Woody Dr., Apt. 4, 59102.
Hruska, Eugene P., 2621 15th Ave. S., 59405.
Kelly, Frank F., 2147 Eagle Rock Dr., 59101.
Lobo, Benjamin, Ben's Ark, Alake, Mangalore 575 003 India.
McInnis, Francis L., 1701-26th St. S. #3, 59404-5173.
Nyquist, Raymond J., 2003 Woody Dr., Apt. 1, 59102.
O'Hanlon, Michael A., Danesfort, Dromahane Mallow, County Cork 022-50140 Ireland.
Osterman, Richard, P.O. Box 1093, Red Lodge, 59068-1093.
Regan, Terrence P., 2805 3rd Ave. N., 59401.
Schuster, Anthony J., 2003 Wood Dr, Apt. 3, 59102.
Shinnick, Edward P., 11499 Hwy. 2, Savage, 59262-9420.
Tarrant, Patrick J., P.O. Box 275, Yarmouth Port, MA 02675-0275.

Leave of Absence:
Rev.—
Yurkovic, Dale E., 735 Nottingham Cir., 59105.

Permanent Deacons:
Birkle, Timothy J., 3820 Towhee Ln., 59102-7723.
Daem, Robert W., 220 34th St. W., 59102-4473.
Kristufek, Joseph M., P.O. Box 100, Lame Deer, 59043-0100.
Medved, William, 410 22nd Ave., N.E., 59404.
Melius, Melvin A., 1437 Ave. D, 59102-3124.
Pico, Lee, 39 Jardine Rd., Gardiner, 59030.
Zenner, Mark, P.O. Box 1399, 59403.

INSTITUTIONS LOCATED IN THE DIOCESE

[A] COLLEGES AND UNIVERSITIES

GREAT FALLS. *University of Great Falls* (1932) 1301 20th St. S., 59405. Tel: 406-791-5300; Fax: 406-791-5391. Email: rsanne01@ugf.edu. Web: www.ugf.edu. Richard McDowell, Provost; Eugene J. McAllister, Pres.; David Agans, Campus Min.; Rev. James R. Sikora, Academic Dean; Oliver Pflug, Library Dir.; Stacy Eve, Vice Pres. Admin. & Finance. Sponsored by the Sisters of Providence, Mother Joseph Province Sisters 1; Lay Teachers 49; Students 1,075.
Associate Professors of Theology & Ministry: Revs. James R. Sikora, Academic Dean; Jon Taylor; Dan McGuire, Asst. Prof. Theology & Ministry; Sr. Mary Kaye Nealen, S.P., Prof. Theology & Ministry & Dir. Mission Intergration.

[B] HIGH SCHOOLS, DIOCESAN

GREAT FALLS. *Great Falls Central Catholic High School*, 2800-18th Ave. S., 59405. Tel: 406-216-3344; Fax: 406-216-3343. Email: hsmith@greatfallscentral.org. Web: greatfallscentral.org. Hugh Smith, Prin.; Sarah Zook, Asst. Prin.; Rev. Francis McInnis, Chap.; Noel Osterman, Librarian. Lay Teachers 18; Students 102.

BILLINGS. *Central Catholic High School*, 3 Broadwater Ave., 59101. Tel: 406-245-6651; Fax: 406-259-3124. Email: shelhanser@billingscatholicschools.org; jhawbaker@billingscatholicschools.org. Web: www.billingscatholicschools.org. Sheldon Hanser, Prin.; Jim Hawbaker, Assoc. Prin. Lay Teachers 32; Students 324.

[C] HIGH SCHOOLS, PRIVATE

ASHLAND. *St. Labre Indian Catholic High School*, P.O. Box 216, 59003. Tel: 406-784-4500; Fax: 406-784-4565. Email: bbailey@stlabre.org. Web: www.stlabre.org. Ivan Small, Dir. Schools; Bart Bailey, Prin. Lay Teachers 21; Students 139.

[D] ELEMENTARY SCHOOLS, DIOCESAN

BILLINGS. *St. Francis Intermediate School*, (Grades 3-5), 1734 Yellowstone Ave., 59102. Tel: 406-656-2300; Fax: 406-656-2301. Email: cread@billingscatholicschools.org. Web: billingscatholicschools.org. Chris Read, Prin.; Jennifer Nieva, Librarian. Lay Teachers 20; Students 169.

St. Francis Primary School, (Grades PreK-2), 511 Custer Ave., 59101. Tel: 406-259-6421; Fax: 406-245-0176. Email: kpetermann@billingscatholicschools.org. Web: www.billingscatholicschools.org. Karen Petermann, Prin.; Amy Brown, Librarian. Lay Teachers 18; Students 214.

St. Francis Upper School, (Grades 6-8), 205 N. 32nd St., 59101. Tel: 406-259-5037; Fax: 406-259-7981. Email: jstanton@billingscatholicschools.org. Jim Stanton, Prin.; Donna Petriccione, Librarian. Lay Teachers 21; Students 197.

[E] ELEMENTARY SCHOOLS, PRIVATE

ASHLAND. *St. Labre Indian Catholic Elementary School*, (Grades PreK-4), P.O. Box 216, 59003. Tel: 406-784-4500; Fax: 406-784-4565. Email: twendt@stlabre.org. Ivan Small, Dir. of Schools; Toni Wendt, Prin. Lay Teachers 15; Students 171.

St. Labre Academy (Grades 5-8) Tel: 406-784-4500; Fax: 406-784-4565. Email: linda@stlabre.org. Linda Pease-Brien, Prin. Lay Teachers 11; Students 107.

PRYOR. *St. Charles Mission School*, (Grades PreK-8), P.O. Box 29, 59066. Tel: 406-259-9976; Fax: 406-259-7092. Email: dfritzler@stlabre.org. Web: www.stlabre.org. Dell Fritzler, Prin.; Jane Giard, Librarian. Priests 1; Lay Teachers 28; Students 111.

ST. XAVIER. *Pretty Eagle Catholic Academy*, (Grades K-8), P.O. Box 310, 59075. Tel: 406-666-2215; Fax: 406-666-2245. Email: gwilliamson@stlabre.org. Web: www.stlabre.org. Garla Williamson, Prin.; Anne Smith, Librarian. Clergy 1; Lay Teachers 34; Students 154.

[F] CHILD CARE & YOUTH SERVICES

GREAT FALLS. *St. Thomas Child and Family Center*, 1710 Benefis Ct., 59405. Tel: 406-761-6538; Fax: 406-727-0670. Email: carrie@stthomaskids.org. Web: stthomaskids.org. Carrie Doty, Exec. Dir. Sisters of Providence, Mother Joseph Province. Lay Staff 30; Child Care & Pre-School Children 106.

BILLINGS. *Little Flower Day Care*, 120 S. 34th St., P.O. Box 31158, 59107. Tel: 406-867-8050; Fax: 406-252-5697. Email: kseibel@billingscatholicschools.org. Web: www.billingscatholicschools.org. Katie Seibel, Dir. Children ages infant-12 years 22.

St. Francis Primary Early Childcare Center, 511 Custer Ave., 59101. Tel: 406-254-7548; Fax: 406-252-5697. Katie Seibel, Dir. Children ages 3-8 years 112.

Wm. R. Lowe Childcare, 2630 Normal Ave., 59102. Tel: 406-896-5820; Fax: 406-252-5697. Katie Seibel, Dir. Children ages infant-12 years 62.

Saint Francis West Childcare, 2821 Augusta Ln., 59102. Tel: 406-256-3562; Fax: 406-252-5697. Katie Seibel, Dir. Children ages 2-12 years 48.

[G] GENERAL HOSPITALS

BILLINGS. *St. Vincent Healthcare*, 1233 N. 30th St., P.O. Box 35200, 59107-5200. Tel: 406-237-7000; Fax: 406-237-3078. Web: svhhc.org. Jason Barker, Pres. & CEO; Sr. Catrina Bones, S.C.L., Vice Pres. Mission Integration. Sisters of Charity of Leavenworth, Kansas. Sisters 4; Bed Capacity 314; Patients Assisted Annually 423,611; Total Staff 2,051.

MILES CITY. *Holy Rosary Healthcare* (Critical Access Hospital), 2600 Wilson St., 59301. Tel: 406-233-2600; 800-843-3820; Fax: 406-233-2611. Web: www.holyrosaryhealthcare.org. Paul Lewis, Interim CEO. Sponsored by Sisters of Charity of Leavenworth. Beds: Acute Care 25; Extended Care 74; Patients Assisted Annually 11,428; Total Staff 353.

[H] CONVENTS AND RESIDENCES FOR SISTERS

GREAT FALLS. *Poor Clares of Montana, Inc.*, 3020-18th Ave. S., 59405. Tel: 406-453-7891; Fax: 406-453-8689. Email: sisters@poorclaresmt.org. Web: www.poorclaresmt.org. Sisters 4.

Ursuline Convent, 2300 Central Ave., 59401. Tel: 406-452-8585; Fax: 406-452-8586. Email: ursuline@in-tch.com. Sr. Francis Xavier Porter, O.S.U., Ursuline Archivist. Ursuline Sisters 2.

BILLINGS. *Sisters of Charity of Leavenworth*, 2703 Gregory Dr. S., 59102. Tel: 406-252-2508. Sisters 2.

[I] RETREAT HOUSES

GREAT FALLS. *Ursuline Retreat & Conference Centre*, 2300 Central Ave., 59401. Tel: 406-452-8585; Fax: 406-452-8586. Email: ursuline@in-tch.com. Web: www.ursulinecentre.com. Harry J. Tholen, Dir.

[J] MISCELLANEOUS LISTINGS

GREAT FALLS. *Big Sky Cum Christo/Cursillo*, P.O. Box 1399, 59403-1399. Web: www.bigskycumchristo.org. Rev. Gregory Staudinger. Tel: 406-322-5541; Bob Meyers. Tel: 406-453-5304 (Great Falls, MT); Carolyn Miller. Tel: 406-245-5440 (Billings/Laurel, MT); Mary Miller. Tel: 406-377-7973 (Glendive, MT); Dan Williams, (Landusky, MT).

Big Sky Marriage Encounter, c/o Holy Rosary Church, 521 Cluster Ave., 59101. Web: www.wwmemontana.org. Rev. Barton K. Stevens; Rebecca Stevens.

**Cascade County Council of the St. Vincent de Paul Society*, 426 Central Ave. W., P.O. Box 1562, 59403. Tel: 406-761-0870. Email: svdp@in-tch.com. Dione Leidholt, Opers. Dir.

Catholic Foundation of Eastern Montana, Inc., P.O. Box 1399, 59403-1399. Tel: 406-727-6683; Fax: 406-454-3480. Web: www.dioceseofgfb.org.

Engaged Encounter, c/o P.O. Box 1399, 59403-1399. Web: www.engagedencounter.org. Robert Dean; Adrea Dean.

Frank & Isabell Stites Memorial Center (Retired Priests & Lay People Living), *Pastoral Center*, P.O. Box 1399, 59403. Tel: 406-727-6683; Fax: 406-454-3480. Email: business@dioceseofgfb.org. Web: www.dioceseofgfb.org.
1701 26th St. S., 59403. Joseph Loncki, Contact Person.

Heisey Memorial Trust Fund, 313 Seventh St. N., 59401. Tel: 406-453-1211; Fax: 406-453-0607. Sandra Fermo, Exec. Dir.

Heisey Memorial Youth Center, 313 Seventh St. N., 59401. Tel: 406-453-1211; Fax: 406-453-0607. Email: info@theheisey.org. Web: www.theheisey.org. Sandra Fermo, Exec. Dir. Recreation center serving the adults and youth of the community.

Holy Spirit Catholic School Endowment Trust, 2820 Central Ave., 59401-3412. Tel: 406-761-5775; Fax: 406-761-5887. Email: wingerter@holyspiritschool.net. Marge Sitzman, Contact Person.

St. Joseph's Education Trust, 410 22nd Ave., 59404. Tel: 406-453-6546. Deacon William Medved.

**St. Martin De Porres Mission of Great Falls*, P.O. Box 141, 59403-0141. Tel: 406-868-0528.

Retrouvaille of Montana, P.O. Box 4, 59403-0004. Tel: 800-470-2330; 406-761-4830. Email: retrovaille@larc-ent.com. Rev. Robert Noonan. Tel: 406-544-5681; Larry Cutrone, Co-Coord.; Rose Cutrone, Co-Coord.

Tekakwitha Conference National Center, P.O. Box 6768, 59406-6768. Tel: 406-727-0147; 800-842-9635; Fax: 406-452-9845. Email: tekconf@gmail.com. Web: www.tekconf.org. Sr. Kateri Mitchell, S.S.A., Exec. Dir.

BILLINGS. *Billings Area Catholic Education Trust* (BACET), P.O. Box 31158, 59107-1158. Tel: 406-252-0252; Fax: 406-252-5731. Janyce Haider, Exec. Dir.; Eileen McDonald, Chair.

Billings Catholic Schools Foundation, P.O. Box 31158, 59107. Tel: 406-252-0252; Fax: 406-252-5731. Janyce Haider, Exec. Dir.; Eileen McDonald, Chm.

Regina Cleri, Pastoral Center: P.O. Box 1399, 59403. Tel: 406-727-6683; Fax: 406-454-3480. Email: business@dioceseofgfb.org. Web: www.dioceseofgfb.org. 2003 Woody Dr., 59102. Joseph Loncki, Contact Person. (Retired Priests Living).

St. Vincent Healthcare Foundation, 1106 N. 30th St., 59101. Tel: 406-237-3600; Fax: 406-237-3619. Email: david.irion@svh-mt.org. Web: www.svfoundation.org. David Irion, Pres. & CEO; Dr. Neal Sorenson, Chm.

ASHLAND. *St. Labre Indian School Educational Association*, P.O. Box 77, 59003. Tel: 406-784-4500; Fax: 406-784-4512. Email: executivedirector@atlabre.org. Web: www.stlabre.org. Curtis Yarlott, Pres. & Exec. Dir. A Nonprofit Corporation.; Four Catholic schools for Native Americans: St. Labre Indian School at Ashland (PreK-8 Students 278); (High School Students 139); Pretty Eagle Catholic Academy, St. Xavier (Students 154); St. Charles Mission School, Pryor (Students 111).

St. Labre Youth & Family Services, P.O. Box 458, 59003. Tel: 406-784-4521; 877-785-4457; Fax: 406-784-4527. Email: vanderson@stlabre.org. Web: www.stlabre.org. Vicki Anderson, Dir. Residential Group Homes:; Shilo Home for Native American Children; Licensed for 8 children.; Other Services: St. Labre Clothes Room Thrift Store; St. Labre Daycare Center; St. Labre Outreach Services (food, gas, heating, medical, funeral)

HAVRE. *St. Jude's Education Trust*, P.O. Box 407, 59501. Tel: 406-265-4261; Fax: 406-265-4408. Email: stjude@ttc.cmc.net. Web: stjudehavre.catholicweb.com. Rev. Daniel Wathen.

LEWISTOWN. *St. Leo's Catholic Education Trust*, P.O. Box 421, 59457. Tel: 406-538-9306; Fax: 406-538-7624. Email: stleos@midrivers.com. Rev. Daniel O'Rourke, Chm.

MALTA. *St. Mary's Catholic Education Trust*, P.O. Box 70, 59538. Tel: 406-654-1446; Fax: 406-654-1467. Web: www.saintmarysmalta.org. Rev. Cory D. Sticha.

MILES CITY. **Custer County Conference of the Society of Saint Vincent de Paul and Thrift Store*, 407 Main St., 59301. Tel: 406-234-3011. Linda Life, Exec. Dir.

Holy Rosary Healthcare Foundation, 2600 Wilson St., 59301. Tel: 406-233-4043; Fax: 406-233-4214. Web: holyrosaryhealthcare.org. Jackie Muri, Dir.

MONARCH. *Thieltges-St. Thomas Camp*, P.O. Box 46, 59463. Tel: 406-236-5385. Email: jimhoxter@3rivers.net.

RELIGIOUS INSTITUTES OF MEN REPRESENTED IN THE DIOCESE

For further details refer to the corresponding bracketed number in the Religious Institutes of Men or Women section.

[0200]—*Benedictine Monks* (Assumption Abbey, Richardton, ND; Cleveland, OH)—O.S.B.

[0200]—*Benedictine Monks* (St. Anselm's Abbey, Washington, DC)—O.S.B.

[0200]—*Benedictine Monks* (St. Andrew Abbey)—O.S.B.

[0470]—*The Capuchin Friars* (Prov. of St. Joseph, Detroit)—O.F.M.Cap.

[0690]—*Jesuit Fathers and Brothers* (Oregon Prov.)—S.J.

RELIGIOUS INSTITUTES OF WOMEN REPRESENTED IN THE DIOCESE

[2100]—*Congregation of the Humility of Mary* (Davenport, IA)—C.H.M.

[1730]—*Congregation of the Sisters of the Third Order of St. Francis* (Oldenburg, IN)—O.S.F.

[1070-14]—*Dominican Congregation of Our Lady of the Sacred Heart* (Grand Rapids, MI)—O.P.

[1115]—*Dominican Sisters of Peace*—O.P.

[1070-11]—*Dominican Sisters, Congregation of Our Lady of the Rosary* (Sparkill, NY)—O.P.

[3760]—*Order of St. Clare, Holy Name Federation* (Great Falls, MT)—O.S.C.

[0480]—*Sisters of Charity of Leavenworth, Kansas*—S.C.L.

[2575]—*Sisters of Mercy of the Americas* (Omaha, NE)—R.S.M.

[3350]—*Sisters of Providence* (Spokane, WA)—S.P.

[]—*Sisters of Sainte Anne* (Victoria, BC, Canada)—S.S.A.

[1720]—*Sisters of the Third Order Regular of St. Francis of the Congregation of Our Lady of Lourdes* (Rochester, MN)—O.S.F.

[4110]—*Ursuline Nuns* (Santa Rosa, CA)—O.S.U.

DIOCESAN CEMETERIES

BILLINGS. *Holy Cross*

GREAT FALLS. *Calvary*

Mount Olivet

NECROLOGY

† Arbanas, Harold P., (Retired)—Died Dec. 4, 2010
† Dobbin, Jay D., (Retired)—Died Nov. 8, 2011
† Tokarski, Stephen L., Billings, MT St. Pius X Church—Died Oct. 4, 2011

An asterisk (*) denotes an organization that has established tax-exempt status directly with the IRS and is not covered by the USCCB Group Ruling.

Diocese of Green Bay

(Dioecesis Sinus Viridis)

Most Reverend

ROBERT J. BANKS, D.D.

Retired Bishop of Green Bay; ordained December 20, 1952; consecrated September 19, 1985; appointed Auxiliary Bishop to the Archbishop of Boston and Titular Bishop of Taraqua on June 26, 1985; appointed to Green Bay October 16, 1990; installed December 5, 1990; retired December 12, 2003. *Office: 1825 Riverside Dr., Green Bay, WI 54301. Mailing Address: P.O. Box 23825, Green Bay, WI 54305-3825.*

Most Reverend

DAVID LAURIN RICKEN, D.D., J.C.L.

Bishop of Green Bay; ordained September 12, 1980; appointed Coadjutor Bishop of Cheyenne December 14, 1999; Episcopal Ordination January 6, 2000; succeeded to See September 26, 2001; appointed Bishop of Green Bay July 9, 2008; installed August 28, 2008. *Office: 1825 Riverside Dr., Green Bay, WI 54301. Mailing Address: P.O. Box 23825, Green Bay, WI 54305-3825.*

Chancery: 1825 Riverside Dr., Green Bay, WI 54301. Tel: 920-437-7531; Fax: 920-435-1330. *Mailing Address: P.O. Box 23825, Green Bay, WI 54305-3825*

Web: www.gbdioc.org

Most Reverend

ROBERT F. MORNEAU, D.D.

Auxiliary Bishop of Green Bay; ordained May 28, 1966; appointed Auxiliary Bishop of Green Bay and Titular Bishop of Massa Lubrense December 19, 1978; consecrated February 22, 1979. *Res.: 333 Hilltop Dr., Green Bay, WI 54301-2713. Office: 1825 Riverside Dr., Green Bay, WI 54301.* Tel: 920-437-7531. *Mailing Address: P.O. Box 23825, Green Bay, WI 54305-3825.*

ESTABLISHED MARCH 3, 1868.

Square Miles 10,728.

Incorporated January 16, 1907.

Comprises these 16 Counties: Brown, Calumet, Door, Florence, Forest, Kewaunee, Langlade, Manitowoc, Marinette, Menominee, Oconto, Outagamie, Shawano, Waupaca, Waushara and Winnebago in the State of Wisconsin.

Legal Title: Catholic Diocese of Green Bay, Inc.
For legal titles of parishes and diocesan institutions, consult the Chancery Office.

STATISTICAL OVERVIEW

Personnel	
Bishop	1
Auxiliary Bishops	1
Retired Bishops	1
Abbots	1
Retired Abbots	1
Priests: Diocesan Active in Diocese	78
Priests: Diocesan Active Outside Diocese	7
Priests: Diocesan in Foreign Missions	2
Priests: Retired, Sick or Absent	93
Number of Diocesan Priests	180
Religious Priests in Diocese	99
Total Priests in Diocese	279
Extern Priests in Diocese	12
Ordinations:	
Diocesan Priests	2
Transitional Deacons	2
Permanent Deacons	4
Permanent Deacons in Diocese	133
Total Brothers	34
Total Sisters	457
Parishes	
Parishes	157
With Resident Pastor:	
Resident Diocesan Priests	59
Resident Religious Priests	17
Without Resident Pastor:	
Administered by Priests	48
Administered by Deacons	12
Administered by Religious Women	10
Administered by Lay People	10
Missions	2
Pastoral Centers	18
Professional Ministry Personnel:	
Sisters	48
Lay Ministers	169
Welfare	
Catholic Hospitals	8
Total Assisted	943,303
Homes for the Aged	13
Total Assisted	1,005
Day Care Centers	2
Total Assisted	98
Specialized Homes	4
Total Assisted	9,579
Special Centers for Social Services	8
Total Assisted	217,325
Educational	
Diocesan Students in Other Seminaries	24
Seminaries, Religious	1
Students Religious	8
Total Seminarians	32
Colleges and Universities	2
Total Students	3,532
High Schools, Diocesan and Parish	5
Total Students	1,470
High Schools, Private	1
Total Students	736
Elementary Schools, Diocesan and Parish	54
Total Students	8,458
Catechesis/Religious Education:	
High School Students	6,364
Elementary Students	14,120
Total Students under Catholic Instruction	34,712
Teachers in the Diocese:	
Sisters	16
Lay Teachers	940
Vital Statistics	
Receptions into the Church:	
Infant Baptism Totals	3,408
Adult Baptism Totals	135
Received into Full Communion	209
First Communions	3,555
Confirmations	3,007
Marriages:	
Catholic	787
Interfaith	293
Total Marriages	1,080
Deaths	2,989
Total Catholic Population	332,200
Total Population	1,006,668

Former Bishops—Rt. Revs. JOSEPH MELCHER, D.D., ord. March 27, 1830; cons. July 12, 1868; died Dec. 20, 1873; FRANCIS XAVIER KRAUTBAUER, D.D., ord. July 16, 1850; cons. June 29, 1875; died Dec. 17, 1885; FREDERICK XAVIER KATZER, D.D., ord. Dec. 21, 1866; appt. July 13, 1886; cons. Sept. 21, 1886; appt. Archbishop of Milwaukee, Jan. 30, 1891; died July 20, 1903; SEBASTIAN GEBHARD MESSMER, D.D., ord. July 23, 1871; cons. Bishop of Green Bay, March 27, 1892; appt. Archbishop of Milwaukee, Nov. 28, 1903; died Aug. 4, 1930; JOSEPH J. FOX, D.D., ord. June 7, 1879; cons. Bishop of Green Bay, July 25, 1904; resigned Dec. 4, 1914; appt. Titular Bishop of Ionopolis; died March 14, 1915; Most Revs. PAUL P. RHODE, D.D., ord. June 17, 1894; cons. Titular Bishop of Barca and Auxiliary to the Archbishop of Chicago, July 29, 1908; transferred to the See of Green Bay, July 5, 1915; died March 3, 1945; STANISLAUS V. BONA, D.D., ord. Nov. 1, 1912; appt. Bishop of Grand Island, NE Dec. 18, 1931; cons. Feb. 25, 1932; appt. Coadjutor Bishop of Green Bay, Dec. 2, 1944; succeeded to See, March 3, 1945; died Dec. 1, 1967; ALOYSIUS J. WYCISLO, D.D., ord. April 7, 1934; appt. Titular Bishop of Stadia and Auxiliary Bishop of Chicago Oct. 17, 1960; cons. Dec. 21, 1960; appt. to Green Bay, March 8, 1968; retired May 10, 1983; died Oct. 11, 2005; ADAM J. MAIDA, J.C.L., J.D., S.T.L., ord. May 26, 1956; appt. to Green Bay, Nov. 8, 1983; cons. Jan. 25, 1984; installed as Archbishop of Detroit, June 12, 1990; created Cardinal on Nov. 26, 1994; ROBERT J. BANKS, D.D., J.C.D. (Retired), ord. Dec. 20, 1952; cons. Sept. 19, 1985; appt. Auxiliary Bishop to the Archbishop of Boston and Titular Bishop of Taraqua on June 26, 1985; appt. to Green Bay Oct. 16, 1990; installed Dec. 5, 1990; retired Dec. 12, 2003; DAVID A. ZUBIK, ord. May 3, 1975; appt. Auxiliary Bishop of Pittsburgh and Titular Bishop of Jamestown Feb. 18, 1997; cons. April 6, 1997; appt. Bishop of Green Bay Oct. 10, 2003; installed Dec. 12, 2003; appt. Bishop of Pittsburgh July 18, 2007.

Vicars General—Most Rev. ROBERT F. MORNEAU, D.D.; Very Revs. JOHN F. DOERFLER, S.T.D., J.C.L.; DANIEL J. FELTON.

Chancery—1825 Riverside Dr., Green Bay, 54301. Tel: 920-437-7531; Fax: 920-435-1330. *Mailing Address: P.O. Box 23825, Green Bay, 54305-3825.* Office Hours: Mon.-Fri. 8-4:30; other times by appointment only.

General Director of the Diocesan Curia—Deacon TIMOTHY G. REILLY. Tel: 920-272-8171.

Associate Director of the Curia—Mrs. DORIS V. VINCENT. Tel: 920-272-8175.

Chancellor—Very Rev. JOHN F. DOERFLER, S.T.D., J.C.L. Tel: 920-272-8180.

Vice-Chancellor—Rev. Msgr. BRIAN P. COLEMAN, J.C.L. (Retired).

Archivist—Mr. JOHN LEDOUX. Tel: 920-272-8186.

Secretaries to Bishop—Mrs. NANCY LUCAS. Tel: 920-272-8194; Mrs. GLADYS POWELL. Tel: 920-272-8167.

Executive Assistant to General Director of the Curia—Mrs. TERRI WICKMAN. Tel: 920-272-8189.

Executive Assistant to Chancellor—Mrs. MARY JO KRUEGER. Tel: 920-272-8188.

Diocesan Tribunal—1825 Riverside Dr., Green Bay,

54301. Tel: 920-437-7531. *Mailing Address: P.O. Box 23825, Green Bay, 54305-3825.*

Judicial Vicar—Very Rev. ROBERT J. KABAT, J.C.L. Tel: 920-272-8172.

Adjutant Judicial Vicars—Rev. Msgr. BRIAN P. COLEMAN, J.C.L. (Retired); Very Rev. RICHARD GETCHEL, J.C.L.

Judges—Most Rev. ROBERT J. BANKS, D.D., J.C.D. (Retired); Rev. Msgr. BRIAN P. COLEMAN, J.C.L. (Retired); Rev. JAMES B. HERRING, O.Praem., J.C.D.; Very Rev. ROBERT J. KABAT, J.C.L.; Rt. Rev. GARY J. NEVILLE, O.Praem., J.C.D.; Rev. WILLIAM L. VAN DE KREEKE, J.C.L. (Retired); Very Rev. RICHARD GETCHEL, J.C.L.

Promoter of Justice—Sr. ANN F. REHRAUER, J.C.L., M.A.

Defenders of the Bond—Rev. LEE J. KAHRS, B.A. (Retired); Sr. ANN F. REHRAUER, J.C.L., M.A.

Notaries—JOANN VANDER LOOP; Mrs. GLADYS POWELL.

Diocesan Health Services—Very Rev. RICHARD H. KLINGEISEN, Coord., 601 N. 8th St., Manitowoc, 54220-3919. Tel: 920-684-3718.

College of Consultors—Most Revs. DAVID L. RICKEN, D.D., J.C.L.; ROBERT F. MORNEAU, D.D.; Rev. RONALD C. BELITZ; Very Rev. DANIEL J. FELTON; Revs. JAMES R. JUGENHEIMER; ROBERT KOLLATH; CARL E. SCHMITT; MATHEW J. SIMONAR; Very Revs. JOHN F. DOERFLER, S.T.D., J.C.L.; JOHN W. GIROTTI.

Regional Vicars—Very Revs. JOSEPH E. DORNER, Vicariate I - North; CELESTINE BYEKWASO, Asst. Vicar, Vicariate I - North; JOHN BERGSTADT, Vicariate II - Mid-North; DOUGLAS E. LECAPTAIN, Vicariate III - Southwest; DONALD M. ZULEGER, Vicariate IV - Mid-South; RICHARD H. KLINGEISEN, Vicariate V - Southeast; RICHARD GETCHEL, J.C.L., Vicariate VI - Mid-East; ANTHONY J. BIRDSALL, Vicariate VII - Peninsula (Retired).

Diocesan Pastoral Council—Most Rev. DAVID L. RICKEN, D.D., J.C.L., Chm.

Ecumenical Liaison—Rev. JAMES P. MASSART (Retired).

Presbyteral Council Membership—

President—Most Rev. DAVID L. RICKEN, D.D., J.C.L.

Appointed Members—Revs. GERALD J. FOLEY (Retired); PATRICK LLOYD, S.C.J.; ROBERT KOLLATH; Very Rev. DANIEL J. FELTON.

Elected Members—Vicariate: Revs. MATTHEW W. SETTLE, I - North; DANE RADECKI, O.Praem., II - Mid-North; JAMES R. JUGENHEIMER, III - Southwest; JAMES A. HABLEWITZ, IV - Mid-South; THOMAS J. REYNEBEAU, V - Southeast; RONALD C. BELITZ, VI - Mid-East; CARL E. SCHMITT, VII - Peninsula.

Ex Officio—Most Rev. ROBERT F. MORNEAU, D.D.; Very Revs. JOHN F. DOERFLER, S.T.D., J.C.L.; W. THOMAS LONG.

Resource—Deacon TIMOTHY G. REILLY.

Bishop's Finance Council—Most Rev. DAVID L. RICKEN, D.D., J.C.L.; Rev. ROBERT K. FINNEGAN, O.Praem.; Mrs. JOANN COTTER; Mr. W. PAUL JONES; Mr. MICHAEL ARIENS; Mr. ROBERT C. GALLAGHER; Mr. PAUL GEHL; Mr. THOMAS VORPAHL; Mr. JOSEPH VARKOLY; Deacon TIMOTHY G. REILLY; Most Rev. ROBERT F. MORNEAU, D.D.; Mr. PAUL KOLBACH, Resource.

Censores Librorum—Revs. GORDON J. GILSDORF; MILTON M. SUESS.

Ministry Formation

Vicar for Ministers—Very Rev. W. THOMAS LONG, Mailing Address: P.O. Box 23825, Green Bay, 54305-3825. Tel: 920-272-8165.

Vocations—Revs. DANIEL J. SCHUSTER, Dir.; QUENTIN A. MANN, Assoc. Dir.

Administrative Assistants—DEBBIE RUSCH; VERONICA CORTES.

Representative for Religious—Sr. FLORENCE YOUNGWIRTH, A.N.G.

Department of the Permanent Diaconate—Deacons PAUL K. GRIMM, Dir., Prog. Coord.; KURT L. GRUBE, Personnel Assoc. Dir., Mailing Address: P.O. Box 23825, Green Bay, 54305-3825. Tel: 920-272-8290.

Lay Ministry Formation—Mr. TONY PICHLER, Dir., Mailing Address: P.O. Box 23825, Green Bay, 54305-3825. Tel: 920-272-8268.

Hispanic Ministry—Sr. MELANIE MACZKA, Coord.; ELIZABETH KOSTICHKA, Formation Facilitator.

Safe Environment—Ms. ANN FOX, Assistance Coord. Tel: 920-272-8174; Ms. KAREN R. BASS, Asst. Tel: 920-272-8198.

Diocesan Department of Education

Director—Dr. JOSEPH BOUND. Tel: 920-272-8266.

Management Support Coordinator—DEBBIE LINNANE. Tel: 920-272-8266.

Catholic Schools—JANE SCHUELLER, Dir. Curriculum & Instruction. Tel: 920-272-8284; JACALYN VANKAUWENBERG, Administrative Asst. Tel: 920-272-8279.

Religious Education—Sr. JACQUELINE SPANIOLA, O.S.F., Dir. Tel: 920-272-8288; CAROL FOUNTAIN, Administrative Asst. Tel: 920-272-8270.

Youth Ministry—ERIC BLUMREICH, Dir. Tel: 920-272-8162.

Camp Tekawitha Retreat and Conference Center—ERIC BLUMREICH, Camp Dir. Tel: 715-526-2316.

Adult Faith Formation and Young Adult Ministry—JULIANNE DONLON-STANZ, Dir. Tel: 920-272-8270; SHEILA SCHAUT, Administrative Asst. Tel: 920-437-7531, Ext. 8276.

Evangelization, Living Justice and Worship

Evangelization, Living Justice and Worship—Sr. ANN REHRAUER, Dir. Tel: 920-272-8292. Administrative Assistants: NANCY MOOREN. Tel: 920-272-8310; TANYA WOLLENBERG. Tel: 920-272-8291.

Campus Ministry—SAM WOOD, Dir., Newman Center of Oshkosh, Inc., 514 Scott Ave., Oshkosh, 54901-3741. Tel: 920-233-5555; Ms. BETTY SCHWANDT, Campus Min., Univ. of Wisconsin - Green Bay, 2420 Nicolet Dr., Green Bay, 54311-7003.

Family & Married Life—VACANT, Dir. Tel: 920-272-8315.

Dignity of Human Life—CHRISTINA PALLINI, Volunteer Consultant. Tel: 920-272-8286.

Evangelization and Welcoming Director—Dr. KRISTINA DENEVE. Tel: 920-272-8304.

Worship and Sacraments—CLARE STURM, Dir. Tel: 920-272-8311.

Holy Name Retreat House—BARBARA CONDER, Exec. Dir.

Stewardship and Pastoral Services

Stewardship and Pastoral Services—1825 Riverside Dr., Green Bay, 54301. Tel: 920-437-7531; Fax: 920-437-0694. Email: pastserv@gbdioc.org. *Mailing Address: P.O. Box 23825, Green Bay, 54305-3825.* MARK MOGILKA, Dir. Tel: 920-272-8297. Email: mmogilka@gbdioc.org; MARY SHERMAN, Asst. Dir. Tel: 920-272-8300; PATTY YOUNG, Administrative Svcs. Supvr. Tel: 920-272-8295.

Consultants—

Hispanic Ministry—CARLOS HERNANDEZ. Tel: 920-272-8308.

Pastoral Care—MARY SHERMAN. Tel: 920-272-8300; 920-272-8307.

Parish Planning & Collaboration—DEBORAH WEGNER-HOHENSEE. Tel: 920-272-8286.

Prison Ministry—MARY SHERMAN. Tel: 920-272-8300; Deacon ROBERT VINCENT. Tel: 920-731-0356.

Rural Life—VACANT.

Social Concerns—VACANT.

Stewardship and Special Projects—MARY ANN OTTO. Tel: 920-272-8301.

Community Services

Catholic Charities—KAREN JOHNSTON, Dir., 1825 Riverside Dr., Green Bay, 54301. Tel: 920-272-8234; Fax: 920-437-0694. Mailing Address: P.O. Box 23825, Green Bay, 54305-3825.

Apostleship of the Sea—Deacon GLENN TESKE, Port Chap., 2839 S. Broadway, Green Bay, 54304-5309. Tel: 920-499-0035.

Communications—Mailing Address: P.O. Box 23825, Green Bay, 54305-3825. Tel: 920-272-8213. Deacon RAYMOND L. DUBOIS, Dir. Tel: 920-272-8213.

Diocesan Newspaper— "The Compass" *Mailing Address: P.O. Box 23825, Green Bay, 54305-3825.* Tel: 920-437-7531. *Appleton Area.* Tel: 920-233-5555. SAM LUCERO, Editor. Tel: 920-272-8210.

Computer Services—Deacon RAYMOND L. DUBOIS, Mailing Address: Box 23825, Green Bay, 54305-3825. Tel: 920-272-8214; ROY VERSTEGEN, Database Mgr. Tel: 920-272-8255; NICK GRIFFIE, Intranet Coord. Tel: 920-272-8245; SEAN MASSEY, Network Admin.; MATTHEW LIVINGSTONE, Web & Social Media Admin.; AMBER BACKUS, Communications Coord.

Financial Services—Mr. PAUL KOLBACH, Dir., Mailing Address: P.O. Box 23825, Green Bay, 54305-3825. Tel: 920-272-8206. Accounting Managers: MIKE SPEEL. Tel: 920-272-8259; CATHERINE HOEFT. Tel: 920-272-8267. Financial Systems Consultants: PAULA NAULT; KEN JUNGWIRTH. Accounting Supervisors: TERRY SELISSEN; JEAN JOHNSON.

Facilities, Properties and Cemeteries—Ms. TAMMY BASTEN, Dir. Diocesan Properties, Mailing Address: P.O. Box 23825, Green Bay, 54305-3825. Tel: 920-272-8260.

Human Resources—JACQUELYN MATHEIN, Dir. Tel: 920-272-8216; BARBARA WIEGAND, Coord., Mailing Address: P.O. Box 23825, Green Bay, 54305-3825. Tel: 920-272-8216.

Medical Insurance and Benefits—AMY TREICHEL, Mailing Address: Box 23825, Green Bay, 54305-3825. Tel: 920-272-8201. Employee Relations Coordinator: JENNIFER BUECHEL. Tel: 920-272-8200. Administrative Assistant: BETTY ALLEN. Tel: 920-272-8200.

Sacred Heart Seminary, Corp.—Mailing Address: P.O. Box 23825, Green Bay, 54305-3825. Tel: 920-437-7531.

St. Joseph Corporation and Central Services—Ms. TAMMY BASTEN, Mailing Address: P.O. Box 23825, Green Bay, 54305-3825. Tel: 920-272-8260.

The Catholic Foundation for the Diocese of Green Bay, Inc.—CINDI BRAWNER, Mailing Address: P.O. Box 23825, Green Bay, 54305-3825. Tel: 920-272-8173.

Department of World Mission Services—CINDI BRAWNER, Dir. Tel: 920-272-8173; MARGIE SUMNICHT, Coord. Mission Svcs., Mailing Address: P.O. Box 23825, Green Bay, 54305-3825. Tel: 920-272-8192; Fax: 920-435-1330.

Agencies— Propagation of the Faith, St. Peter the Apostle, Holy Childhood Association, Catholic Relief Services

Annual Bishop's Appeal—JOSH DIEDRICH, Dir. Tel: 920-272-8197.

Priests' Personnel Board—Mailing Address: P.O. Box 23825, Green Bay, 54305-3825. Tel: 920-437-7531. Most Revs. DAVID L. RICKEN, D.D., J.C.L.; ROBERT F. MORNEAU, D.D., Resource Person; Very Rev. W. THOMAS LONG; Revs. JOHN J. BECKER, Chm.; BRIAN S. BELONGIA; MICHAEL E. BETLEY; Very Rev. JOHN F. DOERFLER, S.T.D., J.C.L.; Rev. Msgr. JAMES B. FEELY (Retired); Very Rev. DANIEL J. FELTON; Rev. Msgr. DENNIS M. LALLY, B.A.; Very Rev. DOUGLAS E. LECAPTAIN; Sr. PAMELA A. BIEHL, O.S.F.

Leo Benevolent Association—Rev. Msgr. MARK J. SCHOMMER, Chm. (Retired), N2614 Bughs Lake Rd., Wautoma, 54982-7130. Tel: 920-787-1666.

CLERGY, PARISHES, MISSIONS AND PAROCHIAL SCHOOLS

CITY OF GREEN BAY

(BROWN COUNTY)

1—ST. FRANCIS XAVIER CATHEDRAL, Also serves St. John, Green Bay. Rev. John W. Girotti; Deacon Thomas Mahoney. In Res., Rev. Richard L. Thomas (Retired).

Res.: 139 S. Madison St., 54301-4501. Tel: 920-432-4348; Fax: 920-435-5068. Email: sfxavier@sbcglobal.net.

School—St. Thomas More, (Part of the GRACE System, Inc.), 650 S. Irwin Ave., 54301-3398. Tel: 920-432-8242; Fax: 920-432-1562. Email: stmore@stmoregb.org. Eric Weydt, Prin. (Consolidated with SS. Peter & Paul and St. Mary of the Angels.)

Catechesis/Religious Program—Mrs. Connie Demeuse, D.R.E. Associated with Ss Peter & Paul, Green Bay.

2—ST. AGNES Rev. Dane J. Radecki, O.Praem.; Deacon James R. Gauthier.

Res.: 1484 9th St., 54304-3061. Tel: 920-494-2534; Fax: 920-617-3118. Email: stagnesparishoffice@netnet.net.

School—Holy Family, (Part of GRACE System, Inc.), 1204 S. Fisk St., 54304-2299. Tel: 920-494-1931; Fax: 920-494-4942. Pamela S. Otto, Prin.

Catechesis/Religious Program—Tel: 920-494-6450. Email: religioused@stagnesgreenbay.org. Mrs. Carrie A. Aimers, D.R.E.; Peter J. Leitermann, D.R.E. Students 377.

3—ANNUNCIATION OF THE BLESSED VIRGIN MARY, Served from St. Joseph, Green Bay. Revs. Donald E. Everts; Callistus I. Elue, Parochial Vicar; Rev. Msgr. Roy M. Klister, Sacramental Min.; Deacons Michael J. Mervilde; Daniel Wagnitz.

Mailing Address: 1420 Division St., 54303-3122. Tel: 920-496-2160; Fax: 920-496-2167. Email: lverheyden@allofuswestgb.org.

Catechesis/Religious Program—Combined with St. Joseph, Green Bay, St. Jude, Green Bay and St. Patrick, Green Bay., 936 9th St., 54304-3439. Tel: 920-497-7042; Fax: 920-491-0121. Tina Meyer, D.R.E.

4—ST. BERNARD, Also serves St. Philip the Apostle, Green Bay. Revs. David J. Pleier; Jose Castaneda; Deacons Keith P. Holschbach; John H. Laurant; Larry V. Mastalish.

Res.: 2040 Hillside Ln., 54302-4098. Tel: 920-468-4811; Fax: 920-468-1396. Email: dave@stbernardcong.org.

School—(Part of GRACE System, Inc.), 2020 Hillside Ln., 54302-4099. Tel: 920-468-5026; Fax: 920-468-3478. Kay L. Franz, Prin.

Catechesis/Religious Program—Tel: 920-468-4390.

Email: amy@stbernardcong.org. Mrs. Amy M. Weigand, D.R.E.; Ms. Holly Meyer, D.R.E.; Ms. Stephanie Rottier, D.R.E.

5—ST. ELIZABETH ANN SETON Rev. Paul E. Demuth; Deacon Steven J. Meyer.
Res.: 2771 Oakwood Dr., 54304-1618. Tel: 920-499-1546; Fax: 920-499-2207. Email: seas@seasgb.org.
School: See Holy Family, Green Bay under St. Agnes, Green Bay for details.
Catechesis/Religious Program—Judy A. Brown, D.R.E.; Ms. Kathleen A. Brooks, D.R.E.

6—HOLY MARTYRS OF GORCUM, [CEM] Merged with Holy Trinity, Pine Grove to form Prince of Peace, Green Bay.

7—ST. JOHN, Served from St. Francis Xavier Cathedral, Green Bay. Rev. John W. Girotti; Deacon Thomas Mahoney.
Res.: 413 St. John St., 54301-4116. Tel: 920-436-6380; Fax: 920-436-6382. Email: stjevan@sbcglobal.net.
Catechesis/Religious Program—Susan K. Perrault, D.R.E.

8—ST. JOSEPH, Also serves Annunciation, Green Bay, St. Jude, Green Bay & St. Patrick, Green Bay. Revs. Donald E. Everts; Callistus I. Elue, Parochial Vicar; Rev. Msgr. Roy M. Klister, Sacramental Min.; Deacons Michael J. Mervilde; Daniel Wagnitz.
Res.: 1420 Division St., 54303-3122. Tel: 920-496-2160; Fax: 920-496-2167. Email: lverheyden@allofuswestgb.org.
Catechesis/Religious Program—Combined with Annunciation of the Blessed Virgin Mary, Green Bay, St. Jude, Green Bay and St. Patrick, Green Bay., 936 9th St., 54304-3439. Tel: 920-497-7042; Fax: 920-491-0121. Tina Meyer, D.R.E.

9—ST. JUDE, Served from St. Joseph, Green Bay. Revs. Donald E. Everts; Callistus I. Elue, Parochial Vicar; Rev. Msgr. Roy M. Klister, Sacramental Min.; Deacons Michael J. Mervilde; Daniel Wagnitz.
Res.: 1420 Division St., 54303-3122. Tel: 920-496-2160; Fax: 920-496-2167. Email: lverheyden@allofuswestgb.org.
Catechesis/Religious Program—Combined with Annunciation of the Blessed Virgin Mary, Green Bay, St. Joseph, Green Bay and St. Patrick, Green Bay., 936 9th St., 54304-3439. Tel: 920-497-7042. Tina Meyer, D.R.E.

10—ST. MARY OF THE ANGELS Rev. Patrick M. Gawrylewski, O.F.M.; Deacon Paul P. Umentum.
Res.: 645 S. Irwin Ave., 54301-3303. Tel: 920-437-1979; Fax: 920-965-9127. Email: stmarygb@gmail.com.
School: See St. Thomas More, Green Bay under St. Francis Xavier Cathedral, Green Bay for details.
Catechesis/Religious Program—Tel: 920-432-2747. Email: stmaryangel@att.net. Mary S. Sedlacek, D.R.E.

11—ST. MATTHEW Rev. Philip Dinh-Van-Thiep; Deacons Paul J. Cibula; Michael W. Dabeck.
Res.: 130 St. Matthews St., 54301-2999. Tel: 920-435-6811; Fax: 920-435-0065. Email: parishoffice@stmattsgb.org.
School—(Part of GRACE System, Inc.), 2575 S. Webster Ave., 54301-2998. Tel: 920-432-5223; Fax: 920-432-5139. Email: stmatthews1@new.rr.com. Ms. Heidi Potts, Prin.
Catechesis/Religious Program—Michael Westenberg, D.R.E.

12—NATIVITY OF OUR LORD Rev. John H. Harper; Deacon Michael E. Schmidt.
Res.: 2270 S. Oneida St., 54304-4712. Tel: 920-499-5156; Fax: 920-490-9285. Email: natscene@nativityparish.com.
Catechesis/Religious Program—Tel: 920-499-6012. Email: natjw@nativityparish.com. Mr. James R. Whalen, D.R.E.; Andrea Sabor, D.R.E.

13—ST. PATRICK, Served from St. Joseph, Green Bay. Revs. Donald E. Everts; Callistus I. Elue, Parochial Vicar; Rev. Msgr. Roy M. Klister, Sacramental Min.; Deacons Michael J. Mervilde; Daniel Wagnitz.
1420 Division St., 54303-3122.
Res.: 211 N. Maple Ave., 54303-2749. Tel: 920-496-2160; Fax: 920-437-3274. Email: lverheyden@allofuswestgb.org.
Catechesis/Religious Program—Combined with Annunciation of the Blessed Virgin Mary, Green Bay, St. Joseph, Green Bay and St. Jude, Green Bay., 936 9th St., 54304-3439. Tel: 920-497-7042; Fax: 920-491-0121. Tina Meyer, D.R.E.

14—SS. PETER AND PAUL Revs. Anthony Cirignani, O.F.M.; Harry G. Hafeman, Sacramental Min.; Deacons Michael C. Vincent; Robert F. Ellis.
Res.: 710 N. Baird St., 54302-1997. Tel: 920-435-7548; Fax: 920-432-1321. Email: cfsspp@sbcglobal.net.
School: See St. Thomas More, Green Bay under St. Francis Xavier Cathedral, Green Bay for details.
Catechesis/Religious Program—720 N. Baird St., 54302-1902. Tel: 920-437-0651. Michael F. Lee, D.R.E.; Mrs. Michael Vincent, D.R.E.

15—ST. PHILIP THE APOSTLE, Served from St. Bernard, Green Bay. Revs. David J. Pleier, Admin.; Jose Castaneda, Parochial Vicar.
Res.: 312 Victoria St., 54302-2818. Tel: 920-468-7848; Fax: 920-468-1025. Email: parishoffice@stphilipcong.org.
Catechesis/Religious Program—Mary A. Peters, D.R.E.

16—PRINCE OF PEACE, Merger of Holy Trinity, Pine Grove & Holy Martyrs of Gorcum, Green Bay. Rev. Ronald C. Belitz; Deacon William J. Burkel.
Mailing Address: 3425 Willow Rd., 54311-8232. Tel: 920-468-5718; Fax: 920-468-5713. Email: kmiller@princeofpeaceparish.com.
School—(Part of GRACE Systems, Inc.), 3542 Finger Rd., 54311-7733. Tel: 920-468-7262. Email: info@princeofpeacecatholicschool.com. Mary McCabe, Prin.
Catechesis/Religious Program—Carolyn Whitcomb, D.R.E.

17—RESURRECTION Most Rev. Robert F. Morneau; Deacons Donald J. Ropson; Timothy G. Reilly.
Res.: 333 Hilltop Dr., 54301-2799. Tel: 920-336-7768; Fax: 920-336-1949. Email: resurrectionparish@gbres.org.
School—(Part of GRACE System, Inc.), Tel: 920-336-3230. Mrs. Kay Gross, Prin.
Catechesis/Religious Program—Rosemary A. Baloun, D.R.E.; Amberly Boerschinger, D.R.E.

18—ST. WILLEBRORD Rev. Andrew G. Cribben, O.Praem.; Deacon Luis Sanchez.
Res.: 209 S. Adams St., 54301-4584. Tel: 920-435-2016; Fax: 920-435-2039. Email: frandy@stwillys.org.
Catechesis/Religious Program—Email: rita@stwillys.org. Ms. Rita M. Bauldry, D.R.E.; Ms. Alma Vazquez, D.R.E.

OUTSIDE THE CITY OF GREEN BAY

ABRAMS, OCONTO CO., ST. LOUIS, [JC] Merged with St. Joseph, Chase and St. John Cantius, Sobieski to form St. Maximilian Kolbe, Sobieski.

ALGOMA, KEWAUNEE CO., ST. MARY (1860) [CEM], Also serves Holy Rosary, Kewaunee. Rev. William D. Swichtenberg.
Mailing Address: 214 Church St., 54201-1035.
Res.: 118 Church St., 54201-1098. Tel: 920-487-5005; Fax: 920-487-5002. Email: wdswitz@sbcglobal.net.
School—Tel: 920-487-5004. Mrs. Laura L. Krzysiak, Prin. & D.R.E.
Catechesis/Religious Program—

ALVERNO, MANITOWOC CO., ST. JOSEPH, Merged with St. Casimir, Northeim; St. Isidore, Osman; and St. Wendel, Cleveland to form St. Thomas the Apostle, Northeim.

AMBERG, MARINETTE CO., ST. AGNES, Served from St. Augustine, Wausaukee. Revs. Ronald C. Belitz, Priest Moderator; Donald R. Burkart, Sacramental Min.; John J. Hephner, Sacramental Min. (Retired); Deacon Patrick J. Whitcomb, Pastoral Coord.
Mailing Address: 507 Church St., Wausaukee, 54177-9749. Tel: 715-856-5276; Fax: 715-856-5276. Email: staugustine@centurytel.net.

ANIWA, SHAWANO CO., ST. BONIFACE, [CEM], Served from St. Philomena, Birnamwood. Rev. Everard Scesney, O.F.M.
Res.: P.O. Box K, Birnamwood, 54414-0911. Tel: 715-449-2104; Fax: 715-449-0029.
Catechesis/Religious Program—

ANTIGO, LANGLADE CO.

1—ST. HYACINTH, Merged with St. Mary, Antigo to form SS. Mary & Hyacinth, Antigo.

2—ST. JOHN, [JC] Revs. David R. Schmidt; William J. Brunner, Parochial Vicar. Also serves St. Mary & Hyacinth, Antigo & St. Wenceslaus, Neva.
Res.: 415 6th Ave., 54409-2104. Tel: 715-623-2024; Fax: 715-627-0234. Email: carolyn@stjohnantigo.com.
School: See All Saints Catholic Schools, Inc., Antigo located under Consolidated Schools Antigo located in the Institution Section for details.
Catechesis/Religious Program—Email: religioused@stjohnantigo.com. Dawn Kratzke, D.R.E.

3—ST. MARY, Merged with St. Hyacinth, Antigo to form SS. Mary & Hyacinth, Antigo.

4—SS. MARY & HYACINTH, [JC], Served from St. John, Antigo. Has records for St. Mary & St. Hyacinth, Antigo. Revs. David R. Schmidt; William J. Brunner, Parochial Vicar; Charles G. Hoffmann, Sacramental Min.
Res.: 819 3rd Ave., 54409-1930. Tel: 715-623-4938; Fax: 715-623-5255. Email: ssmhy@dwave.net.
School: See All Saints Catholic Schools, Inc., Antigo located under Consolidated Schools in the Institution Section for details.
Catechesis/Religious Program—Tel: 715-623-5255. Mrs. Susan Brettingen, D.R.E.

APPLETON, OUTAGAMIE CO.

1—ST. BERNADETTE Very Rev. Donald M. Zuleger; Rev. Anthony Ibekwe, Parochial Vicar; Deacon Michael A. Madden. Also serves Sacred Heart, Appleton
Church: 2331 E. Lourdes Dr., 54915-3615. Tel: 920-739-4157; Fax: 920-739-2795. Email: peichhorst@saint-bernadette.org.
School—ACES/Xavier Education System, Inc. (St. Bernadette Campus), Tel: 920-739-5391; Fax: 920-739-0061. Email: ewatson@acesxavier.k12.wi.us. Web: www.acesys.org/st_bernadette/index.htm. Elizabeth A. Watson, Prin.
Catechesis/Religious Program—Tel: 920-734-7502. Shirley Riley, D.R.E.; Peter J. Gagnon, D.R.E.

2—ST. BERNARD Rev. Dennis M. Ryan; Deacons Michael J. Eash; Maurice F. Reed; Shuying (Joe) Vang.
1617 W. Pine St., 54914-5118. Tel: 920-739-0331; Fax: 920-749-9771. Email: stbernard@stbernardappleton.org.
School—ACES/Xavier Educational System Inc., 101 E. Northland Ave., 54911-2104. Tel: 920-735-9380; Fax: 920-735-1787. Email: tabts@acesys.org. Deacon Anthony J. Abts, Pres.
Catechesis/Religious Program—Tel: 920-739-8912. Maurine Overesch, D.R.E.; Kathleen McDonald, D.R.E.

3—ST. JOSEPH, Also serves St. Mary, Appleton. Revs. James P. Leary, O.F.M.Cap.; David J. Funk, O.F.M.Cap., Parochial Vicar; Deacons Clarence F. Dedman; Mark J. Farrell; Roy J. Baumruk.
Res.: 404 W. Lawrence St., 54911-5855. Tel: 920-734-7195; Fax: 920-734-0227. Email: jpleary@saintjosephparish.org.
School—ACES/Xavier Educational System, Inc. (St. Joseph Middle School Campus), 2626 N. Oneida St., 54911-2099. Tel: 920-730-8849; Fax: 920-703-4147. Email: bnorcross@acesxavier.k12.wi.us. Bradley Norcross, Prin.
Catechesis/Religious Program—Tel: 920-738-7413. Email: iprf@inter-parish.org. Jonathan R. Elmer, D.R.E.; Celia J. McKee, D.R.E.; Andrew J. Russell, D.R.E.; Jennifer R. Schubring, D.R.E. Associated with St. Mary's, Appleton.

4—ST. MARY, [CEM], Served from St. Joseph, Appleton. Revs. James P. Leary, O.F.M.Cap.; David J. Funk, O.F.M.Cap., Parochial Vicar; Deacons Gerard J. Schraufnagel; William J. Burke.
Church: 312 S. State St., 54911-5926. Tel: 920-739-5119; Fax: 920-739-5111. Email: stmary@stmaryparish.org.
School—ACES/Xavier Educational System, Inc (Catholic Central Campus), 313 S. State St., 54911-5929. Tel: 920-733-3709; Fax: 920-733-8142. Email: cwilant@acesxavier.k12.wi.us. Carol Wilant, Prin.
Catechesis/Religious Program—404 W. Lawrence St., 54911-5817. Tel: 920-738-7413. Email: iprf@inter-parish.org. Jonathan R. Elmer, D.R.E.; Celia J. McKee, D.R.E.; Andrew J. Russell, D.R.E.; Jennifer R. Schubring, D.R.E. Associated with St. Joseph-St. Mary Interparish.

5—ST. PIUS X Revs. Thomas J. Farrell; Quentin A. Mann, Parochial Vicar; Deacon Richard S. Simon.
Office:—500 W. Marquette St., 54911-1996. Tel: 920-733-0575; Fax: 920-749-8056. Email: thorson_d@hotmail.com.
School—ACES/Xavier Educational System, Inc. (St. Pius X Campus), Tel: 920-733-4918; Fax: 920-733-7269. Email: scjpeterson@acesxavier.k12.wi.us. Sr. Carol Jean Peterson, C.S.J., Prin.
Catechesis/Religious Program—Tel: 920-733-4919. Kathy Schommer, D.R.E.

6—SACRED HEART Very Rev. Donald M. Zuleger; Rev. Anthony Ibekwe, Parochial Vicar; Deacons Daniel T. Koszalinski; Gilbert Schmidt. Served from St. Bernadette, Appleton
Res.: 222 E. Fremont St., 54915-1890. Tel: 920-739-3196; Fax: 920-739-4062. Email: office@sacredheartappleton.com.
Catechesis/Religious Program—Email: faith@sacredheartappleton.com. Mrs. Kelly Koszalinski, D.R.E.

7—ST. THERESE Rev. William A. Hoffman; Deacon Anthony J. Abts.
Office:—213 E. Wisconsin Ave., 54911-4875. Tel: 920-733-8568; Fax: 920-954-5727. Email: william.hoffman@st-therese.com.
School—ACES/Xavier Educational System, Inc., 101 E. Northland Ave., 54911-2104. Tel: 920-735-9380; Fax: 920-735-1787. Email: tabts@acesys.org. Deacon Anthony J. Abts, Pres.
Catechesis/Religious Program—

8—ST. THOMAS MORE Rev. James W. Lucas; Deacons Donald J. Wetzel; Craig W. Merrick; Timothy E. Downey.
Res.: 1810B N. McDonald St., 54911-3450. Tel: 920-739-7758; Fax: 920-749-3743. Email: stmparish@stmcath.org.
School—ACES/Xavier Educational System, Inc. (St. Thomas More Campus), 1810 N. McDonald St., 54911-3498. Tel: 920-739-7826; Fax: 920-739-2376.

Email: dcallan@acesxavier.k12.wi.us. Mr. David L. Callan, Prin.
Catechesis/Religious Program—Tel: 920-739-8172. Ms. Irene M. Skarban, D.R.E.; Ms. Carolyn M. Coutu, D.R.E.; Ms. Anna M. Donnermeyer, D.R.E.

ARGONNE, FOREST CO., ST. MARY, Merged with St. Joseph, Crandon.

ARMSTRONG CREEK, FOREST CO., ST. STANISLAUS KOSTKA, Also serves St. Joan of Arc, Goodman. Rev. Matthew W. Settle, Priest Mod.; Rev. Msgr. Paul P. Koszarek, Sacramental Min. (Retired); Rev. John J. Hephner, Sacramental Min. (Retired); Deacon Gerald H. Cross, Parish Dir.
Mailing Address: P.O. Box 39, 54103-0039. Tel: 715-336-2334. Email: ststanislausarmstrong@gmail.com.
Catechesis/Religious Program— Associated with St. Joan of Arc, Goodman.

AURORA, FLORENCE CO., SACRED HEART, Served from St. Anthony, Niagara. Rev. Matthew W. Settle.
Mailing Address: 1432 River St., Niagara, 54151-1599. Tel: 715-251-3879; Fax: 715-251-3642. Email: stanthony@borderlandnet.net.

BAILEYS HARBOR, DOOR CO., ST. MARY OF THE LAKE, Merged with St. John the Baptist, Egg Harbor; St. Paul, Fish Creek; St. Michael, Jacksonport and St. Rosalia, Sister Bay to form Stella Maris, Egg Harbor.

BAY SETTLEMENT, BROWN CO., HOLY CROSS, [CEM] Rev. Thomas A. Hagendorf, O.Praem.
Res.: 3009 Bay Settlement Rd., 54311-7301. Tel: 920-468-0595. Email: holycross@new.rr.com.
School—(Part of GRACE System, Inc.), 3002 Bay Settlement Rd., 54311-7302. Tel: 920-468-0625; Fax: 920-468-0625. Email: rjensen@gracesystem.org. Robin J. Jensen, Prin.
Catechesis/Religious Program—Tel: 920-468-6554. Email: faithform@hotmail.com. Martha Burkard, D.R.E.

BEAR CREEK, OUTAGAMIE CO., ST. MARY, [CEM], Served from St. Rose, Clintonville. Mr. Lincoln Wood, Parish Dir.; Revs. John W. Girotti, Priest Mod.; John T. Mullarkey, Sacramental Min. (Retired); Deacons Thomas V. Jozwiak; Joseph M. Lehman; Paul J. Brulla.
Mailing Address: 140 Auto St., Clintonville, 54929-1712. Tel: 715-752-4177; Fax: 715-823-6010. Email: ssrmsborlen@gmail.com.
Catechesis/Religious Program—140 Auto St., Clintonville, 54929-1712. Tel: 715-823-5266. Email: ssrmre@gmail.com. Jennifer Wood, D.R.E.; Julie Minter, D.R.E. Associated with St. Rose, Clintonville.

BIRNAMWOOD, SHAWANO CO., ST. PHILOMENA, [CEM], Also serves St. Boniface, Aniwa. Rev. Everard Scesney, O.F.M.
Res.: P.O. Box K, 54414-0911. Tel: 715-449-0050; Fax: 715-449-0029. Email: eversces@charter.net.
Catechesis/Religious Program—

BLACK CREEK, OUTAGAMIE CO., ST. MARY, [CEM] Rev. Theodore J. Hendricks.
Res.: P.O. Box 217, 54106-0217. Tel: 920-984-3319.
Catechesis/Religious Program—Email: bczahn@charter.net. Rita Theobald, D.R.E.

BRILLION, CALUMET CO.
1—HOLY FAMILY, [JC], Merger of St. Mary, Brillion & St. Mary-St. Patrick, Reedsville/Maple Grove. (Has records for St. Mary, Brillion & St. Mary-St. Patrick, Reedsville/Maple Grove; St. Mary Reedsville & St. Patrick) Rev. Timothy Brandt, Admin.; Deacon Stephen T. Letourneaux.
Res.: 1100 W. Ryan St., 54110-1074. Tel: 920-756-2535; Fax: 920-756-9802. Email: office@holyfamily-parish.org.
School—209 N. Custer St., 54110-1236. Tel: 920-756-2502; Fax: 920-756-9702. Email: holyfamilybrillon@charter.net. Scott Smith, Prin.
Catechesis/Religious Program—Email: theresa@holyfamily-parish.org. Mrs. Maxine Geiger, D.R.E.; Mrs. Theresa Lambrecht, D.R.E.; Ms. Anna Schmidt, D.R.E.
2—ST. MARY, Merged with St. Mary-St. Patrick, Reedsville to form Holy Family, Brillion.

BRUSSELS, DOOR CO.
1—ST. FRANCIS XAVIER, Merged with St. Mary, Namur to form St. Francis-St. Mary, Brussels.
2—ST. FRANCIS-ST. MARY PARISH, [CEM 3], Merger of St. Francis Xavier, Brussels & St. Mary, Namur. (Has records for St. Francis Xavier, Brussels & St. Mary, Namur.) Rev. Pius Cotter, O.F.M.Cap., Admin.
Res.: 9716 Cemetery Rd., 54204-9749. Tel: 920-825-7555; Fax: 920-825-1492. Email: stfrancis@centurytel.net.
Catechesis/Religious Program—Tel: 920-825-7713. Susan M. Johnson, D.R.E.

CASCO/SLOVAN, KEWAUNEE CO., HOLY TRINITY, [CEM] Rev. Milton M. Suess; Deacon Robert J. Miller. Merger of Holy Trinity, Casco & Mission of St. Adalbert, Slovan. (Has records for Holy Trinity, Casco & St. Adalbert, Slovan) Old church was torn down; a new church was built with same address.
Res.: 510 Church Ave., 54205-9712. Tel: 920-837-7531; Fax: 920-837-2361. Email: holytrinitycasco@hotmail.com.
School—510 Church Ave., 54205-9712. Email: htsprincipal@centurytel.net. Ms. Kaye Jacobs, Prin.
Catechesis/Religious Program—

CECIL, SHAWANO CO., ST. MARTIN, [CEM] Deacon Michael G. Grzeca, Parish Dir.; Rev. Leonard M. Evers, Priest Moderator; Very Rev. John F. Doerfler, Sacramental Min.; Deacon Kenneth Banker.
Church: 418 S. Warrington St., 54111-9280. Tel: 715-745-6681; Fax: 715-745-4289. Email: stmartin_cecil@frontiernet.net.
Catechesis/Religious Program—Ms. Lynn Schaal, D.R.E.

CHAMPION, BROWN CO., ST. JOSEPH, [CEM] Rev. William O'Brien.
Mailing Address: 5996 County Rd. K, New Franken, 54229-9456. Tel: 920-866-9961. Email: sttomhum@baycomwi.com. Served from St. Thomas the Apostle, Humboldt.
Catechesis/Religious Program—Email: stjosephchampion@centurytel.net. Ms. Lisa Laurent, D.R.E.; Mrs. Patricia Ratajczak, D.R.E.; Ms. Mary E. Murphy, Contact Person.

CHARLESBURG, CALUMET CO., ST. CHARLES BORROMEO, Merged with St. Augustine, Chilton; St. Mary, Chilton; St. Martin, Charlestown; Holy Trinity, Jericho and St. Elizabeth, Kloten to form Good Shepherd, Chilton.

CHARLESTOWN, CALUMET CO., ST. MARTIN, Merged with St. Augustine, Chilton; St. Mary, Chilton; St. Charles Borromeo, Charlesburg; Holy Trinity, Jericho and St. Elizabeth, Kloten to form Good Shepherd, Chilton.

CHASE, OCONTO CO., ST. JOSEPH, [CEM] Merged with St. Louis, Abrams and St. John Cantius, Sobieski to form St. Maximilian Kolbe, Sobieski.

CHILTON, CALUMET CO.
1—ST. AUGUSTINE, Merged with St. Mary, Chilton; St. Charles Borromeo, Charlesburg; St. Martin, Charlestown; Holy Trinity, Jericho and St. Elizabeth, Kloten to form Good Shepherd, Chilton.
2—GOOD SHEPHERD, [CEM] Rev. Robert Kollath; Deacon Dennis G. Bennin. Merger of St. Augustine, Chilton; St. Mary, Chilton; St. Charles Borromeo, Charlesburg; St. Martin, Charlestown; Holy Trinity, Jericho & St. Elizabeth, Kloten
Res.: 62 E. Main St., 53014-1428. Tel: 920-849-9363; Fax: 920-849-7270. Email: deacondennis@catholic.org.
School—Chilton Area Catholic School, 60 E. Washington St., 53014-1297. Tel: 920-849-4141; Fax: 920-849-9092. Email: lrollmann@mail2school.com. Mrs. Elisabeth Rollmann, Prin.
Catechesis/Religious Program—Ms. Anne P. Stemper, D.R.E.
3—ST. MARY, Merged with St. Augustine, Chilton; St. Charles Borromeo, Charlesburg; St. Martin, Charlestown; Holy Trinity, Jericho and St. Elizabeth, Kloten to form Good Shepherd, Chilton.

CLARKS MILLS, MANITOWOC CO., IMMACULATE CONCEPTION, [CEM], Also serves St. Michael, Whitelaw. Rev. David M. Zimmerman.
Res.: 15 S. County Rd. J, Cato, 54230-8329. Tel: 920-775-4365; Fax: 920-775-4365. Email: stmarycm@tds.net.
School: See St. Mary/St. Michael School, Cato under Consolidated Schools located in the Institution section.
Catechesis/Religious Program—Tel: 920-775-4876. Mrs. Teresa Pederson, D.R.E.

CLEVELAND, MANITOWOC CO., ST. WENDEL, Merged with St. Isidore, Osman; St. Joseph, Alverno; and St. Casimir, Northeim to form St. Thomas the Apostle, Northeim.

CLINTONVILLE, WAUPACA CO., ST. ROSE, [CEM], Also serves St. Mary, Bear Creek. Mr. Lincoln Wood, Parish Dir.; Revs. John W. Girotti, Priest Mod.; John T. Mullarkey, Sacramental Min. (Retired); Deacons Joseph M. Lehman; Thomas V. Jozwiak; Paul J. Brulla.
Res. & Mailing Address: 140 Auto St., 54929-1712. Tel: 715-823-3416; Fax: 715-823-6010. Email: ssrmsborlen@gmail.com.
School—Tel: 715-823-4360. Email: ssrmjwood@gmail.com. Jennifer Wood, Prin.
Catechesis/Religious Program—Tel: 715-823-5266. Email: ssrmre@gmail.com. Jennifer Wood, D.R.E.; Julie Minter, D.R.E.

COLEMAN, MARINETTE CO.
1—ST. ANNE PARISH CORP., Merger of SS. Francis-Wenceslaus, Coleman & Holy Cross, Lena. (Has records for these two parishes in addition to St. Leo, Pound; St. John, Coleman; St. Francis of Assisi Coleman: St. Wenceslaus Klondike.) Very Rev. Celestine Byekwaso, Admin.
228 E. Main St., 54112-9407. Tel: 920-897-3226; Fax: 920-897-3226. Email: stanne1@centurytel.net.
Catechesis/Religious Program—P.O. Box 30, Lena, 54139-0030. Tel: 920-829-5222; Fax: 920-829-6027. Email: churchlady525@yahoo.com. Mrs. Theresa M. Alberts, D.R.E.; Mrs. Kathryn Lieburn, D.R.E.
2—ST. FRANCIS OF ASSISI, Merged with St. Wenceslaus, Klondike to form SS. Francis-Wenceslaus, Coleman.

COMBINED LOCKS, OUTAGAMIE CO., ST. PAUL, [CEM] Rev. Andrew T. Kysely, Admin.; Deacon George J. Schraufnagel.
Res.: 410 Wallace St., 54113-1128. Tel: 920-788-4553; Fax: 920-788-6822. Email: stpaulcl@newbc.rr.com.
Catechesis/Religious Program—Tel: 920-788-5711. Email: stpaulff@newbc.rr.com.

COOPERSTOWN, MANITOWOC CO., ST. JAMES, [CEM], Served from All Saints, Denmark. Revs. Ronald A. Colombo; David J. Koch, Sacramental Min.; Deacon Clarence Naidl.
Res.: 18228 County Rd. R, Denmark, 54208-9554. Tel: 920-863-2585; Fax: 920-863-5445. Email: stjamescoop@tm.net.
Catechesis/Religious Program—Email: recoordinator@tm.net. Mrs. Ann M. Habeck, D.R.E.; Mrs. Katherine A. Styer, D.R.E.

CRANDON, FOREST CO., ST. JOSEPH, (Has records for St. Mary, Argonne & St. Michael Station, Hiles.) Rev. Ralph J. Gillis.
Res.: 208 N. Park Ave., 54520-1351. Tel: 715-478-3396.
Catechesis/Religious Program—

CRIVITZ, MARINETTE CO., ST. MARY, [CEM], Also serves Station at Caldron Falls. Rev. Walter P. Stumpf.
Mailing Address: P.O. Box 159, 54114-0159. Tel: 715-854-2501. Email: stmary's@centurytel.net. Web: www.stmarycrivitz.net.
Catechesis/Religious Program—

DARBOY, OUTAGAMIE CO. (APPLETON P.O.), HOLY ANGELS, [CEM] Merged with Holy Name of Jesus, Kimberly to form Holy Spirit, Kimberly/Darboy.

DE PERE, BROWN CO.
1—ST. BONIFACE, Merged with St. Joseph, De Pere to form Our Lady of Lourdes, De Pere.
2—ST. FRANCIS XAVIER, [JC], Served from St. Mary, De Pere. Very Rev. Richard Getchel; Rev. Patrick C. Beno Jr., Parochial Vicar; Deacon Kevin DeCleene.
Res.: 220 S. Michigan St., 54115-2794. Tel: 920-336-1813; Fax: 920-336-1814. Email: office@stfrancisdepere.org.
School—Notre Dame School, (Part of GRACE System, Inc.), 221 S Wisconsin St., 54115-2797. Tel: 920-337-1115; Fax: 920-337-1117. Email: jkaftan@gracesystem.org. Mr. Jeffrey J. Kaftan, Prin.
Catechesis/Religious Program—P.O. Box 70, 54115-0070. Tel: 920-337-2330. Mr. Michael Lotto, D.R.E.; Ms. Pamela A. McKeefry, D.R.E.
3—ST. JOSEPH, Merged with St. Boniface, De Pere to form Our Lady of Lourdes, De Pere.
4—ST. MARY, [JC], Also serves St. Francis Xavier, De Pere. Very Rev. Richard Getchel; Rev. Patrick C. Beno Jr., Parochial Vicar; Deacon Kevin DeCleene.
Mailing Address: P.O. Box 70, 54115-0070. Tel: 920-337-2330; Fax: 920-337-2332. Email: office@stmarydepere.org.
School—Notre Dame School, 221 S. Wisconsin St., 54115-2797. Tel: 920-337-1115; Fax: 920-337-1117. Email: jkaftan@gracesystem.org. Mr. Jeffrey J. Kaftan, Prin.
Catechesis/Religious Program—Mr. Michael Lotto, D.R.E.; Ms. Pamela A. McKeefry, D.R.E.
5—ST. NORBERT COLLEGE Revs. James T. Baraniak, O.Praem.; Salvatore H. Cuccia, O.Praem., Parochial Vicar.
Mailing Address: 100 Grant St. Dept. 59, 54115-2002. Tel: 920-403-3010; Fax: 920-403-4432. Email: oldstjoseph@snc.edu.
Catechesis/Religious Program—Tel: 920-403-3474. Mrs. Margaret Vande Hey, D.R.E.
6—OUR LADY OF LOURDES (1996) [CEM], (Has records for St. Joseph, De Pere & St. Boniface, De Pere.) Rev. Timothy D. Shillcox, O.Praem.; Deacon Michael D. Vander Bloomen.
Res.: 1307 Lourdes Ave., 54115-1018. Tel: 920-336-4033; Fax: 920-336-3910. Email: parish@lourdesdepere.org.
School—(Part of GRACE Systems, Inc.), 1305 Lourdes Ave., 54115-1018. Tel: 920-336-3091; Fax: 920-337-6806. Email: tsjoberg@gracesystem.org. Mrs. Tammy S. Sjoberg, Prin.
Catechesis/Religious Program—Tel: 920-337-0443. Mrs. Karen Nienhaus, D.R.E.

DENMARK, BROWN CO., ALL SAINTS, [CEM], Also serves St. James, Cooperstown & Holy Trinity Mission, New Denmark. Revs. Ronald A. Colombo; David J. Koch, Sacramental Min.; Deacon Clarence Naidl.
P.O. Box 787, 54208-0787. Email: asden_parish@allsaintsschool.net.
School—Tel: 920-863-2449. Email: vstrecke@allsaintsschool.net. Virginia Streckenbach, Prin.

Catechesis/Religious Program—Mrs. Lori A. Wagner, D.R.E. Associated with Holy Trinity, New Denmark.

DYCKESVILLE, KEWAUNEE CO., ST. LOUIS, [CEM 2] Sr. Marlene M. Dimmerling, O.P., Parish Dir.; Rev. John H. Van Deuren, Priest Mod. & Sacramental Min. (Retired).
Res.: N8726 County Line Rd., Luxemburg, 54217-8629. Tel: 920-866-2410; Fax: 920-866-3591. Email: mardim@greenbaynet.com.
Catechesis/Religious Program—Tel: 920-866-2842; Fax: 920-866-2611. Mrs. Kathleen Cornette, D.R.E.

EATON, BROWN CO., SS. CYRIL AND METHODIUS, Merged with Our Lady Queen of Peace, Humboldt to form St. Thomas the Apostle, Humboldt

EGG HARBOR, DOOR CO.
1—ST. JOHN THE BAPTIST, Merged with St. Mary of the Lake, Baileys Harbor; St. Paul, Fish Creek; St. Michael, Jacksonport and St. Rosalia to form Stella Maris, Egg Harbor.
2—STELLA MARIS, Merger of St. John the Baptist, Egg Harbor; St. Mary of the Lake, Baileys Harbor; St. Paul, Fish Creek; St. Michael, Jacksonport; St. Rosalia, Sister Bay & the Station at Washington Island. (Has records for all 5 parishes) Rev. David C. Ruby; Deacon David J. Kowalski.
Mailing Address: P.O. Box 49, 54209-0049. Tel: 920-868-3241; Fax: 920-868-1481. Email: churchoffice@dcwis.com.
Catechesis/Religious Program—Tel: 920-854-5264. Email: faithchurch@dcwis.com. Mary Ellen Waldvogel, D.R.E.

ELAND, SHAWANO CO., ST. WILLIAM, Merged with Holy Family, Wittenberg to form Holy Family-St. William, Wittenberg.

ELCHO, LANGLADE CO., HOLY FAMILY, [CEM], Also serves St. Mary Parish, Pickerel. Revs. David R. Schmidt, Priest Mod.; Jeremiah F. Worman, Sacramental Min. (Retired); Mrs. Cindy Eultgen, Parish Dir.
Mailing Address: P.O. Box 128, 54428-0128. Tel: 715-275-3750. Email: holyfamilyelcho@frontiernet.net.
Catechesis/Religious Program—Tel: 715-275-4343. Mr. Joel DeNamur, Contact Person; Mrs. Wendy DeNamur, Contact Person.

FISH CREEK, DOOR CO., ST. PAUL, Merged with St. John the Baptist, Egg Harbor; St. Mary of the Lake, Baileys Harbor; St. Michael, Jacksonport and St. Rosalia, Sister Bay to form Stella Maris, Egg Harbor.

FLINTVILLE, BROWN CO., SS. EDWARD AND ISIDORE, [CEM] Rev. David D. Kasperek.
Mailing Address: 3667 Flintville Rd., 54313-8330. Tel: 920-865-7844; Fax: 920-865-4375. Email: clom@stedwardisidore.org.
Catechesis/Religious Program—Tel: 920-865-7677. Email: jingold@stedwardisidore.org. June L. Ingold, D.R.E.

FLORENCE, FLORENCE CO., IMMACULATE CONCEPTION, [CEM] Mrs. Christine Gall, Parish Dir.; Rev. Matthew W. Settle, Priest Mod. & Sacramental Min.
Res.: P.O. Box 166, 54121-0166. Tel: 715-528-3310; Fax: 715-528-3052. Email: stmary@borderlandnet.net.
Catechesis/Religious Program—Tel: 715-582-4992. Dawn M. Schuch, D.R.E.

FRANCIS CREEK, MANITOWOC CO., ST. ANNE, [CEM], Served from Holy Cross, Mishicot. Rev. John J. Becker.
Res.: P.O. Box 218, 54214-0218. Tel: 920-682-6640. Email: holycrossparish@holycrossmishicot.com.
Catechesis/Religious Program—Tel: 920-682-1454. Ms. Amy Trost, D.R.E.

FREEDOM, OUTAGAMIE CO., ST. NICHOLAS, [CEM] Rev. David J. Hoffman; Deacon Gregory J. Humpal.
Res.: W2037 County Rd. S., 54130-7565. Tel: 920-788-1492; Fax: 920-788-1492. Email: parish@stnicholasfreedom.org.
School—W2035 County Rd. S., 54130-7565. Tel: 920-788-9371. Rosemary F. Perrino, Prin.
Catechesis/Religious Program—Tel: 920-788-1451. Ms. Michelle Kettner, D.R.E.

GILLETT, OCONTO CO., ST. JOHN, [CEM], Also serves St. Michael, Suring & Chute Pond Station. Sr. Marla J. Clercx, A.N.G., Parish Dir.; Revs. John J. Becker, Priest Mod.; David S. Barrett, Sacramental Min. (Retired).
Res.: 127 Garden St., 54124-9413. Tel: 920-855-2542; Fax: 920-855-1449. Email: mjclercx@hotmail.com.
Catechesis/Religious Program—Dixie Hall, D.R.E.
Station—Chute Lake, Chute Lake Station P.O. Box 248, Suring, 54174-248.

GLENMORE, BROWN CO., IMMACULATE CONCEPTION, Merged with St. Mary, Stark to form St. Mary, Glenmore/Stark.

GLENMORE/STARK, BROWN CO., ST. MARY, [CEM 2], Merger of Immaculate Conception, Glenmore & St. Mary, Stark. (Has records for St. Mary, Stark); Served from All Saints, Denmark. Rev. Ronald A. Colombo; Deacon Clarence Naidl.
Mailing Address: 5840 Big Apple Rd., De Pere, 54115-9766. Tel: 920-864-7641. Email: kvschmidt6@aol.com.
Catechesis/Religious Program—Tel: 920-863-8307. Denis Lotto, D.R.E.

GOODMAN, MARINETTE CO., ST. JOAN OF ARC, Served from St. Stanislaus Kostka, Armstrong Creek. Deacon Gerald H. Cross, Parish Dir.; Revs. Matthew W. Settle, Priest Mod.; John J. Hephner, Sacramental Min. (Retired); Rev. Msgr. Paul P. Koszarek, Sacramental Min. (Retired).
Church: P.O. Box 218, 54125-0218. Tel: 715-336-2334. Email: stjoanofarcgoodman@gmail.com.
Catechesis/Religious Program—P.O. Box 39, Armstrong Creek, 54103-0039. Vinnie Duda, D.R.E. Associated with St. Stanislaus Kosta, Armstrong Creek.

GREENLEAF, BROWN CO., ST. CLARE CORP., (Merger of St. Mary, Greenleaf; St. Patrick, Askeaton & St. Paul, Wrightstown) Rev. Dennis L. Bergsbaken; Deacon Kenneth J. Kabat.
2218 Day St., 54126-9200. Tel: 920-864-2550; Fax: 920-864-2979. Email: office@stclareagw.org.
School—St. Clare School, 425 Main St., Wrightstown, 54180-1057. Tel: 920-532-4833; Fax: 920-532-0458. Email: stclareschool@stclareagw.org. Laura Barnett, Prin.
Catechesis/Religious Program—Tel: 920-864-2586. Email: stclarere@gmail.org. Mrs. Gloria Kennedy, D.R.E.; Ms. Sarah Heimerl, D.R.E.

GREENVILLE, OUTAGAMIE CO., ST. MARY, [CEM], Also serves St. Edward, Mackville. Rev. Mark P. Vander Steeg; Deacon David L. DeYoung.
Res.: N2385 Municipal Dr., 54942-9713. Tel: 920-757-6555; Fax: 920-757-6560. Email: parish@stmarygreenville.org.
School—(Grades PreK-8), N2387 Municipal Dr., 54942-9713. Debra Fuller, Prin.
Catechesis/Religious Program—Luke Gietman, Contact Person.

GRESHAM, SHAWANO CO., ST. FRANCIS SOLANUS, [CEM], Served from St. Michael, Keshena. Rev. Robert F. Rank.
Mailing Address: P.O. Box 177, 54128-0177. Tel: 715-787-3250. Email: sfrancis@frontiernet.net.
Catechesis/Religious Program—Tel: 715-787-3208. Email: garv@frontiernet.net. Sandra Gawryleski, Contact Person.

HILBERT, CALUMET CO., ST. MARY, [CEM], Served from St. John-Sacred Heart, Sherwood. Rev. Michael E. Betley; Deacon Steven M. Vande Hey.
Res.: P.O. Box 386, 54129-0386. Tel: 920-853-3252; Fax: 920-853-3560. Email: stmary-hilbert@new.rr.com.
School—P.O. Box 249, 54129-0249. Tel: 920-853-3216. Email: chasro@stmaryhilbert.com. Chandra L. Sromek, Prin.
Catechesis/Religious Program—N369 Military Rd., Sherwood, 54169-9661. Tel: 920-989-2400. Email: re@tds.net. Ms. Diane Wickersheim, D.R.E.

HOFA PARK, SHAWANO CO., ST. STANISLAUS, [CEM], Served from Assumption BVM, Pulaski. Rev. Finian Andrew Zaucha, O.F.M.
Res.: W1888 Hofa Park Dr., Seymour, 54165-9510. Tel: 920-822-3279; Fax: 920-822-8030. Email: parishoffice@abvm.org.
Catechesis/Religious Program—109 E. Pulaski St., Pulaski, 54162-9287. Tel: 920-822-5650; Fax: 920-822-8003. Deanne Wilinski, Contact Person.

HOLLANDTOWN, BROWN CO., ST. FRANCIS, [CEM] Merged with St. Mary of the Annunciation, Kaukauna and St. Aloysius, Kaukauna to form St. Katharine Drexel, Kaukauna.

HORTONVILLE, OUTAGAMIE CO., SS. PETER AND PAUL, [CEM] Greg Layton, Parish Dir.; Rev. David J. Lewis, Priest Mod.; Rev. Msgr. James B. Feely, Sacramental Min. (Retired); Deacon Kenneth D. Bilgrien.
Res.: P.O. Box 238, 54944-0238. Tel: 920-779-6133; Fax: 920-779-6164. Email: sspeterandpaul@sbcglobal.net.
See St. Mary School under St. Mary Parish, Greenville.
Catechesis/Religious Program—105 N. Olk St., 54944-9434. Tel: 920-779-0551. Monica Janssen, Contact Person.

HOWARD, BROWN CO., ST. JOHN THE BAPTIST, [CEM] Rev. John P. Bergstadt; Deacons Manuel Torres; Nicholas J. Williams.
Res.: 2597 Glendale Ave., 54313-6899. Tel: 920-434-2145; Fax: 920-434-5015. Email: jbergstadt@sjbh.org.
School—(Part of the GRACE System, Inc.), 2561 Glendale Ave., 54313-6898. Tel: 920-434-3822; Fax: 920-434-5016. Vicki Marotz, Prin.
Catechesis/Religious Program—880 Cardinal Ln., 54313-6816. Tel: 920-434-2417. Sr. Gretchen Krueger, O.P., D.R.E.; Ms. Amy E. Koehler, D.R.E.; Mrs. Margaret Mary Schiffer, D.R.E.

HUMBOLDT, BROWN CO.
1—OUR LADY QUEEN OF PEACE, Merged with SS. Cyril & Methodius, Eaton to form St. Thomas the Apostle, Humbolt.
2—ST. THOMAS THE APOSTLE, [JC 4], Also serves St. Kilian, New Franken & St. Joseph, Champion. Rev. William O'Brien.
Res.: 5930 Humboldt Rd., Luxemburg, 54217-9325. Tel: 920-863-6113; Fax: 920-845-5180. Email: sttomhum@baycomwi.com.
Catechesis/Religious Program—3041 S. County Rd. T, 54311-9429. Tel: 920-863-5297. Email: stthomastheapostlecre@yahoo.com. Mrs. Nancy Metzler, D.R.E.

INSTITUTE, DOOR CO., SS. PETER AND PAUL, [CEM], Served from St. Joseph, Sturgeon Bay. Rev. Robert Konkol, O.F.M., Admin.; Deacon Kenneth D. Kopydlowski.
Res.: 4767 Dunn Rd., Sturgeon Bay, 54235-8822. Tel: 920-743-4842; Fax: 920-743-3885. Email: ssppchurch@charter.net.
See St. John Bosco Catholic School, Inc., Sturgeon Bay under Elementary Schools, Diocesan in the Institution Section.
Catechesis/Religious Program—526 Louisiana St., Sturgeon Bay, 54235-1796. Tel: 920-743-2062; Fax: 920-743-6786. Ms. Penny Biwer, D.R.E.

ISAAR, OUTAGAMIE CO., ST. SEBASTIAN, [CEM], Served from St. John, Seymour. Very Rev. Robert J. Kabat, Admin.; Deacon Richard J. Matuszak.
Res.: N9269 Isaar Rd., Seymour, 54165-9428. Tel: 920-833-2558. Email: stseb2010@centurylink.net.
Catechesis/Religious Program—

JACKSONPORT, DOOR CO., ST. MICHAEL, Merged with St. John the Baptist, Egg Harbor; St. Mary of the Lake, Baileys Harbor; St. Paul, Fish Creek and St. Rosalia, Sister Bay to form Stella Maris, Egg Harbor.

JERICHO, CALUMET CO., HOLY TRINITY, Merged with St. Augustine, Chilton; St. Mary, Chilton; St. Charles Borromeo, Charlesburg; St. Martin, Charlestown and St. Elizabeth, Kloten to form Good Shepherd, Chilton.

KAUKAUNA, OUTAGAMIE CO.
1—ST. ALOYSIUS, Merged with St. Mary of the Annunciation, Kaukauna and St. Francis, Hollandtown to form St. Katharine Drexel, Kaukauna.
2—HOLY CROSS, [CEM] Rev. Thomas Pomeroy; Deacon Bruce H. Corey.
Res.: 309 Desnoyer St., 54130-2187. Tel: 920-766-3773; Fax: 920-766-3774. Email: tschmahl@holycrosskaukauna.org.
School—Kaukauna Catholic Schools System, 220 Doty St., 54130-2188. Tel: 920-766-0186; Fax: 920-759-2428. Lawrence Konetzke, Prin.
Catechesis/Religious Program—212 Doty St., 54130-2108. Tel: 920-766-3510. Ms. Gloria Ackerman, D.R.E.; Ms. Belinda Micke, D.R.E.; Mrs. Jacqueline Wallace, D.R.E.
3—ST. KATHARINE DREXEL Rev. Jerome P. Pastors; Deacons Randall A. Haak; Gerald G. Kuborn.
119 W. 7th St., 54130-2356. Tel: 920-766-1445; Fax: 920-766-1476. Email: stkatharineparish@new.rr.com.
Merger of St. Aloysius, Kaukauna, St. Mary of the Annunciation, Kaukauna & St. Francis, Hollandtown. Has records for all 3 parishes.
School—Kaukauna Catholic Schools System, 2401 Main Ave., 54130-3599. Tel: 920-766-5199; Fax: 920-766-5229. Lawrence Konetzke, Prin.
Catechesis/Religious Program—Tel: 920-766-5977. Email: giftstkatharine@yahoo.com. Mrs. Jean Olson, D.R.E.
4—ST. MARY OF THE ANNUNCIATION, [JC] Merged with St. Aloysius, Kaukauna, and St. Francis, Hollandtown to form St. Katharine Drexel, Kaukauna.

KELLNERSVILLE, MANITOWOC CO., ST. JOSEPH, [CEM 2], Served from All Saints, Denmark. Revs. Ronald A. Colombo, Admin.; David J. Koch, Sacramental Min.; Deacon Clarence Naidl.
Res.: P.O. Box 27, 54215-0027. Tel: 920-732-3770; Fax: 920-732-4612. Email: stjoseph@tm.net.
Catechesis/Religious Program—Tel: 920-905-5282. Cynthia Thelen, Contact Person.

KESHENA, MENOMINEE CO., ST. MICHAEL, (Native American), [CEM], Also serves St. Francis Solanus, Gresham & St. Anthony, Neopit. Rev. Robert F. Rank.
Mailing Address: P.O. Box 610, 54135-0610. Tel: 715-799-3811; Fax: 715-799-5092. Email: saintmichaels@frontiernet.net.
Catechesis/Religious Program—Tel: 715-799-3234. Sandra Gawryleski, D.R.E.

KEWAUNEE, KEWAUNEE CO., HOLY ROSARY, [CEM], Served from St. Mary, Algoma. Rev. William D. Swichtenberg.
Res.: 521 Juneau St., 54216-1397. Tel: 920-388-2285; Fax: 920-388-3822. Email: mrsvan2001@yahoo.com.
School—519 Kilbourn St., 54216-1343. Tel: 920-388-2431. Richard C. Aebly, Prin.

Catechesis/Religious Program—Kathleen E. Zeman, D.R.E.

KIEL, MANITOWOC CO., SS. PETER AND PAUL, [CEM], Also serves Holy Rosary, New Holstein & St. Ann, St. Anna. Joseph Zenk, Parish Dir.; Revs. Robert Kollath, Priest Mod.; Loren Nys, S.D.S., Sacramental Min.; Deacon Bernard (Pat) P. Knier.
Res.: 413 Fremont St., 53042-1398. Tel: 920-894-3553; Fax: 920-894-4462. Email: secretary@sspeternpaul.org.
School—Divine Savior Catholic SchoolKiel Campus, 423 Fremont St., 53042-1316. Tel: 920-894-3533. *New Holstein Campus*, 1814 Madiston St., New Holstein, 53061-1347. Tel: 920-898-4210; Fax: 920-898-4220. Gerard Stepanek, Prin.
Catechesis/Religious Program—409 Fremont St., 53042-1316. Email: faithformationkiel@gmail.com. Mary Jo Meyer, D.R.E.; Danelle Ehlenbeck, Contact Person.

KIMBERLY, OUTAGAMIE CO.

1—HOLY NAME OF JESUS, [CEM] Merged with Holy Angels, Darboy to form Holy Spirit, Kimberly/Darboy.

2—HOLY SPIRIT, [CEM], Merger of Holy Name of Jesus, Kimberly & Holy Angels, Darboy. Rev. David B. Beaudry; Deacon Cyril J. Klister.
Res.: 620 E. Kimberly Ave., 54136-1513. Tel: 920-788-7640; Fax: 920-788-7658. Email: hspkim@holyspirit-parish.org.
School—Holy Spirit School, W2796 County Rd. KK, Appleton, 54915-9407. Tel: 920-733-2651; Fax: 920-733-5440. Carrie Gossens, Prin.
Catechesis/Religious Program—Tel: 920-788-7655. Sr. Elise Cholewinski, O.S.F., D.R.E.

KING, WAUPACA CO., ST. GEORGE, Closed. For inquiries for parish records, please see St. Mary Magdalene, Waupaca.

KLONDIKE, OCONTO CO., ST. WENCESLAUS, Merged with St. Francis of Assisi, Coleman, to form SS. Francis-Wenceslaus, Coleman.

KLOTEN, CALUMET CO., ST. ELIZABETH, Merged with St. Augustine, Chilton; St. Mary, Chilton; St. Charles Borromeo, Charlesburg; St. Martin, Charlestown and Holy Trinity, Jericho to form Good Shepherd, Chilton.

KOSSUTH, MANITOWOC CO., ST. AUGUSTINE, [CEM], Served from Holy Cross, Mishicot. Rev. John J. Becker.
Mailing Address: P.O. Box 218, Francis Creek, 54214-0218. Tel: 920-682-6640. Email: holycrossparish@hoycrossmishicot.com.
Catechesis/Religious Program—Tel: 920-982-1545. Ms. Amy Trost, D.R.E. Associated with St. Anne, Francis Creek.

KRAKOW, SHAWANO CO., ST. CASIMIR, [CEM], Served from Assumption of BVM, Pulaski. Rev. Finian Andrew Zaucha, O.F.M.
Mailing Address: P.O. Box 66, 54137-0066. Tel: 920-899-3621. Email: stcasimir@netnet.net.
Catechesis/Religious Program—Mr. William Mihalski, D.R.E.

KROK, KEWAUNEE CO., ST. JOHN, Merged with St. Joseph, Montpelier to form St. Joseph-St. John, Montpelier.

LAKEWOOD, OCONTO CO., ST. MARY OF THE LAKE, [CEM], Also serves St. Ambrose, Wabeno & stations at Crooked Lake and Silver Cliff. Rev. Jason J. Blahnik, Admin.; Deacon William V. Doran.
Res.: P.O. Box 219, 54138-0219. Tel: 715-276-7364; Fax: 715-276-1414. Email: stmary01@centurytel.net.
Catechesis/Religious Program—Email: stmary01@centurytel.net. Kendra Yingling, D.R.E.
Station—Crooked Lake, Crooked Lake Station
Station—Silver Cliff, Silver Cliff Station

LANGLADE, LANGLADE CO., ST. STANISLAUS KOSTKA, Merged with St. James, White Lake to form SS. James-Stanislaus, White Lake.

LAONA, FOREST CO., ST. LEONARD, [JC], Also serves St. Norbert, Long Lake & St. Hubert Mission, Newald. Rev. Msgr. Paul P. Koszarek, Sacramental Min. & Priest Mod (Retired); Deacon Gerald H. Cross, Parish Dir.
Res.: 5330 Beech St., 54541-9340. Tel: 715-674-3241; Fax: 715-674-3241. Email: stleonardlaona@gmail.com.
Catechesis/Religious Program—Tel: 715-674-3862. Ms. Cynthia Beairl, D.R.E.

LEBANON, DODGE CO., ST. PATRICK, [CEM] Rev. Msgr. Dennis M. Lally, Admin.
Res.: N5705 County Rd. T, New London, 54961-8464. Tel: 920-982-5475. Email: stpatrickslebanon@charter.net.
Catechesis/Religious Program—Ms. Barbara Tate, D.R.E.

LENA, OCONTO CO., ST. CHARLES BORROMEO, Merged with Sacred Heart, Spruce to form Holy Cross, Lena.

LEOPOLIS, SHAWANO CO., ST. MARY, [CEM], Served from St. Anthony, Tigerton. Rev. Patrick Lloyd, S.C.J.; Deacons Patrick G. Berg; Howard R. Bricco; Kenneth F. Sambs; Clay Wildenberg.
Mailing Address: P.O. Box 106, Tigerton, 54486-0106. Tel: 715-535-2571; Fax: 715-535-2953. Email: sacctig@frontiernet.net.
Church: W11842 3rd St., 54948.
Catechesis/Religious Program—Mrs. Sally Korbisch, D.R.E.

LINCOLN, KEWAUNEE CO., ST. PETER, Merged Merged with St. Hubert, Rosiere to become St. Peter and St. Hubert, Rosiere/Lincoln.

LITTLE CHUTE, OUTAGAMIE CO., ST. JOHN NEPOMUCENE, [CEM] Revs. James A. Hablewitz; Lawrence J. Canavera, Parochial Vicar; Deacon David G. Van Eperen.
Res.: 323 Pine St., 54140-1854. Tel: 920-788-9061; Fax: 920-687-0851. Email: sjnparish@stjn.org.
School—328 Grand Ave., 54140-1704. Tel: 920-788-9082; Fax: 920-788-7046. Ms. Jean VanderHeiden, Prin.
Catechesis/Religious Program—325 Pine St., 54140-1854. Tel: 920-788-9033. Email: sjnfaithdev@stjn.org. Ms. Nancy Schmoll, D.R.E.; Mrs. Charlene A. Kilsdonk, D.R.E.

LITTLE SUAMICO, OCONTO CO., ST. PIUS, Served from St. Maximilian Kolbe, Sobieski. Rev. Gerald A. Prusakowski, O.F.M.
Mailing Address: P.O. Box 66, Suamico, 54173-0066. Tel: 920-434-2024; Fax: 920-662-2301. Email: sbsp@wi.twcbc.com.
Catechesis/Religious Program—Tel: 920-434-1219. Ms. Tammi LaLuzerne, D.R.E.

LONG LAKE, FLORENCE CO., ST. NORBERT, Served from St. Leonard, Laona (Laona also serves St. Hubert Mission, Newald). Rev. Msgr. Paul P. Koszarek, Priest Mod. & Sacramental Min. (Retired); Deacon Gerald H. Cross, Parish Dir.
Res.: 5330 Beech St., Laona, 54541-9340. Tel: 715-674-3241; Fax: 715-674-3401.
Catechesis/Religious Program—Tel: 715-674-3862. Ms. Cynthia Beairl, D.R.E.; Sr. Marla J. Clercx, A.N.G., D.R.E. Associated with St. Leonard, Laona.

LUXEMBURG, KEWAUNEE CO., IMMACULATE CONCEPTION, [CEM], Also serves Holy Trinity, Casco/Slovan. Rev. Milton M. Suess; Deacon Robert J. Miller.
Res.: 1412 Main St., 54217-1308. Tel: 920-845-2056. Email: stmaryoffice@itol.com.
School—Immaculate Conception, 1406 Main St., 54217-1308. Tel: 920-845-2224; Fax: 920-845-5581. Mr. William Matchefts, Prin.
Catechesis/Religious Program—Email: stmaryoffice@itol.com. Mr. Lee Treml, D.R.E.

MACKVILLE, OUTAGAMIE CO., ST. EDWARD, [CEM], Served from St. Mary, Greenville. Rev. Mark P. Vander Steeg, Admin.; Deacons Jeffrey J. Hofacker; Raymond G. Ambrosius Jr.
Res.: N2926 State Rd. 47, Appleton, 54913-9564. Tel: 920-733-9266; Fax: 920-733-7964. Email: stedwardparish@new.rr.com.
School—N2944 State Rd. 47, Appleton, 54913-9564. Tel: 920-733-6276; Fax: 920-733-1005. Email: saintedward@catholicweb.com. Ms. Becky Morrin, Prin.
Catechesis/Religious Program—Tel: 920-733-6070. Email: stedwardre@new.rr.com. Ms. Patricia Coonen, D.R.E.

MANAWA, WAUPACA CO., SACRED HEART, [JC], Served from St. Mary Magdalene, Waupaca. Rev. Brian S. Belongia.
Res.: P.O. Box 10, 54949-0010. Tel: 920-596-3323; Fax: 920-596-3323.
Catechesis/Religious Program—Email: shmanawa@wolfnet.net. Ms. JoAnn Schuelke, Contact Person.

MANITOWOC, MANITOWOC CO.

1—ST. ANDREW, Merged with St. Boniface, Manitowoc; Holy Innocents, Manitowoc; St. Mary, Manitowoc; St. Paul, Manitowoc and Sacred Heart, Manitowoc to form St. Francis of Assisi, Manitowoc.

2—ST. BONIFACE, Merged with St. Andrew, Manitowoc; Holy Innocents, Manitowoc; St. Mary, Manitowoc; St. Paul, Manitowoc and Sacred Heart, Manitowoc to form St. Francis of Assisi, Manitowoc.

3—ST. FRANCIS OF ASSISI, [CEM] Very Rev. Daniel J. Felton; Rev. Daniel Viertel, Parochial Vicar; Very Rev. Richard H. Klingeisen, Parochial Vicar; Deacons Robert L. Beehner; Richard D. Bahnaman; Alan L. Boeldt; Paul A. Kieffer; Kenneth R. Nelesen; Michael Dolezal.
Mailing Address: 601 N. 8th St., 54220-3919. Tel: 920-684-3718; Fax: 920-682-1096. Email: dan.felton@sfamanitowoc.com.
Catechesis/Religious Program—Ms. Barbara K. Kratz, D.R.E.

4—HOLY INNOCENTS, Merged with St. Andrew, Manitowoc; St. Boniface, Manitowoc; St. Mary, Manitowoc; St. Paul, Manitowoc and Sacred Heart, Manitowoc to form St. Francis of Assisi, Manitowoc.

5—ST. MARY, Merged with St. Andrew, Manitowoc; St. Boniface, Manitowoc; Holy Innocents, Manitowoc; St. Paul, Manitowoc and Sacred Heart, Manitowoc to form St. Francis of Assisi, Manitowoc.

6—ST. PAUL, Merged with St. Andrew, Manitowoc; St. Boniface, Manitowoc; Holy Innocents, Manitowoc; St. Mary, Manitowoc and Sacred Heart, Manitowoc to form, St. Francis of Assisi, Manitowoc.

7—SACRED HEART, Merged with St. Andrew, Manitowoc; St. Boniface, Manitowoc; Holy Innocents, Manitowoc; St. Mary, Manitowoc and St. Paul, Manitowoc to form St. Francis of Assisi, Manitowoc.

MAPLE GROVE, MANITOWOC CO., ST. PATRICK, Merged with St. Mary, Reedsville to form St. Mary-St. Patrick, Reedsville.

MAPLEWOOD, DOOR CO., ST. MARY, [CEM 2] Deacon Paul T. Zenefski, Parish Dir.; Revs. Carl E. Schmitt, Priest Mod.; Lee J. Kahrs, Sacramental Min. (Retired); Deacon Mark R. Hibbs.
Mailing Address: P.O. Box 308, 54226-0308. Tel: 920-856-6440; Fax: 920-856-6123. Email: holynameofmary@centurytel.net. Also serves St. Peter & St. Hubert Parish, Rosiere/Lincoln.
Catechesis/Religious Program—Ms. Sarah Larson, D.R.E.

MARCHAND, DOOR CO., ST. FRANCIS DE PAUL (Duvall) Closed. For inquiries for parish records contact St. Louis, Dyckesville.

MARINETTE, MARINETTE CO.

1—ST. ANTHONY, Merged with St. Joseph, Sacred Heart, and Our Lady of Lourdes, Marinette to form Holy Family, Marinette.

2—HOLY FAMILY, [CEM 2], Has records for St. Anthony, St. Joseph, Our Lady of Lourdes & Sacred Heart, Marinette. Very Rev. Joseph E. Dorner; Rev. Msgr. John B. Dewane, Temporary Admin. (Retired); Deacons Jerome E. Thetreau; James Dennison.
Office:—2715 Taylor St., 54143-1537. Tel: 715-735-9100; Fax: 715-735-9650. Email: holyfamily@holyfamparish.com.
School—St. Thomas Aquinas Academy, 1045 Water St., 54143-2524. Tel: 715-735-7481; Fax: 715-735-7146. Mr. Peter Mayhew, Prin.
Catechesis/Religious Program—Mrs. Kim M. Duffrin, D.R.E.

3—ST. JOSEPH, Merged with St. Anthony, Our Lady of Lourdes & Sacred Heart, Marinette to become Holy Family Parish.

4—OUR LADY OF LOURDES, Closed. For inquiries for parish records please see Holy Family, Marinette.

5—SACRED HEART CONGREGATION, Merged with St. Anthony, St. Joseph, and Our Lady of Lourdes, Marinette to form Holy Family, Marinette.

MARION, WAUPACA CO., ST. MARY, [CEM], Served from St. Anthony, Tigerton. Rev. Patrick Lloyd, S.C.J.; Deacons Patrick G. Berg; Howard R. Bricco; Clay Wildenberg; Kenneth F. Sambs.
Mailing Address: P.O. Box 106, Tigerton, 54486-0106. Tel: 715-535-2571; Fax: 715-535-2953. Email: sacctig@frontiernet.net.
Catechesis/Religious Program—Mrs. Sally Korbisch, D.R.E. Associated with St. Anthony, Tigerton.

MATTOON, SHAWANO CO., HOLY FAMILY, [CEM] Merged with St. Joseph, Phlox, to form St. Joseph-Holy Family Parish, Phlox. Served from St. Anthony, Neopit.

MENASHA, WINNEBAGO CO.

1—ST. JOHN, [CEM], Served from St. Mary, Menasha. Rev. Paul J. Paider; Deacon Richard B. Dvorak.
Res.: 516 Depere St., 54952-2847. Tel: 920-725-7714; Fax: 920-725-7612. Email: jjulius@tcces.k12.wi.us.
See Twin Cities Catholic Education System (TCCES), Neenah/Mensha under Consolidated Schools, Neenah/Mensha located in the Institution Section for details.
Catechesis/Religious Program—628 5th St., 54952-2308. Tel: 920-722-4830. Mrs. Sally Michalkiewicz, D.R.E.; Mrs. Deborah A. Spielbauer, Contact Person.

2—ST. MARY, [CEM], Also serves St. John and St. Patrick, Menasha. Rev. Paul J. Paider; Deacon Richard B. Dvorak.
Res.: 528 2nd St., 54952-3112. Tel: 920-725-7714; Fax: 920-725-7612. Email: jjulius@tcces.k12.wi.us.
See Twin Cities Catholic Education System (TCCES), Neenah/Mensha under Consolidated Schools, Neenah/Mensha located in the Institution Section for details.
Catechesis/Religious Program—628 5th St., 54952-2308. Tel: 920-722-4830. Mrs. Sally Michalkiewicz, D.R.E.; Mrs. Deborah A. Spielbauer, Contact Person.

3—ST. PATRICK, [JC] Rev. Lawrence E. Abler, O.F.M.Cap., Admin.
Res.: 324 Nicolet Blvd., 54952-3334. Tel: 920-725-8381; Fax: 920-725-5544. Email: stpatmen@gmail.com.
School—Seton Catholic Middle School, 312 Nicolet Blvd., 54952. Tel: 920-727-0279. Monica Bausom,

Prin.
See Twin Cities Catholic Education System (TCCES), Neenah/Mensha under Consolidated Schools, Neenah/Mensha located in the Institution Section for details.
Catechesis/Religious Program—Mrs. Cheryl Stinski, Contact Person.

MISHICOT, MANITOWOC CO., HOLY CROSS, [JC], Also serves St. Anne, Francis Creek & St. Augustine, Kossuth. Rev. John J. Becker.
Res.: 423 S. Main St., 54228-9777. Tel: 920-755-2550. Email: holycrossparish@holycrossmishicot.com.
Catechesis/Religious Program—423 E. Church St., 54228-9688. Tel: 920-755-2487. Email: drecor3hcs@charter.net. Mrs. Marie T. Steeber, D.R.E.

MONTPELIER, KEWAUNEE CO.
1—ST. JOSEPH, Merged with St. John, Krok to form St. Joseph-St. John, Montpelier.
2—ST. JOSEPH-ST. JOHN, Merged with St. Lawrence, Stangelville and St. Hedwig, West Kewaunee to form St. Therese de Lisieux, Stangelville.

NAMUR, DOOR CO., ST. MARY, Merged with St. Francis Xavier, Brussels to form St. Francis-St. Mary, Brussels.

NAVARINO, SHAWANO CO., ST. LAWRENCE, [CEM] Deacon Donald F. Coenen, Pastoral Coord.; Very Rev. Robert J. Kabat, Priest Mod.; Rev. Theodore J. Hendricks, Sacramental Min.
Res.: W5125 State Hwy. 156, Bonduel, 54107-8614. Tel: 715-758-8161; Fax: 715-758-7562. Email: stlawrence@granitewave.com.
Catechesis/Religious Program—Ms. Lisa Tepolt, D.R.E.

NEENAH, WINNEBAGO CO.
1—ST. GABRIEL THE ARCHANGEL, [JC] Very Rev. Larry J. Seidl; Deacon Raymond L. DuBois.
Res.: 900 Geiger St., 54956-2302. Tel: 920-722-4914; Fax: 920-722-2566. Email: stgabriel@tcces.k12.wi.us.
See Twin Cities Catholic Education System (TCCES), Neenah/Mensha under Consolidated Schools, Neenah/Mensha located in the Institution Section for details.
Catechesis/Religious Program—Tel: 920-725-0660. Mr. Stephen C. Pable, D.R.E.; Ms. Jennifer L. Schneider, D.R.E.
2—ST. MARGARET MARY, [JC] Rev. Michael L. Ingold.
Mailing Address: 439 Washington Ave., 54956-3398. Tel: 920-729-4560; Fax: 920-729-4572. Email: sbellile@tcces.k12.wi.us.
Church: 666 Division St., 54956-3398.
See Twin Cities Catholic Education System (TCCES), Neenah/Mensha under Consolidated Schools, Neenah/Mensha located in the Institution Section for details.
Catechesis/Religious Program—Tel: 920-729-4562. Sr. Diane Baumann, A.N.G., D.R.E.; Mrs. Cindy M. Kyles-Werth, D.R.E.

NEOPIT, MENOMINEE CO., ST. ANTHONY, [CEM], Served from St. Michael, Keshena. Rev. Robert F. Rank.
Mailing Address: P.O. Box 241, 54150-0241. Tel: 715-756-2361; Fax: 715-756-2756. Email: chyrl@stanthonyneopit.org.
Catechesis/Religious Program—Tel: 715-756-2218. Email: stare@stanthonyneopit.org. Ms. Charlotte Ann Wagner, D.R.E.

NEVA, LANGLADE CO., ST. WENCESLAUS, [CEM], Served from St. John, Antigo. Revs. David R. Schmidt; William J. Brunner, Parochial Vicar.
Mailing Address: P.O. Box 50, Deerbrook, 54424-0050. Tel: 715-627-2126; Fax: 715-627-2126. Email: stwencelneva@goantigo.com.
Res.: N5340 Church Rd., Deerbrook, 54424-9413. Tel: 715-623-7019.
See All Saints Catholic School, Antigo under SS. Mary & Hyacinth, Antigo for details.
Catechesis/Religious Program—Mrs. Susan Brettingen, D.R.E.; Mrs. Lisa Ourada, D.R.E.

NEW DENMARK, BROWN CO., HOLY TRINITY MISSION, [CEM], Served from All Saints, Denmark. Revs. Ronald A. Colombo; David J. Koch, Sacramental Min.; Deacon Clarence Naidl.
Res.: P.O. Box 787, Denmark, 54208-0787. Tel: 920-863-5256; Fax: 920-863-5425.
Catechesis/Religious Program—Mrs. Lori A. Wagner, D.R.E.

NEW FRANKEN, BROWN CO., ST. KILIAN, [CEM], Served from St. Thomas the Apostle, Humboldt. Rev. William O'Brien.
Res.: P.O. Box 83, 54229-0083. Tel: 920-866-3541; Fax: 920-866-3541. Email: stkilian2508@yahoo.com.
Catechesis/Religious Program—3041 County Rd. T, 54311-9429. Tel: 920-863-5297. Email: stthomastheapostlecre@yahoo.com. Mrs. Nancy Meltzer, D.R.E. Students 122.

NEW HOLSTEIN, CALUMET CO., HOLY ROSARY, [CEM], Served from Ss. Peter & Paul, Kiel. Joseph Zenk, Parish Dir.; Revs. Robert Kollath, Priest Mod.; Harold L. Berryman, Sacramental Min. (Retired); Deacon Bernard (Pat) P. Knier.
Res.: 1724 Madison St., 53061-1389. Tel: 920-898-4884; Fax: 920-898-4884. Email: hrparish_1@charter.net.
School—Divine Savior Catholic School, 1814 Madison St., 53061-1347. Tel: 920-898-4210; Fax: 920-898-4220. Mr. Gary F. Stepanek, Prin.
Catechesis/Religious Program—Tel: 920-898-9248. Ms. Carla Nennig, D.R.E.

NEW LONDON, WAUPACA CO., MOST PRECIOUS BLOOD, [CEM] Rev. David J. Lewis.
Res.: 712 S. Pearl St., 54961-1861. Tel: 920-982-2346; Fax: 920-982-8381. Email: parish@mpbnewlondon.org.
School—120 E. Washington St., 54961-1891. Tel: 920-982-2134; Fax: 920-982-1572. Email: jstaddler@mpbnewlondon.org. Mr. Jeffrey Staddler, Prin.
Catechesis/Religious Program—Tel: 920-982-9025. Mrs. Ellen E. Clarke, D.R.E.; Mrs. Tina L. Noel, Contact Person.

NEWALD, ARGONNE CO., ST. HUBERT MISSION, Served from St. Leonard, Laona. Rev. Msgr. Paul P. Koszarek, Priest Mod. & Sacramental Min. (Retired); Deacon Gerald H. Cross, Parish Dir.
Res.: 5330 Beech St., Laona, 54541-9340. Tel: 715-674-3241; Fax: 715-674-3241. Email: stleonard@ez-net.com.
Catechesis/Religious Program—Tel: 715-674-3862. Ms. Cynthia Beairl, D.R.E.

NEWTON, MANITOWO CO., ST. THOMAS THE APOSTLE (2000) [CEM], Merger of St. Joseph, Alverno; St. Wendel, Cleveland; St. Isidore, Osman & St. Casimir, Northeim. Has records for all 4 parishes. Sr. Marlita Henseler, Parish Dir.; Very Rev. Daniel J. Felton, Priest Mod.; Rev. Thomas Long, Sacramental Min.
Res.: 8100 Brunner Rd., 53063-9607. Tel: 920-726-4228; Fax: 920-726-4229. Email: marlita@lakefield.net.
Catechesis/Religious Program—Mrs. Pamela Fischer, D.R.E.

NIAGARA, MARINETTE CO., ST. ANTHONY, Also serves St. Margaret, Pembine & Sacred Heart, Aurora. Rev. Matthew W. Settle; Deacon Gerald A. Nardi.
Res.: 1432 River St., 54151-1599. Tel: 715-251-3879; Fax: 715-251-3642. Email: stanthony@borderlandnet.net.
Catechesis/Religious Program—Email: stanthony@borderlandnet.net. Ms. Rebecca S. Adedrman, D.R.E.; Ms. Debra Maszka, D.R.E.

NORMAN, KEWAUNEE CO., ST. JOSEPH, Merged with Nativity of the Blessed Virgin Mary, Tisch Mills to form St. Isidore the Farmer, Tisch Mills.

NORTHEIM, MANITOWOC CO., ST. CASIMIR, Merged with St. Joseph, Alverno; St. Wendel, Cleveland; and St. Isidore, Osman to form St. Thomas the Apostle, Northeim.

OCONTO, OCONTO CO.
1—HOLY TRINITY (1996) [CEM], Also serves Oconto Falls and Stiles. Rev. Joel A. Sember, Admin.; Deacon Walter P. Kaszynski.
Res.: 716 Madison St., 54153-1668. Tel: 920-835-5900; Fax: 920-835-5907. Email: holytrinity@netnet.net.
Catechesis/Religious Program—Ms. Emma Janssen, D.R.E.
2—ST. JOSEPH, Merged with St. Peter, Oconto to form Holy Trinity, Oconto.
3—ST. PETER, Merged with St. Joseph, Oconto to form Holy Trinity, Oconto.

OCONTO FALLS, OCONTO CO., ST. ANTHONY, [CEM], Served from Holy Trinity, Oconto. Rev. Joel A. Sember, Admin.
Church: 253 N. Franklin St., 54154-1042. Tel: 920-846-2276; Fax: 920-846-2180. Email: admsec@plbb.us.
School—Email: stant84@plbb.us. Ms. Rosemary Marifke, Prin.
Catechesis/Religious Program—Ms. Lynn Beaumier, D.R.E. Associated with St. Patrick, Stiles.

OMRO, WINNEBAGO CO., ST. MARY, Served from St. Mary, Winneconne. Sr. Pamela A. Biehl, O.S.F., Parish Dir.; Very Rev. Douglas E. LeCaptain, Priest Mod. & Sacramental Min.; Rev. Luke A. Ferris, Sacramental Min.
Res.: 730 Madison Ave., 54963-1630. Tel: 920-685-2258; Fax: 920-685-7343. Email: stmaryomro@charter.net.
Catechesis/Religious Program—Ms. Janet Abalan, D.R.E.

ONEIDA, BROWN CO., ST. JOSEPH, [CEM], Also serves Immaculate Conception, Oneida. Rev. David J. Hoffman, Temporary Admin.; Deacons Everett L. Doxtator; James P. Heider.
145 Saint Joseph Dr., 54155-8914.
Res.: N5589 County Rd. E., De Pere, 54115-8529. Tel: 920-869-2244; Fax: 920-869-2219. Email: ruthboyea@aol.com.
Catechesis/Religious Program—Mrs. Mary Van Schyndel, D.R.E.; Mrs. Jennie Le Mere, D.R.E.

ONEIDA TOWNSHIP, OUTAGAMIE CO., IMMACULATE CONCEPTION, [CEM], Served from St. Joseph, Oneida. Rev. David J. Hoffman, Temporary Admin.; Deacons Everett L. Doxtator; James P. Heider.
Res.: N5589 County Rd. E., De Pere, 54115-8529. Tel: 920-869-2281; Fax: 920-869-2219. Email: ruthboyea@aol.com.
Catechesis/Religious Program—Tel: 920-869-2950. Mrs. Jennie Le Mere, Contact Person; Mrs. Mary Van Schyndel, D.R.E.

OSHKOSH, WINNEBAGO CO.
1—ST. JOHN, [JC] Merged with Sacred Heart, Oshkosh and St. Vincent de Paul, Oshkosh to form St. Jude the Apostle, Oshkosh.
2—ST. JOSAPHAT, Merged with St. Mary, Oshkosh and St. Peter, Oshkosh to form Most Blessed Sacrament, Oshkosh.
3—ST. JUDE THE APOSTLE Rev. Mathew J. Simonar; Deacons Frederick C. Fischer; G. Patrick Gelhar; Robert Penzenstadler.
1025 W. 5th Ave., 54902-5725. Tel: 920-235-7412; Fax: 920-651-9826. Email: office@stjudeoshkosh.org.
Merger of St. John, Oshkosh, St. Vincent de Paul, Oshkosh & Sacred Heart, Oshkosh. Has records for all 3 parishes.
See Unified Catholic Schools of Oshkosh, Oshkosh under Consolidated Schools located in the Institution section.
Catechesis/Religious Program—Ms. Michele Zowin, Contact Person.
4—ST. MARY, Merged with St. Josaphat, Oshkosh and St. Peter, Oshkosh to form Most Blessed Sacrament, Oshkosh.
5—MOST BLESSED SACRAMENT Very Rev. James R. Jugenheimer; Deacons Peter A. Cheskie; Richard A. Hocking.
449 High Ave., 54901-4708. Tel: 920-231-9782; Fax: 920-231-9808. Email: lpollack@mbsoshkosh.org.
Merger of St. Josaphat, Oshkosh, St. Mary, Oshkosh & St. Peter, Oshkosh. Has records for all 3 parishes.
See Unified Catholic Schools of Oshkosh, Oshkosh under Consolidated Schools located in the Institution section.
Catechesis/Religious Program—Mrs. Mary Wichmann, Contact Person; Mrs. Kristin Bird, D.R.E.
6—ST. PETER, [JC] Merged with St. Josaphat, Oshkosh and St. Mary, Oshkosh to form Most Blessed Sacrament, Oshkosh.
7—ST. RAPHAEL THE ARCHANGEL, [JC] Very Rev. Douglas E. LeCaptain; Rev. Luke A. Ferris, Parochial Vicar; Deacons Gregory A. Grey; John Ingala.
Church & Mailing Address: 830 S. Westhaven Dr., 54904-7977. Tel: 920-233-8044; Fax: 920-233-2360. Email: parish.office@raphael.org.
See Unified Catholic Schools of Oshkosh, Oshkosh under Consolidated Schools located in the Institution section.
Catechesis/Religious Program—Mr. Rich F. Curran, Contact Person; Mrs. Debbie Peters, D.R.E.
8—SACRED HEART, [CEM] Merged with St. John, Oshkosh and St. Vincent de Paul, Oshkosh to form St. Jude the Apostle, Oshkosh.
9—ST. VINCENT DE PAUL, [JC] Merged with St. John, Oshkosh and Sacred Heart, Oshkosh to form St. Jude the Apostle, Oshkosh.

OSMAN, MANITOWOC CO., ST. ISIDORE, Merged with St. Wendel, Cleveland; St. Joseph, Alverno; and St. Casimir, Northeim to form St. Thomas the Apostle, Northeim.

PEMBINE, MARINETTE CO., ST. MARGARET, Served from St. Anthony, Niagara. Rev. Matthew W. Settle.
Mailing Address: P.O. Box 235, 54156-0235. Tel: 715-324-5849; Fax: 715-324-6571. Email: stanthony@borderlandnet.net.
Catechesis/Religious Program—Tel: 715-324-5595. Ms. Rebecca S. Aderman, D.R.E.

PESHTIGO, MARINETTE CO., ST. MARY, Also serves SS. Joseph & Edward, Walsh. Sr. Helen M. Plum, S.S.N.D., Parish Dir.; Revs. Dean W. Dombroski, Priest Mod. (Retired); Richard L. Allen, Sacramental Min. (Retired); Deacon Charles R. Schumacher.
Res.: 171 S. Wood Ave., 54157-1426. Tel: 715-582-3876; Fax: 715-582-0970. Email: cte47017@centurytel.net.
School—141 S. Wood Ave., 54157-1426. Tel: 715-582-4041; Fax: 715-582-1165. Email: cte46995@centurytel.net. Mr. Peter Mayhew, Prin.
Catechesis/Religious Program—Tel: 715-582-4897. Mr. Darren Eultgen, D.R.E.

PHLOX, LANGLADE CO.
1—ST. JOSEPH, [CEM] Merged with Holy Family, Mattoon to form St. Joseph-Holy Family Parish, Phlox. Served from St. Anthony, Neopit.
2—ST. JOSEPH-HOLY FAMILY PARISH, Merger of St. Joseph, Phlox & Holy Family, Mattoon. Has records for both parishes. Revs. David R. Schmidt, Priest Mod.; Charles G. Hoffmann, Sacramental Min.; Deacon Thomas W. Hartman, Pastoral Coord.

Mailing Address: P.O. Box 73, 54464-0073. Tel: 715-489-3330. Email: sjhfphlox@granitewave.com.
Catechesis/Religious Program—Mrs. Patricia Koeppel, D.R.E.

PICKEREL, LANGLADE CO., ST. MARY, [CEM], Served from Holy Family, Elcho. Revs. David R. Schmidt, Priest Mod.; Jeremiah F. Worman, Sacramental Min. (Retired); Mrs. Cindy Eultgen, Parish Dir.
Mailing Address: P.O. Box 77, 54465-0077. Tel: 715-484-4300. Email: holyfamilyelcho@frontiernet.net.
Catechesis/Religious Program—Lynn Verhagen, D.R.E.

PINE GROVE, BROWN CO., HOLY TRINITY, [CEM] Merged with Holy Martyrs of Gorcum, Green Bay to form Prince of Peace, Green Bay.

PLAINFIELD, WAUSHARA CO., ST. PAUL (1898) [CEM] Deacon Robert L. Precourt, Parish Dir.; Very Rev. Robert Stegmann, Priest Mod.
Res.: 622 S. Beach St., 54966-9637. Tel: 715-335-4314; Fax: 715-335-6016. Email: stpaul@uniontel.net.
Catechesis/Religious Program—Mrs. Heather Burns, D.R.E.; Mrs. Cheryl Pionke, D.R.E.; Mrs. Kate Drmolka, Contact Person.

POY SIPPI, WAUSHARA CO., SACRED HEART OF JESUS (1920), Served from St. Mark, Redgranite. Karen J. Nesbit, Parish Dir.; Very Rev. Robert Stegmann, Priest Mod.; Rev. Joseph A. Mattern, Sacramental Min. (Retired).
Mailing Address: P.O. Box 273, Redgranite, 54970-0273. Tel: 920-566-4442; Fax: 920-566-4559. Email: sacredheartps@centurytel.net.
Catechesis/Religious Program—Mrs. Barbara M. Breest, Contact Person.

PULASKI, BROWN CO., ASSUMPTION OF THE BLESSED VIRGIN MARY (1887) [CEM], Also serves St. Stanislaus, Hofa Park and St. Casimir, Krakow. Rev. Finian Andrew Zaucha, O.F.M.; Deacon Dennis G. Majewski.
Res.: P.O. Box 379, 54162-0379. Tel: 920-822-3279; Fax: 920-822-8030. Email: parishoffice@abvm.org.
School—109 E. Pulaski St., 54162-9287. Tel: 920-822-5650; Fax: 920-822-8003. Deanne Wilinski, Prin.
Catechesis/Religious Program—Deanne Wilinski, D.R.E.

REDGRANITE, WAUSHARA CO., ST. MARK (1906) [CEM], Also serves Sacred Heart of Jesus, Poy Sippi. Karen J. Nesbit, Parish Dir.; Very Rev. Robert Stegmann, Priest Mod.; Rev. Joseph A. Mattern, Sacramental Min. (Retired).
Mailing Address: P.O. Box 273, 54970-0273. Tel: 920-566-4442; Fax: 920-566-4559. Email: stmarkredgranite@centurytel.net.
Catechesis/Religious Program—Mrs. Barbara M. Breest, D.R.E.

REEDSVILLE, MANITOWOC CO.
1—ST. MARY, Merged with St. Patrick's, Maple Grove to form St. Mary-St. Patrick, Reedsville.
2—ST. MARY-ST. PATRICK, Merged with St. Mary, Brillion to form Holy Family, Brillion.

ROSIERE, KEWAUNEE CO., ST. HUBERT, Merged with St. Peter, Lincoln to form St. Peter & St. Hubert, Rosiere/Lincoln.

ROSIERE/LINCOLN, KEWAUNEE CO., ST. PETER-ST. HUBERT (1994) [JC 4] Deacon Paul T. Zenefski, Parish Dir.; Revs. Carl E. Schmitt, Priest Mod.; Lee J. Kahrs, Sacramental Min. (Retired); Deacon Mark R. Hibbs. Served from St. Mary, Maplewood.
Res.: E3085 County Rd. X, Casco, 54205-9787. Tel: 920-837-2852; Fax: 920-837-2671. Email: stpnh@centurytel.net.
Catechesis/Religious Program—Ms. Tammy Barta, Contact Person.

SAINT ANNA, CALUMET CO., ST. ANN (1851) [CEM], Served from Ss. Peter & Paul, Kiel. Joseph Zenk, Parish Dir.; Revs. Robert Kollath, Priest Mod.; Harold L. Berryman, Sacramental Min. (Retired); Deacon Bernard (Pat) P. Knier.
Res.: N188 School St., New Holstein, 53061-9776. Tel: 920-894-3147; Fax: 920-894-3147. Email: stann@bertramwireless.com.
Catechesis/Religious Program—Tel: 920-418-4104. Email: wisco_02@hotmail.com. Ms. Abigail Schoeborn, D.R.E.; Mrs. Susan Mintner, Contact Person.

SAINT JOHN, CALUMET CO., ST. JOHN THE BAPTIST, Merged with Sacred Heart, Sherwood, to form St. John-Sacred Heart, Sherwood.

SAINT NAZIANZ, MANITOWOC CO., ST. GREGORY (1854) [CEM], Also serves Holy Trinity, School Hill. Rev. Patrick Nelson, S.D.S., Admin.; Deacon James E. Steffen.
Mailing Address: P.O. Box 199, St. Nazianz, 54232-0199. Tel: 920-773-2511; Fax: 920-773-3086. Email: stgregory100@hotmail.com.
School—Tel: 920-773-2530. Email: stgregs100@hotmail.com. Ms. Rita A. Steffen, Prin.
Catechesis/Religious Program—Mrs. Rosemary G. Bartel, D.R.E.

SCHOOL HILL, MANITOWOC CO., HOLY TRINITY (1869) [CEM], Served from St. Gregory, St. Nazianz. Rev. Patrick Nelson, S.D.S., Admin.; Deacon James E. Steffen.
Res.: 11928 Marken Rd., Kiel, 53042-9750. Tel: 920-773-2380. Email: holytrinityparish@tds.net.
Catechesis/Religious Program—Mrs. Rosemary G. Bartel, D.R.E.

SEYMOUR, OUTAGAMIE CO., ST. JOHN (1873) [CEM] Very Rev. Robert J. Kabat; Deacons Paul K. Grimm; Orvell A. DeBruin; Richard J. Matuszak.
Res. & Mailing Address: 915 Ivory St., 54165-1629. Tel: 920-833-6140; Fax: 920-833-7098. Email: office@stjohnseymour.com.
Catechesis/Religious Program—Tel: 920-833-2122. Mrs. Mary P. Carter, D.R.E.

SHAWANO, SHAWANO CO., SACRED HEART (1867) [CEM 2] Rev. Leonard M. Evers.
Office & Mailing Address: 321 S. Sawyer St., 54166-2437. Tel: 715-526-2023; Fax: 715-526-4105. Email: reevers@sacredheartofshawano.org.
School—124 E. Center St., 54166-2499. Tel: 715-526-5328; Fax: 715-526-4107. Email: principal@shcscardinals.org. Mr. Daniel W. Minter, Prin.
Catechesis/Religious Program—Tel: 715-526-4104. Email: shdre@sacredheartofshawano.org. Ms. Mindy Wegner, D.R.E.

SHERWOOD, CALUMET CO.
1—ST. JOHN-SACRED HEART (1995), Merger of St. John the Baptist, Saint John& Sacred Heart, Sherwood. Has records for both parishes. Also serves St. Mary, Stockbridge & St. Mary, Hilbert (Has records for St. John the Baptist, Saint John). Rev. Michael E. Betley; Deacon Steven M. Vande Hey.
Res.: N369 Military Rd., 54169-9661. Tel: 920-989-1515; Fax: 920-989-8585. Email: triparish@tds.net.
School—N361 Military Rd., 54169-9661. Tel: 920-989-1373; Fax: 920-989-1689. Email: heart@tds.net. Mr. Kerry Sievert, Prin.
Catechesis/Religious Program—Tel: 920-989-2400. Email: re@tds.net. Ms. Diane Wickersheim, Contact Person.
2—SACRED HEART, Merged with St. John the Baptist, St. John to form St. John-Sacred Heart, Sherwood.

SHIOCTON, OUTAGAMIE CO., ST. DENIS (1898) [CEM], Served from St. Patrick, Stephensville. Sr. Pauline Feiner, S.D.S., Parish Dir.; Revs. Patrick M. Gawrylewski, O.F.M., Priest Moderator; John P. Kastenholz, O.Praem., Sacramental Min.
Mailing Address: N3686 State Rd. 76, Hortonville, 54944-8320. Tel: 920-757-5090; Fax: 920-757-5010. Email: stpatdenis@new.rr.com.
Catechesis/Religious Program—Ben Wolf, D.R.E.

SISTER BAY, DOOR CO., ST. ROSALIA, Merged with St. John the Baptist, Egg Harbor; St. Mary of the Lake, Baileys Harbor; St. Paul, Fish Creek and St. Michael, Jacksonport to form Stella Maris, Egg Harbor.

SLOVAN, KEWAUNEE CO., ST. ADALBERT, Merged with Holy Trinity, Casco.

SOBIESKI, OCONTO CO.
1—ST. JOHN CANTIUS, [CEM] Merged with St. Louis, Abrams and St. Joseph, Chase to form St. Maximilian Kolbe, Sobieski.
2—ST. MAXIMILIAN KOLBE Rev. Gerald A. Prusakowski, O.F.M.
6051 Noble St., 54171-9724. Tel: 920-822-5255; Fax: 920-822-5255. Email: frg33ofm6051@netnet.net. Also serves St. Benedict, Suamico & St. Pius, Little Suamico.
Catechesis/Religious Program—Tel: 920-822-8795. Mrs. Donna Rae VanKauwenbergh, D.R.E.

SOUTH BRANCH, MENOMINEE RESERVATION, ST. JOSEPH OF THE LAKE, Closed. For inquiries for parish records contact the chancery.

SPRUCE, OCONTO CO., SACRED HEART OF JESUS, Merged with St. Charles Borromeo, Lena to form Holy Cross, Lena.

STANGELVILLE, KEWAUNEE CO.
1—ST. LAWRENCE, Merged with St. Joseph-St. John, Montpelier and St. Hedwig, West Kewaunee to form St. Therese de Lisieux, Stangelville.
2—ST. THERESE DE LISIEUX (2000) [JC], Also serves St. Isidore the Farmer, Tisch Mills. Rev. Dennis G. Drury; Deacon Robert J. Pribek.
Mailing Address: N2085 County Rd. AB, Denmark, 54208-7705. Tel: 920-863-8747; Fax: 920-863-5768. Email: parish@sttheresеonline.com.
Catechesis/Religious Program—Mrs. Sandy Salentine, D.R.E.

STEPHENSVILLE, OUTAGAMIE CO., ST. PATRICK (1867) [CEM], Also serves St. Denis, Shiocton. Sr. Pauline Feiner, S.D.S., Parish Dir.; Revs. Patrick M. Gawrylewski, O.F.M., Priest Moderator; John P. Kastenholz, O.Praem., Sacramental Min.
Res.: N3686 State Rd. 76, Hortonville, 54944-8320. Tel: 920-757-5090; Fax: 920-757-5010. Email: stpatdenis@new.rr.com.
Catechesis/Religious Program—Ben Wolf, D.R.E.

STILES, OCONTO CO., ST. PATRICK (1870) [JC], Served from Holy Trinity, Oconto. Rev. Joel A. Sember, Admin.
Mailing Address: 253 N. Franklin St., Oconto Falls, 54154-1042.
Res.: 5246 St. Patrick's Rd., Lena, 54139-9105. Tel: 920-846-2276; Fax: 920-846-2180. Email: admsec@plbb.us.
Catechesis/Religious Program—Email: relcoor@plbb.us. Ms. Lynn Beaumier, D.R.E. Associated with St. Anthony, Oconto Falls.

STOCKBRIDGE, CALUMET CO., ST. MARY (1882) [CEM], Served from St. John-Sacred Heart, Sherwood/Saint John. Rev. Michael E. Betley; Deacon Steven M. Vande Hey.
Res.: P.O. Box 8, 53088-0008. Tel: 920-439-1515. Email: stmarystockbridge@tds.net.
Catechesis/Religious Program—N369 Military Rd., Sherwood, 54169-9661. Tel: 920-898-2400. Email: re@tds.net. Ms. Diane Wickersheim, Contact Person.

STURGEON BAY, DOOR CO.
1—CORPUS CHRISTI (1904) [JC] Rev. Carl E. Schmitt; Deacon Raymond G. Ambrosius Jr.
Mailing Address: 25 N. Elgin Ave., 54235-2963.
Oratory— [JC] Mailing Address & Oratory: 25 N. Elgin Ave., 54235-2963. Tel: 920-743-4716; Fax: 920-743-3711. Email: christiparish@corpuschristiparish.us.
Res.: 722 W. Maple St., 54235.
See St. John Bosco Catholic School, Inc., Sturgeon in the Institution Section under Elementary Schools, Diocesan.
Catechesis/Religious Program—Tina Lauder-Boucher, D.R.E.
2—ST. JOSEPH (1865), Serves Ss. Peter & Paul Parish, Institute. Rev. Robert Konkol, O.F.M., Admin.; Deacon Kenneth D. Kopydlowski.
Church & Office Address: 526 Louisiana St., 54235-1796. Tel: 920-743-2062; Fax: 920-743-6786. Email: mvandertie@hotmail.com.
See St. John Bosco Catholic School, Inc., Sturgeon Bay in the Institution Section under Elementary Schools, Diocesan.
Catechesis/Religious Program—Ms. Penny Biwer, D.R.E.

SUAMICO, BROWN CO., ST. BENEDICT (1917) [CEM], Served from St. Maximilian Kolbe, Sobieski. Rev. Gerald A. Prusakowski, O.F.M.
Mailing Address: P.O. Box 66, 54173-0066. Tel: 920-434-2024; Fax: 920-662-2301. Email: sbsp@wi.twcbc.com.
Catechesis/Religious Program—Tel: 920-434-1219. Mrs. Elizabeth Nier, D.R.E.

SURING, OCONTO CO., ST. MICHAEL (1906) [CEM], Served from St. John, Gillett, with Station at Chute Pond. Sr. Marla J. Clercx, A.N.G., Parish Dir.; Revs. John J. Becker, Priest Mod.; David S. Barrett, Sacramental Min. (Retired).
Mailing Address: P.O. Box 248, 54174-0248. Tel: 920-842-2580; Fax: 920-842-9825. Email: stmikesuring@centurytel.net.
Catechesis/Religious Program—Sheelagh School, D.R.E.

THIRY DAEMS, KEWAUNEE CO., ST. ODILE, Closed. For inquiries for parish records, please see St. Joseph, Champion.

TIGERTON, SHAWANO CO., ST. ANTHONY (1881), Also serves St. Mary, Marion St. Mary, Leoplis & Holy Family-St. William, Wittenberg. Rev. Patrick Lloyd, S.C.J.; Deacons Patrick G. Berg; Howard Bricco; Kenneth F. Sambs; Clay Wildenberg.
Mailing Address: P.O. Box 106, 54486-0106. Tel: 715-535-2571; Fax: 715-535-2953. Email: sacctig@frontiernet.net.
Catechesis/Religious Program—Mrs. Sally Korbisch, D.R.E.

TISCH MILLS, MANITOWOC CO.
1—ST. ISIDORE THE FARMER (2002), Merger of Nativity of the Blessed Virgin Mary & St. Joseph, Norman. Has records for both parishes. Served from St. Therese de Lisieux Parish, Stangelville. Rev. Dennis G. Drury; Deacon Robert J. Pribek.
Mailing Address: 18424 Tisch Mills Rd., Denmark, 54208-9508. Tel: 920-776-1555; Fax: 920-776-1814. Email: st.isidore@tm.net.
Catechesis/Religious Program—Christal Wavrunek, D.R.E.; Barbara Zipperer, D.R.E.
2—NATIVITY OF THE BLESSED VIRGIN MARY, Merged with St. Joseph, Norman to form St. Isidore the Farmer, Tisch Mills.

TONET, KEWAUNEE CO., ST. MARTIN, Closed. For inquiries for parish records, please see St. Joseph, Champion.

TWO RIVERS, MANITOWOC CO.
1—HOLY REDEEMER - SACRED HEART (2000) Merged with St. Luke and St. Mark, Two Rivers to form St. Peter the Fisherman, Two Rivers.
2—ST. LUKE, Merged with St. Mark and Holy Redeemer-Sacred Heart, Two Rivers to form St.

Peter the Fisherman, Two Rivers.
3—ST. MARK, Merged with St. Luke and Holy Redeemer-Sacred Heart, Two Rivers to form St. Peter the Fisherman, Two Rivers.
4—MOST HOLY REDEEMER, Merged with Sacred Heart, Two Rivers to form Holy Redeemer-Sacred Heart, Two Rivers.
5—ST. PETER THE FISHERMAN (2002) [CEM], Merger of St. Luke, St. Mark and Holy Redeemer-Sacred Heart, Two Rivers. (Has records for St. Luke, St. Mark, Most Holy Redeemer.) Rev. Thomas J. Reynebeau; Deacons Paul J. Gleichner; Kurt L. Grube.
Mailing Address: 3218 Tannery Rd., 54241-1648. Tel: 920-793-4531; Fax: 920-793-8067. Email: parish@stpeterthefisherman.org.
School—1322 33rd St., 54241-1747. Tel: 920-794-7622; Fax: 920-553-7625. Mrs. Karolyn Efferson, Prin.
Catechesis/Religious Program—Roxanne Dyzak, D.R.E.; Mrs. Gail Eichhorn, D.R.E.; Ms. Kari R. Kruser, D.R.E.
6—SACRED HEART, Merged with Most Holy Redeemer, Two Rivers to form Holy Redeemer-Sacred Heart, Two Rivers.
WABENO, FOREST CO., ST. AMBROSE (1905) [CEM], Served from St. Mary of the Lake, Lakewood. Rev. Jason J. Blahnik, Admin.; Deacon Harold R. Orlowski.
Mailing Address: P.O. Box 280, 54566-0280. Tel: 715-473-2511. Email: stambrose@centurylink.net.
Catechesis/Religious Program—Ms. Linda McEwen, D.R.E.
WAGNER, MARINETTE CO., ST. EDWARD, [CEM] Merged with St. Joseph, Walsh to form SS. Joseph & Edward, Walsh. For inquiries for parish records contact St. Joseph & Edward, Walsh.
WALHAIN, KEWAUNEE CO., ST. AMAND, Closed. For inquiries for parish records, please see St. Joseph, Champion.
WALSH, MARINETTE CO.
1—ST. JOSEPH, Merged with St. Edward, Wagner to form SS. Joseph & Edward, Walsh. For inquiries for parish records contact St. Joseph & Edward, Walsh.
2—SS. JOSEPH & EDWARD (1894), Served from St. Mary, Peshtigo. (Has records for St. Edward, Wagner & St. Joseph, Walsh.) Sr. Helen M. Plum, S.S.N.D., Parish Dir.; Revs. Dean W. Dombroski, Priest Moderator (Retired); William J. Stengel, Sacramental Min. (Retired); Deacon Charles R. Schumacher.
Mailing Address: W3308 County Road G, Porterfield, 54159-9736. Tel: 715-789-2254; Fax: 715-789-2293. Email: stsjosed@centurytel.net.
Catechesis/Religious Program—Tel: 715-582-4897. Mr. Darren Eultgen, D.R.E.
WAUPACA, WAUPACA CO., ST. MARY MAGDALENE (1890) [CEM], Also serves Sacred Heart, Manawa & Ss. Pter & Paul, Weyauwega. Has records for St. George, King. Rev. Brian S. Belongia.
Office & Mailing Address: P.O. Box 409, 54981-0409. Tel: 715-258-2088; Fax: 715-258-5708. Email: info@smm-waupaca.org.
Catechesis/Religious Program—Mrs. Elizabeth Manion, D.R.E.; Mrs. Catherine Miller, D.R.E.
WAUSAUKEE, MARINETTE CO., ST. AUGUSTINE (1890), Also serves St. Agnes, Amberg. Deacon Patrick J. Whitcomb, Pastoral Coord.; Revs. Ronald C. Belitz, Priest Moderator; John J. Hephner, Sacramental Min. (Retired); Donald R. Burkart, Sacramental Min.
Mailing Address: 507 Church St., 54177-9749. Tel: 715-856-5276; Fax: 715-856-5276. Email: staugustine@centurytel.net.
Catechesis/Religious Program—Ms. Linda Suzawith, D.R.E.
WAUTOMA, WAUSHARA CO., ST. JOSEPH (1885) [CEM] Very Rev. Robert Stegmann.
Res.: 364 S. Cambridge St., 54982-8101. Tel: 920-787-3848; Fax: 920-787-4781. Email: sjcc@centurytel.net.
Catechesis/Religious Program—Ms. Nancy Reilly, D.R.E.
WEST KEWAUNEE, KEWAUNEE CO., ST. HEDWIG, Merged with St. Joseph-St. John, Montpelier and St. Lawrence, Stangelville to form St. Therese de Lisieux, Stangelville.
WEYAUWEGA, WAUPACA CO., SS. PETER AND PAUL (1890) [CEM] Rev. Brian S. Belongia. Served from St. Mary Magdalene, Waupaca.
Res.: P.O. Box 548, 54983-0548. Tel: 920-867-2179; Fax: 920-867-2074. Email: sspeterpaul@charter.net.
Catechesis/Religious Program—Tel: 920-867-2170. Email: peterpauled@charter.net. Ms. Sabrina Danke, D.R.E.
WHITE LAKE, LANGLADE CO.
1—ST. JAMES, Merged with St. Stanislaus Kostka, Langlade to become SS. James & Stanislaus, White Lake/Langlade.
2—SS. JAMES-STANISLAUS (1992) [CEM 2] Revs. Walter P. Stumpf, Temporary Admin.; Roger W. Strebel, Sacramental Min. (Retired).
Mailing Address: P.O. Box 36, 54491-0036. Tel: 715-882-2551.
Res.: 252 Bissell St., 54491.
Catechesis/Religious Program—Sr. Marie A. Miszewski, S.S.N.D., D.R.E.
WHITELAW, MANITOWOC CO., ST. MICHAEL (1872) [CEM], Served from Immaculate Conception, Clarks Mills. Rev. David M. Zimmerman.
Mailing Address: P.O. Box 206, 54247-0206. Tel: 920-732-3901. Email: stmichaelwzipperer@yahoo.com.
See St Mary/St. Michael School, Cato under Consolidated Schools located in the Institution Section.
Catechesis/Religious Program—15 S. County Rd. J, Cato, 54230-8329. Tel: 920-775-4876; Fax: 820-775-4365. Mrs. Teresa Pederson, D.R.E.
WINNECONNE, WINNEBAGO CO., ST. MARY (1884) [JC], Also serves St. Mary Omro. Sr. Pamela A. Biehl, O.S.F., Parish Dir.; Very Rev. Douglas E. LeCaptain, Priest Mod. & Sacramental Min.; Rev. Luke A. Ferris, Sacramental Min.
Res.: P.O. Box 487, 54986-0487. Tel: 920-582-7712; Fax: 920-582-0181. Email: stmarywinneconne@sbcglobal.net.
Catechesis/Religious Program—Ms. Andrea Krueger, Contact Person.
WITTENBERG, SHAWANO CO., HOLY FAMILY, Merged with St. William, Eland to form Holy Family & St. William, Wittenberg/Eland. Has records for both parishes.
WITTENBERG/ELAND, SHAWANO CO., HOLY FAMILY-ST. WILLIAM (2000) [CEM], Merger of Holy Family, Wittenberg & St. William, Eland. Has records for both parishes. Rev. Patrick Lloyd, S.C.J.; Deacons Patrick G. Berg; Howard R. Bricco; Clay Wildenberg; Kenneth F. Sambs.
Mailing Address: P.O. Box 106, Tigerton, 54486-0106. Tel: 715-535-2571; Fax: 715-535-2953. Email: sacctig@frontiernet.net.
Res.: 106 N. Ellms St., 54499-9099.
Catechesis/Religious Program—Mrs. Sally Korbisch, D.R.E.

Special Assignment:
Very Revs.—
Doerfler, John F., S.T.D., J.C.L., P.O. Box 23825, 54305-3825.
Long, W. Thomas, P.O. Box 23825, 54305-3825.
Revs.—
Gilsdorf, Gordon J., 3788 Cottage Row, Suamico, 54173-8254.
Hafeman, Harry G., 703 N. Locust St., 54303.
Koch, David J., Chap., 145 St. Joseph Dr., Oneida, 54155.
Mann, Quentin A., Assoc. Vocs. Dir., 500 W. Marquette St., Appleton, 54911.
Schuster, Daniel J., Dir., Vocations, P.O. Box 23825, 54305-3825.
Weber, Frank N., St. Paul Villa, 312 E. 14th St., Apt. 214, Kaukauna, 54130.

On Duty Outside the Diocese:
Revs.—
Ashbeck, David K., (Diocese of Phoenix, AZ)
Reuter, John F., Apartado 46, Tlaxiaco, Oaxaca 69800 Mexico.
Schiavone, Robert W., Sacred Heart School of Theology, P.O. Box 429, Hales Corners, 53130-0429. Tel: 414-425-0630
Seis, Michael, 8400 N.W. 25th St., Suite 110, Doral, FL 33122.
Sember, Benjamin, J.C.L., Villa Stritch, Via della Nocetta, 63 00164, Rome, Italy.
Vander Heyden, William F., Chap., V.A. Medical Center, 3001 Green Bay Rd., North Chicago, IL 60064-3049.

Military Chaplains:
Revs.—
Dory, Michael, Lt. Cmdr., 16113 W. Quail Creek Ln., Surprise, AZ 85374-4910.
LaCombe, Terrence, 5252 Balboa Arms Dr., Unit 117, San Diego, CA 92117.
Schuetze, John W., Chap. U.S.A.F., 113 Curtiss Dr., Biloxi, MS 39531.

Absent on Leave, Sick or Disabled:
Revs.—
Carroll, Michael
Duffeck, David A.
Mastalir, Peter
Radetski, Paul J.
Schneider, Ronald
Somers, Michael

Retired:
Most Rev.—
Banks, Robert J., D.D., J.C.D., P.O. Box 23825, 54305-3825.
Rev. Msgrs.—
Coleman, Brian P., J.C.L., 224 Iroquois Ave., #14, 54101.
Dewane, John B., M.A., S.T.L., D.Min., 1435 N. McCarthy Rd., Apt. 3, Appleton, 54913-8285.
Dillenburg, James E., 704 Baumeister Rd., Kewaunee, 54216.
Feely, James B., 2785 Taurus Rd., 54311.
Klauck, Peter N., 224 Iroquois Ave., #2, 54301-1994.
Koszarek, Paul P., 2788 W. Shore Ln., Crandon, 54520.
Rose, Donald, 865 Mill Rd., Sturgeon Bay, 54235-9267.
Schommer, Mark J., N2614 Bughs Lake Rd., Wautoma, 54982.
Schuh, John H., 226 S. Walnut St., Kimberly, 54136.
Vanden Hogen, James, 925 Wilson St., Little Chute, 54140.
Very Rev.—
Birdsall, Anthony J., 2105 Shiloh Rd., Sturgeon Bay, 54235.
Revs.—
Allen, Richard L., 3220 E. Parkside Blvd., Apt. 82, Appleton, 54915. Tel: 920-213-0985
Barrett, David S., N6772 Black Oak Cir., Shawano, 54166.
Bernardy, Patrick, 1341 Wilson St., Niagara, 54151.
Berryman, Harold L., 1724 Madison St., New Holstein, 53061-1326.
Bestler, Joseph, 5319B Sunset Bluff Dr., Unit B, 54311-9133.
Brooks, Charles R., 4721 Everbreeze Cir., Unit C, Appleton, 54913.
Browne, Stanley, 224 Iroquois Ave., #11, 54301.
Buhl, Wilbert L., 224 Iroquois Ave., #1, 54301.
Burkardt, Donald, N7374 Birchwood Rd., Crivitz, 54114.
Cerkas, John W., 4308 River Trail Rd., Cavour, 54511.
Clifford, Michael J., 1110 10th Ave., Apt. 222, Menominee, MI 49858.
Conard, Ray J., 2961 St. Anthony Dr., 54311.
Conrad, John F., 1039 Covington Dr., Sheboygan Falls, 53085.
Dantinne, Gary J., 1305 Sorrento Dr., 54304-1433.
Dewane, Daniel, 3723 Mackert St., Apt. 1, Manitowoc, 54220-4254.
Dombroski, Dean W., 1878 Guns St., 54311.
Dowling, Raymond, 11300 W. Parmer Ln., #1114, Cedar Park, TX 78613.
DuCharme, Paul, 224 Iroquois Ave., #8, 54301-1998.
Falk, Gerald R., 1825 N. McDonald St., Appleton, 54911.
Foley, Gerald J., 1700 S. 18th St., #214, Manitowoc, 54220.
Fox, Martin F., 224 Iroquois Ave., #16, 54301.
Frozena, Kenneth R., W5045 Golf Course Rd., Sherwood, 54169.
Gallagher, John M., 224 Iroquois Ave., #7, 54301-1998.
Geiser, Allen A., 224 Iroquois Ave., #4, 54301.
Gerend, Lawrence, 216 Catherine St., Kaukauna, 54130-2136.
Gilsdorf, Daniel C., N518 Robinhood Way, Sherwood, 54169-9660.
Groher, Robert C., 5082 Lucas Rd., Oconto, 54153-9408.
Hephner, John J., N15211 Beazley Rd., Amberg, 54102-9177.
Heymen, Richard, 3400 Yorkshire Ln., Apt. 318, Manitowoc, 54220.
Hoffman, Charles, 426 Hudson St., Antigo, 54409.
Hoffman, Philip, 313 E. Allouez Ave., 54301.
Kahrs, Lee J., B.A., 1751 Eldorado Dr., #13, 54302.
Karuhn, Robert J., 8170 Hogsback Rd., Oconto, 54153.
Kelley, Omer C., 918 Elm St., Antigo, 54409-1525.
Kerscher, Francis, 2005 Division St., Rm. 2066, Manitowoc, 54220.
Koch, Michael R., 224 Iroquois Ave, #7, 54301-1994.
Krutzik, Norman, 622 Pershing St., Appleton, 54911-2870.
Kuhr, William, 631 Haylett St., Neenah, 54956.
Kutiuk, Casimir, 1246 W. 20th Ave., Oshkosh, 54902-6620.
Lenzner, George, 1157 Packerland Dr., 54304-1376.
Lessard, Leo, 17725 Munger Lake Ln., Lakewood, 54138-9615.
Lexa, Robert, 232 S. Pleasant Dr., Appleton, 54914-4205.
Marquardt, Donald, 224 Iroquois Ave., #3, 54301-1994.
Massart, James P., 625 N. Broadway, De Pere, 54115.
Mattern, Joseph A., 320 N. Webster Ave., Omro, 54963.

Mauthe, Richard, Old Orchard Apts., 3001 S. Webster Ave., #216, 54301.
Mayefske, Thomas J., 1017 Florida St. S.E., Albuquerqe, NM 87108-4823.
Melchior, Frank, E2783 Rockledge Rd., Casco, 54205.
Merkatoris, Ralph, 2808 Taurus Rd., 54311-4600.
Mullarkey, John T., 1409 Alcan Dr., Menasha, 54952.
Neuser, John, St. Mary's Home, 1635 S. 21st St., Rm 327, Manitowoc, 54220.
Nickel, Leander, 224 Iroquois Ave., # 6, 54301-1998.
Nowakowski, Edward S., 224 Iroquois Ave., #10, 54301.
O'Brien, John, 502 N. Front St., Apt. 4, De Pere, 54115-2546.
Reinke, Francis P., 1820 Ridgeway Dr., Apt. 12B, De Pere, 54115.
Rhyner, Robert E., 340 W. St. Joseph St., #5, 54301.
Rickert, William, 224 Iroquois Ave., #5, 54301-1998.
Sammut, Tito, P.O. Box 23825, 54305-3825.
Samter, James W., 1600 Rustic Oaks Ct., #11, 54301-2465.
Shebuski, Charles J., 224 Iroquois Ave., #9, 54301.
Smet, Leroy R., N3640 Rocky Mountain Dr., New London, 54961.
Stencil, Rallen, 493 Alpine Dr., 54302.
Stengel, William J., W8445 Germantown Rd., Crivitz, 54114.
Strebel, Roger W., 17444 Riggins St., Townsend, 54175.
Taddy, Jerome J., 6106 Hwy. O, Two Rivers, 54241.
Taylor, Peter, 224 Iroquois Ave., #15, 54301-1969.
Thomas, Richard L., 139 S. Madison St., 54301.
Van De Kreeke, William L., J.C.L., 376-A Wyldewood Dr., Oshkosh, 54904.
Van De Loo, Willard J., 825 E. River Dr., #4, De Pere, 54115.
Van Deuren, John H., 1490 Capitol Dr., #12, 54303.
Vanden Hogen, Paul, 1030 County Rd. QQ, Apt. 6, Waupaca, 54981.
Vandenberg, Robert H., 705 Kramer Lane, Keshena, 54135.
Vennix, James J., E1277 Cleghorn Rd., Waupaca, 54981-9552.
Werner, Justin, N1682 Ridgeway Dr., Greenville, 54942.
Worman, Jeremiah F., N9065 Waterpower Rd., Deerbrook, 54424.
Worzalla, Dennis A., 224 Iroquois Ave., #13, 54301.

Permanent Deacons:
Abts, Anthony J., St. Therese, Appleton
Ambrosius, Raymond G., Jr., Corpus Christi, Sturgeon Bay
Asmuth, James, (Retired), Neenah
Bahnaman, Richard D., St. Francis of Assisi Church, Manitowoc
Banker, Kenneth, St. Martin Church, Cecil
Baumruk, Roy J., St. Joseph Church, Appleton
Beehner, Robert, St. Francis of Assisi Church, Manitowoc
Bennin, Dennis G., Good Shepherd Church, Chilton
Berg, Patrick G., St. Anthony, Tigerton; St. Mary, Marion; Holy Family-St. William, Wittenberg; St. Mary, Leopolis
Bilgrien, Kenneth, SS. Peter & Paul Church, Hortonville
Boeldt, Alan L., St. Francis of Assisi Church, Manitowoc
Boucher, Paul, (Retired), Gresham
Brandenstein, Raymond L., (Retired), Oshkosh
Bricco, Howard, St. Anthony, Tigerton; St. Mary, Marion; Holy Family-St. William, Wittenberg; St. Mary, Leopolis
Brulla, Paul J., St. Rose, Clintonville; St. Mary, Bear Creek
Burke, William, St. Mary Church, Appleton
Burkel, William J., Prince of Peace Church, Green Bay
Charlier, Earl, (Retired), Green Bay
Cheskie, Peter A., Most Blessed Sacrament Church, Oshkosh
Cibula, Paul J., St. Matthew Church, Green Bay
Clark, Kenneth, Green Bay
Coenen, Donald F., Parish Coord., St. Lawrence Church, Navarino
Corey, Bruce H., Holy Cross, Kaukauna
Craig, Thomas M., (Retired), Wausaukee
Cross, Gerald H., Par. Dir., St. Stanislaus Kostka, Armstrong Creek; St. Joan of Arc, Goodman; St. Leonard, Laona; St. Norbert, Long Lake; St. Hubert Mission, Newald
Dabeck, Michael W., St. Matthew, Green Bay
Dahlen, Joseph, Hortonville
De Bruin, Orvell, St. John Church, Seymour
De Groot, Vincent M., (Retired), Little Chute
DeCleene, Kevin, St. Mary Church, St. Francis Xavier, DePere
Dedman, Clarence F., St. Joseph, Appleton
Dennison, James, Parish Dir., Holy Family, Marinette
DeYoung, David L., St. Mary Church, Greenville
Dolezal, Michael, St. Francis of Assisi, Manitowoc
Doran, William V., St. Mary of the Lake, Lakewood
Downey, Timothy E., St. Thomas More, Appleton
Doxtator, Everett L., St. Joseph Church, Oneida; Immaculate Conception, Oneida
Drobka, Robert F., St. Francis of Assisi Church, Manitowoc
DuBois, Raymond L., St. Gabriel the Archangel Church, Neenah + Dir. Communications For Diocese
Dvorak, Richard B., St. Mary Church, Menasha; St. John Church, Menasha
Eash, Michael J., St. Bernard, Appleton
Ellis, Robert F., St. Peter and Paul Church, Green Bay
Farrell, Mark J., St. Joseph Church, Appleton
Fischer, Frederick, St. Jude the Apostle, Oshkosh
Garcia, Benjamin, (Retired), Shawano
Gauthier, James R., St. Agnes Church, Green Bay
Gelhar, G. Patrick, St. Jude the Apostle Church, Oshkosh
Gigure, Donald J., (Retired), Appleton
Gleichner, Paul J., St. Peter the Fisherman Church, Two Rivers; Silver Lake College, Manitowoc
Grey, Gregory A., St. Raphael the Archangel, Oshkosh
Gribowski, Mark A., 4106 106th Dr., Phoenix, AZ 85037. (Diocese of Phoenix, AZ)
Grimm, Paul K., Dir. Office of Permanent Diaconate, St. John Church, Seymour
Grube, Kurt L., St. Peter the Fisherman, Two Rivers
Grzeca, Michael G., Pastoral Coord., St. Martin, Cecil
Haak, Randall A., St. Katharine Drexel Church, Kaukauna
Hanley, Thomas J., Milwaukee, WI
Hartman, Thomas W., Pastoral Coord., St. Joseph/Holy Family Church, Plox
Hayek, Hilary W., (Retired), Tigerton
Heider, James P., St. Joesph and Immaculate Conception, Oneida
Hibbs, Mark R., St. Mary, Maplewood; St. Peter & St. Hubert, Rosiere/Lincoln
Hocking, Richard A., Most Blessed Sacrament, Oshkosh
Hofacker, Jeffrey J., St. Edward Church, Mackville
Holschbach, Keith, St. Bernard Church, Green Bay
Humpal, Gregory J., St. Nicholas Church, Freedom
Ingala, John, St. Raphael the Archagel, Oshkosh
Jacqmin, Robert, (Retired), Green Bay
Jozwiak, Thomas V., St. Rose Church, Clintonville; St. Mary Church, Bear Creek
Kabat, Kenneth, St. Clare Church, Greenleaf
Kaszynski, Walter, Holy Trinity Church, Oconto
Kieffer, Paul A., St. Francis of Assisi Church, Manitowoc
Klister, Cyril, Holy Spirit Church, Kimberly/Darboy
Knier, Bernard (Pat) P., SS. Peter & Paul Church, Kiel; Holy Rosary, New Holstein & St. Ann, St. Anna
Kopydlowski, Kenneth D., St. Joseph, Sturgeon Bay; SS. Peter & Paul, Institute
Koszalinski, Daniel T., Sacred Heart Church, Appleton
Kowalski, David J., Stella Maris, Egg Harbor (Door County)
Kuborn, Gerald G., St. Katharine Drexel Church, Kaukauna
Laurant, John H., St. Bernard Church, Green Bay
Le Mere, David, Gresham
Lehman, Joseph M., St. Mary Church, Bear Creek; St. Rose Church, Clintonville
Letourneaux, Stephen T., Holy Family, Brillion
Lowe, Russ, (Retired), Waupaca
Madden, Michael, St. Bernadette Church, Appleton
Mahoney, Thomas, St. Francis Xavier Cathedral & St. John, Green Bay
Majewski, Dennis, Assumption of the BVM Church, Pulaski
Maloney, John R., (Retired), Suamico
Mastalish, Larry V., St. Bernard Church, Green Bay
Matuszak, Richard J., St. John, Seymour; St. Sebastian, Isaar
Meidl, Richard, Peoria, AZ
Merrick, Craig, St. Thomas More Church, Appleton
Mervilde, Michael J., St. Joseph, St. Jude, Annunciation & St. Patrick, Green Bay
Meyer, Steven J., St. Elizabeth Ann Seton, Green Bay
Miech, Richard M., (Richmond, VA)
Miller, Robert J., Immaculate Conception, Luxemburg; Holy Trinity, Casco
Naidl, Clarence, All Saints, Denmark; Holy Trinity, New Denmark; St. James, Cooperstown; St. Joseph, Kellnersville; St. Mary, Glenmore/Stark
Nardi, Gerald A., St. Anthony, Niagara
Nass, Donald, (Retired), Redgranite
Nelesen, Ken, St. Francis of Assisi Church, Manitowoc
Newhouse, Don, St. Nicholas Church, Freedom
Nooker, Robert L., Green Bay
Nowak, Richard, (Retired), Green Bay
Orlowski, Harold R., St. Ambrose Church, Wabeno
Otradovec, Byron A., (Retired), Florida
Penzenstadler, Robert, St. Jude the Apostle, Oshkosh
Plantico, Paul, (Retired), Marietta, GA
Precourt, Robert L., Parish Dir., St. Paul Church, Plainfield
Pribek, Robert J., St. Therese de Lisieux, Stangelville; St. Isidore the Farmer, Tisch Mills
Quinette, Harvey J., (Retired), De Pere
Reed, Maurice F., St. Bernard Church, Appleton
Reilly, Timothy G., General Dir., Diocesan Curia & Resurrection Church, Green Bay
Reinl, Peter M., Appleton
Rocchi, Steven, (Retired), Wild Rose
Ropson, Donald J., Resurrection Church, Green Bay
Sambs, Kenneth F., St. Anthony Church, Tigerton; St. Mary Church, Marion; Holy Family-St. William, Wittenberg; St. Mary, Leopolis
Sanchez, Luis, St. Willebrord Church, Green Bay
Schmidt, Gilbert, Sacred Heart Church, Appleton
Schmidt, Michael, Nativity of Our Lord Church, Green Bay
Schraufnagel, George J., St. Paul Church, Combined Locks
Schraufnagel, Gerard J., St. Mary, Appleton
Schumacher, Charles R., St. Mary Church, Peshtigo; SS. Joseph & Edward, Walsh
Simon, Richard S., St. Pius X, Appleton
Spielbauer, Norman, Neenah
Steffen, James E., Holy Trinity Church, School Hill; St. Gregory Church, St. Nazianz
Sustman, James, Mishicot
Teske, Glenn, Port Chap., Apostleship of the Sea, Green Bay
Thetreau, Jerome E., Holy Family Church, Marinette
Torres, Manuel, St. John the Baptist, Howard; Episcopal/Diocesan Master of Ceremonies
Umentum, Paul, St. Mary of the Angels Church, Green Bay; Asst. Episcopal & Diocesan Master of Ceremonies
Van Eperen, David G., St. John Nepomucene, Little Chute
Vande Hey, Steven, St. John - Sacred Heart, Sherwood; St. Mary, Hilbert; St. Mary, Stockbridge
Vander Bloomen, Michael D., Our Lady of Lourdes Church, DePere
Vang, Shuying (Joe), St. Bernard, Appleton
Vincent, John, Manitowoc
Vincent, Michael C., SS. Peter & Paul Church, Green Bay
Vincent, Robert, (Retired), Appleton
Wagnitz, Daniel, Annunciation of the BVM, St. Joseph, St. Jude & St. Patrick, Green Bay
Wetzel, Donald J., (Retired), Appleton
Whitcomb, Patrick, Coord.; St. Augustine, Wausankee & St. Agnes, Amberg
Wildenberg, Clay, St. Anthony, Tigerton; St. Mary, Marion; Holy Family-St. William, Wittenberg; St. Mary, Leopolis
Williams, Nicholas J., St. John the Baptist Church, Howard
Zenefski, Paul T., Parish Dir., St. Mary, Maplewood; St. Peter & St. Hubert, Rosiere/Lincoln

INSTITUTIONS LOCATED IN THE DIOCESE

[A] SEMINARIES, RELIGIOUS OR SCHOLASTICATES

GREEN BAY. *St. Mary of the Angels Friary*, 645 S. Irwin Ave., 54301-3303. Tel: 920-437-7411; Fax: 920-437-7411. Rev. Richard Tulko, O.F.M., Guardian & Librarian. Priests 4; Lay Teachers 7.

DE PERE. *St. Norbert Abbey*, 1016 N. Broadway, 54115-2697. Tel: 920-337-4300; Fax: 920-337-4328. Email: john.kastenholz@snc.edu. Web: www.norbertines.org. Rt. Revs. Gary J. Neville, O.Praem., J.C.D., Abbot; John P. Kastenholz, O.Praem., Sec. & Treas.; E. Thomas De Wane, O.Praem., Abbot Emeritus; Jerome G. Tremel, O.Praem., Abbot Emeritus; Very Rev. James B. Herring, O.Praem., J.C.D., Prior; Revs. John M.

Tourangeau, O.Praem., Vocation Coord.; Conrad J. Kratz, O.Praem., Dir. Norbertine Center for Spirituality. Priests 57; Brothers 3; Novices 8; Total Staff 68.

[B] COLLEGES AND UNIVERSITIES

DE PERE. *St. Norbert College* (1898) 54115-2099. Tel: 920-403-3165; Fax: 920-403-4063. Email: amy.sorenson@snc.edu. Web: www.snc.edu. Mr. Thomas Kunkel, Pres.; Dr. Jeffrey Frick, Vice Pres. Academic Affairs & Dean of College; Ms. Eileen Jahnke, C.P.A., Vice Pres. Business & Finance; Revs. Jay J. Fostner, O.Praem., Ph.D., Vice Pres. Mission & Student Affairs; James T. Baraniak, O.Praem., Pastor, St. Norbert College Parish; Salvatore H. Cuccia, O.Praem., Assoc. Pastor, St. Norbert College.

St. Norbert College, Inc. Priests 6; Sisters 1; Lay Teachers 166; Lay Staff 449; Students 2,241.

Faculty: Revs. John Bostwick, O.Praem.; Jay J. Fostner, O.Praem., Ph.D.; David R. McElroy, O.Praem.; James P. Neilson, O.Praem.; Sr. Shawn Madigan.

St. Norbert College Tel: 920-403-3005; Fax: 920-403-4096. Email: admit@snc.edu. Web: www.snc.edu. Ms. Kristin Vogel, Dir. Library.

MANITOWOC. *Silver Lake College of the Holy Family* (1935) 2406 S. Alverno Rd., 54220-9319. Tel: 920-684-6691; Fax: 920-684-7082. Email: george.arnold@sl.edu. Web: www.sl.edu. George Arnold, Pres.; Sr. Ritarose Stahl, Librarian; Thomas Nelson, Dir. Campus Ministry. Sponsored by the Franciscan Sisters of Christian Charity. Sisters 29; Lay Faculty 25; Students 1,291.

[C] HIGH SCHOOLS, DIOCESAN

APPLETON. *Xavier High School* (1959) Coed, 1600 W. Prospect Ave., 54914. Tel: 920-733-6632; Fax: 920-733-5513. Email: mreynebeau@acesxavier.k12.wi.us. Web: www.acesxavier.k12.wi.us. Mr. Matt Reynebeau, Prin.; Mrs. Donna Fahrenkrug, Assoc. Prin.; Mr. Andrew Mahoney, Dir. Guidance Dept.; Ms. Sarah Simon, Campus Min.; Mrs. Mary Micke, Librarian. (Part of ACES Xavier Educational System, Inc.) Lay Teachers 36; Students 584.

MANITOWOC. *Roncalli High School* (1965) 2000 Mirro Dr., 54220-6799. Tel: 920-682-8801; Fax: 920-686-8110. Mr. John Stelzer, Pres.; Mr. Tim Olson, Prin.; Mr. Frank Birr, Campus Min.; Mrs. Sue Rohrer, Librarian. Christian Brothers and Franciscan Sisters of Christian Charity. Sisters 3; Lay Teachers 30; Students 370.

MARINETTE. *St. Thomas Aquinas Academy (Secondary Campus)*, 1200 Main St., 54143-2594. Tel: 715-735-7481; Fax: 715-735-3375. Email: hssec.staa@gmail.com. Anita Folgert, Librarian. Lay Teachers 14; Students 57.

NEENAH/MENASHA. *St. Mary Central High School*, 1050 Zephyr Dr., 54956-1389. Tel: 920-722-7796; Fax: 920-722-5940. Email: pbatey@tcces.k12.wi.us. Web: www.smc.k12.wi.us. Mr. Patrick Batey, Prin.; Jane Sturn, Contact Person; Anne Shelley, Librarian. (part of Twin City Catholic Education System) Lay Teachers 25; Students 238.

OSHKOSH. *Lourdes High School* (1959) (Coed.), 110 N. Sawyer St., 54902. Tel: 920-235-5670; Fax: 920-235-7453. Web: www.lourdes.k12.wi.us. Mr. Jim LaDue, Prin.; Mary Mueller, Librarian. (Part of Unified Catholic Schools of Oshkosh) Lay Teachers 22; Students 221.

[D] HIGH SCHOOLS, PRIVATE

GREEN BAY. *Notre Dame de la Baie Academy*, 610 Maryhill Dr., 54303-2092. Tel: 920-429-6100; Fax: 920-429-6168. Email: rpauly@notredameacademy.com. Web: www.notredameacademy.com. Robert C. Pauly, Pres.; Dr. John Ravizza, Prin.; Mr. Greg Masarik, Assoc. Prin.; Mr. Ken Flaten, Business Mgr.; Mary Schmidt, Librarian. Priests 1; Lay Teachers 48; Students 736.

[E] ELEMENTARY SCHOOLS, DIOCESAN

NEW HOLSTEIN/KIEL. *Divine Savior Catholic Elementary School, Inc.*, 1814 Madison St., 53061. Tel: 920-898-4210; Fax: 920-898-4220. Email: info@divinesaviorschool.org. Rev. Harold L. Berryman, Admin. (Retired); Mr. Gary F. Stepanek, Prin.

STURGEON BAY. *St. John Bosco Catholic School, Inc.*, (Grades PreK-8), 15 N. Elgin Ave., 54235. Tel: 920-743-4144; Fax: 920-743-3711. Sr. Patricia Beckman, O.P., Prin. Priests 2; Sisters 1; Lay Teachers 15.

[F] CONSOLIDATED SCHOOLS

GREEN BAY. *Green Bay Area Catholic Education, Inc., (GRACE), Admin. Office*, 1087 Kellogg St., P.O. Box 33084, 54303-3058. Tel: 920-499-7330; Fax: 920-272-6564. Email: apatek@gracesystem.org. Allan R. Patek, System Pres.

ANTIGO. *All Saints Catholic Schools, Inc.* (1998) 419 6th Ave., 54409. Tel: 715-623-4835; 715-623-2211; Fax: 715-623-3202. Email: pgaluska@ascscrusaders.org. Web: www.ascscrusaders.org. Paul Galuska, Admin. & Prin.; Michele Nagel, Librarian. Lay Teachers 15; Total Enrollment 182.

APPLETON. *ACES Xavier Educational System, Inc.*, 101 E. Northland Ave., 54911. Tel: 920-735-9380; Fax: 920-735-1787. Email: aces@acesxavier.k12.wi.us. Web: acesxavier.k12.wi.us. Deacon Anthony J. Abts, Pres. Sisters 1; Lay Teachers 133; Total Enrollment 1,772.

CATO. *St. Mary/St. Michael School*, (Grades PreSchool-8), 19 S. County Rd. J, 54230-8329. Tel: 920-775-4366; Fax: 920-775-4365. Email: lstmarysschoo2@new.rr.com. Lori Scheffler, Admin.; Ronald Nesper, Prin.; Carol Wetenkamp, Librarian. Priests 1; Sisters 1; Lay Staff 8.

MANITOWOC. *St. Francis of Assisi School*, 601 N. 8th St., 54220. Tel: 920-683-6880; Fax: 920-683-6881. Email: bob.beehner@sfamanitowoc.com. Deacon Bob Beehner, Dir. of Admin.; Mr. James Clark, Middle School Prin.; Mrs. Linda Bender, Elementary Sch. Prin. Sisters 2; Lay Teachers 31; Total Enrollment 415.

NEENAH/MENASHA. *Twin Cities Catholic Educational System (TCCES)*, 1050 Zephyr Dr., 54956. Tel: 920-967-0021; Fax: 920-722-5940. Email: msullivan@tcces.k12.wi.us. Michael Sullivan, System Dir.; Shelley Wautlet, Contact Person. (Consolidation of St. Gabriel, St. Margaret Mary, Neenah and St. Mary, St. John, St. Patrick, Menasha.) Lay Teachers 87; Total Enrollment 942.

OSHKOSH. *Unified Catholic Schools of Oshkosh*, 110 N. Sawyer St., 54902. Tel: 920-426-3626; Fax: 920-303-6682. Mr. Tony Blando, Pres. Sisters 3; Lay Teachers 51; Total Enrollment 800.

TWO RIVERS. *St. Peter the Fisherman Catholic School*, (Grades PreSchool-8), 1322 33rd St., 54241. Tel: 920-794-7622; Fax: 920-553-7625. Email: spfcs@stpeterthefisherman.org. Sr. Mary Lee Schommer, O.S.F., Prin. (Consolidation of St. Luke and St. Mark. Holy Redeemer Schools.) Sisters 3; Lay Teachers 18; Students 182.

[G] GENERAL HOSPITALS

GREEN BAY. *St. Mary's Hospital-Medical Center*, 1726 Shawano Ave., 54303-3282. Tel: 920-498-4200; Fax: 920-497-3707. Email: cbecker@stmgb.org. Web: www.stmgb.org. Mr. Larry Connors, COO; Ms. Cynthia L. Becker, Dir. Pastoral Care; Deacon Nick Williams, Chap.; Rev. David J. Koch, Chap.; Sisters Rita Schmidt, S.S.J.-T.O.S.F., Chap.; Madonna Swintkoske, O.S.F., Pastoral Care Assoc.; Kathy Kitslaar, Pastoral Care Assoc. Hospital Sisters of Third Order of St. Francis. Bed Capacity 158; Total Staff 515; Patients Assisted Annually 108,788.

St. Vincent Hospital (1888) P.O. Box 13508, 54307-3508. Tel: 920-433-0111; 920-433-8155; Fax: 920-431-3215. Email: cbecker@smg.hshs.org. Web: www.stvgb.org. Thomas R. Bayer, COO; Ms. Cynthia L. Becker, Dir. Pastoral Care; Sisters Paulette Hupfauf, O.S.F., Chap.; Monica Bongert, O.S.F., Chap.; Marilyn Herr, O.S.F., Chap.; John Viste, Chap.; Barb Malueg, Chap. Hospital Sisters of the Third Order of St. Francis. Bassinets 24; Bed Capacity 547; Patients Assisted Annually 98,303; Total Staff 1,693.

ANTIGO. *Langlade Hospital - Hotel Dieu of St. Joseph of Antigo Wisconsin*, 112 E. 5th Ave., 54409. Tel: 715-623-2331; Fax: 715-623-9359. Email: jbricco@langhosp.org; rhsj@antigopro.net. Web: www.langladehospital.org. Sr. Dolores Demulling, Mission & Philosophy Advocate & Trustee, Dir. of LeRoyer Hospice; Mr. David Schneider, Exec. Dir.; Sisters Jean Bricco, Dir. Pastoral Care, Trustee & Contact Person; Adele Demulling, R.H.S.J., Supr., Coord. LeRoyer Hospice; Rev. Omer C. Kelley, Part-time Chap. (Retired). Religious Hospitallers of St. Joseph. Bed Capacity 25; Total Assisted Annually 80,000; Total Staff 550.

Religious Hospitalliers of St. Joseph (1636) Sisters Res.: 650 Langlade Rd., 55409. Tel: 715-623-4615; Fax: 715-623-4615. Email: rhsj@antigopro.net. Web: www.rhsj.org/. Sisters 3; Priests 1; Staff 525; Bed Capacity 25; Patients Assisted Annually 75,000.

APPLETON. *St. Elizabeth Hospital, Inc.*, 1506 S. Oneida St., 54915-1305. Tel: 920-831-8913; Fax: 920-831-8916. Email: dschoono@affinityhealth.org. Web: www.affinityhealth.org. Daniel Neufelder, CEO; Travis Andersen, Pres.; Revs. Karin Derenne, Dir. Clinical Svcs. & Clinical Ethics; Roy Rogers, Chap.; Calvin Reyburn, Chap.; Sisters Gerri Krautkramer, Chap.; Anne Arthur Klinker, Chap.; Annette Johnson, Chap.; Teri Wagner, Chap.; Debra Langacker, Contact Person.

St. Elizabeth Hospital, Inc., Corporate Sponsors: Wheaton Franciscan Services, Inc. (Wheaton, IL) and Affinity Health System (Menasha, WI) Franciscan Sisters, Daughters of the Sacred Hearts of Jesus and Mary (Wheaton, IL) 1; Bed Capacity 205; Total Staff 1,139; Patients Assisted Annually 148,059.

CHILTON. *Calumet Medical Center, Inc.*, 614 Memorial Dr., 53014-1568. Tel: 920-849-2386; Fax: 920-849-7510. Timothy Richman, Pres.& CEO. Email: timothy.richman@affinity.org. Affinity Health System, Spiritual Services Dept: Chaplain support from St. Elizabeth Hospital, Appleton. Bed Capacity 25; Total Staff 187; Patients Served 33,967.

MANITOWOC. *Holy Family Memorial, Inc.* (1898) 2300 Western Ave., P.O. Box 1450, 54221-1450. Tel: 920-320-2011; Fax: 920-320-3042. Email: services@hfmhealth.org. Web: www.hfmhealth.org. Mr. Mark Herzog, Pres. & CEO; Rev. Joel Szydlowski, O.F.M., Dir. Pastoral Care & Chap.; John Vincent, Chap.; Rahlf Proulx, Chap.; Molly La Fond, Chap. Franciscan Sisters of Christian Charity 9; Licensed Beds 167; Maternity Rooms 7; Patients Assisted Annually 202,778; Total Staff 1,225.

OSHKOSH. *Mercy Medical Center of Oshkosh, Inc.*, 500 S. Oakwood Rd., P.O. Box 3370, 54903-3370. Tel: 920-223-0504; Fax: 920-223-0508. Email: wcalhoun@affinityhealth.org. Web: www.affinityhealth.org. Daniel Neufelder, CEO; Bill Calhoun, COO; Sr. Johnette Marek, S.S.M., Chap.; Revs. Karin Derenne, Dir., Spiritual Svcs. & Clinical Ethics; Phil Dewitt, Chap.; Donna Greischar, Chap.; Ronald Michels, Chap.

Mercy Medical Center of Oshkosh, Inc. Corporate Sponsors: Ministry Health Care, Inc. (Milwaukee, WI) and Affinity Health System (Menasha, WI). Sisters of the Sorrowful Mother 1; Bed Capacity 162; Total Staff 828; Bassinets 25; Patients Assisted Annually 91,526.

STURGEON BAY. **Door County Memorial Hospital* (1943) 323 S. 18th Ave., 54235-1495. Tel: 920-743-5566; Fax: 920-743-8165. Email: Gerald.Worrick@ministryhealth.org. Web: www.ministryhealth.org. Gerald M. Worrick, Pres. & CEO; Susan Johnson, Contact Person & Spiritual Svcs. Dir. Corporate Sponsor: Ministry Health Care, Inc. (Milwaukee, WI); Sponsored by Sisters of the Sorrowful Mother. Bed Capacity, Critical Access Hospital 25; Patients Assisted Annually 179,612; Total Staff 650.

[H] PROTECTIVE INSTITUTIONS

GREEN BAY. *Libertas Treatment Center for Chemically Dependent*, 1701 Dousman St., 54303-3282. Tel: 920-498-8600; Fax: 920-496-2027. Joan M. Coffman, Pres. & CEO; Patrick W. Ryan, Prog. Dir. St. Joseph's Hospital of the Hospital Sisters of the Third Order of St. Francis., Hospital Sisters Health System. Bed Capacity 24; Patients Assisted Annually 9,514; Total Staff 35.

McClosky Program, Inc., 2560 Shawano Ave., P.O. Box 10357, 54313. Tel: 920-434-8208; Fax: 920-662-0047. Sr. Barbara Jean Arnsmeyer, O.L.C., Dir. A Community based residential facility for women 18 years old and over who are pregnant or in a crisis situation and in need of transitional supervision and guidance. Needs addressed are personal and family problems. Also, shelter offered during crisis or unemployment. Bed Capacity 4; Total Staff 2; Total Assisted 4.

Our Lady of Charity Center, Inc., 2560 Shawano Ave., P.O. Box 10357, 54313. Tel: 920-434-8208; Fax: 920-662-0047. Sr. Donna Truckey, Admin. Total Staff 2; Total Assisted 2.

OSHKOSH. *The Convent Project, Inc.*, 449 High Ave., 54901. Tel: 920-233-1894. Email: baker8983@sbcglobal.net. Barbara Baker, Treas. For victims of domestic abuse. Bed Capacity 32; Total Assisted 59; Total Staff 1.

[I] HOMES FOR AGED

GREEN BAY. *The McCormick Memorial Home for the Aged* (1921) 212 Iroquois Ave., 54301-1918. Tel: 920-437-0883; Fax: 920-437-2696. Email: jim@mmhgb.com. James Genrich, Admin.; Rev. Michael R. Koch, Chap. (Retired). Bed Capacity 56; Total Staff 27; Nursing Staff 6; Residents 44; Total Assisted Annually 62.

KAUKAUNA. *St. Paul Elder Services, Inc.*, 316 E. Fourteenth St., 54130. Tel: 920-766-6020; Fax: 920-766-7945. Email: jimf@stpaulelders.org. Web: stpaulelders.org. James J. Fett, Pres.; Sondra Norder, COO & Admin. Bed Capacity 218; Total Assisted Annually 305; Total Staff 350.

St. Paul Home, 316 E. 14th St., 54130. Tel: 920-766-6020; Fax: 920-766-9161. Rev. Frank N. Weber, Asst. Chap. Bed Capacity 129.

St. Paul Villa, 312 E. Fourteenth St., 54130. Tel: 920-766-6020; Fax: 920-766-7945. Total Apartments 89.

MANITOWOC. *Felician Village* Tel: 920-684-7171; Fax: 920-684-0240. Web: www.felicianvillage.org.

Felician Village Inc. dba The Gardens at Felician Village 1635 S. 21st St., 54220-5652. Tel: 920-684-7171; Fax: 920-684-0240. Email: pkaldor@felicianvillage.org. Web: felicianvillage.org. Patricia Kaldor, CEO. Apartments 122.

St. Mary's Home for the Aged, Inc. dba St. Mary's at Felician Village 1635 S. 21st St., 54220-5652. Tel: 920-684-7171; Fax: 920-684-0240. Email: pkaldor@felicianvillage.org. Web: felicianvillage.org. Patricia Kaldor, CEO. Sisters 5; Aged Residents 84.

St. Mary's Home for the Aged, Inc. dba The Court at Felician Village 1635 S. 21st St., 54220-5652. Tel: 920-684-7171; Fax: 920-684-0240. Email: pkaldor@felicianvillage.org. Web: felicianvillage.org. Patricia Kaldor, CEO. Total Apartments 48.

St. Mary's Home for the Aged, Inc. dba The Villas at Felician Village 1635 S. 21st St., 54220-5652. Tel: 920-684-7171; Fax: 920-684-0240. Email: pkaldor@felicianvillage.org. Web: felicianvillage.org. Beds 32.

NEENAH. *Assisi Homes of Neenah, Inc.* (1989) 210 Byrd Ave., 54956. Tel: 920-729-1771; Fax: 920-729-1797. Web: www.fm-inc.org. *Assisi Homes of Neenah, Inc.*, 26W171 Roosevelt Rd., Wheaton, IL 60187. Susan M. Dillberg, Chm. & Contact. (An independent living community for Seniors.) Total Staff 3; Total in Residence 38; Housing Units 38.

Villa St. Clare, Inc. (1993) 130 Byrd Ave., 54946. Tel: 920-722-5100; Fax: 920-722-5171. Web: www.wfs-inc.org. 26W71 Roosevelt Rd., Wheaton, IL 60189. Susan M. Dillberg, Chm. & Contact. Special care facility, affordable housing with supportive accommodations in an independent setting for seniors 55+. Bed Capacity 45; Total in Residence 41; Total Assisted 45; Total Staff 31; Housing Units 45.

NEW LONDON. *St. Joseph Residence, Inc., New London*, 107 E. Beckert Rd., 54961. Tel: 920-982-5354; Fax: 920-982-5420. Robert Fietsch, CEO. Residents 107.

Trinity Terrace, 107 E. Beckert Rd., 54961. Tel: 920-982-9354. Total in Residence 32.

Marion Heights Apartments, 101 E. Beckert Rd., 54961. Tel: 920-982-5354. Residents 26.

St. Joseph Residence - The Washington Center, Inc., 500 Washington St., 54961. Tel: 920-982-9200. Robert Fietsch, CEO. Apartments 33.

NIAGARA. *Maryhill Manor (SNF)*, 501 Madison Ave., 54151. Tel: 715-251-3172; Fax: 715-251-1193. Email: maryhill@borderlandnet.net. Web: www.maryhillmanor.org. Joan Roehrig, Admin., Pres. & CEO. Sponsored by School Sisters of St. Francis, Milwaukee. Bed Capacity 75; Nursing Care Residents 75; Total Staff 113; Total Assisted Annually 175.

[J] MONASTERIES AND RESIDENCES OF PRIESTS AND BROTHERS

GREEN BAY. *St. Mary of the Angels Friary*, 645 S. Irwin Ave., 54301-3303. Tel: 920-437-7411; 920-437-1979 (Res.); Fax: 920-437-7411. Email: RJTOFM@aol.com. Bro. Paul Belco, Guardian. Franciscan Friars, Assumption of the Blessed Virgin Mary Province (Order of Friars Minor). Priests 6; Brothers 3. In Res. Revs. Thomas Wojciechowski, O.F.M.; Bede Hepnar; Joel Szydlowski, O.F.M.; Bro. Joseph Molinari, O.F.M. *St. Thomas More*, 650 S. Irwin Ave., 54301. Fax: 920-432-1562. Administrators 1; Lay Teachers 15; Students 161.

APPLETON. *St. Fidelis Friary*, 1100 N. Ballard Rd., 54911-5100. Tel: 920-954-8954; Fax: 920-954-1095. Web: www.thecapuchins.org. Revs. William Alcuin, O.F.M.Cap. (Retired); Silas Baumann, O.F.M.Cap. (Retired); David Belongea, O.F.M.Cap.; Donald Brody, O.F.M.Cap. (Retired); Ralph Fellenz, O.F.M.Cap. (Retired); Leopold Gleissner, O.F.M.Cap. (Retired); Gilbert Hemauer, O.F.M.Cap. (Retired); Kieran Hickey, O.F.M. (Retired); John Francis Samsa, O.F.M.Cap. (Retired); Giles Soyka, O.F.M.Cap. (Retired); Ambrose Simon, O.F.M.Cap. (Retired); Robert Udulutsch, O.F.M.Cap. (Retired); Ellis Zimmer, O.F.M.Cap. (Retired); Bros. John Gau, O.F.M.Cap., (Retired); Conrad Heinen, O.F.M.Cap., (Retired); Rob Roemer, O.F.M.Cap., Local Minister; Kenneth Stewart, O.F.M.Cap., (Retired); Cyrus Toschik, O.F.M.Cap., (Retired). Order of Friars Minor Capuchin. Priests 13; Brothers 5; Total Staff 5.

St. Joseph Friary, 404 W. Lawrence St., 54911-5855. Tel: 920-734-7195; Fax: 920-734-0227. Web: www.saintjosephparish.org. Revs. James P. Leary, O.F.M.Cap., Pastor; David J. Funk, O.F.M.Cap., Assoc. Pastor. Order of Friars Minor Capuchin.

DE PERE. *St. Joseph Priory*, 103 Grant St., 54115-2001. Tel: 920-403-3572 (Office); Fax: 920-403-4430. Revs. James T. Baraniak, O.Praem.; John Bostwick, O.Praem.; Rowland C. De Peaux, O.Praem.; Kenneth DeGroot, O.Praem.; Conrad J. Kratz, O.Praem., House Supr.; Alfred A. McBride, O.Praem.; Brendan J. McKeough, O.Praem.; Gery G. Meehan, O.Praem.; Brian J. Prunty, O.Praem.; Joseph S. Rekasi, O.Praem.; Peter J. Renard, O. Praem.; Timothy D. Shillcox, O.Praem. Residence for Norbertine Community. Priests 11.

St. Norbert Abbey (1898) 1016 N. Broadway, 54115-2697. Tel: 920-337-4300; Fax: 920-337-4328. Email: john.kastenholz@snc.edu. Web: www.norbertines.org. Rt. Revs. Gary J. Neville, O.Praem., J.C.D., Abbot; Jerome G. Tremel, O.Praem., Abbot Emeritus; Revs. Bartholomew A. Agar, O.Praem.; Robert E. Carson, O.Praem.; Xavier G. Colavechio, O.Praem.; Joseph R. Coopmans, O.Praem.; Salvatore H. Cuccia, O.Praem.; Mark D. Falcone, O.Praem; Angelo J. Feldkamp, O.Praem.; Robert M. Feller, O.Praem.; Roderick R. Fenzl, O.Praem.; Robert K. Finnegan, O.Praem.; Michael F. Frisch, O.Praem.; Very Rev. James B. Herring, O.Praem., J.C.D., Prior; Revs. Gilbert H. Jacobs, O.Praem.; John P. Kastenholz, O.Praem., Treas.; David R. McElroy, O.Praem.; Gilbert Mihayli, O.Praem.; Conan P. Mulrooney, O.Praem.; James P. Neilson, O.Praem.; William H. Ribbens, O.Praem.; Stephen J. Rossey, O.Praem.; John M. Tourangeau, O.Praem.; Roman R. Vanasse, O.Praem.; Steven J. Vanden Boogard, O.Praem.; Michael J. Weber, O.Praem.; Bros. Robert J. Craanen, O.Praem.; Steven J. Herro, O.Praem.

The Premonstratensian Fathers

NORBERT & CO., a nominee of The Premonstratensian Fathers, Norbertine Fathers

St. Norbert Abbey, Inc.

Augustine Stewardship Fund Trust

Norbertine Retirement Fund Trust

St. Norbert Abbey Seminary and Education Fund Trust

The Walnut Markets, Inc.

Los Amigos del Peru, Inc. Canons Regular of Premontre. Brothers 3; Priests 57; Priests 27; Novices 8.

Priests serving in foreign countries: Rev. John P. MacCarthy, O.Praem., Archdiocese of Iquitos, Peru, Santa Clotilde, Rio Napo, Apartado 216, Iquitos, Peru. Tel: 011-51-94-25-1932; Fax: 011-51-94-25-1922.

NEW HOLSTEIN. *Salvatorian Residence*, 1303 Milwaukee Dr., 53061-1443. Tel: 920-898-5898; Fax: 920-898-4736. Brothers 2. *Salvatorian Public Relations*, Salvatorian Center, 53062. Tel: 920-898-5605; Fax: 920-898-4736. Rev. Gregory Coulthard, S.D.S. *Salvatorian Mission Warehouse*, 53061. Tel: 920-898-5898; Fax: 920-898-4736. Bro. Regis Fust, S.D.S., Dir. Mission Supply Prog.

OSHKOSH. *Community of Our Lady* (1968) (Diocesan Pious Union), 2804 Oakwood Ln., 54904-8406. Tel: 920-233-5633; Fax: 920-233-5604. Very Rev. Regis N. Barwig, Prior; Revs. Eugene E. Kalinski; Augustine Serafini; Bro. Joseph G. Le Sanche. Priests 3; Brothers 1.

PULASKI. *Assumption of B.V.M. Friary* (1887) 143 E. Pulaski St., P.O. Box 100, 54162-0100. Tel: 920-822-8125; Fax: 920-822-5423. Email: blwofm@aol.com. Web: www.ofm.abvm.org. (Order of Friars Minor). *Friary*, 54162. Tel: 920-822-8125; Fax: 920-822-5423. Revs. Anthony Chojnacki, O.F.M., Vice-Guardian; Sebastian Kus, O.F.M.; Joachim Swarick, O.F.M. (Retired); Melvin Wierzbicki, O.F.M.; Brendan Wroblewski, O.F.M., Guardian; Bros. James Buda, O.F.M.; Anthony Gancarz, O.F.M.; Andrew Giba, O.F.M.; Henry Kolbok, O.F.M.; Jude Lustyk, O.F.M.; Austin Mysliwiec, O.F.M.; Gerald Tokarz, O.F.M.; Peter Rydza, O.F.M.; Robert Sembrat, O.F.M.; Gregory Stasinski, O.F.M.; David Typek, O.F.M.; Didacus Weber. *Villa Alverna*, N. 11450 Rademaker Rd., Wausaukee, 54177. Tel: 715-732-6612.

Outside of Diocese: Revs. James Esser, O.F.M.; Adam Szufel, O.F.M.; Patrick M. Gawrylewski, O.F.M.; Gerald A. Prusakowski, O.F.M.; Everard Scesney, O.F.M.

[K] CONVENTS AND RESIDENCES FOR SISTERS

GREEN BAY. *The Sisters of St. Francis of the Holy Cross, Inc.* (1881) 3110 Nicolet Dr., 54311-7212. Tel: 920-468-1828; Fax: 920-468-1207. Email: CommSecretary@gbfranciscans.org. Web: www.gbfranciscans.org. Sr. Donna Koch, Pres. Sisters 65; In Diocese 65.

Union of Our Lady of Charity United States Province (1882) 2560 Shawano Ave., P.O. Box 10357, 54307-0357. Tel: 920-434-8208; Fax: 920-662-0047. Web: www.nauolc.org. Sr. Donna Truckey, Supr. Sisters 8.

DENMARK. *Monastery of the Holy Name of Jesus, Ltd.* (1992) Discalced Carmelite Nuns, *Monastery of the Holy Name of Jesus, Ltd.*, 6100 Pepper Rd., 54208. Tel: 920-863-5055. Email: holynamecarmel@catholic.org. Sr. Mary Elizabeth, O.C.D., Prioress. Total 11.

MANITOWOC. *St. Clare Convent*, 3 Riverview Dr., 54220. Tel: 920-682-5145. Sr. Michael Majeskie, Dir. Franciscan Sisters of Christian Charity. Sisters 7.

St. Francis Convent (1869) 6835 Calumet Ave., 54220. Tel: 920-684-7884; Fax: 920-682-4195. Web: www.sl.edu/FSCC. Sr. June Smith, Sec. Franciscan Sisters of Christian Charity. Sisters 38.

Holy Family Convent of Franciscan Sisters of Christian Charity (1869) Motherhouse and Novitiate dedicated to the Holy Family, 2409 S. Alverno Rd., 54220-9320. Tel: 920-682-7728; Fax: 920-682-4195. Email: slouise@fscc-calledtobe.org. Web: www.fscc-calledtobe.org. Revs. Nathan Jaskulski, O.F.M., Chap.; Samuel D. Jadin, O.Praem., Chap.; Sr. Louise Hembrecht, Community Dir. Sisters 307; In Diocese 239; Novices 3; Postulants 1; Total in Residence 157.

OSHKOSH. *SSM Franciscan Courts*, 815 S. Westhaven Dr., 54904-7978. Tel: 920-426-2440; Fax: 920-426-3196. Email: jbelongie@ssm-courts.org. Sisters of the Sorrowful Mother. Sisters 41.

SSM US/Caribbean Provincial Administration, 815 S. Westhaven Dr., Ste. 100, 54904. Sr. Marilyn Vollmer, S.S.M., Provincial.

Sisters of the Sorrowful Mother, 2185 Abbey Ave., 54904. Tel: 920-426-1757.

Sisters of the Sorrowful Mother, Holy Cross Community, 800 S. Westhaven Dr., 54904. Tel: 920-385-1627.

Sisters of the Sorrowful Mother, Epiphany House, 1145 Devonshire Dr., 54904. Tel: 920-303-1432.

Sisters of the Sorrowful Mother, 103 E. Irving, 54901-4617. Tel: 920-426-0441.

[L] SHRINES

CHILTON. *St. Peregrine Shrine* 62 E. Main St., 53014. Tel: 920-849-9363; Fax: 920-849-7270. Rev. Robert Kollath, Pastor Good Shepherd, Chilton.

NEW FRANKEN. *The Shrine of Our Lady of Good Help, Inc.*, 4047 Chapel Dr., 54229. Tel: 920-866-2571. Email: info@shrineofourladyofgoodhelp.com. Web: www.shrineofourladyofgoodhelp.com. P.O. Box 23825, 54305-3825. Revs. Peter Stryker, C.P.M., Rector; Jewel Aytona, C.P.M., Chap.

[M] RETREAT HOUSES

APPLETON. *Monte Alverno Retreat & Spirituality Center*, 1000 N. Ballard Rd., 54911-5198. Tel: 920-733-8526; Fax: 920-733-7562. Email: montealverno@juno.com. Web: www.montealverno.org. Revs. Keith Clark, O.F.M.Cap., Dir.; Adrian Staehler, O.F.M.Cap.; Bro. John Kocian, O.F.M.Cap.; Sr. Marsaia Kaster; Bro. Carl Schaefer, O.F.M.Cap. The Province of St. Joseph of the Capuchin Order, Inc. Priests 2; Brothers 2; Retreatants Annually 3,000; Total in Residence 4; Total Staff 17.

CHAMBERS ISLAND. *Holy Name Retreat House* (1951) 1825 Riverside Dr., 54301. Mailing Address: P.O. Box 23825, 54305-3825. Tel: 920-437-7531; Fax: 920-437-0694. Mrs. Doris V. Vincent, Assoc. Dir. Admin.; Barbara Conder, Exec. Dir. Conducted by Diocese of Green Bay.

DENMARK. *The Bridge-Between Retreat Center, Inc.*, 4471 Flaherty Ln., 54208. Tel: 920-864-7230; Fax: 920-864-7044. Email: info@bridge-between.com. Web: www.bridge-between.com. Mary Failey, Business Mgr. & Contact Person; Sr. Caroline Sullivan, O.P., Dir.

DE PERE. *Norbertine Center for Spirituality* (1979) (An Apostolate of the Norbertine Fathers), St. Norbert Abbey, 1016 N. Broadway, 54115-2697. Tel: 920-337-4315; Fax: 920-337-4385. Email: norbertinecenter@yahoo.com. Web: www.norbertines.org. Rev. Conrad J. Kratz, O.Praem., Dir. Total in Residence 1; Total Staff 6.

MENASHA. *Mount Tabor Center* (1983) 522 2nd St., 54952-3112. Tel: 920-722-8918; Fax: 920-722-8918. Email: mttabor1@sbcglobal.net. Web: mttabor.net. Eden Foord, Dir.; Katherine Foord, Asst. Dir. Total Staff 7.

OSHKOSH. *Jesuit Retreat House* (1961) 4800 Fahrnwald Rd., 54902-7598. Tel: 920-231-9060; Fax: 920-231-9094. Email: office@jesuitretreathouse.org. Web: www.jesuitretreathouse.org. Revs. John Schwantes, S.J., Dir.; Eugene Donahue, S.J., Retreat Dir.; Sr. Kerry Larkin, O.S.M., Assoc. Dir.; Rev. Thomas Schloemer, S.J., Retreat Dir. Society of Jesus.

SHAWANO. *Camp Tekawitha Retreat and Conference Center, Inc.*, W5248 Lake Dr., 54166. Tel: 920-272-8162. Email: eblumreich@gbdioc.org. Web: www.gbdioc.org. P.O. Box 23825, 54305-3825. Eric Blumereich, Dir. & Contact Person; Mrs. Doris V.

Vincent, Assoc. Dir. Admin.

[N] NEWMAN CENTERS

GREEN BAY. *Ecumenical Center-UWGB* P.O. Box 23825, 54305-3825. Tel: 920-366-3661; Fax: 920-465-0128. Email: info@ecumenical-center.org. Web: www.ccm-uwgb.blogspot.com. Rev. Daniel J. Schuster, Chap.; Carol Jensen, Contact Person.

Lawrence University Newman Center , (Appleton)

University of Wisconsin Oshkosh, Newman Center 800 Elmwood Ave., Oshkosh, 54901-3518. Tel: 920-233-5555; Fax: 920-233-5556. Rev. Quentin A. Mann, Chap.

[O] MISCELLANEOUS LISTINGS

GREEN BAY. *The Catholic Foundation for the Diocese of Green Bay, Inc.* (1998) 1825 Riverside Dr., 54301. Mailing Address: P.O. Box 22128, 54305-2128. Tel: 920-272-8173; Fax: 920-272-8435. Email: catholicfoundation@gbdioc.org. Web: www.catholicfoundationgb.org. Cindi Brawner, Exec. Dir.

The Diocesan Charismatic Renewal Center, 1087-A Kellog St., 54303. Tel: 920-405-1960. Email: dcrc@att.net. Judy Goolsbey, Office Mgr.

St. Francis Xavier Investment Corp. (1998) 1825 Riverside Dr., 54301. Mailing Address: P.O. Box 23825, 54305-3825. Tel: 920-437-7531, Ext. 8206; Fax: 920-437-0694. Web: gbdioc.org.

Green Bay Area Catholic High School Foundation, L.T.D., P.O. Box 23825, 54305-3825. Tel: 920-272-8166. Mr. Thomas Olejniczak, Pres.

Green Bay Diocese Cemetery Corporation, 2121 Riverside Dr., P.O. Box 23825, 54305-3825. Tel: 920-432-7585; Fax: 920-432-0425. Email: tbasten@gbdioc.org. Web: www.gbdioc.org. Ms. Tammy Basten, Dir., Facilities & Properties.

St. John the Evangelist Homeless Shelter, Inc., 411 St. John St., P.O. Box 1743, 54305. Tel: 920-436-9765. Email: mary.kelly@stjohnhomelessshelter.org. Mary Kelly, Exec. Dir.

St. Joseph Real Estate Services Corporation, Diocesan Central Offices, P.O. Box 23825, 54305-3825. Tel: 920-272-8260; Fax: 920-437-0694. Email: tbasten@gbdioc.org. Web: www.gbdioc.org. Ms. Tammy Basten, Dir., Facilities & Properties.

A New Genesis (ANG) An Association of the Faithful, P.O. Box 8642, 54308. Tel: 920-729-4562; 715-752-3374; Fax: 920-729-4572. Email: dbaumann@tcces.k12.wi.us. Web: groups.yahoo.com/group/angmembers. Sr. Diane Baumann, A.N.G., Coord. Total Members 25; In Diocese 22; Vowed in Diocese 17.

Notre Dame de la Baie Foundation, Inc., 610 Maryhill Dr., 54303. Tel: 920-429-6100; Fax: 920-429-6140. Robert C. Pauly, Pres.

Oratory of St. Joseph Institute of Christ the King, 211 N. Maple Ave., 54303. Tel: 920-437-9660; Fax: 920-437-5154. Email: stjoseph@institute-christ-king.org. Web: institute-christ-king.org/greenbay/. Rev. Canon Andreas Hellmann, Rector.

Sacred Heart Seminary Corporation, P.O. Box 23825, 54305-3825. Tel: 920-437-7531; Fax: 920-435-1330. Deacon Timothy G. Reilly, Gen. Dir. & Diocese Curia; Very Rev. John F. Doerfler, S.T.D., J.C.L., Chancellor.

Society for Faith and Children's Education, Inc., 423 Woodfield Dr., 54313. Tel: 920-434-2420. Email: sfacegreenbay@yahoo.com. Web: www.sfacemission.org. June L. Ingold, Pres. & Contact Person; Rev. Savio J. Samala, Sec. & Treas.

St. Luke Benefit & Insurance Services Corp., 1825 Riverside Dr., P.O. Box 23825, 54305-3825. Tel: 920-272-8216; Fax: 920-437-9296. Email: jmathein@gbdioc.org. Web: www.gbdioc.org. Jacquelyn Mathein, Contact Person.

**Starboard Media Foundation, Inc. dba Relevant Radio* 1496 Bellevue St., Ste. 202, 54311. Tel: 877-291-0123; Fax: 920-465-9986. Web: www.relevantradio.com. Margaret Kleinschmidt, O.C.D.S., Exec. Asst. to CEO. Total Staff 45.

Teens Encounter Christ (TEC), Green Bay Chapter, P.O. Box 23825, 54305-3825. Tel: 920-437-7531; Fax: 920-272-8431. Email: tec1978@anchorofhopetec.org. Rev. Thomas Long, Spiritual Dir.

St. Therese of the Little Flower, Inc., 1825 Riverside Dr., 54305-3825. Tel: 920-272-8206; Fax: 920-437-0694. Web: gbdioc.com.

St. Thomas More Society of the Roman Catholic Diocese of Green Bay, Inc., P.O. Box 23825, 54305-3825. Web: www.stmsgb.com. Paul P. Umentum, Pres.

ANTIGO. *Religious Hospitallers of St. Joseph Health Corporation "RHSJ Health Corporation"*, 112 E. Fifth Ave., 54409. Tel: 715-623-2331; Fax: 715-623-9440.

APPLETON. *Catholic Youth Expeditions, Inc.*, 1000 W. Wisconsin Ave., 54914. Tel: 920-312-0070. Email: fatherquinn@cyexpeditions.org. Web: www.cyexpeditions.org. Rev. Quentin A. Mann, Chm. & Treas.

St. Elizabeth Hospital Community Foundation, Inc., 1506 S. Oneida St., 54915-1397. Tel: 920-831-1475; Fax: 920-738-2061. Daniel Neufelder, CEO Affinity Health System; Tonya L. Dedering, Exec. Dir. Franciscan Sisters, Daughters of the Sacred Heart of Jesus and Mary (Wheaton, IL) & Ministry Health Care (Sisters of the Sorrowful Mother).

Global Outreach, Inc. (1994) 4815 Whitetail Way, 54914. Tel: 920-734-5967. Email: boryczkabb@sbcglobal.net. Web: www.globaloutreachprogram.com. Barbara Tota-Boryczka, Exec. Dir.; Jerry Greany, Pres.; Tom Kropidlowski, Vice Pres.; Gary Elmer, Treas.; Jerry Greany, Co-Treas.; Connie Babler, Sec.

DE PERE. *Augustine Stewardship Fund Trust* (1986) 1016 N. Broadway, 54115-2697. Tel: 920-337-4300; Fax: 920-337-4328. Email: john.kastenholz@snc.edu. Web: www.norbertines.org.

Canons Regular of Magnovarad, Ltd. (1981) 1016 N. Broadway, 54115-2697. Tel: 920-337-4300; Fax: 920-337-4328. Email: rkfinn@netnet.net. Web: www.norbertines.org. Rt. Rev. Jerome G. Tremel, O.Praem., Pres.; Revs. Joseph S. Rekasi, O.Praem.; Robert K. Finnegan, O.Praem., Sec. & Treas.

Los Amigos del Peru, Inc. (1991) 1016 N. Broadway St., 54115-2697. Tel: 920-337-4300; Fax: 920-337-4328. Email: john.kastenholz@snc.edu. Web: www.norbertines.org.

NORBERT & CO. (1978) A nominee of The Premonstratensian Fathers, 1016 N. Broadway, 54115-2697. Tel: 920-337-4300; Fax: 920-337-4328. Email: john.kastenholz@snc.edu. Web: www.norbertines.org. Rt. Rev. Gary J. Neville, O.Praem., J.C.D., Abbot; Very Rev. James B. Herring, O.Praem., J.C.D., Prior; Rev. John P. Kastenholz, O.Praem., Sec.& Treas.

St. Norbert Abbey Seminary and Education Fund Trust (1989) 1016 N. Broadway, 54115-2697. Tel: 920-337-4300; Fax: 920-337-4328. Email: john.kastenholz@snc.edu. Web: www.norbertines.org.

Norbertine Generalate, Inc. (1989) 1016 N. Broadway, 54115-2697. Tel: 920-337-4300; Fax: 920-337-4328. Email: rkfinn@netnet.net. Web: www.premontre.org. Rt. Revs. Thomas A. Handgratinger, O.Praem., Pres., Rome, Italy; Gary J. Neville, O.Praem., J.C.D., Vice Pres.; Rev. Robert K. Finnegan, O.Praem., Sec. & Treas.

Norbertine Retirement Fund Trust (1986) 1016 N. Broadway, 54115-2697. Tel: 920-337-4300; Fax: 920-337-4328. Email: john.kastenholz@snc.edu. Web: www.norbertines.org.

Thea Bowman Spirituality Center, Inc. (2001) 1016 N. Broadway, 54115. Tel: 920-337-4300; Fax: 920-337-4328. Email: gjn@netnet.net. Rt. Rev. Gary J. Neville, O.Praem., J.C.D., Abbot.

DEERBROOK. **Living Waters International, Inc.* (1996) N7544 County Rd. S., 54424. Tel: 715-627-4782; Fax: 715-627-4782. Email: livingh2o@livingwatersinternational.org. Web: www.livingwatersinternational.org. Dr. Stephen L. Zimmerman, Ph.D., Pres.

MANITOWOC. *Franciscan Sisters of Christian Charity HealthCare Ministry, Inc.* (1985) 1415 S. Rapids Rd., 54220-9302. Tel: 920-684-7071; Fax: 920-684-6417. Email: lwolf@fhcm.org. Web: www.fhcm.org. Sr. Laura J. Wolf, O.S.F., Pres.

MENASHA. **Affinity Health System*, 1570 Midway Pl., 54952. Tel: 920-720-1713; Fax: 920-720-1720. Email: dneufeld@affinityhealth.org. Web: www.affinityhealth.org. Daniel Neufelder, Pres. & CEO. Sponsored by Wheaton Franciscan Services, Inc. (Wheaton, IL) and Ministry Health Care, Inc. (Milwaukee, WI).

**Network Health System, Inc.*, 1570 Midway Pl., 54952-8005. Tel: 920-720-1734. Web: www.affinityhealth.org. Daniel Neufelder, CEO. Total Staff 1,109; Total Assisted 143,905.

NEENAH. *St. Mary High School Foundation, Inc.*, 1050 Zephyr Dr., 54956-1389. Tel: 920-722-7796; Fax: 920-722-5940. Web: www.smc.k12.wi.us.

OSHKOSH. *Christ Child Society, Oshkosh Chapter, c/o St. Raphael the Archangel*, 830 Westhaven Rd., 54904. Tel: 920-232-9453. Marie Combs, Contact Person.

SSM US/Caribbean Provincial Administration, 815 S. Westhaven Dr., Ste. 100, 54904-7978. Tel: 920-230-2040; Fax: 920-230-2041. Sr. Marilyn Vollmer, S.S.M., Provincial. Tel: 920-230-2045.

STURGEON BAY. *Christ Child Society of Door County* (1996) P.O. Box 572, 54235. Tel: 920-823-2200. Diane Stracka, Pres.

[P] CLOSED AND MERGED PARISHES

GREEN BAY. *Green Bay Diocesan Archives*, 1910 S. Webster Ave., P.O. Box 23825, 54305-3825. Tel: 920-437-7531, Ext. 8186; Fax: 920-435-1330. Email: jledoux@gbdioc.org. Web: www.gbdioc.org. Parish sacramental records for parishes that have closed or merged can be found at the locations listed below. As the location of sacramental records can change periodically, inquiries for records of parishes on this list should be directed to the above address.

St. Louis, Abrams Please see St. Maximilian Kolbe, Sobieski.

St. Joseph, Alverno Tel: 920-726-4228; Fax: 920-726-4229. Please see St. Thomas the Apostle, Newton.

St. Hyacinth, Antigo Please see SS. Mary & Hyacinth, Antigo.

St. Mary, Antigo Please see SS. Mary & Hyacinth, Antigo.

St. Mary, Argonne Tel: 715-478-3396. Please see St. Joseph, Crandon.

St. Patrick, Askeaton Please see St. Clare Corp., Greenleaf.

St. Mary of the Lake, Baileys Harbor Please see Stella Maris, Egg Harbor.

St. Mary, Brillion Tel: 920-753-2535; Fax: 920-753-9802. Please see Holy Family, Brillion.

St. Charles Borromeo, Charlesburg Please see Good Shepherd, Chilton.

St. Martin, Charlestown Please see Good Shepherd, Chilton.

St. Joseph, Chase Please see St. Maximilian Kolbe, Sobieski.

St. Augustine, Chilton Please see Good Shepherd, Chilton.

St. Mary, Chilton Please see Good Shepherd, Chilton.

St Wendel, Cleveland Tel: 920-726-4228; Fax: 920-726-4229. Please see St. Thomas the Apostle, Newton.

St. John the Baptist, Coleman Tel: 920-897-3226; Fax: 920-897-4677. Please see St. Anne Parish, Corp., Coleman.

St. Francis of Assisi, Coleman Tel: 920-897-3226; Fax: 920-897-4677. Please see St. Anne Parish, Corp., Coleman.

SS. Francis-Wenceslaus, Coleman Please see St. Anne Parish Corp., Coleman.

Holy Angels, Darboy Tel: 920-788-7640; Fax: 920-788-7658. Please see Holy Spirit, Kimberly.

St. Boniface, De Pere Tel: 920-336-4033; Fax: 920-336-3910. Please see Our Lady of Lourdes, De Pere.

St. Joseph, De Pere Tel: 920-336-4033; Fax: 920-336-3910. Please see Our Lady of Lourdes, De Pere.

SS. Cyril and Methodius, Eaton Tel: 920-863-2593; Fax: 920-845-5180. Please see St. Thomas the Apostle, Humboldt.

St. John the Baptist, Egg Harbor Please see Stella Maris, Egg Harbor.

St. William, Eland Tel: 715-253-2050; Fax: 715-253-3020. Please see Holy Family-St. William, Wittenberg.

St. Paul, Fish Creek Please see Stella Maris, Egg Harbor.

Holy Marytrs of Gorcum, Green Bay See Prince of Peace, Green Bay.

St. Mary, Greenleaf Please see St. Clare Corp., Greenleaf.

St. Michael, Hiles Tel: 715-478-3396. Please see St Joseph, Crandon.

St. Francis, Hollandtown Please see St. Katharine Drexel, Kaukauna.

Our Lady Queen of Peace, Humboldt Tel: 920-863-2593; Fax: 920-845-5180. Please see St. Thomas the Apostle, Humboldt.

St. Michael, Jacksonport Please see Stella Maris, Egg Harbor.

Holy Trinity, Jericho Please see Good Shepherd, Chilton.

Holy Trinity, Kasson Please see Holy Family, Brillion.

St. Aloysius, Kaukauna Please see St. Katharine Drexel, Kaukauna.

St. Mary of the Annunciation, Kaukauna Please see St. Katharine Drexel, Kaukauna.

Holy Name of Jesus, Kimberly Please see Holy Spirit, Kimberly.

St. George, King Tel: 715-258-3000; Fax: 715-258-5708. Please see St. Mary Magdalene, Waupaca.

St. Wenceslaus, Klondike Tel: 920-897-3226; Fax: 920-897-4677. Please see St. Anne Parish, Corp., Coleman.

St. Elizabeth, Kloten Please see Good Shepherd, Chilton.

St. John, Krok Tel: 920-863-8747; Fax: 920-863-5768. Please see St. Therese de Lisieux, Stangelville.

St. Stanislaus Kostka, Langlade Tel: 715-882-2551. Please see SS. James and Stanislaus, White Lake.

St. Charles Borromeo, Lena Tel: 920-829-5222. Please see Holy Cross, Lena.

Holy Cross, Lena Please see St. Anne Parish Corp., Coleman.

St. Peter, Lincoln Tel: 920-837-2852. Please see St. Peter and St. Hubert, Rosiere.
St. Andrew, Manitowoc Please see St. Francis of Assisi, Manitowoc.
St. Boniface, Manitowoc Please see St. Francis of Assisi, Manitowoc.
Holy Innocents, Manitowoc Please see St. Francis of Assisi, Manitowoc.
St. Mary, Manitowoc Please see St. Francis of Assisi, Manitowoc.
St. Paul, Manitowoc Please see St. Francis of Assisi, Manitowoc.
Sacred Heart, Manitowoc Please see St. Francis of Assisi, Manitowoc.
St. Patrick, Maple Grove Tel: 920-756-2535; Fax: 920-756-9802. Please see Holy Family, Brillion/ Reedsville.
St. Francis De Paul, Marchand (Duvall) Tel: 920-866-2410; Fax: 920-866-3591. Please see St. Louis, Dyckesville.
Our Lady of Lourdes, Marinette Tel: 715-735-9100; Fax: 715-735-9650. Please see Holy Family, Marinette.
Sacred Heart of Jesus, Marinette Tel: 715-735-9100; Fax: 715-735-9650. Please see Holy Family, Marinette.
St. Anthony, Marinette Tel: 715-735-9100; Fax: 715-735-9650. Please see Holy Family, Marinette.
St. Joseph, Marinette Tel: 715-735-9100; Fax: 715-735-9650. Please see Holy Family, Marinette.
Holy Family Church, Mattoon Please see St. Joseph-Holy Family, Phlox.
St. Joseph, Montpelier Tel: 920-863-8747; Fax: 920-863-5768. Please see St. Therese de Lisieux, Stangelville.
St. Joseph-St. John, Montpelier Tel: 920-863-8747; Fax: 920-863-5768. Please see St. Therese de Lisieux, Stangelville.
St. Mary, Namur Tel: 920-825-7555; Fax: 920-825-1492. Please see St. Francis and St. Mary, Brussels.
St, Joseph, Norman Tel: 920-776-1555; Fax: 920-776-1555. Please see St. Isidore the Farmer, Tisch Mills
St. Casimir, Northeim Tel: 920-726-4228; Fax: 920-726-4229. Please see St. Thomas the Apostle, Newton.
St. Joseph, Oconto Tel: 920-835-5900; Fax: 920-835-5907. Please see Holy Trinity, Oconto.
St. Peter, Oconto Tel: 920-835-5900; Fax: 920-835-5907. Please see Holy Trinity, Oconto.
St. John, Oshkosh Please see St. Jude the Apostle, Oshkosh.
St. Josaphat, Oshkosh Please see Most Blessed Sacrament, Oshkosh.
St. Mary, Oshkosh Please see Most Blessed Sacrament, Oshkosh.
St. Peter, Oshkosh Please see Most Blessed Sacrament, Oshkosh.
Sacred Heart, Oshkosh Please see St. Jude the Apostle, Oshkosh.
St. Vincent De Paul, Oshkosh Please see St. Jude the Apostle, Oshkosh.
St. Isidore, Osman Tel: 920-726-4228; Fax: 920-726-4229. Please see St. Thomas the Apostle, Newton.
Holy Trinity, Pine Grove See Prince of Peace, Green Bay.
St. Leo, Pound Tel: 920-897-3226; Fax: 920-897-4677. Please see St. Anne Parish, Corp., Coleman.
St. Mary, Reedsville Tel: 920-756-2535; Fax: 920-756-9802. Please see Holy Family, Brillion.
St. Mary-St. Patrick, Reedsville/ Maple Grove Tel: 920-756-2535; Fax: 920-756-9802. Please see Holy Family, Brillion.
St. Rosalia, Sister Bay Please see Stella Maris, Egg Harbor.
St. Adalbert, Slovan Tel: 920-837-7234; Fax: 920-837-2361. Please see Holy Trinity, Casco.
St. John Cantius, Sobieski Please see St. Maximilian Kolbe, Sobieski.
St. Joseph of the Lake, South Branch Tel: 715-799-3811; Fax: 715-799-5092. Please see St. Michael, Keshena.
Sacred Heart, Spruce Tel: 920-829-5222. Please see Holy Cross, Lena.
St. John the Baptist, St. John Tel: 920-989-1515; Fax: 920-989-8585. Please see St. John-Sacred Heart, Sherwood.
St. Lawrence, Stangelville Tel: 920-863-8747; Fax: 920-863-5768. Please see St. Therese de Lisieux, Stangelville.
St. Mary, Stark Tel: 920-864-7641. Please see St. Mary, Glenmore.
St. Odile, Thiry Daems Tel: 920-866-9961. Please see St. Joseph, Champion.
Nativity of the BVM, Tisch Mills Tel: 920-776-1555; Fax: 920-776-1555. Please see St. Isidore the Farmer, Tisch Mills.
St. Martin, Tonet Tel: 920-866-9961. Please see St. Joseph, Champion.
Holy Redeemer-Sacred Heart, Two Rivers Tel: 920-793-4531; Fax: 920-793-8067. Please see St. Peter the Fisherman, Two Rivers.
Sacred Heart, Two Rivers Tel: 920-793-4531; Fax: 920-793-8067. Please see St. Peter the Fisherman, Two Rivers.
St. Luke, Two Rivers Tel: 920-793-4531; Fax: 920-793-8067. Please see St. Peter the Fisherman, Two Rivers.
St. Mark, Two Rivers Tel: 920-793-4531; Fax: 920-793-8067. Please see St. Peter the Fisherman, Two Rivers.
St. Edward, Wagner See St. Joseph & Edwards, Walsh.
St. Amand, Walhain Tel: 920-866-9961. Please see St. Joseph, Champion.
St. Joseph, Walsh Please see SS. Joseph & Edward, Walsh.
St. Hedwig, West Kewaunee Tel: 920-863-8747; Fax: 920-863-5768. Please see St. Therese de Lisieux, Stangelville.
St. James, White Lake Please see SS. James & Stanislaus, White Lake/Langlade.
St. Paul, Wrightstown Please see St. Clare Corp., Greenleaf.

RELIGIOUS INSTITUTES OF MEN REPRESENTED IN THE DIOCESE

For further details refer to the corresponding bracketed number in the Religious Institutes of Men or Women section.

[0330]—*Brothers of the Christian Schools* (Midwest Province), Burr Ridge, IL—F.S.C.
[0900]—*Canons Regular of Premontre*—O.Praem.
[0470]—*The Capuchin Friars* (Province of St. Joseph)—O.F.M.Cap.
[1130]—*Congregation of the Priests of the Sacred Heart*—S.C.J.
[0690]—*Franciscan Friars*—O.F.M.
[0305]—*Institute of Christ the King*—I.C.
[0690]—*Jesuit Fathers and Brothers* (Wisconsin Province)—S.J.
[0910]—*Oblates of Mary Immaculate*—O.M.I.
[1200]—*Society of the Divine Savior*—S.D.S.

RELIGIOUS INSTITUTES OF WOMEN REPRESENTED IN THE DIOCESE

[3710]—*Congregation of the Sisters of St. Agnes*—C.S.A.
[0420]—*Discalced Carmelite Nuns*—O.C.D.
[1070-03]—*Dominican Sisters* Adrian, MI—O.P.
[1070-09]—*Dominican Sisters* Racine, WI—O.P.
[1070-14]—*Dominican Sisters* Sinsinawa, WI—O.P.
[1115]—*Dominican Sisters of Peace*—O.P.
[1170]—*Felician Sisters*—C.S.S.F.
[]—*Felician Sisters (Congregation of the Sisters of St. Felix)*—C.S.S.F.
[1230]—*Franciscan Sisters of Christian Charity*—O.S.F.
[]—*Franciscan Sisters of Perpetual Adoration*—F.S.P.A.
[1240]—*Franciscan Sisters, Daughters of the Sacred Hearts of Jesus and Mary*—O.S.F.
[]—*Handmaids of the Divine Redeemer*—H.D.R.
[1820]—*Hospital Sisters of the Third Order of St. Francis*—O.S.F.
[3070]—*North American Union Sisters of Our Lady of Charity*—N.A.U.-O.L.C.
[3440]—*Religious Hospitallers of Saint Joseph*—R.H.S.J.
[2970]—*School Sisters of Notre Dame*—S.S.N.D.
[1680]—*School Sisters of St. Francis*—S.S.S.F.
[]—*Servants of Mary*—O.S.M.
[]—*Sisters of St. Elizabeth*—S.S.E.
[1705]—*The Sisters of St. Francis of Assisi*—O.S.F.
[1550]—*Sisters of St. Francis of the Holy Cross*—O.S.F.
[3840]—*Sisters of St. Joseph of Carondelet* (Prov. of St. Louis)—C.S.J.
[3930]—*Sisters of St. Joseph of the Third Order of St. Francis*—S.S.J.-T.O.S.F.
[1030]—*Sisters of the Divine Savior*—S.D.S.
[4100]—*Sisters of the Sorrowful Mother (Third Order of St. Francis)*—S.S.M.
[]—*Society of Sisters for the Church*—S.S.C.

DIOCESAN CEMETERIES

GREEN BAY. *Diocesan Cemeteries*, P.O. Box 23825, 54305-3825. Tel: 920-437-7531, Ext. 8229. Ms. Tammy Basten, Diocesan Dir.

Allouez Catholic Cemetery and Mausoleum, 2121 Riverside Dr., 54301.

Queen of Peace Cemetery & Mausoleum, 101 6th St., P.O. Box 535, Antigo, 54409.

Calvary Cemetery & Calvary Chapel Mausoleum, 2601 S. 14th St., Manitowoc, 54220-6467.

Oshkosh Catholic Cemeteries, 1905 Roosevelt Ave., Oshkosh, 54901.

NECROLOGY

† Baeten, David, (Retired)—Died Nov. 27, 2010
† Beerntsen, Harold A., (Retired)—Died Jan. 24, 2011
† Dolski, V. Anthony, (Retired)—Died Sept. 17, 2011
† Jacobs, James T., (Retired)—Died Feb. 12, 2011
† Kiefer, R. David, (Retired)—Died May 21, 2011

An asterisk (*) denotes an organization that has established tax-exempt status directly with the IRS and is not covered by the USCCB Group Ruling.

Diocese of Greensburg

(Dioecesis Greensburgensis)

Most Reverend

LAWRENCE E. BRANDT, J.C.D., PH.D.

Bishop of Greensburg; ordained December 19, 1969; appointed Bishop of Greensburg January 2, 2004; installed March 4, 2004. *Office: 723 E. Pittsburgh St., Greensburg, PA 15601.*

Most Reverend

ANTHONY G. BOSCO, D.D., J.C.L.

Retired Bishop of Greensburg; ordained June 7, 1952; appointed Auxiliary Bishop of Pittsburgh and Titular Bishop of Labico May 14, 1970; consecrated June 30, 1970; appointed Bishop of Greensburg April 14, 1987; installed June 30, 1987; retired January 2, 2004.

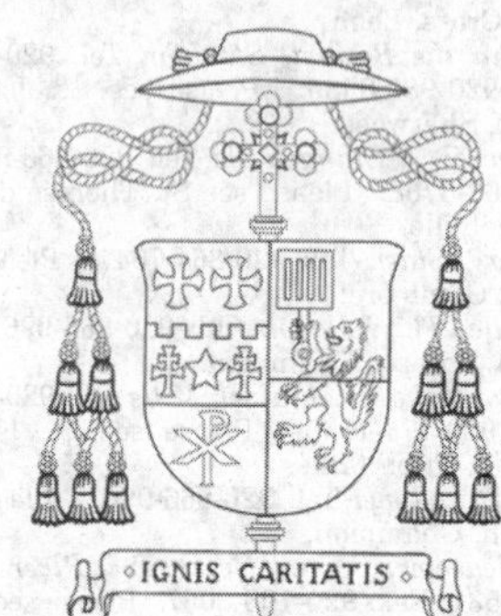

Pastoral Center: 723 E. Pittsburgh St., Greensburg, PA 15601. Tel: 724-837-0901; Fax: 724-837-0857.

Web: www.catholicgbg.org

ESTABLISHED MARCH 10, 1951.

Square Miles 3,334.

Comprises the Counties of Armstrong, Fayette, Indiana and Westmoreland in the State of Pennsylvania.

For legal titles of parishes and diocesan institutions, consult the Chancery Office.

STATISTICAL OVERVIEW

Personnel	
Bishop	1
Retired Bishops	1
Abbots	1
Priests: Diocesan Active in Diocese	70
Priests: Retired, Sick or Absent	37
Number of Diocesan Priests	107
Religious Priests in Diocese	65
Total Priests in Diocese	172
Extern Priests in Diocese	2
Permanent Deacons in Diocese	2
Total Brothers	32
Total Sisters	196
Parishes	
Parishes	85
With Resident Pastor:	
Resident Diocesan Priests	58
Resident Religious Priests	6
Without Resident Pastor:	
Administered by Priests	21
Professional Ministry Personnel:	
Sisters	13
Lay Ministers	69
Welfare	
Homes for the Aged	2
Total Assisted	194
Special Centers for Social Services	6
Total Assisted	16,398
Residential Care of Disabled	1
Total Assisted	90
Educational	
Diocesan Students in Other Seminaries	7
Seminaries, Religious	1
Students Religious	24
Total Seminarians	31
Colleges and Universities	2
Total Students	4,166
High Schools, Diocesan and Parish	2
Total Students	679
Elementary Schools, Diocesan and Parish	14
Total Students	2,421
Elementary Schools, Private	3
Total Students	258
Catechesis/Religious Education:	
High School Students	1,876
Elementary Students	7,153
Total Students under Catholic Instruction	16,584
Teachers in the Diocese:	
Priests	31
Brothers	4
Sisters	7
Lay Teachers	440
Vital Statistics	
Receptions into the Church:	
Infant Baptism Totals	1,235
Minor Baptism Totals	32
Adult Baptism Totals	53
Received into Full Communion	321
First Communions	1,502
Confirmations	675
Marriages:	
Catholic	347
Interfaith	209
Total Marriages	556
Deaths	2,213
Total Catholic Population	152,689
Total Population	659,596

Former Bishops—Most Revs. HUGH L. LAMB, S.T.D., First Bishop of Greensburg; ord. May 29, 1915; appt. Titular Bishop of Helos and Auxiliary of Philadelphia Dec. 19, 1935; cons. March 19, 1936; promoted to Greensburg May 28, 1951; installed Jan. 16, 1952; died Dec. 8, 1959; WILLIAM G. CONNARE, D.D., ord. June 14, 1936; appt. Feb. 23, 1960; cons. May 4, 1960; retired Jan. 20, 1987; died June 12, 1995; ANTHONY G. BOSCO, D.D., J.C.L., ord. June 7, 1952; appt. Auxiliary Bishop of Pittsburgh and Titular Bishop of Labico May 14, 1970; cons. June 30, 1970; appt. Bishop of Greensburg April 14, 1987; installed June 30, 1987; retired Jan. 2, 2004.

Pastoral Center—723 E. Pittsburgh St., Greensburg, 15601-2697. Tel: 724-837-0901; Fax: 724-837-0857. Office Hours: Mon.-Fri. 8:45-5.

Vicar General/Chancellor—Rev. Msgr. LAWRENCE T. PERSICO, J.C.L., V.G. Tel: 724-837-0901.

Chief Financial Officer—Mrs. SHEILA R. MURRAY, CPA, M.B.A.

Deaneries—Rev. Msgr. JAMES T. GASTON, V.F., Deanery 1; Very Revs. LAWRENCE L. MANCHAS, V.F., Deanery 2; KENNETH G. ZACCAGNINI, V.F., Deanery 3; DANIEL C. MAHONEY, V.F., Deanery 4; Rev. Msgr. MICHAEL W. MATUSAK, V.F., Deanery 5.

Director for Religious—VACANT, Office, 723 E. Pittsburgh St., Greensburg, 15601-2697. Tel: 724-837-0901.

Tribunal— Address all correspondence to *723 E. Pittsburgh St., Greensburg, 15601-2697.* Tel: 724-837-0901.

Judicial Vicar—Rev. Msgr. WILLIAM R. RATHGEB, J.C.L.

Defender of Bond—Rev. Msgr. LAWRENCE T. PERSICO, J.C.L., V.G.

Judges—Rev. RICHARD J. KOSISKO, J.C.L.; Rev. Msgr. WILLIAM G. CHARNOKI, P.A., J.C.L.; Rev. ANTHONY J. CARBONE, J.C.L.

Advocate—VACANT.

Notaries—Mrs. CINDY J. OZZELLO; Ms. KATHLEEN POLOSKY.

Tribunal Coordinator and Auditor—Ms. KATHLEEN POLOSKY.

Advisory Bodies

College of Consultors—Most Rev. LAWRENCE E. BRANDT, J.C.D., Ph.D.; Rev. Msgr. LAWRENCE T. PERSICO, J.C.L., V.G.; Very Rev. KENNETH G. ZACCAGNINI, V.F.; Rev. Msgr. MICHAEL W. MATUSAK, V.F.; Revs. JOHN A. MOINEAU; PAUL A. LISIK; Very Rev. LAWRENCE L. MANCHAS, V.F.

Diocesan Pastoral Council—VACANT.

Bishop's Priests Council—Rev. Msgr. LAWRENCE T. PERSICO, J.C.L., V.G.; Very Rev. LAWRENCE L. MANCHAS, V.F.; Rev. Msgr. JAMES T. GASTON, V.F.; Very Revs. DANIEL C. MAHONEY, V.F.; KENNETH G. ZACCAGNINI, V.F.; Revs. JOHN A. MOINEAU; JOHN M. FORISKA; JAMES D. TRINGHESE; MICHAEL J. CROOKSTON; Rev. Msgr. MICHAEL W. MATUSAK, V.F.; Rev. RICHARD J. KOSISKO, J.C.L.

Finance Council—Most Rev. LAWRENCE E. BRANDT, J.C.D., Ph.D.; Rev. Msgr. LAWRENCE T. PERSICO, J.C.L., V.G.; Mrs. NORMA F. SCHERER; Rev. THADDEUS J. KACZMAREK; Mr. CHARLES A. FAGAN III; Mr. B. PATRICK COSTELLO; Mr. WILLIAM MCCABE; Ms. MARIE HUSS; Mrs. RUTH GRANT.

Diocesan Offices, Commissions and Special Programs

The Catholic Foundation for the Diocese of Greensburg— The Catholic Foundation for the Diocese of Greensburg (the Foundation) is a not-for-profit, tax-exempt corporation established by the Diocese of Greensburg (diocese) in 1986. Effective July 1, 2009, Bishop Lawrence E. Brandt announced the restructuring of The Catholic Foundation and new by-laws were adopted for the Foundation. These by-laws provide for a three-tier management structure designed to enhance monitoring of policies and procedures, and ensure effective accomplishment of the Foundation's mission. As the philanthropic arm of the Diocese, the Foundation exists to support the pastoral, educational, and social service ministries of the Diocese of Greensburg. This includes, but is not exclusive to parishes, Catholic schools, Catholic Charities, Catholic Cemeteries, and other Diocesan ministries. *723 E. Pittsburgh St., Greensburg, 15601.*

Members of the Corporation—Most Rev. LAWRENCE

E. BRANDT, J.C.D., Ph.D., Chm.; Rev. Msgr. LAWRENCE T. PERSICO, J.C.L., V.G., Vice Chm.; VACANT, Assoc. Vice Chm.

Board of Trustees—Mr. LAWRENCE S. BUSCH, Pres.; VACANT, Vice Pres.; Mr. MARC B. ROBERTSHAW, Sec.; Mr. DANIEL L. CHESS, CPA, C.V.A., Treas.; Mr. LEO N. HITT; Mr. RAYMOND J. HANLEY.

Ex-Officio Trustees—

College of Deans—Rev. Msgr. JAMES T. GASTON, V.F., Deanery I; Very Revs. LAWRENCE L. MANCHAS, V.F., Deanery II; KENNETH G. ZACCAGNINI, V.F., Deanery III; DANIEL C. MAHONEY, V.F., Deanery IV; Rev. Msgr. MICHAEL W. MATUSAK, V.F., Deanery V.

Diocese of Greensburg - Managing Directors—Mrs. SHEILA R. MURRAY, CPA, M.B.A., CFO; Mr. TRENT D. BOCAN, Supt. Catholic Schools; Rev. Msgr. RAYMOND E. RIFFLE, M.S.W., M.P.A., Catholic Charities; Mr. ROBERT A. SHERWIN, Evangelization & Faith Formation; VACANT, The Catholic Foundation; Mr. JEROME ZUFELT, Communications.

Diocese of Greensburg - Development Personnel—Mrs. JUDY M. MODECKI, MPPM, Catholic Charities.

The Catholic Institute of Greensburg— A Corporation, not-for-profit, incorporated under the law of the Commonwealth of Pennsylvania on the 4th day of June, 1954 having as its purpose the support of any Roman Catholic benevolent, charitable, educational or missionary undertaking.

Board of Members of the Corporation—Most Rev. LAWRENCE E. BRANDT, J.C.D., Ph.D., Pres.; Rev. Msgr. LAWRENCE T. PERSICO, J.C.L., V.G., Sec.

Board of Trustees—Mr. PAUL D. PULEO, Pres.; Mr. MARK E. LOPUSHINSKY; Mr. JOHN N. STEVENS; Rev. Msgr. J. EDWARD MCCULLOUGH; Mrs. SHEILA R. MURRAY, CPA, M.B.A., CFO. Staff: Ms. MARA BRADFORD, CPA, Dir. Financial Oper.; Mrs. CARLA C. PELLIS, Catholic Inst./Accounts Receivable Accountant.

Greensburg Catholic Accent and Communications, Inc.— A corporation, not-for-profit, under the laws of the Commonwealth of Pennsylvania having as its purpose the support of any Roman Catholic benevolent, charitable, educational or missionary undertaking. Most Rev. LAWRENCE E. BRANDT, J.C.D., Ph.D.; Rev. Msgr. LAWRENCE T. PERSICO, J.C.L., V.G.; VACANT, Treas., 723 E. Pittsburgh St., Greensburg, 15601-2697. Tel: 724-837-0901; Fax: 724-837-0857.

Catholic Charities of the Diocese of Greensburg, PA, Inc.— A corporation not-for-profit incorporated under the law of the Commonwealth of Pennsylvania on the 27th day of August, 1954, having as its purpose, the support of any Roman Catholic benevolent, charitable, educational or missionary undertaking. Most Rev. LAWRENCE E. BRANDT, J.C.D., Ph.D., Chm. Bd. Members of the Corp.; CHARLES DELUZIO, Pres. Bd. of Trustees; Rev. Msgr. RAYMOND E. RIFFLE, M.S.W., M.P.A., Mng. Dir., 711 E. Pittsburgh St., Greensburg, 15601-2636. Tel: 724-837-1840; Fax: 724-837-4077.

Archives—723 E. Pittsburgh St., Greensburg, 15601. Tel: 724-837-0901.

Catholic Charities—Rev. Msgr. RAYMOND E. RIFFLE, M.S.W., M.P.A., Mng. Dir.; Mr. ROBERT MCHENRY, Dir. Oper. & Finance; Mrs. JUDY M. MODECKI, MPPM, Dir., Coordinated Svcs. & Devel., 711 E. Pittsburgh St., Greensburg, 15601-2636. Tel: 724-837-1840; Fax: 724-837-4077.

Catholic Relief Services Representative—Rev. Msgr. J. EDWARD MCCULLOUGH, 723 E. Pittsburgh St., Greensburg, 15601-2697. Tel: 724-837-0901.

The Catholic Accent & Media Relations—Mr. JERRY ZUFELT, Mng. Dir. Communications & Editor, Catholic Accent; Mrs. ELIZABETH FAZZINI, Asst. Dir., 725 E. Pittsburgh St., P.O. Box 850, Greensburg, 15601-2697. Tel: 724-834-4010; Fax: 724-836-5650.

Diocesan Ecumenical Office—Rev. THOMAS A. FEDERLINE, 820 Carbon Rd., Greensburg, 15601. Tel: 724-834-6880; Fax: 724-834-1492.

Office of Information Technology—Ms. KAREN CORNELL, Dir.; Mr. BRIAN LOOSZ, Network Analyst; Mr. TONY KRANCE, Internet/Lotus Notes System Admin.; Mr. GREGG WHITFIELD, Client Technology Analyst & Telecommunication Specialist; Mr. DARREN DORN, Client Technology Specialist; JORDAN GOVI, Database & System Admin.; KATHERINE FINFROCK, Instructional Technology Analyst; Mrs. CINDY STICKLE, IT Asset Management & Contract Admin.

Office for Planning—Rev. WILLIAM J. LECHNAR, Dir., 723 E. Pittsburgh St., Greensburg, 15601-2697. Tel: 724-837-0901; Fax: 724-837-0857.

Office of Catholic Schools—Mr. TRENT D. BOCAN, Supt. Schools; Mrs. BARBARA SABO, Dir.; Mr. DONALD M. FAVERO, Scholarship Partners Foundation.

Office for Worship—Rev. MICHAEL P. SIKON, Dir.

Office for Faith Formation—Mr. ROBERT A. SHERWIN, Mng. Dir.

Youth & Young Adult Ministry and Adult Initiation—CHRISTINA M. SMITH.

Marriage Preparation and Enrichment Trainers—Coordinators: RICHARD RYBA; LEEANNA RYBA.

Consultant for Catechesis of the Good Shepherd—BONNIE MILAN.

Athletics—Mrs. AMANDA IWINSKI, CYO Athletic Dir.

Diocesan Catholic Scoutmaster—Rev. E. GEORGE SALETRIK, 723 E. Pittsburgh St., Greensburg, 15601-2697. Tel: 724-837-0901; Fax: 724-837-0857.

Office for Lay Ecclesial Ministry—Ms. MARSHA KABLE, Dir., 723 E. Pittsburgh St., Greensburg, 15601-2697. Tel: 724-837-0901; Fax: 724-837-0857.

Office for Clergy Vocations—Revs. LARRY J. KULICK, Dir.; JONATHAN J. WISNESKI, M.Div., M.A., J.C.L., Co Dir. Tel: 724-837-0901; Fax: 724-837-0857.

Office for the Permanent Diaconate—Rev. Msgr. ROGER A. STATNICK, S.T.L., Ph.D., Dir.; Ms. MARSHA KABLE, 723 E. Pittsburgh St., Greensburg, 15601. Tel: 724-837-0901; Fax: 724-837-0857.

Missions— Society for the Propagation of the Faith and Holy Childhood, Rev. Msgr. J. EDWARD MCCULLOUGH, 723 E. Pittsburgh St., Greensburg, 15601-2697. Tel: 724-837-0901; Fax: 724-837-0857.

Newspaper— "The Catholic Accent" *Mailing Address: 725 E. Pittsburgh St., P.O. Box 850, Greensburg, 15601-2697.* Tel: 724-834-4010; Fax: 724-836-5650. Mr. JEROME ZUFELT, Editor; Mrs. ELIZABETH FAZZINI, Asst. Dir.

Engineering and Facility Management Office—Mr. EDGAR R. TURNER, Dir., 723 E. Pittsburgh St., Greensburg, 15601-2697. Tel: 724-837-0901; 724-552-2570; Fax: 724-836-5592.

SPECIAL PROGRAMS

Apostleship of Prayer—Rev. Msgr. J. EDWARD MCCULLOUGH, Dir., 459 Ranch Rd., Dunbar, 15431. Tel: 724-277-4236; Fax: 724-277-0192.

Apostolate for the Deaf—VACANT, Diocese of Greensburg, 723 E. Pittsburgh St., Greensburg, 15601. Tel: 724-837-0901.

Catholic Business and Professional Women's Association—Rev. LARRY J. KULICK, Spiritual Moderator, 723 E. Pittsburgh St., Greensburg, 15601-2697. Tel: 724-837-0901; Fax: 724-837-0857.

Catholic Daughters of America—VACANT, c/o Diocese of Greensburg, 723 E. Pittsburgh St., Greensburg, 15601. Tel: 724-837-0901; Fax: 724-837-0857.

Cemeteries—723 E. Pittsburgh St., Greensburg, 15601-2697. Tel: 724-837-0901.

Charismatic—Sr. ANN INFANGER, S.C., Moderator, Seton Hill College, Greensburg, 15601. Tel: 724-834-2200, Ext. 374.

Cursillo—c/o Diocese of Greensburg, 723 E. Pittsburgh St., Greensburg, 15601. Tel: 724-837-0901; Fax: 724-837-0857.

Diocesan Council of Catholic Women—Rev. Msgr. DONALD J. MONDELLO, Dir., Villa Angela, 685 Angela Dr., Greensburg, 15601. Tel: 724-834-2409.

Holy Childhood Association—Rev. Msgr. J. EDWARD MCCULLOUGH, Dir., 723 E. Pittsburgh St., Greensburg, 15601-2697. Tel: 724-837-0901; Fax: 724-837-0857.

Holy Name Society—Rev. RICHARD P. KARENBAUER, Dir., St. Florian, P.O. Box 187, United, 15689. Tel: 724-423-4431; Fax: 724-423-4438.

Legion of Mary—Rev. ALAN W. GROTE, 857 Kenneth Ave., New Kensington, 15068. Tel: 724-335-8212. Email: agrote@dioceseofgreensburg.org.

Pilgrimages—VACANT, c/o Diocese of Greensburg, 723 E. Pittsburgh St., Greensburg, 15601. Tel: 724-837-0901; Fax: 724-837-0857.

Priests' Eucharistic League—Rev. Msgr. J. EDWARD MCCULLOUGH, 459 Ranch Rd., Dunbar, 15431. Tel: 724-277-4236.

St. Luke Society for Health Care Professionals—Rev. Msgr. LAWRENCE T. PERSICO, J.C.L., V.G., Chap., 723 E. Pittsburgh St., Greensburg, 15601. Tel: 724-837-0901; Fax: 724-837-0857.

St. Thomas More Society for Lawyers—Rev. TIMOTHY J. KRUTHAUPT, Chap., Mailing Address: 349 Morris St., Clymer, 15728. Tel: 724-254-3041; Fax: 724-254-3045.

St. Vincent de Paul Society—Rev. JOHN A. SEDLAK, Spiritual Dir., Mailing Address: St. Joseph Church, P.O. Box 3, Everson, 15631. Tel: 724-887-6714.

Bishop's Delegate—Rev. Msgr. LAWRENCE T. PERSICO, J.C.L., V.G Tel: 724-837-0901, Ext. 221. Email: lpersico@dioceseofgreensburg.org.

Victim Assistance Coordinators—Rev. Msgr. RAYMOND E. RIFFLE, M.S.W., M.P.A. Email: rriffle@dioceseofgreensburg.org; Dr. PAUL NIEMIEC. Email: pniemiec@dioceseofgreensburg.orgTel: 724-837-1840.

CLERGY, PARISHES, MISSIONS AND PAROCHIAL SCHOOLS

CITY OF GREENSBURG

(WESTMORELAND COUNTY)

1—BLESSED SACRAMENT CATHEDRAL, [CEM] Rev. Msgr. Raymond E. Riffle, Rector; Rev. Alan N. Polczynski; Sandi Kocian, Pastoral Assoc.; Christopher Pardini, Dir. Liturgy & Music.
Res.: 300 N. Main St., 15601. Tel: 724-834-3710; Fax: 724-834-1518.
See Aquinas Academy, Greensburg under Elementary Schools, Inter-Parochial located in the Institution section.
Catechesis/Religious Program—Sara Thomas, C.R.E.; Kathi Probo, Dir. Faith Formation. Students 307.

2—ST. BRUNO (1919) Rev. Martin R. Bartel, O.S.B.
Res.: 1715 Poplar St., 15601. Tel: 724-836-0690; Fax: 724-834-9980.
See Aquinas Academy, Greensburg under Elementary Schools, Inter-Parochial located in the Institution section.
Catechesis/Religious Program—Tel: 724-836-0690, Ext. 11; Fax: 724-834-9980. Christine Gannon, D.R.E. Students 108.

3—OUR LADY OF GRACE (1910) Rev. Paul A. Lisik; Hollie Uccellini, Pastoral Min.; Greg Petrucci, Dir. Faith Formation; Marisa Cazden, Music Min. In Res., Rev. Larry J. Kulick.
Res.: 1011 Mount Pleasant Rd., 15601. Tel: 724-838-9480; Fax: 724-838-1842.
See Aquinas Academy, Greensburg under Elementary Schools, Inter-Parochial located in the Institution section.
Catechesis/Religious Program—Tel: 724-832-6730. Katrina Coleman, Dir. Young Adult & Youth Min. Students 254.

4—ST. PAUL (1955) Rev. Thomas A. Federline. In Res., Rev. Msgr. William R. Rathgeb.
Res.: 820 Carbon Rd., 15601. Tel: 724-834-6880; Fax: 724-834-1492.
See Aquinas Academy, Greensburg under Elementary Schools, Inter-Parochial located in the Institution section.
Catechesis/Religious Program—Students 123.

OUTSIDE THE CITY OF GREENSBURG

APOLLO, ARMSTRONG CO., ST. JAMES THE GREATER Rev. John T. Euker.
Res.: 109 Owens View Ave., 15613. Tel: 724-478-4958; Fax: 724-478-3551.
Catechesis/Religious Program—Megan Krachanko, Rel. Educ. Coord. Students 77.

ARNOLD, WESTMORELAND CO., ALL SAINTS, (Slovak), Closed. For inquiries for parish records, see St. Joseph, New Kensington.

AVONMORE, WESTMORELAND CO., ST. AMBROSE Rev. Salvatore R. Lamendola.
Res.: 505 Cambria Ave., P.O. Box 617, 15618. Tel: 724-697-4129; Fax: 724-697-4484.
Catechesis/Religious Program—Grace Sikora, D.R.E. Students 42.

BELLE VERNON, WESTMORELAND CO., ST. SEBASTIAN Rev. Msgr. Roger A. Statnick.
801 Broad Ave., 15012.
Res.: 712 Henry St., 15012. Tel: 724-929-9300; Fax: 724-930-7611.
Catechesis/Religious Program—Mr. Scott J. Martin, D.R.E. Students 126.

BLAIRSVILLE, INDIANA CO., SS. SIMON AND JUDE (1830) Rev. Chester J. Raimer; Elaine Scherer, Pastoral Assoc.
Res.: 155 N. Brady St., 15717. Tel: 724-459-7103; Fax: 724-459-5314.
Catechesis/Religious Program—Students 71.

BOVARD, WESTMORELAND CO., ST. BEDE, Closed. For inquiries for parish records, see Blessed Sacrament Cathedral, Greensburg.

BRADY'S BEND, ARMSTRONG CO., ST. PATRICK, [CEM 2] Rev. Ronald L. Cyktor Jr.
Res.: 915 State Rte. 68, 16028. Tel: 724-526-5079; Fax: 724-526-3028.
Catechesis/Religious Program—Mrs. Mary Anne Seybert, D.R.E. Students 84.
Chapel—Sugar Creek, Chapel of St. Patrick, Brady's Bend [CEM]

BROWNSVILLE, FAYETTE CO.

1—ST. MARY, (Slovak), [CEM] Closed. For inquiries for parish records please see St. Peter Parish.

2—ST. PETER, [CEM 2] Rev. Micah E. Kozoil.
Office: 118 Church St., 15417. Tel: 724-785-7781; Fax: 724-785-0844.
Church: 300 Shaffner Ave., 15417.
Res.: 304 Shaffner Ave., 15417.
Catechesis/Religious Program—Amy Guty, D.R.E. Students 60.

CADOGAN, ARMSTRONG CO., ST. LAWRENCE, [CEM] Rev. Bryan F. Summers, C.O., Admin.

Res. & Church: 114 Main St., P.O. Box 114, 16212. Tel: 724-763-1089.
Catechesis/Religious Program—Tel: 724-763-7973. Patricia Shevchuk, D.R.E. Students 64.
Chapel—Nicholson Run, Guardian Angel Cemetery and Chapel Cadogan-Slatelick Rd., Kittanning, 16201.

CALUMET, WESTMORELAND CO., ST. STANISLAUS, (Polish), [CEM] Closed. For inquiries for parish records, see Saint Florian, United.

CARDALE, FAYETTE CO., MADONNA OF CZESTOCHOWA, (Polish), [CEM] Rev. William C. McGuirk, Admin.
Res.: 1043 Main St., Republic, 15475. Tel: 724-246-9639; Fax: 724-246-8081. In Res., Rev. James W. Clark.
Catechesis/Religious Program—Kathleen Dunlevy, D.R.E. Students 18.

CLYMER, INDIANA CO., CHURCH OF THE RESURRECTION, [CEM] Very Rev. Lawrence L. Manchas; Revs. Timothy J. Kruthaupt; Rudolph J. Koser.
Administration Center—349 Morris St., 15728-1266. Tel: 724-254-3041; Fax: 724-254-3045.
Catechesis/Religious Program—Students 165.
Chapel—Camerons Bottom, Chapel of Church of the Resurrection, Clymer, Suppressed June 21, 1995.

CONNELLSVILLE, FAYETTE CO.

1—HOLY TRINITY, (Polish), [CEM] Closed. For inquiries for parish records, see Immaculate Conception, Connellsville.

2—IMMACULATE CONCEPTION, [CEM 5] Rev. Joseph E. Bonafed; Deacon William J. Hisker.
Res.: 148 E. Crawford Ave., 15425. Tel: 724-628-6840 (Bus. Office); Fax: 724-628-0838.
See Conn-Area Catholic School, Connellsville under Elementary Schools, Inter-Parochial located in the Institution section.
Catechesis/Religious Program—Sr. Donna Mulligan, S.C., D.R.E. Students 65.
Chapel—Dawson, Sacred Heart Chapel, Suppressed April 16, 2007.

3—ST. JOHN THE EVANGELIST, (Slovak), [CEM] Rev. Joseph E. Bonafed, Admin.; Deacon William J. Hisker. In Res., Rev. Dennis A. Bogusz.
Res.: 908 W. Crawford Ave., 15425. Tel: 724-628-6840 Office; 724-626-0736 Rectory Phone; Fax: 724-628-0838.
See Conn-Area Catholic School, Connellsville under Elementary Schools, Inter-Parochial located in the Institution section.
Catechesis/Religious Program—Students 42.

4—ST. RITA, (Italian), [CEM] Rev. Joseph E. Bonafed, Admin.; Deacon William J. Hisker.
Partner Parishes Offices: 116 S. Second St., 15425. Tel: 724-628-6840; Fax: 724-628-0838.
See Conn-Area Catholic School, Connellsville under Elementary Schools, Inter-Parochial located in the Institution section.
Catechesis/Religious Program—Students 61.

CORAL, INDIANA CO.

1—ST. FRANCIS, [CEM] Merged with St. Louis, Lucernemines to form Our Lady of the Assumption, Coral.

2—OUR LADY OF THE ASSUMPTION Rev. Terry A. Hercik.
Res.: 403 Lucerne Rd., P.O. Box 197, Lucernemines, 15754. Tel: 724-479-0983; Fax: 724-479-1130.
Church: 2434 Neal Rd., P.O. Box G, 15731. Tel: 724-479-9542; Fax: 724-479-1130.
Catechesis/Religious Program—Celeste Stolte-Jones, D.R.E. Students 125.

CRABTREE, WESTMORELAND CO., ST. BARTHOLOMEW, [CEM] Rev. Leon Hont, O.S.B.
Res.: 2538 State Rte. 119, P.O. Box A, 15624. Tel: 724-834-0709; Fax: 724-832-3768.
Catechesis/Religious Program—Eric Kocian, D.R.E. Students 48.

DELMONT, WESTMORELAND CO., ST. JOHN BAPTIST DE LA SALLE Rev. Michael P. Sikon.
Res.: 497 Athena Dr., 15626. Tel: 724-461-7129; Fax: 724-325-3784.
Catechesis/Religious Program—Students 13.

DERRY, WESTMORELAND CO., ST. JOSEPH, [CEM] Rev. Stephen C. West.
Rectory—117 S. Ligonier St., 15627. Tel: 724-694-5359; Fax: 724-694-6215.
Catechesis/Religious Program—Betty Wechtenhiser, D.R.E. Students 66.

DONEGAL, WESTMORELAND CO., ST. RAYMOND OF THE MOUNTAINS (1919) [CEM] Rev. Anthony W. Ditto.
Res.: 170 School House Ln., P.O. Box 330, 15628. Tel: 724-593-7479; Fax: 724-593-5934.
Catechesis/Religious Program—Toni T. Terretti, D.R.E. Students 52.

DUNBAR, FAYETTE CO., ST. ALOYSIUS, [CEM] Rev. Msgr. J. Edward McCullough.
Res.: 459 Ranch Rd., 15431. Tel: 724-277-4236.
Catechesis/Religious Program—Jane Laurion, D.R.E. Students 72.

EAST VANDERGRIFT, WESTMORELAND CO., OUR LADY, QUEEN OF PEACE Rev. John T. Euker, Admin. In Res., Rev. Michael J. Sciberras.
Res.: 400 Kennedy Ave., P.O. Box 429, 15629. Tel: 724-567-7603; Fax: 724-568-3365.
Catechesis/Religious Program—Fax: 724-568-3365. Carol Hollenbaugh, D.R.E. Students 10.

ERNEST, INDIANA CO., CHURCH OF THE ASSUMPTION, Closed. For inquiries for parish records contact Church of the Resurrection, Clymer.

EVERSON, FAYETTE CO., ST. JOSEPH, (Polish), [CEM] Rev. John A. Sedlak.
Mailing Address: P.O. Box 3, 15631.
Res.: 201 Painter St., 15631. Tel: 724-887-6714; Fax: 724-887-8180.
Catechesis/Religious Program—Students 42.

EXPORT, WESTMORELAND CO., ST. MARY Rev. Michael P. Sikon, Admin.; Maureen Wygonik, Dir. Liturgy & Music.
Res.: 497 Athena Dr., Delmont, 15626. Tel: 724-327-0647; Fax: 724-325-3784.
Catechesis/Religious Program—Students 96.

FAIRCHANCE, FAYETTE CO., SS. CYRIL AND METHODIUS, [CEM] Rev. Andrew M. Kawecki.
Res.: 50 Morgantown St., 15436. Tel: 724-564-7436; Fax: 724-564-7435.
Catechesis/Religious Program—Tel: 724-438-5271. Rita Kennison, C.R.E. Students 12.
Chapel—Shoaf, Chapel of SS. Cyril & Methodius, Fairchance, Suppressed Oct. 1, 2007.

FARMINGTON, FAYETTE CO., ST. JOAN OF ARC, [CEM] Rev. James L. Popochock.
Res.: 3521 National Pike, P.O. Box 92, 15437. Tel: 724-329-4522; Fax: 724-329-4955.
Catechesis/Religious Program—Mary Judd, D.R.E. Students 43.

FAYETTE CITY, FAYETTE CO., HOLY SPIRIT, Closed. For inquiries for parish records, see Saint Sebastian, Belle Vernon.

FOOTEDALE, FAYETTE CO., ST. THOMAS, (Polish), [CEM] Rev. Peter L. Peretti, Admin.
Res.: 528 Footedale Rd., P.O. Box 547, New Salem, 15468. Tel: 724-245-9244; Fax: 724-245-9289.
Catechesis/Religious Program—Students 24.

FORBES ROAD, WESTMORELAND CO., ST. MARY, Closed. For inquiries for parish records, see St. Bartholomew, Crabtree.

FORD CITY, ARMSTRONG CO.

1—CHRIST, PRINCE OF PEACE PARISH Rev. Bryan F. Summers, C.O.
718 Fourth Ave., 16226.
Res.: 736 Fifth Ave., 16226. Tel: 724-763-9141; Fax: 724-763-9142.
Catechesis/Religious Program—Tel: 724-763-2521. Joann Kochman, D.R.E. Students 58.

2—ST. FRANCIS OF PAOLA, (Polish), Merged with St. Mary and Holy Trinity, Ford City to form Christ, Prince of Peace Parish, Ford City.

3—HOLY TRINITY, (Slovak), Merged St. Mary and St. Francis of Paola, Ford City to form Christ, Prince of Peace Parish, Ford City.

4—ST. MARY, Merged with St. Francis of Paola and Holy Trinity, Ford City to form Christ, Prince of Peace Parish, Ford City.

FREEPORT, ARMSTRONG CO., ST. MARY (1826) [CEM] Rev. Edward Volz, O.S.P.P.E.
Res.: 608 High St., 16229. Tel: 724-295-2281; Fax: 724-295-3090.
Catechesis/Religious Program—610 High St., 16229. Students 170.

GLEN CAMPBELL, INDIANA CO., ST. MICHAEL, Closed. For inquiries for parish records contact Church of the Resurrection, Clymer.

GRINDSTONE, FAYETTE CO., ST. CECILIA, (Slovak), Rev. Micah E. Kozoil, Admin.
Mailing Address: c/o 118 Church St., Brownsville, 15417. Tel: 724-785-7781; Fax: 724-785-0844.
Catechesis/Religious Program—Amy Guty, D.R.E. Students 5.

HARRISON CITY, WESTMORELAND CO., ST. BARBARA, [CEM] Very Rev. Kenneth G. Zaccagnini; Rev. Jaime Sullan Ozoa.
Mailing Address: 111 Raymaley Rd., 15636.
Res.: 91 Raymaley Rd., 15636. Tel: 724-744-7474; Fax: 724-744-3056.
Catechesis/Religious Program—Tel: 724-744-4885. Joseph M. Killian, D.R.E. Students 474.

HEILWOOD, INDIANA CO., ST. JOHN THE BAPTIST, Closed. For inquiries for parish records contact Church of the Resurrection, Clymer.

HERMINIE, WESTMORELAND CO., ST. EDWARD Rev. John J. Harrold.
Res.: 120 St. Edward Ln., 15637. Tel: 724-446-5197; Fax: 724-446-1433.
Catechesis/Religious Program—Mrs. Kathleen Topolosky, D.R.E. Students 216.

INDIANA, INDIANA CO.

1—ST. BERNARD OF CLAIRVAUX, [CEM] Rev. William J. Kiel.
Res.: 200 Clairvaux Dr., 15701. Tel: 724-465-2210; Fax: 724-465-0422.
Catechesis/Religious Program—Tel: 724-349-9145. Students 182.

2—ST. THOMAS MORE UNIVERSITY PARISH, (Newman Center) Rev. William J. Lechnar; Lynne Jones, Dir., Liturgy & Music; Bill Mrozowski, Office & Business Mgr.; Cindy Schillinger, Pastoral Assoc. & Dir. Campus Min.
Catechesis/Religious Program—Mary Beth Paeko, Coord. Faith Formation. Students 137.
Indiana University of PA—1200 Oakland Ave., 15701. Tel: 724-463-2277; Fax: 724-463-7116.

IRWIN, WESTMORELAND CO., IMMACULATE CONCEPTION (1868) [CEM] Rev. John A. Moineau.
Res.: 308 Second St., 15642. Tel: 724-863-9550; Fax: 724-863-9552.
See Queen of Angels Regional Catholic School, under Elementary Schools, Inter-Parochial located in the Institution section.
Catechesis/Religious Program—Ginny McConnell, D.R.E. Students 370.

ISELIN, INDIANA CO., HOLY CROSS, Closed. For inquiries for parish records contact Church of the Good Shepherd, Kent.

JEANNETTE, WESTMORELAND CO.

1—ASCENSION (1918), (Italian), Revs. John M. Foriska, Admin.; Joseph L. Sredzinski.
Res.: 615 Division St., 15644. Tel: 724-523-6567; 724-523-6568; Fax: 724-523-5199.
Catechesis/Religious Program—John Ridilla, D.R.E. Students 98.

2—SACRED HEART (1889) [CEM] Rev. John M. Foriska. In Res., Rev. Joseph L. Sredzinski.
Office: 504 Cowan Ave., 15644. Tel: 724-523-2560; Fax: 724-523-9400.
Catechesis/Religious Program—Students 155.

KENT, INDIANA CO., CHURCH OF THE GOOD SHEPHERD Rev. Charles P. Esposito.
Res.: 100 Good Shepherd Dr., P.O. Box 99, 15752. Tel: 724-479-3881; Fax: 724-479-3882.
Catechesis/Religious Program—Mrs. Denise Pencola, Coord. Faith Formation. Students 128.

KITTANNING, ARMSTRONG CO., ST. MARY, OUR LADY OF GUADALUPE (1854) [CEM] Rev. Daniel L. Blout.
Office: 348 N. Water St., 16201. Tel: 724-548-7649.
Res.: 101 W. High St., 16201.
Catechesis/Religious Program—Sr. Jacqueline Trzeciak, C.S.J., D.R.E. Students 72.

LATROBE, WESTMORELAND CO.

1—ST. BONIFACE, (Chestnut Ridge) Rev. Anthony W. Ditto, Admin. Tel: 724-593-7479.
Mailing Address: c/o 170 School House Ln., P.O. Box 330, Donegal, 15628. Tel: 724-593-7479.
See Christ the Divine Teacher School, Latrobe under Elementary Schools, Inter-Parochial located in the Institution section.
Catechesis/Religious Program—Fax: 724-593-5934. Toni T. Terretti, D.R.E. Students 18.

2—HOLY FAMILY, [CEM] Very Rev. Daniel C. Mahoney.
Res.: 1200 Ligonier St., 15650. Tel: 724-539-9751; Fax: 724-539-8044.
See Christ the Divine Teacher School, Latrobe under Elementary Schools, Inter-Parochial located in the Institution section.
Catechesis/Religious Program—Tel: 724-539-3638. Erin Colcombe, Dir., Faith Formation. Students 105.

3—ST. JOHN THE EVANGELIST Rev. Anthony J. Carbone.
Res.: 306 St. John Dr., 15650. Tel: 724-537-8909; Fax: 724-537-2788.
See Christ the Divine Teacher School, Latrobe under Elementary Schools, Inter-Parochial located in the Institution section.
Catechesis/Religious Program—Erin Colcombe, D.R.E. Students 56.

4—ST. ROSE (1893) [CEM] Rev. William P. Donahue.
Res.: 4969 Rte. 982, 15650. Tel: 724-537-3709.
See Christ the Divine Teacher School, Latrobe under Elementary Schools, Inter-Parochial located in the Institution section.
Catechesis/Religious Program—Eva Japalucci, D.R.E. Students 93.

5—ST. VINCENT BASILICA, [CEM] Revs. Thomas P. Curry, O.S.B.; Daniel Paul O'Keefe, O.S.B.
Res.: 300 Fraser Purchase Rd., 15650. Tel: 724-539-8629; Fax: 724-539-3810.
See Christ the Divine Teacher School, Latrobe under Elementary Schools, Inter-Parochial located in the Institution section.
Catechesis/Religious Program—Tel: 724-539-8629, Ext. 16. Sharon Bogusz, D.R.E. Students 192.

LECKRONE, FAYETTE CO., OUR LADY OF PERPETUAL HELP (ST. MARY) (1902) [CEM] Rev. John M. Butler.
Res.: 304 Leckrone High House Rd., P.O. Box 248, 15454. Tel: 724-737-5736; Fax: 724-737-1042.
Catechesis/Religious Program—Anita Olesh, D.R.E. Students 13.

LEECHBURG, ARMSTRONG CO.

1—ST. CATHERINE OF ALEXANDRIA, Closed. For inquiries for parish records contact Christ the King, Leechburg.

2—CHRIST THE KING, [CEM] Rev. Joseph V. Trupkovich.
Administrative Center—630 Second St., 15656. Tel:

724-845-8191; 724-842-1791; Fax: 724-845-5480.
Catechesis/Religious Program—Jim Peterman, D.R.E. Students 71.
3—CHURCH OF THE ASSUMPTION, Closed. For inquiries for parish records contact Christ the King, Leechburg.
4—ST. MARTHA, (Slovak), Closed. For inquiries for parish records contact Christ the King, Leechburg.
LEISENRING, FAYETTE CO., ST. VINCENT DE PAUL, [CEM] Closed. For inquiries for parish records, see Saint Aloysius, Dunbar.
LIGONIER, WESTMORELAND CO., HOLY TRINITY, [CEM] Rev. Msgr. William G. Charnoki; Mrs. Carol A. Serafin, Pastoral Assoc.
Res.: 342 W. Main St., 15658. Tel: 724-238-6434; Fax: 724-238-6688.
Catechesis/Religious Program—Tel: 724-238-6341. Students 81.
LOWER BURRELL, WESTMORELAND CO., ST. MARGARET MARY Rev. Msgr. James T. Gaston; Mr. John Kane, Coord. Ministry.
Mailing Address: 3055 Leechburg Rd., 15068. Tel: 724-335-2336; Fax: 724-335-1945.
Res.: 231 Park Dr., 15068.
Catechesis/Religious Program—Joan Duncan, Dir. Faith Formation. Students 475.
LUCERNEMINES, INDIANA CO., ST. LOUIS, [CEM] Merged with St. Francis, Coral to form Our Lady of the Assumption, Coral.
MARGUERITE, WESTMORELAND CO., ST. BENEDICT (1901) Rev. Martin R. Bartel, O.S.B., Admin.
Mailing Address: 260 Bruno Rd., 15601. Tel: 724-836-0690; Fax: 724-834-9980.
Res.: 1715 Poplar St., 15601.
Catechesis/Religious Program—Lynette DiDonato, D.R.E. Students 63.
MASONTOWN, FAYETTE CO., ALL SAINTS, [CEM] Rev. John M. Butler.
Res.: 101 W. Church Ave., 15461. Tel: 724-583-7866; Fax: 724-583-0373.
Catechesis/Religious Program—Ms. Wanda Wokulich, D.R.E. Students 49.
Chapel—McClellandtown, Chapel of All Saints, Masontown
MAXWELL, FAYETTE CO., ST. JAMES, Closed. For inquiries for parish records, see Saint Peter, Brownsville.
MONESSEN, WESTMORELAND CO., THE EPIPHANY OF OUR LORD, [CEM 2] Rev. David Nazimek.
Res.: 618 Knox Ave., 15062. Tel: 724-684-7661; Fax: 724-684-8981.
Catechesis/Religious Program—Mr. Scott J. Martin, D.R.E. Students 65.
MOUNT PLEASANT, WESTMORELAND CO.
1—ST. PIUS X, [CEM] Rev. Richard J. Kosisko; Cindy Copeland, Pastoral Assoc.
Res.: 216 Spruce St., 15666. Tel: 724-547-1911; Fax: 724-547-2630.
Catechesis/Religious Program—Students 89.
2—TRANSFIGURATION, (Polish), [CEM] Closed. For inquiries for parish records contact the chancery.
3—VISITATION OF THE BLESSED VIRGIN MARY, (Slovak), [CEM] Rev. Richard J. Kosisko, Admin.
Mailing Address: 740 Walnut St., 15666. Tel: 724-547-1911; Fax: 724-547-2630.
Res.: 216 Spruce St., 15666.
Catechesis/Religious Program—Students 54.
MURRYSVILLE, WESTMORELAND CO., MOTHER OF SORROWS (1939) Rev. Thaddeus J. Kaczmarek.
Res.: 4202 Old William Penn Hwy., 15668. Tel: 724-733-8870; Fax: 724-733-8108. Email: pastoralcenter2@mosparish.org. Web: www.mosparish.org.
Catechesis/Religious Program—Jason Stanislaw, D.R.E. Tel: 724-733-1887. Students 443.
NEW ALEXANDRIA, WESTMORELAND CO., ST. JAMES Rev. Msgr. Lawrence T. Persico.
Res.: 306 Saint James Ln., 15670. Tel: 724-668-2829; Fax: 724-668-7327.
Catechesis/Religious Program—William J. D'Angelo, D.R.E. Students 28.
NEW DERRY, WESTMORELAND CO., ST. MARTIN, [CEM] Rev. Stephen C. West, Admin.
Res.: 5684 Rte. 982, 15671-1008. Tel: 724-694-5716; Fax: 724-694-5716.
Catechesis/Religious Program—Betty Wechtenhiser, D.R.E. Students 19.
NEW KENSINGTON, WESTMORELAND CO.
1—ST. JOSEPH (1891) Revs. John S. Szczesny; Alan W. Grote, Parochial Vicar.
Res.: 1125 Leishman Ave., 15068. Tel: 724-337-6412; Fax: 724-337-4022.
See Mary Queen of Apostles, New Kensington, located under Inter-Parochial Schools in the Institution Section.
Catechesis/Religious Program—Students 105.
2—ST. MARY OF CZESTOCHOWA, (Polish), [CEM] Revs. John S. Szczesny, Admin.; Alan W. Grote, Parochial Vicar; Sr. Mary Carol Kardell, C.S.S.F., Pastoral Min.
Res.: 857 Kenneth Ave., 15068. Tel: 724-335-8212; Fax: 724-335-1314.
Catechesis/Religious Program—Deborah Discello, D.R.E. Students 105.
3—MT. ST. PETER, (Italian), Rev. Msgr. Michael J. Begolly; Rev. Douglas E. Dorula, Parochial Vicar Pro Tem.
Res.: 100 Freeport Rd., 15068. Tel: 724-335-9877; Fax: 724-335-9138.
Catechesis/Religious Program—Sisters Susan Jenny, S.C., Faith First Coord.; Valerie Zottola, Coord. Youth & Young Adult Ministry. Students 161.
NEW SALEM, FAYETTE CO., ST. PROCOPIUS, [CEM] Rev. Peter L. Peretti.
Res.: 20 Church St., P.O. Box 547, 15468. Tel: 724-245-9244; Fax: 724-245-9289.
Catechesis/Religious Program—Students 23.
NORTH HUNTINGDON, WESTMORELAND CO.
1—ST. AGNES Rev. Msgr. V. Paul Fitzmaurice; Rev. Joseph D. Armamento, Parochial Vicar. In Res., Rev. Jonathan J. Wisneski.
Res.: 11400 St. Agnes Ln., 15642. Tel: 724-863-2626; 724-863-2630; Fax: 724-863-1057.
See Queen of Angels Regional Catholic School, North Huntingdon under Elementary Schools, Inter-Parochial located in the Institution section.
Catechesis/Religious Program—Tel: 724-864-5393. Mary Blythe, D.R.E. Students 424.
2—ST. ELIZABETH ANN SETON Rev. Leonard W. Stoviak.
Res.: 119 Katherine Dr., 15642. Tel: 724-864-6364; Fax: 724-864-4580.
Catechesis/Religious Program—Sr. Charlene Ozanick, C.S.S.F., D.R.E. Students 176.
PALMER, FAYETTE CO., ST. ALBERT, Closed. For inquiries for parish records, see St. Mary, Our Lady of Perpetual Help, Leckrone.
PARKER, ARMSTRONG CO., ST. MARY, OUR LADY OF THE SNOWS, Closed. For inquiries for parish records, see Saint Patrick, Brady's Bend.
PENN, WESTMORELAND CO., ST. BONIFACE, [CEM] Closed. For inquiries for parish records, see Sacred Heart, Jeannette.
PERRYOPOLIS, FAYETTE CO., ST. JOHN THE BAPTIST, [CEM] Rev. Robert T. Lubic.
Res.: P.O. Box 606, 15473. Tel: 724-736-4442; Fax: 724-736-8403.
Catechesis/Religious Program—Tel: 724-736-0158; Fax: 724-736-0158. Sr. Loretta Topper, D.R.E. Students 114.
POINT MARION, FAYETTE CO., ST. HUBERT Rev. Andrew M. Kawecki, Admin.
Res.: c/o 50 N. Morgantown St., Fairchance, 15436. Tel: 724-725-3655; Fax: 724-564-7435.
Catechesis/Religious Program—Students 5.
REPUBLIC, FAYETTE CO., HOLY ROSARY (1916) [CEM] Rev. William C. McGuirk.
Res.: 1043 Main St., P.O. Box 400, 15475. Tel: 724-246-9639; Fax: 724-246-8081.
Catechesis/Religious Program—Kathleen Dunlevy, D.R.E. Students 37.
ROSSITER, INDIANA CO., ST. FRANCIS OF ASSISI, Closed. For inquiries for parish records contact the Church of the Resurrection, Clymer.
ROSTRAVER, WESTMORELAND CO., ST. ANNE Rev. Vincent J. Gigliotti.
Res.: 1870 Rostraver Rd., Belle Vernon, 15012. Tel: 724-872-3555; Fax: 724-872-3373.
Catechesis/Religious Program—Tel: 724-872-3486. Barbara Zucconi, D.R.E. Students 209.
SAGAMORE, ARMSTRONG CO., SACRED HEART, [CEM] Closed. Parish closed Oct. 1, 2007. For inquiries for parish records, see St. Mary, Yatesboro.
SALTSBURG, INDIANA CO., ST. MATTHEW, (Italian), [CEM] Rev. Salvatore R. Lamendola, Admin.
Mailing Address: 505 Cambria Ave., P.O. Box 617, Avonmore, 15618.
Res.: 505 Cambria Ave., Avonmore, 15618. Tel: 724-697-4129; Fax: 724-697-4484.
Catechesis/Religious Program—703 Indiana Ave., 15687. Students 55.
SCOTTDALE, WESTMORELAND CO., ST. JOHN THE BAPTIST (1878) [CEM] Rev. E. George Saletrik; Sr. Susanne Chenot, O.S.B., Pastoral Assoc.
Res.: 416 S. Broadway, 15683. Tel: 724-887-6321; Fax: 724-887-6324.
Catechesis/Religious Program—Dr. Joseph Dreliszak, D.R.E. Students 60.
Convent—Benedictine Sisters, 408 S. Broadway, 15683. Tel: 724-887-6612.
SEWARD, WESTMORELAND CO., HOLY FAMILY (1907) [CEM 3] Rev. Robert M. Washko.
Res.: 425 Bridge St., 15954. Tel: 814-446-5759.
Catechesis/Religious Program—Gail Smyder, D.R.E. Students 147.
SLICKVILLE, WESTMORELAND CO., ST. SYLVESTER Rev. Salvatore R. Lamendola, Admin. In Res., Rev. James M. Goldberg, Senior Priest.
Res.: 3028 Rt. 819, Box 307, 15684. Tel: 724-468-5794; Fax: 724-468-5765.
Catechesis/Religious Program—
SMITHTON, WESTMORELAND CO., ST. TIMOTHY, [CEM] Closed. For inquiries for parish records, see St. Ann, Rostraver.
SMOCK, FAYETTE CO., ST. HEDWIG, (Slovak), [CEM 2] Revs. Robert T. Lubic, Admin.; James F. Petrovsky, Sr. Priest.
Res.: Box 251, 15480. Tel: 724-677-2110; Fax: 724-677-0146.
Catechesis/Religious Program—Students 14.
STARFORD, INDIANA CO., ST. ELIZABETH, Closed. For inquiries for parish records contact Church of the Resurrection, Clymer.
SUTERSVILLE, WESTMORELAND CO., ST. CHARLES BORROMEO, Closed. For inquiries for parish records, see Holy Family, West Newton.
TRAFFORD, WESTMORELAND CO., ST. REGIS Rev. James D. Tringhese.
Res.: 517 Homewood Ave., 15085. Tel: 412-372-4577; Fax: 412-373-5979.
Catechesis/Religious Program—Tel: 412-372-7609. Kathy Wawrzeniak, D.R.E. Students 163.
TRAUGER, WESTMORELAND CO., FORTY MARTYRS, (Hungarian), [CEM] Closed. For inquiries for parish records, see St. Florian, United.
UNIONTOWN, FAYETTE CO.
1—ST. JOHN THE EVANGELIST Rev. Michael J. Crookston.
Res.: 50 Jefferson St., 15401. Tel: 724-437-7569; Fax: 724-437-6277.
Catechesis/Religious Program—Students 62.
2—ST. JOSEPH, (Polish), [CEM] Rev. Ronald L. Simboli.
Res.: 180 Old Walnut Hill Rd., 15401. Tel: 724-437-3927; Fax: 724-437-5354.
Catechesis/Religious Program—Tel: 724-438-2341. Marlene Bandzuch, D.R.E. Students 58.
3—NATIVITY OF THE BLESSED VIRGIN MARY (1903), (Slovak), [CEM] Rev. Stephen R. Bugay; Nancy Blake, Pastoral Assoc.
Res.: 61 N. Mount Vernon Ave., 15401. Tel: 724-437-1513; Fax: 724-437-7482.
Catechesis/Religious Program—Students 101.
Convent—Vincentian Sisters of Charity of Nazareth & Sisters of Charity of Seton Hill, 7 Gilmore St., 15401. Tel: 724-437-5478.
4—ST. THERESE, THE LITTLE FLOWER OF JESUS, (Italian), Rev. Msgr. Michael W. Matusak.
Res.: 61 Mill St., 15401. Tel: 724-438-2341; Fax: 724-438-2361.
Catechesis/Religious Program—Marlene Bandzuch, D.R.E. Students 240.
UNITED, WESTMORELAND CO., ST. FLORIAN, [CEM] Rev. Richard P. Karenbauer.
Res.: 4261 Rt. 981, P.O. Box 187, 15689. Tel: 724-423-4431; Fax: 724-423-4438.
School—(Grades PreSchool), 4257 Rt. 981, Mount Pleasant, 15666. Tel: 724-423-4437. Lay Teachers 2; Students 40.
Catechesis/Religious Program—Toni Chovanec, D.R.E. Students 70.
VANDERGRIFT, WESTMORELAND CO., ST. GERTRUDE, [CEM] Rev. James H. Loew, O.S.B.
Res.: 303 Franklin Ave., 15690. Tel: 724-568-2331; Fax: 724-568-2030.
Catechesis/Religious Program—James Peterman, D.R.E. Students 50.
WEST NEWTON, WESTMORELAND CO., HOLY FAMILY Rev. John T. Sweeney.
Res.: 225 N. Second St., 15089. Tel: 724-872-6123.
Catechesis/Religious Program—Tel: 724-872-2106. Michalene Lovato, D.R.E. Students 60.
WHITNEY, WESTMORELAND CO., ST. CECILIA Rev. Peter Augustine H. Pierjok, O.S.B., Admin.
Res.: 218 St. Cecilia Rd., P.O. Box 80, 15693. Tel: 724-423-3777; 724-423-2289; Fax: 724-423-3778.
Catechesis/Religious Program—William Smith, C.R.E. Students 45.
YATESBORO, ARMSTRONG CO., ST. MARY (1903) [CEM] Rev. Daniel L. Blout, Admin.
Mailing Address: 111 Second St., P.O. Box 327, 16263.
Res.: 109 Second St., P.O. Box 327, 16263. Tel: 724-783-7191; Fax: 724-783-7783.
Catechesis/Religious Program—Students 77.
YOUNGSTOWN, WESTMORELAND CO., SACRED HEART Rev. Peter Augustine H. Pierjok, O.S.B.
Res.: c/o 218 St. Cecelia Rd., P.O. Box 80, Whitney, 15693. Tel: 724-537-7358; Fax: 724-537-6988.
Catechesis/Religious Program—William Smith, C.R.E. Students 28.
YOUNGWOOD, WESTMORELAND CO., HOLY CROSS Rev. William G. Berkey.
Res.: 711 Depot St., 15697. Tel: 724-925-7811; Fax: 724-925-6170.
Catechesis/Religious Program—Tel: 724-925-8206. John Zombar, D.R.E. Students 77.
YUKON, WESTMORELAND CO., SEVEN DOLORS (1909) [CEM] Very Rev. Kenneth G. Zaccagnini, Admin.
Res.: 102 Center St., P.O. Box 308, 15698. Tel: 724-722-3141; 724-722-3150 (Hall); Fax: 724-722-3140.
Catechesis/Religious Program—Lauretta B. Stanley,

D.R.E. Parish of Seven Dolors. Students 24.

Chaplains of Public Institutions

GREENSBURG. *Excela Health - Westmoreland Hospital*, Tel: 724-832-4000; 724-832-4447 (Chaplain's Office). Revs. Robert R. Byrnes, Assoc. Chap., Justin Withrow, O.S.B., Assoc. Chap.

BROWNSVILLE. *Brownsville General Hospital*. Attended by St. Peter, Brownsville, Tel: 724-785-7200; 724-785-7781 (Res.).

CONNELLSVILLE. *Highlands Hospital & Health Center*, Tel: 724-628-1500. Rev. Dennis A. Bogusz, Chap. Tel: 724-626-0736.

INDIANA. *Indiana Hospital*, Tel: 724-357-7000. Rev. Timothy J. Kruthaupt, Chap. Tel: 724-254-3041; 724-465-5840. Attended by Church of Resurrection, Clymer, Tel: 724-465-3900 (Indiana County Home); 724-465-5840 (Res.).

KITTANNING. *Armstrong County Hospital*, Tel: 724-543-8500. Rev. Raphael K. Glinkowski, O.S.P.P.E., Chap. Tel: 724-763-1375 (Res.).

LATROBE. *Excela Health - Latrobe Area Hospital*, Tel: 724-537-1000. Revs. Jacques de Paul Daley, O.S.B., Assoc. Chap. Tel: 724-539-9761, Dominic J. Petroy, O.S.B., Assoc. Chap. Tel: 724-539-9761.

MOUNT PLEASANT. *Frick Community Health Center*, Tel: 724-547-1500 (Hospital). Rev. Dennis A. Bogusz, Chap. Tel: 724-626-0736.

NEW KENSINGTON. *Citizens General Hospital*, Tel: 724-337-3541. Attended by St. Mary, New Kensington, Tel: 724-335-8212 (Res.); St. Joseph, New Kensington, Tel: 724-337-6412 (Res.); Mount St. Peter, New Kensington, Tel: 724-335-9877 (Res.).

TORRANCE. *Torrance State Hospital*, Tel: 724-459-8000. Rev. Chester J. Raimer, Chap. Tel: 724-459-7103 (Res.).

UNIONTOWN. *Uniontown Hospital*, Tel: 724-430-5000 (Res.); 724-246-9657. Rev. James W. Clark, Chap. Tel: 724-246-9657.

Priests On Leave:
Rev.—
Trupkovich, Thomas S.

Retired:
Rev. Msgrs.—
Conway, John L., V.F., St. Margaret Mary Church, 3055 Leechburg Rd., Lower Burrell, 15068.
Dylag, Michael R., 1 Kenberton Dr., Pleasant Ridge, MI 48069.
McCarren, Stephen A., 307 Avenue of Dukes, Nokomis, FL 34275.
Revs.—
Bratus, Walter N., 723 E. Pittsburgh St., 15601.
Bucci, Michael J., 1319 Walnut St., South Connellsville, 15425.
Cheatham, Louis W., Neumann House, 2900 Seminary Dr., 15601.
Higgins, Edward F., St. Anne Home, 685 Angela Dr., 15601.
Kacinko, Elmer A., 1987 Centurion Dr., Apt. 601, Pittsburgh, 15221.
Lukac, Thomas M., St. Anne Home, 685 Angela Dr., 15601.
Mandock, Patrick H., P.O. Box 497, Elephant Butte, NM 87935.
Minsterman, Joseph, 510 S. Chestnut St., Scottdale, 15683.
O'Connor, Patrick J., Villa Angela, 685 Angela Dr., 15601.
Pleban, Alexander L., S.T.L., Neumann House, 2900 Seminary Dr., 15601.
Rutkowski, Ronald J., 231 Rocky Branch Rd., Blountville, TN 37617.
Weiksner, Jerome M., Villa Angela, 685 Angela Dr., 15601.

INSTITUTIONS LOCATED IN THE DIOCESE

[A] SEMINARIES, RELIGIOUS OR SCHOLASTICATES

LATROBE. *St. Vincent Seminary*, 300 Fraser Purchase Rd., 15650. Tel: 724-805-2592; Fax: 724-532-5052. Email: justin.matro@email.stvincent.edu. Web: www.benedictine.stvincent.edu/seminary. Very Rev. Justin M. Matro, O.S.B., Rector; Revs. Aaron N. Buzzelli, O.S.B., Dir. Spiritual Formation; Cyprian G. Constantine, O.S.B., Liturgy Director; John Mary Tompkins, O.S.B., Vice Rector & Dir. of Pastoral Formation; Patrick T. Cronauer, O.S.B., Dir. Rel. Ordination Students; Bro. David Kelly, O.S.B., Dir. Library; Dr. Michel Therrien, S.T.D., Academic Dean; Ms. Denise A. Hegeman, Lattimer Family Library Public Svcs. Librarian. Professors 33; Lay Students 12; Seminarians 57; Benedictines 21; Other Religious 1.

[B] COLLEGES AND UNIVERSITIES

GREENSBURG. *Seton Hill University* 15601. Tel: 724-834-2200; Fax: 724-830-4611. Email: admit@setonhill.edu. Web: www.setonhill.edu. Dr. JoAnne W. Boyle, Pres.; Mary Ann Gawelek, Ed.D., Provost & Dean of Faculty; Mr. David Stanely, Dir. Reeves Library. Sisters of Charity of Seton Hill. Sisters 7; Lay Teachers 94; Students 2,237.

LATROBE. *Saint Vincent College*, 300 Fraser Purchase Rd., 15650-2690. Tel: 724-532-6600; Fax: 724-532-5065. Rt. Rev. Douglas R. Nowicki, O.S.B., Chancellor; Bros. Norman W. Hipps, O.S.B., Pres.; David Kelly, O.S.B., Dir. of Libraries.
Saint Vincent College Corporation Priests 15; Brothers 6; Lay Teachers 104; Students 1,929.

[C] HIGH SCHOOLS, DIOCESAN

GREENSBURG. *Greensburg Central Catholic High School/Greensburg Central Catholic Jr. High School*, (Grades 7-12), 911 Armory Dr., 15601. Tel: 724-834-0310; Fax: 724-834-2472. Email: info@gcchs.org. Web: www.gcchs.org. Rev. William G. Berkey, Chap. & Rel. Instructor; Mrs. Denise Myers, Prin.; Carol Whalen, Librarian. Priests 1; Sisters 1; Lay Teachers 40; Students 516.

CONNELLSVILLE. *Geibel Catholic Junior-Senior High School*, (Grades 7-12), 611 E. Crawford Ave., 15425. Tel: 724-628-5600; Fax: 724-626-5700. Web: www.geibelcatholic.org. Rev. Robert T. Lubic, Chap. & Rel. Instructor; Mr. Donald M. Favero, Prin. Priests 1; Lay Teachers 14; Students 163.

[D] ELEMENTARY SCHOOLS, INTER-PAROCHIAL

CONNELLSVILLE. *Conn-Area Catholic School*, 613 E. Crawford Ave., 15425. Tel: 724-628-5090; Fax: 724-628-1745. Email: connarea@cvzoom.net. Web: www.connareacatholic.org. Mrs. Cecilia Solan, Prin. Lay Teachers 11; Students 100.

NEW KENSINGTON. *Mary Queen of Apostles*, (Grades PreK-8), (Regional School), 1129 Leishman Ave., 15068. Tel: 724-339-4411; Fax: 724-337-6457. Catherine M. Collett, Prin. Lay Teachers 19; Students 245.

[E] ELEMENTARY SCHOOLS - REGIONAL

GREENSBURG. *Aquinas Academy*, (Grades PreK-7), 340 N. Main St., 15601. Tel: 724-834-7940; Fax: 724-836-0497. Email: info@aquinasacademy.org. Mr. Scott Manns, M.Ed., Prin.; Mrs. Michelle Finoli, Librarian. Lay Teachers 28; Students 245.

BELLE VERNON. *St. Sebastian Regional School*, 815 Broad Ave., 15012. Tel: 724-929-5143; Fax: 724-929-3038. Mr. Steven J. Dorko, Prin. Lay Teachers 21; Students 268.

FORD CITY. *Divine Redeemer School*, (Grades PreSchool-6), 726 Fourth Ave., 16226. Tel: 724-763-3761; Fax: 724-763-4112. Nicalena Carlesi, Prin. Lay Teachers 8; Students 150.

INDIANA. *St. Bernard Regional School*, 300 Clairvaux Dr., 15701. Tel: 724-465-7139; Fax: 724-465-0803. Denise Swope, Prin. Lay Teachers 12; Students 122.

LATROBE. *Christ the Divine Teacher School*, (Grades PreK-6), 323 Chestnut St., 15650. Tel: 724-539-1561; Fax: 724-532-3873. Email: cdt@cdtschool.org. Web: www.cdtschool.org. J. Kevin Frye, Prin.; Cathie Ortiz, Librarian. Lay Teachers 16; Students 235.

LIGONIER. *Holy Trinity School*, 327 W. Vincent St., 15658. Tel: 724-238-6430; Fax: 724-238-6402. Mrs. Connie Beam, Prin. Lay Teachers 11; Students 103.

MASONTOWN. *All Saints Regional School*, 100 S. Washington St., 15461. Tel: 724-583-2141; Fax: 724-583-2141. Mr. Steven J. Dorko, Prin. Lay Teachers 8; Students 91.

MURRYSVILLE. *Mother of Sorrows School*, 3264 Evergreen Dr., 15668. Tel: 724-733-8840; Fax: 724-325-1144. Email: jrice@mosschool.org. Web: www.mosschool.org. Joseph J. Rice, Prin. Lay Teachers 25; Students 287.

NORTH HUNTINGDON. *Queen of Angels School/The Bishop Anthony G. Bosco Center*, One Main St., 15642. Tel: 724-978-0144; Fax: 724-978-0171. Email: info@queenofangelssch.org. Web: www.queenofangelssch.org. Mrs. Linda L. Holsopple, Prin.; Jennifer Cunningham, Librarian. Lay Teachers 20; Students 305.

SCOTTDALE. *St. John the Baptist Regional Catholic School*, 504 S. Broadway, 15683. Tel: 724-887-9550; Fax: 724-887-9553. Dr. Joseph Dreliszak, Prin. Lay Teachers 13; Students 85.

UNIONTOWN. *St. John the Evangelist Regional Catholic School*, (Grades PreK-8), 52 Jefferson St., 15401. Tel: 724-438-8598; Fax: 724-438-8585. Christine Roskovensky, Prin. Lay Teachers 12; Students 214.

VANDERGRIFT. *The Cardinal Maida Academy*, (Grades PreSchool-8), 315 Franklin Ave., 15690. Tel: 724-568-3304; Fax: 724-567-1900. Patrice Majeran, Prin. Lay Teachers 9; Students 99.

[F] SPECIAL EDUCATION

GREENSBURG. *Clelian Heights School for Exceptional Children*, (Grades K-12), 135 Clelian Heights Ln., 15601. Tel: 724-837-8120; Fax: 724-837-6480. Email: clelian@aol.com. Web: www.clelianheights.org. Sisters Ritamary Schulz, A.S.C.J., Exec. Dir.; Charlene Celli, A.S.C.J., Prin.; Rev. Bernard Survil, Chap. Apostles of the Sacred Heart of Jesus. Sisters 13; Lay Teachers 11; Students 90.
Elizabeth Seton Montessori School of Westmoreland County, Inc., 294 Frye Farm Rd., P.O. Box 268, 15601. Tel: 724-837-8500; Fax: 724-836-0772. Email: esmontessori@comcast.net. Sr. Anita Schulte, S.C., Admin.; Mrs. Linda M. Fidazzo, Dir. & Teacher in Charge. Sisters of Charity. Sisters 1; Lay Teachers 3; Students 40.

MOUNT PLEASANT. *Verna Montessori School*, 268 Prittstown Rd., 15666. Tel: 724-887-8810; Fax: 724-887-2977. Email: vmsami@zoominternet.net. Sisters M. Letizia Tribuzio, S.C.I.C., Prin.; Donatella Garreffa, Admin. Ivrea Sisters of Charity of the Immaculate Conception of Ivrea Sisters 9; Lay Teachers 9; Students 137.

[G] HOMES FOR AGED

GREENSBURG. *St. Anne Home*, 685 Angela Dr., 15601. Tel: 724-837-6070; Fax: 724-837-6099. Email: jlong@stannehome.org. Web: www.stannehome.org. Felician Sisters 5; Daughters of Mary 4; Assisted Living 55; Capacity for Intermediate Skilled Care 125; Independent Living 4.
Neumann House, 2900 Seminary Dr., 15601. Tel: 724-834-7350; Fax: 724-834-7351. Email: jbertig@dioceseofgreensburg.org. Residence for retired Priests. In Res. Rev. Msgrs. Lawrence R. Kiniry; John A. Regoli (Retired); Revs. Louis W. Cheatham (Retired). Tel: 724-850-7619; Emil S. Payer; Lawrence Hoppe; Alexander L. Pleban, S.T.L. (Retired); Henry S. Preneta (Retired); Donald P. Trexler; Anthony A. Wozniak.

[H] MONASTERIES AND RESIDENCES OF PRIESTS AND BROTHERS

BOLIVAR. *Mount Carmel Hermitage*, 244 Baileys Rd., 15923. Tel: 724-238-0423; Fax: 724-238-0423. Revs. Bede J.K. Mulligan, O.Carm., Prior; Simeon D. Marro, O.Carm., Procurator. Email: smarr@winbeam.com; Bro. Robert Ryba, O.Carm. Priests 2; Brothers 1.

KITTANNING. *Pauline Fathers Monastery*, 543 Bunker Hill Rd., P.O. Box 66, 16201. Tel: 724-763-1375; Fax: 724-763-8100. Revs. Sebastian J. Hanks, O.S.P.P.E., Supr.; Edward Volz, O.S.P.P.E.; Raphael K. Glinkowski, O.S.P.P.E., Admin. Priests 3.

LATROBE. *Saint Vincent Archabbey*, 300 Fraser Purchase Rd., 15650-2690. Tel: 724-532-6600; Fax: 724-539-2110. Email: archabbot@stvincent.edu. Web: www.saintvincentarchabbey.org. Rt. Revs. Douglas R. Nowicki, O.S.B., Archabbot; Paul R. Maher, O.S.B., Archabbot (Retired); Joaquim F. De Arruda Zamith, O.S.B. (Retired), (Mosteiro de Sao, Vinhedo, SP Brasil); Most Rev. Rembert G. Weakland, O.S.B. (Retired); Very Rev. Earl J. Henry, O.S.B., Prior; Bro. Anthony Kirsch, O.S.B., Subprior; Revs. Edward M. Mazich, O.S.B., Master of Novices; Philip M. Kanfush, O.S.B., Procurator; Thomas Acklin, O.S.B.; Joseph M. Adams, O.S.B.; Filipe R.J. de Almeida, O.S.B.; Benoit Alloggia, O.S.B.; Shawn Matthew Anderson, O.S.B.; Martin R. Bartel, O.S.B.; William A. Beaver, O.S.B.; Kurt J. Belsole, O.S.B.; Jeremy J. Bolha, O.S.B.; Brian D. Boosel, O.S.B.; Jude Brady, O.S.B.; Cristiano E. Brito, O.S.B.; Ananias G. Buccicone, O.S.B.; Gilbert J. Burke, O.S.B., Dir. Alumni St. Vincent Seminary & St. Vincent Devel. Club; Aaron N. Buzzelli, O.S.B.; Frederick Byrne, O.S.B.; Andrew S. Campbell, O.S.B.; Cornelius P. Chang, O.S.B.; Athanasius C. Cherry, O.S.B.; Richard Chirichiello, O.S.B.; Wulfstan F. Clough, O.S.B.; Stephen P. Concordia, O.S.B.; Cyprian G. Constantine, O.S.B.; Lucas Torrell deAlmeida Costa, O.S.B.; Patrick T. Cronauer, O.S.B., Master of Juniors, St. Vincent Archabbey; Vincent R. Crosby, O.S.B.; Thomas P. Curry, O.S.B.; Bonaventure J. Curtis, O.S.B.; Jacques de Paul Daley, O.S.B.; Demetrius R. Dumm, O.S.B.; Mauro N. de Souza Fernandes, O.S.B.; Chad R. Ficorilli, O.S.B.; Augustine A. Flood, O.S.B.; Job J. Foote, O.S.B.; Mario A. Fulgenzi, O.S.B.; Michael J. Gabler, O.S.B.;

Ronald Gatman, O.S.B.; Campion P. Gavaler, O.S.B.; Joseph U. Gerg, O.S.B.; David R. Griffin, O.S.B.; Anthony J. Grossi, O.S.B.; Mark F.X. Gruber, O.S.B.; Thomas M. Hart, O.S.B.; Bede J. Hasso, O.S.B.; Boniface Hicks, O.S.B.; David Liang Ho, O.S.B.; Vernon A. Holtz, O.S.B.; Stephen Honeygoskey, O.S.B.; Leon Hont, O.S.B.; Cuthbert A. Jack, O.S.B.; Myron M. Kirsch, O.S.B.; Paschal N. Kneip, O.S.B.; Rene M. Kollar, O.S.B.; Matthew T. Laffey, O.S.B.; Meinrad J. Lawson, O.S.B.; James H. Loew, O.S.B.; Stanley T. Markiewicz, O.S.B.; Matthias Martinez, O.S.B.; Very Rev. Justin M. Matro, O.S.B., Rector of Seminary; Revs. Paschal A. Morlino, O.S.B.; Maurus B. Mount, O.S.B.; Nathan J. Munsch, O.S.B.; Jonathan J. Murrman, O.S.B.; Warren D. Murrman, O.S.B.; Justin Nolan, O.S.B.; Jeffrey Nyardy, O.S.B.; Daniel Paul O'Keefe, O.S.B.; Very Rev. Paulo Sergio Panza, O.S.B.; Revs. Alfred Patterson, O.S.B.; John Peck, O.S.B.; Dominic J. Petroy, O.S.B.; Peter Augustine H. Pierjok, O.S.B.; James Podlesny, O.S.B.; Luke E. Policicchio, O.S.B.; Jerome J. Purta, O.S.B.; Donald Raila, O.S.B.; Blane L. Resko, O.S.B.; Thaddeus E. Rettger, O.S.B.; Robert J. Roche, O.S.B.; Noel H. Rothrauff, O.S.B., Dir. of Foreign Missions; Paul E. Rubadue, O.S.B.; Sebastian A. Samay, O.S.B.; Chrysostom V. Schlimm, O.S.B.; Paul-Alexander Shutt, O.S.B.; Thomas More Sikora, O.S.B.; Ralph Tajak, O.S.B.; Paul R. Taylor, O.S.B.; John Mary Tompkins, O.S.B.; Richard Ulam, O.S.B.; Eric Vogt, O.S.B.; Damian J. Warnock, O.S.B.; Mark Edward Wenzinger, O.S.B.; Anthony Wesolowski, O.S.B.; Justin Withrow, O.S.B.; Daniel C. Wolfel, O.S.B.; Lee R. Yoackam, O.S.B.; Vincent E. Zidek, O.S.B.; Frank Ziemkiewicz, O.S.B.

The Benedictine Society of Westmoreland County

Saint Vincent College Corporation

The Wimmer Corporation

The Saint Vincent Cemetery Corporation Priests in Archabbey 66; Priests in Community 106; Brothers 32; Deacons 4; Junior Professed Monks 12; Choir Novices 6.

Priests of the Archabbey Serving Abroad: Rt. Rev. Joaquim de Arruda Zamith, O.S.B. (Retired); Revs. Lucas Torrell deAlmeida Costa, O.S.B.; Felipe R.J. del Almeida, O.S.B.; Very Rev. Paulo Sergio Panza, O.S.B., Prior; Rev. David Liang Ho, O.S.B.

Priests on Loan: Revs. Cornelius P. Chang, O.S.B., Archdiocese of New York; Lee R. Yoakam, O.S.B., Chap., US Army: Active Duty, Fort Leavenworth, KS 66027; Mauro N. de Souza Fernandes, O.S.B., Archdiocese of Campinas, Brazil.

Priests on Leave for Study and Teaching: Revs. Shawn Matthew Anderson, O.S.B., Virginia Commonwealth University, Richmond, VA; Kurt J. Belsole, O.S.B., North American College, Rome, Italy; Brian D. Boosel, O.S.B., Catholic University, Washington, DC; Maurus B. Mount, O.S.B., University of Illinois, Champaign, IL.

UNIONTOWN. *St. Anthony Friary*, 115 Oakland Ave., 15401-2800. Tel: 724-438-0500; Fax: 724-438-4251. Revs. Matthew R. Brozovic, O.F.M., Sacramental Min.; John Joseph Gonchar, O.F.M., Guardian & Sacramental Min.; Bros. Damien Murkley, O.F.M., Vicar; Bill Spond, O.F.M., Asst. Fraternal Ministry.

[I] CONVENTS AND RESIDENCES FOR SISTERS

GREENSBURG. *Apostles of the Sacred Heart of Jesus, Clelian Heights Convent*, 135 Clelian Heights Ln., 15601-6665. Tel: 724-837-8120; Fax: 724-837-6480. Email: clelian@aol.com. Web: www.clelianheights.org. Sr. Ritamary Schulz, A.S.C.J., Local Supr.; Rev. Bernard Survil, Chap. Sisters 13.

Benedictine Nuns, St. Emma Monastery, 1001 Harvey Ave., 15601-1494. Tel: 724-834-3060; Fax: 724-834-5772. Email: benedictinenuns@stemma.org. Web: www.stemma.org. Sr. Mary Anne Noll, O.S.B., Prioress; Revs. Jacques de Paul Daley, O.S.B., Chap.; Jeffrey Nyardy, O.S.B., Chap. Sisters 11.

Doran Hall, 441 Mount Thor Rd., 15601. Tel: 724-837-8645. Web: www.scsh.org. Sisters of Charity 12.

Ennis Hall, 443 Mount Thor Rd., 15601. Tel: 724-836-7940. Sisters of Charity 8.

Regina House (Sisters of Charity), 469 Mt. Thor Rd., 15601. Tel: 724-836-0406; Fax: 724-836-8280. Web: www.scsh.org. Sr. Vivien Linkhauer, S.C., Prov. Supr.

Sisters of Charity, Caritas Christi, Motherhouse, 129 DePaul Center Rd., 15601. Tel: 724-853-7948; Fax: 724-838-1512. Web: www.scsh.org. Sr. Jane Mary Kelly, Sister Servant. Sisters 84.

Sisters of Charity, Marian Hall, 449 Mount Thor Rd., 15601. Tel: 724-837-5863. Web: www.scsh.org. Sisters of Charity 2.

Sisters of Charity of Seton Hill, Greensburg, Pennsylvania (DePaul Center), 144 DePaul Center Rd., 15601. Tel: 724-836-0406; Fax: 724-836-8280. Web: www.scsh.org. Sisters 422; Novices 8; Postulants 2.

Sisters of Charity of Seton Hill, Caritias Christi Motherhouse, 129 DePaul Center Rd., 15601. Tel: 724-853-7948; Fax: 724-838-1512. Web: www.scsh.org. Sisters 84.

Sisters of Charity of Seton Hill, Marian Hall Novitiate, 449 Mt. Thor Rd., 15601. Tel: 724-837-5863. Web: www.scsh.org. Sisters 2.

Bayley House Tel: 724-836-6398. A Pennsylvania nonprofit corporation. Sisters 3.

Doran Hall Tel: 724-837-8645. Sisters 12.

Ennis Hall Tel: 724-836-7940. Sisters 8.

Regina House, Regina House: 469 Mt. Thor Rd., 15601. Tel: 724-836-0406; Fax: 724-836-8280. Sisters 3.

LATROBE. *Discalced Carmelite Nuns, Carmel of the Assumption*, 5206 Center Dr., 15650. Tel: 724-539-1056; Fax: 724-539-0752. Email: carmelite.monastery@verizon.net. Professed Nuns of Solemn Vows 13.

LEECHBURG. *Catechist Sisters of Mary Immaculate Help of Christians*, 118 Park Rd., 15656. Tel: 724-845-2828; Fax: 724-845-1658. Email: lbgsmi@comcast.net. Sisters 6.

MOUNT PLEASANT. *Sisters of Charity of the Immaculate Conception of Ivrea*, Immaculate Virgin of Miracles Convent, 268 Prittstown Rd., 15666. Tel: 724-887-6753; Fax: 724-887-0220. Email: scicusa@zoominternet.net. Sr. M. Letizia Tribuzio, S.C.I.C., Local Supr. Sisters 9.

[J] RETREAT HOUSES

GREENSBURG. *St. Emma Retreat House*, 1001 Harvey Ave., 15601. Tel: 724-834-3060; Fax: 724-834-5772. Email: benedictinenuns@stemma.org. Web: www.stemma.org. Revs. Jacques de Paul Daley, O.S.B., Chap.; Jeffrey Nyardy, O.S.B., Chap.; Sr. Mary Anne Noll, O.S.B., Prioress. Benedictine Nuns.

[K] MISCELLANEOUS LISTINGS

GREENSBURG. *The Bishop William G. Connare Center*, 2900 Seminary Dr., 15601. Tel: 724-834-7350; Fax: 724-834-7351. Email: jbertig@dioceseofgreensburg.org. Web: www.bishopconnarecenter.org. Mr. Gerald R. Bertig, Dir. Facilities Mgmt. In Res. Revs. Robert R. Byrnes; John R. Cindric; Rev. Msgr. Richard G. Curci.

Congregations of Religious Women Charitable Trust, 144 DePaul Center Rd., 15601. Tel: 724-836-0406; Fax: 724-836-8280. Email: rhildenbrand@scsh.org. Robert M. Hildenbrand, Chm., CRWCT Committee.

Gilbert Straub Plaza, 620 Reamer Ave., 15601. Tel: 724-832-2280; Fax: 724-832-9511. Email: jgrindle@scsh.org. Sr. Mary Janice Grindle, S.C., Mgr. Sisters of Charity. Sisters 1.

Magnificat - Greensburg, PA, 931 Mace St., 15601. Email: pattiron@netzero.net. Jeannette Hernandez, Treas.

CONNELLSVILLE. *Ladies of Charity*, c/o St. Joseph Church, P.O. Box 3, Everson, 15631. Tel: 724-887-6714; Fax: 724-887-8180. Email: jsedlak@dioceseofgreensburg.org. Rev. John A. Sedlak, Spiritual Advisor; Sr. Mary Price, S.C., Sister Moderator.

DUNBAR. *Rendu Services, Inc.*, 453 Pechin Rd., 15431. Tel: 724-277-8680; Fax: 724-277-8681. Email: maryfranb@yahoo.com. Web: www.renduservices.org. Sr. Mary Francis Bassick, D.C., Exec. Dir.

INDIANA. *Clairvaux Commons*, 100 Clairvaux Dr., 15701. Tel: 724-349-2920; Fax: 724-349-1355. Sisters of St. Joseph 2.

LEECHBURG. *Bishop Morrow Personal Care Home, Inc.*, 118 Park Rd., 15656. Tel: 724-845-2828; Fax: 724-845-1658. Email: lbgsmi@comcast.net. Sr. Mercy F. Anchalakal, S.M.I. Sisters of Mary Immaculate.

RELIGIOUS INSTITUTES OF MEN REPRESENTED IN THE DIOCESE

For further details refer to the corresponding bracketed number in the Religious Institutes of Men or Women section.

[0200]—*Benedictine Monks* (St. Vincent Archabbey)—O.S.B.

[0270]—*Carmelite Fathers and Brothers*—O.Carm.

[0520]—*Franciscan Friars*—O.F.M.

[1010]—*Pauline Fathers*—O.S.P.P.E.

RELIGIOUS INSTITUTES OF WOMEN REPRESENTED IN THE DIOCESE

[0130]—*Apostles of the Sacred Heart of Jesus*—A.S.C.J.

[0190]—*Benedictine Sisters*—O.S.B.

[0230]—*Benedictine Sisters of Pontifical Jurisdiction*—O.S.B.

[0420]—*Discalced Carmelite Nuns*—O.C.D.

[1070]—*Dominican Sisters, St. Mary of the Springs* (Columbus, OH)—O.P.

[1170]—*Felician Sisters*—C.S.S.F.

[2575]—*Institute of the Sisters of Mercy of the Americas* (Pittsburgh, PA)—R.S.M.

[1690]—*School Sisters of the Third Order of St. Francis*—O.S.F.

[0570]—*Sisters of Charity of Seton Hill, Greensburg, Pennsylvania*—S.C.

[0450]—*Sisters of Charity of the Immaculate Conception of Ivrea*—S.C.I.C.

[0990]—*Sisters of Divine Providence* (St. Peter Prov.)—C.D.P.

[2440]—*Sisters of Mary Immaculate*—S.M.I.

[1660]—*Sisters of Saint Francis of the Providence of God*—O.S.F.

[1620]—*Sisters of Saint Francis, Millvale, Pennsylvania*—O.S.F.

[3830-13]—*Sisters of St. Joseph*—C.S.J.

[2040]—*Sisters of the Holy Spirit*—S.H.S.

[3730]—*Sisters of the Order of St. Basil the Great*—O.S.B.M.

[4160]—*Vincentian Sisters of Charity*—V.S.C.

NECROLOGY

† McAlpin, Leonard J., (Retired)—Died May 29, 2011

† Murphy, Harry J., (Retired)—Died May 30, 2011

An asterisk (*) denotes an organization that has established tax-exempt status directly with the IRS and is not covered by the USCCB Group Ruling.

Diocese of Harrisburg

(Dioecesis Harrisburgensis)

Most Reverend

JOSEPH P. MCFADDEN

Bishop of Harrisburg; ordained May 16, 1981; appointed Auxiliary Bishop of Philadelphia and Titular Bishop of Horreomargum June 8, 2004; consecrated July 28, 2004; appointed Bishop of Harrisburg June 22, 2010; installed August 18, 2010. *Office: 4800 Union Deposit Rd., Harrisburg, PA 17111-3710.*

Diocesan Center: 4800 Union Deposit Rd., Harrisburg, PA 17111-3710. Tel: 717-657-4804; Fax: 717-657-2453.

Web: www.hbgdiocese.org

Email: general@hbgdiocese.org

ESTABLISHED MARCH 3, 1868.

Square Miles 7,660.

Comprises the Counties of Dauphin, Lebanon, Lancaster, York, Adams, Franklin, Cumberland, Perry, Juniata, Mifflin, Snyder, Northumberland, Union, Montour and Columbia in the State of Pennsylvania.

Patron of Diocese: St. Patrick, Bishop and Confessor.

Legal Title: The Diocese of Harrisburg and each parish in the diocese are organized as separate Pennsylvania Charitable Trusts. For further information, consult the Office of the Vicar General.

STATISTICAL OVERVIEW

Personnel	
Bishop	1
Priests: Diocesan Active in Diocese	96
Priests: Diocesan Active Outside Diocese	5
Priests: Retired, Sick or Absent	36
Number of Diocesan Priests	137
Religious Priests in Diocese	35
Total Priests in Diocese	172
Extern Priests in Diocese	11
Ordinations:	
Diocesan Priests	1
Transitional Deacons	1
Permanent Deacons in Diocese	69
Total Brothers	1
Total Sisters	335
Parishes	
Parishes	89
With Resident Pastor:	
Resident Diocesan Priests	73
Resident Religious Priests	13
Without Resident Pastor:	
Administered by Priests	3
Missions	8
Professional Ministry Personnel:	
Brothers	1
Sisters	16
Lay Ministers	77
Welfare	
Catholic Hospitals	1
Total Assisted	248,646
Homes for the Aged	3
Total Assisted	272
Residential Care of Children	1
Total Assisted	611
Specialized Homes	4
Total Assisted	264
Special Centers for Social Services	14
Total Assisted	2,872
Educational	
Diocesan Students in Other Seminaries	31
Total Seminarians	31
High Schools, Diocesan and Parish	7
Total Students	3,391
Elementary Schools, Diocesan and Parish	39
Total Students	8,133
Elementary Schools, Private	2
Total Students	82
Catechesis/Religious Education:	
High School Students	1,445
Elementary Students	15,188
Total Students under Catholic Instruction	28,270
Teachers in the Diocese:	
Priests	1
Sisters	29
Lay Teachers	750
Vital Statistics	
Receptions into the Church:	
Infant Baptism Totals	2,024
Minor Baptism Totals	529
Adult Baptism Totals	326
Received into Full Communion	418
First Communions	2,738
Confirmations	2,817
Marriages:	
Catholic	402
Interfaith	316
Total Marriages	718
Deaths	2,255
Total Catholic Population	249,238
Total Population	2,224,542

Former Bishops—Rt. Revs. JEREMIAH F. SHANAHAN, D.D., ord. July 3, 1859; cons. July 12, 1868; died Sept. 24, 1886; THOMAS MCGOVERN, D.D., ord. Dec. 27, 1861; cons. March 11, 1888; died July 25, 1898; JOHN W. SHANAHAN, D.D., ord. Jan. 2, 1869; cons. May 1, 1899; died Feb. 19, 1916; Most Revs. PHILIP R. MCDEVITT, D.D., cons. Sept. 21, 1916; died Nov. 11, 1935; GEORGE L. LEECH, D.D., J.C.D., appt. Auxiliary of Harrisburg July 6, 1935; cons. Oct. 17, 1935; succeeded to See Dec. 19, 1935; retired Oct. 19, 1971; died March 12, 1985; JOSEPH T. DALEY, D.D., cons. Jan. 7, 1964; appt. Coadjutor Bishop July 31, 1967; succeeded to See Oct. 19, 1971; died Sept. 2, 1983; WILLIAM H. KEELER, ord. July 17, 1955; cons. Sept. 21, 1979; appt. Bishop of Harrisburg, Nov. 10, 1983; succeeded to See Jan. 4, 1984; transferred to Baltimore May 23, 1989; NICHOLAS C. DATTILO, D.D., ord. May 31, 1958; appt. Eighth Bishop of Harrisburg Nov. 21, 1989; cons. Jan. 26, 1990; died March 5, 2004; KEVIN C. RHOADES, ord. July 9, 1983; appt. Ninth Bishop of Harrisburg Oct. 14, 2004; cons. Dec. 9, 2004; appt. Bishop of Fort Wayne-South Bend Nov. 14, 2009; installed Jan. 13, 2010.

Diocese of Harrisburg Officials

Administrative Assistant to the Bishop and Liturgical Coordinator—Rev. JOSHUA R. BROMMER, Mailing Address: 4800 Union Deposit Rd., Harrisburg, 17111-3710. Tel: 717-657-4804; Fax: 717-657-2453.

Vicar General—Rev. Msgr. WILLIAM J. KING, J.C.D., V.G., 4800 Union Deposit Rd., Harrisburg, 17111-3710. Tel: 717-657-4804; Fax: 717-657-2453.

Assistant to the Vicar General—Ms. MARY T. SHRIVER, M.A. Tel: 717-657-4804, Ext. 325. Email: mshriver@hbgdiocese.org.

Moderator of the Curia—Rev. Msgr. WILLIAM J. KING, J.C.D., V.G., Mailing Address: 4800 Union Deposit Rd., Harrisburg, 17111-3710.

Secretary for Catholic Charities—MARK A. TOTARO, Ph.D., MBA, Mailing Address: 4800 Union Deposit Rd., Harrisburg, 17111-3710. Tel: 717-657-4804; Fax: 717-657-8683.

Secretary for Administrative Services—Mr. DONALD J. KAERCHER, CPA, CFO, Mailing Address: 4800 Union Deposit Rd., Harrisburg, 17111-3710. Tel: 717-657-4804; Fax: 717-671-7021.

Secretary for Clergy and Consecrated Life—Very Rev. PHILIP G. BURGER, V.F., Mailing Address: 4800 Union Deposit Rd., Harrisburg, 17111-3710. Tel: 717-657-4804; Fax: 717-657-2453.

Office of Communications—Mr. JOSEPH G. APONICK, Dir., Mailing Address: 4800 Union Deposit Rd., Harrisburg, 17111-3710. Tel: 717-657-4804; Fax: 717-657-7673.

Secretary for Education—Very Rev. EDWARD J. QUINLAN, M.Div., M.A., M.S., Mailing Address: 4800 Union Deposit Rd., Harrisburg, 17111-3710. Tel: 717-657-4804; Fax: 717-657-3790.

Secretary for Catholic Life and Evangelization—VACANT, Mailing Address: 4800 Union Deposit Rd., Harrisburg, 17111-3710. Tel: 717-657-4804; Fax: 717-657-4041.

Judicial Vicar—Very Rev. EDWARD C. MALESIC, J.C.L., M.Div., J.V., Mailing Address: 4800 Union Deposit Rd., Harrisburg, 17111-3710. Tel: 717-657-4804; Fax: 717-657-1573.

Chancellor—CAROL HOUGHTON, S.T.D., J.C.D., Mailing Address: 4800 Union Deposit Rd, Harrisburg, 17111-3710. Tel: 717-657-4804; Fax: 717-657-1573.

Diocesan Offices, Commissions, Boards and Programs

Adult Education and Catechist Formation, Office of—Mr. RYAN BOLSTER, Dir., Mailing Address: 4800 Union Deposit Rd., Harrisburg, 17111-3710. Tel: 717-657-4804, Ext. 225; Fax: 717-657-3790.

Catholic History and Archives, Office of—Rev. Msgr. THOMAS J. KUJOVSKY, Dir. (Retired); Dr. LINDA V. ITZOE, Archivist & Asst. Chancellor Archives, 4800 Union Deposit Rd., Harrisburg, 17111-3710. Tel: 717-657-4804.

Black Catholic Apostolate—Ms. GWEN SUMMERS, Coord., 4800 Union Deposit Rd., Harrisburg, 17111-3710. Tel: 717-657-4804.

Buildings and Properties—Mr. TERRY CONNER, Dir., 4800 Union Deposit Rd., Harrisburg, 17111-3710. Tel: 717-657-4804; Fax: 717-657-6208.

Campus Ministry—Mr. ROBERT J. WILLIAMS, Dir., Mailing Address: 4800 Union Deposit Rd., Harrisburg, 17111-3710. Tel: 717-657-4804.

Catholic Charities Administration, Department for—MARK A. TOTARO, Ph.D., MBA, Exec. Dir. & CEO; PETER A. BIASUCCI, L.S.W., Asst. Exec. Dir.; CAROLE A. KLINGER, M.B.A., Dir. Admin.; CHRISTOPHER MEEHAN, Dir. Devel., Mailing Address: 4800 Union Deposit Rd., Harrisburg, 17111-3710.

Catholic Charities Counseling/Field Services, Department for—Associate Executive Directors: ANNETTE MARTIN, M.H.S.; KIRK REIDER, A.C.S.W, L.C.S.W.; CHRISTOPHER VANDENBERG, M.H.S.; NICHOLAS GIAMPIETRO, M.A.

Catholic Physicians League—Rev. DAVID L. DANNEKER, Ph.D., Liaison, 1840 Marshall Dr., Elizabethtown, 17022.

Catholic Schools, Department for—Mrs. LIVIA ANN RILEY, Supt., Mailing Address: 4800 Union Deposit Rd., Harrisburg, 17111-3710. Tel: 717-657-4804; Fax: 717-657-3790.

The "Catholic Witness"—Ms. JENNIFER REED, Mng. Editor, 4800 Union Deposit Rd., Harrisburg, 17111-3710. Tel: 717-657-4804; Fax: 717-657-7673.

Catholic Women, Diocesan Council of—Mrs. BONNIE ONOMASTICO, 6480 Fairway Dr. W., Fayetteville, 17222. Tel: 717-352-3514.

Cemeteries—Mr. DONALD J. KAERCHER, CPA, Diocesan Finance Officer & Sec. for Admin. Svcs., 4800 Union Deposit Rd., Harrisburg, 17111-3710. Tel: 717-657-4804.

Charismatic Renewal—Rev. FRANCIS J. KARWACKI, V.F., Liaison, 47 S. Market St., Mount Carmel, 17851. Tel: 570-339-1036.

Consultors, College—Very Revs. PHILIP G. BURGER, V.F.; ROBERT M. GILLELAN, V.F.; Rev. PETER I. HAHN; Very Rev. EDWARD C. MALESIC, J.C.L., M.Div., J.V.; Rev. RAYMOND J. LAVOIE; Very Rev. KENNETH F. LAWRENCE, V.F.; Revs. LAWRENCE J. MCNEIL, D.Min., M.Div.; LOUIS P. OGDEN; ROBERT F. SHARMAN, S.T.L. Contact: Rev. Msgr. WILLIAM J. KING, J.C.D., V.G., Vicar Gen. & Moderator of the Curia, 4800 Union Deposit Rd., Harrisburg, 17111-3710. Tel: 717-657-4804; Fax: 717-657-2453.

Continuing Formation of Priests, Office of—VACANT, Dir., 4800 Union Deposit Rd., Harrisburg, 17111-3710. Tel: 717-657-4804; Fax: 717-657-4042.

Cursillo Movement—Rev. Msgr. THOMAS H. SMITH, V.F., Moderator.

Deans—Very Revs. JOSEPH F. GOTWALT, Adams Deanery; WILLIAM C. FORREY, V.F., Cumberland/Perry Deanery; Rev. Msgr. JAMES M. LYONS, M.Div., M.Ed., V.F., Dauphin Deanery; Very Revs. JOHN B. BATEMAN, V.F., Franklin Deanery; KENNETH F. LAWRENCE, V.F., North Lancaster Deanery; Rev. Msgr. RICHARD A. YOUTZ, J.C.L., South Lancaster Deanery; Very Rev. MICHAEL P. REID II, V.F., Lebanon Deanery; Rev. Msgr. WILLIAM M. RICHARDSON, V.F., Northern Deanery; Very Revs. ALFRED P. SCESKI, V.F., Northumberland Deanery; ROBERT M. GILLELAN JR., V.F., York Deanery.

Diocesan Center—Mrs. DONNAJOAN MATTIS, Coord., 4800 Union Deposit Rd., Harrisburg, 17111-3710. Tel: 717-657-4804; Fax: 717-671-7146.

Development, Office of—Ms. PAULA M. LASECKI, Dir., 4800 Union Deposit Rd., Harrisburg, 17111-3710. Tel: 717-657-4804; Fax: 717-657-8757.

Ecumenical and Interreligious Affairs, Office for—Deacon CHARLES CLARK, Dir., 4800 Union Deposit Rd., Harrisburg, 17111-3710. Tel: 717-657-4804; Fax: 717-657-4041.

Evangelization and Special Ministries, Office of—LUCIA C.R. MURPHY, Ph.D., Dir., 4800 Union Deposit Rd., Harrisburg, 17111-3710. Tel: 717-657-4804; Fax: 717-657-4041.

Family Ministries, Office of—VICTORIA LASKOWSKI, J.D., Dir., 4800 Union Deposit Rd., Harrisburg, 17111-3710. Tel: 717-657-4804; Fax: 717-657-4041.

Finance Council—

Harrisburg Catholic Administrative Services, Inc.—Mr. DONALD J. KAERCHER, CPA, Diocesan Finance Officer & Sec. for Admin., 4800 Union Deposit Rd., Harrisburg, 17111-3710. Tel: 717-657-4804; Fax: 717-671-7021.

Health Care Ministry—LUCIA C.R. MURPHY, Ph.D., Dir., 4800 Union Deposit Rd., Harrisburg, 17111-3710. Tel: 717-657-4804; Fax: 717-657-4041.

Holy Name Societies—Deacon THOMAS AUMEN, Liaison, 15 Oak Hill Dr., Hanover, 17331. Tel: 717-637-6491.

Korean Ministry—Rev. JOSEPH J. YANG, 329 Lowther St., Lemoyne, 17043. Tel: 717-774-2728.

Knights of Columbus—Mr. BERT LANGENDIJK, 34 Riverview Dr., Enola, 17025. Tel: 717-732-4086.

Human Resources, Department for—Mrs. JANET E. JACKSON, M.C.I.P.D., 4800 Union Deposit Rd., Harrisburg, 17111-3710. Tel: 717-657-4804.

Legion of Mary—Rev. PAUL R. SHUDA, Moderator (Retired), 675 Rutherford Rd., Harrisburg, 17109. Tel: 717-657-3147.

Mater Dei Community— (Traditional Latin Mass Community) *110 State St., Harrisburg, 17101.* Tel: 717-234-4184. Rev. FRANK PARRINELLO, F.S.S.P.

Mediation Services, Office of—Mrs. BARBARA A. ROTH, Clerk, 4800 Union Deposit Rd., Harrisburg, 17111-3710. Tel: 717-657-4804.

Missions, Office of (Home and Foreign)—Rev. ROBERT F. SHARMAN, S.T.L., Dir., 4800 Union Deposit Rd., Harrisburg, 17111-3710. Tel: 717-657-4804; Fax: 717-657-4042.

Ministry with People with Disabilities, Office for—Mrs. GINNY DUNCAN, Dir., 4800 Union Deposit Rd., Harrisburg, 17111-3710. Tel: 717-657-4804; Fax: 717-657-4041.

Natural Family Planning, Office of—4800 Union Deposit Rd., Harrisburg, 17111-3710. Tel: 717-657-4804; Fax: 717-657-4041.

Pastoral Council, Diocesan—Contact: Ms. MARY T. SHRIVER, M.A., Asst. to Vicar Gen. Tel: 717-657-4804, Ext. 325. Email: mshriver@hbgdiocese.org.

Permanent Diaconate, Office for—Very Rev. PHILIP G. BURGER, V.F., Dir., 4800 Union Deposit Rd., Harrisburg, 17111-3710. Tel: 717-657-4804; Fax: 717-657-2453; Deacon MICHAEL A. GRELLA, Ed.D., Dir. Continuing Formation of Deacons. Tel: 717-657-4804; Fax: 717-657-4042.

Presbyteral Council—Rev. LAWRENCE J. MCNEIL, D.Min., M.Div., Adams; Very Rev. WILLIAM C. FORREY, V.F., Cumberland/Perry; Rev. LOUIS P. OGDEN, Dauphin; Very Revs. JOHN B. BATEMAN, V.F., Franklin; KENNETH F. LAWRENCE, V.F., North Lancaster; Revs. PETER I. HAHN, South Lancaster; JOSEPH T. SCANLIN, Lebanon; THOMAS A. SCALA, Northern; Very Revs. ALFRED P. SCESKI, V.F., Northumberland; ROBERT M. GILLELAN JR., V.F., York; Rev. Msgr. THOMAS J. KUJOVSKY (Retired).

Appointed—Rev. RAYMOND J. LAVOIE; Very Rev. EDWARD C. MALESIC, J.C.L., M.Div., J.V.; Revs. DANIEL C. MITZEL; TIMOTHY D. MARCOE; ROBERT F. SHARMAN, S.T.L.

Prison Ministry—VACANT, Dir., 4800 Union Deposit Rd., Harrisburg, 17111-3710. Tel: 717-657-4804; Fax: 717-657-4041.

Senior Adult Ministry—VICTORIA LASKOWSKI, J.D., Coord., 4800 Union Deposit Rd., Harrisburg, 17111-3710. Tel: 717-657-4804; Fax: 717-657-4041.

Respect Life, Office for—Rev. PAUL C.B. SCHENCK, Dir., 4800 Union Deposit Rd., Harrisburg, 17111-3710. Tel: 717-657-4804; Fax: 717-657-2453.

Media Relations—Mr. JOSEPH G. APONICK, 4800 Union Deposit Rd., Harrisburg, 17111-3710. Tel: 717-657-4804; Fax: 717-657-7673.

Religious Education (CCD), Department for—Mr. JAMES GONTIS, 4800 Union Deposit Rd., Harrisburg, 17111-3710. Tel: 717-657-4804; Fax: 717-657-3790.

Consecrated Life, Department for—4800 Union Deposit Rd., Harrisburg, 17111-3710. Tel: 717-657-4804; Fax: 717-657-2453.

Saint Thomas More Society—ANDREW CLARK, Esq., Pres., 4800 Union Deposit Rd., Harrisburg, 17111-3710. Tel: 717-657-4804, Ext. 305.

Saint Vincent de Paul Society—VACANT.

Hispanic Apostolate—LUCIA C.R. MURPHY, Ph.D., 4800 Union Deposit Rd., Harrisburg, 17111-3710. Tel: 717-657-4804; Fax: 717-657-4041.

Tribunal—4800 Union Deposit Rd., Harrisburg, 17111-3710. Tel: 717-657-4804; Fax: 717-657-1573.

Judicial Vicar—Very Rev. EDWARD C. MALESIC, J.C.L., M.Div., J.V.

Case Services Administrator—Mrs. BARBARA A. ROTH.

Diocesan Judges—Rev. Msgr. RICHARD A. YOUTZ, J.C.L.; Dr. CAROL L. HOUGHTON, S.T.D., J.C.D.; Rev. JORDAN HITE, T.O.R.

Defenders of the Bond—Revs. EDWARD R. LAVELLE; PAUL M. CLARK, J.C.L.

Promoter of Justice—Rev. PAUL M. CLARK, J.C.L.

Advocates—Mr. ROBERT F. O'DONNELL; Mrs. BARBARA A. ROTH; Mrs. CONSTANCE T. HESS; Mrs. ANITA M. PAYNTER.

Notary—Mrs. MARLENE M. RAUDENSKY.

Victim Assistance Coordinator—MARK A. TOTARO, Ph.D., MBA. Tel: 717-657-4804. Email: mtotaro@hbgdiocese.org.

Vietnamese Ministry—Rev. HOA VAN NGUYEN, Coord., 929 N. Duke St., Lancaster, 17602. Tel: 717-392-2225.

Vocations, Office for—Rev. RAYMOND J. LAVOIE, Dir., 4800 Union Deposit Rd., Harrisburg, 17111-3710. Tel: 717-657-4804; Fax: 717-657-4042.

World Apostolate of Fatima—Rev. JOHN A. SZADA JR., Spiritual Moderator, St. Vincent de Paul, 224 Third St., Hanover, 17331. Tel: 717-637-5190.

Youth and Young Adult Ministry, Office for—Mr. ROBERT J. WILLIAMS, Dir., 4800 Union Deposit Rd., Harrisburg, 17111-3710. Tel: 717-657-4804; Fax: 717-657-4041.

Youth Protection Program—Rev. Msgr. WILLIAM J. KING, J.C.D., V.G.; Mrs. JANET E. JACKSON, M.C.I.P.D., Compliance Coord., 4800 Union Deposit Rd., Harrisburg, 17111-3710. Tel: 717-657-4804; Fax: 717-657-2453.

CLERGY, PARISHES, MISSIONS AND PAROCHIAL SCHOOLS

CITY OF HARRISBURG

(DAUPHIN COUNTY)

1—CATHEDRAL PARISH OF ST. PATRICK (1995) Rev. Thomas J. Rozman; Deacons Charles W. Clark; Lawrence R. Crudup. In Res., Rev. Michael C. Letteer.
Res.: 212 State St., 17101. Tel: 717-232-2169; Fax: 717-232-2799. Email: cathedralparish@comcast.net. Web: www.stpatrickcathedral.com.
Catechesis/Religious Program—Students 74.

2—ST. CATHERINE LABOURE (1948), (Shrine of the Miraculous Medal) Revs. Neil S. Sullivan; Joseph Howard, Parochial Vicar; Deacons Thomas H. Flannery; Thomas A. Fedor; John C. Heil. In Res., Revs. Bernard P. McGinley (Retired); Jordan Hite, T.O.R.; Rev. Msgr. Vincent J. Topper (Retired).
Res.: 4000 Derry St., 17111. Tel: 717-564-1321; Fax: 717-564-8822. Email: parishinfo@sclhbg.org. Web: www.sclhbg.org.
School—4020 Derry St., 17111. Tel: 717-564-1760; Fax: 717-564-3010. Web: www.stcatherinelaboure.org. Jennifer Wicht, Prin.; Tricia McKinney, Dir. Advancement. Sisters of Christian Charity, Mendham, NJ (SCC) 2; Lay Teachers 27; Students 364.
Catechesis/Religious Program— Fatima Roberge, D.R.E. Students 383.
Convent—4010 Derry St., 17111. Tel: 717-745-4134. Email: ihmsisters@sclhbg.org. Web: www.ihmimmaculata.org. Sr. Mary L. Birster, I.H.M., Supr. Sisters, Servants of the Immaculate Heart of Mary

3—ST. FRANCIS OF ASSISI (1901) Very Rev. John F. Bednarik, O.F.M.Cap.; Rev. Leon Leitem, O.F.M.Cap.; Deacon Miguel Marroquin. In Res., Rev. Matthew Palkowski, O.F.M.Cap.; Orlando Reyes, O.F.M.Cap.
Res.: 1439 Market St., 17103. Tel: 717-232-1003; Fax: 717-232-4536. Email: cfagan@hbgdiocese.org.
Catechesis/Religious Program—Tel: 717-233-7912. Students 155.

4—HOLY FAMILY (1958) Rev. Robert A. Yohe Jr.
Church: 555 S. 25th St., 17104. Tel: 717-232-4237; Fax: 717-232-9661.
Rectory—2501 Barkley Ln., 17104. Tel: 717-561-8250.
School—Tel: 717-232-2551. Sr. Kathleen Gorman, Prin. Sisters Servants of the Immaculate Heart of Mary 3; Lay Teachers 9; Students 130.
Catechesis/Religious Program—Tel: 717-232-2551. Students 9.
Convent—2473 Adrian St., 17104. Tel: 717-564-7236.

5—HOLY NAME OF JESUS (Lower Paxton Twp.) (1960) Very Rev. Edward J. Quinlan; Rev. Mark M. Speitel, Parochial Vicar; Deacons Jerome T. Foerster; Joseph J. Wrabel.
Res.: 6150 Allentown Blvd., 17112-2603. Tel: 717-652-4211; Fax: 717-652-2033. Email: p036holyname@hbgdiocese.org. Web: www.holynameofjesus.com.
School—(Grades PreK-8), 6190 Allentown Blvd., 17112-2603. Tel: 717-657-1704; Fax: 717-657-9135. Email: s036holyname@hbgdiocese.org. Sr. Rita Smith, S.S.J., Prin.; Mrs. Elaine Tomeck, Librarian. (Lower Paxton Twp.) Sisters of St. Joseph 1; Lay Teachers 26; Students 366.
Catechesis/Religious Program— Sr. Rita Smith, S.S.J., D.R.E. Students 522.
Convent—Tel: 717-545-4357. Email: ssjhnj@ezonline.net. Pastoral Associates 1.

6—ST. LAWRENCE (1859), (German), Closed. See St. Patrick Cathedral, Harrisburg.

7—ST. MARGARET MARY ALACOQUE (Penbrook) (1948) Rev. Daniel F.X. Powell; Mrs. Karen Hurley, Pastoral Assoc.
Res.: 2848 Herr St., 17103-1817. Tel: 717-233-3062; Fax: 717-238-5633. Email: rectory@stmmparish.org. Web: www.stmmparish.org.
Worship Site—2800 Paxton Church Rd., 17110.
School—Tel: 717-232-3771; Fax: 717-232-0776. Web: school.stmmparish.org. Mrs. Jean Fennessy, Prin. Lay Teachers 25; Students 404.
Catechesis/Religious Program— Bonnie Finnerty, C.R.E. Students 180.

8—OUR LADY OF THE BLESSED SACRAMENT (1906) Revs. Paul C.B. Schenck, Admin.; Paul R. Fisher, Parochial Vicar; Deacon James B. Doyle.
Res.: 2121 N. Third St., 17110-1812. Tel: 717-233-1014; Fax: 717-234-5652.
Catechesis/Religious Program—Students 33.

9—SACRED HEART OF JESUS (1901) Closed. See St. Patrick Cathedral, Harrisburg.

OUTSIDE THE CITY OF HARRISBURG

ABBOTTSTOWN, YORK CO., IMMACULATE HEART OF MARY (1809) [CEM] Rev. Kenneth G. Smith; Deacon Raymond J. Smith. In Res., Rev. Msgr. Robert C. Gribbin (Retired).
Res.: 6084 W. Canal Rd., 17301. Tel: 717-259-0611; Fax: 717-259-6371.
Catechesis/Religious Program—Tel: 717-259-9426. Students 154.

ANNVILLE, LEBANON CO., ST. PAUL THE APOSTLE

(1928) Rev. John J. Peck, O.S.B.; Mary Beazley, Music Min.
Res.: 125 S. Spruce St., 17003. Tel: 717-867-1525; Fax: 717-867-5318. Email: p002stpaul@hbgdiocese.org. Web: www.saintpaulsinannville.org.
Catechesis/Religious Program—Tel: 717-867-7471. Sr. Mary Cronin, D.M., D.R.E. Students 285.
Station—Lebanon Valley College, Miller Chapel, Tel: 717-867-6135.

BERWICK, COLUMBIA CO.

1—IMMACULATE CONCEPTION OF THE BLESSED VIRGIN MARY (1906) [CEM] Rev. Francis J. Tamburro.
Res.: 1730 Fowler Ave., 18603-1462. Tel: 570-759-8113; Fax: 570-759-6637.
See Holy Family Consolidated School, Berwick under Consolidated Elementary Schools located in the Institution section.
Catechesis/Religious Program—Tel: 570-759-9225. Students 204.

2—ST. JOSEPH'S (1928) Rev. Dennis G. Dalessandro; Sisters M. Carmel Marie, Pastoral Assoc.; M. Amelia, D.M., Pastoral Assoc.; M. Michael Jean, D.M., Pastoral Assoc.
Res.: 721 Monroe St., 18603. Tel: 570-752-5684; 570-752-7000; Fax: 570-752-5010.
See Holy Family Consolidated School, Berwick under Consolidated Elementary Schools located in the Institution section.
Catechesis/Religious Program—Students 75.
Convent—Daughters of Mercy, 728 Washington St., 18603. Tel: 570-752-2112. Sisters 3.

BLOOMSBURG, COLUMBIA CO., ST. COLUMBA (1882), (Irish), [CEM] Rev. Msgr. Robert E. Lawrence.
Res.: 342 Iron Street, 17815-1824. Tel: 570-784-0801; Fax: 570-387-2604.
School—(Grades PreK-8), 40 E. Third St., 17815. Tel: 570-784-5932; Fax: 570-387-1257. Email: scsprincipal@saintcolumbaschool.org. Mrs. Nancy D. Sheehan-Becker, Prin.; Mrs. Carol Phillips, Librarian. Sisters 2; Lay Teachers 12; Students 118.
Catechesis/Religious Program—Tel: 570-784-0801. Students 189.
Mission—Christ the King Mendenhall Ln., Benton, Columbia Co. 17814. Tel: 570-925-6969. P.O. Box 297, Benton, 17814. Rev. Timothy D. Marcoe, Admin.

BLUE RIDGE SUMMIT, FRANKLIN CO., ST. RITA (1919) [JC] Rev. Michael A. Messaro, M.SS.CC.; Very Rev. Robert P. Malagesi, M.SS.CC., Parochial Vicar.
Mailing Address: *Immaculate Conception*, 256 Tract Rd., Fairfield, 17320. Tel: 717-642-8815; Fax: 717-642-9616. Email: bstaples@hbgdiocese.org.
Catechesis/Religious Program—Tel: 717-794-2067. Students 62.

BONNEAUVILLE, ADAM CO., ST. JOSEPH THE WORKER (1859) [CEM] Rev. Augusty T. Valomchalil, M.S.S.C.C.; Deacon Richard J. Weaver.
Res.: 12 E. Hanover St., Gettysburg, 17325-7750. Tel: 717-334-2510; Fax: 717-337-1968.
Catechesis/Religious Program—Students 42.

BUCHANAN VALLEY, ADAMS CO., ST. IGNATIUS LOYOLA (Orrtanna) (1817) [CEM] Rev. Daniel P. O'Brien.
Res.: 1095 Church Rd., Orrtanna, 17353. Tel: 717-677-8012; Fax: 717-677-6350.
Catechesis/Religious Program—Tel: 717-677-8012. Students 60.

CAMP HILL, CUMBERLAND CO., GOOD SHEPHERD (1951) Rev. Paul C. Helwig; Deacons Francis C. Gorman; Patrick M. Kiley; Derrick Rosenstein, Parish Mgr.
3435 Trindle Rd., 17011. Tel: 717-761-1167; Fax: 717-761-5313. In Res., Very Rev. Philip G. Burger.
School—Elementary, 3400 Market St., 17011. Tel: 717-737-7261; Fax: 717-761-4673. Web: www.gss-chpa.org. Mr. Robert E. Graf, Prin. Lay Teachers 21; Students 275.
Catechesis/Religious Program—3400 Market St., 17011. Tel: 717-737-8216; Fax: 717-737-4673. Amanda Spahr, C.R.E. Students 249.

CARLISLE, CUMBERLAND CO., SAINT PATRICK (1779) [CEM 2] Very Rev. William C. Forrey; Rev. Dwight D. Schlaline. In Res., Revs. Andre J. Meluskey (Retired); Daniel J. Menniti (Retired).
Res.: 152 E. Pomfret St., 17013. Tel: 717-243-4411; Fax: 717-258-9281. Email: po12stpatrickparishcarlisle@hbgdiocese.org. Web: www.saintpatrickchurch.org.
School—87 Marsh Dr., 17015. Tel: 717-249-4826; Fax: 717-245-0522. Web: www.spscarlisle.us. Lay Teachers 32; Students 307.
Catechesis/Religious Program—Tel: 717-243-4891; Fax: 717-245-0552. Joan Ellen Frist, C.R.E.; Mr. Joseph Goodman, Dir. Life Teen & Youth Min. Students 356.
Chapel—Pine Grove Furnace, St. Eleanor Regina
Chapel—St. Katherine Drexel Chapel - Perpetual Adoration

CENTRALIA, COLUMBIA CO., ST. IGNATIUS (1869) Closed. See Our Lady of Mount Carmel, Mount Carmel.

CHAMBERSBURG, FRANKLIN CO., CORPUS CHRISTI (1792) [CEM] Very Rev. James R. O'Brien; Revs. Ignacio Palomino, Parochial Vicar; Keith M. Carroll.
Res.: 320 Philadelphia Ave., 17201. Tel: 717-264-6317; Fax: 717-264-1787.
School—305 N. Second St., 17201. Tel: 717-263-5036; Fax: 717-263-6079. Mr. Robert G. Dortenzo, Prin. Lay Teachers 20; Students 260.
Catechesis/Religious Program—Tel: 717-263-9541. Mr. David C. Cheslock, D.R.E. Students 248.
Mission—Our Lady of Refuge 21169 Cross Rd., Doylesburg, Franklin Co. 17219. Tel: 717-349-7953.

COAL TOWNSHIP, NORTHUMBERLAND CO.

1—OUR LADY OF HOPE (1995) Revs. Adrian Gallagher, O.F.M.Conv.; John Voytek, O.F.M.Conv.; Deacon Robert P. Mack.
Res.: 863 W. Chestnut St., 17866-1995. Tel: 570-648-4432; Fax: 570-648-8944. Email: p130ourladyhope2@hbgdiocese.org.
Catechesis/Religious Program—Students 59.

2—ST. STEPHEN PROTOMARTYR (1898), (Polish), Closed. See Our Lady of Hope, Coal Township.

COLUMBIA, LANCASTER CO.

1—HOLY TRINITY (1860) [CEM] Very Rev. Kenneth F. Lawrence; Sr. Anna Cosgrave, O.S.F., Pastoral Assoc.
Res.: 409 Cherry St., 17512. Tel: 717-684-2711; Fax: 717-684-9612. Email: jreese@hbgdiocese.org.
School—(Consolidated), 404 Cherry St., 17512. Tel: 717-684-2664; Fax: 717-684-5039. Theresa Burg, Prin. Lay Teachers 14; Students 94.
Catechesis/Religious Program—Tel: 717-684-2232. Students 109.
Convent—Sisters of St. Francis of Philadelphia, 548 Cherry St., 17512. Tel: 717-684-2232.

2—ST. PETER (1828) [CEM 2] Rev. Dominic M. DiBiccaro.
Res.: 121 S. Second St., 17512. Tel: 717-684-7070; Fax: 717-684-3102.
See Our Lady of Angels, Columbia under Consolidated Elementary Schools located in the Institution section.
Catechesis/Religious Program—Tel: 717-684-7070. Corrinne Eck, D.R.E. Students 37.
Mission—Mother of Holy Purity Chapel 217 Maple St., Wrightsville, 17368.

CONEWAGO TOWNSHIP, ADAMS CO., BASILICA OF THE SACRED HEART OF JESUS (1730) [CEM] Rev. Lawrence J. McNeil.
Res.: 30 Basilica Dr., Hanover, 17331-8924. Tel: 717-637-2721; Fax: 717-637-4569.
School—50 Basilica Dr., Hanover, 17331. Tel: 717-632-8715; Fax: 717-632-6596. Crystal Noel, Prin. Sisters of St. Joseph 1; Lay Teachers 9; Students 260.
Catechesis/Religious Program—Students 50.
Convent—Sisters of St. Joseph, 55 Basilica Dr., Hanover, 17331. Tel: 717-637-3370. Sisters 4.

CORNWALL, LEBANON CO., SACRED HEART OF JESUS (1886) [CEM] Rev. Rodrigo A. Arrazola; Becky Broderic, Pastoral Assoc.
Res.: 2596 Cornwall Rd., P.O. Box 136, 17016-0136.
Parish Center—Tel: 717-274-3239; Fax: 717-273-9588.
Catechesis/Religious Program—Tel: 717-273-2160. Students 95.

DALLASTOWN, YORK CO., ST. JOSEPH (1850) [CEM] Rev. John McCloskey, O.F.M.Cap.; Deacon Daniel L. Bernardy.
Res.: 251 E. Main St., 17313. Tel: 717-246-3007; Fax: 717-244-5278. Email: stjosephdtown@comcast.net. Web: www.sjdchurch.com.
School—271 E. Main St., 17313. Tel: 717-244-9386; Fax: 717-244-9478. Web: www.stjoesdallastown.org. Margaret Snyder, Prin. Lay Teachers 10; Students 130.
Catechesis/Religious Program—Tel: 717-246-9959. Email: psivulka@yahoo.com. Students 370.

DANVILLE, MONTOUR CO., ST. JOSEPH (1848) [CEM 3] Rev. Steven W. Fauser.
Res.: 18 E. Center St., 17821. Tel: 570-275-2512; Fax: 570-275-6840.
School—511 Ferry St., 17821. Tel: 717-275-2435; Fax: 570-275-3947. Lay Teachers 11; Students 150.
Catechesis/Religious Program—Students 165.

DAUPHIN, DAUPHIN CO., ST. MATTHEW, APOSTLE AND EVANGELIST (1976) Rev. Paul M. Clark; Deacon Richard Aull.
Res.: 420 Stony Creek Rd., P.O. Box 459, 17018. Tel: 717-921-2363; Fax: 717-921-2364.
Catechesis/Religious Program—Students 31.

DOYLESBURG, FRANKLIN CO., OUR LADY OF REFUGE MISSION (1802) [CEM] Unassigned.21169 Cross Rd., 17219-9707. Tel: 717-349-7953; Fax: 717-349-7953.
Catechesis/Religious Program—Students 12.

ELIZABETHTOWN, LANCASTER CO., ST. PETER (1752) [CEM] Rev. David L. Danneker.
Parish Office—1840 Marshall Dr., 17022. Tel: 717-367-1255; Fax: 717-367-1270. Email: secretary@stpeteretown.org. Web: www.stpeteretown.org.
Res.: 1 Saint Peter's Pl., 17022-1956.
School—61 E. Washington St., 17022. Tel: 717-367-1678; Fax: 717-367-3081. Email: secretary@spschooletown.org. Web: www.spschooletown.org. Mrs. Suzanne Wood, Prin. Lay Teachers 6; Students 64.
Catechesis/Religious Program—Email: cre@stpeteretown.org. Web: www.stpeteretown.org/education.htm. Students 161.

ELYSBURG, NORTHUMBERLAND CO., QUEEN OF THE MOST HOLY ROSARY (1950) [JC] Very Rev. Alfred P. Sceski.
Res.: 599 W. Center St., 17824. Tel: 570-672-2302; Fax: 570-672-3310. Web: www.qmhr.net.
Catechesis/Religious Program—Students 298.

ENHAUT, DAUPHIN CO., ST. JOHN THE EVANGELIST (1902) Closed. See Prince of Peace, Steelton.

ENOLA, CUMBERLAND CO., OUR LADY OF LOURDES (1926) Rev. Michael J. Grab.
Res.: 225 Salt Rd., 17025. Tel: 717-732-9642; Fax: 717-732-8184. Email: olchurch@comcast.net.
Catechesis/Religious Program—Students 287.

EPHRATA, LANCASTER CO., MOTHER OF PERPETUAL HELP (1914) [JC] Revs. John McLoughlin, C.Ss.R.; Robert Harrison, C.S.s.R., Parochial Vicar.
Church Office: 320 Church Ave., 17522. Tel: 717-733-9641; Fax: 717-733-2119. Email: perpetualhelp@dejazzd.com. Web: omphchurch.org.
Res.: 300 W. Pine St., 17522. Tel: 717-733-6596; Fax: 717-733-0502.
School—330 Church Ave., 17522. Tel: 717-738-2414; Fax: 717-738-3280. Email: office@omph.org. Web: www.omph.org. Margaret Gardner, Prin. Lay Teachers 10; Students 221.
Catechesis/Religious Program—Tel: 717-738-4517; Fax: 717-733-2119. Students 500.
Convent—310 Church Ave., 17522. Tel: 717-733-1291.

FAIRFIELD, ADAMS CO., IMMACULATE CONCEPTION OF THE BLESSED VIRGIN MARY (1823) [CEM] [JC] Rev. Michael A. Messaro, M.SS.CC.; Very Rev. Robert P. Malagesi, M.SS.CC., Parochial Vicar.
Res.: 256 Tract Rd., 17320. Tel: 717-642-8815; Fax: 717-642-9616. Email: bstaples@hbgdiocese.org.
Catechesis/Religious Program—Students 76.

GETTYSBURG, ADAMS CO., ST. FRANCIS XAVIER'S (1831) [CEM] Revs. Benardo Pistone; Jonathan P. Sawicki.
Office & Res.: 455 Table Rock Rd., 17325. Tel: 717-334-3919; 717-334-7711; Fax: 717-334-3919; 717-334-7711.
Church: 25 W. High St., 17325.
School—465 Table Rock Rd., 17325. Tel: 717-334-4221; Fax: 717-334-8883. Sisters of Mercy 1; Sisters of St. Joseph 1; Lay Teachers 19; Students 251.
Catechesis/Religious Program—Tel: 717-334-1221. Students 514.
Convent—Sisters of Mercy Convent, Tel: 717-334-4310. Sisters 5.

GREENCASTLE, FRANKLIN CO., ST. MARK THE EVANGELIST (1965) [JC] Rev. Joseph L. Stahura.
Res.: 395 S. Ridge Ave., P.O. Box 218, 17225. Tel: 717-597-2705. Email: stmkstlk@comcast.net.
Catechesis/Religious Program—Tel: 717-597-2705. Students 143.
Mission—St. Luke the Evangelist Overhill Dr. & Black Rd., Mercersburg, Franklin Co. 17236.

HANOVER, YORK CO.

1—ST. JOSEPH (1864) [CEM] Very Rev. Joseph F. Gotwalt; Rev. James E. Lease, Parochial Vicar.
Res.: 5055 Grandview Rd., 17331. Tel: 717-637-5236; Fax: 717-637-6615. Web: www.stjosephparishhanover.org.
School—236 Baltimore St., 17331. Tel: 717-632-1335; Fax: 717-632-5147. Web: www.sjshanover-.org. Mrs. Susan M. Mummert, Prin. Lay Teachers 16; Students 225.
School—Middle School, 5125 Grandview Rd., 17331. Tel: 717-632-0118; Fax: 717-632-0030.
Catechesis/Religious Program—Students 403.

2—ST. VINCENT (1904) [CEM] Rev. Jeffrey Thoms, Admin.
Res.: 220 Third St., 17331. Tel: 717-637-4625; Fax: 717-637-6650. Email: dklinedinst@hbgdiocese.org. Web: www.svparish.org.
Catechesis/Religious Program—Students 38.

HERSHEY, DAUPHIN CO., ST. JOAN OF ARC (1920) Revs. Michael W. Rothan; Brian J. Wayne, Parochial Vicar. In Res., Rev. Chukwubikem Okpechi, O.P., Chap., Hershey Medical Center.
Res.: 359 W. Areba Ave., 17033. Tel: 717-533-7168; Fax: 717-520-0526. Email: sjaoffice@gmail.com. Web: www.stjoanhershey.org.
School—329 W. Areba Ave., 17033. Tel: 717-533-2854; Fax: 717-534-0755. Email: sreileen@stjoanhershey.org. Sr. Eileen M. McGowan, Prin. Daughters of Our Lady of Mercy 1; Lay Teachers 25; Students 337.
Catechesis/Religious Program—Tel: 717-533-8578. Email: stjoanrep@yahoo.com. Students 700.

Convent—Sisters 5.

KULPMONT, NORTHUMBERLAND CO.

1—ASSUMPTION OF THE BLESSED VIRGIN MARY (1909) Closed. See Holy Angels, Kulpmont.

2—ST. CASIMIR (1915) Closed. See Holy Angels, Kulpmont.

3—HOLY ANGELS (1995) [CEM 3] Rev. Andrew J. Stahmer.
Res.: 855 Scott St., 17834. Tel: 570-373-1221; Fax: 570-373-1226.
Catechesis/Religious Program—863 Scott St., 17834. Tel: 570-373-3801. Students 109.

LANCASTER, LANCASTER CO.

1—ST. ANNE (1923) Rev. Norman C. Hohenwarter Jr.
Res.: 929 N. Duke St., 17602. Tel: 717-392-2225; Fax: 717-392-3985.
School—108 E. Liberty St., 17602. Tel: 717-394-6711; Fax: 717-394-8628. Dr. Christopher Kennedy, Prin.
Catechesis/Religious Program—Tel: 717-509-8554. Mrs. Nicole Martin, C.R.E. Students 245.

2—ST. ANTHONY OF PADUA (1870) [CEM] Rev. Daniel C. Mitzel. In Res., Rev. John A. Acri (Retired).
Res.: 501 E. Orange St., 17602. Tel: 717-394-0669; Fax: 717-394-4507.
See Resurrection, Lancaster under Consolidated Elementary Schools located in the Institution section.
Catechesis/Religious Program—Tel: 717-392-2930. Patricia Meyer, D.R.E. Students 154.
Station—Lancaster County Prison, Tel: 717-299-7800.
Station—Conestoga View Nursing Home, Tel: 717-299-7850.

3—ASSUMPTION OF THE BLESSED VIRGIN MARY (1741) Rev. Leo M. Goodman; Mrs. Frances Sescilla, Pastoral Assoc.; Deacon Manuel Velazquez.
Res.: 119 S. Prince St., 17603. Tel: 717-392-2578; Fax: 717-394-6549. Email: p049assumptionlanc@hbgdiocese.org. Web: www.stmaryslancaster.org.
See Resurrection, Lancaster under Consolidated Elementary Schools located in the Institution section.
Catechesis/Religious Program—Anne Barnes, D.R.E. Students 225.

4—IGLESIA CATOLICA SAN JUAN BAUTISTA Revs. Allan F. Wolfe; Jose E. Mera-Vallejos, Parochial Vicar; Deacons Expedito Santos-Santiago; Manuel Velazquez; Felix Ramos; Jose A. Lopez.
425 S. Duke St., 17602. Tel: 717-392-4118; Fax: 717-392-4789. Email: p127sanjuan@hbgdiocese.org.
Catechesis/Religious Program—Armando Torres, D.R.E. Students 324.

5—ST. JOHN NEUMANN (1978) Rev. Msgr. Richard A. Youtz; Revs. Paul Theisz; Michael J. Culkin; Rose M. Toole, Pastoral Assoc.; Mrs. Yolanda Larson, Pastoral Assoc.
Res.: 601 E. Delp Rd., 17601. Tel: 717-569-8531; Fax: 717-569-2135. Email: info@sjnlancaster.org. Web: saintjohnneumannlancaster.org.
Catechesis/Religious Program—Tel: 717-569-8533; 717-581-9156 (Youth Ministry). Mrs. Rose Poet, D.R.E. Students 997.

6—ST. JOSEPH (1849) [CEM] Rev. Msgr. Thomas H. Smith; Deacon Martin C. Light Sr.; Mrs. Patricia Weaver, Pastoral Assoc. In Res., Revs. Joseph C. Hilbert (Retired); Tariq Isaac.
Res.: 440 St. Joseph St., 17603-5298. Tel: 717-397-6921; Fax: 717-397-2120. Email: msgrtsmith@hbgdiocese.org. Web: www.stjosephslanc.com.
See Resurrection, Lancaster under Consolidated Elementary Schools located in the Institution section.
Catechesis/Religious Program—Students 160.

7—SACRED HEART OF JESUS (1900) Rev. Michael E. Messner. In Res., Rev. Arokiaswamy Samson.
Res.: 558 W. Walnut St., 17603. Tel: 717-394-0757; Fax: 717-394-3589. Email: sacredheartlanc@verizon.net. Web: sacredheartlanc.org.
School—235 Nevin St., 17603. Tel: 717-393-8433; Fax: 717-393-1028. Email: shschool@comcast.net. Web: www.sacredheartschoollancaster.com. Sr. Mary Carmel, I.H.M., Prin. Sisters (Servants of the Immaculate Heart of Mary) 3; Lay Teachers 14; Students 164.
Catechesis/Religious Program—Sr. Mary Elizabeth Schmidt, I.H.M., D.R.E. Students 55.
Convent—565 W. Walnut St., 17603. Tel: 717-392-4522.

LEBANON, LEBANON CO.

1—ASSUMPTION OF THE BLESSED VIRGIN MARY (1812) [CEM] Rev. Michael P. Reid II; Deacon Richard Wentzel, Pastoral Assoc. In Res., Rev. Harold F. Dagle (ALN) (Retired).
Office & Res.: 2 N. Eighth St., 17046-5008. Tel: 717-272-5674; Fax: 717-270-2734. Email: abvmleb@comcast.net.
Catechesis/Religious Program—Students 78.
Mission—Our Lady of Fatima US 22 & N. Mill St., Jonestown, Lebanon Co. 17038. Tel: 717-865-7439.
Catechesis/Religious Program—Students 59.

2—ST. BENEDICT THE ABBOT (1995) Rev. Walter F. Guzman.
Res.: 1300 Lehman St., 17046-3331. Tel: 717-450-4506; Fax: 717-270-6926. Web: www.sbaclpa.com.
Catechesis/Religious Program—Students 45.

3—ST. CECILIA (1995) [CEM] Rev. Joseph T. Scanlin.
Res.: 202 E. Lehman St., 17046. Tel: 717-272-4412; Fax: 717-272-3966. Email: scecilia@nbn.net.
Catechesis/Religious Program—Tel: 717-272-4352. Sisters 1; Students 133.
Convent—202 E. Lehman St., 2nd Fl., 17046.

4—SS. CYRIL AND METHODIUS (1905), (Slovak), Closed. See St. Benedict the Abbot, Lebanon.

5—ST. GERTRUDE (1906) Closed. See St. Cecilia, Lebanon.

6—ST. GREGORY THE GREAT (1965) Closed. See St. Cecilia, Lebanon.

LEWISBURG, UNION CO., SACRED HEART OF JESUS (1935) Rev. Msgr. William M. Richardson.
Res.: 814 St. Louis St., 17837. Tel: 570-523-3104; Fax: 570-523-3157.
Catechesis/Religious Program—Amanda Ciccocioppo, Youth Min.; Sr. Thomas More Dzurnak, SS.C.M., D.R.E., Pastoral Asst. Students 310.
Mission—Saint George Church 775 Forest Hill Rd., Mifflinburg, Union Co. 17844. Tel: 570-966-3088.

LEWISTOWN, MIFFLIN CO., SACRED HEART OF JESUS (1830) [CEM] Revs. William M. Weary; Fidelis Umukoro, O.P.
Office: 9 N. Brown St., 17044. Tel: 717-242-2781; Fax: 717-447-0058. Email: mbender@sacredheartlewistown.com. Web: www.sacredheartlewistown.com.
Res.: 106 N. Dorcas St., 17044. Tel: 717-447-0727.
School—110 N. Dorcas St., 17044. Tel: 717-248-5351; 717-447-2002; Fax: 717-248-1516. Email: shsoffice@sacredheartlewistown.com. Web: www.sacredheartschool.com. Lay Teachers 10; Students 88.
Catechesis/Religious Program—Email: shparishoffice@sacredheartlewistown.com. Students 88.

LITITZ, LANCASTER CO., ST. JAMES (1977) [CEM 3] Rev. James O'Blaney, C.Ss.R.
Res.: 505 Woodcrest Ave., 17543. Tel: 717-626-5580; Fax: 717-626-2146. Email: p060stjames@hbgdiocese.org. Web: www.stjameslititz.org.
Catechesis/Religious Program—Tel: 717-626-0244. Email: re060@hbgdiocese.org. Rose Barnas, D.R.E. Students 319.

LITTLESTOWN, ADAMS CO., ST. ALOYSIUS (1884) [CEM] Rev. James M. Sterner.
Res.: 29 S. Queen St., 17340. Tel: 717-359-4513; Fax: 717-359-0683.
Catechesis/Religious Program—Cynthia Baughman, C.R.E. Students 57.

LOCUST GAP, NORTHUMBERLAND CO., ST. JOSEPH (1870) Closed. See Our Lady of Mount Carmel, Mount Carmel.

LOCUSTDALE, COLUMBIA CO., ST. JOSEPH (1913) Closed. See Our Lady of Mount Carmel, Mount Carmel.

LYKENS, DAUPHIN CO., OUR LADY HELP OF CHRISTIANS (1853) [CEM 2] [JC 3] Rev. C. Anthony Miller.
Res.: 732 E. Main St., 17048. Tel: 717-453-7895; Fax: 717-453-9426.
Catechesis/Religious Program—Students 104.
Mission—Sacred Heart of Jesus 140 E. Market St., Williamstown, Dauphin Co. 17098.

MANHEIM, LANCASTER CO., ST. RICHARD (1957) [JC] Rev. Francis Menei; Deacons William J. Jordan; Donovan A. Mann.
Res.: 201 Adele Ave., 17545. Tel: 717-665-2465; Fax: 717-665-7119.
Catechesis/Religious Program—Students 70.

MARIETTA, LANCASTER CO., PRESENTATION OF THE BLESSED VIRGIN MARY (1869) Closed. See Mary, Mother of the Church, Mount Joy.

MARION HEIGHTS, NORTHUMBERLAND CO., OUR LADY OF PERPETUAL HELP (1905) Closed. See Holy Angels, Kulpmont.

MARYSVILLE, PERRY CO., OUR LADY OF GOOD COUNSEL (1965) Rev. John P. Trigilio Jr.
Res.: 121 William St., 17053. Tel: 717-957-2662; Fax: 717-957-4247. Email: church@olgcsb.org. Web: www.olgcsb.org.
Catechesis/Religious Program—Tel: 717-957-9218. Mary Olley, D.R.E. Students 20.
Mission—St. Bernadette (1954) 901 High St., Duncannon, Perry Co. 17020. Tel: 717-834-4519.
Catechesis/Religious Program—Emily VisLocky, D.R.E. Students 35.

MCSHERRYSTOWN, ADAMS CO., ANNUNCIATION OF THE BLESSED VIRGIN MARY (1899) [CEM] Rev. Lawrence W. Sherdel; Deacon Joseph F. Lawrence.
Res.: 26 N. Third St., 17344. Tel: 717-637-1191; Fax: 717-637-1715.
School—316 North St., 17344. Tel: 717-637-3135. Email: abvmbusoff@abvmschool.org. Web: www.abvmschool.org. Ms. Amy McNeill, Prin. Lay Teachers 21; Students 262.
Catechesis/Religious Program—Students 50.

MECHANICSBURG, CUMBERLAND CO.

1—ST. ELIZABETH ANN SETON (1977) Rev. Msgr. William J. King; Rev. Tri M. Luong, Parochial Vicar. In Res., Rev. Msgr. William J. King.
Res.: 310 Hertzler Rd., 17055. Tel: 717-697-2614; Fax: 717-795-0800. Web: www.steas-mech.org.
Catechesis/Religious Program—Tel: 717-697-3545. Email: cstrakaseas@comcast.net. Candice Straka, C.R.E.; Judy Olinger, C.R.E. Students 393.

2—ST. JOSEPH (1950) Revs. Chester P. Snyder; David M. Hereshko, Parochial Vicar; Deacon Jack Paruso; John Durle, Parish Mgr.
410 E. Simpson St., P.O. Box 2012, 17055. In Res., Rev. William J. Sullivan (Retired).
Res.: P.O. Box 2012, 17055. Tel: 717-766-9433 (Office); Fax: 717-795-9123. Email: parishoffice@stjosephmech.org.
Church: 400 E. Simpson St., 17055.
School—420 E. Simpson St., 17055. Tel: 717-766-2564; Fax: 717-766-1226. John Cominsky, Prin. Lay Teachers 26; Students 392.
Catechesis/Religious Program—Tel: 717-766-2472. Richard Groff, D.R.E. Students 367.

3—SAINT KATHARINE DREXEL (1988) Rev. Stephen D. Weitzel; Jodi M. Bova, Parish Mgr.; John Frye III, Dir. Music.
Mailing Address: One Peter Dr., 17050. Web: skdparish.com. In Res., Rev. Msgr. Vincent J. Smith (Retired).
Res.: 87 Skyline Dr., 17050. Tel: 717-697-8716; Fax: 717-697-3702.
Catechesis/Religious Program—(Grades K-8) Tel: 717-795-8572. Julie A. Worhach, D.R.E.; Michael E. Creavey, Dir., Youth & Young Adult Ministry; Suzanne Bruzga, Pastoral Assoc. Students 332.

MIDDLETOWN, DAUPHIN CO., SEVEN SORROWS OF THE BLESSED VIRGIN MARY (1855) Rev. Louis P. Ogden; Deacon Thomas A. Lang. In Res., Rev. Edward R. Lavelle.
Res.: 280 N. Race St., 17057. Tel: 717-944-3133; Fax: 717-944-1170. Email: church@sevensorrows.org. Web: www.sevensorrows.org.
School—(Grades PreK-8), 360 E. Water St., 17057. Tel: 717-944-5371; Fax: 717-944-5419. Mrs. Loretta Miller, Prin. Lay Teachers 14; Students 208.
Catechesis/Religious Program— Ray Kerwin, D.R.E. Students 161.

MIFFLINTOWN, JUNIATA CO., ST. JUDE (1959) Revs. William M. Weary; Fidelis Umukoro, O.P.
P.O. Box 187, 17059.
Res.: 106 N. Dorcas St., Lewistown, 17044. Tel: 717-242-2781. Email: rectory@stjudemifflintown.org. Web: www.stjudemifflintown.org. Res.: 9 N. Brown St., Lewistown, 17044.
Catechesis/Religious Program—Students 34.
Mission—St. Jude Thaddeus William Penn Hwy., 17059.

MILLERSBURG, DAUPHIN CO., QUEEN OF PEACE (1952) Rev. Darius G. C. Moss. Email: fatherdariusmoss@yahoo.com.
Res.: 202 Zimmerman Rd., 17061. Tel: 717-692-3504; Fax: 717-692-5723.
Catechesis/Religious Program—Tel: 717-692-3504. Mrs. J. Roadcap, C.R.E. Students 61.

MILLERSVILLE, LANCASTER CO., ST. PHILIP THE APOSTLE (1965) Rev. Mark E. Weiss; Deacon Ross Beighley; Susan C. Havey, Parish Mgr.
Res.: 2111 Millersville Pike, Lancaster, 17603. Tel: 717-872-2166; Fax: 717-872-2587.
Catechesis/Religious Program—Tel: 717-872-5653 (Sundays only). Miss Christine M. Miller, D.R.E.; Stephen Sauer, Dir. Music. Students 260.

MILTON, NORTHUMBERLAND CO., ST. JOSEPH (1805) [CEM] Rev. Thomas A. Scala.
Res.: 109 Broadway, 17847. Tel: 570-742-4356; Fax: 570-742-3475.
Catechesis/Religious Program—854 Cemetery Rd., 17847. Tel: 570-724-4302. Harold Prentiss, C.R.E. Students 39.

MOUNT CARMEL, NORTHUMBERLAND CO.

1—DIVINE REDEEMER (1995) [CEM 4] Rev. John A. Szada Jr.
Res.: 438 West Ave., 17851. Tel: 570-339-3450; Fax: 570-339-5759. Email: divredeemr@verizon.net.
Catechesis/Religious Program—47 S. Market St., 17851. Tel: 570-339-1317; Fax: 570-339-4814. Students 58.

2—HOLY CROSS (1892), (Lithuanian), Closed. See Divine Redeemer, Mount Carmel.

3—ST. JOHN THE BAPTIST (1892), (Slovak), Closed. See Divine Redeemer, Mount Carmel.

4—ST. JOSEPH (1875), (Polish), Closed. See Our Lady of Mount Carmel, Mount Carmel.

5—OUR LADY OF MOUNT CARMEL (1886) [JC 4] Rev. Francis J. Karwacki; Deacon Martin P. McCarthy.
Res.: 47 S. Market St., 17851. Tel: 717-339-1031; Fax: 717-339-4814.

Catechesis/Religious Program—Tel: 717-339-1317. Karen Harris, C.R.E. Students 157.

6—OUR MOTHER OF CONSOLATION (1895), (Polish), Closed. See Divine Redeemer, Mount Carmel.

7—ST. PETER (1905), (Italian), Closed. See Divine Redeemer, Mount Carmel.

MOUNT JOY, LANCASTER CO.

1—ASSUMPTION OF B.V.M. (1979) Closed. See Mary, Mother of the Church, Mount Joy.

2—MARY, MOTHER OF THE CHURCH (1995) Rev. Luis R. Rodriguez.
Mailing Address: 625 Union School Rd., 17552-9712.
Res.: 530 St. Mary Dr., 17552-9712. Tel: 717-653-4903; Fax: 717-653-4915. Email: p138marymother@hbgdiocese.org.
Catechesis/Religious Program—Students 152.

MYERSTOWN, LEBANON COUNTY, MARY, GATE OF HEAVEN (1926) Rev. Robert F. Berger.
Res.: 188 W. McKinley Ave., P.O. Box 227, 17067. Tel: 717-866-5640; Fax: 717-866-5951.
Catechesis/Religious Program—Students 96.

NEW BLOOMFIELD, PERRY CO., ST. BERNARD (1942) Rev. Robert F. Sharman.
Res.: 811 Shermans Valley Rd., P.O. Box 25, 17068. Tel: 717-582-4113; Fax: 717-582-3797.
Catechesis/Religious Program— Alice Vilk, D.R.E. Students 150.

NEW CUMBERLAND, CUMBERLAND CO., ST. THERESA OF THE INFANT JESUS (1928) Revs. J. Michael McFadden; Tiburtis Antony Raja (India), Parochial Vicar. In Res., Rev. T. Ronald Haney (Retired).
Res.: 1300 Bridge St., 17070. Tel: 717-774-5918; Fax: 717-774-5915.
School—1200 Bridge St., 17070. Tel: 717-774-7464; Fax: 717-774-3154. Matthew Shore, Prin. (Elementary). Lay Teachers 32; Students 496.
Catechesis/Religious Program—Tel: 717-774-7296. Students 430.

NEW FREEDOM, YORK CO., ST. JOHN THE BAPTIST (1841) [CEM] Revs. Sylvan P. Capitani; Bernard Wamayose, A.J., Parochial Vicar; Deacons Michael Bahn, Pastoral Assoc.; Frederick C. Horn, Pastoral Assoc. In Res., Rev. C. Robert Nugent, S.D.S.
Res.: 315 N. Constitution Ave., 17349. Tel: 717-235-2156; Fax: 717-235-8595.
School—(Grades PreK-6) Tel: 717-235-3525. Sue Mareck, Prin.
Catechesis/Religious Program—Tel: 717-235-2439. Nelle Bailey, Dir. Music. Students 482.

NEW HOLLAND, LANCASTER CO., OUR LADY OF LOURDES (1972) Rev. John D. Schmalhofer.
Res.: 737 Walnut St., 17557. Tel: 717-354-2540; Fax: 717-354-4170.
Catechesis/Religious Program—Tel: 717-354-3338. Students 209.

NEW OXFORD, ADAMS CO., IMMACULATE CONCEPTION OF THE BLESSED VIRGIN MARY (1852) [CEM] Rev. Charles L. Persing.
Res.: 106 Carlisle St., 17350. Tel: 717-624-4121; Fax: 717-624-4221.
School—101 N. Peter St., 17350. Tel: 717-624-2061; Fax: 717-624-9711. Mrs. Donna Hoffman, Prin. Lay Teachers 13; Students 110.
Catechesis/Religious Program—Tel: 717-321-3939; Fax: 717-624-4221. Kimberly DePaulis, D.R.E. Students 70.

NORTHUMBERLAND, NORTHUMBERLAND CO., ST. THOMAS MORE (1955) Closed. See St. Monica, Sunbury.

PALMYRA, LEBANON CO., CHURCH OF THE HOLY SPIRIT (1955) Rev. James F. Podlesny, O.S.B.
Res.: 245 W. Pine St., 17078. Tel: 717-838-3369; Fax: 717-838-3065. Email: church@holyspiritrcchurch.com. Web: holyspiritrcchurch.com.
Catechesis/Religious Program— Marcie Warner, D.R.E. Students 323.

QUARRYVILLE, LANCASTER CO., ST. CATHERINE OF SIENA (1843) [CEM] Rev. Ronald J. Moratelli.
Res.: 955 Robert Fulton Hwy., 17566-9543. Tel: 717-786-2695; Fax: 717-786-0374. Email: p096stcatherinesiena@hbgdiocese.org.
Catechesis/Religious Program—Mrs. Diane Dalgaard, D.R.E. Students 130.

RANSHAW, NORTHUMBERLAND CO., ST. ANTHONY OF PADUA (1919) Closed. See Mother Cabrini, Shamokin.

ROARING CREEK, COLUMBIA CO., OUR LADY OF MERCY (1923) [CEM] Rev. Thomas Ignatius Mannion.
Res.: 304 Slabtown Rd., Catawissa, 17820. Tel: 570-799-5642.
Catechesis/Religious Program—Mrs. Margaret Jessick, D.R.E. Students 54.

ROHRERSTOWN, LANCASTER CO., ST. LEO THE GREAT (1964) Rev. Peter I. Hahn; Deacon Eugene Vannucci.
Res.: 2427 Marietta Ave., Lancaster, 17601. Tel: 717-394-1742; Fax: 717-394-1779. Email: secretary@stleos.org. Web: www.stleos.org.
School—(Grades K-8) Tel: 717-392-2441; Fax: 717-392-4080. Email: secretary@stleoschool.org. Web: www.stleoschool.org. Mrs. Georgia Steinbacher, Prin. Lay Teachers 18; Students 241.
Catechesis/Religious Program—Tel: 717-394-7354. Email: psr@stleos.org. Sr. Dorothy Wilkinson, S.S.C., D.R.E. Students 347.

SELINSGROVE, SNYDER CO., ST. PIUS X (1964) Rev. Edward J. Keating Jr.
Res.: 112 Fairview Dr., 17870-9406. Tel: 570-374-4113; Fax: 570-374-0156.
Catechesis/Religious Program—Students 252.
Mission—Susquehanna University, Snyder Co. 17870.
Mission—Selinsgrove Center, Snyder Co. 17870. Tel: 570-374-4113.
Mission—Snyder County Prison, Snyder Co.

SHAMOKIN, NORTHUMBERLAND CO.

1—ASSUMPTION OF THE BLESSED VIRGIN MARY (1892), (Slovak), Closed. See Mother Cabrini, Shamokin.

2—ST. EDWARD (1866) Closed. See Mother Cabrini, Shamokin.

3—ST. JOSEPH (1913) Closed. See Our Lady of Hope, Coal Township.

4—ST. MICHAEL ARCHANGEL (1894), (Lithuanian), Closed. See Mother Cabrini, Shamokin.

5—MOTHER CABRINI (1995) [JC 4] Revs. Martin Kobos, O.F.M.Conv.; Adam Ziolkowski, O.F.M.Conv.
Res.: 106 N. Cherry St., 17872. Tel: 570-644-0335; Fax: 570-644-0806.
Catechesis/Religious Program—Students 84.

6—ST. STANISLAUS KOSTKA (1874), (Polish), Closed. See Mother Cabrini, Shamokin.

SHIPPENSBURG, CUMBERLAND CO., OUR LADY OF THE VISITATION (1950) Rev. David A. Hillier.
Res.: 305 N. Prince St., 17257. Tel: 717-532-2912; Fax: 717-532-3905. Email: ourlady106@yahoo.com.
Catechesis/Religious Program—Students 117.

SOUTH MOUNTAIN, FRANKLIN CO., MOST HOLY ROSARY, Closed. See St. Ignatius, Buchanan Valley.

SPRING GROVE, YORK CO., SACRED HEART (1976) Rev. Thomas C. Marickovic.
Res.: 152 N. Main St., Box 42, 17362. Tel: 717-225-1704; Fax: 717-225-9570. Email: sacredheart07@comcast.net. Web: www.sacredheartsg.org.
Catechesis/Religious Program—Sacred Heart Parish Center, 1031 Sprenkle Rd., 17362. Tel: 717-225-1997. Marianne Harbold, C.R.E.; Kristine Trettel, C.R.E. Students 112.

STEELTON, DAUPHIN CO.

1—ST. ANN (1901), (Italian), Closed. See Prince of Peace, Steelton.

2—ASSUMPTION OF THE BLESSED VIRGIN MARY (1898), (Croatian), Closed. See Prince of Peace, Steelton.

3—ST. JAMES (1878) Closed. See Prince of Peace, Steelton.

4—ST. PETER (1909), (Slovenian), Closed. See Prince of Peace, Steelton.

5—PRINCE OF PEACE (1995) Rev. Msgr. James M. Lyons; Deacon Michael Grella, Dir. Office Continuing Formation of Deacons. In Res., Rev. Raymond J. LaVoie.
Res.: 815 S. Second St., 17113. Tel: 717-985-1330; Fax: 717-985-1333. Email: pop.parish@comcast.net.
Catechesis/Religious Program—(Grades K-8), 245 Reynders Ave., 17113. Students 68.

SUNBURY, NORTHUMBERLAND CO.

1—ST. MICHAEL ARCHANGEL (1863) Closed. See St. Monica, Sunbury.

2—ST. MONICA (1995) Rev. Donald W. Cramer; Linda Walborn, Pastoral Assoc.
Res.: 20 N. Front St., 17801. Tel: 570-286-0761; Fax: 570-286-8588. Email: p141stmonica@hbgdiocese.org.
School—109 Market St., 17801. Tel: 570-286-5983; Fax: 570-286-7351. Email: office@saintmonica.sunbury.pa.us. Web: saintmonicasunbury.com. Susan Bickhart, Prin. Lay Teachers 13; Students 135.
Catechesis/Religious Program—Email: 141stmonica@hbgdiocese.org. Suzanne Erhardt, C.R.E. Students 46.

TREVORTON, NORTHUMBERLAND CO., ST. PATRICK (1850) [CEM] Revs. Adrian Gallagher, O.F.M.Conv.; John Voytek, O.F.M.Conv.
Res.: 331 W. Shamokin St., 17881-1523. Tel: 570-797-8251; Fax: 570-797-3990. Email: stpats@ptd.net.
Catechesis/Religious Program—Students 43.

WAYNESBORO, FRANKLIN CO., ST. ANDREW (1893) [CEM] Very Rev. John B. Bateman.
Res.: 12 N. Broad St., 17268. Tel: 717-762-1914; Fax: 717-762-3319. Email: office.standrew@embarqmail.com. Web: www.standrewwbo.org.
School—213 E. Main St., 17268. Tel: 717-762-3221; Fax: 717-762-8474. Email: standrewschool@embarqmail.com. Web: www-.saintandrewschool.org. Mr. Pat McDonald, Prin. Lay Teachers 13; Students 113.
Catechesis/Religious Program—Fax: 717-762-3319. Email: peg.standrew@embarqmail.com. Margaret E. Wagaman, D.R.E. Students 136.

WILLIAMSTOWN, DAUPHIN CO., SACRED HEART OF JESUS (1875) [CEM] [JC] Rev. C. Anthony Miller.
Church: 140 E. Market St., 17098. Tel: 717-453-7895; Fax: 717-453-9426.
Res.: 732 Main St., Lykens, 17048.
Catechesis/Religious Program—Tel: 717-647-2645. Earl Roberts, D.R.E. Students 104.

YORK, YORK CO.

1—IMMACULATE CONCEPTION OF THE BLESSED VIRGIN MARY (1852) [CEM] [JC] Very Rev. Robert M. Gillelan Jr.; Deacon Catalino Gonzalez, Pastoral Assoc. In Res., Rev. L. Frederick Nkwasibwe, A.J.
Res.: 309 S. George St., 17401. Tel: 717-845-7629; Fax: 717-845-2433. Email: stmarysyork@comcast.net.
Catechesis/Religious Program—Tel: 717-846-6001. Ms. Mollie Luginski, D.R.E. Students 244.

2—ST. JOSEPH (1913) [JC] Revs. Louis Petruha, O.F.M.Cap.; Dennis Klemash, O.F.M.Cap.; Zenon Maszczyk, O.F.M.Cap. (Poland); Deacon Neil A. Crispo. In Res., Rev. John McCloskey, O.F.M.Cap.; Bro. Michael Rubus, O.F.M.Cap.
Res.: 2935 Kingston Rd., 17402-4003. Tel: 717-755-7503; Fax: 717-757-1900. Web: www.sjy.org.
School—2945 Kingston Rd., 17402. Tel: 717-755-1797; Fax: 717-751-0136. Mrs. Patricia A. Byrnes, Prin. Lay Teachers 25; Students 348.
Catechesis/Religious Program—Bernadette L. Snook, C.R.E. Students 638.

3—ST. PATRICK (1776) [CEM] Rev. Samuel E. Houser; Deacons Michael V. DeVivo; Sabino Moschella; Sr. Monica Imgrund, R.S.M., Pastoral Assoc. In Res., Rev. William M. Cawley (GF).
Res.: 231 S. Beaver St., 17401. Tel: 717-848-2007. Email: rectoryoffice@stpatrickyork.org. Web: www.stpatrickyork.org.
School—235 S. Beaver St., 17401. Tel: 717-854-8263; Fax: 717-846-6049. Email: schooloffice@stpatrickyork.org. Sr. Mary Elizabeth Muir, I.H.M., Prin. Lay Teachers 13; Students 155.
Catechesis/Religious Program—219 S. Beaver St., 17401. Tel: 717-854-6653. Email: stpatrick_re@yahoo.com. Susan Varholy, C.R.E. Students 189.

4—ST. ROSE OF LIMA (1907) [JC] Rev. Thomas R. Hoke. In Res., Rev. Carl T. Tancredi.
Res.: 950 W. Market St., 17401. Tel: 717-846-4935; Fax: 717-699-0715.
School—115 N. Biesecker Rd., Thomasville, 17364. Tel: 717-792-0889; Fax: 717-792-3959. Peggy Rizzuto, Prin. Lay Teachers 14; Students 100.
Catechesis/Religious Program—Tel: 717-843-3043. Sr. Jane Keller, S.S.J., D.R.E. Students 222.
Convent—Sisters of St. Joseph, 944 W. Market St., 17401. Tel: 717-854-0378. Sisters 3.

YORK HAVEN, YORK CO., HOLY INFANT (1972) Very Rev. Edward C. Malesic; Rebecca Papa, Pastoral Asst.; Deacon Joseph J. Kramer.
Res.: 34 Third St., P.O. Box 398, 17370. Tel: 717-266-5286. Email: holyinfantyh@comcast.net. Web: www.holyinfantparish.com.
Catechesis/Religious Program—Students 157.

Chaplains of Public Institutions

HARRISBURG. *Community General Osteopathic Hospital*. Rev. Matthew Palkowski, O.F.M.Cap.
Pinnacle Health System, Tel: 717-782-5208. Rev. Matthew Palkowski, O.F.M.Cap.
Polyclinic Medical Clinic, Tel: 717-782-4141. Rev. Matthew Palkowski, O.F.M.Cap.

CAMP HILL. *State Correctional Institution*, P.O. Box 200, 17011. Tel: 717-737-4531, Ext. 4439. Deacon Epifanio DeJesus.

DANVILLE. *Geisinger Medical Center*, Tel: 717-275-2512. Rev. Dominic Azagbor, O.P.
State Hospital, P.O. Box 219, 17821. Tel: 717-275-7011. Rev. Steven W. Fauser. Tel: 570-275-7011.

HERSHEY. *Milton J. Hershey Medical Center*, 500 University Blvd., 17033. Tel: 717-534-8177. Rev. Chukwubikem Okpechi, O.P.

LANCASTER. *Lancaster County Prison*, 625 E. King St., 17602. Tel: 717-534-8177. Deacon Expedito Santos-Santiago, Rev. Allan F. Wolfe.
Lancaster General Hospital and Lancaster Community Hospital. Rev. Arokiaswamy Samson.

LEBANON. *Veterans Administration Hospital*, 17 S. Lincoln Ave., 17042. Tel: 717-272-6621. Rev. Harold Dagle.

LEWISBURG. *U.S. Penitentiary*, Tel: 570-523-1251. Rev. Ngozi Osuji.

SELINSGROVE. *Selinsgrove Center*, Box 500, 17870. Tel: 717-374-2911, Ext. 425. Rev. Edward J. Keating Jr.

SOUTH MOUNTAIN. *Restoration Center*, Tel: 717-749-5773. Rev. Joseph C. Carolin.

YORK. *York Hospital*, 1001 S. George St., 17405. Tel: 717-771-2345. Rev. L. Frederick Nkwasibwe, A.J.

On Duty Outside the Diocese:
Revs.—
Bennett, Michael X., 2446 Bank St., Ottawa ON KIV 1A8 Canada.

Blackwell, Edward A., 3637 S.W. 22nd St., Fort Lauderdale, FL 33312.
Hoke, John R., U.S. Navy
Kemper, John C., S.S., Provincial House, 5408 Roland Ave., Baltimore, MD 21210.
Moran, Martin O., III, Cincinnati, OH
Topper, Charles J., 303 Tunxis Rd., West Hartford, CT 06107.

Retired:
Rev. Msgrs.—
Bierster, Leo N.
Brenner, Thomas R.
Fregapane, Mercurio A.
Gribbin, Robert C.
Kujovsky, Thomas J.
Overbaugh, Hugh A.
Rost, George W.
Smith, Vincent J.
Topper, Vincent J.
Revs.—
Acri, John A.
Devine, Patrick A.
Farace, Frederick A., P.O. Box 276, Mount Carmel, 17851.
Fennessy, Joseph H.
Fontanella, Andrew J.
Haney, T. Ronald
Haviland, William T.
Heintzelman, Gerard T.
Hilbert, Joseph C.
Langan, Thomas
Lytle, Gerald A.
Mammarella, Dominick
Marinak, Andrew P.
Meluskey, Andre J.
Menniti, Daniel J.
Olszewski, Clarence A.
Orloski, Raymond J.
Rindos, Paul T., Bishop Dattilo Retirement Residence for Priests.
Sempko, Walter A.
Shuda, Paul R.
Steffan, Carl J.
Sullivan, William J., St. Joseph, Mechanicsburg

Permanent Deacons:
Amarante, Gregory M., St. Joseph, Danville
Anders, Joseph L., St. Anne, Lancaster
Aull, Richard H., St. Matthew, Dauphin
Aumen, Thomas M., St. Joseph, Hanover
Bahn, Michael P., St. John the Baptist, New Freedom
Baylor, Jeffrey A., St. Peter, Columbia
Beighley, Ross W., St. Philip the Apostle, Lancaster
Bernardy, Daniel L., St. Joseph, Dallastown
Bertollo, Edward L., Jr., (Retired)
Boucek, Thomas E., St. Theresa, New Cumberland
Clark, Charles W., St. Patrick Cathedral, Harrisburg
Conlin, Thomas J., Jr., St. Columba, Bloomsburg
Crispo, Neil A., St. Joseph, York
Crudup, Lawrence R., St. Patrick Cathedral, Harrisburg
Deleon, Joseph, A.B.D., St. Francis of Assisi, Harrisburg
DeVivo, Michael V., St. Patrick, York
Doyle, James B., Our Lady of the Blessed Sacrament, Harrisburg
Eckman, Frank M., (Retired)
Enderle, Frank X.
Fedor, Thomas A., St. Catherine Laboure, Harrisburg
Fine, Andrew V., (Retired)
Flannery, Thomas H., St. Catherine Laboure, Harrisburg
Foerster, Jerome T., Holy Name of Jesus, Harrisburg
Garber, George M., Our Lady Help of Christians, Lykens; Sacred Heart, Williamstown
Gonzales, Catalino, Immaculate Conception BVM, York
Gorini, Joseph B., Our Lady of Good Counsel, Marysville
Gorman, Francis C., Holy Spirit Hospital, Camp Hill
Grella, Michael A., Ed.D., Prince of Peace, Steelton
Heil, John C., St. Catherine Laboure, Harrisburg
Horn, Frederick C., St. John the Baptist, New Freedom
Jordan, William J., St. Richard, Manheim
Jupin, Peter J., St. John Neumann, Lancaster
Kearney, Anthony A., St. Paul the Apostle, Annville
Kenski, Francis G., (Retired)
Kiley, Patrick M., Good Shepherd, Camp Hill
Kramer, Joseph J., Holy Infant, York Haven
Ladouceur, Philip J., St. Theresa, New Cumberland
Lang, Thomas A., Seven Sorrows BVM, Middletown
Lawrence, Joseph F., Annunciation BVM, McSherrystown
Light, Martin C., Sr., St. Philip, Millersville
Lopez, Jose A., San Juan Bautista, Lancaster
Mack, Robert P., Our Lady of Hope, Coal Twp.
Mann, Donovan A., St. Richard, Manheim
Marroquin, Miguel, St. Francis of Assisi, Harrisburg
McCarthy, Martin P., Our Lady of Mt. Carmel, Mount Carmel
Miller, Gene R., (Retired)
Mortel, Rodrigue, St. Joan of Arc, Hershey
Moschella, Sabino E., St. Patrick, York
Mowery, John A., (Retired)
Owen, Richard D., Sacred Heart of Jesus, Lewisburg
Parr, Frank J., (Retired)
Paruso, John L., St. Joseph, Mechanicsburg
Paynter, Arthur F., Mary, Mother of the Church, Mount Joy
Ramos, Felix, San Juan Bautista, Lancaster
Ramsey, Richard W., Corpus Christi, Chambersburg
Robinson, Gerald P., St. Bernard, New Bloomfield
Rush, James J., Our Lady of Good Counsel, Marysville; St. Bernadette, Duncannon
Ryan, Richard A., (Retired)
Santos-Santiago, Expidito, San Juan Bautista, Lancaster
Shultis, Timothy J., St. Vincent dePaul, Hanover
Smith, Raymond, Immaculate Heart of Mary, Abbottstown
Vannucci, Eugene D., St. Leo the Great, Rohrerstown
Velazquez, Manuel, Assumption BVM & San Juan Bautista, Lancaster
Walter, James K., St. John Neumann, Lancaster
Weaver, Richard J., St. Joseph, Bonneauville
Weaver, Robert E., Lancaster Regional Medical Center, Lancaster
Wentzel, Richard W., Assumption BVM, Lebanon
Whale, William E., Our Lady of Lourdes, Daytona Beach, FL
Wrabel, Joseph J., Holy Name of Jesus, Harrisburg

INSTITUTIONS LOCATED IN THE DIOCESE

[A] HIGH SCHOOLS

HARRISBURG. *Bishop McDevitt High School of Harrisburg*, 2200 Market. St., 17103. Tel: 717-236-7973; Fax: 717-234-1270. Email: smaryanneb@bishopmcdevitt.org. Sr. Mary Anne Bednar, I.H.M., Prin.; Rev. Raymond J. LaVoie, Chap.; Mrs. Claire Bianchi, Librarian. Sisters 6; Lay Teachers 48; Students 670.

CAMP HILL. *Trinity High School*, 3601 Simpson Ferry Rd., 17011. Tel: 717-761-1116; Fax: 717-761-7309. Email: dbouton@trinityhs.k12.pa.us. Web: www.trinityhs.k12.pa.us. Dr. David Bouton, Prin.; Rev. David M. Hereshko, Chap.; Mrs. Dolores Kirkpatrick, Librarian. Priests 1; Sisters 3; Full-Time Lay Teachers 45; Students 616.

COAL TOWNSHIP. *Our Lady of Lourdes Regional School*, (Grades PreK-12), 2001 Clinton Ave., 17866-1699. Tel: 570-644-0375; Fax: 570-644-7655. Email: lourdes@ptd.net. Web: www.lourdes.k12.pa.us. Deacon Martin P. McCarthy, Admin. & Prin., High School; Very Rev. Alfred P. Sceski, V.F., Chap. Lay Teachers 32; Students 354.

LANCASTER. *Lancaster Catholic High School*, 650 Juliette Ave., 17601. Tel: 717-509-0315; Fax: 717-509-0312. Email: tfertal@lchsyes.org. Mr. Thomas Fertal, Prin.; Miss Susan Martin, Librarian. Lay Teachers 46; Students 778.

LEBANON. *Lebanon Catholic School* (1859) (Grades PreK-12), 1400 Chestnut St., 17042. Tel: 717-273-3731; Fax: 717-274-5167. Email: mambrosia@lebanoncatholicschool.org; lebanoncatholic@hbgdiocese.org. Web: www.lebanoncatholicschool.org. Rose Kury, Prin.; Mrs. Cynthia Williams, Asst. Prin.; Rev. Michael W. Rothan, Chap.; Mrs. Nancy Pelepko, Librarian. Sisters 1; Lay Teachers 37; Students 385.

MCSHERRYSTOWN. *Delone Catholic High School*, 140 S. Oxford Ave., 17344. Tel: 717-637-5969; Fax: 717-637-0442. Email: information@delonecatholic.org. Web: www.delonecatholic.org. Dr. Maureen Thiec, Prin.; Sr. Jackie Staub, S.S.J., Librarian. Sisters 1; Lay Teachers 39.

YORK. *York Catholic High School*, 601 E. Springettsbury Ave., 17403. Tel: 717-846-8871; Fax: 717-843-4588. Email: info@yorkcatholic.org. Web: www.yorkcatholic.org. George E. Andrews Jr., Prin.; Revs. William M. Cawley (GF), Teacher; James E. Lease, Chap.; Sr. Gilmary Beagle, Teacher. Priests 1; Sisters 1; Lay Teachers 44; Total Staff 87; Students 638.

[B] CONSOLIDATED ELEMENTARY SCHOOLS

HARRISBURG. *Cathedral School* (1873) 212 State St., 17101. Tel: 717-234-3797; Fax: 717-213-2000. Email: secretary@cathedralschoolharrisburg.com. Web: www.cathedralschoolharrisburg.com. Mr. David Rushinski, Prin. Lay Teachers 13; Total Enrollment 177.

Upper School (Grades PreK-8), St. Patrick's Building: Tel: 717-234-3797; Fax: 717-213-2000. Lay Teachers 7.

Lower School, St. Lawrence Bldg.: Tel: 717-234-3797. Mr. David Rushinski, Prin. Sisters 1; Lay Teachers 3; Total Enrollment 177.

BERWICK. *Holy Family Consolidated School*, 728 Washington St., 18603. Tel: 570-752-2021; Fax: 570-752-2914. Craig Lehnowsky, Prin.; Elaine Miknich, Librarian. Lay Teachers 5; Sisters 1.

COLUMBIA. *Our Lady of the Angels School* (1998) *Primary Bldg.*, 215 Union St., 17512. Tel: 717-684-2433; Fax: 717-684-5039. *Elementary Bldg.*, 404 Cherry St., 17512. Tel: 717-684-2664. Email: tburg@ourladyoftheangels.org. Mrs. Theresa M. Burg, Prin.

LANCASTER. *Resurrection Catholic School, School*, 521 E. Orange St., 17602. Tel: 717-392-3083; Fax: 717-735-7793. Email: bweaver@resurrectioncatholicschool.net. Miss Brenda Weaver, Prin.; Mrs. Mary Weaver, Librarian. Lay Teachers 10.

[C] PRESCHOOLS AND DAY NURSERIES

MCSHERRYSTOWN. *St. Joseph Academy Preschool*, 90 Main St., 17344. Tel: 717-630-9990. Email: sjaprek@gmail.com. Sr. Anne Leonard Freed, S.S.J., M.S.Ed., Dir. Sisters of St. Joseph. Sisters 1; Students 36; Aides 2.

[D] CATHOLIC CHARITIES COUNSELING & FIELD SERVICES

HARRISBURG. *Department for Catholic Charities Administrative Office*, 4800 Union Deposit Rd., 17111-3710. Tel: 717-657-4804; Fax: 717-657-8683. Web: www.hbgdiocese.org. 4800 Union Deposit Rd., 17111-3710. Tel: 717-657-4804; Fax: 717-657-8683. Mark A. Totaro, Ph.D., MBA, Exec. Dir. & CEO; Peter A. Biasucci, L.S.W., Asst. Exec. Dir.

Adoption Services, 939 E. Park Dr., Ste. 103, 17111. Tel: 717-564-7115; Fax: 717-564-7180. Kelly M. Bolton, M.S.W., L.S.W., Dir. Adoption & Specialized Foster Care.

Capital Region Office, 939 E. Park Dr., Ste. 101, 17111. Tel: 717-233-7978; Fax: 717-233-4194. Kirk Reider, A.C.S.W, L.C.S.W., Assoc. Exec. Dir. of Behavioral Health Svcs.

Evergreen House Program, 100 Evergreen St., 17104. Tel: 717-238-6343; Fax: 717-238-4161. Lydia Porter, M.S., CCDP-DIP, Prog. Dir.

Specialized Foster Care, 939 E. Park Dr., Ste. 103, 17111. Tel: 717-654-7115; Fax: 717-564-7180. Kelly M. Bolton, M.S.W., L.S.W., Prog. Mgr.

Immigration and Refugee Services, 939 E. Park Dr., Ste. 102, 17111. Tel: 717-232-0568; Fax: 717-234-1742. Mira Lukic, Assoc. Exec. Residential Svcs.

English As A Second Language Tel: 717-232-0568; Fax: 717-234-7142. Sara Beck, B.A., Mgr.

Employment Services Tel: 717-232-0568; Fax: 717-234-7142. Sinisa Jovic.

Resettlement Services Tel: 717-232-0568; Fax: 717-909-0968. Mira Lukic, Mgr.

Interfaith Shelter for Homeless Families, 1002 Hemlock Dr., 17110-3588. Tel: 717-236-6783; Fax: 717-236-3271. Hilary Hoover, Prog. Dir.

Lourdeshouse Maternity Services, 1611 Boas St., 17103. Tel: 717-236-3417; Fax: 717-236-4548. Annette Martin, M.H.S., Assoc. Exec. Residential Svcs.

Paradise School, 6156 West Canal Rd., Abbottstown, 17301-8982. Tel: 717-259-9537; Fax: 717-259-9262. Greg Landi, Prog. Dir.

Chambersburg Office, 1331 S. 7th St., Bldg. 2, Ste. 203, Chambersburg, 17201. Tel: 717-263-3765; Fax: 717-263-3226. Sr. Maria Theresa Mulieri, L.C.S.W., Prog. Dir.

Lancaster Office, 925 N. Duke St., Lancaster, 17602. Tel: 717-299-3659; 717-392-2113 (Spanish); Fax: 717-299-1328. Michelle Maddon, M.Ed., Prog. Dir.

Intensive Day Treatment, 47 S. Mulberry St., Lancaster, 17603. Tel: 717-295-9630; Fax: 717-295-9525. Rebecca Diamondstone, M.S., Prog. Dir.

Lancaster In-Home Intensive Services, 417 Poplar St., Lancaster, 17603. Tel: 717-392-3619; Fax: 717-392-4198. Christopher Vandenberg, M.H.S., Assoc. Exec. Dir.

Lebanon Office, 503 Cumberland St., Lebanon, 17042. Tel: 717-273-8514; Fax: 717-273-5942. Kirk Reider, A.C.S.W, L.C.S.W., Dir.

Northern Offices, 112 Market St., Sunbury, 17801.

Tel: 570-988-2860 (Voice); Fax: 570-988-2861. Michael McGranaghan, M.S., Prog. Dir.

York Office, 253 E. Market St., York, 17403. Tel: 717-845-2696; Fax: 717-843-3941. Kirk Reider, A.C.S.W, L.C.S.W., Assoc. Exec. Dir. Behavioral Health Svcs.

York/Adams Family Based Program, c/o Paradise School, 6156 W. Canal Rd., Abbottstown, 17301-8982. Tel: 717-845-3373; Fax: 717-845-4101. Rebecca Jacoby, Prog. Dir.

York Intensive Family Services, 26 E. College Ave., York, 17401. Tel: 717-843-7986; Fax: 717-699-0020. Nick Giampietro, Assoc. Exec. Dir.

HOPE House, 1509 Crescent Ave., Lancaster, 17601. Tel: 717-293-9089; Fax: 717-293-1425. Carol Carp, Prog. Dir.

Dauphin/Cumberland/Perry County Family Based Program, 939 E. Park Dr., Ste. 104, 17111. Tel: 717-564-9450; Fax: 717-564-9456. Sandra Holland, M.Div., Prog. Dir.

[E] GENERAL HOSPITALS

CAMP HILL. *Holy Spirit Health System*, 503 N. 21st St., 17011-2288. Tel: 717-763-2100; Fax: 717-763-2183. Email: jfegan@hsh.org. Web: www.hsh.org. Sr. Romaine Niemeyer, S.C.C., Pres. & CEO.
Sisters of Christian Charity Health Care Corporation.
Holy Spirit Ventures, Inc.
Holy Spirit Corporation.
West Shore ALS, Inc.
Holy Spirit Hospital.
Spirit Physician Services, Inc. Sisters of Christian Charity. Inpatient Admissions 16,097; Outpatient Visits 197,634; Bed Capacity 316; Bassinets 15; Sisters 22; Total Staff 2,236.

[F] CONVALESCENT & RETIREMENT HOMES

HARRISBURG. *Bishop Dattilo Retirement Residence for Priests* (2001) 675 Rutherford Rd., 17109. Tel: 717-657-3147; Fax: 717-657-3167. Email: retirementresidence@hbgdiocese.org.

COLUMBIA. *St. Anne's Retirement Community* (1954) 3952 Columbia Ave., 17512-9715. Tel: 717-285-5443; Fax: 717-285-5950. Email: mturnbaugh@stannesrc.org. Mary Turnbaugh, Pres. Adorers of the Blood of Christ. Total Staff 273; Personal Care Staff 20; Residents 121; Cottages 37; Apartments 34; Bed Capacity 245; Residents in Retirement Village 35; Residents in Apartments 31; Personal Care 48; Total Assisted Annually 70.

DANVILLE. *Holy Family Convent and Infirmary*, One Montour St., 17821. Tel: 570-275-3141; Fax: 570-275-9511. Email: sccbronxsb@juno.com. Web: www.scceast.org. Sr. Barbara Armstrong, S.C.C., Local Coord.; Rev. Michael Laicha, Chap. Tel: 717-275-0103. Home for the Aged Sisters of Christian Charity. Sisters of Christian Charity 59; Bed Capacity 95; Total Staff 44; Patients Assisted Annually 50.

Maria Hall, Inc., 1 Maria Hall Dr., 17821. Tel: 570-275-1120; Fax: 570-275-1134. Email: mariahalljobs@yahoo.com. Sr. M. Philothea Fabian, S.S.C.M., Admin.; Rev. Gerard T. Heintzelman (Retired). Home for retired Sisters of SS. Cyril and Methodius; Dominican Sisters of St. Catherine de 'Ricci; Discalced Carmelites of Danville Sisters 44; Total Assisted 20; Total Staff 19.

Maria Joseph Manor, 875 Montour Blvd., 17821. Tel: 570-275-4221; Fax: 570-275-4711. Fran Crucci, Admin.; Mr. Thomas Conlin Jr., COO. Sisters 9; Religious 10; Bed Capacity 190; Total Assisted Annually 455; Total Staff 220.

The Meadows at Maria Joseph Manor, 875 Montour Blvd., 17821. Tel: 570-271-1000; Fax: 570-271-0848. Sr. M. Christopher Godlewski, Dir. Independent Living Units 112; Total Staff 6; Residents 151.

YORK. *Misericordia Nursing & Rehabilitation Center* (1943) 998 S. Russell St., 17402. Tel: 717-755-1964; Fax: 717-840-0010. Email: mbittner@mnrc.org. Marion Bittner, N.H.A., Admin. Daughters of Our Lady of Mercy. Priests 1; Sisters 7; Bed Capacity 50; Total Assisted 84; Total Staff 90.

[G] MONASTERIES AND RESIDENCES OF PRIESTS AND BROTHERS

EPHRATA. *St. Clement's Mission House*, 300 W. Pine St., 17522-2072. Tel: 717-733-6596; Fax: 717-733-0502. Email: ledger@ptd.net. Revs. Patrick McGarrity, C.Ss.R.; James O'Blaney, C.Ss.R.; James Small, C.Ss.R. (Retired); Thomas Loftus, C.Ss.R. (Retired); John McLoughlin, C.Ss.R.; Richard Knappik, C.S.s.R.; Robert Harrison, C.S.s.R.; Clement Cahill, C.S.s.R.; Lawrence Murphy, C.S.s.R.; Charles Brinkmann, C.S.s.R.; Bros. Stephen E. Lendvay; Robert P. Skinner. Redemptorist Fathers and Brothers. Total in Residence 12.
Mission Preaching Band: Rev. Paul Bryan, C.Ss.R.

[H] CONVENTS AND RESIDENCES FOR SISTERS

ELYSBURG. *Carmel of Jesus, Mary and Joseph in Elysburg, PA, Inc.*, 430 Monastery Rd., 17824. Tel: 570-672-2122.

HARRISBURG. *Sisters of IHM Saint Catherine Laboure Convent*, 4010 Derry St., 17111. Tel: 717-745-4134. Email: ihm4010@comcast.net. Sr. Mary L. Birster, I.H.M., Supr. Sisters, Servants of the Immaculate Heart of Mary 7.

COLUMBIA. *Adorers of the Blood of Christ* (1834) *Columbia Center of the Adorers of the Blood of Christ*, 3950 Columbia Ave., 17512-9714. Tel: 717-285-4536; Fax: 717-285-9789. Web: www.adorers.org. Sr. Martha Wachtel, A.S.C., Dir. Comm. Life & Mission. St. Joseph Convent

DANVILLE. *Discalced Carmelite Nuns of Danville, PA* (1953) One Maria Hall Dr., 17821-1237. Tel: 570-275-4682; Fax: 570-275-4684. Sr. Angela Pikus, O.C.D., Prioress. Discalced Carmelite Nuns. Nuns in Solemn Vows 10.

Sisters of Saints Cyril and Methodius (1909) 17821-1698. Tel: 570-275-3581; 570-275-4929; Fax: 570-275-5997. Email: smtmsscm@hotmail.com. Web: www.sscm.org. Sr. Linda Marie Bolinski, SS.C.M., Gen. Supr. Motherhouse of the Sisters of Saints Cyril and Methodius. Sisters 89.

Villa Sacred Heart Formation Center Tel: 570-275-3581, Ext. 331; Fax: 570-275-5997. Web: www.sscm.org. *Vocation Office/SCA Spiritual Center* Sr. Deborah Marie, SS.C.M., Vocation Dir.

Villa Sacred Heart Music Conservatory, 17821-1698. Tel: 570-275-3581, Ext. 311; Fax: 570-275-5997. Email: smlsscm@hotmail.com. Sr. M. Michaelette, SS.C.M., Dir.

St. Cyril Academy Preschool and Kindergarten, 17821-1698. Tel: 570-275-3581, Ext. 160; Fax: 570-275-5997. Email: scpandk@hotmail.com. Web: www.sscm.org; www.stcyril1.vpweb.com. Sr. Donna Marie, SS.C.M., Dir.

St. Cyril Academy Spiritual Center, 17821-1698. Tel: 570-275-3581, Ext. 320; Fax: 570-275-5997. Email: jeanholupsscm@yahoo.com. Web: www.sscm.org. Sr. Jean Marie Holup, SS.C.M., Dir.

LANCASTER. *Dominican Nuns of the Perpetual Rosary, Incorporated* (1927) 1834 Lititz Pike, 17601-6585. Tel: 717-569-2104; Fax: 717-569-1598. Email: monlanc@aol.com. Sr. Mary Albert, O.P., Prioress; Rev. Edward M. Gaffney, O.P., Chap. Solemnly Professed Nuns 10.

[I] NEWMAN CENTERS

HARRISBURG. *Catholic Campus Ministry* 4800 Union Deposit Rd., 17111-3710. Tel: 717-657-4804; Fax: 717-657-4041. Web: www.hbgdiocese.org. Mr. Robert J. Williams, Dir. Tel: 717-657-4804.

Lebanon Valley College 125 S. Spruce St., Annville, 17003. Tel: 717-867-1525. Rev. John J. Peck, O.S.B.

Bloomsburg University of Pennsylvania 353 E. Second St., College Hill, Bloomsburg, 17815. Tel: 570-784-3123; Fax: 570-784-3583. Rev. Timothy D. Marcoe, Campus Min.; Elizabeth Trexler.

Dickinson College 152 E. Pomfret St., Carlisle, 17013. Tel: 717-243-4411; Fax: 717-258-9281. Rev. Dwight D. Schlaline.

Elizabethtown College 1840 Marshall Dr., Elizabethtown, 17022. Tel: 717-367-1255. Rev. David L. Danneker, Ph.D.; Mrs. Angela Sedun, Asst.

Gettysburg College 300 N. Washington St., Box 427, Gettysburg, 17325-0136. Tel: 717-337-6284; Fax: 717-337-6284. Rev. Augusty T. Valomchalil, M.S.S.C.C.; Susan Collinge.

Messiah College One College Ave., P.O. Box 3006, Grantham, 17027. Tel: 717-766-2511, Ext. 7192; Fax: 717-796-2349. Cathy Poiesz.

Franklin and Marshall College, Lancaster 558 W. Walnut St., Lancaster, 17603. Tel: 717-394-0757. Rev. Michael E. Messner; Bradley Fischer, Campus Min.

Bucknell University Newman Center, 610 St. George St., Lewisburg, 17837. Tel: 570-577-3766; Fax: 570-577-2760. Rev. Fred Wangwe, A.J. (Africa).

Millersville University Newman Center, 227 N. George St., Millersville, 17551. Tel: 717-872-3350; Fax: 717-872-3668. Rev. Pang S. Tcheou, Campus Min.

Susquehanna University Catholic Campus Ministry 112 Fairview Dr., Selinsgrove, 17870. Tel: 570-374-4113. Rev. Edward J. Keating Jr.

**Shippensburg University Cora I Grove Spiritual Center*, 1871 Old Main Dr., Rm. 215, Shippensburg, 17257. Tel: 717-532-2912. Rev. David A. Hillier; Roxanne Dennis.

Penn State University, Mont Alto Campus, South Mountain 12 N. Broad St., Waynesboro, 17268. Tel: 717-762-1914. Very Rev. John B. Bateman, V.F.

Penn State University, York Campus 950 W. Market St., York, 17401. Tel: 717-873-5163. Rev. Carl T. Tancredi.

York College 950 W. Market St., York, 17401. Tel: 717-873-5163. Rev. Carl T. Tancredi.

[J] MISCELLANEOUS LISTINGS

HARRISBURG. *Harrisburg Catholic Administrative Services, Inc.*, 4800 Union Deposit Rd., 17111. Tel: 717-657-4804; Fax: 717-671-7021.

Kolbe Catholic Publishing, Inc., 4800 Union Deposit Rd., 17111-3710. Tel: 717-657-4804, Ext. 387; Fax: 717-657-6208. Email: pkielwein@hbgdiocese.org. Mr. Patrick Kielwein, Print Broker.

The Neumann Scholarship Foundation, 4800 Union Deposit Rd., 17111-3710. Tel: 717-657-4804; Fax: 717-657-3790. Very Rev. Edward J. Quinlan, M.Div., M.A., M.S., Sec. for Educ.

Pennsylvania Catholic Conference, 223 North St., P.O. Box 2835, 17105. Tel: 717-238-9613; Fax: 717-238-1473. Email: info@pacatholic.org. Web: www.pacatholic.org.

Pennsylvania Catholic Conference Scholarship Foundation, 223 North St., P.O. Box 2835, 17105. Tel: 717-238-9613; Fax: 717-238-1473. Email: info@pacatholic.org. Web: www.pacatholic.org. Dr. Robert J. O'Hara Jr., Exec. Dir.

Pennsylvania Catholic Health Association (1963) 223 North St., P.O. Box 2835, 17105. Tel: 717-238-9613; Fax: 717-238-1473. Email: PCHA@pacatholic.org. Web: www.pacatholic.org/pcha. Sr. Clare Christi Schiefer, O.S.F., Pres.

Roman Catholic Diocese of Harrisburg Charitable Trust, 4800 Union Deposit Rd., 17111. Tel: 717-657-4804; Fax: 717-657-2453.

Roman Catholic Diocese of Harrisburg Real Estate Trust, 4800 Union Deposit Rd., 17111. Tel: 717-657-4804; Fax: 717-657-2453.

ELIZABETHTOWN. *The Cor Project*, 48 Industrial Rd., 17022. Tel: 717-826-3533. Email: jason@thecorporject.org. Web: www.corporject.org. Jason Clark, Contact Person.

**Stewardship: A Mission of Faith*, 48 Industrial Rd., 17022. Tel: 717-367-0100.

FAIRFIELD. *Missionaries of the Sacred Hearts of Jesus & Mary House of Studies*, 350 Tract Rd., 17320. Tel: 717-457-0114; Fax: 717-457-0094. Email: msscc5@yahoo.com. Very Rev. Robert P. Malagesi, M.SS.CC., Delegate, USA Supr. Gen.

LANCASTER. *St. Joseph Health Ministries*, 1929 Lincoln Hwy. E., Ste. 150, 17602. Tel: 717-397-7625; Fax: 717-397-6057. Email: sjhm@catholichealth.net. Web: www.sjhm.org. (An affiliate of Catholic Health Initiatives)

MCSHERRYSTOWN. *St. Joseph Village Corporation* Sisters of St. Joseph., Residence for Senior Citizens

Village Location (1995) 50 Academy St., 17344. Tel: 717-637-4441; Fax: 717-637-2441. Sr. Joanne Fehrenbach, S.S.J., Gen. Sec. Total Staff 3; Total in Residence 40.

RELIGIOUS INSTITUTES OF MEN REPRESENTED IN THE DIOCESE

For further details refer to the corresponding bracketed number in the Religious Institutes of Men or Women section.

[]—*Apostles of Jesus*—A.J.

[]—*Benedictine Monks of Saint Vincent Archabbey, Latrobe*—O.S.B.

[]—*Capuchin Franciscan Fathers* (Prov. of Saint Augustine)—O.F.M. Cap.

[]—*Conventual Franciscans* (Prov. of Saint Anthony of Padua)—O.F.M. Conv.

[1120]—*Missionaries of the Sacred Hearts of Jesus and Mary*—M.SS.CC.

[]—*Order of Preachers* (Prov. of Nigeria)—O.P.

[]—*Order of Preachers* (Prov. of Saint Joseph)—O.P.

[]—*Priestly Fraternity of Saint Peter*—F.S.S.P.

[1070]—*Redemptorist Fathers* (Baltimore Prov.)—C.SS.R.

[]—*Society of Jesus*—S.J.

[1060]—*Society of the Precious Blood* (Cincinnati Prov.)—C.PP.S.

[0560]—*Third Order Regular of Saint Francis* (Prov. of the Most Sacred Heart of Jesus)—T.O.R.

RELIGIOUS INSTITUTES OF WOMEN REPRESENTED IN THE DIOCESE

[0100]—*Adorers of the Blood of Christ*—A.S.C.

[ ]—*Bernardine Franciscan Sisters*—O.S.F.

[]—*Carmel of Jesus, Mary and Joseph* (Elysburg)—O.C.D.

[0890]—*Daughters of Our Lady of Mercy*—D.M.

[ ]—*Discalced Carmelite Nuns of Danville*—O.C.D.

[ ]—*Dominican Nuns of the Perpetual Rosary*—O.P.

[]—*Dominican Sisters, Congregation of Saint Catherine de Ricci*—O.P.

[ ]—*Holy Union Sisters*—S.U.S.C.

[]—*Missionary Servants of the Most Holy Trinity*—M.S.B.T.

[]—*Missionary Sisters of Saint Benedict*—O.S.B.

[0660]—*Sisters of Christian Charity*—S.C.C.

[2575]—*Sisters of Mercy of the Americas*—R.S.M.
[]—*Sisters of Saint Joseph of Chestnut Hill*—S.S.J.
[3780]—*Sisters of Saints Cyril and Methodius*—SS.C.M.
[1650]—*The Sisters of St. Francis of Philadelphia*—O.S.F.
[]—*Sisters, Servants of the Immaculate Heart of Mary (Philadelphia)*—I.H.M.
[]—*Sisters, Servants of the Immaculate Heart of Mary (Scranton)*—I.H.M.
[]—*Society of the Sisters of the Church*—S.S.C.

NECROLOGY

(No Deaths)

An asterisk (*) denotes an organization that has established tax-exempt status directly with the IRS and is not covered by the USCCB Group Ruling.

Archdiocese of Hartford

(Archidioecesis Hartfortiensis)

Most Reverend

HENRY J. MANSELL, D.D.

Archbishop of Hartford; ordained December 19, 1962; appointed Titular Bishop of Marazane and Auxiliary of New York November 24, 1992; ordained January 6, 1993; appointed Bishop of Buffalo April 18, 1995; installed June 12, 1995; appointed Archbishop of Hartford October 20, 2003; installed December 18, 2003. *Office: 134 Farmington Ave., Hartford, CT 06105-3784.* Tel: 860-541-6491; Fax: 860-541-6293. *Res.: 1109 Prospect Ave., West Hartford, CT 06105.*

The Hartford Roman Catholic Diocesan Corporation-Chancery Office: 134 Farmington Ave., Hartford, CT 06105-3784. Tel: 860-541-6491; Fax: 860-541-6309.

Web: www.archdioceseofhartford.org

Most Reverend

DANIEL A. CRONIN, D.D., S.T.D.

Archbishop Emeritus of Hartford; ordained December 20, 1952; appointed Titular Bishop of Egnatia and Auxiliary Bishop of Boston June 10, 1968; ordained Bishop September 12, 1968; appointed Bishop of Fall River October 30, 1970; installed December 16, 1970; appointed Archbishop of Hartford December 10, 1991; installed January 28, 1992; retired October 20, 2003. *Office: 469 Bloomfield Ave., Bloomfield, CT 06002.* Tel: 860-242-5628.

Most Reverend

CHRISTIE ALBERT MACALUSO, D.D., V.G.

Auxiliary Bishop of Hartford; ordained May 22, 1971; appointed Auxiliary Bishop of Hartford and Titular Bishop of Grass Valley March 18, 1997; ordained Bishop June 10, 1997. *Office: 134 Farmington Ave., Hartford, CT 06105-3784.* Tel: 860-541-6491; Fax: 860-541-6293.

Most Reverend

PETER A. ROSAZZA, D.D., V.G.

Auxiliary Bishop Emeritus of Hartford; ordained June 29, 1961; appointed Auxiliary Bishop of Hartford and Titular Bishop of Oppido Nuovo February 28, 1978; ordained Bishop June 24, 1978; retired June 30, 2010. *Office: 467 Bloomfield Ave., Bloomfield, CT 06002-2999.* Tel: 860-761-7430; Fax: 860-242-4886. Email: prosazza@aol.com.

Square Miles 2,288.

Established November 28, 1843; created Archdiocese August 6, 1953.

Corporate Title: "The Hartford Roman Catholic Diocesan Corporation."

Comprises the Counties of Hartford, Litchfield and New Haven in the State of Connecticut.

For legal titles of parishes and archdiocesan institutions, consult the Chancery Office.

STATISTICAL OVERVIEW

Personnel	
Archbishops	1
Retired Archbishops	1
Auxiliary Bishops	1
Retired Bishops	1
Priests: Diocesan Active in Diocese	184
Priests: Diocesan Active Outside Diocese	11
Priests: Retired, Sick or Absent	106
Number of Diocesan Priests	301
Religious Priests in Diocese	85
Total Priests in Diocese	386
Extern Priests in Diocese	46
Ordinations:	
Diocesan Priests	5
Transitional Deacons	9
Permanent Deacons in Diocese	289
Total Brothers	31
Total Sisters	645
Parishes	
Parishes	213
With Resident Pastor:	
Resident Diocesan Priests	162
Resident Religious Priests	14
Without Resident Pastor:	
Administered by Priests	37
Missions	1
Professional Ministry Personnel:	
Brothers	4
Sisters	25
Lay Ministers	96
Welfare	
Catholic Hospitals	3
Total Assisted	879,972
Health Care Centers	2
Total Assisted	2,772
Homes for the Aged	6
Total Assisted	2,974
Residential Care of Children	2
Total Assisted	171
Day Care Centers	9
Total Assisted	456
Special Centers for Social Services	18
Total Assisted	31,756
Residential Care of Disabled	10
Total Assisted	34
Other Institutions	2
Total Assisted	51,025
Educational	
Seminaries, Diocesan	1
Diocesan Students in Other Seminaries	48
Seminaries, Religious	1
Students Religious	80
Total Seminarians	128
Colleges and Universities	2
Total Students	4,733
High Schools, Diocesan and Parish	4
Total Students	2,025
High Schools, Private	5
Total Students	2,647
Elementary Schools, Diocesan and Parish	52
Total Students	10,991
Elementary Schools, Private	2
Total Students	215
Catechesis/Religious Education:	
High School Students	11,962
Elementary Students	42,368
Total Students under Catholic Instruction	75,069
Teachers in the Diocese:	
Priests	9
Brothers	4
Sisters	29
Lay Teachers	991
Vital Statistics	
Receptions into the Church:	
Infant Baptism Totals	5,710
Minor Baptism Totals	257
Adult Baptism Totals	162
Received into Full Communion	291
First Communions	7,006
Confirmations	6,763
Marriages:	
Catholic	1,149
Interfaith	192
Total Marriages	1,341
Deaths	7,725
Total Catholic Population	600,040
Total Population	1,946,413

Former Bishops—Rt. Revs. WILLIAM TYLER, D.D., ord. June 3, 1829; first Bishop; cons. March 17, 1844; died June 18, 1849; BERNARD O'REILLY, D.D., ord. Oct. 13, 1831; second Bishop; cons. Nov. 10, 1850; perished at sea, Jan., 1856.; FRANCIS P. MCFARLAND, D.D., ord. May 18, 1845; third Bishop; cons. March 14, 1858; died Oct. 12, 1874; THOMAS GALBERRY, D.D., ord. Dec. 20, 1856; fourth Bishop; cons. March 19, 1876; died Oct. 10, 1878; LAWRENCE S. MCMAHON, D.D., ord. March 24, 1860; fifth Bishop; cons. Aug. 10, 1879; died Aug. 21, 1893; MICHAEL TIERNEY, D.D., ord. May 26, 1866; sixth Bishop; cons. Feb. 22, 1894; died Oct. 5, 1908; Most Revs. JOHN J. NILAN, D.D., ord. Dec. 2, 1878; seventh Bishop; cons. April 28, 1910; died April 13, 1934; MAURICE F. MCAULIFFE, D.D., eighth Bishop; ord. July 29, 1900; appt. Auxiliary to the Bishop of Hartford, Dec. 17, 1925; cons. April 28, 1926; appt. Bishop of Hartford, April 25, 1934; installed May 29, 1934; died Dec. 15, 1944; HENRY J. O'BRIEN, D.D., ninth Bishop, first Archbishop; ord. July 8, 1923; appt. Titular Bishop of Sita and Auxiliary to Bishop of Hartford, March 19, 1940; cons. May 14, 1940; appt. Bishop of Hartford, April 7, 1945; appt. Archbishop of Hartford, Aug. 6, 1953; appt. at Pontifical Throne, April 29, 1955; resigned and appt. Titular Archbishop of Utina, Nov. 20, 1968; Given title "Former Archbishop of Hartford", Nov. 14, 1970; died July 23, 1976; JOHN F. WHEALON, D.D., S.T.L., S.S.L., tenth Bishop, second Archbishop; ord. May 26, 1945; appt. Titular Bishop of Andrapa and Auxiliary of Cleveland, June 2, 1961; consecrated July 6, 1961; appt. Bishop of Erie, Nov. 30, 1966; installed March 7, 1967; appt. Archbishop of Hartford, Dec. 28, 1968; installed March 19, 1969; died Aug. 2, 1991; DANIEL A. CRONIN, D.D., S.T.D., ord. Dec. 20, 1952; appt. Titular Bishop of Egnatia and Auxiliary Bishop of Boston June 10, 1968; ord. Bishop Sept. 12, 1968; appt. Bishop of Fall River Oct. 30, 1970; installed Dec. 16, 1970; appt. Archbishop of Hartford Dec. 10, 1991; installed Jan. 28, 1992; retired Oct. 20, 2003.

Vicar General—Most Rev. CHRISTIE ALBERT MACALUSO, D.D., V.G.

Episcopal Vicars—Rev. Msgrs. JOHN P. CONTE, New Haven Vicariate; JAMES G. COLEMAN, Waterbury Vicariate (Retired); Rev. LAWRENCE R. BOCK, Hartford Vicariate.

Chancery Office—134 Farmington Ave., Hartford, 06105-3784. Tel: 860-541-6491; Fax: 860-541-6293 (Bishop's Office); 860-541-6309 (Chancery). All applications for dispensations and correspondence on diocesan business should be sent to this address. Office Hours: Mon.-Fri. 8:30-4:30.

Moderator of the Curia—Most Rev. CHRISTIE ALBERT MACALUSO, D.D., V.G.; SHARON ANDERSON, Sec.

Chancellor—Rev. Msgr. JOHN J. MCCARTHY, J.C.D., J.D.; HELEN A. FORTIN, Sec.; MARION VALENTI, Part-time Sec.

Assistant Chancellor—Rev. JEFFREY V. ROMANS; DIANA TIERINNI, Sec.

Office of Communications—MARIA ZONE, Dir. Fax: 860-560-0031. Email: mzone@aohct.org.

Archivist—F. MARIA MEDINA, M.L.S.

Finance Office—

Finance Officer—Most Rev. CHRISTIE A. MACALUSO, D.D., V.G.

Director of Finance—MATTHEW A. BYRNE, CPA, M.B.A.; LINDA CARROLL, Administrative Asst.

Assistant Director of Finance—TIMOTHY F. DERBY, CPA. *Accounting Manager*, THERESA MROCZKOWSKI. *Accounts Payable*, DONNA SHREVE. *Accounts Receivable*, CHERYL A. ROAIX. *Accounting Manager - Offices & Corporations*, KEVIN L. BEECHER. *Offices and Corporations Support, Staff Accountants*, ELAINE RUFFINO; DEAN WALFORD. *Risk Management, Workers Compensation, General Insurance - Claims Processing*, BRENDA ROCK.

Director of Parish Financial Services—NANCY H. STUPIK, CPA. *Parish Support Administrator*, PATRICK EGAN. *Assurance Review Coordinator*, ROBERT KEATING.

Director of Facilities & Construction—KEN MUCHERINO.

Development Office—

Director of Development—ROBERT MCTIERNAN, Interim Dir.

Administrative Assistant—KATHLEEN CHRIST.

Planned Giving Manager—ROBERT MCTIERNAN.

Secretary to the Archbishop—Rev. JEFFREY V. ROMANS.

Human Resources—

Director—KAREN A. KEAN.

Employee and Priest Benefits, Pension, and Payroll—LESLI ANDERSON.

Metropolitan Tribunal—467 Bloomfield Ave., Bloomfield, 06002-2999. Tel: 860-541-6491.

Judicial Vicar (Officialis)—Rev. ROBERT B. VARGO, J.C.L.

Adjutant Judicial Vicar—Rev. JAMES F. KINNANE, J.C.L.

Defender of the Bond—Rev. CHRISTOPHER M. FORD, J.C.L.

Promoter of Justice—Rev. Msgr. JOHN J. MCCARTHY, J.C.D., J.D.

Judges—Revs. CHRISTOPHER M. FORD, J.C.L.; JAMES F. KINNANE, J.C.L.; ALVIN J. LEBLANC, J.C.L.

Experts—Deacon RONALD BIAMONTE, M.A. (NCC Bd. Eligible); DONALD PAGLIA, M.S., C.A.G.S.; ROBERT SWORDS, M.D.

Assessor—Sr. PATRICK MARIE DOHERTY, I.H.M.

Secretary—NANCY C. SCOTT.

Notary—CAROL M. HATTEN.

College of Consultors—Most Revs. CHRISTIE ALBERT MACALUSO, D.D., V.G.; PETER A. ROSAZZA, D.D.; Rev. Msgrs. JAMES G. COLEMAN (Retired); JOHN P. CONTE; JOHN J. MCCARTHY, J.C.D., J.D.; Revs. LAWRENCE R. BOCK; SHAWN T. DALY; GERALD H. DZIEDZIC; DANIEL G. KEEFE.

Consultors - Canon 1742—Rev. Msgrs. JAMES G. COLEMAN (Retired); JOHN P. CONTE; GERARD G. SCHMITZ; Revs. LAWRENCE R. BOCK; JOHN J. GEORGIA; GENE E. GIANELLI; JOHN S. GOLAS; THOMAS R. MITCHELL; LAWRENCE S. SYMOLON.

Deans—Hartford Vicariate: Rev. JOHN S. GOLAS, Farmington Valley; Rev. Msgr. DANIEL J. PLOCHARCZYK, New Britain; Revs. JOSEPH T. DEVINE, Hartford; JAMES F. LEARY, Suburban Hartford; KEVIN P. CAVANAUGH, Manchester; ROBERT A. O'GRADY, Enfield. New Haven Vicariate: Rev. DANIEL G. KEEFE, Hamden-North Haven; Rev. Msgr. DAVID M. WALKER, East Shore Line; Revs. SHAWN T. DALY, Meriden; GENE E. GIANELLI, West Shore Line; DANIEL J. MCLEAREN, New Haven. Waterbury Vicariate: Revs. JOHN M. COONEY, Suburban Waterbury; LEONARD J. KVEDAS, Ansonia-Derby; PAUL J. PACE, Waterbury; CHRISTOPHER M. TIANO, Litchfield; JOSEPH V. DISCIACCA, Bristol; EUGENE J. CHARMAN, Naugatuck-Cheshire.

Presbyteral Council—

Ex Officio Members—Most Rev. CHRISTIE A. MACALUSO, D.D., V.G., Auxiliary Bishop; Rev. Msgrs. JOHN J. MCCARTHY, J.C.D., J.D., Chancellor; JAMES G. COLEMAN, Vicar for Waterbury (Retired); JOHN P. CONTE, Vicar for New Haven; Rev. LAWRENCE R. BOCK, Vicar for Hartford.

Elected Members—

Ansonia-Derby Deanery—Rev. STEPHEN H. BZDYRA.

Bristol Deanery—Rev. ALVIN J. LEBLANC.

Cheshire-Naugatuck Deanery—Rev. MICHAEL J. SLUSZ.

East Shore Deanery—Rev. Msgr. DAVID M. WALKER.

Enfield Deanery—Rev. MICHAEL C. DEVITO.

Farmington Valley Deanery—Rev. MICHAEL G. WHYTE.

Hamden-North Haven Deanery—Rev. DANIEL G. KEEFE.

Hartford Deanery—Rev. EMMANUEL I. IHEMEDU.

Litchfield Deanery—Rev. JOHN L. LAVORGNA.

Manchester Deanery—Rev. VINCENT J. CURRAN.

Meriden Deanery—Rev. SHAWN T. DALY.

New Britain Deanery—Rev. THOMAS J. WALSH.

New Haven Deanery—Rev. THOMAS B. SHEPARD.

Suburban Hartford Deanery—Rev. Msgr. DOUGLAS P. CLANCY.

Suburban Waterbury Deanery—Rev. JOSEPH T. DONNELLY.

Waterbury Deanery—Rev. Msgr. THOMAS M. GINTY.

West Shore Line Deanery—Rev. GENE E. GIANELLI.

Appointed Members—Most Rev. PETER A. ROSAZZA, D.D.; Revs. DAVID C. CAREY; DAIRO E. DIAZ; GERALD H. DZIEDZIC; Rev. Msgr. JOHN D. REGAN (Retired); Rev. JACK HOAK, O.F.M.

Ecumenical Affairs, Commission for—Rev. AIDAN N. DONAHUE, Ecumenical Officer, Sacred Heart Church, 26 Wintonbury Ave., Bloomfield, 06002-2488. Tel: 860-242-4142.

Office of Stewardship—VACANT. Tel: 860-242-4777.

Holy Childhood Association—MARY CHRISTINAT, Assoc. Dir., 467 Bloomfield Ave., Bloomfield, 06002-2999. Tel: 860-761-7440; Fax: 860-243-0661.

Office for Divine Worship—Rev. DAVID J. BARANOWSKI, Dir.; LUCY ZOCCO, Assoc. Dir., 467 Bloomfield Ave., Bloomfield, 06002-2999. Tel: 860-761-7442; Fax: 860-243-0661.

Newspaper— "The Catholic Transcript" Most Rev. HENRY J. MANSELL, D.D., Pres. & Publisher; Rev. Msgr. DAVID Q. LIPTAK, Exec. Editor, 467 Bloomfield Ave., Bloomfield, 06002-2999. Tel: 860-286-2828; 800-726-2391; Fax: 860-726-0000. Email: info@catholictranscript.org; ROBERTA TUTTLE, Mng. Editor; JACK SHEEDY, News Editor; MARY CHALUPSKY, Staff Reporter; JEFFREY GUERRETTE, Advertising Representative; CAROLE CRONSELL, Business Mgr. Graphic Designers: LESLIE DIVENERE; JOSEPH BROWN; JOYCE H. BOUDREAU, Circulation Supvr.

Office for Black Catholic Ministries—Deacon ARTHUR L. MILLER, Dir. St. Thomas Seminary, 467 Bloomfield Ave., Bloomfield, 06002-2999. Tel: 860-243-0648; Fax: 860-243-0649.

Office of Ministry Enrichment for Priests—Rev. THOMAS J. SAS, Dir., St. Peter Claver Church, 47 Pleasant St., West Hartford, 06107-1625. Tel: 860-561-4235, Ext. 5; Fax: 860-561-0552.

Office of Radio and Television—Rev. JOHN P. GATZAK, Exec. Dir., 15 Peach Orchard Rd., Prospect, 06712-1052. Tel: 203-758-7367; Fax: 203-758-7371. Web: www.ortv.org. Email: ortv@ortv-hartford.org. Radio Stations: WJMJ-FM 88.9 Hartford, 93.1 Hamden, 107.1 New Haven. Tel.: 860-242-8800. Licensed by St. Thomas Seminary, Bloomfield (Hartford).

Office of WJMJ-FM—Rev. JOHN P. GATZAK, Gen. Mgr. Fax: 860-242-5556. Web: www.wjmj.org. Email: wjmj@ortv-hartford.org.

Office of Family Life, Marriage and Family Apostolate—Co-Directors: DONALD PAGLIA, M.S., C.A.G.S.; CHRISTINE PAGLIA, 412 Ridge Rd., Hamden, 06517-2941. Tel: 203-230-2460; Fax: 203-230-2472.

Archbishop's Annual Appeal—Rev. Msgr. JAMES G. COLEMAN, Pastors' Advisory Committee Chm. (Retired); JIM GALLAGHER, Dir., Mailing Address: P.O. Box 28, Hartford, 06141. Tel: 860-243-3800; Fax: 860-242-4553. Email: aaa2@stseminary.org.

Office of Religious Education—Rev. Msgr. MICHAEL J. MOTTA, Dir.; Ms. PATRICIA KECK, Asst. Dir., St. Thomas Seminary, 467 Bloomfield Ave., Bloomfield, 06002-2999. Tel: 860-243-9465; Fax: 860-243-9690. Web: www.orehartford.org.

Catholic Biblical School—Ms. BARBARA JEAN DALY HORELL, Coord.

Catechesis for Hispanics—MIRIAM HIDALGO, Coord.

Lay Ministry, RCIA, Adult Formation—Ms. MARY E. MARSAN, Coord.

Youth and Young Adult Ministry—Ms. SHAWNEE BALDWIN, Coord.

Catholic Scouting—Ms. JENNIFER MCCLINTOCK, Coord.

Evangelization—Rev. Msgr. MICHAEL J. MOTTA, Dir.

Commission for Priests' Retreats—Revs. DAVID CINQUEGRANI, C.P.; RONALD P. MAY; THOMAS J. SAS.

Ministry for Healing and Assistance—Sr. MARY KELLY, C.S.J., Dir., 134 Farmington Ave., Hartford, 06105-3784. Tel: 860-541-6491; Fax: 860-541-6293.

Safe Environment Program—Sr. MARY KELLY, C.S.J., Victims' Assistance Coord.; THERESA HATFIELD, Background Check Coord.; DOLORES SKOVICH, VIRTUS Prog. Coord.; KIMBERLEE DONAHUE, Child Lures Prevention Prog. Coord.; TRACEY MILLER; LISA M. STEVENS.

Office of Ministry for Priests—Rev. JOSEPH V. DISCIACCA, Min. for Priests, St. Joseph Rectory, 149 Goodwin St., Bristol, 06010-5115. Tel: 860-202-6013; Fax: 860-589-5374.

Mission Cooperative Planning Office—MARY CHRISTINAT, Assoc. Dir., 467 Bloomfield Ave., Bloomfield, 06002-2999. Tel: 860-761-7440; Fax: 860-243-0661.

Priests Retirement Plan for Secular Priests of the Archdiocese of Hartford— The Secular Priests of the Archdiocese of Hartford Retirement Trust. 134 Farmington Ave., Hartford, 06105-3784. Tel: 860-541-6491. Ex Officio: Rev. Msgr. GERARD G. SCHMITZ; Rev. JOSEPH V. DISCIACCA. Appointed: Revs. THOMAS E. BERBERICH; JOHN C. BLACKALL (Retired); ARTHUR J. DUPONT (Retired); RONALD P. MAY; ROBERT P. ROY; RONALD R. YELLE (Retired); MATTHEW A. BYRNE, CPA, M.B.A.

Pro-Life Activities—Rev. ROBERT J. ROUSSEAU, Dir., 30 Caputo Rd., North Branford, 06471-1027. Tel: 203-484-0403; Fax: 203-484-0132; Sr. SUZANNE GROSS, F.S.E., Prog. Coord., 271 Finch Ave., Meriden, 06451-2715. Tel: 203-639-0833. Email: prolife@flcenter.org. Web: www.prolifeministry.org.

Mission Office, The— (The Catholic Mission Aid Society of Hartford, Holy Childhood Assoc., Mission Cooperative Planning Office, Propagation of the Faith) MARY CHRISTINAT, Assoc. Dir., 467 Bloomfield Ave., Bloomfield, 06002-2999. Tel: 860-761-7440; Fax: 860-243-0661; Sr. LORETTA FRANCIS MANN, O.S.F., Mission Coord. for Educ.

Office of Catholic Schools—Mr. DALE R. HOYT, Supt. Assistant Superintendents: Sr. KATHLEEN FITZSIMONS, C.N.D.; Mrs. MARIA T. MAYNARD, 467 Bloomfield Ave., Bloomfield, 06002-2999. Tel: 860-242-4362; Fax: 860-242-8683. Web: catholicschoolshartford.org.

Diocesan Labor Institute—Rev. DANIEL E. JOHNSON, Dir. (Retired).

Social Service—LOIS M. NESCI, CEO, 839-841 Asylum Ave., Hartford, 06105. Tel: 860-493-1841; Fax: 860-548-1930.

Vocations—Rev. MICHAEL J. DOLAN, Dir.; NANCY SMYTH LASTRINA, Administrative Asst., St. Thomas Seminary, 467 Bloomfield Ave., Bloomfield, 06002-2999. Tel: 860-761-7456; Fax: 860-243-0661.

Office of the Permanent Diaconate—Deacon ROBERT M. PALLOTTI, Dir., 467 Bloomfield Ave., Bloomfield, 06002-2999. Tel: 860-761-7445; Fax: 860-243-0661. Email: deaconofc@aol.com.

Office for Religious—Rev. JAMES F. KINNANE, J.C.L., Vicar; Sr. MARY KELLY, C.S.J., Dir., 134 Farmington Ave., Hartford, 06105-3784. Tel: 860-541-6491; Fax: 860-541-6293.

Office of Vicar For Priests—Rev. Msgr. GERARD G. SCHMITZ, 467 Bloomfield Ave., Bloomfield, 06002-2999. Tel: 860-242-2510; Fax: 860-242-3785. Email: vicar@stseminary.org.

Office of Coordinator for Retired Priests—Rev. Msgr. GERARD G. SCHMITZ, Dir., 467 Bloomfield Ave., Bloomfield, 06002-2999. Tel: 860-242-2510; Mrs. MARY FITZPATRICK, Coord. Svcs. for Retired Priests. Tel: 860-761-7449; Fax: 860-242-3785.

Censor Librorum—Rev. Msgr. DAVID Q. LIPTAK.

Archdiocesan Offices and Directors

Archdiocesan Dispute Resolution Office—Most Rev. CHRISTIE ALBERT MACALUSO, D.D., V.G., Moderator of the Curia, 134 Farmington Ave., Hartford, 06105-3784. Tel: 860-541-6491.

Office for Catholic Social Justice Ministry—RONALD SHEA, Acting Dir., 81 Saltonstall Ave., New Haven, 06513-4356. Tel: 203-777-7279; Fax: 203-776-3233. Email: ocsjm@catholicsocialjustice.org. Web: www.catholicsocialjustice.org.

Office for Hispanic Evangelization—Rev. JOSE A. MERCADO, Dir.; LUZ YUNEZ, Dir. Asst., 467 Bloomfield Ave., Bloomfield, 06002-2999. Tel: 860-243-0940; Fax: 860-286-2797.

Cana Conferences—DONALD PAGLIA, M.S., C.A.G.S.; CHRISTINE PAGLIA, 412 Ridge Rd., Hamden, 06517-2941. Tel: 203-230-2460; Fax: 203-230-2472.

Catholic Cemeteries Association—Rev. Msgr. DAVID M. WALKER, Dir.; CRAIG S. NEAL, Exec. Dir., 700 Middletown Ave., P.O. Box 517, North Haven, 06473-0517. Tel: 203-239-2557; Fax: 203-239-5035.

Catholic Deaf Apostolate—VACANT.

Catholic Library and Information Center - Catholic Book Store—Deacon ROBERT M. PALLOTTI, Dir.; ANNEMARIE HUTCHINSON, Mgr., 467 Bloomfield Ave., Bloomfield, 06002-2999. Tel: 860-246-5628; Fax: 860-247-3490. Email: catholicbkstore@aol.com.

Connecticut Catholic Public Affairs Conference—(Connecticut Catholic Conference) MICHAEL C.

CULHANE, Exec. Dir.; Deacon DAVID W. REYNOLDS, Legislative Liaison; LI-LING LAM WALLER, Administrative Asst., 134 Farmington Ave., Hartford, 06105-3784. Tel: 860-524-7882; Fax: 860-525-0750. Email: ccc@ctcatholic.org.

Coordinator of the Hospital Apostolate—VACANT.

Office for People with Disabilities—VACANT. Tel: 860-761-7444.

Small Christian Communities Pastoral Department—Bro. ROBERT K. MORIARTY, S.M., Ph.D., Dir., 467 Bloomfield Ave., Bloomfield, 06002-2999. Tel: 860-761-7450; Fax: 860-760-6116. Email: info@sccquest.org.

Cursillo Movement, Archdiocesan Director of—Rev. JOHN M. COONEY, Dir., St. John the Evangelist, 21 Academy Hill, Watertown, 06795-2101. Tel: 860-274-8836; Fax: 860-274-0667.

Victim Assistance Coordinator—Sr. MARY KELLY, C.S.J., 134 Farmington Ave., Hartford, 06105-3784. Tel: 860-541-6491.

CLERGY, PARISHES, MISSIONS AND PAROCHIAL SCHOOLS

CITY OF HARTFORD

(HARTFORD COUNTY)

1—CATHEDRAL OF ST. JOSEPH (1872) Rev. Msgr. John J. McCarthy, Rector; Sr. Ann Marie Strileckis, C.N.D., Pastoral Assoc. In Res., Rev. Lawrence G. Wrenn (Retired); Rev. Msgr. David Q. Liptak; Rev. Daniel Akho, Ministry to the Burmese Community.
Res.: 140 Farmington Ave., 06105-3708. Tel: 860-249-8431; Fax: 860-249-5910. Web: cathedralofsaintjoseph.com.
Catechesis/Religious Program—Students 75.

2—ST. ANNE (1889), (French), Closed. For inquiries for sacramental records contact St. Anne-Immaculate Conception, Hartford.

3—ST. ANNE-IMMACULATE CONCEPTION (2000), (French—Spanish), Rev. Zacarias Pushpanathan.
Res.: 820 Park St., 06106-2388. Tel: 860-728-7445; 860-525-1522; Fax: 860-728-1973.
Catechesis/Religious Program—Students 70.

4—ST. AUGUSTINE (1902) Revs. Jose A. Mercado; Diego A. Jimenez; Deacon Ramon A. Rosado.
Res.: 10 Campfield Ave., 06114-1832. Tel: 860-522-7128; Fax: 860-246-1753. Email: staugust@staugustinehtfd.org. Web: staugustinehtfd.org.
School—(Grades PreK-8), 20 Clifford St., 06114-1798. Tel: 860-249-5661; Fax: 860-293-2981. Mrs. Cynthia Niedbala, Prin. Lay Teachers 12; Students 200.
Catechesis/Religious Program—Tel: 860-249-3430; Fax: 860-246-1753. Students 60.

5—SS. CYRIL AND METHODIUS (1902), (Polish), Revs. Adam Hurbanczuk (Poland); Andrzej Pogorzelski.
Res.: 55 Charter Oak Ave., 06106-1902. Tel: 860-522-9157; Fax: 860-524-9433.
School—(Grades PreK-8), 35 Groton St., 06106-2799. Tel: 860-522-8490; Fax: 860-493-7409. Mrs. Joy Chlus, Interim Prin. Sisters 4; Lay Teachers 10; Students 124.
Catechesis/Religious Program—Tel: 860-527-3775. Students 110.
Convent—Felician Sisters, 45 Groton St., 06106-2798. Tel: 860-527-3775.

6—HOLY TRINITY (1900), (Lithuanian), Rev. Charles E. Jacobs.
Res.: 53 Capitol Ave., 06106-1798. Tel: 860-246-4162; Fax: 860-246-5662. Email: holytrinity53@yahoo.com.
Catechesis/Religious Program—Mary Beth Murphy, D.R.E. Students 5.

7—IMMACULATE CONCEPTION (1899) Closed. For inquiries for sacramental records contact St. Anne-Immaculate Conception, Hartford.

8—ST. JUSTIN (1924), (African American—West Indian), Linked with St. Michael Parish. Rev. Emmanuel I. Ihemedu; Deacon Isidro DeJesus.
Res.: 230 Blue Hills Ave., 06112-1836. Tel: 860-246-6897; Fax: 860-246-6898. Email: stjustinsrectory@sbcglobal.net.
Catechesis/Religious Program—Tel: 860-522-6184. Students 27.

9—ST. LAWRENCE O'TOOLE (1885) Rev. Joseph T. Devine. In Res., Rev. Jose M. Cavalcante, (Brazilian Ministry).
Res.: 494 New Britain Ave., 06106-3797. Tel: 860-522-1129; Fax: 860-549-4261. Email: 494slot@sbcglobal.net.
Catechesis/Religious Program—Students 196.

10—ST. LUKE (1930) Rev. Msgr. Vittorio Guerrera.
Res.: 66 Bolton St., 06114. Tel: 860-296-8681; Fax: 860-296-1983. Email: saintlukechurch@comcast.net.
Catechesis/Religious Program—

11—ST. MICHAEL (1900), (African American—Hispanic), Linked with St. Justin Parish. Rev. Emmanuel I. Ihemedu; Deacon Isidro DeJesus.
Res.: 98 Capen St., 06120-2010. Tel: 860-522-6184; Fax: 860-278-8410. Email: stmichaelsrectory@sbcglobal.net.
Catechesis/Religious Program—Tel: 860-522-6184; Fax: 860-278-8410. Students 25.

12—OUR LADY OF FATIMA (1958), (Portuguese), Rev. Antonio Jorge Tchingui (Angola).
Res.: 22 Madison Ave., 06106. Tel: 860-236-1443; Fax: 860-232-4455. Email: olfchurch1958@yahoo.com. Web: www.ourladyoffatima.us.
Church: Fatima Sq., 50 Kane St., 06106.
Catechesis/Religious Program—Email: olfcatequese@yahoo.com. Students 220.

13—OUR LADY OF SORROWS (1895) Revs. Francis C. Cooney, M.S.; Thomas J. Huhn, M.S.; Deacons Victor Bilbraut; Valentin Perez.
Res.: 16 Greenwood St., 06106-2109. Tel: 860-233-4424; Fax: 860-236-0149. Email: olsparish@aol.com. Web: ourladyofsorrowsparish.homestead.com.
Church: 79 New Park Ave., 06106-2109.
Catechesis/Religious Program—Students 70.

14—ST. PATRICK-ST. ANTHONY (1829) Revs. Thomas M. Gallagher, O.F.M.; Andrew Giardino, O.F.M.; Cidouane C. Joseph; John J. Leonard, O.F.M.; Patricia Curtis, Pastoral Assoc.
Franciscan Center for Urban Ministry—285 Church St., 06103. Tel: 860-756-4034; Fax: 860-249-6487.
Catechesis/Religious Program—Students 436.

15—ST. PETER (1859), (Irish), Revs. Dairo E. Diaz; Diego Albarracin (Colombia); Deacons Ramon A. Rosado; Adolfo Carrero, Pastoral Assoc. Tel: 860-610-1055.
Res.: 160 Main St., 06106-1894. Tel: 860-525-2683; Fax: 860-548-0202. Email: stpeterhartford@gmail.com.
Catechesis/Religious Program—Tel: 860-525-2684. Students 66.

16—SACRED HEART (1872), (Spanish), Revs. Dairo E. Diaz; Diego Albarracin (Colombia); Deacon Isidro DeJesus.
Res.: 49 Winthrop St., 06103-1030. Tel: 860-527-6459; Fax: 860-527-6450. Email: shparishhartford@comcast.net.
Catechesis/Religious Program—Students 133.

OUTSIDE THE CITY OF HARTFORD

ANSONIA, NEW HAVEN CO.

1—ST. ANTHONY (1915), (Lithuanian), Linked with Holy Rosary Parish. Rev. Joseph V. Napolitano.
Res.: 10 Father Salemi Dr., 06401-3296. Tel: 203-735-7874; Fax: 203-735-7875.
Catechesis/Religious Program—Tel: 203-736-0242. Students 3.

2—ASSUMPTION (1870) Revs. Robert F. Condron; George P. Burnett (Retired).
Res.: 61 N. Cliff St., 06401-1698. Tel: 203-735-7857; Fax: 203-734-8302. Email: chofaspt@aol.com. Web: assumptionansonia.org.
School—(Grades PreK-8), 51 N. Cliff St., 06401-1698. Tel: 203-734-0855; Fax: 203-734-5521. Web: assumption.eduk12.net. Mrs. Kathleen Molner, Prin.; Monica Masiero, Librarian. Lay Teachers 12; Students 250.
Catechesis/Religious Program—Tel: 203-735-2701. Email: annelynch0401@yahoo.com. Students 152.

3—HOLY ROSARY (1908), (Italian), Linked with St. Anthony Parish. Rev. Joseph V. Napolitano; Deacon Richard W. Renker.
Res.: Fr. Salemi Dr., 06401-2396. Tel: 203-735-7874.
Catechesis/Religious Program—Tel: 203-736-0242; Fax: 203-732-2212. Margaret Vernassa, D.R.E. Students 187.

4—ST. JOSEPH (1925), (Polish), Rev. Mitchell Wanat, C.M. In Res., Rev. Waclaw Hlond, C.M. (Retired).
Res.: 32 Jewett St., 06401-2499. Tel: 203-734-0402; Fax: 203-734-4884. Email: josephansonia@snet.net. Web: rc.net/hartford/stjoseph.
Catechesis/Religious Program—Students 63.

AVON, HARTFORD CO., ST. ANN'S (1917) [CEM] Rev. John W. McHugh; Deacons John J. Mylott, (Retired); Jeffrey B. Sutherland; Alan Campbell, (Retired). In Res., Rev. Joseph Cheah, O.S.M.
Res.: 289 Arch Rd., 06001-4209. Tel: 860-673-9858; Fax: 860-675-4350.
Catechesis/Religious Program—Tel: 860-673-2137; Fax: 860-675-4350. Lisa M. Stevens, D.R.E. Students 845.

BANTAM, LITCHFIELD CO., OUR LADY OF GRACE (1970) [CEM] Rev. John H. McCann, S.M.M.
Res.: Rte. 202, 715 Bantam Rd., P.O. Box 427, 06750. Tel: 860-567-9522; Fax: 860-567-5540. Email: ourladyofgrace@optonline.net.
Catechesis/Religious Program—Students 30.

BEACON FALLS, NEW HAVEN CO., ST. MICHAEL (1899) Rev. Leonard J. Kvedas; Deacon Victor M. Lembo.
Res.: 25 Maple Ave., 06403-1145. Tel: 203-729-2504; Fax: 203-723-0710. Email: saint_michaels@sbcglobal.net. Web: www.saintmichaelsonline.org.
Catechesis/Religious Program—Students 365.

BETHLEHEM, LITCHFIELD CO., CHURCH OF THE NATIVITY (1921) Rev. Joseph E. Looney.
Res.: 48 East St., Box 192, 06751-0192. Tel: 203-266-5211; Fax: 203-266-7543. Email: churchofnativity@att.net. Web: churchofthenativity-ct.org.
Catechesis/Religious Program—Tel: 203-266-5212. Students 229.

BLOOMFIELD, HARTFORD CO.

1—CHRIST THE KING (1936) Closed. For inquiries for sacramental records contact Sacred Heart, Bloomfield.

2—SACRED HEART (1878) Rev. Aidan N. Donahue; Deacons Anthony Nwankwo; Richard D. Santos; Bro. Paul L. Gauvin, S.C., Pastoral Assoc.
Rectory—35 Cold Spring Dr., 06002. Tel: 860-242-1942.
Church: 26 Wintonbury Ave., 06002. Tel: 860-242-4142; Fax: 860-286-0044.
Catechesis/Religious Program—Students 53.

BRANFORD, NEW HAVEN CO.

1—ST. ELIZABETH (1966), Linked with St. Clare Parish, East Haven. Rev. Kevin G. Donovan; Deacon George G. Sartor.
Res.: 65 Burban Dr., 06405. Tel: 203-488-1661; Fax: 203-483-9248. Email: secretary@st-elizabethparish.org.
Catechesis/Religious Program—Tel: 203-483-1997; Fax: 203-483-9248. Students 92.

2—ST. MARY (1868) [CEM 2] Revs. Christopher M. Ford; John Kuzhikottayil, S.D.B., Parochial Vicar. In Res., Rev. Robert J. Burbank (Retired).
Res.: 731 Main St., 06405-3693. Tel: 203-488-1607; Fax: 203-483-9208.
School—(Grades PreK-8), 62 Cedar St., 06405-3646. Tel: 203-488-8386; Fax: 203-488-2347. Donna Binkoski, Prin. Lay Teachers 7; Students 87.
Catechesis/Religious Program—Tel: 203-488-7412. Email: stmarybranford@yahoo.com. Web: stmary-branford.org. Students 354.

3—ST. THERESE (1947) Rev. Msgr. David M. Walker; Deacon Gerald S. Walton.
Office: 105 Leetes Island Rd., 06405. Tel: 203-488-2998; Fax: 203-488-8542. Email: sttheresebfd@comcast.net. Web: www.sttheresebranford.4lpi.com.
Res.: 39 Acorn Rd., 06405. Tel: 203-483-9304.
Catechesis/Religious Program—Students 201.

BRISTOL, HARTFORD CO.

1—ST. ANN (1908), (French), Rev. Alvin J. LeBlanc; Deacons Roger R. Albert; John J. Lovett.
Parish Center—180 Laurel St., 06010.
Res.: 215 West St., 06010-5754. Tel: 860-589-9080; Fax: 860-585-7139. Email: saintann180@comcast.net. Web: stann-bristolct.org.
Catechesis/Religious Program—Tel: 860-582-8169. Students 80.

2—ST. ANTHONY (1920), (Italian), Rev. Alphonso R. Fontana.
Res.: 111 School St., 06010-6078. Tel: 860-583-1349; Fax: 860-582-3861. Email: rectorystanthony@gmail.com. Web: stanthonybristolct.com.
School—(Grades PreK-8), 30 Pleasant St., 06010. Tel: 860-582-7874; Fax: 860-582-2440. Dr. Gene Nocera, Prin. Lay Teachers 12; Students 202.
Catechesis/Religious Program—20 Pleasant St., 06010. Tel: 860-583-4495; Fax: 860-582-3861. Students 182.

3—ST. GREGORY THE GREAT (1957) Revs. Gary F. Simeone; Sebastian Kochupurackal, C.M.I. (India); Deacon Stanley J. Piotrowski Jr.
Res. & Mailing Address: St. Gregory Rectory, 235 Maltby St., 06010-3892. Tel: 860-589-2295; Fax: 860-589-6692. Email: st.gregory.rectory@comcast.net. Web: stgregorys-bristol.ct.41pi.com.
Catechesis/Religious Program—1043 Stafford Ave., 06010. Tel: 860-589-4232; Fax: 860-584-4786. Claudia Larson, D.R.E. Students 933.

4—ST. JOSEPH (1864) [CEM] Revs. Joseph V. DiSciacca; Israel Rivera, Parochial Vicar; Deacon Neil B. Richter.
Res.: 149 Goodwin St., 06010-5115. Tel: 860-583-1369; Fax: 860-589-5374. Email: parishoffice@stjosephbristol.org. Web: stjosephbristol.org.
School—(Grades PreK-8), 335 Center St., 06010. Tel: 860-582-8696; Fax: 860-584-9907. Email: schooloffice@stjosephbristol.org. Web: www.school-stjosephbristol.org. Mark J. Monnerat, Prin. Lay Teachers 13; Students 252.
Catechesis/Religious Program—Tel: 860-582-2888. Web: faithformation.stjosephbristol.org. Students 304.

5—ST. STANISLAUS (1919), (Polish), Rev. Raymond S. Smialowski; Deacons Leonard R. Lewandoski, (Retired); Michael P. Szumigala.
Res.: 510 West St., P.O. Box 1860, 06011-1860. Tel: 860-583-4242; Fax: 860-583-9464.
Catechesis/Religious Program—Tel: 860-584-5378. Mary Ann Miecznikowski, D.R.E. Students 220.

BROAD BROOK, HARTFORD CO., ST. CATHERINE (1886) [CEM], Linked with St. Philip Parish, East Windsor. Rev. Paul A. Gotta.
Res.: 6 Windsorville Rd., P.O. Box 359, 06016-0359. Tel: 860-623-4636; Fax: 860-292-8550. Email: stcchurch@att.net.
Catechesis/Religious Program—7 Rye St., 06016. Robert Nadler, D.R.E. Students 275.

CANAAN, LITCHFIELD CO., ST. JOSEPH (1920) [CEM] [JC], Linked with Immaculate Conception Parish, Norfolk. Rev. Brian E. Jeffries; Deacon Stephen M. Beecher Sr.
Mailing Address: P.O. Box 897, 06018-2459.
Res.: 4 Main St., 06018. Tel: 860-824-7078; Fax: 860-824-4925. Email: sacrament@sbcglobal.net. Web: www.rc.net/hartford/saintjoseph.
Catechesis/Religious Program—Denise Dubay, D.R.E. Students 50.

CHESHIRE, NEW HAVEN CO.

1—ST. BRIDGET (1871) [CEM] Rev. Robert P. Ricciardi; Deacon Richard Wilber.
Res.: 175 Main St., 06410-2446. Tel: 203-272-3531; Fax: 203-271-3356.
Parish Center—Tel: 203-271-9994.
School—(Grades PreK-8), 171 Main St., 06410. Tel: 203-272-5860; Fax: 203-271-7031. Web: www-.stbridgetcheshire.org; www.stbridgetschool.org. Mrs. Margaret Whalen, Prin.; Mrs. Lorriane Mikolinski, Librarian. Lay Teachers 37; Students 433.
Catechesis/Religious Program—Tel: 203-272-6504; Fax: 203-272-2807. Students 1,042.

2—CHURCH OF THE EPIPHANY (1967) Rev. John L. Williams; Deacon Thomas F. Johnson.
Res.: 1777 Old Waterbury Rd., 06410-1399.
Church & Parish Center: 1750 Huckins Rd., 06410. Tel: 203-272-4355; Fax: 203-272-4878. Email: church@epiphany.necoxmail.com.
Catechesis/Religious Program—Tel: 203-272-4355. Students 124.

3—ST. THOMAS BECKET (1971) Rev. Eugene J. Charman.
Res.: 435 N. Brooksvale Rd., 06410-3341. Tel: 203-272-5777; Fax: 203-271-9210. Email: stboffice1@cox.net. Web: www.stthomasbecket.org.
Catechesis/Religious Program—Mrs. Phyllis Provost McNeil, C.R.E. Students 398.

COLLINSVILLE, HARTFORD CO., ST. PATRICK (1856) [CEM] [JC 2] Rev. John P. McHugh; Deacon Timothy E. Healy.
Res.: 7 Burlington Ave., P.O. Box 287, 06022-0287. Tel: 860-693-8727; Fax: 860-693-4538.
Catechesis/Religious Program—Fax: 860-693-4538. Peter Fortier, C.R.E. Students 822.

CORNWALL BRIDGE, LITCHFIELD CO., ST. BRIDGET (1883) [CEM], Linked with St. Bernard Parish, Sharon. Rev. Francis R. Fador.
Church: 7 River Rd., 06754. Tel: 860-672-6515; Fax: 860-364-9893.
Res. & Mailing Address: 52 New St., P.O. Box 218, Sharon, 06069-0218. Tel: 860-364-5244; Fax: 860-364-9893. Email: pastor@snet.net. Web: stbridgetschurch.org.
Catechesis/Religious Program—Email: stbern.rel.ed@snet.net. Students 25.

DERBY, NEW HAVEN CO.

1—ST. JUDE (1961) Rev. Grzegorz Jaworowski (Poland).
Res.: 71 Pleasant View Rd., 06418-2455. Tel: 203-735-8725; Fax: 203-735-4402. Email: stjudechurch06401@att.net.
Catechesis/Religious Program—Tel: 203-735-8725; Fax: 203-735-4402. Karen Blake, D.R.E. Students 28.

2—ST. MARY THE IMMACULATE CONCEPTION (1851) Rev. Janusz Kukulka, S.T.L.; Deacon Robert C. Johnson.
Res.: 212 Elizabeth St., 06418-1834. Tel: 203-735-3341; Fax: 203-736-6492. Email: st_mary_s_church@sbcglobal.net. Web: stmaryderbyct.org.
School—St. Mary-St. Michael, (Grades PreK-8), *St. Mary Campus*, 14 Seymour Ave., 06418. Tel: 203-735-6471; Fax: 203-732-9009. Mrs. Linda T. Coppola, Prin. Lay Teachers 13; Students 107.
Catechesis/Religious Program—Students 177.

3—ST. MICHAEL THE ARCHANGEL (1905), (Polish), [CEM] Rev. Roman Gorowski, C.M.
Res.: 75 Derby Ave., 06418-2098. Tel: 203-734-0005.
School—St. Mary-St. Michael, 14 Seymour Ave., 06418-1491. Tel: 203-735-6471; Fax: 203-732-9099. Mrs. Linda T. Coppola, Prin. Lay Teachers 8; Students 113.
Catechesis/Religious Program—Students 183.

EAST BERLIN, HARTFORD CO., SACRED HEART (1896) Rev. Edmund S. Nadolny.
Res.: 48 Cottage St., 06023-1108. Tel: 860-828-0154; Fax: 860-828-5305. Email: fngoodnews@aol.com. Web: www.sacredheartchurchct.com.
Church: 66 Cottage St., 06023-1108.
Catechesis/Religious Program—Students 149.

EAST HARTFORD, HARTFORD CO.

1—BLESSED SACRAMENT (1948), Linked with Our Lady of Peace Parish. Rev. James J. Nock; Deacons Raymond A. Parenteau; Leo R. LaRocque.
Mailing Address: 36 Cambridge Dr., 06118. Tel: 860-568-2747; Fax: 860-568-4133. In Res., Rev. Michael S. Galasso.
Catechesis/Religious Program—Linked with Our Lady of Peace, East Hartford. Students 250.

2—ST. CHRISTOPHER (1965) Rev. Vincent J. Curran; Deacons William J. Gilles; Edward J. Giard. In Res., Rev. Louis D. Cremonie.
Res.: 538 Brewer St., 06118-2305. Tel: 860-568-5240; Fax: 860-568-0673. Email: stchris-eh@sbcglobal.net. Web: stchris-eh.org.
School—(Grades PreK-8), 570 Brewer St., 06118-2305. Tel: 860-568-4100; Fax: 860-568-1070. Web: saintchristopherschool.org. Mrs. Kathleen Madej, Prin. Lay Teachers 18; Students 230.
Catechesis/Religious Program—580 Brewer St., 06118-2305. Tel: 860-895-8692; Fax: 860-568-0242. Students 128.

3—ST. ISAAC JOGUES (1964), Linked with St. Mary Parish and St. Rose Parish. Revs. John P. Rohan; Robert P. Roy; Ivan D. Ramirez; John Kyere; Deacon Julio C. Maturana.
Parish Center & Mailing Address: 15 Maplewood Ave., 06108. Tel: 860-289-7916; Fax: 860-289-3224.
Church: 1 Community St., 06108-2808. Tel: 860-528-6749.
Res.: 33 Church St., 06108. Tel: 860-289-8616; Fax: 860-289-3966.
Catechesis/Religious Program—Mrs. Judy Craig, D.R.E. Students 15.

4—ST. MARY (1873), Linked with St. Isaac Jogues Parish and St. Rose Parish. Revs. John P. Rohan; Robert P. Roy; John Kyere, (Min. to Ghanaian Catholic Community); Ivan D. Ramirez; Deacons Julio C. Maturana; Michael Torres. In Res., Rev. Joseph Naduvilekoot (India).
Res.: 15 Maplewood Ave., 06108-4021. Tel: 860-289-7916; Fax: 860-289-3224. Email: stmaryschurcheasthartford@comcast.net.
Parish Center—30 Maplewood Ave., 06108. Tel: 860-289-7510.
Catechesis/Religious Program—Mrs. Judy Craig, D.R.E. Students 18.

5—OUR LADY OF PEACE (1971), Linked with Blessed Sacrament Parish. Rev. James J. Nock; Deacons Leo R. LaRocque; Raymond A. Parenteau.
Res.: 370 May Rd., 06118-3496. Tel: 860-568-4414.
Catechesis/Religious Program— Twinned with Blessed Sacrament. Students 250.

6—ST. ROSE (1920), Linked with St. Isaac Jogues Parish and St. Mary Parish. Revs. John P. Rohan; Robert P. Roy; Ivan D. Ramirez; John Kyere; Deacon Julio C. Maturana.
Parish Center & Mailing Address: 15 Maplewood Ave., 06108. Email: strosechurcheasthartford@comcast.net.
Res.: 33 Church St., 06108-3728. Tel: 860-289-8616; 860-289-7916; Fax: 860-289-3224.
Catechesis/Religious Program—Mrs. Judy Craig, D.R.E. Students 235.

EAST HAVEN, NEW HAVEN CO.

1—ST. CLARE (1947), Linked with St. Elizabeth Parish, Branford. Rev. Kevin G. Donovan; Deacon George G. Sartor.
Parish Office: 234 Coe Ave., 06512-4112. Tel: 203-467-5136; Fax: 203-469-0241. Web: www.st-clareparish.org.
Catechesis/Religious Program—Tel: 203-467-0600. Email: faithformation@st-clareparish.org. Students 119.

2—OUR LADY OF POMPEII (1947) Rev. John L. Lavorgna; Deacon Norman H. Singer, (Retired).
Res.: 355 Foxon Rd., 06513. Tel: 203-469-0764; Fax: 203-469-3645. Email: ourladyofpompeii@snet.net. Web: pompeiichurch.org.
Catechesis/Religious Program—Tel: 203-468-7071. Email: olopreled@snet.net. Students 640.

3—ST. VINCENT DE PAUL (1915) Rev. Thomas A. Sievel; Deacons Robert J. Macaluso; William H. Parkinson.
Res.: 80 Taylor Ave., 06512. Tel: 203-467-6394; Fax: 203-467-6716.
School—(Grades PreK-8), 35 Bishop St., 06512. Tel: 203-467-1606; 203-467-1607; Fax: 203-467-8851. Email: svdp@snet.net. Web: stvincentdepaulschool.org. Sr. Eugenie Guterchi, R.S.M., Prin. Lay Teachers 10; Students 125.
Catechesis/Religious Program—Mrs. Carol Silva, D.R.E. Students 245.

EAST WINDSOR, HARTFORD CO., ST. PHILIP'S (1959), Linked with St. Catherine Parish, Broad Brook. Rev. Paul A. Gotta.
Res.: 150 S. Main St., 06088-9760. Tel: 860-623-4636; Fax: 860-292-8550.
Catechesis/Religious Program—

ENFIELD, HARTFORD CO.

1—ST. ADALBERT'S (1915), (Polish), [CEM] Rev. Edmund M. O'Brien (Retired); Deacon Robert E. Lambert. In Res., Rev. Anthony J. Bruno. Tel: 860-745-9966.
Res.: 90 Alden Ave., 06082-2865. Tel: 860-745-4837; Fax: 860-745-1787.
Catechesis/Religious Program—Students 136.

2—ST. BERNARD (1870) Rev. John P. Melnick; Deacons Richard F. Boucher; Donald H. Pond; Sr. Theresa Marie Grochowski, C.S.S.F., Pastoral Assoc.
Res.: 426 Hazard Ave., 06082-4719. Tel: 860-749-8353; Fax: 860-749-6456. Email: st.bernards@snet.net.
School—(Grades K-8), 232 Pearl St., 06082-4399. Tel: 860-745-5275; Fax: 860-745-0167. Charlene Mongillo, Prin. Sisters 2; Lay Teachers 18; Students 213.
School—Little Angels Catholic Preschool, 424 Hazard Ave., 06082. Tel: 860-745-6135. Lay Teachers 4; Students 77.
Catechesis/Religious Program—Tel: 860-749-2993; Fax: 860-749-6456. Email: stbernardccd@yahoo.com. Beth Chase, C.R.E. (Grades 1-10). Students 189.

3—HOLY FAMILY (1965) Revs. Francis T. Kerwan; John E. Pahl; Deacons Arthur J. Dickman; F. Robert Linehan, (Retired).
Res.: 23 Simon Rd., 06082-5903. Tel: 860-741-2101; Fax: 860-741-7411.
Catechesis/Religious Program—Karen Zeni, D.R.E.; Carole Frappier, D.R.E. Students 612.

4—ST. MARTHA (1961) Rev. J. Daniel McElheron; Deacons Robert E. Bernd; Joseph S. Sloan.
Res.: 214 Brainard Rd., 06082-2609. Tel: 860-745-5616; Fax: 860-741-6731. Email: rectory@stmartha.necoxmail.com.
School—(Grades K-8) Tel: 860-745-3833; Fax: 860-745-3329. Email: saintmartha.school@snet.net. Web: stmarthaschool-ct.org. Mrs. Ann Theresa Sarpu, Prin. Daughters of Mary of the Immaculate Conception 1; Lay Teachers 9; Students 171.
Catechesis/Religious Program—Tel: 860-749-8457. Brian LeMay, D.R.E.; Jon Barbalich, Confirmation Dir.; Patricia Barbalich, Confirmation Dir. Tel: 860-749-3255. Students 145.

5—ST. PATRICK (1866) [CEM] Rev. John G. Weaver; Deacon Vincent J. Motto.
Church: 64 Pearl St., 06082-3594. Tel: 860-745-2411; Fax: 860-253-9483. Email: stpatricc@aol.com. Web: saintpatrickenfield.org.
Catechesis/Religious Program—Tel: 860-741-0572. Carolyn Dague, D.R.E. Students 187.

FARMINGTON, HARTFORD CO., ST. PATRICK (1871) Rev. Thomas J. Barry; Deacons William A. Farrell; Clifford E. Thermer.
Res.: 110 Main St., P.O. Box 523, 06034-0523. Tel: 860-677-2639; Fax: 860-677-2672. Email: rectory@stpatsfarm.com. Web: stpatsfarm.com.
Catechesis/Religious Program—128 Garden St., 2nd Fl., 06032. Tel: 860-676-0253; Fax: 860-677-2672. Email: religioused@stpatsfarm.com. Eileen Dignazio, D.R.E. Students 451.

FORESTVILLE, HARTFORD CO., ST. MATTHEW (1891) Rev. Msgr. Thomas M. Ginty; Deacons Richard H. Hamel; James P. McCluskey.
Res.: 120 Church Ave., Box 9216, 06011-9216. Tel: 860-583-1833; Fax: 860-582-6152. Web: stmatthewrcc.com.
School—(Grades PreK-8), Welch Dr., 06010. Tel: 860-583-5214; Fax: 860-314-1541. Web: stmatthewsschool.com. Sr. Christina Joseph Dolan, I.H.M., Prin.; Mrs. Mary Ellen Schigas, Librarian. Sisters 4; Lay Teachers 11; Students 242.
Parish Resource Center—101 Church Ave., 06010. Tel: 860-583-1241.
Catechesis/Religious Program—Tel: 860-583-7806. Maryann Wisniewski, D.R.E. Students 442.
Convent—Sisters, Servants of the Immaculate Heart of Mary, 119 Church Ave., 06010. Tel: 860-583-2004.

GLASTONBURY, HARTFORD CO.

1—ST. DUNSTAN (1971) Rev. George M. Couturier; Sr. Mary O'Neill, R.S.M., Pastoral Assoc.; Deacons Peter J. Klein; Ronald R. Daigle; Linda DiCaprio, Parish Mgr.
Mailing Address: 1345 Manchester Rd., 06033. Tel: 860-633-3317.
Res.: 1150 Neipsic Rd., 06033. Tel: 860-633-8159; Fax: 860-659-8611. Email: stdunstanchurch@aol.com. Web: stdunstanchurch.org.
Catechesis/Religious Program—Tel: 860-633-6876. Patricia Kearney, C.R.E.; Rose Slusarczyk, C.R.E. (K-8); Gina Raymond, C.R.E. (9-10) & Youth Min. Students 895.

2—ST. PAUL (1954), Linked with St. Augustine

Parish, South Glastonbury. Revs. John P. Gwozdz; Thomas W. Hickey; Deacon Stephen L. Weaver. In Res., Rev. Edward J. McLean (Retired).
Res.: 2577 Main St., 06033-2023. Tel: 860-633-9419; Fax: 860-633-0040.
Catechesis/Religious Program—Tel: 860-659-3029. Students 711.

GOSHEN, LITCHFIELD CO., ST. THOMAS OF VILLANOVA (1877) [CEM] Rev. Richard M. Taberski; Deacon John R. Maffeo.
Res.: 71 North St., P.O. Box 177, 06756-0177. Tel: 860-491-2756; Fax: 860-491-3780. Email: stthomaschurch@optonline.net. Web: stthomasofvillanovachurch.com.
Catechesis/Religious Program—Tel: 860-491-9276. Students 84.

GRANBY, HARTFORD CO., ST. THERESE (1958) Rev. Thomas E. Ptaszynski.
Res.: 120 W. Granby Rd., 06035-2907. Tel: 860-653-3371; Fax: 860-653-5780. Email: sttheresechurch@att.net.
Catechesis/Religious Program—Tel: 860-844-8627. Students 340.

GUILFORD, NEW HAVEN CO., ST. GEORGE (1870) [CEM] Revs. James A. Shanley; Anthony J. Smith; Deacons P. Terrence Moran; William A. Elder.
Res.: 33 Whitfield St., 06437-2698. Tel: 203-453-2788; Fax: 203-453-1707.
School—Our Lady of Mercy, School for Guilford and Madison., 149 Neck Rd., Madison, 06443-2728. Tel: 203-245-4393; Fax: 203-245-3498. Sr. Carol Sansone, A.S.C.J., Prin. Students 200.
Catechesis/Religious Program—Tel: 203-453-3496. Students 1,308.

HAMDEN, NEW HAVEN CO.

1—ST. ANN (1919), (Italian), Linked with St. John the Baptist Parish, New Haven. Rev. Robert A. Morgewicz II.
Parish Office: 930 Dixwell Ave., 06514-4990. Tel: 203-865-0886; Fax: 203-865-4502.
Catechesis/Religious Program—Linked with St. John the Baptist, New Haven. Students 18.

2—ASCENSION (1964) Rev. Thomas J. O'Rourke.
Res.: 1040 Dunbar Hill Rd., 06514-1410. Tel: 203-288-7516; Fax: 203-288-7516 (Call first).
Catechesis/Religious Program—Tel: 203-288-7516. Donna Olsen, D.R.E. Students 82.

3—BLESSED SACRAMENT (1939) Rev. Donald J. French; Deacon Robert J. Brunell.
Res.: 321 Circular Ave., 06514-3428. Tel: 203-288-1652; Fax: 203-248-0873. Email: bsrectory322@yahoo.com.
Catechesis/Religious Program—306 Circular Ave., 06514. Tel: 203-288-5228. Dominic Lonardo, D.R.E. Students 140.

4—ST. JOAN OF ARC (1971) Rev. Daniel G. Keefe; Deacon Stephen J. Yatcko.
Res.: 450 W. Todd St., 06518. Tel: 203-288-4543; Fax: 203-288-1130. Email: stjofa@comcast.net. Web: www.sjarc.us.
Catechesis/Religious Program—Tel: 203-230-1926. Students 206.

5—OUR LADY OF MT. CARMEL (1869) [CEM] Revs. Daniel James Sullivan; Faron Calumba, C.S. (Philippines); Deacons James H. Stanley, (Retired); John C. O'Donovan, (Retired).
Res.: 2819 Whitney Ave., 06518-2598. Tel: 203-248-0141; Fax: 203-248-8658. Email: olmtcarmel@sbcglobal.net. Web: www.olomc.org.
Parish Center—2809 Whitney Ave., 06518. Tel: 203-287-9017.
Catechesis/Religious Program—Tel: 203-287-9017. Sr. Ann O'Neill, R.S.M., D.R.E. Students 613.

6—ST. RITA (1928) Revs. Philip J. Sharkey; Sebastian K. Kos; Deacon Ronald B. Gurr. In Res., Rev. Geoffrey C. Smith.
Res.: 1620 Whitney Ave., 06517. Tel: 203-248-5513; Fax: 203-248-2684. Email: stritachurchct@sbcglobal.net. Web: stritachurch.org.
School—(Grades PreK-8), 1601 Whitney Ave., 06517. Tel: 203-248-3114; Fax: 203-248-1016. Web: stritaschool.org. Sr. Maureen Fitzgerald, A.S.C.J., Prin.; Linda Kiley, Librarian. Priests 1; Apostles of the Sacred Heart 3; Lay Teachers 26; Students 402.
Catechesis/Religious Program—Tel: 203-281-7522; Fax: 203-248-2684. Mrs. Dianne Breen, D.R.E. Students 338.

7—ST. STEPHEN (1953) Rev. Robert G. Heffernan; Deacon George E. McCarroll.
Res.: 400 Ridge Rd., 06517-2941. Tel: 203-288-6439; Fax: 203-288-4152. Email: rectory@ststephenparishhamden.com. Web: ststephenparishhamden.com.
School—(Grades PreK-8), 418 Ridge Rd., 06517. Tel: 203-288-6792; Fax: 203-287-9158. Web: saintstephenschool.net. Mrs. Maria Testa, Prin. Lay Teachers 13; Students 180.
Catechesis/Religious Program—Tel: 203-288-1305. Eleanor Shaw, C.R.E. Students 49.

HARWINTON, LITCHFIELD CO., IMMACULATE HEART OF MARY (1956), Linked with Immaculate Conception, New Hartford. Revs. Timothy A. O'Brien; Iain R. Highet; Deacon John H. Charles.
Res.: 78 Litchfield Rd., P.O. Box 127, 06791-2230. Tel: 860-485-1588; Fax: 860-485-1004. Web: www.immaculateheartharwinton.org.
Catechesis/Religious Program—Tel: 860-485-9264. Mrs. Christine Rousseau, C.R.E. Students 201.

KENSINGTON, HARTFORD CO., ST. PAUL (1878) Revs. Robert Schlageter, O.F.M. Conv.; Raymond Borowski, O.F.M. Conv.; Martin Breski, O.F.M. Conv.; Deacons Peter Tremblay, O.F.M. Conv.; Carmen Guzzardi.
Res.: 479 Alling St., 06037-2170. Tel: 860-828-0331; Fax: 860-828-7620.
Parish Center—467 Alling St., 06037. Email: ourchurch@stpaulkensington.org.
School—(Grades PreK-8), 461 Alling St., 06037-2170. Tel: 860-828-4343; Fax: 860-828-1226. Email: ourschool@stpaulkensington.org. Web: ourschool.stpaulkensington.org. Laurie Piecewicz, Prin. Lay Teachers 24; Students 241.
Catechesis/Religious Program—Tel: 860-828-1934; Fax: 860-828-7620. Email: religioused@stpaulkensington.org. Annie Molleda, D.R.E. Students 917.

KENT, LITCHFIELD CO., SACRED HEART (1970) [CEM] Rev. Thomas E. Berberich.
Res.: 90 Cobble Rd., P.O. Box 186, 06757-0186. Tel: 860-927-3003; Fax: 860-927-3985. Email: shcsec@hotmail.com.
Church: 17 Bridge St., 06757.
Catechesis/Religious Program—Students 62.

LAKEVILLE, LITCHFIELD CO., ST. MARY (1874) [CEM] Rev. Joseph G.M. Kurnath.
Res.: 76 Sharon Rd., P.O. Box 466, 06039-0466. Tel: 860-435-2659; Fax: 860-435-1042. Email: churchofstmary@snet.net. Web: stmarylakeville.org.
Catechesis/Religious Program—Nancy Hodgkins, D.R.E. Students 52.

LITCHFIELD, LITCHFIELD CO., ST. ANTHONY OF PADUA (1882) [CEM] Rev. Robert F. Tucker.
Res.: 49 South St., P.O. Box 97, 06759-0097. Tel: 860-567-5209; Fax: 860-567-2052. Email: stanthonypadua@optonline.net. Web: stanthonyofpaduachurch.org.
Catechesis/Religious Program—Tel: 860-567-4188. Mitzi Cappello, C.R.E. Students 345.

MADISON, NEW HAVEN CO., ST. MARGARET (1937) Rev. Msgr. John P. Conte; Rev. Robert L. Turner; Deacons Joseph M. Regan, (Retired); Adam J. Michele; Paul Prete, (Retired).
Res.: 24 Academy St., P.O. Box 814, 06443-0814. Tel: 203-245-7301; Fax: 203-245-8568.
School—Our Lady of Mercy, (Grades PreK-8), 149 Neck Rd., 06443-2728. Tel: 203-245-4393; Fax: 203-245-3498. Sr. Carol Sansone, A.S.C.J., Prin.
Catechesis/Religious Program—Tel: 203-245-7971; Fax: 203-245-3387. Lauri Sturwold, D.R.E.; Monica Piombino, Youth Min. Students 1,335.

MANCHESTER, HARTFORD CO.

1—ASSUMPTION (1955), Linked with St. James Parish. Revs. Kevin P. Cavanaugh; Joseph Moonnanappallil (India); Deacon Thomas F. Breen III.
Res.: 285 W. Center St., 06040-4898. Tel: 860-643-2195; Fax: 860-646-4360. Email: info@assumptionmanchester.org.
Church: 29 S. Adams St., 06040.
School—(Grades PreK-8) Tel: 860-649-0889; Fax: 860-643-0559. Marguerite Ouellette, Prin. Sisters 2; Lay Teachers 12; Students 148.
Catechesis/Religious Program—Tel: 860-643-7596. Sr. Colleen Doyle, R.S.M., D.R.E. Students 136.
Convent—Sisters of Charity of Our Lady, Mother of the Church, 21 S. Adams St., 06040. Tel: 860-643-0452.

2—ST. BARTHOLOMEW (1958) Revs. Stephen M. Sledesky; Marcin P. Pluciennik; Deacon William H. Bartlett; Mary Jo Tomsic, Youth Min.; Diane Gluhosky, Business Mgr.
Res.: 45 Ludlow Rd., 06040-4542. Tel: 860-646-1613; Fax: 860-646-7121. Web: stbartparish.org.
Catechesis/Religious Program—Tel: 860-643-9178. Denise Bartlett, D.R.E. Students 410.

3—ST. BRIDGET (1870) Revs. Stephen M. Sledesky; Marcin P. Pluciennik; Mr. John Ryan, Pastoral Assoc.
Res.: 80 Main St., 06042-3140. Tel: 860-643-2403; Fax: 860-646-6936. Email: parishoffice@saintbridget.com. Web: www.saintbridget.com.
School—(Grades PreK-8), 74 Main St., 06042-3140. Tel: 860-649-7731; Fax: 860-646-6936. Web: www.school.saintbridget.com. Mary Alice Nadaskay, Prin. Lay Teachers 18; Students 158.
Catechesis/Religious Program—Tel: 860-643-5454. Kathleen Sinnamon, D.R.E. Students 245.

4—ST. JAMES (1874), Linked with Church of the Assumption, Manchester. Revs. Kevin P. Cavanaugh; Joseph Moonnanappallil (India). In Res., Rev. William L. Burns (Retired).
Res.: 896 Main St., 06040-6079. Tel: 860-643-4129; Fax: 860-643-4130. Email: stjamesmanchester@cox.net. Web: saint-james-church.org.
School—(Grades PreK-8), 73 Park St., 06040. Tel: 860-643-5088; Fax: 860-649-6462. Mrs. Patricia Kanute, Prin.; Barbara Alexander, Librarian. Lay Teachers 26; Students 417.
Catechesis/Religious Program—73 Park St., 06040. Tel: 860-643-9605. Students 85.

MARLBOROUGH, HARTFORD CO., ST. JOHN FISHER (1972) Rev. Arthur J. Audet; Deacon John W. McKaig. In Res., Rev. Mark F. Flynn.
Res. & Mailing Address: 24 Cheney Rd., 06447-1327. Tel: 860-295-0067. Email: stjohnfisher30@yahoo.com.
Church: 30 Jones Hollow Rd., 06447. Tel: 860-295-0001 (Parish Office); Fax: 860-295-8682.
Catechesis/Religious Program—Email: stjohnfisherccd@yahoo.com. Students 327.

MERIDEN, NEW HAVEN CO.

1—THE CORPORATION OF THE CHURCH OF THE HOLY ANGELS (1887) Rev. Lawrence S. Symolon; Deacon Joseph S. Mazurek.
Res.: 585 Main St., 06451-4934. Tel: 203-235-5311 (Rectory); 203-235-3822 (Office); Fax: 203-630-3041. Email: pastor@holyangelschurch.org. Web: www.holyangelschurch.org.
Catechesis/Religious Program—Tel: 203-237-8697. Email: hared@holyangelschurch.org. Geralyn Kogut, D.R.E. Students 130.

2—ST. JOSEPH (1900), Linked with St. Mary Parish. Revs. Shawn T. Daly; Augustine Okoroafor; Deacon John T. Nugent; Sr. Georgeann Vumbaco, R.S.M., Pastoral Assoc.
Res.: 22 Goodwill Ave., 06451. Tel: 203-237-5593.
School—(Grades K-8) Tel: 203-237-6800; Fax: 203-238-2963. Mrs. Katherine A. Spencer, Prin. Lay Teachers 9; Students 178.
Catechesis/Religious Program—Tel: 203-237-5593. Students 206.

3—ST. LAURENT (1880), (French), Linked with Our Lady of Mt. Carmel Parish. Rev. David C. Carey; Deacons Donald H. Smith Jr.; George W. Frederick.
Mailing: *c/o Mt. Carmel*, 109 Goodwill Ave., 06451.
Res.: 121 Camp St., 06450-3279. Tel: 203-634-1583; Fax: 203-238-3629.
Catechesis/Religious Program—Deborah Haggett, D.R.E. Students 119.

4—ST. MARY (1890), (German), [CEM], Linked with St. Joseph Parish. Revs. Shawn T. Daly; Augustine Okoroafor; Deacon John T. Nugent.
Res.: 5 Sherman Pl., 06451. Tel: 203-235-0519.
Catechesis/Religious Program—Students 3.

5—OUR LADY OF MOUNT CARMEL (1894), (Italian), Linked with St. Laurent Parish. Rev. David C. Carey; Deacons Donald H. Smith Jr.; George W. Frederick.
Parish: 109 Goodwill Ave., 06451-3000. Tel: 203-235-6381.
Res.: 17 North St., 06451. Fax: 203-238-3629.
School—(Grades PreK-8), 115 Lewis Ave., 06451. Tel: 203-235-2959. Norine McDermott, Prin. Lay Teachers 13; Students 200.
Catechesis/Religious Program— Deborah Haggett, D.R.E. Students 119.

6—ST. ROSE OF LIMA (1848) Revs. Jack Hoak, O.F.M.; Isaac J. Calicchio, O.F.M.; Deacons Charles E. Cunniff Jr.; Raul Cardona; Roberto L. Lugo.
Res.: 35 Center St., 06450-5685. Tel: 203-235-1644; Fax: 203-235-1360. Email: strosechurch@cox.net.
Catechesis/Religious Program—Tel: 203-235-6887. Students 220.

7—ST. STANISLAUS (1891), (Polish), [CEM] Rev. Edward Ziemnicki.
Res.: 82 Akron St., 06450-5796. Tel: 203-235-6341; Fax: 203-235-6342. Email: ststanislaus@cox.net.
School—(Grades PreK-8), 81 Akron St., 06450. Tel: 203-237-1005; Fax: 203-630-3424. Email: info@ststanislausschool.org. Web: ststanislausschool.org. George Claffey, Prin. Lay Teachers 20; Students 181.
Catechesis/Religious Program—Tel: 203-235-6341. Students 116.

MIDDLEBURY, NEW HAVEN CO., ST. JOHN OF THE CROSS (1904) Rev. Dennis J. Vincenzo; Deacon Michael J. Walsh.
Res.: 1321 Whittemore Rd., P.O. Box 361, 06762-0361. Tel: 203-758-2659; Fax: 203-577-6464. Email: st.john@snet.net.
Catechesis/Religious Program—Tel: 203-758-1326. Mrs. Annette Williams, D.R.E. Students 522.

MILFORD, NEW HAVEN CO.

1—ST. AGNES (1906) Rev. Francis X. Callahan; Deacon Nicholas A. Genovese.
Res.: 400 Merwin Ave., 06460-7198. Tel: 203-878-1617; Fax: 203-878-5545.
Catechesis/Religious Program—Students 356.

2—ST. ANN (1924) Rev. Brian A. Shaw.
Res.: 501 Naugatuck Ave., 06460-5048. Tel: 203-874-0634; Fax: 203-874-1919. Web: www.saintann-parish.com.
Catechesis/Religious Program—Tel: 203-878-8130. Students 90.

3—CHRIST THE REDEEMER (1966) Revs. Cyriac Maliekal; Gerard G. Masters; Deacon George A. Puskas.
Res.: 325 Oronoque Rd., 06461. Tel: 203-878-7431; Fax: 203-878-0677. Web: www.ctrmilford.net.
Catechesis/Religious Program—Students 177.

4—ST. GABRIEL (Wildemere Beach) (1946) Rev. Maurice J. Maroney; Deacon Henry Doyle, (Retired).
Business Office: 26 Broadway, 06460-5926. Tel: 203-877-6096; Fax: 203-878-9700. Email: stgabchurch@aol.com. Web: stgabrielmilford.org.
School—(Grades PreK-8), 1 Tudor Rd., 06460. Tel: 203-874-3811; Fax: 203-874-0416. Dr. Gail Kingston, Prin. Lay Teachers 13; Students 207.
Catechesis/Religious Program—Therese LeFever, D.R.E. Students 264.

5—ST. MARY (1874) [CEM] Revs. James J. Cronin; Nathaniel C. Labarda; Chacko K. Kumplam (India); Deacons Richard M. Sennett; John H. Hoffman.
Res.: 70 Gulf St., Box 230, 06460-0230. Tel: 203-878-3571; Fax: 203-877-8741. Email: kelleystmarymfd@optonline.net.
School—(Grades PreK-8) Tel: 203-878-6539; Fax: 203-878-1866. Web: saintmarysmilford.com. Frank Lacerenza, Prin. Lay Teachers 25; Students 280.
Catechesis/Religious Program—Tel: 203-877-5874. Sue Marra, D.R.E. Students 840.

NAUGATUCK, NEW HAVEN CO.

1—ST. FRANCIS OF ASSISI (1866) Revs. Michael J. Slusz; George S. Mukuka; Deacon Ernest H. Pagliaro Jr.
Res.: 318 Church St., 06770. Tel: 203-729-4543; Fax: 203-729-6216.
School—St. Francis-St. Hedwig School, (Grades PreK-8) Tel: 203-729-2247; Fax: 203-729-0512. Dr. John Salatto, Prin. Lay Teachers 12; Students 255.
Catechesis/Religious Program—Mrs. Joyce Luzio; Jessica Mulligan, D.R.E. Students 378.

2—ST. VINCENT FERRER (1975) Rev. Kevin J. Forsyth.
Res.: 1006 New Haven Rd., 06770-4731. Tel: 203-723-7497; Fax: 203-729-2978. Email: stvincentfer@sbcglobal.net.
Catechesis/Religious Program—Tel: 203-723-0782. Stephen Kenny, D.R.E.; Helen Northrup, Youth Min. Students 257.

NEW BRITAIN, HARTFORD CO.

1—ALL SAINTS (1918), (Slovak), Closed. For inquiries for sacramental records, contact St. Ann, New Britain.

2—ST. ANDREW (1895), (Lithuanian), Linked with St. John the Evangelist Parish. Rev. Ronald T. Smith.
Res.: 396 Church St., Box 515, 06050-0515. Tel: 860-223-3667; Fax: 860-826-6201.
Catechesis/Religious Program—Tel: 860-223-3667.

3—ST. ANN (1938), (Italian), Linked with St. Mary Parish. Revs. Thomas R. Mitchell; Gustavo Lopez.
Res.: 544 Main St., 06051. Tel: 860-225-7625; Fax: 860-224-4283.
Catechesis/Religious Program—Tel: 860-229-1929; Fax: 860-229-1929. Fran Caron, D.R.E. Students 57.

4—ST. FRANCIS OF ASSISI (1941) Rev. Jerzy Auguscik, O.F.M. Conv. (Poland); Deacon Michael E. Cassella.
Res.: 1755 Stanley St., 06053-2099. Tel: 860-225-6449; Fax: 860-225-2315.
Catechesis/Religious Program—Elizabeth Arena, D.R.E. Students 55.
Convent—1757 Stanley St., 06053-2027. Tel: 860-225-7143. School Sisters of Notre Dame 2.

5—HOLY CROSS (1927), (Polish), Revs. Dariusz Gosciniak; Szymon Kurpios, Sch.P.; Deacon Michael Rubitz.
Res.: 31 Biruta St., 06053-2899. Tel: 860-229-2011; Fax: 860-826-5887.
Church: 220 Farmington Ave., 06053.
School—Pope John Paul II School, (Grades PreK-8), 221 Farmington Ave., P.O. Box 1810, 06050-1810. Tel: 860-225-4275; Fax: 860-225-5073. Email: principal@pjp2school.org. Web: www.pjp2school.org. Bohdan Cuprak, Prin. Lay Teachers 12; Students 172.
Catechesis/Religious Program—Pope John Paul II School of Religion, Tel: 860-839-2040. Eva Fadgyas, D.R.E. Students 268.

6—ST. JEROME (1958), Linked with St. Maurice Parish. Rev. Thomas J. Cieslikowski; Deacon Michael J. Ward.
Res.: 1010 Slater Rd., 06053-1698. Tel: 860-224-2411; Fax: 860-224-6838. Email: st.jerome.church@snet.net. Web: www.stjeromenb.org.
Catechesis/Religious Program—Students 93.

7—ST. JOHN THE EVANGELIST (1916), Linked with St. Andrew Parish. Rev. Ronald T. Smith.
Res.: 655 East St., 06051-2108. Tel: 860-223-3667; 860-223-3668; Fax: 860-348-1488.
Catechesis/Religious Program—Cheryl Rusczyk, D.R.E. Students 4.

8—ST. JOSEPH'S (1896), Linked with St. Peter Parish. Rev. Joseph P. Crowley; Deacon Joseph K. Kane.
Res.: 195 S. Main St., 06051-3199. Tel: 860-229-4851; Fax: 860-225-1403.
Catechesis/Religious Program—Students 55.

9—ST. MARY'S (1848), Linked with St. Ann Parish. Revs. Thomas R. Mitchell; Gustavo Lopez; Deacons Pedro Rivera; James F. Papillo.
Res.: 544 Main St., 06051-1814. Tel: 860-229-4894; Fax: 860-223-2756. Email: parish@smnb.org.
Catechesis/Religious Program—Students 219.

10—ST. MAURICE (1946), Linked with St. Jerome Parish. Rev. Thomas J. Cieslikowski; Deacon Michael J. Ward.
Res.: 100 Wightman Rd., 06052-1597. Tel: 860-225-8419; Fax: 860-224-1947. Email: stmauricechurch@att.net.
Catechesis/Religious Program—Tel: 860-225-4477. Students 38.

11—ST. PETER (1873), (German—French), Linked with St. Joseph Parish. Rev. Joseph P. Crowley; Deacon Joseph K. Kane.
Res.: 98 Franklin Sq., 06051-2607. Tel: 860-224-1446; Fax: 860-223-8717.
Catechesis/Religious Program—Students 2.

12—SACRED HEART OF JESUS (1894), (Polish), [CEM] Rev. Msgr. Daniel J. Plocharczyk; Rev. Stanislaus Dudek, O.F.M. Conv. (Poland).
Res.: 158 Broad St., 06053-4195. Tel: 860-229-0081. Email: sercaj@aol.com.
School—(Grades PreK-8), 35 Orange St., 06053. Tel: 860-229-7663; Fax: 860-832-6098. Katherine Muller, Prin. Daughters of Mary of the Immaculate Conception 3; Lay Teachers 18; Students 243.
Catechesis/Religious Program—Students 254.

NEW HARTFORD, LITCHFIELD CO., IMMACULATE CONCEPTION (1869) [CEM], Linked with Immaculate Heart, Harwinton. Revs. Timothy A. O'Brien; Iain R. Highet; Deacon Robert N. Blair.
Res.: 60 Town Hill Rd., P.O. Box 285, 06057-0285. Tel: 860-379-5215; Fax: 860-379-9587. Email: immaculate.parish@snet.net. Web: immaculate-conceptionnhct.org.
Catechesis/Religious Program—Students 320.

NEW HAVEN, NEW HAVEN CO.

1—ST. AEDAN (1900), Linked with St. Brendan Parish. Rev. Thomas B. Shepard; Deacon Joseph R. Ryzewski.
Res.: 112 Fountain St., 06515-0156. Tel: 203-389-2619; Fax: 203-389-1235. Email: staedan@sbcglobal.net.
School—St. Aedan-St. Brendan Catholic School, (Grades PreK-8) Tel: 203-387-5693; Fax: 203-387-1609. Michael Votto, Prin. Lay Teachers 11; Students 179.
Catechesis/Religious Program—Students 57.

2—ST. ANTHONY (1904), (Italian), Linked with St. Michael Parish, New Haven. Rev. Ralph M. Colicchio.
Res.: 25 Gold St., 06519. Tel: 203-624-1418; Fax: 203-624-3420.
Catechesis/Religious Program—Students 35.

3—ST. BERNADETTE (1938), (Italian), Rev. Francis T. Carter; Deacon Martin J. O'Connor.
Res.: 385 Townsend Ave., 06512-3998. Tel: 203-467-1007; Fax: 203-467-3719. Email: stberndtchurch@sbcglobal.net. Web: www.saintbernadettechurch.org.
School—(Grades PreK-8) Tel: 203-469-2271; Fax: 203-469-4615. Email: sbsoffice@sbcglobal.net. Web: www.saintbernadette.org. Sherry Steines, Prin.; Mrs. Eileen Steele, Librarian. Lay Teachers 18; Students 128.
Catechesis/Religious Program—Tel: 203-467-8763; Fax: 203-467-3719. Tammie Tinari, C.R.E. Students 156.

4—ST. BONIFACE (1868), (German), Closed. For inquiries for sacramental records contact St. Bernadette Parish, New Haven.

5—ST. BRENDAN (1913), Linked with St. Aedan Parish. Rev. Thomas B. Shepard; Deacon Joseph R. Ryzewski.
Res.: 455 Whalley Ave., 06511-3080. Tel: 203-865-0561; Fax: 203-865-0562.
School—St. Aedan-St. Brendan Catholic School, (Grades PreK-8), 351 McKinley Ave., 06515. Tel: 203-387-5693. Michael Votto, Prin. Lay Teachers 15; Students 181.
Catechesis/Religious Program—Students 57.

6—ST. CASIMIR (1912), (Lithuanian), Closed. For inquiries for sacramental records, contact St. Bernadette, New Haven.

7—ST. DONATO (1915), (Italian), Closed. For inquiries for sacramental records, contact St. Francis Parish, New Haven.

8—ST. FRANCIS (1868) Rev. Daniel J. McLearen.
Res.: 397 Ferry St., 06513-3698. Tel: 203-777-5356; Fax: 203-777-0874.
School—St. Francis/St. Rose of Lima School, (Grades PreK-8) Tel: 203-777-5352; Fax: 203-865-1271. Web: www.stfrancischool.org. Mr. Victor Vessicchio, Prin.; Jean Groom, Librarian. Lay Teachers 13; Students 231.
Catechesis/Religious Program—Tel: 203-865-5179. Students 46.

9—ST. JOHN THE BAPTIST (1893), Linked with St. Ann Parish, Hamden. Rev. Robert A. Morgewicz II.
Res.: 782 Dixwell Ave., 06511-1098. Tel: 203-624-3097; Fax: 203-562-0433. Web: www.sjbrcchurch.org.
Parish Center—20 Elizabeth St., 06511. Tel: 203-562-3908.
Catechesis/Religious Program—Tel: 203-562-0433. Twinned with St. Ann, Hamden.

10—ST. JOHN THE EVANGELIST, Closed. For inquiries for sacramental records contact Sacred Heart, New Haven.

11—ST. JOSEPH'S (1900) Rev. John P. Sullivan.
Res.: 129 Edwards St., 06511-2299. Tel: 203-777-2548; Fax: 203-562-0197. Email: st.josephnh@att.net.

12—SAINT MARTIN DE PORRES (1942), (African American), Rev. Joseph M. Elko.
Res.: 136 Dixwell Ave., 06511-3400. Tel: 203-624-9944.
Catechesis/Religious Program—Students 32.

13—ST. MARY'S (1832) Rev. Joseph P. Allen, O.P.
Mailing Address: P.O. Box 1202, 06505-1202. Email: church@stmarys-priory.com. Web: www.stmarys-priory.com. In Res., Very Rev. Vincent G. DeLucia, O.P., Prior; Revs. Jonah Pollock, O.P.; Peter John Cameron, O.P.; Albert A. Caprio, O.P. (Retired); Henry A. Camacho, O.P.; Hugh Vincent Dyer, O.P.; Bro. Patrick Foley, O.P.
Res.: *St. Mary's Priory*, 5 Hillhouse Ave., 06511. Tel: 203-562-6193; Fax: 203-562-1273.
Catechesis/Religious Program—Moira Hambleton, D.R.E. Students 66.
Shrine—The Shrine of the Infant Prague (Inc.), Tel: 203-562-9326; Fax: 203-562-1273.

14—ST. MICHAEL (1889), (Italian), Linked with St. Anthony Parish, New Haven Rev. Ralph M. Colicchio; Deacon Richard L. Santello.
Res.: 29 Wooster Pl., 06511-6998. Tel: 203-562-7178; Fax: 203-752-0157.
Catechesis/Religious Program—Sharon Tartaris, D.R.E. Students 25.

15—ST. PATRICK (1851) Closed. For inquiries for sacramental records, contact St. Michael, New Haven.

16—ST. PETER (1902) Closed. For inquiries for sacramental records contact Sacred Heart, New Haven.

17—ST. ROSE OF LIMA (1907) Rev. James C. Manship; Deacon Emilio Gonzalez.
Res.: 115 Blatchley Ave., 06513-4298. Tel: 203-865-6149; Fax: 203-865-6140. Email: strosechurch@sbcglobal.net.
Catechesis/Religious Program—Students 300.

18—SACRED HEART (1876) Rev. Francis Snell.
Res.: 25 Gold St., 06519-1601. Tel: 203-562-7592; Fax: 203-562-1737. Email: sacredheart06519@yahoo.com.
Catechesis/Religious Program—Students 115.

19—ST. STANISLAUS (1901), (Polish), Revs. Roman Kmiec, C.M.; Marek Sadowski, C.M.; Stanley Miekina, C.M.
Res.: 9 Eld St., 06511-3815. Tel: 203-562-2828; Fax: 203-752-0217. Email: stanislausnewhaven@comcast.net.
Catechesis/Religious Program—Students 70.
St. Gregory Society (Latin Mass Association)—
St. Stanislaus Fraternity, Secular Franciscan Order—

NEW MILFORD, LITCHFIELD CO.

1—ST. FRANCIS XAVIER (1871) [CEM] Revs. Lawrence Parent, O.F.M.; Matthew Morreale, O.F.M.; Deacon Roland G. Miller.
Mailing Address: 1 Elm St., 06776-4009. Tel: 860-354-2202; Fax: 860-355-9485.
Res.: 48 Old Park Lane Rd., 06776-2508. Tel: 860-350-1611. Web: www.sfxnewmilford.org.
Catechesis/Religious Program—Tel: 860-354-5372. Mary Vannucci, C.R.E. (K-5); Susan Pullen, Youth Min. (6-12). Students 940.

2—OUR LADY OF THE LAKES (1990) Rev. Frederick M. Langlois; Deacon Robert E. Muro Sr. Tel: 860-354-9062.
Res.: 3 Old Town Park Rd., 06776-4212. Tel: 860-354-5239; Fax: 860-354-2968. Email: ololnm@sbcglobal.net.
Catechesis/Religious Program—Tel: 860-355-5365. Karen O'Donnell, D.R.E. Students 217.

NEWINGTON, HARTFORD CO.

1—CHURCH OF THE HOLY SPIRIT (1964) Revs. Lawrence R. Bock; James F. Kinnane; Deacons James H. Shiels; Joseph Guzauckas.
Res.: 183 Church St., 06111-4898. Tel: 860-666-5671; Fax: 860-666-9784. Web: www.holyspirit.41pi.com.
Catechesis/Religious Program—Tel: 860-666-3562. Susan Skipp, D.R.E. Students 500.

2—ST. MARY (1924) Rev. Joseph F. Keough; Deacon Bruce R. Thompson; Sr. Rosemary Spodnick, S.S.N.D., Pastoral Min. In Res., Rev. Nicholas J. Cesaro (Retired).

Res.: 626 Willard Ave., 06111. Tel: 860-666-1591; Fax: 860-666-5720.
School—(Grades PreK-8), 652 Willard Ave., 06111-2692. Tel: 860-666-3844; Fax: 860-666-5570. Margaret M. McDonald, Prin. Lay Teachers 12; Students 130.
Catechesis/Religious Program—Tel: 860-666-6347. Mrs. Joan Guerrera, D.R.E. Students 668.

NORFOLK, LITCHFIELD CO., IMMACULATE CONCEPTION (1889) [CEM], Linked with St. Joseph Parish, Canaan. Rev. Brian E. Jeffries; Deacon Stephen M. Beecher Sr.
Mailing Address: P.O. Box 897, Canaan, 06018.
Church: 4 North St., 06058. Tel: 860-542-5442; Fax: 860-824-4925. Email: imconception@sbcglobal.net. Web: www.sacrament7.org.
Catechesis/Religious Program—Robin Gundlach, D.R.E. Students 43.

NORTH BRANFORD, NEW HAVEN CO., ST. AUGUSTINE (1941) Rev. Robert J. Rousseau; Deacons John Hart; William J. Lovelace.
Res.: 30 Caputo Rd., 06471-1027. Tel: 203-484-0403; Fax: 203-484-0132. Email: staugustinenobfdct@sbcglobal.net. Web: staugustine.catholicweb.com.
Catechesis/Religious Program—Bernadette Lysaght, D.R.E. Students 549.

NORTH HAVEN, NEW HAVEN CO.

1—ST. BARNABAS (1922) Revs. Hugh J. MacDonald; John J. Daly (Retired); Deacon Anthony P. Solli.
Res.: 44 Washington Ave., 06473-1799. Tel: 203-239-5378; Fax: 203-239-3510.
Catechesis/Religious Program—Tel: 203-239-3804. Mrs. Karin Tierney, D.R.E.

2—ST. FRANCES CABRINI (1967) Rev. Timothy A. Meehan; Deacons George R. Stephens, (Retired); Julius R. Marcarelli.
Res.: 6 Welch Rd., 06473-2896. Tel: 203-239-5700; Fax: 203-239-6463. Email: st_frances_rector@sbcglobal.net.
Church & Parish Center: 57 Pond Hill Rd., 06473. Tel: 203-239-5644.
Catechesis/Religious Program—90 Chapel Hill Rd., 06473. Tel: 203-985-0424; Fax: 203-985-0236. Students 306.
Nursery School—
Convent—Sisters of the Sacred Heart of Jesus of Ragusa, 94 Chapel Hill Rd., 06473. Tel: 203-239-8012.

3—ST. THERESE (1925) Revs. Timothy A. Meehan; Donald Anyagwa (Nigeria); Deacon Louis J. Florio.
Res.: 555 Middletown Ave., 06473-4000. Tel: 203-239-1671; Fax: 203-234-2220. Web: www.sttheresenoh.com.
School—St. Therese Nursery School, Tel: 203-234-9971; Fax: 203-907-0545. Michele Adinolfi-Lucibello, Dir. Students 90.
Catechesis/Religious Program—Tel: 203-234-9287; Fax: 203-907-0545. Terry Raffone, D.R.E. Students 700.

NORTHFORD, NEW HAVEN CO., ST. MONICA (1964) Rev. Joseph Parel; Deacons Louis P. Fusco; Joseph P. Marenna; William B. Bergers, (Retired); Mrs. Judith Derbacher, Pastoral Assoc. Tel: 203-484-2434.
Res.: 1331 Middletown Ave., Box 160, 06472-0160. Tel: 203-484-9226; Fax: 203-484-1189.
Catechesis/Religious Program—Tel: 203-484-2434. Students 275.

OAKVILLE, LITCHFIELD CO., ST. MARY MAGDALEN (1900) Rev. James T. Gregory; Deacon George M. Pettinico.
Res.: 145 Buckingham St., 06779-1728. Tel: 860-274-9273; Fax: 860-274-2013.
School—(Grades PreK-8), 140 Buckingham St., 06779. Tel: 860-945-0621; Fax: 860-945-6162. Web: www.smmsoakville.org. Thomas Maynard, Prin. Lay Teachers 24; Students 291.
Catechesis/Religious Program—Kelly A. Shamansky, Coord. Faith Formation. Students 270.

ORANGE, NEW HAVEN CO., HOLY INFANT (1952) Revs. Peter S. Dargan; Francois-Xavier Eale; Thomas J. Kelly; Deacon Joseph D. Sullivan.
Res.: 450 Race Brook Rd., 06477. Tel: 203-799-2379; Fax: 203-799-9720.
Catechesis/Religious Program—Tel: 203-777-2417. Connie Gustafson, D.R.E. Students 854.

OXFORD, NEW HAVEN CO., ST. THOMAS THE APOSTLE (1966) Rev. Dominic J. Valla; Sr. Mary Elizabeth Preston, O.S.U., Pastoral Assoc.
Res.: 733 Oxford Rd., 06478. Tel: 203-888-2382; Fax: 203-881-5518.
Catechesis/Religious Program—Christine Troia, Dir. Faith Formation. Students 400.

PLAINVILLE, HARTFORD CO., OUR LADY OF MERCY (1881) [CEM] Revs. John F. Brinsmade; Joseph Savino-Gyimah (Ghana); Deacon Robert A. Berube; Bryan Knorr, Pastoral Assoc.
Res.: 15 S. Canal St., 06062-2756. Tel: 860-747-6825; Fax: 860-747-5407.
Catechesis/Religious Program— Jeanne Gionfriddo, D.R.E. Students 158.

PLANTSVILLE, HARTFORD CO.

1—ST. ALOYSIUS (1961) [JC] Rev. Kevin M. Dillon; Deacon James V. Arena.
Res.: 254 Burritt St., 06479-1426. Tel: 860-276-9208; Fax: 860-628-7650.
Catechesis/Religious Program—Students 700.

2—MARY OUR QUEEN (1961) Rev. A. Waine Kargul; Deacon John L. Crowley.
Res.: 248 Savage St., P.O. Box 46, 06479-0046. Tel: 860-628-4901; Fax: 860-621-0610.
Catechesis/Religious Program—Tel: 860-628-0437. Annelise Fusco, D.R.E. Students 515.

POQUONOCK, HARTFORD CO., ST. JOSEPH'S (1874) [CEM] Rev. Robert B. Vargo; Deacon Ronald Biamonte.
Res.: 1747 Poquonock Ave., P.O. Box 253, 06064-0253. Tel: 860-688-9566; Fax: 860-683-2225. Email: stjoepoquonock@aol.com. Web: home.catholicweb.com/stjosephwinct.
Catechesis/Religious Program—Tel: 860-683-0366. Cyndie Glick, D.R.E. Students 23.

PROSPECT, NEW HAVEN CO., ST. ANTHONY'S (1939) Rev. Mark S. Suslenko; Deacon Domenic N. Stolfi.
Res.: 4 Union City Rd., P.O. Box 7117, 06712-0117. Tel: 203-758-4056; Fax: 203-758-4594.
Catechesis/Religious Program—Tel: 203-758-4848. Students 370.

ROCKY HILL, HARTFORD CO.

1—ST. ELIZABETH SETON (1985) Rev. Stuart H. Pinette; Deacon Michael A. Shelto.
Res.: 280 Brook St., 06067-0485. Tel: 860-529-3222; Fax: 860-529-6421. Email: churchoffice@sesrockyhill.org. Web: www.sesrockyhill.org.
Catechesis/Religious Program—Students 372.

2—ST. JAMES (1880) Rev. David J. Baranowski; Deacon Robert M. Pallotti.
Res.: 767 Elm St., 06067-1902. Tel: 860-529-8655; Fax: 860-257-1754. Web: stjamesrh.org.
Catechesis/Religious Program—Tel: 860-529-1274. Thomas Sacerdote, D.R.E.; Joyce O'Sullivan, Music Min. Tel: 860-529-8655, Ext. 17. Students 479.

SEYMOUR, NEW HAVEN CO.

1—ST. AUGUSTINE (1866) [CEM] Rev. Honore M. Kombo (Congo); Deacons Mario DiRienzo; Frank J. Bevvino Jr.
Res.: 35 Washington Ave., 06483-3124. Tel: 203-888-2081; Fax: 203-888-9681. Email: staugustine@snet.net. Web: staugustine-churchseymour.myownparish.com.
Catechesis/Religious Program—Tel: 203-888-7003. Students 147.

2—GOOD SHEPHERD (1967) Rev. Edward S. Jaksina; Deacons Frank J. Krasnicki; Kenneth E. Ewaskie.
Res.: 135 Mountain Rd., 06483-2038. Tel: 203-888-9243; Fax: 203-888-6016.
Catechesis/Religious Program—Tel: 203-735-3190. Glenn Durette, D.R.E.; Debra Durette, D.R.E. Students 410.

SHARON, LITCHFIELD CO., ST. BERNARD (1885) [CEM], Linked with St. Bridget, Cornwall Bridge. Rev. Francis R. Fador.
Res.: 52 New St., Box 218, 06069-0218. Tel: 860-364-5244; Fax: 860-364-9893. Email: pastor@snet.net.
Catechesis/Religious Program—Students 23.

SIMSBURY, HARTFORD CO., ST. MARY (1921) Rev. William R. Metzler; Deacons Arthur L. Miller; Joseph Gabriele, (Retired).
Res.: 940 Hopmeadow St., P.O. Box 575, 06070-0575.
Parish Office—3 Massaco St., P.O. Box 575, 06070-0575. Tel: 860-658-7627; Fax: 860-658-7626. Web: stmarysimsbury.org.
School—St. Mary School, (Grades PreK-8), 946 Hopmeadow St., 06070. Tel: 860-658-9412; Fax: 860-658-1737. Web: stmarysschoolsimsbury.org. Mrs. Marie Gannatti, Prin.; Susan Ray, Librarian. Lay Teachers 13; Students 223.
Catechesis/Religious Program—Tel: 860-658-5919. Judy Eagen, C.R.E.; Jeannie Carpenter, C.R.E. Students 781.

SOUTH GLASTONBURY, HARTFORD CO., ST. AUGUSTINE (1877) [CEM], Linked with St. Paul Parish, Glastonbury. Revs. John P. Gwozdz; Thomas W. Hickey; Deacon Stephen L. Weaver.
Res.: 55 Hopewell Rd., P.O. Box 175, 06073-0175. Tel: 860-633-9505; Fax: 860-633-1341.
Catechesis/Religious Program—Tel: 860-633-4950. Students 221.

SOUTH WINDSOR, HARTFORD CO.

1—ST. FRANCIS OF ASSISI (1941) Rev. Jeremiah N. Murasso.
Res.: 673 Ellington Rd., 06074-4166. Tel: 860-528-8288 (Parish Office); Fax: 860-528-1685. Web: www.stfrancisofassisisw.org.
Catechesis/Religious Program—Mark F. Cerrato, D.R.E. Students 489.

2—ST. MARGARET MARY (1961) Rev. Daniel Jeremiah Sullivan; Deacons Michael D. Haines; Thomas J. Conklin, (Retired).
Res.: 80 Hayes Rd., 06074-1499. Tel: 860-644-2411; Fax: 860-644-5765. Email: office@smm.necoxmail.com. Web: stmargaretmary-sowindsor-ct4lpi.com.
Catechesis/Religious Program—Tel: 860-644-2549; Fax: 860-644-5765. Email: re@smm.necoxmail.com. Louise Bridge, D.R.E. Students 668.

SOUTHBURY, NEW HAVEN CO., SACRED HEART (1884) [CEM] Rev. Joseph T. Donnelly; Deacon Charles Dietsch, Pastoral Assoc.; Sr. Patricia Torre, D.W., Pastoral Assoc. In Res., Rev. Collins I. Anaeche.
Church: 910 Main St. S., 06488. Tel: 203-264-5071; Fax: 203-264-9562.
Res.: 91 Old Waterbury Rd., 06488.
Catechesis/Religious Program—Tel: 203-264-5065; Fax: 203-264-4271. Ami Conlan, Faith Formation. Students 635.

SOUTHINGTON, HARTFORD CO.

1—ST. DOMINIC (1971) Rev. Ronald P. May; Deacons Paul J. Kulas; Eugene P. Nebiolo, (Retired).
Res.: 1050 Flanders Rd., 06489-1344. Tel: 860-628-0349; Fax: 860-276-8390. Web: saintdominicchurch.com.
School—(Grades PreK-5) Tel: 860-628-4678; Fax: 860-628-6572. Mrs. Patricia O'Neil Tiezzi, Prin. Lay Teachers 12; Students 167.
Catechesis/Religious Program—Tel: 860-628-5159; Fax: 860-620-9246. Theresa Kamradt, D.R.E. Students 770.

2—IMMACULATE CONCEPTION (1915), (Polish), [CEM] Rev. Daniel T. Wojtun; Deacon Wayne F. Griffin.
Res.: 130 Summer St., 06489. Tel: 860-628-2181; Fax: 860-628-0341. Email: immaculateconception06489@gmail.com. Web: www.immaculateconception06489.4lpi.com.
Catechesis/Religious Program—Judy Telesmanick, D.R.E. Students 123.
Father Kolbe Catechetical Center—152 Summer St., Plantsville, 06479. Tel: 860-628-6973.

3—ST. THOMAS (1860) [CEM] Rev. Nicholas P. Melo; Deacon Angelo J. Coppola.
Res.: 99 Bristol St., 06489-4599. Tel: 860-628-4713; Fax: 860-628-7341. Email: stchurch@snet.net.
School—(Grades PreK-8), 133 Bristol St., 06489. Tel: 860-628-2485. Mrs. Mary Pat Wirkus, Prin. Lay Teachers 14; Students 172.
Catechesis/Religious Program—Tel: 860-628-9679. Sr. Marie Roccapriore, M.P.F., D.R.E. Students 190.
Convent—Religious Sisters Filippini, 20 Eden Pl., 06489-4599. Tel: 860-621-1904.

SUFFIELD, HARTFORD CO.

1—ST. JOSEPH (1916), (Polish), [CEM] Rev. William L. Baldyga.
Res.: 140 S. Main St., 06078-2218. Tel: 860-668-2880.
Catechesis/Religious Program—Students 6.

2—SACRED HEART (1884) [JC] Rev. Michael C. DeVito; Sr. Dorothy Connelly, S.N.D.deN., Pastoral Assoc. In Res., Rev. Theodore T. Raczynski (Retired).
Res.: 446 Mountain Rd., P.O. Box 626, 06078-0626. Tel: 860-668-4246; Fax: 860-668-1337. Email: sheart.church@sbcglobal.net. Web: www.sacredheartct.com.
Catechesis/Religious Program—Tel: 860-668-7766; Fax: 860-668-7811. Students 449.

TARIFFVILLE, HARTFORD CO., ST. BERNARD (1878) [CEM] Revs. Aidan N. Donahue; Joseph J. Cretella Jr.
Res.: 7 Maple St., P.O. Box 85, 06081-0085. Tel: 860-658-5142; Fax: 860-658-2804. Email: stbernardschurch@comcast.net. Web: www.stbernardschurch.net.
Catechesis/Religious Program—Students 129.

TERRYVILLE, LITCHFIELD CO.

1—ST. CASIMIR (1906), (Polish), Linked with Immaculate Conception Parish. Rev. Gerald H. Dziedzic; Deacon Leo B. Conard III.
Res.: 21 Maple St., 06786. Tel: 860-583-4697; Fax: 860-584-8656. Email: immclte.cncptn.chrch@snet.net. Web: rc.net/hartford/stcasimir.
Catechesis/Religious Program—Students 118.

2—IMMACULATE CONCEPTION (1882) [CEM 2], Linked with St. Casimir Parish. Rev. Gerald H. Dziedzic; Deacon Leo B. Conard III.
Res. & Mailing Address: 21 Maple St., 06786-1197. Tel: 860-583-4697. Email: immclte.cncptn.chrch@snet.net. Web: rc.net/hartford/icc.
Church: 170 Main St., 06786.
Catechesis/Religious Program—Fax: 860-584-8656. Students 191.

THOMASTON, LITCHFIELD CO., ST. THOMAS (1869) [CEM] Rev. Robert J. Grant; Deacons Kenneth Dos Santos; Victor C. Mitchell Jr.
Parish Center—19 Electric Ave., 06787-1651. Tel: 860-283-5817; Fax: 860-283-1009. Email: stc-office@sbcglobal.net. Web: www.stthomasthomaston.org.
Catechesis/Religious Program—Tel: 860-283-4296. Students 378.

TORRINGTON, LITCHFIELD CO.

1—ST. FRANCIS OF ASSISI (1877) Revs. Christopher M. Tiano; Carlos A. Echavarria; John Granato, S.M.; Deacons John L. Dembishack, (Retired); Roy C. Dungan; David W. Reynolds; James M. Sullivan; Beverly Sesko, Pastoral Min.
Church: Pope John Paul II Pastoral Center, 160 Main St., 06790-5201. Tel: 860-482-5571; Fax: 860-489-4070. Email: torringtoncatholicparishes@yahoo.com. Web: www.torringtoncatholics.org.
School—(Grades PreK-8) Tel: 860-489-4177; Fax: 860-489-1590. Web: spsfschool.org. Mrs. Jo-Anne Gauger, Prin. Franciscan Sisters of the Eucharist 2; Lay Teachers 12; Students 159.
Catholic Youth Ministry of Torrington—
Catechesis/Religious Program— 06790. Tel: 860-482-3121. Marlene Carrier, Coord., Faith Formation (7-8); Donna Puzacke, Confirmation Dir.; Lisa Kelsey, C.R.E. Torrington Cluster of Roman Catholic Parishes Religious Education. Students 141.

2—ST. MARY (1919), (Polish), Revs. Christopher M. Tiano; Carlos A. Echavarria; John Granato, S.M.; Deacons David W. Reynolds; John L. Dembishack, (Retired); Roy C. Dungan; James M. Sullivan; Beverly Sesko, Pastoral Min.
Mailing Address: Pope John Paul II Pastoral Center, 160 Main St., 06790-5201. Tel: 860-482-5047; Fax: 860-482-1972. Email: torringtoncatholicparishes@yahoo.com. Web: www.torringtoncatholics.org.
Church: 85 Pulaski St., 06790-5201.
Catechesis/Religious Program—360 Prospect St., 06790. Tel: 860-482-3121. Marlene Carrier, Coord., Faith Formation (7-8); Donna Puzacke, Confirmation Dir.; Lisa Kelsey, C.R.E. Torrington Cluster of Roman Catholic Parishes Religious Education Students 33.

3—ST. PETER (1910), (Italian), Revs. Christopher M. Tiano; Carlos A. Echavarria; John Granato, S.M.; Deacons Roy C. Dungan; John L. Dembishack, (Retired); David W. Reynolds; James M. Sullivan; Beverly Sesko, Pastoral Min.
Mailing Address: Pope John Paul II Pastoral Center, 160 Main St., 06790-5201.
Church: 107 E. Main St., 06790-5493. Tel: 860-482-4433; Fax: 860-489-4070.
School—(Grades PreK-8), 360 Prospect St., 06790. Tel: 860-489-4177; Fax: 860-489-1590. Mrs. Jo-Anne Gauger, Prin. Franciscan Sisters of the Eucharist 2; Lay Teachers 12; Students 159.
Catechesis/Religious Program—360 Prospect St., 06790. Tel: 860-482-3121. Marlene Carrier, Coord., Faith Formation (7-8); Donna Puzacke, Confirmation Dir.; Lisa Kelsey, C.R.E. Torrington Cluster of Roman Catholic Parishes Religious Education Students 210.

4—SACRED HEART (1910), (Slovak), Revs. Christopher M. Tiano; Carlos A. Echavarria; John Granato, S.M.; Deacons John L. Dembishack, (Retired); Roy C. Dungan; David W. Reynolds; James M. Sullivan; Beverly Sesko, Pastoral Min.
Mailing Address: Pope John Paul II Pastoral Center, 160 Main St., 06790-5047.
Church: 116 Grove St., 06790-5047. Tel: 860-482-8246; Fax: 860-489-4070. Email: torringtoncatholicparishes@yahoo.com. Web: www.torringtoncatholics.org.
Catechesis/Religious Program—360 Prospect St., 06790. Tel: 860-482-3121. Marlene Carrier, Coord., Faith Formation (7-8); Donna Puzacke, Confirmation Dir.; Lisa Kelsey, C.R.E. Torrington Cluster of Roman Catholic Parishes Religious Education Students 16.

UNION CITY, NEW HAVEN CO.

1—ST. HEDWIG (Naugatuck) (1906), (Polish), Linked with St. Mary Parish, Union City. Rev. Adam C. Subocz; Deacon Earle A. Kimball.
Res.: 32 Golden Hill St., 06770-3099. Tel: 203-729-2490; Fax: 203-720-2161. Email: sthedwig.unioncity@gmail.com. Web: www.sthedwigschool.org.
See St. Francis-St. Hedwig School, St Francis of Assisi Parish, Naugatuck.
Catechesis/Religious Program—Students 80.

2—ST. MARY (Naugatuck) (1907), Linked with St. Hedwig, Union City. Rev. Adam C. Subocz; Deacon Earle A. Kimball.
Res.: 338 N. Main St., 06770-3235. Tel: 203-729-2279; Fax: 203-729-1392.
Catechesis/Religious Program—Linked with St. Hedwig, Union City. Students 35.

UNIONVILLE, HARTFORD CO., ST. MARY (1874) [CEM] Rev. John S. Golas; Deacons Thomas S. Sutak; Michael T. Sponzo, (Retired). In Res., Rev. Robert J. St. Martin (Retired).
Res.: 16 Bidwell Sq., 06085-1116. Tel: 860-673-2422; Fax: 860-673-2001. Web: www.stmary-unionville.org.
Catechesis/Religious Program—Tel: 860-675-8522. Email: st.mary.re@sbcglobal.net. Students 625.

WALLINGFORD, NEW HAVEN CO.

1—HOLY TRINITY (1869) Revs. Thomas J. Walsh; James W. Richardson, S.C.; Deacons Eugene C. Riotte; Tullio V. Ossa.
Res.: 68 N. Colony St., 06492-3696. Tel: 203-269-8791; Fax: 203-269-0880.
School—(Grades K-8), 11 N. Whittlesey Ave., 06492. Tel: 203-269-4476; Fax: 203-294-4983. Sr. Kathleen Kelly, R.S.M., Prin. Sisters of Mercy 1; Lay Teachers 9; Students 215.
Catechesis/Religious Program—Tel: 203-265-6300. Frances Selmecki, D.R.E. Students 904.
Convent—Sisters of Mercy, 247 S. Main St., 06492-3619. Tel: 203-265-6999.

2—SS. PETER AND PAUL (1924) [CEM] Rev. Ronald P. Zepecki.
Res.: 139 N. Orchard St., 06492-3617. Tel: 203-269-4617; Fax: 203-265-6751. Email: st_peter_paul@sbcglobal.net. Web: www.stpeterpaulwallingford.org.
Catechesis/Religious Program—Tel: 203-269-0271. Jennifer Perrin, C.R.E. Students 72.

3—RESURRECTION (1963) Rev. John J. Georgia; Mr. Joseph R. Tatta, Pastoral Assoc. In Res., Rev. Arthur J. DuPont (Retired).
Res.: 115 Pond Hill Rd., 06492-4836. Tel: 203-265-1694; Fax: 203-284-9766.
Catechesis/Religious Program—Tel: 203-269-4683; Fax: 203-269-4683. Mrs. Mary Ann Marchitto, D.R.E. Students 446.

WASHINGTON DEPOT, LITCHFIELD CO., OUR LADY OF PERPETUAL HELP (1893) [CEM] Rev. Mathew T. Kappalumakkel; Deacon George H. Streib.
Res.: 34 Green Hill Rd., P.O. Box 303, 06794. Tel: 860-868-2600; Fax: 860-868-7252.
Catechesis/Religious Program—Students 103.
Mission—St. Patrick's Church St., Roxbury, Litchfield Co. 06783.

WATERBURY, NEW HAVEN CO.

1—BASILICA OF THE IMMACULATE CONCEPTION (1847) Revs. John J. Bevins; Peter Kucer, M.S.A.; Stanley Grove, M.S.A.; John R. Lyons, M.S.A.; Susith Silva.
Res.: 74 W. Main St., 06721-1670. Tel: 203-574-0017; Fax: 203-756-8748.
School—St. Mary, (Grades PreK-8), 55 Cole St., 06706-1291. Tel: 203-753-2574; Fax: 203-796-2498. Joseph Kenny, Prin.; Elizabeth Cristoff, Librarian. Lay Teachers 15; Students 297.
Catechesis/Religious Program—Students 178.

2—BLESSED SACRAMENT (1911) Rev. Michael A. Carlson; Deacon Carl H. Gerstung. In Res., Revs. John P. Gatzak; Carmine B. Raneri (Retired).
Res.: 182 Robbins St., 06708. Tel: 203-753-3149; Fax: 203-596-0740.
School—(Grades K-8), 386 Robinwood Rd., 06708-2750. Tel: 203-756-5313; Fax: 203-756-5313. Eileen Omundsen, Prin. Lay Teachers 10; Students 219.
Catechesis/Religious Program—Linda Hendrickson, C.R.E.; Sara Saturno, Youth Min. Students 105.

3—ST. CECILIA (1893), (German), Closed. For inquiries for sacramental records, contact Sacred Heart-Sagrado Corazon, Waterbury.

4—ST. FRANCIS XAVIER (1896) Rev. Paul J. Pace; Deacon Thomas J. Clifford.
Res.: 625 Baldwin St., 06706-1597. Tel: 203-756-7804.
Catechesis/Religious Program—Tel: 203-754-6996. Mrs. Laurie Ciarello, D.R.E. Students 95.

5—ST. JOSEPH (1894), (Lithuanian), Linked with St. Patrick Parish. Rev. Richard P. Okiria (Africa), Admin.
50 Charles St., P.O. Box 271, 06708. Tel: 203-756-8837; Fax: 203-756-4690.

6—ST. LEO THE GREAT (1974), Linked with SS. Peter and Paul Parish. Rev. Msgr. James G. Coleman (Retired); Rev. Cornelius Kelechi Anyanwu; Deacons Modesto A. Rosello; Charles G. Colella. In Res., Rev. Joseph F. Gorman (Retired).
Res.: 14 Bentwood Dr., 06705-3612. Tel: 203-573-0572; Fax: 203-573-9642. Email: cleogr14@sbcglobal.net.
Catechesis/Religious Program—Students 33.

7—ST. LUCY (1926), (Italian), Linked with Our Lady of Lourdes Parish. Rev. Ronald A. Ferraro; Deacon Robert F. Wallin.
Res.: 24 Branch St., 06704-3626. Tel: 203-574-5903.
Catechesis/Religious Program—At Our Lady of Lourdes Parish. Students 9.

8—ST. MARGARET (1910), (Hispanic), Rev. Robert Villa; Deacons Paul P. Iadarola; Edwin Lopez. In Res., Rev. Carlos M. Zapata.
Res.: 289 Willow St., 06710. Tel: 203-754-6101; Fax: 203-754-2006. Email: stmargarets@snet.net.
Catechesis/Religious Program—Tel: 860-567-2394. Jaqueline Boulier Tiul, D.R.E. (Elem & Middle School); Raul Santiago, Confirmation Dir.; Genevieve Santiago, Confirmation Dir. Students 150.

9—ST. MICHAEL (1902) Rev. Roger L. Hall, O.F.M.; Deacon George D. Hajjar.
Res.: 62 St. Michael Dr., 06704-1295. Tel: 203-753-0689; Fax: 203-573-9101.
Catechesis/Religious Program—Students 122.

10—OUR LADY OF FATIMA (1971), (Portuguese), Rev. Francisco Eurico.
Res.: 2071 Baldwin St., 06706. Tel: 203-753-1424; Fax: 203-573-1914. Email: fatimachurchwaterbury@yahoo.com.
Catechesis/Religious Program—Students 245.

11—OUR LADY OF LORETO (1971), Linked with St. Stanislaus Kostka. Rev. Allan J. Hill.
Res.: 12 Ardsley Rd., 06708-1825. Tel: 203-757-6112; Fax: 203-756-9656.
Catechesis/Religious Program—Students 91.

12—OUR LADY OF LOURDES (1899), (Italian), Linked with St. Lucy Parish. Rev. Ronald A. Ferraro; Deacon Robert F. Wallin.
Res.: 309 S. Main St., 06706-1014. Tel: 203-754-4134; Fax: 203-755-0456.
Catechesis/Religious Program—Students 74.

13—OUR LADY OF MT. CARMEL (1923), (Italian), Rev. Frederick M. Aniello; Deacon Nicholas J. Diorio.
Res.: 785 Highland Ave., 06708-4116. Tel: 203-756-8981; Fax: 203-756-2074. Web: olmcwtby.com.
School—(Grades PreK-8), 645 Congress Ave., 06708-4198. Tel: 203-755-6809; Fax: 203-755-5850. Joaquim (Jack) Taveras, Prin.; Karen Kleinschmidt, Librarian. Lay Teachers 18; Students 255.
Catechesis/Religious Program— Edward Owens, Coord., Faith Formation. Students 85.

14—ST. PATRICK (1880), (Irish), Linked with St. Joseph Parish. Rev. Richard P. Okiria (Africa). In Res., Rev. Will-Roger Malave (Retired).
Res.: 50 Charles St., 06708. Tel: 203-756-8837; Fax: 203-756-4690. Email: rectory50@gmail.com.

15—SS. PETER AND PAUL (1920), Linked with St. Leo the Great Parish. Rev. Msgr. James G. Coleman (Retired); Rev. Cornelius Kelechi Anyanwu; Deacon Charles G. Colella.
Res.: 67 Southmayd Rd., 06705. Tel: 203-756-7919; Fax: 203-755-3535. Email: ssppchurch1@juno.com.
School—(Grades PreK-8), 116 Beecher Ave., 06705. Tel: 203-755-0881. Mrs. Janet Curry, Prin. Lay Teachers 14; Students 268.
Catechesis/Religious Program—Frances Walsh, D.R.E. Students 208.

16—SACRED HEART-SAGRADO CORAZON (1885) Revs. Mark S. Suslenko; Carlos M. Zapata; Deacon Alexander Lopez Jr.
Office: 13 Wolcott St., 06702-1790. Tel: 203-757-8737; Fax: 203-754-5862. Email: sacredheartadm@comcast.net.
Catechesis/Religious Program—Students 84.

17—SHRINE OF SAINT ANNE FOR MOTHERS (1886), (French), Rev. Michael A. Carlson, Admin.; Deacon Carl H. Gerstung.
Res.: 515 S. Main St., 06706-1089. Tel: 203-756-4439; Fax: 203-754-3244. Web: www.shrineofsaintanne.org.
Catechesis/Religious Program—Dorothy Mihaliak, C.R.E. Students 35.

18—ST. STANISLAUS KOSTKA (1913), (Polish), Linked with Our Lady of Loreto Parish. Revs. Allan J. Hill; Jose M. Cavalcante, Brazilian Min.
Mailing Address: Parish Office, 12 Ardsley Rd., 06708. Tel: 203-757-6112; Fax: 203-756-9656.
Church: 86 E. Farm St., 06704.

19—ST. THOMAS (1898) Closed. For inquiries for sacramental records contact St. Michael, Waterbury.

WATERTOWN, LITCHFIELD CO., ST. JOHN THE EVANGELIST (1878) [CEM] Revs. John M. Cooney; James George (India); Deacons Robert D. Gordon; Daniel Camerota.
Res. & Mailing Address: 21 Academy Hill, 06795-2101. Tel: 860-274-8836; Fax: 860-274-0667. Web: www.stjohns-wtnct.4lpi.com.
Church: 574 Main St., 06795.
School—(Grades PreK-8), 760 Main St., 06795. Tel: 860-274-9208; Fax: 860-945-1082. Web: www-.stjohnwtn.org. John Petto, Prin. School Sisters of Notre Dame 1; Lay Teachers 14; Students 179.
Catechesis/Religious Program—Theresa N. Morgado, D.R.E. Students 422.
Convent—School Sisters of Notre Dame, 9 Academy Hill, 06795-2101. Tel: 860-274-1820.

WEST HARTFORD, HARTFORD CO.

1—ST. BRIGID (1919) Rev. Msgr. Douglas P. Clancy; Rev. Charles E. Ikwuegbu.
Res.: 1088 New Britain Ave., 06110-2426. Tel: 860-236-5965; Fax: 860-233-8016. Email: stbrigidchurchwhct@sbcglobal.net.
School—(Grades PreK-8), 100 Mayflower St., 06110-1420. Tel: 860-561-2130; Fax: 860-561-0011. Web: www.saintbrigidschool.org. Mrs. Pamela Belury, Prin.; Maureen Wine, Librarian. Lay Teachers 19; Students 193.
Catechesis/Religious Program—Tel: 860-521-8523. Mrs. Penny Hickey, D.R.E. Students 159.

2—THE CHURCH OF ST. TIMOTHY (1958) Rev. Henry P. Cody; Deacon Dennis R. Ferguson; Patricia A. Piano, Pastoral Assoc. Tel: 860-232-8594; Patricia

L. Pruitt, Business Mgr.
Res.: 1116 N. Main St., 06117-1209. Tel: 860-233-5131; Fax: 860-232-2189.
School—St. Timothy Middle School, 225 King Philip Dr., 06117-1497. Tel: 860-236-0614; Fax: 860-920-0293. Dr. Stephen Balkun, Prin. Lay Teachers 10; Students 148.
Catechesis/Religious Program—Tel: 860-232-3952. Bobbi Moran, D.R.E. (Grades 6-10); Stephanie Barney, D.R.E. (Grades PreK-5). Students 293.

3—ST. HELENA (1966) Rev. Msgr. Douglas P. Clancy; Revs. Charles E. Ikwuegbu; Joseph Naduvilekoot (India). Tel: 860-289-7916, Ext. 12 Ministry for the Syro-Malabar Catholic Community.; Deacon Robert J. Hilliard. In Res., Revs. Francis P. Johnson (Retired); Eugene M. Kilbride (Retired); Zigford J. Kriss (Retired). Tel: 860-521-1908.
Res.: 30 Echo Ln., 06107-3698. Tel: 860-521-1921; Fax: 860-521-1129.
Catechesis/Religious Program—Tel: 860-521-3661. Paula Krompinger, C.R.E. Students 205.

4—ST. JOHN THE EVANGELIST (1942) Closed. For inquiries for sacramental records contact St. Lawrence O'Toole, Hartford.

5—ST. MARK THE EVANGELIST (1942) Rev. Msgr. Michael J. Motta; Deacon Raymond J. Fugere Jr.
Res.: 467 S. Quaker Ln., 06110-1042. Tel: 860-233-1269; Fax: 860-233-5791. Email: st_marks_church@snet.net. Web: stmarkwesthartford.com.
Catechesis/Religious Program—Tel: 860-236-3545. Lou Ann Warren, D.R.E. Students 289.

6—ST. PETER CLAVER (1966) Revs. James F. Leary; Thomas J. Sas; Deacon James E. Hickey Jr.
Res.: 47 Pleasant St., 06107-1625. Tel: 860-561-4235; Fax: 860-561-0552. Email: st.peterclaver@sbcglobal.net. Web: www.stpeterclaverparish.com.
Catechesis/Religious Program—Tel: 860-521-2904. Email: spcreled@sbcglobal.net. Janine Cote, D.R.E. Students 472.

7—ST. THOMAS THE APOSTLE (1921) Revs. Edward M. Moran, Admin.; Arthur J. Murphy, Pastor Emeritus (Retired); Samuel Seyd (Pakistan); Deacon Kevin M. Monahan.
Res.: 872 Farmington Ave., 06119-1499. Tel: 860-233-8269; Fax: 860-523-8794. Email: stawh@comcast.net.
School—(Grades PreK-5), 25 Dover Rd., 06119-1298. Tel: 860-236-6257; Fax: 860-236-8865. Mrs. Colleen DiSanto, Prin.; Janet Cashman, Librarian. Lay Teachers 16; Students 225.
Catechesis/Religious Program—Tel: 860-523-4209; Fax: 860-570-0273. Mrs. Elizabeth B. Kiselica, D.R.E. Students 195.

WEST HAVEN, NEW HAVEN CO.

1—ST. JOHN VIANNEY (1965), Linked with Our Lady of Victory Parish. Rev. Joseph R. Cronin; Deacons Paul E. Sabo; Robert P. Tartaris; Sr. Ellen McNulty, O.P., Pastoral Assoc. In Res., Rev. Gregory M. Altermatt.
Parish Office: 600 Jones Hill Rd., 06516.
Res.: 300 Capt. Thomas Blvd., 06516-5974. Tel: 203-934-6000; Fax: 203-931-8747.
Catechesis/Religious Program—Attended at Our Lady of Victory., Tel: 203-933-0044. Angela Pietrowski, D.R.E.

2—ST. LAWRENCE (1886), Linked with St. Paul, West Haven. Rev. Mark R. Jette; Deacon Edward J. Mancini.
Res.: 207 Main St., 06516-4599. Tel: 203-934-8351; Fax: 203-937-7858.
School—(Grades PreK-8), 231 Main St., 06516. Tel: 203-933-2518; Fax: 203-932-2058. Mr. Paul De Fronzo, Prin. Lay Teachers 11; Students 200.
Catechesis/Religious Program—231 Main St., 06516. Tel: 203-933-2519. Students 170.

3—ST. LOUIS (1886), (French Territorial), Rev. Jeffrey Gubbiotti; Deacon Salvatore A. DeFilippo.
Res.: 89 Bull Hill Ln., 06516-3925. Tel: 203-934-5249; Fax: 203-934-1055. Email: st.louischurch@catholicweb.com. Web: www.saintlouischurch.catholicweb.com.
Catechesis/Religious Program—Students 285.

4—OUR LADY OF VICTORY (1935), Linked with St. John Vianney Parish. Rev. Joseph R. Cronin; Deacons Paul E. Sabo; Robert P. Tartaris; Sr. Ellen McNulty, O.P., Pastoral Assoc. In Res., Rev. Gregory M. Altermatt.
Res.: 600 Jones Hill Rd., 06516-6399. Tel: 203-934-6357; Fax: 203-932-3315. Email: olovrectory@yahoo.com. Web: www.olov.org.
School—(Grades PreK-8), 620 Jones Hill Rd., 06516-6397. Tel: 203-932-6457; Fax: 203-932-6456. Ardell Bartolotta, Prin. Lay Teachers 12; Students 177.
Catechesis/Religious Program—Twinned with St. John Vianney Parish., Tel: 203-933-0044. Email: olovore@sbcglobal.net. Angela Pietrowski, D.R.E. Students 562.
Convent—Ursuline Sisters of Tildonk, 634 Jones Hill Rd., 06516-6398. Tel: 203-934-8601.

5—ST. PAUL'S (1916), (Italian), Linked with St. Lawrence, West Haven. Rev. Mark R. Jette; Deacon Edward J. Mancini. In Res., Revs. Titus Ibe; Augustine Mangalath (India).
Parish Office & Rectory: 41 Alling St., 06516-2799. Tel: 203-933-1024; Fax: 203-931-9416.
Parish Center: 45 Alling St., 06516-2798.
Catechesis/Religious Program—Tel: 203-934-1357. Clarice Purcell, C.R.E. Students 130.

WEST SIMSBURY, HARTFORD CO., ST. CATHERINE OF SIENA (1971) Rev. Michael G. Whyte.
Res.: Box 184, 06092. Tel: 860-658-1642; Fax: 888-297-3134. Email: stcathy@comcast.net.
Catechesis/Religious Program—Tel: 860-658-4737. Mrs. Kathi Bonner, D.R.E. Students 615.

WETHERSFIELD, HARTFORD CO.

1—CORPUS CHRISTI (1941), Linked with Sacred Heart Parish. Revs. Thomas B. Campion (Retired); Stanley R. Staron; Deacon Seth M. English.
Res.: 84 Somerset St., 06109-3068. Tel: 860-529-2545; Fax: 860-529-5861. Email: corpuschristi1@cox.net. Web: www.corpuschristiparish.net.
Church: 601 Silas Deane Hwy., 06109.
School—(Grades PreK-8), 581 Silas Deane Hwy., 06109. Tel: 860-529-5487; Fax: 860-257-9106. Email: corpuschristisch@yahoo.com. Web: corpuschristis-choolct.com. Mrs. Eileen Sampiere, Prin. Lay Teachers 28; Students 385.
Catechesis/Religious Program—581 Silas Deane Hwy., 06109. Tel: 860-721-9419; Fax: 860-721-9418. Students 760.

2—INCARNATION (1963) Rev. James M. Moran.
Res.: 544 Prospect St., 06109-3609. Tel: 860-529-2533; Fax: 860-721-6595. Email: cincarnation@sbcglobal.net.
Catechesis/Religious Program—Tel: 860-529-6765. Noranne Wamester, D.R.E. Students 586.

3—SACRED HEART (1876), Linked with Corpus Christi Parish. Revs. Thomas B. Campion (Retired); Stanley R. Staron; John Hoon Gyeom Kim (Korea, South) (Korean Catholic Community Office: 860-529-1456).
Res.: 56 Hartford Ave., 06109-1805. Tel: 860-529-1991 (Office & Rectory); Fax: 860-529-0815. Email: sacred_church@sbcglobal.net.
Catechesis/Religious Program—Tel: 860-257-0740. Lynne Lantagne, C.R.E.; Candace Detrich, C.R.E. Students 146.

WINDSOR, HARTFORD CO.

1—ST. GABRIEL (1894) Revs. Richard J. Neumann; Edmund K. Karwowski, Parochial Vicar; Deacon R. Carl Lickwar.
Res.: 379 Broad St., 06095-3004. Tel: 860-688-4905; Fax: 860-688-2638. Email: gabrielchurch@comcast.net. Web: www.stgabes.org.
School—(Grades K-8), 77 Bloomfield Ave., 06095. Tel: 860-688-6401; Fax: 860-298-8668. Web: www-.stgabrielschool.org. Patricia Martin, Prin.; Jane Dunn, Librarian. Lay Teachers 17; Students 204.
Catechesis/Religious Program—Mrs. Janet Alampi, D.R.E. Students 100.

2—ST. GERTRUDE (1947) Rev. Maurice J. Barry.
Res.: 550 Matianuck Ave., 06095-3599. Tel: 860-522-6163; Fax: 860-525-2320. Email: stgertrudechurch@sbcglobal.net.
Catechesis/Religious Program—Teri Coughlin, D.R.E. Students 65.

WINDSOR LOCKS, HARTFORD CO.

1—ST. MARY (1852) [CEM], Linked with St. Robert Bellarmine Parish, Windsor Locks. Revs. Robert A. O'Grady; George Vellaplackil (India); Deacons Donald Norton; Benedict L. Winiarski.
Res.: 42 Spring St., 06096-2311. Tel: 860-623-2524; Fax: 860-623-5684.
Parish Center—45 Church St., 06096. Tel: 860-627-9469.
Catechesis/Religious Program—Marilyn Stratton, D.R.E. Students 479.

2—ST. ROBERT BELLARMINE (1962), Linked with St. Mary Parish, Windsor Locks. Revs. Robert A. O'Grady; George Vellaplackil (India); Deacons Donald Norton; Benedict L. Winiarski.
Office: 52 S. Elm St., P.O. Box 315, 06096-0315. Tel: 860-623-0240.
Catechesis/Religious Program—Twinned with St. Mary, Windsor Locks, *St. Mary Parish Center*, 45 Church St., 06096. Tel: 860-627-9469.

WINSTED, LITCHFIELD CO., ST. JOSEPH (1853) [CEM] Revs. Dennis Arambasick, O.F.M.; Louis M. Pintye, O.F.M.; Deacon William H. Wilcox, (Retired).
Res.: 66 Oak St., 06098. Tel: 860-379-8375.
School—St. Anthony, (Grades PreK-8), 55 Oak St., 06098. Tel: 860-379-7521; Fax: 860-379-7522. Mrs. Patricia Devanney, Prin. Lay Teachers 10; Students 240.
Catechesis/Religious Program—Tel: 860-379-5968. Students 116.

WOLCOTT, NEW HAVEN CO.

1—ST. MARIA GORETTI (1973) Rev. William R. Sokolowski.
Res.: 1300 Woodtick Rd., P.O. Box 6291, 06716-0291. Tel: 203-879-4608; Fax: 203-879-4609. Email: donna@smgchurch.org.
Catechesis/Religious Program—Tel: 203-879-5242. Carmelina Calabrese, D.R.E. Students 213.

2—ST. PIUS X (1955) Rev. Henry A. Balchunas; Deacon Emil P. Croce.
Res.: 525 Woodtick Rd., 06716-2898. Tel: 203-879-2544; Fax: 203-879-2545.
Catechesis/Religious Program—Tel: 203-879-9030. Angela Engaratt, D.R.E. Students 323.

WOODBRIDGE, NEW HAVEN CO., CHURCH OF THE ASSUMPTION (1924) Rev. Gene E. Gianelli; Deacons William J. Sayles; John J.M. Conte Jr., (Retired).
Res.: 81 Center Rd., 06525-1699. Tel: 203-387-7119; Fax: 203-387-4281. Email: gassumptionchurch@sbcglobal.com. Web: www.assumptionchurch.com.
Catechesis/Religious Program—Tel: 203-389-9863. Sr. Dorellen Sullivan, R.S.M., D.R.E.; Mr. Jonathan Galo, Youth Min. Students 554.

WOODBURY, LITCHFIELD CO., ST. TERESA (1902) Rev. Robert M. Kwiatkowski; Deacons Ralph Rescildo; Terence M. Nolan; Horace G. Hamor; Sr. Marilyn Cullina, C.N.D., Pastoral Min.
Parish Office: 494 Main St. S., P.O. Box 5001, 06798-5001.
Res.: 11 Washington Ave., P.O. Box 5001, 06798-5001. Tel: 203-263-2008; Fax: 203-263-7259. Email: saintteresas@aol.com. Web: www.saintteresaofavila.org.
Catechesis/Religious Program—Mrs. Carol Moriarty, D.R.E. Students 510.

YALESVILLE, NEW HAVEN CO., OUR LADY OF FATIMA (1956) Rev. Salvatore F. Cavagnuolo; Deacon James P. Taylor.
Res.: 382 Hope Hill Rd., P.O. Box 4518, 06492-7565. Tel: 203-265-0961; Fax: 203-269-9386.
Catechesis/Religious Program—Tel: 203-265-6818; Fax: 203-269-5343. Tracy Blum, D.R.E. Tel: 203-265-6426, Ext. 4; Corinne Sommo, Youth Min. Students 569.

Chaplains of Public Institutions

HARTFORD. *Hartford Correctional Institution*, 177 Weston St., 06120. Tel: 860-240-1857. Rev. Robert A. O'Grady, Chap., Sr. Jerilyn Hunihan, A.S.C.J., Chap.
Hartford Hospital, 80 Seymour St., 06102-5037. Tel: 860-545-2251; Fax: 860-545-3594.

BRISTOL. *Bristol Hospital*, Brewster Rd., 06011-0977. Tel: 860-585-3431. Rev. J. Richard Fowler, Interfaith Chap. (United Church of Christ).

CHESHIRE. *Cheshire Correctional Institution*, 900 Highland Ave., 06410-1698. Tel: 203-250-2787. Revs. Stephen A. Krugel, Chap., Robert Vujs, M.M., Chap., Deacons George Hajjar, Chap., Rene Kieda, Chap., Carl Vecca, Chap.
Manson Youth Institution, 42 Jarvis St., 06410-1545. Tel: 203-806-2508. Rev. Robert Vujs, M.M., Chap., Deacon Carl Vecca, Chap.

ENFIELD. *Carl Robinson Correctional Institution*, P.O. Box 1400, 06083-1400. Tel: 860-763-6387. Deacon Robert E. Lambert, Chap., Rev. Thomas Plathottam, C.S.T.
Enfield Correctional Institute, 289 Shaker Rd., 06083. Tel: 860-763-7318. Rev. Thomas Plathottam, C.S.T., Deacon Benedict L. Winiarski.
Willard-Cybulski Correction Institute, 391 Shaker Rd., P.O. Box 2400, 06082. Tel: 860-763-6140. Rev. Stephen A. Krugel, Chap., Deacon Leo B. Conard III, Chap.

MANCHESTER. *Manchester Memorial Hospital*, 71 Haynes St., 06040-4188. Tel: 860-646-1222, Ext. 2137. Rev. Louis D. Cremonie, Chap.

NEW BRITAIN. *The Hospital of Central Connecticut (New Britain General Hospital)*, 100 Grand St., 06050-2016. Tel: 860-224-5011; Fax: 860-224-5740. Rev. Ronald T. Smith, Chap.
Res.: 396 Church St., P.O. Box 515, 06050-0515. Tel: 860-224-0341.

NEW HAVEN. *Yale-New Haven Hospital*, 20 York St., 06504-1001. Tel: 203-688-2151; Fax: 203-688-3478. Rev. Geoffrey C. Smith, Chap. Tel: 203-688-7031, Sr. Carole Hermann, O.P. Tel: 203-688-7032.

ROCKY HILL. *Veterans' Home and Hospital*, 287 West St., 06067-3902. Tel: 860-529-2571, Ext. 2386. Rev. Francis J. Kulas, M.S. Tel: 860-257-3368.

SUFFIELD. *Macdougall - Walker Correctional Institute*, 1153 E. St. S., 06080-0002. Tel: 860-627-2148 Mac Dougall; 860-292-3429 Walker; Fax: 860-627-2152 Mac Dougall. Deacon Richard F. Boucher, Rev. Stephen A. Krugel, Chap.

WATERBURY. *Waterbury Hospital*, 64 Robbins St., 06721-2600. Tel: 203-573-7213; Fax: 203-573-7326; 203-573-6000.

WEST HAVEN. *V.A. CT Health Care System*, 950 Campbell Ave., 06516-2700. Tel: 203-932-5711, Ext. 2422. Rev. Cosmas Archibong.

WETHERSFIELD. *Connecticut Department of Correction*, 24 Wolcott Hill Rd., 06109-1152. Tel: 860-692-7577; Fax: 860-692-6263. Rev. Anthony J. Bruno, Dir. Religious Svcs.
Res.: 90 Alden Ave., Enfield, 06082-2865. Tel: 860-745-9966.

Special and other Archdiocesan Assignment:
Rev. Msgrs.—
Liptak, David Q., Editor, "The Catholic Transcript", 467 Bloomfield Ave., Bloomfield, 06002.
McCarthy, John J., J.C.D., J.D., Chancellor & Rector, 134 Farmington Ave., 06105. Cathedral of St. Joseph, 140 Farmington Ave., 06105.
Motta, Michael J., Dir., Office of Religious Education, 467 Bloomfield Ave., Bloomfield, 06002.
Schmitz, Gerard G., St. Thomas Seminary, 467 Bloomfield Ave., Bloomfield, 06002. Vicar for Priests and Pres./Rector.
Walker, David M., Dir., Catholic Cemeteries Association, P.O. Box 517, North Haven, 06473-0517.
Revs.—
Altermatt, Gregory M., Hospital of St. Raphael, 1450 Chapel St., New Haven, 06511.
Baranowski, David J. Office for Divine Worship 467 Bloomfield Ave., Bloomfield, 06002.
Beloin, Robert L., Ph.D., More House, Yale University, 268 Park St., New Haven, 06511-4714.
Brockett, Norman L., St. Mary Home, 2021 Albany Ave., West Hartford, 06117-2796.
Bruno, Anthony J., Connecticut Department of Correction, 24 Wolcott Hill Rd., 06109-1152.
Cremonie, Louis D., Manchester Memorial Hospital, 71 Haynes St., Manchester, 06040.
DiSciacca, Joseph V., Office of Minister for Priests, 467 Bloomfield Ave., Bloomfield, 06002-2999.
Dolan, Michael J., Campus Min. & Dir. Vocations, 467 Bloomfield Ave., Bloomfield, 06002. Tel: 860-297-2015. Email: mjdofr@aol.com
Donahue, Aidan N., Diaconate Continuing Formation, 35 Cold Spring Dr., Bloomfield, 06002.
Gatzak, John P., Exec. Dir., 15 Peach Orchard Rd., Prospect, 06712-1052. Office of Radio/Television.
Kinnane, James F., J.C.L., 134 Farmington Ave., 06105-3784. Vicar for Religious and Adjutant Judicial Vicar.
Krugel, Stephen A., Cheshire Correctional Institution, P.O. Box 3260, Milford, 06460.
Mercado, Jose A., Office for Hispanic Evangelization, 467 Bloomfield Ave., Bloomfield, 06002-2999.
O'Brien, Timothy A., Coord. Restructuring Committee, P.O. Box 285, New Hartford, 06057-0285.
O'Grady, Robert A., Hartford Correctional Institution, 117 Weston St., 06120.
Romans, Jeffrey V., Asst. Chancellor & Sec. Archbishop, 134 Farmington Ave., 06105-3784.
Rousseau, Robert J., Pro-Life Activities, 271 Finch Ave., Meriden, 06451-2715.
Sas, Thomas J., Office of Ministry Enrichment, 467 Bloomfield Ave., Bloomfield, 06002-2999.
Smith, Geoffrey C., Yale - New Haven Hospital, 20 York St., New Haven, 06510-3202.
Smith, Ronald T., The Hospital of Central Connecticut, 100 Grand St., New Britain, 06050-2016.
Vargo, Robert B., J.C.L., Judicial Vicar (Officialis), Chancery, 467 Bloomfield Ave., Bloomfield, 06002-2999.

On Duty Outside the Archdiocese:
Rev. Msgr.—
Sokolowski, Robert S., Catholic University of America, School of Philosophy, Washington, DC 20064.
Revs.—
Cwiekowski, Frederick J., S.S., St. Patrick Seminary, 320 Middlefield Rd., Menlo Park, CA 94025.
Dietrich, John J., Mt. St. Mary Seminary, Emmitsburg, MD 21727-7797.
Leavitt, Robert F., S.S., St. Mary Seminary, 5400 Roland Ave., Baltimore, MD 21210.
Matera, Frank J., M.A., Ph.D., Catholic University of America, Dept. of Theology, Washington, DC 20064.
McBrien, Richard P., University of Notre Dame, Notre Dame, IN 46556.
McKearney, James L., S.S., St. Patrick Seminary, 320 Middlefield Rd., Menlo Park, CA 94025.
Smolenski, Stanley, 300C Ashton Ave., Kingstree, SC 29556.
Thayer, David D., S.S., Theological College of Catholic University of America, 401 Michigan Ave., N.E., Washington, DC 20064.

Military Chaplains:
Revs.—
Hanley, Dennis P., PSC 2, Box 15047, Apo, AE 09012. U.S. Air Force
Hellwig, Lee W., RELMIN Dept., USS Peleliu (LHA 5), FPO, AP 99624-1620. Tel: 619-556-4200 U.S. Navy

Medical Leave:
Revs.—
Hinkley, Michael F.X., S.T.D.
Mangiafico, Paul J.

Leave of Absence:
Revs.—
Bzdyra, Stephen H.
Manna, David
Warnakulasuriya, Edward Tissera (Sri Lanka)

Unassigned:
Revs.—
Gingras, Dennis C.
Van Nguyen, Thanh, (Retired), Portland in Maine, 115 F Beachwood Dr., Bristol, 06010. Tel: 860-585-6663

Retired:
Rev. Msgrs.—
Daly, Charles W., Archbishop Daniel A. Cronin Retirement Residence, 467 Bloomfield Ave., Bloomfield, 06002.
Regan, John D., Archbishop Daniel A. Cronin Retirement Residence, 467 Bloomfield Ave, Bloomfield, 06002.
Revs.—
Ahern, John S., The Village of Mariner's Point, 111 South Shore Dr., East Haven, 06512.
Archambault, James H., 2003 49th St. W., Bradenton, FL 34209.
Barry, Raymond J., P.O. Box 257, Westbrook, 06498.
Baylis, Thomas J., 7 Jensen Ct., Southington, 06489.
Birmingham, Robert F., P.O. Box 177, Shenorock, NY 10587.
Blackall, John C., 1027 Farmington Ave., West Hartford, 06107.
Blackall, Randall L., 1027 Farmington Ave., West Hartford, 06107.
Bonadies, Kenneth P., 5402 Glenn Ivy Place, Pinellas Park, FL 33782.
Borino, David J., 45 Francis St., East Haven, 06512-2808.
Burbank, Robert J., St. Mary Rectory, 731 Main St., Branford, 06405-3693.
Burnett, George P., Assumption Rectory, 61 N. Cliff St., Ansonia, 06401-1698.
Burns, William L., St. James Rectory, 896 Main St., Manchester, 06040.
Campion, Thomas B., Corpus Christi Rectory, 84 Somerset St., 06109-3031.
Cesaro, Nicholas J., St. Mary Rectory, 626 Willard Ave., Newington, 06111-2614.
Chow, Louis Y., 4 E. 5th St., Corning, NY 14830.
Cockayne, John E., P.O. Box 716, Southington, 06489.
Connaghan, Daniel H., 38325 Wilderness Ct., Box 232, Beaver Island, MI 49782.
Daly, John J., St. Barnabas Rectory, 44 Washington Ave., North Haven, 06473-1799.
DeCarolis, Joseph R., P.O. Box 1325, Naugatuck, 06770.
DeCarolis, Vito C., Box 1325, Naugatuck, 06770.
Dery, Henry R., Archbishop Daniel A. Cronin Retirement Residence, 467 Bloomfield Ave., Bloomfield, 06002.
Dilion, Joseph A., 13 Leeway Dr., Westbrook, 06498.
DuPont, Arthur J., Church of the Resurrection Rectory, 115 Pond Hill Rd., Wallingford, 06492.
Evangelisto, Louis Anthony, 37 Cairo Ave., Northport, NY 11768.
Fanelli, James G., Archbishop Daniel A. Cronin Retirement Residence, 467 Bloomfield Ave., Bloomfield, 06002.
Frascadore, Henry C., Bushnell Towers, 1 Gold St., Apt. 4C, 06103. Tel: 860-904-7817
Genua, Ronald L.
Gorman, Joseph F., St. Leo the Great Rectory, 14 Bentwood Dr., Waterbury, 06705.
Gunnoud, James B., Southington Care Center, 45 Meriden Ave., Southington, 06489.
Hagearty, Charles B., 39 Carriage Dr., Naugatuck, 06770. Tel: 203-592-7749. Email: liturgy@cisbek.net
Heinrich, Harold D., 216 Bristol St., Southington, 06489.
Johnson, Daniel E., 67 Crumpstone Rd., Hamden, 06518-2424.
Johnson, Francis P., St. Helena Rectory, 30 Echo Ln., West Hartford, 06107-3698.
Kaminsky, Joseph T., 4930 Coquina Crossing Dr., Elkton, FL 32033.
Karpiey, Daniel J., Archbishop Daniel A. Cronin Retirement Residence, 467 Bloomfield Ave., Bloomfield, 06002.
Karvelis, Francis V., 14 Deepwood Dr., Southington, 06489-3442.
Keane, John J., 205 Hazard Ave., Enfield, 06082.
Kenefick, Paul F., Archbishop Daniel A. Cronin Retirement Residence, 467 Bloomfield Ave., Bloomfield, 06002.
Kilbride, Eugene M., St. Helena Rectory, 30 Echo Ln., West Hartford, 06107-3698.
Killeen, William J., 185 Ridge Rd., Hamden, 06517-3511.
Kriss, Zigford J., St. Helena Rectory, 30 Echo Ln., West Hartford, 06107.
Krupnik, Marion I., 548 Eddy Glover Blvd., New Britain, 06053.
Ladamus, Robert G., 38 Marshall St., Milford, 06460.
Ladish, Robert W., 255 W. Shore Rd., New Preston, 06777.
Laliberte, George G., 948 Villeroy Greens Dr., Sun City Center, FL 33573.
LaPlante, Roland M., Archbishop Daniel A. Cronin Retirement Residence, 467 Bloomfield Ave., Bloomfield, 06002.
Lauretti, George F., 6 Father Crudele Dr., Bristol, 06010.
Lewandowski, David J., 24 Woodhaven Rd., Bristol, 06010.
Lonergan, David W., 3155 E. Main St., Apt. A-5, Waterbury, 06705.
Lord, Robert J., 5460 N. Ocean Dr., #12D, Singer Island, FL 33404-2503.
Malave, Will-Roger, St. Patrick Rectory, 50 Charles St., Waterbury, 06708.
McLean, Edward J., St. Paul Rectory, 2577 Main St., Glastonbury, 06033-2023.
Mitchell, Peter G., 275 Steele Rd., Apt. B322, West Hartford, 06117.
Montgomery, Joseph T., 30 Royal Oak Rd., New Britain, 06053.
Morrison, Douglas A., 24 Courthouse Sq., Apt. 805, Rockville, MD 20850.
Moskus, John T., 42 Maplewood Ave., Storrs, 06268.
Murphy, Arthur J., St. Thomas the Apostle Rectory, 872 Farmington Ave., West Hartford, 06119-1499.
O'Brien, Edmund M., St. Adalbert Rectory, 90 Alden Ave., Enfield, 06082-2865.
O'Keefe, William F., Archbishop Daniel A. Cronin Retirement Residence, 467 Bloomfield Ave., Bloomfield, 06002.
Padelli, Emilio P., 43 Old Farm Rd., Somers, 06071.
Parzymies, Joseph K., 140 Poland Brook Rd., Terryville, 06786.
Pettit, Joseph H., 433 Lakeview Dr., Southington, 06489.
Pfnausch, Edward G., J.C.D., 2148 Setting Sun, El Paso, TX 79938.
Pilon, James F., 331 Songbird Ln., Southington, 06489.
Raczynski, Theodore T., Sacred Heart Rectory, 446 Mountain Rd., P.O. Box 626, Suffield, 06078-0626.
Raneri, Carmine B., Blessed Sacrament Rectory, 182 Robbins St., Waterbury, 06708.
Rosa, Salvatore J., Archbishop Daniel A. Cronin Retirement Residence, 467 Bloomfield Ave., Bloomfield, 06002.
Rush, James C., 161 Brunswick Ave., West Hartford, 06107-1715.
Russell, Richard R., Archbiship Daniel A. Cronin Retirement Residence, 467 Bloomfield Ave., Bloomfield, 06002.
Russo, Robert T., Archbishop Daniel A. Cronin Retirement Residence, 467 Bloomfield Ave, Bloomfield, 06002.
Sheridan, Philip A., 20 Carmel Ridge Estates, Trumbull, 06611-2072.
Sikora, Stanley J., Archbishop Daniel A. Cronin Retirement Residence, 467 Bloomfield Ave., Bloomfied, 06002-2999.
Smith, James H., 101 S. Raleigh Ave., Atlantic City, NJ 08401.
Sobiecki, Peter S., 49 Hillhurst Ave., New Britain, 06053.
Spodnik, A. Leo, P.O. Box 456, Higganum, 06441.
St. Martin, Robert J., St. Mary Rectory, 16 Bidwell Sq., Unionville, 06085-1116.
Testa, Genaro J., 2179 Herman Drake Rd., Young Harris, GA 30582.
Toscano, Pasquale A., St. Joseph Residence, 1365 Enfield St., Enfield, 06082-4900.
Tracy, John P.
Traxl, William L., P.O. Box 1031, Westbrook, 06498.
Ventura, Anthony C.
Vujs, Joseph E., 14 Hawley St., Newington, 06111.
Wrenn, Lawrence G., 8941 Veranda Way, #522, Sarasota, FL 34238-3372.
Yelle, Ronald R., 281 Chauncey Walker St., L50, Belchertown, MA 01007.
Ziezulewicz, George F., 5 Whitewood Rd., Killingworth, 06419.

Permanent Deacons:
Abdalla, John, (Retired)
Albert, Roger R., St. Ann, Bristol

Arena, James V., St. Aloysius, Plantsville
Bailey, Thomas
Bandeira, Francis X., (Retired)
Bartlett, William H., St. Bartholomew, Manchester; St. Bridget, Manchester
Battiston, Donald, (Retired)
Beecher, Stephen M., Sr., St. Joseph Canaan: Immaculate Conception, Norfolk
Bergers, William B., (Retired)
Bernd, Robert E., St. Martha, Enfield; Chap., Northern Complex of State of CT Correctional System
Berube, Robert A., Catholic Chap., Dept. of Veteran Affairs for State of CT, Rocky Hill; Our Lady of Mercy, Plainville
Bevvino, Frank J., Jr., St. Augustine, Seymour
Biamonte, Ronald, M.A., St. Joseph, Poquonock
Bichi, Americo, (Retired)
Bilbrault, Victor C., Our Lady of Sorrows, Hartford
Blair, Robert N., Immaculate Conception, New Hartford
Borland, Joseph P., (Retired)
Boucher, Richard F., St. Bernard, Enfield
Brady, John F., Jr., (Retired)
Breen, Thomas F., III, Assumption, Manchester
Brown, George S., (Retired)
Brunell, Robert J., Blessed Sacrament, Hamden
Camerota, Daniel A., (Retired)
Campbell, Alan D., (Retired)
Cardona, Raul, St. Rose of Lima, Meriden
Carrero, Adolfo G., St. Peter, Hartford
Cassella, Michael E., St. Francis of Assisi, New Britain
Cassidy, Vincent, (Retired)
Charles, John H., Immaculate Heart of Mary, Harwinton
Chope, Robert C.
Clifford, Thomas J., St. Francis Xavier, Waterbury
Colella, Charles G., SS. Peter and Paul, Waterbury; St. Leo the Great, Waterbury
Conard, Leo B., III, Immaculate Conception & St. Casimir, Terryville
Conklin, Thomas J., St. Margaret Mary, South Windsor
Conte, John J.M., Jr., (Retired)
Cooke, Joseph J., (Retired)
Coppola, Angelo J., St. Thomas, Southington
Cornell, Thomas, (Retired)
Cote, Laurent L., (Retired)
Coyne, Joseph F., (Retired)
Croce, Emil P., St. Pius X, Wolcott
Croll, Calvin S., (Retired)
Crowley, John L., Mary Our Queen, Plantsville
Cruess, Donald E., (Retired)
Culhane, Neil, (Retired)
Cunniff, Charles E., Jr., (Retired)
D'Efemia, Robert J., (Retired)
Daigle, Ronald R., St. Dunstan, Glastonbury
Davis, Thomas J., Jr., Bi-ritual faculties
DeFilippo, Salvatore A., St. Louis, West Haven
DeHippolytis, Albert J., (Retired)
DeJesus, Isidro, St. Justin, St. Michael, & Sacred Heart, Hartford
Delehanty, Thomas F., (Retired)
Delgado, Domingo, St. Lawrence O'Toole, Hartford
Delmonte, Richard F., (Retired)
Dembishack, John L., (Retired)
Dempsey, John F., (Retired)
Dickman, Arthur J., Holy Family, Enfield
Dietsch, Charles C., Sacred Heart, Southbury
Diorio, Nicholas J., Our Lady of Mt. Carmel, Waterbury
DiPiro, Joseph L., (Retired)
DiRienzo, Mario, St. Augustine, Seymour
Dlugokinski, Jose L., (Retired)
DosSantos, Kenneth, St. Thomas, Thomaston
Doyle, Henry, (Retired)
Driscoll, Frank M., (Inactive)
Dudzic, Anthony
Dungan, Roy C., Torrington Clustered Parishes
Elder, William A., St. George, Guilford
English, Seth M., (Retired)
Eschrich, Paul C., (Retired)
Ewaskie, Kenneth E., Good Shepherd, Seymour
Eyles, William H., (Retired)
Falbo, Anthony
Farrell, William A., St. Patrick, Farmington
Ferguson, Dennis R., St. Timothy, West Hartford
Florio, Louis J., (Retired)
Fracasso, Robert G., (Retired)
Frederick, George W., St. Laurent & Our Lady of Mt. Carmel, Meriden
Fugere, Raymond J., Jr., St. Mark the Evangelist, West Hartford
Fusco, Louis P., St. Monica, Northford
Gabriele, Joseph G., (Retired)
Gallucci, Donald, (Retired)
Genovese, Nicholas A., St. Agnes, Milford
Gerstung, Carl H., St. Anne & Blessed Sacrament, Waterbury
Giaimo, Thomas J.
Giard, Edward J., St. Christopher, East Hartford
Gilles, William J., St. Christopher, East Hartford
Giusto, Oreste M., (Retired)
Gluhosky, Frank
Godlewsky, Robert H., (Retired)
Gonzalez, Emilio, St. Rose of Lima, New Haven
Gordon, Robert D., St. John the Evangelist, Watertown
Grant, Frederick M., (Retired)
Griffin, Wayne F., Immaculate Conception, Southington
Gurr, Ronald B., St. Rita, Hamden
Guzauckas, Joseph, Holy Spirit, Newington
Guzzardi, Carmelo A., (Retired)
Haines, Michael D., St. Margaret Mary, South Windsor
Hajjar, George D., St. Michael, Waterbury
Hamel, Richard H., St. Matthew, Forestville
Hamor, Horace G., St. Teresa, Woodbury
Hart, John L., St. Augustine, North Branford
Healy, Timothy E., St. Patrick, Collinsville
Hernandez, Carmelo, St. Anne - Immaculate Conception, Hartford
Hickey, James E., Jr., St. Peter Claver, West Hartford
Higgs, Kenneth
Hilliard, Robert J., (Retired)
Hoffman, Harold J., Jr., St. Mary, Milford
Iadarola, Paul P., St. Margaret, Waterbury
Iassogna, Nicholas J., Jr., St. Francis of Assisi, Naugatuck
Jacob, James M., (Retired)
Jacques, J. Martin, (Retired)
Johnson, Robert C., St. Mary, Derby
Johnson, Thomas F., Church of the Epiphany, Cheshire
Kane, Joseph K., St. Joseph & St. Peter Parishes, New Britain
Kelly, Stephen J., (Retired)
Kieda, Rene J., Catholic Prison Chap.
Kimball, Earle A., St. Mary & St. Hedwig, Union City
Klein, Peter J., Jr., St. Dunstan, Glastonbury
Klimanowski, Peter J.
Krasnicki, Frank J., Good Shepherd, Seymour
Kraussman, George A., (Retired)
Kulas, Michael J., (Retired)
Kulas, Paul J., St. Dominic, Southington
Lafleur, Carl
Lambert, Robert E., St. Adalbert, Enfield
LaPierre, Joseph W., (Retired)
LaRocque, Leo R., Blessed Sacrament & Our Lady of Peace, East Hartford
Lauer, Paul B., (Retired)
Lavoie, Joseph V., (Retired)
Lawson, Thomas L., (Retired)
LeBlanc, Gaspard D., (Retired)
Lembo, Victor M., St. Michael, Beacon Falls
Lepkowski, Henry M., (Retired)
Lewandoski, Leonard R., (Retired)
Lickwar, R. Carl, St. Gabriel, Windsor
Linehan, F. Robert, (Retired)
Lopez, Alexander, Jr., Sacred Heart-Sagrado Corazon, Waterbury
Lopez, Edwin, St. Margaret, Waterbury
Lovelace, William J., St. Augustine, North Branford
Lovetre, Arthur
Lovett, John J., St. Ann, Bristol
Lozier, Albert J., (Retired)
Lugo, Roberto L., St. Rose of Lima, Meriden
Macaluso, Robert J., St. Vincent de Paul, East Haven
Maffeo, John R., St. Thomas of Villanova, Goshen
Mahoney, Patrick
Makara, John W., (Leave of Absence)
Mancini, Edward J., St. Lawrence, West Haven; St. Paul, West Haven
Marcarelli, Julius R., (Retired)
Marenna, Joseph P., St. Monica, Northford
Maturana, Julio C., St. Rose of Lima, East Hartford; St. Isaac Jogues, East Hartford; St. Mary Parishes, East Hartford
Mazurek, Joseph S., Holy Angels, Meriden
McCarroll, George E., St. Stephen, Hamden
McCluskey, James P., St. Matthew, Forestville
McGivney, Raymond J., Jr., (Inactive)
McGrath, William M., (Retired)
McInnis, John P., (Retired)
McKaig, John W., St. John Fisher, Marlborough
Michaele, Adam J., St. Margaret, Madison
Miller, Arthur L., St. Mary, Simsbury; Dir., Office for Black Catholic Ministry; Campus Min., Capital Community College.
Miller, Roland G., St. Francis Xavier, New Milford
Mitchell, Richard
Mitchell, Victor C., Jr., St. Thomas, Thomaston
Moemeka, Andrew A., (Medical Leave)
Monahan, Kevin M., St. Thomas the Apostle, West Hartford
Monahan, William
Morales, Jose A.
Moran, Patrick T., St. George, Guliford; Campus Min., Southern Connecticut State University
Motto, Vincent J., St. Patrick, Enfield
Muro, Robert E., Sr., Our Lady of the Lakes, New Milford
Murray, Thomas A., (Retired)
Mylott, John J., (Retired)
Nebiolo, Eugene P., (Retired)
Neris, Susano, (Retired)
Newbery, Robert D., (Retired)
Nolan, Terence M., St. Teresa, Woodbury
Norton, Donald E., St. Mary, Windsor Locks; St. Robert Bellamine, Windsor Locks
Nugent, John T., St. Joseph, Meriden; St. Mary, Meriden
Nwankwo, Anthony, Sacred Heart, Bloomfield
O'Connor, Martin J., St. Bernadette, New Haven; Campus Min., Univ. of New Haven
O'Donovan, John C., (Retired)
O'Neill, James F., (Retired)
O'Toole, Michael J., (Retired)
Ortiz, Edwin, Sacred Heart, Hartford
Ortiz, Jacinto
Ossa, Tullio V., Most Holy Trinity, Wallingford
Pagliaro, Ernest H., Jr., St. Francis of Assisi, Naugatuck
Pallotti, Robert M., St. James, Rocky Hill; Dir Office for Permanent Diaconate
Pantalena, Edward J., (Retired)
Papillo, James F., St. Mary & St. Ann, New Britain
Parenteau, Raymond A., (Retired)
Parkinson, William H., St. Vincent de Paul, East Haven
Parlee, Charles, (Retired)
Perez, Valentin, (Unassigned)
Pettinico, George M., St. Mary Magdalen, Oakville
Phaneuf, Eugene E., (Retired)
Philip, Donald, Franciscans Sisters of the Eucharist, Meriden
Piotrowski, Stanley J., Jr., St. Gregory the Great, Bristol
Pond, Donald H., Jr., St. Bernard, Enfield
Poulin, Gerald L.
Prete, Paul V., (Retired)
Probulis, Gerard J.
Puskas, George A., Christ the Redeemer, Milford
Quinn, James P., (Retired)
Ramos, Edmund J., (Retired)
Regan, Joseph M., Jr., (Retired)
Renker, Richard W., Holy Rosary, Ansonia; St. Anthony, Ansonia
Rescildo, Ralph, St. Teresa, Woodbury
Reynolds, David W., Cluster of Roman Catholic Parishes, Torrington
Richter, Neil B., St. Joseph, Bristol
Riotte, Eugene C., (Retired)
Rivera, José A., (Retired)
Rivera, Pedro L., St. Ann & St. Mary, New Britain
Rosado, Ramon A., St. Augustine, Hartford
Rosello, Modesto A., (Retired)
Roy, Reginald, (Retired)
Rubitz, Michael, Holy Cross, New Britain
Ryan, Richard A.
Ryzewski, Joseph R., St. Aedan & St. Brendan, New Haven
Sabo, Paul E., Our Lady of Victory & St. John Vianney, West Haven
Sandford, Wayne E., (Inactive)
Santello, Richard L., St. Michael & St. Anthony, New Haven
Santos, Richard D., Sacred Heart, Bloomfield
Sartor, George G., St. Clare, East Haven; St. Elizabeth, Branford
Sayles, William J., Church of the Assumption, Woodbridge
Scanlon, Thomas P., (Retired)
Sennett, Richard M., (Retired)
Shelto, Michael A., St. Elizabeth Seton, Rocky Hill
Shiels, James H., Holy Spirit, Newington
Singer, Norman H., (Retired)
Skipp, Barry T., Sacred Heart, Wethersfield; Corpus Christi, Wethersfield
Sloan, Daniel A., (Retired)
Sloan, Joseph S., St. Martha, Enfield
Smith, Donald H., Jr., Our Lady of Mt. Carmel and St. Laurent, Meriden
Solli, Anthony P., St. Barnabas, North Haven
Sponzo, Michael T., (Retired)
Stadtlander, Hobart T., (Retired)
Stanley, James H., (Retired)
Stephens, George R., (Retired)
Stolfi, Domenic N., St. Anthony, Prospect
Streib, George H., Our Lady of Perpetual Help, Washington Depot
Sullivan, James M., Cluster of Roman Catholic Parishes, Torrington
Sullivan, Joseph D., Holy Infant, Orange
Sutak, Thomas S., St. Mary, Unionville
Sutherland, Jeffrey B., St. Ann, Avon
Sweeney, John M., (Leave of Absence)

Szewczyk, Edward J., (Retired)
Szumigala, Michael P., St. Stanislaus, Bristol
Taddei, Edward D., (Retired)
Talbot, Oral A., (Retired)
Tartaris, Robert P., Our Lady of Victory & St. John Vianney, West Haven
Taylor, James P., Our Lady of Fatima, Yalesville
Thayer, John E.
Thermer, Clifford E., St. Patrick, Farmington
Thompson, Bruce R., (Retired)
Thorney, Vincent M., (Retired)
Tolassi, Bernard, (Retired)
Toner, James H.
Torres, Michael, St. Isaac Jogues, St. Mary & St. Rose, East Hartford
Twerago, John P., (Retired)
Vazquez, Julio, (Retired)
Vecca, Carl M., Chap., Cheshire Correctional Facility
Violette, Carroll, (Inactive)
Wallin, Robert F., St. Lucy & Our Lady of Lourdes, Waterbury
Walsh, Michael J., St. John of the Cross, Middlebury
Walton, Gerald S., (Retired)
Ward, Michael J., St. Jerome & St. Maurice, New Britain
Weaver, Stephen L., St. Augustine, South Glastonbury; St. Paul Glastonbury
Wilber, Richard, St. Bridget, Cheshire
Wilcox, William H., (Retired)
Winiarski, Benedict L., St. Mary & St. Robert Bellarmine, Windsor Locks
Yatcko, Stephen J., St. Joan of Arc, Hamden

INSTITUTIONS LOCATED IN THE ARCHDIOCESE

[A] SEMINARIES, ARCHDIOCESAN

BLOOMFIELD. *St. Thomas Seminary*, 467 Bloomfield Ave., 06002-2999. Tel: 860-242-5573; Fax: 860-242-4886. Email: info@stseminary.org. Web: stseminary.org. Rev. Msgr. Gerard G. Schmitz, Rector & Contact; Karen Lesiak, Library Dir. Priests 16. In Res. Most Rev. Christie A. Macaluso, D.D., V.G.; Rev. Michael J. Dolan In Res. at the Archbishop Daniel A. Cronin Retirement Residence at St. Thomas Seminary Most Rev. Peter A. Rosazza, D.D.; Rev. Msgrs. Charles W. Daly (Retired); John D. Regan (Retired); Revs. Henry R. Dery (Retired); James G. Fanelli (Retired); Daniel J. Karpiey (Retired); Paul F. Kenefick (Retired); Roland M. LaPlante (Retired); William F. O'Keefe (Retired); Salvatore J. Rosa (Retired); Richard R. Russell (Retired); Robert T. Russo (Retired); Stanley J. Sikora (Retired); John P. Tracy (Retired).

[B] SEMINARIES, RELIGIOUS OR SCHOLASTICATES

CHESHIRE. *Novitiate of the Legion of Christ*, 475 Oak Ave., 06410. Tel: 203-271-0805; Fax: 203-271-3845. Email: cheshire@legionaries.org. Web: www.thebrothersincheshire.org; www.facebook.com/lccheshire. Revs. Christopher Brackett, L.C., Rector; Oscar Capilla, L.C., Chap.; Joseph Brickner, L.C., Novice Instructor; Christopher O'Connor, L.C., Prof.; Tarsicio Samaniego, L.C., Prof.; Juan Pablo Duran, Vice Rector; Simon Devereux, L.C. Priests 10; Religious 10; Students 80.

Studies: Revs. Owen Kearns, L.C.; Andreas Kramarz, L.C., Dean Studies; Walter Schu, L.C., Prof.; Justin Kielhorn, L.C., Vocational Dir.

[C] COLLEGES AND UNIVERSITIES

HAMDEN. *Mt. Sacred Heart College*, 295 Benham St., 06514-2801. Tel: 203-248-4225; Fax: 203-230-8341. Email: lretort@ascjus.org. Sisters Maureen Martin, A.S.C.J., Pres.; Lisa Retort, A.S.C.J., Dean. Chartered by the State of Connecticut for Sisters of Community of Apostles of the Sacred Heart of Jesus.

CHESHIRE. *Legion of Christ College, Inc.*, 475 Oak Ave., 06410. Tel: 203-271-0805; Fax: 203-271-3845. Rev. Jose Felix Ortega, L.C., Contact Person.

NEW HAVEN. *Albertus Magnus College* (1925) 700 Prospect St., 06511-1189. Tel: 800-578-9160; Fax: 203-773-5248. Email: admissions@albertus.edu. Web: www.albertus.edu. Dr. Julia M. McNamara, Pres.; Dr. John Donahue, Vice Pres. Academic Affairs & Provost; Sr. Helen Kieran, O.P., Dir., Campus Ministry; Jeanne Mann, Vice Pres., Fin. & Treas.; Claudia Schiavone, Registrar; Maureen Morrison, Dean Student Svcs.; Anne Leeny-Panagrossi, Librarian. Dominican Sisters (St. Mary of the Springs, Columbus, OH). Sisters 4; Lay Teachers 36; Total Enrollment 1,900.

WEST HARTFORD. *Saint Joseph College* (1932) 1678 Asylum Ave., 06117. Tel: 860-232-4571; Fax: 860-233-5695. Email: admissions@sjc.edu. Web: www.sjc.edu. Pamela Trotman Reid, Ph.D., Pres.; Michelle Kalis, Ph.D., Provost; Gary Sherman, M.S., Vice Pres. Enrollment Mgmt.; Doug Nelson, M.B.A., Vice Pres. Inst. Advancement; Shawn Harrington, Vice Pres. Finance; Allison Misky, Registrar; Linda Geffner, Dir. Library. Sisters of Mercy., Women's College-Undergraduates; Graduate School-Co-ed.; Chartered by the State of Connecticut. Priests 1; Sisters 2; Lay Teachers 107; Students 2,592; Undergraduates Men 13; Undergraduates Women 1,026; Graduates Coed 1,553; School for Young Children 149; Gengras Center for Exceptional Children 125.

[D] HIGH SCHOOLS, ARCHDIOCESAN

BRISTOL. *St. Paul Catholic High School*, 1001 Stafford Ave., 06010-3894. Tel: 860-584-0911; Fax: 860-585-8815. Web: www.spchs.com. Mr. Cary Dupont, Pres. & Chief Admin.; Sharon Mielcarz, Dean of Academic Life; Albert Wallace, Dean of Student Life; Rev. Isreal Rivera, Chap.; Dawn Zillich, Librarian. Faculty 33; Lay Teachers 33; Students 329.

MANCHESTER. *East Catholic High School*, 115 New State Rd., 06042-1898. Tel: 860-649-5336; Fax: 860-649-7191. Web: ECHS.com. Jason S. Hartling, Prin. & Chief Admin.; Geoffrey Andrews, Vice Prin., Student Life; Elena Gostic, Vice Prin., Academics; Constance Jurczak, Library/Media Dir.; Rev. Marcin P. Pluciennik, Chap. Sisters of Notre Dame de Namur 3; Lay Teachers 53; Students 684.

WATERBURY. *Sacred Heart High School*, 142 S. Elm St., 06706. Tel: 203-753-1605; Fax: 203-597-1686. Email: aazzara@sacredhearthighschool.org; eileenregan@snet.net. Web: sacredhearthighschool.org. Anthony R. Azzara, Prin.; Mrs. Eileen Regan, Pres. & Chief Admin.; Debra Taylor, Dir. Student Activities; Rev. James T. Gregory, Chap.; Jane Scully-Parshall, Librarian. Priests 1; Lay Teachers 28; Students 349.

WEST HARTFORD. *Northwest Catholic High School* (1961) 29 Wampanoag Dr., 06117-1299. Tel: 860-236-4221; Fax: 860-586-0911. Email: callahan@nwcath.org. Web: www.nwcath.org. Mrs. Margaret R. Williamson, Prin. & Chief Admin.; Mr. Richard Callahan, Vice Prin.; Mr. John Cusson, Academic Dean; Kristina Gillespie, Dir., Campus Ministry; Rev. Joseph P. Crowley, Chap.; Mrs. Helga Phillips, Librarian. Priests 2; Sisters 1; Lay Teachers 53; Students 640.

[E] HIGH SCHOOLS, PRIVATE

HAMDEN. *Sacred Heart Academy*, 265 Benham St., 06514-2833. Tel: 203-288-2309; Fax: 203-230-9680. Web: www.sha-excelsior.org. Sisters Sheila O'Neill, A.S.C.J., Pres.; Maureen Flynn, A.S.C.J., Prin. & Contact; Maureen Hayes, Librarian. Apostles of the Sacred Heart of Jesus. Sisters 9; Lay Teachers 45; Students 494.

MILFORD. *Academy of Our Lady of Mercy*, Lauralton Hall, 200 High St., 06460-3262. Tel: 203-877-2786; Fax: 203-876-9760. Email: cmonk@lauraltonhall.org. Web: www.lauraltonhall.org. Antoinette Iadarola, Ph.D., Pres. & Contact; Ann Pratson, Prin.; Theresa Lawler, Librarian. Sisters of Mercy of the Americas, N.E. Community Sisters 2; Lay Teachers 43; Students 431.

NEW MILFORD. *Canterbury School*, Aspetuck Ave., 06776-1739. Tel: 860-210-3800; Fax: 860-350-4425. Email: tsheehy@cbury.org. Web: www.cbury.org. Thomas J. Sheehy III, Headmaster; Patricia L. Hiro, Headmaster's Asst. & Contact; Rev. Sebastian Leonard, O.S.B., Chap. Coed. Boarding and day students Priests 1; Lay Teachers 75; Students 350.

WATERBURY. *Holy Cross High School* (1968) 587 Oronoke Rd., 06708. Tel: 203-757-9248; Fax: 203-757-3423. Email: tmcdonald@holycrosshs-ct.com. Web: HolyCrosshs-ct.com. Mr. Timothy McDonald, Pres. & Contact; Mrs. Margaret Leger, Prin.; Louis Howe, Dir. Campus Min.; Jessica Lobner, Library & Media. Brothers of the Congregation of Holy Cross, conducted in cooperation with Sisters of the Congregation of Notre Dame. Brothers 1; Sisters 1; Lay Teachers 71; Students 700.

WEST HAVEN. *Notre Dame High School*, 24 Ricardo St., 06516-2499. Tel: 203-933-1673; Fax: 203-933-2474. Email: pclifford@notredamehs.com. Web: www.notredamehs.com. Bro. James J. Branigan, C.S.C., B.A., M.S., Pres.; Mr. Patrick Clifford, Prin.; Mr. Ralph Proto, Exec. Vice. Pres., Faculties Mgmt. & Planning; Mr. Thomas Marcucci, Athletic Dir.; Adam Laput, Asst. Prin.; Mr. Joseph Ramirez, Asst. Prin.; Mrs. Gail Bellucci, Campus Min.; Lisa Mierzejewski, Librarian. Congregation of Holy Cross. Brothers 4; Sisters 2; Lay Teachers 55; Students 650.

Notre Dame Loyalty & Endowment Fund, Inc., 24 Ricardo St., 06516. Tel: 203-933-1673; Fax: 203-933-2474.

[F] SPECIALIZED CHILD CARING HOME

NEW HAVEN. *St. Francis Home for Children, Inc.* (1852) 651 Prospect St., 06511-2003. Tel: 203-777-5513; Fax: 203-777-0644. Email: psalerno1@aol.com. Mr. Peter T. Salerno, Exec. Dir. & Contact. Provides an array of residential programs for youth and community-based services for families and youth including preschool, extended day treatment, life skills, and family support center. Lay Staff 135; Children 52; Extended Day Treatment 25; Preschool 25; Special Education School 70.

[G] DAY CARE CENTER

HAMDEN. *Clelian Adult Day Center* (1988) 261 Benham St., 06514-2898. Tel: 203-288-4151; Fax: 203-288-0551. Email: cscaduto@ascjus.org. Web: www.clelianadultdaycenter.com. Sr. Cecelia Marie Scaduto, R.S.M., Dir. & Contact. Apostles of the Sacred Heart of Jesus., A day health care facility for the elderly (interdenominational). Total Assisted 175; Total Staff 20; Capacity 100.

Sacred Heart Manor Nursery and Kindergarten, 261 Benham St., 06514. Tel: 203-230-4889. Email: sealat@yahoo.com. Sr. Elaine Ann Lattanzi, A.S.C.J., Prin. & Contact. Apostles of the Sacred Heart of Jesus 1; Lay Teachers 7; Students 70; Total Assisted 70.

[H] GENERAL HOSPITALS

HARTFORD. *Saint Francis Hospital and Medical Center*, 114 Woodland St., 06105-1299. Tel: 860-714-4000; Fax: 860-714-8030. Email: pastoralcare@stfranciscare.org. Web: www.stfranciscare.com. Christopher M. Dadlez, Pres. & CEO; Sr. Judith A. Carey, R.S.M., Ph.D., Vice Pres. Mission Integration; Suzanne Nolan, Dir. Pastoral Care & Chap.; Suzanne Carnes, Chap.; Rev. Mark Bonsignore, Chap.; Roy McAlpin, Chap.; Tina Varona, Media Rels. Mgr. Licensed Beds 617; Bassinets 65; Outpatient Visits 315,344; Inpatient Visits 33,057; Observation 2,181; Staff 3,882. In Res. Rev. Elias Menuba, Chap.

The Women's Auxiliary of Saint Francis Hospital and Medical Center Tel: 860-714-4558; Fax: 860-714-7809. Barbara Colli, Pres.

Asylum Hill Family Medicine Center, Inc. Tel: 860-714-4212; Fax: 860-714-8079. Web: stfranciscare.org.

Saint Francis Care Medical Group, P.C. Web: stfranciscare.org.

Saint Francis Hospital and Medical Center Foundation, Inc., 95 Woodland St., 06105-1299. Tel: 860-714-4900; Fax: 860-714-8069. Web: stfranciscare.org. Lynn Rossini, Interim Pres. & Chief Devel. Officer.

Mount Sinai Rehabilitation Hospital, Inc., 480 Blue Hills Ave., 06112. Tel: 860-714-3500; Fax: 860-714-8550. Web: stfranciscare.org.

NEW HAVEN. *Hospital of St. Raphael* (1907) 1450 Chapel St., 06511. Tel: 203-789-3000; Fax: 203-789-3328. Email: jgranville@srhs.org. Web: www.srhs.org. Christopher M. O'Connor, Pres. & CEO; Sr. Joan Granville, S.C., Vice Pres. Missions & Contact; Revs. Gregory M. Altermatt, Chap.; Augustine Mangalath (India), Chap.; William West, UCC & Chap.; Rev. Sandy Alves Belcher, Episcopal Priest & Chap.; Rabbi Steve Steinberg, Chap.; J. Kendall Palladino, Dir. Pastoral Care. Sisters of Charity of St. Elizabeth., Legal Holdings: Saint Raphael Healthcare System; Saint Raphael Foundation, Inc.; DePaul Health Services Corporation; Saint Regis Health Center, Inc. (Nonprofit charitable corporations affiliated with the Hospital of Saint Raphael). Chaplains 9; Sisters 3; Bed Capacity 511; Bassinets 22; Patients Assisted Annually 300,000; Total Staff 3,500; CPE Residents 5.

Saint Regis Health Center, Inc. dba Sister Anne Virginia Grimes Health Center 1354 Chapel St., 06511. Tel: 203-867-8300; Fax: 203-867-8345. Email: jtarutis@srhs.org. Web: www.srhs.org. John Tarutis, Exec. Dir.; Donna Wade, Dir., Nursing; Lisa Irish, Chap. 122-bed skilled nursing facility.; Religious Community: Srs. of Charity of St. Elizabeth Total Assisted Annually 800; Total Staff 152.

WATERBURY. *Saint Mary's Hospital*, 56 Franklin St., 06706-1200. Tel: 203-709-6000; Fax: 203-709-3238. Email: community@stmh.org. Web: stmh.org. Chad W. Wable, Pres. & CEO; Revs. Joseph

Pullikattil, Chap.; William Platt, Chap.; Geralyn Abbott, M.A., L.P.C., Chap. & Mgr. Pastoral Care; Mary Ellen Kindelan, Pastoral Care Asst. Saint Mary's Health System, Inc., Saint Mary's Hospital Foundation, Inc., (Nonprofit corporations for the exclusive benefit of Saint Mary's Hospital). Sisters 2; Bed Capacity 202; Licensed 347; Bassinets 32; Neonatal ICU 8; Patients Assisted Annually 230,000; Total Staff 1,600.

Saint Mary's Hospital Foundation, Inc., 56 Franklin St., 06706. Tel: 203-709-6390; Fax: 203-709-3272. Peg Lawlor, Pres.

Saint Mary's Health System, Inc., 56 Franklin St., 06706. Tel: 203-709-6000; Fax: 203-709-3238. Email: community@stmh.org. Chad W. Wable, Pres. & CEO.

Saint Mary's Hospital Auxiliary, 56 Franklin St., 06706. Tel: 203-709-3732; Fax: 203-709-3703.

[I] SPECIAL HOSPITALS

HARTFORD. **Malta House of Care, Inc.*, 19 Woodland St., Ste. 37, 06105. Tel: 860-725-0171; Fax: 860-725-0191. Web: www.maltahouseofcare.org. Robert Voight, Chm.; Luis Diez-Morales, M.D., Board Pres.; Laurel Baldwin-Ragaven, Medical & Exec. Dir. To deliver charitable primary and/or preventative medical health care to the needy uninsured of the Greater Hartford region. Total Staff 6; Total Assisted 4,500.

WEST HARTFORD. *Saint Agnes Home, Inc* (1914) 104 Mayflower St., 06110-1425. Tel: 860-521-7516; Fax: 860-521-1756. Email: info@stagneshome.org. Web: www.stagneshome.org. Lorna Little, M.S.W., Exec. Dir.; Kathleen M. Costello, Exec. Asst. For adolescent single mothers and their infants. Bed Capacity 16; Patients Assisted Annually 53; Total Staff 40.

[J] HOMES FOR AGED

ENFIELD. *The Home for the Aged of the Little Sisters of the Poor* (1839) Incorporated Operating as St. Joseph's Residence, 1365 Enfield St., 06082-4925. Tel: 860-741-0791; Fax: 860-265-1891. Email: enmothersuperior@littlesistersofthepoor.org. Sr. Genevieve Nugent, L.S.P., Supr. & Contact; Rev. Lech Kuna (Poland), Chap. Little Sisters of the Poor 10; Lay Staff 109; Residents 80; Bed Capacity 80; Total Assisted Annually 90.

NEW BRITAIN. *St. Lucian's Residence, Inc.*, 532 Burritt St., 06053-3699. Tel: 860-223-2123; Fax: 860-612-0321. Email: stlucian.res.inc@snet.net. Sr. Mary Jennifer Carroll, D.M., Admin. & Contact; Rev. Joseph Tran, Chap. Daughters of Mary of the Immaculate Conception. Residents 42; Total Staff 22; Total Assisted Annually 42.

Monsignor Bojnowski Manor, Inc. (1974) 50 Pulaski St., 06053. Tel: 860-229-0336; Fax: 860-229-3252. Carol Ann E. Salvietti, Admin. Owned and operated by the Daughters of Mary of the Immaculate Conception. Skilled Nursing Beds 60; Total Staff 85.

WEST HARTFORD. *Saint Mary Home*, 2021 Albany Ave., 06117-2796. Tel: 860-570-8200; Fax: 860-570-8205. Web: www.saintmaryhome.org. Peter Madden, Admin.; Christopher Johnson, Asst. Admin.; Mrs. Aysha Kuhlor, Dir. Nursing Svcs. Sisters of Mercy 19; Sisters in Residence 9; Residents (Frances Warde Apts.) 97; Patients Assisted Annually 652; Bed Capacity 256; Skilled Nursing 256; Total Staff 360. In Res. Rev. Norman L. Brockett, Resident Chap.

[K] HEALTH CARE CENTERS FOR AGED

WEST HARTFORD. *McAuley Center, Inc.* (1988) 275 Steele Rd., 06117. Tel: 860-920-6300; Fax: 860-232-4077. Stephen Surprenant, Sr. Vice Pres., CEO & Contact. Continuing care retirement community; Sisters of Mercy. 229 residential apartment units for individuals age 62 and over. Nursing care at St. Mary's Home included.

[L] MONASTERIES AND RESIDENCES OF PRIESTS AND BROTHERS

HARTFORD. *Missionaries of LaSalette Province of Mary, Mother of the Americas*, 915 Maple Ave., 06114-2330. Tel: 860-956-8870; Fax: 860-956-8849. Email: mlsadmin@aol.com. Web: www.lasalette.org. Very Rev. Joseph G. Bachand, M.S., Prov. Supr.; Revs. James H. Kuczynski, M.S., Vicar; William Kaliyadan, M.S., Asst.; Brian D. Schloth, M.S., Pro. Treas.

The Missionaries of La Salette Corporation.

MLS Religious Trust Province of Mary, Mother of the Americas. Priests 4. *Missionaries of LaSalette*, 85 New Park Ave., 06106-2184. Tel: 860-523-8275; Fax: 860-586-0754. Revs. Salvatore D. Altavista, M.S.; Gerald Biron, M.S.; Richard R. Boucher, M.S.; Robert J. Campbell, M.S.; Emery N. DesRochers, M.S.; Frederick R. Flaherty, M.S.; Michael J. Flanagan, M.S.; Rene Gelinas, M.S.; Clifford P. Hasler, M.S.; Peter D. Kohler, M.S.; Denis A. Kolumber, M.S.; Maurice F. Linehan, M.S.; James T. Lowery, M.S.; John J. McCarthy, M.S.; Patrick R. McCarthy, M.S.; Alan B. McGuirk, M.S.; William W. Mulcair, M.S.; Joseph J. Nolan, M.S.; Claudius S. Nowinski, M.S.; Louis M. Ouellette, M.S.; Theodule J. Richard, M.S.; Donald D. Simonds, M.S.; Donald K. Thomas, M.S.; Bros. Robert J. Belliveau, M.S.; Gerald B. Buraczewski, M.S.; Jean Paul Champagne, M.S.; G. Peter Collins, M.S.; David J. Cook, M.S.; Mark L. Gallant, M.S.; Andre J. Hamel, M.S.; Paul Maceyka, Oblate; Leonard Melanson, M.S.; Thomas C. Murphy, M.S.; Edmund A. Normantowicz, M.S. Priests 23; Brothers 10; Oblates 1.

Priests-Brothers of Province Serving Abroad: Missionaries in Argentina: Revs. Norman H. Butler, M.S.; Robert R. Butler, M.S.; John M. Garvey, M.S.; James M. Weeks, M.S.

Bolivia: Rev. John F. Higgins, M.S. *Our Lady of Sorrows Rectory*, 16 Greenwood St., 06106-2109. Tel: 860-233-4424; Fax: 860-236-0149. Revs. Francis C. Cooney, M.S.; Thomas J. Huhn, M.S. *North American La Salette Mission Center*, 915 Maple Ave., 06114-2330. Tel: 860-956-8870; Fax: 860-956-8849. Rev. Thomas Vellappallil, M.S., Dir.; Mrs. Connie Evans, Sec.

St. Patrick-St. Anthony Friary (Holy Name Prov.), 285 Church St., 06103-1196. Tel: 860-756-4034; Fax: 860-249-6487. Web: stpatrick-stanthony.org. Franciscan Friars. Priests 4.

BLOOMFIELD. *Brothers of the Sacred Heart* (1821) 1153 Blue Hills Ave., 06002-1901. Tel: 860-242-3342. Email: plgauvinsc@hotmail.com. Bro. Paul L. Gauvin, S.C. Total in Residence 4.

CHESHIRE. *Legionaries of Christ*, 475 Oak Ave., 06410. Tel: 203-271-0805; Fax: 203-271-3845. Email: cheshire@legionaries.org. Web: www.legionofchrist.org. 393 Derby Ave., Orange, 06477. Tel: 203-974-6000; Fax: 203-795-2808.

LITCHFIELD. *Montfort Missionaries*, 83 Montfort Rd., P.O. Box 667, 06759. Tel: 860-567-8434; Fax: 860-567-9670. Email: lourdesshrinect@gmail.com. Web: www.shrinect.org. Revs. James Brady, S.M.M., Admin.; Bernard Brault, S.M.M.; William Considine, S.M.M., Supr. Priests 3. *Lourdes in Litchfield* Tel: 860-567-1041; Fax: 860-567-9670.

Lourdes Shrine Guild, Inc. Montfort House (Center for Spiritual Renewal) Tel: 860-567-8434; Fax: 860-567-9670.

MANCHESTER. *DePaul Provincial Residence* (1995) 234 Keeney St., 06040-7048. Tel: 860-643-2828; Fax: 860-533-9462. Email: nepcm1@cox.net. Revs. A. Rafal Kopystynski, C.M., Prov. & Contact; Edmund Gutowski, C.M.; Chester R. Mrowka, C.M.; Stanley Staniszewski, C.M.; Bro. Joseph S. Zurowski, C.M.

The New England Province of the Congregation of the Mission Incorporated Congregation of the Mission, New England Province., (Vincentian Fathers and Brothers)

Charitable Trust of the New England Province of the Congregation of the Mission

Special Assignments: Revs. George J. Dabrowski, C.M. (Retired); Julian Szumilo, C.M. (Retired). *St. Joseph Rectory* (1926) 32 Jewett St., Ansonia, 06401-2499. Tel: 203-734-0402; Fax: 203-734-4884. *St. Michael the Archangel*, 75 Derby Ave., Derby, 06418-2098. Tel: 203-734-0005; Fax: 203-736-2044. *St. Stanislaus Rectory* (1904) 9 Eld St., New Haven, 06511-3899. Tel: 203-562-2828; Fax: 203-752-0217.

MERIDEN. *Franciscan Brothers of the Eucharist*, 173 Goodspeed Ave., 06451. Tel: 203-237-3601; Fax: 203-237-4217. Email: brothers@fbecommunity.org. Web: www.fbecommunity.org. Bro. Leo Maneri, F.B.E., Pres.

NEW BRITAIN. *Conventual Franciscans* (1979) 532 Burritt St., 06053-2869. Tel: 860-225-5786. Daughters of Mary Motherhouse.

in res. Rev. Joseph Tran. *St. Paul Friary* (1985) 479 Alling St., Kensington, 06037-2100. Tel: 860-828-0331; Fax: 860-828-7620.

NEW HAVEN. *St. Mary Priory*, 5 Hillhouse Ave., 06511. Tel: 203-562-6193; Fax: 203-562-1273. Email: church@stmarys-priory.com. Web: www.stmarys-priory.com. Order of Preachers (Dominicans). Total in Residence 9.

Priests of the Congregation of Holy Cross, 203 Maple St., 06511. Tel: 203-776-2405; Fax: 203-366-7886. Email: jlmyoung@pol.net. Rev. John L. Young, C.S.C.

NORTH GUILFORD. *Our Lady of Grace Monastery* (1947) 11 Race Hill Rd., 06437-1099. Tel: 203-457-0599; Fax: 203-457-1248. Web: www.ourladyofgracemonastery.org. Sr. Mary Ann, O.P., Prioress & Contact. Order of Preachers (Dominicans). Total in Residence 30.

WATERBURY. *Basilica of the Immaculate Conception Rectory*, 74 W. Main St., 06702. Tel: 203-574-0017; Fax: 203-756-8748. Email: iccsms@sbcglobal.net. Web: www.TheImmaculate.com. Missionaries of the Holy Apostles

St. Michael Rectory (1902) 62 St. Michael Dr., 06704-1295. Tel: 203-753-0689; Fax: 203-573-9101. Web: www.stmichaelwtby.com. Rev. Roger L. Hall, O.F.M. (Immaculate Conception Prov.)

WEST HARTFORD. *Holy Family Monastery/Retreat*, 303 Tunxis Rd., 06107. Tel: 860-521-0440; Fax: 860-521-0883 (Community); 860-521-1929 (Retreat Center). Email: holyfamilyretreat@cpprov.org. Web: www.holyfamilyretreat.org. Revs. David Cinquegrani, C.P., Local Leader & Retreat Dir.; Terence J. Kristofak, C.P.; Ronan Callahan, C.P. Congregation of the Passion of Jesus Christ.

Monastery Staff: Retreat Center. Revs. William Maguire, C.P.; Gregory Paul, C.P.; John Baptist Pesce, C.P.; Columkille Regan, C.P.; Simon Paul Wood, C.P.; Vincent Youngberg, C.P.; Bros. Frederick Barton, C.P.; William Drotar, C.P.; Michael Moran, C.P.; Terence Skorka, C.P.

WEST HAVEN. *Brothers of Holy Cross*, 24 Ricardo St., 06516-2499. Tel: 203-932-2101; Fax: 203-933-2474. Bro. Thomas Gorman, C.S.C. Brothers of Holy Cross.

[M] CONVENTS AND RESIDENCES FOR SISTERS

HARTFORD. *The Community of the Dominican Daughters of Our Lady of Nazareth Corporation*, 510 New Britain Ave., 06106. Tel: 860-249-2912. Sr. Lucia Silva Cardenas, Pres.

SS. Cyril & Methodius Convent, 45 Groton St., 06106. Tel: 860-527-3775; Fax: 860-493-7409. Rev. Adam C. Subocz. Felician Sisters of the Order of St. Francis of Connecticut.

Medical Mission Sisters (1925) 92 Sherman St., 06105. Tel: 860-233-0875; Fax: 860-509-9509. Email: mtwinter@hartsem.edu; mms@hartsem.edu. Web: mtwinter.hartsem.edu. Sisters Mary Elizabeth Johnson, M.M.S.; Miriam Therese Winter, M.M.S., Ph.D.

Mercyhouse (2002) 102 Putnam St., 06106-1390. Tel: 860-560-9590. Email: mercyhouse@juno.com. Sisters of Mercy of the Americas.

Sisters of Mercy of the Americas Northeast Community (1831) *Mercyhouse*, 102 Putnam St., 06106-1390. Tel: 860-560-9590.

Sisters of St. Joseph of Chambery (1650) West Hartford, 06119. Tel: 860-233-5126; Fax: 860-232-4649. Email: csjusa@yahoo.com. Web: sistersofsaintjoseph.org. 27 Park Rd., West Hartford, 06119. Tel: 860-233-5126; Fax: 860-232-4649. 145 Elizabeth St., 06105. Tel: 860-523-5704. 73 Cannon Rd., East Hartford, 06108. Tel: 860-291-8998. *Formation House*, 40 Clifford St., 06114. Tel: 860-246-4083.

Shalom Community, 33 Freeman St., 06114. Tel: 860-956-9247. 14 Ringgold St., West Hartford, 06119. Tel: 860-231-8272. 35B Freeman St., 06114. Tel: 860-956-1939.

Spirit of Mercy Community, 410 Campfield Ave., 06114-2807. Tel: 860-956-3030. Sisters of Mercy.

BETHLEHEM. *Abbey of Regina Laudis* (1946) 237 Flanders Rd., 06751. Tel: 203-266-7727; Fax: 203-266-5915. Web: www.abbeyofreginalaudis.com. Sr. David Serna, O.S.B., Abbess & Mailing Contact. Benedictine Nuns of the Primitive Observance. Professed Nuns 29; In First Vows 4; Novices 3; Postulants 1.

BLOOMFIELD. *Sisters of Mercy of the Americas Northeast Community*, 5 Garrison Ter., 06002-3005. Tel: 860-243-8524. Sr. Irene Holowesko, R.S.M., Contact.

Sisters of Notre Dame de Namur (Connecticut Province), 5 Garrison Ter., 06002. Tel: 860-243-8524; Fax: 860-683-1351. Email: sndbloom@aol.com. Total in Residence 3.

BRANFORD. *Benedictines of Jesus Crucified, Monastery of the Glorious Cross*, 61 Burban Dr., 06405-4003. Tel: 203-315-9964; Fax: 203-483-5829. Email: monasterygc@juno.com. Sisters Marie Rita Syn, O.S.B., Prioress. Tel: 203-483-4235; Mary Zita Wenker, O.S.B., Vocation Dir.

BRISTOL. *St. Joseph Convent*, 470 East Rd., 06010. Tel: 860-584-2183.

CHESHIRE. *Sisters of St. Joseph of Chambery*, 441 E. Mitchell Ave., 06410. Tel: 203-699-9421; Fax: 203-272-2807. Email: luscata@aol.com. Sr. Lucy Scata, C.S.J., 145 Main St., 06410. Tel: 203-272-6504; Fax: 203-271-3356.

EAST HARTFORD. *Sisters of Notre Dame de Namur*, 21 Highview St., 06108-2983. Tel: 860-289-5295. Sr. Marion Raymond Hurley, S.N.D., Contact. 50 Larrabee St., #G, 06108. Tel: 860-289-2421. 908 Forbes St., 06118. Tel: 860-568-6958.

Sisters of Notre Dame de Namur, 908 Forbes St., 06118-1924. Tel: 860-568-6958. Email: ellisnd@aol.com. Sr. Mary Rose Crowley, S.N.D., Contact. Total in Residence 4.

EAST HAVEN. *Provincial House*, 32 Tuttle Pl., 06512. Tel: 203-469-7872; Fax: 203-469-8819. Email: scmm@comcast.net. Web: www.sistersofcharity.net. Sr. Barbara Connell, S.C.M.M., Contact. 87 Gerrish Ave., 06512. Tel: 203-468-9112.

ENFIELD. *Felician Sisters - Our Lady of the Angels Convent*, 1315 Enfield St., 06082-4929. Tel: 860-745-7791; 860-745-4946; Fax: 860-741-0819. Email: sconnret@feliciansisters.org. 1315 Enfield St, 06082-4929. Tel: 860-745-4946; Fax: 860-741-7871. Sr. Mary Christopher Moore, C.S.S.F., Prov. Min. Felician Sisters of the Order of St. Francis of Connecticut.

Enfield Convent (1932) Tel: 860-745-7791; Fax: 860-741-0819. Sr. Mary Christopher Moore, C.S.S.F., Prov. Min.; Rev. Noel Danielewicz, O.F.M.Conv. Felician Sisters. Professed Sisters 67; (Total Felician Sisters in North America, Our Lady of Hope Province) 823.

Felician Adult Day Care (1990) 1333A Enfield St., 06082-4929. Tel: 860-745-2542; Fax: 860-745-2542. Email: fadcmail@juno.com. Joy Mason, Dir. Felician Sisters., A day respite health care facility for Caregivers of the Frail, elderly and Alzheimer Clients. Total Assisted 20; Total Staff 10.

Felician Sisters Infirmary (1938) 1315 Enfield St., 06082-4929. Tel: 860-745-0217; Fax: 860-741-6474. Email: snancypiecewicz@feliciansisters.org.

Mother Angela Residence (1964) 1333-B Enfield St., 06082-4929. Tel: 860-745-5705. Email: maresidence@sbcglobal.net.

Child Jesus Convent (1965) 1370 Enfield St., 06082-5526. Tel: 860-745-5847; Fax: 860-745-2010.

Enfield Montessori School (1965) 1370 Enfield St., 06082-5526. Tel: 860-745-5847; Fax: 860-745-2010. Email: montessorischool@cox.net. Cliora Beaulieu, Dir. & Contact. Students 113.

Little Sisters of the Poor (1839) 1365 Enfield St., 06082-4925. Tel: 860-741-0791; Fax: 860-741-3982. Email: enmothersuperior@littlesistersofthepoor.org. Sr. Genevieve Nugent, L.S.P., Pres., Supr. & Contact. Sisters 10.

FARMINGTON. *Maryknoll Sisters of St. Dominic* (1920) 275 Main St. #A1, 06032-2930. Tel: 860-678-1971. Email: kmageemm@yahoo.com. Web: mklsisters.org.

Sisters of the Cross and Passion (1852) St. Gabriel's House, 31 Colton St., 06032-2381. Tel: 860-678-7274; Fax: 860-677-2873. Web: www.cptryon.org/scp; passionistsisters.org. Sr. Mary O'Brien, C.P., Contact. Sisters 4.

FORESTVILLE. *St. Matthew Convent*, 119 Church Ave., 06010-6799. Tel: 860-583-2004; Fax: 860-314-1541 (School). Email: matthewct1@home.com. Sisters, Servants of the Immaculate Heart of Mary.

Sisters of St. Joseph of the Third Order of St. Francis, 82 Kenney St., 06010. Tel: 860-584-2985.

HAMDEN. *Mary, Mother of the Church Convent*, 115 Denslow Hill Rd., 06514. Tel: 203-407-1042. Sr. Sheila O'Neill, A.S.C.J., Religious Supr. Sisters 5.

Mount Sacred Heart Provincial House and Formation House, 295 Benham St., 06514-2801. Tel: 203-248-4225; Fax: 203-230-8341. Email: lretort@ascjus.org. Web: www.ascjus.org. Sisters Maureen Martin, A.S.C.J., Prov. Supr.; Anne Walsh, A.S.C.J., Vicaress; Lisa Retort, A.S.C.J., Sec. & Contact. Sisters in Province 130; Professed 125; Novices 5.

Sisters of Mercy of the Americas Northeast Community, 2809 Whitney Ave., 06518-2544. Tel: 203-287-9017. Sr. Ann O'Neill, R.S.M., Contact Person.

LITCHFIELD. *Daughters of Wisdom* (1949) 229 E. Litchfield Rd., 06759. Tel: 860-567-3163; Fax: 860-567-3166. Email: rg@wisdomhouse.org. Web: www.wisdomhouse.org. Sisters Rosemarie Greco, D.W., Contact; Jo-Ann Iannotti, O.P.

Daughters of Wisdom, 12 Clark Rd., 06759-2808. Tel: 860-529-8419; Fax: 860-529-8419. Web: daughtersofwisdom.org. Sisters 3.

MADISON. *Sisters of Mercy of the Americas Northeast Community*, 167 Neck Rd., P.O. Box 191, 06443-0191. Tel: 203-245-4261. Email: emmanuel115@juno.com. Sr. Lillian Pannozza, R.S.M., Contact.

MANCHESTER. *Assumption Convent* (1961) 21 S. Adams St., 06040. Tel: 860-643-0452; Fax: 860-643-0559. Email: assumption.school@snet.net. Web: www.assumption-parish.com. Sisters Mary Bernard, S.C.M.C., Supr. & Contact; Joan Marie, S.C.M.C.; Joan Clare, S.C.M.C. Sisters of Charity of Our Lady, Mother of the Church.

Sisters of Notre Dame de Namur, 9 Plano Pl., 06040-4907. Tel: 860-647-8544; Fax: 860-647-8544. Email: frandall01@aol.com. Web: www.snadden.org. Sr. Frances Randall, S.N.D., Contact.

MERIDEN. *Generalate of the Franciscan Sisters of the Eucharist* (1973) Mailing Address: *Motherhouse of the Franciscan Sisters of the Eucharist*, 405 Allen Ave., 06451. Tel: 203-238-2243; Fax: 203-237-3734. Email: fseinfo@fsecommunity.org. Web: fsecommunity.org. Sisters Shaun Vergauwen, F.S.E., Mother Gen.; Suzanne Gross, F.S.E., Sec. & Contact.

Franciscan Sisters of the Eucharist, Inc. The Institute of the Franciscan Sisters of the Eucharist. Professed 21; Novices 3. 275 Finch Ave., 06451. Tel: 203-238-2400; Fax: 203-237-3739. 269 Finch Ave., 06451. Tel: 203-630-1771; Fax: 203-630-1776.

St. Joseph Convent, 19 Goodwill Ave., 06451. Tel: 203-686-0559. Email: sr.georgeann@cox.net. Sr. Georgeann Vumbaco, R.S.M., Contact.

Mt. Carmel Convent, 109 Goodwill Ave., 06451. Tel: 203-235-3622.

MILFORD. *Sisters of Mercy of the Americas Northeast Community*, 23 Jones Ct., 06460-5110. Tel: 203-877-1171. Email: Patsio@sbcglobal.net. Sr. Patricia J. Rooney, R.S.M., Fundraising Consultant, Contact.

NEW BRITAIN. *Cana*, 1190 Slater Rd., 06053-1614. Tel: 860-826-1655. Sisters of St. Joseph of Chambery. Total in Residence 2.

St. Francis of Assisi Convent, School Sisters of Notre Dame, 1757 Stanley St., 06053. Tel: 860-225-7143. Email: stfrancis@snet.net. Sisters 2.

Motherhouse of Daughters of Mary of the Immaculate Conception (1904) 314 Osgood Ave., 06053. Tel: 860-225-9406; Fax: 860-225-4321. Web: www.crossfire.org/daughtersofmary/. Sisters Mary Jennifer Carroll, D.M., Supr. Gen.; Mary Clare, D.M., Sec. Daughters of Mary of the Immaculate Conception. Sisters in Community 38.

Marian Heights, 314 Osgood Ave., 06053.

Sacred Heart Convent (1904) 23 Orange St., 06053. Tel: 860-225-3989.

Msgr. Bojnowski Manor (1974) 50 Pulaski St., 06053. Tel: 860-229-0336; Fax: 860-229-3252.

St. Lucian's Residence, 532 Burritt St., 06053. Tel: 860-223-2123; Fax: 860-612-0321.

Sisters of Mercy of the Americas Northeast Community, 37 Carlton St., 06053. Tel: 860-229-7575. Sr. Barbara Kowalski, R.S.M., Contact.

Sisters of the Cross and Passion (1849) 25 Streamside Ln., 06052. Tel: 860-224-1193. Sr. Ann Rodgers, C.P., Contact.

NEW HARTFORD. *Missionary Servants of the Most Blessed Trinity*, 595 Town Hill Rd., 06057. Tel: 860-379-4329; Fax: 860-379-4329. Email: trinita@charter.net. Total in Residence 4.

NEW HAVEN. *Dominican Sisters of Peace* (1901) *St. Mary's Convent*, 15 Lincoln St., 06511. Tel: 203-865-7305. Sisters Mary Faith Dargan, O.P.; Barbara DeCrosta, O.P., Contact; Mary Ellen Boyle, O.P.; Ellen McNulty, O.P.; Maureen O'Brien, O.P.; Patricia Twohill, O.P., Vocation Dir.

St. Joseph Convent, 135 Edwards St., 06511. Tel: 203-562-9202. Email: chermann8@juno.com. Web: www.columbusdominicans.org. Sisters Helen Kieran, O.P., Contact; Melanie Hannigan, O.P., Dominican Sister, St. Mary of the Springs; Sheila O'Brien, O.P. 15 Lincoln St., 06511. Tel: 203-865-7305. Email: melboyle1@juno.com. 1914 Chapel St., 06515. Tel: 203-389-9428.

Sisters of Charity of St. Elizabeth, Convent Station, 1450 Chapel St., 06511. Tel: 203-789-3000. 450 Central Ave., 06515. Tel: 203-397-5243.

Sisters of Notre Dame de Namur 311 Eastern St., 1916 E., 06513. Tel: 203-469-8385.

St. Mary's Convent, 15 Lincoln St., 06511. Tel: 203-865-7305. Email: melboylel@juno.com. Dominican Sisters of Peace (Columbus, OH).

NORTH GUILFORD. *Monastery of Our Lady of Grace* (1947) 11 Race Hill Rd., 06437-1099. Tel: 203-457-0599; Fax: 203-457-1248. Web: www.ourladyofgracemonastery.org. Dominican Contemplative Nuns (Cloistered). Professed Sisters 30.

A contemplative community with solemn vows and papal enclosure. Perpetual Adoration. Sr. Mary Ann, O.P., Prioress & Contact.

Dominican Contemplative Nuns (Cloistered). Sr. Mary Ann, O.P., Prioress & Contact.

NORTH HAVEN. **St. Frances Cabrini Convent*, 94 Chapel Hill Rd., 06473. Tel: 203-239-8012; Fax: 203-985-0236. Sisters of the Sacred Heart of Jesus of Ragusa. Total in Residence 4.

WALLINGFORD. *Holy Trinity Convent*, 247 S. Main St., 06492. Tel: 203-265-6999; Fax: 203-294-4983. Sisters of Mercy of the Americas of Connecticut.

WATERBURY. *Holy Land Convent*, 60 Slocum St., 06706. Tel: 203-755-2456. Religious Teachers Filippini.

St. Mary Hospital, 56 Franklin St., 06706-1200. Tel: 203-574-6455. Sr. Patricia Corcoran, C.S.J., Contact. Sisters of St. Joseph of Chambery. 284 Windy Dr., 06705-2543. Tel: 203-574-6374. 31 Marita Dr., 06705-2527. Tel: 203-574-6482.

Notre Dame Convent, 119 Southmayd Rd., 06705. Tel: 203-753-1095; Fax: 203-753-4431. Sr. Eleanor Verrastro, C.N.D., Contact. Sisters of the Congregation of Notre Dame. Sisters 4. 587 Oronoke Rd., 06708. Tel: 203-755-8828. Sisters 7.

Sisters of Notre Dame de Namur (1804) 131 Herschel Ave., 06708. Tel: 203-757-1444. Sr. Mary Beth Johnson, S.N.D., Contact. 38 Summer St., 06704. Tel: 203-755-0012.

Visitation Plaza, 100 Jefferson Sq., #7J, 06706. Tel: 203-755-7236. Sr. Mary Etta Higgins, R.S.M., Life & Ministry Admin., (Srs. of Mercy).

WATERTOWN. *St. John the Evangelist Convent*, 9 Academy Hill, 06795-2101. Tel: 860-274-1820; Fax: 860-945-6418. Email: bvaluckas@gmail. com. School Sisters of Notre Dame. Sisters 2.

WEST HARTFORD. *Convent of Mary Immaculate, Provincial House of the Sisters of St. Joseph of Chambery* (1650) (North American Province), 27 Park Rd., 06119. Tel: 860-233-5126; Fax: 860-232-4649. Email: csjusa@yahoo.com. Web: www.sistersofsaintjoseph.org. Sr. Dolores Lahr, C.S.J., Prov.; Mrs. Mary D'Arcangelo, Admin. Asst. & Contact.

The Sisters of St. Joseph Corporation Sisters of St. Joseph of Chambery., In Community: Professed Sisters 106.

Religious Trust of the Sisters of St. Joseph of Chambery (the "Trust")

Dominican Sisters, 78 Westpoint Ter., 06107. Tel: 860-521-8296; Fax: 860-521-8296. Sr. Magdalene Nguyen, O.P., Supr. & Contact. Total in Residence 2.

Saint Mary Home, 2021 Albany Ave., 06117. Tel: 860-570-8200; Fax: 860-570-8205. Web: www.mchct.org. Patricia Hamill, Admin. & Contact.

Sisters of Mercy of the Americas - Northeast Community, Inc., 55 E. Cedar St., Newington, 06111. Tel: 860-594-8619; Fax: 860-665-0532. Sr. Mary Etta Higgins, R.S.M., Life & Ministry Admin.

Life and Ministry Office, 55 E. Cedar St., Newington, 06111. Tel: 860-594-8619; Fax: 860-665-0532. Sr. Mary Etta Higgins, R.S.M., Life & Ministry Admin. Sisters in Community 156.

Sisters of Mercy of the Americas of Connecticut, 132 Milton St., 06119-1218. Tel: 860-523-0707.

St. Joseph College, Lourdes Hall, 1678 Asylum Ave., 06117-2791. Tel: 860-232-6730.

St. Paul Convent, 243 Steele Rd., 06117-2741. Tel: 860-232-7745.

Trocaire, 243 Steele Rd., 06117-2796. Tel: 860-233-2195.

Sacred Heart Convent, 243 Steele Rd., 06117-2797. Tel: 860-236-3503.

Maranatha, 243 Steele Rd., 06117-2797. Tel: 860-236-9448. 54 Boulanger Ave. #1, 06110-1103. Tel: 860-231-8472. 54 Boulanger Ave. #2, 06110-1103. Tel: 860-233-6679.

Sisters of Mercy of the Americas of Vermont, 54 Clifford Dr., 06107-1208. Tel: 860-586-8402.

WEST HAVEN. *Our Lady of Victory Convent*, 634 Jones Hill Rd., 06516-6398. Tel: 203-934-8601. Sr. Denise Farrands, O.S.U. Ursuline Sisters of the Congregation of Tildonk, Belgium.

WINCHESTER CENTER. *Villa Ferretti, Religious Teachers Filippini*, 438 Winchester Rd., Box 55, 06094. Tel: 860-379-3279; Fax: 860-379-6479.

WINDSOR. *Sisters of Notre Dame de Namur*, Province Center, 468 Poquonock Ave., 06095-2473. Tel: 860-688-1832; Fax: 860-683-1741. Email: sndct@aol.com. Web: www.sndden.org. Sisters Ellen Agritelley, S.N.D., Leadership Team & Contact; Mary Rose Crowley, S.N.D., Leadership Team. Tel: 860-285-8901; Elizabeth McLaughlin, S.N.D., Leadership Team. Tel: 860-285-8441.

Community, 468 Poquonock Ave., 06095-2473. Tel: 860-285-0038; Fax: 860-683-1741.

Julie House Residential Care Home, 425 Poquonock Ave., 06095-2465. Tel: 860-298-8320; Fax: 860-683-1351. Assisted living home for S.N.D.'s only. Residents 12; Total Staff 4.

Sisters of St. Joseph of Chambery, 67 Bloomfield Ave., 06095. Tel: 860-285-0890. Email: windwomen@att.net.

WOLCOTT. *Contemplative Sisters of the Good Shepherd*, 5 Carriage Hill Dr., 06716. Tel: 203-879-6330; Fax: 203-879-5920. Email: gdshep620@sbcglobal.net. Web: www.goodshepherdsisters.org. Sr. Mary Edith Olaguer, C.G.S., Contact Person & Coord.

Daughters of Wisdom, 18 Munson Rd., #2, 06716. Tel: 203-879-3432. Email: dguerettedw@comcast.net.

[N] COUNSELING CENTERS

MERIDEN. *Franciscan Life Center*, 271 Finch Ave., 06451. Tel: 203-237-8084; Fax: 203-639-1333. Web: www.flcenter.org. Sr. Barbara Johnson, F.S.E., Exec. Dir.

Franciscan Life Center Network, Inc. Franciscan Sisters of the Eucharist 7; Total Assisted 3,000; Total Staff 20.

[O] ADOPTION SERVICES-HOME CARE

MERIDEN. *Franciscan Family Care Center* (1979) 267 Finch Ave., 06451. Tel: 203-238-1441; Fax: 203-686-0807. Email: ssuzanne@franciscanhc.org. Sr. Suzanne Gross, F.S.E., Admin. Franciscan Home Care & Contact. Tel: 203-237-8084; Fax: 203-639-1333.

Franciscan Family Care Center, Inc. (dba Franciscan Home Care and Hospice Care) Franciscan Sisters of the Eucharist 6; Total Assisted 650; Total Staff 91.

[P] RETREAT HOUSES-RENEWAL CENTERS

FARMINGTON. *Our Lady of Calvary Retreat Center*, 31 Colton St., 06032. Tel: 860-677-8519; Fax: 860-677-2873. Email: olcretreat@sbcglobal.net. Web: www.ourladyofcalvary.com. Conducted by the Sisters of the Cross and Passion for Religious and Lay Persons.

Staff: Sisters Ann Rodgers, C.P., Prog. Dir.; Pauline Semkow, R.S.M.; Theresina Scully, C.P., Admin. & Contact; Maria Descy, Retreat Team.

LITCHFIELD. *Wisdom House Retreat Center* (1949) 229 E. Litchfield Rd., 06759-3002. Tel: 860-567-3163; Fax: 860-567-3166. Email: rg@wisdomhouse.org. Web: www.wisdomhouse.org. Sisters Rosemarie Greco, D.W., Admin. & Contact; Jo-Ann Iannotti, O.P., Art & Spirituality Coord. A retreat center which presents programs in spirituality, education & the arts. Use of space is available for nonprofit organizations when their purpose corresponds to the Mission of Wisdom House. The Center is a sponsored ministry of the Daughters of Wisdom.

MADISON. *Mercy Center, Incorporated*, 167 Neck Rd., P.O. Box 191, 06443. Tel: 203-245-0401; Fax: 203-245-8718. Email: info@mercybythesea.org. Web: www.mercybythesea.org. Charles Frey, Exec. Dir. Sisters of Mercy-Northeast Community Sisters 3; Total in Residence 3; Total Staff 10.

WEST HARTFORD. *Holy Family Passionist Retreat Center*, 303 Tunxis Rd., 06107. Tel: 860-521-0440; Fax: 860-521-1929. Email: holyfamilyretreat@cpprov.org. Web: www.holyfamilyretreat.org. Revs. David Cinquegrani, C.P., Retreat Dir.; Terence J. Kristofak, C.P., Retreat Team; Gregory Paul, C.P., Retreat Team; John Baptist Pesce, C.P., Retreat Team; Sisters Eileen Dooling, R.S.M., Retreat Team; Elissa Rinere, C.P., Retreat Team; Liza Peters, M.Div., Dir. & Youth & Young Adult Ministry; Joan Kelly, D.Min., Retreat Team; Brandon Nappi, D.Min., Assoc. Dir.; Kasia Owczarek, Special Events & Conference Coord.; Alice Smith, M.A., Retreat Team; Bill Walsh, M.A., Retreat Team. For laymen and laywomen. Conducted by the Passionist Community Priests 3; Sisters 2; Lay Staff 4.

[Q] NEWMAN CENTERS

HARTFORD. *Capital Community College* 950 Main St., 06103. Tel: 860-906-5000. Web: www.ccc.commnet.edu. Deacon Arthur L. Miller, Chap.

University of Hartford Newman Center 200 Bloomfield Ave., 06117-1599. Tel: 860-768-4899. Email: uhacatholicmin@aol.com. Rev. Michael J. Dolan, Chap.

Trinity College Chapel 300 Summit St., 06106-3186. Tel: 860-297-2015. Email: campusministry5@aol.com. Web: www.trincoll-edu/orgs/newman-club. Rev. Michael J. Dolan, Chap.

HAMDEN. *Catholic Community at Quinnipiac University* 275 Mt. Carmel Ave., 06518-1908. Tel: 203-582-8257. Web: www.qubranches.org. Rev. Hugh Vincent Dyer, O.P., Chap. & Contact, Res.: St. Mary's Priory, 5 Hillhouse Ave., New Haven, 06505. Tel: 203-562-6193; Fax: 203-562-1273.

St. Mary's Priory, 5 Hillhouse Ave., New Haven, 06505. Tel: 203-562-6193; Fax: 203-562-1273.

NEW BRITAIN. *Central Connecticut State University Newman House* 145 Paul J. Manafort Dr., 06053-2552. Tel: 860-832-3795; Fax: 860-225-2315.

St. Francis of Assisi Friary 1755 Stanley St., 06053-2099. Tel: 860-225-6449; Fax: 860-225-2315.

NEW HAVEN. *Southern Connecticut State University Catholic Center* 129 Edwards St., 06511. Tel: 203-392-5331; 203-624-5297. Email: furlongj1@southernct.org. Deacon Patrick T. Moran, Campus Min.; James Furlong, Inter Faith Office.

Yale University-St. Thomas More Catholic Center and Chapel (1957) 268 Park St., 06511-4714. Tel: 203-777-5537; Fax: 203-777-0144. Email: morehouse@yale.edu. Web: www.yale.edu/stm. Revs. Robert L. Beloin, Ph.D., Chap. & Contact; Eddie DeLeon, Asst. Chap.; Kathleen Byrnes, Campus Minister.

[R] ORGANIZED CHARITIES

HARTFORD. *Catholic Charities, Inc. (Archdiocese of Hartford)* Administrative Office, 839-841 Asylum Ave., 06105. Web: www.ccaoh.org. Alyson Karpiej, Contact.

839-841 Asylum Ave., 06105. Tel: 860-493-1841; Fax: 860-548-1930. Lois M. Nesci, CEO.

Ansonia Office, 205 Wakelee Ave., Box 364, Ansonia, 06401. Tel: 203-735-7481; Fax: 203-735-5021.

Hartford Office, 896 Asylum Ave., 06105. Tel: 860-522-8241; Fax: 860-527-1919.

Meriden Office, 61 Colony St., Meriden, 06451. Tel: 203-235-2507; Fax: 203-639-6509.

Milford Office, 203 High St., Milford, 06460. Tel: 203-874-6270; Fax: 203-874-3301.

New Britain Office, 90 Franklin Sq., New Britain, 06051. Tel: 860-225-3561; Fax: 860-225-2558.

New Haven Office, 501 Lombard St., New Haven, 06513. Tel: 203-787-2207; Fax: 203-773-1331.

Torrington Office, 132 Grove St., Torrington, 06790. Tel: 860-482-5558; Fax: 860-489-2984.

Waterbury Office, 56 Church St., Waterbury, 06702. Tel: 203-755-1196; Fax: 203-575-9675.

13 Wolcott St., Waterbury, 06702. Tel: 203-596-9359; Fax: 203-757-9753.

Migration and Refugee Service, 125 Market St., 06103. Tel: 860-548-0059; Fax: 860-549-8697.

Institute for the Hispanic Family, 45 Wadsworth St., 06106. Tel: 860-527-1124; Fax: 860-724-2539.

St. Agnes Family Center, St. Agnes Home, 104 Mayflower St., West Hartford, 06110-1425. Tel: 860-521-7516; Fax: 860-521-6160. Email: info@stagneshome.org. Web: www.stagneshome-.org. Lorna Little, M.S.W., Exec. Dir. Residential Home for teen mothers and babies.

St. Francis Home for Children, Inc., 651 Prospect St., New Haven, 06511-2003. Tel: 203-777-5513; Fax: 203-777-0644. Paula Moody, Exec. Dir.

[S] SOCIAL SERVICE CENTERS FOR SPANISH-SPEAKING AND BLACK PEOPLE

BLOOMFIELD. *Office for Hispanic Evangelization*, 467 Bloomfield Ave., 06002-2999. Tel: 860-243-0940; Fax: 860-243-0649. Email: hispanic.off@hotmail.com. Rev. Jose A. Mercado, Dir.; Luz Yunes, Asst. to Dir. & Program Coord.; Deacon Ramon A. Rosado, Hispanic Youth Coord.; Consuelo Gomez, Office Sec.

WATERBURY. *Spanish-Speaking Center*, 13 Wolcott St., 06702-1790. Tel: 203-757-8737. Rev. Mark S. Suslenko, Contact Person. Total Assisted 350; Total Staff 1.

[T] SOCIETY OF ST. VINCENT DE PAUL

WATERBURY. **St. Vincent de Paul Mission of Waterbury, Inc.*, P.O. Box 1612, 06721. Tel: 203-754-0000; Fax: 203-756-0865. Email: st.vincent.depaul@snet.net. Deacon Paul P. Iadarola, Exec. Dir. & Contact Person.

[U] MISCELLANEOUS

HARTFORD. *Cathedral Green, Inc.*, 839-841 Asylum Ave., 06105. Tel: 860-728-2562. Rose Alma Senatore, Contact Person. Providing housing opportunities for low income and homeless persons, potentially homeless persons or elderly, disabled or otherwise disadvantaged persons.

**Connecticut Federation of Catholic School Parents, Inc.*, 134 Farmington Ave., 06105-3784. Tel: 860-541-6310. John L. Cattelan, Dir.

Hartford Educational Broadband, Inc., 134 Farmington Ave., 06105-3784. Tel: 860-541-6491; Fax: 860-541-6309. Matthew A. Byrne, CPA, M.B.A., Dir. Finance. Purpose: to provide broadband capacity to archdiocesan educational institutions, license the excess broadband capacity and provide funds generated for the support of the Archdiocesan educational mission.

**House of Bread, Inc.*, 1453 Main St., 06120-2726. Tel: 860-549-4188; Fax: 860-249-4656. Sisters Maureen Faenza, C.S.J., Co-Dir.; Theresa Fonti, C.S.J., Co-Dir.

**Jubilee House, Inc.*, 40 Clifford St., 06114. Tel: 860-247-3030; Fax: 860-548-9635. Sr. Susan Cunningham, C.S.J., Exec. Dir.

**Malta House of Care Foundation, Inc.*, 19 Woodland St., Ste. 37, 06105. Tel: 860-548-1593; Fax: 860-548-1593. Web: www.maltahouseofcare.org. Peter G. Kelly, Board Chm.; Jean-Pierre van Rooy, Hospitaller of Hartford of the Federal Assn. of the Order of Malta; Filomena Soyster, Board Pres.; Barbara "Bobbie" Bartucca, Dir. Philanthropy & Organizational Advancement.

Mercy Housing and Shelter Corporation, 211 Wethersfield Ave, 06114. Tel: 860-808-2040; Fax: 860-548-0692. Email: pmckeon@mercyhousingct.org. Web: www.mercyhousingct.org. Patricia McKeon, R.S.M., Pres. & Exec. Dir.; Stephen Abshire, Treas. & Dir. Finance; Henrietta Rand, Sec. & Exec. Asst. Homeless Services Total Assisted 9,700; Total Staff 106.

MLS Religious Trust, 915 Maple Ave., 06114-2330. Tel: 860-956-8870; Fax: 860-956-8849. Sr. Katherine Baker, C.S.J., Contact.

North American La Salette Mission Center, Inc. (1996) 915 Maple Ave., 06114-2330. Tel: 860-956-8870; Fax: 860-956-8849. Email: lsmc2@charter.net. Web: www.lsmc.org. Rev. Thomas Vellappallil, M.S., Exec. Dir. & Contact; Mrs. Connie Evans, Sec.

**Tabor House, Inc.*, 67 Brownell Ave., 06106. Tel: 860-244-3876; Fax: 860-525-2439. Sr. Anne Kane, C.S.J., Exec. Dir.

The Archdiocese of Hartford Investment Trust, 134 Farmington Ave., 06105-3784. Tel: 860-541-6491; Fax: 860-541-6309. Email: mab@aohct.org. Matthew A. Byrne, CPA, M.B.A., Dir. Fin. & Investment Officer.

The Benevolent Association for Priests of The Archdiocese of Hartford, Incorporated, 134 Farmington Ave., 06105-3784. Tel: 860-541-6491; Fax: 860-541-6309. Email: mab@aohct.org. Matthew A. Byrne, CPA, M.B.A., Dir. Finance.

CHESHIRE. *Horizons Institute, Inc.*, 475 Oak Ave., 06410. Tel: 203-271-0805; Fax: 203-271-3845. Rev. Jose Felix Ortega, L.C., Asst. Sec.

Logos, Inc., 475 Oak Ave., 06410. Tel: 203-271-0805; Fax: 203-271-3845. Email: sellis@legionaries.org. Rev. Jose Felix Ortega, L.C., Asst. Sec.

LUX ET VITA, INC., 475 Oak Ave., 06410. Tel: 203-271-0805; Fax: 203-271-3845. Rev. Jose Felix Ortega, L.C.

Racebrook, Inc., 475 Oak Ave., 06410. Tel: 203-271-0805; Fax: 203-271-3845. Rev. Jose Felix Ortega, L.C., Asst. Sec.

Rossotto, Inc. (1992) 475 Oak Ave., 06410. Tel: 203-271-0805; Fax: 203-271-3845. Rev. Jose Felix Ortega, L.C.

The Legion of Christ, Incorporated (1971) 475 Oak Ave., 06410. Tel: 203-271-0805; Fax: 203-271-3845. Rev. Jose Felix Ortega, L.C., Contact. Priests 4; Religious 4.

HAMDEN. *U.S. Apostolic Visitation Corporation*, P.O. Box 4328, 06514-9998. Tel: 203-287-5467. Web: www.apostolicvisitation.org. Sr. Mary Clare Millea, A.S.C.J., Pres.

BLOOMFIELD. *Foundation for the Advancement of Catholic Schools*, 467 Bloomfield Ave., 06002-2999. Tel: 860-761-7499; Fax: 860-242-8683. Cynthia Basil Howard, Exec. Dir.; Shirley Ziolkowski, F.A.C.S. Coord.

BRISTOL. *Magnificat-Mother of Divine Mercy Corporation, Bristol, CT*, 12 Pleasant St., 06010. Tel: 860-584-8803. Ms. Gloria Brophy, Pres. Purpose: to foster the work of intercession; to conduct prayer focused meetings and to serve the needy.

LITCHFIELD. *Lourdes Shrine Guild, Inc.* (1946) 83 Montfort Rd., P.O. Box 667, 06759. Tel: 860-567-1041; Fax: 860-567-9670. Email: lourdesshrinect@gmail.com. Revs. William Considine, S.M.M., Supr., Dir. & Contact Person; James Brady, S.M.M., Admin. Priests 3.

MERIDEN. *Franciscan Life Center Network, Incorporated*, 405 Allen Ave., 06451. Tel: 203-237-8084; Fax: 203-639-1333. Web: www.flcenter.org.

Franciscan Life Center, 271 Finch Ave., 06451. Tel: 203-237-8084; Fax: 203-639-1333. Sr. Barbara Johnson, F.S.E., Exec. Dir.

Franciscan Life Process Center, 11650 Downes St., Lowell, MI 49331. Tel: 616-897-7842; Fax: 616-897-7054. Sr. Colleen Ann Nagle, F.S.E., Dir.

Franciscan Montessori Earth School, 14750 S.E. Clinton St., Portland, OR 97236. Tel: 503-760-8220; Fax: 503-760-8333. Sr. Kathleen Ann Cieslak, F.S.E., Admin.

Franciscan Northwoods Computer Center, 5601 Lilac Hill Rd., Duluth, MN 55810. Tel: 218-624-5478; Fax: 218-624-4649.

Franciscan Family Life Center, 1745 Pocatello Creek Rd., Pocatello, ID 83201. Tel: 208-233-9383; Fax: 208-233-2707. Sr. Mary Paul Moller, F.S.E., Dir.

NEW BRITAIN. *Marian Heights, Incorporated*, 314 Osgood Ave., 06053. Tel: 860-225-9406. Web: www.crossfire.org. Sr. Mary Jennifer Carroll, D.M., Contact Person. Purpose: home is limited for low income elderly, adult day care, child day care, convent.

NEW HAVEN. *Apostle Immigrant Services, Corporation*, 81 Saltonstall Ave., 06513. Tel: 203-752-9068; Fax: 203-752-9136. Sr. Mary Ellen Burns, A.S.C.J., Dir. & Contact Person.

The Children's Foundation at St. Francis Home, Inc., 651 Prospect St., 06511. Tel: 203-777-5513; Fax: 203-777-0644. Email: psalerno1@aol.com. Mr. Peter T. Salerno, Exec. Dir.

NEW MILFORD. *Our Lady of the Lakes Corporation* (1990) 3 Old Town Park Rd., 06776-4212. Tel: 860-354-5239; Fax: 860-354-2968. Email: ololnm@

sbcglobal.net. Rev. Frederick M. Langlois, Pastor & Contact.

WATERBURY. *Francis Xavier Plaza, Inc.*, 605 Baldwin St., 06706-1501. Tel: 860-728-2562. Providing housing opportunities for low income and homeless persons, potentially homeless persons or elderly, disabled or otherwise disadvantaged persons.

WEST HARTFORD. **Intensive Education Academy, Inc.*, 840 N. Main St., 06117-2026. Tel: 860-236-2049; Fax: 860-231-2843. Jim O'Donnell, Dir. of Education.

Mercy Community Health, Inc., 2021 Albany Ave., 06117-2796. Tel: 860-570-8300; Fax: 860-233-8849. Web: www.mchct.org. William J. Fiocchetta, Pres. & CEO.

Mercy Community Home Care Services, Inc., 275 Steele Rd., 06117. Tel: 860-586-8318; Fax: 860-586-8418. Email: lstpierre.mchc@mchct.org. Web: www.mercycommunityhomecare.org. Linda St. Pierre, Admin.

Mercy Services, Inc., 2021 Albany Ave., 06117-2796. Tel: 860-570-8300; Fax: 860-233-8849. Web: www.mchct.org. William J. Fiocchetta, Pres. & CEO.

WINDSOR. *The Connecticut Province of the Sisters of Notre Dame de Namur, Inc.*, 468 Poquonock Ave., 06095-2473. Tel: 860-688-1832; Fax: 860-683-1741. Email: sndct@aol.com. Web: www.sndden.org. Sisters Ellen Agritelley, S.N.D., Contact Person & Leadership Team; Mary Rose Crowley, S.N.D., Leadership Team; Elizabeth McLaughlin, S.N.D., Leadership Team.

RELIGIOUS INSTITUTES OF MEN REPRESENTED IN THE ARCHDIOCESE

For further details refer to the corresponding bracketed number in the Religious Institutes of Men or Women section.

[0200]—*Benedictine Monks*—O.S.B.
[0600]—*Brothers of Holy Cross* (Notre Dame, IN)—C.S.C.
[1100]—*Brothers of the Sacred Heart*—S.C.
[0275]—*Carmelites of Mary Immaculate*—C.M.I.
[0610]—*Congregation of the Holy Cross*—C.S.C.
[1330]—*Congregation of the Mission (Vincentian Fathers)*—C.M.
[1000]—*Congregation of the Passion* (Prov. of St. Paul of the Cross)—C.P.
[0480]—*Conventual Franciscans* (St. Anthony of Padua Prov.)—O.F.M.Conv.
[]—*Franciscan Brothers of the Eucharist*—F.B.E.
[0520]—*Franciscan Friars* (Immaculate Conception, Holy Name Provs.)—O.F.M.
[0730]—*Legionaries of Christ*—L.C.
[0780]—*Marist Fathers*—S.M.
[0800]—*Maryknoll*—M.M.
[0720]—*The Missionaries of Our Lady of La Salette* (Prov. O.L. of Seven Dolors)—M.S.
[0590]—*Missionaries of the Holy Apostles*—M.S.A.
[0870]—*Montfort Missionaries*—S.M.M.
[0910]—*Oblates of Mary Immaculate*—O.M.I.
[093]—*Oblates of St. Joseph*—O.S.J.
[0430]—*Order of Preachers-Dominicans* (Eastern Prov.)—O.P.
[1190]—*Salesians of St. John Bosco*—S.D.B.
[1240]—*Servites (Order of Friar Servants of Mary)*—O.S.M.
[0760]—*Society of Mary (Marianists)*—S.M.
[]—*Sons of Charity*—S.C.

RELIGIOUS INSTITUTES OF WOMEN REPRESENTED IN THE ARCHDIOCESE

[0130]—*Apostles of the Sacred Heart of Jesus*—A.S.C.J.
[0180]—*Benedictine Nuns of the Primitive Observance*—O.S.B.
[2250]—*Congregation of Benedictines of Jesus Crucified*—O.S.B.
[1830]—*Contemplative Sisters of the Good Shepherd*—C.G.S.
[0860]—*Daughters of Mary of the Immaculate Conception*—D.M.
[0820]—*Daughters of the Holy Spirit*—D.H.S.
[0960]—*Daughters of Wisdom*—D.W.
[1050]—*Dominican Contemplative Nuns*—O.P.
[]—*Dominican Oblates of Jesus* (Madrid, Spain)—D.O-O.P.
[]—*Dominican Sisters (Congregation of St. Catherine of Siena)*—O.P.
[]—*Dominican Sisters of Fatima*—O.P.
[1070-15]—*Dominican Sisters of Hope*—O.P.
[1115]—*Dominican Sisters of Peace*—O.P.
[1170]—*Felician Sisters* (Our Lady of the Angels Province)—C.S.S.F.
[1250]—*Institutes of the Franciscan Sisters of the Eucharist*—F.S.E.
[2340]—*Little Sisters of the Poor*—L.S.P.
[2470]—*Maryknoll Sisters of St. Dominic*—M.M.
[2490]—*Medical Mission Sisters*—M.M.S.
[2790]—*Missionary Servants of the Most Blessed Trinity*—M.S.B.T.
[2519]—*Religious Sisters of Mercy of Alma* (MI)—R.S.M.
[3430]—*Religious Teachers Filippini*—M.P.F.
[2970]—*School Sisters of Notre Dame*—S.S.N.D.
[]—*Sisters Minor of the Mary Immaculate*—S.M.M.I.
[0520]—*Sisters of Charity of Our Lady, Mother of Mercy*—S.C.M.M.
[0530]—*Sisters of Charity of Our Lady, Mother of the Church*—S.C.M.C.
[0590]—*Sisters of Charity of Saint Elizabeth, Convent Station*—S.C.
[2575]—*Sisters of Mercy of the Americas* (Albany, Vermont, Detroit & Connecticut)—R.S.M.
[3000]—*Sisters of Notre Dame de Namur* (Connecticut, Boston, California & Base Community)—S.N.D.deN.
[1650]—*Sisters of St. Francis of Philadelphia*—O.S.F.
[3850]—*Sisters of St. Joseph of Chambery*—C.S.J.
[3930]—*Sisters of St. Joseph of the Third Order of St. Francis*—S.S.J.-T.O.S.F.
[2980]—*Sisters of the Congregation de Notre Dame*—C.N.D.
[3180]—*Sisters of the Cross and Passion*—C.P.
[]—*Sisters of the Sacred Heart of Jesus of Ragusa*—S.S.H.J.
[2170]—*Sisters, Servants of the Immaculate Heart of Mary*—I.H.M.
[]—*Society of the Sisters of the Church*—S.S.C.
[4060]—*Society of the Holy Child Jesus*—S.H.C.J.
[4130]—*Ursuline Sisters of The Congregation of Tildonk, Belgium*—O.S.U.

ARCHDIOCESAN CEMETERIES

HARTFORD. *Catholic Cemeteries Association of the Archdiocese of Hartford, Inc.*, 700 Middletown Ave., P.O. Box 517, North Haven, 06473-0517. Tel: 203-239-2557; Fax: 203-239-5035. Email: ccahart@aol.com. Web: cathcemhartford.com. Rev. Msgr. David M. Walker, Dir.
Holy Trinity
St. Patrick

ANSONIA. *St. Mary*
Old St. Mary

BLOOMFIELD. *Mount Saint Benedict*

DERBY. *Mount St. Peter*
Old St. Mary Cemetery

EAST HARTFORD. *St. Mary*

GLASTONBURY. *Holy Cross*

MANCHESTER. *St. Bridget*
St. James

MERIDEN. *St. Patrick*
Sacred Heart

NAUGATUCK. *St. Francis* (New Haven Region)
St. James

NEW BRITAIN. *St. Mary*
Old St. Mary

NEW HAVEN. *St. Bernard*

NORTH HAVEN. *All Saints*

TORRINGTON. *St. Francis*
Old St. Francis
St. Peter

WALLINGFORD. *Holy Trinity*
St. John

WATERBURY. *Calvary*
St. Joseph
Old St. Joseph

WATERTOWN. *Mount Olivet*

WEST HAVEN. *St. Lawrence*

NECROLOGY

† Johnson, Rev. Msgr. Charles B., (Retired)—Died Sept. 22, 2011
† Mullen, Rev. Msgr. William J., (Retired)—Died Feb. 2, 2011
† Bollea, Richard C., (Retired)—Died Nov. 19, 2011
† Brenza, William J., Plantsville, CT Mary Our Queen—Died Dec. 22, 2010
† Casey, John D., (Retired)—Died Oct. 20, 2011
† Clarkin, Herbert J., (Administrative Leave)—Died Dec. 29, 2010
† Farrell, Thomas F., (Retired)—Died Jan. 11, 2011
† LeClair, Lawrence J., (Retired)—Died Feb. 21, 2011
† McDonnell, Francis P., (Retired)—Died Nov. 30, 2011
† Proulx, Raymond G.—Died May 2, 2011
† Shaw, Charles E., (Retired)—Died Nov. 18, 2011
† Stack, John J., (Retired)—Died Feb. 3, 2011
† Thuer, William J., (Retired)—Died April 21, 2011

An asterisk (*) denotes an organization that has established tax-exempt status directly with the IRS and is not covered by the USCCB Group Ruling.

Diocese of Helena

(Dioecesis Helenensis)

Most Reverend

GEORGE LEO THOMAS, D.D., PH.D.

Bishop of Helena; ordained May 22, 1976; appointed Auxiliary Bishop of Seattle November 19, 1999; appointed Bishop of Helena March 23, 2004; installed June 4, 2004.

Chancery: 515 N. Ewing, P.O. Box 1729, Helena, MT 59624-1729. Tel: 406-442-5820; Fax: 406-442-5191.

Web: www.diocesehelena.org

Email: chancery@diocesehelena.org

ERECTED MARCH 7, 1884.

Square Miles 51,922.

Comprises the western part of the State of Montana, and is made up of the following Counties: Lewis and Clark, Glacier, Pondera, Flathead, Lake, Lincoln, Missoula, Mineral, Sanders, Powell, Granite, Ravalli, Deer Lodge, Silver Bow, Jefferson, Broadwater, Gallatin, Madison, Beaverhead, Meagher, Wheatland and parts of Teton and Toole.

Diocesan Legal Title--Roman Catholic Bishop of Helena, Montana, a Corporation Sole.

For legal titles of parishes and diocesan institutions, consult the Chancery Office.

STATISTICAL OVERVIEW

Personnel	
Retired Archbishops	1
Bishop	1
Priests: Diocesan Active in Diocese	41
Priests: Diocesan Active Outside Diocese	5
Priests: Diocesan in Foreign Missions	1
Priests: Retired, Sick or Absent	25
Number of Diocesan Priests	72
Religious Priests in Diocese	6
Total Priests in Diocese	78
Extern Priests in Diocese	4
Ordinations:	
Diocesan Priests	1
Permanent Deacons in Diocese	26
Total Brothers	2
Total Sisters	31
Parishes	
Parishes	57
With Resident Pastor:	
Resident Diocesan Priests	35
Resident Religious Priests	4
Without Resident Pastor:	
Administered by Priests	11
Administered by Deacons	2
Administered by Religious Women	3
Administered by Lay People	2
Missions	39
Pastoral Centers	14
Professional Ministry Personnel:	
Brothers	2
Sisters	17
Welfare	
Catholic Hospitals	2
Total Assisted	275,685
Day Care Centers	3
Total Assisted	97
Educational	
Seminaries, Diocesan	1
Diocesan Students in Other Seminaries	12
Total Seminarians	12
Colleges and Universities	1
Total Students	1,428
High Schools, Diocesan and Parish	2
Total Students	300
Elementary Schools, Diocesan and Parish	4
Total Students	814
Catechesis/Religious Education:	
High School Students	1,121
Elementary Students	3,184
Total Students under Catholic Instruction	6,859
Teachers in the Diocese:	
Brothers	2
Sisters	1
Lay Teachers	151
Vital Statistics	
Receptions into the Church:	
Infant Baptism Totals	457
Minor Baptism Totals	160
Received into Full Communion	69
First Communions	652
Confirmations	634
Marriages:	
Catholic	92
Interfaith	41
Total Marriages	133
Deaths	722
Total Catholic Population	45,278
Total Population	579,983

Former Bishops—Rt. Revs. JOHN B. BRONDEL, cons. Bishop of Victoria, V.I., Dec. 14, 1879; appt. Vicar Apostolic of Montana, April 17, 1883; Bishop of Helena, March 7, 1884; died Nov. 3, 1903; JOHN P. CARROLL, D.D., cons. Bishop of Helena, Dec. 21, 1904; died Nov. 4, 1925; Most Revs. GEORGE J. FINNIGAN, C.S.C., D.D., cons. Bishop of Helena, Aug. 1, 1927; died Aug. 14, 1932; RALPH L. HAYES, D.D., cons. Bishop of Helena, Sept. 21, 1933; transferred to Rectorship North American College, Rome, Italy, Sept. 11, 1935; transferred to Titular See of Hierapolis, Oct. 26, 1935; transferred to Davenport, Nov. 16, 1944; appt. Assistant at the Pontifical Throne, April 30, 1958; transferred to Titular See of Naraggara and retired, Oct. 20, 1966; died July 4, 1970; JOSEPH M. GILMORE, S.T.D., cons. Bishop of Helena, Feb. 19, 1936; died April 2, 1962; RAYMOND G. HUNTHAUSEN, ord. June 1, 1946; appt. July 8, 1962; cons. Bishop of Helena, Aug. 30, 1962; transferred to Archdiocese of Seattle, Feb. 25, 1975; installed Archbishop of Seattle, May 22, 1975; retired Aug. 21, 1991; ELDEN F. CURTISS, D.D., ord. May 24, 1958; appt. March 4, 1976; cons. Bishop of Helena, April 28, 1976; transferred to Archdiocese of Omaha, May 4, 1993; installed Archbishop of Omaha, June 25, 1993; ALEXANDER J. BRUNETT, Ph.D., ord. July 13, 1958; appt. April 19, 1994; cons. Bishop of Helena, July 6, 1994; transferred to Archdiocese of Seattle Oct. 28, 1997; installed Archbishop of Seattle Dec. 18, 1997; ROBERT C. MORLINO, ord. June 1, 1974; cons. Bishop of Helena Sept. 21, 1999; transferred to Diocese of Madison May 23, 2003; installed Bishop of Madison Aug. 1, 2003.

Vicar General—Rev. Msgr. KEVIN S. O'NEILL, V.G. Email: koneill@diocesehelena.org.

Episcopal Vicar for Clergy—Rev. GARY W. RELLER, Mailing Address: 217 Tremont St., Missoula, 59801. Tel: 406-543-3129. Email: greller@diocesehelena.org.

Director for Ministry to Priests—Rev. THOMAS P. HAFFEY, 2100 Farragut, Butte, 59701. Tel: 406-723-4303. Email: thaffey@diocesehelena.org.

Episcopal Vicar for Senior Status Priests—Rev. Msgr. JOSEPH D. HARRINGTON (Retired), Carroll College, 1601 N. Benton Ave., Helena, 59625. Tel: 406-447-4459.

Episcopal Vicar for Canonical Services—Rev. JOHN W. ROBERTSON, Mailing Address: P.O. Box 1729, Helena, 59624. Tel: 406-442-5820; Fax: 406-442-1085. Email: jrobertson@diocesehelena.org.

Chancery Services—515 N. Ewing St., P.O. Box 1729, Helena, 59624. Tel: 406-442-5820; Fax: 406-442-5191. Email: chancery@diocesehelena.org. Web: www.diocesehelena.org.

Director—Sr. RITA MCGINNIS, S.C.L.

Chancellor—Rev. JOHN W. ROBERTSON.

Pastoral and Renewal Services—MARK FREI.

Pastoral Planning Services—Sr. RITA MCGINNIS, S.C.L.

Archivist—Sr. DOLORES BRINKEL, S.C.L.

Financial Services—PETER MCNAMEE, Diocesan Financial Svcs. Officer, 515 N. Ewing St., P.O. Box 1729, Helena, 59624. Tel: 406-442-5820; Fax: 406-442-5191.

Development and Stewardship Services—GLENDA SEIPP, Dir. Stewardship & Annual Giving, Mailing Address: P.O. Box 1729, Helena, 59624. Tel: 406-442-5820; Fax: 406-442-5191.

Foundation for the Diocese of Helena, Inc.—JIM KANEY, Pres.; BETH YEAKEL, Exec. Dir., Mailing Address: P.O. Box 1729, Helena, 59624. Tel: 406-442-5820; Fax: 406-442-5191.

Diocesan Tribunal—Rev. JOHN W. ROBERTSON, Mailing Address: P.O. Box 1729, Helena, 59624. Tel: 406-442-5820; Fax: 406-442-1085.

Judicial Vicar—Rev. JOHN W. ROBERTSON.

Associate Judges—Revs. THOMAS P. HAFFEY; MATTHEW P. HUBER; PATRICK C. MCGURK (Retired).

Promoter of Justice—Rev. ROBERT GROSCH, J.C.L.

Defenders of the Bond—Revs. JEFFREY M. FLEMING; ROBERT C. NOONAN (Retired); GARY W. RELLER.

Notaries—PEGGY PETRINO; MARY MICHAEL SZADERA; VICKI LAFOND-SMITH.

Diocesan Consultors—Rev. Msgr. KEVIN S. O'NEILL, V.G.; Revs. JOHN DARRAGH; MICHAEL DRURY; EDWARD HISLOP; THOMAS P. HAFFEY; ROBERT HALL; LEO J. PROXELL; MARC J. LENNEMAN; THOMAS M. O'DONNELL.

Presbyteral Council—Rev. Msgr. KEVIN S. O'NEILL, V.G.; Revs. JAMES CONNOR; JOHN DARRAGH; MICHAEL DRURY; ROBERT HALL; MARC J. LENNEMAN; THOMAS P. HAFFEY; EDWARD HISLOP; THOMAS M. O'DONNELL; LEO J. PROXELL; ANDREW MADDOCK, S.J.; DANIEL B. SHEA.

Diocesan Finance Council—PETER MCNAMEE; SUSAN BJERKE; MARK CROSS; CHUCK TURNER; LORI MURPHY-MOULLET; Rev. Msgrs. KEVIN S. O'NEILL, V.G.; JOSEPH D. HARRINGTON (Retired); MAUREEN STOHL, Chair; CARMAE FAWAZ; DENNIS LOVELESS; Rev. JOHN W. ROBERTSON; SHERI BROUDY; Sr. RITA MCGINNIS, S.C.L.

Deaneries—Rev. EDWARD KOHLER, Conrad; Rev. Msgr. KEVIN S. O'NEILL, V.G., Helena; Revs. EDWARD HISLOP, Missoula; JOHN P. MILLER, Kalispell; THOMAS P. HAFFEY, Butte; LEO J. PROXELL, Bozeman.

Personnel Board—Rev. Msgr. KEVIN S. O'NEILL, V.G.; Revs. GARY W. RELLER; JAMES CONNOR; JEFFREY

M. FLEMING; BART TOLLESON; VALENTINE D. ZDILLA; MARC J. LENNEMAN; THOMAS P. HAFFEY.

Interdiocesan Organizations

Montana Catholic Conference—Mailing Address: 1313 11th Ave., P.O. Box 1708, Helena, 59624. Tel: 406-442-5761; Fax: 406-442-9047. Email: director@montanacc.org. Web: www.montanacc.org. MOE WOSEPKA, Exec. Dir.; SUZANNE JOHNSON, Exec. Asst.; JAMES ZIEGLER, Bd. Pres.

Catholic Social Services for Montana, Inc.—ROSEMARY MILLER, Exec. Dir., 1301 11th Ave., P.O. Box 907, Helena, 59624. Tel: 406-442-4130; Fax: 406-442-4192. Email: rosemary@cssmt.org. Web: www.cssmt.org. Coordinates and supervises all Catholic Social welfare in the State of Montana; Dr. CRAIG EDDY, Bd. Pres.

Helena Office—ROSEMARY MILLER, Dir., Adoptions; HELEN BEAUSOLEIL, Social Worker; LESLIE MARTIN, Social Worker; SHIRLEY COLE, Prog. Asst., Mailing Address: P.O. Box 907, Helena, 59624. Tel: 406-442-4130; SUSAN GLIKO, Rachel's Hope Prog. Coord.

Billings Office—1048 N. 30th St., Billings, 59101. Tel: 406-252-3399. Social Workers: BECKY HUBBERT, (Billings); LINDA CLADIS, (Billings); SAM HUBBERT, (Columbus).

Great Falls Office—KYLA WRIGHT, Social Workers, 410 Central Ave., #601, Great Falls, 59401. Tel: 406-771-7805.

Missoula Office—BETSY ROBEL, Social Worker, 420 W. Pine St., Missoula, 59802. Tel: 406-728-5429.

Montana Association of Churches—Rev. PETER SHOBER, 25 S. Ewing St., Ste. 408, Helena, 59601. Tel: 406-449-6010; Fax: 406-449-6657; JOHN FENCIK, Diocesan Ecumenical Officer, Mailing Address: Diocese of Helena, P.O. Box 1729, Helena, 59624. Tel: 406-442-5820. Email: jfencik@diocesehelena.org.

Diocesan Offices and Organizations

Borromeo Pre-Seminary Program—Rev. MARC J. LENNEMAN, Carroll College, 1601 N. Benton Ave., Helena, 59625. Tel: 406-447-4869.

Catholic Campaign for Human Development—MARK FREI, Mailing Address: Diocese of Helena, P.O. Box 1729, Helena, 59624. Tel: 406-442-5820.

Catholic Committee on Scouting—MIKE MORGAN, Mailing Address: 23 Laurin Loop, Sheridan, 59749. Tel: 406-842-5085.

Catholic Youth Coalition—DOUG TOOKE, Contact, Mailing Address: P.O. Box 1729, Helena, 59624. Tel: 406-442-5820.

Charismatic Renewal—MARK FREI, Mailing Address: Diocesan Pastoral Office, P.O. Box 1729, Helena, 59624. Tel: 406-442-5820.

Christian Family Movement—MARK FREI, Contact, Diocesan Pastoral Office, P.O. Box 1729, Helena, 59624.

Continuing Formation of the Clergy—Rev. THOMAS P. HAFFEY, Dir., 2100 Farragut, Butte, 59701. Tel: 406-723-4303.

Assembly of Women Religious—Sr. RITA MCGINNIS, S.C.L., Delegate for Rel., Mailing Address: P.O. Box 1729, Helena, 59624. Tel: 406-442-5820.

Cursillo Movement, Journey and Search—MARK FREI, Mailing Address: Diocesan Pastoral Office, P.O. Box 1729, Helena, 59624. Tel: 406-442-5820.

Daughters of Isabella—ANTOINETTE ALEXANDER, Regent, Mailing Address: P.O. Box 603, Bonner, 59823. Tel: 406-258-5378.

Diocesan Attorney—WILLIAM DRISCOLL, Mailing Address: Franz & Driscoll, P.L.L.P., P.O. Box 1155, Helena, 59624. Tel: 406-442-0005.

Diocesan Buildings—Mr. SCOTT FITZPATRICK, Mgr., Mailing Address: P.O. Box 1729, Helena, 59624.

Diocesan Council of Catholic Women—KITT ADAMS, Pres., Mailing Address: P.O. Box 130, Dayton, 59914. Tel: 406-849-5613.

Diocesan Ecumenical Officer—JOHN FENCIK, Diocese of Helena, P.O. Box 1729, Helena, 59624-1729. Tel: 406-442-5820. Email: jfencik@diocesehelena.org.

Friends of The Catholic University—Rev. Msgr. JOSEPH D. HARRINGTON, Chm. (Retired), Carroll College, 1601 N. Benton Ave., Helena, 59625. Tel: 406-447-4459.

Guatemala Missions—MARK FREI, Mailing Address: P.O. Box 1729, Helena, 59624. Tel: 406-442-5820.

Holy Childhood Association—VACANT.

Legendary Lodge (Diocesan Summer Camp)—JOHN FENCIK, Mailing Address: P.O. Box 1729, Helena, 59624. Tel: 406-442-5820.

Marriage Encounter—BILL OLSEN; LYNNE OLSEN, 9825 Cougar Dr., Bozeman, 59718.

Office of Due Process—Rev. JOHN W. ROBERTSON, Mailing Address: P.O. Box 1729, Helena, 59624. Tel: 406-442-5820.

Permanent Deacons—Rev. JOHN W. ROBERTSON, Dir., Mailing Address: P.O. Box 1729, Helena, 59624. Tel: 406-442-5820.

Program of Formation for Lay Ministry—JOHN FENCIK, Mailing Address: P.O. Box 1729, Helena, 59624. Tel: 406-442-5820.

Program of Formation for the Permanent Diaconate—Rev. JOHN W. ROBERTSON, Mailing Address: P.O. Box 1729, Helena, 59624. Tel: 406-442-5820.

Liturgical Commission—Rev. EDWARD HISLOP, Chm., 1475 Eaton St., Missoula, 59801. Tel: 406-721-2405. Members: JOSEPH BEAUSOLEIL; Deacon JAMES BUTTS; DALE FLECK; Rev. JEFFREY M. FLEMING; Sr. MARY AGNES HOGAN, S.C.L.; LORRAINE TUCKER; KATHY WALTER; Sr. MARY JO QUINN, S.C.L.; VICKI BURGMEIER; Rev. VALENTINE D. ZDILLA. Consultant: Rev. MICHAEL DRISCOLL.

Propagation of the Faith—Rev. JOHN ROBERTSON, Diocesan Dir., Mailing Address: Diocese of Helena, P.O. Box 1729, Helena, 59624-1729. Tel: 406-442-5820.

Christian Formation Department—JOHN FENCIK, Dir., 515 N. Ewing St., P.O. Box 1729, Helena, 59624. Tel: 406-442-5820.

Resource Center—KATHY WARD, Mgr., 515 N. Ewing St., P.O. Box 1729, Helena, 59624. Tel: 406-442-5820.

Superintendent of Schools—PATRICK HAGGARTY, Ed.D., Supt., 515 N. Ewing St., P.O. Box 4851, Missoula, 59806. Tel: 406-594-1461; Fax: 406-442-5191.

Third Order of St. Francis—TONY POELMAN, 1702 Peosta, Helena, 59601.

Victim Assistance Coordinator—HELEN BEAUSOLEIL. Tel: 406-459-0513. Mailing Address: P.O. Box 1729, Helena, 59624. Tel: 406-442-5820, Ext. 77. Email: victimassistant@diocesehelena.org.

Vocations Office—Mailing Address: P.O. Box 1729, Helena, 59624. Tel: 406-442-5820. Rev. MARC J. LENNEMAN, Mailing Address: 1601 N. Benton Ave., Helena, 59625. Tel: 406-447-4869.

"The Montana Catholic" (Diocesan Newspaper)—RENEE ST. MARTIN-WIZEMAN, Editor; SUSAN GALLAGHER, Staff Writer & Copy Editor; ERIC CONNOLLY, Multimedia Specialist, 515 N. Ewing St., P.O. Box 1729, Helena, 59624. Tel: 406-442-5820; Fax: 406-442-5191.

CLERGY, PARISHES, MISSIONS AND PAROCHIAL SCHOOLS

CITY OF HELENA

(LEWIS AND CLARK COUNTY)

1—CATHEDRAL OF ST. HELENA (1866) Rev. Msgr. Kevin S. O'Neill; Rev. David Severson, Parochial Vicar; Michael Vreeberg, Pastoral Assoc.; Valarie Krause, Pastoral Assoc.
Office: 530 N. Ewing St., 59601. Tel: 406-442-5825; Fax: 406-449-5113. Email: koneill@sthelenas.org.
Catechesis/Religious Program—Bob Fishman, D.R.E.; Joannie Volesky, Parish Youth Min. & Parish Junior High Coord. Students 260.
Good Samaritan Thrift Store—3067 N. Montana Ave., 59601. Tel: 406-442-0780. Theresa Ortega, Dir. (Assistance to those in need.)
Mission—St. Theodore Avon, Powell Co. 59713.

2—ST. MARY (1910) Rev. Richard Francesco.
Office: 1700 Missoula Ave., 59601. Tel: 406-442-5268; Fax: 406-449-0860. Email: smcc@stmaryhelena.org.
Catechesis/Religious Program—Deb Kralicek, D.R.E. Students 66.

3—OUR LADY OF THE VALLEY Rev. Daniel B. Shea; Deacon Randy Fraser; David Casey, Youth Min.
Office: 1502 Shirley Rd., 59602. Tel: 406-458-6114; Fax: 406-458-8179. Email: olv@mt.net.
Catechesis/Religious Program—Students 148.
Mission—Sacred Heart Wolf Creek, Lewis and Clark Co.

OUTSIDE THE CITY OF HELENA

ANACONDA, DEER LODGE CO.

1—ANACONDA CATHOLIC COMMUNITY (1980), Serves the entire community of Anaconda. Rev. Timothy J. Moriarty.
Office:—217 W. Pennsylvania, 59711. Tel: 406-563-8406; Fax: 406-563-5912. Email: anacondacatholic@qwestoffice.net.
Holy Family: 217 W. Pennsylvania, 59711.
St. Peter: 405 Alder St., 59711.
Catechesis/Religious Program—Students 125.
Station—Georgetown Lake

2—ST. JOSEPH'S (1957) Closed. 1977. For inquiries for parish records contact Anaconda Catholic Community, Anaconda.

3—ST. PAUL'S (1888) Closed. 1980. For inquiries for parish records contact Anaconda Catholic Community, Anaconda.

4—ST. PETER'S (1898) Closed. 1980. For inquiries for parish records contact Anaconda Catholic Community, Anaconda.

BIGFORK, FLATHEAD CO., POPE JOHN PAUL II (1958) Rev. Msgr. Donald Shea; Deacons James Butts, Pastoral Assoc.; Anthony Martin.
Mailing Address: P.O. Box 277, 59911. Email: johnpaul2@centurytel.net.
Church & Office: 195 Coverdell Rd., 59911.
Catechesis/Religious Program—Deacon James Butts, D.R.E.; Jean Tegoli, Parish Youth & Elementary Coord. Students 65.

BONNER, MISSOULA CO., ST. ANN (1940) Rev. Michael P. Poole.
Res.: P.O. Box 1008, 59823. Tel: 406-258-6815; Fax: 406-258-2943. Email: mpoole@diocesehelena.org.
Catechesis/Religious Program—Students 12.
Mission—Living Water 152 S.O.S. Rd., Seeley Lake, Missoula Co. 59868.

BOULDER, JEFFERSON CO., ST. CATHERINE (1894) Rev. William Greytak.
Res.: 214 S. Elder St., P.O. Box 205, 59632. Tel: 406-225-3222; Fax: 406-225-9152.
Catechesis/Religious Program—Students 32.
Mission—St. John the Evangelist Boulder Valley, Jefferson Co.

BOZEMAN, GALLATIN CO.

1—HOLY ROSARY (1885) Rev. Leo J. Proxell.
Office: 220 W. Main St., P.O. Box 96, 59771-0096. Tel: 406-587-4581; Fax: 406-582-0248. Email: hrp@bridgeband.com.
Catechesis/Religious Program—Laura Kuntz, Parish Elementary Coord.; Kelly Ruby, Parish Youth Ministry Coord. Students 166.

2—RESURRECTION (1965), (Newman Parish) Rev. Valentine D. Zdilla; Diane Dwyer, Admin.
Office:—1725 S. 11th Ave., 59715. Tel: 406-586-9243; Fax: 406-586-2886. Email: resparadmin@bresnan.net.
Catechesis/Religious Program—Students 99.

BROWNING, GLACIER CO., CHURCH OF THE LITTLE FLOWER (1904) Rev. Edward Kohler; Deacons John Gobert; Ronald Running Crane.
Office: P.O. Box 529, 59417. Tel: 406-338-5775; Fax: 406-338-5506. Email: lfp@3rivers.net.
Church: 204 First St. N.W., 59417.
School—De La Salle Blackfeet Middle School, (Grades 4-8), P.O. Box 1489, 59417. Tel: 406-338-5290. Bro. Paul Ackerman, F.S.C., Pres.; Mr. Neal Wedum, Prin.
Catechesis/Religious Program—Toni Running Fisher, D.R.E. Students 100.
Mission—St. Mary, Queen of the World Babb, Glacier Co.
Mission—Sacred Heart Starr School.
Mission—Chapel of the Ascension East Glacier, Glacier Co.

BUTTE, SILVER BOW CO.

1—ST. ANN (1917) Rev. Thomas P. Haffey; Sr. Mary Jo McDonald, S.C.L., Pastoral Admin.
Res.: 2100 Farragut Ave., 59701. Tel: 406-723-4303; Fax: 406-723-5172. Email: stannparish@bresnan.net.
Catechesis/Religious Program—Rosie Stimatz-Richards, D.R.E. Students 221.

2—BUTTE CATHOLIC COMMUNITY NORTH, Includes Immaculate Conception, St. Joseph, and St. Patrick Parishes. See individual listings. Rev. Robert Hall.
Office & Res.: 102 S. Washington St., 59701. Tel: 406-723-5407; Fax: 406-723-5408. Email: bccn@diocesehelena.org.
Catechesis/Religious Program—Seaneen Prendergast, D.R.E. Students 46.

3—ST. HELENA (1921) Closed. 1966. For inquiries for parish records contact Butte Catholic Community North, Butte.

4—HOLY SAVIOR (1904) Closed. Closed in 1974. For inquiries for parish records contact Butte Catholic Community North, Butte.

5—HOLY SPIRIT (1978) Revs. William Dornbos; Thomas P. Haffey, Sacramental Min.; Deacon Dan McGrath, Pastoral Admin.
Office: 3930 E. Lake St., 59701. Tel: 406-494-5078; Fax: 406-494-5726. Email: holyspiritbutte@q.com.
Catechesis/Religious Program—Students 57.

6—IMMACULATE CONCEPTION (1907), (Butte Catholic Community North) Rev. Robert Hall.
Office & Res.: 102 S. Washington, 59701. Tel: 406-723-5407; Fax: 406-723-5408.
Church: Western & Caledonia St., 59701.

7—ST. JOHN THE EVANGELIST (1917) Revs. Thomas P. Haffey, Pastoral Admin.; Frank Wright, S.M.A., Sacramental Min.
Office: 1500 Cobban St., 59701. Tel: 406-782-8349. Email: stjohnparish@bresnan.net.
Church: 1500 Majors Ave., 59701.
Catechesis/Religious Program—Kathy Walter, D.R.E.

8—ST. JOSEPH (1905), (Butte Catholic Community North) Rev. Robert Hall.
Office & Res.: 102 S. Washington, 59701. Tel:

406-723-5407 (Office); Fax: 406-723-5408.
Church: Utah & Second St., 59701.
Catechesis/Religious Program—Seaneen Prendergast, D.R.E. Students 24.

9—ST. MARY (1903) Closed. 1986. For inquiries for parish records contact Butte Catholic Community North, Butte.

10—ST. PATRICK (1881), (Butte Catholic Community North) Rev. Robert Hall.
Mailing Address: 102 S. Washington St., 59701.
Church: 329 W. Mercury, 59701. Tel: 406-723-5407; Fax: 406-723-5408.

11—SACRED HEART PARISH (1903) Closed. 1970. For inquiries for parish records contact Butte Catholic Community North, Butte.

CHOTEAU, TETON CO., ST. JOSEPH (1898) Rev. Dougald McCallum.
Res.: P.O. Box 640, 59422. Tel: 406-466-2961; Fax: 406-466-5157.
Church: 320 Main St., 59422.
Catechesis/Religious Program—Lisa Stott, D.R.E. Students 46.

COLUMBIA FALLS, FLATHEAD CO., ST. RICHARD (1941) Rev. John P. Miller; Deacon Robert Pearce; Floyd McCubbins, Pastoral Assoc.; Doug Cordier, Pastoral Assoc.
Mailing Address: P.O. Box 2073, 59912. Church: 1210 9th St. W., 59912. Tel: 406-892-5142; Fax: 406-892-2147. Email: strichards@bresnan.net.
Catechesis/Religious Program—Students 46.
Mission— West Glacier, Flathead Co.
Station—Apgar

CONRAD, PONDERA CO., ST. MICHAEL (1909) Rev. Stanislaw Rog, Pastoral Admin.
Res.: 106 S. Maryland St., 59425. Tel: 406-278-7517; Fax: 406-278-9106. Email: stmike@3rivers.net.
Catechesis/Religious Program—Kathy Hauer, D.R.E. Students 66.

CUT BANK, GLACIER CO., ST. MARGARET (1914) Rev. Michael Drury.
Res.: 129 Second Ave., S.E., P.O. Box 207, 59427. Tel: 406-873-4413; Fax: 406-873-5002. Email: stmarg207@gmail.com.
Catechesis/Religious Program—Juanita Meeks, D.R.E. Students 56.

DEER LODGE, POWELL CO., IMMACULATE CONCEPTION (1911) Rev. Robert G. Porter; Chris Dubay, Pastoral Assoc.
Res.: 605 Clark St., P.O. Box 786, 59722. Tel: 406-846-1444; Fax: 406-846-1999. Email: icchurch_2@msn.com.
Catechesis/Religious Program—Joan Sewell, Parish Youth Min. Coord. Students 27.

DILLON, BEAVERHEAD CO., ST. ROSE OF LIMA (1901) Rev. Herbert J. Pins.
Office: 226 S. Atlantic St., 59725. Tel: 406-683-4391; Fax: 406-683-6244. Email: strosedillon@gmail.com.
Catechesis/Religious Program—Michael Thornton, D.R.E.; Vicki Thornton, Parish Youth Min. Coord. Students 20.
Mission—St. John The Apostle Melrose, Silver Bow Co.
Mission—Our Lady of Wisdom Wisdom, Beaverhead Co.
Station— Lima, Beaverhead Co.

DRUMMOND, GRANITE CO., ST. MICHAEL (1919) Vicki Burgmeier, Parish Admin.
Res.: P.O. Box 329, 59832. Tel: 406-288-3463. Email: vburgmeier@blackfoot.net.
Catechesis/Religious Program—Students 11.
Mission—St. Mary Goldcreek, Powell Co.

DUTTON, TETON CO., ST. WILLIAM (1962) Rev. Stanislaw Rog, Pastoral Admin.; Frank Loch, Pastoral Assoc.; Marie Loch, Pastoral Assoc.
Church: 20 1st Ave., N.E., P.O. Box 18, 59433. Tel: 406-476-3327.
Catechesis/Religious Program—Students 7.
Mission—Guardian Angel Power, Teton Co.

EAST HELENA, LEWIS AND CLARK CO., SS. CYRIL AND METHODIUS (1907) Rev. Thomas M. O'Donnell; Deacon Robert J. Miller.
Res.: 120 W. Riggs St., P.O. Box 1110, 59635. Tel: 406-227-5334; Fax: 406-227-5891. Email: denice@sscyril.org.
Catechesis/Religious Program—Marie Moran, D.R.E.; Rachael Schwaller, Parish Youth Min. Coord. Students 238.
Mission—Our Lady of the Lake Canyon Ferry, Lewis and Clark Co.
Mission—St. John's Clancy, Jefferson Co.

EUREKA, LINCOLN CO., OUR LADY OF MERCY (1916) Rev. Gregory Lively.
Res.: 500 Dewey Ave., P.O. Box 626, 59917. Tel: 406-297-2118; Fax: 406-297-5247. Email: olm@interbel.net.
Catechesis/Religious Program—Students 21.

FAIRFIELD, TETON CO., ST. JOHN THE EVANGELIST (1941) Rev. Dougald McCallum.
Res.: 519 First Ave. S., P.O. Box 397, 59436. Tel: 406-466-2961; Fax: 406-466-5157.
Catechesis/Religious Program—Susan Kalanick, D.R.E. Students 31.
Mission—St. Matthias Augusta, Lewis and Clark Co.

FRENCHTOWN, MISSOULA CO., ST. JOHN THE BAPTIST (1884) [CEM] Rev. William Barton Tolleson.
Mailing Address: P.O. Box 329, 59834.
Res.: 16680 Main St., P.O. Box 329, 59834. Tel: 406-626-4492; Fax: 406-626-1970. Email: stjohnthebaptist@hotmail.com.
Catechesis/Religious Program—Jodi Todd, D.R.E. Students 25.
Mission—St. Mary Queen of Heaven Superior, Mineral Co.
Mission—St. Albert the Great Alberton, Mineral Co.

HAMILTON, RAVALLI CO., ST. FRANCIS (1896) Rev. John J. Darragh; Sr. Margaret Hogan, S.C.L., Pastoral Assoc.
Mailing Address: P.O. Box 593, 59840.
Res.: 411 S. 5th St., 59840. Tel: 406-363-1385; Fax: 406-363-1451. Email: francis@montana.com.
Catechesis/Religious Program—Sara Morin, D.R.E. Students 107.
Mission—St. Philip Benizi 312 Miles Ave., Darby, Ravalli Co. 59829.

HARLOWTON, WHEATLAND CO., ST. JOSEPH (1909) Rev. Richard Kluk.
Res.: 26 Third St., N.W., Box 286, 59036. Tel: 406-632-5538. Email: jbenusa@diocesehelena.org.
Catechesis/Religious Program—Kristi Lane, D.R.E. Students 6.
Mission—Immaculate Conception Judith Gap, Wheatland Co.
Mission—Blessed Sacrament Shawmut, Wheatland Co.

HEART BUTTE, GLACIER CO., ST. ANNE (BLACKFEET RESERVATION) (1911) Rev. Daniel Powers, S.J.; Bev Bullshoe, Pastoral Assoc.; Deacon Melvin Rutherford, Pastoral Assoc.
Mailing Address: P.O. Box 160, 59448. Tel: 406-338-2312; Fax: 406-338-2362. Email: dpowers@3rivers.net.
Mission—Holy Family Mission [CEM], Glacier Co.

HELMVILLE, POWELL CO., ST. THOMAS (1889) [CEM] Rev. John W. Robertson.
Res.: 108 Main St., P.O. Box 90, 59843. Tel: 406-793-5697. Email: hlm5843@blackfoot.net.
Catechesis/Religious Program—Maureen Mannix, D.R.E. Students 15.
Mission—St. Jude's P.O. Box 802, Lincoln, Lewis and Clark Co. 59639.

KALISPELL, FLATHEAD CO.

1—ST. MATTHEW (1895) Rev. Roderick Ermatinger.
Office: 602 S. Main St., 59901. Tel: 406-752-6788; Fax: 406-756-8248. Email: parish@stmattsaints.org.
Catechesis/Religious Program—Sage Dorrington, D.R.E. Students 53.

2—RISEN CHRIST (1978) Rev. Rudolph Bullman.
Res.: 65 W. Evergreen Dr., 59901. Tel: 406-752-4219; Fax: 406-752-4226. Email: rcparish@montanasky.us.
Catechesis/Religious Program—James Miller, Parish Elementary Coord.; Suzanne Johnson, Parish Youth Ministry Coord. Students 78.

LIBBY, LINCOLN CO., ST. JOSEPH (1911) Rev. Jozef Perehubka (Poland).
Res.: 719 Utah Ave., P.O. Box 1467, 59923. Tel: 406-293-4322; Fax: 406-293-7231. Email: stjosephlibby@gmail.com.
Catechesis/Religious Program—Helen Barnett, D.R.E. Students 46.
Mission—Immaculate Conception Troy, Lincoln Co.

MISSOULA, MISSOULA CO.

1—ST. ANTHONY (1921) Rev. Gary W. Reller; Terry Jimmerson, Pastoral Assoc.
Office: 217 Tremont St., 59801. Tel: 406-543-3129; Fax: 406-549-6009. Email: office@saintanthonyparish.com.
Catechesis/Religious Program— Jeanette Borrelli, D.R.E. Students 75.

2—BLESSED TRINITY PARISH (1971) Rev. Edward Hislop; Deacon Thomas McCarthy.
Office: 1475 Eaton St., 59801. Tel: 406-721-2405; Fax: 406-721-0025. Email: office@blessedtrinitymissoula.org.
Catechesis/Religious Program—Louise Yamasaki, D.R.E. Students 24.
Mission—Spirit of Christ 5475 Farm Ln., Lolo, Missoula Co. 59847.

3—CHRIST THE KING (1966), (Newman Parish) Rev. Jeffrey M. Fleming; Sr. Doris Faber, O.P., Pastoral Assoc.; Suzanne A. Monroe, Office Mgr.
Office: 1400 Gerald Ave., 59801. Tel: 406-728-3845; Fax: 406-829-8797. Email: ctkccm@christthekingccm.org.
Catechesis/Religious Program—Patti Cassidy, D.R.E. Students 50.

4—ST. FRANCIS XAVIER (1881) Revs. Richard Perry, S.J.; Joseph Carver, S.J.; Deacons Michael Bloomdahl, Parish Admin.; Carlton Quamme. In Res., Rev. George J. Dumais, S.J.
Office:—420 W. Pine St., 59802. Tel: 406-542-0321; Fax: 406-327-8537. Email: sfx@montanadsl.net.
Catechesis/Religious Program—Debra Johnson, D.R.E.; Jennifer Deeds, Parish Youth Min. Coord. Students 90.

5—HOLY FAMILY (1972) Closed. For inquiries for parish records contact the chancery.

PHILIPSBURG, GRANITE CO., ST. PHILIP (1892) Vicki Burgmeier, Parish Admin.
Mailing Address: P.O. Box 329, Drummond, 59832.
Church: 308 W. Kearney, 59858. Tel: 406-241-3604.
Catechesis/Religious Program—Students 12.

PLAINS, SANDERS CO., ST. JAMES (1889) Rev. Jeffrey M. Benusa; Deacon Lynn F. McAtee.
Res.: 109 W. Meany St., P.O. Box 745, 59859. Tel: 406-826-3668. Email: jbenusa@diocesehelena.org.
Catechesis/Religious Program—Tel: 406-741-3026 (Sacred Heart Mission).
Mission—Sacred Heart Hot Springs, Sanders Co.

POLSON, LAKE CO., IMMACULATE CONCEPTION (1909) [CEM 3] Rev. James Connor; Deacons Wesley Vert; Daniel Gullotta.
Res. & Church: 1002 4th Ave. E., P.O. Box 1477, 59860. Tel: 406-883-2506 (Office); Fax: 406-883-4649. Email: icparish59860@gmail.com.
Catechesis/Religious Program—Marjorie Shrider, D.R.E. Students 65.

RONAN, LAKE CO., SACRED HEART (1911) Rev. James Connor; Sr. Barbara Brown, O.P., Pastoral Assoc.
Res.: 35933 Round Butte Rd. W., 59864. Tel: 406-676-4511; Fax: 406-676-4515. Email: sacredheart@ronan.net.
Catechesis/Religious Program—Students 26.
Mission—St. Joseph's Charlo, Lake Co.

ST. IGNATIUS, LAKE CO., ST. IGNATIUS MISSION (1854) Rev. Andrew Maddock, S.J.; Sr. Mary Stauder, O.P., Pastoral Assoc.
Res.: P.O. Box 667, 59865. Tel: 406-745-2768; Fax: 406-745-0010. Email: mission7@blackfoot.net.
Catechesis/Religious Program—Students 161.
Mission—Sacred Heart 112 Taelman, Arlee, Lake Co. 59821. Tel: 406-726-3450; Fax: 406-726-3540.
Mission—St. John Berchman's Jocko, Lake Co.

SHELBY, TOOLE CO., ST. WILLIAM (1924) Rev. Michael Drury.
Res.: 531 Main St., 59474. Tel: 406-434-2988; Fax: 406-434-9133. Email: saintwm@3rivers.net.
Catechesis/Religious Program—Diane Abrahamson, Parish Youth Ministry Coord.; Sr. Gretchen Wagner, D.R.E. Students 48.
Mission—St. Thomas Aquinas (1917) 120 1st St., S., Sunburst, 59482.

SHERIDAN, MADISON CO., MADISON COUNTY CATHOLIC COMMUNITY, Comprised of St. Mary of the Assumption, Laurin; St. Joseph, Sheridan; and St. Patrick, Ennis. Deacon Andrew Dorrington, Pastoral Admin.
Res.: 105 Poppleton, P.O. Box 17, 59749. Tel: 406-842-5588; Fax: 406-842-7433. Email: kootenai@catholic.org.
Catechesis/Religious Program—Margaret Stecker, Parish Youth Ministry & Parish Junior High Coord. Students 20.

STEVENSVILLE, RAVALLI CO., ST. MARY (1842) [CEM] Rev. Matthew P. Huber.
Res.: 333 Charlos St., 59870. Tel: 406-777-5257; Fax: 406-777-1032. Email: st_marys_stevi@q.com.
Catechesis/Religious Program—Rita Pfau, D.R.E. Students 83.
Mission—St. Joseph Florence, Ravalli Co.

SWAN VALLEY, LAKE CO., OUR LADY OF SWAN VALLEY MISSION Michelle Jenkins, Pastoral Assoc.
Mailing Address: *The Sycamore Tree*, 21592 Sycamore Tree Ln., Swan Lake, 59911. Tel: 406-754-2429; Fax: 406-754-2429. Email: sycamoretree@blackfoot.net.
Church: 201 E. Beck Rd., Condon, 59826.

THOMPSON FALLS, SANDERS CO., ST. WILLIAM (1955) Rev. Jeffrey M. Benusa; Deacon Ronald Kazmierczak.
Res.: 416 Preston Ave., P.O. Box 186, 59873. Tel: 406-827-4433; Fax: 406-827-4433. Email: stwilliam@blackfoot.net.
Catechesis/Religious Program—Students 7.
Mission— Noxon.

THREE FORKS, GALLATIN CO., HOLY FAMILY (1886) Rev. Eric C. Gilbaugh; Deacon Robert Lane.
Church: 104 E. Birch St., P.O. Box 99, 59752. Tel: 406-285-3592.
Catechesis/Religious Program—Margaret Babits, D.R.E. Students 113.
Mission—Valley of Flowers 609 Quaw Blvd., Belgrade, Gallatin Co. 59714.

TOWNSEND, BROADWATER CO., HOLY CROSS (1903) Rev. Joseph L. Byrne.
Res.: 101 S. Walnut, P.O. Box 610, 59644. Tel: 406-266-4811. Email: holycrossparish@mt.net.
Catechesis/Religious Program—Students 37.

VALIER, PONDERA CO., ST. FRANCIS (1909) Rev. Michael Drury; Mary Jean Brophy, Pastoral Assoc.; Sr. Gretchen Wagner, Pastoral Assoc.
Res.: 616 4th St., P.O. Box 338, 59486. Tel:

406-279-3327.
Catechesis/Religious Program— Janet Stokes, D.R.E. Students 56.
Mission—Holy Cross Dupuyer, Pondera Co.
WALKERVILLE, SILVER BOW CO., ST. LAWRENCE O'TOOLE (1896) Closed. 1986. For inquiries for parish records contact Butte Catholic Community North, Butte.
WEST YELLOWSTONE, GALLATIN CO., OUR LADY OF THE PINES Rev. Joseph B. Oblinger (Retired); Sr. Patricia Toeckes, S.C.L., Pastoral Admin.
Res.: 437 Madison Ave., P.O. Box 577, 59758. Tel: 406-646-7755. Email: ptoeckes@mcn.net.
Catechesis/Religious Program—Students 19.
Mission—St. Joseph of Big Sky Big Sky, Gallatin Co.
WHITE SULPHUR SPRINGS, MEAGHER CO., ST. BARTHOLOMEW (1916) Rev. Richard Kluk; AnnaLee Kiff, Pastoral Assoc.
Res.: 407 Second Ave., S.E., P.O. Box 422, 59645. Tel: 406-547-3737.
Catechesis/Religious Program—Gail Weitz, D.R.E. Students 10.
WHITEFISH, FLATHEAD CO., ST. CHARLES BORROMEO (1890) Rev. Kenneth E. Fortney.
Res.: 230 Baker Ave., P.O. Box 128, 59937. Tel: 406-862-2051; Fax: 866-948-8416. Email: stcharles@bresnan.net.
Catechesis/Religious Program—Lynn Beck, D.R.E. Students 64.
WHITEHALL, JEFFERSON CO., ST. TERESA OF AVILA (1911) Rev. Daniel Driscoll.
Res.: 107 Second Ave. E., P.O. Box 337, 59759. Tel: 406-287-3893; Fax: 406-287-9213. Email: stteresa6@q.com.
Catechesis/Religious Program—Students 50.
Mission—Notre Dame Twin Bridges, Jefferson Co.

DIOCESAN MISSIONS

GUATEMALA, SANTO TOMAS Rev. Kevin Christofferson; Sisters Mary Waddell, B.V.M.; Anna Priester, B.V.M., D.R.E.; Sheila McShane, Clinic Dir.
Guatemula Missions, P.O. Box 1729, 59624.
HELENA, LEWIS AND CLARK CO.
GUATEMALA MISSION MEDICAL FUND—P.O. Box 1729, 59624.

Chaplains of Public Institutions

HELENA. *U.S. Veteran's Hospital*, Fort Harrison, 59626. Served by Helena Area Parishes.
BOULDER. *Boulder River School and Hospital*. Rev. William Greytak. Attended from St. Catherine, Boulder.
DEER LODGE. *Montana State Prison*. Attended from Immaculate Conception Parish, Deer Lodge. Rev. Robert G. Porter.
WARM SPRINGS. *Warm Springs State Hospital*. Rev. Herbert J. Pins.

Special Assignments:
Revs.—
Dornbos, William, 100 E. Broadway, Butte, 59701.
Dumais, George J., S.J., Dir., Loyola Sacred Heart High School, 1700 Madeline, Missoula, 59801.
Malnar, Stan, 4220 W. Fremont Rd., Spokane, WA 99224.
Robertson, John W., Vicar for Canonical Svcs., Chancellor & Judicial Vicar, P.O. Box 1729, 59624.

On Duty Outside the Diocese:
Rev. Msgr.—
McCarthy, John F., P.A., Oblates of Wisdom, P.O. Box 13230, St. Louis, MO 63157.
Revs.—
Christofferson, Kevin, Santo Tomas La Union, Departmento Suchitepuez 10017 Guatemala.
Driscoll, Michael, Notre Dame University, Department of Theology, South Bend, IN 46617.
Flynn, Thomas, Emory University, 1278 Oakdale Rd., N.E., Atlanta, GA 30307.

Military Chaplains:
Rev.—
Diphe, Juan M., U.S. Air Force

Health Leave:
Revs.—
Long, Stuart, 2475 Winnie Ave., 59601.
Moran, Joseph P., 4307 Gharrett, Missoula, 59803.

Retired:
Rev. Msgr.—
Harrington, Joseph D., 1726 Cannon St., 59601.
Revs.—
Burke, Gregory, 105 Rampart Dr., Butte, 59701.
Finnegan, Joseph, P.O. Box 503, Whitehall, 59759.
Hannigan, Raymond, 848 S. 79th Pl., Mesa, AZ 85208.
Hazelton, James
Hogan, James J., 901 S. Higgins # 301, Missoula, 59801.
Hunthausen, John F., Carroll College, 59625.
Langhans, Victor E., P.O. Box 153, Bigfork, 59911.
Lowney, Jeremiah, 1601 N. Benton Ave., 59625.
McCormick, Frank, 2409 Mary Jane Blvd., Missoula, 59808.
McGurk, Patrick C., 534 Gold Creek Rd., Gold Creek, 59733.
Murray, John E., 901 Pennsylvania Ave., Deer Lodge, 59722.
Noonan, Robert C., 720A Missy's Way, Missoula, 59801.
Oblinger, Joseph B., 2400 Durston Rd., #37, Bozeman, 59718.
Roman, Charles, 2250 Merganser Dr., Kalispell, 59901.
Smith, Michael M., 4309 Gharrett St., Missoula, 59803.
Sodja, Richard H., 915 Saddle Dr., 59601.
Stupca, Edward L., 100 E. Broadway, Butte, 59701.
Sullivan, James M., 1100 Le Grande Cannon Blvd., 59601.
Sullivan, Jeremiah, 1601 N. Benton, 59625.
Tallman, Stephen, 5630 Lower Woodchuck Rd., Florence, 59833.
Wang, John, 425 Ford St., Missoula, 59801.

Permanent Deacons:
Bloomdahl, Michael, St. Francis Xavier, Missoula
Bremner, Robert, Little Flower, Browning
Butts, James, Pope John Paul II, Bigfork
Casazza, Dan, Our Lady of Mercy, Eureka
Dorrington, Andrew, Madison County Catholic Community
Duvernay, J. Anthony, (Retired)
Fournier, Ronald, St. John Parish, Butte
Fraser, Randall, Our Lady of the Valley, Helena
Gobert, John, Little Flower, Browning
Gullotta, Daniel, Immaculate Conception, Polson
Kazmierczak, Ronald, St. William, Thompson Falls
Kuhl, Gerald, St. Mary Queen of Heaven Mission, Superior
Lane, Robert, Holy Family, Three Forks
Marks, Donald, (Retired)
Martin, Anthony, Pope John Paul II, Bigfork
McAtee, Lynn F., St. James, Plains
McCarthy, Thomas, Blessed Trinity, Missoula
McGrath, Daniel, Holy Spirit, Butte
Miller, Richard, Helena
Miller, Robert J., Sts. Cyril and Methodius, East Helena
Pearce, Robert, St. Richard, Columbia Falls
Quamme, Carlton, St. Francis Xavier, Missoula
Running Crane, Ronald, Little Flower, Browning
Rutherford, Melvin, Little Flower, Browning
Vert, Wesley, Immaculate Conception, Polson

INSTITUTIONS LOCATED IN THE DIOCESE

[A] SEMINARIES, DIOCESAN

HELENA. *Carroll College*, 1601 N. Benton Ave., 59625. Tel: 406-447-4300; Fax: 406-447-4533. Email: mlenneman@carroll.edu. Rev. Marc J. Lenneman, Dir. Diocesan Pre-Seminary Prog.

[B] COLLEGES AND UNIVERSITIES

HELENA. *Carroll College* (1909) 1601 N. Benton Ave., 59625. Tel: 406-447-4300; Fax: 406-447-4533. Web: www.carroll.edu. Rev. Marc J. Lenneman, Chap. & Campus Min.; Dr. Thomas Trebon, Pres.; Lori Peterson, Vice Pres. Finance & Admin.; Mr. Thomas J. McCarvel, Vice Pres. Community Rels.; Dr. James Hardwick, Vice Pres. Student Life; Dr. Paula McNutt, Sr. Vice Pres. Academic Affairs & Dean College; Colleen Dunne, Dir. Campus Ministry Programs; Rev. Daniel B. Shea; Christian Frazza, Dir. Library. Four-year Diocesan College of Liberal Arts and Sciences. Priests 2; Lay Professors 81; Students 1,502; Total Staff 137.

[C] HIGH SCHOOLS, DIOCESAN

BUTTE. *Central High School* (1924) 9 S. Idaho St., 59701. Tel: 406-782-6761; Fax: 406-723-3873. Email: tim.norbeck@buttecentralschools.org. Timothy Norbeck, Prin. Lay Teachers 20; Students 131.
MISSOULA. *Loyola Sacred Heart High School* (Missoula Catholic Schools), 320 Edith St., 59801. Tel: 406-549-6101; Fax: 406-542-1432. Email: info@missoulacatholicschools.org. Web: www.missoulacatholicschools.org. Patrick Haggarty, Ed.D., Supt., Schools; Jeremy Beck, Pres.; Kathy Schneider, Prin.; Patrice Schwenk, Librarian. Priests 1; Lay Teachers 27; Students 169.

[D] SCHOOLS, ELEMENTARY

BROWNING. *De La Salle Blackfeet School*, (Grades 4-8), P.O. Box 1489, 59417. Tel: 406-338-5290; Fax: 406-338-7900. Email: info@dlsbs.org. Web: www.dlsbs.org. Bro. Paul Ackerman, F.S.C., Pres.; Roonie Leittem-Murrell, Prin. Brothers 2; Lay Teachers 11; Students 66.
BUTTE. *Butte Central Elementary Junior High School*, (Grades PreK-8), 1100 Delaware, 59701. Tel: 406-782-4500; Fax: 406-723-4845. Email: carolyn.trudnowski@buttecentralschools.org. Carolyn Trudnowski, Prin. Sisters 1; Lay Teachers 18; Students 264.
After School Care Students (Ages 5-12), Tel: 406-782-4500; Fax: 406-723-4845.
Central Junior High School, (Grades 6-8), 1100 Delaware, 59701. Tel: 406-782-4500; Fax: 406-723-4845. Carolyn Trudnowski, Prin.; Colleen Stillwagon, Librarian.
KALISPELL. *St. Matthew School* (1917) (Grades PreSchool-8), 602 S. Main St., 59901. Tel: 406-752-6303; Fax: 406-756-8248. Email: office@stmattsaints.org. Web: www.stmattsaints.org. Joanna Eichner, Prin.; Myrna Matulevich, Librarian. Clergy 1; Sisters 1; Lay Teachers 16; Preschool (Age 4) 23; Students 198.
Day Care Center Tel: 406-756-6807; Fax: 406-756-8248. Marlene Stevens, Dir. (Ages 2-6) Students 60.
MISSOULA. *St. Joseph Elementary School* (1873) (Grades K-8), (Missoula Catholic Schools), 503 Edith St., 59801. Tel: 406-549-1290; Fax: 406-543-4034. Email: rhyland@missoulacatholicschools.org. Web: www.missoulacatholicschools.org. Rick Hyland, Prin.; Anne Wright, Librarian. Lay Teachers 42; Students 286.
Child Care Center Tel: 406-549-1290; Fax: 406-543-4034. Evalie Hankinson, Dir. (Ages 2-12) Students 45.

[E] GENERAL HOSPITALS

BUTTE. *St. James Health Care, Sisters of Charity of Leavenworth Health System*, 400 S. Clark St., 59701. Tel: 406-723-2500; Fax: 406-723-2443. Web: www.sjh-mt.org. P.O. Box 3300, 59702. Charles Wright, CEO; Mary Patricia Campbell, Dir. Spiritual Care & Mission Svcs.; Rev. Gregory Burke, Chap. & Pastoral Care (Retired). Bed Capacity 100; Sisters of Charity of Leavenworth 2; Lay Staff 575; Patients Assisted Annually 86,122.
MISSOULA. *St. Patrick Hospital and Health Sciences Center, Sisters of Providence of Montana Corporation*, 500 W. Broadway, 59802. Tel: 406-543-7271; Fax: 406-329-5693. Email: info@saintpatrick.org. Web: www.saintpatrick.org. P.O. Box 4587, 59806. Jeff Fee, Pres. & CEO; Sr. Elizabeth Olsen, B.V.M., Pastoral Care. Sisters 1; Lay Staff 1,600; Bed Capacity 253; Patients Assisted Annually 160,000.
POLSON. *St. Joseph Medical Center* (1916) #6 Thirteenth Ave. E., P.O. Box 1010, 59860. Tel: 406-883-5377. Email: jkiser@saintjoes.org. Web: saintjoes.org. James R. Kiser II, CEO; Rev. James Connor, Chap.; Deacon Wes Vert. Bed Capacity 22; Lay Staff 213; Patients Assisted Annually 38,090.

[F] HOUSES OF PRAYER

SWAN LAKE. *The Sycamore Tree Contemplative Prayer Center*, 21592 Sycamore Tree Ln., 59911. Tel: 406-754-2429; Fax: 406-754-2429. Email: sycamoretree@blackfoot.net. Michelle Jenkins, Contact Person.

[G] NEWMAN CHAPLAINS

BOZEMAN. *Montana State University* , (Newman Program), Office: 1725 S. Eleventh, 59715-4218. Tel: 406-586-9243; Fax: 406-586-2886. Web: www.resurrectionbozeman.org. Rev. Valentine D. Zdilla.
BUTTE. *Montana College of Mineral Science and Technology* Office: 102 S. Washington St., 59701. Tel: 406-723-5407; Fax: 406-723-5408. Email: bccn@diocesehelena.org. Web: www.diocesehelena.org. Rev. Robert Hall, Chap.; Seaneen Prendergast, Campus Min.
DILLON. *University of Montana - Western* 226 S. Atlantic St., 59725. Tel: 406-683-4391; Fax: 406-683-6244. Email: strosedillon@gmail.com. Rev. Herbert J. Pins.
MISSOULA. *University of Montana* , (Christ the King Parish), 1400 Gerald Ave., 59801-4230. Tel: 406-728-3845; Fax: 406-829-8797. Email: ctkccm@christthekingccm.org. Web:

www.christthekingccm.org. Rev. Jeffrey M. Fleming; Sr. Doris Faber, O.P., Pastoral Assoc.; Suzanne A. Monroe, Admin. Asst.

[H] FOUNDATIONS

HELENA. *Cathedral of St. Helena Historic Preservation Trust*, 530 N. Ewing St., 59601-4001. Tel: 406-442-5825; Fax: 406-449-5113.

BUTTE. *St. James Healthcare Foundation*, 425 W. Porphyry, 59701. Tel: 406-782-5640; Fax: 406-782-5643. Email: foundation@sjh-mt.org.

MISSOULA. *St. Patrick Hospital and Health Foundation*, 900 N. Orange, P.O. Box 4587, 59806. Tel: 406-329-5640; Fax: 406-329-5693. Email: lankford@stpatrick.org. Michael Bullard, Exec. Dir.; Marian Maxwell, Pharm.D., Chairperson.

[I] MISCELLANEOUS

BROWNING. *St. Vincent de Paul Thrift Store*, 112 First Ave., N.W., P.O. Box 974, 59417. Tel: 406-338-5403. Mona Kipling, Mgr.

BUTTE. *Central Education Foundation*, P.O. Box 634, 59703-0634. Tel: 406-723-6706; Fax: 406-782-4026. Email: buttecentraldev@yahoo.com. Don Peoples Jr., Exec. Dir.

**Maternal Life International* (1996) 326A S. Jackson St., 59701-8804. Tel: 406-782-1719; Fax: 406-782-1719 (Call First). Email: usacares@in-tch.com. Web: www.MLIonline.org.

MISSOULA. *Loyola Sacred Heart High School Foundation* (1960) Serving Missoula Catholic Schools., 300 Edith St., 59801. Tel: 406-728-2367; Fax: 406-542-9900. Email: jgeer@missoulacatholicschools.org. Rob T. Bell, Chm.; Becky Byrne, Vice Chair.

STEVENSVILLE. *Historic St. Mary's Mission*, P.O. Box 211, 59870-0211. Tel: 406-777-5734; Fax: 406-777-5734. Email: stmary@cybernet1.com. Web: saintmarysmission.org. Colleen Meyer, Dir.

RELIGIOUS INSTITUTES OF MEN REPRESENTED IN THE DIOCESE

For further details refer to the corresponding bracketed number in the Religious Institutes of Men or Women section.

[0330]—*Brothers of the Christian Schools* (Midwest Prov.)—F.S.C.

[0690]—*Jesuit Fathers and Brothers* (Oregon Prov.)—S.J.

RELIGIOUS INSTITUTES OF WOMEN REPRESENTED IN THE DIOCESE

[1070-03]—*Dominican Sisters*—O.P.

[1070-11]—*Dominican Sisters*—O.P.

[1070-13]—*Dominican Sisters*—O.P.

[2575]—*Institute of the Sisters of Mercy of the Americas* (Cedar Rapids, IA)—R.S.M.

[0440]—*Sisters of Charity of Cincinnati, Ohio*—S.C.

[0480]—*Sisters of Charity of Leavenworth, Kansas*—S.C.L.

[0430]—*Sisters of Charity of the Blessed Virgin Mary*—B.V.M.

[]—*Sisters of St. Joseph of Carondelet*

DIOCESAN CEMETERIES

HELENA. *Resurrection Cemetery*, 3700 N. Montana Ave., P.O. Box 5029, 59604. Tel: 406-442-1782; Fax: 406-443-7036. Mr. Scott Fitzpatrick, Dir. Cemeteries; Delisa Pearson, Office Mgr.

Resurrection Cemetery Association, 3700 N. Montana Ave., P.O. Box 5029, 59604. Tel: 406-442-1782; Fax: 406-443-7036. Mr. Scott Fitzpatrick, Exec. Dir.; Delisa Pearson, Office Mgr. (Corporate Name for Diocesan Cemeteries)

BUTTE. *Holy Cross Cemetery*, Office: 4700 Harrison Ave., 59701. Tel: 406-494-3812. Kenny Martz, Mgr.

St. Patrick Cemetery, Office: 4700 Harrison Ave., 59701. Tel: 406-494-3812. Kenny Martz, Mgr.

MISSOULA. *St. Mary Cemetery*, Office: 641 Turner St., 59802. Tel: 406-543-7951. Mike Hamlin, Mgr.

NECROLOGY

† Lynam, Gerald J., (Retired)—Died Dec. 15, 2010

An asterisk (*) denotes an organization that has established tax-exempt status directly with the IRS and is not covered by the USCCB Group Ruling.

Diocese of Honolulu

(Dioecesis Honoluluensis)

Most Reverend

CLARENCE R. SILVA

Bishop of Honolulu; ordained May 2, 1975; appointed Bishop of Honolulu May 17, 2005; ordained July 21, 2005. *Bishop's Office: 1184 Bishop St., Honolulu, HI 96813.*

Chancery Office: 1184 Bishop St., Honolulu, HI 96813. Tel: 808-585-3300; Fax: 808-521-8428.

Web: www.catholichawaii.org

Square Miles 6,435.

Corporate Title: The Roman Catholic Church In The State Of Hawaii.

Comprises all of the Hawaiian Islands.

The Hawaiian Islands were annexed as a Territory of the United States in 1898. Hawaii became the 50th State of the Union on August 21, 1959.

In 1826, a Prefecture-Apostolic was erected for the Hawaiian Islands, then called Sandwich Islands, and entrusted to the Fathers of the Sacred Hearts of Jesus and Mary (Picpus). The Very Rev. Alexis Bachelot, SS.CC., was the first Prefect-Apostolic. He arrived with his companions in Honolulu on the 7th of July, 1827. In 1844, the Islands were erected a Vicariate. Diocese erected Sept. 10, 1941.

For legal titles of parishes and diocesan institutions, consult the Chancery Office.

STATISTICAL OVERVIEW

Personnel	
Bishop	1
Priests: Diocesan Active in Diocese	38
Priests: Diocesan Active Outside Diocese	6
Priests: Retired, Sick or Absent	21
Number of Diocesan Priests	65
Religious Priests in Diocese	56
Total Priests in Diocese	121
Extern Priests in Diocese	25
Ordinations:	
Diocesan Priests	4
Permanent Deacons in Diocese	57
Total Brothers	32
Total Sisters	169
Parishes	
Parishes	66
With Resident Pastor:	
Resident Diocesan Priests	38
Resident Religious Priests	24
Without Resident Pastor:	
Administered by Priests	2
Missions	26
Professional Ministry Personnel:	
Brothers	1
Sisters	9
Lay Ministers	49
Welfare	
Health Care Centers	3
Total Assisted	1,815
Homes for the Aged	6
Total Assisted	459
Specialized Homes	1
Total Assisted	56
Special Centers for Social Services	1
Total Assisted	24,939
Educational	
Students from This Diocese	2
Diocesan Students in Other Seminaries	9
Total Seminarians	11
Colleges and Universities	1
Total Students	2,850
High Schools, Diocesan and Parish	3
Total Students	838
High Schools, Private	4
Total Students	2,107
Elementary Schools, Diocesan and Parish	20
Total Students	5,447
Elementary Schools, Private	3
Total Students	777
Catechesis/Religious Education:	
High School Students	2,117
Elementary Students	5,162
Total Students under Catholic Instruction	19,309
Teachers in the Diocese:	
Priests	7
Brothers	13
Sisters	37
Lay Teachers	769
Vital Statistics	
Receptions into the Church:	
Infant Baptism Totals	2,570
Minor Baptism Totals	232
Adult Baptism Totals	162
Received into Full Communion	190
First Communions	1,882
Confirmations	1,307
Marriages:	
Catholic	325
Interfaith	129
Total Marriages	454
Deaths	1,606
Total Catholic Population	222,822
Total Population	1,360,301

Former Prelates—Very Revs. ALEXIS BACHELOT, SS.CC., Pref. Apost.; died Dec. 5, 1837; LOUIS MAIGRET, SS.CC. ord. Sept. 23, 1828; Pref. Apost. till 1844; Rt. Revs. VINCENT FERRIER DUBOIZE, SS.CC., resigned before he was consecrated; LOUIS MAIGRET, SS.CC., ord. Sept. 23, 1828; Titular Bishop of Arathia; consecrated at Santiago, Nov. 28, 1847; died June 11, 1882; HERMAN KOECKEMANN, SS.CC., ord. May 31, 1862; Titular Bishop of Olba; cons. at San Francisco Aug. 21, 1881; died Feb. 22, 1892; GULSTAN ROPERT, SS.CC., ord. May 26, 1866; Titular Bishop of Panopolis; cons. at San Francisco, Sept. 25, 1892; died Jan. 4, 1903; LIBERT H. BOEYNAEMS, SS.CC., ord. Sept. 11, 1881; Titular Bishop of Zeugma; cons. at San Francisco, July 25, 1903; died May 13, 1926; Most Revs. STEPHEN P. ALENCASTRE, SS.CC., ord. April 5, 1902; Titular Bishop of Arabissus; cons. at Los Angeles, Aug. 24, 1924; died Nov. 9, 1940; JAMES J. SWEENEY, D.D., ord. June 20, 1925; appt. May 20, 1941; cons. at San Francisco, July 25, 1941; died June 19, 1968; JOHN J. SCANLAN, D.D., Retired Bishop of Honolulu; ord. June 22, 1930; succeeded to see March 6, 1968; retired June 30, 1981; died Jan. 31, 1997; JOSEPH A. FERRARIO, D.D., Retired Bishop of Honolulu; ord. May 19, 1951; succeeded to see June 25, 1982; retired Oct. 12, 1993; died Dec. 12, 2003; FRANCIS X. DILORENZO, ord. May 18, 1968; appt. Titular Bishop of Tigia and Auxiliary Bishop of Scranton Jan. 26, 1988; cons. March 8, 1988; appt. Apostolic Admin. Oct. 12, 1993; succeeded to See November 29, 1994; appt. Bishop of Richmond March 31, 2004; installed May 24, 2004.

Office of the Bishop

Office of the Bishop—1184 Bishop St., Honolulu, 96813-2858. Tel: 808-585-3300; Fax: 808-521-8428. Office Hours: Mon.-Fri. 8-4.

Administrative Assistant to the Bishop—JOY BULOSAN, M.P.A.

Vicar General and Moderator of the Curia—Very Rev. GARY L. SECOR, V.G.

Administrative Secretary/Public Notary—ELINA SIMON.

Censor Liborum—Rev. Msgr. JOHN MUTISO MBINDA.

Episcopal Vicar for Clergy—Rev. MANUEL HEWE.

Vocations Director—Rev. PETER DUMAG.

Administrative Secretary—DARLENE CACHOLA.

Director of Permanent Deacons—Deacon CLARENCE DECAIRES.

Diocesan Ecumenical Interfaith Director—Rev. JACK RYAN.

College of Consultors—Most Rev. CLARENCE R. SILVA, Ex Officio; Very Rev. GARY L. SECOR, V.G., Ex Officio; Revs. KONELIO FALETOI; WILLIAM J. KUNISCH II; DENNIS KOSHKO; THOMAS P. JOSEPH, Ph.D.; WILLIAM SHANNON; SCOTT BUSH; EFREN A. TOMAS, M.S.

Vicars Forane—Revs. DENNIS KOSHKO, East Oahu; WILLIAM J. KUNISCH II, West Oahu; PASCUAL ABAYA, Central Oahu; MICHEL DALTON, O.F.M.Cap., Leeward Oahu; HERMAN GOMES, SS.CC., Windward Oahu; KONELIO FALETOI, West Hawaii; MICHAEL G. SCULLY, S.J., East Hawaii; WILLIAM SHANNON, Kauai; EFREN A. TOMAS, M.S., Maui, Molokai, Lanai.

Business Office—1184 Bishop St., Honolulu, 96813-2858. Tel: 808-585-3300; Fax: 808-521-8428. Office Hours: Mon.-Fri. 8-4.

Diocesan Finance Officer—LISA SAKAMOTO.

Hawaii Catholic Herald—1184 Bishop St., Honolulu, 96813-2858. Tel: 808-533-1791; Fax: 808-585-3381. Most Rev. CLARENCE R. SILVA, Publisher; PATRICK DOWNES, Editor.

Facilities Management—VINCENT A. VERNAY, Diocesan Svcs. Mgr., 1184 Bishop St., Honolulu, 96813. Tel: 808-585-3334.

Human Resources—DARA PERREIRA, PHR, Dir., 1184 Bishop St., Honolulu, 96813. Tel: 808-585-3306.

Land Asset Management—MARLENE DECOSTA, Diocesan Dir., 1184 Bishop St., Honolulu, 96813. Tel: 808-585-3332.

St. Stephen Diocesan Center—6301 Pali Hwy., Kaneohe, 96744-5224. Tel: 808-203-6700; Fax: 808-261-7022. Office Hours: Mon.-Fri. 8-4.

Chancellor and Archivist—Deacon WALTER H. YOSHIMITSU. Tel: 808-203-6735.

Ecclesiastical Notary and Secretary for the Chancellor/Archives—NETTIE LOU PEILER.

Administrator's Assistant for St. Stephen Diocesan Center—SABRINA IZAGUIRRE. Tel: 808-203-6724.

Tribunal and Canonical Affairs—

Judicial Vicar and Director of Canonical Affairs—Very Rev. MARVIN SAMIANO, J.C.L. Tel: 808-203-6766; Fax: 808-263-8518.

Judge—Rev. STEVE NGUYEN, J.C.L.

Defender of the Bond—Rev. MARK J. GANTLEY, J.C.L.; ANNE KIRBY; Rev. HERMAN LEONG, J.C.L.

Promoter of Justice—Rev. MARK J. GANTLEY, J.C.L.

Moderator of the Tribunal Chancery—MARY L. DUDDY. Email: mary_duddy@rcchawaii.org.

Ecclesiastical Notary and Secretary—LORI J. GRESS.

Mission Cooperative Program—Very Rev. MARVIN SAMIANO, J.C.L., Dir. Tel: 808-203-6741. Email: msamiano@rcchawaii.org.

Hawaii Catholic Schools—MICHAEL M. ROCKERS,

Ed.D., Supt. Tel: 808-203-6764; LOVEY ANN DEREGO, Assoc. Supt. Tel: 808-203-6755.

Office of Worship—Rev. WILLIAM KUNISCH, Dir. Tel: 808-203-6728.

Administrative Secretary—VACANT.

Office of Religious Education—JAYNE MONDOY, M.A., P.L., Dir. Tel: 808-203-6745.

Safe Environment, Shield the Vulnerable and Back Ground Screening—DARA PERREIRA, PHR, Coord. Tel: 808-585-3306.

Victim Assistance—EDWINA REYES, Coord. Tel: 808-527-4981.

Diocesan Adult Faith Formation—Deacon MODESTO R. CORDERO, Coord.

Office for Youth & Young Adult Ministry—LISA GOMES, Dir. Tel: 808-203-6743.

Office of Development and Stewardship—CYNTHIA LALLO, Dir. Tel: 808-203-6723.

Office for Parish Resources—SHARON CHIARUCCI, Dir. Tel: 808-203-6733.

Hospital Ministry—Chaplains: Revs. TEODULO GAQUIT; JON CABICO.

Deacon Formation Office—Deacon JOHN A. COUGHLIN, Dir. Tel: 808-203-6729; KATHLEEN COUGHLIN, Co Dir. Tel: 808-203-6717.

Prison Ministry—Tel: 808-203-6735. Deacon WALTER H. YOSHIMITSU, Diocesan Rep.

Respect Life Office—Deacon WALTER H. YOSHIMITSU, Dir. Tel: 808-203-6735.

Administrative Secretary—PAULETTE VERNAY. Tel: 808-203-6722.

Natural Family Planning—EDWARD CODA; BETTY CODA; Deacon WALTER H. YOSHIMITSU; FRANCES YOSHIMITSU; Deacon RONALD NELSON; LUCI NELSON.

Office for Social Ministry—1315 Kalanianaole Ave., Hilo, 96720. Tel: 808-935-3050; 877-935-3050 (Toll Free); Fax: 808-935-3794. CAROL IGNACIO, Diocesan Dir.

Parish Social Ministry—St. Stephen Diocesan Center, 6301 Pali Hwy., Kaneohe, 96744-5224. Tel: 808-203-6702. IWIE TAMASHIRO, Program Dir.

Catholic Relief Services—IWIE TAMASHIRO, Dir.

Catholic Campaign for Human Development—Deacon LAUREN S. WONG, Interim Diocesan Dir. Tel: 808-203-6734.

Housing and Homeless—Resource Developer/ Community Organizer: Rev. ROBERT STARK, S.S.S. Housing Development Director: KENT ANDERSON.

Councils, Committees and Commissions

Presbyteral Council—Most Rev. CLARENCE R. SILVA, Ex-Officio; Very Rev. GARY L. SECOR, V.G., Ex-Officio; Revs. MANUEL HEWE, Ex-Officio; HERMAN GOMES, SS.CC., Chair; LANE AKIONA, SS.CC., Vice Chair; ALAPAKI KIM, Sec.; PASCUAL ABAYA; GARY P. COLTON; MICHEL DALTON, O.F.M.Cap.; KONELIO FALETOI; GREGORIO S. HONORIO, M.S.; DONG MIN (PAUL) LI; DENNIS KOSHKO; WILLIAM J. KUNISCH II; JACK RYAN; MICHAEL G. SCULLY, S.J.; WILLIAM SHANNON; EFREN A. TOMAS, M.S.

Diocesan Finance Council—Most Rev. CLARENCE R. SILVA, Ex-Officio; Very Rev. GARY L. SECOR, V.G., Ex-Officio; LISA SAKAMOTO, Ex-Officio; MARLENE DE COSTA, Consultant, Ex Officio; ROBERT S. HARRISON, Chair; Sr. DAVILYN AHCHICK, O.S.F., Sec.; PAUL DE VILLE; JANESSA BONIFACIO; VERCY PASCUAL; LAWRENCE LASUA; TARYN SCHUMAN; JAMES M. SEVERSON; TODD TANIGUCHI; BRENDAN PORICK, Staff Representative.

Diocesan Pastoral Council—TRACY HOEVEL, Windward Oahu Representative; Deacon JERRY L. TOKARS, M.A., Deacons Representative; DALLAS CARTER JR., Central Oahu Vicariate Representative; MAUREEN SATURNIO, East Hawaii Vicariate Representative; JOSEPH MITCHELL, Maui Vicariate Representative; MARJORIE FUJIMOTO, West Hawaii Vicariate Representative; Rev. ALAPAKI KIM, Presbyteral Council Representative; Sr. MALIA DOMINICA WONG, O.P., D.Min., Rel. Women Representative; ALDA MAE TAKABAYASHI, West Honolulu Vicariate Representative; Bro. JOHN CAMPBELL, S.M., Rel. Men Representative & Co Chair; SOANE UIAGALELEI, East Honolulu Vicariate Representative; JANEEL T. T. HEW, Molokai/Lanai Vicariate Representative; ELIZABETH FREITAS, Kauai Vicariate Representative, Chair; Rev. JAMES ORSINI, Priest Representative (Retired); KRISTINE CABUDOL, Leeward Oahu Vicariate Representative; GABRIEL GANIBE, Young Adults Representative; Most Rev. CLARENCE R. SILVA, Ex Officio; Very Rev. GARY L. SECOR, V.G., Ex Officio; SHARON CHIARUCCI, Staff Representative.

Bishops Administrative Advisory Council—Very Rev. GARY L. SECOR, V.G.; Revs. MICHEL DALTON, O.F.M.Cap.; MANUEL HEWE; Deacon WALTER H. YOSHIMITSU; DARA PERREIRA, PHR; JAYNE MONDOY, M.A., P.L.; LISA SAKAMOTO.

Clergy Personnel Board—Most Rev. CLARENCE R. SILVA, Ex Officio; Very Rev. GARY L. SECOR, V.G., Ex-Officio; Revs. MANUEL HEWE, Chair; WILLIAM KUNISCH; PASCUAL ABAYA; MICHEL DALTON, O.F.M.Cap.; HERMAN GOMES, SS.CC.; EFREN A. TOMAS, M.S.; KONELIO FALETOI; MICHAEL G. SCULLY, S.J.; WILLIAM SHANNON; DENNIS KOSHKO; DARLENE CACHOLA, Staff Representative.

Deacon Council—Deacons THOMAS P. CONTRADES, Chair; BILLY WHITFIELD, Vice Chair; CORA CONSTANTINO, Treas.; Deacon MODESTO R. CORDERO, Sec.

Members—West Hawaii: Deacon THOMAS J. ADAMS; EVIE ADAMS. East Hawaii: Deacon LEROY ANDREWS; ROSE NUNOGAWA. Maui: Deacon STEPHEN MAGLENTE; CORA CONSTANTINO. Kauai: Deacons THOMAS CONTRADES; JAMES BOSTICK. Central Oahu: Deacons EFRAIN ANDREWS; MODESTO R. CORDERO; ALICIA BORJA. Leewad Oahu: Deacon KEITH GALANG; BERNADETTE GALANG. Windward Oahu: Deacons CLARENCE DECAIRES JR.; BILLY WHITFIELD. East Honolulu: Deacons ANDREW GERAKAS; HENRY MINER. West Honolulu: Deacon GEORGE THORP JR.; Most Rev. CLARENCE R. SILVA, Ex Officio; Rev. MANUEL HEWE, Ex Officio; Deacon JOHN A. COUGHLIN, Ex Officio; KATHLEEN COUGHLIN, Ex Officio.

Permanent Diaconate Formation Core Team—Co Directors: Deacon JOHN A. COUGHLIN; KATHLEEN COUGHLIN. Members: Deacon EFRAIN ANDREWS; PAMELA ANDREWS; Deacon THOMAS P. CONTRADES; JACQUELYN CONTRADES; Deacon MODESTO R. CORDERO; NYDIA-AILEEN CORDERO; Deacon FREDERICO CARAHASEN JR.; LINA CARAHASEN; Deacon KEITH GALANG, Coord. Field Educ.; Rev. MANUEL HEWE, Ex Officio.

Office of Clergy Priest Retirement Committee—Rev. DENNIS KOSHKO, Chm.; DARA PERREIRA, PHR, Co Chair. Members: STELLA M. WONG, M.S.W.; Very Rev. GARY L. SECOR, V.G.; Revs. LANE AKIONA, SS.CC.; GORDON COMBS, O.F.M.Cap. (Retired); CLARENCE L. FISCHER; THOMAS P. JOSEPH, Ph.D.; MANUEL HEWE; Sr. PATTY CHANG, C.S.J.

Office of Clergy - Diocesan Screening Committee—Rev. MANUEL HEWE, Chair; Very Rev. GARY L. SECOR, V.G., Ex Officio. Members: Dr. ALFRED M. ARENSDORF, M.D., F.A.A.C.A.P.; Revs. CLARENCE L. FISHER (Retired); MARK DEL ROSARIO, S.S.S.; CARMELO REY LIM.

Hawaii Catholic Conference Board—Most Rev. CLARENCE R. SILVA, Chair. Members: Very Rev. GARY L. SECOR, V.G.; Rev. ROBERT STARK, S.S.S.; Deacon WALTER H. YOSHIMITSU; KENT ANDERSON; DAVID COLEMAN, M.A., Ph.D.; PATRICK DOWNES; JEROME E. RAUCKHORST; ANNE HARPHAM; BETTY LOU LARSON; PEGGY LEONG; JOSEPH LOCATELLI; CAROL IGNACIO; PAMELA WITTY-OAKLAND; ALLEN CARDINES JR., Consultant; EVA MARIE ANDRADE, Coord.

Saint Damien/Blessed Mother Marianne Commission—Most Rev. CLARENCE R. SILVA, Chair. Members: Sisters DAVILYN AHCHICK, O.S.F.; WILLIAM MARIE ELENIKI, O.S.F.; FRANCIS REGIS HADANO, O.S.F.; ALICIA DAMIEN LAU, O.S.F.; Very Rev. CHRISTOPHER KEAHI, SS.CC.; Rev. CLYDE L. GUERREIRO, SS.CC.; Sr. HELENE WOOD, SS.CC.; Deacon WALLACE MITSUI; PATRICK BOLAND; GAIL ANN CHEW; CUMMINS MAHOE III; BARBARA OKAMOTO; JULIE-ANN BICOY.

Diocesan Development Commission—JOAN BICKSON; R. CHARLES BOCKEN; JOHN BROGAN; ROBERT BRUCE GRAHAM JR., ESQ.; STANLEY HONG; JON THOMAS HUNTER; LILA MARANTZ. Ex-Officio: Most Rev. CLARENCE R. SILVA; LISA SAKAMOTO; CYNTHIA LALLO.

Diocesan Liturgical Commission—Ex Officio: Most Rev. CLARENCE R. SILVA; Rev. WILLIAM KUNISCH. Members: ROSE BRITO; DARLENE AH YO; CALVIN LIU, Chair; Rev. GERONIMO CASTRO, M.S.; CECIL FARIN; MARINA PASCUA; Deacons RONALD PAGLINAWAN; BILLY WHITFIELD; CORA BUNO, Sec.; LISA GOMES; GABRIEL GANIBE; SHARON CHIARUCCI, Coord.

Bishop's Advisory Board for Persons with Disabilities—Members: VALERY O'BRIEN; LINDA DEVERA; MICHAEL PAEKUKUI; IWIE TAMASHIRO, Staff Rep.; CAROL IGNACIO, Staff Rep.

Diocesan Board of Education—Most Rev. CLARENCE R. SILVA, Ex Officio; Very Rev. GARY L. SECOR, V.G., Ex Officio; MICHAEL M. ROCKERS, Ed.D., Ex Officio; LOVEY ANN DEREGO, Ex Officio.

Chairman—ANDREA KAUMEHEIWA. Members: WILLIAM BRILHANTE JR.; PATRICIA BERGIN; LISA COLUCCIO; DAVID COLEMAN, M.A., Ph.D.; BETSEY GUNDERSON; CELINA HAIGH; SUSAN CAINDEC-RANCHEZ; BRIDGET OLSEN; Rev. LANE AKIONA, SS.CC.; REGINALD MALDONADO; CINDY OLASO; THOMAS G. PANGILINAN; LINDA ANDRADE WHEELER; CHARLOTTE WHITE.

Diocesan Ecumenical Commission—Revs. JACK RYAN, Ecumenical & Interfaith Officer; CLARENCE L. FISHER (Retired); REGINA PFEIFFER, D.Min.; PETER STEIGER, Ph.D.; GAIL SUGIMOTO-LEONG.

Catholic Campaign for Human Development Commission—Deacon LAUREN S. WONG, Diocesan Dir. Members: LUIS CAMPO; TRINI JONES; Deacon MANUEL PASCUA; JASMINE HIGA; ALLEN PACQUING; MARGARET UIAGALELEI; Deacon JERRY H. NUNOGAWA; CYNTHIA TAYLOR; PETER MATTOON. Ex Officio: CAROL IGNACIO; Rev. ROBERT STARK, S.S.S.

Diocesan Planning and Building Commission—VINCENT A. VERNAY, Chair. Members: Very Rev. GARY L. SECOR, V.G.; Rev. Msgr. TERRENCE A.M. WATANABE; Revs. WILLIAM KUNISCH; WILLIAM SHANNON; Deacon WALTER H. YOSHIMITSU; GARY BATCHELLER; EDWARD ANDRADE; STEPHEN FONG; MARK LIVELY; FRANK FELIX JR.; DOUGLAS DICK; WALTER CLUR; MICHAEL M. ROCKERS, Ed.D., Ex Officio; LISA SAKAMOTO, Ex Officio; MARLENE DE COSTA, Ex Officio; PAULETTE VERNAY, Staff.

Diocesan Youth and Young Adult Ministry Advisor Council—LISA GOMES, Dir. Advisors: EDWINA FUJIMOTO; SALLY GANIRON; DEBRA ARELLANO; GRACE BENITEZ; KEITH FEBRERO; KATHLEEN LEE; BRENT LIMOS; CHARLIE SILVA; MAKA SECRETARIO; CHARLESTON UNCIANO.

Implementation Commission of Diocesan Road Map for Pastoral Program and Facility Needs—COLLEEN SATHRE, Chair; Very Rev. GARY L. SECOR, V.G., Co Chm.; RIANE ASHLEY CARDENAS; SHARON CHIARUCCI; Rev. MICHEL DALTON, O.F.M.Cap.; PATRICK DOWNES; MICHAEL M. ROCKERS, Ed.D.; Rev. MANUEL HEWE; CAROL IGNACIO; Deacon WALLACE MITSUI; DARA PERREIRA, PHR; JAYNE MONDOY, M.A., P.L.; Bro. BERNARD PLOEGER, S.M.; Sr. FLORENCE REMATA, O.S.F.; LISA SAKAMOTO; MARIA SULLIVAN, Esq.; VINCENT A. VERNAY; MICHAEL WEAVER; PATRICK DOWNES; MILDRED CHARGUALAF; LISA GOMES.

CLERGY, PARISHES, MISSIONS AND PAROCHIAL SCHOOLS

ISLAND OF OAHU

CITY OF HONOLULU

1—CATHEDRAL OF OUR LADY OF PEACE (1843) Most Rev. Clarence R. Silva; Rev. John W. Berger, Rector. In Res., Revs. Khanh Hoang; Manuel Hewe; Gordon Combs, O.F.M.Cap. (Retired); Marvin Samian.
Office: 1184 Bishop St., Honolulu, 96813-2838. Tel: 808-536-7036; Fax: 808-585-3383. Email: coolop@rcchawaii.org. Web: www.cathedralofourladyofpeace.com.
School—Cathedral Catholic Academy, (Grades K-8), 1728 Nuuanu Ave., Honolulu, 96817. Tel: 808-533-2069; Fax: 808-533-3040. Mrs. Jaydee Wagner, Prin. Lay Teachers 13; Students 142.
Catechesis/Religious Program—Mr. Mike Bauer, D.R.E. Students 75.

2—ST. ANTHONY (1916) Rev. Manuel C. Dela Cruz, M.S. In Res., Rev. Teodulo Gaquit.
Office: 640 Puuhale Rd., Honolulu, 96819. Tel: 808-845-3255; Fax: 808-842-3664. Email: stanthonyhonolulu@gmail.com.
School—(Grades K-8) Tel: 808-845-2769; Fax: 808-853-2234. Sr. Victoria Lavente, S.P.C., Prin. Sisters 4; Lay Teachers 6; Students 94.
Catechesis/Religious Program—Students 134.
Convent—702 Puuhale Rd., Honolulu, 96819. Tel: 808-845-4888. St. Paul of Chartres 4.

3—ST. AUGUSTINE BY THE SEA (1854) Revs. Lane Akiona, SS.CC.; Lusius Nimu, SS.CC., Parochial Vicar; Deacons Andres J. Calunod; Robert Cobb.
Office: 130 Ohua Ave., Honolulu, 96815. Tel: 808-923-7024; Fax: 808-922-4086. Email: staugustinebythesea@gmail.com. Web: www.staugustinebythesea.com.
Catechesis/Religious Program—Students 47.

4—BLESSED SACRAMENT (1938) Rev. Steve Nguyen; Deacon Ronald Choo.
Office: 2124 Pauoa Rd., Honolulu, 96813. Tel: 808-531-6980. Email: bscpauoa@rcchawaii.org.
Catechesis/Religious Program—Students 26.

5—LATIN MASS COMMUNITY, P.O. Box 30285, Honolulu, 96813.

6—CO-CATHEDRAL OF ST. THERESA OF THE CHILD JESUS (1931) Revs. William J. Kunisch II, Rector; Jon Cabico, Parochial Vicar; Deacon Roy T. Matsuo. In Res., Rev. Peter Dumag (Philippines).
Office: 712 N. School St., Honolulu, 96817. Tel: 808-521-1700; Fax: 808-599-3629. Email: sttheresa@cocathedral.org. Web: www.cocathedral.org.
School—(Grades K-8) Tel: 808-536-4703; Fax: 808-524-6861. Cyril Pires, Prin.; Wanda Pila, Vice Prin. Sisters 4; Lay Teachers 23; Students 376.
Catechesis/Religious Program—Students 220.

Convent—Sisters of St. Joseph of Carondelet, Tel: 808-533-3101.
Vietnamese Catholic Community—Tel: 808-536-0046. Email: vietholymartyrs@gmail.com. Web: www.vietmartyrs-honolulu.net. Rev. Vincent Kien Nguyen, Chap.

7—HOLY FAMILY (1950) Rev. Sebastian V. Chacko.
Office: 830 Main St., Honolulu, 96818. Tel: 808-422-1135; Fax: 808-423-0389. Email: hfc830@gmail.com.
School—(Grades PreK-8) Tel: 808-423-9611; Fax: 808-422-5030. Email: cmalins@hfca-hawaii.org; cmalins@holyfamilycatholicacademy.org. Christina Malins, Prin.; Michele Holl, Librarian. Lay Teachers 40; Students 646.
Catechesis/Religious Program—Tel: 808-839-1876, Ext. 226; Fax: 808-634-6888. Diane Fujinaga, C.R.E.; Michelle Izon, C.R.E. Students 82.

8—HOLY TRINITY (1939) Rev. Dennis Koshko; Deacons Samuel Taylor; Daniel R. Guinaugh; Santiago Gorospe.
Office: 5919 Kalanianaole Hwy., Honolulu, 96821. Tel: 808-396-0551; Fax: 808-396-1380.
Catechesis/Religious Program—Tel: 808-396-0551, Ext. 11; Fax: 808-396-1380. Students 100.

9—ST. JOHN THE BAPTIST (1844) [CEM] Rev. John Fredy Quintero, Admin.; Deacon Peter Soumwei. In Res., Rev. Mario Raquepo.
Office: 2324 Omilo Ln., Honolulu, 96819. Tel: 808-845-0984; Fax: 808-841-6643. Email: sjbkalihi@gmail.com.
School—(Grades PreK-8), 2340 Omilo Ln., Honolulu, 96819. Tel: 808-841-5551; Fax: 808-842-6104. Web: sjbhawaii.net. Sr. Delia Obenza, O.P., Prin. Dominican Sisters 6; Lay Teachers 15; Students 223.
Catechesis/Religious Program—Tel: 808-845-3304. Students 172.
Convent—2330 Omilo Ln., Honolulu, 96819. Tel: 808-551-3309. Web: www.ophawaiiregion.com. Dominican Sisters of the Most Holy Rosary 6.

10—NEWMAN CENTER-HOLY SPIRIT PARISH (1981) Rev. Jack Ryan.
Mailing Address: 1941 East West Rd., Honolulu, 96822-2321. Tel: 808-988-6222; Fax: 808-988-1752.
Res.: 2727 Pamoa Rd., Honolulu, 96822-1838. Tel: 808-988-3464; Fax: 808-988-7627. Web: www.newmanhawaii.org.
Catechesis/Religious Program—Students 72.

11—OUR LADY OF THE MOUNT (1870) [CEM] Rev. Adrian R. Gervacio.
Office: 1614 Monte St., Honolulu, 96819. Tel: 808-845-0828; Fax: 808-845-0826. Email: olmmonte@yahoo.com.
Catechesis/Religious Program—Tel: 808-845-0828. Students 63.

12—ST. PATRICK (1929) Revs. Clarence L. Guerreiro, SS.CC.; Thomas Choo, SS.CC., Parochial Vicar. Please refer to the listing for St. Patrick Monastery under Monasteries and Residences for Priests and Brothers for additional residents.
Office: 1124 Seventh Ave., Honolulu, 96816. Tel: 808-732-5565; Fax: 808-737-2477.
School—(Grades K-8), 3320 Harding Ave., Honolulu, 96816. Tel: 808-734-8979; Fax: 808-732-2851. Sr. Anne Clare De Costa, SS.CC., Parish Dir. Educ. Sisters 1; Lay Teachers 23; Students 313.
Catechesis/Religious Program—Students 91.

13—SS PETER AND PAUL (1969) Revs. David O. Travers, S.J., Admin.; Sydney Fernandes, Parochial Vicar; Deacons Richard Port; Richard Abel.
Mailing Address: 800 Kaheka St., Honolulu, 96814. Tel: 808-941-0675; Fax: 808-945-0689. Email: sspeterpaul@hawaii.rr.com. Web: www.sspeterpaulhawaii.org.
Res.: 1561 Kanunu St., #1006, Honolulu, 96814. Tel: 808-955-8830.
Catechesis/Religious Program—Students 46.

14—ST. PHILOMENA (1942) Rev. Peter Miti.
Office: 3300 Ala Laulani St., Honolulu, 96818-2837. Tel: 808-839-1876; Fax: 808-834-6888. Email: sp.hawaii.receptionist@gmail.com. Web: www.stphilomenahawaii.org.
School & Early Learning Center—Tel: 808-833-8080; Fax: 808-834-3438. Nicole M. Darity, Dir. Lay Teachers 12; Students 193.
Catechesis/Religious Program—Tel: 808-839-1876. Kurt Meyer, C.R.E. Students 92.

15—ST. PIUS X (1958) Revs. Gordian Carvalho; Edmundo N. Barut Jr., Parochial Vicar; Deacons Sidney Townsley, (Retired); Vince Wozniak; Ronald Nelson.
Res. & Mailing Address: 2821 Lowrey Ave., Honolulu, 96822-1644. Tel: 808-988-3308; Fax: 808-973-2209. Email: general@mp-cc.net. Web: www.mp-cc.net.
Catechesis/Religious Program—Students 38.
Korean Catholic Community—2949 Kahawai St., Honolulu, 96822. Tel: 808-988-9678; Fax: 808-988-6047. Revs. Maryjoseph Kwangseog Han, Chap.; John Chrysostom Seugwook Lim, Chap.

16—SACRED HEART (1914) Revs. Gordian Carvalho; Edmundo N. Barut Jr., Parochial Vicar; Deacons Sidney Townsley, (Retired); Vince Wozniak; Ronald Nelson.
Office: 1701 Wilder Ave., Honolulu, 96822. Tel: 808-973-2211; Fax: 808-973-2209. Email: general@mp-cc.net. Web: www.mp-cc.net.
School—Maryknoll School, (Grades PreK-12), 1526 Alexander St., Honolulu, 96822. Tel: 808-952-8400; 808-952-7100; Fax: 808-972-7101. Shana Tong, Grade School Prin.; Glenn Madeiros, Grade School Vice Prin.; Betsey H. Gunderson, High School Prin.; Darcie Kawamura, High School Vice Prin.; Virginia Koo, Librarian (Grade School); Jennifer Tseu, Librarian (High School). Lay Teachers 130; Students 1,434.
Catechesis/Religious Program—Tel: 808-952-7120; Fax: 808-952-2009. Becky Kotake, D.R.E. Students 111.

17—STAR OF THE SEA (1946) Revs. Mark del Rosario, S.S.S.; Wilbert A. Laroga, Parochial Vicar; Bro. Salvador Yanzon, S.S.S.; Deacons Andrew Gerakas; Henry Miner; Leslie Victor; Fernando V. Ona.
Office: 4470 Aliikoa St., Honolulu, 96821. Tel: 808-734-0396; Fax: 808-744-2008.
School—4469 Malia St., Honolulu, 96821. Tel: 808-734-0208; Fax: 808-735-9790. Email: star@starofthesea.org. Web: www.starofthesea.org. Carola A. Souza, Prin. Lay Teachers 22; Students 236.
Early Learning Center—4470 Aliikoa St., Ste. 100, Honolulu, 96821. Tel: 808-734-3840; Fax: 808-732-1738. Email: elc@starofthesea.org. Web: www.starofthesealc.org. Lisa Foster, Prin. Lay Teachers 11; Students 157.
Catechesis/Religious Program—Tel: 808-735-0259. Darlene Ah Yo, D.R.E. Students 14.

18—ST. STEPHEN CATHOLIC PARISH (1932) Rev. Khanh Pham Nguyen.
Office: 2747 Pali Hwy., Honolulu, 96817. Tel: 808-595-3105. Email: ssccpali@rcchawaii.org.
Catechesis/Religious Program—Students 29.

OUTSIDE THE CITY OF HONOLULU

County of Honolulu

AIEA, ST. ELIZABETH (1926) Rev. Thomas P. Joseph; Deacon Joaquin Borja.
Office: 99-312 Moanalua Rd., 96701. Tel: 808-487-2414; Fax: 808-487-2168. Web: www.stelizabethaiea.org.
School—(Grades K-8), 99-310 Moanalua Rd., 96701. Tel: 808-488-5322; Fax: 808-486-0856. Email: info@steliz-hi.org. Web: www.steliz-hi.org. Sr. Bernarda Sindol, O.P., Prin. Sisters 5; Lay Teachers 14; Students 233.
Catechesis/Religious Program—Tel: 808-487-7994; Fax: 808-487-2168. Manette Kokubun, D.R.E. Students 188.
Convent—Dominican Sisters of the Most Holy Rosary 5.

EWA, IMMACULATE CONCEPTION CHURCH (1929) Rev. Michel Dalton, O.F.M.Cap.
Office: 91-1298 Renton Rd., 96706. Tel: 808-681-3701; Fax: 808-681-3117. Web: www.immaculateconceptionewa.com.
Catechesis/Religious Program—Students 173.

EWA BEACH, OUR LADY OF PERPETUAL HELP (1969) Revs. Scott Bush; Cosmenio Rosimo Jr., Parochial Vicar; Deacon Ron Paglinawan.
Office: 91-1004 North Rd., 96706-2796. Tel: 808-689-8681; Fax: 808-689-1954. Email: olph@rcchawaii.org.
School—(Grades K-8), 91-1010 North Rd., 96706. Tel: 808-689-0474; Fax: 808-689-4847. Sr. Davilyn AhChick, O.S.F., Prin. Lay Teachers 9; Students 188.
Catechesis/Religious Program—Remi Cabrera, C.R.E.; Julia Torres, D.R.E. Students 347.

KAHUKU, ST. ROCH (1917) [CEM] Rev. Dong Min (Paul) Li.
Mailing Address: P.O. Box 295, 96731.
Res.: 56-350 Kamehameha Hwy., 96731. Tel: 808-293-5026; Fax: 808-293-1737. Email: saintrocc001@hawaii.rr.com. Web: saintrochkahuku.com.
Catechesis/Religious Program—Tel: 808-293-5026. Students 53.
Mission—St. Joachim (1917) P.O. Box 295, Honolulu Co. 96731.

KAILUA

1—ST. ANTHONY OF PADUA (1933) Revs. Clarence Zamora, Admin.; Exsequel Tuyor, Parochial Vicar; Deacons Ernest F. Carlbom; George Thorp Jr.
Office: 148 Makawao St., Ste. A, 96734-2334. Tel: 808-266-2222; Fax: 808-266-2229. Email: frontdesk@stanthonyskailua.org. Web: www.stanthonyskailua.org.
Res.: 116 Makua St., 96734.
School—(Grades K-8), 148 Makawao St., 96734-2334. Tel: 808-261-3331; Fax: 808-263-3518. Bridget Olsen, Prin. Sisters 1; Lay Teachers 29; Students 397.
Early Learning Center—Lay Teachers 4; Students 69.
Catechesis/Religious Program—Tel: 808-791-6525. Donna Estomago, C.R.E. Students 139.

2—ST. JOHN VIANNEY (1962) Rev. Thomas L. Gross; Deacons Walter H. Yoshimitsu; Clarence DeCaires; Jerry L. Tokars; Lauren S. Wong.
Office: 920 Keolu Dr., 96734-3842. Tel: 808-262-8317; Fax: 808-772-5634. Email: sjv920@hawaii.rr.com. Web: www.sjvhawaii.org.
School—(Grades PreK-8), 940 Keolu Dr., 96734-3842. Tel: 808-261-4651; Fax: 808-263-0505. Email: achee@hawaii.rr.com. Web: sjv-school.org. Mr. Michael Busekrus, Prin. Lay Teachers 34; Students 260.
Catechesis/Religious Program—Students 157.

KANEOHE, ST. ANN (1841) [CEM] Revs. Herman Gomes, SS.CC.; Benny Kosasih, SS.CC., Parochial Vicar; Deacon Billy Whitfield. In Res., Revs. John Keenan, S.S.S.; Robert Stark, S.S.S.
Office: 46-129 Haiku Rd., 96744. Tel: 808-247-3092; Fax: 808-235-0717.
School—46-125 Haiku Rd., 96744. Tel: 808-247-3092; Fax: 808-235-0717. Email: dkauhane@hawaii.rr.com; vdesilva@stannshi.org. Daphne Kauhane, Parish Dir. Educ.; Victoria DeSilva, Prin. (School). Sisters 1; Lay Teachers 24; Students 246.
Early Learning Center—Mandy Thronas-Brown, Prin. Lay Teachers 11; Students 157.
Catechesis/Religious Program—Students 287.

KAPOLEI, ST. JUDE (1988) Rev. Joseph A. Diaz, Admin.; Deacons Edward Vargas; John A. Coughlin. Res.: 92-104 Leipapa Way, 96707. Tel: 808-672-9041. Church: 92-455 Makakilo Dr., 96707. Tel: 808-672-8669; Fax: 808-672-3779. Email: info@stjudehawaii.org; pastor@stjudehawaii.org. Web: www.stjudehawaii.org.
Catechesis/Religious Program—Tel: 808-672-8669, Ext. 212. Bonnie Boquer, D.R.E. Students 221.

MILILANI TOWN, ST. JOHN APOSTLE AND EVANGELIST (1969) Rev. Msgr. John Mutiso Mbinda; Rev. Cletus Mooya, Parochial Vicar; Deacons Wally Mitsui; Modesto R. Cordero.
Office: 95-370 Kuahelani Ave., 96789. Tel: 808-623-3332, Ext. 100; Fax: 808-623-3286. Email: info@sjmililani.com. Web: www.sjmililani.com.
St. John Catholic Preschool—Tel: 808-623-3332, Ext. 200; Fax: 808-623-6496. Email: mscat@sjcpmililani.org. Catherine Awong, Dir. Lay Teachers 3; Students 55.
Catechesis/Religious Program—Tel: 808-623-3332, Ext. 204,. Sr. Caridad Alma Esmero, S.P.C., D.R.E. Students 363.

NANAKULI, ST. RITA (1963) Rev. Alapaki Kim; Deacon Harold S. Levy Jr.
Office: 89-318 Farrington Hwy., 96792. Tel: 808-668-7833; Fax: 808-668-7716. Email: strita_nanakuli@rcchawaii.org. Web: www.stritananakuli.org.
Catechesis/Religious Program—Tel: 808-668-5634. Brenda Levy, D.R.E. Students 75.

PEARL CITY, OUR LADY OF GOOD COUNSEL (1958) [CEM] Revs. Pascual Abaya; Arthur Amian, Parochial Vicar; Deacons Thomas Miyashiro; Efrain Andrews. In Res., Rev. Msgr. Thaddeus F. Mercado. Office & Rectory: 1525 Waimano Home Rd., 96782. Tel: 808-455-3012; Fax: 808-456-9443. Email: olgc@hawaii.rr.com. Web: www.olgc.moki.org.
School—(Grades PreSchool-8), 1530 Hoolana St., 96782. Tel: 808-455-4533; Fax: 808-455-5587. Cindy Olaso, Prin. Lay Teachers 11; Students 247.
Catechesis/Religious Program—Pamela Falasco, D.R.E.; Eulerson Pajimula, Coord., Youth Min. Students 184.

WAHIAWA, OUR LADY OF SORROWS (1939) Rev. Edgar B. Brillantes; Deacons Benjamin A. Awana; Celestino Enwalu.
Office: 1403-A California Ave., 96786-2595. Tel: 808-621-5109; Fax: 808-622-5073. Email: ols@hawaiiantel.net.
Catechesis/Religious Program— Shirley Caban, C.R.E. Students 102.

WAIALUA, ST. MICHAEL (1853) [CEM] Revs. Bertram Lock, SS.CC.; Johnathan Hurrell, SS.CC., Parochial Vicar.
Office: 67-390 Goodale Ave., 96791. Tel: 808-637-4040; Fax: 808-637-4287. Email: stsmichaelpeter_paul@hawaii.rr.com. Web: www.stsmichaelpeterpaul.com.
School—(Grades PreK-8), 67-340 Haona St., 96791. Tel: 808-637-7772; Fax: 808-637-7722. Deanna Arecchi, Prin.; Nanilisa Pascua, Librarian. Lay Teachers 14; Students 220.
Catechesis/Religious Program—Tel: 808-637-4040. Students 47.
Mission—SS. Peter and Paul 67-390 Goodale Ave., Honolulu Co. 96791.

WAIANAE, SACRED HEART (1838) [CEM] Rev. Carmelo Rey Lim, Admin.; Deacons Jerome Vito; Misa Sewen.
Office: 85-786 Old Government Rd., 96792. Tel:

808-696-3773; Fax: 808-696-2242. Email: shcwaianae@hawaii.rr.com. Web: www.sacredheartwaianae.org.
Catechesis/Religious Program—Tel: 808-696-2242. Students 134.

WAIKANE, OUR LADY OF MT. CARMEL (1867) [CEM] Rev. Paulo R. Kosaka, O.F.M.Cap., Admin.
Office: P.O. Box 6581, 96744.
Res.: 48-422 Kamehameha Hwy., 96744. Tel: 808-239-9269; Fax: 808-239-8561. Email: olmc001@hawaii.rr.com. Web: www.mtcarmelhawaii.wordpress.com.
Catechesis/Religious Program—Students 32.

WAIMANALO, ST. GEORGE (1954) Rev. Robert Maher, O.F.M.Cap., Admin.; Deacon Edward Cho.
Office: 41-1323 Kalanianaole Hwy., 96795. Tel: 808-259-7188; Fax: 808-259-0169. Email: stgeorge96795@aol.com. Web: www.stgeorgechurchwaimanalo.com.
Catechesis/Religious Program—Tel: 808-259-8979. Students 105.

WAIPAHU, ST. JOSEPH (1940) [CEM] Revs. Gregorio S. Honorio, M.S.; Napoleon Andres, M.S., Parochial Vicar; Wilfredo Iminga, M.S., Parochial Vicar; Deacon Keith Galang.
Office: 94-675 Farrington Hwy., 96797. Tel: 808-677-4276; Fax: 808-671-3215.
School—(Grades PreK-8), 94-651 Farrington Hwy., 96797. Tel: 808-677-4475; Fax: 808-677-8937. Email: sjs@stjosephwaipahu.org. Web: www.stjosephwaipahu.org. Miss Beverly Sandobal, Prin.; Vivian Sua, Librarian. Sisters 2; Lay Teachers 23; Students 417.
Catechesis/Religious Program—Tel: 808-676-3493; Fax: 808-676-3493. Geraldine Simbahon, D.R.E. Students 654.

WAIPIO, RESURRECTION OF THE LORD (1986) Rev. Paul L. Minchak, O.F.M.Cap., Admin.; Deacon Ernest Libarios Sr.
Mailing Address: 94-1260 Lumikula St., Waipahu, 96797. Tel: 808-676-4700; Fax: 808-676-4534. Email: resurrect001@hawaii.rr.com.
Catechesis/Religious Program— Yuko D. Ornellas, D.R.E. Students 136.

ISLAND OF HAWAII

County of Hawaii

HAWI, SACRED HEART (1905) [CEM 2] Rev. Raymond R. Elam, O.S.A., Admin.; Deacon Thomas J. Adams.
Mailing Address: P.O. Box 220, 96719. Email: sacredhearthawi@hawaiiantel.net.
Res.: 55-3374 Akonipule Hwy., 96719. Tel: 808-889-6436; Fax: 808-889-5698. Email: sacredhearthawi@hawaiiantel.net.
Catechesis/Religious Program—Tel: 808-889-0674. Students 100.

HILO, ST. JOSEPH (1860) [CEM] Revs. Samuel E. Loterte, S.S.S.; Clifford Barrios, S.S.S., Parochial Vicar; Deacons Don Aanavi; Jerry H. Nunogawa.
Office: 43 Kapiolani St., 96720. Tel: 808-935-1465; Fax: 808-969-1665. Email: stjosephchurch@stjoehilo.com. Web: stjoehilo.org.
School—(Grades PreK-12), 1000 Ululani St., 96720. Tel: 808-935-4935 (Elementary); 808-935-4936 (High School); Fax: 808-935-6894 (Elementary); 808-969-9019 (High School). Victoria Torcolini, Prin.; Janin Malinowski, Elem. School Librarian; Miri Sumida, Jr./Sr. High School Librarian. Deacons 1; Lay Teachers 32; Students 281.
Catechesis/Religious Program—Chrislyn Villena, C.R.E. & Youth Adult Min. Students 181.

HONAUNAU, ST. BENEDICT (1899) [CEM 4] [JC 4] Rev. Alfred Rebuldela.
Office: 84-5140 Painted Church Rd., Captain Cook, 96704. Tel: 808-328-2227; Fax: 808-328-8482.
Catechesis/Religious Program—Cheryline Ono, D.R.E. Students 59.
Mission—St. John the Baptist Kealakekua, Hawaii Co.
Mission—St. Peter Milolii, Honaunau Co.

HONOKAA, OUR LADY OF LOURDES (1870) [CEM 6] Rev. Raymund Ellorin.
Mailing Address: P.O. Box 129, 96727. Tel: 808-775-9591; Fax: 808-775-0591. Email: ourladyof001@hawaii.rr.com.
Res.: 45-5028 Plumeria St., 96727.
Catechesis/Religious Program—Students 105.

KAILUA-KONA, ST. MICHAEL THE ARCHANGEL (1840) [CEM 4] Revs. Konelio Faletoi; Juan Pablo Galeano, Parochial Vicar. In Res., Rev. John B. Stawasz (Retired).
Office: 75-5769 Alii Dr., 96740. Tel: 808-326-7771. Email: info@onecatholicohana.org. Web: www.onecatholicohana.org.
Catechesis/Religious Program—Students 127.
Mission—Holy Rosary Kalaoa, Hawaii Co.
Mission—Immaculate Conception Holualoa, Hawaii Co.
Mission—St. Paul Honalo, Hawaii Co.
Mission—St. Peter by the Sea Kahaluu, Hawaii Co.

KAMUELA, CHURCH OF THE ANNUNCIATION (1965) [CEM] Rev. Robert W. Schwarzhaupt; Deacon Larry Ignacio.
Mailing Address: P.O. Box 301, 96743.
Res.: 65-1235 Kawaihae Rd., 96743. Tel: 808-885-4196 (Rectory); Fax: 808-887-1220 (Office).
Catechesis/Religious Program—Tel: 808-887-1203. Students 85.
Mission—Church of the Ascension, Puako Puako, Hawaii Co. 96743.

KEAUKAHA, HILO, MALIA PUKA O' KALANI (MARY GATE OF HEAVEN) (1929) Revs. Khanh Hoang, Temporary Admin.; Joseph Hennen, Parochial Vicar.
Office: 326 Desha Ave., Hilo, 96720. Tel: 808-935-9338; Fax: 808-935-3865.
Catechesis/Religious Program—Students 23.

LAUPAHOEHOE, ST. ANTHONY (1926) [CEM 2] Rev. Michael G. Scully, S.J., Admin.
Office: P.O. Box 339, 96764. Tel: 808-962-6538; Fax: 808-962-6971.
Catechesis/Religious Program—Dorothy DeConte, D.R.E. Students 7.

MOUNTAIN VIEW, ST. THERESA (1930) Rev. Carmelito Redondo, Admin.
Office: P.O. Box 37, 96771. Tel: 808-968-6233; Fax: 808-968-6215. Email: stcmv@hawaii.rr.com.
Catechesis/Religious Program—Students 66.
Mission—Holy Rosary Keaau, Hawaii Co.

NAALEHU, SACRED HEART (1846) [CEM] Rev. Joel Barut, Admin.
Office: P.O. Box 150, 96772. Tel: 808-929-7474 (Rectory); 808-928-8208 (Office); Fax: 808-928-8208. Email: hrc.shc@gmail.com.
Street Address: 95-5558 Mamalahoa Hwy., 96772.
Catechesis/Religious Program—Jo Ann Moseley, C.R.E. Students 18.

PAHALA, HOLY ROSARY (1885) [CEM] Rev. Joel Barut, Admin.
Office: P.O. Box 760, 96777. Tel: 808-928-8208; Fax: 808-928-8208. Email: hrc.shc@gmail.com.
Church: 96-3143 Pikake St., 96777.
Catechesis/Religious Program—Students 10.

PAHOA, SACRED HEART (1882) [CEM 2] Rev. Carlito Ranjo, Admin.; Deacons Robert Cyr; Julio Akapito.
Mailing Address: 15-3003 Pahoa Village Rd., 96778. Tel: 808-965-8202; Fax: 808-965-5144. Email: shpahoa@hotmail.com.
Catechesis/Religious Program—Debra Bulosan, C.R.E. Students 61.

PAPAIKOU, IMMACULATE HEART OF MARY (1923) [CEM] Rev. Michael G. Scully, S.J., Admin.; Deacon LeRoy Andrews.
Church: P.O. Box 79, 96781. Tel: 808-964-1240; 808-963-5434; Fax: 808-964-5313.
Catechesis/Religious Program—Oarlene Wingate, D.R.E. Students 58.
Mission—Good Shepherd [CEM] Honomu, Hawaii Co. 96728.

ISLAND OF KAUAI

County of Kauai

KALAHEO, HOLY CROSS (1909) [CEM] Rev. Edison Pamintuan, M.S.
Mailing Address: P.O. Box 487, 96741. Tel: 808-332-8011; Fax: 808-332-7749.
Res.: 2-2370 Kaumualii Hwy., 96741. Tel: 808-332-8011; Fax: 808-332-7749.
Catechesis/Religious Program—Students 108.
Mission—Sacred Heart P.O. Box 487, Eleele, Kauai Co. 96741.

KAPAA, ST. CATHERINE (1887) [CEM 2] Revs. Romelo Somera, Admin.; Robbie Deka, Parochial Vicar; Deacon Manuel Pascua.
Office: 5021-A Kawaihau Rd., 96746. Tel: 808-822-4804; 808-822-7900 (Office); Fax: 808-822-3014. Email: kauaistcatherine@hawaiiantel.net. Web: www.stcatherinekauai.org.
School—(Grades PreK-8) Tel: 808-822-4212; Fax: 808-823-0991. Celina Haigh, Prin.; Gloria Aqui, Librarian. Lay Teachers 12; Students 148.
Catechesis/Religious Program—Students 64.
Mission—St. Sylvester 2390 Kolo Rd., Kilauea, Kauai Co. 96754.
Mission—St. William 5292 Kuhio Hwy., Hanalei, Kauai Co. 96714. Tel: 808-822-7900.

KEKAHA, ST. THERESA (1944) [JC] Revs. Arnel Soriano, M.S.; Enrique C. Lapuebla Jr., M.S., Parochial Vicar; Deacon James Bostick.
Mailing Address: P.O. Box 159, 96752. Tel: 808-337-1548 (Office); Fax: 808-337-1548. Email: sttheresac@yahoo.com.
School—(Grades PreK-8), 8320 Elepaio Rd., 96752. Tel: 808-337-1351; Fax: 808-337-1714. Email: sttheresa_kekaha@yahoo.com. Mary Jean Buza-Sims, Prin.; Adela Chavez, Librarian. Sisters 3; Lay Teachers 6; Students 110.
Catechesis/Religious Program—Tel: 808-338-1725. Raynette Kagawa, C.R.E. Students 23.
Convent—P.O. Box 489, 96752. Tel: 808-337-9661. Sr. Georgellen Vissers, Supr. Franciscan Sisters of Christian Charity 4.
Mission—Sacred Hearts of Jesus & Mary 9496 Kaumualii Hwy., Waimea, Kauai Co. 96796.

KOLOA, ST. RAPHAEL (1841) [CEM 2] Rev. Augustine Uthuppu; Deacon Thomas P. Contrades, Parochial Vicar. In Res., Rev. Rene Bisaillon, M.S. (Retired).
Office: 3011 Hapa Rd., 96756. Tel: 808-742-1955; Fax: 808-742-1845. Email: st.raphael@hawaiiantel.net.
Catechesis/Religious Program—Students 106.

LIHUE, IMMACULATE CONCEPTION (1884) [CEM 2] Revs. William Shannon; Anthon W. Rapozo; Deacon William A. Farias.
Mailing Address: 4453 Kapaia Rd., 96766. Tel: 808-245-2432; Fax: 808-246-2571.
Catechesis/Religious Program—Sr. Florence Remata, O.S.F., Pastoral Assoc.; MaryAnn Bode, C.R.E. Students 154.

ISLAND OF LANAI

LANAI CITY, SACRED HEARTS OF JESUS AND MARY PARISH (1930) [JC] Rev. Reginald Paul S. Pira, Admin.
Mailing Address: P.O. Box 630784, 96763. Tel: 808-565-6837; Fax: 808-565-9052. Email: sacredheartslanai@yahoo.com.
Catechesis/Religious Program—Tel: 808-565-6051. Jessie Myers, D.R.E.; Wilma Koep, Asst. D.R.E. Students 60.

ISLAND OF MAUI

County of Maui

HAIKU, ST. RITA (1922) Rev. Patrick Freitas.
Office: 655 Haiku Rd., 96708. Tel: 808-575-2601; Fax: 808-575-2063.
Catechesis/Religious Program—Students 33.
Mission—St. Gabriel, Keanae.

HANA, ST. MARY (1859) [CEM] [JC 2] Rev. Jose Macoy.
Church: 5065 Hana Hwy., 96713.
Office: P.O. Box 219, 96713. Tel: 808-248-8030; Fax: 808-248-8042. Email: hanastmary@gmail.com.
Catechesis/Religious Program—Tel: 808-248-7417. Esse Sinenci, D.R.E. Students 25.
Mission—St. Peter Puuiki, Maui Co.
Mission—St. Paul Kipahulu, Maui Co.
Mission—St. Joseph Kaupo, Maui Co.

KAHULUI, CHRIST THE KING (1932) [CEM] Revs. Efren A. Tomas, M.S.; Adondee Arrellano, M.S., Parochial Vicar; Deacons Cornelio Pulido; Kenneth Bissen Jr.
Office: 20 W. Wakea Ave., 96732. Tel: 808-877-6098; Fax: 808-871-6296. Web: www.ctkchurchmaui.org.
School—(Grades PreK-4), 211 S. Kaulawahine St., 96732. Tel: 808-877-6618; Fax: 808-871-8101. Bernadette Lopez, Teacher in Charge. Lay Teachers 4; Students 54.
Catechesis/Religious Program—Tel: 808-877-3674. Sr. Angela Laurenzo, C.S.J, D.R.E. Students 213.
Convent—Sisters of St. Joseph of Carondelet

KIHEI, MAUI CO., ST. THERESA (1928) Rev. Msgr. Terrence A.M. Watanabe; Rev. Victor Mauricio Valez, Hispanic Ministry; Deacon Lawrence S. Franco. In Res., Rev. James Orsini (Retired).
Office: 25 W. Lipoa St., 96753. Tel: 808-879-4844; Fax: 808-879-0045. Email: info@saint-theresa.com. Web: www.saint-theresa.com.
Catechesis/Religious Program—Sr. Candelaria Angela Pinula, F.S.P., D.R.E. & Pastoral Assoc. Students 179.

KULA, HAWAII CO., OUR LADY QUEEN OF THE ANGELS (1944) [CEM 2] Rev. Bruno L. Genilla, Admin.
Office: 9177 Kula Hwy., 96790-9464. Tel: 808-878-1261; Fax: 808-878-3105. Email: kcchurch@hawaii.rr.com. Web: www.kulacathliccommunity.org.
Catechesis/Religious Program—Tel: 808-878-3838. Mary Jean Bega, D.R.E. Students 80.
Mission—Holy Ghost 4300 Lower Kula Rd., Waiakoa, Maui Co. 96790-9464.
Mission—St. James the Less Ulupalakua, Maui Co.

LAHAINA, MAUI CO., MARIA LANAKILA (1846) [CEM] Revs. Gary P. Colton; Joseph Pathiyil, Parochial Vicar.
Office: 712 Wainee St., 96761-1511. Tel: 808-661-0552; Fax: 808-661-1670. Email: info@marialanakila.org. Web: www.marialanakila.org.
School—Sacred Hearts School, (Grades PreK-8), 239 Dickenson St., 96761. Tel: 808-661-4720; Fax: 808-667-5363. Email: principal@sacredheartschool.net. Web: www.sacredheartsschool.net. Susan Hendricks, Interim Prin. Lay Teachers 20; Students 190.
Catechesis/Religious Program—Students 115.
Mission—Sacred Hearts of Jesus and Mary Office Rd., Honokahua (Kapalua), Maui Co. 96761.

MAKAWAO, HONOLULU, ST. JOSEPH (1851) [CEM] Rev. Geronimo Castro, M.S.
Res. & Office: 1294 Makawao Ave., 96768. Tel: 808-572-7652; Fax: 808-573-2278.
School—St. Joseph Early Learning Center, (Grades PreSchool) Tel: 808-572-6235; Fax: 808-572-0748.

Helen Souza, Dir. Sisters 2; Lay Teachers 6; Students 57.
Catechesis/Religious Program— Sr. Georgina Delgado, O.P., D.R.E. Students 90.
Convent—Dominican Sisters of the Most Holy Rosary 3.

PAIA, MAUI CO., HOLY ROSARY (1866) [CEM] Rev. Elias F. Escanilla, Admin.; Deacon Patrick Constantino.
Church: 954 Baldwin Ave., 96779-9605. Tel: 808-579-9551; Fax: 808-575-2063.
Catechesis/Religious Program—Tel: 808-579-9551.

WAIHEE , HONOLULU, ST. ANN (1935) [CEM] [JC] Rev. Ramon J. Francisco, Admin.
Office: 40 Kuhinia St., 96793-9216. Tel: 808-244-3284; Fax: 808-244-3284.
Catechesis/Religious Program—Students 75.
Mission—St. Francis Xavier [CEM] [JC] Kahakuloa, Maui Co. 96793.

WAILUKU, MAUI CO., ST. ANTHONY OF PADUA (1846) [CEM] Revs. Roland Bunda, S.M.; Gerald Pleva, S.M., Parochial Vicar; Deacons Hiram Haupu; Stephen Maglente.
Office: 1627 B Mill St., 96793-1999. Tel: 808-244-4148; Fax: 808-242-9375.
School—(Grades PreK-6) Tel: 808-244-4976; 808-242-9024 (PreK); Fax: 808-244-7950. Winona Martinez, Prin.; Carlene Santos, Dir. (PreK). Lay Teachers 8; Students 151.
School—(Grades 7-12) Tel: 808-244-4190; Fax: 808-242-8081. Patricia Rickard, Prin.; Sr. Sara Sanders, C.S.J., Librarian. Sisters 1; Lay Teachers 14; Students 140.
Catechesis/Religious Program—Tel: 808-242-6040. Sr. Eva Joseph Mesina, C.S.J., D.R.E. Students 189.

ISLAND OF MOLOKAI

KALAUPAPA, KALAWAO LAHAINA CO., ST. FRANCIS (1873) Revs. Ambrosius Sanar Sapa, SS.CC.; Clyde L. Guerreiro, SS.CC., Parochial Vicar.
Mailing Address: P.O. Box 9, 96742. Tel: 808-567-6238.
Mission—St. Philomena

KAUNAKAKAI, MAUI CO., SAINT DAMIEN OF MOLOKAI CHURCH (1874) [CEM 2] Attended by Our Lady of Sorrows, Kalua'aha; St. Joseph, Kamalo (Shrine); St. Sophia, Kaunakakai; and St. Vincent Ferrer, Maunaloa. Revs. Clyde L. Guerreiro, SS.CC.; Ambrosius Sanar Sapa, SS.CC., Parochial Vicar; Deacon Michael K. Shizuma.
Mailing Address: P.O. Box 1948, 96748-1948. Tel: 808-553-5220; Fax: 808-553-3534. Email: molocathl@hawaiiantel.net. Web: www.blesseddamienchurch.org.
Office: 115 Ala Malama St., 96748.
Catechesis/Religious Program—Students 67.

Chaplains of Public Institutions

HONOLULU. *Apostleship of the Sea*. Deacon Edward Vargas, Port Chap.
Diocesan Hospital Ministry. Revs. Teodulo Gaquit, Dir., Jon Cabico, Deacon Vincent Wozniak.
Prison Ministry, 6301 Pali Hwy, 96744. Tel: 808-203-6735. Deacon Walter H. Yoshimitsu, Diocesan Representative.

Military Chaplains:
Revs.—
Brzeck, Jon, U.S. Navy
Coe, Austin, U.S. Army
Deichert, Joseph, U.S. Air Force
Delis, Robert, U.S. Marines
Voyt, Steve, U.S. Air Force

On Duty Outside the Diocese:
Revs.—
Blazek, Eugene
Butler, John
Coughlin, Thomas
Evers, Paul H., U.S. Marines
Lanuevo, Victor
Mamo, Nathan
Santry, Robert

On Leave of Absence:
Revs.—
Alexander, Marc, S.T.D., V.G.
Pacudan, Roland

Retired:
Rev. Msgr.—
Nagai, Alan A., 801 S. King St., #1001, 96813.
Revs.—
Bolger, Anthony
Burke, Ronald
Carroll, Joseph, 801 S. King St. #1007, 96813.
Ching, Herbert, 86-660 Lualualei Homestead, Maili, 96792.
DeCosta, George
Fisher, Clarence L., 99-727 Malae Pl., Aiea, 96701.
Grimaldi, Joseph A., J.C.L., M.A., 801 S. King St., 96813.
Heinzel, Thomas R., 7669 Fieldfare Dr., North Las Vegas, NV 89084.
Ky, Joseph T., S.S., The Congregation of the Mother Co-Redemptrix, 1900 Grand Ave., Carthage, MO 64836-3500.
McNeeley, Maurice, 3700 Las Vegas Blvd., # 1124B, Las Vegas, NV 89109.
Sabog, Henry, 2909 Kalihi St., 96819.
Siu, Robert K.C., P.O. Box 1047, Lander, WY 82520.
Stawasz, James, 75-5769 Alii Dr., Kailua-Kona, 96740.
Yim, Louis H., 801 S. King St. #1002, 96813.

Permanent Deacons:
Aanavi, Don, St. Joseph-Hilo, P.O. Box 165, Ninole, 96773.
Abel, Richard, Sts. Peter and Paul, 2116 Lime St. #202, 96826.
Adams, Thomas J., Sacred Heart-Hawi, P.O. Box 1048, Kapaau, 96755.
Akapito, Julio, Sacred Heart, Pahoa
Andrews, Efrain, Our Lady of Good Counsel, 98-1366 Oni Kiniki Pl., Aiea, 96701.
Andrews, LeRoy, Immaculate Heart of Mary, 136 Ululani St., Hilo, 96720.
Awana, Benjamin A., 89-104 A Haleakala Ave., Nannakuli, 96792. Our Lady of Sorrows, Wahiawa
Bissen, Kenneth, Jr., Christ the King, P.O. Box 331208, Kahului, 96732.
Borja, Joaquin, St. Elizabeth, 98-1613 Hoomaike St., Pearl City, 96782.
Bostick, James E., (Retired), P.O. Box 894, Kekaha, 96752.
Calunod, Andres J., St. Augustine By the Sea, 1434 Gregory St., 96817.
Carahasen, Frederico, Jr., St. Elizabeth, 98-1040 Moanalua Rd. #1-101, Aiea, 96701.
Carlbom, Ernest F., St. Anthony, Kailua, 41-865 Mahailua St., Waimanalo, 96795.
Cho, Edward, St. George, 41-1403 Kumuula St., Waimanalo, 96795.
Choo, Ronald T.Y., Blessed Sacrament, 46-144 Hilinama St., Kaneoha, 96744.
Cobb, Robert C., (Retired), 2500 Kalakaua Ave., #1003, 96815.
Constantino, Patrick R., 3188 Kilani Pl., Pukalani, 96734. Holy Rosary, Maui
Contrades, Thomas P., 171 A Lani Alii Pl., Kapaa, 96746. St. Raphael
Cordero, Modesto R., St. John Baptist, 91-1015 Keoneula Blvd., Ewa Beach, 96706.
Coughlin, John A., St. Jude, 92-1041 Makakilo Dr. #80, Kapolei, 96707.
Cyr, Robert, 15-2811 Opakapaka St., Pahoa, 96778-8611. Sacred Heart, Pahoa
DeCaires, Clarence, Jr., St. John Vianney, 1131 Kupau St., Kailua, 96734.
Emwalu, Celestino, Our Lady of Sorrows, Wahiawa
Farias, William A., Immaculate Conception, 4696 Hoomana Rd., Lihue, 96766.
Franco, Lawrence Stanley, St. Theresa - Maui, 452 Kaiola Pl., Kihei, Maui 96753.
Galang, Keith, St. Joseph, 94-595 Kaiewa St., Waipahu, 96797.
Gerakas, Andrew J., Star of the Sea, 4524 Waikui St., 96821.
Gorospe, Santiago, Holy Trinity
Guinaugh, Daniel R., Holy Trinity, 520 Lunalilo Home Rd., 96825.
Haupu, Hiram B., St. Anthony, 4 Nakea Way, Wailuku, 96793.
Ignacio, Lawrence, Annunciation Parish, Kamuela, P.O. Box 317, Paauilo, 96776.
Kang, Dominic S., (Retired)
Levy, Harold S., Jr., St. Rita, 87-2214 Farrington Hwy., Waianae, 96792.
Libarios, Ernest, Sr., Resurrection of the Lord, 98-1470 Kaonohi St., Aiea, 96701.
Maglente, Stephen, St. Anthony Maui, 50 E. Waiko Rd., Wailuku, 96793-9319.
Matsuo, Roy T., Co-Cathedral, 1755 Mahani Loop, 96819.
Miner, Henry, Star of the Sea, 1438 Hunakai St., 96816.
Mitsui, Wallace M., St. John Apostle & Evangelist, 95-690 Lewanuu St., Mililani, 97689.
Miyashiro, Thomas H., Our Lady of Good Counsel, 2054 Hoohai St., Pearl City, 96782.
Nelson, Ronald, 66 Queen St., #2301, 96813. Sacred Heart, Honolulu; St. Pius X
Nunogawa, Jerry H., 1673 Haleloke St., Hilo, 96720. St. Joseph, Hilo; Malia Puka O'Kalani
Ona, Fernando V., M.D., Star of the Sea, 1350 Ala Moana Blvd., 96814.
Paglinawan, Ronald, Our Lady of Perpetual Help, 94-348 Kioele Pl., Miliani, 96789.
Pascua, Manuel, 380 Kaima Pl., Kapaa, 96746. St. Catherine, Kauai
Phillips, Albert C., (Retired), 3297 Haleakala Hwy., Makawao, 96768.
Port, Richard J., Sts. Peter and Paul, 1600 Ala Moana Blvd., #3100, 96815.
Pulido, Cornelio, Christ the King, 624 Molokai Hema St., Kahului, 96732.
Sewen, Misa, Sacred Heart, 85-186 McArthur St., G-304, Waianae, 96792.
Shizuma, Michael K., Saint Damien Catholic Parish, P.O. Box 1311, Kaunakakai, 96748.
Soumwei, Peter, St. John the Baptist, Honolulu
Taylor, Samuel, (Retired), Holy Trinity, 7218 Pikoni Pl., 96825.
Thorp, George, Jr., St. Anthony-Kailua, 1459 Akamai St., Kailua, 96734.
Tokars, Jerry L., M.A., St. John Vianney, 748 Iana St., Kailua, 96734.
Townsley, Sidney J., (Retired), 4389 Malia St., Apt. 225, 96821. Sacred Heart, Honolulu; St. Pius X
Vargas, Edward, 92-1051 Makakilo Dr. #96, Kapolei, 96707. St. Jude
Victor, Leslie, Star of the Sea, 7255 Kuhono St., 96825.
Vito, Jerome, Sacred Heart-Waianae, 87-150 Helelua St.#6, Waianae, 96792.
Whitfield, Billy, P.O. Box 530, Kaaawa, 96730. St. Ann, Kaneohe
William, Chitaro, Our Lady of Sorrows, Wahiawa
Wong, Lauren S.F., St. John Vianney, 1309 Kupau St., Kailua, 96734.
Wozniak, Vincent, Sacred Heart; St. Pius X, 1524 Halekula Way #D, 96822-4918.
Yoshimitsu, Walter H., St. John Vianney, 681 Akoakoa St., Kailua, 96734.

INSTITUTIONS LOCATED IN THE DIOCESE

[A] COLLEGES AND UNIVERSITIES

HONOLULU. *Chaminade University of Honolulu (1955) 3140 Waialae Ave., 96816. Tel: 808-735-4711; Fax: 808-735-7748. Email: admissions@chaminade.edu. Web: www.chaminade.edu. Rev. George Cerniglia, S.M., Rector; Bro. Bernard Ploeger, S.M., Pres. Priests 6; Brothers 10; Lay Teachers 90; Students 2,850; Total Staff 223; Total Enrollment 2,850.

[B] SCHOOLS

ISLAND OF OAHU. *Blessed Marianne Cope Preschool* (1999) (Grades PreSchool), 2707 Pamoa Rd., Honolulu, 96822. Tel: 808-988-6528; Fax: 808-988-5497. Email: sjasouza@stfrancis-oahu.org. Sr. Joan of Arc Souza, O.S.F., Prin. Students 43; Teachers 4.

Damien Memorial School (1962) (Grades 6-12), 1401 Houghtailing St., Honolulu, 96817. Tel: 808-841-0195; Fax: 808-847-1401. Email: zawot@damien.edu; bho@damien.edu. Web: www.damien.edu. Mr. Bernard A.K.S. Ho, Pres. & CEO; Bro. Peter E. Zawot, C.F.C., Prin.; Ms. Cheryle O'Brien, Librarian.
The Congregation of Christian Brothers of Hawaii, Inc. Christian Brothers of Ireland, Inc. Priests 1; Brothers 3; Lay Teachers 30; Students 370.

St. Francis School (1924) (Grades PreK-12), 2707 Pamoa Rd., Honolulu, 96822. Tel: 808-988-4111; Fax: 808-988-5497. Email: admin@stfrancis-oahu.org; lgerboc@stfrancis-oahu.org. Web: www.stfrancis-oahu.org. Sr. Joan of Arc Souza, O.S.F., Prin.; Louise Gerboc, Contact Person; Jennifer Mylett, Librarian. Sisters 5; Lay Teachers 71; Girls 339; Boys 159.

Holy Family Catholic Academy Early Learning Center, 830 Main St., Honolulu, 96818. Tel: 808-421-1265; Fax: 808-422-5030. Email: ELC@holyfamilycatholicacademy.org. Kalei DeMello, Dir. Lay Teachers 4; Students 96.

St. John's Catholic Preschool (1979) 95-370 Kuahelani Ave., Mililani Town, 96789. Tel: 808-623-3332, Ext. 200; Fax: 808-623-6496. Email: preschool@sjmililani.com. Web: sjmililani.com. Catherine Awong, Dir. Total Staff 11; Lay Teachers 3; Students 55.

**Saint Louis School*, (Grades 6-12), 3142 Waialae Ave., Honolulu, 96816-1578. Tel: 808-739-7777; Fax: 808-739-4853. Email: info@saintlouishawaii.org. Web: www.saintlouishawaii.org. Walter Kirimitsu, Pres.; Derrick Ligsay, Dir. Middle School; Patricia Hamamoto, Prin.; Kevin Allen, Librarian. Lay Teachers 50; Boys 652.

Maryknoll School, (Grades K-8), 1526 Alexander St., Honolulu, 96822. Tel: 808-952-8400; Fax: 808-952-7101. Email: admission@maryknollschool.org. Web: www.maryknollschool.org. Perry K. Martin, Pres.; Shana Tong, Prin. Lay Teachers 56; Students 837.

Maryknoll School, 1526 Alexander St., Honolulu, 96822. Tel: 808-952-7200; Fax: 808-952-7201. Email: admission@maryknollschool.org. Web: www.maryknollschool.org. Perry K. Martin, Pres.; Betsey H. Gunderson, Prin. Lay Teachers 44; Students 597.

St. Philomena Early Learning Center (1978) 3300 Ala Laulani St., Honolulu, 96818. Tel: 808-833-8080; Fax: 808-834-3438. Email: admin@spelc-hawaii.com. Nicole M. Darity, E.L.C. Dir. Lay Teachers 10; Teacher Aides 22; Students 175.

Sacred Hearts Academy (1909) (Grades PreK-12), 3253 Waialae Ave., Honolulu, 96816. Tel: 808-734-5058; Fax: 808-737-7867. Email: bwhite@sacredhearts.org. Web: www.sacredhearts.org. Mrs. Betty White, Head of School; Linde Debo, Vice Prin.; Mary Roy, Librarian; Laurel Taylor, Librarian. Sisters 2; Lay Teachers 80; Girls 1,042; Support Staff, Counselors, Administrators 30.

Star of the Sea Early Learning Center, 4470 Aliikoa St., Ste. 100, Honolulu, 96821. Tel: 808-734-3840; Fax: 808-732-1738. Email: postmaster@staroftheseaelc.org. Web: www.staroftheseaelc.org. Lisa Foster, Dir. Lay Teachers 11; Students 157.

ISLAND OF HAWAII. *St. Joseph Montessori Based Preschool and Elementary School* (1948) (Grades PreK-6), 999 Ululani St., Hilo, 96720. Tel: 808-935-4935; Fax: 808-935-6894. Email: sjshilo.principal@gmail.com. Web: www.sjeshilo.org. Victoria Torcolini, Prin.; Janan Malinowski, Librarian. Lay Teachers 14; Students 180; Total Staff 5.

St. Joseph Jr.-Sr. High School (1949) (Grades 7-12), 1000 Ululani St., Hilo, 96720. Tel: 808-935-4936; Fax: 808-969-9019. Email: sjshilo.principal@gmail.com. Web: www.sjhshilo.org. Victoria Torcolini, Prin.; Miri Sumida, Librarian. Deacons 1; Lay Teachers 16; Students 101; Total Staff 10.

ISLAND OF MAUI. *St. Anthony Grade School*, (Grades PreK-6), 1627-A Mill St., Wailuku, 96793. Tel: 808-244-4976; Fax: 808-244-7950. Email: office@sagsmaui.com. Winona Martinez, Prin. Lay Teachers 8; Students 151.

St. Anthony Junior-Senior High School, (Grades 7-12), 1618 Lower Main St., Wailuku, 96793. Tel: 808-244-4190; Fax: 808-242-8081. Email: sas@sasmaui.org. Web: www.sasmaui.org/. Patricia Rickard, Prin.; Sr. Sara Sanders, C.S.J., Librarian. Sisters 1; Lay Teachers 14; Students 140.

St. Anthony Pre-School, 1627-B Mill St., Wailuku, 96793. Tel: 808-242-9024; Fax: 808-986-0654. Email: sap@hawaii.rr.com. Carlene Santos, Dir. Lay Teachers 5; Students 46.

[C] HEALTHCARE INSTITUTES

HONOLULU. *St. Francis Healthcare System of Hawaii*, 2226 Liliha St., Ste. 227, 96817. Tel: 808-547-6883; Fax: 808-547-8018. Web: www.stfrancishawaii.org. Sr. Agnelle Ching, CEO; Rev. Mario Raquepo, Chap.; Rev. Msgr. Thaddeus F. Mercado, P.A., STh.D., Chap.; Rev. Arthur Amian, Chap.; Sisters Patricia Schofield, O.S.F., Chap.; Candida Oroc, O.S.F., Chap.; Miriam Dionise Cabacungan, O.S.F., Chap.; Jovita Agustin, O.S.F., Chap.; Joan Souza, O.S.F., Office Mgr.-Spiritual Svcs.; Mary Rose Atuu, Chap.; Grace Michael Souza, O.S.F., Spiritual Svcs. Coord. Total Staff 332.

St. Francis Development Corporation, 91-2135 Fort Weaver Rd., Ste. 502, Ewa Beach, 96706. Tel: 808-676-1200; Fax: 808-676-1202. Email: pwittyoakland@stfrancishawaii.org. Web: stfrancishawaii.org. Pamela Witty-Oakland, Chief Admin.

St. Francis Home Care Services, 91-2135 Fort Weaver Rd., Ste 506, Ewa Beach, 96706. Tel: 808-534-0777; Fax: 808-676-1300. Corinne Suzuka, Exec. Dir.

St. Francis Home Care Services-Kauai, 4473 Pahee St., Ste. N, Lihue, 96766. Tel: 808-245-6430; Fax: 808-246-8620. Maile Ballesteros, Dir.

St. Francis Hospice Home Setting Program Patients Assisted Annually 1,239.

Healthy Lifestyles Program Tel: 808-547-6035; Fax: 808-595-6996.

St. Francis Lifeline Tel: 808-547-6120; Fax: 808-248-1220. Persons Served Annually 248.

St. Francis Medical Center, 2226 Liliha St., 96817.

St. Francis Medical Center West, 2226 Liliha St., 96817.

St. Francis Residential Care Community dba Franciscan Vistas 91-2135 Ft. Weaver Rd., #502, Ewa Beach, 96706. Tel: 808-676-1200; Fax: 808-676-1202. Total Staff 3.

St. Francis Healthcare Foundation of Hawaii, 2228 Liliha St., Ste. 205, 96817. Tel: 808-547-8030; Fax: 808-547-8034. Sr. William Marie Eleniki, O.S.F., Chief Admin. Total Staff 4.

St. Francis Community Health Services, 2251 Mahalo St., 96817. Tel: 808-595-7566; Fax: 808-547-8149. Sr. Agnelle Ching, CEO.

St. Francis Hospitals Hawaii, 2226 Liliha St., Ste. 227, 96817.

St. Francis Hospital Liliha, 2226 Liliha St., Ste. 227, 96817.

St. Francis Hospital West, 2226 Liliha St., Ste. 227, 96817.

Franciscan Care Services, 2226 Liliha St., Ste. 227, 96817.

Health Services for Senior Citizens, 2228 Liliha St., 96817. Tel: 808-547-6121; Fax: 808-676-1220. Patients Assisted Annually 464.

Sister Maureen Intergenerational Learning Environment aka Franciscan Adult Day Center 2715 Pamoa Rd., 96822. Tel: 808-988-5678; Fax: 808-988-1179. Theresa Basta, Dir. Total Staff 8; Capacity 35; Patients Assisted Annually 130.

The Sister Maureen Keleher Center (Hospice), 24 Puiwa Rd., 96817. Tel: 808-595-7580; Fax: 808-595-0220. Gary Simon, Exec. Dir. Bed Capacity 12; Patients Assisted Annually 128.

The Maurice J. Sullivan Family Hospice Center, 91-2127 Fort Weaver Rd., Ewa Beach, 96706. Tel: 808-678-7580; Fax: 808-678-7597. Gary Simon, Exec. Dir. Bed Capacity 24; Patients Assisted Annually 318.

Our Lady of Kea'au, P.O. Box 1475, Waianae, 96792. Tel: 808-696-7255; Fax: 808-696-5672. Sr. Beatrice Tom, O.S.F., Chief Admin.

KALAUPAPA. *Kalaupapa Nursing Facility* (Molokai), P.O. Box 3333, 96742. Tel: 808-567-6911; Fax: 808-567-6916. Carol Franko, Nursing Supvr.; Dr. Kalani Brady, Settlement Medical Dir.; Dr. John Buzanoski, Dept. Medical Dir. Operated by the State Dept. of Health for Hansen's Disease Branch. Franciscan Sisters of the Third Order 1; Bed Capacity 5; Patients Assisted Annually 17; Total Staff 10.

[D] MONASTERIES AND RESIDENCES OF PRIESTS AND BROTHERS

HONOLULU. *The Christian Brothers of Ireland, Inc.*, 1401 Houghtailing St., 96817. Tel: 808-845-2330; Fax: 808-847-1401. Email: cullerton@damien.edu. Bros. B. John Cullerton, C.F.C.; Liam V. Nolan, C.F.C., School Counselor; Patrick L. O'Hare, C.F.C., (Retired); F. M. Popish, C.F.C., (Retired); K. J. Reilly, C.F.C., Contact Person; Bernard S. Samp, C.F.C; Peter E. Zawot, C.F.C. Brothers 7.

Marianist Communities 3140 Waialae Ave., 96816-1578. Rev. Francis Nakagawa, S.M.; Bro. Robert G. Hoppe, S.M., Vice Pres., Marianist Center of Hawaii. *Center Marianist Community*, 3140 Waialae Ave., 96816. Tel: 808-739-8500; 808-739-8517; Fax: 808-739-8501. Bro. Dennis Schmitz, S.M., Community Dir.; Revs. Timothy Eden, S.M.; Kenneth A. Templin, S.M. (Retired); Joseph Lackner, S.M.; George Cerniglia, S.M.; John Thompson, S.M. Priests 5; Brothers 7; Total in Residence 12. *Marianist Hall Community*, 3140 Waialae Ave., 96816. Tel: 808-739-8300; Fax: 808-739-8320. Revs. Joseph Priestly, S.M.; Paul Fitzpatrick, S.M.; Bro. Frank Damm, Community Dir. Priests 2; Brothers 4. *Chaminade Pohaku Marianist Community*, 3140 Waialae Ave., 96816. Tel: 808-735-4857; Fax: 808-739-8333. Bro. Gary Morris, Dir.; Rev. Robert Bouffier, S.M. Priests 1; Brothers 2. *Wailuku Marianist Community*, 1627 B Mill St., Wailuku, 96793. Tel: 808-244-4148; Fax: 808-242-9375. Revs. Roland Bunda, S.M.; John Klobuka, S.M., Community Dir.; Bros. Jim Vorndran, S.M.; Frank Gomes, S.M. Priests 2; Brothers 3.

KANEOHE. *Congregation of the Sacred Hearts of Jesus and Mary (Hawaii Province SS.CC.)* (1800) P.O. Box 1365, 96744-1365. Tel: 808-247-5035; Fax: 808-235-8849. Email: sacredhearts@hawaii.rr.com. Very Rev. Christopher Keahi, SS.CC., Pres. Prov. Priests 14; Brothers 6.

Sacred Hearts Center, P.O. Box 1365, 96744-1365. Tel: 808-247-5035; Fax: 808-235-8849. Email: sacredhearts@hawaii.rr.com. Very Rev. Christopher Keahi, SS.CC., Prov. Supr.; Revs. Albert Garcia, SS.CC., Supr.; Paul Zaccone, SS.CC.; Bro. Charles Kaahanui, SS.CC., (Molokai). Total in Residence 3; Total Staff 2. *St. Patrick's Monastery*, 1124-A Seventh Ave., Honolulu, 96816. Tel: 808-732-0281; Fax: 808-737-2477. Revs. Thomas Choo, SS.CC.; Clarence L. Guerreiro, SS.CC.; Stephen Van den Eynde, SS.CC., Foster Care Home, 96-137B Waiawa Rd., Pearl City, 96782; James Anguay, SS.CC. (Philippines); Bros. Richard Kupo, SS.CC.; Leo Vendiola, SS.CC.; Patrick Hughes, SS.CC; William Dunn, SS.CC.; George Apo, SS.CC. Total in Residence 6; Total Staff 4.

WAIALUA, OAHU. *Benedictine Monastery of Hawaii/ Retreat Center* (1984) 67-290 Farrington Hwy., P.O. Box 490, 96791. Tel: 808-637-7887; Fax: 808-637-8601. Email: monastery@hawaiibenedictines.org. Web: www.hawaiibenedictines.org. Revs. Michael Sawyer, O.S.B., Treas.; Timothy Ottman, O.S.B.; David Barfknecht, O.S.B., Supr. & Pres.; Sisters Mary Jo McEnany, O.S.B., Vice Pres.; Celeste Cabral, O.S.B.; Geralyn Spaulding, O.S.B.; Bros. Gregory Foret, O.S.B., Sec.; Isidore Derouen, O.S.B.; Sr. Ann Cic, O.S.B. Benedictine Congregation of Our Lady of Mounte Oliveto, O.S.B.

[E] CONVENTS AND RESIDENCES FOR SISTERS

HONOLULU. *Congregation of the Sacred Hearts and of Perpetual Adoration* (1800) 1120 Fifth Ave., 96816. Tel: 808-737-5822; Fax: 808-735-0878. Web: www.ssccpicpus.com. (Sisters of the Congregation of the Sacred Hearts of Jesus and Mary of Perpetual Adoration, SS.CC.).

Regina Pacis Community, 1120 Fifth Ave., 96816. Tel: 808-737-5822; Fax: 808-735-0878. Sisters Regina Mary Jenkins, SS.CC., Pres. & Prov. Supr.; Helene Wood, SS.CC., Vice Pres., Vicar Prov., Supr., & Contact Person; Katherine Francis Miller, SS.CC., Sec.; Irene Barboza, SS.CC., Treas. Sisters 5.

Puawakea Community, 3351 Kalihi St., 96819. Tel: 808-845-4353; Fax: 808-848-2696. Sr. Anne Clare DeCosta, SS.CC., Contact Person. Sisters 3.

Paewalani Community, 45-901 Wailele Rd., 96744. Tel: 808-247-3688; Fax: 808-235-0717. Sr. Anne Clare DeCosta, SS.CC., Contact Person. Sisters 2.

Malia o ka Malu Community, 1117 Fourth Ave., 96816. Tel: 808-734-2048. Sr. Helene Wood, SS.CC., Supr. & Contact Person. Sisters 14.

Na Leo Ho'onani Community, 2151 Kauhana St., 96816. Tel: 808-739-5566. Sisters Katherine Francis Miller, SS.CC., Supr.; Irene Barboza, SS.CC., Contact Person. Sisters 4.

Ho'omaluhia Community, 1735 Ala Aolani St., 96819-1413. Sisters 2.

Maryknoll Sisters of St. Dominic Central Pacific Region 125 Ainoni St., Kailua, 96734-2138. Tel: 808-261-6356 (Res.); 808-261-0267. Email: mkainoni@lava.net. Sr. Joan Chatfield, M.M., Contact Person. Sisters 2. 2880 Oahu Ave., 96822-1732. Tel: 808-988-6540; Fax: 808-988-8089. Email: mkmanoa@hawaii.rr.com. Sisters 3. 1570 Mokulua Dr., Kailua, 96734-3254. Tel: 808-261-1674. Email: mksrslan@hawaiiantel.net. Sisters 2.

The Sisters of St. Francis of the Neumann Communities (1883) St. Francis Convent, 2715 Pamoa Rd., 96822-1885. Tel: 808-988-4432; Fax: 808-687-8695. Email: fregis@stfrancis-oahu.org. Sr. Francis Regis Hadano, O.S.F., Contact Person & Region Min. Sisters of St. Francis of the Neumann Communities (O.S.F.); St. Francis Healthcare System of Hawaii; St. Francis School. Sisters 43.

Sisters of St. Joseph of Carondelet CSJ, Hawaii Vice-Province, Administration Center, 5311 Apo Dr., 96821-1829. Tel: 808-373-3850; Fax: 808-373-8801. Email: smlp@hawaiiantel.net. Sr. Claudia Wong, C.S.J., Dir.

The following are listings of residences and the number of sisters residing at each:

Carondelet Community, 5311 Apo Dr., 96821-1829. Tel: 808-373-3850; Fax: 808-373-5341. Email: pachang@verizon.net. Sisters 7.

Mana'olana Community, 1046 6th Ave., 96816-1644. Tel: 808-737-2130; Fax: 808-732-2851. Email: rsm@hawaii.rr.com. Sisters 3.

St. Joseph by the Sea Community, 206 Kailua Rd., Kailua, 96734-2398. Tel: 808-262-0575. Email: sjbts@hawaii.rr.com. Sisters 4.

St. Theresa Community, 712 N. School St. B, 96817-3098. Tel: 808-533-3101. Email: stccsj@pixi.com. Sisters 3.

Christ the King Community, 211 A. South Kaulawahine St., Kahului, 96732-2200. Tel: 808-877-0790. Email: LePuycsj@aol.com. Sisters 5.

KAILUA. *Hale Medaille Community*, 1160 Akipola St., 96734. Sisters 2.

KANEOHE. *Carmel of the Holy Trinity (Carmelite Monastery)*, 6301 Pali Hwy., 96744-5224. Tel: 808-261-6542. Sr. Agnes Marie Wong, Prioress. Order of Discalced Carmelite Nuns of Our Lady of Mount Carmel (O.C.D.). Sisters 6.

WAIPAHU. *Dominican Center Hawaii*, 94-1249 Lumikula St., 96797. Tel: 808-676-1452; 808-677-1202; Fax: 808-677-1202. Email: srmauraliaop@juno.com. Web: www.ophawiiregion.com. Sisters M. Aurelia Sanchez, O.P., Regl. Sec. & Councilor; Dominica Wong, O.P., Contact Person. Please refer to the following parish convents for additional residences: St. Elizabeth, Aiea; St.

John, Honolulu; St. Joseph, Makawao; House of Aloha Convent, Waianae. Sisters 7.

St. Elizabeth Convent, 99-310 Moanalua Rd., Aiea, 96701. Tel: 808-487-3131. Sr. Emilie Basitas, O.P., Contact Person. Sisters 5.

Hale Iokepa Community, 828 Analio St., Wailuku, 96793-9610. Sisters 4.

St. John the Baptist Convent, 2330 Omilo Ln., Honolulu, 96819. Tel: 808-845-2622. Email: srmgenevierebinas@yahoo.com. Sr. M. Candelara Perania, O.P., Contact Person. Sisters 6.

St. Joseph Convent, 57 Dominican Ln., Makawao, 96768. Tel: 808-572-8454. Sr. Georgina Delgado, O.P., Contact Person. Sisters 3.

[F] CATHOLIC CHARITIES

HONOLULU. **Catholic Charities Hawaii*, 1822 Keeaumoku St., 96822. Tel: 808-524-4673; Fax: 808-527-4879. Members of the Corporation: Most Rev. Clarence R. Silva; Very Rev. Gary L. Secor, V.G.; Sr. Alicia Damien Lau, O.S.F.; James E. Dannemiller, Dir.; Lisa Sakamoto; Michael Magaoay Board of Directors: Jerry Rauckhorst, Pres.; Kim Tomlinson, Vice Pres.; Leigh-Ann Miyasato, Sec.; Dan Colin, Treas.; Chuck Jones, Chm. Members: Rix Maurer III, Chm.; Dr. Leslie Correa, Ed.D., Dir.; Mary Fastenau, Dir.; Derek Baughman, Dir.; Ruth Ann Becker, Dir.; Gae Bergquist Trommald, Dir.; Clementine Ceria-Ulep, Ph.D., Dir.; Dan Colin, Dir.; James E. Dannemiller, Dir.; Phyllis B. Dendle, Dir.; Koren Dreher, Dir.; Michael Erne, Dir.; Brandt Farias, Dir.; Bonnie Fong, Dir.; Wesley Fong, Dir.; Terri Fujii, Dir.; James Hasselman, Dir.; Clifton Kagawa, Dir.; David Kostecki, Dir.; Alan Ito, Dir.; Chuck Jones, Dir.; Dew-Anne Langcaon, Dir.; Caron Ling, Dir.; Marianita Lopez Esq., Esq., Dir.; Richard E. Meiers, Dir.; Leigh-Ann Miyasato, Dir.; John Myrdal, Dir.; Debbie Ng-Furuhashi, Dir.; Jerry Rauckhorst, Dir.; Kim Tomlinson, Dir.; Roger J. Wall, Dir.; Dara Young, Dir.

Hope Services Hawaii, Inc. Brandee Menino, Program Admin.

[G] RETREAT AND SPIRITUAL CENTERS

HONOLULU. *St. Anthony Retreat Center* (1909) 3351 Kalihi St., 96819. Tel: 808-845-4353; Fax: 808-848-2696. Sr. Anne Clare DeCosta, SS.CC., Admin. Sisters 4.

**Marianist Center of Hawaii* (1986) 3140 Waialae Ave., 96816. Tel: 808-738-5887; Fax: 808-732-3374. Email: baldschmitz@aol.com. Bros. Robert G. Hoppe, S.M., Vice Pres.; Dennis Schmitz, S.M., Dir. Special Ministry. Total Staff 2.

Our Lady the Mystical Rose Chapel , (Oratory), c/o Marianist Center of Hawaii, 3140 Waialae Ave., 96816. Tel: 808-739-4738; 808-738-5887 (direct line); Fax: 808-732-3374. Email: baldschmitz@aol.com. Rev. Timothy Eden, S.M., Chap.; Bro. Robert G. Hoppe, S.M. Tel: 808-738-5887.

KANEOHE. *Saint Stephen Diocesan Center*, 6301 Pali Hwy., 96744-5298. Tel: 808-203-6700; Fax: 808-261-7022. Email: sizaguirre@rcchawaii.org. Deacon Walter H. Yoshimitsu, Admin. In Res. Rev. Michael J. Owens.

WAIALUA, OAHU. *Benedictine Monastery of Hawaii / Retreat Center* (1984) 67-290 Farrington Hwy., P.O. Box 490, 96791. Tel: 808-637-7887; Fax: 808-637-8601. Rev. Michael Sawyer, O.S.B., Treas. Benedictine Congregation of Our Lady of Mounte Oliveto, O.S.B.

[H] ASSOCIATIONS OF THE FAITHFUL

HONOLULU. *Hawaii Catholic Charismatic Renewal Services*, 520 Lunalilo Home Rd., #6215, 96825. Deacon Daniel Guinaugh, Contact Person; Rita Guinaugh, Contact Person.

Nocturnal Adoration Society, 6770 Hawaii Kai Dr. #505, 96825. Tel: 808-395-1112. John Lyons, Contact Person.

KANEOHE. **INHIM Ministries, Inc.*, 6301 Pali Hwy., 96744. Tel: 808-497-7386. Email: information@inhimhawaii.org.

KAPOLEI. *Diocesan Catholic Congress of Filipino Catholic Clubs*, P.O. Box 700606, 96709. Tel: 808-672-8100. Estrella Estillore, Contact Person.

MILILANI. *Missionary Basic Christian Community*, 95-761 Pulehulehu St., 96789. Rodney Kekina, Contact Person.

PEARL CITY. **Society of St. Vincent DePaul Honolulu District Council*, 920 Keolu Dr., Kailua, 96734-3842. Tel: 808-262-8317. Dennis Sasaki, Contact Person.

WAIALUA. *Basic Christian Community of Hawaii, Benedictine Monastery*, P.O. Box 490, 96791. Tel: 808-674-1853. Raul Perez, Contact Person; Francis Sauser, Contact Person.

Legion of Mary, 86-281 Kawili St., Waianae, 96792. Suzanna Jones-Hart, Contact Person.

[I] FOUNDATIONS

HONOLULU. **Hawaii Catholic Community Foundation, c/o Ashford & Wriston LLP*, 1099 Alakea St., Ste. 1400, 96813. Most Rev. Clarence R. Silva; Very Rev. Gary L. Secor, V.G.; Lisa Sakamoto; Irene Lee, Pres.; John Brogen, Vice Pres.; George Fontaine, Sec.; Mark Pillori, Treas.; Linda Nishigaya; Chuck Furr.

KANEOHE. *Augustine Educational Foundation* (1984) St. Stephen Diocesan Center, 6301 Pali Hwy., 96744. Tel: 808-203-6736; Fax: 808-230-2441. Email: aef@aloha.net. Web: www.augustinefoundation.org. Most Rev. Clarence R. Silva, Pres.; Very Rev. Gary L. Secor, V.G., Vice Pres.; Susan Ferandin, Exec. Dir.

WAILUKU. *Maui Helio Endowment Fund*, 1885 Main St., Ste. 404, 96793. Email: lksodetani@aol.com. Patrick K. Wong, Pres. & Contact Person; John Kim, Vice Pres.; Kara Shimizu, Treas.; Paul Harikawa, Sec.

RELIGIOUS INSTITUTES OF MEN REPRESENTED IN THE DIOCESE

For further details refer to the corresponding bracketed number in the Religious Institutes of Men or Women section.

[]—*The Augustinians*—O.S.A.
[0200]—*Benedictine Monks* (Olivetan)—O.S.B.
[]—*Blessed Sacrament Fathers*—S.S.S.
[0470]—*The Capuchin Friars*—O.F.M.Cap.
[0310]—*Congregation of Christian Brothers*—C.F.C.
[]—*Congregation of the Blessed Sacrament*—S.S.S.
[1140]—*Fathers of the Sacred Hearts* (Hawaii Prov.)—SS.CC.
[0690]—*Jesuit Fathers*—S.J.
[]—*La Salette Fathers*—M.S.
[0720]—*The Missionaries of Our Lady of La Salette* (Pacific Region)—M.S.
[0760]—*Society of Mary* (Prov. of the Pacific)—S.M.

RELIGIOUS INSTITUTES OF WOMEN REPRESENTED IN THE DIOCESE

[]—*Benedictine Congregation of Our Lady of Mounte Oliveto*—O.S.B.
[0950]—*Daughters of Saint Paul*—F.S.P.
[0420]—*Discalced Carmelite Nuns*—O.C.D.
[1070-03]—*Dominican Sisters of the Most Holy Rosary*—O.P.
[1230]—*Franciscan Sisters of Christian Charity*—O.S.F.
[2470]—*Maryknoll Sisters of St. Dominic*—M.M.
[]—*Missionary Sisters of Mary Help of Christians*—M.S.M.H.C.
[]—*Sinsinawa Dominicans*—O.P.
[]—*Sisters for Christian Community*—S.F.C.C.
[0430]—*Sisters of Charity of the Blessed Virgin Mary*—B.V.M.
[]—*Sisters of Divine Providence*—C.D.P.
[]—*Sisters of St. Francis of Philadelphia*—O.S.F.
[]—*Sisters of St. Paul of Chartres*—S.C.P.
[]—*Sisters of St. Francis of the Neumann Communities*—O.S.F.
[3840]—*Sisters of St. Joseph of Carondelet*—C.S.J.
[1960]—*Sisters of the Holy Family*—S.H.F.
[3690]—*Sisters of the Sacred Hearts and of Perpetual Adoration*—SS.CC.

NECROLOGY

† Dever, Rev. Msgr. Daniel J., (Retired)—Died Oct. 19, 2011
† McNichol, Daniel, (Retired)—Died July 29, 2011
† Peterson, Francis, (Retired)—Died April 14, 2011

An asterisk (*) denotes an organization that has established tax-exempt status directly with the IRS and is not covered by the USCCB Group Ruling.

Diocese of Houma-Thibodaux

(Dioecesis Humensis-Thibodensis)

Most Reverend

SAM G. JACOBS, D.D.

Bishop of Houma-Thibodaux; ordained June 6, 1964; appointed Bishop of Alexandria July 1, 1989; ordained and installed August 24, 1989; appointed third Bishop of Houma-Thibodaux August 1, 2003; installed October 10, 2003. *Office: 2779 Hwy. 311, Schriever, LA 70395.*

Chancery: P.O. Box 505, Schriever, LA 70395. Tel: 985-868-7720; Fax: 985-868-7727.

Email: jbaker@htdiocese.org

ERECTED JUNE 5, 1977.

Square Miles 3,440.

Comprises the parishes of Lafourche, Terrebonne, parts of St. Mary and Jefferson.

For legal titles of parishes and diocesan institutions, consult the Chancery Office.

STATISTICAL OVERVIEW

Personnel	
Bishop	1
Priests: Diocesan Active in Diocese	39
Priests: Retired, Sick or Absent	22
Number of Diocesan Priests	61
Religious Priests in Diocese	9
Total Priests in Diocese	70
Ordinations:	
Diocesan Priests	1
Permanent Deacons	9
Permanent Deacons in Diocese	40
Total Brothers	4
Total Sisters	23
Parishes	
Parishes	39
With Resident Pastor:	
Resident Diocesan Priests	38
Without Resident Pastor:	
Administered by Priests	3
Missions	3
Professional Ministry Personnel:	
Sisters	3
Lay Ministers	22
Welfare	
Homes for the Aged	1
Total Assisted	60
Day Care Centers	1
Total Assisted	87
Specialized Homes	2
Total Assisted	45
Special Centers for Social Services	4
Total Assisted	11,474
Educational	
Diocesan Students in Other Seminaries	15
Total Seminarians	15
High Schools, Diocesan and Parish	3
Total Students	1,873
Elementary Schools, Diocesan and Parish	10
Total Students	3,846
Catechesis/Religious Education:	
High School Students	2,438
Elementary Students	4,997
Total Students under Catholic Instruction	13,169
Teachers in the Diocese:	
Brothers	2
Lay Teachers	374
Vital Statistics	
Receptions into the Church:	
Infant Baptism Totals	1,194
Minor Baptism Totals	48
Adult Baptism Totals	33
Received into Full Communion	45
First Communions	1,174
Confirmations	909
Marriages:	
Catholic	247
Interfaith	38
Total Marriages	285
Deaths	1,225
Total Catholic Population	106,305
Total Population	202,000

Former Bishops—Most Revs. WARREN L. BOUDREAUX, J.C.D., D.D., First Bishop of Houma-Thibodaux; ord. May 30, 1942; retired Dec. 29, 1992; died Oct. 6, 1997; MICHAEL JARRELL, D.D., Second Bishop of Houma-Thibodaux; ord. June 3, 1967; appt. Dec. 29, 1992; cons. and installed March 4, 1993; appt. 6th Bishop of Lafayette, Louisiana Nov. 8, 2002.

Chancery

Chancery—Address all correspondence to: P.O. Box 505, Schriever, 70395. Office: 2779 Hwy. 311, Schriever, 70395. Tel: 985-868-7720; Fax: 985-868-7727. Office Hours: Mon.-Fri. 8:30-4:30.

Vicar General—Very Rev. JAY BAKER.

Chancellor—Deacon JIM SWILER.

Finance Officer—Rev. Msgr. FREDERIC J. BRUNET.

Judicial Vicar—Very Rev. VICENTE DELA CRUZ.

Director of Tribunal—VACANT.

Diocesan Tribunal— Address all correspondence to: VERONICA SONGE, Mailing Address: P.O. Box 505, Schriever, 70395. Office: 2779 Hwy. 311, Schriever, 70395. Tel: 985-850-3126.

Departments of the Diocesan Curia

Department of Administration Ministries

Judges—Very Revs. VICENTE DELA CRUZ; JAY BAKER.

Defender of the Bond—Very Rev. DANIEL M. POCHE.

Counselor—Mrs. NANCY DIEDRICH, L.P.C., L.M.F.T.

Priests Council—Revs. JOSEKUTTY VARGHESE; MIKE TRAN; Very Rev. DEAN DANOS, V.F.; Revs. JOSHUA RODRIGUE; EVELIO BUENAFLOR JR.; RONILO VILLAMOR; THANKACHAN (JOHN) NAMBUSSERIL, C.M.I.; Very Rev. CARL COLLINS; Rev. ROBERT C. ROGERS; Very Rev. JAY BAKER, Ex Officio, Mailing Address: P.O. Box 505, Schriever, 70395. 2779 Hwy. 311, Schriever, 70395.

College of Consultors—Rev. JOSEKUTTY VARGHESE; Very Revs. CARL COLLINS; DANIEL M. POCHE; JAY BAKER, Ex-Officio.

Deans—

Upper Lafourche Deanery—Very Rev. DEAN F. DANOS, 815 Barbier Ave., Thibodaux, 70301.

South Lafourche Deanery—Rev. ROBERT C. ROGERS, 612 Main St., Lockport, 70374.

Terrebonne Deanery—Very Rev. CARL COLLINS, 8594 Main St., Houma, 70363.

Diocesan Finance Council—GLENN J. LANDRY; Rev. Msgr. FREDERIC J. BRUNET; Very Rev. JAY BAKER; ANGELIQUE BARKER; RODNEY WHITNEY; PHILIP MCMAHON; A. J. CHAMPAGNE JR.; ROBERT NAQUIN.

Coordinator—GLENN J. LANDRY, 2779 Hwy. 311, Schriever, 70395. Mailing Address: P.O. Box 505, Schriever, 70395. Tel: 985-868-7720.

Accounting, Business Office, Finance—GLENN J. LANDRY, Business Mgr., 2779 Hwy. 311, Schriever, 70395. Mailing Address: P.O. Box 505, Schriever, 70395. Tel: 985-868-7720.

Archives and Historical Research Center—KEVIN ALLEMAND, 205 Audubon St., Thibodaux, 70301. Tel: 985-446-2383.

Building Commission—JAMES J. DANOS, Dir., 2779 Hwy. 311, Schriever, 70395. Mailing Address: P.O. Box 505, Schriever, 70395. Tel: 985-868-7720.

Cemeteries—GEORGE COOKE, Dir., 949 Menard St., Thibodaux, 70301. Tel: 985-446-0280.

Legal Services—Very Rev. JAY BAKER, Dir., 2779 Hwy. 311, Schriever, 70395. Mailing Address: P.O. Box 505, Schriever, 70395. Tel: 985-868-7720. Attorneys: KENNETH WATKINS; DANIEL WALKER, Mailing Address: 501 Roussell St., P.O. Box 5095, Houma, 70361. Tel: 985-868-2333.

Stewardship and Development—JEREMY T. BECKER, CFRE, 2779 Hwy. 311, Schriever, 70395. Mailing Address: P.O. Box 505, Schriever, 70395. Tel: 985-868-7720.

Human Resources & Employment Benefits—MELISSA R. ROBERTSON, 2779 Hwy. 311, Schriever, 70395. Mailing Address: P.O. Box 505, Schriever, 70395. Tel: 985-868-7720.

Insurance - Property, Casualty & Liability—KELLY GUILLOT, Asst. Dir., 2779 Hwy. 311, Schriever, 70395. Mailing Address: P.O. Box 505, Schriever, 70395. Tel: 985-868-7720.

Operations - Computers & Technology—HOLLY BECNEL, Dir., 2779 Hwy. 311, Schriever, 70395. Mailing Address: P.O. Box 505, Schriever, 70395. Tel: 985-868-7720.

Department for Clergy and Religious

Coordinator—Very Rev. JAY BAKER, 2779 Hwy. 311, Schriever, 70395. Mailing Address: P.O. Box 505, Schriever, 70395. Tel: 985-868-7720.

Clergy Personnel—Very Rev. JAY BAKER, Mailing Address: P.O. Box 505, Schriever, 70395. Tel: 985-868-7720.

Continuing Education of the Clergy-Ministry to Priests Program—Rev. GLENN LECOMPTE, Mailing Address: P.O. Box 505, Schriever, 70395. Tel: 985-868-7720.

Vicar for Priests—Rev. ROGER VILLARRUBIA JR. (Retired), 8594 Main St., Houma, 70363. Tel: 985-876-7652.

Permanent Diaconate—Deacon DOUGLAS AUTHEMENT, 123 Fane St., Houma, 70364. Tel: 985-876-0842. 2779 Hwy. 311, Schriever, 70395. Mailing Address: P.O. Box 505, Schriever, 70395. Tel: 985-868-7720.

Vocations—Rev. JOSHUA JOHN RODRIGUE, Mailing Address: P.O. Box 505, Schriever, 70395. Tel: 985-868-7720.

Seminarians—Rev. MARK TOUPS, P.O. Box 505, Schriever, 70395. Tel: 985-868-7720.

Women Religious—VACANT, Mailing Address: P.O. Box 505, Schriever, 70395. Tel: 985-850-3122.

Department of Formation Ministries

Coordinator—LOUIS G. AGUIRRE, 2779 Hwy. 311, Schriever, 70395. Mailing Address: P.O. Box 505, Schriever, 70395. Tel: 985-868-7720.

Campus Ministry—Rev. JOSEPH PILOLA, Dir., N.S.U., Mailing Address: Box 2051, Thibodaux, 70310. Tel: 985-446-6201.

Catholic Schools—MARIAN FERTITTA, Supt., 2779 Hwy.

311, Schriever, 70395. Mailing Address: P.O. Box 505, Schriever, 70395. Tel: 985-868-7720.

Communications, Public Relations, Publications, Radio & Television—LOUIS G. AGUIRRE, Dir., 2779 Hwy. 311, Schriever, 70395. Mailing Address: P.O. Box 505, Schriever, 70395. Tel: 985-868-7720.

Religious Education—Dr. FAITH ANN SPINELLA, Dir., 2779 Hwy. 311, Schriever, 70395. Mailing Address: P.O. Box 505, Schriever, 70395. Tel: 985-868-7720.

New Evangelization and Pastoral Services—SUSAN BLANCHARD, Assoc. Dir. Pastoral Svcs.; TIM BOGAN, Coord. Evangelization, 2779 Hwy. 311, Schriever, 70395. Mailing Address: P.O. Box 505, Schriever, 70395. Tel: 985-868-7720.

"The Bayou Catholic"— (Diocesan Newspaper)-- LOUIS G. AGUIRRE, Editor, 2779 Hwy. 311, Schriever, 70395. Mailing Address: P.O. Box 505, Schriever, 70395. Tel: 985-868-7720.

Youth Ministries—MICHAEL DISALVO, 2779 Hwy. 311, Schriever, 70395. Mailing Address: P.O. Box 505, Schriever, 70395. Tel: 985-868-7720.

Family Ministries—CATHERINE KLINGMAN, 2779 Hwy. 311, Schriever, 70395. Mailing Address: P.O. Box 505, Schriever, 70395. Tel: 985-868-7720.

Worship—Rev. GLENN LECOMPTE, 2779 Hwy. 311, Schriever, 70395. 1220 Aycock St., Houma, 70360. Tel: 985-876-0490.

Rite of Chiristian Initiation of Adults—LILLIE BRUNET; Deacon STEPHEN BRUNET, 4012 Kerr Dr., Bourg, 70343. Tel: 985-232-3218.

Young Adult Ministries—PAUL GEORGE, Dir., Mailing Address: P.O. Box 4174, Houma, 70361. Tel: 985-876-4132.

Conference Office—Mailing Address: P.O. Box 505, Schriever, 70395. Tel: 985-868-7720. Deacon JIM SWILER, Coord.; SHAWN LAPEYROUSE, Dir.

Department of Social Ministries

Coordinator—Deacon JIM SWILER, 2779 Hwy. 311, P.O. Box 505, Schriever, 70395. Tel: 985-850-3122.

Assisi Bridge House—Mr. ROBERT GORMAN, A.C.S.W., B.C.S.W., Dir., 600 Bull Run Rd., Schriever, 70395. Tel: 985-872-5529.

Catholic Campaign for Human Development—Mr. ROBERT GORMAN, A.C.S.W., B.C.S.W., Diocesan Dir., 1220 Aycock St., Houma, 70360. Tel: 985-876-0490.

Catholic Relief Service Director—Mr. ROBERT GORMAN, A.C.S.W., B.C.S.W.

Catholic Charities Diocese of Houma-Thibodaux Justice & Peace—ROBERT D. GORMAN, A.C.S.W., B.C.S.W., Dir.; GERMAINE JACKSON, Assoc. Dir., 1220 Aycock St., Houma, 70360. Tel: 985-876-0490.

Disaster Relief—ROBERT D. GORMAN, A.C.S.W., B.C.S.W., Exec. Dir.; GERMAINE JACKSON, Dir., 1220 Aycock St., Houma, 70360. Tel: 985-876-0490.

St. Lucy's Day Care Center—CARLEEN FITCH, C.D.A., Mgr., 1224 Aycock St., Houma, 70360. Tel: 985-876-1246.

Other Offices and Commissions

Charismatic Renewal—PAUL MACLEAN, Charismatic Renewal Liaison, Mailing Address: P.O. Box 3620, Houma, 70361. Tel: 985-856-5345.

Cursillo—Rev. ROCH R. NAQUIN, Dir., 539 Island Rd., Montegut, 70377. Tel: 985-594-5144; Fax: 985-594-6960.

Ecumenism—Rev. GLENN LECOMPTE, P.O. Box 505, Schriever, 70395. Tel: 985-868-7720.

Pontifical Societies for the Propagation of the Faith—Holy Childhood Association; Society of St. Peter the Apostle. Rev. ROBERT JOEL CRUZ, Dir., 1220 Aycock St., Houma, 70360. Tel: 985-850-0035; Fax: 985-850-0063.

Scouting—MICHAEL J. DISALVO, Dir., 2779 Hwy. 311, Schriever, 70395. Mailing Address: P.O. Box 505, Schriever, 70395. Tel: 985-868-7720; Fax: 985-850-3215.

Organizations

Catholic Daughters of the Americas—Rev. CHARLES PERKINS, Spiritual Advisor, 409 Funderburk Ave., Houma, 70364.

Diocesan Council of St. Vincent de Paul Societies—NORMAN SIMON, Pres., 901 Liberty St., Houma, 70360. Tel: 985-872-9373.

Knights of Columbus—Rev. CLYDE MAHLER, Diocesan Chap., Mailing Address: 246 Corporate Dr., Houma, 70360. Tel: 985-876-3313.

Legion of Mary—Mrs. JERRALINE SERPAS, Pres., 129 Magnolia Courtyard, Houma, 70364; VACANT, Spiritual Dir.

St. Vincent de Paul Store—Mr. PETE CAVALIER, Pres.; Mr. ROY BURNS, Vice Pres.; Mr. CULLEN BOUDREAUX, Treas. Store Managers: JIM LAGARDE; PHYLLIS LAGARDE, 107 Point St., Houma, 70360. Tel: 985-872-9373; Fax: 985-223-1931.

Serra Club of South Lafourche—VACANT.

Serra Club of Thibodaux—Rev. JOSHUA JOHN RODRIGUE, Spiritual Advisor; Mr. DON HARRIS, Pres.; Mr. GIBBENS ROBICHAUX, Treas.

Anawim—EVELYN RUCKSTUHL, Pres., 501 Grinage St., Houma, 70360. Tel: 985-850-3129.

Victim Assistance Coordinator—Mrs. NANCY DIEDRICH, L.P.C., L.M.F.T. Tel: 985-850-3129. Email: ndiedrich@htdiocese.org.

CLERGY, PARISHES, MISSIONS AND PAROCHIAL SCHOOLS

CITY OF HOUMA

(PARISH TERREBONNE)

1—CATHEDRAL OF ST. FRANCIS DE SALES (1847) [CEM 2] Very Rev. Vicente DeLa Cruz, Rector; Rev. Andre Melancon; Deacons Douglas Authement; Joseph Weigand Jr.
Res.: 500 Goode St., Houma, 70360. Tel: 985-876-6904; Fax: 985-851-4204.
School—(Grades PreSchool-7), 300 Verret St., Houma, 70360. Tel: 985-868-6646; Fax: 985-851-5896. Brenda Tanner, Prin.; Celeste Cancienne, Asst. Prin. Lay Teachers 34; Students 803.
Catechesis/Religious Program—Students 224.

2—ANNUNZIATA (1963) Rev. Michael A. Bergeron; Sr. Paula Richard, O.P., Pastoral Assoc.; Deacon Raymond Bourg Jr.
Res.: 2011 Acadian Dr., Houma, 70363. Tel: 985-876-2971; Fax: 985-868-6414.
Catechesis/Religious Program—Students 183.

3—ST. BERNADETTE (1958) Revs. Charles Perkins; Alexis Lazarra; Kathy Lirette, Pastoral Assoc.; Deacons Gerald Rivette; James Brunet Jr. In Res., Rev. Jerod Duet.
Res.: 409 Funderburk Ave., Houma, 70364. Tel: 985-851-6629; Fax: 985-876-9654.
School—(Grades PreSchool-7), 309 Funderburk Ave., Houma, 70364. Tel: 985-872-3854; Fax: 985-872-5780. Joan LeBouef, Prin.; Lydia Landry, Admin. Asst.; Dale Ford, Librarian. Lay Teachers 26; Students 408.
Catechesis/Religious Program—Wanda Fos, C.R.E. Students 618.

4—ST. GREGORY BARBARIGO (1963) Rev. Evelio Buenaflor Jr.; Deacon Dennis Dupre.
Res.: 439 Sixth St., Houma, 70364. Tel: 985-873-7770.
Administration Bldg.—1005 Williams Ave., Houma, 70364. Tel: 985-876-2047; Fax: 985-876-0628.
School—(Grades PreSchool-7), 441 Sixth St., Houma, 70364. Tel: 985-876-2038; Fax: 985-879-2789. Elizabeth Scurto, Prin. Lay Teachers 10; Students 184.
Catechesis/Religious Program—Students 83.

5—ST. LOUIS (1965) [CEM] Rev. Carlos Talavera.
Res.: 2226 Bayou Blue Rd., Houma, 70364. Tel: 985-876-3449.
Catechesis/Religious Program—Tel: 985-876-6686; Fax: 985-876-6810. Email: stlouisch@comcast.net. Catherine Butler, D.R.E. Students 301.

6—ST. LUCY Rev. Glenn LeCompte, Sacramental Min.
Mailing Address: 1214 Aycock St., Houma, 70361. Tel: 985-879-2632; Fax: 985-879-2402.
Church: 1224 Aycock St., Houma, 70360.
Catechesis/Religious Program—Willie Glaze Jr., D.R.E. Students 36.

7—MARIA IMMACOLATA (1963) Revs. Clyde Mahler; Joseph Henry Sabastian.
Administration Office—246 Corporate Dr., Houma, 70360. Tel: 985-876-3313; Fax: 985-879-2137.
Res.: 326 Estate Dr., Houma, 70364. Tel: 985-868-4915.
School—(Grades PreSchool-7), 324 Estate Dr., Houma, 70364. Tel: 985-876-1631; Fax: 985-876-1608. Mrs. Yvonne Weimer, Prin.; Karen DeBlieux, Librarian. Lay Teachers 14; Students 183.
Catechesis/Religious Program—Students 308.

8—OUR LADY OF THE MOST HOLY ROSARY (1948) [CEM], (Holy Rosary Church) Very Rev. Carl Collins. In Res., Rev. Roger Villarrubia Jr. (Retired).
Res.: 8594 Main St., Houma, 70363. Tel: 985-876-7652; Fax: 985-876-7647.
Catechesis/Religious Program—Tel: 985-879-2815; Fax: 985-876-0591. Students 120.

CITY OF THIBODAUX

(LAFOURCHE PARISH)

1—ST. CHARLES BORROMEO (1912) [CEM] Rev. Michael Manase.
Res.: 1027 Hwy. 308, Thibodaux, 70301. Tel: 985-446-6663; Fax: 985-447-3348.
Catechesis/Religious Program—Students 164.

2—CHRIST THE REDEEMER (1983) [CEM] Rev. John Gallen; Deacon Charles Giroir.
Res.: 720 Talbot Ave., Thibodaux, 70301. Tel: 985-447-2013; Fax: 985-447-4422. Email: ctrstaff@bellsouth.net.
Catechesis/Religious Program—Students 227.

3—ST. GENEVIEVE (1959) Very Rev. Dean F. Danos; Rev. Philip Vathyiakaril-Eapen, C.M.I.; Deacon Irving Daigle.
Res.: 815 Barbier Ave., Thibodaux, 70301. Tel: 985-446-5571; Fax: 985-449-1939.
School—(Grades K-7), 807 Barbier Ave., Thibodaux, 70301. Tel: 985-447-9291; Fax: 985-447-9883. Chris Knobloch, Prin.; Cheryl Thibodaux, Asst. Prin.; Jere Shields, Librarian. Lay Teachers 30; Students 496.
Catechesis/Religious Program—Tel: 985-449-1939. Students 109.

4—ST. JOHN THE EVANGELIST (1919) [CEM] Rev. Guy Zeringue; Sheryl Chauvin, Pastoral Assoc.
Res.: 2085 St. Mary St., Thibodaux, 70301. Tel: 985-447-3995; Fax: 985-447-2092.
Catechesis/Religious Program—Fax: 985-447-2092. Susie Richard, D.R.E. Students 117.

5—ST. JOSEPH CO-CATHEDRAL (1817) Very Rev. Jay Baker; Revs. Joseph P. Chacko, I.M.S.; Joseph Minh Nguyen, S.D.D.; Deacons Ambrose J. Ayzinne; Pedro Pujals, (Retired).
Res.: 721 Canal Blvd., P.O. Box 966, Thibodaux, 70302. Tel: 985-446-1387; Fax: 985-446-6571.
School—(Grades PreSchool-7), 501 Cardinal Dr., Thibodaux, 70301. Tel: 985-446-1346; Fax: 985-449-0760. Gerard Rodrigue Jr., Prin.; Nadine Delatte, Librarian. Lay Teachers 41; Students 666.
Catechesis/Religious Program—Students 157.

6—ST. LUKE (1923), (African American), Rev. Glenn LeCompte, Sacramental Min.
Office:—300 E. 11th St., Thibodaux, 70301. Tel: 985-446-0487; Fax: 985-446-0480.
Catechesis/Religious Program—Students 37.

7—ST. THOMAS AQUINAS (1970) Rev. Joseph Pilola. Nicholls Sta.: NSU Box 2051, Thibodaux, 70310. Tel: 985-446-6201; Fax: 985-449-0710. Email: st.thomas@htdiocese.org.
Catechesis/Religious Program—Tel: 985-446-6201; Fax: 985-449-0710. Students 74.

OUTSIDE THE CITIES OF HOUMA AND THIBODAUX

AMELIA, ST. MARY PARISH

1—ST. ANDREW (1965) [CEM] Rev. Joseph P. Chacko, I.M.S.
Res.: P.O. Box 310, 70340. Tel: 985-631-2333; Fax: 985-631-2334.
Catechesis/Religious Program—Students 110.

2—THANH GIA (1981), Personal Parish for Vietnamese Community. Rev. Anthony Tin Nguyen.
Res.: 711 Magnolia St., Morgan City, 70380. Tel: 985-631-3194; Fax: 985-631-2634.
Catechesis/Religious Program—Students 38.
Mission—Vietnam's Martyrs 406 N. Main Project Rd., 70395.
Mission—St. Holy Rosary 3593 Friendswood Dr., Houma, 70363.
Mission—St. Peter 13040 Hwy. 308, Larose, 70373. Tel: 985-693-5575.

BAYOU BLACK, TERREBONNE PARISH, ST. ANTHONY OF PADUA (1876) Rev. Joshua John Rodrigue; Deacons Jesse LeCompte; Brent Bergeron.
Res.: 3897 Bayou Black Dr., Houma, 70360. Tel: 985-872-0922; Fax: 985-872-2001.
Catechesis/Religious Program—Students 264.

BOURG, TERREBONNE PARISH, ST. ANN (1908) [CEM] Rev. Ty Van Nguyen; Deacon Stephen Brunet.
Res.: 4355 Hwy. 24, 70343. Tel: 985-594-3548; Fax: 985-594-3570.
Catechesis/Religious Program—Tel: 985-594-5088. Students 360.

CHACAHOULA, TERREBONNE PARISH, ST. LAWRENCE (1858) [CEM 2] Rev. Josekutty Varghese.
Res.: 2128 Bull Run Rd., 70395. Tel: 985-448-2165; Fax: 985-448-2166. Email: saintlawch@htdiocese.org.
Catechesis/Religious Program—Students 37.

CHACKBAY, LAFOURCHE PARISH, OUR LADY OF PROMPT SUCCOR (1892) [CEM 2] Rev. Robert Joel Cruz.
Res.: 529 Hwy. 20, Thibodaux, 70301. Tel: 985-633-2903; Fax: 985-633-9225.
Catechesis/Religious Program—Students 369.

CHAUVIN, TERREBONNE PARISH, ST. JOSEPH (1948) [CEM] Rev. Msgr. Frederic J. Brunet.
Res.: 5232 Hwy. 56, 70344. Tel: 985-594-5859; Fax: 985-594-2116. Email: saintjosephchurch@charter.net. Web: stjosephchauvin.parishesonline.com.
Catechesis/Religious Program—Jamie Robichaux, D.R.E. Students 365.

CUT-OFF, LAFOURCHE PARISH, SACRED HEART (1923) [CEM] Revs. Wilfredo Decal; Rholando Grecia; Deacons Sam J. Burregi; Eldon Frazier.
Res.: 15300 W. Main, 70345. Tel: 985-632-3858; Fax: 985-632-4452.
Catechesis/Religious Program—Tel: 985-632-6322; Fax: 985-632-4452. Students 429.

GALLIANO, LAFOURCHE PARISH, ST. JOSEPH (1958) [CEM] Rev. Joseph Pereira.
Res.: P.O. Box 519, 70354. Tel: 985-632-7321; Fax: 985-632-7345.
Catechesis/Religious Program—Students 249.

GHEENS, LAFOURCHE PARISH, COMMUNITY OF ST. ANTHONY (1987) [CEM], (Quasi Parish) Revs. Sabino B. Rebosura II; Arnold B. Baura.
Res.: 333 Twin Oaks Dr., Raceland, 70394. Tel: 985-537-6002; Fax: 985-537-4408.
Catechesis/Religious Program—Tel: 985-537-6002. Students 51.

GIBSON, TERREBONNE PARISH

1—MOST BLESSED SACRAMENT FAITH COMMUNITY Rev. Van Constant, Chap.
P.O. Box 587, 70356. Tel: 985-575-3551.

2—ST. PATRICK (1920) Merged with St. Lawrence, Chacahoula.

GOLDEN MEADOW, LAFOURCHE PARISH, OUR LADY OF PROMPT SUCCOR (1916) [CEM] Rev. Ronilo Villamor.
Res.: 723 N. Bayou Dr., 70357. Tel: 985-475-5428; Fax: 985-475-7699.
Catechesis/Religious Program—Tel: 985-475-5886; Fax: 985-475-7699. Students 190.

GRAND CAILLOU, TERREBONNE PARISH, HOLY FAMILY (1952) [CEM 2] Rev. Justino Estoque Jr.; Deacon Bernard A. Harold Fanguy.
Res.: P.O. Box 87, Dulac, 70353. Tel: 985-563-2325; Fax: 985-563-4980.
Catechesis/Religious Program—Students 119.

GRAND ISLE, WEST JEFFERSON PARISH, OUR LADY OF THE ISLE (1933) [CEM] Rev. Peter Tai Le. Email: petertaile66@yahoo.com.
Res.: P.O. Box 885, 70358. Tel: 985-787-2385; Fax: 985-787-4530.
Catechesis/Religious Program—Tel: 985-787-4530. Students 55.

KRAEMER, LAFOURCHE PARISH, ST. LAWRENCE THE MARTYR (1962) [JC 2] Rev. Baby V. Kuruvilla.
Res.: 3723 Hwy. 307, Thibodaux, 70301. Tel: 985-633-9431; Fax: 985-633-5706.
Mission—St. James [CEM] Thibodaux. 3086 Choctaw Rd., Choctaw, Lafourche Parish 70301. Tel: 985-633-9855.
Catechesis/Religious Program—Tel: 985-633-5714. Students 177.

LAROSE, LAFOURCHE PARISH, OUR LADY OF THE ROSARY (1873) [CEM] Revs. Rholando Grecia; Alberto Santiago; Deacons Michael Cantrelle; Davis Doucet.
Res.: 12937 E. Main, P.O. Box 10, 70373. Tel: 985-693-3433; Fax: 985-693-7551.
School—Holy Rosary, (Grades PreK-8), P.O. Box 40, 70373. Tel: 985-693-3342; Fax: 985-693-3348. Scott Bouzigard, Prin.; Connie Callais, Librarian. Lay Teachers 21; Students 299.
Catechesis/Religious Program—Jennifer Sanamo, D.R.E. Students 317.

LOCKPORT, LAFOURCHE PARISH, HOLY SAVIOR (1850) [CEM] Rev. Robert C. Rogers.
Res.: 612 Main St., 70374. Tel: 985-532-3533; Fax: 985-532-2010.
School—(Grades N-8), 201 Church St., 70374. Tel: 985-532-2536; Fax: 985-532-2269. Blaine Degruise, Prin.; Talisha Chiquet, Librarian. Lay Teachers 12; Students 253.
Catechesis/Religious Program—Tel: 985-532-6111; Fax: 985-532-2010. Students 239.

MONTEGUT, TERREBONNE PARISH, SACRED HEART (1864) [CEM 2] Rev. Thankachan (John) Nambusseril, C.M.I.
Res.: P.O. Box 2, 70377. Tel: 985-594-5856; Fax: 985-594-8087.
Catechesis/Religious Program—Tel: 985-594-5856; Fax: 985-594-8087. Students 78.

MORGAN CITY, ST. MARY PARISH

1—HOLY CROSS (1964) Rev. Daniel M. Poche; Deacons Andrew Dragna; Vic Bonnaffee.
Res.: 2100 Cedar St., Unit 3, 70380. Tel: 985-384-3551; Fax: 985-384-5790. Email: holycrosschurch@htdiocese.org.
School—(Grades PreSchool-6), 2100 Cedar St., Unit 2, 70381. Tel: 985-384-1933; Fax: 985-384-3270. Mamie Bergeron, Prin. Lay Teachers 18; Students 302.
Catechesis/Religious Program—Tel: 985-384-3551; Fax: 985-384-5970. Students 223.
Mission—St. Rosalie 1315 Stephensville Rd., St. Mary Parish 70380. Tel: 985-385-5713.

2—SACRED HEART OF JESUS (1859) Rev. Gregory Fratt.
Res.: 415 Union St., P.O. Box 632, 70381. Tel: 985-385-0770; Fax: 985-384-7176.
Catechesis/Religious Program—Tel: 985-384-8108. Students 242.

POINTE-AUX-CHENES, LAFOURCHE PARISH, ST. CHARLES BORROMEO (1971) [CEM] Rev. Thomas Kuriakose.
Mailing Address: P.O. Box 54, Montegut, 70377.
Res.: 1237 Hwy. 665, Montegut, 70377. Tel: 985-594-6801; Fax: 985-594-6802.
Catechesis/Religious Program—Fax: 985-594-6802. Students 81.

RACELAND, LAFOURCHE PARISH

1—ST. HILARY OF POITIERS (1965) Revs. Sabino B. Rebosura II; Arnold B. Baura.
Res.: 333 Twin Oaks, 70394. Tel: 985-537-6002; Fax: 985-537-4408.
Catechesis/Religious Program—Fax: 985-537-4408. Students 262.

2—ST. MARY'S NATIVITY (1850) [CEM] Rev. Mike Tran; Deacon Brent P. Bourgeois.
Res.: 3500 Hwy. 1, 70394. Tel: 985-537-3204; Fax: 985-537-3235.
School—(Grades PreK-8), 3492 Nies St., 70394. Tel: 985-537-7544; Fax: 985-537-4020. Marissa Bagala, Prin.; Jackie Jackson, Librarian. Lay Teachers 19; Students 252.
Catechesis/Religious Program—Students 136.

SCHRIEVER, TERREBONNE PARISH, ST. BRIDGET (1911) [CEM] Rev. Domingo Cruz; Deacon Lloyd Duplantis.
Res.: 100 Hwy. 311, 70395. Tel: 985-446-6801; Fax: 985-448-2764.
Catechesis/Religious Program—Tel: 985-446-1985. Students 180.

THERIOT, TERREBONNE PARISH, ST. ELOI (1875) [CEM] Rev. Florentino F. Santiago; Deacons Daniel Bascle; Glenn Porche.
Res.: 1335 Bayou Dularge Rd., 70397. Tel: 985-872-2946; Fax: 985-872-9961.
Catechesis/Religious Program—Tel: 985-851-6893. Students 106.

Chaplains of Public Institutions

HOUMA. *Chabert Medical Center*. Deacon Linwood Liner, Chap.
Terrebonne General Medical Center. Rev. Joseph Tu Tran.
Terrebonne Parish Sheriff Police and Fire Departments. Deacon Linwood Liner, Chap.

THIBODAUX. *Lafourche Parish Sheriff, Police and Fire Departments*. Vacant.
Thibodaux Regional Medical Center. Rev. Philip Vathyiakaril-Eapen, C.M.I.

On Duty Outside the Diocese:
Revs.—
Boquet, Shenan J.
Bouterie, Thomas

Administrative Leave:
Revs.—
Duet, Jared
Dugas, Scott

Retired:
Rev. Msgrs.—
Amedee, Francis, 725 St. Philip St., 70301.
Bergeron, Albert G., Hollywood Park Apartments, 546 Ave. B, Marrero, 70072.
Ledet, Donald, 1201 Cardnial Dr., 70301.
Songy, James B., 410 Ninth St., Lockport, 70374.
Revs.—
Broussard, Hubert C., Chateau Creole, 273 Monarch Dr., Apt. J13, Houma, 70364.
Chassaniol, Warren F., 4642 Hwy. 1, Raceland, 70394.
Foley, Brendan P., 182 E. 110th St., Galliano, 70354.
Hayes, Gerard C., 316 Hawthorne Dr., Houma, 70360.
LeBlanc, Etienne
Naquin, Roch, 539 Island Rd., Montegut, 70377.
Nguyen, Joseph Luu, P.O Box 29451, New Orleans, 70189.
O'Brien, Patrick, 409 Funderburk Ave., Houma, 70364.
Ruiz, John, Audubon Guest House, 2110 Audubon Ave., 70301.
Timbre, Roland
Todd, Wilmer, 267 Klondyke Rd., Bourg, 70343.
Villarrubia, Roger, Jr., 8594 Main St., Houma, 70363.

Permanent Deacons:
Andy, Malcom, Our Lady of the Most Holy Rosary, Houma
Authement, Douglas, Cathedral of St. Francis de Sales, Houma
Ayzinne, Ambrose Joseph, St. Joseph, Thibodaux
Bascle, Daniel, St. Eloi, Theriot
Belanger, Gerald, (Retired), Bourg
Bergeron, Brent, St. Anthony, Bayou Black
Bonnaffee, Vic, Holy Cross, Morgan City
Bourg, Raymond, Annunziata, Houma
Bourgeois, Brent P., St. Mary's Nativity, Raceland
Brunet, James, Jr., St. Bernadette, Houma
Brunet, Stephen, St. Ann, Bourg
Burregi, Sam J., Sacred Heart, Cut-Off
Cantrelle, Michael, Holy Rosary, Larose
Daigle, Irving, St. Genevieve, Thibodaux
Dickerson, Martin, St. Luke, Thibodaux
Doucet, Davis, Our Lady of the Rosary, Larose
Dragna, Andrew J., Holy Cross, Morgan City
Dufrene, Roland, St. Hilary of Poitiers, Mathews
Dunkelman, William, St. Thomas Aquinas, Thibodaux
Duplantis, Connely, Annunziata, Houma
Duplantis, Lloyd, St. Bridget, Schriever
Dupre, Dennis, St. Gregory, Houma
Duthu, James, (Retired), Houma
Fanguy, Bernard A. Harold, Holy Family, Grand Caillou
Frazier, Eldon, Cut-Off; Sacred Heart
Giroir, Charles, Christ the Redeemer, Thibodaux
Haddad, Gregory, Gray
Jennings, Randall, Sacred Heart, Morgan City
Landry, Alduce, (Retired), Thibodaux
Lapeyrouse, Gary, St. Joseph, Chauvin
LeCompte, Jesse, St. Anthony of Padua, Bayou Black
Liner, Linwood Paul, Sr., St. Lucy, Houma
Marts, Melvin, Shalom Catholic Ministries
Mattingly, John, Our Lady of the Rosary, Houma
Porche, Glenn, St. Eloi, Theriot
Prestenback, Chris A., Maria Immacolata, Houma
Pujals, Pedro P., (Retired), Thibodaux
Rivette, Gerald, St. Bernadette, Houma
Swiler, Jim, Chancellor, Diocese of Houma-Thibodaux
Uzee, Dickey, (Retired), Raceland
Weigand, Joseph, Jr., Cathedral of St. Francis de Sales, Houma

INSTITUTIONS LOCATED IN THE DIOCESE

[A] HIGH SCHOOLS, DIOCESAN

HOUMA. *Vandebilt Catholic High*, (Grades 8-12), 209 S. Hollywood Rd., 70360. Tel: 985-876-2551; Fax: 985-868-9774. Email: vandebilthi@htdiocese.org. Web: www.vandebiltcatholic.org. Mr. James Reiss, Prin.; Patricia Chiasson, Librarian. Brothers of the Sacred Heart. Lay Teachers 71; Students 933.

THIBODAUX. *Edward Douglas White Catholic High*, (Grades 8-12), (Coed), 555 Cardinal Dr., 70301. Tel: 985-446-8486; Fax: 985-448-1275. Email: edwhitehi@htdiocese.org. Michelle Chiasson, Prin.; Mr. David Boudreaux, Pres.; Lozia Richard, Librarian. Brothers of the Sacred Heart. Brothers 2; Lay Teachers 51; Students 724.
E.D. White Catholic High School Foundation, Inc. Tel: 985-446-8486; Fax: 985-446-5444.
E.D. White Catholic High School Alumni Assn. Tel: 985-446-8486; Fax: 985-448-1275.

MORGAN CITY. *Central Catholic High*, (Grades 7-12), 2100 Cedar St., Unit 1, 70380. Tel: 985-385-5372; Fax: 985-385-3444. Email: centcathi@htdiocese.org. Web: www.cchseagles.com. Deacon Vic Bonnaffee, Prin.; Karen Tycer, Senior High & Guidance Counselor; Anna Saleme, Librarian. Lay Teachers 27; Students 216.

[B] DAY CARE CENTERS

HOUMA. *St. Lucy Child Development Center*, 1220 Aycock St., 70360. Tel: 985-876-1246; Fax: 985-876-7751. Email: stlucycdc@htdiocese.org. Germaine Jackson, Dir. Catholic Charities; Carleen Fitch, C.D.A., Mgr. Total Staff 9; Children 42.

[C] RETREAT CENTERS

SCHRIEVER. *Lumen Christi Retreat Center*, 100 Lumen Christi Ln., Hwy. 311, 70395. Tel: 985-868-1523; Fax: 985-868-1525.

[D] CONVENTS

LOCKPORT. *Monastery of the Heart of Jesus*, 155 Church St., 70374. Tel: 985-532-2411. Sr. Mary Valerie Dupree, O.P. Dominican Contemplative Sisters of the Heart of Jesus of the Diocese of Houma-Thibodaux.

[E] PRIVATE ASSOCIATIONS OF THE FAITHFUL

THIBODAUX. *Marian Servants of the Word*, 506 Cardinal Dr., 70301. Tel: 985-447-6564; Fax: 985-447-5734. Email: marianservants@att.net. Very Rev. Michael Bergeron, Chap.; Claire Joller, Dir.; Brenda Fremin, Sec.; Mrs. Sally Sobert, Treas.

[F] PIUS ASSOCIATION

THIBODAUX. *Daughters of St. Joseph - Pius Association*, 113 Lafaye Ave., 70301. Tel: 985-446-7525. Debra McCullough, Contact Person. Daughters 4.

[G] MISCELLANEOUS

THIBODAUX. **Adore Ministries, Inc.*, P.O. Box 4174, Houma, 70361. Tel: 985-876-4132; Fax: 985-876-4171.

The Diocese of Houma-Thibodaux Historical Research Center, 205 Audubon Ave., 70301. Tel: 985-446-2383; Fax: 985-449-0574. Email: kallemand@htdiocese.org.

St. Joseph Manor (Retirement Community), 1201 Cardinal Dr., 70301. Tel: 985-446-9050; Fax: 985-449-0047. Email: annt@stjosephmanor.org. Web: www.stjosephmanor.org. Ann Thibodaux, Admin.

Magnificat of the Houma-Thibodaux Diocese, P.O. Box 702, 70302. Tel: 985-446-5001; Fax: 985-447-4261. Mrs. Mina McKee, Coord., Bayou River Chapter.

SCHRIEVER. *Cemeteries Trust*, P.O. Box 505, 70395. Tel: 985-850-3112; Fax: 985-868-7727. Email: glandry@htdiocese.org.

RELIGIOUS INSTITUTES OF MEN REPRESENTED IN THE DIOCESE

For further details refer to the corresponding bracketed number in the Religious Institutes of Men or Women section.

[1350]—*Brothers of St. Francis Xavier*—C.F.X.

[1100]—*Brothers of the Sacred Heart*—S.C.

RELIGIOUS INSTITUTES OF WOMEN REPRESENTED IN THE DIOCESE

[]—*Benedictine*—O.S.B.

[2410]—*Congregation of the Marianites of Holy Cross*—M.S.C.

[]—*Daughters of Our Lady of the Holy Rosary*

[]—*Dominican Contemplative Sisters*—O.P.

[]—*Dominican Sisters of St. Rose of Lima*

[]—*Guadalupan Missionaries of the Holy Spirit*

[2970]—*School Sisters of Notre Dame*—S.S.N.D.

[]—*Sisters for Christian Community*

[3830]—*Sisters of St. Joseph*—C.S.J.

[2050]—*Sisters of the Holy Spirit and Mary Immaculate*—S.H.Sp.

NECROLOGY

(No Deaths)

An asterisk (*) denotes an organization that has established tax-exempt status directly with the IRS and is not covered by the USCCB Group Ruling.

Archdiocese of Indianapolis

(Archidioecesis Indianapolitana)

Square Miles 13,758.

Established a Diocese in 1834; established an Archdiocese December 19, 1944 by decree of Pope Pius XII.

Comprises the Counties of Bartholomew, Brown, Clark, Clay, Crawford, Dearborn, Decatur, Fayette, Floyd, Franklin, Hancock, Harrison, Hendricks, Henry, Jackson, Jefferson, Jennings, Johnson, Lawrence, Marion, Monroe, Morgan, Ohio, Orange, Owen, Parke, Perry, Putnam, Ripley, Rush, Scott, Shelby, Switzerland, Union, Vermillion, Vigo, Washington and Wayne, and the township of Harrison in Spencer County, in the southern part of Indiana.

For legal titles of parishes and archdiocesan institutions, consult the Chancery Office.

Most Reverend

CHRISTOPHER J. COYNE, S.L.D.

Apostolic Administrator; ordained June 7, 1986; appointed Auxiliary Bishop of the Archdiocese of Indianapolis January 14, 2011; ordained and installed as Auxiliary Bishop of Indianapolis March 2, 2011; appointed Apostolic Administrator September 21, 2011.

(VACANT SEE)

The Archbishop Edward T. O'Meara Catholic Center: 1400 N. Meridian St., Indianapolis, IN 46202-2367. Tel: 317-236-1400; Fax: 317-236-1401.

Web: www.archindy.org

Email: chancery@archindy.org

STATISTICAL OVERVIEW

Personnel	
Retired Archbishops	1
Bishop	1
Abbots	1
Retired Abbots	3
Priests: Diocesan Active in Diocese	94
Priests: Diocesan Active Outside Diocese	3
Priests: Retired, Sick or Absent	46
Number of Diocesan Priests	143
Religious Priests in Diocese	85
Total Priests in Diocese	228
Extern Priests in Diocese	22
Ordinations:	
Diocesan Priests	1
Permanent Deacons in Diocese	30
Total Brothers	30
Total Sisters	574
Parishes	
Parishes	138
With Resident Pastor:	
Resident Diocesan Priests	92
Resident Religious Priests	12
Without Resident Pastor:	
Administered by Priests	22
Administered by Deacons	1
Administered by Religious Women	8
Administered by Lay People	3
Missions	12
Closed Parishes	1
Professional Ministry Personnel:	
Brothers	2
Sisters	45
Lay Ministers	175
Welfare	
Catholic Hospitals	2
Total Assisted	1,467,102
Homes for the Aged	3
Total Assisted	372
Day Care Centers	1
Total Assisted	72
Specialized Homes	2
Total Assisted	909
Special Centers for Social Services	16
Total Assisted	179,920
Residential Care of Disabled	1
Total Assisted	322
Educational	
Seminaries, Diocesan	1
Students from This Diocese	9
Students from Other Diocese	26
Diocesan Students in Other Seminaries	19
Seminaries, Religious	1
Total Seminarians	28
Colleges and Universities	2
Total Students	3,960
High Schools, Diocesan and Parish	7
Total Students	3,586
High Schools, Private	5
Total Students	2,372
Elementary Schools, Diocesan and Parish	58
Total Students	16,871
Elementary Schools, Private	1
Total Students	70
Catechesis/Religious Education:	
High School Students	3,146
Elementary Students	12,291
Total Students under Catholic Instruction	42,324
Teachers in the Diocese:	
Priests	1
Brothers	2
Sisters	21
Lay Teachers	1,539
Vital Statistics	
Receptions into the Church:	
Infant Baptism Totals	4,131
Minor Baptism Totals	444
Adult Baptism Totals	374
Received into Full Communion	545
First Communions	3,990
Confirmations	3,105
Marriages:	
Catholic	626
Interfaith	429
Total Marriages	1,055
Deaths	1,947
Total Catholic Population	227,699
Total Population	2,621,455

The Diocese of Vincennes (now Indianapolis) was established by decree of Pope Gregory XVI, May 6, 1834, and the See was fixed at Vincennes. The territory then comprised the entire State of Indiana and the eastern third of Illinois. By decree of Pope Pius IX, January 8, 1857, the northern half of the State became the Diocese of Fort Wayne. The southern half of the State remained the Diocese of Vincennes.

The second Bishop of Vincennes, by Apostolic Brief, was permitted to establish his residence either at Vincennes, Madison, Lafayette or Indianapolis; the See City, however, was to remain at Vincennes. This permission was renewed to the fourth Bishop, with the exception of Lafayette. On the appointment of the fifth Bishop, he was directed to fix his residence at Indianapolis, but the Cathedral and title of the See were continued at Vincennes. By an Apostolic Brief dated March 28, 1898, the title of the Diocese was changed to that of "Diocese of Indianapolis" with the city of Indianapolis as the Episcopal See. By the same Brief the Patron Saint of the Diocese was to remain St. Francis Xavier, the title of the old Cathedral in Vincennes.

On December 19, 1944, Most Reverend Amleto Giovanni Cicognani, Apostolic Delegate to the United States, solemnly proclaimed the Papal Decree of Pope Pius XII in SS. Peter and Paul Cathedral, Indianapolis, elevating Indianapolis to the status of an Archdiocese, the State of Indiana being the Metropolitan Area. The Dioceses of Evansville and Lafayette-in-Indiana were created by the same decree and were made Suffragan Sees of Indianapolis. Upon the establishment of the Diocese of Gary on December 17, 1956, it too became a Suffragan See.

Former Bishops—Rt. Revs. SIMON GUILLAUME GABRIEL BRUTE DE REMUR, S.S., D.D., ord. 1808; cons. 1834; died 1839; CELESTIN DE LA HAILANDIERE, D.D., ord. 1825; cons. 1839; resigned 1847; died in France, 1882; JOHN S. BAZIN, D.D., ord. 1822; cons. 1847; died 1848; MAURICE DE SAINT PALAIS, D.D., ord. 1836; cons. Jan. 14, 1849; died June 28, 1877; FRANCIS SILAS CHATARD, D.D., ord. 1862; cons. May 12, 1878; died Sept. 7, 1918; Most Revs. JOSEPH CHARTRAND, D.D., ord. Sept. 24, 1892; cons. Titular Bishop of Flavias and Coadjutor Bishop, Sept. 15, 1910; succeeded to the See of Indianapolis, Sept. 7, 1918; died Dec. 8, 1933; JOSEPH ELMER RITTER, S.T.D., ord. May 30, 1917; cons. Titular Bishop of Hippo and Auxiliary Bishop, March 28, 1933; succeeded to the See March 24, 1934; installed as Archbishop Dec. 19, 1944; transferred to Metropolitan See of St. Louis, July 20, 1946; named Cardinal, Jan. 16, 1961; died June 10, 1967; PAUL C. SCHULTE, D.D., ord. June 11, 1915; cons. Bishop of Leavenworth, Sept. 21, 1937; appt. Archbishop of Indianapolis, July 20, 1946; installed Oct. 10, 1946; resigned Jan. 14, 1970; died Feb. 17, 1984; GEORGE J. BISKUP, ord. March 19, 1937; cons. Titular Bishop of Hemeria and Auxiliary of Dubuque, April 24, 1957; transferred to Des Moines Feb. 3, 1965; transferred to Indianapolis "cum jure successionis," July 26, 1967; succeeded to See Jan. 14, 1970; resigned March 26, 1979; died Oct. 17, 1979; EDWARD T. O'MEARA, S.T.D., ord. Dec. 21, 1946; appt. Titular Bishop of Thisiduo and Auxiliary of St. Louis Jan. 28, 1972; consecrated in the Basilica of St. Peter, Rome, Feb. 13, 1972; appt. Archbishop of Indianapolis Nov. 27, 1979; installed Jan. 10, 1980; died Jan. 10, 1992; DANIEL MARK BUECHLEIN, O.S.B., ord. May 3, 1964; appt. to Memphis Jan. 16, 1987; cons. Bishop March 2, 1987; installed March 2, 1987; appt. Archbishop of Indianapolis July 14, 1992; installed Sept. 9, 1992; retired Sept. 21, 2011.

Archdiocesan Administration— Secretariats/ Vicariates/Agencies and Offices can be contacted through The Archbishop Edward T. O'Meara Catholic Center. *Mailing Address: 1400 N. Meridian St., Indianapolis, 46202.* Tel: 317-236-1400; Fax: 317-236-1401.

Chancellor—ANNETTE "MICKEY" LENTZ.

Assistant Chancellor—Rev. STEPHEN W. GIANNINI, M.Div., M.A., M.S.

Chief Financial Officer—JEFFREY D. STUMPF.

Board of Consultors—Most Rev. CHRISTOPHER J. COYNE, S.L.D., Chm.; Rev. Msgrs. JOSEPH F. SCHAEDEL, M.S., M.Div.; WILLIAM F. STUMPF, Ph.D.; Revs. CLIFFORD R. VOGELSANG (Retired); STEPHEN W. GIANNINI, M.Div., M.A., M.S.; Rev. Msgr. PAUL D. KOETTER, V.F.; Revs. GERALD J. KIRKHOFF; VINCENT LAMPERT, M.Div.

Deaneries and Deans—Rev. GUY R. ROBERTS, V.F., Indianapolis North; Rev. Msgr. PAUL D. KOETTER, V.F., Indianapolis East; Revs. JAMES R. WILMOTH, V.F., Indianapolis South; KENNETH TAYLOR, V.F., Indianapolis West; DANIEL J. STAUBLIN, V.F., Seymour; MICHAEL C. FRITSCH, M.Div., V.F., Bloomington; STANLEY J. HERBER, M.A., V.F., Connersville; WILFRED E. DAY, V.F., New Albany; JOHN A. MEYER, V.F., Batesville; DENNIS M. DUVELIUS, V.F., Tell City; RICHARD M. GINTHER, V.F., Terre Haute.

Finance Council—Most Rev. CHRISTOPHER J. COYNE, S.L.D., Chm.; Rev. Msgr. WILLIAM F. STUMPF, Ph.D.; JEFFREY D. STUMPF, CFO; DANIEL DEBARD, Pres.; TIMOTHY ROBINSON, Vice Pres.; JERRY WILLIAMS, Sec.; MARY HORN; KENNETH J. HEDLUND; PHILIP B. MCKEIRNAN; SCOTT NICKERSON; GREG MONTE; DANIEL RILEY.

Priests' Personnel Board—Most Rev. CHRISTOPHER J. COYNE, S.L.D.; Revs. NOAH J. CASEY, M.Div., M.A., D.Min.; PATRICK DOYLE; JOHN P. MCCASLIN; H. MICHAEL HILDERBRAND, M.A., M.Div., M.S., Ed.S.; GERALD J. KIRKHOFF, Chm.; Rev. Msgr. PAUL D. KOETTER, V.F.; Revs. PAUL M. SHIKANY, J.C.L.; STEPHEN W. GIANNINI, M.Div., M.A., M.S.; RANDALL R. SUMMERS, M.B.A., M.A., M.Div.

Deacons' Personnel Board—Rev. STEPHEN W. GIANNINI, Chm.; Deacon MICHAEL EAST, Vice Chair; DARLENE DAVIS; Deacon DAVID HENN; MARY HODGES; Deacons WILLIAM JONES; THOMAS WARD.

Archdiocesan Review Board—ANN M. DELANEY; EILEEN AHRENS; MARY HORTY; EDMUND C. HASKINS, Ph.D.; JOHN "JACK" M. WHELAN; Rev. Msgr. ANTHONY R. VOLZ.

Bishop Simon Brute College Seminary—Rev. ROBERT J. ROBESON, Ph.D., Rector. Tel: 317-924-4100.

Secretariat for Catholic Charities and Family Ministries—DAVID J. SILER, L.C.S.W., Exec. Dir. Tel: 317-236-7325.

Catholic Campaign for Human Development—TERESA CHAMBLEE, Dir. Tel: 317-473-0413.

Deaf Ministry—DAVID BETHURAM, M.A., M.Min, Contact Person. Tel: 317-236-1595.

Office of Family Ministries—DAVID BETHURAM, M.A., M.Min, Exec. Dir. Tel: 317-236-1596.

Commission for Multicultural Ministry—Rev. KENNETH TAYLOR, V.F., Dir. Tel: 317-236-1562.

Office for Pro-Life Ministry—Sr. DIANE CAROLLO, S.G.L., Dir. Tel: 317-236-1569.

Catholic Charities Indianapolis—DAVID BETHURAM, M.A., M.Min, Indianapolis Agency Dir. Tel: 317-236-1500.

Catholic Charities Terre Haute—JOHN C. ETLING, Terre Haute Agency Dir. Tel: 812-232-1447.

Catholic Charities New Albany—MARK CASPER, New Albany Agency Dir. Tel: 812-949-7305.

Catholic Charities Bloomington—MARSHA MCCARTY, Bloomington Agency Dir. Tel: 812-332-1262.

Catholic Charities Tell City—JOAN HESS, Tell City Agency Dir. Tel: 812-547-0903.

St. Elizabeth Coleman Pregnancy and Adoption Services—DAVID BETHURAM, M.A., M.Min, Agency Dir. Tel: 317-787-3412.

St. Elizabeth's Regional Maternity Center—MARK CASPER, Agency Dir. Tel: 812-949-7305.

Secretariat for Catholic Education and Faith Formation—HARRY PLUMMER, Exec. Dir. Tel: 317-236-1440.

Catholic Education—G. JOSEPH PETERS, Assoc. Exec. Dir. Tel: 317-236-1430.

Faith Formation—KEN OGOREK, Dir. Catechesis. Tel: 317-236-1446.

Catholic Education, School Improvement—RONALD COSTELLO, Supt. Catholic Schools. Tel: 317-236-1486.

SPRED—KARA FAVATA, Asst. Dir. Tel: 317-236-1448.

Mother Theodore Catholic Academies—CONNIE ZITTNAN, Exec. Dir. Tel: 317-236-7322; DENNIS SPONSEL, Chm. Bd. Tel: 317-236-1421.

Catholic Youth Organization—EDWARD TINDER, Dir., 580 E. Stevens St., Indianapolis, 46203. Tel: 317-632-9311.

Youth Ministry—KAY SCOVILLE, Dir. Tel: 317-236-1477.

Young Adult and College Campus Ministry—Rev. RICK NAGEL.

St. Mary's Child Center—CONSTANCE SHERMAN, Dir., 901 Dr. Martin Luther King, Jr. St., Indianapolis, 46202. Tel: 317-635-1491.

Secretariat for Communications—GREG A. OTOLSKI, Exec. Dir. Tel: 317-236-1585.

Archdiocesan Newspaper, "The Criterion"—Most Rev. CHRISTOPHER J. COYNE, S.L.D., Apostolic Admin. & Publisher; GREG A. OTOLSKI, Assoc. Publisher; MICHAEL A. KROKOS, Editor. Tel: 317-236-1570.

Catholic Communications Center—GREG A. OTOLSKI, Exec. Dir. Tel: 317-236-1585.

Secretariat for Finance and Administrative Services—JEFFREY D. STUMPF, CFO & Exec. Dir. Tel: 317-236-1410.

Accounting Services—JULIE SHEWMAKER, Controller. Tel: 317-236-1410.

Information Services— Dast Consulting LLC Tel: 317-236-1420.

Management Services—ERIC L. ATKINS, Dir. Tel: 317-236-1452.

Purchasing Office—STEPHEN M. JAMES, Dir. Tel: 317-236-1451.

Catholic Cemeteries Assoc.—TONY LLOYD, Buchanan Group, 9001 N. Haverstick Rd., Indianapolis, 46240. Tel: 317-574-8898.

Roman Catholic Archdiocese of Indianapolis Properties—Most Rev. CHRISTOPHER J. COYNE, S.L.D., Pres.; ANNETTE "MICKEY" LENTZ, Sec.; JEFFREY D. STUMPF, Treas. Tel: 317-236-1410.

Secretariat for Lay Ministry and Pastoral Services—ANNETTE "MICKEY" LENTZ, Exec. Dir.

Archives—KAREN ODDI, Assoc. Archivist. Tel: 317-236-1429; TERESA LAW, Records Mgmt. Coord.

Archdiocesan Historian—Rev. JACK W. PORTER (Retired).

Human Resources—ED ISAKSON, Dir. Tel: 317-236-1594.

Lay Ministry—ED ISAKSON, Dir.

Parish Planning and Organizational Development—ANNETTE "MICKEY" LENTZ, Dir.

Secretariat for Spiritual Life and Worship—CHARLES GARDNER, Exec. Dir. Tel: 317-236-1483.

Archdiocesan Cathedral—Rev. NOAH J. CASEY, M.Div., M.A., D.Min., Pastor & Rector.

Archdiocesan Office of Ecumenism—Rev. JOHN BEITANS, Dir.

Evangelization Commission—PEG MCEVOY, Assoc. Dir., Evangelization & Family Catechesis.

Office of Worship—CHARLES GARDNER, Exec. Dir. Tel: 317-236-1483.

Retreat & Renewal Ministries and Fatima Retreat House—Rev. JAMES M. FARRELL, S.T.B., Dir., 5353 E. 56th St., Indianapolis, 46226. Tel: 317-545-7681; Fax: 317-545-0095.

Secretariat for Stewardship and Development—DAVID MILROY, Exec. Dir. Tel: 317-236-1415.

Office of Stewardship and Development—KENT J. GOFFINET, Dir. Stewardship & Devel. Tel: 317-236-1465; RON GREULICH, Dir. Stewardship Educ. Tel: 317-236-1426; JOLINDA MOORE, Dir. Annual Major Giving. Tel: 317-236-1462; DENA PERRY, Dir. Communications. Tel: 317-236-1578; DANA TOWNSEND, Dir., Donor Svcs. Tel: 317-236-1498; MICHAEL KIRK, Assoc. Dir. Annual Major Giving. Tel: 317-236-1546.

Catholic Community Foundation, Inc.—Most Rev. CHRISTOPHER J. COYNE, S.L.D., Chm.; ELLEN M. BRUNNER, Dir. Planned Giving. Tel: 317-236-1427.

Mission Office—Rev. Msgr. JOSEPH F. SCHAEDEL, M.S., M.Div., Dir. Tel: 317-236-1485.

Vicariate for Clergy and Parish Life Coordinators: Formation and Personnel—Rev. STEPHEN W. GIANNINI, M.Div., M.A., M.S., Vicar. Tel: 317-236-1495.

Deacons, Office of—Deacon MICHAEL EAST, Dir.

Deacon Formation, Office of—Deacon KERRY BLANDFORD, Dir. Tel: 317-236-1490.

Vicariate for Advocacy to Priests—Revs. GERALD J. KIRKHOFF, Vicar. Tel: 317-236-1489; JOSEPH F. RAUTENBERG, Ethics & Bioethics Consultant. Tel: 317-236-1449.

Personnel: Priests and Parish Life Coordinators—Rev. STEPHEN W. GIANNINI, M.Div., M.A., M.S., Dir. Tel: 317-236-1495.

Priestly and Religious Vocations—Rev. ERIC MATTHEW JOHNSON, Dir. Tel: 317-236-1490.

Vicariate Judicial Metropolitan Tribunal—Rev. STANLEY PONDO, J.D., J.C.D., M.Div., Vicar Judicial. Tel: 317-236-1460.

Adjunct Vicars Judicial—Revs. ROBERT J. GILDAY, S.T.B.; PAUL M. SHIKANY, J.C.L.; Rev. Msgr. FREDERICK EASTON, J.C.L., Adjunct Vicar Judicial, Judicial Vicar Emeritus.

Judge Instructors and Assessors—Ms. ANN TULLY, B.S., M.T.S.; Ms. MARY ELLEN HAUCK, B.A.

Defenders of the Bond—Revs. JAMES R. BONKE, J.C.L.; PATRICK COONEY, O.S.B., J.C.L.; Ms. PATRICIA JEFFERS, B.A.; LYNDA ROBITAILLE, J.C.D.

Promoter of Justice—Rev. JAMES R. BONKE, J.C.L.

Archdiocesan Judges—Revs. CLIFFORD R. VOGELSANG (Retired); CLEMENT T. DAVIS, M.Div.; NICHOLAS J. DANT, M.Div., S.T.L.; VINCENT LAMPERT, M.Div.; DANIEL B. DONOHOO, M.A., M.Div.; STEPHEN W. GIANNINI, M.Div., M.A., M.S.

Auditor—Sr. PAULA MODAFF, S.P., J.C.L.

Notaries—Ms. KAY SUMMERS, B.A.; NANCY THOMPSON; Ms. ROSEANNE L. HUCKLEBERRY, B.A.

Victim Assistance Coordinator—CARLA HILL. Tel: 317-236-1548; 800-382-9836, Ext. 1548.

CLERGY, PARISHES, MISSIONS AND PAROCHIAL SCHOOLS

CITY OF INDIANAPOLIS

(MARION COUNTY)

1—SS. PETER AND PAUL CATHEDRAL, INDIANAPOLIS, INC. (1892) [JC] Rev. Noah J. Casey, Rector. In Res., Revs. James R. Bonke; Daniel B. Donohoo.
Res.: 1347 N. Meridian St., 46202. Tel: 317-634-4519; Fax: 317-630-9621. Web: www.ssppc.org.

2—ST. ANDREW THE APOSTLE CATHOLIC CHURCH, INDIANAPOLIS, INC. (1946) Deacon Robert W. Decker, Parish Life Coord.; Revs. James M. Farrell, Priest Mod.; William G. Munshower, Sacramental Min. (Retired); Clifford R. Vogelsang, Sacramental Min. (Retired).
Parish Office—4052 E. 38th St., 46218-1444. Tel: 317-546-1571; Fax: 317-549-6311. Email: lakers@standrewindy.org. Web: www.standrewindy.org.
Catechesis/Religious Program—Email: rdecker@standrewstrita.org. Students 17.

3—ST. ANN CATHOLIC CHURCH, INDIANAPOLIS, INC. (1917) [JC] Rev. Glenn L. O'Connor; Deacon Wesley Jones.
Office & Mailing Address: 6350 S. Mooresville Rd., 46221-4519. Tel: 317-821-2909; Fax: 317-821-2929. Email: saintannchurc@aol.com. Web: www.st-ann-rcindy.org.
Catechesis/Religious Program—Email: saintannindy@sbcglobal.net. Kelly O'Brien, C.R.E. Students 74.

4—ST. ANTHONY CATHOLIC CHURCH, INDIANAPOLIS, INC. (1891), (Irish—German), [JC] Revs. John P. McCaslin; Robert J. Robeson, Sacramental Min.; Patrick J. Beidelman, Sacramental Min.; Thomas C. Widner, S.J., Sacramental Min.
337 N. Warman Ave., 46222-4094. Tel: 317-636-4828; Fax: 317-636-3140.
Catechesis/Religious Program—Students 204.

5—ST. BARNABAS CATHOLIC CHURCH, INDIANAPOLIS, INC. (1965) Revs. Anthony R. Voltz; Sean R. Danda; Deacon Patrick Bower.
Res.: 8300 Rahke Rd., 46217-4999. Tel: 317-882-0724; Fax: 317-887-8932.
School—(Grades K-8) Tel: 317-881-7422; Fax: 317-887-8933. Debra Perkins, Prin. Lay Teachers 33; Students 530.
Catechesis/Religious Program—Students 336.

6—ST. BERNADETTE CATHOLIC CHURCH, INDIANAPOLIS, INC. (1952) [CEM] Rev. J. Nicholas Dant; Deacon Donald Dearman.
Church & Parish Office: 4838 Fletcher Ave., 46203. Tel: 317-356-5867; Fax: 317-356-4184. Email: parishoffice@stb-indy.org. Web: www.stb-indy.org.
Res.: 4720 E. 13th St., 46203. Tel: 317-357-8352.
Catechesis/Religious Program—Students 20.

7—CHRIST THE KING CATHOLIC CHURCH, INDIANAPOLIS, INC. (1939) Revs. Stephen T. Jarrell; James R. Bonke. In Res., Rev. Jeffrey H. Godecker.
Parish Office—5884 Crittenden Ave., 46220. Tel: 317-255-3666; Fax: 317-475-6579. Email: ctk@ctk-indy.org. Web: www.christtheking-indy.org.
Res.: 1827 E. Kessler Blvd., 46220.
School—5858 Crittenden Ave., 46220. Tel: 317-257-9366; Fax: 317-475-6581. Lay Teachers 25; Students 395.
Catechesis/Religious Program—Tel: 317-255-3666; Fax: 317-475-6579. Students 89.

8—ST. CHRISTOPHER CATHOLIC CHURCH, INDIANAPOLIS, INC. (Speedway City) (1937) Revs. D. Michael Welch; David Lawler, Assoc. Pastor; Sisters Kathleen Morrissey, O.P., Pastoral Assoc.; Mary DeFazio, S.P., Pastoral Assoc. Faith Formation; Mr. Bill Szolek Van Valkenburgh, Pastoral Assoc.
Res.: 5301 W. 16th St., 46224-6497. Tel: 317-241-6314; Fax: 317-241-6587.

School—5335 W. 16th St., 46224. Fax: 317-244-6678. Vincent Schurgar, Prin. Lay Teachers 16; Students 222.
Catechesis/Religious Program—Thomas Steiner, Youth Min. Students 312.

9—THE CHURCH OF THE HOLY CROSS, INDIANAPOLIS, INC. (1895) Rev. Carlton J. Beever.
Church: 125 N. Oriental St., 46202-3886. Tel: 317-637-2620; Fax: 317-637-0112. Email: parish@holycrossindy.org. Web: www.holycrossindy.org.
School—Tel: 317-638-9068; Fax: 317-638-0116. Email: school@holycrossindy.org. Ruth Tinsley, Prin. Lay Teachers 15; Students 172.
Catechesis/Religious Program—Students 14.

10—ST. GABRIEL THE ARCHANGEL CATHOLIC CHURCH, INDIANAPOLIS, INC. (1963) Rev. Larry P. Crawford; Deacon Oscar Morales, Pastoral Assoc.
Parish Center:—6000 W. 34th St., 46224. Tel: 317-291-7014; Fax: 317-297-6455. Email: info@stgabrielindy.org. Web: www.stgabrielindy-.org.
See School under St. Michael the Archangel, Indianapolis for details.
Catechesis/Religious Program—Tel: 317-299-9924. Mrs. Teresa Keith, Dir. Faith Formation. Students 159.

11—GOOD SHEPHERD ROMAN CATHOLIC CHURCH, INDIANAPOLIS, INC. (1993) [JC], (St. Catherine, 1909, and St. James the Greater, 1951, were closed, merged, and renamed in 1993.) Rev. Gerald J. Kirkhoff.
Church & Parish Office: 2905 S. Carson Ave., 46203-5216. Tel: 317-783-3158; Fax: 317-781-5961.
School—Central Catholic School, (Grades K-8), 1155 E. Cameron St., 46203. Tel: 317-783-7759; Fax: 317-781-5964. Sara Browning, Prin. Students 169.
Catechesis/Religious Program—Students 11.

12—HOLY ANGELS CATHOLIC CHURCH, INDIANAPOLIS, INC. (1903), (African American), Rev. Kenneth Taylor.
Res.: 740 W. 28th St., 46208-5099. Tel: 317-926-3324; Fax: 317-926-3325. Email: holyangelsbulletin@hotmail.com. Web: www.holyangelsindy.org.
School—(Grades K-6), 2822 Dr. Martin Luther King, Jr. St., 46208. Tel: 317-926-5211; Fax: 317-926-5219. Sherlynn Pillow, Prin.; Michael Joseph, Campus Dir.; Mrs. Jude Mitchell, Librarian. Sisters of I.H.M. Reparatrix 1; Lay Teachers 12; Students 130.
Catechesis/Religious Program—Students 33.

13—HOLY SPIRIT CATHOLIC CHURCH, INDIANAPOLIS, INC. (1946) Rev. Msgr. Paul D. Koetter; Rev. Christopher Wadelton.
Res.: 7243 E. 10th St., 46219-4990. Tel: 317-353-9404; Fax: 317-351-1707. Web: www.holyspirit-indy.org.
School—(Grades PreK-8), 7241 E. 10th St., 46219. Tel: 317-352-1243; Fax: 317-351-1822. Rita Parsons, Prin. Lay Teachers 23; Students 379.
Catechesis/Religious Program—Tel: 317-357-6915. Students 500.

14—HOLY TRINITY CHURCH, INDIANAPOLIS, INC. (1906) [JC] Rev. John P. McCaslin, Admin.
Parish Office: 337 N. Warman Ave., 46222-4094.
Church: N. Holmes Ave. & W. St. Clair St., 46222.
Res.: 379 N. Warman Ave., 46222. Tel: 317-631-2939; Fax: 317-636-3140. Email: holytrinityindy@catholicweb.com. Web: www.holytrinityindy.catholicweb.com.
Catechesis/Religious Program—Students 6.

15—IMMACULATE HEART OF MARY CATHOLIC CHURCH, INDIANAPOLIS, INC. (1946) [JC] Rev. Robert W. Sims.
Parish Center—5692 Central Ave., 46220-3012. Tel: 317-257-2266; Fax: 317-475-7380. Web: ihmindy.org.
School—317 E. 57th St., 46220. Tel: 317-255-5468; Fax: 317-475-7379. Peggy Elson, Prin. Lay Teachers 30; Students 434.
Catechesis/Religious Program—Students 190.

16—ST. JOAN OF ARC CATHOLIC CHURCH, INDIANAPOLIS, INC. (1921) [JC] Rev. Guy R. Roberts.
Res.: 4217 Central Ave., 46205. Tel: 317-283-5508; Fax: 317-283-5511.
School—(Grades PreK-8), 500 E. 42nd St., 46205. Tel: 317-283-1518; Fax: 317-931-3380. Mary Pat Sharpe, Prin.; Sarah Batt, Librarian. Lay Teachers 9; Students 239.
Catechesis/Religious Program—Fax: 317-283-5511. Students 65.

17—ST. JOHN THE EVANGELIST CATHOLIC CHURCH, INDIANAPOLIS, INC. (1837) Rev. Rick Nagel.
Res.: 126 W. Georgia St., 46225. Tel: 317-635-2021; Fax: 317-635-2014. Email: office@stjohnsindy.org. Web: www.stjohnsindy.org.
Catechesis/Religious Program—Students 9.

18—ST. JOSEPH CATHOLIC CHURCH, INDIANAPOLIS, INC. (1949) [JC] Rev. Glenn L. O'Connor.
Res.: 1375 S. Mickley Ave., 46241-3219. Tel: 317-244-9002; Fax: 317-244-0278. Email: glo1375@aol.com.
Catechesis/Religious Program—Students 65.

19—ST. JUDE CATHOLIC CHURCH, INDIANAPOLIS, INC. (1959) Rev. Stephen Banet.
Res.: 5353 McFarland Rd., 46227-7098. Tel: 317-786-4371; Fax: 317-780-7592. Web: www.stjudeindy.org.
School—5375 McFarland Rd, 46227. Tel: 317-784-6828; Fax: 317-780-7594. Mr. Joseph Shelburn, Prin. Sisters of Providence 1; Lay Teachers 26; Students 510.
Catechesis/Religious Program—Tel: 317-780-7591. Students 206.

20—ST. LAWRENCE CATHOLIC CHURCH, LAWRENCE, INC. (1949) Revs. Thomas L. Schliessmann; Jae Peter Choi, Korean Community; Deacon Thomas Ward.
Office: 6944 E. 46th St., 46226-3704. Tel: 317-546-4065; Fax: 317-543-4926.
Res.: 4650 N. Shadeland Ave., 46226.
School—6950 E. 46th St., 46226. Tel: 317-543-4923; Fax: 317-543-4929. Yolanda D. McCormick, Prin. Lay Teachers 22; Students 225.
Catechesis/Religious Program—Email: tbrydon@archindy.org. Students 190.

21—SAINT LUKE CATHOLIC CHURCH, INDIANAPOLIS, INC. (1961) [JC] Rev. Msgr. Joseph F. Schaedel.
Res.: 7550 Holliday Dr. E., 46260. Tel: 317-259-4373; Fax: 317-254-3210. Web: www.stluke.org.
School—7650 N. Illinois St., 46260. Tel: 317-255-3912. Stephen Weber, Prin. Lay Teachers 35; Students 604.
Catechesis/Religious Program—Students 150.

22—ST. MARK THE EVANGELIST CATHOLIC CHURCH, INDIANAPOLIS, INC. (1946) Rev. George F. Plaster; Deacon Kerry Blanford.
Res.: 535 E. Edgewood Ave., 46227-2099. Tel: 317-787-8246; Fax: 317-781-6466. Email: ksweeney@stmarkindy.org. Web: www.stmarkindy.org.
School—541 E. Edgewood Ave., 46227. Tel: 317-786-4013; Fax: 317-783-9574. Rusty Albertson, Prin. Lay Teachers 19; Students 249.
Catechesis/Religious Program—Tel: 317-784-7155. Email: mlcav@stmarkindy.org. Students 167.

23—SAINT MARY OF THE IMMACULATE CONCEPTION CATHOLIC CHURCH, INDIANAPOLIS, INC. (1858), (Hispanic), [JC] Rev. Michael E. O'Mara; Mr. Juan Manuel Guzman, Pastoral Assoc.
Res.: 311 N. New Jersey St., 46204-2174. Tel: 317-637-3983; Fax: 317-637-0111. Email: parish@saintmarysindy.org. Web: www.saintmarysindy.org.
Catechesis/Religious Program—The Marian Center Students 200.

24—ST. MATTHEW CATHOLIC CHURCH, INDIANAPOLIS, INC. (1958) Rev. Paul M. Shikany. In Res., Rev. Robert T. Hausladen.
Res.: 4100 E. 56th St., 46220. Tel: 317-257-4297; Fax: 317-479-2381. Email: ahaage@saintmatt.org. Web: www.saintmatt.org.
School—(Grades K-8) Tel: 317-251-3997. Email: principal@saintmatt.org. Web: www.saintmatt.org/school. David Smock, Prin. Religious 1; Lay Teachers 29; Students 316.
Catechesis/Religious Program—Tel: 317-257-4297, Ext. 1005. Email: jnoll@saintmatt.org. Students 160.

25—ST. MICHAEL THE ARCHANGEL CATHOLIC CHURCH, INDIANAPOLIS, INC. (1948) Rev. Varghese Maliakkal, Admin.
Res.: 3354 W. 30th St., 46222. Tel: 317-926-7359; Fax: 317-921-3282. Email: rectory@indyarchangel.org. Web: www.saintmichaelindy.org.
School—3352 W. 30th St., 46222. Tel: 317-926-0516; Fax: 317-921-3280. Sarah Watson, Prin. Lay Teachers 24; Students 276.
Catechesis/Religious Program—Tel: 317-921-3284. Email: bildanner@att.net. Students 65.

26—ST. MONICA CATHOLIC CHURCH, INDIANAPOLIS, INC. (1956) Revs. Todd Michael Goodson; Dustin M. Boehm.
Res.: 6131 N. Michigan Rd., 46228-1298. Tel: 317-253-2193; Fax: 317-253-3342. Email: parishoffice@stmonicaindy.org. Web: www.stmonicaindy.org.
School—Tel: 317-255-7153; Fax: 317-259-5570. Lay Teachers 33; Students 507.
Catechesis/Religious Program—Students 503.

27—NATIVITY OF OUR LORD JESUS CHRIST CATHOLIC CHURCH, INDIANAPOLIS, INC. (1947) [JC] Rev. Patrick Doyle.
7225 Southeastern Ave., 46239-1209. Tel: 317-357-1200. Email: tmarlin@nativityindy.org. Web: www.nativityindy.org.
School—3310 S. Meadow Dr., 46239. Tel: 317-357-1459; Fax: 317-357-9175. Lay Teachers 25; Students 313.
Catechesis/Religious Program—Tel: 317-359-6075. Email: rhawthorne@nativityindy.org. Students 150.

28—OUR LADY OF LOURDES CATHOLIC CHURCH, INDIANAPOLIS, INC. (1909) Rev. J. Nicholas Dant.
5333 E. Washington St., 46219-6492. Tel: 317-356-7291; Fax: 317-356-2358. Email: parishsecretary@ollindy.org. Web: www.ollindy.org.
School—30 S. Downey Ave., 46219. Tel: 317-357-3316; Fax: 317-357-0980. Lay Teachers 23; Students 272.
Catechesis/Religious Program—Email: marmbrust@ollindy.org. Mary Armbrust, D.R.E. & Pastoral Assoc. Students 15.

29—OUR LADY OF THE MOST HOLY ROSARY CATHOLIC CHURCH, INDIANAPOLIS, INC. (1909), (Italian), [JC] Rev. Michael W. Magiera, F.S.S.P., Admin.
Office: 520 Stevens St., 46203-1737. Tel: 317-636-4478; Fax: 317-636-2522. Email: holyrosaryc@cs.com. Web: www.holyrosaryindy.org.
Catechesis/Religious Program—Teresa Gorsage, C.R.E.

30—ST. PATRICK CATHOLIC CHURCH, INDIANAPOLIS, INC. (1865), (Irish—Hispanic), Rev. Arturo M. Ocampo, O.F.M.
Church: 950 Prospect St., 46203. Tel: 317-631-5824; Fax: 317-631-5828.
See Central Catholic Consolidated, Indianapolis under Good Shepherd, Indianapolis for details.
Catechesis/Religious Program—Students 174.

31—ST. PHILIP NERI CATHOLIC CHURCH, INDIANAPOLIS, INC. (1909), (Irish—Hispanic), [JC] Rev. Carlton J. Beever.
Res.: 550 N. Rural St., 46201-2497. Tel: 317-631-8746; Fax: 317-632-8161.
School—545 Eastern Ave., 46201. Tel: 317-636-0134; Fax: 317-636-3231. Mary McCoy, Prin. Lay Teachers 14; Students 205.
Catechesis/Religious Program—Students 175.

32—ST. PIUS X CATHOLIC CHURCH, INDIANAPOLIS, INC. (1955) Revs. James M. Farrell; Peter A. Marshall.
Res.: 7200 Sarto Dr., 46240-3599. Tel: 317-255-4534; Fax: 317-466-3354. Web: www.spxparish.org.
School—Tel: 317-466-3361. Bill Herman, Prin. Lay Teachers 28; Students 431.
Catechesis/Religious Program—Tel: 317-257-1085; Fax: 317-466-3377. Students 165.

33—ST. RITA CATHOLIC CHURCH, INDIANAPOLIS, INC. (1919), (African American), [JC] Rev. Eusebius Mbidoaka.
1733 Dr. Andrew J. Brown Ave., 46202-1998. Web: www.stritachurch-indy.org.
Catechesis/Religious Program—Students 42.

34—ST. ROCH CATHOLIC CHURCH, INDIANAPOLIS, INC. (1922) [JC] Rev. James R. Wilmoth.
Res.: 3600 S. Pennsylvania St., 46227-1299. Tel: 317-784-1763; Fax: 317-783-9617.
School—3603 S. Meridian St., 46217. Tel: 317-784-9144. Lay Teachers 21; Students 277.
Catechesis/Religious Program—Students 81.

35—SACRED HEART OF JESUS CATHOLIC CHURCH, INDIANAPOLIS, INC. (1875), (German), [CEM 2] [JC] Rev. Lawrence R. Janezic, O.F.M.; Bros. Gary Jeriha, O.F.M.; Moises Gutierrez, O.F.M. In Res., Revs. Arturo M. Ocampo, O.F.M.; Justin Belitz, O.F.M., P.O. Box 30248, 46230.
Res.: 1530 S. Union St., 46225-1697. Tel: 317-638-5551; Fax: 317-637-9741.
See Central Catholic School, Indianapolis under Good Shepherd, Indianapolis and Roncalli High School in the Institution Section for details.
Catechesis/Religious Program—Students 35.

36—ST. SIMON THE APOSTLE CATHOLIC CHURCH, INDIANAPOLIS, INC. (1961) Rev. William G. Marks.
Church & Office: 8155 Oaklandon Rd., 46236-8578. Tel: 317-826-6000; Fax: 317-826-6010.
School—(Grades PreSchool-8) Tel: 317-826-6000, Ext. 107; Fax: 317-826-6020. Donovan Yarnall, Prin. Lay Teachers 37; Students 755.
Catechesis/Religious Program—Tel: 317-826-6000, Ext. 113. Students 420.

37—ST. THERESE OF THE INFANT JESUS CATHOLIC CHURCH, INDIANAPOLIS, INC. (1925) [JC] Rev. Robert J. Gilday.
Res.: 4720 E. 13th St., 46201-1798. Tel: 317-357-8352; Fax: 317-357-5316. Web: www.littleflowerparish.org.
School—(Grades PreSchool-8), 1401 N. Bosart Ave, 46202. Tel: 317-353-2282; Fax: 317-322-7702. Web: www.littleflowerparish.org/school. Kevin Gawrys, Prin. Lay Teachers 16; Students 200.
Catechesis/Religious Program—Students 60.

38—SAINT THOMAS AQUINAS CATHOLIC CHURCH, INDIANAPOLIS, INC. (1939) Rev. Steven C. Schwab.
Office: 4625 N. Kenwood Ave., 46208-3599. Tel: 317-253-1461; Fax: 317-253-1410. Email: mhuelsman@sta-indy.org. Web: www.staindy.org.
Res.: 4650 N. Illinois St., 46208.
School—4600 N. Illinois St., 46208. Tel: 317-255-6244; Fax: 317-255-6106. Email: rsochacki@staschool-indy.org. Web: www.staschool-indy.org. Jerry Flynn, Prin. Lay Teachers 21; Students 212.
Catechesis/Religious Program—Students 40.

OUTSIDE THE CITY OF INDIANAPOLIS

AURORA, DEARBORN CO., ST. MARY IMMACULATE CONCEPTION CATHOLIC CHURCH, AURORA, INC. (1857) Rev. Stephen D. Donahue.
Parish Office—203 Fourth St., 47001-1298. Tel: 812-926-0060; Fax: 812-926-4439. Email: stmarychurch@uswebmail.biz. Web: www.stmarychurchaurora.com.
School—(Grades K-8), 211 Fourth St., 47001. Tel: 812-926-1558; Fax: 812-926-4439. Email: stmary@uswebmail.biz. Web: www.stmaryschoolaurora.com. James Tush, Prin. Lay Teachers 9; Students 136.
Catechesis/Religious Program—Email: carolynmeyer@uswebmail.biz.

BATESVILLE, RIPLEY CO., ST. LOUIS CATHOLIC CHURCH, BATESVILLE, INC. (1868), (German), [CEM] Rev. Randall R. Summers.
Res.: 13 St. Louis Pl., 47006-1393. Tel: 812-934-3204; Fax: 812-933-0667. Web: www.stlouis-batesville.org.
School—Preschool, 200 S. Walnut St., 47006. Tel: 812-932-1731.
School—17 St. Louis Pl., 47006. Tel: 812-934-3310; Fax: 812-934-6202. Chad M. Moeller, Prin. Lay Teachers 28; Students 398.
Catechesis/Religious Program—Tel: 812-934-3204, Ext. 249. Email: tmeyer@stlouisschool.org. Terri Meyer, D.R.E. Students 188.

BEDFORD, LAWRENCE CO., ST. VINCENT DE PAUL CATHOLIC CHURCH, BEDFORD, INC. (1864) Rev. Richard W. Eldred; Deacon David Reising.
Parish/Mailing Office: 1723 I St., 47421-4284.
Rectory—St. Mary of the Assumption: 777 S. 11th St., Mitchell, 47446. Tel: 812-275-6539; Fax: 812-275-3493.
School—(Grades PreK-8), 923 18th St., 47421. Tel: 812-279-2540; Fax: 812-276-4880. Rebecca Floyd, Prin. Lay Teachers 12; Students 176.
Catechesis/Religious Program—Students 53.

BEECH GROVE, MARION CO., HOLY NAME OF JESUS CATHOLIC CHURCH, INDIANAPOLIS, INC. (1908) [JC] Rev. William M. Williams.
Res.: 89 N. 17th Ave., 46107-1531. Tel: 317-784-5454 (Parish Office); Fax: 317-784-1834 (Parish Office). Web: www.holyname.cc.
School—21 N. 17th Ave., 46107. Tel: 317-784-9078 (Office); 317-788-3617; 317-788-3618; Fax: 317-788-3616. Email: gfleming@holyname.cc. Web: www.holyname.cc/school.htm. Gina Kuntz Fleming, Prin. Lay Teachers 20; Students 261.
Catechesis/Religious Program—Tel: 317-784-5454, Ext. 4. Email: jchamblee@holyname.cc. Web: www.holyname.cc. Students 57.

BLOOMINGTON, MONROE CO.

1—ST. CHARLES BORROMEO CATHOLIC CHURCH, BLOOMINGTON, INC. (1864) [JC] Rev. Thomas G. Kovatch; Deacon Marc Kellams.
Mailing Address: 2222 E. 3rd St., 47401-5385.
Res.: 2001 Southdowns Dr., 47401-5385. Tel: 812-336-6846; Fax: 812-331-6732.
School—(Grades PreK-8), 2224 E. 3rd St., 47401. Tel: 812-336-5853; Fax: 812-349-0300. Alec Mayer, Prin.; Ruth Gleason, Librarian. Lay Teachers 32; Students 456.
Catechesis/Religious Program—Tel: 812-334-1664. Janis Dopp, D.R.E. Students 230.

2—ST. JOHN THE APOSTLE CATHOLIC CHURCH, BLOOMINGTON, INC. (1970) Rev. Michael C. Fritsch.
Res.: 4607 W. State Rd. 46, 47404-9255. Tel: 812-876-1974; Fax: 812-876-9494. Email: info@sjabloomington.org. Web: sjabloomington.org.
Catechesis/Religious Program—Tel: 812-876-0718, Ext. 203. Lynn Hansen, D.R.E. Students 112.

3—ST. PAUL CATHOLIC CENTER, BLOOMINGTON, INC. (1969) Revs. John J. Meany, O.P., Admin.; Stanley Drongowski, O.P.; Cassian Sama, O.P.; Stephanie Hudson, Business Mgr.
Res.: 1413 E. 17th St., 47408-1602. Tel: 812-339-5561; Fax: 812-333-4846. Web: www.hoosiercatholic.org.
Catechesis/Religious Program—Email: faithformation@hoosiercatholic.org. Students 215.

BRADFORD, HARRISON CO., ST. MICHAEL CATHOLIC CHURCH, BRADFORD, INC. (1835) [CEM] Rev. John L. Fink.
Mailing Address: 11400 Farmers Ln., N.E., P.O. Box 22, 47107-0022. Tel: 812-364-6646; Fax: 812-364-6614. Web: saintmichaelschurch.net.
Catechesis/Religious Program—Tel: 812-364-6173. Email: johnjacobi@insightbb.com. Students 105.

BRAZIL, CLAY CO., ANNUNCIATION CATHOLIC CHURCH, BRAZIL, INC. (1866) Rev. Harold W. Rightor II.
Office: 19 N. Alabama St., 47834-2399. Tel: 812-448-1901; Fax: 812-448-1901. Email: annunciationchurch@msn.com.
Preschool—415 E. Church St., 47834. Fax: 812-443-2403. Jane Osborn, Admin.
Catechesis/Religious Program—Students 26.

BRIGHT, DEARBORN CO., ST TERESA BENEDICTA OF THE CROSS, BRIGHT, INC. (2000) Rev. Aaron M. Jenkins; Deacon Tim Heller.
Parish Office: 23455 Gavin Ln., Lawrenceburg, 47025-8372. Tel: 812-656-8700; Fax: 812-656-8777.
Catechesis/Religious Program—Students 225.

BROOKVILLE, FRANKLIN CO.

1—ST. MICHAEL THE ARCHANGEL CATHOLIC CHURCH, BROOKVILLE, INC. (1845), (German), [CEM] Rev. C. Ryan McCarthy.
Church: 145 St. Michael Blvd., 47012. Tel: 765-647-5462; Fax: 765-647-1634.
School—Tel: 765-647-4961; Fax: 765-647-4961. Gary Ferguson, Prin. Sisters of the Third Order Regular of St. Francis 2; Lay Teachers 13; Students 199.
Catechesis/Religious Program—Students 48.

BROWNSBURG, HENDRICKS CO., ST. MALACHY CATHOLIC CHURCH, BROWNSBURG, INC. (1869), (Irish), [CEM 2] Revs. Joseph M. Feltz; John J. Hollowell.
Parish Center—Tel: 317-852-3195; Fax: 317-852-8939.
Church & Mailing Address: 9833 E. Co. Rd. 750 N., 46112-1099. Web: www.saintmalachyparish.org.
School—(Grades K-8), 330 N. Green St., 46112. Tel: 317-852-2242; Fax: 317-852-3604. Angela Bostrom, Prin. Lay Teachers 30; Students 396.
Catechesis/Religious Program—Students 448.

BROWNSTOWN, JACKSON CO., OUR LADY OF PROVIDENCE CATHOLIC CHURCH, BROWNSTOWN, INC. (1934) Attended by St. Ambrose, Seymour. Rev. Daniel Staublin, Admin.; Deacon Michael East.
Church: Hwy. 50, P.O. Box 342, 47220.
Catechesis/Religious Program—Students 22.

CAMBRIDGE CITY, WAYNE CO., ST. ELIZABETH OF HUNGARY CATHOLIC CHURCH, CAMBRIDGE CITY, INC. (1852) Rev. Joseph F. Rautenberg.
333 W. Maple St., 47327-1130. Tel: 765-478-3242; Fax: 765-478-3585.
Catechesis/Religious Program—Email: meekerchristine@yahoo.com. Students 53.

CANNELTON, PERRY CO., ST. MICHAEL CATHOLIC CHURCH, CANNELTON, INC. (1859) [CEM] Rev. Barnabas Gillespie, O.S.B.
Parish Office—c/o Catholic Ministry Center, 824 Jefferson St., Tell City, 47586-2114. Tel: 812-547-7994; Fax: 812-547-6985. Email: stpaulch@psci.net.
Res.: 814 Jefferson St., Tell City, 47586. Tel: 812-547-9901.
Church: Eighth St., 47520.
Catechesis/Religious Program—Students 20.

CEDAR GROVE, FRANKLIN CO., HOLY GUARDIAN ANGELS CATHOLIC CHURCH, CEDAR GROVE, INC. (1874), (German), [CEM] Rev. C. Ryan McCarthy.
Mailing Address: 145 St. Michael Blvd., Brookville, 47012. Tel: 765-647-6981; Fax: 765-647-1634. Email: churchhga@verizon.net.
Church: 405 U.S. Hwy. 52, P.O. Box 38, 47016-0186.
Catechesis/Religious Program—Students 115.

CHARLESTOWN, CLARK CO., ST. MICHAEL CATHOLIC CHURCH, CHARLESTOWN, INC. (1860) [CEM] Rev. Steven Schaftlein.
Res.: 101 St. Michael Dr., 47111-1635. Tel: 812-256-3200; Fax: 775-307-6142. Email: michaelsecretary@insightbb.com.
Child Care Center—102 St. Michael Dr., 47111. Tel: 812-256-3503; Fax: 775-307-6142. (PreK-K) Students 59.
Catechesis/Religious Program—Students 79.

CLARKSVILLE, CLARK CO., ST. ANTHONY OF PADUA CATHOLIC CHURCH, CLARKSVILLE, INC. (1851) [CEM] Rev. Joseph West, O.F.M.Conv. In Res., Revs. John Elmer, O.F.M.Conv.; Robert St. Martin, O.F.M.Conv.
Res.: 316 N. Sherwood Ave., 47129-2724. Tel: 812-282-8515. Web: www.stanthonychurch.us.
School—320 N. Sherwood Ave., 47129. Tel: 812-282-2144; Fax: 812-282-2169. Sheila Noon, Prin. Lay Teachers 24; Students 315.
Catechesis/Religious Program—Email: stadre@insightbb.com. Students 70.

CLINTON, VERMILLION CO., SACRED HEART CHURCH, CLINTON, INC. (1891) Rev. Joseph L. Villa.
610 S. 6th St., 47842-2016. Tel: 765-832-8468; Fax: 765-832-5092. Email: sacredheartclinton@sbcglobal.net.
Rectory—558 Nebeker St., 47842.
Catechesis/Religious Program—Students 59.
Mission—St. Joseph (1920) 270 E. Wood Ave., Universal, Vermillion Co. 47884.

COLUMBUS, BARTHOLOMEW CO., ST. BARTHOLOMEW CATHOLIC CHURCH, COLUMBUS, INC. (1994), St. Bartholomew (1841) and St. Columba (1963) were closed, merged, and renamed St. Bartholomew. Rev. Clement T. Davis; Deacon William Jones.
Mailing Address: 1306 27th St., 47201-6375. Tel: 812-379-9353; Fax: 812-375-0720. Web: www.saintbartholomew.org.
School—(Grades K-8), 1306 27th St., 47201. Fax: 812-376-0377. Kathy Schubel, Prin. Lay Teachers 26; Students 406.
Catechesis/Religious Program—Students 980.

CONNERSVILLE, FAYETTE CO., ST. GABRIEL CATHOLIC CHURCH, CONNERSVILLE, INC. (1851) [JC] Rev. Stanley J. Herber; Pamela S. Rader, Business Mgr.
Res.: 232 W. Ninth St., 47331-2099. Tel: 765-825-8578; Fax: 765-825-7060.
School—(Grades PreK-6), 224 W. Ninth St., 47331. Tel: 765-825-7951; Fax: 765-827-4347. Email: sbarth@stgabrielconnersville.org. Web: www.stgabriel.k12.in.us. Sue Barth, Prin. Lay Teachers 8; Students 138.
Catechesis/Religious Program—Students 45.

CORYDON, HARRISON CO., ST. JOSEPH CATHOLIC CHURCH, CORYDON, INC. (1896) [CEM] Rev. Robert Jason Hankee.
Res.: 312 E. High St., 47112-1299. Tel: 812-738-2742; Fax: 812-738-2718. Email: parish.office@catholic-community.org. Web: www.triparishcommunity.com.
School—512 N. Mulberry St., 47112. Tel: 812-738-4549; Fax: 812-738-2722. Heidi Imberi, Prin. Lay Teachers 12; Students 105.
Catechesis/Religious Program—Tel: 812-738-2759. Students 140.
Mission—Most Precious Blood (1880) [CEM] Corydon-New Middletown Rd., New Middletown, Harrison Co. 47160.
Mission—St. Peter (1849) [CEM] Buena Vista Rd., Elizabeth, Harrison Co. 47117.

DANVILLE, HENDRICKS CO., MARY. QUEEN OF PEACE CATHOLIC CHURCH, DANVILLE, INC. (1939) Rev. Bernard Cox; Austin Rahill, Youth Min.
Res.: 1005 W. Main St., 46122-1025. Tel: 317-745-4284; Fax: 317-745-7090. Web: www.maryqueenofpeacedanville.org.
Catechesis/Religious Program—Tel: 317-745-4284, Ext. 13. Email: polycarp11@iquest.net. Peg Klein, D.R.E. Students 181.

DOVER, DEARBORN CO., ST. JOHN THE BAPTIST CATHOLIC CHURCH, DOVER, INC. (1824) [CEM] Revs. Scott E. Nobbe; Sengole Thomas Gnanaraj (India).
Church & Mailing Address: 25743 State Rd. 1, Guilford, 47022-8979. Tel: 812-576-4302; Fax: 812-576-2324.
Catechesis/Religious Program—Students 50.

EDINBURGH, JOHNSON CO., HOLY TRINITY CATHOLIC CHURCH, EDINBURGH, INC. (1851) Rev. John Beitans.
100 Keeley St., P.O. Box 216, 46124-0216.
Res.: 114 Lancelot Dr., Franklin, 46131. Tel: 317-738-3929; Fax: 812-526-2477. Email: hilltop3@sbcglobal.net.
Catechesis/Religious Program—Tel: 812-526-9470. Students 28.

ENOCHSBURG, DECATUR CO., ST. JOHN THE EVANGELIST CATHOLIC CHURCH, ENOCHSBURG, INC. (1844), (German), [CEM] Rev. George Joseph Nangachiveettil (India).
Mailing Address: 5267 N. Hamburg Rd., Oldenburg, 47036. Tel: 812-934-2880; Fax: 812-934-2880.
Church: 9995 E. Base Rd., Greensburg, 47240.
Catechesis/Religious Program—Fax: 812-934-2880. Students 68.

FORTVILLE, HANCOCK CO., ST. THOMAS THE APOSTLE, FORTVILLE, INC. (1869) Rev. Joseph G. Pesola.
Res.: 523 S. Merrill St., 46040-1428. Tel: 317-485-5101; Fax: 317-485-0022. Email: stthomas@iquest.net. Web: www.stthomasfortville.com.
Catechesis/Religious Program—Tel: 317-485-5103; Fax: 317-485-0022. Students 155.

FRANKLIN, JOHNSON CO., ST. ROSE OF LIMA CATHOLIC CHURCH, FRANKLIN, INC. (1868) Rev. John Beitans; Jean Martin, Pastoral Assoc. Tel: 317-738-2965.
Res.: 114 Lancelot Dr., 46131-8806. Tel: 317-738-3929; Fax: 317-738-3583.
School—(Grades PreK-8) Tel: 317-738-3451. Kelly England, Prin.; Shelley Sargent, Librarian.
Catechesis/Religious Program—Tel: 317-736-6754. Students 117.

FRENCH LICK, ORANGE CO., OUR LADY OF THE SPRINGS CATHOLIC CHURCH, FRENCH LICK, INC. (1887) Revs. Joseph B. Moriarty; John M. Hall, Admin.
Res.: 8796 W. State Rd. 56, 47432-9391. Tel: 812-936-4568; Fax: 812-936-4561. Email: ols936@bluemarble.net.
Catechesis/Religious Program—Tel: 812-936-2434.
Mission—Our Lord Jesus Christ the King (1948) Hwy 150, E., Paoli, Orange Co. 47454.
Catechesis/Religious Program—Students 37.

FRENCHTOWN, HARRISON CO., ST. BERNARD CATHOLIC CHURCH, FRENCHTOWN, INC. (1849) [CEM] Rev. John L. Fink.
Church: 7600 Hwy. 337, Depauw, 47115. Tel: 812-347-2326; Fax: 812-347-2172.
Res.: 7600 Hwy. 337 N.W., Depauw, 47115-8558.
Res.: 11400 Farmers Ln., P.O. Box 22, Bradford, 47107. Tel: 812-364-6646; Fax: 812-364-6614.
Catechesis/Religious Program—Students 47.
Mission—St. Joseph (1855) 341 S. State Rd. 66, Marengo, Crawford Co. 47140.

FULDA, SPENCER CO., ST. BONIFACE CATHOLIC CHURCH, FULDA, INC. (1847) [CEM] Rev. Anthony Vinson, O.S.B., Admin.
Mailing Address: P.O. Box 8, Saint Meinrad,

47577-0008. Tel: 812-357-5533; Fax: 812-357-2862. Church: 15529 N. State Rd. 545, 47536.
Catechesis/Religious Program—Students 48.

GREENCASTLE, PUTNAM CO., ST. PAUL THE APOSTLE CATHOLIC CHURCH, PUTNAM COUNTY, INC. (1853) Rev. Darvin E. Winters.
Res.: 202 E. Washington St., 46135-1549. Tel: 765-653-5678; Fax: 765-653-4377.
Catechesis/Religious Program—Students 118.

GREENFIELD, HANCOCK CO., ST. MICHAEL CATHOLIC CHURCH, GREENFIELD, INC. (1860) Rev. Severin Messick, O.S.B.
Res.: 519 Jefferson Blvd., 46140-1899. Tel: 317-462-4240; Fax: 317-462-2571. Email: lnewett@stmichaelsgrfld.org. Web: www.stmichaelsgrfld.org.
School—(Grades PreK-8), 515 Jefferson Blvd., 46140. Tel: 317-462-6380; Fax: 317-467-2864. Theresa Slipher, Prin.; Emily Capen, Librarian. Lay Teachers 21; Students 311.
Catechesis/Religious Program—Email: prichey@stmichaelsgrfld.org. Students 220.

GREENSBURG, DECATUR CO., ST. MARY CATHOLIC CHURCH, GREENSBURG, INC. (1858) [CEM] Rev. John A. Meyer.
Res.: 302 E. McKee St., 47240-2197. Tel: 812-663-8427; Fax: 812-663-6088.
School—(Grades PreK-6), 210 S. East St., 47240. Tel: 812-663-2804. Nancy Buening, Prin. Lay Teachers 16; Students 111.
Catechesis/Religious Program—Students 273.

GREENWOOD, JOHNSON CO.

1—SS. FRANCIS AND CLARE OF ASSISI CATHOLIC CHURCH, GREENWOOD, INC. (1993) Rev. Vincent Lampert; Deacon Stephen Hodges.
Church & Parish Office: 5901 Olive Branch Rd., 46143-8181. Tel: 317-859-4673; Fax: 317-859-4678. Web: www.francisandclare.org.
School—(Grades PreK-3) Betty Popp, Prin. Students 347.
Catechesis/Religious Program—

2—OUR LADY OF THE GREENWOOD CATHOLIC CHURCH, INC. (1948) [JC] Rev. Msgr. Mark Svarczkopf; Rev. Mauro G. Rodas, Hispanic Min. (Retired).
Res.: 101 Orchard Ave., 46143. Tel: 317-888-2861; Fax: 317-885-5006. Email: info@olgreenwood.org. Web: www.olgreenwood.org.
School—(Grades PreK-8), 399 S. Meridian St., 46143. Tel: 317-881-1300. Kent Clady, Prin. Lay Teachers 28; Students 402.
Catechesis/Religious Program—Students 310.

HAMBURG, FRANKLIN CO., ST. ANNE CATHOLIC CHURCH, HAMBURG, INC. (1869) [CEM] Rev. George Joseph Nangachiveettil (India).
5267 N. Hamburg Rd., Oldenburg, 47036-9708.
Res.: 9995 E. Base Rd., Greensburg, 47240. Tel: 812-934-5854; Fax: 812-934-5854. Email: stanne@etczone.com.
Catechesis/Religious Program—Students 26.

HENRYVILLE, CLARK CO., ST. FRANCIS CATHOLIC CHURCH, HENRYVILLE, INC. (1869) Rev. Steven Schaftlein.
Mailing Address: 101 St. Michael Dr., Charlestown, 47111. Tel: 812-294-4682. Email: michaelsecretary@insightbb.com.
Church: 101 N. Ferguson Dr., 47126. Fax: 775-307-6142. Email: francissecretary@insightbb.com.
Catechesis/Religious Program—Students 50.

JEFFERSONVILLE, CLARK CO.

1—ST. AUGUSTINE CATHOLIC CHURCH, JEFFERSONVILLE, INC. (1851) [CEM] Rev. Thomas E. Clegg.
Res.: 315 E. Chestnut St., P.O. Box 447, 47131-0447. Tel: 812-282-2677; Fax: 812-282-8821. Email: saintaug@insightbb.com. Web: www.saintaug.org.
Catechesis/Religious Program—316 E. Maple St. Tel: 812-282-1231; Fax: 812-282-1605. Students 118.

2—SACRED HEART CATHOLIC CHURCH, JEFFERSONVILLE, INC. (1953) Rev. Thomas E. Clegg.
Church & Parish Office: 1840 E. 8th St., 47130-4897. Tel: 812-282-0423; Fax: 812-284-6678.
School—1842 E. 8th St., 47130. Tel: 812-283-3123. Becky Spitznagel, Prin. Lay Teachers 15; Students 203.
Catechesis/Religious Program—Students 104.

KNIGHTSTOWN, HENRY CO., ST. ROSE OF LIMA CATHOLIC CHURCH, KNIGHTSTOWN, INC. (1872) Russell B. Woodard, Parish Life Coord.; Revs. Joseph F. Rautenberg, Sacramental Min.; Stanley J. Herber, Priest Mod.
Mailing Address: P.O. Box 209, 46148-0209. Tel: 765-345-5595.
Church: 8144 W. U.S. Hwy. 40, 46148. Tel: 765-345-5595; Fax: 765-345-5595. Email: strosewilla@centurylink.net.
Catechesis/Religious Program—Students 29.

LANESVILLE, HARRISON CO., ST. MARY CATHOLIC CHURCH, LANESVILLE, INC. (1843), (German), [CEM] Rev. Juan Jose Valdes, Admin.
Res.: 2500 St. Mary's Dr., 47136. Tel: 812-952-2853 (Parish Office); 812-952-0060; Fax: 812-952-2852. Email: stmarys@insightbb.com. Web: stmaryslanesville.org.
Catechesis/Religious Program—Tel: 812-952-2854. Email: smlff@insightbb.com. Students 124.

LAWRENCEBURG, DEARBORN CO., ST. LAWRENCE CATHOLIC CHURCH, LAWRENCEBURG, INC. (1842), (German), Rev. John Peter Gallagher.
Parish Office—542 Walnut St., 47025-1861. Tel: 812-537-3992.
Rectory—526 Walnut St., 47025. Tel: 812-537-1297.
School—524 Walnut St., 47025. Tel: 812-537-3690; Fax: 812-537-9685. Karen White, Prin. Lay Teachers 18; Students 263.
Catechesis/Religious Program—Tel: 812-537-1112. Students 94.

LEOPOLD, PERRY CO., ST. AUGUSTINE CATHOLIC CHURCH, LEOPOLD, INC. (1837) [CEM] Rev. Brian G. Esarey.
Res.: 18020 Lafayette St., 47551. Tel: 812-843-5143.
Catechesis/Religious Program—Students 60.

LIBERTY, UNION CO., ST. BRIDGET CATHOLIC CHURCH, LIBERTY, INC. (1854) [CEM] Rev. Stanley J. Herber, Admin.
Mailing Address: P.O. Box 112, 47353.
Res.: 404 E. Vine St., 47353-1446.
Catechesis/Religious Program—Tel: 765-458-5412. Students 40.

MADISON, JEFFERSON CO., PRINCE OF PEACE CATHOLIC CHURCH, MADISON, INC. (1993) [CEM 3], St. Michael (1837), St. Mary (1851), St. Patrick (1853), Madison, and St. Anthony, China (1861) were closed, merged and renamed Prince of Peace. Rev. Christopher A. Craig.
Mailing Address: *Catholic Community Center*, 305 W. State St., 47250. Tel: 812-265-4166; Fax: 812-273-3427. Web: www.popeace.org.
Res.: 413 E. Second St., 47250-2830. Tel: 812-265-4166.
School—Pope John XXIII, (Grades PreSchool-6), 221 State St., 47250. Tel: 812-273-3957; Fax: 812-265-4566. Jill Mires, Prin. Students 294.
High School—Shawe Memorial Junior-Senior High School, Tel: 812-273-2150; Fax: 812-273-2013. Jerry Bomholt, Prin. See High Schools, Inter-Parochial, under Institutions Located in the Archdiocese. Students 161.
Catechesis/Religious Program—Students 50.

MARENGO, CRAWFORD CO., ST. JOSEPH CATHOLIC CHURCH, MARENGO, INC. (1855) [CEM] Attended by St. Bernard, Frenchtown. Rev. John L. Fink, Admin.
Mailing Address: 7600 Hwy. 337 N.W., Depauw, 47115. Tel: 812-347-2326.
Church: 341 S. State Rd. 66, 47140.
Catechesis/Religious Program—Students 23.

MARTINSVILLE, MORGAN CO., ST. MARTIN OF TOURS CATHOLIC CHURCH, MARTINSVILLE, INC. (1848) [CEM] Rev. John M. Hall.
Res.: 1709 E. Harrison St., 46151-1844. Tel: 765-342-6379.
Catechesis/Religious Program—Tel: 765-352-0602; Fax: 765-342-1263. Students 136.

MILAN, RIPLEY CO., ST. CHARLES CATHOLIC CHURCH, MILAN, INC. (1908) Rev. Shaun P. Whittington, Admin.
Mailing Address: *c/o St. John*, 331 S. Buckeye St., Osgood, 47037. Fax: 812-689-5035.
Church: 213 Ripley St., 47031. Tel: 812-623-8007.
Catechesis/Religious Program—Tel: 812-744-3882. Karen Dole, D.R.E. Students 82.

MILLHOUSEN, DECATUR CO., IMMACULATE CONCEPTION CATHOLIC CHURCH, MILLHOUSEN, INC. (1834) [CEM] Sr. Christine Ernstes, O.S.F., Parish Life Coord.; Revs. William J. Turner, Sacramental Min. (Retired); John F. Geis, Sacramental Min. (Retired); Paul E. Landwerlen, Priest Mod.
Mailing Address: 2081 E. County Rd., 820 S., Greensburg, 47240-9636. Tel: 812-591-2362; Fax: 812-591-2362. Email: icchurchm@gmail.com. Web: icsdchurches.com.
Mission—St. Denis (1894) [CEM] Church: 12155 N. County Rd., 600 E., St. Denis, Jennings Co. 47283.
Catechesis/Religious Program—Students 72.

MITCHELL, LAWRENCE CO., ST. MARY OF THE ASSUMPTION CATHOLIC CHURCH, MITCHELL, INC. (1869) Rev. Richard W. Eldred.
Res.: 777 S. 11th St., 47446-1643. Tel: 812-849-3570; Fax: 812-849-6024. Email: stmarysmitchell@frontier.com. Web: www.catholiccommunityoflawrencecounty.com.
Catechesis/Religious Program—Fax: 812-849-6024. Students 23.

MOORESVILLE, MORGAN CO., ST. THOMAS MORE CATHOLIC CHURCH, MOORESVILLE, INC. (1967) Rev. Mark Gottemoeller.
Res.: 1200 N. Indiana St., 46158. Tel: 317-831-4142; Fax: 317-834-2947. Email: kphillips@stm-church.org.
Catechesis/Religious Program—Students 215.

MORRIS, RIPLEY CO., ST. ANTHONY OF PADUA CATHOLIC CHURCH, MORRIS, INC. (1856) [CEM] Rev. Pascal E. Nduka, Admin.; Deacon John J. Chlopecki.
Mailing Address: P.O. Box 3, 47033. Tel: 812-934-6218; Fax: 812-934-5936.
Parish Office:—4781 E. Morris Church St., 47033.
Catechesis/Religious Program—Students 112.

NAPOLEON, RIPLEY CO., ST. MAURICE CATHOLIC CHURCH, NAPOLEON, INC. (1848) [CEM] Sr. Shirley Gerth, O.S.F., Parish Life Coord.; Revs. John F. Geis, Sacramental Min. (Retired); William J. Turner, Sacramental Min. (Retired).
Mailing Address: 8874 Harrison St., P.O. Box 17, 47034-0017. Tel: 812-852-4237.
Catechesis/Religious Program—Fax: 812-852-4237. Students 99.

NASHVILLE, BROWN CO., ST. AGNES CATHOLIC CHURCH, NASHVILLE, INC. (1940) [JC] Sr. Eileen Flavin, C.S.C., Parish Life Coord.; Rev. Eric Matthew Johnson, Sacramental Min.; Rev. Msgr. William F. Stumpf, Priest Mod.
Mailing Address: 1008 McLary Rd., P.O. Box 577, 47448-0577. Tel: 812-988-2778; Fax: 812-988-2778. Email: stagnes5@iquest.net. Web: www.stagneschurchnashville.org.
Catechesis/Religious Program—Tel: 812-988-1432. Students 104.

NAVILLETON, FLOYD CO., ST. MARY OF THE ANNUNCIATION CATHOLIC CHURCH, NAVILLETON, INC. (1845), (German), [CEM] Rev. Pius Poff, O.F.M.Conv.
Res.: 7500 Navilleton Rd., Floyds Knobs, 47119. Tel: 812-923-5419; Fax: 812-923-3430. Email: stmarynavilleton@insightbb.com. Web: www.stmarysnavilleton.com.
Catechesis/Religious Program—Students 120.

NEW ALBANY, FLOYD CO.

1—HOLY FAMILY CATHOLIC CHURCH, NEW ALBANY, INC. (1954) [JC] Rev. J. Daniel Atkins.
Res.: 129 W. Daisy Ln., 47150-4598. Tel: 812-944-8283; Fax: 812-945-0180. Web: www.holyfamilynewalbany.org. Email: hfna@insightbb.com.
School—(Grades PreSchool-8), 217 W. Daisy Ln., 47150. Tel: 812-944-6090; Fax: 812-944-7299. Web: www.school.holyfamilyeagles.com. Gerald Ernstberger, Prin. Lay Teachers 23; Students 401.
Catechesis/Religious Program—Students 119.

2—ST. MARY OF THE ANNUCIATION CATHOLIC CHURCH, NEW ALBANY, INC. (1858), (German), [CEM] [JC] Rev. Henry F. Tully.
Res.: 415 E. Eighth St., 47150-3299. Tel: 812-944-0417; Fax: 812-944-9557. Email: info@stmarysna.org. Web: www.stmarysna.org.
School—(Grades PreSchool-8), 420 E. 8th St., 47150. Tel: 812-944-0888; Fax: 812-945-4770. Email: cougars@iglou.com. Web: www.smconline.com. Jeffrey Purichia, Prin. Lay Teachers 13; Students 122.
Catechesis/Religious Program—Students 35.

3—OUR LADY OF PERPETUAL HELP CATHOLIC CHURCH, NEW ALBANY, INC. (1950) Rev. Eric Augenstein; Tom Yost, Pastoral Assoc.
Res.: 1752 Scheller Ln., 47150-2423. Tel: 812-944-1184; Fax: 812-944-3326. Email: lslusser@olphna.org. Web: olphna.org.
School—Tel: 812-944-7676; Fax: 812-948-2944. Theresa Horton, Prin. Lay Teachers 27; Students 347.
Catechesis/Religious Program—Tel: 812-948-0185. Students 260.

NEW ALSACE, DEARBORN CO., ST. PAUL CATHOLIC CHURCH, NEW ALSACE, INC. (1833) [CEM] Rev. Scott E. Nobbe.
Mailing Address: 8044 Yorkridge Rd., Guilford, 47022. Tel: 812-623-3408; Fax: 812-623-4879.
Res.: 25743 State Rd. 1, Guilford, 47022. Tel: 812-623-3408; Fax: 812-576-2324.
School—(Grades PreSchool-6), 9788 N. Dearborn Rd., Guilford, 47022. Tel: 812-623-2631. Kathy Mortaugh, Librarian. Lay Teachers 5; Students 45.
Catechesis/Religious Program—Tel: 812-623-2662. Students 50.

NEW CASTLE, HENRY CO., ST. ANNE CATHOLIC CHURCH, NEW CASTLE, INC. (1873) [CEM] Russell B. Woodard, Parish Life Coord.; Revs. Joseph F. Rautenberg, Sacramental Min.; Stanley J. Herber, Priest Mod.
Parish Office—102 N. 19th St., 47362-3999. Tel: 765-529-0933; 765-529-3395. Email: stannechurch@hotmail.com. Web: saintanne.us.to. Church: Tel: 765-529-7413; Fax: 765-529-2879.
Catechesis/Religious Program—Tel: 765-529-8976. Email: lwelch.st.anne@hotmail.com. Students 73.

NEW MARION, RIPLEY CO., ST. MARY MAGDALEN CATHOLIC CHURCH, NEW MARION, INC. (1847) [CEM] Attended by St. John, Osgood. Rev. Shaun P. Whittington.
Office & Rectory: 331 S. Buckeye St., Osgood, 47037. Tel: 812-689-4244; Fax: 812-689-5035. Email: info@stjohnsosgood.org.
Church: 4613 S. Old Michigan Rd., Holton, 47023.
Catechesis/Religious Program—Tel: 812-689-6670. Rita Jansing, D.R.E. Students 7.

NEW MIDDLETOWN, HARRISON CO., MOST PRECIOUS BLOOD CATHOLIC CHURCH, NEW MIDDLETON,INC. (1880) [CEM], Attended from St. Joseph, 312 E.

High St., Corydon, IN 47112. Tel: 812-738-2742. Rev. Robert Jason Hankee.
Mailing Address: *c/o St. Joseph*, 312 E. High St., Corydon, 47112.
Church: Corydon-New Middletown Rd., 47160. Tel: 812-738-2742; Fax: 812-738-2718. Email: joecorydon@yahoo.com. Web: www.triparishcommunity.com.
Catechesis/Religious Program—Tel: 812-738-2759. Combined with St. Joseph, Corydon Students 10.

NORTH VERNON, JENNINGS CO., ST. MARY CATHOLIC CHURCH, NORTH VERNON, INC. (1861) [CEM] Rev. Jonathan P. Meyer; Deacon Lawrence French.
212 Washington St., 47265-1199. Tel: 812-346-3604; Fax: 812-346-3506. Web: www.stmarysce.org.
School—(Grades K-8), 209 Washington St., 47265. Tel: 812-346-3445; Fax: 812-346-5930. Email: stmarys@seidata.com. Web: www.stmarysnv.com. Sr. Joanita Koors, O.S.F., Prin. Lay Teachers 8; Students 207.
Catechesis/Religious Program—Students 130.

OAK FOREST, FRANKLIN CO., SS. PHILOMENA AND CECILIA CATHOLIC CHURCH, BROOKVILLE, INC. (2010) Rev. Karl Piku, F.S.S.P., Admin.
Mailing Address: 16194 St. Mary's Rd., Brookville, 47012.
Church: Tel: 765-647-0310. Web: www.spcfssp.org.

OLDENBURG, FRANKLIN CO., HOLY FAMILY CATHOLIC CHURCH, OLDENBURG, INC. (1837) [CEM] Rev. David Kobak, O.F.M. In Res., Rev. Carl Hawver, O.F.M., Chap., Sisters of St. Frances; Bro. Tim Lamb, O.F.M.
Res.: Main St., P.O. Box 98, 47036-0098. Tel: 812-934-3013; Fax: 812-933-0728. Web: web.me.com/dkobakofm/hfcoldenburgIN/Welcome.html.
Catechesis/Religious Program—Students 189.

OSGOOD, RIPLEY CO., ST. JOHN THE BAPTIST CATHOLIC CHURCH, OSGOOD, INC. (1867) [CEM] Rev. Shaun P. Whittington.
Res.: 331 S. Buckeye St., 47037-1305. Tel: 812-689-4244; Fax: 812-689-5035. Email: info@stjohnsosgood.org. Web: www.stjohnsosgood.org.
Mission—St. Mary Magdalen (1847) [CEM] Holton, Ripley Co. 47023.
Catechesis/Religious Program—Tel: 812-689-6670; Fax: 812-689-6670. Email: formation@stjohnsosgood.org. Rita Jansing, D.R.E. Students 40.

PAOLI, ORANGE CO., OUR LORD JESUS CHRIST THE KING CATHOLIC CHURCH, PAOLI, INC. (1948), Attended from Our Lady of the Springs, French Lick. Revs. John M. Hall, Admin.; Joseph B. Moriarty, Sacramental Min.
Mailing Address: 8796 W. State Rd. 56, French Lick, 47432.
Church: Hwy. 150 E., 47454. Tel: 812-936-4568.
Catechesis/Religious Program—Tel: 812-723-5506. Jim O'Connell, D.R.E. Students 37.

PLAINFIELD, HENDRICKS CO., ST. SUSANNA CATHOLIC CHURCH, PLAINFIELD, INC. (1953) Rev. Kevin Morris.
Res.: 1210 E. Main St., 46168. Tel: 317-839-3333; Fax: 317-839-0732. Web: www.saintsusanna.com.
School—(Grades PreSchool-8), 1212 E. Main St., 46168. Tel: 317-839-3713; Fax: 317-838-7718. Krista Keith, Prin. Lay Teachers 28; Students 315.
Catechesis/Religious Program—Tel: 317-838-7722; Fax: 317-838-7720. Email: gaughan2kelly@sbcglobal.net. Katherine Vandenbergh, D.R.E. Students 405.

RICHMOND, WAYNE CO.

1—ST. ANDREW CATHOLIC CHURCH, RICHMOND, INC. (1846) [JC] Revs. Todd M. Riebe; Gerald Okeke (Nigeria).
Res.: 720 A North St., 47374. Tel: 765-962-3569.
Church: 235 S. 5th St., 47374-5418.
Parish Center & Mailing Address: 240 S. 6th St., 47374. Fax: 765-966-0820.
See Seton Catholic High School, Richmond under High Schools, Inter-Parochial in the Institution section.
Catechesis/Religious Program—Marcy Valentini, C.R.E. Students 64.

2—HOLY FAMILY CATHOLIC CHURCH, RICHMOND, INC. (1953) Revs. Todd M. Riebe; Gerald Okeke (Nigeria).
Mailing Address: 240 S. 6th St., 47374. Tel: 765-962-3902; Fax: 765-966-0820.
Res.: 720 N. A St., 47374. Tel: 765-962-3569.
Church: 815 W. Main St., 47374-5418.
School—St. Elizabeth Ann Seton, (Grades 3-6), 801 W. Main St., 47374. Tel: 765-962-4877; Fax: 765-962-5381. Kimberley Becker, Prin. Lay Teachers 11; Students 293.
See Seton Catholic High School, Richmond under High Schools, Inter-Parochial in the Institution section.
Catechesis/Religious Program—Tel: 765-962-3902. Marcy Valentini, C.R.E. Students 16.

3—ST. MARY CATHOLIC CHURCH, RICHMOND, INC. (1859) [JC] Revs. Todd M. Riebe; Gerald Okeke (Nigeria).
Mailing Address: 240 S. 6th St., 47374. Tel: 765-962-3902; Fax: 765-966-0820. Email: rcco@richmondcatholiccommunity.com.
Church & Res.: 720 N. A St., 47374-5418. Tel: 765-962-3569.
School—St. Elizabeth Ann Seton, (Grades PreK-2), 700 N. A St., 47374. Tel: 765-962-5010; Fax: 765-962-3692. Kimberley Becker, Prin. Lay Teachers 7; Students 293.
See Seton Catholic High School, Richmond under High Schools, Inter-Parochial in the Institution section.
Catechesis/Religious Program—Marcy Valentini, C.R.E. Students 34.

ROCKVILLE, PARKE CO., ST. JOSEPH CATHOLIC CHURCH, ROCKVILLE, INC. (1867) [CEM] Rev. Joseph L. Villa.
Res.: 217 E. Ohio St., 47872. Tel: 765-569-5406. Email: stjoerockville@yahoo.com.
Catechesis/Religious Program—Tel: 765-597-2474. Twinned with Sacred Heart, Clinton. Students 22.

RUSHVILLE, RUSH CO., ST. MARY CATHOLIC CHURCH, RUSHVILLE, INC. (1857) [CEM] Rev. Jeremy M. Gries, Admin.
Res.: 512 N. Perkins St., 46173. Tel: 765-932-2588; Fax: 765-932-2458.
School—(Grades PreK-6), 226 E. 5th St., 46173. Tel: 765-932-3639; Fax: 765-938-1322. Web: www.stmaryrushville.net. Stephanie Hasecuster, Prin. Lay Teachers 7; Students 80.
Catechesis/Religious Program—Students 155.

ST. ANN, JENNINGS CO., ST. ANN CATHOLIC CHURCH, JENNINGS COUNTY, INC. (1841) [CEM], Attended from St. Joseph, North Vernon. Rev. Jonathan P. Meyer, Admin.
Mailing Address: 1875 S. County Rd. 700 W., North Vernon, 47265.
Church: 4570 N. Co. Rd. 150 E., North Vernon, 47265-7564. Tel: 812-346-4783; Fax: 812-352-9033. Email: rectory@stjoefourcorners.org. Web: www.stjoefourcorners.org.
Catechesis/Religious Program—Students 19.

ST. CROIX, PERRY CO.

1—HOLY CROSS CATHOLIC CHURCH, ST. CROIX, INC. (1860) [CEM] Rev. Brian G. Esarey.
Mailing Address: 12239 State Rd. 62, 47576-9999.
Res.: 18020 Lafayette St., Leopold, 47551. Tel: 317-625-6329. Web: www.catholic-church.org/holycrossparish.
Catechesis/Religious Program—Students 3.

2—ST. ISIDORE THE FARMER CATHOLIC CHURCH, BRISTOW, INC. (1968) [CEM], St. John, (1875), and St. Joseph, (1891), Perry Co., were closed, merged and renamed St. Isidore in 1968. Rev. Guy Mansini, O.S.B.
Res.: 6501 St. Isidore Rd., Bristow, 47515. Tel: 812-843-5713; Fax: 812-843-3103. Email: saintisidore@psci.net.
Catechesis/Religious Program—Students 86.

ST. DENIS, JENNINGS CO., ST. DENIS CATHOLIC CHURCH, JENNINGS COUNTY, INC. (1894) [CEM] Attended by Immaculate Conception, Millhousen. Revs. William J. Turner, Sacramental Min. (Retired); John F. Geis, Sacramental Min. (Retired); Paul E. Landwerlen, Priest Mod.; Sr. Christine Ernstes, O.S.F., Parish Life Coord.
Mailing Address: 2081 E. County Rd. 820S, Greensburg, 47240. Tel: 812-591-2362. Email: icchurchm@gmail.com. Web: www.icsdchurches.com.
Church: 12155 N. County Rd. 600E, Westport, 47283.
Catechesis/Religious Program— Clustered with Immaculate Conception, Milhousen.

ST. JOSEPH, JENNINGS CO., ST. JOSEPH CATHOLIC CHURCH, JENNINGS COUNTY, INC. (1850) [CEM 2] Rev. Jonathan P. Meyer, Admin.
Mailing Address: 1875 S. County Rd. 700 W., North Vernon, 47265-7564. Tel: 812-346-4783; Fax: 812-352-9033. Email: rectory@stjoefourcorners.org. Web: www.stjoefourcorners.org.
Mission—St. Ann (1841) 150 E. 450 N., North Vernon, Jennings Co. 47265.
Catechesis/Religious Program—Students 45.

ST. JOSEPH HILL, CLARK CO., ST. JOSEPH HILL CATHOLIC CHURCH, SELLERSBURG, INC. (1853) [CEM] Rev. Robert St. Martin, O.F.M.Conv.
Res.: 2605 St. Joe Rd. W., Sellersburg, 47172-9661. Tel: 812-246-2512; Fax: 812-246-2671. Email: parishoffice@stjoehill.org. Web: www.stjoehill.org.
Catechesis/Religious Program—Tel: 812-246-3969. Lisa Whitaker, C.R.E. Students 120.

ST. LEON, DEARBORN CO., ST. JOSEPH CATHOLIC CHURCH, ST. LEON, INC. (1841) [CEM] Rev. Scott E. Nobbe.
Res.: 7536 Church Ln., West Harrison, 47060-6824. Tel: 812-576-4302; Fax: 812-576-2304.
Catechesis/Religious Program—

ST. MARK, PERRY CO., ST. MARK'S CATHOLIC CHURCH, PERRY COUNTY, INC. (1863), (German), [CEM] [JC] Rev. Dennis M. Duvelius.
Res.: 5377 Acorn Rd., Tell City, 47586-9738. Tel: 812-836-2481. Email: stmark@psci.net.
Catechesis/Religious Program—Students 40.

ST. MARY-OF-THE-KNOBS, FLOYD CO., ST. MARY-OF-THE-KNOBS CATHOLIC CHURCH, FLOYDS KNOBS, INC. (1823) [CEM] Rev. H. Michael Hilderbrand.
Res.: 3033 Martin Rd., Floyds Knobs, 47119-9107. Tel: 812-923-3011; Fax: 812-923-1431. Web: www.stmaryoftheknobs.org.
School—(Grades PreSchool-6) Tel: 812-923-1630; Fax: 812-923-0310. Students 176.
Catechesis/Religious Program—Students 205.

ST. MARY-OF-THE-ROCK, FRANKLIN CO., ST. MARY-OF-THE-ROCK BATESVILLE, INC. (1844) [CEM] Sr. Margie Niemer, O.S.F., Parish Life Coord.
Office: 17440 St. Mary's Rd., Batesville, 47006-9319. Tel: 812-934-4165; Fax: 812-934-4165.
Catechesis/Religious Program—Students 34.

ST. MARY-OF-THE-WOODS, VIGO CO., ST. MARY-OF-THE-WOODS CATHOLIC CHURCH, INC. (1837) [CEM] Sr. Joan Slobig, S.P., Parish Life Coord.; Rev. Bernard Head, Sacramental Min. & Priest Mod. (Retired).
Mailing Address: N. Arms Pl., P.O. Box 155, Saint Mary Of The Woods, 47876-0155. Tel: 812-535-1261; Fax: 812-535-1561.
Catechesis/Religious Program—Diana Bird, C.R.E. Students 63.

ST. MAURICE, DECATUR CO., ST. MAURICE CATHOLIC CHURCH, ST. MAURICE, INC. (1859) [CEM] Rev. George Joseph Nangachiveettil (India), Admin.
Church: 1963 N. St. John St., Greensburg, 47240. Tel: 812-663-4754; Fax: 812-663-4754. Email: stmauricechrch@yahoo.com.
Catechesis/Religious Program—Students 133.

SAINT MEINRAD, SPENCER CO., ST. MEINRAD CATHOLIC CHURCH, INC. (1854) [CEM] Rev. Anthony Vinson, O.S.B., Admin.
Mailing Address: P.O. Box 8, 47577-0008. Tel: 812-357-5533; Fax: 812-357-2862.
Church: 19630 N. 4th St., 47577.
Catechesis/Religious Program—Students 58.

ST. NICHOLAS, RIPLEY CO., ST. NICHOLAS CATHOLIC CHURCH, SUNMAN, INC. (1836) [CEM] Sr. Linda Bates, O.S.F., Parish Life Coord.
6461 E. St. Nicholas Dr., Sunman, 47041. Tel: 812-623-2964; Fax: 812-623-8007.
School—(Grades K-8), 6459 E. St. Nicholas Dr., Sunman, 47041. Tel: 812-623-2348; Fax: 812-623-2964. Judy Luhring, Prin.; Lisa Weisbrod, Librarian. Lay Teachers 11; Students 137.
Catechesis/Religious Program—Students 73.

ST. PETER, FRANKLIN CO., ST. PETER CATHOLIC CHURCH, FRANKLIN COUNTY, INC. (1838), (German), [CEM] Sr. Margie Niemer, O.S.F., Parish Life Coord.; Rev. Msgr. William F. Stumpf, Priest Mod.; Rev. Humbert Moster, O.F.M., Sacramental Min.
Res.: 1207 East Rd., Brookville, 47012-9365. Tel: 812-623-3670; Fax: 812-623-3670. Email: stpeter@nalu.net.
Catechesis/Religious Program—Tel: 812-623-4051. Students 69.

ST. PETER, HARRISON CO., ST. PETER CATHOLIC CHURCH, ELIZABETH, INC. (1849) [CEM], Attended from St. Joseph, Corydon, St. Peter, 312 E. High St., Corydon, Harrison Co., IN 47112. Rev. Robert Jason Hankee.
Mailing Address: *c/o St. Joseph*, 312 E. High St., Corydon, 47112. Tel: 812-738-2742; Fax: 812-738-2718. Email: joecorydon@yahoo.com. Web: www.triparishcommunity.com.
Church: Buena Vista Rd., Elizabeth, 47117.
Catechesis/Religious Program—Tel: 812-738-2759. Religious education program held at St. Joseph, Corydon. Students 13.

ST. PIUS, RIPLEY CO., ST. PIUS V CATHOLIC CHURCH, SUNMAN, INC. (1859) [CEM], Attended from St. Charles Borromeo, Milan. Rev. Shaun P. Whittington, Admin.
Mailing Address: *c/o St. John*, 331 S. Buckeye St., Osgood, 47037. Tel: 812-689-4244.
County Rd. 500, Sunman, 47041. Fax: 812-689-5035.
Catechesis/Religious Program—Ed King, D.R.E.

ST. VINCENT DE PAUL, SHELBY CO., ST. VINCENT DE PAUL CATHOLIC CHURCH, SHELBY COUNTY, INC. (1837) Rev. Paul E. Landwerlen.
Res.: 4218 E. Michigan Rd., Shelbyville, 46176-9242. Tel: 317-398-4028.
Catechesis/Religious Program—Tel: 317-392-3879; Fax: 317-392-3879. Students 61.

SALEM, WASHINGTON CO., ST. PATRICK CATHOLIC CHURCH, SALEM, INC. (1942) [CEM] Rev. Louis Manna.
208 S. Shelby St., P.O. Box 273, 47167-0273. Tel: 812-752-3693.
Catechesis/Religious Program—Tel: 812-883-3589. Students 41.

SCOTTSBURG, SCOTT CO., CHURCH OF THE AMERICAN MARTYRS, SCOTTSBURG, INC. (1938) Rev. Louis Manna.
Mailing Address: 270 S. Bond St., 47170-2009. Tel: 812-752-3693; Fax: 812-752-0969. Email: amartyrs@frontier.com. Web: www.amartyrs.org.

Parish Office: 262 W. Cherry St., 47170-2013.
Catechesis/Religious Program—Students 38.
Mission—St. Patrick (1942) 208 S. Shelby St., P.O. Box 273, Salem, Washington Co. 47167. Tel: 812-883-3589.

SEELYVILLE, VIGO CO., HOLY ROSARY CATHOLIC CHURCH, SEELYVILLE, INC. (1908) Rev. Harold W. Rightor II.
Church & Mailing Address: 2585 N. Main, P.O. Box 151, 47878-0151. Tel: 812-877-1279.
Catechesis/Religious Program—

SELLERSBURG, CLARK CO., ST. PAUL CATHOLIC CHURCH, SELLERSBURG, INC. (1949) Rev. Paul F. Richart.
Church: 218 Schellers Ave., 47172-1241. Tel: 812-246-3522; Fax: 812-246-7635. Email: bsmith@stpaulsellersburg.org. Web: www.stpaulsellersburg.org.
School—(Grades K-6), 105 St. Paul St., 47172. Tel: 812-246-3266; Fax: 812-246-7632. Email: office@stpaulkg.org. Web: www.stpaulk6.org. Karen Haas, Prin. Lay Teachers 19; Students 236.
Catechesis/Religious Program—216 Schellers Ave., 47172. Tel: 812-246-5088. Email: dsnyder@stpaulsellersburg.org. Students 83.

SEYMOUR, JACKSON CO., ST. AMBROSE CATHOLIC CHURCH, SEYMOUR, INC. (1860) [CEM] Rev. Daniel Staublin; Deacon Michael East.
Res.: 325 S. Chestnut St., 47274-2329. Tel: 812-522-5304; Fax: 812-522-8959.
School—(Grades PreK-7), 301 S. Chestnut St., 47274. Tel: 812-522-3522. Michelle Neibert-Levine, Prin. Lay Teachers 13; Students 145.
Catechesis/Religious Program—Tel: 812-522-2686. Students 80.
Mission—Our Lady of Providence (1934) 325 S. Chestnut St., Brownstown, Jackson Co. 47274.

SHELBYVILLE, SHELBY CO., ST. JOSEPH CATHOLIC CHURCH, SHELBYVILLE, INC. (1868) [CEM] [JC] Rev. Aaron J. Pfaff.
Res.: 220 E. Hendricks St., 46176-1498. Tel: 317-398-8227; Fax: 317-392-7820. Web: www.stjosephshelby.org.
School—(Grades PreK-5), 127 E. Broadway, 46176. Tel: 317-398-4202; Fax: 317-398-0270. Email: stjoe@lightbound.com. Lay Teachers 10; Students 144.
Catechesis/Religious Program—Tel: 317-398-0530; Fax: 317-392-7820. Students 190.

SIBERIA, PERRY CO., ST. MARTIN OF TOURS CATHOLIC CHURCH, SIBERIA, INC. (1869) [CEM] Rev. Brian G. Esarey.
Mailing Address: P.O. Box 8, Saint Meinrad, 47577. Tel: 812-357-5533; Fax: 812-357-2862.
Church: 27246 Perry St., 47515.
Catechesis/Religious Program—Students 6.

SPENCER, OWEN CO., ST. JUDE CATHOLIC CHURCH, SPENCER, INC. (1951) Rev. William L. Ehalt.
300 W. Hillside Ave., P.O. Box 317, 47460-0317. Tel: 812-829-3082; Fax: 812-829-0888. Email: stjudespencer@sbcglobal.net.
Catechesis/Religious Program—Students 23.

STARLIGHT, CLARK CO., ST. JOHN THE BAPTIST CATHOLIC CHURCH, STARLIGHT, INC. (1861), (German), [CEM] [JC] Rev. Wilfred E. Day.
Res.: 8310 St. John Rd., Floyds Knobs, 47119-8518. Tel: 812-923-5785; Fax: 812-923-2015.
Catechesis/Religious Program—Students 24.

TELL CITY, PERRY CO., ST. PAUL CATHOLIC CHURCH, TELL CITY, INC. (1859) [CEM] Rev. Dennis M. Duvelius. In Res., Rev. Barnabas Gillespie, O.S.B.
Parish Office—Catholic Ministry Center, 824 Jefferson St., 47586. Tel: 812-547-7994; Fax: 812-547-6985. Email: stpaulch@psci.net.
Church: 814 Jefferson St., 47586. Tel: 812-547-9901.
Catechesis/Religious Program—Tel: 812-547-7102. Students 256.

TERRE HAUTE, VIGO CO.
1—ST. ANN CATHOLIC CHURCH, TERRE HAUTE, INC. (1876) [JC] Sr. Constance Kramer, S.P., Parish Life Coord.; Rev. Robert T. Hausladen, Sacramental Min.
Res.: 1440 Locust St., 47807-1698. Tel: 812-232-6832; Fax: 812-232-2444. Email: stannchurch@stannchurchth.org.
Catechesis/Religious Program—Students 27.
2—ST. BENEDICT CATHOLIC CHURCH, TERRE HAUTE, INC. (1865), (German), [JC] Rev. Edmund Goldbach, O.F.M.Conv.
Church & Parish Office: 111 S. Ninth St., 47807-3711. Tel: 812-232-8421; Fax: 812-238-9203. Web: www.stbenedictth.org.
Catechesis/Religious Program—Students 88.
3—ST. JOSEPH UNIVERSITY CATHOLIC CHURCH, TERRE HAUTE, INC. (1837) [JC] Revs. Mark Weaver, O.F.M.Conv.; John Bammon, O.F.M.Conv.
Res.: 118 S. 9th St., 47807. Tel: 812-232-5075. Web: www.stjoeup.org.
Church & Mailing Address: 113 S. 5th St., 47807-3577.
Catechesis/Religious Program—Email: reled@stjoeup.org. Students 246.
4—ST. MARGARET MARY CATHOLIC CHURCH, TERRE HAUTE, INC. (1920) [JC] Rev. Richard Ginther; Deacon Michael Stratman.
Mailing Address: 2405 S. Seventh St., 47802-3599.
Res.: 2421 S. Seventh St., 47802. Tel: 812-232-3512; Fax: 812-232-6921.
Catechesis/Religious Program—Students 96.
5—ST. PATRICK CATHOLIC CHURCH, TERRE HAUTE, INC. (1881) Rev. Richard Ginther; John Fuller, Business Mgr.
Church: 1807 Poplar St., 47803-2196. Tel: 812-232-8518; Fax: 812-234-3312. Web: www.saintpat.org.
School—(Grades PreK-8), 449 S. 19th St., 47803. Tel: 812-232-2157; Fax: 812-478-9384. Amy McClain, Prin.; Tammy Kikta, Librarian. Lay Teachers 19; Students 293.
Catechesis/Religious Program—Tel: 812-232-2827. Students 107.
6—SACRED HEART OF JESUS CATHOLIC CHURCH, TERRE HAUTE, INC. (1924) Barbara Black, Parish Life Coord.; Rev. Stephen W. Giannini.
Res.: 2322 N. 13 1/2 St., 47804-2498. Tel: 812-466-1231; Fax: 812-466-9683.
Catechesis/Religious Program—Students 65.

TROY, PERRY CO., ST. PIUS V CATHOLIC CHURCH, TROY, INC. (1849) [CEM 2] Rev. Barnabas Gillespie, O.S.B.
Parish Office & Mailing Address: Catholic Ministry Center, 824 Jefferson St., Tell City, 47586. Tel: 812-547-7994; Fax: 812-547-6985. Email: stpaulch@psci.net.
Church: State Rd. 66, 47588.
Catechesis/Religious Program—Students 28.

UNIVERSAL, VERMILLION CO., ST. JOSEPH CATHOLIC CHURCH, UNIVERSAL, INC. (1920), Attended from Sacred Heart, 619 S. Fifth St., Clinton, IN 47842-2016. Tel: 765-832-8468. Rev. Joseph L. Villa, Admin.
Church: 270 E. Wood Ave., 47884-0132.
Catechesis/Religious Program—Students 4.

VEVAY, SWITZERLAND CO., MOST SORROWFUL MOTHER OF GOD CATHOLIC CHURCH, VEVAY, INC. (1876) Rev. Christopher A. Craig.
Mailing Address: *Catholic Community Center*, 305 W. State St., Madison, 47250. Tel: 812-265-4166; Fax: 812-273-3427.
Church: Ferry St., 47043.

YORKVILLE, DEARBORN CO., ST. MARTIN CATHOLIC CHURCH, YORKVILLE, INC. (1850) [CEM] Rev. Scott E. Nobbe.
Res.: 8044 Yorkridge Rd., Guilford, 47022-9758. Tel: 812-487-2096; 812-623-3408; Fax: 812-576-2324. Email: flobraun@etczone.com.
Catechesis/Religious Program—Tel: 812-623-2662. Email: paquette5@comcast.net. Donn Paquette, C.R.E.; Michelle Paquette, C.R.E. Students 48.

Chaplains of Public Institutions

INDIANAPOLIS. *Indianapolis Fire Department*. Rev. John P. McCaslin.
Indianapolis International Airport. Rev. Glenn L. O'Connor.
Indianapolis Metropolitan Police Department. Rev. Steven C. Schwab.
Veterans' Administration Hospital. Rev. Joachim Kiene, O.F.M.Conv.

PUTNAMVILLE. *Putnamville Correctional Facility*. Rev. Darvin E. Winters.

RICHMOND. *Richmond State Hospital*. Revs. Dustin M. Boehm, Todd M. Riebe.

Unassigned:
Revs.—
Ashmore, Ronald M.
Schafer, Raymond E.

Graduate Studies:
Revs.—
Kappes, Christiaan W., St. Dionysius Catholic Cathedral, Athens, Greece
Newton, Joseph L., Catholic University of America, Washington D.C.

On Special or Other Archdiocesan Assignment:
Revs.—
Bramlage, Gregory D., Diocese of Houma-Thibodaux, Louisiana for Missionary Ministry
Porter, Jack W., Archdiocesan Historian (Retired)

Retired:
Rev. Msgrs.—
Easton, Frederick C., 3315 S. Commons Dr., Bloomington, 47401.
Knueven, Harold L., 1339 Indiana Ave., Connersville, 47331.
Moran, Lawrence J., 89 Allendale, Terre Haute, 47802.
Riedman, Joseph G., V.F., 1413 Westwood Blvd., Connersville, 47331.
Wright, John M., CHC, USN, 5385 Toscana Way, Apt. 348, San Diego, CA 92122.
Revs.—
Bryan, Francis E., 1746 W. Morris St., 46221.
Buchanan, Donald E., LCDR, CHC, USN, P.O. Box 367, Austin, 47102-0367.
Burkert, Gerald F., 501 N. 17th Ave., Beech Grove, 46107.
Burwinkel, Elmer J., 501 N. 17th Ave., Beech Grove, 46107.
Ciano, Kenneth J., 1465 E. Crossing Blvd., Apt. 227, Terre Haute, 47802.
Dede, Paul M., 2442 Stonelake Cir., Bloomington, 47404.
Dennison, Frederick J., 50 Lawson Ct., Brandenburg, KY 40108.
Eckstein, Francis J., P.O. Box 336, Milan, 47031.
Ernst, William W., 1118 Creekview Cir., New Albany, 47150.
Evard, Paul A., 718 Bitterbark Ln., 46227.
Geis, John F., 853 N. County Rd., 950 E., Greensburg, 47240.
Hartzer, John, 909 Ridge Ave., Lawrenceburg, 47025.
Head, Bernard, P.O. Box 116, Saint Mary Of The Woods, 47876.
Kraeszig, Charles J., 7901 Castle Dr., Lakewood Estates, New Port Richey, FL 34653.
Luerman, John H., 823 S.W. 15th St., 47374.
Lutz, Herman, St. Paul Hermitage, 501 N. 17th Ave., Beech Grove, 46107-1196.
Mader, Joseph E., 144 N. County Rd., Palm Beach, FL 33480.
Maung, John S., 4524 Wentworth Blvd., 46201.
Mazzola, Robert E., S.T.B., 313 Mary Kay Ln., Connersville, 47331.
McNally, Joseph J., 219 E. Eagle Dr., Ninevah, 46164.
Meny, Hilary G., 111 N. Race St., Haubstadt, 47639.
Munshower, William G., 5353 E. 56th St., 46226.
Murphy, Thomas J., St. Paul Hermitage, 501 N. 17th Ave., Beech Grove, 46107.
Peter, Martin A., 12935 Sawmill Rd., Columbus, 47201.
Porter, Jack W., 7432-D Lions Head Dr., 46260-3445.
Reidman, Joseph G.
Richardt, J. Lawrence, 2026 N. Erin Ct., Huntingburg, 47542-9520.
Ripperger, Harold A., 8403 St. John's Rd., Floyds Knobs, 47119.
Ripperger, William, 38220 Boxwood Dr., Zephyrhills, FL 33542.
Rodas, Mauro G., 4002 Oakfield Dr., 46237.
Sheets, Joseph B., 436 Mutton Creek Dr., Seymour, 47274.
Stepanski, Thomas K., 687 Aspen Ct., Danville, 46122.
Turner, William J., 7972 W. County Rd. 350 N., Saint Paul, 47272.
Vogelsang, Clifford R., 9140 Cinnebar Dr., 46268.

Permanent Deacons:
Deacons—
Alunday, Arthur, St. Mary, Greensburg
Blandford, Kerry, Dir., Deacon Formation, St. Mark the Evangelist, Indianapolis; Village Oaks at Greenwood
Bower, Patrick, St. Barnabas; Methodist Hospital, Indianapolis
Chlopecki, John J., St. Anthony of Padua, Morris
Collier, Daniel, St. Malachy, Brownsburg; Indianapolis Juvenile Correction Facility
Davis, Wayne, St. Michael, Greenfield; Hancock Regional Hospital
Dearman, Donald, St. Bernadette, Marion County Jail #1 and #2, Indianapolis
Decker, Robert W., PLC of St. Andrew the Apostle, Indianapolis
East, Michael, Dir., Deacons, St. Ambrose, Seymour; Our Lady of Providence, Brownstown; Jackson County Jail
Ferrer-Soto, Emilio, St. Patrick; Wishard Hopsital, Indianapolis
French, Lawrence, St. Joseph, Jennings County; St. Mary, North Vernon; St. Vincent Hospital, North Vernon; Patriot Academy, Muscatatuck Urban Training Center, Butlerville
Gardner, Michael, Prince of Peace, Madison; Most Sorrowful Mother of God, Vevay; Madison State Hospital
Gretencord, Steven, Sacred Heart; Ryves Youth Center of Catholic Charities Terre Haute, Terre Haute
Heller, Timothy, St. Teresa Benedicta of the Cross, Bright; Dearborn County Jail, Lawrenceburg
Henn, David, Our Lady of the Greenwood; Kindred Hospital Indianapolis South, Greenwood
Hodges, Stephen, SS. Francis & Clare, Greenwood, Chaplain for Courage Ministry
Jones, Wesley, Ph.D., St. Ann, Indianapolis; Catholic Charities Indianapolis

Jones, William, St. Bartholomew, Columbus; Substance Addiction Ministry
Kellams, Marc, JD, St. Charles Borromeo, Bloomington
Klauder, Francis C., St. Thomas the Apostle, Fortville; police chap., Greenfield Police Dept.
Morales, Oscar, St. Gabriel the Archangel; Marion County Jail #2, Indianapolis
Reimer, Ronald, St. Rose of Lima, Franklin & Johnson County Jail
Reising, David, St. Vincent de Paul, Bedford; St. Mary, Mitchell; Lawrence County Jail, Bedford
Stratman, Michael, St. Patrick, St. Margaret Mary, Union Hospital, Terre Haute
Thompson, John, St. Augustine, Jeffersonville; Clark County Jail
Ward, Thomas, St. Lawrence

INSTITUTIONS LOCATED IN THE ARCHDIOCESE

[A] SEMINARIES, RELIGIOUS OR SCHOLASTICATES

INDIANAPOLIS. *Bishop Simon Bruté College Seminary*, 2500 Cold Spring Rd., 46222. Tel: 317-924-4100; Fax: 317-924-4140. Revs. Robert J. Robeson, Ph.D., Rector; Patrick J. Beidelman, Vice Rector; Thomas C. Widner, S.J., Dir. Spiritual Formation; Jonathan Fassero, O.S.B., Spiritual Dir.; Dr. Ed Mitchell, Dir. Counseling. Seminarians 36.

SAINT MEINRAD. *Saint Meinrad School of Theology*, 200 Hill Dr., 47577. Tel: 812-357-6611; Fax: 812-357-6964. Email: rector@saintmeinrad.edu. Web: www.saintmeinrad.edu. Revs. Denis Robinson, O.S.B., Pres. & Rector; Bede Cisco, O.S.B., Dir. Inst. Research; Patrick Cooney, O.S.B., J.C.L., Dir., Pastoral Formation; Tobias Colgan, O.S.B., Dir., Human Formation; Cyprian Davis, O.S.B., Prof. Church History; Guerric DeBona, O.S.B.; Damian Dietlein, O.S.B. (Assumption Abbey); Jonathan Fassero, O.S.B., Assoc. Dir. Spiritual Formation; Harry Hagan, O.S.B.; Eugene Hensell, O.S.B.; Columba Kelly, O.S.B.; J. Ronald Knott, D.Min. (L), Dir. Institute for Priests & Presbyterates; Guy Mansini, O.S.B.; Joseph B. Moriarty, Dir. Spiritual Formation; Brendan Moss, O.S.B., M.Div., Dir., Enrollment; Godfrey Mullen, O.S.B., Vice Rector; Paul Nord, O.S.B.; Mark O'Keefe, O.S.B.; Thomas Richstatter, O.F.M. (Province of St. John the Baptist); Kurt Stasiak, O.S.B., Prior; Julian Peters, O.S.B., Dir. Permanent Deacon Formation; Bros. Zachary Wilberding, O.S.B., Assoc. Dir. Pastoral Formation; John Mark Falkenhain, O.S.B.; Sr. Diane Pharo, S.C.N., Dir. Counseling Ctr.; Dan Kolb, Ph.D., Library Dir. School of Theology. Priests 16; Brothers 2; Sisters 3; Lay Teachers 11; Other Faculty and Staff 29; Seminarians 140; Lay Degree Students 128.

[B] COLLEGES AND UNIVERSITIES

INDIANAPOLIS. *Marian University* (Coed), 3200 Cold Spring Rd., 46222. Tel: 317-955-6000; Fax: 317-955-6448. Email: admit@marian.edu. Web: www.marian.edu. Sr. Jean Marie Cleveland, O.S.F., Vice Pres. Mission Effectiveness; Dr. Thomas Enneking, Ph.D., Provost; Daniel J. Elsener, Pres.; Revs. Robert J. Robeson, Ph.D.; Leopold Keffler, O.F.M.Conv.; Ms. Kelley Griffith, Librarian. Sisters of the Third Order Regular of St. Francis. Priests 2; Sisters 4; Lay Teachers 101; Students 2,554.

SAINT MARY-OF-THE-WOODS. *Saint Mary-of-the-Woods College* (1840). Saint Mary Of The Woods, 47876. Tel: 812-535-5151; Fax: 812-535-5005. Email: smeier@smwc.edu. Web: www.smwc.edu. Dr. Dottie King, Ph.D., Pres.; Judy Tribble, Librarian. Sponsored by the Sisters of Providence, St. Mary-of-the-Woods. Priests 1; Sisters 4; Lay Teachers 65; Lay Staff 88; Students 1,441.

[C] HIGH SCHOOLS, INTER-PAROCHIAL

INDIANAPOLIS. *Bishop Chatard High School* (1961) 5885 Crittenden Ave., 46220. Tel: 317-251-1451; Fax: 317-254-5427. Email: president@bishopchatard.org. Web: www.bishopchatard.org. William "Bill" Sahm, Pres.; Dr. John Atha, Prin.; Rev. Robert T. Hausladen, Chap. Priests 1; Sisters of St. Benedict 3; Lay Teachers 59; Students 724.

Cardinal Ritter High School, 3360 W. 30th St., 46222. Tel: 317-924-4333; Fax: 317-927-7822. Greg Perkins, Pres.; E. Jo Hoy, B.S., M.S., Prin.; Rev. John J. Hollowell, Chap.; Elizabeth Jessen, Librarian. Priests 1; Sisters 1; Lay Teachers 42; Students 585.

Father Thomas Scecina Memorial High School, 5000 Nowland Ave., 46201-1836. Tel: 317-356-6377; Fax: 317-322-4287. Email: tdavis@scecina.org. Web: www.scecina.org. Mr. Joseph Therber, Pres.; Mr. John M. Hegarty, Prin.; Rev. Robert T. Hausladen, Chap.; Sr. Sheila Hackett, Librarian. Priests 1; Lay Teachers 28; Students 343.

Roncalli High School, 3300 Prague Rd., 46227. Tel: 317-787-8277; Fax: 317-788-4095. Email: cweisenbach@roncallihs.org. Web: www.roncalli.org. Mr. Joseph D. Hollowell, Pres.; Charles Weisenbach, Prin.; Rev. James R. Wilmoth, V.F., Chap. Priests 1; Lay Teachers 75; Students 1,142.

CLARKSVILLE. *Our Lady of Providence Junior - Senior High School*, 707 Providence Way, 47129. Tel: 812-945-2538; Fax: 812-945-3460. Email: mernstberger@providencehigh.net. Web: www.providencehigh.net. Dr. Melinda Ernstberger, Prin.; Mrs. Joan Hurley, Pres.; Rev. Eric Augenstein, Chap. Priests 1; Lay Teachers 39; Students (9-12) 453; Students (7-12) 531.

MADISON. *Shawe Memorial Junior-Senior High School* (1954) 201 W. State St., 47250. Tel: 812-273-2150; Fax: 812-273-2013. Email: shaweprincipal@popeace.org. Phil Kahn, Pres.; Jerome Bomholt, Prin.; Rev. Christopher A. Craig, V.F., Chap. Priests 1; Chaplains 1; Lay Teachers 18; Students 162.

RICHMOND. *Seton Catholic High School*, 233 S. 5th St., 47374. Tel: 765-965-6956; Fax: 765-966-0820. Email: dmusial@setoncatholichighschool.org. Rick Ruhl, Prin.; Rev. Todd Riebe. Priests 1; Lay Teachers 10; Students 155.

[D] HIGH SCHOOLS, PRIVATE

INDIANAPOLIS. *Brebeuf Jesuit Preparatory School, Inc.* (1962) 2801 W. 86th St., 46268-1926. Tel: 317-524-7050; Fax: 317-524-7142. Web: www.brebeuf.org. Dr. Matthew Hayes, Pres.; Mrs. LaTonya Turner, Vice Pres., Student Life & Leadership; Rev. Michael Christiana, S.J., Vice Pres. Mission & Identity; Greg VanSlambrook, Vice Pres., Academics; Revs. Frederick J. Deters, S.J., A.B., M.A., S.T.D.; George R. Menke, S.J.; Paul Peterson, S.J.; Mrs. Ann Sharp, Librarian. Society of Jesus Community. Priests 4; Lay Teachers 68; Students 789.

Cathedral High School (Cathedral Trustees, Inc.) (1918) 5225 E. 56th St., 46226. Tel: 317-542-1418; Fax: 317-542-1484. Email: dworland@cathedral-irish.org. Web: www.cathedral-irish.org. Revs. William G. Munshower, Chap. (Retired); John Zahn, Chap.; Stephen J. Helmich, M.S., Pres.; David Worland, Prin.; Julie Barthel, Librarian. Sisters 3; Lay Teachers 97; Students 1,247.

Providence Cristo Rey Corporate Work Study Program, Inc., 75 N. Belleview Pl., 46222-4145. Tel: 317-236-1430. Email: jhagelskamp@archindy.org. Sr. Jeanette Hagelskamp, S.P., Pres.

Providence Cristo Rey High School, Inc., 75 N. Belleview Pl., 46222-4145. Tel: 317-860-1000; Fax: 317-860-1004. Web: www.pcrhs.org. Joseph Heidt, Pres.; Sr. Jeanette Hagelskamp, S.P., Prin.

OLDENBURG. *Oldenburg Academy of the Immaculate Conception*, One Twister Cir., P.O. Box 200, 47036-0200. Tel: 812-934-4440; Fax: 812-934-4838. Email: tgillman@oldenburgacademy.org. Web: www.oldenburgacademy.org. Sr. Therese Gillman, O.S.F., Pres.; Mrs. Bettina Rose, Prin. Lay Teachers 19; Students 213.

[E] DAY CARE

SAINT MARY-OF-THE-WOODS. *Woods Day Care/ Preschool, Inc.* (1987) Saint Mary Of The Woods, 47876-1099. Tel: 812-535-4610; Fax: 812-535-4674. Children 72; Total Staff 24.

[F] RELIGIOUS EDUCATION CENTERS

CLARKSVILLE. *Aquinas Center for Continuing Religious Education*, 707 Providence Way Side, 47129. Tel: 812-945-0354; Fax: 812-945-2929. Email: dcmnad@sbcglobal.net. Web: aquinascenter.org. Ms. Christina Flum, Dir. Catechetical Ministry.

TERRE HAUTE. *Terre Haute Deanery Pastoral Center*, 1801 Poplar St., 47803. Tel: 812-232-8400; Fax: 812-232-8400 (Call First). Email: director@thdeanery.org. Web: www.thdeanery.org. Sr. Mary Montgomery, S.P., Dir. Total Staff 2.

[G] GENERAL HOSPITALS

INDIANAPOLIS. *Central Indiana Health System Cardiac Services, Inc.* (1991) 8425 N. Harcourt Rd., 46260. Tel: 317-583-3289; Fax: 317-583-3285. Email: jbford@stvincent.org. Mailing Address: 10330 N. Meridian St., 46290. Tel: 317-583-3289; Fax: 317-583-3285. Vincent C. Caponi, Chm.

St. Vincent Hospital and Health Care Center, Inc. (1884) 10330 N. Meridian St., 46290. Tel: 317-583-3289; Fax: 317-583-3285. Email: jbford@stvincent.org. Web: www.stvincent.org. J. Albert Smith Jr., Chairperson; Vincent C. Caponi, CEO, St. Vincent Health, Inc.; Kyle DeFur, Pres.; Ron L. Mead, Vice Pres. Mission Svcs.; Rev. Ben Okonkwo; Rick Renzi, Interim Dir. Pastoral Care. Daughters of Charity of St. Vincent de Paul. Sisters 8; Chaplains 18; Bed Capacity 783; Total Staff 5,662; Inpatient Admissions 34,270; Outpatient Visits 893,832; Emergency Visits 70,285.

**St. Vincent New Hope, Inc.* (1988) 8450 N. Payne Rd., 46268. Tel: 317-872-4210; Fax: 317-338-4585. Email: jbford@stvincent.org. Web: www.stvincent.org. Daughters of Charity of St. Vincent de Paul. Bed Capacity 73; Total Assisted Annually 322; Total Staff 517.

**St. Vincent Pediatric Rehabilitation Center, Inc.* (A member of St. Vincent Health & Ascension Health.), 1707 W. 86th St., 46260. Tel: 317-415-5500; Fax: 317-415-5595. Email: akmott@stvincent.org. Jeff Poltawski, CEO; Andrea Mott, CFO.

BEDFORD. *St. Vincent Dunn Hospital Inc.*, 1600 23rd St., 47421. Tel: 812-275-3331; Fax: 812-276-1211. Web: www.stvincent.org. Deborah A. Bruner, Admin.

BEECH GROVE. *Franciscan St. Francis Health* (1914) 1600 Albany St., 46107. Tel: 317-787-3311; Fax: 317-782-6731. Web: www.stfrancishospitals.org. Mr. Robert J. Brody, B.A., M.H.A., Pres. & CEO; Sr. Marlene Shapley, B.S., R.N., Vice Pres., Mission Integration Svcs.; Revs. Frederick J. Deters, S.J., A.B., M.A., S.T.D., Chap.; Mike O. Onwuegbuzie, B.D., M.Ed., M.Admin., Chap.; John H. Mannion, B.S., M.Div. (LFT), Chap.; Constantine L. Silayo, Chap. Sisters of St. Francis Health Services, Inc. Sisters 5; Priests 4; Staff 4,163; Bed Capacity 600; Patients Assisted Annually 539,000.

(1995) 8111 S. Emerson Ave., 46237. Tel: 317-528-5000; Fax: 317-528-5061. Web: www.stfrancishospitals.org.

1201 Hadley Rd., Mooresville, 46158. Tel: 317-834-1160; Fax: 317-831-9315. Web: www.stfrancishospitals.org.

Franciscan Alliance Foundation St. Francis, 5255 E. Stop 11 Rd., Ste. 245, 46237. Tel: 317-528-8949. Email: bob.brody@franciscanalliance.org.

BRAZIL. **St. Vincent Clay Hospitals, Inc.* (A member of St. Vincent Health & Ascension Health.), 1206 E. National Ave., P.O. Box 489, 47834. Tel: 812-442-2500; Fax: 812-442-2605. Email: jrlau@stvincent.org. Jerry R. Laue, CEO. Bed Capacity 25; Total Staff 158.

NORTH VERNON. *St. Vincent Jennings Hospital Foundation, Inc.*, 301 Henry St., 47265. Tel: 812-352-4200; Fax: 812-352-4201.

**St. Vincent Jennings Hospital, Inc.* (A member of St. Vincent Health & Ascension Health.), 301 Henry St., 47265. Tel: 812-352-4200; Fax: 812-352-4201. Email: jclines@stvincent.org. Joseph E. Roche, CEO; John Lines, CFO. Inpatients 603; Outpatients 76,539; Total Staff 197.

SALEM. *St. Vincent Salem Hospital, Inc.*, 911 N. Shelby St., 47167. Tel: 812-883-5881; Fax: 812-883-8563. Lee Jaeger, Admin.

[H] PROTECTIVE INSTITUTIONS

TERRE HAUTE. *Gibault Children's Services*, 6401 S. U.S. Hwy. 41, 47802-0316. Tel: 812-299-1156; Fax: 812-298-3044. Email: gibault@gibault.org. Web: www.gibault.org. Mr. James M. Sinclair, M.S.S.W., J.D., Pres. & C.E.O. Residential treatment facility for males and females between the ages of 8 and 18, sponsored by the Knights of Columbus of Indiana. Licensed Youth 147; Total Staff 287; Total Assisted Annually 302.

[I] HOMES FOR AGED

INDIANAPOLIS. *St. Augustine Home, Little Sisters of the Poor* (1873) 2345 W. 86th St., 46260. Tel: 317-872-6420; Fax: 317-875-9883. Sr. Mary Vincent Mannion, L.S.P., Admin.; Rev. Msgr. Joseph Duncan, Chap. Sisters 11; Bed Capacity 96; Residents 94; Total Staff 109; Total Assisted Annually 210.

BEECH GROVE. *St. Paul Hermitage*, 501 N. 17th Ave., 46107. Tel: 317-786-2261; Fax: 317-782-1411. Email: rebeccamarie@benedictine.com. Revs. Herman Lutz (Retired); James Rogers, (Evansville Diocese); Gerald F. Burkert, Chap. (Retired); Thomas Murphy; Elmer J. Burwinkel (Retired); Sr. Rebecca Marie Fitterer, O.S.B., Admin.

Sisters of St. Benedict of Beech Grove, Ind., Inc. Sisters 6; Bed Capacity 122; Total Assisted Annually 128; Residents 100; Total Staff 108.

NEW ALBANY. *Mercy Long Term Care Initiatives dba Providence Retirement Home* 4915 Charlestown Rd., 47150. Tel: 812-945-5221; Fax: 812-945-2614. Email: ttodd@lourdes-pad.org. Web: www.prhonline.org. Amy D. Brown, Exec. Dir. Sisters of Mercy. Priests 1; Sisters 1; Total Staff

186; Residents 172; Adult Day Care clients 32.

Providence Retirement Home Auxiliary, Inc., 4915 Charlestown Rd., 47150.

[J] RETREAT HOUSES

INDIANAPOLIS. *Our Lady of Fatima Retreat House, Inc.* (1950) 5353 E. 56th St., 46226. Tel: 317-545-7681; Fax: 317-545-0095. Email: fatima@archindy.org. Web: www.archindy.org/fatima. Revs. James M. Farrell, S.T.B., Dir.; William G. Munshower (Retired). Used by both clergy and laity. Priests 1; Total in Residence 1; Served 9,500; Total Staff 21.

BEECH GROVE. *Benedict Inn Retreat & Conference Center* (1981) 1402 Southern Ave., 46107-1197. Tel: 317-788-7581; Fax: 317-782-3142. Email: benedictinn@benedictinn.org. Web: www.benedictinn.org. Sr. Carol Falkner, O.S.B., Admin. Retreats and workshops for clergy, religious, and laity. Sisters 5.

MOUNT SAINT FRANCIS. *Mount Saint Francis Friary and Retreat Center* (1896) 101 St. Anthony Dr., Mount St. Francis, 47146-9999. Tel: 812-923-8817; Fax: 812-923-0177. Rev. Wayne Hellmann, O.F.M.Conv., Prof., St. Louis Univ. Total Staff 11; Total in Residence 11. In Res. Bro. Robert Baxter, O.F.M.Conv., Guardian & Dir. Retreats; Rev. Conrad Sutter, O.F.M.Conv.; Bro. Paul Clark, O.F.M.Conv., Province Sec.; Revs. Maurus Hauer, O.F.M.Conv.; Ken Bartsch, O.F.M.Conv.; Simon Sauer, O.F.M.Conv.; Don Halpin, O.F.M.Conv.; David Lenz, O.F.M.Conv.; Kenneth Gering, O.F.M.Conv.; Kenneth Davis, O.F.M.Conv.

Province of Our Lady of Consolation, Inc., 101 St. Anthony Dr., Mount St. Francis. Tel: 812-923-8444; Fax: 812-923-8145. Revs. James Kent, O.F.M.Conv., Prov.; John Stowe, O.F.M.Conv., Vicar Prov.; Bro. Paul Clark, O.F.M.Conv., Province Sec.; Revs. Martin Day, O.F.M.Conv., Province Treas.; Mark Weaver, O.F.M.Conv., Definitor; Camillus Gott, O.F.M.Conv., Definitor; Wayne Hellmann, O.F.M.Conv., Definitor. (Provincial Office)

SAINT MEINRAD. *Archabbey Guest House & Retreat Center*, 200 Hill Dr., 47577. Tel: 812-357-6585; 800-581-6905; Fax: 812-357-6841. Email: mzoeller@saintmeinrad.edu. Web: www.saintmeinrad.edu. Bro. Maurus Zoeller, O.S.B., Retreat Dir. & Guest Master. Retreat House for Men, Women, Couples Rooms 31.

[K] MONASTERIES AND RESIDENCES OF PRIESTS AND BROTHERS

BLOOMINGTON. *Marian Friary of Our Lady Coredemptrix, Franciscans of the Immaculate*, 8210 W. State Rd. 48, 47404-9735. Tel: 812-825-4642, Ext. 232; 812-825-4742. Revs. Elias Mary Mills, F.I., Father Guardian; Joachim Mary Mudd, F.I. Priests 2.

MOUNT SAINT FRANCIS. *Provincial Headquarters, Our Lady of Consolation Province, Conventual Franciscans*, 101 Anthony Dr., Mount St. Francis, 47146. Tel: 812-923-8444; Fax: 812-923-8145. Email: ProvOffOLC@aol.com. Web: www.franciscansusa.org. Rev. James Kent, O.F.M.Conv., Prov.; Bro. Paul Clark, O.F.M.Conv., Province Sec.

Province of Our Lady of Consolation Priests 1; Brothers 1. *Development Office*, 103 St. Francis Blvd., Mount St. Francis, 47146. Tel: 812-923-5250; Fax: 812-923-3200. Rev. John Elmer, O.F.M.Conv., Devel. Spiritual Dir. Priests 1; Total Staff 5. *Vocation Office - Our Lady of Consolation Province* Tel: 502-933-4439; Fax: 502-933-7747. Rev. Paul Schloemer, O.F.M.Conv., Dir., Vocation, St. Francis of Assisi Friary, 2225 Lower Hunters Trace, Louisville, KY 40216. Tel: 502-447-5566. Priests 1; Total Staff 2. *St. Paul Parish*, 6901 Dixie Hwy., Pleasure Ridge Park, KY 40258. Tel: 502-933-4439; Fax: 502-933-7747. *Curia Generalizia*

SAINT MEINRAD. *St. Meinrad Archabbey* (1854) 100 Hill Dr., 47577-1010. Tel: 812-357-6611; Fax: 812-357-6551. Email: abbot@saintmeinrad.edu. Web: www.saintmeinrad.edu. Rt. Revs. Justin DuVall, O.S.B., Archabbot; Lambert Reilly, O.S.B., Resigned Archabbot; Bonaventure Knaebel, O.S.B., Resigned Archabbot; Revs. Kurt Stasiak, O.S.B., Prior; Guerric DeBona, O.S.B., Subprior, Master of Novices & Junior Master; Gavin Barnes, O.S.B.; Aurelius Boberek, O.S.B.; Meinrad Brune, O.S.B.; Adrian Burke, O.S.B., V.F., P.O. Box 8, 47577. Tel: 812-357-5533; Fax: 812-357-2862; Bede Cisco, O.S.B., St. Michael Parish, 3354 W. 30th St., 46222; Aelred Cody, O.S.B.; Tobias Colgan, O.S.B.; Patrick Cooney, O.S.B., J.C.L.; Joseph Cox, O.S.B.; Simeon Daly, O.S.B.; Augustine Davis, O.S.B.; Cyprian Davis, O.S.B.; Jonathan Fassero, O.S.B.; Colman Grabert, O.S.B.; Harry Hagan, O.S.B.; Warren Heitz, O.S.B.; Eugene Hensell, O.S.B.; Richard Hindel, O.S.B.; Gabriel Hodges, O.S.B.; Sean Hoppe, O.S.B., St. Augustine Church, General Delivery, Leopold, 47551; Columba Kelly, O.S.B.; Jeremy King, O.S.B.; Pius Klein, O.S.B., St. Mary Rectory, 313 Washington St., Huntingburg, 47542; Eric Lies, O.S.B.; Guy Mansini, O.S.B.; Benedict Meyer, O.S.B.; Brendan Moss, O.S.B., M.Div.; Noel Mueller, O.S.B.; Louis Mulcahy, O.S.B.; Godfrey Mullen, O.S.B.; Rupert Ostdick, O.S.B.; Julian Peters, O.S.B.; Denis Robinson, O.S.B., Pres. & Rector, School Theology; Timothy Sweeney, O.S.B., Parish of the Immaculate, 2516 Christie Pl., Owensboro, KY 42301; Germain Swisshelm, O.S.B.; Vincent Tobin, O.S.B.; Donald Walpole, O.S.B. Archabbey of the Order of St. Benedict, including School of Theology (St. Meinrad Seminary). Priests 67; Brothers 28.

Priests of the Archabbey Teaching, Studying at Universities, or on Special Assignment: Revs. Ephrem Carr, O.S.B., Collegio Sant' Anselmo, Piazza Cavalieri di Malta 5, Rome I-00153 Italy; Gregory D. Chamberlin, O.S.B., St. Benedict Church, 1328 Lincoln Ave., Evansville, 47714-1598; Cassian Folsom, O.S.B., Monastero San Benedetto, Comunita di Maria Sedes Sapientias, Via Reguardati, 22, Norcia (pg) 06046 Italy; Barnabas Gillespie, O.S.B., St. Paul Church, 802 Ninth St., Tell City, 47586; Thomas Gricoski, O.S.B.; Louis Hackev, O.S.B.; Harold Hammerstein, O.S.B., 701 S. Boeke, Evansville, 47714; Boniface Hardin, O.S.B., 2171 Avondale Pl., P.O. Box 18567, 46218; Micheas Langston, O.S.B., The Hollows, 1300 Longcreek Dr., Apt. 713, Columbia, SC 29210; Sebastian Leonard, O.S.B., Canterbury School, Aspetuck Ave., New Milford, CT 06776; Edward Linton, O.S.B., St. James Parish, 2942 S. Wabash, Chicago, IL 60616; Severin Messick, O.S.B., M.Div., St. Michael Church, 519 Jefferson Blvd., Greenfield, 46140; Matthias Neuman, O.S.B., 1414 Southern Ave., Beech Grove, 46107; Paul Nord, O.S.B.; Mark O'Keefe, O.S.B.; Mel Patton, O.S.B., Sacred Heart Monastery, 1005 W. Eighth St., Yankton, SD 57078; David Rabenecker, O.S.B., P.O. Box 3394, Terre Haute, 47803; Damian Schmelz, O.S.B., St. Henry Parish, 1311 W. 1100 S., Ferdinand, 47532; Stephen Snoich, O.S.B.; Raymond Studzinski, O.S.B., Curley Hall, Catholic University of America, Washington, DC 20064; Anthony Vinson, O.S.B.; Samuel Weber, O.S.B., Wake Forest Divinity School, P.O. Box 7719, Winston Salem, NC 27109-7719.

[L] CONVENTS AND RESIDENCES FOR SISTERS

INDIANAPOLIS. *Servants of the Gospel of Life, Inc.*, 1400 N. Meridian St., 46202. Tel: 317-236-1521. Email: dcarollo@archindy.org. Sr. Diane Carollo, S.G.L., Sister Servant.

BEECH GROVE. *Our Lady of Grace Monastery*, 1402 Southern Ave., 46107-1197. Tel: 317-787-3287; Fax: 317-780-2368. Email: olgprioress@benedictine.com. Web: www.benedictine.com.

Sisters of St. Benedict of Beech Grove, Ind., Inc. 1414 Southern Ave., 46107-1197. Tel: 317-786-0338; Fax: 317-780-2368. Email: mneuman204@att.net. Rev. Matthias Neuman, O.S.B., Chap. Sisters 68.

GREENWOOD. *F.I.H. Convent - Franciscan Sisters of the Immaculate Heart of Mary* (1998) 345 S. Meridian St., 46143. Tel: 317-865-6013; Fax: 317-885-5006. Email: srushatta@gmail.com. Sr. Ushatta Mary, F.I.H., Supr. Franciscan Sisters of the Immaculate Heart of Mary. Sisters 12.

OLDENBURG. *Motherhouse of the Congregation of the Sisters of the Third Order of St. Francis* 47036. Tel: 812-934-2475; Fax: 812-933-6403. Email: osf@oldenburgosf.com. Web: www.oldenburgfranciscans.org. Sr. Barbara Piller, O.S.F., Congregational Min.; Rev. Carl Hawver, O.F.M. Professed Sisters in Congregation 234; Professed Sisters in Archdiocese 162; Total in Residence 123.

Sisters of St. Francis Community Support Trust Tel: 812-934-2475.

Michaela Farm, 47036. Tel: 812-933-0260.

Oldenburg Franciscan Center, 47036. Tel: 812-933-6437.

Sisters of Our Lady of Mount Carmel Carmelite Monastery (1922) *Carmelite Sisters*, P.O. Box 260, 47036. Tel: 812-932-2075; Fax: 812-932-2076. Email: indycarmelites@yahoo.com. Sr. Jean Alice McGoff, O.C.D., Prioress. Professed Religious 8.

SAINT MARY-OF-THE-WOODS. *Sisters of Providence General Administration*, Saint Mary Of The Woods, 47876-1007. Tel: 812-535-4193; Fax: 812-535-1011. Web: www.sistersofprovidence.org. Sr. Denise Wilkinson, S.P., Gen. Supr.; Rev. Daniel R. Hopcus, Chap. Professed in Congregation 361; Professed Residing in Archdiocese 236; Novices 4; Postulants 2.

TERRE HAUTE. *Sisters of Our Lady of Mount Carmel of Terre Haute, Carmelite Monastery* (1947) Carmelite Monastery, 59 Allendale, 47802-4751. Tel: 812-299-1410; Fax: 812-299-5820. Email: carmelth@heartsawake.org. Web: www.heartsawake.org. Sr. Mary Clare, O.C.D., Prioress. Solemnly Professed 12.

[M] ARCHDIOCESAN CHARITIES

INDIANAPOLIS. *Adult Day Services*, 1400 N. Meridian, P.O. Box 1410, 46206. Tel: 317-466-0015; Fax: 317-261-3375. Email: sdinnin@fairviewpresbyterian.org. Sr. Susan Dinnin, Prog. Dir.

A Caring Place - Adult Day Services, c/o Fairview Presbyterian Church, 4609 N. Capitol Ave., 46208. Tel: 317-466-0015; Fax: 317-475-3093. Sr. Susan Dinnin, Prog. Dir. Total Staff 13.

Catholic Charities Indianapolis, The Catholic Center, 1400 N. Meridian St., P.O. Box 1410, 46206. Tel: 317-236-1500; Fax: 317-261-3375. Email: vsperka@archindy.org. Web: www.catholiccharitiesindpls.org. David Bethuram, M.A., M.Min, Agency Dir.

St. Elizabeth/Coleman Pregnancy & Adoption Services, 2500 Churchman Ave., 46203. Tel: 317-787-3412; Fax: 317-787-0482. Email: stelizabeths@stelizabeths.org. Web: www.stelizabeths.org. David Bethuram, M.A., M.Min, Agency Dir.

Holy Family Services, 907 N. Holmes Ave., 46222. Tel: 317-635-7830; Fax: 317-684-9702. Email: bbickel@archindy.org. Web: www.catholiccharitiesindpls.org. Bill Bickel, M.T.S., Dir. Total Staff 16; Total Assisted 1,000.

BLOOMINGTON. *Catholic Charities Bloomington*, 631 N. College Ave., 47404. Tel: 812-332-1262; Fax: 812-334-8464.

NEW ALBANY. *St. Elizabeth's Regional Maternity Center*, 601 E. Market St., 47150. Tel: 812-949-7305; Fax: 812-941-7008. Email: info@stelizabethcatholiccharities.org. Web: www.stelizabethcatholicharities.org. Mark Casper, Dir. Full-range maternity home and adoption agency offering residential and outreach services. Total Staff 26; Total Assisted 607.

St. Elizabeth - Catholic Charities, 601 E. Market St., 47150. Tel: 812-949-7305; Fax: 812-941-7008. Email: info@stelizabethcatholiccharities.org. Web: www.stelizabethcatholiccharities.org. Total Staff 26; Total Assisted 607.

TELL CITY. *Catholic Charities Tell City*, 802 9th St., 47586. Tel: 812-547-0903; Fax: 812-547-0903. Email: info@catholiccharitiestellcity.org. Web: www.catholiccharitiestellcity.org. Joan Hess, Agency Dir.

TERRE HAUTE. *Catholic Charities Terre Haute*, 1801 Poplar St., 47803. Tel: 812-232-1447; Fax: 812-478-1363. Email: jetling@catholiccharitiesterrehaute.org. Web: www.catholiccharitiesterrehaute.org. John C. Etling, Dir. Total Staff 25.

Catholic Charities Terre Haute, 1801 Poplar St., 47803. Tel: 812-232-1447; Fax: 812-478-1363. John C. Etling, Agency Dir.

Bethany House, 1402 Locust Ave., 47807. Tel: 812-232-4978. Dottye Crippen, Prog. Dir. Total Staff 5; Total Assisted 13,000.

Christmas House, 829 N. 14th St., 47807. Tel: 812-234-7242. Georgia Nardini, Prog. Dir. Total Staff 1; Total Assisted 3,740.

Household Exchange, 829 N. 14th St., 47807. Tel: 812-234-7242. Georgia Nardini, Prog. Dir. Total Staff 1; Total Assisted 3,140.

Ryves Youth Center at Etling Hall, 1356 Locust St., 47807. Tel: 812-235-1265. Jim Edwards, Prog. Dir. Total Staff 6; Total Assisted 1,917.

Terre Haute Catholic Charities Foodbank, 1356 Locust St., 47807. Tel: 812-235-3424. Tom Kuhl, Prog. Dir. Total Staff 7; Total Assisted 82,000.

[N] CATHOLIC YOUTH ORGANIZATIONS

INDIANAPOLIS. *Catholic Youth Organization*, Related Ministries, 580 E. Stevens St., 46203. Tel: 317-632-9311. Web: www.cyoarchindy.org. Mr. Edward J. Tinder, Exec. Dir.; Mr. Gerald R. Ross, Asst. Exec. Dir. Monsignor Downey Athletic Field Perkins & Raymond St., 46203.

NASHVILLE. *C.Y.O. Camp Rancho Framasa* (1946) 2230 N. Clay Lick Rd., 47448-8638. Tel: 888-988-2839; Fax: 812-988-4842. Email: info@campranchoframasa.org. Web: www.campranchoframasa.org. Mr. Kevin Sullivan, Camp Dir.

[O] CAMPUS MINISTRIES

INDIANAPOLIS. *Butler University c/o Center for Faith and Vocation*, 4600 Sunset Ave., 46208. Tel: 317-509-6012. Rev. Jeffrey H. Godecker.

University of Indianapolis Newman Center c/o St. Barnabas Parish, 8300 Rahke Rd., 46217. Rev. Sean R. Danda.

BLOOMINGTON. *Indiana University, Bloomington c/o*

St. Paul Catholic Center, 1413 E. 17th St., 47408. Tel: 812-339-5561; Fax: 812-333-4846. Web: www.hoosiercatholic.org. Rev. Thomas R. Poulsen, O.P.

FRANKLIN. *Franklin College* (1834) *c/o St. Rose of Lima Parish*, 114 Lancelot Dr., 46131. Tel: 317-738-3929; Fax: 317-738-3583. Rev. John Beitons.

GREENCASTLE. *DePauw University c/o St. Paul the Apostle Parish*, 202 E. Washington St., 46135. Tel: 765-653-5678. Rev. Darvin E. Winters.

MADISON. *Hanover College c/o Prince of Peace Parish*, 305 W. State St., 47250. Tel: 812-265-4166; Fax: 812-273-3427. Rev. Christopher A. Craig, V.F.

RICHMOND. *Earlham College c/o St. Andrew Parish*, 240 S. 6th St., 47374. Tel: 765-962-3902. Rev. Todd M. Riebe.

TERRE HAUTE. *Indiana State University/Rose-Hulman Institute c/o St. Joseph University Parish*, 113 Fifth St., 47807. Tel: 812-232-7011. Jeff Schaffer, Pastoral Assoc. for College Students; Carol Schaffer, Pastoral Assoc. for College Students.

[P] MISCELLANEOUS

INDIANAPOLIS. **The Catholic Writers Guild Inc.*, P.O. Box 39326, 46239-0326. Tel: 877-829-5500. Paula Harrell, Contact Person.

Hearts and Hands Corporation of Indiana, 1400 N. Meridian St., 46202-2367. Rev. Msgr. Joseph F. Schaedel, M.S., M.Div.

**Inter Mirifica, Inc.*, 7340 E. 82nd St., Ste. A, 46256. Tel: 317-598-6700; Fax: 317-598-6701. Email: bob@teipencpa.com. Web: www.catholicradioindy.org. Robert C. Teipen, Chm.

Society of St. Vincent de Paul, Archdiocesan Council of Indianapolis, Inc., 3001 E. 30th St., 46218. Tel: 317-924-5769; Fax: 317-924-5781. Web: www.svdpindy.org. Mr. Jake Asher, Pres. Total Assisted 67,000.

SVSM, Inc. (2001) 10330 N. Meridian St., 46290. Tel: 317-583-3289; Fax: 317-583-3285. Email: jbford@stvincent.org. Web: www.stvincent.org. Mailing Address: 10330 N. Meridian St., 46290. Vincent Caponi, CEO, St. Vincent Health, Inc.

**St. Vincent Health, Inc.*, 10330 N. Meridian St., 46290. Tel: 317-583-3289; Fax: 317-583-3285. Email: jbford@stvincent.org. Web: www.stvincent.org. Mailing Address: 10330 N. Meridian St., 46290. Vincent Caponi, CEO; Joseph B. Ford, Mgr. Finance & Contact Person.

BEECH GROVE. *Charitable Trust of the Monastery of Our Lady of Grace* (1989) 1402 Southern Ave., 46107-1197. Tel: 317-787-3287; Fax: 317-780-2368. Email: olgprioress@benedictine.com. Web: www.benedictine.com.

Charitable Trust of the Monastery of Our Lady of Grace, Sisters of the Order of St. Benedict

Franciscan Alliance Information Services, 1300 Albany St., 46107. Tel: 317-532-7800; Fax: 317-532-7801. Email: william.laker@franciscanalliance.org. Web: www.franciscanalliance.org. Mr. William G. Laker, Senior Vice Pres. & CIO. Sponsored by Franciscan Alliance, Inc.

Mary's King's Village Schoenstatt Center, Inc., 501 N. 17th Ave., 46107. Rev. Elmer J. Burwinkel, Pres. & Dir. (Retired).

CLARKSVILLE. *New Albany Deanery-Catholic Youth Ministries*, 707 Providence Way Side, 47129. Tel: 812-945-2000; Fax: 812-945-2995. Email: marlene@nadyouth.org. Web: www.nadyouth.org.

GEORGETOWN. *Providence Self-Sufficiency Ministries, Inc.* (1994) 8037 Unruh Dr., 47122-8759. Tel: 812-951-1878; Fax: 812-951-1659. Email: sbarannz@insightbb.com. Web: www.pssm.org. Sr. Barbara Ann Zeller, Pres. & CEO. Sponsored by The Sisters of Providence, Saint Mary-of-the-Woods. Total Assisted 2010-2011 11,263; Total Assisted Historically 112,031; Volunteers 204; Personnel 78.

MOORESVILLE. *St. Thomas More Free Clinic, Inc.*, 1125 N. Indiana St., POB 935, 46158. Tel: 317-831-1697. Email: jbuckner@crowntech.com. Jeff Buckner, Bd. Member.

MOUNT SAINT FRANCIS. *Mount Saint Francis Sanctuary, Inc., Sec. Mailing Address: Marian College*, 3200 Cold Spring Rd., 46222. Tel: 812-923-8817; Fax: 812-923-0177. Samuel L. Smith, Pres.; Chris Jones, Vice Pres.; Thomas A. Smith, O.F.M.Conv., Treas.; Rev. Leopold Keffler, O.F.M.Conv., Sec.

NORTH VERNON. *St. Vincent Jennings Hospital Foundation Inc.*, 301 Henry St., 47265.

OLDENBURG. *Association of Contemplative Sisters, Carmelite Sisters*, P.O. Box 260, 47036-0260. Tel: 812-932-2075; Fax: 812-932-2076. Email: jeanmcgoff@yahoo.com. Mary Lyons, Pres. Membership 363.

SAINT MARY OF THE WOODS. **Guerin Outreach Ministries, Inc., Sisters of Providence, Owens Hall*, 1 Sisters of Providence, 47876-1007. Tel: 812-535-2864; Fax: 812-535-1011.

Providence Health Care, Inc., Owens Hall, 1 Sisters of Providence, 47876-1007. Tel: 812-535-2864; Fax: 812-535-1011. Sponsored by the Sisters of Providence of Saint Mary-of-the-Woods.

Sisters of Providence Community Support Trust 47876-1007. Tel: 812-535-4193; Fax: 812-535-1011. Web: www.sistersofprovidence.org. Sr. Rosemary Schmalz, S.P., Gen. Sec.

Women of Providence in Collaboration, Inc., 1 Sisters of Providence, 47876. Tel: 812-535-2502; Fax: 812-535-1011.

SAINT MEINRAD. *Swiss-American Benedictine Congregation, Inc.*, Saint Meinrad Archabbey, 100 Hill Dr., 47577. Fax: 630-897-7086. Email: vbataille@marmion.org. Web: www.osb.org/swissam. Rt. Rev. Vincent Bataille, O.S.B., Abbot Pres.

TERRE HAUTE. *St. Ann Community Outreach Services of Terre Haute*, 1440 Locust St., 47807. Tel: 812-232-6832; Fax: 812-232-2442. Email: stannchurch@gmail.com. Mailing Address: 1440 Locust St., 47807. Sr. Constance Kramer, S.P., Dir.

[Q] CLOSED PARISHES, SCHOOLS AND OTHER INSTITUTIONS

INDIANAPOLIS. *Archives of the Archdiocese of Indianapolis*, 1400 N. Meridian St., 46202. Tel: 317-236-1429; Fax: 317-236-1406. Email: archives@archindy.org. Sacramental and other records may be found where indicated.

Closed Parishes and Missions:

Indianapolis:

Assumption (1894-1994) Merged with St. Anthony, where sacramental records are kept.

St. Bridget (1880-1994) Merged with SS. Peter & Paul, where sacramental records are kept.

St. Catherine of Siena (1909-1993) Merged with St. James and renamed Good Shepherd, where sacramental records are kept.

St. Francis de Sales (1881-1983) Merged with four neighboring parishes. Sacramental records are located in the archives.

St. James the Greater (1951-1993) Merged with St. Catherine and renamed Good Shepherd, where sacramental records are kept.

St. Joseph (1873-1949) Sacramental records kept at the new St. Joseph parish.

Acton:

St. John the Evangelist (1855-1936) Sacramental records are located in the archives.

Adyeville:

St. Jude Thaddeus (1889-1898)

Bainbridge:

St. Patrick (1865-1973)

Blanford:

Queen of the Most Holy Rosary (1917-1942)

Cannelton:

St. Patrick (1847-1902) Merged with St. Michael, Cannelton, where sacramental records are kept.

Carbon:

St. Joseph (1870-1970) Sacramental records are located in the archives.

Centenary:

St. Anthony (1917-1942)

China:

St. Anthony (1861-1993) Merged with Prince of Peace, Madison, where sacramental records are kept.

Columbus:

St. Columba (1963-1994) Merged with St. Bartholomew, Columbus, where sacramental records are kept.

Cypress Dale:

Sacred Heart (1868-1918)

Derby:

St. Mary (1824-1973) Sacramental records kept at St. Augustine, Leopold.

Diamond:

St. John Baptist (Greek Uniate Catholic) (1897-1926) Sacaramental records are located in the archives.

St. Mary (1897-1991) Sacramental records are located in the archives.

Dogwood:

St. Michael (1820-1928)

Dugger:

Our Lady of Perpetual Help (1911-1982) Sacramental records kept at St. Mary, Sullivan Co., Diocese of Evansville.

Ellsworth:

St. John (1910-1912)

Eureka:

Mattingly Chapel (1874-1886)

Fontanet:

St. Augustine (1891-1980) Sacramental records are located in the archives.

Hovey:

All Souls Chapel (1900-1915)

Indian Creek:

St. Columban (1848-1868)

Knightsville:

St. Patrick (1868-1890)

Laconia:

Sacred Heart of Mary (1854-1922)

Laurel:

St. Raphael (1869-1958) Sacramental records kept at St. Gabriel, Connersville.

Lexington:

Mother of God (1854-1941)

Locust Point:

St. Joachim (1888-1930)

Madison:

St. Mary (1851-1993) Merged with St. Patrick (1853-1993) and St. Michael (1837-1993) and renamed Prince of Peace, where sacramental records are kept.

Magnet:

Sacred Heart Sacramental records kept at St. Augustine, Leopold.

McCutcheonville:

St. Patrick (1842-1881)

Mecca:

St. Mary (1905-1936)

Milltown:

St. Joseph (1855-1974) Sacramental records kept at St. Joseph, Crawford Co.

Montezuma:

Parke Co., Immaculate Conception (1867-2001) Sacramental records kept at St. Joseph, Rockville.

Mount Erin:

St. John the Baptist (1852-1885)

Mount Pleasant:

St. Rose (1821-1883)

Nebraska:

St. Bridget (1845-1936)

New Albany:

Holy Trinity (1836-1975) Merged with St. Mary, New Albany, where sacramental records are kept.

Oak Forest:

Franklin Co., St. Cecilia of Rome (Formerly St. Philomena) (1844-2000) Sacramental records are kept at St. Mary of the Rock.

Rome:

St. Peter (1868-1885) Sacramental records are located in the archives.

St. Catherine (1841-1871) Sacramental records are located in the archives.

St. James (1844-1850) Merged with St. Joseph, Perry Co. (1891-1968) and renamed St. Isidore, Perry Co., where sacramental records are kept.

St. Magdalen (1847-1941) Sacramental records kept at St. John, Osgood.

St. Paul (1859-1996) Sacramental records kept at St. Vincent, Shelby Co.

Perry Co.:

St. Peter (See Rome, IN St. Peter.)

St. Rose (1840-1903) Merged with St. Thomas, Knox Co., Diocese of Evansville, where sacramental records are kept.

Salem

St. Mary (1871-1902)

Scipio:

St. Patrick (1841-1958) Sacramental records are located in the archives.

Shelburn:

St. Ann (1909-1978) Sacramental records kept at St. Mary, Sullivan, Diocese of Evansville.

Shirley:

Mother of God (1900-1920) Sacramental records are located in the archives.

Taylorsville (Selvin):

St. Thomas (1845-1875)

Valley Mills:

St. John the Baptist (1855-1903) Sacramental records are located in the archives.

West Baden Springs:

Our Lady of Lourdes (1900-1929)

WEST TERRE HAUTE

St. Leonard of Port Maurice (1912-2011)

Willow Valley:

St. Stephen (1906-1944)

Closed Parish Grade Schools:

Indianapolis:

Assumption, St. Anthony (Consolidated) School, 75 N. Belleview Pl., 46222. Tel: 317-636-3739.

Cathedral, Holy Cross Central School, 125 N. Oriental St., 46201. Tel: 317-638-9068.

Holy Rosary, Holy Rosary Rectory, 520 Stevens St., 46203. Tel: 317-636-4478.

Holy Trinity, St. Anthony (Consolidated) School, 75 N. Belleview Pl., 46222. Tel: 317-636-3739.

Sacred Heart, Sacred Heart Rectory, 1530 Union St., 46225. Tel: 317-638-5551.

St. Ann, St. Ann Rectory, 2862 S. Holt Rd., 46241. Tel: 317-244-3750.

St. Anthony, All Saints Catholic School, 75 N. Belleview Pl., 46222. Tel: 317-636-3739.

St. Bernadette

St. Bridget Sacramental records are located in the archives.

St. Catherine, Central Catholic School, 1155 Cameron St., 46203. Tel: 317-783-7759.

St. Francis de Sales Sacramental records are located in the archives.

St. James the Greater, Central Catholic School, 1155 Cameron St., 46203. Tel: 317-783-7759.

St. Joseph, St. Anthony (Consolidated) School, 75 N. Belleview Pl., 46222. Tel: 317-636-3739.

St. Mary, Holy Cross Central School, 125 N. Oriental St., 46201. Tel: 317-638-9068.

St. Patrick, Central Catholic School, 1155 Cameron St., 46203. Tel: 317-783-7759.

Madison:

St. Mary; St. Michael, Pope John XXIII Grade School, 221 State St., Madison, 47250. Tel: 812-273-3957.

Morris:

St. Anthony, St. Anthony Rectory, P.O. Box 3, Morris, 47033. Tel: 812-934-6218.

New Castle:

St. Anne, St. Anne Rectory, 102 N. 19th St., New Castle, 47362. Tel: 765-529-0933.

Richmond:

Holy Family; St. Andrew; St. Mary, Elizabeth Ann Seton School, 801 W. Main St., Richmond, 47374. Tel: 765-962-4877.

Terre Haute:

St. Ann; St. Joseph, Student Services, Vigo County School Corp., P.O. Box 3703, Terre Haute, 47803. Tel: 812-462-4224.

St. Benedict, Terre Haute. Sacramental records are located in the archives.

St. Margaret Mary, St. Margaret Mary Rectory, 2405 S. Seventh St., Terre Haute, 47802. Tel: 812-232-3512.

Closed High Schools and Academies.

Indianapolis:

Bruté Latin School School records are located in the archives.

Chartrand; Kennedy; Sacred Heart, Roncalli High School, 3300 Prague Rd., 46227. Tel: 317-787-8277.

St. John; St. Agnes; Ladywood; Ladywood / St. Agnes Academies, Sisters of Providence, Records Office - Owens Hall, Saint Mary Of The Woods, 47876. Tel: 812-535-3131.

St. Mary Academy, Registrar, Franciscan Motherhouse. Tel: 812-934-2475.

Beech Grove:

Our Lady of Grace Academy, Our Lady of Grace Monastery, 1402 Southern Ave., Beech Grove, 46107. Tel: 317-787-3287.

Terre Haute:

Central Catholic High School for Girls

St. Patrick High School for Girls

St. Vincent Academy Renamed St. Joseph Academy.

Schulte High School, Student Services, Vigo County School Corp., P.O. Box 3703, Terre Haute, 47803. Tel: 812-462-4224.

Other Closed Institutions:

Indianapolis:

Sisters of the Good Shepherd Convent Sacramental records are located in the archives.

Angel Guardian School for Orphans Entrance records, 1924-1937, are located in the archives.

Marydale School For Girls Sacramental records, 1875-1953, are located in the archives. School records are located in the archives of the Archdiocese of Indianapolis.

New Albany:

St. Edward Hospital, New Albany, Box 766, Mishawaka, 46546. Tel: 219-259-5427.

Terre Haute:

St. Anthony Hospital Baptismal records are located in the archives.

RELIGIOUS INSTITUTES OF MEN REPRESENTED IN THE ARCHDIOCESE

For further details refer to the corresponding bracketed number in the Religious Institutes of Men or Women section.

[0200]—*Benedictine Monks of St. Meinrad*—O.S.B.

[0480]—*Conventual Franciscans* (Our Lady of Consolation Prov.)—O.F.M.Conv

[0520]—*Franciscan Friars (St. John the Baptist & Sacred Heart Province)*—O.F.M.

[]—*Franciscans of the Immaculate*—F.I.

[]—*Glenmary Home Missioners* (Cincinnati, OH)—G.H.M.

[0690]—*Jesuit Fathers and Brothers* (Chicago Prov.)—S.J.

[0430]—*Order of Preachers Central Province*—O.P.

[1065]—*Priestly Fraternity of Saint Peter*—F.S.S.P.

[0420]—*Society of the Divine Word* (Chicago Province)—S.V.D.

RELIGIOUS INSTITUTES OF WOMEN REPRESENTED IN THE ARCHDIOCESE

[0230]—*Benedictine Sisters of Pontifical Jurisdiction* (Ferdinand, IN)—O.S.B.

[]—*Congregation of St. Joseph* (Tipton, IN)—C.S.J.

[1920]—*Congregation of the Sisters of the Holy Cross*—C.S.C.

[1730]—*Congregation of the Sisters of the Third Order of St. Francis, Oldenburg, IN*—O.S.F.

[0760]—*Daughters of Charity of St. Vincent De Paul* (Evansville, IN)—D.C.

[]—*Daughters of Mary Mother of Mercy* (Umuahia, Abia State, Nigeria)—D.M.M.M.

[0420]—*Discalced Carmelite Nuns*—O.C.D.

[1070-03]—*Dominican Sisters*—O.P.

[]—*Franciscan Sisters of the Immaculate Heart of Mary* (Kerala, India)—F.I.H.

[2340]—*Little Sisters of the Poor* (Baltimore, MD)—L.S.P.

[2710]—*Missionaries of Charity*—M.C.

[2820]—*Missionary Sisters of Our Lady of Africa* (American Headquarters, Winooski, VT)—M.S.O.L.A.

[]—*New Evangelization Sisters of Mother of Perpetual Help*—N.E.S.

[]—*Servants of the Gospel of Life*—S.G.L.

[0440]—*Sisters of Charity of Cincinnati, Ohio* (Central Region)—S.C.

[0500]—*Sisters of Charity of Nazareth* (Nazareth, KY)—S.C.N.

[]—*Sisters of Loretto at the Foot of the Cross* (Littleton, CO)

[2990]—*Sisters of Notre Dame* (Toledo, Ohio)—S.N.D.

[3360]—*Sisters of Providence of Saint Mary-of-the-Woods*—S.P.

[]—*Sisters of St. Benedict of Our Lady of Grace Monastery* (Beech Grove, IN)—O.S.B.

[1640]—*Sisters of St. Francis of Perpetual Adoration*—O.S.F.

[3840]—*Sisters of St. Joseph Carondelet* (St. Louis, MO)—C.S.J.

[]—*Sisters Of The Immaculate Heart of Mary Reparatrix* (Kisubi, Uganda)—(I.H.M.R.)

[1720]—*Sisters of the Third Order Regular of St. Francis of the Congregation of Our Lady of Lourdes* (Rochester, MN)—O.S.F.

ARCHDIOCESAN CEMETERIES

INDIANAPOLIS. *Catholic Cemeteries*, 9001 Haverstick Rd., 46240.

Indianapolis South Deanery

Holy Cross Indianapolis

St. Joseph Indianapolis

Calvary Indianapolis

Indianapolis North Deanery

Our Lady of Peace Indianapolis

Indianapolis West Deanery

St. Malachy Brownsburg

St. Malachy Pittsboro

BATESVILLE. *Batesville Deanery*

St. Ann Hamburg

St. Anthony Morris

St. Cecilia Oak Forest

Cemetery (North end of Brookville) Brookville

St. Charles Milan

Holy Family Oldenburg

Holy Family Shrine Oldenburg

Holy Guardian Angels Cedar Grove

Immaculate Conception Millhousen

St. John Dover

St. John Enochsburg

St. John Osgood

St. Joseph St. Leon

St. Joseph Shelbyville

St. Louis Batesville

St. Martin Yorkville

St. Mary Greensburg

St. Mary of the Rock St. Mary of the Rock

St. Maurice Napoleon

St. Maurice St. Maurice

St. Michael Brookville

St. Paul New Alsace

St. Paul St. Paul

St. Peter St. Peter

St. Pius St. Pius

St. Raphael Laurel

St. Vincent de Paul St. Vincent de Paul

BLOOMINGTON. *Bloomington Deanery*

Catholic South of Martinsville

St. Martin Martinsville

Our Lady of Springs French Lick

CONNERSVILLE. *Connersville Deanery*

St. Anne New Castle

St. Andrew Richmond

St. Bridget Liberty

Calvary Rushville

St. Mary Richmond

NEW ALBANY. *New Albany Deanery*

St. Anthony Jeffersonville

St. Bernard Frenchtown

St. Bernard, Old Frenchtown

Cemetery Southwest of Bradford

St. Francis Henryville

Holy Trinity New Albany

St. Joachim Locust Point

St. John Starlight

St. Joseph Corydon

St. Joseph St. Joseph Hill

St. Mary Lanesville

St. Mary New Albany

St. Mary Navilleton

St. Mary of the Knobs Floyds Knobs

Mary, Queen of Heaven Jeffersonville

St. Michael Bradford

St. Michael Charlestown

St. Michael Dogwood

Most Precious Blood New Middleton

St. Peter Taylor Township

SEYMOUR. *Seymour Deanery*

St. Ambrose Seymour

St. Anne Jennings Co.

St. Anthony China

St. Bridget Nebraska

St. Catherine of Siena St. Catherine

St. Dennis Jennings Co.

St. Joseph Madison

St. Joseph St. Joseph

St. Magdalen Madison

St. Mary North Vernon

Old St. James St. James

St. Patrick Madison

St. Patrick Salem

St. Patrick Scipio

TELL CITY. *Tell City Deanery*

St. Augustine Leopold

St. Boniface Fulda

Cemetery, St. Croix. Cemetery on original parish site. St. Croix

Holy Cross St. Croix

St. Isidore Bristow

St. John St. John

St. Joseph Milltown

St. Joseph St. Croix

St. Joseph St. Joseph

St. Martin Siberia

St. Mary Derby

St. Mary Tell City

St. Meinrad St. Meinrad

St. Michael Cannelton

Old St. Patrick Cannelton

St. Paul Cemetery Tell City

St. Peter Cannelton

TERRE HAUTE. *Terre Haute Deanery*

Annunciation Brazil

Catholic Armiesburg

Calvary Terre Haute

Greek Catholic Perth

Immaculate Conception Montezuma

St. John Greek Diamond

St. Joseph Terre Haute

St. Mary-of-the-Woods St. Mary-of-the-Woods

NECROLOGY

† Kern, Rev. Msgr. Joseph R., (Retired)—Died April 16, 2011

† Arneson, James E., (Retired)—Died Oct. 23, 2011

† Quinn, Donald A., Greenwood IN Our Lady Of The Greenwood Catholic Church, Inc.—Died Nov. 13, 2011

Diocese of Jackson

(Dioecesis Jacksoniensis)

Most Reverend

JOSEPH N. LATINO

Bishop of Jackson; ordained May 25, 1963; appointed Bishop of Jackson January 3, 2003; consecrated March 7, 2003. *Mailing Address: P.O. Box 2248, Jackson, MS 39225-2248.*

Most Reverend

WILLIAM R. HOUCK, D.D.

Retired Bishop of Jackson; ordained May 19, 1951; appointed Auxiliary Bishop of Jackson and Titular Bishop of Allessano on March 28, 1979; consecrated May 27, 1979; appointed Bishop of Jackson April 24, 1984; installed June 5, 1984; retired January 3, 2003. *Mailing Address: Catholic Diocese of Jackson, P.O. Box 2248, Jackson, MS 39225-2248.*

Chancery Office: 237 E. Amite St., P.O. Box 2248, Jackson, MS 39225-2248. Tel: 601-969-1880; Fax: 601-960-8455.

Web: www.jacksondiocese.org

Email: chancery@jacksondiocese.org

Square Miles 37,643.

Established July 28, 1837 as Diocese of Natchez. Name changed to Diocese of Natchez-Jackson, March 7, 1957. Name changed to Diocese of Jackson, June 6, 1977.

Comprises 65 Counties in the State of Mississippi, namely: Adams, Alcorn, Amite, Attala, Benton, Bolivar, Calhoun, Carroll, Chickasaw, Choctaw, Claiborne, Clarke, Clay, Coahoma, Copiah, De Soto, Franklin, Grenada, Hinds, Holmes, Humphreys, Issaquena, Itawamba, Jasper, Jefferson, Kemper, Lafayette, Lauderdale, Leake, Lee, Leflore, Lincoln, Lowndes, Madison, Marshall, Monroe, Montgomery, Neshoba, Newton, Noxubee, Oktibbeha, Panola, Pike, Pontotoc, Prentiss, Quitman, Rankin, Scott, Sharkey, Simpson, Smith, Sunflower, Tallahatchie, Tate, Tippah, Tishomingo, Tunica, Union, Warren, Washington, Webster, Wilkinson, Winston, Yalobusha and Yazoo.

Legal Title: "Catholic Diocese of Jackson".

STATISTICAL OVERVIEW

Personnel	
Bishop	1
Retired Bishops	1
Priests: Diocesan Active in Diocese	34
Priests: Diocesan Active Outside Diocese	1
Priests: Retired, Sick or Absent	16
Number of Diocesan Priests	51
Religious Priests in Diocese	33
Total Priests in Diocese	84
Extern Priests in Diocese	1
Ordinations:	
Transitional Deacons	1
Permanent Deacons in Diocese	7
Total Brothers	7
Total Sisters	156
Parishes	
Parishes	75
With Resident Pastor:	
Resident Diocesan Priests	29
Resident Religious Priests	12
Without Resident Pastor:	
Administered by Priests	16
Administered by Deacons	1
Administered by Religious Women	3
Administered by Lay People	7
Administered by Pastoral Teams, etc.	4
Completely Vacant	3
Missions	23
Professional Ministry Personnel:	
Brothers	1
Sisters	9
Lay Ministers	29
Welfare	
Catholic Hospitals	1
Total Assisted	134,279
Health Care Centers	1
Total Assisted	8,458
Homes for the Aged	1
Total Assisted	450
Residential Care of Children	2
Total Assisted	342
Day Care Centers	2
Total Assisted	202
Specialized Homes	6
Total Assisted	4,877
Special Centers for Social Services	17
Total Assisted	17,897
Residential Care of Disabled	3
Total Assisted	63
Other Institutions	3
Total Assisted	78
Educational	
Diocesan Students in Other Seminaries	9
Total Seminarians	9
Colleges and Universities	2
Total Students	20
High Schools, Diocesan and Parish	4
Total Students	1,210
Elementary Schools, Diocesan and Parish	15
Total Students	3,355
Catechesis/Religious Education:	
High School Students	1,310
Elementary Students	4,097
Total Students under Catholic Instruction	10,001
Teachers in the Diocese:	
Brothers	3
Sisters	10
Lay Teachers	437
Vital Statistics	
Receptions into the Church:	
Infant Baptism Totals	826
Minor Baptism Totals	94
Adult Baptism Totals	76
Received into Full Communion	208
First Communions	853
Confirmations	364
Marriages:	
Catholic	95
Interfaith	108
Total Marriages	203
Deaths	437
Total Catholic Population	48,831
Total Population	2,111,593

Former Bishops—Rt. Revs. JOHN J. CHANCHE, S.S., D.D., ord. June 5, 1819; cons. March 14, 1841; died July 22, 1852; J. O. VAN DE VELDE, S.J., D.D., ord. Sept. 25, 1827; appt. Bishop of Chicago Dec. 1, 1848; ord. Feb. 11, 1849; appt. Bishop of Natchez July 29, 1853; died Nov. 13, 1855.; Most Revs. WILLIAM HENRY ELDER, D.D., cons. May 3, 1857; transferred to Cincinnati, 1880; died Oct. 31, 1904; FRANCIS JANSSENS, D.D., cons. May 1, 1881; transferred to New Orleans, Aug. 7, 1888; died June 9, 1897; Rt. Revs. THOMAS HESLIN, D.D., ord. Sept. 18, 1869; cons. June 18, 1889; died Feb. 22, 1911; JOHN EDWARD GUNN, S.M., D.D., ord. Feb. 2, 1890; cons. Aug. 29, 1911; died Feb. 19, 1924; Most Revs. RICHARD OLIVER GEROW, LL.D., S.T.D., ord. June 5, 1909; appt. June 25, 1924; cons. Oct. 15, 1924; retired Dec. 2, 1967; died Dec. 20, 1976; JOSEPH B. BRUNINI, D.D., LL.D., J.C.D., ord. Dec. 5, 1933; cons. Jan. 29, 1957; appt. Bishop, Dec. 2, 1967; installed Jan. 29, 1968; retired Jan. 24, 1984; died Jan. 7, 1996; WILLIAM R. HOUCK, D.D. (Retired), ord. May 19, 1951; appt. Auxiliary Bishop of Jackson and Titular Bishop of Allessano on March 28, 1979; cons. May 27, 1979; appt. Bishop of Jackson April 24, 1984; installed June 5, 1984; retired Jan. 3, 2003.

Chancery Office—237 E. Amite St., P.O. Box 2248, Jackson, 39225-2248. Tel: 601-969-1880; Fax: 601-960-8455. The telephone number for all Diocesan Offices is 601-969-1880, unless otherwise listed. Office Hours: 8:30-4:30.

Office of the Bishop—Most Rev. JOSEPH N. LATINO, 237 E. Amite St., P.O. Box 2248, Jackson, 39225-2248.

Office of Vicar General—Rev. Msgrs. ELVIN SUNDS; MICHAEL FLANNERY, J.C.L.

Department of Ecclesiastical Affairs—

Chancellor—Rev. Msgr. ELVIN SUNDS, 237 E. Amite St., P.O. Box 2248, Jackson, 39225-2248.

Vice Chancellor—Very Rev. JEFFREY WALDREP, S.T.L., J.C.L.

Office of Child Protection—Mrs. VICKIE CAROLLO.

Office of Vocations—Revs. ANTHONY QUYET, Dir.; LENIN VARGAS, Asst. Dir.

Youth Ministry—Ms. KATHIE CURTIS, Diocesan Dir.

Campus Ministry—FRAN LAVELLE, Dir.

Parish Pastoral Councils—Rev. Msgr. ELVIN SUNDS, Dir.

Black Catholic Ministry—Mr. WILL JEMISON, Dir.

Hispanic Ministry—Bro. THEODORE DAUSCH, C.F.C., Dir.

Director of Permanent Diaconate—VACANT.

Propagation of the Faith—Rev. Msgr. ELVIN SUNDS, Dir., Mailing Address: P.O. Box 2248, Jackson, 39225-2248.

Archivist—Miss MARY WOODWARD.

Judicial Vicar—Very Rev. JEFFREY WALDREP, S.T.L., J.C.L.

Adjutant Judicial Vicar—Rev. KEVIN SLATTERY, J.C.L.

Engaged Encounter—Very Rev. JEFFREY WALDREP, S.T.L., J.C.L., Dir.

Ecumenism—Miss MARY WOODWARD.

Continuing Formation Committee—Revs. DAVID O'CONNOR, Chm.; GERARD HURLEY; JOHN BOHN; KEVIN SLATTERY, J.C.L.; SCOTT THOMAS; BRIAN KASKIE; Rev. Msgr. ELVIN SUNDS, Ex Officio; Mrs. PAMELA MINNINGER; Miss MARY WOODWARD.

Promoter of Justice—Rev. Msgr. MICHAEL FLANNERY, J.C.L.
Defenders of the Bond—Rev. Msgr. MICHAEL FLANNERY, J.C.L.; Rev. THOMAS MCGING, J.C.L. at First Instance; Sr. JOYCE HOBEN, S.N.D.N., J.C.L.
Notaries—Rev. MICHAEL O'BRIEN; MARYBETH RABERT.
Diocesan Judges—Very Rev. JEFFREY WALDREP, S.T.L., J.C.L.; Rev. KEVIN SLATTERY, J.C.L.; MARY TARVER, J.C.L.
Approved Advocate and Auditors—Rev. Msgr. PATRICK FARRELL; Revs. JOHN BOHN; CHARLES BUCCIANTINI; FRANCIS J. COSGROVE; BRIAN KASKIE; JOSEPH TONOS; MATTHEW P. SIMMONS.
Priests' Council—Most Rev. JOSEPH N. LATINO, Pres.; Rev. Msgr. ELVIN SUNDS, Sec.; Very Rev. JEFFREY WALDREP, S.T.L., J.C.L., Treas.; Revs. MICHAEL O'BRIEN; JOSEPH DYER; LINCOLN DALL; THOMAS LALOR; DAVID O'CONNOR; SAMUEL MESSINA, Chm.; GREGORY PLATA, O.F.M.; SCOTT THOMAS; KENT BOWLDS; BRIAN KASKIE; FRANCIS J. COSGROVE.
Diocesan Consultors—Most Rev. JOSEPH N. LATINO, Pres.; Rev. Msgr. MICHAEL FLANNERY, J.C.L.; Revs. FRANCIS J. COSGROVE; THOMAS LALOR; MICHAEL O'BRIEN; KEVIN SLATTERY, J.C.L.; Rev. Msgrs. ELVIN SUNDS, (Ex Officio); PATRICK FARRELL.
Association of Priests—Most Revs. JOSEPH N. LATINO, Co-Chm.; ROGER P. MORIN, Co-Chm.; Rev. Msgr. MICHAEL THORNTON, Pres.; Rev. THOMAS MCGING, J.C.L., Sec.-Treas. & Pres.-Elect. Trustees: Revs. CHARLES BUCCIANTINI; THOMAS CONWAY; PATRICK MOCKLER; Rev. Msgr. PATRICK FARRELL.
Diocesan Pastoral Council—Most Rev. JOSEPH N. LATINO, Pres.
Personnel Board—Rev. Msgr. ELVIN SUNDS, Personnel Dir.; Revs. BRIAN KASKIE; WILLIAM F. HENRY; MICHAEL O'BRIEN; THOMAS MCGING, J.C.L.; GERARD HURLEY.
Department of Administration & Finance—Mr. AAD DE LANGE, Dir., Admin. Affairs, 237 E. Amite St., P.O. Box 2248, Jackson, 39225-2248.
Department of Stewardship - Development—Mrs. REBECCA HARRIS, Dir.
Catholic Foundation—Mrs. REBECCA HARRIS, Dir., 237 E. Amite St., P.O. Box 2248, Jackson, 39225-2248.
Department of Catholic Charities and Community Services—
Catholic Charities, Inc.—Mr. GREGORY PATIN, Dir., 200 N. Congress, Ste. 100, Jackson, 39201. Tel: 601-355-8634; Fax: 601-960-8493. Mailing Address: P.O. Box 2248, Jackson, 39225-2248.
Parish-Based Ministries—MICHAEL ANN OROPEZA, Dir. Parish Social Ministry. Tel: 601-355-8634; JENNIFER EIDT, Dir. Family Ministry.
Peace and Justice—Mr. GREGORY PATIN, Dir., Mailing Address: P.O. Box 2248, Jackson, 39225-2248.
Victim Assistance Coordinator—Ms. VALERIE MCCLELLAN. Tel: 601-326-3728.
Department of Formational Ministries—Sr. DEBORAH HUGHES, S.S.J., Dir., 237 E. Amite St., P.O. Box 2248, Jackson, 39225-2248.
Superintendent of Schools—Sr. DEBORAH HUGHES, S.S.J.
Assistant Superintendent—Ms. CATHERINE D. COOK.
Director of Faith Formation—Ms. JEANNE HOWARD.
Director of Spring Hill Theology Program—Ms. JEANNE HOWARD.
Holy Childhood Pontifical Association—Ms. CATHERINE D. COOK, Dir.
Early Child Development, Health and Education Projects—Sr. DEBORAH HUGHES, S.S.J.
Department of Evangelization—Miss MARY WOODWARD, Dir.
Charismatic Renewal—Rev. WILLIAM F. HENRY.
Cursillo Movement—Rev. DANIEL GALLAGHER, Spiritual Dir.
"Mississippi Catholic"—JANNA AVALON, Editor.

CLERGY, PARISHES, MISSIONS AND PAROCHIAL SCHOOLS

CITY OF JACKSON

(HINDS COUNTY)

1—ST. PETER CATHEDRAL (1846) Very Rev. Jeffrey Waldrep, Rector.
Res.: 123 N. West St., P.O. Box 57, 39205-0057. Tel: 601-969-3125; Fax: 601-969-3130. Web: cathedralsaintpeter.org.
Catechesis/Religious Program—Ferrell Tadlock, D.R.E. Students 50.

2—CHRIST THE KING (1945) Revs. Anthony Quyet; Mario Solorzano; Rhoda Kalscheur, Pastoral Min.
Res.: 2303 John R. Lynch St., 39209. Tel: 601-948-8867.
School—Sister Thea Bowman School, (Grades PreK-6), 1217 Hattiesburg St., 39209-7411. Tel: 601-352-5441; Fax: 601-352-5136. Gladys Shae Goodman-Robinson, Prin. Students 40.
Catechesis/Religious Program—Mrs. Frankie Bradley, D.R.E. Students 28.

3—HOLY FAMILY (1957) Revs. Darrell C. Kelly, S.V.D.; Francis Damoah, S.V.D.; Sr. Eileen Hauswald, O.S.F., Pastoral Assoc.
Church: 820 Forest Ave., 39206-3299. Tel: 601-362-1888; Fax: 601-362-1134. Email: holyfamilycc@comcast.net. Web: www.holyfamilyccjackson.org.
Catechesis/Religious Program—Joyce Adams, C.R.E.; Gladys Russell, C.R.E. Students 52.

4—HOLY GHOST (1908) Revs. Darrell C. Kelly, S.V.D.; Francis Damoah, S.V.D.
Res.: 1151 Cloister St., 39202. Tel: 601-353-1339; Fax: 601-353-9607.

5—ST. MARY (1948) Revs. Anthony Quyet; Mario Solorzano.
Res.: 653 Claiborne Ave., 39209. Tel: 601-353-2292; Fax: 601-354-3716.
Catechesis/Religious Program—Mrs. Frankie Bradley, D.R.E. Students 32.

6—ST. RICHARD OF CHICHESTER (1953) Revs. Michael O'Brien; Brian Carroll, Senior Priest. In Res., Rev. Msgr. Elvin Sunds.
Church: 1242 Lynnwood Dr., P.O. Box 16547, 39206. Tel: 601-366-2335; Fax: 601-366-0438. Web: www.saintrichard.com.
School—(Grades PreK-6), 100 Holly Dr., 39206. Tel: 601-366-1157; Fax: 601-366-4344. Web: www-.strichardschool.com. Jules Michel, Prin.; Paulette Cockrell, Librarian. Lay Teachers 52; Students 392.
St. Richard's School Special Kids Program— Lay Teachers 4; Students 11.
Catechesis/Religious Program—Kimberly Turner, C.R.E. Students 182.

7—ST. THERESE (1955) Rev. William F. Henry.
Church: 309 McDowell Rd., P.O. Box 8642, 39284-8642. Tel: 601-372-4481; Fax: 601-376-0094.
School—(Grades PreK-7) Tel: 601-372-3323; Fax: 601-372-3365. Carol McWilliams, Prin.; Julie Owen, Librarian. Lay Teachers 10; Students 101.
Catechesis/Religious Program—Ingrid Piernas, C.R.E. Students 24.

OUTSIDE THE CITY OF JACKSON

ABERDEEN, MONROE CO., ST. FRANCIS OF ASSISI (1977) Rev. Vincent Burns; Susan Sweet, Pastoral Assoc.
Res. & Church: 108 S. James St., P.O. Box 134, 39730-0134. Tel: 662-319-6657. Email: stfa@juno.com.
Catechesis/Religious Program—Students 7.
Mission—Immaculate Heart of Mary (1942) P.O. Box 309, Houston, Chickasaw Co. 38851. Tel: 662-456-5450. Sr. Pat Hinton, O.S.F., Pastoral Min.; Walter Fircowycz, Hispanic Min.
Chapel—St. Theresa 116 N. Fleming St., Okolona, Chickasaw Co. 38860.

AMORY, MONROE CO., ST. HELEN (1977) Sr. Lael Niblick, C.S.A., Lay Ecclesial Min.
Res.: 401 Eighth Ave. S., P.O. Box 97, 38821-0097. Tel: 662-256-8392; Fax: 662-256-8392 (call first).
Catechesis/Religious Program—Nancy Hoang, D.R.E. Students 33.

BATESVILLE, PANOLA CO., ST. MARY (1960) Rev. Samuel Messina.
Res.: 120 Hwy. 35 N., P.O. Box 569, 38606-0569. Tel: 662-563-2273; Fax: 662-563-9788. Email: saintmarycc@bellsouth.net. Web: www.stmarysstjohn.org.
Catechesis/Religious Program—Tel: 662-563-1197. Sharon Hodge, C.R.E. Students 44.
Mission—St. John the Baptist 110 N. Main St., Sardis, Panola Co. 38666.

BELZONI, HUMPHREYS CO., ALL SAINTS (1953) Rev. Lincoln Dall.
Church: 200 Bowles St., 39038-3602. Tel: 662-247-1408.
Catechesis/Religious Program—Joy Bellipanna, D.R.E. Students 6.

BOONEVILLE, PRENTISS CO., ST. FRANCIS OF ASSISI (1962) Rev. Richard Smith; Sheila B. Przesmicki, Pastoral Min.
Church: 721 N. College St., P.O. Box 654, 38829. Tel: 662-728-7509; Fax: 662-728-7509. Email: stfrancisbv@att.net. Web: stfrancisbooneville.com.
Res.: 200 Washington St., 38829. Tel: 662-728-2257.
Catechesis/Religious Program—Students 11.
Mission—St. Mary 205 Eastport St. E., P.O. Box 651, Iuka, Tishomingo Co. 38852. Tel: 662-423-9358; Fax: 662-423-9358.

BROOKHAVEN, LINCOLN CO., ST. FRANCIS (1887) Rev. Matthew P. Simmons.
Res.: 227 E. Cherokee St., P.O. Box 196, 39602. Tel: 601-833-1799. Web: www.stfrancisbrookhaven.org.
Catechesis/Religious Program—Tel: 601-833-2709. Sue Junkin, D.R.E. Students 86.
Mission—St. Ann Meadville, Franklin Co.

BRUCE, CALHOUN CO., ST. LUKE THE EVANGELIST (1997) Deborah A. Holmes, Lay Ecclesial Min.
Church: 209 W. Calhoun St., P.O. Box 230, 38915-0230. Tel: 662-983-4600; Fax: 662-983-4600. Web: catholicweb.com.
Catechesis/Religious Program—Students 23.

CAMDEN, MADISON CO., SACRED HEART (1850) Rev. Michael Barth, S.T.
Res.: 1493 Hwy. 17, 39045-9524. Tel: 662-468-2354; 662-468-0550; Fax: 662-468-2488. Web: www.sacredheartcamden.com.
Parish Center - Sacred Heart Family Center: 1493 Hwy. 17, 39045.
Catechesis/Religious Program—Students 50.

CANTON, MADISON CO.

1—HOLY CHILD JESUS (1946) Revs. Michael Barth, S.T.; Onwuham Akpa, O.Praem.
Church: 315 Garrett St., P.O. Box 366, 39046. Tel: 601-859-2957; Fax: 601-859-8011. Email: schccanton@bellsouth.net.
School—(Grades PreK-2), 315 Garrett St., 39046. Tel: 601-859-4168; Fax: 601-859-4140. Ms. Jacqueline Smith Lacey, Prin. Sisters 1; Lay Teachers 3; Students 50.
Catechesis/Religious Program—Sacred Heart Parish Center, 238 E. Center St., 39046. Sr. Mary Anne Poeschl, R.S.M., D.R.E.

2—SACRED HEART (1859) Revs. Kevin Slattery; Onwuham Akpa, O.Praem.
Res.: 238 E. Center St., P.O. Box 361, 39046-0361. Tel: 601-859-3749; Fax: 601-859-8011. Email: schccanton@bellsouth.net.
Catechesis/Religious Program—Sr. Mary Anne Poeschl, R.S.M., D.R.E. Students 282.

CARTHAGE, LEAKE CO., ST. ANNE (1954) [CEM] Sr. Patricia Godri, S.C., Lay Ecclesial Min.; Rev. Jeremy Tobin, O.Praem., Sacramental Min.
Res.: 207 Red Dog Rd., 39051. Tel: 601-267-7190; Fax: 601-267-7190.
Catechesis/Religious Program—Students 115.

CHARLESTON, TALLAHATCHIE CO., ST. JOHN (1973) Bro. Senan Gallagher, S.T., Deacon Ecclesial Min.
Church: 304 W. Cypress St., P.O. Box 30, 38921-0030. Tel: 662-647-3170.
Catechesis/Religious Program—Students 2.

CHATAWA, PIKE CO., ST. TERESA (1868) Rev. Brian Kaskie.
Church: P.O. Box 67, 39632-0067. Tel: 601-684-5648.
Mission—St. James Bay St., Magnolia, Pike Co. 39652.

CLARKSDALE, COAHOMA CO.

1—ST. ELIZABETH (1891) Rev. Scott Dugas.
Res.: 130 Florence Ave., 38614-2720. Tel: 662-624-4301; Fax: 662-627-7856.
School—(Grades PreK-6), 150 Florence Ave., 38614-2720. Tel: 662-624-4239; Fax: 662-624-2072. Email: stliz1@bellsouth.net. Mrs. Elizabeth Scarbrough, Prin.; Georgette Sabbatini, Librarian. Lay Teachers 9; Students 103.
Catechesis/Religious Program—Maria Fyfe, D.R.E. Students 60.

2—IMMACULATE CONCEPTION (1945) Rev. Scott Dugas.
Res.: 510 Ritchie Ave., 38614. Tel: 662-624-4029.

CLEVELAND, BOLIVAR CO., OUR LADY OF VICTORIES (1924) Rev. Kent Bowlds.
Res.: 215 Bishop Rd., P.O. Box 1450, 38732-1450. Tel: 662-846-6273; Fax: 662-846-6270. Email: olvcc@tecinfo.ocm.
Catechesis/Religious Program—Melanie Bray, D.R.E. Students 143.
Station—Delta State University

CLINTON, HINDS CO., HOLY SAVIOR (1966) Rev. Thomas McGing.
Church: 714 Lindale St., P.O. Box 85, 39060-0085. Tel: 601-924-6344; Fax: 601-924-6344. Web: www.exceedtech.net/~holysavior.
Catechesis/Religious Program—Tel: 601-924-6344; Fax: 601-924-6344. Dena Kinsey, D.R.E. Students 117.
Mission—Immaculate Conception Raymond, Hinds Co. Rev. Richard P. Chiles, O.Praem.

COLUMBUS, LOWNDES CO., ANNUNCIATION (1863) Rev. Robert Dore.
Res.: 823 College St., 39701. Tel: 662-328-2927; Fax: 662-329-8270.
School—(Grades K-7), 223 N. Browder St., 39702-5236. Tel: 662-328-4479; Fax: 662-328-0430. Mrs. Joni House, Prin. Lay Teachers 14; Students 128.

CORINTH, ALCORN CO., ST. JAMES (1956) Rev. Richard Smith.
Church: 3189 Harper Rd., P.O. Box 660, 38835-0660. Tel: 662-287-1051; Fax: 662-287-1051 (call ahead). Email: stjamesc@comcast.net. Web: www.stjamescorinth.org.
Res.: 3187 Harper Rd., P.O. Box 660, 38835-0660. Tel: 662-287-1385.
Catechesis/Religious Program—Linda Gunther, D.R.E.; Peggie Clapp, C.R.E. Students 60.

CRYSTAL SPRINGS, COPIAH CO., ST. JOHN THE EVANGELIST (1953) Rev. Thomas Delaney, Sacramental Min.; Janice Stansell, Lay Ecclesial Min.
Church: 221 E. Georgetown St., P.O. Box 167, 39059-0167. Tel: 601-892-1717; Fax: 601-892-0746.
Rectory—221 E. Georgetown St., 39059.
Catechesis/Religious Program—Students 21.
Mission—St. Martin 113 E. Conway, Hazlehurst, Copiah Co. 39083.

EUPORA, WEBSTER CO., ST. JOHN NEUMANN (1990) Sr. Alies Therese, Lay Ecclesial Min.; Mr. Lorenzo Aju, Pastoral Min.
Church: 2620 W. Roane Ave., 39744. Tel: 662-258-7539; Fax: 662-258-7539 (call ahead). Email: stjohnseupora@yahoo.com.
Catechesis/Religious Program—Mr. Lorenzo Aju, D.R.E. Students 20.

FAYETTE, JEFFERSON CO., ST. ANNE (1969) Very Rev. James Fallon, S.S.J.; Rev. George Burden, S.S.J., Parochial Vicar.
Church: 89 Harriston Rd., P.O. Box 159, 39069. Tel: 601-445-5700; Fax: 601-442-6030.
Catechesis/Religious Program—Belinda Nickels, D.R.E. Students 12.

FLOWOOD, RANKIN CO., ST. PAUL (1978) Rev. Gerard Hurley.
Church: 5971 Hwy. 25, 39232-7101. Tel: 601-992-9547; Fax: 601-992-9972. Email: office@saintpaulcatholicchurch.com. Web: www.saintpaulcatholicchurch.com.
Res.: 108 Twin Oaks Dr., Brandon, 39047.
Learning Center—5969 Hwy. 25, 39232. Tel: 601-992-2876; Fax: 601-992-8741. Darlene Scanlon, Dir. Students 115.
Catechesis/Religious Program—Sarah O'Donnell, C.R.E. Students 300.

FOREST, SCOTT CO., ST. MICHAEL (1957) Rev. Joseph Dyer.
Church: P.O. Box 388, 39074. Tel: 601-469-1916; Fax: 601-469-1815.
Res.: 1352 E. Third St., 39074.
Catechesis/Religious Program—Students 40.
Mission—St. Anne 608 Decatur St., Newton, Newton Co. 39045.
Station—Centro San Martin De Porres Hwy. 80 W., Morton, 39117.

GLUCKSTADT, MADISON CO., ST. JOSEPH (1905) Rev. Kevin Slattery, Sacramental Min.; Mrs. Pamela Minninger, Lay Ecclesial Min.
127 Church Rd., 39110. Tel: 601-856-2054; Fax: 601-856-2029. Email: stjoegluckstadt@bellsouth.net. Web: stjosephgluckstadt.com.
Catechesis/Religious Program—Karen Worrell, C.R.E. Students 133.

GREENVILLE, WASHINGTON CO.

1—ST. JOSEPH (1868) Rev. Richard Somers. In Res., Rev. Frank Corcoran (Retired).
Res.: 410 Main St., P.O. Box 1220, 38702-1220. Tel: 662-335-5251; Fax: 662-332-1178.
School—Our Lady of Lourdes, (Grades PreK-6), 1600 E. Reed St., 38703-7229. Tel: 662-334-3287; Fax: 662-332-9877. Mrs. Michelle Gardiner, Prin. Sisters 2; Lay Teachers 23; Students 285.
High School—Junior & Senior High School, (Grades 7-12), 1501 VFW Rd., 38701-5841. Tel: 662-378-9711; Fax: 662-378-3496. Mr. Paul Artman, Prin. Students 245.

2—SACRED HEART (1913) Revs. Thomas A. Mullally, S.V.D.; Pius Lawe, S.V.D.
Res.: 560 E. Gloster St., 38701-3836. Tel: 662-332-0891; Fax: 662-332-0891. Email: mullally42@yahoo.com. Web: www.shcc-greenville.org.
Catechesis/Religious Program—Students 30.

GREENWOOD, LEFLORE CO.

1—ST. FRANCIS OF ASSISI (1951) Revs. Gregory Plata, O.F.M.; Robert Konopa, O.F.M. In Res., Rev. William Stout, O.F.M.
Res.: 2613 Hwy. 82 E., 38930-5966. Tel: 662-453-0623; Fax: 662-453-1366. Email: themission@bellsouth.net.
School—(Grades PreK-6), 2607 Hwy. 82 E., 38930-5966. Tel: 662-453-9511. Email: stfran@bellsouth.net. Web: www.stfrancisassisi-.com. Sr. Mary Ann Tupy, O.S.F., Prin.; Sandra Sims, Librarian. Sisters 2; Lay Teachers 10; Students 120.
Catechesis/Religious Program—(Combined with Immaculate Heart of Mary, Greenwood)
Convent—Franciscan Sisters of Christian Charity, 2603 Hwy. 82 E., 38930-5966. Tel: 662-453-1221; Fax: 662-453-9060.

2—IMMACULATE HEART OF MARY (1909) Revs. Gregory Plata, O.F.M.; William Stout, O.F.M.
Church: 511 W. Washington St., P.O. Box 313, 38935-0313. Tel: 662-453-3980.
Parish Center/Church Office—310 Henderson St., 38935-0313. Fax: 662-453-0399.
Catechesis/Religious Program—Students 51.

GRENADA, GRENADA CO., ST. PETER (1943) Rev. Martin Ruane.
Res.: 320 College Blvd., 38901-3808. Tel: 662-226-2490.
Catechesis/Religious Program—Donna Mumme, D.R.E. Students 85.

HERNANDO, DESOTO CO., HOLY SPIRIT (1961) Revs. Robert Tucker, S.C.J., Moderator; Gregory Schill, S.C.J.; Edward J. Zemlik, S.C.J.
Church: 545 E. Commerce St., P.O. Box 424, 38632-0424. Tel: 662-429-7851; Fax: 662-429-7882. Email: holyspiritchurch@shsm.org. Web: www.holyspirit-catholic.com.
Catechesis/Religious Program—Tel: 662-429-3467. Amanda Ready, C.R.E. Students 124.

HOLLY SPRINGS, MARSHALL CO., ST. JOSEPH (1857) Rev. Leonard F. Elder, S.C.J.
Church: 305 E. Van Dorn Ave., P.O. Box 430, 38635-0430. Tel: 662-252-3138; Fax: 662-252-3138.
School—Holy Family School, (Grades PreK-8), 395 N. West St., 38635-1922. Tel: 662-252-1612; Fax: 662-252-3694. Clara Isom, Prin. Sisters 1; Lay Teachers 20; Students 185.
Catechesis/Religious Program—Students 196.

INDIANOLA, SUNFLOWER CO.

1—ST. BENEDICT THE MOOR (1953) Rev. Tarsisius Puling, S.V.D.
Res.: 403 Church Ave., P.O. Box 407, 38751. Tel: 662-887-4659.
Catechesis/Religious Program—Rosemary Miller, D.R.E. Students 11.

2—IMMACULATE CONCEPTION (1955) Rev. Tarsisius Puling, S.V.D.
Res.: 700 N. Sunflower Ext. Hwy. 448, P.O. Box 944, 38751-9665. Tel: 662-887-4659.
Catechesis/Religious Program—Rosemary Miller, D.R.E. Students 26.

KOSCIUSKO, ATTALA CO., ST. THERESE (1956) Barbara A. Sturbaum, Lay Ecclesial Min.
Res.: 108 Bell St., P.O. Box 628, 39090. Tel: 662-289-1193.
Catechesis/Religious Program—Students 20.

LELAND, WASHINGTON CO., ST. JAMES (1944) Rev. Charles Bucciantini.
Res.: 312 E. Third St., P.O. Box 352, 38756-0352. Tel: 662-686-7352; Fax: 662-686-7352. Email: stjamesch@yahoo.com.
Catechesis/Religious Program—Students 5.
Mission—Immaculate Conception Hwy. 12 E., Hollandale, Washington Co. 38748.
Mission—Our Mother of Mercy 119 Jefferson St., Anguilla, Sharkey Co. 38721.

LEXINGTON, HOLMES CO., ST. THOMAS (1966) Rev. Gregory Plata, O.F.M., Admin.
Church: 200 Boulevard St., 39095. Tel: 662-283-9092; Fax: 662-453-9060.
Catechesis/Religious Program—Students 11.
Mission—Sacred Heart 304 Jones St., Winona, Montgomery Co. 38967. Rev. Gregory Plata, O.F.M., Sacramental Min.; Mr. Marvin Edwards, Lay Ecclesial Min.
Station—Mississippi State Penitentiary Parchman, 38738.

LOUISVILLE, WINSTON CO., SACRED HEART (1966) Barbara A. Sturbaum, Lay Ecclesial Min.
Res.: 410 Spring Ave., 39339. Tel: 662-773-6062.
Catechesis/Religious Program—Students 7.

MADISON, MADISON CO., ST. FRANCIS OF ASSISI (1983) Rev. Msgr. Michael Flannery; Rev. Scott Thomas. In Res., Rev. Alfred L. Camp (Retired).
Office: 4000 W. Tidewater Ln., 39110-8942. Tel: 601-856-5556; Fax: 601-856-2849. Web: www.stfrancismadison.org.
School—St. Anthony Catholic School, (Grades PreK-6), 1585 Old Mannsdale Rd., 39110. Tel: 601-607-7054; Fax: 601-853-9687. Angela Brunini, Prin.; Vicki Moorehead, Librarian. Lay Teachers 41; Students 283.
Learning Center—Tel: 601-856-9494. Sr. Paula Blouin, S.S.N.D., Dir. Students 168.
Catechesis/Religious Program—Mary Catherine George, D.R.E.; Theresa Prejean, D.R.E. & RCIA Coord. Students 300.

MAGEE, SIMPSON CO., ST. STEPHEN (1968) Mrs. Eula Purvis, Lay Ecclesial Min.
Res.: 594 Simpson Hwy. 149, P.O. Box 427, 39111-0427. Tel: 601-849-3237; Fax: 601-849-3398.
Catechesis/Religious Program—Alicia Keith, D.R.E. Tel: 601-849-3539. Students 24.

MCCOMB, PIKE CO., ST. ALPHONSUS (1876) Rev. Brian Kaskie.
Church: 509 Delaware Ave., P.O. Box 1105, 39649. Tel: 601-684-5648; Fax: 601-684-1924.
Elementary and Preschool—(Grades PreK-6), 104 S. 5th St., 39648. Tel: 601-684-1843; Fax: 601-684-1831. Mrs. Tammy Mabile, Prin. Students 200.
Catechesis/Religious Program—Annette Gabler, D.R.E. Students 231.

MERIDIAN, LAUDERDALE CO.

1—ST. JOSEPH (1910) Rev. Francis J. Cosgrove; Edgar Hernandez, Pastoral Min.
Church & Mailing Address: 1914 18th Ave., P.O. Box 532, 39302-0532. Tel: 601-485-5349; Fax: 601-484-8953. Web: www.stpatsofmeridian.org.
Catechesis/Religious Program—Students 21.

2—ST. PATRICK (1865) Rev. Francis J. Cosgrove; Edgar Hernandez, Pastoral Min.
Church & Mailing Address: 2601 Davis St., P.O. Box 529, 39302. Tel: 601-693-1321; Fax: 601-484-8953. Web: www.stpatsofmeridian.org.
Res.: 204-39th Ct., 39301. Tel: 601-693-2574.
School—(Grades PreK-6), 2700 Davis St., 39301. Tel: 601-482-6044; Fax: 601-485-2762. Email: jaxsp@people.com. Web: www.stpatrickcatholic-school.org. Julie Bordelon, Prin.; Sheri Wall, Librarian. Lay Teachers 9; Students 123.
Catechesis/Religious Program—Students 185.

MOUND BAYOU, BOLIVAR CO., ST. GABRIEL (1949) [CEM] Rev. Scott Dugas, Sacramental Min.
Mailing Address: P.O. Box 53, 38762-0053.
Res. & Church: 501 Martin Luther King St., 38762-0053. Tel: 662-741-2439.

NATCHEZ, ADAMS CO.

1—ASSUMPTION OF THE B.V.M. (1957) Rev. David O'Connor.
Res.: 10 Morgantown Rd., 39120-2788. Tel: 601-442-7250; Fax: 601-442-7250.
Catechesis/Religious Program—Students 17.

2—HOLY FAMILY (1891) Very Rev. James Fallon, S.S.J.; Rev. George Burden, S.S.J., Parochial Vicar.
Res.: 16 Orange Ave., 39120. Tel: 601-445-5700; Fax: 601-442-6030.
School—(Grades PreK-K), 8 Orange Ave., 39120-3647. Tel: 601-442-3947; Fax: 601-442-3973. Mrs. Ira Young, Co-Dir.; Sr. Bernadette McNamara, Co-Dir. Sisters 3; Lay Teachers 5; Students 95.
Catechesis/Religious Program—Sr. Kathleen Higgins, S.H.Sp., D.R.E. Students 26.
Convent—Sisters of the Holy Spirit, 26 Orange Ave., 39120. Tel: 601-445-6785; Fax: 601-442-3973.
Mission—St. John the Baptist Cranfield, Adams Co.

3—ST. MARY BASILICA (1842) Rev. David O'Connor.
Res.: 107 S. Union St., P.O. Box 1044, 39121-1044. Tel: 601-445-5616; Fax: 601-445-9631. Email: stmarybasilica@cableone.net. Web: www.stmarybasilica.org.
Catechesis/Religious Program—(Grades K-12) Ruth Powers, D.R.E. Students 665.

NEW ALBANY, UNION CO., ST. FRANCIS OF ASSISI (1949) Rev. Ricardo M. Phipps.
Res.: 1507 S. Central Ave., P.O. Box 887, 38652-0887.
Church: 650 Hwy. 15 S., P.O. Box 887, 38652-0887. Tel: 662-534-4654; Fax: 662-534-4654.
Catechesis/Religious Program—Leonard Bowen, D.R.E. Students 64.
Mission—St. Christopher 431 Pineridge Dr., P.O. Box 67, Pontotoc, Pontotoc Co. 38863-0067. Tel: 662-489-7749. Rev. Timothy Murphy.

OLIVE BRANCH, DESOTO CO., QUEEN OF PEACE (1983) Rev. Terence Langley, S.C.J.; Deacon Henry Babin.
Res.: 8455 Germantown Rd., P.O. Box 65, 38654-0065. Tel: 662-895-5007; Fax: 662-895-5036.
Catechesis/Religious Program—Mrs. Victoria Stirek, D.R.E. Students 212.

OXFORD, LAFAYETTE CO., ST. JOHN THE EVANGELIST (1943) Rev. Joseph Tonos.
Church: 416 S. 5th St., 38655-3806. Tel: 662-234-6073; Fax: 662-234-6079.
Catechesis/Religious Program—Susan Kelly, D.R.E. Students 169.

PAULDING, JASPER CO., ST. MICHAEL (1843) Rev. Joseph Dyer.
Mailing Address: P.O. Box 388, Forest, 39074-0388. Tel: 601-469-1916.
Church: Star Rte., P.O. Box 15, 39348. Tel: 601-469-1916.
Catechesis/Religious Program—

PEARL, RANKIN CO., ST. JUDE (1962) Rev. Lenin Vargas.
Rectory—399 Barrow St., P.O. Box 5526, 39288-5526. Tel: 601-939-3181 (Office); 601-939-1863; Fax: 601-939-3160. Web: stjudepearl.org.
Catechesis/Religious Program—Stacy Wolf, C.R.E. Students 129.
Station—Mississippi State Mental Hospital Whitfield.

PHILADELPHIA, NESHOBA CO.

1—HOLY CROSS (1860) Unassigned.
Res.: 406 Wilson St., 39350-2906. Tel: 601-656-1841; Fax: 601-650-9098.

2—HOLY ROSARY (Tucker Community) (1884) Rev. Robert Goodyear, S.T.
Res.: 10131 Holy Rosary Rd., P.O. Box 37, 39350. Tel: 601-656-2880; Fax: 601-656-9998.
Catechesis/Religious Program—Students 40.
Mission—St. Catherine 9857 Hwy. 489, Conehatta, Newton Co. 39057.
Mission—St. Theresa, Neshoba Co.

PORT GIBSON, CLAIBORNE CO., ST. JOSEPH (1849) [CEM] Rev. Faustin Misakabo, O.Praem.
Church: 411 Coffee St., P.O. Box 1012, 39150. Tel: 601-437-5790; 601-437-8414.
Catechesis/Religious Program—Students 1.

RIPLEY, TIPPAH CO., ST. MATTHEW (1997) Mr. Sigifredo Bonilla, Lay Ecclesial Min.
Res.: 15710 Hwy. 15 N., P.O. Box 452, 38663. Tel: 662-993-8862; Fax: 662-993-8862.
Catechesis/Religious Program—Students 124.

ROBINSONVILLE, TUNICA CO., GOOD SHEPHERD CATHOLIC CHURCH (2009) Revs. Robert Tucker, S.C.J., Moderator; Gregory Schill, S.C.J.; Edward J. Zemlik, S.C.J.; Duy Nguyen, S.C.J.
Church: 1329 Casino Center Dr. Ext., P.O. Box 70, 38664-0070. Tel: 662-357-0250; 662-342-1073 (Southaven); Fax: 662-342-7733 (Southaven).
Mission—Sacred Heart 6473 Hwy. 161 N., P.O. Box 60, Walls, DeSoto Co. 38680-0060. Tel: 662-781-0450; Fax: 662-429-8423.

ROSEDALE, BOLIVAR CO., SACRED HEART (1968) Rev. Kent Bowlds, Sacramental Min.; Dr. James Tomek, Lay Ecclesial Min.
Res.: 113 Railroad St., P.O. Box 307, 38769. Tel: 662-846-7136.

SENATOBIA, TATE CO., ST. GREGORY THE GREAT (1978) Revs. Robert Tucker, S.C.J., Moderator; Gregory Schill, S.C.J.; Edward J. Zemlik, S.C.J.
Church: 705 Strayhorn St., P.O. Box 129, 38668-0129. Tel: 662-562-5318; Fax: 662-429-8423.

SHAW, BOLIVAR CO., ST. FRANCIS OF ASSISI (1949) Rev. Thomas A. Mullally, S.V.D.; Dr. Florence Louise Ouzts, Pastoral Min.
Res.: 303 Dean Blvd., P.O. Box 239, 38773. Tel: 662-754-5561; Fax: 662-754-5561.

SHELBY, BOLIVAR CO., ST. MARY (1905) Sr. Jo Ann Villademoros, S.S.N.D., Lay Ecclesial Min.
Church: 700 Second St., P.O. Box 208, 38774-0208. Tel: 662-398-7964.

SOUTHAVEN, DESOTO CO., CHRIST THE KING (1974) Revs. Robert Tucker, S.C.J., Moderator; Gregory Schill, S.C.J.; Edward J. Zemlik, S.C.J.
Office: 785 Church Rd. W., 38671. Tel: 662-342-1073; Fax: 662-342-7733. Email: ctkshaven@aol.com. Web: www.ctkshaven.com.
School—Sacred Heart Elementary School, (Grades PreK-8), 5150 Tchulahoma Rd., 38671. Tel: 662-349-0900; Fax: 662-349-0690. Ms. Bridget Martin, Prin.
Catechesis/Religious Program—Donna Williamson, D.R.E.

STARKVILLE, OKTIBBEHA CO., ST. JOSEPH (1930) Rev. John Bohn.
Res.: 607 University Dr., 39759. Tel: 662-323-2257; Fax: 662-323-2258.
Catechesis/Religious Program—Mr. Jeff Artiques, D.R.E. Students 186.
Mission—Corpus Christi P.O. Box 533, Macon, Noxubee Co. 39341.
Chaplaincy—Mississippi State University, 39760.

TUPELO, LEE CO., ST. JAMES (1908) Rev. Thomas Lalor.
Church: 845 Lakeshire Dr., P.O. Box 734, 38804. Tel: 662-842-4881; Fax: 662-844-0327. Email: st_james_parish@comcast.net. Web: www.saint-james.net.
Res.: 757 Lakeshire Dr., 38804. Tel: 662-840-7628.
Catechesis/Religious Program—Jennifer Chase, D.R.E.; Laine Gregory, C.R.E. Students 281.
Mission—St. Thomas Aquinas Saltillo, Lee Co.
Mission—Christ the King 100 E. Main St., P.O. Box 614, Fulton, Itawamba Co. 38843-0614. Tel: 662-862-2239; Fax: 662-862-2239. Don Stephan, Lay Ecclesial Min.

VICKSBURG, WARREN CO.
1—ST. MARY (1906) Rev. Malcolm O'Leary, S.V.D., Admin.
Res.: 1512 Main St., 39183. Tel: 601-636-0115; Fax: 601-661-0677.
Catechesis/Religious Program—Tel: 601-638-3890; Fax: 601-638-3822. Leona Barnes Stringer, D.R.E. Students 43.
2—ST. MICHAEL (1966) Rev. Patrick Curley.
Res.: 100 St. Michael Pl., 39180-8246. Tel: 601-636-3445; Fax: 601-636-3534.
3—ST. PAUL (1848) [CEM] Rev. Msgr. Patrick Farrell.
Res.: 713 Crawford St., 39180-0646. Tel: 601-636-0140; Fax: 601-638-5021. Email: stpaulvick@att.net.
High School—Vicksburg Catholic School, (Grades PreK-12) Tel: 601-636-2256; Fax: 601-631-0430. Mrs. Michele Connelly, Prin. See High Schools, Inter-Parochial under Institutions Located in the Diocese.
Catechesis/Religious Program—Terri Booth, D.R.E. Students 84.

WALLS, DESOTO CO., SACRED HEART (1944), See Good Shepherd, Robinsonville.
Church: 6473 Hwy. 161 N., P.O. Box 60, 38680-0060. Tel: 662-781-0450; Fax: 662-429-8423.
Convent—School Sisters of St. Francis, P.O. Box 237, 38680. Tel: 662-781-0807. School Sisters of St. Francis 1; Sisters of Mercy 1.

WEST POINT, CLAY CO., IMMACULATE CONCEPTION (1965) Rev. Robert Dore, Sacramental Min.; Ms. Loretta Duquette, Lay Ecclesial Min.
Res.: 617 E. Main, 39773-3007. Tel: 662-494-3486. Email: immaculatecon904@bellsouth.net.
Catechesis/Religious Program—Students 43.

WOODVILLE, WILKINSON CO., ST. JOSEPH (1873) Unassigned.
Res.: 338 Church St., P.O. Box 668, 39669. Tel: 601-888-3261; Fax: 601-888-3129. Email: stjoewms@bellsouth.net.
Mission—St. Patrick Fort Adams, Wilkinson Co.
Mission—Holy Family P.O. Box 548, Gloster, Amite Co. 39638. Tel: 601-225-4171.

YAZOO CITY, YAZOO CO.
1—ST. FRANCIS (1940) Rev. Lincoln Dall.
Res.: 735 E. Powell St., 39194-4398. Tel: 662-746-1680.
2—ST. MARY (1851) Rev. Lincoln Dall.
Church: 129 N. Washington St., P.O. Box 27, 39194-0027. Tel: 662-746-1680.

Chaplains of Public Institutions

JACKSON. *Institute for the Blind, Institute for the Deaf and Speech Impaired*. Rev. Michael O'Brien.
University of Mississippi Medical Center. Vacant.
Veterans Administration Hospital. Rt. Rev. E. Thomas DeWane, O.Praem.

MERIDIAN. *East Mississippi State Hospital*. Rev. Francis J. Cosgrove.

PEARL. *Rankin County Prison*. Rev. Lenin Vargas.

SANATORIUM. *Boswell Retardation Center*. Mrs. Eula Purvis, Chap.

WHITFIELD. *Mississippi State Hospital*. Rev. Lenin Vargas.

Serving Outside the Diocese:
Rev.—
Daniels, Jerrell Michael

Retired:
Most Rev.—
Houck, William R., D.D.
Rev. Msgr.—
Koury, Joseph A.
Revs.—
Balser, Edward
Camp, Alfred L.
Corcoran, Frank
Cullen, William
Derivaux, Donald F.
Johnson, Howard
Lopez, Jose
Niemira, Thomas
Noonan, Patrick
O'Riordan, James
Pentony, Liam
Prendergast, Noel
Rietti, John
Shelton, Henry
Smith, Patrick

Permanent Deacons:
Agosta, Frank
Babin, Henry, Queen of Peace, Olive Branch
Baglioni, Victor, (Retired)
Baker, Sam, (Retired)
Campbell, Lawrence M., (Retired)
Klingen, Dr. Theodore, (Retired)
Pancratz, Arnold, (Retired)

INSTITUTIONS LOCATED IN THE DIOCESE

[A] HIGH SCHOOLS, INTER-PAROCHIAL

GREENVILLE. *St. Joseph Catholic School* (1888) (Grades 7-12), (Coed), 1501 VFW Road, 38701. Tel: 662-378-9711; Fax: 662-378-3496. Web: stjoeirish.com. Mr. Paul Artman, Prin.; Donna Goss, Librarian/Media Specialist. Lay Teachers 22; Students 225.

MADISON. *St. Joseph Catholic School* (1870) (Grades 7-12), (Coed), 308 New Mannsdale Rd., P.O. Box 2027, 39130-2027. Tel: 601-898-4800; Fax: 601-898-4689. Email: info@stjoebruins.com. Web: www.stjoebruins.com. Mr. William M. Heller, Prin.; Rachel Hill, Librarian. Brothers 2; Sisters 1; Lay Teachers 63; Students 462.

NATCHEZ. *Cathedral School*, (Grades PreK-12), (Coed), 701 Martin Luther King, Jr. St., 39120. Tel: 601-442-2531; Fax: 601-442-0960. Mr. Patrick Sanguinetti, Prin. Lay Teachers 57; Students 666.

VICKSBURG. *Vicksburg Catholic School*, (Grades PreK-12), (Coed), 1900 Grove St., 39183. Tel: 601-636-2256; Fax: 601-631-0430. Web: www.vicksburgcatholic.org. Mrs. Michele Connelly, Prin. Lay Teachers 47; Students 638.

[B] ELEMENTARY SCHOOLS INTER-PAROCHIAL

JACKSON. *Sister Thea Bowman School*, (Grades PreK-5), 1217 Hattiesburg St., 39209-7411. Tel: 601-352-5441; Fax: 601-352-5136. Mrs. Shae Goodman-Robinson, Prin.; Caryn West, Office Mgr. Lay Teachers 5.

SOUTHAVEN. *Sacred Heart School* (1947) (Grades PreK-8), 5150 Tchulahoma Rd., 38671. Tel: 662-349-0900; Fax: 662-349-0690. Email: cwarwick@shsm.org. Ms. Bridget Martin, Prin. Sisters 2; Lay Teachers 23; Students 350.

[C] GENERAL HOSPITALS

JACKSON. *St. Dominic-Jackson Memorial Hospital* (1946) 969 Lakeland Dr., 39216. Tel: 601-200-2000; Fax: 601-200-6800. Email: charbarger@stdom.com. Web: www.stdom.com. Sr. Kristin Rever, Prioress; Mr. Claude W. Harbarger, Pres.; Rev. Daniel Gallagher, Resident Chap. Sisters of St. Dominic of Springfield, IL 7; Bed Capacity 535; Patients Assisted Annually 134,279; Total Staff 2,929.

TUTWILER. *Tutwiler Clinic, Inc.* (1983) 205 Alma St., P.O. Box 462, 38963-0462. Tel: 662-345-8334; Fax: 662-345-6300. Email: sannebrooks@bellsouth.net. Sr. Anne Brooks, S.N.J.M., D.O., Dir. Patients Assisted Annually 8,458; Total Staff 30.

[D] ORPHANAGES AND INFANT HOMES

JACKSON. *D'Evereaux Hall Home, Inc.*, P.O. Box 2248, 39225. Tel: 601-355-8634; Fax: 601-960-8493. Email: greg.patin@catholiccharitiesjackson.org. Mr. Gregory Patin, Exec. Dir.
St. Mary Orphan Home, Inc., P.O. Box 2248, 39225. Tel: 601-355-8634; Fax: 601-960-8493. Email: greg.patin@catholiccharitiesjackson.org. Mr. Gregory Patin, Exec. Dir.

[E] MONASTERIES AND RESIDENCES OF PRIESTS AND BROTHERS

JACKSON. *Christian Brothers Residence*, 653 Claiborne Ave., 39209. Tel: 601-665-4656. Bros. John Brennan, C.F.C.; Theodore Dausch, C.F.C.; Lucian Knapp, C.F.C.; Daniel Lauber, C.F.C.; Dennis Gunn, C.F.C. Congregation of Christian Brothers.
Priory of St. Moses the Black, 7100 Midway Rd., Raymond, 39154. Tel: 601-857-0157; Fax: 601-857-5076. Rt. Rev. E. Thomas DeWane, O.Praem., Abbot/Prior; Revs. Onwuham Akpa, O.Praem.; Richard P. Chiles, O.Praem.; Norbert N'Zilamba, O.Praem.; Jeremy Tobin, O.Praem.; Sebastian Schalk, O.Praem. Canons Regular of Premontre (The Premonstratensian Fathers). Priests 6.

NESBIT. *St. Michael Community House*, 1360 Nesbit Rd., P.O. Box 38, 38651. Tel: 662-429-8424; Fax: 662-429-8423. Revs. Leonard F. Elder, S.C.J., Coord.; Jack Kurps, S.C.J., Exec. Dir.; Duy Nguyen, S.C.J.; Thomas Lind, S.C.J.; Gregory Schill, S.C.J.; Robert Tucker, S.C.J.; Edward J. Zemlik, S.C.J.; Bro. Michael Fette, S.C.J.

[F] CONVENTS AND RESIDENCES FOR SISTERS

JACKSON. *St. Dominic Convent*, 969 Lakeland Dr., 39216. Tel: 601-200-6729; Fax: 601-944-0096. Email: kfrever@yahoo.com. Web: www.stdom.com. Dominican Sisters (Springfield, IL) 7.
Our Lady of Mount Carmel and Little Flower Monastery (1951) 2155 Terry Rd., 39204. Tel: 601-373-1460; Fax: 601-372-1369. Email: jm2155jt@aol.com. Sr. Margaret Mary Flynn, O.C.D., Prioress. Discalced Carmelites. Nuns with Solemn Vows 6.

CHATAWA. *St. Mary of the Pines*, 3167 Old Hwy. 51 S., P.O. Box 38, 39632. Tel: 601-783-3494; Fax: 601-783-5758. Sr. Georgiann Wildhaber, S.S.N.D., Admin.; Rev. Thomas Potts, S.V.D., Chap. Home for the Retired Sisters of the Dallas Province of the School Sisters of Notre Dame. Retreat Center for Lay and Religious Groups. Sisters in Residence 52.

GREENVILLE. *Our Lady of Lourdes Convent* (1964) 1600 E. Reed Rd., 38703-7229. Tel: 662-334-4337; 662-334-3287 (School); Fax: 662-332-9877. Email: alspaughm@suddenlink.com. Web: lourdes.greenville.ms.us. Sisters of St. Joseph.

GREENWOOD. *St. Francis Convent*, 2603 Hwy. 82 E., 38930-5966. Tel: 662-453-1221; Fax: 662-453-9060. Web: www.stfrancisassisi.com. Franciscan Sisters of Christian Charity 5.

[G] RETREAT CENTERS

BROOKSVILLE. *The Dwelling Place*, 2824 Dwelling Place Rd., 39739-9796. Tel: 662-738-5348; Fax: 662-738-5345. Email: dwellpl@gmail.com. Web: www.dwellingplace.com. Clare Van Lent, Dir.

CHATAWA. *St. Mary of the Pines*, 3167 Old Hwy. 51 S., P.O. Box 38, 39632. Tel: 601-783-3494; Fax: 601-783-5758. Sr. Georgiann Wildhaber, S.S.N.D., Admin.; Rev. Thomas Potts, S.V.D., Chap. Home for the Retired Sisters of the Dallas Province of the School Sisters of Notre Dame. Retreat Center for Lay and Religious Groups. Sisters in Residence 52.

[H] NEWMAN CENTERS

JACKSON. *Belhaven College Newman Center* P.O. Box 57, 39205-0057. Very Rev. Jeffrey Waldrep, S.T.L., J.C.L.

Jackson State University Newman Center c/o Christ the King, 2303 John R. Lynch St., 39209-7498. Tel: 601-948-8867.

Millsaps College Newman Center P.O. Box 57, 39205-0057. Very Rev. Jeffrey Waldrep, S.T.L., J.C.L.

Tougaloo College Newman Center Holy Ghost Church, 1151 Cloister St., 39202. Tel: 601-353-1339. Rev. Darrell C. Kelly, S.V.D.

University of Mississippi Medical Center - Newman Center P.O. Box 57, 39205-0057. Very Rev. Jeffrey Waldrep, S.T.L., J.C.L.

BOONEVILLE. *Northeast Mississippi Community College Catholic Student Center St. Francis of Assisi*, P.O. Box 654, 38829. Tel: 662-728-7509. Email: stfrancisbv@att.net. Web: www.stfrancisbooneville.com. Sheila B. Przesmicki.

BROOKHAVEN. *Lincoln Junior College Newman Center* P.O. Box 196, 39602-0196. Tel: 601-833-1799. Rev. Matthew P. Simmons.

CLEVELAND. *Delta State University Newman Center Our Lady of Victories*, 215 Bishop Rd., P.O. Box 1450, 38732-1450. Tel: 662-846-6273. Rev. Kent Bowlds.

CLINTON. *Mississippi College Newman Center Holy Savior Church*, P.O. Box 85, 39060. Tel: 601-924-6344. Email: holysavior@att.net. Rev. Thomas McGing, J.C.L.

COLUMBUS. *Mississippi University for Women Student Center* Annunciation Church, 823 College St., 39701. Tel: 662-328-2927; Fax: 662-329-8270. Email: annunchr@bellsouth.net. Web: www.annunciationcatholicchurch.com. Rev. Robert Dore.

FOREST. *East Central Community College Newman Center St. Michael's Church*, P.O. Box 388, 39074. Tel: 601-469-1916; Fax: 601-469-1815. Rev. Joseph Dyer.

GOODMAN. *Holmes Community College Newman Center St. Thomas*, 200 Boulevard St., Lexington, 39095. Tel: 662-453-0623; Fax: 662-453-9060. Rev. Gregory Plata, O.F.M.

HOLLY SPRINGS. *Rust College Newman Center St. Joseph's*, P.O. Box 430, 38635. Tel: 662-252-3138; Fax: 662-252-3138. Mr. James Rayford Sr.

OXFORD. *Ole Miss Campus Ministries St. John Church*, 416 S. 5th St., 38655. Tel: 662-234-6073; Fax: 662-234-6079. Email: office@stjohnoxford.org. Rev. Joseph Tonos.

RAYMOND. *Hinds Community College Catholic Student Organization* 7100 Midway Rd., 39154. Tel: 601-857-0157. Rev. Jeremy Tobin, O.Praem.

STARKVILLE. *Mississippi State University Catholic Student Association* St. Joseph Church, 607 University Dr., 39759. Tel: 662-323-2257; Fax: 662-323-2258. Email: falavelle@hotmail.com. Web: www.msstate.edu/org/csa. Rev. John Bohn; Fran Lavelle, Campus Min.

[I] MISCELLANEOUS

JACKSON. *Jackson Diocese Educational Services, Inc.*, P.O. Box 2248, 39225-2248. Tel: 601-969-2742; Fax: 601-960-8469. Email: education.office@jacksondiocese.org. Sr. Deborah Hughes, S.S.J., Dir. Formational Ministries, Supt. Schools.

Parroquia De San Miguel Arcangel, P.O. Box 2248, 39225-2248. Saltillo Mission Sponsored by Dioceses of Jackson and Biloxi.

Av. Central 4649 y Calle 44, Col. Vista Hermosa, Saltillo, Coahuila C.P. 25010 Mexico. Tel: 011-52-84-44-82-2207. Rev. Benjamin Piovan.

Pax Christi Franciscans (1952) LaVerna House, 2108 Alta Woods Blvd., 39204. Tel: 601-373-4463. Kathleen Feyen, Pres.; Rhoda Kalscheur, House Dir. A Private Association of the Christian faithful, living a consecrated life, engaged in social and educational works. Consecrated Members 6.

ABERDEEN. *Catholic Committee of the South, Inc., St. Christopher Church*, P.O. Box 67, Pontotoc, 38863. Tel: 662-489-7749. Email: stchristopher@juno.com. Sr. Mary Priniski, O.P., Coord.

CANTON. *Notre Dame Education Center, Inc.*, 3142 S. Liberty St., P.O. Box 505, 39046. Tel: 601-859-6826; Fax: 601-859-6898. Email: ndec@netdoor.com.

GREENWOOD. *Pax Christi Franciscans*, St. Francis Information Center, 709 Ave. I, 38930. Tel: 662-453-1465. Email: stfrancis_center@bellsouth.net. Genevieve Feyen, Pres.; Bessie Willburn, Center Dir. A Private Association of the Christian faithful, living a consecrated life, engaged in social and educational works. Consecrated Members 6.

JONESTOWN. *Jonestown Family Center for Education and Wellness*, 401 Main St., P.O. Box 248, 38639. Tel: 662-358-4651; Fax: 662-358-4671. Sr. Teresa Shields, S.N.J.M., Exec. Dir.

MADISON. **St. Catherine's Village, Inc.* (1988) 200 Dominican Dr., 39110. Tel: 601-856-0100; Fax: 601-200-0823. Web: www.stcatherinesvillage.com. Assisted Annually 450.

MOUND BAYOU. *St. Gabriel Mercy Center, Inc.*, P.O. Box 0824, 38762-0824. Tel: 662-741-3255; Fax: 662-741-3494. Email: mavish@stgabrielmc.org. Sisters Donald Mary Lynch, R.S.M., Exec. Dir.; Donella Hartman, R.S.M., Asst. Dir.; Ms. LaToya Lee, Development Dir.; Mrs. Dwana Lyles, Coord., Senior Outreach Prog.; Mrs. Myrtle Lucas, Coord. GED Prog.; Ms. Nekedra Blockett, Coord. Emergency Assistance Prog.; Ms. Bobbie DuLaney, Coord. Sewing Prog.; Ms. Martha Black, Coord. Parenting Prog. Outreach Program of the Sisters of Mercy Health System (Mercycare); Mercy Computer Learning Lab, Mound Bayou, MS 38762, Ms. Mavis Honorable, Coord.

ROSEDALE. *Delta Catholic Ministries*, 113 Railroad St., P.O. Box 307, 38769-0307. Sisters Kay Burton, S.N.J.M., Vice Pres. & Dir.; Joanne Blomme, O.P., Bd. Member; Jo Ann Villademoros, S.S.N.D., Bd. Member; Manette Durand, C.S.J., Bd. Member.

WALLS. *Sacred Heart League* (1955) 6050 Hwy. 161 N., P.O. Box 300, 38680-0300. Tel: 662-781-1360; Fax: 662-781-3340. Email: jkurps@shsm.org. Web: www.shsm.org. Rev. Jack Kurps, S.C.J., Exec. Dir.; Mr. Stephen Koepke, Dir. Devel.

Sacred Heart Southern Missions Housing Corporation, P.O. Box 365, 38680-0365. Tel: 662-781-1516; Fax: 662-781-0886. Mr. Ed Savage, Dir. Programs; Rev. Jack Kurps, S.C.J., Pres.

Sacred Heart Southern Missions, Inc. (1942) 6050 Hwy. 161 N., P.O. Box 190, 38680-0190. Tel: 662-781-1360; Fax: 662-342-3390. Email: jkurps@shsm.org. Web: www.shsm.org. Rev. Jack Kurps, S.C.J., Exec. Dir.

RELIGIOUS INSTITUTES OF MEN REPRESENTED IN THE DIOCESE

For further details refer to the corresponding bracketed number in the Religious Institutes of Men or Women section.

[0900]—*Canons Regular of Premontre*—O.Praem.
[0310]—*Congregation of Christian Brothers*—C.F.C.
[1130]—*Congregation of the Priests of the Sacred Heart*—S.C.J.
[0520]—*Franciscan Friars* (Pulaski, WI)—O.F.M.
[0570]—*Glenmary Home Missioners*—G.H.M.
[0840]—*Missionary Servants of the Most Holy Trinity*—S.T.
[0420]—*Society of the Divine Word*—S.V.D.
[0700]—*St. Joseph's Society of the Sacred Heart*—S.S.J.

RELIGIOUS INSTITUTES OF WOMEN REPRESENTED IN THE DIOCESE

[3710]—*Congregation of the Sisters of Saint Agnes*—C.S.A.
[3832]—*Congregation of the Sisters of St. Joseph* (La Grange Park, IL)—C.S.J.
[1780]—*Congregation of the Sisters of the Third Order of St. Francis of Perpetual Adoration*—F.S.P.A.
[0760]—*Daughters of Charity of St. Vincent de Paul*—D.C.
[0420]—*Discalced Carmelite Nuns*—O.C.D.
[1070-03]—*Dominican Sisters* (Sinsinawa, WI)—O.P.
[1070-09]—*Dominican Sisters* (Racine, WI)—O.P.
[1070-10]—*Dominican Sisters* (Springfield, IL)—O.P.
[1070-13]—*Dominican Sisters* (Adrian, MI)—O.P.
[1115]—*Dominican Sisters of Peace*—O.P.
[1230]—*Franciscan Sisters of Christian Charity*—O.S.F.
[1310]—*Franciscan Sisters of Little Falls, Minnesota*—O.S.F.
[1845]—*Guadalupan Missionaries of the Holy Spirit*—M.G.Sp.S.
[2970]—*School Sisters of Notre Dame* (Baltimore & Dallas Provs., St. Louis)—S.S.N.D.
[1680]—*School Sisters of St. Francis*—O.S.F.
[0430]—*Sisters for Charity of the Blessed Virgin Mary* (Dubuque, IA)—B.V.M.
[0500]—*Sisters of Charity of Nazareth* (Kentucky)—S.C.N.
[]—*Sisters of Christian Community*—S.F.C.C.
[0990]—*Sisters of Divine Providence*—C.D.P.
[2100]—*Sisters of Humility of Mary*—C.H.M.
[2575]—*Sisters of Mercy of the Americas* (Belmont, NC)—R.S.M.
[3893]—*Sisters of Saint Joseph of Chestnut Hill, Philadelphia*—S.S.J.
[1570]—*Sisters of St. Francis of the Holy Family* (Dubuque)—O.S.F.
[3840]—*Sisters of St. Joseph of Carondelet* (St. Louis & St. Paul Provs.)—C.S.J.
[1990]—*Sisters of the Holy Names of Jesus and Mary* (U.S. - Ontario)—S.N.J.M.
[2050]—*Sisters of the Holy Spirit and Mary Immaculate*—S.H.Sp.
[2350]—*Sisters of the Living Word*—S.L.W.
[2160]—*Sisters, Servants of the Immaculate Heart of Mary*—I.H.M.

NECROLOGY

† Atkinson, Sean, (Retired)—Died Oct. 4, 2011
† Vollor, John, Clarksdale, MS St. Elizabeth.—Died Jan. 11, 2011

An asterisk (*) denotes an organization that has established tax-exempt status directly with the IRS and is not covered by the USCCB Group Ruling.

Diocese of Jefferson City

(Dioecesis Civitatis Jeffersoniensis)

Most Reverend

JOHN RAYMOND GAYDOS

Bishop of Jefferson City; ordained December 20, 1968; appointed June 25, 1997; consecrated August 27, 1997. *Res.: P.O. Box 104900, Jefferson City, MO 65110-4900.*

Catholic Center: Alphonse J. Schwartze Memorial, 2207 W. Main St., P.O. Box 104900, Jefferson City, MO 65110-4900. Tel: 573-635-9127; Fax: 573-635-0386.

Web: www.diojeffcity.org

ESTABLISHED JULY 2, 1956.

Square Miles 22,127.

Comprises the Counties of Adair, Audrain, Benton, Boone, Callaway, Camden, Chariton, Clark, Cole, Cooper, Crawford, Gasconade, Hickory, Howard, Knox, Lewis, Linn, Macon, Maries, Marion, Miller, Moniteau, Monroe, Montgomery, Morgan, Osage, Pettis, Phelps, Pike, Pulaski, Putnam, Ralls, Randolph, Saline, Schuyler, Scotland, Shelby and Sullivan in the State of Missouri.

For legal titles of parishes and diocesan institutions, consult the Chancery Office.

STATISTICAL OVERVIEW

Personnel	
Bishop	1
Priests: Diocesan Active in Diocese	57
Priests: Diocesan Active Outside Diocese	3
Priests: Retired, Sick or Absent	27
Number of Diocesan Priests	87
Religious Priests in Diocese	9
Total Priests in Diocese	96
Extern Priests in Diocese	12
Ordinations:	
Diocesan Priests	1
Transitional Deacons	3
Permanent Deacons in Diocese	69
Total Brothers	1
Total Sisters	44
Parishes	
Parishes	95
With Resident Pastor:	
Resident Diocesan Priests	45
Resident Religious Priests	5
Without Resident Pastor:	
Administered by Priests	38
Administered by Deacons	1
Administered by Religious Women	3
Administered by Lay People	1
Completely Vacant	2
Missions	15
Professional Ministry Personnel:	
Brothers	1
Sisters	9
Lay Ministers	47
Welfare	
Catholic Hospitals	1
Total Assisted	120,756
Health Care Centers	14
Total Assisted	115,844
Special Centers for Social Services	2
Total Assisted	48,073
Educational	
Diocesan Students in Other Seminaries	20
Total Seminarians	20
High Schools, Diocesan and Parish	3
Total Students	937
Elementary Schools, Diocesan and Parish	37
Total Students	6,206
Catechesis/Religious Education:	
High School Students	1,841
Elementary Students	3,634
Total Students under Catholic Instruction	12,638
Teachers in the Diocese:	
Priests	9
Brothers	1
Sisters	1
Lay Teachers	545
Vital Statistics	
Receptions into the Church:	
Infant Baptism Totals	1,140
Minor Baptism Totals	123
Adult Baptism Totals	153
Received into Full Communion	256
First Communions	1,285
Confirmations	1,195
Marriages:	
Catholic	239
Interfaith	199
Total Marriages	438
Deaths	785
Total Catholic Population	82,516
Total Population	910,356

Former Bishops—Most Revs. JOSEPH M. MARLING, C.PP.S., D.D., ord. Feb. 21, 1929; appt. Auxiliary of Kansas City, June 9, 1947; cons. Aug. 6, 1947; appt. Bishop of Jefferson City, Aug. 24, 1956; retired July 2, 1969; died Oct. 2, 1979; MICHAEL F. MCAULIFFE, S.T.D., ord. May 31, 1945; appt. July 2, 1969; cons. Aug. 18, 1969; retired Aug. 27, 1997; died Jan. 9, 2006.

Vicar General—Rev. Msgr. GREGORY L. HIGLEY, V.G., Mailing Address: P.O. Box 104900, Jefferson City, 65110-4900.

Episcopal Vicars—Rev. Msgrs. MICHAEL T. FLANAGAN, E.V.; MICHAEL J. WILBERS, E.V.

Chancery Office—2207 W. Main St., P.O. Box 104900, Jefferson City, 65110-4900. Tel: 573-635-9127; Fax: 573-635-0386. All offices are at this address unless noted otherwise.

Chancellor—Sr. KATHLEEN WEGMAN, S.S.N.D.

Secretary to the Bishop—Rev. JEREMY A. SECRIST.

Vice-Chancellors—Rev. Msgr. ROBERT A. KURWICKI; Revs. BRENDAN DOYLE; JEREMY A. SECRIST.

Moderator of the Curia—Rev. Msgr. GREGORY L. HIGLEY, V.G.

Diocesan Tribunal— All marriage papers should be sent to the attention of Diocesan Tribunal Office.

Judicial Vicar—Rev. BRENDAN DOYLE.

Adjutant Judicial Vicar—Rev. Msgr. GREGORY L. HIGLEY, V.G.

Defenders of the Bond—Rev. ROBERT W. DUESDIEKER; Deacon JAMES R. BUTLER; Mrs. CONSTANCE SCHEPERS.

Promoter of Justice—Rev. MARK A. PORTERFIELD, J.C.L.

Judges—Revs. J. JAMES OFFUTT; MARK A. PORTERFIELD, J.C.L.; MICHAEL F. QUINN; P. GREGORY OLIGSCHLAEGER; MARK S. SMITH, J.C.L.

Notary—Mrs. SHERYL NOVOTNEY.

Diocesan Consultors—Rev. Msgrs. MICHAEL T. FLANAGAN, E.V.; GREGORY L. HIGLEY, V.G.; DAVID D. COX; Revs. MICHAEL P. MURPHY; PHILIP E. NIEKAMP; P. GREGORY OLIGSCHLAEGER; Rev. Msgr. MICHAEL J. WILBERS, E.V.

Deans—I. Columbia: Rev. ROBERT H. FIELDS Dean: Boonville, Columbia, Fayette, Moberly, Pilot Grove, Brunswick, Glasgow, Indian Grove, Salisbury, Slater, Marshall. II. Hannibal: Rev. R. WILLIAM PECKMAN Dean: Canton (La Grange), Ewing, Hannibal, Indian Creek, Kahoka (Wayland), Louisiana (Clarksville), Monroe City, Palmyra, Perry (Paris), St. Clement, St. Patrick, Vandalia (Laddonia). III. Jefferson City: Rev. GREGORY C. MEYSTRIK Dean: California, Holts Summit, Jefferson City, Russellville, St. Martins, Taos, Wardsville. IV. Kirksville: Rev. CHRISTOPHER L. CORDES Dean: Baring, Edina, Kirksville (Novinger), Memphis, Milan (Unionville), Brookfield, Clarence, Macon (Bevier), Marceline, Shelbina. V. Mexico: Rev. FRANK A. BUSSMANN Dean: Centralia, Fulton, Hermann, Jonesburg, Martinsburg, Mexico, Mokane, Montgomery City, Rhineland, Wellsville. VI. Rolla: Rev. Msgr. MARION J. MAKAREWICZ Dean: Belle, Bourbon, Brinktown, Crocker, Cuba, Dixon, Owensville, Richland, Rolla, Rosati, St. James, Steelville, Vienna, St. Robert. VII. Sedalia/Lake Ozark: Rev. DANIEL I.J. LUECKENOTTE Dean: Camdenton, Eldon, Laurie (Versailles), Hermitage (Climax Springs), Lake Ozark, Mary's Home, St. Anthony, St. Elizabeth, Sedalia, Tipton, Warsaw. VIII. Westphalia: Rev. IGNAZIO C. MEDINA Dean: Argyle (Koeltztown), Bonnots Mill, Chamois, Folk, Frankenstein, Freeburg, Linn, Loose Creek, Meta, Rich Fountain, Westphalia, Morrison, Osage Bend, St. Thomas.

Masters of Ceremonies—

To The Bishop—Revs. MICHAEL W. PENN; JEREMY A. SECRIST; NICHOLAS J. REID.

Personnel Board—Most Rev. JOHN RAYMOND GAYDOS; Revs. J. DAVID MAHER; ROBERT W. DUESDIEKER; Rev. Msgrs. MICHAEL T. FLANAGAN, E.V.; ROBERT A. KURWICKI; GREGORY L. HIGLEY, V.G.; DONALD W. LAMMERS; MICHAEL J. WILBERS, E.V.

Presbyteral Council—Most Rev. JOHN RAYMOND GAYDOS, Pres. Senators: Revs. MICHAEL P. MURPHY; CHRISTOPHER L. CORDES, Vice Chm.; LOUIS E. DORN; WILLIAM D. DEBO; MARK S. SMITH, J.C.L.; Rev. Msgr. ROBERT A. KURWICKI; Rev. PATRICK J. SHORTT. Appointed Members: Revs. P. GREGORY OLIGSCHLAEGER, Chair; PHILIP E. NIEKAMP, Treas.; EDWIN A. SCHMIDT; PAUL M. HARTLEY. Ex Officio Members: Rev. Msgrs. MICHAEL J. WILBERS, E.V.; MICHAEL T. FLANAGAN, E.V.; GREGORY L. HIGLEY, V.G.

Diocesan Offices and Directors

Buildings and Properties—Rev. Msgr. MICHAEL J. WIBERS, E.V.; Mr. BRAD COPELAND, Dir.

Campus Ministry—Mrs. ANGELLE HALL, Dir.

Cemeteries—Rev. JEREMY A. SECRIST, Dir.

Charismatic Renewal Program—Deacon KENNETH BERRY, Diocesan Representative, 201 N. Cottey, Edina, 63537. Tel: 660-397-2636.

Communication—Mr. MARK D. SAUCIER, Dir., 600 Clark Ave., P.O. Box 1022, Jefferson City, 65102.

Cursillo Movement—Ms. TERRIE FOLTZ, Lay Dir.; Rev. JOSEPH S. COREL, Spiritual Dir.

Chief Financial Officer—Deacon JOSEPH M. BRADDOCK.

Diaconate Office—Rev. FREDERICK J. ELSKAMP, Vicar; Deacon RAYMOND L. PURVIS.

Engaged Encounter—Coordinators: BURDETT WILSON; JOYCE WILSON, 4755 County Rd. 2130, Huntsville, 65259; Rev. MICHAEL F. QUINN, Spiritual Dir.

Pro-Life—Dr. STEPHANA LANDWHER.

Finance—Deacon JOSEPH BRADDOCK, CFO.

Stewardship—Mrs. E. JANE RUTTER, Dir.

Finance Committee—Most Rev. JOHN RAYMOND GAYDOS; Deacon JOSEPH M. BRADDOCK; Mr. CHARLES CASSMEYER; Mrs. E. JANE RUTTER; Rev. Msgr. MICHAEL T. FLANAGAN, E.V.; Mr. GEORGE CASEY; Rev. Msgr. GREGORY L. HIGLEY, V.G.; Mr. MICHAEL KELLY; Mr. RODNEY LOESCH; Mr. MATTHIAS TOLKSDORF; Mr. JAMES E. WESTBROOK; Rev. GREGORY C. MEYSTRIK; Rev. Msgr. MICHAEL J. WILBERS, E.V.; Mrs. BETTY ZIMMER; Sr. KATHLEEN WEGMAN, S.S.N.D.

Hispanic Ministry—Mr. ENRIQUE CASTRO, Dir.

Historical Archives—Rev. JEREMY A. SECRIST, Dir.

Leadership Services—Sr. KATHLEEN WEGMAN, S.S.N.D., Chancellor; Mr. MIKE BERENDZEN, Assoc. to Chancellor.

Legion of Mary—Rev. WILLIAM L. KORTE, 301 W. Williams, Salisbury, 65281. Tel: 660-388-5590.

Liturgical Commission—Rev. DANIEL J. MERZ.

Mediation and Arbitration Board—Rev. LOUIS E. DORN.

Marriage Encounter—Chair Couple: Mr. BRIT SMITH; Mrs. CANDI SMITH, 215 Boonville Rd., Jefferson City, 65109. Tel: 573-636-3712; Rev. GREGORY C. MEYSTRIK, Spiritual Dir., 6410 Rt. W, Jefferson City, 65101. Tel: 573-636-4925.

Marriage Tribunal—Mrs. CONSTANCE SCHEPERS, Admin.

Ministry Formation—Rev. JOSEPH S. COREL.

Ministry to Priests—Most Rev. JOHN RAYMOND GAYDOS; Revs. FRANK A. BUSSMANN; DONALD J. ANTWEILER; R. WILLIAM PECKMAN; MICHAEL F. QUINN; Rev. Msgr. MARION J. MAKAREWICZ, Chm.; Revs. JEREMY A. SECRIST, Sec.; MARK S. SMITH, J.C.L.

Mission Office—Mr. MARK D. SAUCIER, Dir.

Newspaper--"The Catholic Missourian"—Mr. JAY NIES, Editor, Mailing Address: P.O. Box 104900, Jefferson City, 65110-4900.

Priestly and Religious Vocations Committee—Revs. JOSEPH S. COREL, Chair; DAVID J. VEIT; MARK S. SMITH, J.C.L.; JOHN J. SCHMITZ; R. WILLIAM PECKMAN; CHRISTOPHER L. CORDES; WAYNE M. BOYER; Rev. Msgrs. DAVID D. COX; GREGORY L. HIGLEY, V.G.; Rev. P. GREGORY OLIGSCHLAEGER.

Priests' Mutual Benefit Society—Board of Trustees: Most Rev. JOHN R. GAYDOS; Revs. CHRISTOPHER L. CORDES, Sec.; GREGORY C. MEYSTRIK, Chair; Rev. Msgrs. MICHAEL T. FLANAGAN, E.V.; GREGORY L. HIGLEY, V.G.; MICHAEL J. WILBERS, E.V.

Religious Education Office—Mr. JAMES M. KEMNA, Dir.; Mrs. CAROLYN A. SAUCIER, Assoc.

School Office—Mr. DONALD F. NOVOTNEY, Supt.

Diocesan Schools Technology Foundation—Mr. DONALD F. NOVOTNEY, Supt., 2207 W. Main St., P.O. Box 104900, Jefferson City, 65110-4900. Tel: 573-635-9127; Fax: 573-635-2286.

Scouting—Deacon ANTHONY J. VALDES, Chap., 825 Cari Ann, Jefferson City, 65109. Tel: 573-761-5524.

Stewardship—Mrs. E. JANE RUTTER, Dir.

Teens Encounter Christ (TEC)—Mr. STEVE MAXWELL, Lay Dir., 364 County Rd. 634, Freeburg, 65035; Rev. MICHAEL A. COLEMAN, Spiritual Dir., P.O. Box 310, Moberly, 65270.

Risk Management—MARY JANE BEXTEN, Contact; Deacon JOSEPH M. BRADDOCK, CFO & Contact.

Victim Assistance Coordinator—Mrs. NANCY HOEY. Tel: 573-644-6128. Email: nhoey@diojeffcity.org.

Youth Ministry—Mr. STEPHEN W. JONES.

CLERGY, PARISHES, MISSIONS AND PAROCHIAL SCHOOLS

JEFFERSON CITY

(COLE COUNTY)

1—ST. JOSEPH CATHEDRAL (1959) [JC] Rev. Msgr. Robert A. Kurwicki; Rev. Nicholas J. Reid; Deacons Robert J. Rackers, (Retired); Joseph M. Braddock; Alvin J. Brand; Dana K. Joyce; James L. Kliethermes.
2305 W. Main St., 65109.
Tel: 573-635-7991; Fax: 573-635-0842. Email: stjosephb@juno.com. Web: www.cathedraljc.org.
School—(Grades PreK-8), 2303 W. Main St., 65109. Tel: 573-635-5024; Fax: 573-635-5238. Email: spencer.allen@cathedralschooljc.com. Web: www.cathedralschooljc.com. Spencer L. Allen, Prin.; Ruth Ann Stratman, Librarian. Lay Teachers 30; Students 514.
Catechesis/Religious Program—Students 99.

2—IMMACULATE CONCEPTION (1913) [JC] Rev. Msgr. David D. Cox; Revs. Hillary Andebo; Dylan Schrader. In Res., Rev. Brendan Doyle; Deacons Mark Aulbur; Philip Garcia; Raymond L. Purvis.
Res.: 1206 E. McCarty St., 65101. Tel: 573-635-6143; 573-635-6144; Fax: 573-635-6036. Email: icchurch3@mchsi.com. Web: www.icangels.com.
School—(Grades PreK-8), 1208 E. McCarty St., 65101. Tel: 573-636-7680; Fax: 573-635-1833. Email: jstruemph@icangels.com. Web: www.icangels.com. Jill Struemph, Prin.; Charlene Connor, Librarian. Sisters 1; Lay Teachers 34; Students 433.
Catechesis/Religious Program—Students 50.

3—ST. PETER (1846) [JC] Revs. J. David Maher; Basil Eruo; Francis W. Doyle; Deacons Robert L. Dulle; Anthony J. Valdes; Thomas M. Whalen; Fred Schmitz; Thomas M. Fischer.
Res.: 216 Broadway, 65101. Tel: 573-636-8159; Fax: 573-634-6079. Email: parish@stpeterjc.org. Web: www.stpeterjc.org.
School—(Grades K-8), 314 W. High St., 65101. Tel: 573-636-8922; Fax: 573-636-8410. Email: spsmc@socket.net. Dr. Joseph Gulino, Prin.; Heather Luebbert, Librarian. Sisters 2; School Sisters of Notre Dame 1; Sisters of Charity of the Incarnate Word 1; Lay Teachers 32; Students 451.
Catechesis/Religious Program—Students 70.

OUTSIDE JEFFERSON CITY

ARGYLE, OSAGE CO., ST. ALOYSIUS (1910) [CEM 2] Rev. Msgr. Marion J. Makarewicz.
Mailing Address: P.O. Box 6, 65001. Tel: 573-728-6212; Fax: 573-728-6217.
Catechesis/Religious Program—Students 71.
Mission—St. Boniface (1866) P.O. Box 226, Vienna, 65582. Tel: 573-728-6919.

BARING, KNOX CO., ST. ALOYSIUS (1894) [CEM] Attended by Edina Rev. Joseph Hoi; Deacon Kenneth Berry.
Res.: 509 N. Main St., Edina, 63537-1239. Tel: 660-397-2183; Fax: 660-397-3680. Email: stjoeal@marktwain.net. Web: knoxcountycatholic.org.
Catechesis/Religious Program—Twinned with St. Joseph, Edina. Students 3.

BELLE, MARIES CO., ST. ALEXANDER (1910) [CEM] Attended by Immaculate Conception, Owensville. Rev. Jeremy A. Secrist.
Mailing Address: 400 W. Third St., P.O. Box 606, 65013. Tel: 573-859-6231.
Catechesis/Religious Program—Students 16.

BONNOTS MILL, OSAGE CO., ST. LOUIS (1905) [CEM] Rev. Donald J. Antweiler, Admin.
Mailing Address: P.O. Box 8, Loose Creek, 65054. Tel: 573-897-2922.
Church: 211 Church Hill, P.O. Box 8, Loose Creek, 65054. Tel: 573-897-2922; Fax: 573-897-4271.
Catechesis/Religious Program—

BOONVILLE, COOPER CO., SS. PETER AND PAUL (1856) [CEM] Rev. Robert W. Duesdieker; Deacon David Miller.
Res.: 322 7th St., 65233. Tel: 660-882-6468; Fax: 660-882-7920. Email: ssppchurch@socket.net. Web: www.catholic-forum.com/churches/0865sspeterpaul.
School—(Grades PreK-8), 502 7th St., 65233. Tel: 660-882-2589; Fax: 660-882-2476. Mr. Alan Lammers, Prin. Lay Teachers 11; Students 204.
Catechesis/Religious Program—Email: ssppreled@socket.net. Students 95.

BOURBON, CRAWFORD CO., ST. FRANCIS (1915) [CEM 2] Rev. James Finder.
Mailing Address: 415 W. School, Cuba, 65453.
Church: 1098 Old Hwy. 66 W., 65441. Tel: 573-885-3520; Fax: 573-885-3501. Email: hccc@fidmail.com.

BRINKTOWN, MARIES CO., HOLY GUARDIAN ANGELS (1891) [CEM] Attended by Visitation, Vienna. Rev. Msgr. Marion J. Makarewicz.
Res. & Mailing Address: P.O. Box 226, Vienna, 65582. Tel: 573-422-3950; Fax: 573-422-3950. Email: bvmchurch@att.net. Web: www.vi-ps.org.
Church: 37515 Hwy., 65443. Tel: 573-422-3105.
Catechesis/Religious Program—Students 15.

BROOKFIELD, LINN CO., IMMACULATE CONCEPTION (1859) [CEM] Rev. Gerald J. Kaimann, Canonical Pastor & Sacramental Min.; Sr. Donna Eggering, O.S.F., Pastoral Admin.
Res.: 313 N. Livingston St., 64628. Tel: 660-258-2507; Fax: 660-258-5637. Email: rectory@icbrookfield.org. Web: www.icbrookfield.org.
Catechesis/Religious Program—Students 81.

BRUNSWICK, CHARITON CO., ST. BONIFACE (1860) [CEM] Revs. Robert H. Fields, Canonical Admin.; Gerald J. Kaimann, Canonical Pastor.
Res.: 203 E. Harrison St., 65236. Tel: 660-548-3267.
Catechesis/Religious Program—Students 20.
Mission—St. Joseph (1870) Hurricane Branch, Chariton Co.

CALIFORNIA, MONITEAU CO., ANNUNCIATION (1872) [CEM] Rev. Frederick J. Elskamp; Sr. Mary Ruth Wand, S.S.N.D., Pastoral Min.
Res.: 310 S. Mill St., 65018. Tel: 573-796-4842; Fax: 573-796-4842 (*51). Email: annunciati@socket.net. Web: www.annunciationcatholicchurch.org.
Catechesis/Religious Program—Tel: 573-796-4842. Students 150.

CAMDENTON, CAMDEN CO., ST. ANTHONY (1946) Rev. Daniel I.J. Lueckenotte, Admin.; Deacons Richard A. Von Gunten, (Retired); David Lovell.
Church & Mailing: 1874 N. Business Rte. 5, 65020. Tel: 573-346-2716; Fax: 573-346-0625. Email: stanthonys@sbcglobal.net.
Catechesis/Religious Program—Students 225.

CANTON, LEWIS CO., ST. JOSEPH (1865) Unassigned.
Res.: 812 Lewis St., 63435. Tel: 573-288-3198; Fax: 573-288-3198. Email: stjosephcanton@centurytel.net.
Catechesis/Religious Program—Students 44.
Mission—Notre Dame (1868) Rte. C, La Grange, Lewis Co. 63448. Tel: 573-655-4296.
Catechesis/Religious Program—Students 9.

CENTRALIA, BOONE CO., HOLY SPIRIT (1897) Rev. J. James Offutt.
Res.: 404 S. Rollins St., 65240. Tel: 573-682-2815. Email: hsoffice@socket.net. Web: members.socket.net/~holyspirit.
Catechesis/Religious Program—Students 73.

CHAMOIS, OSAGE CO., MOST PURE HEART OF MARY (1865) [CEM 2] Rev. David A. Means, Canonical Admin.
Res.: 106 W. 2nd St., P.O. Box 156, 65024. Tel: 573-763-5345; Fax: 573-763-5345. Email: mphparish@centurytel.net. Web: www.mostpureheart.org.
Catechesis/Religious Program—Students 17.

CLARENCE, SHELBY CO., ST. PATRICK (1884) [CEM] Rev. Donardo S. Bermejo, Canonical Admin.
Res. & Mailing Address: 307 E. Chestnut, P.O. Box 306, Shelbina, 63468. Tel: 573-588-4498; Fax: 573-588-4728. Email: marypat@socket.net.
Church: 201 Grand St., 63437. Tel: 573-699-3805.
Catechesis/Religious Program—Students 22.

COLUMBIA, BOONE CO.

1—OUR LADY OF LOURDES (1958) Rev. Msgr. Michael T. Flanagan; Rev. Ron Kreul, O.P.; Deacons Fred Fritsch, (Retired); Joseph Puglis; James Leyden; Thomas Miller.
Res.: 903 Bernadette Dr., 65203. Tel: 573-445-7915; Fax: 573-446-7402. Email: office2@ourladyoflourdes.org. Web: www.ourladyoflourdes.org.
School—(Grades K-8), 817 Bernadette Dr., 65203. Tel: 573-445-6516; Fax: 573-445-9887. Email: pkirk@ccsk8.org. Web: ccsk8.org. Patricia Kirk, Prin.; Julie Barnett, Librarian. Lay Teachers 42; Students 588.
Catechesis/Religious Program—Email: reddirector@ourladyoflourdes.org. Students 380.

2—SACRED HEART (1876) Rev. Thomas Saucier, O.P.; Deacons John D. Weaver; Bill Caubet.
Mailing Address: 105 Waugh St., 65201.
Office: 1115 Locust St., 65201. Tel: 573-443-3470; Fax: 573-442-1082. Email: sbauer@sacredheart-church.org. Web: sacredheart-church.org.
Catechesis/Religious Program—Students 50.

3—ST. THOMAS MORE NEWMAN CENTER, UNIVERSITY OF MISSOURI (1963) Revs. Thomas Saucier, O.P.; Simon Felix Michalski, O.P.; Patrick D. Tobin, O.P.; Deacons Francis Ruggiero; Gene Kazmierczak.
Res.: 905 S. Greenwood, 65203. Tel: 573-442-6044. Email: chris.temporal@newmancentercolumbia.org. Web: www.newmancentercolumbia.org.
Church: 602 Turner Ave., 65201. Tel: 573-449-5424; Fax: 573-874-2777.
Catechesis/Religious Program—Students 227.

CROCKER, PULASKI CO., ST. CORNELIUS (1966) [CEM] Attended by St. Theresa, Dixon. Rev. Walter J. Reisinger, C.M.
Res.: P.O. Box 310, Dixon, 65459. Tel: 573-759-7521.
Catechesis/Religious Program—Students 3.

CUBA, CRAWFORD CO., HOLY CROSS (1880) [CEM] Rev. James Finder.
Res.: 415 W. School Ave., 65453. Tel: 573-885-3520; Fax: 573-885-3501. Email: hccc@fidmail.com.
School—(Grades PreK-8), 407 W. School Ave., 65453. Tel: 573-885-4727. Email: holycrossschoolcuba@gmail.com. Cate Sanazaro, Prin. Lay Teachers 6; Students 53.
Catechesis/Religious Program—Students 53.

DIXON, PULASKI CO., ST. THERESA (1928) [CEM] Rev. Walter J. Reisinger, C.M.
Res.: 506 Oak St., P.O. Box 310, 65459. Tel: 573-759-7521.
Catechesis/Religious Program—Students 4.

EDINA, KNOX CO., ST. JOSEPH (1844) [CEM 2] Rev. Joseph Hoi; Deacon Kenneth Berry.
Res.: 509 N. Main St., 63537-1239. Tel: 660-397-2183; Fax: 660-397-3680. Email:

stjoeal@marktwain.net. Web: www.knoxcountycatholic.org.
Catechesis/Religious Program—Fax: 660-397-3680. Students 75.

ELDON, MILLER CO., SACRED HEART (1910) Rev. Msgr. Donald W. Lammers; Deacon Gary Christoff.
Res.: 540 N. Mill St., 65026. Tel: 573-392-5334; Fax: 573-392-3493. Email: sacred540@sbcglobal.net.
Catechesis/Religious Program—Students 64.

EWING, LEWIS CO., QUEEN OF PEACE (1887) [CEM 2] Unassigned.
Res.: P.O. Box 347, 63440. Tel: 573-209-3343. Email: qofpeace@marktwain.net.
Catechesis/Religious Program—Students 29.

FAYETTE, HOWARD CO., ST. JOSEPH (1956) Rev. Robert W. Duesdieker.
Res.: 300 S. Cleveland Ave., 65248. Tel: 660-248-2439; Fax: 660-248-2439. Email: stjoseph-fayette@socket.net. Web: www.stjosephcath.org.
Catechesis/Religious Program—Students 27.

FOLK, OSAGE CO., ST. ANTHONY OF PADUA (1905) [CEM] Rev. Mark S. Smith.
Mailing Address: P.O. Box 157, Westphalia, 65085. Tel: 573-455-2888. Email: folkchurch@osageconnect.net. In Res., Rev. Roberto M. Ike.
Catechesis/Religious Program—Students 32.

FRANKENSTEIN, OSAGE CO., OUR LADY HELP OF CHRISTIANS (1863) [CEM 3] Rev. Ignazio C. Medina.
Church & Mailing Address: 1665 Hwy. C, Bonnots Mill, 65016. Tel: 573-897-2587.
School—(Grades 1-8) Tel: 573-897-2567; Fax: 573-897-4143. Tatia Taylor, Prin. Sisters 2; Lay Teachers 2; Students 43.
Catechesis/Religious Program—Students 15.

FREEBURG, OSAGE CO., HOLY FAMILY (1904) [CEM] Rev. Philip E. Niekamp.
Res.: 104 Oliver St., P.O. Box 9, 65035. Tel: 573-744-5254; Fax: 573-744-9201. Email: cathedralofozarks@att.net.
School—(Grades K-8) Tel: 573-744-5200. Email: djcc05@earthlink.net. Debbie Reinkemeyer, Prin. Sisters 1; Lay Teachers 5; Students 76.
Catechesis/Religious Program—Students 14.

FULTON, CALLAWAY CO., ST. PETER (1875) Rev. Frank A. Bussmann; Deacon John L. Nuedecker.
Parish Center—700 State Rd. Z, 65251. Tel: 573-642-5562; Fax: 573-642-2839. Email: stpeterparishoffice@stpeterfultonmo.org. Web: stpeterfultonmo.org.
School—(Grades K-8) Tel: 573-642-2839; Fax: 573-642-2839. Email: mrscnewman@sbcglobal.net. Cynthia Newman, School Admin. Lay Teachers 11; Students 108.
Catechesis/Religious Program—Students 70.

GLASGOW, HOWARD CO., ST. MARY (1866) [CEM] Rev. Richard W. Frank.
Res.: 421 Third St., 65254. Tel: 660-338-2053; Fax: 660-338-2598. Email: glasgowcatholicchurch@yahoo.com.
School—(Grades K-8), 501 3rd St., 65254. Tel: 660-338-2258; Fax: 660-338-9930. Email: kentmonnig@att.net. Kent Monnig, Prin.; Melissa Morrison, Librarian. Lay Teachers 11; Students 107.
Catechesis/Religious Program—Students 9.

HANNIBAL, MARION CO., HOLY FAMILY (1845) [JC] Rev. Michael F. Quinn.
Office: 2103 Broadway, 63401. Tel: 573-221-1078; Fax: 573-248-1662. Email: hfparish@sbcglobal.net. Web: www.myholyfamily.com.
School—(Grades PreK-8), 1113 Broadway, 63401. Tel: 573-221-0456; Fax: 573-221-6357. Mrs. Joy Hayward, Prin. Lay Teachers 18; Students 183.
Catechesis/Religious Program—Students 75.

HERMANN, GASCONADE CO., ST. GEORGE (1845) [CEM] Rev. William D. Debo.
Res.: 128 W. 4th St., 65041-1099. Tel: 573-486-2723; Fax: 573-486-3062. Email: bdd@stgeorgeschool-hermann.com. Web: www.stgeorge-hermann.com.
School—(Grades PreK-8) Tel: 573-486-5914; Fax: 573-486-2434. Email: jclingman@stgeorgeschool-hermann.com. Web: www.school.stgeorge-hermann.com. Julie Clingman, Prin. Lay Teachers 12; Students 156.
Catechesis/Religious Program—Students 59.

HERMITAGE, HICKORY CO., ST. BERNADETTE (1973) Rev. Daniel I.J. Lueckenotte, Canonical Admin.
Church: Hwy. 254, P.O. Box 167, 65668. Tel: 417-745-6361. Email: stbernadettechurch@hotmail.com.
Catechesis/Religious Program—Students 7.
Mission—Our Lady of the Snows (1990)Tel: 573-345-4548.

HOLTS SUMMIT, CALLAWAY CO., ST. ANDREW (1975) [CEM] Rev. Msgr. Gregory L. Higley; Deacons Daniel J. Ramsay; David Thompson.
Church: 400 St. Andrew Dr., 65043. Tel: 573-896-5010. Email: standrew@embarqmail.com. Web: www.standrewholtssummit.com.
Catechesis/Religious Program—Students 99.

ILASCO, RALLS CO., HOLY CROSS, Closed. For inquiries for parish records please see Holy Family, Hannibal.

INDIAN CREEK, MONROE CO., ST. STEPHEN (1833) [CEM] Rev. Michael W. Penn.
Res.: 27519 Monroe Rd. 533, Monroe City, 63456. Tel: 573-735-4033. Email: swinkeypat@gmail.com. Web: www.missouri.edu/~tmk5f7/swinkey.
Catechesis/Religious Program—

INDIAN GROVE, CHARITON CO., ST. RAPHAEL (1886) [CEM] Attended by St. Boniface, Brunswick. Revs. Gerald J. Kaimann, Canonical Pastor; Robert H. Fields, Canonical Admin.
Mailing Address: 203 E. Harrison St., Brunswick, 65236. Tel: 660-548-3267.

JONESBURG, MONTGOMERY CO., ST. PATRICK (1862) [CEM] Rev. P. Gregory Oligschlaeger, Canonical Pastor; Ms. Kristin Roth, Pastoral Admin.
Res.: 505 First St., 63351. Tel: 636-488-5623; Fax: 636-488-5629. Email: stpats@centurytel.net.
Catechesis/Religious Program—Students 23.

KAHOKA, CLARK CO.
1—ST. MICHAEL THE ARCHANGEL (1891) Rev. Paul M. Hartley.
Church: 622 W. Exchange St., 63445. Tel: 660-727-3472. Email: stmichel@centurytel.net.
Catechesis/Religious Program—
Mission—St. Martha (1887) 202 S. Main St., Wayland, Clark Co. 63472.
Catechesis/Religious Program—Students 26.
2—THE SHRINE OF ST. PATRICK (1839) [CEM] Attended by Kahoka. Rev. Paul M. Hartley.
Res.: 622 W. Exchange, 63445. Tel: 660-727-3472. Email: stmichel@centurytel.net.
Catechesis/Religious Program—

KIRKSVILLE, ADAIR CO., MARY IMMACULATE (1888) [CEM] Rev. Christopher L. Cordes; Deacon David D. Ream.
716 E. Washington St., 63501. Tel: 660-665-2466; Fax: 660-665-8955. Email: marie.wiskirchen@miparish.org. Web: www.miparish.org.
School—(Grades PreK-8), 712 E. Washington St., 63501. Tel: 660-665-1006; Fax: 660-665-3621. Email: srklauser@miparish.org. Web: www.miparish.org. Sr. Ruth Ann Klauser, S.S.N.D., Prin. Lay Teachers 6; Students 65.
Catechesis/Religious Program—Tel: 660-665-2466. Students 101.
Mission—St. Rose of Lima (1903) Hwy. 149, Novinger, Adair Co. 63559.

LAKE OZARK, MILLER CO., OUR LADY OF THE LAKE (1940) Rev. Msgr. Michael J. Wilbers.
Church: 2411 Bagnell Dam Blvd., P.O. Box 2390, 65049. Tel: 573-365-2241; Fax: 573-365-4458. Email: ourladylake@sbcglobal.net.
Catechesis/Religious Program—Students 100.

LAURIE, MORGAN CO., SHRINE OF ST. PATRICK (1870) [CEM] Revs. Patrick G. Dolan; C. Duane Ryan.
Office: 176 Marian Dr., P.O. Box 1098, 65038-1098. Tel: 573-374-7855; Fax: 573-374-0627. Email: parishsecretary@shrineofstpatrick.com.
Catechesis/Religious Program—Students 43.
Mission—St. Philip Benizi (1963) 17034 Hwy. D, Versailles, Morgan Co. 65084. Tel: 573-378-5958; Fax: 573-378-4002. Email: stphilip@yhti.net.
Catechesis/Religious Program—(Combined with Shrine of St. Patrick, Laurie) Students 12.
Shrine—The National Shrine of Mary, Mother of the Church P.O. Box 1250, 65038. Tel: 573-374-6279; Fax: 573-374-0627.

LINN, OSAGE CO., ST. GEORGE (1866) [CEM] Rev. Ignazio C. Medina.
Res.: 613 E. Main St., P.O. Box 49, 65051. Tel: 573-897-2293. Email: reynoldsgerri@yahoo.com.
School—(Grades K-8) Tel: 573-897-3645; Fax: 573-897-2148. Sr. Celly Ann Amparano, S.S.N.D., Prin. Religious 3; Lay Teachers 11; Students 195.
Catechesis/Religious Program—Tel: 573-897-3203. Students 67.

LOOSE CREEK, OSAGE CO., IMMACULATE CONCEPTION (1845) [CEM 2] Rev. Donald J. Antweiler, Admin.
Res.: 121 County Rd. 402, P.O. Box 8, 65054. Tel: 573-897-2922; Fax: 573-897-4271. Email: frda47@gmail.com.
School—(Grades K-8), 147 Co. Rd. 402, P.O. Box 68, 65054. Tel: 573-897-3516. Rita Stiefermann, Prin. School Sisters of Notre Dame 1; Lay Teachers 9; Students 123.
Catechesis/Religious Program—Students 27.

LOUISIANA, PIKE CO., ST. JOSEPH (1865) [CEM] Rev. Louis E. Dorn; Deacon Mark J. Dobelmann.
Res.: 508 N. 3rd St., 63353. Tel: 573-754-4757.
Catechesis/Religious Program—Tel: 573-754-6609. Students 38.
Mission—Mary Queen of Peace (1951) South Second St., Clarksville, Pike Co. 63336. Tel: 573-242-3730.

MACON, MACON CO., IMMACULATE CONCEPTION (1857) [CEM] Rev. David J. Veit; Deacons Bernhard Toll; Lloyd Collins; William B. Tull III.
Res.: 402 N. Rollins St., 63552. Tel: 660-385-3792; Fax: 660-385-3792. Email: imchurch2004@yahoo.com.
School—(Grades K-8) Tel: 660-385-2711; Fax: 660-385-2839. Sr. Barbara Rose Koch, C.PP.S., Prin. Lay Teachers 5; Students 68.
Catechesis/Religious Program—Students 58.
Mission—Sacred Heart (1880) Bevier, Macon Co. 63532.

MARCELINE, LINN CO., ST. BONAVENTURE (1888) [CEM 2] Rev. Gerald J. Kaimann.
Res.: 409 S. Kansas Ave., 64658-1301. Tel: 660-376-3239. Email: stbon@mcmsys.com. Web: www.stbon.net.
School—Fr. McCartan Memorial School, (Grades PreK-8), 327 S. Kansas Ave., 64658. Tel: 660-376-3580; Fax: 660-376-2836. Richard K. Davis, Prin. Lay Teachers 7; Students 72.
Catechesis/Religious Program—Students 48.

MARSHALL, SALINE CO., ST. PETER (1870) [CEM] Revs. Kevin Gormley; Thomas L. Alber, Senior Priest; Deacons Richard H. Luebbering; Joseph R. Mitchell.
Res.: 1801 S. Miami Ave., P.O. Box 220, 65340. Tel: 660-886-7960; Fax: 660-831-1723. Email: stpeter.office@att.net. Web: www.stpeterchurch-marshallmo.org.
School—(Grades PreK-8), 368 S. Ellsworth St., 65340. Tel: 660-886-6390; Fax: 660-866-6606. Email: garlittrell@stpeterchurch-marshallmo.org. Gary Littrell, Prin. Lay Teachers 15; Students 194.
Catechesis/Religious Program—Students 140.
Mission—Holy Family (1945) 200 Ruby St., Sweet Springs, Saline Co. 65351.

MARTINSBURG, AUDRAIN CO., ST. JOSEPH (1876) [CEM] Revs. P. Gregory Oligschlaeger; Benedict Ayodi, O.F.M.Cap.
Res.: 408 E. Kellett, 65264. Tel: 573-492-6595; Fax: 573-492-6105. Email: joseph@socket.net.
School—(Grades K-8) Tel: 573-492-6283. Email: stjoeschool@socket.net. Kathleen Robnett, Prin. Lay Teachers 7; Students 65.
Catechesis/Religious Program—Students 22.

MARY'S HOME, MILLER CO., OUR LADY OF THE SNOWS (1883) [CEM] Rev. Patrick J. Shortt.
Res.: 274 Hwy. H, Eugene, 65032-4231. Tel: 573-498-3820; Fax: 573-498-3779. Email: frpjshortt@gmail.com.
School—(Grades PreK-8) Tel: 573-498-3574; Fax: 573-498-3776. Email: gaylet@radiowire.net. Web: www.oloscougars.com. Gayle Trachsel, Prin. Lay Teachers 7; Students 91.
Catechesis/Religious Program—Students 151.

MEMPHIS, SCOTLAND CO., ST. JOHN (1952) [CEM] Rev. Joseph Hoi.
Mailing Address: Rt. 3, Box 34-H, 63555.
Res.: 509 N. Main St., Edina, 63537. Tel: 660-465-7130. Email: stjohns@nemr.net.
Catechesis/Religious Program—Students 15.

META, OSAGE CO., ST. CECILIA (1904) [CEM] Rev. Mark A. Porterfield.
Res.: P.O. Box 146, St. Thomas, 65076. Tel: 573-477-3315; Fax: 573-477-0177. Email: stthomasoffice@embarqmail.com.
Catechesis/Religious Program—Students 73.

MEXICO, AUDRAIN CO., ST. BRENDAN (1857) [CEM] Rev. John J. Schmitz.
Res.: 615 S. Washington St., 65265-2658. Tel: 573-581-4720; Fax: 573-581-7711. Email: stbrendn@swbell.net.
School—(Grades PreK-8) Tel: 573-581-2443; Fax: 573-581-2571. Email: bgleeson@saintbrendans.org. Bill Gleeson, Prin. Lay Teachers 12; Students 143.
Catechesis/Religious Program—Students 30.

MILAN, SULLIVAN CO., ST. MARY (1868) [CEM 2] Revs. Gerald J. Kaimann, Canonical Pastor; M. Brendan Griffey, Sacramental Min.; Sr. Loretta Sigler, C.PP.S., Pastoral Admin.
Res.: 101 W. Baker St., P.O. Box 147, 63556. Tel: 660-265-4110; Fax: 660-265-4110. Email: stmarys@nemr.net. Web: www.stmarymilan.parishesonline.com.
Catechesis/Religious Program—Tel: 660-265-4110. Students 58.
Mission—St. Mary (1868) 1118 Main St. Hwy. 136 E., Unionville, Putnam Co. Tel: 660-947-2599.
Catechesis/Religious Program—Students 15.

MOBERLY, RANDOLPH CO., ST. PIUS X (1870) [CEM] Rev. Michael A. Coleman; Deacon David F. Ritter.
Res.: 217 S. Williams St., P.O. Box 310, 65270. Tel: 660-263-5243; Fax: 660-263-0101. Email: frmike@mcmsys.com. Web: www.stpiuschurch.com.
School—(Grades PreK-8), 210 S. Williams St., 65270. Tel: 660-263-5500; Fax: 660-263-5744. Email: jjasper@st-pius.com. Web: st-pius.com. Julie Jasper, Prin.; Margaret Creed, Librarian. Lay Teachers 13; Students 154.
Catechesis/Religious Program—Students 90.

MOKANE, CALLAWAY CO., ST. JUDE THADDEUS (1900) Rev. Frank A. Bussmann.
Rectory—700 State Hwy. Z, Fulton, 65251.

Church: 401 Adams St., 65059. Tel: 573-676-3238.
Catechesis/Religious Program—Students 18.

MONROE CITY, MONROE CO., HOLY ROSARY (1884) [CEM] Rev. Michael W. Penn.
Res.: 405 S. Main St., 63456. Tel: 573-735-4718; Fax: 573-735-0713. Email: hrosary@mywdo.com. Web: www.holyrosarymc.org.
School—(Grades K-8) Tel: 573-735-2422; Fax: 573-735-3091. Email: hrssw@socket.net. Sr. Suzanne Walker, O.P., Prin. Sisters 1; Lay Teachers 10; Students 170.
Catechesis/Religious Program—Students 81.

MONTGOMERY CITY, MONTGOMERY CO., IMMACULATE CONCEPTION (1861) [CEM 2] Revs. P. Gregory Oligschlaeger; Benedict Ayodi, O.F.M.Cap.
Res.: 307 N. Walker, 63361. Tel: 573-564-2375; Fax: 573-564-2375. Email: imm-con@sbcglobal.net.
School—(Grades PreK-8), 407 W. Third St., 63361. Tel: 573-564-2679; Fax: 573-564-2305. Email: jfrankenberg@icschool-mc.org. Web: www.ic-school.org. Jaime Frankenberg, Prin.; Aggie Baldetti, Librarian; Bonnie Walker, Librarian. Lay Teachers 4; Students 41.
Catechesis/Religious Program—Students 54.

MORRISON, GASCONADE CO., ASSUMPTION (1875) [CEM 2] Attended by Most Pure Heart of Mary, Chamois. Rev. David A. Means, Canonical Admin.
Mailing Address: P.O. Box 156, Chamois, 65024. Tel: 573-763-5345. Email: mphparish@centurytel.net. Web: www.assumptionmorrison.org.
Catechesis/Religious Program—Students 1.

OSAGE BEND, COLE CO., ST. MARGARET OF ANTIOCH (1907) [CEM] Rev. Gregory C. Meystrik, Canonical Pastor & Sacramental Min.; Deacon Robert Smerek, Pastoral Admin.
12025 Rte. W., 65101. Tel: 573-496-3404. Email: stmargaretosagebend@radiowire.net.
Catechesis/Religious Program—Students 47.

OWENSVILLE, GASCONADE CO., IMMACULATE CONCEPTION (1893) [CEM 2] Rev. Jeremy A. Secrist.
Res.: 404 S. First St., 65066. Tel: 573-437-2494. Email: icchurch@fidnet.com.
Catechesis/Religious Program—Tel: 573-437-3086. Students 120.

PALMYRA, MARION CO., ST. JOSEPH (1866) Revs. Alexuis Ekka, Canonical Admin.; Michael W. Penn, Canonical Pastor; Deacon Robert A. Leake.
Res.: 400 S. Lane St., P.O. Box 606, 63461. Tel: 573-769-3270; Fax: 573-769-4702. Email: stjoepalmyra@yahoo.com.
Catechesis/Religious Program—Students 67.

PERRY, RALLS CO., ST. WILLIAM (1901) [CEM] Rev. John A. Henderson.
Res.: P.O. Box 339, 63462. Tel: 573-565-2852; Fax: 573-565-8012. Email: stwill@rallstech.com.
Catechesis/Religious Program—Students 34.
Mission—St. Frances Cabrini (1953) 25560 Business Hwy. 24, Paris, Monroe Co. 65275.
Mission—St. Paul (Historic Church) 22520 St. Paul Dr., Center, Ralls Co. 63436. Email: stwill@rallstech.com.

PILOT GROVE, COOPER CO., ST. JOSEPH (1894) [CEM 3] Rev. Philip M. Kane.
Res.: 407 Harris St., 65276. Tel: 660-834-5600; Fax: 660-834-5601. Email: secretarypg@catholicweb.com. Web: www.stjosephparishpg.catholicweb.com.
School—405 Harris St., 65276. Tel: 660-834-5600; Fax: 660-834-5601. Email: kentmonnig@att.net. Kent Monnig, Prin. Lay Teachers 6; Students 47.
Catechesis/Religious Program—Students 55.
Station—St. John the Baptist (1840) Clear Creek, 65276. (Mass)
Station—St. Joseph Otterville, 65348. (Mass)

RHINELAND, MONTGOMERY CO., CHURCH OF THE RISEN SAVIOR (1979) [CEM 2] Rev. William D. Debo; Deacons Joseph E. Horton; Gerald W. Korman.
Res.: 605 Bluff St., 65069. Tel: 573-236-4390. Email: risensav@ktis.net. Web: www.historicshrine.org.
Catechesis/Religious Program—
Pilgrimage Site— (1888) Shrine of Our Lady of Sorrows, 65069. Tel: 573-236-4334.

RICH FOUNTAIN, OSAGE CO., SACRED HEART (1838) [CEM] Rev. Philip E. Niekamp.
Church: 4277 Hwy. U, 65035. Tel: 573-744-5987; Fax: 573-744-5761. Email: shrf1838@earthlink.net. Web: www.sacredheartrf.com.
School—(Grades K-8), 4309 Hwy. U, 65035. Tel: 573-744-5898. Email: shsrf@sacredheartrf.com. Web: www.sacredheartrf.com. Linda Neuner, Prin. Sisters of Notre Dame 1; Lay Teachers 5; Students 72.
Catechesis/Religious Program—Students 47.

RICHLAND, PULASKI CO., ST. JUDE (1972) Rev. John W. Groner.
Res. & Mailing Address: 367 Old Hwy. 66, St. Robert, 65584. Tel: 573-336-3662.
Catechesis/Religious Program—Students 9.

ROLLA, PHELPS CO., ST. PATRICK (1862) [CEM] Rev. Michael P. Murphy; Deacons Michael S. Brooks; Thomas C. Manion; Matthew McLaughlin.
Res.: 17 St. Patrick Ln., 65401. Tel: 573-364-1435; Fax: 573-364-2073. Email: dwilly@stpatsrolla.org. Web: stpatsrolla.org.
School—(Grades PreK-8), 19 St. Patrick Ln., 65401. Tel: 573-364-1162; Fax: 573-364-0679. Deacon Michael Brooks, Prin. Lay Teachers 16; Students 175.
Catechesis/Religious Program—Students 135.

ROSATI, PHELPS CO., ST. ANTHONY (1906) [CEM] Rev. Charles D. Pardee.
Res.: 316 E. Scioto St., Saint James, 65559. Tel: 573-265-7247. Email: stanthony@centurylink.net.
Catechesis/Religious Program—Students 2.

RUSSELLVILLE, COLE CO., ST. MICHAEL (1906) [CEM 2] Rev. J. David Maher, Canonical Pastor; Sr. Mary Rost, S.S.N.D., Pastoral Admin.
Res.: 13321 Railroad Ave., 65074-1214. Tel: 573-782-4503; Fax: 573-782-3171. Email: stmrussellville@yahoo.com.
Catechesis/Religious Program—Tel: 573-782-3171. Students 69.

ST. ANTHONY, MILLER CO., ST. ANTHONY (1906) [CEM] Revs. Benjamin Nwosu, Canonical Admin.; Patrick J. Shortt, Canonical Pastor.
Res.: 246 Main St., P.O. Box 128, Saint Elizabeth, 65075.
Church: 132 Main St., Iberia, 65486. Tel: 573-793-6550. Email: stanthonyofpaduachurch@hotmail.com.
Catechesis/Religious Program—Students 49.

ST. CLEMENT, PIKE CO., ST. CLEMENT (1871) [CEM 2] Rev. R. William Peckman.
Res.: 21509 Hwy. 161, Bowling Green, 63334. Tel: 573-324-5545; Fax: 573-324-5155. Email: clement@dishmail.net. Web: www.stclementmo.org.
School—(Grades K-8) Tel: 573-324-2166; Fax: 573-324-6159. Email: stclement@socket.net. Larry Twellman, Prin. Lay Teachers 6; Students 71.
Catechesis/Religious Program—Students 55.

ST. ELIZABETH, MILLER CO., ST. LAWRENCE (1871) [CEM] Revs. Benjamin Nwosu, Canonical Admin.; Patrick J. Shortt, Canonical Pastor.
Res.: 246 Main, P.O. Box 128, 65075. Tel: 573-493-2301. Email: stlawrencegridiron@hotmail.com.
Catechesis/Religious Program—Tel: 573-793-6550. Students 138.

ST. JAMES, PHELPS CO., IMMACULATE CONCEPTION (1870) Rev. Charles D. Pardee.
Rectory—316 E. Scioto, Saint James, 65559. Tel: 573-265-7250; Fax: 573-265-7269. Email: icchurch@socket.net. Web: www.icchurchstjames.org.
Catechesis/Religious Program—Students 52.

ST. MARTINS, COLE CO., ST. MARTIN (1885) [CEM] Rev. Edwin A. Schmidt; Deacons Francis J. Butel; Stephan J. Kliethermes.
Res.: 7148 St. Martins Ave., 65109. Tel: 573-893-2923; Fax: 573-893-3865. Email: stmartin@socket.net.
School—(Grades K-8), 7206 St. Martins Ave., 65109. Tel: 573-893-3519; Fax: 573-893-7404. Email: cwolters3@embarqmail.com. Cathy Wolters, Prin. Lay Teachers 14; Students 226.
Catechesis/Religious Program—Tel: 573-893-2352; Fax: 573-893-9587. Email: BAWasinger@aol.com. Students 72.

ST. ROBERT, PULASKI CO., ST. ROBERT BELLARMINE (1941) [CEM] Rev. John W. Groner.
Res.: 367 Old Hwy. 66, 65584. Tel: 573-336-3662; Fax: 573-336-5648. Email: strobert@fidmail.com. Web: www.strobertcatholic.com.
Catechesis/Religious Program—Students 100.

ST. THOMAS, COLE CO., ST. THOMAS THE APOSTLE (1869) [CEM] Rev. Mark A. Porterfield.
Res.: 14814 Rt. B, P.O. Box 146, 65076. Tel: 573-477-3315; Fax: 573-477-0177. Email: stthomasoffice@embargmail.com.
School—(Grades PreK-8), P.O. Box 211, 65076. Tel: 573-477-3322; Fax: 573-477-3700. Email: sdoerhoff@embarqmail.com. Web: www.stthomasmo-.com. Mr. Sidney Doerhoff, Interim Prin. Lay Teachers 9; Students 106.
Catechesis/Religious Program—Students 58.

SALISBURY, CHARITON CO., ST. JOSEPH (1870) [CEM] Rev. William L. Korte.
Res.: 301 W. Williams, 65281. Tel: 660-388-5590; Fax: 660-388-5590. Email: stjosephchurch@mcmsys.com.
School—(Grades K-8) Tel: 660-388-5518; Fax: 660-388-5518. Email: stjoe@mcmsys.com. Jan Dubbert, Prin.; Carrie Henke, Librarian. Lay Teachers 12; Students 122.
Catechesis/Religious Program—Students 36.

SEDALIA, PETTIS CO.
1—ST. PATRICK (1866) Revs. Mark Miller, C.PP.S; James G. Betzen, C.PP.S.; Deacons Jerome Connery; Mark Yates.
Rectory—415 E. Fourth St., 65301. Tel: 660-826-2062; Fax: 660-829-1085. Email: stpatricks@charter.net.
Catechesis/Religious Program—Students 85.
2—SACRED HEART (1882) [CEM] Revs. Mark Miller, C.PP.S; James G. Betzen, C.PP.S.; Deacons Jerome Connery; Mark Yates.
Res.: 421 W. Third St., 65301. Tel: 660-827-2311; Fax: 660-827-3941. Email: shparish@charter.net.
School—(Grades K-8), 416 W. Third St., 65301. Tel: 660-827-3800; Fax: 660-827-3806. Dr. Mark Register, Prin.; Jinny O'Donnell, Librarian. Lay Teachers 21; Students 266.
High School—(Grades 9-12) Dr. Mark Register, Prin. Lay Teachers 12; Students 122.
Catechesis/Religious Program—Students 109.
Mission—St. John (1845) Bahner, Pettis Co.
Station—St. Patrick (1876) Spring Fork. (Mass)

SHELBINA, SHELBY CO., ST. MARY (1879) [CEM] Rev. Donardo S. Bermejo, Canonical Admin.; Deacons John DeGraff; Bernhard Toll.
Mailing Address: 307 E. Chestnut St., P.O. Box 306, 63468. Tel: 573-588-4498; Fax: 573-588-4498. Email: marypat@socket.net.
Catechesis/Religious Program—Students 88.

SLATER, SALINE CO., ST. JOSEPH (1882) Attended by Glasgow. Rev. Richard W. Frank.
Res.: 325 W. Emma St., 65349. Tel: 660-529-2588. Email: stjoseph1927@sbcglobal.net.
Catechesis/Religious Program—Students 9.

STEELVILLE, CRAWFORD CO., ST. MICHAEL (1949) Rev. James Finder.
Res.: 415 W. School St., Cuba, 65453. Tel: 573-885-3520; Fax: 573-885-3501. Email: hccc@fidmail.com. Church: Hwy. 8 E., 65565.
Catechesis/Religious Program—Students 18.

TAOS, COLE CO., ST. FRANCIS XAVIER (1838) [CEM] Rev. Wayne M. Boyer; Deacon James E. Skahan.
Res.: 7319 Rte. M, 65101. Tel: 573-395-4401; Fax: 573-395-4302. Email: sfxchurch1@embarqmail.com. Web: www.members.socket.net/~SFXschool.
School—(Grades K-8), 7307 Rt. M., 65101. Tel: 573-395-4612; Fax: 573-395-4017. Donna Frazier, Prin. Lay Teachers 16; Students 188.
Catechesis/Religious Program—Students 95.

TIPTON, MONITEAU CO., ST. ANDREW (1857) [CEM] Rev. Frederick J. Elskamp.
Res.: 106 W. Cooper St., 65081-8210. Tel: 660-433-2162. Email: standrewchurch@embarqmail.com. Web: www.standrewtipton.org.
School—(Grades K-8), 118 E. Cooper St., 65081-0617. Tel: 660-433-2232; Fax: 660-433-5432. Email: standr34@embarqmail.com. Helen J. Franken, Prin. Lay Teachers 13; Students 127.
Catechesis/Religious Program—Students 49.

VANDALIA, AUDRAIN CO., SACRED HEART (1891) Rev. Russell R. Judge.
Res.: 203 W. Home, 63382. Tel: 573-594-2717. Email: shccastj@windstream.net.
Catechesis/Religious Program—Students 29.
Mission—St. John (1889) 7th & Elm, Laddonia, Audrain Co. 63352. Tel: 573-373-5351.

VIENNA, MARIES CO., VISITATION OF THE BLESSED VIRGIN MARY (1867) [CEM] Rev. Msgr. Marion J. Makarewicz.
Res.: 105 N. Main St., P.O. Box 171, 65582. Tel: 573-422-3950; Fax: 573-422-3950. Email: bvmchurch@att.net.
School—(Grades K-8), 105 N. Coffey St., P.O. Box 269, 65582. Tel: 573-422-3375; Fax: 573-422-3375. Web: www.vi-ps.org. Linda Stuckenschneider, Prin. Lay Teachers 5; Students 54.
Catechesis/Religious Program—Students 38.

WARDSVILLE, COLE CO., ST. STANISLAUS (1880) [CEM] Rev. Gregory C. Meystrik.
Res.: 6418 Rte. W., 65101. Tel: 573-636-4925; Fax: 573-636-2534. Email: ststan@socket.net. Web: www.ststan.net.
School—(Grades PreK-8), 6410 Rte. W., 65101. Tel: 573-636-7802; Fax: 573-635-4782. Email: nancyh@ststan.net. Web: www.ststan.net. Nancy Heberlie, Prin. Lay Teachers 19; Students 246.
Catechesis/Religious Program—Students 60.

WARSAW, BENTON CO., ST. ANN (1945) [CEM] Rev. Keith Branson, C.PP.S.
Res.: 30455 W. Dam Access Rd., 65355. Tel: 660-438-3844; Fax: 660-438-3844. Email: stannwarsaw1@yahoo.com. Web: stannwarsaw.org.
Catechesis/Religious Program—Tel: 660-438-3843.
Mission—SS. Peter & Paul (1878) P.O. Box 248, Cole Camp, Benton Co. 65325. Tel: 660-668-3468. Email: spap@iland.net.

WELLSVILLE, MONTGOMERY CO., CHURCH OF THE RESURRECTION (1873) [CEM] Revs. P. Gregory Oligschlaeger; Benedict Ayodi, O.F.M.Cap.
Church: 409 E. Bates, 63384.
Res. & Mailing Address: 408 E. Kellett, Martinsburg, 65264. Tel: 573-492-6595; Fax: 573-492-6105. Email: joseph@socket.net.
Catechesis/Religious Program—Students 11.

WESTPHALIA, OSAGE CO., ST. JOSEPH (1835) [CEM 2] Rev. Mark S. Smith.
Res.: P.O. Box 116, 65085-0116. Tel: 573-455-2320; Fax: 573-455-2984. Email: stjo1835@socket.net. Web: www.stjo1835.org.
School—(Grades K-8) Tel: 573-455-2339; Fax: 573-455-2287. Email: sjsw1838@att.net. Deacon James E. Skahan, Prin. Lay Teachers 14; Students 226.

Catechesis/Religious Program—Students 88.

WIEN, CHARITON CO., ST. MARY OF THE ANGELS (1876) [CEM 2] Rev. William L. Korte.

Res.: 12520 St. Mary's Ave., New Cambria, 63558-3418. Tel: 660-226-5243.

Catechesis/Religious Program—Students 8.

Chaplains of Public Institutions Hospitals and Schools

COLUMBIA. *Columbia Catholic Hospital Ministry*. Dr. Eleanor S. Braddock, M.D., Deacon Gene Kazmierczak, Coord. Tel: 573-446-0387, Rev. M. Brendan Griffey, Chap. Tel: 573-338-2199.

On Duty Outside the Diocese:
Revs.—
Merz, Daniel J.
Smith, M. Christopher
Steinhauser, Kenneth B.

Absent on Leave:
Revs.—
Behan, Hugh F.
Hereford, Thomas D.
Schlachter, Eric A.
Seifner, Thomas J.
Shetler, Joseph L.
Tatro, Timothy M.

Retired:
Rev. Msgrs.—
McCorkle, Louis W., P.O. Box 51, Conception, 64433. Tel: 660-944-2898
Sommer, Jerome, Regina Cleri, 10 Archbishop May Dr., St. Louis, 63119. Tel: 314-918-8216
Revs.—
Bauer, Sylvester W., 1899 Hwy. 63, Westphalia, 65085. Tel: 573-455-2280
Buescher, David G., 708 Marshall, 65101. Tel: 573-635-8845
Calasara, Mansuelo, P.O. Box 448, Dixon, 65459. Tel: 573-759-6381
Cronin, Richard, PO Box 44, Westphalia, 65085. Tel: 573-455-2151
Daly, Manus P.
Doyle, Edward F., #9 Garden Place, Montgomery City, 63361. Tel: 573-564-2497
Flanagan, William F., 27519 Monroe Rd. 533, Monroe City, 63456. Tel: 573-735-4033
Fuemmeler, James R., 1567 Resorts Rd., Camdenton, 65020. Tel: 573-873-3263
Jones, Paul W., HC 77, P.O. Box 536, Pittsburg, 65724. Tel: 573-852-4601
Konrad, Erwin, 12440 S. Benck Dr., Apt. 2, Alsip, IL 60803. Tel: 703-388-6803
Kramer, George, P.O. Box 68, Bonnots Mills, 65018. Tel: 573-897-2061
Lawless, P. Brendan, 12120 Conway Rd., Rm. 20, Saint Louis, 63141.
Long, John, Tara Curaheed Rd., Bishops Town, Cork, Ireland. Tel: 011-353-21-4831103
McGrath, Thomas E., 207 Norris Dr., 65109. Tel: 573-761-9180
Pierceall, Patrick L., P.O. Box 561, Hannibal, 63401. Tel: 573-795-6129
Schutty, John J.
Starmann, Joseph W., 25 Ackermann Rd., Winfield, 63389-3106. Tel: 636-566-8420
Stockman, Gerald W., 718 Randolph St., Glasgow, 65254. Tel: 660-338-2188
Stuart, Francis, O.S.B., St. Elizabeth Care Ctr., 649 S. Walnut St., Saint Elizabeth, 65075.
Wallace, Donald L.
Wheeler, Clarence, M.S., M.S., 612 Norris, 65109. Tel: 573-635-0648
Wiederholt, Clarence E., 1818 Almarie Ct., 65101. Tel: 573-636-4303

Permanent Deacons:
Anderberg, Peter K., (Retired)
Aulbur, Mark
Berry, Kenneth
Bilgrien, Kenneth D., (On Duty Outside the Diocese)
Boettger, Kent
Braddock, Joseph M.
Brand, Alvin J.
Breazile, James E., (On Duty Outside the Diocese)
Brooks, Michael
Brucks, Jerome C., (Retired)
Butel, Francis J.
Capuano, Tom, (Retired)
Caubet, William
Chaplin, Mark, (On Duty Outside the Diocese)
Chavaux, Paul, (Leave of Absence)
Christoff, Gary
Collins, Lloyd
Connery, Jerome
Daly, Michael M., (Leave of Absence)
Davis, Howard E., (On Duty Outside the Diocese)
DeGraff, John
DePyper, Robert
Dobelman, Mark J.
Dulle, Robert L.
Fischer, Thomas M.
Fritsch, Frederick, (Retired)
Garcia, Philip
Heidlage, Walter F., (Retired)
Hildebrand, Larry, (On Duty Outside the Diocese)
Horsefield, Earl R.
Horton, Joseph E.
Houston, John D., (Retired)
Joyce, Dana K.
Kazmierczak, Eugene S.
Kliethermes, James L.
Kliethermes, Stephan J.
Korman, Gerald W.
Leake, Robert A.
Leyden, James
Linhardt, Wayne
Long, Michael L.
Lovell, David
Luebbering, Richard H., (Retired)
Manion, Thomas C.
McLaughlin, Matthew
Miller, David
Miller, Thomas
Mitchell, Joseph R.
Neudecker, John L.
Orscheln, Donald W., (Retired)
Parn, Harold L., (Retired)
Pierceall, Eugene E., (Retired)
Poulter, Paul
Puglis, Joseph
Purvis, Raymond L.
Rackers, Robert J., (Retired)
Ramsay, Daniel J.
Ream, David D.
Reibenspies, Terence L., (On Duty Outside the Diocese)
Ritter, David F.
Rohan, Peter
Ruggiero, Frank
Schepers, Edwin
Schmitz, Fred
Schwartze, Stephen
Shumake, Lindell P., (Retired)
Skahan, James E.
Smerek, Robert
Stahl, Theodore E., (Retired)
Thompson, David
Toll, Bernhard F.
Tull, William B.
Valdes, Anthony J.
Visot, Luis R., (On Duty Outside the Diocese)
Von Gunten, Richard A., (Retired)
Warden, Donald E., (Retired)
Watson, G. Robert, (Leave of Absence)
Weaver, John D.
Weber, Lawrence A., (Leave of Absence)
Weisel, Fred M., (Leave of Absence)
Whalen, Tom, (Retired)

INSTITUTIONS LOCATED IN THE DIOCESE

[A] HIGH SCHOOLS, DIOCESAN

JEFFERSON CITY. *Helias Catholic High School*, 1305 Swift's Hwy., 65109. Tel: 573-635-6139; Fax: 573-635-5615. Email: info@heliashighschool.com. Web: www.heliashighschool.com. Mr. Didier Aur, Pres.; Sr. Jean Dietrich, S.S.N.D., Prin.; Mr. Stan Ochsner, Dean of Students; Rev. Brendan Doyle, Spiritual Dir.; Sr. Barbara Neist, S.S.N.D., Supervision & Professional Curriculum Coord.; Mrs. Christina Bockwinkel-Baker, Campus Ministry; Shelley Swoyer, Librarian. Brothers of the Christian Schools 1; School Sisters of Notre Dame 2; Lay Teachers 57; Students 800.

COLUMBIA. *Fr. Augustine Tolton Regional Catholic High School*, (Grades 9-10), 3351 E. Gans Rd., 65201. Tel: 573-445-7700. Email: kwolfe@toltoncatholic.org. Web: www.frtoltonhs.com. Kristie Wolfe, Pres. & Prin.

[B] CATHOLIC HOSPITALS

JEFFERSON CITY. *St. Mary Health Center*, 100 St. Mary's Medical Plaza, 65101. Tel: 573-761-7000; Fax: 573-636-5733. Web: www.stmarys-jeffcity.com. Brent VanConia, Pres.; Mrs. Peggy Van Gundy, Dir., Mission Effectiveness, Bd. Certified Chap.; Revs. James Gearhart, Bd. Certified Chap.; Paul Deutsch, Bd. Certified Chap.; Mark Steffen, Chap.; Randall Bunch, Chap. Member of SSM Health Care. Bed Capacity 167; Patients Assisted Annually 236,600; Clinics 14; Clinic Visits 115,844.

[C] CONVENTS AND RESIDENCES FOR SISTERS

JEFFERSON CITY. *Discalced Carmelite Monastery*, 2201 W. Main St., 65109. Tel: 573-636-3364. Sr. Marie Therese Dubois, O.C.D., Prioress. Professed of Solemn Vows 4.

[D] NEWMAN CENTERS

COLUMBIA. *St. Thomas More Newman Center* 602 Turner Ave., 65201. Tel: 573-449-5424; Fax: 573-874-2777. Email: chris.temporal@newmancentercolumbia.org. Web: www.newmancentercolumbia.org. Revs. Thomas Saucier, O.P., Pastor; Simon Felix Michalski, O.P.; Patrick D. Tobin, O.P.

KIRKSVILLE. *Catholic Newman Center, Truman State University* 709 S. Davis, 63501. Tel: 660-665-4357; Fax: 660-665-3592. Email: tsnewman@socket.net. Web: www.kirksvillenewman.truman.edu. Chris Korte, Dir.; Rev. William P. Kottenstette, Chap.

ROLLA. *Catholic Newman Center, Missouri University of Science and Technology* formerly University of Missouri-Rolla 1607 N. Rolla St., P.O. Box 838, 65402. Tel: 573-364-2133; Fax: 573-368-3560. Email: newman@mst.edu. Web: www.rollanewman.org. Rev. Michael P. Murphy, Chap.; Sr. Laura Spaeth, S.S.N.D., Campus Min.

[E] SOCIAL SERVICES

JEFFERSON CITY. *Samaritan Center*, 1310 E. McCarty St., P.O. Box 1687, 65102. Tel: 573-634-7776; Fax: 573-761-5948. Email: samaritan@midmosamaritan.org. Web: midmosamaritan.org. Marylyn DeFeo, Exec. Dir.

[F] MISCELLANEOUS

JEFFERSON CITY. *Catholic Charities of Central and Northern Missouri*, P.O. Box 104626, 65110. Tel: 573-635-9127, Ext. 233. Web: www.cccnmo.org. Mr. Michael A. Van Gundy, Exec. Dir.; Rev. Louis E. Dorn, Dir., Prison Ministry; Ms. Barbara Ross, Dir., Social Svcs.; Ms. Lorna Tran, Dir., Refugee & Immigration Svcs.

Catholic Charities of Missouri, LLC, P.O. Box 1127, 65102-1127. Tel: 573-634-8568. Web: www.cc-mo.org. Janel Luck, Exec. Dir.

Catholic Diocese of Jefferson City Fund, Inc., P.O. Box 104900, 65110-4900. Tel: 573-635-9127; Fax: 573-635-0386.

Diocesan Excellence in Education Fund, Inc., P.O. Box 104900, 65110-4900. Tel: 573-635-9127; Fax: 573-635-0386.

Diocese of Jefferson City Jubilee Fund, P.O. Box 104900, 65110-4900. Teletype: 573-635-9127; Fax: 573-635-0386.

Diocese of Jefferson City Real Estate Corporation, P.O. Box 104900, 65110-4900. Tel: 573-635-9127; Fax: 573-635-0386.

Diocese of Jefferson City Real Estate Trust, P.O. Box 104900, 65110-4900. Tel: 573-635-9127; Fax: 573-635-0386.

Fr. Augustine Tolton Regional Catholic High School Foundation, P.O. Box 104900, 65110-4900. Tel: 573-635-9127; Fax: 573-635-0386.

Jefferson City Diocese Chancery Building Fund, P.O. Box 104900, 65110-4900. Tel: 573-635-9127; Fax: 573-635-0386.

St. Mary's Health Center, Jefferson City, Missouri, Foundation, 100 St. Mary's Medical Plaza, 65101. Tel: 573-761-7198; Fax: 573-659-2106. Web: www.LetHealingBegin.com. Member of SSM Health Care.

Missouri Catholic Conference, 600 Clark Ave., P.O. Box 1022, 65102. Tel: 573-635-7239; Fax: 573-635-7431. Email: mocatholic@mocatholic.org. Web: www.mocatholic.org. Michael Hoey, Exec. Dir.

St. Peter School Foundation, P.O. Box 104900, 65110-4900. Tel: 573-635-9127; Fax: 573-635-0386.

LINN. *Good Shepherd Center*, 1117 Adams St., P.O. Box 763, 65051. Tel: 573-897-0525. Bill Voss, Volunteer Dir.

RELIGIOUS INSTITUTES OF MEN REPRESENTED IN THE DIOCESE

For further details refer to the corresponding bracketed number in the Religious Institutes of Men or Women section.

[0330]—*Brothers of the Christian Schools* (Midwest Prov.)—F.S.C.

[1330]—*Congregation of the Mission* (Midwest Prov.)—C.M.

[]—*Dominican Order of St. Albert the Great* (Central Province)—O.P.

[1060]—*Society of the Precious Blood* (Kansas City Prov.)—C.PP.S.

RELIGIOUS INSTITUTES OF WOMEN REPRESENTED IN THE DIOCESE

[0460]—*Congregation of the Sisters of Charity of the Incarnate Word* (San Antonio, TX)—C.C.V.I.

[1730]—*Congregation of the Sisters of the Third Order of St. Francis* (Oldenburg, IN)—O.S.F.

[0420]—*Discalced Carmelite Nuns (Second Order of the Carmel)* Jefferson City, MO—O.C.D.

[1070-11]—*Dominican Sisters* (Sparkill, NY)—O.P.

[1415]—*Franciscan Sisters of Mary* (St. Louis, MO)—F.S.M.

[2970]—*School Sisters of Notre Dame* (St. Louis Prov.)—S.S.N.D.

[1680]—*School Sisters of St. Francis* (Milwaukee, WI)—S.S.S.F.

[]—*Sisters of Mercy of the Americas* (Omaha, NE)—R.S.M.

[3270]—*Sisters of the Most Precious Blood* (O'Fallon, MO)—C.PP.S.

DIOCESAN CEMETERIES

JEFFERSON CITY. *St. Peter's Catholic Cemetery Association*, c/o Resurrection Cemetery, 3015 W. Truman Blvd., 65109. Tel: 573-893-2751; Fax: 573-893-5026. Mr. Lawrence Hasenbeck, Pres.

NECROLOGY

† Barnett, Fred J., (Retired)—Died March 19, 2011
† Buhman, Leo T., (Retired)—Died Jan. 9, 2011
† Lawlor, Joseph G., (Retired)—Died March 31, 2011
† Waickman, Thomas L., (Retired)—Died Dec. 9, 2010
† Walsh, Peter, (Retired)—Died Jan. 17, 2011

An asterisk (*) denotes an organization that has established tax-exempt status directly with the IRS and is not covered by the USCCB Group Ruling.

Diocese of Joliet in Illinois

(Dioecesis Joliettensis in Illinois)

Most Reverend

R. DANIEL CONLON

Bishop of Joliet; ordained January 15, 1977; appointed Bishop of Steubenville May 22, 2002; consecrated and installed August 6, 2002; appointed Bishop of Joliet May 17, 2011; installed July 14, 2011. *Chancery: 425 Summit St., Joliet, IL 60435.*

Most Reverend

JOSEPH L. IMESCH, D.D.

Retired Bishop of Joliet; ordained December 16, 1956; ordained Auxiliary Bishop of Detroit April 3, 1973; appointed Bishop of Joliet June 30, 1979; installed August 28, 1979; retired June 21, 2006. *Chancery: 425 Summit St., Joliet, IL 60435.*

Chancery: 425 Summit St., Joliet, IL 60435. Tel: 815-722-6606; Fax: 815-722-6602.

Web: www.dioceseofjoliet.org

Email: jdavies@dioceseofjoliet.org

Most Reverend

JOSEPH M. SIEGEL

Auxiliary Bishop of Joliet; ordained June 4, 1988; appointed Auxiliary Bishop of Joliet and Titular Bishop of Pupiana October 28, 2009; ordained January 19, 2010. *Chancery: 425 Summit St., Joliet, IL 60435.*

ESTABLISHED BY BULL DATED DECEMBER 11, 1948.

Square Miles 4,218.

Canonically Erected March 24, 1949.

Comprises the Counties of Du Page, Kankakee, Will, Grundy, Ford, Iroquois and Kendall in the State of Illinois.

Patron of Diocese: St. Francis Xavier.

For legal titles of parishes and diocesan institutions, consult the Chancery.

STATISTICAL OVERVIEW

Personnel	
Bishop	1
Auxiliary Bishops	1
Retired Bishops	2
Abbots	1
Retired Abbots	2
Priests: Diocesan Active in Diocese	113
Priests: Diocesan Active Outside Diocese	3
Priests: Diocesan in Foreign Missions	1
Priests: Retired, Sick or Absent	62
Number of Diocesan Priests	179
Religious Priests in Diocese	113
Total Priests in Diocese	292
Extern Priests in Diocese	18
Ordinations:	
Diocesan Priests	1
Religious Priests	1
Transitional Deacons	3
Permanent Deacons	19
Permanent Deacons in Diocese	198
Total Brothers	58
Total Sisters	470
Parishes	
Parishes	120
With Resident Pastor:	
Resident Diocesan Priests	97
Resident Religious Priests	15
Without Resident Pastor:	
Administered by Priests	8
Administered by Professed Religious Men	15
Missions	9
Professional Ministry Personnel:	
Sisters	26
Lay Ministers	190
Welfare	
Catholic Hospitals	3
Total Assisted	864,158
Homes for the Aged	16
Total Assisted	3,706
Day Care Centers	4
Total Assisted	2,199
Special Centers for Social Services	5
Total Assisted	64,524
Residential Care of Disabled	1
Total Assisted	124
Educational	
Diocesan Students in Other Seminaries	29
Total Seminarians	29
Colleges and Universities	3
Total Students	16,429
High Schools, Diocesan and Parish	3
Total Students	1,886
High Schools, Private	4
Total Students	3,558
Elementary Schools, Diocesan and Parish	47
Total Students	16,231
Catechesis/Religious Education:	
High School Students	4,572
Elementary Students	38,984
Total Students under Catholic Instruction	81,689
Teachers in the Diocese:	
Priests	17
Brothers	23
Sisters	17
Lay Teachers	466
Vital Statistics	
Receptions into the Church:	
Infant Baptism Totals	7,541
Minor Baptism Totals	200
Adult Baptism Totals	205
Received into Full Communion	836
First Communions	9,154
Confirmations	8,177
Marriages:	
Catholic	1,195
Interfaith	293
Total Marriages	1,488
Deaths	3,529
Total Catholic Population	615,918
Total Population	1,916,361

Former Bishops—Most Revs. MARTIN D. MCNAMARA, D.D., appt. first Bishop of Joliet; ord. Dec. 3, 1922; appt. Dec. 17, 1948; cons. March 7, 1949; died May 23, 1966; ROMEO BLANCHETTE, D.D., appt. Auxiliary Bishop of Joliet and Titular Bishop of Maxita Feb. 8, 1965; cons. April 3, 1965; appt. Bishop of Joliet July 19, 1966; installed Aug. 31, 1966; resigned Jan. 30, 1979; died Jan. 10, 1982; JOSEPH J. IMESCH, D.D., ord. Dec. 16, 1956; ord. Auxiliary Bishop of Detroit April 3, 1973; appt. Bishop of Joliet June 30, 1979; installed Aug. 28, 1979; retired May 16, 2006.; JAMES PETER SARTAIN, D.D., S.T.L., ord. July 15, 1978; appt. Bishop of Little Rock Jan. 4, 2000; cons. and installed March 6, 2000; appt. Bishop of Joliet May 16, 2006; installed June 27, 2006; appt. Archbishop of Seattle Sept. 16, 2010.

Vicar General—Most Rev. JOSEPH M. SIEGEL.

The Chancery

Secretary—Very Rev. JOSEPH TAPELLA, J.C.L.

Chancery—425 Summit St., Joliet, 60435. Tel: 815-722-6606; Fax: 815-722-6602. Office Hours: Mon.-Thurs. 8 a.m.-4:30 p.m., Fri. 8 a.m.-1 p.m.

Executive Assistant to Bishop/Curia Facilitator—Mr. DOUG DELANEY.

Chancellor—Sr. JUDITH A. DAVIES, O.S.F.

Director of Communications—Mr. DOUG DELANEY, Chancery, 425 Summit St., Joliet, 60435. Tel: 815-722-6606.

Christ Is Our Hope Magazine—Mr. CARLOS BRICENO, Editor, St. Charles Borromeo Pastoral Center, 101 W. Airport Rd., Romeoville, 60446. Tel: 815-834-4060; Fax: 815-834-4068.

Board of Conciliation and Arbitration—Sr. JUDITH A. DAVIES, O.S.F.

Diocesan Pastoral Council—Sr. JUDITH A. DAVIES, O.S.F.

Review Committee—Sr. JUDITH A. DAVIES, O.S.F.

Victim Assistance Coordinator—Mrs. JUDITH SPECKMAN. Tel: 815-263-6467.

Deans—Revs. WILLIAM DESALVO, East Dupage Deanery; THOMAS SULARZ, West Dupage Deanery; MICHAEL POWELL, Ford-Iroquois Deanery; ALBERT J. HEIDECKE, Kankakee Deanery; MICHAEL LANE, East Will Deanery; DAVID J. HANKUS, D.Min., West Will Deanery.

Office of Youth Protection—VACANT.

Presbyteral Council—Rev. ERNEST NORBECK, Chair, St. Mary of Gostyn Parish, 444 Wilson St., Downers Grove, 60515. Tel: 630-969-1063; Fax: 630-969-1259.

The Tribunal

Secretary—Very Rev. JOSEPH TAPELLA, J.C.L.

Diocesan Tribunal—310 Bridge St., Joliet, 60435. Tel: 815-722-2256; Fax: 815-722-6692.

Judicial Vicar—Very Rev. JOSEPH TAPELLA, J.C.L.

Notaries—Mrs. BETTY JOUTRAS; Mrs. HOPE DICK; Ms. NANCY HAUCH.

Defender of the Bond—Sr. ELAINE KERSCHER, O.S.F., J.C.L.

Judges—Very Rev. JOSEPH TAPELLA, J.C.L.; Mr. THOMAS E. KERBER, J.C.L.; Revs. DAVID HYNOUS, O.P., J.C.D.; RICHARD L. SMITH, J.C.L.

Advocates—Sisters DOMINIC DYBEL, O.S.F.; CLARE VAN VOOREN, O.S.F.

Diocesan Offices

Unless otherwise indicated, Diocesan Offices and Directors are located at the Chancery, 425 Summit St., Joliet 60435. Tel: 815-722-6606; Fax:

815-722-6602.

Secretariat for Administration

Secretary—Mr. MICHAEL BAVA.

Buildings and Properties—Mr. CHRISTOPHER NYE, Dir.

Catholic Cemeteries—Mr. RICHARD TAPELLA, Dir., Resurrection Cemetery, 200 W. Romeo Rd., Romeoville, 60446. Tel: 815-886-0750; Fax: 815-886-8711.

Development/Stewardship—Mr. TONY BRANDOLINO, Chief Devel. Officer, St. Charles Borromeo Pastoral Center, 101 W. Airport Rd., Romeoville, 60446. Tel: 815-838-8515; Fax: 815-838-8108.

Employee Benefits—Mrs. MARY JO MONROE, Benefits Specialist; Mrs. PAMELA GEARY, Pension Admin. Fax: 815-727-4674.

Finance Officer—Mr. MICHAEL BAVA, Dir.

Human Resources—Mrs. NANCY SIEMERS, Dir., St. Charles Borromeo Pastoral Center, 101 W. Airport Rd., Romeoville, 60446. Tel: 815-834-4077; Fax: 815-588-6006.

Information Services—Mr. MICHAEL SEKULA, Dir., St. Charles Borromeo Pastoral Center, 101 W. Airport Rd., Romeoville, 60446. Tel: 815-834-4085; Fax: 815-834-4087.

Insurance—Mr. JAMES WRIGHT, Catholic Mutual Insurance, St. Charles Borromeo Pastoral Center, 101 W. Airport Rd., Romeoville, 60446. Tel: 815-838-2142; Fax: 815-834-4079.

Legal Services—Mr. JAMES C. BYRNE.

Secretariate for Pastoral Concerns

Secretary—Sr. SHARON MARIE STOLA, O.S.B.

Campus Ministry—Mr. KEVIN O'DONNELL, Dir., St. Charles Borromeo Pastoral Center, 101 W. Airport Rd., Romeoville, 60446. Tel: 815-834-4022; Fax: 815-838-8129.

Council of Catholic Women—Mrs. LINNEA WARDA, Dir., Office: St. Charles Borromeo Pastoral Center, 101 W. Airport Rd., Romeoville, 60446. Tel: 815-834-4080; Fax: 815-838-8129.

Cursillo—Rev. MARK JENDRYSIK, Mod., St. Raphael Parish, 1215 Modaff Rd., Naperville, 60540. Tel: 630-355-4545; Fax: 630-355-7470.

Divine Worship—Sr. SHARON MARIE STOLA, O.S.B., Dir., St. Charles Borromeo Pastoral Center, 101 W. Airport Rd., Romeoville, 60446. Tel: 815-834-4010; Fax: 815-838-8129.

Ecumenism—Rev. JOHN BALLUFF, Dir., St. Mary Parish, 140 N. Oakwood, West Chicago, 60185. Tel: 630-231-0013; Fax: 630-293-2671.

Family Ministry—Dr. JAMES HEALY, Dir., St. Charles Borromeo Pastoral Center, 101 W. Airport Rd., Romeoville, 60446. Tel: 815-838-5334; Fax: 815-834-4045.

Hispanic Ministry—Mr. MIGUEL MORENO, Dir., St. Charles Borromeo Pastoral Center, 101 W. Airport Rd., Romeoville, 60446. Tel: 815-834-4037; Fax: 815-838-8129.

Marriage Encounter—CHUCK WALLACE; NANCY WALLACE, 122 Lawndale, Elmhurst, 60126. Tel: 630-833-1924.

Marriage Preparation—Dr. JAMES HEALY, Dir., St. Charles Borromeo Pastoral Center, 101 W. Airport Rd., Romeoville, 60446. Tel: 815-838-5334; Fax: 814-834-4045.

Office of Youth & Young Adults—Mr. KEVIN O'DONNELL, Dir. Tel: 815-834-4022.

Young Adult Ministry—Mr. PAUL JARZEMBOWSKI, Dir., St. Charles Borromeo Pastoral Center, 101 W. Airport Rd., Romeoville, 60446. Tel: 815-834-4048; Fax: 815-834-4067.

Youth Ministry—Mr. PAUL MACH, Dir., St. Charles Borromeo Pastoral Center, 101 W. Airport Rd., Romeoville, 60446. Tel: 815-834-4048; Fax: 815-834-4067.

Secretariat for Clergy and Religious

Secretary—Rev. BURKE MASTERS.

Life and Formation of Clergy—Rev. JOHN BALLUFF, Dir., St. Mary Parish, 140 N. Oakwood, West Chicago, 60185. Tel: 630-231-0013; Fax: 630-293-2671.

Vicar for Priests—Rev. WILLIAM G. DEWAN, Dir., Chancery: 425 Summit St., Joliet, 60435. Tel: 815-722-6606; Fax: 815-722-6632.

Delegate for Religious—Sr. THERESA GALVAN, C.N.D., St. Charles Borromeo Pastoral Center, 101 W. Airport Rd., Romeoville, 60446. Tel: 815-834-4009; Fax: 815-838-8129.

Permanent Diaconate—Deacon JOHN FREUND, Dir., St. Charles Borromeo Pastoral Center, 101 W. Airport Rd., Romeoville, 60446. Tel: 815-834-4091; Fax: 815-834-4045.

Vocations—Rev. BURKE MASTERS, Dir., St. Charles Borromeo Pastoral Center, 101 W. Airport Rd., Romeoville, 60446. Tel: 815-834-4020; Fax: 815-838-8129.

Secretariat for Evangelization and Catechesis

Secretary—Mr. DAVID SPESIA.

Catholic Education Foundation—Mr. JOSEPH LANGENDERFER, Exec. Dir., St. Charles Borromeo Pastoral Center, 101 W. Airport Rd., Romeoville, 60446. Tel: 815-834-4023; Fax: 815-588-6007.

Catholic Schools Office—Rev. JOHN BELMONTE, S.J., Supt., St. Charles Borromeo Pastoral Center, 101 W. Airport Rd., Romeoville, 60446. Tel: 815-838-2181; Fax: 815-838-2182.

Religious Education Office—Mr. THOMAS QUINLAN, Dir., St. Charles Borromeo Pastoral Center, 101 W. Airport Rd., Romeoville, 60446. Tel: 815-838-6475; Fax: 815-588-6003.

Office of Lay Formation—Mr. DAVID SPESIA, Dir., St. Charles Borromeo Pastoral Center, 101 W. Airport Rd., Romeoville, 60446. Tel: 815-834-4001; Fax: 815-838-8129.

Secretariat for Social Concerns

Secretary—Mr. GLENN VAN CURA.

Campaign for Human Development—Mr. STEPHEN JACKSON, St. Charles Borromeo Pastoral Center, 101 W. Airport Rd., Romeoville, 60446. Tel: 815-834-7283; Fax: 815-838-8129.

Catholic Charities— Legal Title: Catholic Charities of the Diocese of Joliet. Mr. GLENN VAN CURA, Exec. Dir., 203 N. Ottawa St., Joliet, 60432. Tel: 815-723-3405; Fax: 815-723-3452.

Catholic Relief Services—Mr. THOMAS GARLITZ, Dir., St. Charles Borromeo Pastoral Center, 101 W. Airport Rd., Romeoville, 60446. Tel: 815-834-4026; Fax: 815-838-8129.

Coordinator for Health Affairs—Sr. JUDITH A. DAVIES, O.S.F.

Missions Office/Propagation of the Faith—Rev. J. DAMIEN GRAZIANO, Dir. (Retired), 1 S 314 Summit Ave., Oakbrook Terrace, 60181. Tel: 630-629-5810; Fax: 630-953-8251.

Peace and Social Justice—Mr. THOMAS GARLITZ, Dir., St. Charles Borromeo Pastoral Center, 101 W. Airport Rd., Romeoville, 60446. Tel: 815-834-4026.

Respect Life Office—Mr. DAVID SPESIA, Dir., St. Charles Borromeo Pastoral Center, 101 W. Airport Rd., Romeoville, 60446. Tel: 815-834-4065; Fax: 815-838-8129.

Rural Life—VACANT.

Scouts—Deacon RODGER F. ACCARDI, Dir., St. John the Baptist, O.S. 233 Church St., Winfield, 60190-1291. Tel: 630-668-0918; Fax: 630-668-1074.

CLERGY, PARISHES, MISSIONS AND PAROCHIAL SCHOOLS

CITY OF JOLIET

(WILL COUNTY)

1—THE CATHEDRAL OF ST. RAYMOND (1917) Revs. Brad Baker, Rector; Jason Stone, Parochial Vicar. In Res., Very Rev. Joseph Tapella.
Res.: 604 N. Raynor Ave., 60435. Tel: 815-722-6653. Email: bulletin@straymond.net. Web: www.straymond.net.
School—(Grades PreSchool-8), 608 N. Raynor Ave., 60435. Tel: 815-722-6626; Fax: 815-727-4668. Email: straymond60435@yahoo.com. Dr. Jennifer Groves, Prin.; Katlyn Kinsella, Librarian. Lay Teachers 24; Students 535.
Catechesis/Religious Program—Fax: 815-722-3137. Students 264.

2—ST. ANTHONY (1902), (Italian), Rev. Michael Valente, Admin. (Retired).
Res.: 100 N. Scott St., 60432-4210. Tel: 815-722-1057; Fax: 815-722-9805. Email: saintanthonyjoliet@hotmail.com.

3—ST. BERNARD (1921) Rev. Richard Ross; Deacon Frank Juricic.
Res.: 1313 Ridgewood Ave., 60432. Tel: 815-726-4474; Fax: 815-726-4520.
Catechesis/Religious Program—Tel: 815-727-4600; Fax: 815-726-8055. Clustered with St. Mary Magdalene, Joliet. Students 28.

4—SS. CYRIL AND METHODIUS (1900), (Slovak), Closed. For inquiries for parish records contact the chancery.

5—ST. FRANCIS XAVIER (2002) [CEM] Rev. Kevin J. Spiess (CHI).
Mailing Address: 2500 Arbeiter Rd., 60431. Tel: 815-609-8077; Fax: 815-609-8078. Email: missionlands@aol.com. Web: www.st-francis-xavier.com.
Catechesis/Religious Program—Nancy Akin, D.R.E. Students 255.

6—HOLY CROSS (1893), (Polish), [JC] Revs. Ron P. Neitzke; Julian Kaczowka, S.Ch.
901 Elizabeth St., 60435. Tel: 815-722-0785; Fax: 815-723-0679.
School—Please see St. Mary Nativity, Joliet
School—Polish School of Religion, (Grades K-8) Janina Szocinska, Prin. Students 150.
Catechesis/Religious Program—Please see St. Mary Nativity, Joliet.

7—ST. JOHN THE BAPTIST (1852) [CEM] Revs. Fred Radtke, O.F.M.; Juan Rommel Perez, O.F.M., Parochial Vicar; Deacons Jose Lopez; James Janousek. In Res., Revs. Dennis Schafer, O.F.M., Dir. Postulancy Guardian; J. Derran Combs, O.F.M.; John Dombrowski, O.F.M.; Gerald Bleem, O.F.M.
Res.: 404 N. Hickory St., 60435. Tel: 815-727-4788; Fax: 815-727-1729. Email: stjohnbap@church404.comcastbiz.net. Web: www.stjohnsjoliet.org.
Catechesis/Religious Program—403 N. Hickory St., 60435. Tel: 815-727-9077. Students 625.

8—ST. JOSEPH (1891), (Slovenian), [CEM] Rev. Roger Kutzner.
Res.: 416 N. Chicago St., 60432. Tel: 815-727-9378; Fax: 815-727-9580. Email: stjoseph416@stjosephjoliet.org.
Catechesis/Religious Program—Students 61.

9—ST. JUDE (1954) Rev. Michael Lane; Deacon Raymond Clark, (Retired); Paula Bucciferro, Business Mgr.
Res.: 2212 McDonough St., 60436. Tel: 815-725-2209; Fax: 815-741-8844. Email: mlane@catholicexchange.com. Web: www.stjudejoliet.org.
School—(Grades K-8), 2204 McDonough St., 60436. Tel: 815-729-0288; Fax: 815-729-0344. Sr. Mary Elizabeth Sallese, O.P., Prin.; Wendy Bergman, Librarian. Dominican Sisters of St. Cecilia 2; Lay Teachers 8; Students 229.
Catechesis/Religious Program—Email: stjudejolietff@catholicexchange.com. Students 216.

10—ST. MARY CARMELITE, Closed. For inquiries for parish records contact the chancery.

11—ST. MARY MAGDALENE (1953) Rev. Christopher Groh; Deacon John Mele; Margaret Trepal, Pastoral Assoc.
Res.: 127 S. Briggs St., 60433. Tel: 815-722-7653; Fax: 815-724-1720.
Catechesis/Religious Program—201 S. Briggs St., 60433. Tel: 815-727-4600. Susan O'Brien, D.R.E. Students 110.
Convent—209 Siegmund St., 60433. Tel: 815-726-3565. Sisters of Providence 1.

12—ST. MARY NATIVITY (1906), (Croatian), [JC] Revs. Ron P. Neitzke; Lee F. Bacchi, Parochial Vicar; Deacon Daniel Mahoney Sr. In Res., Rev. Julian Kaczowka, S.Ch.
Res.: 706 N. Broadway, 60435. Tel: 815-726-4031; Fax: 815-727-4393. Web: www.stmarynativity.com.
School—(Grades PreSchool-8), 702 N. Broadway, 60435. Tel: 815-722-8518. Mr. Larry White, Prin.; Deborah Shields, Librarian. Franciscan Sisters of the Sacred Heart 1; Lay Teachers 14; Students 240.
Catechesis/Religious Program—Tel: 815-726-4073. Michael Hoyt, D.R.E. Students 140.
Convent—700 N. Hickory St., 60435.

13—MOUNT CARMEL (1939), (Mexican-American), Revs. Jose Luis Torres, O.Carm.; Enrique Varela-Nungaray, O.Carm.
Church Office: 407 Irving St., 60432. Tel: 815-727-7187; Fax: 815-727-7187. Email: montecarmelo@prodigy.net. Web: www.ourladymtcarmel.net.
Weekend Svcs.: 205 E. Jackson St., 60432. Daily Mass: 405 E. Irving St., 60432.
Res.: 409 Irving St., 60432. Tel: 815-726-5208; Fax: 815-727-7225.
Catechesis/Religious Program—Tel: 815-727-6330; Fax: 815-531-8201. Students 750.

14—ST. PATRICK (1838) Rev. Peter G. Jankowski; Deacons Paul Kolodziej; Charles Peterson; Darrell Kelsey.
Res.: 710 W. Marion St., 60436-1556. Tel: 815-727-4746; Fax: 815-727-4798. Email: stpatrectory0710@sbcglobal.net. Web: www.stpatsjoliet.com.
Catechesis/Religious Program—Tel: 815-727-4798; Fax: 815-727-4746. Students 200.

15—ST. PAUL THE APOSTLE (1950) Rev. Gregory Rothfuchs; Deacon William Bevan. In Res., Rev. John Belmonte, S.J.
Res.: 18 Woodlawn Ave., 60435. Tel: 815-725-1527; Fax: 815-730-9907. Email: stpauljoliet@sbcglobal.net. Web: www.stpauljoliet.com.
School—(Grades PreSchool-8), 130 Woodlawn Ave., 60435. Tel: 815-725-3390; Fax: 815-725-3180. Web: www.thestpaulschool.org. Mrs. Mary Kay Robbins, Prin. Lay Teachers 21; Students 385.
Catechesis/Religious Program—120 Woodlawn Ave., 60435. Tel: 815-725-6927. Students 634.

16—SACRED HEART (1886), (African American), Rev. Raymond C. Lescher; Deacon Ralph Bias.

Res.: 337 S. Ottawa St., 60436. Tel: 815-722-0295; Fax: 815-722-6088.
Catechesis/Religious Program—Students 23.
17—ST. THADDEUS (1927), (Polish), Closed. For inquiries for parish records contact the chancery.

OUTSIDE THE CITY OF JOLIET

ADDISON, DU PAGE CO.
1—ST. JOSEPH (1956), (Hispanic), Rev. Luis Gutierrez; Deacon Philip Marrow.
Res.: 330 E. Fullerton, 60101. Tel: 630-279-6553; Fax: 630-279-4925. Email: stjoes@catholic.org. Web: www.stjoeaddison.com.
See Holy Family Catholic School, Bensenville under St. Charles Borromeo, Bensenville for details.
Catechesis/Religious Program—Tel: 630-832-5514. Ms. Dolly Matthews, C.R.E. Students 555.
2—ST. PHILIP THE APOSTLE (1963) Rev. Philip M. Danaher; Deacons Philip Heitz; Sean McGreal.
Res.: 1223 W. Holtz Ave., 60101. Tel: 630-628-0900; Fax: 630-543-9858.
School—(Grades PreSchool-8), 1233 W. Holtz Ave., 60101. Tel: 630-543-4130; Fax: 630-458-8750. Robert Reisenbuechler, Prin. Lay Teachers 15; Students 311.
Catechesis/Religious Program—Tel: 630-543-1754; Fax: 630-543-4672. Mrs. Nancy McKnight, D.R.E. Students 290.
ASHKUM, IROQUOIS CO., ASSUMPTION OF THE BLESSED VIRGIN MARY (1903) [CEM] [JC 2] Rev. James Holup.
Res.: 208 N. Second St., Box 218, 60911. Tel: 815-698-2262.
Mission—St. John the Baptist (1856) Box 218, L'Erable, Iroquois Co. 60911. Tel: 815-698-2262.
Catechesis/Religious Program—Students 95.
AURORA, DU PAGE CO., OUR LADY OF MERCY (1988) Revs. Hugh Fullmer; Tomy Chellakandathil, C.M.I. (India), Parochial Vicar; Deacons Robert Vavra; Philip Rehmer; Timothy Kueper; Arturo Tiongson.
Res.: 701 S. Eola Rd., 60504. Tel: 630-851-3444; Fax: 630-851-3468.
Catechesis/Religious Program—Tel: 630-851-3444, Ext. 222. Students 1,392.
BEAVERVILLE, IROQUOIS CO., ST. MARY (1857), (French), [CEM] Rev. Reynaldo B. Treyes.
Res.: 308 St. Charles St., P.O. Box 152, 60912. Tel: 815-435-2432. Email: stmarys@dioceseofjoliet.org.
Catechesis/Religious Program—Ryan Loy, D.R.E. Students 19.
BENSENVILLE, DU PAGE CO.
1—ST. ALEXIS (1926) Rev. Agustin Ortega-Ruiz; Sr. Laurina Kahne, C.S.J., Pastoral Assoc.
Res.: 400 W. Wood St., 60106. Tel: 630-766-3530; Fax: 630-766-3536.
Catechesis/Religious Program—410 W. Wood St., 60106. Tel: 630-766-4417. Dr. Donna Cascino, D.R.E. Students 307.
2—ST. CHARLES BORROMEO (1959) Rev. John Klein; Deacon Timothy Taylor.
Res.: 1135 Daniel, 60106-3467. Tel: 630-860-1120; Fax: 630-860-5029. Web: www.stcbchurch.org.
School—Holy Family Catholic School, (Grades PreK-8), 145 E. Grand Ave., 60106. Tel: 630-766-0116; Fax: 630-766-0181. Email: officeeast@hfcatholic.org. Web: www.hfcatholic.org. Mrs. Corinne Alimento, Prin.; Dannette Kimmel, Librarian. Lay Teachers 18; Students 171.
Catechesis/Religious Program—Tel: 630-766-8822; Fax: 630-766-3481. Students 194.
BLOOMINGDALE, DUPAGE CO., ST. ISIDORE (1920) [CEM] Revs. James Murphy; Dennis Paul, Parochial Vicar; Felipe Legarreta, Parochial Vicar; Deacons John Freund; Terry Cummiskey; Lawrence Migliorato; Don Randolph; Lupe Villarreal; Tom Norton, Parish Admin.
Res.: 427 W. Army Trail Rd., 60108-1390. Tel: 630-529-3045; Fax: 630-529-2940. Email: general@stisidoreparish.org. Web: www.stisidoreparish.org.
School—(Grades PreSchool-8) Tel: 630-529-9323; Fax: 630-529-8882. Email: school@stisidoreparish.org. Mrs. Cyndi Collins, Prin. Lay Teachers 23; Students 286.
Catechesis/Religious Program—Tel: 630-529-9191. Students 1,249.
BOLINGBROOK, WILL CO.
1—ST. DOMINIC (1964) Revs. David Lawrence; Matthew Pratscher, Parochial Vicar; Deacons Lorenzo Chaidez; David Ritter; Robert Wallace; Paul Walen.
Res.: 408 E. Briarcliff Rd., 60440. Tel: 630-739-5703; Fax: 630-739-2036. Email: stdominic@comcast.net. Web: www.stdombb.org.
School—(Grades PreSchool-8), 420 E. Briarcliff Rd., 60440. Tel: 630-739-1633; Fax: 630-739-5989. Email: stdominicschool@comcast.net. Sr. John Mary Fleming, O.P., Prin.; Susan Meifert, Librarian. Religious 2; Lay Teachers 14; Students 270.
Catechesis/Religious Program—Tel: 630-739-5703, Ext. 21; 630-739-5703, Ext. 23. Students 600.
2—ST. FRANCIS OF ASSISI (1980) Rev. Herbert Essig; Deacons John Blumenstein; Raymond Hamilton; Marco Lovero; Michael McGuire; Genaro Mempin; Gregory Gresik, Pastoral Assoc.
Res.: 1501 W. Boughton Rd., 60490. Tel: 630-759-7588; Fax: 630-759-5257. Web: www.stfrancisbb.org.
Catechesis/Religious Program— Theresa Palicka, D.R.E. Students 890.
BOURBONNAIS, KANKAKEE CO., MATERNITY OF THE BLESSED VIRGIN MARY (1847) [CEM] Revs. Richard Pighini, C.S.V.; Jason Nesbit, C.S.V.; Deacons Euchrist J. Marcotte; Patrick Skelly. In Res., Rev. James E. Michaletz, C.S.V.
Res.: 308 E. Marsile St., 60914. Tel: 815-933-8285; Fax: 815-933-8289. Email: maternitybvm1847@yahoo.com. Web: www.mbvm.org.
School—(Grades PreSchool-8), 324 E. Marsile St., 60914. Tel: 815-933-7758; Fax: 815-933-1884. Mr. Terry Granger, Prin.; Teresa Rigney, Librarian. Lay Teachers 23; Students 312.
Catechesis/Religious Program—Tel: 815-933-8226; Fax: 815-933-1884. Email: mpallissard@mbvm.org. Students 283.
BRADLEY, KANKAKEE CO., ST. JOSEPH (1904) Rev. Anthony A. Nugent; Deacons Leon Fritz; Jerome Gregoire. In Res., Rev. John Antczak.
Res.: 211 N. Center Ave., 60915. Tel: 815-939-3573; Fax: 815-939-3138. Email: rraymond@stjosephbradley.org. Web: www.stjosephbradley.org.
School—(Grades PreSchool-8), 247 N. Center Ave., 60915. Tel: 815-933-8013; Fax: 815-933-2775. Email: mmeier@stjosephbradley.org. Web: www.stjosephbradley.org/school. Sr. Mary Ann Hettel, S.S.C.M., Prin. Sisters 2; Lay Teachers 10; Students 206.
Catechesis/Religious Program—247 N. Center Ave., 60915. Tel: 815-937-9340. Email: mmarcotte@stjosephbradley.org. Students 176.
Convent—235 N. Center Ave., 60915. Tel: 815-932-0112.
BRAIDWOOD, WILL CO., IMMACULATE CONCEPTION (1869), (Irish—Italian), [CEM] Rev. Show Reddy Allam (India).
Res.: 110 S. School St., 60408. Tel: 815-458-2125; Fax: 815-458-2836. Email: imu359@aol.com.
Catechesis/Religious Program—Students 110.
Mission—St. Lawrence O'Toole Essex, Kankakee Co.
CABERY, FORD CO., ST. JOSEPH (1867), (German), [CEM] Rev. Richard F. Kostelz (Retired).
Res.: 112 W. Main St., P.O. Box 77, 60919. Tel: 815-949-1568.
Catechesis/Religious Program—Students 19.
Mission—St. Mary (1899) Reddick, Kankakee Co. 60961.
CAROL STREAM, DU PAGE CO.
1—CORPUS CHRISTI (1989) Rev. Robert A. Hoffenkamp; Deacon Thomas R. Thiltgen; Mrs. Kathleen A. Brewer, Pastoral Assoc.; Deacon William Thomas.
Res.: 1415 W. Lies Rd., 60188. Tel: 630-483-4673; Fax: 630-483-4679. Email: corpuschristicc@sbcglobal.net. Web: www.corpuschristicarolstream.org.
Catechesis/Religious Program—Tel: 630-483-4222 (RE); 630-483-4226 (YM). Email: ccedu@sbcglobal.net. Students 507.
2—ST. LUKE (1963) Rev. Danilo Soriano.
Res.: 421 Cochise Ct., 60188. Tel: 630-668-1325; Fax: 630-668-1356.
Catechesis/Religious Program—Tel: 630-665-2322. Students 60.
CHANNAHON, WILL CO., ST. ANN PARISH (1990) Rev. Jeffery Stoneberg.
Church: 24500 S. Navajo Dr., 60410. Tel: 815-467-6962; Fax: 815-467-2320. Email: stannparish@cbcast.com.
Rectory—25658 Cherokee Tr., 60410.
Catechesis/Religious Program—Tel: 815-467-6992. Students 433.
CHEBANSE, IROQUOIS CO., SS. MARY AND JOSEPH (1869) [CEM] Rev. Vernon Arseneau.
Res.: 525 S. Chestnut, P.O. Box 5, 60922-0005. Tel: 815-697-2654; Fax: 815-694-3507. Email: stspmj@comcast.net.
Catechesis/Religious Program—Students 50.
CLARENDON HILLS, DU PAGE CO., NOTRE DAME (1954) Revs. Patrick M. Mulcahy, Admin.; Venard Kommer, O.F.M.; Steven Borello, Parochial Vicar; Deacons Frank Foys; David Lifka; Alex McConnell; Alan Symonanis.
Res.: 64 Norfolk Ave., 60514. Tel: 630-654-3365; Fax: 630-654-8701. Web: www.notredameparish.org.
School—(Grades PreSchool-8) Tel: 630-323-1642; Fax: 630-654-3255. Ms. Mary Ann Feeney, Prin. Lay Teachers 17; Students 249.
Catechesis/Religious Program—Tel: 630-654-3365, Ext. 237. Students 510.
CLIFTON, IROQUOIS CO., ST. PETER'S (1869) [CEM] Rev. Vernon Arseneau.
Res.: 450 E. Third Ave., P.O. Box 25, 60927-0025. Tel: 815-694-2027; Fax: 815-694-3507.
Catechesis/Religious Program—Tel: 815-694-2970. Email: stspmj@comcast.net. Students 101.
COAL CITY, GRUNDY CO., ASSUMPTION OF THE BLESSED VIRGIN MARY (1889) Rev. Robert Noesen.
Res.: 245 S. Kankakee St., 60416. Tel: 815-634-4171; Fax: 815-634-4186. Web: www.bvmassumption.org.
Catechesis/Religious Program—Tel: 815-634-8020. Pam Middleton, C.R.E. Students 250.
CREST HILL, WILL CO.
1—ST. AMBROSE (1965) Rev. John J. Doyle.
Res.: 1711 Burry Cir., 60403. Tel: 815-722-3748; Fax: 815-722-4950. Email: st.ambrose@sbcglobal.net.
Catechesis/Religious Program—Tel: 815-722-9193. Students 100.
2—ST. ANNE (1953) Rev. John J. Doyle.
Res.: 1702 N. Dearborn St., 60403. Tel: 815-722-3222; Fax: 815-722-1955. Email: stannech@comcast.net.
Catechesis/Religious Program—Students 100.
DARIEN, DU PAGE CO.
1—OUR LADY OF KOREAN MARTYRS MISSION (1999), (Korean), Rev. Hee Chan Do.
7121 Clarendon Hills Rd., 60561. Tel: 630-794-0203; Fax: 630-887-0991.
Catechesis/Religious Program—Email: olkm7121@hotmail.com. Students 23.
2—OUR LADY OF MOUNT CARMEL (1970) Revs. Michael O'Keefe, O.Carm.; Edward Ward, O.Carm.; Deacons John Farrell; Edward Ptacek.
Res.: 8404 Cass Ave., 60561. Tel: 630-852-3303; Fax: 630-852-5227. Web: www.ourladyofmtcarmel.org.
Catechesis/Religious Program—Tel: 630-963-3053. Students 1,200.
3—OUR LADY OF PEACE (1970) Rev. Walter Dziordz, M.I.C.; Deacons Frank Bina; Paul Brachle; Larry Fudacz; Dennis Stolarz.
Res.: 701 Plainfield Rd., 60561. Tel: 630-323-4333; Fax: 630-323-4354.
School—(Grades PreK-8), 709 Plainfield Rd., 60561. Tel: 630-325-9220; Fax: 630-325-1995. Mickey Tovey, Prin. Lay Teachers 25; Students 376.
Catechesis/Religious Program—Tel: 630-986-8430; 630-986-8446; Fax: 630-986-1214. Leslie Krauledis, D.R.E. Students 291.
DOWNERS GROVE, DU PAGE CO.
1—DIVINE SAVIOR (1968) Rev. William Conway; Deacon Paul S. Newey.
Res.: 6700 Main St., 60516. Tel: 630-969-1532; Fax: 630-969-1724. Email: parish@divinesavior.net. Web: www.divinesavior.net.
Catechesis/Religious Program—Tel: 630-969-1673; Fax: 630-969-0201. Students 373.
2—ST. JOSEPH (1907) Revs. Jerome Kish; John Lindsey, Parochial Vicar.
Res.: 4832 Main St., 60515. Tel: 630-964-0216; Fax: 630-964-0867.
School—(Grades K-8), Franklin & Highland, 60515. Tel: 630-969-4306; Fax: 630-969-3946. Sr. Dorothy Randall, C.S.J., Pres.; Rita Stasi, Prin.; Regina McCutheon, Librarian. Lay Teachers 26; Students 462.
Catechesis/Religious Program—Tel: 630-971-1740; Fax: 630-964-0867. Students 488.
3—ST. MARY OF GOSTYN (1891) Revs. Ernest Norbeck; Raed Bader, Parochial Vicar.
Res.: 444 Wilson St., 60515. Tel: 630-969-1063; Fax: 630-969-1259. Email: parish@stmarygostyn.org. Web: www.stmarygostyn.org.
School—(Grades PreSchool-8), 440 Prairie Ave., 60515. Tel: 630-968-6155; Fax: 630-968-6208. Email: school@stmarygostyn.org. Mrs. Dolores Mielzynski, Prin.; Jaime Belcastro, Librarian. Felician Sisters 2; Lay Teachers 24; Students 516.
Catechesis/Religious Program—445 Prairie Ave., 60515. Tel: 630-960-3565; Fax: 630-969-1289. Email: religiouseducation@stmarygostyn.org. Students 660.
ELMHURST, DU PAGE CO.
1—IMMACULATE CONCEPTION (1876) Revs. Thomas Paul; Raymond Garbin, Parochial Vicar; Scott M. McCawley; Deacon John Feely.
Res.: 134 Arthur St., 60126. Tel: 630-530-8515; Fax: 630-530-9346. Web: www.icelmhurst.org.
School—(Grades PreSchool-8), Grade School., 132 Arthur St., 60126. Tel: 630-530-3490; Fax: 630-530-9787. Mrs. Cathy Linley, Prin. Lay Teachers 31; Students 544.
High School—217 Cottage Hill Ave., 60126. Tel: 630-530-3460; Fax: 630-530-2290. Ms. Pamela M. Levar, Prin. Lay Teachers 25; Students 339.
Catechesis/Religious Program—Tel: 630-530-3483; Fax: 630-530-9346. Students 657.
2—MARY, QUEEN OF HEAVEN (1956) Rev. Anthony Taschetta.
Res.: 426 N. West Ave., 60126-2128. Tel: 630-279-5700; Fax: 630-279-4667. Web: www.maryqueen.org.
Catechesis/Religious Program—442 N. West Ave., 60126. Tel: 630-832-8962. Email: mqhreo@juno.com. Students 620.
3—VISITATION (1953) Revs. Scott Huggins; Jan

Krutewicz, Parochial Vicar; Deacons Jay Janousek; Anthony Spatafore; James Eaker.
Res.: 779 S. York St., 60126. Tel: 630-834-6700; Fax: 630-834-6711.
School—(Grades PreSchool-8), 851 S. York, 60126. Tel: 630-834-4931; Fax: 630-834-4936. Sr. Thomas Leo Monahan, O.P., Prin. Sisters of St. Dominican Adrian 3; Lay Teachers 25; Students 540.
Catechesis/Religious Program—851 S. York, 60126. Tel: 630-279-7058; Fax: 630-279-9340. Students 625.

FRANKFORT, WILL CO., ST. ANTHONY (1929) Revs. Greg Skowron; Miroslaw Stepien, Parochial Vicar; Deacons Donald Berkey; Daniel Danahey, Business & Facilities Mgr.; Richard Rosko; William Boucek; Joseph Johnson, Pastoral Assoc.; Anthony Schlott; Donald Higgins. In Res., Rev. Godwin Olugbami.
Res.: 7659 W. Sauk Tr., 60423. Tel: 815-469-3750; Fax: 815-469-6514. Web: www.stanthonyfrankfort.com.
Catechesis/Religious Program—Tel: 815-469-6072; Fax: 815-806-9421. Kathleen Littleton, D.R.E.; Sophie Follenweider, D.R.E. Students 1,051.

GIBSON CITY, FORD CO., OUR LADY OF LOURDES (1875) [JC] Rev. John Phan; Deacon Jeffrey Volker.
Res.: 534 N. Wood St., 60936. Tel: 217-784-4671; Fax: 217-784-4671. Email: pastor@ololgc.org. Web: www.ololgc.org.
Catechesis/Religious Program—Alyce Hafer, D.R.E. Students 54.
Mission—Immaculate Conception Roberts, 60962.

GILMAN, IROQUOIS CO., IMMACULATE CONCEPTION (1872) [CEM] Rev. Michael Pennock.
Res.: 224 N. Secor St., 60938. Tel: 815-265-7236; Fax: 815-265-7236.
Catechesis/Religious Program—Students 187.

GLEN ELLYN, DU PAGE CO.

1—ST. JAMES THE APOSTLE (1965) Rev. John J. Ouper; Deacons John W. Moeller; Matthew Pidgeon.
Res.: 579 Prince Edward Rd., 60137. Tel: 630-469-7540; Fax: 630-469-7590.
School—(Grades PreK-8), 490 S. Park Blvd., 60137. Tel: 630-469-8060; Fax: 630-469-1107. Ms. Nancy James, Prin. Lay Teachers 17; Students 250.
Catechesis/Religious Program—Tel: 630-858-5646; Fax: 630-858-5687. Students 689.

2—ST. PETRONILLE (1925) Revs. James Dougherty; Sundar Raj Kocherla (India), Parochial Vicar; Deacons Ronald Yurcus; John Spiezio; Bob Cassey. In Res., Rev. John D. Sullivan (Retired).
Res.: 420 Glenwood Ave., 60137. Tel: 630-469-0404; Fax: 630-469-0412. Email: office@stpetschurch.org. Web: www.stpetschurch.org.
School—(Grades K-8), 425 Prospect Ave., 60137. Tel: 630-469-5041; Fax: 630-469-5071. Email: office@stpetschool.org. Web: www.stpetschool.org. Dr. Mary Kelly, Prin.; Mrs. Linda Lohr, Librarian. Lay Teachers 35; Students 544.
Catechesis/Religious Program—Tel: 630-858-3796, Ext. 4000; Fax: 630-858-6232. Susan Tutaj, D.R.E.; Therese Stahl, Assoc. Dir. Students 822.

3—QUEENSHIP OF MARY (1993), (Vietnamese), [JC] Rev. Nguyen Huy Quyen.
Church: 219 Armitage, 60137. Tel: 630-668-2333; Fax: 630-752-0275.
Catechesis/Religious Program—Tel: 630-752-0332. Students 179.

GLENDALE HEIGHTS, DU PAGE CO., ST. MATTHEW (1960) Revs. Herman Kinzler, O.Carm.; Kevin Lafey, O.Carm, Parochial Vicar; Deacon Robert Malek; Mr. Ruben Chavez, Hispanic Pastoral Assoc.
Res.: 1555 Glen Ellyn Rd., 60139. Tel: 630-469-6300; Fax: 630-469-6302. Web: www.stmatthewchurch.org.
School—(Grades PreSchool-8) Tel: 630-858-3112; Fax: 630-858-0623. Mrs. Neoma Mastruzzo, Prin. Lay Teachers 19; Students 359.
Catechesis/Religious Program—Tel: 630-469-5178; Fax: 630-469-6302. Mr. Michael Ruddle, Coord., Faith Formation. Students 419.

GOODRICH, KANKAKEE CO., SACRED HEART (1895) [CEM] Revs. Douglas L. Hauber; Richard Jacklin, Sacramental Min.; Thomas G. Henry, Business Mgr.
Res.: 588 S. 10000 W. Road, Bonfield, 60913-7019. Tel: 815-426-2221.
Catechesis/Religious Program—Students 17.

HERSCHER, KANKAKEE CO., ST. MARGARET MARY, [CEM] Rev. Douglas L. Hauber.
Res.: 207 E. Fifth St., 60941. Tel: 815-426-2153; Fax: 815-426-2153.
Catechesis/Religious Program—Tel: 815-426-2550. Students 63.

HINSDALE, DU PAGE CO., ST. ISAAC JOGUES (1930), (Irish—Italian), Revs. William DeSalvo; Stephen Eickhoff, Parochial Vicar.
Res.: 306 W. Fourth St., 60521. Tel: 630-323-1248; Fax: 630-323-6373. Web: www.sij.net.
School—(Grades K-8), 421 S. Clay St., 60521. Tel: 630-323-3244; Fax: 630-655-6676. Mr. Richard Cronquist, Prin.; Vickie Maxwell, Librarian. Religious 1; Lay Teachers 39; Students 585.
Catechesis/Religious Program—427 S. Clay St., 60521. Tel: 630-323-0265. Students 735.

HOMER GLEN, WILL CO.

1—ST. BERNARD (1978) Rev. Martin M. Gabel; Deacons Kevin Ryan; Christopher McCaffrey.
Res.: 14135 Parker Rd., 60491. Tel: 708-301-3020; Fax: 708-301-0738. Email: st.bernardsrectory@comcast.net.
Catechesis/Religious Program—14724 S. Arboretum Dr., 60491. Tel: 708-301-6952; Fax: 708-301-8870. Students 349.

2—OUR MOTHER OF GOOD COUNSEL (1996) Rev. John M. Ohner, O.S.A. In Res., Rev. Jerome M. Heyman, O.S.A.
Church: 16043 S. Bell Rd., 60491. Tel: 708-301-6246; Fax: 708-301-6356. Email: omgcc@comcast.net. Web: omgc.org.
Catechesis/Religious Program—Tel: 708-301-0214. Email: janet.litterio@comcast.net. Students 692.

IRWIN, KANKAKEE CO., ST. JAMES THE APOSTLE, [CEM] Rev. Douglas L. Hauber.
4372 Main St., 60901. Res. & Mailing Address: *St. Margaret Mary Parish*, 207 E. Fifth St., Herscher, 60941. Tel: 815-426-2153.
Catechesis/Religious Program—Tel: 815-933-5443. Students 42.

ITASCA, DU PAGE CO.

1—ST. ANDREW KIM (1981), (Korean), [JC] Rev. Andrew Soo Hong Jeon (Korea, South).
Res.: 1275 N. Arlington Hts. Rd., 60143. Tel: 630-250-0576; Fax: 630-250-2502. Email: info@standrewkimchicago.org. Web: www.standrewkimchicago.org.

2—ST. PETER THE APOSTLE (1956) Rev. Slawomir Ignasik.
Office: 524 N. Rush St., 60143-1698. Tel: 630-773-1272; Fax: 630-773-1720. Email: frslawek@gmail.com.
Catechesis/Religious Program—Tel: 630-773-1272, Ext. 216. Students 300.

KANKAKEE, KANKAKEE CO.

1—ST. MARTIN OF TOURS (1950) [JC] Rev. Mario S. Quejadas.
Res.: 953 S. Ninth Ave., 60901. Tel: 815-933-7177; Fax: 815-933-2171.
School—St. Martin of Tours Religious Education, (Grades PreSchool-4), Consolidated with Aquinas Catholic Academy., 907 S. Ninth Ave., 60901. Tel: 815-932-7911; Fax: 815-932-7296.
Catechesis/Religious Program—Students 208.

2—ST. PATRICK (1893), (Irish), Revs. John N. Peeters, C.S.V.; John E. Eck, C.S.V.; Sr. Theresa Galvan, C.N.D., Pastoral Min.; Marilyn Mulcahy, Pastoral Assoc. In Res., Rev. Donald R. Wehnert, C.S.V. (Retired).
Res.: 428 S. Indiana Ave., 60901. Tel: 815-932-6716; Fax: 815-932-2585. Email: stpatskan@ameritech.net. Web: stpatrickkankakee.org.
School—Aquinas Catholic Academy, Consolidated with St. Patrick, St. Teresa & St. Martin, Kankakee, 366 E. Hickory St., 60901. Tel: 815-932-8124; Fax: 815-932-0485. Sr. Nancy Gannon, S.F.C.C., Prin. Lay Teachers 12; Students 186.
Catechesis/Religious Program—Tel: 815-932-0314. Students 502.

3—ST. ROSE OF LIMA (1857) Rev. Scaria T. Thoppil, C.M.I. (India).
Res.: 486 W. Merchant St., 60901-3631. Tel: 815-933-9391; Fax: 815-933-9393. Email: stroslima@sbcglobal.net.
Catechesis/Religious Program—Students 86.

4—ST. STANISLAUS, (Polish), Closed. For inquiries for parish records contact the chancery.

5—ST. TERESA (1949) [CEM] Rev. Santos Castillo; Deacons Ronald Whitman; David Marlowe; Barbara Staniszeski, Pastoral Assoc.; Silvia Barajas, Hispanic Pastoral Min.
Res. & Parish Office: 361 N. St. Joseph Ave., 60901. Tel: 815-933-7683; Fax: 815-933-7692.
Lisieux Pastoral Center—371 St. Joseph Ave., 60901. Tel: 815-939-2913. Kathy Wade, Dir.
Azzarelli Outreach Clinic—341 St. Joseph Ave., 60901. Tel: 815-928-6093. Mrs. Helen Chigaros, Dir.
School—(Grades PreSchool-8) Sr. Nancy Gannon, S.F.C.C., Prin. Consolidated with Aquinas Catholic Academy.
Catechesis/Religious Program—Mrs. Virginia Wayer, D.R.E. Twinned with St. Patrick, Kankakee.

KINSMAN, GRUNDY CO., SACRED HEART (1880) Rev. John Joseph Hornicak.
Res.: c/o 165 Rice St., P.O. Box 190, South Wilmington, 60474. Tel: 815-237-2230; Fax: 815-237-2201.
Catechesis/Religious Program—Students 69.

LISLE, DU PAGE CO., ST. JOAN OF ARC (1924) Revs. Gabriel Baltes, O.S.B.; Kenneth Zigmond, O.S.B.; Dong Bui, Parochial Vicar; Donald Kocher, Senior Priest (Retired); Deacons Denis Stucko; Carl Gregorich; Thomas Richardt; George Soloy.
820 Division St., 60532. Tel: 630-963-4500; Fax: 630-963-4568. Email: info@sjalisle.org.
School—(Grades PreSchool-8), 4913 Columbia, 60532. Tel: 630-969-1732; Fax: 630-963-9070. Email: stjoanofarcschool@sjalisle.org. Web: www.sjalisle.org. Sr. Carolyn Sieg, O.S.B., Prin. Lay Teachers 45; Students 595.
Catechesis/Religious Program—Email: mbarouski@sjalisle.org; nbrochmann@sjalisle.org. Students 330.

LOCKPORT, WILL CO.

1—ST. DENNIS (1846) Rev. James Curtin; Sr. Joanne Vallaro, C.S.J., Pastoral Assoc.; Deacon Rob Weierman, Pastoral Assoc.; Jackie Bedore, Pastoral Assoc. In Res., Rev. Thomson Panakal.
Res.: 1214 Hamilton St., 60441. Tel: 815-838-2592; Fax: 815-838-2401. Email: church@saint-dennis.org. Web: www.saint-dennis.org.
School—(Grades PreSchool-8), 1201 S. Washington St., 60441. Tel: 815-838-4494; Fax: 815-838-5435. Email: school@saint-dennis.org. Mrs. Lisa Smith, Prin. Lay Teachers 22; Students 238.
Catechesis/Religious Program—Generations of Faith Program, Tel: 815-838-2592, Ext. 113. Email: jbedore@saint-dennis.org. Web: generationsoffaith.us. Participants 192.

2—ST. JOHN VIANNEY (1958) Rev. Stanley Drewniak (Poland), Admin.
Res.: 401 Brassel, 60441. Tel: 815-723-3291; Fax: 815-724-0566.
Catechesis/Religious Program—Students 34.

3—ST. JOSEPH (1868) Rev. Thomas McGivney Jr.; Deacon Jesse Pagliaro.
Res.: 410 S. Jefferson St., 60441. Tel: 815-838-0187; Fax: 815-838-5379.
School—(Grades PreSchool-8), 529 Madison, 60441. Tel: 815-838-8173; Fax: 815-838-0504. Miss Lynne Scheffler, Prin.; Mrs. Angi Andrashak, Librarian. Lay Teachers 13; Students 277.
Catechesis/Religious Program—529 Madison St., 60441. Tel: 815-838-2112; Fax: 815-838-4795. Ms. Nancy Hauch, D.R.E. Students 214.
Convent—531 E. Fourth St., 60441. Tel: 815-838-0186.

LOMBARD, DU PAGE CO.

1—CHRIST THE KING (1960) Rev. Peter Jarosz; Deacons Frank Lillig, Pastoral Assoc.; Peter Robinson.
Res.: 1501 S. Main St., 60148. Tel: 630-629-1717; Fax: 630-705-0692. Email: office@ctklombard.org. Web: www.ctklombard.org.
School—(Grades PreSchool-K), 115 E. 15th St., 60148. Tel: 630-627-0640; Fax: 630-705-0139. Email: ckslombard@comcast.net. Jill Placey, Academy Dir. Lay Teachers 3; Students 32.
Catechesis/Religious Program—Tel: 630-629-1717, Ext. 6076. Email: eileen@ctklombard.org. Students 176.

2—DIVINE MERCY POLISH MISSION (1997) Revs. Tadeusz Winnicki, S.Ch.; Michal Skiba, S.Ch.; Adam Slominski, S.Ch.
21W411 Sunset Ave., 60148. Tel: 630-268-8766; Fax: 630-268-8712. Email: misja@milosierdzie.us. Web: www.milosierdzie.us.
Catechesis/Religious Program—Tel: 630-830-2669. Mrs. Fryderyka Kubica, D.R.E. Students 1,000.

3—ST. PIUS X (1954) Rev. Thomas A. Corbino; Sr. Pauline Schutz, O.S.F., Pastoral Assoc.; Deacons John Chan; Thomas Rachubinski; Ron Knecht; Larry Lissak.
Res.: 1025 E. Madison, 60148. Tel: 630-627-4526; Fax: 630-495-5926. Email: parishoffice@stpiuslombard.org. Web: www.stpiuslombard.org.
School—(Grades PreSchool-8), 601 S. Westmore, 60148. Tel: 630-627-2353; Fax: 630-627-1810. Web: www.stpiusknights.org. Mr. Daniel Flaherty, Prin. Lay Teachers 38; Students 492.
Catechesis/Religious Program—Tel: 630-627-1551. Gina Weidman, Dir. Faith Formation. Students 290.

4—SACRED HEART (1912) Revs. Thomas Botheroyd; James Radek; Deacons Frank Annerino; William H. Crane.
Res.: 114 S. Elizabeth St., 60148. Tel: 630-627-0687; Fax: 630-627-0688.
School—(Grades PreSchool-8), 322 W. Maple St., 60148. Tel: 630-629-0536; Fax: 630-629-4752. Mr. Joseph Benning, Prin. Lay Teachers 11; Students 216.
Catechesis/Religious Program—Tel: 630-495-0843; Fax: 630-627-0688. Students 313.

MANHATTAN, WILL CO., ST. JOSEPH (1891) [CEM 2] Rev. John T. McGeean; Deacons Patrick Forsythe; John Putman.
Res.: 235 W. North, P.O. Box 25, 60442. Tel: 815-478-3341; Fax: 815-478-7046. Web: www.stjoemanhattanil.org.
School—(Grades PreSchool-8) Tel: 815-478-3951; Fax: 815-478-7412. Mrs. Eileen Ramsay, Prin. Lay Teachers 14; Students 150.

Catechesis/Religious Program—Tel: 815-478-4452. Students 421.

MANTENO, KANKAKEE CO., ST. JOSEPH (1855) [CEM] Rev. Albert J. Heidecke; Deacons Richard Balgeman; John Leonas, (Retired).
Res.: 207 S. Main St., 60950. Tel: 815-468-3403; Fax: 815-468-7089. Email: stjoemanteno@sbcglobal.net. Web: www.stjosephmanteno.com.
Catechesis/Religious Program—Tel: 815-468-8116. Email: stjoesre8116@yahoo.com. Students 306.

MARTINTON, IROQUOIS CO., ST. MARTIN (1899) [CEM] Rev. Reynaldo B. Treyes.
Mailing Address: P.O. Box 152, Beaverville, 60912. Res.: 308 St. Charles, Beaverville, 60912. Tel: 815-435-2432.
Catechesis/Religious Program—Ryan Loy, D.R.E. Students 5.

MINOOKA, GRUNDY CO., ST. MARY (1862), (Irish), [CEM] Rev. Mark A. Fracaro.
Res.: 303 W. St. Mary St., P.O. Box 456, 60447. Tel: 815-467-2233; Fax: 815-467-1760.
Catechesis/Religious Program—Tel: 815-467-2769; Fax: 815-521-0266. Students 490.

MOKENA, WILL CO., ST. MARY CHURCH (1864) [CEM] Rev. James Dvorscak; Deacons Robert Kaminski; Gary Bednar; Nabil Halaby.
Res.: P.O. Box 2, 60448-0002. Tel: 708-326-9300; Fax: 708-326-9301. Web: www.stmarymokena.com.
School—(Grades K-8), 11409 W. 195th St., 60448. Tel: 708-326-9330; Fax: 708-326-9331. Beth Cunningham, Prin. Franciscan Sisters of the Sacred Heart 1; Lay Teachers 24; Students 450.
Catechesis/Religious Program—11409 W. 195th St., 60448. Tel: 708-326-9350; Fax: 708-326-9351. Kathy Kowalewski, D.R.E.; Sisters Dolores Zemont, O.S.F., D.R.E.; Rose Marie Surwilo, O.S.F., Coord., Christian Formation. Students 1,600.

MOMENCE, KANKAKEE CO., ST. PATRICK (1859) [CEM] Rev. Daniel Hessling.
Res.: 119 Market St., 60954. Tel: 815-472-2864; Fax: 815-472-3043. Email: stpatsrectory@mchsi.com.
Catechesis/Religious Program—Students 100.
Mission—Sacred Heart P.O. Box 557, Hopkins Park, Kankakee Co. 60944. Tel: 815-944-5562. Email: srmarybeth1@sbcglobal.net.

MONEE, WILL CO., ST. BONIFACE (1868), (Irish—Polish), [JC] Rev. Mark Menezes; Deacon Mark Otten.
Church: 5304 W. Main St., P.O. Box 217, 60449. Tel: 708-534-9682; Fax: 708-534-9683. Email: stboniface@dioceseofjoliet.org.
Catechesis/Religious Program—Students 95.

MORRIS, GRUNDY CO., IMMACULATE CONCEPTION OF THE BLESSED VIRGIN MARY (1852) [CEM] Rev. Edward Howe, C.R.
516 E. Jackson St., 60450.
Res.: 411 E. Jackson St., 60450. Tel: 815-942-0620; Fax: 815-942-3171. Web: www.icmorris.org.
School—(Grades PreSchool-8), 505 E. North St., 60450. Tel: 815-942-4111; Fax: 815-942-5094. Web: www.ics1.org. Mr. Kim DesLauriers, Prin. Lay Teachers 14; Students 222.
Catechesis/Religious Program—Tel: 815-942-4177. Students 270.

NAPERVILLE, DUPAGE CO.

1—ST. ELIZABETH SETON (1986) Rev. Richard L. Smith; Sr. Karen Nykiel, O.S.B., Pastoral Assoc.; Deacons Bart Federici; Thomas Ross; Gary Swauger; Andrew Cirmo; Scott Pace. In Res., Rev. Patrick Murphy.
Res.: 2220 Lisson Rd., 60565. Tel: 630-416-3325; Fax: 630-416-3642. Web: www.sesnaperville.org.
Catechesis/Religious Program—Tel: 630-416-1992; Fax: 630-416-4086. Students 1,103.

2—HOLY SPIRIT CATHOLIC COMMUNITY (1998) Rev. Dennis Lewandowski; Deacons Tom Schroeder; Timothy Rehor.
Res.: 2003 Hassert Blvd., 60564. Tel: 630-922-0081; Fax: 630-922-0085.
Rectory—2228 Snow Creek Rd., 60564.
Catechesis/Religious Program—Students 2,295.

3—ST. MARGARET MARY (1980) Rev. Paul Hottinger; Sr. Madelyn Gould, S.S.S.F., Pastoral Assoc.; Deacons Kenneth J. Miles; Terry Taylor.
1450 Green Trails Dr., 60540. Tel: 630-369-0777; Fax: 630-369-1493.
Catechesis/Religious Program—Tel: 630-369-0833. Students 1,108.

4—STS. PETER AND PAUL (1856) [CEM] Revs. Thomas Milota; Marek Jurzyk (Poland) (CHI), Parochial Vicar; Joshua Miller, Parochial Vicar; Deacons Ronald Brown; Richard Yarshen; Roger Novak; Michael Crowell; Joseph Verdico. In Res., Revs. Joseph Valentine, F.S.S.P.; Rosimar Dias.
Res.: 36 N. Ellsworth St., 60540. Tel: 630-355-1081; Fax: 630-355-1179.
School—(Grades K-8), 201 E. Franklin, 60540. Tel: 630-355-0113; Fax: 630-355-9803. Mr. Frank Glowaty, Prin.; Rose Ann Bowers, Librarian; Pat Sullivan, Librarian. Lay Teachers 35; Students 615.
Catechesis/Religious Program—36 N. Ellsworth St., Ste. 104, 60540. Tel: 630-357-2436; Fax: 630-357-2458. Students 872.

5—ST. RAPHAEL (1963) Revs. Mark Jendrysik; Dindo Billote, Parochial Vicar; Deacons Andrew Repak; Charles Woods; Thomas Marciani; Kurt Lange; Mark Leonardelli.
Mailing Address: 1215 Modaff Rd., 60540-7818. Tel: 630-355-4545; Fax: 630-355-7470. Web: www.st-raphael.com.
School—(Grades K-8) Tel: 630-355-4545, Ext. 135; Fax: 630-428-4974. Mrs. Karen Udell, Prin.; Mary Beth Boland, Librarian. Lay Teachers 19; Students 315.
Catechesis/Religious Program—Tel: 630-355-4545, Ext. 121; Fax: 630-355-7470. Web: www.st-raphael.com. Students 1,829.

6—ST. THOMAS THE APOSTLE (1984) Revs. Joel Fortier; J. Rodolphe Arty, C.S.C. (Haiti); Deacons William Worden; Charles Lane; James Breen; Lawrence Kearney; Michael Barrett. Email: mbarrett@stapostle.org.
Res.: 1500 Brookdale Rd., 60563. Tel: 630-355-8980; Fax: 630-355-0521. Email: mainoffice@stapostle.org. Web: www.stapostle.org.
Catechesis/Religious Program—Tel: 630-305-6318. Email: pdougherty@stapostle.org. Students 1,143.

NEW LENOX, WILL CO., ST. JUDE (1934) Revs. Donald R. Lewandowski, O.S.A.; R. William Sullivan, O.S.A.; Donald J. Bates, O.S.A.; Deacons Robert Fitt; William Ciston; Dennis Theriault; George Goes.
Res.: 241 W. Second Ave., 60451. Tel: 815-485-8049; Fax: 815-485-7754.
School—(Grades PreK-8) Tel: 815-485-2549; Fax: 815-485-0234. Mrs. Luanne Watson, Prin.; Cheryl Meyer, Librarian. Lay Teachers 12; Students 138; Pre-School Lay Teachers 2; Pre-School Students 30.
Catechesis/Religious Program—Tel: 815-485-4852; Fax: 815-485-2623. Students 1,500.

OAKBROOK TERRACE, DUPAGE CO., ASCENSION OF OUR LORD (1967) Rev. William Donnelly; Deacons William J. Tansey; Peter Rooney.
Res.: 1 S. 314 Summit Ave., 60181. Tel: 630-629-5810; Fax: 630-953-8251. Email: nlonis@ascensionofourlord.net.
Catechesis/Religious Program—Tel: 630-629-5810, Ext. 215. Students 127.

OSWEGO, KENDALL CO., ST. ANNE (1963) Rev. David J. Hankus; Deacons David Brockman; Duane Wozek.
Res.: 551 Boulder Hill Pass, P.O. Box 670, 60543. Tel: 630-554-3331; Fax: 630-554-0530. Email: stanne@stanneparish.org. Web: www.stanneparish.org.
Catechesis/Religious Program—Tel: 630-554-1425; Fax: 630-554-9797. Email: reo@stanneparish.org. Students 1,529.

PARK FOREST, WILL CO., ST. MARY (1959) Rev. Tri Van Tran; Deacons John Drechny; Edward Szymanski.
Rectory—212 Monee Rd., 60466. Tel: 708-747-1600; Fax: 708-748-6907.
Church: 227 Monee Rd., 60466. Tel: 708-748-6686. Web: www.stmaryparkforest.org.
Catechesis/Religious Program—Students 26.

PAXTON, FORD CO., ST. MARY (1910) Rev. Jose Kadukunnel, C.M.I.
Res.: 407 W. Pells, 60957-1290. Tel: 217-379-4033.
Mission—St. Joseph
Catechesis/Religious Program—Tel: 217-379-2983. Students 91.

PEOTONE, WILL CO., ST. PAUL THE APOSTLE (1961) Rev. Daniel Hoehn.
511 N. Conrad St., 60468.
Res.: 501 N. Conrad St., 60468. Tel: 708-258-6917; Fax: 708-258-3061. Email: stpauloffice@att.net.
Catechesis/Religious Program—Tel: 708-258-9580. Students 204.

PIPER CITY, FORD CO., ST. PETER (1887) [CEM] Rev. Michael Pennock.
Mailing Address: 224 N. Secor St., Gilman, 60938. Res.: 212 Pine St., 60959. Tel: 815-686-2595.
Catechesis/Religious Program—1245 E. 2800 N., 60959. Tel: 815-686-9270. Students 15.

PLAINFIELD, WILL CO., ST. MARY IMMACULATE (1908) [CEM] Revs. David Medow; Mark Rosenbaum, Parochial Vicar; Stanley Tabor, Parochial Vicar; Deacons James Sossong; Victor Puscas; Patrick Lombardo; Thomas O'Connell; Manuel Guerrero; Thomas Sagenbrecht; Patricia Widlowski, Office Mgr. & Admin. Asst.; Janice Gregoire, Business Mgr.; David Bachtel, Community Dir.
Res.: 15626 S. Frederick Ave., 60544. Tel: 815-436-2651; Fax: 815-436-5017.
School—(Grades PreSchool-8) Tel: 815-436-3953; Fax: 815-439-8045. Mr. John Garvey, Prin.; Jennifer Erthum, Asst. Prin. Lay Teachers 25; Students 544.
Catechesis/Religious Program—Tel: 815-436-4501; Fax: 815-439-2304. Students 1,895.

PLANO, KENDALL CO., ST. MARY (1885) [CEM] Rev. Andy Davy, M.I.C.; Deacons Santos Martinez; William Dunn; Douglas Wells. In Res., Revs. Matthew Lamoureux, M.I.C.; Michael Callea, M.I.C.
Res.: 901 N. Center St., 60545. Tel: 630-552-3448; Fax: 630-552-3450. Web: www.saintmaryplano.com.
School—(Grades K-8), 817 N. Center Ave., 60545. Tel: 630-552-3345; Fax: 630-552-4385. Mr. Michael Nadeau, Prin.; Mrs. Alyson Cass, Librarian. Lay Teachers 20; Students 207.
Catechesis/Religious Program—Tel: 630-552-1505. Students 231.

ROCKDALE, WILL CO., ST. JOSEPH CHURCH (1914) Rev. Joseph Kudilil (India).
Res.: 1329 Belleview Ave., 60436-2577. Tel: 815-725-4469; Fax: 815-725-1820.
Catechesis/Religious Program—Tel: 815-729-9149. Students 40.

ROMEOVILLE, WILL CO., ST. ANDREW THE APOSTLE (1959) Revs. Gregor Gorsic; Grzegorz Podwysocki, Parochial Vicar; Deacons Herb Waldron; Rich Ford; Jerry Clark; Jesse Tagle. In Res., Rev. John Driscoll (Retired).
Parish Offices: 530 Glen Ave., 60446. Tel: 815-886-4165; Fax: 815-886-6119. Email: office@standrewromeoville.com.
School—(Grades PreSchool-8), 505 Kingston Dr., 60446. Tel: 815-886-5953; Fax: 815-293-2016. Web: www.standrewromeoville.com. Joseph Leppert, Prin. Lay Teachers 10; Students 202.
Catechesis/Religious Program—505 Kingston Dr., 60446. Tel: 815-886-5962; Fax: 815-886-6624. Students 517.

ROSELLE, DU PAGE CO., ST. WALTER (1946) Revs. James Schwab; Francis B. McDonald, Pastor Emeritus (Retired); Deacons Ron Searls; Michael Kowalchik; Richard Foy.
Res.: 130 W. Pine Ave., 60172. Tel: 630-894-2461; Fax: 630-582-4206. Web: www.stwalterchurch.com.
School—(Grades PreSchool-8), 201 W. Maple Ave., 60172. Tel: 630-529-1721; Fax: 630-529-9290. Email: stwalterinfo@sbcglobal.net. Web: www.stwalter-school.com. Mrs. Mary Lloyd, Prin. Lay Teachers 29; Students 702.
Catechesis/Religious Program—140 W. Pine, 60172. Tel: 630-894-5880; Fax: 630-582-5192. Kenneth Ortega, Dir. Faith Formation. Students 850.

ST. ANNE, KANKAKEE CO., ST. ANNE (1865), (French-Canadian), [CEM] Rev. James Fanale, C.S.V.
Res.: 230 N. Sixth Ave., P.O. Box 470, 60964. Tel: 815-427-8265; Fax: 815-427-8267.
Catechesis/Religious Program—Students 50.

ST. GEORGE, KANKAKEE CO., ST. GEORGE (1853), (French-Canadian), [CEM] Rev. Daniel R. Belanger, C.S.V.; Deacon Joseph Cotugno.
Res.: 5272 E. 5000 North Rd., Bourbonnais, 60914-9725. Tel: 815-939-1851; Fax: 815-939-2777.
Catechesis/Religious Program—Students 95.

SHOREWOOD, WILL CO., HOLY FAMILY (1959) Rev. William G. Dewan; Deacons Fred Straub; Karl Huebner; Thomas Paluch; Paul Schneider. In Res., Rev. Vytas Memenas, Senior Priest (Retired).
Church: 600 Brook Forest Ave., 60404. Tel: 815-725-6880; Fax: 815-725-2311. Web: www.holyfamilyshorewood.org.
School—(Grades PreSchool-8) Tel: 815-725-8149. Mrs. Judith Strohschein, Prin.; Mrs. Melissa Crisci, Librarian. Lay Teachers 17; Students 325.
Catechesis/Religious Program—Tel: 815-730-8691; Fax: 815-725-8149. Students 1,100.

SOUTH WILMINGTON, GRUNDY CO., ST. LAWRENCE (1904) Rev. John Joseph Hornicak; Deacon Steven Frazier.
Res.: 165 Rice St., Box 190, 60474. Tel: 815-237-2230; Fax: 815-237-2201. Email: stlawrenceswilm@yahoo.com.
Catechesis/Religious Program—Students 67.

STEGER, WILL CO., ST. LIBORIUS (1902) Rev. Dennis Spies.
Res.: 71 W. 35th St., 60475. Tel: 708-754-1363; Fax: 708-754-7577. Email: stliborius@yahoo.com.
School—Mother Teresa Catholic Academy, (Grades PreSchool-8), 24201 S. Kings Rd., Crete, 60417. Tel: 708-672-3093; Fax: 708-367-0640. Sandra Robertson, Prin. (Steger Campus) Lay Teachers 9; Students 300.
Catechesis/Religious Program—Tel: 708-754-3460. Students 170.

VILLA PARK, DU PAGE CO.

1—ST. ALEXANDER (1924) Rev. Tuan Van Nguyen; Deacons Julio Jimenez; Christopher Cochran; James Krueger; John Gibbons; Matthew Tretina.
Res.: 300 S. Cornell Ave., 60181. Tel: 630-833-7730; Fax: 630-833-3127. Email: stavpark@aol.com. Web: www.stalexanderparish.org.
School—(Grades K-8), 136 S. Cornell Ave., 60181. Tel: 630-834-3787; Fax: 630-834-1961. Web: www-.stalexanderschool.org. Glenn Purpura, Prin. Lay Teachers 10; Students 134.
Catechesis/Religious Program—130 S. Cornell Ave., 60181. Tel: 630-832-0506. Students 210.

2—ST. JOHN THE APOSTLE (1959), (Italian—Polish),

Rev. Robert Duda.
Res.: 330 N. Westmore, 60181. Tel: 630-279-7404; Fax: 630-530-9910.
Catechesis/Religious Program—Tel: 630-832-7588; Fax: 630-832-7588. Students 91.

WARRENVILLE, DU PAGE CO., ST. IRENE (1927) Rev. James Antiporek; Deacons William Murphy, Pastoral Assoc.; Robert True, Pastoral Assoc.; Joseph Urso, Pastoral Assoc.; Annette Kubalanza, Pastoral Assoc.
Res.: 28 W. 441 Warrenville Rd., 60555. Tel: 630-393-2400; Fax: 630-393-9680. Email: parishoffice@st-irene.org. Web: www.st-irene.org.
School—(Grades PreSchool-8), 3S601 Warren Ave., 60555. Tel: 630-393-9303; Fax: 630-393-7009. Email: school@st-irene.org. Web: www.st-ireneschool.org. Mrs. Maureen White, Prin. Lay Teachers 14; Students 162.
Catechesis/Religious Program—Tel: 630-393-2400, Ext. 22. Sr. Nancy Ulrich, O.S.F., D.R.E. Students 185.

WATSEKA, IROQUOIS CO., ST. EDMUND (1872) Rev. Michael Powell.
Church: 219 E. Locust St., 60970. Tel: 815-432-3274; Fax: 815-432-3275.
Catechesis/Religious Program—Tel: 815-432-5569. Email: judystedchurch@yahoo.com. Students 113.
Mission—St. Joseph P.O. Box 173, Crescent City, Iroquois Co. 60928.

WAYNE, DU PAGE CO., RESURRECTION CATHOLIC COMMUNITY (1964) Rev. Daniel Bachner.
Pastoral Center: 30W350 Army Trail Rd., 60184. Tel: 630-289-5400, Ext. 203; Fax: 630-289-5407. Email: ressec@sbcglobal.net. Web: www.rescatholiccom.com.
Catechesis/Religious Program—Tel: 630-289-5400, Ext. 215. Email: resff@sbcglobal.net. Students 360.

WEST CHICAGO, DU PAGE CO., ST. MARY (1894) [CEM] Revs. John Balluff; Matthew Nathan; Sr. Rocio Castillo, Pastoral Assoc., Hisp. Min.; Deacons Bruce Carlson; Luis Saltigerald.
Res.: 140 N. Oakwood Ave., 60185. Tel: 630-231-0013; Fax: 630-293-2671. Email: parish.office@stmarywc.org. Web: www.stmarywc.org.
Catechesis/Religious Program—Tel: 630-231-5704. Sr. Maria Romero, D.R.E. Students 573.

WESTMONT, DU PAGE CO., HOLY TRINITY (1938) Revs. Michael Danek, C.R.; Marion Wroblewski, C.R., Parochial Vicar; Deacons William Casey; Thomas Jagielo. In Res., Rev. Gerald Watt, C.R.
Res.: 111 S. Cass Ave., 60559. Tel: 630-968-1366; Fax: 630-968-7846. Email: htparish@comcast.net. Web: www.holytrinitywestmont.org.
School—(Grades PreSchool-8), 108 S. Linden, 60559. Tel: 630-971-0184; Fax: 630-971-1175. Email: snetzel@holytrinitywestmont.org. Mrs. Nicole Noverini, Prin. Lay Teachers 11; Students 180.
Catechesis/Religious Program—Tel: 630-968-5978. Students 312.

WHEATON, DU PAGE CO.
1—ST. DANIEL THE PROPHET CHURCH (1989) Rev. Thomas Sularz; Deacons Ken Jackson, Pastoral Assoc.; James Perry; Anne Sinclair, Dir. Music & Liturgist.
Res.: 101 West Loop Rd., 60189. Tel: 630-682-5003; Fax: 630-682-5004. Web: www.stdaniel.org.
Catechesis/Religious Program—Tel: 630-682-5003, Ext. 121. Diane Ahlemeyer, D.R.E. Students 288.
2—ST. MARK (1962) Rev. John Ducaji.
Res.: 303 E. Parkway Dr., 60187. Tel: 630-665-0030; Fax: 630-665-0303.
Catechesis/Religious Program—300 E. Cole St., 60187. Tel: 630-668-4614. Students 72.
3—ST. MICHAEL (1882) [CEM] Revs. Don E. McLaughlin; Mark Cote, Parochial Vicar; Deacons John Cozzens; William Stroner; David Meador; Kenneth Kubica; Daniel Simmet.
Res.: 310 S. Wheaton Ave., 60187. Tel: 630-665-2250; Fax: 630-510-8891. Web: www.stmichaelcommunity.org.
School—(Grades PreSchool-8), 314 W. Willow Ave., 60187. Tel: 630-653-1454; Fax: 630-665-1491. Marcia Opal, Prin. Lay Teachers 28; Students 564.
Catechesis/Religious Program—317 Willow Ave., 60187. Tel: 630-682-3650; Fax: 630-690-3324. Students 1,339.

WILMINGTON, WILL CO., ST. ROSE (1855) [CEM] Rev. Steven Bondi; Sr. Ann Ellen Quirk, B.V.M., Pastoral Assoc.; Deacon Donald Dyer.
Res.: 603 S. Main St., 60481. Tel: 815-476-7491; Fax: 815-476-1085.
School—(Grades PreSchool-8), 626 Kankakee St., 60481. Tel: 815-476-6220; Fax: 815-476-2154. Linda Bland, Prin. Lay Teachers 9; Students 130.
Catechesis/Religious Program—Students 132.

WILTON CENTER, WILL CO., ST. PATRICK (1905), (Irish), [CEM] Rev. Daniel Hoehn.
Res.: 14936 Wilmington Peotone Rd., Manhattan, 60442. Tel: 815-478-3440; Fax: 815-478-4186.
Catechesis/Religious Program—Students 35.

WINFIELD, DU PAGE CO., ST. JOHN THE BAPTIST (1867) [CEM] [JC 2] Revs. Thomas Cargo; Thomas Theneth, C.M.I., Parochial Vicar; Deacon Rod Accardi. In Res., Rev. Henry Wilkening (Retired).
Res.: O.S. 233 Church St., 60190. Tel: 630-668-0918; Fax: 630-668-1074. Web: www.stjohnwinfield.org.
School—(Grades PreSchool-8), O.S. 259 Church St., 60190. Tel: 630-668-2625; Fax: 630-668-7176. Catherine Kos, Prin. Lay Teachers 21; Students 272.
Catechesis/Religious Program—Tel: 630-682-4400; Fax: 630-668-1074. Maureen Brennan, D.R.E. Students 353.

WOOD DALE, DU PAGE CO., HOLY GHOST (1946) Rev. Kevin R. Farrell; Deacon Dino Franch.
Res.: 254 N. Wood Dale Rd., 60191. Tel: 630-860-2975; Fax: 630-860-9482. Email: tbero@holyghostparish.org. Web: www.holyghostparish.org.
School—(Grades PreSchool-8) Tel: 630-766-4508; Fax: 630-860-7697. Mrs. Diana Mendez, Prin.; Debbie Fillip, Librarian. Lay Teachers 15; Students 200.
Catechesis/Religious Program—Tel: 630-766-1045. Sheri Abel, D.R.E. Students 110.

WOODRIDGE, DU PAGE CO.
1—CHRIST THE SERVANT PARISH (1990) Rev. Frank Vitus; Deacon Thomas Fricke.
Mailing Address: 8700 Havens Dr., 60517. Tel: 630-910-0770; Fax: 630-910-6060. Email: ctsoffice@ctswoodridge.org. Web: www.ctswoodridge.org.
Catechesis/Religious Program—Students 249.
2—ST. SCHOLASTICA (1962) Rev. Gerald Riva; Deacons Gerald G. Christensen; Roger Schmith; Terry Zarembka.
Res.: 7800 S. Janes Ave., 60517. Tel: 630-985-2351; Fax: 630-985-8770. Email: archabbess@aol.com. Web: www.stscholasticaparish.org.
School—(Grades K-8) Tel: 630-985-2515; Fax: 630-985-2395. Gail Kueper, Prin.; Barbara Stance, Librarian. Lay Teachers 11; Students 261.
Catechesis/Religious Program—7720 Janes Ave., 60517. Tel: 630-985-9255. Beth Cartner, Dir. Faith Formation. Students 512.

YORKVILLE, KENDALL CO., ST. PATRICK (1885) [CEM] [JC] Revs. Matthew Lamoureux, M.I.C.; Michael Callea, M.I.C., Parochial Vicar; Deacons Dale Metcalfe; Donald Cyr; Jerome Heitschmidt.
406 Walnut St., 60560. Tel: 630-553-6671; Fax: 630-553-2695. Email: info@stpatrickyorkville.org. Web: www.stpatrickyorkville.org.
Catechesis/Religious Program— Justin Frato, Dir. Faith Formation. Students 702.

Chaplains of Public Institutions

JOLIET. *Dept. of Corrections*, 2848 McDonough St., 60432. Rev. Richard Ross.
Illinois State Penitentiary, P.O. Box 112, 60434. Deacon Charles Peterson.
Illinois Youth Commission, Reception and Diagnostic Center, McDonough St., 60435. Deacon Joseph O'Connor.
Silver Cross Hospital, 1200 Maple Rd., 60432. Vacant.

DOWNERS GROVE. *Good Samaritan Hospital*, 3821 Highland Ave., 60515. Vacant.

ELMHURST. *Elmhurst Memorial Hospital*, 200 Berteau Ave., 60126. Rev. Patrick Murphy, Chap.

HINSDALE. *Hinsdale Hospital*, 120 N. Oak, 60521. Rev. James Walton, O.F.M.

KANKAKEE. *Riverside Medical Center*, 350 N. Wells, 60901. Rev. John Antczak.
Shapiro Development Center, 100 E. Jeffery, 60901. Rev. Richard Jacklin.

NAPERVILLE. *Edward Hospital*, S. Washington St., 60540. Rev. Patrick Murphy, Chap.

WINFIELD. *Central DuPage Hospital*, 0N025 Winfield Rd., 60190. Rev. Henry Wilkening (Retired), Deacon Rod Accardi.

On Duty Outside the Diocese:
Revs.—
Dieter, Thomas M.
Martis, Douglas, Ph.D., S.T.D., Mundelein Seminary, Mundelein, 60060.
Schoenstene, Robert L., M.A., S.S.L., St. Mary of the Lake Seminary, Mundelein, 60060.

Leave of Absence:
Revs.—
Buczyna, Andrew L.
Burnett, James
Collogan, Robert
Flores, Alejandro
Gohlke, Nathan
Infanger, Frank
LaPone, Arthur
Larson, Ryan
Pozen, Matthew
Regan, John
Ryan, F. Lee
Simonelli, Gerald
Sponder, John

Retired:
Most Rev.—
Imesch, Joseph L., 425 Summit St., 60435.
Revs.—
Barrett, John F., 460 Raintree Ct. #1H, Glen Ellyn, 60137.
Best, Richard
Bowden, Lloyd, 115 N. May St., 60435.
Butters, Joseph, 13140 Nassau Dr., Apt. 214B, Seal Beach, CA 90740.
Carlin, Warren, O.Carm.
Coleman, Robert J.
Corkery, Raymond, O.Carm.
Cullen, William, 6267 Trinity Dr., #2D, Lisle, 60532.
Dennerlein, John L.
Dillon, David, O.Carm.
Driscoll, John, St. Andrew the Apostle, 530 Glen Ave., Romeoville, 60446.
Fleming, Thomas, Carmelite Carefree Village, Darien, 60561.
Graziano, J. Damien
Guiney, John, S.M.A., 256 Forest, Glen Ellyn, 60137.
Guz, Leonard J.
Hemrick, Eugene F.
Hurley, George, 5 Oak Brook Club Dr., Oakbrook, 60521-1314.
Kelpsas, A., M.I.C.
Kenny, Donald, Quito, Ecuador
Kloepfer, John S., Box 1742, Clarksville, VA 23927.
Kocher, Donald
Kostelz, Richard F.
Lennon, James M., John Paul II House, 430 N. Center St., 60435.
Maher, Arthur, 1115 Lorraine Rd., #32, Wheaton, 60189.
Maher, Francis, 965-B Tenderfoot Hill Rd., Colorado Springs, CO 80906.
Meis, Anthony
Memenas, Vytas, St. Anthony Parish, 100 Scott St., 60432.
Micka, A., M.I.C.
Moriarty, John J.
Morrissette, Dominic, Nazareth House, 6333 Rancho Mission Rd., San Diego, CA 92108.
Mumper, Edward, 4515 Sawdust Rd., Bruce, WI 54819.
O'Shea, William J.
Pietras, Robert E.
Poff, Edward
Prodehl, Richard B.
Rowland, Edward P.
Ryan, William
Schubert, Gerold, O.F.M.
Sebahar, John, St. John Vianney Villa, Naperville.
Settles, Dennis F.
Stalzer, Joseph
Stempora, Daniel F.
Sullivan, John D.
Testa, Jess
Tivy, Gerald
Valente, Michael, 3633 N. Pacific Ave., Chicago, 60634.
Wehnert, Donald R., C.S.V.
Wheeler, Charles
White, Denis
White, Thomas J.
Wilkening, Henry, St. John the Baptist Parish, OS233 Church St., 60190.
Wolter, Thomas
Yarno, Kenneth, C.S.V.

Permanent Deacons:
Accardi, Rodger F., Central DuPage Hospital and St. John the Baptist, Winfield
Agurkis, Albert, St. Mary of Gostyn, Downers Grove
Anchor, Robert, (On Duty Outside the Diocese)
Anderson, Roy D., (On Duty Outside the Diocese)
Annerino, Frank, Sacred Heart, Lombard
Balgeman, Richard, St. Joseph, Manteno
Barrett, Michael, St. Thomas, Naperville
Beabout, Norman, (On Duty Outside the Diocese)
Bednar, Gary, St. Mary, Mokena
Berkey, Donald, St. Anthony, Frankfort
Bernardin, Donald, (Leave of Absence)
Bevan, William F., III, St. Paul the Apostle, Joliet
Bias, Ralph, Sacred Heart, Joliet
Bina, Frank, Our Lady of Peace, Darien
Blumenstein, John, St. Francis of Assisi, Bolingbrook
Borkowicz, Leo M., (Retired)
Boucek, William, St. Anthony, Frankfort
Bowns, Loren, St. Liborius, Steger (On Duty

Outside the Diocese)
Boyle, John R., St. Alexander, Villa Park
Brachle, Paul L., Jr., Our Lady of Peace, Darien
Brechtel, Scott, (Leave of Absence)
Breen, James, St.Thomas the Apostle, Naperville
Brockman, David, St. Anne, Oswego
Brown, Ronald, Sts. Peter & Paul, Naperville
Bumble, John, St. James Manor, Crete
Carlson, Bruce, St. Mary, West Chicago
Carson, Neill, (Retired)
Casey, William, Holy Trinity, Westmont
Cassey, Robert, St. Petronille, Glen Ellyn
Chaidez, Lorenzo, St. Dominic, Bolingbrook
Chambers, Frank A., (On Duty Outside the Diocese)
Chan, John, St. Pius X, Lombard
Christensen, Gerald G., St. Scholastica, Woodridge
Cirmo, Andrew, St. Elizabeth Seton, Naperville
Ciston, William, St. Jude, New Lenox
Clark, Gordon, St. Andrew, Romeoville
Clark, Raymond, St. Jude, Joliet
Clodi, Gregory, St. Martin of Tours, Kankakee
Cochran, Christopher, St. Alexander, Villa Park
Cole, John, (On Duty Outside the Diocese)
Cook, Michael, (On Duty Outside the Diocese)
Cooley, Stephen, (On Duty Outside the Diocese)
Cotugno, Joseph, St. George, St. George
Cozzens, John, St. Michael, Wheaton
Crane, William H., St. Pius X, Lombard
Crowell, Michael, Sts. Peter & Paul, Naperville
Cummiskey, Terry, St. Isidore, Bloomingdale
Cyr, Donald, St. Patrick, Yorkville
Dalpiaz, Joseph C., Mother of Good Counsel, Homer Glen
Dalton, James, Cathedral of St. Raymond, Joliet
Danahey, Daniel, St. Anthony, Frankfort
Darschewski, Ronald, (On Duty Outside the Diocese)
Dennison, James, (On Duty Outside the Diocese)
Dixon, James A., (On Duty Outside the Diocese)
Drechny, John, St.Mary, Park Forest
Duncan, Robert, St. Ann, Channahon
Dunn, William, St. Mary, Plano
Dyer, Donald L., St. Rose, Wilmington
Eaker, James, Visitation, Elmhurst
Eastburn, Lloyd D., St. Patrick, Momence
Ellman, Edward, (On Duty Outside the Diocese)
Farrell, John, Our Lady of Mt. Carmel, Darien
Federici, Bart, St. Elizabeth Seton, Naperville
Feely, John, Immaculate Conception, Elmhurst
Fitt, Robert, St. Jude, New Lenox
Ford, Richard, St. Andrew, Romeoville
Forsythe, Patrick, St. Joseph, Manhattan
Fox, Steven A., (On Duty Outside the Diocese)
Foy, Richard, St. Walter, Roselle
Foys, Frank F., Notre Dame, Clarendon Hills
Franch, Dino J., Holy Ghost, Wood Dale
Frazier, Steven, St. Lawrence, South Wilmington
Freund, John, St. Isidore, Bloomingdale
Fricke, Thomas E., Christ the Servant, Woodridge
Fritz, Leon P., St. Joseph, Bradley
Fudacz, Larry, Our Lady of Peace, Darien
Gagnon, Ronnie, St. Margaret Mary, Herscher
Gamboa, Gabriel, (Leave of Absence)
Gavin, Philip, (Retired)
Gibbons, John, St. Alexander, Villa Park
Goebel, Thomas, Immaculate Conception, Elmhurst
Goes, George, St. Jude, New Lenox
Gregoire, Jerome, St. Joseph, Bradley
Gregorich, Carl, St. Joan of Arc, Lisle
Grozik, Alexander, Mary Queen of Heaven, Elmhurst
Guerrero, Manuel, St. Mary Immaculate, Plainfield
Hahn, Duane, (Leave of Absence)
Halaby, Nabil, St. Mary, Mokena
Hamilton, Raymond, St. Francis of Assisi, Bolingbrook
Heitschmidt, Jerome, St. Patrick, Yorkville
Heitz, Philip, St. Philip, Addison
Henrissey, Francis R., (Leave of Absence)
Higgins, Donald, St. Anthony, Frankfort
Huebner, Karl, Holy Family, Shorewood
Jackson, Kenneth, St. Daniel the Prophet, Wheaton
Jagielo, Thomas, Holy Trinity, Westmont
Janousek, James, St. John the Baptist, Joliet
Janousek, Jay, Visitation, Elmhurst
Jimenez, Julio, St. Alexander, Villa Park
Johnson, Joseph, St. Anthony, Frankfort
Jossey, Robert, (Retired)
Juricic, Frank, St. Bernard, Joliet
Kaminski, Robert, St. Mary, Mokena
Kearney, Lawrence, St. Thomas, Naperville
Kelly, William, (On Duty Outside the Diocese)
Kim, Paul, St. Andrew Kim, Itasca
Kinsella, James, Cathedral of St. Raymond, Joliet
Knecht, Ronald, St. Pius X, Lombard
Kobs, Dennis, (On Duty Outside the Diocese)
Kolodziej, Paul, St. Patrick, Joliet
Kowalchik, Michael, St. Walter, Roselle
Kowalski, Henry, (Retired)
Koza, Joseph, (On Duty Outside the Diocese)
Kozar, Francis, St. Joseph, Downers Grove
Krueger, James, St. Alexander, Villa Park
Kubica, Kenneth, St. Michael, Wheaton
Kueper, Timothy, Our Lady of Mercy, Aurora
Lamon, John D., (On Duty Outside the Diocese)
LaMotte, Robert, (Retired)
Lane, Charles, St. Thomas, Naperville
Lange, Kurt, St. Raphael, Naperville
Legner, Neil, (On Duty Outside the Diocese)
Leonard, John, Our Lady of Lourdes, Gibson City
Leonardelli, Mark, St. Raphael, Naperville
Leonas, John, (Retired)
Leppert, Milton, St. Patrick, Wilton Center
Lifka, David, Notre Dame, Clarendon Hills
Lillig, Francis, Christ the King, Lombard
Lissak, Lawrence, St. Pius X, Lombard
Lombardo, Patrick, St. Mary Immaculate, Plainfield
Lopez, Jose L., St. John the Baptist, Joliet
Lovero, Marco, St. Francis of Assisi, Bolingbrook
Mahoney, Daniel, Sr., St. Mary Nativity, Joliet
Malek, Robert, St. Matthew, Glendale Heights
Marciani, Thomas, St. Raphael, Naperville
Marcotte, Euchrist, Maternity B.V.M., Bourbonnais
Marlowe, David, St. Theresa, Kankakee
Marrow, Philip, St. Joseph, Addison
Martinez, Santos H., St. Mary, Plano
McCaffrey, Christopher, St. Bernard, Homer Glen
McConnell, Alexander, Notre Dame, Clarendon Hills
McDonnell, Joseph, St. Ann, Channahon
McGreal, Sean, St. Philip, Addison
McGuire, Michael, St. Francis of Assisi, Bolingbrook
Meador, David, St. Michael, Wheaton
Mele, John, St. Mary Magdalene, Joliet
Mempin, Genaro, St. Francis of Assisi, Bolingbrook
Metcalfe, Dale R., St. Patrick, Yorkville
Miciunas, Robert, St. Mary of Gostyn, Downers Grove
Migliorato, Lawrence, St. Isidore, Bloomingdale
Miles, Kenneth J., St. Margaret Mary, Naperville
Moeller, John, St. James, Glen Ellyn
Molinaro, Serafin, Resurrection, Wayne
Monahan, Kevin, (On Duty Outside the Diocese)
Murphy, William E., St. Irene, Warrenville
Neher, Norman, (Retired)
Newey, Paul, Divine Savior, Downers Grove
Nguyen, Anthony, Queenship of Mary, Glen Ellyn
Nolan, Thomas J., Mary, Queen of Heaven, Elmhurst
Novak, Roger, Sts. Peter and Paul, Naperville
Nunez, Charles, (Retired)
O'Connell, Thomas, St. Mary Immaculate, Plainfield
O'Connor, Joseph, St. Joseph, Downers Grove
Otten, Mark, St. Boniface, Monee
Ouska, Gregory, St. Joseph, Downers Grove
Pace, Scott, St. Elizabeth Seton, Naperville
Pagliaro, Jesse, St. Joseph, Lockport
Pallo, Daniel, (On Duty Outside the Diocese)
Paluch, Thomas, Holy Family, Shorewood
Perry, James, St. Daniel the Prophet, Wheaton
Petak, Edwin, Cathedral of St. Raymond, Joliet
Peterson, Charles M., St. Patrick, Joliet
Pidgeon, Matthew, St. James, Glen Ellyn
Pistorio, Charles, St. Ambrose, Crest Hill
Powers, Thomas, (On Duty Outside the Diocese)
Principe, Michael, (Retired)
Ptacek, Edward, Our Lady of Mt. Carmel, Darien
Puscas, Victor, St. Mary Immaculate, Plainfield
Putman, John, St. Joseph, Manhattan
Rachubinski, Thomas, St. Pius X, Lombard
Randolph, Donald, St. Isidore, Bloomingdale
Raskowski, David, St. Joseph, Joliet
Rehmer, Philip, Our Lady of Mercy, Aurora
Rehor, Timothy, Holy Spirit Catholic Community, Naperville
Repak, Andrew, (Retired)
Richardt, Thomas, St. Joan of Arc, Lisle
Riggi, Joseph, (Retired)
Rittenhouse, Daniel, Our Mother of Good Counsel, Homer Glen
Ritter, David, St. Dominic, Bolingbrook
Robinson, Peter, Christ the King, Lombard
Rooney, Peter, Ascension, Oakbrook Terrace
Rosko, Richard, St. Anthony, Frankfort
Ross, Thomas, St. Elizabeth Seton, Naperville
Ryan, Kevin, St. Bernard, Homer Glen
Safko, Terry L., St. Mary Immaculate, Plainfield
Sagenbrecht, Thomas, St. Mary Immaculate, Plainfield
Saltigerald, Luis, St. Mary, West Chicago
Schaper, Ed, (On Duty Outside the Diocese)
Schlott, Anthony, St. Anthony, Frankfort
Schlund, James, (On Duty Outside the Diocese)
Schmith, Roger, St. Scholastica, Woodridge
Schneider, Paul A., Holy Family, Shorewood
Schroeder, Thomas, Holy Spirit Catholic Community, Naperville
Schubert, Anthony, (On Duty Outside the Diocese)
Schumacher, Carl N.J., St. Joseph, Downers Grove
Searls, Ronald, St. Walter, Roselle
Sebastian, John, St. Isaac Jogues, Hinsdale
Sheridan, Thomas, (Leave of Absence)
Simmet, Daniel, St. Michael, Wheaton
Siwek, Raymond, (Retired)
Skelly, Patrick, Maternity BVM, Bourbonnais
Solis, Joseph, (On Duty Outside the Diocese)
Soloy, George, St. Joan of Arc, Lisle
Sossong, James R., St. Mary Immaculate, Plainfield
Spatafore, Anthony, Visitation, Elmhurst
Spiezio, John, St. Petronille, Glen Ellyn
Stevens, Richard R., (On Duty Outside the Diocese)
Stolarz, Dennis, Our Lady of Peace, Darien
Storrs, Wayne, Christ the King, Lombard
Straub, Fred, Holy Family, Shorewood
Stroner, William, St. Michael, Wheaton
Stucko, Denis, St. Joan of Arc, Lisle
Sullivan, Robert, St. Joseph, Downers Grove
Swauger, Gary, (Medical Leave of Absence)
Symonanis, Alan, Notre Dame, Clarendon Hills
Szymanski, Edward, St. Mary, Park Forest
Tagle, Jesse, St. Andrew, Romeoville
Tansey, William, Ascension, Oakbrook Terrace
Taylor, Terrance, St. Margaret Mary, Naperville
Taylor, Timothy, St. Charles Borromeo, Bensenville
Tetrault, Robert L., (On Duty Outside the Diocese)
Theriault, Dennis, St. Jude, New Lenox
Thiltgen, Thomas R., Corpus Christi, Carol Stream
Thomas, William, Corpus Christi, Carol Stream
Tiongson, Arturo, Our Lady of Mercy, Aurora
Tretina, Matthew, St. Alexander, Villa Park
Troy, Daniel, (Retired)
True, Robert, St. Irene, Warrenville
Uffmann, William, (Leave of Absence)
Urso, Joseph, St. Irene, Warrenville
Valdez, George, (Leave of Absence)
Vavra, Robert, Our Lady of Mercy, Aurora
Verdico, Joseph, Sts. Peter & Paul, Naperville
Villarreal, Guadalupe, St. Isidore, Bloomingdale
Volker, Jeffrey, Our Lady of Lourdes, Gibson City
Waldron, Herbert, St. Andrew, Romeoville
Walen, Paul J., Sr., St. Dominic, Bolingbrook
Wallace, Robert, St. Dominic, Bolingbrook
Weierman, Robert, St. Dennis, Lockport
Wells, Douglas, St. Mary, Plano
Wharry, James, (On Duty Outside the Diocese)
Whitman, Ronald, St. Teresa, Kankakee
Winblad, Joseph, Marian Village, Homer Glen
Woods, Charles, St. Raphael, Naperville
Worden, William, St. Thomas the Apostle, Naperville
Wozek, Duane, St. Anne, Oswego
Yarshen, Richard, Sts. Peter & Paul, Naperville
Yurcus, Ronald J., St. Petronille, Glen Ellyn
Zarembka, Terrance, St. Scholastica, Woodridge
Ziomek, Robert, St. Peter the Apostle, Itasca

INSTITUTIONS LOCATED IN THE DIOCESE

[A] COLLEGES AND UNIVERSITIES

JOLIET. *University of St. Francis* (1920) 500 N. Wilcox, 60435. Tel: 800-735-7500; Fax: 815-740-4285. Email: information@stfrancis.edu. Web: www.stfrancis.edu. Dr. Michael J. Vinceguerra, B.S., M.S., Ph.D., Pres.; Sr. Mary Elizabeth Imler, O.S.F., B.S., M.S., M.A., Vice Pres., Mission Integration and Ministry; Mr. Terry Cottrell, B.A., M.S., Librarian; Rev. J. Derran Combs, O.F.M., B.A., M.Div., Th.M., Special Asst. to Provost. A coed residence and commuter school. Priests 1; Fran. Srs. of Sacred Heart 1; Lay Teachers 98; Students 3,385; Total Staff 385.

LISLE. *Benedictine University*, 5700 College Rd., 60532-0900. Tel: 630-829-6600; Fax: 630-960-1126. Web: www.ben.edu. Rt. Rev. Austin Murphy, O.S.B., Chancellor; Dr. William J. Carroll, Pres.; Dr. Donald Taylor, Provost & Vice Pres. Academic Affairs; Mr. Charles Gregory, Exec. Vice Pres.; Rev. David Turner, O.S.B., Asst. Provost for Mission; Dr. Maria De La Camara, Dean, College of Liberal Arts; Dr. Bart S. Ng, Dean, College of Sciences; Dr. Sandra Gill, Dean, College Business; Dr. Alan Gorr, Dean, College Educ. & Health Svcs.; Michael Carroll, Dean Moser, College of Adult & Professional Studies; Jack Fritts, Librarian; Mike Bromberg, Dean, Academic Affairs; Bro. Richard Poro, O.S.B., Asst. Univ. Min.; Revs. Theodore D. Suchy, O.S.B., Dir., Jurica-Suchy Nature Museum; Philip S. Timko, O.S.B., Asst. Dir., Univ. Ministry; John Palmer, C.S.V.; Julian von Duerbeck, O.S.B.; Bro. Augustine Mallak, O.S.B.; Bob Bosanac, Registrar; Mark Kurowski, Dir., Univ. Min.

Fathers 6; Brothers 2; Sisters 1; Lay Teachers 144; Administrators 445; Students 6,650.

Founders Woods, Ltd., 5700 College Rd., 60532.

ROMEOVILLE. *Lewis University* (Coed University), One University Pkwy., 60446-2200. Tel: 815-838-0500; Fax: 815-838-5979. Email: brjgaff@lewisu.edu. Web: www.lewisu.edu/. Bros. James Gaffney, F.S.C., Pres.; Philip Johnson, F.S.C., Dir. University Ministry; Rev. Daniel L. Torson, C.PP.S., Chap.; Fredereike Moskal, Librarian. Priests 2; De La Salle Christian Brothers 16; Lay Teachers 224; Students 6,394.

[B] HIGH SCHOOLS, DIOCESAN

KANKAKEE. *Bishop McNamara Catholic High School* (1922) 550 W. Brookmont Blvd., 60901. Tel: 815-932-7413; Fax: 815-932-0926. Email: glamore@bishop-mcnamara.org. Web: www.bishopmac.com. Kurt Weigt, Prin.; Joanne Bracken, Dir. Fundraising & Spec. Events; Gina La More, Dir. Admissions; Jaclyn Dugan-Roof, Dir., Alumni Rels.; Terri Jones, Librarian. Priests 1; Deacons 1; Lay Teachers 31; Students 369; Total Staff 56.

[C] HIGH SCHOOLS, PRIVATE

JOLIET. *Joliet Catholic Academy* (Coed), 1200 N. Larkin Ave., 60435. Tel: 815-741-0500; Fax: 815-741-9530. Email: jbudz@jca-online.org. Web: www.jca-online.org. Jeffrey Budz, Prin. & CEO; William Pender, Asst. Prin. & COO; Barbara Powers, Librarian. Carmelites & Joliet Franciscans. Priests 1; Sisters 1; Lay Teachers 48; Students 724.

LISLE. *Benet Academy* (1887) 2200 Maple Ave., 60532. Tel: 630-719-2782; Fax: 630-719-2849. Email: smarth@benet.org. Web: www.benet.org. Rev. Jude D. Randall, O.S.B., Pres.; Rt. Rev. Austin Murphy, O.S.B.; Mr. Stephen A. Marth, Prin.; Mr. James Brown, Asst. Prin.; Mr. Paul Pyrcik, Dir. Devel.; Mrs. Barbara Sloan, Business Mgr.; Deborah Sola, Librarian. Priests 3; Brothers 3; Lay Teachers 81; Students 1,354.

LOMBARD. *Montini Catholic High School* (1996) 19 W. 070 16th St., 60148-4797. Tel: 630-627-6930; Fax: 630-627-0537. Web: www.montini.org. James F. Segredo, Pres.; Mrs. Maryann O'Neill, Prin.; Mrs. Estelle Soger, Librarian. De La Salle Christian Brothers 1; Lay Teachers 56; Students 700.

NEW LENOX. *Providence Catholic High School* (1918) (Coed), 1800 W. Lincoln Hwy., 60451. Tel: 815-485-2136; Fax: 815-485-2709. Web: www.providencecatholic.org. Rev. Richard J. McGrath, O.S.A., Ph.D., Pres.; Mr. Donald E. Sebestyen, Prin.; Mrs. Janlyn Auld, Asst. Prin.; Revs. John D. Merkelis, O.S.A., Pastoral Dir.; Gerald Nicholas, O.S.A.; Ms. Soteria Papagiannopoulos, Librarian. Priests 3; Brothers 1; Lay Teachers 91; Students 1,178. In Res. Revs. John A. Kret, O.S.A.; Raymond R. Ryan, O.S.A.

WHEATON. *St. Francis High School* (1956) 2130 W. Roosevelt Rd., 60187. Tel: 630-668-5800; Fax: 630-668-5893. Email: rhuhn@sfhsnet.org. Web: www.sfhsnet.org. Raeann Huhn, Prin.; Judi Rath, Librarian. Sisters 1; Lay Teachers 50; Students 780.

[D] ELEMENTARY SCHOOLS, DIOCESAN

NAPERVILLE. *All Saints Catholic Academy*, (Grades PreK-8), 1155 Aurora Ave., 60540. Tel: 630-961-6125; Fax: 630-961-3771. Email: srenehan@ascacademy.org. Web: ascacademy.org. Revs. Paul Hottinger; Joel Fortier; Dick Smith; Sandy R. Renehan, Ed.D., Prin.; Nancy Kries, Librarian. Teachers 43; Students 532.

[E] AGENCIES AND INSTITUTIONS OF THE CHARITIES OF THE DIOCESE

JOLIET. *Catholic Charities*, 203 N. Ottawa St., 60432. Tel: 815-723-3405; Fax: 815-723-3452. Email: gvancura@cc-doj.org. Web: www.cc-doj.org. Glenn VanCura, Exec. Dir. Diocesan Administrative Office and Regional Office for Will, Grundy and Kendall Counties.

KANKAKEE. *Catholic Charities*, 270 N. Schuyler Ave., 60901. Tel: 815-933-7791; Fax: 815-932-3030. Web: www.cc-doj.org. Regional Office for Kankakee, Ford, and Iroquois Counties.

LOMBARD. *Catholic Charities*, 26 W. St. Charles Rd., 60148. Tel: 630-495-8008; Fax: 630-495-9854. Web: www.cc-doj.org. Regional Office for DuPage County.

[F] PROTECTIVE INSTITUTIONS

MOMENCE. *Good Shepherd Manor* (1971) P.O. Box 260, 60954. Tel: 815-472-6492; 815-472-3700; Fax: 815-472-2160. Email: gsmanor@mchsi.com. Web: www.goodshepherdmanor.org. Mr. Bruce Fitzpatrick, Pres.; Revs. Dennis F. Settles, Chap. (Retired); Wolf V.K. Werling, Asst. Chap.; Bro. Alphonsus Brown, B.G.S., Asst. Admin. Adult Male DD-MR. Brothers of the Good Shepherd 3; Priests 2; Bed Capacity 124; Permanent Residents 124.

[G] DAY CARE

JOLIET. *Vilaseca Josephine Center* (1974) 351 N. Chicago St., 60432. Tel: 815-727-1467; Fax: 815-727-1480. Email: josemvilaseca@hotmail.com. Sisters Araceli Perez, Dir.; Judith Perez, Sub-Dir. Josephine Sisters. Students 91.

[H] LEARNING CENTERS

JOLIET. *Franciscan Learning Center* (1979) (Grades PreSchool-K), 1734 Theodore St., 60435. Tel: 815-744-7634; Fax: 815-744-2152. Email: lilpp140@att.net. Sr. Margaret McGuckin, Co-Dir., Prin. & Teacher. Sisters 2; Lay Staff 4; Students 84.

KANKAKEE. *Provena Fortin Villa*, 1025 N. Washington Ave., 60901. Tel: 815-932-8411; Fax: 815-936-3275. Email: deborah.stampanato@provena.org. Deborah Stampanato, Dir. Childcare with Preschool for children 6 weeks to 12 years. Total Staff 25; Students 124.

[I] GENERAL HOSPITALS

JOLIET. *Provena Saint Joseph Medical Center*, 333 N. Madison St., 60435-6595. Tel: 815-725-7133; 708-478-7678; Fax: 815-741-7579; 708-478-6332. Web: www.provenasaintjoe.org. Beth Hughes, Pres. & CEO; Julie Edwards, Mgr. Pastoral Care; Rev. Robert Lucas, C.M., P.T. Chap.

Provena Hospitals dba Provena St. Joseph Medical Center Sisters 4; Chaplains 6; Bed Capacity 480; Patients Assisted Annually 638,825; Total Staff 2,608.

Provena Industrial Rehabilitation Center, Joliet Tel: 815-741-7416; Fax: 815-741-0774.

Provena Physical Rehab & Sports Injury Center, Joliet Tel: 815-741-7114; Fax: 815-725-6997.

KANKAKEE. *Provena St. Mary's Hospital*, 500 W. Court St., 60901. Tel: 815-937-2400; Fax: 815-937-3535. Web: www.provena.org/stmarys. Sr. Anne Jaeger, S.S.C.M., Vice Pres. Mission Svcs.; Amy LaFine, Interim Pres. & CEO; Rev. Matthias Idyu, Priest Chap.

Provena Hospitals dba Provena St. Mary Hospital Chaplains 4; Sisters (SSCM) 1; Bed Capacity 182; Patients Assisted Annually 218,901; Total Staff 913.

MOKENA. *Provena Health (Jol)* (1997) 19065 Hickory Creek Dr., Ste. 300, 60448. Tel: 708-478-6300; Fax: 708-478-5960. Web: www.provena.org. Priests 1; Total Staff 220.

Provena Hospitals (Jol) (1997) 19065 Hickory Creek Dr., Ste. 300, 60448. Tel: 708-478-6300; Fax: 708-478-5960. Web: www.provena.org.

[J] REHABILITATION CENTERS

WHEATON. *Marianjoy Rehabilitation Hospital & Clinics, Inc.* (1969) 26 W. 171 Roosevelt Rd., P.O. Box 795, 60189. Tel: 630-462-4000; Fax: 630-462-0112. Web: www.marianjoy.org. Kathleen Yosko, Pres. & CEO. Franciscan Sisters, Daughters of the Sacred Hearts of Jesus and Mary (Wheaton, IL). Bed Capacity 120; Patients Assisted Annually 6,432.

[K] HOMES FOR AGED

JOLIET. *Our Lady of Angels Retirement Home*, 1201 Wyoming Ave., 60435. Tel: 815-725-6631; Fax: 815-725-1451. Rev. Benet Fonck, O.F.M., Chap.; Carol Shaw-Burns, Admin. & CEO. Sisters of St. Francis of Mary Immaculate. Sisters 4; Lay Staff 168; (Retired) 38; Residents 137; Total Staff 182. In Res. Sr. Sandra Salois, O.S.F., Local Coord.

Provena Villa Franciscan, 210 N. Springfield Ave., 60435. Tel: 815-725-3400; Fax: 815-725-2160. Ann Dodge, Admin.; Paul Kselman, Dir. Pastoral Care.

Provena Senior Services, Extended, Intermediate, and Skilled Care, Respite Care. Total Staff 240; Bed Capacity 176.

BOURBONNAIS. *Provena Our Lady of Victory*, 20 Briarcliff Ln., 60914. Tel: 815-937-2022; Fax: 815-936-3231. Email: Robin.Gifford@provena.org. Robin Gifford, Admin.; Sr. Martha Harrington, Dir. Pastoral Care.

Provena Senior Services Total Staff 134; Bed Capacity 107.

CLIFTON. *Merkle-Knipprath Countryside Home* (1975) 1190 E. 2900 N Rd., 60927-7103. Tel: 815-694-2306. Bro. Damien DeBraekeleer, O.S.F., Admin. Apartment Community and Nursing Center. Religious 4; Total in Nursing Care 100; Apartment Living 30.

DARIEN. *Carmelite Carefree Retirement Village* (1979) 8419 Bailey Rd., 60561-5361. Tel: 630-960-4060; Fax: 630-960-4071. Email: tcrosby@ccvliving.org. Web: www.ccvliving.org. *Society of Mt. Carmel*, 1317 Frontage Rd., 60561. Tel: 630-971-0050; Fax: 630-971-0195. Sandra Kariotis, Dir.; Revs. Raymond Corkery, O.Carm. (Retired); David Dillon, O.Carm. (Retired); John Hertel, O.Carm. (Retired); Raphael Sutherland (Retired). Residents 96.

HOMER GLEN. *Franciscan Communities, Inc. dba Marian Village* 15624 Marian Dr., 60491. Web: www.franciscancommunities.com. 1055 W. 175th St., Ste. 202, Homewood, 60430. Tel: 708-226-3780; Fax: 708-226-3781. Daniel Bannon, Exec. Dir.

KANKAKEE. *Provena Heritage Lodge*, 995 N. Entrance Ave., 60901. Tel: 815-939-4506; Fax: 815-939-4761. Email: carol.mcintyre@provena.org. Carol McIntyre, Admin.

Provena Senior Services dba Provena Heritage Lodge Total Staff 16; Bed Capacity 26.

Provena Senior Services (Jol), Kankakee Tel: 815-939-4506; Fax: 815-939-4761.

Provena Heritage Village, 901 N. Entrance Ave., 60901. Tel: 815-939-4506; Fax: 815-939-4761. Email: carol.mcintyre@provena.org. Carol McIntyre, Admin.; Carole DiZeo, Chap.

Provena Senior Services dba Provena Heritage Village Bed Capacity 87.

LISLE. *Villa St. Benedict*, 1920 Maple Ave., 60532. Tel: 630-725-7000; Fax: 630-852-3196. Email: kdicristina@villastben.org. Web: www.villastben.org. Ms. Kathy DiCristina, Admin. Continuing Care Retirement Lay Staff 125; Residents 230.

NAPERVILLE. *St. John Vianney Villa*, 1464 Green Trails Dr., 60540-8372. Tel: 630-983-0533; Fax: 630-983-6375. Revs. Ronald Hart; James Nowak (Retired); Robert E. Pietras (Retired); Edward P. Rowland (Retired); John Sebahar (Retired); Daniel F. Stempora (Retired); Jess Testa (Retired); Thomas Wolter (Retired). Retirement home for priests. Residents 10.

St. Patrick's Residence, 1400 Brookdale Rd., 60563-2126. Tel: 630-416-6565; Fax: 630-416-8755. Email: info@stpatricksresidence.org. Web: www.stpatricksresidence.org. Sr. Jeanne Francis Haley, Admin. Carmelite Sisters 6; Bed Capacity 210; Residents 200; Total Staff 250.

OAKBROOK. *Franciscan Tertiary Province of the Sacred Heart, Inc. dba Mayslake Village Inc.* 1801 35th St., Oak Brook, 60523. Tel: 630-850-8232; Fax: 630-850-8233. Email: mayslakevillage@comcast.net. Web: www.mayslake.com. Mr. Michael A. Frigo, Vice Pres., Admin. Senior Citizen Retirement Community.

Mayslake Annex II, NFP, 1801 35th St., Oak Brook, 60523. Tel: 630-850-8232; Fax: 630-850-8233. Email: mayslakevillage@comcast.net. Web: www.mayslake.com. Rev. Larry Dreffein, O.F.M., M.Div., M.P.S., Pres. & Contact Person; Mr. Michael A. Frigo, Vice Pres., Admin.

Mayslake East Wing, Inc., 1801 35th St., Oak Brook, 60523. Tel: 630-850-8232; Fax: 630-850-8233. Email: mayslakvillage@comcast.net. Web: www.mayslake.com. Mr. Michael A. Frigo, Vice Pres., Admin.

WHEATON. *Marian Park, Inc.* (1972) 2126 W. Roosevelt Rd., 60187. Tel: 630-665-9100; Fax: 630-665-9357. Web: www.fm-inc.org. *Mailing Address*, 26 W. 171 Roosevelt Rd., P.O. Box 667, 60189-0667. Units 209.

[L] MONASTERIES AND RESIDENCES OF PRIESTS AND BROTHERS

JOLIET. *St. Elias Carmelites*, 3504 Lake Shore Dr., 60431-8819. Tel: 815-439-8246; Fax: 815-439-8633. Email: steliascarmelites@comcast.net. Revs. Robert Boley, O.Carm.; Donald W. Buggert, O.Carm.; John J. Comerford, O.Carm.; Jeffery Smialek, O.Carm.; John Welch, O.Carm.; Bros. Lawrence Fidelus, O.Carm.; Dominic Saganich. Priests 5; Brothers 2.

St. John the Baptist Friary, 404 N. Hickory St., 60435-7554. Tel: 815-727-9783; Fax: 815-740-1521. Revs. Gerald Bleem, O.F.M., Assoc. Dir., Postulancy; J. Derran Combs, O.F.M., B.A., M.Div., Th.M., Faculty, Univ. of St. Francis.; John Dombrowski, O.F.M.; Fred Radtke, O.F.M.; Rogelio Martinez Ruteaga, O.F.M.; Ildephonse Skorup, O.F.M., Chap. at Franciscan Sisters of the Sacred Heart, Frankfort; Gerold Schubert, O.F.M. (Retired); Dennis Schafer, O.F.M., Dir. Postulancy & Guardian; Thomas Fox, O.F.M., Parochial Vicar; Juan Rommel Perez Florez, O.F.M., Parochial Vicar. Priests 5; Brothers 1.

BURR RIDGE. *Christian Brothers Provincial Office (Midwest Province)* (1995) 7650 S. County Line Rd., 60527-7959. Tel: 630-323-3725; Fax: 630-323-3779. Email: info@cbmidwest.org. Web: www.cbmidwest.org. Bros. Bede Baldry, F.S.C., Prov. Special Projects; Larry Schatz, F.S.C., Prov. & Brother Visitor; Joseph Saurbier, F.S.C., COO & Dir., Admin. & Opers.; Kevin Convey, F.S.C., (Retired); Stephen Markham, Dir., Vocation Min.;

Joseph Martin, F.S.C., Dir. Senior Bros.; Mark Snodgrass, F.S.C., Aux. Prov.; Mr. Leonard Suhadolc, CFO.

DARIEN. *Carmelite Provincial Office*, 1317 Frontage Rd., 60561. Tel: 630-971-0050; Fax: 630-971-0195. Email: provincial@carmelnet.org. Web: www.carmelnet.org. Very Rev. Carl Markelz, O.Carm., Prior Prov.; Rev. Joseph Atcher, O.Carm., Prov. Procurator & Commissary Prov.; Bro. Charles Kwiatkowski, O.Carm.

The Society of Mt. Carmel

Carmelites Serving in Italy: Revs. Mario Loya, O.Carm.; Raul Maravi, O.Carm. Email: rmaravi@carmelnet.org.

Carmelites Serving in Canada: Revs. Thomas Hakala, O.Carm.; Leo Huard, O.Carm.; Stanley Makacinas, O.Carm., Acting Dir. Mt. Carmel Spiritual Center; Anthony McNamara, O.Carm.; Gerard Power, O.Carm.; Jordon Rooney, O.Carm.; Bro. Marc Bell, O.Carm.

Carmelites Serving in Peru: Most Rev. Michael LaFay, O.Carm.; Revs. Edward Adelmann, O.Carm.; Miguel Bacigalupo; Salvador Bartolo, O.Carm.; Enrique Laguna-Vargas, O.Carm.; Gerald Payea, O.Carm.; Jorge Remuzgo, O.Carm.; Eduardo Rivero, O.Carm.; Michael Sgarioto, O.Carm.; Jorge Villegas, O.Carm.; Carlos Valdez, O. Carm.; Bro. Rodolfo Aznaran, O.Carm.

Carmelites Serving in Australia: Bro. Sean Keefe, O.Carm.

Carmelites Serving in Mexico: Revs. Peter Hinde, O.Carm.; Emilio Rodriguez, O.Carm.

Carmelites Serving in El Salvador: Revs. David Blanchard, O.Carm.; Thomas Jordan, O.Carm.; Adolfo Medrano, O.Carm.; Bros. Mario Cadena, O.Carm.; Rogelio Garcia, O.Carm.; Floristan Guerrero, O.Carm.; Jorge Monterroso, O.Carm.; Jose Polanco, O.Carm.; Benjamin Salas, O.Carm.

Carmelites Serving in France: Rev. Terrence Cyr, O.Carm.

Carmelites Serving Elsewhere: Revs. Emil Agostino, O.Carm. (Retired); Benjamin Aguilar, O.Carm.; Timothy Andres, O.Carm.; Nelson Belizario, O.Carm.; Robert Boley, O.Carm.; Peter Byrth, O.Carm.; Kyrin Caggiano, O.Carm. (Retired); Warren Carlin, O.Carm. (Retired); Emeric Carmody, O.Carm. (Retired); Daniel Carroll, O.Carm.; Michael Flynn, O.Carm.; Gregory Houck, O.Carm.; Myron Judy, O.Carm.; Anton Kollar, O.Carm.; Albert P. Koppes, O.Carm.; James Lewis, O.Carm.; Bernard Lickteig, O.Carm.; Blaise McInerney, O.Carm.; Guy McPartland, O.Carm.; Zachary Monet, O.Carm.; James Mueller, O.Carm.; Michael Mulhall, O.Carm.; Henry Ormond, O.Carm.; Clyde Ozminkowski, O.Carm.; Paul Robinson, O.Carm.; Daniel Smith, O.Carm.; Frank Weil, O.Carm.; Bros. David McGinnis, O.Carm.; Daryl Moresco, O.Carm.

St. Simon Stock Priory (1959) 8501 Bailey Rd., 60561. Tel: 630-536-7866. Bro. Charles Kwiatkowski, O.Carm.; Revs. Joseph Atcher, O.Carm.; Bernhard Bauerle, O.Carm.; Robert E. Colaresi, O.Carm., Prior; David L. Simpson, O.Carm. Priests 4; Brothers 1.

LISLE. *St. Procopius Abbey*, 5601 College Rd., 60532. Tel: 630-969-6410; Fax: 630-969-6426. Email: secretary@procopius.org. Web: www.procopius.org. Rt. Revs. Dismas B. Kalcic, O.S.B., Retired Abbot (Retired); Austin Murphy, O.S.B., Abbot; Very Rev. Gregory Perron, Subprior; Bro. Columban Trojan, O.S.B., Prior; Revs. Anthony J. Jacob, O.S.B., Procurator; Thomas Chisholm, O.S.B., Novice Master; Joseph Chang, O.S.B.; Odilo Crkva, O.S.B.; Julian von Duerbeck, O.S.B.; James Flint, O.S.B.; T. Becket Franks, O.S.B.; Edward J. Kucera, O.S.B.; Timothy R. Marceau, O.S.B.; Jude D. Randall, O.S.B., Pres., Benet Academy; Theodore D. Suchy, O.S.B.; Philip S. Timko, O.S.B.; David Turner, O.S.B.; Kenneth Zigmond, O.S.B.; Most Rev. Daniel W. Kucera, O.S.B., Archbishop of Dubuque, IA (Retired); Rt. Rev. Hugh R. Anderson, O.S.B., Abbot Pres. (Retired). Benedictine Monks. Monks 29; Priests 18; Brothers 10; Archbishops 1. *Benedictine Chinese Mission*, 5601 College Rd., 60532. Tel: 630-969-6410; Fax: 630-969-6426. *Slav Missions*, 5601 College Rd., 60532. Tel: 630-969-6410; Fax: 630-969-6426. *Benedictine University*, 5700 College Rd., 60532. Tel: 630-829-6000; Fax: 630-829-6242. Web: www.ben.edu. *Benet Academy*, 2200 Maple Ave., 60532. Tel: 630-969-6550; Fax: 630-719-0929. Web: www.benet.org. *St. Scholastica Mission House*, 1920 Maple Ave., 60532. Tel: 630-852-5360.

St. Procopius Abbey Endowment, 5601 College Rd., 60532. Tel: 630-969-6410; Fax: 630-969-6426.

MOMENCE. *Brother Mathias Barrett Inc. of Illinois*, P.O. Box 736, 60954. Tel: 815-472-3700; Fax: 815-472-2160. Bro. Alphonsus Brown, B.G.S., Pres. Brothers 3.

NEW LENOX. *Augustinian Friary*, 1800 W. Lincoln Hwy., 60451. Tel: 815-485-6880; Fax: 815-485-2709. Rev. Richard M. Jacobs, O.S.A. (See separate listing for Providence High School) In Res. Revs. John A. Kret, O.S.A.; John D. Merkelis, O.S.A.; Richard J. McGrath, O.S.A., Ph.D., Pres.; Raymond R. Ryan, O.S.A.; Gerald Nicholas, O.S.A.

ROMEOVILLE. *La Salle House Community* (1996) 100 Faculty Lane, 60446-1178. Tel: 815-836-5530; Fax: 815-836-5858. Email: johnsoph@lewisu.edu. Bros. Pierre St. Raymond, Dir.; Thomas Dupre, Sub-Dir.; Joel Dolan; Christopher Ford; James Gaffney, F.S.C.; Philip Johnson, F.S.C.; Leo Jones, F.S.C. Email: LJones9911@aol.com; Augustine Kossuth; Joseph Martin; Raphael Mascari; Raymond McManaman; Lawrence Oelschlegel; Bernard Rapp; John Vietoris; William Walz, F.S.C.; Robert Wilsbach. Brothers 16.

WESTMONT. *Westmont North Community* (2002) 222 S. Cass Ave., 60559. Tel: 630-724-1976; Fax: 630-724-1978. Bro. Fred Dillenburg, Dir. Brothers 5.

[M] CONVENTS AND RESIDENCES FOR SISTERS

JOLIET. *St. Clare House of Prayer* (1968) 1320 Franciscan Way, 60435-3956. Tel: 815-725-1455. Email: stclarehouse@aol.com. Sisters of St. Francis of Mary Immaculate 4.

Josephine Sisters (1872) 351 N. Chicago St., 60432. Tel: 815-727-1467; Fax: 815-727-1480. Email: josephinesis@hotmail.com. Josephine Sisters of Mexico (Hermanas Josefinas). Sisters 4.

Sisters of St. Francis of Mary Immaculate (1865) 1433 Essington Rd., 60435-2873. Tel: 815-725-8735; Fax: 815-725-8648. Web: www.jolietfranciscans.org. Sr. Mary Rose Lieb, O.S.F., M.S.Ed., M.S.A., Pres. & Gen. Supr.

Congregation of the Third Order of St Francis of Mary Immaculate, Joliet, IL.

FRANKFORT. *Franciscan Sisters of the Sacred Heart* (1866) St. Francis Woods, 9201 W. St. Francis Rd., 60423-8335. Tel: 815-469-4895; Fax: 815-464-3809. Email: judith.plumb@provena.org. Web: www.fssh.com. Sr. Judith Plumb, O.S.F., Gen. Supr.

An Association of Franciscan Sisters of the Sacred Heart and Franciscan Foundation. Sisters 89.

KANKAKEE. *Servants of the Holy Heart of Mary, Holy Family Prov., U.S.A.* (1889) *Provincial Administration*, 15 Elmwood Dr., 60901. Tel: 815-937-2380; Fax: 815-937-5520. Email: linda.hatton@provena.org. Web: www.sscm-usa.org. Sr. Linda K. Hatton, S.S.C.M., Prov. Supr.

Servants of the Holy Heart of Mary Charitable Trust, Provena Health including 7 hospitals and 13 long term care institutions. Professed Sisters 36.

LISLE. *Benedictine Sisters of the Sacred Heart, Sacred Heart Monastery* (1895) 1910 Maple Ave., 60532-2164. Tel: 630-725-6000; Fax: 630-969-5814. Email: mbratrsovsky@shmlisle.org. Web: www.shmlisle.org. Sr. Mary Bratrsovsky, O.S.B., Prioress.

Benedictine Sisters of the Sacred Heart Charitable Trust Professed Sisters 35.

MINOOKA. *The Poor Clares of Joliet, Annunciation Monastery*, 6200 E. Minooka Rd., 60447. Tel: 815-467-0032; Fax: 815-467-0032. Email: paxbonum@aol.com. Web: www.poorclaresjoliet.org. Sr. M. Dorothy Urschalitz, P.C.C., Contact Person. Cloistered Sisters 14; Extern Sisters 2.

NEW LENOX. *Mother of Good Counsel Monastery*, 440 N. Marley Rd., 60451. Tel: 815-463-9662. Sr. Mary Grace Kuppe, O.S.A., Prioress. Augustinian Nuns. Solemnly Professed Sisters 4; Novices 1.

PLAINFIELD. *Mantellate Sisters Servants of Mary, U.S.A.*, 16949 S. Drauden Rd., 60586-9168. Tel: 815-436-5796; Fax: 815-436-7486. Sr. Louise Staszewski, O.S.M., Regl. Supr. Homes for the Aged and Foreign Missions.; Yr. Founded: Italy-1861; USA-1916; Plainfield-1977; Ministry in the field of Academic Educ., Parish Ministry, Social Work, Nursing, Homes for the Aged, and Foreign Missions. Sisters 7.

WHEATON. *St. Clara Province Charitable Trust*, 26 W. 171 Roosevelt Rd., P.O. Box 667, 60187-0667. Tel: 630-462-7422; Fax: 630-909-6615.

Convent of Our Lady of the Angels Motherhouse and Novitiate (1860) Franciscan Sisters, Daughters of the Sacred Hearts of Jesus and Mary (Wheaton, IL), P.O. Box 667, 60187. Tel: 630-909-6600; Fax: 630-462-7148. Email: cmorgan@wheatonfranciscan.org. Web: www.wheatonfranciscan.org. Sr. Beatrice Hernandez, O.S.F., Prov. Dir.

Wheaton Franciscan Sisters Corp. Sisters 64.

Loretto Convent, Religious of the Institute of the Blessed Virgin Mary, P.O. Box 508, 60187. Tel: 630-653-6113; Fax: 630-653-4886. Email: ibvmjfrye1@aol.com. Web: www.ibvm.us. Sisters 16.

Loretto Center Tel: 630-653-7918; Fax: 630-653-0845. Email: IBVMLC@aol.com. Web: www.lorettocenter.org.

Office of Development Tel: 630-682-9097; Fax: 630-868-8258. Email: development@ibvm.org.

Loretto Extension Service Tel: 630-462-3860; Fax: 630-784-9544. Email: IBVMMBRML@aol.com.

Loretto Early Childhood Center Tel: 630-690-8410; Fax: 630-868-2764. Email: IBVMJULIES@hotmail.com.

Children of God Retreats Tel: 630-588-8501; Fax: 630-653-4886. Email: IBVMMCG@aol.com.

United States Province Administration Tel: 630-665-3814 (Superior); 630-653-6113 (Treas.); 630-868-2904 (Sec.); Fax: 630-868-2852. Email: kfoleyIBVM1@juno.com.

Loretto House Tel: 630-868-2784; Fax: 630-868-2791. Email: ibvmlh@aol.com.

Mary Ward Center Email: mwcmaryhoward@aol.com.

[N] HOUSES OF RETREAT/PRAYER

DARIEN. *Carmelite Spiritual Center*, 8433 Bailey Rd., 60561. Tel: 630-969-4141; Fax: 630-969-3376. Email: cscretreat@aol.com. Revs. Robert E. Colaresi, O.Carm., Dir.; David L. Simpson, O.Carm., Spiritual Dir. Total Staff 16.

FRANKFORT. *Portiuncula Center for Prayer* (1990) 9263 W. St. Francis Rd., 60423-8330. Tel: 815-464-3880; Fax: 815-469-4880. Email: info@portforprayer.org. Web: www.portforprayer.org.

KANKAKEE. *One Heart, One Soul Spirituality Center*, 2041 Rte. 113, 60901. Tel: 815-937-2344. Email: ohos@provena.org. Web: www.sscm-usa.org.

LOMBARD. *Mayslake Ministries, Inc.* (1991) 450 E. 22nd St., Ste. 170, 60148. Tel: 630-268-9000; Fax: 630-268-9001. Email: mamore@mayslakeministries.org. Web: mayslakeministries.org. Revs. Jonathan D. Foster, O.F.M.; Thomas Borkowski (KC); Phil Horrigan; Mary Amore, D.Min., Exec. Dir. Priests 3; Lay Staff 8.

PLANO. *La Salle Manor Christian Brothers Retreat House* (1957) 12480 Galena Rd., 60545. Tel: 630-552-3224; Fax: 630-552-9160. Email: info@lasallemanor.org. Web: www.lasallemanor.org. Robert Dressel, Pres.

WARRENVILLE. *Congregation of Our Lady of the Retreat in the Cenacle* (1939) 3S. 230 Warren Ave., P.O. Box 797, 60555-0797. Tel: 630-393-2976; Fax: 630-393-2646. Web: www.cenacle.org. Sr. Joyce Kemp, r.c. Sisters 1; Personnel 3.

[O] MISCELLANEOUS

JOLIET. *Diocesan Educational Endowment Fund*, 425 Summit St., 60435.

John Paul II House, 430 N. Center St., 60435. Tel: 815-722-7361; Fax: 815-727-4675. Email: vocations@dioceseofjoliet.org. Web: www.vocations.com. Rev. Burke Masters, Dir. Vocations.

Provena Home Health, Inc., 1060 Essington Rd., 60435. Tel: 815-741-7371; Fax: 815-741-7372. Email: janet.cotter@provena.org. Web: www.provenahealth.org. Connie March, Pres. & Contact Person.

**The Upper Room Crisis Hotline (TURCH)*, P.O. Box 3572, 60434. Tel: 815-727-4367; 888-808-8724 (Hotline); Fax: 815-726-5004. Email: turch@sbcglobal.net. Web: www.theupperroomcrisishotline.org. Rev. Peter Jarosz, Pres.; Sr. Mary Frances Seeley, O.S.F., Ph.D., CEO.

AURORA. *Assisi Homes - Constitution House, Inc.* (1995)Mailing Address: 26 W. 171 Roosevelt Rd., P.O. Box 667, Wheaton, 60187-0667. 401 N. Constitution Dr., 60506. Tel: 630-896-2100; Fax: 630-896-0313. Web: www.fm-inc.org. Units 232.

BURR RIDGE. *Christian Brothers Fund, Inc.*, 7650 S. County Line Rd., 60527-4718. Tel: 630-323-3725; Fax: 630-323-3779. Email: info@cbmidwest.org. Web: cbmidwest.org. Bros. Thomas Hetland, F.S.C., Pres.; Fred Dillenburg, Treas.

CAROL STREAM. *Assisi Homes - Colony Park, Inc.* (1995) 550 E. Thornhill Dr., 60188. Tel: 630-682-9000; Fax: 630-682-9008. Web: www.fm-inc.org. Mailing Address: 26 W. 171 Roosevelt Rd., P.O. Box 667, Wheaton, 60187-0667. Tel: 630-462-6900. Units 284.

DARIEN. *Carmelite Mission Office*, 8501 Bailey Rd., 60561. Tel: 630-969-5220; Fax: 630-969-5266. Email: jemalley@juno.com. Web: www.carmelitemissions.org. Rev. John Malley, O.Carm., Dir.

National Shrine of St. Therese, 8501 Bailey Rd., 60561. Tel: 630-969-3311; Fax: 630-969-5536. Email: webmaster@saint-therese.org. Web: www.saint-therese.org. Rev. Bernhard Bauerle, O.Carm., Shrine Dir.

Provincial Office of Lay Carmelites and Scapular Center, 8501 Bailey Rd., 60561. Tel: 630-969-5050; Fax: 630-969-7519. Email: laycarmelites@

carmelnet.org. Web: carmelnet.org. Very Rev. Carl Markelz, O.Carm., Prior Prov.; Rev. Joseph Atcher, O.Carm., Prov. Delegate; Sisters Libby Dahlstrom, O.Carm., Assoc. Dir.; Mary Martin, O.Carm., Prov. Coord.

Society of the Little Flower (1923) 1313 Frontage Rd., 60561-5341. Tel: 630-968-9400; Fax: 630-968-9542. Email: webmaster@littleflower.org. Web: www.littleflower.org. Rev. Robert E. Colaresi, O.Carm., Dir.

FRANKFORT. *Provena Care @ Home Inc.*, 9223 W. St. Francis Rd., 60423-8334. Tel: 708-478-7900; Fax: 708-478-5143. Email: susan.enright@provena.org. Web: www.provenahealth.com. 19065 Hickory Creek Dr., Mokena, 60448-8507. Susan Enright, Vice Pres. & Contact Person.

KANKAKEE. *Lisieux Pastoral Outreach Center*, 371 N. St. Joseph Ave., 60901-2741. Tel: 815-939-2913.

Provena St. Mary's Adult Day Center, 1025 N. Washington, 60901. Tel: 815-937-2447; Fax: 815-936-3245. Email: rebecca.barney@provena.org. Web: www.provena.org. 19065 Hickory Creek Dr., #300, Mokena, 60448. Rebecca Barney, Admin.

LISLE. *Catholic CEO Healthcare Connection (CCHC)* (1985) 3333 Warrenville Rd, Ste. 200, 60532. Tel: 630-799-8315; Fax: 630-799-8316. Email: roger.butler@cchcforum.org. Mr. Roger N. Butler, Exec. Dir.

National Association of Catholic Nurses-U.S.A., c/o Diocese of Joliet, 425 Summit St., 60435. Email: catholicnurses@nacn-usa.org. Web: www.nacn-usa.org. Cheryl Hettman, Ph.D., R.N., Pres.

MOKENA. *Provena Senior Services dba Provena Life Connections* 19065 Hickory Creek Dr., Ste. 310, 60448-8507. Tel: 708-478-7900; Fax: 708-478-5143. Email: connie.march@provena.org. Web: www.provena.org. Connie March, Pres. & CEO.

MOMENCE. *B.G.S. Charitable Trust*, P.O. Box 736, 60954-0736. Tel: 815-472-3131; Fax: 815-472-6914. Michael Brown, Contact Person.

Little Brothers of the Good Shepherd, Inc. of Illinois, 4129 N. State Rt. I-17, P.O. Box 736, 60954. Tel: 815-472-3131; Fax: 815-472-6914. Email: judy@lbgs.org. Web: www.lbgs.org. Bro. Richard MacPhee, Treas. Gen.; Judy Brinkmann, Dir. of Finance.

OAK BROOK. *Mayslake Center II, N.F.P.*, 1801 35th St., 60523. Tel: 630-850-8232; Fax: 630-850-8233.

MV Benevolent Fund, Inc. (2003) 1801 35th St., 60523. Tel: 630-214-1858; Fax: 630-850-8233.

PLAINFIELD. *Housing Options for Religious, Clergy and Laity, NFP*, 15555 Mt. Carmel Dr., Apt. 141, Homer Glen, 60491. Tel: 708-590-8141. Email: SMDMV141@yahoo.com. Sr. Marcian Deisenroth, R.S.M., Chm., Year of final profession: 1953.

ROMEOVILLE. *The Catholic Education Foundation of the Diocese of Joliet*, 101 Airport Rd., 60441. Tel: 815-834-4023; Fax: 815-588-6007.

Charitable Trust of the Brothers of the Christian Schools, 1205 Windham Pkwy., 60446-1679. Tel: 630-378-2900; Fax: 630-378-2501. Email: info@cbservices.org. Web: www.cbservices.org.

Christian Brothers Employee Benefit Trust, 1205 Windham Pkwy., 60446-1679. Tel: 630-378-2900; Fax: 630-378-2501. Email: info@cbservices.org. Web: www.cbservices.org.

Christian Brothers Employee Retirement Plan Trust, 1205 Windham Pkwy., 60446-1679. Tel: 630-378-2900; Fax: 630-378-2501. Email: info@cbservices.org. Web: www.cbservices.org.

Christian Brothers Religious Community Deductible Trust, 1205 Windham Pkwy., 60446-1679. Tel: 630-378-2900; Fax: 630-378-2501. Email: info@cbservices.org. Web: www.cbservices.org.

Christian Brothers Religious Comprehensive Trust, 1205 Windham Pkwy., 60446-1679. Tel: 630-378-2900; Fax: 630-378-2501. Email: info@cbservices.org. Web: www.cbservices.org.

Christian Brothers Retirement Savings Plan Trust, 1205 Windham Pkwy., 60446-1679. Tel: 630-378-2900; Fax: 630-378-2501. Email: info@cbservices.org. Web: www.cbservices.org.

**Christian Brothers Services*, 1205 Windham Pkwy., 60446-1679. Tel: 630-378-2900; Fax: 630-378-2501. Email: info@cbservices.org. Web: www.cbservices.org. Bro. Michael Quirk, F.S.C., Pres. & CEO.

Religious & Charitable Risk Pooling Trust of the Brothers of the Christian Schools, 1205 Windham Pkwy., 60446-1679. Tel: 630-378-2900; Fax: 630-378-2501. Email: info@cbservices.org. Web: www.cbservices.org.

WEST CHICAGO. **The Society of St. Vincent de Paul of the Joliet Diocesan Council, Inc.*, 213 Main St., 60185. Tel: 630-293-9755; Fax: 630-293-9881.

WHEATON. **Assisi Homes - LaSalle Manor Inc.*, 26W171 Roosevelt Rd., 60189-0795.

Assisi Homes of Illinois, Inc. (1974)Mailing Address: 26 W. 171 Roosevelt Rd., P.O. Box 667, 60187-0667. 2126 W. Roosevelt Rd., 60187-0667. Tel: 630-665-9100; Fax: 630-665-9357. Web: www.fm-inc.org. Units 65.

Canticle Ministries, Inc., 26 W. 171 Roosevelt Rd., P.O. Box 667, 60189. Tel: 630-588-9165; Fax: 630-588-9167. Email: info@canticleministries.org. Web: www.canticleministries.org. Jeana Stewart, Co-Dir. Tel: 630-784-2722.

Canticle Place, Inc. (1994) 26 W. 171 Roosevelt Rd., 60187. Tel: 630-665-9100; Fax: 630-665-9357. Web: www.fm-inc.org. Mailing Address: 26 W. Roosevelt Rd., P.O. Box 667, 60187-0667. Units 12.

Clara Pfaender Fund, Inc. (1984) 26 W. 171 Roosevelt Rd., P.O. Box 667, 60187. Tel: 630-909-6900; Fax: 630-462-4977. Sr. Patricia Norton, Chairperson & Pres. Franciscan Sisters, Daughters of the Sacred Hearts of Jesus and Mary (Wheaton, IL).

Franciscan Health & Education Corp., Inc., 26 W. 171 Roosevelt Rd., P.O. Box 667, 60187. Tel: 630-462-7422; Fax: 630-909-6615.

**Franciscan Ministries Community Foundation, Inc.* (2001) 26 W. 171 Roosevelt Rd., 60189. Tel: 630-909-6900; Fax: 630-784-2485. Web: www.fm-inc.org.

Franciscan Ministries, Inc. (1983)Property & Mailing Address: 26 W. 171 Roosevelt Rd., P.O. Box 667, 60187-0667. Tel: 630-909-6900; Fax: 630-784-2485. Web: www.fm-inc.org.

Institute of the Blessed Virgin Mary Charitable Trust, P.O. Box 508, 60187. Tel: 630-653-6113; Fax: 630-653-4886. Email: ibvmjfryel@aol.com. Web: www.ibvm.us.

**Marianjoy Foundation, Inc.* (1986) 26 W. 171 Roosevelt Rd., P.O. Box 1620, 60187. Tel: 630-462-7514; Fax: 630-462-4440. Web: www.marianjoy.org.

Marianjoy Rehabilitation Center Auxiliary, 26 W. 171 Roosevelt Rd., 60187. Web: www.marianjoy.org.

**Marianjoy, Inc.*, 26 W. 171 Roosevelt Rd., P.O. Box 667, 60187.

**Rehabilitation Medicine Clinic, Inc.* (1997) 26 W. 171 Roosevelt Rd., 60187. Tel: 630-462-9271; Fax: 630-462-0112. Web: www.marianjoy.org.

Wheaton Franciscan Services, Inc. (1983) 26 W. 171 Roosevelt Rd., P.O. Box 667, 60187. Tel: 630-909-6900; Fax: 630-462-4977. Web: www.mywheaton.org. Michael J. Murry, Chm.; John D. Oliverio, Pres. & CEO; Rev. Thomas Borkowski (KC), Chap.

RELIGIOUS INSTITUTES OF MEN REPRESENTED IN THE DIOCESE

For further details refer to the corresponding bracketed number in the Religious Institutes of Men or Women section.

[0140]—*The Augustinians* (Mother of Good Counsel Prov.)—O.S.A.

[0200]—*Benedictine Monks*—O.S.B.

[0330]—*Brothers of the Christian Schools* (Midwest Prov.)—F.S.C.

[0580]—*Brothers of the Good Shepherd*—B.G.S.

[0270]—*Carmelite Fathers & Brothers* (Prov. of Pure Heart of Mary)—O.Carm.

[0275]—*Carmelites of Mary Immaculate*—C.M.I.

[0360]—*Claretian Missionaries*—C.M.F.

[1320]—*Clerics of St. Viator*—C.S.V.

[0310]—*Congregation of Christian Brothers*—C.F.C.

[]—*Congregation of the Mission (Vincentians)* (Vincentians)—C.M.

[1130]—*Congregation of the Priests of the Sacred Heart*—S.C.J.

[]—*Congregation of the Resurrection*—C.R.

[0430]—*Dominicans* (Prov. of Albert the Great)—O.P.

[0540]—*Franciscan Missionary Brothers of the Sacred Heart of Jesus*—O.S.F.

[0520]—*Franciscans* (Order of Friars Minor, Sacred Heart Prov.)—O.F.M.

[0740]—*Marian Fathers* (Prov. of St. Casimer)—M.I.C.

[1065]—*Priestly Fraterity of St. Peter*—F.S.S.P.

[0610]—*Priests of the Congregation of Holy Cross*—C.S.C.

[0110]—*Society of African Missions*—S.M.A.

[1260]—*Society of Christ*—S.Ch.

[0690]—*Society of Jesus* (Chicago, St. Louis Prov. & Wisconsin)—S.J.

[2010]—*Society of the Precious Blood*—C.PP.S.

RELIGIOUS INSTITUTES OF WOMEN REPRESENTED IN THE DIOCESE

[160]—*Augustinian Nuns of Contemplative Life*—O.S.A.

[0230]—*Benedictine Sisters of Pontifical Jurisdiction* (Lisle, IL; Ferdinand, IN)—O.S.B.

[0330]—*Carmelite Sisters for the Aged and Infirm* (Germantown, NY)—O.Carm.

[0400]—*Congregation of Our Lady of Mount Carmel* (Lacombe, LA)—O.Carm.

[3110]—*Congregation of Our Lady of the Retreat in the Cenacle*—R.C.

[1070]—*Congregation of St. Cecilia*—O.P

[3710]—*Congregation of the Sisters of Saint Agnes*—C.S.A.

[3832]—*Congregation of the Sisters of St. Joseph*—C.S.J.

[1710]—*Congregation of the Third Order of St. Francis of Mary Immaculate, Joliet, IL*—O.S.F.

[1070-03]—*Dominican Sisters* (Sinsinawa)—O.P.

[1070-13]—*Dominican Sisters* (Adrian)—O.P.

[1070-10]—*Dominican Sisters* (Springfield)—O.P.

[1170]—*Felician Sisters*—C.S.S.F.

[1450]—*Franciscan Sisters of the Sacred Heart* (Frankfort)—O.S.F.

[1240]—*Franciscan Sisters, Daughters of the Sacred Hearts of Jesus and Mary* (Wheaton)—O.S.F.

[1910]—*Hermanas Josefinas*—H.J.

[2370]—*Institute of the Blessed Virgin Mary (Loretto Sisters)*—I.B.V.M.

[2575]—*Institute of the Sisters of Mercy of the Americas* (Chicago, IL)—R.S.M.

[3570]—*Mantellate Sisters, Servants of Mary* (Plainfield, IL)—O.S.M.

[2865]—*Missionaries of the Sacred Heart of Jesus & Our Lady of Guadalupe*—M.S.C.Gpe.

[2084]—*Missionary Sisters of Christ the King*—M.Ch.R.

[]—*Missionary Sisters of the Holy Family* (Komorrow-Warsaw, Poland)—M.S.F.

[3760]—*Order of St. Clare*—P.C.C.

[3230]—*Poor Handmaids of Jesus Christ*—P.H.J.C.

[2970]—*School Sisters of Notre Dame* (Chicago Prov.)—S.S.N.D.

[1680]—*School Sisters of St. Francis* (U.S. Prov.)—O.S.F.

[3590]—*Servants of Mary* (Ladysmith, WI)—O.S.M.

[3520]—*Servants of the Holy Heart of Mary*—S.S.C.M.

[0460]—*Sisters of Charity of Incarnate Word*—C.C.V.I.

[0430]—*Sisters of Charity of the Blessed Virgin Mary*—B.V.M.

[1890]—*Sisters of Helpers*—H.H.S.

[]—*Sisters of Korean Martyrs*—S.K.M.

[2350]—*Sisters of Living Word*—S.L.W.

[3000]—*Sisters of Notre Dame de Namur* (Cincinnati Prov.)—S.N.D.deN.

[3360]—*Sisters of Providence of Saint Mary-of-the-Woods, IN*—S.P.

[1540]—*Sisters of St. Francis* (Clinton, IA)—O.S.F.

[1705]—*The Sisters of St. Francis of Assisi* (St. Francis)—O.S.F.

[1520]—*Sisters of St. Francis of Christ the King*—S.S.F.C.R.

[1570]—*Sisters of St. Francis of Dubuque* (Iowa)—O.S.F.

[3930]—*Sisters of St. Joseph of the Third Order of St. Francis* (Prov. of Immaculate Conception)—S.S.J.-T.O.S.F.

[2980]—*Sisters of the Congregation de Notre Dame*—C.N.D.

[1920]—*Sisters of the Holy Cross*—C.S.C.

[1720]—*Sisters of the Third Order Regular of St. Francis of the Congregation of Our Lady of Lourdes* (Rochester, MN)—O.S.F.

[2150]—*Sisters Servants of the Immaculate Heart of Mary*—I.H.M.

DIOCESAN CEMETERIES

JOLIET. *SS. Cyril and Methodius Cemetery*, Rte. 6 Maple Rd., 60432. Tel: 815-838-0395.

Holy Cross Cemetery, Theodore St., Crest Hill, 60403. Tel: 815-838-0395.

St. John the Baptist Cemetery, 101 W. Airport Rd., Romeoville, 60446. Tel: 815-838-0395.

St. Mary Nativity Cemetery, Caton Farm Rd. & Oakland Ave., Crest Hill, 60435. Tel: 815-838-0395.

Mount Olivet Cemetery, 1320 E. Cass St., 60432. Tel: 815-838-0395.

St. Patrick Cemetery, 710 W. Marion St., Hunter St. & Jefferson St., 60436. Tel: 815-838-0395; Fax: 815-834-4069.

BOURBONNAIS. *All Saints Cemetery, All Saints Cemetery*, 1839 W. Rte. 102, 60914. Tel: 815-936-9378.

Maternity/BVM Cemetery, Canterberry Ln., 60914. Tel: 815-933-2342.

CAROL STREAM. *St. Stephen Cemetery*, St. Charles Rd., 60188. Tel: 630-668-3313.

DOWNERS GROVE. *St. Bernard Cemetery*, Hobson & Belmont Roads, 60517. Tel: 630-668-3313.

ELMHURST. *St. Mary Cemetery*, Alexander Blvd., 60126. Tel: 630-668-3313.

KANKAKEE. *Mt. Calvary Cemetery*, 2000 E. Court St., 60901. Tel: 815-933-2342.

St. Rose Cemetery, Rte. 50, 60901. Tel: 815-933-2342.

LOCKPORT. *Calvary Cemetery*, Rte. 171 & High Rd., 60441. Tel: 815-838-0395.

LOCKPORT SOUTH. *Lockport South Cemetery*, 16th St. & Washington St., 60441. Tel: 815-838-0395.

LOMBARD. *St. Mary Cemetery*, Finley Rd., 60148. Tel: 630-668-3313.

NAPERVILLE. *SS. Peter & Paul Cemetery*, Columbia St. & North Ave., 60563. Tel: 630-668-3313.

OSWEGO. *Risen Lord Cemetery*, 1501 Simons Rd., 60543. Tel: 630-554-7590.

ROMEOVILLE. *Catholic Cemeteries Monument Sales*, 101 W. Airport Rd., 60446-2264. Tel: 815-838-0395.

Resurrection, 200 W. Romeo Rd., 60446. Tel: 815-838-0395.

WHEATON. *Assumption Cemetery*, One S. 510 Winfield Rd., 60187. Tel: 630-668-3313.

WINFIELD. *St. John the Baptist*, OS233 Church St., 60190. Tel: 630-668-0918; Fax: 630-668-1074.

NECROLOGY

† Mahoney, Gordon, (Retired)—Died Feb. 3, 2011
† Maternoski, Robert, (Retired)—Died April 15, 2011
† O'Connor, Donald, (Retired)—Died Nov. 15, 2011
† Schutter, Thomas, (Retired)—Died April 2, 2011
† Zanoni, John, (Retired)—Died Feb. 14, 2011

An asterisk (*) denotes an organization that has established tax-exempt status directly with the IRS and is not covered by the USCCB Group Ruling.

Diocese of Juneau

(Dioecesis Junellensis)

Most Reverend

EDWARD J. BURNS

Bishop of Juneau; ordained June 25, 1983; appointed Bishop of Juneau January 19, 2009; ordained March 3, 2009; installed April 2, 2009. *Office: 415 Sixth St., #300, Juneau, AK 99801.*

Chancery: 415 Sixth St., #300, Juneau, AK 99801. Tel: 907-586-2227; Fax: 907-463-3237.

Web: www.dioceseofjuneau.org

Email: junodio@gci.net

ESTABLISHED JUNE 23, 1951.

Square Miles 37,566.

Corporate Title: "Corporation of the Catholic Bishop of Juneau."

Comprises the entire southeastern part of the State of Alaska known legally as The First Judicial District.

For legal titles of parishes and diocesan institutions, consult the Chancery Office.

STATISTICAL OVERVIEW

Personnel	
Bishop	1
Priests: Diocesan Active in Diocese	7
Priests: Diocesan Active Outside Diocese	1
Priests: Retired, Sick or Absent	3
Number of Diocesan Priests	11
Religious Priests in Diocese	2
Total Priests in Diocese	13
Ordinations:	
Permanent Deacons	3
Permanent Deacons in Diocese	3
Total Sisters	2
Parishes	
Parishes	9
With Resident Pastor:	
Resident Diocesan Priests	7
Resident Religious Priests	2
Missions	17
Professional Ministry Personnel:	
Sisters	2
Lay Ministers	11
Welfare	
Catholic Hospitals	1
Total Assisted	45,000
Day Care Centers	1
Total Assisted	100
Special Centers for Social Services	1
Total Assisted	10,000
Other Institutions	1
Total Assisted	15,000
Educational	
Elementary Schools, Diocesan and Parish	1
Total Students	91
Catechesis/Religious Education:	
High School Students	78
Elementary Students	455
Total Students under Catholic Instruction	624
Teachers in the Diocese:	
Lay Teachers	10
Vital Statistics	
Receptions into the Church:	
Infant Baptism Totals	52
Minor Baptism Totals	5
Adult Baptism Totals	7
Received into Full Communion	6
First Communions	96
Confirmations	75
Marriages:	
Catholic	12
Interfaith	8
Total Marriages	20
Deaths	49
Total Catholic Population	10,000
Total Population	75,000

Former Bishops—Most Revs. DERMOT O'FLANAGAN, D.D., ord. Aug. 27, 1929; appt. Bishop July 9, 1951; cons. Oct. 3, 1951; resigned June 19, 1968; appt. Titular Bishop of Trecalae; died Dec. 31, 1972; FRANCIS T. HURLEY, D.D., ord. June 16, 1951; appt. Titular Bishop of Daimlaig and Auxiliary of Juneau, Feb. 4, 1970; cons. March 19, 1970; Ordinary of See, July 20, 1971; appt. Archbishop of Anchorage, May 4, 1976; MICHAEL H. KENNY, D.D., ord. March 30, 1963; appt. March 20, 1979; cons. May 27, 1979; installed June 15, 1979; died Feb. 19, 1995; MICHAEL W. WARFEL, ord. April 26, 1980; appt. Nov. 19, 1996; installed Dec. 17, 1996; appt. Bishop of Great Falls-Billings Nov. 20, 2007.

Diocesan Pastoral Center

Bishop of Juneau—Most Rev. EDWARD J. BURNS.

Chancery—415 Sixth St., #300, Juneau, 99801. Tel: 907-586-2227; Fax: 907-463-3237.

Chancellor—Rev. PATRICK J. TRAVERS, J.C.L., J.D.

Diocesan Consultors—Revs. PETER GORGES (Retired); JEAN PAULIN LOCKULU; PERRY KENASTON; SCOTT R. SETTIMO; PATRICK J. TRAVERS, J.C.L., J.D.; THOMAS L. WEISE; EDMUND J. PENISTEN.

Tribunal—433 Jackson St., Ketchikan, 99901. Tel: 907-247-2755; Fax: 907-225-2571.

Judicial Vicar—Rev. PATRICK J. TRAVERS, J.C.L., J.D.

Defender of the Bond—Sr. CAROLYN ROEBER, O.P., J.C.L., J.D.

Auditor—Ms. ALETHEA JOHNSON.

Notaries—Mrs. LINDA K. KELLEY; Ms. ALETHEA JOHNSON.

Administration—415 Sixth St., #300, Juneau, 99801. Tel: 907-586-2227; Fax: 907-463-3237.

Business Manager and Finance Officer—JAMES DONAGHEY.

Director of Administrative Services/Assistant to the Bishop—ROBERTA IZZARD.

Assistant to the Finance Officer—MICHELE FANGMAN.

Finance Council—HUGH GRANT; Rev. PATRICK J. TRAVERS, J.C.L., J.D.; JAMES DONAGHEY; Mr. WILLIAM PETERS; MICHELE FANGMAN; Most Rev. EDWARD J. BURNS.

Miscellaneous

Apostleship of the Sea—Port Chaplains: Revs. PATRICK T. CASEY, O.M.I., 416 Fifth St., Juneau, 99801; SCOTT R. SETTIMO, 433 Jackson St., Ketchikan, 99801.

Catholic Community Service, Inc.—ROSEMARY HAGEVIG, Exec. Dir., 419 Sixth St., Juneau, 99801. Tel: 907-463-6151.

Board of Directors—Most Rev. EDWARD J. BURNS, Pres.; JOHN GREELY; LISA PUSICH; LOREN JONES; DOUG SMITH, M.D.; PATRICIA ATKINSON; KEVIN RITCHIE; JAMES CARROLL; TONY YORBA; JON BOLLING; BILL DIEBELS; Dr. LINDY JONES; LEON VANCE.

Catholic Community Service—Program Directors: Ms. MARIANNE MILLS, Southeast Sr. Svcs. (SESS) (seniors and adults with disabilities); Ms. HELEN KALK, Child Care & Family Resources (CCFR) (children and families). Co Directors, Hospice & Home Care of Juneau (HHCJ) (people who need in-home care and end-of-life services): NANCY DAVIS; ROSEMARY GRUENING.

Diocesan Publication "Inside Passage"—KARLA DONAGHEY, Editor, 415 Sixth St., #300, Juneau, 99801. Tel: 907-586-2237, Ext. 32.

Office of Ministries & Missions—Deacon CHARLES ROHRBACHER, Dir., 415 Sixth St., #300, Juneau, 99801. Tel: 907-586-2227.

Permanent Deacon Program—Deacon GARY HORTON, 415 6th St., #300, Juneau, 99801. Tel: 907-586-2227, Ext. 36.

School—CONNIE WINGREN, Prin., Holy Name School, 433 Jackson St., Ketchikan, 99901. Tel: 907-225-2400.

Shrine of St. Therese—RUTH VINCENT, 419 6th St., #300, Juneau, 99801. Tel: 907-780-6112. Caretakers: JOHN JORDAN; JEANNE JORDAN.

St. Vincent de Paul Society—DAN AUSTIN, 8617 Teal St., Juneau, 99801. Tel: 907-789-5535.

Special Collections and Archivist—Deacon GARY HORTON, 415 6th St., #300, Juneau, 99801. Tel: 907-586-2227, Ext. 36.

Victim Assistance Coordinator and Safe Environment Coordinator—ROBERTA IZZARD. Tel: 907-586-2227, Ext. 25. Email: robbiei@gci.net.

Vocations—Most Rev. EDWARD J. BURNS, 415 6th St. #300, Juneau, 99801.

CLERGY, PARISHES, MISSIONS AND PAROCHIAL SCHOOLS

CITY AND BOROUGH OF JUNEAU

1—CATHEDRAL OF THE NATIVITY OF THE BLESSED VIRGIN MARY Rev. Patrick T. Casey, O.M.I.
Res.: 416 Fifth St., 99801. Tel: 907-586-1513; Fax: 907-586-8091.
Catechesis/Religious Program—Katherine Rice, D.R.E. Students 100.

2—ST. PAUL THE APOSTLE Rev. Patrick J. Travers.
Res.: 9055 Atlin Ave., 99801. Tel: 907-789-2648 (Rectory); 907-789-7307 (Office); Fax: 907-790-3430.
Catechesis/Religious Program—Tel: 907-789-7303. Marilyn Monagle, D.R.E. Students 253.

OUTSIDE THE CITY AND BOROUGH OF JUNEAU

HAINES, SACRED HEART Rev. Perry Kenaston.
Res.: Box 326, 99827. Tel: 907-766-2241.
Mission—St. Therese of the Child Jesus P.O. Box 496, Skagway, 99840. Tel: 907-983-2271.

Mission— Kluckwan.

KETCHIKAN, KETCHIKAN GATEWAY CO., HOLY NAME Revs. Scott R. Settimo; Steven P. Gallagher, Parochial Vicar.
Res.: 433 Jackson St., 99901. Tel: 907-225-2570; 907-247-2728 (Rectory); Fax: 907-225-2571.
School—(Grades PreSchool-8) Tel: 907-247-0041. Connie Wingren, Prin. Lay Teachers 10; Students 91.
Catechesis/Religious Program—Tel: 907-225-2120; Fax: 907-225-2570. Mrs. Linda K. Kelley, D.R.E. Students 95.
Mission—Holy Family

KLAWOCK, ST. JOHN BY THE SEA Rev. Jean Paulin Lockulu.
Res.: P.O. Box 245, 99925. Tel: 907-755-2345; Fax: 907-755-2350.
Mission— Thorne Bay, 99919. Tel: 907-828-3324.
Mission— Coffman Cove.
Mission— Hydaburg.
Mission— Naukati.
Mission— Hollis.
Mission— Meyers Chuck.

PETERSBURG, WRANGELL-PETERSBURG(CA) CO., ST. CATHERINE OF SIENA Rev. Thomas L. Weise.
Res.: P.O. Box 508, 99833. Tel: 907-772-3257; Fax: 907-772-3020.

SITKA, SITKA CO., ST. GREGORY OF NAZIANZEN, Unassigned. Rev. James Blaney, O.M.I.
Res.: P.O. Box 495, 99835. Tel: 907-747-8371; 907-747-6997; Fax: 907-747-8401.
Mission— Kake.

SKAGWAY, SKAGWAY-HOONAH-ANGOON (CA) CO., ST. THERESE OF THE CHILD JESUS, Closed. Now a mission of Sacred Heart, Haines, AK.

WRANGELL, WRANGELL-PETERSBURG (CA) CO., ST. ROSE OF LIMA Rev. Thomas L. Weise.
Res.: Box 469, 99929. Tel: 907-874-3771; Fax: 907-874-3744.

YAKUTAT, YAKUTAT CO., ST. ANN Rev. Edmund J. Penisten, Dir. Northern Missions.
Res.: P.O. Box 323, 99689. Tel: 907-784-3406.
Mission— Elfin Cove.
Mission— Gustavus.
Mission— Pelican.
Mission— Tenakee Springs.
Mission— Hoonah.
Mission— Kake.
Mission— Excursion Inlet.

Chaplains of Public Institutions

Hospitals

KETCHIKAN. *Ketchikan General Hospital*. 3100 Tongass, 99901. Tel: 907-225-5171; Fax: 907-228-8322. Sr. Arnadene Bean, C.S.J.P., Chap.
New Horizons Transitional Care Unit

On Duty Outside the Diocese:
Rev.—
Saba, Joseph, 5660 W. Placita Del Risco, Tucson, AZ 85745.

Retired:
Revs.—
Frister, Jerome, Nazareth House, 6333 Rancho Mission Rd., San Diego, CA 92108.
Gorges, Peter, St. Gregory, P.O. Box 495, Sitka, 99835-0495.
Konda, Bernard, Priests Retirement Center, 6900 E. 45th St. N. F-1, Bel Aire, KS 67226.

Permanent Deacons:
Hansen, Vincent G, Sacred Heart, Haines
Horton, Gary, Cathedral of the Nativity of the Blessed Virgin Mary, Juneau
Rohrbacher, Charles, Cathedral of the Nativity of the Blessed Virgin Mary, Juneau

INSTITUTIONS LOCATED IN THE DIOCESE

[A] CONVENTS AND RESIDENCES FOR SISTERS

JUNEAU. *St. Joseph Convent*, Mailing Address: c/o 415 6th St., 99801. 2971 Douglas Hwy., 99801. Tel: 907-586-2085. Intercommunity residence of various religious orders of women.

KETCHIKAN. *Sisters of St. Joseph of Peace, Ketchikan General Hospital*, 3100 Tongass Ave., 99901. Tel: 907-225-5171; Fax: 907-228-8322.

RELIGIOUS INSTITUTES OF WOMEN REPRESENTED IN THE DIOCESE

For further details refer to the corresponding bracketed number in the Religious Institutes of Men or Women section.

[1070]—*Dominican Sisters*—O.P.

[3890]—*Sisters of St. Joseph of Peace*—C.S.J.P.

NECROLOGY

(No Deaths)

An asterisk (*) denotes an organization that has established tax-exempt status directly with the IRS and is not covered by the USCCB Group Ruling.

Diocese of Kalamazoo

(Dioecesis Kalamazuensis)

Most Reverend

PAUL J. BRADLEY

Bishop of Kalamazoo; ordained May 1, 1971; appointed Titular Bishop of Afufenia and Auxiliary Bishop of Pittsburgh December 16, 2004; ordained February 2, 2005; appointed Bishop of Kalamazoo April 6, 2009; installed June 5, 2009.

Most Reverend

JAMES A. MURRAY

Retired Bishop of Kalamazoo; ordained June 7, 1958; appointed Bishop of Kalamazoo November 18, 1997; ordained and installed January 27, 1998; retired April 6, 2009. Email: jmurray@dioceseofkalamazoo.org.

ESTABLISHED JULY 21, 1971.

Square Miles 5,337.

Comprises the following nine Counties in the State of Michigan: Allegan, Barry, Berrien, Branch, Calhoun, Cass, Kalamazoo, St. Joseph and Van Buren.

For legal titles of parishes and diocesan institutions, consult the Diocesan Pastoral Center.

Diocesan Pastoral Center: 215 N. Westnedge Ave., Kalamazoo, MI 49007-3760. Tel: 269-349-8714; Fax: 269-349-6440.

Web: dioceseofkalamazoo.org

STATISTICAL OVERVIEW

Personnel	
Bishop	1
Retired Bishops	1
Priests: Diocesan Active in Diocese	40
Priests: Diocesan Active Outside Diocese	2
Priests: Retired, Sick or Absent	19
Number of Diocesan Priests	61
Religious Priests in Diocese	11
Total Priests in Diocese	72
Extern Priests in Diocese	8
Ordinations:	
Diocesan Priests	1
Permanent Deacons in Diocese	35
Total Brothers	2
Total Sisters	208
Parishes	
Parishes	46
With Resident Pastor:	
Resident Diocesan Priests	36
Resident Religious Priests	7
Without Resident Pastor:	
Administered by Priests	2
Administered by Religious Women	1
Missions	13
Pastoral Centers	1
Professional Ministry Personnel:	
Brothers	2
Sisters	3
Lay Ministers	22
Welfare	
Catholic Hospitals	3
Total Assisted	483,582
Health Care Centers	1
Homes for the Aged	3
Total Assisted	546
Specialized Homes	24
Total Assisted	363
Special Centers for Social Services	7
Total Assisted	40,274
Educational	
Diocesan Students in Other Seminaries	13
Total Seminarians	13
High Schools, Diocesan and Parish	3
Total Students	630
Elementary Schools, Diocesan and Parish	19
Total Students	2,508
Catechesis/Religious Education:	
High School Students	430
Elementary Students	4,929
Total Students under Catholic Instruction	8,510
Teachers in the Diocese:	
Priests	2
Brothers	1
Sisters	1
Lay Teachers	205
Vital Statistics	
Receptions into the Church:	
Infant Baptism Totals	1,291
Minor Baptism Totals	79
Adult Baptism Totals	130
Received into Full Communion	142
First Communions	1,187
Confirmations	1,025
Marriages:	
Catholic	182
Interfaith	122
Total Marriages	304
Deaths	847
Total Catholic Population	104,386
Total Population	948,965

Former Bishops—Most Revs. PAUL V. DONOVAN, D.D., ord. May 20, 1950; appt. Bishop of Kalamazoo June 15, 1971; installed July 21, 1971; resigned Nov. 22, 1994; died April 28, 2011.; ALFRED J. MARKIEWICZ, D.D., ord. June 6, 1953; appt. Titular Bishop of Afufenia and Auxiliary to the Bishop of Rockville Centre, July 7, 1986; ord. Bishop, Sept. 17, 1986; appt. Bishop of Kalamazoo, Nov. 22, 1994; installed Jan. 31, 1995; died Jan. 9, 1997; JAMES A. MURRAY, ord. June 7, 1958; appt. Bishop of Kalamazoo Nov. 18, 1997; ord. and installed Jan. 27, 1998; retired April 6, 2009.

Vicar General—Rev. Msgr. MICHAEL D. HAZARD, V.G., St. Joseph Church, 936 Lake St., Kalamazoo, 49001. Tel: 269-343-6256; Fax: 269-343-1214.

Diocesan Pastoral Center—215 N. Westnedge Ave., Kalamazoo, 49007-3760. Tel: 269-349-8714, Ext. 122; Fax: 269-349-6440. Web: dioceseofkalamazoo.org. Office Hours: 8:30-4.

Chancellor and Executive Director of Administration—Mr. MICHAEL EMMONS, 215 N. Westnedge Ave., Kalamazoo, 49007-3760. Tel: 269-903-0213; Fax: 269-349-6440.

Vicar for Canonical Concerns—Rev. Msgr. THOMAS A. MARTIN, J.C.D., 215 N. Westnedge Ave., Kalamazoo, 49007-3760. Tel: 269-903-0179; Fax: 269-349-6440.

Direct Communications regarding Marriage Dispensations to Vicar for Canonical Concerns. *Diocesan Pastoral Center, 215 N. Westnedge Ave., Kalamazoo, 49007-3760.* Tel: 269-903-0179; Fax: 269-349-6440.

Vicar for Clergy—Rev. Msgr. WILLIAM FITZGERALD (Retired), 602 South St., Kalamazoo, 49007. Tel: 269-226-9726.

Vicar for Education—Very Rev. JOHN D. FLECKENSTEIN, St. Philip Church, 126 Capital Ave., N.E., Battle Creek, 49017. Tel: 269-968-6645.

Vicars Forane—Very Revs. LAWRENCE FARRELL, V.F., Central Deanery; MARK J. VYVERMAN, V.F., Eastern Deanery; WILLIAM JACOBS, V.F., Lakeshore Deanery; CHRISTIAN R. JOHNSTON, V.F., Northern Deanery; GERMAN PEREZ-DIAZ, V.F., Southeast Deanery; JOSEPH MCCORMICK, O.S.A., V.F., Southwest Deanery.

Diocesan Tribunal—215 N. Westnedge Ave., Kalamazoo, 49007-3760. Tel: 269-903-0189; Fax: 269-349-6440.

Judicial Vicar—Rev. Msgr. THOMAS A. MARTIN, J.C.D.

Defender of the Bond—Rev. MICHAEL A. HACK, J.C.D.

Promoter of Justice—Deacon HAL BOHAN.

Judge—Rev. KENNETH W. SCHMIDT, J.C.D., M.A., L.P.C.

Advocates—Rev. ROBERT E. FLICKINGER; Very Rev. LAWRENCE FARRELL, V.F.; Rev. CHARLES H. FISCHER.

Chief Notary and Administrative Assistant—Mrs. MARLENE J. PRANSKATIS.

Ecclesiastical Notary—Mrs. MONICA ZEHNER.

Direct communications regarding Marriage Dispensations to: Vicar for Canonical Concerns *Diocesan Pastoral Center, 215 N. Westnedge, Kalamazoo, 49007-3760.* Tel: 269-903-0179; Fax: 269-349-6440.

Diocesan Consultors—Rev. Msgrs. MICHAEL D. HAZARD, V.G.; THOMAS A. MARTIN, J.C.D.; Rev. JAMES L. BARRETT (Retired); Very Rev. MARK J. VYVERMAN, V.F.

Staff to the Diocesan Consultors—Mr. MICHAEL EMMONS.

Presbyteral Council Members—Most Rev. PAUL J. BRADLEY; Rev. Msgrs. MICHAEL D. HAZARD, V.G.; THOMAS A. MARTIN, J.C.D.; EUGENE A. SEARS (Retired); Very Revs. JOHN D. FLECKENSTEIN; JOSEPH MCCORMICK, O.S.A., V.F.; MARK J. VYVERMAN, V.F.; Revs. JAMES ADAMS; JAMES L. BARRETT (Retired); CHRISTOPHER DERDA; ROBERT E. FLICKINGER; FABIO H. GARZON; DONALD G. POTTS.

Staff to the Presbyteral Council—Mr. MICHAEL EMMONS.

Diocesan Offices and Directors

Campaign for Human Development—Sr. SUSAN RIDLEY, O.P., Dir., 215 N. Westnedge Ave., Kalamazoo, 49007-3760. Tel: 269-903-0195; Fax: 269-349-6440.

Catholic Family Services—Mrs. FRANCES H. DENNY, M.B.A., M.S.W., Exec. Dir., 1819 Gull Rd., Kalamazoo, 49001. Tel: 269-381-9800; Fax: 269-381-2932.

Catholic Relief Services—Sr. SUSAN RIDLEY, O.P., Dir., 215 N. Westnedge Ave., Kalamazoo, 49007-3760. Tel: 269-903-0195; Fax: 269-349-6440.

Cemeteries—Very Rev. JOHN D. FLECKENSTEIN, St. Philip Church, 126 Capital Ave., N.E., Battle Creek, 49017. Tel: 269-968-6645; Fax: 269-968-0632.

Diocesan Cemetery - Kalamazoo—Mt. Olivet.

Evangelization, Catechesis & Initiation—Mr. D. J. FLORIAN, Dir. Tel: 269-903-0167. Associate Directors: LISA IRWIN. Tel: 269-903-0177; Deacon KURT LUCAS. Tel: 269-903-0183. 215 N. Westnedge Ave., Kalamazoo, 49007-3760. Tel: 269-349-8714, Ext. 227; Fax: 269-349-6440.

Christian Service—Sr. SUSAN RIDLEY, O.P., Dir., 215 N. Westnedge Ave., Kalamazoo, 49007-3760. Tel: 269-903-0195; Fax: 269-349-6440.

Communications—Ms. VICKIE CESSNA, Dir., 215 N. Westnedge Ave., Kalamazoo, 49007-3760. Tel: 269-903-0163.

Audiovisual Resources—Mr. D. J. FLORIAN, Coord., 215 N. Westnedge Ave., Kalamazoo, 49007-3760. Tel: 269-903-0167.

Diocesan Council of Catholic Women (D.C.C.W.)—Rev. DONALD P. KLINGLER, Spiritual Dir. (Retired); Ms. CAROLYN MORRISON, Pres.

Diocesan Development and Stewardship Office—VACANT.

Delegate for Ecumenical and Interreligious Concerns—Rev. Msgr. THOMAS A. MARTIN, J.C.D., Dir., 215 N. Westnedge Ave., Kalamazoo, 49007-3760. Tel: 269-349-8714, Ext. 118.

Diocesan Pastoral Council—Mr. D. J. FLORIAN, Staff Contact, 215 N. Westnedge Ave., Kalamazoo, 49007-3760. Tel: 269-903-0167.

Diocesan-Parish Council Ministry—VACANT, 215 N. Westnedge Ave., Kalamazoo, 49007-3760. Tel: 269-349-8714.

Education—Very Rev. JOHN D. FLECKENSTEIN, Vicar for Educ., St. Philip Church, 126 Capital Ave., N.E., Battle Creek, 49017. Tel: 269-968-6645; Fax: 269-968-6645; Mrs. MARGARET ERICH, Supt. of Schools. Tel: 269-903-0165; Ms. SALLY J. AMMAN, Assoc. Supt. Schools, 215 N. Westnedge Ave., Kalamazoo, 49007-3760. Tel: 269-903-0181; Fax: 269-349-6440.

Diocesan Finance Council—Mr. MICHAEL EMMONS, Chancellor/Exec. Dir. of Admin., Diocese of Kalamazoo; Very Revs. WILLIAM JACOBS, V.F., Pastor, SS John - Bernard Catholic Church, Benton Harbor, MI; JOHN D. FLECKENSTEIN, Vicar for Educ., Diocese of Kalamazoo, Pastor, St. Philip Church, Battle Creek; Mr. EDWARD BAUMAN, Retired Sr. Dir. Mktg. Procurement, Kellogg Company, Battle Creek, MI; Mr. T. EDWARD CAREY JR., CFO, Vice Chancellor, Diocese of Grand Rapids; Mr. JERRY B. LOVE, CPA, Arcadia Investment Mgmt. Corp., Kalamazoo; Mrs. BOBBIE OTTO, CPA, South Haven, MI; Mr. LEO A. SWIAT, Pres., Olmsted & Mulhall, Inc.; Mrs. SANDY L. BOOTHBY, Accounting Mgr.

Diocesan Finance Office—VACANT, Dir.; Mrs. SANDY L. BOOTHBY, Accounting Mgr., 215 N. Westnedge Ave., Kalamazoo, 49007-3760. Tel: 269-903-0155. Email: sboothby@dioceseofkalamazoo.org.

Diocesan Historian/Archivist—Rev. ROBERT F. CREAGAN, V.F., St. Catherine of Siena Church, 1150 W. Centre Ave., Portage, 49024. Tel: 269-327-5165; Fax: 269-327-7266.

Holy Childhood Association and Propagation of the Faith—Very Rev. LAWRENCE FARRELL, V.F., Dir., 215 N. Westnedge Ave., Kalamazoo, 49007-3760. Tel: 269-345-4389.

Inner City Ministry—Sisters MAUREEN MCGRATH, O.P.; MARY PUNG, S.S.J., Catholic Community Center, 589 Pearl St., Benton Harbor, 49022. Tel: 269-926-6424; Fax: 269-926-2870.

Jail Ministry—Sr. SUSAN RIDLEY, O.P., Coord., 215 N. Westnedge Ave., Kalamazoo, 49007-3760. Tel: 269-903-0195.

Knights of Columbus—Rev. ROBERT F. CREAGAN, V.F., Diocesan Chap., St. Catherine of Siena Church, 1150 W. Centre Ave., Portage, 49024. Tel: 269-327-5165; Fax: 269-327-7266.

Marriage and Family Ministry, Office of—Deacon JOE SCHMITT, Dir. Tel: 269-903-0199; Mrs. JANE BODWAY, Asst. Dir. Tel: 269-903-0147. 215 N. Westnedge Ave., Kalamazoo, 49007-3760. Fax: 269-349-6440.

Ministry with Persons with Disabilities—Miss ANN SHERZER, Dir., 215 N. Westnedge Ave., Kalamazoo, 49007-3760. Tel: 269-903-0201.

Missions—Very Rev. LAWRENCE FARRELL, V.F., Dir., 215 N. Westnedge Ave., Kalamazoo, 49007-3760. Tel: 269-345-4389; Fax: 269-349-6440.

Natural Family Planning—Mrs. JANE BODWAY, Diocesan Pastoral Center, 215 N. Westnedge Ave., Kalamazoo, 49007. Tel: 269-903-0147.

Permanent Diaconate—Deacons EUGENE HAAS, Dir. Deacon Personnel. Tel: 269-903-0169; JOHN BODWAY, Dir. Deacon Formation, 215 N. Westnedge Ave., Kalamazoo, 49007-3760. Tel: 269-903-0151.

Pilgrimages—Rev. ROBERT F. CREAGAN, V.F., Dir., St. Catherine of Siena Church, 1150 W. Centre Ave., Portage, 49024. Tel: 269-327-5165; Fax: 269-327-7266.

Presbyteral Council Members—Most Rev. PAUL J. BRADLEY; Rev. Msgrs. MICHAEL D. HAZARD, V.G.; THOMAS A. MARTIN, J.C.D.; EUGENE A. SEARS (Retired); Very Revs. JOHN D. FLECKENSTEIN; JOSEPH MCCORMICK, O.S.A., V.F.; MARK J. VYVERMAN, V.F.; Revs. JAMES ADAMS; JAMES L. BARRETT (Retired); CHRISTOPHER DERDA; FABIO H. GARZON; DONALD G. POTTS.

Staff to the Presbyteral Council—Mr. MICHAEL EMMONS.

Priestly Life and Ministry Office—Rev. KENNETH W. SCHMIDT, J.C.D., M.A., L.P.C., Dir., 421 Monroe St., Kalamazoo, 49006. Tel: 269-381-8917; Fax: 269-381-0195.

Respect Life—Sr. SUSAN RIDLEY, O.P., Dir., 215 N. Westnedge Ave., Kalamazoo, 49007-3760. Tel: 269-903-0195; Fax: 269-349-6440.

St. Vincent DePaul Society—Sr. SUSAN RIDLEY, O.P., 215 N. Westnedge, Kalamazoo, 49007-3760. Tel: 269-903-0195; Fax: 269-349-6440.

Office of Immigration Services—Ms. KISH INQUILLA, Dir., 219 N. Westnedge Ave., Kalamazoo, 49007. Tel: 269-903-0135.

Office of Strategic Planning—VACANT, Dir., 215 N. Westnedge Ave., Kalamazoo, 49007-3760. Tel: 269-349-8714.

Scouting Apostolate—Rev. RICHARD L. ALTINE, Chap., St. Rose of Lima, 805 S. Jefferson Ave., Hastings, 49058. Tel: 269-945-4246.

Spanish-Speaking Apostolate—Ms. FANNY TABARES, Dir. Tel: 269-903-0209; Sr. CHELA GONZALEZ, O.P., Hispanic Youth Ministry Coord. Tel: 269-903-0219. 215 N. Westnedge Ave., Kalamazoo, 49007. Fax: 269-349-6440.

Victim Assistance Coordinator—Deacon PATRICK HALL. Tel: 269-903-0175. Email: phall@dioceseofkalamazoo.org.

Vocations and Ongoing Formation—Revs. CHRISTOPHER DERDA, Dir.; CHRISTOPHER ANKLEY, Assoc. Dir., 215 N. Westnedge Ave., Kalamazoo, 49007-3760. Tel: 269-903-0203.

Office of Christian Worship—Mr. DAVID J. REILLY, Dir., 215 N. Westnedge Ave., Kalamazoo, 49007-3760. Tel: 269-903-0193; Fax: 269-349-6440.

Address communications for all other offices to Diocesan Pastoral Center *Diocese of Kalamazoo, 215 N. Westnedge Ave., Kalamazoo, 49007-3760.*

CLERGY, PARISHES, MISSIONS AND PAROCHIAL SCHOOLS

CITY OF KALAMAZOO

(KALAMAZOO COUNTY)

1—ST. AUGUSTINE CATHEDRAL (1856) Rev. Msgr. Thomas A. Martin; Rev. Ted Martin, Parochial Vicar.
Res.: 542 W. Michigan Ave., 49007. Tel: 269-345-5147; Fax: 269-349-0166.
School—600 W. Michigan Ave., 49007. Tel: 269-349-1945; Fax: 269-349-1085. Lay Teachers 23; Students 311.
Catechesis/Religious Program—Students 63.

2—ST. JOSEPH (1904) Rev. Msgr. Michael D. Hazard.
Res.: 936 Lake St., 49001. Tel: 269-343-6256; Fax: 269-343-1214. Email: stjosephkazoo@tds.net.
Catechesis/Religious Program—Students 368.

3—ST. MARY (1935) Rev. Robert Sirico.
Res.: 939 Charlotte, 49048. Tel: 269-385-9933.
Catechesis/Religious Program—Mrs. Anne Holewa, D.R.E. Students 14.

4—ST. MONICA (1955) Very Rev. Lawrence Farrell; Deacons Robert Stevens; Kurt Lucas. In Res., Revs. Robert E. Consani; Wieslaw Lipka (Poland).
Res.: 534 W. Kilgore Rd., 49008. Tel: 269-345-4389. Church Office: 4408 S. Westnedge, 49008. Fax: 269-345-5211.
School—530 W. Kilgore Rd., 49008. Tel: 269-345-2444; Fax: 269-345-8534. Web: sms.csgk.org. Lay Teachers 25; Students 374.
Catechesis/Religious Program—Students 543.

5—ST. THOMAS MORE STUDENT PARISH (1956) Rev. Kenneth W. Schmidt; Sisters Susan McCrery, C.S.J., Pastoral Assoc.; Pam Owens, C.S.J., Pastoral Assoc.; Deacons Patrick Hall, Pastoral Assoc.; Joe Schmitt, Pastoral Assoc.
Office: 421 Monroe St., 49006. Tel: 269-381-8917; Fax: 269-381-0195. Email: sttoms@sttomskazoo.org. Web: www.sttomskazoo.org.
Catechesis/Religious Program—936 Lake St., 49001. Tel: 269-343-6258; Fax: 269-343-1214. Students 95.

OUTSIDE THE CITY OF KALAMAZOO

ALBION, CALHOUN CO., ST. JOHN THE EVANGELIST (1873) [CEM] Rev. Joseph B. Gray.
Office: 1020 Irwin Ave., 49224-9713. Tel: 517-629-4532; Fax: 517-629-5462. Web: stjohn-church.org.
Res.: 879 Finley Dr., 49224. Tel: 517-629-8678.
Catechesis/Religious Program—Students 40.

ALLEGAN, ALLEGAN CO., BLESSED SACRAMENT (1934) [CEM] Rev. Alan P. Jorgensen.
Res.: 422 Hubbard St., 49010-1246. Tel: 616-673-4455; Fax: 616-673-5869. Email: blsacch@frontier.com.
Church: 110 Cedar St., 49010-1244. Tel: 269-673-4455; Fax: 269-673-5869.
Catechesis/Religious Program—Students 105.

AUGUSTA, KALAMAZOO CO., ST. ANN (1958) Rev. Christopher Derda.
Res.: 12648 E. D Ave., 49012. Tel: 269-731-4721; Fax: 269-731-4147. Email: stann_gl@comcast.net.
Catechesis/Religious Program—Tel: 269-731-0295. Students 147.

BANGOR, VAN BUREN CO., SACRED HEART OF JESUS (1932) [CEM] Rev. Charles H. Fischer.
Res.: 201 S. Walnut St., 49013. Tel: 269-427-7514; Fax: 269-302-0133. Email: secretary@sacredheartbangor.org. Web: www.sacredheartbangor.com.
Catechesis/Religious Program—Students 22.

BATTLE CREEK, CALHOUN CO.

1—ST. JEROME (1955) [JC] Rev. Mathew Manalel.
Res.: 242 Collier Ave., 49037. Tel: 269-968-2218; 269-441-2309; Fax: 269-968-2233. Email: stjeromechurch22@aol.com.
Catechesis/Religious Program—Students 10.

2—ST. JOSEPH (1942) [JC] Very Rev. Mark J. Vyverman.
Res.: 61 N. 23rd St., 49015. Tel: 269-962-0165; Fax: 269-962-5937. Web: www.stjosephchurchonline.org.
School—(Grades PreK-8), 47 N. 23rd, 49015. Tel: 269-965-7749; Fax: 269-965-0790. Web: bcacs.org. Lay Teachers 33; Students 398.
Catechesis/Religious Program—Tel: 269-965-4079. Students 291.

3—ST. PHILIP (1869) [CEM] Very Rev. John D. Fleckenstein; Rev. Harold G. Potter; Deacons Hal Bohan; Bernie Mileski; Albert Patrick.
Office: 112 Capital Ave., N.E., 49017. Tel: 269-968-6645; Fax: 269-968-0632. Email: admin@stphilipchurch-bc.org. Web: stphilipchurch-bc.org.
Res.: 126 Capital Ave., N.E., 49017.
School—20 Cherry St., 49017. Tel: 269-963-4503; Fax: 269-963-5590. Lay Teachers 13; Students 138.
Catechesis/Religious Program—Tel: 269-962-9506. Students 118.

BENTON HARBOR, BERRIEN CO.

1—ST. BERNARD, Merged with St. John, Benton Harbor.

2—SS. JOHN & BERNARD (1996) [CEM] Very Rev. William Jacobs; Rev. Michael Revent.
Res.: 600 Columbus Ave., 49022. Tel: 616-925-2425; Fax: 616-925-4678. Email: ssjandb@sbcglobal.net.
Catechesis/Religious Program—220 Church St., St. Joseph, 49085. Tel: 616-983-1575. Students 143.

3—ST. JOHN THE EVANGELIST, Merged with St. Bernard, Benton Harbor.

BRIDGMAN, BERRIEN CO., OUR LADY QUEEN OF PEACE (1939) Rev. Arthur Howard.
Res.: 3903 Lake St., 49106-0747. Tel: 269-465-6252; Fax: 269-465-4930. Email: pastor@queenofpeaceb.org. Web: www.queenofpeaceb.org.
Catechesis/Religious Program—Students 73.
Mission—*St. Gabriel Mission Church* 429 Rose Hill, Berrien Springs, Berrien Co. 49103. Tel: 269-471-2424.

BRONSON, BRANCH CO., ST. MARY'S (1867), (Polish), [CEM] Rev. Richard A. Fritz; Deacons Gerald Smoker; James Lavelline.
Res.: 602 W. Chicago, 49028. Tel: 517-369-2120; Fax: 517-369-9012.
School—204 Albers Rd., 49028. Tel: 517-369-4625; Fax: 517-369-1652. Lay Teachers 6; Students 75.

Mission—St. Barbara Colon, St. Joseph Co. Tel: 616-432-2109.
Catechesis/Religious Program—Tel: 517-278-5408. Students 125.

BUCHANAN, BERRIEN CO., ST. ANTHONY (1941) [JC] Rev. Carl F. Peltz.
Res.: 509 W. 4th St., 49107. Tel: 269-695-3863; Fax: 269-697-8189. Email: saintanthonychurch@gmail.com.
Catechesis/Religious Program—Students 38.

BYRON CENTER, KENT CO., ST. MARY'S VISITATION (1866), (German), [CEM 2] [JC 2] Rev. Stephen Rodrigo, S.J. (India).
Res.: 2459 146th Ave., 49315. Tel: 616-681-9701; Fax: 616-681-9919. Email: gandres@smvchurch.org. Web: www.smvchurch.org.
School—2455 146th Ave., 49315. Email: mmaclachlan@smvschool.org. Web: smvschool.org. Lay Teachers 5; Students 76.
Catechesis/Religious Program—Tel: 616-681-9701, Ext. 203. Email: plaperna@smvchurch.org. Students 107.

CASSOPOLIS, CASS CO., ST. ANN (1915) Rev. Donald G. Potts.
Church & Mailing Address: 421 N. Broadway, P.O. Box 247, 49031. Tel: 269-445-3000; Fax: 269-445-5787.
Res.: 312 N. Disbrow, P.O. Box 247, 49031. Tel: 269-445-3140.
Catechesis/Religious Program—Email: stanncass@frontier.com. Students 15.

COLDWATER, BRANCH CO., ST. CHARLES BORROMEO (1849) Rev. Daniel E. Doctor.
Res.: 150 Taylor St., 49036. Tel: 517-278-2650; Fax: 517-278-5800.
School—79 Harrison St., 49036. Tel: 517-279-0404; Fax: 517-278-0505. Lay Teachers 5; Students 69.
Catechesis/Religious Program—Students 60.
Mission—Our Lady of Fatima Union City, Branch Co. Tel: 517-741-7275.

DECATUR, VAN BUREN CO., HOLY FAMILY (1938) Rev. Patrick H. Craig.
Res.: 500 W. St. Mary St., 49045. Tel: 269-783-4223; Fax: 269-783-4668. Email: holyfamilydecatur@comcast.net.
Catechesis/Religious Program—Students 31.

DELTON, BARRY CO., ST. AMBROSE (1950) Sr. Constance Fifelski, O.P., Parish Coord.
11137 Floria Rd., 49046. Tel: 269-623-2490; Fax: 269-623-2498. Email: stambrose@mei.net.
Res.: 11252 Floria Rd., 49046.
Catechesis/Religious Program—Students 37.
Mission—Our Lady of Great Oak Lacey, Barry Co.

DORR, ALLEGAN CO., ST. STANISLAUS (1892), (Polish), [CEM] Rev. Anthony Bitchapogu (India).
Res.: 1871 136th Ave., 49323. Tel: 269-793-7268; Fax: 269-793-3325.
School—(Grades PreSchool-8), 1861 136th Ave., 49323. Tel: 269-793-7204; Fax: 269-793-3264. Amy Skrycki, Librarian. Lay Teachers 7; Students 98.
Catechesis/Religious Program—Students 70.
Mission—Sacred Heart Allegan, 49010.

DOUGLAS, ALLEGAN CO., ST. PETER (1894) [CEM] Rev. W. Timothy Cuny, O.S.A. In Res., Revs. John F. Flynn, O.S.A. (Retired); James J. Sheridan, O.S.A. (Retired).
Res.: 100 St. Peter Dr., P.O. Box 248, 49406-0248. Tel: 269-857-7951; Fax: 269-857-8164.
Catechesis/Religious Program—Students 80.

DOWAGIAC, CASS CO., HOLY MATERNITY OF MARY (1892) [CEM] Rev. Kevin Covert.
Res.: 210 N. Front St., 49047. Tel: 269-782-2808; Fax: 269-782-3558.
Catechesis/Religious Program—Students 60.

EDWARDSBURG, CASS CO., OUR LADY OF THE LAKE (1923) Very Rev. Joseph McCormick, O.S.A.
Res.: 24832 U.S. 12 E., 49112. Tel: 269-699-5870; Fax: 269-699-5474.
Catechesis/Religious Program—Students 138.

GOBLES, VAN BUREN CO., ST. JUDE (1985) Rev. Joseph Xavier, M.S.F.S.; Deacon John R. Bodway, Parish Coord.
Church & Mailing: 13809 M-40 N., P.O. Box 102, 49055. Tel: 269-628-2219; Fax: 269-628-2219. Email: st.judeparish@frontier.com.
Res.: 2802 Nichols Rd., 49004. Tel: 269-382-2379.
Catechesis/Religious Program—Students 25.

HARTFORD, VAN BUREN CO., IMMACULATE CONCEPTION (1946), (Hispanic), Rev. Fabio H. Garzon; Deacons Arthur Morsaw; James Rauner.
Res.: 63559 60th Ave., 49057. Tel: 269-621-4106; Fax: 269-621-2138.
Catechesis/Religious Program—Students 142.
Mission—San Felipe de Jesus 5586 117th Ave., Pearl, 49408. Tel: 269-561-5029; Fax: 269-561-2192.

HASTINGS, BARRY CO., ST. ROSE OF LIMA (1873) [CEM] Rev. Richard L. Altine.
Res.: 805 S. Jefferson Ave., 49058. Tel: 269-945-4246; Fax: 269-945-0005.
School—707 S. Jefferson St., 49058. Tel: 269-945-3164. Lay Teachers 7; Students 95.
Catechesis/Religious Program—Students 117.
Mission—St. Cyril 203 N. State St., Nashville, Barry Co. 49073. Tel: 517-852-9562.

MARSHALL, CALHOUN CO., ST. MARY (1852) [CEM] Rev. Stephen Naas.
Mailing Address: 212 W. Hanover St., 49068.
Res.: 214 S. Eagle St., 49068. Tel: 269-781-3949.
Catechesis/Religious Program—Tel: 269-781-5656. Students 174.

MATTAWAN, VAN BUREN CO., ST. JOHN BOSCO (1953) Rev. Mathew Illikattil.
Res.: 23830 Front Ave., 49071. Tel: 269-668-3312, Ext. 21; Fax: 269-668-3313. Web: www.stjohnbosco.com.
Catechesis/Religious Program—Tel: 269-668-3312, Ext. 13. Email: kellyepoage@yahoo.com. Students 131.
Mission—St. Margaret Mary 296 E. Dibble St., Marcellus, Cass Co. 49067. Tel: 269-668-3312, Ext. 10; Fax: 269-668-3313. Web: www.stjohnbosco.com.

MENDON, ST. JOSEPH CO., ST. EDWARD (1872) [CEM] Rev. James Vinh Le.
Res.: 332 W. State, P.O. Box 368, 49072. Tel: 269-496-3525; Fax: 269-496-8640. Email: stedwardchurch@msn.com.
Catechesis/Religious Program—Students 46.

NEW BUFFALO, BERRIEN CO., ST. MARY OF THE LAKE (1857) Rev. Craig Lusk.
Res.: 718 W. Buffalo St., 49117. Tel: 269-469-2637; Fax: 269-469-7393. Email: sml-parish@comcast.net.
School—704 W. Merchant St., 49117. Tel: 269-469-1515; Fax: 269-469-3772. Lay Teachers 8; Students 83.
Catechesis/Religious Program—Students 29.

NILES, BERRIEN CO.

1—ST. MARK (1955) Rev. Thomas King, C.S.C.
Res.: 3 N. 19th St., 49120-2117. Email: stmark319@yahoo.com.
Catechesis/Religious Program—Students 24.

2—ST. MARY OF THE IMM. CONCEPTION CHURCH (1870) [CEM 2] Rev. David C. Otto; Deacon Roger Gregorski.
Res.: 211 S. Lincoln Ave., 49120. Tel: 269-683-5087, Ext. 12.
Church: 203 S. Lincoln Ave., 49120.
Parish Center—219 S. State St., 49120. Tel: 269-683-5087; Fax: 269-683-5089.
School—(Grades PreK-5), 217 S. Lincoln Ave., 49120. Tel: 269-683-9191; Fax: 269-683-8118. Lay Teachers 6; Students 99.
Catechesis/Religious Program—Email: stmaryniles@sbcglobal.net. Students 71.

OTSEGO, ALLEGAN CO., ST. MARGARET (1887) [CEM] Rev. Gordon L. Greene.
Res.: 766 S. Farmer St., 49078. Tel: 269-694-9369 (Rectory); 269-694-6311 (Church); Fax: 269-694-5415. Email: st.msec@yahoo.com. Web: www.stmargaret-otsego.org.
School—736 S. Farmer, 49078. Tel: 269-694-2951; Fax: 269-694-4520. Email: ftsander@sbcglobal.net. Lay Teachers 6; Students 65.
Catechesis/Religious Program—Tel: 269-694-6311, Ext. 264. Email: reen@bedl.net. Students 61.

PARCHMENT, KALAMAZOO CO., ST. AMBROSE (1955) Rev. James S. O'Leary.
Res.: 1628 E. G Ave., 49004. Tel: 269-385-4152; Fax: 269-385-2527. Email: ambroseparchment@sbcglobal.net.
Catechesis/Religious Program—Tel: 269-343-0099. Email: ambrosedre@sbcglobal.net. Students 98.

PAW PAW, VAN BUREN CO., ST. MARY (1887) [CEM] Rev. Joseph Xavier, M.S.F.S.
Mailing Address: 500 Paw Paw St., 49079.
Res.: 214 S. Brown St., 49079. Tel: 269-657-4459; Fax: 269-657-4260. Email: stmarypawpawoffice@frontier.com. Web: home.catholicweb.com/stmarypawpaw.
School—508 Paw Paw St., 49079. Tel: 269-657-3750. Email: stmarypp@i2k.com. Lay Teachers 7; Students 130.
Catechesis/Religious Program—Students 136.
Mission—St. Jude's Church 13809 N. M-40, Gobles, Van Buren Co. 49055. Tel: 269-628-2219; Fax: 269-628-7479. Email: stjudeparish@verizon.net.

PEARL, ALLEGAN CO., SAN FELIPE DE JESUS (1986), (Hispanic), Rev. Fabio H. Garzon; Mr. Joseph Marble, Parish Coord.; Deacon Maximino Rodriguez.
Mailing Address: P.O. Box 588, Fennville, 49408. Tel: 269-561-5029; Fax: 269-561-2192.
Res.: 63559 60th Ave., Hartford, 49057. Tel: 269-621-4106; Fax: 269-621-2138.
Catechesis/Religious Program—Students 57.

PORTAGE, KALAMAZOO CO., ST. CATHERINE OF SIENA (1966) Revs. Robert F. Creagan; James Adams, Parochial Vicar; Angela Garcia, Admin.; Judy Bruzza, Sec.
Res.: 1150 W. Centre St., 49024-5385. Tel: 269-327-5165; Fax: 269-327-7266. Email: info@stcatherinesiena.org. Web: www.stcatherinesiena.org.
Catechesis/Religious Program—Tel: 269-327-0861. Paula Mathieu, D.R.E. Students 661.

ST. JOSEPH, BERRIEN CO., ST. JOSEPH (1720) [CEM] Revs. James Morris; Alphonse Savarimuthu (India); Deacon Michael Gallagher.
Res.: 211 Church St., 49085. Tel: 269-983-1575; Fax: 269-983-7798. Email: sjcath1@att.net. Web: www.stjoestjoe.com.
Catechesis/Religious Program—220 Church St., 49085. Tel: 269-983-1575, Ext. 10 (Rel. Educ. & Sacramental Prep.). Email: religioued2@att.net. Students 351.

SILVER CREEK, CASS CO., SACRED HEART OF MARY (1838), (Native American), [CEM] Deacon Frank Wesolowski, Parish Coord.
Res.: 51841 Leach Rd., Dowagiac, 49047. Tel: 269-782-5740; Fax: 269-782-5692. Email: shm@12k.com.
Catechesis/Religious Program—Tel: 269-782-8048. Students 54.

SOUTH HAVEN, VAN BUREN CO., ST. BASIL (1900) [CEM] Rev. Robert E. Flickinger.
Res.: 634 Kentucky Ave., 49090.
Rectory—513 Monroe Blvd., 49090. Tel: 269-637-2404; Fax: 269-637-8374. Email: info@saintbasilcatholicchurch.org.
School—94 Superior St., 49090. Tel: 269-637-3529; Fax: 269-639-1242. Lay Teachers 6; Students 65.
Catechesis/Religious Program—Students 85.

STURGIS, ST. JOSEPH CO., HOLY ANGELS (1879) Very Rev. German Perez-Diaz.
Res.: 402 S. Nottawa St., 49091. Tel: 269-651-5200; Fax: 269-659-8366.
Mission—St. Joseph P.O. Box 344, White Pigeon, St. Joseph Co. 49099. Tel: 269-483-7621; Fax: 269-483-7891.
Catechesis/Religious Program—Students 146.

THREE OAKS, BERRIEN CO., ST. MARY OF THE ASSUMPTION (1880) Rev. Donald Suberlak, C.R.
Res.: 28 W. Ash St., 49128. Tel: 269-756-2041; Fax: 269-756-2212.
Catechesis/Religious Program—Students 31.
Mission—St. Agnes Sawyer, Berrien Co.

THREE RIVERS, ST. JOSEPH CO., IMMACULATE CONCEPTION (1885) Rev. Robert J. Johansen.
Res.: 645 S. Douglas Ave., 49093. Tel: 269-273-8953; Fax: 269-273-2114. Email: iccatholicchurch@catholicweb.com.
School—601 S. Douglas Ave., 49093-2044. Tel: 269-273-2085. Lay Teachers 2; Pre-School Aide 1; Students 15.
Catechesis/Religious Program—Tel: 269-273-8953; Fax: 269-273-2114. Deacon Rick Demars, D.R.E. Students 107.
Mission—St. Clare 229 N. Dean, Centreville, St. Joseph Co. 49032. Tel: 269-273-8953.

VICKSBURG, KALAMAZOO CO., ST. MARTIN OF TOURS (1951) Rev. Christopher Ankley.
Res.: 5855 E. W Ave., P.O. Box 264, 49097-0264. Tel: 269-649-1629; Fax: 269-649-0199. Web: www.stmartinvicksburg.org.
Catechesis/Religious Program—Tel: 269-649-3626. Email: stmartinreleducatn@sbcglobal.net. Students 109.

WATERVLIET, BERRIEN CO., ST. JOSEPH (1896) [CEM] Rev. John Peter Ambrose, M.S.F.S. (India).
Mailing Address: 157 Lucinda Ln., 49098.
Res.: 179 Lucinda Ln., 49098. Tel: 269-463-5470; Fax: 269-463-4642. Email: church@sjcatholic.net. Web: www.sjcatholic.net.
School—Tel: 269-463-3941; Fax: 269-463-4525. Lay Teachers 5; Students 51.
Catechesis/Religious Program—Tel: 269-463-5470, Ext. 101. Students 60.

WAYLAND, ALLEGAN CO.

1—SS. CYRIL AND METHODIUS (1917) [CEM] Very Rev. Christian R. Johnston.
Church: 159 131st Ave., 49348. Tel: 269-792-3543; Fax: 269-792-9062. Email: sscm@triton.net. Web: sscmcc.triton.net.
Catechesis/Religious Program—Students 76.

2—ST. THERESE OF LISIEUX (1942) Very Rev. Christian R. Johnston.
Res.: 128 Cedar St., 49348. Tel: 269-792-2138; 269-792-9315; Fax: 269-792-2908. Web: www.stthiresewayland.org.
School—430 S. Main St., 49348. Tel: 269-792-2016; Fax: 269-792-6778. Email: sttoffice@sbcglobal.net. Web: www.sttschool.com. Lay Teachers 6; Students 72.
Catechesis/Religious Program—Tel: 269-792-2016, Ext. 27. Email: bg14all-dre@yahoo.com. Web: www-.stl.catholicweb.com. Students 80.

WHITE PIGEON, ST. JOSEPH CO., ST. JOSEPH (1832) [CEM] Very Rev. German Perez-Diaz.
Office: 702 E. Chicago Rd., P.O. Box 344, 49099-0344. Tel: 269-483-7621; Fax: 269-483-7891. Email: saintjoewp@comcast.net.
Res.: 402 S. Nottawa St., Sturgis, 49091. Tel: 269-651-5200.

Catechesis/Religious Program—Tel: 269-483-7622. Students 33.

Chaplains of Public Institutions

COLDWATER. *Florence Crane Correctional Facility for Women*. Rev. Daniel E. Doctor, O.D., Volunteer Chap.

Lakeland Correctional Facility for Men. Rev. Daniel E. Doctor, O.D., Volunteer Chap.

Special Assignment:
Rev. Msgr.—
Osborn, Michael A., Faculty, Pontifical College Josephinum

Military Chaplains:
Rev.—
Stanley, Brian L., U.S. Army

Retired:
Rev. Msgrs.—
Bogdan, Leonard A., P.O. Box 5753, Sun City Center, AZ 85376-5753.
Fitzgerald, William, 602 South St., 49007.
Sears, Eugene A., 302 Anchor's Way, Saint Joseph, 49085.
Revs.—
Barrett, James L., 16495 F Dr., Marshall, 49068.
Barth, Raymond J., P.O. Box 186, Baroda, 49101.
Consani, Robert E., 1604 Laughton Pl., Sun City Center, FL 33573.
Grathwohl, John M., Amber Place, 600 Golden Dr., 49001.
Howell, Michael J., 304 Whitcomb, 49001.
Klingler, Donald P., 6309 Overdale Manor, 49009.
Pohl, Leon H., Drew Place, 300 E. Washington Rm. 16, 49036.
Russell, Alfred J., 2615 Sanford Ave, Hillsdale, 49242.
Taubitz, Leo A., 125 Genesee Ave., Gaines, 48436.
Thachet, Joseph, St. Joseph Home, Kenala 686008 India.
Valls, Richard, 10552 Rancho Carmel, San Diego, CA 92128.
Weller, Joseph W., Meadows at Worcester, 463 Founders Village, Lansdale, PA 19446-5869.
Wieber, Donald A., P.O. Box 360, Coloma, 49038.
Young, John, 15485 Blue Star Hwy., South Haven, 49090.

Permanent Deacons:
Barbosa, Juan, Diocese of Brownsville, TX
Bartholomew, David, St. Augustine Cathedral, Kalamazoo
Bell, Alfred, St. Catherine of Sienna, Portage
Bodway, John, St. Jude Mission, Gobles
Bohan, Hal, St. Philip, Battle Creek
Connelly, Bart, Immaculate Conception, Three Rivers
DeMars, Richard, Immaculate Conception, Three Rivers
Gallagher, Michael, St. Joseph, St. Joseph
Gregorski, Roger, St. Mary, Niles
Guido, David, St. Martin of Tours, Vicksburg; St. Edwards, Mendon
Haas, Eugene, St. Rose of Lima, Hastings; St. Margarets, Ostego
Hall, Patrick, St. Thomas More, Kalamazoo
Hermann, Dean, Archdiocese of Chicago, IL
Herrera, Manuel, Diocese of Grand Rapids, MI
Kasuboski, Lawrence M., Holy Angels, Sturgis
Lavelline, James, St. Mary of the Assumption, Bronson
Lohstorfer, John, St. Augustine Cathedral, Kalamazoo; St. Basil, South Haven
Lucas, Kurt, St. Monica, Kalamazoo
Mellen, James, St. Rose of Lima, Hastings
Middleton, Allan, Diocese of Grand Rapids, MI
Mileski, Bernie, St. Philip, Battle Creek
Moreno, Michael, St. Joseph, Battle Creek
Morsaw, Arthur, Immaculate Conception, Hartford
Nelson, James, St. Joseph, Battle Creek
Nethercott, Anthony, St. Peter, Douglas
Patrick, Albert, St. Philip, Battle Creek
Prendergast, Jack, St. Catherine of Sienna, Portage
Radford, Alfred, St. Joseph, Battle Creek
Rauner, James, Immaculate Conception, Hartford
Rodriguez, Maximino, (Retired)
Schmitt, Joe, M.A., St. Thomas More, Kalamazoo
Smoker, Gerald, St. Mary of the Assumption, Bronson
Stevens, Robert, St. Monica, Kalamazoo
Thamann, Thomas, St. Martin of Tours, Vicksburg
Van Dril, William, (Retired)
Vogel, Richard, Holy Maternity of Mary, Dowagiac
Wesolowski, Frank, Sacred Heart Mission, Dowagiac
Whitehouse, Howard, (Retired)
Wright, Gary, (Retired), St. Jerome, Battle Creek

INSTITUTIONS LOCATED IN THE DIOCESE

[A] HIGH SCHOOLS, DIOCESAN

KALAMAZOO. *Msgr. Hackett Catholic Central High School* (1964) 1000 W. Kilgore Rd., 49008. Tel: 269-381-2646; Fax: 269-381-3919. Email: hackett@hackettcc.org. Web: www.hackettcc.org. Rev. James Richardson, M.A., Chap.; Mr. Tim Eastman, Prin.; Terri Luzenske, Librarian. Priests 1; Lay Teachers 23; Students 318.

BATTLE CREEK. *St. Philip Catholic Central High School*, 20 Cherry St., 49017. Tel: 269-963-4503; Fax: 269-965-5590. Donald Shafer, Prin. Teachers 14; Total Staff 20; Students 140.

ST. JOSEPH. *Lake Michigan Catholic Middle and High School*, (Grades 6-12), 915 Pleasant St., 49085. Tel: 269-983-2511; Fax: 269-983-0883. Email: jberlin@lmclakers.org. Web: www.lmclakers.org. John Berlin, Exec. Dir. & Prin. Adrian Dominican Sisters of Immaculate Conception Province 1; Sisters of St. Casimir 1; Lay Teachers 21; Students 271.

[B] GRADE SCHOOLS, INTERPAROCHIAL

ST. JOSEPH. *Lake Michigan Catholic Schools*, (Grades PreK-5), 3165 Washington Ave., 49085. Tel: 269-429-0227; Fax: 269-429-1461. Email: jmaher@lmclakers.org. Web: lmclakers.org. Mrs. Jody G. Maher, Prin.; Janice Mathews, Librarian. Lay Teachers 17; Students 270.

[C] CATHOLIC SOCIAL AGENCIES

KALAMAZOO. *Catholic Family Services*, 1819 Gull Rd., 49048. Tel: 269-381-9800; Fax: 269-381-2932. Email: frandenny@catholicfamilyservices.org. Web: www.catholicfamilyservices.org. Mrs. Frances H. Denny, M.B.A., M.S.W., Exec. Dir.

[D] GENERAL HOSPITALS

KALAMAZOO. *Borgess Medical Center*, 1521 Gull Rd., 49048-1640. Tel: 269-226-7000; Fax: 269-226-7396. Paul Spaude, Pres. & CEO. Bed Capacity 465; Total Staff 1,999; Patients Assisted Annually (Inpatient Discharges plus Outpatient Visits) 483,852.

DOWAGIAC. *Lee Memorial Hospital*, 420 W. High St., 49047. Tel: 269-782-8681; Fax: 269-783-3044. Web: www.borgesslee.com. Joy A. Strand, Admin./COO. Bed Capacity 25; Total Staff 225; Patients Assisted Annually 108,975.

[E] RESIDENCES OF PRIESTS AND BROTHERS

DOUGLAS. *Order of St. Augustine* (Chicago Prov.), 100 St. Peter Dr., Box 248, 49406-0248. Tel: 269-857-7951 (Parish); Fax: 269-857-8164. Rev. W. Timothy Cuny, O.S.A. In Res. Revs. John F. Flynn, O.S.A. (Retired); James J. Sheridan, O.S.A. (Retired).

[F] HOMES FOR SENIOR CITIZENS

KALAMAZOO. *Borgess Gardens*, 3057 Gull Rd., 49048. Tel: 269-552-6500; Fax: 269-552-6510. Email: bethann.brehm@borgess.com. Web: www.borgess.com. Beth Ann Brehm, Admin. Bed Capacity 101; Total Assisted 414; Total Staff 150.

Dillon Complex for Independent Living, Inc. Nonprofit housing corporation, *Dillon Hall*, 3301 Gull Rd., P.O. Box 308, 49048. Tel: 269-342-0263; Fax: 269-342-1814. Email: lwillcutt@pp-mi.com. Sr. Theresa MacIntyre, C.S.J., Sec. & C.S.J. Ministries Liaison. Sponsored by the Congregation of the Sisters of St. Joseph. Total in Residence 72; Total Staff 5; Apartments 72.

OTSEGO. *Otsego Senior Apts., Inc.*, Baraga Manor, 301 Washington St., 49078. Tel: 269-694-9711; Fax: 269-694-5857. Email: dianelooman@catholicfamilyservices.org. Web: catholicfamilyservices.org. Managed by Catholic Family Services, Diocese of Kalamazoo. Rental Units 48; Total Staff 5; Total Assisted Annually 60.

1819 Gull Rd., 49048. Apartments 48.

[G] CONVENTS AND RESIDENCES FOR SISTERS

NAZARETH. *Congregation of the Sisters of St. Joseph* (1889) 49074. Tel: 269-381-6290; Fax: 269-381-4909. Web: www.csjoseph.org. Sr. Mary Joan Walsh, C.S.J., Admin. Ministry in the field of Education; Social Services; Parish and Church-related Ministries; Healthcare, Spirituality Sisters in Community 203.

[H] NEWMAN CENTERS

KALAMAZOO. *Western Michigan University, Kalamazoo College, Kalamazoo Valley Community College* St. Thomas More Catholic Student Parish, 421 Monroe St., 49006. Tel: 269-381-8917; Fax: 269-381-0195. Email: sttoms@sttomskazoo.org. Web: www.sttomskazoo.org. Rev. Kenneth W. Schmidt, J.C.D., M.A., L.P.C.; Sisters Sue McCrery, C.S.J., M.A., D.Min., Pastoral Assoc.; Pam Owens, C.S.J., M.A., D.Min., M.S., Pastoral Assoc.; Deacons Patrick Hall, Pastoral Assoc.; Joe Schmitt, M.A., Pastoral Assoc. Davenport University, Kalamazoo Center for Medical Studies.

[I] MISCELLANEOUS LISTINGS

KALAMAZOO. *Borgess Health* (1889) 1521 Gull Rd., 49048. Tel: 269-226-4800; Fax: 269-226-7396. Web: www.borgess.com. Paul Spaude, Pres. & CEO; Daniel E. Stewart, M.D., Chm. Bd.; Joni Knapper, Sec.; Susan Pozo, Ph.D., Bd. Treas.; James Devlin, Bd. Vice Chair. Borgess Health Care is a Health Care System sponsored by Ascension Health which operates Borgess Ambulatory Care, Inc., Borgess Foundation, Borgess Medical Center, Borgess Nursing Home, Borgess-Pipp Hospital, Borgess-Lee Memorial Hospital, ProMed Healthcare, Borgess Visiting Nurse Services, Borgess Home Care, Borgess Hospice, Textile Systems, Inc. and other related companies. Incorporated in the State of Michigan. Bed Capacity 487; Inpatients 21,015; Outpatients 483,100; Personnel 4,300.

Catholic Schools of Greater Kalamazoo, 1000 W. Kilgore Rd., 49008. Tel: 269-381-2646; Fax: 269-381-3919.

Diocesan Council of St. Vincent dePaul, 513 Eleanor St., 49007. Tel: 269-388-4544; Fax: 269-388-4511. Email: MFC7@home.com. James Heffernen, Pres. Total Assisted 150.

Kalamazoo Regional Catholic Schools Foundation, 1000 W. Kilgore Rd., 49008. Tel: 269-381-2646; Fax: 269-381-3919. Email: sharding@csgk.org. Web: hackettcc.org.

The Cathlic Foundation of Southwestern Michigan, 215 N. Westnedge Ave., 49007. Mr. Michael Emmons, Contact Person.

BATTLE CREEK. *BCACS Foundation, Inc.* (Battle Creek Area Catholic Schools Foundation, Inc.), 63 N. 24th St., 49015. Tel: 269-963-4771; Fax: 269-963-3917. Email: kgallagher@bcacs.org.

HASTINGS. *St. Rose Lima Trust Fund*, 805 S. Jefferson St., 49058. Tel: 269-945-4246; Fax: 269-945-0005.

ST. JOSEPH. *Twin-City Area Catholic School Fund, Inc.* (1971) P.O. Box 32, 49085. Tel: 269-861-3108; Fax: 269-983-5520. Email: tcacsf@comcast.net. Paul Landeck, Pres.

SOUTH HAVEN. *St. Basil Educational Endowment Fund*, 94 Superior St., 49090. Tel: 269-637-3529; Fax: 269-639-1242. Email: principal@saintbasilcatholic.org. Web: www.saintbasilcatholic.org.

STURGIS. **Holy Angels School Foundation, Inc.*, P.O. Box 24, 49091-0024. Tel: 616-467-8114.

Secular Franciscan Order, 25580 Waneta Way, 49091. Tel: 269-467-8114. Mr. James Goethals, Pres.

RELIGIOUS INSTITUTES OF MEN REPRESENTED IN THE DIOCESE

For further details refer to the corresponding bracketed number in the Religious Institutes of Men or Women section.

[0140]—*The Augustinians*—O.S.A.

[1330]—*Congregation of the Mission*—C.M.

[1080]—*Congregation of the Resurrection*—C.R.

[]—*Missionaries of St. Frances de Sales*—M.S.F.S.

[0920]—*Oblates of St. Francis deSales* (Toledo-Detroit Prov.)—O.S.F.S.

[0610]—*Priests of the Congregation of the Holy Cross* (Indiana Prov.)—C.S.C.

[]—*Society of Jesus*—S.J.

RELIGIOUS INSTITUTES OF WOMEN REPRESENTED IN THE DIOCESE

[3832]—*Congregation of the Sisters of St. Joseph*—C.S.J.

[1920]—*Congregation of the Sisters of the Holy Cross*—C.S.C.

[1070-05]—*Dominican Sisters*—O.P.

[1070-13]—*Dominican Sisters*—O.P.

[1070-14]—*Dominican Sisters*—O.P.

[2575]—*Sisters of Mercy of the Americas*—R.S.M.

[3930]—*Sisters of St. Joseph of the Third Order of St. Francis*—S.S.J.-T.O.S.F.

[3260]—*Sisters of the Precious Blood* (Dayton, OH)—C.PP.S.

[2150]—*Sisters, Servants of the Immaculate Heart of Mary* (Monroe, MI)—I.H.M.

NECROLOGY

✠ Donovan, Most Rev. Paul V., Retired Bishop of Kalamazoo.—Died April 28, 2011

† Adams, David C., (Retired)—Died Oct. 13, 2011

An asterisk (*) denotes an organization that has established tax-exempt status directly with the IRS and is not covered by the USCCB Group Ruling.

Archdiocese of Kansas City in Kansas

(Archidioecesis Kansanopolitana in Kansas)

Most Reverend

JOSEPH F. NAUMANN

Archbishop of Kansas City in Kansas; ordained May 24, 1975; appointed Titular Bishop of Caput Cilla and Auxiliary Bishop of St. Louis July 9, 1997; consecrated September 3, 1997; appointed Coadjutor Archbishop of Kansas City in Kansas January 7, 2004; installed March 19, 2004; succeeded to See January 15, 2005.

Most Reverend

JAMES P. KELEHER, S.T.D.

Archbishop Emeritus of Kansas City in Kansas; ordained April 12, 1958; appointed Bishop of Belleville October 23, 1984; consecrated December 11, 1984; appointed Archbishop of Kansas City in Kansas June 28, 1993; installed September 8, 1993; retired January 15, 2005.

Catholic Chancery Offices: 12615 Parallel Pkwy., Kansas City, KS 66109. Tel: 913-721-1570; Fax: 913-721-1577.

Web: www.archkck.org

Email: archkck@archkck.org

Square Miles 12,524.

Established Vicariate Apostolic July 19, 1850. Diocese of Leavenworth established May 22, 1877. See changed to Kansas City in Kansas May 10, 1947; created Archdiocese August 9, 1952.

Comprises the following 21 Counties of Kansas: Anderson, Atchison, Brown, Coffey, Doniphan, Douglas, Franklin, Jackson, Jefferson, Johnson, Leavenworth, Linn, Lyon, Marshall, Miami, Nemaha, Osage, Pottawatomie, Shawnee, Wabaunsee and Wyandotte.

Patrons of the Diocese: I. Blessed Virgin Mary (Immaculate Conception); II. St. John Baptist Vianney.

For legal titles of institutions, please contact the Catholic Chancery Offices.

STATISTICAL OVERVIEW

Personnel	
Archbishops	1
Retired Archbishops	1
Abbots	1
Retired Abbots	2
Priests: Diocesan Active in Diocese	74
Priests: Diocesan Active Outside Diocese	5
Priests: Diocesan in Foreign Missions	1
Priests: Retired, Sick or Absent	26
Number of Diocesan Priests	106
Religious Priests in Diocese	52
Total Priests in Diocese	158
Extern Priests in Diocese	19
Ordinations:	
Diocesan Priests	7
Religious Priests	1
Transitional Deacons	2
Permanent Deacons	17
Permanent Deacons in Diocese	22
Total Brothers	12
Total Sisters	496
Parishes	
Parishes	108
With Resident Pastor:	
Resident Diocesan Priests	60
Resident Religious Priests	10
Without Resident Pastor:	
Administered by Priests	38
Closed Parishes	2
Professional Ministry Personnel:	
Brothers	1
Sisters	15
Lay Ministers	84
Welfare	
Catholic Hospitals	3
Total Assisted	678,671
Health Care Centers	4
Total Assisted	7,968
Homes for the Aged	3
Total Assisted	690
Day Care Centers	2
Total Assisted	94
Special Centers for Social Services	6
Total Assisted	85,000
Residential Care of Disabled	19
Total Assisted	21
Other Institutions	6
Total Assisted	23
Educational	
Diocesan Students in Other Seminaries	27
Students Religious	1
Total Seminarians	28
Colleges and Universities	3
Total Students	4,799
High Schools, Diocesan and Parish	6
Total Students	3,362
High Schools, Private	1
Total Students	184
Elementary Schools, Diocesan and Parish	38
Total Students	11,790
Elementary Schools, Private	3
Total Students	160
Catechesis/Religious Education:	
High School Students	2,686
Elementary Students	12,514
Total Students under Catholic Instruction	35,523
Teachers in the Diocese:	
Sisters	14
Lay Teachers	1,124
Vital Statistics	
Receptions into the Church:	
Infant Baptism Totals	3,295
Minor Baptism Totals	268
Adult Baptism Totals	273
Received into Full Communion	460
First Communions	3,830
Confirmations	3,674
Marriages:	
Catholic	640
Interfaith	280
Total Marriages	920
Deaths	1,350
Total Catholic Population	205,531
Total Population	1,193,425

Predecessors—Most Revs. J. B. MIEGE, S.J., cons. Bishop of Messenia, Vicar-Apostolic, March 25, 1851; resignation accepted by Pope Pius IX Nov. 8, 1874; died July 21, 1884; LOUIS M. FINK, O.S.B., D.D., cons. Bishop of Eucarpia June 11, 1871; appt. first Bishop of Leavenworth May 22, 1877; died March 17, 1904; THOMAS F. LILLIS, O.D., cons. Bishop of Leavenworth, Dec. 27, 1904; appt. Coadjutor Bishop of Kansas City, with right of succession March 14, 1910; succeeded to the See of Kansas City, Feb. 21, 1913; JOHN WARD, D.D., ord. July 17, 1884; appt. Bishop of Leavenworth Nov. 25, 1910; cons. Feb. 22, 1911; died April 20, 1929; FRANCIS JOHANNES, D.D., LL.D., cons. May 1, 1928; succeeded to the See, April 20, 1929; died March 13, 1937; PAUL C. SCHULTE, D.D., ord. June 11, 1915; appt. Bishop of Leavenworth May 29, 1937; cons. Sept. 21, 1937; appt. Archbishop of Indianapolis July 20, 1946; installed Oct. 10, 1946; GEORGE J. DONNELLY, S.T.D., ord. June 12, 1921; appt. Titular Bishop of Coela and Auxiliary of St. Louis March 19, 1940; cons. April 23, 1940; appt. Bishop of Leavenworth Nov. 9, 1946; died Dec. 13, 1950; EDWARD J. HUNKELER, D.D., ord. June 14, 1919; appt. Bishop of Grand Island March 10, 1945; cons. May 1, 1945; transferred to Kansas City March 28, 1951; elevated to Archiepiscopal dignity Aug. 9, 1952; retired Sept. 10, 1969; died Oct. 1, 1970; IGNATIUS J. STRECKER, D.D., S.T.D., ord. Dec. 19, 1942; appt. Bishop of Springfield-Cape Girardeau April 7, 1962; cons. June 20, 1962; transferred to Kansas City Sept. 10, 1969; retired Sept. 8, 1993; died Oct. 16, 2003; JAMES P. KELEHER, S.T.D., ord. April 12, 1958; appt. Bishop of Belleville Oct. 23, 1984; cons. Dec. 11, 1984; appt. Archbishop of Kansas City in Kansas June 28, 1993; installed Sept. 8, 1993; retired Jan. 15, 2005.

Catholic Chancery Offices—12615 Parallel Pkwy., Kansas City, 66109. Tel: 913-721-1570; Fax: 913-721-1577. Office Hours: 8:30-5.

Vicars General—Revs. GARY PENNINGS, V.G.; BRIAN SCHIEBER.

Chancellor—Rev. JOHN A. RILEY.

Metropolitan Tribunal—12615 Parallel Pkwy., Kansas City, 66109. Tel: 913-721-1570; Fax: 913-721-1577.

Judicial Vicar—Rev. Msgr. GARY APPLEGATE, J.C.L.

Judges—Rev. GEORGE BERTELS, J.C.L. (Retired); Rev. Msgr. GARY APPLEGATE, J.C.L.; Revs. DENIS MEADE, O.S.B., J.C.D.; JOSEPH ARSENAULT, S.S.A., J.C.L.; BRUCE ANSEMS, J.C.L.

Defenders of the Bond—Rev. Msgr. RAYMOND BURGER (Retired); Rev. BRUCE ANSEMS, J.C.L.

Advocates— Selected Priests & Selected Lay Advocates

Notary—LUCIA DAVIS.

Archdiocesan Consultors—Rev. Msgr. THOMAS TANK; Rev. GARY PENNINGS, V.G.; Rt. Rev. BARNABAS SENECAL, O.S.B.; Rev. BRIAN SCHIEBER; Rev. Msgrs. MICHAEL MULLEN; CHARLES MCGLINN; Revs. WILLIAM PORTER; MICHAEL KOLLER; JOHN A. RILEY; Rev. Msgr. GARY APPLEGATE, J.C.L.; Rev.

FRANK BURGER.

Archdiocesan Council on Finances—Rev. JOHN A. RILEY, Chancellor; Mr. L. JOSEPH BAUMAN; Mr. FRANK J. BECKER; Mr. GARY DAVIS; Mr. MICHAEL EASTERDAY; Mr. FRED FOSNACHT; Mr. JERRY MAYNE; Mr. JAMES HEINTZ; Mr. JOHN GILLCRIST; Mr. KEVIN KELLY; Mr. L. TRAVIS HICKS; Mr. MEL LAVERY; Ms. KATHLEEN LUSK; Mr. MAL ROBINSON; Revs. RICHARD HALVORSON; GARY PENNINGS, V.G.; Mrs. LESLE KNOP; Ms. JEANNE GORMAN; Mr. JOHN SEITZER; Mr. LARRY STRECKER; Mr. GEORGE REBECK; Ms. THERESA GORDIZICA; Ms. STACEY HOFFMAN; Mr. MICHAEL SCHEOPNER.

Archdiocesan Finance Officer—Mr. JERRY MAYNE.

Regional Pastoral Leaders—Revs. GERARD SENECAL, O.S.B., Atchison; RICHARD STOREY, Johnson Co.; PATRIC RILEY, Lawrence; PHILLIP J. WINKELBAUER, Leavenworth; GERALD VOLZ, Topeka; ANTHONY C. WILLIAMS, Southern; JAMES SHAUGHNESSY, Nemaha-Marshall; HAROLD F. SCHNEIDER, Wyandotte Co.

Archdiocesan Pastoral Council—Most Rev. JOSEPH NAUMANN; MARGARET BLEVINS; DARYL CURRIE; Sr. MARY RACHEL FLYNN; JEFF FOLEY; LAURA FORTMEYER; GERALD FRIETCHEN; JEAN HINMAN; JERRY JEWELL; MARK JIRAK; KATE JIRON; Deacon GEORGE KARNAZE; ALAN CONROY; Rev. KEITH LUNSFORD; Sr. ELENA MORCELLI; DENISE OGILVIE; CARMEN OREGEL; MARY ELLEN REESE; MIGUEL SANCHEZ; CAROL SHOMIN; SCOTT WAGNER; JANE SHRIVER; SHARON WILLIAMS. Ex Officio: Revs. GARY PENNINGS, V.G., Vicar Gen.; JOHN RILEY, Chancellor; Ms. ROSE HAMMES, Dir. Communications & Planning.

Archdiocesan Administrative Team—Mrs. LESLE KNOP; Rev. JOHN RILEY; Dr. KATHLEEN O'HARA; Mr. JERRY MAYNE; Rev. BRIAN SCHIEBER; Mrs. JAN LEWIS; Ms. ROSE HAMMES; Rev. GARY PENNINGS, V.G.

Catholic Foundation of Northeast Kansas—12615 Parallel Pkwy., Kansas City, 66109.

Catholic Education Foundation—12615 Parallel Pkwy., Kansas City, 66109.

Archdiocesan Archivist— (contact Chancellor's Office).

Archdiocesan Offices and Directors

Savior Pastoral Center—12601 Parallel, Kansas City, 66109. Tel: 913-721-1097; Fax: 913-721-2339. Web: www.saviorpastoralcenter.org. Email: savior@archkck.org. Mr. TIMOTHY CHIK, Dir.

Black Catholics—BARBARA BAILEY, 2203 Parallel, Kansas City, 66104. Tel: 913-321-1958.

Department of Parish Ministries—Rev. GARY PENNINGS, V.G., Dir., 12615 Parallel Pkwy., Kansas City, 66109. Tel: 913-721-1570.

Evangelization and Catholic Formation of Youth—Mr. DANA NEARMYER, Lead Consultant; Mr. RICK CHEEK, Consultant.

Evangelization & Catholic Formation of Adults—Mr. MATT KARR, Lead Consultant; Ms. KIMBERLY RODE, Consultant.

Prairie Star Ranch—12615 Parallel Pkwy., Kansas City, 66109. Tel: 913-721-1570; Fax: 913-721-2680. Mr. DANA NEARMYER, Dir.

Deaf Ministry—Mrs. PAT RICHEY.

Marriage and Family Life—Deacon TONY ZIMMERMAN, Lead Consultant. Consultants: BRAD DUPONT; LIBBY DUPONT; SAM MEIER (My House - Freedom from Pornography).

Liturgy and Sacramental Life—Mr. MICHAEL PODREBARAC.

Pro-life/Respect Life—Mr. RON KELSEY.

Social Justice—Mr. BILL SCHOLL.

Hispanic Ministry—Revs. PATRICK MURPHY, C.S.; JESUS OLIVARES, C.S., Assoc.

Administrative Services—Mrs. RITA HERKEN.

Human Resources—Ms. KATHLEEN THOMAS.

Stewardship and Development Office—Mrs. LESLE KNOP, Dir., 12615 Parallel Pkwy., Kansas City, 66109. Tel: 913-721-1570.

Catholic Youth Organization—Mr. PETER PISCITELLO, Dir., 5041 Reinhardt Dr., Mission, 66205. Tel: 913-384-7377.

Catholic Charities of Northeast Kansas, Inc.— See Institution section H.

Council for Catholic Charismatic Renewal—Rev. ANTHONY OUELLETTE.

Archdiocesan Council of Catholic Women (ACCW)—Rev. JOSEPH CRAMER, Spiritual Moderator.

Catholic Charities Foundation of Northeast Kansas—See Institution section H.

Catholic Neighborhood Outreach, Inc.— See Institution section H.

Communications and Pastoral Planning—Ms. ROSE HAMMES, Dir., 12615 Parallel Pkwy., Kansas City, 66109. Tel: 913-721-1570.

Catholic Committee on Scouting—Rev. SHAWN TUNINK, Chap.

Holy Childhood Association—Rev. RICHARD HALVORSON, 12615 Parallel Pkwy., Kansas City, 66109. Tel: 913-721-1570.

Kansas Catholic Conference—MICHAEL SCHUTTLOFFEL, Exec. Dir., 204 S.W. 8th Ave., Topeka, 66603. Tel: 785-227-9247. Web: www.kscathconf.org.

Legion of Mary—Rev. BRIAN KLINGELE, Spiritual Moderator, 514 E. 4th St., Garnett, 66032.

Newspaper "The Leaven"—Rev. MARK GOLDASICH, Editor, Mailing Address: 12615 Parallel Pkwy., Kansas City, 66109. Tel: 913-721-1570; Fax: 913-721-5276.

Nurses Association—VACANT, 16 S. Iowa, Kansas City, 66103.

Priests' Council—Rev. WILLIAM PORTER, Chm.

Pontifical Mission Societies in the United States—Rev. RICHARD HALVORSON, 12615 Parallel Pkwy., Kansas City, 66109.

Safe Envrionment Coordinator—Rev. JOHN RILEY.

Schools—Dr. KATHLEEN O'HARA, Supt.; Mrs. ANN CONNOR, Assoc. Supt.; Mrs. KAREN KROH, Asst. Supt. for Special Needs, 12615 Parallel Pkwy., Kansas City, 66109. Tel: 913-721-1570.

Victim Assistance Coordinator—Dr. DENNIS SCHEMMEL, Ph.D. Tel: 913-909-2740.

Vocations Office—Rev. MITCHEL ZIMMERMAN, Dir. Vocations. Co Directors Seminarians: Rev. Msgr. MICHAEL MULLEN; Rev. MITCHEL ZIMMERMAN, 12615 Parallel Pkwy., Kansas City, 66109. Tel: 913-721-1570.

CLERGY, PARISHES, MISSIONS AND PAROCHIAL SCHOOLS

CITY OF KANSAS CITY

(WYANDOTTE COUNTY)

1—CATHEDRAL OF ST. PETER THE APOSTLE (1907) Rev. Harold F. Schneider.
Office & Res.: 409 N. 15th St., 66102. Tel: 913-371-0840 (Business Office); 913-371-2345; Fax: 913-371-2345.
See Resurrection Catholic School at the Cathedral under Elementary Schools, Interparochial in the Institution Section
Catechesis/Religious Program—Students 11.

2—ALL SAINTS (2007) Rev. Daniel Gardner.
Office: 229 S. 8th St., 66101. Tel: 913-371-1837; Fax: 913-621-2709. Email: allsaintsparish@sbcglobal.net.
Res.: 837 Ridge, 66101. Tel: 913-621-3521.
See Resurrection Catholic School at the Cathedral under Elementary Schools, Interparochial in the Institution Section
Catechesis/Religious Program—Angel Delfin, D.R.E. Students 164.

3—BLESSED SACRAMENT (1899) Rev. Mark Mertes.
Res.: 2203 Parallel Ave., 66104. Tel: 913-321-1958; Fax: 913-321-1997.
Catechesis/Religious Program—1416 N. 62nd St., 66102. Tel: 913-299-9344; Fax: 913-321-1997. Miguel Sanchez, C.R.E. Hispanic Ministry. Students 77.

4—CHRIST THE KING Rev. Mark Mertes. In Res., Rev. Roger Schmit, O.S.B.
Res.: 3024 N. 53rd St., 66104. Tel: 913-287-8823; Fax: 913-287-8711.
School—(Grades PreK-8), 3027 N. 54th St., 66104. Tel: 913-287-8883; Fax: 913-287-7409. Web: www.ct-kcatholicschool.org. Cathy Fithian, Prin.; Elizabeth Rebeck, Librarian. Lay Teachers 13; Students 260.
Catechesis/Religious Program—Miguel Sanchez, D.R.E. Students 35.

5—SS. CYRIL AND METHODIUS (1904), (Slovak), Merged with St. Joseph and St. Benedict, Kansas City to form All Saints, Kansas City.

6—HOLY FAMILY, (Slovenian), Rev. Peter Jaramillo, S.S.A.
Res.: 274 Orchard Ave., 66101. Tel: 913-371-1561.
See Resurrection Catholic School at the Cathedral under Elementary Schools, Interparochial in the Institution Section

7—HOLY NAME (1876) Rev. Jeremiah L. Spencer.
Res.: 16 S. Iowa St., 66103. Tel: 913-236-9219; Fax: 913-403-8834. Email: holynamechurchkck@kc.rr.com.
Church: 1001 S.W. Blvd., 66103.
School—(Grades PreSchool-8), 1007 S.W. Blvd., 66103. Tel: 913-722-1032; Fax: 913-722-4175. Email: holyname@archkckcs.org. Web: www.holynamekck.org. Denise Perry, Prin. Lay Teachers 13; Students 163.
Catechesis/Religious Program—Tel: 913-236-9219; Fax: 913-404-8834. Jennifer Starcke, D.R.E. Students 12.

8—ST. JOHN THE BAPTIST, (Croatian), Revs. Peter Jaramillo, S.S.A., Parochial Admin.; Francis Horvat.
Res.: 708 N. Fourth St., 66101. Tel: 913-371-0627; Fax: 913-342-3324.
See Resurrection Catholic School at the Cathedral under Elementary Schools, Interparochial in the Institution Section

9—ST. JOHN THE EVANGELIST, Merged with Sacred Heart, Kansas City to form Our Lady of Unity, Kansas City.

10—ST. JOSEPH AND ST. BENEDICT, Merged with SS. Cyril and Methodius, Kansas City to form All Saints, Kansas City.

11—ST. MARY-ST. ANTHONY (1858) Revs. Peter Jaramillo, S.S.A.; John Melnick, S.S.A.; Joseph Arsenault, S.S.A.
Res.: 615 N. Seventh St., 66101. Tel: 913-371-1408; Fax: 913-371-4177. Email: smsakcks@sbcglobal.net.
Catechesis/Religious Program—Maria Hayte Sandoval, C.R.E. Students 65.

12—OUR LADY AND ST. ROSE, Attended by Blessed Sacrament, Kansas City. Rev. Mark Mertes.
Office: 2203 Parallel, 66101.
Church: 2300 N. Eighth St., 66101.
Catechesis/Religious Program—Tel: 913-321-1958; Fax: 913-321-1997. Franchiel Nyakatura, D.R.E. Students 19.

13—OUR LADY OF UNITY (2007) Revs. Kent O'Connor; Ciro Hernando, Parochial Vicar; Deacon Keith Geary.
2910 Strong Ave., 66106.
Res.: 2910 Strong Ave., 66106. Tel: 913-677-4621; Fax: 913-677-4625. Email: oluparish@gmail.com.
See Our Lady of Unity School, Kansas City under Elementary Schools, Interparochial located in the Institution section.
Catechesis/Religious Program—Tel: 913-262-7022. Estela Amaya, D.R.E. Students 209.

14—ST. PATRICK'S (1873) Rev. Msgr. Michael Mullen. In Res., Rev. Gary Pennings.
Res.: 1086 N. 94th St., 66112. Tel: 913-299-3370; Fax: 913-788-2644.
School—(Grades K-8), 1066 N. 94th, 66112. Tel: 913-299-8131; Fax: 913-299-2845. Kathy Rhodes, Prin.; Emily Yantz, Librarian. Lay Teachers 18; Students 257.
Catechesis/Religious Program—Tel: 913-299-3728. Susan Buck, D.R.E.; Theresa Smith, Dir. Adult Faith Formation. Students 157.

15—SACRED HEART, Merged with St. John the Evangelist, Kansas City to form Our Lady of Unity, Kansas City.

16—ST. THOMAS THE APOSTLE, Closed. For inquiries for parish records contact the chancery.

OUTSIDE THE CITY OF KANSAS CITY

ALMA, WABAUNSEE CO., HOLY FAMILY (1874) [CEM] Attended by St. Bernard, Wamego. Revs. John Pilcher; Lourdu Marreddy Yeruva (India), Parochial Vicar.
Mailing Address: *c/o St. Bernard*, 1006 Eighth, Wamego, 66547.
Church: 1st & Kansas. Tel: 785-456-7869.
Catechesis/Religious Program—Tel: 785-765-2316. Dan Deiter, D.R.E. Students 24.

ATCHISON, ATCHISON CO.

1—ST. BENEDICT'S (1866) [JC] Rev. Gerard Senecal, O.S.B.
Res.: 1001 N. Second St., 66002. Tel: 913-367-0671; Fax: 913-367-0797.
Church: 1000 N. Second St., 66002. Tel: 913-360-8543.
See Atchison Catholic Elementary, Atchison under Elementary Schools, Interparochial located in the Institution section.
Catechesis/Religious Program—Tel: 913-367-3503. Serena Barnhard, D.R.E. Students 75.
Mission—St. John the Baptist Doniphan, Doniphan Co. (Stational Church)

2—ST. JOSEPH (1949) [JC] Rev. Gabriel Landis, O.S.B.
Res.: 705 Spring Garden St., 66002. Tel: 913-367-4271.
See Atchison Catholic Elementary, Atchison under Elementary Schools, Interparochial located in the Institution section.
Catechesis/Religious Program—Consolidated with St. Benedict's, Tel: 913-367-3503; Fax: 913-367-0797.

3—SACRED HEART (1892) [JC] Rev. Gerard Senecal, O.S.B.
Office: 1001 N. 2nd St., 66002. Tel: 913-367-0387; Fax: 913-367-0797.
Church: 1439 Kansas Ave., 66002.
See Atchison Catholic Elementary, Atchison under Elementary Schools, Interparochial located in the Institution section.
Catechesis/Religious Program—Consolidated with St. Benedict's, Atchison.

AXTELL, MARSHALL CO., ST. MICHAEL Rev. Albert Hauser, O.S.B.
Mailing Address: 504 6th St., P.O. Box K, 66403. Tel: 785-736-2220; Fax: 785-736-2230.
School—(Grades 1-6), 605 Elm St., 66403. Tel:

785-736-2257. Todd Leonard, Prin. Lay Teachers 3; Students 29.
Catechesis/Religious Program—Tel: 785-736-2260. Janice Koch, D.R.E. Students 50.

BAILEYVILLE, NEMAHA CO., SACRED HEART (1912) [CEM] Rev. Edward J. Oen, C.PP.S.
Church: 357 Third St., Box 36, 66404. Tel: 785-336-6464.
Catechesis/Religious Program—Tel: 785-336-6415. Alicia Keegan, D.R.E. Students 83.

BALDWIN, DOUGLAS CO., ANNUNCIATION (1857) [CEM] Attended by Mission: St. Francis of Assisi, Lapeer. Rev. Brandon Farrar.
Church Mailing: 740 N. 6th St., 66006. Tel: 785-594-3700.
Catechesis/Religious Program—Ginny Meinen, D.R.E. Students 73.

BASEHOR, LEAVENWORTH CO., HOLY ANGELS (1866) [CEM] Rev. Richard J. McDonald.
Office: 15438 Leavenworth Rd., 66007. Tel: 913-724-1665. Email: holyangelscatholicchurch@hotmail.com.
Res.: 15440 Leavenworth Rd., 66007. Tel: 913-724-3122; Fax: 913-724-4148. Web: www.HolyAngelsBasehor.org.
Catechesis/Religious Program— Cathy Kern, D.R.E. Students 215.

BEATTIE, MARSHALL CO., ST. MALACHY (1880) Attended by St. Gregory, Marysville. Rev. James Shaughnessy.
Church: 1012 Main St., 66406. Tel: 785-353-2280.
Catechesis/Religious Program—Students 3.

BENDENA, DONIPHAN CO., ST. BENEDICT (1855) [CEM] Attended by St. Joseph, Wathena. Rev. Roderic Giller, O.S.B.
Church & Mailing: 676 St. Benedict Rd., P.O. Box 128, 66008. Tel: 785-359-6725; Fax: 785-989-2313.
Catechesis/Religious Program—Tel: 785-359-6725. Amy Joyce, D.R.E. Students 37.

BLAINE, POTTAWATOMIE CO., ST. COLUMBKILLE, Attended by St. Vincent de Paul, Onaga. Rev. Patrick Sullivan.
Mailing Address: *c/o Annunciation*, 213 E. 5th St., Frankfort, 66427.
Church: 66480.
Catechesis/Religious Program—Sally Olson, D.R.E. Students 27.

BLUE RAPIDS, MARSHALL CO., ST. MONICA - ST. ELIZABETH, Attended by Annunciation, Frankfort. Rev. Patrick Sullivan.
Mailing Address: *c/o Annunciation*, 213 E. 5th St., Frankfort, 66427.
Catechesis/Religious Program—Sarah Toerber, D.R.E. Students 34.

BURLINGTON, COFFEY CO., ST. FRANCIS XAVIER (1871) [CEM] Rev. Marianand Mendem.
Res.: 214 Juniatta, 66839. Tel: 620-364-2416; Fax: 620-364-2000.
Catechesis/Religious Program—Tel: 316-364-5220. Catherine Falmon, D.R.E.; Beth Sloyer, D.R.E. Students 84.

CORNING, NEMAHA CO., ST. PATRICK (1890) [CEM] Attended by St. Vincent de Paul, Onaga. Rev. Balachandra Miriyala, Parochial Admin.
Mailing Address: 6606 Atlantic, 66417.
Catechesis/Religious Program—Ann Stallbaumer, D.R.E. Students 126.

DELIA, JACKSON CO., SACRED HEART OF JESUS, Closed. For inquiries for parish records contact Immaculate Conception, St. Marys.

DONIPHAN, DONIPHAN CO., ST. JOHN, Closed. For inquiries for parish records contact St. Benedict's, Atchison.

EASTON, LEAVENWORTH CO.

1—ST. JOSEPH-ST. LAWRENCE (2009) [CEM] Rev. Mathew Francis, Parochial Admin.; Deacon Guy Berry.
Res. & St. Lawrence Church: 211 W. Riley St., P.O. Box 129, 66020. Tel: 913-773-5712; Fax: 913-773-8401. Web: www.sjslparish.org.
St. Joseph of the Valley Church: 31151 207th St., Leavenworth, 66048.
Catechesis/Religious Program—Tel: 913-773-5614. Chuck Schmidt, D.R.E. Students 63.

2—ST. LAWRENCE (1878) [CEM] Consolidated with St. Joseph of the Valley, Leavenworth to form St. Joseph-St. Lawrence, Easton.

EDGERTON, JOHNSON CO., ASSUMPTION (1857) [CEM] Consolidated with Sacred Heart, Gardner to form Divine Mercy, Gardner.

EFFINGHAM, ATCHISON CO., ST. ANN, [CEM] Rev. Benjamin Tremmel, O.S.B.
Res.: 301 Williams St., Box 54, 66023. Tel: 913-833-5660.
Catechesis/Religious Program—Julie Baker, D.R.E. Students 49.

EMERALD, ANDERSON CO., ST. PATRICK, Served by St. Francis Xavier, Burlington. Rev. Marianand Mendem.
Mailing Address: *c/o St. Francis Xavier*, 214 Juniatta, Burlington, 66839.
Church: 66095. Tel: 620-364-2416; Fax: 620-364-2000.
Catechesis/Religious Program—Cindy Rubick, D.R.E. Students 17.

EMMETT, POTTAWATOMIE CO., HOLY CROSS, Consolidated with Immaculate Conception, St. Marys.

EMPORIA, LYON CO.

1—ST. CATHERINE, [CEM] Attended by Didde Catholic Campus Center, Emporia. Rev. Raymond May Jr.
Church: 205 S. Lawrence St., 66801. Tel: 620-342-1368.
Catechesis/Religious Program—Tel: 620-342-1368. Sr. Aurora Villamar, D.R.E. Students 87.

2—SACRED HEART (1874) [CEM] Rev. Richard Warsnak.
Office: 101 Cottonwood St., 66801. Tel: 620-342-1061; Fax: 620-342-0450. Email: parish@sacredheartemporia.org. Web: www.sacredheartemporia.org.
School—(Grades K-6), 102 Cottonwood St., 66801. Tel: 620-343-7394. Email: school@sacredheartemporia.org. Web: www.shsemporia.eduk12.net. Theresa Lein, Prin. Lay Teachers 7; Students 63.
Catechesis/Religious Program—Tel: 620-342-1061. Linda DeDonder, D.R.E. Students 197.

ESKRIDGE, WABAUNSEE CO., ST. JOHN VIANNEY, Closed. For inquiries on parish records, contact Immaculate Conception, St. Marys.

EUDORA, DOUGLAS CO., HOLY FAMILY, [CEM] Rev. Patric Riley.
Res.: 311 E. 9th St., 66025. Tel: 785-542-2788; Fax: 785-542-1908. Email: hfceudora@sunflower.com. Web: www.holyfamilyeudora.com.
Catechesis/Religious Program—Students 255.

FIDELITY, BROWN CO., ST. AUGUSTINE, [CEM] Attended by Sacred Heart, Sabetha. Rev. Greg Hammes.
Church: 1948 Acorn Rd., Sabetha, 66534. Tel: 785-467-3130; Fax: 785-467-3817.
Catechesis/Religious Program—Tel: 785-284-3152. Denise Plattner, D.R.E. Students 26.

FLUSH, POTTAWATOMIE CO., ST. JOSEPH, Attended by St. Bernard, Wamego. Revs. John Pilcher. Tel: 785-456-7869; Lourdu Marreddy Yeruva (India).
Mailing Address: *c/o St. Bernard*, 1006 8th St., Wamego, 66547. Web: www.sbc-sjc.com. In Res., Rev. Carl Dekat (Retired). Tel: 785-494-8234.
Church: 8965 Flush Rd., Saint George, 66535.
Catechesis/Religious Program—Tel: 785-456-2431. Students 45.

FORT LEAVENWORTH, LEAVENWORTH CO., ST. IGNATIUS Rev. Lee Yoakam, Military Services Army Chap. (LTC).
Mailing Address: 500 Pope Ave., 66027. Tel: 913-684-8991; Fax: 913-684-8994.
Catechesis/Religious Program—Dorothy Ling, D.R.E. Students 365.

FRANKFORT, MARSHALL CO., ANNUNCIATION (1880) [CEM] Rev. Patrick Sullivan.
Office: Tel: 785-292-4462; Fax: 785-292-5095.
Res.: 213 E. Fifth St., 66427. Tel: 785-292-4170; Fax: 785-292-5095.
Catechesis/Religious Program—Tel: 785-292-4462. Linda Roeder, D.R.E.; Jan Stallbaumer, D.R.E. (Elementary). Students 64.

GARDNER, JOHNSON CO., DIVINE MERCY, [CEM], Sacred Heart, Gardner consolidated with Assumption, Edgerton to form Divine Mercy, Gardner. Rev. Joseph Cramer; Deacon Daniel Peterson.
Mailing Address: P. O. Box 267, 66030.
Sacred Heart Church—Church: 555 W. Main, 66030. Tel: 913-856-7781; Fax: 913-856-8893. Web: www.divinemercyks.org.
Assumption Church—114 E. Nelsom, Edgerton, 66021.
Res.: 122 E. Warren, 66030. Tel: 913-856-7780; 913-884-7788 (Parish Center).
Catechesis/Religious Program—Tel: 913-884-7788. Judy Orth, D.R.E. Students 387.

GARNETT, ANDERSON CO., HOLY ANGELS, [CEM] Rev. Brian Klingele.
Office: 520 E. 4th St., 66032. Tel: 785-448-1686.
Res.: 514 E. Fourth, 66032. Tel: 785-448-3846.
See St. Rose Philippine Duchesne School under Elementary Schools, Interparochial located in the Institution Section
Catechesis/Religious Program—Sheila Wilson, D.R.E. Students 22.

GREELEY, ANDERSON CO., ST. JOHN THE BAPTIST (1881) [CEM] Attended by Holy Angels, Garnett. Rev. Brian Klingele.
Mailing Address: P.O. Box 94, 66033.
Res.: 66033. Tel: 785-867-2170.
See St. Rose Philippine Duchesne School under Elementary Schools, Interparochial located in the Institution Section
Catechesis/Religious Program—Tel: 785-448-1686. Sheila Wilson, D.R.E. Students 7.

HARTFORD, LYON CO., ST. MARY, [CEM] Attended by St. Joseph's, Olpe. Rev. Anthony C. Williams.
Mailing Address: *c/o St. Joseph*, P.O. Box 165, Olpe, 66865.
Catechesis/Religious Program—Students 13.

HIAWATHA, BROWN CO., ST. ANN Rev. Sylvester D'Souza (India), Parochial Vicar.
Res.: 800 Hiawatha Ave., 66434. Tel: 785-742-3010.
Catechesis/Religious Program— Brian Lillie, D.R.E.; Kim Lillie, D.R.E.; Kevin Hill, D.R.E.; Ellen Hill, D.R.E. Students 57.

HOLTON, JACKSON CO., ST. DOMINIC (1870) [CEM] Rev. Christopher Rossman.
Res.: 416 Ohio Ave., 66436. Tel: 785-364-3262; Fax: 785-364-1499.
Catechesis/Religious Program—Tel: 785-364-3621. Barbara Berg, D.R.E. Students 159.
Mission—Our Lady of the Snows Oratory Potawatomie Reservation, Mayetta, Jackson Co. 66509.

HORTON, BROWN CO., ST. LEO, [CEM 3] Rev. Earl Dekat.
Res.: 1340 First Ave. E., 66439. Tel: 785-486-3971; Fax: 785-486-3971.
Catechesis/Religious Program—Ronda Smith, D.R.E. Students 93.

KELLY, NEMAHA CO., ST. BEDE (1901) [CEM] Attended by St. Vincent de Paul, Onaga. Rev. Arul Carasala (India). Tel: 785-336-3189.
Mailing Address: 7344 Drought St., 66538.
Catechesis/Religious Program—Colette Allen, D.R.E.; Kim Henry, D.R.E.; Angie Lueger, D.R.E. Students 74.

LACYGNE, LINN CO., OUR LADY OF LOURDES (1982) Attended by St. Philip Neri, Osawatomie. Rev. Reginald Saldanha.
Mailing Address: *c/o St. Philip Neri*, P.O. Box 4, Osawatomie, 66064. Tel: 913-755-2652.
Church: 819 N. 5th St., 66040.
Catechesis/Religious Program—Eric Victor, D.R.E. Students 12.

LANSING, LEAVENWORTH CO., ST. FRANCIS DE SALES Rev. William McEvoy; Deacon David Gaumer; Nancy Nelson, Pastoral Assoc.
Res.: 119 Woodland Rd., 66043. Tel: 913-727-3768. Email: sfds@prodigy.net; parish@stfrancislansing.org. Web: www.stfrancislansing.org.
Church & Mailing Address: 900 Ida St., 66043. Tel: 913-727-3742; Fax: 913-727-1281.
Catechesis/Religious Program—Tel: 913-727-3742; Fax: 913-727-1281. Students 226.

LAPEER, DOUGLAS CO., ST. FRANCIS OF ASSISI, [CEM] Attended by Annunciation, Baldwin City. Rev. Brandon Farrar.
Mailing Address: *c/o St. Patrick*, 309 S. 6th St., Osage City, 66523.
Catechesis/Religious Program—Tel: 785-793-2149. Joy Schmidt, D.R.E. Students 8.

LAWRENCE, DOUGLAS CO.

1—CORPUS CHRISTI (1981) [JC] Rev. Michael Mulvany.
Church & Office: 6001 Bob Billings Pkwy., 66049-5200. Tel: 785-843-6286; Fax: 785-865-3933. Email: christi@cccparish.org. Web: www.ccparish.org.
School—(Grades PreK-7) Tel: 785-331-3374. Mary Mattern, Prin. Lay Teachers 19; Students 300.
Catechesis/Religious Program—Sr. Doris Engeman, F.S.H.F., D.R.E. Students 218.

2—ST. JOHN THE EVANGELIST (1858) [CEM] Revs. John Schmeidler, O.F.M.Cap.; Curtis Carlson, O.F.M.Cap., Parochial Vicar; Deacon Leo Bistak.
Office: 1229 Vermont St., 66044. Tel: 785-843-0109; Fax: 785-749-5064. Email: churchoffice@saint-johns.net. Web: www.saint-johns.net.
School—(Grades PreK-6), 1208 Kentucky, 66044. Tel: 785-843-9511; Fax: 785-843-7143. Web: www.saint-johns.net/school. Patricia Newton, Prin.; Karen Rinke, Librarian. Religious Teachers 1; Lay Teachers 19; Students 301.
Catechesis/Religious Program—Students 311.

LEAVENWORTH, LEAVENWORTH CO.

1—ST. CASIMIR, (Polish), Merged with Sacred Heart, Leavenworth to form Sacred Heart-St. Casimir, Leavenworth.

2—IMMACULATE CONCEPTION (1855) Merged with St. Joseph's, Leavenworth to form Immaculate Conception-St. Joseph, Leavenworth.

3—IMMACULATE CONCEPTION-ST. JOSEPH (2007), (Old Cathedral) Rev. David McEvoy, O.Carm.; Deacons Timothy McEvoy, Pastoral Assoc.; Terrance Mulcare, Pastoral Assoc.
Office & Mailing: 747 Osage, 66048. Tel: 913-682-3953; Fax: 913-682-5599. Web: www.icsj.org.
Immaculate Conception Church: 711 N. 5th St., 66048.
St. Joseph Church: 306 N. Broadway, 66048.
Rectory—300 N. Broadway, 66048. Tel: 913-682-0809.
See Xavier Elementary School, Leavenworth under Elementary Schools, Interparochial located in the Institution section.
Catechesis/Religious Program—Students 79.
Mission—Sacred Heart, Kickapoo Twp. 66048.

4—ST. JOSEPH (1858) Merged with Immaculate

Conception, Leavenworth to form Immaculate Conception-St. Joseph's, Leavenworth.

5—St. Joseph of the Valley (1863) [CEM] Consolidated with St. Lawrence, Easton to form St. Joseph-St. Lawrence, Easton.

6—Sacred Heart of Jesus, [CEM] Merged with St. Casimir, Leavenworth to form Sacred Heart-St. Casimir, Leavenworth.

7—Sacred Heart-St. Casimir (2007) Rev. Phillip J. Winkelbauer; Deacon Robert D. Zbylut.
Office: 521 Linn St., 66048. Tel: 913-772-2424. Web: www.shsc.org.
Res.: 1401 Second Ave., 66048. Tel: 913-772-1787; Fax: 913-651-2150.
Sacred Heart Church: 1405 2nd Ave., 66048.
St. Casimir Church: 715 Pennsylvania, 66048.
See Xavier Elementary School, Leavenworth under Elementary Schools, Interparochial located in the Institution section.
Catechesis/Religious Program—Tel: 913-772-2424; Fax: 913-651-2150. Students 35.

Leawood, Johnson Co.

1—Church of the Nativity (1986) Rev. Francis Hund; Deacon Michael Schrock. In Res., Revs. Michael Hermes; Alfred Rockers (Retired).
Church: 3800 W. 119th St., 66209. Tel: 913-491-5017; Fax: 913-491-5065. Email: info@kcnativity.org. Web: www.kcnativity.org.
School—(Grades K-8), 3700 W. 119th St., 66209. Tel: 913-338-4330; Fax: 913-338-2050. Email: nativityparishschool@kcnativity.org. Maureen Huppe, Prin.; Jean Stump, Librarian. Lay Teachers 37; Students 474.
Catechesis/Religious Program—Sr. Helen Smith, D.R.E. Students 321.
Christian Formation Office—Tel: 913-338-4367; Fax: 913-338-0285.

2—Curé of Ars (1959) Rev. Msgr. Charles McGlinn; Revs. Shawn Tunink, Parochial Vicar; Benedict Gomes, Parochial Vicar.
Res.: 9401 Mission Rd., 66206. Tel: 913-649-1337; Fax: 913-649-1339. Email: cureparish@kc.rr.com. Web: cure-of-ars.org.
School—(Grades K-8), 9403 Mission Rd., 66206. Tel: 913-648-2620; Fax: 913-648-3810. Web: www.archkckcs.org/curears. Mary Jo Gates, Prin. Lay Teachers 36; Students 660.
Catechesis/Religious Program—Sandy Hawekotte, D.R.E. Students 260.

3—St. Michael the Archangel (1999) Revs. William Porter; Michael Peterson, Parochial Vicar; Deacons Mark Stukel; John Weist.
Church: 14251 Nall Ave., Overland Park, 66223. Tel: 913-402-3900; Fax: 913-851-8220.
School—(Grades K-8), 14201 Nall Ave., 66223. Tel: 913-402-3950; Fax: 913-851-8221. Michael Cullinan, Prin.; Janet O'Connell, Asst. Prin.; Kate Walsh, Librarian. Lay Teachers 36; Students 661.
Catechesis/Religious Program—Denise Ogilvie, D.R.E. Students 1,150.

Lenexa, Johnson Co., Holy Trinity (1880) Revs. Michael Koller; Francis Bakyor, Parochial Vicar; Barry Clayton, Parochial Vicar; Deacons Dana Nearmyer; Stuart Holland.
Office: 9150 Pflumm Rd., 66215. Tel: 913-888-2770; Fax: 913-888-4403. Email: holytrinity@htlenexa.org. Web: www.htlenexa.org.
School—(Grades K-8), 13600 W. 92nd St., 66215. Tel: 913-888-3250; Fax: 913-438-2572. Martha Concannon, Prin.; Kelly Kinnan, Librarian. Lay Teachers 39; Students 697.
Catechesis/Religious Program—Tel: 913-492-6068. Students 350.

Lillis, Marshall Co., St. Joseph, [CEM] Closed. For inquiries for parish records contact Annunciation, Frankfort.

Louisburg, Miami Co., Immaculate Conception (1887) [CEM] Rev. Msgr. Robert Bergman; Deacon George Karnaze.
Office: Box 118, 66053. Tel: 913-837-2295; Fax: 913-837-3309. Email: iccc@mokancomm.net.
Res.: 602 S. Elm, 66053.
Catechesis/Religious Program—Linda Roberts, D.R.E. Students 113.

Marysville, Marshall Co., St. Gregory (1862) [CEM] Rev. James Shaughnessy.
Office: 207 N. 14th St., Ste. B, 66508. Tel: 785-562-3302; Fax: 785-562-4039. Email: parishoffice@stgregorychurch.org. Web: www.stgregorychurch.org.
Res.: 206 N. 14th, 66508. Tel: 785-562-2989.
School—(Grades PreK-6), 207 N. 14th, 66508. Tel: 785-562-2831; Fax: 785-562-4039. Barbara Hawkins, Prin. Lay Teachers 10; Students 146.
Catechesis/Religious Program—Allyson Lauer, D.R.E. Students 55.

Mayetta, Jackson Co., St. Francis Xavier, [CEM] Attended by St. Dominic, Holton. Rev. Christopher Rossman.
Mailing Address: *c/o St. Dominic*, 416 Ohio Ave., Holton, 66436. Tel: 785-364-3262.
Catechesis/Religious Program—Tel: 785-966-2690. Barbara Berg, D.R.E. Students 53.

Meriden, Jefferson Co., St. Aloysius (1882) [CEM] Attended by St. Theresa, Perry. Rev. Tom Aduri.
Mailing Address: P.O. Box 364, 66512. Email: stalsmer@yahoo.com.
P. O. Box 42, Perry, 66073. Tel: 785-597-5656.
Church: 615 Wyandotte, 66512. Tel: 785-484-3312; Fax: 785-484-3338.
Catechesis/Religious Program—Heather Roenne, D.R.E. (Grades PreK-5); Mary Naumann, D.R.E. (Grades 6-12). Students 135.

Mission, Johnson Co., St. Pius X (1954) Rev. Kenneth W. Kelly.
Res.: 5601 Woodson Rd., 66202. Tel: 913-432-4855; Fax: 913-432-2086.
See John Paul II School under Elementary Schools, Interparochial located in the Institution Section
Catechesis/Religious Program— Shawna Davidson, D.R.E. Students 80.

Mooney Creek, Jefferson Co., Corpus Christi, [CEM] Attended by St. Joseph, Nortonville. Rev. Jojaiah Mandagiri, M.S.F.S., Parochial Admin.
Mailing Address: 18760 Rogers Rd., Atchison, 66002. Tel: 913-886-2030.
Catechesis/Religious Program— Sara Noll, D.R.E. Students 13.

Mound City, Linn Co., Sacred Heart Shrine to St. Philippine Duchesne (1942) [CEM] Attended by St. Philip Neri, Osawatomie. Rev. Reginald Saldanha; Deacon don Poole.
Mailing Address: *c/o St. Philip Neri*, P.O. Box 4, Osawatomie, 66064. Tel: 913-755-2652.
Church Site: 729 W. Main St., 66056. Tel: 913-795-2724.
Catechesis/Religious Program—Theresa White, D.R.E. Students 39.

Nortonville, Jefferson Co., St. Joseph, [CEM] Rev. Jojaiah Mandagiri, M.S.F.S., Parochial Admin.
Church: 221 N. Sycamore St., 66060. Tel: 913-886-2030.
Catechesis/Religious Program—Shawn Gigstad, D.R.E. Students 60.

Olathe, Johnson Co.

1—St. Paul (1860) [JC] Rev. John Torrez; Deacon Michael Hill.
Office: 900 S. Honeysuckle, 66061. Tel: 913-764-0323; Fax: 913-764-1584. Web: www.spcatholic.org.
Res.: 840 Larkspur, 66061. Tel: 913-782-8999.
School—(Grades PreK-8), 920 W. Honeysuckle, 66061. Tel: 913-764-0619; Fax: 913-768-6040. Web: stpaul.eduk12.net. Tonia Helm, Prin.; Ana Escobar, Librarian. Lay Teachers 12; Students 110.
Catechesis/Religious Program—Tel: 913-764-0323, Ext. 119. Mary Mashek, C.R.E. Students 563.

2—Prince of Peace (1979) Revs. Frank Burger; Andrew Strobl, Parochial Vicar; Anthony Kiplagat (Kenya), Parochial Vicar; Thomas Dolezal (Retired).
Office: Tel: 913-782-8864; Fax: 913-780-9658. Web: www.princeofpeace.info.
School—(Grades K-8), 16000 W. 143rd St., 66062. Tel: 913-764-0650; Fax: 913-393-0819. Email: school@princeofpeace.info. Jane Shriver, Prin.; Mary Beth Hare, Asst. Prin.; Pam Schuetz, Librarian. Lay Teachers 35; Students 615.
Catechesis/Religious Program—Tel: 913-829-1147; Fax: 913-747-7747. Mark Schuetz, D.R.E. (Elementary); Polly Holmes, D.R.E. (Jr. High); Amanda Buttig, D.R.E. (High School); Ted Kepes, Dir. Initiation Programs. Students 1,398.

Olpe, Lyon Co., St. Joseph (1885) [CEM] Rev. Anthony C. Williams.
Res.: 306 Iowa, P.O. Box 165, 66865. Tel: 620-475-3326.
School—(Grades PreK-6) Tel: 620-475-3416. Theresa Lein, Prin. Lay Teachers 4; Students 33.
Catechesis/Religious Program—Rose Redeker, D.R.E. Students 91.

Onaga, Pottawatomie Co., St. Vincent de Paul Rev. Balachandra Miriyala.
Res.: Box 396, 66521. Tel: 785-889-4896.
Church Site: 308 E. 3rd St.
Catechesis/Religious Program—Jackie Valburg, D.R.E. Students 50.

Osage City, Osage Co., St. Patrick, [CEM 3] Rev. Anthony Ouellette; Monica Greenwood, Dir. Parish Min.
Mailing Address: 309 S. 6th St., 66523. Tel: 785-528-3424; Fax: 785-528-3381.
Catechesis/Religious Program—Tel: 785-528-3424. Students 64.

Osawatomie, Miami Co., St. Philip Neri (1889) Rev. Reginald Saldanha.
Church: 500 Parker Ave., 66064. Tel: 913-755-2652.
Catechesis/Religious Program—Brenda Minden, D.R.E. Students 39.
Chaplaincy—State Hospital for Mentally Ill, 66064.

Ottawa, Franklin Co., Sacred Heart, [CEM] Rev. William Fisher.
Res.: 408 S. Cedar St., 66067. Tel: 785-242-2174; Fax: 785-242-0820.
School—(Grades PreK-5), 426 S. Cedar, 66067. Tel: 785-242-4297; Fax: 785-242-0820. Diane Chapman, Prin.; Susan Soph, Librarian. Lay Teachers 6; Students 75.
Catechesis/Religious Program—Tel: 785-242-7258. Cynthia Stone, D.R.E. & RCIA Coord. Students 99.

Overland Park, Johnson Co.

1—Church of the Ascension (1991) Rev. Msgr. Thomas Tank; Rev. Matthew Schiffelbein, Parochial Vicar.
9510 W. 127th St., 66213. Tel: 913-681-3348; Fax: 913-681-3517. Email: ascensionchurch@kcascension.org. Web: www.kcascension.org.
School—(Grades K-8) Tel: 913-851-2531; Fax: 913-851-2518. Email: info@acseagles.org. Web: www.acseagles.org. Margaret Sachs, Prin. Lay Teachers 39; Students 645.
Catechesis/Religious Program—Tel: 913-681-7683; Fax: 913-681-7634. William O'Leary, D.R.E. Students 811.

2—Holy Cross (1968) Revs. Michael C. Stubbs; David Garavito (Colombia), Parochial Vicar.
Office: 8311 W. 93rd St., 66212. Tel: 913-381-2755; Fax: 913-381-2766.
Res.: 8315 W. 93rd St., 66212. Tel: 913-341-5618; Fax: 913-381-2766. Email: churchoffice@holycrossopks.org. Web: www.holycrossopks.org.
School—(Grades K-8), 8101 W. 95th, 66212. Tel: 913-381-7408; Fax: 913-381-1312. Email: gradeschool@hccsmail.com. Bobbie Beverlin, Prin. Lay Teachers 23; Students 279.
Catechesis/Religious Program—Tel: 913-381-2757. Julie Dresser, D.R.E. Students 278.

3—Holy Spirit (1981) Rev. Richard Storey; Deacon Jim Lavin.
Office: 11300 W. 103rd St., 66214. Tel: 913-492-7318; Fax: 913-492-7370. Web: www.holyspiritcatholicchurch.org.
School—(Grades PreK-8) Tel: 913-492-2582; Fax: 913-492-9613. Web: www.hsschool.net. Michele Watson, Prin. Sisters 1; Lay Teachers 31; Students 400.
Catechesis/Religious Program—Tel: 913-492-7382; Fax: 913-492-7370. Sr. M. Teresa Pandl, F.S.G.M., D.R.E. Students 218.

4—Queen of the Holy Rosary (1944) Rev. Donald Cullen.
Res.: 7023 W. 71st St., 66204. Tel: 913-432-4616; Fax: 913-432-0620.
See John Paul II School under Elementary Schools, Interparochial located in the Institution Section
Catechesis/Religious Program—Tel: 913-722-2206; Fax: 913-432-0620. Denise Godinez, D.R.E. Students 183.

Paola, Miami Co., Holy Trinity, [CEM] Rev. Richard Halvorson.
Office: 400 S. East St., 66071. Tel: 913-557-2067; Fax: 913-557-2067. Email: htchurch@catholic.org. Web: www.holytrinity.4lpi.com.
School—(Grades K-8), 601 E. Chippewa, 66071. Tel: 913-294-3286; Fax: 913-294-5286. Ben Chapman, Prin. Lay Teachers 9; Students 141.
Catechesis/Religious Program—Tel: 913-294-5492. Gina Sallman, D.R.E. Students 70.

Paxico, Wabaunsee Co., Sacred Heart (1884) [CEM], Served from St. Bernard, Wamego. Revs. John Pilcher; Lourdu Marreddy Yeruva (India), Parochial Vicar.
Res.: *c/o St. Bernard*, 1006 W. 8th, Wamego, 66547. Tel: 785-456-7869.
Office: 22298 Newbury Rd., 66526. Tel: 785-636-5578; Fax: 785-636-5572.
Catechesis/Religious Program— Michelle Stuhlsatz, D.R.E. Students 57.

Perry, Jefferson Co., St. Theresa, [CEM 2] Rev. Tom Aduri.
Res.: P.O. Box 42, 66073. Tel: 785-597-5656.
Catechesis/Religious Program—Tel: 785-597-5138. Janette Adams, D.R.E. Students 74.

Prairie Village, Johnson Co., St. Ann (1949) [CEM] Rev. Keith Lunsford; Deacon Todd Brower.
Office: 7231 Mission Rd., 66208. Tel: 913-660-1182; Fax: 913-660-1194. Web: www.stannpv.org.
School—(Grades K-8), 7241 Mission Rd., 66208. Tel: 913-660-1101; Fax: 913-660-1132. Becky Akright, Prin.; Janet Postlewait, Librarian. Lay Teachers 27; Students 445.
Catechesis/Religious Program—Tel: 913-660-1195. Maureen Leach, D.R.E. Students 185.

Purcell, Doniphan Co., St. Mary, [CEM] Attended by St. Leo's, Horton. Rev. Earl Dekat.
c/o St. Leo 1340 First Ave. E., Horton, 66439.
Church Site: 446 Hwy. 137, 66041. Tel: 785-486-3971; Fax: 785-486-3971.
Catechesis/Religious Program—Combined program with St. Leo, Horton. Ronda Smith, D.R.E.

READING, LYON CO., ASSUMPTION, Closed. For inquiries for parish records contact the chancery.

RICHMOND, FRANKLIN CO., ST. THERESE (1929) Attended by St. Boniface, Scipio. Rev. J. Gerald Williams, O.Carm.
Mailing & Res.: 32292 N.E. Norton Rd., Garnett, 66032. Tel: 785-835-6273; Fax: 785-835-6112.
544 E. Central, 66080.
Catechesis/Religious Program—Nancy Hermreck, D.R.E. Students 12.

ROELAND PARK, JOHNSON CO., ST. AGNES Revs. Gerardo Arano-Ponce; John H. Wisner.
Res.: 5250 Mission Rd., 66205. Tel: 913-262-2400; Fax: 913-262-1050. Web: www.stagneskc.org.
School—(Grades PreK-8), 5130 Mission Rd., 66205. Tel: 913-262-1686; Fax: 913-384-1567. Stephanie Hill, Prin. Lay Teachers 32; Students 372.
Catechesis/Religious Program—Marielena Aguilar, D.R.E. Students 135.

ROSSVILLE, SHAWNEE CO., ST. STANISLAUS, Attended by Immaculate Conception, St. Marys. Rev. Bruce Ansems.
Mailing Address: P.O. Box 794, 66533.
Catechesis/Religious Program—Tel: 785-584-6612. Connie Fischer, D.R.E. Students 127.

ST. BENEDICT, NEMAHA CO., ST. MARY (1859) [CEM] Attended by Sacred Heart, Baileyville. Rev. Edward J. Oen, C.PP.S.
Res.: 9208 Main St., 66538. Tel: 785-336-3174.
Catechesis/Religious Program—Diane Schmitz, D.R.E. (Elementary); Shauna Engelken, D.R.E. (Jr. High & High School). Students 74.

ST. LOUIS, ATCHISON CO., ST. LOUIS, [CEM] Attended by St. Ann's, Effingham. Rev. Benjamin Tremmel, O.S.B.
Mailing Address: 301 William, Box 54, Effingham, 66023. Tel: 913-833-5660.
Church: 11321 Morton Rd., Atchison, 66002. Tel: 913-847-6849.
Catechesis/Religious Program—Tel: 913-874-5191. Jennifer Miller, D.R.E. Students 39.

ST. MARYS, POTTAWATOMIE CO., IMMACULATE CONCEPTION (1849) [CEM] Rev. Bruce Ansems.
Res. & Church: 208 W. Bertrand, 66536. Tel: 785-437-2408; Fax: 785-437-2938. Email: unity_general@oct.net.
Worship Site: Holy Cross Church—Emmett, 66422.
Catechesis/Religious Program—Peggy Wehner, D.R.E. Students 202.

ST. PATRICK, ATCHISON CO., ST. PATRICK (1857) [CEM] Attended by St. Joseph. Rev. Gabriel Landis, O.S.B.
Mailing Address: *c/o St. Joseph*, 705 Spring Garden, Atchison, 66002.
Catechesis/Religious Program—Consolidated program with St. Benedict's, Atchison

SABETHA, NEMAHA CO., SACRED HEART Rev. Gregory Hammes.
Office: 1031 S. 12th, 66534. Tel: 785-284-0888; Fax: 785-284-2913. Email: sacredheartsabetha@sbcglobal.net.
Res.: 1042 S. 14th, 66534. Tel: 785-284-3068.
Catechesis/Religious Program—Mandy Funk, D.R.E. Students 147.

SCIPIO, ANDERSON CO., ST. BONIFACE (1858) [CEM] Rev. J. Gerald Williams, O.Carm.
Res.: 32292 N.E. Norton Rd., Garnett, 66032. Tel: 785-835-6273; Fax: 785-835-6112.
Catechesis/Religious Program—Nancy Hermreck, D.R.E. Students 64.

SCRANTON, OSAGE CO., ST. PATRICK, [CEM] Attended by St. Patrick's, Osage City. Rev. Anthony Ouellette.
Mailing Address: *c/o St. Patrick*, 309 S. 6th St., Osage City, 66523.
Catechesis/Religious Program—Tel: 785-793-2149. Joy Schmidt, D.R.E. Students 60.

SENECA, NEMAHA CO., SS. PETER AND PAUL (1869) [CEM] Rev. Arul Carasala (India).
Res.: 411 Pioneer, 66538. Tel: 785-336-2128; Fax: 785-336-2307. Email: sppchurch@carsoncomm.com.
School—(Grades PreK-8), 409 Elk St., 66538. Tel: 785-336-2727; Fax: 785-336-3817. Todd Leonard, Prin.; Rosalie Divelbiss, Librarian. Lay Teachers 14; Students 174.
Catechesis/Religious Program—Susan Stallbaumer, D.R.E. Students 155.

SHAWNEE, JOHNSON CO.

1—GOOD SHEPHERD (1973) Rev. James E. Ludwikoski.
Office: 12800 W. 75th St., 66216. Tel: 913-631-7116; Fax: 913-631-3539. Email: church@goodshepherdshawnee.org. Web: www.goodshepherdshawnee.org.
Res.: 12509 W. 73rd Ter., 66216. Tel: 913-631-5661.
Parish Center:—12800 W. 75th St., 66216. Tel: 913-631-7116; Fax: 913-631-3539.
School—(Grades K-8), 12800 W. 75th St., 66216. Tel: 913-631-0400; Fax: 913-631-3539. Ann Mc Guff, Prin.; Staci Rueter, Librarian. Lay Teachers 32; Students 369.
Catechesis/Religious Program—Tel: 913-563-5303. Deb Carmody, D.R.E. Students 331.

2—ST. JOSEPH Revs. Michael Hawken; Scott Wallisch, Parochial Vicar; Deacon Tom Mulvenon.
Office: 5901 Flint St., 66203. Tel: 913-631-5983; Fax: 913-631-5973.
School—(Grades K-8), 11505 Johnson Dr., 66203. Tel: 913-631-7730; Fax: 913-631-3608. Web: www.archkckcs.org/stjoe. Sue Carter, Prin. Lay Teachers 34; Students 530.
Early Education Center—11525 Johnson Dr., 66203. Tel: 913-631-0004; Fax: 913-631-4362. (Day Care & Preschool) Auxiliary Teachers 31; Students 132.
Catechesis/Religious Program—Tel: 913-631-8923; Fax: 913-631-5973. Beth Bracken, D.R.E. Students 165.

3—SACRED HEART (1900) Rev. Craig Maxim. In Res., Rev. John Riley.
Office & Mailing Address: 5501 Monticello Rd., 66226. Tel: 913-422-5700; Fax: 913-422-5723. Web: www.shoj.org.
School—(Grades PreK-8), 21801 Johnson Dr., 66218. Tel: 913-422-5520; Fax: 913-745-0290. Nick Antista, Prin.; Kathy Cleringer, Librarian. Lay Teachers 26; Students 403.
Catechesis/Religious Program—Tel: 913-422-5700; Fax: 913-422-5723. Tracie Kersey, D.R.E. (Elementary); Kyle Kuckelman, Youth Min. (Grades 6-12). Students 575.

SUMMERFIELD, MARSHALL CO., HOLY FAMILY, Attended by St. Michael, Axtell. Rev. Albert Hauser, O.S.B.
Church & Mailing: P.O. Box 136, 66541. Tel: 785-736-2220.
Catechesis/Religious Program—Rosalie Meybrunn, D.R.E. Students 18.

TONGANOXIE, LEAVENWORTH CO., SACRED HEART, [CEM] Rev. Mark Goldasich.
Office: 1100 West St., P.O. Box 539, 66086-0539. Tel: 913-369-2851; Fax: 913-369-8697 (call first). Email: catholicbetty@sunflower.com. Web: www.shcct.com.
Catechesis/Religious Program—Tel: 913-369-8697. Students 249.

TOPEKA, SHAWNEE CO.

1—ASSUMPTION (1862) Consolidated with Holy Name, Topeka to form Mater Dei, Topeka.

2—CHRIST THE KING (1977) Rev. Peter O'Sullivan.
Res.: 5972 S.W. 25th St., 66614. Tel: 785-273-0710; 785-273-0715; Fax: 785-273-4766.
Church: 5973 S.W. 25th St., 66614. Web: www.ctktopeka.org.
School—(Grades K-8) Tel: 785-272-2220; Fax: 785-272-9255. Relynn Reynoso, Prin. Lay Teachers 22; Students 357.
Catechesis/Religious Program—Tel: 785-273-2917. Chris Henderson, D.R.E. Students 263.

3—HOLY NAME, Consolidated with Assumption, Topeka to form Mater Dei, Topeka.

4—ST. JOSEPH (1887) Consolidated with Sacred Heart, Topeka to form Sacred Heart-St. Joseph, Topeka.

5—MATER DEI (2006) Rev. Jon Hullinger; Deacon Chris Seago. In Res., Rev. Peter Nwanekezie (Nigeria).
Office: 1114 W. 10th Ave., 66604. Tel: 785-232-7744; Fax: 785-232-2341. Web: www.materdeiparish.org.
Worship Sites:—
Mater Dei Assumption Church—8th & Jackson St., 66604.
Mater Dei Holy Name Church—10th & Clay St., 66604.
School—Elementary, (Grades PreK-8), 934 S.W. Clay St., 66606. Tel: 785-233-1727; Fax: 785-233-1728. Andrea Hillebert, Prin. (Elementary & Middle School). Lay Teachers 14; Students 245.
Catechesis/Religious Program—John Livingston, D.R.E. Students 121.

6—ST. MATTHEW (1955) Rev. Jerry Volz.
Res.: 2700 S.E. Virginia Ave., 66605. Tel: 785-232-5012; Fax: 785-232-0028. Web: www.saintmatthews.org.
School—(Grades K-8), 1000 S.E. 28th, 66605. Tel: 785-235-2188; Fax: 785-235-2207. Web: www.saintmatthews.org. Heather Huscher, Prin.; Debbie Otting, Librarian. Lay Teachers 12; Students 156.
Catechesis/Religious Program—Cheryl Byrne, Dir. Christian Formation. Students 173.

7—MOST PURE HEART OF MARY (1946) [JC] Revs. Brian Schieber; Nicholas Blaha, Parochial Vicar; Deacon Dan Ondracek.
Office: 1800 S.W. Stone, 66604. Tel: 785-272-5590; Fax: 785-272-2801. Web: www.mphm.com.
Church: 3601 S.W. 17th St., 66604.
School—(Grades K-8), 1750 S.W. Stone, 66604. Tel: 785-272-4313; Fax: 785-272-1138. Eric White, Prin.; Judy Desetti, Librarian. Lay Teachers 28; Students 455.
Catechesis/Religious Program—Tel: 785-272-4727; Fax: 785-272-2801. Lucas Tappan, D.R.E. Students 115.

8—MOTHER TERESA OF CALCUTTA (2004) Rev. William Bruning.
Mailing Address: 2014 N.W. 46th St., 66618. Tel: 785-286-2188; Fax: 785-286-2803. Email: mtcctopeka@att.net.
Res.: 4609 N.W. Kendall Dr., 66618. Tel: 785-286-2113.
Catechesis/Religious Program—Beth Mercer, D.R.E. Students 360.

9—OUR LADY OF GUADALUPE, [CEM] Rev. John Cordes; Deacon Ray Delgado.
Office: 134 N.E. Lake St., 66616. Tel: 785-232-5088; Fax: 785-232-8834. Email: olg134@sbcglobal.net. Web: www.olg-parish.org.
Consolidated with Sacred Heart School and renamed Holy Family School. See Elementary Schools Interparochial located in the Institution section.
Catechesis/Religious Program—Tel: 785-233-4593. Sr. Rebecca Granado, D.R.E. Students 559.

10—SACRED HEART (1919) Consolidated with St. Joseph, Topeka to form Sacred Heart-St. Joseph, Topeka.

11—SACRED HEART-ST. JOSEPH (2006) Rev. Timothy A. Haberkorn.
Res. & St. Joseph Church: 227 S.W. VanBuren, 66603. Tel: 785-232-2863.
Worship Site: Sacred Heart Church—312 N.E. Freeman Ave., 66616.
See Holy Family School under Elementary Schools, Interparochial located in the Institution Section
Catechesis/Religious Program—Tel: 785-357-0293. Paul Allen, D.R.E. Students 100.

TROY, DONIPHAN CO., ST. CHARLES, [CEM] Attended by St. Joseph's, Wathena. Rev. Roderic Giller, O.S.B.
Mailing Address: P.O. Box 456, 66087.
Church: 133 S. Park, P.O. Box 456, 66087. Tel: 785-985-2271.
Catechesis/Religious Program—Barb Greaser, D.R.E. Students 23.

VALLEY FALLS, JEFFERSON CO., ST. MARY'S IMMACULATE CONCEPTION, [CEM] Attended by St. Joseph's, Nortonville. Rev. Jojaiah Mandagiri, M.S.F.S., Parochial Admin.
Mailing Address: *c/o St Joseph Church*, 221 N. Sycamore, Nortonville, 66060. Tel: 913-886-2030.
Church: 905 Broadway, P.O. Box 176, 66088. Tel: 913-945-3544.
Catechesis/Religious Program—Tel: 785-945-3787; Fax: 785-945-4021. Dawna Edmonds, D.R.E. Students 53.

WAMEGO, POTTAWATOMIE CO., ST. BERNARD (1898) [CEM] Revs. John Pilcher; Lourdu Marreddy Yeruva (India), Parochial Vicar.
Res.: 1006 8th St., 66547. Tel: 785-456-7869; Fax: 785-456-7862. Email: saintb@wamego.net. Web: www.sbc-sjc.com.
Catechesis/Religious Program—Students 185.

WATERVILLE, MARSHALL CO., ST. MONICA, Closed. For inquiries see St. Monica - St. Elizabeth, Blue Rapids.

WATHENA, DONIPHAN CO., ST. JOSEPH (1869) [CEM] Rev. Roderic Giller, O.S.B.
Res.: 102 S. 7th St., P.O. Box 159, 66090. Tel: 785-989-4818; Fax: 785-989-2313.
Catechesis/Religious Program— Mary Kay Nold, D.R.E. Students 40.

WAVERLY, COFFEY CO., ST. JOSEPH, Attended by St. Francis Xavier, Burlington. Rev. Marianand Mendem.
Mailing Address: *c/o St. Francis Xavier*, 214 Juniatta, Burlington, 66839. Tel: 620-364-2416; Fax: 620-364-2000.
Catechesis/Religious Program—Tel: 785-733-2278. Michelle Lee, D.R.E. Students 32.

WEA, MIAMI CO., QUEEN OF THE HOLY ROSARY (Bucyrus P.O.) [CEM] Rev. Lawrence Albertson.
Office: 22705 Metcalf Rd., Bucyrus, 66013. Tel: 913-533-2462; Fax: 913-533-2460. Email: holyrosarywea@yahoo.com. Web: www.holyrosarywea.org.
School—(Grades PreK-8), 22705 Metcalf Rd., Bucyrus, 66013. Tel: 913-533-2462; Fax: 913-533-2460. Jane Sullivan, Prin. Lay Teachers 19; Students 212.
Catechesis/Religious Program—Kathy O'Bryan, Adult Faith Formation & D.R.E. Students 165.

WESTPHALIA, ANDERSON CO., ST. TERESA, Attended by St. Francis Xavier, Burlington. Rev. Marianand Mendem.
Mailing Address: *c/o St. Francis Xavier*, 214 Juniatta, Burlington, 66839. Tel: 620-364-2416; Fax: 620-364-2000.
Catechesis/Religious Program—Tel: 785-489-2324. Alice Nolan, D.R.E. Students 40.

WETMORE, NEMAHA CO., ST. JAMES, Attended by Sacred Heart, Sabetha. Rev. Gregory Hammes.
Catechesis/Religious Program—Sue Bloom, D.R.E. Students 45.

WHEATON, POTTAWATOMIE CO., ST. MICHAEL, Closed. For inquiries for parish records contact the chancery.

Chaplains of Public Institutions

KANSAS CITY. *K.U. Medical Center and Chapel*, Holy Name Church, 66160. Vacant, Chap.

LAWRENCE. *Haskell Institute*. Rev. Duane F. Reinert, O.F.M.Cap. (Government Indian School)

Special Assignment:
Revs.—
Chontos, Joseph, 901 N. 52nd St., 66102.
Wait, Dennis, Sanctuary of Hope, 2601 Ridge Ave., 66102-4617.

On Duty Outside the Archdiocese:
Rev.—
Tillia, Marc, Bahia, Brazil

On Sabbatical:
Revs.—
Reynolds, John C.
Ziegler, Michael Tod

On Leave of Absence:
Rev.—
Henson, Darren

Retired:
Rev. Msgrs.—
Burger, Raymond, Olathe, KS
Krische, Vincent E., Lawrence, KS
Revs.—
Bertels, George, J.C.L., Leavenworth, KS
Blaufuss, Tony, Garnett, KS
Burger, Robert, Olathe, KS
Cooper, Leo, Olathe, KS
Cornish, Ron, Overland Park, KS
Dekat, Carl, St. George, KS
Dolezal, Thomas, Leneka, KS
Dunnivan, John, Overland Park, KS
Hasenkamp, Robert, Lecompton, KS
Hayes, Edward, Leavenworth, KS
Hesse, Thomas, Topeka, KS
Kearns, Thomas, Overland Park, KS
Klasinski, George, Topeka, KS
Lickteig, Anthony
Livojevich, Ronald, Overland Park, KS
Melchior, Thomas, Topeka, KS
Pflumm, Robert, Overland Park, KS
Rockers, Alfred, Leawood, KS
Schwalm, Donald, Minnesota
Seuferling, George, Meriden, KS
Sheeds, Gerald E., Kansas City, KS
Wempe, Richard C., Kansas City, KS

INSTITUTIONS LOCATED IN THE ARCHDIOCESE

[A] COLLEGES AND UNIVERSITIES

KANSAS CITY. *Donnelly College*, 608 N. 18th St., 66102. Tel: 913-621-6070; Fax: 913-621-8719. Email: admissions@donnelly.edu. Web: www.donnelly.edu. Steve LaNasa, Ph.D., Pres.; Amber Bloomfield-Martinez, Registrar; Jane Ballagh de Tovar, Librarian. Priests 1; Sisters of Charity 1; Lay Teachers 52; Students 1,302.

ATCHISON. *Benedictine College*, 1020 N. 2nd St., 66002. Tel: 913-367-5340; Fax: 913-367-6566. Web: www.benedictine.edu. Stephen D. Minnis, J.D., Pres.; Ron Olinger, CFO; Pete Helgesen, Dean Enrollment Mgmt.; Kimberly C. Shankman, Ph.D., Dean of College; Joseph Wurtz, Dean of Students; Tom Hoopes, Vice Pres. College Relations; Linda Henry, Vice Pres. Student Life; Kelly J. Vowels, Vice Pres. Advancement; Charlie Gartenmayer, Dir. Athletics; Revs. Denis Meade, O.S.B., J.C.D., Theology; Meinrad Miller, O.S.B., Chap. & Theology; Brendan Rolling, O.S.B., Dir. Mission & Min.; Blaine Schultz, O.S.B., Prof. Emeritus Music; Sisters Linda Herndon, O.S.B., Assoc. Dean of Academic Records & Registrar; Angela Osterman, O.S.B., Health, Phys. Ed. & Recreation; Deborah Peters, O.S.B., English Dept.; Bro. Lawrence Bradford, O.S.B., Biology Dept.; Rev. Marion Charboneau, O.S.B., History Dept.; Bro. Joseph Ryan, O.S.B.; Steven Gromatzky, Librarian. Coed College of St. Benedict's & Mount St. Scholastica. Priests 5; Brothers 2; Benedictine Sisters 3; Lay Persons 87; Students 1,909.

LEAVENWORTH. *University of Saint Mary*, 4100 S. 4th St. Trafficway, 66048. Tel: 913-682-5151; Fax: 913-758-6140. Email: admiss@stmary.edu. Web: www.stmary.edu. Sr. Diane Steele, S.C.L., Ph.D., Pres.; Dr. Bryan LeBeau, Academic Vice Pres.; Penelope Lonergan, Librarian; Rev. William McEvoy, Chap. Sisters of Charity of Leavenworth 5; Lay Teachers 40; Students 1,427.

[B] HIGH SCHOOLS, INTERPAROCHIAL

KANSAS CITY. *Bishop Miege High School* (1958) 5041 Reinhardt Dr., Shawnee Mission, 66205. Tel: 913-262-2700; Fax: 913-262-3754. Email: lgerard@bishopmiege.com. Web: www.bishopmiege.com. Joseph Passantino, Ed.D., Pres.; Bob Ludwikoski, Prin. for Academic Svcs.; Michael Bohaty, Prin. for Student Svcs.; Rev. Shawn Tunink, Chap.; Judi Wollenziehn, Library Media Specialist. Sisters 1; Lay Teachers 55; Students 740.

Bishop Miege High School Foundation Tel: 913-262-2700; Fax: 913-262-3754.

Bishop Ward High School, 708 N. 18th St., 66102. Tel: 913-371-1201; Fax: 913-371-2145. Email: wardhigh@wardhigh.org. Web: www.wardhigh.org. Rev. Michael Hermes, Pres.; Dr. Judy Warren, Prin.; Angie Gregory, Librarian. Benedictines 1; Lay Teachers 31; Students 331.

Bishop Ward High School Foundation Tel: 913-371-1201; Fax: 913-371-2145.

LEAVENWORTH. *Immaculata High School*, 600 Shawnee St., 66048. Tel: 913-682-3900; Fax: 913-682-9036. Email: lcsadmin@archkckcs.org. Mrs. Helen Schwinn, Prin. Lay Teachers 14; Students 119.

LENEXA. *Saint James Academy* (2005) 24505 Prairie Star Pkwy., 66227. Tel: 913-254-4200; Fax: 913-254-4221. Web: www.sjakeepingfaith.org. Karla Leibham, Prin.; Andy Tylicki, Pres.; Rev. Scott Wallisch, Chap. Sisters 1; Lay Teachers 43; Students 690.

OVERLAND PARK. *Saint Thomas Aquinas High School, Inc.* (1988) 11411 Pflumm Rd., 66215. Tel: 913-345-1411; Fax: 913-345-2319. Email: wpford@stasaints.net. Web: www.stasaints.net. Dr. William P. Ford, Pres.; Rev. Andrew Strobl, Chap.; Dr. Michael Sullivan, Prin.; Dr. Rebecca Heidlage, Prin.; Barbara Summerson, Librarian. Priests 1; Lay Teachers 79; Students 982.

St. Thomas Aquinas High School Foundation Tel: 913-345-1411; Fax: 913-345-2319.

TOPEKA. *Hayden High School* (1911) 401 Gage Blvd., 66606. Tel: 785-272-5210; Fax: 785-272-2975. Email: streckerr@haydenhigh.org. Web: www.haydenhigh.org. Mr. Rick Strecker, Pres.; Mr. Mark Madsen, Prin.; Rev. Nicholas Blaha, Chap.; Karen Scheopner, Librarian. Lay Teachers 38; Students 501.

Hayden High School Foundation Tel: 785-272-5210; Fax: 785-272-2975.

[C] HIGH SCHOOLS, PRIVATE

ATCHISON. *Maur Hill - Mount Academy*, 1000 Green St., 66002. Tel: 913-367-5482; Fax: 913-367-5096. Email: admissions@mh-ma.com. Web: www.mh-ma.com. Phil Baniewicz, Pres.; Monika King, Prin.; Courtney Laurie, Librarian. Priests 1; Lay Teachers 20; Students 184.

[D] ELEMENTARY SCHOOLS, INTERPAROCHIAL

KANSAS CITY. *Our Lady of Unity School*, (Grades K-8), 2646 S. 34th, 66106. Tel: 913-262-7022; Fax: 913-262-7836. Email: mneff@archkckcs.org. Micah L. Neff, Prin.; Judy McGarry, Librarian. Lay Teachers 11; Students 141.

Resurrection Catholic School at the Cathedral, (Grades PreK-8), (Merger of Cathedral, St. John/Holy Family and All Saints Schools), 425 N. 15th St., 66102. Tel: 913-371-8101; Fax: 913-371-2151. Lynda Higgins, Prin.; Donna O'Connor, Librarian. Lay Teachers 19; Students 250.

ATCHISON. *Atchison Catholic Elementary*, (Grades PreK-8), 201 Division, 66002. Tel: 913-367-3503; Fax: 913-367-9324. Email: dliebsch@benedictine.edu. Diane Liebsch, Prin. Lay Teachers 18; Students 201.

GARNETT. *St. Rose Philippine Duchesne School*, (Grades K-8), 530 E. Fourth, 66032. Tel: 785-448-3423; Fax: 785-448-3164. Nancy Butters, Prin. Lay Teachers 7; Students 65.

LEAVENWORTH. *Xavier Elementary School*, (Grades PreK-8), Admin. Office, 320 N. Broadway, 66048. Tel: 913-682-7801; Fax: 913-682-6021. Email: lrcsadmin@archkckcs.org. Karen Davis, Prin. Consolidation of the following parishes: St. Casimir; Sacred Heart; St. Joseph; and Immaculate Conception, St. Ignatius, St. Francis de Sales, St. Lawrence, St. Joseph of the Valley, and Holy Angels (Basehor) Religious Teachers 3; Lay Teachers 24; Students 369.

OVERLAND PARK. *John Paul II School*, (Grades PreK-8), 6915 W. 71st., 66204. Tel: 913-432-6350; Fax: 913-432-5081. Web: johnpaul2.eduk12.net. Susie English, Prin.; Michele Kolarik, Librarian. Lay Teachers 20; Students 253.

TOPEKA. *Holy Family School*, (Grades PreSchool-8), (East): 1725 N.E. Seward Ave., 66616. Tel: 785-234-8980; Fax: 785-234-6778. (West): 210 N.E. Branner, 66616. Tel: 785-233-9171. Lee Schmidt, Prin.; Nancy Walker, Librarian. Religious 4; Lay Teachers 12; Students 202.

[E] ELEMENTARY AND SECONDARY SCHOOLS, PRIVATE

MAPLE HILL. *St. John Vianney Preparatory School* (2000) 14611A Waterman Crossing Rd., 66507. Tel: 785-256-4500; Fax: 785-256-4611. Email: school@stjohnv.com. Rev. James Gordon, F.S.S.P., Chap.; John Zapletal, Prin. Priests 2; Lay Teachers 8; Students 75.

SHAWNEE. **Padre Pio Academy*, (Grades K-8), 5901 Flint, 66203. Tel: 913-268-3155. Email: info@padrepioacademy.org. Web: www.padrepioacademy.org. Joanne Hanson, Prin. Lay Teachers 8; Students 53.

[F] GENERAL HOSPITALS

KANSAS CITY. *Providence Medical Center*, 8929 Parallel Pkwy., 66112. Tel: 913-596-4000; Fax: 913-596-4098. Email: george.noonan@providence-health.org. Web: www.providence-health.org. Mr. Randy Nyp, Interim Pres. & CEO. An affiliate of the Sisters of Charity of Leavenworth Health System, Inc. Bed Capacity 400; Bassinets 16; Employees 1,093; Physicians 311; Patients Assisted Annually 121,885.

LEAVENWORTH. *Saint John Hospital*, 3500 S. 4th St., 66048. Tel: 913-680-6000; Fax: 913-680-6013. Daniel F. Sheehan, FACHE, Chief Administrative Officer; Mr. Randy Nyp, Interim Pres. & CEO. Physicians 174; Employees 286; Bassinets 8; Bed Capacity 76; Patients Assisted Annually 29,731.

TOPEKA. *St. Francis Health Center, Inc.*, 1700 W. 7th St., 66606. Tel: 785-295-8000; Fax: 785-295-5479. Robert J. Erickson, Pres. & CEO. Bed Capacity 375; Total Staff 1,479; Patients Assisted Annually 527,055.

[G] NURSING AND REST HOMES

OLATHE. *Villa St. Francis, Inc.* (1945) 16600 W. 126th St., 66062. Tel: 913-829-5201; Fax: 913-829-5399. Email: contactus@villasf.org. Web: www.villasf.org. Mr. John May, Admin. Owned and operated by Villa St. Francis, Inc.; Skilled nursing care; memory care unit, long term care, respite care, rapid recovery with PT/OT speech therapy. Live-in Priest Chaplain 1; Sisters of Charity of Leavenworth 1; Bed Capacity 170; Total Staff 200; Total in Residence 155; Total Assisted 160.

OVERLAND PARK. *Villa Saint Joseph Nursing Home*, 11901 Rosewood, 66209. Tel: 913-345-1745; Fax: 913-345-1346. Email: kensign@carondelet.com. Ms. Katharine Ensign, Admin. Bed Capacity 116; Total Staff 150; Total Assisted 250.

[H] CATHOLIC CHARITIES

KANSAS CITY. *Catholic Charities of Northeast Kansas, Inc.*, 9720 W. 87th St., Overland Park, 66212. Tel: 913-433-2100; Fax: 913-433-2101. Email: info@ccsks.org. Web: www.CatholicCharitiesKS.org. Mrs. Jan Lewis, Pres. & CEO.

Emporia: 702 Commercial, Ste. 3A, Emporia, 66801. Tel: 620-343-2296; Fax: 620-343-9517.

North Johnson County: 9806 W. 87th St., Overland Park, 66212. Tel: 913-384-6608; Fax: 913-384-6610.

South Johnson County: 333 E. Poplar, Olathe, 66061. Tel: 913-782-4077; Fax: 913-782-0983.

Topeka: 234 S. Kansas Blvd., Topeka, 66603. Tel: 785-233-6300; Fax: 785-233-7234.

Lawrence: 1229 Vermont, Lawrence, 66044. Tel: 785-843-0109, Ext. 327; Fax: 785-749-5064.

Leavenworth: 716 N. 5th St., Leavenworth, 66048. Tel: 913-651-8060; Fax: 913-651-9350.

Wyandotte County: 2220 Central Ave., 66102. Tel: 913-621-1504; Fax: 913-621-6586.

Catholic Charities Foundation of Northeast Kansas, 9720 W. 87th St., Overland Park, 66212. Tel: 913-433-2030; Fax: 913-433-2101.

Catholic Neighborhood Outreach, Inc. (2004) 2220 Central Ave., 66102. Tel: 913-648-6795.

Shalom House Men's Shelter (1971) 2100 N. 13th St., 66104. Tel: 913-321-2206.

St. Benedict's Early Education Center, 220 S. 9th St., 66101. Tel: 913-621-7403; Fax: 913-621-0279.

[I] MONASTERIES AND RESIDENCES FOR PRIESTS AND BROTHERS

ATCHISON. *St. Benedict's Abbey* (1857) 1020 N. 2nd St., 66002. Tel: 913-367-7853; Fax: 913-367-6230. Email: bsenecal@kansasmonks.org. Web: www.kansasmonks.org. Rt. Revs. Barnabas Senecal, O.S.B., Abbot; Ralph Koehler, O.S.B., Abbott (Retired); Owen Purcell, O.S.B., (Retired Abbot); Most Rev. Herbert Hermes, O.S.B. Bishop,

Prelacy of Cristalandia; Very Rev. James R. Albers, O.S.B., Prior; Rev. Meinrad Miller, O.S.B., Subprior; Very Rev. Maurice C. Haefling, O.S.B., Business Mgr.; Revs. Jude Burbach, O.S.B. (Retired); Joaquim Carvalho, O.S.B.; Marion Charboneau, O.S.B.; Josias Dias da Costa, O.S.B.; Roderic Giller, O.S.B.; Matthew Habiger, O.S.B.; Albert Hauser, O.S.B.; Jeremy Heppler, O.S.B.; Louis Kirby, O.S.B.; Gabriel Landis, O.S.B.; Bertrand LaNoue, O.S.B.; Daniel McCarthy, O.S.B.; Kieran McInerny, O.S.B.; Denis Meade, O.S.B., J.C.D.; Rodrigo Perissinotto, O.S.B.; Aaron Peters, O.S.B.; Donald Redmond, O.S.B (Retired); Brendan Rolling, O.S.B.; Duane Roy, O.S.B.; Michael Santa, O.S.B. (Retired); Blaine Schultz, O.S.B.; Gerard Senecal, O.S.B.; Ignatius Smith, O.S.B.; Paul Steingreaber, O.S.B.; Bruce Swift, O.S.B.; Benjamin Tremmel, O.S.B.; Camillus Wurtz, O.S.B. (Retired); Michael Zoellner, O.S.B.; Bros. Lawrence Bradford, O.S.B.; Gabriel deFaria Contijo, O.S.B.; Justin Damien Dean, O.S.B.; Haraldo Ferreira; Most Rev. Carlos Nogueira Filho, O.S.B.; Bros. Leven Harton; Kaio Maluf, O.S.B.; Diego Oliviera; John Peto, O.S.B.; Joseph Ryan, O.S.B.; Christopher Start, O.S.B.; Anthony Vorwerk, O.S.B.; Simon Baker, O.S.B. Bishops 1; Priests 36; Brothers 12.

LAWRENCE. *St. Conrad Friary* (1990) (Capuchins), 745 Tennessee, 66044. Tel: 785-843-0188; Fax: 785-843-2214. Web: www.capuchins.org. Total in Residence 3. In Res. Revs. Curtis Carlson, O.F.M.Cap.; Duane F. Reinert, O.F.M.Cap.; John Schmeidler, O.F.M.Cap.

[J] CONVENTS AND RESIDENCES FOR SISTERS

KANSAS CITY. *Little Sisters of the Lamb*, Provincial House: 36 S. Boeke St., 66101. Tel: 913-621-1727; Fax: 913-621-2823. Sr. Benedicte Bertrand, O.P., Prioress.

Servants of Mary, Ministers to the Sick, 800 N. 18th St., 66102. Tel: 913-371-3423; 913-621-1147; Fax: 913-621-4962. Email: mprovincialsdemkc@yahoo.com. Ministers to the Sick, Motherhouse of the Congregation for the United States.; Nurses, private duty, and visiting nurses in the homes. *Cathedral of St. Peter*, St. Peters Cathedral: Sisters Carmela Sanz, S.deM., Prov. Supr.; Claudia Rodriguez, S.deM., Local Supr.; Rev. Daniel Gardner, Chap. Professed 33.

ATCHISON. *Dooley Center, Inc.* (1993) 801 S. Eighth St., 66002. Tel: 913-360-6200; Fax: 913-360-6275. Benedictine Sisters of Mount St. Scholastica, Inc., Atchison, KS., Nursing care facility for the aged/infirm members of this religious community.

Mount St. Scholastica (1863) 801 S. 8th St., 66002. Tel: 913-360-6200; Fax: 913-360-6190. Email: anne@mountosb.org. Web: www.mountosb.org. Sr. Anne Shepard, O.S.B., Prioress. Motherhouse of the Sisters of St. Benedict. Professed Sisters 151; Novices 1; Postulants 1.

LEAVENWORTH. *Motherhouse of the Sisters of Charity of Leavenworth*, 4200 S. 4th St., 66048-5054. Tel: 913-758-6501; Fax: 913-682-2128. Email: mhall@scls.org. Web: www.scls.org. Sisters Maureen Hall, S.C.L., Community Dir.; Lucy Walter, S.C.L., Local Coord.; Margaret Finch, S.C.L., Local Admin.; Rev. Michael Zoellner, O.S.B., Chap. Sisters 277; Total in Residence 106.

OVERLAND PARK. *Association of the Apostles of the Interior Life*, 10300 Cody St., 66214. Tel: 913-261-9692. Email: susanmarie.avi@gmail.com. Web: www.apostlesofil.org. Sr. Susan Pieper, Supr. Sisters 6.

[K] PRIVATE ASSOCIATIONS OF THE FAITHFUL

KANSAS CITY. *Society of St. Augustine - Public Association of the Faithful* (2000) 3008 S. 34th St., 66106. Tel: 913-384-3583. Email: pmjaramillo@msn.com. Web: www.augustinian.us. Revs. Peter Jaramillo, S.S.A., Prior; John Melnick, S.S.A., Dir. Formation; Joseph Arsenault, S.S.A., J.C.L.

SHAWNEE MISSION. *Franciscan Servants of the Holy Family - Public Association of the Faithful* (2001) P.O. Box 7251, 66207. Tel: 785-218-2894. Email: srdoris@aol.com. Sr. Doris Engeman, F.S.H.F., Sister Servant. Mission: Helping families grow in holiness and unity.

[L] CAMPUS MINISTRY

EMPORIA. *Didde Catholic Campus Center, Emporia State University* Office: 1415 Merchant St., 66801. Tel: 620-343-6765; Fax: 620-343-6792. Email: dccc-emp@sbcglobal.net. Web: www.emporia.edu/dccc. 1102 Neosho St., 66801. Tel: 620-342-8727. Rev. Raymond May Jr., Chap. Total Staff 7.

LAWRENCE. *Haskell Catholic Campus Center* (1985) 2301 Barker Ave., 66046-4813. Tel: 785-842-2401. Rev. Duane F. Reinert, O.F.M.Cap., Chap.; Ms. Monica Olivera, Dir. Total Staff 1.

St. Lawrence Catholic Campus Center at the University of Kansas and Residence 1631 Crescent Rd., 66044. Tel: 785-843-0357; Fax: 785-842-2203. Email: slccc@st-lawrence.org. Web: www.st-lawrence.org. Rev. Steven Beseau, S.T.D., Dir. Total Staff 15.

St. Lawrence Center Foundation

TOPEKA. *Catholic Campus Center at Washburn University* 1633 S.W. Jewell, 66604. Tel: 785-233-2204; Fax: 785-233-2205. Email: wucatholic@hotmail.com. Web: www.wucatholic.com. Patti Lyon, S.F.O., Dir.

[M] MISCELLANEOUS LISTINGS

KANSAS CITY. *Catholic Care Campus, Inc. dba Santa Marta* (2004) 13800 W. 116th St., Olathe, 66062. Tel: 913-906-0990; Fax: 913-906-0911. Web: www.santamartaretirement.com. Independent, assisted living, memory support, skilled nursing. Total Assisted 242; Total Staff 160.

The Catholic Foundation of Northeast Kansas, 12615 Parallel, 66109. Tel: 913-647-0325; Fax: 913-647-0333. Email: stewdev@archkck.org. Web: www.archkck.org. (Formerly known as Archdiocesan Foundation)

Catholic Housing of Wyandotte County, 2 S. 14th St., 66101. Tel: 913-342-7580; Fax: 913-342-7581. Web: www.chwconline.com.

Duchesne Clinic (1989) 636 Tauromee, 66101. Tel: 913-321-2626; Fax: 913-321-2651. Email: gloria.guerra@caritasclinics.org. Web: www.duchesneclinic.org. Amy Falk, Exec. Dir.; Gloria Guerra, Mgr. A division of Caritas Clinics, Inc., Leavenworth, KS. Total Staff 16; Total Patient Visits 11,312; Patients Assisted Annually 1,888.

**El Centro, Inc.*, 650 Minnesota Ave., 66101. Tel: 913-677-0100; Fax: 913-362-8513. Web: www.elcentroinc.com. Ms. Mary Lou Jaramillo, Pres. & CEO.

Academy for Children, 608 N. 18th St., 66102.

Academy for Children Child Care Center, 1330 S. 30th St., 66106. Tel: 913-677-1115; Fax: 913-677-7090.

Academy for Children, Choo Choo Child Care, 219 S. Mill St., 66101. Tel: 913-371-1744; Fax: 913-371-1866.

ECI Development, Inc., 2100 Metropolitan Ave., 66106. Tel: 913-677-1120; Fax: 913-677-0051.

El Centro, Inc. Argentine, 1333 S. 27th St., 66106. Tel: 913-677-0177; Fax: 913-362-8250.

El Centro, Inc. Family Center, Johnson County, 9525 Metcalf Ave., Overland Park, 66212. Tel: 913-381-2861; Fax: 913-381-2914.

St. Joseph Adoption Referral Service, Inc. (2001) 8160 Parallel Pkwy., Ste. 103, 66112. Tel: 913-299-5222; 800-752-1737; Fax: 913-299-5111. Email: apeacefulblessing@yahoo.com. Web: www.catholicadoption.info. Sisters Janet Fleischhacker, C.S.J., Pres. & Contact Person; Dolora May, Dir. Staff 3; Total Assisted Annually 15.

Lay Employee's Retirement Plan of the Archdiocese of Kansas City in Kansas (1978) 12615 Parallel Pkwy., 66109. Tel: 913-721-1570; Fax: 913-721-2680. Email: kthomas@archkck.org. Web: www.archkck.org.

Priest's Retirement Plan of the Archdiocese of Kansas City in Kansas (1978) 12615 Parallel Pkwy., 66109. Tel: 912-721-1570; Fax: 912-721-2680. Email: kthomas@archkck.org. Web: www.archkck.org.

Providence Saint John Foundation, 8929 Parallel Pkwy., 66112. Tel: 913-596-4151; Fax: 913-596-3418. Email: karla.kimerer@providence-health.org. Web: www.psjf.org.

ATCHISON. *The Maur Hill Prep School Endowment Association, Inc.*, 1000 Green St., 66002. Tel: 913-367-5482; Fax: 913-367-5096.

EASTON. *Christ's Peace House of Prayer* (1972) 22019 Meagher Rd., 66020. Tel: 913-773-8255. Total in Residence 4; Total Staff 5.

LEAVENWORTH. *Caritas Clinics, Inc.*, 818 N. 7th St., 66048. Tel: 913-651-8860; Fax: 913-682-4409. Email: caritas@caritasclinics.org. Web: www.caritasclinics.org. Amy Falk, Exec. Dir. Sisters of Charity of Leavenworth., Administrative structure for St. Vincent Clinic, Leavenworth, Duchesne Clinic, Kansas City. Total Staff 4.

Catholic School Foundation of the Leavenworth Region, Inc., 320 N. Broadway, 66048. Tel: 913-682-7801; Fax: 913-682-6021. Email: lrcs@archkckcs.org. Barbara Ferrara, Dir.

Saint Vincent Clinic (1986) 818 N. 7th St., 66048. Tel: 913-651-8860; Fax: 913-682-4409. Email: briana.cavinaw@caritasclinics.org. Web: www.saintvincentclinic.org. Amy Falk, Exec. Dir. (A division of Caritas Clinics, Inc., Leavenworth, KS.) Total Staff 7; Total Patients 894; Total Patient Visits 4,366.

LENEXA. *Sisters of Charity of Leavenworth Health System, Inc.*, 9801 Renner Blvd., Ste. 100, 66219. Tel: 913-895-2800; Fax: 913-895-2900. Web: www.sclhealthsystem.org. Mr. Michael A. Slubowski, Pres. & CEO.

MAYETTA. *Our Lady of the Snows Oratory* Potawatomi Reservation, 66509. Mailing Address: c/o St. Dominic, 416 Ohio Ave., Holton, 66436. Tel: 785-364-3262; Fax: 785-364-1499. Attended by: St. Dominic, Holton, KS.

OVERLAND PARK. *Holy Family School of Faith*, 11400 W. 103rd St., 66214. Tel: 913-310-0014. Email: cari@schooloffaith.com. Web: www.schooloffaith.com. Michael Scherschligt, Exec. Dir.

PRAIRIE VILLAGE. *School of Love, Inc.*, 5105 Tomahawk Rd., 66208.

TOPEKA. *The Cursillo Movement of the Archdiocese of Kansas City in Kansas* (1974) 2601 Ridge Ave., 66102. Tel: 913-321-4673. Email: frdennis@sanctuaryofhope.org. Web: www.cursillo.org/kckcursillo. Rev. Dennis Wait, Spiritual Mod.; Bill Welch, Lay Dir.

El Centro de Servicios Para Hispanos dba El Centro of Topeka (1971) 134 N.E. Lake, 66616. Tel: 785-232-8207; Fax: 785-232-8834. Email: lmunoz@elcentrooftopeka.org.

St. Francis Health Center Foundation, 1700 W. 7th St., 66606. Tel: 785-295-5356; Fax: 785-295-5479. Email: wsnodgrass@stfrancistopeka.org. Web: www.stfrancistopeka.org.

Marian Clinic, Inc., 1001 S.W. Garfield Ave., 66604. Tel: 785-233-8081; Fax: 785-233-8952. Web: www.marianclinic.org. Mr. Michael A. Slubowski, Pres., SCLHS; Dr. Jeffrey Martin, Interim Exec. Dir. Affiliate of Sisters of Charity of Leavenworth Health System Total Patients 4,913.

RELIGIOUS INSTITUTES OF MEN REPRESENTED IN THE ARCHDIOCESE

For further details refer to the corresponding bracketed number in the Religious Institutes of Men or Women section.

[0200]—*Benedictine Monks* (St. Benedict's Abbey)—O.S.B.

[0200]—*Benedictine Monks* (Conception Abbey)—O.S.B.

[0470]—*The Capuchin Friars* (Holy Family)—O.F.M.Cap.

[0270]—*Carmelite Fathers & Brothers* (American Prov.)—O.Carm.

[1000]—*Congregation of the Passion*—C.P.

[1210]—*Missionaries of St. Charles-Scalabrinians*—C.S.

[]—*Missionaries of St. Francis de Sales*—M.S.F.S.

[1065]—*Priestly Fraternity of St. Peter*—F.S.S.P.

[]—*Society of Jesus*—S.J.

[1060]—*Society of the Precious Blood*—C.PP.S.

RELIGIOUS INSTITUTES OF WOMEN REPRESENTED IN THE ARCHDIOCESE

[0100]—*Adorers of the Blood of Christ*—A.S.C.

[0230]—*Benedictine Sisters of Pontifical Jurisdiction*—O.S.B.

[3832]—*Congregation of the Sisters of St. Joseph of Wichita*—C.S.J.

[]—*Franciscan Servants of Holy Family (Public Association of the Faithful)*

[1430]—*Franciscan Sisters of Our Lady of Perpetual Help*—O.S.F.

[]—*Little Sisters of the Lamb*—O.P.

[2500]—*Medical Sisters of St. Joseph*—M.S.J.

[]—*Missioneras Guadalupanos de Cristo Rey*

[0480]—*Sisters of Charity of Leavenworth, Kansas*—S.C.L.

[0990]—*Sisters of Divine Providence*—C.D.P.

[]—*Sisters of St. Anne*—C.S.S.A.

[]—*Sisters of St. Francis of the Martyr St. George*—F.S.G.M.

[]—*Sisters of St. Joseph* (Concordia, KS)—C.S.J.

[3840]—*Sisters of St. Joseph of Carondelet* (St. Louis, MO)—C.S.J.

[]—*Sisters of the Apostles of the Interior Life*—A.V.I.

[3600]—*Sisters, Servants of Mary*—S.M.

[4120-05]—*Ursuline Nuns, of the Congregation of Paris*—O.S.U.

ARCHDIOCESAN CEMETERIES

KANSAS CITY. *Gate of Heaven, St. John, Mount Calvary*

SHAWNEE, JOHNSON COUNTY. *Resurrection, Shawnee, St. Joseph's, Shawnee, St. John, Lenexa, Mount Calvery, Olathe*

ATCHISON. *Mount Calvary*

LEAVENWORTH. *Mount Calvary*

TOPEKA. *Mount Calvary*

NECROLOGY

† Horvat, Matthew J., (Retired)—Died Nov. 21, 2011
† Krische, Francis, (Retired)—Died Jan. 12, 2011
† Okoye, Joseph—Died April 7, 2011

An asterisk (*) denotes an organization that has established tax-exempt status directly with the IRS and is not covered by the USCCB Group Ruling.

Diocese of Kansas City-St. Joseph

(Dioecesis Kansanopolitanae Sancti Josephi)

Most Reverend

ROBERT W. FINN, D.D.

Bishop of Kansas City-St. Joseph; born April 2, 1953; ordained July 7, 1979; appointed Coadjutor Bishop of Kansas City-St. Joseph March 9, 2004; installed May 3, 2004; succeeded to See May 24, 2005. *Mailing Address: P.O. Box 419037, Kansas City, MO 64141-6037.*

Most Reverend

RAYMOND J. BOLAND, D.D.

Retired Bishop of Kansas City-St. Joseph; born February 8, 1932; ordained June 16, 1957; appointed Bishop of Birmingham February 2, 1988; consecrated March 25, 1988; appointed Bishop of Kansas City-St. Joseph June 22, 1993; installed September 9, 1993; retired May 24, 2005. *Mailing Address: P.O. Box 419037, Kansas City, MO 64141-6037.*

QUAERITE PRIMUM REGNUM DEI

Chancery: 20 W. 9th St., Ste. 200, Kansas City, MO 64105. Mailing Address: P.O. Box 419037, Kansas City, MO 64141-6037. Tel: 816-756-1850; Fax: 816-756-0878.

Web: www.diocese-kcsj.org

Square Miles 15,429.

Diocese of Kansas City Established September 10, 1880; Diocese of St. Joseph Established March 3, 1868.

Redesignated Diocese of Kansas City-St. Joseph August 29, 1956.

Comprises the Counties of Andrew, Atchison, Bates, Buchanan, Caldwell, Carroll, Cass, Clay, Clinton, Daviess, DeKalb, Gentry, Grundy, Harrison, Henry, Holt, Jackson, Johnson, Lafayette, Livingston, Mercer, Nodaway, Platte, Ray, St. Clair, Vernon and Worth in the State of Missouri.

For legal titles of parishes and diocesan institutions, consult the Chancery Office.

STATISTICAL OVERVIEW

Personnel	
Bishop	1
Retired Bishops	1
Abbots	1
Priests: Diocesan Active in Diocese	63
Priests: Diocesan Active Outside Diocese	3
Priests: Diocesan in Foreign Missions	1
Priests: Retired, Sick or Absent	30
Number of Diocesan Priests	97
Religious Priests in Diocese	82
Total Priests in Diocese	179
Extern Priests in Diocese	9
Ordinations:	
Diocesan Priests	2
Transitional Deacons	9
Permanent Deacons	8
Permanent Deacons in Diocese	64
Total Brothers	33
Total Sisters	219
Parishes	
Parishes	87
With Resident Pastor:	
Resident Diocesan Priests	55
Resident Religious Priests	19
Without Resident Pastor:	
Administered by Priests	11
Administered by Deacons	1
Administered by Lay People	1
Missions	11
Professional Ministry Personnel:	
Brothers	1
Sisters	2
Lay Ministers	107
Welfare	
Catholic Hospitals	3
Total Assisted	290,581
Homes for the Aged	11
Total Assisted	2,335
Day Care Centers	8
Total Assisted	1,307
Special Centers for Social Services	7
Total Assisted	296,285
Residential Care of Disabled	1
Total Assisted	40
Other Institutions	1
Total Assisted	32
Educational	
Seminaries, Diocesan	1
Students from This Diocese	5
Students from Other Diocese	107
Diocesan Students in Other Seminaries	19
Total Seminarians	24
Colleges and Universities	2
Total Students	4,619
High Schools, Diocesan and Parish	4
Total Students	1,084
High Schools, Private	4
Total Students	2,404
Elementary Schools, Diocesan and Parish	26
Total Students	7,519
Elementary Schools, Private	1
Total Students	302
Catechesis/Religious Education:	
High School Students	1,438
Elementary Students	6,732
Total Students under Catholic Instruction	24,122
Teachers in the Diocese:	
Priests	21
Brothers	12
Sisters	10
Lay Teachers	1,095
Vital Statistics	
Receptions into the Church:	
Infant Baptism Totals	2,055
Minor Baptism Totals	189
Adult Baptism Totals	259
Received into Full Communion	461
First Communions	2,242
Confirmations	1,855
Marriages:	
Catholic	389
Interfaith	309
Total Marriages	698
Deaths	1,238
Total Catholic Population	134,173
Total Population	1,513,005

Former Bishops—Most Revs. JOHN JOSEPH HOGAN, D.D., ord. April 10, 1852; cons. Bishop of St. Joseph, MO, Sept. 13, 1868; transferred to Kansas City, Sept. 10, 1880; died Feb. 21, 1913; THOMAS F. LILLIS, D.D., ord. Aug. 15, 1885; cons. Bishop of Leavenworth, Dec. 27, 1904; appt. Coadjutor to the Bishop of Kansas City, "cum jure successionis," March 14, 1910; Bishop of Kansas City, Feb. 21, 1913; appt. assistant at the Pontifical Throne, Aug. 19, 1935; died Dec. 29, 1938; EDWIN V. O'HARA, D.D., ord. June 10, 1905; appt. Bishop of Great Falls, MT, August 1, 1930; cons. Oct. 28, 1930; transferred to the See of Kansas City, April 15, 1939; made assistant at the Pontifical Throne, Jan. 5, 1949; appt. Archbishop "ad personam," June 29, 1954; died Sept. 11, 1956; His Eminence JOHN CARDINAL CODY, D.D., S.T.D., ord. Dec. 8, 1931; appt. Titular Bishop of Appollonia and Auxiliary Bishop of St. Louis, May 14, 1947; cons. July 2, 1947; promoted to coadjutor of St. Joseph "cum jure successionis," Jan. 27, 1954; appt. to Diocese of Kansas City-St. Joseph, Aug. 24, 1956; succeeded to See Sept. 11, 1956; transferred to Archdiocese of New Orleans as Coadjutor Archbishop "cum jure successionis," Aug. 10, 1961; acceded to the See of New Orleans, Nov. 8, 1964; transferred to the Archdiocese of Chicago, June 16, 1965; created Cardinal Priest, June 26, 1967; died April 25, 1982; Most Revs. CHARLES H. HELMSING, D.D., ord. June 10, 1933; appt. Titular Bishop of Axomis and Auxiliary Bishop of St. Louis, March 17, 1949; cons. April 19, 1949; appt. Bishop of Springfield-Cape Girardeau, Aug. 24, 1956; transferred to Diocese of Kansas City-St. Joseph, Jan. 27, 1962; retired Aug. 17, 1977; died Dec. 20, 1993; JOHN J. SULLIVAN, D.D., ord. Sept. 23, 1944; appt. Bishop of Grand Island, July 25, 1972; cons. Sept. 19, 1972; installed Grand Island, Sept. 21, 1972; appt. Bishop of Kansas City-St. Joseph, June 27, 1977; installed Aug. 17, 1977; retired Sept. 9, 1993; died Feb. 8, 2001; RAYMOND J. BOLAND, D.D., born Feb. 8, 1932; ord. June 16, 1957; appt. Bishop of Birmingham Feb. 2, 1988; cons. March 25, 1988; appt. Bishop of Kansas City-St. Joseph June 22, 1993; installed Sept. 9, 1993; retired May 24, 2005.

Former Bishops of Diocese of St. Joseph, MO—Most Revs. JOHN J. HOGAN, D.D., ord. April 10, 1852; appt. first Bishop of St. Joseph, March 3, 1868; consecrated Sept. 13, 1868; transferred to See of Kansas City, Sept. 10, 1880; administrator of St. Joseph until 1893; died Feb. 21, 1913; MAURICE F. BURKE, D.D., born May 5, 1844; ord. May 22, 1875; appt. first Bishop of Cheyenne, WY, Aug. 9, 1887; consecrated Oct. 28, 1887; transferred to St. Joseph, June 19, 1893; died March 17, 1923; FRANCIS GILFILLAN, D.D., born Feb. 16, 1872; ord. June 24, 1895; appt. Titular Bishop of Spigas and Coadjutor with the right of succession to the See of St. Joseph, July 8, 1922; consecrated Nov. 8, 1922; succeeded to the See of St. Joseph, March 17, 1923; died Jan. 13, 1933; CHARLES H. LEBLOND, D.D., ord. Oct. 27, 1909; appt. Bishop of St. Joseph, July 21, 1933; consecrated Sept. 21, 1933; resigned as Bishop of St. Joseph and appointed Titular Bishop of Orcistus, Aug. 24, 1956; died Dec. 30, 1958.

Vicar General—Rev. Msgr. A. ROBERT MURPHY.
Vicar for Clergy—Rev. JOSEPH POWERS.
Chancery—Mailing Address: P.O. Box 419037, Kansas City, 64141-6037. Tel: 816-756-1850; Fax: 816-756-0878. All official matters should be sent to this address.
Chancellor—Rev. Msgr. BRADLEY S. OFFUTT.
Chief of Staff—JUDE HUNTZ.
Vice Chancellors—CLAUDE SASSO, Ph.D.; PAULA MOSS.
Finance Officer—DAVID A. MALANOWSKI.
Tribunal—Mailing Address: P.O. Box 419037, Kansas City, 64141-6037. Tel: 816-756-1850.
Judicial Vicar and Tribunal Director—VACANT.
Judge, Adjutant Judicial Vicar—Rev. C. MICHAEL COLEMAN, J.C.L.
Defender of the Bond—Sr. RITA KILLACKEY, O.S.B., J.C.L.
Procurator—DONETTA K. SHAW.
Associate Director & Procurator—ALLISON TOWNLEY.
Consultors—Revs. J. KENNETH CRIQUI; RONALD J. ELLIOTT; DONALD P. FARNAN; Rev. Msgr. ROBERT S. GREGORY; Rev. THOMAS W. HERMES; Rev. Msgrs. A. ROBERT MURPHY; BRADLEY S. OFFUTT; Revs. ALEXANDER B. SINCLAIR (Retired); JOHN J. VOWELLS, S.J.
Presbyteral Council—Revs. CHARLES ROWE, S.T.D., Chm.; JUSTIN E. HOYE, Vice Chm. & Ordained Ten Years & Under; DAVID L. HOLLOWAY, Sec. & Treas.; Rev. Msgr. JOHN E. LEITNER, Retired Priests' Representative (Retired); Revs. KARL BARMANN, O.S.B.; JOSEPH MILLER, C.PP.S.; JOHN J. VOWELLS, S.J.
Deans—Rev. JOHN J. VOWELLS, S.J., Deanery I; Rev. Msgr. ROBERT S. GREGORY, Deanery II; VACANT, Deanery III; Revs. DONALD P. FARNAN, Deanery IV; DAVID L. HOLLOWAY, Deanery V; MICHAEL CLARY, Deanery VI; PHILIP EGAN, Deanery VII; J. KENNETH CRIQUI, Deanery VIII; ANGELO BARTULICA, Deanery IX; KARL BARMANN, O.S.B., Deanery X; JAMES TARANTO, Deanery XI; JOSEPH TOTTON, Deanery XII; CHARLES ROWE, S.T.D., Deanery XIII; VINCENT M. ROGERS, Deanery XIV.

Diocesan Offices and Directors

Archivist—Rev. C. MICHAEL COLEMAN, J.C.L.
Bishop Helmsing Institute—SCOTT MCKELLAR, Dir.
Building Commission—JOSEPH W. HARRIS, Chm.; PAUL BOSCHI; FRANK COHALLA; BOB DRAKE; BERNARD J. GRAM; BERNARD JACQUINOT; ROBERT JONES; DAVE KOPEK; DAVID A. MALANOWSKI; Rev. Msgr. BRADLEY S. OFFUTT; WAYNE ROY; THOMAS STRAHAN; Deacon RALPH L. WEHNER.
Catholic Charities Foundation—ROZANNE PRATHER, Exec. Dir, 20 W. 9th St., Ste. 650, Kansas City, 64105. Tel: 816-221-4377; Fax: 816-472-5423.
Catholic Charities of Kansas City-St. Joseph, Inc., Caritas Center—20 W. 9th St., Ste. 600, Kansas City, 64105. Tel: 816-221-4377; Fax: 816-472-5423. MICHAEL W. HALTERMAN, CEO; STEPHANIE RAY, COO & Dir. Sr. Care Svcs. Northwest Missouri Branch Office: Deacon MARTIN J. GOEDKEN, Assoc. Dir., 902 Edmond, Ste. 204, St. Joseph, 64501. Tel: 816-232-2885. Heart of Missouri Office: JUDY THOMPSON, Assoc. Dir., 118 W. Hout St., Ste. F, Warrensburg, 64093. Tel: 660-747-2241.
Turnaround Program - Community Re-Entry After Prison—RITA FLYNN, Prog. Mgr., 3100 Main St., Ste. 10, Kansas City, 64111. Tel: 816-561-1835.
The "Catholic Key" Diocesan Newspaper—JACK SMITH, Editor.
Cemeteries (Catholic Cemeteries Associated, Diocese of Kansas City-St. Joseph, Inc.)—JOSEPH W. HARRIS, 7601 Blue Ridge, Kansas City, 64138. Cemeteries: Kansas City, Mt. Olivet; Mt. St. Mary; Resurrection; St. Joseph, Mt. Olivet.
Censor Librorum—Rev. Msgr. WILLIAM J. BLACET, P.A., J.C.L.
Communications—REBECCA SUMMERS, Dir.
Hispanic Ministry—JOANN ROA, Dir.
Religious Education—CLAUDE SASSO, Ph.D.
Bright Futures Fund—KERRY ESSMANN, Exec. Dir.
Consecrated Life Office—Sr. CONNIE BOULCH, O.S.F., Dir.
Ecumenical Officer—Rt. Rev. GREGORY POLAN, O.S.B.
Family Life Office—Deacon KENNETH GREENE, Dir.
Finance Council—Most Rev. ROBERT W. FINN; VINCE ANCH; Rev. STEPHEN M. COOK, J.C.L.; MARYELLEN CONNOR; JOHN CROWE; JOHN DESTEFANO; Rev. Msgr. ROBERT S. GREGORY; JOHN HOULEHAN; THERESA HUPP; EILEEN HUTCHINSON; RON JURY; THOMAS A. MCCULLOUGH; JERRY MEINERS; PAULA MOSS, Non-voting Member; MARGO SHEPARD. Staff Representatives: MONICA ADAMS; DAVID A. MALANOWSKI.
Finance Office—DAVID A. MALANOWSKI, Finance Officer; MONICA ADAMS, Internal Auditor; DONNA LEWIS, Accounting Mgr.
Holy Childhood Association—Rev. ROBERT M. CAMERON, Dir.
Human Resources—RHONDA STUCINSKI, Dir.; ANNE MARIE STUEVE, Benefits Coord.
Human Rights Office—JUDE HUNTZ, Dir.
Insurance Office—MONICA ADAMS, Risk Mgr.
Legion of Mary—Rev. DONALD E. STURM, Dir.
Disability & Deaf Services—JUDY SHUTE, Coord., 4101 E. 105th Ter., Kansas City, 64137. Tel: 816-765-9805.
Permanent Diaconate—Rev. Msgr. A. ROBERT MURPHY, Vicar for Deacons; Rev. JOSEPH CISETTI, Dir. Spiritual Formation; Deacon DWAYNE KATZER, Dir. Diaconate Formation; Rev. RONALD J. ELLIOTT, Dir. Deacons.
Priestly Life and Ministry—Rev. ERNEST P. DAVIS, Dir.
Priests' Pension Plan—Administrative Committee: Revs. JOSEPH SHARBEL; ERNEST P. DAVIS; DONALD P. FARNAN; GAYLE LAPLANTE; DAVID A. MALANOWSKI; Rev. Msgr. A. ROBERT MURPHY; RHONDA STUCINSKI.
Priests' Purgatorial Society—Rev. ROBERT M. CAMERON, Sec.
Propagation of the Faith— (Pontifical Society for the Propagation of the Faith, Missionary Union of the Clergy and Religious, The Pontifical Society of St. Peter the Apostle for Native Clergy, and Daily World missionaries) Rev. ROBERT M. CAMERON, Dir.
Property Management—WAYNE ROY, Diocesan Property Mgr.; GERI SIRNA, Property Mgmt. Coord.; ROBERT JONES, A.I.A., C.S.I., Construction Mgr. Fax: 816-756-5572.
Respect Life Office—BILL FRANCIS, Dir.
Safe Environment—CARRIE COOPER, Dir. Child & Youth Protection; MARY FRANCES HORTON, Coord. Safe Environment Programs. Email: mfhorton@kc.rr.com; JENIFER VALENTI, Ombudsman; LESLIE GUILLOT, Victims' Advocate.
St. Vincent De Paul Particular Council—DAN KOEHNE, Moderator.
School Office—DAN PETERS, Ed.D., Supt.; PAT BURBACH, Assoc. Supt.
Stewardship and Development—PAULA MOSS, Dir.; GREG VRANICAR, Assoc. Dir.
Vocation Office—Revs. RICHARD ROCHA, Vocation Dir.; GREGORY J. LOCKWOOD, Administrative Dir.
Worship Office—Deacon RALPH L. WEHNER, Dir. & Master of Ceremonies; KATIE BEYERS, Assoc. Dir.
Young Adult and Campus Ministry—ALLISON KEEGAN, Dir.
Youth Office—JON SCHAFFHAUSEN, Dir.

CLERGY, PARISHES, MISSIONS AND PAROCHIAL SCHOOLS

KANSAS CITY

(JACKSON COUNTY)

1—CATHEDRAL OF IMMACULATE CONCEPTION (1882) Rev. Msgr. Robert S. Gregory, Rector; Deacon Stephen W. Livingston. In Res., Rev. Msgr. Bradley S. Offutt, Chancellor.
Res.: 416 W. 12th St., 64105. Tel: 816-842-0416; 816-842-0416, Ext. 112 Cathedral Social Services; Fax: 816-842-3849.

2—ST. ALOYSIUS (1886), (Hispanic), Closed. For inquiries for parish records contact Archives, Catholic Chancery.

3—ST. ANTHONY (1991) Rev. Jason Koch, L.C., Admin.
Res.: 318 Benton Blvd., 64124. Tel: 816-231-5445; Fax: 816-231-5446.
Catechesis/Religious Program—Students 83.

4—ST. BERNADETTE'S (1958) Rev. David L. Holloway; Deacons Emory Corrigan, (Retired); David Townley.
Mailing Address: 9020 E. 51st Ter., 64133.
Res.: 9021 E. 51st Ter., 64133. Tel: 816-356-3700; Fax: 816-737-3447. Email: stbernadette@kc.rr.com. Web: www.stbernadettekcmo.com.
Catechesis/Religious Program—Students 14.

5—BLESSED SACRAMENT, Closed. For inquiries for parish records contact Archives, Catholic Chancery.

6—ST. CATHERINE OF SIENA (1926) Rev. Robert Kerr; Deacon William Markey, (Retired); Veronica Ward, Pastoral Assoc. Tel: 816-761-5483, Ext. 110.
Res.: 4101 E. 105th Ter., 64137-1649. Tel: 816-761-5483; Fax: 816-761-8795. Web: www.saintcatherine.com.
Catechesis/Religious Program—Tel: 816-761-5483, Ext. 110.

7—ST. CHARLES BORROMEO (1947) Rev. Kenneth A. Riley; Deacons Jerry Williams; Frank Peak; Joseph Whiston.
Res.: 900 N.E. Shady Lane Dr., 64118-4742. Tel: 816-436-0880; Fax: 816-436-0103. Web: www.stcharleskc.com.
School—804 N.E. Shady Lane Dr., Oakview, 64118. Tel: 816-436-1009; Fax: 816-436-6293. Lay Teachers 31; Students 350.
Catechesis/Religious Program—Students 106.

8—CHRIST THE KING (1938) Rev. Gregory J. Lockwood.
Mailing Address: 8510 Wornall Rd., 64114.
Res.: 504 W. 85th Terr., 64114. Tel: 816-363-4888; Fax: 816-363-2315. Web: www.ctkkcmo.org.
School—(Grades K-8), 425 W. 85th St., 64114. Tel: 816-363-1113; Fax: 816-363-2889. Lay Teachers 12; Students 106.
Preschool—Tel: 816-363-5313. (Infant/Toddler & Preschool) Lay Teachers 17; Students 51.

9—CHURCH OF THE HOLY MARTYRS (1991), (Vietnamese), Rev. Joseph Phan Trong Hanh.
Res.: 7801 Paseo, 64131. Tel: 816-333-3214; Fax: 816-523-8168. Email: hphan43@sbcglobal.net.
Catechesis/Religious Program—Tel: 816-333-5349. Students 300.

10—ST. ELIZABETH'S (1917) Rev. Terry Bruce; Deacon Donald Schmit.
Office: 2 E. 75th St., 64114. Tel: 816-523-2405; Fax: 816-444-9858.
Rectory—7444 Main St., 64114. Tel: 816-523-2155.
School—(Grades PreSchool-8), 14 W. 75th St., 64114. Tel: 816-523-7100; Fax: 816-523-2566. Email: info@stelizabethkc.org. Lay Teachers 32; Students 476.
Catechesis/Religious Program—Students 23.

11—ST. FRANCIS SERAPH, Closed. For inquiries for parish records contact St. Anthony, Kansas City.

12—ST. FRANCIS XAVIER (1909) Revs. John J. Vowells, S.J.; A. James Blumeyer, S.J.
Res.: 1001 E. 52nd St., 64110. Tel: 816-523-5115; Fax: 816-333-0082. Email: parish@sfx-kc.org. Web: www.sfx.kc.org.
Catechesis/Religious Program—Tel: 816-523-5115, Ext. 204. Students 37.

13—ST. GABRIEL ARCHANGEL (1956) Rev. Joseph M. Sharbel; Deacon Larry West.
Res.: 4737 N. Cleveland Ave., 64117. Tel: 816-453-1183; Fax: 816-453-6254. Web: www.stgabriels-kc.org.
School—Tel: 816-453-4443. Lay Teachers 16; Students 160.
Early Childhood Learning Center—Tel: 816-453-4555. Lay Teachers 23.
Catechesis/Religious Program—Tel: 816-453-1183, Ext. 217. Students 187.

14—GUARDIAN ANGELS (1909) Margaret Lima, Pastoral Admin.; Rev. Glenn R. Mueller, S.J.
Parish Office—1310 Westport Rd., 64111. Tel: 816-931-4351; Fax: 816-531-6396. Web: guardianangelsparish.ws.
School—Our Lady of the Angels School, 4232 Mercier, 64111. Tel: 816-931-1693; Fax: 816-931-6713. Email: mcdelac@yahoo.com. Web: www.olakc.org.
School—Our Lady of Guadalupe School, 2310 Madison, 64108. Tel: 816-221-2539; Fax: 816-283-3315. Email: wdejbowman@everestkc.com. Web: olgkc.org.
Catechesis/Religious Program—Students 24.

15—HOLY CROSS (1902) Revs. Jason Koch, L.C.; Arnulfo Contreras (Mexico), Hispanic Ministry; Deacon Daniel Esteban; Janel Lynn Bromberek, Youth Min.
Res.: 5106 St. John Ave., 64123. Tel: 816-231-4845; Fax: 816-483-0900.
Catechesis/Religious Program—Students 161.

16—HOLY FAMILY (1980) Rev. Matthew Brumleve.
Res.: 919 N.E. 96th St., 64155. Tel: 816-436-9200; Fax: 816-436-8049. Web: www.holyfamily.com.
Catechesis/Religious Program—Students 361.

17—HOLY ROSARY (1891), (Italian), Rev. Joseph Vicentini, C.S. In Res., Revs. Patrick Murphy, C.S.; Jesus Olivares, C.S.
Res.: 911 Missouri Ave., 64106. Tel: 816-842-5440; Fax: 816-474-3806. Web: www.holyrosarykc.org.
Catechesis/Religious Program—Tel: 816-842-5440. Students 1.

18—HOLY TRINITY, Closed. For inquiries for parish records contact Our Lady of Peace, Kansas City.

19—ST. JAMES (1906) Rev. Garry Richmeier, C.PP.S.; Deacon Philip Ross Beaudoin, Pastoral Admin.
Res.: 3909 Harrison St., 64110. Tel: 816-561-8512; Fax: 816-561-7950. Email: stjames.kc@sbcglobal.net. Web: www.stjkc.org.
Catechesis/Religious Program—Students 20.

20—ST. JOHN FRANCIS REGIS (1964) Revs. Richard Rocha; Louis Farley.
Res.: 8941 James A. Reed Rd., 64138. Tel: 816-761-1608; Fax: 816-966-1350. Email: cmelchior@regischurch.org. Web: www.regischurch.org.
School—Tel: 816-763-5837. Email: mbachkora@regisschool.org. Lay Teachers 20; Students 271.
Catechesis/Religious Program—Tel: 816-763-1366. Email: sduerr@regischurch.org. Students 30.

21—ST. JOHN THE BAPTIST, Closed. For inquiries for parish records contact St. Anthony, Kansas City, Tel: 816-231-5445.

22—ST. LOUIS (1919), (African American), Rev. Carlos Saligumba, S.O.L.T.
Church & Rectory: 5930 Swope Pkwy., 64130. Tel: 816-444-6535; Fax: 818-444-6027. Email: saint.louis@sbcglobal.net. Web: www.solt3.org.
Catechesis/Religious Program—Fax: 816-444-6027. Students 10.

23—ST. MATTHEW APOSTLE (1964) Rev. Lloyd E. Opoka.
Res.: 8001 Longview Rd., 64134. Tel: 816-763-0208; Fax: 816-765-2617. Web: www.stmatthewapostle.com.
Catechesis/Religious Program—Students 18.

24—ST. MICHAEL ARCHANGEL, Closed. For inquiries for parish records contact Our Lady of Peace, Kansas City, Tel: 816-231-0953.

25—ST. MONICA (1995), (African American), Rev. Terrell Finnell; Deacons Kenneth Greene; Darwin Dupree.
Res.: 1616 The Paseo, 64108. Tel: 816-471-3696; Fax: 816-471-1111. Email: stmonica1616kc@hotmail.com. Web: stmonicacatholicchurch.net.
Catechesis/Religious Program—Maxine G. Myers, D.R.E.

26—ORATORY OF OLD ST. PATRICK (2005), Traditional Latin Mass Community. Rev. Canon William E. Avis, I.C.R.S.S., Rector; Rev. Jean-Pierre Herman, Sacramental Min.
Mailing Address: P.O. Box 414237, 64141-4237. 806 Cherry St., 64106. Tel: 816-931-5612. Email: oldstpatrick@institute-christ-king.org. Web: www.institute-christ-king.org/kansascity/.

27—OUR LADY OF GOOD COUNSEL (1866) Rev. Msgr. William J. Blacet.
Res.: 3934 Washington, 64111-2904. Tel: 816-561-0400; Fax: 816-561-1551.

28—OUR LADY OF GUADALUPE, Closed. For inquiries for parish records contact Sacred Heart - Guadalupe, Kansas City, Tel: 816-842-6146.

29—OUR LADY OF PEACE (1991), (Hispanic), Revs. Francisco Guianan, S.O.L.T.; Lauro Bejo, S.O.L.T.; Deacon Donald L. McCandless.
Res.: 1029 Bennington Ave., 64126-2299. Tel: 816-231-0953; Fax: 816-231-8911. Email: admin@olopkc.org. Web: www.olopkc.org.
Catechesis/Religious Program—Students 85.

30—OUR LADY OF PERPETUAL HELP (1878) Revs. Brian J. Johnson, C.Ss.R.; Dennis Ryan, C.Ss.R.; Robert Lindsey, C.Ss.R.; Bros. Charles Long, C.Ss.R.; John Matthys, C.Ss.R. In Res., Revs. Frank Kriski, C.Ss.R.; Edward Morgan, C.Ss.R.; Patrick Power, C.Ss.R.; John Willett, C.Ss.R.; Richard Quinn, C.Ss.R.
Res.: 3333 Broadway, 64111. Tel: 816-561-3771; Fax: 816-561-3704.
School—Cristo Rey, 211 W. Linwood Blvd., 64111. Tel: 816-457-6044; Fax: 816-457-6046. Mary Kallman, Prin. Sisters 5; Brothers 1; Lay Teachers 21; Students 350.
Catechesis/Religious Program—Students 73.

31—OUR LADY OF SORROWS (1890) Rev. Anthony J. Pileggi.
Res.: 2552 Gillham Rd., 64108. Tel: 816-421-2112; Fax: 816-421-6037. Email: oloskc@att.net.
Catechesis/Religious Program—Attend Our Lady of Perpetual Help Catholic Church, Kansas City.

32—ST. PATRICK (1924) Rev. Justin E. Hoye; Deacon Michael Lewis, Pastoral Assoc.
1357 N.E. 42nd Ter., 64116. Tel: 816-453-5510; Fax: 816-453-4458. Email: stpat1@mindspring.com. Web: saintpatrick-kc.com.
Res.: 4505 NE Carolane, 64116.
School—1401 N.E. 42nd Ter., 64116. Tel: 816-453-0971; Fax: 816-453-5451. Web: stpatrickkc.com. Lay Teachers 10; Students 125.
Catechesis/Religious Program—Students 80.

33—ST. PETER'S (1925) Revs. Stephen M. Cook; Sean McCaffery.
815 E. Meyer Blvd., 64131.
Res.: 6415 Holmes Rd., 64131. Tel: 816-363-2320; Fax: 816-363-8157. Web: www.stpetersparishkcmo.org.
School—6400 Charlotte St., 64131. Tel: 816-523-4899; Fax: 816-523-1248. Sisters 1; Lay Teachers 35; Students 557.
Catechesis/Religious Program—Students 12.

34—ST. RAPHAEL THE ARCHANGEL (1963) Closed. For inquiries for parish records contact Archives, Catholic Chancery.

35—SACRED HEART-GUADALUPE (1887), (Hispanic), Rev. Aloys Ebach, C.PP.S.
Res.: 907 Cesar Chavez Ave., 64108. Tel: 816-842-6146; Fax: 816-471-7540.
Catechesis/Religious Program—Students 72.

36—ST. STANISLAUS, Closed. For inquiries for parish records contact Our Lady of Peace, Kansas City, Tel: 816-231-0953.

37—ST. THERESE LITTLE FLOWER (1925) Rev. Ernest P. Davis.
Res.: 5814 Euclid Ave., 64130. Tel: 816-444-5406; Fax: 816-444-9345. Email: edavis@stthereseke.org. Web: www.stthereseke.org.
Catechesis/Religious Program—Students 35.

38—ST. THERESE PARISH (Kansas City North) (1949) Revs. Michael Roach; Evan Harkins. In Res., Rev. Patrick Tobin (Retired).
Res.: 7207 Hwy. 9, N.W., 64152. Tel: 816-741-2800; Fax: 816-741-4959.
School—7277 Hwy. 9 N.W., 64152. Tel: 816-741-5400; Fax: 816-741-0533. Email: sttheresenorth@sttheresenorth.org. Web: www.sttheresenorth.org. Lay Teachers 42; Students 758.
Catechesis/Religious Program—Tel: 816-741-5400, Ext. 107. Students 656.

39—ST. THOMAS MORE (1964) Rev. Donald P. Farnan; Deacon Kevin Cummings. In Res., Revs. Michael G. O'Connor; Francis J. Schuele (Retired).
Res.: 11822 Holmes St., 64131. Tel: 816-942-2492; Fax: 816-942-8803. Email: information@stmkc.com. Web: www.stmkc.com.
School—Tel: 816-942-5581; Fax: 816-941-2450. Web: www.stmcyclones.org. Lay Teachers 42; Students 634.
Catechesis/Religious Program—Students 32.

40—VISITATION OF THE BLESSED VIRGIN MARY (1909), (Irish), Rev. Patrick J. Rush.
Mailing Address: 5141 Main St., 64112. Tel: 816-753-7422; Fax: 816-753-5505. Email: vis@visitation.org. Web: www.visitation.org.
School—5134 Baltimore, 64112. Tel: 816-531-6200; Fax: 816-531-8045. Lay Teachers 36; Students 565.
Catechesis/Religious Program—Students 83.

CITY OF ST. JOSEPH

(BUCHANAN COUNTY)

ST. JOSEPH

1—CO-CATHERDRAL OF ST. JOSEPH (1845) Rev. Joseph Powers; Deacon Steven Welsh.
Res.: 519 N. 10th St., 64501. Tel: 816-232-7763; Fax: 816-232-2460. Web: www.cathedralofstjoe.com.
School—518 N. 11th St., 65401. Tel: 816-232-8486; Fax: 816-232-8793. Web: www.cathedralschool-stjoseph.org. Lay Teachers 13; Students 154.
Catechesis/Religious Program—Students 15.

2—ST. FRANCIS XAVIER (1890) Rev. Ronald L. Will, C.PP.S. In Res., Rev. William Walter.
Res.: 2618 Seneca St., 64507. Tel: 816-232-8449; Fax: 816-364-5174. Email: jlutz@sfxstjoe.com. Web: sfxstjoe.com.
School—2614 Seneca St., 64507. Tel: 816-232-4911; Fax: 816-364-0263. Lay Teachers 28; Students 338.
Catechesis/Religious Program—Students 23.

3—ST. JAMES (1900) Rev. Joseph Totton.
Res.: 5814 King Hill Ave., 64504. Tel: 816-238-0853; Fax: 816-238-1758.
School—120 Michigan Ave., 64504. Tel: 816-238-0281. Lay Teachers 9; Students 147.
Catechesis/Religious Program—Students 20.

4—ST. MARY'S (1891) Rev. Matthew Benjamin.
Res.: 1606 N. 2nd St., 64505. Tel: 816-279-1154; Fax: 816-279-4078. Email: stmarys91@yahoo.com.
Catechesis/Religious Program—Students 37.

5—OUR LADY OF GUADALUPE (1982) Rev. Thomas K. Ludwig; Jeanne Sample, Business Mgr.
Church: 4503 Frederick Blvd., 64506. Tel: 816-232-2847; Fax: 816-232-0269. Web: www.olog.org.
Catechesis/Religious Program—Tel: 816-232-0112. Toni Hamera, D.R.E.; Jay Martin, Youth Min. Students 104.

6—ST. PATRICK (1869) Rev. Jorge Ramirez, Admin.
Office:—1813 S. 12th St., 64503. Tel: 816-279-2594; Fax: 816-232-7904. Email: stpatrickchurch@stjoelive.com. Web: www.parishesonline.com.
Catechesis/Religious Program—

7—QUEEN OF THE APOSTLES, Closed. For inquiries for parish records contact the Co-Cathedral of St. Joseph, Kansas City, Tel: 816-232-7763.

OUTSIDE THE CITIES OF KANSAS CITY AND ST. JOSEPH

BELTON, CASS CO., ST. SABINA'S (1944) Rev. Charles P. Tobin.
Res.: 700 Trevis Ave., 64012. Tel: 816-331-4713; Fax: 816-322-6196. Web: www.stsabinaparish.org.
Catechesis/Religious Program—Students 217.

BETHANY, HARRISON CO., BLESSED SACRAMENT (1945) [JC 2] Rev. Adam Ryan, O.S.B.
Res.: 1208 S. 25th St., 64424. Tel: 660-425-8160; Fax: 660-425-3109. Email: cathlc@grm.net. Web: www.blessedsacramentbethany.parishesonline.com.
Catechesis/Religious Program—Students 13.

BLUE SPRINGS, JACKSON CO.

1—ST. JOHN LA LANDE (1938) Revs. Ronald J. Elliott; Philip Luebbert.
Res.: 805 NW R.D. Mize Rd., 64015. Tel: 816-229-3378; Fax: 816-229-1362. Web: www.stjohnlalande.com.
School—801 NW R.D. Mize Rd., 64015. Tel: 816-228-5895; Fax: 816-228-8979. Lay Teachers 19; Students 285.
Catechesis/Religious Program—Students 169.

2—ST. ROBERT BELLARMINE (1983) Rev. James E. Healy.
Res.: 4112 S.W. 9th St., 64015. Tel: 816-229-5168; Fax: 816-229-3981. Web: www.robertbellarmine.org.
Catechesis/Religious Program—Students 175.

BUCKNER, JACKSON CO., CHURCH OF THE SANTA FE (1965) Rev. Msgr. Ralph L. Kaiser.
231 Sibley St., 64016.
Res.: P.O. Box 317, 64016. Tel: 816-650-9341.
Catechesis/Religious Program—Students 23.

BUTLER, BATES CO., ST. PATRICK'S (1882) Rev. John J. Bolderson.
Res.: 400 W. Nursery St., 64730. Tel: 660-679-4482.
Catechesis/Religious Program—Students 50.

CAMERON, CLINTON CO., ST. MUNCHIN (1867), (German—Irish), [CEM 2] Rev. Paul Turner.
Mailing Address: 301 N. Cedar St., 64429.
Res.: 316 W. 3rd St., 64429. Tel: 816-632-2768; Fax: 816-632-7997. Email: stmunchin@centurytel.net. Web: www.munchin.net.
Catechesis/Religious Program—Tel: 816-632-6276. Students 75.
Mission—St. Aloysius 301 S. Water, Maysville, DeKalb Co. 64469.

CARROLLTON, CARROLL CO., ST. MARY'S (1867) [CEM] Rev. J. Kenneth Criqui.
Res.: 211 E. Shanklin St., 64633. Tel: 660-542-1259. Email: stmary2007@sbcglobal.net. Web: www.carolnet.com/smcp.
Catechesis/Religious Program—Students 106.
Mission—Sacred Heart 403 S. Walnut, Norborne, Carroll Co. 64668. Tel: 660-593-3536.

CHILLICOTHE, LIVINGSTON CO., ST. COLUMBAN (1857) [CEM 2] Rev. Angelo Bartulica; Deacons Lawrence Schneider, (Retired); Jerry Davis, (Retired).
Res.: 1111 Trenton St., 64601-1499. Tel: 660-646-0190; Fax: 660-646-1802. Web: www.stcolumbanonline.org.
School—Bishop Hogan Memorial School, 1114 Trenton St., 64601. Tel: 660-646-0705. Web: www.bishophogan.org. Lay Teachers 9; Students 60.
Catechesis/Religious Program—Students 135.

CLINTON, HENRY CO., HOLY ROSARY (1875) Rev. Philip Egan; Deacon Steven Carter.
Res.: 610 S. 4th St., 64735. Tel: 660-885-4523; Fax: 660-885-3959.
School—400 E. Wilson, 64735. Tel: 660-885-4412. Lay Teachers 11; Students 127.
Catechesis/Religious Program—Students 20.
Mission—St. Catherine's Hwy. WW, Osceola, St. Clair Co. 64776. Tel: 417-646-2217.
Mission—St. Bartholomew 504 E. Benton, Windsor, Henry Co. 65360. Tel: 660-647-2613.

CONCEPTION JUNCTION, NODAWAY CO., ST. COLUMBA (1860) [CEM] Rev. Allan Stetz, O.S.B.; Deacon Martin Goedken.
Res.: 311 Roosevelt, P.O. Box 127, 64434. Tel: 660-944-2301.
Catechesis/Religious Program—Students 120.

EASTON, BUCHANAN CO., ST. JOSEPH'S (1830), (Irish—German), [CEM] Rev. M. Jeffrey Stephan.
Rectory—107 N. Shortridge, P.O. Box 197, 64443. Tel: 816-473-2011. Email: stjosephchurch@centurytel.net.
Catechesis/Religious Program—Students 20.

EXCELSIOR SPRINGS, CLAY CO., ST. ANN (1889) Rev. Msgr. William Caldwell.
Res.: 1503 Tracy, 64024. Tel: 816-630-6659; Fax: 816-630-9696.
Catechesis/Religious Program—Tel: 816-630-5874 (Connie Davis); 816-630-7790 (Chris Sanders). Connie Davis, D.R.E. (Elementary); Chris Sanders, Youth Min. & Adult Faith Formation. Students 107.

GALLATIN, DAVIESS CO., MARY IMMACULATE (1950) Rev. Robert Rost.
Mailing Address: P.O. Box 188, Hamilton, 64644-0188. 409 S. Main, 64640. Tel: 816-583-1117. Email: shmichurch@centurylink.net.
Catechesis/Religious Program—Mary Jarboe, D.R.E. Students 8.

GLADSTONE, CLAY CO., ST. ANDREW THE APOSTLE (1964) Rev. Vincent M. Rogers.
Res.: 6415 N.E. Antioch Rd., 64119. Tel: 816-453-2089; Fax: 816-453-2442. Email: spalmarine@sataps.com. Web: www.sataps.com.
School—(Grades PreK-8) Tel: 816-454-7377; Fax: 816-453-6393. Email: wwinkler@sataps.com. Sisters 1; Lay Teachers 11; Students 275.
Catechesis/Religious Program—Tel: 816-454-7377, Ext. 107. Students 107.

GRANDVIEW, JACKSON CO., CORONATION OF OUR LADY (1958) Rev. Stephen Hansen; Deacons Kenneth Fuenfhausen; Michael Dennis.
Res.: 13000 Bennington Ave., 64030. Tel: 816-761-8811; Fax: 816-761-8812. Email: coronation@kc.rr.com. Web: www.coronationofourlady.org.

Catechesis/Religious Program—Students 73.

HAMILTON, CALDWELL CO., SACRED HEART (1921) Rev. Robert Rost.
Mailing Address: P.O. Box 188, 64644-0188.
Res.: 202 E. Middle St., P.O. Box 188, 64644-0188. Tel: 816-583-1117. Email: shmichurch@centurylink.net.
Catechesis/Religious Program—Students 9.

HARRISONVILLE, CASS CO., OUR LADY OF LOURDES (1941) Rev. Christian Malewski; Deacon Ronald F. Strong.
Mailing Address: 2700 E. Mechanic, P.O. Box 247, 64701.
Catechesis/Religious Program—Students 211.

HIGGINSVILLE, LAFAYETTE CO., ST. MARY'S (1879), (German—Irish), [CEM] Rev. Thomas J. D. Hawkins.
Res.: 401 W. Broadway, 64037. Tel: 660-584-3038. Email: smhigg@ctcis.net.
Catechesis/Religious Program—Students 52.

HIRLINGEN, BUCHANAN CO., SEVEN DOLORS (1872), (German), [CEM] [JC] Rev. Matthew Benjamin.
Res.: 1606 N. 2nd St., 64505. Tel: 816-279-1154; Fax: 816-279-4078.
Catechesis/Religious Program—

HOLDEN, JOHNSON CO., ST. PATRICK'S (1869) [CEM 2] Rev. Peter M. Savidge.
Res.: 703 S. Olive St., 64040-1443. Tel: 816-850-4999. Email: stpatsholden@embarqmail.com.
Catechesis/Religious Program—Kathleen Bryant, D.R.E. Students 46.
Mission—Holy Trinity 1372 N.W. Graham Rd., Urich, Henry Co. 64788.

INDEPENDENCE, JACKSON CO.

1—ST. ANN'S (1917) Rev. Bernard E. Branson; Deacon James Reynolds III.
Res.: 10113 E. Lexington Ave., 64053. Tel: 816-252-1160; Fax: 816-252-1161. Email: saintanns64053@yahoo.com.
Catechesis/Religious Program—Students 10.

2—ST. JOSEPH THE WORKER (1976) Rev. Joseph H. Matt.
1200 N. Blue Mills Rd., 64058.
Res.: 2102 N. Blue Mills Rd., 64058. Tel: 816-796-6877; Fax: 816-796-6876. Email: stjosephtheworker@hotmail.com. Web: www.sjtw.catholicweb.com.
Catechesis/Religious Program—Janice McQuillan, Faith Formation Coord. Students 53.

3—ST. MARK (1965) Rev. James Taranto.
Res.: 3736 S. Lees Summit Rd., 64055. Tel: 816-373-2600; Fax: 816-373-3816. Web: www.stmarksparish.com.
Catechesis/Religious Program—Joyce Arthur, D.R.E. Students 417.

4—ST. MARY'S (1823) [CEM] Rev. Matthew Rotert; Deacons Michael Elsey; Thomas D. Powell, (Retired).
Res.: 600 N. Liberty St., 64050. Tel: 816-252-0121; Fax: 816-461-8153. Web: saintmarysparish.org.
Catechesis/Religious Program—Email: debbie@saintmarysparish.org. Students 48.

5—NATIVITY OF MARY PARISH (1938) Rev. Robert Stone.
10017 E. 36th Ter., 64052.
Res.: 10015 E. 36th Ter., 64052. Tel: 816-353-2184; Fax: 816-358-4155. Email: parish@nativityofmary.org. Web: www.nativityofmary.org.
School—(Grades PreK-8), 10021 E. 36th Ter., 64052. Tel: 816-353-0284; Fax: 816-356-0286. Email: school@nativityofmary.org. Lay Teachers 28; Students 277.
Catechesis/Religious Program—Students 31.

KEARNEY, CLAY CO., CHURCH OF THE ANNUNCIATION (1980) Rev. John Wolf, C.PP.S.
Mailing Address: 701 N. Jefferson, P.O. Box 599, 64060-0599. Tel: 816-628-5030; Fax: 816-628-4279. Web: annunciationkearney.com.
Catechesis/Religious Program—Tel: 816-628-5030; Fax: 816-628-4279. Students 229.

LEES SUMMIT, JACKSON CO.

1—HOLY SPIRIT (1979) Rev. Michael Clary; Ann Hayles, Pastoral Coord.; Deacons Richard Akins; Don Schmidt.
1800 SW State Rte. 150, 64082.
Res.: 1137 S.W. Georgetown, 64082. Tel: 816-623-9117; Fax: 816-537-8104. Email: parish@holyspiritcatholicchurch.net. Web: www.holyspiritcatholicchurch.net.
Catechesis/Religious Program—Tel: 816-537-6990. Students 428.

2—ST. MARGARET OF SCOTLAND CATHOLIC CHURCH (1999) Rev. Robert H. Stewart; Sue Nichols, Parish Mgr.
Res.: 777 N.E. Blackwell Rd., 64086. Tel: 816-246-6800; Fax: 816-246-9858. Email: snichols@stmargaretsparish.org. Web: www.stmargaretsparish.org.
Catechesis/Religious Program—Email: cliccar@stmargaretsparish.org. Cathie Liccar, D.R.E. Students 203.

3—OUR LADY OF THE PRESENTATION (1896) Rev. Thomas Holder; Deacons Del Wilkinson; Mark Fountain, (Retired); Mike Peterson.
Parish Office—130 N.W. Murray Rd., 64081. Tel: 816-251-1100; Fax: 816-251-1199. Web: www.presentation-parish.org.
School—150 N.W. Murray Rd., 64081. Tel: 816-251-1150; Fax: 816-251-1155. Web: www.presentation-parish.org. Lay Teachers 28; Students 468.
Catechesis/Religious Program—Tel: 816-251-1135. Jo Engert, D.R.E. Students 227.

LEXINGTON, LAFAYETTE CO., IMMACULATE CONCEPTION (1842) [CEM] Rev. M. Christopher Smith.
Res.: 107 N. 18th St., 64067. Tel: 660-259-3043; Fax: 660-259-3043. Email: icccpastor@embarqmail.com.
Catechesis/Religious Program—Students 26.

LIBERTY, CLAY CO., ST. JAMES (1840) Revs. Michael Roach; Timothy Armbruster, C.PP.S.
Res.: 309 S. Stewart Rd., 64068. Tel: 816-781-4343; Fax: 816-792-8691.
School—Tel: 816-781-4428; Fax: 816-781-0747. Lay Teachers 33; Students 405.
Catechesis/Religious Program—Students 607.

MARYVILLE, NODAWAY CO., ST. GREGORY BARBARIGO (1858) [CEM 2] [JC] Rev. Martin DeMeulenaere, O.S.B.
333 S. Davis St., 64468. Tel: 660-582-3833; Fax: 660-582-5914. Web: www.stgregorysmaryville.org.
Res.: 825 E. Edwards St., 64468. Tel: 660-582-2051.
School—315 S. Davis St., 64468. Tel: 660-582-2462; Fax: 660-582-2496. Email: stgregorysg@gmail.com. Susan Martin, Prin. 14 Full-time; 2 Part-time 16; Students 169.
Newman Center— 606 College Ave., 64468. Tel: 660-582-7373. Email: newman@nwmissouri.edu.
Catechesis/Religious Program—Tel: 660-582-5914. Students 143.

MONTROSE, HENRY CO., IMMACULATE CONCEPTION (1876), (German), [CEM] [JC 2] Rev. Thomas W. Hermes.
Res.: 606 Kansas Ave., 64770-9601. Tel: 660-693-4651; Fax: 660-693-4713.
School—St. Mary School, 608 Kansas Ave., 64770. Tel: 660-693-4502. Lay Teachers 4; Students 44.
Catechesis/Religious Program—Students 16.

NEVADA, VERNON CO., ST. MARY (1887) [CEM] Rev. Thomas Albers, C.PP.S.
330 N. Main St., 64772. Tel: 417-667-5604. Email: stmarysnevada@sbcglobal.net. Web: www.stmarysnevada.parishesonline.com.
School—Tel: 417-667-7517; Fax: 417-667-7517. Lay Teachers 4; Students 41.
Catechesis/Religious Program—Students 35.
Mission—St. Bridget's Rich Hill, Bates Co.

ODESSA, LAFAYETTE CO., ST. GEORGE (1882) Rev. John Schuele.
Res.: 716 S. Third, 64076. Tel: 816-230-4127. Email: stgeorge7@hotmail.com.
Mission—St. Jude the Apostle 2001 S. Broadway, P.O. Box 590, Oak Grove, Jackson Co. 64075. Tel: 816-690-3165.
Catechesis/Religious Program—Tel: 816-230-7475. Email: stj2515@earthlink.net. Students 67.

PARNELL, NODAWAY CO., ST. JOSEPH'S (1891) [CEM 2] [JC] Rev. Allan Stetz, O.S.B.
Res.: 411 S. Main, P.O. Box 78, 64475. Tel: 660-986-3305.
Catechesis/Religious Program—Students 53.

PLATTE CITY, PLATTE CO., TWELVE APOSTLES PARISH (2008) Rev. Charles Rowe.
700 Branch St., 64079. Mailing Address: 407 Cherry St., Weston, 64098. Tel: 816-640-2206; Fax: 816-640-2209. Web: www.twelveapostlescatholic.org.
Catechesis/Religious Program—Students 138.

PLATTSBURG, CLINTON CO., ST. ANN'S (1866), (Irish), [CEM] Rev. M. Jeffrey Stephan.
Res.: 700 W. Maple St., 64477. Tel: 816-539-2634. Email: stann001@centurytel.net. Web: www.stannplattsburg.parishesonline.com.
Catechesis/Religious Program—Students 45.

PLEASANT HILL, CASS CO., ST. BRIDGET (1884) Rev. Msgr. Robert Murphy; Deacon Gary Kappler.
Mailing Address: 2103 N. Lexington, P.O. Box 43, 64080. Tel: 816-540-4563; Pager: 816-540-2162. Email: stbridgetparish@embarqmail.com. Web: stbridgetcatholicchurch.org.
Catechesis/Religious Program—Cathy Vogel, D.R.E. Students 109.

RAYTOWN, JACKSON CO., OUR LADY OF LOURDES (1948) Rev. Steven C. Rogers.
Res.: 8812 E. Gregory Blvd., 64133. Tel: 816-353-2380; Fax: 816-353-5737.
Catechesis/Religious Program—Students 50.

RICHMOND, RAY CO., IMMACULATE CONCEPTION (1869) [CEM] Rev. George Ssebadduka.
Res.: 602 S. Camden, 64085. Tel: 816-776-6870.
Catechesis/Religious Program—Students 18.

SAVANNAH, ANDREW CO., ST. ROSE OF LIMA (1898) Rev. Peter Ullrich, O.S.B.
Mailing Address: 707 Hall Ave., 64485. Tel: 816-324-5700; Fax: 816-324-5726. Email: srlp@stjoelive.com.
Res.: 705 S. Hall Ave., 64485. Tel: 816-324-3231.
Catechesis/Religious Program—Students 103.
Mission—St. Patrick 303 Grand Ave., Forest City, Holt Co. 64451. Tel: 660-446-2045.

SMITHVILLE, CLAY CO., CHURCH OF THE GOOD SHEPHERD (1974) Rev. Gregory Haskamp.
Res.: 18601 N. 169 Hwy., 64089. Tel: 816-532-4344 (Church); Fax: 816-532-1157. Email: goodshepherd653@sbcglobal.net. Web: www.goodshepherdmo.org.
Catechesis/Religious Program—Email: sondagron@gmail.com. Students 228.

STANBERRY, GENTRY CO., ST. PETER'S (1880) [CEM] Rev. Karl Barmann, O.S.B.
Res.: 614 N. Alanthus Ave., 64489. Tel: 660-783-2159. Email: stpetersparish@sbcglobal.net.
Catechesis/Religious Program—Students 74.
Mission—St. Patrick's Ford City, MO. 4201 State Hwy. AA, King City, Gentry Co. 64463.
Catechesis/Religious Program—Students 30.

SUGAR CREEK, JACKSON CO., ST. CYRIL (1912), (Croatian—Slovak), Rev. Matthew Bartulica.
Res.: 11231 Chicago Ave., 64054. Tel: 816-252-9564; Fax: 816-252-1161.
Catechesis/Religious Program—Students 1.

TARKIO, ATCHISON CO., ST. PAUL THE APOSTLE (1890) [JC] Rev. Reginald Sander, O.S.B.
Res.: 908 Elm St., 64491. Tel: 660-736-4342.
Catechesis/Religious Program—Students 20.
Mission—St. Benedict Catholic Church Burlington Junction, Nodaway Co. 64428. Tel: 660-725-4407.

TRENTON, GRUNDY CO., ST. JOSEPH'S (1872) [CEM] Revs. Angelo Bartulica; Duc Nguyen.
Mailing Address: 1111 Trenton St., Chillicothe, 64601.
Res.: 1728 St. Joseph St., 64683. Tel: 660-359-2841.
Mission—Immaculate Heart of Mary Church 1728 St. Joseph St., Mercer Co. 64683.
Catechesis/Religious Program—Students 33.

WARRENSBURG, JOHNSON CO., SACRED HEART (1865) Rev. Joseph Miller, C.PP.S.
300 S. Ridgeview Dr., 64093. Email: sacredheartparish@embarqmail.com.
Res.: 109 E. Hale Lake Rd., 64093. Tel: 660-747-6154; Fax: 660-747-7623.
Catechesis/Religious Program—Students 213.

WESTON, PLATTE CO., HOLY TRINITY (1842) [JC] Rev. Charles Rowe.
Res.: 407 Cherry St., 64098. Tel: 816-640-2206; Fax: 816-640-2209. Web: www.holytrinitycatholic.org.
Catechesis/Religious Program—Students 73.

Special Assignment:

Rev. Msgrs.—

Murphy, A. Robert, V.G., P.O. Box 419037, 64141-6037.

Offutt, Bradley S., Chancellor & Moderator of the Curia, P.O. Box 419037, 64141-6037.

Revs.—

Cameron, Robert M., Mission Office Dir., 7601 Blue Ridge, 64138.

Coleman, C. Michael, J.C.L., Adjutant Judicial Vicar & Diocesan Archivist, P.O. Box 419037, 64141-6037.

Lockwood, Gregory J., Administrative Dir., Vocation Office

Powers, Joseph, Vicar for Clergy

Rocha, Richard, Dir. of Vocations, P.O. Box 419037, 64141-6037.

On Duty Outside the Diocese:

Revs.—

Borkowski, Thomas, Wheaton, IL

Lwin, Paw Tun, Laguna Niguel, CA.

Reardon, Daniel, Military Chap.

Mission Duty:

Rev.—

Gillgannon, Michael, Casilla 12162, La Paz, Bolivia.

Retired:

Rev. Msgrs.—

Bauer, Henry, 6425 Woodson, 64133.

Leitner, John E., 12100 Wornall Rd. #357, 64145.

Mancuso, Joseph A., Our Lady of Mercy Country Home, 2115 Maturana Dr., Box 101C, Liberty, 64068.

Revs.—

Blaes, Paul, M.A., Ph.D., 7130 Beneva Rd., Apt. 206, Sarasota, FL 34238.

Cleary, Donald R., 12100 Wornall Rd., #126, 64145.

Cronin, Thomas, 143 Desert Lakes Dr., Fernley, NV 89408.
Deming, Robert N., 9415 Terrace St., 64114.
Eldringhoff, John P., 16504 E. 54th St., Independence, 64055.
Gauthier, Ernest, L.C.S.W., 2920 S.E. Bingham Ct., Lee's Summit, 64063.
Hart, James, 616 E. 120th St., 64145.
Jones, Charles F., 2120 Norton, Independence, 64052.
Karels, Ambrose G., P.O. Box 410834, 64141.
Mahoney, Robert J., Ph.D., 4550 Warwick, #905, 64111.
McCormack, John, M.S., 8300 E. 88th Ter., #2010, 64138-4490.
Moscaritolo, Mario, 4019 Warwick, 64111.
Mullin, Hugh J., 10901 Johnson Blvd. J 712, Seminole, FL 33772.
Rice, Michael D., 1650 Shawnee Bend Rd., Sunrise Beach, 65079.
Rotert, Norman, 121 W. 48th St., Apt. 305, 64112.
Ryan, C. Duane, 310 No Return Rd., Sunrise Beach, 65079.
Saale, Richard T., 8745 James A. Reed Rd., 64138.
Sinclair, Alexander B., 4545 Wornall Rd., #608, 64111.
Tobin, Patrick, 7207 Hwy. 9 N.W., 64152.
Walker, Michael, 67008 E. Miami Rd., Montrose, CO 81401.
Wandless, John H., 5426 Wyandotte St., 64112.
Ward, Thomas, 127 S. W. Hillcrest Ln., Lees Summit, 64063.
Waris, Gerald R., 11710 Jefferson St., 64114.
Wiederholt, Thomas W., 514 W. 26th, 4-N, 64108.

Permanent Deacons:
Adams, Samuel
Akins, Richard
Albers, Kenneth
Beaudoin, Philip Ross
Carter, Steven
Cecil, Charles
Corrigan, Emory S., (Retired)
Cummings, Kevin
Davis, F. Jerry, (Retired)
Dennis, Michael
Dupree, Darwin
Elsey, Michael
Esteban, Daniel
Falcon, Francis L., (Retired)
Fountain, J. Mark, (Retired)
Fuenfhausen, Kenneth
Gates, Michael
Goedken, Martin J.
Greene, Kenneth
Healy, David
Hemke, Douglas
Henggeler, Francis J., (Retired)
Kappler, Gary
Katzer, Dwayne
Koch, John J., (Retired)
Koesterer, Charles
Kopp, George C., Jr., (Retired)
Langdon, Harry, (Retired)
Lauhoff, John D., (Retired)
LeMay, Joseph
Lewis, Michael
Livingston, Stephen W.
Madden, Donald
Markey, William R., (Retired)
McCandless, Donald L., (Retired)
McKay, Clarence W., (Retired)
McLean, Michael
McMenamy, Justin M., (Retired)
McNeal, Ralph Joseph
Muller, Paul
Muraski, Richard J., (Retired)
Myler, Douglas
Peak, Frank L.
Peterson, Mike
Pham, Tuyen
Powell, D. Thomas, (Retired)
Reynolds, James, III
Riead, John T., (Retired)
Rodman, Harold M., (Retired)
Schieber, Martin L., (Retired)
Schmit, Donald A., (Retired)
Schneider, Lawrence, (Retired)
Seipel, Leroy, (Retired)
Strong, Ronald F.
Thompson, John R., (Retired)
Townley, David
Tran, Doan
Van Pham, Hao
Wehner, Ralph L.
Welsh, Steven
West, Larry
Whiston, Joseph
Williams, Jerry
Zimmerman, Tony

INSTITUTIONS LOCATED IN THE DIOCESE

[A] SEMINARIES, RELIGIOUS OR SCHOLASTICATES

KANSAS CITY. *Gaspar Mission House*, 5221 Rockhill Rd., 64110. Tel: 816-333-7980. Revs. Richard Bayuk, C.PP.S.; Aloys Ebach, C.PP.S.; Garry Richmeier, C.PP.S. Priests 3.

CONCEPTION. *Conception Seminary College*, 37174 State Hwy., P.O. Box 502, 64433. Tel: 660-944-3105; Fax: 660-944-2829. Email: seminary@conception.edu. Web: conceptionabbey.org. Rt. Rev. Gregory Polan, O.S.B., Chancellor; Very Rev. Samuel Russell, O.S.B., Pres. & Rector; Revs. Ralph B. O'Donnell (OM), Vice Rector & Dean of Students; Sebastian Allgaier, O.S.B.; Thomas Bailey, O.S.B., Marmion Abbey; Albert Bruecken, O.S.B.; Patrick Caveglia, O.S.B.; Simon Dao, C.M.C., Congregation of the Mother Coredemptrix; Donald Grabner, O.S.B.; Aidan McSorley, O.S.B.; Pachomius Meade, O.S.B.; Xavier Nacke, O.S.B.; Benedict Neenan, O.S.B.; Daniel Petsche, O.S.B.; Frowin Reed, O.S.B.; Duane F. Reinert, O.F.M.Cap.; John Rini (ELP) (Retired); Adam Ryan, O.S.B.; Timothy Schoen, O.S.B.; Bro. Thomas Sullivan, O.S.B. Priests 23; Brothers 10; Sisters 1; Lay Professors 8; Total Staff 50; Students 107.

LIBERTY. *Society of the Precious Blood Provincial Offices* (1965) P.O. Box 339, 64069-0339. Tel: 816-781-4344; Fax: 816-781-3639. Email: sec@kcprov.org. Revs. James G. Betzen, C.PP.S., 3rd Councilor; Joseph Nassal, C.PP.S., Prov. Dir.; Richard Bayuk, C.PP.S., Vice Provincial; Ronald L. Will, C.PP.S., 2nd Councilor; Thomas Welk, C.P.P.S., 4th Councilor. Bishops 1; Priests 48; Brothers 2; Candidates 6.

[B] COLLEGES AND UNIVERSITIES

KANSAS CITY. *Avila University*, 11901 Wornall Rd., 64145-1698. Tel: 816-942-8400; Fax: 816-501-2451. Email: ron.slepitza@avila.edu. Web: www.avila.edu. Ronald A. Slepitza, Ph.D., CSJA, Pres.; Sr. Marie Joan Harris, C.S.J., Ph.D., Provost & Vice Pres. for Academic Affairs; Paul G. Bookmeyer, Vice Pres. for Finance & Admin. Svcs.; Sue King, Ph.D., Vice Pres. Information Svcs. & Vice Provost; David Armstrong, Dir. Campus Ministry & Mission Effectiveness; Darby Peoples, Dean of Students; Angie Heer, Vice Pres., Advancement & External Rels. Lay Teachers 71; Students 1,818.

Rockhurst University (1910) 1100 Rockhurst Rd., 64110-2561. Tel: 816-501-4000; Fax: 816-501-4293. Email: kathy.soloducha@rockhurst.edu. Web: www.rockhurst.edu. James G. Castellano, Chm. Bd. of Trustees; Rev. Thomas B. Curran, O.S.F.S., Pres.; Dr. Sharon M. Homan, Vice Pres., Academic Affairs; Guy Swanson, Vice Pres. Finance & Admin; Laurie Hathman, Dir. of the Library; Rachael Lierz, Controller; Rev. William T. Oulvey, S.J., Interim Asst., Pres. for Mission & Ministry; Matthew Quick, Vice Pres., Student Devel., Athletics, & Campus Ministry & Dean of Students; Matt Heinrich, Assoc. Vice Pres., Facilities & Tech.; Lane Ramey, Assoc. Vice Pres., Enrollment. Priests 4; Lay Professors 222; Students 3,425.

College of Arts and Sciences Tel: 816-501-4075; Fax: 816-501-4169. Web: www.rockhurst.edu/academic/deansoffice/index.asp. Timothy L. McDonald, Dean.

School of Graduate and Professional Studies Tel: 816-501-4686; Fax: 816-501-4615. Web: www.rockhurst.edu/academic/SGPS/index.asp. Jeffrey R. Breese, Dean.

Helzberg School of Management Tel: 816-501-4087; Fax: 816-501-4650. Web: www.rockhurst.edu/HSOM/index.asp. James Daley, Dean.

Research College of Nursing, 2525 E. Meyer Blvd., 64132. Tel: 816-995-2800; Fax: 816-995-2817. Web: www.researchcollege.edu: Nancy DeBasio, Pres. & Dean.

[C] HIGH SCHOOLS, DIOCESAN

KANSAS CITY. *Archbishop O'Hara High School* (Coed), 9001 James A. Reed Rd., 64138. Tel: 816-763-4800; Fax: 816-765-5008. Email: postmaster@oharahs.org. Web: www.oharahs.org. John O'Connor, Prin.; Denise Crawford, Librarian. Christian Brothers 3; Lay Teachers 31; Students 353.

St. Pius X High School, 1500 N.E. 42nd Ter., 64116. Tel: 816-453-3450; Fax: 816-452-7099. Email: jmonachino@stpiusxhs-kc.com. Web: www.stpiusxhs-kc.com. Joseph Monachino Jr., Prin.; Sue Johnson, Librarian. Lay Teachers 33; Students 389.

ST. JOSEPH. *Bishop LeBlond High School*, 3529 Frederick Ave., 64506. Tel: 816-279-1629; Fax: 816-279-5488. Email: shaynes@bishopleblondhs.com. Web: bishopleblond.com. Dr. Solon Haynes, Prin.; Rev. Timothy Guthridge, C.PP.S., Chap.; Peggy Leone, Librarian. Lay Teachers 20; Students 228.

INDEPENDENCE. *St. Mary's Diocesan High School-Bundschu Memorial* (1853) 622 N. Main St., 64050. Tel: 816-252-8733; Fax: 816-252-2780. Email: jlynch@stmhs.org. Web: www.stmhs.org. Mr. Jeff Lynch, Prin. Lay Teachers 11; Students 113.

[D] HIGH SCHOOLS, PRIVATE

KANSAS CITY. *Cristo Rey Kansas City High School*, 211 W. Linwood Blvd., 64111. Tel: 816-457-6044; Fax: 816-457-6046. Email: khanlon@cristorey.org. Web: www.cristoreykc.org. Kathleen M. Hanlon, Ph.D., Pres.; Mary Kallman, Prin. Brothers 1; Sisters 4; Lay Staff 45; Students 350.

Notre Dame de Sion High School (1912) 10631 Wornall Rd., 64114-5096. Tel: 816-942-3282; Fax: 816-942-4052. Email: general@ndsion.edu. Web: www.ndsion.edu. Alice Munninghoff, Head of School; Michelle Olson, Prin.; Jennifer Campbell, Librarian. Affiliated with Sisters of Notre Dame de Sion. Lay Teachers 37; Students 403.

Rockhurst High School (1910) 9301 State Line Rd., 64114-3229. Tel: 816-363-2036; Fax: 816-363-3764. Web: www.rockhursths.edu. Revs. Terrence A. Baum, S.J., Pres.; Ian R. Gibbons, S.J.; William T. Sheahan, S.J.; Gregory Harkness, Prin.; Amy Gansner, Librarian. Jesuit Priests 3; Lay Teachers 74; Students 1,089.

St. Teresa's Academy, 5600 Main St., 64113-1298. Tel: 816-501-0011; Fax: 816-523-0232. Email: nbone@stteresasacademy.org. Web: www.stteresasacademy.org. Mrs. Nan Bone, Pres.; Mary Anne Hoecker, M.A., Prin.; Barbara McCormick, M.A., Prin.; Jackie Hershewe, Librarian. Affiliated with Sisters of St. Joseph of Carondelet. Sisters 1; Lay Teachers 46; Students 562.

[E] CONSOLIDATED SCHOOLS

KANSAS CITY. *Holy Cross School*, 121 N. Quincy, 64123-1399. Tel: 816-231-8874; Fax: 816-231-7258. Jean T. Ferrara, Prin. Lay Teachers 12; Students 197.

Our Lady of Guadalupe School (1915) 2310 Madison, 64108. Tel: 816-221-2539; Fax: 816-283-3315. Email: wdcjbowman@everestkc.net. Web: olgkc.net. Connie Bowman, Prin. Lay Teachers 6; Total Staff 11; Students 103.

Our Lady of the Angels School, (Grades PreK-8), 4232 Mercier, 64111. Tel: 816-931-1693; Fax: 816-931-6713. Email: mcdelac@yahoo.com. Mary Delac, Prin. Sisters 1; Lay Teachers 11; Students 158.

[F] ELEMENTARY SCHOOLS, PRIVATE

KANSAS CITY. *Notre Dame de Sion Elementary School* (1912) 3823 Locust St., 64109-2697. Tel: 816-753-3810; Fax: 816-753-0806. Email: general@ndsion.edu. Web: www.ndsion.edu. Alice Munninghoff, Head of School; Catherine Butel, Prin.; Kathy Parker, Librarian. Affiliated with Sisters of Notre Dame de Sion. Lay Teachers 30; Students 301.

[G] GENERAL HOSPITALS

KANSAS CITY. *St. Joseph Medical Center*, 1000 Carondelet Dr., 64114. Tel: 816-942-4400; Fax: 816-943-2840. Web: www.stjosephkc.com. Michael Dorsey, CEO. Sponsored by the Sisters of St. Joseph of Carondelet. Sisters 4; Bed Capacity 310; Nurses 503; Total Staff 1,102; Patients Assisted Annually 137,799.

Parent Corporation:

Carondelet Health, 1000 Carondelet Dr., 64114. Tel: 816-943-5678; Fax: 816-943-2840. Web: www.carondelethealth.org. Fleury Yelvington, Pres. & CEO. Parent Co. Sponsored by the Sisters of St. Joseph of Carondelet.

Divisions:

St. Joseph Medical Center Foundation, 1000 Carondelet Dr., 64114. Tel: 816-942-4400; Fax: 816-943-2786. Web: www.carondelethealth.org. Dorene Shipley, Exec. Dir.; Fleury Yelvington, Pres. & CEO. Sponsored by the Sisters of St. Joseph of Carondelet.

11050 Roe Ave., Ste. 120, Overland Park, KS 66211. Tel: 816-529-4800; Fax: 913-345-9129. Web: www.carondelethealth.org. Home health agency affiliated with Carondelet Health.

BLUE SPRINGS. *St. Mary's Medical Center*, 201 NW R.D. Mize Rd., 64014. Tel: 816-228-5900; Fax: 816-655-5408. Web: www.stmaryskc.com. Annette

Small, CEO. Sponsored by the Sisters of St. Joseph of Carondelet. Acute care facility, having medical, surgical and obstetrical. Nurses 249; Bed Capacity 146; Patients Assisted Annually 94,782; Total Staff 520.

MARYVILLE. *St. Francis Hospital & Health Services* (1894) 2016 S. Main, 64468. Tel: 660-562-2600; Fax: 660-562-7911. Web: www.stfrancismaryville.com. H. Gray Cox, Pres. Member of SSM Health Care. Sponsored by Franciscan Sisters of Mary, St. Louis, MO. Acute care facility. Bed Capacity 81; Total Staff 500; Patients Assisted Annually 58,000.

[H] SPECIAL CARE UNITS

KANSAS CITY. *Carondelet Manor*, 621 Carondelet Dr., 64114. Tel: 816-943-4777; Fax: 816-941-7007. Rick Blim, Admin. Owned and operated by Carondelet Long Term Care Facilities, Inc. Sponsored by Sisters of St. Joseph of Carondelet and Benedictine Health System. Bed Capacity 162.

BLUE SPRINGS. *St. Mary's Manor* (1987) 111 Mock Ave., 64014. Tel: 816-228-5655; Fax: 816-228-8480. Email: pkelley@carondelet.com. Patricia Kelley, Admin.

Carondelet Long Term Care Facilities, Inc., Long term care facility with skilled nursing care and residential care. Sponsored by Sisters of St. Joseph of Carondelet. Managed by Benedictine Health System. Skilled Care 132; Residential Care 57; Total Assisted 189.

LIBERTY. *Immacolata Manor* (1981) 2135 Manor Way, 64068-9397. Tel: 816-781-4332; Fax: 816-781-8820. Email: info@imanor.org. Dale R. Herrick, Exec. Dir.; Karen Sage, Pres. Residential and day habilitation services for people with developmental disabilities; Operated by the Immacolata Board of Directors. Residents 34; Total Staff 63; Total Assisted Annually 40.

[I] HOMES FOR THE ELDERLY

KANSAS CITY. *Brighton Place*, 1905 Hardesty, 64127. Tel: 816-483-6233; Fax: 816-483-1142. Email: nowlin01@kc.rr.com. 32 units 236, S/8 housing for family. Total Assisted 32; Total Staff 3.

Cathedral Square Towers, 444 W. 12th St., 64105. Tel: 816-471-6555; Fax: 816-421-1279. Email: cathedral01@kc.rr.com. Jan Carson, Mgr.; Susan Engel, Diocesan Liaison. Apartment residence for the elderly and handicapped. Units 156; Total in Residence 160; Total Staff 10.

Columbus Park Plaza, 801 Pacific, 64106. Tel: 816-472-0887; Fax: 816-472-6105. Catherine Huntsucker, Mgr.; Susan Engel, Diocesan Liaison. Apartment residence for elderly and handicapped. Units 56; Total in Residence 55; Total Staff 4.

Jeanne Jugan Center, 8745 James A. Reed Rd., 64138. Tel: 816-761-4744; Fax: 816-761-8313. Email: mskansascity@littlesistersofthepoor.org. Sr. Rose Marie Mayock, L.S.P., Pres.; Rev. John McCormack, M.S., Chap. (Retired).

Little Sisters of the Poor Little Sisters of the Poor. Apartments 33; Bed Capacity 76; Total in Residence 109; Total Staff 94; Total Assisted 117; Sisters 11.

Marlborough Manor, 1818 E. 79th St., 64132. Tel: 816-333-7761; Fax: 816-523-2388. Email: marlborough01@kc.rr.com. Louise Shepherd, Mgr. Rental housing for low income (a 31-unit apartment residence for the elderly and disabled). Total in Residence 31; Total Staff 3.

Red Bridge Place, 11300 Colorado, 64137. Tel: 816-761-4667; Fax: 816-761-4769. Email: redbridge01@kc.rr.com. Linda Barber, Mgr. Total Staff 3; Total Assisted 45.

Tremont Place (1994) 6161 N. Chatham, 64151. Tel: 816-587-7707; Fax: 816-587-7637. Email: tremont01@kc.rr.com. Holly Humphrey, Mgr.; Susan Engel, CEO & Diocesan Liaison. A 50-unit apartment residence for the elderly and disabled. Must be sixty-two or over.

ST. JOSEPH. *The Living Community of St. Joseph* (2004) 1202 Heartland Rd., 64506. Tel: 816-671-8500; Fax: 816-671-8571. Email: chris.kerns@bhshealth.org. Web: www.lcosj.com. Christine Kerns, Admin./CEO. Bed Capacity 131; Total Assisted Annually 944; Total Staff 230.

CAMERON. *St. Patrick's Manor*, 514 Northland Dr., 64429. Tel: 816-632-1684; Fax: 816-632-7624. Email: cpp61587@centurytel.net. Nancy Williams, Property Mgr.; Susan Engel, Diocesan Dir. A 31-unit apartment residence for the elderly and disabled. Total Staff 3.

LIBERTY. *Our Lady of Mercy Country Home*, 2115 Maturana Dr., 64068. Tel: 816-781-5711; Fax: 816-781-7276. Email: dtrimmer@ourladyofmercy.net. Web: ourladyofmercy.net. Sr. Sandra Thibodeaux, M.M.B., Regl. Moderator. Mercedarian Missionaries of Berriz. Guest Capacity 106; Sisters 15; Bed Capacity 106; Total Assisted Annually 525; Total Staff 54.

[J] MONASTERIES AND RESIDENCES OF PRIESTS

KANSAS CITY. *Redemptorists Fathers of Kansas City, Missouri*, 3333 Broadway Blvd., 64111. Tel: 816-561-3771; Fax: 816-561-3704. Revs. Frank Kriski, C.Ss.R.; Brian J. Johnson, C.Ss.R.; John Willett, C.Ss.R.; Patrick Power, C.Ss.R.; Edward Morgan, C.Ss.R.; Denis Ryan; Richard Quinn, C.Ss.R; Bros. Charles Long, C.Ss.R.; John Matthys, C.Ss.R.; Rev. Robert Lindsey, C.Ss.R. Priests 8; Brothers 2.

Rockhurst Jesuit Community, 5133 Forest Ave., 64110-2513. Tel: 816-501-3300; Fax: 816-501-3250. Web: www.rockhurst.edu/jesuitcommunity. Revs. William T. Oulvey, S.J., Rector; Terrence A. Baum, S.J.; A. James Blumeyer, S.J.; Martin J. Bredeck, S.J.; Max D. Buehler, S.J.; Revs. Luke J. Byrne, S.J.; John V. Craig, S.J.; Thomas B. Curran, O.S.F.S.; Dirk J. Dunfee, S.J.; Ian R. Gibbons, S.J.; Vernon R. Heinsz, S.J.; Glenn R. Mueller, S.J.; Louis J. Oldani, S.J.; William T. Sheahan, S.J.; John J. Vowells, S.J.; James D. Wheeler, S.J. Total in Residence 16.

Society of Our Lady of the Most Holy Trinity, 3705 Tracy Ave., 64109. Tel: 816-753-3068; Fax: 816-753-3068. Email: soltlaity@gmail.com. Web: www.solt3.org. Priests 2; Brothers 1; Deacons 1; Sisters 4; Laity 50.

CONCEPTION. *Conception Abbey* 64433. Tel: 660-944-3100; Fax: 660-944-2800. Email: communications@conception.edu. Web: www.ConceptionAbbey.org. Rt. Rev. Gregory Polan, O.S.B., Abbot; Rev. Kenneth Reichert, O.S.B.; Bro. Bernard Montgomery, O.S.B., Subprior; Revs. Sebastian Allgaier, O.S.B.; Albert Bruecken, O.S.B.; Patrick Caveglia, O.S.B.; Donald Grabner, O.S.B.; Aidan McSorley, O.S.B.; Benedict Neenan, O.S.B.; Very Rev. Samuel Russell, O.S.B., Seminary Pres. & Rector; Revs. Norbert Schappler, O.S.B.; Joachim Schieber, O.S.B.; Timothy Schoen, O.S.B.; Anthony Shidler, O.S.B.; Hugh Tasch, O.S.B.; Paschal Thomas, O.S.B.; Isaac True, O.S.B. Benedictine Monks. Priests 36; Brothers 22. Priests Elsewhere Revs. Karl Barmann, O.S.B. Tel: 660-783-2159 St. Peter, Stanberry; Martin DeMeulenaere, O.S.B. Tel: 660-582-3833 St. Gregory Barbarigo, Maryville; Xavier Nacke, O.S.B. Tel: 816-324-5700 St. Rose of Lima, Savannah, MO; Adam Ryan, O.S.B. Tel: 660-425-8160 Blessed Sacrament, Bethany; Reginald Sander, O.S.B. Tel: 660-736-4342 St. Paul the Apostle, Tarkio; Allan Stetz, O.S.B., St. Columba, Conception Junction. Tel. 660-944-2301; St. Joseph, Parnell. Tel. 660-986-3305; Peter Ullrich, O.S.B. Tel: 816-324-5700 St. Rose of Lima, Savannah, MO.

INDEPENDENCE. *Vincentian Parish Mission Center*, 2100 N. Noland Rd., 64050. Tel: 816-254-3000; Fax: 816-254-2204. Email: mm@vpmc.net. Web: www.vpmc.net. Revs. Richard Gielow, C.M., Supr. Tel: 816-254-3700; Michael Mulhearn, C.M.; Carl G. Schulte, C.M.; Thomas Cawley, C.M. Total in Residence 4.

LIBERTY. *Precious Blood Center* (1991) 2130 Saint Gaspar Way, 64068-7941. Tel: 816-781-4344; Fax: 816-781-3639. Rev. Michael Goode, C.PP.S.; Bros. Stephen Ohnmacht, C.PP.S.; Daryl Charron, C.PP.S.

Society of the Precious Blood Provincial Office (1965) P.O. Box 339, 64069-0339. Tel: 816-781-4344; Fax: 816-781-3639. Email: sec@kcprov.org. Revs. Joseph Nassal, C.PP.S., Prov. Dir.; Ronald L. Will, C.PP.S., Prov. Sec.; Richard Bayuk, C.PP.S., Prov. Treas.

[K] CONVENTS AND RESIDENCES FOR SISTERS

KANSAS CITY. *Benedictines of Mary, Queen of Apostles* Priory of Our Lady of Ephesus, 8005 NW 316th St., Gower, 64454. Web: benedictinesofmary.orgTel: 816-424-3194; Fax: 866-848-1880. Sr. Cecilia Snell, O.S.B., Prioress of Our Lady of Ephesus. Professed 13; Novices 6; Postulants 2.

Sisters of the Society of Our Lady of the Most Holy Trinity (1958) 3738 Tracy Ave., 64109. Tel: 816-561-8849. Society of Apostolic Life. Sisters 6; Novices 4.

CLYDE. *Benedictine Convent of Perpetual Adoration* (1874) 31970 State Hwy. P, 64432. Tel: 660-944-2221; Fax: 660-944-2152. Email: sister@benedictinesisters.org. Web: www.benedictinesisters.org. Sr. Patricia Nyquist, Prioress Gen. Attended by Conception Abbey; Two other interdependent monasteries: Tucson, AZ; and Dayton, WY. Membership in Clyde Community 56; Total in Congregation 81; Sisters 80.

INDEPENDENCE. *St. Francis Convent Novitiate and Prayer Center* (Switzerland 1378, U.S. 1892) 2100 N. Noland Rd., 64050. Tel: 816-252-1673; Fax: 816-252-5574. Email: STFRAN2100@aol.com. Web: www.osfholyeucharist.org. Sr. M. Lucy Lang, O.S.F., Supr. Motherhouse of the Sisters of St. Francis of the Holy Eucharist. Sisters 15; Postulants 1.

LIBERTY. *Mercedarian Missionaries of Berriz*, U.S. Regional Headquarters, 2115 Maturana Dr., #101B, 64068-7985. Tel: 816-781-8202; Fax: 816-781-8205. Email: mmbus@sbcglobal.net. Web: mmberriz.com. Sr. Sandra Thibodeaux, M.M.B., Regl. Coord. Mercedarian Mission. Mercedarian Missionaries of Berriz 12.

Mercedarian Missionaries of Berriz (M.M.B.), 2116 Maturana Dr., 64068. Tel: 816-415-3024. Sr. Linda Teegarden, M.M.B., Local Coord. Mercedarian Mission. Sisters 3.

Mercedarian Missionaries of Berriz (M.M.B.), 2120 Maturana Dr., 64068. Tel: 816-415-3133. Email: thibfay@sbcglobal.net. Sr. Sandra Thibodeaux, M.M.B., Local Coord. Mercedarian Mission. Sisters 2.

Queen of Angels Monastery - Benedictine Sisters, 23615 N.E. 100th St., 64068-8716. Tel: 816-750-4618; Fax: 816-750-4620. Email: sisters@libertyosb.org. Web: libertyosb.org. Sr. Agnes Helgenberger, O.S.B., Prioress. Sisters 6; Total in Residence 9.

RAYTOWN. *Sisters in Jesus the Lord*, 7049 Blue Ridge Blvd., 64133-5679. Tel: 816-353-2177. Web: www.cjd.cc. Sr. Julia Mary Kubista, Supr. Sisters 2; Sisters in Temporary Profession 2; Postulants 2.

SAVANNAH. *Sisters of St. Francis Provincial House* (1922) 908 S. Third St., Box 488, 64485-0488. Tel: 816-324-3179; Fax: 816-324-7264. Web: sistersofstfrancis.org. Rev. Hugh Tasch, O.S.B. Sisters of St. Francis of Savannah, MO. Motherhouse and Novitiate. Sisters 8.

Maintenance and Custodial Care Trust of the Franciscan Sisters of Savannah, MO Tel: 816-324-3179; Fax: 816-324-7264.

[L] SERVICES

KANSAS CITY. *Bishop Sullivan Center* (1972) 6435 Truman Rd., 64126. Tel: 816-231-0984; Fax: 816-231-3096. Email: tturner@bishopsullivan.org. Web: www.bishopsullivan.org. Rev. Thomas W. Turner, Dir. Total Assisted 21,000; Total Staff 20.

Redemptorist Social Services Center, Inc., 207 W. Linwood Blvd., 64111-1327. Tel: 816-931-9942; Fax: 816-531-0583. Email: info@kcsocialservices.org. Web: www.kcsocialservices.org. Diana Kennedy, Dir. Total Assisted 4,100; Total Staff 7.

**Seton Center Family & Health Services*, 2816 E. 23 St., 64127. Tel: 816-231-3955; Fax: 816-231-7455. Web: www.setonkc.org. Sr. Loretto Marie Colwell, S.C.L., Exec. Dir. Total Assisted 17,541; Total Staff 18.

[M] NEWMAN CENTERS

KANSAS CITY. *Avila University Campus Ministry* 11901 Wornall Rd., 64145. Tel: 816-501-2423; Fax: 816-501-2454. Email: david.armstrong@avila.edu. Web: www.avila.edu. David Armstrong, Dir. Campus Ministry. Total Assisted 1,200; Staff 1.

MARYVILLE. *Newman Catholic Center, Northwest Missouri State University* 606 College Ave., 64468. Tel: 660-582-7373; Fax: 660-582-7397. Email: newman@nwmissouri.edu. M. Bridget Brown, Campus Min. Total Staff 1; Total Assisted 250.

WARRENSBURG. *Newman Center Catholic Campus Ministry for University of Central Missouri* 106 Broad St., 64093. Tel: 660-747-6997; Fax: 660-362-0243. Email: ucmnewman@gmail.com. Michael McCormick, Dir. Total Assisted 200; Total Staff 1.

[N] MISCELLANEOUS

KANSAS CITY. *St. Anthony's Home*, 20 W. 9th St., Ste. 200, P.O. Box 419037, 64141-6037. Tel: 816-756-1850.

Bishop Boland Institute for Housing and Community Development, 20 W. 9th St., Ste. 600, 64105. Tel: 816-221-4377; Fax: 816-472-5423. Email: sengel@ccharities.com. Web: www.catholiccharities-kcsj.org. Susan Engel, Dir.

Camp Little Flower, 20 W. 9th St., Ste. 200, P.O. Box 419037, 64141-6037. Tel: 816-756-1850. Rose-Mary Montemore, Pres.

Catholic Charities Foundation, 20 W. 9th St., Ste. 650, 64105. Tel: 816-221-4377; Fax: 816-472-5423. Email: rprather@ccharities.com. Web: www.catholiccharities-kcsj.org. Rozanne Prather, Exec. Dir.

Cristo Rey Kansas City Corporate Internship Program, 211 W. Linwood Blvd., 64111. Tel: 816-457-6044; Fax: 816-457-6046. Email: khanlon@cristoreykc.org. Web: www.cristoreykc.org. Kathleen M. Hanlon, Ph.D., Pres. & Contact Person; Mary Kallman, Prin.

Cursillo, 20 W. 9th St., 64105. Tel: 816-756-1850; Fax: 816-756-5221. Email: greene@diocesekcsj.org. Web: www.diocese-kcsj.org/igm/familylife/index.htm. Deacon Kenneth Greene, Spirtual Advisor.

De La Salle Academy, 3732 Paseo, 64109. Tel: 816-531-6561; Fax: 816-756-3916. Email: mooney81@hotmail.com. Christian Brothers, F.S.C. and LaSallian Volunteers., Special Lasallion Volunteer Program. Christian Brothers 2; LaSallian Volunteers 2.

**De La Salle Alumni Association*, P.O. Box 380083, 64138. Tel: 816-767-9800; Fax: 816-767-9800.

Diocesan Council of Catholic Women, 20 W. 9th St., Ste. 200, P.O. Box 419037, 64141-6037. Tel: 816-756-1850. Elizabeth Dietrich, Contact Person.

Endowment Trust Fund for Catholic Education (1989) 20 W. 9th St., Ste. 200, 64105. Tel: 816-756-1850; Fax: 816-756-5089. Email: moss@diocesekcsj.org. Web: www.diocese-kcsj.org. Paula Moss, Contact Person.

Friends, Inc., 20 W. 9th St., Ste. 200, P.O. Box 419037, 64141-6037. Tel: 816-756-1850.

Immacolata Retreat Center, 20 W. 9th St., Ste. 200, P.O. Box 419037, 64141-6037. Tel: 816-756-1850.

St. John's Seminary, Inc., P.O. Box 419037, 64141-6037.

Knights of St. Peter Claver (K.P.C.), 1600 Paseo, St. Monica Parish, 64108. Tel: 816-471-3696; Fax: 816-471-1100. Ladies Auxiliary of St. Peter Claver.

Ladies of Charity of Metropolitan Kansas City (1952) P.O. Box 480753, 64148-0753. Web: www.lockc.org. Gwen Brooks, Pres. A group of volunteers who work and raise money to help the poor and those in need through Seton Center and other agencies in the greater Kansas City area.

Marillac Home for Children, P.O. Box 419037, 64141-6037.

Our Lady of Perpetual Help Charitable Trust (1978) 3333 Broadway, 64111. Tel: 816-561-3771; Fax: 816-561-3704. Email: bjohnson@olphkc.org. Web: www.redemptoristkc.org. Rev. Brian J. Johnson, C.Ss.R., Contact Person.

Siena Club, 20 W. 9th St., Ste. 200, P.O. Box 419037, 64141-6037. Tel: 816-756-1850.

CONCEPTION. **The St. Benedict Education Foundation, Conception Abbey Office*, P.O. Box 16, 64433. Tel: 660-944-2820; Fax: 660-944-2885. Email: patrick@conception.edu. Web: www.stbenedictfoundation.org. Rev. Patrick Caveglia, O.S.B.

LIBERTY. **St. Gaspar Society* (1991) P.O. Box 339, 64069. Tel: 816-781-4344; Fax: 816-781-3639. Email: sec@kcprov.org. Revs. Joseph Nassal, C.PP.S., Pres.; Michael Goode, C.PP.S., Treas.; Bro. Stephen Ohnmacht, C.PP.S., Sec.; Rev. Richard Bayuk, C.PP.S.

Our Lady of Mercy Home, 2115 Maturana Dr., 64068-9469. Tel: 816-781-5711; Fax: 816-781-7276.

**Queen of Angels Foundation, Inc.*, 23615 N.E. 100th St., 64068. Tel: 816-750-4618; Fax: 816-750-4620. Email: sisters@libertyosb.org.

MARYVILLE. *St. Francis Hospital Foundation*, 2016 S. Main, 64468. Tel: 660-562-7933; Fax: 660-562-7982. Web: www.stfrancismaryville.com.

RAYMORE. *St. Francis de Sales Association*, 1800 N. Jeter Rd., 64083. Tel: 816-331-4831. Barbara McClung, Group Dir. Tel: 816-331-4831.

RELIGIOUS INSTITUTES OF MEN REPRESENTED IN THE DIOCESE

For further details refer to the corresponding bracketed number in the Religious Institutes of Men or Women section.

[0200]—*Benedictine Monks* (Conception Abbey)—O.S.B.

[]—*Benedictine Monks* (St. Gregory's Abbey)—O.S.B.

[0330]—*Christian Brothers of the Midwest, Burr Ridge*—F.S.C.

[1330]—*Congregation of the Mission* (Western Province)—C.M.

[1210]—*Congregation of the Missionaries of St. Charles*—C.S.

[0305]—*Institute of Christ the King-Sovereign Priest*—I.C.

[0690]—*Jesuit Fathers and Brothers* (Missouri Prov.)—S.J.

[]—*Legionaries of Christ*—L.C.

[0920]—*Oblates of St. Francis de Sales*—O.S.F.S.

[1070]—*Redemptorist Fathers of Kansas City, Missouri* (Denver Prov.)—C.SS.R.

[0975]—*Society of Our Lady of Most Holy Trinity*—S.O.L.T.

[1060]—*Society of the Precious Blood* (Kansas City Prov.)—C.PP.S.

RELIGIOUS INSTITUTES OF WOMEN REPRESENTED IN THE DIOCESE

[0230]—*Benedictine Sisters of Pontifical Jurisdiction* (Atchinson, KS; Liberty, MO)—O.S.B.

[]—*Benedictines of Mary, Queen of Apostles*—O.S.B.

[0397]—*Congregation of Mary Queen* (Springfield, MO)—C.M.R.

[0220]—*Congregation of the Benedictine Sisters of Perpetual Adoration of Pontifical Jurisdiction*—O.S.B.

[3832]—*Congregation of the Sisters of St. Joseph* (Wichita, KS)—C.S.J.

[1115]—*Dominican Sisters of Peace* (Columbus, OH)—O.P.

[2575]—*Institute of the Sisters of Mercy of the Americas* (Omaha, NE)—R.S.M.

[2340]—*Little Sisters of the Poor*—L.S.P.

[2510]—*Mercedarian Missionaries of Berriz*—M.M.B.

[2960]—*Notre Dame Sisters* (Omaha, NE)—N.D.

[]—*School Sisters of Christ the King*—C.K.

[2150]—*Sister Servants of Immaculate Heart of Mary* (Monroe, MI)—I.H.M.

[]—*Sisters in Jesus the Lord*—C.J.D.

[0480]—*Sisters of Charity of Leavenworth, Kansas*—S.C.L.

[0430]—*Sisters of Charity of the Blessed Virgin Mary*—B.V.M.

[2360]—*Sisters of Loretto at the Foot of the Cross*—S.L.

[1670]—*Sisters of St. Francis of Savannah, MO*—O.S.F.

[1560]—*Sisters of St. Francis of the Holy Eucharist* (Independence, MO)—O.S.F.

[]—*Sisters of St. Francis of the Holy Eucharist Foundation*

[3830-15]—*Sisters of St. Joseph* (Concordia, KS)—C.S.J.

[3840]—*Sisters of St. Joseph of Carondelet*—C.S.J.

[3105]—*Society of Our Lady of the Most Holy Trinity*—S.O.L.T.

DIOCESAN CEMETERIES

KANSAS CITY. *Mount Olivet & Mount St. Mary*

ST. JOSEPH. *Mount Olivet*

KANSAS CITY NORTH. *Resurrection*

NECROLOGY

† Bauman, William A., (Retired)—Died April 17, 2011

An asterisk (*) denotes an organization that has established tax-exempt status directly with the IRS and is not covered by the USCCB Group Ruling.

Diocese of Knoxville

Most Reverend

RICHARD F. STIKA

Third Bishop of Knoxville; ordained December 14, 1985; appointed third Bishop of Knoxville January 12, 2009; ordained and installed March 19, 2009. *Office: 805 Northshore Dr., S.W., Knoxville, TN 37919.*

Chancery Office: 805 Northshore Dr., S.W., Knoxville, TN 37919. Tel: 865-584-3307.

Web: www.dioknox.org

ESTABLISHED SEPTEMBER 8, 1988.

Square Miles 14,242.

Comprises the Counties of Anderson, Bledsoe, Blount, Bradley, Campbell, Carter, Claiborne, Cocke, Cumberland, Fentress, Grainger, Greene, Hamblen, Hamilton, Hancock, Hawkins, Jefferson, Johnson, Knox, Loudon, McMinn, Marion, Meigs, Monroe, Morgan, Pickett, Polk, Rhea, Roane, Scott, Sequatchie, Sevier, Sullivan, Unicoi, Union and Washington in the State of Tennessee.

For legal titles of parishes and diocesan institutions, consult the Chancery Office.

STATISTICAL OVERVIEW

Personnel	
Bishop	1
Priests: Diocesan Active in Diocese	47
Priests: Diocesan Active Outside Diocese	3
Priests: Retired, Sick or Absent	12
Number of Diocesan Priests	62
Religious Priests in Diocese	13
Total Priests in Diocese	75
Extern Priests in Diocese	7
Ordinations:	
Diocesan Priests	1
Transitional Deacons	1
Permanent Deacons in Diocese	59
Total Brothers	11
Total Sisters	37
Parishes	
Parishes	47
With Resident Pastor:	
Resident Diocesan Priests	33
Resident Religious Priests	6
Without Resident Pastor:	
Administered by Priests	8
Missions	2
Pastoral Centers	2
Professional Ministry Personnel:	
Sisters	2
Lay Ministers	30
Welfare	
Catholic Hospitals	1
Total Assisted	99,681
Health Care Centers	1
Total Assisted	278
Homes for the Aged	1
Total Assisted	600
Specialized Homes	2
Total Assisted	133
Special Centers for Social Services	7
Total Assisted	62,776
Educational	
Diocesan Students in Other Seminaries	17
Total Seminarians	17
High Schools, Diocesan and Parish	2
Total Students	1,101
Elementary Schools, Diocesan and Parish	8
Total Students	2,192
Catechesis/Religious Education:	
High School Students	1,005
Elementary Students	3,408
Total Students under Catholic Instruction	7,723
Teachers in the Diocese:	
Priests	2
Sisters	13
Lay Teachers	200
Vital Statistics	
Receptions into the Church:	
Infant Baptism Totals	1,094
Minor Baptism Totals	94
Adult Baptism Totals	82
Received into Full Communion	243
First Communions	1,116
Confirmations	655
Marriages:	
Catholic	165
Interfaith	113
Total Marriages	278
Deaths	415
Total Catholic Population	61,827
Total Population	2,364,692

Former Bishops—Most Revs. ANTHONY J. O'CONNELL, ord. 1963; appt. Bishop of Knoxville May 27, 1988; installed Sept. 8, 1988; appt. Bishop of Palm Beach Nov. 11, 1998; JOSEPH E. KURTZ, ord. 1972; appt. Bishop of Knoxville Oct. 26, 1999; ord. and installed Dec. 8, 1999; appt. Archbishop of Louisville June 12, 2007.

Vicars General—Rev. Msgr. FRANCIS XAVIER MANKEL, S.T.L., V.G.; Very Rev. DAVID BOETTNER, V.G.

Episcopal Vicar for Priests—Rev. Msgr. G. PATRICK GARRITY, V.E., Dean.

Deans of the Diocese—Rev. Msgrs. ROBERT J. HOFSTETTER, Five Rivers Deanery; GEORGE E. SCHMIDT JR., Chattanooga Deanery; G. PATRICK GARRITY, V.E., Cumberland Mtn. Deanery; Rev. CHRIS MICHELSON, Smoky Mtn. Deanery.

Chancery Office—805 Northshore Dr., S.W., Knoxville, 37919. Tel: 865-584-3307; Fax: 865-584-7538. Office Hours: Mon.-Fri. 9-5; All official business should be directed to this office.

Moderator of the Curia—Very Rev. DAVID BOETTNER, V.G.

Chancellor and Chief Operating Officer—Deacon SEAN K. SMITH.

Assistant to the Bishop—Deacon SEAN K. SMITH.

Vice Chancellor—Rev. J. DAVID CARTER, J.C.L.

Auditors— All priests on assignment in the diocese.

Presbyteral Council—Rev. BEDE C. ABOH; Very Rev. DAVID BOETTNER, V.G.; Revs. J. DAVID CARTER, J.C.L.; MICHAEL E. CUMMINS; CHARLES DONAHUE, C.S.P.; GILBERT M. DIAZ; Rev. Msgrs. G. PATRICK GARRITY, V.E., Dean & Chm.; ROBERT J. HOFSTETTER, Dean; T. ALLEN HUMBRECHT; FRANCIS XAVIER MANKEL, S.T.L., V.G.; Revs. CHRISTIAN MATHIS, Recording Sec.; CHRIS MICHELSON, Dean & Vice Chm.; MICHAEL F. NOLAN; Rev. Msgr. GEORGE E. SCHMIDT JR., Dean; Rev. RAGAN SCHRIVER.

Diocesan Consultors—Rev. PATRICK P. BROWNELL; Rev. Msgrs. G. PATRICK GARRITY, V.E.; ROBERT J. HOFSTETTER, Dean; T. ALLEN HUMBRECHT; FRANCIS XAVIER MANKEL, S.T.L., V.G.; Rev. MICHAEL F. NOLAN; Very Rev. DAVID BOETTNER, V.G.; Rev. CHARLES DONAHUE, C.S.P.

Diocesan Finance Council—HERBERT ADAMS; DORMAN BLAINE; JERRY BODIE; J. MICHAEL CONNOR, Chm.; Very Rev. DAVID BOETTNER, V.G., Ex-Officio, Vicar Gen.; Deacon DAVID J. LUCHEON, Ex Officio, Diocesan Finance Officer; SHARON FOLK; GEORGE HAGGARD; RUDY HOGAN; Rev. Msgr. FRANCIS XAVIER MANKEL, S.T.L., V.G., Ex Officio; Revs. WILLIAM L. MCKENZIE; CHRIS MICHELSON, Dean; EDWARD PHILLIPS, Ex Officio, Diocesan Attorney; PAUL PREMO; SOCRATES SABATER; Rev. Msgr. GEORGE E. SCHMIDT JR., Dean; SUZANNE SCHRIVER; Deacon SEAN K. SMITH, Ex Officio; BILL SWAIN; FRAN THIE, Vice Chm.

Diocesan Offices and Directors

Archives—Deacon SEAN K. SMITH, 805 Northshore Dr., S.W., Knoxville, 37919. Tel: 865-584-3307.

Campus Ministries—

East Tennessee State University—Rev. MICHAEL E. CUMMINS, Chap., Catholic Center, 734 W. Locust St., Johnson City, 37604. Tel: 423-926-7061.

University of Tennessee-Chattanooga—Rev. JAMES MALLETT, Dir., 514 Palmetto St., Chattanooga, 37403. Tel: 423-779-2400.

University of Tennessee-Knoxville—Rev. CHARLES DONAHUE, C.S.P., Dir., 1710 Melrose Pl., Knoxville, 37916. Tel: 865-523-7931.

Catholic Schools Office—Sr. MARY MARTA ABBOTT, R.S.M., Ed.S., Supt., 805 Northshore Dr., S.W., Knoxville, 37919. Tel: 865-584-3307.

Catholic Charities of East Tennessee, Inc.—Rev. RAGAN SCHRIVER, Exec. Dir., 3009 Lake Brook Blvd., Knoxville, 37909. Tel: 865-524-9896; Fax: 865-971-3558. Email: info@ccetn.org. The umbrella agency for all Catholic Charities of the diocese.

Catholic Campaign for Human Development—Rev. RAGAN SCHRIVER, Dir., 3009 Lake Brook Blvd., Knoxville, 37909. Tel: 865-524-9896.

Catholic Charities (Chattanooga Area)—CHRISTINE WILLINGHAM, Site Coord., 859 McCallie Ave., Chattanooga, 37403. Tel: 423-267-1297; Fax: 423-265-4923.

Catholic Charities (Knoxville Area)—VACANT, 3009 Lake Brook Blvd., Knoxville, 37909. Tel: 865-524-9896.

Catholic Charities (Upper East Tennessee Area)—BRENDA DUNN, Site Coord., 703 E. Jackson Blvd., P.O. Box 323, Jonesborough, 37659. Tel: 423-753-3001; Fax: 423-753-5260.

Cemeteries—Deacon SEAN K. SMITH, Dir., 805 Northshore Dr., S.W., Knoxville, 37919. Tel: 865-584-3307; Rev. Msgr. GEORGE E. SCHMIDT JR., Dean, Contact: Mt. Olivet Cemetery, 4159 Ringgold Rd., Chattanooga, 37412. Tel: 423-266-1618; Rev. RONALD A. FRANCO, C.S.P., Contact, Calvary Cemetery in Knoxville, 2000 Martin Luther King, Jr. Blvd., Knoxville, 37915. Mailing Address: c/o Immaculate Conception Church, 414 W. Vine Ave., Knoxville, 37902-1327. Tel: 865-522-1508.

Chancellor and Chief Operating Officer—Deacon SEAN K. SMITH, 805 Northshore Dr., S.W., Knoxville, 37919. Tel: 865-584-3307.

Censor Librorum—Rev. Msgr. ROBERT J. HOFSTETTER, Dean, 308 Lou Ellen St., Newport, 37821. Tel:

423-237-6419.

Christian Formation—Sr. MARY TIMOTHEA ELLIOTT, R.S.M., Dir.; Rev. RICHARD G. ARMSTRONG JR., Asst. Dir., 805 Northshore Dr., S.W., Knoxville, 37919. Tel: 865-584-3307.

Diaconate and Deacon Formation—Deacon TIM ELLIOTT, Dir., 805 Northshore Dr., S.W., Knoxville, 37919. Tel: 865-584-3307.

Diocesan Council of Catholic Women—Rev. Msgr. FRANCIS XAVIER MANKEL, S.T.L., V.G., Diocesan Spiritual Moderator, 111 Hinton Ave., Knoxville, 37927. Tel: 865-522-2205.

Ecumenism—Rev. Msgr. T. ALLEN HUMBRECHT, Dir., 805 Northshore Dr., S.W., Knoxville, 37919. Tel: 865-584-3307.

Employment Services and Benefits—MARCY MELDAHL, Dir., Chancery Office, 805 Northshore Dr., S.W., Knoxville, 37919. Tel: 865-584-3307.

Finance Office—Deacon DAVID J. LUCHEON, Diocesan Finance Officer, 805 Northshore Dr., S.W., Knoxville, 37919. Tel: 865-584-3307.

Hispanic Ministry—LOURDES GARZA, Dir., Chancery Office: 805 Northshore Dr., S.W., Knoxville, 37919. Tel: 865-637-4769.

Justice and Peace Office—PAUL SIMONEAU, Dir., Chancery Office: 805 Northshore Dr., S.W., Knoxville, 37919. Tel: 865-584-3307.

Marriage Tribunal—Very Rev. DEXTER BREWER, J.C.L., J.V., 2400 21st Ave. S., Nashville, 37212-5387. Tel: 615-383-6393 Diocesan marriage tribunal is shared with the Diocese of Nashville.

Ministries of the Chattanooga Deanery—Rev. Msgr. GEORGE E. SCHMIDT JR., Dean; JANE HUBBARD, Deanery Coord., 859 McCallie Ave., Ste. 302, Chattanooga, 37403. Tel: 423-267-9878.

Ministries of the Five Rivers Deanery—Rev. Msgr. ROBERT J. HOFSTETTER, Dean, 308 Lou Ellen St., Newport, 37821. Tel: 423-237-6419.

Ministries of the Cumberland Mtn. Deanery—Rev. Msgr. G. PATRICK GARRITY, V.E., Dean, 633 St. John Court, Knoxville, 37934. Tel: 865-966-4540.

Ministries of the Smoky Mtn. Deanery—Rev. CHRIS MICHELSON, Dean, 7200 Brickey Lane, Knoxville, 37918. Tel: 865-689-7011.

Moderator of the Curia—Very Rev. DAVID BOETTNER, V.G., 805 Northshore Dr., S.W., Knoxville, 37919. Tel: 865-584-3307.

Priestly Life and Ministry—Rev. Msgr. G. PATRICK GARRITY, V.E., Dean & Dir., 633 St. John Ct., Knoxville, 37934. Tel: 865-966-4540.

Propagation of the Faith—PAUL SIMONEAU, Dir., 805 Northshore Dr., S.W., Knoxville, 37919. Tel: 865-584-3307.

Scouting—Deacon OTTO PRESKE, Scout Chap., 535 Buckhorn Rd., Gatlinburg, 37738. Tel: 865-436-5339.

Diocesan Catholic Committee on Scouting—GEORGE C. LECRONE SR., Chm., 10700 Leeward Ln., Knoxville, 37934. Tel: 865-974-0050.

Stewardship, Planned Giving and Development—ANGIE CONNORS, Asst. Dir., 805 Northshore Dr., S.W., Knoxville, 37919. Tel: 865-584-3307. Email: aconnors@dioknox.org.

"The East Tennessee Catholic"— (Diocesan Newspaper). MARY C. WEAVER, Editor, 805 Northshore Dr., S.W., Knoxville, 37919. Tel: 865-584-3307. Email: mweaver@dioknox.org.

Victim Assistance Coordinator—MARLA LENIHAN, 400 Laboratory Rd., Ste. 103, Oak Ridge, 37830. Tel: 865-482-1388.

Vocations—Revs. MICHAEL E. CUMMINS, Vocation Dir.; J. DAVID CARTER, J.C.L., Assoc. Dir., 805 Northshore Dr., S.W., Knoxville, 37919. Tel: 865-584-3307; Sr. MARY CHRISTINE CREMIN, R.S.M., Diocesan Coord. Vocation Promotion for Rel., 815 Hansmore Pl., Knoxville, 37919. Tel: 865-690-9266. Email: srmarychristine@dioknox.org.

Vocation Discernment Office—Rev. MICHAEL E. CUMMINS, Dir., 734 W. Locust St., Johnson City, 37604. Tel: 423-926-7061.

Worship and Liturgy—Rev. RANDY STICE, Dir., 805 Northshore Dr., S.W., Knoxville, 37919. Tel: 865-584-3307.

Youth and Young Adult Ministry—AL FORSYTHE, Diocesan Coord., 805 Northshore Dr., S.W., Knoxville, 37919. Tel: 865-584-3307; DONNA L. JONES, Coord. Chattanooga Deanery, 859 McCallie Ave., Ste. 302, Chattanooga, 37403. Tel: 423-267-9878; Deacons G. JAMES FAGE II, Coord., Five Rivers Deanery, 780 Roddy Dr., Morristown, 37814. Tel: 423-587-4925; DAN HOSFORD, Coord. Cumberland Mtn. and Smoky Mtn. Deanery, 102 Pheasant Rd., Clinton, 37716. Tel: 865-603-9682.

CLERGY, PARISHES, MISSIONS AND PAROCHIAL SCHOOLS

CITY OF KNOXVILLE

(KNOX COUNTY)

1—CATHEDRAL OF THE SACRED HEART OF JESUS (1956) [JC] Very Rev. David Boettner, Rector; Revs. Andres Cano-Ramirez; Randy Stice; Deacons James Lawson, Pastoral Assoc.; Ben Johnston.
Res.: 711 Northshore Dr., S.W., 37919. Tel: 865-588-0249; Fax: 865-558-9671. Web: www.shcathedral.org.
School—(Grades PreK-8) Tel: 865-588-0415; Fax: 865-558-4139. Web: www.shcschool.org. Sedonna Prater, Prin. Lay Teachers 45; Students 617; Religious 1.
Catechesis/Religious Program—Tel: 865-584-4528. Brigid Johnson, D.R.E. Students 197.

2—ST. ALBERT THE GREAT CHURCH (2007) Rev. Chris Michelson; Deacons Michael Eiffe; Patrick Murphy-Racey.
7200 Brickey Ln., 37918. Tel: 865-689-7011; Fax: 865-689-9905. Email: office@satgknox.org. Web: www.satgknox.org.
See Saint Joseph School of Knoxville under Elementary Schools Regional located in the Institution Section.
Catechesis/Religious Program—Students 108.

3—ALL SAINTS CATHOLIC CHURCH (1994) [JC] Revs. Michael Woods; J. David Carter; Miguel Velez-Cardona; Deacons Tim Elliott; David J. Lucheon.
Mailing Address: 620 N. Cedar Bluff Rd., 37923. Tel: 865-531-0770; Fax: 865-531-1009. Email: allsaintsknox@bellsouth.net. Web: www.allsaintsknoxville.org. In Res., Rev. Kwaku John Appiah.
Catechesis/Religious Program—Students 509.

4—BLESSED JOHN XXIII UNIVERSITY PARISH/ CATHOLIC CENTER (1968) [CEM], (Non-territorial parish for the University of Tennessee at Knoxville). Rev. Charles Donahue, C.S.P.; Ruth Queen Smith, Pastoral Assoc.
Office: 1710 Melrose Pl., 37916. Tel: 865-523-7931; Fax: 865-523-7979.
Catechesis/Religious Program—Students 38.

5—HOLY GHOST (1908) [JC] Rev. Msgr. Francis Xavier Mankel; Rev. John Arthur Orr.
1041 N. Central St., 37917.
Res.: 111 Hinton Ave., 37917. Tel: 865-522-2205; Fax: 865-525-6051. Email: hgchurch@bellsouth.net. Web: holyghostknoxville.org.
See Saint Joseph School of Knoxville under Elementary Schools Regional located in the Institution Section.
Catechesis/Religious Program—Kathleen Kramer, D.R.E. Students 76.

6—IMMACULATE CONCEPTION (1852), (Irish), [CEM] Revs. Ronald A. Franco, C.S.P.; Gerard P. Tully, C.S.P.; Deacons Joseph Hieu Vinh; Joe Stackhouse.
Office: 414 W. Vine Ave., 37902-1327. Tel: 865-522-1508; Fax: 865-524-8514. Email: icoffice@bellsouth.net. Web: www.icknoxville.org.
Res.: 707 E. Scott Ave., 37917. Tel: 865-637-6451.
See Saint Joseph School of Knoxville under Elementary Schools Regional located in the Institution Section.
Catechesis/Religious Program— Kathleen Kramer, D.R.E. Students 44.

7—ST. JOHN NEUMANN (1977) Rev. Msgr. G. Patrick Garrity, Dean; Rev. Douglas Owens; Deacons Donald Amelse; Marquis Syler; Michael Gouge.
Mailing Address: 633 St. John Ct., 37934-1555.
Church: 645 St. John Ct., 37934-1555. Tel: 865-966-4540; Fax: 865-675-6815. Email: neumanncc@tds.net. Web: www.sjnknox.org.
School—(Grades K-8), 625 St. John Ct., 37934-1555. Tel: 865-777-0077; Fax: 865-777-0087. Web: www.sjncs-knox.org. Bill Derbyshire, Prin.; Mary Sue Kosky, Academic Dean; Diane Schukman, Librarian. Lay Teachers 28; Students 294.
Catechesis/Religious Program—Students 268.

OUTSIDE THE CITY OF KNOXVILLE

ALCOA, BLOUNT CO., OUR LADY OF FATIMA (1950) Revs. William L. McKenzie; William J. McNeeley; Deacon Kenneth Long.
Res. & Rectory: 860 Louisville Rd., 37701.
Office: 858 Louisville Rd., 37701. Tel: 865-982-3672; Fax: 865-977-4183. Web: www.ourladyoffatima.org.
Catechesis/Religious Program—Fax: 865-983-3563. Students 278.

ATHENS, MCMINN CO., ST. MARY (1968) Rev. William Dickson Oruko, A.J. (Kenya).
Res. & Office: 1291 E. Madison Ave., 37303. Tel: 423-745-4277; Fax: 423-745-9706. Email: stmaryathens@att.net. Web: www.stmaryathenstn.org.
Catechesis/Religious Program—Tel: 423-263-1217. Paulette Croteau, D.R.E. Students 94.

CHATTANOOGA, HAMILTON CO.

1—BASILICA OF STS. PETER AND PAUL (1852) [JC] Rev. Msgr. George E. Schmidt Jr.; Deacon James Wilson. In Res., Rev. Bertin Glennon, S.T.
Res.: 214 E. 8th St., 37402. Tel: 423-266-1618.
Catechesis/Religious Program—Tel: 706-935-4518. Ann May, D.R.E. Students 80.

2—ST. JUDE (1958) [JC] Revs. Charles Burton; Moises Morena-Urzua (LAV); Deacons Gaspar DeGaetano; Brian Gabor; Thomas McConnell; Paul Nelson. In Res., Rev. Paul J. Valleroy (Retired).
Res.: 930 Ashland Ter., 37415. Tel: 423-870-2386; Fax: 423-876-8960. Email: info@stjudechattanooga.org. Web: www.stjudechattanooga.org.
School—(Grades PreSchool-8) Tel: 423-877-6022; Fax: 423-875-8920. Jamie Goodhard, Prin.; Sandra Newton, Librarian. Lay Teachers 29; Students 387.
Catechesis/Religious Program—Kyra Ross, D.R.E. Students 144.

3—OUR LADY OF PERPETUAL HELP (1937) Revs. James L. Vick; Michael Creson; Deacon Mark Gang Jr.
Res.: 501 S. Moore Rd., 37412. Tel: 423-622-7232; Fax: 423-624-2686. Web: www.myolph.com.
School—(Grades K-8), 505 S. Moore Rd., 37412. Tel: 423-622-1418; Fax: 423-622-2016. Mrs. Jeri McInturff, Prin.; Patsy Duenas, Librarian. Lay Teachers 26; Students 320.
Catechesis/Religious Program—Tel: 423-622-7232; Fax: 423-624-2686. Corinne Hennen, D.R.E. Students 142.

4—ST. STEPHEN (1961) [JC] Rev. Gilbert M. Diaz; Deacons Dan Alexander; Charles Lee; Anna C. Anthony, Pastoral Assoc. In Res., Rev. Augustine Idra, A.J. (Sudan).
Res. & Office: 7111 Lee Hwy., 37421. Tel: 423-892-1261; Fax: 423-892-3242. Email: info@ststephenchattanooga.com. Web: www.ststephenchattanooga.com.
Catechesis/Religious Program—Tel: 423-892-2957. Marilyn St. Pierre, D.R.E. Students 108.

CLEVELAND, BRADLEY CO., ST. THERESE OF LISIEUX (1914) Revs. Albert C. Sescon (Philippines), Parochial Admin.; Thomas W. Moser; Deacon Gary Brinkworth.
Res.: 900 Clingan Ridge Dr., N.W., 37312. Tel: 423-476-8123; Fax: 423-479-3339.
Catechesis/Religious Program—Email: sttherese@charter.net. Sandra J. Hartert-Forshee, D.R.E. Students 23.

CLINTON, ANDERSON CO., ST. THERESE (1971) Rev. William H. Gahagan; Sr. Yvette Gillen, R.S.M., Pastoral Assoc. & D.R.E.
Church & Res.: 701 S. Charles G. Seivers Blvd., 37716. Tel: 865-457-4073 (Church); 865-463-8935 (Res.); Fax: 865-463-9734.
Catechesis/Religious Program—Students 30.

COPPERHILL, POLK CO., ST. CATHERINE LABOURE (1977) Rev. William Patrick Resen.
Mailing Address: 115 E. Main St., P.O. Box 1165, 37317. Tel: 423-496-3498. Email: sclc@bellsouth.net.
Catechesis/Religious Program— Kathy Ross, D.R.E. Students 32.

CROSSVILLE, CUMBERLAND CO., ST. ALPHONSUS (1948) Rev. Antony Punnackal, C.M.I. (India), Parochial Admin.; Deacon Joseph Solis.
Res.: 151 St. Alphonsus Way, 38555. Tel: 931-484-2358 (Office); 931-456-5005 (Res.); Fax: 931-484-7407. Email: stalphonsus@frontiernet.net. Web: www.stalphonsuscrossville.org.
Catechesis/Religious Program—Tel: 931-456-5227; Fax: 931-484-7407. Sara Carey, D.R.E. Students 108.

DAYTON, RHEA CO., ST. BRIDGET (1968) Rev. Samuel L. Sturm; Deacon Tom Kiefer.
Res.: 320 Walnut Grove Church Rd., P.O. Box 106, 37321. Tel: 423-775-2664 (Church); 423-775-5542 (Rectory); Fax: 423-775-2664. Email: rosa@saintbridget.net; tina@saintbridget.net. Web: www.saintbridget.net. Students 47.
Catechesis/Religious Program—Christina Mugridge, D.R.E. Students 45.

DUNLAP, SEQUATCHIE CO., SHEPHERD OF THE VALLEY (1997) Rev. Mark A. Scholz.
Res.: 6191 Hwy. 28, P.O. Box 1747, 37327-1747. Tel: 423-949-6903; Fax: 423-837-7793.
Catechesis/Religious Program—Students 58.

ELIZABETHTON, CARTER CO., ST. ELIZABETH (1923) Rev. Dennis Kress; Deacon J. Michael Frazier.
Res.: 510 W. C St., P.O. Box 7, 37644-0007. Tel: 423-543-3412; Fax: 423-542-2961. Email: stelizabeth@chartertn.net.
Catechesis/Religious Program—Students 29.

FAIRFIELD GLADE, CUMBERLAND CO., ST. FRANCIS OF ASSISI (1983) [CEM] Rev. John R. Dowling; Deacons Mark A. Fredrick, (Retired); Mark F. White; Keith S. Farber. In Res., Rev. Msgr. Philip F. Thoni, CH (LTC) (Retired).
Res.: 7505 Peavine Rd., 38558. Tel: 931-456-0415; Fax: 931-707-0186. Email: stfrancis@frontiernet.net. Web: www.saintfrancisfairfield.org.
Church: 7503 Peavine Rd., 38558. Tel: 931-484-3628.
Catechesis/Religious Program—Students 6.

GATLINBURG, SEVIER CO., ST. MARY (1935) Rev.

Joseph J. Brando (Retired).
Res.: 304 Historic Nature Tr., 37738. Tel: 865-436-4907; Fax: 865-430-3623.
Catechesis/Religious Program—Students 11.

GREENEVILLE, GREENE CO., NOTRE DAME (1955) Rev. James P. Harvey II.
Res.: 212 Mt. Bethel Rd., 37745. Tel: 423-639-9381; Fax: 423-638-5219. Email: notredametn@embarqmail.com. Web: notredamechurchtn.org.
Catechesis/Religious Program—Tel: 423-639-9382. Susan Collins, D.R.E. Students 82.

HARRIMAN, ROANE CO., BLESSED SACRAMENT (1908) Rev. Michael Sweeney.
Res.: 535 Margrave Dr., 37748. Tel: 865-882-9838; Fax: 865-882-3786 (Rectory); 865-882-5491 (Sec.). Email: blessedsacramentoffice@gmail.com (Office); fmsdok@gmail.com (Rectory).
Catechesis/Religious Program—Students 50.
Station—Morgan County State Prison Wartburg. Tel: 423-346-1300.
Station—Morgan County Correctional Complex Wartburg.

HELENWOOD, SCOTT CO., ST. JUDE PARISH (1982) Rev. William H. Gahagan; Sr. Patricia Soete, R.S.M., Pastoral Assoc.
Mailing Address: 13067 Scott Hwy., P.O. Box 555, 37755. Tel: 423-569-9584 (Church).
Catechesis/Religious Program—

JAMESTOWN, FENTRESS CO., ST. CHRISTOPHER CATHOLIC CHURCH (1975) Rev. Michael Sweeney.
Mailing Address: P.O. Box 797, 38556-5221. 160 Holt Spur Rd., 38556-5221. Tel: 931-879-4146.

JEFFERSON CITY, JEFFERSON CO., HOLY TRINITY CATHOLIC CHURCH (1997) Rev. Dan G. Whitman; Deacons Gordon Lowery; Jim Prosak; John Riehl.
Office: 475 N. Hwy. 92, P.O. Box 304, 37760. Tel: 865-471-0347; Fax: 865-471-0349. Email: holytrinity.jeffcity@gmail.com.
Catechesis/Religious Program—Students 60.

JOHNSON CITY, WASHINGTON CO., ST. MARY (1906) Revs. Peter J. Iorio; Manuel Perez (Mexico); Deacons Richard Carner; George Fredericks III; Michael Jacobs; Katherine Angulo, Dir. Pastoral Min.
Res.: 2211 E. Lakeview Dr., 37601. Tel: 423-282-6367; Fax: 423-282-6145. Web: www.stmarysjc.org.
School—(Grades K-8) Tel: 423-282-3397; Fax: 423-282-0224. Randi McKee, Prin.; Polly Theobald, Librarian. Lay Teachers 17; Students 199.
Catechesis/Religious Program—Shannon Bryant, Children Faith Formation. Students 280.

KINGSPORT, SULLIVAN CO., ST. DOMINIC (1941) Rev. Michael F. Nolan; Deacons Robert Lange; Frank Fischer.
Res.: 2517 John B. Dennis Hwy., 37660. Tel: 423-288-8101; Fax: 423-288-7183. Web: www.saintdominicchurch.org.
School—(Grades K-5), 1474 E. Center St., 37664. Tel: 423-245-0362; Fax: 423-245-2907. Debbie DePollo, Prin.; Dusty Newman, Librarian. Lay Teachers 15; Students 64.
Catechesis/Religious Program—Tel: 423-288-8101. Karen Lewicki, D.R.E.; Paul Vachon, Youth Min. Students 217.

LA FOLLETTE, CAMPBELL CO., OUR LADY OF PERPETUAL HELP (1904) Rev. Joe Campbell.
Mailing Address: 1142 E. Elm St., 37766. Tel: 423-562-0312.
Catechesis/Religious Program—Students 15.

LANCING, MORGAN CO., ST. ANN (1982) Attended by Blessed Sacrament, Harriman. Rev. Michael Sweeney; Deacon Norman Amero.
Mailing Address: P.O. Box 77, 37770-0077. Tel: 865-346-6260; Fax: 865-882-5491.
Catechesis/Religious Program—Tel: 865-882-9838; Fax: 865-882-3786.

LENOIR CITY, LOUDON CO., ST. THOMAS THE APOSTLE (1973) Revs. Christian Mathis; Jesus Antonio Giraldo (Colombia); Deacons Jose Rivera; Sean K. Smith; Thomas Bomkamp; David E. Pecot.
Res.: 1580 St. Thomas Way, 37772. Tel: 865-986-9885; Fax: 865-988-8230. Email: ourparish@sthomaslc.com. Web: www.sthomaslc.com.
Catechesis/Religious Program—Email: jill@sthomaslc.com. Jill St. Ives, D.R.E. Students 221.

MADISONVILLE, MONROE CO., ST. JOSEPH THE WORKER (1992) [CEM] Revs. P. J. McGinnity; William Patrick Resen.
Mailing Address: 649 Old Tellico Hwy. N., 37354. Tel: 423-442-7273; Fax: 423-442-7272. Email: sjtwrcc@bellsouth.net.
Catechesis/Religious Program—Students 42.

MAYNARDVILLE
MISSION—BLESSED TERESA OF CALCUTTA CATHOLIC MISSION 4365 Maynardville Hwy., 37807. Mailing Address: P.O. Box 1076, 37807.

MORRISTOWN, HAMBLEN CO., ST. PATRICK (1959) Revs. Joseph Hammond (Ghana); Alex Waraksa; Deacons Gerald James Fage; Robert Smearing.
Res.: 2518 W. Andrew Johnson Hwy., 37814. Tel: 423-586-9174; Fax: 423-318-7044. Email: saintpat@charter.net. Web: www.stpatrickmorristown.net.
Catechesis/Religious Program—Tel: 423-586-4091. Kathleen DeAngelis, D.R.E.; Colleen Jacobs, Youth Minister (Elementary & Middle School). Students 236.

MOUNTAIN CITY, JOHNSON CO., ST. ANTHONY OF PADUA CATHOLIC CHURCH (1995) Rev. Dennis Kress, Parochial Admin.; Deacons Donald F. Hathaway; John Hackett.
Res.: 513 Hickory, 37683. Tel: 423-543-3412; Fax: 423-542-2961.
Church: 833 W. Main St., 37683. Tel: 423-727-5156; Fax: 423-727-5017.
Catechesis/Religious Program—

NEWPORT, COCKE CO., GOOD SHEPHERD (1967) Rev. Msgr. Robert J. Hofstetter; Deacon Otto Preske.
Mailing Address: 2361 Cosby Hwy., P.O. Box 1894, 37822. Tel: 423-623-5051.
Catechesis/Religious Program—Students 13.

NORRIS, ANDERSON CO., ST. JOSEPH (1949) Rev. William H. Gahagan; Deacon Dan Hosford.
Res.: P.O. Box 902, 37828. Tel: 865-494-9964; Fax: 865-494-7702. Email: stjosephnorris1@comcast.net. Web: www.rc.net/knoxville/stjoseph/index.htm.
Church: 3425 Andersonville Hwy. 61, P.O. Box 387, 37828. Tel: 865-494-7746.
Catechesis/Religious Program—Lynnette Currie, D.R.E. Students 63.

OAK RIDGE, ANDERSON CO., ST. MARY (1943) Revs. Bede C. Aboh (Nigeria); Christopher Riehl; Deacons Gary Sega; W. Joseph Armento.
Res.: 327 Vermont Ave., 37830. Tel: 865-482-2875; Fax: 865-766-8435. Email: office@smcor.org. Web: www.stmarysoakridge.org.
School—(Grades PreK-8), 323 Vermont Ave., 37830. Tel: 865-483-9700; Fax: 865-483-8305. Web: www-.stmarysoakridge.org. Sr. Andrea Marie Graham, O.P., Prin.; Megan Gallagher, Librarian. Sisters 4; Lay Teachers 21; Students 205.
Catechesis/Religious Program—Tel: 865-766-8386. Karen Wilkins-Butz, D.R.E. Students 248.

PIGEON FORGE, SEVIER CO., HOLY CROSS (1992) Rev. Vijayan Joseph (India); Deacon James Larry West.
Church: 144 Wears Valley Rd., 37863. Tel: 865-429-5587; Fax: 865-453-8951. Web: www.holycrossinthesmokies.org.
Catechesis/Religious Program—Students 79.

ROGERSVILLE, HAWKINS CO., ST. HENRY (1981) Rev. Michael T. Jennings.
Res.: 112-114 Hwy. 70 N., 37857. Tel: 423-272-6897.
Catechesis/Religious Program—Students 7.

RUTLEDGE
MISSION—BLESSED JOHN PAUL II CATHOLIC MISSION 7735 Rutledge Pike, 37861. Mailing Address: P.O. Box 1076, Maynardville, 37807.

SEYMOUR, SEVIER CO., HOLY FAMILY (1984) Rev. Ragan Schriver; Deacons Dean Burry; William Jacobs.
Mailing Address: 307 Black Oak Ridge Rd., 37865. Tel: 865-573-1203; Fax: 865-579-3645.
Catechesis/Religious Program—Cathy Qualls, D.R.E. Students 120.

SIGNAL MOUNTAIN, HAMILTON CO., ST. AUGUSTINE (1938) [CEM] Rev. Joseph Kuzhupil, M.S.F.S. (India); Deacon Gordon Kilburn.
Res.: 1716 Anderson Pike, 37377. Tel: 423-826-0429; Fax: 423-886-3451. Email: parishoffice@staugustinecatholic.org. Web: www.staugustinecatholic.org.
Catechesis/Religious Program—Students 120.

SNEEDVILLE, HANCOCK CO., ST. JAMES THE APOSTLE (1982) Attended by St. Henry, Rogersville. Rev. Michael T. Jennings.
Res. & Mailing Address: P.O. Box 93, 37869. Tel: 423-272-6897.

SODDY DAISY, HAMILTON CO., HOLY SPIRIT CATHOLIC CHURCH (1999) Rev. Msgr. T. Allen Humbrecht; Deacons Michael Kucharzak; Noel W. Spencer Jr.
Mailing Address: P.O. Box 1015, 37384.
Church: 10768 Dayton Pike, 37379. Tel: 423-332-5300; Fax: 423-332-5391. Email: forhscc@yahoo.com. Web: www.holyspiritsoddydaisy.com.
Res.: 10812 Dayton Pike, 37379. Tel: 423-332-8283.
Catechesis/Religious Program—Students 101.

SOUTH PITTSBURG, MARION CO., OUR LADY OF LOURDES (1899) Rev. Mark A. Scholz.
Church: 704 Holly Ave., 37380. Tel: 423-837-7068; Fax: 423-837-7793.
Mission—Virgin of the Poor Shrine New Hope, Marion Co.
Catechesis/Religious Program—Students 16.

TAZEWELL, CLAIBORNE CO., CHRIST THE KING (1990) Attended by Our Lady of Perpetual Help Church, LaFollette Rev. Joseph Campbell.
Res. & Mailing Address: 1142 E. Elm St., La Follette, 37766. Tel: 423-562-0312.
Catechesis/Religious Program—Students 22.

TOWNSEND, BLOUNT CO., ST. FRANCIS OF ASSISI (1961) Rev. James Brent Shelton, Parochial Admin.; Deacon Michael Nestor.
Mailing Address: 7719 River Rd., 37882. Tel: 423-448-6070.
Catechesis/Religious Program—Students 8.

Retired:
Rev. Msgr.—
Thoni, Philip F., CH (LTC), 7503 Peavine Rd., Fairfield Glade, 38558.
Revs.—
Brando, Joseph J., 2146 Floyd Porter Rd., Maryville, 37803.
Brett, Frank X., P.O. Box 510401, Melbourne Beach, FL 32951.
Hostettler, Paul A., Villa Maria Manor, 32 White Bridge Rd., Apt. 225, Nashville, 37205.
Neuzil, Gregory, 10510 Buckeye Rd., Cleveland, OH 44104.
O'Connell, Thomas P., 806 Villa View Way, 37920.
Valleroy, Paul J.

Permanent Deacons:
Alexander, Dan, St. Stephen, Chattanooga
Amelse, Donald, M.P.S., St. John Neumann, Knoxville
Amero, Norman, St. Ann, Lancing
Armento, W. Joseph, St. Mary, Oak Ridge
Bomkamp, Thomas, St. Thomas the Apostle, Lenoir City
Bresler, Thomas, St. Augustine Chapel, Signal Mountain; Alexian Village
Brinkworth, Gary, St. Therese of Lisieux, Cleveland
Burry, Dean, Holy Family, Seymour
Carner, Richard, St. Mary, Johnson City
DeGaetano, Gaspar, St. Jude, Chattanooga
Diesing, William
Eiffe, Michael, St. Albert the Great, Knoxville
Elliott, Tim, All Saints, Knoxville
Fage, G. James, II, St. Patrick, Morristown
Farber, Keith S., St. Francis of Assisi, Fairfield Glade
Fischer, Frank, St. Dominic, Kingsport
Fischer, Robert W., (Retired)
Frazier, J. Michael, St. Elizabeth, Elizabethton
Fredericks, George, III, St. Mary, Johnson City
Fredrick, Mark A., (Retired)
Gabor, Brian, St. Jude, Chattanooga
Gang, Mark, Jr., Our Lady of Perpetual Help, Chattanooga
Gouge, Mike, St. John Neumann, Knoxville
Hackett, John, St. Anthony of Padua, Mountain City
Hathaway, Donald F., St. Anthony, Mountain City
Hosford, Dan, St. Joseph, Norris
Jacobs, Michael, St. Mary, Johnson City
Jacobs, William, Holy Family, Seymour
Johnston, Ben, Cathedral of the Sacred Heart of Jesus, Knoxville
Kiefer, Thomas, St. Bridget, Dayton
Kilburn, Gordon, St. Augustine, Signal Mountain
Kucharzak, Michael, Holy Spirit, Soddy Daisy
Lange, Robert, St. Dominic, Kingsport
Lawson, James, Cathedral of the Sacred Heart of Jesus
Lee, Charles, St. Stephen, Chattanooga
Long, Kenneth, Our Lady of Fatima, Alcoa
Lowery, Gordon, Holy Trinity, Jefferson City
Lucheon, David J., All Saints, Knoxville
McConnell, Thomas, St. Jude, Chattanooga
Murphy-Racey, Patrick, St. Albert the Great, Knoxville
Nelson, Paul, St. Jude, Chattanooga
Nestor, Michael, St. Francis of Assisi, Townsend
Pecot, David E., (Retired), St. Thomas the Apostle, Lenoir City
Preske, Otto F., Good Shepherd, Newport
Prosak, Jim, Holy Trinity, Jefferson City
Riehl, John, Holy Trinity, Jefferson City
Rivera, Jose, (Retired), St. Thomas the Apostle, Lenoir City
Sega, Gary, St. Mary, Oak Ridge
Smearing, Robert, St. Patrick, Morristown
Smith, Sean K., St. Thomas the Apostle, Lenoir City
Solis, Joseph, St. Alphonsus, Crossville
Spencer, Noel W., Jr., Ph.D., Holy Spirit, Soddy Daisy
Stackhouse, Joe, Ph.D., Immaculate Conception, Knoxville
Syler, Marquis E., St. John Neumann, Knoxville
Vinh, Joseph, Immaculate Conception, Knoxville
Volek, Ronald J., (Retired)
West, James Larry, Holy Cross, Pigeon Forge
White, Mark F., St. Francis of Assisi, Fairfield Glade
Wilson, James E., Basilica of Sts. Peter and Paul, Chattanooga

INSTITUTIONS LOCATED IN THE DIOCESE

[A] HIGH SCHOOLS, DIOCESAN

KNOXVILLE. *Knoxville Catholic High School* (1932) 9245 Fox Lonas Rd., 37923. Tel: 865-560-0313; Fax: 865-560-0314. Email: info@knoxvillecatholic.com. Web: knoxvillecatholic.com. Mr. Dickie Sompayrac, Prin. Tel: 865-560-0518; Fax: 865-560-0591; Mr. Mark Balog, Campus Min. Tel: 865-560-0529; Fax: 865-560-0314; Rev. Kwaku John Appiah, Chap.; Dawn Harbin, Librarian. Tel: 865-560-0313; Fax: 865-560-0314. Priests 1; Sisters 2; Lay Teachers 53; Total Staff 55; Students 694.

Knoxville Catholic High School Development Board of Trust Tel: 865-560-0509; Fax: 865-560-0314.

CHATTANOOGA. *Notre Dame High School* (1876) 2701 Vermont Ave., 37404. Tel: 423-624-4618; Fax: 423-624-4621. Email: storeyp@myndhs.com. Web: www.myndhs.com. Mr. Perry Storey, Prin.; Nancy Trice, Librarian; Rev. Augustine Idra, A.J. (Sudan), Spiritual Dir. Priests 1; Sisters 4; Lay Teachers 31; Students 408; Total Staff 16.

Notre Dame High School Financial Board of Trustees

[B] ELEMENTARY SCHOOL, REGIONAL

KNOXVILLE. *Saint Joseph School of Knoxville*, (Grades PreK-8), Parochial-Regional School for Holy Ghost Church, Immaculate Conception Church & St. Albert the Great Church., 1810 Howard Dr., 37918. Tel: 865-689-3424; Fax: 865-687-7885. Web: www.sjsknox.com. Rev. Chris Michelson, Pres.; Sr. Mary Elizabeth Ann McCullough, R.S.M., Prin.; Charles Walden, Librarian. Lay Teachers 19; Students 177.

[C] GENERAL HOSPITALS

CHATTANOOGA. *Memorial Health Care System, Inc.* (1952) 2525 deSales Ave., 37404. Tel: 423-495-2525; Fax: 423-495-7726. Web: memorial.org. James M. Hobson, Pres. & CEO. (Member of Catholic Health Initiatives) Sisters 2; Bed Capacity 405; Patients Assisted Annually 99,681; Total Staff 4,001.

Memorial Health Care System Foundation, Inc. (2001) 2525 deSales Ave., 37404. Tel: 423-495-2525; Fax: 423-495-7726.

[D] SPECIAL HOSPITALS

SIGNAL MOUNTAIN. *Alexian Village Health Care Center* (1938) 671 Alexian Way, 37377. Tel: 423-886-0338; Fax: 423-886-0488. Email: mfox@alexianbrothers.net. Web: www.alexianvillage.com. Matthew Fox, Pres. & CEO; Bro. John Howard, C.F.A., Dir. Community; Rev. Augustine Joseph, M.S.F.S. (India), Assoc. Chap.; Bro. Lawrence Krueger, C.F.A., Sponsor Liaison. Licensed Skilled & Intermediate Care Nursing Home. Brothers 8; Bed Capacity 114; Patients Assisted Annually 278; Assisted Living 32; Total Staff 105.

[E] HOMES FOR THE AGED

SIGNAL MOUNTAIN. *Alexian Village of Tennessee* (1983) 437 Alexian Way, 37377. Tel: 423-886-0100; Fax: 423-886-0470. Email: mfox@alexianbrothers.net. Web: www.alexianvillage.com. Matthew Fox, Pres. & CEO; Revs. Valerie Carnes, Chap.; Augustine Joseph, M.S.F.S. (India), Assoc. Chap.; Camilius Blazek, Assoc. Chap. Retirement Community & Healthcare Center. Life Care Units 322; Total in Residence 600; Total Staff 300.

[F] PROTECTIVE INSTITUTIONS

KNOXVILLE. *Columbus Home*, 3227 Division St., 37919. Tel: 865-971-3560; Fax: 865-544-0538. Total Assisted Annually 22; Total Staff 12.

[G] MONASTERIES AND RESIDENCES OF PRIESTS AND BROTHERS

SIGNAL MOUNTAIN. *Alexian Brothers*, 198 James Blvd., 37377. Tel: 423-886-0380; Fax: 423-886-0381. Email: jhoward@alexianbrothers.net. Web: www.alexianbrothers.org/. Bros. Edward Walsh, C.F.A., Supr. Gen.; John Howard, C.F.A., Provincial Councilor & Community Dir.; Simeon Pytel, C.F.A., Sec. (Generalate); Andrew Thome, C.F.A., Patient Visitor: Alexian Brothers PACE Program; Philip Kennedy, C.F.A., (Retired); Lawrence Krueger, C.F.A., Prov. Councilor; James Darby, C.F.A., (Retired); Ronald Ruberg, C.F.A. Brothers 8.

[H] CONVENTS AND RESIDENCES FOR SISTERS

KNOXVILLE. *St. Justin Convent*, 815 Hansmore Pl., 37919. Tel: 865-690-9266. Religious Sisters of Mercy of Alma, Michigan (R.S.M.) Sisters 4.

Sisters of Mercy (1831) (South Central Region), 900 E. Oak Hill Ave., 37917. Tel: 865-545-8128; 865-545-8265; Fax: 865-545-7915. Email: mnaber@mercysc.org.

CLINTON. *St. Therese Convent*, 701 S. Charles G. Seivers Blvd., 37716. Tel: 865-463-8935; Fax: 865-463-9734. Email: ygillen@bellsouth.net. Sr. Mary Yvette Gillen, R.S.M., Pastoral Assoc. & D.R.E.

COPPERHILL. *Monastery of Our Lady of Little Citeaux* (1997) 255 Golf Course Rd., 37317. Tel: 423-496-7373.

HELENWOOD. *Sisters of Mercy*, 13071 Scott Hwy., P.O. Box 555, 37755. Tel: 423-569-3492.

St. Jude Church, 13067 Scott Hwy., 37755. Tel: 423-569-9584. Email: pasoete@highland.net. Sr. Patricia Soete, R.S.M., Pastoral Assoc. Tel: 423-569-3492.

OAK RIDGE. *Dominican Sisters (St. Cecilia Congregation)* (1860) St. Mary's Convent, 323 Vermont Ave., 37830. Tel: 865-483-9700; Fax: 865-483-8305. Web: nashvilledominican.org. Sisters 8.

[I] NEWMAN CENTERS

KNOXVILLE. *UT-Knoxville, Newman Foundation, Inc.* (1968) *Blessed John XXIII University Parish / Catholic Center*, 1710 Melrose Pl., 37916. Tel: 865-523-7931; Fax: 865-523-7979. Email: john23@utk.edu. Web: www.john23rd.org. Rev. Charles Donahue, C.S.P.

CHATTANOOGA. *Newman Foundation of Chattanooga, Inc.* Catholic Student Center, 514 Palmetto St., 37403. Tel: 423-267-3064. Email: cathstudentctr@chattanooga.net. Web: www.catholicdeaneryofchattanooga.org/utcx.html. Rev. James Mallett. Total Staff 2.

JOHNSON CITY. *ETSU-Catholic Center* 734 W. Locust St., 37604. Tel: 423-926-7061. Email: etsucatholiccenter@yahoo.com. Web: www.etsu.edu/newman. Rev. Michael E. Cummins. Total Staff 1.

[J] FOUNDATIONS AND ENDOWMENTS

KNOXVILLE. *The Catholic Diocese of Knoxville Foundation, Inc.*, 805 Northshore Dr., S.W., 37919. Tel: 865-584-3307; Fax: 865-584-7538.

Catholic Foundation of East Tennessee, 805 Northshore Dr., S.W., 37919. Tel: 865-584-3307; Fax: 865-584-7538.

St. Mary's Legacy Foundation of East Tennessee, Inc., 805 Northshore Dr., S.W., 37919. Members of the Corporation Most Rev. Richard F. Stika; Very Rev. David Boettner, V.G.; Deacons Sean K. Smith; David J. Lucheon; Clara Mathien Board of Directors Most Rev. Richard F. Stika, Chm.; George Haggard, Pres.; Sally Sefton, Sec.

[K] MISCELLANEOUS

KNOXVILLE. *Diocesan Council of Catholic Women*, 805 Northshore Dr., S.W., 37919. Tel: 865-482-7449. Rev. Msgr. Francis Xavier Mankel, S.T.L., V.G., Diocesan & Deanery Spiritual Moderator; Rev. Dan G. Whitman, Deanery Spiritual Moderator, Five Rivers; Rev. Msgr. T. Allen Humbrecht, Deanery Spiritual Moderator, Chattanooga; Rev. Michael Woods, Deanery Spiritual Moderator, Cumberland Mountain.

Ladies of Charity (1942) 120 W. Baxter Ave., 37917. Tel: 865-247-5790 Thrift Shop; 865-474-9329 Emergency Assistance; Fax: 865-474-9367. Email: ladiesofcharityknox@gmail.com. Web: ladiesofcharityknox.org/Ladies_of_Charity/Home.html. Rev. Msgr. Francis Xavier Mankel, S.T.L., V.G., Spiritual Moderator. Total Assisted Annually 39,000; Total Staff 8.

Ladies of Charity- Pantry, 120 W. Baxter Ave., 37917. Tel: 865-474-9329; Fax: 865-474-9367.

CHATTANOOGA. *Ladies of Charity*, 2821 Rossville Blvd., 37407. Tel: 423-624-3222; Fax: 423-698-8048. Rev. Msgr. T. Allen Humbrecht, Spiritual Mod. Emergency assistance through referrals from area churches and social service agencies in the form of food, medicine, clothing, Lifeline, meals on wheels, layettes for newborns, payment on utilities, rent, glasses, dental work, etc. Total Assisted Annually 4,832.

RELIGIOUS INSTITUTES OF MEN REPRESENTED IN THE DIOCESE

For further details refer to the corresponding bracketed number in the Religious Institutes of Men or Women section.

[0120]—*Alexian Brothers*—C.F.A.

[]—*Apostles of Jesus*—A.J.

[]—*Carmelites of Mary Immaculate*—C.M.I.

[]—*Crusaders of the Holy Spirit*—C.H.S.

[0570]—*The Glenmary Home Missioners*—Glmy.

[0840]—*Missionary Servants of the Most Holy Trinity*—S.T.

[]—*Order of Missionaries of St. Francis de Sales*—M.S.F.S.

[1030]—*Paulist Fathers*—C.S.P.

RELIGIOUS INSTITUTES OF WOMEN REPRESENTED IN THE DIOCESE

[1920]—*Congregation of Sisters of Holy Cross*—C.S.C.

[1070-07]—*Dominican Sisters (St. Cecilia Congregation)*—O.P.

[2575]—*Institute of the Sisters of Mercy of the Americas* (South Central)—R.S.M.

[]—*Missionary Congregation of the Evangelizing Sisters of Mary* (Uganda)

[]—*Missionary Sisters of the Sacred Heart of Jesus "Ad Gentes"*—M.A.G.

[2519]—*Religious Sisters of Mercy of Alma, Michigan*—R.S.M.

[0500]—*Sisters of Charity of Nazareth*—S.C.N.

[]—*Sisters of St. Francis of the Martyr St. George*—F.S.G.M.

[3930]—*Sisters of St. Joseph, Third Order of St. Francis*—S.S.J.-T.O.S.F.

[0970]—*Sisters of the Divine Compassion*—R.D.C.

INTERPAROCHIAL CEMETERIES

KNOXVILLE. *Calvary Cemetery*, 2000 Martin Luther King Jr. Blvd., 37915. Tel: 865-522-1508. *c/o Immaculate Conception Church*, 414 West Vine Ave., 37902-1327. Rev. Ronald A. Franco, C.S.P.

CHATTANOOGA. *Mount Olivet Cemetery*, One Mount Olivet Dr., 37412. Tel: 423-622-0728; Fax: 509-693-8902. Email: encompass@prodigy.net. Rev. Msgr. George E. Schmidt Jr., Dean; David E. Hale, Supt.

NECROLOGY

(No Deaths)

Diocese of La Crosse

(Dioecesis Crossensis)

Most Reverend

WILLIAM P. CALLAHAN, O.F.M.CONV.

Bishop of La Crosse; ordained April 30, 1977; appointed Auxiliary Bishop of Milwaukee and Titular Bishop of Lares October 30, 2007; ordained December 21, 2007; appointed Bishop of La Crosse June 11, 2010; installed August 11, 2010. *Chancery Office: 3710 East Ave. S., P.O. Box 4004, La Crosse, WI 54602-4004.*

Chancery Office: 3710 East Ave. S., P.O. Box 4004, La Crosse, WI 54602-4004. Tel: 608-788-7700; Fax: 608-788-8413.

Web: www.dioceseoflacrosse.com

Email: mailbox@dioceseoflacrosse.com

Square Miles 15,078.

Erected March 3, 1868. Subdivided May 3, 1905. Subdivided January 15, 1946.

Comprises the following 19 Counties in the State of Wisconsin: Adams, Buffalo, Chippewa, Clark, Crawford, Dunn, Eau Claire, Jackson, Juneau, La Crosse, Marathon, Monroe, Pepin, Pierce, Portage, Richland, Trempealeau, Vernon and Wood.

For legal titles of parishes and diocesan institutions, consult the Chancery Office.

STATISTICAL OVERVIEW

Personnel	
Bishop	1
Priests: Diocesan Active in Diocese	90
Priests: Diocesan Active Outside Diocese	8
Priests: Diocesan in Foreign Missions	3
Priests: Retired, Sick or Absent	54
Number of Diocesan Priests	155
Religious Priests in Diocese	12
Total Priests in Diocese	167
Extern Priests in Diocese	38
Permanent Deacons in Diocese	51
Total Brothers	3
Total Sisters	393
Parishes	
Parishes	165
With Resident Pastor:	
Resident Diocesan Priests	103
Resident Religious Priests	5
Without Resident Pastor:	
Administered by Priests	57
Professional Ministry Personnel:	
Sisters	13
Lay Ministers	40
Welfare	
Catholic Hospitals	9
Total Assisted	603,842
Homes for the Aged	10
Total Assisted	1,084
Day Care Centers	2
Total Assisted	143
Specialized Homes	5
Total Assisted	7,462
Special Centers for Social Services	2
Total Assisted	5,678
Educational	
Seminaries, Diocesan	1
Diocesan Students in Other Seminaries	33
Total Seminarians	33
Colleges and Universities	1
Total Students	3,000
High Schools, Diocesan and Parish	7
Total Students	1,565
Elementary Schools, Diocesan and Parish	63
Total Students	7,138
Catechesis/Religious Education:	
High School Students	3,798
Elementary Students	12,471
Total Students under Catholic Instruction	28,005
Teachers in the Diocese:	
Priests	10
Sisters	17
Lay Teachers	832
Vital Statistics	
Receptions into the Church:	
Infant Baptism Totals	1,991
Adult Baptism Totals	142
Received into Full Communion	219
First Communions	2,329
Confirmations	2,323
Marriages:	
Catholic	447
Interfaith	208
Total Marriages	655
Deaths	1,992
Total Catholic Population	180,305
Total Population	901,157

Former Bishops—Most Rev. MICHAEL HEISS, D.D., cons. Sept. 6, 1868; appt. Titular Archbishop of Hadrianople, and coadjutor to the Metropolitan of Milwaukee March 14, 1880; promoted to Milwaukee, Sept. 1881; died March 26, 1890; Rt. Revs. KILIAN CASPAR FLASCH, D.D., cons. Aug. 24, 1881; died Aug. 3, 1891; JAMES SCHWEBACH, D.D., cons. Feb. 25, 1892; died June 6, 1921; Most Revs. ALEXANDER J. MCGAVICK, D.D., LL.D., cons. Titular Bishop of Marcopolis and Auxiliary Bishop of Chicago, May 1, 1899; transferred to See of La Crosse, Nov. 21, 1921; died Aug. 25, 1948; JOHN P. TREACY, S.T.D., cons. Titular Bishop of Metelis and Coadjutor of La Crosse "cum jure successionis," Oct. 2, 1945; succeeded to the See, July 23, 1946; died Oct. 11, 1964; FREDERICK W. FREKING, D.D., J.C.D., cons. Bishop of Salina, KS, Nov. 30, 1957; transferred to the See of La Crosse, Dec. 30, 1964; installed La Crosse, Feb. 24, 1965; retired May 10, 1983; died Nov. 28, 1998; JOHN J. PAUL, appt. Titular Bishop of Lambese and Auxiliary Bishop of La Crosse, May 17, 1977; cons. Aug. 4, 1977; appt. to the Residential See of La Crosse, Oct. 18, 1983; installed as Bishop of La Crosse, Dec. 5, 1983; retired Dec. 10, 1994; died March 5, 2006; RAYMOND L. BURKE, D.D., J.C.D., appt. to the Residential See of La Crosse Dec. 10, 1994; cons. Jan. 6, 1995; installed as Eighth Bishop of La Crosse Feb. 22, 1995; appt. Archbishop of the Archdiocese of St. Louis Dec. 2, 2003; installed Jan. 26, 2004; JEROME E. LISTECKI, D.D., J.C.D., ord. May 14, 1975; appt. Auxiliary Bishop of Chicago and Titular Bishop of Nara Nov. 7, 2000; cons. Jan. 8, 2001; appt. Bishop of La Crosse Dec. 29, 2004; installed March 1, 2005; appt. Archbishop of Milwaukee Nov. 14, 2009; installed Jan. 4, 2010.

Chancery Office—3710 East Ave. S., P.O. Box 4004, La Crosse, 54602-4004. Tel: 608-788-7700; Fax: 608-788-8413. Office Hours: Mon.-Fri. 8-4:30.

Chancellor—Very Rev. FRANCIS ABUAH-QUANSAH, J.C.D.

Vice-Chancellor—Rev. LEON A. POWELL.

Vicars General—Very Revs. MICHAEL J. GORMAN, V.G., J.C.L.; JOSEPH G. DIERMEIER, V.G., J.C.L.

Moderator of the Curia—Very Rev. MICHAEL J. GORMAN, V.G., J.C.L.

Archivist—Rev. ROBERT T. ALTMANN (Retired).

Finance Officer—SONDRA RIEDER.

Ecclesiastical Notaries—Very Rev. MICHAEL J. GORMAN, V.G., J.C.L.; Rev. LEON A. POWELL; KELLY MCCARTHY; AARON NIELSEN; SUSAN VLASAK, Mailing Address: P.O. Box 4004, La Crosse, 54602-4004.

Diocesan Tribunal—3710 East Ave. S., P.O. Box 4004, La Crosse, 54602-4004. Tel: 608-788-7700. (Address all rogatory commissions to the Chancellor).

Judicial Vicar—Rev. Msgr. ROBERT P. HUNDT, J.C.L.

Promoter of Justice—Very Rev. JOSEPH G. DIERMEIER, V.G., J.C.L.

Defensor Vinculi—Very Rev. FRANCIS ABUAH-QUANSAH, J.C.D.

Auditor—AARON NIELSEN.

Diocesan Judges—Rev. Msgr. ROBERT P. HUNDT, J.C.L.; Very Rev. MICHAEL J. GORMAN, V.G., J.C.L.

Deans—Very Revs. WOODROW H. PACE, Arcadia Deanery; EDWARD J. SHUTTLEWORTH, Chippewa Falls Deanery; THOMAS J. KRIEG, Durand Deanery; BRIAN D. KONOPA, Eau Claire Deanery; ROBERT A. SCHALLER, La Crosse Deanery; ERIC R. BERNS, Marshfield Deanery; Rev. Msgr. RICHARD W. GILLES, V.G., J.C.L., Mauston-Sparta Deanery; Very Revs. THOMAS M. HUFF, Prairie du Chien Deanery; ROGER J. SCHECKEL, Richland Center Deanery; THOMAS F. LINDNER, Stevens Point Deanery; DANIEL H. HACKEL, Thorp Deanery; ALLAN L. SLOWIAK, Wausau Deanery; JOHN W. STEINER, Wisconsin Rapids Deanery.

Diocesan Offices and Directors

Apostolate for Native Americans—ELEANOR ST. JOHN, Coord.

Boy Scouts—Rev. JAMES T. ALTMAN; Mr. ROBERT J. COOPER, Chm., Mailing Address: P.O. Box 4004, La Crosse, 54602-4004. Tel: 608-791-2667.

Building Commission—CHRISTOPHER CARSTENS; Very Rev. FRANCIS ABUAH-QUANSAH, J.C.D.; SONDRA RIEDER; TRAVIS J. SIMPSON.

Catholic Women, Diocesan Council of—DIANE ANDRASKA, Pres.

Department of Catholic Education—ANN C. LANKFORD, Dir. Catechesis & Evangelization; SUSAN HOLMAN, Acting Dir. Schools; VACANT, La Crosse Area Hmong Catechist, 3710 East Ave. S., P.O. Box 4004, La Crosse, 54602-4004. Tel: 608-788-7707.

Office of Family Life—JEFFREY HEINZEN, Dir.; Deacon MARK C. ARNOLD, Asst. Dir., Mailing Address: P.O. Box 4004, La Crosse, 54602-4004. Tel: 608-791-2665.

Natural Family Planning Program—JEFFREY HEINZEN, Educator; ALICE HEINZEN, Coord., 711

24th St. N.E., Menomonie, 54751. Tel: 715-235-6226.

Holy Childhood Association—Very Rev. ROGER J. SCHECKEL, Dir., Mailing Address: P.O. Box 4004, La Crosse, 54602-4004. Tel: 608-788-7700.

Hospitals and Health Affairs—VACANT.

International Priests—Tel: 608-791-2679. Very Rev. DAVID C. KUNZ On Behalf of the Diocesan Bishop, responsible for the recruitment and retention of international priests who serve in the Diocese; Oversees all legal aspects of hosting international priests including visas, travel documents and residency; Facilitates initial and ongoing orientation within parishes and the Diocese; Maintains relationships with foreign bishops and religious superiors to ensure fruitful, pastoral rapport.

Newman Campus Ministry—VACANT.

Office of Communications and Public Relations—Mr. STANTON R. GOULD, Acting Dir., Mailing Address: P.O. Box 4004, La Crosse, 54602-4004. Tel: 608-791-2655.

Office of Diocesan Buildings and Grounds—TRAVIS J. SIMPSON, Dir., Mailing Address: P.O. Box 4004, La Crosse, 54602-4004. Tel: 608-791-2692.

Office of the Consecrated Life—VACANT.

Office of Ecumenism—Rev. SAMUEL A. MARTIN, Diocesan Officer, Ecumenical Questions.

Office of Ministries and Social Concerns—CHRISTOPHER J. RUFF, Dir.; Deacon MATTHEW LUDDICK, Asst. Dir., Mailing Address: P.O. Box 4004, La Crosse, 54602-4004. Tel: 608-791-2667 Office of Ministries consists of Permanent Diaconate, Lay Ministries.

Office of Sacred Worship—Mr. CHRISTOPHER J. CARSTENS, Dir., Mailing Address: P.O. Box 4004, La Crosse, 54602-4004. Tel: 608-791-2675 Sacred Worship Commission-Confer Office.

Office of Youth Ministry—CHRISTOPHER J. ROGERS, Dir., Mailing Address: P.O. Box 4004, La Crosse, 54602-4004.

Pastoral Council—Rev. Msgr. RICHARD W. GILLES, V.G., J.C.L., Exec. Sec., Mailing Address: P.O. Box 4004, La Crosse, 54602-4004.

Personnel Council—Very Rev. DAVID C. KUNZ, Chm.; Revs. THOMAS J. DONALDSON (Retired); ALLEN F. JAKUBOWSKI; Very Rev. WOODROW H. PACE, Mailing Address: P.O. Box 4004, La Crosse, 54602-4004. Tel: 608-788-7700. Ex Officio: Rev. JOSEPH W. HIRSCH.

Presbyteral Council—Most Rev. WILLIAM P. CALLAHAN, O.F.M.Conv., Pres. Appointed Members: Revs. CHARLES J. HIEBL; ROBERT A. STREVELER; DONALD L. MEURET; RICHARD C. DICKMAN; DAVID P. OLSON; SAMUEL A. MARTIN; WILLIAM A. DHEIN; JESSE D. BURISH; LAWRENCE B. BERGER (Retired); Very Rev. FRANCIS ABUAH-QUANSAH, J.C.D.; Rev. RICHARD TULKO, O.F.M.

Ex Officio—Very Revs. JOSEPH G. DIERMEIER, V.G., J.C.L.; MICHAEL J. GORMAN, V.G., J.C.L.; Revs. WILLIAM N. GREVATCH; EUGENE A. KLINK; Very Revs. DAVID C. KUNZ; DELBERT J. MALIN (Retired); Revs. JOHN A. POTACZEK; ALAN P. WIERZBA. Consultors: Very Rev. FRANCIS ABUAH-QUANSAH, J.C.D.; Revs. LAWRENCE B. BERGER (Retired); WILLIAM A. DHEIN; Very Revs. JOSEPH G. DIERMEIER, V.G., J.C.L.; MICHAEL J. GORMAN, V.G., J.C.L.; Revs. WILLIAM N. GREVATCH; EUGENE A. KLINK; DONALD L. MEURET; JOHN A. POTACZEK; ALAN P. WIERZBA.

Propagation of the Faith—Very Rev. ROGER J. SCHECKEL, Dir., Mailing Address: P.O. Box 4004, La Crosse, 54602-4004. Tel: 608-788-7700.

St. Joseph's Priest Fund, Inc., (Benevolent Society)—Very Revs. ERIC R. BERNS, Pres.; MICHAEL J. GORMAN, V.G., J.C.L., Exec. Sec., Mailing Address: P.O. Box 4004, La Crosse, 54602-4004. Tel: 608-788-7700.

"Catholic Times" Diocesan Newspaper—Mr. STANTON R. GOULD, Editor; DENIS DOWNEY, Asst. Editor, Mailing Address: P.O. Box 4004, La Crosse, 54602-4004. Tel: 608-788-1524.

Victim Assistance Coordinator—VACANT.

CLERGY, PARISHES, MISSIONS AND PAROCHIAL SCHOOLS

CITY OF LA CROSSE

(LA CROSSE COUNTY)

1—ST. JOSEPH THE WORKMAN CATHEDRAL (1860) [CEM 2] Rev. Charles D. Stoetzel, Rector. In Res., Rev. Todd A. Mlsna; Deacon Joseph Richards.
Res.: 530 Main St., 54601. Tel: 608-782-0322; Fax: 608-782-8228. Email: ejones@centurytel.net. Web: www.cathedralsjworkman.org.
See Coulee Catholic Schools, LaCrosse under Unified Catholic School Systems located in the Institution section.
Catechesis/Religious Program—Tel: 608-782-2953; Fax: 608-785-1064. Students 195.

2—BLESSED SACRAMENT (1937) [CEM 2] Revs. David P. Olson; Jesse D. Burish.
Res.: 130 Losey Blvd. S., 54601. Tel: 608-782-2953; Fax: 608-785-1064.
See Aquinas Catholic Schools, LaCrosse under Unified Catholic School Systems located in the Institution section.

3—HOLY CROSS, Closed. For inquiries for parish records contact the Diocesan Archive, P.O. Box 4004, La Crosse, WI 54602-4004 Tel: 608-788-7700.

4—HOLY TRINITY (1887) [JC] Rev. G. Richard Roberts.
Res.: 1333 S. 13th St., 54601. Tel: 608-782-2028.
Catechesis/Religious Program—Jeannie M. Weber, D.R.E. Students 160.

5—ST. JAMES THE LESS (1886) Very Rev. Robert A. Schaller.
Res.: 1032 Caledonia St., 54603. Tel: 608-782-7557; Fax: 608-796-0086. Web: www.saintjameschurch.net.
Catechesis/Religious Program—Students 64.

6—ST. JOHN THE BAPTIST, Closed. For inquiries for parish records contact Diocesan Archives, P.O. Box 4004, La Crosse, WI 54602-4004 Tel: 608-788-7700.

7—ST. MARY, Closed. For inquiries for parish records contact The Diocesan Archives, P.O. Box 4004, La Crosse, WI 54602-4004 Tel: 608-788-7700.

8—MARY, MOTHER OF THE CHURCH (2000) Rev. Douglas C. Robertson.
Res.: 2006 Weston St., 54601. Tel: 608-788-5483; Fax: 608-788-4070. Web: www.mmoclacrosse.org.
See Aquinas Catholic Schools, LaCrosse under Unified Catholic School Systems located in the Institution section.

9—ST. PIUS X, Closed. For inquiries for parish records contact Mary, Mother of the Church, La Crosse, WI 54602-4004 Tel: 608-788-7700.

10—RONCALLI NEWMAN PARISH (1976) Rev. Alan P. Wierzba; Deacon Kevin Ray.
Res.: 1732 State St., 54601. Tel: 608-784-4994; Fax: 608-784-0230. Email: roncallinewman@roncallinewmancenter.org. Web: www.roncallinewman.com.
Catechesis/Religious Program—Kathleen M. Nicklaus, D.R.E. Students 164.

11—ST. THOMAS MORE, Closed. For inquiries for parish records contact Mary, Mother of the Church, La Crosse, WI 54602-4004. Tel: 608-788-7700.

12—ST. WENCESLAUS, Closed. For inquiries for parish records contact The Diocesan Archives, P.O. Box 4004, La Crosse, WI 54602-4004 Tel: 608-788-7700.

OUTSIDE THE CITY OF LA CROSSE

ABBOTSFORD, CLARK CO., ST. BERNARD (1904) [JC] Very Rev. Daniel H. Hackel.
Res.: 208 S. 3rd St., Colby, 54421-0436. Tel: 715-223-3048.
Catechesis/Religious Program—Therese Geiger, D.R.E. Students 177.

ADAMS, ADAMS CO., ST. JOSEPH (1884) [CEM], Also serves St. Ann, Brooks. Rev. James P. McNamee; Deacon David Kennedy.
Res.: 166 N. Main, P.O. Box 310, 53910. Tel: 608-339-3485; Fax: 608-339-3485. Email: stjosephcc@verizon.net.
Catechesis/Religious Program—Students 81.

ALMA CENTER, JACKSON CO., IMMACULATE CONCEPTION (1882) [CEM] Rev. Emmanuel Famiyeh.
Mailing Address: Box 188, 54611. Tel: 715-964-5201.
Res.: 341 W. Main, 54611.

ALMA, BUFFALO CO., ST. LAWRENCE (1867), Served from Immaculate Conception, Fountain City. Rev. Brian J. Jazdzewski.
Res.: One Wall St., P.O. Box 218, Fountain City, 54629. Tel: 608-687-3496.
Catechesis/Religious Program—Bernice Semling, C.R.E. Students 30.

ALMOND, PORTAGE CO., HOLY GUARDIAN ANGELS, Closed. For inquiries for parish records contact St. Maximilian Maria Kolbe, Southeastern Portage County.

ALTDORF, WOOD CO., ST. JOSEPH, Closed. For inquiries for parish records contact St. Joachim, Pittsville.

ALTOONA, EAU CLAIRE CO., ST. MARY (1902) [JC] Rev. Damian Joseph Redfern.
Rectory—1728 Lynn Ave., 54720. Tel: 715-835-6202; Fax: 715-855-8664.
Church & Office: 1812 Lynn Ave., 54720. Tel: 715-855-1294. Email: stmarypar@gmail.com.
See Regis Catholic Schools, Eau Claire under Unified Catholic School Systems located in the Institution section.
Catechesis/Religious Program—Tel: 715-855-1294. Mary Kneer, D.R.E. Students 332.

AMHERST, PORTAGE CO., ST. JAMES (1905) [CEM] Rev. Jude T. Dioka (Nigeria), Parochial Admin.
Res.: 453 S. Main, Box 28, 54406-0280. Tel: 715-824-4484; Fax: 715-824-3455. Email: sjsm@triver.com.
Catechesis/Religious Program—Barbara Lepak, D.R.E.; Dorene Stolpa, D.R.E. Students 181.

ARCADIA, TREMPEALEAU CO.

1—HOLY FAMILY (2000) [CEM] Rev. Amalraj Arockiam; Sr. Rosemary Rombalski, Pastoral Min.
Res.: 223 E. Maple St., 54612. Tel: 608-323-7116; Fax: 608-323-8346. Email: secretary@holyfamily.com. Web: www.holyfam.com.
School—Holy Family Catholic School, (Grades K-8), 532 McKinnley St., 54612. Tel: 608-323-3676; Fax: 608-323-7386. Karla Leavitt, Librarian.
Catechesis/Religious Program—Students 112.

2—OUR LADY OF PERPETUAL HELP, Closed. For inquiries for parish records contact Holy Family, Arcadia.

3—ST. STANISLAUS, Closed. For inquiries for parish records contact Holy Family, Arcadia.

ARKANSAW, PEPIN CO., ST. JOSEPH (1913) [CEM 2], Served from: St. John the Baptist, Plum City. Rev. Paul G. Czerwonka.
Res.: 212 Church St., Plum City, 54761. Tel: 715-647-2910. Email: saintjoseph@nelson-tel.net.
Church: W7805 City Rd. Z, 54721. Tel: 715-285-5313.
Catechesis/Religious Program—Tel: 715-285-5849. Darlene Huppert, C.R.E. Students 51.

ARPIN, WOOD CO., ST. FRANCIS, Closed. For inquiries for parish records contact St. James, Vesper.

ATHENS, MARATHON CO., ST. ANTHONY DE PADUA (1881) [JC] Rev. Charles J. Hiebl.
Res.: 417 Caroline St., P.O. Box 206, 54411-0206. Tel: 715-257-7684; Fax: 715-257-7791. Email: stanthonyathens@gmail.com.
School—Tel: 715-257-7541. Sisters 1; Lay Teachers 8; Students 101.

AUBURNDALE, WOOD CO., NATIVITY OF THE BLESSED VIRGIN MARY (1886) [CEM 2], Also serves St. Michael, Hewitt, and St. Kilian, Blenker. Rev. Peter Raj.
Res.: 5866 Main St., P.O. Box 177, 54412-0177. Tel: 715-652-2806; Fax: 715-652-8020.

AUGUSTA, EAU CLAIRE CO., ST. ANTHONY DE PADUA, Closed. For inquiries for Parish Records contact St. Raymond of Penafort, Southern Eau Claire County.

BABCOCK, WOOD CO., ALL SAINTS, Closed. For inquiries for Parish Records contact Sacred Heart of Jesus, Nekoosa.

BAKERVILLE, WOOD CO., CORPUS CHRISTI, Attended by Sacred Heart, Marshfield. Rev. Peter M. Manickam.
Res. & Mailing Address: 112 E. 11th St., Marshfield, 54449. Tel: 715-676-3658 (Mail); 715-384-3213 (Res.).
Church: 10075 Hwy. BB, Marshfield, 54449.
See Marshfield Area Catholic Schools (MACS), Marshfield under Unified Catholic School Systems located in the Institution section.

BANGOR, LA CROSSE CO., ST. MARY (1899) [CEM] Attended by St. Leo the Great, West Salem. Rev. Robert S. Hegenbarth.
Mailing Address: 303 16th Ave. S., P.O. Box 290, 54614. Tel: 608-786-0610.

BEAR VALLEY, RICHLAND CO., ST. KILIAN, Closed. For inquiries for parish records contact Nativity, B.V.M., Keyesville.

BEVENT, MARATHON CO., ST. LADISLAUS (1886) [CEM] Attended by St. Joseph, Galloway. Rev. Augustine Kofi Bentil (Ghana); Sr. Mary Ellen Diermeier, S.S.J.-T.O.S.F., Pastoral Assoc.; Deacon David Ashenbrenner.
Mailing Address: 6455 State Hwy. 153, Hatley, 54440. Tel: 715-446-3060; Fax: 715-446-2668.

BIG RIVER, PIERCE CO., NATIVITY OF THE BLESSED VIRGIN MARY (1872) [CEM 2] Rev. William J. Matzek.
Res.: W10137 570th Ave., River Falls, 54022. Tel: 715-425-5806; Fax: 715-425-5806.

BLACK RIVER FALLS, JACKSON CO., ST. JOSEPH (1857) [CEM 2] Rev. Emmanuel Famiyeh.
Res.: 507 Main St., 54615-1647. Tel: 715-284-5613; Fax: 715-284-8159.
Catechesis/Religious Program— Denise Cook, C.R.E. Students 95.

BLAIR, TREMPEALEAU CO., ST. ANSGAR (1961) Attended by St. Bridget, Ettrick Rev. Sebastian Venni, Parochial Admin.
Mailing Address: 22650 Washington St., Ettrick, 54627. Tel: 608-525-3811.
Catechesis/Religious Program—Judt Haase-Hardie, D.R.E. Students 21.

BLENKER, WOOD CO., ST. KILIAN (1882) [CEM] Attended by St. Wenceslaus, Milladore. Rev. Peter Raj.
Mailing Address: Box 100, Milladore, 54454. Tel: 715-457-2314.

BLOOMER, CHIPPEWA CO., ST. PAUL (1902) [CEM 3] Rev. John A. Potaczek; Deacon Richard Kostner.

Res.: 1222 Main St., 54724. Tel: 715-568-3255.
School—1210 Main St., 54724. Tel: 715-568-3233; Fax: 715-568-3244. Sisters 2; Lay Teachers 11; Students 187.
Catechesis/Religious Program—Tel: 715-568-3256. Barbara Kostner, D.R.E. Students 192.
Convent—1205 13th Ave., 54724. Tel: 715-568-3266.

BOYCEVILLE, DUNN CO., ST. LUKE (1964) [JC] Attended by St. Joseph, Rockfalls Rev. Sengol Rajan Arockasaimy.
Mailing Address: 919 Center St., P.O. Box 316, 54725. Tel: 715-643-3081. Email: stlukebv@yahoo.com.

BOYD, CHIPPEWA CO., SACRED HEART OF JESUS-ST. JOSEPH (1996) [CEM 2] Attended by Holy Family, Stanley. Rev. William P. Felix. In Res., Rev. Eugene P. Smith (Retired). Tel: 714-667-3038.
Res.: 719 Patten St., P.O. Box 10, 54726-0010. Tel: 715-861-1374.

BRACKETT, EAU CLAIRE CO., HOLY GUARDIAN ANGELS, Closed. For inquiries for Parish Records contact St. Raymond of Penafort, Southern Eau Claire County.

BROOKS, ADAMS CO., ST. ANN, [CEM] Attended by St. Joseph, Adams. Rev. James P. McNamee.
Mailing Address: P.O. Box 310, Adams, 53910. Tel: 608-584-4900.

BUENA VISTA, PORTAGE CO., ST. MARTIN, Closed. For inquiries for parish records contact St. Maximilian Maria Kolbe, Southeastern Portage County.

CADOTT, CHIPPEWA CO., ST. ROSE OF LIMA, [CEM], Also serves Sacred Heart, Jim Falls.
Res.: 415 N. Maple St., P.O. Box 160, 54727. Tel: 715-289-4551; Fax: 715-289-4551.
School—Tel: 715-289-4985. Lay Teachers 6; Students 48.

CAMP DOUGLAS, JUNEAU CO., ST. JAMES (1857) [CEM], Also serves St. Michael, Indian Creek. Rev. John Ofori-Domah.
Res.: 100 Bartell St., Box 199, 54618. Tel: 608-427-6762; Fax: 608-427-2004.

CASHTON, MONROE CO., SACRED HEART OF JESUS (1918) [CEM 3] Attended by Nativity of the Blessed Virgin Mary, St. Mary's Ridge. Very Rev. Michael E. Klos; Deacon Samuel Schmirler.
School—Sacred Heart of Jesus School, 710 Kenyon St., 54619. Tel: 608-654-7733; Fax: 608-654-7733. Lay Teachers 5; Students 50.

CASSEL, MARATHON CO., SACRED HEART, [CEM], Served from St. Patrick, Halder. Rev. Barnabas Kyeah.
Rectory—3372 County Rd. S., Marathon, 54448. Tel: 715-443-3675.

CASTLE ROCK LAKE, JUNEAU CO., OUR LADY OF THE LAKE, [CEM] Attended by St. Paul, New Lisbon. Rev. George Nelson Graham.
Res.: 408 W. River St., New Lisbon, 53950. Tel: 608-562-3125.

CAZENOVIA, RICHLAND CO., ST. ANTHONY DE PADUA (1857) [CEM] [JC], Also serves Sacred Heart, Lone Rock and St. Mary, Keyesville. Rev. Wesley Janowski (Poland).
Res.: 32505 CTH V, 53924. Tel: 608-983-2367.

CHILI, CLARK CO., ST. STEPHEN, Closed. For inquiries for Parish Records contact St. Mary's Parish, Neillsville, WI.

CHIPPEWA FALLS, CHIPPEWA CO.

1—ST. CHARLES BORROMEO (1884) [JC], Also serves St. Peter, Tilden. Very Rev. Edward J. Shuttleworth; Rev. Robert M. Letona; Deacons Thomas Kinnick; Daniel Rider.
Res.: 810 Pearl St., 54729. Tel: 715-723-4088; Fax: 715-723-2195.
See Chippewa Falls Area Catholic Schools, Chippewa Falls under Unified Catholic School Systems located in the Institution section.

2—HOLY GHOST (1886) [JC], Also serves St. Bridget, Springfield. Revs. Victor Inbaraj; Justin Kizewski.
Res.: 412 S. Main St., 54729. Tel: 715-723-4890; Fax: 715-723-7358. Email: hgparish@charter.net.
See Chippewa Falls Area Catholic Schools, Chippewa Falls under Unified Catholic School Systems located in the Institution section.
Catechesis/Religious Program—Tel: 715-723-4890. Sr. Donna Snyder, D.R.E. Students 466.

3—NOTRE DAME (1856) [JC] Rev. Mark R. Pierce.
Res.: 117 Allen St., 54729-2899. Tel: 715-723-7108; Fax: 715-723-7523. Email: cfnotredame@yahoo.com.
See Chippewa Falls Area Catholic Schools, Chippewa Falls under Unified Catholic School Systems located in the Institution section.
Catechesis/Religious Program—Dori Loomis, C.R.E. Students 79.

COLBY, CLARK CO., ST. MARY HELP OF CHRISTIANS (1877) [CEM] Very Rev. Daniel H. Hackel.
Res.: 205 S. 2nd St., P.O. Box 436, 54421. Tel: 715-223-3048; Fax: 715-223-0223.
School—Tel: 715-223-3033. Lay Teachers 11; Students 86.
Catechesis/Religious Program—Tel: 715-223-4926. Diane Feiten, D.R.E. Students 106.

COOKS VALLEY, CHIPPEWA CO., ST. JOHN THE BAPTIST (1884) [CEM] Rev. John A. Potaczek.
Mailing Address: 4540 State Hwy. 40, Bloomer, 54724. Tel: 715-568-3778; Fax: 715-568-9778. In Res., Rev. Albert W. Sonnberger (Retired).
Res.: 1222 Main St., Bloomer, 54724. Tel: 715-568-3255.

COON VALLEY, VERNON CO., ST. MARY, [CEM], Served from St. Joseph, St. Joseph's Ridge. Rev. Joseph C. Nakwah, Parochial Admin.
Res.: 904 Central Ave., 54623. Tel: 608-452-3841. Email: stmaryscv@mwt.net.
Catechesis/Religious Program—Jodie Holdorf, D.R.E. Students 32.

CORNELL, CHIPPEWA CO., HOLY CROSS (1915) [CEM 2] Rev. Jeremiah Cashman; Deacon Dennis Rivers.
Res.: 107 S. 8th St., P.O. Box 68, 54732. Tel: 715-239-6826.
Catechesis/Religious Program—Tel: 715-239-6759. Pamela Herrell, D.R.E.; Betty Rivers, C.R.E. Students 58.

CUSTER, PORTAGE CO., IMMACULATE CONCEPTION (1875) [CEM], Served from St. James, Amherst. Rev. Jude T. Dioka (Nigeria).
Res.: 7176 Esker Rd., 54423. Tel: 715-592-4330; Fax: 715-344-6277.

CZESTOCHOWA, CLARK CO., ST. MARY OF CZESTOCHOWA, Closed. For inquiries for parish records contact Holy Family, Stanley.

DE SOTO, CRAWFORD CO., SACRED HEART, Closed. For inquiries for parish records contact St. Charles Borromeo, Genoa.

DILLY, VERNON CO., ST. JOHN NEPOMUCENE, Closed. For inquiries for parish records contact Diocesan Archives, P.O. Box 4004, La Crosse,WI 54602-4004 Tel: 608-788-7700.

DORCHESTER, CLARK CO., ST. LOUIS (1878) [JC], Served from St. Mary's Help of Christians, Colby. Very Rev. Daniel H. Hackel.
Res.: 208 S. 3rd St., Colby, 54421.
Catechesis/Religious Program—Tel: 715-654-5467. Therese Geiger, D.R.E. Students 50.

DRYWOOD, CHIPPEWA CO., ST. ANTHONY (1886) [CEM] Attended by St. Rose of Lima, Cadott. Deacon Mark C. Arnold, Parish Dir.
Mailing Address: P.O. Box 160, Cadott, 54727.

DURAND, PEPIN CO., ST. MARY'S ASSUMPTION (1860) [CEM] Revs. Allen F. Jakubowski; Eric G. Linzmaier; Deacons James Weingart; Robert Hansen.
Mailing Address: 911 W. Prospect St., P.O. Box 188, 54736-1049. Tel: 715-672-5640; Fax: 715-672-4193. Web: www.triparish.41pi.com.
School—901 W. Prospect St., 54736. Tel: 715-672-5617; Fax: 715-672-3931. Lay Teachers 10; Students 109.

EASTMAN, CRAWFORD CO., ST. WENCESLAUS (1883) [CEM] Very Rev. Thomas M. Huff.
Res.: 28075 State Hwy. 27, P.O. Box 109, 54626-0109. Tel: 608-874-4151; Fax: 608-874-4151.
Catechesis/Religious Program—Tel: 608-874-4221. Barbara Martin, D.R.E. Students 71.

EAU CLAIRE, EAU CLAIRE CO.

1—IMMACULATE CONCEPTION (1945) Rev. Eugene A. Klink.
Res.: 1712 Highland Ave., 54701. Tel: 715-835-9935; Fax: 715-835-9459.
See Regis Catholic Schools, Eau Claire under Unified Catholic School Systems located in the Institution section.
Catechesis/Religious Program—Tel: 715-835-7721; Fax: 715-830-9846. Linda Corey, D.R.E.; Barb Brandner, D.R.E. Students 269.

2—ST. JAMES THE GREATER (1948) [JC] Rev. John A. Schultz; Jacky Miller, Pastoral Min.
Res.: 2502 Eleventh St., Ste. 1, 54703-2700. Tel: 715-835-5887; Fax: 715-835-3110. Email: stjameseac@aol.com. Web: www.stjameseauclaire-.catholicweb.com.
See Regis Catholic Schools, Eau Claire under Unified Catholic School Systems located in the Institution section.
Catechesis/Religious Program—Tel: 715-835-5887, Ext. 120. Jan Legge, C.R.E.; Kelly Beaudrie, C.R.E. Students 149.

3—NEWMAN COMMUNITY (1969) [JC] Rev. George R. Szews.
Res.: 110 Garfield Ave., 54701-4042. Tel: 715-834-3399.
Catechesis/Religious Program—Tel: 715-834-3399. Ryan Luedtke, D.R.E. Students 74.

4—ST. OLAF, [JC] Very Rev. Brian D. Konopa; Deacon Robert Chittendon.
Mailing Address: P.O. Box 1203, 54702-1203. Tel: 715-832-2504; Fax: 715-832-0742.
Church: 3220 Monroe St., 54703.
See Catholic Area Schools of the Eau Claire Deanery (C.A.S.E.), Eau Claire under Unified Catholic School Systems located in the Institution section.

5—ST. PATRICK, Merged with Sacred Heart of Jesus, Eau Claire to form Sacred Heart of Jesus-St. Patrick, Eau Claire. For inquiries for parish records contact Sacred Heart of Jesus-St. Patrick, Eau Claire.

6—SACRED HEART OF JESUS, Merged with St. Patrick, Eau Claire to form Sacred Heart of Jesus-St. Patrick, Eau Claire. For inquiries for parish records contact Sacred Heart of Jesus-St. Patrick, Eau Claire.

7—SACRED HEART OF JESUS-ST. PATRICK (1999) [CEM 2] Rev. William A. Dhein; Deacon Larry Agema.
Res.: 416 N. Dewey St., 54703. Tel: 715-832-0925; Fax: 715-832-0366. Email: sacrdhrt@charter.net. Web: www.sacredheartsaintpatrick.org.
Parish Office: 322 Fulton St., 54703.
Rectory—318 Fulton St., 54703.

EAU GALLE, DUNN CO., ST. HENRY (1856) [CEM] Rev. Jerome G. Hoeser.
Res.: N460 CTH D, 54737. Tel: 715-283-4448.
Catechesis/Religious Program—Tel: 715-283-4255. Orpha Baier, C.R.E. Students 34.

EDGAR, MARATHON CO., ST. JOHN THE BAPTIST (1900), (German—Polish), [CEM], Also serves Holy Family, Poniatowski. Rev. Robert A. Streveler.
Res.: 207 N. 3rd Ave., 54426-0386. Tel: 715-352-3444.
Church: 103 N. Fourth Ave., P.O. Box 35, 54426.
School—125 N. 4th Ave., P.O. Box 66, 54426-0066. Tel: 715-352-3000; Fax: 715-352-7517. Lay Teachers 9; Students 77.
Catechesis/Religious Program—Tel: 715-352-2216. Susan Schraufnagel, C.R.E. Students 156.

EDSON, CHIPPEWA CO., SACRED HEART OF JESUS, Merged with St. Joseph, Boyd to form Sacred Heart of Jesus-St. Joseph, Boyd.

ELK MOUND, DUNN CO., ST. JOSEPH (1959) [CEM] Rev. Sengol Rajan Arockasaimy. In Res., Rev. Henry R. Hoerburger (Retired).
Res.: P.O. Box 275, 54739. Tel: 715-879-5332. Email: stjosephem@centurytel.net.
Catechesis/Religious Program—Sharon Biegel, D.R.E. Students 71.

ELLSWORTH, PIERCE CO., ST. FRANCIS OF ASSISI (1897) [CEM] [JC 4] Rev. Roy R. Witucki.
Res.: 264 S. Grant St., P.O. Box 839, 54011. Tel: 715-273-4774; Fax: 715-723-4066.
School—Box 250, 54011. Tel: 715-273-4391; Fax: 715-273-4066. Lay Teachers 7; Students 145.

ELMWOOD, PIERCE CO., SACRED HEART, [CEM], Also serves Sacred Heart of Jesus, Spring Valley. Rev. Varkey V. Joseph.
114 W. Wilson Ave., 54740. Tel: 715-639-2741; Fax: 715-639-6031.

ELROY, JUNEAU CO., ST. PATRICK (1877) [CEM] Attended by St. Joseph, Kendall. Rev. Richard C. Dickman.
Res.: 307 Spring St., Box 155, Kendall, 54638. Tel: 608-463-7120; Fax: 608-462-5876. Email: stjosephkendall@centurytel.net.
Catechesis/Religious Program—Tel: 608-462-5067. Jayne Beaver, C.R.E. Students 36.

ETTRICK, TREMPEALEAU CO., ST. BRIDGET (1869) [CEM], Also serves St. Ansgar, Blair. Rev. Sebastian Venni.
Res.: 22650 Washington St., 54627. Tel: 608-525-3811; Fax: 608-525-2909. Email: stbridgets@centurytel.net.

FAIRCHILD, EAU CLAIRE CO., ST. JOHN CANTIUS, [CEM] Attended by St. Joseph, Fairview. Rev. Varkey Velickakathu.
Res.: N13740 Fairview Rd., 54741-8514. Tel: 715-334-2202; Fax: 715-334-2202.
Church: 306 2nd St., 54741.

FAIRVIEW, JACKSON CO., ST. JOSEPH (1870) [CEM], Also serves Immaculate Conception, Alma Center and St. John Cantius, Fairchild. Rev. Varkey Velickakathu.
Res.: N13740 Fairview Rd., Fairchild, 54741-8514. Tel: 715-334-2202; Fax: 715-334-2202.

FALL CREEK, EAU CLAIRE CO.

1—ST. JOHN THE APOSTLE, Closed. For inquiries for Parish Records contact St. Raymond of Penafort, Southern Eau Claire County.

2—ST. RAYMOND OF PENAFORT (1998) [CEM] Rev. James Kurzynski; Deacon Larry Agema.
S10444 Hwy. 53, 54742. Tel: 715-878-4183.

FANCHER, PORTAGE CO., ST. MARY OF MOUNT CARMEL (1884) [CEM] Attended by St. James, Amherst. Rev. Jude T. Dioka (Nigeria).
Mailing Address: 3995 Cty. K, P.O. Box 280, Amherst, 54406. Tel: 715-824-3455; Fax: 715-824-3455.
Res.: Amherst, 54406.
Catechesis/Religious Program—Cindy Klish, D.R.E. Students 150.

FOUNTAIN CITY, BUFFALO CO., IMMACULATE CONCEPTION (1857) [CEM], Also serves St. Lawrence, Alma. Rev. Brian J. Jazdzewski.
Res.: 1 Wall St., P.O. Box 218, 54629-0218. Tel: 608-687-3496.

GALESVILLE, TREMPEALEAU CO., ST. MARY (1904) Attended by St. Bartholomew, Trempealeau. Rev. Edmund J. Doerre.

Res. & Mailing Address: 11646 South St., Trempealeau, 54461-8238. Tel: 608-534-6652. Web: www.saintbartholomew.net.

GALLOWAY, MARATHON CO., ST. JOSEPH (1921) [CEM], Also serves St. Ladislaus, Bevent. Rev. Augustine Kofi Bentil (Ghana); Sr. Mary Ellen Diermeier, S.S.J.-T.O.S.F., Pastoral Assoc.; Deacon David Ashenbrenner.
Res.: 8846 CTH C, Wittenberg, 54499-8936. Tel: 715-454-6431.
Catechesis / Religious Program—Tel: 715-454-6432. Kent Jacobson, C.R.E. Students 50.

GAYS MILLS, CRAWFORD CO., ST. MARY (1908) [JC], Also serves St. Philip, Rolling Ground. Rev. Zacharie Beya-Tshingimba.
Res.: 121 School St., 54631. Tel: 608-735-4420; Fax: 608-735-4427.
Catechesis / Religious Program—Students 7.

GENOA, VERNON CO., ST. CHARLES BORROMEO, [CEM] Rev. Robert J. Cook, Priest Mod. (Retired); Deacon Richard Sage, Parish Dir.
Mailing Address: 701 Walnut St., P.O. Box 130, 54632. Tel: 608-689-2646; Fax: 608-689-2811.
School—Tel: 608-689-2642; Fax: 608-689-2811. Lay Teachers 4; Students 32.

GREENWOOD, CLARK CO., ST. MARY HELP OF CHRISTIANS (1903) [CEM], Also serves Holy Family, Willard. Rev. A. Joseph Follmar.
Res.: 123 N. Main St., P.O. Box 129, 54437. Tel: 715-267-6282.
School—Tel: 715-267-6477; Fax: 715-267-6477. Lay Teachers 3; Students 27.

HALDER, MARATHON CO., ST. PATRICK, [CEM], Also serves Sacred Heart, Cassel. Rev. Barnabas Kyeah.
Rectory—3158 Halder Dr., Mosinee, 54455. Tel: 715-693-2765. Email: stpats@mtc.net.

HATLEY, MARATHON CO., ST. FLORIAN (1885) [CEM], Also serves St. Agnes, Weston. Rev. Alan T. Burkhardt.
Res.: 500 Church Ln., P.O. Box 100, 54440. Tel: 715-446-2252; 715-446-3085 (Office); Fax: 715-446-2756.

HEFFRON, PORTAGE CO., ST. JOHN THE BAPTIST, Closed. For inquiries for parish records contact St. Maximilian Maria Kolbe, Southeastern Portage County.

HEWITT, WOOD CO., ST. MICHAEL (1888) [JC] Attended by St. Mary, Auburndale. Rev. Peter Raj.
Parish Office: 11100 Main St., 54441. Tel: 715-384-7676; Fax: 715-384-7675. Email: stmichaelhewitt@gmail.com.
Res.: 5866 Main St., Box 177, Auburndale, 54412. Tel: 715-652-2806; Fax: 715-652-8020. Email: revlinz@tds.net.

HILLSBORO, VERNON CO., ST. ALOYSIUS (1905) [JC] Very Rev. Donald J. Bauer.
Res.: 545 Prairie Ave., P.O. Box 466, 54634. Tel: 608-489-2580; Fax: 608-489-2580.
Catechesis / Religious Program—Tel: 608-489-3544; Fax: 608-489-2580. Students 57.

HOLMEN, LA CROSSE CO., ST. ELIZABETH ANN SETON (1983) Rev. John L. Parr; Sr. Bridget Donaldson, O.S.B., Pastoral Assoc.; Deacon Matthew Luddick.
Office: 515 N. Main St., 54636-9387. Tel: 608-526-4424; Fax: 608-526-3177.
Res.: 704 Hillcrest Dr., 54636-9745.
Catechesis / Religious Program—Students 441.

INDEPENDENCE, TREMPEALEAU CO., SS. PETER AND PAUL (1875) [CEM], Also serves St. John the Apostle, Whitehall. Very Rev. Woodrow H. Pace; Rev. Timothy L. Oudenhoven.
Res.: 36028 Osseo Rd., P.O. Box 430, 54747-0430. Tel: 715-985-2227; Fax: 715-985-2649.
School—Tel: 715-985-3719. Lay Teachers 9; Students 113.

INDIAN CREEK, MONROE CO., ST. MICHAEL (1869) [CEM] Attended by St. James, Camp Douglas. Rev. John Ofori-Domah.
Mailing Address: P.O. Box 199, Camp Douglas, 54618. Tel: 608-427-6762.

JIM FALLS, CHIPPEWA CO., SACRED HEART OF JESUS Deacon Mark C. Arnold.
Res.: 13989 195th St., Box 68, 54748. Tel: 715-382-4422.

JUNCTION CITY, PORTAGE CO., ST. MICHAEL (1884) [CEM] Attended by St. Wenceslaus, Milladore. Rev. Andrzej K. Panek.
Res.: 146 Main St., P.O. Box 100, Milladore, 54454. Tel: 715-457-2314; Fax: 715-457-6255.
Church: 324 Main St., 54443.

KENDALL, MONROE CO., ST. JOSEPH (1883) [CEM], Also serves St. Patrick, Elroy, and St. John the Baptist, Wilton. Rev. Richard C. Dickman.
Res.: 307 Spring St., P.O. Box 155, 54638. Tel: 608-463-7120. Email: stjosephkendall@centurytel.net.
Catechesis / Religious Program—Tel: 608-463-7649. Mary Skolos, C.R.E. Students 35.

KEYESVILLE, RICHLAND CO., NATIVITY OF THE BLESSED VIRGIN MARY, [CEM] Attended by St. Anthony, Cazenovia. Rev. Wesley Janowski (Poland).
Mailing Address: 32605 Durst Ln., Richland Center, 53581. Tel: 608-585-4846.
Res.: 32505 Hwy. V, Cazenovia, 53924. Tel: 608-983-2367.

KNOWLTON, MARATHON CO., ST. FRANCIS XAVIER (1853) [CEM], Also serves St. John the Baptist, Peplin. Rev. Joseph A. Grassl.
Res.: 651 Mead Ln., Mosinee, 54455. Tel: 715-693-3120; Fax: 715-693-3120. Email: sfknowl@mtc.net.

LANARK, PORTAGE CO., ST. PATRICK, Closed. For inquiries for parish records contact St. Maximilian Maria Kolbe, Southeastern Portage County.

LIMA, PEPIN CO., HOLY ROSARY, [CEM], Served from: St. Mary's Assumption, Durand. Revs. Allen F. Jakubowski; Eric G. Linzmaier; Deacons James Weingart; Robert Hansen.
Mailing Address: 911 W. Prospect St., Box 188, Durand, 54736-1048. Tel: 715-672-5640; Fax: 715-672-4193.
School—Tel: 715-672-4276. Lay Teachers 4; Students 57.

LONE ROCK, RICHLAND CO., SACRED HEART, Attended by St. Anthony, Cazenovia. Rev. Wesley Janowski (Poland).
Mailing Address: 32505 Hwy. V, Cazenovia, 53924. Tel: 608-983-2367.

LOYAL, CLARK CO., ST. ANTHONY OF PADUA (1893) [CEM] Rev. Keith Kitzhaber.
Res.: 407 N. Division St., P.O. Box 69, 54446-0069. Tel: 715-255-8017; Fax: 715-255-8017.
School—212 W. Spring St., 54446. Tel: 715-255-8636; Fax: 715-255-8636. Lay Teachers 7; Students 76.
Catechesis / Religious Program—Tel: 715-255-9938. Mary Ann Olson, D.R.E. Students 112.

LYNDON STATION, JUNEAU CO., ST. MARY, [CEM], Served from St. Patrick, Mauston. Rev. Valentine Joseph.
Res.: 117 Juneau St. N., P.O. Box 303, 53944. Tel: 608-666-2421; Fax: 608-666-2421. Email: stmaryslyndon@charter.net.
Catechesis / Religious Program—Vicki McGowan, C.R.E. Students 22.

MARATHON CITY, MARATHON CO., NATIVITY OF THE BLESSED VIRGIN MARY (1856) [CEM] Very Rev. Joseph G. Diermeier.
Res.: 712 Market St., Box 7, 54448-0007. Tel: 715-443-2045; Fax: 715-443-3045. Email: bvmparish@stmarymara.org.
School—Tel: 715-443-3430. Lay Teachers 14; Students 180.
Catechesis / Religious Program—Tel: 715-443-2433; Fax: 715-443-2575. Students 90.

MARSHFIELD, WOOD CO.

1—ST. JOHN THE BAPTIST (1877) [JC], Also serves Christ the King, Spencer. Revs. Samuel A. Martin; Victor C. Feltes.
Res.: 201 W. Blodgett St., 54449-2400. Tel: 715-384-3252; Fax: 715-384-3252. Web: www.stjohnsmarshfield.org.
See Columbus Catholic Schools, Marshfield under Unified Catholic School Systems located in the Institution section.
Catechesis / Religious Program—Tel: 715-384-3919. Richard Hoffman, D.R.E. Students 155.

2—OUR LADY OF PEACE (1947) [JC] Unassigned.
Res.: 1414 W. 5th St., 54449. Tel: 715-384-9414; Fax: 715-384-6606.
See Columbus Catholic Schools, Marshfield under Unified Catholic School Systems located in the Institution section.
Catechesis / Religious Program—Tel: 715-676-2549; Fax: 715-384-6606. Corinne Johnson, D.R.E. Students 217.

3—SACRED HEART OF JESUS (1916) [JC], Also serves Corpus Christi, Bakerville. Rev. Peter M. Manickam.
Res.: 112 E. 11th St., 54449-4216. Tel: 715-384-3213; Fax: 715-384-6929. Email: sacred_heart@verizon.net. Web: www.sacredheartmarshfield.org.
See Columbus Catholic Schools, Marshfield under Unified Catholic School Systems located in the Institution section.

MAUSTON, JUNEAU CO., ST. PATRICK (1901) [CEM 2], Also serves St. Mary, Lyndon Station. Rev. Gasparraj Valentine Joseph.
Res.: 401 Mansion St., 53948-1393. Tel: 608-847-6054; Fax: 608-847-3288. Email: stpatsparish@btsmailbox.com. Web: www.stpatricksmauston.com.
School—325 Mansion St., 53948. Tel: 608-847-5844; Fax: 608-847-4103. Lay Teachers 14; Students 177.

MELROSE, JACKSON CO., ST. KEVIN, [JC] Attended by St. Joseph, Black River Falls Rev. Emmanuel Famiyeh.
813 N. Washington St., 54642.

MENOMONIE, DUNN CO., ST. JOSEPH (1861) [CEM] Very Rev. Thomas J. Krieg.
Res.: 910 Wilson Ave., 54751. Tel: 715-232-4922; Fax: 715-232-4923.
School—Tel: 715-232-4920. Lay Teachers 14; Students 143.
Catechesis / Religious Program—Emily Revak, D.R.E.; Pam Sirinek, Youth Min. Students 260.

MIDDLE RIDGE, LA CROSSE CO., ST. PETER (1869) [CEM], Also serves St. Joseph, St. Joseph Ridge, and St. Mary, Coon Valley. Rev. Joseph C. Nakwah.
Res.: W697 State Rd. 33, Rockland, 54653. Tel: 608-486-2180; Fax: 608-486-2181.

MILAN, MARATHON CO., ST. THOMAS (1913) [CEM] Attended by St. Anthony, Athens. Rev. Charles J. Hiebl.
Mailing Address: 417 Caroline St., P.O. Box 206, Athens, 54411. Tel: 715-257-7684; Fax: 715-257-7791.

MILL CREEK, PORTAGE CO., ST. BARTHOLOMEW, [CEM] Attended by Milladore. Rev. Andrzej K. Panek; Deacon Richard Rozumalski.
Res.: 2493 County Rd. M, Stevens Point, 54481. Tel: 715-344-3003; Fax: 715-344-0331. Email: stbartholomew@g29.net.

MILLADORE, WOOD CO., ST. WENCESLAUS (1883) [CEM], Also serves St. Bartholomew, Mill Creek, and St. Michael, Junction City. Rev. Andrzej K. Panek.
Res.: 146 Main St., Box 100, 54454. Tel: 715-457-2314; Fax: 715-457-6255.

MONDOVI, BUFFALO CO., SACRED HEART OF JESUS (1896) [JC] Attended by St. Mary's Assumption, Durand Revs. Allen F. Jakubowski; Eric G. Linzmaier; Deacon Robert Hansen.
Mailing Address: P.O. Box 188, Durand, 54736. Tel: 715-672-5640; Fax: 715-672-4193.

MOSINEE, MARATHON CO., ST. PAUL (1878) [CEM] Rev. Donald L. Przybylski.
Res.: 603 Fourth St., 54455. Tel: 715-693-2650; Fax: 715-692-2650. Email: parish@stpaulmosinee.org. Web: www.stpaulmosinee.org.
School—404 High St., 54455. Tel: 715-693-2675; Fax: 715-693-1332. Lay Teachers 6; Students 48.
Catechesis / Religious Program—Tel: 715-693-4030; Fax: 715-693-1332. Kathryn Lesniak, D.R.E. Students 299.

NECEDAH, JUNEAU CO., ST. FRANCIS OF ASSISI (1876) [CEM] Rev. Hector C. Moreno; Deacon Glen Heinzl.
Res.: 2001 S. Main St., 54646-8273. Tel: 608-565-2488; Fax: 608-565-6722.

NEILLSVILLE, CLARK CO., ST. MARY (1878) [CEM], Also serves: St. John, Fairchild, St. Joseph, Fairview. Rev. Varkey Velickakathu.
Res.: 1813 Black River Rd., 54456. Tel: 715-743-3840; Fax: 715-743-7963. Email: stmaryneillsville@tds.net.

NEKOOSA, WOOD CO., SACRED HEART OF JESUS (1900) [JC], Also serves St. Alexander, Port Edwards. Rev. R. John Swing.
Res.: 711 Prospect Ave., 54457. Tel: 715-886-3422; Fax: 715-886-3954.
See Wisconsin Rapids Area Catholic Schools, Wisconsin Rapids under Unified Catholic School Systems located in the Institution section.

NEW AUBURN, CHIPPEWA CO., ST. JUDE, Closed. For inquiries for parish records contact the chancery.

NEW LISBON, JUNEAU CO., ST. PAUL (1862) [CEM], Also serves Our Lady of the Lake, Castle Rock Lake. Rev. George Nelson Graham.
Res.: 408 W. River St., 53950. Tel: 608-562-3125; Fax: 715-562-6225. Email: st.paul@mwt.net.
Catechesis / Religious Program—Tel: 608-562-5482. Chris Popp, C.R.E. Students 33.

NORTH CREEK, TREMPEALEAU CO., ST. MICHAEL (1875) Closed. For inquiries for parish records contact the chancery.

NORWALK, MONROE CO., ST. AUGUSTINE OF HIPPO (1903) [CEM] Attended by Nativity of the Blessed Virgin Mary, St. Mary's Ridge. Very Rev. Michael E. Klos; Deacon Samuel Schmirler. In Res., Rev. James H. Miller (Retired).
Res.: 26400 CTH U, Cashton, 54619-8621. Tel: 608-823-7906; Fax: 608-823-7272. Email: smr1856@centurytel.net.

ONALASKA, LA CROSSE CO., ST. PATRICK (1949) [JC] Rev. Steven J. Kachel; Deacon Frank Abnet.
Res.: 1031 Main St., 54650. Tel: 608-783-5535.
See Aquinas Catholic Schools, LaCrosse under Unified Catholic School Systems located in the Institution section.
Catechesis / Religious Program—Tel: 608-783-1099. Cathryn Olson, D.R.E.; Nina Long, D.R.E. Students 533.

OWEN, CLARK CO., HOLY ROSARY (1953), Served from: St. Mary Help of Christians, Colby. Very Rev. Daniel H. Hackel.
Parish Office: 415 W. 3rd St., P.O. Box 309, 54460-0309. Tel: 715-229-2348. Email: catholiccentral@gmail.com.

PEPLIN, MARATHON CO., ST. JOHN THE BAPTIST (1916) [CEM] Attended by St. Francis Xavier, Knowlton. Rev. Joseph A. Grassl.
Mailing Address: 651 Mead Ln., Mosinee, 54455. Tel: 715-693-3120. In Res., Rev. Wladyslaw J.

Kowalski (SUP) (Retired).

PINE CREEK, TREMPEALEAU CO., MOST SACRED HEART (1864) [CEM] Rev. Joseph M. O'Hara.
Res.: N20555 CTH G, Dodge, 54625-9721. Tel: 608-539-3704; Fax: 608-539-3704. Email: sacredheartparis@centurytel.net.

PITTSVILLE, WOOD CO., ST. JOACHIM, [CEM], Also serves St. James, Vesper, and Holy Rosary, Sigel. Rev. Robert W. Nelson.
Res.: 5312 Third Ave., P.O. Box 69, 54466-0069. Tel: 715-884-6815; Fax: 715-884-6160.
Catechesis/Religious Program—Tel: 715-884-2115. Judy Gachnang, D.R.E. Students 129.

PLOVER, PORTAGE CO., ST. BRONISLAVA (1896) [JC] Revs. James F. Trempe; Gregory J. Bohren; Deacons Vernon R. Linzmaier; Richard Zietlow.
Res.: 3200 Plover Rd., P.O. Box 158, 54467-0158. Tel: 715-344-4326; Fax: 715-344-6121.
School—3301 Willow Dr., 54467. Tel: 715-342-2015; Fax: 715-342-2016.
Catechesis/Religious Program—Tel: 715-341-6700. Jody Glodowski, C.R.E.; Julie Studinski, Dir. Youth Min. Students 653.

PLUM CITY, PIERCE CO., ST. JOHN THE BAPTIST (1872) [JC], Also serves: St. Joseph, Arkansaw. Rev. Paul G. Czerwonka.
Res.: 212 Church Rd., P.O. Box 206, 54761-0206. Tel: 715-647-2301; Fax: 715-647-2901.

POLONIA, PORTAGE CO., SACRED HEART, [CEM] Attended by St. Adalbert, Rosholt Rev. Gregory A. Michaud; Deacon James Maciejewski.
Res.: 7375 Church St., Custer, 54423. Tel: 715-592-4221; Fax: 715-592-4189.
School—7379 Church St., Custer, 54423. Tel: 715-592-4902. Lay Teachers 4; Students 48.
Convent—7381 Church St., Custer, 54423. Tel: 715-592-4213.

PONIATOWSKI, MARATHON CO., HOLY FAMILY (1877) [CEM 2] Attended by St. John the Baptist, Edgar. Rev. Robert A. Streveler; Deacon LeRoy Knauf, Pastoral Assoc.
Mailing Address: 417 Caroline St., P.O. Box 206, Athens, 54411-0206.
Church: R444 CTHU, Edgar, 54426. Tel: 715-443-2527.
Catechesis/Religious Program—Deacon LeRoy Knauf, D.R.E. Students 73.

PORT EDWARDS, WOOD CO., ST. ALEXANDER (1941) [JC], Served from Sacred Heart, Nekoosa. Rev. R. John Swing. In Res., Sr. Catherine Kaiser, F.S.P.A., Pastoral Assoc.
Church & Res.: 880 First St., 54469. Tel: 715-887-3012; Fax: 715-887-3748. Email: stalex@wctc.net.

PRAIRIE DU CHIEN, CRAWFORD CO.

1—ST. GABRIEL (1817) [CEM 2], Served from St. Nepomucene, Prairie du Chien. Rev. James C. Weighner.
Office: 506 N. Beaumont Rd., P.O. Box 176, 53821-0176. Tel: 608-326-2404.
School—Prairie Catholic Schools, 515 N. Beaumont Rd., 53821. Tel: 608-326-8624. Lay Teachers 22; Students 240.

2—ST. JOHN NEPOMUCENE (1891), Also serves St. Gabriel, Prairie du Chien. Rev. James C. Weighner.
Res.: 710 S. Wacouta St., P.O. Box 28, 53821-0028. Tel: 608-326-6511; Fax: 608-326-4876.
School—Prairie Catholic Schools, 720 S. Wacouta St., 53821. Tel: 608-326-4400.

PRESCOTT, PIERCE CO., ST. JOSEPH, [CEM] Rev. John Robert; Deacon Gerald Rynda.
Res.: 269 Dakota St. S., P.O. Box 245, 54021-0245. Tel: 715-262-5310; Fax: 715-262-4543. Email: stjosephprescott@comcast.net. Web: stjosephprescott.com.
School—281 Dakota St. S., 54021. Tel: 715-262-5912; Fax: 715-262-5901. Franciscan Sisters of Perpetual Adoration 2; Lay Teachers 10; Students 120.
Convent—268 Dakota St. S., 54021. Tel: 715-262-5105.

RICHLAND CENTER, RICHLAND CO., ST. MARY (ASSUMPTION OF B.V.M.), [CEM] Very Rev. Roger J. Scheckel; Deacon Edward Wendt.
160 W. 4th St., P.O. Box 456, 53581. Tel: 608-647-2621; Fax: 608-647-6029.
School—155 W. 5th St., 53581. Tel: 608-647-2422. Lay Teachers 12; Students 124.
Catechesis/Religious Program—Tel: 608-647-4210. Denise Gainor, D.R.E. Students 180.
Convent—789 N. Central Ave., 53581. Tel: 608-647-4210.

RISING SUN, CRAWFORD CO., ST. JAMES, Closed. For inquiries for parish records contact The Diocesan Archive, P.O. Box 4004, La Crosse, WI, 54602-4004.

ROCK FALLS, DUNN CO., ST. JOSEPH (1905) [CEM] Rev. Sengol Rajan Arockasaimy.
Res.: E. 9265 State Rd. 85, Mondovi, 54755-8857. Tel: 715-875-4539; Fax: 715-875-4539. Email: stjosephrf@yahoo.com.
Catechesis/Religious Program—Amy Mayer, C.C.D. Coord. Tel: 715-875-4527. Students 23.

ROLLING GROUND, CRAWFORD CO., ST. PHILIP (1857) [CEM] Attended by St. Mary, Gays Mills. Rev. Zacharie Beya-Tshingimba.
Mailing Address: 115 E. School St., Gays Mills, 54631-7211. Tel: 608-735-4420; Fax: 608-735-4427.
Church: 42668 Church Rd., Soldiers Grove, 54655.
Catechesis/Religious Program—Students 31.

ROSHOLT, PORTAGE CO., ST. ADALBERT (1898) [CEM], Also serves Sacred Heart, Polonia. Rev. Gregory A. Michaud; Deacon James Maciejewski.
Res.: 3315 St. Adalbert Rd., 54473. Tel: 715-677-4519; Fax: 715-677-6943.
School—3314 St. Adalbert Rd., 54473. Tel: 715-677-4517. Lay Teachers 5; Students 36.
Catechesis/Religious Program—Patty Lawson, D.R.E. Students 59.

ROTHSCHILD, MARATHON CO.

1—ST. MARK (1960) Very Rev. Allan L. Slowiak; Deacon Patrick McKeough.
Res.: 602 Military Rd., 54474-1523. Tel: 715-359-5206; Fax: 715-355-8904. Email: stmarkroths@smproths.org.
See Newman Area Catholic Schools, Wausau under Unified Catholic School Systems located in the Institution section.
Catechesis/Religious Program—Fax: 715-355-8904. Mary Hart, D.R.E. Students 212.

2—ST. THERESE OF THE CHILD JESUS, [CEM] Rev. Janusz Kowalski.
Res.: 113 W. Kort St., 54474-1094. Tel: 715-359-2421; Fax: 715-355-3088.
See Wausau Area Catholic Schools, Wausau under Unified Catholic School Systems located in the Institution section.
Catechesis/Religious Program—112 W. Kort St., Schofield, 54476. Tel: 715-359-9006. Students 224.

ROZELLVILLE, MARATHON CO., ST. ANDREW, [CEM] Attended by St. Joseph, Stratford. Very Rev. Eric R. Berns. In Res., Rev. Arthur S. Redmond (Retired). Tel: 715-384-7932.
Res.: Box 106, Stratford, 54484. Tel: 715-687-2404.
Rectory—D 1876 CTH C., Stratford, 54484.

RUDOLPH, WOOD CO., ST. PHILIP, [CEM] Attended by St. Lawrence, Wisconsin Rapids. Rev. Timothy J. Welles.
Parish Office: 6957 Grotto Ave., Box 165, 54475. Tel: 715-435-3286.
Res.: 530 Tenth Ave. N., Wisconsin Rapids, 54495. Tel: 715-421-5777.
See Wisconsin Rapids Area Catholic Schools, Wisconsin Rapids under Unified Catholic School Systems located in the Institution section.

SAINT JOSEPH RIDGE, LA CROSSE CO., ST. JOSEPH (1866) [CEM], Also serves: St. Peter, Middle Ridge, and St. Mary, Coon Valley. Rev. Joseph C. Nakwah.
Res.: W2601 Hwy. 33, 54601. Tel: 608-788-1646.

SAINT MARY'S RIDGE, MONROE CO., NATIVITY OF THE BLESSED VIRGIN MARY (1856) [CEM], Also serves St. Augustine, Norwalk, and Sacred Heart, Cashton. Very Rev. Michael E. Klos; Deacon Samuel Schmirler.
Res.: 26400 CTH U, Cashton, 54619-9157. Tel: 608-823-7906; Fax: 608-823-7272.
School—Tel: 608-823-7577. Lay Teachers 5; Students 27.

SENECA, CRAWFORD CO., ST. PATRICK (1872) [CEM] Very Rev. Thomas M. Huff.
Res.: 21150 State Hwy. 27, P.O. Box 18, 54654. Tel: 608-734-3931.

SIGEL, WOOD CO., HOLY ROSARY (1881) [CEM] Attended by Joachim, Pittsville. Rev. Robert W. Nelson.
Mailing Address: P.O. Box 69, Pittsville, 54466-0069.

SOUTHEASTERN PORTAGE COUNTY, PORTAGE CO., ST. MAXIMILIAN MARIA KOLBE (1996) [CEM 4] Unassigned.Mailing Address: 8611 State Hwy. 54, Almond, 54909. Tel: 715-824-3380.

SPARTA, MONROE CO., ST. PATRICK (1876) [CEM], Also serves St. John the Baptist, Summit Ridge. Rev. John Selva Manohar.
Res.: 319 W. Main St., 54656-2143. Tel: 608-269-2655; Fax: 608-269-3084. Web: www.stpatricksparish.41pi.com.
School—100 S. L St., 54654. Tel: 608-269-4748; Fax: 608-269-4748. Lay Teachers 11; Students 150.
Catechesis/Religious Program—Tel: 608-269-7500. Students 248.

SPAULDING-CITY POINT, JACKSON CO., NORTH AMERICAN MARTYRS, Closed. For inquiries for parish records contact St. Joachim, Pittsville.

SPENCER, MARATHON CO., CHRIST THE KING (1938) [JC] Attended by St. John, Marshfield. Revs. Samuel A. Martin; Victor C. Feltes.
Res.: 201 W. Blodgett, Marshfield, 54449-2004. Tel: 715-659-4480; Fax: 715-384-3252.
Catechesis/Religious Program—101 Wendell St., P.O. Box 156, 54479-0156. Fax: 715-384-3252. Students 126.

SPRING VALLEY, PIERCE CO., SACRED HEART OF JESUS (1884) [CEM 2] Attended by Sacred Heart, Elmwood. Rev. Kevin C. Louis.
Res.: S. 105 Sabin Ave., P.O. Box 456, 54767-0456. Tel: 715-778-5519; Fax: 715-778-5599. Email: shp@svtel.net.

SPRINGFIELD, EAU CLAIRE CO., ST. BRIDGET (1859) [CEM] Attended by Holy Ghost, Chippewa Falls. Revs. Victor Inbaraj; Justin Kizewski.
Office: 412 S. Main, Chippewa Falls, 54729. Tel: 715-723-4890. Email: hgparish@charter.net.

STANLEY, CHIPPEWA CO., HOLY FAMILY (1896) [CEM], Also serves Sacred Heart of Jesus-St. Joseph, Boyd. Rev. William P. Felix.
Office: 226 E. 3rd Ave., P.O. Box 125, 54768. Tel: 715-644-5435; Fax: 715-709-0022.
Res.: 239 S. Franklin St., P.O. Box 125, 54768. Tel: 715-644-3561.

STEVENS POINT, PORTAGE CO.

1—ST. CASIMIR (1871) [CEM], Served from St. Peter, Stevens Point. Rev. V. Arul Joseph.
Res.: 203 W. Casimir Rd., 54481. Tel: 715-344-9582. Email: stcasimir@localnet.com.

2—ST. JOSEPH (1884) [JC] Rev. Jerzy Rebacz; Deacon Arthur Schaller.
Res.: 1709 Wyatt Ave., 54481-3699. Tel: 715-341-1617; Fax: 715-341-2623. Web: www.togetherinfaith.org.
See Stevens Point Area Catholic Schools, Stevens Point under Unified Catholic School Systems located in the Institution section.
Catechesis/Religious Program—1901 Lincoln Ave., 54481. Tel: 715-341-1617, Ext. 115; Fax: 715-341-2623. Lynn Meyer, C.R.E.; Teresa Loepfe, Youth Min.; Kris Hansen, Pastoral Min. Students 179.

3—NEWMAN UNIVERSITY PARISH (1970) [JC] Very Rev. Thomas F. Lindner.
Office: 2108 Fourth Ave., 54481. Tel: 715-345-6500; Fax: 715-345-5303.
Catechesis/Religious Program—Bonnie Seidl Bauman, D.R.E. Students 101.

4—ST. PETER (1876) [JC] Rev. Arul Joseph Visuvasam.
Res.: 800 4th Ave., 54481-1627. Tel: 715-344-6115; Fax: 715-344-6277. Web: www.saintpetercatholic.com.
Catechesis/Religious Program—Philip Lawson, D.R.E. Students 110.
See Stevens Point Area Catholic Schools, Stevens Point under Unified Catholic School Systems located in the Institution section.

5—ST. STANISLAUS (1917) [JC] Rev. George Kutty Thayilkuzhithottu, M.S.F.S.; Deacon Donald Borski.
Res.: 838 Fremont St., 54481. Tel: 715-344-9117; Fax: 715-344-1771. Email: ststans@charter.net. Web: www.saintstans.net.
See Stevens Point Area Catholic Schools, Stevens Point under Unified Catholic School Systems located in the Institution section.

6—ST. STEPHEN (1852) [CEM], Served from: St. Joseph, Stevens Point. Rev. Jerzy Rebacz; Deacons Arthur Schaller; Richard Rozumalski.
Res.: 1401 Clark St., 54481. Tel: 715-344-3319; Fax: 715-344-6101. Email: ststephenparish@att.net. Web: www.saintstephenparish.com.
See Stevens Point Area Catholic Schools, Stevens Point under Unified Catholic School Systems located in the Institution section.
Catechesis/Religious Program—1335 Clark St., 54481. Tel: 715-344-6433. Students 130.

STRATFORD, MARATHON CO., ST. JOSEPH (1900) [CEM 3], Also serves St. Andrew, Rozellville. Very Rev. Eric R. Berns.
Res.: 420 Larch St., P.O. Box 6, 54484. Tel: 715-687-2404.
School—P.O. Box 6, 54484. Tel: 715-687-4145; Fax: 715-687-4343. Lay Teachers 11; Students 116.
Catechesis/Religious Program—Tel: 715-687-3392. Ruth Gawlikoski, D.R.E. Students 134.

SUMMIT, MONROE CO., ST. JOHN THE BAPTIST (1877) [CEM] Attended by St. Patrick, Sparta. Rev. John Selva Manohar; Deacon Samuel Schmirler.
Mailing Address: 319 W. Main St., Sparta, 54656. Tel: 608-269-2655; Fax: 608-269-3084.

THORP, CLARK CO., ST. BERNARD-ST. HEDWIG PARISH (1884) [CEM] Rev. Donald L. Meuret.
Res.: 109 N. Church St., Box 329, 54771. Tel: 715-669-5526; Fax: 715-669-5754.
School—411 E. School St., Box 369, 54771. Tel: 715-669-5530. Lay Teachers 10; Students 77.
Catechesis/Religious Program—Tel: 715-669-7302. Leeann Klapatauskas, D.R.E. Students 229.

TILDEN, CHIPPEWA CO., ST. PETER (1869) [CEM], Attended by St. Charles Borromeo, Chippewa Falls. Very Rev. Edward J. Shuttleworth; Deacons Thomas Kinnick; Daniel Rider.
Mailing Address: 11358 CTH Q, Chippewa Falls, 54729-6115. Tel: 715-288-6484; Fax: 715-723-2195.
Res.: 11358 CTU Q, Chippewa Falls, 54729-6115. Tel: 715-723-4088; Fax: 715-723-2195.
School—11370 CTH Q, Chippewa Falls, 54729. Tel: 715-288-6250; Fax: 715-288-6250. Lay Teachers 6; Students 60.

TOMAH, MONROE CO., ST. MARY (IMMACULATE CONCEPTION) (1867) [CEM], Also serves St. Andrew,

Warrens. Rev. Msgr. Richard W. Gilles.
Office: 303 W. Monroe St., 54660. Tel: 608-372-4516.
Res.: 516 W. Foster, 54660.
School—315 W. Monroe St., 54660. Tel: 608-372-5765; Fax: 608-372-4440. Lay Teachers 12; Students 173.
Catechesis/Religious Program—Tel: 608-372-0825. Wanda Thorson, D.R.E. Students 179.

TORUN, PORTAGE CO., ST. MARY, [CEM], Served from St. Adalbert, Rosholt. Rev. Gregory A. Michaud, Parochial Admin.
Office: 5589 Dewey Dr., Stevens Point, 54482. Tel: 715-344-2599; Fax: 715-345-1377.
Res.: 203 W. Casimir Rd., Stevens Point, 54481.

TREMPEALEAU, TREMPEALEAU CO., ST. BARTHOLOMEW (1869) [CEM 2], Also serves St. Mary, Galesville. Rev. Edmund J. Doerre.
Res.: 11646 South St., 54661-8238. Tel: 608-534-6652. Web: www.saintbartholomew.net.

UNION CENTER, JUNEAU CO., ST. THERESA OF AVILA, Closed. For inquiries for parish records contact St. Jerome, Wonewoc.

VESPER, WOOD CO., ST. JAMES, [CEM] Attended by St. Joachim, Pittsville. Rev. Robert W. Nelson.
6623 N. Church St., Box 68, 54489. Tel: 715-569-4412.
Res.: P.O. Box 69, Pittsville, 54489.
Catechesis/Religious Program—Annette Molepske, D.R.E. Students 58.

VIROQUA, VERNON CO., ANNUNCIATION OF THE BLESSED VIRGIN MARY (1906) Very Rev. Francis Abuah-Quansah.
Res.: 400 Congress Ave., 54665-1309. Tel: 608-637-7711; Fax: 608-637-6914. Email: rjc1965@frontiernet.net. Web: www.saintmaryviroqua.org.
Catechesis/Religious Program—Tel: 608-634-3033. Dennis Olson, C.R.E. Students 211.

WARRENS, MONROE CO., ST. ANDREW, Attended by St. Mary (Immaculate Conception), Tomah. Rev. Msgr. Richard W. Gilles.
Mailing Address: 24798 Atlas Ave., 54666. Tel: 608-378-4397.
Office: 203 W. Monroe St., Tomah, 54660. Tel: 608-372-4516.

WAUMANDEE, BUFFALO CO., ST. BONIFACE (1867) [CEM 2], Served from Holy Family, Arcadia. Rev. Brian J. Jazdzewski.
Res.: 52026 Cty. Rd. U, 54622-0962. Tel: 608-626-2621.
School—Tel: 608-626-2611. Students 39.

WAUSAU, MARATHON CO.
1—ST. ANNE (1949) [JC] Rev. Steven J. Brice; Deacon Robert G. Anderson.
Res.: 700 W. Bridge St., 54401. Tel: 715-849-3930; Fax: 715-849-4679. Email: frsteve@stanneswausau.org. Web: www.stanneswausau.org.
See Newman Catholic Schools, Wausau under Unified Catholic School Systems located in the Institution section.
Catechesis/Religious Program—Tel: 715-849-3520. Barbara Ceranski, D.R.E. Students 755.
2—CHURCH OF THE RESURRECTION (1998) [JC] Revs. William N. Grevatch; John Robert Alphonse; Deacon Peter Burek.
Mailing Address: 621 2nd St., 54403. Tel: 715-845-6715; 715-845-5379; Fax: 715-845-4120.
3—HOLY NAME OF JESUS (1946) Rev. David G. Rybicki.
Res.: 1104 S. 9th Ave., 54401. Tel: 715-842-4543; Fax: 715-845-5059. Email: hnoffice@charter.net.
See Newman Catholic Schools, Wausau under Unified Catholic School Systems located in the Institution section.
4—ST. JAMES THE GREATER, Closed. For inquiries for Parish Records contact Resurrection of Our Lord Jesus Christ, Wausau.
5—ST. MARY (IMMACULATE CONCEPTION), Closed. For inquiries for Parish Records contact Resurrection of Our Lord Jesus Christ, Wausau.
6—ST. MATTHEW (1958) Rev. Robert C. Thorn.
Res.: 229 S. 28th Ave., 54401. Tel: 715-842-3148; Fax: 715-842-3209.
Catechesis/Religious Program—Sandy Grabko, D.R.E. Students 110.
St. Matthew Parish Center—221 S. 28th Ave., 54401. Tel: 715-842-3148.
7—ST. MICHAEL (1887) [CEM] Revs. William N. Grevatch; John Robert Alphonse.
611 Stark St., 54403-3577.
Res.: Tel: 715-842-4283; 715-842-2344; Fax: 715-849-2509.
See Newman Catholic Schools, Wausau under Unified Catholic School Systems located in the Institution section.
Convent—Tel: 715-845-6885; Fax: 715-849-2509.

WAUZEKA, CRAWFORD CO., SACRED HEART (1881) [CEM] Attended by St. Wenceslaus, Eastman. Very Rev. Thomas M. Huff.
Mailing Address: 711 E. Main St., P.O. Box 237, 53826.

WEST SALEM, LA CROSSE CO., ST. LEO THE GREAT (1957), Also serves St. Mary, Bangor. Rev. Robert S. Hegenbarth.
Res.: 210 W. Hamlin St., 54669. Tel: 608-786-0610.

WESTON, MARATHON CO., ST. AGNES (1910) [CEM], Served from St. Florian, Hatley. Rev. Alan T. Burkhardt.
Office: 6101 Zinser St., Schofield, 54476. Tel: 715-359-5675; Fax: 715-359-4392.
Catechesis/Religious Program—Students 215.

WHITEHALL, TREMPEALEAU CO., ST. JOHN THE APOSTLE (1948), Served from SS. Peter & Paul, Independence. Very Rev. Woodrow H. Pace.
Office: 35900 Lee St., 54773. Tel: 715-538-4607; Fax: 715-538-2224.

WILLARD, CLARK CO., HOLY FAMILY (1912) [CEM] Attended by St. Mary Help of Christians, Greenwood. Rev. A. Joseph Follmar.
Res.: 123 N. Main St., Greenwood, 54437. Tel: 715-267-6905.

WILSON, EAU CLAIRE CO., ST. PETER, Closed. For inquiries for parish records contact Sacred Heart-St. Joseph, Boyd.

WILTON, MONROE CO., ST. JOHN THE BAPTIST (1875) [CEM] Attended by St. Joseph, Kendall. Rev. Richard C. Dickman.
Res.: Box 155, Kendall, 54638. Tel: 608-463-7120.
Catechesis/Religious Program—Tel: 608-463-7649. Mary Skolos, D.R.E. Students 50.

WISCONSIN RAPIDS, WOOD CO.
1—ST. LAWRENCE, [JC], Also serves St. Philip, Rudolph. Rev. Timothy J. Welles; Deacon James L. Landry.
Res.: 530 10th Ave. N., 54495. Tel: 715-421-5777; 715-424-2651; Fax: 715-421-2478.
See Wisconsin Rapids Area Catholic Schools, Wisconsin Rapids under Unified Catholic School Systems located in the Institution section.
2—OUR LADY, QUEEN OF HEAVEN (1947) [JC] Revs. Sahayanathan Nathan; Paul Hoffman.
Res.: 750 10th Ave. S., 54495. Tel: 715-423-1251; Fax: 715-423-9407. Email: ourladyqueenofheaven@hotmail.com. Web: www.our-lady.org.
See Assumption Catholic Schools, Wisconsin Rapids under Unified Catholic School Systems located in the Institution section.
3—SS. PETER AND PAUL (1837) [CEM] Rev. James F. Altman.
Mailing Address: 1150 2nd St. N., 54494.
Catechesis/Religious Program—Tel: 715-423-1351. Julie Pisula, C.R.E. Students 240.
4—ST. VINCENT DE PAUL (1956) Very Rev. John W. Steiner.
Res.: 820 13 St. S., 54494-5336. Tel: 715-423-2111; Fax: 715-423-4227.
See Assumption Catholic Schools, Wisconsin Rapids under Unified Catholic School Systems located in the Institution section.
Catechesis/Religious Program—Tel: 715-423-2540; Fax: 715-423-4227. Mary Jo Sigourney, D.R.E. Students 108.

WONEWOC, JUNEAU CO., ST. JEROME, [CEM] Attended by St. Aloysius, Hillsboro. Very Rev. Donald J. Bauer.
Office:—528 N. Center St., R.R. 2, Box 87A, 53968. Tel: 608-464-7713; 608-462-5875.

WUERZBURG, MARATHON CO., ST. JOHN THE BAPTIST (1904) Closed. For inquiries for parish records contact the Diocesan Archives.

YUBA, RICHLAND CO., ST. WENCESLAUS, Closed. For inquiries for parish records contact The Diocesan Archives.

Chaplains of Public Institutions

OXFORD. *Federal Correctional Institute*, Tel: 608-584-5511. Vacant.

TOMAH. *Veterans Administration Medical Center* 54660. Tel: 608-372-3971.

WAUSAU. *Wausau Hospital Center*, 333 Pine Ridge Blvd., 54401. Tel: 715-847-2121; 715-847-2840.
Res.: 4303 Lake Shore Dr., 54401. Tel: 715-355-4499.

Special Assignment:
Very Revs.—
Gorman, Michael J., V.G., J.C.L., Vicar Gen., P.O. Box 4004, 54602-4004. Tel: 608-788-7700
Kunz, David C., Vicar for Clergy, P.O. Box 4004, 54602-4004. Tel: 608-788-7700
Malin, Delbert J., Vicar for Senior Priests (Retired), Holmen, 54636.
Revs.—
Apfelbeck, Keith B., Chap. of Hmong Catholics of the Diocese of LaCrosse
Genovesi, James
Hirsch, Joseph W., Dir., Vocations, Holy Cross Seminary House of Formation, P.O. Box 4004, 54602-4004. Tel: 608-788-7700
Powell, Leon A., Vice Chancellor, P.O. Box 4004, 54602-4004. Tel: 608-788-7700
Thorn, Robert C., Diocesan Chap. of Spanish Speaking Catholics, St. Matthew Rectory, 2700 Westwood Dr., 54403. Tel: 715-842-3148; 608-788-6594

On Duty Outside the Diocese:
Revs.—
Burrill, Jeffrey D., Dir., Apostolic Formation, (Pontifical North American College, Rome)
Fliss, Richard L. (Retired), 8531 S.W. 185th Ter., Miami, FL 33157. Tel: 305-969-9964
Heagle, John L., P.O. Box 510, Lincoln City, OR 97367. Tel: 541-764-2982

Foreign Missions:
Revs.—
Flock, Robert H., Parroquia de la Santa Cruz, Casilla 713, Santa Cruz, Bolivia. Tel: 011-591-332-6302
Kolodziejczyk, Sebastian J., Casa Hogar Juan Pablo II, Lurin 16, Peru. Tel: 011-5114-30-5646

Graduate Studies:
Rev.—
Sakowski, Derek (WH), Casa Santa Maria, Via Del'Umilta 30, Rome 00187 Italy.

Leave of Absence:
Revs.—
Apfelbeck, Kurt J.
Bauer, Scott A.
Benzmiller, James T.
Kiedinger, Daniel J.
Konopacky, Joseph R.
Neis, William P.
Olson, Randy G.
Stashek, Brian E.
Waldbilling, Brian T.
Wolf, Anthony J.

Retired:
Rev. Msgrs.—
Blecha, Charles A., 420 Heller Rd., Apt. 322, Menomonie, 54751. Tel: 715-235-1860
Malnar, Matthew G., Holy Cross Diocesan Center, P.O. Box 4004, 54602-4004.
McGarty, Bernard O., 109 S. 14th St., 54601. Tel: 608-784-4473
Very Rev.—
Malin, Delbert J., 909 Western Ave., Holmen, 54636. Tel: 608-526-4908
Revs.—
Altmann, Robert T., 10080 County Rd. F, P.O. Box 103, Blenker, 54415-0103.
Beckfelt, John W., Westwood Benedictine Health Center, 925 Kenwood Ave., Apt. 2142, Duluth, MN 55811. Tel: 218-279-7654
Berg, Donald M., Renaissance Rm. 224, 4602 Barbican Ave., Weston, 54476. Tel: 715-352-3444
Berger, Lawrence B., 518 10th Pl. N., Onalaska, 54650.
Blazewicz, William J., 2904 East Ave. S. #112, 54601. Tel: 608-787-0982
Blenker, Ambrose J., Holy Cross Diocesan Center, P.O. Box 4004, 54602-4004.
Boneck, Norman D., 113 W. Kort St., Rothschild, 54474. Tel: 715-842-7852
Cassidy, John V., 3325 Solaris Ln., 54601. Tel: 608-788-1196
Cook, Robert J., 100 N. 6th St. #406, 54601.
Donaldson, Thomas J., W7805 Co. Rd. Z, Arkansaw, 54721-9469. Tel: 715-273-4774
DuChez, Daniel B., Holy Cross Diocesan Center, P.O. Box 4004, 54602-4004.
Faber, Emmet N., 162 Cynthia Dr., Bastrop, TX 78602-9530.
Finucan, J. Thomas, 2904 East Ave. S., 54601. Tel: 608-785-3167
Fliss, Richard L., 16843 S. Octillo View Pl., Corona De Tucson, AZ 85641. Tel: 520-762-0494
Gerum, Jerome G., P.O. Box 673, Marshfield, 54449-0673. Tel: 715-387-4783
Greatorex, Robert W., St. Joseph Convent, 1300 Maria Dr., Stevens Point, 54481. Tel: 715-344-8346
Herrmann, Richard J., 309 W. Blodgett St., Marshfield, 54449. Tel: 715-305-7565
Hoerburger, Henry R., St. Joseph Parish, P.O. Box 275, Elk Mound, 54739. Tel: 715-879-5332
Jablonske, William, 15419 W. Victory Hts. Cir., Stone Lake, 54876.
Keating, Joseph R., Meadowwood Assisted Living, 2904 E. Ave. S., 54601.
Kelly, Daniel J., 1547 Raymond Dr., Naperville, IL 60563. Tel: 630-355-4696
Leszczynski, James J., 2883 City Rd. Z., Adams, 53910. Tel: 608-565-2488
Logan, James J., 706 S. Palmetto Ave., Marshfield, 54449. Tel: 715-389-1396

McInnis, Thomas J., 19660 Bluffview Pl., P.O. Box 368, Galesville, 54630-6085. Tel: 608-582-2012
Menzel, William G., 2511 8th St. S., PMB 136, Wisconsin Rapids, 54494.
Mertens, Michael G., Holy Cross Diocesan Center, P.O. Box 4004, 54602-4004. Tel: 608-788-0311
Miller, James H., 109 CTH U W., Norwalk, 54648. Tel: 608-823-7561
Mish, Roy L., 107 4th Ave. N., Apt. 2, Strum, 54770. Tel: 715-695-2748
Monti, Robert M., 3333 N.E. 34th St., Apt. 1616, Fort Lauderdale, FL 33309.
Osowski, Chester J., St. Philip Rectory, P.O. Box 165, Rudolph, 54475. Tel: 715-435-4183
Pedretti, Raymond J., W7796 County Rd. Zn, Onalaska, 54650. Tel: 608-779-0972
Pedretti, Robert F., 491 Red Tail Dr., Amherst, 54406.
Penchi, Edward J., Casilla 713, Santa Cruz, Bolivia. Tel: 011-591-343-0302
Rafacz, Joseph J., 1202 Jefferson St., 54403. Tel: 715-359-5675
Redmond, Arthur S., St. Andrew Rectory, D1868 County Rd. C, Stratford, 54484-9380. Tel: 715-384-3859
Reuter, Arnold F., Holy Cross Diocesan Center, P.O. Box 4004, 54602-4004. Tel: 608-963-5903
Rudolph, Thomas J., 10075 County Rd. BB, Marshfield, 54449-8544. Tel: 715-884-6154
Sankoorikal, Paul L., c/o Karla Hansen, 3428 S. Kinney Coulee Rd., Onalaska, 54650.
Schaefer, James F., P.O. Box 1552, 54402-1552.
Schelble, T. Michael, 902 E. Garland St., West Salem, 54669. Tel: 608-787-8283
Schulte, Lyle L., P.O. Box 287, Junction City, 54443-0287.
Smith, Eugene P., 756 Irvine St, Apt. 102, Chippewa Falls, 54729. Tel: 715-667-3038
Smith, Thomas J., 2904 East Ave. S. #227, 54601. Tel: 608-788-4555
Sonnberger, Albert W., St. John the Baptist Rectory, 4540 State Hwy. 40, Bloomer, 54724. Tel: 715-568-5429
Stanchik, Dennis P., St. Bartholomew Rectory, 2493 CTHM, Stevens Point, 54481. Tel: 715-344-3003
Thome, Edwin J., Holy Cross Diocesan Center, P.O. Box 4004, 54602-4004. Tel: 608-796-9048
Wagner, Robert J., Holy Cross Diocesan Center, P.O. Box 4004, 54602-4004. Tel: 608-797-8758
Wolf, Eugene J., Holy Cross Diocesan Center, P.O. Box 4004, 54602-4004.
Ziegelmaier, David A., N3180 Vista Ct. N., 54601.
Zimmerman, Rex A., 823 Indiana Ave., Stevens Point, 54481-2208.
Zoromski, Herbert P., 2100 Townline Rd., Apt. 226, 54403-8794. Tel: 715-454-6994

Permanent Deacons:
Abnet, Frank, St. Patrick, Onalaska
Agema, Larry, Sacred Heart, St. Patrick, Eau Claire
Allen, David, Blessed Sacrament, La Crosse
Anderson, Robert, St. Anne, Wausau
Arnold, Mark C., Asst. Dir., Office of Family Life, Diocesan Curia, La Crosse
Ashenbrenner, David, St. Joseph, Galloway, St. Ladislaus, Bevent
Austin, Jeffrey, Christ the King, Spencer; St. John the Baptist, Marshfield
Borski, Donald, St. Stanislaus, Stevens Point
Brunner, Norbert, St. Vincent de Paul, Wisconsin Rapids
Burek, Peter, Church of the Resurrection, Wausau, WI
Chittendon, Robert, St. Olaf, Eau Claire
Delgado, Juan, Mauston
Draeger, Raymond, Corpus Christi, Bakerville; Sacred Heart, Marshfield
Gannon, Daniel, Nativity of the Blessed Virgin Mary, Big River
Hansen, Robert, N5904 Albany N., Mondovi, 54755.
Heinzl, Glen, St. Francis of Assisi, Necedah
Hensen, Robert, (Retired)
Hurrish, Florian, (Retired), Mesa, AZ
Hutzler, Jason, St. James the Less, La Crosse
Jansing, Richard, 5625 Sandpiper Dr., Stevens Point, 54481.
Jirous, Thomas, St. James, Amherst, St. Mary of Mt. Carmel, Fancher
Jolliffe, Garry, Chandler, AZ
Kennedy, David, St. Joseph, Adams
Kinnick, Thomas, St. Charles Borromeo, Chippewa Falls; St. Peter, Tilden
Knauf, LeRoy, Holy Family, Poniatowski
Kostner, Richard, St. Paul, Bloomer, St. Jude, New Auburn
Koza, J. Michael, La Crescent, MN
Landry, James, St. Lawrence, Wisconsin Rapids
Limzmeier, Vernon, St. Bronislava, Plover
Ludick, Matthew, St. Elizabeth Ann Seton, Holmen
Maciejewski, James, Sacred Heart, Polonia; St. Adalbert, Rosholt
McKeough, Patrick, St. Mark, Rothschild
Nusse, John, St. Aloysius, Hillsboro; St. Jerome, Wonewoc
Quayhackx, Mark, St. Francis of Assisi, Ellsworth
Ray, Kevin, Roncalli Newman Parish, Hillsboro
Richards, Joseph, St. Joseph the Workman Cathedral, La Crosse
Rider, Daniel, St. Charles Borromeo, Chippewa Falls; St. Peter, Tilden
Rivers, Dennis, Holy Cross, Cornell
Rozumalski, Richard, St. Stephen, Stevens Point; St. Bartholomew, Mill Creek
Rynda, Gerald, St. Joseph, Prescott
Sage, Richard, Exec. Dir., Catholic Charities of The Diocese of La Crosse
Schaller, Arthur, St. Maximilian Kolbe, Southeastern Portage County.
Schaper, Edward, Black River Falls, WI
Schmirler, Samuel, Sacred Heart, Cashton; Nativity of the BVM, St. Mary's Ridge; St. Augustine, Norwalk; St. John the Baptist, Summit Ridge
Trzinski, James, St. Maximilian Kolbe, Southeastern Portage County
Walker, Hugh, (Retired)
Weingart, James, St. Mary's Assumption, Durand; Holy Rosary, Lima; Sacred Heart, Mondovi
Wendt, Edward, 29445 Town Hall Rd., Muscoda, 53573.
Willkom, Ned, St. Rose of Lima, Cadott; St. Anthony de Padua, Drywood
Zietlow, Richard, St. Bronislava, Plover

INSTITUTIONS LOCATED IN THE DIOCESE

[A] SEMINARIES, DIOCESAN

LA CROSSE. *Holy Cross Seminary House of Formation*, 3710 East Ave. S., P.O. Box 4004, 54602-4004. Tel: 608-788-9095; Fax: 608-788-8413. Rev. Joseph W. Hirsch, Dir. Students 5.

[B] COLLEGES AND UNIVERSITIES

LA CROSSE. *Viterbo University*, 900 Viterbo Dr., 54601-8804. Tel: 608-796-3000; Fax: 608-796-3050. Email: admission@viterbo.edu. Web: www.viterbo.edu. Dr. Richard Artman, Pres.; Barbara Gayle, Vice Pres. Academic Affairs; Diane Brimmer, Vice Pres. Student Devel.; Todd M. Ericson, C.P.A., Vice Pres. Finance; Patrick G. Kerrigan, Vice Pres. Communications & Mktg.; Amy Gleason, Registrar; Rob Forget, Vice Pres., Admission; Gary Klein, Vice Pres. Institutional Advancement; Gretol Stock-Kupperman, Librarian. Founded in 1890 by the Franciscan Sisters of Perpetual Adoration, Viterbo Univ. is a Catholic, Franciscan Univ. Comprised of Five Undergraduate Schools, A Graduate School, and a Center for Adult Learning. Priests 3; Sisters 4; Lay Teachers 145; Students 3,000.

[C] UNIFIED CATHOLIC SCHOOL SYSTEMS

LA CROSSE. *Aquinas Catholic Schools, Inc.*, 521 S. 13th St., 54601. Tel: 608-784-8585; Fax: 608-784-9988. Web: www.aquinascatholicschools.org. Kurt Nelson, Pres.

Aquinas Middle School (1999) 315 S. 11th St., 54601. Tel: 608-784-0156; Fax: 608-784-0229. Web: www.aquinascatholicschools.org/aquinasms/. Mrs. Patricia A. Gallagher-Kosmatka, Prin. Lay Teachers 16; Students 158.

Aquinas High School, 315 S. 11th St., 54601. Tel: 608-784-0287; Fax: 608-782-8851. Web: www.aquinascatholicschools.org/aquinashs/. Ted Knutson, Prin. Priests 1; Religious 1; Lay Teachers 29; Students 345.

Blessed Sacrament School (Grades 3-6), 2404 King St., 54601. Tel: 608-782-5564; Fax: 608-782-7765. Email: kayberra@pvt.k12.wi.us. Web: www.aquinascatholicschools.org/blessedsacrament/. Kay Berra, Prin. Lay Teachers 18; Students 167.

Mary, Mother of the Church Early Childhood Center (Grades PreK-K), 2000 Weston St., 54601. Tel: 608-788-5225; Fax: 608-788-5230. Web: www.aquinasschools.org/ecc/. Val Breidel, Dir. Students 99.

St. Joseph Cathedral School (Grades PreK-2), 1319 Ferry St., 54601. Tel: 608-782-5998; Fax: 608-784-9933. Web: www.aquinascatholicschools.org/cathedral/. John Stellflue, Prin. Lay Teachers 14; Students 130.

St. Patrick School (Grades PreK-6), 127 11th Ave. N., Onalaska, 54650. Tel: 608-783-5483; Fax: 608-783-5483. Web: www.aquinasschools.org/stpats/. Greg Wesely, Prin. Lay Teachers 19; Students 195.

CHIPPEWA FALLS. *McDonell Area Catholic Schools* Central Office, 1316 Bel Air Blvd., 54729. Tel: 715-723-0538; Fax: 715-723-1501. Web: www.macs.k12.wi.us. Bro. Roger Betzold, Pres.

Holy Ghost Elementary School (Grades 4-6), 436 S. Main St., 54729. Tel: 715-723-6478; Fax: 715-723-8990. Mary Selz, Prin. Lay Teachers 8; Students 96.

McDonell Central Catholic High School, 1316 Bel Air Blvd., 54729. Tel: 715-723-9126; Fax: 715-723-1501. Bro. Roger Betzold, Prin.; Rev. Justin Kizewski, Chap. & Instructor. Priests 1; Christian Brothers 1; Lay Teachers 18; Students 175.

Notre Dame Middle School (Grades 7-8), 1316 Bel Air Blvd., 54729. Tel: 715-723-4777; Fax: 715-723-3353. Bro. Roger Betzold, Prin. Lay Teachers 2; Students 50.

St. Charles Primary School (Grades PreK-3), 429 W. Spruce St., 54729. Tel: 715-723-5827; Fax: 715-723-2109. Mary Selz, Prin. Lay Teachers 12; Students 112.

EAU CLAIRE. *Catholic Area Schools of the Eau Claire Deanery (C.A.S.E.)* Central Office:, 448 N. Dewey St., 54703. Tel: 715-830-2273; Fax: 715-835-4658. Email: chofacker@case.kiz.wi.us. Web: www.case.kiz.wi.us. Cynthia Hofacker, Pres.

Genesis Child Development Center, 418 N. Dewey St., 54701. Tel: 715-830-2275. Gayle Flaig, Dir.

Immaculate Conception School (Grades K-6), 1703 Sherwin Ave., 54701. Tel: 715-830-5816; Fax: 715-835-9459. Sr. Dorothy Brenner, F.S.P.A., Prin. Lay Teachers 18; Students 270.

Regis Child Devel. Center, 2100 Fenwick Ave., 54701. Tel: 715-830-2274; Fax: 715-830-2270. Gayle Flaig, Dir.

Regis Middle School (Grades 7-8), 2100 Fenwick Ave., 54701. Tel: 715-830-1327; Fax: 715-835-4658. Renee Cassidy, Prin.; Rev. William A. Dhein, Chap. Lay Teachers 10; Students 125.

Regis High School, 2100 Fenwick Ave., 54701. Tel: 715-830-2271; Fax: 715-830-5461. Thomas Saporito, Prin.; Rev. William A. Dhein, Chap. Priests 1; Lay Teachers 17; Students 209.

St. James School (Grades K-6), 2502 Eleventh St., 54703. Tel: 715-830-2277; Fax: 715-830-9861. Lay Teachers 9; Students 116.

St. Mary School (Grades K-5), 1828 Lynn Ave., Altoona, 54720. Tel: 715-830-2278; Fax: 715-830-9573. Lay Teachers 9; Students 73.

St. Olaf School (Grades K-6), 2407 North Ln., 54703. Tel: 715-830-2279; Fax: 715-832-0742. Faculty 10; Students 123.

MARSHFIELD. *Columbus Catholic Schools (MACS)*, 710 S. Columbus Ave., 54449. Tel: 715-387-1177; Fax: 715-384-4535. Email: catalanog@mfldacs.net. Mr. David Eaton, Pres.

Columbus High School, 710 S. Columbus Ave., 54449-3413. Tel: 715-387-1177; Fax: 715-384-4535. Email: catalanog@mfldacs.net. Web: www.columbus.marshfield.wi.us. Barbara Billings, Prin.; Rev. Victor C. Feltes, Chap. Priests 1; Lay Teachers 27; Students 150.

Columbus Catholic Middle School, 710 S. Columbus Ave., 54449. Tel: 715-384-7184; Fax: 715-384-4535. Email: hfms@wctc.net. Web: www.columbus.marshfield.wi.us/hfms. Steven Van Wyhe, Prin.; Rev. Victor C. Feltes, Chap. Priests 1; Lay Teachers 8; Students 110.

Our Lady of Peace School (Grades 4-6), 1300 W. Fifth St., 54449. Tel: 715-384-5474; Fax: 715-387-8697. Sr. Mary Ann Wutkowski, S.S.N.D., Prin. Students 153.

St. John the Baptist School (Grades PreK-3), 307 Walnut Ave., 54449. Tel: 715-384-4989; Fax: 715-384-5131. Sr. Mary Ann Wutkowski, S.S.N.D., Prin. Students 115.

STEVENS POINT. *Stevens Point Area Catholic Schools* Central Office:, 1004 First St., 54481. Tel: 715-341-2445; Fax: 715-342-2001. Email: jdyer@spacs.k12.wi.us. Web: www.spacs.k12.wi.us. Mr. James Dyer, Pres.

St. Bronislava School (Grades PreK-5), 3301 Willow Dr., Plover, 54467. Tel: 715-342-2015; Fax: 715-342-2016. Mr. James Dyer, Prin. Lay Teachers 7; Students 127.

Pacelli High School, 1301 Maria Dr., 54481. Tel: 715-341-2442; Fax: 715-341-6799. Mr. Jeff Brengman, Prin.; Rev. Robert M. Letona, Chap. & Instructor. Priests 1; Sisters 2; Lay Teachers 25; Students 241.

St. Joseph School Early Childhood Center, 1901 Lincoln Ave., 54481. Tel: 715-341-2878; Fax: 715-342-2013. Lori Shafranski, Dir. Lay Teachers 1; Students 89.

St. Peter Middle School (Grades 6-8), 708 First St., 54481. Tel: 715-344-1890; Fax: 715-342-2005. Ellen Lopas, Prin.; Rev. Robert M. Letona, Chap. Lay Teachers 15; Students 168.

St. Stanislaus School (Grades K-2), 2150 High St., 54481. Tel: 715-344-3086; Fax: 715-342-2014. Mr. Gregg Hansel, Prin. Lay Teachers 10; Students 115.

St. Stephen School (Grades 3-5), 1335 Clark St., 54481. Tel: 715-344-3751; Fax: 715-342-2013. Mr. Gregg Hansel, Prin. Lay Teachers 9; Students 152.

WAUSAU. *Newman Catholic Schools*, 619 Stark St., 54403. Tel: 715-845-5735; Fax: 715-848-3582. Web: www.newmancatholicschools.com. Janet M. Klosinski, Pres. Central Office:

Newman Catholic High School, 1130 W. Bridge St., 54401. Tel: 715-845-8274; Fax: 715-842-1302. Lawrence Theiss, Prin.; Rev. Gregory A. Michaud, Chap. Priests 1; Lay Teachers 20; Students 188.

Newman Catholic Elementary School at St. Anne Parish (Grades PreK-5), 604 N. 6th Ave., 54401. Tel: 715-845-5754; Fax: 715-842-4021. Emily Miller, Prin. Sisters 1; Lay Teachers 16; Students 239.

Newman Catholic Elementary School at St. Mark Parish, 602 Military Rd., Rothschild, 54474. Tel: 715-359-9662; Fax: 715-355-8904. Jeanne Lang, Prin. Sisters 1; Lay Teachers 19; Students 118.

Newman Catholic Middle School at St. Matthew Parish, 225 S. 28th Ave., 54401. Tel: 715-842-4857; Fax: 715-845-2937. Tina Meyer, Prin.; Rev. Robert C. Thorn, Chap. Lay Teachers 15; Students 149.

Newman Catholic Elementary School at St. Michael Parish (Grades PreK-5), 615 Stark St., 54403. Tel: 715-848-0206; Fax: 715-845-6852. Jeanne Lang, Prin. Felician Sisters 1; Lay Teachers 8; Students 85.

WISCONSIN RAPIDS. *Assumption Catholic Schools, Inc.* Central Office, 1120 Lincoln Ave., Ste. B, 54494. Tel: 715-422-0900; Fax: 715-422-0903. Email: colson@wracs.org. Web: wracs.org. Carol Olson, Pres.

Assumption Middle School, 440 Mead, 54494. Tel: 715-422-0950; Fax: 715-422-0955. Joan Bond, Prin.; Revs. James T. Altman, Chap.; Paul Hoffman, Chap. Students 103.

Assumption High School, 445 Chestnut St., 54494. Tel: 715-422-0910; Fax: 715-422-0912. Email: jbond@wracs.org. Joan Bond, Prin.; Revs. James T. Altman, Chap.; Paul Hoffman, Chap. Priests 1; Lay Teachers 21; Students 186.

Our Lady Queen of Heaven School, 750 Tenth Ave. S., 54495. Tel: 715-422-0980; Fax: 715-424-2972. Email: pfochs@wracs.org. Pam Fochs, Prin. Lay Teachers 9; Students 94.

St. Lawrence Early Childhood Center, 551 Tenth Ave. N., 54495. Tel: 715-422-0990; Fax: 715-422-0993. Lay Teachers 5; Students 87.

St. Vincent de Paul School, 831 12th St. S., 54494. Tel: 715-422-0960; Fax: 715-422-0963. Brenda Walczak, Prin. Lay Teachers 16; Students 142.

[D] GENERAL HOSPITALS

LA CROSSE. *Mayo Clinic Health System - Franciscan Healthcare, La Crosse Campus Medical Center*, 700 West Ave. S., 54601-4796. Tel: 608-785-0940; Fax: 608-791-9429. Web: www.mayohealthsystem.org. Timothy Johnson, M.D., Pres. & CEO; Rev. Todd A. Mlsna, Chap. Franciscan Sisters of Perpetual Adoration and Mayo Foundation. Sisters 1; Total Staff 1,568; Bed Capacity 170; Patients Assisted Annually 29,885.

CHIPPEWA FALLS. *St. Joseph's Hospital* (1888) 2661 County Hwy. I, 54729. Tel: 715-717-7200; Fax: 715-717-7204. Web: www.stjoeschipfalls.com. Joan M. Coffman, Pres. & CEO; Revs. Frank Corradi, Mission Educator, Pastoral Care Dir.; William Jablonske (Retired). Hospital Sisters of the Third Order of St. Francis., Hospital Sisters Health System. Total Staff 590; Bed Capacity 193; Patients Assisted Annually 58,669.

EAU CLAIRE. *Sacred Heart Hospital*, 900 W. Clairemont Ave., 54701-6122. Tel: 715-717-4131; Fax: 715-717-6076. Web: www.sacredhearthospital-ec.org. Rev. James Arthur, Chap. Hospital Sisters of the Third Order of St. Francis 3; Bed Capacity 344; Patients Assisted Annually 117,700.

MARSHFIELD. *Saint Joseph's Hospital of Marshfield, Inc.*, 611 St. Joseph Ave., 54449. Tel: 715-387-1713; Fax: 715-387-8601. Web: www.ministryhealth.org. Brian Kief, Pres. & CEO; Michael Kryda. Corporate Sponsor: Ministry HealthCare, Inc. (Milwaukee, WI); Sponsored by the Sisters of the Sorrowful Mother., Training School for Nurses (Affiliated with U.W.-Eau Claire).

Spiritual Services Dept. Tel: 715-387-7753. Michael Adamson, Dir., Spiritual Svcs.; Rita Austin, Pastoral Care Staff; Robert Cassidy, Pastoral Care Staff; Rev. Linden Nelson, Coord., Spiritual Svcs.; Mary Jane Lipinski, Pastoral Care Staff; Sr. Jeanine Retzer, S.S.M., Pastoral Care Staff; Doug Rogers, Protestant Chap.; Jeff Siegel, Pastoral Care Staff; Randy Van DeLoo, Protestant Chap. Sisters of the Sorrowful Mother 2; Bed Capacity 504; Patients Assisted Annually 104,100; Total Staff 1,848.

SPARTA. **Mayo Clinic Health System - Franciscan Healthcare, Sparta Campus Hospital*, 310 W. Main St., 54656-2142. Tel: 608-269-2132; Fax: 608-269-4562. Web: www.mayohealthsystem.org. 700 West Ave., S., 54601. Robert M. Tracey, Admin.; Curtis Miller, Chap. Pastoral Care. Franciscan Sisters of Perpetual Adoration and Mayo Foundation. Total Staff 166; Bed Capacity 25; Patient Days 830.

STANLEY. **Our Lady of Victory Hospital*, 1120 Pine St., 54768-0220. Tel: 715-644-5571; Fax: 715-644-6221. Email: eichmanc@olvh.org. Web: www.ministryhealth.org. Mrs. Cynthia Eichman, Pres.; Sr. Pat Belongia, Dir. Spiritual Svcs. Corporate Sponsor: Ministry Healthcare, Inc. (Milwaukee, WI); Sponsored by Sisters of the Sorrowful Mother. Hospital 24; Total Staff 135; Patients Assisted Annually 47,000.

STEVENS POINT. *St. Michael's Hospital of Stevens Point, Inc.*, 900 Illinois Ave., 54481. Tel: 715-346-5000; Fax: 715-346-5088. Email: jeff.martin@ministryhealth.org. Web: www.ministryhealth.org. Jeffrey L. Martin, FACHE, Pres. & CEO; Rev. Dennis J. Lynch, Chap.; Mrs. Janet Jacoby, Spiritual Svcs. & Chap.; Martin Lieber, Spiritual Svcs. & Chap. Corporate Sponsor: Ministry Health Care, Inc. (Milwaukee, WI); Sponsored by Sisters of the Sorrowful Mother. Licensed Bed Capacity 181; Patients Assisted Annually 183,564; Total Staff 1,219.

Ministry Medical Group, Inc., 824 Illinois Ave., 54481. Tel: 715-342-7500; Fax: 715-346-5088. Email: chuck.fehring@ministryhealth.org. Web: www.ministryhealth.org. Mark L. Fenlon, M.D., Regl. Vice Pres.; Anne Rifleman, Regl. Admin. Total Staff 400; Patients Assisted Annually 250,000.

WESTON. *Saint Clare's Hospital of Weston, Inc.* (2002) 3400 Ministry Pkwy., 54476. Tel: 715-393-2501; Fax: 715-359-1087. Web: www.ministryhealth.org. Mary Krueger, Pres. (Ministry Health Care)Tel: 715-393-2500. Corporate Sponsor: Ministry Health Care, Inc. (Milwaukee, WI). Sponsored by Sisters of the Sorrowful Mother.

[E] REHABILITATION FACILITIES

CHIPPEWA FALLS. *L.E. Phillips Libertas Treatment Center* (1977) 2661 County Hwy. I, 54729. Tel: 715-723-5585; 800-680-4578; Fax: 715-726-3504. Email: ddachel@sjcf.hshs.org. Web: www.stjoeschipfalls.com. David B. Fish, Exec. Vice Pres.; Dr. Shawna T. Kovach, Prog. Coord. Hospital Sisters Health System, Hospital Sisters of the Third Order of St. Francis. Bed Capacity 48; Patients Assisted Annually 1,200; Total Staff 60.

[F] HOMES FOR AGED

LA CROSSE. *Bethany St. Joseph Care Center*, 2501 Shelby Rd., 54601. Tel: 608-788-5700. Eric Jacobson, Admin. Bed Capacity 172; Patients Assisted Annually 350.

St. Joseph's Rehabilitation Center, 2902 East Ave. S., 54601. Tel: 608-788-9870; Fax: 608-787-8889. Daniel Meyer, Admin. Operated by Catholic Residential Services, Inc. Units 80; Patients Assisted Annually 186; Total Staff 177.

ARCADIA. *Mayo Clinic Health System - Franciscan Healthcare, Arcadia Campus Nursing Home*, 464 S. St. Joseph Ave., 54612. Tel: 608-323-3341; Fax: 608-323-3694. 700 West Ave., S., 54601. Darlene Goehner, Admin.; Sisters Rose Grabowski, S.S.J.-T.O.S.F., Chap.; Arlene Melder, F.S.P.A., Chap. Franciscan Sisters of Perpetual Adoration and Mayo Foundation. Bed Capacity 75; Total Staff 44; Patient Days 25,044.

EAU CLAIRE. *St. Francis Apartments* (1986) 851 University Dr., 54701. Tel: 715-834-1388; Fax: 715-717-1602. Email: cwerner@shec.hshs.org. Cathy Werner, Managing Agent.

Hospital Sisters Health Care-West, Inc. Units 60; Total in Residence 75.

WAUSAU. *Marywood Convalescent Center*, 1821 N. 4th St., 54401. Tel: 715-675-9451; Fax: 715-675-4051. Jerry Frese, Admin. Operated by Catholic Residential Services, Inc. Units 90; Patients Assisted Annually 257; Total Staff 172.

[G] RETREAT HOUSES

LA CROSSE. *Franciscan Spirituality Center*, 920 Market St., 54601-8809. Tel: 608-791-5295; Fax: 608-782-6301. Email: fscenter@fspa.org. Web: www.franciscanspiritualitycenter.org. Vince Hatt, Dir. Sisters of the Third Order of St. Francis of Perpetual Adoration.

MARATHON CITY. *St. Anthony Spirituality Center*, 300 E. 4th St., 54448-9602. Tel: 715-443-2236; Fax: 715-443-2235. Email: info@sarcenter.com. Web: www.sarcenter.com. Rev. Dan Crosby, O.F.M.Cap., Dir. The Province of St. Joseph of the Capuchin Order, Inc. Priests 2.

[H] MONASTERIES AND RESIDENCES OF PRIESTS AND BROTHERS

LA CROSSE. *Holy Cross (Seminary) Diocesan Center*, 3710 East Ave. S., P.O. Box 4004, 54602-4004. Tel: 608-788-7700; Fax: 608-788-8413. Deacon Joseph Richards, Dir. In Res. Very Rev. Michael J. Gorman, V.G., J.C.L.; Revs. Robert T. Altmann (Retired); Joseph W. Hirsch. Tel: 608-343-0627; Rev. Msgr. Robert P. Hundt, J.C.L.; Revs. Michael G. Mertens (Retired). Tel: 608-788-0311; Leon A. Powell. Tel: 608-788-4625; Arnold F. Reuter (Retired). Tel: 608-788-0717; Thomas J. Smith (Retired). Tel: 608-788-4555; Edwin J. Thome (Retired); Robert J. Wagner (Retired).

SPRING VALLEY. *Brothers of St. Pius X*, S. 105 Sabin, P.O. Box 284, 54767. Tel: 715-778-4999. Bro. Charles Bisenius, C.S.P.X. Dir.

WAUSAU. *St. Mary's Roman Catholic Oratory*, 26384 County Hwy. U, Cashton, 54646. Tel: 715-842-9995; Fax: 715-842-9995. Email: stmarysoratory@aol.com. Web: www.institute-christ-king.org. Institute of Christ the King-Sovereign Priest.

[I] CONVENTS AND RESIDENCES FOR SISTERS

LA CROSSE. *St. Rose Convent*, 912 Market St., 54601-4782. Tel: 608-782-5610; Fax: 608-782-6301. Email: fspa@fspa.org. Web: www.fspa.org. Sr. Linda Mershon, F.S.P.A., Pres. Motherhouse and Novitiate of the Congregation of the Franciscan Sisters of Perpetual Adoration. In Community: Professed 302; In Motherhouse 79.

Villa St. Joseph, W2658 State Rd. 33, 54601-2625. Tel: 608-788-5100; Fax: 608-788-7360. Email: jmtreba@villastj.org. Web: www.fspa.org. Sr. Jean Michael Treba, F.S.P.A., Admin. Franciscan Sisters of Perpetual Adoration., A Retirement home for aged and convalescent Franciscan Sisters of Perpetual Adoration. Sisters 10; Lay Staff 130; Under Care 103.

CUSTER. *St. Clare Convent* (1874) 7381 Church St., Polonia, 54423. Tel: 715-592-4213; Fax: 715-592-4099. Felician Sisters 3.

STEVENS POINT. *St. Joseph Motherhouse* (1901) 1300 Maria Dr., 54481. Tel: 715-344-2830; Fax: 715-344-2380. Email: jsmolinski@ssj-tosf.org. Rev. Robert W. Greatorex, Chap. (Retired). Tel: 715-344-8346; Sr. Janet Smolinski, S.S.J.-T.O.S.F., Coord. Residence of the Sisters of St. Joseph of the Third Order of St. Francis. Sisters 54.

[J] SOCIAL SERVICE AGENCIES

LA CROSSE. *Catholic Charities of the Diocese of La Crosse, Inc.* (1932) 3710 East Ave. S., P.O. Box 266, 54602-0266. Tel: 608-782-0710; Fax: 608-782-0702. Email: info@catholiccharitieslax.org. Web: www.cclse.org. Deacon Richard Sage, Exec. Dir. Fin. Counseling, Pregnancy & Parenting Svcs., Adoption Placement, Emergency Svcs., Immigration Svcs, In Home Support Svcs. Total Staff 74.

Catholic Residential Services, Inc., 3710 East Ave., S., P.O. Box 2394, 54602-2394. Tel: 608-784-5323; Fax: 608-784-7522. Mr. Jim Gajewski, Exec. Dir.; John Prince, Bd. Pres.; Glenn Horessi, Bd. Vice Pres.; Barbara Smith, Bd. Sec. Total Staff 300; Patients Assisted Annually 420.

WAUSAU. *Northland House*, 102 McClellan St., 54402-0231. Tel: 715-845-4898; Fax: 715-848-0498. Email: nhgh@dwave.net. Web: www.crsinc.org/northland. Janet R. Nissen, Admin. Operated by Catholic Residential Services, Inc., Diocese of La Crosse.; Residential Care of Children.

[K] NEWMAN CAMPUS MINISTRY

LA CROSSE. *Roncalli Newman Parish* 1732 State St., 54601. Tel: 608-784-4994; Fax: 608-784-0230. Email: roncallinewman@roncallinewmancenter.org. Web: www.roncallinewman.com. Rev. Alan P. Wierzba, Pastor; Jon Stuttgen, Campus Min. Serving Univ. of Wisconsin-La Crosse and Western Technical College.

EAU CLAIRE. *Newman Parish* 110 Garfield Ave., 54701-4042. Tel: 715-834-3399. Email: georgeszews@charterinternet.com. Web: www.newmanec.com. Rev. George R. Szews, Pastor. Serving Univ. of Wisconsin-Eau Claire and Chippewa Valley Technical College.

MENOMONIE. *Newman Center of Stout* 108 3rd Ave. W., 54751. Tel: 715-235-4258; Fax: 715-235-4258. Very Rev. Thomas J. Krieg, Chap.; Sr. Kathy Wiesneski, S.C.S.C., M.A., Dir. Campus Min.

STEVENS POINT. *Newman University Parish* 2108 Fourth Ave., 54481. Tel: 715-345-6500. Email: newmanuwsp@aol.com. Web:

www.newmanuwsp.org. Very Rev. Thomas F. Lindner, Pastor. Serving Univ. of Wisconsin-Stevens Point.

[L] FOUNDATIONS, FUNDS & TRUSTS

LA CROSSE. *Aquinas High School and Aquinas Schools Foundation*, 315 S. 11th St., 54601. Tel: 608-784-0287; 608-784-0707 (Foundation); Fax: 608-782-8851.

Bishop John J. Paul Scholarship Endowment Trust, P.O. Box 4004, 54602-4004.

Bishop's Education Endowment Trust, P.O. Box 4004, 54602-4004. Tel: 608-788-7700.

Blessed Sacrament Parish Endowment Trust, 130 S. Losey Blvd., 54601. Tel: 608-782-2953; Fax: 608-785-1064. Email: blessedsacrament@centurytel.net. Web: www.blessedsacramentlacrosse.com.

Caritas Endowment Trust, 3710 East Ave. S., P.O. Box 266, 54602-0266. Tel: 608-782-0710; Fax: 608-782-0702.

Cathedral of St. Joseph the Workman Endowment Trust, 530 Main St., 54601. Tel: 608-782-0322; Fax: 608-782-8228.

Diocese of La Crosse Youth Ministry Endowment Trust, Office of Youth Ministry, P.O. Box 4004, 54602-4004.

Father Joseph Walijewski Orphanage Endowment Trust, 3710 E. Ave S., 54601. Tel: 608-788-7700; Fax: 608-788-8413. Very Rev. Roger J. Scheckel, Exec. Sec.

Holy Cross Seminary Education Fund Endowment Trust, P.O. Box 4004, 54602-4004. Tel: 608-788-7700; Fax: 608-788-8413.

Holy Trinity Catholic Church Endowment Trust, 1333 S. 13th St., 54601. Tel: 608-782-2028; Fax: 608-784-2029.

St. James Parish Endowment Trust, 1032 Caledonia St., 54603. Tel: 608-782-7557; Fax: 608-796-0086. Email: scheckel@charter.net.

La Crosse Deanery Catholic Education Endowment Trust, P.O. Box 4004, 54602-4004.

Mary, Mother of the Church Parish Endowment Trust, 2006 Weston St., 54601. Tel: 608-788-5483; Fax: 608-788-4070.

Mayo Clinic Health System - Franciscan Healthcare Foundation, Inc., 700 West Ave. S., 54601-4796. Tel: 608-784-6449; Fax: 608-791-9799. Email: grabow.peter@mayo.edu. Web: www.mayohealthsystem.org. Peter Grabow, Dir.

Roncalli Newman Parish Student Endowment Trust, 1732 State St., 54601. Tel: 608-784-4994; Fax: 608-784-0230. Email: roncallinewman@roncallinewmancenter.org. Web: www.roncallinewman.com.

ALMOND. *St. Maximilian Kolbe Church Endowment Trust*, 8611 State Hwy. 54, 54909.

ALTOONA. *St. Mary Parish Endowment Trust*, 1812 Lynn Ave., 54720. Tel: 715-855-1294; Fax: 715-855-8664. Email: stmarypar@gmail.com.

ARCADIA. *Arcadia Catholic School Endowment Trust Fund*, 341 S. Washington St., 54612. Tel: 608-323-3676; Fax: 608-323-3786. Email: acs@triwest.net. Web: www.holyfam.com.

Franciscan Skemp Foundation of Arcadia, Inc., 464 S. St. Joseph Ave., 54612. Tel: 608-323-3341; Fax: 608-323-3694. Email: feltes.darlene@mayo.edu. Web: www.mayohealthsystem.org. 700 West Ave., S., 54601. Darlene Feltes, Ex-Officio.

ATHENS. *Saint Anthony Parish Endowment Trust*, 417 Caroline St., P.O. Box 206, 54411. Tel: 715-257-7684; Fax: 715-257-7791.

AUBURNDALE. *St. Mary Education Endowment Trust*, Box 177, 54412-0177. Tel: 715-652-2806; Fax: 715-652-8020.

BIG RIVER. *The St. Mary's-Big River Endowment Trust*, W10137 570th Ave., River Falls, 54022. Tel: 715-425-5806.

BLAIR. *The St. Ansgar Catholic Church Endowment Trust*, 35900 Lee St., Whitehall, 54773. Tel: 715-538-4607; Fax: 715-538-2224.

BLOOMER. *St. Paul Catholic Parish of Bloomer Wisconsin Endowment Trust*, 1222 Main St., 54724. Tel: 715-568-3255.

CADOTT. *St. Rose of Lima Catholic Church Endowment Trust*, Box 160, 54727. Tel: 715-289-4551.

CASHTON. *Sacred Heart of Jesus Education Endowment Trust*, 26400 CTH U, 54619-8627. Tel: 608-823-7906; Fax: 608-823-7272.

CHIPPEWA FALLS. *St. Charles Future Fund Trust*, 810 Pearl St., 54729. Tel: 715-723-4088; Fax: 715-723-2195.

The Chippewa Area Catholic Schools Endowment Trust, 1316 Bel Air Blvd., 54729. Tel: 715-723-0538; Fax: 715-723-1501.

The Education/Sustaining Endowment Trust, 412 Main St., 54729. Tel: 715-723-4890; Fax: 715-723-7358.

Friends of St. Joseph's, 2661 County Hwy. I, 54729. Tel: 715-717-7392; Fax: 715-717-7258. Email: bgiles@sjcf.hshs.org. Web: www.stjoeschipfalls.com.

Notre Dame Children's Endowment Trust, 117 Allen St., 54729-2899. Tel: 715-723-7108; Fax: 715-723-7523. Email: cfnotredame@gmail.com.

Notre Dame Parish Endowment Trust, 117 Allen St., 54729-2899. Tel: 715-723-7108; Fax: 715-723-7523. Email: cfnotredame@gmail.com.

COLBY. *St. Mary's Catholic School, Colby Endowment Trust*, P.O. Box 436, 54421. Tel: 715-223-3033; Fax: 715-223-0223.

CUSTER. *Sacred Heart School, Polonia Endowment Trust*, 7379 Church St., 54423.

DURAND. *St. Mary Catholic School Endowment Trust*, 901 W. Prospect St., 54736-1049. Tel: 715-672-5617.

EAU CLAIRE. *Catholic Area Schools of Eau Claire Deanery Foundation*, 2100 Fenwick Ave., 54701.

Catholic Area Schools of the Eau Claire Deanery Endowment Fund (Case Endowment Fund), 2100 Fenwick Ave., 54701. Tel: 715-830-2273; Fax: 715-835-4658.

Friends of St. James the Greater Catholic School at Eau Claire Tuition Endowment Trust, 2502 11th St., 54703-2700. Tel: 715-835-5887; Fax: 715-835-3110. Email: stjameseac@aol.com.

Hospital Sisters of St. Francis Foundation, Inc., 900 Clairemont Ave., 54701. Friends of Sacred Heart Hospital (a division of Hospital Sisters of St. Francis Foundation, Inc.)

The St. James the Greater Catholic Church Endowment Trust, 2502 11th St., 54703-2700. Tel: 715-835-5887; Fax: 715-835-3110. Email: stjameseac@aol.com. Web: www.stjameseauclaire.catholicweb.com.

The Newman Parish - Eau Claire Endowment Trust, 110 Garfield Ave., 54701-4042. Tel: 715-834-3399. Email: georgeszews@charterinternet.com. Web: www.newmanec.com.

St. Olaf Parish Endowment Trust, 3220 Monroe St., P.O. Box 1203, 54703-1203. Tel: 715-832-2504; Fax: 715-832-0742. Email: solaf@execpc.com. Web: www.saintolafparish.com.

St. Patrick Parish of Eau Claire Endowment Trust, 322 Fulton St., 54703-5323. Tel: 715-832-0925; Fax: 715-832-0366. Email: sacrdhrt@charter.net.

Regis High School Foundation, 2100 Fenwick Ave., 54701-4498. Tel: 715-830-2271; Fax: 715-830-5461.

The Sacred Heart Parish Endowment Trust, 322 Fulton St., 54703. Tel: 715-832-0925; Fax: 715-832-0366. Email: sacrdhrt@charter.net.

ELLSWORTH. *The St. Francis Parish Endowment Trust*, 264 S. Grant, Box 839, 54011. Tel: 715-273-4774; Fax: 715-273-4066. Email: francis@warpdriveonline.com.

HATLEY. *St. Ladislaus Parish Bevent Endowment Trust*, 6455 State Rd. 153, 54440. Tel: 715-446-3060; Fax: 715-446-2668.

HOLMEN. *St. Elizabeth Ann Seton Endowment Trust*, 515 N. Main St., 54636. Tel: 608-526-4424; Fax: 608-526-3177. Email: office@seasholmen.org.

INDEPENDENCE. *The SS. Peter & Paul Parish-Independence Education Endowment Trust*, 36028 Osseo Rd., P.O. Box 430, 54747-0430. Tel: 715-985-2227; Fax: 715-985-2649.

LYNDON STATION. *Troy Quasi-Endowment Trust*, P.O. Box 303, 53944. Tel: 608-666-2421.

MARATHON CITY. *Nativity of the Blessed Virgin Mary, Marathon Endowment Trust*, 712 Market, Box 7, 54448-0007. Tel: 715-443-2045.

MARSHFIELD. *Columbus High School Foundation*, 710 S. Columbus Ave., 54449. Tel: 715-387-2444; Fax: 715-384-4535. Email: keffer.michelle@columbusdons.org. Web: www.columbuscatholicschools.org. Michelle Keffer, Devel. Coord.

Foundation of Saint Joseph's Hospital of Marshfield, Inc., 611 St. Joseph Ave., 54449. Tel: 715-389-4072; Fax: 715-389-3993. Email: ann.boson@ministryhealth.org. Web: www.ministryhealth.org.

St. John the Baptist Educational Endowment Trust, 201 W. Blodgett, 54449. Tel: 715-384-3252; Fax: 715-384-3252.

St. John the Baptist Maintenance Endowment Trust, 201 W. Blodgett, 54449. Tel: 715-384-3252; Fax: 715-384-3252.

Marshfield Area Catholic Schools Endowment Trust, 710 S. Columbus Ave., 54449.

The Our Lady of Peace Endowment Trust, 1414 W. 5th St., 54449. Tel: 715-384-9414; Fax: 715-384-6606. Email: peacerectory@charter.net. Web: www.olpmarshfield.org.

MAUSTON. *St. Patrick's Congregation Trust*, 401 Mansion St., 53948-1393. Tel: 608-847-6054; Fax: 608-847-3288. Email: stpatsparish@btsmailbox.com. Web: www.stpatrickmauston.com.

MENOMONIE. *The St. Joseph School at Menomonie Endowment Trust*, 910 Wilson Ave., 54751. Tel: 715-232-4920; Fax: 715-232-4923.

MOSINEE. *St. Paul Parish Endowment Trust*, 603 4th St., 54455. Tel: 715-693-2650; Fax: 715-692-2650.

NEILLSVILLE. *The St. Mary's Catholic Church Endowment Trust*, 1813 Black River Rd., 54456. Tel: 715-743-3840; Fax: 715-743-7963. Email: stmaryneillsville@tds.net.

ONALASKA. *Charles Simpson of St. Patrick Parish, Onalaska Endowment Trust*, 1031 Main St., 54650.

Father John Rossiter and Friends Endowment Trust of St. Patrick Parish, 1031 Main St., 54650. Tel: 608-783-5535.

PITTSVILLE. *St. Joachim's Parish Endowment Trust*, P.O. Box 69, 54466-0069. Tel: 715-884-6815.

PLOVER. *St. Bronislava Parish, Plover Endowment Trust*, 3200 Plover Rd., P.O. Box 158, 54467-0158. Tel: 715-344-4326; Fax: 715-344-6121. Web: stbrons.com.

PORT EDWARDS. *St. Alexander's Church, Port Edwards Endowment Trust*, 880 First St., 54469. Tel: 715-887-3012; Fax: 715-887-3748. Rev. R. John Swing.

PRAIRIE DU CHIEN. *The St. Gabriel's Endowment Trust*, 506 N. Beaumont Rd., P.O. Box 176, 53821-0176. Tel: 608-326-2404.

The St. John's Endowment Trust, 710 S. Wacouta St., P.O. Box 28, 53821-0028. Tel: 608-326-6511; Fax: 608-326-4876.

RICHLAND CENTER. *The Assumption of the Blessed Virgin Mary Parish Endowment Trust*, 160 W. 4th St., Box 456, 53581. Tel: 608-647-2621; Fax: 608-647-6029. Email: parishsec@mwt.net. Web: www.stmarysrc.4LPI.COM.

ROTHSCHILD. *The St. Mark Catholic Parish Endowment Trust*, 602 Military Rd., 54474-1523. Tel: 715-359-5206; Fax: 715-355-8904.

St. Therese Catholic Church Endowment Fund, 113 W. Kort St., 54474. Tel: 715-359-2421; Fax: 715-355-3088.

ST. JOSEPH RIDGE. *St. Joseph Endowment Trust*, W260 Hwy. 33, 54601. Tel: 608-788-1646.

ST. MARY'S RIDGE. *Holy Family Endowment Trust Fund*, Rectory: 26400 CTH U, Cashton, 54619-9757. Tel: 608-823-7906; Fax: 608-823-7272. Email: SMR1856@centurytel.com.

SPARTA. *Endowment Trust of the Friends and Parishioners of St. Patrick Parish*, 319 W. Main St., 54656-2143. Tel: 608-269-2655.

Franciscan Skemp Foundation of Sparta, Inc., 310 W. Main St., 54656-2142. Tel: 608-269-2132; Fax: 608-269-4562. Web: www.mayohealthsystem.org. 700 West Ave., S., 54601. Kimberly A. Hawthorne, Admin.

STEVENS POINT. *Catholic Schools Endowment Trust in Portage County, Wisconsin*, 1004 First St., 54481. Tel: 715-341-2445; Fax: 715-342-2001. Email: jdyer@spacs.k12.wi.us. Web: www.spacs.k12.wi.us.

Community Foundation of Saint Michael's Hospital of Stevens Point, Inc., 900 Illinois Ave., 54481. Tel: 715-346-5337; Fax: 715-343-3330. Email: stmichaelsfoundation@ministryhealth.org. Kristin Duckart, Dir.

St. Joseph's Congregation, Stevens Point Endowment Trust, 1709 Wyatt Ave., 54481-3699. Tel: 715-341-1617; Fax: 715-341-2623. Web: www.togetherinfaith.org.

Newman Campus Ministry Endowment Trust, 2108 Fourth Ave., 54481.

Pacelli High School Foundation, 1301 Maria Dr., 54481. Tel: 715-341-2445; Fax: 715-342-2001.

St. Stanislaus Kostka Congregation, Stevens Point Endowment Trust, 838 Fremont St., 54481. Tel: 715-344-9117; Fax: 715-344-1771. Email: ststans@charter.net.

St. Stephen Parish Endowment Trust, 1401 Clark St., 54481. Tel: 715-344-3319; Fax: 715-344-6101. Email: ststephenparish@att.net. Web: www.saintstephenparish.com.

STRATFORD. *St. Joseph Parish Endowment Trust*, Box 6, 54484. Tel: 715-687-2404; Fax: 715-687-4343.

TILDEN. *St. Peter Parish Endowment Trust*, 11358 CTH Q, 54729. Tel: 715-288-6484; Fax: 715-723-2195.

TOMAH. *The St. Mary's Catholic Church Educational Endowment Trust*, 303 W. Monroe St., 54660. Tel: 608-372-4516; Fax: 608-372-4440.

VIROQUA. *St. Mary's Parish Viroqua Endowment Trust*, 400 Congress Ave., 54665. Tel: 608-637-7711; Fax: 608-637-6914.

WAUMANDEE. *St. Boniface Parish Catholic School Endowment Trust Fund*, 52026 Cty. Rd. U, 54622-8111. Tel: 608-626-2621. Email: stbon@mwt.net. Web: www.mwt.net/~stbon.

WAUSAU. *Church of the Resurrection Parish Church Building Endowment Trust*, 621 Second St., 54403. Tel: 715-845-6715; Fax: 715-845-4120.

St. Michael Parish Endowment Trust, 611 Stark St., 54403-3577. Tel: 715-842-4283; Fax: 715-849-2509. Email: frbill@eastsideparishes.org.

**Newman Catholic Schools Endowment Trust*, 619 Stark St., 54403. Tel: 715-845-5735; Fax: 715-848-3582. Janet M. Klosinski, Pres.

WESTON. *Foundation of Saint Clare's Hospital of Weston, Inc.*, 3400 Ministry Pkwy., 54476. Tel: 715-393-2604; Fax: 715-393-2645. Web: www.ministryhealth.org. Matt Ruppert, Foundation Dir.

WHITEHALL. *St. John Parish Endowment Trust*, 35900 Lee St., 54773. Tel: 715-538-4607; Fax: 715-538-2224. Email: bettyhalama@tcc.coop.

WILLARD. *Holy Family Parish, Willard Endowment Trust* 54493. Tel: 715-267-6905.

WISCONSIN RAPIDS. *St. Lawrence Parish, Wisconsin Rapids Endowment Trust*, 530 10th Ave. N., 54495-2566. Tel: 715-421-5777.

Our Lady Queen of Heaven Parish Endowment Trust, 750 10th Ave. S., 54495. Tel: 715-423-1251; Fax: 715-423-9407. Email: olqs@solarus.net.

St. Vincent de Paul Parish, Wisconsin Rapids Endowment Trust, 820 13th St., S., 54494-5336. Tel: 715-423-2111; Fax: 715-423-4227. Email: stvin@wctc.net.

Wisconsin Rapids Area Catholic Schools Endowment Trust, 711 Hill St., 54494.

[M] ASSOCIATIONS OF THE FAITHFUL

EASTMAN. *Marian Academy of the Oblates of Holy Tradition*, P.O. Box 109, 54626. Very Rev. Msgr. John F. McCarthy, P.A., Contact Person.

Society of the Oblates of Wisdom, P.O. Box 109, 54626-0109. Tel: 608-874-4733.

TILDEN. *Institute of St. Joseph*, 31360 Cty. Hwy. MM, Boyd, 54726. Tel: 715-288-6272. Email: srpetra@centurytel.net. Revs. William P. Felix, Moderator Gen.; John Mary Gilbert, Chap., 11358 Cty. Hwy. Q, Chippewa Falls, 54729.

[N] MISCELLANEOUS LISTINGS

LA CROSSE. *St. Ambrose Financial Services, Inc.*, 3710 East Ave., S., P.O. Box 4004, 54602-004.

La Crosse Guild of the Catholic Medical Association, W5560 County Rd. MM, 54601. Tel: 608-788-5052.

The Marian Catechist Apostolate, 1032 Caledonia St., 54603. Tel: 608-782-0011; Fax: 608-796-0086. Theresa Ann Knothe, National Coord.

Mater Redemptoris House of Formation, 3730 East Ave. S., 54601. Tel: 608-788-4530; Fax: 608-788-4571.

**Mayo Clinic Health System - Franciscan Healthcare, Inc., Corporate Office*, 700 West Ave. S., 54603. Tel: 608-785-9710; Fax: 608-791-9429. Web: www.mayohealthsystem.org. Timothy Johnson, M.D., Pres. & CEO, Integrated Healthcare Delivery System. Sponsored by the Congregation of the Sisters of the Third Order of St. Francis of Perpetual Adoration (Franciscan Sisters of Perpetual Adoration) and Mayo Foundation.

**Mayo Clinic Health System - Franciscan Medical Center, Inc.*, 700 West Ave. S., 54601-4796. Tel: 608-785-0940; Fax: 608-791-9429. Timothy Johnson, M.D., Pres. & CEO; Rev. Todd A. Mlsna, Chap. Sisters 1; Total Staff 1,568; Bed Capacity 170.

Gerard Hall Tel: 608-791-3985; Fax: 608-791-7802. 8 bed home for women with AODA, MH, or Pregnancy and Parenting Issues. Total Staff 5; Patients Days 1,862.

Mens LAAR House Tel: 608-782-7700; Fax: 608-791-9431. 18 bed home for chemically dependent adults. Total Staff 4; Patient Days 2,106.

Scarseth House Tel: 608-785-1270; Fax: 608-784-7084. 8 bed home for chemically dependent male adolescents. Total Staff 4; Patient Days 1,785.

Siena Hall Tel: 608-784-6010; Fax: 608-784-7084. 20 bed home for mentally ill adults. Total Staff 11; Patient Days 5,861.

Village on Cass, 225 S. 24th St., 54601. Tel: 608-791-9487; Fax: 608-782-2779. 30 bed assisted living unit for elderly. Total Staff 7.

Village on 9th, 621 S. 9th St., 54601. Tel: 608-791-9505; Fax: 608-782-2779. 24 bed independent living unit for elderly

Villa Success, Prairie du Chien, 53821. Tel: 608-326-8424; Fax: 608-326-8638. 12 bed halfway house for AODA and AODA outpatient and Detox programs. Total Staff 7; Patient Days 2,316.

Womens LAAR House Tel: 608-791-6147; Fax: 608-791-9511. 9 bed home for chemically dependent adults. Total Staff 5; Patient Days 2,817.

Shrine of Our Lady of Guadalupe, Inc., 5250 Justin Rd., P.O. Box 1237, 54602-1237. Tel: 608-782-5440; Fax: 608-782-3104. Email: larvidson@shrineofourlady.com. Web: www.guadalupeshrine.org. Mr. Leif E. Arvidson, Exec. Dir.

We Belong To Christ Campaign, Inc., P.O. Box 4004, 54602-4004. Tel: 608-791-2685; Fax: 608-788-3854.

CHIPPEWA FALLS. *Northern Wisconsin Center for the Developmentally Disabled*, East Park Ave., 54729. Tel: 715-723-5542. State Institution for the Developmentally Disabled.

EAU CLAIRE. *Hospital Sisters Health Care-West, Inc.*, St. Francis Apartments, 851 University Dr., 54701. Tel: 715-834-1338; Fax: 715-717-1602. Email: cwerner@shec.hshs.org.

GENOA. *The Hermitage of St. Mary, Inc.* (1997) W1498 Spring Coulee Rd., 54632. Tel: 608-689-2753; Fax: 608-689-2753. Email: godshermitess@hotmail.com. Sr. Mary Dawiczyk, Pres. & Treas.

MARSHFIELD. **Ministry Home Care*, 611 St. Joseph Ave., 54449. Tel: 715-389-3802; Fax: 715-387-9950. Web: www.ministryhomecare.org.

STEVENS POINT. *Ministry Behavioral Health of St. Michael's Hospital, Inc.*, 209 Prentice St. N., 54481. Tel: 715-344-4611; Fax: 715-344-8127. Email: giffinj@smhosp.org. Web: www.ministrybehavioralhealth.org. JoAnne Griffin, Exec. Dir. Corporate Sponsor: Ministry Health Care, Inc. (Milwaukee, WI); Sponsored by Sisters of the Sorrowful Mother.

WILLARD. *The Christine Center*, W8303 Mann Rd., 54493. Tel: 715-267-7507; Fax: 715-267-7512. Email: christinecenter@ceas.cood. Web: www.christinecenter.org. Sr. Cecilia Corcoran, F.S.P.A., Pres.

RELIGIOUS INSTITUTES OF MEN REPRESENTED IN THE DIOCESE

For further details refer to the corresponding bracketed number in the Religious Institutes of Men or Women section.

[1180]—*Brothers of Saint Pius X* (La Crosse)—C.S.P.X.

[0470]—*The Capuchin Friars* (St. Joseph's Prov., Detroit)—O.F.M.Cap.

[]—*Congregation of the Blessed Sacrament*

[]—*Missionaries of St. Francis de Sales*

RELIGIOUS INSTITUTES OF WOMEN REPRESENTED IN THE DIOCESE

[1010]—*Congregation of Divine Providence* (San Antonio, TX)—C.D.P.

[0470]—*Congregation of Sisters of Charity of the Incarnate Word* (San Antonio, TX)—C.C.V.I.

[1170]—*Congregation of the Sisters of St. Felix of Cantalice, of the III Order of St. Francis* (Chicago, IL)—C.S.S.F.

[1780]—*Congregation of the Sisters of the Third Order of St. Francis of Perpetual Adoration* (La Crosse, WI)—F.S.P.A.

[1310]—*Franciscan Sisters of Little Falls, Minnesota*—O.S.F.

[1820]—*Hospital Sisters of the Third Order of St. Francis* (Springfield, IL)—O.S.F.

[]—*Presentation Sisters of the Blessed Virgin Mary* (Philippines)

[2970]—*School Sisters of Notre Dame* (Milwaukee Prov.)—S.S.N.D.

[1680]—*School Sisters of St. Francis* (Milwaukee, WI)—O.S.F.

[3590]—*Servants of Mary* (Ladysmith, WI)—O.S.M.

[1070-03]—*Sinsinawa Dominican Congregation of the Most Holy Rosary*—O.P.

[2630]—*Sisters of Mercy of the Holy Cross* (Merrill, WI)—S.C.S.C.

[]—*Sisters of St. Francis of the Martyr St. George* (Alton, IL, Prov. of St. Elizabeth)—O.S.F.

[1720]—*Sisters of St. Francis of the Third Order Regular of St. Francis of the Congregation of Our Lady of* (Rochester, MN)—O.S.F.

[3930]—*Sisters of St. Joseph - Third Order Regular* (Stevens Point, WI)—S.S.J.-T.O.S.F.

[1030]—*Sisters of the Divine Savior* (Milwaukee, WI)—S.D.S.

[4100]—*Sisters of the Sorrowful Mother* (U.S./Caribbean Prov.)—S.S.M.

[1705]—*Sisters of the Third Order of St. Francis of Assisi of Penance and Charity* (Milwaukee, WI)—O.S.F.

DIOCESAN CEMETERIES

LA CROSSE. *Catholic Cemetery*, 519 Losey Blvd. S., 54601. Tel: 608-782-0238. Jeffrey Reinhart, Supt. Gate of Heaven Cemetery; French Island Cemetery.

Woodlawn, 3636 Mormon Coulee Rd., 54601. Tel: 608-788-0980. John Reinhart, Supt.

CHIPPEWA FALLS. *Hope Cemetery and Mausoleum*, 418 N. State St., 54729. Tel: 715-723-0792. Walter Hurt, Supt.

EAU CLAIRE. *Calvary Cemetery and Mausoleum*, P.O. Box 633, 54702-0633. Tel: 715-552-8195. Peter J. Wagemen, Mgr.

MARSHFIELD. *Gate of Heaven*, 1803 S. Maple Ave., 54449. Tel: 715-384-5815. Richard DeJarlais, Pres.; Monica Herman, Sec.

STEVENS POINT. *Stevens Point Area Catholic Cemetery Association, Inc.*, P.O. Box 497, 54481. Tel: 715-341-3236. Jack Okonek, Supt.; Shirley Suplicki, Exec. Sec. & Treas.

NECROLOGY

† Dunklee, Lawrence G., (Retired)—Died Jan. 7, 2011
† Farley, Daniel H., (Retired)—Died Dec. 18, 2011
† Hogan, John P., (Retired)—Died July 19, 2011
† Kidd, Wayne R., (Retired)—Died March 16, 2011
† Wilger, Norbert J., (Retired)—Died March 2, 2011
† Wisneski, John A., (Retired)—Died July 27, 2011

An asterisk (*) denotes an organization that has established tax-exempt status directly with the IRS and is not covered by the USCCB Group Ruling.

Diocese of Lafayette

(Dioecesis Lafayettensis)

Most Reverend

MICHAEL JARRELL, D.D.

Bishop of Lafayette; ordained June 3, 1967; ordained to the episcopacy and installed as second Bishop of Houma-Thibodaux March 4, 1993; appointed sixth Bishop of Lafayette November 8, 2002; installed December 18, 2002. *Office: 1408 Carmel Dr., Lafayette, LA 70501.*

Administrative Offices: Diocesan Office Building, 1408 Carmel Dr., Lafayette, LA 70501. Tel: 337-261-5500; Fax: 337-261-5635.

Web: www.diolaf.org

Email: rstevenson@diolaf.org

ESTABLISHED JANUARY 11, 1918.

Square Miles 5,777.

Comprises the civil parishes (Counties) of Acadia, Evangeline, Iberia, Lafayette, St. Landry, St. Martin and St. Mary (west of Atchafalaya River) and Vermilion in the south central part of the State of Louisiana.

For legal titles of Diocese, parishes and diocesan institutions, consult the Chancery Office.

STATISTICAL OVERVIEW

Personnel	
Bishop	1
Priests: Diocesan Active in Diocese	111
Priests: Diocesan in Foreign Missions	1
Priests: Retired, Sick or Absent	46
Number of Diocesan Priests	158
Religious Priests in Diocese	43
Total Priests in Diocese	201
Extern Priests in Diocese	11
Ordinations:	
Diocesan Priests	4
Transitional Deacons	1
Permanent Deacons in Diocese	67
Total Brothers	13
Total Sisters	136
Parishes	
Parishes	121
With Resident Pastor:	
Resident Diocesan Priests	82
Resident Religious Priests	16
Without Resident Pastor:	
Administered by Priests	22
Administered by Professed Religious Men	1
Missions	29
Professional Ministry Personnel:	
Sisters	1
Lay Ministers	977
Welfare	
Catholic Hospitals	1
Total Assisted	94,065
Homes for the Aged	32
Total Assisted	4,117
Specialized Homes	15
Total Assisted	7,783
Special Centers for Social Services	6
Total Assisted	56,798
Educational	
Diocesan Students in Other Seminaries	29
Seminaries, Religious	1
Students Religious	17
Total Seminarians	46
High Schools, Diocesan and Parish	9
Total Students	3,496
High Schools, Private	1
Total Students	135
Elementary Schools, Diocesan and Parish	29
Total Students	10,492
Elementary Schools, Private	2
Total Students	744
Catechesis/Religious Education:	
High School Students	13,489
Elementary Students	6,352
Total Students under Catholic Instruction	34,754
Teachers in the Diocese:	
Sisters	1
Lay Teachers	977
Vital Statistics	
Receptions into the Church:	
Infant Baptism Totals	3,603
Minor Baptism Totals	138
Adult Baptism Totals	80
Received into Full Communion	212
First Communions	3,630
Confirmations	2,850
Marriages:	
Catholic	886
Interfaith	136
Total Marriages	1,022
Deaths	3,259
Total Catholic Population	304,921
Total Population	568,154

Former Bishops—Most Revs. JULES B. JEANMARD, D.D., LL.D., ord. June 11, 1903; appt. first Bishop of Lafayette, July 18, 1918; cons. Dec. 8, 1918; installed as first Bishop of Lafayette, Dec. 12, 1918; appt. Assistant at the Pontifical Throne, Dec. 8, 1943; resigned and named Titular Bishop of Bareta, March 13, 1956; died Feb. 23, 1957; ROBERT E. TRACY, D.D., LL.D., Auxiliary Bishop of Lafayette, March 18, 1959; appt. first Bishop of Baton Rouge, Aug. 10, 1961; died April 4, 1980; WARREN L. BOUDREAUX, D.D., J.C.D., Auxiliary Bishop of Lafayette, May 19, 1962; appt. second Bishop of Beaumont, Texas, June 4, 1971; died Oct. 6, 1997; MAURICE SCHEXNAYDER, D.D., ord. April 11, 1925; appt. Titular Bishop of Tuscamia and Auxiliary of Lafayette, Dec. 11, 1950; cons. Feb. 22, 1951; appt. second Bishop of Lafayette, March 13, 1956; installed May 24, 1956; resigned Nov. 7, 1972; died Jan. 23, 1981; GERARD L. FREY, D.D., appt. third Bishop of Lafayette, Nov. 7, 1972; installed Jan. 7, 1973; resigned May 13, 1989; died Aug. 16, 2007; HARRY J. FLYNN, D.D., ord. May 28, 1960; appt. Coadjutor Bishop of Lafayette, April 19, 1986, fourth Bishop of Lafayette, May 13, 1989; appt. Coadjutor Archbishop of St. Paul and Minneapolis, Feb. 22, 1994; EDWARD JOSEPH O'DONNELL, D.D. (Retired), ord. April 6, 1957; appt. Titular Bishop of Britonia and Auxiliary Bishop of St. Louis Dec. 6, 1983; cons. Feb. 10, 1984; appt. fifth Bishop of Lafayette Nov. 8, 1994; installed Dec. 16, 1994; retired Nov. 8, 2002; died Feb. 1, 2009.

Bishop's Office—Mailing Address: Diocesan Office Building, P.O. Box 3387, Lafayette, 70502-3387. Tel: 337-261-5614; Fax: 337-261-5603.

Administrative Offices—Diocesan Office Building, 1408 Carmel Dr., Lafayette, 70501-5298. Tel: 337-261-5500; Fax: 337-261-5635.

Vicars General—Very Rev. Msgr. H. ALEXANDRE LARROQUE, J.C.D., V.G.; Very Rev. W. CURTIS MALLET, J.C.L., V.G. Tel: 337-261-5613; Fax: 337-261-5603.

Chancellor & Vicar for Priests—Very Rev. Msgr. RUSSELL J. HARRINGTON, V.E., Mailing Address: P.O. Box 3387, Lafayette, 70502-3387. Tel: 337-261-5611; Fax: 337-261-5603.

Council of Priests—Rev. GARY SCHEXNAYDER.

Diocesan Pastoral Council—Mailing Address: 1408 Carmel Dr., Lafayette, 70501. Tel: 337-261-5551.

Clergy Personnel Advisory Board—Very Rev. Msgr. ROBIE E. ROBICHAUX, J.C.L., Mailing Address: P.O. Box 3387, Lafayette, 70502-3387. Tel: 337-261-5623; Fax: 337-261-5646.

Finance Officer—Deacon JEFF TRUMPS, Diocesan Finance Officer & Dir., Mailing Address: P.O. Box 3387, Lafayette, 70502-3387. 1408 Carmel Dr., Lafayette, 70501-5298. Tel: 337-261-5632.

Victims Assistance Coordinator—Sr. KATHLEEN FARRELLY, O.Carm., L.C.S.W., S.S.W.S. Tel: 337-298-2987. Email: kfarrelly@diolaf.org.

Abuse Review Board—Mailing Address: P.O. Box 3387, Lafayette, 70502-3387. Tel: 337-261-5611 Chancellor's Office of the Diocese of Lafayette.

Tribunal

Tribunal—Mailing Address: P.O. Box 3387, Lafayette, 70502-3387. Tel: 337-261-5623; Fax: 337-261-5646.

Judicial Vicar—Very Rev. Msgr. ROBIE E. ROBICHAUX, J.C.L. Tel: 337-261-5623; Fax: 337-261-5646.

Adjutant Judicial Vicar—VACANT.

Assessors—Rev. HERBERT J. MAY, J.C.L.; Mrs. JANE JOY; Sr. MARIE BRIETENBECK, J.C.D. Instructors: Rev. Msgr. RICHARD VON PHUL MOUTON (Retired); Mr. PHIL LIZOTTE.

Promoter of the Justice—Very Rev. Msgr. H. ALEXANDRE LARROQUE, J.C.D., V.G. Tel: 337-261-5613.

Judges—Very Rev. Msgr. H. ALEXANDRE LARROQUE, J.C.D., V.G. Tel: 337-261-5613; Rev. HERBERT J. MAY, J.C.L.; Very Rev. W. CURTIS MALLET, J.C.L., V.G.

Defenders of the Bond—Revs. OVERTON JOSEPH BREAUX; KEN BROUSSARD; JAMES BRADY, J.C.L.

Notary—Mrs. LINDA W. SAVOY.

Diocesan Consultors—Very Rev. Msgrs. RUSSELL J. HARRINGTON, V.E.; H. ALEXANDRE LARROQUE, J.C.D., V.G.; Very Rev. W. CURTIS MALLET, J.C.L., V.G.; Rev. Msgr. RICHARD VON PHUL MOUTON (Retired); Revs. GARY SCHEXNAYDER; CHESTER C. ARCENEAUX; ALBERT GAYLE NUNEZ; JASON VIDRINE; THOMAS P. VOORHIES; JAMES BRADY, J.C.L.

Diocesan Secretariats, Offices and Directors

Secretariat of Community Services—MAUREEN K. FONTENOT, Dir.

"Acadiana Catholic" Newspaper—VACANT, Editor, 1408 Carmel Dr., Lafayette, 70501-5298. Tel: 337-261-5513.

Archives - Research and Information—BARBARA C.

DEJEAN, Dir., 1408 Carmel Dr., Lafayette, 70501-5298. Tel: 337-261-5639; 337-261-5667.
Catholic Schools—ANNA LARRIVIERE, Supt., 1408 Carmel Dr., Lafayette, 70501-5298. Tel: 337-261-5529.
Christian Formation, Adult Catechesis and Youth Ministry—ANN BROUSSARD, Dir., 1408 Carmel Dr., Lafayette, 70501-5298. Tel: 337-261-5550.
College Ministry—Rev. BRYCE SIBLEY, Pastor & Dir., Mailing Address: Our Lady of Wisdom Catholic Student Center, P.O. Box 42371, Lafayette, 70504-2371. Tel: 337-232-8742.
Human Resources - Safe Environment—MAUREEN K. FONTENOT, Dir., 1408 Carmel Dr., Lafayette, 70501-5298. Tel: 337-261-5526.
Pro-Life Apostolate—KAROL MEYNARD, Dir., 1408 Carmel Dr., Lafayette, 70501-5298. Tel: 337-261-5607.
Radio-TV—DAVID MERGIST, Producer & Dir., 1408 Carmel Dr., Lafayette, 70501-5298. Tel: 337-261-5626.
Secretariat of Pastoral Services—Deacon JAMES (JIM) KINCEL, Dir.
Black Catholic Ministry—STEPHANIE BERNARD, Dir., 1408 Carmel Dr., Lafayette, 70501-5298. Tel: 337-261-5694.
Catholic Social Services—PAULA MILNER, Dir., 1408 Carmel Dr., Lafayette, 70501-5298. Tel: 337-261-5654.
Marriage and Family Life Ministry—Rev. JUDE HALPHEN, Ph.D., Dir., Mailing Address: 1408 Carmel Dr., Lafayette, 70501-5298. Tel: 337-261-5653.
Hispanic Ministry—CRISTINA LEBLANC, Dir., 1408 Carmel Dr., Lafayette, 70501-5298. Tel: 337-261-5544.
Office of Justice and Peace—ED BOUSTANY, Dir., 1408 Carmel Dr., Lafayette, 70501-5298. Tel: 337-261-5545.
Migration and Refugee Services—TINA QUESADA, Dir., 1408 Carmel Dr., Lafayette, 70501-5298. Tel: 337-261-5535.
Persons with Disabilities and Deaf Apostolate—VACANT, 1408 Carmel Dr., Lafayette, 70501-5298. Tel: 337-232-3463; 337-261-5548.
Vietnamese Catholic Ministry—Rev. THOMAS H. VU, Dir., Mailing Address: 601 Magnolia St., Franklin, 70538. Tel: 337-828-1714.
Office of Worship—Rev. Msgr. KEITH J. DEROUEN, Dir.; FAYE DROBNIC, Asst. Dir., 1408 Carmel Dr., Lafayette, 70501-5298. Tel: 337-261-5554.
Secretariat of Religious Personnel—Very Rev. Msgr. RUSSELL J. HARRINGTON, V.E., Dir.
Continuing Formation of Priests—Rev. KEVIN BORDELON, Dir., 1408 Carmel Dr., Lafayette, 70501. Tel: 337-735-9451; Fax: 337-261-5693.
Minister to Priests—Rev. MICHAEL GUIDRY, Mailing Address: P.O. Box 319, Morrow, 71356-0319. Tel: 318-346-7010.
Permanent Diaconate—Deacon JAMES (JIM) KINCEL, Dir., 1408 Carmel Dr., Lafayette, 70501-5298. Tel: 337-261-5607.
Religious Brothers and Sisters—Sr. JUDITH COREIL, M.S.C., Dir., 1408 Carmel Dr., Lafayette, 70501-5298. Tel: 337-261-5430.
Seminarians—Rev. KEVIN BORDELON, Dir., 1408 Carmel Dr., Lafayette, 70501-5298. Tel: 337-261-5690.
Vicar for Priests—Very Rev. Msgr. RUSSELL J. HARRINGTON, V.E., 1408 Carmel Dr., Lafayette, 70501-5298. Tel: 337-261-5611; Fax: 337-261-5603.
Vocations—Rev. KEVIN BORDELON, Dir., 1408 Carmel Dr., Lafayette, 70501-5298. Tel: 337-261-5690.
Secretariat of Stewardship—Deacon JEFF TRUMPS, Dir. & Diocesan Finance Officer, 1408 Carmel Dr., Lafayette, 70501-5298. Tel: 337-261-5632.
Building & Renovations—AL LANDRY, AIA, Coord., 1408 Carmel Dr., Lafayette, 70501-5298. Tel: 337-735-9429.
General Manager—ANTHONY BOUDREAUX, 1408 Carmel Dr., Lafayette, 70501-5298. Tel: 337-261-5605.
Community Development—J. BERNEL FONTENOT, Dir., 1408 Carmel Dr., Lafayette, 70501-5298. Tel: 337-261-5650.
Information Technology—ROBIN STEVENSON, Dir., 1408 Carmel Dr., Lafayette, 70501-5298. Tel: 337-261-5516.
Financial Affairs—Deacon JEFF TRUMPS, Diocesan Finance Officer & Dir., Mailing Address: P.O. Box 3387, Lafayette, 70502-3387. 1408 Carmel Dr., Lafayette, 70501-5298. Tel: 337-261-5632.
Auxiliary Services—PATSY ARWOOD, Dir., 1408 Carmel Dr., Lafayette, 70501-5298. Tel: 337-261-5600.
Bishop's Services Appeal—CONNIE B. BABIN, Dir., 1408 Carmel Dr., Lafayette, 70501-5298. Tel: 337-261-5641.
Controller—THOMAS D. LANDRY, CPA, 1408 Carmel Dr., Lafayette, 70501-5298. Tel: 337-261-5627.
Development Office—CONNIE B. BABIN, Dir., 1408 Carmel Dr., Lafayette, 70501-5298. Tel: 337-261-5641.

Miscellaneous

Catholic Charismatic—GRAHAM SMITH, Ph.D., Coord., Office: 1408 Carmel Dr., Lafayette, 70501.
Catholic Daughters of America—Diocesan Co Chaplains: Revs. HERBERT BENNERFIELD. Tel: 337-685-4426; CEDRIC SONNIER. Tel: 337-457-8107.
Knights of Columbus—Rev. MARK DERISE, State Chap., Mailing Address: P.O. Box 10110, New Iberia, 70562-0110. Tel: 337-365-5481.
Catholic Relief Services—ED BOUSTANY, Diocesan Coord., 1408 Carmel Dr., Lafayette, 70501. Tel: 337-261-5545.
Credit Union—*St. Jules Credit Union, 1600 N. Bertrand Dr., Lafayette, 70506*. Tel: 337-261-1151.
Cursillo—Rev. THEODORE BROUSSARD JR., Spiritual Dir. to Secretariat of the Cursillo & Dir. Women's Cursillo. Tel: 337-543-7425.
Ecumenism—Very Rev. Msgr. RICHARD GREENE, V.E., Mailing Address: 2514 Old Jeanerette Rd., New Iberia, 70563. Tel: 337-364-4439; Fax: 337-364-4474.
Hospitals—Rev. M. KEITH LABOVE, Coord. Health Affairs, Mailing Address: 406 E. Pinhook Rd., Lafayette, 70501. Tel: 337-237-0988.
Pontifical Mission Societies—Rev. Msgr. RICHARD VON PHUL MOUTON (Retired), 1408 Carmel Dr., Lafayette, 70501-5298. Tel: 337-261-5536.
Holy Childhood—Rev. Msgr. RICHARD VON PHUL MOUTON (Retired), 1408 Carmel Dr., Lafayette, 70501. Tel: 337-261-5536.
Retreats—Mr. JIMMY L. DAUZAT, Dir. Our Lady of the Oaks Retreat House, Grand Coteau, LA. Mailing Address: P.O. Box D, Grand Coteau, 70541-1003. Tel: 337-662-5410.
Scouting—Rev. GARY SCHEXNAYDER, Chap., Mailing Address: St. Michael Church, P.O. Box 406, Crowley, 70527-0406. Tel: 337-783-7394; ROBERT T. CLEMENTS, Lay Chm., 204 Crawford, Lafayette, 70506-6028. Tel: 337-981-2519.

CLERGY, PARISHES, MISSIONS AND PAROCHIAL SCHOOLS

CITY OF LAFAYETTE

(LAFAYETTE PARISH)

1—CATHEDRAL OF ST. JOHN THE EVANGELIST (1821) [CEM] Revs. Chester C. Arceneaux; Kevin P. Bordelon. In Res., Rev. Msgr. Richard von Phul Mouton (Retired); Rev. Cyprian Eze.
Res. & Mailing Address: 515 Cathedral St., 70501. Tel: 337-232-1322; Fax: 337-232-1379. Email: sjclaf@bellsouth.net. Web: www.saintjohncathedral.org.
Church: 914 St. John St., 70501. Email: sjc@bellsouth.net.
School—Cathedral-Carmel Elementary, (Grades PreK-8), 848 St. John St., 70501. Tel: 337-235-5577; Fax: 337-261-9493. Web: cathedralcarmel-.com. Mary Catherine "Kay" Aillet, Prin.; Erin Soignier, Librarian. Sisters of Mt. Carmel 1; Lay Teachers 65; Students 779.
Catechesis/Religious Program—Tel: 337-232-1325. Email: sjcreligiouseducation@yahoo.com. Students 213.

2—ST. ANTHONY (1955), (African American), [JC] Rev. Lambert Lein, S.V.D.; Deacon Albert Marcel.
Mailing Address: P.O. Box 92708, 70509. Tel: 337-234-5855; Fax: 327-264-1507.
Church: 615 Edison St., 70501.
Catechesis/Religious Program—Students 120.

3—ST. EDMOND (1974) Rev. Gilbert J. Dutel; Deacon Frank Cormier.
Res.: 4131 W. Congress St., 70506. Tel: 337-981-0874; Fax: 337-989-1417. Web: www.st-edmond.org.
Catechesis/Religious Program—Carol Broglio. Students 385.

4—ST. ELIZABETH SETON (1975) Rev. Martin Borcherding; Deacon Nelson Joseph Schexnayder Jr.
Office: 610 Raintree Tr., 70507. Tel: 337-235-1483; Fax: 337-235-9645. Email: pastor@setonchurch.org. Web: www.setonchurch.org.
Catechesis/Religious Program—Students 117.

5—ST. GENEVIEVE (1929) [CEM] Very Rev. W. Curtis Mallet; Rev. Thomas E. Habetz.
Res.: 417 E. Simcoe St., 70501. Tel: 337-234-5147; Fax: 337-234-8654. Email: stgenevieve@cox.net.
School—Elementary School, (Grades PreK-5), 201 Elizabeth St., 70501. Tel: 337-234-5257; Fax: 337-237-6065. Email: sgscardinals@stgen.net. Web: www.stgen.net. Becky Trouille, Prin. Lay Teachers 18; Students 356.
School—Middle School, (Grades 6-8), 91 Teurlings Dr., 70501. Tel: 337-266-5553; Fax: 337-266-5775. Mrs. Julie Champagne, Prin. Lay Teachers 10; Students 177.
See Teurlings Catholic High under High Schools, Interparochial located in the Institution section.
St. Genevieve School Foundation, Inc.—
Catechesis/Religious Program—Tel: 337-234-5147, Ext. 104; Fax: 337-234-8654. Students 90.

6—HOLY CROSS (1965) Rev. Howard Blessing; Deacons Michael Clark; Richard Picard.
Res.: 415 Robley Dr., 70503. Tel: 337-984-9636; Fax: 337-988-3790. Web: www.holycrosslafayette.com.
Catechesis/Religious Program—Tel: 337-984-9643. Students 719.

7—IMMACULATE HEART OF MARY (1934), (African American), [CEM] Very Rev. Thomas James, S.V.D.; Rev. Anderson Luis de Sousa; Deacon Anthony Ozene. In Res., Rev. Ryszard Kalinowski, S.V.D.
Res.: 818-12th St., P.O. Box 2398, 70502. Tel: 337-235-4618; Fax: 337-235-4775. Email: ihm818@bellsouth.net. Web: www.ihmch.homestead.com.
School—(Grades K-8), 800-12th St., 70502. Tel: 337-235-7843; Fax: 337-233-0070. Dr. Edith White, Prin. Sisters of the Holy Family 3; Lay Teachers 17; Students 176.
Catechesis/Religious Program—Tel: 337-235-6323; Fax: 337-235-6321. Students 257.

8—ST. JULES (1962) Rev. J. Daniel Edwards; Deacon Reginald A. Bollich. In Res., Rev. Jairo Castano, S.D.S.
Res.: 116 St. Jules St., 70506. Tel: 337-234-2727; Fax: 337-232-1544. Email: stjuleschurch@lusfiber.net.
Catechesis/Religious Program—Students 60.

9—ST. LEO THE GREAT (1960) Very Rev. Msgr. Robie E. Robichaux.
Res.: 300 W. Alexander St., 70501. Tel: 337-232-2404; Fax: 337-261-0801.
School—Sts. Leo-Seton, (Grades PreK-8), 502 St. Leo St., 70501. Tel: 337-234-5510; Fax: 337-234-3676. Kimberly Gothreaux, Prin.; Trisha Badeaux, Librarian. Sisters 1; Lay Teachers 34; Students 553.
Catechesis/Religious Program—Tel: 337-257-2132. Students 51.

10—ST. MARY MOTHER OF THE CHURCH (1975) Rev. Harold Trahan.
Res.: 419 Doucet Rd., 70503. Tel: 337-981-3379; Fax: 337-981-5445. Email: stmarych@cox-internet.com. Web: www.stmarych.com.
St. Mary Early Learning Center—Tel: 337-984-3750. Amy Robideaux, Prin. Students 178.
Catechesis/Religious Program—Students 202.

11—OUR LADY OF FATIMA (1949) Rev. Michael Russo; Deacon Timothy Maragos.
Res.: 2319 Johnston St., 70503. Tel: 337-232-8945; Fax: 337-232-0323. Web: fatimalafayette.org.
School—(Grades PreK-8), 2315 Johnston St., 70503. Tel: 337-235-2464; Fax: 337-235-1320. Web: www.fatimawarrior.com. Mr. Herb Boasso, Prin.; Mrs. Lois Sellers, Asst. Prin.; Mrs. Joni Duos, Asst. Prin.; Lorraine Allain, Librarian; Diane Legnon, Librarian. Special Ed. offered Lay Teachers 63; Students 915.
Catechesis/Religious Program—Email: education@fatimalafayette.org. Students 19.

12—OUR LADY OF WISDOM, UNIVERSITY OF LOUISIANA (1942) Rev. Bryce Sibley.
Mailing Address: P.O. Box 42371, 70504-2371. Tel: 337-232-8741; Fax: 337-236-6737. Email: wisdom@ourladyofwisdom.org. Web: www.ourladyofwisdom.org.
Catechesis/Religious Program—Students 100.

13—OUR LADY QUEEN OF PEACE (1969), (African American), [CEM] Rev. F. Hampton Davis III.
Mailing Address: P.O. Box 90740, 70509.
Church: 145 Martin Luther King Jr. Dr., 70501. Tel: 337-233-1591; Fax: 337-232-5961.
Rectory—415 Cooper St., 70501. Tel: 337-233-0598.
Catechesis/Religious Program—Students 160.

14—ST. PATRICK (1952) Rev. M. Keith LaBove.
Res.: 406 E. Pinhook Rd., 70501. Tel: 337-237-0988; Fax: 337-233-8868. Email: stpat.org@gmail.com.

15—ST. PAUL THE APOSTLE (1911), (African American), Rev. Robert Seay; Bro. Juniper Crouch, O.F.M.
Res.: 326 S. Washington St., 70501. Tel: 337-235-0272; Fax: 337-235-3100.
Catechesis/Religious Program—Students 130.
Mission—Our Lady of Good Hope, Lafayette Parish. Tel: 337-235-0272; Fax: 337-235-3100.

16—ST. PIUS X (1968) [JC] Revs. Steven C. LeBlanc; Corey Campeaux.
Res.: 200 E. Bayou Pkwy., P.O. Box 80489, 70598-0489. Tel: 337-232-4656; Fax: 337-233-9468. Web: www.stpiusxchurch.org.
School—(Grades PreK-8), 205 E. Bayou Pkwy., 70508. Tel: 337-237-3139; Fax: 337-232-3455. Web: www.stpiuselementary.org. Miss Donna Lemaire,

Prin. Lay Teachers 53; Students 730.
Catechesis/Religious Program—Tel: 337-232-4672. Students 338.

OUTSIDE THE CITY OF LAFAYETTE

ABBEVILLE, VERMILION PARISH

1—ST. MARY MAGDALEN (1844) [CEM 2] Revs. William C. Blanda; J. Scott Desormeaux; Deacons Randy E. Hyde; Tam Tran.
Mailing Address: P.O. Box 1507, 70511. Tel: 337-893-0244; Fax: 337-893-0427. Web: www.st-marymagdalenparish.org. Email: parish@stmarymagdalenparish.org.
School—Mt. Carmel Elementary, (Grades K-8), 405 Park Ave., 70510. Tel: 337-898-0859; Fax: 337-893-5968. Email: carmel@mceschool.org. Web: www.mceschool.org. Sr. Janet LeBlanc, O.Carm., Prin.; Tiffany Abshire, Librarian. Sisters 2; Lay Teachers (K-8) 24; Lay Teachers (PS) 3; Students (K-8) 397; Students (PS) 49.
High School—Vermilion Catholic, 425 Park Ave., 70510. Tel: 337-893-6636; Fax: 337-898-0394. Web: www.vermilioncatholic.com. Mr. Mike Guilbeaux, Prin. Lay Teachers 22; Students 173.
St. Mary Magdalen Christian Service Center—701 Chevis St., 70510. Tel: 337-893-9756; Fax: 337-893-1532.
Catechesis/Religious Program—Tel: 337-893-0244; Fax: 337-893-0427. Students 218.

2—ST. THERESA OF THE CHILD JESUS (1959) Rev. Kenneth Mayne.
Mailing Address: P.O. Box 609, 70511. Tel: 337-893-5631; Fax: 337-893-9168.
Catechesis/Religious Program—Students 219.

ARNAUDVILLE, ST. LANDRY PARISH

1—ST. CATHERINE (1949), (African American), Rev. Keenan Wynn Brown; Deacon James B. Davis, Pastoral Assoc.
Mailing Address: P.O. Box 53, 70512. Tel: 337-754-7754; Fax: 337-754-7754.
Catechesis/Religious Program—Tel: 337-754-5912; Fax: 337-754-7754.

2—ST. JOHN FRANCIS REGIS (1853) [CEM] Rev. Keenan Wynn Brown.
Mailing Address: P.O. Box 649, 70512. Tel: 337-754-5912; Fax: 337-754-7203. Email: johnfrancisregis@hotmail.com.
Catechesis/Religious Program—Tel: 337-754-5912; Fax: 337-754-7203. Students 287.

BALDWIN, ST. MARY PARISH, SACRED HEART (1906) [CEM] Rev. Gregory P. Cormier; Deacons Harry Darce; Gerald Bourg.
Mailing Address: P.O. Box 308, 70514. Tel: 337-923-7781; Fax: 337-923-4966.
Catechesis/Religious Program—Twinned with St. Peter the Apostle, Baldwin. Joland Charpentier, D.R.E. Students 51.

BASILE, EVANGELINE PARISH, ST. AUGUSTINE (1921) [CEM] Rev. Brian Taylor.
Res.: 2717 Third St., 70515. Tel: 337-432-6817; Fax: 337-432-5203.
Catechesis/Religious Program—Tel: 337-432-5608. Students 230.
Mission—Assumption, Evangeline Parish. Tel: 337-432-6817; Fax: 337-432-5203.

BAYOU VISTA, ST. MARY PARISH, ST. BERNADETTE (1963) [CEM] Rev. William G. Rogalla.
Res.: 1112 Saturn Rd., Morgan City, 70380. Tel: 985-395-2470; Fax: 985-395-6514. Email: stbern@teche.net. Web: stbern-bv.org.
Catechesis/Religious Program—Tel: 985-395-6517. Students 149.

BERWICK, ST. MARY PARISH, ST. STEPHEN (1950) Rev. Msgr. J. Douglas Courville.
Res.: 3217 Second St., 70342. Tel: 985-385-1280; Fax: 985-385-1279.
Catechesis/Religious Program—Tel: 985-385-1283. Students 205.

BREAUX BRIDGE, ST. MARTIN PARISH

1—ST. BERNARD (1847) [CEM 2] [JC 2] Revs. Paul J. LaFleur; Donald Pousson; Deacons Jim Davis; Marcel P. Hebert Jr.
Mailing Address: *Admin. Bldg.*, 219 E. Bridge St., 70517.
Res.: 204 N. Main St., 70517. Tel: 337-332-2159; Fax: 337-332-2276. Web: stbernardch.net.
School—(Grades PreK-8), 251 E. Bridge St., 70517. Tel: 337-332-5350; Fax: 337-332-5894. Raymond Latiolais Jr., Prin. Lay Teachers 34; Students 463.
Catechesis/Religious Program—219 E. Bridge St., 70517. Tel: 337-332-4488; Fax: 337-332-4488. Students 387.

2—ST. FRANCIS OF ASSISI (1923), (African American), [CEM] Rev. Joseph J. Campion, S.S.J. In Res., Rev. Charles Moffatt, S.S.J.
Res.: 610 N. Main St., 70517. Tel: 337-332-2250; Fax: 337-332-5026.
Catechesis/Religious Program—Students 181.

BROUSSARD, LAFAYETTE PARISH

1—ST. JOSEPH (1952), (African American), [CEM 2] Rev. Arockiam Arockiam, S.V.D. (India).
Mailing Address: P.O. Box 278, 70518.
Res.: 232 St. DePorres St., 70518. Tel: 337-837-6218; Fax: 337-837-2072.
Catechesis/Religious Program—Students 104.
Mission—St. Anthony Cade, St. Martin Parish.

2—SACRED HEART OF JESUS (1883) [CEM] Revs. Louis J. Richard; Edward J. Duhon Jr.
Mailing Address: 200 W. Main St., P.O. Box 737, 70518. Tel: 337-837-1864; Fax: 337-837-1703. Email: pastor@shbroussard.org. Web: shbroussard.org.
School—St. Cecilia, (Grades PreK-8), P.O. Box 309, 70518. Tel: 337-837-6363; Fax: 337-837-3688. Web: scsbluejays.org. Mr. George Fontenot, Prin.; Sonya Renard, Librarian. Lay Teachers 31; Students 490.
Catechesis/Religious Program—Students 434.

CANKTON, ST. LANDRY PARISH, ST. JOHN BERCHMANS (1925) [CEM] Rev. Henry J. Broussard.
Res.: 552 Main St., 70584-9722. Tel: 337-668-4413; Fax: 337-668-4505. Email: stjb@centurytel.net.
Catechesis/Religious Program—Students 176.

CARENCRO, LAFAYETTE PARISH

1—OUR LADY OF THE ASSUMPTION (1925), (African American), [CEM] Rev. Peter Emusa.
Res.: 410 N. Michaud St., P.O. Box 130, 70520-0130. Tel: 337-896-8304; Fax: 337-896-5874. Email: officemanager@assumptiononline.com. Web: www.assumptiononline.com.
Catechesis/Religious Program—Students 66.

2—ST. PETER (1874) [CEM] Revs. Mark Ledoux; Johnathan J. Janise.
Mailing Address: P.O. Box 40, 70520. Tel: 337-896-9408; Fax: 337-896-9414. Web: www.sprcc.org.
School—Carencro Catholic, (Grades PreK-8), 200 W. St. Peter St., 70520. Tel: 337-896-8973; Fax: 337-896-1931. Web: www.carencrocatholic.org. Andrea Angelle, Prin.; Sandie Enland, Librarian. Lay Teachers 28; Students 427.
Catechesis/Religious Program—Tel: 337-896-8488. Students 249.

CATAHOULA, ST. MARTIN PARISH, ST. RITA (1952) [CEM] Rev. Richard Fabre.
Res.: 1006 St. Rita Hwy., St. Martinville, 70582. Tel: 337-394-4679; Fax: 337-394-7020. Email: church@strita.brcoxmail.com.
Catechesis/Religious Program—Students 188.

CECILIA, ST. MARTIN PARISH

1—ST. JOSEPH (1893) [CEM] [JC] Rev. Michael L. Delcambre.
Mailing Address: P.O. Box 279, 70521. Tel: 337-667-6344; Fax: 337-667-7073.
Catechesis/Religious Program—Students 215.

2—ST. ROSE OF LIMA (1944), (African American), [CEM] Rev. Michael L. Delcambre.
Mailing Address: P.O. Box 126, 70521. Tel: 337-667-6555; Fax: 337-667-6686.
Catechesis/Religious Program—Students 78.

CENTERVILLE, ST. MARY PARISH, ST. JOSEPH (1953) [CEM] Rev. Salvino Primor.
Mailing Address: P.O. Box 280, 70522. Tel: 337-836-5659; Fax: 337-836-5659.
Catechesis/Religious Program—P.O. Box 280, 70522. Students 44.

CHARENTON, ST. MARY PARISH, IMMACULATE CONCEPTION (1844) [CEM] Rev. Gregory P. Cormier.
Mailing Address: P.O. Box 278, 70523. Tel: 337-923-4281.
Catechesis/Religious Program—

CHATAIGNIER, EVANGELINE PARISH, OUR LADY OF MOUNT CARMEL (1869), (French), [CEM] Rev. Darren J. Eldridge.
Mailing Address: P.O. Box 100, 70524. Tel: 337-885-3223; Fax: 337-885-3223.
Catechesis/Religious Program—Students 34.

CHURCH POINT, ACADIA PARISH

1—OUR LADY OF THE SACRED HEART (1873) [CEM 3] [JC] Very Rev. Msgr. Jefferson J. DeBlanc Jr.; Rev. Stephen Ugwu. In Res., Rev. Randall Moreau.
Res.: 118 N. Rogers St., P.O. Box 403, 70525. Tel: 337-684-5494; Fax: 337-684-2133.
School—Our Mother of Peace, (Grades K-8), 218 N. Rogers St., 70525. Tel: 337-684-5780; Fax: 337-684-5780. Donald Courville, Prin. Lay Teachers 18; Students 301.
Catechesis/Religious Program—Students 251.
Chapel—Lewisburg, St. John, Tel: 337-684-5494; Fax: 337-684-2133.

2—OUR MOTHER OF MERCY (1941), (African American), [JC] Rev. Francis Butler, S.S.J.
Res.: 693 N. Main St., P.O. Box 237, 70525. Tel: 337-684-2319; Fax: 337-684-3086.
Catechesis/Religious Program—Students 42.

COTEAU HOLMES, ST. MARTIN PARISH, ST. ELIZABETH (1956) [CEM] Rev. Joseph L.F. Padinjarepeedika, C.M.I. (India).
Office: 1006 St. Elizabeth St., St. Martinville, 70582. Tel: 337-394-6684; Fax: 337-394-6684.
Catechesis/Religious Program—Students 36.

COTEAU, IBERIA PARISH, OUR LADY OF PROMPT SUCCOR (1934) [CEM] Rev. Barry F. Crochet.
Res.: 2409 Coteau Rd., New Iberia, 70560. Tel: 337-369-6993; Fax: 337-560-4475. Email: secretary@opls-coteau.org.
Catechesis/Religious Program—Students 327.

COW ISLAND, VERMILION PARISH, ST. ANNE (1933) [CEM] [JC 3] Rev. Michael Keith Landry.
Res.: 17315 Lionel Rd., Abbeville, 70510. Tel: 337-643-7714; Fax: 337-643-1021.
Catechesis/Religious Program—Students 184.
Mission—Sacred Heart Pecan Island, Vermilion Parish.

CROWLEY, ACADIA PARISH

1—IMMACULATE HEART OF MARY (1959) Rev. Matthew P. Higginbotham.
Res.: 825 E. Elm St., 70526.
Rectory—901 E. Elm St., 70526. Tel: 337-783-3498; Fax: 337-783-7444. Email: ihmcatholicchurch@cox-internet.net.
School—Redemptorist Catholic Elementary School, (Grades PreK-8), 606 South Ave. N., 70526. Tel: 337-783-4466; Fax: 337-788-0961. Web: www.rcsraider.org. Louis Cramer, Prin.; Priscilla Leonards, Librarian. Lay Teachers 14; Students 205.
Catechesis/Religious Program—Tel: 337-783-7444. Students 108.

2—ST. MICHAEL ARCHANGEL (1895) Revs. Gary Schexnayder; Jared Suire.
Mailing Address: P.O. Box 406, 70527. Tel: 337-783-7394; Fax: 337-788-0237.
School—(Grades PreK-8), 805 E. Northern Ave., 70526. Tel: 337-783-1410; Fax: 337-783-8547. Mrs. Myra Broussard, Prin. Lay Teachers 26; Students 425.
Catechesis/Religious Program—Students 120.

3—ST. THERESA (1920), (African American), Rev. Godwin Imoru.
Res.: 417 W. 3rd St., 70526. Tel: 337-783-1880; Fax: 337-783-9676.
Catechesis/Religious Program—Tel: 337-783-1311; Fax: 337-783-9676. Students 103.

DELCAMBRE, VERMILION PARISH

1—SAINT MARTIN DE PORRES (1948), (African American), [JC] Rev. Herbert Bennerfield.
Res.: 206 W. Church St., 70528. Tel: 337-685-4426; Fax: 337-685-4424.
Catechesis/Religious Program—Castel School of Religion, 208 S. Peter St., 70528. Tel: 337-685-2549. Students 21.

2—OUR LADY OF THE LAKE (1897) [CEM] Rev. Herbert Bennerfield.
Res.: 206 W. Church St., 70528. Tel: 337-685-4426; Fax: 337-685-4424.
Catechesis/Religious Program—Castel School of Religion, 208 South St. Peter St., 70528. Tel: 337-685-2549. Students 270.

DURALDE, EVANGELINE PARISH, ANNUNCIATION OF THE B.V.M. (1964), (Acadian), Rev. Msgr. J. Robert Romero; Rev. Nathan A. Comeaux; Deacon James Cormier, Pastoral Assoc.
Res.: 4476 Duralde Hwy., Eunice, 70535. Tel: 337-457-4849; Fax: 337-457-4502.
Catechesis/Religious Program—Students 95.

DUSON, LAFAYETTE PARISH

1—ST. BENEDICT THE MOOR, (African American), [CEM] Revs. Martin C. Leonards; Allen Breaux.
Mailing Address: P.O. Box 8, 70529. Tel: 337-873-6772; Fax: 337-873-3023.
Catechesis/Religious Program—Tel: 337-873-6772; Fax: 337-873-3023. Students 98.

2—ST. THERESA OF THE CHILD JESUS (1928) [CEM] Revs. Martin C. Leonards; Allen Breaux; Deacon Steve Simon.
Mailing Address: P.O. Box 8, 70529. Tel: 337-873-4962; Fax: 337-873-3023.
Catechesis/Religious Program—Tel: 337-873-4488. Students 118.

ERATH, VERMILION PARISH, OUR LADY OF LOURDES (1928) [CEM 2] Rev. Bill Melancon.
Res.: 700 S. Broadway, 70533. Tel: 337-937-6888; Fax: 337-937-8650. Email: frmelancon@aol.com. Web: ololcatholic.com.
Catechesis/Religious Program—Email: ftoups@ololcatholic.com. Students 417.

EUNICE, ST. LANDRY PARISH

1—ST. ANTHONY OF PADUA (1902) [CEM] Rev. Msgr. J. Robert Romero; Rev. Nathan A. Comeaux; Deacon Gary Gaudin.
Mailing Address: 310 W. Vine Ave., P.O. Box 31, 70535. Tel: 337-457-5285; Fax: 337-457-7904. Email: stanthony@stanthonyeunice.org.
School—St. Edmund Elementary, (Grades PreK-6), 331 N. 3rd St., 70535. Tel: 337-457-5988; 337-457-3777; Fax: 337-457-5989. Email: elementary@stedmund.com. Web: stedmund.com. Mrs. Elizabeth Christ, Prin.; Mr. James Wallett, Asst. Prin.; Mrs. Katie Cormier, Librarian; Mrs. Beth Langley.
High School—St. Edmund High, (Grades 7-12), 351 W. Magnolia St., 70535. Tel: 337-457-2592; Fax: 337-457-2510. Mrs. Karen Rougeau, Librarian. Lay Teachers 43; Students 582.
Catechesis/Religious Program—Tel: 337-457-7505; Fax: 337-457-7904. Students 172.

2—ST. MATHILDA (1939), (African American), [CEM] Rev. Darren J. Eldridge.
Mailing Address: P.O. Box 346, 70535. Tel: 337-457-3286; Fax: 337-457-3274. Email: stmathildaeunice@gmail.com.
Res.: 130 N. Martin L. King Dr., 70535.
Church: 800 E. Laurel Ave., 70535.
Catechesis/Religious Program—Tel: 337-457-0108. Students 75.

3—ST. THOMAS MORE (1967) Rev. Cedric Sonnier; Deacon David Guillory.
Mailing Address: P.O. Box 1022, 70535. Tel: 337-457-8107; Fax: 337-457-1735. Email: pastor@stm-eunice.com.
Catechesis/Religious Program—Tel: 337-457-8101. Email: stm-eunice@charterinternet.com. Students 274.

EVANGELINE, ACADIA PARISH, ST. JOSEPH (1938) [CEM 2] Rev. Blaine Cement.
Mailing Address: P.O. Box 183, 70537. Tel: 337-824-4995; Fax: 337-824-4995.
Catechesis/Religious Program—Tel: 337-824-8352. Students 104.
Mission—St. Jules Petit Mamou, Acadia Parish 70537.

FOUR CORNERS, ST. MARY PARISH, ST. PETER THE APOSTLE (1960) Rev. Dismas Mauk, S.V.D.
Mailing Address: 1325 Big Four Corners Rd., Franklin, 70538. Tel: 337-276-5256; Fax: 337-276-5256.
Catechesis/Religious Program—lue Pearl Washington, D.R.E. Students 26.
Mission—St. Joan of Arc, (Closed), Glencoe, St. Mary Parish.

FRANKLIN, ST. MARY PARISH

1—ASSUMPTION B.V.M. (1852) Rev. Lloyd F. Benoit Jr.; Deacon Douglas Hebert.
Mailing Address: 211 Iberia St., 70538. Tel: 337-828-3869; Fax: 337-828-3872. Email: marysassumption@yahoo.com. Web: www.churchofassumption.com.
School—St. John Elementary, (Grades PreK-5), 924 Main St., 70538. Tel: 337-828-2648; Fax: 337-828-2112. Email: stjohn@msis.net. Web: www-.stjohnelem.com. Mrs. Sheri Higdon, Prin. Lay Teachers 14; Students 165.
High School—Hanson High School, (Grades 6-12), 903 Anderson St., 70538. Tel: 337-828-3487; Fax: 337-828-7431. Web: www.hansonmemorial.com. Mrs. Kim Adams, Prin. Lay Teachers 23; Students 275.
Catechesis/Religious Program—Tel: 337-828-9499. Students 45.

2—ST. JULES (1950) [CEM] Rev. Thomas H. Vu; Deacon Joseph Thomas.
Res.: 601 Magnolia St., 70538. Tel: 337-828-1714; Fax: 337-828-1734. Email: stjules1943@yahoo.com.
Catechesis/Religious Program—Students 134.
Mission—Immaculate Conception 601 Magnolia, Verdunville, St. Mary Parish.

GRAND COTEAU, ST. LANDRY PARISH, ST. CHARLES BORROMEO (1819) [CEM] [JC] Revs. James L. Lambert, S.J.; Ferdinand Derrera, S.J.; Deacons Samuel Henry; Herd Guilbeau; James (Jim) Kincel.
Mailing Address: P.O. Box A, 70541. Tel: 337-662-5279; Fax: 337-662-5270. Web: www.st-charles-borromeo.org.
Res.: 174 Church St., 70541.
School—St. Ignatius, (Grades K-8), P.O. Drawer J, 70541. Tel: 337-662-3325; Fax: 337-662-3349. Web: stignatiusschool.us. Mrs. Cindy Prather, Prin. Lay Teachers 25; Students 330.
Catechesis/Religious Program—Tel: 337-662-5271. Students 210.
Mission—Christ the King Opelousas. 369 Christ the King Rd., Opelousas, St. Landry Parish 70570.

GRAND PRAIRIE, ST. LANDRY PARISH, ST. PETER (1951) [CEM 2] [JC] Rev. Richard Vidrine.
Res. & Mailing Address: 1074 Hwy. 748 (Grand Prairie), Washington, 70589-4541. Tel: 337-826-3870; Fax: 337-826-5635.
Catechesis/Religious Program—Students 117.

GUEYDAN, VERMILION PARISH, ST. PETER THE APOSTLE (1907) [JC] Rev. Jason Vidrine.
Res.: 603 Main St., P.O. Box 28, 70542. Tel: 337-536-9258; Fax: 337-536-0071.
School—(Grades PreK-8), 513 6th St., 70542. Tel: 337-536-7930; Fax: 337-536-9460. Lay Teachers 10; Students 80.
Catechesis/Religious Program—Students 81.
Mission—St. David Mulvey, Vermilion Parish.

HENDERSON, ST. MARTIN PARISH, OUR LADY OF MERCY (1962) [CEM] [JC] Rev. Lawrence N. Abara.
Mailing Address: P.O. Box 587, Breaux Bridge, 70517. Tel: 337-228-2352; Fax: 337-228-2372.
Res.: 1454 Henderson Hwy., 70517.
Catechesis/Religious Program—Tel: 337-228-2234. Students 153.
Mission—Sacred Heart Butte La Rose, St. Martin Parish.

HENRY, VERMILION PARISH, ST. JOHN (1939), (French-Acadian), [CEM] Rev. Emmanuel Fernandez.
Res. & Mailing: 18534 La. Hwy. 689, Erath, 70533. Tel: 337-937-5108; Fax: 337-937-0002.
Catechesis/Religious Program—Students 137.
Mission—St. James 21125 LA Hwy. 333, Abbeville, 70510.

IOTA, ACADIA PARISH, ST. JOSEPH (1892) [CEM] Rev. Mikel Anthony Polson.
Mailing Address: 604 St. Joseph Ave., 70543. Tel: 337-779-2627; Fax: 337-779-2632. Email: stjosephiota@charter.net.
School—St. Francis, 490 St. Joseph Ave., 70543. Tel: 337-779-2527. Cindy D. Habetz, Prin. Lay Teachers 12; Students 189.
Catechesis/Religious Program—Students 329.
Mission—St. Michael Egan, Acadia Parish. Tel: 337-788-0529.

JEANERETTE, IBERIA PARISH

1—ST. JOHN THE EVANGELIST (1879) [CEM] Rev. Jody Simoneaux.
Res.: 1510 Church St., 70544. Tel: 337-276-4576; Fax: 337-276-5804. Email: stjohnev@yahoo.com. Web: www.stjohnjeanerette.com.
Catechesis/Religious Program—Tel: 337-276-6944. Students 104.

2—OUR LADY OF THE ROSARY (1945), (African American), [CEM] [JC] Rev. Dismas Mauk, S.V.D.
Res.: 11200 Old Jeanerette Rd., 70544. Tel: 337-276-6900; Fax: 337-276-6931.
Catechesis/Religious Program—Students 42.

JUDICE, LAFAYETTE PARISH, ST. BASIL (1970) [CEM 2] Rev. A. Rex Broussard Jr.
Res.: 1803 Duhon Rd. (Judice), Duson, 70529. Tel: 337-984-2179.
Catechesis/Religious Program—Tel: 337-988-2655; Fax: 337-988-3793. Email: stbasil@cox.net. Students 132.

KAPLAN, VERMILION PARISH, OUR LADY OF THE HOLY ROSARY (1896) [JC] Rev. F. David Broussard. Email: hrcc3@kaplantel.net; Deacons Paul Eleazar; David L. Vaughn.
Mailing Address: 603 N. Herbert Ave., 70548. Tel: 337-643-6472; Fax: 337-643-2516.
School—Maltrait Memorial, (Grades PreK-8), One Crusader Square, 70548. Tel: 337-643-7765; Fax: 337-643-7765. Mrs. Renee C. Meaux, Prin. Lay Teachers 14; Students 150.
Catechesis/Religious Program—Students 529.
Mission—St. Frances Xavier Cabrini 901 N. Frederick Ave., Vermilion Parish 70548.

KROTZ SPRINGS, ST. LANDRY PARISH, ST. ANTHONY OF PADUA (1958) Rev. Chanh Nguyen, Admin.
Mailing Address: 219 Eighth Ave., P.O. Box 425, 70750. Tel: 337-566-3527; Fax: 337-566-2803.
Catechesis/Religious Program—Students 90.

LAWTELL, ST. LANDRY PARISH

1—ST. BRIDGET (1920) [CEM 2] Rev. Ted Broussard.
Mailing Address: P.O. Box 156, 70550. Tel: 337-543-7591; Fax: 337-543-7593.
Catechesis/Religious Program—Students 96.
Mission—Sacred Heart Prairie Ronde, St. Landry Parish.

2—HOLY FAMILY (1953), (African American), Rev. Justin Arockiasamy, S.V.D.
Mailing Address: P.O. Box 310, 70550. Tel: 337-543-2366; Fax: 337-543-8281. 283 Thibodeaux St., 70550.
Catechesis/Religious Program—Twinned with St. Ann, Mallet.

LEBEAU, ST. LANDRY PARISH, IMMACULATE CONCEPTION (1897), (African American), [CEM] Rev. John O'Hallaran, S.S.J., Admin.
Mailing Address & Office: 103 Lebeau Church Rd., 71345. Tel: 337-623-0838 (Rectory); 337-623-0303 (Office); Fax: 337-623-0675.
Rectory—P.O. Box 6, 71345.
Catechesis/Religious Program—Students 25.

LEONVILLE, ST. LANDRY PARISH

1—ST. CATHERINE (1952), (African American), [JC] Rev. Kenneth J. Domingue.
Mailing Address: P.O. Box 547, 70551. Tel: 337-879-2365; Fax: 337-879-3050.
Catechesis/Religious Program—Twinned with St. Leo the Great, Leonville., Tel: 337-879-2347; Fax: 337-879-9717.
Mission—St. Jules Prairie Laurent, St. Landry Parish.

2—ST. LEO THE GREAT (1896) [CEM] [JC] Rev. Kenneth J. Domingue.
Mailing Address: P.O. Box 544, 70551. Tel: 337-879-2365; Fax: 337-879-3050.
Catechesis/Religious Program—Twinned with St. Catherine, Leonville. Students 422.

LEROY, VERMILION PARISH, OUR LADY OF PERPETUAL HELP (1922) [CEM] Rev. Gregory M. Simien.
Res.: 12995 Louisiana Hwy. 699, Maurice, 70555. Tel: 337-893-0610; Fax: 337-893-6412.
Catechesis/Religious Program—Students 101.

LOREAUVILLE, IBERIA PARISH

1—ST. JOSEPH (1873) [CEM] [JC 2] Rev. John G. Breaux.
Mailing Address: P.O. Box 365, 70552. Tel: 337-229-4254; Fax: 337-229-4255.
Catechesis/Religious Program—Tel: 337-229-6728. Students 315.

2—OUR LADY OF VICTORY (1953), (African American), [CEM 2] [JC] Rev. Paul Onuegbe.
Mailing Address: 120 Daigre St., P.O. Box 387, 70552. Tel: 337-229-8284; Fax: 337-229-8254. Email: olv-loreauville@yahoo.com.
Catechesis/Religious Program—Tel: 337-229-6329. Students 94.

LOUISA, ST. MARY PARISH, ST. HELENA (1890) [CEM] Rev. Thomas Thanh Nguyen.
Res.: 108 St. Helen's Church Ln., Franklin, 70538. Tel: 337-867-4378; Fax: 337-867-5223.
Chapel—St. Francis Cypremort Point.

LYDIA, IBERIA PARISH, ST. NICHOLAS (1867) [CEM 2] Rev. Gregory Chauvin.
Mailing Address: P.O. Box 369, 70569. Tel: 337-364-5228; Fax: 337-364-5251.
Catechesis/Religious Program—Tel: 337-367-0562; Fax: 337-364-5251. Students 297.

LYONS POINT, ACADIA PARISH, ST. JOHN THE BAPTIST (1952) [CEM] Rev. Clint James Trahan.
Mailing Address: 8021 Lyons Point Hwy., Crowley, 70526. Tel: 337-783-2457; Fax: 337-783-9015.
Catechesis/Religious Program—Tel: 337-783-2457. Students 48.

MALLET, ST. LANDRY PARISH, ST. ANN (1856), (African American), [CEM] Rev. Justin Arockiasamy, S.V.D.
Mailing Address: P.O. Box 310, Lawtell, 70550. Tel: 337-543-2385; Fax: 337-543-8281. 8348 Hwy. 190, Lawtell, 70550.
Catechesis/Religious Program—Combined with Holy Family, Lawtell., Tel: 337-543-2366. Students 104.

MAMOU, EVANGELINE PARISH, ST. ANN (1914) [CEM] Rev. Mark Melancon.
Parish Center—716 Sixth St., 70554. Tel: 337-468-3159; Fax: 337-468-3427.
Catechesis/Religious Program—Students 307.
Mission—Holy Spirit

MAURICE, VERMILION PARISH

1—ST. ALPHONSUS (1893) [CEM] Rev. Overton Joseph Breaux.
Res.: 8700 Maurice Ave., P.O. Box 190, 70555. Tel: 337-893-4099; Fax: 337-893-2474. Email: stalphonsus@cox-internet.com. Web: www.stalphonsus-maurice.org.
Catechesis/Religious Program—Tel: 337-893-0923; Fax: 337-893-2474. Students 493.

2—ST. JOSEPH (1948), (African American), [JC] Rev. Michael M. Sucharski, S.V.D.
Mailing Address: P.O. Box 250, 70555-0250. Tel: 337-893-5428; Fax: 337-893-5441. Email: stjosephchurchmaurice@yahoo.com. Web: www.stjoseph-maurice.org. 8005 Maurice Ave., 70555.
Catechesis/Religious Program—Students 57.

MELVILLE, ST. LANDRY PARISH, ST. JOHN THE EVANGELIST (1931) [CEM] Rev. James Bam Nguyen.
Mailing Address: 318 First St., P.O. Box 256, 71353-0256. Tel: 337-623-4957; Fax: 337-623-4970. Email: stjohndioceselaf@att.net.
Catechesis/Religious Program—Students 28.
Mission—St. Thomas, the Apostle Palmetto, St. Landry Parish.

MERMENTAU, ACADIA PARISH, ST. JOHN THE EVANGELIST (1882) [CEM] Rev. Neil McNeill.
Mailing Address: P.O. Box 340, 70556. Tel: 337-824-2278; Fax: 337-824-9624.
Catechesis/Religious Program—Tel: 337-824-2278; Fax: 337-824-9624.
Mission—St. Margaret 311 Miller St., Estherwood, Acadia Parish 70534.

MILTON, LAFAYETTE PARISH, ST. JOSEPH (1977) [CEM] Rev. J. Aaron Melancon; Deacon Cody Miller.
Mailing Address: P.O. Box 299, 70558. Tel: 337-856-5997; Fax: 337-856-5955. Email: pastor@stjo-milton.org. Web: www.stjo-milton.org.
Catechesis/Religious Program—Tel: 337-856-5997; Fax: 337-856-5955. Email: dre@stjo-milton.org. Students 480.

MIRE, ACADIA PARISH, ASSUMPTION OF THE BLESSED VIRGIN MARY (1954) [CEM] Very Rev. Msgr. Russell J. Harrington.
Res.: 6080 Mire Hwy., Church Point, 70525. Tel: 337-873-6574; Fax: 337-873-3777.
Catechesis/Religious Program—Tel: 337-873-3777. Students 283.

MORROW, ST. LANDRY PARISH, ST. PETER (1947), (French), [CEM] Rev. Michael Guidry.
Mailing Address: P.O. Box 319, 71356. Tel: 318-346-7010. Email: stpeters319@att.net.
Catechesis/Religious Program—Students 5.
Mission—Resurrection Whiteville.

MORSE, ACADIA PARISH, IMMACULATE CONCEPTION (1956) Rev. Clint James Trahan.

Mailing Address: P.O. Box 297, 70559-0297. Tel: 337-783-2968; Fax: 337-783-2965.
Catechesis/Religious Program—Tel: 337-783-2968. Students 89.
Mission—St. Aloysius Midland. Tel: 337-783-2968.

MOWATA, ACADIA PARISH, ST. LAWRENCE (1905) [CEM 2] Rev. Joseph T. Sai Tran, S.V.D.
Res.: 29031 Crowley-Eunice Hwy., Eunice, 70535. Tel: 337-457-2739; Fax: 337-457-2739.
Catechesis/Religious Program—Students 82.

NEW IBERIA, IBERIA PARISH

1—ST. EDWARD (1917) [CEM] [JC] Very Rev. Msgr. Ronald Broussard; Deacons Raymond Charles Derouen; Nolton Senegal.
Mailing Address: 175 Ambassador W. Lemelle Dr., 70560. Tel: 337-369-3101; Fax: 337-369-3118. Email: stedwardcc@cox.net.
School—(Grades K-3), 175 Porter St., 70560. Tel: 337-369-6764; Fax: 337-369-9534. Mrs. Karen Bonin, Prin. Lay Teachers 15; Students 353.
Catechesis/Religious Program—Tel: 337-365-3762. Students 168.
Mission—St. Jude, Iberia Parish 70560.

2—NATIVITY OF OUR LADY (1964) [CEM] Rev. Michael Arnaud.
Res.: Richelieu Circle, 70560. Tel: 337-364-8360; Fax: 337-364-1509. Email: nativity@cox.net.
Catechesis/Religious Program—Tel: 337-365-3759; Fax: 337-364-1509. Students 237.

3—OUR LADY OF PERPETUAL HELP (1949) [JC] Revs. Mark Derise; Jude W. Thierry.
Res.: 1303 St. Jude Ave., 70560. Tel: 337-365-5481; Fax: 337-365-5483. Email: olphni@bellsouth.net.
Catechesis/Religious Program—Students 124.

4—ST. PETER (1838), (Hispanic—Acadian), [CEM] [JC] Revs. Charles Langlois; Jude Halphen; Deacons Wade Joseph Broussard; Patrick D. Burke. Email: deaconburke.stpeters@yahoo.com.
Mailing Address: P.O. Box 12507, 70562. Tel: 337-369-3816; Fax: 337-369-3192. Email: stpeter@cox-internet.com.
Catechesis/Religious Program—Students 200.

5—SACRED HEART OF JESUS (1960) Very Rev. Msgr. Richard Greene. In Res., Rev. Juan Luis Gandara (Mexico) Office of Hispanic Ministry.
Res.: 2514 Old Jeanerette Rd., 70563. Tel: 337-364-4439; Fax: 337-364-4474.
Rectory—4000 Walnut Dr., 70563.
Catechesis/Religious Program—Students 172.

OPELOUSAS, ST. LANDRY PARISH

1—HOLY GHOST (1920), (African American), [JC] Revs. Jaison Mangalath, S.V.D. (India); Stanley Jawa, S.V.D.; Bartlomiej Jasilek, S.V.D. (Poland), Pastoral Assoc.
Mailing Address: P.O. Box 1785, 70571-1785. Web: holyghostcatholic.org.
Res.: 747 N. Union St., 70570. Tel: 337-942-2732; Fax: 337-948-4108.
Catechesis/Religious Program—Students 276.

2—ST. LANDRY (1776) [CEM] [JC] Rev. James Brady; Deacons Samuel Diesi; John W. Miller.
Res.: 1020 N. Main St., 70570. Tel: 337-942-6552; Fax: 337-948-1295. Email: stlandrychurch@att.net. Web: www.stlandrycatholicchurch.org.
Catechesis/Religious Program—Students 49.

3—OUR LADY OF MERCY (1942) Rev. Paul G. Bienvenu; Deacons Ulysse Joubert; Thomas Lindsey.
Office: 207 N. Camille St., 70570. Tel: 337-942-4174; Fax: 337-942-1476. Email: ourladymercy@aol.com. Web: ourladymercy.org.
Res.: 124 N. Camille St., 70570.
Catechesis/Religious Program—Tel: 337-942-9404. Students 133.

4—OUR LADY QUEEN OF ANGELS (1967) [JC] Rev. Msgr. Keith J. DeRouen; Deacon Jerome Collins.
Office & Res.: 2125 S. Union St., 70570-5742. Tel: 337-942-5628; Fax: 337-942-9708. Web: www.queenofangelschurch.org.
Catechesis/Religious Program—Tel: 337-942-7831; Fax: 337-942-9708. Email: jerome@queenofangelschurch.org. Students 289.

PARKS, ST. MARTIN PARISH, ST. JOSEPH (1938) Rev. Brad D. Guillory.
Mailing Address: 1034 Bridge St., 70582. Tel: 337-845-4168; Fax: 337-845-5079.
Catechesis/Religious Program—Students 178.
Mission—St. Louis, Tel: 337-845-4168.

PATTERSON, ST. MARY PARISH, ST. JOSEPH (1848) [CEM] Rev. Donavan J. Labbe.
Res.: P.O. Box 219, 70392-0219. Tel: 985-395-3616; Fax: 985-395-9129. Email: stjoepat@cox-internet.com.
Catechesis/Religious Program—Students 152.

PINE PRAIRIE, EVANGELINE PARISH, ST. PETER (1924) [CEM 2] Rev. Richard Dale Broussard.
Mailing Address: 1325 1st St., P.O. Box 709, 70576. Tel: 337-599-2224; Fax: 337-599-3003.
Mission—St. Theresa 2117 St. Landry Hwy., Evangeline Parish, LA.
Catechesis/Religious Program—Students 162.

PLAISANCE, ST. LANDRY PARISH, ST. JOSEPH (1949), (African American), [CEM] Rev. Jude M. Obiechina, C.M.F. (Nigeria).
Res.: 3283 Hwy. 167, Opelousas, 70570. Tel: 337-826-3395; Fax: 337-826-3550.
Catechesis/Religious Program—Students 31.
Mission—St. Ann Frilot Cove, Evangeline Parish.

PORT BARRE, ST. LANDRY PARISH

1—ST. MARY (1952), (African American), [CEM] [JC] Rev. Godwin O. Nzeh, C.M.F., Admin.
Mailing Address: P.O. Box 338, 70577. Tel: 337-585-2315; Fax: 337-585-5860.
Catechesis/Religious Program—Tel: 337-585-2863; 337-585-2703; Fax: 337-585-5860. Students 52.

2—SACRED HEART OF JESUS (1871) [CEM] [JC] Rev. Daniel Picard.
Mailing Address: P.O. Box 129, 70577. Tel: 337-585-2279; Fax: 337-585-5377.
Catechesis/Religious Program—Fax: 337-585-5317. Students 225.

RAYNE, ACADIA PARISH

1—ST. JOSEPH (1872) [CEM 2] [JC 2] Revs. William Paul Ruskoski; Kendal Faulk.
Mailing Address: P.O. Box 199, 70578. Tel: 337-334-2193; Fax: 337-334-2199.
School—Rayne Catholic Elementary, (Grades PreK-8), 407 S. Polk St., 70578. Tel: 337-334-5657; 337-334-5658; Fax: 337-334-3301. Email: raynecatholicelem@bellsouth.net. Web: www.raynecatholic.org. Fred Menard, Prin.; Sharon Chatelain, Librarian. Lay Teachers 37; Students 443.
Catechesis/Religious Program—Tel: 337-334-9849; Fax: 337-334-5665. Students 290.

2—OUR MOTHER OF MERCY (1924), (African American), [CEM] Rev. Richard F. Wagner, S.S.J.
Res. & Mailing Address: 707 Lyman Ave., 70578. Tel: 337-334-3516.
Catechesis/Religious Program—Students 102.

RICHARD, ACADIA PARISH, ST. EDWARD (1939) [CEM] [JC] Unassigned.
Res.: 1463 Charlene Hwy., Church Point, 70525. Tel: 337-684-5991; Fax: 337-684-0189.
Catechesis/Religious Program—Students 176.
Mission—St. Thomas Savoy, St. Landry Parish.

ROBERTS COVE, ACADIA PARISH, ST. LEO IV (1883), (German), [CEM] Rev. Paul Broussard.
Res.: 7166 Roberts Cove Rd., Rayne, 70578-8912. Tel: 337-334-5056; Fax: 337-334-0832.
Catechesis/Religious Program—Tel: 337-334-7458. Students 53.
Mission—St. Edmund Chapel Branch, Acadia Parish.

RYNELLA, IBERIA PARISH, ST. MARCELLUS (1960) [CEM] Rev. Eugene R. Tremie.
Res.: 6100 Avery Island Rd., New Iberia, 70560. Tel: 337-364-0818; Fax: 337-364-0824. Email: stmarcellusc@aol.com.
Catechesis/Religious Program—Tel: 337-364-9419. Students 174.

ST. MARTINVILLE, ST. MARTIN PARISH

1—ST. MARTIN OF TOURS (1765) [CEM] Revs. Rusty P. Richard; Kenneth A. Bienvenu (Retired); Deacon Douglas J. Melancon.
Res.: 133 S. Main St., P.O. Drawer 10, 70582. Tel: 337-394-6021; Fax: 337-394-6020.
Catechesis/Religious Program—Tel: 337-394-4203. Students 181.

2—NOTRE DAME DE PERPETUEL SECOURS (1938), (African American), [CEM] [JC] Revs. Augustinus Seran, S.V.D.; Stanley Jawa, S.V.D.; Deacon David Chambers.
Res.: 201 Gary St., 70582. Tel: 337-394-3084; Fax: 337-394-5380.
Catechesis/Religious Program—Tel: 337-394-3084. Students 259.

SCOTT, LAFAYETTE PARISH

1—SAINT MARTIN DE PORRES (1961), (African American), [CEM] Rev. Peter Emusa, Sacramental Min.; Deacon Louis J. Lloyd, Parish Life Coord.
Mailing Address: P.O. Box 1347, 70583-1347. Tel: 337-232-1968; Fax: 337-266-8922. Email: deporres@bellsouth.net.
Catechesis/Religious Program—Students 63.

2—STS. PETER AND PAUL (1904) [CEM] Revs. Thomas P. Voorhies; David B. Hebert.
Mailing Address: 1110 Old Spanish Tr., 70583. Tel: 337-235-2433; Fax: 337-233-4868. Email: stspeterandpaulscott@hotmail.com.
School—Sts. Peter and Paul Catholic School, (Grades PreK-6), 1301 Old Spanish Tr., 70583. Tel: 337-504-3400. Dr. Robert Richard, Prin.; Etta Tarver, Librarian.
Catechesis/Religious Program—Tel: 337-232-6167. Students 471.

VILLE PLATTE, EVANGELINE PARISH

1—ST. JOSEPH (1947), (African American), [CEM] Revs. Joshua P. Guillory; Garrett K. McIntyre; Sr. Rita Darensbourg, S.S.F., Pastoral Assoc.
Res.: 1107 Martin L. King Dr., 70586. Tel: 337-363-1051.
Catechesis/Religious Program—Students 23.

2—OUR LADY QUEEN OF ALL SAINTS (1969) Rev. Marion P. Romero; Deacon Eugene Le Boeuf.
1220 W. Dardeau St., 70586.
Rectory—1135 Parkview St., 70586. Tel: 337-363-5167; Fax: 337-363-5179.
Catechesis/Religious Program—Students 120.

3—SACRED HEART OF JESUS (1854) [CEM] Revs. Joshua P. Guillory; Garrett K. McIntyre, Parochial Vicar.
Res.: 708 E. Main St., 70586. Tel: 337-363-2989; Fax: 337-363-3500. Email: sacredheart-vp@centurytel.net. Web: www.geocities.com/sacredheart-vp.
School—Sacred Heart Elementary, (Grades K-8), 532 E. Main St., 70586. Tel: 337-363-3445; Fax: 337-363-3551. Diane Fontenot, Prin. Lay Teachers 22; Students 521.
High School—Sacred Heart High School, 114 Trojan Ln., 70586. Tel: 337-363-1475; Fax: 337-363-0348. Diane Fontenot, Prin.; Mrs. Dawn C. Shipp, Asst. Prin. Lay Teachers 20; Students 237.
Catechesis/Religious Program—Tel: 337-363-7788; Fax: 337-363-3500. Students 77.
Chapel—Belarie Cove Chapel 2003 Belaire Cove Rd., 70586. Tel: 337-363-2989; Fax: 337-363-3500.

WASHINGTON, ST. LANDRY PARISH

1—HOLY TRINITY (1950), (African American), Rev. Albert Gayle Nunez.
Mailing Address: P.O. Box 186, 70589. Tel: 337-826-3376; Fax: 337-826-3376.
Catechesis/Religious Program—Students 24.

2—IMMACULATE CONCEPTION (1756), (French—German), Rev. Albert Gayle Nunez.
Mailing Address: P.O. Box 116, 70589. Tel: 337-826-7396; Fax: 337-826-0099. Email: immaculate123@charterinternet.com.
Catechesis/Religious Program—Students 92.

YOUNGSVILLE, LAFAYETTE PARISH, ST. ANNE (1859) [CEM] Rev. Thomas Jason Mouton.
Mailing Address: P.O. Box 410, 70592. Tel: 337-856-8212; Fax: 337-856-8277. Email: stanne@bellsouth.net.
Catechesis/Religious Program—Tel: 337-856-8242. Students 435.

On Special Assignment:
Revs.—
Akalawa, Ambrose, Chap., Our Lady of Lourdes.
Boyer, Millard G., Chap. Tel: 337-289-7483 Lafayette General Medical Center, Lafayette
Castano, Jairo, S.D.S., Hispanic Ministry.
Eze, Cyprian, Hospital Ministry - Central Region.
Finley, John Thomas, Chap., Bethany Health Care, Lafayette
Gandara, Juan Luis (Mexico), Hispanic Ministry.
Guidry, Mitchell
Vaniyepurackal, George, Chap., Our Lady of Lourdes, Hospital Ministry.

Graduate Studies:
Revs.—
Broussard, Ken, Canada
Guillory, Joshua P., Rome.
Sensat, Clinton M., New Hampshire

Absent on Sick Leave:
Revs.—
Delauney, Herbert C.
Downs, Gregory Todd, P.O. Box 432, Natchitoches, 71458-0432.
Moreau, Randall
Romero, Marion

On Leave:
Rev. Msgr.—
Herpin, Michael
Revs.—
Alexander, Joseph
Arceneaux, Jules
Gearheard, William

Retired:
Rev. Msgrs.—
Angelle, Robert G., 205 N. Anita St., 70501.
Mallet, Charles J., 40 Audobon Oaks Blvd., 70506.
Metrejean, Paul, 136 Metrejean Ln., Opelousas, 70570.
Mouton, Richard von Phul, 515 Cathedral St., 70501.
Revs.—
Bergeron, C. Paul, 402 Wayside Dr., Houma, 70360.
Betrand, Conley, 1804 W. University Ave., 70506.
Bienvenu, Kenneth A., 1017 Alan Dr., St. Martinville, 70582.
Bourgeois, Francis L., P.O. Box 52, Mamou, 70554-0052.
Brennan, Joseph F., 203 Bocage Circle, 70503.
Brown, Wilbur J., Eunice, LA
Calais, Floyd J., 313 Rue Louis XIV, Apt. H, 70508.

Courville, Robert, 1111 Greenbriar St., Alexandria, 71301.
Cremaldi, Angelo, Patterson, LA
Degeyter, Edward, P.O. Box 923, Saint Martinville, 70582.
DeLeeuw, John, 526 Raintree Tr., 70507.
Dugas, Willard, 520 Dugas Rd., 70507-3010.
Dutra, Luis C., 1522 Carmel Dr., 70501. (Extern-Diocesan)
Estilette, Grady J.
Frey, Jerome V.
Hebert, T. J., 411 Hanover Sq., 70508.
Landry, Oneil Anthony, P.O. Box 202, Centerville, 70522.
Landry, Ralph James, 2603 Bodin Rd., New Iberia, 70560.
Ledoux, Louis Vernon, (Retired Armed Forces), 205-21 115th Rd., Jamaica, NY 11412-2907.
Leger, Austin, 1906 George Dr., Opelousas, 70570.
Matt, J. Wilson, 2319 E. Main St., New Iberia, 70560.
Montelaro, Thomas, 5485 Charleston Blvd., Las Vegas, NV 89142.
Pelous, Donald
Robitaille, Raymond, 2319 Main St., New Iberia, 70560-4096.
Simon, George Howard, 238 Edgewood Dr., 70503.
Stemmann, Joseph, 2319 Main St., New Iberia, 70560.
Theriot, Donald C., 2004 W. Summers Dr., Abbeville, 70510.
Thibodeaux, Paul, 222 Bombardier Ln., Eunice, 70535.
Thychery, George, India.
Trahan, Charles N.
Warren, Arthur, 3305 N.W. Evangeline Thruway, 70507.

Permanent Deacons:
Arnaud, John Kenneth, St. Francis Regis, Arnaudville
Bakeler, Arthur Francis, Jr., Sts. Peter & Paul, Scott
Bergeron, Harris, St. Rita, Catahoula
Besse, Daniel Lee, St. Joseph, Rayne
Bollich, Reginald A., St. Jules, Lafayette
Borbas, Timothy, Houston, TX
Boudreaux, Francis, St. Leo, Leonville
Bourg, Gerald J., Exec. Asst. to Regl. Vicar, South, Sacred Heart, Baldwin
Broussard, Wade, St. Peter, New Iberia
Burke, Patrick Douglas, St. Peter, New Iberia
Chambers, David Brodrick, Notre Dame, St. Martinville
Clark, Michael, Holy Cross, Lafayette
Collins, Jerome, Our Lady Queen of Angels, Opelousas
Comeaux, Joseph, (Retired)
Cormier, Frank Alex, St. Edmond, Lafayette
Cormier, James, Annunciation Bvm, Duralde
Darce, Harry, Sacred Heart, Baldwin
Davis, James, St. Catherine, Arnaudville
DeJean, Alvin Ray, (Unassigned)
Derouen, Raymond Charles, St. Edward, New Iberia
Diesi, Samuel Charles, St. Landry, Opelousas Church
Doumit, Christopher, St. Joseph, Loreauville
Eleazar, Paul, (Retired)
Gaudin, Gary Michael, St. Anthony, Eunice
Guilbeau, Joseph Herd, St. Charles Borromeo, Coteau
Guillory, David, St. Thomas More, Eunice
Hebert, Clifford Mitchell, Jr., Sacred Heart of Jesus, Port Barre
Hebert, Douglas, (Retired)
Hebert, Marcel, St. Bernard, Breaux Bridge
Henry, Samuel, St. Charles, Grand Coteau
Hyde, Randy Eugene, St. Mary Magdalen, Abbeville
Joubert, Ulysse, Our Lady of Mercy, Opelousas
Judice, Julian, (Retired)
Kincel, James (Jim), Dir. & Permanent Diaconate, St. Charles Borromeo, Grand Coteau
Landry, Theodule, St. Nicholas, Lydia
Lebouef, Eugene J., Queen of All Saints, Ville Platte
Ledet, Timothy Francis, St. Joseph, Rayne
Lee, Carlton J., Sr., Notre Dame, St. Martinville
Leger, Robert Lee, St. Mathilda, Eunice
Lejeune, Joseph L., St. Peter, Gueydan
Leleux, Rodless, St. Michael, Crowley
Lindsey, Thomas, Our Lady of Mercy, Opelousas
Lloyd, Louis, St. Martin de Porres, Scott
Maragos, Timothy Alan, Our Lady of Fatima, Lafayette
Marcel, Albert, St. Anthony, Lafayette
Matte, Paul, Not Assigned
McDonner, Robert, Not Assigned
Melancon, Douglas J., St. Martin de Tours, St. Martinville
Miller, Cody, St. Joseph, Milton
Miller, John W., St. Landry, Opelousas
Mouton, Chris, (Leave of Absence)
Nguyen, Tuan Anh, Vietnamese Ministry, Lafayette
Ortego, Charles, Ol Mt. Carmel, Chataignier
Ozene, Anthony, Immaculate Heart of Mary, Lafayette
Perron, Roderick P., (Retired)
Picard, Richard, Holy Cross, Lafayette
Rabailais, Bert, (Retired)
Richard, Thomas, (Retired)
Sarkies, John, (Retired)
Schexnayder, Nelson Joseph, Jr., St. Elizabeth Seton, Lafayette
Senegal, Nolton, St. Edwards, New Iberia
Simon, Steve, St. Theresa, Duson
Smith, Charles J., Cathedral of St. John the Evangelist, Lafayette (Extern)
Soignier, Kenneth Earl, St. Joseph, Cecilia; St. Rose of Lima, Cecilia
Soileau, Harris, (Retired)
Sommers, Thomas Richard, St. John the Baptist, Lyons Point
Thibodeaux, John, (Retired)
Thomas, Joseph, St. Jules, Franklin
Trahan, Joseph, Sacred Heart, Broussard
Tran, Tam, St. Mary Magdalen, Abbeville
Trumps, Jeffrey Paul, Diocesan Finance Officer; Sacred Heart, Broussard
Vaughn, David Lee, St. Anne, Cow Island
Waguespack, Eugene, (Retired)
Waguespack, Kenneth, (Retired)
Winn, Byrne James, St. John Berchmans Cankton
Yenik, Michael Robert, Houston, TX

INSTITUTIONS LOCATED IN THE DIOCESE

[A] SEMINARIES, RELIGIOUS OR SCHOLASTICATES

GRAND COTEAU. *St. Charles College*, P.O. Box C, 70541-1003. Tel: 337-662-5251; Fax: 337-662-3187. Revs. Mark E. Thibodeaux, S.J., Novice Dir.; Daniel White, S.J., Asst. Novice Dir. Novitiate of Missouri and New Orleans Provinces of the Society of Jesus. Priests 2; Novices 11.

[B] HIGH SCHOOLS, INTERPAROCHIAL

LAFAYETTE. *Teurlings Catholic High School* (1955) 139 Teurlings Dr., 70501. Tel: 337-235-5711; Fax: 337-234-8057. Email: mboyer@tchs.net. Web: www.tchs.net. Mr. Michael H. Boyer, Prin.; Mrs. Toni Dueitt, Librarian. Lay Teachers 39; Students 654.

St. Thomas More, 450 E. Farrel Rd., 70508. Tel: 337-988-3700; Fax: 337-988-2911. Web: www.stmcougars.com. Audrey Menard, Prin. Lay Teachers 86; Students 1,048.

CROWLEY. *Notre Dame High School of Acadia Parish*, 910 N. Eastern Ave., 70526. Tel: 337-783-3519; Fax: 337-788-2115. Email: cistre@ndpios.com. Web: www.ndpios.com. Ms. Cindy M. Istre, Prin.; Donna R. Fruge, Librarian. Lay Teachers 36; Students 436.

NEW IBERIA. *Catholic High School*, (Grades 4-12), 1301 DeLaSalle Dr., 70560. Tel: 337-364-5116; Fax: 337-364-5041. Email: rsimon@chspanthers.com. Web: chspanthers.com. Mr. Ray Simon, Prin.; Roberta Landry, Librarian. Lay Teachers 54; Total Staff 72; Students 835.

OPELOUSAS. *Opelousas Catholic School* (1971) (Grades PreK-12), Elementary: (PreK-5); High School: (6-12), 428 E. Prudhomme St., 70570. Tel: 337-942-5404; Fax: 337-942-5922. Email: ocsvikings@yahoo.com. Mr. Perry Fontenot, Prin.; Leslie Carlos, Librarian. Lay Teachers 50; Students 726.

[C] ELEMENTARY SCHOOLS, INTERPAROCHIAL

LAFAYETTE. *Holy Family School* (1903) (Grades PreK-7), 200 St. John St., 70501. Tel: 337-235-0267; Fax: 337-235-0558. Email: hfs98@aol.com. Roger Griffin, Prin.; Dorothy Navarre, Librarian. Sisters of the Holy Family. Sisters 4; Lay Teachers 14; Students 224.

ST. MARTINVILLE. *Trinity Catholic School* (1971) (Grades PreK-8), 242 Gary St., 70582. Tel: 337-394-6693; Fax: 337-394-3394. Email: rpierre@trinitycatholicschoolla.org. Miss Rosemary Pierre, Prin.; Karen Olivier, Librarian. Lay Teachers 17; Total Staff 31; Students 266.

[D] ELEMENTARY SCHOOLS, PRIVATE

ABBEVILLE. *Mt. Carmel Elementary School* (1885) (Grades K-8), 405 Park, 70510. Tel: 337-898-0859; Fax: 337-893-5968. Email: srjanet@mceschool.com. Web: www.mceschool.org. Sr. Janet LeBlanc, O.Carm., Prin.; Jackie Trahan, Asst. Prin.; Tiffany Abshire, Librarian. Sisters of Mt. Carmel 2; Lay Teachers 22; Students 446.

[E] HIGH AND ELEMENTARY SCHOOLS, PRIVATE

GRAND COTEAU. *Academy of the Sacred Heart*, (Grades PreK-12), P.O. Box 310, 70541. Tel: 337-662-5275; Fax: 337-662-3011. Email: llieux@sshcoteau.org. Web: www.sshcoteau.org. Sr. Lynne Lieux, R.S.C.J., Head Mistress; Gail Dack, Ed.D., Prin. (Elementary); Carol Boudreaux, Prin. (High School); Mae Ludeau, Librarian. Day School for both divisions (girls-boys) are single gender. Boarding facilities for girls 7th-12th grade. Religious of the Sacred Heart 1; Lay Teachers 51; Students 355.

Berchmans Academy of the Sacred Heart (Grades PreK-9), (Day school for boys) Lay Teachers 28; Students 127.

[F] GENERAL HOSPITALS

LAFAYETTE. *Our Lady of Lourdes Regional Medical Center, Inc.* (1949) 4801 Ambassador Caffery Pkwy., P.O. Box 4027, 70508. Tel: 337-470-2100; Fax: 337-470-2574. Email: padgettd@lourdesrmc.com. Web: www.lourdes.net. Gerald R. Boudreaux, Chm. of the Governing Bd.; Mr. W.F. "Bud" Barrow, Pres. & CEO. Bed Capacity 186; Total Staff 1,306; Patients Assisted Annually 94,065.

[G] HOMES FOR THE AGED INFIRM

LAFAYETTE. *Bethany M.H.S. Health Care Center* (1962) P.O. Box 2308, 70502. Tel: 337-234-2459; Fax: 337-234-9483. Sisters of the Most Holy Sacrament 5; Total Staff 55; Bed Capacity 42; Total Assisted 49.

Village du Lac, Inc., 1404 Carmel Dr., 70501. Tel: 337-234-5106; Fax: 337-234-2630. J. Bernel Fontenot, Dir. Community housing for the handicapped and elderly with low income. Sponsored by the Diocese. Bed Capacity 200; Total Assisted Annually 197; Total Staff 11.

NEW IBERIA. *Consolata Home* (1960) 2319 E. Main St., 70560. Tel: 337-365-8226; Fax: 337-365-8626. Email: chasdel@cox-internet.com. Charles L. Delahoussaye, Admin.; Rev. Joseph Stemmann, Chap. (Retired). Tel: 337-365-7477. Clergy Apartments 6; Residents 98; Bed Capacity 120; Total Assisted 107; Total Staff 114.

OPELOUSAS. *C'est La Vie Center of the Sisters Marianites of Holy Cross dba C'est la Vie Independent Living Apartments* 960 E. Prudhomme St., 70570. Tel: 337-942-8154; Fax: 337-942-8279. Email: mike@promptsuccor.com. Web: www.promptsuccor.com. Michael Purser, Admin. Independent living for the elderly and handicapped. Sisters 3; Total Staff 6; Bed Capacity 34; Patients Assisted Annually 50.

Our Lady of Prompt Succor Nursing Home dba Our Lady of Prompt Succor Nursing Facility 954 E. Prudhomme St., 70570. Tel: 337-948-3634; Fax: 337-942-8279. Email: mike@promptsuccor.com. Web: www.promptsuccor.com. Michael Purser, Admin. Sisters 30; Patients Assisted Annually 200; Bed Capacity 120; Total Staff 135.

[H] MONASTERIES AND RESIDENCES OF PRIESTS AND BROTHERS

LAFAYETTE. *De La Salle Christian Brothers*, 1522 Carmel Dr., 70501. Tel: 337-235-3576; Fax: 337-261-0765. Email: arthurcsf@aol.com. Bro. Arthur Carroll, F.S.C., Dir.; Rev. Luis C. Dutra, Chap. (Retired). Retired Brothers Home. Brothers 13.

De La Salle Christian Brothers Provincialate, 1530 Carmel Dr., 70501. Tel: 337-234-1973; Fax: 337-261-1014. Email: coldwellnosf@cox.net. Bros. Timothy Coldwell, F.S.C., Prov.; Arthur Carroll, F.S.C., Local Supr.; David Sinitiere, F.S.C., Auxiliary Prov. & Ed. Dir.; Peter Tripp, Prov. & Dir., Resource Mgmt. Headquarters for the New Orleans-Santa Fe District.

OPELOUSAS. *Mother of the Redeemer Monastery* (1990) 168 Monastery Ln., 70570. Tel: 337-543-2237; Fax: 337-543-7752. Revs. James Liprie, O.S.B., Supr.; Bernard V. Lebiedz, O.S.B.; Bro. Mark Bordelon; Rev. Joseph Brasseaux, O.S.B.; Bro. Gabriel Wadlington, O.S.B. Priests 3; Brothers 2.

[I] CONVENTS AND RESIDENCES FOR SISTERS

LAFAYETTE. *Discalced Carmelites* Monastery of Mary, Mother of Grace., 1250 Carmel Dr., 70501-5299. Tel: 337-232-4651; Fax: 337-232-3540. Sr. Regina Mullins, O.C.D., Prioress; Very Rev. Msgr. H. Alexandre Larroque, J.C.D., V.G., Chap. Cloistered Nuns 15; Solemnly Professed 12; Novices 2; Postulants 1.

Franciscan Missionaries of Our Lady, 611 St. Landry St., 70506. Tel: 337-289-2110; Fax: 337-289-2574.

Marianites of Holy Cross, 1417 St. John St., 70506. Tel: 337-234-5454. Email: judithmsc@cs.com. Sisters 3.

Missionaries of Charity, 904 Jack St., 70501. Tel: 337-233-3929. Sisters 4.

School Sisters of Notre Dame, 105 Dogwood, 70501. Tel: 337-504-4360. Email: landrylor@cox.net.

Sisters of Divine Providence (1866) 317 Guilbeau Rd., Apt. 101-E, 70506. Tel: 337-984-8520. Email: mildredleonards@peoplepc.com. Sisters 2.

Sisters of Mt. Carmel (1846) 309 Evangeline Dr., 70501. Tel: 337-235-8687. Sisters 4.

Sisters of the Most Holy Sacrament (1872) *Convent, Generalate & Administrative Offices*, 313 Corona Dr., P.O. Box 90037, 70509-0037. Tel: 337-981-8475; Fax: 337-981-9128. Sr. Judine Theriot, M.H.S., Major Supr. Sisters 28.

CROWLEY. *Marianites of the Holy Cross*, 516 N. Ave. E, 70526. Tel: 337-783-1550; Fax: 337-783-1550. Marianites of Holy Cross 2.

DUSON. *Dominican Sisters of Peace*, P.O. Box 725, 70529. Tel: 337-873-4159; Fax: 337-873-4159. Sisters 11.

GRAND COTEAU. *Religious of the Sacred Heart*, P.O. Box 438, 70541. Tel: 337-662-5526. Email: tdowney@rscj.org. Web: www.rscj.org. Sisters 6.

Sisters of the Holy Spirit, P.O. Box 115, Lebeau, 71345. Tel: 337-623-5540.

NEW IBERIA. *Sisters of Providence*, 213 Oak Hill Rd., 70563. Tel: 337-364-3142.

Sisters of the Blessed Sacrament, 720 Providence St., 70560. Tel: 337-369-9534; Fax: 337-369-9534. Email: stedwards@cox-internet.com. Sisters also reside in Rayne 5.

OPELOUSAS. *Sisters of the Holy Family*, 708 N. Union St., 70570. Tel: 337-942-2052; Fax: 337-942-2052. Email: sr.antonia@charter.net. Sisters 4.

[J] RETREAT HOUSES

GRAND COTEAU. *Jesuit Spirituality Center (St. Charles College)*, P.O. Box C, 70541-1003. Tel: 337-662-5251; Fax: 337-662-3187. Email: office@jesuitspiritualitycenter.org. Web: jesuitspiritualitycenter.org. Revs. Thomas J. Madden, S.J.; Hernando J. Ramirez, S.J.; Anthony H. Ostini, S.J., Supr. of St. Charles & Dir.; Bros. Lawrence J. Huck, S.J.; A. Joseph Martin, S.J.; Sisters Consuelo Champagne, M.S.C.; Marlene Labbe, M.S.C. Year-round directed retreats of 3, 5, 8, or 30 days plus a variety of weekend retreats and/or programs open to men and women. Priests 4; Brothers 1; Sisters 2.

Our Lady of the Oaks Retreat House, P.O. Box D, 70541. Tel: 337-662-5410; Fax: 337-662-5331. Email: oloaks@centurytel.net. Web: www.ourladyoftheoaks.com. Mr. Jimmy L. Dauzat, Dir.; Revs. Jerome H. Neyrey, S.J.; Paul B. Patin, S.J. Jesuit Fathers., Preached retreats for men, women and married couples.

[K] CURSILLO CENTERS

OPELOUSAS. *Cursillo Center*, 3651 Hwy. 104 (Prairie Ronde), 70570. Tel: 337-543-7425; Fax: 337-543-2100. Email: rctomlinson@bellsouth.com. Web: www.whowillsit.com. Rev. Theodore Broussard Jr., Dir.

[L] NEWMAN CENTERS

LAFAYETTE. *Our Lady of Wisdom Catholic Student Center Univ. of Louisiana*, P.O. Box 43271, 70504. Tel: 337-232-8741; 337-232-8742; Fax: 337-236-6737. Email: wisdom@ourladyofwisdom.org. Web: ragincajuncatholic.org. Rev. Bryce Sibley, S.T.L.

EUNICE. *Catholic Student Center-Louisiana State Univ.* P.O. Box 1129, 70535. Tel: 337-457-8668; Cell: 337-580-1129; Fax: 337-457-7298. Email: yogisittig@att.net. Deborah "Yogi" Sittig, Dir. Total Staff 1; Total in Residence 1.

[M] MISCELLANEOUS

LAFAYETTE. *Magnolia Lafayette, Inc.*, 1522 Carmel Dr., 70501. Tel: 504-899-4567. Bros. Timothy Coldwell, F.S.C.; Arthur Carroll, F.S.C.

St. Augustine Trust Fund, P.O. Box 90037, 70509-0037. Tel: 337-981-8475; Fax: 337-981-9128. Sisters of the Most Holy Sacrament.

Brothers of the Christian Schools of Lafayette - Retirement Trust (1988) 1522 Carmel Dr., 70501. Tel: 337-234-1973; Fax: 337-261-1014. Email: coldwellnosf@cox.net; bacomb@joneswalker.com.

Come Lord Jesus! Inc. (1974) 1804 W. University Ave., 70506. Tel: 337-233-6277; Fax: 337-233-6144. Email: comelordjesusprogram@gmail.com. Web: www.comelordjesus.com. Rev. Conley Bertrand, Dir. Priests 3; Total Staff 6.

Community of Jesus Crucified, 421 1/2 Carmel Dr., 70501. Tel: 337-232-7491; Fax: 337-261-5294. Email: cjc_ols@att.net. Revs. Jerome V. Frey, Spiritual Dir. (Retired); Michael Champagne.

St. La Salle Auxiliary (1921) 1522 Carmel Dr., 70501. Tel: 337-234-1973; Fax: 337-261-1014. Email: coldwellnosf@cox.net. The St. LaSalle Auxiliary is a development project of "De La Salle Christian Brothers," a nonprofit organization.

Lourdes Foundation, Inc., 4801 Ambassador Caffery Pkwy., 70508. Tel: 337-470-4610; Fax: 337-470-2574. Web: www.lourdes.net. Jeigh O. Stipe, Exec. Dir.; Ian Macdonald, Chm. & Pres. of Governing Board.

Sisters of the Eucharistic Covenant, 105 Upperline Ave., 70501. Tel: 337-233-2226; Fax: 337-233-2226. Sr. Celeste D. Larroque, S.E.C., Pres.

NEW IBERIA. *Progressive Education Program, Inc.* (1976) P.O. Box 10237, 70562-0237. Tel: 337-365-0933; Fax: 337-364-2555. Email: pepitc1990@gmail.com. Sr. Barbara Kraus, S.S.N.D., Dir.

[N] CATHOLIC SOCIAL SERVICE CENTERS

LAFAYETTE. *Lafayette Catholic Service Centers, Inc.* (1973) 405 St. John St., P.O. Box 3177, 70502-3177. Tel: 337-235-4972; Fax: 337-234-0953. Email: kjames@catholicservice.org. Web: www.catholicservice.org. Total Assisted Annually 51,589.

Service Centers: Kimberly James Boudreaux, Exec. Dir.

Bishop O'Donnell Transitional Housing Tel: 337-233-7788; Fax: 337-234-0953. Email: kjames@catholicservice.org. Web: www.catholicservice.org. Cynthia Herring, Housing Spec.

Msgr. A. O. Sigur Service Center, 401 St. John St., 70501. Tel: 337-233-7788; Fax: 337-234-0953. Web: www.catholicservice.org. Autumn delaHoussaye, Dir.

St. Joseph Shelter for Men, 425 St. John St., 70501. Tel: 337-233-6816; Fax: 337-233-6829. Web: www-.catholicservice.org. Eric Gammons, Dir.

St. Joseph Diner, 613 W. Simcoe, 70501. Tel: 337-232-8434; Fax: 337-234-0953. Web: www.catholicservice.org. Autumn delaHoussaye, Dir.

St. Bernadette Clinic Tel: 337-264-6292; Fax: 337-261-5276.

New Life Center, 411 E. Landry, Opelousas, 70570. Tel: 337-948-3161; Fax: 337-948-0011. Email: mhinman@catholicservice.org. Web: www.catholicservice.org. Michelle Hinman, Dir. Total Assisted Annually 359.

St. Michael Center for Veterans, 425 St. John St., 70501. Tel: 337-233-6816; Fax: 337-233-6829. Web: www.catholicservice.org. Jonathan Linzer, Dir.

CROWLEY. *Crowley Christian Care Center* (1987) 726 W. 7th St., P.O. Box 686, 70527-0686. Tel: 337-783-5811; Fax: 337-783-5811. Total Staff 53; Total Assisted 4,800.

NEW IBERIA. *Social Service Center* (1975) 432 Bank Ave., 70560. Tel: 337-369-6384; Fax: 337-369-7522. Shirley DeClouet, Dir. Total Staff 30; Total Families Assisted 5,000.

OPELOUSAS. *New Life Center*, 411 E. Landry St., P.O. Box 3177, 70502. Tel: 337-948-3161; Fax: 337-948-0011. Email: mhinman@catholicservice.org. Web: www.catholicservice.org. Michelle Hinman, Dir. Emergency Shelter Transitional Housing and Child Care Center for women & children operated under the direction of the Lafayette Catholic Services Centers, Inc. Staff 18; Total Assisted 329.

VILLE PLATTE. *Christian Care and Share Center* (1985) 129 W. Main St., P.O. Box 901, 70586. Tel: 337-363-8041. Mr. Eugene S. Fontenot, Chm. Total Staff 12.

RELIGIOUS INSTITUTES OF MEN REPRESENTED IN THE DIOCESE

For further details refer to the corresponding bracketed number in the Religious Institutes of Men or Women section.

[0200]—*Benedictines (Olivetan, Subiaco Congregation)*—O.S.B.

[0330]—*Brothers of the Christian Schools* (New Orleans Prov.)—F.S.C.

[]—*Carmelites of Mary Immaculate*—C.M.I.

[]—*Claretians*—C.M.F.

[0520]—*Franciscan Friars*—O.F.M.

[]—*Holy Ghost Fathers*—C.S.Sp.

[0690]—*Jesuit Fathers and Brothers* (New Orleans Prov.)—S.J.

[]—*Missionaries of St. Paul* (Nigeria)—M.S.P.

[0610]—*Priests of the Congregation of Holy Cross*—C.S.C.

[]—*Society of the Divine Savior*—S.D.S.

[0420]—*Society of the Divine Word*—S.V.D.

[0700]—*St. Joseph's Society of the Sacred Heart* (Baltimore Prov.)—S.S.J.

RELIGIOUS INSTITUTES OF WOMEN REPRESENTED IN THE DIOCESE

[0400]—*Congregation of Our Lady of Mount Carmel*—O.Carm.

[2410]—*Congregation of the Marianites of Holy Cross*—M.S.C.

[1950]—*Congregation of the Sisters of the Holy Family*—S.S.F.

[0420]—*Discalced Carmelite Nuns*—O.C.D.

[]—*Dominican Rural Missionaries*—O.P.

[1115]—*Dominican Sisters of Peace*—O.P.

[1380]—*Franciscan Missionaries of Our Lady*—O.S.F.

[2710]—*Missionaries of Charity* (Bronx, NY)—M.C.

[4070]—*Religious of the Sacred Heart*—R.S.C.J.

[2970]—*School Sisters of Notre Dame* (South Central)—S.S.N.D.

[0990]—*Sisters of Divine Providence* (San Antonio, TX)—C.D.P.

[]—*Sisters of Our Lady of Sorrows*—O.L.S.

[]—*Sisters of Providence*—S.P.

[2050]—*Sisters of the Holy Spirit and Mary Immaculate*—S.H.Sp.

[2940]—*Sisters of the Most Holy Sacrament*—M.H.S.

NECROLOGY

† Benefiel, Rev. Msgr. Harry E., (Retired)—Died March 13, 2011

An asterisk (*) denotes an organization that has established tax-exempt status directly with the IRS and is not covered by the USCCB Group Ruling.

Diocese of Lafayette in Indiana

(Dioecesis Lafayettenis in Indiana)

Most Reverend

TIMOTHY L. DOHERTY

Bishop of Lafayette in Indiana; ordained Priest June 26, 1976; appointed Sixth Bishop of Lafayette in Indiana May 12, 2010; ordained and installed as Bishop July 15, 2010. *Office: P.O. Box 260, Lafayette, IN 47902-0260.*

Office of Bishop and Chancery: P.O. Box 260, Lafayette, IN 47902-0260. Tel: 765-742-0275; Fax: 765-742-7513.

Web: www.dioceseoflafayette.org

Most Reverend

WILLIAM L. HIGI, D.D.

Bishop Emeritus of Lafayette in Indiana; ordained May 30, 1959; appointed Bishop of Lafayette in Indiana April 7, 1984; consecrated and installed June 6, 1984; retired May 12, 2010. *Res.: 610 Lingle Ave., P.O. Box 260, Lafayette, IN 47902-0260.*

CANONICALLY ERECTED OCTOBER 21, 1944.

Square Miles 9,832.

Comprises the Counties of Benton, Blackford, Boone, Carroll, Cass, Clinton, Delaware, Fountain, Fulton, Grant, Hamilton, Howard, Jasper, Jay, Madison, Miami, Montgomery, Newton, Pulaski, Randolph, Tippecanoe, Tipton, Warren and White in the State of Indiana.

For legal titles of parishes and diocesan institutions, consult the Bishop's Office (Chancery).

STATISTICAL OVERVIEW

Personnel	
Bishop	1
Retired Bishops	1
Priests: Diocesan Active in Diocese	66
Priests: Diocesan Active Outside Diocese	26
Priests: Retired, Sick or Absent	25
Number of Diocesan Priests	117
Religious Priests in Diocese	15
Total Priests in Diocese	132
Extern Priests in Diocese	6
Ordinations:	
Diocesan Priests	4
Transitional Deacons	3
Permanent Deacons in Diocese	17
Total Brothers	3
Total Sisters	54
Parishes	
Parishes	62
With Resident Pastor:	
Resident Diocesan Priests	45
Resident Religious Priests	6
Without Resident Pastor:	
Administered by Priests	11
Professional Ministry Personnel:	
Brothers	3
Sisters	9
Lay Ministers	52
Welfare	
Catholic Hospitals	7
Total Assisted	1,008,547
Homes for the Aged	1
Total Assisted	590
Educational	
Diocesan Students in Other Seminaries	22
Total Seminarians	22
Colleges and Universities	3
Total Students	9,554
High Schools, Diocesan and Parish	2
Total Students	1,017
Elementary Schools, Diocesan and Parish	18
Total Students	3,820
Catechesis/Religious Education:	
High School Students	2,934
Elementary Students	8,928
Total Students under Catholic Instruction	26,275
Teachers in the Diocese:	
Priests	1
Brothers	3
Sisters	7
Lay Teachers	353
Vital Statistics	
Receptions into the Church:	
Infant Baptism Totals	1,791
Minor Baptism Totals	114
Adult Baptism Totals	138
Received into Full Communion	274
First Communions	2,163
Confirmations	1,660
Marriages:	
Catholic	254
Interfaith	161
Total Marriages	415
Deaths	777
Total Catholic Population	95,619
Total Population	1,296,384

Former Bishops—Most Rev. JOHN GEORGE BENNETT, D.D., LL.D., ord. June 27, 1914; appt. First Bishop of Lafayette Nov. 11, 1944; cons. Jan. 10, 1945; died Nov. 20, 1957; His Eminence JOHN CARDINAL CARBERRY, D.D., S.T.D., J.C.D., Ph.D., ord. July 28, 1929; appt. Coadjutor with Right of Succession Aug. 22, 1956; appt. Bishop of Lafayette in Indiana Nov. 20, 1957; transferred to Diocese of Columbus, Jan. 20, 1965; transferred to the Archdiocese of St. Louis March 24, 1968; created Cardinal April 28, 1969; retired July 31, 1979; died June 17, 1998; Most Revs. RAYMOND J. GALLAGHER, D.D., ord. March 25, 1939; appt. Bishop of Lafayette in Indiana June 23, 1965; cons. Aug. 11, 1965; installed Aug. 23, 1965; resigned Oct. 26, 1982; retired April 13, 1983; died March 7, 1991; GEORGE A. FULCHER, S.T.D., D.D., ord. Feb. 28, 1948; appt. Auxiliary Bishop of Columbus, OH and Titular Bishop of Morosbido May 24, 1976; cons. July 18, 1976; appt. Bishop of Lafayette in Indiana Feb. 8, 1983; installed April 14, 1983; died Jan. 25, 1984; WILLIAM L. HIGI, ord. May 30, 1959; appt. Bishop of Lafayette in Indiana April 7, 1984; cons. and installed June 6, 1984; retired May 12, 2010.

Vicar General—Rev. Msgr. ROBERT L. SELL III, J.C.L., V.G.

Chancellor and Moderator of the Curia—Rev. Msgr. ROBERT L. SELL III, J.C.L., V.G.

Office of Bishop and Chancery—Mailing Address: P.O. Box 260, Lafayette, 47902-0260. Tel: 765-742-0275; Fax: 765-742-7513.

Deans—Revs. DANIEL B. GARTLAND, V.F., Lafayette Deanery; ROBERT L. WILLIAMS, V.F., Anderson Deanery; DONALD L. GROSS, V.F., Fowler Deanery; THEODORE D. ROTHROCK, V.F., Carmel Deanery; FRANCIS I. KILCLINE III, V.F., Logansport Deanery; ROBERT E. MORAN, V.F., Muncie Deanery.

Diocesan Consultors—Rev. Msgr. ROBERT L. SELL III, J.C.L., V.G.; Revs. DANIEL B. GARTLAND, V.F.; THEODORE D. ROTHROCK, V.F.; MICHAEL A. MCKINNEY; DONALD L. GROSS, V.F.; FRANCIS I. KILCLINE III, V.F.; ROBERT L. WILLIAMS, V.F.

Diocesan Pastoral Office for Administration—Mr. ROBERT H. QUINN, Finance Officer; EILEEN HATKE, Financial Svcs. Mgr.; MARILYN DEHNE, Accounts Coord.; KATHY ASKINS, Admin. Asst.; KENT MIKESELL, Maintenance; ANDREW A. GULJAS, Facilities Mgmt. Coord., Mailing Address: P.O. Box 260, Lafayette, 47902-0260. Tel: 765-742-4852. Email: aguljas@dioceseoflafayette.org. Conducts the financial affairs of the diocese; oversees employee benefit program.

Diocesan Pastoral Office for Planning and Communication—KEVIN CULLEN, Dir., Mailing Address: P.O. Box 1603, Lafayette, 47902-1603. Tel: 765-742-2050. Shipping Address: 610 Lingle Ave., Lafayette, 47901-1740.

Publisher- "The Catholic Moment"—KEVIN CULLEN, Editor; LAURIE CULLEN, Asst. Editor; CAROLINE MOONEY, Contributing Editor; CAROLYN MCKINNEY, Advertising/Circulation, Coordinates pastoral planning; serves the communications needs of the diocese primarily through "The Catholic Moment"; maintains the diocesan web page on the world wide web.

Pastoral Office for Family Life—Catholic Pastoral Center, 2300 S. Ninth St., Lafayette, 47909-2400. Tel: 765-474-6644; Fax: 765-474-3403. VACANT, Dir.

Associates for Hispanic Ministry—Deacons DOMINGO CASTILLO; JOSE MUNOZ. Tel: 888-544-1684.

Administrative Assistant—CHARLENE KUHN, Promotes the dignity of the family and all human life through promotion and coordination of programs dealing with family life, marriage preparation and pro-life activities.

Pastoral Office for Worship & RCIA—Catholic Pastoral Center, 2300 S. Ninth St., Lafayette, 47909-2400. Tel: 765-474-6644; Fax: 765-474-3403. JULIE MALES, Dir.; JUDY HANSELL, Receptionist, Provides direction, consultation and staff development opportunities for pastors, principals, directors of religious education, teachers and catechists of the schools and parishes.

Associate Director for Music—ROSE HALLBERG.

Associate Director for Liturgical Resources—BETH BERGER.

Pastoral Office for Catechesis—Dr. ANNE D. ROAT, Dir.; PAUL SHIREMAN, Assoc. Dir. Lay Ministry Formation, Provides formational opportunities for adults; prepares men and women for lay ministry in the diocese and the catholic church through human, spiritual, pastoral and intellectual formation.; EVELYN BURTON, Assoc. Dir. Youth Formation; NAN CLAIRE ROSS, Assoc. Dir. Faith Formation; TRICIA MULLER, Administrative Asst.

Pastoral Office for Stewardship and Development—ROBERT MCCREARY, Dir. Planned Giving; KATHY WALDREP, Assoc. Dir.; KARLA SAMPLES, Administrative Asst., Oversees the Biennial Fruitful Harvest Appeal; organizes and presents estate planning programs, the Annual Seminary Fund Appeal and Diocesan Capital Campaigns.

Pastoral Office for Education and Youth Catechesis—Dr. MARIE WILLIAMS, Supt.; MARY BANTA, Assoc. for Educ.; LOUISE SMITH, Admin. Asst.

Diocesan Tribunal—Catholic Pastoral Center, 2300 S. Ninth St., Lafayette, 47909-2400. Tel: 765-474-0506.

Officialis—Rev. TIMOTHY M. ALKIRE, J.C.L.

Vice Officialis—VACANT.

First Instance—

Presiding Judge—Rev. TIMOTHY M. ALKIRE, J.C.L.

Associate Judges—Revs. PETER J. VANDERKOLK; SAMUEL JOSEPH KALU, J.C.L.; DAVID L. RASNER, J.C.L.

Defenders of the Bond—Revs. DONALD L. GROSS, V.F.; DAVID J. BUCKLES, J.C.L.; WILLIAM R. VATH, Appelate Court.

Ecclesiastical Notary—VERNA S. MEEK.

Full-Time Advocates—BRIDGET O'BRIEN; LOU CUFFING.

Periti—VERONICA GIBBS, M.S.

Second Instance—

Presiding Judge—Rev. DAVID L. RASNER, J.C.L.

Associate Judges—Revs. DAVID J. BUCKLES, J.C.L.; PETER J. VANDERKOLK; TIMOTHY M. ALKIRE, J.C.L.; Rev. Msgrs. JOHN C. DUNCAN; FRED E. POTTHOFF (Retired); Very Rev. GERALD J. BORAWSKI; Revs. JAMES R. GOODRUM (Retired); PAUL W. COCHRAN; EDWARD F. DHONDT (Retired); DAVID J. NEWTON.

Defender of the Bond—Rev. WILLIAM R. VATH.

Ecclesiastical Notary—VERNA S. MEEK.

Advocates— Refer to the Court of First Instance.

Periti— Refer to the Court of First Instance.

Administrative Causes—Rev. Msgr. ROBERT L. SELL III, J.C.L., V.G.

Diocesan Offices and Directors

Archivist—VACANT.

Building Commission—NORBERT STRANSKY, Chm.; Rev. THEODORE D. ROTHROCK, V.F.; Rev. Msgr. ROBERT L. SELL III, J.C.L., V.G., Ex Officio; ANDREW A. GULJAS, Ex Officio; MICHAEL GIBSON; EUGENE HATKE; STEPHAN GOFFINET; Dr. DOUGLAS SUTTON; WILL WRIGHT; DENNIS G. PAGE; ANDRE MAUE.

Office of the Permanent Diaconate—Rev. THEODORE C. DUDZINSKI, Episcopal Vicar. Associate Directors: Deacons STEPHEN MILLER, Dir. Formation; JOHN JEZIERSKI, Assoc. Dir. Formation & Coord. Academics; MIKE GRAY, Assoc. Dir. Personnel; WILLIAM REID, Coord. Pastoral Field Educ. & Vocation Recruitment; Rev. DALE W. EHRMAN, Dir. Spiritual Formation. Administrative Assistants: CHRISTINA ANDERSON; SUZANNE KEARNEY, Mailing Address: 3155 S. County Rd., 200 W., Kokomo, 46902-9611. Tel: 765-865-6688; Fax: 765-865-6683.

Office of the Ecclesial Lay Ministry Program—Dr. ANNE D. ROAT, Dir.; PAUL SHIREMAN, Assoc.; LINDA HARMON, Administrative Asst., Mailing Address: 2300 S. 9th St., Lafayette, 47909-2400. Tel: 765-474-6644; 888-544-1684; Fax: 765-474-3403.

Finance Officer—Mr. ROBERT H. QUINN, Mailing Address: P.O. Box 260, Lafayette, 47902-0260. Tel: 765-742-4852.

Administration— Refer to Diocesan Pastoral Office.

Corporation— Roman Catholic Diocese of Lafayette in Indiana, Inc. (Incorporated, March 21, 1958). Most Rev. TIMOTHY L. DOHERTY, Ph.D., D.D., Pres. & Treas.; Rev. Msgr. ROBERT L. SELL III, J.C.L., V.G., Vice Pres. & Sec.; Mr. ROBERT H. QUINN, Asst. Sec. & Treas.

Director of Planned Giving—ROBERT MCCREARY, Mailing Address: Bishop's Office, P.O. Box 1687, Lafayette, 47902-1687. Tel: 765-742-7000; Fax: 765-742-7513.

Fruitful Harvest Office—Mailing Address: P.O. Box 1687, Lafayette, 47902. Tel: 765-742-4852.

Finance Council—Most Rev. TIMOTHY L. DOHERTY, Ph.D., D.D.; Rev. Msgr. ROBERT L. SELL III, J.C.L., V.G.; Mr. ROBERT H. QUINN, Dir. Pastoral Office for Admin.; LEON CYR; LEO DIERCKMAN; LYNN LAYDEN; MARIANNE MCLEAN; LEE SNIDER; DON GOETZ; EDWARD LOPKE; MARY PIANTEK; TOM PARENT, Legal Advisor.

Human Resources Department—HELEN BENDER, Dir.; CAROL MALLETT, Administrative Asst., Mailing Address: P.O. Box 260, Lafayette, 47902-0260. Tel: 765-742-4852.

Legal Council—JOHN C. DUFFEY, Mailing Address: Life Building, P.O. Box 1010, Lafayette, 47902. Tel: 765-423-1561; Fax: 765-742-8175.

Presbyteral Council—Revs. THEODORE D. ROTHROCK, V.F., Chm.; ROBERT L. WILLIAMS, V.F., Vice Chm.

Members—Rev. Msgr. ROBERT L. SELL III, J.C.L., V.G.; Revs. BRIAN A. DUDZINSKI; THEODORE D. ROTHROCK, V.F.; MICHAEL A. MCKINNEY; PATRICK BAIKAUSKAS, O.P.; DANIEL B. GARTLAND, V.F.; DONALD L. GROSS, V.F.; ROBERT E. MORAN, V.F.; ROBERT J. BERNOTAS; FRANCIS I. KILCLINE III, V.F.; DAVID A. HOYING, C.PP.S.

Catholic Relief Services—VACANT.

Censor Librorum—Rev. DAVID L. RASNER, J.C.L., Catholic Pastoral Center, 2300 S. Ninth St., Lafayette, 47909-2400. Tel: 765-474-0506.

Aquinas Educational Foundation, Inc.—Rev. PATRICK BAIKAUSKAS, O.P., Res. Agent, 535 State St., West Lafayette, 47906. Tel: 765-743-4653.

Catholic Charities Central Office— Refer to Diocesan Pastoral Office.

Superintendent for Catholic Schools—Dr. MARIE WILLIAMS, The Catholic Pastoral Center, 2300 S. Ninth St., Lafayette, 47909-2400. Tel: 765-474-6644.

Liturgical Commission— Refer to Diocesan Pastoral Office.

Eucharistic League—The Chancery, P.O. Box 260, Lafayette, 47902.

Greater Lafayette Catholic School Board—Rev. TIMOTHY M. ALKIRE, J.C.L. Tel: 765-742-5064.

Greater Lafayette Catholic School Foundation, Inc.—WILLIAM BURNS, P.O. Box 1493, Lafayette, 47902.

Holy Childhood Association—VACANT.

Diocesan Board of Education— Refer to Diocesan Pastoral Office.

D.C.C.W.—BETH KEELE, Pres., 1016 Coin Dr., Frankfort, 46041.

Ministry to Priests' Program—Rev. CHRISTOPHER J. WELDON, Dir., St. Francis of Assisi, 1200 W. Riverside Ave., Muncie, 47303-3692. Tel: 765-288-6180.

Newman Apostolate, Purdue University—Rev. PATRICK BAIKAUSKAS, O.P., Dir., 535 State St., West Lafayette, 47906. Tel: 765-743-4652.

Newman Foundation, Ball State, Inc.—Rev. CHRISTOPHER J. WELDON, Dir., 1200 Riverside Ave., Muncie, 47303. Tel: 765-288-6180.

Newspaper "The Catholic Moment"—KEVIN CULLEN, Editor; LAURIE CULLEN, Asst. Editor; CAROLINE MOONEY, Contributing Editor; CAROLYN MCKINNEY, Advertising, Editorial Office, P.O. Box 1603, Lafayette, 47902. Tel: 765-742-2050.

Office of the Apostolate to the Spanish Speaking—Deacon DOMINGO CASTILLO, Assoc. Dir., 1404 Ironwood Dr., Marion, 46952. Tel: 317-662-6078. Res.: Guadalupe Center. Tel: 765-664-3710.

Propagation of the Faith—Rev. Msgr. ROBERT L. SELL III, J.C.L., V.G., Refer to the Bishop's Office.

Religious Education Dept.— Refer to Pastoral Office for Formation.

Rural Life Program—VACANT, Dir.

Schools— See Superintendent listing.

St. Joseph Memorial Hospital Foundation, Inc.—PEGGY CALDWELL, Exec. Dir., 1907 W. Sycamore St., Kokomo, 46901. Tel: 765-456-5425.

Vicar for Clergy—Rev. DALE W. EHRMAN, Sacred Heart of Jesus, 429 Main St., Cicero, 46034-9658.

Vicar for Hispanic Ministry in White County—Rev. CHRISTOPHER T. MILLER, 600 St. Mary's Ave., Frankfort, 46041-2735.

Vicar for Religious—VACANT.

Victim Assistance Coordinator—TIMOTHY HECK, Ph.D. Tel: 800-533-7018.

Conduct in Ministry Officer—CHARLES "MAX" LAYDEN. Tel: 765-463-2242.

Vocation Director—Rev. DAVID JOSEPH HASSER, St. Alphonsus Ligouri, 1870 W. Oak St., Zionsville, 46077-1894. Tel: 765-513-1800.

CLERGY, PARISHES, MISSIONS AND PAROCHIAL SCHOOLS

CITY OF LAFAYETTE

(TIPPECANOE COUNTY)

1—ST. MARY CATHEDRAL (1843) [JC] Revs. Daniel B. Gartland, Rector; Eric Christopher Underwood; Matthew J. Arbuckle; Andrew DeKeyser.
Res.: 1207 Columbia St., 47901-1522. Tel: 765-742-4440; Fax: 765-742-8933.
School—(Grades PreK-3) Tel: 765-742-6302. Lay Teachers 10; Preschool 65; Students 134.
Catechesis/Religious Program—Tel: 765-742-8336. Students 154.

2—ST. ANN (1884) [JC] Rev. Dominic G. Young.
Res.: 612 Wabash Ave., 47905-1096. Tel: 765-742-7031; Fax: 765-429-5690. Email: dominic.stannli@frontier.com.
Catechesis/Religious Program—Tel: 765-423-4635. Students 60.

3—ST. BONIFACE (1853), (German), [CEM] Revs. Timothy M. Alkire; Jeffrey D. Martin; Deacons Ron Nevinger; Jose Munoz. In Res., Revs. William R. Vath; Gustavo Lopez (Mexico).
Res.: 318 N. Ninth St., 47904-2597. Tel: 765-742-5063; Fax: 765-742-5018. Email: bonioffice@comcast.net. Web: www.stboniface.org.
School—St. Boniface Middle School, (Grades 4-6) Tel: 765-742-7913; Fax: 765-423-4988. Email: srlenore@lcss.org. Web: lcss.org. Sr. M. Lenore Schwartz, O.S.F., Prin. Sisters 1; Lay Teachers 6; Students 129.
Catechesis/Religious Program—Tel: 765-742-1351. Email: religioused@maxkolbe.net. Judy Edwards, D.R.E.; Jenny Haro, Asst. D.R.E.; Jessica Hickey, Dir. Catechesis. Students 346.

4—ST. LAWRENCE (1895) Revs. Daniel B. Gartland; Matthew J. Arbuckle; Eric Christopher Underwood; Andrew DeKeyser; Michael Gray; John Jezierski.
Res.: 1916 Meharry St., 47904-1442. Tel: 765-742-2107; Fax: 765-742-1347.
School—1902 Meharry St., 47904-1497. Tel: 765-742-4450. Jody Williams, Prin. Lay Teachers 13; Students 284.
Catechesis/Religious Program—Tel: 765-423-2396. Carl Wagner, D.R.E. Students 224.

OUTSIDE THE CITY OF LAFAYETTE

ALEXANDRIA, MADISON CO., ST. MARY (1896) Rev. Alejandro Paternoster, Admin.
Res.: 820 W. Madison St., 46001-1520. Tel: 765-724-2483; 765-724-4459; Fax: 765-724-9711.
School—Tel: 765-724-4459. Sisters 1; Lay Teachers 6; Students 89.
Catechesis/Religious Program—Students 39.

ANDERSON, MADISON CO.

1—ST. AMBROSE (1947) Rev. Robert L. Williams. In Res., Rev. Edward F. Dhondt (Retired).
Res.: 2801 Lincoln St., 46016-5067. Tel: 765-644-5956; Fax: 765-642-9439. Web: www.st.ambrosechurch.com.
School—2825 Lincoln St., 46016. Tel: 765-642-8428; Fax: 765-642-7348. Email: stan.warner@ambrosechurch.com. Lay Teachers 13; Students 120.
Catechesis/Religious Program—Students 174.

2—ST. MARY (1858) [CEM] Rev. Robert L. Williams; Janice Storey, Pastoral Min.
Res.: 1115 Pearl St., 46016-1789. Tel: 765-644-8467; Fax: 765-648-4000. Email: stoner@catholicweb.com. Web: www.stmary.catholicweb.com.
School—Tel: 765-642-1848; Fax: 765-642-1828. Email: stmarys.school@catholicweb.com. Web: www.smschool.catholicweb.com. Ms. Elizabeth Richards, Prin. Lay Teachers 19; Students 166.
Station—St. John Medical Center Chapel 46016. Tel: 765-649-2511.
Catechesis/Religious Program—Tel: 765-644-8467. Email: stmarys.minister@catholicweb.com. Students 117.

ATTICA, FOUNTAIN CO., ST. FRANCIS XAVIER (1863) [CEM] Rev. David L. Rasner.
Res.: 407 S. Perry St., P.O. Box 55, 47918-0001. Tel: 765-762-3330.
Catechesis/Religious Program—Students 70.

BRYANT, JAY CO., HOLY TRINITY (1861), (German), [CEM] Rev. David A. Hoying, C.PP.S.
Res.: 7321 E. SR 67, 47326-9636. Tel: 219-997-6450. Email: dahht@watchtv.net.
Catechesis/Religious Program—Tel: 219-997-6450. Students 142.

CARMEL, HAMILTON CO.

1—ST. ELIZABETH ANN SETON (1981) Revs. Theodore D. Rothrock; Brendan O. Mbagwu; Sean V. Pogue; Deacon William Reid.
Res.: 10655 Haverstick Rd., 46033-3800. Tel: 317-846-3850; Fax: 317-846-3710. Email: parish@seas-carmel.org. Web: www.seas-carmel.org.
Catechesis/Religious Program—Tel: 317-816-0045. Students 696.

2—OUR LADY OF MOUNT CARMEL (1955) Rev. Richard J. Doerr; Rev. Msgr. John C. Duncan; Revs. Adam Mauman; Mark Walter; Raymond A. Akeriwe; Deacon William Rahill.
Office: 14598 Oak Ridge Rd., 46032-1198. Tel: 317-846-3475; Fax: 317-846-3477. Web: www.olmc1.org.
School—14596 Oak Ridge Rd., 46032-1198. Tel: 317-846-1118; Fax: 317-582-2375. Web: www.olmc-school.org. Dominican Sisters of St. Cecilia 4; Lay Teachers 39; Students 672.
Catechesis/Religious Program—Tel: 317-846-3878. Students 1,039.

CICERO, HAMILTON CO., SACRED HEART OF JESUS

(1898), (German—Irish), Rev. Dale W. Ehrman.
Res.: 429 S. Main St., 46034-9680. Tel: 317-984-5117; Fax: 317-984-5117. Web: www.sacredheartcicero.org.
Catechesis/Religious Program—Tel: 317-984-2115. Students 54.

COVINGTON, FOUNTAIN CO., ST. JOSEPH (1861) [CEM] Rev. David L. Rasner.
Res.: 308 Pearl St., 47932-1062. Tel: 765-793-3289.
Catechesis/Religious Program—Tel: 765-793-4628. Students 25.

CRAWFORDSVILLE, MONTGOMERY CO., ST. BERNARD (1859) [CEM] Rev. Dennis A. Faker.
Res.: 1306 E. Main St., 47933-0719. Tel: 765-362-6121; Fax: 765-361-0796. Email: stbernardchurch@sbcglobal.net.
Catechesis/Religious Program—Tel: 765-362-6121, Ext. 17. Email: amy.huff@sbcglobal.net. Amy Huff, D.R.E. & Youth Min. Students 110.

DE MOTTE, JASPER CO., ST. CECILIA (1952) [CEM] Rev. Msgr. Robert L. Sell III.
Mailing Address: P.O. Box 700, 46310-0700.
Res.: 334 Fifteenth St., S.W., 46310-9269. Tel: 219-987-3511.
Catechesis/Religious Program—Tel: 219-987-3514. Students 152.

DELPHI, CARROLL CO., ST. JOSEPH (1859) [CEM] Rev. Peter J. Vanderkolk.
Res.: 207 N. Washington St., 46923-1297. Tel: 765-564-2407.
Catechesis/Religious Program—Tel: 765-564-3601. Students 153.

DUNKIRK, JAY CO., ST. MARY (1896) Rev. David J. Newton.
Res.: 346 S. Broad St., P.O. Box 286, 47336-0286. Tel: 765-768-6157.
Catechesis/Religious Program—Students 31.

DUNNINGTON, BENTON CO., ST. MARY (1876) [CEM] Rev. Donald L. Gross.
Mailing Address: 2961 South SR71, Ambia, 47917. Tel: 765-884-1818.
Catechesis/Religious Program—Students 28.

EARL PARK, BENTON CO., ST. JOHN THE BAPTIST (1888) [CEM] Rev. Robert J. Bernotas.
Mailing Address: P.O. Box 131, Kentland, 47951-0131.
Catechesis/Religious Program— Combined with Sacred Heart, Fowler

ELWOOD, MADISON CO., ST. JOSEPH (1889), (Irish—German), [CEM] [JC] Rev. Alejandro Paternoster, Admin.
Res.: 1306 S. A St., 46036-1941. Tel: 765-552-6753.
Catechesis/Religious Program—Tel: 765-552-6753. Elaine Bowers, D.R.E. Students 55.

FISHERS, HAMILTON CO.

1—HOLY SPIRIT CHURCH (1991) Rev. Phillip T. Bowers.
Res.: 10350 Glaser Way, 46037. Tel: 317-849-9245; Fax: 317-849-9388.
Catechesis/Religious Program—Tel: 317-849-8016. Students 1,848.

2—ST. JOHN VIANNEY PARISH (2005) Rev. Brian A. Dudzinski.
15176 Blessed Mother Blvd., 46037. Tel: 317-485-0150; Fax: 317-485-0153. Web: stjohnvianney-fishers.com.
Catechesis/Religious Program—Timothy O'Donnell, D.R.E.; Jim Stroud, D.R.E. Students 88.

3—ST. LOUIS DE MONTFORT (1978) Revs. Patrick R. Click; John D. Kiefer.
Res.: 11441 Hague Rd., 46038-1876. Tel: 317-842-6778; Fax: 317-576-1932. Email: info@sldmfishers.org. Web: sldmfishers.org.
School—11421 Hague Rd., 46038. Tel: 317-842-1125; Fax: 317-842-1126. Email: ajones@sldmfishers.org. Annette Jones, Prin. Lay Teachers 28; Students 483.
Catechesis/Religious Program—Students 614.

FOWLER, BENTON CO., SACRED HEART OF JESUS (1872) [CEM] Rev. Donald L. Gross.
Res.: 107 E. Main St., 47944-1148. Tel: 765-884-1818; Fax: 765-884-1583.
School—Tel: 765-884-0710; Fax: 765-884-0710. Mrs. Terri Goodman, Prin. Lay Teachers 10; Students 95.
Catechesis/Religious Program—Students 80.
Mission—St. Mary's Church 2961 S. State Rd. 71, Ambia, 47917-8516.

FRANCESVILLE, PULASKI CO., ST. FRANCIS SOLANO (1867) Rev. Paul R. White, C.PP.S., Admin. (Retired). St. Joseph's College: P.O. Box 852, Rensselaer, 47978. Tel: 219-866-6271.
Catechesis/Religious Program—Students 3.

FRANKFORT, CLINTON CO., ST. MARY (1875) [CEM] Rev. Christopher T. Miller.
Res.: 600 St. Mary's Ave., 46041-2735. Tel: 765-654-5796; Fax: 765-654-6589. Email: stmarysfkt@sbcglobal.net.
Preschool—Tel: 765-659-3914.
Catechesis/Religious Program—Tel: 765-654-2913. Email: stmarysjohnpaul@sbcglobal.net. Students 277.

GAS CITY, GRANT CO., HOLY FAMILY (1908) Rev. Richard J. Weisenberger.
Res.: 325 E. North A St., 46933-1431. Tel: 765-674-2605; Fax: 765-674-3875. Email: hcatholicchurch@indy.rr.com.
Catechesis/Religious Program—Students 40.

GOODLAND, NEWTON, SS. PETER AND PAUL (1880) [CEM] Rev. Robert J. Bernotas.
Church: 421 S. Newton St., 47948-8156.
Catechesis/Religious Program— Combined with St. Joseph, Kentland

HARTFORD CITY, BLACKFORD CO., ST. JOHN THE EVANGELIST (1865) Rev. David J. Newton.
Res.: 209 S. Spring St., 47348-2551. Tel: 765-348-3123; Fax: 765-348-4399.
Catechesis/Religious Program—Students 42.

KENTLAND, NEWTON, ST. JOSEPH (1864) [CEM] Rev. Robert J. Bernotas.
P.O. Box 131, 47951-1322.
St. Joseph School Foundation, Inc.—Tel: 219-474-5514.
Catechesis/Religious Program—Students 53.

KEWANNA, FULTON CO., ST. ANN (1857) [CEM] Rev. Herbert Woolson, Admin.
Mailing Address: 1310 Main St., Rochester, 46975.
Catechesis/Religious Program—Tel: 574-223-2808; Fax: 574-224-2808.

KOKOMO, HOWARD CO.

1—ST. JOAN OF ARC (1927) Revs. Theodore C. Dudzinski; David Huemmer; Joshua T. Bennett; Anthony T. Rowland.
3155 S. 200 W., 46902-9611.
School—Sts. Joan of Arc & Patrick, (Grades PreSchool-8) Jan Underwood, Librarian. (Consolidated School) Lay Teachers 14; Students 149.
Catechesis/Religious Program—Students 236.

2—ST. PATRICK (1859) [JC] Revs. Theodore C. Dudzinski; David Huemmer; Anthony T. Rowland; Joshua T. Bennett. Email: frbennett@saintjoan.org.
Office & Mailing Address: 320 W. Broadway, 46901-2898. Tel: 765-452-6021; Fax: 765-868-8384. Web: www.stpatrick-kokomo.org.
Res.: 1229 N. Washington, 46901-2898.
School—Sts. Joan of Arc & Patrick, 1230 N. Armstrong St., 46901. Tel: 765-459-4769; Fax: 765-457-3096. Web: www.stsjp.org. Lay Teachers 12; Students 187.
Catechesis/Religious Program—Students 121.

LAKE VILLAGE, NEWTON, ST. AUGUSTA (1947) [JC] Rev. Stephen Snoich, O.S.B.
Res.: 3228 W. St. Rd. 10, 46349-9706. Tel: 219-992-3220; Fax: 219-992-9332. Email: staugusta@sbcglobal.net.
Catechesis/Religious Program—Students 45.

LEBANON, BOONE CO., ST. JOSEPH (1862) [CEM] Rev. Timothy Kroeger; Norma DeLaRosa, Youth Min.
Mailing Address: P.O. Box 309, 46052-0309. Tel: 765-482-5558; Fax: 765-482-1436. Email: stjoe@stjoeleb.org. Web: www.stjoeleb.org.
Res.: 310 E. Pearl St., 46052-2684. Tel: 765-482-5558.
Catechesis/Religious Program—Email: religioused@stjoeleb.org. Caroline VanAtter, D.R.E. Students 220.

LOGANSPORT, CASS CO., ALL SAINTS (1985) [JC], Consolidation of the following three parishes (Legal Titles): St. Bridget (1875); St. Joseph (1868); and St. Vincent de Paul (1838). Rev. Michael A. McKinney; Deacon Juan Rodriguez.
Parish Office—112 E. Market St., 46947-3428. Tel: 574-722-4080; Fax: 574-722-5426. Web: www.allsaintslogansport.com.
School—All Saints Elementary, (Grades PreSchool-6), 121 Eel River Ave., 46947-3188. Tel: 574-753-3410; Fax: 574-753-1608. Lay Teachers 10; Students 167.
Catechesis/Religious Program—Tel: 574-722-4080; Fax: 574-722-5426. Students 308.

LUCERNE, CASS CO., ST. ELIZABETH (1953) Closed. For inquiries for parish records, please see All Saints Church, Logansport.

MARION, GRANT CO.

1—OUR LADY OF GUADALUPE, (Hispanic), Closed. For inquiries for parish records contact St. Paul, Marion.

2—ST. PAUL (1868) Rev. Richard J. Weisenberger.
Res.: 1031 W. Kem Rd., 46952-2048. Tel: 765-664-6345; Fax: 765-668-3518. Email: stpaul@stpaulcatholicmarion.com. Web: www.stpaulcatholicmarion.com.
School—1009 Kem Rd., 46952. Tel: 765-662-2883; Fax: 765-664-5953. Email: jpcertain@stpaulcatholicmarion.com. Elisha Schlabach, Prin. Lay Teachers 9; Students 108.
Catechesis/Religious Program—Email: nreynolds@stpaulcatholicmarion.com. Students 96.

MEDARYVILLE, PULASKI CO., ST. HENRY (1868) [CEM] Rev. Paul R. White, C.PP.S., Admin. (Retired).
St. Joseph's College: P.O. Box 852, Rensselaer, 47978. Tel: 219-866-6271.
Catechesis/Religious Program—Students 11.

MONTEREY, PULASKI CO., ST. ANNE (1851), (German), [CEM 2] Rev. Herbert Woolson.
Mailing Address: 6894 N. Walnut St., P.O. Box 96, 46960-0096.
Res.: 2122 E. 250 N., Winamac, 46996. Tel: 574-946-3453; Fax: 574-946-3563. Email: woolson@winamac.tv. Web: www.parishesonline.com/holytrinitycluster.
Catechesis/Religious Program—Tel: 219-542-4711. Students 15.

MONTICELLO, WHITE CO., OUR LADY OF THE LAKES (1948) Very Rev. Gerald J. Borawski; Deacon Edward Cleary.
Res.: 543 S. Main St., 47960-2948. Tel: 574-583-5724; Fax: 574-583-4112.
Catechesis/Religious Program—Tel: 574-583-6790. Students 171.

MONTPELIER, BLACKFORD CO., ST. MARGARET OF SCOTLAND (1864) [CEM] Closed. For sacramental records contact 209 S. Spring St., Hartford City, IN 47348.

MUNCIE, DELAWARE CO.

1—ST. FRANCIS OF ASSISI (1973), (Ball State University Parish) Rev. Christopher J. Weldon.
Res.: 1200 W. Riverside Ave., 47303-3650. Tel: 765-288-6180; Fax: 765-288-7777. Email: admin.stfrancis@comcast.net. Web: www.stfrancisnewman.org.
Catechesis/Religious Program—Students 168.

2—ST. LAWRENCE (1869) Rev. Dennis J. Goth.
Res.: 820 E. Charles St., 47305-2699. Tel: 765-288-9223; Fax: 765-289-9262. Email: parish@stlawrence.com. Web: www.stlawrencemuncie.com.
School—2801 E. 16th St., 47302. Tel: 765-282-9353; Fax: 765-282-0457. Lay Teachers 7; Students 101.
Catechesis/Religious Program—Tel: 765-284-2673. Students 26.

3—ST. MARY (1930) Rev. Andrew J. Dudzinski; Deacon Gary Kuenz, Pastoral Assoc.; Carol Kuenz, Pastoral Assoc.; Cathie Snider, Business Mgr. In Res., Rev. James T. Keane.
Res.: 2300 W. Jackson St., 47303-4797. Tel: 765-288-5308; Fax: 765-288-6357. Web: www.stmarymuncie.org.
School—(Grades K-5), 2301 W. Gilbert St., 47303-4797. Tel: 765-288-5878; Fax: 765-284-3685. Lay Teachers 8; Students 134.
School—Pope John Paul II Middle School, (Grades 6-8)
Catechesis/Religious Program—Email: maburford@stmarymuncie.org. Mary Burford, C.R.E. Students 138.

NOBLESVILLE, HAMILTON CO., OUR LADY OF GRACE (1944) Revs. Thomas H. Metzger; Christopher R. Shocklee; Michael J. Witka, Dir. Business & Admin.; Barb Leap, Dir. Music & Liturgy.
Res.: 9900 E. 191st St., 46060-1520. Tel: 317-773-4275; Fax: 317-773-9344. Web: www.ologn.org.
School—Tel: 317-770-5660; Fax: 317-770-5663. Web: www.ologs.org. Maureen Clerkin, Prin. Lay Teachers 25; Students 363.
Catechesis/Religious Program—Tel: 317-773-0297. Stacy Costa, Youth Ministry Coord. (High School); Jake Teitgen, Youth Ministry Coord. (Junior High); Becky Hampton, D.R.E. Coord. (Elementary). Students 454.

OTTERBEIN, BENTON CO., ST. CHARLES (1902) [JC] Rev. Robert Klemme.
Res. & Mailing: 502 S. Michigan St., Oxford, 47971-8562. Tel: 765-385-2587; Fax: 765-385-0225. Church: 108 N. Meadow St., 47970-0661. Tel: 765-583-4641.
Catechesis/Religious Program—Students 86.

OXFORD, BENTON CO., ST. PATRICK (1867), (Irish), [CEM] [JC] Rev. Robert Klemme.
Res.: 502 S. Michigan St., 47971-8562. Tel: 765-385-2587; Fax: 765-385-0225. Email: spchurch@localline.com.
Catechesis/Religious Program—Students 45.

PERU, MIAMI CO., ST. CHARLES BORROMEO (1860) [CEM] Rev. Francis I. Kilcline III; Deacon Truman Stevens.
Church & Office: 58 W. Fifth St., 46970-2100. Tel: 765-473-5543; Fax: 765-472-2692. Web: www.stcharlesperu.org.
Catechesis/Religious Program—Tel: 765-473-5544; Fax: 765-472-2692. Students 98.

PORTLAND, JAY CO., IMMACULATE CONCEPTION (1876), (German), Rev. Robert E. Moran.
Res.: 506 E. Walnut St., 47371-1599. Tel: 260-726-7341.
Catechesis/Religious Program—Tel: 260-726-7055. Students 202.

REMINGTON, JASPER CO., SACRED HEART (1875), (German—French), [CEM] Rev. Thomas E. Fox.
Res.: 124 New York St., P.O. Box 159, 47977-0159. Tel: 219-261-2302; Fax: 219-261-2934. Email: shremin@embarqmail.com.
Catechesis/Religious Program—Tel: 219-279-2910. Students 40.

RENSSELAER, JASPER CO., ST. AUGUSTINE (1883) [CEM]

Rev. Donald Davison, C.PP.S.
Res.: 318 N. McKinley Ave., 47978-2599. Tel: 219-866-5351; Fax: 219-866-4310. Email: stachurch@rhsi.tv.
School—328 N. Mckinley Ave., 47978. Tel: 219-866-5480; Fax: 219-866-5663. Religious 1; Lay Teachers 7; Students 118.
Catechesis/Religious Program—Tel: 219-866-5351. Students 81.

REYNOLDS, WHITE CO., ST. JOSEPH (1866) [CEM] Rev. John J. Cummings, Admin.
Res.: 601 S. Kenton St., 47980-8098. Tel: 219-984-5401; Fax: 219-984-5443.
Catechesis/Religious Program—Students 40.

ROCHESTER, FULTON CO., ST. JOSEPH (1900) Rev. Herbert Woolson, Pastor & Admin.
Rectory—1310 Main St., 46975-2108. Tel: 574-223-2808; Fax: 574-224-2808. Web: www.parishesonline.com/holytrinitycluster.
Catechesis/Religious Program—Tel: 574-223-3246. Students 49.
Mission—St. Ann Kewanna, Fulton Co.

STAR CITY, PULASKI CO., ST. JOSEPH (1851) [CEM 2] Rev. Ronald J. Schiml, C.PP.S.
Res.: 5895 S. SR 119, 46985-8826. Tel: 574-595-7198.
Catechesis/Religious Program—Students 18.

TIPTON, TIPTON CO., ST. JOHN THE BAPTIST (1866) [CEM] Rev. Leroy G. Kinnaman.
Res.: 340 N. Mill St., 46072-1403. Tel: 765-675-2422. Email: baptizer@tiptontel.com. Web: www.stjohnstipton.com.
School—(Grades PreK-5), 323 Mill St., 46072. Tel: 765-675-4741; Fax: 765-675-2163. Email: principal@stjohnstipton.com. Web: www.stjohnstipton.com/school/school.htm. Lay Teachers 8; Students 87.
Catechesis/Religious Program—Email: dsmithmar@aol.com. Students 93.

UNION CITY, RANDOLPH CO., ST. MARY (1865), (Irish—German), [CEM] Rev. Michael J. McKinley.
Rectory—425 W. Hickory St., 47390-1301. Tel: 765-964-4202. Email: www.stmaryuc@embarqmail.com.
Catechesis/Religious Program—Kathy DeBolt, D.R.E. Tel: 765-964-4767; Sheila Reichard, D.R.E. Tel: 765-964-5561. Students 46.

WEST LAFAYETTE, TIPPECANOE CO.
1—BLESSED SACRAMENT (1957) Rev. David J. Buckles.
Res.: 2224 Sacramento Dr., 47906-1998. Tel: 765-463-5733; Fax: 765-497-7866. Email: info@blessedsacramentwl.org. Web: www.bscwl.org.
Catechesis/Religious Program—Students 327.
Station—Indiana Veterans' Home, Tel: 765-463-1502.

2—ST. THOMAS AQUINAS (1951), (Purdue University Parish) Revs. Patrick Baikauskas, O.P., Pastor & Dir Campus Ministry; Michail Ford, O.P.; Joseph Minuth, O.P.
Office: 535 W. State St., 47906-3541. Tel: 765-743-4652; Fax: 765-743-0426. Email: mailbox@boilercatholics.org. Web: www.boilercatholics.org.
Catechesis/Religious Program—Michael Plake, D.R.E. Students 306.

WESTFIELD, HAMILTON CO., ST. MARIA GORETTI (1995) Revs. Kevin J. Haines; Daniel Joseph Duff; Deacon Steve Miller, Pastoral Assoc.; Pat Gorman, Financial Controller.
Res.: 17102 Spring Mill Rd., 46074. Tel: 317-867-5694 (Rectory); Fax: 317-867-3263. Web: www.smgonline.org.
School—(Grades PreK-8), 17104 Spring Mill Rd., 46074. Tel: 317-896-5582; Fax: 317-867-0783. Vince Barnes, Prin. Lay Teachers 23; Students 431.
Catechesis/Religious Program—Connie Anderson, D.R.E.; Caitie Rose Beardnore, Youth Min. Students 854.

WHEATFIELD, JASPER CO., SORROWFUL MOTHER (1887) [CEM] Rev. Alejandro Paternoster.
Res.: 165 Grace St., P.O. Box 248, 46392-0248. Tel: 219-956-3343; Fax: 219-956-3343.
Church Hall: Tel: 219-956-4648.
Catechesis/Religious Program—Tel: 219-956-3347. Students 67.

WINAMAC, PULASKI CO., ST. PETER (1859) [CEM] Rev. Martin J. Sandhage.
Res.: 401 N. Monticello St., 46996-1327. Tel: 574-946-4906; Fax: 574-946-4962. Email: stpete4906@embarqmail.com.
Catechesis/Religious Program—424 N. Market St., 46996. Tel: 574-946-6804. Email: stpeterswinamac@yahoo.com. Students 92.

WINCHESTER, RANDOLPH CO., ST. JOSEPH (1952) Rev. Michael J. McKinley.
St. Mary's Rectory: 425 W. Hickory St., Union City, 47390-1301. Tel: 765-964-4202. Email: www.stmaryuc@embarqmail.com.
Church: 514 W. Washington St., 47394.
Catechesis/Religious Program—Paula Dirksen, D.R.E. Students 32.

ZIONSVILLE, BOONE CO., ST. ALPHONSUS (1945) [JC] Revs. Dennis J. O'Keeffe; Christopher George Roberts. In Res., Rev. David Joseph Hasser.
Res.: 1870 W. Oak St., 46077-1894. Tel: 317-873-2885; Fax: 317-873-8746. Email: parishsecretary@zionsvillecatholic.com.
Catechesis/Religious Program—Kim Overmyer, Dir Faith Formation; Paul Sifuentes, Dir. Youth Ministry; Sandra Santucci, Dir. Worship & Sacred Music. Students 733.

Chaplains of Public Institutions

LAFAYETTE. *Indiana Veterans' Home, Queen of the Universe Chapel*. Attended from Blessed Sacrament Church, West Lafayette.

GRISSOM. *Grissom Air Force Base, St. Michael's Chapel* 46971. Tel: 765-688-2191. Rev. Philip S. Hascinger, Auxiliary Civilian Chap.

LOGANSPORT. *Logansport State Hospital*. Vacant.

MARION. *U.S. Veteran's Hospital*. Revs. James Rose (FTW), Chap. (Retired), Joseph W. Grace, Auxiliary Chap. (Retired).

PENDLETON. *Correctional Industrial Complex Ecumenical Chapel*, P.O. Box 601, 46064. Tel: 765-778-8011. Rev. Joseph Pesola.
Indiana State Reformatory, St. Christopher Chapel, P.O. Box 28, 46064. Tel: 765-778-2107. Rev. Joseph Pesola.

Special Assignment:
Rev. Msgr.—
Sell, Robert L., III, J.C.L., V.G., Vicar Gen., Chancellor & Moderator of the Curia, 1128 E. State St., 47905. Tel: 765-742-1665
Revs.—
Buckles, David J., J.C.L., Diocesan Tribunal, 2300 S. 9th St., 47905. Tel: 765-474-0506
Miller, Christopher T., Vicar for Hispanics, 600 St. Mary's Ave., Frankfort, 46041-2735. Tel: 765-654-5796. Email: frchris93@yahoo.com
Vath, William R., Diocesan Tribunal, 2300 S. 9th St., 47905. Tel: 765-474-0506; 317-742-4440

On Duty Outside the Diocese:
Revs.—
Clegg, Timothy, 3635 Westchester Dr., Holiday, FL 34691.
Comeau, Ronald R., 6 Johnson Rd., Aurora ON L4C 2A2 Canada. Tel: 416-772-1965
Cover, Phillip B., 1600 S. Eads St., #923-S, Arlington, VA 22202.
Doerr, Brian M., Mt. St. Mary Seminary, 16300 Old Emmittsburg Rd., Emmitsburg, MD 21727-7797. Tel: 301-447-5295
Gross, Barry, 1601 Georgia Ave., Wheaton, MD 20902.
Mannion, John H., B.S., M.Div., 1600 Albany St., Beechgrove, 46107. Tel: 317-787-3311 St. Francis Hospital, Pastoral Care Department
Westfall, Joseph B., P.O. Box 45715, Kansas City, MO 64171.

Military Chaplains:
Revs.—
Kinney, John M., 2520 Crested Hills, Schertz, TX 78154. Tel: 210-658-6825
Mahalic, Philip A., 172 Artillery Loop Apt. D, San Antonio, TX 78234-2629. Tel: 810-289-0573

Unassigned:
Revs.—
Courtney, Patrick E.
Hagan, Paul

Retired:
Rev. Msgr.—
Potthoff, Fred E., 37 Wea Oaks St., 47905-3406. Tel: 765-474-7152
Revs.—
Askar, George F., 901 Edison Blvd., Port Huron, MI 48060-2117. Tel: 810-982-0516
Bates, James R., 5016 Allisonville Rd., Apt. D, Indianapolis, 46205-1536. Tel: 317-257-5569
Bruetsch, Joseph J., St. Mary Cathedral, 1212 South St., 47901-1576. Tel: 765-742-4440
Cox, Alan B., 56 Fulton Rd., Salmon, ID 83467-5099.
Dhondt, Edward F., St. Ambrose, 2801 Lincoln St., Anderson, 46016. Tel: 765-644-5956
Douglas, David M., 1700 Lindberg Rd., Apt. 1130, West Lafayette, 47906-7317.
Eder, Donald, 3056 N. State Rd. 17, Logansport, 46947-8746. Tel: 574-732-1509
Goodrum, James R., 112B Williams St., Monticello, 47960-1675. Tel: 574-583-5755
Grace, Joseph W., Bishop Gallagher Manor, 100 N. Celia Ave., Muncie, 47303-4607. Tel: 765-289-7415
Heitz, Louis S., 120 Red Oak Dr., Cridersville, OH 45806. Tel: 419-645-4157
Holbrook, William M., 6210 W. Bell Plaine, Chicago, IL 60634.
Hosey, P. Keith, St. Joseph Center, 1440 W. Division Rd., Tipton, 46072-8584. Tel: 765-675-4146
Matuszak, Edward S., 400 E. Gord Rd., Erie, PA 16509-3726. Tel: 814-455-1166
Ondo, Michael A., 6765 State Rd., Parma, OH 44134-4581. Tel: 440-663-1296
Puetz, Richard W., St. Elizabeth Healthcare Center, 701 Armory Rd., Rm. 409, Delphi, 46923-1915. Tel: 765-564-2182
Ruffing, Joseph R., 317 E. Pinetree Blvd., Thomasville, GA 31792-6858. Tel: 229-228-7356
Schiavone, Jeldo J., 1701 Pinehurst Rd., Apt. 20E, Dunedin, FL 34698-3627.
Wicklum, Paul R., 11385 N. 540 E., Roselawn, 46310-8945.
Ziegler, Ambrose M., 3118 Longlois Rd., 47904-1716. Tel: 765-447-5458

Permanent Deacons:
Cain, Jerry, Blessed Sacrament, West Lafayette
Castillo, Domingo, St. Paul, Marion
Cleary, Edward, Our Lady of the Lakes, Monticello
Gallagher, Patrick, St. Joseph, Lebanon
Gray, D. Michael, St. Lawrence, Lafayette
Jezierski, John, Cathedral, Lafayette
Kuenz, Gary, St. Mary, Muncie
MacDougall, James, St. Lawrence, Muncie
Miller, Mark, Our Lady of Grace, Noblesville
Miller, Stephen, St. Maria Goretti, Westfield
Morrow, Ronald, St. Patrick, Kokomo
Munoz, Jose, St. Boniface, Lafayette
Nevinger, Ronald, St. Boniface, Lafayette
Rahill, William, Our Lady of Mount Carmel, Carmel
Reid, William, St. Elizabeth Seton, Carmel
Rodriguez, Juan, All Saints, Logansport
Stevens, Truman, St. Patrick, Kokomo
Van Schepen, Joe, St. Cecilia, DeMotte

INSTITUTIONS LOCATED IN THE DIOCESE

[A] COLLEGES AND UNIVERSITIES

RENSSELAER. *Saint Joseph's College* (1889) P.O. Box 909, 47978. Tel: 219-866-6000; Fax: 219-866-6100. Web: www.saintjoe.edu. F. Dennis Riegelnegg, Ed.D., Pres.; Revs. Philip F. Gilbert, C.PP.S., M.S.; Jeffrey S. Kirch, C.PP.S., Rel. Advisor to Pres.; Leonard J. Kostka, C.PP.S., J.C.L. (Retired); Timothy D. McFarland, C.PP.S., Ph.D., Asst. Vice Pres. Academics; William J. Stang, C.PP.S., M.D., Rel. Supr.; Paul R. White, C.PP.S., M.A. (Retired); Kevin Scalf, C.PP.S., M.A., M.Div., Chap.; Bros. Timothy P. Hemm, C.PP.S.; Robert Reuter, C.PP.S., Ph.D.; Cathy Salyers, Librarian. The Society of the Precious Blood. Priests 5; Brothers 2; Lay Teachers 85; Students 1,099; Total Staff 212.

[B] HIGH SCHOOLS, INTER-PAROCHIAL

LAFAYETTE. *Central Catholic Junior-Senior High School*, 2410 S. Ninth St., 47909-2499. Tel: 765-474-2496; Fax: 765-474-8752. Email: Brettnacher@lcss.org. Web: www.lcss.org. Mr. Joseph A. Brettnacher, Prin.; Grant Freeman, Campus Min. Campus Minister 1; Religious 2; Lay Teachers 25; Administrators 3; Lay Staff 8; Students 360.

NOBLESVILLE. *Saint Theodore Guerin High School*, 15300 N. Gray Rd., 46062. Tel: 317-582-0120; Fax: 317-582-0140. Email: plunsford@guerincatholic.org. Web: www.guerincatholic.org. Rev. Joshua M. Sanko, Dir. Catholic Mission; Richard J. Wagner, Prin.; Marcia M. Murphy, Librarian. Faculty 46; Students 658.

[C] GENERAL HOSPITALS

LAFAYETTE. *Franciscan St. Elizabeth Health-Lafayette Central* (1874) 1501 Hartford St., P.O. Box 7501, 47903. Tel: 765-423-6011; Fax: 765-502-4455. Email: ste.pr@franciscanalliance.org. Web: www.franciscanste.org. Terrance E. Wilson, Pres. & CEO; Sr. M. Ann Kathleen Magiera, O.S.F., Vice Pres. Mission Integration; Revs. Paul Graf; Cajetan Ebuziem. Franciscan Alliance, Inc. Sisters 4; Operational Beds 116; Patients Assisted Annually 185,000; Total Staff 668.
St. Elizabeth School of Nursing Tel: 765-423-6408; Fax: 765-423-6364. Web: www.franciscanste.org. Students 230.
Franciscan St. Elizabeth Health-Lafayette East, 1701 S. Creasy Ln., 47905. Tel: 765-502-4000; Fax: 765-502-4455. Email: ste.pr@

franciscanalliance.org. Web: www.franciscanste.org. Terrance E. Wilson, Pres. & CEO. Owned by the Sisters of Franciscan Alliance, Inc. Operational Beds 150; Patients Assisted Annually 188,000; Total Staff 902.

St. Vincent Seton Specialty Hospital (1996) 1501 Hartford St., 47904. Tel: 765-423-6650; Fax: 765-423-6648. Email: cxschech@stvincent.org. Web: seton.stvincent.org. Sr. Raphael Kochert, O.S.F., Certified Chap. (A member of St. Vincent Health, Inc. and Ascension Health.) Bed Capacity 30; Total Patient Visits Per Year 400; Total Staff 95.

ANDERSON. *Saint John's Health System*, 2015 Jackson St., 46016. Tel: 765-646-8373; Fax: 765-646-8504. Email: tjvanosd@sjhsnet.org. Web: www.stjohns.stvincent.org. Mr. Thomas VanOsdol, Pres.; Sr. Kathleen Reilly, C.S.C., Vice Pres. Mission. Sisters of the Holy Cross 3; Bed Capacity 225; Total Assisted 257,000; Total Staff 1,500.

CARMEL. *St. Vincent Carmel Hospital, Inc.* (1985) 13500 N. Meridian St., 46032-1903. Tel: 317-582-7137; Fax: 317-582-7744. Email: jclandry@stvincent.org. Web: www.stvincent.org. Carey Landry, Certified Chap. (A member of St. Vincent Health, Inc. and Ascension Health.) Bed Capacity 135; Total Assisted Annually by Pastoral Care 5,000; Total Pastoral Care Staff 1; Total Hospital Staff 850.

CRAWFORDSVILLE. *Franciscan St. Elizabeth Health-Crawfordsville*, 1710 Lafayette Rd., 47933. Tel: 765-362-2800; Fax: 765-364-3189. Email: tom.peck@franciscanalliance.org. Web: www.ste.org/crawfordsville. Thomas R. Peck, Exec. Dir. Franciscan Alliance, Inc. Sisters of St. Francis of Perpetual Adoration 1; Bed Capacity 71; Licensed Beds 103; Patients Assisted Annually 99,840; Total Staff 399.

ELWOOD. *St. Vincent Mercy Hospital, Inc.* (1926) 1331 South A St., 46036-1942. Tel: 765-552-4600; Fax: 765-552-4700. Email: ACYates@stvincent.org. Web: mercy.stvinent.org. Ann C. Yates, R.N., Dir., Patient Care. Bed Capacity 25; Total Assisted Annually 34,822; Total Staff 210.

(1999) Tel: 765-552-4600; Fax: 765-552-4700. Bed Capacity 25; Patients Assisted Annually 52,128; Total Staff 230.

KOKOMO. *St. Joseph Hospital & Health Center*, 1907 W. Sycamore St., 46901. Tel: 765-452-5611; 765-456-5300 (Administration); Fax: 765-456-5038. Email: vlmason@stjoseph.stvincent.org. Web: www.stjoseph.stvincent.org. P.O. Box 9010, 46904-9010. Kathlene Young, M.S., F.A.C.H.E., Pres. & CEO; Sr. Catherine Kelly, D.C., M.T.S., M.S.-H.S., Vice Pres., Mission Integration, Clinical Leader, & Palliative Care; Marcia Jewsbury, B.A., M.Div., Mgr., Pastoral Care. Sisters 1; Total Staff 962; Bed Capacity 167; Patients Assisted Annually 167,885.

Saint Joseph Foundation of Kokomo, Indiana, Inc. Tel: 765-456-5406; Fax: 765-456-5387. Email: tmoser@stjoseph.stvincent.org. Web: stjoseph.stvincent.org. Todd Moser, Dir. St. Joseph Foundation.

WILLIAMSPORT. *St. Vincent Williamsport Hospital*, 412 N. Monroe St., 47993-1097. Tel: 765-762-4000; Fax: 765-762-4126. Web: www.stvincent.org. Jane Craigin, CEO. Priests 1; Bed Capacity 16; Patients Assisted Annually 76,000; Total Staff 200.

[D] NURSING HOMES

LAFAYETTE. *St. Anthony Health Care*, 1205 N. 14th St., 47904. Tel: 765-423-4861; Fax: 765-742-8790. Email: admin@sahc.net. Web: www.sahc.net. Bed Capacity 120; Residents 115; Total Assisted Annually 590; Total Staff 147.

[E] MONASTERIES AND RESIDENCES OF PRIESTS AND BROTHERS

LAFAYETTE. *Emmaus House*, 2500 S. Ninth St., 47909. Tel: 765-477-6441. Revs. Cajetan Ebuziem, Hospital Chap.; Samuel Joseph Kalu, J.C.L. Priests 2.

[F] CONVENTS AND RESIDENCES FOR SISTERS

ANDERSON. *Congregation of the Sisters of the Holy Cross*, 2115 Meridian St., 46016. Tel: 765-642-2427.

Sisters of the Holy Cross, Inc. Sisters 2.

KOKOMO. *Maria Regina Mater Monastery* (1959) 1175 N. 300 W., 46901-1799. Tel: 765-457-5743. Web: www.thepoorclares.org. Sr. Miriam, P.C.C., Abbess. Monastery of Poor Clares of the Reform of St. Colette. Solemnly Professed Nuns in Cloister 9; Perpetually Professed Extern Sisters 1; Junior Professed 1.

TIPTON. *St. Joseph Center: Congregation of the Sisters of St. Joseph* (1888) 1440 W. Division Rd., 46072-8584. Tel: 765-675-4146; 765-675-6203; Fax: 765-675-6205. Email: tmacintyre@csjoseph.org. Web: www.csjoseph.org. Sr. Theresa MacIntyre, C.S.J., Asst. Sec./Admin. Sisters Resident at Motherhouse 14; Total in Residence 31; Total Staff 40.

Sisters of St. Joseph of Tipton, Indiana, Inc., 1440 W. Division Rd., 46072. Tel: 765-675-4146; Fax: 765-675-6205.

[G] RETREAT HOUSES

HARTFORD CITY. *John XXIII Center*, 407 W. McDonald St., 47348. Tel: 765-348-4008; Fax: 765-348-5819. Email: john23rd@sbcglobal.net. Web: www.john23rdretreatcenter.com. Sr. Joetta Huelsmann, P.H.J.C., Dir.; Dorothy Stewart, Office Mgr.; Beth Adams, Devel. Mktg. Coord.

[H] NEWMAN CENTERS

MUNCIE. *Newman Foundation-Ball State University* (1973) 1200 W. Riverside Ave., 47303. Tel: 765-288-6180; Fax: 765-288-7777. Email: admin.stfrancis@comcast.net. Web: www.stfrancisnewman.org. Rev. Christopher J. Weldon.

WEST LAFAYETTE. *St. Thomas Aquinas Parish and Foundation for Catholic Students Attending Purdue University* (1951) 535 W. State St., 47906-3541. Tel: 765-743-4652; Fax: 765-743-0426. Email: mailbox@boilercatholics.org. Web: www.boilercatholics.org. Revs. Patrick Baikauskas, O.P., Pastor & Dir. Campus Ministry; Michail Ford, O.P.; Joseph Minuth, O.P. Michael Plake, D.R.E. Students 8,000.

[I] MISCELLANEOUS

LAFAYETTE. *Caregiver Companion, Inc.*, 612 Wabash Ave., 47905. Tel: 765-423-1879. Email: caregiver95@gmail.com. Web: www.caregivercompanion.org. Helen Klemme, Exec. Dir. & Contact Person.

Catholic Foundation of Northcentral Indiana, Inc., P.O. Box 1687, 47902-1687. Tel: 765-742-7000; Fax: 765-742-7513. Email: rmccreary@dol-in.org. Web: www.dol-in.org/staff-development.html. Robert McCreary, Dir., Pastoral Office for Stewardship & Devel.; Joseph Bonner, Chm. Bd. Total Staff 3.

ANDERSON. *Saint John's Foundation, Inc.*, 2015 Jackson St., 46016. Tel: 765-646-8373; Fax: 765-646-8504. Email: tjvanosd@sjhsnet.org. Web: www.saintjohns.stvincent.org. Mr. Thomas VanOsdol, Pres.

CARMEL. *Our Lady of Mount Carmel Parochial School*, 14596 Oak Ridge Rd., 46032. Tel: 317-846-1118; Fax: 317-582-2375. Email: OLMCprincipal@olmc1.org. Web: olmc1.org. Rev. Richard J. Doerr, Contact Person.

NOBLESVILLE. *Hamilton County Catholic High School Corporation dba St. Theodore Guerin Catholic High School* 15300 N. Gray Rd., 46062. Tel: 317-582-0120; Fax: 317-582-0140. Email: plunsford@guerincatholic.org. Web: www.guerincatholic.org. Most Rev. Timothy L. Doherty, Ph.D., D.D., Bishop, Diocese of Lafayette in Indiana Board Members: Rev. Msgr. Robert L. Sell III, J.C.L., V.G.; Dr. Marie Williams; G. Gary Malone; Robert Quinn.

Hamilton County Catholic High School Corporation, Blessed Theodore Guerin High School, 15300 N. Gray Rd., 46062. Tel: 317-582-0120; Fax: 317-582-0140. Web: www.guerincatholic.org. Rev. Dale W. Ehrman, Vicar for Catholic Mission; Paul S. Lunsford, Pres. Priests 1; Total Staff 35.

PERU. *St. Charles Conference of the Society of St. Vincent DePaul, Inc.*, P.O. Box 1332, 46970. Tel: 317-472-1855.

WEST LAFAYETTE. *Dominicans, Community of St. Thomas Aquinas, Inc.*, 2535 Newman Rd., 47906-4537. Tel: 765-743-3795. Rev. Benjamin Joseph Russell, O.P., Pres.

RELIGIOUS INSTITUTES OF MEN REPRESENTED IN THE DIOCESE

For further details refer to the corresponding bracketed number in the Religious Institutes of Men or Women section.

[0520]—*Order of St. Francis Minors*—O.F.M.

[1060]—*Society of the Precious Blood*—C.PP.S.

RELIGIOUS INSTITUTES OF WOMEN REPRESENTED IN THE DIOCESE

[3832]—*Congregation of the Sisters of St. Joseph*—C.S.J.

[1920]—*Congregation of the Sisters of the Holy Cross*—C.S.C.

[1070-09]—*Dominican Sisters*—O.P.

[1780]—*Franciscan Sisters of Peace*—F.S.P.A.

[4150]—*Irish Ursuline Union*—O.S.U.

[0240]—*Olivetan Benedictine Sisters*—O.S.B.

[3230]—*Poor Handmaids of Jesus Christ*—P.H.J.C.

[2970]—*School Sisters of Notre Dame*—S.S.N.D.

[0110]—*Sisters Adorers of the Precious Blood*—A.P.B.

[0430]—*Sisters of Charity of the Blessed Virgin Mary*—B.V.M.

[2990]—*Sisters of Notre Dame* (Toledo Prov.)—S.N.D.

[3000]—*Sisters of Notre Dame de Namur*—S.N.D.deN.

[3360]—*Sisters of Providence of Saint Mary-of-the-Woods, IN*—S.P.

[]—*Sisters of St. Francis* (Sylvania, OH)—O.S.F.

[1640]—*Sisters of St. Francis of Perpetual Adoration*—O.S.F.

[3260]—*Sisters of the Precious Blood* (Dayton, Ohio)—C.PP.S.

NECROLOGY

† Bennett, Melvin J., Carmel, IN St. Elizabeth Ann Seton.—Died April 19, 2011

† Miller, Maurice R., (Retired)—Died June 1, 2011

An asterisk (*) denotes an organization that has established tax-exempt status directly with the IRS and is not covered by the USCCB Group Ruling.

Diocese of Lake Charles

Most Reverend

GLEN JOHN PROVOST

Bishop of Lake Charles; ordained June 29, 1975; appointed Bishop of Lake Charles March 6, 2007; ordained April 23, 2007. *Chancery Office: 414 Iris St., P.O. Box 3223, Lake Charles, LA 70602.* Tel: 337-439-7400; Fax: 337-439-7413.

ESTABLISHED APRIL 25, 1980.

Square Miles 5,313.

Comprises the civil parishes (or counties) of Allen, Beauregard, Calcasieu, Cameron and Jefferson Davis in the State of Louisiana.

For legal titles of parishes and diocesan institutions, consult the Chancery Office.

Chancery Office: 414 Iris St., P.O. Box 3223, Lake Charles, LA 70602. Tel: 337-439-7400; Fax: 337-439-7413.

Web: lcdiocese.laol.net

Email: lcdiocese@laol.net

STATISTICAL OVERVIEW

Personnel	
Bishop	1
Retired Bishops	1
Priests: Diocesan Active in Diocese	35
Priests: Diocesan Active Outside Diocese	2
Priests: Retired, Sick or Absent	10
Number of Diocesan Priests	47
Religious Priests in Diocese	13
Total Priests in Diocese	60
Extern Priests in Diocese	5
Ordinations:	
Diocesan Priests	2
Transitional Deacons	1
Permanent Deacons in Diocese	26
Total Brothers	1
Total Sisters	12
Parishes	
Parishes	38
With Resident Pastor:	
Resident Diocesan Priests	27
Resident Religious Priests	8
Without Resident Pastor:	
Administered by Priests	3
Missions	8
Professional Ministry Personnel:	
Brothers	1
Sisters	3
Lay Ministers	70
Welfare	
Catholic Hospitals	1
Total Assisted	81,969
Homes for the Aged	1
Total Assisted	118
Day Care Centers	3
Total Assisted	97
Special Centers for Social Services	3
Total Assisted	10,021
Educational	
Diocesan Students in Other Seminaries	7
Students Religious	2
Total Seminarians	9
High Schools, Diocesan and Parish	1
Total Students	647
Elementary Schools, Diocesan and Parish	7
Total Students	2,019
Catechesis/Religious Education:	
High School Students	1,809
Elementary Students	5,040
Total Students under Catholic Instruction	9,524
Teachers in the Diocese:	
Sisters	1
Lay Teachers	174
Vital Statistics	
Receptions into the Church:	
Infant Baptism Totals	913
Adult Baptism Totals	69
Received into Full Communion	323
First Communions	928
Confirmations	758
Marriages:	
Catholic	191
Interfaith	77
Total Marriages	268
Deaths	817
Total Catholic Population	72,999
Total Population	292,619

Former Bishops—Most Revs. JUDE SPEYRER, D.D., ord. July 25, 1953; appt. First Bishop of Lake Charles Jan. 29, 1980; ord. and installed April 25, 1980; resigned Dec. 12, 2000; EDWARD K. BRAXTON, ord. May 13, 1970; appt. Auxiliary Bishop of St. Louis March 28, 1995; ord. Auxiliary Bishop of St. Louis May 17, 1995; appt. Bishop of Lake Charles Dec. 12, 2000; installed Feb. 22, 2001; appt. Bishop of Belleville March 15, 2005.

Diocesan Board of Administration— (Legal Title - Society of the Roman Catholic Church of the Diocese of Lake Charles, LA) Deacon GEORGE A. STEARNS; Rev. Msgr. JACE F. ESKIND.

Bishop's Office—414 Iris St., P.O. Box 3223, Lake Charles, 70602. Tel: 337-439-7400, Ext. 204.

Chancery Office—414 Iris St., P.O. Box 3223, Lake Charles, 70602. Tel: 337-439-7400; Fax: 337-439-7413. Office Hours: Mon.-Fri. 8:30-4:30.

Bishop Perry Building—411 Iris St., Lake Charles, 70601. Tel: 337-439-7426; Fax: 337-439-7428. Office Hours: Mon.-Fri. 8:30-4:30.

Vicar General and Moderator of the Curia—Rev. Msgr. DANIEL A. TORRES, V.G., Mailing Address: P.O. Box 3223, Lake Charles, 70602. Tel: 337-439-7400.

Chancellor—Deacon GEORGE STEARNS, Mailing Address: P.O. Box 3223, Lake Charles, 70602. Tel: 337-439-7400, Ext. 22.

Vicar Judicial—Rev. Msgr. JACE F. ESKIND, Mailing Address: P.O Box 3223, Lake Charles, 70602. Tel: 337-439-7400, Ext. 210.

Tribunal—414 Iris St., P.O. Box 3223, Lake Charles, 70602. Tel: 337-439-7400, Ext. 210.

Judges—Rev. Msgrs. JACE F. ESKIND; VINCENT SEDITA (Retired); Ms. BONNIE LANDRY, J.C.L.; Rev. ALBERT BOREL, J.C.L.

Advocates—Revs. JOHN POERIO (Retired); THEOPHILUS L. HERLONG (Retired); Deacon GEORGE K. CARR.

Defenders of the Bond—Rev. Msgr. HARRY D. GREIG II; Rev. JAMES DOYLE.

Notary—Mrs. DEBRA FOREMAN.

Promoter of Justice—Rev. Archimandrite HERBERT J. MAY, J.C.L.

Deans—Very Revs. AUBREY V. GUILBEAU, West Deanery; ANTHONY M. FONTENOT, East Deanery; MARCUS JOHNSON, Central Deanery.

Presbyteral Council—Very Rev. ANTHONY M. FONTENOT, Chm.; Rev. ALAN P. TROUILLE; Very Rev. MARCUS JOHNSON; Revs. WHITNEY MILLER; JOSEPH G. AQUINO, M.S.; Rev. Msgr. RONALD GROTH; Rev. ALBERT BOREL, J.C.L.; Very Rev. AUBREY V. GUILBEAU; Revs. FRED RUSSI (Retired); CELSIUS OFFOR; Rev. Msgrs. DANIEL A. TORRES, V.G.; JACE F. ESKIND; Rev. JACOB SCOTT CONNER.

Diocesan Consultors—Rev. FRED RUSSI (Retired); Very Revs. AUBREY V. GUILBEAU; MARCUS JOHNSON; Revs. SUSIL FERNANDO; TIMOTHY GOODLY; DON PIRARO; ROMMEL P. TOLENTINO; Rev. Archimandrite HERBERT J. MAY, J.C.L.; Rev. Msgrs. RONALD GROTH; DANIEL A. TORRES, V.G.; JACE F. ESKIND; Very Rev. ANTHONY M. FONTENOT.

Offices, Boards, Commissions, Committees

Black Catholics—Deacon EDWARD LAVINE, Mailing Address: P.O. Box 3223, Lake Charles, 70601. Tel: 337-439-7436, Ext. 11.

Clergy Formation—Rev. NATHAN LONG, 411 Iris St., Lake Charles, 70601. Tel: 337-439-7400.

Communications—MORRIS LEBLEU, Mailing Address: P.O. Box 3223, Lake Charles, 70601. Tel: 337-439-7400, Ext. 304.

Counseling—Rev. WHITNEY MILLER, St. Charles Retreat Center, 2151 Sam Houston Jones Pkwy., Moss Bluff, 70611.

Deaf Apostolate—Very Rev. AUBREY V. GUILBEAU, 418 Iris St., Lake Charles, 70601. Tel: 337-439-4373.

Development Office—Rev. Msgr. RONALD GROTH, Dir. Tel: 337-439-7400, Ext. 307; MORRIS LEBLEU, Assoc. Dir., Mailing Address: P.O. Box 3223, Lake Charles, 70602. Tel: 337-439-7400, Ext. 304.

Diocesan Building Commission—Deacon GEORGE STEARNS, Chm., Mailing Address: P.O. Box 3223, Lake Charles, 70602. Tel: 337-439-7400, Ext. 204.

Director of Seminarians—Rev. Msgr. DANIEL A. TORRES, V.G., Vocation Dir. & Dir. Seminarians, 414 Iris St., Lake Charles, 70601. Tel: 337-439-7400.

Education—Mrs. KIMBERLEE GAZZOLO, Supt., Mailing Address: P.O. Box 3223, Lake Charles, 70602. Tel: 337-439-7426, Ext. 18.

Evangelization—BERNEL EZELL, 411 Iris St., Lake Charles, 70601. Tel: 337-439-7426, Ext. 300.

Fiscal Administration—Ms. PATRICIA MYERS, Mailing Address: P.O. Box 3223, Lake Charles, 70602. Tel: 337-439-7400, Ext. 203.

Hispanic Ministry—VACANT, Mailing Address: St. Henry Catholic Church, 1021 8th Ave., Lake Charles, 70601. Tel: 337-436-7223; Fax: 337-436-4614.

Office For Worship—Rev. Msgr. JACE F. ESKIND. Tel: 337-439-7400, Ext. 210; Rev. RUBEN J. BULLER, Assoc. Dir., 414 Iris St., Lake Charles, 70601. Tel: 337-439-7400, Ext. 217.

Parish Boundaries Commission—Rev. Msgr. DANIEL A. TORRES, V.G., Chm., Mailing Address: P.O. Box 3223, Lake Charles, 70602. Tel: 337-439-7400, Ext. 204.

Permanent Diaconate—Deacon GLENN VIAU, 221 Aqua Dr., Lake Charles, 70605.

Personnel Board—Rev. Msgr. DANIEL A. TORRES, V.G., Vicar Gen.

Propagation of the Faith & Holy Childhood Association—Rev. WAYNE LEBLEU, Dir., Mailing Address: 7680 Gulf Hwy., Lake Charles, 70607. Tel: 337-478-0213; Fax: 337-478-0793.

Religious Education—Mrs. DENISE DONAHOE, 411 Iris St., Lake Charles, 70601. Tel: 337-439-7426, Ext. 302.

Relief Services Catholic—Rev. WAYNE LEBLEU.

St. Charles Retreat Center—Rev. WHITNEY MILLER, Dir., 2151 Sam Houston Jones Pkwy., Lake Charles, 70611. Tel: 337-855-1232.

Sea, Apostleship of the—Rev. ROMMEL P. TOLENTINO, Chap.; Deacon PATRICK LAPOINT, 160 Marine St., Lake Charles, 70601. Tel: 337-436-1315.

Catholic Charities—Mrs. TRISH TREJO, Dir., 612 Louisiana Ave., Lake Charles, 70601. Tel: 337-439-7436.

Pastoral Services, Catholic—Rev. WAYNE LEBLEU.

Scouting—Rev. NATHAN LONG, Our Lady Queen of Heaven, Lake Charles, 70601.

Seminary Advisory Board—Rev. Msgr. DANIEL A. TORRES, V.G., Vicar Gen.

Vocation Director—Rev. Msgr. DANIEL A. TORRES, V.G., Vicar Gen. Vocation Recruiters: Revs. NATHAN LONG; RUBEN J. BULLER; SUSIL FERNANDO; Very Rev. MARCUS JOHNSON, 411 Iris St., Lake Charles, 70601. Tel: 337-439-7400, Ext. 308.

CLERGY, PARISHES, MISSIONS AND PAROCHIAL SCHOOLS

LAKE CHARLES

(CALCASIEU PARISH)

1—IMMACULATE CONCEPTION CATHEDRAL (1869) [CEM] Rev. Msgr. Jace F. Eskind.
Mailing Address: P.O. Box 1029, 70602. Tel: 337-436-7251; Fax: 337-436-7240.
Church: 935 Bilbo, 70601.
School—(Grades PreK-8), 1536 Ryan St., 70601. Tel: 337-433-3497; Fax: 337-433-5056. Mrs. Dinah Bradford, Prin.; Ms. Tena Fuselier, Librarian. Lay Teachers 36; Students 439.

2—CHRIST THE KING (2002) Rev. Wayne LeBleu.
Res.: 7680 Gulf Hwy., 70607. Tel: 337-478-0213; Fax: 337-478-0793.
Catechesis/Religious Program—Students 164.

3—ST. HENRY (1958) [JC] Rev. Msgr. Daniel A. Torres; Rev. Ruben J. Buller, Parochial Vicar; Deacon Ray Granger.
Res.: 1021 Eighth Ave., 70601. Tel: 337-436-7223; Fax: 337-436-4614.
Catechesis/Religious Program—Tel: 337-433-6119. Phyllis Kittling, D.R.E. Students 205.

4—IMMACULATE HEART OF MARY (1953), (African American), Very Rev. Marcus Johnson; Deacon Joseph Bushnell. In Res., Rev. Msgr. Ronald Groth.
Res.: 2031 Opelousas St., 70601. Tel: 337-436-8093; Fax: 337-436-8033. Email: ihmchurch@suddenlink.net.
Catechesis/Religious Program—Tel: 337-433-0158. Students 231.
Mission—Our Lady of Fatima Chapel 1700 Graham St., Calcasieu Parish 70601.

5—ST. MARGARET (1940) Revs. William Miller; Jacob Scott Conner; Deacons Dan Landry; Raymond Menard.
Res.: 2500 Enterprise Blvd., 70601. Tel: 337-439-4585; Fax: 337-433-3186.
School—(Grades PreK-8) Tel: 337-436-7959; Fax: 337-436-9932. Mrs. Brenda Dufrene, Prin.; Ms. Monica Guidry, Librarian. Lay Teachers 25; Students 261.
Catechesis/Religious Program—Tel: 337-436-6358. Myrtle Wren, D.R.E.; Joanne Schwem, D.R.E. Students 184.

6—ST. MARTIN DEPORRES (2002) Rev. Keith Pellerin. 5326 Elliott Rd., 70605. Mailing Address: P.O. Box 4386, 70606.
Res.: 2503 Vogue Dr., 70605. Tel: 337-478-3845; Fax: 337-477-2828.
Catechesis/Religious Program—Students 34.

7—OUR LADY OF GOOD COUNSEL (1957) Rev. Alan P. Trouille; Deacon Glenn Viau.
Res.: 221 Aqua Dr., 70605. Tel: 337-477-1434; Fax: 337-479-2129. Web: www.mcneesecatholic.com.
Catechesis/Religious Program—Students 99.

8—OUR LADY QUEEN OF HEAVEN (1957) [CEM] Rev. Msgr. James Gaddy; Rev. John B. Huckaby; Deacon George K. Carr.
Res.: 617 W. Claude St., 70605. Tel: 337-477-1236; Fax: 337-478-3451. Email: olqh@lcdiocese.org.
School—(Grades PreK-8), 3908 Creole St., 70605. Tel: 337-477-7349; Fax: 337-477-7384. Ms. JoAnn Wallwork, Prin.; Jackie Bohdan, Librarian. Lay Teachers 45; Students 664.
Catechesis/Religious Program—3909 Creole St., 70605. Tel: 337-477-3937. Pamela Alston, D.R.E. (Grades 7-12); Mrs. Robin Suire, D.R.E. (Grades 1-6). Students 664.

9—SACRED HEART OF JESUS (1919), (African American), [CEM] Rev. Msgr. Ronald Groth; Deacon Ed Lavine.
Res.: 1102 Mill St., 70601. Tel: 337-439-2646; Fax: 337-439-2650.
School—Tel: 337-436-3588; Fax: 337-433-1761. Mrs. Hattie Ashton, Prin. Lay Teachers 15; Students 74.
Catechesis/Religious Program—Jacqueline Mathews, D.R.E. Students 98.

10—ST. THEODORE (1974) Rev. Msgr. Charles J. Dubois; Deacon Jack Reynolds, (Retired).
Mailing Address: 785 Sam Houston Jones Pkwy., 70611. In Res., Rev. James Doyle.
Res.: 713 Longleaf Dr., 70611. Tel: 337-855-6662; Fax: 337-855-6663.
School—(Grades PreK-8) Tel: 337-855-9465; Fax: 337-855-2809. Mrs. Jennifer Bellon, Interim Prin.; Ms. Barbara Phillips, Librarian. Lay Teachers 17; Students 130.
Catechesis/Religious Program—Tel: 337-855-6664. (St. Theodore & St. Pius) 1,253.
Mission—St. Pius X Mission 16816 Hwy. 171, Ragley, 70657. Tel: 337-725-6248; Fax: 337-725-3719.

OUTSIDE THE CITY OF LAKE CHARLES

BELL CITY, CALCASIEU PARISH, ST. JOHN VIANNEY (1939) [CEM] Rev. Emanuel Tanu, S.V.D.
Mailing Address: 7120 Hwy. 14 E., 70630.
Res. & Office: 7128 Hwy. 14 E., 70630. Tel: 337-622-3255; Fax: 337-622-3337.
Catechesis/Religious Program—Paige Myers, D.R.E. Students 210.

BIG LAKE, CAMERON PARISH, ST. MARY OF THE LAKE (1938) Rev. Msgr. Harry D. Greig II.
Res.: 11054 Hwy. 384 (Big Lake), 70607. Tel: 337-598-3101; Fax: 337-598-4298.
Catechesis/Religious Program—Students 175.
Mission—St. Patrick's Sweet Lake, Cameron Parish.

CAMERON, CAMERON PARISH, OUR LADY STAR OF THE SEA (1961) Rev. Timothy Goodly.
Church & Res.: 5250 W. Creole Hwy., 70631. Tel: 337-542-4795; Fax: 337-542-4641.
Catechesis/Religious Program—Students 14.

CREOLE, CAMERON PARISH, SACRED HEART OF JESUS (1890) [CEM 3] Rev. Timothy Goodly.
Church & Res.: 5250 W. Creole Hwy., Cameron, 70631. Tel: 337-542-4795; Fax: 337-542-4641.
Catechesis/Religious Program—Stephanie Rodrigue, D.R.E. Students 54.

DEQUINCY, CALCASIEU PARISH, OUR LADY OF LA SALETTE (1955) Rev. Edward J. Brunnert, M.S.
Res.: 203 S. Grand, 70633. Tel: 337-786-3500; Fax: 337-786-4222. Email: ourladyoflasalette@centurytel.net.
Catechesis/Religious Program—Tel: 337-786-3205. Students 77.

DE RIDDER, BEAUREGARD PARISH, ST. JOSEPH'S (1938) Rev. Jude Brunnert, M.S.; Deacon Sumner Kohlhund.
Res.: 1125 Blankenship Dr., 70634. Tel: 337-463-6878; Fax: 337-463-6875.
Catechesis/Religious Program—Mrs. Theresa Pendley, D.R.E. Students 201.

ELTON, JEFFERSON DAVIS PARISH

1—ST. JOSEPH'S (1950), (African American), [CEM] Rev. Babasino Fernandes; Deacon John Eaves.
Mailing Address: P.O. Box 789, 70532.
Res.: 209 N. Washington St., P.O. Box 789, 70532. Tel: 337-584-2038; Fax: 337-584-3997.
Catechesis/Religious Program—Tel: 337-584-2642. Carroll Sue Gobert, D.R.E. Students 7.

2—ST. PAUL (1913) [CEM] Rev. Marshall Boulet; Deacon John Eaves.
Mailing Address: P.O. Box 129, 70532.
Res.: 1100 Saint Mary St., P.O. Box 129, 70532. Tel: 337-584-2818; Fax: 337-584-3246. Web: www.saintpaul-elton.com.
Catechesis/Religious Program—Lezlie LaFosse, D.R.E. Students 146.

FENTON, JEFFERSON DAVIS PARISH, ST. CHARLES BORROMEO (1980) Rev. Roland G. Vaughn.
Res.: P.O. Box 309, 70640. Tel: 337-756-2529; Fax: 337-756-2706.
Catechesis/Religious Program—Susan Augustine, D.R.E. Students 46.
Mission—St. John the Evangelist P.O. Box 124, Lacassine, Jefferson Davis Parish 70647.
Catechesis/Religious Program—Cindy Scharff, D.R.E. Students 130.

GRAND CHENIER, CAMERON PARISH, ST. EUGENE (1962) [CEM 3] Rev. Richard U. Adiukwu.
Res.: 5035 Grand Chenier Hwy., 70643. Tel: 337-538-2245; Fax: 337-538-2246.
Catechesis/Religious Program—Students 28.

HACKBERRY, CAMERON PARISH, ST. PETER APOSTLE (1955) [CEM] Rev. Rommel P. Tolentino.
Res.: 1210 Main St., P.O. Box 372, 70645. Tel: 337-762-3365; Fax: 337-762-3160.
Catechesis/Religious Program—Tel: 337-762-3160. Tamra Welch, D.R.E. Students 113.
Mission—Our Lady of the Assumption Johnson Bayou.

IOWA, CALCASIEU PARISH, ST. RAPHAEL (1931) Rev. Andreas A. Kedati, S.V.D.
Mailing Address: P.O. Drawer 849, 70647. In Res., Rev. Benignus Lambertus Wego, S.V.D.
Res.: 918 Dorothy St., P.O. Drawer 849, 70647. Tel: 337-582-3503; Fax: 337-582-6326. Email: straphael-iowa@hotmail.com.
Catechesis/Religious Program—Students 228.
Mission—St. Joseph P.O. Box 849, Le Bleu Settlement, Calcasieu Parish 70647-0849. Tel: 337-582-3483.

JENNINGS, JEFFERSON DAVIS PARISH

1—IMMACULATE CONCEPTION (1956) Very Rev. Anthony M. Fontenot; Deacon Bennett McNeal.
Res.: 515 Bryan St., P.O. Box 358, 70546. Tel: 337-824-1164; Fax: 337-824-1717.
Catechesis/Religious Program—Deacon Bennett McNeal, D.R.E. Students 170.

2—OUR LADY HELP OF CHRISTIANS (1891) [CEM] Revs. Charles McMillin; Jeffery Paul Starkovich, Parochial Vicar; Deacon Edward McNally.
Res.: 710 State St., P.O. Drawer 1170, 70546. Tel: 337-824-0168; Fax: 337-824-7597. Web: www.olhc.catholicweb.com.
School—600 Roberts Ave., 70546. Tel: 337-824-1743; Fax: 337-824-1752. Nicole Reeves, Prin. Lay Teachers 23; Students 270.
Catechesis/Religious Program—Tel: 337-824-0168. Florence McNally, C.R.E. Students 267.

3—OUR LADY OF PERPETUAL HELP (1941) [CEM] Rev. Celsius Offor (Nigeria).
Res.: 920 S. Broadway, P.O. Box 1331, 70546. Tel: 337-824-3182; 337-824-3186; Fax: 337-824-3186.
Catechesis/Religious Program—Tel: 337-824-3703. Ella D. Williams, D.R.E. Students 42.

KINDER, ALLEN PARISH, ST. PHILIP NERI (1937), (Acadian—French), [CEM] Rev. Carlos Garcia Cardona; Deacon Roy Nash.
Res.: P.O. Box 146, 70648. Tel: 337-738-5612; Fax: 337-738-2728.
Catechesis/Religious Program—Troy Fuselier, D.R.E. Students 341.

LAKE ARTHUR, JEFFERSON DAVIS PARISH, OUR LADY OF THE LAKE (1922) [CEM] [JC 3] Rev. Clyde Thomas.
Res.: 203 Commercial Ave., P.O. Drawer P, 70549. Tel: 337-774-2614; Fax: 337-774-3793.
Catechesis/Religious Program—203 Commercial St., 70549. Tel: 337-774-2675. Students 130.

OAKDALE, ALLEN PARISH, SACRED HEART (1948) [CEM] Rev. Jose Vattakunnel.
Mailing Address: P.O. Box 926, 71463-0926.
Res.: 1208 E. Seventh Ave., 71463. Tel: 318-335-3780; Fax: 318-335-0708.
Catechesis/Religious Program—Students 52.
Mission—St. Frances 204 Poplar St., P.O. Box 926, Elizabeth, Allen Parish 70638.

OBERLIN, ALLEN PARISH, ST. JOAN OF ARC (1920) [CEM] Rev. Felix Anyikwa, Admin.; Deacons Norris Chapman, (Retired); James Dale Deshatel.
Res.: 110 W. Fifth Ave., P.O. Box 479, 70655. Tel: 337-639-4399; 337-639-4798; Fax: 337-639-4799.
Catechesis/Religious Program—Freddy Gorman, D.R.E. Students 192.

RAYMOND, JEFFERSON DAVIS PARISH, ST. LAWRENCE (1951) Rev. Babasino Fernandes.
Res.: 5505 Pine Island Hwy., Jennings, 70546. Tel: 337-584-2700.
Catechesis/Religious Program—Tel: 337-584-2002; Fax: 337-584-3990. Students 189.

SULPHUR, CALCASIEU PARISH

1—IMMACULATE CONCEPTION OF THE B.V.M. (1959) Very Rev. Aubrey V. Guilbeau.
Res.: 2700 Maplewood Dr., 70663. Tel: 337-625-3364; Fax: 337-625-9547.
Catechesis/Religious Program—Tel: 337-625-9719. Vicki Cordell, D.R.E. (Elementary); Sherry Miller, D.R.E. (Middle & H.S.). Students 332.

2—OUR LADY OF LASALETTE (1961) Rev. James M. Winiarski, M.S.; Deacons Johnny Mounce; Maurice Serice. In Res., Rev. Lawrence A. Kohler, M.S.; Bro. Donald V. Smith, M.S.
Res.: 602 N. Claiborne St., 70663. Tel: 337-527-6722; Fax: 337-527-0909.
Catechesis/Religious Program—Tel: 337-527-8307. Cay Gibson, D.R.E. Students 190.

3—OUR LADY OF PROMPT SUCCOR (1919) Revs. Edward J. Richard, M.S.; Thomas J. Hunh, M.S., Parochial Vicar. In Res., Revs. Egidio Vecchio, M.S. (Retired); Sibi Kunninu, MS.
Res.: 1109 Cypress St., 70663. Tel: 337-527-5261; Fax: 337-528-2991.
School—1111 Cypress St., 70663. Tel: 337-527-7828; Fax: 337-528-3778. Mr. Trevor Donnelly,

Prin.; Ms. Stephanie Viator, Librarian. Lay Teachers 25; Students 211.
Catechesis/Religious Program—1029 Lasalette Dr., 70663. Tel: 337-527-9964. Patsy Hebert, D.R.E.; Terry Sittig, D.R.E. Students 259.

4—ST. THERESA (1971) Rev. Joseph G. Aquino, M.S.; Ann Guidry, Office Admin. & Bookkeeper. In Res., Rev. Ernest Corriveau, M.S.
Res.: 4822 Carlyss Dr., 70665. Tel: 337-583-4800; Fax: 337-583-4818.
Catechesis/Religious Program—Tel: 337-583-4010. Angie Clark, D.R.E. Students 387.

VINTON, CALCASIEU PARISH, ST. JOSEPH (1920) Rev. Susil Fernando.
Res.: 1502 Industrial, 70668. Tel: 337-589-7358; Fax: 337-589-7843.
Catechesis/Religious Program—Tel: 337-589-2982. Students 173.

WELSH, JEFFERSON DAVIS PARISH

1—ST. JOSEPH (1941), (African American), [JC] Rev. Celsius Offor (Nigeria).
Res.: P.O. Box 607, 70591. Tel: 337-734-3673.
Mission—St. Peter Claver 400 W. 2nd St., Iowa, Calcasieu Parish 70547. Fax: 337-734-4435.
Catechesis/Religious Program—Patrick Guillony, D.R.E. Students 15.

2—OUR LADY OF SEVEN DOLORS (1904) [CEM] [JC] Rev. Archimandrite Herbert J. May; Deacons Richard Hinchee; Wayne Chapman.
Res.: P.O. Box 515, 70591. Tel: 337-734-3446; Fax: 337-734-3697.
Catechesis/Religious Program—Tel: 337-734-3848. Betty LaBouve, D.R.E. Students 271.

WESTLAKE, CALCASIEU PARISH, ST. JOHN BOSCO (1955) Rev. Albert Borel; Deacons Fred Reed Jr.; Garrett Caraway Jr. In Res., Rev. Michael J. Barras.
Res.: 1301 Sampson St., 70669. Tel: 337-433-2467; Fax: 337-436-9766.
Catechesis/Religious Program—Tel: 337-439-6585; Fax: 337-493-8579. Fred Reed, D.R.E.; Judy Reed, D.R.E. Students 328.

Chaplains of Public Institutions

LAKE CHARLES. *Lake Charles Memorial Hospital*. Rev. Benignus Lambertus Wego, S.V.D.

DEQUINCY. *Phelps Correctional Facility*. Deacon Edward Lavine.

SULPHUR. *West Calcasieu Cameron Hospital*. Rev. Michael J. Barras.

On Duty Outside the Diocese:
Revs.—
Covert, Derek Scott, Pontifical North American College, Casa Santa Maria, Via Dell'Umilta 30 00187, Rome, Italy.
DesOrmeaux, Scott, St. Mary Magdalen Church, 300 Pere Megret, Abbeville, 70511-1507.

On Leave:
Revs.—
Fuselier, Karl, 2781 N. Hwy. 171, 70611.
Harris, Whitney G., Wells Fargo Place, 30 7th St. E., Ste. 350, St. Paul, MN 55101-7804. Tel: 651-201-1800
Miles, James, 115 Gladys Ave., Lansdowne, MD 21227.

On Medical Leave:
Rev.—
McGrath, Joseph, 805 Willow Springs Rd., 70663.

Retired:
Rev. Msgrs.—
Bourque, Joseph A., 2960 Lake St., Apt. 142, 70601.
Melancon, Louis, P.O. Box 508, Opelousas, 70571.
Revs.—
Herlong, Theophilus L., 5635 B Welcome Rd., 70611.
Mancuso, Henry, 858 Kirby St., 70601.
Marco, Alfredo, #9 Std. Domingo St., Bombon, Camarines Sur Philippines. Tel: 011-63-54-471-65-24
Mullen, Thomas G., 15115 Interlachen Dr., Unit 712, Silver Spring, MD 20906-5642. Tel: 301-598-1922. Email: waverlywoods@earthlink.net
Poerio, John, 8656 Big Lake Rd., 70605.
Russi, Fred, 16012 Hwy 102, Jennings, 70546.
Smit, Gerard C., 105 Justice Way, Elkton, MD 21921.

Permanent Deacons:
Bushnell, Joseph, Immaculate Heart of Mary, LC
Caraway, Julius G., Jr., St. John Bosco Church, Westlake
Carr, George K., Our Lady Queen of Heaven, LC
Chapman, Norris, St. Joan of Arc, Oberlin
Chapman, Wayne, Our Lady of Seven Dolors, Welsh
Deshotel, Dale, St. Joan of Arc, Oberlin
Eaves, John, St. Paul, Elton
Granger, James R., St. Henry, Lake Charles
Harmon, Glenn, St. Theodore, LC
Hinchee, Richard, Our Lady of Seven Dolors, Welsh
Kohlhund, Sumner, St. Joseph, De Ridder
Landry, Dan, St. Margaret, Lake Charles
LaPoint, Patrick Our Lady of Prompt Succor, Sulphur
Lavine, Edward, Sacred Heart, Lake Charles
McNally, Edward, Immaculate Conception, Jennings
McNeal, Bennett, Immaculate Conception, Jennings
Menard, Raymond, St. Margaret, LC
Mounce, Johnny, Our Lady of LaSalette, Sulphur
Nash, Roy, St. Philip Neri, Kinder
Reed, Frederick, (Retired), St. John Bosco, Westlake
Reynolds, Jack J., (Retired), St. Theodore's, Lake Charles
Serice, Maurice, Our Lady of LaSalette, Sulphur
Stearns, George, Chancellor & Archivist
Tramel, Michael, St. Lawrence, Jennings
Viau, Glenn, Our Lady of Good Counsel, Lake Charles
Wagner, Harry E., Jr., Immaculate Conception, Sulphur

INSTITUTIONS LOCATED IN THE DIOCESE

[A] HIGH SCHOOLS, INTERPAROCHIAL

LAKE CHARLES. *St. Louis Catholic High School*, 1620 Bank St., 70601. Tel: 337-436-7275; Fax: 337-436-6792. Web: www.slchs.org. Very Rev. Marcus Johnson, Rector; Ms. Deborah Frank, Pres.; Rev. Jacob Scott Conner, Chap.; Ted Nixon, Prin.; Jennifer Guillory, Librarian. Lay Teachers 51; Students 647.

[B] GENERAL HOSPITALS

LAKE CHARLES. *CHRISTUS Health Southwestern Louisiana*, 524 Dr. Michael DeBakey Dr., 70601. Tel: 337-436-2511; Fax: 337-491-7157. Email: brian.king@christushealth.org. Web: www.sph.christushealth.org. Mr. Stephen F. Wright, CEO, Northern Region; Revs. Brian Madison King, Dir. Pastoral Care & Vice Pres. Mission Integration; Charles Okorougo; Sr. Leonie Iweh, D.M.M.M., Chap. Sponsored by Christus Health System, Dallas, TX. Sisters 3; Bed Capacity 266; Patients Assisted Annually 81,969; Total Staff 1,174.

[C] RETREAT HOUSES

LAKE CHARLES. *Holy City Community*, 5611 Welcome Rd., 70611. Tel: 337-855-2871. Email: selma01@localnet.com. Deacon Edward McNally, Moderator & Admin.; Selma Thompson, Sec. & Treas.

MOSS BLUFF. *St. Charles Center*, 2151 Sam Houston Jones Pkwy., 70611. Tel: 337-855-1232; Fax: 337-855-9062. Revs. Whitney Miller, Dir.; Don Piraro, Dir. Emeritus.

[D] MONASTERIES AND RESIDENCES OF PRIESTS AND BROTHERS

OAKDALE. **Herald of Good News, Inc.*, P.O. Box 926, 71463. Tel: 318-335-3780; Fax: 318-335-0708. Rev. Jose Vattakunnel.

[E] SPECIAL RESIDENCES

LAKE CHARLES. *Our Lady Queen of Heaven Manor*, Villa Maria, 3905 Kingston St., 70605. Tel: 337-478-4780; Fax: 337-474-8822. Email: villamaria@suddenlinkmail.com. Units 61; Bed Capacity 118; Total Staff 32.

[F] NEWMAN CENTERS

LAKE CHARLES. *Catholic Student Center* McNeese State University, 221 Aqua Dr., 70605. Tel: 337-477-1434; Fax: 337-479-2129. Web: www.mcneesecatholic.com. Rev. Alan P. Trouille; Sr. Shirley Gobert, S.E.C., Campus Min.; Deacon Glenn Viau, Pastoral Assoc.

[G] SOCIAL SERVICE CENTERS

LAKE CHARLES. *Catholic Service Center*, 1225 2nd St., 70601. Tel: 337-439-7436; Fax: 337-439-7435. Mrs. Trish Trejo, Dir.

[H] MISCELLANEOUS

LAKE CHARLES. *Catholic Daughters of America*, 2117 Constance Ln., 70605.
CHRISTUS St. Patrick Home Care Mr. Stephen F. Wright, CEO.
School Food Services of Lake Charles, Inc., 1112 Bilbo St., 70601. Tel: 337-433-9640, Ext. 202; Fax: 337-433-9685. Email: edrie.durio@lcdiocese.org.

RELIGIOUS INSTITUTES OF MEN REPRESENTED IN THE DIOCESE

For further details refer to the corresponding bracketed number in the Religious Institutes of Men or Women section.

[]—*Missionaries of Compassion*

[0720]—*The Missionaries of Our Lady of La Salette* (Prov. of Mary Queen)—M.S.

[]—*Society of the Divine Word*—S.V.D.

RELIGIOUS INSTITUTES OF WOMEN REPRESENTED IN THE DIOCESE

[0470]—*Congregation of the Sisters of Charity of the Incarnate Word, Houston, Texas*—C.C.V.I.

[]—*Daughters of Mary, Mother of Mercy*

NECROLOGY

† Alers, Juan, (Retired)—Died Feb. 1, 2011
† Okolie, Maxwell, Elton, LA St. Joseph's.—Died Oct. 3, 2011
† Soileau, Charles, (Retired)—Died June 6, 2011

An asterisk (*) denotes an organization that has established tax-exempt status directly with the IRS and is not covered by the USCCB Group Ruling.

Diocese of Lansing

(Dioecesis Lansingensis)

Most Reverend

EARL A. BOYEA

Bishop of Lansing; ordained May 20, 1978; appointed Auxiliary Bishop of Detroit and Titular Bishop of Siccenna July 22, 2002; consecrated September 13, 2002; appointed Bishop of Lansing February 27, 2008; installed April 29, 2008. *Chancery: 228 N. Walnut St., Lansing, MI 48933.* Tel: 517-342-2452; Fax: 517-342-2505.

Most Reverend

CARL F. MENGELING, D.D., S.T.D.

Retired Bishop of Lansing; ordained May 25, 1957; appointed Bishop of Lansing November 7, 1995; consecrated and installed January 25, 1996; retired February 27, 2008. *Chancery, 228 N. Walnut St., Lansing, MI 48933.* Tel: 517-342-2452; Fax: 517-342-2505.

Chancery: 228 N. Walnut St., Lansing, MI 48933. Tel: 517-342-2440; Fax: 517-342-2519.

Web: www.dioceseoflansing.org

Email: chancery@dioceseoflansing.org

ESTABLISHED MAY 22, 1937.

Square Miles 6,218.

Canonically Erected August 4, 1937.

Comprises the Counties of Clinton, Eaton, Genesee, Hillsdale, Ingham, Jackson, Lenawee, Livingston, Shiawassee and Washtenaw, in the State of Michigan.

For legal titles of parishes and diocesan institutions, consult the Chancery Office.

STATISTICAL OVERVIEW

Personnel	
Bishop	1
Retired Bishops	1
Priests: Diocesan Active in Diocese	87
Priests: Diocesan Active Outside Diocese	10
Priests: Retired, Sick or Absent	69
Number of Diocesan Priests	166
Religious Priests in Diocese	45
Total Priests in Diocese	211
Extern Priests in Diocese	21
Ordinations:	
Diocesan Priests	3
Transitional Deacons	1
Permanent Deacons	10
Permanent Deacons in Diocese	103
Total Brothers	3
Total Sisters	329
Parishes	
Parishes	84
With Resident Pastor:	
Resident Diocesan Priests	65
Resident Religious Priests	8
Without Resident Pastor:	
Administered by Priests	4
Administered by Deacons	1
Administered by Professed Religious Men	3
Administered by Religious Women	2
Administered by Lay People	1
Pastoral Centers	2
Professional Ministry Personnel:	
Sisters	5
Lay Ministers	275
Welfare	
Catholic Hospitals	6
Total Assisted	3,727,806
Health Care Centers	7
Total Assisted	104,537
Homes for the Aged	3
Total Assisted	330
Day Care Centers	1
Total Assisted	100
Specialized Homes	3
Total Assisted	173
Special Centers for Social Services	11
Total Assisted	322,032
Residential Care of Disabled	1
Total Assisted	60
Educational	
Diocesan Students in Other Seminaries	29
Total Seminarians	29
Colleges and Universities	1
Total Students	2,630
High Schools, Diocesan and Parish	4
Total Students	2,019
Elementary Schools, Diocesan and Parish	30
Total Students	6,806
Elementary Schools, Private	2
Total Students	193
Catechesis/Religious Education:	
High School Students	2,810
Elementary Students	14,964
Total Students under Catholic Instruction	29,451
Teachers in the Diocese:	
Priests	2
Sisters	5
Lay Teachers	528
Vital Statistics	
Receptions into the Church:	
Infant Baptism Totals	2,307
Minor Baptism Totals	201
Adult Baptism Totals	285
Received into Full Communion	508
First Communions	3,285
Confirmations	2,800
Marriages:	
Catholic	468
Interfaith	303
Total Marriages	771
Deaths	1,969
Total Catholic Population	207,023
Total Population	1,793,060

Former Bishops—Most Revs. JOSEPH H. ALBERS, D.D., J.C.D., appt. Titular Bishop of Lunda and Auxiliary to the Archbishop of Cincinnati, Dec. 16, 1929; cons. Dec. 27, 1929; appt. first Bishop of Lansing, Aug. 4, 1937; died Dec. 1, 1965; ALEXANDER M. ZALESKI, D.D., S.S.L., appt. Titular Bishop of Lyrbe and Auxiliary of Detroit, March 28, 1950; cons. May 23, 1950; transferred to Lansing Oct. 7, 1964; acceded to the See Dec. 1, 1965; died May 16, 1975; KENNETH J. POVISH, D.D., appt. Bishop of Crookston, July 28, 1970; cons. Sept. 29, 1970; appt. Bishop of Lansing, Oct. 8, 1975; installed Dec. 11, 1975; retired Nov. 7, 1995; died Sept. 5, 2003; CARL F. MENGELING, D.D., S.T.D., ord. May 25, 1957; appt. Bishop of Lansing Nov. 7, 1995; cons. and installed Jan. 25, 1996; retired Feb. 27, 2008.

Chancery—228 N. Walnut St., Lansing, 48933. Tel: 517-342-2440; Fax: 517-342-2519. (see Diocesan Departments for additional Fax numbers); Office Hours: Mon.-Fri. 8-12 & 1-4:30; Address all communications to this office.

Bishop's Office—228 N. Walnut St., Lansing, 48933. Tel: 517-342-2452; Fax: 517-342-2505. Rev. Msgrs. STEVEN J. RAICA, J.C.D., Chancellor & Administrative Asst. to the Bishop. Tel: 517-342-2454; GEORGE C. MICHALEK, J.C.L., Vice Chancellor. Tel: 517-485-9902.

Vicar General—Rev. Msgr. RICHARD GROSHEK (Retired), 4381 Springbrook Dr., Swartz Creek, 48473. Tel: 810-630-2042.

Regional Vicars—Revs. JOHN P. KLEIN, Lansing; DENNIS J. HOWARD, Clinton/Shiawassee; ANDREW A. CZAJKOWSKI, Genesee; JAMES R. SHAVER, Jackson; DANIEL WHEELER, Lenawee; ROBERT H. MCGRAW, Livingston; BRENDAN J. WALSH, Washtenaw.

College of Consultors—Rev. Msgrs. MICHAEL D. MURPHY (Retired); STEVEN J. RAICA, J.C.D.; Revs. THOMAS FIRESTONE; DAVID HUDGINS; JEFFREY A. POLL; BERNARD REILLY; DAVID J. SPEICHER; FREDERICK H. TAGGART, O.S.A.; THOMAS W. THOMPSON (Retired).

Vicar for Charismatic Communities—Rev. PETER J. CLARK, St. Mary Church, 157 High St., Williamston, 48895. Tel: 517-655-2620; Fax: 517-655-3933.

Vicar for Religious—Sr. MARY ANN FOGGIN, S.G.L., 4399 Ford Rd., Ann Arbor, 48105. Tel: 734-663-6128.

Ecumenical Officer—Rev. WILLIAM WEGHER, St. Mary, 10601 Dexter Pinckney Rd., Pinckney, 48169. Tel: 734-878-3161; Fax: 734-878-2383.

Commissions and Councils—

Presbyteral Council—Revs. THOMAS FIRESTONE, Pres., St. John Vianney, 2415 Bagley St., Flint, 48504. Tel: 810-235-1812; Fax: 810-235-4911; BERNARD REILLY, Vice Pres., St. Mary Cathedral, 219 Seymour, Lansing, 48933. Tel: 517-484-5331; Fax: 517-484-0475; JEFFREY A. POLL, Sec. & Treas., St. Mary Church, 700 Columbia Dr., Durand, 48429. Tel: 855-288-6704; Fax: 989-288-0295.

Board of Education and Catechesis—MICHAEL MCCARTHY, Pres. Tel: 810-519-4056.

Building Commission—Rev. JONATHAN WEHRLE, St.

Martha Church, 1100 W. Grand River, Okemos, 48864. Tel: 517-349-1763; Fax: 517-347-3536.

Cursillo—Rev. Msgr. SYLVESTER L. FEDEWA, Spiritual Dir. (Retired), 120 N. Willow St., Box 412, Westphalia, 48894. Tel: 989-587-4379.

Finance Council—Rev. DANIEL WHEELER, St. Elizabeth, 506 N. Union St., Tecumseh, 49286. Tel: 517-423-2447.

Priest Pension Board—Rev. JONATHAN WEHRLE, St. Martha, 1100 W. Grand River, Okemos, 48864. Tel: 517-349-1763.

Priests' Assignment Commission—Revs. WILLIAM A. ASHBAUGH; BERNARD REILLY; DAVID E. FISHER; ROY HORNING; JOHN KLEIN; THOMAS BUTLER; KARL L. PUNG; TIMOTHY NELSON; DAVID HUDGINS; ROBERT J. PIENTA.

Diocesan Offices And Departments

Office of Child & Youth Protection—SALLY ELLIS, Coord. Tel: 517-342-2551; Fax: 517-342-2505.

Victim Assistance Coordinator—ADRIENNE ROWLAND, LMSW, ACSW. Tel: 888-308-6252. Email: arowlandvac@dioceseoflansing.org.

Diocesan Archivist—Rev. Msgr. GEORGE C. MICHALEK, J.C.L., 228 N. Walnut St., Lansing, 48933. Tel: 517-342-2540; Fax: 517-342-2544.

Diocesan Mission Office— (Includes Propagation of the Faith, Holy Childhood Assoc., Inter-Parish Sharing) DAWN LAWLESS, Dir., 228 N. Walnut St., Lansing, 48933. Tel: 517-342-2541; Fax: 517-342-2542.

Legal Advisor and Chief of Staff—Deacon MICHAEL MURRAY. Tel: 517-342-2456; Fax: 517-342-2527.

Director of Human Resources—LISA KUTAS. Tel: 517-342-2511; Fax: 517-342-2527.

Diocesan Tribunal—

Judicial Vicar—Rev. Msgr. GEORGE C. MICHALEK, J.C.L., 228 N. Walnut St., Lansing, 48933. Tel: 517-342-2560; Fax: 517-342-2561 (Address all rogatory commissions to the Diocesan Tribunal).

Tribunal Judges—Rev. Msgrs. RAYMOND J. GOEHRING, J.C.L.; STEVEN J. RAICA, J.C.D.; EILEEN JARAMILLO, J.C.L.; Rev. Msgr. GEORGE C. MICHALEK, J.C.L.; Revs. PHILLIP SCHWEDA, J.C.L.; NATHANIEL SOKOL, J.C.L.

Defender of the Bond—Deacon JOHN CAMERON, J.C.L.

Promoter of Justice—Rev. CHARLES IRVIN (Retired).

Court Experts—RICHARD G. STRIFE, Ph.D.; LINDA BLOHM, Ph.D.; Ms. CAROLE BEAUCHAMP, L.M.S.W.; Dr. ROBERT L. SAIN, Ph.D.

Notary—AVA JO PUNG.

Office of Pastoral Planning—Sr. RITA WENZLICK, O.P., Dir. Tel: 517-342-2502; Fax: 517-342-2468.

Christian Initiation Advisory Committee—MICHAEL ANDREWS, Chm. Tel: 517-342-2479.

Faith Magazine— See Miscellaneous Listings: Faith Publishing Service.

Department of Catholic Charities—CHRISTOPHER ROOT, Chm. Tel: 517-342-2462; Fax: 517-342-2446.

Bishop's Council on Alcoholism-Chemical Dependency—VINCENT GALE. Tel: 517-342-2471.

Befriender Ministry—VINCENT GALE. Tel: 517-342-2471.

Campaign for Human Development—VINCENT GALE. Tel: 517-342-2471.

Catholic Relief Services—VINCENT GALE. Tel: 517-342-2471.

Courage and Encourage—VINCENT GALE. Tel: 517-342-2471.

Family Life—VINCENT GALE. Tel: 517-342-2471.

Natural Family Planning—CHRISTINE BACKLUND. Tel: 517-342-2587.

Life Justice—VACANT. Tel: 517-342-2469.

Restorative Justice—JOE DIONISE, Dir. Tel: 517-342-2495.

Separated & Divorced Ministry—VINCENT GALE. Tel: 517-342-2471.

Project Rachel (Post-Abortion Counseling)—VINCENT GALE. Tel: 517-342-2471.

Multicultural Evangelization—RONALD LANDFAIR, Dir. Tel: 517-342-2496.

Ministry with Persons with Disabilities—VACANT. Tel: 517-342-2497.

Catholic Deaf Ministry—ROSE SMITH, Dir. Tel: 517-342-2532; Rev. BOSCO PADAMATTUMMAL, Chap. Tel: 810-769-2550.

Hispanic/Migrant Ministry—RONALD LANDFAIR, Dir. Tel: 517-342-2496.

Department of Communication—MICHAEL DIEBOLD, Chm. Tel: 517-853-7660; Fax: 517-853-7616.

Department of Education and Catechesis—Rev. STEVEN M. MATTSON, Chm. Tel: 517-342-2481; Fax: 517-342-2515.

Superintendent of Schools—Rev. STEVEN M. MATTSON. Tel: 517-342-2481.

Associate Superintendent—SEAN COSTELLO. Tel: 517-342-2483.

Evangelization—PATRICK RINKER. Tel: 517-342-2485.

Catechesis—MICHAEL ANDREWS, Dir. Tel: 517-342-2479.

Youth Ministry and Young Adult Ministry—PATRICK RINKER. Tel: 517-342-2485.

Campus Ministry—PATRICK RINKER. Tel: 517-342-2485.

Worship Office—RITA THIRON, Dir. Tel: 517-342-2476.

Worship Commission—Rev. WILLIAM R. LUGGER. Tel: 517-482-1346.

Department of Finance—THOMAS PASTULA, Chm. & Finance Officer. Tel: 517-342-2442; Fax: 517-342-2527.

Accounting Services—ANDREA RATHWELL. Tel: 517-342-2445; Fax: 517-342-2519.

Development—PATRICIA O'HEARN, Dir. Tel: 517-342-2503; Fax: 517-342-2519; LISA WEBER, Assoc. Dir. Tel: 517-342-2535.

Property & Parish Cemeteries—PAUL GARRIEPY, Dir. Tel: 517-342-2534; Fax: 517-342-2468.

Diocesan Cemeteries—VICKIE YANKEE, Dir. Tel: 517-484-2500.

Technology Administrator—SHARON BYERS. Tel: 517-342-2538; Fax: 517-342-2519.

Department of Formation and Lay Ministry—Rev. JOHN LINDEN, Chm. Tel: 517-342-2507; Fax: 517-342-2468.

Director of Seminarians—Rev. JOHN LINDEN. Tel: 517-342-2507.

Joseph H. Albers Trust Fund for Diocesan Vocations—Rev. JOHN LINDEN. Tel: 517-342-2507.

Lay Ecclesial Ministry—DEBORAH AMATO, Dir. Tel: 517-342-2512.

Permanent Diaconate—Deacon GERALD BRENNAN. Tel: 517-342-2451.

Priestly Life and Ministry—Rev. KARL L. PUNG, Dir. Tel: 810-229-9863; Fax: 810-220-0730.

Vocations/Vicar for Consecrated Life—DAWN HAUSMANN, Dir. Tel: 517-342-2506.

Discernment Houses—

Emmaus House—Rev. JOHN LINDEN, Dir., 320 M.A.C. Ave., East Lansing, 48823. Tel: 517-351-1543.

Father McGiveny House—Rev. WILLIAM A. ASHBAUGH, Dir., St. Thomas the Apostle Church, 530 Elizabeth St., Ann Arbor, 48104. Tel: 734-761-8606.

St. Catherine House—Rev. WILLIAM A. ASHBAUGH, Dir., St. Thomas the Apostle Church, 530 Elizabeth St., Ann Arbor, 48104. Tel: 734-761-8606.

CLERGY, PARISHES, MISSIONS AND PAROCHIAL SCHOOLS

CITY OF LANSING

(INGHAM COUNTY)

1—ST. MARY CATHEDRAL (1866) Rev. Bernard Reilly. In Res., Rev. Msgrs. George C. Michalek, Vice Chancellor, Diocese of Lansing; Steven J. Raica, Chancellor, Diocese of Lansing.
Res.: 219 Seymour, 48933. Tel: 517-484-5331; Fax: 517-484-0475. Web: http://stmarycathedrallansing.catholicweb.com.
Catechesis/Religious Program—Jennifer Nelson, D.R.E. Students 32.

2—ST. ANDREW DUNG-LAC (1998), (Vietnamese), Rev. Joseph S. Kim (Retired).
Res.: 1611 W. Oaklnad Ave., 48915. Tel: 517-272-3276; 517-580-7557; Fax: 517-580-7557.
Catechesis/Religious Program—Chuong Thanh Nguyen, D.R.E. Students 79.

3—ST. CASIMIR (1921) Rev. William R. Lugger.
Mailing Address: 815 Sparrow Ave., 48910-8003. Tel: 517-482-1346; Fax: 517-482-1313. Email: office@stcas.org. Web: www.stcas.org.
Catechesis/Religious Program—Students 81.

4—CRISTO REY (1961), (Hispanic), Rev. Frederick L. Thelen; Deacon Rogelio Alfaro.
Office: 201 W. Miller Rd., 48911. Tel: 517-394-4639; Fax: 517-394-8090. Web: www.cristoreychurch.org.
Res.: 6121 Rosedale Rd., 48911. Tel: 517-394-0676.
Catechesis/Religious Program—Students 230.

5—ST. GERARD (Delta Township, Eaton Co.) (1958) [JC] Revs. John P. Klein; Pieter vanRooyen; Deacons Richard Savage; Jim Corder.
Res.: 1304 Maycroft, 48917. Tel: 517-323-2379; Fax: 517-886-1394. Web: stgerard.org.
School—4433 W. Willow Hwy., 48917. Tel: 517-321-6126; Fax: 517-323-8046. Email: mpiecuch@stgerard.org. Web: stgerardlansing.org. Michelle Piecuch, Prin. Lay Teachers 30; Students 523.
Catechesis/Religious Program—Tel: 517-321-4179. Students 361.

6—HOLY CROSS (1924) Closed. For inquiries for parish records contact the chancery.

7—IMMACULATE HEART OF MARY (1949) Revs. John Byers; George Daisy; Deacons William Fudge III; John Cameron.
Office:—3815 S. Cedar, 48910. Tel: 517-393-3030; Fax: 517-393-0855. Email: smithb@ihmlansing.org. Web: immaculateheartofmarylansing.catholicweb.com.
School—3830 Rosemont St., 48910-4525. Tel: 517-882-6631; Fax: 517-882-5536. Email: wilcoxc@ihmlansing.org. Web: www.ihmlansing.org. Angela Johnston, Prin. Lay Teachers 10; Students 160.
Catechesis/Religious Program—Tel: 517-393-3033. Students 235.

8—RESURRECTION (1922) Revs. John M. Fain; Pankratius Kerketta. In Res., Rev. Msgr. Raymond J. Goehring.
Res.: 1531 E. Michigan Ave., 48912. Tel: 517-482-4749; Fax: 517-484-4740. Email: resurrection1531@sbcglobal.net. Web: resurrectionlansing.org.
School—1527 E. Michigan Ave., 48912. Tel: 517-487-0439; Fax: 517-487-3198. Email: resurrectionschool@comcast.net. Web: resschool.com. Jack Von Achen, Prin. Lay Teachers 11; Students 153.
Catechesis/Religious Program—1527 E. Michigan Ave., 48912. Tel: 517-482-2605. Students 44.

9—ST. THERESE (1949) [CEM] Rev. Michael J. Williams; Deacon David Borzenski; Anthony Sperendi, Adult Faith Formation Dir.
Res.: 102 W. Randolph St., 48906. Tel: 517-487-3749; Fax: 517-487-3755. Email: staff@sttherese.org. Web: www.sttherese.org.
Catechesis/Religious Program—Tel: 517-487-3730. Ms. Patricia Droste, D.R.E. Students 82.

OUTSIDE THE CITY OF LANSING

ADRIAN, LENAWEE CO.

1—ST. JOSEPH (1863) [CEM] Revs. David Hudgins; Thomas Wasilewski, Parochial Vicar; Deacon Leonard C. Brown.
Res.: 415 Ormsby St., 49221. Tel: 517-265-8938; Fax: 517-265-1987. Email: office@stjosephadrian.com. Web: www.stjosephadrian.com.
Catechesis/Religious Program—Email: aimee@stjosephadrian.com. Students 100.

2—ST. MARY OF GOOD COUNSEL (1853) [CEM] Rev. Robert Schramm, O.S.F.S.; Deacons Richard Bayes Jr.; Calistro Torres. In Res., Rev. Louis A. Komorowski, O.S.F.S.
Office: 305 Division St., 49221. Tel: 517-263-4681; Fax: 517-263-4682. Email: stmarys@tc3net.com. Web: www.stmarysadrian.com.
Res.: 320 Division St., 49221. Tel: 517-265-6543.
Catechesis/Religious Program—Fax: 517-263-4682. Students 100.

ANN ARBOR, WASHTENAW CO.

1—CHRIST THE KING (1981) Rev. Edward O. Fride; Deacons Daniel R. Foley; Gerald P. Holowicki; Louis J. Russello, Pastoral Assoc.; Larry Randolph; Gregory VandeVoorde.
4000 Ave Maria Dr., 48105. Tel: 734-665-5040; Fax: 734-663-3735. Email: thofer@ctkcc.net. Web: www.ctkcc.net.
Catechesis/Religious Program—Tel: 734-929-0981; Fax: 734-663-3735. Email: bmorgan@ctkcc.net. Students 425.

2—ST. FRANCIS OF ASSISI (1950) [CEM] Revs. James G. McDougall; Bosco Padamattummal (India).
Res.: 2150 Frieze Ave., 48104. Tel: 734-769-2550; Fax: 734-821-2102. Email: parishoffice@stfrancisa2.org. Web: www.stfrancisa2.com. In Res., Rev. Terrence J. Dumas (Retired).
School—(Grades K-8) Tel: 734-821-2200; Fax: 734-821-2202. Email: school@stfrancisaa.org. Sara Collins, Prin.; Julie Rick, Librarian. Lay Teachers 39; Students 420.
Catechesis/Religious Program—Tel: 734-821-2130. Email: stfreled@stfrancisa2.org. Students 750.

3—ST. MARY STUDENT PARISH (1915), Serving students, faculty, and staff at the University of Michigan. Revs. Benjamin B. Hawley, S.J.; Dennis T. Dillon, S.J.; Dennis T. Glasgow, S.J.; Daniel T. Reim, S.J., Campus Min.; Steve Wolbert, Devel. Dir.; Sr. Catherine Morgan, O.P., Campus Min.; Anita M. Bohn, Music Dir.; Patrick J. Waters, Opers. Dir./Pastoral Assoc.; Sr. Dorothy Ederer, O.P., Campus Min.; Deacon Romolo J. Leone, Pastoral Assoc.; Kelly Dunlop, Campus Min.
Office: 331 Thompson St., 48104-2295. Tel: 734-663-0557; 734-663-0558; Fax: 734-663-2756. Email: stmarys@umich.edu. Web: www.stmarystudentparish.org.
Catechesis/Religious Program—Students 290.

4—ST. PATRICK (1831) [CEM] Rev. Gerald Gawronski.
Res.: 5671 Whitmore Lake Rd., 48105. Tel: 734-662-8141; 734-663-1851; Fax: 734-994-9136. Email:

carlap@parishmail.com. Web: www.oldstpatrick-annarbor.com.
Catechesis/Religious Program—Students 90.

5—ST. THOMAS THE APOSTLE (1835) [CEM] Revs. William A. Ashbaugh; Nithyaselvam Arokiaselvam; Glen D. Johnston, Business Mgr.; Deacons James Miles; Warren Hecht.
Mailing Address: 530 Elizabeth St., 48104. Tel: 734-761-8606; Fax: 734-997-8432. Web: www.sta2.org.
School—Tel: 734-769-0911; Fax: 734-769-9078. Tony Moskus, Prin. Lay Teachers 20; Students 267.
Catechesis/Religious Program—Tel: 734-761-8606; Fax: 734-997-8432. Monica Pope, Dir. Faith Formation; Beth Spizarny, Coord., Youth Ministry. Students 169.

BELLEVUE, EATON CO., ST. ANN (1923) Rev. Francis D. Mossholder.
Res.: 312 S. Main St., P.O. Box 33, 49021. Tel: 269-763-9372; Fax: 269-763-9372. 807 Saint Marys Blvd., Charlotte, 48813.
Catechesis/Religious Program—Students 30.

BLISSFIELD, LENAWEE CO., ST. PETER THE APOSTLE (1910) Merged with St. Alphonsus Parish, Deerfield to form Light of Christ Parish, Deerfield

BRIGHTON, LIVINGSTON CO.

1—HOLY SPIRIT (1979) Rev. John George Rocus; Deacon Gerald Brennan.
Res.: Tel: 810-231-9199, Ext. 219; Fax: 810-231-6129. Email: parishoffice@holyspiritbrighton.com. Web: www.hsrcc.net.
School—9565 Musch Rd., 48116. Tel: 810-231-9199, Ext. 214. Email: piccira@holyspiritbrighton.com. Anna Piccirillo-Loewe, Prin.
Catechesis/Religious Program—Tel: 810-231-9199, Ext. 209. Katherine Jean, Dir. Faith Formation. Students 55.

2—ST. MARY MAGDALEN CHURCH (1993) Rev. David F. Howell; Deacons H. David Scharf; James M. Chevalier; Gary W. Prise.
Res.: 2201 Old U.S. 23, 48114. Tel: 810-229-0646; 810-229-8624; Fax: 810-229-6471. Email: info@saintmarymagdalen.org. Web: www.saintmarymagdalen.org.
Catechesis/Religious Program—Students 674.

3—ST. PATRICK (1832), (Irish), [CEM] Revs. Karl L. Pung; Mark J. Rutherford; Deacons David Lawrence; Patrick A. McDonald; Sr. Theresa M. Fifer, O.S.F., Pastoral Min.; Margaret Mullally-Henne, Pastoral Min.; Glenna Diskin, Pastoral Min.; Robert Wolf, Pastoral Min.; H. William Smeal, Pastoral Min.
711 Rickett Rd., 48116.
Res.: 129 Becker, 48116-9863. Tel: 810-229-9863; Fax: 810-220-0730. Web: http://home.catholicweb.com/stpatchurch.
School—1001 Orndorf Dr., 48116. Tel: 810-229-7946; Fax: 810-229-6206. Jeanine Kenny, Prin. Lay Teachers 26; Students 459.
Catechesis/Religious Program—710 Rickett Rd., 48116. Tel: 810-229-4221; Fax: 810-229-6206. Email: secre@stpatchurch.org. Sr. Theresa M. Fifer, O.S.F., D.R.E. Students 1,005.

BROOKLYN, LENAWEE CO., ST. JOSEPH SHRINE (Irish Hills) (1854) [CEM] Revs. David Hudgins; Thomas Wasilewski; Deacons John Amthor; Gene Hausmann.
Office: 8743 U.S. 12, 49230. Tel: 517-467-2183; Fax: 517-467-4285. Email: sjshrine@frontiernet.net. Web: www.stjosephshrinebrooklyn.catholicweb.com.
Catechesis/Religious Program—Tel: 517-467-2106. Students 87.

BURTON, GENESEE CO.

1—BLESSED SACRAMENT (1957) Rev. Andrew A. Czajkowski.
Res.: 6340 Roberta, 48509. Tel: 810-742-3151; Fax: 810-742-1409. Email: blesssacrament@comcast.net.
Catechesis/Religious Program—Rev. Andrew A. Czajkowski, D.R.E. Students 35.

2—HOLY REDEEMER (1940) Rev. Steven D. Anderson.
Res.: 1227 E. Bristol Rd., 48529. Tel: 810-743-3050; Fax: 810-743-4381. Email: info@holyredeemerburton.org. Web: holyredeemerburton.com.
Catechesis/Religious Program—Tel: 810-742-9460. Paul Schlegelmilch, D.R.E.; Emily Frybarger, RCIA / Adult Faith Formation. Students 201.

CHARLOTTE, EATON CO., ST. MARY (1868) Rev. Francis D. Mossholder; Deacon Thomas Fogle.
807 St. Mary Blvd., 48813. Tel: 517-543-4319; Fax: 517-543-9078. Email: stmaryschurch807@att.net. Web: stmarycharlotte.catholicweb.com.
Res.: 812 St. Mary Blvd., 48813. Tel: 517-541-2755; Fax: 517-543-9078.
School—905 St. Mary Blvd., 48813. Tel: 517-543-3460; Fax: 517-541-9798. Email: smschar@sbcglobal.net. Web: stmaryschoolcharlotte.catholicweb.com. Linda Yeager, Prin. Lay Teachers 5; Students 67.
Catechesis/Religious Program—Email: stmarydre@sbcglobal.net. Students 112.

CHELSEA, WASHTENAW CO., ST. MARY (1845) [CEM] [JC] Rev. William J. Turner; Deacon Thomas Franklin.
Res.: 14200 E. Old U.S. Hwy. 12, 48118. Tel: 734-475-7561; Fax: 734-475-3207. Email: smcch@aol.com. Web: www.stmarychelsea.org.
Catechesis/Religious Program—Tel: 734-475-8164; Fax: 734-475-5835. Students 533.

CLARKLAKE, JACKSON CO., ST. RITA (1916) [JC] Rev. Lehr Barkenquest, O.S.F.S.; Deacon Louis Weitzel.
Res.: 10720 Hayes Rd., 49234. Tel: 517-592-5470; Fax: 517-592-5470 (Call First). Email: stritascatholicchurch@frontiernet.net. Web: catholicweb.com/stritaclarklake.
Catechesis/Religious Program—Tel: 517-592-5718. Students 252.

CLINTON, LENAWEE CO., ST. DOMINIC ORATORY (1853) [CEM] Revs. Daniel Wheeler; Paul Ruddy, O.S.F.S., Sacramental Min.
Res.: 506 N. Union, Tecumseh, 49286. Tel: 517-423-2447.
Catechesis/Religious Program—Tel: 517-423-2447, Ext. 6. Students 10.

CLIO, GENESEE CO., SS. CHARLES AND HELENA (1953) Rev. Thomas Butler.
Res.: 230 E. Vienna St., 48420-1423. Tel: 810-686-9861; Fax: 810-686-8070. Email: sscharlesandhelena@catholicweb.com. Web: www.sscharlesandhelena.org.
Catechesis/Religious Program—Tel: 810-686-6720. Students 178.

CONCORD, JACKSON CO., ST. CATHERINE LABOURE (1953) Rev. Denis R. Spitzley; Deacon Carol Franssen.
211 Harmon Ave., 49237.
Res.: 312 Kryst St., 49237. Tel: 517-524-7578; 517-524-6261; Fax: 517-524-7518. Web: http://home.catholicweb.com/stcatherinelaboureconcord.
Catechesis/Religious Program—Students 60.

DAVISON, GENESEE CO., ST. JOHN THE EVANGELIST (1871) [CEM] Revs. Andrew A. Czajkowski; Carl Simon; Deacon Dan Fairweather.
404 N. Dayton St., 48423-1397.
Res.: 316 N. Dayton St., 48423-1397. Tel: 810-653-2377; 810-653-8015; 810-658-4776 (Voice Mail); Fax: 810-658-1123. Web: www.stjohndavison.org.
Catechesis/Religious Program—505 N. Dayton, 48423. Tel: 810-653-4056. Elaine Davis, D.R.E.; Elaine Ouellette, D.R.E.; Paul Schlegelmilch, D.R.E., Youth Ministry. Students 594.

DEWITT, CLINTON CO., ST. JUDE (1971) Rev. Dwight M. Ezop.
Res.: 409 Wilson, De Witt, 48820. Tel: 517-669-8335; Fax: 517-669-8343. Email: catholic.stjude@comcast.net. Web: www.stjudedewitt.com.
Catechesis/Religious Program—Tel: 517-669-8341. Students 515.

DEERFIELD, LENAWEE CO., LIGHT OF CHRIST PARISH (2010) Rev. John J. Loughran, O.S.F.S.; Margaret O'Malley, Liturgist.
Church Office: 222 Carey St., 49238. Tel: 517-447-3500; 517-447-3766 (Rectory); Fax: 517-447-3210. Email: lightofchristparish@gmail.com. Web: www.lightofchristparish.com.
Worship Sites—
St. Alphonsus— (1864), with St. Peter the Apostle Parish, Blissfield to form Light of Christ Parish, Deerfield, 222 Carey St., 49238.
St. Peter the Apostle—309 S. Lane, Blissfield, 49228-1244. Tel: 517-486-2156; Fax: 517-486-2157.
Catechesis/Religious Program—Deanna Burke, D.R.E.; Sara Smith, Youth Min.; Mary Quick, RCIA Adult Faith Formation. Students 169.

DEXTER, WASHTENAW CO., ST. JOSEPH (1840) [CEM] Rev. Brendan J. Walsh; Deacon Romolo Leone.
Office: 3430 Dover St., 48130. Tel: 734-426-8483; Fax: 734-426-6451. Email: info@stjos.com. Web: www.stjos.com.
Church: 6805 Mast Rd., 48130.
Catechesis/Religious Program—Tel: 734-426-2674; Fax: 734-426-6451. Email: marinell_high@stjos.com. Students 546.

DURAND, SHIAWASSEE CO., ST. MARY (1900) Rev. Jeffrey A. Poll.
Res.: 700 Columbia Dr., 48429. Tel: 855-288-6704; Fax: 989-288-0295. Web: www.stmarydurand.catholicweb.com.
Catechesis/Religious Program—Students 128.

EAST LANSING, INGHAM CO.

1—ST. JOHN THE EVANGELIST CHURCH AND STUDENT CENTER (1958) Revs. Mark Inglot; Joseph J. Krupp; Matt Eldred, Dir. Music; Katie Diller, Campus Min.; Denise Waytes, Dir. Worship; Al Weilbaecher, Dir. Adult Faith Formation; Katie Cervenak, Dir. Communications; Keith Tharp, Business Mgr.
327 M.A.C. Ave., 48823.
Res.: 955 Alton Rd., 48823. Tel: 517-351-7215; Fax: 517-337-8358. Email: sjsecretary@elcatholics.org. Web: www.stjohnmsu.org.

2—ST. THOMAS AQUINAS (1940) Revs. Mark Inglot; Anthony Strouse, Parochial Vicar; Joseph J. Krupp, Dir. Campus Min.; Deacons James Kasprzak; Michael Murray.
Res.: 955 Alton Rd., 48823. Tel: 517-351-7215; Fax: 517-351-7271. Web: www.elcatholics.org.
School—915 Alton Rd., 48823. Tel: 517-332-0813; Fax: 517-332-9490. Rod Murphy, Prin. Lay Teachers 25; Students 413.
Catechesis/Religious Program—Tel: 517-351-5460. Students 488.

EATON RAPIDS, EATON CO., ST. PETER (1891) Rev. Bennett P. Constantine; Deacon Gideon Marsal.
Res.: 405 E. Knight St., 48827. Tel: 517-663-4735; Fax: 517-663-7110. Email: office@cathlicstpeter.com. Web: www.catholicstpeter.com.
Catechesis/Religious Program—Tel: 517-663-2088; Fax: 517-663-7110. Email: dre@catholicstpeter.com. Web: www.catholicstpeter.com. Students 102.

FENTON, GENESEE CO., ST. JOHN THE EVANGELIST (1843) [CEM 2] Revs. David W. Harvey; Kurian Kollapallil, M.S.F.S. (India); Deacons Terry Carsten; Ronald Kenney.
Res.: 600 N. Adelaide St., 48430. Tel: 810-629-2251; Fax: 810-629-2302. Web: www.stjohnfenton.org.
School—514 Lincoln St., 48430. Tel: 810-629-6551; Fax: 810-629-2213. Mrs. Kit White, Prin. Lay Teachers 25; Students 406.
Catechesis/Religious Program—512 N. Adelaide St., 48430. Tel: 810-629-1850. Students 617.

FLINT, GENESEE CO.

1—ST. AGNES (1928) Closed. For inquiries for parish records contact St. John Vianney, Flint.

2—ALL SAINTS (1910), (Polish), [CEM] Rev. Anthony P. Majchrowski.
Res.: G-4063 W. Pierson Rd., 48504. Tel: 810-787-0491.
Catechesis/Religious Program—Students 20.

3—CHRIST THE KING (1929), (African American), Rev. Philip Schmitter.
1811 Seymour Ave., 48503. Tel: 810-233-0402; Fax: 810-233-0466. Email: ccatholic@att.net. Web: www.christthekingflint.catholicweb.com.
Rectory—Res.: 1832 Seymour Ave., 48503. Tel: 810-233-8810.
Catechesis/Religious Program—Students 31.

4—ST. FRANCIS OF ASSISI, Closed. For inquiries for parish records contact the diocesan archives.

5—HOLY ROSARY (1951) Rev. George Puthenpeedika (India).
Res.: 5199 Richfield Rd., 48506. Tel: 810-736-4040; Fax: 810-736-9129. Email: holyrosaryflint@yahoo.com. Web: www.holyrosary-flint.catholicweb.com; www.holyrosaryflint.org.
School—5191 Richfield Rd., 48506. Tel: 810-736-4220; Fax: 810-736-0164. Email: hrschool@comcast.net. Deborah Hodges, Prin. Lay Teachers 5; Students 92.
Catechesis/Religious Program—Tel: 810-736-4040, Ext. 30. Students 73.

6—ST. JOHN VIANNEY (1941) Rev. Thomas Firestone.
Res.: 2415 Bagley St., 48504-4613. Tel: 810-235-1812; Fax: 810-235-4911.
School—2319 Bagley St., 48504. Tel: 810-235-5687; Fax: 810-235-2811. Web: www.sjvkids.com. Mrs. Mary Allen LAN, Prin. Lay Teachers 13; Total Staff 13; Students 221.
Catechesis/Religious Program—Students 107.

7—ST. LEO THE GREAT (1957) Closed. For inquiries for parish records contact Holy Rosary, Flint.

8—ST. LUKE (1950) Closed. For inquiries for parish records contact St. John Vianney, Flint.

9—ST. MARY (1919) Rev. Santhiyagu Arockiyasamy, M.S.F.S. (India).
Res.: 2500 N. Franklin Ave., 48506. Tel: 810-232-4012; Fax: 810-232-3889. Email: stmaryflint@hotmail.com.
Catechesis/Religious Program—Deacon Michael McCrandall, D.R.E. Students 14.

10—ST. MATTHEW (1911) Revs. Frederick H. Taggart, O.S.A.; Ronald E. Scheible, O.S.A.; James G. Ryan, O.S.A.
Res.: 706 Beach St., 48502. Tel: 810-232-0880; Fax: 810-232-4148. Web: www.stmatthewflint.org.
Catechesis/Religious Program—Students 18.

11—ST. MICHAEL (1843) Deacon Michael Dear, Pastoral Coord.
Res.: 609 E. Fifth Ave., 48503. Tel: 810-238-2679; Fax: 810-232-6820. Email: stmichael_flint@hotmail.com.
Catechesis/Religious Program—Tel: 810-238-7931; Fax: 810-232-6820. Students 53.

12—OUR LADY OF GUADALUPE (1957), (Spanish), Rev. Cecilio C. Reyna.
Res.: G-2316 W. Coldwater Rd., 48505. Tel: 810-787-5701; Fax: 810-787-3198. Email: reyna64@gmail.com. Web: www.ologflint.org.
Catechesis/Religious Program—Students 123.

13—ST. PIUS X (1955) Rev. Robert F. Copeland; Deacon Gary A. Gallagher.
Res.: G-3139 Hogarth Ave., 48532. Tel: 810-235-8574. Email: stpiuschurch@comcast.net. Web: www.saintpiusxparish.com.

School—Tel: 810-235-8572; Fax: 810-235-2675. R.J. Kaplan, Prin. Sisters 1; Lay Teachers 13; Students 218.
Catechesis/Religious Program—Students 23.
Convent—G-3165 Hogarth Ave., 48532. Tel: 810-233-8956.

14—SACRED HEART (1928) Closed. For inquiries for parish records contact St. John Vianney, Flint.

FLUSHING, GENESEE CO., ST. ROBERT (1875) [CEM] Revs. Roy Theodore Horning; Louis T. Ekka; Deacon Dennis Pennell.
Res.: 310 N. Cherry St., 48433. Tel: 810-659-2501; Fax: 810-659-2564. Email: jrymar@parishmail.com. Web: www.strobertparish.org.
School—St. Robert School, 214 E. Henry, 48433. Tel: 810-659-2503; Fax: 810-659-4002. Email: srsoffice@aol.com. Web: www.strobertschool.com. Susan C. Sharp, Prin. Lay Teachers 12; Students 253.
Catechesis/Religious Program—Tel: 810-659-8556. Students 190.

FOWLER, CLINTON CO., MOST HOLY TRINITY (1881), (German), [CEM] Rev. Dennis J. Howard.
Res.: 545 N. Maple St., 48835. Tel: 989-593-2162; Fax: 989-593-2171. Email: office@mhtparish.com. Web: www.mhtparish.com.
School—11144 Kent St., 48835. Tel: 517-593-2616; Fax: 989-593-2801. Email: anneh@mhtparish.com. Anne K. Hufnagel, Prin. Lay Teachers 7; Students 81.
Catechesis/Religious Program—Tel: 517-593-3174; Fax: 517-593-2801. Email: halfmanandrew@hotmail.com. Students 295.

FOWLERVILLE, LIVINGSTON CO., ST. AGNES (1891) [CEM] Rev. Robert H. McGraw; Deacons Roger Cahaney; Peter Guditas.
Res.: 855 E. Grand River Ave., 48836. Tel: 517-223-8684; Fax: 517-223-0813. Email: stagnesfowlerville@sbcglobal.net. Web: www.stagnesfowlerville.parishesonline.com.
Catechesis/Religious Program—Tel: 517-223-8684. Students 320.

GAINES, GENESSEE CO., ST. JOSEPH (1871) [CEM] Revs. David W. Harvey, Canonical Pastor; Robert McKeon, Sacramental Min. (Retired); Sr. Ann Marie Petri, O.P., Pastoral Coord.
Mailing Address: 9450 Duffield Rd., P.O. Box 145, 48436.
Res.: 118 E. Lord St., P.O. Box 145, 48436. Tel: 989-271-8434; Fax: 989-271-3017. Email: stjosephgaines@gmail.com. Web: stjosephgaines.catholicweb.com.
Catechesis/Religious Program—Tel: 989-288-0548; Fax: 989-288-6130. Sandy Corrion, D.R.E. Students 81.

GOODRICH, GENESEE CO., ST. MARK THE EVANGELIST (1978) Rev. Michael W. Kuchar.
Church: 7296 Gale Rd., P.O. Box 131, 48438. Tel: 810-636-2216; Fax: 810-636-3221. Email: stmarkslink@hotmail.com. Web: home.catholicweb.com/stmarktheevangelistgoodrich.
Catechesis/Religious Program—Email: stmarksdre@hotmail.com. Students 150.

GRAND BLANC, GENESEE CO., HOLY FAMILY (1946) Rev. Kenneth F. Coughlin; Deacon Jack Daunt; Rev. Jonathan P. Perrotta, Parochial Vicar.
Res.: 11804 S. Saginaw, 48439. Tel: 810-694-4891; Fax: 810-694-1583. Email: info@holyfamilygrandblanc.org. Web: www.holyfamilygrandblanc.catholicweb.com.
School—(Grades PreK-8), 215 Orchard St., 48439. Tel: 810-694-9072; Fax: 810-694-9405. Michele Jahn, Prin. Lay Teachers 23; Students 465.
Catechesis/Religious Program—Tel: 810-694-9072, Ext. 101. Students 345.

GRAND LEDGE, EATON CO., ST. MICHAEL (1901) Rev. James F. Eisele.
Res.: 405 Edwards St., 48837. Tel: 517-627-8493, Ext. 26; Fax: 517-627-1289. Web: www.stmichaelgl.org.
Church: 345 Edwards St., 48837.
School—325 Edwards St., 48837. Tel: 517-627-2167. Mitzi Luttrull, Prin. Lay Teachers 10; Students 207.
Catechesis/Religious Program—Tel: 517-627-8493. Students 271.

HILLSDALE, HILLSDALE CO., ST. ANTHONY (1853) [CEM] Rev. Jeffrey Njus.
Res.: 11 N. Broad St., 49242. Tel: 517-437-3305; Fax: 517-437-0034. Email: stanthonycatholicchurch@dmcibb.net. Web: http://home.catholicweb.com/stanthonypadua.
Catechesis/Religious Program—Tel: 517-437-2777. Students 267.

HOWELL, LIVINGSTON CO.

1—ST. AUGUSTINE (1843) [CEM], (Quasi Parish) Rev. Gregg A. Pleiness; Deacon William Sirl.
Church: 6481 Faussett Rd., 48855. Tel: 517-546-9807.
Res.: 8011 Faussett Rd., Fenton, 48430.
Parish House—Tel: 810-750-0354.
Catechesis/Religious Program—Students 122.

2—ST. JOHN THE BAPTIST (1843), (Irish—German), [CEM] Rev. Francis M. George; Deacon David Piggot.
Res.: 2099 N. Hacker Rd., 48855. Tel: 517-546-7200; Fax: 517-546-0403. Web: www.stjohnthebaptisthowell.catholicweb.com.
Catechesis/Religious Program—Tel: 517-548-2540; Fax: 517-546-0403. Students 587.

3—ST. JOSEPH (1888) [CEM] Revs. David J. Speicher; Prabhu Lakra, Parochial Vicar; Deacons Endre Doran; Frank Wines Sr., Dir. Faith Formation; Ray Kunik.
Res.: 440 E. Washington St., 48843. Tel: 517-546-0090; Fax: 517-546-3126. Web: www.stjosephhowell.com.
School—425 E. Washington, 48843. Tel: 517-546-0090, Ext. 200; Fax: 517-546-8939. Judy Meerschaert, Prin. Lay Teachers 21; Students 260.
Catechesis/Religious Program—Tel: 517-546-0090, Ext. 400. Students 358.

HUDSON, LENAWEE CO., SACRED HEART (1846) [CEM] Rev. Richard Eberle, O.S.F.S.
Res.: 207 S. Market St., 49247. Tel: 517-448-3811; Fax: 517-448-2401. Email: rteberle@tc3net.com. Web: www.laforestnet.com/church.
School—Tel: 517-448-6405. Web: www.sacredhearthudson.com. April McCaskey, Prin. Lay Teachers 4; Students 51.
Catechesis/Religious Program—Web: www.sacredhearthudson.com/catechism. Students 42.

JACKSON, JACKSON CO.

1—ST. JOHN THE EVANGELIST (1856) [CEM] [JC] Revs. James R. Shaver; Robert J. Pienta; Deacons Joseph A. Kratofil; John Epley; Albert Krieger; Michael McCormick.
Res.: 711 N. Francis St., 49201. Tel: 517-784-0553; Fax: 517-788-5381. Email: stjohnjackson@catholicweb.com. Web: www.stjohntheevangelistjackson.catholicweb.com.
School—(Grades PreSchool-6), 405 E. North St., 49202. Tel: 517-784-1714; Fax: 517-788-5382. Kristi Blair, Prin. Lay Teachers 12; Students 237.
Catechesis/Religious Program—717 N. Waterloo at St. Joseph, 49202. Tel: 517-784-5746. Students 300.
Oratory—St. Joseph the Worker Oratory (1902) 705 N. Waterloo Ave., 49202.
Rectory—705 N. Waterloo Ave., 49202. Tel: 517-784-9716; Fax: 517-784-5411.
Catechesis/Religious Program— Joint with St. Johns (at our school) Students 300.

2—ST. JOSEPH, See separate listing. Became an oratory of St. John the Evangelist, Jackson.

3—ST. MARY STAR OF THE SEA (1881) Rev. Timothy Nelson; Deacons Vincent C. Genco; Matthew Shannon.
Res.: 301 S. Mechanic St., 49201. Tel: 517-784-7184; Fax: 517-783-2571. Web: www.stmaryjackson.catholicweb.com.
School—116 E. Wesley St., 49201. Tel: 517-784-8811; Fax: 517-788-3425. Email: stmaryschool@tds.net. Julia Hurlburt, Prin. Lay Teachers 13; Students 125.
Catechesis/Religious Program—Tel: 517-788-6153. Email: stmaryjacksondre@tds.net. Students 70.
Oratory—St. Stanislaus Kosta 608 S. Elm Ave., 49203.

4—QUEEN OF THE MIRACULOUS MEDAL (1934) Revs. Timothy E. MacDonald; Mathias Thelen; Deacons David Barrett; Ken Spaulding; Jack Kowalski.
Res.: 606 S. Wisner, 49203. Tel: 517-783-2748; Fax: 517-788-4528. Web: www.queenschurch.com.
School—811 S. Wisner, 49203. Tel: 517-782-2664; Fax: 517-782-3570. Elizabeth Harley, Prin. Lay Teachers 20; Students 305.
Catechesis/Religious Program—Students 123.

5—ST. STANISLAUS KOSTKA (1920), Now an oratory of St. Mary Star of the Sea, Jackson.

LAINGSBURG, SHIAWASSEE CO., ST. ISIDORE (1902) [CEM] Rev. Duaine H. Pamment.
Res.: 310 Crum St., 48848. Tel: 517-651-6617; 517-651-6722 (Office); Fax: 517-651-6617. Web: www.stisidorelaingsburg.catholicweb.com. Email: parishhq1@juno.com.
Catechesis/Religious Program—Tel: 517-651-6722. Students 105.

LESLIE, INGHAM CO., SS. CORNELIUS AND CYPRIAN (Bunker Hill) (1863) [CEM] Rev. Michael A. Petroski; Deacon Tom Rea.
Res.: 1320 Catholic Church Rd., 49251. Tel: 517-589-8492; Fax: 517-589-8470. Email: bnkrhlch@acd.net. Web: sscorneliusandcyprianleslie.catholicweb.com.
Catechesis/Religious Program—Students 64.

MANCHESTER, WASHTENAW CO., ST. MARY (1871) [CEM] Rev. Timothy D. Krzyzaniak; Deacon R. Dennis Walters.
Res.: 210 W. Main St., P.O. Box 249, 48158. Tel: 734-428-8811; Fax: 734-428-1393. Email: stmaryofc@rc.net. Web: www.stmarymanchester.catholicweb.com.
Catechesis/Religious Program—Students 47.

MANITOU BEACH, LENAWEE CO., ST. MARY ON THE LAKE (1956) Mrs. Jean Schaub, Pastoral Coord.; Revs. Paul F. Grehl, O.S.F.S., Sacramental Min.; Richard Eberle, O.S.F.S., Canonical Pastor.
Res.: 450 Manitou Rd., 49253. Tel: 517-547-7496; Fax: 517-547-4162.
Catechesis/Religious Program—Students 27.

MASON, INGHAM CO., ST. JAMES (1942) Rev. Kusitino Cobona; Deacons Thomas Feiten; Albert Turkovich.
Office: 1010 S. Lansing St., 48854. Tel: 517-676-9111; Fax: 517-676-1343.
Catechesis/Religious Program—Rose Robertson, D.R.E. Students 201.

MICHIGAN CENTER, JACKSON CO., OUR LADY OF FATIMA (1954) Rev. Timothy E. MacDonald, Temporary Admin.
Res.: 913 Napoleon Rd., 49254. Tel: 517-764-2088; 517-764-2112; Fax: 517-764-0461. Email: olf_parish@tds.net.
Catechesis/Religious Program—Tel: 517-764-1321. Email: olf_reled@tds.net. Students 75.

MILAN, WASHTENAW CO., IMMACULATE CONCEPTION (1854) Rev. Vincent VanDoan; Deacon John Flanagan.
Church: 420 North St., 48160. Tel: 734-439-2030; Fax: 734-439-5659.
Catechesis/Religious Program—Tel: 734-439-2030. Students 204.

MONTROSE, GENESEE CO., GOOD SHEPHERD (1979) Revs. Roy Horning; Louis T. Ekka, Parochial Vicar.
400 N. Saginaw, P.O. Box 3274, 48457-0974.
Res.: 314 Genesee, 48457-0974. Tel: 810-639-3245. Email: goodshep@centurytel.net. Web: www.goodshepherdmontrose.catholicweb.com.
Catechesis/Religious Program—Students 71.

MORRICE, SHIAWASSEE CO., ST. MARY (1875) [CEM] Rev. John M. Bosco (India).
Res.: 509 N. Main St., P.O. Box 310, 48857. Tel: 517-625-4260; Fax: 517-625-3050. Email: cgarrison@catholicweb.com (parish secretary); lnebo@catholicweb.com (bookkeeper). Web: www.stmarymorrice.catholicweb.com.
Catechesis/Religious Program—Tel: 517-625-6140. Students 96.

MOUNT MORRIS, GENESEE CO., ST. MARY (1867) [CEM] Rev. Thomas D. Nenneau.
Res.: 11110 Saginaw St., 48458. Tel: 810-686-3920; Fax: 810-686-0759. Web: stmarymountmorris.catholicweb.com.
School—11208 N. Saginaw, 48458. Tel: 810-686-4790; Fax: 810-686-4749. Web: www.saintmaryscatholic.com. Diane Martindale, Prin. Lay Teachers 12; Students 80.
Catechesis/Religious Program—Students 56.

OKEMOS, INGHAM CO., ST. MARTHA (1988) Rev. Jonathan Wehrle. In Res., Rev. Phillip Schweda.
Church: 1100 W. Grand River, 48864. Tel: 517-349-1763; Fax: 517-347-3536.
School—Tel: 517-349-3322; Fax: 517-349-3322. Francie Herring, Prin. Sisters of Charity 2; Lay Teachers 9; Students 142.
Catechesis/Religious Program—Students 343.

OTISVILLE, GENESEE CO., ST. FRANCIS XAVIER (1947) Revs. Thomas W. Butler, Canonical Pastor; Francis Faraci, Sacramental Min. (Retired); Sr. Elaine LaBell, O.P., Pastoral Coord.
212 Center St., 48463. Tel: 810-631-6305; Fax: 810-631-4412. Email: sfranotisville@aol.com. Web: stfrancisxavierotisville.catholicweb.com.
Catechesis/Religious Program—Email: dre_grace@yahoo.com. Students 71.

OVID, SHIAWASSEE CO., HOLY FAMILY (1966) Rev. Raymond J. Urbanek.
Res.: 510 N. Mabbitt Rd., P.O. Box 612, 48866. Tel: 989-834-5855; Fax: 989-834-1208. Email: holy_family_church@frontier.com. Web: http://holyfamilyovid.catholicweb.com.
Catechesis/Religious Program—Tel: 989-834-2138. Students 57.

OWOSSO, SHIAWASSEE CO.

1—ST. JOSEPH (1923) Rev. David E. Fisher.
Res.: 915 E. Oliver St., 48867. Tel: 989-725-5215; Fax: 989-725-1519. Email: nancyann@sjowosso.com. Web: www.catholicweb.com.
St. Joseph Child Care Services—Child Care 81.
Catechesis/Religious Program—811 E. Oliver St., 48867. Tel: 989-723-4765. Email: slhrdnbrgh@gmail.com. Students 95.

2—ST. PAUL (1871) [CEM 2] Revs. Michael O'Brien; Nonatus Lakra, Parochial Vicar; Deacon Gary Edington.
Res.: 111 N. Howell St., 48867. Tel: 989-723-4277; Fax: 989-723-9503. Email: spcowosso@aol.com. Web: www.stpaulowosso.org.
School—738 W. Main St., 48867. Tel: 989-725-7766; Fax: 989-725-9824. Email: spsowosso@aol.com. Merry Jane Robertson, Prin. Lay Teachers 12; Students 140.
Catechesis/Religious Program—718 W. Main St., 48867. Tel: 989-723-1400. Students 177.

PINCKNEY, LIVINGSTON CO., ST. MARY (1867) [CEM]

Rev. William Wegher.
Res.: 10601 Dexter-Pinckney Rd., 48169. Tel: 734-878-3161; Fax: 734-878-2383. Email: hshamp@stmarypinckney.org. Web: www.stmarypinckney.org.
School—Tel: 734-878-5616. Email: mrskinsey@stmarypinckey.org. Web: www.stmarypinckney.org/school. Veronica Kinsey, Prin. Lay Teachers 14; Students 158.
Catechesis/Religious Program—Tel: 734-878-2217. Email: rkeiser@stmarypinckney.org. Students 203.

ST. JOHNS, CLINTON CO., ST. JOSEPH (1874) Rev. Eoin Murphy (Ireland); Deacons Marvin Robertson; Gerald Fust.
Res.: 109 Linden St., 48879. Tel: 989-224-8994; Fax: 989-224-3475. Email: stjoechurch@mutualdata.com. Web: www.stjoecatholic.com.
School—201 E. Cass St., Saint Johns, 48879. Tel: 989-224-2421; Fax: 989-224-1900. Web: www.stjoecatholic.com. Tomi Ann Schultheiss, Prin. Lay Teachers 13; Students 255.
Catechesis/Religious Program—Tel: 989-224-8537. Students 283.

SALINE, WASHTENAW CO., ST. ANDREW THE APOSTLE (1968) Revs. William J. Stevenson; David B. Rosenberg; Deacons Paul Ellis; Douglas Cummings; Kendra Serrico, Music Dir.
Res.: 910 Austin Dr., 48176. Tel: 734-429-5210; Fax: 734-429-0680. Email: standrew@comcast.net. Web: www.standrewsaline.parishesonline.com.
Catechesis/Religious Program—Tel: 734-429-7776. Margaret Greca, D.R.E.; Nancy Carter, Coord. Youth Ministry Grades 7-8. Students 743.

SWARTZ CREEK, GENESEE CO., ST. MARY (1912), (Czech), [CEM] Revs. Steven M. Mattson; Daniel J. Kogut, Parochial Vicar; Deacon Rodney Amon.
Mailing Address: 4413 Morrish Rd., 48473.
Res.: 7563 Mary St., 48473. Fax: 810-630-1630.
Catechesis/Religious Program—Tel: 810-635-3240. Students 138.

TECUMSEH, LENAWEE CO., ST. ELIZABETH (1947) Rev. Daniel Wheeler; Deacons James Nicholson; Ray Pizana.
Res.: 506 N. Union St., 49286. Tel: 517-423-2447. Email: steliz50@aol.com. Web: www.stelizabethstdominic.org.
Catechesis/Religious Program—512 N. Union St., 49286. Monica Bauer, D.R.E.; Heather Marsh, Youth Min. Students 291.

WESTPHALIA, CLINTON CO., ST. MARY (1836), (German), [CEM] Rev. James P. Conlon; Deacons Bernard Pohl; Chuck Thelen.
Res.: 201 N. Westphalia St., P.O. Box 267, 48894. Tel: 989-587-4201; Fax: 989-587-3838. Email: office@stmarychurch.net. Web: www.stmarychurch.net.
School—209 N. Westphalia St., P.O. Box 270, 48894. Tel: 989-587-3702; Fax: 989-587-3706. Raymond Rzepecki, Prin. Lay Teachers 13; Students 262.
Catechesis/Religious Program—Tel: 989-587-4201. Students 283.

WILLIAMSTON, INGHAM CO., ST. MARY (1869) [CEM] Rev. Peter J. Clark.
Res.: 157 High St., 48895. Tel: 517-655-2620; Fax: 517-655-3933.
School—220 Cedar St., 48895. Tel: 517-655-4038; Fax: 517-655-3855. Suzanne Penn, Prin. Lay Teachers 6; Students 107.
Catechesis/Religious Program—Tel: 517-655-2520. Adam Janke, D.R.E. Students 207.

YPSILANTI, WASHTENAW CO.

1—ST. ALEXIS, Closed. For inquiries for parish records contact Transfiguraton Catholic Church.

2—HOLY TRINITY STUDENT PARISH (1965) Revs. Phillip Mayfield, P.I.M.E.; Joseph Ngidjoi, P.I.M.E.; Deacon Stanley Kukla.
Res.: 315 Benjamin Dr., 48198. Tel: 734-480-4392. Church: 511 W. Forest, 48197. Tel: 734-482-1400; Fax: 734-482-0542. Email: holytrinity@emich.edu. Web: www.catholicsoncampus.org.
Catechesis/Religious Program—

3—ST. JOHN (1858) [CEM] Rev. Robert Roggenbuck; Deacons Wayne Charlton; Stephen A. Thomashefski.
Res.: 410 W. Cross St., 48197. Tel: 734-483-3360; Fax: 734-483-0712. Email: stjohnypsilanti@parishmail.com. Web: www.ypsilanticatholic.com.
Catechesis/Religious Program—Students 235.
Convent—411 Florence St., 48197.

4—ST. JOSEPH (1889) [CEM] Rev. Edmond L. Ertzbischoff.
Res.: 9425 Whittaker Rd., 48197. Tel: 734-461-6555; Fax: 734-461-1444.
Catechesis/Religious Program—Tel: 734-461-1800. Students 85.

5—TRANSFIGURATION CATHOLIC CHURCH (1994) Closed. For inquiries for parish records contact the chancery.

6—ST. URSULA, Closed. For inquiries for parish records contact Transfiguration Catholic Church.

Chaplains of Public Institutions

Hospitals

LANSING. *Ingham Regional Medical Center, Sparrow Hospital*, Tel: 517-646-6850. Vacant.

ANN ARBOR. *University of Michigan Hospitals/Pastoral Dept.* Rev. Lewis Eberhart, Deacon Wayne Charlton. Tel: 734-434-2546.

FLINT. *Hurley Regional Medical Center*. Rev. Paul Schwermer. Tel: 810-252-6979.
McLaren Regional Medical Center. Rev. Paul Schwermer. Tel: 810-252-6979.

GRAND BLANC. *Genesys Regional Medical Center*. Rev. L. Harold Sanford, S.J.

JACKSON. *Allegiance Health*, 205 N. East Ave., 49201. Vacant.

Prisons

ADRIAN. *Gus Harrison Regional Facility*. Joseph Serafin, Chap. Tel: 517-265-3900, Ext. 3550, Deacons Calistro Torres. Tel: 517-265-8927, James Hashman, Catholic Coord. Tel: 517-486-2083, Gene Hausmann. Tel: 517-423-7451.
Parr Hwy. Correctional Facility (Consolidated with Gus Harrison). Rev. Thomas J. Helfrich, O.S.F.S., Deacons Ray Pizana. Tel: 517-467-7621, Jim Nicholson. Tel: 517-467-2072, Gene Hausmann. Tel: 517-423-7451.

JACKSON. *Cotton Facility*. Rev. James R. Shaver. Tel: 517-784-0553, Paul Young, Chap. Tel: 517-780-5009.
Egeler Correctional Facility. Rev. Gary McInnis. Tel: 810-232-3639, Isa Basir, Chap. Tel: 517-780-5909.
Parnall Facility. Deacons Vincent Genco. Tel: 517-750-3759, Matthew Shannon. Tel: 517-789-6260, James Burrus, Chap. Tel: 517-780-6295.

MILAN. *Federal Correctional Institution*. Deacons Calistro Torres. Tel: 517-265-8927, James Hashman. Tel: 517-486-2083.

Special Alternative Incarceration

CHELSEA. *Camp Cassidy Lake*. Revs. Fortunato Turati, S.C. Tel: 734-475-8430, William J. Turner. Tel: 734-475-1697.

WHITMORE LAKE. *W. J. Maxey Boys Training School*. Rev. John George Rocus. Tel: 810-231-9199, Deacon Joseph Lennon. Tel: 734-663-7213.

On Duty Outside the Diocese:
Revs.—
Bui, Vincent, S.S., Laframboise Hall, 249 Main St., Ottawa ON KIS 1C5 Canada.
Canoy, Charles, Sacred Heart Major Seminary, 2701 Chicago Blvd., Detroit, 48206.
Gerl, Robert, P.O. Box 19225, Kalamazoo, 49019.
Irish, Robert, 8280 W. Warm Springs Rd., Las Vegas, NV 89113.
Kersten, Jay J., Navy Chap.
Kropf, Richard, Star Rte. 1, P.O. Box 629, Johannesburg, 49751.
Madey, Louis, Ss. Cyril & Methodius Seminary, 3535 Indian Trail, Orchard Lake, 48324.
Sessions, Phillip D., St. Catherine Laboure, 4124 Mt. Abraham Ave., San Diego, CA 92111.
Vincke, Gerald L., Pontifical North American College 00120 Vatican City State.
Weber, Eric Christopher, Sacred Heart Major Seminary, 2701 Chicago Blvd., Detroit, 48206.

On Leave of Absence:
Revs.—
Carlos, Miguel
Dehetre, Mark
Munley, J. Thomas
Thomsen, Steven (New Zealand)

Retired:
Rev. Msgrs.—
Fedewa, Sylvester L., 120 N. Willow St., Box 412, Westphalia, 48894.
Goehring, Raymond, 1531 E. Michigan, 48912.
Groshek, Richard, 4381 Springbrook Dr., Swartz Creek, 48473.
Howard, Vincent, 1849 Pierce Rd., Chelsea, 48118.
Lunsford, Robert D., 401-A E. Madison, Dewitt, 48820.
Murphy, Michael D., 703 E. Main St., #100, Dewitt, 48820.
Revs.—
Aubin, Joseph, 402 E. Madison, #B, Dewitt, 48820.
Beiter, Eugene J., 402 E. Madison #D, Dewitt, 48820.
Bettendorf, James B., 1139 Creekside Ct., Burton, 48509.
Brennan, Thomas, 468 Lancaster Ct., Saline, 48176.
Cummings, Paul J., 711 N. Francis St., Jackson, 49201.
Czarnota, Stanislaus, 401 Madison, Apt. C, Dewitt, 48820.
Dougherty, C. Peter, P.O. Box 14062, 48901.
Dumas, Terrence J., 2150 Frieze Ave., Ann Arbor, 48104.
Dupuis, Philip, 13280 Friendly Dr., Wolverine, 49799.
Eder, Donald, 6290 Oak Creek Dr., Swartz Creek, 48473.
Faraci, Francis, 2214 Blackthorn, Burton, 48509.
Fedewa, Matthew, 395 E. Madison, Apt. B, Dewitt, 48820.
Foglio, John, P.O. Box 4098, East Lansing, 48826.
Gallagher, Philip P., 3375 N. Linden Rd., Apt. 350, Flint, 48504.
Irvin, Charles, 402 E. Madison, Apt. A, Dewitt, 48820.
Kim, Joseph S., Okemos Health & Rehabilitation Center, 5211 Marsh Rd., Rm. 203, Okemos, 48864.
Koenigsknecht, William J., 10809 E. 3rd St., Fowler, 48835.
Kolenski, Robert D., 3375 N. Linden Rd., #205, Flint, 48504.
Ledwidge, Brendan, The Village Woodland, 7533 Grand River Ave., Apt. 201, Brighton, 48114.
Lorenzo, Eduardo, 6073 Ballard, Flint, 48505.
Lothamer, James, 8455 Lamoreaux Rd., Fowlerville, 48836.
Makranyi, Steven F., 3096 Vineyard Ln., Flushing, 48433.
McDonald, Kenneth, 401-D E. Madison, DeWitt, 48820.
McInnis, Gary, 1125 S. Franklin, Flint, 48503.
McKeon, Robert, 10018 Lehring Rd., Box 132, Byron, 48418-0132.
Murray, Francis J., 2146-3 Robinson Rd., Jackson, 49203-8620.
Osborn, Douglas, 402-C E. Madison, Dewitt, 48820.
Ploof, Gerald, 395 E. Madison, Apt. D, Dewitt, 48820.
Robert, Darin T., 1020 Wing Dr., Ann Arbor, 48103.
Rusch, Donald, P.O. Box 399, East Pointe, 48021.
Schmitt, James, Jr., The Marquette, 5968 Park Lake Rd., Rm. 314, East Lansing, 48823.
Swiat, James R., 3903 Ruthin Rd., Kalamazoo, 49008.
Taylor, Jon, 5594 Livingston Ave., Eugene, OR 97402.
Thompson, Thomas W., 395 E. Madison, Apt. C, Dewitt, 48820.
Tyler, Bernard L. (GLD), 112 McKee St., Houghton, 48629.
Wakefield, Alan, 4512 Glenberry Dr., Holt, 48842.
Werner, Benjamin, 2123 Robinson Rd., Apt. 230, Jackson, 49203.
Williams, Francis, 401-B E. Madison, DeWitt, 48820.
Wyszynski, Darius W., 2235 Cascade Ridge, Jackson, 49203.

Permanent Deacons:
Alfaro, Rogelio, Cristo Rey, Lansing
Amon, Rodney, St. Mary Queen of Angels, Swartz Creek
Amthor, John, St. Joseph Shrine, Brooklyn
Arquette, Lester, St. Thomas the Apostle, Ann Arbor
Badics, Richard, St. Francis of Assisi, Ann Arbor
Barrett, David, Queen of the Miraculous Medal, Jackson
Bayes, Richard, St. Mary of Good Counsel, Adrian
Borzenski, David, St. Therese, Lansing
Brennan, Gerald, Director of Deacons; Holy Spirit, Hamburg
Brown, James, St. Mary, Flint
Brown, Leonard C., St. Joseph, Adrian
Cahaney, Roger, St. Agnes, Fowlerville
Cameron, John, J.C.L., Diocese of Lansing Tribunal; Immaculate Heart of Mary, Lansing
Carsten, Terry, St. John the Evangelist, Fenton
Charlton, Wayne, St. John the Baptist, Ypsilanti
Chevalier, James M., St. Mary Magdalen, Brighton
Coffelt, Randy, St. Mary, Pinckney
Corder, James, St. Gerard, Lansing
Corrion, Wayne, St. Joseph, Gaines
Cummings, Doug, St. Andrew, Saline
Daunt, Jack, Holy Family, Grand Blanc
Dear, Michael, St. Michael, Flint
Doran, Endre, St. Joseph, Howell
Edington, Gary, St. Paul, Owosso
Ellingson, Raymond, SS. Charles & Helena, Clio
Ellis, Paul, St. Andrew, Saline
Epley, John, St. John the Evangelist, Jackson
Fairweather, Daniel, St. John the Evangelist, Davison
Feiten, Thomas, St. James, Mason
Fitch, John, II, St. Casimir, Lansing
Flanagan, John, Immaculate Conception, Milan
Fogle, Thomas, St. Mary, Charlotte
Foley, Daniel R., Christ the King, Ann Arbor
Franklin, Thomas, St. Mary, Chelsea
Franssen, Carol, St. Catherine Laboure, Concord

Fudge, William, Immaculate Heart of Mary, Lansing
Fust, Gerald, St. Joseph, St. Johns
Gallagher, Gary, St. Pius X, Flint
Genco, Vincent, St. Mary Star of the Sea, Jackson
Giesige, Richard, St. Joseph, Ypsilanti
Gudaitis, Peter, St. Agnes, Fowlerville
Hashman, James, St. Peter, Blissfield
Hausmann, Gene, St. Joseph Shrine, Brooklyn
Hecht, Warren, St. Thomas the Apostle, Ann Arbor
Heutsche, Ted, St. Jude, Dewitt
Hilker, Stephen, St. Mary, Williamston
Holowicki, Gerry, Christ the King, Ann Arbor
Kazprzak, James, St. Thomas Aquinas, East Lansing
Kenney, Ronald, St. John, Fenton
Kowalski, John, Queen of the Miraculous Medal, Jackson
Kratofil, Joseph, St. John the Evangelist, Jackson
Krieger, Albert, St. Joseph, Jackson
Kukla, Stanley, Holy Trinity, Ypsilanti
Kunik, Ray, St. Joseph, Howell
Lawrence, Dave, St. Patrick, Brighton
Leone, Romolo, St. Joseph, Dexter
Marsal, Gideon, St. Peter, Eaton Rapids
McCarthy, John, St. Michael, Grand Ledge
McCormick, Michael, St. John the Evangelist, Jackson
McCrandall, Michael, St. Mary, Flint
McDonald, Patrick, St. Patrick, Brighton
Michael, Donald, St. Anthony, Hillsdale
Middleton, Greg, St. Mary, Durand
Miles, James, St. Thomas the Apostle, Ann Arbor
Murray, Michael, St. Thomas Aquinas, East Lansing
Nguyen, Chuong, St. Andrew Dung Lac, Lansing
Nicholson, James, St. Elizabeth, Tecumseh
Novak, Edwin, St. Thomas, Ann Arbor
Omar, Joseph, Our Lady of Guadalupe, Flint
Papp, Frank, St. Patrick, Ann Arbor
Pennell, Dennis, St. Robert Bellarmine, Flushing
Petersen, Aaron, St. Anthony of Padua, Hillsdale
Piggot, David, St. John the Baptist, Hartland
Pigott, David, SS. Charles & Helena, Clio
Pizana, Eulalio, St. Elizabeth, Tecumseh
Pohl, Bernard, St. Mary, Westphalia
Poole, Gregory, St. Mary, Charlotte
Prise, Gary W., St. Mary Magdalen, Brighton
Randolph, Larry, Christ the King, Ann Arbor
Rea, Tom, SS. Cornelius & Cyprian, Leslie
Robertson, Marvin, St. Joseph, St. Johns
Rowe, Ronald, St. Michael, Flint
Russello, Lou, Christ the King, Ann Arbor
Savage, Richard, St. Gerard Majella, Lansing
Scharf, David, St. Mary Magdalen, Brighton
Shaneyfelt, Richard, St. Mary, Chelsea
Shannon, Matthew, St. Mary Star of the Sea, Jackson
Simmon, Mark, Most Holy Trinity, Fowler
Sirl, William, St. Augustine, Deerfield Twp.
Spaulding, Kenneth, Queen of the Miraculous Medal, Jackson
Stanford, Richard, St. Mary Cathedral, Lansing
Sundwick, John, St. John Vianney, Flint; Our Lady of Guadalupe, Flint
Tardif, Andy, St. Michael, Grand Ledge
Thelen, Chuck, St. Mary, Westphalia
Thomashefski, Stephen A., St. John the Baptist, Ypsilanti
Torres, Calistro, St. Mary, Adrian
Turkovich, Al
VandeVoorde, Gregory, Christ the King, Ann Arbor
Verdun, Anthony, Sacred Heart, Flint
Walters, Dennis, St. Mary, Manchester
Washington, Oliver
Weitzel, Louis, St. Rita, Clarklake
Wines, Frank, Sr., St. Joseph, Howell

INSTITUTIONS LOCATED IN THE DIOCESE

[A] COLLEGES AND UNIVERSITIES

ADRIAN. *Siena Heights University*, 1247 E. Siena Heights Dr., 49221-1796. Tel: 517-263-0731; Fax: 517-264-7702. Web: www.sienaheights.edu. Sisters Peg Albert, O.P., Ph.D., Pres.; Sharon R. Weber, O.P., Ph.D., Vice Pres., Academics; Robert Gordon, Ph.D., Dir. Library. Sponsored by the Adrian Dominican Sisters. Sisters 8; Faculty 75; Total Staff 165; Students 2,630.

[B] HIGH SCHOOLS, DIOCESAN

LANSING. *Lansing Catholic Central High School*, 501 Marshall St., 48912. Tel: 517-267-2100; Fax: 517-267-2135. Email: draminski@lansingcatholic.org. Web: www.lansingcatholic.org. Thomas P. Maloney, Prin.; Rev. Gordon P. Reigle, Chap.; Liz Webster, Librarian. Lansing Catholic Central Board of Education Priests 1; Lay Teachers 30; Students 487.

ANN ARBOR. *Father Gabriel Richard High School* (1867) 4333 Whitehall Dr., 48105. Tel: 734-662-0496; Fax: 734-662-4133. Email: fgoffice@fgrhsaa.org. Web: www.fgrhsaa.org. Brian Wolcott, Prin.; Catherine Weber, Librarian; Rev. Richard C. Lobert, Chap. Gabriel Richard Board of Education Priests 1; Sisters 1; Lay Teachers 41; Students 507.

FLINT. *Luke M. Powers Catholic High School*, G-2040 W. Carpenter Rd., 48505. Tel: 810-591-4741; Fax: 810-591-0383. Email: tfurnas@powerscatholic.org. Web: www.powerscatholic.org. Mr. Thomas Furnas, M.A., Prin.; Carolyn Matthei, Librarian; Rev. Daniel J. Kogut, Chap. Powers Catholic Board of Education Priests 1; Sisters 2; Lay Teachers 29; Total Staff 62; Other 30; Students 541.

JACKSON. *Lumen Christi Catholic High School*, 3483 Spring Arbor Rd., 49203. Tel: 517-787-0630; Fax: 517-787-1066. Web: www.jcslumenchristi.org. Patrick R. Kalahar, M.S., Prin.; Revs. Paul F. Grehl, O.S.F.S.; Geoff Rose, O.S.F.S.; Bro. John W. Bailey, O.S.F.S.; Martha Artz, Librarian. Oblates of St. Francis de Sales. Priests 2; Brothers 1; Lay Teachers 39; Students 473.

[C] ELEMENTARY & MIDDLE SCHOOLS, DIOCESAN

JACKSON. *Jackson Catholic Middle School*, 915 Cooper, 49202. Tel: 517-784-3385; Fax: 517-782-7883. Email: jacksoncatholicms@jcmjcms.org. Web: www.jcsjcms.org. Anthony Shaughnessy, Prin.; Mrs. Elizabeth Norkey, Librarian. Lay Teachers 10; Students 186.

[D] SCHOOLS, PRIVATE

ADRIAN. **St. Joseph Academy* (1896) (Grades PreK-4), 1267 E. Siena Heights Dr., 49221. Tel: 517-263-4898; Fax: 517-265-6240. Email: info@sjaschool.org. Web: sjaschool.org. Sr. Patricia Fischer, O.P., Prin. Sisters of St. Dominic, Congregation of the Most Holy Rosary (Adrian, MI). Sisters 1; Lay Teachers 5; Assistants 7; Administrators 1; Students 116; Total Staff 14.

ANN ARBOR. **Spiritus Sanctus Academy*, (Grades PreSchool-8), 4101 E. Joy Rd., 48105. Tel: 734-996-3855; Fax: 734-996-4270. Web: www.spiritussanctus.org. Sr. John Dominic Rasmussen, O.P., Prin.; Rev. Charles Kibirige, Chap.; Ruta Guska, Librarian. Priests 1; Sisters 2; Lay Teachers 12; Students 185; Staff 4.

BURTON. *St. Thomas More Academy* (1989) (Grades K-12), 6456 E. Bristol Rd., 48519. Tel: 810-742-2411; Fax: 810-742-4803. Email: stma2003@sbcglobal.net. Web: stma-mi.org. Dan Le Blanc, Prin. Priests 1; Lay Teachers 12; Administrators 4; Students (K-8) 66; (9-12) 45 111; Total Staff 16.

PLYMOUTH. **Spiritus Sanctus Academy*, 10450 Joy Rd., 48170. Tel: 734-414-8430; Fax: 734-414-8495. Email: srmariaguadalupe@spiritussanctus.org. Web: www.spiritussanctus.org. Sr. Maria Guadalupe, O.P., Prin.; Rev. Charles Muwonge, Chap. Priests 1; Sisters 4; Lay Teachers 12; Students 194.

YPSILANTI. **HVS Corp. (Huron Valley Catholic School)* (2000) (Grades PreK-8), 1300 N. Prospect, 48198-3087. Tel: 734-483-0366; Fax: 734-483-0372. Timothy F. Kotyuk, Prin.; Barb Oas, Librarian. Sisters 2; Lay Teachers 11; Students 170; Total Staff 16.

[E] SPECIALIZED CHILD CARE FACILITIES & SCHOOLS

CHELSEA. *St. Louis Center for Exceptional Children & Adults*, 16195 Old U.S. 12, 48118. Tel: 734-475-8430; Fax: 734-475-0310. Email: frjoe@stlouiscenter.org. Web: www.stlouiscenter.org. Revs. Joseph Rinaldo, S.C., Prov. Treas.; Satheesh C. Alphonse, Asst. Admin.; Fortunato Turati, S.C., Chap.; Enzo Addari, M.Div., M.Ed, Admin.; David Stawasz, S.C., R.N., Medical Program. Operated by the Servants of Charity. Priests 5; Total Staff 55; Residents 60.

CLINTON. *Boysville Campus/Holy Cross Children's Services*, 8744 Clinton-Macon Rd., 49236. Tel: 517-423-7556; Fax: 517-423-5442. Email: fboylan@hccsnet.org. Web: www.hccsnet.org. Bro. Francis Boylan, C.S.C., Exec. Dir.; Mr. James Chludzinski, Prin. Residential and community based treatment programs for troubled youth and their families with facilities located throughout the state of Michigan under the auspices of the Brothers of Holy Cross & Notre Dame. Brothers 1; Boys 100; Total Staff 160.

JACKSON. *St. Joseph Home for Children, Inc.*, 1000 E. Porter, 49202. Tel: 517-787-3320; Fax: 517-787-3704. Sr. Mary Renetta Rumpz, C.S.S.F., Admin. Asst.; Lezlie Bowles, Prog. Dir. Felician Sisters (C.S.S.F.)., Day Care Center for Children Pre-school. Children 100; Sisters 2; Lay Teachers 1; Lay Caregivers 17; Lay Director 1.

MOUNT MORRIS. *Boysville of Michigan/Holy Cross Children's Services: Corcoran House*, 8212 N. Jennings Rd., 48458. Tel: 810-687-5100; Fax: 810-687-5020. Email: fboylan@hccsnet.org. Web: www.hccsnet.org. Bro. Francis Boylan, C.S.C., Exec. Dir.; Ms. Sharon Berkobien, Regl. Dir. A day treatment program for 13 boys and girls. Total Assisted 33; Total Staff 27; Total in Residence 6.

[F] CATHOLIC CHARITIES & SERVICE AGENCIES

LANSING. **Cristo Rey Community Center*, 1717 N. High St., 48906. Tel: 517-372-4700; Fax: 517-372-8499. Email: castillojohnroycrcc@earthlink.net. Web: www.cristo-rey.org. John Roy Castillo, J.D., Exec. Dir. Total Assisted 32,000; Total Staff 49.

St. Vincent Catholic Charities (1948) 2800 W. Willow, 48917. Tel: 517-323-4734; Fax: 517-886-1150. Email: kitchep@stvcc.org. Web: www.stvcc.org. Andrea E. Seyka, CEO. Total Assisted 6,015; Total Staff 180.

Adoption, 2800 W. Willow, 48917. Tel: 517-323-4734; Fax: 517-886-1168. Email: snoeyig@stvcc.org.

Children's Home, 2828 W. Willow St., 48917. Tel: 517-323-4734; Fax: 517-323-0257. Email: snoeyig@stvcc.org. Residents 40.

Counseling Services, 2800 W. Willow, 48917. Tel: 517-323-4734; Fax: 517-886-1158. Email: millerk@stvcc.org.

Family Preservation, 2800 W. Willow, 48917. Tel: 517-323-4734; Fax: 517-886-1168. Email: snoeyig@stvcc.org.

Foster Care ` Includes case management and licensing., 2800 W. Willow, 48917. Tel: 517-323-4734; Fax: 517-886-1168. Email: snoeyig@stvcc.org.

Immigration Law Clinic, 2800 W. Willow, 48917. Tel: 517-323-4734; Fax: 517-886-1150. Email: glennol@stvcc.org. Lesley Glennon, Dir.

Volunteer Opportunities, 2800 W. Willow, 48917. Tel: 517-323-4734; Fax: 517-886-1150. Email: phamt@stvcc.org.

Refugee Resettlement, 2800 W. Willow, 48917. Tel: 517-323-4734; Fax: 517-853-0031. Email: harrisj@stvcc.org. (Includes Reception, Placement, Health & Employment).

Housing Services for the Homeless, 2800 W. Willow St., 48917. Tel: 517-323-4734; Fax: 517-853-0031. Email: williap@stvcc.org.

ADRIAN. *Catholic Charities of Jackson, Lenawee & Hillsdale Counties* (1958) 199 N. Broad St., 49221. Tel: 517-263-2191; Fax: 517-264-6080. Email: cssdir@tc3net.com. Web: www.catholiccharitiesjacksonlenaweehillsdale.org. Sue Lewis, B.A., Exec. Dir. Total Assisted Annually 7,460; Total Staff 53.

1522 Joy Ave., Jackson, 49203. Tel: 517-782-2551; Fax: 517-783-1986. Email: cssdir@tc3net.com. Web: ccjhc.org. 405 Mechanic St., Jackson, 49203. Total Assisted Annually 6,100; Total Staff (Jackson Site) 26.

ANN ARBOR. *C.S.S. of Washtenaw County*, 4925 Packard Rd., 48108. Tel: 734-971-9781; Fax: 734-971-2730. Email: info@csswashtenaw.org. Web: www.csswashtenaw.org. Lawrence J. Voight, A.C.S.W. Total Assisted Annually 8,500; Total Staff 150.

Catholic Charities of Michigan (2000) 4925 Packard St., 48108. Tel: 734-223-1844; Fax: 734-973-2138. Email: ceo@catholiccharities-mi.org. Web: www.catholiccharities-mi.org. Roberto M. Javier, M.H.A., CEO.

DAVISON. *Outreach East*, 425 N. Genesee St., P.O. Box 61, 48423. Tel: 810-653-7711; Fax: 810-658-0891. Jan Lebert, Dir. Total Assisted 7,256; Total Staff 1.

FLINT. *Catholic Charities of Shiawassee & Genessee Counties - North End Soup Kitchen Programs*, 901 Chippewa St., 48503. Tel: 810-232-9950; Fax: 810-232-9110. Email: givehope@ccsgc.org. Web: www.ccsgc.org. Vicky L. Schultz, Pres. & CEO. Total Meals 155,557; Total Assisted Annually 217,175; Total Staff 9.

Catholic Charities of Shiawassee and Genesee Counties (1941) 901 Chippewa St., 48503. Tel: 810-232-9950; Fax: 810-232-9110. Email: givehope@ccsgc.org. Web: www.ccsgc.org. Vicky L. Schultz, Pres. & CEO. Total Assisted Annually 30,000; Total Staff 90.

Catholic Outreach, 509 N. Grand Traverse, P.O. Box 815, 48501. Tel: 810-234-4693; Fax: 810-234-1717. Gregg T. Berent, Dir. Total Assisted Annually 9,200; Total Staff 25.

HOWELL. *Livingston County Catholic Charities* (1985) 2020 E. Grand River Ave., Ste. 104, 48843. Tel: 517-545-5944; Fax: 517-545-7390. Email: mark@livingstoncatholiccharities.org. Mark T. Robinson,

A.C.S.W., Exec. Dir. Total Assisted Annually 2,400; Total Staff 28.

OWOSSO. *Catholic Charities of Shiawassee & Genesee Counties*, 120 W. Exchange, Ste. 300, 48867. Tel: 989-723-8239; Fax: 989-723-8230. Email: givehope@ccsgc.org. Web: www.ccsgc.org. Vicky L. Schultz, Pres. & CEO. Total Assisted Annually 2,096; Total Staff 15.

[G] GENERAL HOSPITALS

LANSING. **Migrant Clinic-Cristo Rey Community Center*, 1717 N. High St., 48906. Tel: 517-371-1700; Fax: 517-371-4245. Email: castillojohnroycrcc@earthlink.net. Web: www.cristo-rey.org. Dr. Peter Cooke, Medical Dir. Total Assisted 100; Total Staff 3.

ANN ARBOR. *Catherine McAuley Health Services Corporation* (Subsidiary of Trinity Health), 5305 E. Huron River Dr., P.O. Box 992, 48106. Tel: 734-712-4986; Fax: 734-712-5459. Health Care Center, Ancillary Care Systems: (Primary Care Physician Practices) Total Staff 94; Total Assisted Annually 86,945.

Saint Joseph Mercy Health System (A Member of Trinity Health), 5305 E. Huron River Dr., Box 992, 48106. Tel: 734-712-4986; Fax: 734-712-5459. Garry C. Faja, Pres. & CEO. General Hospitals 5; Bed Capacity 1,164; Total Staff 9,541; Total Assisted Annually 1,977,499.

St. Joseph Mercy Hospital, 5301 E. Huron River Dr., P.O. Box 995, 48106. Tel: 734-712-4986; Fax: 734-712-5459. Email: soler@trinityhealth.org. Robert Casalou, Pres. & CEO; Rev. Timothy Dombrowski, Chap. General Hospitals 1; Bed Capacity 537; Total Staff 5,186; Patients Assisted Annually 1,161,799.

CHELSEA. *Chelsea Community Hospital* (A member of Trinity Health), 775 S. Main, 48118. Tel: 734-475-3912; Fax: 734-475-4066. Email: soler@trinity-health.org. Web: trinity-health.org. Kathleen Griffiths, Pres. & CEO; Kathy Schell, Chap. Bed Capacity 113; Patients Assisted Annually 161,700; Total Staff 1,054.

GRAND BLANC. *Center for Gerontology* An affiliate of Genesys Health System., 5445 Ali Dr., 48439-5193. Tel: 810-603-8682; Fax: 810-603-8906. Email: cbruett@genesys.org. Web: genesys.org. Linda Gibson, Dir. Provides adult day care, care management programs, and educational training. Adult Day Care Days 7,325; Total Assisted 94; Total Staff 18.

Genesys Ambulatory Health Services, Inc. (1981) An affiliate of Genesys Health System., 5445 Ali Dr., 48439-5193. Tel: 810-603-8682; Fax: 810-603-8906. Email: cbruett@genesys.org. Web: genesys.org. Jo Anne Herman, Vice Pres. Provides private duty home care services and manages shared services. Total Staff 166; Total Assisted Annually 5,127.

Genesys Health System, 5445 Ali Dr., 48439. Tel: 810-603-8682; Fax: 810-603-8906. Email: cbruett@genesys.org. Web: genesys.org. Betsy Aderholdt, Pres. & CEO. Total Staff 3,979.

Genesys Regional Medical Center An affiliate of Genesys Health System. Acute care hospital., 5445 Ali Dr., 48439. Tel: 810-603-8682; Fax: 810-603-8906. Email: cbruett@genesys.org. Web: www.genesys.org. Betsy Aderholdt, CEO & Pres. Bed Capacity 410; Total Staff 3,398; Total Assisted Annually 239,539.

HOWELL. *Saint Joseph Mercy Livingston Hospital* (A member of Trinity Health), 620 Byron Rd., 48843-1093. Tel: 517-545-6000; Fax: 517-545-6192. Email: markelm@trinity-health.org. Web: trinity-health.org. Michael J. Markel Jr., R.N., M.S.N., M.S.B.A., Exec. Dir. Opers. & CNO. Bed Capacity 136; General Hospitals 1; Patients Assisted Annually 114,735; Total Staff 730.

SALINE. *Saint Joseph Mercy Saline Hospital*, 400 W. Russell, 48176. Tel: 734-429-1600; Fax: 734-429-4662. Garry Faja, Pres. & CEO. (A unit of Saint Joseph Mercy Health System) General Hospitals 1; Bed Capacity 74; Patients Assisted Annually 72,534; Total Staff 124.

[H] HOMES FOR THE AGED & CONVALESCENT

ANN ARBOR. *Servants of God's Love Ministries: Emmanuel House* (1999) 475 Evergreen, 48103. Tel: 734-669-8825; Fax: 734-669-8261. Email: emmanuelhse@juno.com. Sr. Fran DePuydt, S.G.L., Admin. Bed Capacity 7; Total Assisted 6; Volunteers 90.

GRAND BLANC. *Genesys Convalescent Center-Grand Blanc, Inc.* (1980) An affiliate of Genesys Health System., 8481 Holly Rd., 48439-1899. Tel: 810-603-8682. Web: genesys.org. One Genesys Pkwy., 48439. Robert Stevens, Admin. Skilled Nursing Facility Bed Capacity 140; Patients Assisted Annually 318; Total Staff 198.

YPSILANTI. *Emmanuel House II* (2002) 3341 Hillside Dr., 48197. Tel: 734-528-9031; Fax: 734-528-9086. Email: ehypsi@juno.com. Sr. Mary Zielinski, Admin. Bed Capacity 4; Total Assisted 5; Total Staff 45.

[I] HOSPICES

LANSING. **Mother Teresa House for the Care of the Terminally Ill*, 308 N. Walnut St., 48933. Tel: 517-484-5494; Fax: 866-678-5053. Web: motherteresahouse.org. Karen Bussey, Dir. & Contact Person. Total Staff 4; Total Assisted 24.

GOODRICH. *Genesys Hospice* (Affiliate of Genesys Health System), 7280 S. State Rd., 48438. Tel: 810-636-5000; Fax: 810-636-5019. Email: lmccombs@genesys.org. LaVerne McCombs, Admin. & Contact Person. Provides in-home and residential hospice care. Inpatient hospice care for symptom management and respite care. Bed Capacity 22; Care Center Patients Assisted Annually 267; Home Program Patients Assisted Annually 519; Total Assisted Annually 633; Total Staff 88.

GRAND BLANC. *Genesys Home Health & Hospice* (1997) An affiliate of Genesys Health System., 5445 Ali Dr., Dept. 500, 48439. Tel: 810-603-8600; Fax: 810-695-8318. Email: rstevens@genesys.org. Web: www.genesys.org. Robert Stevens, Vice Pres. Continuum Care Svcs. Provides professional home care and rehabilitation services. Home Health Staff 110; Total Assisted 3,350.

[J] MONASTERIES AND RESIDENCES OF PRIESTS AND BROTHERS

ANN ARBOR. *Detroit Province of the Society of Jesus - Jesuit Residence*, 1250 Ferdon Rd., 48104. Tel: 734-663-0557; Fax: 734-663-2756. Revs. Daniel T. Reim, S.J., Supr.; Dennis T. Dillon, S.J.; Dennis T. Glasgow, S.J.; Benjamin B. Hawley, S.J.

BROOKLYN. *Oblate Fathers of St. Francis De Sales, Inc.*, 1124 Ventura Dr., 49230. Tel: 517-592-8218; Fax: 517-592-8218. Email: jmslc@earthlink.net. Web: www.desales.org. Total in Residence 4.

Thorrez Vocational Trust, Ltd., 1124 Ventura Dr., 49230. Tel: 517-592-8218. Email: jmslc@earthlink.net. Web: www.desales.org. Rev. James McHugh, O.S.F.S., Contact Person.

[K] CONVENTS AND RESIDENCES FOR SISTERS

LANSING. *Congregation of the Passion* (1984) St. Therese Convent, 109 E. Randolph, 48906-4042. Tel: 517-372-5849. Sr. Marcella Oloarte, C.F.P., Prioress. Sisters 4.

ADRIAN. *Adrian Dominican Office of Development* (1987) 1257 E. Siena Heights. Dr., 49221-1793. Tel: 517-266-3400; Fax: 517-266-3545. Email: devoffad@aol.com. Web: www.adriandominicans.org. Adrian Dominican Sisters.

Dominican Sisters of Adrian, MI, Inc. (1998) 1257 E. Siena Heights Dr., 49221. Tel: 517-266-3570. Sr. Attracta Kelly, O.P., Pres.

Motherhouse of the Sisters of St. Dominic, Congregation of the Most Holy Rosary (1923) 1257 E. Siena Heights Dr., 49221-1793. Tel: 517-266-3400; Fax: 517-266-3545. Web: www.adriandominicans.org. Sr. Attracta Kelly, O.P., Prioress; Rev. Robert Kelly, O.P., Dir. Liturgy & Chap. Total in Congregation 781.

Dominican Life Center (1926) 1277 E. Siena Heights Dr., 49221-1755. Tel: 517-266-3650; Fax: 517-266-3656. Sr. Karen Rossman, O.P., Admin.

ANN ARBOR. *Benedictine Sisters of Corpus Christi Monastery*, 4485 Earhart Rd., 48105-9710. Tel: 734-995-3876; Fax: 734-930-9471. Email: benedictines@sbcglobal.net. Sr. Regina Mary Kust, O.S.B., Supr.

Dominican Sisters of Mary, Mother of the Eucharist (1997) 4597 Warren Rd., 48105. Tel: 734-994-7437; Fax: 734-994-7438. Email: sjab@sistersofmary.org. Web: www.sistersofmary.org. Sr. Mary Assumpta Long, O.P., Prioress Gen. Final Professed 35; Temporary Professed 41; Novices 29; Postulants 16.

Dominican SMME Corporation (2002) *c/o Dominican Sisters of Mary, Mother of the Eucharist*, 4597 Warren Rd., 48105. Tel: 734-994-7437; Fax: 734-994-7438. Email: sjab@sistersofmary.org. Sr. Mary Assumpta Long, O.P., Pres.

**Servants of God's Love* (1975) 4399 Ford Rd., 48105. Tel: 734-663-6128; Fax: 734-663-6128. Email: sgl@att.net. Web: www.servantsofgodslove.catholicweb.net. Sr. Dorcee Clarey, Supr.

DE WITT. *St. Albert the Great House of Studies*, 217 Schavey Rd., 48820. Tel: 517-669-2277; Fax: 517-669-8123. Email: saintalberts@rsmofalma.org. Web: rsmofalma.org. Sr. Mary Rachel Nerbun, R.S.M., Supr. Religious Sisters of Mercy, Alma Michigan 3.

[L] PASTORAL CENTERS

FLUSHING. *Mt. Zion Catholic Community* (1988) 8228 N. McKinley Rd., 48433. Tel: 810-639-7175; Fax: 810-639-5262. Email: mtzion@centurytel.net. Web: youthtoyouthcatholic.com; www.mtzioncatholiccommunity.com.
Res.: 8236 N. McKinley Rd., 48433. Fax: 810-639-5262.

JACKSON. *Sacred Heart Chapel c/o St. Stanislaus Oratory*, 608 Elm Ave., 49203. Tel: 517-783-2772. Email: sacredchapel@aol.com. Sr. Marcella Oloarte, C.F.P., Pastoral Assoc.; Angela Medina, Treas.

[M] RETREAT CENTERS

ADRIAN. *Weber Retreat Center* (1970) 1257 E. Siena Heights Dr., 49221-1793. Tel: 517-266-4000; Fax: 517-266-4004. Email: webercenter@adriandominicans.org. Web: www.adriandominicans.org/weber. Sr. Margaret O'Flynn, O.P., Dir.

BROOKLYN. *Lake Vineyard Camps, Inc., (De Sales Center)*, 1124 Ventura, 49230-9078. Tel: 517-592-8218; Fax: 517-592-8218. Email: jmslc@earthlink.net. Web: www.desales.org. Rev. James McHugh, O.S.F.S., Dir. De Sales Center is a Catholic Retreat Center operated by Lake Vineyard Camps, Inc. for the Oblates of St. Francis de Sales, Inc. Also on the property is the Novitiate House for the Toledo-Detroit Province of the Oblates of St. Francis de Sales. Priests 3; Total Staff 40; Total Assisted 1,160.

DE WITT. *St. Francis Retreat Center*, 703 E. Main St., 48820. Tel: 517-669-8321; 866-669-8321 (Toll Free); Fax: 517-669-2708. Email: information@stfrancis.ws. Web: www.stfrancis.ws. Rev. Lawrence Delaney, Dir.; Deacon Richard Savage, Operations Mgr. Total in Residence 1; Total Staff 35.

Bethany House (Spiritual Life Center for Youth) (2001) St. Francis Retreat Center, 703 E. Main St., DeWitt, 48820. Tel: 517-669-8321; Fax: 517-669-2708.

[N] CAMPUS MINISTRY

ADRIAN. *Siena Heights University* 1247 E. Siena Heights Dr., 49221. Tel: 517-264-7192; Fax: 517-264-7745. Email: tpuszcze@sienaheights.edu. Web: www.sienaheights.edu. Tom Puszczewicz, Dir. Campus Ministry; Rev. Thomas J. Helfrich, O.S.F.S., Chap. Tel: 517-264-7198. Email: thelfric@sienaheights.edu. Campus Ministry.

ANN ARBOR. *St. Mary Student Parish* 331 Thompson St., 48104-2295. Tel: 734-663-0557; Fax: 734-663-2756. Email: stmarys@umich.edu. Web: www.stmarystudentparish.org. Rev. Benjamin B. Hawley, S.J. Serving the University of Michigan. Total Staff 19.
Refer to the parish section for complete campus ministry staff.

BELLEVUE. *St. Ann* (1923) 312 S. Main St., P.O. Box 38, 49021. Tel: 269-763-9372; Fax: 269-763-9372. Web: stannbellevue.catholicweb.com.

EAST LANSING. *St. John the Evangelist Church and Student Center* 327 M.A.C. Ave., 48823-4388. Tel: 517-337-9778; Fax: 517-337-8358. Email: sjsecretary@elcatholics.org. Web: www.elcatholics.org. Revs. Mark Inglot; Joseph J. Krupp, Dir. Campus Ministry; Denise Zakerski, Sec.; Keith Tharp, Business Mgr.; Colleen Tinsey, Opers. Asst.; Katie Diller, Campus Min. Serving Michigan State University
Refer to the parish section for complete campus ministry staff.

HILLSDALE. *St. Anthony Family Center* 11 Broad St., 49242. Tel: 517-439-1316; Fax: 517-437-0034. Email: stanthony@dmci.net. (Serving Hillsdale College and all of Hillsdale Co.) Total Assisted 1,500; Total Staff 1.

YPSILANTI. *Holy Trinity Student Parish* (1965) 511 W. Forest, 48197. Tel: 734-482-1400; Fax: 734-482-0542. Email: holytrinity@emich.edu. Web: www.catholicsoncampus.org. Revs. Phillip Mayfield, P.I.M.E.; Joseph Ngidjoi, P.I.M.E.; Sr. Carmen Gillick, S.F.C.C., Dir., Campus Ministry. Serving Eastern Michigan University and Washtenaw Community College.

[O] ENDOWMENTS AND TRUSTS

LANSING. *Chancery Office*, 300 W. Ottawa, 48933. Tel: 517-342-2440.

Blessed Sacrament Educational Trust Fund Tel: 810-742-3151; Fax: 810-742-1409. Rev. Joseph Sy Kim. (Blessed Sacrament Parish, Burton)

Camilla Madden Charitable Trust (Adrian)

Church of the Resurrection Educational Trust Fund (Church of the Resurrection, Lansing) Tel: 517-482-4749; Fax: 517-484-4740.

Father Al Miller Educational Trust Fund (St. Mary Parish, Westphalia) Tel: 517-587-4201; Fax: 517-587-3838.

Father Gabriel Richard High School Trust Fund (Fr. Gabriel Richard H.S., Ann Arbor) Tel: 734-662-0496; Fax: 734-662-4133.

Greater Lansing Catholic Education Foundation (Lansing) Tel: 517-485-8333; Fax: 517-484-8880.

Immaculate Heart of Mary St. Casimir School Mary Goeddeke Educational Trust Fund Tel: 517-882-6631. (IHM-St. Casimir School, Lansing)

Luke M. Powers Educational Trust Fund (Flint) Tel: 810-591-4741; Fax: 810-591-0383.

Lumen Christi High School Endowment Fund (Lumen Christi H.S., Jackson) Tel: 517-787-0630; Fax: 517-787-1066.

Most Holy Trinity Educational Trust Fund (Most Holy Trinity Church, Fowler) Tel: 517-593-2616; Fax: 517-593-2801.

Msgr. Lawrence H. Soest Educational Trust Fund (St. Mary Parish, Flint) Tel: 810-232-4012; Fax: 810-232-4013.

Rev. Joseph R. Robb Educational Trust Fund (Holy Rosary Parish, Flint) Tel: 810-736-4040; Fax: 810-736-9129.

Sacred Heart Educational Fund (Sacred Heart Parish, Hudson) Tel: 517-448-3811.

St. Francis of Assisi Educational Trust Fund (St. Francis of Assisi Parish, Ann Harbor) Tel: 734-821-2200; Fax: 734-821-2202.

St. John the Evangelist Parish Educational Trust Fund (St. John the Evangelist Parish, Jackson) Tel: 517-784-0553; Fax: 517-788-5381.

St John School Educational Foundation, Inc. (St. John Parish, Fenton) Tel: 810-629-2251; Fax: 810-629-2302.

St. John Vianney Educational Trust Fund (St. John Vianney Parish, Flint) Tel: 810-235-1812; Fax: 810-235-4911.

St. Joseph Church of Howell Trust Fund (St. Joseph Church, Howell) Tel: 517-546-0090.

St. Joseph Educational Trust Fund (St. Joseph Church, Owosso) Tel: 517-725-5215; Fax: 517-725-1519.

St. Joseph Educational Trust Fund (St. Joseph Church, St. Johns) Tel: 517-224-8994; Fax: 517-224-3475.

St. Louis Center for Exceptional Children & Adults Endowment Trust Agreement (St. Louis Center, Chel Tel: 734-475-8430; Fax: 734-475-0310.

St. Mary Educational Trust Fund (St. Mary Parish, Mt. Morris) Tel: 810-686-3920; Fax: 810-686-0759.

St. Mary Parish Educational Trust Fund (St. Mary Parish, Charlotte) Tel: 517-543-4319; Fax: 517-543-9078.

St. Mary Star of the Sea Educational Trust Fund (St. Mary Star of the Sea Parish, Jackson) Tel: 517-784-7184; Fax: 517-783-2571.

St. Michael's School Endowment Fund Policy (St. Michael School, Grand Ledge) Tel: 517-627-2167.

St. Paul's School Education Trust Fund (St. Paul Parish, Owosso) Tel: 517-723-4277; Fax: 517-723-9503.

St. Pius X Church Educational Trust Fund (St. Pius X Church, Flint) Tel: 810-235-8574; Fax: 810-235-8580.

St. Robert Bellarmine/Fr. Charles Jacobs Educational Trust Fund (St.Robert Bellarmine Parish, Flushing Tel: 810-659-2501; Fax: 810-659-2564. (St. Robert Bellarmine Parish, Flushing)

St. Therese Educational Trust Fund (St. Therese Parish, Lansing) Tel: 517-487-3749; Fax: 517-487-3755.

St. Thomas Aquinas Educational Foundation Trust (St. Thomas Aquinas Parish, East Lansing) Tel: 517-351-7215; Fax: 517-351-7271.

St. Thomas Grade School Trust Agreement (St. Thomas the Apostle Parish, Ann Arbor) Tel: 734-761-8606; Fax: 734-997-8432.

St. Thomas Scholarship Trust for Father Gabriel Richard H.S., 517 Elizabeth St., Ann Arbor, 48104. Tel: 734-769-0911; Fax: 734-997-8432. (St. Thomas the Apostle Parish, Ann Arbor)

St. Patrick Parish Educational Trust Fund (St. Patrick Parish, Brighton) Tel: 810-229-9863; Fax: 810-220-0730.

St. Gerard Educational Trust Fund (St. Gerard Parish, Lansing) Tel: 517-323-2379; Fax: 517-886-1394.

Holy Redeemer Educational Trust Fund (Holy Redeemer Parish, Burton) Tel: 810-743-3050; Fax: 810-743-4381.

[P] PRIVATE ASSOCIATION OF THE FAITHFUL

ANN ARBOR. *Catholic Men's Movement* (1997) 1 Ave Maria Dr., P.O. Box 466, 48106. Tel: 734-930-4524. Email: cmmdesk@catholic-men.org. Web: www.catholic-men.org. Peter Ziolkowski, Dir.; Bob Roleke, Admin. Tel: 734-930-4524; Rev. Patrick Egan, M.A., M.S., S.T.B., Chap. Tel: 734-930-3246.

[Q] PUBLIC ASSOCIATIONS OF THE FAITHFUL

LANSING. *Blessed John XXIII Community* (2010) 219 Seymour St., 48933. Tel: 517-589-8211. Email: bj23@getholy.com. Web: www.getholy.com. Rev. Jeffrey Robideau, Chap.

Catholic Lay Association of the Holy Spirit Oratory (1999) *Immaculate Heart of Mary*, 3815 S. Cedar St., 48910. Tel: 517-393-3030; Fax: 517-393-0855. Rev. John Byers, Chap.

FENTON. *Alma Redemptoris Mater*, 7381 Turner Rd., 48430. Tel: 810-735-6578; Fax: 734-663-2756. Email: tmf734@netzero.com. Rev. Thomas Firestone, Contact Person; Bro. Gary Pearce.

[R] MISCELLANEOUS LISTINGS

LANSING. *Charismatic Renewal Diocesan Service Committee* (Catholic Charismatic Renewal), 835 Maycroft Rd., 48917. Tel: 517-321-8661. Email: rstamford@hotmail.com. Rev. Peter J. Clark, Bishop's Liaison, St. Mary, Williamston; Ralph Stamford, Assoc. Liaison & Treas.; Patricia Stamford, Sec. Communications & Assoc. Liaison; Alan Pittel, Representative to Michigan Svc. Committee; Debbie Hawley, Flint Area Representative & Chairperson; Susan Tyle, Livingston Co. Area Representative.

FAITH Publishing Service, 1500 E. Saginaw St., 48906. Tel: 517-853-7600; Fax: 517-853-7616. Email: pobrien@faithcatholic.com. Web: www.faithcatholic.com. Patrick O'Brien, Pres. & CEO.

Catholic Event Finder Web: www.catholiceventfinder.com.

Diocesan Communications Tel: 517-853-7660. Michael Diebold, Dir. Communications, Diocese of Lansing.

FAITH Magazine Rev. Dwight M. Ezop, Editor-in-Chief; Patrick O'Brien, Mng. Editor & Creative Dir.; Elizabeth Solsburg, Editorial Dir. & Dir. Custom Publishing.

Liturgical Products Michael Marshall, Dir. Liturgical Products.

Ministry Marketing

Michigan Catholic Conference (1963) 510 S. Capitol Ave., 48933. Tel: 517-372-9310; Fax: 517-372-3940. Web: www.micatholicconference.org. Paul A. Long, Pres. & CEO.

ADRIAN. *Adrian Dominican Montessori Teacher Education Institute*, 1257 E. Siena Heights Dr., 49221. Tel: 517-266-3415; Fax: 517-266-3545. Email: info@admtei.org. Web: www.admtei.org. Sr. Leonor J. Esnard, O.P., Ph.D., Dir.

Adrian Rea Literacy Center, 1257 E. Siena Heights Dr., 49221-1793. Tel: 517-266-4260; Fax: 517-266-4235. Sr. Carleen Maly, O.P., Dir.

ANN ARBOR. *The Marnee and John DeVine Foundation*, 4925 Packard, 48108. Tel: 734-971-9781; Fax: 734-971-2730. Email: development@csswashtenaw.org. Web: www.csswashtenaw.org. Jan Wisniewski, Contact Person. Philanthropic arm of Catholic Social Services of Washtenaw County.

Renewal Ministries Inc. (1980) 230 Collingwood Blvd., Ste. 250, 48103. Tel: 734-662-1730; Fax: 734-662-4697. Email: gseromik@renewalministries.net. Web: www.renewalministries.net. Ralph Martin, Pres. Total Staff 10.

CHELSEA. *The Franciscan Project, Inc.*, Office: 14228 E. Old U.S. Hwy. 12, 48118. Tel: 734-475-9005. Mailing Address: P.O. Box 9, 48118-0009. Sisters Patricia Mary Hackett, S.A., Pres. & Treas.; Ann Francis Mahany, S.A.

FLINT. *St. Luke N.E.W. Life Center*, 3115 Lawndale Ave., 48504. Tel: 810-239-8710; Fax: 810-239-8726.

GRAND LEDGE. *Catholic Lawyers Guild* (1985) P.O. Box 66, 48837. Tel: 517-627-8700; Fax: 517-627-3950.

GRASS LAKE. *The Pious Union of St. Joseph*, 953 E. Michigan Ave., 49240-9210. Tel: 517-522-8017 (Voice/TDD); Fax: 517-522-8387. Email: piousunion@pusj.org. Web: www.piousunionofstjoseph.org. Revs. Joseph Rinaldo, S.C., Admin.; Fortunato Turati, S.C., Dir.; Sr. Margaret Mary Schissler, D.S.M.P., Prog. Dir.

"Now and at the Hour" Magazine: Tel: 517-522-8017; Fax: 517-522-8387. Email: piousunion@pusj.org. Web: pusj.org.

[S] CLOSED PARISHES & INSTITUTIONS

The Sacramental Records of the following Parishes and Institutions are kept at the Archives of the Diocese of Lansing with the exceptions as listed. The Archives address is: 228 N. Walnut St., Lansing, MI 48933. Tel: 517-342-2450; Fax: 517-342-2544. Available on Tuesdays only from 9:30 a.m. to 4:30 p.m.

LANSING. *Holy Cross Church* Sept. 1924-July 2009 (Baptisms after Dec. 31, 1967 at St. Mary Cathedral)

Lansing & Olivet Newman Centers Jan. 1974-Oct. 1976

St. Lawrence Hospital Aug. 1936-Feb. 1998

GENESEE. *St. Agnes Church, Flint* July 1928-Aug. 2008 (Baptisms after Sept. 1972 at St. John Vianney, Flint)

St. Francis of Assisi Church, Flint July 1949-June 1985

St. Joseph Church, Flint Aug. 1921-March 1973 (All records at Blessed Sacrament, Burton)

St. Leo the Great Church, Flint June 1957-Dec. 2008 (Baptisms after Aug. 1973 at Holy Rosary, Flint)

St. Luke Church, Flint July 1950-Aug. 2008 (Baptisms after March 1973 at St. John Vianney, Flint)

Sacred Heart Church, Flint July 1928-Aug. 2008 (Baptisms after July 1959 at St. John Vianney, Flint)

INGHAM. *St. Joseph Church, Leslie* 1869-1904 (Always a Mission, request assistance from Archives)

JACKSON. *St. Agnes, Brooklyn* 1913-1931 (Records at St. Joseph Shrine, Brooklyn)

LIVINGSTON. *St. Joseph Church, Cohoctah* 1880-1904 (Records at St. Joseph, Howell)

St. Joseph/St. Patrick Church, Green Oak Township 1838-1856 (Records at St. John, Fenton)

SHIAWASSEE. *Annunciation to the Blessed Virgin Mary Church, Corunna* 1857-1907 (Records at St. Paul, Owosso

St. Patrick Church, Woodhull Township 1847-1932 (Always a Mission, request assistance from Archives)

WASHTENAW. *St. Alexis Church Ypsilanti* June 1966-Jan.1994

St. Francis Borgia Church, Freedom Township 1874-1938 (Records at St. Mary, Manchester)

Transfiguration Church, Ypsilanti Jan. 1994-Sept. 2009 (All Baptism records at St. John the Baptist, Ypsilanti)

St. Ursula Church, Ypsilanti June 1960-Jan. 1994 (Baptisms after Aug. 1978 at St. John the Baptist, Ypsilanti)

[T] CLOSED HIGH SCHOOLS

All surviving high school student records of the following were transferred to the regional high schools.

LANSING. *St. Mary Cathedral High School, Lansing* 1904-1963 (Records at Lansing Catholic Central High School, Lansing)

Msgr. John A. Gabriels High School, Lansing 1964-1970 (Records at Lansing Catholic Central High School, Lansing)

Msgr. John A. Rafferty High School, Lansing 1964-1970 (Records at Lansing Catholic Central High School, Lansing)

Resurrection High School, Lansing 1939-1963 (Records at Lansing Catholic Central High School, Lansing)

GENESEE. *St. Agnes High School, Flint* 1954-1970 (Records at Fr. Luke M. Powers High School, Flint)

All Saints High School, Flint 1939-1954 (Records at Fr. Luke M. Powers High School, Flint)

Holy Redeemer High School, Burton 1956-1970 (Records at Fr. Luke M. Powers High School, Flint)

Holy Rosary High School, Flint 1964-1992 (Records at Fr. Luke M. Powers High School, Flint)

St. John Vianney High School, Flint 1955-1970 (Records at Fr. Luke M. Powers High School, Flint)

St. Mary High School, Flint 1929-1971 (Records at Fr. Luke M. Powers High School, Flint)

St. Mary High School, Mt. Morris 1930-1970 (Records at Fr. Luke M. Powers High School, Flint)

St. Matthew High School, Flint 1919-1970 (Records at Fr. Luke M. Powers High School, Flint)

St. Michael High School, Flint 1919-1970 (Records at Fr. Luke M. Powers High School, Flint)

Sacred Heart High School, Flint 1946-1967 (Records at Fr. Luke M. Powers High School, Flint)

JACKSON. *St. John the Evangelist High School, Jackson* 1892-1968 (Records at Lumen Christi High School, Jackson)

St. Mary Star of the Sea High School, Jackson 1892-1968 (Records at Lumen Christi High School, Jackson)

WASHTENAW. *St. John the Baptist High School, Ypsilanti* 1961-1970 (Records at Fr. Gabriel Richard High School, Ann Arbor)

St. Thomas the Apostle High School, Ann Arbor 1887-1977 (Records at Fr. Gabriel Richard High School, Ann Arbor)

The following high schools have no succeeding institutions. Contact the local parish for records.

Adrian Catholic Central High School, Adrian 1955-1969 (Records at St. Mary, Adrian)
Sacred Heart High School, Hudson 1933-1946
St. Joseph High School, Adrian 1927-1954
St. Mary High School, Adrian 1933-1954
St. Mary, Chelsea 1916-1934
St. Alphonsus High School, Deerfield 1918-1937
St. Joseph High School, Dexter 1926-1927
St. Paul High School, Owosso 1905-1971
St. Mary High School, Westphalia 1936-1961

RELIGIOUS INSTITUTES OF MEN REPRESENTED IN THE DIOCESE

For further details refer to the corresponding bracketed number in the Religious Institutes of Men or Women section.

[]—*Alma Redemptoris Mater*—A.R.M.
[0140]—*The Augustinians*—O.S.A.
[]—*Detroit Province of the Society of Jesus*—S.J.
[0485]—*Missionaries of St. Francis de Sales*—M.S.F.S.
[0920]—*Oblates of St. Francis de Sales*—O.S.F.S.
[0940]—*Oblates of the Virgin Mary*—O.M.V.
[]—*Order of Preachers*—O.P.
[1050]—*Pontifical Institute for Foreign Missions, Inc.*—P.I.M.E.
[]—*Priests of the Congregation of Holy Cross*—C.S.C.
[1220]—*Servants of Charity*—S.D.C.
[]—*Society of the Priests of Saint Sulpice*—S.S.
[]—*Work of Mary Mediatrix*—O.M.M.

RELIGIOUS INSTITUTES OF WOMEN REPRESENTED IN THE DIOCESE

[]—*Benedictine Nuns of Corpus Christi*—O.S.B.
[]—*Congregation of the Passion*—C.F.P.
[3832]—*Congregation of the Sisters of St. Joseph*—C.S.J.
[0940]—*Daughters of St. Mary of Providence*—D.S.M.P.
[1070-13]—*Dominican Sisters* (Adrian)—O.P.
[1070-14]—*Dominican Sisters* (Grand Rapids)—O.P.
[]—*Dominican Sisters of Mary, Mother of the Eucharist* (Ann Arbor)—O.P.
[1170]—*Felician Sisters*—C.S.S.F.
[2575]—*Institute of the Sisters of Mercy of the Americas*—R.S.M.
[]—*Servants of God's Love*—S.G.L.
[3580]—*Servants of Mary*—O.S.M.
[0440]—*Sisters of Charity of Cincinnati, Ohio*—S.C.
[1560]—*Sisters of St. Francis of the Holy Eucharist*—O.S.F.
[3830]—*Sisters of St. Joseph*—C.S.J.
[2260]—*Sisters of the Lamb of God*—A.D.
[2350]—*Sisters of the Living Word*—S.L.W.
[3260]—*Sisters of the Precious Blood (Dayton, OH)*—C.PP.S.
[3320]—*Sisters of the Presentation of the Blessed Virgin Mary*—P.B.V.M.
[2150]—*Sisters Servants of the Immaculate Heart of Mary*—I.H.M.
[]—*Society of the Atonement*—S.A.

DIOCESAN CEMETERIES

LANSING. *St. Joseph*
LAINGSBURG. *St. Patrick*
FLINT. *St. Michael Byzantine*
New Calvary
Old Calvary

NECROLOGY

† Lesniak, Marian J., (Retired)—Died Oct. 9, 2011
† Martin, Francis T., (Retired)—Died Sept. 23, 2011
† Miller, Randall J., Jackson, MI St. John the Evangelist—Died March 28, 2011
† Ritter, Nicholas J., (Retired)—Died April 24, 2011

An asterisk (*) denotes an organization that has established tax-exempt status directly with the IRS and is not covered by the USCCB Group Ruling.

Diocese of Laredo

Most Reverend

JAMES A. TAMAYO, D.D.

Bishop of Laredo; ordained Priest June 11, 1976; appointed Titluar Bishop of Ita and Auxiliary Bishop of Galveston-Houston January 26, 1993; consecrated March 10, 1993; appointed first Bishop of Diocese of Laredo July 3, 2000; installed August 9, 2000. *Office: 1901 Corpus Christi St., Laredo, TX 78043.* Tel: 956-727-2140; Fax: 956-727-2777.

Chancery Office: 1901 Corpus Christi St., Laredo, TX 78043. Tel: 956-727-2140; Fax: 956-727-2777. *Mailing Address: P.O. Box 2247, Laredo, TX 78044-2247*

ESTABLISHED AUGUST 9, 2000.

Square Miles 10,905.

Comprises the Counties of Webb, Zapata, Jim Hogg, La Salle, Maverick, Zavala and Dimmitt.

STATISTICAL OVERVIEW

Personnel	
Bishop	1
Priests: Diocesan Active in Diocese	27
Priests: Retired, Sick or Absent	3
Number of Diocesan Priests	30
Religious Priests in Diocese	21
Total Priests in Diocese	51
Extern Priests in Diocese	29
Permanent Deacons in Diocese	31
Total Brothers	7
Total Sisters	74
Parishes	
Parishes	32
With Resident Pastor:	
Resident Diocesan Priests	21
Resident Religious Priests	10
Without Resident Pastor:	
Administered by Priests	1
Missions	17
Professional Ministry Personnel:	
Brothers	1
Sisters	3
Lay Ministers	13
Welfare	
Health Care Centers	1
Total Assisted	25,000
Residential Care of Children	1
Total Assisted	49
Specialized Homes	1
Total Assisted	855
Special Centers for Social Services	3
Total Assisted	314,159
Other Institutions	1
Total Assisted	319
Educational	
Diocesan Students in Other Seminaries	5
Total Seminarians	5
High Schools, Diocesan and Parish	1
Total Students	390
Elementary Schools, Diocesan and Parish	5
Total Students	1,223
Elementary Schools, Private	1
Total Students	500
Catechesis/Religious Education:	
High School Students	4,208
Elementary Students	8,829
Total Students under Catholic Instruction	15,155
Teachers in the Diocese:	
Priests	2
Brothers	2
Sisters	11
Lay Teachers	145
Vital Statistics	
Receptions into the Church:	
Infant Baptism Totals	2,672
Minor Baptism Totals	223
Adult Baptism Totals	63
Received into Full Communion	94
First Communions	3,073
Confirmations	1,715
Marriages:	
Catholic	441
Interfaith	11
Total Marriages	452
Deaths	1,051
Total Catholic Population	299,573
Total Population	352,439

Chancery—1901 Corpus Christi St., Laredo, 78043. Tel: 956-727-2140; Fax: 956-727-2777. *Mailing Address: P.O. Box 2247, Laredo, 78044-2247.*

Vicar General—Rev. R. ANTHONY MENDOZA, St. Joseph, 628 Burton St., La Pryor, 78872-0436. Tel: 830-365-4107; Fax: 830-365-9367.

Chancellor—MARIA DE LA LUZ R. CARDENAS, M.A., 1201 Corpus Christi St., Laredo, 78040. Tel: 956-727-2140; Fax: 956-764-7842.

Vice Chancellor—Rev. IDEN JOSE BELLO MIQUILENA, 1201 Corpus Christi St., Laredo, 78040. Tel: 956-727-2140; Fax: 956-764-7842.

Tribunal—Rev. OLIVER ANGEL, J.C.L., Judicial Vicar, 1901 Corpus Christi St., Laredo, 78043. Tel: 956-727-2140; Fax: 956-712-1343.

Fiscal Officer—LOURDES MARTINEZ, CPA, 1901 Corpus Christi St., Laredo, 78043. Tel: 956-727-2140; Fax: 956-523-0828.

Presbyteral Council—Most Rev. JAMES ANTHONY TAMAYO, D.D., Pres. Ex Officio Members: Rev. R. ANTHONY MENDOZA, Dean/Northern; VACANT, Dean/Central; Revs. FRANCISCO LEON, O.S.A., Dean/San Agustin; JAN ZIEMNIAK, Dean/Southern; IDEN JOSE BELLO MIQUILENA, Vice Chancellor; JERZY KRZYWDA; LESZEK J. WACLAWIK; JAMES A. LOIACONO, O.M.I.; JACINTO OLGUIN; ALIRIO CORRALES; JOHN JESUS MOLONEY, C.S.J.

College of Consultors—Revs. IDEN JOSE BELLO MIQUILENA; JOSE MARIA GUEVARA; R. ANTHONY MENDOZA; JAN ZIEMNIAK.

Diocesan Offices and Directors

Campus Ministry— Congregation of St. John; Laredo Community College; Texas A&M International University. Rev. MICHAEL THERESE SCHEERGER, C.S.J., 505 Century Dr. S., Laredo, 78046. Tel: 956-722-3399, Ext. 26. Web: www.newmanclub.us.

Laredo Catholic Communications, Inc.—BENNETT MCBRIDE, Exec. Vice Pres. & Gen. Mgr., 1901 Corpus Christi St., Laredo, 78043. Tel: 956-722-4167; Fax: 956-722-4464. Email: khoy@khoy.org. Web: www.khoy.org.

Communications Department—BENNETT MCBRIDE, Dir.; GREGORIO M. LOPEZ, Editor, La Fe Magazine, 1901 Corpus Christi St., Laredo, 78043. Tel: 956-722-4167; Fax: 956-722-4464. Email: glopez@dioceseoflaredo.org.

Stewardship and Development—REBECCA C. SEPULVEDA, Dir., 1901 Corpus Christi St., Laredo, 78043. Tel: 956-727-2140; Fax: 956-523-0828.

Catholic Social Services—REBECCA SOLLOA, Dir., 1919 Cedar St., Laredo, 78040. Tel: 956-722-2443; Fax: 956-725-2238.

Emergency Assistance Program—CHRISTINA RODRIGUEZ. Tel: 956-722-2443.

Immigration Services—MYRNA GONZALEZ, Servicios Para Inmigrantes, 1919 Cedar St., Laredo, 78040. Tel: 956-722-2443. Email: mgonzalez@csslaredo.org.

Catholic Social Services Senior Center—Sr. CARMEL RANGEL, O.S.U., 1717 Callaghan Ave., Laredo, 78040. Tel: 956-722-3629.

Calvary Catholic Cemetery—ROSA ALDAPE, Mgr., 3600 McPherson, P.O. Box 2366, Laredo, 78040. Tel: 956-723-6811; Fax: 956-723-8726.

Our Lady of Refuge Cemetery—Tel: 830-773-4247. *1679 Flowers, Eagle Pass, 78852.*

Sacred Heart Church Cemetery—51 N. IH 35, Cotulla, 78014. Tel: 830-879-2658.

Charismatic Renewal—Deacon ANASTACIO BERNAL, Mailing Address: P.O. Box 671, Laredo, 78042. Tel: 956-724-2659.

Cursillo Movement—Rev. TORIBIO C. GUERRERO, Spiritual Dir., 1510 Matamoros St., Laredo, 78040. Tel: 956-723-3850; Fax: 956-725-6544.

Finance Council—J. PAT HEARN, Chm.; SABAS ZAPATA III; Rev. WOJCIECH KOSOWICZ, Ph.D.; HECTOR J. CERNA; SAUL FERNANDEZ; PEDRO SAENZ JR., J.D.; TORIBIO SAUCEDO, CPA.

Human Resources—MELINDA MENDOZA, Dir., 1901 Corpus Christi St., Laredo, 78043. Tel: 956-727-2140; Fax: 956-523-0828.

Family Life Ministry—MARTHA E. MILLER, Dir., 1201 Corpus Christi St., Laredo, 78040. Tel: 956-727-2140; Fax: 956-764-7842.

Natural Family Planning and Understanding Sexuality—Family Life Office, 1201 Corpus Christi St., Laredo, 78040. Tel: 956-727-2140; Fax: 956-764-7842.

Office of Respect Life—Rev. R. ANTHONY MENDOZA, Spiritual Dir., 1201 Corpus Christi St., Laredo, 78040. Tel: 956-727-2140; Fax: 956-764-7842.

Religious Education for Children—Sr. LUZ MARIA MONDRAGON, M.R.F., 1201 Corpus Christi St., Laredo, 78040. Tel: 956-727-2140; Fax: 956-764-7842.

Persons with Special Needs—Sr. LUZ MARIA MONDRAGON, M.R.F., 1201 Corpus Christi St., Laredo, 78040. Tel: 956-727-2140; Fax: 956-764-7842.

Religious Education for Adults—REYNALDO MONTEMAYOR, Dir., 1201 Corpus Christi St., Laredo, 78040. Tel: 956-727-2140; Fax: 956-764-7842.

Priests Personnel Board—Revs. FRANCISCO LEON, O.S.A.; R. ANTHONY MENDOZA; JAN ZIEMNIAK.

Youth Ministry—CHRISTOPHER OSGOOD, Dir., 1201 Corpus Christi St., Laredo, 78040. Tel: 956-727-2140; Fax: 956-764-7842.

Archives—MARIA DE LA LUZ R. CARDENAS, M.A., Chancellor; ESTHER DELGADILLO, Asst. Archivist, 1919 Cedar St., Laredo, 78040. Tel: 956-727-0700; Fax: 956-727-1530.

Catholic Schools—

Superintendent's Office—Dr. ROSA MARIA VIDA, Ph.D., Supt.

Safe Environment Coordinator—MELINDA MENDOZA, 1901 Corpus Christi St., Laredo, 78043. Tel: 956-727-2140.

Victim Assistance Coordinator—MARIA DE LA LUZ R. CARDENAS, M.A., Dir., 1201 Corpus Christi St., Laredo, 78040. Tel: 956-764-7825; Fax: 956-764-7842. Email: mchancellor3@dioceseoflaredo.org.

Vocations Office—

Casa Guadalupe House of Discernment—Rev. IDEN JOSE BELLO MIQUILENA, Dir., 2302 Corpus Christi St., Laredo, 78043. Tel: 956-568-0463; Fax: 956-764-7842.

Equestrian Order of the Holy Sepulcher of Jerusalem—

Southwestern Lieutenancy—Sir TOMAS M. RODRIGUEZ JR., KC HS; Lady DIANA E. C. RODRIGUEZ, LC HS. Email: dcrodriguez1948@yahoo.com.

Knights of Columbus—JAVIER F. CABELLO, Master of 4th Degree. Email: jfcabello@sbcglobal.net.

Catholic Daughters of the Americas—ANNA CHAPMAN, District Deputy #15, Court St. Joan of Arc #1224, 202 Silver Sage Dr., Del Rio, 78840. Tel: 830-774-7081.

International Order of the Alhambras-Zahara Caravan No. 64—JORGE DE LA GARZA, Grand Commander, 1117 Laredo St., Laredo, 78040. Tel: 956-724-8644.

Sultanas—ROSA IMELDA DE LA GARZA, Sultana, 1117 Laredo St., Laredo, 78040. Tel: 956-724-8644.

CLERGY, PARISHES, MISSIONS AND PAROCHIAL SCHOOLS

CITY OF LAREDO

(WEBB COUNTY)

1—SAN AGUSTIN CATHEDRAL (1762), (Hispanic), Revs. Francisco J. Hernandez, Admin.; Miguel Ortiz Uribe, Parochial Vicar.
200 San Agustin Ave., 78040. Tel: 956-722-1382; Fax: 956-722-0441. Email: san_agustine@sbcglobal.net.
Parish Office: 214 San Bernardo Ave., 78040.
Catechesis/Religious Program—Students 225.

2—BLESSED SACRAMENT (1950), (Hispanic), [CEM 2] Rev. Wojciech Przystasz, Admin.; Deacons David Vargas; Larry Sandlin.
2219 Galveston St., 78043. Tel: 956-722-1231; Fax: 956-722-2823. Email: blessedsacrament@prodigy.net.
Catechesis/Religious Program—Students 197.

3—SAN CARLOS MISSION (1993) Unassigned. Attended by Christ the King, Laredo., c/o 146 Northpoint Dr., 78041. *San Carlos Mission*, 1105 Tilden Ave., 78040. Tel: 956-723-4267; Fax: 956-791-8034. Email: melcan_3333@yahoo.com.
Catechesis/Religious Program—Laura Villalobos, D.R.E. Students 131.

4—CHRIST THE KING (1954) Rev. Jose Luis Balderas; Deacon Guillermo De la Garza.
1105 Tilden Ave., 78040. Tel: 956-723-4267; Fax: 956-791-8034.
Catechesis/Religious Program—Tel: 956-722-7821. Students 313.
Mission—San Carlos Mission (1993)

5—DIVINE MERCY (1998) Rev. Michael De Leon; Deacon Raymundo Guevara Jr.
Parish Office: 9350 Amber Ave., 78045. Tel: 956-726-9972; Fax: 956-726-1286.
Catechesis/Religious Program—Students 196.

6—ST. FRANCES CABRINI (1958), (Hispanic), [CEM] Rev. Jose Alfredo Gaytan, S.O.L.T.
3018 Davis Ave., 78040. Tel: 956-722-2919; Fax: 956-724-5232. Email: mothercabrinichurch@bizlaredo.rr.com.
Catechesis/Religious Program—Tel: 956-722-8315; Fax: 956-724-5232. Students 112.

7—HOLY FAMILY (1984), (Hispanic), Rev. P. Nolasco Hinojosa Jr.; Deacon Hector D. Hernandez.
2705 McPherson, 78040. Tel: 956-724-6881; Fax: 956-724-5581. Email: hfccl_oc@yahoo.com.
Catechesis/Religious Program—Tel: 956-724-5581. Students 60.

8—HOLY REDEEMER (1940), (Hispanic), [JC] Rev. Francisco Leon, O.S.A.; Deacon Edmundo Lopez Jr.
Mailing Address: P.O. Box 1087, 78040. 1602 Garcia St., 78040. Tel: 956-723-7171; Fax: 956-723-7194. Email: holyredeemer@laredohrc.org. Web: www.laredohrc.org.
Mission—Santa Cruz 2002 Lee Ave., Webb Co. 78040.
Catechesis/Religious Program—Students 171.

9—ST. JOHN NEUMANN (1979) Rev. Daniel Ramirez-Portugal; Rev. Msgr. James E. Harris, Parochial Vicar; Deacon Gerardo Morales.
102 W. Hillside Rd., 78041. Tel: 956-726-9488; Fax: 956-726-0540.
Catechesis/Religious Program—Tel: 956-726-9452. Students 121.

10—ST. JOSEPH (1953) Rev. Leszek J. Waclawik; Deacon Crispin O. Soto.
109 N. Meadow, 78040. Tel: 956-723-4172; Fax: 956-728-8824.
Catechesis/Religious Program—Tel: 956-791-6664; Fax: 956-728-8824. Students 159.

11—ST. JUDE (1984) Rev. Jose Maria Guevara.
Mailing Address: 2031 Lowry Rd., 78045. Tel: 956-722-2280; Fax: 956-722-0209.
Catechesis/Religious Program—Students 550.

12—NUESTRA SENORA DEL ROSARIO (2000) Revs. Jan Ziemniak; Gustavo Ortega Rodriguez, O.F.M., Parochial Vicar.
420 Sierra Vista Blvd., 78046. Tel: 956-753-8764; Fax: 956-753-9972.
Catechesis/Religious Program—Diana Salazar, D.R.E. Students 543.

13—OUR LADY OF GUADALUPE (1926) [JC] Revs. Juan Ayala Jr., O.M.I.; Edward J. Vrazel, O.M.I.; David Munoz, O.M.I., Parochial Vicar; Deacon Anastacio Bernal.
Mailing Address: P.O. Box 671, 78042. 1718 San Jorge Ave., 78040. Tel: 956-723-6954; Fax: 956-723-6047. Email: petraolog@sbcglobal.net. Web: www.ologlaredo.com.
Catechesis/Religious Program—Students 146.

14—ST. PATRICK (1970) Revs. Wojciech Kosowicz, Admin.; Jacinto Olguin, Parochial Vicar; Deacons Roderick Bordelon; Joe Longoria.
555 E. Del Mar Blvd., 78041. Tel: 956-722-6215; Fax: 956-764-7842. Email: stpatlaredotx@yahoo.com.
Catechesis/Religious Program—Tel: 956-722-6215, Ext. 15. Students 566.
Mission—Apostolate Missions in Northern Mexico

15—ST. PETER THE APOSTLE (1897) Rev. Toribio C. Guerrero.
Mailing Address: 1510 Matamoros St., 78040. Tel: 956-723-6301; Fax: 956-723-6321.
Catechesis/Religious Program—Students 51.

16—SAGRADO CORAZON DE JESUS MISSION (1994) Rev. Gustavo Ortega Rodriguez, O.F.M., Admin.
Res.: 2570 Cassata Ln., 78046. Tel: 956-725-0508; 956-744-4899 Cell Phone; Fax: 956-417-3325.
Catechesis/Religious Program—Students 54.

17—SAN FRANCISCO JAVIER (1966), (Hispanic), Rev. William Davis, O.M.I.; Deacon Ignacio Valdez.
Mailing Address: P.O. Box 1175, 78042-1175. 2502 Zaragoza St., 78042-1175. Tel: 956-723-3850; Fax: 956-725-6544. Email: chaqui6@aol.com.
Catechesis/Religious Program—Students 96.

18—SAN LUIS REY (1958), (Hispanic), Revs. Michael J. Gergen, S.D.B.; Raul Acosta-Zunini, S.D.B., Parochial Vicar; Deacon Jose Rodriguez.
Church: 3502 Sanders Ave., 78040. Tel: 956-723-6587; Fax: 956-723-6825. Email: sanluisreychurch@yahoo.com.
Catechesis/Religious Program—Tel: 956-722-3323. Students 480.

19—SAN MARTIN DE PORRES (1979), (Hispanic), Rev. Salvador Pedroza; Deacons Leonel San Miguel; Joel Perez De la Fuente.
Mailing Address: 1704 Sandman St., P.O. Box 2666, 78041. Tel: 956-723-5215; Fax: 956-723-9443. Web: www.san-martin.org.
Catechesis/Religious Program—Tel: 956-725-2440; Fax: 956-725-2440. Email: smartinccd@hotmail.com. Students 401.
Mission—Santa Teresita (1996)

20—SANTA ANITA MISSION, Closed.

21—SANTA MARGARITA DE ESCOCIA (1991), (Hispanic), Rev. Alirio Corrales, Admin.
320 Segovia Dr., 78046. Tel: 956-724-9669; Fax: 956-791-2167. Email: stmargaritachurch@att.net.
Catechesis/Religious Program—Students 197.

22—SANTO NINO (1985), (Hispanic), Rev. Santiago Domingo, Admin.
2717 Cross St., 78046. Tel: 956-724-6638; Fax: 956-712-8096. *Santo Nino Church*, 2801 Cross, 78046.
Catechesis/Religious Program—Students 138.

23—SANTA TERESITA MISSION (1996) Rev. Salvador Pedroza.
1704 Sandman St., P.O. Box 2666, 78041. Tel: 956-723-4172; Fax: 956-728-8824. P.O. Box 2666, 78044. Tel: 956-723-5215; Fax: 956-723-9443.
Catechesis/Religious Program—Students 28.

24—ST. VINCENT DE PAUL (1969), (Hispanic), Revs. Leonel Martinez, O.S.A.; Edgar Guadarrama, O.S.A., Pastoral Assoc.; Deacon Miguel Vallarta.
2710 Boulanger St., 78043. Tel: 956-722-3034; Fax: 956-722-4829.
Catechesis/Religious Program—Tel: 956-726-4134. Students 850.

OUTSIDE THE CITY OF LAREDO

ASHERTON, DIMMIT CO., IMMACULATE CONCEPTION (1918), (Hispanic), Rev. Oscar Ramirez Martinez, Admin.
Mailing Address: 579 Crocket & 6th St., P.O. Box 8, 78827.
Mission—St. Michael P.O. Box 266, Big Wells, Dimmit Co. 78830-0266. Tel: 830-457-2693; Fax: 830-457-0100.
Mission—St. Henry P.O. Box 15, Catarina, Dimmit Co. 78836. Tel: 830-468-3343.
Catechesis/Religious Program—Students 120.

CARRIZO SPRINGS, DIMMIT CO., OUR LADY OF GUADALUPE (1881) Rev. Jerzy Krzywda, Admin.; Deacons Jose F. Perez; Juan Sauceda.
Mailing Address: 1003 N. 6th St., 78834. Tel: 830-876-2239; Fax: 830-876-5023.
Catechesis/Religious Program—Tel: 830-876-0153; Fax: 830-876-5023. Students 347.

COTULLA, LA SALLE CO., SACRED HEART (1882) [JC] Rev. Francisco Stodola; Deacon Jose Patterson.
Mailing Address: 307 S. Main St., P.O. Box 560, 78014. Tel: 830-879-2658; Fax: 830-879-4916. Email: sagradocorazon@sbcglobal.net.
Catechesis/Religious Program—Tel: 930-879-3196. Students 148.

CRYSTAL CITY, ZAVALA CO., SACRED HEART (1917), (Hispanic), Rev. Jozef Glabinski, Admin.; Deacons Frank Huerta; Jose Luis Lopez; Antonio Rivera; Frank Solansky.
115 E. Kinney St., 78839. Tel: 830-374-3148; Fax: 830-374-2211. Email: sacredheartchurchcc@yahoo.com.
Catechesis/Religious Program—Students 157.

EAGLE PASS, MAVERICK CO.

1—ST. JOSEPH (1967), (Hispanic), Rev. Richard Kulwiec, O.M.I.
Mailing Address: 800 Comal St., 78852-4029. Tel: 830-773-6114; Fax: 830-773-6608.
Catechesis/Religious Program—Tel: 830-773-6515; Fax: 830-773-6608. Students 300.

2—OUR LADY OF REFUGE (1859) [CEM] Rev. James A. Loiacono, O.M.I.; Deacon Efren Maldonado.
Mailing Address: 815 Webster, 78852. Tel: 830-773-8451 (Office); 830-773-8421 (Res.).
Our Lady of Refuge Cemetery—1679 Flowers, 78852. Tel: 830-773-4247.
Mission—Our Lady of Lourdes Seco Mines, Maverick Co. Tel: 830-773-8288.
Mission—Our Lady of Guadalupe Quemado, Maverick Co. Tel: 830-758-1888.
Catechesis/Religious Program—Tel: 830-773-8915 (Res.); 830-773-7744 (Office). Students 585.

3—SACRED HEART (1966), (Hispanic), Rev. Paul Wilhelm, O.M.I.; Deacons Manuel Rene Cardona; Victor Carrillo Jr.; Leandro Contreras Jr.; Hector Ricardo Martinez.
Church: 2055 Williams St., 78852. Tel: 830-773-2451; Fax: 830-773-0643.
Catechesis/Religious Program—Tel: 830-758-1681. Students 587.
Mission—Our Lady of San Juan El Indio, Maverick Co.

ENCINAL, LA SALLE CO., IMMACULATE HEART OF MARY (1898), (Hispanic), Rev. Noel Davis.
Mailing Address: P.O. Box 5, 78019-0005. 400 Santa Fe St., 78019-0005. Tel: 956-948-5328; Fax: 956-948-5328. Email: ihmcce@yahoo.com.
Catechesis/Religious Program—Students 58.

HEBBRONVILLE, JIM HOGG CO., OUR LADY OF GUADALUPE (1926) [CEM] Revs. Flavio Sanchez de la Torre, O.F.M.; Silvestre Rodriguez Rivas, O.F.M., Parochial Vicar; Juan Jose Villa Barriga, O.F.M., Parochial Vicar.
504 E. Santa Clara St., 78361. Tel: 361-527-3865; Fax: 361-527-5548. Email: gpeheb@hotmail.com.
Mission—St. Agnes 324 Liner St., Mirando City, Jim Hogg Co. 78369.
Mission—St. Bridget 115 Laurel Ave., Oilton, Jim Hogg Co. 78371.
Mission—Sacred Heart 211 N. Ave. G, Bruni, Jim Hogg Co. 78344.
Mission—Inmaculada 202 W. Draper, Jim Hogg Co. 78361.
Catechesis/Religious Program—Tel: 361-231-0003 (After 6:00 P.M.); Fax: 361-527-5548. Clemencia Villanueva, D.R.E. Students 170.

LA PRYOR, ZAVALA CO., ST. JOSEPH (1917), (Hispanic), Rev. R. Anthony Mendoza; Deacons Gene Corrigan; Juan Gallegos.
Mailing Address: 628 Burton St., P.O. Box 436, 78872-0436. Tel: 830-365-4107; Fax: 956-764-7824.
Mission—St. Patrick P.O. Box 83, Batesville, Zavala Co. 78829.
Catechesis/Religious Program—Students 159.

RIO BRAVO, WEBB CO., SANTA RITA DE CASIA (1986) Rev. Janusz Glabinski; Deacon Juan Cerda.
1001 Espejo Molina, 78046. Tel: 956-725-7215; Fax: 956-728-8539.
Catechesis/Religious Program—Students 148.
Mission—Santa Monica Mission 507 Morales (El Cenizo), Webb Co. 78046. Tel: 956-724-4413.

ZAPATA, ZAPATA CO., OUR LADY OF LOURDES (1940), (Spanish), Revs. Agustin Escalante, Admin.; Gerardo Silos, Parochial Vicar.
Mailing Address: 1609 Hidalgo Blvd., 78076. Tel: 956-765-4216; Fax: 956-765-6188.

Res.: 1610 Hidalgo Blvd, 78076.
Catechesis/Religious Program—Students 427.
Mission—Our Lady of Refuge San Ignacio, Zapata Co. Tel: 950-765-4940.
Mission—San Pedro Lopeno, Zapata Co.
Mission—Santa Ana Falcon, Zapata Co.

Chaplains of Public Institutions

LAREDO. *Webb County Jail*, 4402 Tilden Ave., 78041. Tel: 956-723-5029. Deacon Jose Rodriguez, Prison Chap. Chaplaincy Apostolate to Refugees & Jail Ministry.

INSTITUTIONS LOCATED IN THE DIOCESE

[A] HIGH SCHOOLS

LAREDO. *St. Augustine High School* (Diocesan), 1300 Galveston St., 78040. Tel: 956-724-8131; Fax: 956-724-8770. Email: ogentry@st-augustine.org. Web: st-augustine.org. Mrs. Olga P. Gentry, Prin. Sisters 2; Lay Teachers 20; Students 390; Administration 2.

[B] JUNIOR HIGH AND ELEMENTARY SCHOOLS

LAREDO. *St. Augustine (Elementary School)* (1927) (Diocesan), 1300 Galveston St., 78040. Tel: 956-724-1176; Fax: 956-724-9891. Email: tcortez@st-augustine.org. Web: www.st-augustine.org. Sylvia F. Cortez, Prin. Lay Teachers 21; Students 384; Part time Priest 1.

Blessed Sacrament School, 1501 N. Bartlett Ave., 78043. Tel: 956-722-1222; Fax: 956-712-2002. Email: ebgutierrezbss@yahoo.com. Esther B. Gutierrez, Prin.; Maria del Carmen Alaniz, Librarian. Lay Teachers 13; Students 268.

Mary Help of Christians School, (Grades PreK-8), (Private) , 10 E. Del Mar Blvd., 78045. Tel: 956-722-3966; Fax: 956-722-1413. Web: www.mhsoul.org. Sr. Marie Gannon, F.M.A., Prin. Sisters 6; Lay Teachers 45; Students 500.

Our Lady of Guadalupe School (1904) 400 Callaghan St., 78040-3834. Tel: 956-722-3915; Fax: 956-727-2840. Email: hrlndmartinez@yahoo.com. Herlinda Martinez, Prin.; Mrs. Raquel Bradley, Librarian. Sisters 1; Lay Teachers 9; Students 108.

St. Peter Memorial (Diocesan), 1519 Houston St., P.O. Box 520, 78040. Tel: 956-723-6302; Fax: 956-725-2671. Dr. Linda G. Mitchell, Ed.D., Prin.; Eladia Martinez, Library Mgr. Sisters 1; Lay Teachers 13; Students 170.

EAGLE PASS. *Our Lady of Refuge* (1950) 577 Washington St., 78852. Tel: 830-773-3531; 830-773-1800; Fax: 830-773-7310. Email: olive2005bush@yahoo.com. Web: oloroschool.org. Adolfo Olivares Jr., Prin.; Anna Saucedo, Librarian; Rosantina Zamarripa, Contact Person. Sisters 1; Lay Teachers 17; Students 293.

[C] ORPHANAGES AND INFANT HOMES

LAREDO. *Sacred Heart Children's Home* (1907) 3310 S. Zapata Hwy., 78046. Tel: 956-723-3343; Fax: 956-723-3409. Sr. Maria Teresa Grajeda, S.S.H.J.P., Supr. Sisters 16; Children 49.

[D] MONASTERIES AND RESIDENCES OF PRIESTS AND BROTHERS

LAREDO. *St. John Priory, F.J.* Congregation of St. John, 505 Century Dr., South, 78046. Tel: 956-242-6623; Fax: 956-242-6623. Email: laredo@stjean.com. Web: www.communityofstjohn.com. Revs. John Jesus Moloney, C.S.J., Prior; Michael Therese Scheerger, C.S.J.; Salvador E. Uribe Ramirez, C.S.J.; Jean Frederic Plateaux, C.S.J.; Bros. Esteban Gonzalez; Gabriel Maria; Malachi Patcho; Miguel Angel Valadez. Tel: 956-290-2913. Priests 4; Brothers 3; Total in Residence 7.

Marist Brothers, 1511 Cherry Hill Dr., 78041-3807. Tel: 956-724-2651; Fax: 956-724-1963. Email: fmslaredo@prodigy.net. Bros. Joseph E. Herrera, F.M.S., Dir.; Philip R. Degagne, F.M.S.; Thomas W. Coyne, F.M.S. Marist Brothers 3.

[E] CONVENTS AND RESIDENCES FOR SISTERS

LAREDO. *Eucharistic Missionary Society (EMS)*, 1101 Cortez St., 78040. Tel: 956-726-4085; Fax: 956-726-4085. Email: emisoc@laredo.globalpc.net. Sr. Maria Manuela Susana Pedroza, E.M.S. Sisters 1.

Mary Help of Christians Convent (1935) 10 E. Del Mar Blvd., 78045. Tel: 956-791-8617; Fax: 956-722-1413. Email: srgannon@mhsoul.org. Web: www.mhsoul.org. Sr. Marie Gannon, F.M.A., Supr. & Prin. Daughters of Mary Help of Christians (Salesian Sisters). Sisters 6.

Misioneras del Rosario de Fatima, 1415 N. Jarvis Ave., 78043. Tel: 956-693-9986. Sisters 3.

Mother of the Eucharist Convent Felician Sisters (1855) 705 Dellwood Dr., 78045. Telian: 956-568-1502. Email: feliciansisters@stx.rr.com. Web: feliciansisters.org. Sisters 2.

Sacred Heart Children's Home Convent (1907) 3310 S. Zapata Hwy., 78046. Tel: 956-723-3343; Fax: 956-723-3409. Sr. Maria Yolanda Fernandez, S.S.H.J.P., Supr. Servants of the Sacred Heart of Jesus and of the Poor. Sisters 16.

School Sisters of Notre Dame, 1802 San Francisco, 78040. Tel: 956-568-5820. Sr. Leah Couvillion, S.S.N.D., Contact Person. Sisters 3.

Sisters of Mercy Convent, 1901 Guerrero St., 78043. Tel: 956-724-5512. Email: oobregop@mercysc.org; ktinnel@mercysc.org. Sr. Kathleen Marie Tinnel, R.S.M., Contact Person. Sisters 2.

Sisters of Our Lady of the Most Holy Trinity, 2454 Colonia Loop, 78046. Tel: 956-727-3965. Sr. Leticia Venegas, S.O.L.T., Migrant Min. Dir. Sisters 2.

Sisters of St. John (1992) 504 Century Dr., S., 78046. Tel: 956-727-1028; Fax: 956-727-1028. Sr. Jean Marthe, Supr. Total in Residence 15.

Ursuline Sisters, 136 Palencia, 78046. Tel: 956-722-1101. Sisters Carmel Rangel, O.S.U., Treas.; Karen Schwane, O.S.U. Sisters 3.

EAGLE PASS. *Benedictine Sisters* Nurse Employed by Fort Duncan Regional Medical Center., 1080 Vista Hermosa, 78852. Tel: 830-758-0812. Sisters 2.

Missionary Sisters of Our Lady of Perpetual Help (1934) 895 Webster, 78852. Tel: 956-727-2140; Fax: 956-764-7842. Sisters 6.

[F] RETREAT HOUSES

LAREDO. *Holy Spirit Retreat and Conference Center*, 501 Century Dr., S., 78046. Tel: 956-242-6223; Fax: 956-242-6623. Email: lhsrc@sbcglobal.net. Web: www.communityofstjohn.com. Rev. John Jesus Moloney, C.S.J., Prior. Priests 4; Brothers 4.

[G] MISCELLANEOUS

LAREDO. *St. Augustine School Endowment Fund, Inc.*, 1300 Galveston, 78040. Tel: 956-724-8131; Fax: 956-724-8770. Email: ogentry@st-augustine.org. Web: www.st-augustine.org. Mrs. Olga P. Gentry, Prin.

Bethany House (1982) 819 Hidalgo St., 78040. Tel: 956-722-4152; Fax: 956-791-1102. Email: info@bethanyhouseoflaredo.org. Web: bethanyhouseoflaredo.org. Evelyn Sames, Vice Pres.; Beatriz Saldana, Dir., Opers.

Casa de Misericordia (1998) P.O. Box 430175, 78043-0175. Tel: 956-712-9590; 877-782-2722; Fax: 956-791-1364. Email: misericordia@stx.rr.com. Maria Elena Arambula, Shelter Admin. Domestic Violence Shelter for Women and Children.

Diocese of Laredo Deposit and Loan Fund, Inc., 1901 Corpus Christi St., 78043. Tel: 956-727-2140; Fax: 956-523-0828.

Diocese of Perpetual Benefit Endowment Fund, Inc., 1901 Corpus Christi St., 78043. Tel: 956-727-2140; Fax: 956-523-0828.

Mercy Ministries of Laredo (2003) 2500 Zacatecas, 78046. Tel: 956-718-6810; Fax: 956-721-7405. Email: mercy.laredo@mercy.net. Web: mercylaredo.com. Sr. Maria Luisa Vera, R.S.M., Pres.

RELIGIOUS INSTITUTES OF WOMEN REPRESENTED IN THE DIOCESE

For further details refer to the corresponding bracketed number in the Religious Institutes of Men or Women section.

[]—*Benedictine Sisters*
[]—*Eucharistic Missionary Society*—E.M.S.
[]—*Hijas de San Jose*
[]—*Mary Help of Christians Convent*—F.M.S.
[]—*Misioneras del Rosario de Fatima*
[]—*Missionary Sisters of Our Lady of Perpetual Help*
[]—*Mother of the Eucharist Convent Felician Sisters*
[]—*School Sisters of Notre Dame*—S.S.N.D.
[]—*Sisters of Mercy Convent*—R.S.M.
[]—*Sisters of Our Lady of the Most Holy Trinity*—S.O.L.T.
[]—*Sisters of St. John*
[]—*Ursuline Sisters*—O.S.U.

NECROLOGY

(No Deaths)

An asterisk (*) denotes an organization that has established tax-exempt status directly with the IRS and is not covered by the USCCB Group Ruling.

Diocese of Las Cruces

(Dioecesis Las Cruces)

Most Reverend

RICARDO RAMIREZ, C.S.B., D.D.

Bishop of Las Cruces; ordained December 10, 1966; appointed Titular Bishop of Vatarba and Auxiliary of San Antonio October 27, 1981; consecrated December 6, 1981; appointed First Bishop of Las Cruces August 31, 1982; installed October 18, 1982. *Res.: 5625 Spanish Pointe Rd., Las Cruces, NM 88007.*

The Pastoral Center: 1280 Med Park Dr., Las Cruces, NM 88005. Tel: 575-523-7577; Fax: 575-524-3874.

Web: www.dioceseoflascruces.org

Email: pastoralcenter@dioceseoflascruces.org

ESTABLISHED OCTOBER 18, 1982.

Square Miles 44,483.

Comprises the Counties of Dona Ana, Hidalgo, Grant, Luna, Sierra, Otero, Lincoln, Chaves, Eddy and Lea in the State of New Mexico.

For legal titles of parishes and diocesan institutions, consult The Pastoral Center.

STATISTICAL OVERVIEW

Personnel	
Bishop	1
Priests: Diocesan Active in Diocese	20
Priests: Retired, Sick or Absent	14
Number of Diocesan Priests	34
Religious Priests in Diocese	40
Total Priests in Diocese	74
Extern Priests in Diocese	8
Ordinations:	
Transitional Deacons	2
Permanent Deacons	7
Permanent Deacons in Diocese	46
Total Brothers	1
Total Sisters	45
Parishes	
Parishes	46
With Resident Pastor:	
Resident Diocesan Priests	21
Resident Religious Priests	15
Without Resident Pastor:	
Administered by Priests	8
Administered by Deacons	2
Missions	45
Pastoral Centers	1
Professional Ministry Personnel:	
Brothers	1
Sisters	2
Lay Ministers	25
Welfare	
Day Care Centers	1
Total Assisted	85
Educational	
Diocesan Students in Other Seminaries	8
Total Seminarians	8
High Schools, Private	2
Total Students	357
Elementary Schools, Private	3
Total Students	228
Catechesis/Religious Education:	
High School Students	2,556
Elementary Students	5,904
Total Students under Catholic Instruction	9,053
Teachers in the Diocese:	
Lay Teachers	41
Vital Statistics	
Receptions into the Church:	
Infant Baptism Totals	1,828
Minor Baptism Totals	274
Adult Baptism Totals	74
Received into Full Communion	246
First Communions	1,969
Confirmations	1,554
Marriages:	
Catholic	278
Interfaith	31
Total Marriages	309
Deaths	1,092
Total Catholic Population	132,646
Total Population	549,219

The Pastoral Center—1280 Med Park Dr., Las Cruces, 88005. Tel: 575-523-7577; Fax: 575-524-3874. Office Hours: Mon.-Fri. 8:00-12:00 & 1:00-5:00.

Bishops Administrative Council—Most Rev. RICARDO RAMÍREZ, C.S.B., D.D.; Deacon LOUIS A. ROMAN, Chancellor; Very Rev. Msgr. JOHN E. ANDERSON, V.G., P.A.; DEBBIE ISHAM MOORE; DAVID MCNAMARA; GRACE CASSETTA.

Vicar General—Very Rev. Msgr. JOHN E. ANDERSON, V.G., P.A.

Episcopal Vicar for Clergy and Personnel—Very Rev. Msgr. ROBERT L. GETZ, P.A. (Retired).

Chancellor—Deacon LOUIS A. ROMAN.

Vice Chancellor—DEBBIE ISHAM MOORE.

Director of Clergy Personnel—Very Rev. Msgr. JOHN E. ANDERSON, V.G., P.A.

Diocesan Tribunal—Rev. JOSE ROGELIO MARTINEZ, J.C.L., Judicial Vicar, 1280 Med Park Dr., Las Cruces, 88005.

Promoter of Justice—Rev. ENRIQUE LOPEZ.

Judges—Revs. GILES CARIE, O.F.M.Conv.; JOHN S. WEBER, J.C.L.; JOSE ROGELIO MARTINEZ, J.C.L.; IRENE VALLES.

Defenders of the Bond—Very Rev. Msgr. JOHN E. ANDERSON, V.G., P.A.; Revs. RICHARD CATANACH; MICHAEL P. LINDSAY.

Administrative Director for Tribunal—IRENE VALLES.

Assesor—NORMA SPINA, M.A.

Advocate—IRENE VALLES.

Notary—DOROTHY MEDINA.

Vicars—Revs. RICHARD CATANACH; JAMES JOSHE DUPLISSEY; VALENTINE M. JANKOWSKI, O.F.M.Conv.; ANDRES ALAVA, O.A.R.; CHARLIE MARTINEZ, O.F.M.; ALFRED GALVAN.

Diocesan Consultors—Most Rev. RICARDO RAMIREZ, C.S.B.; Very Rev. Msgrs. JOHN E. ANDERSON, V.G., P.A.; ROBERT L. GETZ, P.A. (Retired); Revs. MARTIN G. CORDERO; RAYMOND J. FLORES; ENRIQUE LOPEZ; JOSE ROGELIO MARTINEZ, J.C.L.; WILLIAM MCCANN; VALENTINE M. JANKOWSKI, O.F.M.Conv.; MARCOS REYNA.

Presbyteral Council—Very Rev. Msgr. JOHN E. ANDERSON, V.G., P.A.; Revs. JAMES JOSHE DUPLISSEY; MITCHELL DOWALGO, C.S.B.; CHARLIE MARTINEZ, O.F.M.; MICHAEL WILLIAMS; ELEAZAR PEREZ; MARTIN G. CORDERO; Deacon LOUIS A. ROMAN; Rev. JOSE ROGELIO MARTINEZ, J.C.L.; Deacon ROBERT BROTHERTON; Revs. RICHARD CATANACH; RICARDO BAUZA; RAYMOND J. FLORES; VALENTINE M. JANKOWSKI, O.F.M.Conv.; ANDRES ALAVA, O.A.R.; ALFRED GALVAN; JUAN CARLOS RAMIREZ; CYPRIAN ULINE, O.F.M.Conv.; Most Rev. RICARDO RAMIREZ, C.S.B.; Revs. ENRIQUE LOPEZ; WILLIAM MCCANN; PAUL BOTENHAGEN, O.F.M.

Clergy Personnel Board—Very Rev. Msgrs. JOHN E. ANDERSON, V.G., P.A.; ROBERT L. GETZ, P.A. (Retired); Most Rev. RICARDO RAMIREZ, C.S.B.; Revs. RICHARD CATANACH; WILLIAM MCCANN; MARCOS REYNA; MANUEL IBARRA; ENRIQUE LOPEZ; RAYMOND J. FLORES; Deacons LOUIS A. ROMAN; ROBERT BROTHERTON.

Priestly Life and Ministry Committee—Revs. RICHARD CATANACH, Chm.; MARCOS REYNA; PAUL BOTENHAGEN, O.F.M.; RAYMOND J. FLORES.

Priests Retirement Fund Committee—Very Rev. Msgr. ROBERT L. GETZ, P.A. (Retired); Revs. MICHAEL LINDSAY; WILLIAM MCCANN; Very Rev. Msgr. JOHN E. ANDERSON, V.G., P.A.; Rev. RICHARD CATANACH; Mr. DANIEL DOLAN.

Permanent Deacon Council—Deacons RICHARD RODRIGUEZ, Chm.; MARIANO MELENDREZ, Sec.; JESUS HERRERA; ROBERT BROTHERTON; EMILIO RAMOS; HOWARD HERRING.

Director of Deacon Formation—Rev. MICHAEL P. CERRETTO, C.S.B.; Deacon LOUIS A. ROMAN.

Director of Deacons—Deacon ROBERT BROTHERTON.

Comptroller—VACANT.

Human Resources—DEBBIE ISHAM MOORE, Dir.; PATRICIA RAMOS, HR Asst. & Office Mgr.

Finance Council—Most Rev. RICARDO RAMÍREZ, C.S.B., D.D.; Judge MANUEL SAUCEDO; Very Rev. Msgr. JOHN E. ANDERSON, V.G., P.A.; Deacon LOUIS A. ROMAN; Rev. WILLIAM MCCANN; DAN DOLAN, Diocesan Attorney; Rev. RICARDO BAUZA; TIM FLYNN; DAVID MCNAMARA; TOM MCCARTY; Rev. JOHN S. WEBER, J.C.L.; SUSAN ROBERTS; BILL QUINONES; CONNIE PRIETO; MARGARET FLORES; MICHAEL GRANO; RICK KOLL; ELOY ORTEGA.

Office of Development, Stewardship and Foundation—SUSAN ROBERTS, Exec. Dir.; CHRISTINA VILLEGAS, Devel. Assoc.

Office of Insurance—MARTA ROMERO, Insurance Dir.

Office of Buildings and Properties—MANUEL LEYVA, Dir.

Diocesan Ministries Offices and Directors

Office of Education and Formation—DAVID MCNAMARA, Dir.

Office of Adult Catechesis—DAVID MCNAMARA, Dir.

Office of Vocations—Revs. RICARDO BAUZA; RAYMOND J. FLORES.

Art and Environment Committee—JOANNA HASTON.

Attorneys—Mr. DANIEL DOLAN; MIKE LILLEY; DAVID MCNEILL; Mr. CARLOS MARTINEZ.

Campus Ministry—Rev. MITCHELL DOWALGO, C.S.B.

Judicial Vicar—Rev. JOSE ROGELIO MARTINEZ, J.C.L.

Cursillo Secretariat—VICTOR RODRIGUEZ, Pres.; BLANCA LUNA, Treas.; VICENTE LUNA, Sec.

Office of Elementary Catechesis—MARY HELEN LLANEZ, Dir.

Lay Ministry Formation—DAVID MCNAMARA, Dir.

Ecumenical Liaison—VACANT.

Hispanic Ministry—VACANT.

Holy Childhood Association—Very Rev. Msgr. JOHN E. ANDERSON, V.G., P.A.

Office of Liturgical Education—JOANNA HASTON.

Propagation of the Faith—Very Rev. Msgr. JOHN E. ANDERSON, V.G., P.A.

Order of Christian Initiation—DAVID MCNAMARA, Children; JOANNA HASTON; ROMELIA ENRIQUEZ; VENITA CHELGREN; SALLY HARPER.

Office of Adolescent Catechesis and Youth Ministry—GRACE CASSETTA, Dir.

Diocesan Pastoral Council—Most Rev. RICARDO RAMIREZ, C.S.B. Members: EZEQUIO NAVARETTE; LYNNE YBARRA; LUCIANO MONTES; Deacon DAVID MCNEIL; JESSE SANCHEZ, Chm.; Sr. ROBERT ANN HECKER, O.S.F.; Rev. BRIAN GUERRINI; JOHNNY ALDAZ; ANDY WEISS; JESSICA TRUJILLO; GARY MONTOYA; MARY SALAZAR-HIGHTOWER; LOUIS A. ROMAN, Chancellor; DEBBIE ISHAM MOORE, Sec.

Office of Pastoral Planning and Outreach—DEBBIE ISHAM MOORE.

Catholic Lending Library—DAVID MCNAMARA, Coord.

Diocesan Archives—Deacon LOUIS A. ROMAN, Archivist; DONNA VARGAS.

Charismatic Renewal Liaisons—Rev. MARTIN G. CORDERO; Mr. SAM TOME, (West); Mrs. ENEDINA TOME, (West).

Agua Viva—CHRISTINA ANCHONDO, Editor; DAVID MCNAMARA, Special Projects.

Agua Viva Editorial Advisory Board—Most Rev. RICARDO RAMIREZ, C.S.B.; CHRISTINA ANCHONDO; MANUEL LEYVA; DAVID MCNAMARA; MARY CARTER; Dr. WAYNE E. PRIBBLE; LINDA PRIBBLE; LOURDES RAMOS; CHRISTINA VILLEGAS; Rev. MICHAEL P. CERRETTO, C.S.B.; Deacon LOUIS A. ROMAN.

Office of Prison and Jail Ministry—Deacon EMILIO RAMOS.

Office of Marriage and Family Life—MARY HELEN LLANEZ, Coord.

Office of Catholic Schools—BEN TRUJILLO, Supt.

Pro-Life Coordinators—JOSEPH BEHNKE; ELIZABETH BEHNKE.

Victim Assistance Coordinators—Dr. WAYNE E. PRIBBLE. Tel: 575-653-4415. Email: sanpatricioretreat@gmail.com; Deacon LOUIS A. ROMAN. Tel: 575-523-7577. Email: lroman@dioceseoflascruces.org.

CLERGY, PARISHES, MISSIONS AND PAROCHIAL SCHOOLS

CITY OF LAS CRUCES

(DONA ANA COUNTY)

1—CATHEDRAL OF THE IMMACULATE HEART OF MARY (1953) Revs. William McCann, Rector; Rene Espejel, C.S.B., Parochial Vicar; Deacons Louis A. Roman; Edward Misquez; Robert Brotherton. In Res., Revs. Michael P. Cerretto, C.S.B.; Ed Heidt, C.S.B.
1240 S. Espina St., 88001. Tel: 575-524-8563; Fax: 575-523-2252.

2—ST. ALBERT THE GREAT NEWMAN PARISH (1986), Serving New Mexico State University. Rev. Mitchell G. Dowalgo, C.S.B.; Deacon David McNeill Jr.
Res.: 2615 S. Solano, 88001. Tel: 575-522-6202; Fax: 575-521-3453.

3—ST. GENEVIEVE (1859) [CEM] Rev. Ricardo Bauza. In Res., Rev. Juan Moreno.
Res.: 100 S. Espina, 88001. Tel: 575-524-9649; Fax: 575-524-3263.

4—HOLY CROSS (1970) Very Rev. Msgr. John E. Anderson; Deacons Paul Lederman, Pastoral Assoc.; Steve Apodaca, Pastoral Assoc.; Francisco Gurrola. In Res., Rev. Sergio Balderrama.
Office: 1327 N. Miranda St., 88005. Tel: 575-523-0167; Fax: 575-523-8023.

5—OUR LADY OF HEALTH (1956) Revs. Ricardo Hinojal, O.A.R.; Francisco Oviedo, O.A.R., Parochial Vicar.
Res.: 1178 N. Mesquite, 88001. Tel: 575-526-9545; Fax: 575-526-9545.
Catechesis/Religious Program—Sr. Marie-Paule Willem, F.M.M., D.R.E. Students 250.

6—SANTA ROSA DE LIMA (1982) Rev. Jesus Martinez de Esponceda, O.A.R.
Church: 5035 Holsome Rd., 88011. Tel: 575-382-8123; Fax: 575-382-5481. Email: santarosadelimachurch@yahoo.com.

OUTSIDE THE CITY OF LAS CRUCES

ALAMOGORDO, OTERO CO.

1—IMMACULATE CONCEPTION (1900) [CEM] Rev. Carlos Espinosa; Deacon Peter Schumacher; Bro. Bill Spirk, Pastoral Assoc.
Res.: 705 Delaware Ave., 88310. Tel: 575-437-3291; Fax: 575-437-3239.
Mission—Our Lady of the Desert, (Closed), Boles Acres, Otero Co.
Mission—Sacred Heart Cloudcroft, Otero Co. Tel: 575-682-2228.

2—ST. JUDE (1965) Revs. Wayne D. Herpin, S.J.; Thomas W. Hoffman, S.J., Parochial Vicar.
Office: 1404 College Ave., 88310-4860. Tel: 575-437-0238; Fax: 575-437-0267.

ANTHONY, DONA ANA CO., ST. ANTHONY'S (1899) [CEM] Revs. Andres Alava, O.A.R.; Juan Almarza, O.A.R., Parochial Vicar; Deacons Robert Diaz; Luis Padilla.
Church: 224 Lincoln St., P.O. Box 2624, 88021. Tel: 575-882-2239; Fax: 575-882-7343.
Convent—Hermanas Dominicas de la Doctrina Cristiana, 124 Tornillo, Chaparral, 88081. Tel: 575-824-0508.
Mission—Our Lady of Refuge 1320 Mercantil, La Union, Dona Ana Co. 88021. Tel: 505-589-0542. Deacon Jesse Sanchez, Admin.
Mission—Immaculate Conception San Benito Rd., P.O. Box 2624, Dona Ana Co. 88021.

ARTESIA, EDDY CO.

1—ST. ANTHONY (1905) Rev. Paul Murtagh, SS.CC.; Deacon Antonio Torrez.
Res.: 502 S. Ninth St., 88210. Tel: 575-746-4471; Fax: 575-748-1049.

2—OUR LADY OF GRACE (1942) Revs. Paul Murtagh, SS.CC.; Brian Guerrini, Parochial Vicar.
Res.: 709 N. Roselawn, 88210.
Church: 1111 N. Roselawn Ave., 88210. Tel: 575-748-1356; Fax: 575-748-1049.

BAYARD, GRANT CO., OUR LADY OF FATIMA (1950) Rev. Paulus Kao.
Church: 340 Mayo St., P.O. Box 1425, 88023. Tel: 575-537-2421.
Mission—St. Anthony c/o Our Lady of Fatima, P.O. Box 1425, 88023. Fierro, NM, Grant Co.
Mission—Holy Family P.O. Box 67, Hanover, Grant Co. 88043.
Mission—San Lorenzo-Black Range Station San Lorenzo, Grant Co. Tel: 575-313-4126.

CARLSBAD, EDDY CO.

1—ST. EDWARD (1893) Rev. Cyprian Uline, O.F.M.Conv. In Res., Rev. Regis Schladheck, O.F.M.Conv.; Deacon Antonio Dominguez.
Office:—209 N. Guadalupe St., 88220. Tel: 575-885-6600; Fax: 575-885-9992. Email: workingforjesus@saint-edward.net. Web: www.saint-edward.net.
Res.: 610 W. Stevens, 88220. Tel: 575-887-6486.

2—SAN JOSE (1902) Rev. Valentine M. Jankowski, O.F.M.Conv.; Deacon Melvin Balderrama.
Church: 1002 DeBaca, 88220. Tel: 575-885-5792; Fax: 575-887-3553.
Religious Education Center—Tel: 575-887-1346. Patsy Grantner, D.R.E.

CARRIZOZO, LINCOLN CO., ST. RITA (1850) [CEM] Rev. Anthony Basso, S.D.V., Admin.
Church: 213 Birch St., Box 727, 88301. Tel: 575-648-2853; Fax: 888-779-1103. Email: santaritachurch@yahoo.com.
Mission—Sacred Heart Capitan, Lincoln Co.
Mission—St. Therese of the Little Flower Corona, Lincoln Co.

CHAMBERINO, DONA ANA CO., SAN LUIS REY (1959) Rev. Robert Villegas, C.S.C.
Church: 206 S. San Luis Ave., P.O. Box 230, 88027. Tel: 575-882-2045.

CHAPARRAL, DONA ANA CO., ST. THOMAS MORE CHURCH (1977) Rev. Miguel Echeverria, O.A.R.; Deacon Roberto Mata.
112 Lisa Dr., PMB 119, 88081. Tel: 575-824-4433; Fax: 575-842-4433.

DEMING, LUNA CO.

1—ST. ANN'S (1918) Rev. Enrique Lopez.
Res.: 400 S. Ruby St., 88030. Tel: 575-546-3343; Fax: 575-546-3444.
Catechesis/Religious Program—Tel: 575-546-3905. Alexandra Vigil, D.R.E.; Kiley Giacomelli, Youth Min. Students 347.

2—HOLY FAMILY (1905) Rev. James Joshe Duplissey.
Res.: 612 S. Copper St., 88030-4114. Tel: 575-546-9783; Fax: 575-546-9815.
Catechesis/Religious Program—615 S. Copper St., 88030. Students 91.
Mission— P.O. Box 1498, Columbus, Luna Co. Tel: 575-531-2373; Fax: 575-546-8192.

DEXTER, CHAVEZ CO., IMMACULATE CONCEPTION (1953) Deacon Jesus Herrera, Admin.
Church: 400 W. Sixth St., P.O. Box 189, 88230. Tel: 575-734-5478.
Mission—Our Lady of Guadalupe 204 Broadway, Lake Arthur, Chavez Co. 88253.
Mission—St. Catherine 200 S. Texas, Hagerman, Chavez Co. 88232.

DONA ANA, DONA ANA CO., OUR LADY OF THE PURIFICATION (1860) [JC] Rev. Miguel Macaya.
Mailing Address: 5525 Cristo Rey, P.O. Box 706, 88032. Tel: 575-526-2114. In Res., Deacon Rigoberto Chavez.
Mission—San Isidro San Isidro, Dona Ana Co.

GARFIELD, DONA ANA CO., SAN ISIDRO (1945) [CEM] Rev. Martin Cornejo, O.F.M.
Res.: 2003 Loma Parda, HC 31, Box 43, 87936-9701. Tel: 575-267-5111; Fax: 575-267-1887.
Mission—San Jose Arrey, Sierra Co.
Mission—Our Lady of Guadalupe Hillsboro, Sierra Co.

HATCH, DONA ANA CO., OUR LORD OF MERCY (1889) Rev. Raymond J. Flores.
Church: 117 Hartman St., Box 321, 87937. Tel: 575-267-4983; Fax: 575-267-4299.
Mission—Our Lady of All Nations 1992 Rincon Rd., Rincon, Dona Ana Co.

HOBBS, LEA CO.

1—ST. HELENA (1951) Rev. Juan Carlos Ramirez, Admin.
Office: 100 E. Bender Blvd., 88240. Tel: 575-392-7551; 575-392-7552; Fax: 575-392-3333.

2—OUR LADY OF GUADALUPE (1981) Rev. Ruben Romero, Admin.; Deacon Samuel Navarrette.
Office: 914 S. Selman, 88240. Tel: 575-393-4991; Fax: 575-397-1480.

HURLEY, GRANT CO., INFANT JESUS (1916) Revs. Paulus Kao; Roberto Barreto, Parochial Vicar.
Church: 204 Cortez St., Box 97, 88043. Tel: 575-537-3691; Fax: 575-537-3514.
Mission—San Juan San Juan, Grant Co.
Mission—San Jose Faywood, Luna Co.

JAL, LEA CO., ST. CECILIA (1941) Rev. Martin G. Cordero.
Res.: 300 W. Merryman St., P.O. Box 430, 88252. Tel: 575-395-2431; Fax: 575-395-2238.
Mission—St. Clare 3000 N. Main St., Eunice, 88252. Tel: 575-392-2198.

LA LUZ, OTERO CO.

1—OUR LADY OF THE LIGHT, P.O. Box 236, 88337. Tel: 575-434-9460.

LA MESA, DONA ANA CO., SAN JOSE, [JC] Rev. Jose Rogelio Martinez; Deacons Tom Baca; Leopoldo Moreno.
Church: 353 Josephine St., P.O. Box 278, 88044. Tel: 575-233-3191; Fax: 575-233-2204.
Mission—San Pedro (Del Cerro) P.O. Box 278, Dona Ana Co. 88044.

LORDSBURG, HIDALGO CO., ST. JOSEPH (1900) Rev. John S. Weber.
Res.: 416 E. Second St., 88045. Tel: 575-542-3268.
Mission—St. Jude Cotton City, Hidalgo Co.
Mission—San Felipe de Neri Rodeo, Hidalgo Co.

LOVING, EDDY CO., OUR LADY OF GRACE (1937) Rev. Valentine M. Jankowski, O.F.M.Conv.
Office: 301 4th St., P.O. Box 428, 88256. Tel: 575-745-3341.
Res.: 610 W. Stevens, Carlsbad, 88220. Tel: 575-887-6486.
Mission—Cristo Rey P.O. Box 69, Malaga, Eddy Co. 88263.

LOVINGTON, LEA CO., ST. THOMAS AQUINAS (1919) Rev. Manuel Ibarra.
Res.: 1301 N. Ninth St., 88260. Tel: 575-396-4206; Fax: 575-396-4116.
Mission—Our Lady of the Holy Rosary Tatum, Lea Co.

MESCALERO, OTERO CO., ST. JOSEPH (1895), (Native American), Rev. Paul Botenhagen, O.F.M.; Sr. Robert Ann Hecker, O.S.F.
Res.: Box 187, 88340. Tel: 575-464-4473; Fax: 575-464-1511.
Mission—Our Lady of Guadalupe Hwy. 70, Bent, Otero Co. 88340.
Mission—St. Patrick Three Rivers, Otero Co.

MESILLA PARK, DONA ANA CO., SHRINE AND PARISH OF OUR LADY OF GUADALUPE Rev. Vincent Petersen, O.F.M.Conv.
Church: 3600 Parroquia St., Box 298, 88047. Tel: 575-526-8171; Fax: 575-523-1175.

MESILLA, DONA ANA CO., BASILICA OF SAN ALBINO (1852) [CEM] Rev. Richard Catanach.
Church: 2280 Calle Principal, P.O. Box 26, 88046. Tel: 575-526-9349; Fax: 575-647-1619.
Mission—San Jose Mission P.O. Box 502, Fairacres, Dona Ana Co. 88033. Tel: 505-647-1979. Deacon Daniel Check, Admin.

ROSWELL, CHAVES CO.

1—ASSUMPTION OF THE BLESSED VIRGIN MARY (1963) Rev. Joseph Pacquing, Admin.; Deacon Christopher Gutierrez.
Res.: 2808 N. Kentucky, 88201. Tel: 575-622-9895; Fax: 575-622-6845.

2—ST. JOHN THE BAPTIST (1903), (Hispanic), Rev. Juan Antonio Enrique Gutierrez, O.F.M.; Deacons Louis Romero; Enrique Salas; Ernesto Martinez.
Res.: 510 S. Lincoln, 88203. Tel: 575-622-3531; Fax: 575-623-8933.

3—ST. PETER (1903) Rev. Charlie Martinez, O.F.M.; Deacons Howard Herring, Pastoral Assoc.; Frank Pitman.
Church: 111 E. Deming, 88203. Tel: 575-622-5092; Fax: 575-623-9228.

RUIDOSO, LINCOLN CO., ST. ELEANOR (1939) Rev. Alfred Galvan; Deacon Robert G. Racicot.
Res.: 207 Junction Rd., P.O. Box 8300, 88345. Tel: 575-257-2330; Fax: 575-257-7062.
Mission—St. Jude Thaddeus [CEM] San Patricio,

Lincoln Co.
Mission—San Juan Lincoln, Lincoln Co.
Mission—Sacred Heart Fort Stanton, Lincoln Co.
Mission—St. Joseph Picacho, Lincoln Co.
Mission—San Ysidro Glencoe, Lincoln Co.

SAN MIGUEL, DONA ANA CO., SAN MIGUEL (1927) Deacon Emilio Ramos.
Res.: Drawer E, 88058. Tel: 575-233-2453; Fax: 575-233-2453.
Mission—Our Lady of Perpetual Help P.O. Box 48, Mesquite, Dona Ana Co. 88048. Tel: 575-233-4695.

SANTA CLARA, GRANT CO., SANTA CLARA (1888) Rev. Robert L. Becerra; Deacon Richard Rodriguez.
Church: 207 S. Bayard, P.O. Box 215, 88026. Tel: 575-537-3713; Fax: 575-537-3517.

SILVER CITY, GRANT CO.
1—ST. FRANCIS NEWMAN CENTER PARISH (1964), Serving Western New Mexico University. Rev. Michael Williams.
Res.: 914 W. 13th St., 88061. Tel: 575-538-3662; Fax: 575-534-1059.
2—ST. VINCENT DE PAUL (1874) Rev. Roderick Nichols; Deacons William Holguin; Johnnie Perez; Jeremiah Bustillos; Joseph Arellano.
Res.: 414 Bayard St., P.O. Box 1189, 88062. Tel: 575-538-9373; Fax: 575-388-0870.
Mission—St. Isidore Gila, Grant Co.
Mission—Holy Cross Pinos Altos, Grant Co.
Parish Retreat Center: *St. Mary Theotokos Retreat Center*, 5202 Hwy. 152, 88062. Tel: 575-537-4839.

SUNLAND PARK, DONA ANA CO., ST. MARTIN DE PORRES (1964) Rev. Eleazar Perez Rodriguez, Admin.; Deacons Jesus Favela; Rogelio Montes.
Res.: 1885 McNutt Rd., 88063. Tel: 575-589-2106.
Mission—Santa Teresa de Avila Santa Teresa, Dona Ana Co.

TRUTH OR CONSEQUENCES, SIERRA CO., OUR LADY OF PERPETUAL HELP (1916) Revs. Marcos Reyna; Donald F. Hyatt, C.S.B., Parochial Vicar; Deacon Adam L. Sanchez.
Res.: 103 E. Sixth Ave., 87901. Tel: 575-894-7804; Fax: 575-894-0451.
Mission—St. Jose Cuchillo, Sierra Co.
Mission—San Ysidro Las Palomas, Sierra Co.
Mission—St. Ignatius Montecello, Sierra Co.
Mission—San Lorenzo Placitas, Sierra Co.
Chapel—St. Gregory, Chapels Chiz
Chapel—San Miguel, Rancho de San Miguel
Station—St. Jude Winston.

TULAROSA, OTERO CO., ST. FRANCIS DE PAULA (1868) [CEM] [JC] Rev. Maximilian J. Hottle, O.F.M.; Deacon Mariano Melendrez. In Res., Revs. Peter A. Verheggen, O.F.M.; Clifford Herle, O.F.M.
Res.: 303 Encino, 88352. Tel: 575-585-2793; Fax: 575-585-3005.
Mission—Santo Nino

Absent On Leave:
Revs.—
Amezaga, Louis
Beggane, Thomas
Fountain, Dennis
Herrera, Edward
Montoya, Juan Camilo
Valdez, Jose Pedro

On Leave for Military:
Rev.—
Nguyen, Gan, C.Ss.R., Sierra Chapel, WSMR, NM

Retired:
Very Rev. Msgr.—
Getz, Robert L., P.A.
Revs.—
Bergs, David
Burke, Ronald
Clark, Anthony
Colgan, John
Reitmeyer, Larry

Permanent Deacons:
Albin, Richard, Holy Cross, Las Cruces
Apodaca, Steve, Holy Cross, Las Cruces
Arellano, Joseph, St. Vincent de Paul, Silver City
Baca, Tom, San Jose, La Mesa
Balderrama, Mel L., San Jose, Carlsbad
Brotherton, Bob, IHM, Las Cruces; Dir. of Permanent Deacons
Bustillos, Jeramiah Gomes, St. Vincent de Paul, Silver City
Castanon, David M., Santa Clara, Santa Clara
Chavez, Rigoberto, Our Lady of Purification, Dona Ana
Check, Daniel, Admin., St. Joseph, Fairacres
Diaz, Robert, St. Anthony, Anthony
Dickman, Donald, Our Lady of the Light, La Luz
Dominguez, Antonio, St. Edward, Carlsbad
Favela, Jesus, San Martin de Porres, Sunland Park
Gurrola, Francisco, Holy Cross, Las Cruces
Gutierrez, Christopher, Assumption of the Blessed Virgin Mary, Roswell
Herrera, Jesus, Immaculate Conception, Dexter
Herring, Howard, St. Peter, Roswell
Holguin, William, St. Vincent de Paul, Silver City
Lederman, Paul, Holy Cross, Las Cruces
Martinez, Ernesto, St. John the Baptist, Roswell
Mata, Roberto, St. Thomas More, Chaparral
McNeill, David, Jr., Albert the Great Newman Center, Las Cruces
Melendrez, Mariano C., St. Francis de Paula, Tularosa
Merjil, Pablo, Our Lady of Grace, Artesia
Miller, Jerry Our Lady of Fatima, Bayard
Misquez, Edward, IHM, Las Cruces
Montes, Rogelio, San Martin de Porres, Sunland Park
Moreno, Leopoldo, San Jose, La Mesa
Narvaez, Arthur, (Retired)
Navarrette, Sam, Our Lady of Guadalupe, Hobbs
Padilla, Luis, St. Anthony, Anthony
Pena, Daniel S., St. Ann, Deming
Perez, Johnnie, (Retired)
Pitman, Frank, St. Peter, Roswell
Racicot, Robert G., St. Eleanor, Ruidoso
Ramos, Emilio, Admin., San Miguel, San Miguel; Dir., Prison & Jail Ministry
Rodriguez, Richard Alires, Santa Clara, Santa Clara
Roman, Louis A., IHM, Las Cruces; Chancellor & Co-Dir., Deacon Formation
Romero, Louis, St. John the Baptist, Roswell
Sanchez, Adam L., Our Lady of Perpetual Help, Truth or Consequences
Sanchez, Jesse, Our Lady of Refuge, La Union
Schretlen, Frank, (Retired)
Schumacher, Peter, Immaculate Conception, Alamogordo
Shuster, John, St. Joseph, Mescalero
Torrez, Antonio, St. Anthony, Artesia

INSTITUTIONS LOCATED IN THE DIOCESE

[A] ELEMENTARY SCHOOLS, PRIVATE

LAS CRUCES. *Las Cruces Catholic School*, (Grades PreK-12), 1331 N. Miranda, 88005. Tel: 575-526-2517; Fax: 575-524-0544. Web: www.lascrucescatholicschool.org. Connie Limon, Prin.; Catherine Cisneros, Librarian. Lay Teachers 30; Students 265.

ALAMOGORDO. *Fr. James B. Hay, Inc.* (1956) (Grades PreK-9), 1000 E. Eighth St., 88310. Tel: 575-437-7821; Fax: 575-443-6129. Email: jbhay@tularosa.net. Web: www.fatherhay.org. Mr. Wallace Moore, Admin.; Diolanda Moore, Librarian; Maria Quade, Sec. Lay Teachers 9; Students 92.

CARLSBAD. *St. Edward School, Inc.*, (Grades PreK-6), 805 Walter, 88220. Tel: 575-885-4620; Fax: 575-885-7706. Jack Litschke, Prin.; Janice Parrott, Librarian. Lay Teachers 7; Students 90.

HOBBS. *St. Helena School of Hobbs, Inc.*, (Grades PreK-6), 105 E. St. Anne St., 88240. Tel: 575-392-5405; Fax: 575-392-0128. Mrs. Sheila Fuentes, Prin.; Ernestina Harmston, Librarian. Lay Teachers 7; Students 71.

ROSWELL. *All Saints Catholic School*, (Grades PreK-8), 2700 N. Kentucky, 88201. Tel: 575-627-5744; Fax: 575-622-6845. Email: principal@allsaintsschool.us. Web: www.allsaintsschool.us. Sonia Raftery, Prin.; Rosella Romero, Librarian. Lay Teachers 9; Students 77.

[B] MONASTERIES & RESIDENCES OF PRIESTS AND BROTHERS

LAS CRUCES. *Basilian Fathers*, 1682 Alta Vista Pl., 88011. Tel: 575-521-4269. Web: www.basilian.org. Revs. Sean M. Garrity, C.S.B., Supr. (Sabbatical); Ed Heidt, C.S.B., 1st Councilor; Michael P. Cerretto, C.S.B., Supr.; Mitchell G. Dowalgo, C.S.B.; Rene Espejel, C.S.B.; Donald F. Hyatt, C.S.B.; David O. Klein, C.S.B.; David L. Sharp, C.S.B.

MESILLA. *Augustinian Recollect Fathers* Province of St. Nicholas of Tolentine, Provincial Delegation in the South of U.S.A., *San Alypius House*, P.O. Box 310, 88046. Tel: 575-523-7030. Revs. Ricardo Hinojal, O.A.R.; Jesus Martinez de Esproncеda, O.A.R., Supr. San Alypius House; Antonio Martinez, O.A.R.; Francisco Oviedo, O.A.R.

[C] CONVENTS AND RESIDENCES FOR SISTERS

LAS CRUCES. *Franciscan Missionaries of Mary*, 2119 Laredo Ave., 88011. Tel: 575-523-9083.

CHAPARRAL. *Dominicas De La Doctrina Cristiana*, 124 Tornillo, 88081. Tel: 575-824-0508. Professed 5; Novices 2.
Religious of the Assumption (2001) 300-2 McCombs Rd., PMB #43, 88081. Tel: 575-824-2850. Email: rachaparral@juno.com. Sr. Maria Isabel Galbe Sada, R.A., Contact Person, Supr.

DEMING. *Daughters of the Heart of Mary*, P.O. Box 1531, 88030. Tel: 575-546-7599. Email: nazhouse@swnm.com.

ROSWELL. *The Community of Poor Clares of New Mexico, Inc.* (1948) 809 E. 19th St., 88201. Tel: 575-622-0868; Fax: 575-627-2184. Web: www.poorclaresroswell.com. Sisters Angela Kelly, P.C.C., Abbess; Mary Jeannine, P.C.C., Vicaress. Professed Nuns 21.

SILVER CITY. *Sisters of St. Joseph*, St. Mary's Center, 1801 N. Alabama, 88061. Tel: 575-538-3350. Email: rkfarrell@q.com.

[D] RETREAT CENTERS

MESILLA PARK. *Holy Cross Retreat and Friary*, 600 Holy Cross Rd., 88047. Tel: 575-524-3688; Fax: 575-524-3811. Email: director@holycrossretreat.org. Web: www.holycrossretreat.org. Rev. Thomas A. Smith, O.F.M.Conv., Dir.

SAN PATRICIO. *San Patricio Retreat Center*, 119 La Mancha, P.O. Box 102, 88348. Tel: 575-653-4415. Email: sanpatricioretreat@gmail.com. Web: www.sanpatricioretreat.org. Dr. Wayne E. Pribble, Dir.; Linda Pribble, Dir.

[E] MISCELLANEOUS

LAS CRUCES. *Catholic Charities of the Diocese of Las Cruces, Inc.*, 1280 Med Park Dr., 88005. Tel: 575-523-7577; Fax: 575-524-3874.
Catholic Diocese of Las Cruces Foundation, Inc., 1280 Med Park Dr., 88005. Tel: 575-523-7577; Fax: 575-524-3874. Email: cvillegas@dioceseoflascruces.org. Web: dioceseoflascruces.org. Susan Roberts, Exec. Dir.
**Order of Secular Discalced Carmelites* (1989) 6100 Robledo Rd., 88012-9566. Tel: 575-382-3795. Email: annunez@zianet.com. Carolyn Nunez, Pres.; Therese Mastrantuono, Contact Person.
Our Lady of Guadalupe Prayer Center, Inc., 5480 Lassiter Rd., 88001. Tel: 575-647-1117. Email: olgprayerctr@gmail.com. Web: olgpclascruces.blogspot.com. P.O. Box 1135, Mesilla Park, 88047.
The Priests' Retirement Plan of the Catholic Diocese of Las Cruces, Inc., 1280 Med Park Dr., 88005. Tel: 575-523-7577; Fax: 575-524-3874.
Secular Institute of Missionaries of the Kingship of Christ, 1012 Ivydale Dr., Apt. A, 88005-1260.

ALAMOGORDO. *Shroud Exhibit and Museum, Inc.*, 3199 N. White Sands Blvd., Ste. D-1, 88310. Tel: 575-446-2113. Web: shroudNM.com.

CARLSBAD. *San Jose Child Care Inc.*, 421 W. Fox St., 88220.

CLOUDCROFT. **Mount Subasio Hermitage* (1997) P.O. Box 845, 88317. Tel: 651-216-0558. Email: mtsubasio@yahoo.com. Ms. Helen Riegger, Dir. & Trustee.

MESILLA. *Magnificat-Our Lady of the Cross Chapter, Inc.*, P.O. Box 1387, 88046. Tel: 575-541-1625. Olivia McDonald, Chapter Coord.; Isabel L. Gallegos, Sec. & Treas.

RELIGIOUS INSTITUTES OF MEN REPRESENTED IN THE DIOCESE

For further details refer to the corresponding bracketed number in the Religious Institutes of Men or Women section.

[0170]—*Basilian Fathers*—C.S.B.
[1140]—*Congregation of the Sacred Hearts of Jesus and Mary*—SS.CC.
[0480]—*Conventual Franciscans* (Our Lady of Guadalupe Custody)—O.F.M.Conv
[0520]—*Franciscan Friars* (St. John the Baptist, Our Lady of Guadalupe, St. Barbara Provs.)—O.F.M.
[0690]—*Jesuit Fathers and Brothers* (New Orleans, Wisconsin Provs.)—S.J.
[0150]—*Order of the Augustinian Recollects*—O.A.R.
[0610]—*Priests of the Congregation of Holy Cross* (Southwest Prov.)—C.S.C.
[]—*U.S. Vocationist Fathers*—S.D.V.

RELIGIOUS INSTITUTES OF WOMEN REPRESENTED IN THE DIOCESE

[0810]—*Daughters of the Heart of Mary*—D.H.M.
[]—*Discalced Carmelites*
[1110]—*Dominican Sisters of Our Lady of the Rosary and of Saint Catherine of Siena, Cabra*—O.P.
[1070]—*Dominicas de la Doctrina Cristiana*—O.P.
[]—*ECCE Franciscan Sisters*

[1370]—*The Franciscan Missionaries of Mary*—F.M.M.
[]—*Franciscan Sisters*
[1430]—*Franciscan Sisters of Our Lady of Perpetual Help*—O.S.F.
[]—*Los Consagrados, dba Mission Helpers of the Holy Savior*
[2490]—*Medical Mission Sisters*—M.M.S.
[3760]—*Poor Clares Monastery of Our Lady of Guadalupe*—P.C.C.
[]—*Religious of the Assumption*—R.A.
[]—*Sisters of Loretto*—S.L.
[2575]—*Sisters of Mercy of the Americas* (Omaha, Vermont, Cincinnati, New Jersey)—R.S.M.
[3830-15]—*Sisters of St. Joseph*—C.S.J.
[]—*Sisters of the Sacred Hearts of Jesus and Mary*—SS.CC.
[4100]—*Sisters of the Sorrowful Mother*—S.S.M.

NECROLOGY

† Lafrenz, James, (Retired)—Died Aug. 24, 2011

An asterisk (*) denotes an organization that has established tax-exempt status directly with the IRS and is not covered by the USCCB Group Ruling.

Diocese of Las Vegas

(Dioecesis Campensis)

Most Reverend

JOSEPH A. PEPE

Bishop of Las Vegas; ordained May 16, 1970; appointed Bishop of Las Vegas April 6, 2001; ordained and installed May 31, 2001. *Mailing Address: P.O. Box 18316, Las Vegas, NV 89114-8316*. Tel: 702-735-3500; Fax: 702-735-8941.

Catholic Center: 336 Cathedral Way, Las Vegas, NV 89109. Mailing Address: P.O. Box 18316, Las Vegas, NV 89114-8316. Tel: 702-735-3500; Fax: 702-735-8941.

Square Miles 39,688.

Erected by His Holiness Pope Pius XI March 27, 1931.

Redesignated Diocese of Reno-Las Vegas by Pope Paul VI, October 13, 1976.

Redesignated Diocese of Las Vegas by His Holiness Pope John Paul II March 21, 1995.

For legal titles of parishes and diocesan institutions, consult the Chancery Office.

STATISTICAL OVERVIEW

Personnel	
Bishop	1
Priests: Diocesan Active in Diocese	19
Priests: Diocesan Active Outside Diocese	3
Priests: Retired, Sick or Absent	15
Number of Diocesan Priests	37
Religious Priests in Diocese	18
Total Priests in Diocese	55
Extern Priests in Diocese	34
Ordinations:	
Transitional Deacons	1
Permanent Deacons	19
Permanent Deacons in Diocese	32
Total Brothers	3
Parishes	
Parishes	29
With Resident Pastor:	
Resident Diocesan Priests	9
Resident Religious Priests	2
Without Resident Pastor:	
Administered by Priests	18
Missions	6
Professional Ministry Personnel:	
Brothers	1
Lay Ministers	28
Welfare	
Special Centers for Social Services	21
Total Assisted	7,500,000
Other Institutions	1
Total Assisted	4,587
Educational	
Diocesan Students in Other Seminaries	7
Total Seminarians	7
High Schools, Diocesan and Parish	1
Total Students	1,268
Elementary Schools, Diocesan and Parish	7
Total Students	2,704
Catechesis/Religious Education:	
High School Students	3,274
Elementary Students	9,775
Total Students under Catholic Instruction	17,028
Teachers in the Diocese:	
Priests	1
Lay Teachers	229
Vital Statistics	
Receptions into the Church:	
Infant Baptism Totals	5,967
Minor Baptism Totals	765
Adult Baptism Totals	168
Received into Full Communion	312
First Communions	4,177
Confirmations	1,664
Marriages:	
Catholic	436
Interfaith	129
Total Marriages	565
Deaths	948
Total Catholic Population	643,900
Total Population	1,951,000

Former Bishop—Most Rev. DANIEL F. WALSH, D.D., ord. March 30, 1963; appt. Titular Bishop of Tigia and Auxiliary of San Francisco Sept. 24, 1981; appt. Bishop of Reno-Las Vegas June 9, 1987; installed Aug. 6, 1987; appt. Bishop of Las Vegas March 21, 1995; installed July 28, 1995; appt. Bishop of Santa Rosa in California, April 11, 2000; installed May 22, 2000.

Catholic Center—336 Cathedral Way, Las Vegas, 89109. Tel: 702-735-3500; Fax: 702-735-8941. Web: www.lasvegas-diocese.org. *Mailing Address: P.O. Box 18316, Las Vegas, 89114-8316*. Office Hours: Mon.-Fri. 8-12 & 1-4.

Chancellor and Moderator of the Curia—Very Rev. ROBERT STOECKIG, V.G. Tel: 702-697-3903; Fax: 702-735-8941.

Vicar General—Very Rev. ROBERT STOECKIG, V.G. Tel: 702-697-3903; Fax: 702-735-8941.

Diocesan Tribunal Office-Judicial Vicar—Rt. Rev. Archimandrite FRANCIS M. VIVONA, S.T.M., J.C.L. Tel: 702-735-1210; Fax: 702-735-5146.

Notary-Secretary—Mrs. PAM MORLEY, A.A.

Promoter of Justice—Rev. THOMAS J. FRANSISCUS, C.SS.R., J.C.L.

Defender of the Bond—Rev. KURT BURNETTE, J.C.D.

Diocesan Judges—Revs. THOMAS J. FRANSISCUS, C.SS.R., J.C.L.; THOMAS F. DONOVAN, J.C.D.; Very Rev. LANGES J. SILVA, J.C.D.; Revs. KURT BURNETTE, J.C.D.; DAVID H. SCHUYLER, S.M., J.C.D.

Diocesan Advocates—Mr. ROBERT HANDCOX, J.D.; Mrs. PAM MORLEY, A.A.; Revs. THOMAS J. FRANSISCUS, C.SS.R., J.C.L.; MARK GOMORI; Mr. SAM MARTINEZ; Mrs. MARGARITA HERNANDEZ; Rev. JOHN T. ASSALONE, M.Div.; Deacon JACOB FAVELLA.

Presbyteral Council for the Diocese of Las Vegas—Rt. Rev. Archimandrite FRANCIS M. VIVONA, S.T.M., J.C.L., Ex Officio; Very Revs. ROBERT STOECKIG, V.G.; PATRICK W. RENDER, C.S.V., V.F., Ex Officio; Rev. RON ZANONI, V.F., Ex Officio; Rev. Msgr. PATRICK LEARY; Revs. WILLIAM F. HAESAERT, C.S.V.; JOHN T. ASSALONE, M.Div.; ROBERT W. PUHLMAN; DAVID E. CASALEGGIO; GERALD GRUPCZYNSKI, S.Ch.; GUSTAVO CRUZ; JAMES JANKOWSKI, O.F.M.Cap.

Diocesan Offices and Directors

Building Committee—Revs. RON ZANONI, V.F.; STEVEN R. HOFFER; Bro. JOHN J. DODD, C.S.V.; GIA NGUYEN; HARRY SHULL.

Catholic Charities of Southern Nevada—

CEO—Rev. Msgr. PATRICK LEARY, 1501 Las Vegas Blvd. N., Las Vegas, 89101. Tel: 702-385-2662.

Chief Financial Officer—Bro. JOHN J. DODD, C.S.V. Tel: 702-735-7865.

Director of Clergy Education—Very Rev. ROBERT STOECKIG, V.G.

St. Thomas Aquinas Catholic Newman Community at UNLV—Rev. ALBERT FELICE-PACE, O.P., Dir. & Campus Minister, 4765 Brussels St., Las Vegas, 89119. Tel: 702-736-0887; Fax: 702-891-0615. Email: info@unlvnewman.com. Web: newman.unlv.edu.

Human Resources Department—Tel: 702-735-4570. JUDITH KOHL, Esq.

Legal Department—Tel: 702-735-2512. JUDITH KOHL, Esq., Gen. Counsel.

Department of Faith & Ministry Formation

Director for Faith and Ministry Formation—MARC GONZALEZ, D.Min. Tel: 702-735-6044.

Coordinator for Catholic Campaign for Human Development, Catholic Relief Services, Respect Life—Deacon TIM O'CALLAGHAN, Dir. Social Justice, Mailing Address: P.O. Box 18316, Las Vegas, 89114-8316. Tel: 702-293-7500. Email: lvsocialaction@gmail.com.

Home and Foreign Missions—Very Rev. ROBERT STOECKIG, V.G. Tel: 702-697-3903.

Hospital Apostolate—Revs. REY SALDITOS. Tel: 702-870-2767; VICENTE PANALIGAN. Tel: 702-870-2767.

Information, Communications and Media—Very Rev. ROBERT STOECKIG, V.G. Tel: 702-697-3903; Deacon TIM O'CALLAGHAN. Tel: 702-293-7500.

Italian Catholic Federation—Rev. SAMUEL J. FALBO.

Native American and Colored People Commission—Very Rev. ROBERT STOECKIG, V.G.

Pontifical Association of the Holy Childhood—VACANT.

Propagation of the Faith—Very Rev. TIMOTHY WEHN, V.E. Tel: 702-697-3903.

Priests' Pension Board—Bro. JOHN J. DODD, C.S.V.; Very Rev. ROBERT STOECKIG, V.G.; Revs. ROBERT W. PUHLMAN; GUSTAVO CRUZ; MANUEL QUINTERO; Very Rev. TIMOTHY WEHN, V.E.

Property Management—Bro. JOHN J. DODD, C.S.V.

Vocations—Rev. MUGAGGA LULE, Dir.

Respect Life Liaison—Mrs. KATHLEEN MILLER, 3510 Leor Ct., Las Vegas, 89121. Tel: 702-212-6472; 702-737-1672.

Natural Family Planning/Fertility Care—MICKEY BACHMAN, R.N., C.N.F.P.P. Tel: 702-616-7550.

Diocesan Finance Committee Members—PATRICIA MULROY; LEO FALKENSAMMER; CHUCK KERZETSKI; TED ATENCIO; ED SKONICKI; JELINDO TIBERTI.

Diocesan Loan Committee—PAT MULROY; RANDY GARCIA; ARTHUR DEJOYA; ED SKONICKI.

Catholic Charities of Southern Nevada—Board of Trustees: Most Rev. JOSEPH ANTHONY PEPE, D.D., J.C.D.; Rev. Msgr. PATRICK LEARY, Exec. Dir. Catholic Charities, 1501 Las Vegas Blvd. N., Las Vegas, 89101. Tel: 702-385-2662; Very Rev. ROBERT STOECKIG, V.G.; PATRICIA MORRISEY, Pres.; TERESSA CONLEY; KEVIN J. HIGGINS; TERRI JANISON; Rev. MARC C. HOWES; T. J. MATTHEWS; VICTORIA FOUCE-OTTER; TOM MCCORMICK; LARRY BROWN; JILL BLANCHETTE; FRANK GARGANO; JOHN PAGE; SHAUNDELL NEWSOME; JOHN D. SELI; JENNIFER LOGAN.

Victim Advocate & Safe Environment Coordinator—Mr. RONALD VALLANCE. Tel: 702-235-7723.

Archivist—ARGIA KOPA. Tel: 702-697-5918.

CLERGY, PARISHES, MISSIONS AND PAROCHIAL SCHOOLS

CITY OF LAS VEGAS

(CLARK COUNTY)

1—GUARDIAN ANGEL CATHEDRAL (1963) Very Rev. Timothy Wehn, Rector; Deacon Patrick Cater.
Office: 336 Cathedral Way, 89109. Tel: 702-735-5241; Fax: 702-734-7086.
Rectory—

2—ST. ANNE (1948) Revs. David E. Casaleggio; Gregorio Leon.
Office & Res.: 1901 S. Maryland Pkwy., 89104. Tel: 702-735-0510; Fax: 702-735-5582.
School—(Grades PreK-8), 1813 S. Maryland Pkwy., 89104. Tel: 702-735-2586; Fax: 702-735-8357. Mrs. Elizabeth Flanagan, Prin.; Rick Valois, Librarian. Lay Teachers 11; Students 280.
Catechesis/Religious Program—Tel: 702-866-0008; Fax: 702-866-0006. Students 1,485.

3—ST. ANTHONY OF PADUA (2006) Revs. Samuel J. Falbo, Admin.; Richard Philiposki, S.Ch., Parochial Vicar.
4275 N. Rancho Dr., Ste. 120/125, 89130.
Rectory—5605 Rainbow Springs, 89149. Tel: 702-399-6897; Fax: 702-645-9975. Email: stanthony@saplv.org.
Catechesis/Religious Program—Robin Vitiello, D.R.E. Students 380.

4—ST. BRIDGET ROMAN CATHOLIC CHURCH (1945) Rev. Jesse Cortes, Admin.
Office: 220 N. 14th St., 89101-4312. Tel: 702-384-3382; Fax: 702-382-9467. Email: sbcclv@earthlink.net. Web: sbcclv.e-paluch.com.
Res.: 215 N. 14th St., 89101. Tel: 702-489-2877.
Catechesis/Religious Program—Students 307.

5—CHRIST THE KING (1978) Rev. William J.M. Kenny; Deacons Jacob Favela; Richard Green; Richard Minch.
Mailing Address: 4925 S. Torrey Pines, 89118. Tel: 702-871-1904; Fax: 702-251-4935.
Catechesis/Religious Program—Tel: 702-871-1904, Ext. 230. Beth Thompson, D.R.E. Students 549.
Mission—St. Catherine of Siena Jean. P.O. Box 19789, Sandy Valley, Clark Co. 89019. Tel: 702-723-5454.

6—ST. ELIZABETH ANN SETON (1992) Rev. James Jankowski, O.F.M. Conv.; Deacons Joseph Deegan; Steve Doucet; Francis Pemper. In Res., Rev. Mark Gomori.
Office & Mailing Address: 1811 Pueblo Vista Dr., 89128. Tel: 702-228-8311; Fax: 702-228-8310. Email: seas@dioceseoflasvegas.org.
Res.: 2109 Golden Lotus Dr., 89134.
School—(Grades K-8), 1807 Pueblo Vista Dr., 89128. Tel: 702-804-8328; Fax: 702-228-8906. Email: school@seaslv.org. Dr. Cary Roybal-Benson, Prin.; Julie Krueger, Librarian. Lay Teachers 24; Students 482.
Catechesis/Religious Program—Tel: 702-228-8311; Fax: 702-228-2154. Mary Del Giorno, D.R.E. Students 559.

7—ST. FRANCIS DE SALES (1964) Revs. Manuel Quintero; Michael Conway, O.SS.T.
Mailing Address: 1111 Michael Way, 89108. Tel: 702-647-3440; Fax: 702-646-3587.
Res.: 1628 Desert Fort, 89128. Tel: 702-341-7009.
School—(Grades K-8) Tel: 702-647-2828; Fax: 702-647-0284. Web: www.sfdslv.org. Mrs. Catherine Thompson, Prin. Lay Teachers 20; Students 305.
Catechesis/Religious Program—Tel: 702-646-2266; Fax: 702-647-6701. Students 786.

8—HOLY FAMILY (1975) Revs. M. Eugene Kinney, Admin.; Innocent Anyanwu; Ruben D. Bedoya Sanchez.
Mailing Address: 4490 Mountain Vista, 89121.
Res.: 4528 E. Harmon Ave., 89121-6548. Tel: 702-458-2211 (Office); Fax: 702-458-0966 (Office).
Catechesis/Religious Program—Tel: 702-458-3575. Students 550.

9—HOLY SPIRIT CATHOLIC CHURCH (2007) Rev. William J.M. Kenny, Admin.
5959 S. Hualapai Way, 89148. Tel: 702-459-7778; Fax: 702-437-9548. Email: holyspiritlv@embarqmail.com. Web: www.holyspiritlv.org.
Catechesis/Religious Program—Len Urso, D.R.E. (K-8); Louie Latina, D.R.E. (9-12). Students 396.

10—ST. JAMES THE APOSTLE (1942), (African American), Rev. Henry Salditos, Admin.
Office & Church: 1920 N. Martin Luther King Blvd., 89106. Tel: 702-648-6606; Fax: 702-648-0352. Email: stjameschurch@lvcoxmail.com.
Catechesis/Religious Program—Tel: 702-648-6606; Fax: 702-648-0352. Arsenia Eagan, D.R.E. Students 112.

11—ST. JOAN OF ARC (1908) [CEM] Rev. David E. Casaleggio.
Office & Res.: 315 S. Casino Center Blvd., 89101. Tel: 702-382-9909; Fax: 702-382-6655.
School—(Grades K-8), 1300 Bridger Ave., 89101. Tel: 702-384-6909; Fax: 702-386-0249. Dr. James Machinski, Prin. Lay Teachers 15; Students 153.
Catechesis/Religious Program—Clustered with St. Bridget's, Las Vegas. Students 4.

12—ST. JOSEPH, HUSBAND OF MARY (1989) Revs. Marc C. Howes; Thomas E. Gallenbach; Cassian Lewinski, O.P., Parochial Vicar; Deacons Tom Bast; Thomas Roberts; Al Paduano; Barbara Finn, Music Min.; Vince Murone, Finance; Greg Sinclair, Pastoral Assoc.
Office & Mailing Address: 7260 W. Sahara Ave., 89117. Tel: 702-363-1902; Fax: 702-363-7976. Web: www.stjosephhom.org.
Res.: 7761 Via Olivero Ave., 89117.
Catechesis/Religious Program—Fax: 702-363-0142. Cynthia O'Connell, D.R.E.; Jennifer Hill, Youth Min. Students 775.

13—ST. MARY THE VIRGIN (1983) Closed. For inquiries for parish records contact the chancery.

14—OUR LADY OF LA VANG (2003), (Vietnamese), Rev. Quang Minh Dong.
Vietnamese Community, 4835 S. Pearl St., 89121. Tel: 702-821-1459. Web: www.lavanglasvegas.com.
Catechesis/Religious Program—Mai Le, D.R.E.; Ron Tran, D.R.E. Students 117.

15—OUR LADY OF LAS VEGAS (1957) Revs. Gerald Grupczynski, S.Ch., Admin.; Frank Yncierto, Parochial Vicar; Rey Salditos, Hospital Min.; Vicente Panaligan, Hospital Min.
Office: 3050 Alta Dr., 89107. Tel: 702-870-2767; Fax: 702-870-1267. Email: ollvparish@ollv.org. Web: www.ollv.org.
Res.: 3104 Alta Dr., 89107.
School—(Grades PreK-8), 3046 Alta Dr., 89107. Tel: 702-878-6841; Fax: 702-880-5758. Phyllis Joyce, Prin. Lay Teachers 26; Students 610.
Catechesis/Religious Program—Tel: 702-870-1882. Email: lizwilliams1234@hotmail.com. Students 180.

16—ST. PAUL JUNG-HA-SANG (1987), (Korean), Rev. Hee Ook Chung, Chap.
Korean Community, 6080 S. Jones Blvd., 89118. Tel: 702-222-4349; Fax: 702-227-8817.
Catechesis/Religious Program—Eun-Mi Park, D.R.E.

17—PRINCE OF PEACE (1981) Revs. Gustavo Cruz; Juan Antonio Perez, O.SS.T.
Office: 5485 E. Charleston Blvd., 89142. Tel: 702-431-2233; Fax: 702-431-2234. Web: www.lasvegas-diocese.org.
Res.: 653 Los Feliz, 89110.
Catechesis/Religious Program—Students 1,607.

18—SHRINE OF THE MOST HOLY REDEEMER (1991) Rev. Msgr. Francis M. Vivona, Rector.
Office: 55 E. Reno Ave., 89119. Tel: 702-891-8600; Fax: 702-891-0339. Email: mostholyredeemer3@embarqmail.com.

19—ST. VIATOR (1954) Revs. Richard A. Rinn, C.S.V.; William F. Haesaert, C.S.V.; Bro. Michael Rice, C.S.V.; Anita Taylor, Business Mgr.
Office: 2461 E. Flamingo Rd., 89121. Tel: 702-733-8323; Fax: 702-733-8154. Web: www.stviator.org.
School—(Grades PreK-8), 4246 S. Eastern Ave., 89119-5426. Tel: 702-732-4477; Fax: 702-732-4418. Mrs. Kathleen Daulton, Prin. Lay Teachers 32; Students 660.
Catechesis/Religious Program—Tel: 702-733-0392. Rosy Hartz, D.R.E. Students 221.

OUTSIDE THE CITY OF LAS VEGAS

AMARGOSA VALLEY, NYE CO., CHRIST OF THE DESERT CATHOLIC CHURCH (1984), (Hispanic), Mission of Our Lady of the Valley, Pahrump. Rev. John McShane.
Whitesands Ave., H 69 Box 450 E, 89020.
Catechesis/Religious Program—Students 19.

BOULDER CITY, CLARK CO., ST. ANDREW'S (1931) [JC] Rev. Robert E. Stoeckig; Deacon Tim O'Callaghan, Pastoral Min.
1399 San Felipe Dr., 89005. Tel: 702-293-7500; Fax: 702-989-4789. Email: standrewbc@gmail.com.
Catechesis/Religious Program— Jenifer Jefferies, D.R.E. Students 122.

CALIENTE, LINCOLN CO., HOLY CHILD (1870) [CEM] Rev. John McShane, Chap.; Deacon Patrick R. Fitzsimons.
Mailing Address: P.O. Box 748, 89008-0748. Tel: 775-726-3669; Fax: 775-726-3669.
Church: 80 Tennille St., 89008.
Catechesis/Religious Program—Students 20.

ELY, WHITE PINE CO., SACRED HEART (1869) Rev. Paul Oye, O.P., Admin.; Nancy Marich, Pastoral Assoc.
Mailing Address & Office: 900 E. 11th St., P.O. Box 151026, 89315. Tel: 775-289-2201; Fax: 775-289-2207.
Res.: 515 Murry St., 89301. Tel: 775-289-3606.
Catechesis/Religious Program—Students 85.
Mission—St. Michael's

HENDERSON, CLARK CO.

1—ST. FRANCIS OF ASSISI (2003) Revs. John T. Assalone, Admin.; Steven R. Hoffer, Parochial Vicar.
2300 Sunridge Heights, 89052. Tel: 702-914-2175; Fax: 702-914-2178. Email: sfa@sfahdnv.org. Web: www.sfahdnv.org.
Rectory—725 Waltham Hills St., 89052.
Catechesis/Religious Program—Tel: 702-914-3529; Fax: 702-914-3563. Email: king@sfahdnv.org. Students 897.

2—ST. PETER THE APOSTLE (1943) Revs. Bruno Mauricci (Peru); Mugagga Lule, Parochial Vicar; Donald A. Casey (Retired); Deacons Daniel De Pozo; Bill Davis.
Office: 204 S. Boulder Hwy., 89015. Tel: 702-565-8406; Fax: 702-565-8731. Email: info@stpahend.org.
Rectory—179 Mount St. Helen Dr., 89012.
Catechesis/Religious Program—Tel: 702-565-0284; Fax: 702-565-3809. Students 455.

3—ST. THOMAS MORE (1986) Very Rev. Patrick W. Render, C.S.V.; Revs. Michael P. Keliher, C.S.V.; Robert T. Bolser, C.S.V.; Deacons Eugene Krzeminski; Richard Daluga.
130 N. Pecos Rd., 89074. Tel: 702-361-3022; Fax: 702-361-7784. Email: stmlv02@aol.com. Web: www.stmlv.org.
Catechesis/Religious Program—Tel: 702-361-8840; Fax: 702-361-5992. Juliann Dwyer, D.R.E.; Dorothy Distel, D.R.E. Students 1,338.

LAUGHLIN, CLARK CO., ST. JOHN THE BAPTIST CATHOLIC CHURCH (1992) Rev. Charles B. Urnick, Admin.; Deacon Daniel McHugh.
Office & Mailing Address: 3055 El Mirage Way, P.O. Box 31230, 89028. Tel: 702-298-0440. Email: stjohn@cmaaccess.com. Web: www.stjohnthebaptistlaughlin.com.
Res.: 3115 Terrace View, 89029.
Catechesis/Religious Program—Students 10.

MESQUITE, CLARK CO., LA VIRGEN DE GUADALUPE (1992) Rev. Robert W. Puhlman; Deacon John Lawrence Smith.
Mailing Address: P.O. Box 300, 89024. 401 Canyon Crest Blvd., 89027.
Office: 93 W. 1st S., Bunkerville, 89007. Tel: 702-346-7065; Fax: 702-345-2280. Email: lvdgoffice@mesquiteweb.com.
Res.: 121 Falcon St., 89027.
Education Center—Tel: 702-346-4460; Fax: 702-346-6077. Email: floresnev@yahoo.com.
Catechesis/Religious Program—Students 238.

NORTH LAS VEGAS, CLARK CO.

1—ST. CHRISTOPHER (1953) [JC] Revs. Ron Zanoni; Alberto Alzate (Colombia).
Mailing Address: 1840 N. Bruce St., 89030. Tel: 702-642-1154; Fax: 702-642-0719. Email: cfierro@stchrisnlv.org.
Res.: 1401 Flower Ave., 89030.
School—(Grades K-8) Tel: 702-657-8008; Fax: 702-642-2461. Email: pmertzman@stchrisnlv.org. Web: www.saintchristophernlv.org. Paul Mertzman, Prin. Lay Teachers 13; Students 214.
Catechesis/Religious Program—Tel: 702-657-6779; Fax: 702-657-8406. Victoria Gonzales, D.R.E. Students 1,020.

2—ST. JOHN NEUMANN (1999) Rev. Bede Wevita; Deacons Frank Oettinger; Andre Richard.
Mailing Address: 2575 W. El Campo Grande Ave., 89031. Tel: 702-657-0200; Fax: 702-648-2327. Email: secretary@sjnc.org. Web: www.sjnc.org.
Res.: 912 Whitehollow Ave., 89031. Tel: 702-642-6750.
Catechesis/Religious Program—Tel: 702-657-0200, Ext. 210. Email: dre@sjnc.org. Students 667.

OVERTON, CLARK CO., ST. JOHN THE EVANGELIST (1959) Rev. Robert W. Puhlman, Admin.
Mailing Address: P.O. Box 457, 89040.
Church & Office: 2955 St. Joseph St., Logandale, 89021. Tel: 702-398-3998; Fax: 702-398-3995. Email: stjohn@mvdsl.com.
Res.: 3228 Taylor St., Logandale, 89021. Tel: 702-398-7275.
Catechesis/Religious Program—Students 57.

PAHRUMP, NYE CO., OUR LADY OF THE VALLEY (1985) Rev. Anthony Hughes, Admin.
Mailing Address: 781 E. Gamebird, 89048.
Rectory—3031 S. Blagg Rd., 89048.
Catechesis/Religious Program—Students 131.

TONOPAH, NYE CO., ST. PATRICK (1902) Rev. Gemnoli Bandivas.
Mailing Address: P.O. Box 325, 89049.
Res.: 144 South St., 89049. Fax: 775-482-6746. Email: stpatrickstonopah@frontier.com.
Catechesis/Religious Program—Students 25.
Mission—St. Barbara 91 Hadley Cir., Round Mountain, 89045.
Mission—Our Lady of Guadalupe SR 264, Fish Lake Community Center, Dyer, Esmeralda Co. 89010.

On Duty Outside the Diocese:
Rev. Msgr.—
Gordon, Gregory W., Apostolic Nunciature, 3339 Massachusetts Ave., N.W., Washington, DC 20008.
Rev.—
Anthony, Joseph, P.O. Box 295042, Kerrville, TX 78029.

Military Chaplains:
Rev.—
Beale, Kenneth, Chap., Our Lady of the Skies, 4302 N. Washington Blvd., Nellis AFB, 89191.

Unassigned:
Revs.—
Audet, Phil
Petekiewicz, Robert P.
Waters, Bernard F. (New Zealand)

Administrative Leave:
Rev.—
Chaanine, George

Retired:
Revs.—
Annese, Joseph P.
Bevan, James J., Jr.
Caviglia, Caesar J.
Franzinell, Benjamin
McVeigh, John J.
Nguyen, Joseph Trong
O'Donnell, Philip
Savial, Joseph Clarence
Slatterie, Leo
Timoney, Francis

Permanent Deacons:
Bast, Thomas
Breeden, John
Cater, Patrick
Cormier, Joseph
Daluga, Richard
Davis, William
Deegan, Joseph
Depozo, Dan
Doucet, Steve
Favela, Jacobo, Jr.
Fitzsimons, Patrick R.
Green, Richard
Guerrero, Santiago
Krzeminski, Eugene
Maier, Daniel
Marek, James
McHugh, Daniel
McManus, William
Minch, Richard
O'Callaghan, Tim
Oettinger, Frank F.
Paduano, Al
Pemper, Frank
Richard, Andre
Roberts, Thomas
Rodriguez Tarango, Jose
Rudloff, Robert, Jr.
Smith, John Lawrence
Torres, G. Miguel
Underwood, Michael
Wiggins, Jim L.
Wilson, Tracy

INSTITUTIONS LOCATED IN THE DIOCESE

[A] HIGH SCHOOLS, DIOCESAN

Las Vegas. *Bishop Gorman High School* (1954) 5959 S. Hualapai, 89148. Tel: 702-732-1945; Fax: 702-732-8830. Web: www.bishopgorman.org. Kevin Kiefer, Prin.; Mr. John Kilduff, Pres. Priests 1; Lay Teachers 88; Students 1,268.

[B] GENERAL HOSPITALS

Henderson. *St. Rose Dominican Hospital, Rose de Lima Campus dba Catholic Healthcare West* (1947) 102 E. Lake Mead Pkwy., 89015. Tel: 702-564-2622; Fax: 702-616-4699. Web: www.strosehospitals.org. Rod Davis, Pres., NV Svc. Area. Sponsored by Sisters of St. Dominic, Congregation of the Most Holy Rosary Adrian, MI. Priests 1; Sisters 5; Beds 129; Patients Assisted Annually 49,498; Total Staff 762.

St. Rose Dominican Hospital, San Martin Campus dba Catholic Healthcare West 8280 W. Warm Springs Rd., 89113. Tel: 702-492-8000; Fax: 702-492-8511. Web: www.strosehospitals.org. Vicky VanMeetren, Pres. Sisters of St. Dominic, Congregation of the Most Holy Rosary, Adrian, MI. Priests 1; Bed Capacity 147; Patients Assisted Annually 41,529; Total Staff 784.

St. Rose Dominican Hospital, Siena Campus dba Catholic Healthcare West (2000) 3001 St. Rose Pkwy., 89052-6178. Tel: 702-616-5000; Fax: 702-616-5511. Web: www.strosehospitals.org. Rod Davis, Pres., NV Svc. Area. Sponsored by Sisters of St. Dominic, Congregation of the Most Holy Rosary Adrian, MI. Sisters 1; Bed Capacity 219; Patients Assisted Annually 89,844; Total Staff 1,804.

[C] MONASTERIES AND RESIDENCES OF PRIESTS AND BROTHERS

Las Vegas. *Clerics of St. Viator Retirement Home*, 4219 Pinecrest Cir. E., 89121. Tel: 702-456-8512. Revs. Edward C. Anderson, C.S.V; William F. Haesaert, C.S.V. Priests 3.

Dominican Rectory, Fra Angelico House (1998) 1701 Chapman Dr., 89104-3516. Tel: 702-369-1215; Fax: 702-369-3742. Rev. Albert Felice-Pace, O.P., Supr.; Bro. Frederick W. Narbares, O.P., Prof.; Revs. Joseph O'Brien, O.P.; Cassian Lewinski, O.P. (Western Dominican Province) Priests 3; Brothers 1.

[D] CONVENTS AND RESIDENCES FOR SISTERS

Las Vegas. *The Franciscan Sisters of Perpetual Adoration* (1979) 1304 E. St. Louis Ave., 89104-3466. Tel: 702-735-5285. Email: lorforster1@aol.com. Sr. Lorraine Forster, Contact Person.

[E] NEWMAN CENTERS

Las Vegas. *St. Thomas Aquinas Catholic Newman Community at UNLV*, 4765 Brussels St., 89119. Tel: 702-736-0887; Fax: 702-891-0615. Email: info@unlvnewman.com. Web: newman.unlv.edu. Rev. Albert Felice-Pace, O.P., Dir. & Campus Min.; David Zeamer, Assoc. Dir. & Devel. Dir.

[F] MISCELLANEOUS

Las Vegas. *Bishop Gorman Development Corp.*, P.O. Box 18316, 89114-8316. Tel: 702-735-7865; Fax: 702-735-2996. Email: witkowski@dioceseoflasvegas.org. Bro. John J. Dodd, C.S.V., Exec. Dir.

Catholic Charities of Southern Nevada (1941) 1501 Las Vegas Blvd., N., 89101. Tel: 702-385-2662; Fax: 702-384-0677. Web: www.catholiccharities.com. Rev. Msgr. Patrick Leary, CEO.

Adoption Program (1941) Tel: 702-385-3351; Fax: 702-388-8723. Web: www.catholiccharities.com.

Crossroads Transitional Program for Senior Men (1995) Tel: 702-387-2282; Fax: 702-383-8243. Web: www.catholiccharities.com.

Immigration Services (1984) Tel: 702-387-2229; Fax: 702-436-1579. Web: www.catholiccharities.com.

Marian Transitional Program for Senior Women (1995) Tel: 702-565-5388; Fax: 702-565-7711. Web: www.catholiccharities.com.

Migration and Refugee Services (1975) Tel: 702-387-2229; Fax: 702-436-1579. Web: www.catholiccharities.com.

Respite Care Referral Service (1995) Tel: 702-382-0721; Fax: 702-385-3206. Web: www.catholiccharities.com.

RSVP (Retired & Senior Volunteer Program) (1975) Tel: 702-382-0721; Fax: 702-307-1203. Web: www.catholiccharities.com.

Senior Community Employment Service (1977) Tel: 702-215-4701; Fax: 702-366-2066. Web: www.catholiccharities.com.

Senior Companion (1974) Tel: 702-382-0721; Fax: 702-307-1203. Web: www.catholiccharities.com.

Senior Foster Grandparent Program Tel: 702-382-0721; Fax: 702-307-1203. Web: www.catholiccharities.com.

Senior Nutrition & Meals-on-Wheels (1975) Tel: 702-385-5284; Fax: 702-385-3206. Web: www.catholiccharities.com.

Social Services (1941) Tel: 702-387-2291; Fax: 702-383-9031. Web: www.catholiccharities.com.

St. Vincent Lied Dining Facility (1965) Tel: 702-366-2072; Fax: 702-385-1173. Web: www.catholiccharities.com.

Resident Empowerment Program (1985) Tel: 702-387-2282; Fax: 702-366-2066. Web: www.catholiccharities.com.

Employment Services Center

Catholic Charities Thrift Stores (1961) Tel: 702-385-2662; Fax: 702-384-0677. Web: www.catholiccharities.com.

NCWB Housing, Inc. (1978) Tel: 702-878-5398; Fax: 702-878-4579.

CCSN Mojave Project, Inc. (1985) Tel: 702-384-2643; Fax: 702-384-8759.

CCSN McFarland Housing Development Corporation, Inc. (1997) Tel: 702-878-5398; Fax: 702-878-4597.

CCSN McFarland Housing, Inc., 4988 Jeffreys St., 89119. Tel: 702-736-9596; Fax: 702-736-9597.

Women, Infants, and Children (WIC) Tel: 702-366-2069; Fax: 702-366-9551. Web: www.catholiccharities.com.

Catholic Diocese of Las Vegas Capital Funding Corporation, 336 Cathedral Way, 89109.

Catholic Diocese of Las Vegas Capital Management Corporation, 336 Cathedral Way, 89109.

Serra House (Formation Residence), 9308 Harrow Rock St., 89143-1385. Tel: 702-538-9048. Email: frmugaggalule@yahoo.com. Rev. Mugagga Lule, Vocations Dir.

Service Campaign Corporation, P.O. Box 18316, 89114-8316.

Henderson. *Diocesan Residence* (1999) 507 Chestnut View Pl., 89052-2821. Tel: 702-735-7865; Fax: 702-735-2996. Lee Liguori, Vice Chancellor.

St. Rose Dominican Health Foundation, 3001 St. Rose Pkwy., 89052. Tel: 702-616-5750; Fax: 712-616-5751. Web: www.strosehospitals.org.

Saint Therese Center (1998) HIV/AIDS Outreach Program, 100 E. Lake Mead Pkwy., 89015. Tel: 702-564-4224; Fax: 702-564-0604. Email: aidsproject@dioceseoflasvegas.org. Web: sainttheresecenter.org. Rev. Joseph O'Brien, O.P., Exec. Dir.; Bro. Frederick Naberes, O.P.

West Las Vegas Satellite, 8280 W. Warm Springs Rd., San Martin Hospital G3022, 89113. Tel: 702-564-4224; Fax: 702-564-0604.

Laughlin Satellite, 3055 El Mirage Way, St. John the Baptist Mission Church, Laughlin, 89028. Tel: 702-564-4224; Fax: 702-564-0604.

RELIGIOUS INSTITUTES OF MEN REPRESENTED IN THE DIOCESE

For further details refer to the corresponding bracketed number in the Religious Institutes of Men or Women section.

[1320]—*Clerics of St. Viator*—C.S.V.
[]—*Congregation of the Holy Spirit*—C.S.Sp
[]—*Order of Friars Minor Conv.*—O.F.M.Conv.
[]—*Order of the Holy Trinity*—O.SS.T.
[]—*Society of Christ*—S.Chr.
[]—*Western Dominican Province*—O.P.

RELIGIOUS INSTITUTES OF WOMEN REPRESENTED IN THE DIOCESE

[1780]—*Congregation of the Sisters of the Third Order of St. Francis of Perpetual Adoration*—F.S.P.A.
[1070-04]—*Dominican Sisters*—O.P.
[]—*Franciscan Sisters*—O.S.F.
[1960]—*Sisters of the Holy Family*—S.H.F.

NECROLOGY

† Lavoy, Rev. Msgr. Elwood, (Retired)—Died April 15, 2011

An asterisk (*) denotes an organization that has established tax-exempt status directly with the IRS and is not covered by the USCCB Group Ruling.

Diocese of Lexington

Most Reverend

RONALD W. GAINER

Bishop of Lexington; ordained May 19, 1973; appointed Bishop of Lexington December 13, 2002; consecrated February 22, 2003. *Office: The Catholic Center, 1310 W. Main St., Lexington, KY 40508-2048.*

The Catholic Center: 1310 W. Main St., Lexington, KY 40508-2048. Tel: 859-253-1993; Fax: 859-254-6284.

Web: www.cdlex.org

Email: webmaster@cdlex.org

ESTABLISHED MARCH 2, 1988.

Square Miles 16,423.

Comprises the counties of Anderson, Bath, Bell, Bourbon, Boyd, Boyle, Breathitt, Carter, Clark, Clay, Elliott, Estill, Fayette, Floyd, Franklin, Garrard, Greenup, Harlan, Jackson, Jessamine, Johnson, Knott, Knox, Laurel, Lawrence, Lee, Leslie, Letcher, Lincoln, McCreary, Madison, Magoffin, Martin, Menifee, Mercer, Montgomery, Morgan, Nicholas, Owsley, Perry, Pike, Powell, Pulaski, Rockcastle, Rowan, Scott, Wayne, Whitley, Wolfe and Woodford.

For legal titles of parishes and diocesan institutions, consult the Chancellor.

STATISTICAL OVERVIEW

Personnel	
Bishop	1
Retired Bishops	1
Priests: Diocesan Active in Diocese	37
Priests: Diocesan Active Outside Diocese	3
Priests: Retired, Sick or Absent	12
Number of Diocesan Priests	52
Religious Priests in Diocese	21
Total Priests in Diocese	73
Extern Priests in Diocese	2
Ordinations:	
Diocesan Priests	2
Transitional Deacons	1
Permanent Deacons in Diocese	53
Total Brothers	3
Total Sisters	74
Parishes	
Parishes	49
With Resident Pastor:	
Resident Diocesan Priests	31
Resident Religious Priests	9
Without Resident Pastor:	
Administered by Deacons	2
Administered by Professed Religious Men	1
Administered by Religious Women	5
Administered by Lay People	1
Missions	14
Professional Ministry Personnel:	
Sisters	14
Lay Ministers	29
Welfare	
Catholic Hospitals	11
Total Assisted	1,249,529
Health Care Centers	4
Total Assisted	56,000
Homes for the Aged	1
Total Assisted	210
Special Centers for Social Services	1
Total Assisted	8,000
Educational	
Diocesan Students in Other Seminaries	12
Total Seminarians	12
High Schools, Diocesan and Parish	1
Total Students	807
High Schools, Private	1
Total Students	95
Elementary Schools, Diocesan and Parish	15
Total Students	3,045
Catechesis/Religious Education:	
High School Students	986
Elementary Students	2,481
Total Students under Catholic Instruction	7,426
Teachers in the Diocese:	
Priests	5
Sisters	7
Lay Teachers	334
Vital Statistics	
Receptions into the Church:	
Infant Baptism Totals	821
Minor Baptism Totals	70
Adult Baptism Totals	82
Received into Full Communion	197
First Communions	994
Confirmations	759
Marriages:	
Catholic	125
Interfaith	70
Total Marriages	195
Deaths	285
Total Catholic Population	42,056
Total Population	1,578,749

Former Bishop—Most Rev. JAMES K. WILLIAMS, D.D., ord. May 25, 1963; appt. Titular Bishop of Catula and Auxiliary Bishop of Covington on April 15, 1984; cons. June 19, 1984; appt. Bishop of Lexington Jan. 14, 1988; installed March 2, 1988; resigned June 11, 2002.

The Catholic Center—1310 W. Main St., Lexington, 40508-2048. Tel: 859-253-1993; Fax: 859-254-6284. Office Hours: Mon.-Fri. 8:30-4:30.

Vicar General—Very Rev. MARK DREVES.

Chancellor—KAREN ABBEY.

Chief Administrative Officer—DOUG CULP.

Executive Administrative Assistant To The Bishop—KAREN ABBEY.

Secretariat for Stewardship—Deacon BILL WAKEFIELD, CFO, 1310 W. Main St., Lexington, 40508-2048.

College of Consultors—Revs. JOHN MORIARTY; THOMAS P. FARRELL; MICHAEL CHOWNING, O.F.M.; JOHN P. NOE; DANIEL J. NOLL; FRANK C. OSBURG (Retired), 1310 W. Main St., Lexington, 40508-2048.

Regional Councillors—Fayette: Rev. JOHN MORIARTY. Bluegrass West: Rev. THOMAS P. FARRELL. Bluegrass East: Rev. JAMES W. SICHKO. Mountain West: Rev. MICHAEL J. RAMLER. Mountain East: Rev. REYNOLDS GARLAND, O.F.M. Big Sandy/ Licking: Rev. JOHN P. NOE.

Diocesan Tribunal—1310 W. Main St., Lexington, 40508-2048. Tel: 859-253-1993; Fax: 859-259-0951.

Judicial Vicar—Rev. JOHN E. LIST, J.C.L. Email: jlist@cdlex.org.

Tribunal Director—RENATA BABICZ-BARATTO, J.U.D., J.C.L. Email: ribabicz@cdlex.org.

Associate Judges—Revs. THOMAS P. KOONS, J.C.L.; VICTOR FINELLI, J.C.L.; BARRY WINDHOLTZ, J.C.L.

Defenders of the Bond—Revs. THOMAS V. THAI, Ph.D. (Retired); MICHAEL WEGLICKI; PAUL PRABELL; MARCO RAJKOVICH, J.D.; AROKODIAS DAS, J.C.L.

Case Instructor—CAROLYN G. SNOWDEN.

Promoter of Justice—Rev. PAUL PRABELL.

Notaries—CAROLYN G. SNOWDEN; LORRAINE LEE.

Ministry Admissions Board—Most Rev. RONALD WILLIAM GAINER.

Priests' Retirement Committee—Revs. DENNIS KNIGHT; LAWRENCE W. HEHMAN (Retired); FRANK C. OSBURG (Retired); MICHAEL J. RAMLER; CHRIS CLAY; MICHAEL FLANAGAN; Mr. JOHN D. PRICE; JOHN DOWELL; JOB D. TURNER; Deacon BILL WAKEFIELD.

Diocesan Offices And Directors

Secretariat of the Vicar General—Very Rev. MARK DREVES, Vicar Gen., 1310 W. Main St., Lexington, 40508. Tel: 859-253-1993. Email: mdreves@cdlex.org.

Archives—KAREN ABBEY, 1310 W. Main St., Lexington, 40508-2048. Tel: 859-253-1993.

Campus Ministry— Newman Center Dir., Contact The Catholic Center, *1310 W. Main St., Lexington, 40508-2048*. Tel: 859-253-1993. MICHELE FAUGHT, Dir.

Catholic Scouting—Rev. MICHAEL WEGLICKI, Diocesan Dir. Tel: 606-464-3357.

Secretariat for Social Services—Tel: 859-253-1993. Mrs. RUSLYN CASE-COMPTON, Dir., Lexington. Tel: 859-253-1993. Email: rcasecompton@cdlex.org.

Catholic Charities of Lexington—Mrs. RUSLYN CASE-COMPTON, Dir., 1310 W. Main St., Lexington, 40508-2048. Tel: 859-253-1993, Ext. 215. Email: charities@cdlex.org.

Father Beiting Appalachian Mission Center—Rev. Msgr. RALPH BEITING, Founder, Mailing Address: 332 River Bend Rd., Louisa, 41230. Tel: 606-638-0219.

Deaf Ministry— Masses: Sun. 11 am every other week at Mary, Queen of the Holy Rosary, Lexington; Sun. 11:15 am at Sts. Peter and Paul, Danville.

Secretariat for Stewardship—Deacon BILL WAKEFIELD, CFO, 1310 W. Main St., Lexington, 40508-2048. Tel: 859-253-1993, Ext. 238.

Mission Office, Propagation of the Faith and The Holy Childhood—NANCY BAILEY, 1310 W. Main St., Lexington, 40508-2048. Tel: 859-253-1993.

Ecumenical Liaison—Rev. NICK A. PAGANO, 4001 Victoria Way, Lexington, 40515. Tel: 859-273-9999.

R.C.I.A.—KAREN ROOD, Coord., 1310 W. Main St., Lexington, 40508-2048. Tel: 859-253-1993, Ext. 251.

Healthcare—Deacon BILL WAKEFIELD, Diocesan Coord., 1310 W. Main St., Lexington, 40508-2048. Tel: 859-253-1993, Ext. 238.

Secretariat for Pastoral Life—DOUG CULP, 1310 W. Main St., Lexington, 40508-2048. Tel: 859-253-1993, Ext. 220.

Secretariat for Catholic Schools—Mr. TIM WEAVER, 1310 W. Main St., Lexington, 40508-2048. Tel: 859-253-1993, Ext. 219.

Director of Religious Formation & Adult Faith Formation—ROD STERN, 1310 W. Main St., Lexington, 40508-2048. Tel: 859-253-1993, Ext. 221.

Cliffview Retreat Center—Co-Directors: DAVID WELLS; SHARLA WELLS. Tel: 859-792-3333.

Communications—THOMAS SHAUGHNESSY, Dir., 1310 W. Main St., Lexington, 40508-2048. Tel: 859-253-1993, Ext. 258.

Hispanic Ministry—Sr. SANDRA DELGADO, O.P., Dir.; Revs. JOSEPH VON HANDORF; EULICES GODINEZ.

Buen Pastor - Centro Catolico—1310 W. Main St., Lexington, 40508. Tel: 859-254-5507. Staff: DANNY HERNANDEZ-SILVA, Youth Min.; YOLANDA PINILLA, Prog. Coord.; LINNETTE HACKER, Families & Youth Activities Coord.

Peace & Justice—POLLY DUNCAN-COLLUM, Dir., 1310 W. Main St., Lexington, 40508. Tel: 859-253-1993, Ext. 224. Email: pduncancollum@cdlex.org.

Director of Family Life—MICHAEL ALLEN. Tel: 859-253-1993, Ext. 212.

Director of Youth & Young Adult Ministry—MICHELE FAUGHT, 1310 W. Main St., Lexington, 40508. Tel: 859-253-1993, Ext. 218. Email: mfaught@cdlex.org.

HIV/AIDS Ministry—Rev. JOHN C. CURTIS, Diocesan Coord.

Commission for African American Catholic Concerns—Contacts: Mrs. BARBARA DEHAAN; Mrs. CHRISTINA WEATHERS, Mailing Address: 410 Jefferson St., Lexington, 40508. Tel: 859-223-3703; 859-254-0030.

Rural Life—The Catholic Center, 1310 W. Main St., Lexington, 40508-2048. Tel: 859-253-1993.

Regina Pacis Community— (Traditional Latin Mass Community) *177 St. Ann Dr., Lexington, 40502*. Tel: 859-983-6729; 859-268-5159. Rev. JOHN RICKERT, F.S.S.P., Chap. Email: jrickert@cdlex.org.

Liturgy—KAREN ROOD, Dir., 1310 W. Main St., Lexington, 40508-2048. Tel: 859-253-1993, Ext. 251.

Newspaper "Cross Roads"—THOMAS F. SHAUGHNESSY, Editor, 1310 W. Main St., Lexington, 40508-2048. Tel: 859-253-1993, Ext. 258; Fax: 859-259-0951.

Permanent Diaconate—Co-Directors: ARDEN WOLTERMAN; BETTY WOLTERMAN, 3 Lansdowne Estate, Lexington, 40502-3321. Tel: 859-276-4123.

Magnificat-Lexington—SUE SOPALA, Coord., 3852 Heimbaugh Ln., Lexington, 40514. Tel: 859-224-4908. Email: mngr@championfactorydirect.com.

Ministry for Persons with Disabilities—JOE PETRY; Mrs. MARY PETRY, 124 Rolling Hills, Danville, 40422. Tel: 859-936-8656.

Priests' Personnel—Rev. DANIEL J. NOLL, 601 Hill N Dale Rd., Lexington, 40503-2116. Tel: 859-983-2643.

Prison Ministry—Mrs. RUSLYN CASE-COMPTON, Diocesan Coord., 1310 W. Main St., Lexington, 40508. Tel: 859-253-1993, Ext. 215. Email: rcasecompton@cdlex.org.

Religious—Sr. MARIA GORETTI BROWNE, O.P., Delegate, 327 Duke Rd., No. 2, Lexington, 40502. Tel: 859-266-9809.

Respect Life—PEGGY SHEIKO, Diocesan Coord.

Victim Assistance Coordinator—Mrs. NELDA JACKSON. Tel: 859-253-1993, Ext. 214. Email: njackson@cdlex.org.

Vocations—Rev. STEPHEN ROBERTS, Dir. Tel: 859-253-1993, Ext. 249. Email: sroberts@cdlex.org.

Coordinator of Vocation Programs—BRET HUNTERBRINKER, 1310 W. Main St., Lexington, 40508. Tel: 859-253-1993, Ext. 248. Email: bhunterbrinker@cdlex.org.

CLERGY, PARISHES, MISSIONS AND PAROCHIAL SCHOOLS

CITY OF LEXINGTON

(FAYETTE COUNTY)

1—CATHEDRAL OF CHRIST THE KING (1945) Very Rev. Mark Dreves, Rector; Revs. Gino Donatelli, S.J., Parochial Vicar; Richard Watson, Parochial Vicar; Deacons Arden Wolterman; Mark Stauffer; Raoul Ouellette; Timothy Weinmann; Patricia Dimon, Business Mgr.; Deborah Goonan, Outreach Min.; Robert Whitaker, Music Min.; Brian Hunt, Asst. Music Min.; Brenda Psotka, Dir. of Advancement.
Res.: 299 Colony Blvd., 40502. Tel: 859-268-2861; Fax: 859-268-8061. Web: cathedral.cdlex.org.
School—(Grades K-8), 412 Cochran Rd., 40502. Tel: 859-266-5641; Fax: 859-266-4547. Karen Thomas, Prin. Lay Teachers 33; Students 510.
Catechesis/Religious Program—John Molloy, Dir. Faith Formation; Elena Beauregard, Youth Min. Students 230.

2—ST. ELIZABETH ANN SETON (1980) Rev. John Moriarty; Sr. Eileen Golby, O.S.F., Pastoral Assoc.; Deacons Robert S. Joice; Matthew C. Coriale; Mark T. Woelfel.
Res.: 1750 Summerhill Dr., 40515. Tel: 859-273-0134.
Parish Center—Tel: 859-273-1318; Fax: 859-272-6988. Email: seasparish@cdlex.org. Web: seas.cdlex.org.
School—Seton Catholic School, (Grades PreK-8), 1740 Summerhill Dr., 40515. Email: lcoomer@cdlex.org. Web: setonschool.cdlex.org. Lee Coomer, Prin.; Susan Whalen, Librarian. Lay Teachers 33; Students 462.
Education Office—Tel: 859-273-7827; Fax: 859-272-0115. Jayne Morris, D.R.E.

3—MARY, QUEEN OF THE HOLY ROSARY (1960) Revs. Daniel J. Noll; Jeffrey Estacio, Parochial Vicar; Deacons Jim Paris; Bob Kotzbauer; Bill Rood.
Church & Res.: 601 Hill'N Dale Rd., 40503. Tel: 859-278-7432; Fax: 859-278-2453.
School—(Grades PreK-8), 605 Hill 'N Dale Rd., 40503. Tel: 859-277-3030; Fax: 859-277-1784. Email: lkeeney@mq.cdlex.org. Web: maryqueenschool.cdlex-.org. Rebecca Brown, Prin.; Betsy Tibe, Librarian. Lay Teachers 38; Students 402.
Catechesis/Religious Program—Students 893.

4—THE NEWMAN CENTER, HOLY SPIRIT (1963), Parish for Students, Faculty and Staff of the University of Kentucky. Revs. Albert J. DeGiacomo; Stephen Roberts, Parochial Vicar.
Res.: 320 Rose Ln., 40508. Tel: 859-255-8566; Fax: 859-254-7519.
Catechesis/Religious Program—Sr. Ellen Kehoe, S.P., D.R.E. Students 143.

5—ST. PAUL (1865) [JC] Rev. Charles W. Niehaus, S.J.; Sr. Clara Fehringer, O.S.U., Parish Life Dir.; Deacon Raymond D. Martorano.
Res.: 501 W. Short St., 40507-1254. Tel: 859-252-0738; Fax: 859-225-6127. Email: saintpaul@cdlex.org. Web: saintpaul.cdlex.org.
Catechesis/Religious Program—Carey Parker, D.R.E. Students 126.
See Inter-Parish Elementary - Sts. Peter and Paul, Lexington under St. Peter, Lexington for details.

6—PAX CHRISTI CATHOLIC CHURCH (1994) [CEM] Rev. Nicholas A. Pagano Jr.; Deacons Ralph B. Jahnige; Michael Rupinen; Melissa Holland, Pastoral Assoc.
Res.: 4001 Victoria Way, 40515. Tel: 859-273-2465; Fax: 859-245-8123.
Catechesis/Religious Program—Debra Rouholiman, C.R.E.

7—ST. PETER (1812) [JC] Rev. John E. List; Deacon Bill Wakefield; Pam Berger, Pastoral Assoc. In Res., Rev. Theodore A. Keller (Retired).
Res.: 125 Barr St., 40507-1321. Tel: 859-252-7551; Fax: 859-252-1853.
School—Inter-Parish Elementary - Sts. Peter and Paul School, (Grades PreK-8) Tel: 859-254-9257; Fax: 859-254-9050. Catherine Cybriwsky, Prin. Lay Teachers 44; Students 477.
Catechesis/Religious Program—Students 64.

8—ST. PETER CLAVER (1887) Rev. Norman Fischer; Deacon James Weathers, Parish Life Dir.
Res.: 410 Jefferson St., 40508-1319. Tel: 859-254-0030; Fax: 859-253-6740.
Catechesis/Religious Program—Fax: 859-253-6740. Nita Clarke, C.R.E. Students 52.

OUTSIDE THE CITY OF LEXINGTON

ASHLAND, BOYD CO., HOLY FAMILY (1860) [CEM] Rev. John P. Noe; Deacon Bob Maher.
Res.: 900 Winchester Ave., 41101-7497. Tel: 606-329-1607; Fax: 606-329-1806.
School—(Grades PreK-8), 932 Winchester Ave., 41101. Tel: 606-324-7040; Fax: 606-324-6288. Mrs. Mary Lou Chandler, Prin. Lay Teachers 13; Students 146.
Catechesis/Religious Program—Students 52.
Mission—St. Lawrence Greenup.

BARBOURVILLE, KNOX CO., ST. GREGORY (1910) Rev. Anthony Muthu, H.G.N.; Deacon Jack Raymond.
Church: 329 N. Sycamore Dr., 40906-1540. Tel: 606-546-4461; Fax: 606-546-4461.
Catechesis/Religious Program—Kathy Greene, D.R.E. Students 11.

BEATTYVILLE, LEE CO., QUEEN OF ALL SAINTS (1965) Rev. Joseph N. Koury Jr.; Sr. Alice Retzner, O.S.F., Pastoral Assoc.
Mailing Address: P.O. Box 563, 41311-0563. Tel: 606-464-8695; Fax: 606-464-3357 (Call First).
Res.: 88 Railroad St., 41311. Tel: 606-464-3357. Email: queenas1@bellsouth.net.
Mission—Booneville Catholic Church of the Holy Family (1984) 1439 KY 11 S., Booneville, Owsley Co. 41314. Tel: 606-593-6948; Fax: 606-593-6948. Email: meilermanosf@yahoo.com. Sisters Angie Keil, O.S.F., Pastoral Assoc.; Marge Eilerman, O.S.F, Pastoral Assoc.
Catechesis/Religious Program—Tel: 606-593-6948. Students 11.
Oratory—St. Therese (1948) P.O. Box 563, Heidelberg, Lee Co. 41311. Tel: 606-464-3357.

BEREA, MADISON CO., ST. CLARE (1950) Rev. Michael Flanagan; Mr. John Roche, Pastoral Assoc.
Res.: 622 Chestnut St., 40403. Tel: 859-228-0937; Fax: 859-985-8413. Email: stclare@cdlex.org.
Catechesis/Religious Program—Students 51.
Mission—Our Lady of Mt. Vernon (1954) P.O. Box 1006, Mt. Vernon, Rockcastle Co. 40456. Tel: 859-985-8413.
Mission—St. Paul (1973) P.O. Box 189, McKee, Jackson Co. 40456. Tel: 606-287-7601. Email: stpaulmk@prtnet.org. Rebecca Koury, Pastoral Assoc.

CARLISLE, NICHOLAS CO., SHRINE OF OUR LADY OF GUADALUPE (1962) Rev. John C. Curtis.
Church: 617 E. Main St., 40311. Tel: 859-289-5502.
Res.: 1007 Main St., Paris, 40361-1709. Tel: 859-987-1571; Fax: 859-987-7367.
Catechesis/Religious Program—Tel: 859-289-5586. Sr. Dorothy Bondi, O.S.U., D.R.E. Students 24.

CORBIN, KNOX CO., SACRED HEART (1902) Rev. Michael Weglicki; Deacon Jack Raymond.
Res.: 703 Masters St., P.O. Box 455, 40702. Tel: 606-528-5222; Fax: 606-523-9901. Email: sacredheartparish@newwavecomm.net. Web: corbin.cdlex.org.
School—St. Camillus Academy, (Grades 8-8), 709 Roy Kidd Ave., 40701. Tel: 606-528-5077; Fax: 606-526-0106. Email: stcam@bellsouth.net. Web: homeforangels.org. Ms. Patty Beckert, Prin. Sisters 2; Lay Teachers 8; Students 119.
Catechesis/Religious Program—Students 67.

CUMBERLAND, HARLAN CO., ST. STEPHEN (1940) Rev. Mani George Thellikalayil, M.C.
Res.: 304 Central St., 40823. Tel: 606-589-5616; Fax: 606-589-4549. Email: sstephen@windstream.net.

DANVILLE, BOYLE CO., SS. PETER & PAUL (1807) Rev. Thomas P. Farrell; Deacon Jeremiah Noe.
Res.: 117 W. Main St., 40422. Tel: 859-236-2111; Fax: 859-236-2922. Email: ssppchurch@cdlex.org. Web: danville.cdlex.org.
Catechesis/Religious Program—Students 156.

DAVID, FLOYD CO., **SAINT VINCENT MISSION INC.*, 6359 Hwy. 404, P.O. Box 232, 41616.

FRANKFORT, FRANKLIN CO., GOOD SHEPHERD (1845) Rev. Charles W. Howell; Deacon Thomas Snyder.
Church & Office: 72 Shepherd Way, Hwy. 421 S., 40601. Tel: 502-227-4511 (Office); Fax: 502-875-9854 (Office).
School—(Grades K-8), 75 Shepherd Way, 40601. Tel: 502-223-5041; Fax: 502-223-2755. Stephanie Sims, Prin.; Dee Depenbrock, Librarian. Lay Teachers 15; Students 142.
Catechesis/Religious Program—Students 110.

GEORGETOWN, SCOTT CO., SS. FRANCIS & JOHN CATHOLIC CHURCH (1869) [CEM] Rev. Linh Nguyen; Deacons John Calandrella; Skip Olson.
Res.: 509 E. Main St., 40324. Tel: 502-863-3404; Fax: 502-863-3402. Email: parishoffice@ssfrancisjohn.org.
School—(Grades PreK-8), 106 Military St., 40324. Tel: 502-863-2607; Fax: 502-863-2259. Rebecca Elswerky, Prin. Lay Teachers 14; Students 182.
Catechesis/Religious Program—Tel: 502-863-1213. Carmen Garcia, D.R.E. Students 121.

GRAYSON, CARTER CO., SS. JOHN & ELIZABETH (1964) Sr. Marie Colette Gerry, O.S.F., Parish Life Dir.; Rev. Bruce C. Brylinski, G.H.M.
Church: 799 State Hwy. 1947, 41143. Tel: 606-474-9979; Fax: 606-474-9979. Email: sje1947@gmail.com.
Res.: P.O. Box 841, 41143. Tel: 606-474-9897.
Catechesis/Religious Program—Tel: 606-474-6440. Nancy Kozee, D.R.E. Students 16.

HARLAN, HARLAN CO., HOLY TRINITY (1948) Marjorie D. Grieshop, Parish Life Dir.; Rev. Mani George Thellikalayil, M.C.
Res.: 2536 S. U.S. Hwy. 421, 40831-1798. Tel: 606-573-6311; Fax: 606-574-0093. Email: holytrinity@bellsouth.net.
The Learning Center—Tel: 606-573-3570. Email: holytrinitylearningcenter@harlanonline.net.
Catechesis/Religious Program—Students 30.

HARRODSBURG, MERCER CO., ST. ANDREW (1858) [CEM] Rev. Noel Zamora; Deacon Richard L. Abbey.
Res.: 1125 Danville Rd., P.O. Box 648, 40330-0648. Tel: 859-734-4270; Fax: 859-733-9770. Email: standrewschurch2@bellsouth.net.
Catechesis/Religious Program—Mary Jane Trimble, D.R.E. Students 133.
Mission—St. Mary (1949) 307 S. Buell St., Perryville, Boyle Co. 40468.

HAZARD, PERRY CO., MOTHER OF GOOD COUNSEL (1913) Rev. Michael Chowning, O.F.M.; Ms. Patricia Riestenberg, Pastoral Assoc.
Res.: 329 Poplar St. & Cedar St., 41701. Tel: 606-436-2533; Fax: 606-435-0171.
Catechesis/Religious Program—Students 20.

JACKSON, BREATHITT CO., HOLY CROSS (1923) Bro. Jerome Beetz, O.F.M., Parish Life Dir.; Rev. Reynolds Garland, O.F.M.
Church: 51 Brewers Dr., 41339-9616. Tel: 606-666-7871; Fax: 606-666-7370.
Mission—Catholic Church of the Good Shepherd (1987) P.O. Box 742, Campton, Wolfe Co. 41301. Tel: 606-668-3731. (A Mission of Holy Cross,

Jackson, KY).

JELLICO, WHITLEY CO., KY & CAMPBELL CO., TN, ST. BONIFACE (1886) [CEM] Rev. Michael Weglicki; Deacon John C. Coe; Sr. Margaret Verhoff, C.D.P., Parish Life Dir.
Res.: 76 W. Sycamore St., Williamsburg, 40769. Tel: 606-549-2156.
Catechesis/Religious Program—Students 3.

JENKINS, LETCHER CO., ST. GEORGE (1912) Rev. Santosh Madanu, H.G.N.
Res.: P.O. Box 787, 41537. Tel: 606-832-2409.
Catechesis/Religious Program—
Mission—Holy Angels (1960) McRoberts, Letcher Co.

LANCASTER, GARRARD CO., ST. WILLIAM (1951) Rev. Peter Joseph, H.G.N.
Res.: 224 Lexington St., P.O. Box 269, 40444. Tel: 859-792-4009; Fax: 859-792-4009. Email: stwlcath@windstream.net.
Catechesis/Religious Program—Tel: 859-792-4578. Joni Jordan, D.R.E. Students 16.

LAWRENCEBURG, ANDERSON CO., ST. LAWRENCE (1873) Rev. Catesby Clay Jr.
Res.: 120 Gatewood Ave., 40342. Tel: 502-839-6381; Fax: 502-859-2419. Email: stlawrencecathol@bellsouth.net. Web: lawrenceburg.cdlex.org.
Catechesis/Religious Program—Angela Pike, C.R.E. Students 73.

LONDON, LAUREL CO., ST. WILLIAM (1905) [CEM] Rev. Patrick F. Stewart.
Res.: 521 W. 5th St., 40741. Tel: 606-864-7500; Fax: 606-864-8263. Email: stwilliam@windstream.net. Web: london.cdlex.org.
Catechesis/Religious Program—Sr. Marjorie Manning, C.S.C. Students 70.
Mission—St. Ann (1952) 222 Town Branch Rd., Manchester, Clay Co. 40962-1322. Tel: 606-598-2718; Fax: 606-598-2718. Email: saint_ann@windstream.net.
Oratory—St. Sylvester, East Bernstadt

LOUISA, LAWRENCE CO., ST. JUDE (1982) Rev. Msgr. Ralph Beiting; Rev. M. Maria Salethu Jesuraj, H.G.N., Parochial Vicar.
Res.: 1121 Meadowbrook Ln., 41230. Tel: 606-638-3409; Fax: 606-638-0220. Email: churchstjude@yahoo.com. Web: www.louisa.cdlex.org.
Catechesis/Religious Program—Sr. Pat Cataldi, C.P.S., C.R.E. Students 20.
Mission—St. John Neumann (1980) Rte. 292, Hode, Martin Co. 41223. Tel: 606-395-5316. Mailing Address: P.O. Box 132, Beauty, 41203.

LYNCH, HARLAN CO., CHURCH OF THE RESURRECTION (1917) Rev. Mani George Thellikalayil, M.C.
Res.: 304 Central St., Cumberland, 40823. Tel: 606-589-5616; Fax: 606-589-4549. Email: sstephen@windstream.net.
Catechesis/Religious Program—Mrs. Anna Carruba, D.R.E.

MIDDLESBORO, BELL CO., ST. JULIAN (1890) Rev. Thobias Sabariar, M.C.
Res.: 118 E. Chester Ave., 40965-1256. Tel: 606-248-2068; Fax: 606-248-2207. Email: saintjuliancatho@bellsouth.net.
School—(Grades K-6), 116 E. Chester Ave., 40965. Tel: 606-248-8309; Fax: 606-248-8309. Kim Honeycutt, Prin. Lay Teachers 4; Students 64.
Catechesis/Religious Program—Theresa Tanner, D.R.E. Tel: 423-869-9555; Barry Tanner, D.R.E. Tel: 423-869-9255. Students 33.
Mission—St. Anthony (1889) c/o 118 E. Chester Ave., 40965.

MONTICELLO, WAYNE CO., ST. PETER (1967) Deacon Thomas Wagner, Parish Life Dir.; Rev. John L. Kieffer, S.J.
Office: P.O. Box 669, 42633. Tel: 606-348-9416. Web: monticello.cdlex.org.
Res.: 455 Michigan Ave., 42633. Tel: 606-348-0086.
Catechesis/Religious Program—Students 14.

MOREHEAD, ROWAN CO., CHURCH OF JESUS OUR SAVIOR (1961) Rev. Paul Prabell; Deacons William T. Buelterman; William R. Grimes.
Res.: 315 Battson-Oates, P.O. Box 307, 40351. Tel: 606-784-4392; Fax: 606-783-0190.
Catechesis/Religious Program—Sr. Rosemary McCormack, D.R.E. Students 95.
Mission—St. Julie Catholic Church (1969) P.O. Box 382, Owingsville, 40360. Tel: 606-674-3261.
Chapel—Morehead, St. Claire Medical Center, Tel: 606-783-6500.

MOUNT STERLING, MONTGOMERY CO., ST. PATRICK (1868) [CEM] Rev. Frank Brawner.
Office: 139 W. Main St., 40353. Tel: 859-498-0300; Fax: 859-499-1742. Email: stpatmtsterling@bellsouth.net.
Catechesis/Religious Program—Diana Ingram, C.R.E. Students 57.

NICHOLASVILLE, JESSAMINE CO., ST. LUKE (1867) Revs. William C. Bush; Patrick Fitzsimons, Parochial Vicar; Deacon Frank Keller.
Res.: 304 S. Main St., 40356. Tel: 859-885-4892; Fax: 859-885-6762. Email: nicholasville@catholicweb.com. Web: nicholasville.cdlex.org.
Catechesis/Religious Program—Marquita Stafford, D.R.E. Students 54.

OTTENHEIM, LINCOLN CO., ST. SYLVESTER (1885) [CEM] Rev. Peter Joseph, H.G.N.
Res.: 224 Lexington St., P.O. Box 269, Lancaster, 40444. Tel: 859-792-4009; Fax: 859-792-4009. Email: stwlcath@windstream.net.
Catechesis/Religious Program—Tel: 606-365-2902. Carrie Adams, D.R.E. Students 8.

PAINTSVILLE, JOHNSON CO., ST. MICHAEL CATHOLIC CHURCH (1941) Rev. Terence E. Hoppenjans; Deacons John M. Lewis; Paul David Brown.
Res.: 720 Washington Ave., 41240. Tel: 606-789-4455; Fax: 606-789-4455. Email: stmike@bellsouth.net.
School—Our Lady of the Mountains, (Grades PreK-8), 405 Third St., 41240. Tel: 606-789-3661; Fax: 606-789-3661. Sr. Lillian Jordan, Prin. Lay Teachers 12; Students 62.
Catechesis/Religious Program—Kelli Salyers, D.R.E. Students 28.

PARIS, BOURBON CO., ANNUNCIATION OF THE BLESSED VIRGIN MARY (1856) [CEM] Rev. John C. Curtis.
Res.: 1007 Main St., 40361. Tel: 859-987-1571; Fax: 859-987-7367.
School—St. Mary, (Grades PreK-8), 1121 Main St., 40361. Tel: 859-987-3815; Fax: 859-987-3815. Melody Thompson, Prin. Lay Teachers 9; Students 76.
Catechesis/Religious Program—Jennifer Frye, D.R.E. Students 64.

PIKEVILLE, PIKE CO., ST. FRANCIS OF ASSISI (1949) Rev. Daniel Fister.
Office & Res.: 132 Bryan St., 41501. Tel: 606-437-6822; Fax: 606-437-6822.
Church: 136 S. College St., 41501.
School—(Grades K-6), 147 Bryan St., 41501. Tel: 606-437-6117. Craig Chapman, Prin. Lay Teachers 5; Students 77.
Catechesis/Religious Program—Sr. Beth Carrender, O.S.F., D.R.E. Students 41.
Mission—St. Joseph the Worker (1985) P.O. Box 55, Elkhorn City, Pike Co. 41522. Tel: 606-754-5225; Fax: 606-754-5294. Sr. Margie Zureick, C.P.P.S., Pastoral Assoc.
Mission—Jesus of the Mountains Catholic Church (1988) 38 Birch Ct., Phelps, Pike Co. 41553. Tel: 606-456-7907. Sr. Beth Carrender, O.S.F., Pastoral Assoc.

PRESTONSBURG, FLOYD CO., ST. MARTHA (1984) Rev. Robert Damron.
Res.: 60 Martha Vineyard, 41653. Tel: 606-874-9526. Email: stmarthas@bellsouth.net. Web: www.home.catholicweb.com/prestonsburg.
Catechesis/Religious Program—Patty McBride, D.R.E. Students 30.
Chapel—Martin, St. Joseph Hospital, Tel: 606-285-6400.

RAVENNA, ESTILL CO., ST. ELIZABETH OF HUNGARY (1932) Rev. Albert Fritsch, S.J.
Res.: 316 5th St., 40472-1812. Tel: 606-723-4705.
Catechesis/Religious Program—Students 6.

RICHMOND, MADISON CO., ST. MARK (1867) Rev. James W. Sichko; Deacon James D. Bennett.
Res.: 608 W. Main St., 40475. Tel: 859-623-2989; Fax: 859-623-4652.
School—(Grades PreK-3) Tel: 859-623-2989, Ext. 4; Fax: 859-623-9947. Connie Fischer, Prin. Lay Teachers 8; Students 72.

SALYERSVILLE, MAGOFFIN CO., ST. LUKE (1982) Rev. Robert Damron.
1221 Parkway Dr., 41465. Tel: 606-349-5320. Email: stluke41465@hotmail.com. Mailing Address: P.O. Box 129, 41465.
Catechesis/Religious Program—Students 4.

SOMERSET, PULASKI CO., ST. MILDRED (1887) Revs. Michael J. Ramler; Carlos Martinez, Parochial Vicar; Deacons G. A. Weigel; Vincent E. Cheshire; Larry Cranfill.
203 S. Central Ave., 42501. Tel: 606-678-5051. Email: saintmildred@windstream.net. Web: somerset.cdlex.org.
Catechesis/Religious Program—Students 65.
Mission—Good Shepherd Chapel 130 N. Main St., Whitley City, 42653. Tel: 606-376-8728.

STANTON, POWELL CO., OUR LADY OF THE MOUNTAINS (1984) Rev. Albert Fritsch, S.J.; Sr. Mary Jane Kreidler, Parish Life Dir.
1093 E. College Ave., P.O. Box 727, 40380-2354. Tel: 606-663-5919.
Catechesis/Religious Program—Fax: 606-663-5915. Students 17.

VERSAILLES, WOODFORD CO., ST. LEO (1891) Rev. Daniel P. Schwendeman.
Res. & Church: 295 Huntertown Rd., 40383. Tel: 859-879-8481; 859-873-4573 (Church); Fax: 859-873-1495 (Church). Email: stleo@cdlex.org. Web: versailles.cdlex.org.
School—(Grades K-8), 255 Huntertown Rd., 40383. Tel: 606-873-4591. Email: stleoschool@catholicweb.com. Web: stleoschool.cdlex-.org. George Pressey, Prin. Lay Teachers 14; Students 163.
Catechesis/Religious Program—Pat Newell, D.R.E. Students 143.

WEST LIBERTY, MORGAN CO., PRINCE OF PEACE (1963) Rev. M. Daniel Edelen.
Res.: Pine Acres Dr., P.O. Box 393, 41472. Tel: 606-743-3266.
Rectory—Tel: 606-743-4817.

WILLIAMSBURG, WHITLEY CO., OUR LADY OF PERPETUAL HELP (1963) Rev. Anthony Muthu, H.G.N.; Sisters Mary Joyce Moeller, C.D.P., Parish Min.; Margaret Verhoff, C.D.P., Parish Life Dir.; Deacon John C. Coe.
Office: 76 W. Sycamore St., 40769. Tel: 606-549-2156. Email: olph.boniface@gmail.com. Web: williamsburg.cdlex.org.
Catechesis/Religious Program—Students 7.

WINCHESTER, CLARK CO., ST. JOSEPH (1872) Rev. Frank Brawner; Deacon Anthony R. Fritz.
Office: 248 S. Main St., 40391.
Res.: 254 S. Main St., 40391. Tel: 859-744-4917; Fax: 859-744-0994. Email: stjoseph@cdlex.org.
School—St. Agatha Academy, (Grades K-8), 244 S. Main St., 40391. Tel: 859-744-6484; Fax: 859-744-0268. Email: stagatha@bellsouth.net. John Pica, Prin. (Montessori) Lay Teachers 21; Students 144.
Catechesis/Religious Program—Kathie Schweikart, D.R.E. Students 34.

Chaplains of Public Institutions

LEXINGTON. *Federal Medical Center*, 3301 Leestown Rd., 40507. Rev. David Rabenecker, O.S.B.
Veterans' Administration Hospital, Leestown Pk., 40511. Tel: 859-233-4511. Vacant.

ASHLAND. *Federal Correctional Institution*. Vacant.

MANCHESTER. *Federal Correction Institute*. Vacant.

Special Assignment:
Revs.—
Aduaka, Anthony, (On Duty Outside of Diocese)
Fedders, William, (On Administrative Leave)
Johnson, Carl, Allenwood Correctional Complex, Allenwood, PA
Molina, Arturo, (On Duty Outside of Diocese)
Sichko, James W., Asst. to the Bishop, Special Projects

Retired:
Rev. Msgr.—
Rolf, John J., 15 Lemans Dr., Naples, FL 34112.
Revs.—
Dane, John, 193 Barnsley Rd., Wombwell, Barnsley, South Yorkshire S73 8DR, England.
Fraenzle, Wilfred, 1750 Summerhill Dr., 40515.
Hehman, Lawrence W., 1332 Viley Rd., 40504.
Imfeld, Thomas J., 200 Red Oak St., Corbin, 40702.
Keller, Theodore A., 153 Barr St., 40507.
McDonald, Charles J., 2725 Bay Cedar Cove, 40511.
Nieberding, Robert, 2716 Green Vally Ct., 40511.
Osburg, Frank C., 2717 Bay Cedar Cove, 40511.
Poole, William G., 2724 Green Valley Ct., 40511.
Stratman, Raymond, 2720 Green Valley Ct., 40511.
Thai, Thomas V., Ph.D., 4698 Long Dr., Hamilton, OH 45011.

Permanent Deacons:
Abbey, Richard L.
Agnoli, Frank
Bennett, James D.
Boduch, Robert
Brown, David
Buelterman, William
Burns, Michael
Calandrella, John
Cheshire, Vincent
Coe, John C.
Coriale, Matthew C.
Cox, James H.
Cranfill, Larry
Daukas, Michael R.
Downey, Richard C.
Flowers, Don K.
Fritz, Anthony R.
Fugazzi, Frederick E., Jr.
Greenwell, William
Grimes, William R.
Horine, James, (Retired)
Jahnige, Ralph B.
Joice, Robert S.
Keller, William F.
Kotzbauer, Robert N.
Lackney, Robert R., (Retired)
Lewis, John M.
Maher, Robert J.
Marshall, Boyd, (Retired)

Martorano, Raymond D.
Mellenger, Karl, (Retired)
Noe, Jeremiah
O'Neil, Dennis J., (Retired)
Olson, Paul E.
Ouellette, Guy R.
Paris, Jim
Raymond, Jack
Rohan, Thomas, (Retired)
Rood, William A.
Root, Paul S.
Ross, Carter, Jr., (Retired)
Rupinen, Michael
Schueneman, Joseph T., (Retired)
Snyder, Thomas, (Retired)
Strauffer, Mark B.
Wagner, Thomas
Wakefield, Bill
Weathers, James
Weigel, Gerard A.
Weinmann, Timothy E.
Woelfel, Mark T.
Wolterman, Arden J.
Young, Melvin, (Retired)
Zeigler, John F.

PARISH PILGRIMAGE SHRINES

CARLISLE. *Our Lady of Guadalupe Shrine*, 617 E. Main St., 40311.

INSTITUTIONS LOCATED IN THE DIOCESE

[A] HIGH SCHOOLS, DIOCESAN

LEXINGTON. *Lexington Catholic High School*, 2250 Clays Mill Rd., 40503. Tel: 859-277-7183; Fax: 859-276-5086. Web: www.lexingtoncatholic.com. Dr. Steven Angelucci, Pres.; Mrs. Sally Stevens, Prin.; Karen McDavid, Librarian. Lay Teachers 63; Students 807.

[B] HIGH SCHOOLS, PRIVATE

MARTIN. *The Piarist School* (1990) (Grades 7-12), Rte. 80, P.O. Box 870, 41649. Tel: 606-285-3950; Fax: 606-285-3950. Email: piarist@bellsouth.net. Web: www.piaristschool.org. Rev. Thomas R. Carroll, Sch.P., Prin. College Prep High School. Priests 2; Lay Teachers 11; Students 95.

[C] ELEMENTARY SCHOOLS

CORBIN. *St. Camillus Academy* (1914) (Grades PreK-8), 709 Roy Kidd Ave., 40701. Tel: 606-528-5077; Fax: 606-526-0106. Email: stcam@bellsouth.net. Web: homeforangels.org. Ms. Patty Beckert, Prin. Sisters 2; Lay Teachers 8; Students 119.

[D] GENERAL HOSPITALS

LEXINGTON. *Continuing Care Hospital, Inc.* (2001) 150 N. Eagle Creek Dr., 40509. Tel: 859-967-5744; Fax: 859-967-5616. Email: willto@sje.sjhlex.org. Tonja Williams, Pres. & CEO.

St. Joseph Health System, Inc. dba St. Joseph East 150 N. Eagle Creek Dr., 40509. Tel: 859-967-5000; Fax: 859-967-5766. Web: www.sjhlex.org/east. Bruce Klockars, Interim CEO. Bed Capacity 152; Patients Assisted Annually 98,941.

St. Joseph Hospital, One St. Joseph Dr., 40504. Tel: 859-313-1000; Fax: 859-313-3000. Bruce Klockars, Pres. & CEO. (Member of Catholic Health Initiatives). Congregation of Divine Providence 1; Sister Servants of the Immaculate Heart of Mary 1; Bed Capacity 468; Patients Assisted Annually 129,648.

ASHLAND. *Our Lady of Bellefonte Hospital, Inc.*, 1000 St. Christopher Dr., 41101. Tel: 606-833-3333; Fax: 606-833-3593. Web: www.olbh.com. Kevin Halter, Interim CEO; Marguerite P. Gilner, Vice Pres., Mission; Rev. John P. Noe, Chap.; Sandy Adams, Chap. (Member of Bon Secours Kentucky Health System, Inc.) Bed Capacity 214; Patients Assisted Annually 189,000.

BEREA. *Saint Joseph-Berea*, 305 Estill St., 40403. Tel: 859-986-3151; Fax: 859-986-6768. Email: greggerard@catholichealth.net. A member of Catholic Health Initiatives. Bed Capacity 25.

IRVINE. *Marcum and Wallace Memorial Hospital*, 60 Mercy Ct., 40336. Tel: 606-723-2115; Fax: 606-723-2951. Email: sstarling@marcumandwallace.org. Web: www.marcumandwallace.org. Susan Starling, Pres. & CEO. (Member of Mercy Health System, Cincinnati, OH). Bed Capacity 25; Patients Assisted Annually 53,354.

LONDON. *Saint Joseph-London*, 1001 Saint Joseph Ln., 40741. Tel: 606-330-6000; Fax: 606-330-6020. Email: vbdempsey@sj-london.org. Web: saintjoseph-london.org. Virginia B. Dempsey, Pres. (Member of Catholic Health Initiatives). Bed Capacity 120; Patients Assisted Annually 246,302.

MARTIN. *Saint Joseph-Martin*, Box 910, 41649. Tel: 606-285-6400; Fax: 606-285-6409. Email: judithparsons@catholichealth.net. Web: www.saintjoseph-martin.org. Ms. Kathy Stumbo, Pres. Member of Catholic Health Initiatives. Bed Capacity 25; Patients Assisted Annually (Patient Visits) 31,302.

MOREHEAD. *Saint Claire Regional Medical Center*, 222 Medical Cir., 40351. Tel: 606-783-6500; Fax: 606-783-6503. Email: mjneff@st-claire.org. Web: st-claire.org. Mr. Mark Neff, Pres. & CEO. Sisters of Notre Dame. Sisters 5; Bed Capacity 159; Bassinets 10; Patients Assisted Annually 375,421; Patients with Primary Care Centers 80,162.

MOUNT STERLING. *St. Joseph Hospital Mt. Sterling*, 225 Falcon Dr., 40353. Tel: 859-497-5000. Email: bennynolan@catholichealth.net. Mr. Benny Nolan, Pres. Bed Capacity 63; Patients Assisted Annually 100,806.

[E] PRIMARY HEALTH CARE SERVICES

FRENCHBURG. *St. Claire Regional Family Medicine-Frenchburg*, 732 Hwy. 36, 40322. Tel: 606-768-2191; Fax: 606-768-6130. Email: mjgulley@st-claire.org. Web: st-claire.org. Mary Jane Humkey, Medical Dir. (Div. of St. Claire Regional Medical Center). Patients Assisted Annually 12,000.

OLIVE HILL. *St. Claire Regional Family Medicine-Olive Hill*, 155 Bricklayer St., P.O. Box 1268, 41164. Tel: 606-286-4152; Fax: 606-286-2385. Janie Zornes, Clinic Coord. (Div. of St. Claire Medical Center). Patients Assisted Annually 14,000.

OWINGSVILLE. *St. Claire Regional Family Medicine - Owingsville*, 632 Slate Ave., P.O. Box 1120, 40360. Tel: 606-674-6386; Fax: 606-674-3096. Levonda Thomas, Clinic Coord. (Div. of St. Claire Medical Center). Patients Assisted Annually 16,000.

SANDY HOOK. *St. Claire Regional Family Medicine-Sandy Hook*, P.O. Box 748, 41171. Tel: 606-738-5155; Fax: 606-738-5420. Lisa Goldstein M.D., Clinic Medical Dir. (Div. of St. Claire Medical Center). Patients Assisted Annually 14,000.

[F] NURSING HOMES

VERSAILLES. *Taylor Manor Nursing Home*, 300 Berry Ave., 40383. Tel: 859-873-4201; Fax: 859-873-4856. Email: tmnh1958@msn.com. Sr. Mary Faustina Zugelder, S.J.W., Admin.; Rev. Brice Bahouamio, Chap. Sisters of St. Joseph the Worker 5; Patients Assisted Annually 210.

[G] RESIDENCES OF PRIESTS

PRESTONSBURG. *Piarist Fathers* (1989) P.O. Box 870, Martin, 41649. Tel: 606-285-3950; Fax: 606-285-3950. Rev. Thomas R. Carroll, Sch.P. Priests 2.

[H] MONASTERIES FOR SISTERS

MARTIN. *Mt. Tabor Benedictines-The Dwelling Place Monastery* (1982) 150 Mt. Tabor Rd., 41649. Tel: 606-886-9624; Fax: 606-886-9624. Email: mtabor150@hotmail.com. Web: www.geocities.com/athens/9871. Sr. Judy Yunker, O.S.B., Prioress. Total number in Community (Perpetually Professed) 5.

[I] SECULAR INSTITUTES

LEXINGTON. *Society of St. Vincent de Paul*, 1730 Summerhill Dr., 40515. Tel: 859-266-8003. Email: svdplex@yahoo.com. Tim Lewis, Pres. District Council of Lexington.

[J] SOCIAL SERVICES

MOUNT VERNON. **Appalachia Science in the Public Interest*, 50 Lair St., 40456. Tel: 606-256-0077; Fax: 606-256-2779. Email: aspi@a-spi.org. Web: www.a-spi.org. Rev. John L. Kieffer, S.J.

[K] RENEWAL CENTERS

HAZARD. *Father Farrell Spiritual Life Center*, 329 Poplar at Cedar, 41701. Tel: 606-436-2533; Fax: 606-435-0171. Email: mike.chowning@mgccc.org. Rev. Michael Chowning, O.F.M., Dir.; Pat Riestenberg, Assoc. Dir.

LANCASTER. *Cliffview Retreat Center*, 789 Bryants Camp Rd., 40444. Tel: 859-792-3333; 877-792-3330; Fax: 859-792-1223. Email: cliffctr@cdlex.org. Web: www.cliffview.org. David Wells, Co-Dir.; Sharla Wells, Co-Dir.

MARTIN. *Mt. Tabor Retreat Center*, 150 Mt. Tabor Rd., 41649. Tel: 606-886-9624; Fax: 606-886-6598. Email: mtabor150@hotmail.com. Staff Sisters 5.

[L] NEWMAN CENTERS

LEXINGTON. *The Newman Center Holy Spirit Parish University of Kentucky* 320 Rose Ln., 40508. Tel: 859-255-8566; Fax: 859-254-7519. Email: timenewman@aol.com. Revs. Albert J. DeGiacomo; Stephen Roberts, Parochial Vicar.

BARBOURVILLE. *St. Gregory Church-Union College* 329 N. Sycamore St., 40906-1540. Tel: 606-546-4461; Fax: 606-546-4461. Email: stgreg@barbourville.com. Web: barbourville.catholicweb.com. Rev. Anthony Muthu, H.G.N.

BEREA. *St. Clare Church-Berea College* 711 Chestnut St., Ste. 3, 40403. Tel: 859-986-4633; Fax: 859-756-3408. Email: stclare@cdlex.org. Rev. Michael Flanagan.

MOREHEAD. *Catholic Student Center-Morehead State University* P.O. Box 307, 40351. Tel: 606-784-4392; Fax: 606-783-0190. Email: joscc@roadrunner.com. Web: www.cdlex.org/morehead. Rev. Paul Prabell.

RICHMOND. *Catholic Campus Ministry of St. Mark* Eastern Kentucky University, 405 University Dr., 40475-2154. Tel: 859-623-2989 (Center); Fax: 859-623-4652. Email: alanna.siniger@saintmarkcatholicchurch.net. Web: stmark-richmond.org/newman. Rev. James W. Sichko; P. Brian Walsh, Campus Min.

[M] MISCELLANEOUS

LEXINGTON. *Catholic Way Bible Study*, P.O. Box 22324, 40522-2324. Tel: 859-552-6484. Email: teachingleader@cwbs.org. Web: www.cwbs.org. Lavinia Spirito, Teaching Leader.

ASHLAND. *Bon Secours Kentucky Health System Foundation, Inc. dba Our Lady of Bellefonte Hospital Foundation* 1000 St. Christopher Dr., 41101. Tel: 606-833-3333. Web: www.careyoucantrust.com. Mr. Chuck Charles, Vice Pres., Foundation.

Bon Secours Kentucky Health System, Inc., 1000 St. Christopher Dr., 41101. Tel: 606-833-3333. Web: www.careyoucantrust.com. Kevin Halter, Int. CEO.

IRVINE. *Marcum & Wallace Memorial Hospital Foundation Inc.*, 60 Mercy Ct., 40336. Tel: 606-723-2115, Ext. 152; Fax: 606-723-2951. Email: sstarling@marcumandwallace.org. Web: www.marcumandwallace.org.

STANTON. *The Catholic Committee of Appalachia* (1970) 150 Mt. Tabor Rd., Martin, 41649. Tel: 606-886-9624. Email: janibosb@hotmail.com. Rev. John Rausch, G.H.M., Dir.

RELIGIOUS INSTITUTES OF MEN REPRESENTED IN THE DIOCESE

For further details refer to the corresponding bracketed number in the Religious Institutes of Men or Women section.

[]—*Benedictine Monks* (Swiss-American Congregations)—O.S.B.
[0520]—*Franciscan Friars* (St. John Baptist Prov.)—O.F.M.
[0570]—*Glenmary Home Missioners*—G.H.M.
[0585]—*Heralds of Good News* (India)—H.G.N.
[0690]—*Jesuit Fathers and Brothers* (Chicago & Detroit Provs.)—S.J.
[]—*Missionaries of Compassion* (India)—M.C.
[1040]—*Piarist Fathers* (U.S. Prov.)—Sch.P.
[]—*Priestly Fraternity of St. Peter*—F.S.S.P.

RELIGIOUS INSTITUTES OF WOMEN REPRESENTED IN THE DIOCESE

[0230]—*Benedictine Sisters of Pontifical Jurisdiction* (Pittsburgh, PA; Covington, KY; Martin, KY)—O.S.B.
[2100]—*Congregation of Humility of Mary*—C.H.M.
[2230]—*Congregation of the Infant Jesus*—C.I.J.
[3832]—*Congregation of the Sisters of St. Joseph*—C.S.J.
[1920]—*Congregation of the Sisters of the Holy Cross*—C.S.C.
[1730]—*Congregation of the Sisters of the Third Order of St. Francis* (Oldenburg, IN)—O.S.F.
[1070-13]—*Dominican Sisters* (Adrian, MI)—O.P.
[1070-14]—*Dominican Sisters* (Grand Rapids, MI)—O.P.
[2080]—*Home Mission Sisters of America (Glenmary)*—G.H.M.S.
[2710]—*Missionaries of Charity*—M.C.
[2850]—*Missionary Sisters of the Precious Blood*—C.P.S.
[2070]—*Religious of the Holy Union of the Sacred Hearts*—S.U.S.C.
[2970]—*School Sisters of Notre Dame* (Baltimore)—S.S.N.D.
[1680]—*School Sisters of St. Francis*—O.S.F.
[0430]—*Sisters of Charity of Blessed Virgin Mary* (Dubuque, IA)—B.V.M.
[0500]—*Sisters of Charity of Nazareth*—S.C.N.

[0580]—*Sisters of Charity of St. Augustine* (Rienfield, OH)—C.S.A.

[1000]—*The Sisters of Divine Providence of Kentucky*—C.D.P.

[]—*Sisters of Mercy of the Americas* (Belmont, NC)—R.S.M.

[2990]—*Sisters of Notre Dame* (Covington Prov.)—S.N.D.

[3360]—*Sisters of Providence of St. Mary-of-the-Woods, Indiana*—S.P.

[1540]—*Sisters of St Francis* (Clinton, IA)—O.S.F.

[3830-05]—*Sisters of St. Joseph* (Brentwood, NY)—C.S.J.

[3850]—*Sisters of St. Joseph of Chambery*—C.S.J.

[3920]—*Sisters of St. Joseph the Worker*—S.J.W.

[1760]—*Sisters of the Third Order of St. Francis of Penance and Charity* (Tiffin, OH)—O.S.F.

[2150]—*Sisters, Servants of the Immaculate Heart of Mary*—I.H.M.

[]—*Ursuline Sisters of Louisville* (Louisville, KY)—O.S.U.

[4120-04]—*Ursuline Sisters of the Immaculate Conception* (Cleveland, OH)—O.S.U.

DIOCESAN CEMETERIES

LEXINGTON. *Calvary*

ASHLAND. *Calvary*

MT. STERLING. *St. Thomas*

NECROLOGY

† Edelen, Richard, (Retired)—Died Feb. 28, 2011

An asterisk (*) denotes an organization that has established tax-exempt status directly with the IRS and is not covered by the USCCB Group Ruling.

Diocese of Lincoln

(Dioecesis Lincolnensis)

Most Reverend

FABIAN W. BRUSKEWITZ, D.D., S.T.D.

Bishop of Lincoln; ordained July 17, 1960; appointed Bishop of Lincoln March 24, 1992; consecrated May 13, 1992. *Mailing Address: P.O. Box 80328, Lincoln, NE 68501-0328.*

ERECTED AUGUST 2, 1887.

Square Miles 23,844.

Comprises that part of the State of Nebraska south of the Platte River.

Legal Title: "The Catholic Bishop of Lincoln." For legal titles of parishes and diocesan institutions, consult the Chancery.

Chancery: P.O. Box 80328, Lincoln, NE 68501-0328. Tel: 402-488-0921; Fax: 402-488-3569.

STATISTICAL OVERVIEW

Personnel	
Bishop	1
Priests: Diocesan Active in Diocese	122
Priests: Diocesan Active Outside Diocese	8
Priests: Retired, Sick or Absent	20
Number of Diocesan Priests	150
Religious Priests in Diocese	10
Total Priests in Diocese	160
Extern Priests in Diocese	1
Ordinations:	
Diocesan Priests	3
Religious Priests	2
Transitional Deacons	2
Permanent Deacons in Diocese	3
Total Sisters	148
Parishes	
Parishes	134
With Resident Pastor:	
Resident Diocesan Priests	84
Resident Religious Priests	1
Without Resident Pastor:	
Administered by Priests	49
Missions	1
Pastoral Centers	6
New Parishes Created	1
Professional Ministry Personnel:	
Sisters	148
Lay Ministers	2
Welfare	
Catholic Hospitals	4
Total Assisted	170,435
Homes for the Aged	3
Total Assisted	221
Day Care Centers	1
Total Assisted	45
Specialized Homes	1
Total Assisted	46
Special Centers for Social Services	22
Total Assisted	27,439
Residential Care of Disabled	1
Total Assisted	13
Other Institutions	1
Total Assisted	2,768
Educational	
Seminaries, Diocesan	1
Students from This Diocese	20
Students from Other Diocese	14
Diocesan Students in Other Seminaries	22
Seminaries, Religious	1
Students Religious	77
Total Seminarians	119
High Schools, Diocesan and Parish	6
Total Students	1,704
Elementary Schools, Diocesan and Parish	27
Total Students	5,257
Non-residential Schools for the Disabled	1
Total Students	13
Catechesis/Religious Education:	
High School Students	1,722
Elementary Students	5,312
Total Students under Catholic Instruction	14,127
Teachers in the Diocese:	
Priests	24
Sisters	36
Lay Teachers	458
Vital Statistics	
Receptions into the Church:	
Infant Baptism Totals	1,088
Minor Baptism Totals	268
Adult Baptism Totals	100
Received into Full Communion	184
First Communions	1,535
Confirmations	1,515
Marriages:	
Catholic	242
Interfaith	156
Total Marriages	398
Deaths	693
Total Catholic Population	96,625
Total Population	588,641

Former Bishops—Most Revs. THOMAS BONACUM, D.D., Bishop of Lincoln; cons. Nov. 20, 1887; died Feb. 4, 1911; J. HENRY TIHEN, D.D., cons. Bishop of Lincoln, July 6, 1911; transferred to the See of Denver, Sept. 21, 1917; died Jan. 14, 1940; CHARLES J. O'REILLY, D.D., cons. Bishop of Baker City, Aug. 24, 1903; transferred to the See of Lincoln, March 20, 1918; died Feb. 4, 1923; FRANCIS J. L. BECKMAN, S.T.D., D.D., cons. Bishop of Lincoln, May 1, 1924; elevated to the Metropolitan See of Dubuque, Jan. 17, 1930; died Oct. 17, 1948; LOUIS B. KUCERA, D.D., cons. Bishop of Lincoln, Oct. 28, 1930; died May 9, 1957; JAMES V. CASEY, appt. Auxiliary of Lincoln April 5, 1957; cons. April 24, 1957; appt. Bishop of Lincoln June 14, 1957; promoted to Archbishop of Denver, Feb. 22, 1967; died March 14, 1986; GLENNON P. FLAVIN, D.D., appt. Titular Bishop of Joannina and Auxiliary Bishop of St. Louis April 24, 1957; cons. May 30, 1957; promoted to See of Lincoln, May 29, 1967; retired March 24, 1992; died Aug. 27, 1995.

Chancery—3400 Sheridan Blvd., Lincoln, 68506. Mailing Address: P.O. Box 80328, Lincoln, 68501-0328. Tel: 402-488-0921; Fax: 402-488-3569. Office Hours: 8:30-5.

Moderator of the Curia—Rev. Msgr. TIMOTHY J. THORBURN, J.C.L.

Vicar General—Rev. Msgr. TIMOTHY J. THORBURN, J.C.L.

Chancellor—Rev. DANIEL J. RAYER, J.C.L.

Diocesan Tribunal—3400 Sheridan Blvd., Lincoln, 68506. Mailing Address: P.O. Box 80328, Lincoln, 68501-0328.

Officialis—Rev. Msgr. MARK D. HUBER, J.C.L., V.F.

Adjutant Judicial Vicars—Revs. MAURICE H. CURRENT, J.C.L.; CRAIG A. DOTY, J.C.L.

Promoters Justitiae—Rev. Msgr. TIMOTHY J. THORBURN, J.C.L.; Rev. GARY COULTER, J.C.L.

Defensores Vinculi—Rev. Msgr. TIMOTHY J. THORBURN, J.C.L.; Rev. GARY COULTER, J.C.L.

Judge—Rev. DANIEL J. RAYER, J.C.L.

Advocates—Very Rev. THOMAS Y. AU; Revs. CRAIG J. CLINCH; ADAM M. SUGHROUE; MATTHEW J. ZIMMER; THOMAS D. MCGUIRE; MICHAEL J. MORIN; RAFAEL RODRIGUEZ-FUENTES; BENJAMIN P. HOLDREN; CHRISTOPHER J. MILLER; Very Rev. MICHAEL K. HOULIHAN, V.F.; Revs. JAMES W. COOPER; ANDREW J. KURZ; JOSEPH J. FAULKNER; SEAN P. KILCAWLEY; BRENDAN R.J. KELLY; ANTHONY O. STAMMITTI; DAVID F. BOUREK; THOMAS M. BUSH; SCOTT M. COURTNEY; RAMON E. DECAEN; MATTHEW J. VANDEWALLE; JEREL A. SCHOLL; JAMIE S. HOTTOVY; THOMAS S. MACLEAN; JOSEPH J. BERNARDO; DAVID A. OLDHAM; SEAN M. TIMMERMAN; JAY M. BUHMAN; MARK L. CYZA; CHRISTOPHER P. GOODWIN; PAUL G. FRANK; LEE T. JIROVSKY; NICHOLAS A. KIPPER; LOTHAR M. GILDE; JONATHAN J. HASCHKE; ANDREW J. HEASLIP; DOMINIC T.H. PHAN; PATRICK F. BARVICK; MATTHEW M. ROLLING; STEVEN W. THOMLISON; KENNETH J. WEHRS.

Notaries—Rev. Msgr. JOHN T. FOLDA; Rev. CHRISTOPHER L. BARAK; Sr. COLLETTE BRUSKEWITZ, O.S.F.; Mrs. MARILYN L. FRIESEN.

Diocesan Consultors—Rev. Msgr. TIMOTHY J. THORBURN, J.C.L.; Revs. DANIEL J. RAYER, J.C.L.; MARK L. CYZA; THOMAS BROUILLETTE; Rev. Msgr. JOHN J PERKINTON; Rev. HARLAN D. P. WASKOWIAK; Rev. Msgr. MARK D. HUBER, J.C.L., V.F.; Rev. ROBERT A. MATYA.

Presbyteral Council—Rev. Msgrs. TIMOTHY J. THORBURN, J.C.L.; ROBERT A. ROH, V.F., M.A., S.T.L.; JAMES M. REINERT; Revs. MICHAEL J. MORIN; JOSEPH S. STEELE; LAWRENCE J. STOLEY; CHRISTOPHER P. GOODWIN; JARED MCCAMBRIDGE, F.S.S.P.; MARK S. PFEIFFER; JOHN R. SULLIVAN; Rev. Msgr. JOHN J PERKINTON; Revs. JOSEPH M. WALSH; DANIEL J. RAYER, J.C.L.; Rev. Msgr. MARK D. HUBER, J.C.L., V.F.; Rev. ROBERT A. MATYA.

Vicars For Religious—Rev. Msgr. JOHN T. FOLDA; Rev. CRAIG A. DOTY, J.C.L.

Deaneries and Deans—Rev. Msgr. MARK D. HUBER, J.C.L., V.F., Crete; Very Revs. JOHN C. ROONEY, V.F., David City; RUDOLF F. OBORNY, V.F., Fairbury; Rev. Msgr. ROBERT A. ROH, V.F., M.A., S.T.L., Falls City; Very Revs. MARK E. SEIKER, M.Div., Indianola; VALERIAN BARTEK, Grant; MICHAEL K. HOULIHAN, V.F., Hastings; JAMES C. SCHRADER JR., V.F., Lawrence; Rev. Msgr. LIAM M. BARR, Lincoln; Very Revs. NICHOLAS J. BAKER, V.F., Orleans; THOMAS Y. AU, Plattsmouth; Rev. Msgr. PAUL K. WITT, V.F., Wahoo; Very Rev. M. JAMES DIVIS, S.T.L., V.F., York.

Diocesan Offices and Directors

Apostleship of Prayer—Rev. MICHAEL J. MORIN, Dir.

Apostolate to the Elderly—Rev. ANTHONY O. STAMMITTI, Asst.

Apostolate to the Spanish Speaking—Revs. RAMON E. DECAEN, Dir.; WILLIAM D. GRANT, Asst. Dir.; JOHN J. KEEFE; THOMAS B. DUNAVAN; JAMES BENTON; JULIUS TVRDY; MARK L. CYZA; MATTHEW M. ROLLING.

Apostolate of Suffering—Rev. CHRISTOPHER K. KUBAT, 3700 Sheridan Blvd., Lincoln, 68506. Tel: 402-489-1834; Fax: 402-489-2046.

Archivist—Sr. KATHRYN MANEY, M.S.

Bishop's Lay Committee for Vocations—Rev. ROBERT A. MATYA, Chap.

Bishop's Pastoral Plan for Pro-Life Activities—GREG SCHLEPPENBACH, State Dir., 215 Centennial Mall S., Ste. 310, Lincoln, 68508.

Building Commission—Rev. Msgrs. JOHN J PERKINTON, Chm.; ADRIAN F. HERBEK, V.F. (Retired); IVAN F. VAP (Retired); TIMOTHY J. THORBURN, J.C.L.; Rev. LEO V. SEIKER; Rev. Msgr. MARK D. HUBER, J.C.L., V.F.; Revs. JAMIE S. HOTTOVY; THOMAS S. MACLEAN; Very Rev. JOHN C. ROONEY, V.F.

Catholic Relief Services—Rev. DANIEL J. RAYER, J.C.L., Dir.

Cemeteries—Rev. Msgr. DAVID R. HINTZ, Dir.

Censores Librorum—Very Rev. M. JAMES DIVIS, S.T.L., V.F.; Rev. Msgrs. JOHN T. FOLDA; TIMOTHY J. THORBURN, J.C.L.

Catholic Social Services—Rev. CHRISTOPHER K. KUBAT, Dir., Catholic Social Services: Pregnancy & Counseling Services, 3700 Sheridan Blvd., Lincoln, 68506. Tel: 402-489-1834; Fax: 402-489-2046. Administrative, Food Pantry, Housing Refugee & Emergency Services, 2241 O St., Lincoln, 68510. Tel: 402-474-1600; Fax: 402-474-1612. Email: curtkrueger@csshope.org; Catholic Social Services, 333 W. 2nd St., Hastings, 68901. Tel: 402-463-2112. Thrift Store, 325 W. 2nd St., Hastings, 68901. Tel: 402-463-2151. Email: pgibson@csshope.org; Catholic Social Services, 1014 Central Ave., Auburn, 68305. Tel: 402-274-4818. Catholic Social Services Thrift Store, 746 Broadway St., Imperial, 69033. Tel: 308-882-3065.

Clergy Relief Society--The Saint John Vianney Association—Rev. Msgr. TIMOTHY J. THORBURN, J.C.L., Sec. & Treas., Mailing Address: P.O. Box 80328, Lincoln, 68501-0328.

Commission on Alcohol and Drug Abuse—Very Revs. M. JAMES DIVIS, S.T.L., V.F., Dir.; JOHN C. ROONEY, V.F., 3400 Sheridan Blvd., Lincoln, 68506. Tel: 402-483-1941.

Commission for Sacred Liturgy and Sacred Music—Rev. Msgr. JOSEPH J. NEMEC, Chm.; Revs. CHRISTOPHER L. BARAK; ROBERT K. BARNHILL; MAURICE H. CURRENT, J.C.L.; LAWRENCE J. STOLEY; MATTHEW EICKHOFF; LEO D. KOSCH; Sr. COLLETTE BRUSKEWITZ, O.S.F.

Catholic Lawyers Guild—Rev. GARY COULTER, J.C.L.

Catholic Planned Giving Office—Mr. MICHAEL L. HENKENIUS, Dir., Mailing Address: P.O. Box 80328, Lincoln, 68501-0328. Tel: 402-488-2142.

Catholic Physicians Guild—Rev. Msgr. JOHN T. FOLDA, Spiritual Dir., 800 Fletcher Rd., Seward, 68434-7541. Tel: 402-643-4052.

Office of Religious Education (CCD)—Rev. CHRISTOPHER L. BARAK, Diocesan Dir. Tel: 402-488-2040. Diocesan Area CCD Directors: Revs. THOMAS BROUILLETTE; KENNETH F. HOESING; LEO D. KOSCH; JEREL A. SCHOLL; BERNARD A. LORENZ; THOMAS R. WALSH; Very Rev. NICHOLAS J. BAKER, V.F.; Revs. LORAS K. GRELL; THOMAS KUFFEL; THOMAS D. MCGUIRE; Very Rev. RUDOLF F. OBORNY, V.F.; Rev. MICHAEL S. STEC.

Cursillo—Very Rev. MARK E. SEIKER, M.Div., Dir.; JOHN SPRINGER, Asst.

Deaf Ministry—Revs. ROBERT K. BARNHILL, Dir. Tel: 402-488-2040 (TTY); MICHAEL S. STEC, Asst. Dir.

Diocesan Council of Catholic Women—Mrs. KRIS SARVER, Pres.; Revs. THOMAS J. LUX, Moderator; THOMAS D. MCGUIRE, Asst. Moderator.

Diocesan Director of Liturgy—Rev. Msgr. JOSEPH J. NEMEC, 735 S. 36th St., Lincoln, 68510.

Bishop Bruskewitz Charity and Stewardship Appeal (DDP)—Rev. KENNETH A. BOROWIAK, Dir., Mailing Address: P.O. Box 80328, Lincoln, 68501-0328.

Diocesan Finance Council—Most Rev. FABIAN WENDELIN BRUSKEWITZ, D.D., S.T.D.; Rev. Msgr. TIMOTHY J. THORBURN, J.C.L.; Rev. JOHN R. SULLIVAN, Finance Officer. Members: Rev. Msgrs. ADRIAN F. HERBEK, V.F. (Retired); JOHN T. FOLDA; Rev. MICHAEL G. MCCABE.

Diocesan Health Ministries, Inc.—Most Rev. FABIAN WENDELIN BRUSKEWITZ, D.D., S.T.D., Pres.; Rev. Msgrs. TIMOTHY J. THORBURN, J.C.L., Vice Pres.; JOHN T. FOLDA, Sec., Mailing Address: P.O. Box 80328, Lincoln, 68501-0328. Tel: 402-488-0921; Fax: 402-488-3569.

Diocesan Housing Ministries, Inc.—Most Rev. FABIAN WENDELIN BRUSKEWITZ, D.D., S.T.D., Pres.; Rev. Msgrs. TIMOTHY J. THORBURN, J.C.L.; JOHN T. FOLDA; JOHN J PERKINTON; Revs. DANIEL J. RAYER, J.C.L.; CHRISTOPHER K. KUBAT, Mailing Address: P.O. Box 80328, Lincoln, 68501-0328. Tel: 402-488-0921.

Ecumenical Affairs, Commission for—Revs. DOUGLAS D. DIETRICH, Chm.; MATTHEW EICKHOFF; Very Rev. M. JAMES DIVIS, S.T.L., V.F., Chm.; Rev. Msgr. PAUL K. WITT, V.F.; Rev. MAURICE H. CURRENT, J.C.L.

Engaged Encounter—Rev. MATTHEW EICKHOFF.

Evangelization Office—Rev. MATTHEW EICKHOFF, Chm.

Evangelization Committee—Rev. MATTHEW EICKHOFF, Chm. Tel: 402-488-2040; Rev. Msgrs. TIMOTHY J. THORBURN, J.C.L.; MYRON J. PLESKAC (Retired); JAMES D. DAWSON (Retired); PAUL K. WITT, V.F.; Revs. CHRISTOPHER L. BARAK; WILLIAM DAVID GRANT; Rev. Msgr. JOSEPH J. NEMEC.

Family Life Office—Rev. MATTHEW EICKHOFF, Dir., Mailing Address: P.O. Box 80328, Lincoln, 68501-0328. Tel: 402-488-2040.

Holy Childhood, Pontifical Association—Rev. K. WILLIAM HOLOUBEK, Dir., Mailing Address: P.O. Box 80328, Lincoln, 68501-0328.

Health Care Facilities—Revs. STEPHEN A. COONEY, 5401 South St., Lincoln, 68506; EDWIN L. STANDER, Mailing Address, 555 S. 70th St., Lincoln, 68510; JOSEPH P. FINN; CASEY PORADA; ANTHONY O. STAMMITTI; THOMAS S. MACLEAN.

Office of Information and Media—Rev. KENNETH A. BOROWIAK, Dir., Mailing Address: P.O. Box 80329, Lincoln, 68501. Tel: 402-488-0090.

Insurance—Rev. Msgr. TIMOTHY J. THORBURN, J.C.L., Dir.; Mrs. MARSHA BARTEK, Mailing Address: P.O. Box 80328, Lincoln, 68501-0328.

Legion of Mary—Revs. JEREMY L. HAZUKA, Spiritual Dir.; MARK L. CYZA, Asst. Spiritual Dir.; JOYCE RICHTER, Pres.

Liturgical Ministries—Rev. DANIEL J. RAYER, J.C.L.

Marriage Encounter—Rev. MATTHEW EICKHOFF, Dir.

Missionary Union of the Clergy—Rev. K. WILLIAM HOLOUBEK.

Natural Family Planning—Rev. MATTHEW EICKHOFF, Diocesan Dir.; MICHELLE CHAMBERS, Diocesan Coord. Tel: 402-488-2040.

Nebraska Catholic Conference—JAMES R. CUNNINGHAM, Exec. Dir., 215 Centennial Mall S., Ste. 310, Lincoln, 68508. Tel: 402-477-7517; Fax: 402-477-1503.

Newman Center University of Nebraska—Rev. ROBERT A. MATYA, Chap., 320 N. 16th St., Lincoln, 68508. Tel: 402-474-7914.

Newspaper— "The Southern Nebraska Register" Revs. NICHOLAS A. KIPPER, Editor; KENNETH A. BOROWIAK, Sr. Editorial Advisor, 3700 Sheridan Blvd., Lincoln, 68506. Tel: 402-488-0090. Mailing Address: P.O. Box 80329, Lincoln, 68501.

Office of Stewardship & Development—Rev. Msgr. LIAM M. BARR, Delegate; Mrs. KRIS LANIK, Asst., Mailing Address: P.O. Box 80328, Lincoln, 68501. Tel: 402-488-0921; Fax: 402-488-3569.

Permanent Deacon Continuing Education Committee—Revs. DANIEL J. RAYER, J.C.L.; LEO V. SEIKER; DOUGLAS D. DIETRICH.

PREP—Rev. MATTHEW EICKHOFF.

Priests' Continuing Education Committee—Rev. LAWRENCE J. STOLEY; Rev. Msgrs. TIMOTHY J. THORBURN, J.C.L.; JOHN T. FOLDA; Revs. DANIEL J. RAYER, J.C.L.; CHRISTOPHER L. BARAK; MAURICE H. CURRENT, J.C.L.; Rev. Msgrs. JOHN J PERKINTON; DANIEL J. SEIKER, J.C.L.; MARK D. HUBER, J.C.L., V.F.; Revs. ROBERT A. MAYTA; JOHN R. SULLIVAN.

Pro Life—Revs. JEFFREY R. EICKHOFF, Dir.; LEO V. SEIKER, Asst. Dir.

Project Rachel—Catholic Social Services. Tel: 800-964-3787.

Propagation of the Faith—Rev. K. WILLIAM HOLOUBEK, Dir., Mailing Address: P.O. Box 80328, Lincoln, 68501-0328.

Retreat Program—Rev. LAWRENCE J. STOLEY, Dir., Our Lady of Good Counsel Retreat House. Tel: 402-786-2705.

Rural Life Conference—Rev. DAVID F. BOUREK, Mailing Address: P.O. Box 80328, Lincoln, 68501-0328. Tel: 402-488-0921.

Serra Club—Rev. ROBERT A. MATYA, Chap. & Spiritual Dir. Tel: 402-474-7914.

Schools—Rev. Msgr. JOHN J PERKINTON, Supt.; Rev. LAWRENCE J. STOLEY; Sr. COLLETTE, O.S.F., Asst. Supt., 3400 Sheridan Blvd., Lincoln, 68506. Mailing Address: P.O. Box 80328, Lincoln, 68501-0328.

Scouting—Rev. ROBERT K. BARNHILL.

Society of St. Vincent de Paul - Lincoln Council—Rev. THOMAS R. WALSH, Spiritual Advisor; Mr. RONALD LEE, Pres.; JOYCE BURGESS, Council Sec. & Res. Agent, Sacred Heart Church, 3128 S St., Lincoln, 68503. Tel: 402-476-2610.

Teens Encounter Christ (TEC)—Rev. MATTHEW EICKHOFF.

1962 Mass Apostolate—Rev. JARED MCCAMBRIDGE, F.S.S.P., St. Francis of Assisi Church, 1145 South St., Lincoln, 68502. Tel: 402-477-5145.

Victim Assistance Coordinator—Rev. LEO D. KOSCH. Tel: 402-784-2511.

Vocations—Revs. ROBERT A. MATYA, Dir.; BENJAMIN P. HOLDREN, Asst., St. Thomas Aquinas Church, 320 N. 16th St., Lincoln, 68508. Tel: 402-474-7914.

CLERGY, PARISHES, MISSIONS AND PAROCHIAL SCHOOLS

CITY OF LINCOLN

(LANCASTER COUNTY)

1—CATHEDRAL OF THE RISEN CHRIST (1932) [JC] Rev. Msgr. Robert G. Tucker; Rev. Steven W. Thomlison, Parochial Vicar. In Res., Rev. James J. Meysenburg. Res.: 3500 Sheridan Blvd., 68506. Tel: 402-488-0948; Fax: 402-488-7895.
School—(Grades PreK-8) Tel: 402-489-9621. Lay Teachers 24; Students 378.
Catechesis/Religious Program—Students 113.

2—BISHOP BONACUM CHANCERY (1961) Rev. Msgr. Timothy J. Thorburn, Moderator of the Curia. Res.: 3400 Sheridan Blvd., P.O. Box 80328, 68501. Tel: 402-488-0921; Fax: 402-488-3569.

3—BLESSED SACRAMENT (1922) [JC] Revs. John R. Sullivan; Jonathan J. Haschke. In Res., Rev. Casey Porada.
Res.: 1720 Lake St., 68502. Tel: 402-474-4249; Fax: 402-474-4258.
School—(Grades PreK-8) Tel: 402-476-6202; Fax: 402-476-0232. Priests 3; Sisters 1; Lay Teachers 13; Students 239.
Catechesis/Religious Program—Students 91.

4—CRISTO REY (2002), (Hispanic), Revs. Ramon E. Decaen; William David Grant.
4245 J St., 68510. Tel: 402-327-2170 (Rectory); 402-488-5087 (Parish Office).
Catechesis/Religious Program—Students 556.

5—IMMACULATE HEART OF MARY (1979), (Vietnamese), Rev. Hilary M. Khanh Hia Nguyen, C.M.C.
Res.: 6345 Madison Ave., 68507. Tel: 402-464-0111; Fax: 402-464-0111.
Catechesis/Religious Program—Students 176.

6—ST. JOHN THE APOSTLE (1959) [JC] Revs. Lyle Johnson; Adam M. Sughroue, Parochial Vicar.
Res.: 7601 Vine St., 68505. Tel: 402-489-1946; Fax: 402-486-4762. Email: stjohn@inebraska.com.
School—(Grades PreK-8) Tel: 402-486-1860. Lay Teachers 20; Students 285.
Catechesis/Religious Program—Students 161.

7—ST. JOSEPH (1976) [JC] Rev. Msgr. Liam M. Barr; Rev. Patrick F. Barvick, Parochial Vicar.
Res.: 7900 Trendwood Dr., 68506. Tel: 402-483-2288; Fax: 402-483-2336. Web: www.stjosephlnk.org.
School—(Grades PreK-8), 1940 S. 77th St., 68506. Tel: 402-489-0341; Fax: 402-489-3260. Sisters 3; Lay Teachers 32; Students 460.
High School—Pius X High School, 6000 A St., 68510. Students 190.
Catechesis/Religious Program—Students 369.

8—ST. MARY (1867) [JC] Rev. Douglas D. Dietrich. In Res., Rev. Joseph P. Finn.
Res.: 1420 K St., 68508. Tel: 402-435-2125. Web: www.stmarylincoln.org.
School—(Grades K-8), 1434 K St., 68508. Tel: 402-476-3987; Fax: 402-476-0838. Lay Teachers 10; Students 144.
Catechesis/Religious Program—Students 13.

9—ST. MICHAEL (1909) [CEM] Rev. Kenneth A. Borowiak. In Res., Rev. Nicholas A. Kipper.
Res.: 9101 S. 78th St., 68506. Tel: 402-328-8480 (Rectory). Web: www.stmichaelcheney.org.
School—St. Michael School, (Grades K-6) Tel: 402-488-1313. Sisters 1; Lay Teachers 9; Students 136.
Catechesis/Religious Program—Students 171.

10—NORTH AMERICAN MARTYRS (1993) [JC] Revs. Brian P. Connor; Matthew J. Zimmer, Parochial Vicar.
Res.: 1101 Isaac Dr., 68521. Tel: 402-476-8088. Email: julie-crawford@cdolinc.net.
School—(Grades PreK-8), 1101 Issac Dr., 68521. Tel: 402-476-7373. Web: www.namartyrs.org. Sr. Patricia Heirigs, O.S.B., Prin. Priests 2; Sisters 4; Lay Teachers 20; Students 570.
Catechesis/Religious Program—Students 239.

11—ST. PATRICK'S (1893) [JC] Rev. Troy J. Schweiger. In Res., Rev. Rayappa Konka.
Res.: 6111 Morrill Ave., 68507. Tel: 402-466-2752; Fax: 402-466-3572.
School—Tel: 402-466-3710; Fax: 402-466-3752. Marian Sisters (Waverly, NE) 1; Lay Teachers 10; Students 129.
Catechesis/Religious Program—Students 121.

12—ST. PETER (1990) [JC] Revs. Michael R. Christensen; Christopher J. Miller, Parochial Vicar.
Res.: 4500 Duxhall Dr., 68516. Tel: 402-423-1239; Fax: 402-421-6507. Web: www.saintpeterslincoln.com.
School—(Grades PreK-8) Tel: 402-421-6299. Priests 2; School Sisters of Christ the King 3; Lay Teachers 25; Students 482.
Catechesis/Religious Program—Students 332.

13—SACRED HEART (1919) [JC] Revs. Michael J. Morin; Dominic T.H. Phan, Parochial Vicar.
Res.: 3128 S St., 68503. Tel: 402-476-2610.
School—Tel: 402-476-1783; Fax: 402-476-3040. Sisters 2; Lay Teachers 12; Students 200.
Catechesis/Religious Program—Students 115.

14—ST. TERESA'S (1926) [JC] Rev. Msgr. Joseph J. Nemec; Rev. Gerald Rush, O.F.M., Parochial Vicar.
Res.: 735 S. 36th St., 68510. Tel: 402-477-3979.
School—(Grades PreK-8), 616 S. 36th St., 68510. Tel: 402-477-3358; Fax: 402-477-3361. Sisters 3; Lay Teachers 20; Students 296.
Catechesis/Religious Program—Students 82.

15—ST. THOMAS AQUINAS (1958) [JC] Revs. Robert A. Matya; Benjamin P. Holdren.
Res.: 320 N. 16th St., 68508. Tel: 402-474-7914; Fax: 402-476-2620.

OUTSIDE THE CITY OF LINCOLN

ASHLAND, SAUNDERS CO., ST. MARY'S (1900) Rev. Gary Coulter.
Res.: 1625 Adams St., 68003. Tel: 402-944-3554; Fax: 402-944-3554. Email: stmaryashland@windstream.net.
Catechesis/Religious Program—Students 80.
Mission—St. Joseph's Greenwood, Cass Co.

AUBURN, NEMAHA CO., ST. JOSEPH'S (1881) [CEM] Rev. Gregory P. Pawloski.
Res.: 1306 23rd St., P.O. Box 406, 68305. Tel: 402-274-3733; Fax: 402-274-3733. Email: stjoseph@windstream.net.
Catechesis/Religious Program—Students 111.
Mission—St. Clara Peru, Nemaha Co.

AURORA, HAMILTON CO., ST. MARY'S (1888) Rev. Dennis M. Hunt.
Res.: 1419 10th St., P.O. Box 291, 68818. Tel: 402-694-3427; Fax: 402-694-2455. Email: stmarys@hamilton.net.
Catechesis/Religious Program—Students 122.
Mission—St. Joseph's [CEM] Giltner, Hamilton Co.

BEATRICE, GAGE CO., ST. JOSEPH'S (1869) [CEM] Rev. Steven P. Major.
Res.: 612 High St., 68310. Tel: 402-223-2923. Email: rectory-office@cdolinc.net.
School—Tel: 402-223-5033. Lay Teachers 9; Students 90.
Catechesis/Religious Program—Students 218.

BEAVER CROSSING, SEWARD CO., SACRED HEART (1890) Rev. Maurice H. Current.
Res.: 401 Dimery, P.O. Box 208, 68313. Tel: 402-532-2545.
Catechesis/Religious Program—Students 61.
Mission—St. Patrick's [CEM 2] Utica, Seward Co.

BELLWOOD, BUTLER CO.

1—ST. PETER'S (1889) [JC] Rev. Jay M. Buhman.
Res.: 211 Esplanade St., 68624-2402. Tel: 402-538-3135.
Catechesis/Religious Program—Students 30.
Mission—St. Joseph's, Butler Co.

2—PRESENTATION (1874) [JC] Rev. Joseph S. Steele.
Res.: 1291 41 Rd., 68624. Tel: 402-367-3666.
Catechesis/Religious Program—Students 34.

BENKELMAN, DUNDY CO., ST. JOSEPH'S (1911) [CEM] Rev. Thomas L. Wiedel.
Res.: 813 Cheyenne St., P.O. Box 447, 69021. Tel: 308-423-2329.
Catechesis/Religious Program—Students 65.
Mission—St. Joseph's Stratton, Hitchcock Co.

BRAINARD, BUTLER CO., HOLY TRINITY (1888) [CEM] Rev. Matthew Eickhoff.
Res.: P.O. Box 39, 68626. Tel: 402-545-2691.
Catechesis/Religious Program—Students 52.

BRUNO, BUTLER CO., ST. ANTHONY (1899) [CEM] Rev. Ronald G. Homes.
Res.: 405 Pine St., 68014. Tel: 402-543-2233.
Catechesis/Religious Program—Tel: 402-543-2465. Students 49.
Mission—SS. Peter and Paul [CEM 2] Abie, Butler Co.

CAMBRIDGE, FURNAS CO., ST. JOHN'S (1883) [CEM] Rev. Robert K. Barnhill.
Res.: 815 Nelson, P.O. Box F, 69022. Tel: 308-697-3722.
Catechesis/Religious Program—Students 62.
Mission—St. Germanus Arapahoe, Furnas Co.

CAMPBELL, FRANKLIN CO., ST. ANNE (1880) [CEM] Very Rev. James C. Schrader Jr.
Res.: 518 S. Stewart, P.O. Box 156, 68932-0156. Tel: 402-756-8006.
Catechesis/Religious Program—Students 54.
Mission—Holy Trinity 513 S. Liberty, Blue Hill, Webster Co. 68930.

COLON, SAUNDERS CO., ST. JOSEPH'S (1919) [CEM] Rev. Matthew J. Vandewalle.
Res.: 111 Cherry St., P.O. Box 58, 68018. Tel: 402-647-4901.
Catechesis/Religious Program—Students 65.
Mission—St. Mary [CEM] Cedar Bluffs, Saunders Co.

CORTLAND, GAGE CO., ST. JAMES (1882) [CEM] Rev. Leo V. Seiker.
Res.: 255 W. First St., 68331. Tel: 402-798-7335. Email: leoseiker@windstream.net.
Catechesis/Religious Program—Students 92.

CRETE, SALINE CO., SACRED HEART (1873) [CEM] Rev. Julius Tvrdy. In Res., Rev. John J. Keefe.
Res.: 515 E. 14th St., 68333. Tel: 402-826-2044; Fax: 402-826-2318.
School—(Grades K-6) Tel: 402-826-2318. Sisters 3; Lay Teachers 6; Students 129.
Catechesis/Religious Program—Students 137.

CURTIS, FRONTIER CO., ST. JAMES (1914) Rev. Harlan D. P. Waskowiak.
Res.: 313 E. 6th St., P.O. Box 144, 69025. Tel: 308-367-4280.
Catechesis/Religious Program—Students 16.
Mission—St. Joseph's Farnam, Dawson Co.
Mission—St. William's Wellfleet, Lincoln Co.

DAVEY, LANCASTER CO., ST. MARY'S (1876) [CEM] Rev. Joseph J. Bernardo.
Res.: 17630 N. 3rd St., P.O. Box 37, 68336. Tel: 402-785-3445.
Catechesis/Religious Program—Students 96.

DAVID CITY, BUTLER CO.

1—ST. FRANCIS (Center) (1878) [CEM] Rev. Sean M. Timmerman.
Res.: 3071 P Rd., 68632. Tel: 402-367-4202.
Catechesis/Religious Program—Students 45.

2—ST. MARY'S (1877) [CEM] Revs. Bernard Kimminau; Kenneth J. Wehrs, Parochial Vicar.
Res.: 580 I St., 68632. Tel: 402-367-3579; Fax: 402-367-3570.
School—(Grades K-5) Tel: 402-367-3669. Priests 1; Sisters 3; Lay Teachers 13; Students 209.
Catechesis/Religious Program—Students 25.
Mission—Assumption (1878), Butler Co. 68632.

DAWSON, RICHARDSON CO., ST. MARY'S (1873) [CEM] Rev. Kenneth F. Hoesing.
Res.: 312 4th St., P.O. Box 96, 68337. Tel: 402-855-3595.
Catechesis/Religious Program—Students 50.
Mission—St. Anne's [CEM 2] Shubert, Richardson Co.

DENTON, LANCASTER CO., ST. MARY'S (1906) Rev. Msgr. Mark D. Huber.
Res.: 7105 Cass, P.O. Box 406, 68339. Tel: 402-797-2105. Email: stmary@inebraska.com.
Catechesis/Religious Program—Students 82.

DONIPHAN, HALL CO., ST. ANN'S (1888) [CEM] Rev. Andrew J. Kurz.
Res.: 404 Cedar, Box 407, 68832. Tel: 308-390-8266.
Catechesis/Religious Program—Students 98.

DWIGHT, BUTLER CO., ASSUMPTION (1899) [CEM]
Res.: 336 W. Pine, P.O. Box 70, 68635. Tel: 402-566-2765.
Catechesis/Religious Program—Students 79.
Mission—St. Wenceslaus [CEM] 350 Elm St., Bee, Seward Co. 68314.

EXETER, FILLMORE CO., ST. STEPHEN'S (1871) [JC] Rev. Thomas Kuffel.
Res.: 207 N. Union Ave., P.O. Box 57, 68351. Tel: 402-266-5581.
Catechesis/Religious Program—Students 42.
Mission—St. Patrick's [CEM] 305 E. M St., Mc Cool Junction, York Co. 68401.
Catechesis/Religious Program—Students 20.

FAIRBURY, JEFFERSON CO., ST. MICHAEL'S (1885) [CEM] Rev. John B. Birkel.
Res.: 807 F St., P.O. Box 406, 68352. Tel: 402-729-2058.
Catechesis/Religious Program—Students 68.
Mission—St. Mary's 511 Amanda, Alexandria, Thayer Co. 68303.

FALLS CITY, RICHARDSON CO., SS. PETER AND PAUL (1871) [CEM 2] Rev. Msgr. Robert A. Roh.
Res.: 1820 Fulton St., 68355. Tel: 402-245-3002; Fax: 402-245-3002. Email: fr_roh@sentco.net.
School—(Grades PreK-12) Tel: 402-245-4151; Fax: 402-245-5217. Lay Teachers 18; Students 215.
Catechesis/Religious Program—Students 37.

FRIEND, SALINE CO., ST. JOSEPH'S (1874) [CEM] Rev. David F. Bourek.
Res.: 405 S. Main St., 68359. Tel: 402-947-3651.
Catechesis/Religious Program—Tel: 402-947-3657. Students 72.
Mission—St. Wenceslaus (1874) Milligan, Fillmore Co.

GENEVA, FILLMORE CO., ST. JOSEPH'S (1898) [CEM 2] Rev. Thomas R. Walsh.
Res.: 831 E St., P.O. Box 383, 68361. Tel: 402-759-3225; Fax: 402-759-3225. Email: saint_joseph@windstream.net.
Catechesis/Religious Program—Students 93.
Mission—St. Mary Shickley, Fillmore Co.

GRANT, PERKINS CO., MOTHER OF SORROWS (1928) Rev. Mark S. Pfeiffer.
Res.: 739 Garfield Ave., P.O. Box 536, 69140. Tel: 308-352-4803. Email: motherofsorrows@gpcom.net.
Catechesis/Religious Program—Students 39.

HARVARD, CLAY CO., ST. JOSEPH'S (1878) Rev. James Benton, Admin.
Res.: 605 N. Kearney, P.O. Box 70, 68944. Tel: 402-772-3511.
Catechesis/Religious Program—Students 65.

HASTINGS, ADAMS CO.

1—ST. CECILIA'S (1878) [JC] Revs. Joseph M. Walsh; Andrew J. Heaslip, Parochial Vicar. In Res., Rev. Lee T. Jirovsky.
Res.: 301 W. 7th St., 68901. Tel: 402-463-1336; Fax: 402-463-1336. Email: frjwalsh@mac.com.
Catechesis/Religious Program—Hastings Catholic Schools, Tel: 402-462-2105; Fax: 402-462-2106. Students 282.

2—ST. MICHAEL'S (1945) [JC] Very Rev. Michael K. Houlihan; Rev. Joseph J. Faulkner, Parochial Vicar.
Res.: 715 Creighton Ave., 68901. Tel: 402-463-1023.
Catechesis/Religious Program—Hastings Catholic Schools, 721 Creighton Ave., 68901. Tel: 402-462-6310; Fax: 402-462-6035. Students 659.

HEBRON, THAYER CO., SACRED HEART (1878) [CEM] Very Rev. Rudolf F. Oborny.
Res.: 436 N. 3rd St., 68370. Tel: 402-768-6293. Email: robornyhebron@yahoo.com.
Catechesis/Religious Program—Students 80.

HOLDREGE, PHELPS CO., ALL SAINTS (1902) Rev. Thomas J. Lux, Pastor.
Res.: 1308 Logan St., 68949. Tel: 308-995-9561.
School—(Grades PreK-4), 1206 Logan St., 68949. Tel: 308-995-8931. Lay Teachers 4; Students 55.
Catechesis/Religious Program—Tel: 308-995-4590. Students 97.
Mission—St. John's Smithfield, Gosper Co.

IMPERIAL, CHASE CO., ST. PATRICK'S (1903) Rev. Bernard A. Lorenz.
Res.: 126 E. 7th St., P.O. Box 96, 69033. Tel: 308-882-4995; Fax: 308-882-4995. Email: frblorenz@hotmail.com.
Catechesis/Religious Program—Students 117.

INDIANOLA, RED WILLOW CO., ST. CATHERINE'S (1888) [CEM] Rev. Thomas D. McGuire.
Res.: 815 D St., P.O. Box O, 69034. Tel: 308-364-2428; Fax: 308-364-2428.
Catechesis/Religious Program—Students 71.

KENESAW, ADAMS CO., SACRED HEART (1908) Rev. Andrew J. Kurz.
Res.: 404 Cedar, Box 407, Doniphan, 68832. Tel: 308-390-8266 (Pastor).
Catechesis/Religious Program—Tel: 402-752-8149. Students 31.

LAWRENCE, NUCKOLLS CO., SACRED HEART (1893) [CEM 3] Rev. Loras K. Grell.
Res.: 141 E. 2nd St., P.O. Box 247, 68957. Tel: 402-756-7393. Email: fathergrell@gmail.com.
School—Tel: 402-756-7043. Lay Teachers 3; Students 15.
Catechesis/Religious Program—Students 116.
Mission—Assumption 506 Liberty St., Deweese, Clay Co. 68934.
Mission—St. Stephen's 1838 Road 2600, Nuckolls Co. 68957.

LOMA, BUTLER CO., ST. LUKE'S CZECH CATHOLIC SHRINE (1912), (Czech), [CEM], Mailing Address: *c/o Rev. Msgr. Myron J. Pleskac, Admin.*, 4100 S.W. 56th St., 68522. Email: msgr.myron-pleskac@cdolinc.net.

MANLEY, CASS CO., ST. PATRICK'S (1881) [CEM] Rev. Patrick F. Murphy.
Res.: 101 N. Broadway, P.O. Box 27, 68403. Tel: 402-234-3595.
Catechesis/Religious Program—Students 132.
Mission—St. Mary's [CEM] 505 W. G St., Elmwood, Cass Co. 68349. Tel: 402-994-2485.

MCCOOK, RED WILLOW CO., ST. PATRICK (1886) [CEM] Revs. Gary G. Brethour; Lothar M. Gilde, Parochial Vicar. In Res., Rev. John L. Copenhaver.
Res.: 612 E. 4th St., P.O. Box 1040, 69001. Tel: 308-345-6734; Fax: 308-345-6734.
School—(Grades PreK-8), 401 E. F St., 69001. Tel: 308-345-4546; Fax: 308-345-4546. Priests 2; Lay Teachers 15; Students 144.
Catechesis/Religious Program—Students 75.
Mission—Sacred Heart, Red Willow Co.
Mission—St. Ann's [CEM], Red Willow Co.

MEAD, SAUNDERS CO., ST. JAMES (1882) [CEM 2] Rev. Brian P. Kane.
Res.: 213 E. 8th St., 68041. Tel: 402-624-3555.
Catechesis/Religious Program—Students 94.

MINDEN, KEARNEY CO., ST. JOHN THE BAPTIST (1882) Very Rev. Nicholas J. Baker.
Res.: 624 N. Garber Ave., P.O. Box 245, 68959. Tel: 308-832-1245; Fax: 308-832-1626. Email: baptiststjohn0@gmail.com.
Catechesis/Religious Program—Tel: 308-832-1626. Students 92.
Mission—Holy Family Heartwell, Kearney Co.

MORSE BLUFF, SAUNDERS CO., ST. GEORGE (1945) Rev. Jeremy L. Hazuka.
Res.: 260 Short St., P.O. Box 98, 68648. Tel: 402-666-5280.
Catechesis/Religious Program—Students 16.
Mission—Sacred Heart [CEM] Cedar Hill, Saunders Co.

NEBRASKA CITY, OTOE CO.
1—ST. BENEDICT'S (1856) [CEM] Rev. Mark L. Cyza.
Res.: 411 5th Rue, 68410. Tel: 402-873-3047.
See Lourdes Elementary and Lourdes Primary, Nebraska City under Elementary Schools, Interparochial located in the Institution section.
Catechesis/Religious Program—Students 19.
2—ST. MARY'S (1869) [CEM] Revs. Michael G. McCabe; Matthew M. Rolling, Parochial Vicar. In Res., Rev. Peter M. Mitchell.
Res.: 218 N. 6th St., 68410. Tel: 402-873-3024.
Catechesis/Religious Program—Students 74.

NORTH PLATTE, LINCOLN CO., ST. ELIZABETH ANN SETON (1994) Very Rev. Mark E. Seiker.
Res.: 3301 Echo Dr., 69101. Tel: 308-534-5461; Fax: 308-534-0914.
Catechesis/Religious Program—Students 40.

ORLEANS, HARLAN CO., ST. MARY'S (1878) [CEM] Rev. Jamie S. Hottovy.
Res.: 109 W. Linn, P.O. Box 446, 68966. Tel: 308-473-3475.
Catechesis/Religious Program—Students 45.
Mission—St. Michael's Oxford, Furnas Co.
Mission—St. Joseph's (1909) 810 4th, P.O. Box 764, Alma, Harlan Co. 68920. Tel: 308-928-2575.
Catechesis/Religious Program—Students 24.

OSCEOLA, POLK CO., ST. VINCENT FERRER (1946) Rev. James W. Cooper.
Res.: 751 S. Nance, P.O. Box 212, 68651. Tel: 402-747-3491; Fax: 402-747-4221.
Catechesis/Religious Program—Students 80.
Mission—St. Mary's (1893), Polk Co.

PALMYRA, OTOE CO., ST. LEO'S (1874) [CEM 2] Rev. Christopher L. Barak.
Res.: 330 W. 8th St., 68418-2537. Tel: 402-780-5535.
Catechesis/Religious Program—Students 40.
Mission—St. Martin's Douglas, Otoe Co.

PAUL, OTOE CO., ST. JOSEPH'S (1871) [CEM] Rev. Thomas M. Bush.
Res.: 5592 O Rd., Nebraska City, 68410. Tel: 402-873-4569.
Catechesis/Religious Program—Students 6.
Mission—St. Bernard's [CEM] Julian, Nemaha Co.

PLATTSMOUTH, CASS CO., CHURCH OF THE HOLY SPIRIT (1862) [CEM] Very Rev. Thomas Y. Au.
Res.: 520 S. 18th St., 68048. Tel: 402-296-3139; Fax: 402-296-2408. Email: mcdan@stjohnplt.org.
School—(Grades K-8) Tel: 402-296-6230. Lay Teachers 13; Students 153.
Catechesis/Religious Program—Students 52.

PRAGUE, SAUNDERS CO., ST. JOHN'S (1901) [CEM] Rev. Leo D. Kosch.
Res.: 122 Center Ave., P.O. Box 96, 68050. Tel: 402-663-4615.
Catechesis/Religious Program—Students 35.
Mission—SS. Cyril and Methodius [CEM] Plasi, Saunders Co.

RED CLOUD, WEBSTER CO., SACRED HEART (1883) [CEM] Rev. Paul G. Frank.
Res.: 413 N. Seward St., 68970. Tel: 402-746-3750.
Catechesis/Religious Program—Students 21.
Mission—St. Kathrine Drexel Franklin, Franklin Co. 68939.

ROSELAND, ADAMS CO., SACRED HEART (1921) Rev. Thomas Brouillette.
Res.: 11818 W. Alexander, P.O. Box 67, 68973. Tel: 402-756-6251.
Catechesis/Religious Program—Students 66.
Mission—Assumption [CEM] Juniata, Adams Co.

RULO, RICHARDSON CO., IMMACULATE CONCEPTION (1863) [CEM] Rev. David A. Oldham.
Res.: 601 W. Rouleau St., 68431. Tel: 402-245-4731.
School—Tel: 402-245-4151. Priests 1; Lay Teachers 6; Students 35.
Catechesis/Religious Program—Tel: 402-245-3002. Students 7.
Mission—St. Mary's Arago, Richardson Co.

SEWARD, SEWARD CO., ST. VINCENT DE PAUL (1878) Revs. Randall L. Langhorst; Rafael Rodriguez-Fuentes.
Res.: 152 Pinewood Ave., 68434. Tel: 402-643-3421; Fax: 402-643-2594.
School—(Grades K-4) Tel: 402-643-9525. Students 84.
Catechesis/Religious Program—Tel: 402-643-3521. Students 255.

SHELBY, POLK CO., SACRED HEART (1898) [CEM] Very Rev. John C. Rooney.
Res.: 200 S. Walnut St., P.O. Box 340, 68662. Tel: 402-527-5425; Fax: 402-527-5849. Web: www.shelbysacredheart.com.
Catechesis/Religious Program—Students 54.

STEINAUER, PAWNEE CO., ST. ANTHONY (1882) [CEM] Rev. Scott M. Courtney.
Res.: 310 Hickory St., 68441. Tel: 402-869-2256.
Catechesis/Religious Program—Students 78.
Mission—Sacred Heart [CEM] Burchard, Pawnee Co.

SUPERIOR, NUCKOLLS CO., ST. JOSEPH'S (1934) Rev. Bradley Zitek.
Res.: 1415 California, 68978-1019. Tel: 402-879-3735; Fax: 402-879-4495.
Catechesis/Religious Program—Students 66.
Mission—Sacred Heart Nelson, Nuckolls Co.

SUTTON, CLAY CO., ST. MARY'S (1876) [CEM] Rev. K. William Holoubek.
Res.: 312 S. Saunders Ave., P.O. Box 406, 68979. Tel: 402-773-5346.
Catechesis/Religious Program—Students 90.
Mission—St. Helena's 172 Jackson St., Grafton, Fillmore Co. 68365.

SYRACUSE, OTOE CO., ST. PAULINUS (1906) Rev. Michael S. Stec.
Mailing Address: 863 5th St., 68446-9504. Tel: 402-269-3382.
Catechesis/Religious Program—Students 104.
Mission—Holy Trinity [CEM] 4456 Arbor Rd., Avoca, Cass Co. 68307.

TECUMSEH, JOHNSON CO., ST. ANDREW'S (1866) [CEM] Rev. Thomas B. Dunavan.
Res.: 186 N. 5th St., P.O. Box 656, 68450. Tel: 402-335-3742; Fax: 402-335-2234. Email: fr.thomas-dunavan@hotmail.com.
School—(Grades K-6) Tel: 402-335-2234. Sisters 1; Lay Teachers 2; Students 22.
Catechesis/Religious Program—Students 53.
Mission—St. Mary's [CEM] St. Mary, Johnson Co.

TRENTON, HITCHCOCK CO., ST. JAMES (1894) [CEM] Very Rev. Valerian Bartek.
Res.: 117 W. B St., P.O. Box 488, 69044. Tel: 308-334-5328.
Catechesis/Religious Program—Students 43.
Mission—Holy Family Palisade, Hitchcock Co.
Mission—St. John's [CEM] Wauneta, Chase Co. Tel: 308-394-5440 (Church).

ULYSSES, BUTLER CO., IMMACULATE CONCEPTION (1915) [CEM] Rev. Raymond L. Jansen.
Res.: 215 S. 6th St., P.O. Box 128, 68669. Tel: 402-549-2437.
Catechesis/Religious Program—Students 24.

VALPARAISO, SAUNDERS CO., STS. MARY AND JOSEPH'S (1975) [CEM] Rev. Msgr. Paul K. Witt.
Res.: 601 Iver St., 68065. Tel: 402-784-2511. Email: maherbek@windstream.net.
Catechesis/Religious Program—Students 146.

WAHOO, SAUNDERS CO., ST. WENCESLAUS (1877) [CEM 2] Revs. Charles L. Townsend; Craig J. Clinch, Parochial Vicar.
Res.: 214 E. 2nd St., 68066. Tel: 402-443-4235; Fax: 402-443-4275.
School—(Grades K-6), 108 N. Linden, 68066-1953. Tel: 402-443-3336; Fax: 402-443-5551. Sisters 1; Lay Teachers 17; Students 310.
Catechesis/Religious Program—Students 605.

WALLACE, LINCOLN CO., ST. MARY'S (1909) Rev. Mark S. Pfeiffer.
Res.: 221 N. Commercial Ave., P.O. Box 191, 69169. Tel: 308-387-4441. Email: stmary@nebnet.net.
Catechesis/Religious Program—Students 37.
Mission—Resurrection of Our Lord Elsie, Perkins Co.

WESTON, SAUNDERS CO., ST. JOHN NEPOMUCENE (1885) [CEM 2] Rev. Christopher P. Goodwin.
Res.: 110 Front St., P.O. Box 10, 68070. Tel: 402-642-5245.
School—(Grades PreK-6) Tel: 402-642-5234. Lay Teachers 6; Students 70.
Mission—St. Vitus [CEM] Touhy, Saunders Co.

WILBER, SALINE CO., ST. WENCESLAUS (1878) Rev. Craig A. Doty.
Res.: 501 N. Wilson, P.O. Box 706, 68465. Tel: 402-821-2689.
Catechesis/Religious Program—Students 100.
Mission—St. Joseph's Tobias, Saline Co.

WYMORE, GAGE CO., ST. MARY'S (1881) [CEM 3] Rev. Ferdinand J. Boehme.
Res.: 107 N. 11th St., P.O. Box 295, 68466. Tel: 402-645-3051.
Catechesis/Religious Program—Students 53.
Mission—St. Joseph's Barneston, Gage Co.
Mission—St. Mary's [CEM] Odell, Gage Co.

YORK, YORK CO., ST. JOSEPH'S (1878) [CEM] Rev. Msgr. James M. Reinert. In Res., Rev. Melvin Rempe.
Res.: 505 N. East Ave., 68467. Tel: 402-362-4595.
School—(Grades K-8) Tel: 402-362-3021; Fax: 402-362-4067. Franciscan Apostolic Sisters 2; Lay Teachers 12; Students 85.
Catechesis/Religious Program—Students 145.

Shrines

CRETE, SALINE CO., SCHOENSTATT SHRINE (2001) Sr. M. Veronica Muniz, I.S.S.M., Supr.
Shrine— 340 Hwy. 103, 68333. Tel: 402-826-3346. Web: www.schoenstattne.org.

LOMA, BUTLER CO., ST. LUKE'S CZECH CATHOLIC SHRINE Rev. Msgr. Myron J. Pleskac, Dir. (Retired). P.O. Box 80328, 68501.

Chaplains of Public Institutions

LINCOLN. *Nebraska Penal Complex*, 1420 K St., 68508. Tel: 402-742-4421. Rev. Msgr. James M. Reinert, Revs. Thomas B. Dunavan, Thomas S. MacLean, Thomas R. Walsh.

On Duty Outside the Diocese:
Rev. Msgr.—
Fucinaro, Thomas J., Villa Stritch, Via della Nocetta, 63, 00164 Rome, Italy.
Revs.—
Gross, Gary, Military Duty, 1296 Kapiolani Blvd., Apt. 3007, Honolulu, HI 96814.
Gyhra, Richard A., Apartado Postal 312, Avenida Maximo Gomez 27, Santo Domingo, Dominican Republic. Apostolic Nunciature in the Dominican Republic
Menke, Andrew V., Villa Stritch, Via della Nocetta 63, 00164 Rome, Italy.
Panzer, Joel, Military Duty, St. John Church, 95-370 Kuahelani Ave., Mililani, HI 96789.

Graduate Studies:
Revs.—
Kilcawley, Sean P., (Casa Santa Maria)
Snitily, Steven P., (Casa Santa Maria)

Retired:
Rev. Msgrs.—
Dawson, James D., Bonacum House, 3301 Sheridan Blvd., 68506.
Hain, Raymond B., Bonacum House, 3301 Sheridan Blvd., 68506.
Pleskac, Myron J., 4100 S.W. 56th St., 68522.
Pohl, Daniel J., Bonacum House, 3301 Sheridan Blvd., 68506.
Vap, Ivan F., 1301 E. 9th, Hastings, 68901.
Very Rev.—
O'Byrne, Patrick J., West End Millstreet, Co. Cork Ireland.
Revs.—
Cooper, John A., Bonacum House, 3301 Sheridan Blvd., 68506.
Gadient, Peter J., Madonna Rehabilitation Hospital, 5401 South St., 68506.
Hebert, John M., 9 Perralena Ln., Hot Springs, AR 71909.
Hotovy, Dennis W., 2211 Sunset Dr., Beatrice, 68310.
Kalin, William A., Bonacum House, 3301 Sheridan Blvd., 68506.
Lyons, Patrick J., Bonacum House, 3301 Sheridan Blvd., 68506.
Mroczkowski, Joseph A., P.O. Box 238, Cedar Creek, 68016.
Murphy, Francis J., #1 West End, Millstreet, Co. Cork Ireland.
O'Connor, James M., 2110 30th Ave., #32, Kearney, 68845.
Rauth, Philip J., 13305 William Cir., Omaha, 68144.
Rutten, Paul J., Bonacum House, 3301 Sheridan Blvd., 68506.
Zastrow, John A., Bonacum House, 3301 Sheridan Blvd., 68506.

INSTITUTIONS LOCATED IN THE DIOCESE

[A] SEMINARIES, RELIGIOUS OR SCHOLASTICATES

DENTON. *Our Lady of Guadalupe Seminary*, 7880 W. Denton Rd., P.O. Box 147, 68339. Tel: 402-797-7700; Fax: 402-797-7705. Email: seminary@fsspolgs.org. Very Rev. Josef Bisig, F.S.S.P., Rector; Revs. Robert Fromageot, F.S.S.P.; Calvin R. Goodwin, F.S.S.P.; James B. Buckley, F.S.S.P.; Robert Ferguson, F.S.S.P.; William Lawrence, F.S.S.P.; Joseph Lee, F.S.S.P.; Sr. Stephen Larson, O.S.B., Librarian. Priests 8; Sisters 1; Lay Staff 11; Adjunct 3; Students 74.

SEWARD. *St. Gregory the Great Seminary*, 800 Fletcher Rd., 68434. Tel: 402-643-4052; Fax: 402-643-6964. Email: sggs@stgregoryseminary.edu. Web: www.stgregoryseminary.edu. Rev. Msgr. John T. Folda, Rector; Very Rev. M. James Divis, S.T.L., V.F., Spiritual Dir.; Rev. Jeffrey R. Eickhoff, Academic Dean; Rev. Msgr. David R. Hintz, Dean of Men; Dr. Terrence Nollen, Ph.D., Librarian. Priests 11; Sisters 3; Lay Staff 5; Students 34.

[B] ELEMENTARY SCHOOLS, INTERPAROCHIAL

HASTINGS. *St. Michael's Elementary, Hastings Catholic Schools*, 721 Creighton Ave., 68901. Tel: 402-462-6310; Fax: 402-462-6035. Email: sr.hedwig-kortte@cdolinc.net. Sisters M. Hedwig Kortte,

F.S.G.M., Prin.; M. Francesca Santacroce, F.S.G.M., Librarian. Priests 6; Sisters 2; Lay Teachers 21; Students 244.

NEBRASKA CITY. *Lourdes Elementary*, (Grades PreK-5), 412 2nd Ave., 68410. Tel: 402-873-3739; Fax: 402-873-3154. Mrs. Valerie Able, Prin. Lay Teachers 10; Students 199.

[C] HIGH SCHOOLS, INTERPAROCHIAL

LINCOLN. *Pius X Catholic High School*, 6000 A St., 68510. Tel: 402-488-0931; Fax: 402-488-1061. Email: webmaster@piusx.net. Web: www.piusx.net. Rev. James J. Meysenburg, B.A., M.A., M.Div., M.Ed., Supt.; Mr. Tom Korta, Prin.; Mr. Greg Lesiak, Asst. Prin.; Mrs. Jan Frayser, Dir. of Guidance; Mr. Tim Aylward, Dir. Activities; Karen Buckley, Librarian. Priests 12; Sisters 3; Lay Teachers 61; Students 1,057.

DAVID CITY. *Aquinas/St. Mary's Schools* (1899) (Grades PreK-12), 3420 MN Rd., P.O. Box 149, 68632. Tel: 402-367-3175; Fax: 402-367-3176. Email: fr.sean-timmerman@cdonlinc.net. Web: www.aquinas.esu7.org. Rev. Sean M. Timmerman, Supt.; Mr. David G. McMahon, Prin. (Aquinas High School); Miss Carmelita Fiala, Prin. (St. Mary's); Rev. Joseph S. Steele, Guidance Dir.; Bobbi Schmid, Career Counselor. Priests 6; Sisters 3; Lay Teachers 34; Students 514.

FALLS CITY. *Sacred Heart School*, 1820 Fulton St., 68355. Tel: 402-245-4151; Fax: 402-245-5217. Email: doug-goltz@fcsacredheart.org. Web: www.sacredheart.esu6.org/. Rev. Msgr. Robert A. Roh, V.F., M.A., S.T.L., Supt.; Mr. Douglas Goltz, M.A., Prin.; Rev. David A. Oldham, Dir., Guidance; Linda Barnhill, Librarian.

High School Email: robert.roh@fcsacredheart.org. Web: www.sacredheart.esu6.org/. Priests 3; Lay Teachers 9; Students 66.

Elementary School Priests 3; Lay Teachers 18; Students 180.

HASTINGS. *St. Cecilia's Middle School/High School*, (Grades 6-12), 521 N. Kansas, 68901. Tel: 402-462-2105; Fax: 402-462-2106. Email: fr.tom-brouillette@cdolinc.net. Web: www.hastingscatholicschools.org. Revs. Thomas S. Brouillette, Supt.; Lee T. Jirovsky, Prin.; Mrs. Marilyn Zysset, Librarian. Priests 5; Sisters 2; Lay Teachers 22; Students 256.

NEBRASKA CITY. *Lourdes Central Catholic Schools*, (Grades K-12), 412 2nd Ave., 68410. Tel: 402-873-6154; Fax: 402-873-3154. Email: lourdes-office@cdolinc.net. Revs. Michael G. McCabe, Supt.; Mark L. Cyza, High School Prin.; Mr. Andy Fedoris, Middle School Prin.; Mrs. Valerie Able, Elementary Prin. Priests 6; Sisters 3; Lay Teachers 28; Students 315.

WAHOO. *Bishop Neumann Jr.-Sr. High School*, 202 S. Linden, 68066. Tel: 402-443-4151; Fax: 402-443-5551. Web: bishopneumann.com. Revs. Brian P. Kane, Supt.; Jeremy L. Hazuka, Prin. Priests 5; Sisters 3; Lay Teachers 22; Students 295.

[D] GENERAL HOSPITALS

LINCOLN. *St. Elizabeth Regional Medical Center* (1889) 555 S. 70th St., 68510. Tel: 402-219-8000; Fax: 402-219-8973. Email: blanik@stez.org. Web: www.saintelizabethonline.com. Mr. Robert Lanik, Pres.; Rev. Edwin L. Stander, Chap. Affiliate of Catholic Health Initiatives. Priests 1; Sisters 2; Bed Capacity 265; Total Staff 1,850; Patients Assisted Annually 124,760.

Nebraska Heart Hospital, 7500 S. 91st St., 68526. Tel: 402-328-3711; Fax: 402-483-8708. Web: www.neheart.com. Affiliate of Catholic Health Initiatives Bed Capacity 63; Patients Assisted Annually 9,052; Staff 328.

NEBRASKA CITY. *St. Mary's Community Hospital*, 1314 3rd Ave., 68410. Tel: 402-873-3321; Fax: 402-873-9033. Email: dkelly@stez.org. Web: www.stmaryshospitalnecity.org. Daniel J. Kelly, Pres., C.E.O., Admin. Affiliate of Catholic Health Initiatives. Bed Capacity 18; Total Staff 147; Patients Assisted Annually 32,375.

[E] HOMES FOR AGED

LINCOLN. *Bonacum House* (1987) 3301 Sheridan Blvd., 68506. Tel: 402-483-0391; Fax: 402-483-0391. Rev. Msgrs. Raymond B. Hain (Retired); James D. Dawson (Retired); Daniel J. Pohl (Retired); Adrian F. Herbek (Retired); Revs. John A. Cooper (Retired); William A. Kalin (Retired); Patrick J. Lyons (Retired); Paul J. Rutten (Retired); John A. Zastrow (Retired). Residence for retired priests.

Madonna Rehabilitation Hospital, 5401 South St., 68506. Tel: 402-489-7102; Fax: 402-483-9460. Email: feedback@madonna.org. Web: www.madonna.org. Physical Medicine and Rehabilitation, Outpatient Services, Long-Term Care, Adult Day Care and Supportive Inpatient Hospice, Alzheimers Care. Sisters 7; Bed Capacity 303; Patients Assisted Annually 33,218.

DAVID CITY. *St. Joseph's Court, Inc.* (2000) 646 I St., 68632. Tel: 402-367-4337; Fax: 402-367-4345. Email: stoutva@hotmail.com. Web: saintjosephsvilla.org. Assisted Living Residents 26; Total Assisted 26.

St. Joseph's Villa, Inc., 927 7th St., 68632. Tel: 402-367-3045; Fax: 402-367-3730. Email: stoutva@hotmail.com. Joyce Stewart, Admin.; Vicki Stout, Admin. Sisters Adorers of the Blood of Christ (St. Louis, MO). Residents 58; Total Assisted 72; Total Staff 103.

[F] RETREAT HOUSES

WAVERLY. *Our Lady of Good Counsel Retreat House*, 7303 N. 112th St., 68462. Tel: 402-786-2705; Fax: 402-786-7211. Email: goodcounsel@cdolinc.net. Web: www.goodcounselretreat.com. Rev. Lawrence J. Stoley, Dir. Private Rooms 50. In Res. Rev. Msgr. John J Perkinton.

[G] CONVENTS AND RESIDENCES FOR SISTERS

LINCOLN. *Adoration Convent and Church of Christ the King*, 1040 S. Cotner Blvd., 68510. Tel: 402-489-0765; Fax: 402-489-0864. Sr. Mary Henrita Robillard, Supr.; Rev. Msgr. Joseph J. Nemec, Chap. Sister Servants of the Holy Spirit of Perpetual Adoration. Professed Sisters 8.

St. Agnes Convent, 3405 Sheridan Blvd., 68506. Tel: 402-484-7348. Professed Sisters 2.

Congregation of Missionary Sisters of the Blessed Virgin Mary, Queen of Mercy, P.O. Box 30917, 68503. 1313 Eldon Dr., 68503. Tel: 402-421-1704; Fax: 402-421-1704. Email: srsqueenmercy@hotmail.com. Professed Sisters 10.

Guadalupan Missionaries of the Holy Spirit (1924) Hispanic Apostolate, 110 W. "E" St., 68508-3087. Tel: 402-477-1190 (U.S. Delegation Headquarters, Miami, FL). Email: hijasespsto@alltel.net. Sr. Manuela de Jesus Gutierrez, Supr. Sisters 4.

School Sisters of Christ the King, Villa Regina Motherhouse & Novitiate (1976) 4100 S.W. 56th St., 68522-9261. Tel: 402-477-5232; Fax: 402-477-0464. Email: M.Joan-Paul@cdolinc.net. Web: www.cksisters.org. Sr. Joan Paul, C.K., Supr. Sisters 24; Novices 3; Postulants 2. In Res. Rev. Msgr. Myron J. Pleskac (Retired). Tel: 402-477-1768.

CRETE. *Secular Institute of the Schoenstatt Sisters of Mary, ISSM*, 340 Hwy. 103, 68333. Tel: 402-826-3346; Fax: 402-826-4390. Sr. M. Veronica Muniz, I.S.S.M., Supr.

NEBRASKA CITY. *The Franciscan Sisters of the Sorrowful Mother*, 1503 4th Corso, 68410-2628. Tel: 402-873-3052. Email: fs93813@gmail.com. Sr. Ana Maria Solis, O.S.F., Supr.

TECUMSEH. *Benedictine Sisters of Mt. Scholastica - Atchison, KS, St. Andrew Convent*, 179 N. 6th, P.O. Box 386, 68450. Tel: 402-335-2034. Email: sr.mary-ellen@standrewtecumseh.org. Sr. Mary Ellen Auffert, Contact Person.

VALPARAISO. *Carmel of Jesus, Mary, and Joseph*, 9300 W. Agnew Rd., 68065. Tel: 402-784-0375; Fax: 402-784-0375. Sr. Teresa of Jesus, O.C.D., Prioress.

WAVERLY. *Marian Sisters of the Diocese of Lincoln Motherhouse and Novitiate*, 6765 N. 112th St., 68462-9762. Tel: 402-786-2750; Fax: 402-786-7256. Sr. Jacquelyn Darner, M.S., Supr. Professed 31; Postulants 3.

[H] SPECIAL EDUCATION

LINCOLN. *Villa Marie School and Home for the Educable Mentally Handicapped* (1964) P.O. Box 80328, 68501. Tel: 402-786-3625; Fax: 402-488-6525. Sr. Peggy Kucera, M.S., Head Teacher; Rev. Msgr. John J Perkinton, Dir. Marian Sisters (Waverly, NE). Sisters 3; Students 13.

[I] NEWMAN CENTERS

LINCOLN. *University of Nebraska, Newman Club* 320 N. 16th St., 68508. Tel: 402-474-7914; Fax: 402-476-2620. Email: newmancenter@unl.edu. Web: newmancenter.unl.edu. Revs. Robert A. Matya, Vocation Dir.; Benjamin P. Holdren. See also: St. Thomas Aquinas, Lincoln, NE.

[J] FUNDS, FOUNDATIONS AND TRUSTS

LINCOLN. *Chancery*, 3400 Sheridan Blvd., P.O. Box 80328, 68501. Tel: 402-488-0921; Fax: 402-488-3569.

Mass Stipends Rev. Daniel J. Rayer, J.C.L.

Mission Office Fund

The Catholic Foundation of the Diocese of Lincoln, P.O. Box 80328, 68501-0328. Tel: 402-488-2142; Fax: 402-488-3569. Rev. Msgr. Timothy J. Thorburn, J.C.L.

Crossing the Threshold Campaign, Crossing the Threshold Campaign, 3400 Sheridan Blvd., 68506. Tel: 402-488-0921; Fax: 402-488-3569. Rev. Msgr. Timothy J. Thorburn, J.C.L.

Charity and Stewardship Appeal (DDP), Charity and Stewardship Appeal (DDP), 3400 Sheridan Blvd., 68506. Tel: 402-488-0921; Fax: 402-488-3569. Rev. Msgr. Timothy J. Thorburn, J.C.L.

[K] CATHOLIC SOCIAL SERVICES

LINCOLN. *Catholic Social Services*, Admin. Offices 2241 O St., 68510. Tel: 402-474-1600; Fax: 402-474-1612. Email: frckubat@cssisus.org. Web: www.cssisus.org. Rev. Christopher K. Kubat, Dir. (Housing Services & Social Services)

Other Addresses:

Apostolate of Suffering, 2241 O St., 68510. Tel: 402-474-1600; Fax: 402-474-1612. Email: frckubat@cssisus.org.

Counseling Svcs. 3700 Sheridan Blvd., 68506. Tel: 402-489-1834; 800-961-6277; Fax: 402-489-2046.

Catholic Social Svcs. 515 W. Third St., Hastings, 68901. Tel: 402-463-2112; 888-826-9629; Fax: 402-463-2322. Email: tschik@csshope.org.

1014 Central Ave., Auburn, 68305. Tel: 402-274-4818.

[L] MISCELLANEOUS LISTINGS

LINCOLN. *Blessed John XXIII Diocesan Center* (2001) 3700 Sheridan Blvd., 68506. Tel: 402-488-2040; Fax: 402-488-6525. Email: joan-penn@cdolinc.net. Rev. Msgr. John J Perkinton.

Calvary Cemetery and Mausoleum, 145 S. 40th St., 68510. Tel: 402-476-8787. Rev. Msgr. David R. Hintz, Dir. Joint cemetery for Lincoln parishes.

Camp Kateri, P.O. Box F, Mc Cool Junction, 68401. Tel: 402-499-4082. Rev. Thomas Kuffel, Dir.

St. Francis of Assisi Church, 3400 S. 17th St., 68502. Tel: 402-477-5145; Fax: 402-477-5159. Rev. Jared McCambridge, F.S.S.P., Chap. In Res. Rev. Robert Fromageot, F.S.S.P.

Holy Family Convent, 5720 A St., 68510. Tel: 402-486-3706.

Magnificat-Lincoln, 7221 South St. #4, 68506. Tel: 402-476-1880. Email: mharper55@yahoo.com. Mary Harper, Coord.

Pius X Foundation and Pius X Endowment Fund, 6000 A St., 68510. Tel: 402-488-1046; Fax: 402-488-1061. Email: michelle.birkel@piusx.net. Web: www.piusx.net. Rev. James J. Meysenburg, B.A., M.A., M.Div., M.Ed., Sec. & Treas.

Vietnamese Martyrs Catholic Community, 3400 Sheridan Blvd., 68506.

CRETE. *Schoenstatt Shrine* 340 State Hwy. 103, 68333. Tel: 402-826-3346; Fax: 402-826-3346. Web: www.schoenstattne.org.

DAVID CITY. *Aquinas High School Endowment Fund*, 3420 MN Rd., 68632. Tel: 402-367-3175; Fax: 402-367-3176. Email: fr.kenneth-hoesing@cdolinc.net. Web: aquinas.esu7.org. Rev. Sean M. Timmerman.

FALLS CITY. *Sacred Heart High School Endowment Fund*, 1820 Fulton St., 68355. Tel: 402-245-4151; Fax: 402-245-3002. Email: fr_roh@sentco.net. Rev. Msgr. Robert A. Roh, V.F., M.A., S.T.L., Sec. & Treas.

HASTINGS. *St. Cecilia High School Endowment Fund* (1981) 521 N. Kansas, 68901. Tel: 402-462-2105; Fax: 402-462-2106. Web: www.hastingscatholicschools.org. Rev. Thomas S. Brouillette, Sec. & Treas.

NEBRASKA CITY. *Lourdes Central High School Endowment Fund*, 412 Second Ave., 68410. Tel: 402-873-6154; Fax: 402-873-3154. Email: sm22100@navix.net. Rev. Michael G. McCabe, Sec. & Treas.

WAHOO. *Bishop Neumann High School Endowment Fund*, 202 S. Linden, 68066. Tel: 402-443-4151; Fax: 402-443-5551. Web: bishopneumann.com. Revs. Charles L. Townsend, Sec. & Treas.; Brian P. Kane, Contact Person.

RELIGIOUS INSTITUTES OF MEN REPRESENTED IN THE DIOCESE

For further details refer to the corresponding bracketed number in the Religious Institutes of Men or Women section.

[]—*Congregation of the Mother Coredemptrix* (Vietnamese)—C.M.C.

[1065]—*Priestly Fraternity of St. Peter*—F.S.S.P.

RELIGIOUS INSTITUTES OF WOMEN REPRESENTED IN THE DIOCESE

[0100]—*Adorers of the Blood of Christ*—A.S.C.

[]—*Benedictine Sisters of Mount St. Scholastica*—O.S.B.

[0230]—*Benedictine Sisters of Pontifical Jurisdiction* (Yankton)—O.S.B.

[]—*Benedictine Sisters of the Sacred Hearts* (Tulsa, OK)—O.S.B.

[0420]—*Carmelite Monastery of Jesus, Mary, and Joseph*—O.C.D.

[]—*Congregation of Missionary Sisters of the Blessed Virgin Mary, Queen of Mercy* (Vietnam)

[1115]—*Dominican Sisters of Peace*—O.P.

[]—*Franciscan Apostolic Sisters*—F.A.S.

[]—*Franciscan Sisters of Christian Charity* (Manitowoc, WI)—O.S.F.

[]—*Franciscan Sisters of the Sorrowful Mother*—O.S.F.

[1845]—*Guadalupan Missionaries of the Holy Spirit*—M.G.Sp.S.

[]—*Handmaids of the Holy Child of Jesus* (Ikot Ekpene, Nigeria)—H.H.C.J.

[]—*Holy Family Sisters of the Needy*—H.F.S.N.

[2575]—*Institute of the Sisters of Mercy of the Americas*—R.S.M.

[2400]—*Marian Sisters of the Diocese of Lincoln*—M.S.

[2960]—*Notre Dame Sisters*—N.D.

[]—*Schoenstatt Sisters of Mary*

[]—*School Sisters of Christ the King*—C.K.

[1680]—*School Sisters of St. Francis*—O.S.F.

[3540]—*Sister Servants of the Holy Spirit of Perpetual Adoration*—S.Sp.S.deA.

[1600]—*Sisters of St. Francis of Martyr St. George*—O.S.F.

[1640]—*Sisters of St. Francis of Perpetual Adoration* (Prov. of St. Joseph)—O.S.F.

NECROLOGY

† Holoman, Rev. Msgr. Thomas L., (Retired)—Died March 19, 2011

† Keenan, Rev. Msgr. Charles J., (Retired)—Died July 9, 2010

An asterisk (*) denotes an organization that has established tax-exempt status directly with the IRS and is not covered by the USCCB Group Ruling.

Diocese of Little Rock

(Dioecesis Petriculana)

Most Reverend

ANTHONY BASIL TAYLOR

Bishop of Little Rock; ordained August 2, 1980; appointed seventh Bishop of Little Rock March 18, 2008; consecrated & installed June 5, 2008. *Res.: 30 Sherrill Rd., Little Rock, AR 72202.* Tel: 501-664-0340. *Mailing Address: P.O. Box 7565, Little Rock, AR 72217. Office: 2500 N. Tyler St., Little Rock, AR 72207.*

Most Reverend

ANDREW J. McDONALD, D.D., J.C.D.

Bishop Emeritus of Little Rock; ordained May 8, 1948; appointed Bishop of Little Rock July 4, 1972; consecrated September 5, 1972; installed September 7, 1972; retired January 4, 2000. *Res.: St. Joseph's Home for the Elderly, 80 W. Northwest Hwy., Palatine, IL 60067.* Tel: 847-358-5700; Fax: 847-934-6979.

Chancery: 2500 N. Tyler St., P.O. Box 7565, Little Rock, AR 72217. Tel: 501-664-0340.

Web: www.dolr.org

ESTABLISHED NOVEMBER 28, 1843.

Square Miles 52,068.

Comprises the State of Arkansas.

For legal titles of parishes and diocesan institutions, consult the Chancery Office.

STATISTICAL OVERVIEW

Personnel	
Bishop	1
Retired Bishops	1
Abbots	1
Priests: Diocesan Active in Diocese	53
Priests: Diocesan Active Outside Diocese	1
Priests: Retired, Sick or Absent	19
Number of Diocesan Priests	73
Religious Priests in Diocese	33
Total Priests in Diocese	106
Extern Priests in Diocese	24
Ordinations:	
Transitional Deacons	4
Permanent Deacons in Diocese	82
Total Brothers	24
Total Sisters	171
Parishes	
Parishes	89
With Resident Pastor:	
Resident Diocesan Priests	54
Resident Religious Priests	15
Without Resident Pastor:	
Administered by Priests	19
Administered by Deacons	1
Missions	38
Pastoral Centers	1
Professional Ministry Personnel:	
Sisters	16
Lay Ministers	93
Welfare	
Catholic Hospitals	11
Total Assisted	876,711
Health Care Centers	5
Total Assisted	24,435
Homes for the Aged	28
Total Assisted	1,027
Day Care Centers	26
Total Assisted	1,288
Specialized Homes	1
Total Assisted	202
Special Centers for Social Services	5
Total Assisted	44,257
Other Institutions	9
Total Assisted	22,955
Educational	
Diocesan Students in Other Seminaries	33
Total Seminarians	33
High Schools, Diocesan and Parish	4
Total Students	1,029
High Schools, Private	2
Total Students	637
Elementary Schools, Diocesan and Parish	28
Total Students	5,456
Catechesis/Religious Education:	
High School Students	1,808
Elementary Students	7,225
Total Students under Catholic Instruction	16,188
Teachers in the Diocese:	
Priests	1
Brothers	3
Sisters	7
Lay Teachers	571
Vital Statistics	
Receptions into the Church:	
Infant Baptism Totals	2,830
Minor Baptism Totals	222
Adult Baptism Totals	220
Received into Full Communion	501
First Communions	3,017
Confirmations	1,804
Marriages:	
Catholic	384
Interfaith	211
Total Marriages	595
Deaths	915
Total Catholic Population	137,137
Total Population	2,915,918

Former Bishops—Rt. Revs. ANDREW BYRNE, D.D., cons. March 10, 1844; died in Helena, June 10, 1862; EDWARD FITZGERALD, D.D., preconized June 22, 1866; cons. Feb. 3, 1867; died in Hot Springs, Feb. 21, 1907; Most Revs. JOHN B. MORRIS, D.D., ord. June 11, 1892; cons. June 11, 1906; died in Little Rock, Oct. 22, 1946; ALBERT L. FLETCHER, D.D., ord. June 4, 1920; cons. April 25, 1940; appt. Bishop of Little Rock Dec. 7, 1946; retired July 3, 1972; died Dec. 6, 1979; ANDREW J. MCDONALD, D.D., J.C.D. (Retired), ord. May 8, 1948; appt. Bishop of Little Rock July 4, 1972; cons. Sept. 5, 1972; installed Sept. 7, 1972; retired Jan. 4. 2000; JAMES PETER SARTAIN, D.D., S.T.L., ord. July 15, 1978; appt. Bishop of Little Rock Jan. 4, 2000; cons. and installed March 6, 2000; transfer to Joliet in Illinois June 27, 2006; transfer to Seattle Dec. 1, 2010.

Pastoral Center—2500 N. Tyler St., P.O. Box 7565, Little Rock, 72217. Tel: 501-664-0340; Fax: 501-664-9075. Office Hours: Mon.-Fri. 8:30-5.

Vicar General—Rev. Msgr. R. SCOTT FRIEND, V.G.

Chancellor for Ecclesial Affairs—Very Rev. Msgr. FRANCIS I. MALONE, J.C.L., P.A., V.F.

Chancellor for Canonical Affairs—Deacon JOHN M. MCALLISTER, J.D., J.C.L., This office also handles Archives.

Assistant Chancellor for Canonical Affairs—CATHERINE A. GILLIGAN, J.C.L.

Chancellor for Administrative Affairs—Mr. DENNIS P. LEE.

Finance Officer—Mr. GREGORY C. WOLFE, CFO.

Diocesan Tribunal—Fax: 501-664-4583.

Judicial Vicar—Very Rev. Msgr. FRANCIS I. MALONE, J.C.L., P.A., V.F. Adjutant Judicial Vicar: Very Rev. GREGORY T. LUYET, J.C.L., V.F.

Judges—Very Rev. GREGORY T. LUYET, J.C.L., V.F.; Deacon JOHN M. MCALLISTER, J.D., J.C.L.

Defenders of the Bond—Rev. Msgr. JOHN KORDSMEIER (Retired); CATHERINE A. GILLIGAN, J.C.L.; Mrs. BARBARA ANHALT.

Promoter of Justice—CATHERINE A. GILLIGAN, J.C.L.

Notaries—Mrs. LIZ PARKER; MARIAN GRANT-SWIFT; LAZETH NOVAK; TERI TRIBBY; SUSI BLANCO; MARIA PENA.

Minister for Religious—Sr. JOAN PYTLIK, D.C.

Diocesan Consultors—Rev. Msgr. R. SCOTT FRIEND, V.G.; Very Rev. Msgr. FRANCIS I. MALONE, J.C.L., P.A., V.F.; Rev. Msgr. SCOTT L. MARCZUK, J.C.L.; Rev. MARK WOOD; Very Rev. GREGORY T. LUYET, J.C.L., V.F.; Rev. JOHN E. MARCONI; Very Rev. WARREN HARVEY, V.F.; Rev. JOHN M. CONNELL; Very Rev. Msgr. DAVID LESIEUR, V.F.; Very Rt. Rev. JEROME KODELL, O.S.B., V.F.

Deans—Very Rev. Msgr. FRANCIS I. MALONE, J.C.L., P.A., V.F., Central Deanery; Very Rev. PAUL F. WORM, Ouachita Deanery; Very Rev. Msgr. JACK D. HARRIS, D.Min., North Delta Deanery; Very Rev. JAMES M. FANRAK, V.F., North Ozark Deanery; Very Rt. Rev. JEROME KODELL, O.S.B., V.F., River Valley Deanery; Very Rev. WARREN HARVEY, V.F., South Delta Deanery; Very Rev. Msgr. DAVID LESIEUR, V.F., West Ozark Deanery; Very Rev. GREGORY T. LUYET, J.C.L., V.F., West River Valley Deanery.

Diocesan Offices and Directors

Unless otherwise indicated all Diocesan Offices and Directors are located at: *St. John Catholic Center, 2500 N. Tyler St., Little Rock, 72207.* Tel: 501-664-0340; Fax: 501-664-9075. *Mailing Address: P.O. Box 7565, Little Rock, 72217-7565.*

Adoption Services, Inc.—ANTJE HARRIS, Dir. Fax: 501-664-9186.

Diocesan Council for Black Catholics—Very Rev. WARREN HARVEY, V.F., Bishop's Liaison, P.O. Box

7434, Pine Bluff, 71611. Tel: 870-534-4701.

Building Commission—JIM DRIEDRIC, Exec. Sec. Fax: 501-664-1310.

Catholic Charities of Arkansas—PATRICK GALLAHER, Exec. Dir. This office also handles: Alcohol and Chemical Addiction Ministry; Adoption Services; Catholic Campaign for Human Development; Catholic Immigration Services - N.W. Arkansas; Catholic Immigration Services - Little Rock; Catholic Relief Services; Disaster Response; Parish Social Ministry; Prison Ministry; Refugee Resettlement; Social Action; Westside Free Medical Clinic.Fax: 501-664-9186.

Catholic Campus Ministry—LIZ TINGQUIST, Dir.

Catholic Immigration Services - Little Rock Office—MARICELLA GARCIA, Dir. Fax: 501-664-9186.

Catholic Immigration Services - NW Arkansas Office—FRANK HEAD JR., Dir. Refugee Resettlement Program 2022 W. Sunset Ave., Springdale, 72762. Tel: 479-927-1996; Fax: 479-927-2979.

Catholic Women, Diocesan Council of—VACANT, Moderator. Contact: KEM DRAKE, Pres., 115 S. 14th St., Paragould, 72450. Tel: 870-236-2937.

Catholic Youth Ministry—LIZ TINGQUIST, Dir.

Calvary Cemetery, Greater Little Rock—MICHAEL CAGLE, Supt., W. Charles Bussey Ave. & S. Woodrow St., Little Rock, 72207. Mailing Address: Calvary Cemetery, Diocese of Little Rock, 2500 N. Tyler St., Little Rock, 72207. Tel: 501-664-0340; Fax: 501-664-1310. Email: smullins@dolr.org.

Charismatic Movement—Rev. Msgr. JAMES E. MANCINI, Bishop's Liaison (Retired). Email: jammanci@aol.com. Web: www.arkcc.org.

Clergy Welfare Advisory Board—Rev. MARK WOOD, Chm.

Continuing Education for the Clergy—Very Rev. Msgr. DAVID LESIEUR, V.F., Dir.

Cursillo Movement—Revs. MARK WOOD; RUBEN QUINTEROS, Spiritual Dir., Spanish Cursillo; Deacon WILLIAM G. BRANDON JR., Spiritual Dir., English Cursillo Office; VACANT, Dir. English Cursillo Office, Contact: Tel: 501-664-0340; Fax: 501-664-5835. Email: lrcursillo@dolr.org; JAMIE TORRES, Dir. Spanish Cursillo Office. Fax: 501-664-9075; LAZETH NOVAK, Administrative Asst.

Information Systems—Rev. Msgr. THOMAS SEBAUGH, Dir.

Stewardship and Development Office—DIANNE BRADY, Dir.

Diaconate Office—Deacon JOHN JACOB MARSCHEWSKI, Min. to Permanent Deacons.

Diaconate Formation (English)—Deacon ROBERT E. WANLESS.

Diaconate Formation (Spanish)—Deacon MARCELINO LUNA.

Ecumenical and Interreligious Affairs Office—Deacon JOHN JACOB MARSCHEWSKI, Dir.

Family Life Office: (Pre-Cana, Marriage Encounter, Retrouvaille, Natural Family Planning)—ELIZABETH REHA, Dir.

Hispanic Ministry—Deacon MARCELINO LUNA, Dir.

Hospitals—Very Rev. Msgr. FRANCIS I. MALONE, J.C.L., P.A., V.F.

Library—TERESA HAYDEN, Librarian.

Office of Divine Worship—Rev. Msgr. RICHARD S. OSWALD, V.F.

Minister to Priests—Very Rev. Msgr. DAVID LESIEUR, V.F.

Newspaper "Arkansas Catholic"—MALEA HARGETT, Editor, P.O. Box 7417, Little Rock, 72217.

Presbyteral Council—Rev. Msgrs. RICHARD S. OSWALD, V.F.; R. SCOTT FRIEND, V.G.; Very Rev. Msgr. FRANCIS I. MALONE, J.C.L., P.A., V.F.; Very Revs. GREGORY T. LUYET, J.C.L., V.F.; JAMES M. FANRAK, V.F.; WARREN HARVEY, V.F.; Revs. ERIK POHLMEIER; JOHN E. MARCONI; PIUS AJUNWA IWU, J.C.D.; Rev. Msgr. J. GASTON HEBERT; Rev. ERNEST L. HARDESTY; Very Rev. PAUL F. WORM; Revs. LEONARD WANGLER, O.S.B.; MARK WOOD; Very Rt. Rev. JEROME KODELL, O.S.B., V.F.; Very Rev. Msgr. DAVID LESIEUR, V.F.

Clergy Personnel Advisory Board (Diocesan)—Rev. Msgr. R. SCOTT FRIEND, V.G.; Very Rev. Msgrs. FRANCIS I. MALONE, J.C.L., P.A., V.F.; DAVID LESIEUR, V.F.; Revs. JOHN E. MARCONI; CHARLES THESSING; ERIK POHLMEIER; JASON TYLER, S.T.L.; Very Rev. GREGORY T. LUYET, J.C.L., V.F.; Rev. Msgrs. J. GASTON HEBERT; SCOTT L. MARCZUK, J.C.L.

Project Rachel—ANNE DIERKS, Dir., 2500 N. Tyler St., Little Rock, 72207. Tel: 501-664-0340, Ext. 357.

Propagation of the Faith—Very Rev. Msgr. FRANCIS I. MALONE, J.C.L., P.A., V.F. Fax: 501-664-5835.

Refugee Resettlement Program—FRANK HEAD JR., Dir.

Religious Education Department/Christian Initiation—CHUCK ASHBURN.

Respect Life Office—MARIANNE LINANE, Dir.

St. John's Catholic Center/Office Services—PATRICK SWEENEY, Mgr.

Schools—VERNELL BOWEN, Supt. Fax: 501-603-0518.

Little Rock Scripture Study—CACKIE UPCHURCH, Dir.; LILLY HESS, Assoc. Dir., Administration & Production; CLIFF YEARY, Assoc. Dir., Devel. of Study Materials.

Monsignor James E. O'Connell Diocesan Seminarian Fund, Inc.—Rev. Msgr. R. SCOTT FRIEND, V.G., Dir.

Social Action and Prison Ministry, Catholic Campaign for Human Development Alcohol and Chemical Addiction Ministry—TOM NAVIN, Dir. Fax: 501-664-9186.

Parish Social Ministry and Disaster Response—PATRICK GALLAHER, Exec. Dir., 2500 N. Tyler St., Little Rock, 72207. Tel: 501-664-0340; Fax: 501-664-9186.

Victim Assistance Coordinators—Dr. GEORGE SIMON; Dr. SHERRY SIMON. Cell: 501-766-6001. Email: vacoord@dolr.org.

Vocations—Rev. Msgr. R. SCOTT FRIEND, V.G., Dir. Assistant Directors: Rev. ERIK POHLMEIER; Rev. Msgr. JOHN F. O'DONNELL (Retired).

Westside Free Medical Clinic—KAREN DIPIPPA, Dir. Fax: 501-664-9186.

CLERGY, PARISHES, MISSIONS AND PAROCHIAL SCHOOLS

GREATER LITTLE ROCK

(PULASKI COUNTY)

1—CATHEDRAL OF ST. ANDREW (1845) [JC] Rev. G. Matthew Garrison, Rector; Deacon William J. Bowen.
617 Louisiana St., 72201. Tel: 501-374-2794; Fax: 501-375-3292. Email: cathedralstandrew@sbcglobal.net. Web: www.cathedralsaintandrew.org.
Catechesis/Religious Program—Andrea Cordell, D.R.E. Students 58.

2—ST. ANNE (North Little Rock) (1935) [JC] Revs. Michael F. Walsh, C.M.; Luis A. Ramirez.
Mailing Address: 6150 Remount Rd., North Little Rock, 72118. Tel: 501-753-3977; Fax: 501-753-3991. Email: info@saintannenlr.org. Web: www.saintannenlr.org.
Catechesis/Religious Program—Belinda Kaye Ortner, D.R.E. Students 211.

3—ST. AUGUSTINE (1929), (African American), [JC] Rev. Bartholomew N. Okere.
1421 E. Second, North Little Rock, 72114. Tel: 501-375-9617; Fax: 501-375-9617.
Catechesis/Religious Program—Rosalyn G. Pruitt, D.R.E. Students 18.

4—ST. BARTHOLOMEW (1907), (African American), Rev. Ryszard Zawadzki, S.V.D. (Poland); Deacon Kirke Leo Herman.
1622 Marshall St., 72202. Tel: 501-372-4682. Email: fr.richard@goodcounsellr.com.
Catechesis/Religious Program—Students 35.

5—CHRIST THE KING (1966) [JC] Very Rev. Msgr. Francis I. Malone; Rev. Jason Sharbaugh; Deacons William Melville Hartmann, (Retired); John M. McAllister; Richard Lewis Patterson; Dan Charles Cashman; Curtis Don Greenway; William Johnson; John Jacob Marschewski.
4000 N. Rodney Parham Rd., 72212. Tel: 501-225-6774; Fax: 501-225-7169. Web: www.ctkLr.org.
School—(Grades PreK-8), 4002 N. Rodney Parham Rd., 72212. Tel: 501-225-7883; Fax: 501-225-1315. Mrs. Kathy House, Prin. Lay Teachers 41; Students 691.
Catechesis/Religious Program—Students 184.
Msgr. Hebert Endowment Fund—Tel: 501-225-7883; Fax: 501-225-1315.

6—ST. EDWARD (1884) [JC] Rev. Jason Tyler; Deacon Daniel James Hennessey III; Rev. Msgr. Richard S. Oswald; Deacon Marcelino Luna.
815 Sherman St., 72202. Tel: 501-374-5767; Fax: 501-374-5839. Email: office@saintedwards.net. Web: www.saintedwards.net.
School—(Grades PreK-8), 805 Sherman St., 72202. Tel: 501-374-9166. Jason Pohlmeier, Prin.; Karen Stoltz, Librarian. Lay Teachers 20; Students 186.
Catechesis/Religious Program— Lilia Hernandez, D.R.E. Students 380.

7—IMMACULATE CONCEPTION (1948) [JC] Rev. Thomas A. Elliott; Deacon Chuck Arthur Farrar.
7000 John F. Kennedy Blvd., North Little Rock, 72116. Tel: 501-835-4323; Fax: 501-834-5598. Email: secretary@iccnlr.org. Web: www.iccnlr.org.
School—(Grades PreK-8) Tel: 501-835-0771; Fax: 501-834-8652. Email: mbru@icsnlr.org. Web: icsnlr.org. Marcia Brucks, Prin. Lay Teachers 19; Students 187.
Catechesis/Religious Program—Tel: 501-835-4323, Ext. 30. Phyllis Eubanks, D.R.E. Students 130.
Immaculate Conception School Endowment Fund—Fax: 501-834-0165.

8—IMMACULATE HEART OF MARY (Marche) (1878), (Polish), [CEM] Rev. Thomas Joseph Hart; Deacon Brunon John Strozyk.
7006 Jasna Gora Dr., North Little Rock, 72118. Tel: 501-851-2763; Fax: 501-851-4769. Email: ihmparish@ihmparishschool.org. Web: www.ihmparishschool.org.
School—(Grades PreK-8) Tel: 501-851-2760; Fax: 501-851-4769. Email: ihmschool@sbcglobal.net. Mr. Daniel Smith, Prin. Lay Teachers 15; Students 145.
Catechesis/Religious Program—Students 29.
Immaculate Heart of Mary Educational Trust Fund for Immaculate Heart of Mary School—Tel: 501-851-2763.

9—ST. MARY (North Little Rock) (1897), (Polish), Rev. Frank V. DuPreez (South Africa).
1516 Parker St., North Little Rock, 72114. Tel: 501-374-7123; Fax: 501-372-2995. Email: stmaryschurchnlr@comcast.net.
School—North Little Rock Catholic Academy, (Grades PreK-8), 1518 Parker St., North Little Rock, 72114. Tel: 501-374-5237; Fax: 501-374-5237. Denise Troutman, Admin.; Sandra Naylor, Librarian. Lay Teachers 21; Students 212.
Catechesis/Religious Program—Denise Troutman, D.R.E. Students 170.
St. Mary's School Endowment Fund—Tel: 501-758-2220; Fax: 501-753-6623.

10—OUR LADY OF GOOD COUNSEL (1894) Rev. Ryszard Zawadzki, S.V.D. (Poland).
1321 S. Van Buren St., 72204. Tel: 501-666-5073; Fax: 501-664-1964. Email: olgc_parishoffice@sbcglobal.net. Web: www.goodcounselchurch.org.
Msgr. Scheper Endowment Fund for Our Lady of Good Counsel Catholic School—
Catechesis/Religious Program—Email: olgc_debbie@sbcglobal.net. Students 32.

11—OUR LADY OF THE HOLY SOULS (1947) Revs. Erik Pohlmeier; L. Dhanraj Narla (India); Deacons Lawrence H. Jegley; Timothy Massanelli.
Church & Office: 1003 N. Tyler St., 72205. Tel: 501-663-8632; Fax: 501-663-8699. Email: office@holysouls.org. Web: www.holysouls.org.
School—(Grades PreK-8), 1001 N. Tyler St., 72205. Tel: 501-663-4513; Fax: 501-663-1014. Email: hss@holysouls.org. Web: arcathsch.org/hs/. Ileana Dobbins, Prin.; Ellie Stewart, Librarian. Lay Teachers 42; Students 531.
Catechesis/Religious Program—Anne Thomisee, D.R.E. Students 83.

12—ST. PATRICK (1880) [JC] Rev. Frank V. DuPreez (South Africa); Deacon Ron Stager.
211 W. 19th St., North Little Rock, 72114. Tel: 501-758-1155; Fax: 501-753-8251. Email: linda@stpatricknlr.comcastbiz.net.
Catechesis/Religious Program—
St. Patrick's Educational Endowment Fund—Tel: 501-605-0008; Fax: 501-753-8251.

13—ST. THERESA (1954) [JC] Revs. D. Mark Wood; Michael E. Bass; Deacon Donald Joseph Francis.
6219 Baseline Rd., 72209. Tel: 501-565-9198; Fax: 501-565-3949. Email: abirge@stclr.org. Web: www.stclr.org.
School—(Grades PreK-8) Tel: 501-565-3855; Fax: 501-565-9522. Marguerite Olberts, Prin. Lay Teachers 8; Students 179.
St. Theresa Catholic School Endowment Fund—
Catechesis/Religious Program—Tel: 501-565-5647. Students 455.

OUTSIDE THE CITY OF LITTLE ROCK

ADONA, CONWAY CO., ST. ELIZABETH (Oppelo) (1884), (German), [CEM] Attended by St. Boniface Church, New Dixie. Rev. Richard P. Davis.
Mailing Address: 20 St. Boniface Dr., Bigelow, 72016. Tel: 501-354-0631; Fax: 501-759-2152.
Catechesis/Religious Program—Students 47.

ALTUS, FRANKLIN CO., ST. MARY (1879) [CEM] Rev. Aaron Pirrera, O.S.B.; Deacon Matthew Joseph Post.
5118 St. Mary's Ln., 72821. Tel: 479-468-2585.
Catechesis/Religious Program—(Attended from St. Benedict, Subiaco) Students 57.

ARKADELPHIA, CLARK CO., ST. MARY (1971) Rev. Innocent Okore (Nigeria); Deacon Edward Carl "Bud" Daven.
Church: P.O. Box 26, 71923. Tel: 870-246-7575.
Catechesis/Religious Program—Students 40.

ASHDOWN, LITTLE RIVER CO., ST. ELIZABETH ANN SETON CHURCH (1991) Attended by St. Edward, Texarkana. Very Rev. Paul F. Worm.
Mailing Address: 1910 Rankin St., P.O. Box 966, 71822. Tel: 870-898-8529.
Catechesis/Religious Program—Students 1.

ATKINS, POPE CO., ASSUMPTION B.V.M. (1878),

(German), [CEM] Rev. Ernest L. Hardesty.
Mailing Address: P.O. Box 337, 72823. Tel: 479-641-7179.
Catechesis/Religious Program—Students 9.

BALD KNOB, WHITE CO., ST. RICHARD CHURCH, Attended by St. James, Searcy. Rev. Mathew Vianney Malapati Santhaiah (India).
Mailing Address: P.O. Box 172, Searcy, 72145. Tel: 501-268-5252 (Searcy).
Church: 101 W. Cleveland St., 72010.

BARLING, SEBASTIAN CO., SACRED HEART OF MARY (1902) [CEM] Revs. Henry B. Mischkowiuski; Peter Quang Le, (Vietnamese Catholic Community).
1301 Frank St., 72923. Tel: 479-452-1795; Fax: 479-452-0571.
Catechesis/Religious Program—Edwina Schwarz, D.R.E.; Dottie Hunter, D.R.E. Students 33.
Mission—SS. Sabina & Mary Church, (See listing under Fort Smith), Jenny Lind. Dr. Thomas Bonin, D.R.E.

BATESVILLE, INDEPENDENCE CO., ST. MARY (1909) Rev. Phillip A. Reaves; Deacon Mike Comnock.
3800 Harrison St., 72501. Tel: 870-793-7717 (Office); 870-793-7464 (Rectory); Fax: 870-793-7717. Email: stmarys@suddenlinkmail.com.
Catechesis/Religious Program—Patricia Hinds, D.R.E. Students 121.
Mission—St. Cecilia 2475 Galleria Dr., Newport, Jackson Co. 72112. Tel: 870-523-6542.

BELLA VISTA, BENTON CO., ST. BERNARD OF CLAIRVAUX (1980) [CEM] Rev. Barnabas Maria Susai, I.M.S.
Office: One St. Bernard Ln., 72715. Tel: 479-855-9069; Fax: 479-855-9067. Email: office@bvstbernard.org. Web: www.bvstbernard.org.
Catechesis/Religious Program—Kathy Smith, Rel. Educ. Coord. Students 55.

BENTON, SALINE CO., OUR LADY OF FATIMA (1942) Rev. Joseph Ejimofor (Nigeria); Deacon John Charles Duke.
900 W. Cross St., 72015. Tel: 501-315-5186. Email: olfchurch@swbell.net.
School—(Grades K-8), 818 W. Cross St., 72015. Tel: 501-315-3398; Fax: 501-315-0927. Web: www.ourladyoffatimaschool.com. Jan Cash, Prin.; Loretta Stehle, Librarian. Lay Teachers 13; Students 70.
Our Lady of Fatima School Endowment Trust Fund—
Catechesis/Religious Program—Kath Dunlap, D.R.E. Students 195.
Station—Arkansas Health Center, Tel: 501-860-0500.

BENTONVILLE, BENTON CO., ST. STEPHEN (1989) [CEM] Rev. Msgr. Scott L. Marczuk.
Mailing Address: 1300 N.E. J St., 72712. Tel: 479-273-1240; Fax: 479-464-0969. Email: ststephen@cox-internet.com. Web: www.ststephenbentonville.com.
Rectory—1208 N.E. J St., 72712. Tel: 479-273-1240; Fax: 479-464-0969.
Catechesis/Religious Program—Students 623.

BERRYVILLE, CARROLL CO., ST. ANNE (1958) Attended by St. Elizabeth of Hungary, Eureka Springs. (See listing for Eureka Springs). Rev. Shaun C. Wesley.
614 S. Main, 72616. Tel: 870-423-3927. Email: stannes@windstream.net. Web: www.stanneschurchberryville.org.
Res.: 30 Crescent Dr., Eureka Springs, 72632. Tel: 479-253-9853.
Catechesis/Religious Program—Students 145.

BIGELOW, PERRY CO., ST. BONIFACE (1879), (German), [CEM] Rev. Richard P. Davis.
20 St. Boniface Dr., 72016. Tel: 501-759-2371; Fax: 501-759-2152. Email: stboniface@tcworks.net.
Catechesis/Religious Program—Students 49.
Mission—St. Francis of Assisi Little Italy, Pulaski Co.
Mission—St. Elizabeth Adona, Conway Co.

BLYTHEVILLE, MISSISSIPPI CO., IMMACULATE CONCEPTION (1894) Rev. Thomas C. Marks; Deacons William G. Brandon Jr.; Kenneth Klinger.
Mailing Address: 1301 W. Main St., P.O. Box 747, 72316.
Office: 1301 Main St., 72315. Tel: 870-762-2506; Fax: 870-762-2506.
Catechesis/Religious Program—Tel: 870-561-4120. Students 51.
Mission—St. Matthew Osceola, 72370.
Mission—St. Norbert Marked Tree, 72365.

BOONEVILLE, LOGAN CO., CHURCH OF OUR LADY OF THE ASSUMPTION (1953) Rev. Don Tranel, G.H.M.
Mailing Address: P.O. Box 298, 72927. Tel: 479-675-3371.
Church: 616 N. Cherry Ave., 72927.
Catechesis/Religious Program—Students 58.

BRINKLEY, MONROE CO., ST. JOHN THE BAPTIST (1875) [CEM] Attended by St. Mary, Helena. Also attends St. Francis of Assisi, Forrest City; St. Mary of the Lake, Horseshoe Lake; and St. Andrew, Marianna. Revs. Benoit Mukamba, C.S.Sp.; Martin Vu, C.S.Sp.; Honest Munishi, C.S.Sp.
203 W. Ash, 72021-3201. Tel: 870-734-1202.
Catechesis/Religious Program—Tel: 870-734-3392. Carl Frein, D.R.E. Students 4.
Mission—St. Francis of Assisi Forrest City.
Mission—St. Mary of the Lake, See St. St. Mary of the Lake, Horseshoe Lake for complete listing., Horseshoe Lake, Crittenden Co. 72348.

CAMDEN, OUACHITA CO., ST. LOUIS (1923) Rev. Anthony Robbins.
Mailing Address: 202 Adams, N.W., 71701. Tel: 870-836-2426.
Res.: 2114 N. Jackson St., Magnolia, 71753. Email: stlouiscc6674@sbcglobal.net.
Catechesis/Religious Program—Tel: 870-231-4554. Mrs. Deb Murray, D.R.E. Students 29.
Mission—Immaculate Heart of Mary 2114 N. Jackson St., Magnolia, Columbia Co. 71753. Tel: 870-234-2710. Mailing Address: P.O. Box 365, Magnolia, 71754.

CARLISLE, LONOKE CO., ST. ROSE OF LIMA CHURCH (1895) Rev. Thomas W. Keller; Deacon William Cunningham Jr.
603 E. Park, P.O. Box M, 72024. Tel: 870-552-3601. Email: strose011@centurytel.net. Mailing Address: P.O. Box M, 72024.
Catechesis/Religious Program—Beth Plafcan, D.R.E. Students 22.
Mission—Holy Trinity, (See listing under England), England, Lonoke Co.

CENTER RIDGE, CONWAY CO., ST. JOSEPH (1881), (Italian), [CEM] Rev. Silvio D'Ostilio, C.S.Sp.
Mailing Address: 343 Catholic Point Rd., 72027. Tel: 501-893-2887; Fax: 501-893-2887. Email: stjoseph343@hotmail.com.
Catechesis/Religious Program—Annette May, D.R.E. Students 49.

CHARLESTON, FRANKLIN CO., SACRED HEART (1879) [CEM] Rev. Patrick Watikha, A.J. (Uganda).
18 Prairie St., 72933-9334. Tel: 479-965-2532. Email: sacredheartchurch@gmail.com.
Catechesis/Religious Program—Tel: 479-965-2771. Anita Collier, D.R.E. Students 126.

CHEROKEE VILLAGE, SHARP CO., ST. MICHAEL (1939) Rev. Linus Ukomadu (Nigeria).
Mailing Address: P.O. Box 970, 72525. Tel: 870-257-2850. Email: stmichaelcv@yahoo.com. Web: www.stmichaelscv.org. 49 Tekakwitha Dr., 72529.
Res.: 12 Micanopy Circle, 72529. Tel: 870-257-4456.
Catechesis/Religious Program—Students 23.
Mission—St. Mary of the Mount Church 401 E. Church St., Horseshoe Bend, Izard Co. 72512. Tel: 870-670-5896.
St. Michael Memorial Garden (Columbarium)—Tel: 870-257-2850.

CLARKSVILLE, JOHNSON CO., HOLY REDEEMER (1879) [CEM] Rev. William Wewers, O.S.B.
103 E. Main St., 72830. Tel: 479-754-3610. Email: wgwosb@suddenlinkmail.com.
Catechesis/Religious Program—Students 370.

CLINTON, VAN BUREN CO., ST. JUDE CHURCH (1988) Attended by St. Francis of Assisi, Fairfield Bay. Rev. Oliver Ochieze (Nigeria).
Mailing Address: P.O. Box 526, 72031. Tel: 501-745-5716; Fax: 501-745-5716. Email: grakme@clinton.cable.
Catechesis/Religious Program—David Adams, D.R.E. Students 19.

CONWAY, FAULKNER CO., ST. JOSEPH (1878) [CEM] Revs. John E. Marconi; James P. Melnick; Deacons David Kirby Westmoreland; Richard John Papini; Gerald Joseph Harrison.
Parish Business Office: 1115 College Ave., 72032. Tel: 501-327-6568; Fax: 501-327-6607. Email: sjbusoff@hotmail.com. Web: www.sjparish.org.
School—(Grades PreK-12), 502 Front St., 72032. Tel: 501-329-5741; Fax: 501-513-6804. Web: www.stjosephconway.org. Joe Mallett, Prin.; Matt Tucker, Asst. Prin. (PreK-3); Susie Freyaldenhoven, Asst. Prin. (Grades 4-6); Karen Wilson, Librarian; Myra Book, Librarian. Lay Teachers 46; Students 450.
Catechesis/Religious Program—Tel: 501-513-6812. Jean Leffler, D.R.E. Students 361.

CORNING, CLAY CO., ST. JOSEPH THE WORKER CHURCH (1968) Attended by St. Paul the Apostle, Pocahontas. Rev. Athanasius N. Okeiyi (Nigeria).
Mailing Address: c/o 2CR 186, 72422. Tel: 870-857-6607.
Church Site: 1415 Harb S., 72422.
Catechesis/Religious Program—Fran Black, D.R.E. Students 7.

CRAWFORDSVILLE, CRITTENDEN CO., SACRED HEART CHURCH, Attended by St. Michael, West Memphis. Very Rev. Msgr. Jack D. Harris.
Mailing Address: *c/o St. Michael*, P.O. Box 899, West Memphis, 72303. Tel: 870-733-1212 (West Memphis); Fax: 870-732-4808. Email: stmichaels899@sbcglobal.net.
Church: 216 S. Main St., 72327.

CROSSETT, ASHLEY CO., HOLY CROSS, Attended by St. Mary, McGehee. Rev. Theophilus Okpara (Nigeria).
Mailing Address: 2400 S. Main St., 71635.
Catechesis/Religious Program—204 Mareus Saline Rd., 71635. Tel: 870-364-4584. Pat Hubbard, D.R.E. Students 22.

DANVILLE, YELL CO., SAINT ANDREW CHURCH (1996) Attended by St. Jude Thaddeus, Waldron. Rev. Francois Pellissier, G.H.M.
Mailing Address: P.O. Box 1262, 72833.
Catechesis/Religious Program—David Henley, D.R.E.

DARDANELLE, YELL CO., ST. AUGUSTINE (1925) Rev. Clayton Gould.
P.O. Box 460, 72834.
Church: 1001 N. 2nd., 72834. Tel: 479-229-3972.
Catechesis/Religious Program—Students 94.

DE QUEEN, SEVIER CO., ST. BARBARA (1911) [CEM] [JC] Rev. Edward P. D'Almeida.
Mailing Address: P.O. Box 86, 71832. Tel: 870-642-5559; Fax: 870-642-3426. Email: st.barbar@hotmail.com.
Catechesis/Religious Program—Students 389.

DUMAS, DESHA CO., HOLY CHILD CHURCH, (Hispanic), Attended by St. Mark, Monticello. Rev. Rajasekhar Chappidi (India).
Mailing Address: *c/o St. Mark*, 1016 N. Hyatt St., Monticello, 71655. Tel: 870-367-2848 (Monticello); Fax: 870-367-5868.
Church: 807 E. Waterman St., 71639.
Catechesis/Religious Program—

EL DORADO, UNION CO., HOLY REDEEMER (1923) Rev. Gregory Pilcher, O.S.B.
Church: 440 W. Main St., 71730-5757. Tel: 870-863-3620; Fax: 870-863-7537. Email: holyredeemer@suddenlinkmail.com. Web: www.holyredeemereldorado.org.
Catechesis/Religious Program—Students 101.
El Dorado Holy Redeemer School Endowment Fund—1103 W. Cedar St., 71730. Tel: 870-863-8677; Fax: 870-863-7779.

ENGELBERG, RANDOLPH CO., ST. JOHN THE BAPTIST (Pocahontas P.O.) (1885), (German), [CEM] Attended by St. Paul the Apostle, Pocahontas. Rev. Athanasius N. Okeiyi (Nigeria).
4650 Engelberg Rd., Pocahontas, 72455. Tel: 870-892-3319.
Catechesis/Religious Program—Tel: 870-647-1141. David Helms, D.R.E. Students 24.

ENGLAND, LONOKE CO., HOLY TRINITY CHURCH (1976) Attended by St. Rose of Lima, Carlisle. Rev. Thomas W. Keller.
Mailing Address: P.O. Box 243, 72046.
Church: 1240 AR Hwy 161 W., 72046. Tel: 870-552-3601 (Carlisle).

EUREKA SPRINGS, CARROLL CO., ST. ELIZABETH OF HUNGARY (1909) Rev. Shaun C. Wesley.
Mailing Address: 232 Passion Play Rd., 72632. Tel: 479-253-2222; Fax: 479-253-6616. Email: stelizabeth@vrc4u.com.
Res.: #30 Crescent Dr., 72632. Tel: 479-253-9853.
Catechesis/Religious Program—Tel: 479-253-6742. Margaret Bartell, D.R.E.; Kathy Tromburg, D.R.E. Students 13.
Mission—St. Anne, (See listing for Berryville), 614 S. Main St., Berryville, 72616. Tel: 870-423-3927.

FAIRFIELD BAY, VAN BUREN CO., ST. FRANCIS ASSISI (1976) Rev. Oliver Ochieze (Nigeria); Deacon Frank Joseph Zanoff.
Res.: 250 Woodlawn Dr., 72088. Tel: 501-884-3349; Fax: 501-884-4852. Email: stfrancis@artelco.com.
Catechesis/Religious Program—Tel: 501-884-7272. Deacon Frank Joseph Zanoff, D.R.E.
Mission—St. Jude, (See listing under Clinton), Clinton, Van Buren Co.

FAYETTEVILLE, WASHINGTON CO.

1—ST. JOSEPH (1844) [CEM] Revs. John K. Antony; Ravi Gudipalli (India); Deacons Bud Baldwin III; Al Genna.
Church & Office: 1722 N. Starr Dr., 72701. Tel: 479-442-0890; Fax: 479-442-7887. Email: bbarber@sjfay.com. Web: www.sjfay.com.
School—(Grades PreK-7) Tel: 479-442-4554. Web: www.sjfay.com. Marcia Diamond, Prin.; Jenny Brown, Librarian. Lay Teachers 24; Students 316.
St. Joseph Endowment and Educational Trust Fund—1722 N. Starr Dr., 72701. Tel: 479-442-4554.
Catechesis/Religious Program—Tel: 479-442-0890, Ext. 256. Email: skrumpelman@sjfay.com. Suzanne Krumpelman, D.R.E. Students 638.

2—ST. THOMAS AQUINAS UNIVERSITY PARISH (1960) Rev. Joseph Patrick Marconi.
603 N. Leverett Ave., 72701-3220. Tel: 479-444-0223; Fax: 479-442-2633.

FORDYCE, DALLAS CO., GOOD SHEPHERD (1977) Attended by St. Mark, Monticello.

FOREMAN, LITTLE RIVER CO., SACRED HEART CHURCH, A mission of St. Edward, Texarkana. Very Rev. Paul F. Worm.
Mailing Address: P.O. Box 43, 71836. Tel: 870-542-6574; Fax: 870-542-6715.
Catechesis/Religious Program—Students 10.

FORREST CITY, ST. FRANCIS CO., ST. FRANCIS OF ASSISI (1876) [JC] Attended by St. Mary, Helena. Also attends St. John the Baptist, Brinkley; St. Mary of

the Lake, Horseshoe Lake; and St. Andrew, Marianna. Revs. Benoit Mukamba, C.S.Sp.; Martin Vu, C.S.Sp.; Honest Munishi, C.S.Sp.
621 S. Washington St., P.O. Box 786, 72336-0786. Tel: 870-633-1665; Fax: 870-633-6307. Email: stfrancis21@gmail.com.
Catechesis/Religious Program—
FORT SMITH, SEBASTIAN CO.
1—ST. BONIFACE (1886) [JC] Rev. H. Jon McDougal; Deacon John Joseph Burns.
1820 North B St., 72901. Tel: 479-783-6711; Fax: 479-783-7423. Email: stbface@aol.com. Web: www.saintboniface.com.
School—(Grades PreK-6), 201 N. 19th St., 72901. Tel: 479-783-6601; Fax: 479-783-6605. Web: www-.stbonifaceschool.org. Karen Hollenbeck, Prin.; Cindy Foss, Librarian. Lay Teachers 18; Students 154.
Catholic Education Endowment Trust of Fort Smith, Arkansas—
Catechesis/Religious Program—Rowena Gran, D.R.E. Students 61.
2—CHRIST THE KING (1928) [CEM] [JC] Very Rev. Kevin Atunzu (Nigeria).
2112 S. Greenwood Ave., 72901. Tel: 479-783-7745; Fax: 479-783-7075. Email: ctkpastor@christ-king.org. Web: www.christ-king.org.
School—(Grades PreK-6), 1918 S. Greenwood, 72901. Tel: 479-782-0614; Fax: 479-782-1098. Email: principal@christ-king.org. Web: www.ctk-school.com. Diana Redding, Prin. & Librarian. Lay Teachers 22; Students 289.
Christ the King Catholic School Trust and Endowment Fund—Tel: 479-783-1937.
Catechesis/Religious Program—Tel: 479-783-5305. Jennifer Briselden, Youth Min.; Beth Roberts, D.R.E. Students 210.
3—IMMACULATE CONCEPTION (1849) [JC] Very Rev. Gregory T. Luyet; Rev. Joseph Archibong; Deacon Greg Pair.
Mailing Address: P.O. Box 1866, 72902-1866.
Church: 22 North 13th, 72901. Tel: 479-783-7963; Fax: 479-783-7865.
School—(Grades PreK-6), 223 South 14th St., 72901. Tel: 479-783-6798; Fax: 479-783-0510. Web: www.icschoolfs.org. Sharon Blentlinger, Prin.; Sr. Mary Sarto Gaffrey, Librarian. Sisters of Mercy 1; Lay Teachers 30; Students 322.
Immaculate Conception School Educational Trust—
Catechesis/Religious Program—Tel: 479-783-7497. Surennah Werley, D.R.E. Students 635.
Mission—St. Leo's P.O. Box 1866, Hartford, Sebastian Co. 72902.
4—SS. SABINA & MARY CHURCH, Attended by Sacred Heart of Mary, Barling. Rev. Henry B. Mischkowiuski.
Mailing Address: 14304 Old Jenny Loop Rd., 72919. Tel: 479-452-1795 (Barling); Fax: 501-452-0571.
Catechesis/Religious Program—Dr. Thomas Bonin, D.R.E. Students 30.
GLENWOOD, PIKE CO., OUR LADY OF GUADALUPE CHURCH, Attended by St. Agnes, Mena. Rev. Norbert F. Rappold.
Mailing Address: P.O. Box 426, 71943.
Church: Mountain View & Kennedy Cutoff, 71943. Tel: 870-356-5185.
Catechesis/Religious Program—Students 120.
GRADY, LINCOLN CO., BLESSED SACRAMENT CHURCH, (Hispanic), Attended by St. Justin, Star City. Sr. Kathleen Miles, D.C., Pastoral Admin.
Mailing Address: P.O. Box 128, Star City, 71667.
Res.: 1207 S. Main, 71644. Tel: 870-628-3092; Fax: 870-628-3092.
HAMBURG, ASHLEY CO., HOLY SPIRIT CHURCH (1987), (Hispanic), Attended by Our Lady of the Lake, Lake Village. Rev. Theophilus Okpara (Nigeria).
Mailing Address: P.O. Box 272, Lake Village, 71653. Tel: 870-265-5439; Fax: 870-265-5439.
Church: 110 E. Franklin, 71646. Tel: 870-853-8991.
Catechesis/Religious Program—Students 70.
HARRISON, BOONE CO., MARY, MOTHER OF GOD (1919) Very Rev. James M. Fanrak.
Mailing Address: P.O. Box 2150, 72602. Tel: 870-741-5234; Fax: 870-741-4234. Email: mmgchurch@hotmail.com.
Church: Hwy. 43 E. & Maplewood Rd., 72602.
Catechesis/Religious Program—Fax: 870-741-4234. Karen Rezabek, D.R.E. Students 105.
Mission—St Andrews Catholic Church, (See listing under Yellville), Yellville, Marion Co.
HARTFORD, SEBASTIAN CO., ST. LEO'S (1901), A mission of Immaculate Conception, Fort Smith. Very Rev. Gregory T. Luyet; Rev. Joseph Archibong.
Mailing Address: P.O. Box 1866, Fort Smith, 72902. Tel: 479-783-7963; Fax: 479-783-7865.
Catechesis/Religious Program—
HEBER SPRINGS, CLEBURNE CO., ST. ALBERT CHURCH, Attended by St. James, Searcy. Rev. Mathew Vianney Malapati Santhaiah (India); Deacon Robert L. Morris.
Mailing Address: 21 Park Rd., 72543. Tel: 501-362-2914; Fax: 501-362-8942. Email: stalbert21@suddenlinkmail.com.
Catechesis/Religious Program—Students 57.
HELENA, PHILLIPS CO., ST. MARY (1858) [CEM], Also attends St. John the Baptist, Brinkley; St. Francis of Assisi, Forrest City; St. Mary of the Lake, Horseshoe Lake; and St. Andrew, Marianna. Revs. Benoit Mukamba, C.S.Sp.; Martin Vu, C.S.Sp.; Honest Munishi, C.S.Sp.
123 Columbia St., 72342. Tel: 870-338-6990; Fax: 870-338-6990.
Catechesis/Religious Program—Students 29.
Mission—St. Andrew, (See listing for Marianna), 54 W. Tennessee St., P.O. Box 724, Marianna, Lee Co. 72360.
HOPE, HEMPSTEAD CO., OUR LADY OF GOOD HOPE (1875) [CEM] Rev. Alphonse Gollapalli (India); Deacon Robert V. Regan, (Retired).
Mailing Address: P.O. Box 517, 71802-0517.
Office: 315 S. Walker St., 71801. Tel: 870-777-3202; Fax: 870-777-8533. Email: ourladyofgoodhope@sbcglobal.net.
Catechesis/Religious Program—Karen Barham, D.R.E. Students 137.
HORSESHOE BEND, IZARD CO., ST. MARY OF THE MOUNT (1974) [CEM] Attended by St. Michael, Cherokee Village. Rev. Linus Ukomadu (Nigeria).
1002 First St., 72512. Tel: 870-670-5896. Email: mounts@centurytel.net.
Catechesis/Religious Program—
HORSESHOE LAKE, CRITTENDEN CO., ST. MARY OF THE LAKE CHURCH, Attended by St. Mary, Helena; also attends St. John the Baptist, Brinkley; St. Francis of Assisi, Forrest City; and St. Andrew, Marianna. Revs. Benoit Mukamba, C.S.Sp.; Martin Vu, C.S.Sp.; Honest Munishi, C.S.Sp.
Mailing Address: 123 Columbia St., Helena, 72342. Tel: 870-734-1202.
Church: 1713 Horseshoe Cr., 72348.
HOT SPRINGS NATIONAL PARK, GARLAND CO.
1—ST. JOHN THE BAPTIST (1907) Revs. James P. West; Alan Rosenau; Deacon Patrick McCruden.
Res.: 589 W. Grand Ave., 71901. Tel: 501-623-6201; Fax: 501-318-0328.
School—(Grades PreK-8), 583 W. Grand Ave., 71901. Tel: 501-624-3147; Fax: 501-624-3141. Mrs. Elizabeth Shackelford, Prin. Sisters of Mercy 3; Lay Teachers 24; Students 122.
St. John's School Endowment—Tel: 501-624-3171.
Catechesis/Religious Program—Students 150.
2—ST. MARY OF THE SPRINGS (1869) [JC] Rev. William F. Thomas; Deacons Joe Dale Harrison; Lee Leckner.
100 Central Ave., 71901. Tel: 501-623-3233. Email: stmcc@hotsprings.net.
Catechesis/Religious Program—Students 64.
HOT SPRINGS VILLAGE, GARLAND CO., SACRED HEART OF JESUS (1979) Rev. William Elser; Deacons Bernard Louis Bauer; Larry Lipsmeyer; William Friedman.
Rectory—293 Balearic Rd., 71909. Tel: 501-922-4024.
Church & Mailing Address: 295 Balearic Rd., 71909. Tel: 501-922-2062; Fax: 501-922-4153. Email: sacredheart@hsvsacredheart.com. Web: www.hsvsacredheart.com.
HUNTSVILLE, MADISON CO., ST. JOHN THE EVANGELIST (1963) [JC], Attended from St. Joseph, Tontitown Revs. John K. Antony; Ravi Gudipalli (India).
Mailing Address: P.O. Box 755, 72740.
Church: 411 Crossbow Rd., 72740. Tel: 479-559-2826.
Catechesis/Religious Program—Tel: 479-232-5790. Susan Rivera, D.R.E. Students 15.
JACKSONVILLE, PULASKI CO., ST. JUDE THE APOSTLE (1966) Rev. W. Andrew Smith; Deacons James M. Alberson; Max R. Elliott.
2403 McArthur Dr., 72076. Tel: 501-982-4891; Fax: 501-982-0821. Email: stjude982@aol.com.
Catechesis/Religious Program—Tel: 501-843-9467. Paula Price, D.R.E. Students 309.
JONESBORO, CRAIGHEAD CO.
1—BLESSED JOHN NEWMAN UNIVERSITY PARISH, Attended by Blessed Sacrament, Jonesboro. Rev. Jack Vu; Deacon David Emory England; Mary Ruth Stuadt, Dir.
Mailing Address: 2800 E. Johnson Ave., 72401. Tel: 870-972-1888; Fax: 870-972-6294. Email: cnc28@sbcglobal.net. Web: www.clt.astate.edu/cnc.
2—BLESSED SACRAMENT (1885) [CEM] Rev. Jack Vu; Deacons Victor J. Stepka, (Retired); David Emory England.
614 S. Church St., P.O. Box 1735, 72401. Tel: 870-932-2529. Email: office@catholicjonesboro.com. Web: www.catholicjonesboro.com.
School—(Grades K-6), 1105 E. Highland Dr., 72401. Tel: 870-932-3684. Email: pillow@tdn.to. Carol Stoverink, Prin. Lay Teachers 7; Students 123.
Catechesis/Religious Program—Tel: 870-931-7079. Students 350.
Blessed Sacrament Educational Endowment Fund—Tel: 870-935-2871.
LAKE VILLAGE, CHICOT CO., OUR LADY OF THE LAKE (1869), (Italian), [CEM 2] Rev. Theophilus Okpara (Nigeria).
Mailing Address: P.O. Box 272, 71653. Tel: 870-265-5439; Fax: 870-265-5663.
School—(Grades PreK-6) Tel: 870-265-2921; Fax: 870-265-2921. Mary Belle Tonos, Prin. Lay Teachers 7; Students 59.
Catechesis/Religious Program—Deborah Vaughn, D.R.E.; Terry Lee, D.R.E. Students 65.
St. Mary's Educational Trust Fund—
Mission—Holy Spirit, See Holy Spirit, Hamburg for complete listing., Hamburg, Ashley Co. 71646.
LEOLA, GRANT CO., BLESSED JUAN DIEGO CHURCH, Closed. For inquiries for parish records contact the chancery.
LITTLE ITALY, PULASKI CO., ST. FRANCIS OF ASSISI CHURCH (1922) Attended by St. Boniface, Bigelow. Rev. Richard P. Davis.
Mailing Address: *c/o St. Boniface*, 20 St. Boniface, Bigelow, 72016. Tel: 501-759-2371.
Catechesis/Religious Program—
MAGNOLIA, COLUMBIA CO., IMMACULATE HEART OF MARY (1946) Attended by St. Louis Church, Camden. Rev. Anthony Robbins.
Mailing Address: P.O. Box 365, 71754. Tel: 870-234-2710.
Catechesis/Religious Program—Students 30.
MALVERN, HOT SPRING CO., ST. JOHN THE BAPTIST (1949) Rev. Innocent Okore (Nigeria).
Mailing Address: 1121 McBee St., P.O. Box 6, 72104. Tel: 501-332-6244; Fax: 501-332-7100.
Catechesis/Religious Program—Carolyn Paul, D.R.E. Students 3.
MARIANNA, LEE CO., ST. ANDREW, Attended by St. Mary, Helena. Also attends St. John the Baptist, Brinkley; St. Francis of Assisi, Forrest City; and St. Mary of the Lake, Horseshoe Lake. Revs. Benoit Mukamba, C.S.Sp.; Martin Vu, C.S.Sp.; Honest Munishi, C.S.Sp.
54 W. Tennessee St., P.O. Box 724, 72360. Tel: 870-338-6990 (Helena); Fax: 870-338-6990 (Helena).
Catechesis/Religious Program—
MARKED TREE, POINSETT CO., ST. NORBERT (1947) Rev. Thomas C. Marks.
Mailing Address: 42 Frisco St., 72365. Tel: 870-358-2135; Fax: 870-358-4055.
Church: 501 Normandy St., 72365.
MCCRORY, WOODRUFF CO., ST. MARY CHURCH, Attended by St. Peter, Wynne. Rev. Arokiasamy Madhichetty Irudayaraj (India).
Mailing Address: c/o 1695 N. Falls Blvd., P.O. Box 517, Wynne, 72396. Tel: 870-731-0048; Fax: 870-238-2613 (Wynne).
Catechesis/Religious Program—
MCGEHEE, DESHA CO., ST. MARY (1906) Attended by St. Mark, Monticello. Rev. Rajasekhar Chappidi (India).
401 N. 3rd St., 71654. Tel: 870-222-3389 (call for fax).
MENA, POLK CO., ST. AGNES (1896) [CEM] Rev. Norbert F. Rappold; Deacon Larry Hatch.
203 8th St., 71953. Tel: 479-394-1017; Fax: 479-394-2088. Email: saintagnesmena@sbcglobal.net.
Catechesis/Religious Program—Students 74.
Mission—All Saints, (See listing Mount Ida), Mount Ida, Montgomery Co.
Mission—Our Lady of Guadalupe, (See listing Glenwood), Glenwood, Pike Co.
MONTICELLO, DREW CO., ST. MARK (1975) Rev. Rajasekhar Chappidi (India).
Mailing Address: 1016 N. Hyatt St., 71655. Tel: 870-367-2848; Fax: 870-367-5868.
Rectory—452 W. Jefferson, 71655. Tel: 870-367-5974.
Catechesis/Religious Program—Tel: 870-460-9919. Hope Bragg, D.R.E. Students 64.
Mission—Holy Child, (See listing under Dumas), Dumas, Desha Co.
MORRILTON, CONWAY CO., SACRED HEART (1879) [CEM] Rev. Charles Thessing.
506 E. Broadway, 72110. Tel: 501-354-4181; Fax: 501-354-4181. Email: sacred_heart@hotmail.com.
School—(Grades K-6) Tel: 501-354-8113; Fax: 501-354-2001. Brian Bailey, Prin.; Katherine Etris, Librarian. Lay Teachers 8; Students 129.
High School—(Grades 7-12), 106 N. St. Joseph, 72110. Brian Bailey, Prin.; Katherine Etris, Librarian. Lay Teachers 11; Students 95.
Catechesis/Religious Program—Students 72.
Sacred Heart School Endowment—
MORRISON BLUFF, LOGAN CO., SS. PETER AND PAUL (1878) Rev. Josely Dhyan Kalathil, I.M.S.
Mailing Address: P.O. Box 87, Scranton, 72863.
Res.: 108 E. Main St., Scranton, 72863. Tel: 479-938-2821.
Catechesis/Religious Program—Ruth Beshoner, D.R.E. Students 22.
MOUNT IDA, MONTGOMERY CO., ALL SAINTS CHURCH, Attended by St. Agnes, Mena. Rev. Norbert F. Rappold.

Mailing Address: P.O. Box 724, 71957. Tel: 479-867-4644; Fax: 479-867-4644 (Mena).
Catechesis / Religious Program—Students 3.

MOUNTAIN HOME, BAXTER CO., ST. PETER THE FISHERMAN (1959) Revs. Stan Swiderski; Christopher Okeke (Nigeria); Deacons John Thomas Krug, (Retired); Richard Linstad; Robert Crawford; Paul Poulosky.
249 Dyer St., P.O. Box 298, 72654. Tel: 870-425-2832; Fax: 870-424-5172.
Catechesis / Religious Program—Students 115.
Mission—St. Mary Church (1983), (See listing under Mountain View), Mountain View, Stone Co.

MOUNTAIN VIEW, STONE CO., ST. MARY CHURCH (1982) Attended by St. Peter the Fisherman, Mountain Home. Revs. Stan Swiderski; Christopher Okeke (Nigeria).
Mailing Address: P.O. Box 926, Stone Co. 72560.
Res. & Church: 17068 Hwy. 66 W., 72560. Tel: 870-269-5194; Fax: 870-269-5194. Email: stmarychurch@mvtel.net.
Catechesis / Religious Program—Loreena Hegenbart, D.R.E. Students 7.

NASHVILLE, HOWARD CO., ST. MARTIN CHURCH, Attended by Our Lady of Good Hope, Hope. Rev. Alphonse Gollapalli (India).
Mailing Address: 1011 Leslie St., P.O. Box 1039, 71852. Tel: 870-845-1271.
Catechesis / Religious Program—Nona Broussard, D.R.E. Students 47.

NEWPORT, JACKSON CO., ST. CECILIA, Attended by St. Mary's, Batesville. Rev. Phillip A. Reaves.
Church: 2475 Galeria Subdivision, 72112. Tel: 870-793-7464; 870-523-6542; Fax: 870-793-7717.
St. Mary Church: 3800 Harrison St., Batesville, 72501. Tel: 870-793-7717.
Catechesis / Religious Program—Students 15.

OSCEOLA, MISSISSIPPI CO., ST. MATTHEW (1879) Attended by Immaculate Conception, Blytheville. Rev. Thomas C. Marks.
Mailing Address: P.O. Box 583, 72370.
Res.: 1301 W. Main St., Blytheville, 72315. Tel: 870-762-2506; Fax: 870-762-2506.
Church: S. Ermen St., 72370.
Catechesis / Religious Program—800 Betty Lynn, 72370. Tel: 870-563-4889.

PARAGOULD, GREENE CO., ST. MARY (1883) [CEM] Rev. Michael Sinkler; Deacon Rex A. Bouldin.
Church, Office & Mailing Address: 220 N. Second St., 72450. Tel: 870-236-2568; Fax: 870-236-8675. Email: stmryoff@grnco.net. Web: www.stmarysparagould.org.
School—(Grades PreK-6) Tel: 870-236-3681; Fax: 870-236-1073. Sharon Warren, Prin.; Jennifer King, Librarian. Lay Teachers 8; Students 50.
Catechesis / Religious Program—Tel: 870-239-3976. Karen Ussery, D.R.E. Students 56.
Mission—Immaculate Heart of Mary, (See listing under Walnut Ridge)
St. Mary Educational Trust Fund—

PARIS, LOGAN CO., ST. JOSEPH (1879), (German), [CEM] Rev. Eugene Luke, O.S.B.; Deacon Thomas J. Pohlmeier.
15 S. Spruce St., 72855. Tel: 479-963-2131.
School—(Grades PreK-8), 25 S. Spruce St., 72855. Tel: 479-963-2119; Fax: 479-963-8039. Kimberlee Felix, Prin. Lay Teachers 7; Students 88.
Catechesis / Religious Program—Students 10.
St. Joseph Endowment Fund—

PINE BLUFF, JEFFERSON CO.

1—ST. JOSEPH (1858) [CEM 5] [JC] Rev. L. Warren Harvey; Deacon Noel F. "Bud" Bryant.
412 W. 6th Ave., P.O. Box 7434, 71611. Tel: 870-534-4701; Fax: 870-534-4703. Web: www.stjosephpinebluff.org.
See St. Joseph Catholic Jr./Sr. High School, Pine Bluff under High Schools, Diocesan located in the Institution section.
Catechesis / Religious Program—Tel: 870-536-6699. Brynn Koschel, D.R.E. Students 69.
Mission—St. Mary Plum Bayou P.O. Box 7434, Jefferson Co. 71611-7434.
Mission—Good Shepherd 410 W. Oak St., Fordyce, 71742. Tel: 870-352-2328.
St. Joseph's Education Fund—Tel: 870-879-4217. David Schimmel, Pastoral Council Pres.
Junior High Endowment Fund—
Senior High Trust Fund—

2—ST. PETER (1894), (African American), Rev. Anil Thomas, S.V.D.; Deacon Elton Harrison.
207 E. 16th Ave., 71601. Tel: 870-534-6418. Email: dmsppb@aristotle.net.
School—(Grades PreK-6) Tel: 870-535-4017; Fax: 870-535-4017. Carol A. Beeman, Prin. Lay Teachers 9; Students 70.
Catechesis / Religious Program—Nola Harrison, D.R.E.
Convent—Tel: 870-534-2316.
Mission—St. Raphael, Jefferson Co.
St. Peter Catholic School Foundation—

POCAHONTAS, RANDOLPH CO., ST. PAUL THE APOSTLE (1868) [CEM], Attended from St. John the Baptist, Engelberg (see listing for Engelberg); St. Joseph the Worker, Corning (see listing for Corning). Rev. Athanasius N. Okeiyi (Nigeria); Deacon George Joseph Edwards.
1002 Convent St., 72455. Tel: 870-892-3319. Email: saintpaul@suddenlink.net. Web: saintpaulscatholic.com.
School—(Grades PreK-6), 311 Cedar St., 72455. Tel: 870-892-5639. Email: stpaulsch@suddenlink.net. Rebecca Jansen, Prin. Lay Teachers 18; Students 130.
Catechesis / Religious Program—Sr. Laura Cathcart, O.S.B., D.R.E. Students 106.

PRAIRIE VIEW, LOGAN CO., ST. MEINRAD CHURCH (1913) Attended by St. Ignatius, Scranton. Rev. Josely Dhyan Kalathil, I.M.S.
Mailing Address: 108 Main St., P.O. Box 87, Scranton, 72863.
35 Saint Meinrad Loop, Scranton, 72863. Tel: 479-938-2821; Fax: 479-938-2821 (Scranton).
Catechesis / Religious Program—Heath Spellers, D.R.E. Students 23.

RATCLIFF, LOGAN CO., ST. ANTHONY (1879), (German), [CEM] Rev. Don Tranel, G.H.M., Sacramental Min.; Deacon Bob Grierson Cowie, Pastoral Admin.
470 W. Wilson St., 72951. Mailing Address: c/o N. Carbon City Rd., Paris, 72855. Tel: 479-963-3990.
Catechesis / Religious Program—Jana Stengel, D.R.E. Students 15.

ROGERS, BENTON CO., ST. VINCENT DE PAUL (1941) [CEM] Very Rev. Msgr. David LeSieur; Rev. Jose Antonio Galvez-Orellana; Deacons Clarence Arthur Leis; John Ray Pate.
Church: 1416 W. Poplar St., 72758. Tel: 479-636-4020. Web: www.svdprogers.com.
School—(Grades PreK-8), 1315 W. Cypress St., 72758. Tel: 479-636-4421; Fax: 479-636-5812. Web: www.svdpschool.net. Joe Sine, Prin.; Carolyn Pio, Asst. Prin.; Alice Stautzenberger, Librarian. Lay Teachers 24; Students 314.
St. Vincent de Paul Endowment Fund—Tel: 479-621-1723; Fax: 479-621-1723.
Catechesis / Religious Program—Students 1,013.

RUSSELLVILLE, POPE CO.

1—ST. JOHN (1950) Rev. Chuma P. Ibebuike (Nigeria).
Mailing Address: 1900 W. Main St., 72801. Tel: 479-967-3699; Fax: 479-967-6215. Email: stjcatholic@suddenlinkmail.com. Web: www.saintjohnrussellville.org.
School—(Grades PreK-5), 1912 W. Main St., 72801. Tel: 479-967-4644; Fax: 479-967-6215. Mark Tyler, Librarian. Lay Teachers 14; Students 89.
Catechesis / Religious Program—Patricia Joselin, D.R.E. & Youth Min. Students 117.
St. John's Educational Trust—1912 W. Main St., 72801.

2—ST. LEO THE GREAT UNIVERSITY PARISH, Attended by Assumption of the Blessed Virgin Mary, Atkins. Rev. Ernest L. Hardesty.
Mailing Address: P.O. Box 9033, 72811. 509 W. "L" St., 72801. Tel: 479-968-8249. Email: stleos@hotmail.com. Web: www.stleoatu.homestead.com.

ST. VINCENT, CONWAY CO., ST. MARY (1880) [CEM] Rev. James Burnie, C.S.Sp.
11 Kaufman Ln., Hattieville, 72063. Tel: 501-354-3206; Fax: 501-354-4132.
Catechesis / Religious Program—Students 62.

SCRANTON, LOGAN CO., ST. IGNATIUS (1913), (German), [CEM] Rev. Josely Dhyan Kalathil, I.M.S.
Mailing Address: P.O. Box 87, 72863.
Church: 108 E. Main St., 72863. Tel: 479-938-2821.
Catechesis / Religious Program—Tel: 479-938-7474. Students 60.
Mission—St. Meinrad, (See listing under Prairie View), Prairie View, Logan Co.
Mission—SS. Peter & Paul Church Hwy. 109, Morrison Bluff, Logan Co. Tel: 479-938-2200.

SEARCY, WHITE CO., ST. JAMES (1915) Rev. Mathew Vianney Malapati Santhaiah (India); Deacon Robert L. Morris.
1102 Pioneer Rd., P.O. Box 172, 72143. Tel: 501-268-5252 (Office); Fax: 501-268-2388. Email: stjames172@sbcglobal.net. Web: www.stjamescatholicsearcy.org.
Catechesis / Religious Program—Theresa Gillram, D.R.E. Students 194.
Mission—St. Albert, (See listing under Heber Springs), Heber Springs, Cleburne Co.
Mission—St. Richard, (See listing under Bald Knob), Bald Knob, White Co.

SHERIDAN, GRANT CO., HOLY CROSS (1949) Attended by St. Joseph, Pine Bluff. Rev. L. Warren Harvey.
Res.: 910 W. Vine St., P.O. Box 624, 72150-0624.
Catechesis / Religious Program—Tel: 870-942-8366. Mary Hale, D.R.E. (Attended from St. Joseph, Pine Bluff).

SHOAL CREEK, LOGAN CO., ST. SCHOLASTICA (New Blaine) (1878), (German), Rev. Denis Soerries, O.S.B.
288 St. Scholastica Rd., New Blaine, 72851. Tel: 479-938-7566.
Catechesis / Religious Program—Students 21.

SILOAM SPRINGS, BENTON CO., ST. MARY (1963) Rev. Salvador Marquez-Munoz.
Mailing Address: P.O. Box 118, 72761. Tel: 479-524-8526 (rectory); Fax: 479-524-5677.
Catechesis / Religious Program—Tel: 479-524-3120. Leticia Zavala, D.R.E. Students 248.

SLOVAK, PRAIRIE CO., SS. CYRIL AND METHODIUS, [CEM] Attended by Holy Rosary, Stuttgart. Rev. Pius Ajunwa Iwu (Nigeria).
Mailing Address: 1852 Hwy. 86 W., Stuttgart, 72160. Tel: 870-241-3359; Fax: 870-673-6701.
Catechesis / Religious Program—Students 28.

SPRINGDALE, WASHINGTON CO., ST. RAPHAEL (1949) [JC] Rev. John M. Connell; Very Rev. Leslie A. Farley; Rev. Ruben Quinteros; Deacon Chuck Marino.
Church: 1386 S.West End St., 72764. Tel: 479-756-6711; Fax: 479-756-8818. Email: info@straphaelcc.org. Web: www.straphaelcc.org.
School—(Grades PreSchool), 1721 W. Sunset St., 72762. Karen LaMendola, Prin. Staff 21; Students 130.
Catechesis / Religious Program—Students 1,541.

STAMPS, LAFAYETTE CO., ST. VINCENT DE PAUL, Closed. For inquiries for parish records contact the chancery.

STAR CITY, LINCOLN CO., ST. JUSTIN (1986) [CEM] [JC] Sr. Kathleen Miles, D.C., Admin.
Mailing Address: 400 N. Drew St., P.O. Box 128, 71667. Tel: 870-628-3092; Fax: 870-628-3092.
Catechesis / Religious Program—Students 8.
Mission—Blessed Sacrament, (See listing under Gary), Grady, Lincoln Co.

STUTTGART, ARKANSAS CO., HOLY ROSARY (1887) [CEM] Rev. Pius Ajunwa Iwu (Nigeria).
1815 S. Prairie St., 72160. Tel: 870-673-8351; Fax: 870-673-6701.
School—(Grades PreK-6), 920 W. 19th St., 72160. Tel: 870-673-3211. Kathy Lorince, Prin. Lay Teachers 5; Students 51.
Catechesis / Religious Program—Polly Franzen, D.R.E. Students 30.

SUBIACO, LOGAN CO., ST. BENEDICT (1878) [CEM] Rev. Aaron Pirrera, O.S.B.
Church & Res.: 81 W. Parish Dr., 72865. Tel: 479-934-4321. Email: stbensubi@yahoo.com.
Catechesis / Religious Program—(Also attended by St. Mary Altus)., Tel: 479-934-4106. Donna Forst, D.R.E. Students 85.

TEXARKANA, MILLER CO., ST. EDWARD (1903) [CEM] Very Rev. Paul F. Worm; Rev. Salvador Vega-Alvarenga (El Salvador); Deacons Joe Lawrence Bruick; David Fowler.
Mailing Address: P.O. Box 1186, 71854.
Office: 410 Beech St., 71854. Tel: 870-772-1115; Fax: 870-773-2890. Email: office@saintedwardstexarkana.com. Web: www.saintedwardstexarkana.com.
Rectory—407 Beech St., P.O. Box 1186, 71854.
Catechesis / Religious Program—Tel: 870-772-7098. Kelli Nugent, D.R.E. Students 219.
Mission—St. Elizabeth Ann Seton, (See listing under Ashdown), Ashdown, Little River Co.
Mission—Sacred Heart, (See listing under Foreman), Foreman, Little River Co.

TONTITOWN, WASHINGTON CO., ST. JOSEPH (1898), (Italian), [CEM] Rev. Gregory G. Hart.
Mailing Address: P.O. Box 39, 72762. Tel: 479-361-2612; Fax: 479-361-9271. Email: stjoetontitown1@att.net. Web: www.stjoetontitown.org. 154 E. Henri de Tonti Blvd., 72770.
Catechesis / Religious Program—Tel: 479-521-4978. Shannon Stowe, D.R.E. Students 252.

VAN BUREN, CRAWFORD CO., ST. MICHAEL (1872) Rev. Timothy Donnelly, O.S.B.
1019 Pointer Tr. E., 72956. Tel: 479-471-1211; Fax: 479-471-1219. Email: stmichael@sbcglobal.net. Web: www.stmichaelcatholicchurch.com.
Catechesis / Religious Program—Tel: 479-471-1211. Students 227.
Shrine—Our Lady of the Ozarks Shrine 22741 N. Hwy. 71, Winslow, Crawford Co. 72959.

WALDRON, SCOTT CO., ST. JUDE THADDEUS CHURCH (1947) Rev. Francois Pellissier, G.H.M., Sacramental Min.
Mailing Address: P.O. Box 1688, 72958. Tel: 479-207-0485. Web: www.waldronar.catholicweb.com.
Catechesis / Religious Program—Students 75.
Mission—St. Andrew Danville, Yell Co. 72833.

WALNUT RIDGE, LAWRENCE CO., IMMACULATE HEART OF MARY (1925) Rev. Michael Sinkler; Deacon Marlyn Glenn Tate.
320 Free St., P.O. Box 70, 72476. Tel: 870-886-2119.
Catechesis / Religious Program—Students 6.

WARREN, BRADLEY CO., ST. LUKE CHURCH, Attended by St. Mark, Monticello. Rev. Anthony Robbins.

508 W. Pine St., 71671. Tel: 870-367-2848 (Monticello); Fax: 870-367-5868 (Monticello). Mailing Address: *c/o St. Mark*, 1016 N. Hyatt, Monticello, 71656.
Catechesis/Religious Program—Students 46.

WEINER, POINSETT CO., ST. ANTHONY (1902) [CEM], Attended from St. Mary, Batesville. Rev. Phillip A. Reaves.
Mailing Address: P.O. Box 76, 72479. Tel: 870-684-2656; Fax: 870-684-2656.
Church: 407 Kings Hwy., 72479.
Catechesis/Religious Program—Tel: 870-578-4255. Students 23.

WEST MEMPHIS, CRITTENDEN CO., ST. MICHAEL (1914) Very Rev. Msgr. Jack D. Harris.
Mailing Address: P.O. Box 899, 72303.
Res.: 208 W. Cooper Ave., 72301.
Church: 411 Missouri, P.O. Box 899, 72303. Tel: 870-733-1212; 870-735-7983; Fax: 870-732-4808. Email: stmichaels899@sbcglobal.net.
School—(Grades PreK-6), 405 Missouri, P.O. Box 899, 72303. Tel: 870-735-1730; Fax: 870-735-3017. Elizabeth Haney, Prin. Olivetan Benedictine Sisters 2; Lay Teachers 10; Students 95.
Catechesis/Religious Program—Libby Burroughs, D.R.E. Students 70.
St. Michael's School Endowment and Charitable Trust—Tel: 870-735-2683. Robert Gross, CPA.
Mission—Sacred Heart, (See listing under Crawfordsville), Crawfordsville, Crittenden Co.

WINSLOW, CRAWFORD CO., OUR LADY OF THE OZARKS SHRINE (1946) [CEM] Rev. Timothy Donnelly, O.S.B.; Deacon Dan Joseph Daily, Pastoral Admin.
Mailing Address: 22741 N. Hwy. 71, 72959. Tel: 479-634-2181.
Catechesis/Religious Program—1832 Seminole Ct., Fayetteville, 72701. Tel: 479-521-4536. Students 8.

WYNNE, CROSS CO., ST. PETER (1921) Rev. Arokiasamy Madhichetty Irudayaraj (India).
Mailing Address: P.O. Box 517, 72396. Tel: 870-238-2613; Fax: 870-238-2613.
Church: 1695 N. Falls Blvd., 72396.
Catechesis/Religious Program—Students 60.
Mission—St. Mary, (See listing under McCrory), McCrory, Woodruff Co.

YELLVILLE, MARION CO., ST. ANDREW CHURCH (1980) Attended by Mary Mother of God, Harrison. Very Rev. James M. Fanrak.
Mailing Address: P.O. Box 197, 72687. Tel: 870-449-4850; Fax: 870-741-4234 (Harrison).
Church: 1486 Hwy. 62 W., 72687.
Catechesis/Religious Program—Pat Goulet, D.R.E. Students 13.

Chaplains of Public Institutions

LITTLE ROCK. *John L. McClellan Memorial Hospital, VA Medical Center*, 4300 W. 7th St., 72205. Tel: 501-257-2151; Fax: 501-257-2157. Vacant.

FAYETTEVILLE. *U.S. Veterans Administration Hospital*. Attended from St. Joseph Church.

NORTH LITTLE ROCK. *Fort Roots VA Medical Center*, Tel: 501-257-2151; Fax: 501-257-2157. Vacant.

On Special or Other Diocesan Assignment:
Rev. Msgr.—
Sebaugh, Thomas, Dir. Information Systems, 2500 N. Tyler St., P.O. Box 7565, 72217. Tel: 501-664-0340; Fax: 501-664-9075

Leave of Absence:
Rev.—
Kerr, John W.

Retired:
Rev. Msgrs.—
Kordsmeier, John, St. John Manor, Apt. 306, 2414 N. Tyler St., 72207.
Malone, Bernard G., St. John Manor, 2414 N. Tyler St., 72207.
Mancini, James E., St. John Manor, 2414 N. Tyler St., 72207.
O'Donnell, John F., St. John Manor, 2414 N. Tyler St., 72207.
Revs.—
Dienert, Robert T.
Do, Nho Duy, St. John Manor, 2414 N. Tyler St., 72207.
Esposito, Ralph J., 220 Hillcrest Ave., New Castle, PA 16105.
Lange, Milton R., P.O. Box 6037, Springdale, 72766.
Oswald, John, St. John Manor, Apt. 304, 2414 N. Tyler St., 72207.
Pallo, Joseph L.
Preske, Venantius, 1716 Court Loop, Horseshoe Bend, 72512.
Rossi, Raymond R., P.O. Box 21817, Hot Springs, 71913.
Savary, James, 6720 Brentwood Rd., 72205.
Strock, Richard M., St. John Manor, 2414 N. Tyler St., 72207.

Permanent Deacons:
Deacons—
Alberson, James M., St. Jude the Apostle, Jacksonville
Anderson, Arthur John, (Leave of Absence)
Baldwin, Warren Thomas, St. Joseph & St. Thomas Aquinas, Fayetteville
Bauer, Bernard Louis, (Retired)
Bouldin, Rex A., St. Mary, Paragould
Bowen, William Joseph, Cathedral of St. Andrew, Little Rock
Brandon, William G., Jr., Immaculate Conception, Blytheville
Briselden, David Lee, St. John the Baptist, Hot Springs
Bruick, Joe Lawrence, (Retired), St. Edward, Texarkana
Brust, Raymond Edward, (Retired)
Bryant, Noel F. "Bud", St. Joseph, Pine Bluff
Burns, John Joseph, St. Boniface, Fort Smith
Cashman, Dan Charles, Christ the King, Little Rock
Connell, John Michael, (Retired)
Cook, William Renee, (Retired)
Cowie, Bob Grierson, St. Anthony, Ratcliff
Cumnock, Thomas Michael, St. Mary, Batesville; St. Cecelia, Newport
Cunningham, William Wayne, St. Rose, Carlisle
Daily, Dan Joseph, Our Lady of the Ozarks, Winslow
Daven, Edward Carl "Bud", St. John the Baptist, Malvern; St. Mary, Arkadelphia
Duke, John Charles, (Retired)
Edwards, George Joseph, (Retired)
Elliott, Max Robert, St. Jude the Apostle, Jacksonville; Little Rock Air Force Base
England, David Emory, Blessed Sacrament, Jonesboro
Farrar, Chuck Arthur, Immaculate Conception, North Little Rock
Fowler, David, St. Edward, Texarkana
Francis, Donald Joseph, St. Theresa, Little Rock
Genna, Al, St. Joseph, Fayetteville
Gieringer, Wallace Arnold, (Retired)
Goetz, Roy E., St. Benedict, Subiaco
Greenway, Curtis Don, Christ the King, Little Rock
Hankins, Chuck Elden, (On Duty Outside the Diocese)
Harrison, Elton Clement, St. Peter, Pine Bluff
Harrison, Gerald Joseph, St. Joseph, Conway
Harrison, Joe Dale, St. Mary of the Springs, Hot Springs
Hartmann, William Melville, (Retired)
Hartnedy, John Augustine, Our Lady of Good Counsel, Little Rock
Hennessey, Daniel James, III, St. Edward, Little Rock
Herman, Kirke Leo, (Retired)
Jegley, Lawrence H., (Retired)
Johnson, Robert Joseph, St. Michael, Van Buren
Johnson, William Albert, Christ the King, Little Rock
Klingler, Kenneth Arlie, Immaculate Conception, Blytheville
Krug, John Thomas, (Retired)
Leckner, Leland Paul, St. Mary of the Springs, Hot Springs
Leis, Clarence Arthur, (Retired)
Lipsmeyer, Lawrence Joseph, Sacred Heart of Jesus, Hot Springs Village
Luna, Marcelino, St. Edward, Little Rock
Marino, Charles, Jr., St. Raphael, Springdale
Marschewski, John Jacob, Christ the King, Little Rock
Massanelli, Garland Edward, (Retired)
Mattingly, Johnson Smith, (Retired)
McAllister, John M., J.D., J.C.L., Christ the King, Little Rock
Miller, Thomas Ervin, (Out of Diocese)
Morris, Robert L., (Retired)
Pair, Greg, Immaculate Conception, Fort Smith
Papini, Richard John, St. Joseph, Conway
Pate, John Ray, St. Vincent de Paul, Rogers
Patterson, Richard Lewis, Christ the King, Little Rock
Pohlmeier, Thomas J., St. Joseph, Paris
Post, Matthew Joseph, (Retired)
Rohlman, Oscar Aloys, (Retired)
Smith, James, (On Duty Outside the Diocese)
Stager, Ronald F., Immaculate Conception, North Little Rock
Stepka, Victor J., (Retired)
Strozyk, Brunon John, Immaculate Heart of Mary, North Little Rock
Tate, Marlyn Glenn, Immaculate Heart of Mary, Walnut Ridge
Wanless, Robert E., St. John the Baptist, Hot Springs
Westmoreland, David Kirby, St. Joseph, Conway
Wrape, William Robert, (Retired)
Zanoff, Frank Joseph, St. Francis of Assisi, Fairfield Bay; St. Jude, Clinton

INSTITUTIONS LOCATED IN THE DIOCESE

[A] SEMINARIES, RELIGIOUS OR SCHOLASTICATES

LITTLE ROCK. *Marylake - Carmelite Novitiate* (1952) 5151 Marylake Dr., 72206. Tel: 501-888-3052; Fax: 501-888-3080. Revs. Sam Anthony Morello, O.C.D., Supr.; Raphael Kitz, O.C.D., Novice Master; John Magdalene Suenram, O.C.D., Dir. Devel.; Bros. Joseph Le, O.C.D.; Bernard Joseph O'Neil, O.C.D. Discalced Carmelite Friars of the Province of St. Therese, Little Rock. Priests 4.

SUBIACO. *Subiaco Abbey*, 405 N. Subiaco Ave., 72865. Tel: 479-934-1000; Fax: 479-934-4328. Web: www.subi.org. Rev. Richard Walz, O.S.B., Novice Master, Formation Dir.; Very Rt. Rev. Jerome Kodell, O.S.B., V.F., Abbot; Revs. David Bellinghausen, O.S.B., Prior; Hugh Assenmacher, O.S.B.; Bruno Fuhrman, O.S.B.; Brendan Miller, O.S.B.; Nicholas Fuhrmann, O.S.B.; Leonard Wangler, O.S.B.; Mark Stengel, O.S.B.; Sebastian Beshoner, O.S.B.; Bro. Ephrem O'Bryan, O.S.B., Subprior. Abbots 1; Priests 19; Brothers 24; Novices 2.

[B] HIGH SCHOOLS, DIOCESAN

LITTLE ROCK. *Catholic High School*, 6300 Father Tribou St., 72205. Tel: 501-664-3939; Fax: 501-664-6549. Email: chs@lrchs.org. Mr. Steve Straessle, Prin.; Rev. Msgr. Lawrence A. Frederick, Rector.
Catholic High School of Little Rock, AR Priests 1; Brothers 1; Lay Teachers 38; Total Staff 42; Students 713.

CONWAY. *St. Joseph High School*, (Grades 7-12), 502 Front St., 72032-5408. Tel: 501-329-5741; Fax: 501-513-6804. Web: www.stjosephconway.org. Joe Mallett, Prin.; Matthew Tucker, Asst. Prin. (Grades K-3); Susie Freyaldenhoven, Asst. Prin. (Grades 4-6); Myra Book, Librarian (Grades K-6); Karen Wilson, Librarian (Grades 7-12). Lay Teachers 18; Students 205.

FORT SMITH. *Trinity Junior High*, (Grades 7-9), 1205 S. Albert Pike, 72903. Tel: 479-782-2451; Fax: 479-782-7263. Web: www.trinitycatholicjh.org. Very Rev. Kevin Atunzu, V.F. (Nigeria), Admin.; Dr. Jim Hattabaugh, Prin.; Bonnie Gondolfi, Librarian. Lay Teachers 25; Total Staff 25; Students 240.
Trinity Educational Trust Fund Tel: 479-782-2451; Fax: 479-782-7263.

MORRILTON. *Sacred Heart Catholic School*, 106 N. St. Joseph St., 72110. Tel: 501-354-8113; Fax: 501-354-2001. Email: shcsbailey@cox-internet.com. Brian Bailey, Prin. Lay Teachers 11; Total Staff 11; Students 56.

PINE BLUFF. *St. Joseph Catholic Jr./Sr. High School*, (Grades 7-12), 1501 W. 73rd Ave., 71603. Tel: 870-540-0413; Fax: 870-540-0345. Email: stjosephhighschool@cablelynx.com. Web: www.stjosephschool.cc. Very Rev. Warren Harvey, V.F.; Brenda Costello, Prin.; Ann Talbot, Librarian. Total Staff 10; Students 34.

[C] HIGH SCHOOLS, PRIVATE

LITTLE ROCK. *Mount St. Mary Academy* (Girls), 3224 Kavanaugh Blvd., 72205. Tel: 501-664-8006; Fax: 501-666-4382. Web: www.mtstmary.edu. Mrs. Diane Wolfe, Prin.; Sr. Lisa Griffith, R.S.M., Dean Academics; Alice W. Jones, Librarian. Priests 1; Sisters of Mercy 2; Lay Teachers 30; Students 485.
Mount St. Mary Foundation Corporation Tel: 501-664-8006; Fax: 501-664-4382.

SUBIACO. **Subiaco Academy*, (Grades 7-12), 405 N. Subiaco Ave., 72865. Tel: 479-934-1005; 800-364-7824 (Toll Free); Fax: 479-934-1033; 800-364-7824. Web: www.subi.org. Michael Burke, Headmaster; Rev. Leonard Wangler, O.S.B., Prin. Priests 2; Brothers 2; Lay Teachers 30; Students 173.

[D] GENERAL HOSPITALS

LITTLE ROCK. *St. Vincent Infirmary Medical Center* (1888) No. 2 St. Vincent Circle, 72205. Tel: 501-552-3664; Fax: 501-552-8614. Sisters 1; Total Staff 2,048; Bed Capacity 615; Patients Assisted Annually 121,720.

FORT SMITH. *St. Edward Mercy Medical Center* (1905)

7301 Rogers Ave., 72917. Tel: 479-314-6000; Fax: 479-314-1770. Web: www.StEdwardMercy.com. P.O. Box 17000, 72917-7000. Rev. Vincent Flusche, Chap.; Sr. Chabanel Finnegan, R.S.M., Dir. Ethics; Jared H. Bryson, M.Div., Vice Pres., Mission; John McIntosh, Dir. Mktg & Planning. Total Staff 1,400; Bed Capacity 343; Patients Assisted Annually 180,000.

St. Edward Mercy Foundation, 5401 Ellsworth Rd., 72903. Tel: 479-314-1133.

HOT SPRINGS NATIONAL PARK. *St. Joseph's Mercy Health Center*, P.O. Box 29001, 71903-9001. Tel: 501-622-1000; Fax: 501-622-1199. Email: patrickmccruden@mercy.net. Web: www.saintjosephs.com. Timothy J. Johnsen, Pres. & CEO; Rev. Alan Rosenau, Priest Chap.; Deacon Patrick McCruden, Vice Pres. Mission & Ethics, Contact Person. Lay Staff 1,950; Total Staff 1,950; Patients Assisted Annually 45,000; Bed Capacity 309.

Sisters of Mercy of St. Joseph Convent of Hot Springs, Arkansas, Inc. Tel: 501-321-1554.

JONESBORO. *St. Bernard Medical Center* (1900) 225 E. Jackson #84, 72401. Tel: 870-972-4100; Fax: 870-974-7040. Email: sbrown@sbrmc.org. Web: stbernards.info. Chris Barber, Pres. & CEO. Olivetan Benedictine Sisters 13; Total Staff 2,047; Patients Assisted Annually 251,354; Bed Capacity 438.

MORRILTON. *St. Vincent Morrilton* (1925) #4 Hospital Dr., 72110-4510. Tel: 501-977-2300; Fax: 501-977-2400. Email: llyarbrough@stvincenthealth.com. Christy Hockaday, Admin. & CEO.

St. Anthony's Hospital Association, Sponsored by St. Vincent Health System, a division of Catholic Health Initiatives. Total Staff 175; Patients Assisted Annually 32,478; Bed Capacity 25.

OZARK. *St. Edward Health Facilities of Franklin County dba Mercy Hospital/Turner Memorial* 801 W. River St., 72949. Tel: 479-667-4138; Fax: 479-667-4751; 479-667-9778 (Asst. Admin.). Email: steve.loveless@mercy.net. Doug Gantier, Vice Pres. Total Staff 57; Patients Assisted Annually 13,500; Bed Capacity 25.

PARIS. *St. Edward Health Facilities of Logan Co. dba North Logan Mercy Hospital* 500 E. Academy, 72855. Tel: 479-963-6101; Fax: 479-963-6155. Email: steve.loveless@mercy.net. Steve Loveless, C.O.O.; Jared H. Bryson, M.Div., Vice Pres. Total Staff 46; Patients Assisted Annually 12,500; Bed Capacity 16.

ROGERS. *St. Mary-Rogers Memorial Hospital dba Mercy Medical Center* 2710 Rife Medical Ln., 72756. Tel: 479-338-2903; Fax: 479-338-2906. Email: scott.street@mercy.net. Web: www.mercy4u.com. Scott Street, CEO. Total Staff 810; Bed Capacity 165; Patients Assisted Annually 122,871.

St. Mary Hospital Foundation Tel: 479-338-8000; Fax: 479-338-2906.

SHERWOOD. *St. Vincent Medical Center/Sherwood* (1999) 2215 Wildwood Ave., 72120. Tel: 501-552-3664; Fax: 501-552-8614. Bed Capacity 69; Total Assisted Annually 43,688; Total Staff 188.

WALDRON. *St. Edward Health Facilities of Scott County dba Mercy Hospital* 1341 W. 6th St., 72958. Tel: 479-637-4135; Fax: 479-637-3523. Email: dede.obar@mercy.net. Greta Wilcher-McDonald, C.O.O.; Dorothy (Dede) O'Bar, Asst. Admin.; Jared H. Bryson, M.Div., Vice Pres. Mission. Total Staff 56; Patients Assisted Annually 32,000; Bed Capacity 24.

WYNNE. *St. Bernard Community Hospital Corporation dba Crossridge Community Hospital* 310 S. Falls Blvd., 72396. Tel: 870-238-3300; Fax: 870-238-7432. 225 E. Jackson, Jonesboro, 72401. Bed Capacity 25; Total Staff 152; Patients Assisted Annually 21,600.

[E] PROTECTIVE INSTITUTIONS

LITTLE ROCK. *ABBA House, Missionaries of Charity*, 1014 S. Oak St., 72204. Tel: 501-666-9718 (Abba House); 501-663-3596 (convent). Home for expectant mothers, homeless women & children. Missionaries of Charity 4; Staff 4; Bed Capacity 13; Monthly food distribution assisted 1,363; Total Assisted 202.

[F] HOMES FOR AGED

BARLING. *Mercy Crest Housing, Inc. aka Mercy Crest Retirement Living* 1300 Strozier Ln., 72923. Tel: 479-478-3000; Fax: 479-452-8382. Web: www.mercycrest.com. Sandra Presson, R.N., Admin. Sponsored by the Religious Sisters of Mercy. Total Staff 49; Bed Capacity 102; Assisted & Independent Living 102; Patients Assisted Annually 136.

BERRYVILLE. *Mercy Home Health Berryville*, 804 W. Freeman, Ste. 4, 72616. Tel: 866-433-6078 (toll free); Fax: 870-423-4367. Total Staff 16; Total Assisted Annually 298.

JONESBORO. *Benedictine Manor I*, 312 Bridge St., 72401. 225 E. Jackson, 72401. Bed Capacity 20; Total Staff 1; Total Assisted Annually 23.

Benedictine Manor II, 312 Bridge St., 72401. 225 E. Jackson, 72401. Bed Capacity 20; Total Staff 1; Total Assisted Annually 22.

St. Bernard Village, Inc., 1606 Heern Dr., 72401. Tel: 870-932-8141; Fax: 870-933-5563. Web: www.stbernards.info. Kevin Hodges, Vice Pres., Senior Svcs.; Mr. Brian Rega, Dir. (Affiliated with Olivetan Benedictine Sisters, Inc., Jonesboro, AR) Patients Assisted Annually 250; Total Staff 36; Bed Capacity 142.

[G] RESIDENCES FOR PRIESTS

LITTLE ROCK. *St. John Manor*, 2414 N. Tyler St., 72207. Tel: 501-664-0340; Fax: 501-664-9075. Email: psweeney@dolr.org. Rev. Msgrs. John Kordsmeier (Retired); Bernard G. Malone (Retired); James E. Mancini (Retired); John F. O'Donnell (Retired); Rev. John Oswald (Retired); Mr. Jinho Zyung, Res. Mgr.; Revs. Robert T. Dienert (Retired); Nho Duy Do (Retired); Richard M. Strock (Retired). Priests 7.

[H] CONVENTS AND RESIDENCES FOR SISTERS

LITTLE ROCK. *Discalced Carmelite Nuns*, 7201 W. 32nd St., 72204-4716. Tel: 501-565-5121; Fax: 501-565-3877. Email: Lrcarmel@comcast.net. Web: www.littlerockcarmel.org. Sr. Cecilia Chun, O.C.D., Prioress.

Discalced Carmelite Nuns of Little Rock, Attended from Catholic High School, Little Rock. Sisters 15; Nuns with Solemn Vows 12.

Mt. St. Mary's Convent (1851) 3508 Kavanaugh Blvd., 72205. Tel: 501-664-5977; Fax: 501-666-4382. Email: jkonecny@mercysc.org. Sisters 2.

BARLING. *McAuley Convent and Retirement Residence*, 1300 Strozier Ln., 72923. Tel: 479-478-3002; Fax: 479-478-3006. Email: dallen@mercysc.org. Sisters of Mercy 20; Bed Capacity 30; Number Served 23.

FORT SMITH. *St. Scholastica Monastery-Motherhouse* (1879) 1301 S. Albert Pike, P.O. Box 3489, 72913. Tel: 479-783-4147; Fax: 479-782-4352. Email: monastery@stscho.org. Web: www.stscho.org. Sisters Maria Goretti DeAngeli, O.S.B., Prioress; Cecelia Marie Brickell, Archivist; Rev. David McKillin, O.S.B., Chap. Benedictine Professed Sisters 59.

Sisters of Mercy of St. Edward Convent (1905) 7315 Riviera Dr., 72903. Tel: 479-314-6097; Fax: 479-452-1699. Email: srsjm@yahoo.com. Sisters of Mercy 2.

JONESBORO. *Holy Angels Convent-Motherhouse* 72403-0130. Tel: 870-935-5810; Fax: 870-935-4210. Email: olivben@olivben.org. Web: www.olivben.org. Sr. Lilian Marie Reiter, O.S.B., Prioress; Rev. Udochukwu Vincent Ogbuji (Nigeria). Olivetan Benedictine Sisters. Sisters 39; Postulants 1.

[I] NEWMAN CENTERS

LITTLE ROCK. *Catholic Campus Ministry* 2500 N. Tyler St., 72207. Tel: 501-664-0340; Fax: 501-664-0119. Email: ltingquist@dolr.org.

Univ. of Arkansas at Little Rock Catholic Campus Ministry 725 Adams Dr., Jacksonville, 72076. Tel: 501-319-2013. Email: ualrcatholics@gmail.com. Web: ualr.edu/catholic/. Deacon Ron Stager, Campus Min.

BATESVILLE. *Lyons College Catholic Campus Ministry* Deacon Thomas Michael Cumnock.

CLARKSVILLE. *University of Ozarks Catholic Campus Ministry (Clarksville)* 1068 CR 2305, Hartman, 72840. Tel: 479-979-1434. Email: mlstickl@ozarks.edu. Melodye Stickley, Campus Min.

CONWAY. *University of Central Arkansas & Hendrix College Catholic Campus Ministry* 2204 Bruce St., 72034. Tel: 501-336-9091; Fax: 501-336-9091. Email: catholic@cyberback.com. Web: www.uca.edu/org/ccm. Rev. John E. Marconi, Campus Min.; Deacon Richard John Papini, Campus Min. (Conway)

FAYETTEVILLE. *University of Arkansas, St. Thomas Aquinas University Parish* 603 N. Leverett Ave., 72701. Tel: 479-444-0223; Fax: 479-442-2633. Email: ccm@uark.edu. Rev. Joseph Patrick Marconi; Nora Bryant, Administrative Asst.; Lance Dufour, Campus Min.; Kasey Miller, Campus Min.

FORT SMITH. *University of Arkansas at Fort Smith, Catholic Campus Ministry* 4313 S. P St., 72903. Tel: 479-208-0449. Email: skispert@gmail.com.

JONESBORO. *Arkansas State University, Blessed John Newman University Parish* 2800 E. Johnson Ave., 72401. Tel: 870-972-1888; Fax: 870-972-6294. Email: cnc28@sbcglobal.net. Web: www.astatecnc.com. Rev. Jack Vu; Mary Ruth Staudt, Dir. & Campus Min.; Elizabeth Wiederkehr Huss, Campus Min.; Patricia McCaughan, Bookkeeper & Sec.; Deacon David Emory England.

MAGNOLIA. *Southern Arkansas University Catholic Campus Ministry, Immaculate Heart of Mary Church*, 2114 N. Jackson St., 71753. Tel: 870-234-2710. Rev. Anthony Robbins.

RUSSELLVILLE. *St. Leo the Great University Parish* 509 W. L St., 72801. Tel: 479-968-8249. Email: stleos@hotmail.com. Web: www.stleoatu.homestead.com/homepage. P.O. Box 9033, 72811. Rev. Ernest L. Hardesty, Pastor; Mrs. Pat Buford, Dir. Campus Ministry.

SEARCY. *Harding University In Searcy/Arkansas State University at Beebe, Campus Ministry* 109 Campbell Dr., Beebe, 72012. Tel: 501-230-2890; Fax: 501-882-5465. Email: flo.fitch@badger.k12.ar.us. Flo Fitch, Campus Min.

[J] RETREAT CENTERS

BERRYVILLE. *Little Portion Hermitage* (Public Association of the Faithful), 350 CR 248, 72616-8505. Tel: 479-253-7710; Fax: 888-420-5678. Email: info@littleportion.org. Web: www.LittlePortion.org. John Michael Talbot, B.S.C., Gen. Min.; Viola Talbot, B.S.C., Vicar Gen. Min.

Brothers and Sisters of Charity at Little Portion, Inc.

EUREKA SPRINGS. *Little Portion Retreat and Training Center at MORE Mt.*, 171 Hummingbird Ln., 72632. Tel: 479-253-7379; Fax: 479-253-8227. Email: retreatinfo@littleportion.org. Web: www.littleportion.org. John Michael Talbot, B.S.C., Exec. Dir.; Peggy Lodewyks, B.S.C.D., Contact Person & Mgr.

FORT SMITH. *St. Scholastica Center*, 1205 S. Albert Pike, P.O. Box 3489, 72913. Tel: 479-783-1135; Fax: 479-783-8138. Email: retreats@stscho.org. Web: stscho.org. Cathy Smeltzer, Center Dir.; Sisters Madeline Bariola, O.S.B., Dir. Maintenance & Hospitality; Macrina Wiederkehr, O.S.B., Retreats & Spiritual Dir. Conducted by Benedictine Sisters.

SHOAL CREEK. *Hesychia House of Prayer* (1981) 204 St. Scholastica Rd., New Blaine, 72851. Tel: 479-938-7375. Email: hesychia@centurytel.net. Web: www.stscho.org. Sr. Louise Sharum, O.S.B., Dir.; Rev. Denis Soerries, O.S.B. Attended from Subiaco Abbey, Subiaco, AR. Benedictine Sisters 3.

[K] MISCELLANEOUS LISTINGS

LITTLE ROCK. *"Arkansas Catholic"* (1911) Published by Arkansas Catholic, Inc. of the Diocese of Little Rock., 2500 N. Tyler St., P.O. Box 7417, 72217. Tel: 501-664-0340; 501-664-0125; Fax: 501-664-6572. Email: mhargett@dolr.org. Web: www.arkansas-catholic.org. Malea Hargett, Editor.

Christopher Homes of Arkansas, Inc., 2417 N. Tyler St., 72207. Tel: 501-664-1881; Fax: 501-664-1631. Email: jmckinnon@dolr.org. Jimmy McKinnon, Exec. Dir. Total in Residence 568.

Christopher Homes, Inc.

Augusta (1989) 900 Carver N. St., Augusta, 72006. Tel: 870-347-2388; Fax: 870-347-2388. Units 20.

Brinkley (1987) 900 W. 6th St., Brinkley, 72021. Tel: 870-734-2201; Fax: 870-734-2201. Units 20.

Camden (1988) 900 Sharp Ave., Camden, 71701. Tel: 870-837-1911; Fax: 870-837-1914. Units 20.

Clarendon (1989) 400 Meadow Ln., Clarendon, 72029. Tel: 870-747-5441; Fax: 870-747-1345. Units 20.

DeQueen (1986) 119 S. Lakeside Dr., De Queen, 71832. Tel: 870-642-6211; Fax: 870-642-6211. Units 20.

DeValls Bluff (1990) 119 W. Sycamore, De Valls Bluff, 72041. Tel: 870-998-7280; Fax: 870-998-7285. Units 15.

Elaine (1988) 500 N. Pecan, P.O. Box 43, Elaine, 72333. Tel: 870-827-3705; Fax: 870-827-3705. Units 20.

El Dorado (1985) 1323 W. 5th St., El Dorado, 71730. Tel: 870-862-9711; Fax: 870-862-9714. Units 40.

Forest City (1986) 805 Dawson Rd., Forrest City, 72335. Tel: 870-633-4804; Fax: 870-633-4804. Units 20.

Horatio (1988) 408 Bruce St., Horatio, 71842. Tel: 870-832-4014; Fax: 870-832-4014. Units 20.

Jonesboro (1988) 2204 Crescendo Dr., Jonesboro, 72401. Tel: 870-931-9575; Fax: 870-931-9575. Units 19.

Mariana (1986) 238 Christopher Cove #1, Marianna, 72360. Tel: 870-295-6345; Fax: 870-295-6345. Units 20.

Paragould (1990) 1612 S. 9th St., Paragould, 72450. Tel: 870-239-8609; Fax: 870-239-8609. Units 18.

Parkin (1990) 100 College St., P.O. Box 586, Parkin, 72373. Tel: 870-755-2939; Fax: 870-755-2939. Units 20.

Searcy (1985) 17 Christopher Cr., Searcy, 72143. Tel: 501-268-7804; Fax: 501-268-7805. Units 40.

West Helena (1984) 13 Christopher Pl., West Helena, 72390. Tel: 870-572-9433; Fax: 870-572-9433. Units 62.

Wynne (1991) 21 Christopher Pl., Wynne, 72396. Tel: 870-238-3388; Fax: 870-238-3915. Units 20.

Christopher Homes of Hot Springs, Inc. (1997) 1010 Cones Rd., Hot Springs, 71901. Tel: 501-318-1317; Fax: 501-318-1317. Units 20.

Christopher Homes of Monette, Inc. (1993) 21 Christopher Pl., Monette, 72447. Tel: 870-486-2748; Fax: 870-486-2748. Units 20.

Christopher Homes of North Little Rock, Inc. (1996) 656 Donovan Briley Blvd., North Little Rock, 72118. Tel: 501-758-8582; Fax: 501-758-4466. Units 55.

Christopher Homes of Palestine, Inc. (1993) 21 Christopher Pl., Palestine, 72372. Tel: 870-581-2023; Fax: 870-581-2057. Units 20.

Christopher Homes of Strong, Inc. (1994) 21 Christopher Pl, Strong, 71765. Tel: 870-797-7525; Fax: 870-797-7525. Units 20.

The Cottages at Delta Acres Inc., 721 N. 7th St., Clarendon, 72029. Tel: 870-747-5150; Fax: 870-747-5151. Units 19.

Clergy Welfare Fund, Inc., P.O. Box 7565, 72217-7565. Tel: 501-664-0340; Fax: 501-664-1310. Email: gwolfe@dolr.org. Mr. Gregory C. Wolfe, Dir. Finance.

Diocese of Little Rock Catholic Schools Education Trust, 2500 N. Tyler St., 72207. Tel: 501-664-0340. Email: vbowen@dolr.org. Vernell Bowen, Supt.

Diocese of Little Rock House of Formation, 2500 N. Tyler St., 72207.

John Gazzola Trust, P.O. Box 7565, 72217. Tel: 501-664-0340; Fax: 501-664-1310. Mr. Gregory C. Wolfe, Trustee; Mr. Charles Baker, Trustee; Mr. Dale Wintroath, Trustee.

Ladies of Charity of Arkansas, 2500 N. Tyler St., 72207. Tel: 501-664-0340; Fax: 501-664-9075.

Little Rock Scripture Study (1974) 2500 N. Tyler St., P.O. Box 7565, 72217. Tel: 501-664-0340; 501-664-6102; Fax: 501-664-9075. Email: lrss@dolr.org. Web: www.littlerockscripture.org. Cackie Upchurch, Dir.

The Mary Raymond Trust, P.O. Box 7565, 72217-7565. Tel: 501-664-0340; Fax: 501-664-1310. Email: gwolfe@dolr.org. Mr. Gregory C. Wolfe, Dir. Finance.

Monsignor James E. O'Connell Diocesan Seminarian Fund, Inc., P.O. Box 7565, 72217. Tel: 501-664-0340, Ext. 331; Fax: 501-664-9075. Email: sfriend@dolr.org.

St. Thomas More Society of Arkansas, Inc., 4801 North Hills Blvd., Ste. 1550, North Little Rock, 72116. Tel: 501-753-4800; Fax: 501-753-7477. Email: haleyoung@aristotle.net. Milas "Butch" Hale III, Pres.

BERRYVILLE. **Society of St. Vincent De Paul, St. Anne's Conference Inc.*, 1844 Hwy. 62 W., 72616.

BLYTHEVILLE. *Immaculate Conception Trust Fund* (1894) 1301 W. Main St., 72315. Tel: 870-762-2506; Fax: 870-762-2506. P.O. Box 747, 72316. Rev. Thomas C. Marks, V.F.

CHEROKEE VILLAGE. *Magnificat - Mary Ark of the Covenant Corp.*, P.O. Box 970, 72525.

DUMAS. *Daughters of Charity Services*, 145 W. Waterman, P.O. Box 158, 71639. Tel: 870-382-4878; Fax: 870-382-4895. Email: kmusholt@dcsark.org. *Administrative Offices*, 161 S. Main St., P.O. Box 158, 71639. Tel: 870-382-3080; Fax: 870-382-3085. Kathryn Musholt, CEO. Patients Assisted Annually 4,365; Total Staff 32.

Clinics:

St. Elizabeth Health Center, P.O. Drawer 370, Gould, 71643. Tel: 870-263-4317; Fax: 870-263-4782. 407 S. Gould Ave., Gould, 71643.

DePaul Health Center, P.O. Box 158, 71639. Tel: 870-382-4878; Fax: 870-382-4895. 140 W. Waterman St., 71639.

Wellness Center, 405 N. Gould Ave., Gould, 71643. Tel: 870-263-4748; Fax: 870-263-4233.

JONESBORO. *St. Bernard Healthcare*, 225 E. Jackson Ave., 72401. Tel: 870-972-4429; Fax: 870-974-7040. Web: www.stbernards.info. Mr. Robert S. Jones, Attorney.

Jonesboro Real Estate Holding Company, Inc., 225 E. Jackson St., 72401. Tel: 870-972-4301; Fax: 870-974-7040. Email: cbarber@sbrmc.org. Ralph Waddell, Legal Counsel.

Total Life Healthcare, Inc., 225 E. Jackson #92, 72401. Tel: 870-336-5000; Fax: 870-336-5001. Staff 13; Total Assisted 70.

NORTH LITTLE ROCK. *Priestly Fraternity of St. Peter*, 1921 Maple St., 72114. Tel: 501-812-9155; Fax: 501-812-9155. Email: fssp_arkansas@sbcglobal.net. Web: www.arkansaslatinmass.org. Revs. Laurent Demets, F.S.S.P., Chap.; Charles Ryan, F.S.S.P., Chap.

POCAHONTAS. *St. Paul the Apostle Catholic Church - Capital Improvement Trust Fund*, 1002 Convent St., 72455. Tel: 870-892-3319; Fax: 870-892-5199. Email: saintpaul@suddenlink.net. Web: saintpaulcatholic.com. Rev. Athanasius N. Okeiyi (Nigeria), Pastor.

STUTTGART. *Holy Rosary Catholic School "Vision 2000" Educational Trust Fund*, 1815 S. Prairie St., 72160. Tel: 870-673-8351; Fax: 870-673-6701. Email: holyrose@centurytel.net. Rev. Pius Ajunwa Iwu, J.C.D. (Nigeria).

RELIGIOUS INSTITUTES OF MEN REPRESENTED IN THE DIOCESE

For further details refer to the corresponding bracketed number in the Religious Institutes of Men or Women section.

[]—*Apostles of Jesus*

[0200]—*Benedictine Monks* (Conception Abbey, MO)—O.S.B.

[0200]—*Benedictine Monks* (Subiaco Abbey)—O.S.B.

[0460]—*Brothers of the Poor of St. Francis*—C.F.P.

[1330]—*Congregation of the Mission*—C.M.

[0260]—*Discalced Carmelite Friars* (St. Therese Prov.)—O.C.D.

[0570]—*Glenmary Home Missioners*—G.H.M.

[0650]—*Holy Ghost Fathers* (Western Vice Prov.)—C.S.Sp.

[]—*Indian Missionary Society*—I.M.S.

[1065]—*Priestly Fraternity of St. Peter*—F.S.S.P.

[0420]—*Society of the Divine Word* (Techny, IL)—S.V.D.

RELIGIOUS INSTITUTES OF WOMEN REPRESENTED IN THE DIOCESE

[0230]—*Benedictine Sisters of Pontifical Jurisdiction* (Fort Smith, AR)—O.S.B.

[0760]—*Daughters of Charity of St. Vincent de Paul* (West Central Prov.)—D.C.

[0793]—*Daughters of Divine Love*—D.D.L.

[]—*Daughters of Mary Mother of Mercy*—D.M.M.M.

[]—*Daughters of Mary of the Cross*—D.M.C.

[0420]—*Discalced Carmelite Nuns* (Little Rock, AR)—O.C.D.

[1070-10]—*Dominican Sisters*—O.P.

[2575]—*Institute of the Sisters of Mercy of the Americas* (St. Louis, MO)—R.S.M.

[2710]—*Missionaries of Charity*—M.C.

[0390]—*Missionary Carmelites of St. Teresa*—C.M.S.T.

[]—*Missioneras Catequestas de los Pobres*—M.C.P.

[0240]—*Olivetan Benedictine Sisters* (Jonesboro, AR)—O.S.B.

[0500]—*Sisters of Charity of Nazareth*—S.C.N.

CEMETERIES

LITTLE ROCK. *Calvary*

FORT SMITH. *Calvary*

NECROLOGY

† Enderlin, Joseph J., (Retired)—Died Dec. 14, 2011

An asterisk (*) denotes an organization that has established tax-exempt status directly with the IRS and is not covered by the USCCB Group Ruling.

Archdiocese of Los Angeles

(Archidioecesis Angelorum in California)

His Eminence

ROGER CARDINAL MAHONY, D.D., V.G.

Archbishop Emeritus of Los Angeles; ordained May 1, 1962; appointed Titular Bishop of Tamascani and Auxiliary Bishop of Fresno January 7, 1975; consecrated March 19, 1975; appointed Bishop of Stockton February 26, 1980; installed as the third Bishop of Stockton April 17, 1980; appointed Archbishop of Los Angeles July 16, 1985; installed as the fourth Archbishop of Los Angeles September 5, 1985; Created Cardinal June 28, 1991; retired March 1, 2011. *Res.: 10834 Moorpark St., North Hollywood, CA 91602-2206.* Tel: 818-290-2286.

Most Reverend

THOMAS J. CURRY, D.D., PH.D., V.G.

Auxiliary Bishop of Los Angeles; ordained June 18, 1967; appointed Titular Bishop of Ceanannus Mor and Auxiliary Bishop of Los Angeles February 8, 1994; ordained Bishop March 19, 1994. *Office: Santa Barbara Pastoral Region, 3240 Calle Pinon, Santa Barbara, CA 93105.* Tel: 805-682-0442; Fax: 805-682-7509.

Most Reverend

JOSEPH M. SARTORIS, D.D., V.G.

Retired Auxiliary Bishop of Los Angeles; ordained May 30, 1953; appointed Titular Bishop of Oliva and Auxiliary Bishop of Los Angeles February 8, 1994; ordained Bishop March 19, 1994; retired December 31, 2002. *1988 Rolling Vista Dr., #21, Lomita, CA 90717.*

Most Reverend

GERALD E. WILKERSON, D.D., V.G.

Auxiliary Bishop of Los Angeles; ordained May 1, 1965; appointed Titular Bishop of Vincennes and Auxiliary Bishop of Los Angeles November 5, 1997; ordained Bishop January 21, 1998. *Office: San Fernando Pastoral Region, 15101 San Fernando Mission Blvd., Mission Hills, CA 91345-1109.* Tel: 818-361-6009; Fax: 818-361-6270.

Most Reverend

JOSÉ H. GOMEZ

Archbishop of Los Angeles; ordained August 15, 1978; appointed Auxiliary Bishop of Denver and Titular See of Belali January 23, 2001; ordained March 26, 2001; appointed Archbishop of San Antonio December 29, 2004; installed February 15, 2005; Pallium conferred June 29, 2005; appointed Coadjutor Archbishop of Los Angeles April 6, 2010; Succeeded to the See March 1, 2011. *Office: 3424 Wilshire Blvd., Los Angeles, CA 90010-2241.* Tel: 213-637-7534; Fax: 213-637-6510.

Archdiocesan Catholic Center Office: 3424 Wilshire Blvd., Los Angeles, CA 90010-2241. Tel: 213-637-7000; Fax: 213-637-6000.

Web: www.LA-Archdiocese.org

Email: info@LA-Archdiocese.org

Most Reverend

EDWARD W. CLARK, D.D., S.T.D., V.G.

Auxiliary Bishop of Los Angeles; ordained May 27, 1972; appointed Titular Bishop of Gardar and Auxiliary Bishop of Los Angeles January 16, 2001; ordained March 26, 2001. *Office: Regional Bishop, Our Lady of the Angels Pastoral Region, 5835 W. Slauson, Culver City, CA 90230.* Tel: 310-215-0703; Fax: 310-215-0749.

Most Reverend

OSCAR AZARCON SOLIS, D.D., V.G.

Auxiliary Bishop of Los Angeles; ordained April 28, 1979; appointed Titular Bishop of Urci and Auxiliary Bishop of Los Angeles December 11, 2003; ordained February 10, 2004. *Office: San Pedro Pastoral Region, 3555 St. Pancratius Pl., Lakewood, CA 90712-1416.* Tel: 562-634-0456; Fax: 562-531-4783.

Most Reverend

ALEXANDER SALAZAR, D.D., V.G.

Auxiliary Bishop of Los Angeles; ordained June 16, 1984; appointed Titular Bishop of Nesqually and Auxiliary Bishop of Los Angeles September 7, 2004; ordained November 4, 2004. *Office: Ethnic Ministry, Justice and Peace, 3424 Wilshire Blvd., Los Angeles, CA 90010-2241.* Tel: 213-637-7356; Fax: 213-637-6356.

Square Miles 8,762.

Diocese Established 1840; an Archbishopric July 11, 1936.

Comprises the Counties of Los Angeles, Santa Barbara and Ventura in the State of California.

Patroness of the Diocese: St. Vibiana.

Legal Titles:
The Roman Catholic Archbishop of Los Angeles, a Corporation Sole.
Archdiocese of Los Angeles Education and Welfare Corporation.
Our Lady Queen of Angels.
St. John's Seminary College.
St. John's Seminary in California.
The Cardinal McIntyre Fund for Charity.
Catholic Charities of Los Angeles, Inc.
Catholic Charities Community Development Corporation.
The Tidings.
Vida Nueva.
Catholic Education Foundation.
Opus Caritatis.
Cathedral of Our Lady of the Angels.
For legal titles of parishes and archdiocesan institutions, consult the Chancery Office.

STATISTICAL OVERVIEW

Personnel	
Retired Cardinals	1
Archbishops	1
Auxiliary Bishops	5
Retired Bishops	1
Abbots	1
Retired Abbots	1
Priests: Diocesan Active in Diocese	327
Priests: Diocesan Active Outside Diocese	11
Priests: Retired, Sick or Absent	181
Number of Diocesan Priests	519
Religious Priests in Diocese	530
Total Priests in Diocese	1,049
Extern Priests in Diocese	120
Ordinations:	
Diocesan Priests	6
Religious Priests	10
Transitional Deacons	8
Permanent Deacons	16
Permanent Deacons in Diocese	324
Total Brothers	79
Total Sisters	1,793
Parishes	
Parishes	287
With Resident Pastor:	
Resident Diocesan Priests	166
Resident Religious Priests	57
Without Resident Pastor:	
Administered by Priests	45
Administered by Deacons	1
Administered by Religious Women	2
Administered by Lay People	5
Administered by Pastoral Teams, etc.	11
Missions	9
Pastoral Centers	14
Professional Ministry Personnel:	
Brothers	8
Sisters	102
Lay Ministers	596
Welfare	
Catholic Hospitals	14
Total Assisted	2,500,850
Health Care Centers	5
Total Assisted	9,804
Homes for the Aged	9
Total Assisted	3,756
Residential Care of Children	2
Total Assisted	577
Day Care Centers	6
Total Assisted	490
Specialized Homes	1
Total Assisted	7,093
Special Centers for Social Services	33
Total Assisted	232,649
Residential Care of Disabled	6
Total Assisted	805
Other Institutions	12
Total Assisted	360
Educational	
Seminaries, Diocesan	1
Students from This Diocese	43
Students from Other Diocese	28
Seminaries, Religious	11
Students Religious	24
Total Seminarians	67
Colleges and Universities	4
Total Students	12,427
High Schools, Diocesan and Parish	26
Total Students	14,431
High Schools, Private	24
Total Students	13,000
Elementary Schools, Diocesan and Parish	209
Total Students	49,224
Elementary Schools, Private	9
Total Students	2,248
Catechesis/Religious Education:	
High School Students	38,748
Elementary Students	84,720
Total Students under Catholic Instruction	214,865
Teachers in the Diocese:	
Priests	26
Scholastics	2
Brothers	13
Sisters	104
Lay Teachers	4,177
Vital Statistics	
Receptions into the Church:	
Infant Baptism Totals	76,661
Minor Baptism Totals	2,588
Adult Baptism Totals	1,403
Received into Full Communion	6,278
First Communions	44,895
Confirmations	24,907
Marriages:	
Catholic	6,784
Interfaith	846
Total Marriages	7,630
Deaths	11,165

Total Catholic Population. . . . . 4,233,010 Total Population. 11,758,360

Former Bishops—Rt. Revs. FRANCIS GARCIA DIEGO Y MORENO, O.F.M., D.D., cons. Oct. 4, 1840; Bishop of both Californias; died at Santa Barbara, April 30, 1846; JOSEPH SADOC ALEMANY, O.P., D.D., cons. June 30, 1850; Bishop of Monterey; transferred to San Francisco, July 29, 1853; died in Valencia, Spain, April 14, 1888; THADDEUS AMAT, C.M., D.D., cons. March 12, 1854; died May 12, 1878; FRANCIS MORA, D.D., cons. Titular Bishop of Mosynopolis and Coadjutor to Bishop Amat, Aug. 3, 1873; resigned May 6, 1896; died Aug. 3, 1905 in Sarria, Barcelona, Spain; GEORGE MONTGOMERY, D.D., cons. April 8, 1894, Bishop of Tmul and Coadjutor-Bishop of Monterey and Los Angeles cum jure successionis; succeeded to May 6, 1896; appt. Coadjutor-Archbishop of San Francisco, Jan. 1, 1903; died in San Francisco, Jan. 10, 1907; THOMAS JAMES CONATY, D.D., ord. 1872; cons. Nov. 24, 1901, Titular-Bishop of Samos; appt. Bishop of Monterey and Los Angeles, March 27, 1903; died at Coronado, CA, Sept. 18, 1915; Most Rev. JOHN J. CANTWELL, D.D., LL.D., appt. Bishop of Monterey-Los Angeles, Sept. 21, 1917; cons. Dec. 5, 1917; appt. Assistant to the Pontifical Throne, Sept. 30, 1929; transferred to Los Angeles, June 1, 1922; elevated to Archepiscopal dignity, July 11, 1936; installed Dec. 3, 1936; died Oct. 30, 1947, at Los Angeles, CA; His Eminence JAMES FRANCIS MCINTYRE, D.D., appt. Auxiliary Bishop of New York, Nov. 16, 1940; cons. Jan. 8, 1941; promoted to Coadjutor Archbishop, July 20, 1946; appt. Archbishop of Los Angeles, Feb. 7, 1948; installed March 19, 1948; created Cardinal Priest, Jan. 12, 1953; resigned Jan. 21, 1970; died July 16, 1979; TIMOTHY CARDINAL MANNING, D.D., J.C.D., appt. Titular Bishop of Lesvi and Auxiliary Bishop of Los Angeles, Aug. 3, 1946; cons. Oct. 15, 1946; installed as first Bishop of Fresno, Dec. 15, 1967; appt. Titular Bishop of Capri and Coadjutor Archbishop of Los Angeles, May 26, 1969; appt. Archbishop of Los Angeles, Jan. 21, 1970; created a Cardinal Priest, March 5, 1973; retired Sept. 4, 1985; died June 23, 1989 at Los Angeles, CA; ROGER CARDINAL MAHONY, D.D., V.G. (Retired), ord. May 1, 1962; appt. Titular Bishop of Tamascani and Auxiliary Bishop of Fresno Jan. 7, 1975; cons. March 19, 1975; appt. Bishop of Stockton Feb. 26, 1980; installed as the third Bishop of Stockton April 17, 1980; appt. Archbishop of Los Angeles July 16, 1985; installed as the fourth Archbishop of Los Angeles Sept. 5, 1985; Created Cardinal June 28, 1991; retired March 1, 2011.

Archdiocesan Catholic Center Office—3424 Wilshire Blvd., Los Angeles, 90010-2241. Tel: 213-637-7000; Fax: 213-637-6000.

Office of the Archbishop—Most Rev. JOSE H. GOMEZ; Rev. BRIAN CASTANEDA, Priest Sec. & Master of Ceremonies; LUCIANE URBAN, Exec. Sec. to the Archbishop, 3424 Wilshire Blvd., Los Angeles, 90010-2241. Tel: 213-637-7534.

Office of the Cardinal—His Eminence ROGER CARDINAL MAHONY, D.D., V.G., Archbishop Emeritus (Retired), 10834 Moorpark St., North Hollywood, 91602-2206. Tel: 818-290-2286.

Moderator of the Curia and Vicar General—Rev. Msgr. ROYALE M. VADAKIN, P.A., V.G. Tel: 213-637-7255.

Chancellor—Sr. MARY ELIZABETH GALT, B.V.M. Tel: 213-637-7460.

Vice Chancellor—Rev. Msgr. JOSEPH F. HERNANDEZ. Tel: 213-637-7426.

Canonical Services, Vicar for—Rev. THOMAS C. ANSLOW, C.M., J.C.L. Tel: 213-637-7888.

Director of Special Services—JUDY DEROSA BROOKS. Tel: 213-637-7520.

General Counsel—MARGARET G. GRAF. Tel: 213-637-7511.

Chief Financial Officer—RANDOLPH E. STEINER. Tel: 213-637-7218.

Archdiocesan Pastoral Regions

Santa Barbara Region—Most Rev. THOMAS J. CURRY, D.D., Ph.D., V.G., 3240 Calle Pinon, Santa Barbara, 93105-2760. Tel: 805-682-0442; Fax: 805-682-7509.
- *Deanery 1*—Rev. CHARLES L. HOFSCHULTE, C.J., V.F.
- *Deanery 2*—Rev. RAFAEL MARIN-LEON, V.F.
- *Deanery 3*—Rev. Msgr. JON F. MAJARUCON, V.F.
- *Deanery 4*—Rev. Msgr. PAUL M. ALBEE, V.F.

San Fernando Region—Most Rev. GERALD E. WILKERSON, D.D., V.G., Mailing Address: P.O. Box 7608, Mission Hills, 91346-7608. 15101 San Fernando Mission Blvd., Mission Hills, 91345-1109. Tel: 818-361-6009; Fax: 818-361-6270.
- *Deanery 5*—Rev. ROBERT L. MILBAUER, V.F.
- *Deanery 6*—Rev. EDWARD R. DOVER, V.F.
- *Deanery 7*—Rev. Msgr. ROBERT J. GALLAGHER, V.F.
- *Deanery 8*—Rev. THOMAS E. BAKER, V.F.

San Gabriel Region—
- *Deanery 9*—Rev. Msgr. JOHN T. MORETTA, V.F.
- *Deanery 10*—Rev. Msgr. RICHARD G. KREKELBERG, V.F.
- *Deanery 11*—Rev. Msgr. NESTOR D. REBONG, V.F.
- *Deanery 12*—Rev. Msgr. JAMES J. LOUGHNANE, V.F., P.A.

Our Lady of the Angels Pastoral Region—Most Rev. EDWARD W. CLARK, D.D., S.T.D., V.G., 5835 Slauson Ave., Culver City, 90230-6505. Tel: 310-215-0703; Fax: 310-215-0749.
- *Deanery 13*—Rev. Msgr. NORMAN F. PRIEBE, V.F.
- *Deanery 14*—Rev. Msgr. TERRANCE L. FLEMING, S.T.D., V.F.
- *Deanery 15*—Rev. PAUL J. SPELLMAN, V.F.
- *Deanery 16*—Rev. Msgr. DAVID G. O'CONNELL, V.F.

San Pedro Pastoral Region—Most Rev. OSCAR A. SOLIS, D.D., V.G., 3555 St. Pancratius Pl., Lakewood, 90712-1416. Tel: 562-634-0456; Fax: 562-531-4783.
- *Deanery 17*—Rev. ANTONIO GARNICA, M.S.C., V.F.
- *Deanery 18*—Rev. PEDRO J. LOPEZ, V.F.
- *Deanery 19*—Rev. Msgr. JOHN F. BARRY, V.F., P.A.
- *Deanery 20*—Rev. Msgr. BERNARD M. LEHENY, V.F.

Archdiocesan Catholic Center

Unless otherwise listed, all ACC offices are located at: *3424 Wilshire Blvd., Los Angeles, 90010-2241.* Tel: 213-637-7000; Fax: 213-637-6000.

African-American Catholic Center for Evangelization—ANDERSON SHAW, 9505 Haas Ave., Los Angeles, 90047-3439. Tel: 323-777-2106; Fax: 323-777-2151. Email: aaccfe@shcglobal.net.

AIDS/HIV Ministry—Rev. CHRISTOPHER D. PONNET, Liaison, 1911 Zonal Ave., Los Angeles, 90033. Tel: 323-223-9047. Email: cponnet@stcamillus.ftml.net. Web: www.stcamilluscenter.org.

Alcohol and Substance Abuse—Rev. Msgr. TERRENCE RICHEY, Dir. (Retired). Tel: 213-637-7644.

Annual Catholic Appeal—Mr. JOSEPH HINDLEY, Dir. Tel: 213-637-7672; Fax: 213-637-6111.

Apostleship of the Sea—Rev. HENRY L. HERNANDO, Maritime Chap., 870 W. Eighth St., San Pedro, 90731-3091. Tel: 310-833-3541.

Applied Technology—DAVID SCHMITT, Dir. Tel: 213-637-7526; QUI TRAN, Network Admin. Tel: 213-637-7784; JAMES R. CELONI, Technology Evangelist. Tel: 213-637-7271.

Archives—KEVIN FEENEY, Archivist, 15151 San Fernando Mission Blvd., Mission Hills, 91345-2617. Tel: 818-365-1501; Fax: 818-361-3276.

Brothers Council, Religious—Bro. LARRY MOEN, C.M.F. Tel: 323-337-6776.
- *ACC Liaison to Brothers' Council*—Rev. Msgr. JOSEPH F. HERNANDEZ, Vice Chancellor. Tel: 213-637-7426.

Canonical Services, Vicar for—Rev. THOMAS C. ANSLOW, C.M., J.C.L. Tel: 213-637-7888; Fax: 213-637-6178.
- *Canonical Services Coordinator*—Rev. PATRICK J. HILL, J.C.L., D.Min. Tel: 213-637-7888.
- *Legal Secretary*—ELVIA MACDONALD. Tel: 213-637-7888.

Cardinal Manning House of Prayer for Priests—Rev. JOHN D. STOEGER, Dir., 3441 Waverly Dr., Los Angeles, 90027-2526. Tel: 323-662-7966; Fax: 323-953-4802.

Cardinal McIntyre Fund for Charity—Rev. Msgr. JOSEPH F. HERNANDEZ, Interim Dir. Tel: 213-637-7438; Fax: 213-637-6438.

Cathedral of Our Lady of the Angels Mausoleum—FRED BALAK, Dir. Tel: 213-680-5226.

Catholic Campaign for Human Development—JAIME HUERTA, Coord. Tel: 213-637-7560.

Catholic Charities of Los Angeles, Inc.—1531 James M. Wood Blvd., P.O. Box 15095, Los Angeles, 90015-0095. Tel: 213-251-3400; Fax: 213-380-4603.
- *Executive Director*—Rev. Msgr. GREGORY A. COX, M.S.W., M.B.A., M.Div. Tel: 213-251-3464.
- *Chief Administrative Officer*—RONALD G. LOPEZ, M.S.W. Tel: 213-251-3413.
- *Chief Financial Officer*—JAMES E. BATHKER, M.B.A. Tel: 213-251-3410.
- *Department of Resource Development*—ALEXANDRIA "SANDI" ARNOLD, M.S., Dir. Tel: 213-251-3495.
- *Department of Human Resources*—LELAND RATLEFF, Dir. Tel: 213-251-3414.
- *Adeste--Child Care Services*—ARMINE LALAIAN, Quality Assurance Mgr. Tel: 213-251-3468.
- *Central Intake Unit*—BRENDA THOMAS, Prog. Dir. Tel: 818-502-2002.
- *Immigration and Refugee Services*—LOC NAM NGUYEN, Prog. Dir. Tel: 213-251-3489.
- *CCLA Continuous Quality Improvement*—EDWARD NELSON, Ph.D., Performance Quality Improvement Dir.
- *CYO*— JAMES MCGOLDRICK, Prog. Dir., 1530 James M. Wood Blvd., Los Angeles, 90015. Tel: 213-251-3553.
- *Youth Employment Services*—ROBERT L. GUTIERREZ, Prog. Dir., 3250 Wilshire Blvd., Ste. 1010, Los Angeles, 90010. Tel: 213-736-5456.
- *Esperanza Immigrant Rights Project*—CAITLIN C. WILLIAMS, J.D., Project Dir. Tel: 213-251-3505.

Regional Offices and Community Centers—
- *Our Lady of the Angels Pastoral Region*—
  - *Metro Area*—HECTOR MANUEL BRIONES, J.D., Regl. Dir. Tel: 310-392-8701.
  - *Western Area*—HECTOR MANUEL BRIONES, J.D., Regl. Dir. Tel: 310-392-8701.
- *San Fernando Pastoral Region*—MOEED KHAN, M.S.W., Regl. Dir. Tel: 818-883-6015.
- *San Gabriel Pastoral Region*—MARY ROMERO, Regl. Dir. Tel: 323-266-3130.
- *San Pedro Pastoral Region*—ANNA R. TOTTA, M.S., Regl. Dir. Tel: 562-591-1641.
- *Santa Barbara Pastoral Region*—
  - *Santa Barbara County*—FRANK BOGNAR, D.P.A., Regl. Dir. Tel: 805-965-7045.
  - *Ventura County*—FRANK BOGNAR, D.P.A., Regl. Dir.; PATRICIA ESSEFF, Prog. Dir. Tel: 805-643-4784.

Catholic Education Foundation—KATHLEEN ANDERSON, Exec. Dir. Tel: 213-637-7576.

Catholic Relief Services—JAIME HUERTA, Coord. Tel: 213-637-7560.

Cemeteries, Catholic—Tel: 213-637-7801; Fax: 213-637-6800.
- *Pastoral Relations*—Deacon SAM FRIAS. Tel: 213-637-7807.
- *Director of Administrative Services*—BRIAN MCMAHON. Tel: 213-637-7815.

Clergy, Vicar for—Rev. Msgr. LORENZO MIRANDA, Vicar; Rev. FRANCIS HICKS, Assoc. Vicar. Tel: 213-637-7284.
- *Archdiocesan Personnel Board*—Chairman: Rev. Msgr. JAMES J. LOUGHNANE, V.F., P.A. Tel: 909-861-7106; Fax: 909-861-2697. Members: Rev. Msgrs. GREGORY A. COX, M.S.W., M.B.A., M.Div.; ROBERT J. GALLAGHER, V.F.; Rev. RAFAEL MARIN-LEON, V.F.; Sr. MARY ELIZABETH GALT, B.V.M.; Rev. FRANCIS MENDOZA; Rev. Msgr. TERRANCE L. FLEMING, S.T.D., V.F.; Rev. PEDRO J. LOPEZ, V.F.; Rev. Msgr. SABATO "SAL" A. PILATO; Most Rev. ALEXANDER SALAZAR, D.D., V.G.; Ms. KATHERINE ENRIGHT; Mr. LOUIS VELASQUEZ. Ex Officio: Rev. Msgr. LORENZO MIRANDA, Vicar for Clergy; Rev. FRANCIS J. HICKS, Assoc. Vicar for Clergy.
- *Continuing Formation for Clergy*—Rev. Msgr. JOSEPH F. HERNANDEZ, Dir. Tel: 213-637-7426.
- *Alcohol and Substance Abuse Ministry*—Rev. Msgr. TERRENCE RICHEY, Dir. (Retired). Tel: 213-637-7644.
- *Ministry to Retired and Ill Priests*—Sr. ANGELICA RAMOS, S.deM. Tel: 213-637-7238.
- *Orientation and Support Programs*—Mr. ANDREW RIVAS, Spec. Asst. Tel: 213-637-7240; Mr. LOUIS VELASQUEZ, Spec. Projects. Tel: 213-637-7575; Ms. LUCILLE MILLER, Exec. Asst. Tel: 213-637-7284; Ms. MARGARITA FRANCO, Admin. Asst. Tel: 213-637-7573; Mr. JESUS ARELLANO, Database/ Immigration. Tel: 213-637-7274.
- *Continuing Formation*—Rev. Msgr. JOSEPH F. HERNANDEZ, Dir. Tel: 213-637-7426; GERALDINE SPRAY, Administrative Asst. Tel: 213-637-7479.

Construction—JOHN CHEE, Dir. Tel: 213-637-7858; CECILIA URIBE, Asst. Dir. Tel: 213-637-7855.

Council of Catholic Women, Archdiocesan—Tel: 213-637-7394.

Cursillo Movement—Rev. MODESTO LEWIS PEREZ, J.C.D., Archdiocesan Spiritual Dir. Tel: 626-281-0466; Rev. Msgr. JUAN MATAS, Spanish Spiritual Advisor (Retired). Tel: 323-722-5861; Deacon PETER CHU, Chinese Spiritual Advisor. Tel: 909-598-4710; Revs. JOSE FERNANDO LAMBELHO, Portugese Spiritual Advisor. Tel: 213-637-7482; PETER T.C. NGO, J.C.L., Vietnamese Spiritual Advisor. Tel: 909-626-9513; Rev. Msgr. NESTOR D. REBONG, V.F., Filipino Spiritual Advisor. Tel: 626-960-1805; Revs. GAEL SULLIVAN, S.D.B., English Spiritual Advisor. Tel: 323-920-7796; BRIAN CHUNG, Korean Spiritual Advisor.

Deacons in Ministry—Deacon MANUEL MARTINEZ, f.s.p., Dir. Tel: 213-637-7734.

Diaconate, Formation Office—Deacons CRAIG SIEGMAN, Dir. Tel: 213-637-7282; VALENTIN SAUCEDO, Assoc. Dir. Tel: 213-637-7754. Coordinators: Dr. WILLIAM SHAULES. Tel: 213-637-7738; Mrs. JENNIFER OCEGUEDA-REYNOSA. Tel: 213-637-7747.

Ecumenical and Interreligious Affairs—Rt. Rev. ALEXEI R. SMITH, Dir., c/o St. Andrew's Church,

538 Concord St., El Segundo, 90245. Tel: 310-322-1892; Fax: 310-322-1919.

Ethnic Ministry—Most Rev. ALEXANDER SALAZAR, D.D., V.G., Vicar; MARIA GUADALUPE GARRIDO, Exec. Sec. Tel: 213-637-7356.

Family Life Office—JOAN T. VIENNA, Dir. Tel: 213-637-7227; Fax: 213-637-6681. Email: familylife@la-archdiocese.org.

Coordinators, Marriage Preparation and Natural Family Planning—CANDY METOYER. Tel: 213-637-7250 (English); GRACIELA VILLALOBOS. Tel: 213-637-7561 (Spanish).

Filipino Ministry—Rev. ALBERT H. AVENIDO, Spiritual Mod., 320 W. Garvey Ave., Monterey Park, 91754. Tel: 213-587-2226; Fax: 626-288-0620. Email: fr.albert@yahoo.com.

Financial Services—Information Desk. Tel: 213-637-7500. SANDRA SMITH, CPA, M.B.A., Controller. Tel: 213-637-7622; ELISITA LANDRY, Accounts Receivable & Payable. Tel: 213-637-7291; EDNA CRISTOBAL, CPA, M.B.A., Investments. Tel: 213-637-7292; ROSA R. PADILLA, Payroll. Tel: 213-637-7544; DOREEN RODRIGUEZ, Exec. Asst. Tel: 213-637-7267.

Government Funded Programs—LILIA CHAVEZ, Dir. Tel: 213-637-7915; Fax: 213-637-6900.

Youth Employment Programs—ROBERT L. GUTIERREZ, Prog. Dir., 3250 Wilshire Blvd., #1010, Los Angeles, 90010. Tel: 213-736-5456.

Health Affairs—Sr. ANGELA HALLAHAN, C.H.F., Dir. Tel: 213-637-7531.

Holy Childhood Association— (See Mission Office)

Holy Name Union—JESUS MENDEZ, Pres., Mailing Address: Archdiocesan Union of Holy Name Societies, 430 S. Fresno St., Los Angeles, 90063-3160. Tel: 323-265-1740.

Moderator—Rev. Msgr. PAUL M. MONTOYA. Tel: 323-465-7605.

Human Resources—WILLIAM HEINEN, Dir. Tel: 213-637-7596; Fax: 213-637-6116; MARGARET M. ANTCZAK, Archdiocesan Catholic Center Human Resources Mgr. Tel: 213-637-7625; MARGIE RODRIGUEZ, H.R. Specialist. Tel: 213-637-7371.

Human Resources Representative—TERESA BARRY. Tel: 213-637-7242.

Information—MARIA VARGAS, Archdiocesan Catholic Center Switchboard. Tel: 213-637-7000.

Instructional Television—DAVID G. MOORE, Dir. Tel: 213-637-7312; FERNANDO DIAZ, Studio Technician. Tel: 213-637-7399.

Insurance—LEVONTINE TOMACAN, Dir. Tel: 213-637-7279; GUADALUPE A. GARIBAY, Priests' Pension. Tel: 213-637-7320; BERTHA MIER, Benefits Admin. Tel: 213-637-7671.

Office of Justice and Peace—Most Rev. ALEXANDER SALAZAR, D.D., V.G., Dir. Tel: 213-637-7356; Sr. GAIL YOUNG, S.S.S., Prog. Coord. Tel: 213-637-7690; JAIME HUERTA, Prog. Consultant. Tel: 213-637-7560.

Knights of Columbus—California State Council Office, 15808 Arrow Blvd., Ste. A, Fontana, 92335. Tel: 909-434-0460; Fax: 909-434-0465.

State Deputy—ROBERT J. VILLALABOS. Email: state.deputy@kofc-california.org.

State Chaplain—Rev. CHUCK FULD. Tel: 858-490-8279. Email: frchuckfuld@aol.com.

Ladies of Charity of St. Vincent de Paul—2131 W. Third St., Seton Hall, Los Angeles, 90057-0992. Tel: 213-413-3688.

Marriage Encounter—Contacts: BOON HAZBOUN; GINNY HAZBOUN, 12506 Dolan Ave., Downey, 90242. Tel: 562-861-7562. Web: www.geocities.com/melawest. Marriage Encounter Weekends are offered in English, Spanish and Korean in the Archdiocese of Los Angeles.

Marriage Tribunal—(See Tribunal)

Media Relations—Mr. TOD TAMBERG, Dir. Tel: 213-637-7215; Fax: 213-637-6215; CAROLINA GUEVARA, Assoc. Dir. Tel: 213-637-7253; MARIA RODRIGUEZ, Sec. Tel: 213-637-7215.

Mission Office—Rev. Msgr. TERRANCE L. FLEMING, S.T.D., V.F., Dir.; LYDIA GAMBOA, Assoc. Dir. Tel: 213-637-7223; Fax: 213-637-6223. Email: missionoffice@la-archdiocese.org.

Holy Childhood Association—Rev. KEN DEASEY. Tel: 213-637-7229.

Mission Circles—Tel: 213-637-7223.

Propagation of the Faith—Rev. Msgr. TERRANCE L. FLEMING, S.T.D., V.F. Tel: 213-637-7223.

Operations—Director of Archdiocesan Catholic Center Facilities and Operations: EILEEN O'BRIEN. Tel: 213-637-7618.

Parish Life Office—Ms. KATHERINE ENRIGHT, Dir. Tel: 213-637-7533.

Priest Pension Plan—GUADALUPE A. GARIBAY. Tel: 213-637-7320.

Project Rachel—CONNIE MARTIN, 1028 N. Lake, Ste. 207, Pasadena, 91104. Tel: 626-398-6100.

Purchasing/Mail Center—JOHN MARMOLEJO, Purchasing Agent/Office Svcs. Supvr. Tel: 213-637-7281.

Real Estate—MICHAEL T. DAVITT, Dir. Tel: 213-637-7273; Fax: 213-637-6273.

Escrows—MARIE A. URBACH. Tel: 213-637-7505.

Leases—ADRIANA LOPEZ. Tel: 213-637-7270.

Property Taxes—ALICIA PINKLEY. Tel: 213-637-7516.

Religious Education—Sr. EDITH PRENDERGAST, R.S.C., Dir. Tel: 213-637-7309; Fax: 213-637-6574. Web: ore.la-archdiocese.org.

Adult Education—DOUGLAS LEAL. Tel: 213-637-7498.

Adult Education, Spanish—MARTHA NUNEZ. Tel: 213-637-7705; ERNESTO VEGA. Tel: 213-637-7345.

Advanced Cathechetical Ministries and Formation—English—DIONE GRILLO. Tel: 213-637-7654.

Spanish—LOURDES GONZALES-RUBIO. Tel: 213-637-7344.

Confirmation, Junior High and Youth Ministry—J. MICHAEL NORMAN, Assoc. Dir. Tel: 213-637-7674; HEATHER MACDONALD, Santa Barbara Region. Tel: 805-682-5500; KATHRYN ZEIGLER. Tel: 213-637-7616.

Early Childhood—JAN PEDROZA. Tel: 213-637-7352.

Elementary—DIONE GRILLO, (English). Tel: 213-637-7410; MARTHA NUNEZ, (Spanish). Tel: 213-637-7705.

Ministry to the Spanish Speaking—ERNESTO VEGA. Tel: 213-637-7345.

Religious Education Congress—Coordinators: PAULETTE SMITH. Tel: 213-637-7332; JAN PEDROZA. Tel: 213-637-7352. Web: recongress.org.

Ministry with Young Adults—DOUGLAS LEAL. Tel: 213-637-7498; ALBERTO EMBRY, (Spanish). Tel: 213-637-7355.

ORE Regional Offices—Our Lady of the Angels Region: Mr. DAVID LARA, 5835 W. Slauson Ave., Culver City, 90230. Tel: 310-216-9587. San Fernando Region: MARGARET SARDO, San Fernando Pastoral Region, 15101 San Fernando Mission Blvd., Mission Hills, 91345. Tel: 818-365-5123; Fax: 818-361-4133. Mailing Address: P.O. Box 7608, Mission Hills, 91346. San Gabriel Region: CHRISTINA LUJAN, San Gabriel Pastoral Region, 16009 E. Cypress Ave., Irwindale, 91706. Tel: 626-962-7707; Fax: 626-962-0455. San Pedro Region: KARINA PLASCENCIA, San Pedro Pastoral Region, 3555 St. Pancratius Pl., Lakewood, 90712. Tel: 562-630-6272; Fax: 562-531-4783. Santa Barbara Region: SUE SPIES, Santa Barbara Pastoral Region, Bishop Garcia Diego Center, 4032 La Colina Rd., Santa Barbara, 93110. Tel: 805-569-1135; Fax: 805-569-2746.

Respect Life Office—Rev. Msgr. TIMOTHY P. O'CONNELL, Coord. (Retired), 2100 S. Western Ave., Apt. 9, San Pedro, 90732-4331. Tel: 310-547-1930. Email: respectlife1@aol.com.

Restorative Justice—Rev. GEORGE E. HORAN, Dir. Adult Facilities. Tel: 213-438-4820, Ext. 14; JAVIER E. STAURING, Dir. Juvenile Facilities. Tel: 213-438-4820, Ext. 13.

Safeguard the Children—JOAN T. VIENNA, Dir. Tel: 213-637-7227.

Schools, Department of Catholic—Tel: 213-637-7300; Fax: 213-637-6140.

Superintendent Elementary Schools—Dr. KEVIN BAXTER. Tel: 213-637-7328.

Elementary School Supervisors—Tel: 213-637-7328. CARLA COTTON; KATHERINE BARRANTES; LELANA MORAN; Sisters DOLORES MADDEN, C.H.F.; JILL NAPIER, C.S.J.; CARMEN VADILLO.

WASC Certification for Elementary Schools—PATRICIA LIVINGSTON. Tel: 213-637-7328.

Director of Personnel (K-8)—LOU ANNE INSPRUCKER. Tel: 213-637-7436.

Finance Consultant: Elementary—Sr. JILL NAPIER, C.S.J. Tel: 213-637-7328.

Superintendent Secondary Schools—Rev. Msgr. SABATO "SAL" A. PILATO. Tel: 213-637-7265.

Secondary Supervisor/WCEA/WASC—JAMES MCCLUNE, Secondary Regl. Supvr.; Dr. BETH POLITO. Tel: 213-637-7701.

Finance Consultant: Secondary—LOURDES "LUDY" SANTA MARIA. Tel: 213-637-7701.

High School Religion Certification Director—Sr. ANGELA HALLAHAN, C.H.F. Tel: 213-637-7701.

Federal and State Programs—Sr. PATRICIA SUPPLE, C.S.J., Dir. Tel: 213-637-7436; PATRICIA S. ACEVEDO, Assoc. Coord. Preschool Programs. Tel: 213-637-7902.

Scouting, Camp Fire Ministry—Web: www.ccsala.org. ROBERT B. TARN, Chm., Los Angeles Catholic Committee on Scouting, 29475 Fountainwood St., Agoura, 91301. Tel: 818-314-8340; Deacon STEVEN R. MARSH, Chap. Tel: 626-334-1688; SHARON SHELLMAN, Chm. Girls & Camp Fire Groups. Tel: 626-825-6436.

Society of St. Vincent de Paul—JAMES R. WEISS, Pres., 210 N. Ave. 21, Los Angeles, 90031-1713. Tel: 323-224-6287; 800-974-3571; JOSE J. ROSSIER, Exec. Dir. Tel: 800-974-3571.

Synod Implementation/Stewardship—Tel: 213-637-7542. Deacon DAVID ESTRADA, Exec. Dir. Tel: 213-637-7474.

"The Tidings" (Archdiocesan Newspaper)—Tel: 213-637-7360; Fax: 213-637-6360.

Executive Publisher—DAVID G. MOORE. Tel: 213-637-7312.

Editor—MICHAEL NELSON, Editor. Tel: 213-637-7543; JOSE VELASQUEZ, Production Mgr. Tel: 213-637-7380; HERMINE LEES, Directory. Tel: 213-637-7392; CHRISTOPHER KRAUSE, Directory. Tel: 213-637-7378; CORA LEUTERIO, Business Mgr. Tel: 213-637-7391.

Tribunal—Main Office, 3424 Wilshire Blvd., Los Angeles, 90010-2241. Tel: 213-637-7245; Fax: 213-637-6245. *Santa Barbara/Ventura Branch, P.O. Box 2215, Oxnard, 93034*. Tel: 805-486-6553; Fax: 805-486-3884.

Judicial Vicar—Rev. Msgr. CHARLES J. CHAFFMAN, J.C.D. Tel: 213-637-7209.

Adjutant Judicial Vicar—Rev. REYNALDO B. MATUNOG, J.C.L. Tel: 213-637-7220.

Judges—Rev. Msgr. CHARLES J. CHAFFMAN, J.C.D.; Rev. REYNALDO B. MATUNOG, J.C.L.

Defenders of the Bond—Revs. TRUC Q. NGUYEN; REYNALDO B. MATUNOG, J.C.L.

Advocate—LOUIS A. SHAPIRO.

Notaries and Other Officials—MYRIAM WAGNER; Sr. ROSA GONZALEZ, F.M.I.; HELEN GULLIVER; Sr. M. DOMNIC JONES, S.N.D.; BOBBIE LOPEZ; SARAH FIERRO; OLIVIA ALVAREZ; CECILIA GARCIA; MARIA ROCIO ZAMBRANO.

Trusts and Estates Programs—H. RICHARD CLOSSON, Dir. Tel: 213-637-7472.

Victims Assistance Ministry—SUZANNE HEALY. Tel: 800-355-2545 (Hotline); 213-637-7650 (Office). Email: sdhealy@la-archdiocese.org.

"Vida Nueva" (Archdiocesan Spanish Newspaper)—Tel: 213-637-7360; Fax: 213-637-6360. DAVID G. MOORE, Exec. Publisher. Tel: 213-637-7599; VICTOR ALEMAN, Editor. Tel: 213-637-7310; JOSE VELASQUEZ, Production Dir. Tel: 213-637-7380.

Vocations—Tel: 213-637-7248. Web: www.vocations.la-archdiocese.org. Rev. Msgr. JAMES FORSEN, Dir. Email: frjrforsen@la-archdiocese.org; Rev. JAMES M. ANGUIANO, Dir. House of Formation. Tel: 310-516-6671.

Women Religious, Vicar for—Sr. CECILIA CANALES, O.P. Tel: 213-637-7592; Fax: 213-637-6592.

Association of Women Religious—3424 Wilshire Blvd., Los Angeles, 90010-2241. Tel: 213-637-7592.

Coordinating Council—Sisters CECILIA CANALES, O.P.; M. ANNCARLA COSTELLO, S.N.D.; CAROLYN MCCORMACK, O.P.; CARMEN MALDONADO, S.S.C.; MARY ELIZA MARTIN, C.S.C.; JEAN MORNINGSTAR, S.N.J.M.; MARGARET SPILLER, S.N.J.M.; MARY JOSEPH SUTER, D.C.; DARLENE YOUNG, S.C.R.H.

Worship—Sr. ROSANNE BELPEDIO, C.S.J., Dir. Tel: 213-637-7262. Email: worship@la-archdiocese.org.

Hispanic Liturgy and Ministry Coordinator—Rev. MANUEL SANAHUJA, Sch.P. Tel: 213-637-7588.

Archdiocesan Advisory Boards

Unless otherwise indicated, mailing address for all offices is: *3424 Wilshire Blvd., Los Angeles, 90010-2241*.

HIV/AIDS Council and Executive Committee—Co Chair: FRANK GALVAN; MANUEL TORREZ; NICK ROCCA; DAVID KENNEDY; Rev. CHRISTOPHER D. PONNET, Dir. HIV/AIDS Ministry. Ex Officio: ELIZABETH BREEN, Ph.D.; Most Rev. JOSE H. GOMEZ.

Cardinal McIntyre Fund for Charity Board of Directors—Most Rev. JOSE H. GOMEZ, Chm.; Rev. Msgr. ROYALE M. VADAKIN, P.A., V.G., Pres.; Sr. MARY ELIZABETH GALT, B.V.M., Sec.; Rev. JOSEPH P. SHEA, V.F., Treas.; Rev. Msgrs. JOSEPH F. HERNANDEZ, Exec. Dir.; ANTONIO CACCIAPUOTI; GREGORY A. COX, M.S.W., M.B.A., M.Div.; Rev. PAUL K. FITZPATRICK; Rev. Msgr. BERNARD M. LEHENY, V.F.; Revs. JOSEPH QUAN NGUYEN; GUSTAVO J. RAMON.

Clergy Misconduct Oversight Board—FERNANDO L. AENLLE-ROCHA, Chm.; Rev. JAMES M. ANGUIANO; RICHARD P. BYRNE; ADRIENNE CEDRO-HAMENT; ANNE DAVIDSON; JACK HOURIGAN; JAMES J. MCGOUGH, M.D.; KATHERINE MORET; Dr. INES MONGUIO; Sr. GENEVIEVE VIGIL, S.J.C.; JERRY YSLAS; ROSE ANN RASIC, Admin.

Commission for Catholic Life Issues—Chairman and Coordinator of Activities: Rev. Msgr. TIMOTHY P. O'CONNELL (Retired), 2100 S. Western Ave., Apt. 9, San Pedro, 90732-4331. Tel: 310-547-1930. Commission Members: WILLIAM ANDERSON, Esq.; ASTRID BENNETT-GUTIERREZ; DENNIS DI PIETRO; RACHEL DI PIETRO; DAN MANSUETO; BETTY ODELLO, R.N., M.S.N.; Rev. Msgr. SABATO "SAL" A. PILATO; JENNIFER SHAW; ROSALINDA TANDOC. Advisory Members to the Commission: ANDREA BURMAN, M.A.; MARIAN BURMAN, M.A.; VINCENT

FORTANASCE, M.D.; Rev. MARCOS GONZALEZ; LICIA NICASSIO; KATHERINE DOWLING SCHLAERTH, M.D.; MARY V. SHERIDAN; Sr. PAULA VANDEGAER, S.S.S., L.C.S.W.; GERMAINE WENSLEY, R.N.

College of Consultors—President: Most Rev. JOSE H. GOMEZ. Members: Most Revs. EDWARD W. CLARK, D.D., S.T.D., V.G., (Our Lady of the Angels Pastoral Region).; THOMAS J. CURRY, D.D., Ph.D., V.G., (Santa Barbara Pastoral Region).; ALEXANDER SALAZAR, D.D., V.G., (Ethnic Ministry).; OSCAR A. SOLIS, D.D., V.G., (San Pedro Pastoral Region).; GERALD E. WILKERSON, D.D., V.G., (San Fernando Pastoral Region).; Rev. Msgrs. TIMOTHY J. DYER, V.F., (Our Lady of the Angels Pastoral Region).; RICHARD MARTINI, (Chair, Council of Priests).; ROYALE M. VADAKIN, P.A., V.G., (Vicar General/Moderator of the Curia).

Council of Deacons—Our Lady of the Angels: VICKIE RACE, Regl. Representative. Email: vrace06@yahoo.com; Deacons MARK RACE, Regl. Representative. Tel: 310-844-1970. Email: deaconmark07@yahoo.com; GREGORY PATTERSON, Alternate Representative. Tel: 323-857-1051. Santa Barbara: KIM TORTI, Regl. Representative; Deacon JOSEPH FELIX TORTI, Regl. Representative & Sec. Tel: 805-445-9555; 805-216-1866. Email: joe@jtorti.net; CELIA GONZALEZ, Alternate Representative. Email: celigon1@aol.com; Deacon ART GONZALEZ, Alternate Representative. Tel: 805-450-4973. San Fernando: LALLY GUIAO, Regl. Representative; Deacon REY GUIAO, Regl. Representative & Chair. Tel: 818-421-1890. Email: dcnguiao@olpeace.org; ELOISA PASOS, Alternate Representative; Deacon JESUS S. PASOS, Alternate Representative. Tel: 818-510-1239. Email: epasos@sbcglobal.net. San Gabriel: RITA AUSTIN, Regl. Representative. Email: rital@uia.net; Deacon AL AUSTIN, Regl. Representative. Tel: 909-593-9403. Email: aaustin@californiasteel.com; ROSE SALCIDO, Alternate Representative; Deacon MICHAEL SALCIDO, Alternate Representative. Tel: 626-358-2151. Email: msalcido2@juno.com. San Pedro: PAT ROBERTO, Regl. Representative; Deacons TIMOTHY J. ROBERTO, Regl. Representative. Tel: 562-944-7741. Email: deacontim2000@verizon.net; CIRO AUGUSTO GARZA, Alternate Representative. Tel: 323-646-8546. Email: cirogarza@sbcglobal.com.

Spirituality—MARGE PATTERSON; Deacon GARY PATTERSON. Tel: 626-331-8846. Email: deaconngp@gmail.com.

Education—PON SEIDLER; Deacon ROBERT SEIDLER. Tel: 818-517-1656. Email: bobandpon@sbcglobal.net. Synod Executive Director: RITA ESTRADA; Deacon DAVID ESTRADA. Tel: 562-942-1300. Email: dndjestrada@la-archdiocese.org. Vicar for Clergy: Rev. Msgr. LORENZO MIRANDA. Tel: 213-637-7284. Email: frlmiranda@la-archdiocese.org. Assistant Vicar Clergy: Rev. FRANCIS HICKS. Tel: 213-637-7284. Email: bikerprt@yahoo.com. Hispanic Deacon Representatives: ELEANA BENALCAZAR. Email: ebenalcazar@sbcglobal.net; Deacon EUDORO G. BENALCAZAR. Tel: 626-808-2815. Email: ebenalcazar@hdrinc.com; ELBA VILLACORTA; Deacon RICARDO VILLACORTA. Tel: 323-559-3645. Email: nery1990@hotmail.com. Deacon Director: Deacon MANUEL MARTINEZ, f.s.p. Tel: 213-637-7734; 310-592-0740. Email: dnmmartinez@la-archdiocese.org.

Council of Priests—President: Most Rev. JOSE H. GOMEZ. Chairman: Rev. Msgr. RICHARD MARTINI, 3424 Wilshire Blvd., Los Angeles, 90010-2241. Tel: 213-637-7479. Vice Chairman: Rev. ANTONIO GARNICA, M.S.C., V.F. Secretary/Treasurer: Rev. SAMUEL W. WARD.

Elected Members—Santa Barbara Region: Rev. Msgr. JON F. MAJARUCON, V.F.; Rev. STEPHEN V. DAVOREN; Rev. Msgr. MICHAEL J. JENNETT, S.T.D. San Fernando Region: Rev. THOMAS E. BAKER, V.F.; Rev. Msgrs. RICHARD MARTINI; ANTONIO CACCIAPUOTI. San Gabriel Region: Rev. Msgr. JOHN T. MORETTA, V.F.; Revs. ALEX ACLAN; GUSTAVO CASTILLO. San Pedro Region: Revs. ANTONIO GARNICA, M.S.C., V.F.; JAMES L. HALLEY; SAMUEL W. WARD. Our Lady of the Angels Region: Rev. Msgr. TIMOTHY J. DYER, V.F.; Rev. BRIAN CASTANEDA; Rev. Msgr. TERRANCE L. FLEMING, S.T.D., V.F. Ex Officio Members: Most Revs. JOSE H. GOMEZ, D.D., S.T.D., V.G.; EDWARD W. CLARK, D.D., S.T.D., V.G.; THOMAS J. CURRY, D.D., Ph.D., V.G.; ALEXANDER SALAZAR, D.D., V.G.; OSCAR A. SOLIS, D.D., V.G.; Rev. Msgr. ROYALE M. VADAKIN, P.A., V.G.; Most Rev. GERALD E. WILKERSON, D.D., V.G.

Archdiocesan Finance Council Members 2011-2012—Mr. PAUL WATSON, (Chair), Retired Vice Chm./Wells Fargo Bank; Mr. MICHAEL ENRIGHT, (Vice Chair), Exec. Vice Pres./Chartwell Partners, LLC; Mr. RICHARD CORGEL, Exec. Dir./Ernst & Young, LLP; Mr. WILLIAM WARDLAW, Esq., Attorney/Freeman, Spogli & Company; Mr. DAVID S. DEVITO, CFO & Mng. Dir./Trust Company of the West (TCW); Mr. ALLEN LUND, Pres. & CEO/Allen Lund Company; Ms. SUSAN M. WEGLEITNER, Mng. Dir./JP Morgan Chase; Mr. THOMAS CONDON, Chm./Condon Family Foundation; Ms. DIANA NISHIURA, Sr. Counsel/California Dept. of Fin. Institutes; Mr. ROBERT BERRY, Retired Exec. Vice Pres./Lockheed Credit Union; Mr. SALVADOR VILLAR, Chm. & CEO/Banamex USA; Most Rev. ALEXANDER SALAZAR, D.D., V.G., Auxiliary Bishop & Vicar for Ethnic Ministry/Archdiocese of Los Angeles; Rev. Msgrs. PAUL M. ALBEE, V.F., Pastor/Holy Cross, Moorpark; JOHN F. BARRY, V.F., P.A., Pastor/American Martyrs, Manhattan Beach; ROBERT J. GALLAGHER, V.F., Pastor/St. Charles Borromeo, North Hollywood; NESTOR D. REBONG, V.F., Pastor/St. Christopher, West Covina; DAVID G. O'CONNELL, V.F., Pastor, St. Michael, Los Angeles. Ex Officio Members: Most Rev. JOSE H. GOMEZ, Archbishop of Los Angeles; Rev. Msgr. ROYALE M. VADAKIN, P.A., V.G., Mod. of the Curia & Vicar Gen. Archdiocese of Los Angeles; Mr. RANDOLPH STEINER, CFO, Archdiocese of Los Angeles.

Office of Justice and Peace—Most Rev. ALEXANDER SALAZAR, D.D., V.G., Dir. Tel: 213-637-7356; Sr. GAIL YOUNG, S.S.S., Prog. Coord. Tel: 213-637-7690; JAIME HUERTA, Assoc. Dir. Tel: 213-637-7560.

Justice and Peace Commission Members 2011-2012—ANTHONY FADALE, Chair; ALLIS DRUFFEL; ANDERSON SHAW; BERNADETTE ROBERT; Bro. ANDRES RIVERA, S.T.; CHRISTOPHER GABRIELE; Deacons GUY WAUTHY; JAIME ABRERA; FRANCES JONTE; Rev. FRANCISCO VALDOVINOS, S.T.; JOSEPH DOMOND; LUCY BOUTTE; RICHARD SCHOLTZ; RAMON J. POSADA; ROCKY T. DOMINGO; Sr. PATRICIA KROMMER, C.S.J. Ex Officio Members: Most Rev. ALEXANDER SALAZAR, D.D., V.G., Dir.; JAIME HUERTA, Assoc. Dir.; Sr. GAIL YOUNG, S.S.S., Prog. Coord.

Spirituality Commission—Rev. JAMES CLARKE, Ph.D.; Rt. Rev. ALEXEI R. SMITH; Sisters THOMAS BERNARD MACCONNELL, C.S.J.; LAURA GORMLEY, S.S.L.; JUDY ALVAREZ.

Theological Commission—Co Chairmen: Revs. THOMAS P. RAUSCH, S.J., Ph.D.; MARIUSZ BECZEK, O.S.J., M.A., S.T.D.; Most Rev. EDWARD W. CLARK, D.D., S.T.D., V.G.; Rev. Msgr. CRAIG A. COX, J.C.D., D.Min.; Revs. LUKE DYSINGER, O.S.B., M.D., D.Phil.; GUILLERMO C. GARCIA, Ph.D.; Dr. ELIZABETH DIVELY LAURO, Ph.D.; Sr. MARY MCKAY, C.S.J., Ph.D.; Dr. DANIEL SMITH-CHRISTOPHER, Ph.D., Consultant.

Liturgical Commission—Ex Officio: Most Rev. ALEXANDER SALAZAR, D.D., V.G.; Rev. MANUEL SANAHUJA, Sch.P.; Sr. ROSANNE BELPEDIO, C.S.J.

Appointed Membership—Mr. DAN WHITE; Ms. MARY LOU VANDERLIP; Mr. DALE SIEVERDING; Rev. BRIAN NUNES; Ms. KIM NGUYEN; Ms. JANIS NELSON; Ms. FE MUSGRAVE; Revs. KEVIN MCCRACKEN, C.M.; PEDRO J. LOPEZ, V.F.; Mr. DAVID LARA; Ms. LILIANA HSUEH-GUTIERREZ; Ms. ROSE M. HERNANDEZ; Rev. JOEL HENSON; Rev. Msgr. HELMUT A. HEFNER, J.C.L.; Dr. PAUL F. FORD, Ph.D.; Ms. GABRIELA ESPARZA-REITZELL; Mr. JAMES DROLLINGER; Ms. SYLVIA DEVILLERS; Rev. CHRISTOPHER BAZYOUROS; Deacon ARTURO BARRAGAN; Ms. DONNA BARNES; Mr. VINCENT ADAMS.

CLERGY, PARISHES, MISSIONS AND PAROCHIAL SCHOOLS

CITY OF LOS ANGELES

(LOS ANGELES COUNTY)

1—CATHEDRAL OF OUR LADY OF THE ANGELS (2002) Rev. Msgr. Kevin J. Kostelnik; Most Rev. Jose H. Gomez; Revs. Brian Castaneda; Angel Castro; Deacon Manny Martinez.
Church: 555 W. Temple St., 90012. Tel: 213-680-5200; Fax: 213-620-1982. Email: ebonaduce@olacathedral.org. Web: www.olacathedral.org.
Catechesis/Religious Program—Michelle-Marie Youssef, D.R.E. Students 16.

2—ST. AGATHA (1923) Sr. M. Karen Collier, S.S.L., Parish Life Dir. In Res., Revs. William Axe, O.SS.T.; Frank Whatley, O.SS.T.
Res.: 2610 S. Mansfield Ave., 90016. Tel: 323-935-8127; Fax: 323-939-3547. Email: st.agatha@stagathas.org. Web: www.stagathas.org.
Catechesis/Religious Program—Tel: 323-933-0963. Email: religiousedstagathas.org. Students 317.

3—ST. AGNES (1903), (Hispanic—Korean), Revs. John J. Franck, C.PP.S.; William J. Delaney, C.PP.S., Senior Priest; Joseph J. Grilliot, C.PP.S, Parochial Vicar. In Res., Rev. DaeJe Choi, S.J., Chap., Korean Catholic Community.
Res.: 2625 S. Vermont Ave., 90007. Tel: 323-731-2464; Fax: 323-731-6186.
School—1428 W. Adams Blvd., 90007. Tel: 323-731-2464, Ext. 140; Fax: 323-735-7719. Lay Teachers 9; Students 240.
Catechesis/Religious Program—Mrs. Miriam Oliva, D.R.E. Students 396.

4—ALL SAINTS (1926), (Hispanic), Revs. Jose L. Vega, O.M.; Gino Vanzillotta, O.M.; Mario Pisano, O.M.; Deacon Pedro Rojas.
Rectory—3431 Portola Ave., 90032-2215. Tel: 323-223-1101; Fax: 323-223-9592.
School—(Grades K-8), 3420 Portola Ave., 90032. Tel: 323-225-7264; Fax: 323-225-1240. Lay Teachers 9; Students 117.
Catechesis/Religious Program—Tel: 323-225-5193; Fax: 323-225-5193. Students 222.

5—ST. ALOYSIUS GONZAGA (1908), (Hispanic), [CEM] Rev. Pedro Antonio Esteban.
Res.: 7814 Crocket Blvd., 90001. Tel: 323-585-4485; Fax: 323-589-8485.
School—2023 E. Nadeau St., 90001. Tel: 323-582-4965; Fax: 323-585-4938. Mrs. Nicole Johnson, Prin. Lay Teachers 9; Students 197.
Catechesis/Religious Program—2023 E. Nadeau St. Tel: 323-277-7824. Students 427.

6—ST. ALPHONSUS (1935), (Hispanic), Revs. Enrique De Los Rios; Chongkuk Carlos Kim; J. Jesus Garcia (Mexico). In Res., Rev. Frank Tinajero, S.V.D.
Res.: 5223 Hastings St., 90022-2625. Tel: 323-264-3353; Fax: 323-264-4858.
School—552 S. Amalia Ave., 90022-2625. Tel: 323-268-5165; Fax: 323-268-7784. Email: khughes@stalphonsusschool.org. Lay Teachers 6; Students 169.
Catechesis/Religious Program—552 South Amalia Ave., 90022. Tel: 323-266-0855. Students 350.

7—ST. ANASTASIA (1953) Rev. Msgr. Gabriel Gonzales; Rev. Thomas F. King, Pastor Emeritus (Retired); Rev. Msgr. Royale M. Vadakin, Pastor Emeritus. In Res., Rev. Msgr. Gregory A. Cox.
Res.: 7390 W. Manchester Ave., 90045. Tel: 310-670-2243; Fax: 310-670-5052. Email: parish@st-anastasia.org. Web: www.st-anastasia.org.
School—8631 S. Stanmoor Dr., 90045. Tel: 310-645-8816; Fax: 310-645-6923. Mrs. Rosemary Connolly, Prin. Lay Teachers 13; Students 292.
Catechesis/Religious Program—Students 195.

8—ST. ANN (1937) Revs. Marco Antonio Ortiz; Hugh Crowe, Pastor Emeritus (Retired).
Office: 1365 Blake Ave., 90031.
Res.: 2310 Riverdale Ave., 90031. Fax: 323-222-6871.
Catechesis/Religious Program—Tel: 323-222-9749. Sr. Margarita Montoya, E.E.P., D.R.E. Students 90.

9—ST. ANSELM (1924) Rev. Lawrence Shelton.
Res.: 2222 W. 70th St., 90043. Tel: 323-758-6729; Fax: 323-758-8455. Email: tcanselm@aol.com.
Catechesis/Religious Program—Students 101.

10—ST. ANTHONY (1910), (Croatian), [CEM] Rev. Mate Bizaca, Admin.
Res.: 712 N. Grand Ave., 90012. Tel: 213-628-2938; Fax: 213-628-1635. Email: croatsvantela@sbcglobal.net. Web: croatianchurch.org/la.

11—ASCENSION (1923), (Hispanic—African American), Rev. Humberto Bernabe.
Res.: 517 W. 112th St., 90044. Tel: 323-754-2978; Fax: 323-754-3905. Email: ascens@pacbell.net.
School—500 W. 111th Pl., 90044. Tel: 323-756-4064; Fax: 323-756-1060. Dr. Karen Kallay, Prin. Lay Teachers 10; Students 260.
Catechesis/Religious Program—Tel: 323-777-6356. Students 450.

12—ASSUMPTION (1926), (Hispanic), Rev. Gustavo J. Ramon. In Res., Rev. Paul L. O'Donnell.
Res.: 2832 Blanchard St., 90033. Tel: 323-269-8171; Fax: 323-269-0106. Email: assumptionchurch@sbcglobal.net.
School—(Grades K-8), 3016 Winter St., 90063. Tel: 323-269-4319; Fax: 323-269-2434. Carolina Gomez, Prin. Lay Teachers 8; Students 182.
Catechesis/Religious Program—Tel: 213-269-5920; Fax: 323-269-7786. Students 122.
Mission—Assumption 414 N. Fresno St., Old Co. 90063.

13—ST. BASIL'S (1920) Revs. Francis J. Hicks; Ki-Jun Lawrence Pak. In Res., Rev. Msgr. Terrence Richey (Retired); Revs. Cornelius Noel Phelan (Retired); Dennis P. Marrell.
Res.: 637 S. Kingsley Dr., 90005. Tel: 213-381-6191; Fax: 213-382-5883.
Catechesis/Religious Program—Students 130.

14—ST. BERNADETTE (1947), (African American), Rev. Allan Roberts; Deacons Emile Adams; Mark Race.
Res.: 3825 Don Felipe Dr., 90008. Tel: 323-293-4877; Fax: 323-293-2838. Email: stbernadette@earthlink.net.*School*—4196 Marlton

Ave., 90008. Tel: 323-291-4284; Fax: 323-291-0839. Mrs. Barbara M. Davis, Prin. Lay Teachers 10; Students 215.
Catechesis/Religious Program—Students 65.

15—ST. BERNARD (1924) Rev. Gerald Hugh McSorley (Retired); Rev. Msgr. Patrick McNulty, Pastor Emeritus (Retired).
Res.: 2500 W. Ave. 33, 90065. Tel: 323-255-6142; Fax: 323-255-2351. Email: stbla@aol.com. Web: stbernardla.cc.
School—3254 Verdugo Rd., 90065. Tel: 323-256-4989; Fax: 323-256-4963. Email: sstbernard3@aol.com. Mrs. Margaret Samaniego, Prin. Lay Teachers 9; Students 158.
Catechesis/Religious Program—2515 W. Ave. 33, 90065. Tel: 323-478-0001; Fax: 323-256-6242. Students 274.

16—BLESSED SACRAMENT (1904) Revs. Michael J. Mandala, S.J.; Wayne Negrete, S.J.; Leo P. Prengaman, S.J.; Joseph G. Spieler, S.J.; Anastacio Rivera, S.J.; Allen Reese, Exec. Dir., Social Svcs.; Yolanda Lichtman, Dir. Social Svcs.
Res.: 6657 Sunset Blvd., 90028. Tel: 323-462-6311; Fax: 323-462-0113. Email: church@blessedsacramenthollywood.org. Web: www.blessedsacramenthollywood.org.
School—6641 Sunset Blvd., 90028. Tel: 323-467-4177; Fax: 323-467-6099. Email: blssdsacsch@gmail.com. Lay Teachers 13; Students 120.
Catechesis/Religious Program—Tel: 323-463-9820. Email: religioused@blessedsacramenthollywood.org. Virginia Cipres, D.R.E. Students 160.

17—ST. BRENDAN (1915) Rev. Msgr. Terrance L. Fleming; Rev. Kenneth Deasy.
Res.: 310 S. Van Ness Ave., 90020. Tel: 323-936-4656; Fax: 323-936-9058. Email: info@stbrendanmail.org. Web: www.stbrendanchurch.org.
School—238 S. Manhattan Pl., 90004. Tel: 213-382-7401; Fax: 213-382-8918. Sisters 3; Lay Teachers 18; Students 305.
Catechesis/Religious Program—Students 95.

18—ST. BRIDGET'S CHINESE CATHOLIC CHURCH (1940), (Chinese), [JC] Rev. John Lam, S.D.B.
445 Cottage Home St., 90012-1418. Tel: 323-222-5518. Web: www.stbridgetccc.com.
Res.: 448 Cottage Home St., 90012. Tel: 323-276-8587; Fax: 323-222-0814.
Church: 510 Cottage Home, 90012-1418.
Catechesis/Religious Program—Sr. Grace Yip, S.P.S.H., D.R.E. Students 60.

19—ST. BRIGID'S (1920), (African American—Hispanic), Revs. Roger J. Caesar, S.S.J.; Kenneth Keke, S.S.J.
Res.: 5214 S. Western Ave., 90062. Tel: 323-292-0781; Fax: 323-290-1254. Email: stbrigidchurch@sbcglobal.net.
Catechesis/Religious Program—Students 64.

20—ST. CAMILLUS CENTER FOR SPIRITUAL CARE (1954), (Center for Pastoral Care). Rev. Christopher D. Ponnet, Pastor, Dir. & Chap.; His Eminence Cardinal Roger Michael Mahony, Chap. (Retired); Revs. Robert J. Jones, C.M., Chap.; Mark Martinez, Chap.; Sisters Mary Jean Ferry, B.V.M., Chap.; Theresa Hann, O.S.F., Chap.; Janet Husung, C.S.J., Chap.; Nadine McGiness, C.S.J., Chap.; Angela Pacheco, C.S.J., Chap.; Martha Vega, S.S.S., Chap.; Mr. Frederico Gianelli, Chap.; Mr. Luis Lupercio, Chap.; Mr. Symeon Rendall Yee, Chap.; Mr. William Rice, Chap.; Mr. Rene Valle, Chap.; Leticia Delgado, Chap.; Christopher Stephan, Admin. Asst.
Res.: 1911 Zonal Ave., 90033-1032. Tel: 323-225-4461; Fax: 323-225-9096. Web: www.stcamilluscenter.org.
Catholics Against the Death Penalty Center—Tel: 323-225-4461, Ext. 221.
Catholic HIV/AIDS Office—Tel: 323-225-4461, Ext. 221.
Pax Christi Los Angeles—Tel: 323-225-4461, Ext. 221.
Ministry with Gay & Lesbian Catholics—Tel: 323-225-4461, Ext. 221.
Consistent Life Ethics Institute—Tel: 323-225-4461, Ext. 221.
Catechesis/Religious Program—Rambhoru Brinkmann, C.P.E. (Clinical Pastoral Educ.).

21—ST. CASIMIR (1946), (Lithuanian), Rev. Tomas Karanauskas.
Res.: 2718 St. George St., 90027. Tel: 323-664-4660; Fax: 323-664-8729.
Catechesis/Religious Program—Tel: 818-248-4046.

22—CATHEDRAL CHAPEL (1927) Rev. Truc Q. Nguyen, Admin.; Most Rev. Edward W. Clark, Auxiliary Bishop OLA Region.
Mailing Address: 927 S. La Brea Ave., 90036.
Office: 926 S. Detroit St., 90036. Tel: 323-930-5976; 323-930-5977; Fax: 323-935-7308. Email: parish@cathedralchapel.org. Web: cathedralchapel.org.
Church: 923 S. La Brea Ave., 90036.
Res.: 922 S. Detroit St., 90036. Tel: 323-930-5978; Fax: 323-935-7308.
School—755 S. Cochran Ave., 90036. Tel: 323-938-9976; Fax: 323-938-9930. Web: cathedralchapelschool.org. Lay Teachers 15; Students 285.
Catechesis/Religious Program—Students 47.

23—ST. CECILIA (1909), (African American—Hispanic), Rev. Jorge Ochoa, M.C.C.J., Admin. In Res., Rev. Aldo Pozza, M.C.C.J.
Res.: 4230 S. Normandie Ave., 90037. Tel: 323-294-6628; Fax: 323-294-3310. Email: parish@stcecilia-la.org.
School—4224 S. Normandie Ave., 90037. Tel: 323-293-4266; Fax: 323-293-5556. Lay Teachers 9; Students 190.
Catechesis/Religious Program—Students 650.

24—CHRIST THE KING (1926) Rev. Msgr. Antonio Cacciapuoti. In Res., Rev. Msgr. Charles J. Chaffman.
Res.: 624 N. Rossmore Ave., 90004. Tel: 323-465-7605; Fax: 323-463-4895. Email: christtheking@sbcglobal.net. Web: www.ctk-ca.org.
School—617 N. Arden Blvd., 90004. Tel: 323-462-4753; Fax: 323-462-8475. Lay Teachers 9; Students 232.
Catechesis/Religious Program—Tel: 323-465-7084. Students 314.

25—ST. COLUMBAN (1945), (Filipino), Rev. John Brannigan, S.S.C.; Deacon Felix Dumlao.
Res.: 125 Loma Dr., 90026-5712. Tel: 213-250-8818; Fax: 213-975-9398.
Catechesis/Religious Program—

26—ST. COLUMBKILLE (1921), (Hispanic—African American), Revs. Francis Mendoza; Jesus Eduardo Martinez (CHI). In Res., Rev. Msgr. James Forsen.
Res.: 6315 S. Main St., 90003. Tel: 323-758-5540; Fax: 323-758-8108.
School—145 W. 64th St., 90003. Tel: 323-758-2284; Fax: 323-750-7141. Sisters 1; Lay Teachers 8; Students 250.
Catechesis/Religious Program—Tel: 323-789-3344. Students 420.

27—CRISTO REY (1939), (Hispanic), [CEM] Revs. Galo Espinoza, O.A.R. (Ecuador); Michael Stechmann, O.A.R.
Res.: 4343 Perlita Ave., 90039. Tel: 323-245-4585; Fax: 818-247-8831.
Catechesis/Religious Program—Students 302.

28—DIVINE SAVIOUR (1907), (Hispanic), Rev. Marco Antonio Ortiz.
Res.: 610 Cypress Ave., 90065. Tel: 323-225-9181; Fax: 323-225-1099. Email: office@divinesaviour.com. Web: www.divinesaviour.com.
School—Tel: 323-222-6077; Fax: 323-222-6494. Email: principaldss@yahoo.com. Lay Teachers 7; Students 115.
Catechesis/Religious Program—Tel: 323-225-9181 Ext. 127, 128. Email: reled@divinesaviour.com. Sr. Estela Pina, E.E.P., D.R.E. Students 411.

29—DOLORES MISSION (1945), (Hispanic), Revs. Scott Santarosa, S.J.; Ted Gabrielli, S.J.; Ellie Hidalgo, Pastoral Assoc.; Jody Lozano, Bookkeeper; Dana Valenzuela, Devel. Dir.; Jo Ann McLaughlin, Youth Min. In Res., Revs. Tri M. Dinh, S.J.; Gregory Boyle, S.J.; Mark Torres.
Res.: 1901 E. 4th St., 90033. Tel: 323-881-0039 (Church); Fax: 323-881-0034. Web: www.dolores-mission.org.
School—Tel: 323-881-0001; Fax: 323-881-0003. Karina Moreno, Prin. Lay Teachers 9; Students 230.
Catechesis/Religious Program—Students 205.

30—ST. DOMINIC (1921) Very Rev. Peter Rogers, O.P.; Revs. Michael Carey, O.P.; Jerome Cudden, O.P.; Dismas Sayre, O.P. In Res., Very Rev. Jude Eli, O.P.; Revs. Dominic DeLay, O.P.; Paul Scanlon, O.P.
Res.: 2002 Merton Ave., 90041. Tel: 323-254-2519; Fax: 323-255-3067. Email: st.dominic@sbcglobal.net. Web: dominicla.org.
School—Tel: 323-255-5803; Fax: 323-255-2817. Ms. Elida Lujan, Prin. Sisters of Notre Dame 1; Lay Teachers 11; Students 197.
Catechesis/Religious Program—Tel: 323-255-6373. Students 178.

31—ST. EUGENE (1942) Mailing Address: 9505 Haas Ave., 90047. Pastoral Team:, Rev. Jude Umeobi, Admin.; Martin Hicks, Dir. Pastoral Svcs.
Church: 9506 S. Van Ness Ave., 90047. Tel: 323-757-3121; Fax: 323-757-8872. Email: steugenechurch@sbcglobal.net.
Catechesis/Religious Program—Students 60.

32—FORMER CATHEDRAL OF ST. VIBIANA (1876) Closed. For inquiries for Sacramental Records contact 555 W. Temple St., Los Angeles, CA 90012.

33—ST. FRANCES XAVIER CABRINI (1946), (African American—Latino), Rev. Cesar Raffo.
Res.: 1440 W. Imperial Hwy., 90047. Tel: 323-757-0271; Fax: 323-757-9267.
School—1428 W. Imperial Hwy., 90047. Tel: 323-756-1354; Fax: 323-756-1157. Email: school-8650@la-archdiocese.org. Web: ohartcabrinila.weebly.com. Mrs. Carmen A. Orinoco-Hart, Prin. Lay Teachers 9; Students 170.
Catechesis/Religious Program—Students 393.

34—ST. FRANCIS OF ASSISI (1920) Revs. Richard Juzix, O.F.M.; Alberto Villafan, O.F.M. In Res., Bro. Hajime Okuhara, O.F.M.
Res.: 1523 Golden Gate Ave., 90026. Tel: 323-664-1305; Fax: 323-664-4975.
School—1550 Maltman Ave., 90026. Tel: 323-665-3601; Fax: 323-665-4143. Lay Teachers 11; Students 215.
Catechesis/Religious Program—Tel: 323-662-3345. Students 124.

35—ST. FRANCIS XAVIER CHAPEL *dba Maryknoll Japanese Catholic Center* (1921), (Japanese), Rev. Richard Hoynes.
Res.: 222 S. Hewitt St., 90012. Tel: 213-626-2279; Fax: 213-628-1757. Email: info@sfxcjcc.org. Web: www.sfxcjcc.org.
Catechesis/Religious Program—Students 57.

36—ST. GERARD MAJELLA (1952) Rev. Martin Slaughter.
Res.: 4439 Inglewood Blvd., 90066. Tel: 310-390-5034; Fax: 310-397-0964. Email: stgerardmajella@ca.rr.com. Web: stgerardla.com.
Catechesis/Religious Program—Tel: 310-391-9637. Students 450.

37—ST. GREGORY NAZIANZEN (1923) Rev. Alex Chung.
Res.: 900 S. Bronson Ave., 90019. Tel: 323-935-4224; Fax: 323-934-0016.
School—911 S. Norton Ave., 90019. Tel: 323-936-2542; Fax: 323-936-1690. Email: la154e@aol.com. Web: www.stgregorylaschool.com. Linda Guzman, Prin. Lay Teachers 7; Students 92.
Catechesis/Religious Program—Tel: 323-935-4701. Sr. Jini Yang, O.S.B., C.R.E. Students 85.

38—HOLY CROSS (1906), (African American—Hispanic), Revs. Luis Cananza Cervantes, M.C.C.J. (Mexico); Modi Abil Nairki, M.C.C.J.; Robert Kleiner, M.C.C.J.
Res.: 4705 S. Main St., 90037. Tel: 323-234-5984; Fax: 323-234-0130.
Catechesis/Religious Program—Students 860.

39—HOLY NAME OF JESUS (1921), (African American), Rev. Paul J. Spellman; Deacons Hosea Alexander Sr.; Alejandro Marin; Douglass R. Johnson Sr.
Res.: 2190 W. 31st St., 90018. Tel: 323-734-8888; Fax: 323-734-8430. Web: www.holynameofjesus-la.org.
School—Tel: 323-731-2255; Fax: 323-730-0321. Mrs. Marva Belisle, Prin. Lay Teachers 10; Students 190.
Catechesis/Religious Program—Students 90.

40—HOLY SPIRIT (1926) Rev. Victor J. Ruvalcaba.
Res.: 1425 S. Dunsmuir Ave., 90019-4031. Tel: 323-935-1333; Fax: 323-935-7741.
School—(Grades K-4), 1418 S. Burnside Ave., 90019. Tel: 323-933-7775; Fax: 323-933-7453. Lay Teachers 7; Students 94.
Catechesis/Religious Program—Students 328.

41—HOLY TRINITY (1925), (Filipino—Hispanic), Revs. Maurice D. Harrigan; Thomas James Peacha, Pastor Emeritus (Retired); John J. Daly, Pastor Emeritus (Retired); James Bong-Won Choe (Korea, South); Deacon Rolando Bautista.
Res.: 3722 Boyce Ave., 90039. Tel: 323-664-4723; Fax: 323-664-2581.
School—3716 Boyce Ave., 90039. Tel: 323-663-2064; Fax: 323-663-0732. Email: holytrinityla@yahoo.com. Lay Teachers 12; Students 251.
Catechesis/Religious Program—Students 115.

42—ST. IGNATIUS OF LOYOLA (1911) Rev. Edwin C. Duyshart.
Res.: 322 N. Ave. 61, 90042. Tel: 323-256-3041; Fax: 323-256-0105. Web: saintignatiusparish.com.
School—6025 Monte Vista St., 90042. Tel: 323-255-6456; Fax: 323-255-0959. Web: www.sifalcons.net. Dominican Sisters, San Jose Mission 1; Lay Teachers 14; Students 203.
Catechesis/Religious Program—Tel: 323-254-9073; Fax: 323-254-9073. Email: stignatiusre@yahoo.com. Students 442.

43—IMMACULATE CONCEPTION (1908), (Hispanic), Revs. Alfonso Amezcua (Mexico); Jose Cruz (Mexico); Rafael Ochoa (Mexico); Octavio Mata.
Res.: 1433 James M. Wood Blvd., 90015. Tel: 213-384-1019; Fax: 213-384-0437. Email: immaconc@sbcglobal.net.
School—830 Green St., 90017. Tel: 213-382-5931; Fax: 213-382-4563. Ms. Mary Ann Murphy, Prin. Lay Teachers 14; Students 240.
Catechesis/Religious Program—832 Green Ave., 90017. Tel: 213-389-7277. Students 416.

44—IMMACULATE HEART OF MARY (1910) Revs. Rodel G. Balagtas; Mateo H. Hicarte (Retired); Deacon George Asmar.
Res.: 4954 Santa Monica Blvd., 90029. Tel: 323-660-0034; Fax: 323-660-0047.
School—1055 N. Alexandria Ave., 90029. Tel: 323-663-4611; Fax: 323-663-6216. Lay Teachers 11; Students 260.
Catechesis/Religious Program—4954 W. Santa

Monica Blvd., 90029. Tel: 323-660-0034, Ext. 17. Students 225.

45—ST. JEROME (1949) Rev. Msgr. Norman F. Priebe; Rev. Samuel Okafor.
Res.: 5550 Thornburn St., 90045. Tel: 310-348-8212; Fax: 310-417-3577.
School—Tel: 310-670-1678; Fax: 310-670-2170. Web: www.stjeromewestchester.org. Sisters of St. Joseph of Carondelet 2; Lay Teachers 14; Students 269.
Catechesis/Religious Program—Tel: 310-645-8318; Fax: 310-645-8318. Students 180.
Convent—5570 Thornburn St., 90045. Tel: 310-670-8838.

46—ST. JOAN OF ARC (1943), (Spanish), Revs. James H. Barnes; Frederick Byaruhanga (Uganda).
Res.: 11534 Gateway Blvd., 90064. Tel: 310-479-5111; Fax: 310-479-2513. Email: sjachurchwla@msn.com. Web: www.stjoanofarcla.com.
School—11561 Gateway Blvd., 90064. Tel: 310-479-3607; Fax: 310-478-1398.
Catechesis/Religious Program—Students 240.

47—ST. JOHN, THE EVANGELIST (1909), (Hispanic—African American), Revs. Damian Kabot, S.V.D. (Poland); Anthaiah Madanu, S.V.D. (India).
Res.: 6028 S. Victoria Ave., 90043. Tel: 323-758-9161; Fax: 323-758-0112. Email: saint_john_evangelist@yahoo.com. Web: www.johnevangelist.org.
Catechesis/Religious Program—Students 113.

48—ST. JOSEPH (1888), (Hispanic), Rev. Rafael Casillas; Deacon Miguel Cruz.
Res.: 218 E. 12th St., 90015. Tel: 213-748-5394; Fax: 213-748-4793.
School—Tel: 213-749-8894; Fax: 213-749-0424. Claudia Moreno, Prin. Lay Teachers 9; Students 147.
Catechesis/Religious Program—Tel: 213-748-5394; 626-813-0763. Students 233.
Mission—St. Turibius 1524 Essex, Los Angeles Co. 90021. Tel: 213-749-8894; Fax: 213-749-0424.

49—ST. KEVIN (1923), (Hispanic—Filipino), Revs. Manuel Gacad, M.J.; Melanio Viuya, M.J.; Enrique Ymson, M.J.; Deacon Carlos Magos.
Res.: 4072 Beverly Blvd., 90004. Tel: 213-909-1801; Fax: 213-381-3255.
Catechesis/Religious Program—Students 207.

50—ST. LAWRENCE OF BRINDISI (1908), (African American—Hispanic), Capuchin Franciscan Friary. Revs. Jesus Vela, O.F.M.Cap.; John De La Riva, O.F.M.Cap.; James L. Cleary, O.F.M.Cap.; Ron Talbott, O.F.M.Cap.
Res.: 10122 Compton Ave., 90002. Tel: 323-567-1439; Fax: 323-564-4050.
School—10044 Compton Ave., 90002. Tel: 323-564-3051. Lay Teachers 9; Students 285.
Catechesis/Religious Program—Tel: 323-567-4698. Students 1,125.

51—ST. LUCY (1981), (Hispanic), [CEM] Revs. Ramon Novell, Sch.P.; Miguel Mascorro, Sch.P.
Res.: 1419 N. Hazard Ave., 90063. Tel: 323-266-0451; Fax: 323-266-4907.
Catechesis/Religious Program—Tel: 323-266-0456.

52—ST. MALACHY (1926), (Hispanic), Revs. Abel Loera; Victor Raul Ramos. In Res., Rev. David Ocran.
Res.: 1221 E. 82nd St., 90001. Tel: 323-585-1437; Fax: 323-277-4776. Email: st.malachychurch@gmail.com.
School—Saint Malachy Pre-School, 1232 E. 81st St., 90001. Tel: 323-582-1096; Fax: 323-582-9972. Lay Teachers 2; Students 20.
School—Saint Malachy Elementary School, 1200 E. 81st St., 90001. Tel: 323-582-3112; Fax: 323-582-9340. Email: stmalachyschl@sbcglobal.net. Lay Teachers 8; Students 163.
Catechesis/Religious Program—Tel: 323-582-0203. Sr. Virginia Sandoval, M.J.C., D.R.E. Students 315.
Convent—Missionaries of Jesus Crucified, St. Malachy Convent, 1228 E. 81st St., 90001. Tel: 323-582-2992. Sisters 3.

53—ST. MARCELLINUS (1957) Humberto Ramos, Parish Life Dir.
Res.: 2349 Strong Ave., Commerce, 90040. Tel: 323-269-2733.
Catechesis/Religious Program—Tel: 323-266-4938. Students 200.

54—ST. MARTIN OF TOURS (1946) Rev. Ben Le; Rev. Msgr. Lawrence O'Leary, Pastor Emeritus (Retired); Rev. Donal Keohane (Ireland).
Res.: 11967 Sunset Blvd., 90049. Tel: 310-476-7403; Fax: 310-476-0290. Email: info@saintmartinoftours.com. Web: www.saintmartinoftours.com.
Church: 11967 Sunset Blvd., 90049.
School—11955 Sunset Blvd., 90049. Tel: 310-472-7419; Fax: 310-440-2298. Email: coswald@smtschool.net. Web: smtschool.net. Sisters 1; Lay Teachers 27; Students 237.
Catechesis/Religious Program—Tel: 310-472-1757, Ext. 235. Email: smtchurchlady@aol.com. Students 75.

55—ST. MARY (1896) Revs. Juan Francisco Munoz, S.D.B.; Marc Rougeau, S.D.B.
Res.: 407 S. Chicago St., 90033. Tel: 323-268-7432; Fax: 323-268-8076. Email: stmarysela@aol.com.
School—(Grades K-8), 416 S. St. Louis St., 90033. Tel: 323-262-3395; Fax: 323-262-4738. Email: stmary_la@yahoo.com. Daughters of Mary Help of Christians 2; Lay Teachers 10; Students 195.
Catechesis/Religious Program—Tel: 323-268-2351. Email: stmarysccd@yahoo.com. Students 376.

56—ST. MARY MAGDALEN (1930) Rev. Victor J. Ruvalcaba.
Res.: 1241 Corning St., 90035. Tel: 310-652-2444; Fax: 310-652-4885. Email: saintmarymagdalen@sbcglobal.net. Web: stmarymagdalenla.org.
School—1223 Corning St., 90035. Tel: 310-652-4723. Lay Teachers 6; Students 141.
Catechesis/Religious Program—

57—ST. MICHAEL (1907), (Hispanic—African American), Rev. Msgr. David G. O'Connell. In Res., Rev. Stan Bosch, S.T.
Res.: 1016 W. Manchester Ave., 90044. Tel: 323-753-2696; Fax: 323-753-3475. Email: parish-5630@la-archdiocese.org.
School—(Grades K-8), 1027 W. 87th St., 90044. Tel: 323-752-6101; Fax: 323-752-6785. Lay Teachers 11; Students 200.
Catechesis/Religious Program—Tel: 323-753-2976. Students 450.

58—MOTHER OF SORROWS (1923), (Hispanic—African American), Revs. Abel Loera; Victor Raul Ramos. In Res., Rev. Cletus Madu.
Res.: 114 W. 87th St., 90003. Tel: 323-758-7697; Fax: 323-758-7853.
School—(Grades PreSchool-8) Tel: 323-758-6204; Fax: 323-758-6203. Jennifer Beltramo, Prin. Lay Teachers 14; Students 230.
Catechesis/Religious Program—Tel: 323-789-6316. Sr. Rosa Lidia Orellana, C.S.J., D.R.E. Students 364.

59—NATIVITY (1920), (Hispanic—African American), Rev. Francis Mendoza.
Res.: 953 W. 57th St., 90037. Tel: 323-759-1562; Fax: 323-759-7716.
School—944 W. 56th St., 90037. Tel: 323-752-0720; Fax: 323-752-1945. Lay Teachers 8; Students 320.
Catechesis/Religious Program—Tel: 323-752-1770. Students 2.
Loretto Literary & Benevolent Institution—

60—NATIVITY OF BLESSED VIRGIN MARY (1947), (Ukrainian—Byzantine), Rev. Myron Mykyta.
Res.: 5154 De Longpre Ave., 90027. Tel: 323-663-6307; Fax: 323-663-0369.

61—ST. ODILIA (1926), (Hispanic), Rev. Francis Eldridge, S.A.
Res.: 5222 Hooper Ave., 90011-4807. Tel: 323-231-5930; Fax: 323-231-9714.
School—5300 S. Hooper Ave., 90011. Tel: 323-232-5449; Fax: 323-233-6154. Sima Saravia-Perez, Prin. Lay Teachers 11; Students 260.
Catechesis/Religious Program—Tel: 323-233-2651. Students 248.
Mission—St. John Bosco 5516 Duarte St., Los Angeles Co. 90058. Tel: 323-581-3345.

62—OUR LADY HELP OF CHRISTIANS (MARIA AUXILIADORA) (1923), (Hispanic), Revs. Hilario Flores, Sch.P., Parish Admin.; Roberto Morales, Sch.P. In Res., Rev. Manuel Sanahuja, Sch.P.
Res.: 512 S. Ave. 20, 90031. Tel: 323-223-4153; Fax: 323-223-1427.
School—2024 Darwin Ave., 90031. Tel: 323-222-3913; Fax: 323-222-2561. Maria G. Negrete, Prin. Lay Teachers 5; Students 57.
Catechesis/Religious Program—Tel: 323-225-2846. Students 120.

63—OUR LADY OF GUADALUPE (1923), (Hispanic), Rev. Peter T.C. Ngo.
Res.: 4018 Hammel St., 90063. Tel: 323-261-8051; Fax: 323-261-1259.
School—436 Hazard Ave., 90063. Tel: 323-269-4998; Fax: 323-780-7001. Lay Teachers 9; Students 170.
Catechesis/Religious Program—Tel: 323-262-7957. Students 180.
Mission—San Felipe 738 N. Geraghty Ave., Los Angeles Co. 90063. Tel: 213-266-1433; Fax: 323-261-1259.

64—OUR LADY OF GUADALUPE (Rosehill) (1928), (Hispanic), Revs. Nelson Trinidad; Pio Antonio C. Yllana.
Res.: 4509 Mercury Ave., 90032. Tel: 323-225-4201; Fax: 323-225-3668.
School—4522 Browne Ave., 90032. Tel: 323-221-8187. Lay Teachers 10; Students 140.
Catechesis/Religious Program—4504 Brown Ave., 90032. Tel: 323-223-1777. Students 213.

65—OUR LADY OF GUADALUPE SANCTUARY (1929), (Hispanic), Rev. Leslie N. Delgado (Panama).
Res.: 4100 E. Second St., 90063. Tel: 323-261-4365; Fax: 323-261-2735.
Catechesis/Religious Program—Students 215.

66—OUR LADY OF LORETTO (1905) Revs. Richard Casillas, S.V.D.; Stephen Ayisu. In Res., Rev. Frank Drzaic.
Res.: 250 N. Union Ave., 90026. Tel: 213-483-3013; Fax: 213-484-0187. Email: ollsvd@aol.com.
School—258 N. Union Ave., 90026. Tel: 213-483-5251; Fax: 213-483-6709. Email: olloretto@hotmail.com. Web: olloretto.catholicweb-.com. Michelle Sarmiento, Prin. Lay Teachers 9; Students 184.
Catechesis/Religious Program—Tel: 213-483-8137. Students 378.

67—OUR LADY OF LOURDES (1910) Revs. Eamonn Donnelly, S.V.D.; Tinh Nguyen, S.V.D.
Res.: 3772 E. Third St., 90063-2408. Tel: 323-526-3800; Fax: 323-526-3807.
School—315 S. Eastman Ave., 90063. Tel: 323-526-3813; Fax: 323-526-3814. Lay Teachers 4; Students 85.
Catechesis/Religious Program—Students 240.

68—OUR LADY OF SOLITUDE (1925), (Hispanic), Revs. Benito Rojas, M.S.P.; Saul A. Garcia, M.S.P.; Deacon Sergio A. Perez.
Res.: 4561 Cesar Chavez Ave., 90022. Tel: 323-269-7248; Fax: 323-269-3600.
Catechesis/Religious Program—Tel: 323-261-1083. Students 345.

69—OUR LADY OF THE BRIGHT MOUNT (1925), (Polish), Rev. Rafal Dygula.
Res.: 3424 W. Adams Blvd., 90018. Tel: 323-734-5249; Fax: 323-734-0046. Email: biuletynla@gmail.com. Web: www.polskaparafiala.org.
Catechesis/Religious Program—Students 126.
Convent—Tel: 323-734-6754. Missionary Sisters of Christ the King for Polonia 2.

70—OUR LADY OF THE ROSARY OF TALPA (1928), (Spanish), Revs. Margarito Severino Martinez, C.M.; Luis Arreola, C.M.
Res.: 2914 E. Fourth St., 90033. Tel: 323-268-9176; Fax: 323-268-4026. Email: talpachurch@sbcglobal.net.
School—411 S. Evergreen Ave., 90033. Tel: 323-261-0583; Fax: 323-261-0352. Daughters of Charity of St. Vincent de Paul 2; Lay Teachers 9; Students 215.
Catechesis/Religious Program—Tel: 323-261-2956. Students 283.
Convent—427 S. Evergreen St., 90033. Tel: 323-268-7731.
Mission—La Purisima Chapel 3236 Inez St., Los Angeles Co. 90023.

71—OUR LADY OF VICTORY (1966), (Spanish), Rev. Pedro G. Valdez.
Res.: 1316 S. Herbert Ave., 90023. Tel: 323-268-9502; Fax: 323-780-1719. Email: elavictory@adelphia.net.
Catechesis/Religious Program—1317 S. Herbert Ave., 90023. Tel: 323-262-2101. Students 280.

72—OUR LADY QUEEN OF ANGELS PARISH (1781), (Spanish), Very Rev. Roland Lozano, C.M.F.; Revs. Paschal Amagba, C.M.F.; Domingo Zuniga, C.M.F.; Richard Estrada, C.M.F.; Deacon Hernan Ramirez-Chavez.
Res.: 535 N. Main St., 90012. Tel: 213-629-3101; Fax: 213-629-1951. Email: placita@pacbell.net. Web: www.laplacita.org.
Catechesis/Religious Program—Students 256.

73—OUR LADY QUEEN OF MARTYRS, (Armenian), Rev. Antoine Panossian, P.I.A.
Res.: 1327 Pleasant Ave., 90033. Tel: 323-261-9898; Fax: 323-261-0522.

74—OUR MOTHER OF GOOD COUNSEL (1925) Rev. James A. Mott, O.S.A. In Res., Rev. James P. Retzner, O.S.A.; Deacon Fernando Lopez, O.S.A.
Res.: 2060 N. Vermont Ave., 90027-1919. Tel: 323-664-2111; Fax: 323-664-0556. Web: www.omogc.org.
School—4622 Ambrose Ave., 90027. Tel: 323-664-2131; Fax: 323-664-1906. Allison Essman, Prin. Lay Teachers 9; Students 135.
Catechesis/Religious Program—Students 205.

75—OUR SAVIOUR CATHOLIC CENTER (1957) Rev. Lawrence Seyer.
3163 S. Hoover St., 90007. Email: info@catholictrojan.org. Web: www.catholictrojan.org.
Res.: Transfiguration, 2515 Martin Luther King Jr. Blvd., 90008. Tel: 323-291-1136; Fax: 323-291-1136. Email: frlawrence@catholictrojan.org.
Catechesis/Religious Program—Anthony Heim, D.R.E.

76—ST. PATRICK (1904), (Hispanic), Revs. Francisco X. Ramirez; Moises R. Apolinar Jr.
Res.: 1046 E. 34th St., 90011. Tel: 323-234-5963; Fax: 323-234-6725. Email: spatricio@aol.com.
Catechesis/Religious Program—Tel: 323-232-5460. Students 760.

77—ST. PAUL (1917) Revs. Jose Navarro Gonzalez,

M.G.; Julio Ramos, M.G.; Maurilio Franco, M.G.
Office: 1920 S. Bronson Ave., 90018. Tel: 323-730-9490; Fax: 323-734-5266. Email: stpaulschurch@hotmail.com. Web: www.stpaulla.org.
Res.: 4112 W. Washington Blvd., 90018. Tel: 323-730-9491.
School—1908 S. Bronson Ave., 90018. Tel: 213-734-4022; Fax: 323-734-5057. Mrs. Michelle Wechsler, Prin. Lay Teachers 9; Students 178.
Catechesis/Religious Program—Tel: 323-737-1784. Sr. Antonia Lopez, D.R.E. Students 435.

78—ST. PAUL THE APOSTLE (1928) Revs. John B. Ardis, C.S.P., Supr.; Joe Scott, C.S.P.; Dat Tran, C.S.P. In Res., Revs. Thomas J. Clerkin, C.S.P., Chap. UCLA Medical Center; Theodore A. Vierra (Retired); Edward D. Wrobleski, C.S.P. (Retired); Patrick E. Hensy, C.S.P. (Retired); Brett C. Hoover, C.S.P., (Faculty at LMU); Edward Donovan, C.S.P. (Retired); Peter Abdella, C.S.P., Chap. UCLA Catholic Center & Dir. Campus Ministry; Eric Andrews, C.S.P.; Paul Rospond, C.S.P.
Res.: 10750 Ohio Ave., 90024. Tel: 310-474-1527; Fax: 310-474-2897. Email: parishoffice@sp-apostle.org. Web: sp-apostle.org.
School—1536 Selby Ave., 90024. Tel: 310-474-1588; Fax: 310-474-4272. Daughters of Mary and Joseph 3; Lay Teachers 33; Students 540.
Catechesis/Religious Program—Tel: 310-689-6212. Students 157.

79—ST. PETER (1904), (Italian), Rev. Raniero Alessandrini, C.S.
Res. & Mailing Address: 1039 N. Broadway, 90012-1429. Tel: 323-225-8119; Fax: 323-225-0085. Email: stpeterit@yahoo.com. Web: www.stpeterschurchla.org.
Catechesis/Religious Program—Liz Staley, D.R.E. Students 40.
Mission—San Conrado 1820 Bouett St., Los Angeles Co. 90012. Tel: 323-223-6581.
Scalabrini House of Discernment (Seminary)—
Scalabrini Vocation Center—

80—PRECIOUS BLOOD (1923) Revs. Manuel Gacad, M.J.; Enrique Ymson, M.J.; Melanio Viuya, M.J.; Deacon Carlos Magos.
Res.: 435 S. Occidental Blvd., 90057. Tel: 213-389-8439; Fax: 213-389-1951. Email: preciousblood.cc@gmail.com.
School—307 S. Occidental Blvd., 90057. Tel: 213-382-3345; Fax: 213-382-2078. Email: pbtigers@netscape.net. Web: www.pbschool:us. Lay Teachers 12; Students 180.
Catechesis/Religious Program—Students 210.

81—PRESENTATION OF MARY PARISH (1925), (Hispanic), Revs. Jose Rafael Lara, Admin.; Ramon Orozco; Deacon Valentin Saucedo.
Res.: 6406 Parmelee Ave., 90001. Tel: 323-585-0570; Fax: 323-585-8148.
Catechesis/Religious Program—Students 550.

82—ST. RAPHAEL (1924), (Hispanic—African American), Revs. Tracy O'Sullivan, O.Carm.; Thomas John Alkire, O.Carm.; Deacons Hernan Ramirez-Chavez; Miguel Angel Martinez; Mr. Harry Wiley, Dir. African American Ministry.
Res.: 942 W. 70th St., 90044. Tel: 323-758-7100; Fax: 323-758-7134.
School—Mrs. Barbara Curtis, Prin. Lay Teachers 11; Students 270.
Catechesis/Religious Program—Tel: 323-752-5965; Fax: 323-752-5955. Mrs. Maria Moran, D.R.E.; Ms. Carolina Hernandez, C.R.E. (Confirmation Coord.). Students 295.

83—RESURRECTION (1923), (Mexican), Rev. Msgr. John T. Moretta; Rev. Gustavo Mejia; Deacon Hernando Rodriguez.
Res.: 3324 E. Opal St., 90023. Tel: 323-268-1141; Fax: 323-268-1143. Email: resurrectionla@yahoo.com. Web: resurrectionla.com.
School—3360 E. Opal St., 90023. Tel: 323-261-5750; Fax: 323-261-1463. Angelica Figueroa, Prin. Franciscan Sisters of Mary Immaculate 2; Lay Teachers 10; Students 220.
Catechesis/Religious Program—Tel: 323-264-1963. Students 677.
Convent—3346 Opal St., 90023. Tel: 323-261-6957.

84—SACRED HEART (1887), (Hispanic), Rev. Tesfaldet Asghedom. In Res., Revs. George E. Horan; Reynaldo B. Matunog (Philippines).
Res.: 2210 Sichel St., 90031-3030. Tel: 323-221-3179; Fax: 323-221-3613. Email: sacredheart2210@sbcglobal.net.
School—2109 Sichel St., 90031. Tel: 323-225-4177; Fax: 323-225-2615. Dominican Sisters of Mission San Jose 2; Lay Teachers 10; Students 216.
Catechesis/Religious Program—Tel: 323-223-7571. Students 424.
Convent—2222 Sichel St., 90031. Tel: 323-222-5157; Fax: 323-276-9431.

85—SAN ANTONIO DE PADUA (1926), (Hispanic), Revs. Gustavo J. Ramon; Paul L. O'Donnell.
Res.: 555 N. Fairview Ave., 90033. Tel: 323-225-1301; Fax: 323-225-2534.
Catechesis/Religious Program—Students 167.

86—SAN CONRADO MISSION (1966) See separate listing. (See St. Peter, Los Angeles for details.)

87—SAN FRANCISCO CHURCH (1982), (Hispanic), [CEM] [JC] Rev. Severiano Castaneda.
Res.: 4800 E. Olympic Blvd., 90022. Tel: 323-262-4253; Fax: 323-268-8246. Email: sfchurch@attglobal.net.
Catechesis/Religious Program—Tel: 323-261-2447. Students 647.

88—SAN MIGUEL (1927), (Hispanic), Rev. Jose Valdez Romo, M.S.C.
Res.: 2214 E. 108th St., 90059. Tel: 323-569-5951; Fax: 323-567-1850.
School—2270 E. 108th St., 90059. Tel: 323-567-6892; Fax: 323-567-4065. Lay Teachers 11; Students 206.
Catechesis/Religious Program—Students 188.

89—SANTA ISABEL (1915), (Mexican), Revs. Genaro Zavala; Juan Diego Vallejof, M.S.P.
Res.: 918 S. Soto St., 90023. Tel: 323-268-4065; Fax: 323-268-4180.
School—2424 Whittier Blvd., 90023. Tel: 323-263-3716. Lay Teachers 11; Students 242.
Catechesis/Religious Program—Tel: 323-268-3019. Students 245.
Mission—Hermanas Misioneras Servidoras de la Palabra 90023. Tel: 323-268-7063.

90—SANTA TERESITA (1923), (Hispanic), Revs. Augustin Arriola, Sch.P.; Ramon Novell, Sch.P.; Miguel Mascorro, Sch.P.; Raymond Farre, Sch.P.
Res.: 2645 Zonal Ave., 90033. Tel: 323-221-2446; Fax: 323-221-2216. Email: steresita38@yahoo.com.
School—(Grades K-8), 2646 Zonal Ave., 90033. Tel: 323-221-1129; Fax: 323-221-6339. Email: santa@msjdominicans.org. Dominican Sisters 2; Lay Teachers 9; Students 228.
Catechesis/Religious Program—Tel: 213-221-2511. Students 184.
Convent—1375 Murchison St., 90033. Tel: 323-221-6663.

91—ST. SEBASTIAN (1924) Rev. German Sanchez, Admin.
Res.: 1453 Federal Ave., 90025-2301. Tel: 310-479-7421.
Church: 1425 Federal Ave., 90025.
Parish Center—11607 Ohio Ave., 90025. Tel: 310-478-0136; Fax: 310-479-5121. Email: office@stsebastian.net.
School—1430 Federal Ave. W., 90025. Tel: 310-473-3337; Fax: 310-473-3178. Email: info@saintsebastian.com. Web: saintsebastianschool.com.
Catechesis/Religious Program—Tel: 310-479-7380. Sr. Catalina Avila, O.S.F., D.R.E. Students 160.

92—ST. STEPHEN OF HUNGARY (1928), (Hungarian—German), Rev. Francisco X. Ramirez.
Res.: 1046 E. 34th St., 90011. Tel: 323-234-5963; Fax: 323-234-6725.
Catechesis/Religious Program—

93—ST. TERESA OF AVILA (1921) Rev. Msgr. Joseph F. Hernandez; Rev. Mariano Garrido (Philippines).
Res.: 2216 Fargo St., 90039. Tel: 323-664-8426; Fax: 323-665-3115.
School—(Grades K-8), 2215 Fargo St., 90039. Tel: 323-662-3777; Fax: 323-662-3420. Email: cdbfc@stteresaofavilala.org. Web: www.stapanthers.org. Lay Teachers 8; Students 190.
Catechesis/Religious Program—Students 145.
Convent—2223 Fargo St., 90039. Tel: 323-913-1510.

94—ST. THOMAS THE APOSTLE (1903), (Hispanic), Revs. Arturo Corral; William Rodriguez; Leo Ortega; Deacons Juan Bautista Cantillo; Daniel Bernal.
Res.: 2727 W. Pico Blvd., 90006. Tel: 323-737-3325; Fax: 323-737-2665.
Church: 2760 W. Pico Blvd., 90006.
School—Tel: 323-737-4730; Fax: 323-737-6348. Lay Teachers 10; Students 295.
Catechesis/Religious Program—2632 W. 15th St., 90006. Tel: 323-737-5624; Fax: 323-737-2582. Students 985.

95—ST. TIMOTHY (1943) Rev. Paul E. Vigil.
Rectory—10425 W. Pico Blvd., 90064. Tel: 310-474-1216; Fax: 310-475-6047. Email: stc.la@verizon.net. Web: sttimothyla.org.
School—Tel: 310-474-1811; Fax: 310-470-1391. Web: sttimothy.org. Lena Rowland, Prin. Lay Teachers 13; Students 165.
Catechesis/Religious Program—Students 73.

96—TRANSFIGURATION (1923), (African American), Rev. Michael Tang. In Res., Revs. Michael P. McCullough; Lawrence Seyer.
Res.: 2515 W. Martin Luther King Blvd., 90008-2728. Tel: 323-291-1136; Fax: 323-291-8216. Web: transfigchurchla.com.
School—4020 Roxton Ave., 90008. Tel: 323-292-3011; Fax: 323-292-1527. Web: transfigschool.com. Lay Teachers 10; Students 185.
Catechesis/Religious Program—Tel: 323-292-5112. Students 20.

97—ST. VINCENT DE PAUL (1887), (Hispanic), Bro. Anthony B. Wiedemer, C.M., Admin.; Revs. Ruben D. Restrepo, C.M.; Prudencio Rodriguez, C.M.; Jerome Herff, C.M.
Res.: 621 W. Adams Blvd., 90007. Tel: 213-749-8950; Fax: 213-749-9137.
School—2333 S. Figueroa St., 90007. Tel: 213-748-5367; Fax: 213-748-5347. Email: svs1911@pacbell.net. Web: home.pacbell.net/svs1911. Sisters 3; Lay Teachers 11; Students 270.
Catechesis/Religious Program—Tel: 213-741-9347. Students 510.
Mission—Santo Nino 601 E. 23rd St., Los Angeles Co. 90011. Tel: 213-748-5246.

98—VISITATION (1943) [JC] Rev. William J. Brelsford. In Res., Revs. James F. O'Grady, Pastor Emeritus (Retired); James L. Kolling (Retired).
Res.: 6561 W. 88th St., 90045. Tel: 310-216-1145; Fax: 310-216-1002. Email: visitationchurch497@gmail.com.
School—8740 Emerson Ave., 90045. Tel: 310-645-6620; Fax: 310-645-4407. Lay Teachers 16; Students 253.
Catechesis/Religious Program—Tel: 310-216-1145, Ext. 20; Fax: 310-216-1002. Students 90.

OUTSIDE THE CITY OF LOS ANGELES

ALHAMBRA, LOS ANGELES CO.

1—ALL SOULS (1912) Revs. Joseph Kim Dang Nguyen; Joseph Dass.
29 S. Electric Ave., 91801. In Res., Rev. Msgr. William P. O'Toole (Retired).
Res.: 29 S. Electric Ave., 91801. Tel: 626-281-0466; Fax: 626-281-2163. Email: allsoulscc@allsouls-la.org. Web: www.allsouls-la.org.
Pastoral Ministry Center—
School—29 S. Electric Ave., 91801. Tel: 626-282-5695; Fax: 626-282-2260.
Catechesis/Religious Program—29 S. Electric Ave., 91801. Tel: 626-281-0466, Ext. 214. Students 290.

2—ST. THERESE (1924), (Little Flower) Revs. Jan Lundberg, O.C.D.; Robert Barcelos, O.C.D.; David Guzman, O.C.D. In Res., Rev. Jerome Lantry, O.C.D.
Res.: 510 N. El Molino St., 91801. Tel: 626-282-2744; Fax: 626-282-7560. Web: mysttherese.org.
School—1106 E. Alhambra, 91801. Tel: 626-289-3364; Fax: 626-284-6700. Web: stthereseschoolalhambra.org. Lay Teachers 18; Students 260.
Catechesis/Religious Program—Tel: 626-284-0020. Students 171.

3—ST. THOMAS MORE (1948) Sandra E. Elizondo, Parish Life Dir.; Lucy Lai, Accounting Mgr.; Sisters Margaret Devlin, S.S.C., Pastoral Assoc.; Andrea Johnson, C.S.H., Liturgy Dir. In Res., Rev. Jeremiah O'Neill, Pastor Emeritus (Retired).
Res.: 2510 S. Fremont Ave., 91803. Tel: 626-284-8333; Fax: 626-282-4459.
School—Tel: 626-284-5778; Fax: 626-284-3303. Mrs. Judith Jones, Co-Prin.; Mrs. Jennifer Schmidt, Co-Prin. Lay Teachers 9; Students 216.
Catechesis/Religious Program—Tel: 626-457-5302. Mae Ho, D.R.E. Students 210.

ALTADENA, LOS ANGELES CO.

1—ST. ELIZABETH OF HUNGARY (1918) Rev. Modesto Lewis Perez; Deacons Jose Gallegos; Charles A. Mitchell.
Office:—1879 N. Lake Ave., 91001. Tel: 626-797-1167; Fax: 626-797-9245. Web: saintelizabethchurch.org.
School—1840 N. Lake Ave., 91001. Tel: 626-797-7727; Fax: 626-797-6541. Web: saint-elizabeth.org. Lay Teachers 15; Students 270.
Catechesis/Religious Program—Students 279.

2—SACRED HEART (1935), (African American—Hispanic), Rev. Jose Vaughn Banal, Admin.; Rev. Msgr. Jerome L. Schmit, Pastor Emeritus (Retired); Rev. Gilbert Cruz.
Church: 2889 N. Lincoln Ave., 91001. Tel: 626-794-2046; Fax: 626-794-8315. Email: sacredheartchurch@att.net. Web: www.sacredheartaltadena.org.
Catechesis/Religious Program—600 W. Mariposa. Tel: 626-798-6961; Fax: 626-798-2616. Students 310.

ARCADIA, LOS ANGELES CO., HOLY ANGELS (1935) Revs. Michael J. Evans; John Hoa Nguyen; Blaise N. Brockman; Deacon Arnaldo Lopez.
Res.: 370 Campus Dr., 91007. Tel: 626-447-1671; Fax: 626-447-7617. Email: ha@holyangelsarcadia.org. Web: www.holyangelsarcadia.org.
School—360 Campus Dr., 91007. Tel: 626-447-6312; Fax: 626-447-2843. Email: admin@holyangelsarcadia.org. Lay Teachers 20; Students 292.
Catechesis/Religious Program—Tel: 626-445-2967. Students 278.

ARTESIA, LOS ANGELES CO., HOLY FAMILY (1931) Revs. Raymond Decipeda, M.M.H.C.; Thomas F. Asia, M.M.H.C.; Joachim E. Ablanida.

Res.: 18708 S. Clarkdale Ave., 90701. Tel: 562-865-2185; Fax: 562-860-0718.
School—Our Lady of Fatima, 18626 S. Clarkdale Ave., 90701. Tel: 562-865-1621; Fax: 562-403-0409. Lay Teachers 9; Students 177.
Catechesis/Religious Program—Tel: 562-860-5973. Students 894.

AVALON, LOS ANGELES CO., ST. CATHERINE OF ALEXANDRIA (1902) Rev. John Nghi Tran.
Res.: 800 Beacon St., 90704. Tel: 310-510-0192; Fax: 310-510-8360. Email: stcatherineofavalon@gmail.com.
Catechesis/Religious Program—Students 150.

AZUSA, LOS ANGELES CO., ST. FRANCES OF ROME (1908), (Hispanic), [CEM] Revs. Gustavo Castillo; Aloysius Ezeonyeka, O.S.B.; Edward Joseph Landreau, Pastor Emeritus (Retired); Roque A.D. Fernandes (Retired); Deacons Ernesto Vital; Juan Rogelio Garcia.
Res. 5: 501 E. Foothill Blvd., P.O. Box 637, 91702. Tel: 626-969-1829; Fax: 626-815-2755.
School—734 N. Pasadena Ave., 91702. Tel: 626-334-2018; Fax: 626-815-2760. Lay Teachers 12; Aides 3; Students 219.
Catechesis/Religious Program—508 N. Soldano, 91702. Tel: 626-334-3500. Students 830.

BALDWIN PARK, LOS ANGELES CO., ST. JOHN THE BAPTIST (1946), (Hispanic—Filipino), Revs. Michael D. Gutierrez; Erasmus B. Soriano; Antonio M. Aldaz; Rev. Msgr. Joseph W. Herres.
Res.: 3848 Stewart Ave., 91706. Tel: 626-960-2795; Fax: 626-960-5085.
School—3870 Stewart Ave., 91706. Tel: 626-337-1421; Fax: 626-337-3733. Sisters of the Love of God 5; Lay Teachers 15; Students 361.
Catechesis/Religious Program—Tel: 626-962-1004. Students 1,151.
Convent—3963 Baldwin Park Blvd., 91706. Tel: 626-337-0527.

BELL GARDENS, LOS ANGELES CO., ST. GERTRUDE (1938) Revs. Randy Raul Campos; Sigifredo Martin Roque-Torres.
Res.: 7025 Garfield Ave., 90201. Tel: 562-927-4495; Fax: 562-927-5826. Web: www.saintgertrudechurch.org.
School—6824 Toler Ave., 90201. Tel: 562-927-1216; Fax: 562-927-5607. Lay Teachers 7; Students 108.
Catechesis/Religious Program—Tel: 562-927-3185. Students 846.

BELLFLOWER, LOS ANGELES CO.

1—ST. BERNARD (1923) Revs. Michael Ume; Gaylord Reyes.
Res.: 9647 E. Beach St., 90706. Tel: 562-867-2337; Fax: 562-867-4863.
School—9626 Park St., 90706. Tel: 562-867-9410; Fax: 310-866-2310. Mrs. Melissa Oswald, Prin. Lay Teachers 11; Students 156.
Catechesis/Religious Program—Tel: 562-925-9886. Students 325.

2—ST. DOMINIC SAVIO (1954) Revs. Ted Montemayor, S.D.B.; Avelino Lorenzo, S.D.B.; Thinh Nguyen, S.D.B.
13400 Bellflower Blvd., 90706.
Res.: 9720 Foster Rd., 90706. Tel: 562-920-7796; Fax: 562-920-0149.
School—9750 Foster Rd., 90706. Tel: 562-866-3617; Fax: 562-867-0887. Salesian Sisters of St. John Bosco 7; Lay Teachers 24; Students 382.
Catechesis/Religious Program—Tel: 562-920-7796, Ext. 317. Students 800.

BEVERLY HILLS, LOS ANGELES CO., GOOD SHEPHERD (1924) Rev. Msgr. Thomas Welbers; Deacon Eric Stoltz. In Res., Revs. George O'Brien; Colm O'Ryan (Retired).
Res.: 504 N. Roxbury Dr., 90210. Tel: 310-285-5425; Fax: 310-285-5433. Email: info@goodshepherdbh.org. Web: www.goodshepherdbh.org.
School—148 S. Linden Dr., 90212. Tel: 310-275-8601; Fax: 310-275-0366. Email: goodshepherdbh@aol.com. Web: www.goodshepherd-beverlyhills.com. Terry Miller, Prin. Lay Teachers 17; Students 170.
Catechesis/Religious Program—Students 55.

BURBANK, LOS ANGELES CO.

1—ST. FINBAR (1938) Rev. Albert M. Bahhuth.
Res.: 2010 W. Olive Ave., 91506. Tel: 818-846-6251; Fax: 818-846-1703. Web: www.stfinbarburbank.org.
School—2120 W. Olive Ave., 91506. Tel: 818-848-0191; Fax: 818-848-4315. Lay Teachers 19; Students 302.
Catechesis/Religious Program—Students 320.

2—ST. FRANCIS XAVIER (1954) Revs. Richard Albarano; Benny George, C.M.I. (India); Deacon Jaime Abrera; Rita Recker, Pastoral Assoc. & Business Mgr. In Res., Rev. John D. Murray (Retired).
Res.: 3801 Scott Rd., 91504. Tel: 818-504-4400; Fax: 818-767-5096. Email: rectory@sfxrccburbank.org. Web: www.sfxrccburbank.org.
School—Tel: 818-504-4422; Fax: 818-504-4424. Lay Teachers 19; Students 285.
Catechesis/Religious Program—Tel: 818-504-4411. Email: religioused@sfxrccburbank.org. Rosie Roope, C.R.E. Students 171.

3—ST. ROBERT BELLARMINE (1907) Rev. John Collins; Rev. Msgrs. Patrick Reilly (Retired); Francis T. Wallace (Retired); Peter C. Healy (Retired).
Ministry Center (Offices):—520 E. Orange Grove Ave., 91501. Email: srbcc@srbburbank.org. Web: srbburbank.org.
Res.: 133 N. Fifth St., 91501. Tel: 818-846-3443; Fax: 818-954-9441.
Church: Fifth St. and E. Orange Grove Ave., 91501.
School—154 N. Fifth St., 91501. Tel: 818-842-5033; Fax: 818-842-9789. Email: info@strobertbellarmineburbank.com. Web: strobertbellarmineburbank.com. Lay Teachers 13; Students 200.
Catechesis/Religious Program—Tel: 818-845-3521. Students 317.

CAMARILLO, VENTURA CO.

1—BLESSED JUNIPERO SERRA (1988), Liturgies celebrated at: Padre Serra Parish, 5205 Upland Rd., Camarillo, CA 93012. Rev. Patrick Mullen; Deacons Isaac Edie; Bob Fargo; Genaro Gacasan; Neil Joseph Kingsley; Luc Papillon; John Picard; Jack William Redmond II; Arnold Peter Reyes; William Spies; Joseph Felix Torti.
Office & Mailing Address: 5205 Upland Rd., 93012. Tel: 805-482-6417; Fax: 805-987-8100. Email: parish@padreserra.org. Web: www.padreserra.org.
Catechesis/Religious Program—Students 650; Preschool 35.

2—ST. MARY MAGDALEN (1940) Rev. James Stehly; Rev. Msgr. John Charles Hughes, Pastor Emeritus (Retired); Rev. John Neiman; Deacons George Bednar; George J. Esseff Jr.; Johnnie Hammonds; Larry Modugno; Anh Quoc Vu; Ronald Dale Moon.
Res.: 2532 Ventura Blvd., 93010. Tel: 805-484-0532; Fax: 805-987-2941.
School—2534 Ventura Blvd., 93010. Tel: 805-482-2611; Fax: 805-987-8211. Lay Teachers 13; Students 201.
Catechesis/Religious Program—Tel: 805-482-1219. Students 415.

CANOGA PARK, LOS ANGELES CO., OUR LADY OF THE VALLEY (1921) Revs. Arturo Velasco; Roman Arzate; Leo Del Carmen; Sr. Estela del Bando, C.H.S.
Pastoral Center—22021 Gault St., 91303-1804. Tel: 818-592-2880; Fax: 818-592-0299. Web: www.ourladyofthevalley.org.
School—Tel: 818-592-2894; Fax: 818-592-2896. Web: www.olvcrusaders.org. Lay Teachers 15; Students 195.
Catechesis/Religious Program—Students 646.

CARPINTERIA, SANTA BARBARA CO., ST. JOSEPH (1933) Rev. Adalberto Blanco.
Mailing Address: 1532 Linden Ave., 93013. Tel: 805-684-2181; Fax: 805-684-0534.
Catechesis/Religious Program—Students 176.
Chapel— 7th & Ash, 93013.

CARSON, LOS ANGELES CO., ST. PHILOMENA (1956) [CEM] Revs. Demetrio L. Bugayong; William E. Ruther; Jozef Mitek; Niko F. Leota.
Res.: 21900 S. Main St., 90745. Tel: 310-835-7161; Fax: 310-830-5494. Email: stphilomenacatholicchurch@yahoo.com.
School—21832 S. Main St., 90745. Tel: 310-835-4827; Fax: 310-835-1655. Email: stphilomenasch@aol.com. Carmelite Sisters 3; Lay Teachers 7; Students 299.
Catechesis/Religious Program—Tel: 310-830-6180; Fax: 310-830-4287. Email: replupe@yahoo.com. Students 1,232.
Convent—21832 1/2 S. Main St., 90745. Tel: 310-834-9180.

CHATSWORTH, LOS ANGELES CO., ST. JOHN EUDES (1963) Revs. Gerard Lecomte, C.J.M.; William McLean, Senior Priest; Deacons Robert Seidler, Pastoral Admin.; Michael A. Perez; Reymundo Melgar.
Church Office & Res.: 9901 Mason Ave., 91311. Tel: 818-341-3680 (Office); Fax: 818-882-4326 (Office). Web: stjohneudes.org.
School—9925 Mason Ave., 91311. Tel: 818-341-1454; Fax: 818-341-3093. Barbara Danowitz, Prin. Sisters of the Pious Schools 1; Lay Teachers 14; Students 305.
Catechesis/Religious Program—9933 Mason Ave., 91311. Tel: 818-882-9323; Fax: 818-700-5142. Students 250.

CLAREMONT, LOS ANGELES CO., OUR LADY OF THE ASSUMPTION (1947) Revs. Charles J. Ramirez; Joseph Quan Nguyen; Christopher Troxell; Deacons Arthur Escovedo, (Retired); Robert Steighner; John Tullius. In Res., Rev. Msgr. Peter A. O'Reilly (Retired).
Res.: 435 Berkeley Ave., 91711. Tel: 909-626-3596; Fax: 909-624-3680. Email: ola@olaclaremont.org. Web: www.olaclaremont.org.
School—611 E. Bonita Ave., 91711. Tel: 909-626-7135; Fax: 909-398-1395. Web: www.ola-ca.org. Administrators 1; Lay Teachers 18; Students 395.
Catechesis/Religious Program—Tel: 909-624-1360. Email: ffoffice@olaclaremont.org. Students 407.

COMPTON, LOS ANGELES CO.

1—ST. ALBERT THE GREAT (1949), (Hispanic—African American), [CEM] Revs. Christopher Bazyouros; Cristobal Guardado Gonzalez.
Res.: 804 E. Compton Blvd., Rancho Dominguez, 90220. Tel: 310-329-7548; Fax: 310-464-8666.
School—Tel: 310-323-4559; Fax: 310-323-4825. Lay Teachers 11; Students 177.
School—823 E. Compton Blvd., Rancho Dominguez, 90220. Tel: 310-515-3891. Teachers 3; Students 103.
Catechesis/Religious Program—Tel: 310-323-1599. Arturo Gallardo, D.R.E. Students 320.

2—OUR LADY OF VICTORY (1920), (Hispanic—African American), Rev. Francisco Valdovinos, S.T. (Mexico). In Res., Rev. John Seymour, S.T.
Res.: 519 E. Palmer St., 90221. Tel: 310-631-3233; Fax: 310-886-5681.
School—601 E. Palmer St., 90221. Tel: 310-631-1320; Fax: 310-631-4280.
Catechesis/Religious Program—Tel: 310-631-1831. Students 150.

3—SAGRADO CORAZON, SACRED HEART (1956), (Hispanic), Margarita Flores, Parish Life Dir.; Rev. Msgr. John S. Woolway, Priest Min.
Res.: 1720 North Culver Ave., 90222. Tel: 310-635-5436; Fax: 310-635-2121.
Catechesis/Religious Program—Tel: 310-635-8483. Students 536.

COVINA, LOS ANGELES CO.

1—ST. LOUISE DE MARILLAC (1963) Revs. Robert P. Fulton; Robert A. Folbrecht.
Mailing Address: 1720 E. Covina Blvd., 91724.
Res.: 1770 E. Covina Blvd., 91724. Tel: 626-915-7873; Fax: 626-332-4431.
School—1728 E. Covina Blvd., 91724. Tel: 626-966-2317; Fax: 626-967-7947. Lay Teachers 12; Students 305.
Catechesis/Religious Program—Tel: 626-332-5822. Students 389.

2—SACRED HEART (1927) Revs. William T. Easterling; Brian M. Cavanagh (Retired); Jeffrey Deikel; James J. Kelly; Deacons John G. Horn; Ronald Butler; Rodolfo R. Leyva.
Res.: 344 W. Workman St., 91723. Tel: 626-332-3570; Fax: 626-967-4884. Email: admin@sacredheart.cc. Web: www.sacredheart.cc.
School—360 W. Workman St., 91723. Tel: 626-332-7222; Fax: 626-967-8836. Web: www.shs.cc. Lay Teachers 18; Students 289.
Catechesis/Religious Program—Tel: 626-331-7914; Fax: 626-966-7165. Students 571.

CUDAHY, LOS ANGELES CO., SAGRADO CORAZON Y SANTA MARIA DE GUADALUPE (1991), (Hispanic), [JC] Revs. Antonio Garnica Lopez, M.S.C.; Florentino Victorino, M.S.C.
4235 Clara St., 90201. Tel: 323-562-3356; Fax: 323-562-3332. Email: sagrado_cudahy@yahoo.com.
Catechesis/Religious Program—Fax: 323-562-3332. Students 240.

CULVER CITY, LOS ANGELES CO., ST. AUGUSTINE (1919) Revs. Kevin L. Nolan; Christopher B. Fagan; Richard J. Gleason; Deacon Rafael A. Victorin.
Res.: 3850 Jasmine Ave., 90232. Tel: 310-838-2477; Fax: 310-838-3070.
School—3819 Clarington Ave., 90232. Tel: 310-838-3144; Fax: 310-838-7479. Daughters of Mary and Joseph 1; Lay Teachers 15; Students 290.
Catechesis/Religious Program—Tel: 310-836-6561; Fax: 310-838-2477. Students 403.

DIAMOND BAR, LOS ANGELES CO., ST. DENIS (1971) Rev. Msgr. James J. Loughnane; Revs. Sebastian Vettickal, C.M.I. (India); Dennis Mongrain; Deacon Tom Le Donne. In Res., Rev. Donald William Potthoff, Pastor Emeritus (Retired).
Res.: 2151 S. Diamond Bar Blvd., 91765-2981. Tel: 909-861-7106; Fax: 909-861-2697. Web: stdenis91765.parishworld.net.
Catechesis/Religious Program—Tel: 909-861-8018. Students 733.

DOWNEY, LOS ANGELES CO.

1—OUR LADY OF PERPETUAL HELP (1909) Revs. Mark Warnstedt; Joseph Magdaong; Deacons Charles Denisac; Carlos Origel.
Res.: 10727 S. Downey Ave., 90241. Tel: 562-923-3246; Fax: 562-862-7020. Email: olphoffice@ca.rr.com. Web: olphdowney.parishesonline.com.
School—10441 S. Downey Ave., 90241. Tel: 562-869-9969; Fax: 562-923-0659. Web: ourladyschool.com. Lay Teachers 16; Students 312.
Catechesis/Religious Program—Tel: 562-862-7268. Theresa Nicholas, D.R.E. Students 600.

2—ST. RAYMOND (1956) Revs. John Higgins; Francis Osana Kalathil, O.C.D.; Deacons Ralph Riera; Mario Guerra. In Res., Rev. Joseph Ambrose, O.C.D.

Res.: 12348 Paramount Blvd., 90242. Tel: 562-923-4509; Fax: 562-869-3359. Email: straydny@aol.com. Web: www.st-raymond-downey.org.
School—12320 Paramount Blvd., 90242. Tel: 562-862-3210; Fax: 562-862-6328. Sisters of the Holy Faith 1; Lay Teachers 16; Students 310.
Catechesis/Religious Program—Tel: 562-862-6959. Sr. Paula Strohfus, C.H.F., D.R.E. Students 600.
Convent—12322 Paramount Blvd., 90242.
Mission—Rancho Los Amigos Hospital 7601 Imperial Hwy., Los Angeles Co. 90242. Tel: 562-401-7111.
Mission—Los Padrinos Juvenile Hall 7285 Quill Dr., Los Angeles Co. 90242. Tel: 562-940-8711.

EL MONTE, LOS ANGELES CO.

1—NATIVITY (1923) Revs. Alberto Villalobos; Doan The Pham; Luis R. Lucchetti (Peru).
Res.: 3743 N. Tyler Ave., 91731. Tel: 626-444-2511; Fax: 626-443-1417. Email: parish@mynativity.org.
School—10907 St. Louis Dr., 91731. Tel: 626-448-2414; Fax: 626-448-2763. Web: www.school.mynativity.org. Sisters of St. Louis 3; Lay Teachers 9; Students 215.
Catechesis/Religious Program—Tel: 626-448-8895; Fax: 626-443-2495. Students 313.

2—OUR LADY OF GUADALUPE (1973), (Hispanic), Revs. Nicolas Sanchez Toledano; Jesus Castrillo, C.M.F. (Spain).
Res.: 11359 Coffield Ave., 91731. Tel: 626-448-1795; Fax: 626-448-9507. Email: ologpe@pacbell.net. Web: ologpeelmonte.org.
Catechesis/Religious Program—Tel: 626-448-7131; Fax: 626-448-8376. Email: ologpe@pacbell.net. Students 2,100.

EL SEGUNDO, LOS ANGELES CO.

1—ST. ANDREW (1936), (Russian—Greek), Rt. Rev. Alexei R. Smith.
Res.: 538 Concord St., 90245. Tel: 310-322-1892; Fax: 310-322-1919.
Catechesis/Religious Program—Students 9.

2—ST. ANTHONY (1925) Rev. Robert Victoria.
Mailing Address: 215 Lomita St., 90245.
Res.: 710 E. Grand Ave., 90245. Tel: 310-322-4392; Fax: 310-322-0797. Email: administration@stanthonyes.com. Web: www.stanthonyes.com.
School—233 Lomita St., 90245. Tel: 310-322-4218; Fax: 310-322-2659. Lay Teachers 11; Students 179.
Catechesis/Religious Program—Tel: 310-322-4392, Ext. 450. Email: dre@stathonyes.com. Students 270.

ENCINO, LOS ANGELES CO.

1—ST. CYRIL (1949) Rev. Larry S. Neumeier, Admin.; Rev. Msgr. Carl F. Bell, Pastor Emeritus (Retired).
Res.: 4601 Firmament Ave., 91436. Tel: 818-986-8234; Fax: 818-986-3310. Email: st-cyril-encino@sbcglobal.net.
School—4548 Haskell Ave., 91436. Tel: 818-501-4155; Fax: 818-501-8480. Lay Teachers 14; Students 304.
Catechesis/Religious Program—Tel: 818-789-5947. Students 125.

2—OUR LADY OF GRACE (1945) Rev. Msgr. Jarlath Cunnane; Revs. Thomas Feltz, Senior Priest; Ernesto Jaramillo.
Res.: 5011 White Oak Ave., 91316. Tel: 818-342-4686; Fax: 818-342-6579. Web: www.ourladyofgrace.org.
School—Tel: 818-344-4126; Fax: 818-344-1736. Web: www.ourladyofgrace.org. Sisters 2; Lay Teachers 14; Students 266.
Catechesis/Religious Program—Students 240.

FILLMORE, VENTURA CO., ST. FRANCIS OF ASSISI (1926) [JC] Revs. Bernard Gatlin; Artur Gruska.
Church: 1048 W. Ventura St., 93015. Web: www.stfrancisfillmore.com.
Catechesis/Religious Program—Tel: 805-524-2865. Email: stfrancisoffice@sbcglobal.net. Students 150.
Mission—San Salvador 4045 E. Center St., P.O. Box 805, Piru, Ventura Co. 93040.

GARDENA, LOS ANGELES CO.

1—ST. ANTHONY OF PADUA (1910) Revs. George Aquilera; Alfonso Borgen; Deacon Antonio Huerta.
Res.: 1050 W. 163rd St., 90247. Tel: 310-327-5830; Fax: 310-327-6440.
School—1003 W. 163rd St., 90247. Tel: 310-329-7170; Fax: 310-329-9843. Lay Teachers 14; Students 220.
Catechesis/Religious Program—Tel: 310-323-0860. Students 1,200.
Mission—St. Francis Korean Catholic Center 2040 W. Artesia Blvd., Los Angeles Co. 90504. Tel: 310-324-8159; Fax: 310-769-1882.

2—MARIA REGINA (1956) [CEM] Rev. Leo W. Alberg; Deacon Phuoc Van Nguyen. In Res., Rev. Msgr. Thomas M. Acton, Pastor Emeritus (Retired).
Res.: 2150 W. 135th St., 90249. Tel: 310-323-0030; Fax: 310-323-8081. Email: mariaregina56@sbcglobal.net.
School—13510 S. Von Ness, 90249. Tel: 310-327-9133; Fax: 310-327-2636. Lay Teachers 15; Students 245.
Catechesis/Religious Program—Tel: 310-323-0030; Fax: 310-323-8081. Students 475.

GLENDALE, LOS ANGELES CO.

1—CHURCH OF THE INCARNATION (1927) Rev. Msgrs. Steven B. Zak; Eugene P. Frilot, Pastor Emeritus (Retired); Deacon Restie Noriega. In Res., Rev. Msgr. Patrick G. Thompson (Retired); Rev. Thomas Schweitzer.
Res.: 1001 N. Brand Blvd., 91202-2979. Tel: 818-242-2579; Fax: 818-507-4976.
School—123 W. Glenoaks, 91202-2908. Tel: 818-241-2269; Fax: 818-241-4734. Lay Teachers 16; Students 277.
Pre-School—214 W. Fairview, 91202. Tel: 818-241-2264; Fax: 818-241-0876. Teachers 2; Students 43.
Catechesis/Religious Program—Tel: 818-241-7045. Students 303.

2—HOLY FAMILY (1907) Revs. James M. Bevacqua; Michael Perucho; Marcial Juan; John Bosco Musinguzi; Deacon John Steele.
Res.: 209 E. Lomita Ave., 91205. Tel: 818-247-2222; Fax: 818-247-4780. Web: www.hfglendale.org.
School—Holy Family Grade School, (Grades K-8), 400 S. Louise, 91205. Tel: 818-243-9239; Fax: 818-243-0976. Web: www.hfgsglendale.org. Lay Teachers 12; Students 285.
High School—(Grades 9-12), (Girls) College Prep, 400 E. Lomita Ave., 91205. Tel: 818-241-3178; Fax: 818-241-7753. Web: hfhsglendale.org. Ms. Nancy O'Sullivan, Prin.; Paulina Fuster, Bookkeeper. Lay Teachers 14; Girls 208.
Catechesis/Religious Program—Tel: 818-240-6551, Ext. 220; Fax: 818-243-2560. Students 410.

GLENDORA, LOS ANGELES CO., ST. DOROTHY (1958) Revs. John J. Vogel; Michael J. Carcerano; Deacons William Bolduc; Steve Marsh. In Res., Revs. Lawrence Joseph; Leszek Semik.
Res.: 241 S. Valley Center, 91741-3854. Tel: 626-914-3941; Fax: 626-335-0059. Web: www.stdorothy.org.
School—215 S. Valley Center, 91741. Tel: 626-335-0772. Lay Teachers 14; Students 247.
Catechesis/Religious Program—Tel: 626-335-2811; Fax: 626-335-0057. Students 520.

GOLETA, SANTA BARBARA CO.

1—ST. MARK UNIVERSITY PARISH (1966) [CEM] Rev. John W. Love.
Res.: 6550 Picasso Rd., 93117. Tel: 805-968-1078; Fax: 805-968-3965. Web: www.saint-marks.net.
Catechesis/Religious Program—Sr. Eva Duarte, D.R.E. Students 130.

2—ST. RAPHAEL (1896) Revs. Bruce Correio; J. Lawrence Santos; Deacons Wayne Rascati; Stephen Montross; Noel Fuentes, Pastoral Assoc.
Res.: 5444 Hollister Ave., Santa Barbara, 93111-2308. Tel: 805-967-5641; Fax: 805-964-2988. Email: raphstgo@yahoo.com. Web: www.straphaelsb.com.
School—160 St. Joseph St., Santa Barbara, 93111. Tel: 805-967-2115; Fax: 805-683-9765. Email: sraph@sbceo.org. Web: www.sbceo.k12.ca.us/~sraph. Michelle Limb, Prin. Lay Teachers 12; Students 295.
Catechesis/Religious Program—Tel: 805-967-1641. Ana Solis-Cervantes, C.R.E. (Bilingual); Karen Froelicher, C.R.E. (English); John Vasellina, Youth Ministry. Students 562.

GRANADA HILLS, LOS ANGELES CO.

1—ST. EUPHRASIA (1963) Rev. Msgr. James C. Gehl.
Res.: 11766 Shoshone Ave., 91344. Tel: 818-360-4611; Fax: 818-360-2755. Email: karencolletti@hotmail.com. Web: www.steuphrasia.org.
School—Tel: 818-363-5515; Fax: 818-832-6678. Web: www.steuphrasiaschool.org. Lay Teachers 10; Students 257.
Catechesis/Religious Program—Tel: 818-368-4512. Email: resecretary@hotmail.com. Students 315.

2—ST. JOHN BAPTIST DE LA SALLE (1953) Revs. Robert L. Milbauer; Altaire Fernandez; Deacon Samuel Frias.
Res.: 10738 Hayvenhurst Ave., 91344. Tel: 818-363-2535; Fax: 818-360-7407.
School—16535 Chatsworth St., 91344. Tel: 818-363-2270; Fax: 818-832-8950. Web: www.dlsschool.com. Lay Teachers 22; Students 450.
Catechesis/Religious Program—Tel: 818-368-1514. Students 550.

GUADALUPE, SANTA BARBARA CO., OUR LADY OF GUADALUPE (1867), (Hispanic), [JC] Rev. Miguel B. Java (Philippines).
Res.: 1164 Obispo St., P.O. Box 897, 93434. Tel: 805-343-2181; Fax: 805-343-6642.
Catechesis/Religious Program—Tel: 805-343-4404. Students 330.

HACIENDA HEIGHTS, LOS ANGELES CO., ST. JOHN VIANNEY (1965) Rev. Msgr. Timothy E. Nichols; Revs. Ricardo De Alba, M.Sp.S.; Ricardo Henry Viveros; Deacons Jesse Martinez; Richard Noon. In Res., Rev. Michael J. Sezzi.
Res.: 1345 Turnbull Canyon Rd., 91745. Tel: 626-330-2269; Fax: 626-330-0220. Web: sjvhh.org.
Catechesis/Religious Program—Students 866.

HAWAIIAN GARDENS, LOS ANGELES CO., ST. PETER CHANEL (1986), (Mexican—Filipino), Revs. Lawrence T. Darnell, O.M.V.; Edward Broom, O.M.V.; Fernando Cuenca, O.M.V.; Vincenzo Antolini, O.M.V.; Craig MacMahon, O.M.V.
Res. & Church: 12001 E. 214th St., 90716-1117. Tel: 562-924-7591; Fax: 562-402-9411. Email: spcparish@yahoo.com. Web: www.spcomv.com.
Catechesis/Religious Program—Tel: 562-860-3637 (Spanish); 562-865-6498 (English). Students 1,304.

HAWTHORNE, LOS ANGELES CO., ST. JOSEPH (1915) Revs. Gregory C. King; Eugene S. Buhr (Retired); Edgardo Espinoza Puga (Peru). In Res., Rev. Edward C. Benioff.
Res.: 11901 Acacia Ave., 90250. Tel: 310-679-1139; Fax: 310-679-3034.
School—11886 Acacia Ave., 90250. Tel: 310-679-1014; Fax: 310-679-1310. Lay Teachers 21; Students 402.
Catechesis/Religious Program—Students 918.

HERMOSA BEACH, LOS ANGELES CO., OUR LADY OF GUADALUPE (1927) [CEM] Revs. Raymond Mallett, O.F.M.Conv.; Lazaro Sandoval, O.F.M.Conv. In Res., Revs. Peter Mallin, O.F.M.Conv.; Kevin Schindler-McGraw, O.F.M.Conv.; Steve Gross, O.F.M.Conv.; Allen Ramirez, O.F.M.Conv.
Res.: 244 Prospect Ave., 90254. Tel: 310-372-7077; Fax: 310-798-4051. Web: ourladyofguadalupechurch.org.
School—340 Massey Ave., 90254. Tel: 310-372-7486. Web: ourladyofguadalupeschool.org. Mrs. Cheryl Hunt, Prin. Lay Teachers 13; Students 171.
Catechesis/Religious Program—Students 300.

HUNTINGTON PARK, LOS ANGELES CO.

1—ST. MARTHA (1913), (Hispanic), Revs. Manuel Vazquez, M.Sp.S.; Mario Rodriguez, M.Sp.S.; Enrique Espinosa Ramirez, M.Sp.S.; Deacons Ciro Augusto Garza; Juan Antonio Romero.
6012 Seville Ave., 90255. In Res., Most Rev. Jose De Jesus Madera, M.Sp.S.
Res.: 6019 Stafford Ave., 90255. Tel: 323-585-0386; Fax: 323-585-4560. Email: stamartha@aol.com. Web: www.christthepriest.org.
Catechesis/Religious Program—Tel: 323-585-4941, Ext. 25 (Confirmation). Students 528.

2—ST. MATTHIAS (1913), (Latino), [JC] Rev. Mario Torres. In Res., Revs. Rody Ignatius Gorman (Retired); David Ochoa (Mexico).
Res.: 3095 E. Florence Ave., 90255. Tel: 323-588-2134; Fax: 323-588-4519. Email: parish-5850@la-archdiocese.org; stmatthias7125@gmail.com. 7125 Mission Pl., 90255.
School—7130 Cedar St., 90255. Tel: 323-588-7253; Fax: 323-588-1136. Email: stmatthiaspanthers@hotmail.com. Lay Teachers 12; Students 200.
Catechesis/Religious Program—Students 2,200.

INGLEWOOD, LOS ANGELES CO., ST. JOHN CHRYSOSTOM (1923), (Hispanic), Revs. Marcos Gonzalez; Javier Altuna, S.J. (Retired); Roberto Pirrone; Deacon Roberto Vasquez. In Res., Rev. Msgr. Sabato "Sal" A. Pilato.
Res.: 546 E. Florence Ave., 90301. Tel: 310-677-2736; Fax: 310-677-0584. Email: stjohnchrysostom@sbcglobal.net. Web: www.stjohnchrysostomparish.org.
School—530 E. Florence Ave., 90301. Tel: 310-677-5868; Fax: 310-677-3429. Email: sjcnet@earthlink.net. Religious Teachers 3; Lay Teachers 15; Students 260.
Catechesis/Religious Program—Tel: 310-674-3733. Email: dresjc@gmail.com. Students 801.

IRWINDALE, LOS ANGELES CO., OUR LADY OF GUADALUPE (1964) Rev. Joseph Canna; Deacons Gary Patterson; Roberto I. Chevez.
Res.: 16025 E. Cypress St., 91706-2199. Tel: 626-962-3649, Ext. 231; Fax: 626-337-3318.
Catechesis/Religious Program—Students 1,227.

LA CANADA FLINTRIDGE, LOS ANGELES CO., ST. BEDE THE VENERABLE (1951) Rev. Msgr. Antonio Cacciapuoti; Rev. Kevin A. Kester.
Res.: 215 Foothill Blvd., 91011. Tel: 818-949-4300; Fax: 818-790-9520. Web: www.bede.org.
School—(Grades K-8), 4524 Crown Ave., 91011. Tel: 818-949-4388; Fax: 818-790-7887. Email: stbedeeducationcenter@yahoo.com. Web: stbedeschool.net. Lay Teachers 18; Students 261.
Catechesis/Religious Program—Tel: 818-949-4322; Fax: 818-949-7887. Moira Arjani, D.R.E.; Joshua Godson, Teen Spirituality; Theresa Costanzo, Confirmation Coord. Students 516.

LA CRESCENTA, LOS ANGELES CO., ST. JAMES THE LESS (1955) Rev. Edward R. Dover; Deacons Joe Hegenbart; Raymond Lim.
Res.: 4625 Dunsmore Ave., 91214. Tel: 818-248-3442; Fax: 818-248-9332. Email: stjameschurch4@hotmail.com. Web: www.saintjamescatholicchurch.net.
School—(Grades K-5), 4635 Dunsmore Ave., 91214.

Tel: 818-248-7778; Fax: 818-248-5242. Lay Teachers 7; Students 93.
Catechesis/Religious Program—Students 175.

LA MIRADA, LOS ANGELES CO.

1—BEATITUDES OF OUR LORD (1964) Rev. Anthony J. Page; Deacon Hector M. Hidalgo.
Res.: 13013 S. Santa Gertrudes Ave., 90638. Tel: 562-943-1521; Fax: 562-902-7627. Email: beatitudeschurch@ca.rr.com. Web: beatitudesofourlord.org.
School—Tel: 562-943-3218; Fax: 562-943-9718. Web: bolschool.org. Lay Teachers 14; Students 252.
Catechesis/Religious Program—Tel: 562-943-5678; Fax: 562-943-9419. Email: beatitudesreo@ca.rr.com. Students 317.

2—ST. PAUL OF THE CROSS (1956) Revs. Joseph Visperas; Emmanuel Wharren Banico; Deacons Mark Orcutt; Timothy J. Roberto.
Res.: 14020 Foster Rd., 90638. Tel: 562-921-2914; Fax: 562-926-1514. Email: splamir@msn.com. Web: www.stpaulofthecross.org.
School—14030 Foster Rd., 90638. Tel: 562-921-2118; Fax: 562-802-2048. Lay Teachers 9; Students 163.
Catechesis/Religious Program—Tel: 562-921-4911. Students 205.

LA PUENTE, LOS ANGELES CO.

1—ST. JOSEPH (1919) Revs. Matthew T. Cumberland; Mario Arrellano, O.S.F.; Deacon Luis Gonzalez. In Res., Rev. Msgr. Patrick Joseph Staunton (Retired).
Res.: 550 N. Glendora Ave., 91744. Tel: 626-336-2001; Fax: 626-336-6010.
School—15650 E. Temple Ave., 91744. Tel: 626-336-2821; Fax: 626-369-8921. Carmelite Sisters 3; Lay Teachers 7; Students 200.
Catechesis/Religious Program—15650 E. Temple Ave., 91744. Tel: 626-336-1191; Fax: 626-934-7371. Students 302.

2—ST. LOUIS OF FRANCE (1955) Revs. Cesar A. Fernandez; Pedro A. Cobenas; Miguel B. Java (Philippines); Deacons Oscar Valeriano Jr.; Jaime S. Guerrero; Bernardo Zavala. In Res., Rev. Eric Anthony Lewis.
Res.: 13935 E. Temple, 91746-2098. Tel: 626-918-8314; Fax: 626-917-8413. Email: stlouis91746@roadrunner.com. Web: www.stlouisoffrance.org.
School—13901 E. Temple Ave., 91746-2021. Tel: 626-918-6210; Fax: 626-918-9549. Web: www.saint-louisoffrance.org. Lay Teachers 11; Students 199.
Catechesis/Religious Program—Tel: 626-918-7002; Fax: 626-917-8434. Email: stlouisre@roadrunner.com. Students 1,250.

LAKEWOOD, LOS ANGELES CO., ST. PANCRATIUS (1953) Rev. Msgr. Joseph F. Greeley.
Res.: 3519 St. Pancratius Pl., 90712. Tel: 562-634-6111; Fax: 562-634-7817. Email: stpanrectory@sbcglobal.net.
School—3601 St. Pancratius Pl., 90712. Tel: 562-634-6310; Fax: 562-633-0731. Lay Teachers 10; Students 174.
Catechesis/Religious Program—Tel: 562-634-1611; Fax: 562-634-2524. Email: stpanre@sbcglobal.net. Students 219.

LANCASTER, LOS ANGELES CO.

1—BLESSED JUNIPERO SERRA (Quartz Hill) (1987) Revs. Leo Dechant, C.S.J.; Ernest Candelaria, C.S.J., Parochial Vicar; Sylvan Schiavo, C.S.J., Parochial Vicar; Deacons Gary D. Poole; Paul Schwerdt; Rito R. Lopez. In Res., Rev. Giampietro Gasparin, C.S.J.
Res.: 6122 Azalea Dr., 93536-3700. Tel: 661-943-6475 (Res.); Fax: 661-943-6863.
Office: 42121 60th St. W., 93536-3767. Tel: 661-943-9314. Email: info@fatherserra.org. Web: www.fatherserra.org.
School—Father Serra Mission Bell Preschool, 42121 60th St. W., 93536-3767. Tel: 661-802-6375; Fax: 661-943-6863. Email: cespinosa@fatherserra.org.
Catechesis/Religious Program—Tel: 661-943-5912. Email: rmosich@fatherserra.org. Students 751.
Mission—St. Elizabeth 13845 Johnson Rd., Lake Hughes, Los Angeles Co. 93532. Tel: 661-724-9911.

2—SACRED HEART (1886) Revs. Thomas E. Baker; Hieu Chi Tran; Deacons John Charters; Ron Routolo; Dale Reynolds; Fermin Herrera. In Res., Rev. Michael Ohanete (Nigeria).
Res.: 565 W. Kettering St., 93534. Tel: 661-942-7122; Fax: 661-945-4255. Web: www.sacredheartlancaster.org.
School—625 W. Kettering St., 93534. Tel: 661-948-3613; Fax: 661-948-4486. Web: www.shsav.org. Lay Teachers 11; Students 313.
Catechesis/Religious Program—565 W. Kettering St., 93534. Tel: 661-948-3011; Fax: 661-948-2697. Students 1,083.

LOMITA, LOS ANGELES CO., ST. MARGARET MARY ALACOQUE (1937) Rev. Msgr. Marc V. Trudeau; Revs. Juan Silva; Bao Huy Nguyen; Deacons Craig Siegman; Rick Soria; Dan Wallace. In Res., Rev. Rowland Nwokocha.
Res.: 25429 Eshelman Ave., 90717.
Parish Center—25511 Eshelman Ave., 90717. Tel: 310-326-3364; Fax: 310-539-1570. Email: smmchur@yahoo.com.
School—(Grades K-8), 25515 Eshelman Ave., 90717. Tel: 310-326-9494; Fax: 310-326-2711. Linda Areyan, Librarian. Lay Teachers 13; Students 312.
Catechesis/Religious Program—Tel: 310-326-3364, Ext. 17. Email: smmcym@yahoo.com. Students 708.

LOMPOC, SANTA BARBARA CO.

1—LA PURISIMA CONCEPCION (1787) Rev. Thomas S. Cook.
Pastoral Center: 213 W. Olive Ave., 93436. Tel: 805-735-3068; Fax: 805-735-7649. Email: lapurcon@impulse.net. Web: www.lapurisima.org.
Rectory—324 S. I Street, 93436.
School—219 W. Olive Ave., 93436. Tel: 805-736-6210. Email: marcy.tijerina@lapurisima.org. Lay Teachers 11; Students 135.
Catechesis/Religious Program—Tel: 805-735-3068, Ext. 23. Email: suzann.oseguera@lapurisima.org. Students 209.

2—OUR LADY QUEEN OF ANGELS (1972) Rev. Msgr. John G. Fitzgerald.
Res.: 3495 Rucker Rd., 93436. Tel: 805-733-2735; Fax: 805-733-1235.
Catechesis/Religious Program—Tel: 805-733-3155. Students 250.

LONG BEACH, LOS ANGELES CO.

1—ST. ANTHONY (1902) Rev. Jose L. Magana.
Mailing Address: 600 Olive Ave., 90802. In Res., Rev. Brian D. Doran (Retired).
Res.: 540 Olive Ave., 90802. Tel: 562-590-9229; Fax: 562-590-9048. Email: community@stanthonylb.org. Web: stanthonylb.org.
School—855 E. 5th St., 90802. Tel: 562-432-5946; Fax: 562-435-8606. Email: elementary@stanthonylb.org. Lay Teachers 12; Students 215.
Catechesis/Religious Program—Tel: 562-590-9229, Ext. 34. Students 960.
Mission—Our Lady of Mt. Carmel Cambodian Catholic Center 600 Olive Ave., Los Angeles Co. 90806.

2—ST. ATHANASIUS (1933) Rev. Jose Luis Cuevas.
Res.: 5390 Linden Ave., 90805. Tel: 562-423-7986; Fax: 562-422-0306. Email: athanasius@charter.net. Web: www.stathanasius.us.
School—5369 Linden Ave., 90805. Tel: 562-428-7422. St. Francis Mission Community 3; Lay Teachers 9; Students 190.
Catechesis/Religious Program—Tel: 562-428-3494. Students 1,400.

3—ST. BARNABAS (1939) Rev. Msgr. Loreto Gonzales; Rev. George Reynolds; Deacons Carlito De Los Reyes; Alden Bohlig.
Res.: 3955 Orange Ave., 90807. Tel: 562-424-8595; Fax: 562-595-7875. Email: stbarnabaschurch@verizon.net. Web: www.stbarnabaslb.org.
School—(Grades PreK-8), 3980 Marron Ave., 90807. Tel: 562-424-7476; Fax: 562-981-3351. Lay Teachers 11; Students 242.
Catechesis/Religious Program—Tel: 562-988-6855; Fax: 562-981-8792. Email: religioused@sblb.org. Students 460.

4—ST. BARTHOLOMEW (1937) Rev. Msgr. Bernard M. Leheny.
Rectory—252 Granada Ave., 90803. Tel: 562-438-3826; Fax: 562-438-2227. Email: stbarts@sblb.org. Web: www.sblb.org.
Church: 5100 E. Broadway, 90803.
Catechesis/Religious Program—4545 E. 4th St., 90814. Tel: 562-439-1802. Students 322.

5—ST. CORNELIUS (1951) Revs. Michael Gleeson (Ireland); Pat Sheary, S.J.; Deacon Richard Boucher.
Res.: 5500 Wardlow Rd., 90808. Tel: 562-421-8966; Fax: 562-421-5096.
School—3330 Bellflower Blvd., 90808. Tel: 562-425-7813; Fax: 562-425-2743. Lay Teachers 14; Students 313.
Catechesis/Religious Program—Tel: 562-420-7613; Fax: 562-420-7613. Students 362.

6—ST. CYPRIAN (1944) Rev. Jason Souza.
Res.: 4714 Clark Ave., 90808. Tel: 562-421-9487; Fax: 562-496-1024.
School—5133 Arbor Rd., 90808. Tel: 562-425-7341; Fax: 562-421-1642. Email: info@stcyprianschool.org. Web: www.stcyprianschool.org. Lay Teachers 9; Students 210.
Catechesis/Religious Program—Tel: 562-420-6885; Fax: 562-421-1422. Students 247.

7—HOLY INNOCENTS (1923) Revs. G. Peter Irving III; Gilberto Monico.
Res.: 425 E. 20th St., 90806. Tel: 562-591-6924; Fax: 562-685-0556. Email: holyinnocents@gmail.com. Web: www.holyinnocentslongbeach.blogspot.com.
School—2500 Pacific Ave., 90806. Tel: 562-424-1018; Fax: 562-424-9250. Carmelite Sisters of the Most Sacred Heart 3; Lay Teachers 7; Students 162.
Catechesis/Religious Program—Students 250.

8—ST. JOSEPH (1955) Rev. James L. Halley; Deacons Shane Cuda; Don Gath; Thomas L. Halliwell. In Res., Rev. Harold LeRoy Ford (Retired).
Res.: 6220 E. Willow St., 90815. Tel: 562-594-4657; Fax: 562-431-7424.
School—6200 E. Willow St., 90815. Tel: 562-596-6115; Fax: 562-596-6725. Lay Teachers 20; Students 290.
Catechesis/Religious Program—6180 E. Willow St., 90815. Tel: 562-598-0519; Fax: 562-598-8720. Email: religioused@stjoseph.org. Students 240.

9—ST. LUCY (1944) Revs. Michael Roebert; John Quy V. Tran; Antonio Rodriguez; Deacon Victor Lopez.
Res.: 2344 Cota Ave., 90810. Tel: 562-424-9051; Fax: 562-988-0376. Email: lucy2344@gmail.com.
School—2320 Cota Ave., 90810. Tel: 562-424-9062; Fax: 562-424-8572. Lay Teachers 9; Students 200.
Catechesis/Religious Program—Tel: 562-997-0511. Students 493.

10—ST. MARIA GORETTI (1955) Rev. John Schiavone.
Res.: 3954 Palo Verde Ave., 90808-2298. Tel: 562-425-7459; Fax: 562-421-0475.
School—3950 Palo Verde Ave., 90808-2298. Tel: 562-425-5112. Email: principal@smgschool.com. Web: www.smgschool.com. Lay Teachers 9; Students 126.
Catechesis/Religious Program—3950 Palo Verde Ave., 90808-2298. Tel: 562-420-1321. Students 87.

11—ST. MATTHEW (1920) Revs. Guillermo Rodriguez (El Salvador); Gerald A. Meisel, Pastor Emeritus (Retired).
Res.: 672 Temple Ave., 90814. Tel: 562-439-0931; Fax: 562-434-7621. Email: stmatt@stmatthewlb.org. Web: stmatthewlb.org.
Catechesis/Religious Program—Tel: 562-434-6402. Students 243.

12—OUR LADY OF REFUGE (1948) Rev. Raymond D. Morales; Rev. Msgr. William J. O'Keeffe, Pastor Emeritus; Rev. Thomas Joseph Glynn (Retired); Deacon Roger Faubert.
Res.: 5195 Stearns St., 90815. Tel: 562-498-6641; Fax: 562-498-3344. Email: parish@olrs.org. Web: www.ourladyofrefuge.org.
School—5210 Los Coyotes Diagonal, 90815. Tel: 562-597-0819; Fax: 562-597-1419. Email: admin@olrs.org. Web: www.olrs.org. Lay Teachers 9; Students 129.
Catechesis/Religious Program—Tel: 562-597-3102; Fax: 562-494-4381. Email: sre@olrs.org. Students 275.

LOS NIETOS, LOS ANGELES CO., OUR LADY OF PERPETUAL HELP (1958), (Hispanic), Revs. Michael Sears; Josef Draugialis.
Res.: 8545 S. Norwalk Blvd., 90606. Tel: 562-692-3758; Fax: 562-695-4068.
Catechesis/Religious Program—Tel: 562-463-3389. Students 800.

LYNWOOD, LOS ANGELES CO.

1—ST. EMYDIUS (1924) Rev. Msgr. Emigdio Herrera; Revs. Mario F. Cabrera; Long Nguyen; Marco D. Reyes.
Res.: 10900 California Ave., P.O. Box 100, 90262-2094. Tel: 310-637-7095; Fax: 310-637-3319.
School—10990 California Ave., 90262. Tel: 310-635-7184; Fax: 310-605-3041. Sisters of the Holy Faith 1; Lay Teachers 14; Students 300.
Catechesis/Religious Program—Tel: 310-639-1249. Students 1,500.
Convent—10950 California Ave., 90262. Tel: 310-635-3264. Missionaries of Charity 6.

2—ST. PHILIP NERI (1948), (Hispanic), Revs. Juan Enriquez; Jose Mejia.
Res.: 4311 Olanda St., 90262. Tel: 310-632-7179; Fax: 310-632-5119. Email: parish-5860@la-archdiocese.org.
Pastoral Center—12435 Cookacre Ave., 90262.
School—12522 Stoneacre Ave., 90262. Tel: 310-638-0341; Fax: 310-638-9805. Lay Teachers 8; Students 176.
Catechesis/Religious Program—Students 1,446.

MALIBU, LOS ANGELES CO., OUR LADY OF MALIBU (1946) Rev. William F. Kerze.
Res.: 3625 Winter Canyon Rd., 90265. Tel: 310-456-2361; Fax: 310-456-3942. Email: parish@olmalibu.org. Web: www.olmalibu.org.
School—Tel: 310-456-8071; Fax: 310-456-7767. Lay Teachers 12; Students 95.
Catechesis/Religious Program—Tel: 310-456-8813. Students 77.

MANHATTAN BEACH, LOS ANGELES CO., AMERICAN MARTYRS (1930) Rev. Msgr. John F. Barry; Revs. Nicholas Assi; Joseph Kammerer; Deacons Chris Amantea; Derek A. Brown; Fred Rose; Richard (Dick) Williams.
Res.: 624 15th St., P.O. Box 3639, 90266. Tel: 310-545-5651; Fax: 310-546-9209. Email: rectory@americanmartyrs.org. Web: www.americanmartyrs.org.

School—1701 Laurel Ave., 90266-4805. Tel: 310-545-8559; Fax: 310-546-7219. Email: ams@americanmartyrs.org. Web: americanmartyrsschool.org. Lay Teachers 33; Students 671.
Catechesis/Religious Program—1701 Laurel Ave., 90266-4805. Tel: 310-546-4734; Fax: 310-546-9104. Students 1,380.
Spirituality Center—770 17th St., 90266-4805.

MAYWOOD, LOS ANGELES CO., ST. ROSE OF LIMA (1922), (Hispanic), Revs. Dario R. Miranda; Edward P. Soto (Retired); Primitivo Gonzalez; Daniel M. Martinez (Mexico).
Res.: *Rectory Office*, 4430 E. 60th St., 90270. Tel: 323-560-2381; Fax: 323-560-8537.
School—4422 E. 60th St., 90270. Tel: 323-560-3376; Fax: 323-560-8539. Lay Teachers 8; Students 170.
Catechesis/Religious Program—4430 E. 60th St., 90270. Tel: 323-560-0187. Students 702.

MISSION HILLS, LOS ANGELES CO., SAN FERNANDO REY MISSION (1797) Rev. Msgr. Francis J. Weber, Dir. Emeritus (Retired); Kevin Feeney, Dir.
Res.: 15151 San Fernando Mission Blvd., 91345. Tel: 818-361-0186; Fax: 818-361-3276.

MONROVIA, LOS ANGELES CO.

1—ANNUNCIATION (1949) Rev. Eugene Herbert; Deacon Gilbert Chavez. In Res., Rev. Msgr. Roland George Zimmerman (Retired), Pastor Emeritus; Revs. Ramon Marti, Sch.P.; Michael G. Callanan, M.M. (Retired).
Church Office & Mailing Address: 2701 S. Peck Rd., 91016. Tel: 626-447-6202; Fax: 626-447-9834.
Res.: 1307 E. Longden Ave., Arcadia, 91006.
School—(Grades K-8) Tel: 626-447-8262; Fax: 626-447-3841. Lay Teachers 5; Students 112.
Catechesis/Religious Program—Tel: 626-447-9834. Arcie Reza, D.R.E. Students 210.

2—IMMACULATE CONCEPTION (1904) Revs. Luis R. Lucchetti (Peru); Hung Ba Tran; Deacons Fred Conrey; Michael Salcido; Ronald Sanchez. In Res., Rev. Francis J. Cassidy (Retired).
Res.: 740 S. Shamrock Ave., 91016. Tel: 626-358-1166; Fax: 626-358-6466. Web: www.icmonrovia.org.
School—(Grades K-4), 726 S. Shamrock Ave., 91016. Tel: 626-358-5129; Fax: 626-358-3933. Web: www.icsmonrovia.org. Lay Teachers 5; Students 79.
Catechesis/Religious Program—Tel: 626-357-3010; Fax: 626-357-5299. Students 660.

MONTEBELLO, LOS ANGELES CO.

1—ST. BENEDICT (1906) Revs. Domingos A. Machado, O.A.R.; Felizardo J. Daganta, O.A.R.; John A. Gruben, O.A.R.; James D. McGuire, O.A.R.; Deacons David J. Estrada; Alfonso Castillo.
Res.: 1022 W. Cleveland Ave., 90640. Tel: 323-721-1184; Fax: 323-721-5075.
School—Tel: 323-721-3348; Fax: 323-721-8698. Frank Loya, Prin. Lay Teachers 21; Students 568.
Catechesis/Religious Program—1009 W. Madison Ave., 90640. Tel: 323-720-5760, Ext. 100. Raymundo Garcia, D.R.E. Students 599.

2—OUR LADY OF THE MIRACULOUS MEDAL (1950) Rev. Msgr. Juan Matas (Retired); Revs. Jude Umeobi; Roland Astudillo; Deacons Fred Rios; Frederick Peter Lara. In Res., Rev. Brian Delaney.
Res.: 820 N. Garfield Ave., 90640. Tel: 323-725-7578; Fax: 323-722-2654. Web: olmmparish.com.
School—840 N. Garfield Ave., 90640. Tel: 323-728-5435; Fax: 323-728-8038. Web: olmmschool.com. Daughters of Charity of St. Vincent de Paul 2; Lay Teachers 21; Aides 7; Students 491.
Catechesis/Religious Program—Tel: 213-725-6962; Fax: 323-722-2654. Email: maria@olmmparish.com. Students 41.

MONTEREY PARK, LOS ANGELES CO.

1—ST. STEPHEN MARTYR (1921) Rev. Albert H. Avenido, Priest Min.; Sr. Susan M. Slater, S.H.C.J., Parish Life Coord. In Res., Rev. Gregorius Tulus Sudarto, Indonesian Community Chap.
Res.: 320 W. Garvey Ave., 91754. Tel: 626-573-0427; Fax: 626-288-0260.
School—119 S. Ramona, 91754. Tel: 626-573-1716; Fax: 626-573-3251. Lay Teachers 9; Students 118.
Catechesis/Religious Program—Tel: 626-573-4517. Students 121.
Convent—122 S. Ramona Ave., 91754. Tel: 626-573-2417.

2—ST. THOMAS AQUINAS (1960) Rev. Gabriel Lui.
Res.: 1501 S. Atlantic Blvd., 91754. Tel: 323-264-4447; Fax: 323-264-2524. Email: saintthomasaquinas@sbcglobal.net.
School—Tel: 323-261-6563; Fax: 323-261-5972. Email: sta-eagles@yahoo.com.
Catechesis/Religious Program—Tel: 323-264-1338. Students 172.

MONTROSE, LOS ANGELES CO., HOLY REDEEMER (1925) Rev. Edward R. Dover; Rev. Msgr. John Kieran Foley, Pastor Emeritus (Retired); Rev. Timothy McGowan.
Res.: 2411 Montrose Ave., 91020. Tel: 818-249-2008; Fax: 818-249-5642. Email: hrccoffice@aol.com.
School—2361 Del Mar Rd., 91020. Tel: 818-541-9005; Fax: 818-541-9006. Web: holyredeemerschool.net. Lay Teachers 6; Students 87.
Catechesis/Religious Program—Tel: 818-249-2008, Ext. 443. Students 176.

MOORPARK, VENTURA CO., HOLY CROSS (1982) Rev. Msgr. Paul M. Albee; Rev. Paul Velazquez; Deacons J. Trinidad Andrade; Eduardo Castillo; Patrick Coulter; Derrel Craig; Dennis Flemming; Michael Kromm; Kevin Barry Mauch; Joseph Tumbarello.
Res., Parish Church & Administration Bldg.: 13955 Peach Hill Rd., 93021. Tel: 805-529-1397; Fax: 805-529-3939.
Catechesis/Religious Program—Tel: 805-529-0283; Fax: 805-529-5897. Students 739.

NEW CUYAMA, SANTA BARBARA CO., IMMACULATE CONCEPTION (1969) Deacon Ricardo Barragan, Parish Dir.
Res.: 4793 Cebrian St., P.O. Box 265, 93254. Tel: 661-766-2741; Fax: 661-766-2919.
Catechesis/Religious Program—Students 41.

NEWBURY PARK, VENTURA CO., ST. JULIE BILLIART (1969) Rev. Msgr. J. Michael Bunny (Retired); Rev. Michael Carrol; Deacons Louis Henschel; Barry Harper; David Nicholas Smith.
Res. & Church: 2475 Borchard Rd., 91320. Tel: 805-498-3602; Fax: 805-376-2332. Email: parish@stjuliesnp.org. Web: www.stjuliesnp.org.
Catechesis/Religious Program—Tel: 805-499-0979. Email: heather@stjuliesnp.org. Students 364.

NORTH HILLS, LOS ANGELES CO., OUR LADY OF PEACE (1944) Revs. Alexander Joseph Lewis; Peter Ha; Rodolfo Prado; Deacons Doug Jones; Rey Guiao; J. Francisco Sanchez; Ms. Rose M. Hernandez, Pastoral Assoc.
Res.: 15444 Nordhoff St., 91343. Tel: 818-894-1176; Fax: 818-894-3838. Email: olpeace@olpeace.org. Web: www.olpeace.org.
School—9022 Langdon Ave., 91343. Tel: 818-894-4059; Fax: 818-894-6759. Email: school@olpeace.org. Lay Teachers 11; Students 183.
Catechesis/Religious Program—Tel: 818-891-3578; Fax: 818-894-5498. Email: religioused@olpeace.org. Students 616.

NORTH HOLLYWOOD, LOS ANGELES CO.

1—ST. CHARLES BORROMEO (1921) Rev. Msgr. Robert J. Gallagher; Revs. Preston P. Passos; Julio Gonzalez. In Res., His Eminence Cardinal Roger Michael Mahony (Retired); Rev. Msgr. Lorenzo Miranda.
Res.: 10828 Moorpark St., 91602. Tel: 818-766-3838.
Parish Center—10834 Moorpark St., 91602. Tel: 818-766-3838; Fax: 818-766-5711. Email: generalinfo@scbnh.com.
School—10850 Moorpark St., 91602. Tel: 818-508-5359; Fax: 818-508-4511. Email: scbsoffice@pacbell.net. Web: www.stcharlescatholicschool.org. Lay Teachers 12; Students 274.
Catechesis/Religious Program—Tel: 818-980-1826. Students 358.

2—ST. JANE FRANCES DE CHANTAL (1948) Rev. Peter J. Liuzzi, O.Carm.; Deacons Richard Morgan; John Sprissler, O.Carm., Business Mgr.; Miss Gladys S. Rodriguez, Vicar of Pastoral/Spiritual Life. In Res., Rev. Thomas Batsis, O.Carm.
Priory: 13001 Victory Blvd., 91606.
Parish Center—12930 Hamlin St., 91606. Tel: 818-985-8600; Fax: 818-985-0606. Web: www.dechantalparish.org.
School—12950 Hamlin St., 91606. Tel: 818-766-1714. Mr. Edgar Sedano, Prin. Lay Teachers 10; Students 340.
Catechesis/Religious Program—Students 190.

3—ST. PATRICK (1948) Revs. Nicolas Sanchez, Admin.; Oliver Ortega.
Res. & Office: 6153 Cahuenga Blvd., 91606-5117. Tel: 818-752-3240; Fax: 818-769-6174.
School—10626 Erwin St., 91606. Tel: 818-761-7363; Fax: 818-761-6349. Email: razar@stpatrickcatholicschool.com. Web: stpatrickcatholicschool.com. Lay Teachers 11; Students 199.
Catechesis/Religious Program—Tel: 818-769-0263. Students 640.

4—ST. PAUL ASSYRIAN-CHALDEAN (1980), (Assyrian-Chaldean), [JC] Chorbishop Samuel Dinkha; Rev. Tomy Tomikeh (SPA).
13050 Vanowen St., 91605.
Res.: 6628 Alcove Ave., 91605. Tel: 818-765-3665; Fax: 818-765-0493.

5—SACRED HEART SYRIAC CATHOLIC PARISH (1996), (Jesus Sacred Heart Antiochene Syrian Catholic Mission, Antiochean Syriac Rite). Chorbishop Yousif Habash.
10837 Collins St., 91601. Tel: 818-766-7001; Fax: 818-766-7254.
Catechesis/Religious Program—Layla Toma, D.R.E. Students 42.

NORTHRIDGE, LOS ANGELES CO., OUR LADY OF LOURDES (1958) Rev. David C. Loftus, Admin.; Rev. Msgr. Peter C. Moran, Pastor Emeritus (Retired); Revs. Jeremiah E. O'Keeffe, Senior Priest; Ramon G. Valera, Pastoral Assoc.; Deacon Juan Galido.
Church: 18405 Superior St., 91325. Tel: 818-349-1500; Fax: 818-349-2516. Email: parishcenter@ollnr.org. Web: www.ollnr.org/parish.
Res.: 9800 Canby Ave., 91325.
School—18437 Superior St., 91325. Tel: 818-349-0245; Fax: 818-349-4156. Web: ollnr.org/school. Lay Teachers 14; Students 285.
Catechesis/Religious Program—Tel: 818-349-1285. Email: re@ollnr.org. Students 345.

NORWALK, LOS ANGELES CO.

1—ST. JOHN OF GOD (1950) Revs. Edward J. Dober; Laurence Gallagher, C.Ss.R.; John Moloney.
Res.: 13819 S. Pioneer Blvd., 90650. Tel: 562-863-5721; Fax: 562-406-3927. Web: www.sjogparish.org.
School—13817 S. Pioneer Blvd., 90650. Tel: 562-863-5721, Ext. 228; Fax: 562-406-3928. Web: www.sjogschool.com. Lay Teachers 11; Students 225.
Catechesis/Religious Program—Tel: 562-863-5721, Ext. 231. Students 627.

2—ST. LINUS (1961) Revs. Anthony J. Gomez; Huy Nguyen; Deacons Chuck Baker; John T. Cunneen; Mario Mejia.
Mailing Address: 13915 Shoemaker Ave., 90650. In Res., Rev. Brian Delaney.
Res.: 13921 Shoemaker Ave., 90650. Tel: 562-921-6649; Fax: 562-921-5150. Email: stlinus@stlinus.org. Web: www.stlinus.org.
School—13913 Shoemaker Ave., 90650. Tel: 562-921-0336; Fax: 562-926-9077. Lay Teachers 12; Students 261.
Catechesis/Religious Program—Tel: 562-921-5179. Students 345.

OJAI, VENTURA CO., ST. THOMAS AQUINAS (1919) Revs. Steven Ochoa, O.S.A.; William Tom Davis, O.S.A., Pastor Emeritus; Deacon Chris Gorman.
Res.: 185 St. Thomas Dr., 93023. Tel: 805-646-4338; Fax: 805-646-5928.
Catechesis/Religious Program—Tel: 805-646-0307. Students 200.

OXNARD, VENTURA CO.

1—ST. ANTHONY (1959) Revs. Albert Sang V. Tran; Porfirio Alvarez; Deacons Andrew Cottam; Oscar Duke; George Angel Garcia; James Henry; Joe Kennedy; Jon McPheeters; Donald Pinedo; Roy Edward Sadowski.
Res.: 2511 S. C St., 93033. Tel: 805-486-7301; Fax: 805-486-3142.
School—2421 S. C. St., 93033. Tel: 805-487-5317; Fax: 805-486-1537. Lay Teachers 12; Students 200.
Catechesis/Religious Program—Students 76.

2—MARY STAR OF THE SEA (1963), (Filipino—Mexican), Rev. Fidel Hernandez, O.A.R.; Deacon Harold "Hal" Parish; Revs. John Michael Rafferty, O.A.R.; Frank T. Wilder, O.A.R.; Deacons Alfonso Flores; Dante Tibor Manalo; Noe Jose Morales.
Res.: 463 W. Pleasant Valley Rd., 93033. Tel: 805-486-6133; Fax: 805-483-6913.
Catechesis/Religious Program—Tel: 805-483-9313. Students 1,021.

3—OUR LADY OF GUADALUPE PARISH (1958), (Hispanic), Revs. Roberto Saldivar, M.Sp.S.; Agustin Rodriguez, M.Sp.S.; Guillermo Flores, M.Sp.S.; Deacons Arturo Godinez; Francisco Lopez; Henry Barajas; Alejandro Zendejas Marron.
Res.: 500 N. Juanita Ave., P.O. Box 272, 93030. Tel: 805-483-0987; 805-483-1481; Fax: 805-486-2434. Email: olgpar@aol.com.
School—530 N. Juanita Ave., 93030. Tel: 805-483-5116; Fax: 805-385-7242. Lay Teachers 12; Students 339.
Catechesis/Religious Program—Tel: 805-487-4737; Fax: 805-486-2434. Students 747.
Mission—Christ the King 535 Cooper Rd., Ventura Co. 93030. Tel: 805-483-3499.

4—SANTA CLARA (1885) Rev. Msgrs. Jon F. Majarucon; Charles Francis O'Gorman, Senior Priest (Retired); Revs. Michael S. Grieco; Lucio Juarez; Deacons Jerome Bettencourt; John G. Castorena; Vince Crawford; Michael Holguin; Vincent Charles Kelch; Leo Lacbain; Lawrence James Lopez; Fidel Ramirez; Dano L. Ramos; Milton Rosenberg; Raymond Vasquez Jr.
Res.: 323 S. E St., 93030. Tel: 805-487-3891; Fax: 805-487-4733. Email: parish@santaclaraparish.org. Web: www.santaclaraoxnard.parishesonline.com.
School—324 S. E St., 93030. Tel: 805-483-6935; Fax: 805-487-6686. Lay Teachers 14; Students 222.
Catechesis/Religious Program—Tel: 805-487-6742. Students 1,249.
Mission—Santa Clara Chapel 1333 Ventura Blvd., Ventura Co. 93030. Tel: 805-485-7335; Fax: 805-981-1183.

PACIFIC PALISADES, LOS ANGELES CO., CORPUS CHRISTI (1950) Rev. Msgrs. Liam J. Kidney; Richard Affrim.
Parish Office: 880 Toyopa Dr., 90272. Tel: 310-454-1328; Fax: 310-573-5021. Email: parishmail@corpuschristichurch.com. Web: corpuschristichurch.com.
Rectory—887 Toyopa Dr., 90272.
School—890 Toyopo Dr., 90272. Tel: 310-454-9411; Fax: 310-454-3776. Sisters of St. Louis (Monaghan)

1; Lay Teachers 25; Students 255.
Catechesis/Religious Program—Tel: 310-454-1328, Ext. 226. Students 137.
Convent—875 Toyopa Dr., 90272. Tel: 310-454-6262.

PACOIMA, LOS ANGELES CO.

1—GUARDIAN ANGEL (1956), (Hispanic), Revs. Steven Guitron; Fredy B. Rosales.
Res.: 10886 Lehigh Ave., 91331. Tel: 818-899-2345; Fax: 818-899-2537. Email: guardianangelchurch1@yahoo.com.
School—10919 Norris Ave., 91331. Tel: 818-896-1113; Fax: 818-834-4014. Lay Teachers 9; Students 212.
Catechesis/Religious Program—Tel: 818-899-8907. Students 370.

2—MARY IMMACULATE (1954), (Spanish), Revs. William Antone, O.M.I.; Porfirio Garcia, O.M.I.; John M. Curran, O.M.I.
Res.: 10390 Remick Ave., 91331. Tel: 818-899-0278; Fax: 818-890-9878. Email: maryimmaculateparish@yahoo.com. Web: www.maryimmaculateparish.org.
School—Tel: 818-834-8551; Fax: 818-896-7996. Web: miseagles.org. Lay Teachers 10; Students 258.
Catechesis/Religious Program—Tel: 818-899-2111. Students 1,013.

PALMDALE, LOS ANGELES CO., ST. MARY (1890) Revs. Vaughn P. Winters; Fidelis C. Omeaku; Roland Astudillo; Deacons Elvys C. Perez; Ed Caputo. In Res., Rev. Thomas White, State Prison Chap.
Res.: 1600 E. Ave., R-4, 93550. Tel: 661-947-3306; Fax: 661-947-8687.
School—Tel: 661-273-5555; Fax: 661-273-3845. Kate Laferriere, Prin. Lay Teachers 13; Students 278.
Catechesis/Religious Program—Tel: 661-273-5554; Fax: 661-273-5525. Students 1,775.
Mission—Our Lady of the Desert 35647 87th St. E, Littlerock, Los Angeles Co3620 Antelope Valley Rd., Acton, 93543. Tel: 661-269-8837.

PANORAMA CITY, LOS ANGELES CO., ST. GENEVIEVE (1950) Revs. Alden J. Sison; John Kyebasuuta.
Res.: 14061 Roscoe Blvd., 91402. Tel: 818-894-2261; Fax: 818-893-4284. Web: www.stgenevievechurch.org.
School—St. Genevieve Elementary School, 14024 Community St., 91402. Tel: 818-892-3802; Fax: 818-893-8143. Web: spartansonline.org. Sisters 2; Lay Teachers 25; Students 625.
High School—13967 Roscoe Blvd., 91402. Tel: 818-894-6417; Fax: 818-892-9853. Lay Teachers 35; Students 600.
Catechesis/Religious Program—Tel: 818-892-7177. Students 630.

PARAMOUNT, LOS ANGELES CO., OUR LADY OF THE ROSARY (1913), (Hispanic—Tongan), Rev. Jesse C. Galaz; Deacons Oscar A. Corcios; Jorge Perez. In Res., Revs. Alojzy Gryszko, S.D.B. (Poland); William A. Gil Londono.
Res.: 14815 S. Paramount Blvd., 90723. Tel: 562-633-1126; Fax: 562-633-3192. Email: olrspr@aol.com.
School—Our Lady of the Rosary School, 14813 S. Paramount Blvd., 90723. Tel: 562-633-6360; Fax: 562-633-2641. Sisters of the Daughters of Mary and Joseph 1; Lay Teachers 8; Students 200.
Catechesis/Religious Program—Tel: 562-602-0086. Students 884.

PASADENA, LOS ANGELES CO.

1—ST. ANDREW (1886), (Hispanic), Revs. Paul A. Sustayta; Jose Corral. In Res., Rev. Msgr. Tobias P. English, Pastor Emeritus (Retired).
Res.: 311 N. Raymond Ave., 91103. Tel: 626-792-4183; Fax: 626-792-4456.
School—(Grades K-8), 42 Chestnut St., 91103. Tel: 626-796-7697; Fax: 626-796-1931. Sisters of the Holy Names of Jesus and Mary 3; Lay Teachers 10; Students 205.
Catechesis/Religious Program—140 Chestnut St., 91103. Tel: 626-792-8153, Ext. 201; Fax: 626-792-4456. Students 430.

2—ASSUMPTION OF THE BLESSED VIRGIN MARY (1950) Revs. Gerard O'Brien; Joseph C. Wah; Deacon Jim Crowley.
Res.: 2640 E. Orange Grove Blvd., 91107. Tel: 626-792-1343; Fax: 626-792-0052. Web: assumptionchurch.net.
School—2660 E. Orange Grove Blvd., 91107. Tel: 626-793-2089; Fax: 626-793-4070. Web: abvmschool-.net. Ms. Christine Hunter, Prin. Lay Teachers 19; Students 313.
Catechesis/Religious Program—Tel: 626-792-6844; Fax: 626-792-6844. Email: mhuckler@abvmpasadena.org. Students 225.

3—ST. PHILIP THE APOSTLE (1921) Revs. Joseph V. Moniz; Dennis P. Marrell; Deacons William Landa; Richard J. Medina.
151 S. Hill Ave., 91106.
Res.: 1462 E. Del Mar Ave., 91106. Tel: 626-793-0693; Fax: 626-793-0733. Email: cjurecki@stphiliptheapostle.org. Web: www.stphiliptheapostle.org/church.
School—1363 Cordova St., 91106. Tel: 626-795-9691; Fax: 626-795-9946. Email: jramirez@stphiliptheapostle.org. Web: www.stphiliptheapostle.org/school. Lay Teachers 29; Students 533.
Catechesis/Religious Program—Students 335.

PICO RIVERA, LOS ANGELES CO.

1—ST. FRANCIS XAVIER (1939) Revs. Enrique Huerta; Jorge A. Penaloza, Pastor Emeritus (Retired); Arturo Valadez; Deacon Carlos R. Rivas.
Res.: 4245 S. Acacia Ave., 90660. Tel: 562-699-8527; Fax: 562-699-5331.
Catechesis/Religious Program—Students 711.

2—ST. HILARY (1950) Rev. Joshua Peter Lee.
Res.: 5465 Citronell Ave., 90660. Tel: 562-942-7300; Fax: 562-948-3760.
School—Tel: 562-942-7361; Fax: 562-801-9131. Web: sthilaryschool.org. School Sisters of Notre Dame 1; Lay Teachers 10; Students 243.
Catechesis/Religious Program—5401 S. Citronell Ave., 90660. Tel: 562-942-7018. Email: st.hilarydre@yahoo.com. Students 415.
Convent—5333 S. Citronell Ave., 90660. Tel: 562-942-7151.

3—ST. MARIANA DE PAREDES (1951), (Hispanic), Revs. David Gallardo; Lazaro Garcia Revilla.
Res.: 7922 S. Passons Blvd., 90660. Tel: 562-949-8240; Fax: 562-942-2405. Email: parish@stmariana.org. Web: www.stmariana.org.
School—7911 Buhman Ave., 90660. Tel: 562-949-1234; Fax: 562-948-3855. Web: www.smschargers.org. Karen Lloyd, Prin. Lay Teachers 11; Students 250.
Catechesis/Religious Program—Tel: 562-949-5653; Fax: 562-949-9277. Rebecca Salcido, C.R.E. Students 500.

POMONA, LOS ANGELES CO.

1—ST. JOSEPH (1886) Revs. Roberto Jaranilla Jr.; Anh-Tuan Dominic Nguyen. In Res., Rev. Richard Van De Water.
Res.: 1150 W. Holt Ave., 91768. Tel: 909-629-4101; Fax: 909-623-0265. Email: stjosephpomona@verizon.net. Web: mysite.verizon.net/stjosephpomona.
School—1200 W. Holt Ave., 91768. Tel: 909-622-3365; Fax: 909-469-5146. Lay Teachers 11; Students 194.
Catechesis/Religious Program—Tel: 909-629-1404. Students 650.
Convent—1180 W. Holt Ave., 91768-3429. Tel: 909-629-1308.

2—ST. MADELEINE (1963) Rev. Alejandro Aclan; Rev. Msgr. Andrew Stanislaus Tseu, Pastor Emeritus (Retired); Rev. Wayne E. Noble.
Res.: 931 E. Kingsley Ave., 91767. Tel: 909-629-9495; Fax: 909-623-7148.
Catechesis/Religious Program—Students 452.

3—SACRED HEART (1935) Rev. Alberto Arreola, O.M.I.; Deacon Carlos Madrigal; Sr. Theresa F.M. DeFeo, C.S.S.F., Pastoral Assoc.
Res.: 1215 S. Hamilton Blvd., 91766. Tel: 909-622-4553; Fax: 909-623-0841.
Catechesis/Religious Program—Students 1,000.

RANCHO PALOS VERDES, LOS ANGELES CO., ST. JOHN FISHER (1961) Rev. Msgrs. David A. Sork; Eugene A. Gilb, Pastor Emeritus (Retired); Rev. Khoa Luong Mai.
Res.: 5448 Crest Rd., 90275. Tel: 310-377-5571; Fax: 310-377-6303. Email: info@sjf.org. Web: www.sjf.org.
School—5446 Crest Rd., 90275. Tel: 310-377-2800; Fax: 310-377-3863. Email: principal@sjf.org. Lay Teachers 21; Students 235.
Catechesis/Religious Program—5400 Crest Rd., 90275. Tel: 310-377-4573. Email: religioused@sjf.org. Margaret Johnson, D.R.E. Students 625.

REDONDO BEACH, LOS ANGELES CO.

1—ST. JAMES (1892) Rev. Msgr. Michael M. Meyers, Pastor Emeritus; Rev. John Lee; Deacon Robert J. Miller. In Res., Rev. James F. Kavanagh (Retired).
Parish Office & Mailing Address: 124 N. Pacific Coast Hwy., 90277. Tel: 310-372-5228; Fax: 310-379-5552.
Res.: 124 N. Pacific Coast Hwy., 90277.
School—4625 Garnet St., Torrance, 90503. Tel: 310-371-0416; Fax: 310-371-8377. Sisters of St. Joseph of Carondelet 3; Lay Teachers 12; Students 328.
Catechesis/Religious Program—Tel: 310-379-3221. Diana Holly, D.R.E. Students 302.

2—ST. LAWRENCE MARTYR (1955) Rev. Msgr. Paul J. Dotson; Rev. Richard Sunwoo; Deacons Frank Dieter; James A. Egnatuk; Dale Sheckler.
Res.: 1900 S. Prospect Ave., 90277-6099. Tel: 310-540-0329; Fax: 310-540-8999.
School—1950 Prospect Ave., 90277-6003. Tel: 310-540-3049; Fax: 310-316-0888. Lay Teachers 15; Students 306.
Catechesis/Religious Program—Tel: 310-316-4460. Students 617.

RESEDA, LOS ANGELES CO., ST. CATHERINE OF SIENA (1949) Revs. Paul Gerard Griesgraber; Raul Cortes; Jose Humberto Pineda; Hernan Canete; Deacon Pedro Lira.
Res.: 18115 Sherman Way, 91335. Tel: 818-343-2110; Fax: 818-343-1018.
School—18125 Sherman Way, 91335. Tel: 818-343-9880; Fax: 818-343-6851. Lay Teachers 15; Students 310.
Catechesis/Religious Program—Tel: 818-996-4588. Students 650.

ROWLAND HEIGHTS, LOS ANGELES CO., ST. ELIZABETH ANN SETON (1981) Revs. John H. Keese; Antony J. Gaspar; Peter Zhai, S.V.D.; Rev. Msgr. Michael F. Killeen, Pastor Emeritus (Retired); Deacons Steven V. Hillman; Peter K. Chu.
Res.: 18090 Via Amorosa, 91748. Tel: 626-964-3629. Email: stelizabethannseton@yahoo.com.
Church & Mailing Address: 1835 Larkvane Rd., 91748. Tel: 626-964-3629; Fax: 626-913-2209.
Catechesis/Religious Program—Tel: 626-965-5792; Fax: 626-513-0580. Students 558.

SAN DIMAS, LOS ANGELES CO., HOLY NAME OF MARY (1957) Revs. Richard J. Danyluk, SS.CC., Admin.; Peadar Cronin, SS.CC.; Deacons Alfred H. Austin; Marv Estey; Jose Guadamuz; Mario Lopez; Ron Hale, Business Mgr.
724 E. Bonita Ave., 91773.
Res.: 764 Dickens Ln., La Verne, 91750. Tel: 909-599-1243; Fax: 909-599-4230. Web: www.hnmparish.org.
School—Tel: 909-542-0449, Ext. 224; Fax: 909-592-3884. Web: holynamemaryschool.org. Lay Teachers 16; Students 324.
Catechesis/Religious Program—Tel: 909-599-1243, Ext. 232. Charles Martinez, D.R.E. Students 681.

SAN FERNANDO, LOS ANGELES CO.

1—ST. FERDINAND (1902) Revs. Thomas Coughlin, O.M.I.; Manuel "Meme" Villarreal, O.M.I.
Office: 1109 Coronel St., 91340. Tel: 818-365-3967; Fax: 818-365-0067.
School—1012 Coronel St., 91340. Tel: 818-361-3264; Fax: 818-361-5894. Sisters of St. Joseph of Carondelet 1; Religious Sisters of Charity 1; Lay Teachers 10; Students 220.
Catechesis/Religious Program—Tel: 818-361-1813. Students 412.

2—SANTA ROSA (1927), (Hispanic), Revs. Stanislaw Zowada, O.M.I. (Poland); Jose Antonio Ponce, O.M.I.
Res.: 668 S. Workman St., 91340. Tel: 818-361-4617; Fax: 818-365-8599.
School—Santa Rosa Bishop Alemany Catholic School, 1316 Griffith St., 91340. Tel: 818-361-5096; Fax: 818-361-2259. Lay Teachers 10; Students 155.
Catechesis/Religious Program—Students 760.

SAN GABRIEL, LOS ANGELES CO.

1—ST. ANTHONY (1945), (Hispanic—Filipino), Revs. Austin C. Doran; Patrick Mbazuigwe.
Res.: 1901 S. San Gabriel Blvd., 91776. Tel: 626-288-8912; Fax: 626-288-3730.
School—1905 S. San Gabriel Blvd., 91776. Tel: 626-280-7255; Fax: 626-280-3870. Maria Christina Buckowski, Prin. Lay Teachers 11; Students 170.
Catechesis/Religious Program—Tel: 626-288-5511; Fax: 626-288-5210. Stephanie Ramos, D.R.E.; Lizette Bermudez, Confirmation Coord. Students 486.
Convent—626 E. Marshall St., 91776. Tel: 626-288-2200.

2—SAN GABRIEL MISSION (1771) [CEM], (Old Mission) Revs. Stephen Niskanen, C.M.F.; Theo Fuentes, C.M.F.; Arnold J. Gonzalez, C.M.F.; Tony Diaz, C.M.F.; Anthony Quyen Nguyen, C.M.F.; James Curran, O.M.I.
Church and Res.: 428 S. Mission Dr., 91776. Tel: 626-457-3035; Fax: 626-282-5308.
School—San Gabriel Mission Elementary School, 416 S. Mission Dr., 91776. Tel: 626-281-2454; Fax: 626-281-4817. Dominican Sisters 2; Lay Teachers 13; Students 240.
High School—San Gabriel Mission High School, 254 S. Santa Anita St., 91776. Tel: 626-282-3181; Fax: 626-282-4209. Girls College Prep. Parish School Sisters 4; Lay Teachers 17; Girls 249.
Catechesis/Religious Program—Tel: 626-457-3041. Students 30.
Convent—412 S. Mission Dr., 91776. Tel: 626-284-9585.

SAN MARINO, LOS ANGELES CO., SAINTS FELICITAS AND PERPETUA (1938) Rev. Paul K. Fitzpatrick; Sr. Eva Bryan, R.S.C.
Res.: 1190 Palomar Rd., 91108. Tel: 626-796-0432; Fax: 626-796-0363. Web: www.ssfp.org.
School—2955 Huntington Dr., 91108. Tel: 626-796-8223. Lay Teachers 14; Students 248.
Catechesis/Religious Program—Students 159.

SAN PEDRO, LOS ANGELES CO.

1—HOLY TRINITY (1924) Rev. Msgr. Joseph Brennan; Revs. Augustine Chang; Joseph Van Vu.
Parish Center:—209 N. Hanford Ave., 90732. Tel: 310-548-6535; Fax: 310-833-1134.
Church: 1292 W. Santa Cruz St., 90732.

School—1226 W. Santa Cruz St., 90732. Tel: 310-833-0703; Fax: 310-833-5219. Mrs. Linda Wiley, Prin. Lay Teachers 28; Students (incl. preschool) 558.
Catechesis/Religious Program—Tel: 310-833-3500. Students 580.

2—MARY, STAR OF THE SEA (1889) Revs. John F. Provenza; Lorenzo De Dominici (Retired); Brian Nunes; Deacon William Garcia.
Res.: 870 W. 8th St., 90731. Tel: 310-833-3541; Fax: 310-833-9254. Email: office@marystar.org. Web: www.marystar.org.
School—Tel: 310-831-0875; Fax: 310-831-0877. Email: marystarelementary@sbcglobal.net. Lay Teachers 10; Students (incl. preschool) 263.
High School—Tel: 310-547-1138; Fax: 310-547-1827. Email: marystarhigh@aol.com. Web: www-.marystarhigh.com. Priests 4; Lay Teachers 25; Students 510.
Catechesis/Religious Program—810 W. 8th St., 90731. Tel: 310-833-3933; Fax: 310-832-1257. Students 352.

3—ST. PETER (1965), (Hispanic), Revs. Claudio De Agostini, C.S.J.; Bruno De Santi, C.S.J.; Joseph Scalco, C.S.J.
Res.: 338 N. Grand Ave., 90731-2006. Tel: 310-831-5360; Fax: 310-831-0415.
Catechesis/Religious Program—Tel: 310-561-2153. Students 385.

SANTA BARBARA, SANTA BARBARA CO.

1—HOLY CROSS (1973) Revs. Ludo DeClippel, C.J. (Belgium); Alfred Verstreken, C.J. (Belgium); Deacons Nicholas Curran; Randy Saake; Rodolfo Naranjo Cabello.
Res.: 1740 Cliff Dr., 93109. Tel: 805-962-0411; Fax: 805-564-6921. Email: parish@holycross.sbcoxmail.com. Web: www.rc.net/losangeles/holycross.
Catechesis/Religious Program—Tel: 805-962-7311. Email: dirreled@holycross.sbcoxmail.com. Students 191.

2—OLD MISSION SANTA BARBARA (1786) [CEM] Rev. Daniel Barica, O.F.M.
Res.: 2201 Laguna St., 93105. Tel: 805-682-4151; Fax: 805-687-7841. Email: stbabs@yahoo.com. Web: www.saintbarbaraparish.org.
Catechesis/Religious Program—Tel: 805-682-4713, Ext. 140. Students 75.

3—OUR LADY OF GUADALUPE (1928), (Hispanic), Rev. Rafael Marin-Leon.
Mailing Address: 227 N. Nopal St., 93103.
Res.: 801 Jennings Ave., 93103. Tel: 805-965-4060; Fax: 805-965-3386.
Catechesis/Religious Program—Tel: 805-962-4441. Students 374.

4—OUR LADY OF MOUNT CARMEL (1856) Rev. Msgr. Stephen N. Downes; Revs. Maurice K. O'Mahony (Retired); Carrol O'Sullivan (Retired).
Res.: 1300 E. Valley Rd., 93108. Tel: 805-969-6868; Fax: 805-565-5959. Email: dellastrada1300@gmail.com. Web: www.olmc-montecito.com.
School—530 Hot Springs Rd., 93108. Tel: 805-969-5965; Fax: 805-565-9841. Lay Teachers 15; Students 210.
Catechesis/Religious Program—Tel: 805-969-4868. Students 151.

5—OUR LADY OF SORROWS (1856) Revs. Paul Devot, S.J.; Denis E. Collins, S.J.; Michael W. Ravenkamp, S.J.; Joseph Morris, S.J.; Augusto Berrio, S.J.; Deacons William Sangster; Luis Cabello; Gregory Robert Calderon; Arturo Gonzalez; Jose Ascencion Ramirez; Jose Antonio Trujillo. In Res., Rev. Christopher Soh, S.J.
Res.: 21 E. Sola St., 93101. Tel: 805-963-1734; Fax: 805-965-6461.
School—Notre Dame, 33 E. Micheltorena St., 93101. Tel: 805-965-1033; Fax: 805-965-1034. Anne Chenoweth, Prin. Lay Teachers 10; Students 148.
Catechesis/Religious Program—Tel: 805-966-4941. Students 310.

6—SAN ROQUE (1953) [JC] Rev. Msgr. Michael J. Jennett.
Res.: 325 Argonne Cir., 93105. Tel: 805-687-5215; Fax: 805-682-9778. Email: office@sanroqueparish.org.
Catechesis/Religious Program—Tel: 805-682-1097. Email: education@sanroqueparish.org. Students 150.

SANTA CLARITA, LOS ANGELES CO.

1—BLESSED KATERI TEKAKWITHA (1998) Rev. Msgr. Michael J. Slattery; Rev. David L. Whorton, Admin.; Deacon Edward Littleton.
Mailing Address: 22508 Copper Hill Dr., 91350-4299.
Res.: 28142-28130 Seco Canyon Rd., 91390. Tel: 661-296-3180; Fax: 661-296-7854. Email: secretary@blessedkateriparish.org. Web: www.blessedkateriparish.org.
Catechesis/Religious Program—Tel: 661-296-6945. Email: re@blessedkateriparish.org. Students 1,215.

2—ST. CLARE (1977) Rev. Olin Mayfield; Rev. Msgr. Edmond M. Renehan, Pastor Emeritus (Retired); Rev. Malcolm Ambrose.
Res.: 27341 Camp Plenty Rd., 91351. Tel: 661-252-3353; Fax: 661-252-1539. Web: www.st-clare.org.
Catechesis/Religious Program—Tel: 661-252-6950; Fax: 661-299-6594. Peggy Pigors, D.R.E.; Nancy Fishwick, Youth Min. Students 722.

3—OUR LADY OF PERPETUAL HELP (1944) Rev. Msgr. Richard Martini; Revs. Donatus Ekenachi (Nigeria); Raymond Marquez; Deacon Richard Karl.
Res.: 23233 Lyons Ave., 91321-2632. Tel: 661-259-2276; Fax: 661-259-1873. Email: olphnewhall@la.twcbc.com. Web: www.olph-church.org.
School—Tel: 661-259-1141; Fax: 661-259-8254. Lay Teachers 11; Students 261.
Catechesis/Religious Program—Tel: 661-259-4266; Fax: 661-259-2084. Students 1,400.

SANTA FE SPRINGS, LOS ANGELES CO., ST. PIUS X (1954), (Hispanic), Revs. Pedro J. Lopez; Peter Duc Tran; Francis V. Aguilar.
Res.: 10827 Pioneer Blvd., 90670. Tel: 562-863-8734; Fax: 562-868-0051. Email: stpiusx10@aol.com. Web: www.stpiusx10.org.
School—Tel: 562-864-4818; Fax: 562-864-7120. Lay Teachers 11; Students 200.
Catechesis/Religious Program—Tel: 562-868-2389. Students 619.

SANTA MARIA, SANTA BARBARA CO.

1—ST. JOHN NEUMANN (Santa Barbara) (1986) Rev. Msgr. Emigdio Herrera; Rev. Rolando A. Sierra, C.Ss.R. (Venezuela); Deacons Ricardo Berumen; Jose Ojeda; Roberto Lupian Valdez.
Res.: 966 W. Orchard, 93458-2063. Tel: 805-922-7099; Fax: 805-346-1747.
Catechesis/Religious Program—Tel: 805-922-5288. Students 866.

2—ST. LOUIS DE MONTFORT (Santa Barbara) (1963) [JC] Revs. Charles L. Hofschulte, C.J.; Mark L. Newman, C.J.; John A. Mayhew, C.J.; Alidor Mikobi, C.J. (Democratic Republic of Congo); Franklin Minzaki, C.J. (Democratic Republic of Congo); Deacons Raul Blanco; Christopher Boerger; Richard Carmody; Alfredo Espinoza; Douglas Halvorsen; Robert Maciel; Antonio Mejia; Robert Schaefer. Email: rmshaefer@live.com; Shawn Stanley Vedro.
Res.: 5075 Harp Rd., 93455. Tel: 805-937-4555; Fax: 805-934-2805. Email: sldmchurch@sldm.org. Web: www.sldm.org.
School—5095 Harp Rd., 93455. Tel: 805-937-5571; Fax: 805-937-3181. Email: school_office@sldmschool.org. Web: www.sldm-school.org. Lay Teachers 9; Students 260.
Catechesis/Religious Program—Tel: 805-937-8363. Email: ckuhbander@sldm.org. Students 730.
Mission—St. Anthony's Church 270 Helena St., Los Alamos, 93440. Tel: 805-344-1604.

3—ST. MARY OF THE ASSUMPTION (1905) [JC] Rev. Riz J. Carranza; Rev. Msgrs. James Philip Colberg, Pastor Emeritus (Retired); John Ukaegbu; Deacons Francisco Javier Lopez; Zenon Nawrocik; Dennis Pearson; Steven Pent.
Res.: 414 E. Church St., 93454. Tel: 805-922-5826; Fax: 805-922-1986. Email: parish@stmary-sm.org. Web: www.stmary-sm.org.
School—424 E. Cypress St., 93454. Tel: 805-925-6713; Fax: 805-925-3815. Email: stmsch@verizon.net. Web: stmarysm.ca.campusgrid-.net.home. Lay Teachers 10; Students 207.
Preschool—209 S. School St., 93454. Tel: 805-346-6541; Fax: 805-347-7658. Email: stmpresch@verizon.net. Teachers 4; Students 39.
Catechesis/Religious Program—Tel: 805-925-2007. Email: osf@stmary-sm.org (First Communion Prog.); meliwar@aol.com (Confirmation & Youth Min.). Students 556.

SANTA MONICA, LOS ANGELES CO.

1—ST. ANNE (1951) Rev. Rafael Venegas. In Res., Rev. Christopher Onyenobi (Nigeria).
Res.: 2011 Colorado Ave., 90404. Tel: 310-829-4411; Fax: 310-829-9006. Email: stanneschurch@yahoo.com. Web: www.stanneshrine.org.
School—2015 Colorado Ave., 90404. Tel: 310-829-2775; Fax: 310-829-3945. Lay Teachers 9; Students 219.
Catechesis/Religious Program—Tel: 310-829-4040. Students 200.

2—ST. CLEMENT (1904) Rev. Anthony Gonzalez.
Res.: 3102 Third St., 90405. Tel: 310-396-2679; Fax: 310-396-4239. Email: pastoraloffice@stclementscc.org.
Catechesis/Religious Program—Students 90.

3—ST. MONICA (1886) Rev. Msgr. Lloyd A. Torgerson; Rev. Timothy Clement Klosterman.
725 California Ave., 90403. Tel: 310-393-9287; Fax: 310-319-9758. Email: info@stmonica.net. Web: www.stmonica.net. In Res., Revs. Willie Raymond, C.S.C.; David Guffey, C.S.C.
School—Elementary School., 1039 Seventh St., 90403. Tel: 310-451-9801; Fax: 310-394-6001. Email: lynda.auer@stmonicaelem.com. Web: www.stmonicaelem.com. Lay Teachers 12; Students 302.
High School—1030 Lincoln Blvd., 90403. Tel: 310-394-3701; Fax: 310-458-1353. Web: www.stmonicahs.org. Sisters 2; Lay Teachers 45; Students 550.
Catechesis/Religious Program—Tel: 310-395-8903; Fax: 310-458-2064. Students 510.

SANTA PAULA, VENTURA CO.

1—OUR LADY OF GUADALUPE (1929), (Hispanic), [CEM] Rev. Charles R. Lueras, C.R.I.C.
Res.: 427 N. Oak St., 93060. Tel: 805-525-3716; Fax: 805-525-3788.
Catechesis/Religious Program—423 N. Oak St., 93060. Tel: 805-525-2225. Students 620.
Convent—432 N. Oak St., 93060. Tel: 805-525-9207; Fax: 805-933-2729. Email: opolgs@aol.com. Web: crmsdusadelegation.org.

2—ST. SEBASTIAN (1896) Revs. Pasquale Vuoso, C.R.I.C.; Thomas J. Dome, C.R.I.C.; Deacon Alfonso A. Guilin.
Res.: 235 N. Ninth St., 93060. Tel: 805-525-2149; Fax: 805-933-5520.
School—325 E. Santa Barbara St., 93060. Tel: 805-525-1575; Fax: 805-933-0190. Lay Teachers 20; Students 176; Preschool 44.
Catechesis/Religious Program—Tel: 805-525-3201. Email: stsebastianccd@verizon.net. Students 129.

SHERMAN OAKS, LOS ANGELES CO., ST. FRANCIS DE SALES (1938) Revs. Michael Wakefield; Kevin John Larkin, Pastor Emeritus (Retired); Mario Pacheco.
Res.: 13360 Valleyheart Dr., S., 91423. Tel: 818-784-0105; Fax: 818-784-4807.
Church: Moorpark St. at Dixie Canyon Ave., 91423.
School—13368 Valleyheart Dr., 91423. Tel: 818-784-9573; Fax: 818-784-9649. Lay Teachers 18; Students 340.
Catechesis/Religious Program—Tel: 818-782-1907. Students 300.

SIERRA MADRE, LOS ANGELES CO., ST. RITA (1908) Rev. Msgr. Richard G. Krekelberg; Deacons John Hull; Manuel Valencia.
Res.: 50 E. Alegria Ave., 91024. Tel: 626-355-1292; Fax: 626-355-2290. Web: st-rita.org.
School—322 N. Baldwin Ave., 91024. Tel: 626-355-6114; Fax: 626-355-0713. Lay Teachers 15; Students 275.
Catechesis/Religious Program—Tel: 626-355-3841; Fax: 626-355-3841. Students 197.

SIMI VALLEY, VENTURA CO.

1—ST. PETER CLAVER (1972) Rev. Msgr. Gary P. Bauler; Rev. William R. Crowe; Deacons Brian Clements; Melecio Zamora.
Res.: 5649 E. Pittman St., 93063. Tel: 805-526-6499; Fax: 805-526-7233. Email: saintpeterclaver@aol.com. Web: www.saintpeterclaver.org.
School—(Grades PreSchool-K), 5670 Cochran St, 93063. Tel: 805-526-2244. Lay Teachers 11; Students 90.
Catechesis/Religious Program—Tel: 805-526-0680; Fax: 805-526-3658. Email: pspcre@aol.com. Students 624.

2—ST. ROSE OF LIMA (1921) Revs. Joseph P. Shea; Budi Wardhana; Deacons Peter Wilson Jr.; Terence Reibenspies; Louis Homero Fernandez.
Res.: 1305 Royal Ave., 93065. Tel: 805-526-1732; Fax: 805-526-0067. Email: parish@strosesv.com.
School—1325 Royal Ave., 93065. Tel: 805-526-5304; Fax: 805-526-0939. Web: srls.org. Lay Teachers 18; Students 252.
Catechesis/Religious Program—Tel: 805-526-5513; Fax: 805-520-7638. Students 525.

SOLVANG, SANTA BARBARA CO., OLD MISSION SANTA INES (1804), (Spanish), Revs. Gerald Barron, O.F.M-.Cap.; Brendan P. Buckley, O.F.M.Cap.; Deacon Ancelmo Aguirre. In Res., Revs. Peter Banks, O.F.M.Cap.; Harold Snider, O.F.M.Cap.
Res.: 1760 Mission Dr., P.O. Box 408, 93464. Tel: 805-688-4815; Fax: 805-686-4468. Email: office@missionsantaines.org. Web: www.missionsantaines.org.
Catechesis/Religious Program—Tel: 805-688-4138. Students 225.

SOUTH EL MONTE, LOS ANGELES CO., EPIPHANY (1956), (Hispanic), Revs. Juan Francisco Gonzalez; Jose A. Ortiz (El Salvador); Jose Jesus Martinez; Deacon Doroteo Gonzalez.
Res.: 10911 Michael Hunt Dr., 91733. Tel: 626-442-6262; Fax: 626-575-1738. Email: epiphanysem@att.net. Web: epiphanychurchsem.com.
School—10915 Michael Hunt Dr., 91733. Tel: 626-442-6264; Fax: 626-442-6074. Lay Teachers 9; Students 137.
Catechesis/Religious Program—Tel: 626-448-3636; Fax: 626-448-0894. Students 541.

SOUTH GATE, LOS ANGELES CO., ST. HELEN (1931) Revs. Samuel W. Ward; Jaime M. Villalobos (Peru); Deacon Cecilio G. Pena.

Res.: 3170 Firestone Blvd., 90280. Tel: 323-563-3522; Fax: 323-563-0161.
School—9329 Madison Ave., 90280. Tel: 323-566-5491; Fax: 323-566-2810. Sisters of Notre Dame 1; Lay Teachers 10; Students 361.
Catechesis/Religious Program—9314 Madison Ave., 90280. Tel: 323-569-9550; Fax: 323-569-5103. Students 1,000.

SOUTH PASADENA, LOS ANGELES CO., HOLY FAMILY (1910) Rev. Jose Parathanal; Rev. Msgr. Clement J. Connolly, Pastor Emeritus (Retired); Rev. Niall Finbarr O'Leary, Dir. of Spirituality (Retired); Cambia Smith, Parish Life Dir.
Pastoral Center—1527 Fremont Ave., 91030. Tel: 626-799-8908; Fax: 626-799-0423.
School—1301 Rollin St., 91030. Tel: 626-799-4354; Fax: 626-403-6180. Web: www.holyfamily.net/school. Carolyn Strong, Prin. Lay Teachers 16; Students 320.
Catechesis/Religious Program—Tel: 626-403-6118; Fax: 626-403-6199. Students 570.

SUN VALLEY, LOS ANGELES CO., OUR LADY OF THE HOLY ROSARY (1937), (Hispanic—Filipino), Revs. Richard Zanotti, C.S.; Ariel Durian, C.S.
Res.: 7800 Vineland Ave., 91352-4596. Tel: 818-765-3350; Fax: 818-765-3170.
School—7802 Vineland Ave., 91352. Tel: 818-765-4897; Fax: 818-765-5791. Servant Sisters of the Blessed Sacrament 4; Lay Teachers 9; Students 224.
Catechesis/Religious Program—Tel: 818-982-4248. Diana Cruz, D.R.E. Students 600.
Mission—Our Lady of Zapopan 7824 Lankershim Blvd., North Hollywood, Los Angeles Co. 91605. Tel: 818-503-8920.

SYLMAR, LOS ANGELES CO., ST. DIDACUS (1957), (Hispanic), Rev. Robert E. J. Garon; Deacon Raymond Camacho. In Res., Rev. Msgr. Peter L. Amy, Pastor Emeritus (Retired); Rev. Norman A. Supancheck.
Res.: 14339 Astoria St., 91342. Tel: 818-367-6181; Fax: 818-367-0604. Email: sdparish@stdidacus.org. Web: www.stdidacus.org.
School—14325 Astoria St., 91342. Tel: 818-367-5886; Fax: 818-364-5486. Lay Teachers 10; Students 215.
Catechesis/Religious Program—Tel: 818-367-4155. Students 740.

TEMPLE CITY, LOS ANGELES CO., ST. LUKE THE EVANGELIST (1946) Revs. Mark A. Strader; Joseph Yang.
Mailing Address: *Parish Administrative Center*, 5605 Cloverly Ave., 91780.
Res.: 9451 E. Broadway, 91780. Tel: 626-291-5900; Fax: 626-287-2332. Email: web@stluketemplecity.org. Web: www.stluketemplecity.org.
School—5521 Cloverly Ave., 91780. Tel: 626-291-5959; Fax: 626-285-5367. Lay Teachers 13; Students 185.
Catechesis/Religious Program—Tel: 626-291-5925. Students 220.

THOUSAND OAKS, VENTURA CO., ST. PASCHAL BAYLON (1960) Revs. David Heney; Thai Le; Deacons Mitchell Ito; David Lawrence; James Robinson; Guillermo Rodriguez.
Res.: 155 E. Janss Rd., 91360. Tel: 805-496-0222; Fax: 805-379-2506. Email: parish@stpaschal.org. Web: www.stpaschal.org.
School—(Grades K-8), 154 E. Janss Rd., 91360. Tel: 805-495-9340; Fax: 805-778-1509. Email: school@stpaschal.org. Suzanne Duffy, Prin. Lay Teachers 16; Students 350.
Catechesis/Religious Program—Tel: 805-496-0222, Ext. 115. Students 500.

TORRANCE, LOS ANGELES CO.

1—ST. CATHERINE LABOURE (1947) Revs. John O'Byrne; John K. Vo (Vietnam); Tovia Lui.
Res.: 3846 Redondo Beach Blvd., 90504. Tel: 310-323-8900; Fax: 323-321-0486. Email: parish-6140@la-archdiocese.org. Web: stcatchurch.org.
School—Tel: 310-324-8732; Fax: 310-324-2471. Mrs. Kathleen Gorze, Prin. Lay Teachers 19; Students 400.
Catechesis/Religious Program—16831 Ainsworth, 90504. Tel: 310-515-6033; Fax: 310-515-5619. Students 565.

2—NATIVITY (1924) Revs. Alfred Hernandez; Gerhart Habison.
Res.: 1447 Engracia Ave., 90501-3234. Tel: 310-328-2776; Fax: 310-328-0508.
School—2371 Carson, 90501. Tel: 310-328-5387; Fax: 310-328-5365. Lay Teachers 9; Students 269.
Catechesis/Religious Program—Tel: 310-320-6673. Students 419.

TUJUNGA, LOS ANGELES CO., OUR LADY OF LOURDES (1920) Revs. Freddie T. Chua; Ronald Schmidt, S.J.
Res.: 10321 Tujunga Canyon Blvd., 91042.
Parish Business Office: 7344 Apperson St., 91042. Tel: 818-352-3218; Fax: 818-352-2738.
School—7324 Apperson St., 91042. Tel: 818-353-1106; Fax: 818-951-4276. Lay Teachers 13; Students 220.
Catechesis/Religious Program—Tel: 818-353-3053. Email: rosieramos.oll@gmail.com. Students 275.

VALINDA, LOS ANGELES CO., ST. MARTHA (1958), (Hispanic—Filipino), Revs. Mauricio O. Goloran III (Philippines); Ornoldo Cherrez (Ecuador); Rolando Clarin, O.S.C. (Philippines); Deacon Victor Tiambeng. In Res., Rev. Msgr. Aidan M. Carroll.
Res.: 444 N. Azusa Ave., 91744-4299. Tel: 626-964-4313; Fax: 626-913-2953. Email: spirit@stmarthaval.org. Web: www.stmarthaval.org.
School—Tel: 626-964-1093; Fax: 626-912-2014. Sisters of the Love of God 5; Lay Teachers 4; Students 210.
Catechesis/Religious Program—Tel: 626-912-2581. Students 894.
Youth Ministry Confirmation Program—Tel: 626-964-1903; Fax: 626-965-7034. Students 279.

VAN NUYS, LOS ANGELES CO.

1—ST. BRIDGET OF SWEDEN (1955) Revs. Paul Gerard Griesgraber; Jose Humberto Pineda; Deacon Ramon Rivera.
Res.: 16711 Gault St., 91406. Tel: 818-782-7180; Fax: 818-782-7184. Web: www.sbos.org.
School—7120 Whitaker, 91406. Tel: 818-785-4422; Fax: 818-785-0490. Email: stbridgetof1@yahoo.com. Lay Teachers 9; Students 200.
Catechesis/Religious Program—Liz Cruz, D.R.E. Students 225.

2—ST. ELISABETH (1919), (Hispanic), Revs. John Bruno, R.C.J.; Rodolfo D'Agostino, R.C.J.; Vito Di Marzio, R.C.J.; Deacon Salvador Espana.
Res.: 6635 Tobias Ave., 91405. Tel: 818-779-1756; Fax: 818-785-4492.
School—Tel: 818-779-1766; Fax: 818-779-1768. Lay Teachers 11; Students 245.
Catechesis/Religious Program—Tel: 818-779-1772. Students 653.

VENICE, LOS ANGELES CO., ST. MARK (1923) Rev. Michael Rocha. In Res., Rev. Daniel C. White.
Res.: 940 Coeur d'Alene Ave., 90291. Tel: 310-821-5058; Fax: 310-821-7031. Email: info@st-mark.net. Web: www.st-mark.net.
School—912 Coeur d'Alene Ave., 90291. Tel: 310-821-6612; Fax: 310-822-6101. Lay Teachers 20; Students 180.
Catechesis/Religious Program—Tel: 310-822-1201. Students 300.

VENTURA, VENTURA CO.

1—OUR LADY OF THE ASSUMPTION (1954) Revs. Stephen V. Davoren; Steven Correz; Deacons Rodger Adams; Daniel Bojorquez; Michael Burns; James M. Farley; Raul Gonzalez; Donald Huntley; Philip Joerger; Aurelio Robles Macias; Ed Mlls; Charles Philip Wessler; Bill Wilson. In Res., Rev. Msgr. Donal Mulcahy, Pastor Emeritus (Retired).
Res.: 3175 Telegraph Rd., 93003-3283. Tel: 805-642-7966; Fax: 805-642-7635. Email: parish@olavta.org. Web: olaventura.com.
School—3169 Telegraph Rd., 93003-3282. Tel: 805-642-7198; Fax: 805-642-7110. Lay Teachers 14; Students 320.
Catechesis/Religious Program—Tel: 805-642-7966, Ext. 118. Students 450.

2—SACRED HEART (1966) Revs. Cyprian Carlo; Daniel A. O'Sullivan, Pastor Emeritus (Retired); Bill Bolton; Deacons John William Barry; Philip Conforti; Fernando M. Flores; Humberto Guzman.
Res.: 10800 Henderson Rd., 93004. Tel: 805-647-3235; Fax: 805-647-8087. Email: rectory@sacredheartventura.org. Web: www.sacredheartventura.org.
School—(Grades K-8), 10770 Henderson Rd., 93004. Tel: 805-647-6174; Fax: 805-647-2291. Email: office@sacredheartventura.org. Lay Teachers 10; Students 217.
Catechesis/Religious Program—Tel: 805-647-3235, Ext. 306. Email: re@sacredheartventura.org. Students 335.

3—SAN BUENAVENTURA MISSION (1782), (Hispanic), Revs. Thomas J. Elewaut; Peter Damian Fernando, Senior Priest; Jiwan A. Kim, O.F.M.Conv.; Deacons Mark Lawrence Banda; Teodoro Landeros; Alfonso Cruz Mendez.
Res.: 211 E. Main St., 93001. Tel: 805-643-4318; Fax: 805-643-7831. Email: mission@sanbuenaventuramission.org. Web: www.sanbuenaventuramission.org.
School—Tel: 805-643-1500. Lay Teachers 10; Students 142.
Catechesis/Religious Program—Students 513.

VERNON, LOS ANGELES CO., HOLY ANGELS PARISH OF THE DEAF (1987) Rev. Thomas Schweitzer; Deacons David Rose; Lawrence McGloin.
Res.: 4433 Santa Fe Ave., 90058. Tel: 323-587-2096; Fax: 323-587-7193. Web: hacofthedeaf.org. Email: info@hacofthedeaf.org.
Catechesis/Religious Program—Students 80.

WALNUT, LOS ANGELES CO., ST. LORENZO RUIZ (1991) Revs. Tony P. Astudillo; Severo Kuupuo.
Res.: 747 Meadowpass Rd., 91789. Tel: 909-595-9545; Fax: 909-594-3940. Web: www.stlovenzo.org.
Catechesis/Religious Program—Tel: 909-468-1812. Students 512.

WEST COVINA, LOS ANGELES CO., ST. CHRISTOPHER (1954) Rev. Msgr. Nestor D. Rebong; Revs. Francis Dang Hoang, S.J., Chap. (Vietnamese Community); Thomas Han, Chap. (Korean Community); Francisco Ho Seok Jin; Deacons Jesse Batacan; Andrew Cho; Douglas Moloney; Loc Nguyen; Ching Dimaculangan, Business Mgr.
Parish Center—629 S. Glendora Ave., 91790. Tel: 626-960-1805; Fax: 626-851-0595. Web: www.stchriswestcovina.parishesonline.com.
School—900 W. Christopher St., 91790. Tel: 626-960-3079; Fax: 626-338-7910. Web: www.saintchristopherparishschool.com. Mrs. Mary Bachman, Prin. Lay Teachers 12; Students 187.
Catechesis/Religious Program—Tel: 626-338-2937. Elizabeth Hudson, D.R.E. Students 406.

WEST HOLLYWOOD, LOS ANGELES CO.

1—ST. AMBROSE (1922) Rev. William P. Wolfe.
Res.: 1281 N. Fairfax Ave., 90046-5205. Tel: 323-656-4433; Fax: 323-656-6634. Email: stambrosech@aol.com. Web: www.st-ambrose.com.

2—ST. VICTOR (1906) Rev. Msgr. Jeremiah Murphy. In Res., Rev. Msgr. George John Parnassas (Retired).
Res.: 8634 Holloway Dr., 90069. Tel: 310-652-6477; Fax: 310-652-6478. Email: info@saintvictor.org. Web: saintvictor.org.
Catechesis/Religious Program—

WESTLAKE VILLAGE, LOS ANGELES CO., ST. JUDE (1970) Rev. Peter Foran; Deacons Dick Dornan; Joseph Manion; Bill Smith.
Res.: 32032 W. Lindero Canyon Rd., 91361-4270. Tel: 818-889-1279; Fax: 818-889-3405. Email: stjude@saintjudetheapostle.org. Web: stjudeswv.org.
School—32036 W. Lindero Canyon Rd., 91361-4270. Tel: 818-889-9483. Web: www.stjudeschool.org/school. Lay Teachers 15; Students 245.
Catechesis/Religious Program—Tel: 818-889-0612. Email: cindy@stjudeswv.org. Students 311.

WESTLAKE VILLAGE, VENTURA CO., ST. MAXIMILIAN KOLBE (1992) Rev. Jarlath Dolan; Deacons John Kruer; Vince Tomkovicz.
Res.: 5801 Kanan Rd., 91362. Tel: 818-991-3915; Fax: 818-991-7152. Email: kolbe@stmaxchurch.org. Web: www.stmaxchurch.org.
Catechesis/Religious Program—Tel: 818-991-3915, Ext. 112. Students 36.

WHITTIER, LOS ANGELES CO.

1—ST. BRUNO (1955) Revs. Michael Reardon; James Bradley, S.D.S.; Deacon P. Michael Freeman.
Res.: 15740 Citrustree Rd., 90603. Tel: 562-947-5637; Fax: 562-943-3193. Email: stbruno@stbrunochurch.org. Web: www.stbrunochurch.org.
School—15700 Citrustree Rd., 90603. Tel: 562-943-8812; Fax: 562-943-2172. Web: www.saintbrunoschool.com. Lay Teachers 17; Students 313.
Catechesis/Religious Program—Tel: 562-943-2510; 562-947-5637. Email: re@stbrunochurch.org. Students 582.
Convent—10734 S. Widener Ave., 90603. Tel: 562-947-1177.

2—ST. GREGORY THE GREAT (1951) Rev. Ikechukwu Ikeocha. In Res., Rev. Finbarr Divine (Retired).
Res.: 13935 Telegraph Rd., 90604. Tel: 562-941-0115; Fax: 562-941-3785.
School—13925 Telegraph Rd., 90604. Tel: 562-941-0750; Fax: 562-903-7325. Lay Teachers 13; Students 210.
Catechesis/Religious Program—Tel: 562-944-8311; Fax: 562-941-4380. Students 380.

3—ST. MARY OF THE ASSUMPTION (1893) Revs. Jose Luis Chavez, C.Ss.R.; Donald B. Willard, C.Ss.R.; Scott Katzenberger, C.Ss.R. In Res., Revs. Arthur Frost, C.Ss.R. (Retired); William Adams, C.Ss.R. (Retired); Michael McAndrew, C.Ss.R.; Anthony Phuc Nguyen, C.Ss.R.
Res.: 7215 S. Newlin Ave., 90602-1266. Tel: 562-698-0107; Fax: 562-696-1617. Web: st-maryschurch.org.
School—7218 S. Pickering Ave., 90602. Tel: 562-698-0253; Fax: 562-698-0206. Lay Teachers 12; Students 205.
Catechesis/Religious Program—Tel: 562-693-3764. Email: drecruces@yahoo.com. Students 670.

WILMINGTON, LOS ANGELES CO.

1—HOLY FAMILY (1929), (Hispanic), Rev. Ruben Rocha (Mexico).
Res. & Pastoral Center: 1011 E. "L" St., 90744. Tel: 310-834-6333; Fax: 310-834-9038. Email: holyfamily@hfamwil.org.
School—1122 E. Robidoux St., 90744. Tel: 310-518-1440; Fax: 310-518-1257. Email: holyfmly@hfswilm.org. Web: www.hfswilm.org. Mrs. Gabriela Moya, Preschool Dir. Lay Teachers 3; Students 16.
Catechesis/Religious Program—Tel: 310-549-0011. Students 685.

2—SS. PETER AND PAUL (1865) Revs. Raymond L.

Perez, O.Praem.; Michael U. Perea, O.Praem.; Martin Benzoni, O.Praem. In Res., Rev. Patrick Foutts, O.Praem.
Res.: 515 W. Opp St., 90744. Tel: 310-834-5215; Fax: 310-834-4685. Email: sppc@sbcglobal.net. Web: www.sppc.us.
School—706 Bayview Ave., 90744. Tel: 310-834-5574; Fax: 310-834-1601. Email: spp_school@yahoo.com. Web: www.sppcatholicschool-.com. Lay Teachers 10; Students 215.
Catechesis / Religious Program—Students 348.

WINNETKA, LOS ANGELES CO., ST. JOSEPH THE WORKER (1956), (Hispanic—Vietnamese), Revs. Kevin E. Rettig; Hugo R. Neyra; Francis Ty Bui; Deacon Heriberto "Ed" Vega; Mike Stafford, Parish Business Mgr.
Res.: 19808 Cantlay St., 91306. Tel: 818-341-6634; Fax: 818-341-3875.
Parish Center—19808 Cantlay St., 91306. Web: www.sjwchurch.com.
School—19812 Cantlay St., 91306. Tel: 818-341-6616; Fax: 818-341-1102. Web: www.saintjosephtheworkerschool.net. Sr. Barbara Joseph Wilson, C.S.J., Prin. Lay Teachers 17; Students 300.
Catechesis / Religious Program—Tel: 818-998-4166. Web: www.sjwchurch.com. Students 632.

WOODLAND HILLS, LOS ANGELES CO.

1—ST. BERNARDINE OF SIENA (1962) Revs. Robert J. McNamara; Daniel A. Fox; Deacons Jerome Cellner; Dale Taufer; Steven Ellms; Jesus S. Pasos. In Res., Rev. Msgr. Richard Hayes Murray, Pastor Emeritus (Retired).
Res.: 24410 Calvert St., 91367. Tel: 818-888-8200; Fax: 818-888-5046. Web: www.stbernardine.org.
School—6061 Valley Circle Blvd., 91367. Tel: 818-340-2130; Fax: 818-340-3417. Lay Teachers 17; Students 317.
Catechesis / Religious Program—6061 Valley Circle Blvd., 91367. Tel: 818-340-1440. Students 448.

2—ST. MEL (1955) Rev. Msgr. Helmut A. Hefner; Rev. Vivian B. Lima.
Res.: 20870 Ventura Blvd., 91364. Tel: 818-340-6020; Fax: 818-340-0261. Email: parish@stmel.org. Web: www.stmelparish.org.
School—20874 Ventura Blvd., 91364. Tel: 818-340-1924; Fax: 818-347-4426. Web: www.stmel.org. Lay Teachers 35; Students 563.
Catechesis / Religious Program—Tel: 818-340-6020, Ext. 1022. Email: pandre@stmel.org. Students 225.

Chaplains of Public Institutions
Non-Catholic Hospitals/Institutions

LOS ANGELES. *Cedar Sinai Medical Center*. Rev. Lester S. Avestruz, Chap.
8700 Beverly Blvd. Rm. 2508, 90048. Tel: 310-423-8040.
L.A. City Fire Dept., Tel: 213-978-3820.
L.A. County Fire Dept. Rev. Robert A. Folbrecht, Chap. Tel: 626-960-1136.
L.A. County / University of Southern California Hospital.
Norris Cancer and USC University Hospital, St. Camillus Center for Pastoral Care, 1911 Zonal Ave., 90033. Tel: 323-225-4461; 213-223-9047 (AIDS Center); Fax: 323-225-9096. His Eminence Roger Cardinal Mahony, D.D., V.G., Chap. (Retired), Revs. Christopher D. Ponnet, Chap., Mark Martinez, Chap., Bro. Adam Bacerra, F.S.P., Chap., Sisters Mary Jean Ferry, B.V.M., Chap., Theresa Hann, O.S.F., Chap., Angela Pacheco, C.S.J., Chap., Martha Vega, S.S.S., Chap., Yolanda Vega, S.S.S., Chap., Leticia Delgado, Chap., Vu Ngo, Chap., Mr. William Rice, Chap., Manuel Torres, Chap.
L.A. Police Dept. Rev. Michael P. McCullough, Chap.
Employee Assistance Unit, 150 N. Los Angeles St., 90012. Tel: 213-485-0703.
LAC + USC Medical Center. Revs. Robert Jones, C.M., Chap., Christopher Dennis Ponnet, Chap., Los Angeles County-USC Medical Center, Deacon Walter J. Hanson.
Metropolitan Detention Center. (Federal Institution), 535 N. Alameda St., 90012. Tel: 213-253-9575. Rev. Frank Tinajero, S.V.D.
Queenscare / Hollywood Presbyterian Medical Center. Bro. Larry Moen, C.M.F.

CAMARILLO. *Youth Correctional Facility, California Youth Authority*, 3100 Wright Rd., 93010-8307. Catherine Conneally-Salazar, Chap.

DOWNEY. *Rancho Los Amigos Medical Center*, 7601 E. Imperial Hwy., 90242. Deacon Ralph Riera, Chap. Tel: 562-920-3340.

DUARTE. *City of Hope Medical Center*, 1500 E. Duarte Rd., 91010. Tel: 626-256-4673, Ext. 63898.

LANCASTER. *Immigration and Naturalization Service*, Mira Loma Facility, 45100 N. 60th St. W., 93536. Tel: 661-949-3811. Imelda Bermejo, Chap.

LOMPOC. *Lompoc Federal Correctional Institution*, 3600 Guard Rd., 93436-2705. Tel: 805-736-4154, Ext. 725. Federal Intensive Confinement Center.
US Penitentiary, 3901 Klein Rd., 93436. Tel: 805-735-2771, Ext. 450 &.
Vandenberg Air Force Base. Rev. David J. Ivey. 30SW/HC, 587 Utah St., Bldg. 16200, Vandenberg AFB, 93437-6309.

LONG BEACH. *VA Long Beach Healthcare System*Rev. David Craig, Chap.
Veterans Affairs Medical Center. Rev. Craig David, Chap.
5901 E. 7th St., 90822. Tel: 562-494-5418.

NORTHRIDGE. *Northridge Hospital Medical Center.* Rev. Ambrose Udoji, Chap.

NORWALK. *California Youth Authority*. Tom Moletteire, Chap.
Southern Youth Correction Reception, 13200 S. Bloomfield Ave., 90650. Tel: 562-868-9979, Ext. 2467.
Metropolitan State Hospital. Rev. Paul Vung Le, S.V.D. Tel: 310-863-7011.
11400 S. Norwalk Blvd., 90650. Tel: 562-651-4311.

POINT MUGU. *Naval Air Station*. Vacant.
Bldg. 121, Code NASCG, 93042. Tel: 805-989-7967.

POMONA. *Frank D. Lanterman Developmental Center*, 3530 W. Pomona Blvd., 91768. Tel: 909-595-1221, Ext. 7162. P.O. Box 100, 91769. Tel: 909-444-7162. Sr. Nuala Ryan, S.S.L., Chap.

PORT HUENEME. *Naval Construction Battalion Center.*
NCBC Code CBCHP, 1000 23rd Ave., 93042. Tel: 805-982-4358.

SAN PEDRO. *Fort MacArthur Annex.*
Chaplain's Office, 325 Challenger Way, Ste. 1901, LA AFB, El Segundo, 90245-5677. Tel: 310-363-1956.
Immigration and Naturalization Service, San Pedro Service Processing Center, 2001 Seaside Ave., 90731. Tel: 310-241-2347. Imelda Bermejo.

SEPULVEDA. *Veterans Administration Medical Center.* 16111 Plummer St., 91343-2099.

TERMINAL ISLAND. *Federal Correctional Institution.* Rev. Michael D. Kirkness, Contract Chap., 1299 Seaside Ave., San Pedro, 90731. Tel: 626-918-8314.
1299 Seaside Ave., San Pedro, 90731-0207. Tel: 626-918-8314.

TORRANCE. *L.A. County-Harbor-U.C.L.A. Medical Center*, 1000 W. Carson, 90509. Tel: 310-222-2345; 310-222-2167 (Catholic Chap. Office). Rev. Thomas J. Clerkin, C.S.P., Chap., 1000 W. Carson, 90509. Tel: 310-222-2345; 310-222-2167 Catholic Chap. Office.
21900 S. Main St., Carson, 90745. Tel: 310-835-7161 (St. Philomena Parish).
Providence Little Company of Mary Medical Center. Rev. Dan Hudson, Chap.

WEST LOS ANGELES. *VA Greater Los Angeles Health System*, 11301 Wilshire Blvd. 691/125, 90099-5786. Tel: 310-268-3391. Rev. Max E. Saldua, Chap.
Veterans Administration Wadsworth Hospital Center.

Restorative Justice

LOS ANGELES. *L.A. Juvenile Detention Facilities*, Central Juvenile Hall, 1605 Eastlake Ave., 90033. Tel: 323-226-8530. Janne Shirley, Cheryl Bonacci.
MacLaren Hall. Vacant.
Dorothy Kirby Center. Dwain Miller, Chap. Tel: 323-981-4301.
L.A. Men's Central Jail, 441 Bauchet St., 90012. Tel: 213-974-8081. Rev. George E. Horan, Chap., Deacon Paulino Jaurez-Ramirez, Chap., Patricia L. Bartlett, Chap., Sr. Patricia Geoghegan, D.C., Chap.
Metropolitan Detention Center, 535 N. Alameda St., 90053. Tel: 213-253-9575. Vacant. (Federal Institution)
Office of Restorative Justice, 2049 S. Santa Fe Ave., 90021-2919. Tel: 213-438-4820; Fax: 213-438-4830. Rev. George E. Horan, Co-Dir. Tel: 213-438-4820, Ext. 14, Javier E. Stauring, Co-Dir. Tel: 213-438-4820, Ext. 13.
Twin Towers Correctional Facility I, 450 Bauchet St., 90063. Tel: 213-893-5241; Fax: 213-830-0907. Arturo Alvarez.

CAMARILLO. *Department of Juvenile Justice, Ventura Youth Correctional Facility*, 3100 Wright Rd., 93010. Tel: 805-278-3746. Catherine Conneally-Salazar.
Twin Towers Correctional Facility II, 450 Bauchet St., 90063. Tel: 213-893-5152; Fax: 213-830-0907. Dennis Gibbs.

DOWNEY. *Los Padrinos Juvenile Hall*, 7285 Quill Dr., 90242. Tel: 562-940-8711; 562-940-8712. Sr. Teresa Doherty, R.S.C.

LANCASTER. *California State Prison, L.A. County*, 44750 60th St. W., 93536-7620. Tel: 805-729-2000, Ext. 6129. Rev. Thomas White, Chap.
Challenger Youth Memorial Center, 5300 West Ave. I, 93536. Tel: 805-940-4165; 805-940-4166. Samuel Smolinsky, Chap.

LYNWOOD. *Century Regional Detention Facility*, 11705 S. Alameda St., 90262. Tel: 323-357-5114. Sr. Hilda Alfaro, S.A.C., Chap. (Women)

NORWALK. *Southern Youth Correctional Reception*, 13200 S. Bloomfield Ave., 90650. Tel: 562-868-9979, Ext. 2467. Tom Moletteire, Chap.

OJAI. *Ojai Men's Honor Farm*, 370 W. Baldwin Rd., 93023. Tel: 805-649-6020. Margaret Oberon, Chap. Tel: 805-654-5087.
Ojai Women's Jail Farm, 370 W. Baldwin Rd., 93023. Tel: 805-649-3020. Margaret Oberon, Chap. Tel: 805-654-5087.

SANTA BARBARA. *Los Prietos Boy's Camp*, Star Rte., 93105-9722. Tel: 805-898-7008. Marciano Avilla, Chap.
Santa Barbara County Jail, 4436A Calle Real, 93110. Tel: 805-898-7008. Marciano Avilla, Chap.
Santa Barbara Juvenile Hall, 4500 Hollister Ave., 93111. Tel: 805-681-5334. Marciano Avilla, Chap.

SANTA MARIA. *Juvenile Hall*, 812-B W. Foster Rd., 93454. Tel: 805-681-5334. Marciano Avilla, Chap.

SANTA PAULA. *Santa Paula Jail*, 600 S. Todd Rd., 93060. Tel: 805-933-8564. Margaret Oberon, Chap. Tel: 805-654-5087.

SAUGUS. *North County Correctional Facility*, 29340 The Old Rd., 91350. Tel: 661-295-7800, Ext. 5217. Gonzalo De Vivero, Chap., Alfredo Anaya.
Pitchess Detention Center, 29300 The Old Rd., 91350.
Medium South. Gonzalo De Vivero, Chap. Tel: 661-295-8805, Ext. 3020, Alfredo Anaya.
Medium North. Gonzalo De Vivero, Chap., Alfredo Anaya.
Maximum East. Gonzalo De Vivero. Tel: 661-295-8815, Ext. 3337, Alfredo Anaya.

SYLMAR. *Barry J. Nidorf Juvenile Hall*, 16350 Filbert St., 91342. Tel: 818-364-2021. Rev. Michael E. Kennedy, S.J., Chap., Arturo Lopez.

THOUSAND OAKS. *East County Jail*, 2101 E. Olsen Rd., 93162. Tel: 805-933-8564. Margaret Oberon, Chap. Tel: 805-654-5087.

VENTURA. *Colston Treatment Center*, 315 N. Hillmont Ave., 93003. Tel: 805-652-5721. Margaret Oberon, Chap.
Ventura County Jail, 800 S. Victoria Ave., 93009. Margaret Oberon, Chap. Tel: 805-654-5087.
Ventura Juvenile Hall-Clifton Tatum Center, 380 N. Hillmont Ave., 93003. Tel: 805-652-5727. Margaret Oberon, Chap.
Ventura Juvenile Restitution Project, 381 Hospital Rd., 93003. Tel: 805-652-6594. Margaret Oberon, Chap.

Camps

LOS ANGELES. *Juvenile Probation Camps.* Thomas Bleich, Coord. Tel: 818-889-0260.
Camp C.B. Afflerbaugh, 6331 N. Stephens Ranch Rd., La Verne, 91750. Tel: 909-596-0686. Connie Arambula, Chap.
Camp Dorothy Kirby Center, 1500 S. McDonnell Ave., 90022. Tel: 323-981-4301. Dwain Miller, Chap.
Camp David Gonzales, 1301 N. Las Virgines Rd., Calabasas, 91302. Tel: 818-222-1192. Joe Barrera.
Camp Holton, 12653 N. Little Tujunga Canyon Rd., San Fernando, 91342. Vacant.
Camp Kilpatrick, 427 S. Encinal Canyon Rd., Malibu, 90265. Tel: 818-889-1353. Jim Graham, Chap.
Camp McLaren Children's Center. Closed., 4024 Durfee Rd., El Monte, 91732. Tel: 213-438-4820. Vacant.
Camp Kenyon J. Scudder, 287 N. Bouquet Canyon Rd., Saugus, 91350. Tel: 661-296-9811. Aurora Montejano, Chap.
Camp Mendenhall, 42230 Lake Hughes Rd., Lake Hughes, 93532. Tel: 661-724-1211. Alfred E. Miller, Chap.
Camp Miller, 433 S. Encinal Canyon Rd., Malibu, 90265. Tel: 818-889-0260. Thomas Bleich, Chap.
Camp John Munz, 42220 Lake Hughes Rd., Lake Hughes, 93532. Tel: 661-724-1211. Alfred E. Miller, Chap.
Camp Paige, 6601 N. Stephens Ranch Rd., La Verne, 91750. Tel: 909-593-4921. Frank Cunningham, Chap., Cindy Cunningham, Chap.
Camp Rockey, 1900 N. Sycamore Canyon Rd., San Dimas, 91773. Tel: 909-599-2391. Ron Atkinson, Chap.
Camp Routh, 12500 Big Tujunga Rd., Tujunga, 91042. Tel: 818-352-4407. Bro. Kevin Cunniff, C.F.X., Chap.
Camp Scott, 28700 N. Bouquet Canyon Rd., Saugus, 91350. Tel: 661-296-8500. Deacon Pete Wilson, Chap., Cecilia Smith, Chap., Larry Smith, Chap. (Girls)

On Duty Outside the Archdiocese:

Rev. Msgr.—

Spiteri, Laurence J.

Revs.—

Beck, Lawrence J.

O'Shea, Patrick

Vega, Richard

Graduate Studies:
Revs.—
Durazo, Marco Antonio
Montejano, John
Pham, Thinh Duc
Szkredka, Slawomir

Hospital Chaplains:
Rev. Msgr.—
O'Connell, Timothy P., Chap. (Retired), Jeanne Jugan Residence
Revs.—
Arbelaez, Ernesto, S.J., Chap., Santa Teresita Medical Center
Castillo, Carlos C., C.M.F., Chap., St. John of God Hospital, Los Angeles & St. John's Health Center
Chukwu, Kenneth, Chap., Providence Tarzana
Ciccone, Mark, S.J., Chap., Providence St. Joseph Medical Center
Ciccone, Mark, S.J., Chap., Providence St. Joseph Medical Center - Burbank
Comerford, Patrick, Chap., St. John's Health Center, Santa Monica
Comerford, Patrick, Chap., St. John Health Center, Santa Monica
Dow, Emanuel, C.Ss.R., Chap., St. Mary Medical Center CHW Southern California
Gelfer, Peter, O.H., Chap., St. John's Regional Medical Center; St. Joseph's Health & Retirement Center
Griffin-Smolenski, Tomas, S.J., Chap., St. Vincent Medical Center
Kadambukatt, Ambrose Joseph, O.C.D., Chap., St. Francis Medical Center
Kadambukatt, Ambrose, O.C.D., Chap., St. Francis Medical Center
Lewis, Eric Anthony, Chap., Citrus Valley Medical Center-Queen of the Valley Hospital, West Covina
Lewis, Eric Anthony, Chap., Citrus Valley Medical Center - Queen of the Valley Campus
Mallin, Peter, O.F.M.Conv., Chap., Providence Little Company of Mary Hospital
Mallin, Peter, O.F.M.Conv., Chap., Providence Little Company of Mary Medical Center - Torrance
Mayor, Paul, Chap., St. Vincent Medical Center
Onyenobi, Christopher (Nigeria), Chap., Little Company of Mary-San Pedro
Onyenobi, Christopher (Nigeria), Chap., Providence Little Company of Mary Medical Center -San Pedro
Park, Shin-Hwa, Chap., St. Vincent Medical Center
Philip, Thomas, Chap., St. Francis Medical Center
Ponnet, Christopher D., Chap., Los Angeles County-USC Medical Center
Sigler, John William, Chap.
Sundaram, Manuel A., Chap., St. Mary Medical Center CHW Southern California
Tamiian, Calin, Chap., St. John's Regional Medical Center
Thompson, Jerald Wayne, Chap.
Whatley, Francis, O.SS.T., Chap., Nazareth House
Sisters—
DeLeon, Grace, S.S.C., Chap., St. Francis Medical Center
Jones, Janice, C.H.S., Chap., St. Francis Medical Center
Nguyen, Van, L.H.C., Chap., St. Francis Medical Center
Rojo, Marth, S.P., Chap., St. Francis Medical Center
Sanchez, Laura Paz, S.S.P., Chap., St. Francis Medical Center
Bros.—
Bui, Thaddeus, O.H., Chap., St. John of God Retirement & Care Center
Hirbe, Richard A., F.S.P., Chap., St. Francis Medical Center
Deacons—
Nawrocik, Zenon, Chap., Marian Medical Center
Nawrocik, Zenon L., Chap., Marian Medical Center
Abraham, Philip, Chap., Providence Holy Cross Medical Center
Abraham, Philip, Chap., Providence Holy Cross Medical Center - Mission Hills
Bigler, Kelly, Chap., St. Vincent Medical Center
Cosman, Patricia, Chap., Providence Little Company of Mary Hospital
Galan, Cesar, Chap., St. Francis Medical Center
Glynn, Darrah, Chap., Providence Little Company of Mary Hospital
Kiley, Shawn, Chap., Providence Holy Cross Medical Center
Knapp, David, Chap., St. John's Pleasant Valley Hospital
Landry, Tom, Chap., Providence St. Joseph Medical Center
Rev.—
Owen, Renee, Chap., Providence Tarzana Medical Center
Turrentine, Fleeta, Chap., Little Company of Mary Sub Acute Care Center
West, George, Chap., St. John's Pleasant Valley Hospital
Wright, Hillary, Chap., Providence Little Company of Mary Hospital

Military Chaplains:
Revs.—
Bautista, Jose A.
Llanos, Philip S.

On Sick Leave:
Revs.—
Blanco, Jose A.
Cavanagh, James
de Souza, Owen
Dowdel, Lawrence J., Jr.
Fernandez, Cesar A.
Lewis, Alexander Joseph
Marquez, Esteban
McDonnell, Anthony
Nunez, Anthony
Rendon, Samuel (Mexico)
Russo, Frank, Jr.
Wolkovits, Paul Dennis

On Administrative Leave:
Rev. Msgrs.—
Loomis, Richard A.
Van Liefde, Christian M.
Revs.—
Granadino, David F.
Juarez, Robert Jesus
Palomera, Ramon

On Active Leave:
Revs.—
Byrne, Keith
Collins, John Michal
Lui, Gabriel
Tucker, James
Woodland, Stephen

In Transition:
Rev.—
Palacios, Joseph M., Ph.D.

Retired:
His Eminence—
Mahony, Cardinal Roger Michael, St. Charles Borromeo Catholic Church, 10834 Moorpark St., North Hollywood, 91602-2206.
Most Rev.—
Sartoris, Joseph M., D.D., V.G., 1988 Rolling Vista Dr., #21, Lomita, 90717.
Rev. Msgrs.—
Acton, Sean A., 627 Avenida Sevilla, Unit C, Laguna Woods, 92653.
Acton, Thomas M., Maria Regina Catholic Church, 2150 W. 135th St., Gardena, 90249-2498.
Amy, Peter L., St. Didacus Catholic Church, 14339 Astoria St., Sylmar, 91342-4124.
Bell, Carl F., 13821 Fresh Meadow Ln. Apt. #7D, Seal Beach, 90740.
Bunny, J. Michael, V.F., 21621 Sandia Rd. #167, Apple Valley, 92308.
Cokus, Joseph J., 3 La Serena, Irvine, 92612.
Colberg, James Philip, 414 E. Church St., Santa Maria, 93454.
Connolly, Clement J., Holy Family Catholic Church, 1527 Fremont Ave., South Pasadena, 91030-3736.
Cosgrove, Joseph, 7842 Lily Trotter St., North Las Vegas, NV 89084.
Diomartich, Felix S., Nazareth House, 3333 Manning Ave., 90064-4804.
Donnelly, Lawrence Edward, 1065 W. Lomita Blvd., Space 411, Harbor City, 90710.
Doyle, Thomas, St. James the Less Catholic Church, 4651 Dunsmore Ave., La Crescenta, 91214-1812.
English, Tobias P., St. Andrew Catholic Church, 140 Chestnut St., Pasadena, 91103-3896.
Flanagan, Sean B., St. Bartholomew Catholic Church, 252 Granada Ave., Long Beach, 90803-5518.
Foley, John Kieran, Holy Redeemer Catholic Church, 2411 Montrose Ave., Montrose, 91020-1419.
Fosselman, John Anthony, Nazareth House, 3333 Manning Ave., 90064-4804.
Frilot, Eugene P., Incarnation Catholic Church, 1001 N. Brand, Glendale, 91202-2979.
George, Alexander C., 65565 Acoma Ave Spc. 118, Desert Hot Springs, 92240.
George, Joseph S., 65565 Acoma Ave. Spc. 118, Desert Hot Springs, 92240.
Gibson, Lawrence J., 2023 Via Mariposa E., Unit A, Laguna Woods, 92653.
Gilb, Eugene A., St. John Fisher Catholic Church, 5448 Crest Rd., Rancho Palos Verdes, 90274-5097.
Gipson, Robert W., 489 E. Laurel Cir., Palm Springs, 92262.
Gomez, Henry, Proto Notary Apostolic, 1401 Pebbledon St., Monterey Park, 91754.
Healy, Peter C., St. Robert Bellarmine Catholic Church, 133 N. 5th St., Burbank, 91501-2178.
Hernandez, Alfred, 573 S. Boyle Ave., P.O. Box 113, 90033.
Hill, Charles E., 517 E. 220th St., Carson, 90745.
Howard, Robert E., P.O. Box 2354, Palm Springs, 92263-2354.
Hughes, John Charles, St. Mary Magdelen Catholic Church, 2532 Ventura Blvd., Camarillo, 93010-6649.
Johnson, Edward Joseph, Nazareth House, 3333 Manning Ave., 90064-4804.
Killeen, Michael F., St. Elizabeth Ann Seton Catholic Church, 1835 Larkvane Rd., Rowland Heights, 91748-2501.
Leser, William J., C.B., S.T.B., 18550 W. Vincennes St., Apt. 108, Northridge, 91324.
Loftus, Padraic, 22046 Providencia St., Woodland Hills, 91364.
Matas, Juan, 1947 Palm Ave., Monterey Park, 91755.
McCabe, Vincent, 2840 Honolulu Ave., Verdugo City, 91046.
McGovern, Thomas, 564 Bellflower Blvd., #309, Long Beach, 90814.
McNulty, Patrick, 2501 W. Ave. 33, 90065-2892.
Mihan, John A., 635 S. Hobart Blvd., Apt. 101, 90005.
Moran, Peter C., 9801 Canby Ave., Northridge, 91325.
Mulcahy, Donal, Our Lady of the Assumption Catholic Church, 3175 Telegraph Rd., Ventura, 93003-3283.
Murray, Richard Hayes, St. Bernardine of Siena Catholic Church, 24410 Calvert St., Woodland Hills, 91367-1099.
Naughton, John Thomas, 2033 Mayorca Dr., Oxnard, 93035.
Nugent, Peter D., St. John Eudes Catholic Church, 9901 Mason Ave., Chatsworth, 91311-4592.
O'Connell, Timothy P., Jeanne Jugan Residence, 2100 S. Western Ave., San Pedro, 90732.
O'Gorman, Charles Francis, Santa Clara Catholic Church, 323 S. E St., Oxnard, 93030-5835.
O'Keefe, William Joseph, Our Lady of Refuge Catholic Church, 5195 Stearns St., Long Beach, 90815-2901.
O'Leary, Lawrence, St. Martin of Tours Catholic Church, 11967 Sunset Blvd., 90049-4220.
O'Reilly, Peter A., 722 Alden Rd., Claremont, 91711.
O'Toole, William P., All Souls Catholic Church, 29 S. Electric Ave., Alhambra, 91801-1992.
Parnassas, George John, St. Victor Catholic Church, 8634 Holloway Dr., West Hollywood, 90069-2304.
Rawden, John A., Wood Glen Hall, 3010 Foothill Rd., Santa Barbara, 93105.
Reilly, Patrick, St. Robert Bellarmine Catholic Church, 133 N. 5th St., Burbank, 91501-2178.
Renehan, Edmond M., V.F., St. Clare Catholic Church, 27341 Camp Plenty Rd., Santa Clarita, 91351-2645.
Richey, Terrence, St. Basil Catholic Church, 637 S. Kingsley Dr., 90005-2392.
Rodriguez, Benigno Antonio, 12109 Bayla St., Norwalk, 90650.
Royer, Ronald Edmund, 40708-B Balch Park Rd., Springville, 93265.
Saunders, Douglas William, V.F., 6741 Lincoln Ave., #153, Buena Park, 90620-5678.
Schmit, Jerome L., Sacred Heart Catholic Church, 600 W. Mariposa St., Altadena, 91001-4516.
Segaric, John, Trg Sv Stosije 1, Zador 23000 Croatia.
Staunton, Patrick Joseph, St. Joseph Catholic Church, 555 N. Glendora Ave., La Puente, 91744-5112.
Thompson, Patrick G., Incarnation Catholic Church, 1001 N. Brand Blvd., Glendale, 91202-2979.
Tseu, Andrew Stanislaus, St. Madeleine Catholic Church, 931 E. Kingsley Ave., Pomona, 91767-5098.
Wallace, Francis T., J.C.L., St. Robert Bellarmine Catholic Church, 133 N. 5th St., Burbank, 91501-2178.
Weber, Francis J., San Fernando Mission Catholic Church, 15151 San Fernando Mission, Mission Hills, 91345-2617.
Won, John P. H., KKOTT Dogne Center, 37885 Hwy. 79 S., Temecula, 92592.
Young, John Melvin, 1022 N.W. Keasey St., Roseburg, OR 97471.
Zimmerman, Roland George, Annunciation Catholic Church, 1307 E. Longden Ave., Arcadia, 91006-5597.
Revs.—
Bebek, Dominic L., 114 Ocean Ave., Seal Beach, 90740.

Belletty, Emile Ignatius, 22039 Mariposa Ave., Torrance, 90502.
Biroschak, Robert V., J.C.L., 70 Parkwood Rd., Stratford, CT 06614.
Bonner, William J., 5731 Lucretia Ave., Mira Loma, 91752.
Boudreau, Thomas Francis, Nazareth House, 3333 Manning Ave., 90064-4804.
Bradley, Robert M., 108 Courtside Dr., Butler, PA 16001-2466.
Brincat, George, 37 A. Mons. Farrugia St., Victoria Gogo VCT 105 Malta.
Buhr, Eugene S., St. Joseph Catholic Church, 11901 S. Acacia Ave., Hawthorne, 90250-3083.
Carey, Richard W., P.O. Box 678, Tecate, 91980.
Cassidy, Francis J., Immaculate Conception Catholic Church, 740 S. Shamrock Dr., Monrovia, 91016-0510.
Cavanagh, Brian M., Sacred Heart Catholic Church, 344 W. Workman St., Covina, 91723-3345.
Ciordia, Pedro M., Holy Family Catholic Church, 1011 E. "L" St., Wilmington, 90744-2706.
Colborn, Francis R., S.T.D., 333 Old Mill Rd., #236, Santa Barbara, 93110.
Connor, William Joseph, 2500 E. 2nd St., #205, Long Beach, 90803.
Cooley, John Edward, Nazareth House, 3333 Manning Ave., 90064-4804.
Coronado, Genero, 2505 W. Foothill Blvd., Apt. 145, San Bernardino, 92410.
Crowe, Hugh, St. Ann Catholic Church, 2302 Riverdale Ave., 90031-1133.
Daly, John J., Holy Trinity Catholic Church, 3722 Boyce Ave., 90039-1810.
De Dominici, Lorenzo, P.O. Box 6425, San Pedro, 90734.
Delaney, Matthew S., 13700 El Dorado Dr., Seal Beach, 90740.
Devine, Finbarr Columba, St. Gregory the Great Catholic Church, 13935 Telegraph Rd., Whittier, 90604-2597.
Doran, Brian D., St. Anthony Catholic Church, 600 Olive Ave., Long Beach, 90802-1546.
Duc Minh, Joseph N., 432 S. Harbor Blvd., Apt. #37, Santa Ana, 92704-1368.
Elis, Tomas Alfonso, St. Mel Catholic Church, 20870 Ventura Blvd., Woodland Hills, 91364-2396.
Fahey, John Peter, 1111 James Donion Blvd. Apt. 2090, Antioch, 94509.
Fernandes, Roque A.D., St. Frances of Rome Church Catholic Church, 501 E. Foothill Blvd., Azusa, 91702.
Fitzgerald, John B., Nazareth House, 3333 Manning Dr., 90064-4804.
Ford, Harold LeRoy, St. Joseph Catholic Church, 6220 E. Willow St., Long Beach, 90815-2295.
Fremgen, Edward George, 4849 Hersholt Ave., Long Beach, 90808.
Gannon, Patrick J., Nazareth House, 3333 Manning Ave., 90064-4804.
Glynn, Thomas Joseph, Our Lady of Refuge Church Catholic Church, 5195 Stearns St., Long Beach, 90815-2901.
Gorman, Rody Ignatius, St. Matthias Church Catholic Church, 7125 Mission Pl., Huntington Park, 90255-5299.
Guerrini, Roderic M., Nazareth House, 333 Manning Ave., 90064-4804.
Gutting, John C., Nazareth House, 3333 Manning Ave., 90064-4804.
Haefeli, Joaquin C., St. Ignatius Loyola Church Catholic Church, 322 N. Ave. 61, 90042-3499.
Hicarte, Mateo H., 138 S. Pacific Ave., Glendale, 91204.
Iglesias, Fernando Gonzalez, 23505 Evening Snow, Moreno Valley, 92557.
Janowski, Rock J., 1241 S. Petit Ave., #5, Ventura, 93004.
Johnson, Henry Joseph, 4676 Admiralty Way, Ste. 101, Marina Del Rey, 90292.
Joy, Laurence, P.O. Box 435090, San Ysidro, 92143.
Kavanagh, James F., St. James Catholic Church, 124 N. Pacific Coast Hwy., Redondo Beach, 90277-3194.
Kelly, Francis, 700 E. Ocean Blvd., Unit 1806, Long Beach, 90802.
Kelly, Paul Maurice, P.O. Box 129, Pasadena, 91102.
King, Thomas F., 32 Avenue 27, Venice, 90291.
Kolling, James L., Visitation Catholic Church, 6561 W. 88th St., 90045-3716.
Kribs, Don Richard, Nazareth House, 3333 Manning Ave., 90064-4804.
Landreau, Edward Joseph, St. Frances of Rome Catholic Church, 501 E. Foothill Blvd., Azusa, 91702.
Larkin, Kevin John, St. Francis de Sales Catholic Church, 13360 Valleyheart Dr., Sherman Oaks, 91423-3287.
Lee, Joseph P., P.O. Box 1254, Gardena, 90249.
Luck, Robert O., 200 E. Racquet Club Rd., Unit 45, Palm Springs, 92262.
Madrigal, Ildefonso M., Mary Health of the Sick Hospital, 2929 Theresa Dr., Newbury Park, 91320.
Maechler, Edmund Francis, 18401 Delaware St., Huntington Beach, 92648-1415.
Maher, James Joseph, St. Paschal Baylon Catholic Church, 155 E. Janss Rd., Thousand Oaks, 91360-3396.
Mayer, Jules Anthony, Nazareth House, 3333 Manning Ave., 90064-4804.
McNulty, Gerard J., 2722 E. 20th St., Unit 204, Signal Hill, 90755.
McSorley, Gerald Hugh, P.O. Box 2790, Carlsbad, 92018.
Meisel, Gerald A., St. Matthew Catholic Church, 672 Temple Ave., Long Beach, 90814-1297.
Menke, Paul F., P.O. Box 39518, 90039.
Merino, Santiago James, 959 La Deney Dr., Ontario, 91762.
Meskill, Thomas A., Mary Health of the Sick Hospital, 2929 Theresa Dr., Newbury Park, 91320.
Miskella, Richard, Rathimney Gusserane, County Wexford Ireland.
Murray, John D., St. Francis Xavier Catholic Church, 3801 Scott Rd., Burbank, 91504-1799.
Nocero, Pascal Francis, 1503 San Rafael St., Ojai, 93023.
O'Grady, James F., Visitation Catholic Church, 6561 W. 88th St., 90045-3716.
O'Grady, James Francis, GlenKeen, Louisburg, County Mayo, Ireland.
O'Leary, Niall Finbarr, Holy Family Catholic Church, 1527 Fremont Ave., South Pasadena, 91030-3736.
O'Mahony, Maurice K., Our Lady of Mount Carmel Catholic Church, 1300 E. Valley Rd., Santa Barbara, 93108-1294.
O'Neill, Jeremiah, 2100 W. Carlos Ave., Alhambra, 91803-4321.
O'Ryan, Colm, Good Shepherd Catholic Church, 505 N. Bedford Dr., Beverly Hills, 90210-3298.
O'Shea, Michael, 11 Taobh Linn, Kenmare, County Kerry Ireland.
O'Sullivan, Daniel A., Sacred Heart Catholic Church, 10800 Henderson Rd., Ventura, 93004-1895.
O'Sullivan, Thomas Carrol, Our Lady of Mount Carmel Catholic Church, 1300 E. Valley Rd., Santa Barbara, 93108-1294.
Peacha, Thomas James, 13361 St. Andress Dr., 129 C, Seal Beach, 90740.
Penaloza, Jorge A., St. Francis Xavier Catholic Church, 4245 S. Acaia Ave., Pico Rivera, 90660-1679.
Phelan, Cornelius Noel, St. Basil Catholic Church, 637 S. Kingsley Dr., 90005-2392.
Poljicak, Vlatko, Zagrebacka 21, 31 400 Kjakovo, Croatia.
Potthoff, Donald William, St. Denis Catholic Church, 2151 Diamond Bar Blvd., Diamond Bar, 91765-2860.
Rodriguez, Lawrence, Soto y Amio, Santovenio de San Marcos, Leon, CP24125 Spain.
Roman, Julio, P.O. Box 226934, 90022.
Romero, Gilbert Claude, 13220 Southport Ln., #170-E., Seal Beach, 90740-3361.
Romero, Juan R. (SB), 2347 Los Patos Dr., Palm Springs, 92264.
Rothe, James A., P.O. Box 692, Bridgeport, 93517-0692.
Scott, Alfonso A., 6246 Crystal Cove Lot #236, Long Beach, 90803.
Siebenand, Paul Alcuin, 41663 Calle Pampas, Indio, 92203.
Soto, Edward P., St. Rose of Lima Catholic Church, 4450 E. 60th St., Maywood, 90270-3198.
Stehly, Thomas J., 9432 S. Bloomfield Ave., Cypress, 90630.
Steinbock, Leo E., P.O. Box 1950, Covina, 91722.
Suquilvide, Abel, Nazareth House, 3333 Manning Ave., 90064-4804.
Thompson, Jerome H., Windsor Court, 201 Sunrise Way, Palm Springs, 92262.
Tsang, Peter, 1739 Bolanos Ave., Rowland Heights, 91748.
Walker, Gerald Bernard, 2020 Via Mariposa E., Apt. C, Laguna Woods, 92637-0890.
Weible, Thomas C., St. Peter the Apostle Parish, 11 Prince St., Provincetown, MA 02657.
Young, Gerald A., 121 Vista View Dr., Montrose, CO 81401.

Permanent Deacons:
Abalos, Roland, St. Finbar Catholic Church, Burbank
Abrera, Jaime, St. Francis Xavier Catholic Church, Burbank
Acquaviva, Dick, St. Clare Catholic Church, Santa Clarita
Adams, Emile, St. Bernadette Catholic Church, Los Angeles
Adams, Rodger John, Our Lady of the Assumption Catholic Church, Ventura
Aguirre, Ancelmo, Old Mission Santa Ines, Lompoc
Aispuro, Genaro, St. Joseph Catholic Church, Carpinteria
Alexander, Hosea, Sr., (Retired), Holy Name of Jesus Catholic Church, Los Angeles
Allen, John Paul, (Retired), 18053 Bluesail Dr., Pacific Palisades, 90272.
Amantea, Chris, American Martyrs Catholic Church, Manhattan Beach
Andrade, J. Trinidad, Holy Cross Catholic Church, Moorpark
Aranda, Fernando, Jr., San Gabriel Mission Catholic Church, Los Angeles
Arban, Wilfredo, St. Dominic Savio Catholic Church, Bellflower
Ascencio, Juan Francisco, St. Cecilia Catholic Church, Los Angeles
Asmar, George, Immaculate Heart of Mary Catholic Church, Santa Clarita
Austin, Alfred H., Holy Name of Mary Catholic Church, Pomona
Baker, William F., (Retired), 901 Centennial St. #5, 90012.
Banda, Mark Lawrence, San Buenaventura Mission Catholic Church, Port Hueneme
Barajas, Henry, Jr., Our Lady of Guadalupe Catholic Church, Oxnard
Barragan, Arturo, St. John the Baptist Catholic Church, Santa Fe Springs
Barragan, Ricardo, Immaculate Conception Catholic Church, Oxnard
Barrera, Jose Oscar, Sagrado Corazon Catholic Church, Compton
Barry, John William, Sacred Heart Catholic Church, Ventura
Batacan, Jesse, St. Christopher Catholic Church, West Covina
Bautista, Rolando, Holy Trinity Catholic Church, Los Angeles
Benalcazar, Eudoro G., All Souls Catholic Church, Alhambra
Bernal, Daniel, St. Thomas the Apostle Catholic Church, Los Angeles
Berumen, Ricardo, St. John Neumann Catholic Church, Santa Maria
Betliskey, Michael Joseph, St. Joseph Catholic Church, Carpinteria
Blanco, Raul, St. Louis de Montfort Catholic Church, Santa Maria
Bohlig, Alden, (Retired), 1516 Armando Dr., Long Beach, 90807.
Boucher, Richard, St. Cornelius Catholic Church, Long Beach
Brandlin, Thomas E., M.N.A., St. Teresa of Avila Catholic Church, Los Angeles
Bravo, Anthony J., (Retired), 3922 Mesa Dr. #103, Oceanside, 92056.
Brenes, Francisco, St. Finbar Catholic Church, Burbank
Brown, Derek A., American Martyrs Catholic Church, Hermosa Beach
Butler, Ronald, Sacred Heart Catholic Church, Covina
Cabello, Luis, Holy Cross Catholic Church, Santa Barbara
Cabello, Rodolfo Naranjo, Holy Cross Catholic Church, Santa Barbara
Camacho, Raymond, St. Didacus Catholic Church, Sylmar
Cantillo Romero, Juan Bautista, St. Thomas the Apostle Catholic Church, Palmdale
Caputo, Edward E., St Mary Catholic Church , Quartz Hill
Carlson, Dennis Dean, Holy Trinity Catholic Church, San Pedro
Carmody, Richard, St. Louis de Montfort Catholic Church, Santa Maria
Castillo, Alfonso, St. Benedict Catholic Church, El Monte
Castorena, John G., Santa Clara Catholic Church, Oxnard
Catipon, Gus, Cathedral of Our Lady of the Angeles, Los Angeles
Cellner, Jerome, St. Bernardine of Siena Catholic Church, West Hills
Charters, John, Sacred Heart Catholic Church, Lancaster
Chavez, Gilbert M., Annunciation Catholic Church, Temple City
Chavez, Manuel, St. Anthony Catholic Church, Rosemead
Chavez, Raul, Guardian Angel Catholic Church, Sylmar
Chevez, Roberto I., Our Lady of Guadalupe Catholic Church, Baldwin Park
Cho, Tae Jun, St. Christopher Catholic Church, Fontana

Chu, Peter, St. Elizabeth Ann Seton Catholic Church, Rowland Heights
Clements, Brian, St. Peter Claver Catholic Church, Simi Valley
Copon, Ricardo Pareja, Jr., Mary Star of the Sea Catholic Church, Camarillo
Corcios, Oscar A., Our Lady of the Rosary Catholic Church, South Gate
Cordero, Ruben A., Guardian Angel Catholic Church, Granada Hills
Crowley, James, Assumption of the Blessed Virgin Mary Catholic Church, Atladena
Cruz, Miguel, St. Joseph Catholic Church, Fontana
Cuda, Shane, St. Joseph Catholic Church, Long Beach
Cunneen, John T., St. Linus Catholic Church, Cerritos
Curran, Nicholas P., Holy Cross Catholic Church, Santa Barbara
de Jesus, Jose, Mary Immaculate Catholic Church, Panorama City
De Los Reyes, Carlito, St. Barnabas Catholic Church, Long Beach
Denisac, Charles M., Jr., Our Lady of Perpetual Help Catholic Church, Downey
Dieter, Frank, St. Lawrence Martyr Catholic Church, Redondo Beach
Dionne, Ireneaus, (Retired), 231 S. Olive Ave. #F, Alhambra, 91801.
Dornan, Richard, (Retired), St. Jude Catholic Church, Westlake Village
Duke, Oscar M., (Retired), 557 S. "E' St., Oxnard, 93030.
Dumlao, Felix, St. Anthony of Padua Catholic Church, Gardena
Edie, Isaac, Blessed Junipero Serra Catholic Church, Camarillo
Egnatuk, James A., St. Lawrence Martyr Catholic Church, Redondo Beach
Ellms, Steven, St. Bernardine of Siena Catholic Church, Simi Valley
Elsey, Ken, Santa Rosa Catholic Church, Sylmar
Escovedo, Arthur, (Retired), 734 Scripps Dr., Claremont, 91711.
Espana, Salvador, St. Elizabeth Catholic Church, North Hollywood
Estey, Marvin, Holy Name of Mary Catholic Church, Glendora
Estrada, Armando, St. Stephen Catholic Church, Rosemead
Estrada, David J., St. Benedict Catholic Church, Pico Rivera
Fargo, Robert, Blessed Junipero Serra Catholic Church, Camarillo
Farley, James M., (Retired), 248 Agnus Dr., Ventura, 93003.
Faubert, Roger, Our Lady of Refuge Catholic Church, Cypress
Fermin, Gilberto, Our Lady of Guadalupe Catholic Church, Santa Barbara
Fernandez, Jesus, Santa Rosa Catholic Church, Sylmar
Fernandez, Louis Homero, St. Rose of Lima Catholic Church, Simi Valley
Finocchiaro, Michael, St. Dominic Catholic Church, Pasadena
Fitzgerald, James, M.D., St. Agatha Catholic Church, Whittier
Flores, Fernando, Sacred Heart Catholic Church, Ventura
Flores, Ricardo L., (Retired), 4137 McConnell Blvd., 90066.
Freeman, P. Michael, St. Bruno Catholic Church, Whittier
Frias, Sam, St. John the Baptist de la Salle Catholic Church, Granada Hills
Galido, Juan, Jr., Our Lady of Lourdes Catholic Church, Chatsworth
Gallardo, Jose Alberto, Our Lady of Guadalupe Catholic Church, Santa Barbara
Gallegos, Jose, St. Elizabeth Catholic Church, Pasadena
Galvez, Miguel, Sacred Heart Catholic Church, Pomona
Garcia, Armando, St. Camillus Catholic Center for Pastoral Care, Los Angeles
Garcia, George Angel, St. Anthony Catholic Church, Oxnard
Garcia, Rogelio, St. Thomas More Catholic Church, Monterey Park
Garcia, William J., Mary Star of the Sea Catholic Church, San Pedro
Garcia Bejarano, Marco Antonio, Christ the King Catholic Church, Van Nuys
Garcia Cruz, Juan Rogelio, St. Francis of Rome Catholic Church, Azusa
Garza, Ciro Augusto, St. Martha Catholic Church, Huntington Park
Gath, Don, St. Joseph Catholic Church, Long Beach
Gibboney, Carl, St. Bartholomew Catholic Church, Long Beach
Girard, Joseph, St. Mark Catholic Church, Marina del Rey
Godinez, Jose Arturo, Our Lady of Guadalupe Catholic Church, Oxnard
Gonzalez, Arturo, Our Lady of Sorrows Catholic Church, Santa Barbara
Gonzalez, Doroteo, Epiphany Catholic Church, El Monte
Gonzalez, Luis, St. Joseph Catholic Church, La Puente
Gorman, Christopher, St. Thomas Aquinas Catholic Church, Ojai
Guadamuz, Jose, Holy Name of Mary Catholic Church, La Verne
Guerra, Mario, St Raymond Catholic Church, Downey
Guerrero, Jaime S., St. Louis of France Catholic Church, West Covina
Guiao, Rey, Our Lady of Peace Catholic Church, Panorama City
Guilin, Alfonso, St. Sebastian Catholic Church, Santa Paula
Hall, Willard J., Sr., St. John the Evangelist Catholic Church, Los Angeles
Halliwell, Thomas L., St. Joseph Catholic Church, Long Beach
Halvorsen, Douglas A., St. Louis de Montfort Catholic Church, Santa Maria
Hammonds, Johnnie, (Retired), 2250 N. Lyndhurst Ave., Camarillo, 93010.
Hanson, Walter J., St. Charles Borromeo Catholic Church, Studio City
Harper, John Barry, St. Julie Billiart Catholic Church, Newbury Park
Hegenbart, Joseph, St. James the Less Catholic Church, La Crescenta
Henry, James J., (Retired), 3345 Harbor Blvd., Oxnard, 93035. St. Anthony, Oxnard
Henschel, Louis E., St. Julie Billiart Catholic Church, Newbury Park
Hernandez, Roberto, Holy Spirit Catholic Church, Los Angeles
Herrera, Fermin, Sacred Heart Catholic Church, Lancaster
Hidalgo, Hector M., Beatitudes of Our Lord Catholic Church, Whittier
Hillman, Steven V., St. Elizabeth Ann Seton Catholic Church, Walnut
Holderness, Alan, St. Louise de Marillac Catholic Church, Glendora
Holguin, Michael, Santa Clara Catholic Church, Oxnard
Horn, John G., Sacred Heart Catholic Church, Covina
Huerta, Antonio, St. Anthony of Padua Catholic Church, Los Angeles
Huff, David Warren, (Retired)
Hull, John, St. Rita Catholic Church, Sierra Madre
Ito, Mitchell, St. Pascal Baylon Catholic Church, Westlake Village
Johnson, Douglass R., Sr., Holy Name of Jesus Catholic Church, Los Angeles
Jones, Douglas, Our Lady of Peace Catholic Church, North Hills
Juarez, Ernesto Macias, St. Thomas Aquinas Catholic Church, Ojai
Juarez-Ramirez, Paulino, St. Genevieve Catholic Church, Sylmar
Karl, Richard J., Our Lady of Perpetual Help Catholic Church, Valencia
Kelch, Vincent Charles, Santa Clara Catholic Church, Oxnard
Kennedy, Joseph Charles, St. Anthony Catholic Church, Oxnard
Kingsley, Neil Joseph, Blessed Junipero Serra Catholic Church, Camarillo
Kolbash, Frank, St. Finbar Catholic Church, Burbank
Kruer, John, St. Maximilian Kolbe Catholic Church, Westlake Village
Landa, William, St. Philip the Apostle Catholic Church, Pasadena
Landeros, Teodoro, San Buenaventura Mission Catholic Church, Ventura
Lara, Frederick Peter, Our Lady of the Miraculous Medal Catholic Church, Montebello
Lauderdale, Walter John, Holy Trinity Catholic Church, San Pedro
Ledonne, Tom, St. Denis Catholic Church, Diamond Bar
Lee, Paul D., St. Agnes Korean Catholic Community, Buena Park
Leyva, Rodolfo R., Sacred Heart Catholic Church, Covina
Ligot, Romy, St. Pancratius Catholic Church, Lakewood
Lim, Raymond, St. James the Less Catholic Church, Glendale
Lira, Pedro, St. Catherine of Sien Catholic Churcha, Reseda
Littleton, Edward, Blessed Kateri Tekakwitha Catholic Church, Valencia
Lopez, Arnaldo, Holy Angels Catholic Church, Arcadia
Lopez, Francisco Javier, Our Lady of Guadalupe Catholic Church, Oxnard
Lopez, Francisco, St. Mary of the Assumption Catholic Church, Santa Maria
Lopez, Lawrence James, Santa Clara Catholic Church, Oxnard
Lopez, Mario, Holy Name of Mary Catholic Church, Pomona
Lopez, Rito R., Blessed Junipero Serra Catholic Church, Palmdale
Lopez, Victor, St. Lucy Catholic Church, Long Beach
Lumsdaine, Joseph, St. Dominic Savio Catholic Church, Downey
Macias, Aurelio Robles, Sacred Heart Catholic Church, Oxnard
Maciel, Robert, Sr., St. Louis de Montfort Catholic Church, Santa Maria
Madrigal, Carlos, Sacred Heart Catholic Church, Pomona
Magos, Carlos, Precious Blood Catholic Church, Los Angeles
Manalo, Dante Tibor, Mary Star of the Sea Catholic Church, Oxnard
Manion, Joseph M., Sr., (Retired), 779 Cedar Point Pl., Westlake Village, 91362.
Marin, Alejandro, Holy Name of Jesus Catholic Church, Los Angeles
Marron, Alejandro Zendejas, Our Lady of Guadalupe Catholic Church, Oxnard
Marsh, Steven R., St. Dorothy Catholic Church, Azusa
Martinez, Jesse, St. John Vianney Catholic Church, Hacienda Heights
Martinez, Manuel J., f.s.p., Cathedral of Our Lady of the Angels, Los Angeles
Martinez, Miguel Angel, St. Raphael Catholic Church, Los Angeles
Mauch, Kevin Barry, Holy Cross Catholic Church, Moorpark
McGloin, Lawrence, Holy Angels of the Deaf, Gardena
McNamara, Eugene P., (Retired), 1114 14th St. Apt. D, Santa Monica, 90403-5445. St. Monica, Santa Monica
McPheeters, Jon C., St. Anthony Catholic Church, Oxnard
Medina, Richard J., San Fernando Pastoral Region Office, Downey
Mejia, J. Guadalupe, Holy Family Catholic Church, Artesia
Mejia, Mario, St. Linus Catholic Church, Bell Gardens
Melgar, Reymundo, St. John Eudes Catholic Church, Chatsworth
Mendez, Alfonso Cruz, San Buenaventura Mission Catholic Church, Ventura
Miller, Robert J., St. James Catholic Church, Torrance
Mills, Edgar, Our Lady of the Assumption Catholic Church, Ventura
Mitchell, Charles A., St. Elizabeth of Hungary Catholic Church, Pasadena
Mizerski, Joseph R., St. Therese Catholic Church, San Gabriel
Modugno, Larry, St. Mary Magdalen Catholic Church, Camarillo
Molina, Raul, St. Anne Catholic Church, Monterey Park
Moloney, Douglas, St. Christopher Catholic Church, West Covina
Montross, Stephen, St. Raphael Catholic Church, Santa Barbara
Morales, Jose Noe, Mary Star of the Sea Catholic Church, Oxnard
Morgan, T. Richard, St. Jane de Chantal Catholic Church, North Hollywood
Moske, Walter Thomas, St. Joseph Catholic Church, Gardena
Nawrocik, Zenon, Mary of the Assumption Catholic Church, Santa Maria
Nguyen, Loc, St. Christopher Catholic Church, West Covina
Nguyen, Matthew Van, Maria Regina Catholic Church, Torrance
Noon, Richard, St. John Vianney Catholic Church, Hacienda Heights
Noriega, Restie T., Incarnation Catholic Church, Glendale
O'Malley, Thom, St. Finbar Catholic Church, Burbank
Ochoa, Ruben, Guardian Angel Catholic Church, San Fernando
Orcutt, Mark A., St. Paul of the Cross Catholic Church, La Mirada

Origel, Carlos, Our Lady of Perpetual Help Catholic Church, Downey
Ortega, Carlos, St. Basil Catholic Church, Van Nuys
Ortiz, Joe, (Retired), 472 Tanner Cir., Riverside, 92507.
Ortiz Dominguez, David, St. Lawrence of Brindisi Catholic Church, Los Angeles
Palmer, William Scott, Our Lady of Guadalupe Catholic Church, Redondo Beach
Pardo, Rogelio, Our Lady of Perpetual Help Catholic Church, Downey
Parish, Harold "Hal", J.C.D., (Retired), 3504 Ketch Ave., Oxnard, 93035. Mary Star of the Sea, Oxnard
Pasos, Jesus S., St. Bernardine of Siena Catholic Church, Thousand Oaks
Patterson, Gary R., Our Lady of Guadalupe Catholic Church, Covina
Patterson, Gregory, Transfiguration Catholic Church, Los Angeles
Pena, Cecilio G., St. Helen Catholic Church, South Gate
Pepe, Joseph, (Retired), 3327 S. 'E' St., Oxnard, 93033. St. Joseph the Worker, Winnetka
Perez, Elvys C., St. Mary's Catholic Church, Littlerock
Perez, Jorge, Our Lady of the Rosary Catholic Church, Downey
Perez, Michael A., St. John Eudes Catholic Church, Sylmar
Perez, Sergio, Our Lady of Solitude Catholic Church, Hacienda Heights
Pesqueira, Paul, St. Mariana de Paredes Catholic Church, Pico Rivera
Picard, John B., (Retired), 4892 Paseo Montelena, Camarillo, 93012. Blessed Junipero Serra, Camarillo
Pinedo, Donald, St. Anthony Catholic Church, Oxnard
Pomphrey, Richard, St. Bede the Venerable Catholic Church, Altadena
Poole, Gary D., Blessed Junipero Serra Catholic Church, Quartz Hill
Rac, Felix, Christ the King Catholic Church, Los Angeles
Race, Mark, St. Bernadette Catholic Church, Los Angeles
Ramirez, Fidel M., Santa Clara Catholic Church, Oxnard
Ramirez, Jose Ascencion, Our Lady of Sorrows Catholic Church, Santa Barbara
Ramirez, Rogelio, St. Helen Catholic Church, Southgate
Ramirez, Salvador, St. John of God, Norwalk
Ramirez-Chavez, Hernan, St. Raphael Catholic Church, Los Angeles
Ramos, Dano L., Santa Clara Catholic Church, Oxnard
Rascati, Wayne, St. Raphael Catholic Church, Goleta
Recinos, Ricardo, St. Agatha Catholic Church, Inglewood
Redmond, Jack William, II, Blessed Junipero Serra Catholic Church, Camarillo
Reibenspies, Terence L., St. Rosa of Lima Church Catholic Church, Simi Valley
Reiser, Jay, Blessed Kateri Tekakwith Catholic Churcha, Santa Clarita
Reyes, Alberto, St. Rose of Lima Catholic Church, Bellflower
Reyes, Arnold Peter, Blessed Junipero Serra Catholic Church, Camarillo
Reynolds, Harrell Dale, Jr., Sacred Heart Catholic Church, Lancaster
Riera, Ralph, St. Raymond Catholic Church, Bellflower
Rios, Fred, Our Lady of the Miraculous Medal Catholic Church, Montebello
Rivas, Carlos R., St. Francis Xavier Catholic Church, Montebello
Roberto, Timothy J., St. Paul of the Cross Catholic Church, La Mirada
Rodriguez, Hernando, Resurrection Catholic Church, Los Angeles
Rodriguez, Jorge Alberto, Our Lady of Guadalupe Catholic Church, Santa Barbara
Rodriguez, Rodrigo, (Retired), 1813 Dawn Ridge Ct., Palmdale, 93555. St. Mary's, Palmdale
Rodriguez-Hernandez, Federico, St. Paschal Baylon Catholic Church, Thousand Oaks
Rojas, Pedro, All Souls Catholic Church, Los Angeles
Rose, David, Holy Angels Church of the Deaf, Covina
Rose, Frederick, American Martyrs Catholic Church, Manhattan Beach
Ruelas, Hector, St. Lawrence of Brindisi Catholic Church, Los Angeles
Ruotolo, Ronald, Sacred Heart Catholic Church, Lancaster
Ryan, Jack, (Retired), 6260 Guava Ave., Goleta, 93117. Santa Barbara Mission, Santa Barbara
Saake, Randal, Holy Cross Catholic Church, Santa Barbara
Sabol, Thomas A., St. Timothy Catholic Church, Los Angeles
Sadowski, Roy Edward, St. Anthony Catholic Church, Oxnard
Sahagun, Luis, St. Ignatius of Loyola Catholic Church, Los Angeles
Salazar, John Burgos, St. Francis of Assisi Catholic Church, Los Angeles
Salcido, Michael P., Immaculate Conception Catholic Church, Monrovia
Sanchez, Enrique R., St. Mark University Catholic Church, Santa Barbara
Sanchez, J. Francisco, Our Lady of Peace Catholic Church, North Hills
Sanchez, Ronald, Immaculate Conception Catholic Church, Monrovia
Sandner, Christopher Alan, Our Lady of Sorrows Catholic Church, Santa Barbara
Sangster, William B., (Retired), 340 Old Mill Rd., Space 166, Santa Barbara, 93110. Our Lady of Sorrows, Santa Barbara
Saucedo, Valentin, Presentation of Mary Catholic Church, Paramount
Schwerdt, Paul, Blessed Junipero Serra Catholic Church, Lancaster
Sebenius, Wayland "Gus", St. Therese Catholic Church, San Marino
Seidler, Robert, St. John Eudes Catholic Church, Valencia
Sheckler, Dale, St. Lawrence Martyr Catholic Church, Torrance
Shinkle, Richard D., (Retired), 538 Palos Verdes Blvd., Redondo Beach, 90277. St. James, Redondo Beach
Shinn, John, Valley Catholic Korean Center, Sherman Oaks
Siegel, Lawrence, St. Joseph Catholic Church, Carpinteria
Siegman, Craig A., St. Margaret Mary Alacoque Catholic Church, Verdes
Skupnik, Raymond P., St. Cyprian Catholic Church, Seal Beach
Smith, David Nicholas, St. Julie Billiart Catholic Church, Thousand Oaks
Smith, William Richard, St. Jude Catholic Church, Thousand Oaks
Soria, Richard, St. Margaret Mary Alacoque Catholic Church, Lomita
Spies, William, Blessed Junipero Serra Catholic Church, Camarillo
Stalder, Richard, La Purisima Concepcion Catholic Church, Santa Maria
Steele, John, Holy Family Catholic Church, Glendale
Steighner, Robert, Our Lady of the Assumption Catholic Church, Claremont
Stoltz, Eric, Good Shepherd Catholic Church, Los Angeles
Suh, Ignatius Jin, Our Lady of Lourdes Catholic Church, Glendale
Taufer, Wm. Dale, St. Bernardine of Siena Catholic Church, West Hills
Tchoi, Francis, The 103 Saints Korean Catholic Center, San Pedro
Tiambeng, Victor, St. Martha Catholic Church, Corona
Tomkovicz, Vincent, St. Maximilian Kolbe Catholic Church, Simi Valley
Torti, Joseph Felix, Blessed Junipero Serra Catholic Church, Camarillo
Trujillo, Jose Antonio, Our Lady of Sorrows Catholic Church, Santa Barbara
Tullius, John, Our Lady of the Assumption Catholic Church, Claremont
Turner, John, Jr., (Retired), 8711 S. Harvard Blvd. Apt. 522, 90047.
Ulibarri, Ralph J., Nativity Catholic Church, Torrance
Valdez, Roberto Lupian, St. John Neumann Catholic Church, Santa Maria
Valencia, Manuel, St. Rita Catholic Church, Sierra Madre
Valeriano, Oscar J., Jr., St. Louis of France Catholic Church, La Puente
Valles, Al, St. Louise de Marillac Catholic Church, San Dimas
Vasquez, Raymond, Jr., Santa Clara Catholic Church, Oxnard
Vazquez, Roberto L., St. John Chrysostom Catholic Church, Inglewood
Vedro, Shawn Stanley, St. Louis de Montfort Catholic Church, Santa Maria
Vega, Heriberto "Ed", St. Joseph the Worker Catholic Church, West Hills
Victorin, Rafael A., St. Augustine Catholic Church, Los Angeles
Villacorta, Ricardo, Christ the King Catholic Church, Los Angeles
Vital, Ernesto, St. Francis of Rome Catholic Church, Azusa
Vu, Anh Quoc, St. Mary Magdalen Catholic Church, Camarillo
Wallace, Daniel, St. Margaret Mary Alacoque Catholic Church, Lomita
Wauthy, Guy, St. Jerome Catholic Church, Los Angeles
Wessler, Charles Philip, Our Lady of the Assumption Catholic Church, Ventura
Williams, Richard (Dick), American Martyrs Catholic Church, Manhattan Beach
Wilson, Peter, Jr., St. Rose of Lima Catholic Church, Simi Valley
Wilson, William Robert, Jr., Our Lady of the Assumption Catholic Church, Ventura
Won, Augustine Y., St. Bede the Venerable Catholic Church, La Canada
Ye, Young, Holy Trinity Catholic Church, Glendale
Yoque, Leonel, Holy Cross Catholic Church, Los Angeles
Zavala-Dominguez, Bernardo, St. Louis of France Catholic Church, La Puente

INSTITUTIONS LOCATED IN THE ARCHDIOCESE

[A] SEMINARIES, ARCHDIOCESAN

CAMARILLO. *St. John's Seminary*, 5012 Seminary Rd., 93012-2500. Tel: 805-482-2755; Fax: 805-484-4074. Email: ccox@stjohnsem.edu. Web: www.stjohnsem.edu. Rev. Msgr. Craig A. Cox, J.C.D., D.Min., Rector & Pres.; Revs. Mariusz Beczek, O.S.J., M.A., S.T.D.; John P. Brennan, S.M.A., S.T.D.; James Clarke, Ph.D., Dir. of Spiritual Formation; Leon Hutton, Dir. of Human Formation & Evaluations; Vice Rector; Deacon Milton Rosenberg, Ph.D., Dir. Psych. Svcs.; Sisters Leanne Hubbard, S.N.D., Dir. of Pastoral Formation & Field Educ.; Mary Glennon, R.S.M., Assoc. Dir. Spiritual Formation; Ms. Jacquelein Rotter, Dir. Finance; Mr. Greg Julius, Dir. Facilities; Mrs. Mary Bissinger, Dir. Human Resources; Dr. Mark F. Fischer, Ph.D., Dir. Admissions & Pre-Theology Prog.; Dr. Patricia Lyons, M.L.S., Libraries Dir.; Ms. Esme Takahashi, Registrar; Revs. Joel Henson, Academic Dean; Eugenio Cardenas, M.Sp.S.; John Cawley, C.M., Assoc. Dir. of Pastoral Field Educ. & Vice Rector; Kevin McCracken, C.M.; Luke Dysinger, O.S.B., M.D., D.Phil.; Gregory Semeniuk, C.M., Dir. of Students; Steven Thoma, C.R.; Dr. Aurora Mordey, Dir. Language & Cultural Studies; Dr. Alan Vincelette, Dir. Lay Ministry Students; Marilena Christodorescu, M.A.; Dr. Paul F. Ford, Ph.D.; LaDonna Harrison, M.A.; Revs. Anthony S. Lee, Ph.D.; Aelred Niespolo, O.S.B., M.A., B.Th., M.Th. Major Seminary of the Archdiocese of Los Angeles. Priests 14; Sisters 2; Lay Teachers 7; Seminarians 81.

[B] SEMINARIES, RELIGIOUS OR SCHOLASTICATES

LOS ANGELES. *St. Joseph's Novitiate*, 2468 S. St. Andrews Pl., 90018. Tel: 323-734-0233; Fax: 323-731-5987. Email: usaprov-office@sbcglobal.net. Web: hospitallers.org. Bro. Stephen de la Rosa, O.H., Prov. & Formation Dir. Hospitaller Brothers of St. John of God. Brothers 24.

SANTA MARIA. *St. Joseph Seminary (Josephite Fathers' Novitiate)*, 180 Patterson Rd., 93455. Tel: 805-937-5378; Fax: 805-937-5759. Web: www.josephiteweb.org. Revs. Timothy R. Lane, C.J.; John A. Mayhew, C.J.; Alex-Louis Mubenga, C.J.; Edward Jalbert, C.J.; Mark L. Newman, C.J.; Franklin Minzaki, C.J. (Democratic Republic of Congo). Priests 6; Total Staff 1.

SANTA PAULA. *Canons Regular of the Immaculate Conception, (C.R.I.C.) Dom Grea House (House of Formation)* (1871) 984 Monte Vista Dr., 93060-1612. Tel: 805-933-5063; Fax: 805-525-5115. Email: cricusa@yahoo.com. Web: cricusa.org. Rev. Thomas J. Dome, C.R.I.C., Dir. & Novice Master. Priests 1; Postulants 2; Seminarians 2; Novices 1.

SANTA YNEZ. *San Lorenzo Seminary - Retreat Center*, Retreat Center: 1802 Sky Dr., P.O. Box 247, 93460-0247. Tel: 805-688-5630; Fax: 805-686-0775. Email: info@sanlorenzo.org. Web: www.sanlorenzo.org. Revs. Robert A. Barbato, O.F.M.Cap., Guardian & Dir.; Alejandro

Magallenes; James Johnson, O.F.M. Cap.; Bros. Lance Love, O.F.M.Cap, Vicar & Assoc. Dir.; Joseph Slominski, O.F.M.Cap.; Jim Doyle, O.F.M.Cap. Capuchin Franciscan Friars. Priests 3; Brothers 3; Total Staff 6.

SUN VALLEY. *Scalabrini House of Discernment (Seminary)*, 10651 Vinedale St., 91352-2825. Tel: 818-504-9561; Fax: 818-504-9562. Revs. Giovanni Bizzotto, C.S., Vocation Dir.; Ramiro V. Sanchez Chan, C.S., Dir. Discernment Program. Seminarians 9.

Scalabrini Vocation Office Tel: 323-216-6278; Fax: 818-504-9562.

[C] COLLEGES AND UNIVERSITIES

LOS ANGELES. *Loyola Marymount University*, One LMU Dr., Ste. 4844, 90045-2659. Tel: 310-338-2700. Web: www.lmu.edu (Including Law School). Mr. David W. Burcham, Pres.; Rev. Patrick J. Cahalan, S.J., Chancellor; Dr. Joseph Hellige, Senior Vice Pres. & Chief Academic Office; Mr. Thomas O. Fleming Jr., Senior Vice Pres. & CFO; Dennis Slon, Senior Vice Pres. Univ. Rels.; Dr. Lane Bove, Senior Vice Pres. Student Affairs; Rev. Joseph LaBrie, S.J., Special Asst. to the Pres.; Rae Linda Brown, Ph.D., Vice Pres. Undergraduate Educ.; Rev. Robert V. Caro, S.J., Vice Pres. for Mission & Min.; Dr. Abbie Robinson-Armstrong, Vice Pres. for Intercultural Affairs; Ms. Lynne Scarboro, Senior Vice Pres. for Admin.; Kathy Reed, Registrar; Kristine Brancolini, Dean, Univ. Libraries; Dr. Joseph McNicholas, Office of Research & Sponsored Projects; Anne Prisco, Vice Pres. for Enrollment Mgmt.; Rebecca Chandler, Vice Pres. for Human Resources; Rev. Albert P. Koppes, O.Carm., Assoc. Chancellor; Dr. Dennis W. Draper, Dean of Business Admin.; Dr. Richard G. Plumb, Dean of Science & Engineering; Prof. Barbara Busse, Dean, Communication & Fine Arts; Mr. Stephen G. Ujlaki, Dean School of Film & TV; Dr. Shane P. Martin, Dean, School of Educ.; Mr. Victor Gold, Senior Vice Pres. & Dean Loyola Law School. Students 7,911; Full Time: 444; Part Time 402 846; Loyola Marymount & Loyola Law School Staff 1,040.

Jesuit Community, P.O. Box 45041, 90045-0041. Tel: 310-338-7445; Fax: 310-338-3002. Revs. Robert W. Scholla, S.J., Rector; James Erps, S.J., Dir. Campus Min.; John Galvan, S.J., Min.; Marc Reeves, S.J., Min./Theology; Jose Ignacio Badenes, S.J.; James McDermott, S.J.; Jacques Randrianary, S.J. (Madagascar); Albertus Bagus Laksana, S.J.; Sean Dempsey, S.J.; Bro. James Siwicki, S.J., Vocation Dir. In Res. Most Rev. Gordon D. Bennett, S.J.; Revs. Mark Bandsuch, S.J.; Patrick J. Cahalan, S.J.; Robert V. Caro, S.J.; Philip J. Chmielewski, S.J.; Patrick Connolly, S.J.; James Fredericks; William J. Fulco, S.J.; James H. Keene, S.J.; Albert P. Koppes, O.Carm.; Joseph LaBrie, S.J.; Michael Lee, S.J.; Dorian Llywelyn, S.J.; Terrance L. Mahan, S.J.; John D. Murphy, S.J.; Thomas P. Rausch, S.J., Ph.D.; Richard A. Robin, S.J.; Randall Roche, S.J.; Richard W. Rolfs, S.J.; Kenneth Rudnick, S.J.; Robert W. Scholla, S.J.; Robert J. Welch, S.J.

The Sacred Heart of Mary and Sisters of St. Joseph of Orange, One LMU Dr., 90045-2659. Tel: 310-338-2700; 310-641-4682.

Communities of the Religious of the Sacred Heart of Mary and Sisters of St. Joseph of Orange

Loyola School of Law (1920) 919 S. Albany St., P.O. Box 15019, 90015. Tel: 213-736-1000. Web: www.lls.edu. Mr. Victor Gold, Sr. Vice Pres. & Dean. Priests 1; 77 full time; 72 part time 149; Students 1,312.

Mount St. Mary's College (1925)Tel: 310-954-4010; Fax: 310-954-4019. Email: amcelaney@msmc.la.edu. Web: www.msmc.la.edu. Conducted by the Sisters of St. Joseph of Carondelet., Resident and non-resident students.

Chalon Campus, 12001 Chalon Rd., 90049-1599. Tel: 310-954-4000; Fax: 310-954-4019. Web: www.msmc.la.edu.

Doheny Campus, 10 Chester Pl., 90007. Tel: 213-477-2500; Fax: 213-477-2519. Dr. Ann McElaney-Johnson, Pres.; Dr. Jane Lingua, Vice Pres. Student Affairs; Larry Smith, Vice Pres. Info. Support Svcs. & Enrollment; Dr. Eleanor D. Slebert, Provost & Academic Vice Pres.; Dr. Linda Moody, Graduate Dean; Dr. Stephanie Cubba, Vice. Pres. Inst. Advancement; Mr. Dean Kilgour, Asst. Vice Pres. Enrollment Mgmt.; Dr. Karol Dean, Asst. Provost; Chris McAlary, Vice Pres. Admin. & Fin.; Claudia Reed, Librarian. Sisters 5; Priests 2; Lay Teachers 99; Students 2,936.

RANCHO PALOS VERDES. *Marymount College, Palos Verdes, California*, 30800 Palos Verdes Dr., E., 90275-6299. Tel: 310-377-5501; Fax: 310-265-0642. Email: kramsay@marymountpv.edu. Web: www.marymountpv.edu. Michael S. Brophy, Ph.D., M.F.A., Pres.; Dr. Ariane Schauer, Vice Pres. Academic Affairs; Mr. James Reeves, Vice Pres. Finance & Admin.; Mary McMillan, Librarian. An independent and Catholic Co-educational, four-year Liberal Arts College. Priests 1; Sisters 1; Lay Teachers 98; Students 930.

SANTA PAULA. *Thomas Aquinas College* (1969) 10000 N. Ojai Rd., 93060. Tel: 805-525-4417; 800-634-9797; Fax: 805-525-0620. Email: pr@thomasaquinas.edu. Web: www.thomasaquinas.edu. Dr. Michael F. McLean, Pres.; Dr. Brian T. Kelly, Dean; Mr. Peter L. DeLuca III, Vice Pres. Finance & Admin.; Dr. Paul O'Reilly, Vice Pres. Devel.; Revs. Cornelius M. Buckley, S.J., Chap.; Paul Raftery, O.P., Chap.; Viltis Jatulis, Librarian. Four-year undergraduate program in the Liberal Arts leading to the B.A. Degree; Co-educational. Lay Teachers 37; Students 354.

[D] HIGH SCHOOLS, ARCHDIOCESAN

LOS ANGELES. *Bishop Conaty-Our Lady of Loretto High School* (1923) (Girls), 2900 W. Pico Blvd., 90006-3802. Tel: 323-737-0012; Fax: 323-737-1749. Web: www.bishopconatyloretto.org. Richard A. Spicer, Prin.; Lisa J. Gabriel, Vice Prin.; Dennis J. Polito, Dir. Inst. Advancement. Sisters 2; Lay Teachers 21; Students 358; Total Staff 30.

Bishop Mora Salesian High School (Boys), 960 S. Soto St., 90023. Tel: 323-261-7124; Fax: 323-261-9474. Web: salesianmustangs.com. Mr. Samuel Robles, Prin.; Mr. Mark Johnson, Vice Prin. Salesians of Don Bosco. Priests 1; Lay Teachers 35; Students 455.

Sacred Heart High School (Girls), 2111 Griffin Ave., 90031. Tel: 323-225-2209; Fax: 323-225-5046. Email: principal@shhsla.org. Web: www.shhsla.org. Sr. Janice Therese Wellington, O.P., Prin.; Mrs. Muriel Bourhe, Librarian. Sisters 3; Lay Teachers 21; Students 212; Total Staff 5.

Verbum Dei High School (Boys), 11100 S. Central Ave., 90059-1199. Tel: 323-564-6651; Fax: 323-564-9009. Email: wmuller@verbumdei.us. Web: www.verbumdei.us. Revs. William H. Muller, S.J., Pres.; Michael Mandala, S.J., V.F., Dir. Community Rels.; Dr. Daniel J. O'Connell, Prin.; Ms. Cristina Cuellar-Villanueva, Vice Pres. Corp. Work Study Prog.; Mr. Victor M. Cancino, S.J., Teacher; Sr. Marilyn Ficht, R.S.H.M., Teacher. Conducted by the Archdiocese of Los Angeles. Priests 2; Brothers 1; Sisters 1; Lay Teachers 22; Students 300; Total Staff 50.

Verbum Dei High School WorkStudy, Inc., 11100 S. Central Ave., 90059-1199. Tel: 323-564-6651, Ext. 7000; Fax: 323-564-9009.

BURBANK. *Bellarmine-Jefferson High School* (Coed), 465 E. Olive Ave., 91501. Tel: 818-972-1400 (Main Office & Attendance); 818-972-1401 (Athletic); Fax: 818-559-6387. Web: www.bell-jeff.net. Mr. John Matheus, Prin. Brothers 1; Lay Teachers 20; Students 222; Total Staff 25.

DOWNEY. *St. Matthias High School*, 7851 E. Gardendale St., 90242. Tel: 562-861-2271; Fax: 562-869-8652. Email: principal@stmatthiashs.org. Web: www.stmatthiashs.org. Erick A. Rubalcava, Pres.; Michael Wagner, Prin.; Veronica Zozaya, Asst. Prin. Lay Teachers 15; Students 219.

GARDENA. *Junipero Serra High School* (1950) 14830 S. Van Ness Ave., 90249. Tel: 310-324-6675; Fax: 310-352-4953. Email: principal@la-serrahs.org. Web: www.la-serrahs.org. Erick A. Rubalcava, Pres.; Michael Wagner, Prin.; Christian De Larkin, Asst. Prin.; Tamara Shelton, Librarian. Priests 1; Lay Teachers 42; Students 705; Total Staff 15.

LA PUENTE. *Bishop Amat Memorial High School* (Coed), 14301 Fairgrove Ave., 91746. Tel: 626-962-2495; Fax: 626-960-0994. Email: president@bishopamat.org. Web: www.bishopamat.org. Rev. Msgr. Aidan M. Carroll, Pres.; Dr. Merritt V. Hemenway, Prin.; Mr. Richard Beck, Vice Prin.; Ms. Deborah Oswald, Dir. of Finance & Devel.; Mrs. Maria Gover, Asst. Prin.; Mrs. Ivette Salcedo, Asst. Prin. & Student Services; Mrs. Isabelle Selak, Librarian. Conducted by the Archdiocese of Los Angeles. Priests 2; Sisters 1; Lay Teachers 85; Students 1,385; Total Staff 110.

LA VERNE. *Damien High School*, 2280 Damien Ave., 91750. Tel: 909-596-1946; Fax: 909-596-6112. Email: info@damien-hs.edu. Web: www.damien-hs.edu. Rev. Peadar Cronin, SS.CC., Pres.; Mr. Sam Pearsall, Prin.; Mr. Jeff Grant, Dean of Students; Mr. Thomas Carroll, Athletic Dir.; Dr. Michael Williams, Asst. Prin. Academic Affairs; Mr. Casey Yeazel, Asst. Prin. of Guidance; Mrs. Mary Ellen Leggio, Fin. Officer; Alejandro Jimenez, Librarian.

Congregation of the Sacred Hearts, Inc., Conducted by the Archdiocese of Los Angeles. Priests 2; Lay Teachers 57; Students 965; Total Staff 74.

Faculty Res.: 2150 Damien Ave., 91750. Tel: 909-596-1946; Fax: 909-596-6112. Email: info@damien-hs.edu. Web: www.damien-hs.edu.

LAKEWOOD. *Saint Joseph High School* (Girls), 5825 N. Woodruff Ave., 90713. Tel: 562-925-5073; Fax: 562-925-3315. Web: www.sj-jester.org. Dr. Terri Mendoza, Ph.D., Prin.; Revs. John Shevlin, S.V.D.; James Henry, S.V.D.; Mrs. Lisa Lindgren, Librarian. Conducted by Archdiocese of Los Angeles. Priests 2; Sisters 2; Lay Teachers 57; Students 754; Total Staff 75.

LANCASTER. *Paraclete High School* (Coed), 42145 N. 30th St., 93536. Tel: 661-943-3255; Fax: 661-722-9455. Email: janson@paracletehs.org. Web: www.paracletehs.org. John W. Anson, M.Ed., Prin.; Mary Ruth Farrell, Librarian. Tel: 661-943-3255, Ext. 116; Rev. Giampietro Gasparin, C.S.J. Conducted by Archdiocese of Los Angeles. Priests 1; Lay Teachers 44; Students 744.

LONG BEACH. *St. Anthony High School*, 620 Olive Ave., 90802. Tel: 562-435-4496; Fax: 562-437-3055. Gina Maguire, Pres.; Michael Schabert, Prin. Lay Teachers 28; Students 440.

MISSION HILLS. *Bishop Alemany High School*, 11111 N. Alemany Dr., 91345. Tel: 818-365-3925; Fax: 818-365-2064. Email: fferry@alemany.org. Web: www.alemany.org. Mr. Frank Ferry, Prin.; Mrs. Jan Galla, Vice Prin.; Mr. Randy Thompson, Asst. Prin. Student Life; Dr. Juliet Fine, Asst. Prin. Curriculum & Instruction; Mike Purnell, Librarian. Priests 1; Sisters 3; Lay Teachers 94; Students 1,666; Total Staff 150.

MONTEBELLO. *Cantwell Sacred Heart of Mary High School* (1946) (Coed), 329 N. Garfield Ave., 90640. Tel: 323-887-2066; Fax: 323-724-4332. Email: cshm@cshm.org. Web: www.cshm.org. David I. Chambers, Prin.; Sr. Rose Marie Wilson, O.S.F., Librarian. Archdiocesan Institution. Sisters 2; Lay Teachers 32; Students 571; Total Staff 43.

OXNARD. *Santa Clara High School*, 2121 Saviers Rd., 93033. Tel: 805-483-9502; Fax: 805-483-1588. Web: www.santaclarahighschool.com. Mrs. Siobhain O'Reilly-Hill, Prin.; Ms. Nancy O'Sullivan, Vice Prin. Lay Teachers 26; Total Faculty & Staff 39; Students 447.

PLAYA DEL REY. *St. Bernard High School* (Coed), 9100 Falmouth Ave., 90293. Tel: 310-823-4651; Fax: 310-827-3365. Email: malvarez@stbernardhs.com. Web: www.stbernardhs.com. Michael Alvarez, Prin. Conducted by Archdiocese of Los Angeles. Brothers 1; Sisters 1; Lay Teachers 23; Students 380; Total Staff 31.

POMONA. *Pomona Catholic High School* (Girls), 533 W. Holt Ave., 91768. Tel: 909-623-5297; Fax: 909-620-6057. Email: storres@pomonacatholichs.org. Web: www.pomonacatholichs.org. Samuel Torres, Prin.; Sr. Feliz Gil-Jimenez, Vice Prin. Sisters 2; Lay Teachers 15; Students 233; Total Staff 5.

SANTA FE SPRINGS. *St. Paul High School* (1956) 9635 S. Greenleaf Ave., 90670. Tel: 562-698-6246; Fax: 562-696-8396. Email: kaceves@stpaulhs.org. Web: www.stpaulhs.org. Mrs. Kate Aceves, Prin.; Mr. Robert Miller, Asst. Prin. Curriculum & Instruction; Denis O'Sullivan, O.S.F., Librarian. Conducted by Archdiocese of Los Angeles. Priests 1; Brothers 2; Sisters 1; Lay Teachers 40; Students 600; Total Staff 65.

SANTA MARIA. *St. Joseph High School* (1964) (Coed), 4120 S. Bradley Rd., 93455. Tel: 805-937-2038; Fax: 805-937-4248. Email: sjhs@sjhsknights.com. Web: www.sjhsknights.com. Rev. Edward Jalbert, C.J.; Joseph Myers, Prin.; Toni Jetter, Librarian. Conducted by Archdiocese of Los Angeles. Priests 1; Sisters 1; Lay Teachers 26; Students 474.

TORRANCE. *Bishop Montgomery High School* (Coed), 5430 Torrance Blvd., 90503. Tel: 310-540-2021; Fax: 310-792-1273. Email: rlibbon@bmhs-la.org. Web: www.bmhs-la.org. Rosemary Distaso-Libbon, Pres. & Prin.; William Martinez, Librarian. Conducted by the Archdiocese of Los Angeles. Lay Teachers 80; Students 1,100.

VENTURA. *St. Bonaventure High School* (1963) (Coed), 3167 Telegraph Rd., 93003-3281. Tel: 805-648-6836; Fax: 805-648-4903. Email: office@saintbonaventure.com. Web: www.saintbonaventure.com. Marc Groff, Prin.; Ruth McNamara, Librarian. Conducted by Archdiocese of Los Angeles. Lay Teachers 42; Total Staff 46; Students 565.

[E] HIGH SCHOOLS, PAROCHIAL

High Schools are maintained in the following parishes (for particulars refer to the individual parishes):

Glendale: Holy Family; San Gabriel: San Gabriel Mission; San Pedro: Mary Star of the Sea; Santa Monica, St. Monica; Van Nuys: St. Genevieve

[F] HIGH SCHOOLS, PRIVATE

LOS ANGELES. *Cathedral High School of Los Angeles,*

Incorporated (1925) (Boys), 1253 Bishops Rd., 90012. Tel: 323-225-2438; Fax: 323-222-7223. Email: brjohnm@cathedralhighschool.org. Web: www.cathedralhighschool.org. Mr. Martin Farfan, Pres.; Bro. John Montgomery, F.S.C., Prin. Conducted by the Brothers of the Christian Schools (F.S.C.) Brothers 7; Lay Teachers 37; Students 725; Total Staff 52.

Immaculate Heart High School (1906) (Girls), 5515 Franklin Ave., 90028-5999. Tel: 323-461-3651; Fax: 323-462-0610. Email: ihhs1@aol.com. Web: www.immaculateheart.org. Julie Anne McCormick, Pres.; Virginia Hurst, Prin.; Tracie Thomas, Librarian. Conducted by the Immaculate Heart Community. Lay Teachers 48; Students 553.

Loyola High School of Los Angeles, 1901 Venice Blvd., 90006. Tel: 213-381-5121, Ext. 125; Fax: 213-368-1758. Email: ggoethals@loyolahs.edu. Web: loyolahs.edu. Revs. Gregory M. Goethals, S.J., Pres.; Peter F. Filice, S.J., Supr. Jesuit Community; Mr. Frank Kozakowski, Prin.; Revs. Jerry Hayes, S.J., Asst. Dir. Advancement; John Quinn, S.J.; Mrs. April Hannah, Librarian; Mr. William Slocum, Intermin Sr. Dir. of Advancement; Mr. Ike Udoh, S.J., Scholastic; Rev. Stephen A. Barber, S.J., Dir. of Cura Personal's Prog. at Loyola High School. Sponsored by the California Province of the Society of Jesus. Priests 5; Lay Teachers 82; Administrators 9; Total Staff 171; Students 1,254; Scholastics 1. In Res Revs. William H. Muller, S.J., Pres. Verbum Dei High School; Michael Mandala, S.J., V.F., Dir. Community Rels., Verbum Dei High School; Mr. Victor M. Cancino, S.J., Scholastic.

Marymount High School (Girls), 10643 Sunset Blvd., 90077. Tel: 310-472-1205; Fax: 310-476-0910. Email: jbutler@mhs-la.org. Web: www.mhs-la.org. Ms. Jacqueline L. Landry, Head; Michele DeVita, Librarian. Religious of the Sacred Heart of Mary. Sisters 1; Lay Teachers 48; Total Staff 39; Students 369.

Notre Dame Academy (1949) (Girls), 2851 Overland Ave., 90064. Tel: 310-839-5289; Fax: 310-839-7957. Email: nehrmann@ndala.com. Web: www.ndala.com. Ms. Nancy J. Coonis, Pres.; Joan Gumaer Tyhurst, Prin.; Mrs. Gloria Lukacovic, Librarian. Sisters of Notre Dame of Los Angeles 2; Teachers 24; Students 400.

ALHAMBRA. *Ramona Convent Secondary School, Ramona Convent of the Holy Names* (Girls Grades 7-12), 1701 W. Ramona Rd., 91803-3099. Tel: 626-282-4151; Fax: 626-281-0797. Email: ramona@ramonaconvent.org. Web: www.ramonaconvent.org. Ms. Tina Bonacci, Prin.; Sr. Kathleen Callaway, S.N.J.M., Pres. Sisters of the Holy Names of Jesus and Mary 3; Lay Teachers 32; Total Staff 35; Students 375.

BELLFLOWER. *St. John Bosco High School*, 13640 S. Bellflower Blvd., 90706. Tel: 562-920-1734; Fax: 562-867-5322. Email: jnuguyen@bosco.org. Web: www.bosco.org. Revs. Joseph Thinh-Nguyen, S.D.B., Dir.; Tho Bui, S.D.B.; Bros. Joseph Lockwood; Noel De Bruton, S.D.B.; Steve Standard, S.D.B.; Patrick Lee, Prin.; Karen McCoy, Librarian. (Boys) Priests 2; Brothers 2; Lay Teachers 50; Students 760.

BURBANK. *Providence High School* (Coed), 511 S. Buena Vista St., 91505. Tel: 818-846-8141; Fax: 818-843-8421. Email: joesciuto@providencehigh.org. Web: www.providencehigh.org. Mr. Joe Sciuto, Head of School; Joanie Fenstermaker, Dir. Campus Ministry; Claire Hickey, Dean of Studies; Dennis Bullock, Dean of Students; Marina Cedillo, Librarian. Sisters 1; Lay Teachers 47; Total Staff 17; Students 401.

CHATSWORTH. *Chaminade College Preparatory* (1952) Office of the President, 10210 Oakdale Ave., 91311-3533. Tel: 818-366-9284; Fax: 818-363-8492. Email: jadams@chaminade.org. Web: www.chaminade.org. Mr. James V. Adams, Pres.

Chaminade College Preparatory, (Coed Grades 6-12) Priests 2; Brothers 5; Lay Teachers 142; Total Staff 205; Students 2,041.

Chatsworth Campus (Middle School, Grades 6-8), 19800 Devonshire St., 91311. Tel: 818-363-8127; Fax: 818-363-1219. Mr. Michael Valentine, Prin.; Helen Foster, Librarian.

West Hills Campus (High School, Grades 9-12), 7500 Chaminade Ave., West Hills, 91304. Tel: 818-347-8300; Fax: 818-348-8374. Bro. Thomas Fahy, O.S.F., Prin.

Marianist Community Tel: 818-347-8043; Fax: 818-347-2788. Revs. James Mueller, S.M., Chap.; Theodore Ley, S.M., Chap. Priests 2; Brothers 4.

ENCINO. *Crespi Carmelite High School*, 5031 Alonzo Ave., 91316. Tel: 818-345-1672; Fax: 818-705-0209. Web: www.crespi.org. Revs. Thomas Schrader, O.Carm., Pres.; Paul Henson, O.Carm., Prin.; Mr. Jeff Thornton, Vice Prin.; Mr. Jonathan Schild, Vice Prin.; Mr. Brian Banducci, Vice Prin.; Mr. Jason Nevis, Dean; Mrs. Margie Moreno, Dir. Finance; Mr. Greg Cornell, Vice Pres. Inst. Advancement; Mrs. Sharon Barkins-Wasson, Dir. Counseling & Guidance; Mr. Rob Kodama, Dir. Admissions; Mr. Chris Knabenshue, Campus Min.; Mrs. Dona Long, Dir. of Student Activity; Mrs. Janet Nungester, Librarian; Mr. Matthew Luderer, Athletic Dir. For further details about Our Lady of Mount Carmel Priory, Encino please see Monasteries and Residences of Priests and Brothers. Priests 2; Lay Teachers 55; Students 600.

GLENDORA. *St. Lucy's Priory High School* (Girls), 655 W. Sierra Madre Ave., 91741. Tel: 626-335-3322; Fax: 626-335-4373. Email: slphs@aol.com. Web: www.stlucys.com. Sr. Monica Collins, O.S.B., Prin.; Mrs. Marsha Solano, Librarian. Conducted by the Benedictine Sisters. Sisters 2; Lay Teachers 37; Total Staff 39; Students 670.

INGLEWOOD. *St. Mary's Academy* (Girls), 701 Grace Ave., 90301. Tel: 310-674-8470; Fax: 310-674-6255. Web: www.smabelles.org. Dr. Yvonne McNeal, Prin.; Sr. Maureen Dougherty, Librarian. Sisters of St. Joseph of Carondelet 7; Lay Teachers 22; Total Staff 20; Students 350.

LA CANADA FLINTRIDGE. *Flintridge Sacred Heart Academy* (1931) (Girls), 440 St. Katherine Dr., 91011. Tel: 626-685-8500; Fax: 626-685-8555. Email: cmccormack@fsha.org. Web: www.fsha.org. Sr. Celeste Marie Botello, O.P., Prin.; Nora Murphy, Librarian.

Flintridge Sacred Heart Academy, A Corporation Dominican Sisters of Mission San Jose 4; Lay Teachers 44; Students 410.

St. Francis High School of La Canada-Flintridge (Boys), 200 Foothill Blvd., 91011. Tel: 818-790-0325; Fax: 818-790-5542. Web: sfhs.net. Email: martit@sfhs.net. Rev. Antonio Marti, O.F.M.Cap., Pres. St. Francis High School; Mr. Thomas G. Moran, Prin.; Sr. Barbarine Houdek, O.S.F., Librarian; Revs. Hung Nguyen, O.F.M.Cap., Campus Chap.; Chris Thiel, O.F.M.Cap.; Anthony Scannel, O.F.M.Cap.; Michael Walsh; Bro. Tran Vu, O.F.M.Cap.

St. Francis High School of La Canada-Flintridge Priests 3; Brothers 1; Sisters 1; Lay Teachers 48; Teachers 53; Total Staff 69; Students 658.

OJAI. *Villanova Preparatory School in California*, 12096 N. Ventura Ave., 93023-3999. Tel: 805-646-1464; Fax: 805-646-4430. Email: info@villanovaprep.org. Web: www.villanovaprep.org. Carol Hoffer, Headmaster; Rev. Gregory Heidenblut, O.S.A., Pres.

Villanova Preparatory School in California Conducted by Augustinians (Order of St. Augustine). Priests 1; Brothers 1; Sisters 3; Lay Teachers 30; Total Staff 65; Students 305.

PASADENA. *La Salle High School* (1956) 3880 E. Sierra Madre Blvd., 91107. Tel: 626-351-8951; Fax: 626-351-0275. Email: principal@lasallehs.org. Web: lasallehs.org. Mr. Patrick Bonacci, Prin.; Dr. Richard Gray, Pres.; Mrs. Delia Swanner, Librarian. Brothers 1; Lay Teachers 73; Total Staff 93; Students 742.

Mayfield Senior School of the Holy Child Jesus, 500 Bellefontaine St., 91105-2439. Tel: 626-799-9121; Fax: 626-799-8576. Email: rita.mcbride@mayfieldsenior.org. Web: www.mayfieldsenior.org. Thomas Wheatley, Dir. Finance & Opers.; Rita C. McBride, Prin.; Ann Pibel, Librarian. Sisters 1; Lay Teachers 36; Students 300.

**St. Monica Academy, Inc.*, 301 N. Orange Grove Blvd., 91103. Marguerite Grimm, Headmaster.

ROSEMEAD. *Don Bosco Technical Institute* (Boys), 1151 San Gabriel Blvd., 91770-4299. Tel: 626-940-2000; Fax: 626-940-2001. Email: xjimenez@boscotech.edu. Web: www.boscotech.edu. Mr. Alberto M. Pimentel, Pres.; Mr. Xavier E. Jimenez, Prin.; Rev. Mel Trinidad, S.D.B., Dir. & Religious Supr.; Mr. Robert J. Currie, Dean of Academics; Ms. Jeff Krynen, Dean of Technology. Sponsored by Salesians of St. John Bosco., Secondary Section. Priests 4; Brothers 5; Administrators 4; Lay Teachers 39; Students 431; Total Staff 88.

SANTA BARBARA. *Bishop Garcia Diego High School Inc.* (1959) (Coed), 4000 La Colina Rd., 93110. Tel: 805-967-1266; Fax: 805-964-3178. Email: bishop@bishopdiego.org. Web: www.bishopdiego.org. Dr. Paul Harrington, Head of School; Dr. Joe Reiken, Asst. Head of School Cirriculum & Instruction; Ms. Lori Willis, Dir. of Advancement. Email: lwillis@bishopdiego.org; Mrs. Jennifer Winnewisser, Dir., Campus Ministry. Sisters 1; Lay Teachers 28; Students 285; Total Staff 43.

SHERMAN OAKS. *Notre Dame High School* (1947) 13645 Riverside Dr., 91423. Tel: 818-933-3600; Fax: 818-501-0507. Email: connelly@ndhs.org. Web: www.ndhs.org. Mr. Brett A. Lowart, Pres.; Mrs. Stephanie Connelly, Prin. Priests 1; Brothers 1; Lay Teachers 90; Students 1,195; Total Staff 113.

SIERRA MADRE. *Alverno High School* (Girls), 200 N. Michillinda Ave., 91024. Tel: 626-355-3463; Fax: 626-355-3153. Web: Alverno-hs.org. Ann M. Gillick, M.S., Prin. Lay Teachers 26; Students 285; Total Staff 44.

THOUSAND OAKS. *La Reina High School* (Girls, Grades 7-12), 106 W. Janss Rd., 91360. Tel: 805-495-6494; Fax: 805-494-4966. Email: lareina@lareina.com. Web: www.lareina.com. Shannon Gomez, Ed.D., Prin.; Sr. Mary LaReina Kelly, S.N.D., Pres.; Kristine Durand, Dir., Campus Ministry; Heather Neidenbach, Library Media Teacher. Sisters of Notre Dame 4; Lay Teachers 42; Students 582; Total Staff 76.

WOODLAND HILLS. *Louisville High School* (1960) (Girls), 22300 Mulholland Dr., 91364. Tel: 818-346-8812; Fax: 818-346-9483. Email: kvercillo@louisvillehs.org. Web: louisvillehs.org. Kathleen Vercillo, Prin.; Sr. Myra McPartland, S.S.L., Pres.; Mrs. Robbi Horvath, Librarian. Sisters 3; Lay Teachers 36; Total Staff 23; Students 428.

[G] ELEMENTARY SCHOOLS, PRIVATE

LOS ANGELES. *Notre Dame Academy (Elementary)*, 2911 Overland Ave., 90064. Tel: 310-287-3895; Fax: 310-838-8983. Web: www.ndaes.org. Ms. Nancy J. Coonis, Pres.; Lilliam Paetzold, Prin. Sisters of Notre Dame of Los Angeles 1; Lay Teachers 16; Total Staff 24; Students 272.

PASADENA. *Mayfield Junior School*, 405 S. Euclid Ave., 91101. Tel: 626-796-2774; Fax: 626-796-5753. Email: mjs@mayfieldjs.org. Web: www.mayfieldjs.org. Joseph J. Gill, Headmaster; Tina Halpin, Dir. Communications; Tatiana Guyer, Librarian. Lay Teachers 60; Total Staff 25; Students 507.

**St. Monica Academy, Inc.*, 301 N. Orange Grove Blvd., 91103. Marguerite Grimm, Headmaster.

[H] ORPHANAGES AND INFANT HOMES

ROSEMEAD, LOS ANGELES. *Maryvale* (1953) 7600 E. Graves Ave., P.O. Box 1039, 91770-1003. Tel: 626-280-6510; 323-283-9311; Fax: 626-288-8903. Email: maryvale@maryvalle-ca.org. Web: www.maryvale-ca.org. Steve Gunther, M.S.W., Pres. & Exec. Dir. Daughters of Charity 3; Total Assisted 447; Children: Residential Treatment 85; Mental Health Day Treatment 85; Early Education 257; Aftercare Services 17; Transitional Housing Program 3; Total Staff 228.

The Los Angeles Orphan Asylum (1856) 7600 E. Graves Ave., 91770. Tel: 626-280-6510; Fax: 626-288-8903.

Los Angeles Orphanage Guild (1951) 7600 E. Graves Ave., 91770. Tel: 626-280-6510; Fax: 626-288-8903. Email: maryvale@maryvale-ca.org. Web: www.maryvale-ca.org.

[I] DAY NURSERIES

LOS ANGELES. *Divine Providence Pre-school and Kindergarten* (1954) 2620 Monmouth Ave., 90007. Tel: 213-747-3074; Fax: 213-747-6468. Email: divine_providence@sbcglobal.net. Web: www.companyofmary.us. Sr. Mary Gomez, O.D.N., Dir. & Prin.; Belen Rojas, Co-Prin. Sisters of the Company of Mary 4; Lay Teachers 12; Children 168; Total Staff 4.

St. Jeanne de Lestonnac Preschool and Kindergarten, 4001 Venice Blvd., 90019. Tel: 323-737-1217; Fax: 323-737-3672. Email: sjdlsla@gmail.com. Web: www.companyofmary.us. Sisters Teresa Zapata, O.D.N., Prin. & Dir.; Cecilia Duran, O.D.N., Supvr. (Formerly Little Flower Kindergarten & Day Nursery). Sisters 3; Lay Teachers 15; Children 170; Total Staff 21.

GARDENA. *St. Anthony's Day Nursery*, 1044 W. 163rd St., 90247. Tel: 310-329-8654. Sr. Yadira Villalobos, M.C., Prin. Sisters 10; Total Staff 12; Children 90.

SYLMAR. *Poverello of Assisi Preschool* (1964) 13367 Borden Ave., 91342. Tel: 818-364-7446; Fax: 818-364-8596. Sr. Mary Fatima Guevara, Prin. Franciscan Missionary Sisters of the Immaculate Conception. Sisters 12; Total Staff 15; Children 120.

[J] GENERAL HOSPITALS

LOS ANGELES. *St. Vincent Medical Center*, 2131 W. 3rd St., 90057. Tel: 213-484-7111. Web: www.stvincentmedicalcenter.com. Rev. Thomas Griffin, Dir. Spiritual Care. Daughters of Charity Health System.; Sponsored by the Daughters of Charity of St. Vincent de Paul, Province of the West. Bed Capacity 366; Patients Assisted Annually 79,632; Total Staff 1,150.

BURBANK. *Providence Health and Services California Region*, 501 S. Buena Vista St., 91505. Tel: 818-847-4688; Fax: 818-847-4607. Email:

srsheila.browne@providence.org (Mission Dir., Providence St. Joseph Medical Center). Michael Hunn, CEO; Sisters Colleen Settles, O.P., Chief Mission Integration Officer. Tel: 818-847-3350; Sheila Browne, R.S.M., Mission Leader-Providence St. Joseph Medical Center. Sponsored by Providence Ministries.

Providence Saint Joseph Medical Center, 501 S. Buena Vista St., 91505. Tel: 818-843-5111; Fax: 818-525-3444. Web: www.providence.org. Sr. Sheila Browne, R.S.M., Dir., Mission Leadership. Tel: 818-847-3356; Rev. Mark Ciccone, S.J., Mgr., Spiritual Care. Tel: 818-847-4735; Mr. R. Phillip Kiehl, Chap.; D'vorah McDonald, Chap.; W. Diane Gardner-Slater, Chap.; Rev. Kenneth Chukwu, Chap.; Samuel Scriven, Chap.; Sr. Blanca Sagles, S.P., Chap. Bed Capacity 414; Patients Assisted Annually 115,000; Total Staff 2,600.

ALHAMBRA. *Santa Teresita, Inc.* (1930) 920 E. Alhambra Rd., 91801. Tel: 626-359-3243; Fax: 626-357-7166. Email: administration@santa-teresita.org. Web: www.santa-teresita.org. Sr. Mary Clare, O.C.D., CEO. Sisters 50; Bed Capacity Skilled Nursing 120; Patients Assisted Annually 48,917; Beds - Assisted Living 44; Total Staff 180.

CAMARILLO. *St. John's Pleasant Valley Hospital dba Catholic Healthcare West* 2309 Antonio Ave., 93010. Tel: 805-389-5800; Fax: 805-383-7450. Web: www.stjohnshealth.com. John Bibby, Pres. Sponsored by Sisters of Mercy of the Americas West Midwest Community. Sisters 3; Beds 180; Patients Assisted Annually 42,552; Total Staff 519.

INGLEWOOD. *Daniel Freeman Memorial Hospital* Division of Daniel Freeman Hospitals, 333 N. Prairie Ave., 90301. Tel: 310-674-7050; 310-678-0361; Fax: 310-419-8273. Web: www.danielfreeman.org. Joseph W. Dunn, Ph.D., CEO; Nancy J. Lee, R.N., M.S.N., COO; Sr. Regina Clare Salazar, C.S.J., Corp. Vice Pres., Sponsorship & Mission; Daniel J. Ahearn, M.D., Vice Pres. & Medical Dir.; Willard F. Worthen, M.D., Chief of Staff; Rev. Francis X. Chrysostom (Sri Lanka), Chap.; Sisters Loretta Flood, C.S.J., Dir. of Pastoral Care; Kathleen Mary McCarthy, C.S.J., Chm. Sponsored by Sisters of St. Joseph of Carondelet in California. Sisters of St. Joseph of Carondelet 11; Sisters from Other Communities 5; Bed Capacity 364; Patients Assisted Annually 102,115; Total Staff 1,643.

Freeman Hospitals Foundation Tel: 310-419-8292; Fax: 310-419-8248. Sr. Mary Esther McCann, C.S.J., Pres. Emeritus; Brian Gauthier, Vice Pres.; Bernie Sklar, Chm.

LONG BEACH. *St. Mary Medical Center dba Catholic Healthcare West* (1924) 1050 Linden Ave., 90813. Tel: 562-491-9000; Fax: 562-436-6378. Web: www.stmarymedicalcenter.org. Christopher DiCicco, Pres.; Sr. Gerard Earls, C.C.V.I., Vice Pres., Mission Integration & Dir. Spiritual Care. Patients Assisted Annually 251,722; Bed Capacity 389; Total Staff 1,465; Sisters 1.

St. Mary Professional Building, Inc., 1050 Linden Ave., 90813. Christopher DiCicco, Pres.

LYNWOOD. *St. Francis Medical Center*, 3630 E. Imperial Hwy., 90262. Tel: 310-900-8900; Fax: 310-900-8299. Gerald T Kozai, D. Pharm, Pres./CEO; Bro. Richard Hirbe, f.s.p., M.P.C., B.C.C., Division Dir., Spiritual Care & Ethics; Revs. Ambrose Joseph Kadambukatt, O.C.D., Assoc. Chap.; Thomas M. Philip, Assoc. Chap. Sponsored by the Daughters of Charity of St. Vincent de Paul, Province of the West., Daughters of Charity Health System. Patients Assisted Annually 200,000; Bed Capacity 384; Total Staff 2,120.

MISSION HILLS. *Providence Holy Cross Medical Center*, 15031 Rinaldi St., P.O. Box 9600, 91346-9600. Tel: 818-365-8051; Fax: 818-496-4569. Web: www.providence.org/holycross. Larry Bowe, Cheif Exec.; D.W. Donovan, Dir., Mission Leadership and Spiritual Care. Tel: 818-496-5000; Dr. Alya Basher, Chap.; Rev. Christina Chambers, Chap.; Jan Hale, Sr. Chap.; Sr. Teresa While, Chap.; Francis Welch, Chap.; Kristin Michealson, Chap. Bed Capacity 377; 14565 Inpaitent 86,571; Total Staff 2,083.

NORTH HOLLYWOOD. *Providence St. Elizabeth Care Center*, 10425 Magnolia Blvd., 91601. Tel: 818-980-3872; Fax: 818-980-6349. Bed Capacity 52; Patients Assisted Annually 60; Total Staff 50.

OXNARD. *St. John's Regional Medical Center*, 1600 N. Rose Ave., 93030. Tel: 805-988-2500; Fax: 805-981-4440. Web: www.stjohnshealth.com. Laurie Eberst, Pres. Sponsored by Sisters of Mercy of the Americas West Midwest Community. Sisters of Mercy 3; Bed Capacity 265; Patients Assisted Annually 88,218; Total Staff 1,408.

St. John's Healthcare Foundation Oxnard and Pleasant Valley, 1600 N. Rose Ave., 93030. Tel: 805-988-2721; Fax: 805-981-4450. Web: stjohnshealth.org. Arron Peace, Vice Pres. Devel.

SAN PEDRO. *Providence Little Company of Mary Medical Center San Pedro*, 1300 W. 7th St., 90732. Tel: 310-832-3311; Fax: 310-514-5314. Web: www.providence.org/sanpedro. Nancy Carlson, COO; Sr. Nancy Jurecki, O.P., Dir., Mission Leadership & Spiritual Care. Tel: 310-514-4364; Darrah Glynn, Chap. (Protestant); Judith Sommerstein, Chap. (Jewish); Rev. Christopher Onyenobi (Nigeria), Chap. Sponsored by Providence Ministries. Bed Capacity 210; Total Staff 1,150.

Providence Little Company of Mary Peninsula Diagnostic Center, 1360 W. 6th St., Ste. 100, 90732. Tel: 310-831-0371; Fax: 310-514-8920.

Providence Little Company of Mary Peninsula Recovery Center, 1386 W. 7th St., 90732. Tel: 310-832-3311; Fax: 310-514-5376.

Providence Little Company of Mary San Pedro Peninsula Hospital Pavilion, 1322 W. Sixth St., 90732. Tel: 310-832-3311; Fax: 310-514-5332. Julie Theiring, Admin. Dir.; Rev. Joel R. Buchman, M.A., S.T.B., Dir. Spiritual Care; Rev. Frank Gordillo, Chap. (Protestant); Rev. Francis L. Shigo, S.V.D., Chap. Skilled Nursing Facility. Bed Capacity 128.

SANTA MARIA. *Marian Medical Center dba Catholic Healthcare West* 1400 E. Church St., 93454. Tel: 805-739-3000; Fax: 805-739-3060. Web: www.marianmedicalcenter.org. Charles J. Cova, Pres.; Deacon Zenon L. Nawrocik, Dir. Pastoral Care. Sponsored by Sisters of St. Francis of Penance and Christian Charity. Sisters 5; Bed Capacity 262; Patients Assisted Annually 194,213; Total Staff 1,440.

Marian Medical Center Extended Care Facility Tel: 805-739-3650; Fax: 805-922-9067. Skilled Nursing Facility. Beds 95.

Marian Medical Center Day Care Facility for Children Tel: 805-739-3666; Fax: 805-922-9067. Capacity 52.

Marian Residence Retirement Home, 124 S. College Dr., 93454. Tel: 805-922-7731.

Marian Medical Center Foundation, 1406 E. Main St., Ste. E., 93454. Tel: 805-739-3595; Fax: 805-739-3599. Web: www.marianmedicalcenter.org.

SANTA MONICA. *Saint John's Health Center*, 2121 Santa Monica Blvd., 90404. Tel: 310-829-5511; Fax: 310-315-6134. Web: www.stjohns.org. Sr. Marie Madeleine Shonka, S.C.L., Co-Chair of Legacy Project; Ms. Lou Lazatin, CEO; Rev. Patrick Comerford, Chap. Sisters of Charity of Leavenworth. Sisters 6; Bed Capacity 340; Patients Assisted Annually 225,000; Total Staff 1,500.

Saint John's Health Center Foundation
John Wayne Cancer Institute
The Irene Dunne Guild

TARZANA. *Providence Tarzana Medical Center*, 18321 Clark St., 91356. Tel: 818-881-0800. Shawn Kiley, Dir. Mission Leadership Dept. Tel: 818-757-4388; Rev. Kenneth Chukwu, Chap.; Loraine Polacci, Chap.; Rabbi Sara Berman, Chap.

TORRANCE. *Providence Little Company of Mary Foundation*, 4101 Torrance Blvd., 90503. Tel: 310-303-5340; Fax: 310-540-8664. Joseph M. Zanetta, Pres.

Providence Little Company of Mary Medical Center Torrance, 4101 W. Torrance Blvd., 90503. Tel: 310-540-7676; Fax: 310-540-7659. Web: lcmhs.org; providence.org. Michael Hunn, CEO; Paul Makarewicz, Dir., Mission Leadership. Tel: 310-303-6182; Rev. Dan Hudson, Mgr., Spiritual Care. Tel: 310-303-6122; Rev. Jason Cusick, Chap. (Protestant); Revs. Peter Mallin, O.F.M.Conv., Chap.; Christopher Onyenobi (Nigeria), Chap. Sponsored by Providence Ministries. Total Staff 3,700; Bed Capacity 250; Bassinets 35.

Providence Little Company of Mary Sub-Acute Center-South Bay, 1322 W. 6th St., San Pedro, 90732. Tel: 310-732-6700; Fax: 310-732-6719. La Verna McMiller, Admin. Dir.; Rev. Joel R. Buchman, M.A., S.T.B., Dir. Spiritual Care; Margaret O'Leary, Chap. Skilled Nursing Facility.; Sponsored by Providence Ministries. Bed Capacity 120.

WEST COVINA. *Citrus Valley Medical Center, Queen of the Valley Campus*, 1115 S. Sunset Ave., P.O. Box 1980, 91790. Tel: 626-962-4011; Fax: 626-814-2428. Email: catherine@cvhp.com. Web: cvhp.org. Rev. Eric Anthony Lewis; Mr. James T. Yoshioka, CEO. Bed Capacity 325; Patients Assisted Annually 125,000; Total Staff 1,500.

[K] SPECIAL HOSPITALS AND SANATORIA FOR INVALIDS

LOS ANGELES. *Order of Malta Los Angeles Clinic, Inc.*, 2222 W. Ocean View, #112, 90057. Tel: 213-384-4323; Fax: 213-384-4097. Email: freemed112@sbcglobal.net. David Frelinger, M.D., K.M., Medical Dir.; David Johnson, Admin. Conducted by Order of Malta Los Angeles Clinic, Inc., Primary Health Care for the frail elderly, the working poor and medically underserved children. Total Assisted 2,217; Total Staff 12.

CULVER CITY. *Marycrest Manor* (1956) 10664 St. James Dr., 90230-5498. Tel: 310-838-2778; 310-838-0016 (Carmelite Sisters); Fax: 310-838-9647; 310-838-0024 (Carmelite Sisters). Email: marycrestocd@yahoo.com. Sisters Noella, O.C.D., Admin.; Veronica Del Carmen, O.C.D., Asst. Admin. Carmelite Sisters of the Most Sacred Heart of Los Angeles., Skilled Nursing Facility attended by priests from Loyola Marymount University. Carmelite Sisters of the Most Sacred Heart of Los Angeles 7; Pastoral Care Sisters 2; Bed Capacity 57; Residents 57; Total Assisted Annually 600; Total Staff 85.

NEWBURY PARK. *Mary Health of the Sick Convalescent and Nursing Hospital* (1964) 2929 Theresa Dr., 91320. Tel: 805-498-3644; Fax: 805-498-5112. Web: maryhealth.com. Sr. Cristina Juarez, S.deM., Exec. Dir. Sisters Servants of Mary., Skilled Nursing Facility. Sisters 15; Bed Capacity 61; Residents Assisted Annually 85; Total Staff 86.

OJAI. *St. Joseph's Health and Retirement Center*, 2464 E. Ojai Ave., 93023. Tel: 805-646-1466; Fax: 805-646-1013. Email: brmichaeloh@yahoo.com. Bro. Michael Bassemier, O.H., Admin.; Rev. Thaddeus Bui, O.H., Prior & Chap. Hospitaller Brothers of St. John of God. Capacity 28; Independent Living 25; Total Staff 42.

[L] HANDICAPPED

SANTA MONICA. *Saint John's Child Study Center, Saint John's Hospital & Health Center*, 1339 20th St., 90404. Tel: 310-829-8921; Fax: 310-829-8455. Rev. Patrick Comerford, Chap.; Rebecca Refuerza, L.C.S.W., Dir. Conducted by Sisters of Charity of Leavenworth., Affiliated with Saint John's Hospital. Children Treated Annually 1,800.

SUNLAND. **Tierra del Sol Foundation*, 9919 Sunland Blvd., 91040. Tel: 818-352-1419; Fax: 818-353-0777. Web: tierradelsol.org. Stephen J. Miller, Exec. Dir.; Nancy Bissonette-Andrew, Clinical Dir. Community Program/Supported Employment for Adults with Developmental Disabilities. Licensed Capacity 304.

[M] VISITING NURSE SERVICES

LOS ANGELES. *Servants of Mary, Ministers to the Sick*, 2131 W. 27th St., 90018-3018. Tel: 213-731-5747; Fax: 323-731-4251. Sr. Leticia Rodriguez, S.M., Supr. Sisters 13; Total Assisted 41; Total Staff 7.

[N] PROTECTIVE INSTITUTIONS

LOS ANGELES. *St. Anne's*, 155 N. Occidental Blvd., 90026. Tel: 213-381-2931; Fax: 213-381-7804. Email: stannes@stannes.org. Web: www.stannes.org. Tony Walker, M.A., Pres. & CEO. Sponsored by the Franciscan Sisters of the Sacred Heart., Residential Treatment Program; Transitional Housing; Mental Health; Family Based Services; Early Learning Center Services for pregnant parent and at risk children and families. Beds Licensed for Children Under 18 years of age 50; Children Served Annually in Residential Care 125.

Support groups include:
St. Anne's Foundation
St. Anne's Guild
Mabel Mosler Auxiliary
Loretta Young Auxiliary
Sister Winifred Auxiliary Residential 250; Prevention Education 2,000; Total Staff 220.

Convent of the Good Shepherd-Good Shepherd Shelter (1904) Mailing Address: P.O. Box 19487, 90019. Tel: 323-737-6111; Fax: 323-737-6113. Email: llengel@goodshepherdshelter.org. Web: www.goodshepherdshelter.org. Conducted by Sisters of the Good Shepherd., Shelter for Battered Women and Their Children. Sisters 10; Women Assisted Annually 15; Children 58; Total Assisted Annually 73.

CHATSWORTH. *Rancho San Antonio*, 21000 Plummer St., 91311. Tel: 818-882-6400; Fax: 818-882-6404. Bro. John Crowe, C.S.C., Exec. Dir. Directed by the Brothers of Holy Cross., Sponsored by Brothers of Holy Cross Brothers 1; Boys (13-17 yrs.) 106; Total Staff 168; Families Assisted 310.

SANTA BARBARA. *St. Vincent's* (1858) 4200 Calle Real, 93110-1454. Tel: 805-683-6381; Fax: 805-967-7508. Email: info@sv-sb.org. Web: www.stvincents-sb.org. For single moms on welfare and/or very low income. Daughters of Charity of St. Vincent de Paul 5; Mothers 30; Children 40; Total Staff 19.

St. Vincent's Early Childhood Education Center (1999) 4200 Calle Real, 93110-1454. Tel: 805-683-6381, Ext. 211; Fax: 805-967-7508. Email: info@sv-sb.org. Web: www.stvincents-sb.org. For infants, toddlers, and preschoolers. Daughters of Charity of St. Vincent de Paul 5; Day Care 46; Total Staff 18.

[O] HOMES FOR AGED

LOS ANGELES. *St. John of God Retirement and Care Center*, 2468 S. St. Andrews Pl., 90018. Tel: 323-731-0641; Fax: 323-731-1452. Bros. Michael Bassemier, O.H., Admin.; Pablo Lopez, O.H., Provincial; George Tecku, O.H., Prior. Brothers 7; Bed Capacity 287; SNF 131; Residential Care 105; Patients Assisted Annually 280; Total Staff 230; Independent Living 51.
Supporting Organizations:
Hospitaller Foundation of California, Inc. Tel: 323-731-7141; Fax: 323-731-5717. Bro. Patrick Corr, O.H., Pres.
Women's League of St. John of God, Inc., Helpers Club of St. John of God, Inc. Tel: 323-731-7141; Fax: 323-731-5717.
Nazareth House (1946) 3333 Manning Ave., 90064. Tel: 310-839-2361; Fax: 310-839-4204. Email: pmurphy@nazarethhouseja.org. Web: www.nazarethouse.org. Sr. Philomena Murphy, Supr. Congregation of the Sisters of Nazareth. Retired Priests 15; Sisters 6; Total Staff 78; Residents 123.

SAN FERNANDO. *Mother Gertrude Home for Senior Citizens* (Franciscan Missionary Sisters of the Immaculate Conception, Inc.), 11320 Laurel Canyon Blvd., 91340. Tel: 818-898-1546; Fax: 818-365-6646. Capacity 45; Total Staff 19; Total in Residence 36.

SAN PEDRO. *Little Sisters of the Poor* (1979) Jeanne Jugan Residence, 2100 S. Western Ave., 90732. Tel: 310-548-0625; Fax: 310-548-4504. Email: adsanpedro@littlesistersofthepoor.org. Web: www.lspsocal.org. Sr. Paul Magyar, L.S.P., Supr. *Little Sisters of the Poor of Los Angeles. A Corporation* Priests 2; Sisters 10; Lay Associates 15; Total Staff 110; Residents 102; Total Assisted Annually 1,260.

SUN VALLEY. *Villa Scalabrini*, 10631 Vinedale St., 91352. Tel: 818-768-6500; Fax: 818-768-0684. Web: www.villascalabrini.com. Rev. Ermete Nazzani, C.S., Exec. Dir. & Admin. Missionary Fathers of St. Charles., Retirement Center and Special Care Unit; Augustinian Recollect Sisters. Bed Capacity 188; Retirement Center 130; Skilled Nursing Unit 58; Total Staff 115.

[P] MONASTERIES AND RESIDENCES OF PRIESTS AND BROTHERS

LOS ANGELES. *Brothers of John of God, Inc., The*, 2425 S. Western Ave., 90018-2608. Tel: 323-734-0233; Fax: 323-731-5987. Email: usaprov-office@sbcglobal.net. Web: www.hospitallers.org. Bro. Pablo Lopez, O.H., Prov. *Women's League of St. John of God, Inc.*, 90002. Tel: 323-731-7141; Fax: 323-731-5717. *Helper's Club, Inc.* Tel: 323-731-7141; Fax: 323-731-5717. *St. John of God Retirement & Care Center*, 90018. Tel: 323-731-0641; Fax: 323-737-1452. Email: john@stjohnofgodseniors.org. Web: hospitallers.org. *St. Joseph's Health & Retirement Center* Tel: 805-646-1466; Fax: 805-646-1013. Email: igi@ojai.net. Web: hospitallers.org. *Hospitaller Foundation of California, Inc.* Tel: 323-731-7141; Fax: 323-731-5717. Email: arlene@hospitallerfoundation.org. Web: hospitallers.org. *Women's League of St. Joseph's Health & Retirement Center* Tel: 805-646-1466; Fax: 805-646-1013. Web: hospitallers.org. *Grande Apartments-Los Angeles* Tel: 323-730-4100; Fax: 323-737-1452. Email: jpeters@stjohnofgodseniors.org. Web: hospitallers.org. *Hospitaller Brothers Healthcare, Inc.* Tel: 805-734-0233; Fax: 323-737-1452. Email: usaprov-office@sbcglobal.net. Web: hospitallers.org. *St. John of God Health Care Services* Tel: 760-241-4917; Fax: 760-241-8911. Email: brogary@sjghcs.org. Web: hospitallers.org.
Colombiere House Formerly Connolly House., 5322 Franklin Ave., 90027. Tel: 323-466-3723; Fax: 323-466-3826. Email: wdelaney@calprov.org. Revs. Wayne Negrete, S.J., Supr.; Mark Ciccone, S.J.; William K. Delaney, S.J.; Thomas J. Griffin-Smolenski, S.J.; Paul J. Bernadicou, S.J.; Leo P. Preugaman, S.J.; Anastacio Rivera, S.J.; Joseph G. Spieler, S.J. Jesuit Fathers. Priests 8.
Columban Fathers, Procure House, 2600 N. Vermont Ave., 90027-1245. Tel: 323-665-4289; Fax: 323-664-7160. Email: columbanla@aol.com. Web: www.columban.org. Revs. Peter Kenny, S.S.C., Supr. & Contact Person; Thomas Cusack, S.S.C.; Paul White, S.S.C.; Anthony Mortell, S.S.C.; James Shiffer, S.S.C., J.C.L.; John Wanaurny, S.S.C.; Brendan O'Sullivan, S.S.C.
Divine Word Residence, Divine Word Missionaries, 2181 W. 25th St., 90018. Tel: 323-735-8130; Fax: 323-735-8122. Bro. Andrew Hotchkiss, S.V.D., Rector.
Dominic Savio Salesian Residence (1958) 920 Soto St., 90023-1396. Tel: 323-266-6000; Fax: 323-266-3487. Email: sdblosangeles@hotmail.com. Web: www.donboscowest.org. In Res. Revs. John Lam, S.D.B., Pastor St. Bridgit; Lucian B. Lomello, S.D.B. (Retired); Juan Francisco Munoz, S.D.B., Pastor St. Mary's Parish; James Nieblas, S.D.B., Supr. of Community, Salesian High School; Marc Rougeau, S.D.B., Assoc. St. Mary's Parish; Bros. Philip Mandile Salesian Boys & Girls Club, Salesian Family Youth Center & St. Mary's; Tom Mass, S.D.B., Salesian Boy's & Girl's Club, Salesian Family Youth Center & St. Mary's.
Franciscan Brothers of the Third Order Regular, 4522 Gainsborough Ave., 90027-1227. Tel: 323-644-2740. Bro. Paulinus Horkan, O.S.F., Regl. Supr. Brothers 6.
Guadalupe Missioners Procure, 4714 W. 8th St., 90005. Tel: 323-937-2780; Fax: 323-937-2782. Revs. Santiago G. Lara, M.G., Local Supr.; Abraham R. Garcia, M.G., Asst. Priests 2.
Hospitaller Brothers of St. John of God, 2468 S. St. Andrew's Pl., 90018. Tel: 323-731-0641; Fax: 323-731-5987. Email: usaprov-office@sbcglobal.net. Web: www.hospitallers.org. Bro. George Tecku, O.H., Prior. Brothers 10.
St. John of God Retirement and Care Center, 2468 S. St. Andrews Pl., 90018. Tel: 323-731-0641; Fax: 323-737-1452. Email: usaprov-office@sbcglobal.net. Web: www.hospitaller.org. Bros. Pablo Lopez, O.H., Prov.; George Tecku, O.H., Local Supr. Brothers 7.
Maryknoll Fathers and Brothers (Catholic Foreign Mission Society of America), 222 S. Hewitt St. #6, 90012-4309. Tel: 213-747-9676; Fax: 213-908-2317. Email: losangeles@maryknoll.org. Web: www.maryknoll.org. Rev. Joseph J. Donovan, M.M. Tel: 213-808-1002. 2701 S. Peck Rd., Monrovia, 91016-5004. Tel: 626-447-6202, Ext. 32 Annunciation Parish, Arcadia. Rev. Michael G. Callanan, M.M. (Retired). 255 S. Grand Ave., #413, 90012-3017. Tel: 213-625-5702. Rev. James P. Colligan, M.M. (Retired). 340 Norumbega Dr., Monrovia, 91016-2445. Tel: 626-358-1825. Rev. Richard Ouellette, M.M. (Retired), 340 Norumbega Dr., Monrovia, 91016. Tel: 626-358-1825.
Minim Fathers, 3431 Portola Ave., 90032. Tel: 323-223-1101; Fax: 323-223-9592. Email: jvega@earthlink.net. Web: home.earthlink.net/~jvega/. Revs. Mario Pisano, O.M., Supr.; Gino Vanzillotta, O.M.; Jose L. Vega, O.M. Priests 3.
Missionaries of Charity Brothers (1975) 1316 S. Westlake Ave., 90006. Tel: 213-384-6111. Email: brosla@aol.com. Web: www.mcbrothers.org. *Casa Teresa*, 1316 S. Westlake Ave., 90006. Tel: 213-380-5225. Email: brosla@aol.com. Web: www.mcbrothers.org. Hospitality for men. Temporary shelter for sick homeless men. Brothers 5.
**Missionaries of Jesus, Inc.*, 435 S. Occidental Blvd., 90057. Tel: 213-389-8439, Ext. 19; Fax: 213-389-1951. Email: info@missionariesofjesus.com. Web: www.missionariesofjesus.com. Revs. Joseph Ricardo Guerrero, M.J., Prov. Supr.; Manuel Gacad, M.J., Vice Supr.; Michael Montoya, M.J., Councillor; Enrique Ymson, M.J.; Melanio Viuya, M.J., Dir. Mission Promotion Office & Treas.
Our Lady of Mount Carmel Priory, 4966 Alonzo Ave., Encino, 91316. Tel: 818-345-6055. Revs. Augustine W. Carter, O.Carm.; John Coleman, O.Carm., Prior; Stephen Cooley, O.Carm.; Matt J. Ewing, O.Carm.; Paul Henson, O.Carm.; Thomas Schrader, O.Carm.; Barnabas B. Hughes, O.F.M. *Fathers of the Order of Mount Carmel, Corporation* Priests 7.
Piarist Fathers, 512 S. Avenue 20, 90031. Tel: 213-223-4153. Revs. Raul Palma, Sch.P.; Juan Trenchs, Sch.P.; Miguel Campos, Sch.P. Priests 4.
The Society of St. Paul (1914) (Mexican Province), 112 Herbert St., 90063. Tel: 323-269-9814; Fax: 323-269-0242. Email: joerelop@hotmail.com. Revs. Valeriano Giachino, S.S.P.; José Refugio López, S.S.P., Supr.; Antonio Francisco Paredes Monjaras, S.S.P., Seminarian; Marco Antonio Vences, S.S.P.

BALDWIN PARK. *Vietnamese Redemptorist Mission*, 3452 N. Big Dalton Ave., 91706. Tel: 626-851-9020; 626-338-3295. Email: chaqhung@yahoo.com. Revs. Ngo Dinh Thoa, C.Ss.R.; Pham Quoc Hung, C.Ss.R.; Doan Trong Son, C.Ss.R.; Nguyen Van Phan, C.Ss.R.; Tran Gia Dien; Ho Anh Nghia, C.Ss.R.; Ha Quoc Dung, C.Ss.R.; Bros. John M. Viet Hien, C.Ss.R.; Martin Nguyen Van Moi, C.Ss.R.
In Residence Elsewhere: Revs. Dang Phuoc Hoa, C.Ss.R., 8800 E. 22nd St., Tucson, AZ 85710. Tel: 602-751-2060; Tran Dinh Phuc, C.Ss.R., 22 Stone St., Salinas, 93901. Tel: 408-772-8227; Nguyen Duc Mau, C.Ss.R., 2458 Atlantic Ave., Long Beach, 90806. Tel: 562-424-2041; Fax: 562-424-2152; Phan Phat Huon, C.Ss.R., 2458 Atlantic Ave., Long Beach, 90806. Tel: 562-424-2041; Fax: 562-424-2152; Ngo Van Dao, C.Ss.R., 2458 Atlantic Ave., Long Beach, 90806. Tel: 562-424-2041; Fax: 562-424-2152; Nguyen Tat Hai, C.Ss.R., 2458 Atlantic Ave., Long Beach, 90806. Tel: 562-424-2041; Fax: 562-424-2152; Nguyen Truong Luan, 2458 Atlantic Ave., Long Beach, 90806. Tel: 562-424-2041; Fax: 562-424-2152; Bro. Vo Thanh Ha, C.Ss.R., 2458 Atlantic Ave., Long Beach, 90806. Tel: 562-424-2041; Fax: 562-424-2152; Revs. Dinh Minh Hai, C.Ss.R., 3910 S. Ledbetter Dr., Dallas, TX 75236. Tel: 972-438-4082; Bui Quang Tuan, C.Ss.R., 3910 S. Ledbetter Dr., Dallas, TX 75236. Tel: 972-438-4082; Nguyen Phi Long, C.Ss.R., 3910 S. Ledbetter Dr., Dallas, TX 75236. Tel: 972-438-4082; Chau Xuan Bau, C.Ss.R., 3417 W. Little York Rd., Houston, TX 77091. Tel: 214-321-9493; Fax: 713-686-4589; Le Quang Phung, C.Ss.R., 3417 W. Little York Rd., Houston, TX 77091. Tel: 214-321-9493; Fax: 713-686-4589; Nguyen Duc Thanh, C.Ss.R., 3417 W. Little York Rd., Houston, TX 77091. Tel: 214-321-9493; Fax: 713-686-4589; Nguyen Van Thach, C.Ss.R., 3417 W. Little York Rd., Houston, TX 77091. Tel: 214-321-9493; Fax: 713-686-4589; Nguyen Quoc Dung, C.Ss.R.; Nguyen Dinh Trung, C.Ss.R., 3417 W. Little York Rd., Houston, TX 77091. Tel: 214-321-9493; Fax: 713-686-4589; Bro. Nguyen Tran Duc, C.Ss.R.; Revs. Tung Duc Vu, C.Ss.R.; Dominic Pham, C.Ss.R.; Dinh Ngoc Que, C.Ss.R.; Le Trong Hung, C.Ss.R.; Bros. Nguyen Phvoc Hahn, C.Ss.R.; Nguyen Ngoc Khanh, C.Ss.R.

CUDAHY. *Misioneros del Sagrado Corazon y Santa Maria de Guadalupe* (1938) 4235 Clara St., 90201. Tel: 323-562-3356; Fax: 323-562-3332. Email: sagrado_cudahy@yahoo.com. Tony Vienna, Esq., Contact Person. Tel: 213-485-1555; Fax: 213-689-1004; Rev. Antonio Garnica, M.S.C., V.F., Regl. Supr.

CULVER CITY. *Ignatius House, The Novitiate of the California Province, Society of Jesus*, P.O. Box 5166, 90231-5166. Tel: 310-815-0166; Fax: 310-815-0170. Email: mweiler@calprov.org. Web: www.calprov.org. Revs. Michael F. Weiler, S.J., Dir. of Novices; Christopher T. Nguyen, S.J., Asst. Dir. of Novices; John LeVecke, S.J., Christian Life Community Natl. Ecclesial Asst.; Doan T. Hoang, S.J., Dir. of the Apostleship of Prayer; John W. Clark, S.J.; Edward J. Siebert, S.J.; Bro. Michael E. Breault, S.J., Min. of the Jesuit Community. 10775 Deshire Pl., 90230-5017. Tel: 310-815-0166 (Staff); 310-815-0185 (Novices); Fax: 310-815-0170.

LA VERNE. *Congregation of the Sacred Hearts of Jesus and Mary*, 2150 Damien Ave., 91750-5114. Tel: 909-593-5441 (Provincial Office); Fax: 909-593-3971. Email: ssccwest@cpl.net. Web: www.cpl.net/~ssccwest. Very Rev. Donal McCarthy, SS.CC., Prov. Supr., La Verne, CA; Revs. Michael W. Barry, SS.CC., Dir., Mary's Mercy Center, Inc: Mary's Table & Veronica's Home of Mercy, San Bernardino, CA; Peter K. Dennis, SS.CC., La Verne, CA; Patrick J. Crowley, SS.CC., Hemet House of Prayer, Hemet, CA; Kenneth McCabe, SS.CC., Hemet House of Prayer, Hemet, CA; Michael N. Maher, SS.CC, Pastor, St. Louis Church, Cathedral City, CA; William C. Moore, SS.CC., Ministry of the Arts, Pomona, CA; Patrick J. O'Hagan, SS.CC., Pastor, St. Paul the Apostle, Chino Hills, CA; Thomas J. Mullen, SS.CC., (On Sabbatical); John Roche, SS.CC., Assoc. Pastor, Holy Name of Mary, San Dimas, CA; Richard J. Danyluk, SS.CC., Chap., Sisters of St. Joseph of Carondelet, Los Angeles, CA; Vincent Fallon, SS.CC., Our Lady of the Wisdom, NV; Jeremiah Holland, SS.CC., Pastor, Holy Spirit Catholic Church, Hemet, CA; Pasquale V. Laghezza, SS.CC., Chap., NY Harbor Health Care System, NYC; Henry Paul Murtagh, SS.CC., Pastor, Artesia, NM - Our Lady of Grace; Martin P. O'Loghlen, SS.CC., Assoc. Pastor, Holy Name of Mary, San Dimas, CA; Patrick Travers, SS.CC., Prin., Damien High School, La Verne, CA; Michael J. Brooks, SS.CC., La Verne, CA; Peadar Cronin, SS.CC., Assoc. Pastor, Holy Name of Mary, San Dimas, CA; Patrick Argue, SS.CC. (Retired), Co. Cavan, Ireland; Brian Guerrini, SS.CC., Assoc. Pastor, Artesia, NM - Our Lady of Grace; Patrick P. Coyle, SS.CC. (Retired), Twenty-Nine Palms, CA. Priests in Residence 6; Priests not in Residence 16.

MONTEBELLO. *Congregation of the Mission Western Province*, 1105 Bluff Rd., 90640-6198. Tel: 323-721-6050; Fax: 323-887-1765. Email: cmstlouis@vincentian.org. Web: www.vincentian.org.
DePaul Center, a California Corporation; Congregation of the Mission, Western Province, California; Vincentian Province of the West Support Trust Fund; Vincentian Foreign Mission Society
Vincentian Foreign Mission Society DePaul Evangelization Center, 1105 Bluff Rd., 90640-6198. Tel: 323-721-6060; Fax: 323-887-1765. Revs. James Osendorf, C.M., Supr. & Dir.; Kevin S. Collins, C.M.; Binh Van Nguyen, C.M.; Peter J.

Diliberto (Retired); Robert J. Jones, C.M. Priests 7; Brothers 1. *St. Mary's Evangelization Center*, 1964 Las Canoas Rd., Santa Barbara, 93105-2351. Tel: 805-966-4829; Fax: 805-564-1662. Revs. Walter L. Housey, C.M. (Retired); Patrick J. Mullin, C.M., Dir.; Roy A. Persich, C.M. (Retired); John V. Shine, C.M., Supr. (Retired). Priests 4. *Amat Residence 1*, 649 W. Adams Blvd., 90007-2546. Tel: 213-747-1227; Fax: 213-749-4504. Email: amathouse@aol.com. Rev. William R. Piletic, C.M., Vocation Dir., Asst. Prov. & Supr. Priests 1. *Amat Residence II*, 641 W. Adams Blvd., 90007-2546. Tel: 213-748-9829; Fax: 213-748-9829. Revs. Pedro Villarroya, C.M.; Thomas C. Anslow, C.M., J.C.L.; Stafford Poole, C.M. (Retired). Priests 3.

OXNARD. *Order of Augustinian Recollects (O.A.R.), St. Augustine Priory* (1990) 400 Sherwood Way, 93033-7510. Tel: 805-486-7433; Fax: 805-487-2805. Email: saprovince@yahoo.com. Web: augustinianrecollects.org; www.agustinosrecolectos.com. Revs. Marlon Beof, O.A.R., Prior; John Michael Rafferty, O.A.R., Subprior & Vocations Dir. Total in Residence 10; Priests 8; Brothers 1; Deacons 1. In Res. Revs. James V. Brown, O.A.R.; Joaquin Goni, O.A.R.; Paul Goni, O.A.R.; Fidel Hernandez, O.A.R.; Robert Huse, O.A.R.; Frank T. Wilder, O.A.R.; Bro. Mario Alvarez, O.A.R.; Deacon Ascencion Esqueda, O.A.R.

PASADENA. *Legionaries of Christ*, 1041 Rancho Rd., Arcadia, 91006. Tel: 626-244-5020. Web: www.legionofchrist.org. Priests 4. In Res. Revs. Dean Stasell; John Bullock, L.C.; Mariano de Blas, L.C.

SANTA BARBARA. *Franciscan Friary, Order of Friars Minor (Old Mission)* (1786) 2201 Laguna St., 93105. Tel: 805-682-4713; Fax: 805-682-6067. Revs. Richard McManus, O.F.M., Guardian; Nevin Ford, O.F.M.; Maurus Kelly, O.F.M.; Howard Hall, O.F.M.; Leo Sprietsma, O.F.M.; Pedro Vasquez, O.F.M.; Thomas Messner, O.F.M.; Daniel Barica, O.F.M.; John Vaughn, O.F.M.; Jack Clark Robinson, O.F.M.; Bros. Timothy Arthur, O.F.M., Prov. Archivist; Joachim Grant, O.F.M.; Philip Morales, O.F.M.; Ernest LuVisi, O.F.M. Priests 11; Brothers 5.

SANTA MARIA. *American Region of the Josephite Fathers Charitable Trust*, 180 Patterson Rd., 93455. Tel: 805-937-4555. Email: frcharles@sldm.org. Web: www.josephiteweb.org. Rev. Charles L. Hofschulte, C.J., V.F., Contact Person.

SANTA PAULA. *Canons Regular of the Immaculate Conception* (1871) Dom Grea House of Formation & Novitiate, 984 Monte Vista Dr., 93060-1612. Tel: 805-933-5063; Fax: 805-525-5115. Email: cricusa@yahoo.com. Web: cricusa.org. Revs. Pasquale Vuoso, C.R.I.C., Supr. Tel: 805-525-2149; Fax: 805-933-5520; Thomas J. Dome, C.R.I.C., Dir. & Novice Master; Charles R. Lueras, C.R.I.C. Tel: 805-525-2149; Fax: 805-933-5520; William B. Ustaski, C.R.I.C. Tel: 661-252-3353; Fax: 661-252-1539. Priests 4; Postulants 2; Seminarians 2; Novices 1.

SIERRA MADRE. *Passionist Community*, 700 N. Sunnyside Ave., 91024. Tel: 626-355-1740; Fax: 626-355-1744. *Passionist Retreat House*, 700 N. Sunnyside Ave., 91024. Tel: 626-355-7188; Fax: 626-355-0485. Congregation of the Passion, Mater Dolorosa Community. *Passionist Residence*, 700 N. Sunnyside Ave., 91024. Tel: 626-355-1740; Fax: 626-355-1744. Very Rev. Alan Phillip, C.P., Local Supr.; Revs. Patrick Brennan, C.P., Retreat Dir.; Michael Hoolahan, C.P., Retreat Team; Bro. John Rockenbach, C.P. Priests 4; Brothers 1.

VALYERMO. *St. Andrew's Abbey*, 31001 N. Valyermo Rd., P.O. Box 40, 93563-0040. Tel: 661-944-2178; Fax: 661-944-1076. Email: information@saintandrewsabbey.com. Web: www.saintandrewsabbey.com. Rev. Damien Toilolo, O.S.B., Abbot; Rt. Rev. Francis Benedict, O.S.B., Abbot Emeritus; Rev. Simon O'Donnell, O.S.B.; Bro. Patrick Sheridan, O.S.B.; Rev. John Bosco Stoner, O.S.B.; Bros. John Mark Matthews, O.S.B.; Peter Zhou Bang-jiu, O.S.B.; Rev. Philip Edwards, O.S.B.; Bro. Dominic Guillen, O.S.B.; Rev. Gregory Elmer, O.S.B.; Bros. Benedict Dull, O.S.B.; Joseph Iarrobino, O.S.B.; Revs. Luke Dysinger, O.S.B., M.D., D.Phil.; Martin Yslas, O.S.B.; Isaac Kalina, O.S.B.; Carlos Lopez, O.S.B.; Joseph (Dennis) Brennan, O.S.B., Subprior; Aelred Niespolo, O.S.B., M.A., B.Th., M.Th.; Matthew Rios, O.S.B.; Bros. Cassian DiRocco, O.S.B.; Bede Hazlet, O.S.B. Benedictine Monks. Priests 14; Brothers 7.

VAN NUYS. *Rogationist Fathers* (2001) 6635 Tobias Ave., 91405. Tel: 818-782-0184; Fax: 818-782-1794. Email: rogdevoff@aol.com. Web: www.rcj.org; www.vocationsandprayer.org; www.rogationists.org. Revs. John Bruno, R.C.J.; Rodolfo D'Agostino, R.C.J.; Vito Di Marzio, R.C.J., Vocation Dir.

Congregation of Rogationists, Inc.

WHITTIER. *Redemptorists of Whittier*, 7215 S. Newlin Ave., 90602-1266. Tel: 562-698-0107; Fax: 562-696-1617. Web: www.st-maryschurch.org. Revs. Scott Katzenberger, C.Ss.R.; Jose Luis Chavez, C.Ss.R.; Donald B. Willard, C.Ss.R.; Arthur Frost, C.Ss.R. (Retired); William Adams, C.Ss.R. (Retired). Priests 9. In Res Revs. Anthony Phuc Nguyen, C.Ss.R.; Michael McAndrew, C.Ss.R.

[Q] CONVENTS AND RESIDENCES FOR SISTERS

LOS ANGELES. **The Blessed Sacrament Sisters of Charity, Inc.*, 248 S. Mariposa Ave., 90004. Tel: 213-389-7760; Fax: 213-389-1332. Email: ahelga_ahelga@yahoo.com. Sr. Theresa Kong, Local Supr.

California Institute of the Sisters of the Immaculate Heart Mary (1848) 3431 Waverly Dr., 90027-2526. Tel: 323-664-3357, Ext. 114; Fax: 323-664-2215. Sr. Catherine Rose, I.H.M., Dir. & Treas.

California Institute of the Sisters of the Most Holy and Immaculate Heart of the Blessed Virgin Mary Sisters 9.

Congregation of the Sisters of Nazareth Motherhouse, U.S.A., 3333 Manning Ave., 90064. Tel: 310-839-2361; Fax: 310-839-0648. Email: regional@nazarethhousela.org. Web: www.nazarethhouse.org. Sr. Marie McCormack, C.S.N., Regl. Supr. Sisters 8.

Eucharistic Franciscan Missionary Sisters, Motherhouse: 943 S. Soto St., 90023. Tel: 213-264-6556; Fax: 213-526-1655. Email: efms@earthlink.net. Sr. Rose Seraphim, E.F.M.S., Supr. Gen. Sisters 25.

Eucharistic Franciscan Missionary Sisters of Los Angeles, Nativity Convent, 1421 Cota Ave., Torrance, 90501. Tel: 310-328-6725; Fax: 310-328-5248.

Guadalupan Missionaries of the Holy Spirit, 5467 W. 8th St., 90036. Tel: 323-424-7208; Fax: 323-424-7498. Email: gabycastro@guadalupeusa.org. Sisters Ana Gabriela Castro, M.G.Sp.S., Provincial; Oliva Olivares-Gutierrez, M.G.Sp.S., Treas.; Hilda Mateo, M.G.Sp.S., Dir. On-Going Formation; Ofelia Galicia, M.G.Sp.S., Sec.; Elva Mendez, M.G.Sp.S., D.R.E., St. Martha Catholic Church.

Missionary Guadalupanas of the Holy Spirit, Apostolate House. Sisters 5.

Guadalupanas Missionaries of the Holy Spirit (1930) Novitiate., 758 S. Dunsmuir Ave., 90036. Tel: 323-936-0135; Fax: 323-939-8735. Email: niditomgsps@aol.com. Sr. Maria Julia Lozano, Supr.

Hermanas Carmelitas de San Jose (1916) 141 W. 87th Pl., 90003. Tel: 323-758-6840; 323-752-2838. Sr. Enedina de Jesus Hernandez, C.S.J., Regl. Supr. US Community. Sisters 4.

Missionary Benedictine Sisters of Tutzing in Los Angeles, Inc. (2002) 912 Bronson Ave., 90019-1935. Tel: 323-939-3977; Fax: 323-937-7971; 323-935-8985. Email: osbgregory@hanmail.net. Sr. Pachomia Kim, O.S.B., Supr. & Contact Person.

Missionary Sisters of Christ the King (Poland) (1959) 3424 W. Adams Blvd., 90018. Tel: 323-734-5249; Fax: 323-734-0046. Email: plchurchla@earthlink.net. Sisters Anna Kalinowski, M.S.C.K., Local Supr.; Jadwiga Kokolus, M.C.H.R., Parish Sec. Sisters working in Archdiocese of Los Angeles 3.

Monastery of the Angels (Contemplative), 1977 Carmen Ave., 90068. Tel: 323-466-2186; Fax: 323-466-6645. Sr. Mary Raymond, O.P., Prioress; Rev. Emmerch Vogt, O.P., Chap. Nuns of the Order of Preachers. Professed Cloistered Nuns 16.

Pious Disciples of the Divine Master, 501 N. Beaudry Ave., 90012-1509. Tel: 213-250-7962 (Center); 213-977-0893 (Community); Fax: 213-977-0987. Web: www.pddm.us. Sr. M. Lucille Van Hoogmoed, P.D.D.M., Local Supr. Sisters 7.

Servants of the Immaculate Child Mary, E.I.N. (Esclavas de la Inmaculada Nina) (1901) 5135 Dartmouth Ave., 90032-3323. Tel: 323-225-3279; Fax: 323-225-3279. 350 S. Boyle Ave., 90033-3813. Tel: 323-269-7786; Fax: 323-269-7786. Email: ein-la@hotmail.com.

Sisters of Social Service of Los Angeles (1926) *General Motherhouse*, 4316 Lanai Rd., Encino, 91436. Tel: 818-285-3355; Fax: 818-285-3366. Email: ssocialser@aol.com. Web: www.socialservicesisters.com. Sr. Rochelle Mitchell, S.S.S., Gen. Dir.

Sisters of Social Service of Los Angeles, Inc.

Sisters of Social Service Support Trust Fund Sisters 100.

Sisters of Social Service, Formation, 4316 Lanai Rd., Encino, 91436. Tel: 818-285-3355; Fax: 818-285-3366. Email: ssocialser@aol.com. Web: sistersofsocialservice.com. In Formation 2.

Sisters of St. Joseph of Carondelet in California (1850) (St. Mary's Provincialate, Carondelet Center), 11999 Chalon Rd., 90049-1524. Tel: 310-889-2100; Fax: 310-476-8735. Email: provincialate@csjla.org. Web: www.csjla.org. Sisters Barbara Anne Stowasser, C.S.J., Prov. Supr.; Theresa Kvale, C.S.J., Asst. Prov. Supr.; Sandra Williams, C.S.J., Asst. Prov. Supr. Sisters 345.

Sisters of St. Joseph in California Tel: 310-889-2154; Fax: 310-472-5982.

Sisters of St. Joseph Ministerial Services Tel: 310-889-2157; Fax: 310-472-5982.

Sisters of St. Joseph of Orange, 8000 Regis Way, 90045. Tel: 310-645-2514; 310-645-0718. Sisters 5.

Sisters of the Company of Mary, 2634 Monmouth Ave., 90007. Tel: 213-747-3542; Fax: 213-747-6468. Email: divine_providence@sbcglobal.net. Sisters Maria Elena Minjarez, O.D.N., Supr.; Mary Gomez, O.D.N., Prin. & Dir.; Ruth Henchy, O.D.N., Classroom Aide; Mary Raphael Ybarra, O.D.N., Family Svcs.; Zina Onoro, O.D.N., Teacher. Sisters 6. In Res Sr. Claudia L. Romero, O.D.N., Detention Min.

Sisters of the Good Shepherd (1904) 2561 W. Venice Blvd., 90019. Tel: 323-737-6111; Fax: 323-731-5014. Email: rgsla1@aol.com. Web: www.goodshepherdsisters.org. Sisters 10.

Sisters of the Guardian Angel (1838) 4529 New York St., 90022. Tel: 323-266-4431. Email: regipenin@yahoo.com.

Sisters of the Immaculate Heart of Mary of Mirinae, I.H.M.M., 423 S. Commonwealth Ave., 90020. Tel: 213-738-1020; Fax: 213-381-6302. Email: laihmm@hanmail.net. Total in Residence 6.

Sisters of the Society Devoted to the Sacred Heart (1940) 869 S. Rimpau Blvd., 90005. Tel: 323-935-2372; Fax: 323-935-5943. Web: www.sacredheartsisters.com. Sisters 3.

ALHAMBRA. *Carmel of St. Teresa of Los Angeles* (1913) 215 E. Alhambra Rd., 91801. Tel: 626-282-2387; Fax: 626-282-2053. Email: teresacarm@aol.com. Web: www.carmelteresa.org. Sr. Brenda Marie, O.C.D., Prioress. Discalced Nuns of the Order of Our Blessed Lady of Mt. Carmel. Sisters 17.

Carmelite Sisters of the Most Sacred Heart of Los Angeles (1941) 920 E. Alhambra Rd., 91801-2799. Tel: 626-289-1353; Fax: 626-308-1913. Email: carmelitegeneralate@carmelitesistersocd.com. Web: www.carmelitesistersocd.com. Professed Sisters 132; Novices 9; Postulants 4.

Missionary Sisters of St. Columban, 2500 S. Fremont Ave., #E, 91803. Tel: 626-458-1869; 626-570-6187; Fax: 626-570-6101. Web: www.columbansisters.org.

ALTADENA. *Franciscan Sisters of the Sacred Heart* (1866) *Sacred Heart Convent*, 579 W. Mariposa St., 91001. Tel: 626-791-4359. Email: ruthagee@juno.com. Sr. Mary Elizabeth Imler, O.S.F., Gen. Supr. Sisters 2.

Sacred Heart Convent (A California nonprofit corp.), 579 W. Mariposa St., 91001-4509. Tel: 620-791-4359. Web: www.fssh.com. Sr. Judith Plumb, O.S.F., Gen. Supr. Franciscan Sisters of the Sacred Heart, (Frankfort, IL).

BELLFLOWER. **Sisters of the Blessed Korean Martyrs, S.B.K.M.* (1946) 16276 California Ave., 90706. Tel: 562-461-8100. Sisters 5.

BONITA. *Sister Servants of the Blessed Sacrament*, U.S. Provincial House, 3173 Winnetka Dr., 91902. Tel: 619-267-0720; Fax: 619-267-0920. Email: sup@sjsusprovince.sdcoxmail.com. Sisters in the Archdiocese 13.

CHATSWORTH. *Sacred Heart Retreat Apostolate* (2004) 10480 1/2 Winnetka Ave., 91311. Tel: 818-488-1357; Fax: 818-488-1475. Sisters Susan Blaschke, S.D.S.H., Treas. Gen; Jane Stafford, Supr. Gen. Email: mhsdsh2@sbcglobal.net.

CULVER CITY. *Daughters of St. Paul*, 3908 Sepulveda Blvd., 90230. Tel: 310-390-4699; Fax: 310-391-1152. Email: culvercity@paulinemedia.com. Web: pauline.org. Sr. Karen Joseph Hamm, F.S.P., Supr. Sisters 8.

Religious Sisters of Charity (1815) 10668 St. James Dr., 90230-5461. Tel: 310-559-0176; Fax: 310-559-3530. Email: marshamoon.la@gmail.com. Web: www.rsccaritas.org. Sisters 32.

DOWNEY. *Sisters of the Holy Faith in California*, 12322 S. Paramount Blvd., 90242-3538. Tel: 562-869-6092; Fax: 562-869-4609. Email: shfaith@yahoo.com. Web: www.holyfaithsisters.com. Sisters 31.

GARDENA. *Lovers of the Holy Cross Sisters*, 14700 S. Van Ness Ave., 90249. Tel: 310-516-0271; Fax: 310-352-6435. Email: lhcla@yahoo.com; theresahaong@yahoo.com. Web: www.lhcla.org.

St. Anselm Convent, 7023 Arlington Ave., 90043. Tel: 323-752-4405. Email: srmtonga@yahoo.com. Web: www.lhcla.org. *St. Bruno Convent*, 10734 S.

Widener Ave., Whittier, 90603. Tel: 562-947-1177; Fax: 562-947-1177. Email: srtuoi@yahoo.com. Web: www.lhcla.org. Sisters 60; Postulants 2; Aspirants 11; Novices 4.

Poor Clare Missionary Sisters, Inc., 1050 W. 161st St., 90247. Tel: 310-323-9942. Sr. Elvira Duron, M.C., Supr. Sisters 14.

GLENDORA. *St. Lucy's Priory* (1955) 19045 E. Sierra Madre Ave., 91741. Tel: 626-335-1682; Fax: 626-914-9398. Email: stlucysebrown@aol.com. Web: www.stlucys.com. Sr. Elizabeth Brown, Prioress.

St. Lucy's Priory of Glendora California, Inc. Sisters 12.

HAWAIIAN GARDENS. *Lovers of the Holy Cross Nha Trang* (1950) 21618 Juan Ave., 90716. Tel: 562-809-1570; Fax: 562-809-1570. Sr. Mary Men T. Pham, L.H.C.N.T., Reg. Supr. U.S. Community 5.

LONG BEACH. **Little Handmaids of the Most Holy Trinity, M.A.S.T.* (1988) 3716 Arabella St., 90805. Tel: 562-633-0640; Fax: 562-531-8773. Sr. Monica Bermiso, M.A.S.T., Foundress & Mother Supr.

The Medical Sisters of St. Joseph, 3627 Lemon Ave., 90807. Tel: 562-426-8825. Email: msjnirmala.@aol.com. Web: www.msjnirmala.org. Sr. Dennis Punchakunnel, M.S.J.

MONROVIA. *Maryknoll Sisters of St. Dominic, Inc.* (1912) 340 Norumbega Dr., 91016-2445. Tel: 626-358-1825; Fax: 626-358-1227. Email: mkmonrovia2010@yahoo.com. Sr. Joan Delaney, M.M., Team Contact Person. Sisters 39.

MONTEBELLO. *Religious of the Sacred Heart of Mary*, Provincial Center, 441 N. Garfield Ave., 90640-2901. Tel: 323-887-8821; Fax: 323-887-8952. Email: rshmwap@earthlink.net. Web: www.rshm.org.

NORTHRIDGE. *Mother of Mercy Convent*, 9329 Crebs Ave., 91324. Tel: 818-882-4095. Sister of Mercy Burlingame.

Sisters of the Society Devoted to the Sacred Heart (1940) Motherhouse: 9814 Sylvia Ave., 91324. Tel: 818-772-9961; Fax: 818-772-2742. Email: mhsdsh2@sbcglobal.net. Web: www.sacredheartsisters.com. Sr. Jane Stafford, S.D.S.H., Supr. Gen. Sisters 50.

OJAI. *Sisters of Mary Mother of the Church*, 431 Montana Cir., 93023. Tel: 805-640-1798; Fax: 805-640-1798. Email: SRSMMC@aol.com.

OXNARD. *Servants of Mary, Ministers to the Sick*, 140 North G St., 93030-5214. Tel: 805-486-5502; Fax: 805-486-0663. Email: ssofmary_pro_ox@verizon.net. Sr. Felisa Ripa, Mistress of Novices. Professed Sisters 15; Novices 3.

RANCHO PALOS VERDES. *Daughters of Mary & Joseph, D.M.J.* (1817) 5300 Crest Rd., 90275-5004. Tel: 310-377-9968; Fax: 310-541-5967. Email: leadershipteam@dmjca.org. Web: www.daughtersofmaryandjoseph.org. Sisters 46.

Sisters of Charity of Rolling Hills, 28600 Palos Verdes Dr. E., 90275. Tel: 310-831-4104. Sr. Virginia Buchholz, S.C.R.H., Supr. Gen. Sisters 6.

SAN FERNANDO. *Religious Sisters of Charity*, 1608 Eighth St., 91340. Tel: 818-365-7926; Fax: 818-838-1098. Email: michellehrsc@msn.com. Sisters 3.

SAN PEDRO. *Little Sisters of the Poor* (1979) 2100 S. Western Ave., 90732. Tel: 310-548-0625; Fax: 310-548-4504. Email: adsanpedro@littlesistersofthepoor.org. Sr. Paul Magyar, L.S.P., Supr. Priests 2; Sisters 10; Total Staff 110; Total Assisted 1,260; Residents 102; Lay Assocs. 15.

SANTA BARBARA. *Monastery of Poor Clares* (1928) Cloistered Contemplative Monastery, 215 E. Los Olivos St., 93105. Tel: 805-682-7670; Fax: 805-682-8041. Web: www.poorclaressantabarbara.org. Sr. Aimee Marie of the Eucharist, Abbess. Attended by Franciscan Fathers of the Old Mission. Professed 12; Novices 1.

SOLVANG. *Sisters of the Society Devoted to the Sacred Heart* (1940) 1762 Mission Dr., 93463. Tel: 805-688-6158; Fax: 805-688-9247. Sr. Paula Sawhill, S.D.S.H., Supr. Sisters 3.

SYLMAR. *Franciscan Sisters of the Immaculate Conception* (1874) 13367 Borden Ave., Unit A, 91342. Tel: 818-364-6122; 818-364-5557; Fax: 818-362-7536. Email: provstclare@verizon.net.

Franciscan Missionary Sisters of the Immaculate Conception Sisters 100; Novices 2; Postulants 2.

Poor Clare Missionary Sisters, P.O. Box 922046, 91392. Tel: 818-365-8307; Fax: 818-365-8307. Sr. Edelmira Rivera, M.C., Supr. Sisters 7.

THOUSAND OAKS. *Sisters of Notre Dame* (1924) 1776 Hendrix Ave., 91360. Tel: 805-496-3243; Fax: 805-379-3616. Email: smanncarla@yahoo.com. Web: www.sndca.org. Sr. Mary Anncarla Costello, S.N.D., Prov. Supr. Sisters 60.

TORRANCE. *Little Company of Mary Convent*, 20552 Mansel Ave., 90503. Tel: 310-214-3190; Fax: 310-921-3253. Email: srmildred@sbcglobal.net. Web: www.lcmglobal.org. Sisters 2. 20562 Mansel Ave., 90503. Tel: 310-370-3992; Fax: 310-370-8452. Email: terrence.landini@providence.org.

565 W. 36th St., Apt. 2, San Pedro, 90731. Tel: 424-772-1861. Email: gloria.harper@providence.org.

VENTURA. *Congregation of the Sisters of the Holy Cross*, 1931 Poli St., 93001-2360. Tel: 805-652-1700; Fax: 805-653-1354. Sr. Patricia Riley, C.S.C., Supr.

Sisters of the Holy Cross, Inc. St. Catherine-by-the-Sea Convent 20; Holy Cross Convent 3.

Handmaids of the Sacred Heart of Jesus, Mary and Joseph, + J.M.J., P.O. Box 2957, 93002-2957. Tel: 805-653-2379. Email: handmaidsjmj@gmail.com; info@handmaids.org. Web: www.handmaidjmj.org.

WINNETKA. *Sisters of St. Louis*, 20253 Ingomar St., 91306-2521. Tel: 818-772-8959. Ursuline Sisters.Presentation Sisters.Sisters of St. Louis. Sisters 4.

WOODLAND HILLS. *Sisters of St. Louis, Louisville Convent*, 22300 Mulholland Dr., 91364-4933. Tel: 818-883-1678; Fax: 818-346-6109. Email: sslca4@sistersofsaintlouis.com. Web: www.stlouissisters.org. Sr. Judith Dieterle, S.S.L., Regl. Leader. Sisters 11.

[R] SECULAR INSTITUTES

LOS ANGELES. *Society of Our Lady of the Way*, 2339 N. Catalina St., 90027. Tel: 323-661-3315. Email: laffertyjudy@yahoo.com. Web: www.saecimds.com.

Society of Our Lady of the Way of Southern California, Inc.

WEST COVINA. *Fr. Kolbe Missionaries of the Immaculata* (1954) 531 E. Merced Ave., 91790. Tel: 626-917-0040. Email: fkmissionaries@gmail.com. Web: www.kolbemission.org/en.

[S] ASSOCIATIONS OF THE FAITHFUL

LOS ANGELES. **Servants of the Father of Mercy, Inc.*, P.O. Box 42001, 90024. Tel: 310-595-4175.

LONG BEACH. **Friars of the Sick Poor of Los Angeles, Inc.* (2002) 1276 E. Appleton St., 90802-3632. Tel: 562-432-4770; Fax: 310-900-8518. Email: brrichardhirbe@dochs.org. Web: friarsofthesickpoor.org. Bro. Richard A. Hirbe, F.S.P., Min./General-Founder. Friars 7; Novices 1.

TUJUNGA. *Community of the Holy Spirit, C.H.S.*, 10358 Las Lunitas Ave., 91042-1812. Tel: 818-470-2741; 562-596-8423; 818-687-5685. Email: jjhs106@aol.com. Mailing Address: 7239 Hatillo Ave., Winnetka, 91306.

VENTURA. *Trinitas*, 10332 Darling Rd., 93004-2425. Tel: 805-659-4158; Fax: 805-659-4158. Email: trinitascom@juno.com.

[T] RESIDENCES FOR WOMEN

LOS ANGELES. *St. Anne's*, 155 N. Occidental Blvd., 90026. Tel: 213-381-2931, Ext. 218; Fax: 213-381-7804. Email: stannes@stannes.org. Web: www.stannes.org. Group Home transitional housing, child care, mental health and family based services for pregnant, parenting teens, their children & families.

Bethany House, 850 N. Hobart Blvd., 90029. Tel: 323-665-6937; Fax: 323-664-0754. Email: imas.bethania@hotmail.com. Sisters 6; Residents 32.

Good Shepherd Center for Homeless Women and Children (1984) Languille Emergency Shelter, 267 N. Belmont Ave., 90026. Tel: 213-250-5241; Fax: 213-250-5073. Email: srjuliamary@sbcglobal.net. Web: www.thegoodshepherdcenter.com. (A Program of Catholic Charities.) Women in Residence 30; Bed Capacity 130; Women Assisted Annually 2,784; Total Staff 26; Total Assisted Annually 3,124.

Mother-Child Transitional Residence Administrative Site (1992) 267 N. Belmont Ave., 90026. Tel: 213-469-6540; Fax: 213-469-0370. Mother-Children in Residence 30; Mother-Children Sheltered Annually 150.

Hawkes Transitional Residence/Women's Village (1998) 1640 Rockwood St., 90026. Tel: 213-482-0281; Fax: 213-482-0299. Women Sheltered Annually 150.

Angel Guardian Home for Homeless Disabled Mothers with Minor Children (2000) 1660 Rockwood St., 90026. Tel: 213-483-6654; Fax: 213-482-0522. Women-Children Sheltered Annually 40.

St. Joseph's Residence (1957) 1124 W. Adams Blvd., 90007. Tel: 213-749-9577; Fax: 213-747-6468. Email: divine_providence@sbcglobal.net. Web: www.companyofmary.com. Sisters of the Company of Mary. Women 60.

[U] RESIDENCES FOR MEN

LOS ANGELES. *Catholic Kolping House*, 1225 S. Union Ave., 90015. Tel: 213-388-9438; Fax: 213-388-9438. Email: losangeleskolpinghouse@yahoo.com. Web: www.kolping.org. Alma Tamayo, Mgr. Capacity 60.

Missionaries of Charity Brothers (1975) 1325 S. Westlake Ave., 90006. Tel: 213-384-6111. Email: brosla@aol.com. Web: www.mcbrothers.org. Brothers 5.

[V] RETREAT HOUSES

LOS ANGELES. *Immaculate Heart Retreat House* (1971) (Days of Recollection Only), 3431 Waverly Dr., 90027-2526. Tel: 323-664-3357, Ext. 114; Fax: 323-664-2215. Sr. Catherine Rose, I.H.M., Dir. & Treas. Conducted by the Sisters of the Immaculate Heart. Capacity 60; Sisters 9.

ALHAMBRA. *Sacred Heart Retreat House, Inc.*, 920 E. Alhambra Rd., 91801. Tel: 626-289-1353; Fax: 626-281-3546. Email: contact@sacredheartretreathouse.com. Web: www.sacredheartretreathouse.com. Carmelite Sisters of the Most Sacred Heart of Los Angeles. Overnight 85; Day Retreat 200; St. Joseph Campus Day Retreat 400.

ENCINO. *Holy Spirit Retreat Center*, 4316 Lanai Rd., 91436. Tel: 818-784-4515; Fax: 818-784-0409. Email: hsrcenter@earthlink.net. Web: www.hsrcenter.com. Sisters of Social Service.

MALIBU. *Serra Retreat* (1942) 3401 Serra Rd., P.O. Box 127, 90265. Tel: 310-456-6631; Fax: 310-456-9417. Email: frmel@serraretreat.com. Web: www.serraretreat.com. Revs. Melvin A. Jurisich, O.F.M., Dir.; Warren Rouse, O.F.M., Asst. Dir.; Michael Doherty, O.F.M., Retreat Master; Alexander Manville, O.F.M. (Retired); Bro. Samuel Cabot, O.F.M. Franciscan Friars of California. Priests 4; Brothers 1.

MONTEBELLO. *DePaul Evangelization Center* (1987) 1105 S. Bluff Rd., 90640-6143. Tel: 323-721-6060; Fax: 323-887-0765. Email: depaulcenter@att.net. Web: depaulcenter.org. Revs. James Osendorf, C.M., Supr. & Dir.; Andrew E. Bellisario, C.M., Prov.; Peter J. Diliberto (Retired); Robert J. Jones, C.M.; Gary S. Landry, C.M.; Binh Van Nguyen, C.M.; Thomas J. McIntyre, C.M. (Retired); Bro. Edward D. Graham, C.M., (Retired). Formerly St. Vincent's Seminary; Congregation of the Mission (Vincentians); Retreat and Evangelization Center.

RANCHO PALOS VERDES. *Mary and Joseph Retreat Center*, 5300 Crest Rd., 90275-5004. Tel: 310-377-4867; Fax: 310-541-1176. Email: alenneman@maryjoseph.org. Web: www.maryjoseph.org. Daughters of Mary and Joseph. Retreat Center Capacity 70.

ROSEMEAD. *St. Joseph's Salesian Youth Renewal Center* (Boys and Girls), 8301 Arroyo Dr., P.O. Box 1639, 91770. Tel: 626-280-8622; Fax: 626-280-0545. Web: stjoescenter.org. Revs. Paul M. Caporali, S.D.B.; Bill Bolton, S.D.B., Dir. Retreat Center; Ted Montemayor, S.D.B., Dir. & Supr.; Mel Trinidad, S.D.B., Youth Min.; Marc Rougeau, S.D.B., Treas. & Vice Dir.; Christian H. Woerz, S.D.B., Vocation Dir.; Bros. Phil Mandile, S.D.B.; Larry King, S.D.B. Conducted by Salesians of St. John Bosco. Priests 6; Brothers 2; Total Staff 4; Total Assisted Annually 6,000.

SAN FERNANDO. *Poverello of Assisi Retreat House* (1962) 1519 Woodworth St., 91340. Tel: 818-365-1071; Fax: 818-361-2751. Email: poverelloretreathouse@verizon.net. Sr. Mary Jesus, O.S.F., Dir. Franciscan Missionary Sisters of the Immaculate Conception., For men and women. Korean groups, Married couples Spanish. Other Denominations workshops seminars, staff meetings. Priests and Sisters retreats, assemblies and chapters, one day retreats for Grammar and High Schools. Capacity 112.

SANTA BARBARA. *St. Mary's Seminary Center*, 1964 Las Canoas Rd., 93105. Tel: 805-966-4829; Fax: 805-564-1662. Email: stmarysseminary@cox.net. Revs. Patrick J. Mullin, C.M., Dir.; Roy A. Persich, C.M. (Retired); James M. Galvin; Walter L. Housey, C.M. (Retired); John V. Shine, C.M. (Retired). Priests 5.

SIERRA MADRE. *Mater Dolorosa Passionist Retreat Center, Inc.*, 700 N. Sunnyside Ave., 91025. Tel: 626-355-7188; Fax: 626-355-0485. Email: materdolorosa@materdolorosa.org. Web: www.materdolorosa.org. Conducted by the Passionist Community., Lay Retreats for parish men and women. Specialized Retreats. Hosted programs. Priests 3; Brothers 1.

Retreat Team: Revs. Patrick Brennan, C.P., Retreat Dir.; Alfred Pooler, C.P.; Michael Hoolahan, C.P.; Deacon Manuel Valencia; Bro. John Rockenbach, C.P.; Elizabeth Welch Velarde, Admin.

TEMPLE CITY. *Claretian Missionaries - Western Province, Inc.*, 10203 Lower Azusa Rd., 91780. Tel: 626-443-2009; Fax: 626-443-2005. Email: usawestprov@earthlink.net. Web: www.claretian.com. Very Rev. Rosendo Orrabazo, C.M.F., Prov. Supr., San Gabriel Mission, 428 S. Mission Dr., San Gabriel, 91776. Tel: 626-457-3035; Bro. Rene Lepage, C.M.F., Asst. Treas., Dominguez Seminary, 18127 S. Alameda St.,

Rancho Dominguez, 90220. Tel: 323-636-6030. *Tepeyac House*, 6104 York Blvd., 90042. Tel: 323-254-0510. Revs. Paul J. Keller, C.M.F.; Darrin Merlino, C.M.F.; John Raab, C.M.F.; Bro. Larry Moen, C.M.F. *Educational and Renewal Center, Inc.*, 91780. Tel: 626-443-2009; Fax: 626-443-2005. Email: usawestprov@earthlink.net. Web: www.claretian.com. *Dominguez Seminary Inc.*, 18127 S. Alameda St., Rancho Dominguez, 90220. Tel: 310-631-5981; 310-631-8484; Fax: 310-638-1818. Rev. Frank Ferrante, C.M.F., Supr.; Bro. Rene LePage, C.M.F., Econome; Revs. Mark Clarke, C.M.F., Econome & Treas.; Joseph Daries, C.M.F.; Robert Billett, C.M.F., Vicar Supr.; Robert Bishop, C.M.F.; Carlos C. Castillo, C.M.F.; Diego Barrios, C.M.F.; Salvatore Bonano, C.M.F. (Retired); John Corominas, C.M.F.; Milton Alvarez, C.M.F.; Alberto Domingo, C.M.F. (Retired); Joseph Gamm, C.M.F.; Isidor Garcia, C.M.F.; John Gregory Hencier, C.M.F.; Donald Lavelle, C.M.F.; James Overend, C.M.F.; Michael Philen, C.M.F.; Frank Pyka, C.M.F. (Retired); John Hampsch, C.M.F.; Christian Ihedoro, C.M.F.; Bernard O'Connor, C.M.F.; Fernando Vega, C.M.F. (Retired); George Whedbee, C.M.F. (Retired); Bros. Modesto Leon, C.M.F.; Paul Roy, C.M.F. Congregation of Missionaries, Sons of the Immaculate Heart of Mary (Claretian Missionaries)., Retirement Center, Ministries Community. Priests 22; Brothers 3.

VALYERMO. *St. Andrew's Abbey Retreat Center (All Groups)*, 31001 N. Valyermo Rd., P.O. Box 40, 93563. Tel: 661-944-2178, Ext. 0; Fax: 661-944-1076. Email: retreats@valyermo.com. Web: www.saintandrewsabbey.com. Rev. Philip Edwards, O.S.B., Guestmaster. Tel: 661-944-2178, Ext. 0; Rita Jones, Youth Center Contact Person. Tel: 661-944-2734; Cheryl Evanson, Retreat Center Admin. & Youth Center Dir. Conducted by the Benedictine Monks.

[W] PERSONAL PRELATURES

LOS ANGELES. *Prelature of the Holy Cross and Opus Dei* Offices of the Prelature in California, 770 S. Windsor Blvd., 90005. Revs. Matthew A. Bloomer; Paul A. Donlan; Very Rev. Luke Mata; Rev. John R. Meyer.

Tilden Study Center, 655 Levering Ave., 90024-2308. Tel: 310-208-0941; Fax: 310-208-6783. Web: www.tildensc.org.

[X] CATHOLIC CHARITIES OF CALIFORNIA

LOS ANGELES. *Catholic Charities of Los Angeles, Inc.*, 1531 James M. Wood Blvd., P.O. Box 15095, 90015-0095. Tel: 213-251-3400; Fax: 213-380-4603. Web: catholiccharitiesla.org. Most Rev. Jose H. Gomez, D.D., S.T.D., V.G.; Rev. Msgr. Gregory A. Cox, M.S.W., M.B.A., M.Div., Exec. Dir. Tel: 213-251-3464.

Central Administrative Offices, 1531 James M. Wood Blvd., P.O. Box 15095, 90015-0095. Tel: 213-251-3400; Fax: 213-380-4603. Web: CatholicCharitiesLA.org. Rev. Msgr. Gregory A. Cox, M.S.W., M.B.A., M.Div., Exec. Dir. Tel: 213-251-3464; Ronald G. Lopez, M.S.W., Chief Admin. Officer. Tel: 213-251-3413; James E. Bathker, M.B.A., CFO. Tel: 213-251-3410; Alexandria "Sandi" Arnold, M.S., Dir. Dept. Resource Devel. Tel: 213-251-3495; Leland Ratleff, Dir. Human Resources. Tel: 213-251-3414.

Adeste Child Care Services Tel: 213-251-3468; Fax: 213-251-3510. Armine Lalaian, Quality Assurance Mgr. Tel: 213-251-3468.

Archdiocesan Youth Employment Services, 3250 Wilshire Blvd., Ste. 1010, 90010. Tel: 213-736-5456; Fax: 213-736-5654. Robert L. Gutierrez, Prog. Dir.

CYO James McGoldrick, Prog. Dir.

CYO Athletics Tel: 213-251-3553; Fax: 213-251-3510.

Esperanza Immigrant Rights Project, 1530 James M. Wood Blvd., 90015. Tel: 213-251-3505; Fax: 213-487-0986. Caitlin C. Williams, J.D., Prog. Dir.

Immigration & Refugee Services Tel: 213-251-3489; Fax: 213-251-3444. Loc Nam Nguyen, Prog. Dir. Tel: 213-251-3489.

Immigration Reception Tel: 213-251-3411; 213-251-3471; Fax: 213-251-3444.

Refugee Resettlement Tel: 213-251-3470.

Central Intake Unit (CIU) Tel: 213-251-3481; Fax: 213-251-3580. Brenda Thomas, Prog. Dir. Tel: 213-251-3445.

CCLA Continuous Quality Improvement Tel: 213-251-3459; Fax: 213-251-3563. Edward Nelson, Ph.D., Performance Quality Improvement Dir. Tel: 213-251-3459.

Regional Offices and Community Centers:

OUR LADY OF THE ANGELS PASTORAL REGION: METRO AREA, 4665 Willowbrook Ave., 90029. Tel: 323-662-1462; Fax: 323-662-2708. Hector Manuel Briones, J.D., Regl. Dir. (Los Angeles Inner City)

Adeste Child Care, 601 E. 23rd St., 90011. Tel: 213-748-5246.

Community Service Centers:

St. Mary's Center, 4665 Willowbrook Ave., 90029. Tel: 323-662-4391; Fax: 323-662-2708.

El Santo Nino Center, 601 E. 23rd St., 90011. Tel: 213-748-5246; Fax: 213-748-9006.

Shelters & Housing Services:

Angels Flight - Runaway/Homeless Youth Shelter, 357 S. Westlake Ave., 90057. Tel: 213-413-2311; 800-833-2499 (Hotline); Fax: 213-413-5690.

Angels Flight Outreach, 357 S. Westlake Ave., 90057. Tel: 213-413-2311.

Sr. Julia Mary Farley House and the Village Kitchen, Women's Village, 1671 Beverly Blvd., 90026. Tel: 213-235-1460.

Good Shepherd Center for Homeless Women, 267 N. Belmont Ave., 90026. Tel: 213-250-5241; Fax: 213-250-5073. Sr. Anne Tran, L.H.C., Prog. Dir.

Good Shepherd Hawkes Transitional Residence, Women's Village, 1650 Rockwood St., 90026. Tel: 213-482-0281; Fax: 213-482-0299.

My Club After School Program, 8701 S. Vermont Ave., Unit A, 90044. Tel: 213-413-2311.

OUR LADY OF THE ANGELS PASTORAL REGION: WESTERN AREA, 211 Third Ave., Venice, 90291. Tel: 310-392-8701; Fax: 310-399-4097. Hector Manuel Briones, J.D., Regl. Dir. (Inglewood, Crenshaw District, Korea Town, West Los Angeles, Malibu & Los Angeles Airport region)

Adeste Child Care, 211 Third Ave., Venice, 90291. Tel: 310-392-8701; Fax: 310-399-4097.

Community Service Centers:

St. Margaret's Center, 10217 S. Inglewood Ave., Inglewood, 90304. Tel: 310-672-2208; Fax: 310-672-1841.

St. Peter Claver Center, 4502 W. Washington Blvd., 90016. Tel: 323-297-0292; Fax: 323-737-3649.

St. Robert's Center, 211 Third Ave., Venice, 90291. Tel: 310-392-8701; Fax: 310-399-4097.

Citizenship Services & Classes, St. Margaret's Center, 10217 S. Inglewood Ave., Inglewood, 90304. Tel: 310-672-2208.

Catholic Counseling Services, 211 Third Ave., Venice, 90291. Tel: 310-399-1451; Fax: 310-399-4097.

St. Margaret's Thrift Store, 10505 Hawthorne Blvd., Lennox, 90304. Tel: 310-674-9652.

SAN FERNANDO REGION, 21600 Hart St., Canoga Park, 91303. Tel: 818-883-6015; Fax: 818-883-4122. Moeed Khan, M.S.W., Regl. Dir. (Burbank, Glendale, Eagle Rock, Verdugo Hills, Antelope Valley, San Fernando Valley)

Community Service Centers:

Glendale Community Services Center, 4322 San Fernando Rd., Glendale, 91204. Tel: 818-409-3080; Fax: 818-956-1857.

Temporary Skilled Worker Center, 5101 San Fernando Rd., Glendale, 91204. Tel: 818-548-6495.

Guadalupe Community Center, 21600 Hart St., Canoga Park, 91303. Tel: 818-340-2050.

Loaves and Fishes I, 4322 San Fernando Rd., Glendale, 91204. Tel: 818-409-3080.

Loaves and Fishes II, 14640 Keswick St., Van Nuys, 91405. Tel: 818-997-0943; Fax: 818-497-6980.

Loaves and Fishes IV, 21600 Hart St., Canoga Park, 91303. Tel: 818-340-2050.

Temporary Skilled Worker Center, 1190 S. Flower St., Burbank, 91502. Tel: 818-566-7148.

Immigration & Refugee Department, 4322 San Fernando Rd., Glendale, 91204. Tel: 818-409-0057.

Shelter/Housing Services:

Lancaster Community Shelter, 44611 Yucca Ave., Lancaster, 93534. Tel: 661-945-7524.

SAN GABRIEL REGION, 1307 Warren St., 90033. Tel: 323-266-3130; Fax: 323-266-3269. Mary Romero, Regl. Dir. (San Gabriel Valley, Mt. Baldy, Pomona Valley, East Los Angeles).

Adeste Child Care, 1307 Warren Ave., 90033. Tel: 323-264-4981; Fax: 323-266-3269.

Community Service Centers:

The Art of Parenting (Padua School), 1500 E. Bridge St., 90033. Tel: 323-263-4651.

Brownson House Community Center, 1307 Warren Ave., 90033. Tel: 323-264-8700; Fax: 323-266-3269.

Catholic Counseling Services, 1215 S. Hamilton Blvd., Pomona, 91766. Tel: 909-622-2824.

McGill Transitional Housing, Administration: 4171 N. Tyler Ave., El Monte, 91731. Tel: 626-350-5867.

Pomona Community Services, 248 E. Monterey Ave., Pomona, 91769. Tel: 909-629-0472.

Youth Employment Services, 5301 Whittier Blvd., 90022. Tel: 323-832-1232.

San Juan Diego Center, 4171 N. Tyler Ave., El Monte, 91731. Tel: 626-575-7652.

SAN PEDRO REGION, 123 E. 14th St., Long Beach, 90813. Tel: 562-591-1641; Fax: 562-591-2481. Anna R. Totta, M.S., Regl. Dir. (Long Beach, South Bay, Compton, Rio Hondo, Vernon, Huntington Park, Whittier, Pico Rivera).

Community Service Centers:

Long Beach Community Services, 123 E. 14th St., Long Beach, 90813. Tel: 562-591-1351; Fax: 562-591-2481.

Mahar House Community Center, 1115 Mahar Ave., Wilmington, 90744. Tel: 310-834-7265; Fax: 310-834-8813.

Immigration Services Tel: 310-834-7265.

Pico Rivera Family Resource Center, 5014 Passons Rd., Pico Rivera, 90660. Tel: 562-949-0937.

Elizabeth Ann Seton Homeless Services, 2241 Williams St., Long Beach, 90810. Tel: 562-388-7670.

Oasis Community Center, 2045 St. Gabriel Ave., Long Beach, 90810. Tel: 562-480-2166.

Project Achieve Shelter, 1368 Oregon, Long Beach, 90813. Tel: 562-218-9864.

SANTA BARBARA PASTORAL REGION: SANTA BARBARA COUNTY, 609 E. Haley St., Santa Barbara, 93103. Tel: 805-965-7045; Fax: 805-963-2978. Frank Bognar, D.P.A., Regl. Dir. (Lompoc, Santa Maria, Santa Barbara, Carpinteria).

Community Service Centers:

Santa Barbara Community Services, 609 E. Haley St., Santa Barbara, 93103. Tel: 805-965-7045.

Carpinteria Community Services, 941 Walnut St., Carpenteria, 93013. Tel: 805-684-8621; Fax: 805-684-9771.

Lompoc Community Services & Food Pantry, 903 E. Chestnut, Lompoc, 93436. Tel: 805-736-4886.

Santa Maria Community Services, 607 W. Main, Santa Maria, 93458. Tel: 805-922-2059; Fax: 805-925-1979.

Guadalupe Community Services Tel: 805-922-2059.

New Cuyama Community Services Tel: 805-922-2059.

Thrift Stores:

Thrifty Shopper at Catholic Charities, 609 E. Haley St., Santa Barbara, 93103. Tel: 805-966-9659.

Santa Maria Thrift Store, 605 W. Main St., Santa Maria, 93454. Tel: 805-925-8372.

Older Adult Services, 609 E. Haley St., Santa Barbara, 93103. Tel: 805-965-7045.

Catholic Counseling Services, 609 E. Haley St., Santa Barbara, 93103. Tel: 805-965-7045; Fax: 805-963-2978.

SANTA BARBARA PASTORAL REGION: VENTURA COUNTY, 303 N. Ventura Ave., Ste. A, Ventura, 93001. Tel: 805-643-4694; Fax: 805-643-4781. Patricia Esseff, Prog. Dir. (Camarillo, Moorpark, Oxnard, Thousand Oaks, Simi Valley, Ventura, Conejo Valley)

Adeste Child Care, 303 N. Ventura Ave., Ste. A, Ventura, 93001. Tel: 805-643-4784.

Community Service Centers:

Ventura Community Services, 303 N. Ventura Ave., Ste. C, Ventura, 93001. Tel: 805-643-4694.

Oxnard Community Services, 402 N. "A" St., Oxnard, 93030. Tel: 805-486-2900.

Moorpark Community Services, 609 Fitch Ave., Moorpark, 93021. Tel: 805-529-0720.

Handicapables Tel: 805-643-4694.

OASIS - Older Adult Services

OASIS - Older Adult Services, 2532 Ventura Blvd., Camarillo, 93010. Tel: 805-987-2083; Fax: 805-383-1318.

Moorpark/Piru/Fillmore, Santa Paula, 93061. Tel: 805-794-5929.

[Y] SUMMER CAMPS

LOS ANGELES. *Scouting and Camp Fire Ministry/ Catholic Youth Camps*, P.O. Box 91764, Long Beach, 90809-1764. Sharon Shellman, Chm. CLGScf. Tel: 626-967-1815; Fax: 626-966-9610; Bill Cole, Vice Chm. Boys, 2972 Canaan Rd., Thousand Oaks, 91360. Tel: 626-732-2831.

St. Vincent dePaul Ranch Camp, 210 N. Ave. 21st, 90031. Tel: 323-224-6213; Fax: 323-226-4997. Raymond P. Lopez, Dir. Camp. (Boys, Ages 7-13); Sponsored by St. Vincent de Paul Society. Capacity 100.

Camp Mariastella, 1120 Manchester Pl., 90019. Fax: 323-266-4139. (Girls). Coed Program for Developmentally Disabled, Ages 7-Adult.; Owned & Operated by Sisters of Social Service.; Located in Wrightwood. Capacity 140.

Sacred Heart Retreat Camp, 869 S. Rimpau Blvd., 90005. Tel: 323-935-2372. Girls & Boys Sessions, Ages 8-17 years.; Owned and operated by the Sisters of the Society Devoted to the Sacred Heart.; Located at Big Bear Lake.

Camp Office, 896 Cienega Rd., P.O. Box 1795, Big Bear Lake, 92315. Tel: 909-866-5696; Fax: 909-866-5650. Capacity 150.

Lions Camp at Teresita Pines, P.O. Box 98, Wrightwood, 92397. Fax: 760-249-1063. Email: teresitapines@snowline.net. Web: www.lionswildcamp.com. (Girls), Ages 7-15 years.; Owned & Operated by Lions.; Located in Big Pines Area near Wrightwood. Capacity 125.

St. Nicholas Camp, 1170 Frontier Rd., Frazier Park, 93225. Tel: 805-245-3571; Fax: 805-245-0710. Available for year round camps & rates.

[Z] ST. VINCENT DE PAUL SOCIETY

LOS ANGELES. *Society of St. Vincent de Paul*, 210 N. Avenue 21, 90031. Tel: 323-224-6287; Fax: 323-225-4997. Email: olreyes@svdpla.org. Web: www.svdpla.org. David R. Fields, Exec. Dir. Tel: 323-224-6289. Email: dfields@svdpla.org; James Bibb, Dir. Opers. Tel: 323-226-1770. Email: jamesbibb@svdpla.org; Catalina M. Miller, Dir., St. Vincent de Paul Conferences. Tel: 888-552-7872. Email: cmiller@svdpla.org.

St. Vincent de Paul Ranch Camp & Retreat Center, 2550 Hwy. 154, Santa Barbara, 93105. Tel: 323-224-6213; Fax: 323-225-4997. Raymond P. Lopez, Dir.

St. Vincent's Cardinal Manning Center, 231 Winston St., 90013. Tel: 213-229-9963; Fax: 213-620-9141. Joan Sotiros, Dir.

St. Vincent de Paul Stores, 210 N. Avenue 21, 90031. Tel: 323-224-6280; Fax: 323-225-4997.

For Pick Up: 323-224-6280; 800-974-3571. Anthony Terrazas, Store Dir.

[AA] NEWMAN CENTERS

LOS ANGELES. *Campus Ministry c/o Office of the Chancellor* 3424 Wilshire Blvd., 90010-2241. Tel: 213-637-7000; Fax: 213-637-6000.

Loyola Law School 919 S. Albany St., P.O. Box 15019, 90019. Tel: 213-736-1000; Fax: 213-380-3769. Rev. Kenneth Rudnick, S.J., Dir.

Loyola Marymount University One LMU Dr., 90045-2659. Tel: 310-338-2700; Fax: 310-338-1845. Rev. James Erps, Dir.

Mount St. Mary College, Chalon Campus 12001 Chalon Rd., 90049-1599. Tel: 310-954-4125; Fax: 310-954-4119. Gail Gresser, Dir.

Mount St. Mary College, Downtown Campus 10 Chester Pl., 90007-2598. Tel: 213-477-2672, Ext. 2672; Fax: 213-477-2669. Gail Krause, Dir.

Occidental College, Catholic Campus Ministry 1600 Campus Rd., 90041. Tel: 323-259-2500; Fax: 323-255-3067. Rev. Raymond J. Finerty, O.P., Dir.

University of California, Los Angeles, University Catholic Center 633 Gayley Ave., 90024. Tel: 310-208-5015; Fax: 310-208-6077. Rev. Peter Abdella, C.S.P., Dir.

University of Southern California Our Saviour University Parish, 3207 University Ave., 90007. Tel: 213-749-5341; Fax: 213-749-3475. Rev. Lawrence Seyer, Dir.

California Institute of Technology I-88, Pasadena, 91125. Tel: 626-395-6212; Fax: 626-792-0475.

Claremont Colleges McAllister Religious Center, 919 N. Columbia, Claremont, 91711. Tel: 909-621-8000, Ext. 8685; Fax: 909-621-8304. Rev. Joe Fenton, S.M.

University of California Santa Barbara St. Mark University Parish, 6550 Picasso Rd., Goleta, 93117. Tel: 805-968-1078; Fax: 805-968-3965. Rev. John W. Love.

University of La Verne (La Verne) Campus Ministry, 1950 Third St., La Verne, 91750. Tel: 909-593-3511, Ext. 4322; Fax: 909-392-2753.

Marymount College (Rancho Palos Verdes) Campus Ministry, 30800 Palos Verdes Dr. E., Palos Verdes Peninsula, 90274. Tel: 310-377-5501; Fax: 310-377-6223. Web: www.marymountpv.edu. Rev. Mark Villano, Chap.

[BB] MISCELLANEOUS LISTINGS

LOS ANGELES. *Association of Christian Therapists*, 11942 Sunset Blvd., 90049. Tel: 310-403-2844. Email: redsunrise@mac.com. Web: www.actheals.org.

Catholic Big Brothers Big Sisters, Inc., 1530 James M. Wood Blvd., 90015. Tel: 213-251-9800; 213-251-7760 (TTY); Fax: 213-251-9855. Email: info@catholicbigbrothers.org. Web: www.catholicbigbrothers.org. Ken Martinet, Pres. & CEO. Branch offices throughout Los Angeles county.; A mentoring organization for 85 years, its core program matches adult volunteers with children between the ages of 7 and 14. Volunteer mentors provide role modeling and friendship in a one-to-one relationship. Other programs include mentoring among adults, high school youth, and elementary children; school based and site based after-school mentoring.

Catholic Charities Community Development Corporation, Inc., 1531 James M. Wood Blvd., P.O. Box 15095, 90015-0095. Tel: 213-251-3475; Fax: 213-380-4603.

Charisma in Missions, La Porciuncula, 1059 S. Gage Ave., 90023. Fax: 213-260-7221. Catholic Center of Evangelization and renewal ministries. A service for hispanic people through ongoing affirmation and growth seminars and courses; Catholic evangelizers' formation courses; direct evangelization missions; social service programs; prayer hot-line services; television and radio ministries; and a bookstore providing Catholic books, audio and video cassettes.

Collaborative Project for Aging Religious (1992) 2468 S. St. Andrew's Pl., 90018. Tel: 323-735-3625; Fax: 323-737-6320. Email: linkages@cpar.org. Web: www.cpar.org.

Conrad N. Hilton Fund for Sisters, 10100 Santa Monica Blvd., #1000, 90067-4145. Tel: 310-785-0746; Fax: 310-785-0166. Email: info@hiltonfundforsisters.org. Web: www.hiltonfundforsisters.org. Sr. Marcia Sichol, S.H.C.J.

Estrella del Mar de Los Angeles, Inc. dba Regis House Community Center (1949) 2212 W. Beverly Blvd., 90057. Tel: 213-380-8168; Fax: 213-380-8160. Email: regishousecc@att.net. Sisters Albertina Morales, S.S.S., Dir.; Teresita Saavedra, S.S.S., Prog. Dir. Sisters of Social Service 2.

**Federation of Oases of Koinonia John the Baptist*, 1016 W. Manchester Ave., 90044. Tel: 323-759-1070. Sr. Maire S. Close, Contact Person.

The Focolare Movement, Men's Branch (California) (Work of Mary), 8016 Cowan Ave., 90045-1405. Tel: 310-670-6736; Fax: 310-670-8036. Email: focolare.mla@gmail.com. Web: www.focolare.us. Mr. Carlos Bajo, Dir. West Coast. Formation in the Spirituality of Unity.

The Focolare Movement, Women's Branch, 3138 Glendon Ave., 90034-3404. Tel: 310-470-8505; Fax: 310-470-9239. Email: focolare-fla@att.net. Donna Kempt, Co-Dir., Westcoast.

St. Francis Center, 1835 S. Hope St., 90015. Tel: 213-747-5347; Fax: 213-765-8915. Email: info@sfcla.org. Web: www.sfcla.org. Jill Remelski, Exec. Dir.; Jill Remelski, Asst. Exec. Dir. A nonprofit, charitable corporation serving the homeless, children and low income families in downtown Los Angeles.

Franciscan Communications, 1530 James M. Wood Blvd., 90015. Tel: 213-251-9800; Fax: 213-251-9855. Kenneth E. Martinet, Pres. & CEO.

Friends of John Paul II Foundation of Southern California, 3424 W. Adams Blvd., 90018. Tel: 626-281-0516. Email: skcybulski@gmail.com. Stanislaw K. Cybulski, Pres.

Hospitaller Foundation of California, Inc., The, 2468 S. St. Andrew's Pl., 90018. Tel: 323-731-7141; Fax: 323-731-5717. Email: info@hospitallerfoundation.org. Web: www.hospitallerfoundation.org. Bro. Patrick Corr, O.H., Pres., Dir. & Mod. (Fundraising for St. John of God Retirement and Care Center)

Women's League of St. John of God Tel: 323-731-7141; Fax: 323-731-5717.

Helpers Club of St. John of God Tel: 323-731-7141; Fax: 323-731-5717.

Hotel Dieu, Mailing Address: 3663 Martin Luther King Jr. Blvd., Lynwood, 90262. 265 S. Lake St., 90057. Tel: 213-484-7111; Fax: 213-484-0450. Mary McKenna, CFO.

**The Institute for Advanced Catholic Studies, University Religious Center*, 835 W. 34th St., Ste. 102, 90089-0751. Tel: 213-740-3055; 213-740-1864; Fax: 213-740-2179. Email: iacss@comcast.net. Web: www.ifacs.com; www.instituteforadvancedcatholicstudies.com. Rev. James L. Heft, S.M., Contact Person.

Korean Catholic Renewal Movement of Southern California, 1230 San Fernando Rd., 90065. Tel: 323-221-8874. Rev. Constantine Kihyen Bae (Korea, South), Chap.

Lay Mission Helpers Association, 3435 Wilshire Blvd., Ste. 1940, 90010-1901. Tel: 213-368-1870; Fax: 213-368-1871. Email: info@laymissionhelpers.org. Web: www.laymissionhelpers.org. John McKenna, Exec. Dir.; Janice England, Prog. Dir.; Jorenz Campo, Devel. Dir.

**Mission Doctors Association*, 3435 Wilshire Blvd., Ste. 1940, 90010. Tel: 213-368-1875; Fax: 213-368-1871. Elise Frederick, Exec. Dir.

**Niño Jesus de Belen, Inc.* (2003) 141 W. 87th Pl., 90003-3315. Email: njesusdebelen@yahoo.com. Web: www.ninojesusdebeleninc.org.

Opus Caritatis, Inc., 1531 James W. Wood Blvd., 90015-0095. Tel: 213-251-3464. Rev. Msgr. Gregory A. Cox, M.S.W., M.B.A., M.Div., Contact Person.

Salesian Boys & Girls Club of Los Angeles, 3218 Wabash Ave., 90063. Tel: 323-263-7519; Fax: 323-263-8558. Email: wschafer@salesianclubs-la.org. Web: www.salesianclubs-la.org.

Salesian Family Youth Center, 2228 E. 4th St., 90033. Tel: 323-980-8551; Fax: 323-980-8594. The Salesian Family Youth Center is an outreach site of the Salesian Boys and Girls Club of Los Angeles and forms a single corporate entity with the Salesian Boys and Girls Club of Los Angeles.

Serra Ancillary Care, 3424 Wilshire Blvd., 90010. Tel: 213-637-7538.

Serra Institute, 2060 N. Vermont, 90027. Tel: 323-664-9292. Email: gcrye@aol.com. Web: quantumtheology.org.

Servants of the Immaculate Child Mary, 5135 Dartmouth Ave., 90032. Tel: 323-225-3279; Fax: 323-225-3279. Email: ImmaculateAL@.com. Sr. Raquel Sandoval, Contact Person.

Sisters of Nazareth Foundation, Inc., 3333 Manning Ave., 90064.

Sisters of Nazareth of Los Angeles Real Estate Holdings, Inc., 3333 Manning Ave., 90064.

**South Central Los Angeles Ministry Project aka South Central LAMP* (1993) 892 E. 48th St., 90011. Tel: 323-234-1471; Fax: 323-234-1472. Web: www.southcentrallamp.org. Nina Denise Hernandez, Exec. Dir.

Spirituality Center (1983) 10 Chester Pl., 90007. Tel: 213-747-6508; Fax: 213-477-2649. Email: spircenter@msmc.la.edu. Web: www.archdiocese.la/prayer/spirituality. Sr. Patricia Beirne, R.S.M., Dir.

St. Vincent Senior Citizen Nutrition Program, Inc. aka St. Vincent Meals on Wheels (1977) 2131 W. Third St., 90057. Tel: 213-484-7778; Fax: 213-484-7276. Sr. Alice Marie Quinn, D.C., Prog. Dir. Volunteers 300; Total Staff 98; Meals Served Daily 4,700.

Vincentians Province of the West, Support Trust Fund, 3663 Martin Luther King Blvd., Lynwood, 90262. Tel: 310-603-6007; Fax: 310-638-0075. Mike Garko, Contact Person.

Works in New Directions, Inc. (WIND), 4316 Lanai Rd., Encino, 91436. Tel: 818-285-3355; Fax: 818-285-3366. Sr. Grace Boys, S.S.S., Contact Person.

ALHAMBRA. **Carmelite Educational Centers, Inc.*, 920 E. Alhambra Rd., 91801. Tel: 626-289-1353; Fax: 626-308-1913. Email: carmelitegeneralte@carmelitesistersocd.com. Web: www.carmelitesistersocd.com.

Carmelite Sisters Foundation, Inc., 920 E. Alhambra Rd., 91801. Tel: 626-289-1353; Fax: 626-308-1913. Email: carmelitegeneralate@carmelitesistersocd.com.

Flos Carmeli Formation Centers, Inc., 920 E. Alhambra Rd., 91801. Tel: 626-289-1353; Fax: 626-308-1913. Email: carmelitegeneralate@carmelitesistersocd.com.

**Little Flower Center dba Little Flower Missionary House* 920 E. Alhambra Rd., 91801-2704. Tel: 323-221-9248; Fax: 323-221-9831. Email: lflower@catholic.org; carmelitegeneralate@carmelitesistersocd.com. Web: www.littleflowerla.com. Seminarians 8; Lay Teachers 11; Capacity 148; Kindergarten Capacity 25.

ANAHEIM HILLS. *Equestrian Order of the Holy Sepulchre of Jerusalem Western USA Lieutenancy*, 8141 E. Kaiser Blvd., Ste. 300, 92808. Tel: 714-282-9632; Fax: 714-282-1563. Email: awilliams@khswesternusa.org. Web: www.khswesternusa.org. H.E. Patrick D. Powers, Lieutenant.

3424 Wilshire Blvd., 90010-2241. Tel: 213-637-7000; Fax: 213-637-7691. His Eminence Cardinal Roger Michael Mahony, Grand Prior (Retired).

ARTESIA. *Filipino Pastoral Ministry*, 18708 S. Clarkdale Ave., 90701. Tel: 562-865-2185; Fax: 562-860-0718. Email: mac3exodus@aol.com. Rev. Johnny Zulueta, C.M.

BALDWIN PARK. *The Redemptorist Vietnamese Mission Corporation*, 3452 N. Big Dalton Ave., 91706. Tel: 626-338-3295; Fax: 626-851-1280. Email: chaqhung@yahoo.com. Rev. Pham Quoc Hung, C.Ss.R., Pres.

BELLFLOWER. *World Apostolate of Fatima, Blue Army, USA, Los Angeles Division*, 15550 Bellflower Blvd., 90706-3819. Tel: 562-867-8661; Fax: 562-867-8661.

BURBANK. **El Sembrador Ministries*, 2636 N. Ontario St., 91504. Tel: 818-260-0222; Fax: 818-557-7796. Noel Diaz, Contact Person; Salvador Hernandez, Office Mgr.

SCRC (Southern California Renewal Communities), 9795 Cabrini Dr., Ste. 208, 91504-1740. Tel: 818-771-1361; Fax: 818-771-1379. Email: spirit@scrc.org. Web: www.scrc.org. Dominic Berardino, Pres.; Rev. William K. Delaney, S.J., Pastoral Coord. Serving Catholic Charismatic Renewal through annual summer convention, pastoral teaching events, healing masses, retreats, book & tape ministry and a bi-monthly publication.

CARPINTERIA. **International Theological Institute for Studies on Marriage and the Family*, 3299 Padaro Ln., 93013. Tel: 805-649-2346; Fax: 706-867-6216. Betty Hartmann, Contact Person.

COVINA. *Comboni Mission Center*, 645 S. Aldenville Ave., 91723. Tel: 626-339-1914; Fax: 626-974-4238. Email: combonicovin@earthlink.net. Web: www.comboni.com. Revs. Sergio Contran, M.C.C.J. (Italy), Burser; Angelo G. Biancalana, M.C.C.J. (Italy), Community Member; Joseph Forlani, M.C.C.J. (Italy), Community Member.

CULVER CITY. **Loyola Productions, Inc.*, 8505 Washington Blvd., 90232. Tel: 310-815-8542; Fax: 310-815-8758. Email: esiebert@

loyolaproductions.com. Web: www.loyolaproductions.com. Rev. Edward J. Siebert, S.J., Pres.

DOWNEY. *Visitation Congregation of North America*, 7845 Quill Dr., 90242. Tel: 562-862-7472; Fax: 560-862-7472. Sr. Meera Parayil, Contact Person.

DUARTE. *Mount Carmel Health Ministries, Inc.*, 819 Buena Vista St., 91010. Tel: 626-408-7830; Fax: 626-408-7873.

EL MONTE. *Hombre Nuevo*, 12036 Ramona Blvd., 91732. Tel: 626-444-4442; Fax: 626-444-1435. Email: info@hombrenuevo.tv. Web: www.hombrenuevo.net. Rev. Juan Rivas, L.C.

GLENDALE. **Together in Christ* (1998) 311 E. Stocker St. Ste. 102, 91207. Tel: 818-246-5582; Fax: 818-246-5582. Email: TogetherChrist1@yahoo.com. Nancy Barona, Pres.

LA MIRANDA. *World Wide Marriage Encounter*, 16706 Cerise Ave., Torrance, 90504. Tel: 310-515-3522. Web: www.wwme.org. Anthony Mena, Contact; Vel Mena, Contact.

LA VERNE. *Picpus Charitable Trust* (1991) 2150 Damien Ave., 91750. Tel: 909-227-9346; Fax: 760-955-2100. Email: ptravers37@gmail.com. P.O. Box 8228, 91750.

LANCASTER. *Antelope Valley Magnificat*, 6116 Quail Ridge Ln., 93536-3714. Tel: 661-943-6402. Rita Trabold, Contact Person.

Our Lady of Charity, Conference of St. Vincent de Paul Society, P.O. Box 412, 93584. Tel: 661-942-3222. Donald Willey, Pres.

LONG BEACH. *St. Mary Catholic Housing Corp. dba St. Mary Tower* 1050 Linden Ave., 90813. Tel: 562-491-9189; Fax: 562-436-6378.

St. Mary Medical Center Foundation (Catholic Healthcare West), 1050 Linden Ave., P.O. Box 887, 90801. Tel: 562-491-9225; Fax: 562-491-9888. Email: drew.gagner@chw.edu. Web: stmarymedicalcenter.org. Drew Gagner, Pres.

MONTEREY PARK. *Congregation of St. John the Baptist*, 220 S. Ynez Ave., 91754. Tel: 626-280-3430; Fax: 626-280-1590. Email: csjb@gus.net. Web: www2.gus.net/home/c/csjb. Rev. Antonio Ho, C.S.J.B., Contact Person.

Theresian Sisters, 901 W. El Repetto Dr., 91754. Tel: 323-780-8911; Fax: 323-780-8911. Sr. Anna Thaolu, C.S.T., Contact Person.

**United Chinese Apostolate Council*, 1501 S. Atlantic Blvd., 91754. Tel: 323-261-8630.

OJAI. **St. Joseph's H. & RC Foundation* (1996) 2464 Ojai Ave., 93023. Tel: 805-646-1466; Fax: 805-646-1013. Email: igi@ojai.net. Rev. Ignatius Sudol, O.H., CEO & Pres. Priests 2; Total Assisted 50.

PACIFIC PALISADES. *Paulist Pictures* (1985) P.O. Box 1057, 90272. Tel: 310-454-0688; Fax: 310-459-6549. Email: Paulistmail@paulistproduction.org. Web: www.paulistproductions.org.

Paulist Productions (1968) (Insight) 17575 Pacific Coast Hwy., P.O. Box 1057, 90272. Tel: 310-454-0688; Fax: 310-459-6549. Email: Paulistmail@paulistproduction.org. Web: www.paulistproductions.org. Rev. Eric Andrews, C.S.P., Pres.; Barbara Gangi, Vice Pres. Devel.; Enid Sevilla, Gen. Mgr. Financial Officer; Joseph Kim, Vice Pres. Business Affairs.

PASADENA. *Ramona Blvd., Inc.*, P.O. Box 662359, Arcadia, 91106. Tel: 626-445-3511; Fax: 626-792-0475.

Territorial Administrative Office, P.O. Box 162, Thornwood, NY 10594. Tel: 914-773-1368; Fax: 914-773-1438. Rev. Jose Felix Ortega, L.C., Sec. & Treas.

PICO RIVERA. *Margaret Aylward Center*, 4270 Acacia Ave., 90660. Tel: 562-695-6621; Fax: 562-699-6614.

SAN FERNANDO. *Valley Family Center* (1987) 302 S. Brand Blvd., 91340. Tel: 818-365-8588; Fax: 818-898-3382. Email: info@valleyfamilycenter.org. Web: www.valleyfamilycenter.com. Sr. Carmel Somers, R.S.C., Exec. Dir. Religious Sisters of Charity., All Services are in English and Spanish. Counseling is available for individual, marriage, family, children/teen, victims of sexual and physical abuse, and adults molested as children (AMAC). Special Programs include School Counseling; Parent Education; anger management; violence prevention; victims and perpetrators of domestic violence; at risk youth. Learning Center Programs include tutorials; basic skill building for children and adults; and opportunities for gifted students. Fees on sliding scale basis according to income.

SAN PEDRO. *Apostleship of the Sea, Catholic Maritime Ministry*, Mary, Star of the Sea Parish, 870 W. 8th St., 90731. Tel: 310-833-3541; Fax: 310-833-9254. Email: marystar2@aol.com. Rev. Henry L. Hernando, Dir. of Chap. Svcs.

Center, Berth 93A, World Cruise Center, Port of Los Angeles, 90731. Tel: 310-521-1041; Fax: 310-521-1046.

SANTA BARBARA. **The Cause of Blessed Junipero Serra*, Old Mission Santa Barbara, 2201 Laguna St., 93105-3611. Tel: 805-682-4713. Email: epilarcik@aol.com. Rev. John Vaughn, O.F.M., Vice Postulator.

SANTA MARIA. *Servants and Handmaids of the Sacred Heart of Jesus, Mary and Joseph*, P.O. Box 2309, 93457-2309. Tel: 805-524-5890. Email: info@theservantsandhandmaids.net. Web: www.theservantsandhandmaids.net.

SANTA SUSANA KNOLLS. *Magnificat, A Ministry to Catholic Women West San Fernando Valley Chapter* (1984) 6202 Wisteria Dr., 93063. Tel: 805-527-3745. Email: terithompson@sbcglobal.net. Web: www.magnificatsfv.com.

STUDIO CITY. **Catholics in Media Associates* (1992) 12400 Ventura Blvd., PMB #228, 91604. Tel: 818-907-2734; Fax: 323-851-8641. Email: catholicsinmedia@aol.com. Web: www.catholicsinmedia.org. Jane Abbott, Pres.; Andrea Setterstrom, Treas. Tel: 323-997-0055.

VENICE. *St. Joseph Center* (1976) 204 Hampton Dr., 90291-8633. Tel: 310-396-6468; Fax: 310-392-8402. Email: vadams@stjosephctr.com. Web: www.stjosephctr.org. Sr. Catherine Mary Bundon, C.S.J., Contact Person.

VENTURA. *CAREGIVERS: Volunteers Assisting the Elderly* (1984) 1765 Goodyear Ave., #205, 93003. Tel: 805-658-8530; Fax: 805-658-8537. Email: info@caregivers.org. Web: www.vccaregivers.org.

WEST COVINA. *Federation of Filipino Rosary Groups, Inc.*, 2809 Elena Ave., 91792. Eddie B. De Sagun, Contact. Purpose: To provide evangelization of people, particularly the Filipinos, and to aid in building communities of faith through the propagation of the devotion to the Holy Rosary.

Luz De Cristo USA Member of Lumen 2000., 1151 E. Grovecenter St., 91790. Tel: 626-966-7594. Web: www.luzdecristousa.com. Non-profit corporation. Spanish evangelism through modern means of communication.

[CC] LEGAL TITLES

LOS ANGELES. *Archdiocesan Catholic Center*, 3424 Wilshire Blvd., 90010-2241. Tel: 213-637-7000; Fax: 213-637-6000. Email: webmaster@la-archdiocese.org. Web: www.la-archdiocese.org. For further information contact the Chancery. Also see Miscellaneous for additional listings.

Recollect Augustinian Fathers & Brothers, Province of St. Augustine, Inc., O.A.R., Oxnard (1990) Tel: 805-486-7433; Fax: 805-487-2805.

Missionary Oblates of Mary Immaculate Residence, Inc., O.M.I., Arleta Tel: 818-891-0579; Fax: 818-893-9819.

School Sisters of Notre Dame Tel: 314-544-0455; Fax: 314-544-6754. Various Locations in the Archdiocese

Congregation of the Sacred Heart of Jesus & Mary and of Perpetual Adoration, Inc., SS.CC., LaVerne Tel: 909-593-5441; Fax: 909-593-3971.

Sisters of St. Louis Monaghan, Inc., S.S.L., Woodland Hills Tel: 818-883-1678; Fax: 818-346-6109.

Ursulines of the Western Province, Inc., O.S.U., Encino Tel: 650-346-9897.

RELIGIOUS INSTITUTES OF MEN REPRESENTED IN THE ARCHDIOCESE

For further details refer to the corresponding bracketed number in the Religious Institutes of Men or Women section.

[0530]—*Atonement Friars*—S.A.
[150]—*Augustinian Recollect Brothers*—O.A.R.
[0150]—*Augustinian Recollects*—O.A.R.
[0140]—*The Augustinians*—O.S.A.
[200]—*Benedictine Brothers*—O.S.B.
[0200]—*Benedictine Monks*—O.S.B.
[1160]—*Brothers of St. Patrick*—F.S.P.
[330]—*Brothers of the Christian Schools* (De La Salle)—F.S.C.
[600]—*Brothers of the Holy Cross*—C.S.C.
[]—*Canons Regular of the Immaculate Conception*—C.R.I.C.
[0470]—*Capuchin Franciscans*—O.F.M.Cap.
[260]—*Carmelite (Discalced) Fathers*—O.C.D.
[270]—*Carmelite Fathers*—O. Carm.
[0275]—*Carmelites of Mary Immaculate*—C.M.I.
[0360]—*Claretian Missionaries* (Western Prov.)—C.M.F.
[370]—*Columban Fathers (Society of St. Columban)*—S.S.C.
[0380]—*Comboni Missionaries* (Verona)—M.C.C.J.
[1150]—*Congregation of St. Joseph*—C.S.J.
[1080]—*Congregation of the Resurrection*—C.R.
[1140]—*Congregation of the Sacred Hearts of Jesus and Mary*—SS.CC.
[0480]—*Conventual Franciscan Friars* (St. Joseph Cupertino Prov.)—O.F.M.Conv.
[0420]—*Divine Word Missionaries*—S.V.D.
[0430]—*Dominican Friars*—O.P.
[]—*Eudist Fathers*—C.J.M.
[515]—*Franciscan Brothers*—O.S.F.
[]—*Franciscan Brothers* (St. Barbara Province)—o.f.m.
[0520]—*Franciscan Friars* (St. Barbara Prov.)—O.F.M.
[470]—*Franciscans / Capuchin Franciscans*—O.F.M.Cap
[480]—*Franciscans / Conventional Franciscans*—O.F.M.Conv.
[]—*Guadalupe Missioners* (Mexico)—M.G.
[0610]—*Holy Cross Fathers*—C.S.C.
[670]—*Hospitaller Brothers of St. John of God*—O.H.
[690]—*Jesuit Brothers*—S.J.
[0690]—*Jesuits (Society of Jesus)* (California Prov.)—S.J.
[0710]—*Josephite Fathers*—C.J.
[700]—*Josephites (St. Joseph's Society of the Sacred Heart)*—S.S.J.
[0730]—*Legionaries of Christ*—L.C.
[]—*Marian Missionaries of the Holy Cross* (Philippines)—M.M.H.C.
[760]—*Marianist Brothers*—S.M.
[760]—*Marianists (Society of Mary)*—S.M.
[0780]—*Marist Fathers*—S.M.
[0800]—*Maryknoll Missioners*—M.M.
[0835]—*Minim Fathers*—O.M.
[]—*Misioneros del Sagrado Corazon y Santa Maria de Guadalupe* (Mexico)—M.S.C.
[]—*Misioneros Oblatos de la Sagrada Familia*—O.S.F.
[]—*Misioneros Servidores de la Palabra* (Mexico)—M.S.P.
[]—*Missionaries of Jesus* (Philippines)—M.J.
[0660]—*Missionaries of the Holy Spirit*—M.Sp.S.
[]—*Missionary of Charity Brothers*—M.C.
[840]—*Missionary Servants of Most Holy Trinity*—S.T.
[900]—*Norbertine Fathers (Canons Regulars of Premontre)*—O.Praem.
[0910]—*Oblates of Mary Immaculate* (Western Prov.)—O.M.I.
[0930]—*Oblates of St. Joseph*—O.S.J.
[0940]—*Oblates of the Virgin Mary*—O.M.V.
[]—*Operarios del Reino de Cristo* (Mexico)—O.R.C.
[140]—*Order of St. Augustine*—O.S.A.
[1000]—*Passionist Brothers*—C.P.
[1060]—*Passionists (Congregation of the Passion)*—C.P.
[1030]—*Paulist Fathers (Congregation of St. Paul)*—C.S.P.
[1040]—*Piarist Fathers* (California Vice-Province)—Sch.P.
[1070]—*Redemptorist Fathers* (Denver Prov.)—C.SS.R.
[]—*Redemptorist Fathers* (Vietnamese Province)—C.Ss.R.
[1090]—*Rogationist Fathers*—R.C.J.
[1190]—*Salesians of Don Bosco*—S.D.B.
[1190]—*Salesians of St. John Bosco*—S.D.B.
[1210]—*Scalabrinians (Missionaries of St. Charles)*—C.S.
[1260]—*Society of Christ*—S.Ch.
[1020]—*Society of St. Paul (Pauline Fathers)*—S.S.P.
[420]—*Society of the Divine Word*—S.V.D.
[1060]—*Society of the Precious Blood*—C.PP.S.
[840]—*Trinitarians (Missionary Servants of the Most Holy Trinity)*—S.T.
[1310]—*Trinitarians (Order of the Most Holy Trinity)*—O.SS.T
[1070]—*Vietnamese Redemptorists*—C.Ss.R.
[1330]—*Vincentian Brothers (Congregation of the Mission)*—C.M.
[1330]—*Vincentian Fathers*—C.M.
[]—*Vincentian Fathers* (Mexico Province)—C.M.

RELIGIOUS INSTITUTES OF WOMEN REPRESENTED IN THE ARCHDIOCESE

[2120]—*Armenian Sisters of the Immaculate Conception*—C.I.C.
[]—*Augustinian Recollect Sisters*—A.R.
[]—*Benedictine Sisters of Monastery of St. Gertrude*
[0230]—*Benedictine Sisters of St. Lucy's Priory*
[1810]—*Bernardine Franciscan Sisters*—O.S.F.
[]—*Blessed Sacrament Sisters of Charity*
[]—*Caritas Sisters of Miyazaki*
[]—*Carmelitas de San Jose*—C.S.J.
[0370]—*Carmelite Sisters of the Most Sacred Heart*—O.C.D.
[]—*Community of the Holy Spirit*
[3832]—*Congregation of St. Joseph*—C.S.J.
[1940]—*Congregation of the Holy Faith*—C.H.F.
[2100]—*Congregation of the Humility of Mary*—C.H.M.
[0760]—*Daughters of Charity of St. Vincent de Paul* (Prov. of the West)—D.C.
[0860]—*Daughters of Mary*—D.M.
[0880]—*Daughters of Mary and Joseph*—D.M.J.

[0850]—*Daughters of Mary Help of Christians (Salesian Sisters of St. John Bosco)*—F.M.A.
[950]—*Daughters of St. Paul*—F.S.P.
[0420]—*Discalced Carmelites*—O.C.D.
[1050]—*Dominican Nuns of the Order of Preachers*—O.P.
[1070-13]—*Dominican Sisters of Adrian*—P.
[]—*Dominican Sisters of Christian Doctrine*—O.P.
[1070-19]—*Dominican Sisters of Houston*—O.P.
[1070-12]—*Dominican Sisters of Mission San Jose*—O.P.
[1070-03]—*Dominican Sisters of Sinsinawa*—O.P.
[3615]—*Esclavas de la Immaculada Nina (Servants of the Immaculate Child Mary)*—E.I.N.
[1150]—*Eucharistic Franciscan Missionary Sisters*—E.F.M.S.
[]—*Evangelizadores Eucaristicas de los Pobres*—E.E.P.
[1170]—*Felician Sisters (Sisters of St. Felix)*—C.S.S.F.
[]—*Focolare*
[]—*Fr. Kolbe Missionaries of the Immaculata*
[1310]—*Franciscan Sisters of Little Falls*—O.S.F.
[1500]—*Franciscan Sisters of Mary Immaculate*—F.M.I.
[1780]—*Franciscan Sisters of Perpetual Adoration*—O.S.F.
[1630]—*Franciscan Sisters of St. Francis of Penance and Christian Charity*—O.S.F.
[1450]—*Franciscan Sisters of the Sacred Heart*—O.S.F.
[1845]—*Guadalupan Missionaries of the Holy Spirit*—M.G.Sp.S.
[]—*Handmaids of the Sacred Heart of Jesus, Mary and Joseph*—J.M.J.
[]—*Hermanas del Corazon de Jesus Sacramentado* (Srs. of the Sacred Heart of Jesus in the Blessed Sacrament)
[]—*Hermanas Misioneras Servidoras de la Palabra*—H.M.S.P.
[0157]—*Hermanitas de la Annunciacion*
[]—*Immaculate Mary Queen of Haven Missionaries*
[]—*Institute of Our Lady of the Annunciation*
[]—*Institute of the Heart of Jesus, Cor Unum*
[]—*Kkottongnae Sisters of Jesus*
[]—*Koinonia John the Baptist*
[]—*Little Handmaids of the Most Holy Trinity*—M.A.S.T.
[2340]—*Little Sisters of the Poor*—L.S.P.
[2390]—*Lovers of the Holy Cross*—L.H.C.
[2385]—*Lovers of the Holy Cross, Nha Trang Province*—L.H.C.N.T.
[]—*Marian Community of Reconciliation*
[2470]—*Maryknoll Sisters of St. Dominic*—M.M.
[2500]—*Medical Sisters of St. Joseph*—M.S.J.
[]—*Misioneras Eucaristicas De Maria Inmaculada*—M.E.M.I.
[2710]—*Missionaries of Charity*—M.C.
[]—*Missionaries of Jesus Crucified*—M.J.C.
[0210]—*Missionary Benedictine Sisters*—O.S.B.
[2690]—*Missionary Catechists of Divine Providence*—M.C.D.P.
[2715]—*Missionary Sisters of Christ the King*—M.S.C.K.
[2880]—*Missionary Sisters of St. Columban*—S.S.C.
[2750]—*Missionary Sisters of the Immaculate Heart of Mary*—I.C.M.
[]—*Oblates of the Heart of Jesus*
[0240]—*Olivetan Benedictine Sisters of Pusan*—O.S.B.
[3130]—*Our Lady of Victory Missionary Sisters*—O.L.V.M.
[3760]—*Poor Clare Colettines*
[2840]—*Poor Clare Missionary Sisters*—M.C.
[]—*Puso Ng Carmelo Community*
[1145]—*Religious Missionaries of St. Dominic*—O.P.
[3450]—*Religious of Jesus and Mary*—R.J.M.
[3465]—*Religious of the Sacred Heart of Mary*—R.S.H.M.
[3400]—*Religious Sisters of Charity*—R.S.C.
[2970]—*School Sisters of Notre Dame*—S.S.N.D.
[3580]—*Servants of Mary*—O.S.M.
[3580]—*Servants of Mary, Ministers to the Sick*—O.S.M.
[0980]—*Sister Disciples of the Divine Master*—P.D.D.M.
[3499]—*Sister Servants of the Blessed Sacrament*—S.J.S.
[0250]—*Sisters of Bethany*—C.V.D.
[0480]—*Sisters of Charity of Leavenworth, Kansas*—S.C.L.
[0565]—*Sisters of Charity of Rolling Hills*—S.C.R.H.
[570]—*Sisters of Charity of Seton Hill*—S.C.
[0430]—*Sisters of Charity of the Blessed Virgin Mary*—B.V.M.
[]—*Sisters of Charity of the Incarnate Word*
[2360]—*Sisters of Loretto At the Foot of the Cross* (Southern Prov.)—S.L.
[2560]—*Sisters of Mary Reparatrix*
[2575]—*Sisters of Mercy of the Americas*—R.S.M.
[3242]—*Sisters of Nazareth*
[2990]—*Sisters of Notre Dame* (Prov. of Los Angeles)—S.N.D.
[3000]—*Sisters of Notre Dame de Namur*—S.N.D.deN.
[]—*Sisters of Our Lady of Perpetual Help*—S.O.L.P.H.
[3350]—*Sisters of Providence*—S.P.
[3360]—*Sisters of Providence of Saint Mary Of The Woods, Indiana*—S.P.
[4080]—*Sisters of Social Service*—S.S.S.
[1710]—*Sisters of St. Francis of Mary Immaculate* (Joliet)—O.S.F.
[1620]—*Sisters of St. Francis of the Neumann Communities*
[3860]—*Sisters of St. Joseph Congregation*—S.J.C.
[3840]—*Sisters of St. Joseph of Carondelet*—C.S.J.
[3860]—*Sisters of St. Joseph of Cluny*—S.J.C.
[3830]—*Sisters of St. Joseph of Orange*—C.S.J.
[3890]—*Sisters of St. Joseph of Peace*—C.S.J.P.
[3930]—*Sisters of St. Joseph to the Third Order of St. Francis*—S.S.J.-T.O.S.F.
[3935]—*Sisters of St. Louis*—S.S.L.
[3960]—*Sisters of St. Mary of Oregon*—S.S.M.O.
[]—*Sisters of the Blessed Korean Martyrs*—B.K.M.
[0700]—*Sisters of the Company of Mary*—O.D.N.
[1830]—*Sisters of the Good Shepherd*—R.G.S.
[1850]—*Sisters of the Guardian Angel*—S.A.C.
[1920]—*Sisters of the Holy Cross*
[1960]—*Sisters of the Holy Family*—S.H.F.
[1990]—*Sisters of the Holy Names of Jesus and Mary*—S.N.J.M.
[2930]—*Sisters of the Immaculate Heart of Mary* (Waverly)—I.H.M.
[]—*Sisters of the Immaculate Heart of Mary, Mirinae*
[]—*Sisters of the Immaculate Heart of Mary, Mother of the Church*
[2270]—*Sisters of the Little Company of Mary*—L.C.M.
[]—*Sisters of the Love of God*—R.A.D.
[3200]—*Sisters of the Pious Schools*—Sch.P.
[3320]—*Sisters of the Presentation of the Blessed Virgin Mary* (San Francisco, CA)—P.B.V.M.
[3320]—*Sisters of the Presentation of the Blessed Virgin Mary of Aberdeen, SD*—P.B.V.M.
[]—*Sisters of the Sacred Heart of Mary*—C.S.C.M.
[]—*Sisters of the Sick Poor of Los Angeles*
[3499]—*Sisters Servants of the Blessed Sacrament*
[4050]—*Society Devoted to the Sacred Heart*—S.D.S.H.
[]—*Society of Our Lady of the Way*
[4060]—*Society of the Holy Child Jesus*—S.H.C.J.
[1505]—*St. Francis Mission Community* (Joliet)—O.S.F.
[]—*Theresian Sisters*—C.S.T.
[]—*Trinitas*
[3330]—*Union of Sisters of Presentation of the Blessed Virgin Mary*—P.B.V.M.
[4110]—*Ursuline Sisters of the Roman Union*—O.S.U.
[]—*Verbum Dei Missionary Fraternity*—V.D.M.F.
[4200]—*Visitation Congregation*—S.V.M.

ARCHDIOCESAN CEMETERIES

LOS ANGELES. *Calvary Cemetery and Mausoleum*, 4201 Whittier Blvd., 90023. Tel: 323-261-3106. Maria Orozco, Mgr.

CULVER CITY. *Holy Cross Cemetery & Mortuary*, 5835 W. Slauson Ave., 90230. Tel: 310-836-5500; Fax: 310-836-3560.

LANCASTER. *Good Shepherd Cemetery & Mausoleum*, 43121 70th St. West, 93536. Tel: 661-722-0887; Fax: 661-722-5344. Daniel Rejniak, Mgr.

LONG BEACH. *All Souls Cemetery and Mausoleum*, 4400 Cherry Ave., 90807. Tel: 562-424-8601; Fax: 562-426-8065. Maryann McAdams, Mgr.

MISSION HILLS. *San Fernando Mission Cemetery & Mausoleum*, 11160 Stanwood Ave., 91345. Tel: 818-361-7387; Fax: 818-365-6187. Rosalie Castillo, Mgr.

MONTEBELLO. *Resurrection Cemetery & Mausoleum*, 966 N. Potrero Grande Dr., 90640. Tel: 323-887-2024; Fax: 323-722-0874. Web: www.lacatholiccemeteries.org. Sofia V. Sandru, Mgr.

OXNARD. *Santa Clara Cemetery & Mausoleum*, 2370 North "H" St., 93036. Tel: 805-485-5757. Elizabeth Welsh, Mgr.

POMONA. *Holy Cross Cemetery*, P.O. Box 1145, 91769. Tel: 909-627-3602; Fax: 909-465-0690. Birdie Orta, Mgr.

ROWLAND HEIGHTS. *Queen of Heaven Cemetery*, 2161 S. Fullerton Rd., 91748. Tel: 626-964-1291; Fax: 626-964-4325. Norberta Orta, Mgr.

SANTA BARBARA. *Calvary Cemetery & Mausoleum*, 199 N. Hope Ave., 93110. Tel: 805-687-8811; Fax: 805-569-5814. Gwen Hueston, Mgr.

SIMI. *Assumption Cemetery*, 1380 Fitzgerald Rd., Simi Valley, 93065. Tel: 805-583-5825. Rosalie Castillo, Mgr.

NECROLOGY

† Lenihan, Rev. Msgr. Michael, Redondo Beach, CA St. Lawrence Martyr—Died March 23, 2011
† Navin, Rev. Msgr. Cyril, Encino, CA St. Cyril—Died June 24, 2011
† Walsh, Rev. Msgr. Michael, (Retired)—Died April 20, 2011
† Bouska, Jerome Anthony, (Retired)—Died Nov. 20, 2010
† Byrne, Robert Paul, (Retired)—Died July 13, 2011
† Carroll, Michael J., (Retired)—Died May 26, 2011
† Ford, James Michael, (Retired)—Died May 22, 2011
† Gaffney, Joseph P., (Retired)—Died April 12, 2011
† Griffin, Noel, (Retired)—Died Sept. 23, 2011
† Jardiniano, Rolly P., (Retired)—Died Jan. 30, 2011
† McHugh, Patrick Joseph, (Retired)—Died July 27, 2011
† Meskill, Patrick A., (Retired)—Died Aug. 23, 2011
† Toal, James Aloysius—Died June 28, 2011
† Walker, Earl Gordon—Died Oct. 26, 2010

An asterisk (*) denotes an organization that has established tax-exempt status directly with the IRS and is not covered by the USCCB Group Ruling.

Archdiocese of Louisville

(Archidioecesis Ludovicopolitana)

Most Reverend

JOSEPH E. KURTZ

Archbishop of Louisville; ordained 1972; appointed Bishop of Knoxville October 26, 1999; ordained and installed December 8, 1999; appointed Archbishop of Louisville June 12, 2007; installed August 15, 2007. *Office: 212 E. College St., P.O. Box 1073, Louisville, KY 40201.* Tel: 502-585-3291.

Chancery: 212 E. College St., P.O. Box 1073, Louisville, KY 40201. Tel: 502-585-3291; Fax: 502-585-2466.

Web: www.archlou.org

Email: chancery@archlou.org

Square Miles 8,124.

Established at Bardstown April 8, 1808; Transferred to Louisville Feb. 13, 1841; created an Archdiocese Dec. 10, 1937.

Comprises the following twenty-four Counties in central Kentucky: Adair, Barren, Bullitt, Casey, Clinton, Cumberland, Green, Hardin, Hart, Henry, Jefferson, Larue, Marion, Meade, Metcalfe, Monroe, Nelson, Oldham, Russell, Shelby, Spencer, Taylor, Trimble and Washington.

For legal titles of parishes and archdiocesan institutions, consult the Chancery.

STATISTICAL OVERVIEW

Personnel	
Archbishops	1
Abbots	1
Retired Abbots	1
Priests: Diocesan Active in Diocese	76
Priests: Diocesan Active Outside Diocese	6
Priests: Diocesan in Foreign Missions	1
Priests: Retired, Sick or Absent	54
Number of Diocesan Priests	137
Religious Priests in Diocese	44
Total Priests in Diocese	181
Extern Priests in Diocese	1
Ordinations:	
Diocesan Priests	2
Transitional Deacons	3
Permanent Deacons in Diocese	127
Total Brothers	53
Total Sisters	602
Parishes	
Parishes	102
With Resident Pastor:	
Resident Diocesan Priests	74
Resident Religious Priests	7
Without Resident Pastor:	
Administered by Priests	16
Administered by Deacons	4
Administered by Lay People	1
Missions	9
Professional Ministry Personnel:	
Sisters	14
Lay Ministers	173
Welfare	
Catholic Hospitals	2
Total Assisted	263,350
Health Care Centers	1
Total Assisted	5,907
Homes for the Aged	3
Total Assisted	1,000
Residential Care of Children	2
Total Assisted	815
Day Care Centers	6
Total Assisted	300
Special Centers for Social Services	7
Total Assisted	41,000
Educational	
Diocesan Students in Other Seminaries	16
Total Seminarians	16
Colleges and Universities	3
Total Students	6,242
High Schools, Diocesan and Parish	4
Total Students	2,207
High Schools, Private	5
Total Students	3,940
Elementary Schools, Diocesan and Parish	36
Total Students	11,440
Elementary Schools, Private	3
Total Students	514
Non-residential Schools for the Disabled	1
Total Students	65
Catechesis/Religious Education:	
High School Students	758
Elementary Students	5,024
Total Students under Catholic Instruction	30,206
Teachers in the Diocese:	
Priests	7
Brothers	1
Sisters	23
Lay Teachers	1,678
Vital Statistics	
Receptions into the Church:	
Infant Baptism Totals	1,975
Minor Baptism Totals	158
Adult Baptism Totals	162
Received into Full Communion	441
First Communions	2,462
Confirmations	2,350
Marriages:	
Catholic	398
Interfaith	240
Total Marriages	638
Deaths	1,565
Total Catholic Population	192,396
Total Population	1,263,368

Former Bishops—Rt. Revs. BENEDICT JOSEPH FLAGET, S.S., D.D., cons. Bishop of Bardstown, Nov. 4, 1810; died Feb. 11, 1850; JOHN B. DAVID, S.S., D.D., Coadjutor; cons. Aug. 15, 1819; died July 12, 1841; GUY IGNATIUS CHABRAT, S.S., D.D., Coadjutor; cons. July 20, 1834; died Nov. 21, 1868; MARTIN JOHN SPALDING, D.D., Coadjutor with right of succession; cons. Sept. 10, 1848; transferred to Baltimore, May 6, 1864; died Feb. 7, 1872; PETER JOSEPH LAVIALLE, D.D., cons. Sept. 24, 1865; died May 11, 1867; WILLIAM GEORGE MCCLOSKEY, D.D., cons. May 24, 1868; died Sept. 17, 1909; DENIS O'DONAGHUE, D.D., ord. Sept. 6, 1874; cons. Titular Bishop of Pomario and Auxiliary of Indianapolis on April 25, 1900; transferred to Louisville, Feb. 7, 1910; transferred to the Titular See of Lebedus, July 26, 1924; died Nov. 7, 1925; Most Revs. JOHN A. FLOERSH, D.D., ord. June 10, 1911; appt. Titular Bishop of Lycopolis and Coadjutor Bishop of Louisville with right of succession, Feb. 6, 1923; cons. April 8, 1923; succeeded to See July 26, 1924; elevated to Archiepiscopal dignity Dec. 10, 1937; resigned and named to Titular See of Sistroniana, March 1, 1967; died June 11, 1968; THOMAS J. MCDONOUGH, D.D., transferred to Louisville, May 2, 1967; resigned Sept. 29, 1981; died Aug. 4, 1998; THOMAS C. KELLY, ord. June 5, 1958; appt. Titular Bishop of Tusuro July 12, 1977; promoted Archbishop of Louisville Dec. 29, 1981; retired June 12, 2007; died Dec. 14, 2011.

Vicar General—Very Rev. J. MARK SPALDING, J.C.L.

Chancery—212 E. College St., P.O. Box 1073, Louisville, 40201. Tel: 502-585-3291; Fax: 502-585-2466. Office Hours: 8:30-4:30; All applications for dispensations are to be sent to this office.

Chancellor—Dr. BRIAN B. REYNOLDS.

Vice Chancellor—NORMA L. MERRICK.

Secretary to Archbishop—NORMA L. MERRICK.

Vicar for Priests—Rev. JEFFREY P. SHOONER.

Archivist—Rev. R. DALE CIESLIK.

Chief Financial Officer—ROBERT L. ASH.

Metropolitan Tribunal—212 E. College St., P.O. Box 1073, Louisville, 40201. Tel: 502-585-3291.

Judicial Vicar and Director—Very Rev. J. MARK SPALDING, J.C.L.

Adjutant Judicial Vicar—Rev. PHILIP LEE ERICKSON, J.C.L.

Promoter of Justice—Rev. FREDERICK W. KLOTTER, S.T.L., J.C.L.

Defenders of the Bond—Revs. DONALD R. GOETZ; JOHN J. STOLTZ; ANTHONY L. CHANDLER, M.A.; J. WAYNE MURPHY (Retired); ROBERT E. OSBORNE (Retired); PATRICK J. DOLAN, Ph.D., S.T.D.; Deacon WALTON JONES; Dr. ROBERT L. STENGER, S.T.D., J.D.

Associate Judges—Revs. R. PAUL BEACH; KENNETH R. FORTENER; T. MICHAEL TOBIN, S.T.L., J.C.B.; Ms. JACQUELINE RAPP, J.D., J.C.L.

Assessor and Associate Director—PATRICIA A. NORRIS, Ed.D.

Assessor—Deacon P. STEPHAN PHELPS.

Ecclesiastical Notaries—SHARON A. ARCHER; LINDA D. THOMAN; ANN TUMBLIN.

College of Consultors—Very Revs. J. MARK SPALDING, J.C.L.; WILLIAM P. GARROTT, O.P.; Revs. TERRY L. BRADSHAW; JOSEPH M. RANKIN; THOMAS A. SMITH; JEFFREY P. SHOONER.

Deans—Revs. WILLIAM D. HAMMER, Bardstown Deanery; GERALD L. BELL, Lebanon Deanery; CHARLES D. WALKER, Elizabethtown Deanery.

Priest Personnel Commission—Revs. R. DALE CIESLIK; WILLIAM S. GRINER (Retired); BRIAN A. KENNEY; H. ANTHONY OLGES; Very Rev. JEFFREY S. NICOLAS; Rev. JEFFREY P. SHOONER, Dir.

Priests' Council—Most Rev. JOSEPH E. KURTZ, D.D., Presider; Rev. WILLIAM D. HAMMER, Pres.; NORMA L. MERRICK, Sec., 212 E. College St., Louisville, 40203. Ex Officio: Very Rev. J. MARK SPALDING, J.C.L.; Revs. THOMAS L. BOLAND (Retired); THOMAS A. SMITH; JEFFREY G. HOPPER; JOHN T. JUDIE; MARTIN A. LINEBACH; FREDERICK W. KLOTTER, S.T.L., J.C.L.; THOMAS E. GENTILE; LOUIS J. MEIMAN; JOSEPH M. RANKIN; ROBERT E. RAY; JEFFREY P. SHOONER; TERRY L. BRADSHAW; JOHN J. STOLTZ; WILLIAM M. BOWLING; JOHN A. SCHWARTZLOSE; J. WAYNE JENKINS; PATRICK J. DOLAN, Ph.D., S.T.D.; PETER QUAN DO; LAWRENCE J. GELTHAUS; MATTHEW T. HARDESTY; JOHN SCHORK, C.P.; Very Rev. WILLIAM P. GARROTT, O.P.

Archdiocesan Examiners—Revs. WILLIAM L. FICHTEMAN (Retired); THOMAS L. BOLAND

(Retired); GARY T. PADGETT.

Archdiocesan Offices and Directors

Archdiocesan Communications Center—CECELIA PRICE, Chief Communications Officer, Maloney Center, 1200 S. Shelby St., Louisville, 40203. Tel: 502-636-0296; Fax: 502-636-2379.

Byzantine Rite Faithful—Rev. JOHN W. BIRK, Chap. (Retired), 2082 Douglass Blvd., #1, Louisville, 40205. Tel: 502-451-1555.

Catholic Cemeteries Office—JAVIER FAJARDO, Exec. Dir., 1600 Newburg Rd., P.O. Box 4096, Louisville, 40204. Tel: 502-451-7710; Fax: 502-456-9270.

Catholic Charities—Mr. STEVEN E. BOGUS, Exec. Dir., 2911 S. 4th St., Louisville, 40208. Tel: 502-637-9786; Fax: 502-637-9780.

Office of Migration and Refugee Services—Ms. BECKY JORDAN.

Office of Parish Social Ministry—DAVID J. DUTSCHKE.

Priest Personnel Office—Rev. JEFFREY P. SHOONER, Dir., Mailing Address: P.O. Box 1073, Louisville, 40201. Tel: 502-585-3291; Fax: 502-585-2466.

Clerical Aid Society—212 E. College St., P.O. Box 1073, Louisville, 40201. Tel: 502-585-3291.

Continuing Education for Clergy-Ministry to Priests—Rev. JEFFREY P. SHOONER, Mailing Address: P.O. Box 1073, Louisville, 40201. Tel: 502-585-3291.

Cursillo Movement—PATRICIA WILLIAMS, Lay Dir., Flaget Center, 1935 Lewiston Pl., Louisville, 40216. Tel: 502-448-8581.

Due Process Board—JOHN LAUN, Chm., Mailing Address: P.O. Box 1073, Louisville, 40201. Tel: 502-585-3291.

Ecumenical and Interreligious Relations Officer—Rev. MARTIN A. LINEBACH.

Family Ministries Office—SUE BRODFEHRER, Exec. Dir.; THOMAS D. ROBBINS, Ph.D., Clinical Dir., Maloney Center, 1200 S. Shelby St., Louisville, 40203. Tel: 502-636-0296; Fax: 502-636-2379.

Holy Childhood Association—Deacon J. PATRICK WRIGHT, Dir., 212 E. College St., Box 1073, Louisville, 40201. Tel: 502-585-3291.

Holy Name Society—MICHAEL HEEB, Pres., 2302 Bradford Dr., Louisville, 40218. Tel: 502-454-7151.

L.A.M.P.— (Louisville Archdiocesan Mission Promoters), Most Rev. JOSEPH E. KURTZ, D.D.; Very Rev. J. MARK SPALDING, J.C.L., 212 E. College St., P.O. Box 1073, Louisville, 40201. Tel: 502-585-3291.

Office of the Diaconate—Deacon J. PATRICK WRIGHT, Maloney Center, 1200 S. Shelby St., Louisville, 40203. Tel: 502-636-0296; Fax: 502-636-2379.

Office of Lifelong Formation and Education—VACANT, Flaget Center, 1935 Lewiston Pl., Louisville, 40216. Tel: 502-448-8581; Fax: 502-448-5518.

Superintendent of Schools—LEISA SCHULZ.

Director of Youth Ministry—DR. CAROLE GOODWIN.

Director of Faith Formation—SAL DELLA BELLA.

Office of Multicultural Ministry—M. ANNETTE TURNER, Dir., Maloney Center, 1200 S. Shelby St., Louisville, 40203. Tel: 502-636-0296.

Office of Worship—Dr. JUDY BULLOCK, Dir., Maloney Center, 1200 S. Shelby St., Louisville, 40203. Tel: 502-636-0296; Fax: 502-636-2379.

Opportunities for Life—BRENDA THOMPSON, Coord., Louisville/Owensboro Diocese, 600 Locust St., Owensboro, 42301. Tel: 502-683-1545; 800-822-5824; Fax: 270-683-6883.

Personnel and Planning—Dr. BRIAN B. REYNOLDS, Dir., 212 E. College, P.O. Box 1073, Louisville, 40201. Tel: 502-585-3291.

Pro-Life Ministries—SHARON SCHUHMANN, Coord., Maloney Center, 1200 S. Shelby St., Louisville, 40203. Tel: 502-636-0296; Fax: 502-636-2379.

Propagation of the Faith— (Missions Office), Deacon J. PATRICK WRIGHT, Dir., Mailing Address: P.O. Box 1073, Louisville, 40201. Tel: 502-585-3291.

Sacred Heart Enthronement Center—Rev. LAWRENCE H. LINDLE, Dir. (Retired), 3623 Fern Valley Rd., Louisville, 40219.

Stewardship and Development Office—NICHOLAS K. EVE, Dir., 212 E. College St., P.O. Box 1073, Louisville, 40201. Tel: 502-585-3291; Fax: 502-585-2466.

Vicar for Retired Clergy—Rev. J. ROY STILES (Retired), 2040 Buechel Bank Rd., Louisville, 40218. Tel: 502-499-0868.

Victim Assistance Coordinator—THOMAS D. ROBBINS, Ph.D. Tel: 502-636-1044. Email: trobbins@archlou.org; family@archlou.org.

Vocations—Rev. JEFFREY P. SHOONER, Dir., Maloney Center, 1200 S. Shelby St., Louisville, 40203. Tel: 502-636-0296.

CLERGY, PARISHES, MISSIONS AND PAROCHIAL SCHOOLS

CITY OF LOUISVILLE

(JEFFERSON COUNTY)

1—CATHEDRAL OF THE ASSUMPTION (1852) Very Rev. Jeffrey S. Nicolas; Deacon P. Stephan Phelps. In Res., Most Rev. Joseph E. Kurtz.
Res.: 433 S. 5th St., 40202. Tel: 502-582-2971; Fax: 502-582-3919.
Catechesis/Religious Program—Students 69.

2—ST. AGNES (1885) Rev. David Colhour, C.P. In Res., Rev. Joseph Mitchell, C.P.
Res.: 1920 Newburg Rd., 40205. Tel: 502-451-2220; Fax: 502-454-8483. Email: jackicecil@yahoo.com. Web: stagneslouisville.org.
School—(Grades K-8), 1800 Newburg Rd., 40205. Tel: 502-458-2850; Fax: 502-459-5215. Carol Meirose, Prin.; Margi Johnstone, Librarian. Lay Teachers 26; Students 430.
Catechesis/Religious Program—Students 38.

3—ST. ALBERT THE GREAT (1959) Rev. J. Wayne Jenkins; Deacon Michael A. Layman.
Res.: 1395 Girard Dr., 40222. Tel: 502-425-3940; Fax: 502-394-9896. Web: www.stalbert.org.
School—(Grades PreK-8) Tel: 502-425-1804. Bernadette Cooper, Prin. Lay Teachers 44; Students 709.
Catechesis/Religious Program—Tel: 502-423-1590, Ext. 110. Students 155.

4—ASCENSION OF OUR LORD (1965) Rev. Gary T. Padgett; Deacon Michael Edwards.
Res.: 4600 Lynnbrook Dr., 40220. Tel: 502-451-3860; Fax: 502-458-9782. Email: dschabel@ascension-parish.com.
School—(Grades PreK-8) Tel: 502-451-2535; Fax: 502-451-2535. Mary Jo Ellis, Prin.; Elaine Whitehead, Librarian. Lay Teachers 19; Students 203.
Catechesis/Religious Program—Tel: 502-451-3860, Ext. 12. Students 30.

5—ST. ATHANASIUS (1960) Rev. Gary G. Davis; Deacon Jesse E. Schook.
Res.: 5915 Outer Loop Dr., 40219. Tel: 502-969-3332; Fax: 502-966-8948. Email: secretary@staparish.com. Web: www.stathanasiuslouisville.com.
School—(Grades PreK-8) Tel: 502-969-2345; Fax: 502-969-8974. Diane Arrow, Prin.; Anne Bainridge, Librarian. Lay Teachers 25; Students 479.
Catechesis/Religious Program—Students 70.

6—ST. AUGUSTINE (1870) Deacon James Turner, Pastoral Admin.; Rev. Patrick D. Delahanty, Sacramental Moderator; Deacon Keith L. McKenzie.
Res.: 1310 W. Broadway, 40203. Tel: 502-584-4602; Fax: 502-581-0893. Email: staugustine@insightbb.com.
Hines Center—Tel: 502-584-5463.

7—ST. BARNABAS (1953) Rev. Paul A. Scaglione; Deacons Joseph F. Moore; James R. Plummer.
Parish Office: 3042 Hikes Ln., 40220. Tel: 502-459-4251; Fax: 502-459-9815. Email: rtemple@stbarnabaslou.org.
Catechesis/Religious Program—Students 36.

8—ST. BARTHOLOMEW (1941) Rev. Peter Quan Do; Deacons Thomas E. Box; Francisco J. Villalobos; Mrs. Becky Box, Pastoral Assoc. In Res., Rev. J. Roy Stiles (Retired).
Parish Office: 2042 Buechel Bank Rd., 40218. Tel: 502-499-0883; Fax: 502-499-0877. Web: www.stbarths.org.
Res.: 2040 Buechel Bank Rd., 40218. Tel: 502-499-0876.
Catechesis/Religious Program—2825 Klondike Ln., 40218. Mrs. Becky Box, D.R.E. Students 25.

9—ST. BERNADETTE PARISH (2008) Rev. Terry L. Bradshaw; Deacons Patrick Harris; Danny E. Parker.
Parish Office: 6500 St. Bernadette Ave., Prospect, 40059. Tel: 502-425-2210; Fax: 502-425-0941.
Catechesis/Religious Program—Judy Montgomery, D.R.E. Students 237.

10—ST. BERNARD (1963) Rev. Robert L. Stuempel; Deacon Philip Hettich.
Res.: 7500 Tangelo Dr., 40228. Tel: 502-231-8840; Fax: 502-239-9025. Email: stbernardparish@insightbb.com. Web: stbernardlou.com.
School—(Grades PreK-8) Tel: 502-239-5178; Fax: 502-239-9025. Fred J. Klausing III, Prin. Lay Teachers 25; Students 481.
Catechesis/Religious Program—Tel: 502-239-5178, Ext. 125. Jan Redle, D.R.E. Students 54.

11—BLESSED TERESA OF CALCUTTA (2008) Rev. Robert E. Ray; Deacon Kenneth J. Mitchell.
903 Fairdale Rd., Fairdale, 40118. Tel: 502-363-9929; Fax: 502-363-9960.
Catechesis/Religious Program—Lynn McDaniel, D.R.E. Students 45.

12—ST. BONIFACE (1836) Rev. Jeffrey P. Shooner, Sacramental Mod.; Deacons Brian Karley, C.R., Pastoral Admin.; David R. Tomes.
Parish Office: 531 E. Liberty St., 40202-1107. Tel: 502-584-4279; Fax: 502-584-8659. Email: stboniface@insightbb.com. Web: stbonifaceparish.com.

13—ST. BRIGID (1873) Revs. Donald R. Goetz; Joseph H. Voor (Retired); Deacon Louis B. Dugan.
Res.: 1520 Hepburn Ave., 40204. Tel: 502-584-5565; Fax: 502-584-1328. Email: stbrigidlou@stbrigid.org.

14—CHRIST THE KING (1928) Rev. John T. Judie.
Res.: 718 S. 44th St., 40211. Tel: 502-778-5055; Fax: 502-776-5120 (Call first). Email: ctkarchlou@bellsouth.net.
Catechesis/Religious Program—Tel: 502-772-7851. Loueva Moss, D.R.E. Students 36.

15—ST. EDWARD (1884) [CEM] Rev. Joseph T. Graffis; Mrs. Betty Deerwester, Pastoral Assoc.
Res.: 9608 Sue Helen Dr., 40299. Tel: 502-267-7494; Fax: 502-267-7495. Email: churchoffice@stedwardchurch.com.
School—(Grades PreK-8), 9610 Sue Helen Dr., 40299. Tel: 502-267-6633; Fax: 502-267-4474. Susan Jones, Prin.; Diane Walsh, Librarian. Lay Teachers 27; Students 433.
Catechesis/Religious Program—Lynn Ekstrom, D.R.E. Students 92.

16—ST. ELIZABETH ANN SETON (1975) Rev. R. Dale Cieslik; Deacon James C. Olrich; Margee Joseph, Pastoral Assoc.
Res.: 11501 Maple Way, 40229. Tel: 502-969-0004 Parish; 502-966-3164; Fax: 502-969-0553. Email: parishoffice@easeton.com. Web: easeton.com.
Catechesis/Religious Program—Students 106.

17—ST. ELIZABETH OF HUNGARY (1906) Revs. H. Anthony Olges; Robert B. Gray (Retired).
Mailing Address: 3926 Poplar Level Rd., 40213.
Res.: 1020 E. Burnett Ave., 40217. Tel: 502-636-3706; Fax: 502-456-9198. Email: stemain@iglou.com. Web: germantownwcatholiccluster.org.
Catechesis/Religious Program—2931 Pindell Ave., 40217. Tel: 502-635-5813. Students 6.

18—EPIPHANY (1971) Rev. J. Randall Hubbard; Deacon Lucio A. Caruso; Sr. Mary Gowern, C.S.J., Pastoral Assoc.
Parish Office: 914 Old Harrods Creek Rd., 40223. Tel: 502-245-9733; Fax: 502-245-7658. Email: martha@churchofepiphany.com. Web: churchofepiphany.com.
Catechesis/Religious Program—Students 293.

19—ST. FRANCES OF ROME (1887) Rev. Bernard J. Breen; Sr. Carmelita Dunn, S.C.N., Pastoral Assoc.
Res.: 2119 Payne St., 40206. Tel: 502-896-8401; Fax: 502-895-0310. Email: stfranrome@aol.com. Web: stfrancesofrome.org.
Catechesis/Religious Program—Sr. Mary Jo Gramig, O.S.U., D.R.E. Students 36.

20—ST. FRANCIS OF ASSISI (1886) Rev. Louis J. Meiman; Deacon Lawrence Biven. In Res., Rev. Joseph T. Merkt (Retired).
Res.: 1960 Bardstown Rd., 40205-1572. Tel: 502-456-6394; Fax: 502-456-9462. Email: lmeiman@ccsfa.org. Web: ccsfa.org.
School—(Grades K-8), 1938 Alfresco Pl., 40205-1876. Tel: 502-459-3088; Fax: 502-456-9462. Paula Watkins, Prin.; Susan Messerschidt, Librarian. Lay Teachers 24; Students 257.
Catechesis/Religious Program—Tel: 502-456-6394. Students 40.

21—ST. GABRIEL THE ARCHANGEL (1953) Revs. John J. Stoltz; James T. Mudd (Retired); Deacon T. Stephen Bowling.
Res.: 5505 Bardstown Rd., 40291. Tel: 502-239-5481; Fax: 502-239-7717. Email: parish@stgabriel.net. Web: stgabriel.net.
School—(Grades PreK-8), 5503 Bardstown Rd., 40291. Tel: 502-239-5535; Fax: 502-231-1464. Pamela Huelsman, Prin.; Tammy Herbert, Librarian. Lay Teachers 37; Students 798.
Catechesis/Religious Program—Cyndi Marlow, Dir. Children's Formation. Students 135.

22—GOOD SHEPHERD (2009) Rev. John R. Burke; Deacons Paul F. Bissig; Geoffrey Gnau.
Parish Office: 338 N. 25th St., 40212. Tel: 502-772-3694; Fax: 502-772-3695.
Catechesis/Religious Program—Carolyn Denning, D.R.E. Students 15.

23—GUARDIAN ANGELS (1957) Rev. Jeffrey P. Leger.
Res.: 6000 Preston Hwy., 40219. Tel: 502-968-5421; Fax: 502-962-1080. Email: gangelscommunity@bellsouth.net.
Catechesis/Religious Program—

24—HOLY FAMILY (1929) Rev. H. Anthony Olges.
Res.: 3926 Poplar Level Rd., 40213. Tel: 502-459-6066; Fax: 502-456-9198. Email: churchoffice@hofaky.org. Web: hofaky.org.
School—(Grades PreK-8), 3934 Poplar Level Rd., 40213. Tel: 502-458-4531. Gayle Bauch, Prin. Lay Teachers 15; Students 159.
Catechesis/Religious Program—Students 19.

25—HOLY NAME (1891) Rev. David Sanchez.
Res.: 2914 S. 3rd St., 40208. Tel: 502-637-5560.

Email: holynamecatholicchurch@live.com.
Catechesis / Religious Program—Students 29.

26—HOLY SPIRIT (1937) Revs. Thomas A. Smith; John R. Johnson; Deacons Joseph A. Raibert; Robert Hall.
Res.: 3345 Lexington Rd., 40206. Tel: 502-893-3982; Fax: 502-893-8287. Email: office@hspirit.org. Web: hspirit.org.
School—(Grades K-8), 322 Cannons Ln., 40206. Tel: 502-893-7700; Fax: 502-893-8078. Doris Swenson, Prin.; Diane Justice, Librarian. Lay Teachers 27; Students 387.
Catechesis / Religious Program—Students 28.

27—HOLY TRINITY (1882) Very Rev. J. Mark Spalding; Deacons Walton G. Jones; Jeremiah S. Babin.
Pastoral Center—501 Cherrywood Rd., 40207. Tel: 502-897-5207; Fax: 502-897-0962. Web: htparish.org.
School—(Grades K-8), 423 Cherrywood Rd., 40207. Tel: 502-897-2785; Fax: 502-896-0990. Mr. Jack Richards, Prin.; D. Dee Hill, Librarian. Email: dhill@ht-school.org. Lay Teachers 42; Students 712.
Catechesis / Religious Program—Tel: 502-897-5207, Ext. 125. Dinah Tichy, D.R.E. Students 81.

28—ST. IGNATIUS (1963) Rev. David W. Naylor.
Res.: 1818 Rangeland Rd., 40219. Tel: 502-964-5904; Fax: 502-964-5905. Email: stignatius@aol.com.
Catechesis / Religious Program—Students 20.

29—IMMACULATE HEART OF MARY (1953) Rev. John T. Judie.
Office: 1545 S. 34th St., 40211. Tel: 502-774-5772; Fax: 502-774-5899. Email: irectory@bellsouth.net.
Catechesis / Religious Program—Students 2.

30—INCARNATION (1966) Rev. Christian Moore, O.F.M-.Conv.; Deacon Robert Markert; Mary Ann Glaser, Pastoral Assoc.
Res.: 2229 Lower Hunters Trace Rd., 40216. Tel: 502-447-2013; Fax: 502-448-3821. Email: incarnationcatho@bellsouth.net. Web: incarnation-catholicchurch.com.

31—ST. JAMES (1906) Revs. Donald R. Goetz; Joseph H. Voor (Retired); Deacon Louis B. Dugan.
Res.: 1826 Edenside Ave., 40204. Tel: 502-451-1420; Fax: 502-451-1429. Email: stjameslou@stjameslou.org. Web: stjameslou.org.
School—(Grades PreSchool-8), 1818 Edenside Ave., 40204. Tel: 502-454-0330; Fax: 502-454-0330. Tom Schmitt, Prin. Lay Teachers 15; Students 200.
Catechesis / Religious Program—Students 6.

32—ST. JOHN VIANNEY (1951) Rev. Anthony Chinh N'go.
Res.: 4839 Southside Dr., 40214. Tel: 502-366-5517; Fax: 502-366-3544.
Catechesis / Religious Program—Sr. Clare Nguyen, D.R.E.; Mr. Thang Ly, D.R.E. Students 90.

33—ST. JOSEPH (1866) Rev. David Sanchez.
Res.: 1406 E. Washington St., 40206. Tel: 502-583-7401; Fax: 502-589-7465. Email: parish@sjosephcatholic.org. Web: sjosephcatholic.org.
Catechesis / Religious Program—Tel: 502-583-0892. Students 50.

34—ST. LAWRENCE (1953) Rev. Terry L. Langford; Sr. Ann Marie Howard, O.S.B., Pastoral Assoc.; Deacon David Dalton.
Res.: 1925 Lewiston Dr., 40216. Tel: 502-448-2122; Fax: 502-448-2163. Email: secretary.lawrence@gmail.com.
Catechesis / Religious Program— Sr. Ann Marie Howard, O.S.B., D.R.E. Students 157.

35—ST. LEONARD (1953) Rev. Bernard J. Breen; Joy Trimble, Pastoral Assoc.
Res.: 440 Zorn Ave., 40206. Tel: 502-897-2595; Fax: 502-896-8259.
School—(Grades PreK-8) Tel: 502-897-5265; Fax: 502-897-5125. Linda Kinderman, Prin.; Nancy Tomasetti, Librarian. Lay Teachers 16; Students 175.
Catechesis / Religious Program—Students 8.

36—ST. LOUIS BERTRAND (1866) Very Rev. William P. Garrott, O.P., Prior; Revs. William Dominic Fields, O.P.; George G. Christian, O.P.; James B. Muller, O.P.; Elias A. Henritzy, O.P.; Emmanuel Bertrand, O.P.
Res.: 1104 S. 6th St., 40203. Tel: 502-583-4448; Fax: 502-589-0056.
Catechesis / Religious Program—Rob Lewis, D.R.E. Students 25.
Shrine—Lourdes Rosary Shrine, Inc.
Shrine—Blessed Margaret Castello Shrine

37—ST. LUKE (1965) Revs. Joseph M. Rankin; Winson Parekkat, C.M.I.; Deacon K. Michael Burchett.
Res.: 4211 Jim Hawkins Dr., 40229. Tel: 502-969-3291; Fax: 502-969-1718.
Catechesis / Religious Program—Debbie Minton, D.R.E. Students 25.

38—ST. MARGARET MARY (1950) Revs. Stephen A. Pohl; John Miles, C.R.; Deacon Charles T. Bent.
Res.: 7813 Shelbyville Rd., 40222. Tel: 502-426-1588; Fax: 502-426-1503. Email: grace@stmm.org. Web: stmm.org.
School—(Grades K-8) Tel: 502-426-2635; Fax: 502-426-1304. Wendy Sims, Prin. Lay Teachers 38; Students 723.
Catechesis / Religious Program—Students 115.

39—ST. MARTHA (1960) Rev. Mark M. Hamilton; Deacons Ken Ward, Parish Admin.; John P. Maher; Daniel G. Bisig Sr.
Res.: 2825 Klondike Ln., 40218. Tel: 502-491-8535; Fax: 502-491-8536. Email: parishof@bellsouth.net.
School—(Grades PreK-8) Tel: 502-491-3171; Fax: 502-495-6107. Cathy Guizio, Prin.; Carolyn Deckelman, Librarian. Lay Teachers 34; Students 491.
Catechesis / Religious Program—Tel: 502-491-5135. Students 85.

40—ST. MARTIN DE PORRES (1990) Deacon James Turner, Pastoral Admin.; Rev. Patrick D. Delahanty, Sacramental Moderator.
3112 W. Broadway, 40211. Tel: 502-778-1118; Fax: 502-778-0148.
Catechesis / Religious Program—Tel: 502-418-3447. M. Annette Mandley-Turner, D.R.E. Students 104.

41—ST. MARTIN OF TOURS (1853) Rev. Frederick W. Klotter; Deacons Robert C. Bryant; Richard P. Zoldak.
Res.: 639 S. Shelby St., 40202. Tel: 502-582-2827; Fax: 502-582-1780. Email: pastorsoffice@louisville-catholic.net.
Catechesis / Religious Program—Students 141.

42—MARY QUEEN OF PEACE PARISH Rev. Thomas E. Gentile; Deacons Robert M. Kampschaefer; William Niemeier.
Parish Office: 4005 Dixie Hwy., 40216. Tel: 502-448-4008; Fax: 502-448-8546.
Catechesis / Religious Program—Students 20.

43—ST. MICHAEL (1975) Rev. J. Richard Sullivan; Deacons Martin J. Brown; Kenneth J. Carter.
Res.: 3705 Stone Lakes Dr., 40299. Tel: 502-266-5611; Fax: 502-267-4272. Email: frdick@stmichaellouisville.org. Web: stmichaelchurch.org.
School—(Grades PreK-8) Tel: 502-267-6155; Fax: 502-267-1652. Sheila Marstiller, Prin. Email: smarstiller@stmichaellouisville.org; Kathy Geoghegan, Librarian. Lay Teachers 53; Students 642.
Catechesis / Religious Program—Brenda Rickert, D.R.E. Students 155.

44—MOST BLESSED SACRAMENT (1937) Rev. Jeffrey D. Gatlin.
Mailing Address: 4335 Hazelwood Ave., 40215.
Res.: 3509 Taylor Blvd., 40215. Tel: 502-361-0149; Fax: 502-375-1988. Web: mbsparish.com.
Catechesis / Religious Program—Tel: 502-361-0960. Students 20.

45—OUR LADY OF LOURDES (1950) Rev. Scott J. Wimsett; Deacons F. Eugene Waldon; Timothy B. Ayers.
Res.: 508 Breckenridge Ln., 40207. Tel: 502-896-0241; Fax: 502-895-4535. Email: olol@ourlourdes.org. Web: ourlourdes.org.
School—(Grades K-8), 510 Breckenridge Ln., 40207. Tel: 502-895-5122; Fax: 502-893-5051. Laura Glaser, Prin.; Maureen Choate, Librarian. Lay Teachers 27; Students 449.
Catechesis / Religious Program—Tel: 502-896-0241, Ext. 13; Fax: 502-895-4535. Mary Caroline Marchal, S.C., D.R.E.; Ann Pifer, D.R.E. Students 120.

46—OUR LADY OF MOUNT CARMEL (1957) Rev. Philip Lee Erickson.
Parish Office: 5505 New Cut Rd., 40214. Tel: 502-366-5651; Fax: 502-368-9972. Email: parishsecretary@insightbb.com.
Res.: 7333 Southside Dr., 40214.
Catechesis / Religious Program—6105 S. Third St., 40214. Tel: 502-366-1463; Fax: 502-366-1464. Students 43.

47—OUR MOTHER OF SORROWS (1937) Rev. James F. Hackett; Deacon Timothy E. Stewart.
Res.: 747 Harrison Ave., 40217. Tel: 502-637-7442; Fax: 502-637-3794. Email: parishoffice@omos.org. Web: omos.org.

48—ST. PATRICK (1988) Rev. Martin A. Linebach; Deacons Gregory M. Gitschier; Scott R. Haner; Mark J. Rougeux.
Res.: 1000 N. Beckley Station Rd., 40245-4550. Tel: 502-244-6083; Fax: 502-719-0359. Email: ourparish@stpatrick-lou.org. Web: stpatrick-lou.org.
School—(Grades K-8) Tel: 502-244-7083; Fax: 502-719-0369. Michael L. Bratcher, Prin.; Adele Koch, Librarian. Sisters 3; Lay Teachers 40; Students 643.
Catechesis / Religious Program—Tel: 502-254-9472. R. Tim Grove, Dir. Formation. Students 146.

49—ST. PAUL (1851) Rev. Dismas J. Veeneman, O.F.M.Conv.; Deacon Charles Beckmann. In Res., Revs. Adam Bunnell, O.F.M.Conv.; Benjamin Knopp, O.F.M.Conv.
Res.: 6901 Dixie Hwy., 40258. Tel: 502-935-1223; Fax: 502-933-7747. Email: dismasv@aol.com.
School—(Grades PreK-8) Tel: 502-935-5511; Fax: 502-935-5596. Kevin Brever, Prin.; Beth Trusty, Librarian. Lay Teachers 14; Students 186.
Catechesis / Religious Program—Amy Gaekle, D.R.E. Students 50.

50—ST. PETER THE APOSTLE PARISH (2008) Rev. Ronald J. Domhoff; Deacons Wayne Thieneman; Steve Smith; Gregory L. Klinglesmith. In Res., Rev. Bryan Lamberson.
Parish Office: 5431 Johnsontown Rd., 40272. Tel: 502-937-5920; Fax: 502-937-5927.
Catechesis / Religious Program—Catherine Blandford, D.R.E. Students 88.

51—ST. PIUS X (1956) Rev. William P. Burks; Deacon James I. McGoff.
Res.: 3521 Goldsmith Ln., 40220. Tel: 502-451-9300 (Office); 502-451-4124 (Rectory); Fax: 502-458-7109.
Catechesis / Religious Program—Kathleen Stout, D.R.E. Students 45.

52—ST. RAPHAEL THE ARCHANGEL (1947) Rev. Donald M. Hill; Deacon Todd C. Auffrey.
Res.: 2121 Lancashire Ave., 40205. Tel: 502-458-2500.
Parish Offices—2141 Lancashire Ave, 40205. Tel: 502-458-2500; Fax: 502-458-8049.
School—(Grades K-8), 2131 Lancashire Ave., 40205. Tel: 502-456-1541; Fax: 502-451-3632. Paul DeZarn, Prin. Lay Teachers 22; Students 404.
Catechesis / Religious Program—Students 4.

53—ST. RITA (1921) Revs. Joseph M. Rankin; Winson Parekkat, C.M.I.; Deacons K. Michael Burchett; Aurelio A. Puga.
Res.: 8709 Preston Hwy., 40219. Tel: 502-969-4579; Fax: 502-969-3679. Email: lheitz@saintrita.net. Web: saintrita.net.
School—(Grades PreK-8) Tel: 502-969-7067; Fax: 502-969-3679. Mary Lee Lanning, Prin. Lay Teachers 19; Students 241.
Catechesis / Religious Program—Students 150.

54—SS. SIMON AND JUDE (1950) Rev. Jeffrey D. Gatlin.
Res.: 4335 Hazelwood Ave., 40215. Tel: 502-368-4887; Fax: 502-375-1988.
Catechesis / Religious Program—Students 20.

55—ST. STEPHEN, MARTYR (1948) Rev. Harry J. Gelthaus, hgelthaus@ssmartyr.org; Deacons Sylvester Nitzken; Stephen J. DaPonte.
Res.: 2931 Pindell Ave., 40217. Tel: 502-635-5813; Fax: 502-635-5888.
School—(Grades PreK-8), 2931 Pindell, 40217. Tel: 502-635-7141; Fax: 502-635-1576. Margaret Bowen, Prin. Lay Teachers 19; Students 283.
Catechesis / Religious Program—Students 108.

56—ST. THERESE (1908) Revs. H. Anthony Olges. Email: frtony@hofaky.org; Robert B. Gray (Retired).
Mailing Address: 3926 Poplar Level Rd., 40213.
Res.: 1010 Schiller Ave., 40204. Tel: 502-634-3671; Fax: 502-634-3672.
Catechesis / Religious Program—Twinned with Holy Family, Louisville. Barbara Klump, D.R.E. Students 3.

57—ST. THOMAS MORE (1944) Rev. Philip Lee Erickson; Deacons Michael A. Tolbert; Terry Maguire.
Res.: 6105 S. Third St., 40214. Tel: 502-366-1463; Fax: 502-366-1464.
Catechesis / Religious Program—Students 15.

58—ST. WILLIAM (1901) Rev. John R. Burke, Sacramental Mod.; Sharan A. Benton, Pastoral Admin.
Res.: 1226 W. Oak St., 40210. Tel: 502-635-6307; Fax: 502-638-0683 (Call first).
Catechesis / Religious Program—Ryan J. Renoud, D.R.E. Students 50.

OUTSIDE THE CITY OF LOUISVILLE

ALBANY, CLINTON CO., EMMANUEL CATHOLIC (1975) Revs. Joel C. Rogers, C.P.M.; Charles Zmudzinski, C.P.M.; Kenneth Soroko, C.P.M.
Mailing Address: P.O. Box 126, 42602.
Res.: 103 W. Brown St., Glasgow, 42141. Tel: 270-651-5263.
Catechesis / Religious Program—Students 9.
Mission—Holy Cross Catholic 264 Glasgow Rd., P.O. Box 197, Burkesville, Cumberland Co. 42717. Fax: 270-864-4107 (Call First).

BARDSTOWN, NELSON CO.

1—BASILICA OF ST. JOSEPH PROTO-CATHEDRAL (1816) [CEM] Revs. William D. Hammer; Michael T. Wimsatt; Deacons Richard J. Walsh; John Hamilton. In Res., Rev. C. Joseph Batcheldor (Retired).
Res.: 310 W. Stephen Foster Ave., P.O. Box 548, 40004. Tel: 502-348-3126; Fax: 502-349-0941.
School—(Grades PreK-8), 320 W. Stephen Foster Ave., 40004. Tel: 502-348-5994; Fax: 502-348-4694. Michael Bickett, Prin.; Karen Spalding, Librarian. Lay Teachers 26; Students 405.
St. Joseph Montessori Children's Center—161 West Dr., Nazareth, 40048. Tel: 502-348-1548; Fax: 502-331-4050.
Catechesis / Religious Program—Students 122.

2—ST. MONICA (1956) Rev. Jeffrey G. Hopper, Admin.; Deacon Scott R. Turner.
Res.: 407 S. Third St., 40004. Tel: 502-348-5250; Fax: 502-348-3635. Email: stmonica@bardstown.com.
Catechesis / Religious Program—Students 20.

BRANDENBURG, MEADE CO., ST. JOHN THE APOSTLE

(1892) [CEM] Rev. Kevin J. Bryan; Deacons J. Michael Jones; Robert Caspar.
Res.: 515 Broadway, 40108. Tel: 270-422-2196; Fax: 270-422-2471.
Catechesis/Religious Program—Monica Lucas, D.R.E. Students 264.

CALVARY, MARION CO., HOLY NAME OF MARY (1798) [CEM] Revs. Gerald L. Bell, Admin.; William M. Bowling; Deacon Dennis May.
Mailing Address: 235 S. Spalding Ave., Lebanon, 40033.
Res.: 3295 Hwy. 208, Lebanon, 40033. Tel: 270-692-6491; Fax: 270-692-5708. Email: holymary@windstream.net.
Catechesis/Religious Program—Students 118.

CAMPBELLSVILLE, TAYLOR CO., OUR LADY OF PERPETUAL HELP (1879) [CEM] Rev. James M. Reinhart, Admin.
Office: 425 N. Central Ave., 42718. Tel: 270-465-4282; Fax: 270-789-9669.
Catechesis/Religious Program—Students 30.
Mission—Our Lady of Fatima Phillipsburg, Marion Co.

CECILIA, HARDIN CO., ST. AMBROSE (1879) Revs. Charles D. Walker; Matthew T. Hardesty; Deacons William Clark; Karl A. Drerup.
Mailing Address: *St. James Church*, 307 W. Dixie Ave., Elizabethtown, 42701. Tel: 270-765-6268; Fax: 270-234-9598.
Church: 609 Main St., 42724.
Catechesis/Religious Program—Students 3.

CLEMENTSVILLE, CASEY CO., ST. BERNARD (1802) Rev. Patrick J. Dolan.
Res.: 5075 KY 551, Liberty, 42539. Tel: 606-787-7570. Email: stbernard@windstream.net.
Catechesis/Religious Program—Tel: 606-787-6600. Sue Goode, D.R.E. Students 15.
Mission—Sacred Heart c/o 5075 KY 551, Liberty, Casey Co. 42539.

CULVERTOWN, NELSON CO., IMMACULATE CONCEPTION Rev. Troy Overton, Admin.; Deacon William A. Downs.
Mailing Address: 413 First St., New Haven, 40051-6030.
Res.: 8191 New Haven Rd., New Haven, 40051-6030. Tel: 502-331-3467.

EDMONTON, METCALFE CO., CHRIST THE HEALER (1975) Rev. Lawrence J. Gelthaus.
Mailing Address: P.O. Box 599, 42129.
Res.: 506 Skyline, 42129. Tel: 270-432-0686.
Catechesis/Religious Program—Tel: 270-678-6280. Students 4.
Mission—Christ the King P.O. Box 518, Tompkinsville, Monroe Co. 42167. Tel: 270-487-8881.

ELIZABETHTOWN, HARDIN CO., ST. JAMES (1851) [CEM] Revs. Charles D. Walker; Matthew T. Hardesty; Stanley J. Osborne (Retired); Deacons Joseph Chathaparampil; William Clark; Karl A. Drerup.
Res.: 307 W. Dixie Ave., 42701. Tel: 270-765-6268; Fax: 270-234-9598. Email: parishoffice@stjames-etown.org. Web: stjames-etown.org.
School—(Grades PreK-8), 114 N. Miles St., 42701. Tel: 270-765-7011; Fax: 270-769-5745. Sr. Michael Marie Friedman, Prin.; Linda Yates, Librarian. Religious Teachers 1; Lay Teachers 30; Students 412.
Catechesis/Religious Program—Amy Kramer, D.R.E. Students 236.

FAIRFIELD, NELSON CO., ST. MICHAEL (1792) [CEM] Revs. William D. Hammer; Albert J. Hartlage (Retired).
Res.: P.O. Box 27, 40020. Tel: 502-252-8308; Fax: 502-252-0106.
Catechesis/Religious Program—111 Church St., P.O. Box 27, 40020. Tel: 502-252-0106. Gilly Simpson, D.R.E. Students 72.

FINLEY, TAYLOR CO., OUR LADY OF THE HILLS (1908) [CEM] Rev. James M. Reinhart, Admin.
Office: 425 N. Central Ave., Campbellsville, 42718. Tel: 270-465-4282; Fax: 270-789-9669.
Catechesis/Religious Program—Students 15.

FLAHERTY, MEADE CO., ST. MARTIN OF TOURS (1848) [CEM] Rev. Kevin J. Bryan; Deacons John R. Whelan; Robert Caspar.
Res.: 440 Saint Martin Rd., Vine Grove, 40175. Tel: 270-828-2552; Fax: 270-828-2562. Email: martinfl@bbtel.com. Web: stmartinfl.org.
Catechesis/Religious Program—Tel: 270-828-8484; Fax: 270-828-8484. Regina Bennett, D.R.E. Students 141.

GLASGOW, BARREN CO., ST. HELEN (1893) Revs. Joel C. Rogers, C.P.M.; Charles Zmudzinski, C.P.M.; Kenneth Soroko, C.P.M.; Deacons Lee Bidwell; David U. Smith.
Res.: 103 W. Brown St., 42141. Tel: 270-651-5263; Fax: 270-651-1373. Email: sthelen@glasgow-ky.com.
Catechesis/Religious Program—Students 75.
Mission—Our Lady of the Caves Church Rte. 31 W., Horse Cave, Hart Co. 42749. Tel: 270-651-5263.

GREENSBURG, GREEN CO., HOLY REDEEMER (1969) Rev. Paul W. Eve, Admin.
Mailing Address: P.O. Box 247, Jamestown, 42629. Tel: 270-384-4528.
Church: 110 Industrial Rd., 42743.
Catechesis/Religious Program—Students 10.

HODGENVILLE, LARUE CO., OUR LADY OF MERCY (1853) [CEM] Rev. Pablo A. Hernandez; Deacon James A. Cecil.
Res.: 210 Walters Ave., 42748. Tel: 270-358-4697; Fax: 270-358-3601 (Call First). Email: olmparish@windstream.net.
Catechesis/Religious Program—Tel: 270-325-3801. Students 45.

HOLY CROSS, MARION CO., HOLY CROSS (1785) [CEM] Rev. R. Joseph Hemmerle.
Office: 200 School Dr., P.O. Box 74, Loretto, 40037. Tel: 270-865-2521; Fax: 270-865-2071.
Res.: 3560 N. Saint Francis Rd., Loretto, 40037. Tel: 270-865-2075. Email: sfahc@windstream.net. Web: sf-hc.org.
Catechesis/Religious Program—Carol Blanford, D.R.E. Students 39.

HOWARDSTOWN, NELSON CO., ST. ANN (1862) [CEM] Rev. Kenneth R. Fortener, Admin.
Res.: 7490 Howardstown Rd., 40051. Tel: 502-549-3285.
School—Tel: 502-549-7310. Lois Cecil, Prin. Lay Teachers 4; Students 30.

JAMESTOWN, RUSSELL CO., HOLY SPIRIT (1953) Rev. Paul W. Eve, Admin.; Sr. Marian Stenken, S.C.N., Pastoral Assoc.
Res.: 406 N. Main St., P.O. Box 247, 42629. Tel: 270-343-3346.
Catechesis/Religious Program—Students 12.
Mission—Good Shepherd (1964) 1221 Greensburg St., P.O. Box 354, Columbia, Adair Co. 42728. Tel: 270-384-4528.

LAGRANGE, OLDHAM CO., IMMACULATE CONCEPTION (1962) Rev. Anthony L. Chandler; Deacons Charles Brown; Thomas M. McNally.
Res.: 502 N. Fifth St., 40031. Tel: 502-222-0255; Fax: 502-225-9844. Web: iclagrange.org.
Catechesis/Religious Program—Julie Asbeck, Children's Family Min. Students 345.
Station—Luther Luckett Correctional Center, Tel: 502-222-0363.
Station—Kentucky State Reformatory, Tel: 502-222-9441.
Station—Roederer Farm Prison, Tel: 502-222-0173.
Station—Cedar Lake Lodge La Grange, 40032. Tel: 502-222-7157.
Station—Baptist Hospital Northeast, Tel: 502-222-5388.
Station—Richwood Nursing Home La Grange, 40032. Tel: 502-222-3186.

LEBANON JUNCTION, BULLITT CO., ST. BENEDICT (1907) Rev. Brian A. Kenney; Deacon Phillip L. Noltemeyer.
Mailing Address: 187 S. Plum St., Shepherdsville, 40165.
Res.: 139 N. Brook St., 40150. Tel: 502-833-4886. Email: parish@stafalcons.com.
Catechesis/Religious Program—Students 17.

LEBANON, MARION CO., ST. AUGUSTINE (1815) [CEM] Revs. Gerald L. Bell; William M. Bowling; Deacons Joseph R. Dant; Dennis May; Kathy Shannon, Pastoral Assoc.
Res. & Mailing Address: 235 S. Spalding Ave., 40033. Tel: 270-692-3019; Fax: 270-692-5532. Email: staugustinechurch@kyol.net. Web: staugustinechurch.net.
School—(Grades PreK-8), 236 S. Spalding Ave., 40033. Tel: 270-692-2063; Fax: 270-692-6597. Alicia Riggs, Prin. Lay Teachers 9; Students 148.
Catechesis/Religious Program—Mike Luescher, D.R.E. Students 203.

MOUNT WASHINGTON, BULLITT CO., ST. FRANCIS XAVIER (1846) [CEM] Rev. R. Paul Beach; Deacon Gerald J. Mattingly.
Res.: 155 Stringer Ln., 40047. Tel: 502-538-4933; Fax: 502-955-0449. Web: sfxmw.com.
Catechesis/Religious Program—Tel: 502-538-0672. Students 226.
Mission—All Saints Church (1830) [CEM] 410 W. Main St., P.O. Box 531, Taylorsville, Spencer Co. 40071. Tel: 502-477-6676; Fax: 502-477-5278.

NEW HAVEN, NELSON CO., ST. CATHERINE (1844) [CEM] Rev. Troy Overton; Deacon Joseph E. Hutchins.
Res.: 413 First St., 40051. Tel: 502-549-3680; Fax: 502-549-5410.
School—(Grades PreK-8), 413 First St., 40051. Tel: 502-549-3680; Fax: 502-549-5410. Jo Renee O'Bryan, Prin.; Tonia Greenwell, Librarian. Lay Teachers 6; Students 94.

NEW HOPE, NELSON CO., ST. VINCENT DE PAUL (1820) [CEM] Rev. Kenneth R. Fortener.
Mailing Address: P.O. Box 58, 40052. Tel: 502-549-5559; Fax: 502-549-5572.
Church: 104 Church St., 40052.
Catechesis/Religious Program—Norine Masterson, D.R.E. Students 25.

PAYNEVILLE, MEADE CO., ST. MARY MAGDALEN OF PAZZI (1883) [CEM] Rev. Robert M. Abel; Deacon Gregory A. Beavin.
Res.: 110 Hwy. 376, 40157. Tel: 270-496-4333; Fax: 270-496-4790. Email: stmarymag@insightbb.com.
Catechesis/Religious Program—Tel: 270-422-3345. Philip Millay, D.R.E. Students 59.

PEWEE VALLEY, OLDHAM CO., ST. ALOYSIUS (1871) [CEM] Revs. John A. Caldwell; David W. Harris; Deacons Theodore C. Luckett; Thomas L. Roth.
Res.: 212 Mount Mercy Dr., P.O. Box 468, 40056. Tel: 502-241-8452; Fax: 502-243-1740. Email: parishoffice@staloysiuspwv.org.
School—(Grades PreK-8), 122 Mt. Mercy Dr., 40056. Tel: 502-241-8516; Fax: 502-243-2241. Maryann Hayslip, Prin.; Susan Singer, Librarian. Lay Teachers 20; Students 450.
Catechesis/Religious Program—Tel: 502-241-8452, Ext. 1036. Students 281.
Mission—Korean Catholic Community June Brandenburg, Coord.
Station—Kentucky Correctional Institute for Women, Tel: 502-241-8454.
Station—Friendship Manor Nursing Home, Tel: 502-241-8821.

RADCLIFF, HARDIN CO., ST. CHRISTOPHER (1958) [CEM] Rev. Dennis L. Cousens; Deacons Joseph D. Calvert; Harry Prestwood.
Res.: 1225 S. Wilson Rd., 40160. Tel: 270-351-3706; Fax: 270-351-2843. Email: church@stchristopherparish.org.
Catechesis/Religious Program—Students 100.

RAYWICK, MARION CO., ST. FRANCIS XAVIER CHURCH (1837) [CEM] Rev. James W. Graf.
Res.: 108 Main St., 40060. Tel: 270-692-2245; Fax: 270-692-1138. Email: raywickchurch@kyol.net.
Catechesis/Religious Program—Students 74.

RHODELIA, MEADE CO., ST. THERESA (1818) [CEM] Rev. Robert M. Abel; Deacon Gregory A. Beavin.
Res.: 9245 Rhodelia Rd., Payneville, 40157. Tel: 270-496-4343; Fax: 270-496-4416.
Catechesis/Religious Program—Students 56.

ST. FRANCIS, MARION CO., ST. FRANCIS OF ASSISI (1870) [CEM] Rev. R. Joseph Hemmerle.
Office: 200 School Dr., P.O. Box 74, Loretto, 40037. Tel: 270-865-2521; Fax: 270-865-2071.
Res.: 6785 Hwy. 52, 40062. Tel: 270-865-2075. Email: sfahc@windstream.net. Web: sf-hc.org.
Catechesis/Religious Program—Students 73.

ST. JOHN, HARDIN CO., ST. JOHN THE BAPTIST (1829) [CEM] Rev. Daniel L. Lincoln; Deacon Michael J. Vessels.
Res.: 306 E. Main St., Vine Grove, 40175. Tel: 270-862-9816.
Catechesis/Religious Program—Tel: 270-862-3005. Lisa Thomas, D.R.E. Students 70.

ST. MARY, MARION CO., ST. CHARLES (1786) [CEM] Rev. James W. Graf, Admin.
Res.: 675 Hwy. 327, Lebanon, 40033. Tel: 270-692-4513; Fax: 270-692-6204. Email: saintcharles@kyol.net.
Catechesis/Religious Program—Students 68.

ST. THOMAS, NELSON CO., ST. THOMAS (1812) Rev. Jeffrey G. Hopper, Admin.; Deacons Samuel R. Filiatreau; Scott R. Turner.
Res.: 870 Saint Thomas Ln., Bardstown, 40004. Tel: 502-348-3717; Fax: 502-348-1905. Email: stthomas@bardstown.com. Web: st-thomasparish.org.
Catechesis/Religious Program—Students 105.

SAMUELS, NELSON CO., ST. GREGORY (1845) [CEM] Rev. John A. Schwartzlose; Deacons Joseph E. Livers; Joseph H. Filiatreau; Joseph C. Wiechert.
Parish Office:—330 Samuels Loop, Cox's Creek, 40013. Tel: 502-348-6337; Fax: 502-348-5784. Email: stgreg@stgregoryparish.org.
School—(Grades PreK-8), 350 Samuel's Loop, Cox's Creek, 40013. Tel: 502-348-9583; Fax: 502-348-9597. John Westerfield, Prin.; Sr. Rosemary Rule, Librarian. Lay Teachers 9; Students 135.
Catechesis/Religious Program—Students 95.

SHELBYVILLE, SHELBY CO., ANNUNCIATION OF THE BLESSED VIRGIN MARY (1860) Revs. T. Michael Tobin; John Perez; Deacons Brendan Kinsella; Robert J. Hart.
Res.: 105 W. Main St., 40065. Tel: 502-633-1547; Fax: 502-633-1547. Email: parishoffice@ourcoa.org.
Catechesis/Religious Program—Tel: 502-633-1547; Fax: 502-633-0833. Students 235.
Mission—St. John Chrysostom (1873) 122 Penn St., P.O. Box 74, Eminence, Henry Co. 40019. Tel: 502-845-7005.

SHEPHERDSVILLE, BULLITT CO., ST. ALOYSIUS (1911) Rev. Brian A. Kenney; Deacon Phillip L. Noltemeyer.
Res.: 187 S. Plum St., 40165. Tel: 502-543-5918; Fax: 502-543-6615. Email: parish@stafalcons.com.
School—(Grades PreK-8), 197 S. Plum St., 40165. Tel: 502-543-6721; Fax: 502-531-9575. Mrs. Mary Alice Zettel, Prin.; Lori Hart, Librarian. Lay Teachers 9; Students 100.

Catechesis/Religious Program—Tel: 502-543-5918; Fax: 502-955-6370. Students 23.

SPRINGFIELD, WASHINGTON CO.

1—ST. DOMINIC (1843) [CEM] Rev. Trumie C. Elliott; Deacon Donald K. Flowers.
Res.: 303 W. Main St., 40069. Tel: 859-336-3569; Fax: 859-336-3549. Email: stdom@bellsouth.net.
School—309 W. Main St., 40069. Tel: 859-336-7165; Fax: 859-336-7169. Pamela Breunig, Prin. Lay Teachers 12; Students 211.
Catechesis/Religious Program—Students 56.

2—HOLY ROSARY (1929) Rev. Benedict J. Brown, Sacramental Mod.; Deacon Ernest Cooper, Pastoral Admin.
Mailing Address: Box 146, 40069. Tel: 859-336-3898; Fax: 859-336-3898 (Call first). Email: kyholyrosary@bellsouth.net.
Catechesis/Religious Program—378 Rosary Hgts., 40069. Pamela Grundy, D.R.E. Students 52.

3—HOLY TRINITY (1883) [CEM] Rev. John Christopher Allegra.
Res.: 306 Fredericktown Rd., 40069. Tel: 859-284-5242; Fax: 859-284-5224.
Catechesis/Religious Program—Chris Riley, D.R.E. Students 65.
Mission—Holy Rosary-Manton [CEM] 306 Fredericktown Rd., Washington Co. 40069.

4—ST. ROSE (1806) [CEM] Revs. Kevin Anthony McGrath, O.P.; James Stephen Murray, O.P.; Francis Ralph, O.P. In Res., Bro. Peter Osburne, O.P.
Res.: 868 Loretto Rd., P.O. Box 71, 40069. Tel: 859-336-3121; Fax: 859-336-3841. Email: strose3121@att.net.
Catechesis/Religious Program—Students 48.

VINE GROVE, HARDIN CO., ST. BRIGID (1915) [CEM] Rev. Daniel L. Lincoln; Deacon Michael J. Vessels.
Res.: 306 E. Main St., 40175. Tel: 270-877-2461; Fax: 270-877-2523. Email: brigidvg@bbtel.com. Web: stbrigidvg.org.
Catechesis/Religious Program—Students 89.

WHITE MILLS, HARDIN CO., ST. IGNATIUS (1842) [CEM] Revs. Charles D. Walker; Matthew T. Hardesty; Deacons William Clark; Karl A. Drerup.
Mailing Address: P.O. Box 67, 42788. Tel: 270-369-6279.
Res.: 307 W. Dixie Ave., Elizabethtown, 42701. Tel: 270-765-6268; Fax: 270-234-9598.
Catechesis/Religious Program—Students 12.

Chaplains of Public Institutions

LOUISVILLE. *Jewish Hospital*. Rev. Bryan Lamberson, Chap.
Norton Hospitals. Revs. Expedito Muwonge, Conrad Sutter, O.F.M.Conv., Chap.

On Duty Outside the Archdiocese:
Revs.—
Bromwich, James S., Washington, DC
Dittmeier, Charles R., Maryknoll, P.O. Box 632, Phnom Penh, Cambodia.
Do, Tung Minh, Sacred Heart School of Theology, P.O. Box 429, Hales Corners, WI 53130.
Knott, J. Ronald, D.Min., St. Meinrad Seminary, Saint Meinrad, IN 47577.
Stevens, Gladstone H., S.S., St. Patrick Seminary and University, 320 Middlefield Rd., Menlo Park, CA 94025.
Tran, John R., St. Peter the Apostle Church, 7020 Concord Rd., P.O. Box 30859, Savannah, GA 31410.
Whelan, Daniel, Washington, DC

Retired:
Revs.—
Batcheldor, C. Joseph, St. Joseph Church, P.O. Box 548, Bardstown, 40004.
Bindner, Charles J., 1723 Parkridge Pkwy., 40214.
Birk, John W., 2082 Douglass Blvd., #1, 40205.
Boland, Thomas L., 11802 Big Horn Pl., 40299.
Brennan, William J., St. Joseph Home, 15 Audubon Plaza Dr., 40217.
Butler, John J., 3115 Lexington Rd., 40206.
Cecil, Ivo E., 1080 Optimist Rd., Elizabethtown, 42701.
Clark, Thomas R., 407 D S. Third St., Bardstown, 40004.
Craycroft, Bernard L., 388 University Dr., Radcliff, 40160.
Deatrick, John D., 3806 Village Green Dr., 40299.
Dentinger, Roy E., 3030 Breckenridge Ln., Bldg. 1, Apt. 501, 40220.
Eifler, John G., 572 Upland Rd., 40206.
Eimer, Frank J., Nazareth Home, 2000 Newburg Rd., 40205.
Fichteman, William L., 3309 Heather Ln., 40218.
Flynn, James E., Masonic Home Dr., #106, Bldg. 290, Masonic Home, 40041.
Fowler, Joseph M., 3509 Taylor Blvd., 40215.
Gephart, John B., Bishop David Apartments, 5146 Dixie Hwy., 40216.
Gray, Robert B., 1278 Parkway Gardens Ct., 40217.
Griner, William S., 11110 Old Harrods Creek Ct., 40223.
Hall, Joseph S., 4165 Hwy. 52, Loretto, 40037.
Hanrahan, John W., 1170 Castlevale Dr., #3, 40217.
Hartlage, Albert J., P.O. Box 27, Fairfield, 40020.
Hayden, Joseph F., Chimbote, Peru.
Hogan, Timothy A., 407 McCready Ave., 40206.
Hommrich, Thomas A., St. Joseph Home, 17 Audubon Plaza Dr., 40217.
Howard, Clarence J., 7521 Lanfair Dr., 40241.
Jones, John E., 1697 Taylor Wood Rd., Simpsonville, 40067.
Kamber, Kenneth L., 4029 Busath Ave., 40218.
Lindle, Lawrence H., 3623 Fern Valley Rd., Rm. 227, 40219.
Lyon, Joseph A., Sacred Heart Village, 2120 Payne St., 40206.
Magel, John E., Sacred Heart Village, 2120 Payne St., 40206.
Martin, William J., Nazareth Home, 200 Newburg Rd., 40205.
Merkt, Joseph T., 1960 Bardstown Rd., 40205.
Miller, William, 3517 Nanz Ave., 40207.
Mudd, James T., 5505 Bardstown Rd., 40291.
Murphy, James Wayne, 7908 Woodfern Way, 40291.
Osborne, Robert E., 3910 Village Green Dr., 40299.
Osborne, Stanley J., 657 St. John Church Rd., Elizabethtown, 42701.
Reilly, Robert E., Sacred Heart Village, 2120 Payne St., 40206.
Reteneller, Charles E., Nazareth Village, #21, P.O. Box 2000, Nazareth, 40048.
Rice, G. Nicholas, 214 Eline Ave., 40207.
Ryan, Donald P., Bishop David Apts., 5146 Dixie Hwy., 40216.
Scheich, Eugene, 5907 Branden Dunes Dr., P.O. Box 91348, 40228.
Smith, F. Harold, 945 S. 5th St., #814, 40203.
Spalding, Leon C., 506 N. Randolph Ave., Clarksville, IN 47129.
Springman, Donald W., 8028 St. Andrews Village Dr., 40241.
Stiles, J. Roy, 2042 Buechel Bank Rd., 40218.
Timmel, Gerald L., Bishop David Apts., 5146 Dixie Hwy., 40216.
Volpert, Robert C., 3004 Aspenwood Way, 40241.
Voor, Joseph H., St. James Church, 1826 Edenside Ave., 40204.
Wafzig, James E., Sacred Heart Village, 2120 Payne St., 40206.
Wagner, William F., 952 Hinton Hills Loop, Hardinsburg, 40143.
Wilson, Albert L., Bishop David Apts., 5146 Dixie Hwy., 40216.
Zettel, David H., 4011 Shelbyville Rd., 40207.
Zoeller, Eugene, 3920 Manner Dale Dr., 40220.

Permanent Deacons:
Abell, James H., (Retired)
Auffrey, Todd C., St. Raphael, Louisville
Ayers, Timothy B., Our Lady of Lourdes, Louisville
Babin, Jeremiah S., Holy Trinity, Louisville
Beavin, Gregory A., St. Mary Magdalen of Pazzi, Payneville; St. Theresa, Rhodelia
Becker, Gary Earle, (Retired), Santa Barbara, CA
Beckmann, Charles, St. Paul, Louisville
Bell, Kenneth, (On Leave)
Bent, Charles T., St. Margaret Mary, Louisville
Bidwell, Lee G., St. Helen, Glasgow; Our Lady of the Caves, Horse Cave
Bisig, Daniel G., Sr., St. Martha, Louisville
Bissig, Paul F., Good Shepherd, Louisville
Biven, Lawrence, St. Francis of Assisi, Louisville; Nazareth Home, Louisville
Bowling, T. Stephen, St. Gabriel, Louisville
Box, Thomas E., St. Bartholomew, Louisville
Brown, Charles, Immaculate Conception, La Grange
Brown, Martin J., St. Michael, Louisville
Bryant, Robert C., St. Martin of Tours, Louisville
Burchett, K. Michael, St. Rita, St. Luke, Louisville
Burns, Robert L., Central State Hospital, La Grange
Calvert, Joseph D., St. Christopher, Radcliffe
Carney, Edward P., (Retired)
Carter, Kenneth J., St. Michael, Louisville
Caruso, Lucio A., Epiphany, Louisville
Caspar, Robert, St. Martin of Tours, Flaherty; St. John the Apostle, Brandenburg
Cecil, James A., Our Lady of Mercy, Hodgenville
Chathaparampil, Joseph, St. James Church, Elizabethtown
Churchill, John, (Retired)
Clark, George B., (On Leave)
Clark, William, St. James, Elizabethtown
Cooper, Ernest A., Holy Rosary, Springfield
Cottrell, Francis E., (Retired)
Coulter, William D., St. Rose, Springfield
Dalton, David, Dismas Charities, St. Lawrence
Dant, Joseph R., St. Augustine, Lebanon
DaPonte, Stephen J., St. Stephen Martyr, Louisville
Dever, Robert, (Retired)
Diemer, Darryl J., St. Francis of Assisi, Louisville
Downs, William A., Immaculate Conception, Culvertown
Drerup, Karl A., St. James, Elizabethtown; St. Ambrose, Cecilia; St. Ignatius, White Mills
Dugan, Louis B., St. James & St. Brigid, Louisville
Edwards, Michael, Ascension, Louisville
Filiatreau, Joseph H., St. Gregory, Samuels
Filiatreau, Samuel R., St. Thomas, Bardstown
Flowers, Donald K., (Retired)
Gitschier, Gregory M., St. Patrick, Louisville; Metro Police Dept.
Gnau, Geoffrey, Good Shepherd, Louisville
Hall, Robert, Holy Spirit, Louisville
Hamilton, John, St. Joseph, Bardstown
Haner, Scott R., St. Patrick, Louisville
Harris, Patrick, St. Bernadette, Louisville
Hart, Robert J., Annunciation, Shelbyville; St. John Chrysostom, Eminence
Hasson, Anthony P., (Retired)
Hettich, Philip, St. Bernard, Louisville; Jefferson County Jail
Higgins, Frederick, (Retired)
Houck, Peter L., (Retired)
Hutchins, Joseph E., St. Catherine, New Haven
Jackson, Jarvis, (On Leave)
Jones, J. Michael, St. John the Apostle, Brandenburg
Jones, Walton G., Holy Trinity, Louisville
Kampschaefer, Robert M., Mary Queen of Peace, Louisville
Karley, Brian, C.R., St. Boniface, Louisville
Kinsella, Brendan, Annunciation, Shelbyville; St. John Chrysostom, Eminence
Klinglesmith, Gregory L., St. Peter the Apostle, Louisville
Klump, William, St. Louis Bertrand, Louisville
Layman, Michael A., St. Albert, Louisville
Livers, Joseph E., St. Gregory, Samuels
Luckett, Theodore C., St. Aloysius, Pewee Valley
Maguire, Terry, Our Lady of Mt. Carmel; St. Thomas More, Louisville
Maher, John P., St. Martha, Louisville
Markert, Robert, Incarnation, Louisville; Catholic Cemeteries Chaplain
Masterson, Donald E., (On Leave)
Mattingly, Gerald J., St. Francis Xavier, Mt. Washington; All Saints, Taylorsville
Mattingly, Tom, (Retired)
May, Dennis, St. Augustine, Lebanon; Holy Name of Mary, Calvary
McGinty, David L., (retired)
McGoff, James I., St. Pius X, Louisville
McKenzie, Keith L., St. Augustine, Louisville
McNally, Thomas M., Immaculate Conception, La Grange
Miller, Norbert F., (Retired), Vicar For Senior Deacons
Mitchell, Kenneth J., Blessed Teresa, Louisville
Moore, Joseph F., St. Barnabas, Louisville
Mullins, William L., (Retired)
Murphy, Michael, (On Duty Outside the Diocese)
Nevitt, Charles "Mack", (On Leave)
Niemeier, William, Mary Queen of Peace, Louisville
Nitzken, Sylvester, St. Stephen Martyr, Louisville
Noltemeyer, Phillip L., St. Aloysius, Shepherdsville; St. Benedict, Lebanon Junction
Olrich, James C., St. Elizabeth Ann Seton Church, Louisville
Osborne, Kenneth F., (Retired)
Parker, Danny E., St. Bernadette, Louisville
Patterson, Daniel, (Retired)
Phelps, P. Stephan, Cathedral of the Assumption; St. Boniface, Louisville
Plummer, James R., St. Barnabas, Louisville
Prestwood, Harry, St. Christopher, Radcliff
Puga, Aurelio A., St. Rita, Louisville
Raibert, Joseph A., Holy Spirit, Louisville
Ratterman, Cletus A., (Retired)
Roth, Thomas L., St. Aloysius, Pewee Valley
Rougeux, Mark J., St. Patrick, Louisville
Ryan, Thomas, (Retired)
Schook, Jesse E., St. Athanasius, Louisville
Shoulta, John, (Retired)
Simpson, John L., (Retired)
Singer, Ernest, (Retired)
Smith, David U., St. Helen, Glasgow; Our Lady of the Caves, Horse Cave
Smith, Steve, St. Peter the Apostle, Louisville
Stanley, Vincent (Jim) G., (Retired)
Steinmetz, Richard Earl, St. Joseph Home for the Aged
Stewart, Timothy E., Our Mother of Sorrows, Louisville
Sturgeon, James C., Sr., (Retired)
Thieneman, Wayne, St. Peter the Apostle, Louisville

Tolbert, Michael A., St. Thomas More, Louisville
Tomes, David R., St. Boniface, Louisville
Turner, James R., St. Martin de Porres; St. Augustine, Louisville
Turner, Scott R., St. Thomas; St. Monica, Bardstown
Vessels, Michael J., St. John the Baptist, Rineyville; St. Brigid, Vine Grove
Villalobos, Francisco J., St. Bartholomew, Louisville
Waldon, F. Eugene, Our Lady of Lourdes, Louisville
Wall, Joseph, (Retired)
Walsh, Richard J., St. Joseph, Bardstown
Ward, Ken, St. Martha, Louisville
Whelan, John R., St. Martin of Tours, Flaherty
Wiechert, Joseph C., St. Gregory, Samuels
Wright, Joseph P., Dir., Permanent Diaconate Office, Dir., Permanent Diaconate Office, Holy Family, Louisville; St. Therese, Louisville
Young, R. James, (On Leave)
Zoldak, Richard P., St. Martin of Tours, Louisville

INSTITUTIONS LOCATED IN THE ARCHDIOCESE

[A] COLLEGES AND UNIVERSITIES

LOUISVILLE. *Bellarmine University*, 2001 Newburg Rd., 40205-0671. Tel: 502-272-8000; Fax: 502-272-8033. Web: www.bellarmine.edu. John Stemmer, Librarian. Priests 4; Sisters 1; Students 3,090.
Administration Officers: Most Rev. Joseph E. Kurtz, D.D., Archbishop of Louisville, Chancellor; Revs. Clyde F. Crews; George A. Kilcourse; Isaac McDaniel; Adam Bunnell, O.F.M.Conv.; Dr. Michael Mattei, Dean Continuing & Professional Studies; Dr. Dan Bauer, Dean of the Rubel School of Business; Dr. Susan Davis, Dean of the Lansing School of Nursing; Mr. Glenn Kosse, Vice Pres. Devel. & Alumni Rels.; Dr. Joseph J. McGowan, Pres.; Dr. Cindy Gnadinger, Asst. Vice Pres. Academic Affairs; Dr. Fred W. Rhodes, Vice Pres. Student Affairs; Mr. Tim Sturgeon, Dean of Admissions; Dr. Doris Tegart, Provost; Dr. Melanie Prejean Sullivan, Dir. Campus Ministry; Mr. Sean Ryan, Vice Pres. Enrollment Mgmt.; Mr. Robert L. Zimlich, Vice Pres., Admin. & Finance; Mr. Hunt Helm, Vice Pres. Communications & Public affairs; John Stemmer, Dir., Library.
**Spalding University*, 845 S. 3rd St, 40203. Tel: 502-585-9911; Fax: 502-585-7158. Web: www.spalding.edu. Tori Murden McClure, Pres.; Dr. Randy Strickland, Provost; Dr. Beverly Keepers, Dean College of Education; Dr. John James, Dean College of Social Sciences & Humanities; Dr. Richard Hudson, Dean Student Devel. & Campus Life; Bobbie Rafferty, Senior Dir. Advancement & Philanthropy; Joanne Berryman, Dean College of Health & Natural Sciences; Mark Hohman, CFO; Chris Hart, Dean Enrollment Mgmt.; Rick Barney, Exec. Dir. Mktg. & Public Rels.; Ezra Krumhansl, Exec. Dir. Information Technology; Melissa Lowe, Exec. Dir. Human Resources. Sisters 1; Lay Teachers 92; Students 2,069.

ST. CATHARINE. *St. Catharine College*, 2735 Bardstown Rd., 40061. Tel: 859-336-5082; Fax: 859-336-5031. Email: ckays@sccky.edu. Web: www.sccky.edu. Mr. Bill Huston, Pres.; Dr. Don Giles, Vice Pres. & Academic Dean; Roger L. Marcum, Exec. Vice Pres.; Rev. Benedict J. Brown, Chap.; Ilona Burdette, Librarian. Dominican Sisters of Peace Priests 1; Sisters 10; Lay Teachers 45; Students 1,083.

[B] HIGH SCHOOLS, ARCHDIOCESAN

LOUISVILLE. *St. Francis DeSales High School*, 425 Kenwood Dr., 40214. Tel: 502-368-6519; Fax: 502-366-6172. Web: www.desaleshighschool.com. Mr. Douglas Strothman, Pres.; Mrs. Mary Lee McCoy, Prin. Lay Teachers 30; Students 330.
Holy Cross High School, 5144 Dixie Hwy., 40216. Tel: 502-447-4363; Fax: 502-448-1062. Email: holycross@holycrosshs.com. Web: www.holycrosshs.com. Mr. Tim Weihe, Pres.; Ms. Danielle Wiegandt, Prin. Sisters 1; Lay Teachers 22; Students 250.
Trinity High School, 4011 Shelbyville Rd., 40207. Tel: 502-895-9427; Fax: 502-895-6837. Web: trinityrocks.com; www.thsrock.net. Dr. Robert J. Mullen, Pres.; Mr. Daniel J. Zoeller, Prin.; Rev. David H. Zettel, Chap. (Retired); Ms. Charlotte Miller, Librarian. Priests 1; Sisters 1; Lay Teachers 93; Students 1,310.

BARDSTOWN. *Bethlehem High School* 40004. Tel: 502-348-8594; Fax: 502-349-1247. Email: BHS@bethlehemhigh.org. Web: www.bethlehemhigh.org. Tom Hamilton, Prin.; Mrs. Susan Simpson, Librarian. Sisters of Charity of Nazareth. Sisters 1; Lay Teachers 24; Students 317.

[C] HIGH SCHOOLS, PRIVATE

LOUISVILLE. *Academy of Our Lady of Mercy*, 5801 Fegenbush Ln., 40228. Tel: 502-671-2010; Fax: 502-491-0661. Email: mjohnson@mercyacademy.com. Web: www.mercyacademy.com. Mr. Michael C. Johnson, Pres.; Julie H. Crone, Prin.; Karen Alpiger, Asst. Prin.; Kristina Hortert, Librarian. Sisters of Mercy 2; Lay Teachers 55; Students 612.
Assumption High School, 2170 Tyler Ln., 40205. Tel: 502-458-9551; Fax: 502-454-8411. Web: www.ahsrockets.org. Elaine Salvo, Pres.; Rebecca Henle, Prin.; Erica Lasley, Librarian. Sisters of Mercy. Sisters 1; Lay Teachers 84; Students 866.
Presentation Academy, 861 S. 4th St., 40203. Tel: 502-583-5935; Fax: 502-583-1342. Email: mbruder@presentationacademy.org. Web: www.presentationacademy.org. Sr. Christine Beckett, S.C.N., Pres.; Barbara Wine, Prin.; Terry Roberts, Librarian. Sisters 2; Lay Teachers 33; Students 267.
Sacred Heart Academy, 3175 Lexington Rd., 40206. Tel: 502-897-6097; Fax: 502-893-0120. Email: officesha@sacredheartschools.org. Web: www.sacredheartschools.org/academy. Dr. Beverly McAuliffe, Prin.; Linda Lenahan, Librarian. Ursuline Sisters. Sisters 2; Lay Teachers 76; Students 816.
St. Xavier High School, Xaverian Brothers, 1609 Poplar Level Rd., 40217. Tel: 502-637-4712; Fax: 502-634-2171. Email: psangalli@saintx.com. Web: www.saintx.com. Dr. Perry E. Sangalli, Pres.; Frank Espinosa, Prin.; Mrs. Elaine Steinberg, Librarian. Lay Teachers 122; Students 1,390.

[D] ELEMENTARY SCHOOLS, PRIVATE

LOUISVILLE. **Holy Angels Academy, Inc.*, (Grades K-12), 12201 Old Henry Rd., 40223. Tel: 502-254-9440; Fax: 502-254-9907. Joseph M. Norton, Headmaster and Prin., Grade School; Michael A. Monaghan, Prin., High School; Rev. Robert M. Gregor, C.P.M., Chap. Priests 1; Lay Teachers 12; Students 100.
Sacred Heart Model School, (Grades K-8), 3107 Lexington Rd., 40206. Tel: 502-896-3931; Fax: 502-896-3932. Email: mbowling@sacredheartschools.org. Web: www.sacredheartschools.org. Dr. Mary Beth Bowling, Prin.; Mrs. Carol Kraemer, Librarian. Sisters 1; Lay Teachers 36; Students 360.
Sacred Heart Preschool, 3105 Lexington Rd., 40206. Tel: 502-896-3941; Fax: 502-896-3966. Web: www.sacredheartschools.org. Vicki Furlow, Dir. Lay Teachers 40; Students 256.

[E] REGIONAL SCHOOLS

LOUISVILLE. *St. Andrew Academy*, (Grades PreK-8), 7724 Columbine Dr., 40258. Tel: 502-935-4578; Fax: 502-933-2204. Email: office@standrewacademy.com. Jennifer Barz, Prin.; Cathy Wright, Literacy Coord. Lay Teachers 11; Students 212.
John Paul II Academy, (Grades PreK-8), 3525 Goldsmith Ln., 40220. Tel: 502-452-1712; Fax: 502-451-2462. Lynn Wilt, Prin.; Nancy Heady, Librarian. Lay Teachers 25; Students 277.
St. Nicholas Academy, (Grades K-8), 5501 New Cut Rd., 40214. Tel: 502-368-8506; Fax: 502-380-5453. Email: kdelozier@sna-panthers.org. Web: www.sna-panthers.org. Kathy DeLozier, Prin. Lay Teachers 27; Total Enrollment 416.
Notre Dame Academy, (Grades PreK-8), 1927 Lewiston Dr., 40216. Tel: 502-447-3155; Fax: 502-447-5515. Email: b.scherr@ndasaints.org. Web: ndasaints.org. Bernice Scherr, Prin.; Mrs. Daivie Kay, Librarian. Sisters 1; Lay Teachers 26; Students 447.

PROSPECT. *St. Mary Academy*, (Grades PreK-8), 11311 Saint Mary Ln., 40059. Tel: 502-315-2555; Fax: 502-326-3655. Ms. Julie Tobbe, Prin. Lay Teachers 33; Students 540.

[F] SPECIAL SCHOOLS

LOUISVILLE. *St. Joseph Child Development Center*, 2823 Frankfort Ave., 40206. Tel: 502-893-0241; Fax: 502-896-2394. Web: www.sjkids.org. Leanna Mays, Admin. Students 150; Teachers 32.
**Nativity Academy*, 529 E. Liberty St., 40202. Tel: 502-855-3300; Fax: 502-562-2192. Carol Nord, Exec. Dir.; Meghan Weyland, Prin. (Grades 6-8) Students 54; Staff 17.
Pitt Academy, 6010 Preston Hwy., 40219. Tel: 502-966-6979; Fax: 502-962-8878. Email: sdowney@pitt.com. Web: www.pitt.com. Sherry Downey, Prin. Lay Teachers 12; Students 65.
Sacred Heart School for the Arts, 3105 Lexington Rd., 40206. Tel: 502-897-1816; Fax: 502-896-3927. Email: dthurmond@sacredheartschools.org. Web: www.sacredheartschools.org. David X. Thurmond, Dir. Students 400.

[G] ORPHANAGES AND INFANT HOMES

LOUISVILLE. *St. Joseph Catholic Orphan Society*, 2823 Frankfort Ave., 40206. Tel: 502-893-0241; Fax: 502-896-2394. Web: www.sjkids.org. Paul Hirn, Pres. Bd. of Directors.
St. Thomas Orphan Society, Inc., P.O. Box 1073, 40201.
St. Vincent's Orphan Society, Inc., P.O. Box 1073, 40201.

[H] GENERAL HOSPITALS

LOUISVILLE. *SS. Mary and Elizabeth Hospital*, 1850 Bluegrass Ave., 40215. Tel: 502-361-6000; Fax: 502-361-6799. Web: jhsmh.org. James Parobek, Pres. & CEO. Catholic Health Initiatives. Sisters 4; Bed Capacity 298; Patients Assisted Annually 170,000.

BARDSTOWN. *Flaget Healthcare, Inc. dba Flaget Memorial Hospital* 4305 New Shepherdsville Rd., 40004. Tel: 502-350-5000; Fax: 502-350-5039. Email: info@flaget.com. Web: www.flaget.com. Sue Downs, Pres. Catholic Health Initiatives., Attended from St. Joseph Church. Sisters 2; Bed Capacity 52; Bassinets 8; Patients Assisted Annually 93,350.

[I] SPECIAL HOSPITALS

LOUISVILLE. *Our Lady of Peace*, 2020 Newburg Rd., 40205. Tel: 502-451-3330; Fax: 502-479-4140. Email: rebecca.kistler@jhsmh.org. Web: www.jhsmh.org. Jennifer Nolan, Pres. & CEO. Catholic Health Initiatives., Hospital for Psychiatric Illness. Sisters 1; Bed Capacity 396; Patients Assisted Annually 5,907.

[J] PROTECTIVE INSTITUTIONS

LOUISVILLE. *Boys' Haven*, 2301 Goldsmith Ln., 40218. Tel: 502-458-1171; Fax: 502-451-2161. Email: jhadley@boyshaven.org. Web: www.boyshaven.org. Jeff Hadley, CEO. For dependent, neglected, or abused boys and girls, 12 to 23 years of age. Total Assisted 765.
St. Joseph Children's Home, 2823 Frankfort Ave., 40206. Tel: 502-893-0241; Fax: 502-212-1290. Web: www.sjkids.org. Pamela Cotton, L.C.W., M.S.S.W., Exec. Dir. Children 40.

[K] NURSING HOMES

LOUISVILLE. *St. Joseph Home for the Aged*, 15 Audubon Plaza Dr., 40217. Tel: 502-636-2300; Fax: 502-636-2239. Web: www.littlesistersofthepoor.org. Sr. Isabel Londono-Gomez, Pres.
Home for the Aged of the Little Sisters of the Poor Sisters 10; Bed Capacity 77.
Nazareth Home, Inc., 2000 Newburg Rd., 40205. Tel: 502-459-9681; Fax: 502-456-9077. Email: mhaynes@nazhome.org. Web: nazhome.org. Mary Haynes, CEO & Admin.; Bridget Bunning, Dir. Pastoral Care; Deacon Lawrence Biven, Chap. Sisters of Charity of Nazareth. Staff Sisters 2; Residents 168; Personal Care 33; Total Staff 259.

[L] MONASTERIES AND RESIDENCES OF PRIESTS AND BROTHERS

LOUISVILLE. *Bishop David Apartments*, 5146 Dixie Hwy., 40216. Tel: 502-449-2159. Revs. Albert L. Wilson, Dir. (Retired); John B. Gephart (Retired); Donald P. Ryan (Retired); Gerald L. Timmel (Retired). Priests 4.
St. Francis of Assisi Friary, 2225 Lower Hunters Trace, 40216. Tel: 502-447-5566. Revs. Christian Moore, O.F.M.Conv.; Paul Schloemer, O.F.M.Conv.; Bros. Larry Eberhardt, O.F.M.Conv.; John Mauer, O.F.M.Conv.; Dennis Moses, O.F.M.Conv.
St. Louis Bertrand Priory, 1104 S. Sixth St., 40203. Tel: 502-583-4448; Fax: 502-589-0056. Very Rev. William P. Garrott, O.P., Prior; Revs. George G. Christian, O.P.; William Dominic Fields, O.P.; Elias A. Henritzy, O.P.; James B. Muller, O.P.; Emmanuel Bertrand, O.P. Priests: see St. Louis Bertrand Parish Priests 6.
Sacred Heart Retreat, 1924 Newburg Rd., 40205. Tel: 502-451-2330; Fax: 502-451-0192. Web: www.passionist.org. Rev. John Schork, C.P., Local Supr. (Corporate Title: Congregation of the Passion, Sacred Heart Community) Priests 13; Brothers 2. In Res. Revs. Leon Grantz, C.P.; Philip Schaefer, C.P.; Emmet Linden, C.P.; Joseph Mitchell, C.P.; Albert Schwer, C.P.; Frederick Sucher, C.P.; Bernard Weber, C.P.; David Colhour, C.P.; Robert Weiss, C.P.; Alfred Pooler, C.P.; Louis

Doherty, C.P.; Leonard Kosatka, C.P.; Bros. Jerome Milazzo, C.P.; John Monzyk, C.P.

Villa Pacis, Resurrectionist Retirement Home, 512 Breckenridge Ln., 40207. Tel: 502-424-0068; Fax: 502-895-3431. Email: crvillapacis@aol.com. In Res. Revs. Raymond Hofmann, C.R.; John Lesousky, C.R.; John Miles, C.R.; Charles Schoenbaechler, C.R.

TRAPPIST. *Abbey of Our Lady of Gethsemani, of the Order of Cistercians of the Strict Observance*, 3642 Monks Rd., 40051. Tel: 502-549-3117; Fax: 502-549-8281. Email: getabbot@iglou.com. Rev. Elias Dietz, O.C.S.O.; Rt. Revs. Damien Thompson, O.C.S.O., Abbot (Retired); Timothy Kelly, O.C.S.O., Abbot (Retired); Revs. James Conner, O.C.S.O.; Alan Gilmore, O.C.S.O.; Michael Casagram, O.C.S.O.; Peter Tong, O.C.S.O.; Joachim Johnson, O.C.S.O.; Seamus Malvey, O.C.S.O.; Andrew McAughan, O.C.S.O.; Anton Rusnak, O.C.S.O.; Carlos Rodriguez, O.C.S.O.; Mark Scott, O.C.S.O. Priests 12; Brothers 39.

[M] CONVENTS AND RESIDENCES FOR SISTERS

LOUISVILLE. *Monastery of the Discalced Carmelite Nuns*, 1740 Newburg Rd., 40205. Tel: 502-451-6796; Fax: 502-458-5272. Sr. Katherine, O.C.D., Prioress. Professed Nuns 9; In Formation 2.

Sisters of Mercy St. Catherine Convent, 2169 Tyler Ln., 40205. Tel: 502-451-2245; Fax: 502-452-6988. Sr. Paulanne Diebold, R.S.M., Dir. Sisters in Residence 16.

Ursuline Sisters of the Immaculate Conception, 3105 Lexington Rd., 40206. Tel: 502-897-1811; Fax: 502-896-3913. Email: webmaster@ursulineslou.org. Web: www.ursulineslou.org. Sr. Lynn Jarrell, O.S.U., Pres. Total in Congregation 110.

NAZARETH. *Generalate, Motherhouse and Novitiate of the Sisters of Charity of Nazareth*, P.O. Box 172, 40048. Tel: 502-348-1555 (SCN Center & Generalate); 502-348-1500 (Motherhouse); Fax: 502-348-1502. Email: mmiller@scnky.org. Web: www.scnfamily.org. Rev. Gary Young, C.R., Chap., Motherhouse. Sisters at Motherhouse 97; Sisters at David Hall 15; Sisters at SCN Center 2; Nazareth Villages 3; Nazareth Sadan 2; Guest Houses 3.

NERINX. *Motherhouse and Novitiate of the Sisters of Loretto at the Foot of the Cross*, 515 Nerinx Rd., 40049. Tel: 270-865-5811; Fax: 270-865-2200. Email: maryswain@lorettocommunity.org. Web: www.lorettocommunity.org. Sisters Maria Visse, S.L., Svcs. Coord.; Catherine Mueller, S.L., Pres. Sisters in the Motherhouse 87; Total in Congregation 220.

ST. CATHARINE. *Dominican Sisters of Peace*, 2645 Bardstown Rd., 40061. Tel: 859-336-9303; Fax: 859-336-9306. Email: srpeace@oppeace.org. Web: www.oppeace.org. Sisters Helen O'Sullivan, O.P., Mission Group Coord.; Diane Traffas, O.P., Mission Group Coord. St. Catharine Motherhouse Sisters in Motherhouse 45; Total in Archdiocese 108; Total in Congregation 587.

Sansbury Care Center, Inc., 2625 Bardstown Rd., 40061. Tel: 859-336-3974; Fax: 859-336-0401. Sr. Barbara Ann Fava, O.P., Mission Group Coord.; Darlene Herald, Admin.; Revs. John Christopher Allegra; Francis Ralph, O.P. Sisters in Infirmary 48.

[N] HOMES FOR MEN AND WOMEN

LOUISVILLE. *Sacred Heart Village I, Inc.* (Senior Housing Apartments), 2110 Payne St., 40206. Tel: 502-895-6409; Fax: 502-895-8166. Mary Worley, Resident Mgr.

Sacred Heart Village II, Inc. (Senior Housing Apartments), 2108 Payne St., 40206. Tel: 502-895-8085; Fax: 502-895-8039. Brenda L. Thurston, Mgr.

Sacred Heart Village III, Inc. (Senior Housing Apartments), 3101 Wayside Dr., 40216. Tel: 502-776-5004; Fax: 502-772-7695. Bertha Greenwell, Property Mgr.

Sacred Heart Village, Inc. dba Sacred Heart Village 2120 Payne St., 40206. Tel: 502-895-9425; Fax: 502-357-5549. Kim Thieneman, Exec. Dir.

Mercy Sacred Heart, Inc. Sisters of Mercy., Mercy Franciscan Health and Housing Services. Sisters 2; Residents 152; Capacity 172.

[O] RETREAT HOUSES

LOUISVILLE. *Catholic Charismatic Renewal*, Flaget Center, 1935 Lewiston Dr., 40216. Tel: 502-448-8581; Fax: 502-448-5518. Maureen Larison, Contact Person. Tel: 502-448-8581.

Flaget Center, 1935 Lewiston Dr., 40216. Tel: 502-448-8581; Fax: 502-448-5518. Email: dmc@archlou.org. Donna M. McHugh, Admin.

CRESTWOOD. *Lake St. Joseph Center*, 5800 Old LaGrange Rd., 40014. Tel: 502-241-4469.

NERINX. *Knobs Haven*, 515 Nerinx Rd., 40049. Tel: 270-865-2621. Email: knobshaven@yahoo.com. Jo Ann Gates, Dir.

NEW HAVEN. *Bethany Spring-Merton Institute Retreat Center*, 115 Dee Head Rd., 40051. Tel: 502-583-6117.

[P] MISCELLANEOUS LISTINGS

LOUISVILLE. *Archdiocesan Marian Committee*, 3623 Fern Valley Rd., #227, 40219. Tel: 502-968-2933. Rev. Lawrence H. Lindle, Dir. (Retired).

Catholic Bicentennial Initiative Fund, Inc., 212 E. College St., 40203. Very Rev. J. Mark Spalding, J.C.L., Dir.; Dr. Brian B. Reynolds, Dir.; Robert L. Ash, Dir.

**Catholic Education Foundation*, 325 W. Main St., Ste. 1806, 40202. Tel: 502-585-2747; Fax: 502-583-4929. Rosemary Bisig Smith, Exec. Dir.

**Center for Interfaith Relations*, 415 W. Muhammad Ali Blvd., Ste. 101, 40202-2334. Tel: 502-583-3100; Fax: 502-583-8524. Web: interfaithrelations.org. Vicki Warren, Office Admin.

CHI Kentucky, Inc., 1850 Bluegrass Ave., 40215. Tel: 502-361-6000. Email: peggymartin@catholichealth.net. Sr. Peggy Martin, O.P., Sr. Vice Pres.

**The St. Francis de Sales High School Foundation, Inc.*, 425 Kenwood Dr., 40214. Tel: 502-368-6519. Stephen James, Chair.

The Franciscan Foundation, Inc., 6901 Dixie Hwy., 40258. Tel: 502-935-1223; Fax: 502-933-7747. Email: dismasv@aol.com.

Franciscan Shelter House, 748 S. Preston St., P.O. Box 1673, 40201. Tel: 502-589-0140; Fax: 502-589-1134. Email: fsh748@aol.com. Web: www.franciscanshelterhouse.net. Mrs. Patti L. Thompson, Business Mgr.; Chuck Mattingly, Opers. Mgr.

Mass of the Air, 508 Breckenridge Ln., 40207. Tel: 502-893-5120; Fax: 502-896-8128. Email: frnick@ourlourdes.org. Rev. G. Nicholas Rice, Dir. (Retired).

Our Lady's Rosary Makers, 4611 Poplar Level Rd., P.O. Box 37080, 40233. Tel: 502-968-1434; Fax: 502-969-8883. Web: www.olrm.org. Michael Ford, Gen. Mgr.

St. Patrick School Foundation, Inc., 1000 N. Beckley Station Rd., 40245. Tel: 502-244-7083; Fax: 502-719-0359. Web: stpatrick-lou.org. R. Mark Page, Pres.

Perpetual Eucharistic Adoration, 3623 Fern Valley Rd., #227, 40219. Tel: 502-245-5778; 502-968-2933. Rev. Lawrence H. Lindle, Spiritual Dir. (Retired).

Publication: "The Record", Maloney Center, 1200 S. Shelby St., 40203-2600. Tel: 502-636-0296; Fax: 502-636-2379. Email: record@archlou.org. Official newspaper of the Archdiocese of Louisville (Weekly).

Office: Archdiocesan Communications Center Glenn Rutherford, Editor.

Sacred Heart Schools, Inc., 3177 Lexington Rd., 40206. Tel: 502-896-3910; Fax: 502-895-0989. Email: shs@sacredheartschools.org. Web: www.sacredheartschools.org. Dr. Cynthia Crabtree, Pres. Sponsored by Ursuline Sisters.

**Trinity High School Foundation, Inc.*, 4011 Shelbyville Rd., 40207. Tel: 502-736-2100; Fax: 502-736-2190. Phillip J. Stuecker, Chm.

Ursuline Society and Academy of Education, 3105 Lexington Rd., 40206. Tel: 502-897-1811; Fax: 502-896-3913. Email: webmaster@ursulineslou.org. Web: www.ursulineslou.org.

World Apostolate of Fatima (Blue Army), 3623 Fern Valley Rd., #227, 40219. Tel: 502-968-2933. Rev. Lawrence H. Lindle, Spiritual Dir. (Retired).

Sacred Heart Apostolate, 3623 Fern Valley Rd., #227, 40219. Tel: 502-968-2933. Rev. Lawrence H. Lindle, Dir. (Retired).

BARDSTOWN. *Flaget Hospital Foundation, Inc.*, 4305 New Shepherdsville Rd., 40004. Tel: 502-350-5040; Fax: 502-350-5039. Email: info@flaget.com. Web: flaget.com. Sue Downs, Pres. & CEO.

LEBANON. *The Laura*, 1995 Sam Browning Rd., 40033. Tel: 270-692-1790. Email: mheleneking@windstream.net. Sisters Marilyn King, R.S.M., Dir.; Genevieve Durcan, O.C.S.O., Co-Dir.

LORETTO. *Holy Cross Cemetery Trust, Inc.*, 7945 Loretto Rd., 40037. Tel: 502-348-5404.

NAZARETH. *Office of Congregational Advancement*, P.O. Box 9, 40048. Tel: 502-348-1578; Fax: 502-348-1587. Email: potoole@scnky.org. Web: www.scnfamily.org. Sisters of Charity of Nazareth.

Sisters of Charity of Nazareth, Inc., Crimmins Hall, 135 West Dr., P.O. Box 187, 40048. Tel: 502-331-4072; Fax: 502-331-4076. Email: jraley@scnazareth.org. Sr. Judy Raley, S.C.N., Provincial.

NERINX. *Sisters of Loretto Charitable Trust*, 515 Nerinx Rd., 40049-9999. Tel: 270-865-3414; Fax: 270-865-2200. Email: maryswain@lorettocommunity.org. Web: www.lorettocommunity.org. Sr. Mary Swain, S.L., Treas.

NEW HOPE. *St. Martin De Porres Lay Dominican Community*, P.O. Box 10, 40052. Tel: 270-325-3061; Fax: 270-325-3091. Email: stmdp@newhope-ky.org. Web: www.newhope-ky.org. Mary Frances Musk, T.O.P., Prioress.

[Q] CLOSED PARISHES

LOUISVILLE. *St. Aloysius* For parish records please contact the Chancery office.

St. Andrew For parish records please contact the Chancery office.

St. Ann For parish records please contact the Chancery office.

St. Anthony (1867) For inquiries for parish records contact Good Shepherd, Louisville.

St. Basil For records please contact Mary Queen of Peace parish.

St. Benedict For records please contact Martin de Porres parish.

St. Cecilia (1873) For inquiries for parish records contact Good Shepherd, Louisville.

St. Charles Borromeo For records please contact St. Martin De Porres parish.

St. Clement (1956) For inquiries for parish records please see St. Peter the Apostle, Louisville.

St. Columba For parish records please contact the Chancery office.

St. Denis (1916) For inquiries for parish records please see Mary Queen of Peace, Louisville.

St. George For parish records please contact the Chancery office.

St. Helen (1897) For inquiries for parish records please see Mary Queen of Peace, Louisville.

Holy Cross For records contact St. Martin de Porres parish.

St. Jerome (1953) For inquiries for parish records please see Blessed Teresa of Calcutta, Louisville.

St. John For records contact St. Martin of Tours parish.

St. Leo the Great For parish records please contact the Chancery office.

St. Mary (1968) For inquiries for parish records please see Blessed Teresa of Calcutta, Louisville.

St. Mary Magdalen For parish records please contact the Chancery office.

St. Matthias (1950) For inquiries for parish records please see Mary Queen of Peace, Louisville.

Mother of Good Counsel (1959) For inquiries for parish records please see St. Bernadette, Louisville.

Our Lady (1839) For inquiries for parish records contact Good Shepherd, Louisville.

Our Lady Help of Christians (1957) For inquiries for parish records please see St. Peter the Apostle, Louisville.

Our Lady of Consolation (1959) For inquiries for parish records please see St. Peter the Apostle, Louisville.

St. Peter Claver (2008) For parish records please contact the Chancery office.

St. Philip Neri For records please contact Holy Family parish.

St. Polycarp (1960) For inquiries for parish records please see St. Peter the Apostle, Louisville.

Resurrection D.N.J.C. For records please contact Guardian Angels parish.

St. Timothy (1963) For inquiries for parish records please see St. Peter the Apostle, Louisville.

COLESBURG. *St. Clare* For inquiries for parish records contact St. Benedict, Lebanon Junction.

GOSHEN. *Transfiguration of Our Lord* (1983) For inquiries for parish records please see St. Bernadette, Louisville.

ST. JOSEPH. *St. Joseph* For records contact St. Francis Xavier, Raywick.

RELIGIOUS INSTITUTES OF MEN REPRESENTED IN THE ARCHDIOCESE

For further details refer to the corresponding bracketed number in the Religious Institutes of Men or Women section.

[1350]—*Brothers of St. Francis Xavier* (American Central Prov.)—C.F.X.

[0275]—*Carmelites of Mary Immaculate*—C.M.I.

[0350]—*Cistercians Order of the Strict Observance-Trappists*—O.C.S.O.

[0820]—*Congregation of the Fathers of Mercy*—C.P.M.

[1000]—*Congregation of the Passion* (Holy Cross Prov.)—C.P.

[1080]—*Congregation of the Resurrection* (Rome, Italy)—C.R.

[0480]—*Conventual Franciscans* (Prov. of Our Lady of Consolation)—O.F.M.Conv.

[0430]—*Order of Preachers-Dominicans* (St. Joseph Prov.)—O.P.

RELIGIOUS INSTITUTES OF WOMEN REPRESENTED IN THE ARCHDIOCESE

[0230]—*Benedictine Sisters of Pontifical Jurisdiction*—O.S.B.

[2145]—*Congregation of Augustinian Sisters Servants of Jesus and Mary*—O.S.A.

[3832]—*Congregation of the Sisters of St. Joseph*—C.S.J.

[0420]—*Discalced Carmelite Nuns*—O.C.D.

[1070-13]—*Dominican Sisters*—O.P.

[1115]—*Dominican Sisters of Peace*—O.P.

[2575]—*Institute of the Sisters of Mercy of the Americas*—R.S.M.

[2340]—*Little Sisters of the Poor*—L.S.P.

[2490]—*Medical Mission Sisters*—M.M.S.

[0670]—*Order of Trappistines*—O.C.S.O.

[0440]—*Sisters of Charity of Cincinnati, OH*—S.C.

[0500]—*Sisters of Charity of Nazareth*—S.C.N.

[2360]—*Sisters of Loretto At the Foot of the Cross*—S.L.

[3000]—*Sisters of Notre Dame de Namur*—S.N.D.deN.

[3360]—*Sisters of Providence of Saint Mary-of-the-Woods, IN* (St. Gabriel Prov.)—S.P.

[1630]—*Sisters of St. Francis of Penance and Christian Charity*—O.S.F.

[4120-03]—*Ursuline Nuns, of the Congregation of Paris*—O.S.U.

[4120-05]—*Ursuline Sisters of Mt. St. Joseph*—O.S.U.

ARCHDIOCESAN CEMETERIES

Offices for all cemeteries: 1600 Newburg Rd., Louisville, KY 40205; Mailing Address: P.O. Box 4096, Louisville, KY 40204. Tel: 502-451-7710; Fax: 502-456-9270.

LOUISVILLE

Calvary, 1600 Newburg Rd., 40205.

St. John, 2601 Duncan St., 40212. P.O. Box 4096, 40204.

St. Louis, 1215 Barret Ave., 40204.

St. Michael, 1153 Charles St., 40204.

NECROLOGY

✠ Kelly, Most Rev. Thomas C., Retired Archbishop of Louisville.—Died Dec. 14, 2011

† Dickman, John W., (Retired)—Died May 25, 2011

† Sans, Theodore R., (Retired)—Died April 21, 2011

† Smith, Francis H., (Retired)—Died Jan. 27, 2012

An asterisk (*) denotes an organization that has established tax-exempt status directly with the IRS and is not covered by the USCCB Group Ruling.

Diocese of Lubbock

Most Reverend

PLACIDO RODRIGUEZ, C.M.F.

Bishop of Lubbock; ordained May 23, 1968; consecrated December 13, 1983; installed Auxiliary Bishop of Chicago; appointed Second Bishop of Lubbock April 5, 1994; installed June 1, 1994. *Res.: 3505 37th St., Lubbock, TX 79413. Office: The Catholic Pastoral Center, P.O. Box 98700, Lubbock, TX 79499-8700.* Fax: 806-792-2953. Email: prodriguez@catholiclubbock.org.

CARITAS CHRISTI URGET NOS

The Catholic Pastoral Center: P.O. Box 98700, Lubbock, TX 79499-8700. Tel: 806-792-3943; Fax: 806-792-8109.

Web: www.catholiclubbock.org

Email: lflores@catholiclubbock.org

ESTABLISHED AND CREATED A DIOCESE, JUNE 17, 1983.

Square Miles 23,382.

Comprises the Counties of Bailey, Lamb, Hale, Floyd, Motley, Cottle, Cochran, Hockley, Lubbock, Crosby, Dickens, King, Yoakum, Terry, Lynn, Garza, Kent, Stonewall, Haskell, Gaines, Dawson, Borden, Scurry, Fisher and Jones.

Legal Title: Roman Catholic Diocese of Lubbock.

STATISTICAL OVERVIEW

Personnel	
Bishop	1
Priests: Diocesan Active in Diocese	34
Priests: Diocesan Active Outside Diocese	3
Priests: Retired, Sick or Absent	12
Number of Diocesan Priests	49
Religious Priests in Diocese	9
Total Priests in Diocese	58
Ordinations:	
Diocesan Priests	1
Permanent Deacons in Diocese	52
Total Sisters	24
Parishes	
Parishes	62
With Resident Pastor:	
Resident Diocesan Priests	52
Resident Religious Priests	10
Professional Ministry Personnel:	
Sisters	21
Lay Ministers	24
Welfare	
Catholic Hospitals	2
Total Assisted	297,315
Health Care Centers	20
Total Assisted	58,324
Special Centers for Social Services	1
Total Assisted	30,000
Educational	
Diocesan Students in Other Seminaries	6
Total Seminarians	6
High Schools, Diocesan and Parish	1
Total Students	53
Elementary Schools, Diocesan and Parish	2
Total Students	377
Catechesis/Religious Education:	
High School Students	1,516
Elementary Students	4,935
Total Students under Catholic Instruction	6,887
Teachers in the Diocese:	
Sisters	1
Lay Teachers	53
Vital Statistics	
Receptions into the Church:	
Infant Baptism Totals	1,276
Minor Baptism Totals	235
Adult Baptism Totals	84
Received into Full Communion	142
First Communions	1,356
Confirmations	946
Marriages:	
Catholic	253
Interfaith	38
Total Marriages	291
Deaths	639
Total Catholic Population	80,742
Total Population	494,458

Former Bishops—Most Rev. MICHAEL J. SHEEHAN, S.T.L., J.C.D., ord. July 12, 1964; cons. and installed as the first Bishop of Lubbock, June 17, 1983; appt. Apostolic Administrator of Santa Fe, April 6, 1993; installed as the 11th Archbishop of Santa Fe, Sept. 21, 1993.

The Catholic Pastoral Center—4620 Fourth St., Lubbock, 79416. Mailing Address: P.O. Box 98700, Lubbock, 79499-8700. Tel: 806-792-3943; Fax: 806-792-8109; 806-792-2953 (Bishop's Office). Office Hours: Mon.-Fri. 8-5.

Chancellor—Mr. B. MARTY MARTIN, Catholic Pastoral Center, P.O. Box 98700, Lubbock, 79499-8700. Tel: 806-792-3943, Ext. 212; Fax: 806-792-2953.

Moderator of the Curia—Mr. B. MARTY MARTIN.

Chancellor's Administrative Assistant—BELINDA L. AGUIRRE.

Bishop's Administrative Assistant—JUDY LEOS RODRIGUEZ.

Diocesan Tribunal—Mailing Address: P.O. Box 98700, Lubbock, 79499-8700. Tel: 806-792-3943.

Officialis—Rev. JOSE MATTHEW KOCHUPARAMBIL, O.S.B.

Administrative Assistant—RITA ORTIZ.

Promoter of Justice—VACANT.

Defender of the Bond—Rev. Msgr. EUGENE J. DRISCOLL.

Defender of the Bond-Appeal—Rev. Msgr. EUGENE J. DRISCOLL.

Notaries—RITA ORTIZ; JUDY LEOS RODRIGUEZ; BELINDA L. AGUIRRE.

Presbyteral Council—Most Rev. PLACIDO RODRIGUEZ, C.M.F.; Mr. B. MARTY MARTIN, Chancellor; Rev. Msgr. NICOLAS RENDON; Revs. RAYMUNDO MANRIQUEZ; EMILIANO ZAPATA, O.P.; ARSENIO C. REDULLA; PETER D'SOUZA; JOHN SMITH; MICHAEL MELCHER; Rev. Msgr. EUGENE J. DRISCOLL; Rev. RUDY CRASTA.

Priests Personnel Board—Most Rev. PLACIDO RODRÍGUEZ, C.M.F.; Mr. B. MARTY MARTIN; Revs. ARSENIO C. REDULLA; GERALD LEATHAM; Rev. Msgr. EUGENE J. DRISCOLL; Rev. ANDRES MENDOZA; Deacon JUAN CAVAZOS; Rev. Msgr. JAMES O'CONNOR.

Diocesan Vicars—

Vicar General—Rev. Msgr. EUGENE J. DRISCOLL.

Vicar General Finance—Rev. ARSENIO C. REDULLA.

Vicar of Priests—Rev. GERALD LEATHAM.

Vicar of Retired Priests—Rev. Msgr. JAMES O'CONNOR.

Vicars Forane—Revs. RAYMUNDO MANRIQUEZ, Plainview Deanery; JOSEPH KURUMBEL, O.S.B., Brownfield Deanery; ANDRES MENDOZA, Lubbock Deanery; MICHAEL MELCHER, Snyder Deanery.

Superintendent of Schools—Mrs. CHRISTINE WANJURA, Prin., Christ the King Elementary/Middle School, 4011 54th St., Lubbock, 79413. Mailing Address: P.O. Box 98700, Lubbock, 79499; Sr. ANALYN TINDOG, O.S.F., Prin., St. Joseph Elementary School, 20th & W. Division St., Slaton, 79364.

Director of Youth—Sr. MARTHA JANE VENHAUS.

Campus Ministry, Texas Tech University—GREG RAMZINSKI, 2305 Main St., Lubbock, 79401. Tel: 806-762-5225.

Director of Scouting—Rev. Msgr. NICOLAS RENDON.

Priests' Pension Board—Most Rev. PLACIDO RODRÍGUEZ, C.M.F.; Mr. B. MARTY MARTIN; Revs. JAMES MCCARTNEY; GERARD J. KENNEY; GEORGE RONEY; LEONARDO PAHAMTANG; MICHAEL MELCHER; Rev. Msgr. JAMES O'CONNOR; Mr. ANTON BUXKEMPER; Mr. DON BOOK; Mr. DAN CASTRO; Mr. FRED LARA; Mrs. JUANITA PINEDA; Mr. SONNY GARZA.

Diocesan Building Commission—Rev. Msgr. EUGENE J. DRISCOLL; Mr. B. MARTY MARTIN; Mr. MARC CHAPMAN; Mr. MAX GARZA; Mr. BERNARD GRADEL; Mr. LYLE FETTERLY; Mr. JOSEPH RAPIER; JAMES HARGRAVE; Mr. ROLLO GURSS.

Diocesan Pastoral Liturgy Commission—Most Rev. PLACIDO RODRÍGUEZ, C.M.F.; Revs. ERNESTO LOPEZ; RUDY CRASTA; Mr. B. MARTY MARTIN, Chm.; ALICIA ALVAREZ; Mr. ERNESTO ESPARZA; Deacons JUAN CAVAZOS; JOE MORIN; Mrs. JANIE HERNANDEZ.

Office of Christian Formation—ALICIA ALVAREZ, Mailing Address: P.O. Box 98700, Lubbock, 79499. Tel: 806-792-3943.

Catholic Charities, Diocese of Lubbock, Inc.—BETH ZARATE, Dir., 102 Ave. J, Lubbock, 79401. Tel: 806-765-8475.

Director of Hispanic Affairs—VACANT.

Ecumenical Affairs—VACANT.

Diocesan Council of Catholic Women—Rev. GERARD J. KENNEY, Chap.; ANN MCGINTY.

Director of Vocations—Rev. ERNESTO LOPEZ, Seminarian Formation & Dir. Vocations.

Diocesan Attorney—BRIAN E. MURRAY, 913 Texas Ave., Lubbock, 79401.

Diocesan Health Coordinator—VACANT.

Propagation of the Faith—Mr. B. MARTY MARTIN. Tel: 806-792-3943.

Office of Peace & Justice—VACANT.

Catholic Campaign for Human Development—Deacon DARRIS LINDER, 755 S. 20th St., Slaton, 79364. Tel: 806-828-5662.

Director of the Permanent Diaconate—Deacon JUAN CAVAZOS, Mailing Address: P.O. Box 98700, Lubbock, 79499. Tel: 806-792-3943.

Cursillo Movement—Rev. Msgr. DAVID CRUZ.

Newspaper— "South Plains Catholic" Mr. LUCAS FLORES, Editor, Mailing Address: P.O. Box 98700, Lubbock, 79499. Tel: 806-792-3943.

Director of Communications—Mr. LUCAS FLORES.

Office of Evangelization—VACANT.

Office of Stewardship & Development—Mrs. RENEE UNDERWOOD, M.B.A., Mailing Address: P.O. Box 98700, Lubbock, 79499. Tel: 806-792-3943.

Finance Office—ANNABELLE G. OCANAS, Finance Officer, Mailing Address: P.O. Box 98700,

Lubbock, 79499. Tel: 806-797-3943.

Catholic Renewal Center—JUDY RODRIGUEZ, Mailing Address: P.O. Box 98700, Lubbock, 79499. Tel: 806-792-3943.

Family Life—RICHARD YBARRA; ELAINE YBARRA, Dir., P.O. Box 98700, Lubbock, 79499. Tel: 806-792-3943.

Respect Life Office—LAWRENCE D'SOUZA, Mailing Address: P.O. Box 98700, Lubbock, 79499. Tel: 806-792-3943.

Diocesan Rural Life Office—DOUG HLAVATY, 20407 Hwy. 87, Lubbock, 79423.

Victim Assistance Coordinator—Mrs. CHARLOTTE AMATO, 4011 54th St., Lubbock, 79413. Tel: 806-792-6168. Email: camato@ctkcathedral.org.

CLERGY, PARISHES, MISSIONS AND PAROCHIAL SCHOOLS

CITY OF LUBBOCK

(LUBBOCK COUNTY)

1—CATHEDRAL CHRIST THE KING (1958) Rev. William J. Anton.
Res.: 4011 54th St., 79413-4699. Tel: 806-792-6168; Fax: 806-792-1417.
School—(Grades PreK-12) Tel: 806-795-6477; Fax: 806-795-9715. Mrs. Christine Wanjura, Prin. Lay Teachers 48; Students 320.
Catechesis/Religious Program—Mrs. Charlotte Amato, D.R.E. Students 307.

2—ST. ELIZABETH UNIVERSITY PARISH (1935) Revs. Emiliano Zapata, O.P.; Jorge Rativa, O.P., Chap.; Deacon Richard McCann; Greg Ramzinski, Dir. Campus Min. In Res., Deacon Waldo Martinez.
Res. & Office: 2305 Main St., 79401. Tel: 806-762-5225; Fax: 806-741-1962. Email: stelizabeth@nts-online.net.
Catechesis/Religious Program—Sr. Nancy Palanog, M.S.L.T., D.R.E. Students 270.

3—HOLY SPIRIT (1998) Rev. Msgr. Eugene J. Driscoll; Deacons Rick Vasquez; Ralph Rosiles; Nick Trey Davis, Music Min.; Gloria Decker, Sec.
Mailing Address: 9821 Frankford Ave., 79424. Tel: 806-698-6400; Fax: 806-798-0646. Email: parish@holyspiritlubbock.org. Web: www.holyspiritcathparish.org.
Res.: 9819 Frankford Ave., 79424. Tel: 806-698-6400; Fax: 806-798-0646.
Catechesis/Religious Program—Sr. Rosalinda Erispe, M.S.L.T., D.R.E.; Jessica Kelly, C.R.E.; Sr. Maria Carmela Macabanti, M.S.L.T., Youth Min. & Confirmation; Sam Sparkman, Youth Min.; Tami Sparkman, Youth Min.; Tino Gamueda III, Youth Min.; Katie Gamueda, Youth Min.; Tiffany See, Youth Min. Students 600.

4—ST. JOHN NEUMANN (1979) Rev. Gerard J. Kenney; Deacons Richard Wood; Kyle Broderson; Clarke Cochran.
Res.: 5802 22nd, 79407-1721. Tel: 806-799-2649; Fax: 806-799-0037.
Catechesis/Religious Program—Sr. Mary Ann Mishurda, RCIA Dir.; Ellie Contreras, D.R.E. Students 349.

5—ST. JOSEPH'S (1924), (Hispanic), Rev. Martin Pina; Deacons Benny Brito; Joe Martinez.
Res.: 102 N. Ave. P, 79401-1199. Tel: 806-765-9935; Fax: 806-740-0032.
Catechesis/Religious Program—Tel: 806-763-9695. Yolanda Gutierrez, D.R.E. Students 550.

6—OUR LADY OF GRACE (1960), (Hispanic), Rev. Msgr. David Cruz; Rev. Anthony Phelps; Deacons Ernest Hernandez, (Retired); Erasmo Rodriguez, (Retired); Joe Morin; Sylvia Rubio, Business Mgr.
Res.: 3111 Erskine St., 79415-1623. Tel: 806-763-4156; Fax: 806-763-2521.
Catechesis/Religious Program—Tel: 806-763-8727. Soyla Castillo, D.R.E.; Janie D. Lopez, C.R.E. (Elem. School); Maria Trevino Kopel, C.R.E. (Middle School). Students 311.

7—OUR LADY OF GUADALUPE (1980), (Hispanic), [CEM] Rev. Andres Mendoza.
Res.: 1120 52nd St., P.O. Box 3947, 79412. Tel: 806-763-0710; Fax: 806-741-1915.
Catechesis/Religious Program—Tel: 806-763-0732. Tina Narvaiz, D.R.E.; Sr. Mary Jane Alaniz, O.S.F., D.R.E. Students 742.

8—ST. PATRICK (1960) Rev. Msgr. James O'Connor.
Res.: 1603 Cherry Ave., 79403-6001. Tel: 806-765-5123; Fax: 806-765-5123. Email: saintpatrickchurch@yahoo.com.
Catechesis/Religious Program—Tel: 806-765-6979. Cleta Arrellano, D.R.E. Students 135.
Mission—Our Lady Queen of Apostles Main St. N., New Deal, Lubbock Co. 79403. Tel: 806-765-5123.
Catechesis/Religious Program—Students 35.

9—ST. THERESA'S (1961), (Hispanic), Rev. Dennis Prisco.
Res.: 2202 Upland Ave., 79407. Tel: 806-795-2249; Fax: 806-793-4456. Email: agomezstt@gmail.com.
Catechesis/Religious Program—Nancy Sanchez, D.R.E. Students 71.

OUTSIDE THE CITY OF LUBBOCK

ABERNATHY, HALE CO., ST. ISIDORE Rev. Jacob P. Puthuparambil, O.S.B. (India).
Mailing Address: P.O. Box 330, Petersburg, 79250-0330. Tel: 806-667-0063.
Res.: R.R. 2, Box 159A, 79311-6921. Tel: 806-298-4278.
Catechesis/Religious Program—Matthew Dole, D.R.E.; Gloria Garibaly, D.R.E. Students 100.
Mission—Sacred Heart Petersburg.
Catechesis/Religious Program—Santi Garza, D.R.E. Students 40.

ANSON, JONES CO., ST. MICHAEL (1960), (Hispanic), [JC] Rev. Michael Melcher.
Res.: 2010 County Rd. 477, 79501. Tel: 325-823-2777. Email: mike00777@juno.com.
Catechesis/Religious Program—Lisa Ramos, D.R.E.; Eloise Quintanilla, D.R.E. Students 110.
Mission—Holy Trinity (1926) Hwy. 83, Hamlin, Jones Co. 79520. Students 28.

BROWNFIELD, TERRY CO., ST. ANTHONY'S (1952), (Hispanic), Rev. Gerald Leatham; Deacon George Holguin.
Mailing Address: P.O. Box 671, 79316.
Res.: 1902 Levelland Hwy., 79316. Tel: 806-637-6626; 806-637-2344 (Office).
Catechesis/Religious Program—Fax: 806-637-2356. Chris Martinez, D.R.E.; Elsa Martinez, D.R.E. Students 200.
Mission—San Francisco de Asis P.O. Box 92, Ropesville, Hockley Co. 79358.
Catechesis/Religious Program—Anna Ricker, D.R.E. Students 8.

DENVER CITY, YOAKUM CO., ST. WILLIAM (1955) Rev. Joseph Thanavelil, O.S.B. (India).
Res.: 401 Mustang Ave., 79323-2749. Tel: 806-592-2063; Fax: 806-592-2239.
Catechesis/Religious Program— Mr. Angel Hernandez, D.R.E. Students 376.
Mission—Sacred Heart 1305 11th St., Plains, Yoakum Co. 79355. Tel: 806-456-7002.

FLOYDADA, FLOYD CO., ST. MARY MAGDALEN (1928) [JC] Rev. Angelo R. Consemino.
Mailing Address: 309 S. Wall, 79235.
Res.: 809 W. Ross, 79235. Tel: 806-983-5878. Email: stmarymagdalen@att.net.
Catechesis/Religious Program—Lupe De la Fuente, D.R.E. Students 42.
Mission—Our Lady of Guadalupe 701 Bundy St., Matador, Motley Co. 79244.
Mission—St. Elizabeth Second St. & Clare St., Paducah, Cottle Co. 79348. Tel: 806-492-3053.

IDALOU, LUBBOCK CO., ST. PHILIP BENIZI (1979), (Spanish), Rev. Jose Kochuparambil; Deacons Urbano Rodriguez; Jose Rubio.
Res.: 722 Sixth Pl., Box 1337, 79329-1337. Tel: 806-892-2743; 806-892-2928 (Office); Fax: 806-892-9001.
Catechesis/Religious Program—Terri Espinoza, D.R.E. Students 121.
Mission—San Lorenzo Jackson & Monroe, P.O. Box 129, Lorenzo, Crosby Co. 79343.

LAMESA, DAWSON CO., ST. MARGARET MARY (1929) [CEM] Rev. Joseph Kurumbel, O.S.B.; Deacon Daniel Valenzuela; Elva Gutierrez, Parish Sec. In Res., Rev. Joseph Kurumbel, O.S.B.
Res.: 911 S. 2nd St., P.O. Box 599, 79331. Tel: 806-872-7100; Fax: 806-872-3630. Email: stmargaretmary@valornet.com.
Catechesis/Religious Program—Ms. Adriana Sauseda, D.R.E.; Berlinda Ochoa, D.R.E. Students 251.
Mission—Our Lady of Guadalupe 407 N. Hartford, P.O. Box 599, Dawson Co. 79331. Fax: 806-872-7100.

LEVELLAND, HOCKLEY CO., ST. MICHAEL'S (1956) Rev. Rudy Crasta; Deacons Juan Cavazos; Leo Cottenoir.
Res.: 316 E. Washington St., 79336-2611. Tel: 806-894-2268; Fax: 806-894-9348.
Catechesis/Religious Program—Tel: 806-894-9880. Elsa Ramirez, D.R.E.; Sadie McNutt, Dir. Youth Min. Students 464.
Mission—San Isidro 1306 S. Slaughter, P.O. Box 764, Sundown, Hockley Co. 79372-0764.

LITTLEFIELD, LAMB CO., SACRED HEART (1921) [CEM] Rev. James McCartney.
Res.: Eighth & Sunset, P.O. Box 1347, 79339-4234. Tel: 806-385-6043.
Catechesis/Religious Program—Susan Craig, D.R.E. Students 400.

MORTON, COCHRAN CO., ST. ANN (1955) Rev. Heriberto Mercado.
Res.: 105 N.E. Eighth St., 79346-2719. Tel: 806-266-8693; Fax: 806-266-8692.
Catechesis/Religious Program—Alma Ornelas, D.R.E. Students 83.
Mission—St. Philip Neri [CEM] Farm Rd. 303, P.O. Box 395, Pep, Hockley Co. 79353. Tel: 806-933-4355.

MULESHOE, BAILEY CO., IMMACULATE CONCEPTION (1956), (Hispanic), [CEM 2] [JC] Rev. Leonardo Pahamtang (Philippines).
Res.: R.R. 3, Box 247, 79347-2460. Tel: 806-272-4384; 806-272-4389 (Rectory); Fax: 806-272-4384. Email: icchurch@fivearea.com.
Catechesis/Religious Program—Tel: 806-272-4167. Alma Orozco, D.R.E. Students 260.
Mission—St. Mary Magdalen
Catechesis/Religious Program—Patsy Garcia, D.R.E. Students 55.

O'DONNELL, LYNN CO., ST. PIUS X (1959), (Hispanic), [CEM] Rev. Eduardo C. Teo.
Res.: Rte. 1, Box 41-A, 79351. Tel: 806-428-3490; Fax: 806-428-3490.
Catechesis/Religious Program—Students 48.
Mission—St. Jude Thaddeus Catholic Church (1951) P.O. Box 785, Tahoka, Lynn Co. 79373. Tel: 806-561-4420.
Catechesis/Religious Program—Students 96.

OLTON, LAMB CO., ST. PETER THE APOSTLE (1944) Rev. John K. Smith.
Mailing Address: P.O. Box 655, 79064. Fax: 806-285-2140.
Catechesis/Religious Program—Students 119.
Mission—St. Theresa P.O. Box 528, Hale Center, 79041. Tel: 806-839-2892; Fax: 806-839-9938.

PLAINVIEW, HALE CO.

1—ST. ALICE (1911) Rev. Patrick Maher.
Mailing Address: 1114 Houston St., 79072-7124.
Res.: 810 W. 11th St., 79072-7124. Tel: 806-293-1903.
Catechesis/Religious Program—Tel: 806-293-2891. Joann Gamez, D.R.E. Students 103.
Mission—San Jose 303 S.E. Fourth, Lockney, Floyd Co. 79241. Tel: 806-652-2321 (Parish Hall).

2—OUR LADY OF GUADALUPE (1946) [CEM] Rev. Raymundo Manriquez.
Mailing Address: P.O. Box 1269, 79072. Tel: 806-291-0195.
Church: 211 W. Seventh St., 79072. Tel: 806-293-0085; Fax: 806-293-4507.
Catechesis/Religious Program—Tel: 806-293-0086. Jonathan Yanez, D.R.E. (Elem.); Belinda Hinojosa, D.R.E. (H.S.). Students 600.

3—SACRED HEART (1964), (Hispanic), Rev. Arsenio C. Redulla.
Res. & Mailing Address: 400 W. 29th St., 79072-2399. Tel: 806-296-2753; Fax: 806-296-6553.
Catechesis/Religious Program—Tel: 806-296-6553. Students 250.

POST, GARZA CO., HOLY CROSS (1955) [JC] Rev. Hugh Thekkel, O.S.B.
Res.: Box 190, 79356-0190. Tel: 806-495-2791.
Catechesis/Religious Program—Susan Collaso, D.R.E. Students 50.
Mission—Blessed Sacrament P.O. Box 119, Wilson, Lynn Co. 79381-0119. Rev. Hugh Thekkel, O.S.B.

RALLS, CROSBY CO., ST. MICHAEL (1959), (Hispanic), [JC] Rev. Samuel B. Oracion.
Mailing Address: P.O. Box 906, 79357-0906. Tel: 806-253-2008.
Catechesis/Religious Program—Students 93.
Mission—St. Joseph P.O. Box 906, Crosby Co. 79357. Tel: 806-253-2008.

ROTAN, FISHER CO., ST. JOSEPH (1929) Rev. Teresito P. Paqueo, M.S.C.
Res.: 303 E. Lee, 79546-3011. Tel: 325-735-3285; 325-735-2935 (Office); Fax: 325-735-2181.
Catechesis/Religious Program— Rosemary Carrillo, D.R.E. Students 33.
Mission—Sacred Heart [CEM] Ranchito, Fisher Co.
Mission—St. Mary Aspermont, Stonewall Co.

SEMINOLE, GAINES CO., ST. JAMES (1958) Rev. Hugh Thekkel, O.S.B.
Res.: P.O. Box 898, 79360-0898. Tel: 432-758-2371; Fax: 432-758-2766. Email: stjamescatholic@sbcglobal.net.
Catechesis/Religious Program—Veronica Rubio, D.R.E.; Wendy Martinez, D.R.E. Students 705.
Mission—St. Paul's P.O. Box 1321, Seagraves, Gaines Co. 79359-1321. Tel: 806-546-2950.

SHALLOWATER, LUBBOCK CO., ST. PHILIP BENIZI (1967), (Hispanic), [JC] Rev. George Poonely, O.S.B. (India); Deacons Frank Lopez; Tommy Alvarado; Richard Flores.
Res.: 1314 6th St., 79363-0039. Tel: 806-832-5915 (Rectory).
Catechesis/Religious Program—Carmen Behrens, C.R.E.; Natalia Flores, C.R.E. Students 107.
Mission—St. Anthony of Padua (1966) 4th S. Lawrence, Box 545, Anton, Hockley, Co. 79313. Tel: 806-997-2188.

SLATON, LUBBOCK CO.

1—ST. JOSEPH'S (1912), (German), [JC] Rev. Msgr. Nicolas Rendon (Philippines); Deacons Leroy Behnke, Pastoral Assoc.; Darris D. Linder, Pastoral Assoc.
Res.: 205 S. 19th, 79364-3755. Tel: 806-828-3944; Fax: 806-828-3944.
School—(Grades PreK-8), 1305 W. Division St., 79364. Tel: 806-828-6761; Fax: 806-828-5396. Sr. Analyn Tindog, O.S.F., Prin. Sisters 1; Lay Teachers 5; Students 45.
Catechesis/Religious Program—Students 52.

2—OUR LADY OF GUADALUPE (1952) [JC] Rev. Chacko Thadathil, O.S.B.; Deacon Phillip Maldonado; Eva Diaz, Parish Sec.
Res.: 705 S. Fourth, 79363-5406. Tel: 806-828-5108 (Office).
Catechesis/Religious Program—Tel: 806-828-4573. David Ariaz, Youth Min. (H.S.). Students 80.

SNYDER, SCURRY CO.

1—ST. ELIZABETH'S (1952) [CEM] Rev. John Cherolikal.
Res.: 3005 Ave. A, 79549-3909. Tel: 325-573-2590.
Email: snyderstelizabeth@gmail.com.
Catechesis/Religious Program—Tel: 325-573-0999. Students 61.
Mission—St. John

2—OUR LADY OF GUADALUPE (1955), (Hispanic), [CEM] [JC 2] Rev. Roy Jose Badilles.
Res.: 1311 Ave. K, 79549-9533. Tel: 325-573-3866 (Office); 325-573-1569 (Res.); Fax: 325-573-7142.
Email: ologsny@sbcglobal.net.
Catechesis/Religious Program—Tel: 915-573-7142; Fax: 915-573-7142. Irma Guerero, D.R.E.; Melinda Dominguez, Asst. D.R.E. Students 265.

SPUR, DICKENS CO., ST. MARY (1948) Rev. Joseph Chorikavunkal (India); Deacon Pete Garcia.
Res.: Box 189, 79370-0189. Tel: 806-440-0568; Fax: 806-271-4385.
Catechesis/Religious Program—Students 43.
Mission—Epiphany [JC] Jayton, Kent Co.

STAMFORD, JONES CO., ST. ANN (1955) [CEM] Rev. George Roney.
Res.: 104 New Braunfels, 79553-6415. Tel: 325-773-2659.
Catechesis/Religious Program—Students 79.
Mission—St. George 901 N. 16th St., Haskell, Haskell Co. 79521-3340. Tel: 940-864-3171.
Catechesis/Religious Program—Students 35.

WOLFFORTH, LUBBOCK CO., ST. FRANCIS OF ASSISI MISSION, See separate listing. See San Ramon, Woodrow for details. Rev. Rene Perez.

WOODROW, LUBBOCK CO., SAN RAMON (1974) Rev. Rene Perez.
Church: 15706 Loop 493, 79423. Tel: 806-863-2201; Fax: 806-863-3435.
Catechesis/Religious Program—Tel: 806-863-3435. Students 150.
Mission—St. Francis of Assisi P.O. Box 785, Wolfforth, Lubbock Co. 79382. Tel: 806-866-9007.

Retired:

Very Rev. Msgr.—
Kasteel, Ben, V.G.

Rev. Msgrs.—
Buxkemper, Roland
Comiskey, James
Halfmann, Curtis T., P.O. Box 94722, 79493.
James, Joseph W., Our Lady of Mercy Retreat Center, P.O. Box 744, Slaton, 79364.

Revs.—
Diebel, Thomas, Box 10753, 79408.
Hayden, Johnrose, 428 E. Loyola Dr., Tempe, AZ 85282.
Hemp, Lawrence, 705 S. 4th St., Slaton, 79364.
Judd, Timothy, Sacred Heart Mission, P.O. Box 530, Petersburg, 79250-0530.
O'Dwyer, Michael, S.A.C., Ireland.
Ramirez, Cornelio C., S.A.C., 8415 Fremont Ave., 79423.
Vazneparambil, Thomas, Desam P.O., Aluva-Kerala 683103, India.

Permanent Deacons:
Aguilar, Francisco, St. Jude, Tahoka
Almager, Ramon, St. James, Seminole
Alvarado, Tommy, St. Anthony, Anton
Behnke, Leroy, St. Joseph, Slaton
Brito, Benny, St. Joseph, Lubbock
Broderson, Kyle, St. John Neumann, Lubbock
Bustamante, Juan, St. Ann, Stamford
Canale, Randy, Christ the King, Lubbock
Cavazos, Juan, St. Michael, Levelland
Cochran, Clarke E., St. John Neumann, Lubbock
Cottenoir, Leo, St. Michael, Levelland
Duenes, Jerry, On duty outside the Diocese
Esquivel, Jessie, On duty outside the Diocese
Estrada, Julian, St. George, Haskell
Flores, Richard, St. Anthony, Anton
Garcia, Aureliano, St. Michael, Ralls
Garcia, Doroteo, Sacred Heart, Littlefield
Gracia, Pedro, (Retired), St. Mary, Spur
Hernandez, Ernesto, Our Lady of Grace, Lubbock
Holguin, George, St. Anthony, Brownfield
Juarez, Pedro, On duty outside the Diocese
Key, Billy, On Duty Outside the Diocese
Linder, Darris D., St. Joseph's, Slaton
Lopez, Frank, St. Phillip, Shallowater
Maldonado, Phillip, Our Lady of Guadalupe, Slaton
Martinez, Joe, St. Joseph, Lubbock
Martinez, Waldo, St. Elizabeth, Lubbock
McCann, Richard, St. Elizabeth, Lubbock
McDonald, Isaac, Our Lady of Guadalupe, Lubbock
Morales, Eddie, Church of the Epiphany, Jayton
Morin, Joe, Our Lady of Grace, Lubbock
Ortegon, Frank, (Retired), Our Lady of Guadalupe, Snyder
Ramirez, Robert, Our Lady of Guadalupe, Snyder
Rendon, Dario, (Retired), St. Patrick's, Lubbock
Resendez, Simon, St. Pius X, O'Donnell
Revilla, Nash, (Retired), St. Philip Benizi, Shallowater
Rodriguez, Jose Luis, St. Theresa, Lubbock
Rodriguez, Ramiro, St. Patrick's, Lubbock
Rodriguez, Simon, (Retired)
Rosiles, Ralph, Holy Spirit, Lubbock
Rubalcado, Nasario, St. Joseph, Ralls
Rubio, Jose, St. Phillip Benizi, Idalou
Saldana, Isidoro, St. Francis, Lubbock
Thompson, Richard, Sacred Heart, Littlefield
Tjia, Steve, Christ the King, Lubbock
Valenzuela, Daniel, St. Margaret Mary, Lamesa
Vasquez, Enrique, St. Mary Magdalen, Floydada
Wood, Richard, St. John Neumann, Lubbock

INSTITUTIONS LOCATED IN THE DIOCESE

[A] CATHOLIC RENEWAL CENTERS

LUBBOCK. *Catholic Renewal Center*, P.O. Box 98700, 79499-8700. Tel: 806-792-3943, Ext. 214; Fax: 806-687-8668. Web: www.dioceseoflubbock.org. Mr. B. Marty Martin, Center Dir. Total Staff 4.

Office for Cursillo Movement, P.O. Box 98303, 79499-8296. Tel: 806-792-4308. Rev. Msgr. David Cruz, Spiritual Dir.

[B] RETREAT HOUSES

SLATON. *Our Lady of Mercy Retreat Center*, 605 S. 19th St., P.O. Box 744, 79364-0744. Tel: 806-828-6428; Fax: 806-828-3856. Email: mercy@door.net. Web: www.catholiclubbock.org/mercycenter. Rev. Msgr. Joseph W. James, Dir. Emeritus (Retired); Deacon Darris D. Linder, Exec. Dir. Total in Residence 1; Total Staff 8.

[C] CONVENTS AND RESIDENCES FOR SISTERS

LUBBOCK. *Our Lady of Grace Convent*, 3101 Erskine, 79415. Tel: 806-747-7472. Missionary Catechists of the Sacred Hearts of Jesus and Mary 3.

PLAINVIEW. *St. Alice Convent*, 1114 Houston, 79072. Tel: 806-296-5426. St. Francis Mission Community 3.

WOLFFORTH. *St. Francis Mission Community* (1981) Our Lady of the Angels Motherhouse, 8202 CR 7700, 79382. Tel: 806-863-4904; Fax: 806-863-4906. Email: franciscan@erfwireless.net. St. Francis Mission Community 17.

[D] MISCELLANEOUS LISTINGS

LUBBOCK. *Catholic Foundation of the Diocese of Lubbock, Inc.*, P.O. Box 98700, 79499-8700. Tel: 806-792-3943, Ext. 206; Fax: 806-771-7660. Email: foundation@catholiclubbock.org. Web: www.catholicfoundation.org. Mrs. Renee Underwood, M.B.A., Dir.

Christ the King Cathedral School Foundation, 4011 54th St., 79413. Tel: 806-795-8283; Fax: 806-795-9715. Email: cduran@ctkcathedral.org. Web: www.CTKCathederalschool.org. Rev. William J. Anton. Total Staff 50.

RELIGIOUS INSTITUTES OF WOMEN REPRESENTED IN THE DIOCESE

For further details refer to the corresponding bracketed number in the Religious Institutes of Men or Women section.

[]—*Adorers of the Blood of Christ*—A.S.C.

[2700]—*Missionary Cathechists of the Sacred Hearts of Jesus and Mary*—M.C.S.S.C.C.J.M.

[]—*Missionary Sisters of the Lord's Table*—M.S.L.T.

[]—*Sisters of Charity of the Incarnate Word*—C.C.V.I.

[2575]—*Sisters of Mercy of the Americas*—R.S.M.

[1620]—*Sisters of Saint Francis the Neumann Communities*—O.S.F.

[]—*St. Francis Mission Community* (Wolfforth, TX)—O.S.F.

NECROLOGY

† Gonzalez, Rev. Msgr. Antonio, (Retired)—Died Dec. 9, 2011

An asterisk (*) denotes an organization that has established tax-exempt status directly with the IRS and is not covered by the USCCB Group Ruling.

Diocese of Madison

(Dioecesis Madisonensis)

Most Reverend

ROBERT C. MORLINO, D.D., S.T.D.

Bishop of Madison; ordained June 1, 1974; appointed Bishop of Helena July 6, 1999; consecrated and installed September 21, 1999; appointed Bishop of Madison May 23, 2003; installed August 1, 2003. *Chancery: Bishop O'Connor Catholic Pastoral Center, 702 S. High Point Rd., P.O. Box 44983, Madison, WI 53744-4983.*

Chancery: Bishop O'Connor Catholic Pastoral Center, 702 S. High Point Rd., P.O. Box 44983, Madison, WI 53744-4983. Tel: 608-821-3000; Fax: 608-821-3013.

Web: www.madisondiocese.org

Email: diocese@madisondiocese.org

ESTABLISHED 1946.

Square Miles 8,070.

Corporate Title: "Roman Catholic Diocese of Madison."

Comprises the Counties of Columbia, Dane, Grant, Green, Green Lake, Iowa, Jefferson, Lafayette, Marquette, Rock and Sauk in the State of Wisconsin.

For legal titles of parishes and diocesan institutions, consult the Chancery.

STATISTICAL OVERVIEW

Personnel	
Bishop	1
Retired Abbots	1
Priests: Diocesan Active in Diocese	80
Priests: Diocesan Active Outside Diocese	3
Priests: Retired, Sick or Absent	50
Number of Diocesan Priests	133
Religious Priests in Diocese	21
Total Priests in Diocese	154
Extern Priests in Diocese	13
Ordinations:	
Diocesan Priests	2
Transitional Deacons	2
Permanent Deacons in Diocese	20
Total Brothers	8
Total Sisters	399
Parishes	
Parishes	120
With Resident Pastor:	
Resident Diocesan Priests	74
Resident Religious Priests	1
Without Resident Pastor:	
Administered by Priests	45
Pastoral Centers	1
New Parishes Created	4
Closed Parishes	11
Professional Ministry Personnel:	
Brothers	1
Sisters	28
Lay Ministers	616
Welfare	
Catholic Hospitals	3
Total Assisted	488,203
Health Care Centers	2
Total Assisted	145,038
Homes for the Aged	6
Total Assisted	773
Day Care Centers	22
Total Assisted	1,104
Special Centers for Social Services	25
Total Assisted	53,051
Residential Care of Disabled	1
Total Assisted	291
Educational	
Diocesan Students in Other Seminaries	26
Total Seminarians	26
Colleges and Universities	1
Total Students	2,650
High Schools, Private	3
Total Students	685
Elementary Schools, Diocesan and Parish	42
Total Students	6,766
Elementary Schools, Private	3
Total Students	461
Catechesis/Religious Education:	
High School Students	6,168
Elementary Students	12,352
Total Students under Catholic Instruction	29,108
Teachers in the Diocese:	
Brothers	1
Sisters	29
Lay Teachers	699
Vital Statistics	
Receptions into the Church:	
Infant Baptism Totals	2,600
Minor Baptism Totals	107
Adult Baptism Totals	112
Received into Full Communion	200
First Communions	2,598
Confirmations	2,081
Marriages:	
Catholic	436
Interfaith	270
Total Marriages	706
Deaths	1,723
Total Catholic Population	281,438
Total Population	1,015,451

Former Bishops—Most Revs. WILLIAM P. O'CONNOR, D.D., Ph.D., ord. March 10, 1912; appt. Bishop of Superior, Dec. 31, 1941; cons. March 7, 1942; transferred to as first Bishop of Madison, Feb. 22, 1946; resigned Feb. 22, 1967; died July 13, 1973; CLETUS F. O'DONNELL, D.D., J.C.D., ord. May 3, 1941; appt. Titular Bishop of Abrittum and Auxiliary of Chicago, Oct. 26, 1960; cons. Dec. 21, 1960; promoted to Bishop of Madison, Feb. 22, 1967; resigned April 18, 1992; died Aug. 31, 1992; WILLIAM H. BULLOCK, D.D., E.D.S. (Retired), ord. June 7, 1952; appt. Auxiliary Bishop of St. Paul and Minneapolis and Titular Bishop of Natchez June 3, 1980; cons. Aug. 12, 1980; appt. Bishop of Des Moines Feb. 10, 1987; installed April 2, 1987; appt. Bishop of Madison April 13, 1993; installed June 14, 1993; retired May 23, 2003; died April 3, 2011.

Vicar General—Rev. Msgr. JAMES R. BARTYLLA.

Chancery—Bishop O'Connor Catholic Pastoral Center, 702 S. High Point Rd., P.O. Box 44983, Madison, 53744-4983. Office Hours: Mon.-Fri. 8-4:30.

Chancellor—KEVIN R. PHELAN. Tel: 608-821-3162.

Director of Finance—Mr. JOHN C. PHILIPP. Tel: 608-821-3021.

Diocesan Tribunal—Bishop O'Connor Catholic Pastoral Center, 702 S. High Point Rd., P.O. Box 44983, Madison, 53744-4983. Tel: 608-821-3060; Fax: 608-821-3067. Email: tribunal@straphael.org.

Judicial Vicar—Rev. Msgr. MICHAEL E. HIPPEE, J.C.L.

Director of the Tribunal—VACANT.

Judges—Rev. JAMES W. HINNEN, J.C.L.; Rev. Msgr. MICHAEL E. HIPPEE, J.C.L.; Mrs. MARIA YOUNG, J.U.D.

Promoter of Justice—TIM CAVANAUGH, J.C.L.

Defender of the Bond—TIM CAVANAUGH, J.C.L.

Advocate/Procurator (cc.1481-1490)—Revs. BRIAN J. WILK; ERIC G. STERNBERG; TAIT C. SCHROEDER; MICHAEL R. RADOWICZ.

Notaries—SUSAN STACK; BECCA FISCHER; WILLIAM YALLALY.

Diocesan Consultors—Rev. Msgrs. JAMES R. BARTYLLA; MICHAEL L. BURKE, Sec.; DANIEL T. GANSHERT; KEVIN D. HOLMES; Revs. JOHN MEINHOLZ; PAUL U. ARINZE; RICHARD M. HEILMAN; ERIC G. STERNBERG; BART D. TIMMERMAN.

Presbyteral Council—Most Rev. ROBERT CHARLES MORLINO, Pres.; Rev. Msgr. JAMES R. BARTYLLA, Vicar Gen. & Ex Officio. Elected: Revs. DAVID W. TIMMERMAN; RANDY J. TIMMERMAN; STEVEN J. KORTENDICK; GARY L. KRAHENBUHL; JOHN H. HEDRICK; KENT A. SCHMITT; MICHAEL A. RESOP; JAMES M. POSTER; BRIAN J. WILK; STEPHEN J. UMHOEFER; Rev. Msgr. TERRENCE L. CONNORS; Rev. THOMAS E. GILLESPIE. Appointed: Rev. PAUL U. ARINZE; Rev. Msgr. MICHAEL L. BURKE; Rev. RICHARD M. HEILMAN; Rev. Msgrs. MICHAEL E. HIPPEE, J.C.L.; KEVIN D. HOLMES; DANIEL T. GANSHERT; Revs. JARED M. HOOD, S.J.S.; ERIC G. STERNBERG; Rev. Msgr. DELBERT L. SCHMELZER (Retired); Rev. BART D. TIMMERMAN.

Personnel Board—Revs. LAWRENCE M. BAKKE; KENNETH J. FRISCH; THOMAS L. KELLEY; Rev. Msgrs. MICHAEL L. BURKE; TERRENCE L. CONNORS; Rev. BART D. TIMMERMAN; Rev. Msgr. JAMES R. BARTYLLA, Chm.

Vicar for Permanent Deacons—Rev. PATRICK J. WENDLER, Mailing Address: Diocese of Madison, P.O. Box 44983, Madison, 53744-4983.

Vicar for Priests—Rev. Msgr. JAMES L. GUNN, Mailing Address: Diocese of Madison, P.O. Box 44983, Madison, 53744-4983.

Vicar for Religious—VACANT.

Deaneries—Revs. RAYMOND J. DISCHLER, Columbia Deanery; MICHAEL C. RICHEL, East Dane Deanery; VACANT, Grant Deanery; VACANT, Iowa Deanery; Revs. THOMAS P. MARR, Jefferson Deanery (Retired); RANDY J. BUDNAR, Lafayette Deanery; Rev. Msgr. KENNETH J. FIEDLER, Madison Deanery; Rev. DALE W. GRUBBA, Marquette-Green Lake Deanery; VACANT, Rock-Green Deanery; VACANT, Sauk Deanery; Rev. THOMAS L. KELLEY, West Dane Deanery.

Diocesan Offices and Directors

Apostolate to the Handicapped—Rev. LAWRENCE M. BAKKE, Mailing Address: P.O. Box 443, Monroe, 53566. Tel: 608-328-8371.

Apostolate to the Deaf—VACANT.

Archives—Ms. PAT BORN, Archivist, Bishop O'Connor Catholic Pastoral Center, 702 S. High Point Rd., P.O. Box 44983, Madison, 53744-4983. Tel: 608-821-3140; Fax: 608-821-3181.

Catholic Committee on Scouting—Mr. MICHAEL KLECKNER, Chm., 5595 Longford Terr., Madison,

53711. Tel: 608-275-3344. Email: mkleckner@amfam.com.

Building Commission—Rev. Msgrs. MICHAEL E. HIPPEE, J.C.L.; DUANE R. MOELLENBERNDT; JAMES R. BARTYLLA; Mr. JOHN C. PHILIPP, Chm.; Dr. PATRICK GORMAN; Mr. PETER SZOTKOWSKI; Mr. JOHN FELLER; Mr. GRANT R. EMMEL, P.E.

Camp Gray—Co Directors: JEFF HOEBEN; REBECCA HOEBEN, E10213 Shady Lane Rd., Reedsburg, 53959. Tel: 608-356-8200; Fax: 608-356-5855. Email: bigfun@campgray.com.

Catholic Relief Services—VACANT.

Department of Cemeteries, Diocese of Madison—JOHN MILLER, Diocesan Dir., Central Office, 2705 Regent St., Madison, 53705. Tel: 608-238-5561; Fax: 608-238-5768.

Charities--Catholic Charities of the Diocese of Madison, Inc.—Bishop O'Connor Catholic Pastoral Center, 702 S. High Point Rd., P.O. Box 46550, Madison, 53744-6550. Tel: 608-821-3100. BRIAN A. CAIN, Dir. Fax: 608-821-3125. Madison Area Offices, 30 S. Franklin St., Madison, 53703. Tel: 608-256-2358. 426 S. Yellowstone Dr., Ste. 100, Madison, 53719. Tel: 608-833-4800. Beloit District Office, 3311 Prairie Ave., Beloit, 53511. Tel: 608-365-3665. Janesville District Office, 2020 E. Milwaukee St., Ste. 208, Janesville, 53547. Tel: 608-752-4906.

Office for the Continuing Education of Priests—Rev. Msgr. O. CHARLES SCHLUTER, Dir., Bishop O'Connor Catholic Pastoral Center, 702 S. High Point Rd., P.O. Box 44983, Madison, 53744-4983. Tel: 608-821-3006.

Education—PATRICK DELANEY, Acting Dir., Adult & Spec. Educ. Tel: 608-821-3161; MICHAEL LANCASTER, Supt., Schools. Tel: 608-821-3180; RIA SCHMIDT, Ed.D., Asst. Supt., Bishop O'Connor Catholic Pastoral Center, 702 S. High Point Rd., P.O. Box 44983, Madison, 53744-4983. Tel: 608-821-3160.

Saint Raphael Society Clergy Retirement Plan—Rev. Msgr. JAMES R. BARTYLLA, Bishop O'Connor Catholic Pastoral Center, 702 S. High Point Rd., P.O. Box 44983, Madison, 53744-4983. Tel: 608-821-3011.

Council of Catholic Women—Rev. Msgr. DUANE R. MOELLENBERNDT, Moderator, Sacred Hearts of Jesus & Mary, 221 Columbus St., Sun Prairie, 53590-2297. Tel: 608-837-7381; Rev. LORIN M. BOWENS, Co-Moderator, Mailing Address: St. Boniface Parish, P.O. Box 60, Lime Ridge, 53942. Tel: 608-986-2101.

Director of Communications—BRENT KING. Tel: 608-821-3033.

Holy Childhood, Pontifical Association—Rev. Msgr. DELBERT L. SCHMELZER, Dir. (Retired), Bishop O'Connor Catholic Pastoral Center, 702 S. High Point Rd., P.O. Box 44983, Madison, 53744-4983. Tel: 608-821-3052.

Information—BRENT KING, Mailing Address: P.O. Box 44983, Madison, 53744-4983.

Office of Worship—Dr. PATRICK GORMAN, Bishop O'Connor Catholic Pastoral Center, 702 S. High Point Rd., P.O. Box 44983, Madison, 53744-4983. Tel: 608-821-3080.

Office of Justice & Pastoral Outreach—VACANT, Bishop O'Connor Catholic Pastoral Center, 702 S. High Point Rd., P.O. Box 44983, Madison, 53744-4983. Tel: 608-821-3086.

Outreach—

Catholic Multicultural Center—ANDREW RUSSELL, Admin. Tel: 608-661-3512. *Centro Pastoral Guadalupano, Catholic Multicultural Center, 1862 Beld St., Madison, 53713.* Tel: 608-661-3512, Ext. 102. VACANT. *St. Martin House, Catholic Multicultural Center, 1862 Beld St., Madison, 53713.* Tel: 608-661-3512, Ext. 200. STEVE MAURICE, Coord.

Hispanic Ministry—Bishop O'Connor Catholic Pastoral Center, 702 S. High Point Rd., P.O. Box 44983, Madison, 53744-4983. Tel: 608-821-3092.

Evangelization and Catechesis Department— (Youth & Young Adult Ministry; Respect Life - Tel: 608-821-3086; Curriculum and Catechist Development; Newman Apostolate - Madison: Rev. Eric H. Nielsen, Dir.; St. Paul Univ. Catholic Center, 723 State St., Madison, WI, 53703. Tel: 608-258-3140. Platteville: Rev. Faustino Ruiz, S.J.S.; St. Augustine Newman Center, 135 S. Hickory St., Platteville, WI 53818. Tel: 608-348-7530)

Newspaper— "Catholic Herald, Madison Edition" MARY UHLER, Editor, Bishop O'Connor Catholic Pastoral Center, 702 S. High Point Rd., P.O. Box 44983, Madison, 53744-4983. Tel: 608-821-3070.

Office of Planning—Mr. ERIC SCHIEDERMAYER, Dir.; ANNA DELANEY, Spec. Asst., Bishop O'Connor Catholic Pastoral Center, 702 S. High Point Rd., P.O. Box 44983, Madison, 53744-4983. Tel: 608-821-3025.

Diocesan Victim Assistance Program—KEVIN R. PHELAN, Chancellor.

Victim Assistance Coordinator—KEVIN R. PHELAN, Chancellor, Bishop O'Connor Catholic Pastoral Center, 702 S. High Point Rd., P.O. Box 44983, Madison, 53744-4983. Tel: 608-821-3083; Fax: 608-821-3013.

Propagation of the Faith—Rev. Msgr. DELBERT L. SCHMELZER, Dir. (Retired), Bishop O'Connor Catholic Pastoral Center, 702 S. High Point Rd., P.O. Box 44983, Madison, 53744-4983. Tel: 608-821-3052.

St. Vincent de Paul Society—VACANT.

Serra Clubs—Madison: Rev. PAUL U. ARINZE. Janesville: Rev. RANDY J. TIMMERMAN.

Vigilance Council— (The Very Rev. Deans)

Vocations—Rev. PAUL U. ARINZE, Dir., Bishop O'Connor Catholic Pastoral Center, 702 S. High Point Rd., P.O. Box 44983, Madison, 53744-4983. Tel: 608-821-3088.

Wisconsin Catholic Conference—JOHN HUEBSCHER, Exec. Sec., 131 W. Wilson St., Ste. 1105, Madison, 53703. Tel: 608-257-0004.

Office of Human Resources—JOHN MILLER, Dir., Bishop O'Connor Catholic Pastoral Center, 702 S. High Point Rd., P.O. Box 44983, Madison, 53744-4983. Tel: 608-821-3047.

Office of Stewardship and Development—DAUN MAIER, Assoc. Dir., Mailing Address: Bishop O'Connor Catholic Pastoral Center, 702 S. High Point Rd., P.O. Box 44983, Madison, 53744-4983. Tel: 608-821-3040.

CLERGY, PARISHES, MISSIONS AND PAROCHIAL SCHOOLS

CITY OF MADISON

(DANE COUNTY)

1—CATHEDRAL PARISH OF ST. RAPHAEL (1854), (Merger of St. Raphael, Madison, Holy Redeemer, 128 W. Johnson St., Madison & St. Patrick, 410 E. Main St., Madison) Rev. Msgr. Kevin D. Holmes, Rector; Rev. Jose Luis Vazquez (Mexico); Deacon Raymond Lukesic.
Mailing Address: 404 E. Main St., 53703. Tel: 608-257-5000; Fax: 608-257-5565. Email: cathedral@straphael.org. Web: www.isthmuscatholic.org.
Res.: 120 W. Johnson St., 53703. Tel: 608-255-1658.
Catechesis / Religious Program—Students 203.

2—ST. BERNARD (1907) [JC] Rev. Msgr. Michael E. Hippee.
Res.: 2450 Atwood Ave., 53704. Tel: 608-249-9256; Fax: 608-244-3773. Web: www.stbernards.net.
Catechesis / Religious Program—2438 Atwood Ave., 53704. Tel: 608-249-7288, Ext. 230. Email: stb-education@stbernardmadison.com. Students 83.

3—BLESSED SACRAMENT (1922) [JC] Revs. Patrick F. Norris, O.P.; Steven F. Kuhlmann, O.P.
Mailing Address: 2116 Hollister Ave., 53726-3958. Tel: 608-238-3471; Fax: 608-238-4220. Web: www.blsacrament.org.
Priory: 2131 Rowley Ave., 53726. Tel: 608-238-3472. Rev. Jerome Matthias Walsh, O.P.; Bros. Vincent Dirienzo, O.P.; Terrence Bullock, O.P.
School—2112 Hollister Ave., 53726. Tel: 608-233-6155. Lay Teachers 22; Students 317.
Catechesis / Religious Program—Students 273.

4—ST. DENNIS (1956) [JC] Revs. Kent A. Schmitt; Paul U. Arinze, Vocation Dir.; Deacon David Hendrickson; Cheryl Porior-Mayhew, Admin.
Res.: 313 Dempsey Rd., 53714. Tel: 608-246-5124; Fax: 608-246-5138. Email: dns@chorus.net. Web: www.st-dennis.org.
School—Tel: 608-246-5121. Dominican Sisters (Sinsinawa, WI) 5; Lay Teachers 21; Students 284.
Catechesis / Religious Program—Tel: 608-246-5123; Fax: 608-246-5138. Judy Hronek, D.R.E. (Pastoral Ministry); Sr. Mary Therese Dolan, O.P., D.R.E. (RCIA); Joanna Gehrmann, D.R.E. (K-3); Lisa Harms, D.R.E. (4-8); David Hendrickson, D.R.E. (H.S.); Pat Hendrickson, Liturgy Director/Pastoral Ministry. Students 880.

5—GOOD SHEPHERD PARISH (1905) Rev. Msgr. Thomas F. Baxter; Rev. Manuel Mendez-Cobos, Parochial Vicar, Latino Ministry.
Res.: 1128 St. James Ct., 53715-1363. Tel: 608-268-9930; Fax: 608-268-9929. Email: goodshepherdmadison@straphael.org. Web: www.thegoodshepherdmadison.org.
School—1204 St. James Ct., 53715. Tel: 608-268-9935. Web: www.stjamesschool.org. Lay Teachers 20; Students 191.
Catechesis / Religious Program—Tel: 608-268-9931. Michelle Nilsson, D.R.E. & Youth Min. Students 56.

6—HOLY REDEEMER (1857) Merged into Cathedral Parish of St. Raphael, Madison.

7—IMMACULATE HEART OF MARY (1950) [JC] Rev. Bart D. Timmerman.
Res.: 5101 Schofield St., Monona, 53716. Tel: 608-221-1521; Fax: 608-221-1794. Web: www.ihmparishmonona.org.
School—4913 Schofield St., 53716. Tel: 608-222-8831; Fax: 608-221-4492. Lay Teachers 19; Students 197.
Catechesis / Religious Program—Students 151.

8—ST. MARIA GORETTI (1959) [JC] Rev. Msgr. Michael L. Burke; Rev. Chad M. Droessler, Parochial Vicar; Deacons Jerome Buhman; Richard Martin.
Res.: 10 Maria Pl., 53711. Tel: 608-271-7421; Fax: 608-275-6621. Email: parish@stmariagoretti.org. Web: www.stmariagoretti.org.
Church: 5313 Flad Ave., 53711.
School—5405 Flad Ave., 53711. Tel: 608-271-7551; Fax: 608-275-6625. Email: admin@stmariagoretti.org. Lay Teachers 31; Students 430.
Catechesis / Religious Program—Tel: 608-271-8081; Fax: 608-268-2974. Students 597.

9—OUR LADY, QUEEN OF PEACE (1945) [JC] Rev. Msgr. Kenneth J. Fiedler; Sr. Sue Hetebrueg, S.S.N.D., Pastoral Assoc.
Res. & Parish Center: 401 S. Owen Dr., 53711. Tel: 608-231-4600; Fax: 608-231-4606. Web: www.qopc.org.
School—418 Holly Ave., 53711. Tel: 608-231-4580; Fax: 608-231-4589. Web: www.qops.k12.wi.us. Lay Teachers 36; Students 448.
Catechesis / Religious Program—Tel: 608-231-4610. Mary Jo Trapani, D.R.E.; Cheryl Horne, Youth Min. Students 351.

10—ST. PATRICK (1888) [JC] Merged into Cathedral Parish of St. Raphael, Madison.

11—ST. PAUL UNIVERSITY PARISH, [JC] Revs. Eric H. Nielsen; Eric G. Sternberg.
Office: 723 State St., 53703. Tel: 608-258-3140; Fax: 608-258-3141.
Catechesis / Religious Program—

12—ST. PETER (1967) [JC] Rev. Msgr. O. Charles Schluter; Deacon Todd Martin.
Res.: 5001 N. Sherman Ave., 53704. Tel: 608-249-6651; Fax: 608-249-6870. Email: mdillon@stpetersofmadison.org. Web: www.stpetersofmadison.org.
Catechesis / Religious Program—Students 163.

13—ST. THOMAS AQUINAS, [JC] Rev. Msgr. Donald J. Heiar Jr.
Res.: 602 Everglade Dr., 53717. Tel: 608-833-2600; Fax: 608-833-1129. Email: parish@stamadison.org. Web: www.stamadison.org.
Catechesis / Religious Program—Tel: 608-833-2606. Holly Irving, D.R.E.; Kay Schachte, D.R.E. Students 157.

OUTSIDE THE CITY OF MADISON

ARGYLE, LAFAYETTE CO., ST. JOSEPH (1898) [CEM 2], (Linked with St. Michael, Yellowstone; St. John's in South Wayne; St. Joseph's Gratiot) Rev. David A. Wanish.
Res.: 313 N. Lafayette St., P.O. Box 76, 53504. Tel: 608-543-3631.
Catechesis / Religious Program— Judy Zurfluh, D.R.E. Students 34.

ASHTON, DANE CO., ST. PETER'S (1866) [CEM], (Linked with St. Martin of Tours, Martinsville) Rev. Eugene F. Hollfelder (Retired).
Res.: 7121 Co. Trunk K, Middleton, 53562. Tel: 608-831-4843; Fax: 608-831-5377.
School—7129 Hwy. K, Middleton, 53562. Tel: 608-831-4846; Fax: 608-831-6095. Lay Teachers 6; Students 41.
Catechesis / Religious Program—Michelle Leveque, D.R.E. Students 161.

BARABOO, SAUK CO., ST. JOSEPH (1859) [CEM] Revs. James M. Poster, Admin.; Timothy J. Renz, Parochial Vicar.
Mailing Address: 300 2nd St., P.O. Box 70, 53913. Tel: 608-356-4773.
Res.: 314 East St., 53913. Tel: 608-356-3083; Fax: 608-356-4024. Web: stjosephbaraboo.org.
School—Web: www.stjosephbaraboo.org. Lay Teachers 10; Students 135.
Catechesis / Religious Program—Tel: 608-356-5353; Fax: 608-356-4024. Becky Thompson, Dir. Faith Formation. Students 182.

BARNEVELD, IOWA CO., IMMACULATE CONCEPTION (1886) [CEM] [JC] Merged with St. Bridget, Ridgeway to form St. Bernadette, Ridgeway.

BELLEVILLE, DANE CO., ST. FRANCIS OF ASSISI (2008) [CEM 2] Rev. Michael E. Moon.
Mailing Address: 338 S. Harrison St., P.O. Box 349, 53508. Tel: 608-424-3831.
Res.: 221 Frederick St., P.O. Box 349, 53508. Tel:

608-424-3681; Fax: 608-424-3831.
Catechesis/Religious Program—Anne Murray, D.R.E. (7th-11th); Pamela Burke, D.R.E. (Pre-K-6th). Students 319.

BELMONT, LAFAYETTE CO., ST. PHILOMENA (1957) [CEM], (Linked with St. Michael, Calamine and Immaculate Conception, Truman) Rev. Monte E. Robinson.
Res.: 338 Chestnut St., Box 345, 53510. Tel: 608-762-5446.
Catechesis/Religious Program— Also serves these Missions: St. Michael's at Calamine, WI & Immaculate Conception at Truman, WI Students 48.

BELOIT, ROCK CO.
1—ST. JUDE (1908), (Linked With St. Thomas the Apostle, Beloit) Rev. John H. Hedrick; Deacon James Davis.
Res.: 747 Hackett St., 53511. Tel: 608-364-2820; Fax: 608-364-2822. Email: pquinn@stjudebeloit.org. Web: www.stjudebeloit.org.
Catechesis/Religious Program—Students 82.
2—OUR LADY OF THE ASSUMPTION (1953) [JC] Rev. Gary L. Krahenbuhl.
Mailing Address: 2222 Shopiere Rd., 53511. Tel: 608-362-9066. Web: www.olaparish.com.
Res.: 2487 N. Bootmaker Dr., 53511.
School—Tel: 608-365-4014; Fax: 608-368-2832. Lay Teachers 13; Students 178.
Catechesis/Religious Program—Tel: 608-362-1231; Fax: 608-368-2820. Rob Olsen, Dir. Faith Formation; Dominick Meyer, Youth Min. Students 276.
3—ST. PAUL, Closed. 1988. For inquiries for parish records contact St. Thomas the Apostle, Beloit.
4—ST. THOMAS THE APOSTLE (1851), (Linked with St. Jude, Beloit) Rev. John H. Hedrick; Jessica Brey, Pastoral Assoc.
Church & Office: 822 E. Grand Ave., 53511. Tel: 608-362-1034; Fax: 608-363-9931. Email: parishoffice@stthomasbeloit.org. Web: www.stthomasbeloit.org.
Res.: 747 Hackett St., 53511. Tel: 608-364-2820.
Catechesis/Religious Program—Students 130.

BENTON, LAFAYETTE CO., ST. PATRICK (1845) [CEM], (Linked with St. Rose of Lima, Cube City) Rev. David J. Flanagan.
Res.: 237 E. Main St., P.O. Box 3, 53803-0003. Tel: 608-759-2131.
Catechesis/Religious Program—Students 51.

BERLIN, GREEN LAKE CO.
1—ALL SAINTS (2001) [CEM 2] Rev. Jerome J. Maksvytis.
Church: N8566 State Rd. 49, P.O. Box 269, 54923-0269. Tel: 920-361-5252; Fax: 920-361-5255. Web: allsaintsberlin.org.
Res.: 167 N. Wisconsin, 54923. Tel: 920-361-2354.
School—151 S. Grove St., 54923. Tel: 920-361-1781; Fax: 920-361-7379. Email: szangl@allsaintsberlin.org. Web: www.allsaintsberlin.org/school.html. Lay Teachers 16; Students 148.
Catechesis/Religious Program— 54923. Tel: 920-361-0940. Students 225.
2—ST. JOSEPH, Merged with St. Michael, Berlin and St. Stanislaus, Berlin to form All Saints, Berlin.
3—ST. MICHAEL, Merged with St. Joseph, Berlin and St. Stanislaus, Berlin to form All Saints, Berlin.
4—ST. STANISLAUS, Merged with St. Joseph, Berlin and St. Michael, Berlin to form All Saints, Berlin.

BLANCHARDVILLE, LAFAYETTE CO., IMMACULATE CONCEPTION (1898) [CEM], (Linked with St. Patrick, Hollandale and Holy Redeemer, Perry) Rev. Thomas E. Gillespie.
Mailing Address: P.O. Box 37, Hollandale, 53544. 601 Grover St., P.O. Box 37, Hollandale, 53544-0037. Church: 604 East St., 53516. Tel: 608-967-2344; Fax: 608-967-2344. Email: spichr@straphael.org.
Catechesis/Religious Program—Students 15.

BLOOMINGTON, GRANT CO., ST. MARY (1898) [CEM 2], (Linked with St. John, Patch Grove; St. Charles, Cassville; St. Mary, Glen Haven) Rev. John Meinholz.
Res.: 535 Congress St., P.O. Box 35, 53804-0035. Tel: 608-994-2526; Fax: 608-994-2551. Email: sunday7@grant.tds.net.
School—Lay Teachers 7; Students 71.
Catechesis/Religious Program—P.O. Box 35, 53804. Tel: 608-994-2435. Students 137.
Mission—St. John Parish Patch Grove, Grant Co. 53817.

BOSCOBEL, GRANT CO., CORPUS CHRISTI PARISH, BOSCOBEL, WI Rev. Peter Auer, S.O.L.T.
Mailing Address: 405 E. LeGrand St., 53805-1150. Tel: 608-375-4257 (Office in Boscobel); Fax: 608-375-4255.
Res. & Church: 341 N. Wisconsin Ave., Muscoda, 53573.
Catechesis/Religious Program—Tel: 608-721-3206.

BRIGGSVILLE, MARQUETTE CO., ST. MARY HELP OF CHRISTIANS (1851) [CEM], (Linked with St. Mary of the Immaculate Conception, Portage) Rev. James H. Murphy; Sr. Jovita Winkel, C.S.A., Pastoral Min.
Res.: 309 W. Cook St., P.O. Box 216, Portage, 53901-0216. Tel: 608-742-6998; Fax: 608-742-1039. Church: N565 Hwy. A, Box 127, 53920-0127. Tel: 608-981-2282; Fax: 608-981-2282.
Catechesis/Religious Program—Students 51.

BUFFALO TOWNSHIP, MARQUETTE CO., ST. ANDREW (1860) [CEM], (Linked with St. Mary, Pardeeville) Rev. David J. Greenfield.
Mailing Address: 318 S. Main St., Pardeeville, 53954. Tel: 608-429-3030; Fax: 608-429-3129. Email: stmary@jvlnet.com. Web: www.stmary-standrew.net.

CALAMINE, LAFAYETTE CO., ST. MICHAEL (1916) [CEM], (Linked with St. Philomena, Belmont and Immaculate Conception, Truman) Rev. Monte E. Robinson.
Res.: 338 Chestnut St., Box 345, Belmont, 53510. Tel: 608-762-5446.
Catechesis/Religious Program— Twinned with Holy Rosary, Darlington.; (Included in St. Philomena, Belmont)

CAMBRIDGE, DANE CO., ST. PIUS X (1955) Rev. David W. Timmerman, Admin.
Res.: 701 W. Water St., 53523. Tel: 608-423-3015. Email: parishstpiusx@gmail.com.
Catechesis/Religious Program—Tel: 608-423-4699. Bernadette Daggett, C.R.E. Students 163.

CASSVILLE, GRANT CO., ST. CHARLES BORROMEO, [CEM 2], (Linked with St. Mary Help of Christians, Glen Haven) Rev. John Meinholz.
Mailing Address: 605 E. Dewey St., 53806.
Res.: 535 Congress St., Bloomington, 53804. Tel: 608-994-2526; Fax: 608-725-2343.
School—521 E. Dewey St., 53806. Tel: 608-725-5173; Fax: 608-725-5179. Lay Teachers 8; Students 49.
Catechesis/Religious Program—Tel: 608-725-2330. Patricia Ballweg, D.R.E. Students 50.
Mission—St. Mary Help of Christians

CASTLE ROCK, GRANT CO., ST. JOHN NEPOMUCENE (1879) [CEM], (Linked with St. Mary's Parish, Fennimore) Rev. Miguel Galvez, S.J.S.
Mailing Address: 15055 Shemak Rd., Muscoda, 53573.
Res.: 341 N. Wisconsin Ave., Muscoda, 53573. Tel: 608-448-6061.
Catechesis/Religious Program—Students 10.

CLINTON, ROCK CO., ST. STEPHEN (1973) Rev. William Connell.
Mailing Address: 716 Shular Ln., Box 399, 53525.
Res.: 714 Shular Ln., Box 399, 53525. Tel: 608-676-2241; Fax: 608-676-4981.
Catechesis/Religious Program—716 Shular Ln., 53525. Steve Zahn, D.R.E. Students 76.

COLUMBUS, COLUMBIA CO., ST. JEROME (1856) [CEM], (Linked with St. Patrick, Doylestown) Rev. Steven J. Kortendick; Deacon Timothy Byrnes.
Parish Office—1550 Farnham St., 53925. Tel: 920-623-3753; Fax: 920-623-1115. Email: columbussjp@straphael.org.
Res.: 329 Folsom St., 53925. Tel: 920-623-2720.
School—Tel: 920-623-5780. Lay Teachers 13; Students 165.
Catechesis/Religious Program—Students 127.

COTTAGE GROVE, DANE CO., ST. PATRICK (1882) [CEM] Rev. John J. Sasse.
Res.: 434 N. Main St., P.O. Box 400, 53527-0400. Tel: 608-839-3969; Fax: 608-839-3593. Email: info@st-patrick-parish.com. Web: www.st-patrick-parish.com.
Catechesis/Religious Program—Sr. M. Marcella Meadowcroft, F.S.M., D.R.E.; Meredith Meinholz, Youth Min. Students 256.

CROSS PLAINS, DANE CO., ST. FRANCIS XAVIER (1853) [CEM] Rev. Thomas L. Kelley.
Res.: 2947 Thinnes St., 53528. Tel: 608-798-0800; Fax: 608-798-2976. Email: stfrancis@chorus.net.
School—2939 Thinnes St., 53528. Tel: 608-798-2422; Fax: 608-798-0898. Web: www.sfxschool-cp.org. Lay Teachers 16; Students 186.
Catechesis/Religious Program—Tel: 608-798-4824. Cindy Ballweg, C.R.E. Students 268.

CUBA CITY, GRANT CO., ST. ROSE OF LIMA, [CEM], (Linked with St. Patrick, Benton) Rev. David J. Flanagan.
Res.: 519 W. Roosevelt, 53807. Tel: 608-744-2010; Fax: 608-744-3709.
School—Tel: 608-744-2120; Fax: 608-744-8449. Lay Teachers 10; Students 131.
Catechesis/Religious Program—Students 161.

DANE, DANE CO., ST. MICHAEL, [CEM], (Linked with St. Patrick, Lodi) Rev. Francisco Higuera.
Mailing Address: 109 S. Military Rd., 53529.
Res.: 515 Fair St., Lodi, 53555. Tel: 608-592-5711, Ext. 1; 608-592-5711, Ext. 6; Fax: 608-237-1786.
School—Tel: 608-848-5619. Lay Teachers 6; Students 25.

DARLINGTON, LAFAYETTE CO., HOLY ROSARY (1854) [CEM 2] Rev. Randy J. Budnar.
Mailing Address: 730 Wells St., 53530. Tel: 608-766-4059; Fax: 608-766-4059.
Res.: 104 E. Harriet St., 53530. Tel: 608-776-2251. Email: hrosary@centurytel.net. Web: www.holyrosarycatholicchurch.org.
School—744 Wells St., 53530. Tel: 608-776-3710. Email: hrschool@centurytel.net. Web: www.school-.holyrosarycatholicchurch.org. Diane Smith-Hole, Prin. Lay Teachers 8; Students 64.
Catechesis/Religious Program—Students 269.

DE FOREST, DANE CO., ST. OLAF (1948) [CEM], (Linked with St. Joseph, East Bristol) Rev. Robert J. Butz.
Res.: 623 Jefferson St., 53532. Tel: 608-846-3812.
Catechesis/Religious Program—Tel: 608-846-5726. Paula Hill, D.R.E. Students 385.

DICKEYVILLE, GRANT CO., HOLY GHOST, [CEM], (Linked with Immaculate Conception, Kieler) Rev. Bernard E. Rott; Deacon Lawrence Tranel.
Res.: 305 W. Main St., 53808. Tel: 608-568-7519; Fax: 608-568-3872.
School—325 W. Main St. Tel: 608-568-7790; Fax: 608-568-3872. Rita Hesseling, Prin. Consolidated with Immaculate Conception, Kieler. Lay Teachers 11; Students 171.
Catechesis/Religious Program—Angela Snyder, D.R.E., (Grade School). Tel: 608-568-7925; Tina Tranel, D.R.E., (High School). Tel: 608-568-7530. Students 119.

DODGEVILLE, IOWA CO., ST. JOSEPH, [CEM 3] Rev. Patrick J. Wendler.
Res.: 405 S. Dacotah St., 53533-1799. Tel: 608-930-3392; Fax: 608-930-1722. Email: sjoffice@mhtc.net. Web: stjoedodge.org.
School—305 E. Walnut St., 53533. Lay Teachers 12; Students 230.
Catechesis/Religious Program—Students 147.

DOYLESTOWN, COLUMBIA CO., ST. PATRICK (1865) [CEM], (Linked with St. Jerome, Columbus) Rev. Steven J. Kortendick.
Res.: N4085 Bruce St., P.O. Box 40, 53928. Tel: 920-992-3343; Fax: 920-623-1115. Email: doylestownspp@straphael.org.
Catechesis/Religious Program—Students 55.

DURWARD'S GLEN, COLUMBIA CO., ST. CAMILLUS, [CEM] Closed. For inquiries for parish records contact the chancery.

EAST BRISTOL, DANE CO., ST. JOSEPH (1847) [CEM], (Linked with St. Olaf, De Forest) Rev. Robert J. Butz.
Res.: 623 Jefferson St., De Forest, 53532. Tel: 608-846-5726.
Catechesis/Religious Program—1935 Hwy. V, Sun Prairie, 53590. Students 98.

EDGERTON, ROCK CO., ST. JOSEPH, [CEM 2] Rev. David W. Timmerman.
Res.: 590 S. Saint Joseph Cir., 53534-1243. Tel: 608-884-3038; Fax: 608-884-3298.
Catechesis/Religious Program—Tel: 608-884-6231. Students 140.

ELK GROVE, LAFAYETTE CO., ST. PETER, [CEM], (Linked with St. Matthew, Shullsburg and Our Lady of Hope, Seymour) Rev. John Bosco Pudhota.
Res.: 344 N. Judgement St., Shullsburg, 53586. Tel: 608-965-4518.

EVANSVILLE, ROCK CO., ST. PAUL (1906) [CEM], (Linked with St. Augustine, Footville) Rev. Kevin F. Dooley.
Office: 39 Garfield St., 53536-1110. Tel: 608-882-4138. Email: stpaulevans@sbcglobal.net.
Res.: 35 Garfield Ave., 53536. Tel: 608-882-0490.
Catechesis/Religious Program—Students 155.

FENNIMORE, GRANT CO., ST. MARY (1885) [CEM], (Linked to St. John Nepomucene, Castle Rock) Rev. George B. Horath; Deacon Patrick Jozefowicz.
Res.: 930 Jefferson St., 53809. Tel: 608-822-6425.
Catechesis/Religious Program—Tel: 608-822-3520. Students 131.

FOOTVILLE, ROCK CO., ST. AUGUSTINE (1869), (Linked with St. Paul, Evansville) Rev. Kevin F. Dooley.
Mailing Address: 280 Haberdale Dr., 53537-0325. Tel: 608-876-6252; Fax: 608-876-6252.
Res.: 35 Garfield Ave., Evansville, 53536. Tel: 608-882-0490; 608-882-4138 (Office); Fax: 608-882-0690.
Catechesis/Religious Program—Tel: 608-876-6311. Email: amazgr8z@ticon.net. Linked with St. Paul, Evansville. Students 56.

FORT ATKINSON, JEFFERSON CO., ST. JOSEPH (1884) [CEM] Rev. Brian J. Wilk.
Mailing Address: 1660 Endl Blvd., 53538. Tel: 920-563-3029. Web: stjosephfort.org.
Res.: 1512 Dommo Dr., 53538.
School—1650 Endl Blvd., 53538. Fax: 920-563-3150. Email: khomb@stjosephfort.org. Friar Kari Homb, Prin. Lay Teachers 13; Students 150.
Catechesis/Religious Program—Lisa Meitzner, C.R.E. Students 225.

GLEN HAVEN, GRANT CO., ST. MARY HELP OF CHRISTIANS (1864) [CEM 2], (Linked with St. Charles Borromeo, Cassville) Rev. John Meinholz.
Mailing Address: 605 E. Dewey St., Cassville, 53806. Tel: 608-725-5595.
Res.: 635 Congress St., Bloomington, 53804. Tel:

608-994-2526; Fax: 608-725-2343.

GRATIOT, LAFAYETTE CO., ST. JOSEPH (1869) [CEM], (Linked with St. John, South Wayne) Rev. David A. Wanish.
Church: Box 76, Argyle, 53504. Tel: 608-543-3631.
Catechesis/Religious Program—Students 26.

GREEN LAKE, GREEN LAKE CO., OUR LADY OF THE LAKE (1908) Rev. Philip J. Krogman.
Res.: 530 Ruth St., P.O. Box 215, 54941. Tel: 920-294-6440; Fax: 920-294-6550.
Catechesis/Religious Program—Lawrence D. Behlen, D.R.E. Students 52.

HAZEL GREEN, GRANT CO., ST. FRANCIS DE SALES (1845) [CEM], (Linked with St. Joseph, Hazel Green) Rev. Cyril O. Weisensel (Retired).
Parish Center: 2720 N. Percival St., 53811-9681. Tel: 608-854-2391. Email: stfrancisdesales@centurytel.net.
Catechesis/Religious Program—Students 280.

HIGHLAND, IOWA CO., SS. ANTHONY AND PHILIP, [CEM 2], (Linked with St. Thomas, Montfort) Rev. Kenneth J. Frisch.
Res.: 1023 Dodgeville St., P.O. Box 306, 53543. Tel: 608-929-7490; Fax: 608-929-7701. Email: solson@mhtc.net. Web: stsanthonyphilip.com.
Catechesis/Religious Program—Tel: 608-929-7701. Email: deggers@mhtc.net. Delores Eggers, D.R.E. Students 158.

HOLLANDALE, IOWA CO., ST. PATRICK (1844) [CEM], (Linked with Immaculate Conception, Blanchardville and Holy Redeemer, Perry) Rev. Thomas E. Gillespie.
Res.: 601 Grover St., P.O. Box 37, 53544. Tel: 608-967-2344; Fax: 608-967-2344. Email: spichr@straphael.org.
Catechesis/Religious Program—Students 38.

JANESVILLE, ROCK CO.

1—ST. JOHN VIANNEY (1955) Rev. Randy J. Timmerman; Deacon John Houseman.
Mailing Address: 1221 Clark St., 53545.
Res.: 1245 Clark St., 53545. Tel: 608-752-8708; Fax: 608-752-1970. Web: www.sjv.org.
School—1250 E. Racine St., 53545. Tel: 608-752-6802. Lay Teachers 19; Students 255.
Catechesis/Religious Program—1238 E. Racine St., 53545. Tel: 608-755-1476; Fax: 608-758-3321. Students 375.

2—NATIVITY OF ST. MARY (1876) [JC] Rev. Stephen J. Umhoefer; Deacon Steven Hayes.
Res.: 313 E. Wall St., 53545. Tel: 608-752-7861; Fax: 608-758-0720. Email: hrude@nativitymary.org. Web: www.nativitymary.org.
School—Tel: 608-754-5221. Lay Teachers 13; Students 132.
Catechesis/Religious Program— (Family Faith Formation) Students 71.

3—ST. PATRICK (1850) [JC] Rev. James G. Kuhn; Deacon John Houseman, Pastoral Assoc.
Res.: 315 Cherry St., 53548. Tel: 608-754-8193; Fax: 608-754-0357. Email: stpats@straphael.org. Web: www.stpats.org.
School—305 Lincoln St., 53548. Tel: 608-752-0321. Lay Teachers 7; Students 71.
Catechesis/Religious Program—Tel: 608-754-0531. Margaret Clark, D.R.E. Students 107.

4—ST. WILLIAM (1952) [JC] Rev. John R. Auby; Deacon Richard Fischer.
Res.: 1815 Ravine St., 53548. Tel: 608-755-5180; Fax: 608-755-5190. Email: stwill@charterinternet.net. Web: www.stwilliam.net.
School—1822 Ravine St., 53548. Tel: 608-755-5184; Fax: 608-755-5182. Lay Teachers 10; Students 157.
Catechesis/Religious Program—Tel: 608-755-5183. Email: religioused1822@charter.net. Jane Graves, D.R.E. Students 188.

JEFFERSON, JEFFERSON CO.

1—ST. JOHN THE BAPTIST (1859) [CEM], (Linked with St. Lawrence, Jefferson & St. Mary Help of Christians, Sullivan) Rev. Thomas J. Coyle.
Res.: 214 N. Sanborn Ave., 53549. Tel: 920-674-2025; Fax: 920-674-2521.
School—333 E. Church St., 53549. Tel: 920-674-5821. Web: www.stjohnbaptist.net. Lay Teachers 19; Students 203.
Catechesis/Religious Program—Tel: 920-674-5433. Email: stjohnsre@hotmail.com. Julie Endl, C.R.E.; Tiffany Topel, D.R.E. Students 220.

2—ST. LAWRENCE (1850) [CEM], (Linked with St. John the Baptist, Jefferson) Rev. Thomas J. Coyle.
Res.: W. 4975 Hwy. 18, 53549. Tel: 920-674-2822.
Catechesis/Religious Program—W. 4975 Hwy. 18, 53549. Students 12.

JOHNSON CREEK, JEFFERSON CO., ST. MARY MAGDALENE (1906) [CEM], (Linked with St. Francis Xavier, Lake Mills) Rev. Robert W. Hughes.
Res.: 242 Williams St., P.O. Box 202, 53038. Tel: 920-648-2468; Fax: 920-648-2468.
Catechesis/Religious Program—Tel: 920-699-2913. Melissa Cahill, C.R.E. Students 72.

KIELER, GRANT CO., IMMACULATE CONCEPTION, [CEM], (Linked with Holy Ghost, Dickeyville) Rev. Bernard E. Rott, Admin.; Deacon Lawrence Tranel.
Res.: Box 57, 53812. Tel: 608-568-7530; Fax: 608-568-3811. Email: icparish@tds.net.
School—Tel: 608-568-7220. Rita Hesseling, Prin. Consolidated with Holy Ghost, Dickeyville. Lay Teachers 13; Students 171.
Catechesis/Religious Program—3685 County HHH. Twinned with Holy Ghost, Dickeyville. Students 132.

KINGSTON, GREENLAKE CO., ST. MARY (1876) [CEM] Merged with St. Joseph, Markesan to form Holy Family Parish, Pardeeville.

LA VALLE, SAUK CO., HOLY FAMILY (1917) [CEM 2], (Linked with St. Boniface, Lime Ridge and St. Patrick, Loreto) Rev. Lorin M. Bowens; Nora Durst, Pastoral Assoc.
Mailing Address: 310 Bluff St., P.O. Box 166, 53941. Tel: 608-985-7558.
Res.: 105 Church St., P.O. Box 60, Lime Ridge, 53942. Tel: 608-986-2101. Email: holyfamily@mwt.net.
Catechesis/Religious Program—Tel: 608-985-7915. Students 104.

LAKE MILLS, JEFFERSON CO., ST. FRANCIS XAVIER (1912), (Linked with St. Mary Magdalene, Johnson Creek) Rev. Robert W. Hughes.
Res.: 602 College St., 53551. Tel: 920-648-2468; Fax: 920-648-2468.
Catechesis/Religious Program—Tel: 920-648-2815. Lin Cleghorn, C.R.E.; Mary Paulowske, Youth Min. Students 195.

LANCASTER, GRANT CO., ST. CLEMENT (1859) [CEM 2] Rev. William J. Seipp.
Res.: 135 S. Washington St., 53813. Tel: 608-723-4990; Fax: 608-723-4012.
School—330 W. Maple St., 53813. Tel: 608-723-7474; Fax: 608-723-4424. Sisters 2; Lay Teachers 10; Students 134.
Catechesis/Religious Program—Tel: 608-723-7425. Kitty Mumm, D.R.E. Students 174.

LIME RIDGE, SAUK CO., ST. BONIFACE (1912) [CEM], (Linked with Holy Family, La Valle and St. Patrick, Loreto) Rev. Lorin M. Bowens.
Res.: 105 Church St., P.O. Box 85, 53942-0085. Tel: 608-986-2101. Email: boniface@wicw.net.
Catechesis/Religious Program—
Mission—St. Patrick-Loreto Plain. 105 Church St., 53942.
Mission—Holy Family 310 Bluff St., La Valle, 53941. Tel: 608-985-7558. Email: holyfamily@mwt.net.

LODI, COLUMBIA CO., ST. PATRICK (1857) [CEM], (Linked with St. Michael, Dane) Rev. Francisco Higuera.
521 Fair St., 53555.
Res.: 515 Fair St., 53555. Tel: 608-592-5711; Fax: 608-237-1786. Email: fr.higuera@saintpatrickinlodi.org; officemary@saintpatrickinlodi.org. Web: www.saintpatrickinlodi.org.
Catechesis/Religious Program—Tel: 608-592-5711, Ext. 3. Cynthia Fischer, Parish Catechetical Dir.; Blaine Hechimovich, Youth Min. Students 291.

LORETO, MANITOWOC CO., ST. PATRICK (1866), (Irish—German), [CEM 2], (Linked with Holy Family, LaValle and St. Boniface, Lime Ridge) Rev. Lorin M. Bowens.
Res.: 105 Church St., P.O. Box 85, Lime Ridge, 53942-0085. Tel: 608-986-2101.
Catechesis/Religious Program—E. 3460 McCarville Rd., Plain, 53577. Tel: 608-546-3159. Brenda Faber, D.R.E. Students 80.

MARKESAN, GREEN LAKE CO., ST. JOSEPH (1886) Merged with St. Mary, Kingston, to form Holy Family Parish, Pardeeville.

MARSHALL, DANE CO., ST. MARY OF THE NATIVITY, [CEM], (Linked with St. Joseph, Waterloo) Rev. Michael R. Radowicz.
Mailing Address: 205 Milwaukee Ave., Waterloo, 53594. Tel: 608-655-3708.
Church: 120 Beebe St., 53559.
Catechesis/Religious Program—Tel: 920-478-3232. Eileen Bender, C.R.E. Students 80.

MARTINSVILLE, DANE CO., ST. MARTIN OF TOURS (1850) [CEM], (Linked with St. Peter, Ashton) Rev. Eugene F. Hollfelder (Retired).
Res.: 5959 St. Martin Cir., Cross Plains, 53528-9312. Tel: 608-798-2815.
Catechesis/Religious Program—Tel: 608-798-2328. Linda Stafford, D.R.E. Students 98.

MAZOMANIE, DANE CO.

1—ST. BARNABAS (1856) [CEM] Merged with St. John the Baptist, Mill Creek to form Holy Cross Parish, Mazomanie.

2—HOLY CROSS PARISH, [CEM] Rev. George A. Navarro, S.J.S. (Peru).
Mailing Address: 410 Cramer St., P.O Box 68, 53560. Tel: 608-795-4321.
Res.: 115 Madison St., Sauk City, 53583. Tel: 608-643-2449; Fax: 608-643-2440.
Catechesis/Religious Program—Students 29.

MCFARLAND, DANE CO., CHRIST THE KING Rev. D. Stephen Smith.
Res.: 5306 Main St., P.O. Box 524, 53558. Tel: 608-838-9797; Fax: 608-838-6449. Email: ctk@myparish.com. Web: www.myparish.com.
Catechesis/Religious Program—Students 245.

MERRIMAC, SAUK CO., ST. MARY, HEALTH OF THE SICK (1948) Merged with St. Aloysius, Sauk City to form Divine Mercy Parish, Sauk City.

MIDDLETON, DANE CO., ST. BERNARD (1889) [CEM] Rev. Msgr. Douglas L. Dushack.
Res.: 2015 Parmenter St., P.O. Box 620187, 53562-0187. Tel: 608-831-6531; Fax: 608-831-8101. Email: parish@stbmidd.org. Web: www.stbmidd.org.
Catechesis/Religious Program—Students 453.

MILL CREEK, ST. JOHN THE BAPTIST, Merged with St. Barnabas, Mazomanie to form Holy Cross Parish, Mazomanie

MILTON, ROCK CO., ST. MARY (1891) [CEM] Rev. Msgr. James J. Uppena; Sr. Carol Hanus, F.S.P.A., Pastoral Assoc.
837 Parkview Dr., 53563. Tel: 608-868-3338; Fax: 608-868-3345. Web: saintmarymilton.org.
Res.: 836 Neumann Ct., 53563. Tel: 608-868-2338. Email: stmarys@centurytel.net.
Catechesis/Religious Program—Tel: 608-868-3336. Sabrina Elsen, Youth Min. Tel: 608-868-3334; Angela McNally, Coord. Liturgy & Music. Tel: 608-868-3335. Students 394.

MINERAL POINT, IOWA CO., CONGREGATION OF ST. MARY-ST. PAUL (1870) [JC 2] Rev. James W. Hinnen.
Res.: 224 Davis St., 53565. Tel: 608-987-2026; Fax: 608-987-3361.
Catechesis/Religious Program—Tel: 608-987-3361. Students 201.

MONROE, GREEN CO., ST. CLARE OF ASSISI PARISH (1860 St. Victor; 2011 St. Clare of Assisi) Revs. Lawrence M. Bakke; Michael E. Klarer.
1760 14th St., 53566-2149. Tel: 608-325-9506; Fax: 608-325-3115. Email: secretary@stclaregreencty.org. Web: stclaregreencty.org.
School—Students 141.
Catechesis/Religious Program—Students 259.

MONTELLO, MARQUETTE CO., ST. JOHN THE BAPTIST, [CEM], (Linked with Good Shepherd, Westfield) Rev. Michael C. Richel.
Res.: 277 E. Montello St., 53949. Tel: 608-297-2217. Email: sjgs@frontier.com.
Catechesis/Religious Program—Tel: 608-297-7423; Fax: 608-297-8047. Email: sjreled@frontier.com. Students 95.
Mission—Good Shepherd 241 E. 6th St., Westfield, Marquette Co. 53964. Tel: 608-296-3631; Fax: 608-296-2465.

MONTFORT, GRANT CO., ST. THOMAS (1925) [CEM], (Linked with SS. Anthony and Philip, Highland) Rev. Kenneth J. Frisch.
Res.: Box 68, 53569. Tel: 608-943-6944; Fax: 608-943-6944. Email: stthomas@mhtc.net.
Catechesis/Religious Program—Julie Hawes, C.R.E. Students 93.

MOUNT HOPE, GRANT CO., ST. LAWRENCE O'TOOLE (1884) [CEM], (Linked with St. Mary, Fennimore) Rev. George B. Horath.
Mailing Address: P.O. Box 206, Fennimore, 53809. Tel: 608-822-6425.

MOUNT HOREB, DANE CO., ST. IGNATIUS, [CEM], (Linked with St. Mary of Pine Bluff, Pine Bluff) Rev. Richard M. Heilman.
Mailing Address: 107 S. Seventh St., 53572-2050. Tel: 608-437-5195 (Office); Fax: 608-437-7691.
Res.: 3673 Cty. Tk. P, Cross Plains, 53528. Tel: 608-798-4644; Fax: 608-798-2112.
Catechesis/Religious Program—Tel: 608-437-5348. Steve Davies, C.R.E.; Sonja Preimesberger, C.R.E. Students 217.

NESHKORO, MARQUETTE CO., ST. JAMES, [CEM], (Linked with St. John the Baptist, Princeton) Rev. Dale W. Grubba.
Res.: 1211 W. Main St., Princeton, 54968. Tel: 920-295-6209; Fax: 920-295-0231.
Church: 315 N. Main St., 54960. Tel: 920-293-4211; Fax: 920-293-4211.
Catechesis/Religious Program—Students 32.

OREGON, DANE CO., HOLY MOTHER OF CONSOLATION (1856) [CEM] Rev. Gary A. Wankerl.
Res.: 651 N. Main St., 53575. Tel: 608-835-5763; Fax: 608-835-5764. Email: hmoc@charter.net. Web: holymotherchurch.4lpi.com.
Catechesis/Religious Program—Tel: 608-835-5764. Students 642.

PALMYRA, JEFFERSON CO., ST. MARY (1911) [CEM], (Linked with St. Joseph, Fort Atkinson) Rev. Brian J. Wilk.
Res.: 1512 Dommo Dr., Fort Atkinson, 53538. Tel: 920-397-7253 (Rectory).
Church: 919 W. Main St., P.O. Box P, 53156. Tel: 262-495-2395. Email: smarypal@mwt.net.
Catechesis/Religious Program—P.O. Box P, 53156.

Tel: 262-495-2395. Janine Curtin, C.R.E. Students 27.

PAOLI, DANE CO., ST. WILLIAM, [CEM] Merged with St. Andrew, Verona to form St. Christopher, Verona.

PARDEEVILLE, COLUMBIA CO.

1—HOLY FAMILY PARISH Rev. David J. Greenfield.
318 S. Main St., 53954. Tel: 920-398-3146; Fax: 608-429-3129.
Catechesis/Religious Program—45 St. Joseph St., Markesan, 53946. Students 78.

2—ST. MARY OF THE MOST HOLY ROSARY (1903), (Linked with St. Andrew, Buffalo) Rev. David J. Greenfield.
Res.: 318 S. Main St., 53954. Tel: 608-429-3030; Fax: 608-429-3129. Email: stmary@jvlnet.com. Web: stmary-standrew.net.
Catechesis/Religious Program—Maureen Nelson, D.R.E. Students 93.
Mission—St. Andrew N117 State Hwy. 22, Buffalo Twp., WI 53949.

PATCH GROVE, GRANT CO., ST. JOHN (1845) [CEM], (Linked with St. Mary, Bloomington; St. Charles, Cassville; St. Mary's, Glen Haven) Rev. John Meinholz.
Res.: 535 Congress St., P.O. Box 35, Bloomington, 53804. Tel: 608-994-2526; Fax: 608-994-2530. Email: sunday7@grant.tds.net.
Catechesis/Religious Program— Twinned with St. Mary, Bloomington.

PERRY, HOLY REDEEMER (1859) [CEM], (Linked with St. Patrick, Hollandale and Immaculate Conception, Blanchardville) Rev. Thomas E. Gillespie.
Res.: 601 Grover St., P.O. Box 37, Hollandale, 53544. Tel: 608-967-2344; Fax: 608-967-2344.
Catechesis/Religious Program—111 S. Sixth St., Mount Horeb, 53572. Tel: 608-437-5195; Fax: 608-437-7691. Students 27.

PINE BLUFF, DANE CO., ST. MARY OF PINE BLUFF (1854) [CEM] [JC], (Linked with St. Ignatius, Mount Horeb) Rev. Richard M. Heilman.
Res. & Parish: 3673 County Road P, Cross Plains, 53528. Tel: 608-798-4644 (Rectory); 608-798-2115 (School); 608-798-2111 (Parish); Fax: 608-798-2112. Email: catholic@tds.com. Web: www.stmarypb.org.
Catechesis/Religious Program—Tel: 608-437-5348. Beth Ptak, C.R.E. (K-5); Steve Davies, C.R.E. (6-12). Students 30.

PLAIN, SAUK CO., ST. LUKE (1857), (German), [CEM 2] [JC 2], (Linked with St. John the Evangelist, Spring Green) Rev. Michael A. Resop; Sisters Amy Taylor, F.S.P.A., Pastoral Assoc.; Karen Flottmeier, F.S.P.A., Pastoral Ministry.
Res.: 1240 Nachreiner Ave., 53577. Tel: 608-546-2482; Fax: 608-546-2616. Email: stlukesplain@charter.net.
School—Tel: 608-546-2963. Web: http://stlukesplain.org. Lay Teachers 10; Students 90.
Catechesis/Religious Program— Angie Pulvermacher, C.R.E. Students 116.

PLATTEVILLE, GRANT CO.

1—ST. AUGUSTINE UNIVERSITY PARISH (1974), (Linked with St. Mary, Platteville) Revs. Faustino Ruiz, S.J.P. (Spain); John Del Priore, S.J.S., Parochial Vicar; Deacon William Bussan, Pastoral Min.
Res.: 130 W. Cedar St., 53818-2457. Tel: 608-348-9735; Fax: 608-348-9920. Email: jdp@slsonline.org.
Church: 135 S. Hickory St., 53818-3316. Tel: 608-348-7530; Fax: 608-348-7530. Email: migalvez@slsonline.org. Web: www.uwplatt.edu/org/catholicnc; http://mystaugustine.org.
Catechesis/Religious Program—Students 25.

2—ST. MARY (1842), (Linked with St. Augustine University Parish, Platteville) Revs. Faustino Ruiz, S.J.P. (Spain); John Del Priore, S.J.S., Parochial Vicar.
Res.: 130 W. Cedar St., 53818-2457. Tel: 608-348-9735; Fax: 608-348-9920.
School—Tel: 608-348-5806; Fax: 608-348-7883. Lay Teachers 9; Students 115.
Catechesis/Religious Program—Students 147.

PORTAGE, COLUMBIA CO., ST. MARY OF THE IMMACULATE CONCEPTION, [CEM], (Linked with St. Mary Help of Christians, Briggsville) Rev. James H. Murphy; Deacon Dennis Sutter.
Mailing Address: 309 W. Cook St., P.O Box 216, 53901-0216.
Res.: 305 W. Cook St., P.O. Box 216, 53901-0216. Tel: 608-742-6998; Fax: 608-742-1039. Email: parish@stmaryotic.com. Web: www.stmaryotic.com.
School—315 W. Cook St., 53901. Tel: 608-742-4998. Email: jhahn@straphael.com. Lay Teachers 14; Students 121.
Catechesis/Religious Program—Sr. Anita Henning, D.R.E. Students 237.

POYNETTE, COLUMBIA CO., ST. THOMAS (1907) [JC], (Linked with St. Joseph, Rio) Rev. Raymond J. Dischler.
Res.: 655 S. Main, P.O. Box 310, 53955-0310. Tel: 608-635-4326.
Catechesis/Religious Program—651 S. Main St., 53955. Tel: 608-635-4326. Julie Cross, C.R.E.; Anna Niemeyer, C.R.E. Students 136.

PRINCETON, GREEN LAKE CO., ST. JOHN THE BAPTIST (1875) [CEM], (Linked with St. James, Neshkoro) Rev. Dale W. Grubba.
Res.: 1211 W. Main, 54968. Tel: 920-295-6209; Fax: 920-295-0231.
School—125 Church St., 54968. Tel: 920-295-3541; Fax: 920-295-0178. Web: stjohnprince.org. Lay Teachers 6; Students 69.
Catechesis/Religious Program—Students 34.

REEDSBURG, SAUK CO., SACRED HEART (1878) [CEM 3] Rev. Thomas J. Monaghan; Deacons Thomas Hale, Pastoral Assoc.; Ronald Pickar.
Res.: 852 8th St., 53959.
Church: 624 N. Willow St., 53959. Tel: 608-524-2412; Fax: 608-524-3831. Email: sheart@rucls.net. Web: www.sacred-heart-online.org.
School—(Grades PreK-8), 545 N. Oak St., 53959. Tel: 608-524-3611. Email: shs@rucls.net. Lay Teachers 8; Religious Teacher 1; Students 179.
Catechesis/Religious Program—Email: map@rucls.net. Mary Ann Polcyn, D.R.E. Students 275.

RIDGEWAY, IOWA CO.

1—ST. BERNADETTE Rev. Santus K. Ibe.
Mailing Address: 106 North St., 53582.
Res.: 803 W. Main St., 53582-9659. Tel: 608-514-9468; 608-924-2441.
Catechesis/Religious Program—Students 82.
Mission—Immaculate Conception, Barneveld

2—ST. BRIDGET (1850) [CEM] [JC] Merged with Immaculate Conception, Barneveld to form St. Bernadette, Ridgeway.

RIO, COLUMBIA CO., ST. JOSEPH (1902) [CEM 2], (Linked with St. Thomas, Poynette) Rev. Raymond J. Dischler.
Res.: 655 S. Main St., P.O. Box 310, Poynette, 53955-0310. Tel: 608-635-4326.
Catechesis/Religious Program—514 Lincoln Ave., 53960. Tel: 920-992-5185. Janeen Wakeman, C.R.E. Students 31.

ROXBURY, DANE CO., ST. NORBERT (1846) [CEM] Revs. John Patrick Blewett; George A. Navarro, S.J.S. (Peru); Jared M. Hood, S.J.S. (Ecuador); Pedro Escribano.
Res.: 115 Madison St., Sauk City, 53583. Tel: 608-370-3784.
Church: 8944 County Rd. Y, Sauk City, 53583-9510. Tel: 608-643-3661.
Catechesis/Religious Program—Tel: 608-643-6611. Juanita Wipperfurth, C.R.E. Students 252.

SAUK CITY, SAUK CO.

1—ST. ALOYSIUS (1845) [CEM 2] Merged with St. Mary Health of the Sick, Merrimac to form Divine Mercy Parish, Sauk.

2—DIVINE MERCY PARISH, [CEM 2] Revs. Jared M. Hood, S.J.S. (Ecuador); George A. Navarro, S.J.S. (Peru), Parochial Vicar; Pedro Escribano, Parochial Vicar.
Res.: 115 Madison St., 53583. Tel: 608-643-2449; Fax: 608-643-2440. Web: www.divinemercy-parish.org.
School—608 Oak St., 53583. Tel: 608-643-6868. Lay Teachers 14; Students 98.
Catechesis/Religious Program—Students 109.

SEYMOUR, LAFAYETTE CO., OUR LADY OF HOPE, [CEM], (Linked with St. Peter, Elk Grove and St. Matthew, Shullsburg) Rev. John Bosco Pudhota.
Res.: 344 N. Judgement St., Shullsburg, 53586. Tel: 608-965-4518.

SHULLSBURG, LAFAYETTE CO., ST. MATTHEW (1835) [CEM 2] [JC 2], (Linked with St. Peter, Elk Grove and Our Lady of Hope, Seymour) Rev. John Bosco Pudhota.
Res.: 344 Judgment St., 53586. Tel: 608-965-4518.
Catechesis/Religious Program—Students 130.

SINSINAWA, GRANT CO., ST. JOSEPH, [CEM 2], (Linked with St. Francis de Sales, Hazel Green) Rev. Cyril O. Weisensel (Retired).
Res.: 2630 N. Main St., Hazel Green, 53811. Tel: 608-748-4528.
Church: 780 County Hwy. Z, Hazel Green, 53811-9709.
School—Tel: 608-748-4442. Lay Teachers 8; Students 84.
Catechesis/Religious Program—Students 60.

SOUTH WAYNE, LAFAYETTE CO., ST. JOHN (1898) [CEM], (Linked with St. Joseph, Gratiot) Rev. David A. Wanish.
c/o St. Joseph's, Box 76, Argyle, 53504.
Res.: 5695 Main St., Box 37, Gratiot, 53541. Tel: 608-543-3631.
Catechesis/Religious Program—Students 22.

SPRING GREEN, SAUK CO., ST. JOHN THE EVANGELIST, [CEM], (Linked with St. Luke, Plain) Rev. Michael A. Resop; Sisters Amy Taylor, F.S.P.A., Pastoral Assoc.; Karen Flottmeier, F.S.P.A., Pastoral Ministry.
209 W. Daley St., 53588. Tel: 608-588-2028; Fax: 608-588-2648.
Office: 253 N. WashingtonSt., P.O. Box 628, 53588. Tel: 608-588-2028; Fax: 608-588-2648. Email: stjohnsoffice@charter.net.
School—P.O. Box 129, 53588. Tel: 608-588-2021; Fax: 608-588-9372. Web: http://stjohns-springgreen.org. Lay Teachers 8; Students 84.
Catechesis/Religious Program—Tel: 608-582-2425. Angie Pulvermacher, D.R.E. Students 110.

STOUGHTON, DANE CO., ST. ANN, [CEM] Rev. Msgr. Gerard M. Healy.
Res.: 320 N. Harrison St., 53589. Tel: 608-873-7633; Fax: 608-873-6425. Email: weissco@stoughton.k12.wi.us. Web: stannparish.41pi.com.
School—Tel: 608-873-3343. Lay Teachers 13; Students 126.
Catechesis/Religious Program—Students 323.

SULLIVAN, JEFFERSON CO., ST. MARY HELP OF CHRISTIANS (1854) [CEM] Rev. Thomas J. Coyle.
Mailing Address: P.O. Box 418, 53178-0418. Tel: 262-593-2250. Email: smaryhoc@yahoo.com. Web: www.stmaryparishes.org.
Res.: 214 N. Sanborn Ave., Jefferson, 53549. Tel: 920-674-9619.
Catechesis/Religious Program—Tel: 262-593-2721. Edward Paloucek, D.R.E. Students 43.

SUN PRAIRIE, DANE CO.

1—ST. ALBERT THE GREAT Rev. Msgr. Terrence L. Connors; Deacon Joseph Stafford.
Res.: 2420 St. Albert Dr., 53590. Tel: 608-837-3798; Fax: 608-837-8576.
Catechesis/Religious Program—Susan Leet, D.R.E. Students 449.

2—SACRED HEARTS OF JESUS AND MARY, [CEM] Rev. Msgr. Duane R. Moellenberndt; Rev. John D. Putzer, Parochial Vicar; Sr. Anne Raymond Gasser, S.S.N.D., Pastoral Assoc.
221 Columbus St., 53590. Tel: 608-837-7381; Fax: 608-825-9585. Web: www.sacred-hearts.org.
Rectory—227 Columbus St., 53590.
School—219 Columbus St., 53590. Tel: 608-837-8508. Lay Teachers 30; Students 468.
Catechesis/Religious Program—Tel: 608-837-8509; Fax: 608-825-9585. Students 314.

TENNYSON-POTOSI, GRANT CO., SS. ANDREW AND THOMAS (1970) [CEM 2] Rev. Richard J. Leffler.
Res.: 101 Church St., Potosi, 53820. Tel: 608-763-2671. Web: www.ssandrew-thomas.org.
School—100 Hwy. 61 N., P.O. Box 160, Potosi, 53820. Tel: 608-763-2120; Fax: 608-763-4064. Lay Teachers 6; Students 60.
Catechesis/Religious Program—Tel: 608-763-2527 (1-8). Email: ssandrew@pcii.net. Beth Flesch, D.R.E. (1-8). Students 128.

TRUMAN, LAFAYETTE CO., IMMACULATE CONCEPTION (1856) [CEM], (Linked with St. Philomena, Belmont and St. Michael, Calamine) Rev. Monte E. Robinson.
Res.: 338 Chestnut St., Box 345, Belmont, 53510. Tel: 608-762-5446.
Catechesis/Religious Program—(Included in St. Philomena, Belmont)

VERONA, DANE CO.

1—ST. ANDREW (1917) [CEM] Merged with St. William, Paoli to form St. Christopher Parish, Verona.

2—ST. CHRISTOPHER PARISH (2010) [CEM] Rev. William F. Vernon.
Res.: 301 N Main St., 53593. Tel: 608-845-6613; Fax: 608-848-4293.
Catechesis/Religious Program—Laurie Sabbarese, C.R.E. (K-8); Joe Amato, C.R.E. (6-12). Students 303.

3—ST. WILLIAM, Merged with St. Andrew, Verona to form St. Christopher Parish, Verona.

WATERLOO, JEFFERSON CO., ST. JOSEPH (1868) [CEM], (Linked with St. Mary of the Nativity, Marshall) Rev. Michael R. Radowicz.
Res.: 205 Milwaukee Ave., 53594-1329. Tel: 920-478-2032. Email: office@ssmjwi.org. Web: www.ssmjwi.org.
School—387 S. Monroe St., 53594. Tel: 920-478-3221. Lay Teachers 5; Students 45.
Catechesis/Religious Program—Tel: 920-478-3232. Eileen Bender, C.R.E. Students 60.

WATERTOWN, JEFFERSON CO.

1—ST. BERNARD (1843) Rev. Msgr. Daniel T. Ganshert; Terese Markl, Pastoral Assoc.
Parish Center: 114 S. Church St., 53094-4399. Tel: 920-261-5133; Fax: 920-261-8371. Email: church@stbern.org. Web: www.stbern.org.
Rectory—110 S. Church St., 53094.
School—Tel: 920-261-7204. Email: principal@st.bern.org. Jeff Allen, Prin. Lay Teachers 8; Students 157; Religious Ed. Teacher 1.
Catechesis/Religious Program—111 S. Montgomery St., 53094. Tel: 920-261-2582; Fax: 920-261-7215. Email: faithformation@stbern.org. Students 95.

2—ST. HENRY (1853) [CEM] Rev. Msgr. Daniel T. Ganshert; Rev. Jorge A. Miramontes, Parochial

Vicar.
Res.: 412 N. 4th St., 53094. Tel: 920-261-7273; Fax: 920-261-3681.
School—300 Cady St., 53094. Tel: 920-261-2586. Lay Teachers 12; Students 121.
Catechesis/Religious Program—Tel: 920-261-6332. Todd Weissenborn, C.R.E.

WAUNAKEE, DANE CO., ST. JOHN THE BAPTIST (1874) [CEM] Rev. Msgr. James L. Gunn; Revs. David A. Carrano, Parochial Vicar; Gregory S. Ihm, Parochial Vicar; Deacon Norbert Brunner.
Res.: 209 South St., 53597. Tel: 608-849-5121; Fax: 608-849-5866. Email: stjohnparishwau@shraphael.org. Web: www.stjb.org.
School—Tel: 608-849-5325; Fax: 608-849-5342. Email: cstark@straphael.org. Conni Stark, Prin. Lay Teachers 17; Students 198.
Catechesis/Religious Program— Jenny Schmitz, Coord. Faith Formation (Children); Jenna Keller, Youth Min. Students 489.

WESTFIELD, MARQUETTE CO., GOOD SHEPHERD (1961), (Linked with St. John the Baptist, Montello) Rev. Michael C. Richel.
Res.: 277 E. Montello St., Montello, 53949. Tel: 608-296-2217.
Catechesis/Religious Program—241 E. 6th St., 53964. Tel: 608-296-3631; Fax: 608-296-2465. Darlene Duley, D.R.E. Students 84.

WESTPORT, DANE CO., ST. MARY OF THE LAKE (1866) [CEM] Rev. Msgr. James L. Gunn; Revs. Gregory S. Ihm; David Carraro.
Res.: 5460 Mary Lake Rd., Waunakee, 53597-9121. Tel: 608-849-4116; Fax: 608-849-4122.
Catechesis/Religious Program—Tel: 608-849-4376. Jennifer Schultz, C.R.E.; Jenna Keller, Youth Min. Students 69.

WISCONSIN DELLS, COLUMBIA CO., ST. CECILIA, [CEM] Res. & Office: 1612 Pleasant View Dr., 53965. Tel: 608-253-5107; 608-254-8381 (Office); Fax: 608-254-6217. Email: pastor@dellscatholic.com. Web: www.dellscatholic.com.
Church: 604 Oak St., 53965.
Catechesis/Religious Program—Tel: 608-253-5621. Students 214.

YELLOWSTONE, LAFAYETTE CO., ST. MICHAEL (1870) [CEM], (Linked with St. Joseph, Argyle; St. Joseph, Gratiot; St. John's, South Wayne) Rev. David A. Wanish.
Res.: 313 N. Lafayette St., P.O. Box 76, Argyle, 53504. Tel: 608-543-3631.
Catechesis/Religious Program—Classes attended at St. Joseph, Argyle Students 1.

Chaplains of Public Institutions

MADISON. *Columbia County Institution*. Attended from St. Mary's Church, Portage.
Dane County Institution. Attended from St. Christopher, Verona.
Grant County Institution. Attended from St. Clement Church, Lancaster.
Green County Institution. Attended from St. Victor Church, Monroe.
Iowa County Institution. Attended from St. Joseph Church, Dodgeville.
Madison-Meriter General Hospital. Attended from Cathedral Parish of St. Raphael
Mendota State Hospital. Vacant.
University Hospitals. Rev. Diego O. Cuevas, Chap. 302 S. High Point Rd., 53744.

JANESVILLE. *Jefferson County Institution*. Attended from St. John the Baptist Church, Jefferson.
LaFayette County Institution. Attended from Holy Rosary Church, Darlington.
Mercy Hospital. Attended from Janesville Parishes, Janesville.
Rock County Institution. Attended from Janesville Parishes, Janesville.
Sauk County Institution. Attended from St. Boniface Church, Lime Ridge.
Wisconsin State School for the Blind. Attended from St. Patrick's Church, Janesville.

Graduate Studies:
Revs.—
Dulli, Brian
Schroeder, Tait C.

Leave of Absence:
Revs.—
Clauder, J. Gibbs
Vosen, Gerald P.

Medical Leave of Absence:
Rev.—
Klarer, Michael E.

Military Chaplains:
Rev. Msgr.—
Heiar, Donald J., Jr.
Rev.—
Hesseling, Jason E.

Retired:
Rev. Msgrs.—
Hastrich, George M., 501 Bram St., 53713.
Hebl, John H., W8595 Fern Rd., Oxford, 53952.
Higgins, Joseph P., 3424 Maple Grove Rd., 53719.
Kertz, Raymond N.
Schmelzer, Delbert L., Bishop O'Connor Pastoral Center, 702 S. Highpoint Rd., 53719.
Revs.—
Borre, Robert J., 2000 Glenview Rd., Glenview, IL 60025-2850.
Buholzer, Robert E., St. Elizabeth Manor, P.O. Box 217, Footville, 53537.
Cassidy, Kevin W., P.O. Box 391, Mauston, 53948.
Conlon, Philip J., 306 Michael Ave., P.O. Box 326, Hollister, MO 65672.
Cox, Joseph C., 2805 Hunters Tr. #703, Portage, 53901.
Deitelhoff, Bernard H., 204 Buell St., 53704.
Doheny, Thomas R., 1914 Woodsdale Dr., Durham, NC 27703.
Doherty, Patrick J.
Dominic, Francis J., Park Place, 1015 N. Elm St., Platteville, 53818.
Fox, George W., 8202 Highview Dr., Apt. 45, 53719.
Furlong, J. Daryl, 3095 N. Course Dr., #1002, Pompano Beach, FL 33069.
Heitke, Lawrence R., 1022 Chester Ct., Nekoosa, 54457.
Hennington, Bruce M., 120 Rainbow Dr., #2022, Livingston, TX 77399.
Hollfelder, Eugene F., S2518 Vanhy St., Baraboo, 53913.
Hower, William J., 1870 Orchard Ln., Oshkosh, 54902.
Kalscheuer, Henry N., 1017 S. Holiday Dr., Waunakee, 53597.
Kieffer, Lawrence J., 4929 Whitcomb Dr., #6, 53711-2650.
Klink, Kenneth J., 7610 Mid-Town Rd., 53719.
Lange, Donald F., Academy Apts., #103, Hazel Green, 53811.
Lesniak, Richard D., 221 Vista Ct., Waupaca, 54981-1993.
Lins, James R., All Saints Assisted Living, 8210 Highview Dr., 53719.
Marr, Thomas P.
McEnery, James G., 57 Cherokee Cir., #204, 53704-1499.
Meier, Laverne G., Bishop O'Connor Pastoral Center, 702 S. High Point Rd., P.O. Box 44983, 53744-4983.
Murray, Donald J., 8541 Greenway Blvd., #302, Middleton, 53562.
Nilles, Roger G., 57 Cherokee Cir., #204, 53704.
Nolan, William A., 4007 Sandstone Dr., 53546.
Norder, John R., Bishop O'Connor Catholic Pastoral Center, 702 S. High Point Rd., 53719.
Pickarts, Bernard J., River House, Co. Hwy. Y, #10126, Mazomanie, 53560.
Rank, Ronald G., 700 Rosewood Ave., Marshall, 53559.
Runde, David H., Bishop O'Connor Catholic Pastoral Center, 702 S. High Point Dr., 53719.
Runde, Raymond E.
Schmidt, Francis J., 1934 Dolores Dr., 53716.
Schroeder, Thomas H., St. Mary Care Center, 3401 Maple Grove Dr., 53719.
Schumacher, Anthony J., 2976 Chapel Valley, #103, 53711.
Steffen, Francis J., Academy Apts. #110, 511 Co. Rd. Z, Hazel Green, 53811.
Taylor, Roger H., 801 S. Klein Dr., Waunakee, 53597.
Turner, Jerome R., 5658 NE Michael's Way, Poulsbo, WA 98370-8934.
Urban, John L., W 5410 Urban Dr., Johnson Creek, 53038.
Weisensel, Cyril O., Bishop O'Conner Catholic Pastoral Center, 702 S. High Point Dr., 53719.

Permanent Deacons:
Deacons—
Brunner, Norbert, St. John the Baptist, Waunakee
Buhman, Jerome, St. Maria Goretti, Madison
Bussan, William, St. Augustine Univ., Platteville
Davis, James, St. Jude, Beloit
Fernan, John K.
Fischer, Richard, St. William, Janesville
Hale, Thomas, Sacred Heart, Reedsburg
Hayes, Steven, Nativity of Mary, Janesville
Hendrickson, David, St. Dennis, Madison
Houseman, John, St. Patrick, Janesville
Jozefowicz, Patrick, St. Mary, Fennimore
Kraus, John, (Retired)
Lukesic, Raymond, Cathedral Parish of St. Raphael, Madison
Martin, Richard, St. Maria Goretti, Madison
Martin, Todd, St. Peter, Madison
Pickar, Ronald, Sacred Heart, Reedsburg
Stack, William A., (Retired)
Stafford, Joseph, St. Albert the Great, Sun Prairie
Sutter, Dennis, St. Mary of the Immaculate Conception, Portage
Tranel, Lawrence, Holy Ghost, Dickeyville

INSTITUTIONS LOCATED IN THE DIOCESE

[A] COLLEGES

MADISON. *Edgewood College, Inc.*, 1000 Edgewood College Dr., 53711. Tel: 608-663-2262; Fax: 608-663-6717. Email: dcarey@edgewood.edu. Web: www.edgewood.edu. Dr. Daniel Carey, Pres.; Mary Klink, Dir. College Ministries; Sr. Margaret Hopkins, O.P., Asst to the Pres. for Mission; Stephen Bullock, College Ministries; Rev. Anthony J. Schumacher, Chap. (Retired); Tasha Haverkamp, College Ministries. Dominican Sisters, Sinsinawa, WI. Sisters 9; Lay Teachers 245; Students 2,550.

[B] HIGH SCHOOLS, PRIVATE

MADISON. **St. Ambrose Academy*, 602 Everglade Dr., 53717. Tel: 608-827-5863; Fax: 608-833-1129. Email: info@ambroseacademy.org. Web: www.ambroseacademy.org. David Stiennon, Pres.; Scott Schmiesing, Prin. Sisters 3; Lay Teachers 10; Students 69.
Edgewood High School of the Sacred Heart, 2219 Monroe St., 53711. Tel: 608-257-1023; Fax: 608-257-9133. Web: www.edgewoodhs.org. Judd T. Schemmel, Pres.; Mr. Robert Growney, Prin.; Kristin DeLorme, Librarian. Dominican Sisters, Sinsinawa. Lay Teachers 56; Students 678.

[C] ELEMENTARY SCHOOLS, PRIVATE

MADISON. *Edgewood Campus School, Inc.*, 829 Edgewood College Dr., 53711. Tel: 608-663-4100; Fax: 608-663-4101. Web: www.campus-school.edgewood.edu. Sr. Kathleen Malone, O.P., Pres. & Prin.; Vikki Larson, Librarian. Dominican Sisters, Sinsinawa. Sisters 1; Lay Teachers 22; Students 289.

[D] GENERAL HOSPITALS

MADISON. *St. Mary's Hospital*, 700 S. Park St., 53715. Tel: 608-251-6100; Fax: 608-258-6731. Email: paula_mckenzie@ssmhc.com. Dr. Frank Byrne, M.D., Pres. Franciscan Sisters of Mary (St. Louis, MO)., Member of SSM Health Care. Total Staff 2,785; Beds 440; Patients Assisted Annually 128,894.
Pastoral Care Department Chaplains: Rev. Leo Petrimoulx, O.F.M.Cap. (Retired); Rev. Ted Lindquist, Lutheran Min., Evangelical Lutheran Church of America; Rev. Melva Bishop, American Baptist Chap.; Rev. Janet Summers, United Church of Christ, Chap.; Rev. Joanne Whelden, Unitarian Chap.; Sisters Pamela Moehring, S.S.N.D., Chap.; Clement Sabol, V.S.C., Chap.; Sandra Schmitz, O.P., Chap.; Liz Allen, Chap.; Paula McKenzie, Dir. of Pastoral Care; Rev. Jessica Scholten, Reformed Chap.; Rev. Robert Vetter, ELCA Chap.

BARABOO. *St. Clare Hospital*, 707 14th St., 53913. Tel: 608-356-1400; Fax: 608-356-1367. Web: www.stclare.com. Sandra L. Anderson, Pres.; Mary Hess, M.T.S., Chap. Member of SSM Health Care. Bed Capacity 100; Patients Assisted Annually 98,543.

JANESVILLE. *St. Mary's Janesville Hospital* (a division of SSM Health Care of Wisconsin, Inc.), 3400 E. Racine St., 53546. Tel: 608-373-8010; Fax: 608-373-8006. Email: kerry.swanson@ssmhc.com. Web: www.stmarysjanesville.com. Kerry Swanson, Pres. Sponsored by: Franciscan Sisters of Mary (St. Louis, MO).Member of SSM Health Care., Purpose: to provide health care, health education and related facilities and services as a Catholic hospital. Bed Capacity 50; Patients Assisted Annually 19,350; Total Staff 350.

MONROE. *The Monroe Clinic, Inc.*, 515 22nd Ave., 53566. Tel: 608-324-1000; Fax: 608-324-1114. Email: mike.sanders@monroeclinic.org. Web: www.monroeclinic.org. Michael B. Sanders, Pres. & CEO; Julie Wilke, CFO, Vice Pres., Contact Person. Congregation of Sisters of St. Agnes. Bed Capacity 61; Nurses 245; Patients Assisted Annually 219,000; Total Staff 1,123.

PORTAGE. *Divine Savior Healthcare, Inc.*, 2817 New Pinery Rd., 53901. Tel: 608-742-4131; Fax: 608-742-6098. Email: mdnelson@dshealthcare.com. Web: dshealthcare.com. Mr. Michael Decker, Pres. & CEO; Kurt Patrick, Dir. Spiritual Care & Chap.; Monica Holden, Chap. Sisters of the Divine

Savior. Sisters 2; Bed Capacity 52; Patients Assisted Annually 140,689; Total Staff 593.

[E] HOMES FOR THE AGED

MADISON. *St. Mary's Care Center*, 3401 Maple Grove Dr., 53719. Tel: 608-845-1000; Fax: 608-845-1001. William Bender, Admin.; Joe Pichler, Contact Person. Member of SSM Health Care. Total Assisted 687; Total Staff 290; Bed Capacity 184.

BARABOO. *St. Clare Meadows Care Center*, 1414 Jefferson St., 53913. Tel: 608-356-4838; Fax: 608-356-5441. Web: www.stclare.com. Ronnie E. Schaetzl, Admin.; Linda Gamble, Contact Person. Member of SSM Health Care. Total Assisted 20; Total Staff 180; Bed Nursing Home 102.

JANESVILLE. *St. Elizabeth Home*, 109 S. Atwood Ave., 53545. Tel: 608-752-6709; Fax: 608-752-1724. Sr. Marie Julie Saegaert, S.C.M.C., Admin. Aged Residents 43; Bed Capacity 43; Total Assisted Annually 52; Total Staff 85.

PORTAGE. *Divine Savior Healthcare Extended Care*, Mailing Address: 2805 Hunters Trail, P.O. Box 387, 53901-0387. Tel: 608-745-5900; Fax: 608-745-5997. Web: dshealthcare.com. (See Divine Savior Healthcare, Portage.) Aged Residents 100; Bed Capacity 110; Total Assisted Annually 194; Total Staff 124.

[F] MONASTERIES AND RESIDENCES OF PRIESTS

MADISON. *Bishop O'Connor Catholic Pastoral Center*, 702 S. High Point Rd., P.O. Box 44983, 53744-4983. Tel: 608-821-3000; Fax: 608-821-3013. Email: o'connorcenter@straphael.org. Web: www.madisondiocese.org. In Res. Rt. Rev. Marcel Rooney; Rev. Msgr. James R. Bartylla, Vicar Gen.; Rev. Diego O. Cuevas, Hospital Chap.; Rev. Msgr. Delbert L. Schmelzer (Retired); Revs. Laverne G. Meier (Retired); John R. Norder (Retired); David H. Runde (Retired); Cyril O. Weisensel (Retired).

EDGERTON. *Koshkonong Pastoral Center*, 432 Liguori Rd., 53534. Tel: 608-884-3425; Fax: 608-884-9231. Revs. Thomas Moylan, L.C.; Anthony Bailleres, L.C., Asst. to Provincial; Jose Felix Ortega, L.C., Sec.; Bros. Peter DeGoede, L.C.; Anthony Hale, L.C.; Joao Ricardo Macallo, L.C.; Luis Peiret, L.C.

[G] CONVENTS AND RESIDENCES FOR SISTERS

MADISON. *Secular Institute of Schoenstatt Sisters of Mary*, 5901 Cottage Grove Rd., 53718-1397. Tel: 608-222-7208. Email: schoenstattheights@schsrsmary.org. Sr. Ellen Marie Baranek, Supr. Sisters 5.

BELOIT. *Blessed Sacrament Convent*, 916 Bluff St., 53511. Tel: 608-362-3326. Sr. Pauline Labrecque, A.B.S., Regl. Supr. Regional House of the Auxiliaries of the Blessed Sacrament. Sisters in Residence 4.

PRAIRIE DU SAC. *Valley of Our Lady Monastery*, E11096 Yanke Dr., 53578-9737. Tel: 608-643-3520; 608-643-7986 (Altar Breads). Email: volocist@nunocist.org. Web: www.nunocist.org. Sr. M. Bernarda Seferovich, O.Cist., Prioress, Contact Person; Rev. Robert Keffer, Chap. Cistercian Nuns. Solemnly Professed 16; Temporal Professed 2.

SINSINAWA. *Dominican Motherhouse*, 585 County Rd. Z, 53824-9701. Tel: 608-748-4411; Fax: 608-748-4491. Email: gevelinger@aol.com. Web: www.sinsinawa.org. Sisters Mary Ellen Gevelinger, O.P., Prioress of the Congregation; Maryann Tranel, O.P., Sec. of the Congregation; Revs. John C. Risley, O.P., Chap.; John Gerlach, O.P., Chap.; Sisters Sharon Casey, O.P., Prioress - Siena, St. Clara Community; Martha Mary Rohde, O.P., Prioress - Mound; Mary Ann Carroll, O.P., Prioress, St. Dominic Villa; Kathleen Hayes, O.P., Prioress - St. Clara. Sinsinawa Dominican Congregation of the Most Holy Rosary. Sisters in the Congregation 548; Sisters 167.

[H] CHARITABLE INSTITUTIONS

MADISON. *Catholic Charities, Inc.* Diocese of Madison, *Administrative Center*, 702 S. High Point Rd., P.O. Box 46550, 53744-6550. Tel: 608-821-3100; Fax: 608-821-3125. Email: ccharities@ccmadison.org. Web: www.ccmadison.org. Brian A. Cain, Pres.

Central City Counseling Services, 30 S. Franklin St., 53703. Tel: 608-256-2358; Fax: 608-256-2350.

Janesville District Office, 2020 E. Milwaukee St., Janesville, 53545. Tel: 608-752-4906; Fax: 608-752-9699.

Yellowstone Office, 426 S. Yellowstone Dr., Ste. 100, 53719. Tel: 608-833-4800; Fax: 608-833-7897.

Saint Martin House Saint Martin House, 1862 Beld St., 53713. Tel: 608-661-3512, Ext. 200; Fax: 608-661-0363. Email: andy@cmctoday.org. Web: www.cmctoday.org. Rev. Msgr. Kenneth J. Fiedler, Spiritual Dir.; Andrew Russell, Dir.

Society of St. Vincent de Paul (District Council of Madison, Inc.), 2033 Fish Hatchery Rd., P.O. Box 259686, 53725-9686. Tel: 608-442-7200; Fax: 608-442-2711. Email: svdpmad@svdpmadison.org. Web: www.svdpmadison.org. Norbert Rabholz, Council Pres.; Ralph B. Middlecamp, Exec. Dir.

BARABOO. *Society of St. Vincent de Paul (Diocesan Council of Madison)*, 408 8th St., 53913. Tel: 608-356-8549; Fax: 608-356-2018. Email: rlpl@centurytel.net. Roger LaMasney, Council Pres.

JEFFERSON. *St. Coletta of Wisconsin, Inc.*, N4637 Hwy. Y, 53549. Tel: 920-674-4330; Fax: 920-674-4603. Web: www.stcolettawi.org. Anthony LoDuca, Pres. & CEO; Jonathan Berger, Vice Pres. Mktg. & Community Rels. Sponsored by the Sisters of St. Francis of Assisi. Milwaukee. Sisters 1; Brothers 1; Residents 271; Lay Staff 403.

[I] MISCELLANEOUS

MADISON. *All Saints Assisted Living Center, Inc.*, 702 S. High Point Rd., P.O. Box 46550, 53744-6550. Tel: 608-821-3100; Fax: 608-821-3125. Email: bcain@ccmadison.org. Web: www.ccmadison.org. Brian A. Cain, Sec. & Treas. Bed Capacity 58.

All Saints Retirement Center, Inc., 702 S. High Point Rd., P.O. Box 46550, 53744-6550. Tel: 608-821-3100; Fax: 608-821-3125. Email: bcain@ccmadison.org. Web: www.ccmadison.org. Brian A. Cain, Sec. & Treas. Purpose: To own, operate and maintain apartment homes for the aged in the tradition of the Roman Catholic Church, having a Catholic identity, and serving the physical, mental, emotional and spiritual needs of residents of the Diocese of Madison, Wisconsin. Bed Capacity 144.

The Catholic Diocese of Madison Foundation, Inc., 702 S. High Point Rd., P.O. Box 44983, 53744-4983. Tel: 608-821-3000; Fax: 608-821-3028. Rev. Msgr. James R. Bartylla, Pres. Purpose: to operate at all times hereafter, exclusively for religious charitable and educational purposes within the meaning of 501(c)(3) of the Internal Revenue Code of 1986...and to exclusively serve the Roman Catholic Diocese of Madison, its Bishop...

Edgewood College Incorporated, 1000 Edgewood College Dr., 53711. Tel: 608-663-4861; Fax: 608-663-6722. Email: dcarey@edgewood.edu. Web: www.edgewood.edu. Dr. Daniel Carey, Pres. Sponsored by Sinsinawa Dominican Sisters of Sinsinawa, WI.; Purpose: Edgewood College, rooted in the Dominican tradition, engages students within a community of learners committed to building a just and compassionate world. The college educates students for meaningful personal and professional lives of ethical leadership, service and a lifelong search for truth.

**The Evangelical Catholic*, 723 State St., 53703. Tel: 608-258-3140, Ext. 107. Mr. Jason J. Simon, M.Div., Exec. Dir.; Mrs. Grace Simon, M.Div., Asoc. Dir.; Mrs. Katelin Cummins, Administrative Asst.

St. Mary's Janesville Foundation, Inc., 3400 E. Racine St., Janesville, 53546. Tel: 608-373-8015. Web: www.stmarysjanesville.com. Norah L. Jones, Contact Person. Franciscan Sisters of Mary, Purpose: Organized to provide gifts, grants or other payments to SSM Health Care of Wisconsin, Inc. and other charitable, educational, scientific or religious organizations exclusively.

St. Mary's Foundation, Inc., 700 S. Park St., 53715. Tel: 608-258-5600; Fax: 608-229-8495. Email: stmarys_foundation@ssmhc.com. Web: www.stmarysmadison.com. Sandra Lampman, Contact Person & Exec. Dir.; Sarah E. Coyne, Contact Person & Attorney. Sponsored by the Franciscan Sisters of Mary., Purpose: To solicit, manage, invest and expend endowment funds and other gifts, grants and bequests primarily for the maintenance and benefit of St. Mary's Hospital and St. Mary's Care Center of Madison, WI; to support other medical research, educational or charitable programs or activities of St. Mary's in the Madison, WI area. Member of SSM Health Care.

St. Paul University Catholic Foundation, Inc., 723 State St., 53703-1087. Tel: 608-258-3140; Fax: 608-258-3141. Email: om@uwcatholic.org. Web: www.uwcatholic.org. Most Rev. Robert Charles Morlino, Ex-Officio Pres.; John Drake, Treas.; Nate Wlodarchak, Sec.; Mike Varda, Chm.; Rev. Eric H. Nielsen, Exec. Admin. Purpose: to own and maintain the property on which resides the St. Paul University Parish and St. Paul University Catholic Center. Total Staff 51. In Res. Jeffrey J. Karls, Assoc. Dir.

San Damiano Friary, 4123 Monona Dr., 53716. Tel: 608-222-6238; Fax: 608-222-6766. Revs. Lester Bach, O.F.M.Cap. (Retired); Augustin Cops, O.F.M.Cap. (Retired); Rupert Dorn, O.F.M.Cap (Retired); Loran Miller, O.F.M.Cap. (Retired); Leo Petrimoulx, O.F.M.Cap. (Retired); William Frigo, O.F.M. Cap. (Retired). Capuchin Order-Province of St. Joseph., House of Healing and Hospitality.

SSM Health Care of Wisconsin, Inc., 2901 Landmark Pl., Ste. 300, 53713. Tel: 608-258-6120; Fax: 608-258-6218. Steven M. Barney, Interim CEO. Sponsored by: Franciscan Sisters of Mary., Purpose: To provide either directly or in conjunction with other persons or organizations health care, health education and related facilities and services. Member of SSM Health Care.

BARABOO. *St. Clare Health Care Foundation, Inc.*, 707 14th St., 53913. Tel: 608-356-1449; Fax: 608-356-1367. Email: keri_olson@ssmhc.com. Web: www.stclare.com. Keri Olson, Foundation Dir. Sponsored by The Franciscan Sisters of Mary., Purpose: to solicit, manage, invest and expend endowment funds and other gifts, grants and bequests primarily for the maintenance and benefit of St. Clare Hospital and St. Clare Meadows Care Center of Baraboo, WI; to support other medical research, educational or charitable programs or activities in the Baraboo, Wisconsin Dells and Lake Delton, Wisconsin Area. Member SSM Health Care.

Saint Vincent de Paul Society-Baraboo (District Council of Baraboo), P.O. Box 233, 53913. Tel: 608-356-4649; Fax: 608-356-4430. Email: svdpbaraboo@centurytel.net. Tim Nolden, Gen. Mgr. Sponsored by: Saint Vincent de Paul Society., Purpose: To help the poor and needy in a Vincentian spirit and manner.

EDGERTON. *Oaklawn Academy*, 432 Liguori Rd., 53534. Tel: 608-884-3425; Fax: 608-884-8175. Email: oaklawnusa@aol.com. Web: www.oaklawnusa.com. Mr. Javier Valenzuela, Prin. & Contact Person.

Oaklawn Incorporated, 432 Liguori Rd., 53534. Tel: 608-884-3425; Fax: 608-884-8175. Email: oaklawnusa@aol.com. Web: www.oaklawnusa.com. Revs. Thomas Moylan, L.C.; Jose Felix Ortega, L.C., Sec.; Anthony Bailleres, L.C., Asst. to Provincial.

MONROE. **Monroe Clinic and Hospital Foundation, Inc.*, 515 22nd Ave., 53566. Tel: 608-324-2868; Fax: 608-324-1447. Tracey Pederson, Exec. Dir. Sponsored by Congregation of Sisters of St. Agnes (CSA)

PLATTEVILLE. *St. Augustine Newman Center* 135 S. Hickory, 53818-3316. Tel: 608-348-7530; Fax: 608-348-7530. Email: thomasl@uwplatt.edu. Web: www.uwplatt.edu/org/catholicnc. Revs. John Del Priore, S.J.P.; Faustino Ruiz, S.J.P. (Spain). Please refer to St. Augustine University Parish, Platteville. Priests 3; Total Assisted 600; Total Staff 4.

130 W. Cedar St., 53818-2457. Tel: 608-348-9735; Fax: 608-348-9920.

PRAIRIE DU SAC. **St. Vincent de Paul Society of Sauk-Prairie Roxbury Inc.*, 815 19th St., 53578. Tel: 608-643-8905; Fax: 608-643-8905. Email: stvdpmanager@verizon.net. Victor Lochner, Pres. Sponsored by: Saint Vincent de Paul Society., Purpose: To help the poor and needy in a Vincentian spirit and manner.

SINSINAWA. *Mother Samuel Coughlin Charitable Trust*, 585 County Rd. Z, 53824-9701. Tel: 608-748-4411; Fax: 608-748-5501. Email: gevelingerop@aol.com. Web: www.sinsinawa.org. Sr. Anne Sur, O.P., Contact Person. Sponsored by: Sinsinawa Dominicans., Purpose: To provide financial support to the aged, infirm or disabled vowed members of the Sinsinawa Dominicans.

Sinsinawa Housing, Inc., 585 County Rd. Z, 53824-9701. Tel: 608-748-4411; Fax: 608-748-4491. Email: gevelingop@aol.com. Web: www.sinsinawa.org. Sr. Maryann Tranel, O.P., Sec. of the Congregation. Sponsored by the Sinsinawa Dominicans., Purpose: To provide low-to moderate-income housing for senior residents of southwestern Wisconsin.

Sinsinawa Nursing, Inc., 585 County Rd. Z, 53824-9701. Tel: 608-748-4411; Fax: 608-748-4491. Email: gevelingop@aol.com. Web: www.sinsinawa.org. Sr. Maryann Tranel, O.P., Sec. of the Congregation. Sponsored by the Sinsinawa Dominicans., To organize, construct, operate and maintain a care center in southwestern Wisconsin for the elderly and infirm.

[J] CLOSED/MERGED PARISHES

Madison Diocesan Archives, 702 S. High Point Rd., P.O. Box 44983, 53744-4983. Tel: 608-821-3140; Fax: 608-821-3181. As the location of sacramental records can change periodically, inquiries for records of parishes on this list should be directed to the Madison Diocesan Archives.

Holy Redeemer, Madison Merged. Parish records located at St. Raphael Cathedral Parish, Madison.

Immaculate Conception, Barneveld Merged. Parish records located at St. Bernadette Parish, Ridgeway.

Immaculate Conception, Boscobel Merged. Parish records located at Corpus Christi Parish, Boscobel.

Our Lady of Guadalupe, Endeavor Closed. Parish records located at Archives, Diocese of Madison.

Queen of Americas, Cambria Closed. Parish records located at St. Mary, Pardeeville.

St. Aloysius, Sauk City Merged. Parish records located at Divine Mercy Parish, Sauk City.

St. Andrew, Tennyson Merged. Parish records located at SS. Andrew and Thomas, Potosi.

St. Andrew, Verona Merged. Parish records located at St. Christopher Parish, Verona.

St. Anthony, Highland Merged. Parish records located at SS. Anthony and Philip, Highland.

St. Barnabas, Mazomanie Merged. Parish records located at Holy Cross Parish, Mazomanie.

St. Bridget, Ridgeway Merged. Parish records located at St. Bernadette Parish, Ridgeway.

St. Camillus, Durward's Glen Merged. Parish records located at Divine Mercy Parish, Sauk City.

St. Francis Xavier, Adams Closed. Parish records located at St. Joseph, Argyle & St. Victor, Monroe.

St. James, Dayton Closed. Parish records located at St. Francis of Assisi, Belleville.

St. James, Madison (1905) Merged. Parish records located at Good Shepherd Parish, Madison.

St. James, Vermont Closed. Parish records located at St. Mary, Pine Bluff.

St. John the Baptist, Mill Creek Merged. Parish records located at Holy Cross Parish, Mazomanie.

St. John the Baptist, Muscoda (1854) Merged. Parish records located at Corpus Christi Parish, Boscobel.

St. John the Baptist, Union Mills Closed. Parish records located at St. Joseph, Dodgeville.

St. Joseph, Avoca Merged. Parish records located at Corpus Christi Parish, Boscobel.

St. Joseph, Berlin Closed. Parish records located at All Saints, Berlin.

Saint Joseph, Madison Merged. Parish records located at Good Shepherd Parish, Madison.

St. Joseph, Markesan Merged. Parish records located at Holy Family Parish, Markesan.

St. Malachy, Clyde Merged. Parish records located at Corpus Christi Parish, Boscobel.

St. Mary, Kingston Merged. Parish records located at Holy Family Parish, Markesan.

St. Mary, Mineral Point Merged. Parish records located at Cong. of St. Mary's/St. Paul's, Mineral Point.

St. Mary, Monroe Closed. Parish records located at St. Victor, Monroe.

St. Mary Health of the Sick, Merrimac Merged. Parish records located at Divine Mercy Parish, Sauk City.

St. Mary of Lourdes, Belleville Merged. Parish records located at St. Francis of Assisi, Belleville.

St. Michael, Berlin Merged. Parish records located at All Saints, Berlin.

St. Patrick, Albany (1868) Merged. Parish records located at St. Francis of Assisi, Belleville.

St. Patrick, Madison Merged. Parish records located at St. Raphael Cathedral Parish, Madison.

St. Patrick, Princeton Closed. Parish records located at St. James, Neshkoro.

St. Paul, Beloit Closed. Parish records located at St. Thomas the Apostle, Beloit.

St. Paul, Mineral Point Merged. Parish records located at Cong. of St. Mary's/St. Paul's, Mineral Point.

SS. Peter & Paul, Pleasant Ridge Closed. Parish records located at St. Joseph, Dodgeville.

St. Philip, Highland Merged. Parish records located at SS. Anthony & Philip, Highland.

St. Raphael Cathedral, Madison Merged. Parish records located at St. Raphael Cathedral Parish, Madison.

St. Rose of Lima, Brodhead Merged. Parish records located at St. Clare of Assisi, Monroe.

St. Stanislaus Kostka, Berlin Merged. Parish records located at All Saints, Berlin.

St. Thomas, Potosi Merged. Parish records located at SS. Andrew and Thomas, Potosi.

St. Victor, Monroe (1860) Merged. Parish records located at St. Clare of Assisi Parish, Monroe.

St. William, Paoli Merged. Parish records located at St. Christopher Parish, Verona.

RELIGIOUS INSTITUTES OF MEN REPRESENTED IN THE DIOCESE

For further details refer to the corresponding bracketed number in the Religious Institutes of Men or Women section.

[0470]—*The Capuchin Fathers*—O.F.M.Cap.

[0730]—*Legionaries of Christ*—L.C.

[0430]—*Order of Preachers-Dominicans* (Prov. of St. Albert the Great)—O.P.

RELIGIOUS INSTITUTES OF WOMEN REPRESENTED IN THE DIOCESE

[]—*Auxiliaries of the Blessed Sacrament*—A.B.S.

[0230]—*Benedictine Sisters of Pontifical Jurisdiction* (Yorktown, Watertown, SD)—O.S.B.

[3710]—*Congregation of the Sisters of Saint Agnes*—C.S.A.

[1070-03]—*Dominican Sisters*—O.P.

[1070-09]—*Dominican Sisters*—O.P.

[1230]—*Franciscan Sisters of Christian Charity*—O.S.F.

[1415]—*Franciscan Sisters of Mary*—F.S.M.

[2575]—*Institute of the Sisters of Mercy of the Americas*—R.S.M.

[2970]—*School Sisters of Notre Dame*—S.S.N.D.

[1680]—*School Sisters of St. Francis*—O.S.F.

[]—*Secular Institute of Schoenstatt Sisters of Mary*

[3020]—*Sisters Oblates to the Blessed Trinity*—O.B.T.

[0530]—*Sisters of Charity of Our Lady, Mother of the Church*—S.C.M.C.

[3930]—*Sisters of St. Joseph of the Third Order of St. Francis* (Prov. of St. Joseph)—S.S.J.-T.O.S.F.

[1030]—*Sisters of the Divine Savior*—S.D.S.

[1705]—*Sisters of the Third Order of St. Francis of Assisi*—O.S.F.

DEPARTMENT OF CEMETERIES DIOCESE OF MADISON

MADISON. *Resurrection Cemetery*, 2705 Regent St., 53705. Tel: 608-238-5561; Fax: 608-238-5768.

BELOIT. *Calvary Cemetery*, Mailing Address: P.O. Box 1944, Janesville, 53548. Tel: 608-754-3472; Fax: 608-744-8715.

Mount Thabor Cemetery, P.O. Box 1944, Janesville, 53547-1944. Tel: 608-754-3472; Fax: 608-741-8715.

JANESVILLE. *Mount Olivet Cemetery*, P.O. Box 1944, 53547-1944. Tel: 608-754-3472; Fax: 608-744-8715.

NECROLOGY

† Oehrlein, Rev. Msgr. Felix G., Wisconsin Dells, WI St. Cecilia.—Died Nov. 25, 2011

† Schuster, Rev. Msgr. Wilfred J., (Retired)—Died March 12, 2011

† Finnane, Daniel P., Westport, WI St. Mary of the Lake Parish.—Died June 25, 2011

† Grasso, Philip A., (Retired)—Died July 18, 2011

† Klink, Delbert D., (Retired)—Died Jan. 23, 2011

An asterisk (*) denotes an organization that has established tax-exempt status directly with the IRS and is not covered by the USCCB Group Ruling.

Diocese of Manchester

(Dioecesis Manchesteriensis)

Most Reverend

PETER A. LIBASCI

Bishop of Manchester; ordained April 1, 1978; appointed Titular Bishop of Satafis and Auxiliary Bishop of Rockville Centre April 3, 2007; installed June 1, 2007; appointed Bishop of Manchester September 19, 2011; installed December 8, 2011. *Chancery Office: 153 Ash St., P.O. Box 310, Manchester, NH 03105.*

Most Reverend

JOHN B. McCORMACK, D.D.

Retired Bishop of Manchester; ordained February 2, 1960; consecrated December 27, 1995; installed September 22, 1998; retired September 19, 2011.

Most Reverend

ODORE J. GENDRON, D.D.

Retired Bishop of Manchester; ordained May 31, 1947; appointed December 12, 1974; consecrated February 3, 1975. *Mailing Address: P.O. Box 310, Manchester, NH 03105-0310.*

Chancery Office: 153 Ash St., P.O. Box 310, Manchester, NH 03105. Tel: 603-669-3100; Fax: 603-669-0377.

Web: www.catholicnh.org

Email: webmaster@rcbm.org

Most Reverend

FRANCIS J. CHRISTIAN, PH.D.

Auxiliary Bishop of Manchester; ordained June 29, 1968; appointed April 2, 1996; consecrated May 14, 1996. *Res.: St. Joseph Cathedral, 145 Lowell St., Manchester, NH 03104-6135.*

ESTABLISHED 1884.

Square Miles 9,305.

Comprises the State of New Hampshire.

For legal titles of parishes and diocesan institutions, consult the Chancery Office.

STATISTICAL OVERVIEW

Personnel	
Bishop	1
Auxiliary Bishops	1
Retired Bishops	3
Abbots	1
Priests: Diocesan Active in Diocese	83
Priests: Diocesan Active Outside Diocese	7
Priests: Retired, Sick or Absent	77
Number of Diocesan Priests	167
Religious Priests in Diocese	53
Total Priests in Diocese	220
Extern Priests in Diocese	36
Ordinations:	
Diocesan Priests	1
Transitional Deacons	2
Permanent Deacons in Diocese	48
Total Brothers	20
Total Sisters	422
Parishes	
Parishes	90
With Resident Pastor:	
Resident Diocesan Priests	80
Resident Religious Priests	10
Missions	13
New Parishes Created	1
Closed Parishes	3
Welfare	
Catholic Hospitals	2
Total Assisted	399,649
Health Care Centers	7
Total Assisted	1,232
Homes for the Aged	3
Total Assisted	99
Specialized Homes	1
Total Assisted	25
Special Centers for Social Services	13
Total Assisted	96,479
Educational	
Diocesan Students in Other Seminaries	10
Total Seminarians	10
Colleges and Universities	4
Total Students	4,267
High Schools, Diocesan and Parish	3
Total Students	1,420
High Schools, Private	2
Total Students	877
Elementary Schools, Diocesan and Parish	20
Total Students	3,681
Elementary Schools, Private	4
Total Students	885
Catechesis/Religious Education:	
High School Students	5,631
Elementary Students	14,097
Total Students under Catholic Instruction	30,868
Teachers in the Diocese:	
Priests	2
Brothers	1
Sisters	11
Lay Teachers	521
Vital Statistics	
Receptions into the Church:	
Infant Baptism Totals	2,260
Minor Baptism Totals	145
Adult Baptism Totals	168
Received into Full Communion	121
First Communions	3,113
Confirmations	2,280
Marriages:	
Catholic	348
Interfaith	131
Total Marriages	479
Deaths	2,670
Total Catholic Population	282,745
Total Population	1,316,470

Former Bishops—Rt. Revs. DENIS M. BRADLEY, D.D., ord. June 3, 1871; first Bishop of Manchester; cons. June 11, 1884; died Dec. 13, 1903; JOHN B. DELANY, D.D., ord. May 23, 1891; cons. Sept. 8, 1904; died June 11, 1906; Most Revs. GEORGE ALBERT GUERTIN, D.D., cons. March 19, 1907; died Aug. 6, 1931; JOHN B. PETERSON, D.D., cons. Auxiliary Bishop of Boston, Nov. 10, 1927; transferred to See, May 13, 1932; died March 15, 1944; MATTHEW F. BRADY, D.D., cons. Oct. 26, 1938; transferred to See, Nov. 11, 1944; died Sept. 20, 1959; ERNEST J. PRIMEAU, S.T.D., appt. Nov. 27, 1959; resigned Jan. 30, 1974; died June 15, 1989; ODORE J. GENDRON, D.D. (Retired), ord. May 31, 1947; appt. Dec. 12, 1974; cons. Feb. 3, 1975; retired June 12, 1990; LEO E. O'NEIL, D.D., ord. June 4, 1955; appt. Coadjutor Oct. 17, 1989; succeeded to See June 12, 1990; died Nov. 30, 1997; JOHN B. McCORMACK, D.D. (Retired), ord. Feb. 2, 1960; cons. Dec. 27, 1995; installed Sept. 22, 1998; Bishop emeritus Sept. 19, 2011.

Vicar General—Most Rev. FRANCIS J. CHRISTIAN, Ph.D., D.D., 153 Ash St., P.O. Box 310, Manchester, 03105-0310. Tel: 603-669-3100.

Vicar for Priest Personnel—Most Rev. FRANCIS J. CHRISTIAN, Ph.D., D.D.

Vicar for Clergy—Rev. RICHARD B. THOMPSON.

Office of the Permanent Diaconate—Deacon ARNOLD J. A. GUSTAFSON, Dir.

Institutional Ministries Office—Rev. RICHARD B. THOMPSON.

Vicars Forane—Rev. Msgr. JOHN P. QUINN, V.F.; Very Revs. CRAIG I. CHENEY, V.F.; DENNIS J. AUDET, V.F.; DANIEL O. LAMOTHE, V.F.; FREDERICK J. PENNETT JR., V.F.; MARC R. GAGNE, V.F.; AGAPIT H. JEAN JR., V.F.; WILLIAM V. KALIYADAN, M.S., V.F.; RICHARD A. ROBERGE, V.F.

Moderator of the Curia—Rev. ROBERT E. GORSKI.

Propagation of the Faith—Rev. ROBERT E. GORSKI, Dir.

Manchester Mission—CLAIRE AUCOIN, R.N., Dir., Hogarel Buen Samaritano, Calle #20, 6-35, Cartago Valle, Colombia.

Canonical Services and Tribunal—153 Ash St., P.O. Box 310, Manchester, 03105-0310. Tel: 603-669-3101; Fax: 603-669-3102. WINIFRED MCGRATH, M.Th., Dir. Canonical Svcs.

Judicial Vicar—Rev. Msgr. DONALD J. GILBERT, J.C.L.

Promoter of Justice—Rev. Msgr. PAUL L. BOUCHARD, S.T.L., J.C.L.

Advocates—Revs. MICHAEL KERPER, V.F.; ROGER H. CROTEAU; MICHAEL E. GENDRON; ANDRE M. THIBODEAU (Retired).

Defenders of the Bond—Rev. Msgr. PAUL L. BOUCHARD, S.T.L., J.C.L.; Rev. JOHN J. MAHONEY JR., J.C.L. (ad causam).

Diocesan Judges—Revs. FRANCIS L. DEMERS, O.M.I., J.C.D.; JOHN J. MAHONEY JR., J.C.L.; MICHAEL S. TAYLOR, J.C.L.; WINIFRED MCGRATH, M.Th.

Auditors—Revs. VOLNEY J. DEROSIA; JOHN W. FLEMING; JANE COSMO; THOMAS H. KELLY, Ph.D.

Notaries—CHRISTINE MARRA; SHIRLEY PEDRICK; KATHERINE HEBERT.

Experts—THOMAS H. KELLY, Ph.D.; DAVID J. CORRISS, Ph.D.

Presbyteral Council—Rev. PETER A. LIBASCI, D.D., Pres.; Most Rev. FRANCIS J. CHRISTIAN, Ph.D., D.D.; Rev. Msgr. PAUL L. BOUCHARD, S.T.L., J.C.L., Vice Chm.; Rev. PETER P. BOUCHER; Rev. Msgr. JOHN P. QUINN, V.F.; Revs. PAUL B. BOUDREAU JR.; GERALD R. BELANGER; ROBERT F. COLE; MARK E. DOLLARD, V.F.; MICHAEL KERPER, V.F.; Very Rev. FREDERICK J. PENNETT JR., V.F.; Revs. MARCOS A. GONZALEZ-TORRES; EDWARD J. KELLEY (Retired); DAVID STEFFY, L.C.; W. PIERRE BAKER; THOMAS L. DUSTON; STEVEN M. KUCHARSKI; C. PETER DUMONT, Chm. (Retired);

JOHN S. SLEDZIONA, C.M.; ROBERT E. GORSKI; ROBERT G. BIRON; CHARLES E. DESRUISSEAUX, Sec. (Retired); RICHARD B. THOMPSON; BENET C. PHILLIPS, O.S.B.

College of Consultors—Most Rev. FRANCIS J. CHRISTIAN, Ph.D., D.D.; Rev. Msgr. JOHN P. QUINN, V.F.; Revs. GERALD R. BELANGER; ROBERT G. BIRON; PAUL B. BOUDREAU JR.; CHARLES E. DESRUISSEAUX (Retired); C. PETER DUMONT (Retired); ROBERT E. GORSKI; MARCOS A. GONZALEZ-TORRES; RICHARD B. THOMPSON.

Pastoral Council—Rev. PETER A. LIBASCI, D.D., Pres.; Most Rev. FRANCIS J. CHRISTIAN, Ph.D., D.D., Ex Officio; Sr. MARY ELIZABETH WHALEN, S.N.D.deN.; NICHOLAS BOUDREAU; Rev. THOMAS L. DUSTON; JOSEPH M. HORTON; CINDY OSSOLA; Deacon JAMES E. PATTERSON; INNOCENTUS ALHAMIS; Ms. JO-ANN M. ELLISON, Staff; Mr. RONALD CORMIER; Mr. DANIEL TAYLOR; Ms. DIANE FARINA; Mrs. PATRICIA NOLETTE; Ms. KARLEEN S. DELL'OVA; Mr. LAM TRAN; Mr. WILLIAM WHEELER.

Finance Council—Rev. PETER A. LIBASCI, D.D.; Mr. ALBERT ROMERO, Vice Chm.; Rev. JOHN W. FLEMING; Mr. STEPHEN J. KANEB; Mr. STEVEN R. MCMANIS; Mr. THOMAS F. PARKS; Mr. RONALD J. RIOUX; Mr. FRANK TOTH. Staff: GUY D. CHAPDELAINE, CPA, A.B., MBA; DAVID A. GABERT; Rev. ROBERT E. GORSKI; PATRICIA GONNEAU; KIMBERLY LOW; COLLEEN FOOTE.

Diocesan Review Board—RODNEY H. FOREY; Rev. THOMAS CHININIS (Greek Orthodox); SHEILA DEMPSEY; SUSAN N. STONE; Rev. Msgr. DONALD J. GILBERT, J.C.L.; CHRISTINE O. TREMBLAY, Chm.; MARK ATTORRI, Esq. Staff: Deacon GREGORY R. MCGINN; MARY ELLEN D'INTINO; JOSEPH P. NAFF; ANNETTE DESMOND; JAMES LUNDT.

Safe Environment Council—Sr. ELIZABETH ROY, C.S.C.; JACKIE CAPES; NANCY DEFILLIPO; RICHARD PLOURDE; NANCY WILMOT; WILLIAM HOSMER; MAURICE STEBBINS; Deacon RICHARD J. SHANNON; GEORGE SCOLLIN; STEPHEN DONOHUE; VIVIANA DURBIN; SANDRA HAUSER. Staff: MARY ELLEN D'INTINO; EVE MONGEAU.

Priest Personnel Board—Most Rev. FRANCIS J. CHRISTIAN, Ph.D., D.D., Chm.; Rev. Msgr. JOHN P. QUINN, V.F.; Very Revs. DENNIS J. AUDET, V.F.; RICHARD A. ROBERGE, V.F.; Revs. RICHARD B. THOMPSON, Ex Officio; ROBERT E. GORSKI, Ex Officio; ROBERT G. BIRON; GERALD R. BELANGER; ROBERT F. COLE; JOSEPH M. COOPER; ALBERT J. TREMBLAY JR.

Masters of Ceremonies—Rev. JASON Y. JALBERT. Email: jjalbert@rcbm.org; ANTHONY J. HALEY. Email: thaley@rcbm.org.

Cabinet Secretary for Evangelization and Education—Sr. MARY ELIZABETH WHALEN, S.N.D.deN. Email: mwhalen@rcbm.org.

Cabinet Secretary for Human Services—THOMAS E. BLONSKI. Email: tblonski@nh-cc.org.

Cabinet Secretary for Administration and Community Affairs—DIANE MURPHY QUINLAN, Esq. Email: dquinlan@rcbm.org.

Cabinet Secretary for Ministry Formation—Very Rev. DENNIS J. AUDET, V.F. Email: daudet@rcbm.org.

Cabinet Secretary for Communication, Planning, and Development—PATRICK F. MCGEE, A.P.R. Email: pmcgee@rcbm.org.

Cabinet Secretary for Real Estate—PAUL F. HARRINGTON. Email: pharrington@rcbm.org.

Chancellor—DIANE MURPHY QUINLAN, Esq., 153 Ash St., P.O. Box 310, Manchester, 03105-0310. Tel: 603-669-3100. Email: dquinlan@rcbm.org.

Secretary to Bishop—VACANT.

Secretary to the Auxiliary Bishop—FRANCEEN M. MORASSE. Email: fmorasse@rcbm.org.

Secretariat for Evangelization and Education—Sr. MARY ELIZABETH WHALEN, S.N.D.deN., Cabinet Sec. Email: mwhalen@rcbm.org.

Liaison for Religious Congregations—Sr. MARY ELIZABETH WHALEN, S.N.D.deN., Dir. Email: mwhalen@rcbm.org.

Department of Catholic Schools—MARY MORAN, Supt. Email: mmoran@rcbm.org; Sr. CLAIRE THORNTON, Ph.D., Assoc. Supt. Email: cthornton@rcbm.org.

Education and Formation of Laity—PATRICIA GABREE, Exec. Dir. Email: pgabree@rcbm.org.

Sacrament of Matrimony Ministry—PATRICIA GABREE, Dir. Email: pgabree@rcbm.org.

Office of Catechetical Formation—MARY ELLEN MAHON, Dir. Email: memahon@rcbm.org.

Office of Youth Ministry—Sr. MARY ELIZABETH WHALEN, S.N.D.deN., Contact. Tel: 603-669-3100; MARY ANN EDWARDS, Dir. Email: maedwards@rcbm.org.

Catholic Scouting—Rev. RAYMOND A. BALL, Dir.

Catholic Youth Organization Office—CHARLES COOK, Dir.

Office of Evangelization—EILEEN SMITH, Dir.

Charismatic Renewal—JACQUELINE MORGANTI, Contact. Tel: 603-332-3576.

Cursillo—DENNIS TRAYNOR, Lay Dir. Tel: 603-361-7591; Rev. WILFRED H. DESCHAMPS, Spiritual Dir. Tel: 603-532-6634.

Diocesan Camps—GUS PLANCHET, Dir.; MICHAEL DRUMM, Dir. Mktg. & Devel., P.O. Box 206, Gilmanton Iron Works, 03837-0206. Tel: 603-364-5851; Fax: 603-364-5038.

Pastoral Ministry—Sr. MARY ELIZABETH WHALEN, S.N.D.deN., Dir. Email: mwhalen@rcbm.org.

NH Diocesan Council of Catholic Women—EILEEN SMITH; MARILYN AUDET, Pres.

Lay Ministry Formation Commission—JACQUELINE MARA, Chm.; Deacon PAUL R. BOUCHER; Most Rev. FRANCIS J. CHRISTIAN, Ph.D., D.D.; RAYMOND J. BILODEAU; Deacon MARK F. HOBSON, Ph.D.; Rev. STEVEN G. MONTESANTI; JO-ANN FENTON; Rev. BENEDICT M. GUEVIN, O.S.B.; Bro. MARK E. HILTON, S.C.; Sr. AMY HOEY, R.S.M.; Deacon GREGORY MCGINN.

Secretariat for Human Services—THOMAS E. BLONSKI, Cabinet Sec. Email: tblonski@nh-cc.org.

New Hampshire Catholic Charities, Inc.—215 Myrtle St., Manchester, 03104. Tel: 603-669-3030; Fax: 603-626-1252.

Immigration and Refugee Services—CATHY CHESLEY, J.D., Ed.D., Dir.; LAN TRUONG, BIA Accredited Rep.; KIMBERLY GEORGE, Immigration Attorney; MARIA EVELETH, BIA Accredited Rep. Tel: 603-893-1971; FRANCIS AGYARE, Immigration Attorney.

Clinical and Family Services Office—JOSEPH P. NAFF, L.I.C.S.W., Dir.

Diocesan Consultation and Counseling Services—JOSEPH P. NAFF, L.I.C.S.W., Clinical Dir.

Adoption and Maternity Services—JOSEPH P. NAFF, L.I.C.S.W., Adoption Supvr.; ELAINE C. LANGTON, Social Worker.

Project Rachel—JOSEPH P. NAFF, L.I.C.S.W., Coord.

Our Place—JOSEPH P. NAFF, L.I.C.S.W., Dir. & Admin.

Office of Persons with Disabilities—Sr. PAULINE LAFOND, P.M., Coord.

Deaf Ministry—Sr. PAULINE LAFOND, P.M.; Rev. THOMAS L. DUSTON.

Parish and Community Services—Deacon RICHARD J. SHANNON, Dir.

Secretariat for Administration and Community Affairs—DIANE MURPHY QUINLAN, Esq., Cabinet Sec. Email: dquinlan@rcbm.org.

Respect Life Office—Bro. PAUL CRAWFORD, O.F.M.Cap., M.S.W.

Diocesan Public Policy Office—DIANE MURPHY QUINLAN, Esq., Chancellor; Bro. PAUL CRAWFORD, O.F.M.Cap., M.S.W., Dir.

Public Policy Commission—MEREDITH P. COOK, Chm.; Revs. MICHAEL KERPER, V.F.; THOMAS L. DUSTON; RAYMOND J. POTVIN; Bro. ISAAC S. MURPHY, O.S.B.; Deacon GREGORY R. MCGINN; ELIZABETH FEREN; THOMAS E. BLONSKI; EDWARD KENNEDY; DONALD W. AYRES, M.D. Staff: Bro. PAUL CRAWFORD, O.F.M.Cap., M.S.W.; DIANE MURPHY QUINLAN, Esq., Chancellor; ROBERT E. DUNN, Esq.

Ecumenical and Interreligious Affairs—Rev. CHARLES E. DESRUISSEAUX (Retired), Mailing Address: P.O. Box 310, Manchester, 03105. Tel: 603-669-3100.

Office for Ministerial Conduct—Deacon GREGORY R. MCGINN. Email: gmcginn@rcbm.org.

Safe Environment Office—MARY ELLEN D'INTINO, Compliance Officer & Dir.; EVE MONGEAU, Safe Environment Asst.

Operations & Information Systems—Sr. SHEILA GARVEY, R.S.M., Dir. Email: sgarvey@rcbm.org.

Catholic Campaign for Human Development/Operation Rice Bowl—Bro. PAUL CRAWFORD, O.F.M.Cap., M.S.W. Email: pcrawford@rcbm.org.

Catholic Relief Services—Bro. PAUL CRAWFORD, O.F.M.Cap., M.S.W. Email: pcrawford@rcbm.org.

Victim Assistance Coordinator—JOSEPH P. NAFF, L.I.C.S.W. Tel: 603-668-0014; 800-475-5585 (NH).

Brazilian Apostolate—Rev. CRISTIANO G. BORRO BARBOSA (Diocese of Baura, Brazil); JOSE GONCALVES, Coord. Brazilian Apostolate Pastoral Council, Blessed John XXIII Parish, 121 Allds St., Nashua, 03060-6395. Tel: 603-598-2622.

Hispanic Ministry—Deacon RAMON ANDRADE, Diocesan Dir. Tel: 603-889-9431, Ext. 13.

Manchester Hispanic Parish Ministry—Rev. JOSEPH GURDAK, O.F.M.Cap., Pastor, St. Anne-St. Augustine Church, 382 Beech St., Manchester, 03103. Tel: 603-625-5655; Sr. CONSUELA GALVIN, H.M.S.P.

Nashua Hispanic Parish Ministry—Rev. DANIEL A. ST. LAURENT, Pastor (Retired), St. Aloysius Rectory, 48 W. Hollis St., Nashua, 03060-3286. Tel: 603-882-4362; Sr. SARA GRIMALDO, H.M.S.P., Pastoral Min.

Vietnamese Apostolate—Rev. THIEN NGUYEN, St. Christopher Church, 60 Manchester St., Nashua, 03064. Tel: 603-882-0632. St. Anne-St. Augustine Church, 382 Beech St., Manchester, 03103. Tel: 603-625-5655.

Secretariat for Ministry Formation—Very Rev. DENNIS J. AUDET, V.F., Cabinet Sec. Email: daudet@rcbm.org.

Vocations Office—Rev. JASON Y. JALBERT, Dir.

Office of Clergy Formation—Rev. JOHN S. SLEDZIONA, C.M., Dir.

Office for Worship—Rev. JASON Y. JALBERT, Dir. Email: jjalbert@rcbm.org.

Office of Permanent Deacon Formation—Co Directors: Deacon GREGORY R. MCGINN; PATRICIA GABREE.

Secretariat for Communication, Planning and Development—PATRICK F. MCGEE, A.P.R., Cabinet Sec. Email: pmcgee@rcbm.org.

Communications Office—KEVIN J. DONOVAN, Dir.

Development Office—PATRICK F. MCGEE, A.P.R., Dir.

Secretariat for Finance—GUY D. CHAPDELAINE, CPA, A.B., MBA, Cabinet Sec. Email: gchapdelaine@rcbm.og.

Finance Office—GUY D. CHAPDELAINE, CPA, A.B., MBA, Finance Officer. Email: gchapdelaine@rcbm.org; DAVID A. GABERT, Dir. Parish & School Financial Svcs. Email: dgabert@rcbm.org; PATRICIA GONEAU, Controller. Email: pgoneau@rcbm.org.

Risk Management and Insurance Office—MARTHA A. KIPP, Dir. Email: mkipp@riskmgmt.rcbm.org.

Human Resources Office—CHRISTINE L. HAGEN, Dir.

Secretariat for Real Estate—PAUL F. HARRINGTON, Cabinet Sec. Email: pharrington@rcbm.org. Real Estate Board: ARTHUR W. ROSE, P.E.; Rev. ROBERT E. GORSKI, Staff; JOHN E. DOHERTY; FRANCIS X. FRAITZL III; STEPHEN CAMANN; HUGH R. O'NEIL; RAYMOND P. CLEMENT; Rev. JASON Y. JALBERT, Staff; DEBRA KEANE, Sec. & Staff.

Diocesan Cemetery Office—PAUL F. HARRINGTON. Email: pharrington@rcbm.org.

Diocesan Bureau of Housing—Rev. PETER A. LIBASCI, D.D., Pres.; PAUL F. HARRINGTON, Vice Pres.; MARTHA A. KIPP, Exec. Dir. Email: mkipp@dbhnh.org.

Diocesan Bureau of Housing, Inc. d/b/a The Carpenter Center, Inc.—323 Franklin St., Manchester, 03101. Tel: 603-625-5422; Fax: 603-625-1014. (Apartments 96)

DBH Shelter, III, Inc. d/b/a Pillsbury Square Apartments—12 W. Broadway, Derry, 03038. Tel: 603-432-0952; Fax: 603-625-1014. (Apartments 28)

DBH Management, Inc.—323 Franklin St., Manchester, 03101. Tel: 603-625-5422; Fax: 603-625-1014. (Total Staff 7; Total Assisted 132)

Censor Librorum—Most Rev. FRANCIS J. CHRISTIAN, Ph.D., D.D.

Society of Saint Vincent de Paul—RAYMOND RIOUX, Contact. Email: stvincentdepaul1@myfairpoint.net.

CLERGY, PARISHES, MISSIONS AND PAROCHIAL SCHOOLS

CITY OF MANCHESTER

(HILLSBOROUGH COUNTY)

1—ST. JOSEPH CATHEDRAL (1869) [CEM] Rev. Msgr. Anthony R. Frontiero; Deacon Robert R. Potvin. In Res., Most Rev. Francis J. Christian; Rev. Jean M. Lemay.

Res.: 145 Lowell St., 03104-6135. Tel: 603-622-6404; Fax: 603-626-4415.

Chapel—Most Blessed Sacrament Chapel Lowell St., 03104.

Catechesis/Religious Program—Colleen B. Lang, Catechetical Leader.

2—ST. ANNE (1848), Unified in 2004 into St. Anne-St. Augustin, Manchester.

3—ST. ANNE-ST. AUGUSTIN (1871) [CEM] Rev. Joseph Gurdak, O.F.M.Cap.; Deacon Ramon Andrade. In Res., Revs. Bernard J. Campbell, O.F.M.Cap; Patrick Glavin, O.F.M.Cap.; Bro. Paul Crawford, O.F.M.Cap.

Rectory—St. Anne, 231 Merrimack St., 03103.

Office: 383 Beech St., 03103-5350. Tel: 603-623-8809; Fax: 603-626-1517.

Catechesis/Religious Program—Marie Dancy, Catechetical Leader.

4—ST. ANTHONY OF PADUA (1899), (French), Rev.

Richard H. Dion; Deacon Harry A. Kram. In Res., Rev. Patrick K. Njau.
Res.: 172 Belmont St., 03103-4452. Tel: 603-625-6409; Fax: 603-625-0099.
School—(Grades PreK-6), 148 Belmont St., 03103. Tel: 603-622-0414; Fax: 603-669-5212. Jerry Bergeron, Prin.
Catechesis/Religious Program—Colette Lemarier, Catechetical Leader (K-6); Sr. Cindy Sanchez, Catechetical Leader (7-10).

5—BLESSED SACRAMENT (1907) Rev. John Bucchino, O.F.M.; Sisters Olivia Kidney, R.S.M., Pastoral Assoc.; Joan Messier, R.S.M., Pastoral Assoc.; Anne Martineau, R.S.M., Pastoral Assoc.; Bro. Charles Gingerich, O.F.M.
Res.: 14 Elm St., 03103-7242. Tel: 603-622-5445; Fax: 603-627-5983.
Catechesis/Religious Program—Stephen Donohue, Catechetical Leader; Martha Donohue, Catechetical Leader.
Chapel: St. Theresa of Lisieux Adoration Chapel—

6—ST. CATHERINE OF SIENA (1954) Rev. Paul D. Montminy; Sr. Jeannette Landreville, C.S.C., Pastoral Min.; Deacon Edward P. Munz. In Res., Rev. Ray J. Labrie.
Res.: 207 Hemlock St., 03104-3248. Tel: 603-622-4966; Fax: 603-622-0236.
School—(Grades PreK-6), 206 North St., 03104. Tel: 603-622-1711; Fax: 603-624-4935. Sr. Janet Belcourt, C.S.C., Prin.
Catechesis/Religious Program—Leslie Goan, Catechetical Leader.

7—ST. EDMUND (1914) Merged in 2002 with St. John the Baptist parish, Manchester and became Parish of the Transfiguration, Manchester.

8—ST. GEORGE (1890), Unified in 2002 with St. Joseph Cathedral, Manchester.

9—ST. HEDWIG (1902), (Polish), [CEM] Rev. Msgr. Alfred Daniszewski.
Res.: 147 Walnut St., 03104-4225. Tel: 603-623-4835.
School—St. Casimir, (Grades K-8), 456 Union St., 03103. Tel: 603-623-6411. Sr. Frances Marion Bonczar, C.S.S.F., Prin. Felician Sisters 1; Students 146; Lay Teachers 8.

10—ST. JOHN THE BAPTIST (1914) Merged in 2002 with St. Edward parish, Manchester to form Parish of the Transfiguration, Manchester.

11—STE. MARIE (1880), (French), [CEM 2] Revs. Maurice R. Larochelle; Donald E. Clinton; Deacon Frank Gallinaro, Pastoral Assoc. In Res., Revs. Marcel M. Allard (Retired); Richard B. Tetu.
Office: 133 Wayne St., 03102-3740.
Res.: 378 Notre Dame Ave., 03102-3793. Tel: 603-622-4615; Fax: 603-666-4732.
Catechesis/Religious Program—Terry Bolduc, Catechetical Leader.
Chapel—Joseph House 279 Cartier St., 03102. Tel: 603-627-9493.
Chapel—Chapel of North American Martyrs 378 Notre Dame Ave., 03102.
Chapel—St. Joan of Arc 378 Notre Dame Ave., 03102.
Chapel—Mother Rivier Eucharist Adoration Chapel 133 Wayne St., 03102.
Convent—(Sisters of the Presentation of Mary), 133 Wayne St., 03102. Tel: 603-623-0815.

12—OUR LADY OF PERPETUAL HELP (1911), Unified in 2006 with St. Anthony of Padua, Manchester.

13—PARISH OF THE TRANSFIGURATION (2002) Rev. John W. Fleming; Sr. Priscilla Lemire, R.J.M., Pastoral Assoc.; Deacon Richard J. Shannon. In Res., Rev. Msgr. James J. Markham (Retired); Rev. John J. Mahoney Jr.
Res.: 107 Alsace St., 03102-3006. Tel: 603-623-4715; Fax: 603-623-4715.
Catechesis/Religious Program—Tel: 603-622-0504. Sr. Bernadette Turgeon, S.N.D.deN., Catechetical Leader.

14—ST. PATRICK (1898) [CEM] Merged Unified in 2007 with Parish of the Transfiguration, Manchester.

15—ST. PIUS X (1955) Revs. Robert E. Gorski; Richard B. Tetu, Senior Priest; Deacon Mark F. Hobson. In Res., Rev. Richard B. Thompson.
Res.: 575 Candia Rd., 03109-4735. Tel: 603-622-6510; Fax: 603-626-1323.
Catechesis/Religious Program—Donna Dukeshire, Catechetical Leader.

16—ST. RAPHAEL (1888) [CEM] Rev. Jerome J. Day, O.S.B.
Res.: 103 Walker St., 03102-4566. Tel: 603-623-2604. Email: raph103@comcast.net.
Catechesis/Religious Program—Tel: 603-647-2283. Therese Dame, Catechetical Leader.

17—SACRED HEART OF JESUS (1911), (French), Revs. Maurice R. Larochelle; Donald E. Clinton; Deacon Frank Gallinaro.
Mailing Address & Office: 247 S. Main St., 03102-4890.
378 Notre Dame Ave., 03102-3793.
Church: 265 S. Main St., 03102. Tel: 603-625-9525; Fax: 603-666-4732.
Catechesis/Religious Program—Tel: 603-622-3312. Karen Hettrick, Catechetical Leader.

18—ST. THERESA, Unified in 2004 with Blessed Sacrament Manchester.

OUTSIDE THE CITY OF MANCHESTER

ALTON, BELKNAP CO.

1—ST. JOAN OF ARC (1961) Merged in 2003 with St. Cecilia Parish, Wolfelboro to form St. Katharine Drexel, Alton.

2—ST. KATHARINE DREXEL (2003) Rev. Robert F. Cole. Mailing Address: P.O. Box 180, Wolfeboro, 03894-0180. Tel: 603-875-2548; Fax: 603-875-4801.
Res.: 50 Friar Tuck Way, Wolfeboro, 03894.
Church: 40 Hidden Springs Rd., 03809.
Catechesis/Religious Program—Gertrude Hammond, Catechetical Leader.

ASHLAND, GRAFTON CO., ST. AGNES (1904) Merged in 2006 with St. Matthew, Plymouth and St. Timothy, Bristol to form Holy Trinity Parish, Plymouth.

AUBURN, ROCKINGHAM CO., ST. PETER (1948) Rev. Michael E. Gendron.
Res. & Church: 567 Manchester Rd., 03032-3123. Tel: 603-623-5429; Fax: 603-669-5598.
Catechesis/Religious Program—Tel: 603-669-5134.

BEDFORD, HILLSBOROUGH CO., ST. ELIZABETH SETON (1964) Rev. Msgr. John P. Quinn; Sr. Rosemary Crowley, SNDdeN, Pastoral Assoc.
Res.: 190 Meetinghouse Rd., 03110-6027. Tel: 603-669-7444; Fax: 603-644-5371.
Catechesis/Religious Program—Mary Danielson, Catechetical Leader; Carrie Soucy, Catechetical Leader; Susan Foote, Catechetical Leader.

BELMONT, BELKNAP CO., ST. JOSEPH (1949) Rev. Paul B. Boudreau Jr.
Res.: 6 High St., P.O. Box 285, 03220-0285. Tel: 603-267-8174; Fax: 603-267-1170.
Catechesis/Religious Program—Kathy Loiacono, Pastoral Min.

BENNINGTON, HILLSBOROUGH CO., ST. PATRICK (1936) [CEM] Merged in 2006 with St. Denis, Harrisville and St. Peter, Peterborough in 2006 to form Divine Mercy Parish, Peterborough.

BERLIN, COOS CO.

1—ST. ANNE (1885) Merged in 2000 with Guardian Angel, St. Joseph and St. Kieran to form Good Shepherd Parish, Berlin.

2—GOOD SHEPHERD (2000) Revs. Mark E. Dollard; Kyle F. Stanton; Sr. Monique Therriault, R.S.M., Pastoral Assoc.
P.O. Box 570, 03570-0570.
Office: 151 Emery St., P.O. Box 570, 03570-0570. Tel: 603-752-2880; Fax: 603-752-1855.
Res.: 162 Madison Ave., 03570-2065.
Catechesis/Religious Program—140 Blanchard St., P.O. Box 518, 03570. Tel: 603-752-5443; Fax: 603-752-1743. Emilie Stiles, Catechetical Leader. Students 260.

3—GUARDIAN ANGEL (1917) Merged in 2000 with St. Anne, St. Joseph and St. Kieran to form Good Shepherd parish, Berlin.

4—ST. JOSEPH (1943) Merged in 2000 with Guardian Angel, St. Anne and St. Kieran to form Good Shepherd parish, Berlin.

5—ST. KIERAN (1894) Merged in 2000 with Guardian Angel, St. Anne and St. Joseph to form Good Shepherd parish, Berlin.

BRISTOL, GRAFTON CO., ST. TIMOTHY (1953) Merged in 2006 with St. Agnes, Ashland and St. Matthew, Plymouth to form Holy Trinity Parish, Plymouth.

CANDIA, ROCKINGHAM CO., ST. PAUL (1971) Merged with St. Peter, Auburn. For sacramental records see St. Peter, Auburn.

CASCADE, COOS CO., ST. BENEDICT, Closed. in 1991. For Sacramental records contact Good Shepherd, Berlin.

CENTER OSSIPEE, CARROLL CO., ST. JOSEPH (1965) Rev. Edmund A. Babicz; Mary Sullivan, Pastoral Assoc.; Deacon William Rich.
Res.: 23 Moultonville Rd., P.O. Box 248, 03814-0248. Tel: 603-539-5036; Fax: 603-539-6295.
Catechesis/Religious Program—Patricia Swanson, Catechetical Leader.

CHARLESTOWN, SULLIVAN CO.

1—ALL SAINTS PARISH (2007) Rev. Steven M. Lepine; Deacon John Blicharz.
Res. & Office: 285 Main St., P.O. Box 332, 03603-0332. Tel: 603-826-3359; Fax: 603-826-5875.
St. Catherine of Siena Church—290 Main St., 03603.
St. Peter Church—38 Church St., North Walpole, 03609-1715.
Catechesis/Religious Program—Lisa Sweet, Catechetical Leader.
Mission—St. Joseph Elm St., Walpole, 03608.

2—ST. CATHERINE (1904) Merged in 2007 with St. Peter Parish, North Walpole to form All Saints Parish, Charlestown.

CLAREMONT, SULLIVAN CO.

1—ST. JOSEPH (1920), (Polish), Rev. George Majka.
Res.: 58 Elm St., P.O. Box 824, 03743-0824. Tel: 603-542-5732; Fax: 603-542-5732.
Catechesis/Religious Program—46 Elm St., 03743. Tel: 603-542-9933. Jeanne Brooks, Catechetical Leader.

2—ST. MARY (1823) [CEM] Rev. Shawn M. Therrien; Deacon Paul R. Boucher.
Res.: 32 Pearl St., 03743-2552. Tel: 603-542-9518; Fax: 603-542-9614.
Catechesis/Religious Program—32 Pearl St., 03743-2552. Cynthia LaCasce, Catechetical Leader. Students 48.
Chapel—Old St. Mary Old Church Rd., Sullivan Co. 03743.

COLEBROOK, COOS CO.

1—ST. BRENDAN (1953) [CEM] Merged in 2007 with St. Albert Parish, West Stewartstown to form North American Martyrs Parish, Colebrook.

2—NORTH AMERICAN MARTYRS PARISH (2007) Very Rev. Craig I. Cheney.
Res. & Office: 55 Pleasant St., 03576-0065. Tel: 603-237-4342; Fax: 603-237-8580.
St. Albert Church—15 Church St., West Stewartstown, 03597.
St. Brendan Church—
Catechesis/Religious Program—
Mission—St. Pius the Tenth Main St., Errol, 03579. P.O. Box 65, 03576-0065.

CONCORD, MERRIMACK CO.

1—CHRIST THE KING PARISH (2011) Very Rev. Richard A. Roberge; Deacon Winton P. DeRosia.
Office & Rectory: 135 N. State St., 03301-6400. Tel: 603-225-2131; Fax: 603-228-4580.

2—IMMACULATE HEART OF MARY (1956) Rev. Raymond A. Ball; Deacon John Morrow.
Res.: 180 Loudon Rd., 03301-6028. Tel: 603-224-4393; Fax: 603-224-6229.
Catechesis/Religious Program—Tel: 603-225-2026; Fax: 603-224-6229. Denise Mainusch, Catechetical Leader.

3—ST. JOHN THE EVANGELIST (1865) Merged with Sacred Heart, Concord and St. Peter, Concord to form Christ the King Parish, Concord. For sacramental records see Christ the King, Concord.

4—ST. PETER (1946) Merged with Sacred Heart, Concord and St. John the Evangelist, Concord to form Christ the King Parish, Concord. For sacramental records see Christ the King, Concord.

5—SACRED HEART (1892), (French), Merged with St. John the Evangelist, Concord and St. Peter, Concord to form Christ the King Parish, Concord. For sacramental records see Christ the King, Concord.

DERRY, ROCKINGHAM CO.

1—HOLY CROSS (1989) Rev. Roger H. Croteau.
Church & Office: 187 Hampstead Rd., 03038-4835. Tel: 603-437-9544; Fax: 603-537-1208.
Res.: 4 Belle Brook Ln., 03038-4835.
Catechesis/Religious Program—Tel: 603-537-1208. George Strout, Catechetical Leader.

2—ST. THOMAS AQUINAS (1888) Revs. Bruce Czapla, O.F.M.; Christopher Gaffney, O.F.M.
Res.: 26 Crystal Ave., 03038-1799. Tel: 603-432-5000; Fax: 603-434-0518.
Catechesis/Religious Program—Tel: 603-432-7530.
School—(Grades K-8), 3 Moody St., 03038. Tel: 603-432-2712; Fax: 603-432-2179. Paul Rakiey, Prin. Sisters 1; Lay Teachers 9; Students 217.

DOVER, STRAFFORD CO.

1—ST. CHARLES (1893), (French), [CEM] Merged with St. Joseph & St. Mary, Dover to form Parish of the Assumption, Dover.

2—ST. JOSEPH (1945) Merged with St. Charles & St. Mary, Dover to form Parish of the Assumption, Dover.

3—ST. MARY (1833) Merged with St. Charles & St. Joseph, Dover to form Parish of the Assumption, Dover.

4—PARISH OF THE ASSUMPTION (2009) Very Rev. Marc R. Gagne; Deacon Robert J. Gagnon.
Res. & Church: 150 Central Ave., 03820-3464. Tel: 603-742-4837; Fax: 603-749-6779.
St. Charles Borromeo Church: 577 Central Ave., 03820.
St. Joseph Church: 150 Central Ave., 03820.
St. Mary Church: Chestnut St. at Third St., 03820.
Catechesis/Religious Program—Ileana Hoeing, Catechetical Leader; Sheila Cronin, Catechetical Leader; Jeanne Supple, Catechetical Leader.
Mission—Chapel of the Nativity Rte. 9, P.O. Box 163, Barrington, Strafford Co. 03825. Tel: 603-664-9336; Fax: 603-664-2310.

DURHAM, STRAFFORD CO., ST. THOMAS MORE Rev. Andrew W. Cryans; Cheryl Goldthwaite, Campus Min.
Church & Office: 6 Madbury Rd., Box 620, 03824-0620. Tel: 603-868-2666 (Office); Fax: 603-868-3765.
Catechesis/Religious Program—Roxanne Raeside-Wilton, Catechetical Leader.

ENFIELD, GRAFTON CO., ST. HELENA (1899) Rev. Johnny Vadakkan, M.S.

Res.: 36 Shaker Hill Rd., 03748-3524. Tel: 603-632-4263; Fax: 603-632-7874.
Catechesis/Religious Program—Dorothy Campbell, Catechetical Leader.
Mission—St. Mary 1157 Rte. 4, Canaan, Grafton Co. 03741.

EPPING, ROCKINGHAM CO., ST. JOSEPH (1898) [CEM] Rev. Volney J. DeRosia.
Res.: 14 Church St., P.O. Box 337, 03042-0337. Tel: 603-679-8805; Fax: 603-679-5192.
Church: 208 Pleasant St., Rte. 27, P.O. Box 337, 03042-0337.
Catechesis/Religious Program—Ann Ryan, Catechetical Leader.

EXETER, ROCKINGHAM CO., ST. MICHAEL (1859) Revs. Marc R. Montminy; Christopher M. Martel; Leah Grant, Pastoral Min.
Res.: 91 Front St., 03833-3297. Tel: 603-772-2494; Fax: 603-778-1629.
Church: 93 Front St., 03833.
Catechesis/Religious Program—Susan Breton, Catechetical Leader.

FARMINGTON, STRAFFORD CO., ST. PETER (1920) Rev. Daniel J. Sinibaldi; Deacon Richard A. Falardeau; Sr. Lucie Ducas, C.S.C., Pastoral Assoc.
Res.: 88 Central St., P.O. Box 565, 03835-0565. Tel: 603-755-2280.
Catechesis/Religious Program—Margaret O'Brien, Catechetical Leader.

FRANKLIN, MERRIMACK CO., ST. PAUL (1884) [CEM] Rev. Raymond E. Gagnon.
Res.: 110 School St., P.O. Box 490, 03235-0490. Tel: 603-934-5013; Fax: 603-934-3469.
Catechesis/Religious Program—Tel: 603-934-4372. Mary Ellen Shaw, Catechetical Leader.

GOFFSTOWN, HILLSBOROUGH CO., ST. LAWRENCE (1955) Rev. Gerard L. Bertin; Gerald Bergeron, Pastoral Min.
Res.: 51 Main St., 03045-1644. Tel: 603-497-2651; Fax: 603-497-3668.
Church: 1 E. Union St., 03045.
Catechesis/Religious Program—Tel: 603-497-4093. Deborah Fatcheric, Catechetical Leader; Edward Hager, Catechetical Leader.

GONIC, STRAFFORD CO., ST. LEO (1892) [CEM] Revs. Paul M. Gousse; Gerald R. Dunn, Weekend Ministry (Retired).
Res.: 59 Main St., 03839-5220. Tel: 603-332-1863; Fax: 603-330-0865.
St. Leo Catholic Children's Center—59 Main St., 03839-5220.
Catechesis/Religious Program—Tel: 603-332-1863; Fax: 603-330-0365. Robin Langlois, Catechetical Leader (K-5); Jerry Gregoire, Catechetical Leader (6-8); Ann McGregor, Catechetical Leader (Confirmation).

GORHAM, COOS CO., HOLY FAMILY (1876) [CEM] Revs. Mark E. Dollard; Kyle F. Stanton.
Res.: 9 Church St., 03581-1695. Tel: 603-466-2335; Fax: 603-466-3490. Res.: 162 Madison Ave., Berlin, 03570-2065.
Catechesis/Religious Program—Tel: 603-752-1176. Emilie Stiles, Catechetical Leader.

GREENVILLE, HILLSBOROUGH CO., SACRED HEART OF JESUS (1888) [CEM] Rev. Wilfred H. Deschamps.
Res.: 15 High St., 03048-3121. Tel: 603-878-1121.
Catechesis/Religious Program—Tel: 603-878-2274. Lisa Kouropoulos, Catechetical Leader.

GROVETON, COOS CO.
1—ST. FRANCIS XAVIER (1899) [CEM] Merged in 2007 with Sacred Heart, North Stratford to form St. Marguerite d'Youville Parish, Groveton., 11 State St., Box 247, 03582-0247.
2—ST. MARGUERITE D'YOUVILLE PARISH (2007) Rev. Daniel R. Deveau; Sr. Helene Georges, S.G.M., Pastoral Min.
Res. & Office: 11 State St., Box 247, 03582-0247. Tel: 603-636-1047; Fax: 603-636-2549.
Sacred Heart Church—59 Main St., North Stratford, 03590.
St. Francis Xavier Church—11 State St., 03582-0247.
Catechesis/Religious Program—Sr. Marie Mansfield, S.G.M., Catechetical Leader.

HAMPSTEAD, ROCKINGHAM CO., ST. ANNE (1979) Rev. Steven G. Montesanti; Deacon William E. Mullen.
Church: 26 Emerson Ave., P.O. Box 339, 03841-0339. Tel: 603-329-5886; Fax: 603-329-4468.
Res.: 99 Emerson Ave., P.O. Box 339, 03841-0339. Tel: 603-329-5089.
Catechesis/Religious Program—Cheryl Gottwald, Catechetical Leader; Pam Walsh, Catechetical Leader.

HAMPTON BEACH, ROCKINGHAM CO., ST. PATRICK (1914), Open in summer months. For all records contact O.L.M.M. Parish, Hampton Tel: 603-926-2206. Church: 5 Williams St., Hampton, NH 03842-2722 Tel: 603-926-2205. Fax: 603-926-6535. Rev. Msgrs. Charles E. Crosby, Rector (Retired); Edward J. Arseneault, Asst. Rector.

HAMPTON, ROCKINGHAM CO., OUR LADY OF THE MIRACULOUS MEDAL (1949) Rev. Gary J. Kosmowski; Deacon Dennis M. Jacobs; Sisters Doris Ouellette, C.S.C., Pastoral Min.; Theresa Malouin, C.S.C., Pastoral Min. In Res., Rev. Stephen F. Concannon.
Res.: 289 Lafayette Rd., 03842-2109. Tel: 603-926-2206; Fax: 603-926-8602.
School—Sacred Heart School, (Grades PreK-8) Tel: 603-926-3254; Fax: 603-926-1109. Mark Gillis, Prin. Lay Teachers 20; Students 215.
Catechesis/Religious Program—Tel: 603-926-5573. Sherry Impostato, Catechetical Leader.
Mission—St. Elizabeth of Hungary (1956) 1 Lowell St., Seabrook, 03874. Tel: 603-474-3839; Fax: 603-926-8602.

HANOVER, GRAFTON CO., ST. DENIS (1907) Rev. Francis C. Belanger, O.P.
Res.: 8 Sanborn Rd., 03755-2149. Tel: 603-643-2166; Fax: 603-643-9881.
Catechesis/Religious Program—Jannine Walsh, Catechetical Leader.

HARRISVILLE, CHESHIRE CO., ST. DENIS, Merged with St. Patrick, Bennington and St. Peter, Peterborough in 2006 to form Divine Mercy Parish, Peterborough.

HENNIKER, MERRIMACK CO., ST. THERESA (1945) Revs. Thomas L. Duston; Paul T. Gilbert, Weekend Ministry; Deacons Joseph P. Borland; James E. Rock.
Mailing Address: 158 Old West Hopkinton Rd., P.O. Box 729, 03242-0729. Tel: 603-428-3325; Fax: 603-428-4479.
Catechesis/Religious Program—Mary Corsetti, Catechetical Leader.

HILLSBOROGH, HILLSBOROUGH CO., ST. MARY (1892) [CEM] [JC] Revs. Thomas L. Duston; Paul T. Gilbert, Weekend Ministry; Deacons Joseph P. Borland; James E. Rock.
Res.: 38 Church St., P.O. Box 907, Hillsborough, 03244-0907. Tel: 603-464-5565; Fax: 603-428-4479.
Catechesis/Religious Program—
Parish Hall—Tel: 603-464-6021.

HINSDALE, CHESHIRE CO.
1—ST. JOSEPH (1884) [CEM] Merged in 2006 with St. Stanislaus, Winchester to form Mary, Queen of Peace Parish, Hinsdale.
2—MARY, QUEEN OF PEACE PARISH (2006) Very Rev. Daniel O. Lamothe; Revs. Steven M. Kucharski; Michael R. Monette; Deacon Arnold J. A. Gustafson.
Office: 161 Main St., Ste. 201, Keene, 03431-3790. Tel: 603-352-3525; Fax: 603-352-7472.
Res.: 173 Main St., Keene, 03431-3790.
St. Joseph Church—35 Brattleboro Rd., 03451.
St. Stanislaus Church—80 Richmond St., Winchester, 03470.
Catechesis/Religious Program—Ann Whittle, Catechetical Leader.

HOOKSETT, MERRIMACK CO., HOLY ROSARY (1886) [CEM] Rev. Edmund G. Crowley; Deacon David J. Shrader.
Res.: 21 Main St., 03106-1630. Tel: 603-485-3523; Fax: 603-485-8435.
Catechesis/Religious Program—Donna McCormack, Catechetical Leader.

HUDSON, HILLSBOROUGH CO.
1—ST. JOHN THE EVANGELIST (1949) Merged in 2007 with Infant Jesus, Nashua to form Blessed John XXIII Parish, Nashua.
2—ST. KATHRYN (1968) Rev. Joseph M. Cooper; Deacon Raymond V. Marcotte.
Mailing Address & Church: 4 Dracut Rd., 03051-5006. Tel: 603-882-7793; Fax: 603-595-1465.
Catechesis/Religious Program—Deacon Raymond V. Marcotte, Catechetical Leader; Nancy Schulz, Catechetical Leader.

JAFFREY, CHESHIRE CO., ST. PATRICK (1885) [CEM] Rev. Wilfred H. Deschamps.
Res.: 87 Main St., 03452-6139. Tel: 603-532-6634; Fax: 603-532-6633.
Church: 89 Main St., 03452.
School—(Grades PreK-8), 70 Main St., 03452. Tel: 603-532-7676; Fax: 603-532-7476. Sr. Cecile Provost, C.S.C., Prin. Sisters 2; Lay Teachers 10; Students 88.
Catechesis/Religious Program—Laurie Mathieu, Catechetical Leader.

KEENE, CHESHIRE CO.
1—ST. BERNARD (1862) [CEM] Merged with St. Margaret Mary, Keene to form Parish of the Holy Spirit, Keene.
2—ST. MARGARET MARY (1955) Merged with St. Bernard, Keene to form Parish of the Holy Spirit, Keene.
3—PARISH OF THE HOLY SPIRIT (2010) Very Rev. Daniel O. Lamothe; Revs. Michael R. Monette; Steven M. Kucharski; Deacon Arnold J. A. Gustafson.
Office: 161 Main St., Ste. 204, 03431.
Res.: 173 Main St., 03431-3790. Tel: 603-352-3525; Fax: 603-352-7472.
Worship Sites—
St. Bernard Church—185 Main St., 03431.
St. Margaret Mary Church—33-35 Arch St., 03431.
Immaculate Conception Church—37 School St., Troy, 03465.
Catechesis/Religious Program—Joy Davis, Catechetical Leader.

LACONIA, BELKNAP CO., ST. ANDRE BESSETTE (2010) Revs. Marc B. Drouin; Matthew J. Mason; Deacons Russell Morey; William McCarty.
Office: 291 Union Ave., 03246-3122. Tel: 603-524-9609; Fax: 603-524-9620.
Rectory—30 Church St., 03246.
Catechesis/Religious Program—Kathryn Canfield, Catechetical Leader (K-8); Margaret Gibbs, Catechetical Leader (9-10).
Worship Sites:—
St. Joseph— (1871), with Sacred Heart, Laconia and Our Lady of the Lakes, Lakeport to form St. Andre Bessette, Laconia. For sacramental records see St. Andre Bessette, Laconia.
Sacred Heart— (1891), with St. Joseph, Laconia and Our Lady of the Lakes, Lakeport to form St. Andre Bessette, Laconia. For sacramental records see St. Andre Bessette, Laconia.

LAKEPORT, BELKNAP CO., OUR LADY OF THE LAKES (1905) Merged with St. Joseph, Laconia and Sacred Heart, Laconia to form St. Andre Bessette, Laconia. For sacramental records see St. Andre Bessette, Laconia.
Mission—St. Helena Rte. 11B, Weirs Beach, Belknap Co.

LANCASTER, COOS CO.
1—ALL SAINTS (1856) [CEM] Merged with St. Matthew, Whitefield to form Gate of Heaven, Lancaster.
2—GATE OF HEAVEN (2009) Rev. John B. MacKenzie.
Res.: 163 Main St., 03584-3032. Tel: 603-788-2083; Fax: 603-788-5553.
All Saints Church: 161 Main St., 03584.
St. Matthew Cemetery Church: 9 Jefferson Rd., Whitefield, 03598-3101.
Mission—St. Agnes 297 Presidential Hwy. (Rte. 2), Jefferson, Coos Co. 03583.
Mission—St. Patrick Twin Mountain. Rte. 3 & 302, Carroll, Coos Co. 03595.
Shrine—Bretton Woods, Our Lady of the Mountains Bretton Woods.
Catechesis/Religious Program—Diane Caruso, Catechetical Leader; Susan Tibbetts, Catechetical Leader.

LEBANON, GRAFTON CO., SACRED HEART (1876) Very Rev. William V. Kaliyadan, M.S.
Res.: 2 Hough St., P.O. Box 482, 03766-0482. Tel: 603-448-1262; Fax: 603-448-3754.
Catechesis/Religious Program—7 Fairview Ave., 03766. Fax: 603-448-2139. Karen R. Boucher, Catechetical Leader.

LINCOLN, GRAFTON CO., ST. JOSEPH (1902) Rev. David L. Kneeland.
Res.: 25 Church St., P.O. Box 128, 03251-0128. Tel: 603-745-2266; Fax: 603-728-6222. Email: stjlincoln@gmail.com.
Catechesis/Religious Program—Joyce Peterson, Catechetical Leader.

LISBON, GRAFTON CO., ST. CATHERINE OF SIENA (1958) Rev. Jeffrey P. Statz.
Res.: c/o 21 Pine St., Woodsville, 03785-1215. Tel: 603-747-2038; Fax: 603-747-8071.
Church: 28 Highland Ave., 03585.
Catechesis/Religious Program—Marianne Hahr, Catechetical Leader.

LITCHFIELD, HILLSBOROUGH CO., ST. FRANCIS OF ASSISI (1953) Rev. Ray J. Labrie.
Parish Office—9 St. Francis Way, 03052-8050. Tel: 603-424-3456; Fax: 603-424-8603.
School—(Grades K-6) Tel: 603-424-3312; Fax: 603-424-9128. Amy K. Malinowski, Prin. Lay Teachers 9; Students 141.
Catechesis/Religious Program—Tel: 603-424-9061. Vicki Isabelle, Catechetical Leader; Jyl Dittbenner, Catechetical Leader; Joseph Malinowski, Catechetical Leader.

LITTLETON, GRAFTON CO., ST. ROSE OF LIMA (1882) [CEM] Rev. Marcel I. Martel.
Res.: 77 Clay St., 03561-4800. Tel: 603-444-2593; Fax: 603-444-3126.
Catechesis/Religious Program—Nicholas DeMayo, Catechetical Leader.
Mission—Our Lady of the Snows Main St., Franconia, Grafton Co. 03580.

LONDONDERRY, ROCKINGHAM CO.
1—ST. JUDE (1962) Rev. Robert Couto; Deacon Marc G. Payeur.
Res.: 435 Mammoth Rd., 03053-2304. Tel: 603-432-3333; Fax: 603-432-1639.
Catechesis/Religious Program—Tel: 603-437-7026. Trish Woodward, Catechetical Leader.
2—ST. MARK THE EVANGELIST (1981) Very Rev. Frederick J. Pennett Jr.; Deacon Leon Abbott Jr.
Res.: One Griffin Rd., 03053.
Church: One South Rd., 03053-3814. Tel: 603-432-8711; Fax: 603-434-6748.
Catechesis/Religious Program—Tel: 603-432-5711.

Catherine Kinnon, Catechetical Leader.
MARLBOROUGH, CHESHIRE CO., SACRED HEART (1886) [CEM], Unified in 2006 with St. Bernard, Keene.
MEREDITH, BELKNAP CO., ST. CHARLES BORROMEO (1946) Very Rev. Dennis J. Audet.
Res.: 8 Ridge Rd., P.O. Box 237, 03253-0237.
Church: 300 NH Rte. 25, P.O. Box 237, 03253-0237. Tel: 603-279-4403; Fax: 603-279-9924.
Catechesis/Religious Program—Marie Samaha, Catechetical Leader.
MERRIMACK, HILLSBOROUGH CO.
1—ST. JOHN NEUMANN (1982) Very Rev. Agapit H. Jean Jr.
Res.: 208 Naticook Rd., 03054.
Church: 708 Milford Rd. (Rte. 101A), 03054-4612. Tel: 603-880-4689; Fax: 603-881-9668.
Catechesis/Religious Program—Tel: 603-880-0825. Jennifer Lajoie, Catechetical Leader.
2—OUR LADY OF MERCY (1954) Rev. Msgr. Paul L. Bouchard; Christine Patterson, Pastoral Assoc.; Deacon James E. Patterson.
Res.: 16 Baboosic Lake Rd., 03054-3603. Tel: 603-424-3757; Fax: 603-424-1780.
Catechesis/Religious Program—Tel: 603-424-4477. Elaine Lamb, Catechetical Leader.
MILFORD, HILLSBOROUGH CO., ST. PATRICK (1895) [CEM] Rev. John W. Keegan, S.J.; Patti Sigvardson, Pastoral Assoc.
Res.: 34 Amherst St., P.O. Box 27, 03055-0027. Tel: 603-673-1311; Fax: 603-673-3687.
Catechesis/Religious Program—Tel: 603-673-4797. Sue Pasquale, Catechetical Leader; Kathy Frye, Catechetical Leader.
NASHUA, HILLSBOROUGH CO.
1—ST. ALOYSIUS OF GONZAGA (1871), (French), [CEM 3] Rev. Marcos A. Gonzalez-Torres. In Res., Rev. Daniel A. St. Laurent (Retired).
Res.: 48 W. Hollis St., 03060-3286. Tel: 603-882-4362; Fax: 603-886-8923.
Catechesis/Religious Program—Tel: 603-821-5192. Giselle North, Catechetical Leader; Carmen Dussault, Catechetical Leader.
Convent—St. Stanislaus, 5 Green St., 03064.
Chapel—Corpus Christi Chapel 43 Franklin St., 03064.
2—BLESSED JOHN XXIII PARISH (2007) Revs. W. Pierre Baker; Patrick N. Gilbert; Deacons Edmund C. Hilston; John H. St. George.
Res. & Office: 121 Allds St., 03060-6395. Tel: 603-882-2462; Fax: 603-882-7104.
Infant Jesus Church—121 Allds St., 03060-6395.
Catechesis/Religious Program—Tel: 603-886-9725.
St. John the Evangelist Church—25 Library St., Hudson, 03051-4239.
Catechesis/Religious Program—23 Library St., Hudson, 03051-4239. Tel: 603-882-6541. Dawn Gagnon, Catechetical Leader.
School—(Grades PreK-6), 3 Crown St., 03060-6366. Tel: 603-889-2649; Fax: 603-594-9117. Mrs. Estelle LaFleur, Prin.
Convent—St. John the Evangelist Convent, 27 Library St., Hudson, 03051.
Convent—Infant Jesus Convent
Brazilian Outreach Office—Tel: 603-598-2622.
3—ST. CASIMIR, Unified in 2002 with St. Patrick, Nashua.
4—ST. CHRISTOPHER (1950) Rev. Richard J. Kelley; James Dary. In Res., Rev. Bruce W. Collard.
Church: 60 Manchester St., 03064.
Res.: 62 Manchester St., 03064-6296. Tel: 603-882-0632; Fax: 603-881-8728.
School—St. Christopher, (Grades PreK-6), 20 Cushing Ave., 03060. Tel: 603-882-7442; Fax: 603-594-9253. Cynthia Clarke, Prin. Students 326.
Catechesis/Religious Program—Alana Kocsis, Catechetical Leader; Deacon James P. Daly, Catechetical Leader.
5—ST. FRANCIS XAVIER (1885) [CEM], Unified in 2003 with St. Aloysius, Nashua.
6—IMMACULATE CONCEPTION (1968) Revs. Richard E. St. Louis Jr.; Dixon Choolakkal, C.R.S., Weekend Ministry; Eric T. Delisle; Deacon William McDermott; Stephen Kimbell, Pastoral Min./Coord.
Res.: 216 E. Dunstable Rd., 03062-2344. Tel: 603-888-0321; Fax: 603-888-8407.
Catechesis/Religious Program—214 E. Dunstable Rd., 03062-2344. Tel: 603-888-0608; Fax: 603-888-3602. Eileen Bowes, D.R.E.
7—INFANT JESUS (1909) Merged with St. John the Evangelist, Hudson to form Blessed John XXIII Parish, Nashua.
8—ST. JOSEPH THE WORKER (1955) Most Rev. Francis J. Christian; Deacon Raymond A. Wheeler. In Res., Rev. Roger P. Bilodeau (Retired).
Church: 777 W. Hollis St., 03062-3553. Tel: 603-883-0757; Fax: 603-883-8057.
Catechesis/Religious Program—Janice Mercure, D.R.E.
9—PARISH OF THE RESURRECTION (1970) Rev. John M. Grace; Ann M. Cormier, Pastoral Min.
Res.: 23 Parrish Hill Rd., 03063-3412.
Pastoral Center—449 Broad St., 03063-3412. Tel: 603-882-0925; Fax: 603-881-3561.
Catechesis/Religious Program—Tel: 603-889-0012. Terry Root, Catechetical Leader; Charlene Tabat, Catechetical Leader.
10—ST. PATRICK (1855) [CEM 2] Rev. Michael Kerper; Sr. Elizabeth Castro Gonzales, H.M.S.D., Pastoral Min. In Res., Rev. John E. Healey.
Church & Res.: 29 Spring St., 03060-3490. Tel: 603-882-2262; Fax: 603-577-9817.
Catechesis/Religious Program—Tel: 603-882-5417.
11—ST. STANISLAUS (1908), Unified in 2002 with St. Aloysius of Gonzaga, Nashua.
NEW LONDON, MERRIMACK CO., OUR LADY OF FATIMA (1952) Rev. Robert G. Biron; Deacon Gregory R. McGinn.
Res. & Church: 724 Main St., 03257-7821. Tel: 603-526-4484; Fax: 603-526-8055.
Catechesis/Religious Program—Teresa Jackson, Catechetical Leader.
Mission—Immaculate Conception 12 Church Ln., Andover, 03216.
NEWMARKET, ROCKINGHAM CO., ST. MARY (1878) [CEM] Revs. Marc R. Montminy; Christopher M. Martel.
Res.: 182 Main St., P.O. Box 337, 03857-0337. Tel: 603-659-3643.
Catechesis/Religious Program—Tel: 603-659-6474. Rachel Willerer, Catechetical Leader; Nicole Benson, Catechetical Leader.
NEWPORT, SULLIVAN CO., ST. PATRICK (1902) [CEM] Rev. Peter P. Boucher.
Res.: 32 Beech St., 03773-1416. Tel: 603-863-1422; Fax: 603-863-7898.
Catechesis/Religious Program—Assumption Hall, 44 School St., 03773. Tel: 603-863-4085. Bill Mealey, Catechetical Leader.
Mission—St. Joachim 5 Olde Georges Mills Rd., Sunapee, Sullivan Co. 03782.
NEWTON, ROCKINGHAM CO., MARY, MOTHER OF THE CHURCH (1967) Merged with Holy Angels to form St. Luke the Evangelist Parish, Plaistow.
NORTH CONWAY, CARROLL CO., OUR LADY OF THE MOUNTAINS (1902) [CEM 2] Rev. Donald F. Gauthier Jr.; Deacon John Carey.
Office, Res. & Church: 2905 White Mountains Hwy., 03860-5111. Tel: 603-356-2535; Fax: 603-356-2877.
Catechesis/Religious Program—Mary Ann Kesmetis, Catechetical Leader.
NORTH STRATFORD, COOS CO., SACRED HEART (1888), (French), [CEM 2] Merged with St. Francis Xavier, Groveton to form St. Marguerite d'Youville Parish, Groveton.
NORTH WALPOLE, CHESHIRE CO., ST. PETER (1878) [CEM] Merged with St. Catherine of Siena Parish, Charlestown to form All Saints Parish, Charlestown.
PELHAM, HILLSBOROUGH CO., ST. PATRICK (1946) Rev. Anthony F. Kuzia, C.M. In Res., Rev. John S. Sledziona, C.M.
Res. & Church: 12 Main St., 03076-3724. Tel: 603-635-3525; Fax: 603-635-3919.
School—St. Patrick, (Grades K-8), 16 Main St., 03076. Tel: 603-635-2941; Fax: 603-635-9800. Henry Golec, Prin. Lay Teachers 20; Students 238.
Catechesis/Religious Program—Tel: 603-635-1447. Sr. Claire Provost, P.M., Faith Life Coord.
PENACOOK, MERRIMACK CO., IMMACULATE CONCEPTION (1880) [CEM] Rev. Raymond J. Potvin.
Res.: 9 Bonney St., 03303-1654. Tel: 603-753-4413.
Catechesis/Religious Program—Robert Charron, Catechetical Leader.
PETERBOROUGH, HILLSBOROUGH CO.
1—DIVINE MERCY PARISH (2006) Rev. Gerald R. Belanger.
Office: 18 Vine St., 03458-2403. Tel: 603-924-7647 (Church Office); Fax: 603-924-8365.
St. Peter Church—18 Vine St., 03458.
Catechesis/Religious Program—Jackie Capes, Catechetical Leader.
2—ST. PETER (1900) [CEM] Merged in 2006 with St. Denis, Harrisville and St. Patrick, Bennington in 2006 to form Divine Mercy Parish, Peterborough.
PITTSFIELD, MERRIMACK CO., OUR LADY OF LOURDES (1889) Rev. John B. Loughnane.
Res.: 20 River Rd., 03263-3314. Tel: 603-435-6242; Fax: 603-435-9398.
Catechesis/Religious Program—Tel: 603-942-8716. Katrina Allan, Catechetical Leader.
Mission—St. Joseph [CEM] 844 1st NH Turnpike (Rte. 4), Northwood, Rockingham Co. 03261. Tel: 603-435-6242; Fax: 603-435-9398.
PLAISTOW, ROCKINGHAM CO.
1—HOLY ANGELS (1892) [CEM] Merged in 2007 with Mary, Mother of the Church, Newton to form St. Luke the Evangelist Parish, Plaistow.
2—ST. LUKE THE EVANGELIST PARISH (2007) Rev. Albert J. Tremblay Jr.
Office: 8 Atkinson Depot Rd. (Rte. 121), 03865-3103. Tel: 603-382-8324; Fax: 603-382-1113.
Res.: 12 Amesbury Rd., Newton, 03858.
Holy Angels Church—8 Atkinson Depot Rd., 03865.
Mary, Mother of the Church—12 Amesbury Rd., Newton, 03858-3200.
School—Holy Angels Pre-School, Tel: 603-382-9783; Fax: 603-382-9783. Jean Lanctot, Dir.
Catechesis/Religious Program—Joyce Szczapa, Catechetical Leader.
Convent—6 Atkinson Depot Rd., 03865. Tel: 603-382-2744.
PLYMOUTH, GRAFTON CO.
1—HOLY TRINITY PARISH (2006) Rev. Leo A. LeBlanc; Deacon Michael Guy.
Res. & Office: 46 Langdon St., 03264-1438. Tel: 603-536-4700; Fax: 603-536-4709.
St. Agnes Church—19 Hill Ave., Ashland, 03217.
St. Matthew Church—11 School St., 03264.
Catechesis/Religious Program—Maureen Ebner, Catechetical Leader; Amy Ulricson, Catechetical Leader.
Mission—Our Lady of Grace 2 W. Shore Rd., Bristol, 03222.
2—ST. MATTHEW (1916) Merged in 2006 with St. Timothy, Bristol and St. Agnes, Ashland to form Holy Trinity Parish, Plymouth.
PORTSMOUTH, ROCKINGHAM CO.
1—ST. CATHERINE OF SIENA (1951) Merged in 2006 with St. James and Immaculate Conception, Portsmouth to form Corpus Christi Parish, Portsmouth.
2—CORPUS CHRISTI PARISH (2006) Rev. Gary J. Belliveau.
Office: 2075 Lafayette Rd., 03801. Tel: 603-436-4555; Fax: 603-433-4401.
Res.: 98 Summer St., 03801. Tel: 603-436-0048.
Immaculate Conception Church—98 Summer St., 03801-4398.
St. Catherine of Siena Church—845 Woodbury Ave., 03801-3294.
St. James Church—2075 Lafayette Rd., 03801-5697.
School—St. Patrick School, (Grades PreK-8), 125 Austin St., 03801. Tel: 603-436-0739. Sr. Mary J. Walsh, O.L.L., Prin.
Convent—Our Lady of Lourdes, Tel: 603-436-6612.
3—IMMACULATE CONCEPTION (1851) [CEM 2] Merged in 2006 with St. Catherine of Siena and St. James, Portsmouth to form Corpus Christi Parish, Portsmouth.
4—ST. JAMES (1958) [JC] Merged in 2006 with St. Catherine of Siena and Immaculate Conception, Portsmouth to form Corpus Christi Parish, Portsmouth.
ROCHESTER, STRAFFORD CO.
1—ST. MARY (1872) [CEM] Rev. Daniel J. Sinibaldi; Sr. Lucie Ducas, C.S.C., Pastoral Assoc.; Deacon Richard A. Falardeau.
Office: 71 Lowell St., 03867-5002. Tel: 603-332-1869; Fax: 603-332-2040.
Catechesis/Religious Program—Sr. Lucie Ducas, C.S.C., Catechetical Leader; Anna Ingram, Catechetical Leader.
2—OUR LADY OF THE HOLY ROSARY (1883), (French), [CEM] Rev. Paul M. Gousse.
Res. & Church: 189 N. Main St., 03867-1299. Tel: 603-332-1863; Fax: 603-330-0865.
St. Leo Catholic Children's Center—59 Main St., Gonic, 03839-5220.
Catechesis/Religious Program—Robin Langlois, Catechetical Leader; Jerry Gregoire, Catechetical Leader; Ann MacGregor, Catechetical Leader.
ROLLINSFORD, STRAFFORD CO., ST. MARY (1856) [CEM] Rev. Michael S. Taylor.
Holy Trinity—Church & Office: 404 High St., Somersworth, 03878. Tel: 603-692-4367; Fax: 603-692-4454.
Res.: 120 Maple St., P.O. Box 70, Somersworth, 03878. Tel: 603-841-3944.
Catechesis/Religious Program—Tel: 603-749-1666. Laurie Lambert, Catechetical Leader.
RYE BEACH, ROCKINGHAM CO., ST. THERESA (1979) Rev. Maurice D. Lavigne; Anne Hoeing, Pastoral Assoc.
Res.: 815 Central Rd., P.O. Box 482, 03871-0482. Tel: 603-964-6440; Fax: 603-964-4139.
Catechesis/Religious Program—Tel: 603-964-9878. Gary Hodsdon, Catechetical Leader.
SALEM, ROCKINGHAM CO.
1—ST. JOSEPH (1910) Merged with Mary, Queen of Peace, Salem to form Saints Mary and Joseph, Salem. For sacramental records see Saints Mary and Joseph, Salem.
2—SAINTS MARY AND JOSEPH (2010) Revs. John W. Michalowski, S.J.; Thomas J. Frink; Deacon David Costello; Mary Roy, Pastoral Min. In Res., Rev. Thomas J. Fitzpatrick, S.J.
Office: 200 Lawrence Rd., 03079-3978. Tel: 603-893-8661; Fax: 603-890-0292.
Rectory—33 Main St., 03079-1922. Web: www.saintsmaryandjoseph.org. Email: st.joseph@comcast.net.
Mary, Queen of Peace Church—200 Laurence Rd., 03079.
St. Joseph Church—40 Main St., 03079.

Catechesis/Religious Program—Marie Mullen, Catechetical Leader; Susan Levesque, Catechetical Leader.
Convent—St. Joseph, 34 Main St., 03079. Tel: 603-898-1829.
Chapel—Holy Family
3—MARY, QUEEN OF PEACE (1966) Merged with St. Joseph, Salem to form Saints Mary and Joseph, Salem. For sacramental records see Saints Mary and Joseph, Salem.
SANBORNVILLE, CARROLL CO., ST. ANTHONY (1908) [CEM] Rev. Edmund A. Babicz; Mary Sullivan, Pastoral Min.; Deacon William Rich.
Res.: 239 Meadow St., P.O. Box 490, 03872-0490. Tel: 603-522-3304; Fax: 603-522-8273.
Catechesis/Religious Program—Andrea Corso, Catechetical Leader; Beth Kilroy, Catechetical Leader.
SOMERSWORTH, STRAFFORD CO.
1—HOLY TRINITY (1857) [CEM] Merged with St. Martin, Somersworth to form Saint Ignatius of Loyola, Somersworth.
2—SAINT IGNATIUS OF LOYOLA (2009) Rev. Michael S. Taylor.
Office: 404 High St., P.O. Box 70, 03878. Tel: 603-692-2172; Fax: 603-692-2499.
Res.: 120 Maple St., 03878-1999.
Holy Trinity Church: 404 High St., 03878.
St. Martin Church: 120 Maple St. Ext., 03878.
Catechesis/Religious Program—Tel: 603-692-4367. Janet Jacobson, Catechetical Leader.
3—ST. MARTIN (1882), (French), [CEM] Merged with Holy Trinity, Somersworth to form Saint Ignatius Loyola, Somersworth.
SUNCOOK, MERRIMACK CO., ST. JOHN THE BAPTIST (1873) [CEM 2] Rev. Edmund G. Crowley; Deacon David J. Shrader. In Res., Rev. John B. Finnigan (Retired).
Res. & Church: 10 School St., 03275-1917. Tel: 603-485-3113; Fax: 603-485-2113.
Catechesis/Religious Program—Tel: 603-485-3972. Muriel Previe, Catechetical Leader.
TILTON, BELKNAP CO., ST. MARY OF THE ASSUMPTION (1894) [CEM] Rev. Raymond E. Gagnon.
Res.: 16 Chestnut St., P.O. Box 363, 03276-5546. Tel: 603-286-4445; Fax: 603-286-4663.
Catechesis/Religious Program—Tel: 603-286-4554. Mary Lacroix, Catechetical Leader.
TROY, CHESHIRE CO., IMMACULATE CONCEPTION (1903) [CEM] Merged with St. Bernard, Keene. For sacramental records see St. Bernard, Keene.
WEST LEBANON, GRAFTON CO., HOLY REDEEMER (1953), Unified in 2003 with Sacred Heart, Lebanon.
WEST STEWARTSTOWN, COOS CO., ST. ALBERT (1926) [CEM] Merged in 2007 with St. Brendan Parish, Colebrook to form North American Martyrs Parish, Colebrook.
WEST SWANZEY, CHESHIRE CO., ST. ANTHONY (1958), Unified in 2004 with St. Bernard Parish, Keene.
WHITEFIELD, COOS CO., ST. MATTHEW (1886) [CEM 2] Merged with All Saints, Lancaster to form Gate of Heaven, Lancaster.
WILTON, HILLSBOROUGH CO., SACRED HEART (1882) [CEM] Rev. Wilfred H. Deschamps.
Res. & Mailing Address: c/o Sacred Heart of Jesus Rectory, 15 High St., Greenville, 03048-3121. Tel: 603-654-6554 (Parish).
Church: 47 Maple St., 03086.
WINCHESTER, CHESHIRE CO., ST. STANISLAUS (1962) Merged in 2006 with St. Joseph, Hinsdale to form Mary, Queen of Peace Parish, Hinsdale.
WINDHAM, ROCKINGHAM CO., ST. MATTHEW (1962) [JC] Rev. A. Stephen Marcoux III; Deacon Bernard MacDonald.
Office: 2 Searles Rd., 03087. Tel: 603-893-3336; Fax: 603-898-4008.
Res.: 5 Searles Rd., 03087-1206.
Catechesis/Religious Program—Margaret Donahue-Turner, Catechetical Leader.
WOLFEBORO, CARROLL CO., ST. CECILIA, Merged in 2003 with St. Joan of Arc Parish, Alton to form St. Katharine Drexel, Alton.
WOODSVILLE, GRAFTON CO., ST. JOSEPH (1896) [CEM] Rev. Jeffrey P. Statz.
Res.: 21 Pine St., 03785-1215. Tel: 603-747-2038; Fax: 603-747-8071.
Catechesis/Religious Program—Sandy Perry, Catechetical Leader; Marianne Hahr, Catechetical Leader.

Chaplains of Public Institutions

MANCHESTER. *Catholic Medical Center*. Revs. Jean M. Lemay, Donald E. Lafond (Retired), Sr. Eileen Auger, Ms. Gayl Callis.
Elliott Hospital. Revs. Adrien R. Longchamps, Patrick K. Njau.
Hillsborough County Jail. Sr. Andrienne Gendron, P.M., Deacon David J. Shrader.
Veterans Administration Medical Center. Vacant.
Youth Development Center. Vacant.
BERLIN. *Androscoggin Valley Hospital*. Sisters Monique Therriault, R.S.M., Pauline Savageau, P.M.
Northern New Hampshire Correctional Facility. Rev. Mark E. Dollard, V.F.
BRENTWOOD. *Rockingham County House of Corrections*. Rev. Volney J. DeRosia.
CLAREMONT. *Sullivan County House of Corrections*. Rev. Shawn M. Therrien.
CONCORD. *Concord Hospital*. Rev. Paul T. Gilbert.
N.H. Prison for Men. Rev. Bernard J. Campbell, O.F.M.Cap, Deacon James P. Daly, Chap., Very Rev. Richard A. Roberge, V.F.
New Hampshire State Hospital. Vacant.
GOFFSTOWN. *New Hampshire State Prison for Women*. Deacon David J. Shrader.
LACONIA. *Belknap County House of Corrections*. Rev. Marc B. Drouin, V.F.
LEBANON. *Dartmouth-Hitchcock Medical Center*. Rev. Lawrence O. Ejiofo.
NASHUA. *St. Joseph Hospital*. Revs. Eric T. Delisle, John E. Healey.
Southern N.H. Regional Medical Center. Sr. Doris E. Gagnon, P.M., Ph.D., B.A., Revs. Eric T. Delisle, Chap., John E. Healey.
NORTH HAVERHILL. *Grafton County House of Correction*. Rev. Jeffrey P. Statz.
OSSIPEE. *Carroll County House of Correction*. Rev. Edmund A. Babicz.
WEST STEWARTSTOWN. *Coos County House of Corrections*. Very Rev. Craig I. Cheney, V.F.
WESTMORELAND. *Cheshire County House of Corrections*. Very Rev. Daniel O. Lamothe, V.F.

On Duty Outside the Diocese:
Rev. Msgr.—
Arsenault, Edward J., S.T.L. (WDC)
Rev.—
de Laire, Georges F.

Military Chaplains:
Revs.—
Cody, Kevin W., Major, PSC 2 Box 14863, Apo, AE 09012.
Glasgow, Robert K., LTC, Major, USA, 458 Dyea Avenlle, Apt. B, Fort Richardson, AK 99505-1176.

Absent on Leave:
Revs.—
Broussard, Dennis A.
Connor, Kevin T.
Guillemette, Robert C.
Lamy, Raymond J.
Ledoux, Damien C.

Retired:
Rev. Msgrs.—
Blair, Raymond O., 1 Harborside Dr., #4201, Delray Beach, FL 33483.
Burns, Lawrence E., 155 Echo Ave., Unit 1, Portsmouth, 03801.
Crosby, Charles E., 793 Ocean Blvd., Hampton, 03842.
Desmond, Joseph E., Bishop Peterson Residence, 221 Orange St., 03104-4324.
Markham, James J., Parish of The Transfiguration, 107 Alsace St., 03102.
Paradis, Wilfrid H., Bishop Peterson Residence, 221 Orange St., 03104-4324.
Revs.—
Allard, Marcel M., Ste. Marie Rectory, 378 Notre Dame Ave., 03102.
Auger, Gerald E., 235 Alsace St., 03102-3008.
Bellefeuille, Albert A., Bishop Peterson Residence, 221 Orange St., 03104-4324.
Bilodeau, Florent, St. Anthony Parish, 172 Belmont St., 03103-4452.
Bilodeau, Roger P., 1 Gilson Rd., Hollis, 03049.
Blais, Roland O., Bishop Peterson Residence, 221 Orange St., 03104-4324.
Boisvert, Robert G., 6 Faith Ln., Center Barnstead, 03225.
Boucher, Gerard A., Bishop Peterson Residence, 221 Orange St., 03104-4324.
Bresnahan, Thomas J., 1225 20th Ave., Vero Beach, FL 32960.
Bryson, John H., Bishop Peterson Residence, 221 Orange St., 03104-4324.
Coyne, Emmett A., 141 Exeter River Landing, Exeter, 03833.
Demers, Wilfred G., Bishop Peterson Res., 221 Orange St., 03104-4324.
Desjardins, George A., 6 Pleasant St., E-3, Hooksett, 03106-1421.
DesRuisseaux, Charles E., 51 River Front Dr., Apt. 3, 03102.
Di Russo, Anthony, 410 Chase Rd., Lunenburg, MA 01462.
Dumont, C. Peter, P.O. Box 490, Winnisquam, 03289.
Dunn, Gerald R., P.O. Box 7356, Gonic, 03839. Tel: 603-569-5058
Finnigan, John B., St. John the Baptist Parish, 10 School St., Suncook, 03275-1917.
Foisy, Leonard R., Bishop Peterson Residence, 221 Orange St., 03104.
Frechette, Leo L., 5 Tampa Dr., Unit 6, Rochester, 03867.
Gagnon, Andre J., Mt. Carmel Rehab. & Nursing Center, 235 Myrtle St., 03104-4314.
Gagnon, Leo G., Bishop Peterson Residence, 221 Orange St., 03104-4324.
Giroux, Richard M., 918, N. Main St., Unit 1., Laconia, 03246.
Goggin, Cornelius J., 96 River Rd., 03104.
Goodwin, Robert T., Bishop Bradley Apts., 406 Court St., Apt. 103, Laconia, 03246.
Gregoire, Paul L., 377 Wilson St., 03103.
Griffin, Michael J., Bishop Peterson Residence, 221 Orange St., 03104-4324.
Irwin, Patrick F., 77 Israel Head Rd., #17, Ogunquit, ME 03907.
Keenan, Thomas E., 679 Lamoine Beach Rd., Lamoine, ME 04605-4744.
Kelley, Edward J., P.O. Box 416, Dover, 03821-0416.
Kelso, Francis E., 774 Dana Hill Rd., New Hampton, 03256.
Klatka, Joseph S., 53 Claremont Ave., 03103.
Lacroix, Maurice R., Bishop Peterson Residence, 221 Orange St., 03104-4324.
Lafond, Donald E., 3010 Brown Ave., #1, 03103.
Lampron, Maurice W., P.O. Box 717, Wolfeboro Falls, 03896-0717.
Marchand, Robert A., P.O. Box 185, Moody, ME 04054.
McHugh, Paul F., P.O. Box 634, Scarborough, ME 04070.
Oliviera, Humbert, 9 Hollis St., Cambridge, MA 02140.
Piwowar, Stanley J., 223 Winter St., Claremont, 03743.
Polito, Victor V.J., St. Mary Rectory, 156 E. Main St., Amsterdam, NY 12010. Tel: 518-843-2728
Rundzio, Mark A., 745 2nd Ave., Berlin, 03570.
Simoneau, Norman J., 185 Eastern Ave., Unit 202, 03104.
Smith, Richard A., 47 Howard Hill Rd., Apt. 202, Jaffrey, 03452.
Soberick, George J., P.O. Box 310, 03105-0310.
St. Laurent, Daniel A., 48 W. Hollis St., Nashua, 03060.
Szopa, Daniel F., Bishop Peterson Res., P.O. Box 310, 03104.
Thibodeau, Andre M., Bishop Primeau Apts. #304, 519 Bridge St., 03104.
Vickery, Richard F., Bishop Peterson Residence, 221 Orange St., 03104-4324.
Walsh, James P., 103 Forest Park Dr., Auburn, MA 01501-2574.
Wegman, Richard H., 70 Taylor Dr. Back Bay, Wolfeboro, 03894-4356.
Wright, John A., 13 Brandon Ln., Goffstown, 03045.

Permanent Deacons:
Abbott, Leon E., Jr., St. Mark Parish, Londonderry
Albert, Merle M., (Retired)
Anderson, Robert J., Jr., (Retired)
Andrade, Ramon, St. Anne-St. Augustine, Manchester
Blicharz, John, All Saints, Charlestown
Borkush, George J., (Retired)
Borland, Joseph P., St. Mary, Hillsborough; St. Theresa, Henniker
Boucher, Paul R., St. Mary, Claremont
Brown, William, (Retired)
Carey, John J., Our Lady of The Mountains, N. Conway
Cloutier, Richard A., (Retired)
Costello, David T., Saints Mary and Joseph, Salem
Cummins, Clarence R., Parish of the Resurrection, Nabhuce
Daly, James P., St. Christopher Parish, Nashua
DeRosia, Winton P., Sacred Heart & St. Peter, Concord
Esposito, Robert, (Retired)
Falardeau, Richard A., St. Mary, Rochester and St. Peter, Farmington
Fitzpatrick, T. Kelly, (Retired)
Gagnon, Robert J., Parish of the Assumption, Dover
Gallinaro, Frank, Ste. Marie and Sacred Heart, Manchester
Gustafson, Arnold J. A., Parish of the Holy Spirit, Keene; Mary Queen of Peace, Hinsdale
Guy, Michael, Holy Trinity, Plymouth
Hamel, David C., Out of State, Oklahoma
Hilston, Edmund C., Blessed John XXIII, Nashua
Hobson, Mark F., Ph.D., St. Pius X, Manchester
Jacobs, Dennis M., Our Lady of the Miraculous Medal, Hampton
Kram, Harry A., St. Anthony Parish, Manchester
LaBonte, Alfred A., Jr., (Retired)

Long, George H. (Gary), Jr., (Retired)
Marcotte, Raymond V., St. Kathryn, Hudson
Martin, John, (Retired)
Mazzuchelli, Joseph, (On Leave)
McCabe, Mark, St. Elizabeth Seton, Bedford
McCarty, William, St. Andre Bessette, Laconia
McGinn, Gregory R., Our Lady of Fatima, New London
Morey, Russell, St. Andre Bessette, Laconia
Morrow, John, Immaculate Heart of Mary, Concord
Mullen, William E., St. Anne, Hampstead
Munz, Edward P., St. Catherine, Manchester
Patterson, James E., Our Lady of Mercy, Merrimack
Payeur, Marc G., St. Jude, Londonderry
Polcari, Joseph A., (Retired)
Potvin, Robert R., St. Joseph Cathedral, Manchester
Rich, William, St. Joseph, Center Ossipee and St. Anthony, Sanbornville
Rock, James E., St. Theresa, Henniker; St. Mary, Hillsborough
Ross, John F., St. Patrick, Pelham
Shannon, Richard J., Parish of the Transfiguration, Manchester
Shrader, David J., Chaplain of New Hampshire State Prison for Women; Goffstown and Hillsborough County Jail, Manchester; Holy Rosary, Hooksett; St. John the Baptist, Suncook
St. George, John H., Blessed John XXIII, Nashua
Testa, Paul E., (Retired)
Wheeler, Raymond A., St. Joseph the Worker, Nashua

INSTITUTIONS LOCATED IN THE DIOCESE

[A] SEMINARIES, RELIGIOUS OR SCHOLASTICATES

MANCHESTER. *St. Anselm Abbey Seminary*, 100 St. Anselm Dr., 03102. Tel: 603-641-7115; Fax: 603-641-7116. Email: vocations@anselm.edu. Web: www.anselm.edu. Rev. Anselm Smedile, O.S.B., Dir. Vocations. Order of St. Benedict. Faculty 3; Students 2.

CENTER HARBOR. *Immaculate Conception Apostolic School*, 109 Dane Rd., P.O. Box 936, 03226. Tel: 603-253-7728; Fax: 603-253-8740. Revs. David Steffy, L.C., Prin.; Thanh Nguyen, L.C.; Steven Liscinsky, L.C. Priests 3; Brothers 3; Lay Teachers 7; Students 38.

[B] COLLEGES AND UNIVERSITIES

MANCHESTER. *Saint Anselm College* 03102. Tel: 603-641-7000; Fax: 603-641-7284. Email: jdefelice@anselm.edu. Web: www.anselm.edu. Rt. Rev. Matthew K. Leavy, O.S.B., Ph.D., Chancellor; Rev. Jonathan P. DeFelice, O.S.B., J.C.L., Pres. Admin. & Faculty. Order of St. Benedict. Priests 6; Brothers 2; Lay Teachers 208; Students 1,915.

MERRIMACK. *The Thomas More College of Liberal Arts* (1978) 6 Manchester St., 03054. Tel: 603-880-8308; Fax: 603-880-9280. Email: info@thomasmorecollege.edu. Web: www.thomasmorecollege.edu. William E. Fahey, Ph.D., Pres.; Chistopher Blum, Ph.D., Academic Dean. Priests 4; Total Staff 22; Students 87.

NASHUA. *Rivier College* (1933) 03060-5086. Tel: 603-888-1311; Fax: 603-897-8812. Web: www.rivier.edu. Sr. Paula Marie Buley, I.H.M., Pres.; Rev. Paul R. Demers, S.C., Chap.; Daniel Speidel, Dir. of Library. Sisters of the Presentation of Mary. Presentation Sisters 15; Teaching Sisters 2; Lay Teachers 73; Students 2,359.

WARNER. *The College of Saint Mary Magdalen* (1973) 511 Kearsarge Mountain Rd., 03278-9206. Tel: 603-456-2656; Fax: 603-456-2660. Email: administration@magdalen.edu. Web: www.magdalen.edu. George A. Harne, Pres.; Dr. Mark Discher, Academic Dean; R. Daniel Peterson, CFO; Marie Lasher, Librarian. Lay Teachers 7; Total Staff 18; Students 100.

[C] HIGH SCHOOLS, DIOCESAN

MANCHESTER. *Trinity High School*, 581 Bridge St., 03104-5395. Tel: 603-668-2910; Fax: 603-668-2913. Email: webmaster@trinity-hs.org. Web: www.trinity-hs.org. Mr. Denis Mailloux, Prin.; Steven Gadecki, Asst. Prin.; Patrick D. Smith, Dean of Students & Admissions Dir.; Brian Flaherty, Campus Min. Lay Teachers 35; Total Staff 52; Students 417.

CONCORD. *Bishop Brady High School*, 25 Columbus Ave., 03301. Tel: 603-224-7418; Fax: 603-228-6664. Email: info@bishopbrady.edu. Web: www.bishopbrady.edu. Trevor Bonat, Prin.; Neal Casale, Asst. Prin.; Joy Degnan, Asst. Prin. Lay Teachers 35; Students 360.

DOVER. *St. Thomas Aquinas High School* (1960) 197 Dover Point Rd., 03820. Tel: 603-742-3206; Fax: 603-749-7822. Email: sta@stalux.org. Web: www.stalux.org. Kevin Collins, Prin.; Jane O'Leary, Librarian. Lay Teachers 47; Students 641.

[D] HIGH SCHOOLS, PRIVATE

NASHUA. *Bishop Guertin High School* (1963) 194 Lund Rd., 03060. Tel: 603-889-4107; Fax: 603-889-0701. Email: brmark@bghs.org. Web: www.bghs.org. Bro. Mark E. Hilton, S.C., Contact Person, Pres.; Linda Brodeur, Prin.; Bro. Paul Demers, S.C., Chap.; Janis Tunstall, Librarian. Brothers of the Sacred Heart., (Coed) Brothers 7; Lay Teachers 67; Students 880.

SUNAPEE. *Mount Royal Academy*, (Grades PreK-12), 26 Seven Hearths Ln., 03782. Tel: 603-763-9010; Fax: 603-763-5390. Email: dthibault@mountroyalacademy.com. Web: www.mountroyalacademy.com. David A. Thibault, Headmaster. Lay Teachers 17; Students 115.

[E] REGIONAL AND PAROCHIAL ELEMENTARY SCHOOLS

MANCHESTER. *St. Anthony School* (1904) (Grades PreK-6), 148 Belmont St., 03103. Tel: 603-622-0414; Fax: 603-669-5212. Email: info@stanthonyschool-nh.com. Web: www.stanthonyschool-nh.com. Jerry Bergeron, Prin.; Mrs. Sally Green, Contact Person & Admin. Asst. Lay Teachers 14; Boys 97; Girls 87.

St. Benedict Academy (1989) (Grades PreK-6), 85 Third St., 03102. Tel: 603-669-3932; Fax: 603-669-3932. Email: sbaprincipal@comcast.net. Web: stbenedictacademy.org. Sr. Betty Roy, C.S.C., Prin. Lay Teachers 8; Students 148.

St. Casimir School, (Grades K-8), 456 Union St., 03103. Tel: 603-623-6411; Fax: 603-623-3236. Email: stcasimirnh@comcast.net. Web: www.stcasimirnh.org. Sr. Frances Marion Bonczar, C.S.S.F., Prin.; Jennifer Girard, Librarian. Lay Teachers 8; Students 146.

St. Catherine School, (Grades PreK-6), 206 North St., 03104. Tel: 603-622-1711; Fax: 603-624-4935. Email: stcatherinenh@comcast.net. Web: www.saintcatherines.org. Sr. Janet Belcourt, C.S.C., Prin.; Mrs. Alice Gordon, Librarian. Sisters 1; Lay Teachers 22; Students 331.

St. Joseph Regional Junior High, (Grades 7-8), 148 Belmont St., 2nd Fl., 03103. Tel: 603-624-4811; Fax: 603-624-6670. Email: pmartimeau@stjoesjrhs.org. Web: www.stjoesjrhs.org. Mr. Denis Mailloux, Prin. Lay Teachers 10; Students 89.

CONCORD. *St. John Regional School* (1888) (Grades PreK-8), 61 S. State St., 03301. Tel: 603-225-3222; Fax: 603-225-0195. Email: mrdonohue@stjohnregional.org. Stephen Donohue, Prin. Lay Teachers 16; Students 229.

DERRY. *St. Thomas Aquinas School*, (Grades PreK-8), 3 Moody St., 03038. Tel: 603-432-2712; Fax: 603-432-2179. Email: info@staderry.com. Web: www.staderry.com. Paul Rakiey, Prin. Priests 1; Lay Teachers 10; Students 210.

DOVER. *St. Mary Academy*, (Grades PreK-8), 222 Central Ave., 03820. Tel: 603-742-3299; Fax: 603-743-3483. Email: bwhite@stmaryacademy.org. Web: www.saintmaryacademy.org. Roberta White, Prin.; Teresa Zellem, Librarian. Lay Teachers 35; Students 285.

HAMPTON. *Sacred Heart School* (1962) (Grades PreK-8), 289 Lafayette Rd., 03842. Tel: 603-926-3254; Fax: 603-929-1109. Email: prin@shshampton.org. Web: www.OLMMparish.org. Mark Gillis, Prin.; Michelle Ryzewic, Librarian. Lay Teachers 20; Students 215.

JAFFREY. *St. Patrick School* (1962) (Grades PreK-8), 70 Main St., 03452. Tel: 603-532-7676; Fax: 603-532-7476. Email: principal@saintpatschool.org. Web: www.saintpatschool.org. Sr. Cecile Provost, C.S.C., Prin.; Katie Robbins, Adm. Asst. & Bookkeeper. Sisters 2; Lay Teachers 10; Students 88.

KEENE. *St. Joseph Regional School* (1886) (Grades PreK-8), 92 Wilson St., 03431. Tel: 603-352-2720; Fax: 603-358-5465. Email: ldellasanta@stjosephkeene.org. Web: stjosephkeene.org. Sr. Laura Della Santa, R.S.M., Prin. & Contact; Mrs. Kathy Bill, Librarian. Lay Teachers 13; Students 120; Total Staff 24.

LACONIA. *Holy Trinity* (1971) (Grades PreK-8), 50 Church St., 03246. Tel: 603-524-3156; Fax: 603-524-4454. Email: jfortier@holytrinity.pvt.k12.nh.us. Web: holytrinity.pvt.k12.nh.us. Mr. Jack Fortier, Prin. Lay Teachers 12; Total Staff 19; Students 112.

LITCHFIELD. *St. Francis of Assisi School*, (Grades PreSchool-6), 9 St. Francis Way, 03052-8050. Tel: 603-424-3312; Fax: 603-424-9128. Email: sdannible@stfrancisschoolnh.org. Amy K. Malinowski, Prin.; Rose Van Uden, Librarian. Lay Teachers 7; Students 93.

NASHUA. *St. Christopher School* (1963) (Grades PreK-6), 20 Cushing Ave., 03064. Tel: 603-882-7442; Fax: 603-594-9253. Email: principal@stchrisschoolnh.org. Web: www.stchrisschoolnh.org. Cynthia Clarke, Prin.; Patricia Riley, Librarian. Lay Teachers 22; Students 326.

Infant Jesus School (1909) (Grades PreK-6), 3 Crown St., 03060. Tel: 603-889-2649; Fax: 603-594-9117. Email: lafleur@ijschool.org. Web: www.ijschool.org. Estelle LaFleur, Prin.; Mrs. Virginia Dumont, Librarian. Sisters 1; Lay Teachers 20; Students 234.

Nashua Catholic Regional Junior High School (1972) (Grades 7-8), 6 Bartlett Ave., 03064-1602. Tel: 603-883-6707; Fax: 603-882-7011; Fax: 603-594-8955. Email: t_kelleher@comcast.net. Web: www.ncrjhs.org. Thomas Kelleher, Prin. Lay Teachers 20; Students 238.

PELHAM. *St. Patrick School*, (Grades K-8), 16 Main St., 03076. Tel: 603-635-2941; Fax: 603-635-9800. Email: stpatsk8@hotmail.com. Web: www.saintpatrickschool.net. Henry Golec, Prin. & Contact; Traci Gamble, Librarian. Lay Teachers 20; Students 183.

PORTSMOUTH. *St. Patrick* (1888) (Grades PreK-8), 125 Austin St., 03801. Tel: 603-436-0739; Fax: 603-436-1569. Email: a-norris@stpatsportsmouth.com. Web: www.stpatsschool.com. Sr. Mary J. Walsh, O.L.L., Prin.; Mrs. Amanda Norris, Sec. Lay Teachers 25; Students 182.

ROCHESTER. *St. Elizabeth Seton School* (1886) (Grades K-8), 16 Bridge St., 03867. Tel: 603-332-4803; Fax: 603-332-2915. Email: stbrochester@metrocast.net. Web: www.sesschool.org. Suzanne T. Boutin, Prin. Lay Teachers 11; Students 121.

SALEM. *St. Joseph Regional Catholic School* (1959) (Grades PreK-8), 40 Main St., 03079. Tel: 603-893-6811; Fax: 603-893-6811. Email: sjrcsoffice@comcast.net. Web: sjrcs.com. Ruth A. Hassett, Prin.; Lois Powers, Librarian. Lay Teachers 16; Total Staff 33; Students 183.

Kindergarten Marilyn Byron, Dir. Lay Teachers 1; Students 19.

[F] ELEMENTARY SCHOOLS, PRIVATE

MANCHESTER. *St. Augustin Pre-School*, 251 Merrimack St., 03103. Tel: 603-623-8800; Fax: 603-626-1517. Email: sapreschool@comcast.net. Mailing Address: 383 Beech St., 03103. Crystal Elie, Dir. Lay Teachers 6; Boys 25; Girls 13.

Holy Cross Early Childhood Center, 420 Island Pond Rd., 03109-4812. Tel: 603-668-0510. Carol Garhart, Prin. & Admin. Sisters 1; Lay Teachers 3; Students 24.

Mount Saint Mary Academy, (Grades PreK-6), 2291 Elm St., 03104. Tel: 603-623-3155; Fax: 603-621-9254. Email: principal@mtstmary.org. Web: www.mtstmary.org. Patricia Baldissard, Prin.; Kathryn Moran, Contact Person; Gina Noury, Librarian. Sisters 1; Lay Teachers 16; Students 168.

GOFFSTOWN. *Villa Augustina School* (1918) (Grades PreSchool-8), 208 S. Mast St., 03045. Tel: 603-497-2361; Fax: 603-821-9945. Email: info@villaaugustina.org. Web: www.villaaugustina.org. Andrew Maloney, Prin.; Mrs. Deidre Angwin, Librarian. Sisters 1; Aides 4; Lay Teachers 18; Students 176.

HUDSON. *Presentation of Mary Academy* (1926) (Grades PreK-8), 182 Lowell Rd., 03051. Tel: 603-889-6054; Fax: 603-595-8504. Web: www.pmaschool.org. Email: pmaprincipal@comcast.net. Sr. Maria Rosa, P.M., Prin.; Denise Babcock, Librarian. Sisters of the Presentation of Mary. Sisters 3; Lay Teachers 28; Students 469.

SUNAPEE. *Mount Royal Academy*, (Grades PreK-12), 26 Seven Hearths Ln., 03782. Tel: 603-763-9010; Fax: 603-763-5390. Email: dthibault@mountroyalacademy.com. Web: www.mountroyalacademy.com. David A. Thibault, Headmaster.

[G] CATHOLIC CHARITIES

MANCHESTER. *Catholic Charities Administration*, 215 Myrtle St., 03104. Tel: 603-669-3030; Fax: 603-626-1252. Web: www.nh-cc.org. Thomas E. Blonski, Pres. & CEO; Nicholas Boudreau, Dir., Communications; Dominque A. Rust, Vice Pres. & COO; Rosemary Hendrickx, Dir., Devel.; Joanne Hollen, CFO; Joseph P. Naff, L.I.C.S.W., Dir. Clinical & Family Svcs.; Lisa Merrill-Burzak, Vice Pres. Devel.; Michael D. Lehrman, Vice Pres. Healthcare Svcs.; Deacon Richard J. Shannon, Dir. Parish Social Ministry; Melanie A. Gosselin, Exec. Dir. of N.H. Food Bank; Cathy Chesley, J.D., Ed.D., Dir. Immigration & Refugee Svcs. District Offices:

633 Third Ave., P.O. Box 182, Berlin, 03570-0182. Tel: 603-752-1325; Fax: 603-752-6174. Email: berlin@nh-cc.org. Nicole Plourde, Admin. Mgr. & Parish Outreach Coord.

176 Loudon Rd., Concord, 03301-6025. Tel: 603-228-1108; Fax: 603-228-6025. Su McKinnon, M.Ed., Admin. Mgr. & Parish Outreach Coord.

161 Main St., Suite 200, Keene, 03431-3722. Tel: 603-357-3093; Fax: 603-357-7810. Email: keene@nh-cc.org. Sr. Kathleen Haight, R.C.D., P.A., Admin. Mgr. & Parish Outreach Coord.

17 Gilford Ave, Laconia, 03246-2827. Tel: 603-528-3035; Fax: 603-524-7153. Email: laconia@nh-cc.org. Leonard B. Campbell, Admin. Mgr. & Parish Outreach Coord.

24 Hanover St., #8, Lebanon, 03766-1334. Tel: 603-448-5151; Fax: 603-448-5155. Marc Cousineau, Admin. Mgr. & Parish Outreach Coord.

41 Cottage St., P.O. Box 323, Littleton, 03561-0323. Tel: 603-444-7727; Fax: 603-444-7728. Email: littleton@nh-cc.org. Anthony Poekert, Admin. Mgr. & Parish Outreach Coord.

325 Franklin St., 03101-1999. Tel: 603-624-4717; Fax: 603-624-4736. Email: manchester@nh-cc.org. Debra Naff, LCMHC, Admin. Mgr., & Clinical Sup.

261 Lake St., Nashua, 03060-4127. Tel: 603-889-9431; Fax: 603-880-4643. Email: nashua@nh-cc.org. Arlene Cody, M.A., LCMHC, Admin. Mgr. & Clinical Sup.

23 Grant St., Rochester, 03867-3001. Tel: 603-332-7701; Fax: 603-332-9629. Email: rochester@nh-cc.org. Debra Naff, LCMHC, Admin. Mgr., & Clinical Sup.

45 Stiles Rd., Ste. 103, Salem, 03079-4808. Tel: 603-893-1971; Fax: 603-898-8661. Email: salem@nh-cc.org. Arlene Cody, M.A., LCMHC, Admin. Mgr., & Clinical Sup.

Other Programs:

Diocesan Consultation & Counseling Services, 215 Myrtle St., 03104. Tel: 603-668-0014; Fax: 603-623-7676. Email: nbunker@nh-cc.org. Joseph P. Naff, Dir. Clinical & Family Svcs.

Healthcare Services, 215 Myrtle St., 03104. Tel: 603-641-0577; Fax: 603-641-6210. Michael D. Lehrman, Vice Pres. Healtcare Svcs.

Immigration and Refugee Services, 261 Lake St., Nashua, 03060-4127. Tel: 603-889-9431; Fax: 603-880-4643. Email: kgeorge@nh-cc.org. Cathy Chesley, J.D., Ed.D., Dir. Immigration & Refugee Svcs. Legal and case management services for immigrants and refugees.

New Hampshire Food Bank, 700 E. Industrial Park Dr., 03109. Tel: 603-669-9725; Fax: 603-669-0270. Web: www.nhfoodbank.org. Melanie A. Gosselin, Exec. Dir. Statewide food distribution to soup kitchens, food pantries and direct service programs.

Our Place, 16 Oak St., 03104-4319. Tel: 603-647-2244; Fax: 603-647-9933. Karen A. Munsell, Admin. Mgr. & Social Worker. Services for pregnant and parenting teens.

St. Charles Children's Home, 19 Grant St., Rochester, 03867-3001. Tel: 603-332-4768; Fax: 603-332-3948. Email: mpm@stcharleshome.net. Sr. Paul Marie Santa Lucia, S.C.M.C., Admin. Residential services for children who have been removed from unsafe home environments. Total Staff 18; Total Assisted 20.

Trinity Home Care, 593 Maple St., 03104. Tel: 603-627-2100; Fax: 603-627-5521. Trish Chandler, Admin.

Bishop Peterson Residence, 221 Orange St., 03104-4324. Tel: 603-641-6277; Fax: 603-641-0385. Marlene Makowski, Admin.

[H] CHILD CARE INSTITUTIONS

MANCHESTER. *St. Peter's Home* (1902) 300 Kelley St., 03102-3093. Tel: 603-625-9313; Fax: 603-625-1910. Email: sft@stpeterhome.com. Web: www.stpeterhome.com. Sr. Florence Therrien, S.C.S.H., Dir.; Mrs. Donna M. Vachon, Asst. Dir.; Sr. Rita Beaulieu, S.C.S.H., Treas. Sisters of Charity (Grey Nuns) 2.

ALLENSTOWN. *Pine Haven Boys Center* (1963) 133 River Rd., P.O. Suncook, 03275. Tel: 603-485-7141; Fax: 603-485-7142. Email: fr.john@comcast.net. Revs. Paul Riva, C.R.S., Dir.; John Vitali, C.R.S., M.Ed.; Dixon Choolakkal, C.R.S. Somascan Fathers. Children 20; Total Staff 40.

ROCHESTER. *St. Charles Children's Home*, 19 Grant St., 03867-3099. Tel: 603-332-4768; Fax: 603-332-3948. Email: mpm@stcharleshome.net. Web: www.stcharleshome.org. Sr. Paul Marie Santa Lucia, Admin. New Hampshire Catholic Charities. Sisters 7; Dependent Children 10.

[I] GENERAL HOSPITALS

MANCHESTER. *Catholic Medical Center of Manchester, NH, Inc.*, 100 McGregor St., 03102. Tel: 603-668-3545; Fax: 603-663-6850. Web: www.catholicmedicalcenter.org. Alyson Pitman Giles, Pres. & CEO. Sisters 3; Bed Capacity 330; Total Staff 2,194; Inpatient Admissions 10,803; Outpatient Admissions 185,451.

Catholic Medical Center Associates, 100 McGregor St., 03102. Tel: 603-668-3545; Fax: 603-663-6850. Web: www.catholicmedicalcenter.org.

NASHUA. *St. Joseph Hospital*, 172 Kinsley St., 03061. Tel: 603-882-3000; Fax: 603-578-5060. Web: www.stjosephhospital.com. David Ross, Pres. & CEO; Kathleen Rice-Orshak, Vice Pres., Mission. Sponsored by Covenant Health Systems Tewksbury, MA Bed Capacity 208; Patients Assisted Annually 203,395; Total Staff 2,000.

[J] HEALTH CARE FACILITIES

MANCHESTER. *Holy Cross Health Center, Inc.* (1984) 357 Island Pond Rd., 03109-4811. Tel: 603-628-3550; Fax: 603-626-6270. Email: bonnie@holycrosshc.org. Bonnie McMahon, N.H.A., Admin. Nursing home for women religious, managed by Covenant Health Systems, Tewksbury, MA

St. Joseph Residence (1980) 495 Mammoth Rd., 03104-5463. Tel: 603-668-6011; Fax: 603-644-1276. Email: MJMakowski@presmarynh.org. Marlene Makowski, Admin. Sponsored by the Presentation of Mary Sisters., New Hampshire Catholic Charities. Bed Capacity 22; Total Staff 64; Total Assisted Annually 39.

Mt. Carmel Rehabilitation and Nursing Center, 235 Myrtle St., 03104-4314. Tel: 603-627-3811; Fax: 603-626-4696. Email: jbohunicky@nh-cc.org. Joe Bohunicky, Admin. New Hampshire Catholic Charities. Bed Capacity 120; Total Staff 188; Total Assisted Annually 350.

St. Teresa Rehabilitation and Nursing Center (1948) 519 Bridge St., 03104-5337. Tel: 603-668-2373; Fax: 603-668-0059. Email: stt.administrator@nh-cc.org. Andrea Sherwin, NHA, Admin. New Hampshire Catholic Charities Total Staff 69; Bed Capacity 51; Total Assisted Annually 138.

Bishop Primeau Senior Living Community (1986) Tel: 603-668-2373; Fax: 603-668-0059. Linda Illg, Apartment Mgr. Total Staff 3; Bed Capacity 25; Total Assisted Annually 34.

BERLIN. *St. Vincent de Paul Rehabilitation and Nursing Center*, 29 Providence Ave., 03570-3130. Tel: 603-752-1820; Fax: 603-752-7149. Email: stv.administrator@nh-cc.org. Louise Marquis, Admin. New Hampshire Catholic Charities. Residents 80; Total Staff 147; Total Assisted Annually 177.

DOVER. *St. Ann Rehabilitation and Nursing Center* (1958) 195 Dover Point Rd., 03820-4693. Tel: 603-742-2612; Fax: 603-743-3055. Email: sta.administrator@nh-cc.org. Chrystal Durand, Admin.; Rev. Donald McAllister, Chap. (Retired). New Hampshire Catholic Charities. Bed Capacity 54; Total Staff 99; Total Assisted Annually 241.

Bishop Gendron Senior Living Community (1999) Tel: 603-742-2612; Fax: 603-743-3055. Cathy Meattey-Stawarz, Apartment Mgr. Total Staff 2; Bed Capacity 31; Total Assisted Annually 38.

JAFFREY. *Good Shepherd Rehabilitation and Nursing Center*, 20 Plantation Dr., 03452-6631. Tel: 603-532-8762; Fax: 603-593-0006. Ann Nunn, Nursing Home Admin. New Hampshire Catholic Charities. Total Staff 115; Total Assisted 148; Bed Capacity 83.

LACONIA. *Bishop Bradley Senior Living Community*, 406 Court St., 03246. Tel: 603-524-0466; Fax: 603-527-0884. Email: stf.administrator@nh-cc.org. Deb Sturgeon, Apartment Mgr. Apartments 25; Total Staff 4; Total Assisted Annually 31.

St. Francis Rehabilitation and Nursing Center (1948) 406 Court St., 03246-3600. Tel: 603-524-0466; Fax: 603-527-0884. Email: stf.administrator@nh-cc.org. Brenda Buttrick, RNC, NHA, Admin. New Hampshire Catholic Charities. Residents 51; Total Staff 92; Total Assisted Annually 148.

Bishop Bradley Senior Living Community Total Staff 4; Apartments 25.

WINDHAM. *Warde Health Center*, 21 Searles Rd., P.O. Box 420, 03087-1203. Tel: 603-890-1290; Fax: 603-890-1293. Email: adm@wardehealth.com. Susan Denopolous, Admin. & Contact. Sisters of Mercy., Managed by New Hampshire Catholic Charities. Total Staff 86; Bed Capacity 28; Total Assisted Annually 65.

[K] MONASTERIES AND RESIDENCES OF PRIESTS AND BROTHERS

MANCHESTER. *St. Anselm Abbey* Of the Order of St. Benedict including Seminary and Formation Program., 100 St. Anselm Dr., 03102-1310. Tel: 603-641-7651; Fax: 603-641-7267. Email: webmaster@anselm.edu. Web: www.anselm.edu/abbey/index.html. Most Rev. Joseph Gerry, O.S.B., D.D. (Retired); Rt. Rev. Matthew K. Leavy, O.S.B., Ph.D., Abbot & Chancellor; Bro. Isaac S. Murphy, O.S.B., Prior; Very Rev. Peter J. Guerin, O.S.B., Subprior; Revs. Bede G. Camera, O.S.B.; Mark A. Cooper, O.S.B.; Jerome J. Day, O.S.B.; Jonathan P. DeFelice, O.S.B., J.C.L.; Bernard Disco, O.S.B.; Cecil J. Donahue, O.S.B.; Mathias D. Durette, O.S.B.; John R. Fortin, O.S.B.; Jude J. Gray, O.S.B.; Benedict M. Guevin, O.S.B.; Augustine G. Kelly, O.S.B.; Iain G. MacLellan, O.S.B.; Benet C. Phillips, O.S.B.; Laurence Schlegel, O.S.B. (Retired); Anselm Smedile, O.S.B.; Patrick M. Sullivan, O.S.B.; William J. Sullivan, O.S.B.; Bros. John Paul James, O.S.B.; Andrew Thornton, O.S.B. Bishops 1; Priests 19; Brothers 4.

CENTER HARBOR. *L.C. Center Harbor, Inc.*, 109 Dane Rd., P.O. Box 936, 03226. Tel: 603-253-7728; Fax: 603-253-8740. Rev. Jose Felix Ortega, L.C., Sec. & Treas.

COLEBROOK. *Shrine of Our Lady of Grace* 03576. Tel: 603-237-5511; Fax: 603-237-8998. Revs. Robert G. Levesque, O.M.I., Supr.; Henri A. DeLisle, O.M.I. Oblates of Mary Immaculate (United States Province). Priests 2; Brothers 2.

ENFIELD. *Shrine of Our Lady of La Salette*, 410 N.H. Rte. 4A, P.O. Box 420, 03748-0420. Tel: 603-632-4301 (Gift Shop); 603-632-7087 (Business); Fax: 603-632-7648. Email: lasalette-enfield@comcast.net. Revs. Rene J. Butler, M.S., Shrine Dir.; Leo Maxfield, M.S., Chap. (Retired); Roger J. Plante, M.S., Chap.; Joseph Ross, M.S., Chap. (Retired); Bros. Claude Rheaume, M.S., Chap.; David Carignan, M.S., Chap.; Raymond M. Tetreault, M.S.

La Salette of Enfield, Inc. Priests 4; Brothers 3; Total Staff 13.

HANOVER. *Order of Preachers, St. Thomas Aquinas House*, 2 Occum Ridge, P.O. Box 147, 03755. Tel: 603-643-2154; Fax: 603-543-9411. Revs. Jonathan Kalisch, O.P., Dir. & Supr.; C. Francis Belanger, O.P.

NASHUA. *Brothers of the Sacred Heart*, 196 Lund Rd., 03060. Tel: 603-883-3683. Bros. Laurent Beaunoyer, S.C., Dir.; Roger Lemoyne, S.C. Brothers 9.

[L] CONVENTS AND RESIDENCES OF SISTERS

MANCHESTER. *St. George Manor*, 357 Island Pond Rd., 03109. Tel: 603-624-4557; Fax: 603-645-1516. Sr. Eleanor Labranch, C.S.C., Local Animator; Rev. Bruce W. Collard, (Non-residential). Sisters 41.

Monastery of the Precious Blood (1898) 700 Bridge St., 03104-5495. Tel: 603-623-4264; Fax: 603-647-8385. Sr. Mary Therese, A.P.B., Supr.; Rev. Adrien R. Longchamps, Chap. Sisters Adorers of the Precious Blood. Sisters 26.

Missionary Rosebushes of St. Theresa (1922) 700 Bridge St., 03104-5495. Tel: 603-623-4264; Fax: 603-647-8385.

Regional Office of the Sisters of Holy Cross, 377 Island Pond Rd., 03109. Tel: 603-622-9504; Fax: 603-622-9782. Email: degagnon@srsofholycross.com. Web: sistersofholycross.org. Sr. Doris E. Gagnon, P.M., Ph.D., B.A., Regl. Animator. Total Staff 8.

Sisters of the Presentation of Mary Provincial House, 495 Mammoth Rd., 03104-5494. Tel: 603-669-1080; Fax: 603-622-4953. Email: provincialhouse@presmarynh.org. Web: www.presentationofmary.com. Sisters Suzanne Bourret, P.M., M.A., Prov. Supr.; Marie Christilla, Contact Person. Sisters in the Diocese 127; Sisters of the Presentation of Mary 134. *St. Joseph Residence* (1980) 495 Mammoth Rd., 03104-5494. Tel: 603-627-5831; 603-668-6011. *St. Marie Residence* (1959) 495 Mammoth Rd., 03104-5494. Tel: 603-623-0671. *Bethany House* (1989) 25 Garmon St., 03104. Tel: 603-625-1957. *Presentation of Mary Academy* (1926) 182 Lowell Rd., Hudson, 03051-4987. Tel: 603-883-8192; 603-889-6362; Fax: 603-883-8054. *Presentation of Mary House of Formation*, 186 Lowell Rd., Hudson, 03051-4908. Tel: 603-882-1347; Fax: 603-880-0298. *Presentation of Mary Convent* (1989) 633 Third Ave., Berlin, 03570. Tel: 603-752-1176; Fax: 603-752-4115. *Our Lady of Hope House of Prayer* (1990) 400 Temple Rd., New Ipswich, 03071. Tel: 603-878-2346; Fax: 603-878-4552. *Holy Angels Convent* (1996) 6 Atkinson Depot Rd., Rte. 121, Plaistow, 03865. Tel: 603-382-2744. *Emmaus Convent* (1999) 664 Central St., 03103. Tel: 603-647-4083.

Adoramus Community at Blessed John XXIII, 27 Liberty St., Hudson, 03051-4259. Tel: 603-809-4132.

St. Joseph Mission Center (Religious of Jesus and Mary) (2003) 627 Montgomery St., 03102. Tel: 603-232-4121. Sr. Priscilla Lemire, R.J.M., Pastoral Assoc.

CONCORD. *Monastery of Discalced Carmelites* (1946) 275 Pleasant St., 03301-2590. Tel: 603-225-5791; Fax: 603-223-9670. Sr. Claudette M. Blais, O.C.D.,

Prioress; Rev. Paul T. Gilbert, Chap. Professed Sisters 8; Postulants 1.

LITTLETON. *Daughters of the Charity of the Sacred Heart of Jesus, Provincial House*, 226 Grove St., 03561. Tel: 603-444-5346; Fax: 603-444-5348. Web: www.fcscj.org. Sisters Pauline Gratton, F.C.S.C.J., Supr.; Elaine Voyer, F.C.S.C.J., Provincial Supr. Sisters 38.

LONDONDERRY. *Sisters of Holy Cross*, Londonderry House, 68 Mammoth Rd., 03053-4024. Tel: 603-432-2430. Sr. Elaine Theoret, C.S.C.

NEW IPSWICH. *Our Lady of Hope House of Prayer*, 400 Temple Rd., 03071. Tel: 603-878-2346; Fax: 603-878-4552. Email: olhope1@yahoo.com. Web: presentationofmary.com; www.presentationofmary.com/retreatwork.html. Sr. Rita Pay, P.M., Local Supr. Sisters 6.

NASHUA. *Holy Infant Jesus Convent*, 3 Crown St., 03060-6366. Tel: 603-882-0553. Email: mag3cr@yahoo.com. Sr. Marie Anne Grenier, C.S.C., Local Animator. Sisters 4.

PORTSMOUTH. *Our Lady of Lourdes Convent*, 125 Austin St., 03801. Tel: 603-436-6612. Email: lourdesll@comcast.net. Sr. Mary Joan Walsh, O.L.L., Supr. Sisters of Our Lady of Lourdes (O.L.L.).

WINDHAM. *Sisters of Mercy of the Americas-Northeast Community, Inc., Life & Ministry Office*, 21 Searles Rd., P.O. Box 420, 03087-0420. Tel: 603-893-6550; Fax: 603-893-2413. Email: nhsistersofmercy@comcast.net. Sr. Mary Cronin, R.S.M., Life & Ministry Admin.

Mount Saint Mary Corporation of the Sisters of Mercy, Inc., Nashua. Tel: 603-883-7874; Fax: 603-594-4178.

Manchester Convent of the Sisters of Mercy (1858) Tel: 603-893-6550; Fax: 603-893-2413.

Warde Health Center, Inc. Tel: 603-890-1290; Fax: 603-890-1293.

Mount St. Mary Academy, Inc. Tel: 603-623-3155; Fax: 603-621-9254.

Frances Warde House Tel: 603-893-6550; Fax: 603-893-2413.

McAuley Commons, 03087. Tel: 603-893-6550; Fax: 603-893-2413.

[M] ASSOCIATIONS OF THE CHRISTIAN FAITHFUL

PORTSMOUTH. *Portsmouth, Society of Our Lady of Lourdes*, 125 Austin St., 03801-4309. Tel: 603-436-6612. Sr. Mary Joan Walsh, O.L.L., Supr.

ROCHESTER. **Daughters of Mary, Mother of Healing Love*, 19 Grant St., 03867. Tel: 603-332-4768; Fax: 603-332-3948. Email: smr@stcharleshome.net. Web: www.runningnuns.com. Sr. Mary Rose Reddy, D.M.M.L., Sec. & Contact Person. (Private Association of the Christian Faithful)

[N] RETREAT HOUSES

ENFIELD. *Shrine of Our Lady of La Salette*, 417 N.H. Rte. 4A, P.O. Box 420, 03748. Tel: 603-632-7087 (Business); 603-632-4301 (Gift Shop); Fax: 603-632-7648. Email: lasalette-enfield@comcast.net. Web: www.lasaletteofenfield.org; www.eco-mission.info. Revs. Leo Maxfield, M.S., Chap. (Retired); Joseph Ross, M.S., Chap. (Retired); Rene J. Butler, M.S., Shrine Dir.; Roger J. Plante, M.S.; Bros. David J. Carignan, M.S.; Claude Rheaume, M.S.; Raymond M. Tetreault, M.S. Priests 4; Brothers 3; Total Staff 13.

PITTSFIELD. *Berakah*, 96 Fairview Rd., 03263-3817. Tel: 603-435-7271; Fax: 603-435-6670. Email: berakah@aol.com. Web: www.berakah.org.

[O] CAMPUS MINISTRY AND NEWMAN CENTERS

DURHAM. *St. Thomas More Catholic Student Center at the University of New Hampshire* 6 Madbury Rd., P.O. Box 620, 03824-0620. Tel: 603-862-1310; Fax: 603-868-3765. Email: stmdurham@aol.com. Rev. Andrew W. Cryans, Chap.; Cheryl Goldthwaite, Campus Minister; Roberta MacBride, Pastoral Asst.

HANOVER. **The Catholic Student Center at Dartmouth, Aquinas House, Aquinas at Dartmouth, Inc.* (1953) 2 Occom Ridge, P.O. Box 147, 03755. Tel: 603-643-2154; Fax: 603-643-9411. Web: www.dartmouth.edu/~aquinas. Rev. Jonathan Kalisch, O.P., Chap. & Dir.; Brian Trexel, Campus Min.; Katherine Kohler, Campus Min. Total Priests in Residence 2; Total Staff 4.

KEENE. *Catholic Newman Center for Keene State College* 161 Main St., Ste. 11, 03431. Tel: 603-357-1444; Fax: 603-352-7472. Email: ksc.newman.ctr@gmail.com. Marika Donders, Campus Min.

PLYMOUTH. *Plymouth State University Catholic Campus Ministry Plymouth State University*, 19 Highland Ave., Ste. A6, 03264. Tel: 603-535-2673. Email: kmtardif@plymouth.edu. Katherine Tardif, Catholic Campus Min. Tel: 603-535-2673.

[P] SPECIAL APOSTOLATE CENTERS

KEENE. *Catholic Faith Formation Center*, 161 Main St., Ste. 118, 03431. Tel: 603-352-7662; Fax: 603-352-7662. Email: cffc-keene@myfairpoint.net. Web: www.catholicfaithformationcenter.org.

[Q] CAMPS AND COMMUNITY CENTERS

CENTER OSSIPEE. *Camp Marist* (1949) 22 Abel Blvd., Effingham, 03882. Tel: 603-539-4552; Fax: 603-539-8318. Email: office@campmarist.org. Web: www.campmarist.org. Vincent Gschlecht, Summer Camp Dir. Total Staff 100; Total Assisted 250.

GILMANTON IRON WORKS. *Camp Bernadette (Girls)* (1953) *Winter Business Office*, P.O. Box 206, 03837-0206. Tel: 603-364-5851; Fax: 603-364-5038. Email: info@campsfatimabernadette.org. Web: www.campsfatimabernadette.org. Rev. Peter A. Libasci, D.D., Chm. of the Bd.; Sr. Mary Elizabeth Whalen, S.N.D.deN., Pres.; Gus Planchet, Dir. Total Assisted Annually 1,000; Total Staff 80.

Summer Business Office for Camp Bernadette, 83 Richards Rd., Wolfeboro, 03894. Tel: 603-569-1692; Fax: 603-569-2560. Total Staff 80; Total Assisted 1,080.

Camp Fatima (1949) (Boys), *Business Office*, P.O. Box 206, 03837-0206. Tel: 603-364-5851; Fax: 603-364-5038. Email: info@campfatimabernadette.org. Web: www.campfatimabernadette.org. Rev. Peter A. Libasci, D.D., Chm. of the Bd.; Sr. Mary Elizabeth Whalen, S.N.D.deN., Pres.; Gus Planchet, Dir. Total Assisted 1,100; Total Staff 80.

[R] MISCELLANEOUS

MANCHESTER. *Bishop Brady High School Capital Campaign Trust Fund* c/o Roman Catholic Bishop of Manchester, a corporation sole., 153 Ash St., 03104. Tel: 603-669-3100, Ext. 117; Fax: 603-669-0377. Email: gchapdelaine@rcbm.org. Web: www.catholicchurchnh.org. Guy D. Chapdelaine, CPA, A.B., MBA, Finance Officer & Contact Person.

Bishop's Charitable Assistance Fund (2002) 153 Ash St., 03104. Tel: 603-669-3100; Fax: 603-669-0377. Email: menglish@rcbm.org. Walter Gallo, Chm.

Catholic Lawyers Guild of New Hampshire, Inc., 153 Ash St., 03105. Courtney Eschbach, Pres.

CMC Healthcare System, 100 McGregor St., 03102. Tel: 603-668-3545; Fax: 603-663-8850. Guy D. Chapdelaine, CPA, A.B., MBA, Chairperson, Bd. Dirs. Tel: 603-669-3100; Fax: 603-669-0377; Alyson Pitman Giles, Pres.

Catholic Medical Center Tel: 603-668-3545; Fax: 603-663-6850.

Alliance Ambulatory Services, Inc., 100 McGregor St., 03102. Tel: 603-668-3545; Fax: 603-663-6850. Alyson Pitman Giles, Pres. & CEO.

Alliance Resources Inc., 100 McGregor St., 03102. Tel: 603-668-3545; 608-663-6850. Alyson Pitman Giles, Pres. & CEO.

St. Peter's Home, 300 Kelly St., 03102. Tel: 603-669-1219. Sr. Florence Therrien, S.C.S.H., Contact Person.

Diocesan Cemetery Office, 153 Ash St., P.O. Box 310, 03105. Tel: 603-669-3100; Fax: 603-669-0377. Email: pharrington@rcbm.org.

St. Patrick Cemetery, Amherst, 03031. Tel: 603-673-1311; Fax: 603-673-3687.

St. Joseph Cemetery, Bartlett, 03812. Tel: 603-356-2535; Fax: 603-356-2877.

St. Joseph Cemetery, Bath, 03740. Tel: 603-747-2038; Fax: 603-747-8071.

St. Joseph Cemetery, Bedford, 03110. Tel: 603-622-9522; Fax: 603-644-0770.

St. Hedwig Cemetery, Bedford, 03110. Tel: 603-623-4835; Fax: 603-623-4835 (Call first).

Mount Calvary Cemetery, Bennington, 03442. Tel: 603-924-7647; Fax: 603-924-8365.

Calvary Cemetery, Berlin, 03570. Tel: 603-752-2880; Fax: 603-752-1855.

St. Anne Cemetery, Berlin, 03570. Tel: 603-752-2880; Fax: 603-752-1855.

St. Kieran Cemetery, Berlin, 03570. Tel: 603-752-2880; Fax: 603-752-1855.

Mount Calvary Cemetery, Berlin, 03570. Tel: 603-752-2880; Fax: 603-752-1855.

Old Parish Cemetery, Bethlehem, 03574. Tel: 603-444-2593; Fax: 603-444-3126.

St. Margaret Cemetery, Carroll, 03598. Tel: 603-837-2558; Fax: 603-837-2558 (Call first).

St. Catherine Cemetery, Charlestown, 03603. Tel: 603-826-3359; Fax: 603-826-5875.

St. Mary Cemetery, Claremont, 03743. Tel: 603-542-9518; Fax: 603-542-9614.

St. Brendan Cemetery, Colebrook, 03576. Tel: 603-237-8580; Fax: 603-237-4342.

St. Charles Cemetery, Dover, 03822. Tel: 603-742-4837; Fax: 603-749-6779.

St. Mary Cemetery, Dover, 03822. Tel: 603-742-4837; Fax: 603-749-6779.

St. Peter Cemetery (Walpole), Drewsville, 03604. Tel: 603-826-3359; Fax: 603-826-5875.

St. Joseph Cemetery, Epping, 03042. Tel: 603-679-8805; Fax: 603-679-5192.

St. Pius Forest Lawn Cemetery, Errol, 03579. Tel: 603-237-4342; Fax: 603-237-8580.

Holy Cross Cemetery, Franklin, 03235. Tel: 603-934-5013; Fax: 603-934-3469.

Mount Calvary Cemetery, (Gonic), Rochester, 03839. Tel: 603-332-1863; Fax: 603-330-0865.

Holy Family Cemetery, Gorham, 03581. Tel: 603-446-2335; Fax: 603-466-3490.

St. Francis Xavier Cemetery, Groveton, 03582. Tel: 603-636-1047; Fax: 603-636-2549.

St. Denis, Harrisville, 03450. Tel: 603-924-7647; Fax: 603-924-8365.

St. Joseph Cemetery, Hinsdale, 03451. Tel: 603-336-5804; Fax: 603-352-7472.

Holy Rosary Cemetery, Hooksett, 03106. Tel: 603-485-3523; Fax: 603-485-8435.

Holy Cross Cemetery, Hudson, 03051. Tel: 603-881-8131; Fax: 603-557-9817.

St. Patrick Cemetery, Hudson, 03051. Tel: 603-881-8131; Fax: 603-577-9817.

St. Patrick Cemetery, Jaffrey, 03452. Tel: 603-532-6634; 603-532-6484; Fax: 603-532-6633.

St. Joseph Cemetery, Keene, 03435. Tel: 603-357-3967; Fax: 603-352-7472.

Sacred Heart Cemetery, Laconia, 03247. Tel: 603-524-9609; Fax: 603-524-9620.

St. Lambert's Cemetery, Laconia, 03247. Tel: 603-524-1442; Fax: 603-524-9620.

All Saints Cemetery, Lancaster, 03584. Tel: 603-788-2083; Fax: 603-788-5553.

Calvary Cemetery, Lancaster, 03584. Tel: 603-788-2083; Fax: 603-788-5553.

St. Rose of Lima Cemetery, Littleton, 03561. Tel: 603-444-2593; Fax: 603-444-3126.

Holy Cross Cemetery, Londonderry, 03053. Tel: 603-622-3215; Fax: 603-624-8638.

St. Augustine Cemetery, 03111. Tel: 603-860-0386; Fax: 603-626-1517.

Mount Calvary Cemetery, 03111. Tel: 603-622-3215; Fax: 603-624-8638.

Mount Calvary Cemetery, Marlborough, 03455. Tel: 603-357-3967; Fax: 603-352-7472.

St. Louis Cemetery, Nashua, 03064. Tel: 603-886-1302; Fax: 603-886-5361.

St. Francis Xavier Cemetery, Nashua, 03064. Tel: 603-886-1302; Fax: 603-886-5361.

St. Stanislaus Cemetery, Nashua, 03064. Tel: 603-886-1302; Fax: 603-886-5361.

Sacred Heart of Jesus Cemetery, New Ipswich, 03071. Tel: 603-878-1121; Fax: 603-878-4657.

Calvary Cemetery, Newmarket, 03857. Tel: 603-659-3643; Fax: 603-659-8924.

St. Patrick Cemetery, Newport, 03773. Tel: 603-863-1422; Fax: 603-863-7898.

Our Lady of the Mountains Cemetery, North Conway, 03860. Tel: 603-356-2535; Fax: 603-356-2877.

Sacred Heart Cemetery, North Stratford, 03590. Tel: 603-636-1047; 802-962-3364; Fax: 603-636-2549.

Calvary Cemetery, Penacook, 03303. Tel: 603-753-4413; Fax: 603-753-4071.

St. Peter Cemetery (old), Peterborough, 03458. Tel: 603-924-7647; Fax: 603-924-8365.

St. Peter Cemetery (new), Peterborough, 03458. Tel: 603-924-7647; Fax: 603-924-8365.

Mount Calvary Cemetery, Pittsfield, 03263. Tel: 603-435-6242; Fax: 603-435-9398.

Holy Angels Cemetery, Plaistow, 03865. Tel: 603-382-8324; Fax: 603-382-1113.

Calvary Cemetery, Portsmouth, 03804. Tel: 603-436-9239; Fax: 603-433-4401.

St. Mary Cemetery, Portsmouth, 03804. Tel: 603-436-9239; Fax: 603-433-4401.

Holy Rosary Cemetery, Rochester, 03839. Tel: 603-332-1863; Fax: 603-330-0865.

St. Mary's Cemetery, Rochester, 03839. Tel: 603-332-1869; Fax: 603-332-2040.

St. Patrick Cemetery, Rollinsford, 03805. Tel: 603-692-4367; Fax: 603-692-2499.

Mount Calvary Cemetery, Sanbornville, 03872. Tel: 603-522-3304; Fax: 603-522-8273.

Holy Trinity Cemetery, Somersworth, 03878. Tel: 603-692-4367; 603-692-0524; Fax: 603-692-4454.

Mount Calvary Cemetery, Somersworth, 03878. Tel: 603-692-2172; 603-692-0524; Fax: 603-692-2499.

St. John the Baptist Cemetery, Suncook, 03275. Tel: 603-485-3113; Fax: 603-485-2113.

St. John the Baptist Old Cemetery, Suncook, 03275. Tel: 603-485-3113; Fax: 603-485-2113.

St. John's Cemetery, Tilton, 03299. Tel: 603-286-4445; 603-630-0673; Fax: 603-286-4663.

Mount Carmel Cemetery, Troy, 03465. Tel: 603-357-3967; Fax: 603-352-7472.

St. Margaret Cemetery, Twin Mountain, 03595. Tel: 603-837-2558; Fax: 603-837-2558 (Call first).

St. Peter Cemetery (Drewsville), Walpole, 03608. Tel: 603-826-3359; 603-445-5304; Fax: 603-826-5875.

St. Albert Cemetery, West Stewartstown, 03597. Tel: 603-237-4342; Fax: 603-237-8580.

St. Matthew Cemetery, Whitefield, 03598. Tel: 603-837-2558; Fax: 603-837-2558 (Call first).

Mount Calvary Cemetery, Wilton, 03086. Tel: 603-654-6554.

Friends of Saint Patrick School Trust Fund, P.O. Box 310, 03105-0310.

Friends of the St. Thomas Aquinas School Trust Fund c/o Roman Catholic Bishop of Manchester, a corporation sole., 153 Ash St., 03104. Tel: 603-669-3100. Email: gchapdelaine@rcbm.org. Web: www.catholicnh.org. Guy D. Chapdelaine, CPA, A.B., MBA, Finance Officer & Contact Person.

Infant Jesus School Trust Fund (c/o Roman Catholic Bishop of Manchester, a corporation sole), 153 Ash St., 03104. Tel: 603-669-3100. Email: gchapdelaine@rcbm.org. Web: www.catholicnh.org. Guy D. Chapdelaine, CPA, A.B., MBA, Finance Officer & Contact Person.

Saint Jude Parish Capital Campaign Trust c/o Roman Catholic Bishop of Manchester, a corporation sole., 153 Ash St., 03104. Tel: 603-669-3100. Email: gchapdelaine@rcbm.org. Web: catholicnh.org. Guy D. Chapdelaine, CPA, A.B., MBA, Finance Officer & Contact Person.

Priests Retirement Trust Fund, P.O. Box 310, 03105-0310.

St. Thomas Aquinas High School Capital Campaign Trust Fund, P.O. Box 301, 03105-0310.

St. Thomas Aquinas High School Tuition Endowment Trust Fund, P.O. Box 310, 03105-0310.

GILFORD. *The Missionary Servants of Pope John Paul I* (1978) 22 Boyd Hill Rd., 03249. Tel: 603-524-4740; Fax: 603-524-4740. The Missionary Servants of Pope John Paul I is a lay association founded in 1978 to aid established missionaries with help mainly given to Mother Teresa's missions in Haiti.

NASHUA. *Corpus Christi Food Pantry and Assistance, Inc.*, 43 Franklin St., 03064. Tel: 603-882-6372 (Pantry); 603-598-1641 (Assistance); Fax: 603-598-1640. Email: corpuschristifp@aol.com. Web: www.corpuschristifoodpantry.org. Kay Golden, Exec. Dir.

Marguerite's Place, 87 Palm St., 03060. Tel: 603-598-1582; Fax: 603-598-7574. Email: balves@margueritesplace.org. Web: www.margueritesplace.org. Barbara A. Alves, CEO. Total Assisted 26; Total Staff 17; Bed Capacity 30.

RELIGIOUS INSTITUTES OF MEN REPRESENTED IN THE DIOCESE

For further details refer to the corresponding bracketed number in the Religious Institutes of Men or Women section.

[]—*Apostles of Jesus* (Nairobi, Kenya)—A.J.

[0200]—*Benedictine Monks* (St. Anselm Abbey)—O.S.B.

[1100]—*Brothers of the Sacred Heart* (New England Prov.)—S.C.

[1330]—*Congregation of the Mission* (New England Prov.)—C.M.

[0520]—*Franciscan Friars* (Province of the Immaculate Conception)—O.F.M.

[0690]—*Jesuit Fathers and Brothers* (New England Prov.)—S.J.

[0730]—*Legionaries of Christ*—L.C.

[0770]—*Marist Brothers of the Schools* (Esopus Prov.)—F.M.S.

[0720]—*The Missionaries of Our Lady of La Salette* (Immaculate Heart of Mary & Our Lady of Seven Dolors Provinces)—M.S.

[0910]—*Oblates of Mary Immaculate*—O.M.I.

[0470]—*Order of Friars Minor Capuchin*—O.F.M.Cap.

[]—*Order of Preachers* (Prov. of St. Joseph-Eastern Dominican Prov.)—O.P.

[1250]—*Somascan Fathers*—C.R.S.

RELIGIOUS INSTITUTES OF WOMEN REPRESENTED IN THE DIOCESE

[1000]—*Congregation of Divine Providence of Kentucky*—C.D.P.

[]—*Congregation of the Sisters of St. Joseph Boston*—C.S.J.

[0750]—*Daughters of the Charity of the Sacred Heart of Jesus*—F.C.S.C.J.

[0420]—*Discalced Carmelites Nuns*—O.C.D.

[1070-16]—*Dominican Sisters of Hope*—O.P.

[1170]—*Felician Sisters*—C.S.S.F.

[2575]—*Institute of the Sisters of Mercy of the Americas* (Manchester, NH)—R.S.M.

[]—*Little Sisters of St. Francis*—O.S.F.

[2410]—*Marianites of Holy Cross*—M.S.C.

[]—*Missionary Sisters Servant of the Word*—H.M.S.P.

[3450]—*Religious of Jesus and Mary*—R.J.M.

[2970]—*School Sisters of Notre Dame*—S.S.N.D.

[1680]—*School Sisters of St. Francis*—O.S.F.

[0110]—*The Sisters Adorers of the Precious Blood*—A.P.B.

[0490]—*Sisters of Charity of Montreal (Grey Nuns)*—S.G.M.

[0610]—*Sisters of Charity of St. Hyacinthe (Grey Nuns)*—S.C.S.H.

[0640]—*Sisters of Charity of St. Vincent De Paul, Halifax*—S.C.

[1930]—*Sisters of Holy Cross*—C.S.C.

[3000]—*Sisters of Notre Dame de Namur - Boston Province*—S.N.D.deN.

[3000]—*Sisters of Notre Dame de Namur - Ipswich Province*—S.N.D.deN.

[3360]—*Sisters of Providence of Saint Mary-of-the-Woods, IN*—S.P.

[]—*The Sisters of St. Francis of Philadelphia*—O.S.F.

[3310]—*Sisters of the Presentation of Mary*—P.M.

[]—*Society of Sisters for the Church*—S.S.C.

NECROLOGY

† Desjardins, Raymond S., (Retired)—Died Dec., 2010

† Kelly, Martin J., Nashua, NH St. Patrick—Died June 21, 2011

† Kemmery, Robert J., (Retired)—Died April 21, 2011

† O'Connor, Francis J., (Retired)—Died Dec. 1, 2010

† Savage, Thomas J., (Retired)—Died April 28, 2011

An asterisk (*) denotes an organization that has established tax-exempt status directly with the IRS and is not covered by the USCCB Group Ruling.

Diocese of Marquette

(Dioecesis Marquettensis)

Most Reverend

ALEXANDER K. SAMPLE, J.C.L.

Bishop of Marquette; ordained June 1, 1990; appointed Bishop of Marquette December 13, 2005; installed January 25, 2006. *Office: 1004 Harbor Hills Dr., Marquette, MI 49855.* Tel: 906-227-9115.

Chancery Office: 1004 Harbor Hills Dr., Marquette, MI 49855. Tel: 906-225-1141; Fax: 906-225-0437.

Web: www.dioceseofmarquette.org

Most Reverend

JAMES H. GARLAND, M.A., M.S.W., D.D.

Retired Bishop of Marquette; ordained 1959; appointed Titular Bishop of Garriana and Auxiliary Bishop of Cincinnati June 2, 1984; consecrated July 25, 1984; appointed Bishop of Marquette October 6, 1992; installed November 11, 1992; retired December 13, 2005. *Res.: 300 Rock St., Marquette, MI 49855.* Tel: 906-225-1141.

VICARIATE-APOSTOLIC JULY 29, 1853; DIOCESE 1857.

Square Miles 16,281.

Comprises the Upper Peninsula of the State of Michigan.

For legal titles of parishes and diocesan institutions, consult the Pastoral Office.

STATISTICAL OVERVIEW

Personnel	
Bishop	1
Retired Bishops	1
Priests: Diocesan Active in Diocese	43
Priests: Diocesan Active Outside Diocese	3
Priests: Retired, Sick or Absent	31
Number of Diocesan Priests	77
Religious Priests in Diocese	6
Total Priests in Diocese	83
Extern Priests in Diocese	13
Ordinations:	
Transitional Deacons	1
Permanent Deacons in Diocese	47
Total Sisters	45
Parishes	
Parishes	72
With Resident Pastor:	
Resident Diocesan Priests	36
Resident Religious Priests	6
Without Resident Pastor:	
Administered by Priests	27
Administered by Religious Women	3
Missions	22
Pastoral Centers	1
Professional Ministry Personnel:	
Sisters	6
Lay Ministers	16
Welfare	
Catholic Hospitals	1
Total Assisted	213,823
Homes for the Aged	1
Total Assisted	109
Special Centers for Social Services	3
Total Assisted	1,968
Other Institutions	1
Total Assisted	500
Educational	
Diocesan Students in Other Seminaries	10
Total Seminarians	10
Elementary Schools, Diocesan and Parish	9
Total Students	1,081
Catechesis/Religious Education:	
High School Students	852
Elementary Students	4,701
Total Students under Catholic Instruction	4,691
Teachers in the Diocese:	
Sisters	1
Lay Teachers	87
Vital Statistics	
Receptions into the Church:	
Infant Baptism Totals	499
Minor Baptism Totals	29
Adult Baptism Totals	42
Received into Full Communion	123
First Communions	537
Confirmations	159
Marriages:	
Catholic	147
Interfaith	85
Total Marriages	232
Deaths	1,073
Total Catholic Population	50,410
Total Population	292,119

Former Bishops—Most Revs. FREDERIC BARAGA, D.D., first Bishop; cons. Nov. 1, 1853; died Jan. 19, 1868; IGNATIUS MRAK, D.D., cons. Feb. 7, 1869; resigned 1878; transferred to Antinoe 1879; died Jan. 2, 1901; JOHN VERTIN, D.D., cons. Sept. 14, 1879; died Feb. 26, 1899; FREDERICK EIS, D.D., cons. Aug. 24, 1899; made Asst. at the Pontifical Throne July 13, 1922; resigned July 8, 1922; appt. Titular Bishop of Bita; died May 5, 1926; PAUL JOSEPH NUSSBAUM, D.D., cons. Bishop of Corpus Christi May 20, 1913; resigned March 26, 1920; appt. Bishop of Marquette Nov. 14, 1922; died June 24, 1935; JOSEPH CASIMIR PLAGENS, D.D., LL.D., cons. Sept. 30, 1924, Auxiliary Bishop of Detroit; Titular Bishop of Rhodiopolis; appt. to See of Marquette Nov. 16, 1935; transferred to the See of Grand Rapids Dec. 16, 1940; died March 31, 1943; FRANCIS J. MAGNER, D.D., appt. Dec. 21, 1940; cons. Feb. 24, 1941; died June 13, 1947; THOMAS L. NOA, D.D., cons. March 19, 1946; Titular Bishop of Salona and Coadjutor Bishop of Sioux City; appt. Bishop of Marquette Aug. 20, 1947; retired March 25, 1968; died March 13, 1977; CHARLES A. SALATKA, D.D., appt. Titular Bishop of Cariana and Auxiliary of Grand Rapids Dec. 9, 1961; cons. March 6, 1962; appt. Bishop of Marquette Jan. 10, 1968; installed March 25, 1968; appt. Archbishop of Oklahoma City Oct. 11, 1977; installed Dec. 15, 1977; retired Nov. 24, 1992; died March 17, 2003.; MARK F. SCHMITT, D.D. (Retired), appt. Titular Bishop of Kells and Auxiliary of Green Bay May 5, 1970; cons. June 24, 1970; appt. Bishop of Marquette March 21, 1978; installed May 8, 1978; retired Nov. 11, 1992; died Dec. 14, 2011.; JAMES H. GARLAND, M.A., M.S.W., D.D., ord. 1959; appt. Titular Bishop of Garriana and Auxiliary Bishop of Cincinnati June 2, 1984; cons. July 25, 1984; appt. Bishop of Marquette Oct. 6, 1992; installed Nov. 11, 1992; retired Dec. 13, 2005.

Chancery Office—1004 Harbor Hills Dr., Marquette, 49855. Tel: 906-225-1141; Fax: 906-225-0437. Office Hours: Mon.-Thurs. 8-4:30, Fri. 8-12.

Vicar General—Rev. Msgr. MICHAEL J. STEBER.

Moderator of the Curia—Rev. RONALD T. BROWNE.

Chancellor—Rev. BENEDETTO J. PARIS, J.C.L.

Secretary to the Bishop—JUDY M. JASON. Tel: 906-227-9115.

Diocesan Tribunal—1004 Harbor Hills Dr., Marquette, 49855. Tel: 906-227-9143.

Judicial Vicar—Rev. Msgr. PETER OBERTO, J.C.L.

Adjutant Judicial Vicar—VACANT.

Diocesan Judge—Rev. Msgr. PETER OBERTO, J.C.L.

Defensore Vinculi—Rev. JOHN J. SHIVERSKI (Retired).

Advocates—Revs. FRANCIS J. DEGROOT; JAMES M. ROETZER.

Administrator and Notary—Rev. BENEDETTO J. PARIS, J.C.L.

Promoter of Justice—Rev. BENEDETTO J. PARIS, J.C.L.

Priests' Council—

Executive Board—Revs. MARK A. MCQUESTEN, Chm.; LARRY P. VAN DAMME, Vice Chm.

Vicars Forane—Revs. THEODORE J. BRODEUR, Holy Name of Mary Vicariate; ROBB M. JURKOVICH, St. John Neumann Vicariate; JOY JOSEPH ADIMAKKEEL, St. Mary Rockland Vicariate; JOHN E. MARTIGNON, The Most Holy Name of Jesus Vicariate; FRANCIS J. DEGROOT, St. Joseph-St. Patrick Vicariate; BENEDETTO J. PARIS, J.C.L., St. Peter Cathedral Vicariate; MICHAEL A. WOEMPNER, St. Mary Norway Vicariate.

Consultors—Revs. RONALD T. BROWNE; COREY J. LITZNER; MICHAEL A. WOEMPNER; LARRY P. VAN DAMME; Rev. Msgr. MICHAEL J. STEBER; Rev. FRANCIS G. DOBRZENSKI.

Diocesan Offices and Directors

Administration & Finance, Dept. of—TIMOTHY D. THOMAS, Dir.; CAROL J. PARKER, Accountant & Human Resource Coord., 1004 Harbor Hills Dr., Marquette, 49855. Tel: 906-227-9105; Fax: 906-225-0437.

Archives—VACANT, Archivist, 347 Rock St., Marquette, 49855.

Catholic Social Services, Dept. of—Deacon DANIEL B. POWERS, Dir., 347 Rock St., Marquette, 49855. Tel: 906-227-9119; Fax: 906-228-2469 Branch Offices: Escanaba, Iron Mountain.

Communication and Development, Dept. of—LOREENE ZENO KOSKEY, Dir. Tel: 906-227-9129; TERRI GADZINSKI, Develop. Office, 1004 Harbor Hills Dr., Marquette, 49855. Tel: 906-227-9108; Fax: 906-225-0437.

Catholic Schools—MARK SALISBURY, Supt. Schools, Mailing Address: 1004 Harbor Hills Dr.,

Marquette, 49855. Tel: 906-227-9127; Fax: 906-225-0437.

Youth Ministry—GREG GOSTOMSKI, Dir. Tel: 906-227-9125.

Office of Faith Formation—DENISE M. FOYE, Dir. Tel: 906-227-9130.

Newspaper "The U.P. Catholic"—JOHN FEE, Editor, 1004 Harbor Hills, Marquette, 49855. Tel: 906-227-9131; Fax: 906-225-0437.

Ministry Personnel Services, Dept. of—Rev. RONALD T. BROWNE, Dir., 1004 Harbor Hills Dr., Marquette, 49855. Tel: 906-227-9107; Fax: 906-225-0437.

Clergy Support Services—Rev. RONALD T. BROWNE, Mgr., Mailing Address: 1004 Harbor Hills Dr., Marquette, 49855. Tel: 906-227-9107; Fax: 906-225-0437.

Apostleship of the Sea—Rev. BENEDETTO J. PARIS, J.C.L., Port Chap. Marquette, MI. Tel: 906-227-9143.

Bishop Baraga Association Inc.— An international organization to promote the Cause of the Beatification of the Most Rev. Frederic Baraga. *347 Rock St., Marquette, 49855*. Tel: 906-227-9117; Fax: 906-228-2469. Rev. BENEDETTO J. PARIS, J.C.L., Exec. Dir.; Dr. ANDREA AMBROSI, Postulator.

Building Commission, Diocese of Marquette—TIMOTHY D. THOMAS, Sec., 1004 Harbor Hills Dr., Marquette, 49855. Tel: 906-227-9108.

Catholic Relief Services—Rev. LAWRENCE T. GAUTHIER, Dir. (Retired), 1004 Harbor Hills Dr., Marquette, 49855.

Cemeteries—Rev. BENEDETTO J. PARIS, J.C.L., Bishop's Rep. for Catholic Cemeteries, 1004 Harbor Hills Dr., Marquette, 49855. Tel: 906-227-9102.

Charismatic Prayer Groups—Rev. Msgr. MICHAEL J. STEBER, Liaison, St. Peter Cathedral, 311 W. Baraga Ave., Marquette, 49855. Tel: 906-226-6548.

Ongoing Formation of Priests—Rev. JAMES C. ZIMINSKI, Dir., Mailing Address: Marygrove, P.O. Box 38, Garden, 49835. Tel: 906-644-2771.

Cursillo—Rev. JAMES C. ZIMINSKI, Diocesan Moderator, Marygrove, P.O. Box 38, Garden, 49835. Tel: 906-644-2771.

Family Life Office—COLIN JENKINS, Coord., 1004 Harbor Hills Dr., Marquette, 49855. Tel: 906-227-9178.

Holy Childhood Association—Rev. LAWRENCE T. GAUTHIER, Dir. (Retired), 1004 Harbor Hills Dr., Marquette, 49855. Tel: 906-227-9109.

Knights of Columbus—Rev. BENEDETTO J. PARIS, J.C.L., Diocesan Chap., 1004 Harbor Hills Dr., Marquette, 49855. Tel: 906-227-9111.

Panama Mission Fund—Rev. PAUL G. MANDERFIELD, 1004 Harbor Hills Dr., Marquette, 49855. Tel: 906-225-1141.

Permanent Diaconate Formation Program—Deacon SCOTT JAMIESON, Dir., 1004 Harbor Hills Dr., Marquette, 49855. Tel: 906-227-9111; Fax: 906-225-0437.

Propagation of the Faith—Rev. LAWRENCE T. GAUTHIER, Diocesan Dir. (Retired), 1004 Harbor Hills Dr., Marquette, 49855. Tel: 906-227-9109.

Retreats—Rev. JAMES C. ZIMINSKI, Dir., Marygrove Retreat Center, Garden, 49835. Tel: 906-644-2771.

Victim Assistance Coordinator—Sr. COLLEEN SWEETING, O.S.F., 2372 Badger St., Marquette, 49855. Tel: 866-857-6459 (Toll Free).

St. Joseph Association— An Association of the Priests of the Diocese to provide Retirement Benefits. Rev. LARRY P. VAN DAMME, Pres., St. Michael Parish, 401 W. Kaye Ave., Marquette, 49855. Tel: 906-228-8180.

U.P. Catholic Services Appeal—TIMOTHY D. THOMAS, Coord., 1004 Harbor Hills Dr., Marquette, 49855. Tel: 906-227-9101.

Vocation Office—Rev. GREGORY R. HEIKKALA, Dir., 1004 Harbor Hills Dr., Marquette, 49855. Tel: 906-227-9112; 866-375-2643; Fax: 906-225-0437.

Women Religious—Sr. MARCELYN GERVAIS, O.S.F., 2372 Badger St., Marquette, 49855. Tel: 906-226-2265.

CLERGY, PARISHES, MISSIONS AND PAROCHIAL SCHOOLS

CITY OF MARQUETTE

(MARQUETTE COUNTY)

1—ST. PETER CATHEDRAL Rev. Msgr. Michael J. Steber; Rev. Ryan T. Ford; Deacons Scott A. Jamieson; John S. Leadbetter; Lawrence H. Londo; Donald Thoren; Thomas E. Foye; Dean J. Jackson.
Res.: 311 Baraga Ave., 49855. Tel: 906-226-6548; Fax: 906-226-8683. Web: www.stpetercathedral-.org.
See Fr. Marquette Catholic Central Schools System, Marquette under Elementary Interparochial Schools located in the Institution section.
Catechesis / Religious Program—Tel: 906-226-6548, Ext. 207. Students 60.
Mission—St. Mary Big Bay, Marquette Co.

2—ST. CHRISTOPHER Rev. Jeff G. Johnson, Canonical Pastor & Sacramental Min.; Deacon Steven M. Gualdoni.
Res.: 2372 Badger St., 49855. Tel: 906-226-2265; Fax: 906-226-8678.
Catechesis / Religious Program—Sr. Colleen Sweeting, O.S.F., D.R.E. Students 39.

3—ST. JOHN THE BAPTIST (1986) Closed. For inquiries for parish records, contact St. Peter's Cathedral, Marquette.

4—ST. LOUIS THE KING (HARVEY) (1954) Rev. Benedetto J. Paris; Deacons Gregg R. St. John; Warren K. Vonck.
Res.: 264 Silver Creek Rd., 49855. Tel: 906-249-1438; Fax: 906-249-3428.
See Fr. Marquette Catholic Central Schools System, Marquette under Elementary Interparochial Schools located in the Institution section.
Catechesis / Religious Program—Students 77.

5—ST. MICHAEL (1942) Revs. Larry P. Van Damme; Nicholas R. Thompson; Deacons Dennis R. Maki; Robert K. LaCosse.
Res.: 401 W. Kaye Ave., 49855. Tel: 906-228-8180; Fax: 906-228-5502. Email: secretary@stmichaelmqt.org.
See Fr. Marquette Catholic Central Schools System, Marquette under Elementary Interparochial Schools located in the Institution section.
Catechesis / Religious Program—Students 79.

OUTSIDE THE CITY OF MARQUETTE

AHMEEK, KEWEENAW CO., OUR LADY OF PEACE, (Keweenaw Catholic Missions) Rev. Abraham J. Mupparathara, M.C.B.S. (India).
Mailing Address: P.O. Box 546, Calumet, 49913. Tel: 906-337-1966; Fax: 906-337-1966.
Catechesis / Religious Program—Debbie Berryman, D.R.E. Students 4.
Mission—Holy Redeemer Eagle Harbor, Keweenaw Co.
Mission—Our Lady of the Pines Copper Harbor, Keweenaw Co.

ALPHA, IRON CO., ST. EDWARD, Closed. For inquiries for parish records contact the chancery.

ASSININS, BARAGA CO., THE MOST HOLY NAME OF JESUS-BLESSED KATERI TEKAKWITHA Revs. John L. Longbucco; Antony Lukka (India); Deacon John M. Cadeau.
Mailing Address: 16 S. Sixth, Lanse, 49946.
Res.: 14808 Assinins Rd., Baraga, 49908. Tel: 906-524-6424; Fax: 908-524-7585.
Catechesis / Religious Program—Tony Angle, D.R.E. Students 19.

BARAGA, BARAGA CO., ST. ANN Revs. John L. Longbucco; Antony Lukka (India); Deacon Robert L. Wahmhoff.
Mailing Address: 318 Lyons St., 49908.
Res.: 16 S. Sixth, Lanse, 49946. Tel: 906-524-6424; Fax: 906-524-7585.
Catechesis / Religious Program—Students 37.

BARBEAU, CHIPPEWA CO., HOLY FAMILY MISSION Rev. John S. Hascall, O.F.M.Cap.
Res.: 1529 Marquette Ave., Sault Sainte Marie, 49783. Tel: 906-632-3213; Fax: 906-632-8490.
Catechesis / Religious Program—Tel: 906-647-3221. Barbara Ogston, D.R.E. Students 13.

BARK RIVER, DELTA CO., ST. ELIZABETH ANN SETON, [CEM], Formerly St. George, Bark River; Sacred Heart of Jesus, Schaffer; & St. Michael, Perronville. Rev. Mark A. McQuesten.
Res.: 1216 12th Rd., P.O. Box 187, 49807. Tel: 906-466-9938; Fax: 906-466-0194.
Catechesis / Religious Program—Kelley VanLanen, D.R.E. Students 82.
Mission—St. Joseph Foster City, Dickinson Co.

BESSEMER, GOGEBIC CO., ST. SEBASTIAN Rev. Joy Joseph Adimakkeel (India).
Res.: 210 E. Iron St., 49911. Tel: 906-667-0952; Fax: 906-667-0952. Email: pastor@stsebastianparish.com.
Catechesis / Religious Program—Angie Mazurek, D.R.E. Students 58.

BRIMLEY, CHIPPEWA CO., ST. FRANCIS XAVIER Rev. Theodore J. Brodeur; Deacon Joseph A. LaPlante.
Mailing Address: P.O. Box 429, 49715. Tel: 906-248-3443.
Catechesis / Religious Program—Tel: 906-248-5386. Amy Perron, D.R.E. Students 2.
Mission—Blessed Kateri Tekakwitha Bay Mills, Chippewa Co. Fax: 906-248-3443. (Formerly St. Catherine).
Catechesis / Religious Program—Students 23.

CALUMET, HOUGHTON CO.

1—ST. PAUL THE APOSTLE (1908) Rev. Abraham J. Mupparathara, M.C.B.S. (India).
Mailing Address: P.O. Box 546, 49913.
Res.: 301 Eighth St., P.O. Box 546, 49913. Tel: 906-337-2044; Fax: 906-337-2058.
Catechesis / Religious Program—Students 51.

2—SACRED HEART (1868) Rev. Abraham J. Mupparathara, M.C.B.S. (India).
Mailing Address: P.O. Box 546, 49913.
Res.: 301 Eighth St., P.O. Box 546, 49913. Tel: 906-337-0810; Fax: 906-337-6424. Web: www.sacredheartcalumet.org.
Catechesis / Religious Program—Debbie Berryman, D.R.E. Students 67.

CASPIAN, IRON CO., ST. CECILIA (1954) Rev. George L. Veneklase, O.C.D.; Deacon Robert J. Kostka.
Mailing Address: P.O. Box 517, 49915. Tel: 906-265-3777.
Catechesis / Religious Program—Students 16.

CHAMPION, MARQUETTE CO., SACRED HEART, [CEM] Rev. Gregory R. Heikkala, Canonical Pastor; Sisters Margey Schmelzle, O.S.F., Pastoral Coord.; Lois Risch, O.S.F., Pastoral Coord.
Mailing Address: P.O. Box 99, 49814. Tel: 906-376-8475; Fax: 906-376-8475.
Catechesis / Religious Program—

CHANNING, DICKINSON CO., ST. ROSE Rev. Daniel S. Zaloga, Parochial Admin.
Mailing Address: P.O. Box 235, 49815. Tel: 906-542-3215.
Catechesis / Religious Program—Nancy Reese, D.R.E. Students 23.

CHASSELL, HOUGHTON CO., ST. ANNE (1887) Rev. Allen P. Mott; Sr. Ellen Enright, I.B.V.M., Pastoral Assoc.; Deacon Thomas F. Corrigan.
Mailing Address: P.O. Box 407, 49916. Tel: 906-523-4912; Fax: 906-523-4904.
Catechesis / Religious Program—Students 43.
Mission—Sacred Heart Painesdale, Houghton Co. Closed. For inquiries for parish records contact St. Ignatius Loyola, Houghton.
Mission—Immaculate Heart of Mary Donken, Houghton Co. Closed. For inquiries for parish records contact St. Ignatius Loyola, Houghton.

COOKS, SCHOOLCRAFT CO., ST. MARY MAGDALENE, [CEM] Rev. James M. Roetzer; Deacon Rodney Groleau.
Mailing Address: P.O. Box 68, Garden, 49835. Tel: 906-644-2626; Fax: 906-644-2626.
Catechesis / Religious Program—Paula LeFevre, D.R.E. Students 15.

CRYSTAL FALLS, IRON CO., GUARDIAN ANGELS (1887) Rev. Jeffrey A. Kurtz.
Res.: 412 Crystal Ave., 49920. Tel: 906-875-3019; Fax: 906-875-1034. Email: guardang@att.net.
Catechesis / Religious Program—11 N. 5th St., 49920. Jeanne Brown, D.R.E. Students 24.

DAGGETT, MENOMINEE CO., ST. FREDERICK, Closed. For inquiries for parish records contact Precious Blood Parish, Stephenson.

DETOUR, CHIPPEWA CO., SACRED HEART Rev. Janusz Romanek; Deacon Ronald P. Andrzejewski.
Mailing Address: 12841 E. Traynor Rd., Goetzville, 49736. Tel: 906-297-5211; Fax: 906-297-5108. Email: 4parishoffice@centurylink.net.
Catechesis / Religious Program—Kim Aubert, D.R.E. Students 17.
Mission—St. Florence Drummond Island, Chippewa Co. Tel: 906-297-5211.
Catechesis / Religious Program—Lisa McDonald, D.R.E.

ENGADINE, MACKINAC CO., OUR LADY OF LOURDES, Closed. For parish records, contact St. Gregory Parish, Newberry.

ESCANABA, DELTA CO.

1—ST. ANNE (1888) Rev. Francis J. DeGroot; Deacons Lewis Vailliencourt; Michael LeBeau; Terrance J. Saunders.
Res.: 817 S. Lincoln Rd., 49829. Tel: 906-786-1421; Fax: 906-786-5401.
See Holy Name Central Grade School, Escanaba under Elementary Interparochial Schools located in the Institution section.
Catechesis / Religious Program—Sharon Mellinger, C.R.E. Students 104.

2—ST. JOSEPH & ST. PATRICK (1997), (Formerly St. Joseph, Escanaba; Formerly St. Patrick, Escanaba). Rev. Eric E. Olson; Deacon William D. Hemes.
Res.: 709 First Ave. S., 49829. Tel: 906-789-6244; Fax: 906-789-1213.
See Holy Name Central Grade School, Escanaba under Elementary Interparochial Schools located in the Institution section.
Catechesis / Religious Program—Hans Whitmer, D.R.E. Students 43.

3—ST. THOMAS THE APOSTLE Rev. Rick L. Courier.
Res.: 1820 Ninth Ave. N., 49829. Tel: 906-786-4627; Fax: 906-789-5558. Web: dioceseofmarquette.org/

stthomas.org.
See Holy Name Central Grade School, Escanaba under Elementary Interparochial Schools located in the Institution section.
Catechesis/Religious Program—Tel: 906-233-9566. Hans Whitmer, D.R.E. Students 34.

EWEN, ONTONAGON CO., SACRED HEART (1892) Rev. Sebastian Ettolil, M.C.B.S. (India).
Mailing Address: P.O. Box 50, 49925. Tel: 906-988-2310; Fax: 906-988-2310. Email: shewen@charter.net.
Catechesis/Religious Program—Tracy Niemi, D.R.E. Tel: 906-827-3617. Students 19.
Mission—St. Ann Bergland, Ontonagon Co.

GARDEN, DELTA CO., ST. JOHN THE BAPTIST Rev. James M. Roetzer; Deacon Rodney Groleau.
Mailing Address: P.O. Box 68, 49835. Tel: 906-644-2626; Fax: 906-644-2626.
Catechesis/Religious Program—Students 32.

GLADSTONE, DELTA CO.
1—ALL SAINTS Rev. Ronald K. Timock.
Res.: 715 Wisconsin Ave., P.O. Box 392, 49837. Tel: 906-428-3199; Fax: 906-428-2829.
Catechesis/Religious Program—Students 127.
2—HOLY FAMILY Rev. Jose J. Maramattam (India).
Res.: 4011 CO 416-20th Rd., 49837. Tel: 906-786-1209; Fax: 906-786-0846.
Catechesis/Religious Program—Cathy Flagstadt, D.R.E. Students 116.

GOETZVILLE, CHIPPEWA CO., ST. STANISLAUS KOSTKA (1897) [CEM] Rev. Janusz Romanek; Deacon Ronald P. Andrzejewski.
Mailing Address: 12841 E. Traynor Rd., 49736. Tel: 906-297-5211; Fax: 906-297-5108. Email: 4parishoffice@centurylink.net.
Catechesis/Religious Program—Darlene Krzycki, D.R.E. Students 34.
Mission—Our Lady of the Snows Hessel, Mackinac Co. Tel: 906-484-3825; 906-484-2773 (Parish House).

GRAND MARAIS, ALGER CO., HOLY ROSARY CHURCH (1895) [CEM] Rev. Timothy W. Hruska.
Mailing Address: P.O. Box 424, 49839. Tel: 906-494-2589; Fax: 906-494-2589. Email: hrosary@gmail.com.
Catechesis/Religious Program—Jean Rochefort, Administrative Asst.
Mission—St. Therese Germfask, Schoolcraft Co.
Mission—St. Timothy Curtis, Mackinac Co.

GWINN, MARQUETTE CO., ST. ANTHONY Rev. John J. Boyle (England).
Res.: 280 N. Boulder, P.O. Box 1358, 49841. Tel: 906-346-5312; Fax: 906-346-3040. Email: stant@chartermi.net.
Catechesis/Religious Program—Tel: 906-346-9116. Lenora McKeen, D.R.E. Students 40.
Mission—St. Joseph Northland, Marquette Co. Tel: 906-346-3040; Fax: 906-346-5312.

HANCOCK, HOUGHTON CO., RESURRECTION, [CEM] Rev. Brian C. Gerber.
Res.: 900 Quincy St., 49930. Tel: 906-482-0215; Fax: 906-523-5485.
Catechesis/Religious Program—Tel: 906-482-1175. Michael Lorence, D.R.E. Students 76.
Mission—St. Francis of Assisi Dollar Bay, Houghton Co. Tel: 906-482-6489.

HERMANSVILLE, MENOMINEE CO., ST. JOHN NEUMANN (1995) [CEM] [JC], (Formerly St. Mary, Hermansville; St. Francis Xavier, Spalding). Rev. Michael T. Vichich.
Res.: P.O. Box 135, Spalding, 49886. Tel: 906-497-4578 (Rectory); 906-497-5800 (Office); Fax: 906-498-5800.
Catechesis/Religious Program—Lana Scott, D.R.E. Students 59.

HOUGHTON, HOUGHTON CO.
1—ST. ALBERT THE GREAT UNIVERSITY PARISH (1963), (Michigan Technological University) Rev. Allen P. Mott; Sr. Ellen Enright, I.B.V.M., Pastoral Assoc.
Res.: 411 MacInnes Dr., 49931. Tel: 906-482-5530; Fax: 906-482-4828.
2—ST. IGNATIUS LOYOLA Rev. John E. Martignon.
Res.: 305 Portage St., 49931. Tel: 906-482-0212; Fax: 906-482-8110. Email: stignatius@stignatius-houghton.org.
Catechesis/Religious Program—Students 88.
Mission—St. Mary Atlantic Mine, Houghton Co. Closed. For inquiries for parish records contact St. Ignatius Loyola, Houghton.

HUBBELL, HOUGHTON CO., ST. CECILIA, Closed. For parish records, contact St. Joseph, Lake Linden.

IRON MOUNTAIN, DICKINSON CO.
1—IMMACULATE CONCEPTION OF THE BLESSED VIRGIN MARY (1890) Rev. Msgr. James A. Kaczmarek.
Mailing Address: 500 E. Blaine St., 49801-1840. Email: ironmtic@sbcglobal.net.
See Bishop Baraga Catholic School System, Iron Mountain under Elementary Interparochial Schools located in the Institution section.
Catechesis/Religious Program—Students 28.
2—ST. MARY AND ST. JOSEPH (1938) Rev. Daniel S. Zaloga; Deacon Donald R. Christy.
Res.: 411 W. B St., 49801. Tel: 906-774-2046; Fax: 906-774-6015.
See Bishop Baraga Catholic School, Iron Mountain under Elementary Interparochial Schools located in the Institution section.
Catechesis/Religious Program—Mary Kay Cahill, D.R.E.; Cecilia Smith, D.R.E. Students 171.

IRON RIVER, IRON CO., ST. AGNES Rev. George L. Veneklase, O.C.D.; Deacon Robert J. Kostka.
Res.: 702 N. Fourth Ave., 49935-1304. Tel: 906-265-4557; Fax: 906-265-7155. Email: stagnes@up.net. Web: www.stagnes-stcecilia.com.
Catechesis/Religious Program—Students 68.

IRONWOOD, GOGEBIC CO.
1—ST. AMBROSE, Consolidated with Holy Trinity & St. Michael to form Our Lady of Peace Parish, 1986.
2—ST. MICHAEL, Consolidated with St. Ambrose & Holy Trinity to form Our Lady of Peace Parish, 1986.
3—OUR LADY OF PEACE (1986), Consolidated from Holy Trinity, St. Ambrose & St. Michael. Rev. Darryl J. Pepin; Deacon Robert A. Hamen.
Res.: 108 S. Marquette St., 49938-2060. Tel: 906-932-0174; Fax: 906-932-1019.
Catechesis/Religious Program—Patricia Niksich, Dir. Faith Formation. Students 76.

ISHPEMING, MARQUETTE CO.
1—ST. JOHN THE EVANGELIST (1871) Rev. Gregory R. Heikkala.
Res.: 325 S. Pine, 49849. Tel: 906-486-6212; Fax: 906-486-4244. Email: stjohnschurch@charterinternet.com.
Religious Education Center—335 S. Pine St., 49849. Tel: 906-486-9361. Angela Johnson, Dir. Faith Formation. Students 126.
2—ST. JOSEPH Rev. James Challancin; Deacon Steven M. Schaffer.
Office (All Mail):—1889 Prairie Ave., 49849-1045. Tel: 906-485-4200.
Res.: 1890 Prairie Ave., 49849-1044. Tel: 906-485-4626; Fax: 906-485-4185. Email: stjoeoffice@sbcglobal.net.
Catechesis/Religious Program—Angela Johnson, D.R.E. Students 56.
3—ST. PIUS X, Closed. For inquiries for parish records contact St. Joseph Church, 1889 Prairie Ave., Ishpeming, MI 49849.

KINGSFORD, DICKINSON CO.
1—AMERICAN MARTYRS Rev. Joseph O. Gouin.
Res.: 908 W. Sagola Ave., 49802. Tel: 906-774-0630; Fax: 906-774-4417. Email: frjoe@att.net. Web: www.americanmartyrskg.org.
Catechesis/Religious Program—Carol Gayan, D.R.E. Students 190.
2—ST. MARY QUEEN OF PEACE (1945) Rev. Michael A. Woempner.
Church & Office: 600 Marquette Blvd., 49802. Tel: 906-774-6122; Fax: 906-774-2349. Email: stmaryqueenofpeace@chartermi.net. Web: www.stmaryqueenofpeace.org.
Catechesis/Religious Program—Mary Beth Casanova, C.R.E. Students 74.

L'ANSE, BARAGA CO., SACRED HEART (1894) Revs. John L. Longbucco; Antony Lukka (India).
Res.: 16 S. Sixth St., 49946. Tel: 906-524-6424; Fax: 906-524-7585. Email: sachartl@up.net. Web: www.sacredheart-lanse.com.
School—433 E. Baraga Ave., 49946. Tel: 906-524-5157; Fax: 906-524-5154. Web: www.sacredheart-lanse.com/school. Karen Sands, Prin.; Pat Marinich, Librarian. Lay Teachers 3; Students 32.
Catechesis/Religious Program—Tel: 906-524-6425. Tony Angle, D.R.E. Students 58.

LAKE LINDEN, HOUGHTON CO., ST. JOSEPH (1871) Rev. Francis G. Dobrzenski.
Res.: 701 Calumet St., 49945. Tel: 906-296-6851.
Catechesis/Religious Program—Students 60.

MACKINAC ISLAND, MACKINAC CO., STE. ANNE DE MICHILIMACKINAC (1695) Rev. James J. Williams (Retired).
Mailing Address: P.O. Box 537, 49757. Tel: 906-847-3507. Web: steanneschurch.org.
Catechesis/Religious Program—Students 14.

MANISTIQUE, SCHOOLCRAFT CO., ST. FRANCIS DE SALES Rev. Glenn J. Theoret; Deacon Gilbert G. Sablack.
Res.: 330 Oak St., 49854. Tel: 906-341-5355; Fax: 906-341-3984.
School—Tel: 906-341-5512. Lay Teachers 12; Students 226.
Catechesis/Religious Program—Mary Desjarden, D.R.E. Students 66.
Mission—Divine Infant of Prague Gulliver, Schoolcraft Co.

MENOMINEE, MENOMINEE CO.
1—HOLY REDEEMER (Birch Creek) Rev. Corey J. Litzner; Deacon Roland Chaltry.
Res.: W-5541 Birch Creek Rd. No. 6, 49858. Tel: 906-863-6920; Fax: 906-863-7303.
See Menominee Catholic Central, Menominee under Elementary Interparochial Schools located in the Institution section.
Catechesis/Religious Program—Students 59.
2—HOLY SPIRIT (1972) Revs. Robb M. Jurkovich; Michael D. Chenier.
Res.: 1016 10th Ave., 49858. Tel: 906-863-5239; Fax: 906-863-2249. Web: holyspiritonline.org.
Catechesis/Religious Program—Tel: 906-863-2249. Students 27.
3—RESURRECTION Revs. Robb M. Jurkovich; Michael D. Chenier; Deacons Vincent W. Beckley; Gerald G. Roetzer.
Res.: 2607 18th St., 49858. Tel: 906-863-3405; Fax: 906-863-9090. Email: resparish@new.rr.com.
See Menominee Catholic Central, Menominee under Elementary Interparochial Schools located in the Institution section.
Catechesis/Religious Program—Students 32.

MORAN, MACKINAC CO., IMMACULATE CONCEPTION, [CEM] Rev. Pawel J. Mecwel.
Res.: 120 Church St., St. Ignace, 49781. Tel: 906-643-7671; Fax: 906-643-7755.
Catechesis/Religious Program—Students 7.

MUNISING, ALGER CO., SACRED HEART OF JESUS Rev. Christopher B. Gardiner; Deacons James E. Anderson; Thomas W. Moseley Jr.
Office: 110 W. Jewell St., P.O. Box 99, 49862. Tel: 906-387-4900; Fax: 906-387-4422.
Catechesis/Religious Program—Tel: 906-387-4901. Barbara Feldhusen, D.R.E. Students 64.
Mission—St. Therese Autrain, Alger Co. Tel: 906-892-8189.

NADEAU, MENOMINEE CO., ST. BRUNO Rev. Michael T. Vichich.
Res.: P.O. Box 95, 49863. Tel: 906-639-2388; Fax: 906-639-2301.
Catechesis/Religious Program—Nicola DuPont, D.R.E. Students 37.

NAHMA, DELTA CO., ST. ANDREW Rev. James M. Roetzer; Deacon Rodney Groleau.
Mailing Address: P.O. Box 68, Garden, 49835. Tel: 906-644-2626; Fax: 906-644-2626.
Catechesis/Religious Program—Paula LeFevre, D.R.E. Students 19.

NEGAUNEE, MARQUETTE CO., ST. PAUL Rev. Msgr. Peter Oberto.
Res.: 202 W. Case St., 49866. Tel: 906-475-9969; Fax: 906-475-9987. Email: stpaul@chartermi.net. Web: www.stpaulchurchnegaunee.com.
Catechesis/Religious Program—Bill Barrette, D.R.E. Students 81.
Mission—Our Lady Perpetual Help Palmer, Marquette Co. Tel: 906-475-4630.

NEWBERRY, LUCE CO., ST. GREGORY Rev. Francis Ricca.
Office: 212 W. Harrie St., 49868. Tel: 906-293-5511; Fax: 906-293-5560. Email: stgreg@sbcglobal.net.
Res.: 111 W. Harrie St., 49868. Tel: 906-293-5001.
Catechesis/Religious Program—Dawn Stephenson, D.R.E. Students 49.
Mission—Our Lady of Victory Paradise, Chippewa Co.
Mission—St. Stephen Naubinway, Mackinac Co.

NORWAY, DICKINSON CO., ST. MARY (1878) Rev. Timothy M. Ekaitis; Deacon Ronald J. LeMire Sr.
Res.: 401 Main St., 49870. Tel: 906-563-9845; Fax: 906-563-7623. Email: saintmary@norwaymi.com.
See Holy Spirit Central School, Norway under Elementary Interparochial Schools located in the Institution section.
Catechesis/Religious Program—Nancy Degnan, D.R.E. Students 58.

ONTONAGON, ONTONAGON CO., HOLY FAMILY, [CEM] Rev. Michael J. Jacobus; Deacon Matthew P. Weaver.
Res.: 515 Pine St., 49953. Tel: 906-884-2569; Fax: 906-884-6030. Email: hfcc@up.net.
Catechesis/Religious Program—Students 81.

PERKINS, DELTA CO., ST. JOSEPH (1901) Rev. Jacek S. Wtyklo.
Mailing Address: 5803 Hwy. M-35, P.O. Box 99, 49872. Tel: 906-359-4701; Fax: 906-359-4701.
Catechesis/Religious Program—Students 63.

PERRONVILLE, MENOMINEE CO., ST. ELIZABETH ANN SETON, (See Bark River.)

QUINNESEC, DICKINSON CO., ST. MARY, Closed. For inquiries for parish records contact St. Mary Church, 401 Main St., Norway, MI 49870.

RAMSAY, GOGEBIC CO., CHRIST THE KING, Closed. For inquiries for parish records contact St. Sebastian, Bessemer.

RAPID RIVER, DELTA CO., ST. CHARLES BORROMEO Rev. Jacek S. Wtyklo.
Res.: P.O. Box 247, 49878. Tel: 906-474-6606; Fax: 906-474-9087.
Catechesis/Religious Program—Julie Hayes-Moe, D.R.E. Students 26.

REPUBLIC, MARQUETTE CO., ST. AUGUSTINE, [CEM] Revs. Gregory R. Heikkala, Canonical Pastor; James Challancin, Sacramental Min.; Sisters Margey Schmelzle, O.S.F., Pastoral Coord.; Lois Risch, O.S.F., Pastoral Coord.
Mailing Address: 574 Kloman Ave., 49879. Tel:

906-376-8475; Fax: 906-376-8475.
Catechesis/Religious Program—Students 2.

ROCKLAND, ONTONAGON CO., ST. MARY Rev. Michael J. Jacobus.
Mailing Address: Holy Family Parish, 515 Pine St., Ontonagon, 49953. Tel: 906-884-2569; Fax: 906-884-6030.

RUDYARD, CHIPPEWA CO., ST. JOSEPH Rev. Joseph Augustine Vandannoor, M.S.T. (India); Deacon Roger A. Bygrave.
Mailing Address: 11509 W. H-40, 49780. Tel: 906-478-4331; Fax: 906-478-4333. Email: stjoseph@lighthouse.net.
Catechesis/Religious Program—Laura Seifert, D.R.E. Students 49.
Mission—St. Mary Trout Lake, Chippewa Co.
Station—Kinross Correctional Facility Kincheloe.
Station—Chippewa East Correctional Facility Kincheloe.
Station—Chippewa West Correctional Facility Kincheloe.

ST. IGNACE, MACKINAC CO., ST. IGNATIUS LOYOLA, [CEM] Rev. Pawel J. Mecwel; Deacons Thomas McClelland; Donald F. Olmstead.
Res.: 120 Church St., 49781. Tel: 906-643-7671; Fax: 906-643-7755.
Catechesis/Religious Program—Tel: 906-643-8887. Carol Masuga, D.R.E. Students 75.

SAULT SAINTE MARIE, CHIPPEWA CO.

1—HOLY NAME OF MARY Rev. Sebastian Kavumkal, M.S.T. (India).
Res.: 377 Maple St., 49783. Tel: 906-632-3381; Fax: 906-632-0741.
Catechesis/Religious Program—Students 24.
Mission—Sacred Heart Sugar Island, Chippewa Co.

2—ST. ISAAC JOGUES MISSION Rev. John S. Hascall, O.F.M.Cap.
Res.: 1529 Marquette Ave., 49783. Tel: 906-632-3213; Fax: 906-632-8490. Email: jhascall@sbcglobal.net.
Catechesis/Religious Program—Tel: 906-632-2856.

3—ST. JOSEPH Rev. Piotr Zaczynski; Deacon William J. Piche, (Retired).
Res.: 606 E. Fourth Ave., 49783. Tel: 906-632-9625; Fax: 906-632-5122.
Catechesis/Religious Program—Tel: 906-632-9625, Ext. 13. Danna Schmitter, D.R.E. Students 51.

4—NATIVITY OF OUR LORD, Closed. For inquiries for parish records contact St. Joseph, Sault Sainte Marie.

SCHAFFER, DELTA CO., ST. ELIZABETH ANN SETON, See separate listing. Formerly Sacred Heart of Jesus. See Bark River.

SOUTH RANGE, HOUGHTON CO., HOLY FAMILY Rev. John E. Martignon.
Res. & Mailing Address: 305 Portage St., Houghton, 49931. Tel: 906-482-0212; Fax: 906-482-8110.
Church: 107 Atlantic Ave., 49963.
Catechesis/Religious Program—Kim Harris, D.R.E. Students 36.

SPALDING, MENOMINEE CO., ST. FRANCIS XAVIER, See separate listing. St. John Neumann, P.O. Box 135, Spalding, MI 49886.

STEPHENSON, MENOMINEE CO., PRECIOUS BLOOD CHURCH (1880) [CEM] Rev. Corey J. Litzner; Deacon Thomas J. Rivard.
Res.: S. 304 Bluff St., 49887. Tel: 906-753-2562; Fax: 906-753-2811. Email: pbchurch@dreamscp.com.
Catechesis/Religious Program—Tel: 906-753-4771. Sharon Tebo, D.R.E. Students 129.

TRENARY, ALGER CO., ST. RITA (1947) Rev. Jacek S. Wtyklo.
Mailing Address: P.O. Box 207, 49891. Tel: 906-446-3350; Fax: 906-446-3523.
Catechesis/Religious Program—Heidi Swajaneu, D.R.E. Students 44.

VULCAN, DICKINSON CO., ST. BARBARA Rev. Timothy M. Ekaitis; Deacon Ronald J. LeMire Sr.
Mailing Address: P.O. Box 493, 49892. Tel: 906-563-9834; Fax: 906-563-7664.
See Holy Spirit Central School, Norway under Elementary Interparochial Schools located in the Institution section.
Catechesis/Religious Program—401 Main St., Norway, 49870. Students 37.

WAKEFIELD, GOGEBIC CO., IMMACULATE CONCEPTION OF THE BLESSED VIRGIN MARY Rev. Joy Joseph Adimakkeel (India).
Res.: 407 Ascherman St., 49968. Tel: 906-224-7851; Fax: 906-224-9118.
Rectory—210 E. Iron St., Bessemer, 49911. Tel: 906-667-0952.
Mission—St. Catherine Marenisco, Gogebic Co. Tel: 906-787-2258. Rev. Raymond F. Moncher (Retired).
Catechesis/Religious Program—Lucretia Mayer, D.R.E. Students 35.

WATERSMEET, GOGEBIC CO., IMMACULATE CONCEPTION Revs. Sebastian Ettolil, M.C.B.S. (India); George S. Maki.
Mailing Address: E23933 D Ave., P.O. Box 398, 49969. Tel: 906-358-4360.
Catechesis/Religious Program—Students 17.

WELLS, DELTA CO., ST. ANTHONY Rev. Rick L. Courier; Deacon David A. Talford.
Mailing Address: 1820 9th Ave. N., Escanaba, 49829. Tel: 906-786-4627; Fax: 906-789-5558. Web: www.dioceseofmarquette.org/stanthony.org.
Res.: 6596 N. 3rd St., Escanaba, 49829.
Catechesis/Religious Program—Hans Whitmer, D.R.E. Students 25.

WHITE PINE, ONTONAGON CO., ST. JUDE (1956) Rev. Michael J. Jacobus.
Mailing Address: 8 Cedar St., P.O. Box 427, 49971. Tel: 906-885-5763; Fax: 906-885-5763.
Catechesis/Religious Program—Students 7.

Indian Missions

ASSININS, BARAGA CO., THE MOST HOLY NAME OF JESUS-BLESSED KATERI TEKAKWITHA, Indian Mission. Revs. John L. Longbucco; Antony Lukka (India).
Res.: 318 Lyons St., Baraga, 49908.

BAY MILLS, CHIPPEWA CO., BLESSED KATERI TEKAKWITHA Rev. Theodore J. Brodeur.
Mailing Address: P.O. Box 429, Brimley, 49715.
Catechesis/Religious Program—Amy Perron, D.R.E. Students 23.

SAULT SAINTE MARIE, CHIPPEWA CO., ST. ISAAC JOGUES Rev. John S. Hascall, O.F.M.Cap.
1529 Marquette Ave., 49783.

SUGAR ISLAND, CHIPPEWA CO., SACRED HEART, Indian Missionaries, East. Rev. Sebastian Kavumkal, M.S.T. (India).
377 Maple St., Sault Sainte Marie, 49783.

WATERSMEET, GOGEBIC CO., LAC VIEUX DESERT RESERVATION Rev. Sebastian Ettolil, M.C.B.S. (India).
Mailing Address: P.O. Box 398, 49969.

Chaplains of Public Institutions

MARQUETTE. *Marquette General Hospital*, Tel: 906-228-9440. Rev. Jeff G. Johnson.

IRON MOUNTAIN. *Veterans Administration Center*. Rev. Msgr. James A. Kaczmarek, Chap.

On Duty Outside the Diocese:
Revs.—
Hasse, Benjamin J., 1000 E. Maple Ave., Mundelein, IL 60060.
Moll, Daniel J., Casa Santa Maria, Via dell'Umilta 30, Rome 00187 Italy.
Murphy, Patrick E., 5500 Armstrong Rd., (118c), Battle Creek, 49016. Dept. of Veterans Affairs Medical Center.

Special Assignment:
Revs.—
Heikkala, Gregory R., Dir., Vocations
Ziminski, James C., Dir., Marygrove Retreat Center

Leave of Absence:
Rev.—
Schaeffer, Richard C.

Retired:
Rev. Msgrs.—
Desrochers, Timothy H., P.O. Box 693, Gwinn, 49841.
Patrick, John E., V.G., P.O. Box 609, Gwinn, 49841.
Revs.—
Borca, Dennis L., P.O. Box 436, Bardstown, KY 40004-9998.
Bracket, Louis P., 307 Eddy St., Wakefield, 49968.
Clisch, Norman A., 527 Maple St., Iron River, 49935.
Eddy, Corbin, 624 Lake Ave., Hancock, 49930.
Gauthier, Lawrence T., 300 Rock St., 49855.
Grambow, Arnold J.
Landreville, Norbert B., P.O. Box 345, St. Ignace, 49781.
Lehman, John J., Winter: 2425 Privateer Blvd, Barataria, LA 70036. Summer: P.O. Box 1, Sault Sainte Marie, 49783.
Lenz, Frank, 207Z Saux Head Rd., Co. Rd. 550, 49855.
Manderfield, R.P. Geraldo, Apartado 2810, Managua, Nicaragua.
Mayotte, Allan J., 405 'C' St., Wakefield, 49968.
McArdle, John F., 4305 Sixth St., Menominee, 49858.
Menapace, James L., 703 N. Corbridge Rd., Gulliver, 49840.
Minelli, Peter A., 114 Provider, Gwinn, 49841.
Moncher, Raymond F., P.O. Box 175, Marenisco, 49947.
Neurohr, Gilbert N., 900 First Ave., S., Apt. 4, Escanaba, 49829.
Nomellini, Paul J., 3883 Town Rd. A.A., Florence, WI 54121.
Norden, Emmett M., P.O. Box 562, Escanaba, 49829.
Nowacki, Jerome A.
Olivier, John H., S.S., St. Charles Villa, 603 Maiden Choice Ln., Baltimore, MD 21228.
Poisson, Thomas L., 300 Rock St., 49855.
Rupp, Daniel N., P.O Box 771, 49855.
Sartorelli, Otto, P.O. Box 494, Caspian, 49915.
Schiska, Paul A., 1490 15.5 Rd., Bark River, 49807.
Sedlock, David W., P.O. Box 536, Gwinn, 49841.
Shiverski, John J., 415 Forestville Basin Trl., 49855.
Strelick, Charles J., 4420 Devonshire Ave., Spring Hill, FL 34609.
Valerio, Raymond A., 831 E. Grant, 49801.
Wantland, Thomas A., 137 Drifting Sands Dr., Venice, FL 34293.
Williams, James J., 1203 Wenniway, Mackinaw City, 49701.
Zeugner, Raymond L., 5096 Dunns Pt. Rd., Florence, WI 54121.

Permanent Deacons:
Adler, David, St. Louis the King, Marquette
Anderson, James, Sacred Heart of Jesus, Munising
Andrzejewski, Ronald P., St. Stanislaus Kostka, Goetzville; Our Lady of Snows Mission, Hessel; Sacred Heart, DeTour; St. Florence Mission, Drummond Island
Beckley, Vincent W., Resurrection, Menominee
Bygrave, Roger A., St. Joseph, Rudyard; St. Mary Mission, Trout Lake
Cadeau, John M., Holy Name of Jesus/Blessed Kateri Tekakwitha, Assinins
Chaltry, Roland, Holy Redeemer, Menominee
Christy, Donald R., St. Mary-St. Joseph, Iron Mountain
Corrigan, Thomas F., St. Anne, Chassell
Foye, Thomas E., St. Peter Cathedral, Marquette
Green, William, St. Anne, Wausau, WI
Gretzinger, Stephen S., Holy Spirit, Menominee
Groleau, Rodney R., Garden Area Churches, Garden
Gualdoni, Steven J., St. Christopher, Marquette
Hamen, Robert, Our Lady of Peace, Ironwood
Hemes, Dr. Bill D., St. Joseph & St. Patrick, Escanaba
Jackson, Dean J., St. Peter Cathedral, Marquette
Jamieson, Scott A., St. Peter Cathedral, Marquette
Kostka, Robert J., St. Cecilia, Caspian; St. Agnes, Iron River
LaCosse, Robert K., Chancery Office & St. Michael, Marquette; (Incardinated in Archdiocese of Chicago, IL)
LaPlante, Joseph A., St. Francis Xavier, Brimley; Mission of Blessed Kateri Tekakwitha, Bay Mills-;(Incardinated in Diocese of Rockford, IL)
Leadbetter, John S., St. Peter Cathedral, Marquette
LeBeau, Michael, St. Anne, Escanaba
LeMire, Ronald J., Sr., St. Mary, Norway
Londo, Lawrence H., Diocese of Marquette
Maki, Dennis R., St. Michael, Marquette
McClelland, Thomas, St. Ignatius Loyola, St. Ignace
Moseley, Thomas W., Jr., Sacred Heart, Munising
Olmstead, Donald F., St. Ignatius Loyola, St. Ignace
Piche, William J., St. Joseph, Sault Ste. Marie
Powers, Daniel B., Catholic Social Svcs., Marquette (Incardinated in Diocese of San Diego)
Rivard, Thomas J., Precious Blood, Menominee
Roetzer, Gerald G., Resurrection, Menominee
Sablack, Gilbert G., St. Francis de Sales & Divine Infant of Prague, Manistique
Sanders, Claire W., St. Mary, Norway; St. Barbara, Vulcan
Saunders, Terrance J., St. Anne, Escanaba
Schaffer, Steven M., St. Joseph, Ishpeming
St. John, Gregg R., St. Louis the King, Marquette
Stancher, Arthur, St. Paul, Calumet
Talford, David A., St. Anthony of Padua, Wells
Thoren, Donald W., St. Peter Cathedral, Marquette
Vailliencourt, Lewis, St. Anne, Escanaba
Vonck, Warren K., St. Peter Cathedral, Marquette
Wahmhoff, Robert L., St. Ann, Baraga
Weaver, Matthew P., Holy Family, Ontonagon
Wittak, Jay W., Union Grove, WI

INSTITUTIONS LOCATED IN THE DIOCESE

[A] ELEMENTARY INTERPAROCHIAL SCHOOLS

MARQUETTE. *Fr. Marquette Catholic Central Schools System*, 500 S. Fourth St., 49855. Tel: 906-225-1129; Fax: 906-225-1987. Web: fathermarquette.org. Jackie Wright, Prin.; Maryann Ferns, Asst. Prin. Serving the following parishes: St. Peter's Cathedral; St. Louis; St. Michael; St. Christopher. Lay Teachers 25; Students 300.

ESCANABA. *Holy Name Catholic School*, 409 S. 22nd St., 49829. Tel: 906-786-7550; Fax: 906-786-7582. Email: office@holynamecrusaders.com. Web: holynamecrusaders.com. Joseph L. Carlson, Prin. Lay Teachers 16; Students 282.

IRON MOUNTAIN. *Bishop Baraga Catholic School*, 406 W. B St., 49801. Tel: 906-774-2277; Fax: 906-774-8704. Email: office@baragaup.com. Web: www.baragaup.com. Richard Krainz, Prin. Lay Teachers 14; Students 125.

IRONWOOD. *All Saints Catholic Academy*, 106 S. Marquette St., 49938. Tel: 906-932-3200; Fax: 906-932-1019. MaryJo Welch, Lead Teacher. Serving Our Lady of Peace, Ironwood. Lay Teachers 4; Students 40.

L'ANSE. *Sacred Heart School*, (Grades K-6), 433 Baraga Ave., Lanse, 49946. Tel: 906-524-5157; Fax: 906-524-5154. Web: www.sacredheart-lanse.com/school. Karen Sands, Prin.; Pat Marinich, Librarian.

MANISTIQUE. *St. Francis de Sales School*, (Grades PreSchool-8), 210 Lake St., 49854. Tel: 906-341-5512; Fax: 906-341-3984. Kathleen (Kitty) Lovell, Prin.; Karen Mooi, Librarian.

MENOMINEE. *Menominee Catholic Central*, 1406 10th Ave., 49858. Tel: 906-863-3190; Fax: 906-863-3990. Dan Paul, Prin. Lay Teachers 8; Students 102.

NORWAY. *Holy Spirit Central School*, 201 Saginaw St., 49870. Tel: 906-563-8817; Fax: 906-563-8854. Elizabeth A. Stack, Prin. Lay Teachers 10; Students 74.

SAULT SAINTE MARIE. *St. Mary School* Serves the parishes of St. Mary & St. Joseph, Sault Sainte Marie., 360 Maple St., 49783. Tel: 906-635-6141. Maria Farney, Prin. Lay Teachers 7; Students 122; Rel. Teacher 1.

[B] ENDOWMENT FUNDS

MARQUETTE. *Endowment Foundation of the Diocese of Marquette*, 1004 Harbor Hills Dr., 49855. Tel: 906-227-9108; Fax: 906-225-0437. Email: tgadzinski@dioceseofmarquette.org. Web: dioceseofmarquette.org; legacyoffaith.net. Terri Gadzinski, Devel. Dir.

St. John's Memorial Scholarship Committee, 144 Fassbender Rd., 49855. Tel: 906-249-3473. Lori Carlson, Pres.

Marquette Area Catholic Education Fund, 1004 Harbor Hills Dr., 49855. Tel: 906-227-9143.

BESSEMER. *St. Sebastian Endowment Fund*, 210 E. Iron St., 49911. Tel: 906-667-0952; Fax: 906-667-0952. Rev. Joy Joseph Adimakkeel (India).

ESCANABA. *Holy Name Endowment Fund*, 409 S. 22nd St., 49829. Tel: 906-786-7550; Fax: 906-786-7582.

Holy Name Scholarship Foundation, 409 S. 22nd St., 49829. Tel: 906-786-7550; Fax: 906-786-7582.

IRON MOUNTAIN. *Bishop Baraga Catholic School Foundation*, 406 W. B St., 49801. Tel: 906-774-2277; Fax: 906-774-8704.

IRONWOOD. *Our Lady of Peace School Educational Fund*, 108 S. Marquette St., 49938-2060. Tel: 906-932-0174; Fax: 906-932-1019. Rev. Darryl J. Pepin.

MANISTIQUE. *St. Francis de Sales Education Foundation*, 330 Oak St., 49854. Tel: 906-341-5355; Fax: 906-341-3984. Web: stfrancisofmanistique41pi.org.

MENOMINEE. *Menominee Catholic Education Fund*, 1406 Tenth Ave., 49858-2604. Tel: 906-863-2723; Fax: 906-863-3990. Elaine Blair-Klitzke, Office Mgr.

NEGAUNEE. *Negaunee St. Paul Endowment Fund*, 202 W. Case St., 49866. Tel: 906-475-9969. Rev. Msgr. Peter Oberto, J.C.L.

NORWAY. *Holy Spirit Central School Educational Fund*, 201 Saginaw, 49870. Tel: 906-563-8817; Fax: 908-563-8854. Email: holyspirit01@hotmail.com.

SAULT SAINTE MARIE. *Holy Family School Endowment Fund, Inc.*, 377 Maple St., 49783. Tel: 906-632-3381; Fax: 906-632-0741.

St. Mary School Endowment Fund, 377 Maple St., 49783. Tel: 906-632-3381; Fax: 906-632-0741.

[C] GENERAL HOSPITALS

ESCANABA. *O.S.F. St. Francis Hospital* O.S.F. Healthcare System., 3401 Ludington, 49829. Tel: 906-786-3311; Fax: 906-786-4004. Web: www.osfhealthcare.org. Peter G. Jennings, Pres. & CEO; Rev. Emmett M. Norden, Chap. (Retired). Staff 555; Bed Capacity 98; Patients Assisted Annually 213,823.

[D] HOMES FOR THE AGED

ESCANABA. *Bishop Noa Home for Senior Citizens*, 2900 3rd Ave. S., 49829. Tel: 906-786-5810; Fax: 906-786-5372. Web: bishopnoahome.com. Sisters of St. Paul de Chartres. Sisters 7; Residents 109.

[E] CONVENTS AND RESIDENCES OF SISTERS

MARQUETTE. *Provincialate of the Sisters of St. Paul de Chartres*, 1300 County Rd. 492, 49855. Tel: 906-226-3932; Fax: 906-226-2139. Web: sistersofstpaulusa.org. Sr. Gloria J. Schultz, S.P.C., Dist. Supr. Sisters 14.

IRON MOUNTAIN. *Monastery of the Holy Cross*, N4028 Hwy. U.S. 2, P.O. Box 397, 49801. Tel: 906-774-0561; Fax: 906-774-0561. Sr. Maria of Jesus, O.C.D., Prioress; Rev. Daniel L. Malone, Chap. Discalced Carmelite Nuns. Cloistered Nuns: Professed 17; Extern Professed Sisters 2; Novices 2.

[F] RETREAT HOUSES

GARDEN. *Marygrove Retreat Center*, P.O. Box 38, 49835. Tel: 906-644-2771; Fax: 908-644-2463. Email: mgcbox38@centurylink.net. Web: www.marygrove.org. Rev. James C. Ziminski, Dir. Retreats and workshops for priests, religious and laity.

[G] NEWMAN CLUBS

MARQUETTE. *Catholic Campus Ministry-Northern Michigan University* 401 W. Kaye Ave., 49855. Tel: 906-228-3302; Fax: 906-228-5502. Email: ccm@nmu.edu. Web: www.ccmnmu.com. Revs. Larry P. Van Damme; Nicholas R. Thompson; Catherine Hardenbergh, Campus Min.

HOUGHTON. *St. Albert the Great, University Parish* (1963) 411 MacInnes Dr., 49931. Tel: 906-482-5530; Fax: 906-482-4828. Email: fralmott@charterinternet.com. Web: stalbert.students.mtu.edu. Rev. Allen P. Mott, Contact Person.

SAULT SAINTE MARIE. *Lake Superior State University, Newman Center* 517 W. Easterday, 49783. Tel: 906-253-1285. Danna Schmitter, Contact Person.

[H] ASSOCIATIONS OF THE FAITHFUL

PARADISE. *Companions of Christ the Lamb*, P.O. Box 12, 49768. Tel: 906-492-3647; Fax: 906-492-3648. Rev. John Fabian, Moderator.

[I] MISCELLANEOUS

MARQUETTE. *St. Vincent De Paul Society*, 2119 Presque Isle Ave., Rm. 101, 49855. Tel: 906-226-2311; Fax: 906-226-4599. Email: svdp@upstvincent.org. Web: www.stvincentup.org.

RELIGIOUS INSTITUTES OF MEN REPRESENTED IN THE DIOCESE

For further details refer to the corresponding bracketed number in the Religious Institutes of Men or Women section.

[0470]—*The Capuchin Friars* (Detroit, MI)—O.F.M.Cap.

[0520]—*Franciscan Friars* (Cincinnati, OH)—O.F.M.

RELIGIOUS INSTITUTES OF WOMEN REPRESENTED IN THE DIOCESE

[3710]—*Congregation of the Sisters of Saint Agnes*—C.S.A.

[0420]—*Discalced Carmelite Nuns*—O.C.D.

[1070-09]—*Dominican Sisters*—O.P.

[1070-13]—*Dominican Sisters*—O.P.

[1630]—*Franciscan Sisters of Christian Charity*—O.S.F.

[2380]—*Institute of the Blessed Virgin Mary (Sisters of Loretto)*—I.B.V.M.

[2970]—*School Sisters of Notre Dame*—S.S.N.D.

[3840]—*Sisters of St. Joseph of Carondelet*—C.S.J.

[3980]—*Sisters of St. Paul of Chartres*—S.P.C.

[2180]—*Sisters of the Immaculate Heart of Mary*—I.H.M.

[3260]—*Sisters of the Precious Blood*—C.PP.S.

[1770]—*Sisters of the Third Order of St. Francis* (Peoria, Illinois)—O.S.F.

DIOCESAN CEMETERIES

MARQUETTE. *Holy Cross*

ESCANABA. *Holy Cross Catholic Cemetery*

NECROLOGY

✠ Schmitt, Most Rev. Mark F., Retired Bishop of Marquette.—Died Dec. 14, 2011

† Gondek, Joseph A., (Retired)—Died Sept. 13, 2011

† Marcotte, Wayne E., (Retired)—Died April 30, 2011

† Shiroda, Donald L., (Retired)—Died March 16, 2011

† Thoren, S. Guy—Died Dec. 17, 2011

An asterisk (*) denotes an organization that has established tax-exempt status directly with the IRS and is not covered by the USCCB Group Ruling.

Diocese of Memphis

(Memphitana in Tennesia)

Most Reverend

J. TERRY STEIB, S.V.D., D.D.

Bishop of Memphis; ordained January 6, 1967; appointed Titular Bishop of Fallaba and Auxiliary Bishop of St. Louis December 6, 1983; consecrated February 10, 1984; appointed Bishop of Memphis March 23, 1993; installed May 5, 1993.

Catholic Center: P.O. Box 341669, Memphis, TN 38184-1669. Tel: 901-373-1200; Fax: 901-373-1269.

Web: www.cdom.org

ESTABLISHED JANUARY 6, 1971.

Square Miles 10,682.

Comprises the Counties of Benton, Carroll, Chester, Crockett, Decatur, Dyer, Fayette, Gibson, Hardeman, Hardin, Haywood, Henderson, Henry, Lake, Lauderdale, McNairy, Madison, Obion, Shelby, Tipton and Weakley in the State of Tennessee.

For legal titles of parishes and diocesan institutions, consult the Chancery Office.

STATISTICAL OVERVIEW

Personnel	
Bishop	1
Priests: Diocesan Active in Diocese	50
Priests: Diocesan Active Outside Diocese	1
Priests: Retired, Sick or Absent	15
Number of Diocesan Priests	66
Religious Priests in Diocese	13
Total Priests in Diocese	79
Extern Priests in Diocese	5
Ordinations:	
Diocesan Priests	3
Transitional Deacons	5
Permanent Deacons in Diocese	61
Total Brothers	27
Total Sisters	52
Parishes	
Parishes	42
With Resident Pastor:	
Resident Diocesan Priests	36
Resident Religious Priests	6
Missions	5
Professional Ministry Personnel:	
Sisters	5
Lay Ministers	34
Welfare	
Day Care Centers	2
Total Assisted	430
Specialized Homes	3
Total Assisted	100
Special Centers for Social Services	1
Total Assisted	1,200
Residential Care of Disabled	1
Total Assisted	127
Other Institutions	7
Total Assisted	600
Educational	
Diocesan Students in Other Seminaries	28
Total Seminarians	28
Colleges and Universities	1
Total Students	1,641
High Schools, Diocesan and Parish	4
Total Students	1,741
High Schools, Private	3
Total Students	1,210
Elementary Schools, Diocesan and Parish	21
Total Students	4,768
Elementary Schools, Private	1
Total Students	562
Catechesis/Religious Education:	
High School Students	551
Elementary Students	4,648
Total Students under Catholic Instruction	15,149
Teachers in the Diocese:	
Brothers	20
Sisters	8
Lay Teachers	857
Vital Statistics	
Receptions into the Church:	
Infant Baptism Totals	1,260
Minor Baptism Totals	106
Adult Baptism Totals	79
Received into Full Communion	206
First Communions	1,470
Confirmations	1,213
Marriages:	
Catholic	179
Interfaith	126
Total Marriages	305
Deaths	470
Total Catholic Population	59,041
Total Population	1,562,650

Former Bishops—Most Revs. CARROLL T. DOZIER, D.D., ord. March 19, 1937; appt. Nov. 17, 1970; cons. Jan. 6, 1971; retired July 27, 1982; died Dec. 7, 1985; J. FRANCIS STAFFORD, D.D., ord. Dec. 15, 1957; cons. Bishop Feb. 29, 1976; appt. Nov. 16, 1982; appt. to Archdiocese of Denver, June 3, 1986; DANIEL M. BUECHLEIN, O.S.B., D.D., ord. May 3, 1964; appt. Jan. 20, 1987; appt. to Archdiocese of Indianapolis, July 14, 1992.

Vicar General—Rev. Msgr. PETER P. BUCHIGNANI, P.A., J.C.L., V.G., St. Francis of Assisi, 8151 Chimney Rock, Cordova, 38018. Tel: 901-756-1213.

Catholic Center Offices—Mailing Address: P.O. Box 341669, Memphis, 38184-1669. Tel: 901-373-1200; Fax: 901-373-1269. *5825 Shelby Oaks Dr., Memphis, 38134.* Office Hours: Mon.-Fri. 7:45-4:45.

Diocesan Offices & Directors

All diocesan office addresses & phone numbers are the same as mentioned above under Catholic Center Offices unless otherwise noted.

Chief Pastoral Officer—Rev. MICHAEL P. JOYCE, C.M., J.C.D.

Chief Operational Officer—CHRISTOPHER KOCK.

Archives—Rev. RICHARD L. MICKEY, M.Ed., Archivist.

Notaries—MARIANNA BEATY; NANCY HENNESSEY.

Dean of the Jackson Deanery—Rev. Msgr. THOMAS D. KIRK, St. Mary's Church, 1665 Hwy. 45 Bypass, Jackson, 38305-4414. Tel: 731-668-2596.

Catholic Public Policy Commission of Tennessee—Mailing Address: P.O. Box 341669, Memphis, 38184-1669.

College of Consultors—Rev. RUSSELL D. HARBAUGH; Rev. Msgrs. PETER P. BUCHIGNANI, P.A., J.C.L., V.G.; VICTOR P. CIARAMITARO; Revs. RICHARD D. COY (Retired); ERNIE DEBLASIO; Rev. Msgr. JOHN B. MCARTHUR; Revs. ROBERT W. MARSHALL JR.; JAMES J. MARTELL; J. DAVID GRAHAM; Rev. Msgr. ALBERT E. KIRK; Revs. MICHAEL E. WERKHOVEN; RICHARD J. KAUMP JR.

Presbyteral Council—Rev. Msgrs. PETER P. BUCHIGNANI, P.A., J.C.L., V.G.; VICTOR P. CIARAMITARO; Revs. RICHARD D. COY (Retired); ERNIE DEBLASIO; THOMAS M. CONDON, O.P.; RICHARD J. KAUMP JR.; Rev. Msgr. ALBERT E. KIRK; Revs. J. DAVID GRAHAM; RUSSELL D. HARBAUGH; MICHAEL P. JOYCE, C.M., J.C.D.; Rev. Msgr. JOHN B. MCARTHUR; Revs. ROBERT W. MARSHALL JR.; JAMES J. MARTELL; MICHAEL E. WERKHOVEN.

Clergy Personnel Board—Rev. Msgr. VICTOR P. CIARAMITARO; Rev. ROBERT W. MARSHALL JR.; Rev. Msgr. JOHN B. MCARTHUR; Rev. MICHAEL P. JOYCE, C.M., J.C.D.; Rev. Msgr. PETER P. BUCHIGNANI, P.A., J.C.L., V.G.

Media Consultant—SUZANNE AVILES, Dir. Communications.

Tribunal

Judicial Vicar—Rev. MICHAEL P. JOYCE, C.M., J.C.D.

Adjutant Judicial Vicar—Rev. Msgr. PETER P. BUCHIGNANI, P.A., J.C.L., V.G.

Defenders of the Bond—Rev. Msgr. J. EDWIN CREARY; Rev. ROBERT D. PONTICELLO, J.C.L., M.Div.

Promoter of Justice—Rev. ROBERT D. PONTICELLO, J.C.L., M.Div.

Judges—Rev. Msgr. VICTOR P. CIARAMITARO; Rev. MICHAEL L. STEWART (Retired); Deacon J. GERARD QUINN, J.C.L.; ANNA M. DANKS, J.C.L.

Ecclesiastical Notaries—NANCY HENNESSEY; MARIANNA BEATY.

Chief Pastoral Officer—Rev. MICHAEL P. JOYCE, C.M., J.C.D.

Facilities and Risk Management—WILLIAM HECHT, Dir., 5825 Shelby Oaks Dr., Memphis, 38134-1669. Tel: 901-373-1200; Fax: 901-373-1269.

Catholic Cemeteries— Calvary, Memphis; All Saints, Memphis; Mount Calvary, Jackson, TN Mr. PATRICK POSEY, Dir., 1663 Elvis Presley Blvd., Memphis, 38106. Tel: 901-948-1529.

Engineering & Maintenance—WILLIAM HECHT, Dir., 5825 Shelby Oaks Dr., Memphis, 38134-1669. Tel: 901-373-1200; Fax: 901-373-1269.

Human Resources—Mrs. SANDRA GOLDSTEIN, Dir.

Employee Benefits—Mrs. SHARON ICHNIOWSKI.

Office for Professional Responsibilities/Child and Youth Protection—Dr. JAMES B. LATTA, D.Min., Dir. Tel: 901-359-2027. Email: jb2latta@aol.com.

Technical Services—Ms. KATHY SABA, M.C.S.E., Dir.

Department for Social Ministries

Episcopal Vicar for Social Ministry—Rev. TIMOTHY F. SULLIVAN, C.S.P., Dir. & Episcopal Vicar. Tel: 901-722-4747; Fax: 901-722-4791.

Catholic Charities of West Tennessee—1325 Jefferson Ave., Memphis, 38104. Tel: 901-722-4700. Web: www.ccwtn.org. Mr. MICHAEL D. ALLEN, Pres. & CEO. Tel: 901-722-4747; Fax: 901-722-4791; Mrs. ALIE LIFSEY, Campus Coord. & Exec. Asst. Tel: 901-722-4750; Mrs. CAROLYN TISDALE, Exec. Dir. Agency. Tel: 901-722-4727; Fax: 901-722-4791; ALTHEA BURKETT, Administrative Asst. Tel: 901-722-4741; Fax: 901-722-4791.

Finance—Mr. DAVID BARCZAK, Dir. Finance & Admin. Tel: 901-722-4715; Fax: 901-722-4766.

Information Technology—Mr. JAMES DUKES, Systems Admin. Tel: 901-722-4705; Fax: 901-722-4791.

Marketing & Public Relations—Mrs. ANNA KATHRYN WORD, Dir. Devel. Tel: 901-722-4733; Fax: 901-722-4791.

Extended Child Care Services—Mrs. PAMELA O'BRYAN, Dir. Tel: 901-722-4718; Fax: 901-722-4791.
Camp Love & Learn—Ms. ANGELA ATKINS, Camp Dir. Tel: 901-722-4716.
Immaculate Conception Extended Care— (After-School Care) Ms. ANGELA SURIANI, Prog. Dir. Tel: 901-725-2710.
St. Louis Extended Care— (after school care) Ms. LORI TUCKER, Prog. Dir. Tel: 901-626-1268.
St. Mary's Jackson— (after school care) Ms. JANICE BITONDO, Prog. Dir. Tel: 731-616-2341.
Community & Parish Social Services—Mrs. THERESA GUSTAITIS, Dir. Parish Social Ministry. Tel: 901-722-4794.
Homeless Residential Treatment Services Coordinator—MARY JORDAN, Div. Dir. Tel: 901-726-9786; Fax: 901-722-4791.
Genesis House—Ms. MARY JORDON, Prog. Dir., 300 N. Bellevue, Memphis, 38104. Tel: 901-726-9786; Fax: 901-725-1649.
Dozier House—Mr. TONY BROWN, Prog. Dir., 69 N. Cleveland, Memphis, 38104. Tel: 901-722-4734; Fax: 901-728-6171.
Sophia's House—Tel: 901-722-4700. Mrs. CHASSITY TAYLOR, Interim Prog. Dir. Tel: 901-722-4700; Fax: 901-722-4791.
*Diocese of Memphis Housing Corporation—1325 Jefferson Ave., Memphis, 38104*Web: dmhcorp.org. Ms. CHERRY BROOKS, Dir. Asst. Tel: 901-722-4795; Fax: 901-722-4732.
Refugee and Immigration Services—Mrs. VINODINI JAYARAMAN, Div. Dir. Tel: 901-722-4714; Fax: 901-722-4791.
St. Peter Ministries— (Emergency Assistance & Counseling Services) Mrs. KAREN HARDAWAY, Emergency Svcs. Tel: 901-722-4787; Mr. MARK BROWN, Counseling Coord. Tel: 901-722-4768; Fax: 901-722-4791.

Department for Catholic Education

Secretary for Catholic Education—Dr. MARY McDONALD.
Catholic Schools—Dr. MARY McDONALD, Sec. Educ. & Supt. Tel: 901-373-1205; Mrs. JANET M. DONATO, Assoc. Supt. Tel: 901-373-1221; Mrs. DEBBIE BELL, Dir. Curriculum & Instruction. Tel: 901-726-4446; Mrs. SONDRA MORRIS, Dir. Diocesan Athletics. Tel: 901-260-2874; CHARLOTTE PERRY, Dir. School Nutrition. Tel: 901-726-4446; Mrs. SHIRLEY MATHENA, Food Svc. Clerk; Mrs. SHARON MASTERSON, Dir. School Communications. Tel: 901-260-2871; Dr. COLLEEN BUTTERICK, Dir. School Counseling Svcs. Tel: 901-373-1219; Dr. DAVID HILL, Dir. Academics & Student Achievement. Tel: 901-726-4446; Sr. ROSE MARTIN GLENN, S.Sp.S., Dir. Health Svcs. Tel: 901-726-4446; Mrs. MARY HELEN CARMACK, Exec. Asst. to Supt./Community Rels. Tel: 901-373-1205; PATRICK MCCARROLL, Dir. School Progs. & Svcs. Tel: 901-726-4446; Mrs. LAURIE COTROS, Dir. Fine & Performing Arts. Tel: 901-373-1219; Mrs. HARDIE MAE FITZGERALD, Diocesan Dir. School Housekeeping Svcs. Tel: 901-373-1219; Mrs. SHARON JONES, Educ. Initiatives Coord. Tel: 901-373-1254; Mrs. TALLIE HODGES, Administrative Asst. Tel: 901-373-1219.

Department for Finance

Chief Financial Officer—Mr. JAMES ABERNATHY.
Controller—JAMES BREWSTER.
Regional Controller—Ms. KATHY OWINGS.
Continuing Education for Clergy—Rev. CARL J. HOOD, Dir.
Formation of Permanent Deacons—Rev. KEITH STEWART.
Permanent Deacons—Deacon FRANK WILLIAMS, Dir. Tel: 901-388-3509.
Seminarians—Rev. KEITH STEWART, Dir. Tel: 901-323-3817.
Villa Vianney Priests Retirement Residence—Rev. RICHARD L. MICKEY, M.Ed., Dir., 10605 Bishop Dozier Dr., Cordova, 38016. Tel: 901-752-0766.
Vicar for Religious—Sr. CATHY GALASKIEWICZ, O.P.
Vocations—Rev. KEITH STEWART, Dir. Tel: 901-323-3817.
Director Multicultural Ministries—Rev. ANTHONY CLARK, S.V.D., 1325 Jefferson Ave., Memphis, 38104. Tel: 901-722-4760; Fax: 901-722-4766. Mailing Address: P.O. Box 41705, Memphis, 38174-1705.
African American Catholics—Rev. ANTHONY CLARK, S.V.D., Dir. Tel: 901-722-4760; Deacon NORMAN ALEXANDER, 5854 Sun Cove, Memphis, 38134. Tel: 901-372-1030.
Filipino Catholic Ministry—Dr. OLIVIA KABIGAO, Pres. Tel: 901-921-3719.
Hispanic Catholic Ministry—Miss LUPE BALDERAS, 1325 Jefferson Ave., Memphis, 38104. Tel: 901-722-4759; 901-351-4013.
Korean Catholic Ministry—Rev. KAZIMIERZ ABRAHAMCZYK, S.V.D., Dir. Tel: 901-828-6832.
Native American Catholic Ministry—Mr. JASON TERRELL, Chairperson. Tel: 901-730-6706.
Polish Catholic Ministry—Mrs. BARBARA WALKOWC, Pres. Tel: 901-754-1649; Rev. KAZIMIERZ ABRAHAMCZYK, S.V.D., Spiritual Advisor. Tel: 901-754-1649; 901-828-6832.
Vietnamese Catholic Ministry—Rev. JOSEPH DAO VU, S.V.D., Dir. Tel: 901-726-1891.
African Catholic Ministry—Rev. MARTIN M. ORJIANIOKE. Tel: 901-756-1213.

Department for Pastoral Services

Director for Pastoral Services—Ms. ALMA ABUELOUF.
Campus & Young Adult Ministry—3625 Mynders Ave., Memphis, 38111. Tel: 901-323-3051. See Section (J) Newman Centers for additional information
Community Health Ministry— (Ministry to Sick, Ministry for People with Disability and Special Needs, Mid-South Area Assoc. of Catholic Nurses, Health Ministries Network of the Mid-South, Council for Mental Illness Ministry). Ms. ALMA ABUELOUFF, Dir.
Evangelization—Ms. ALMA ABUELOUF, Dir.
Family Ministries—Mrs. PATRICIA MITCHELL PERRY, Dir., 1325 Jefferson Ave., Memphis, 38104. Tel: 901-722-4735. Email: patricia.perry@acc.cdom.org; Mailing Address: 5825 Shelby Oaks Dr., Memphis, 38134.
Active Parenting Training—
Sponsor Couple Training— (Couples working with those preparing for marriage).
FOCCUS Training— (Training for priest and deacons to use this tool with couples preparing for marriage).
Grief Ministry—
Windows Training— (Loss of any kind).
Hispanic Marriage Preparation—
Hispanic Marriage Enrichment—
Individual, Couples & Family Counseling—
Marriage Encounter—
Marriage Enrichment—
Programs for the Engaged—
Project Rachel/Rachel's Vineyard—
Retrouvaille—
Singles 40 Years and Older—
Natural Family Planning & Chastity Education—MARY PAT VAN EPPS, Dir., 5825 Shelby Oaks Dr., Memphis, 38134. Tel: 901-373-1285. Email: marypat.vanepps@cc.cdom.org.
Mother/Daughter and Father/Son Fertility Appreciation & Chastity Programs— (Chastity promotion materials). MARY PAT VAN EPPS, Dir.
Parish Pastoral Councils—Ms. ALMA ABUELOUF, Dir.
Prison Ministries—Deacon WILLIAM DAVIS, Dir.
Resource Library—Mrs. MARY BETH BOLTON, Dir.
Youth Ministries—Mrs. DIANNE DOLAN, Dir.
Leadership Camp—Rev. JOEY KAUMP, Spiritual Dir.
Quest—Rev. JOEY KAUMP, Spiritual Dir.
Voyage—Rev. JOEY KAUMP, Spiritual Dir.
Search—Rev. MICHAEL E. WERKHOVEN, Spiritual Dir.
Scouting—Mr. CHUCK SCHADRACK, Chm.; Rev. WAYNE H. ARNOLD, Chap.
Director for Strategic Planning & Development—Mr. DAVID CREMERIUS, Dir. Devel. Tel: 901-373-1273; Fax: 901-373-1269.
Communications—SUZANNE AVILES, Dir. Tel: 901-373-1231.
Newspaper— "West Tennessee Catholic" Mrs. PAM FLYNN, Mng. Editor. Tel: 901-373-1213.
Planned Giving—Mr. DAVID CREMERIUS, Dir. Tel: 901-373-1273.

Department of Worship and Spiritual Life

Director for Worship & Spiritual Life—Rev. BRUCE CINQUEGRANI, 1325 Jefferson Ave., Memphis, 38104. Tel: 901-722-4744; Fax: 901-722-4791. Mailing Address: P.O. Box 41705, Memphis, 38174-1705.
Office of Catechesis—Sr. CATHY GALASKIEWICZ, O.P., Dir.
Parish Evangelization Team Training—Ms. ALMA ABUELOUF, Dir.
Institute for Liturgy and Spirituality—Rev. BRUCE CINQUEGRANI, Dir. Tel: 901-722-4744.
Liturgical Music—Mrs. BARBARA GOLDSMITH, Dir., 1695 Central Ave., Memphis, 38104. Tel: 901-725-2703.
Ministry with Gay & Lesbian Persons—Co Directors: Mrs. JUDY GRAY. Tel: 901-725-2714; Sr. MAUREEN GRINER, O.S.U. Tel: 901-725-2707.
Our Lady Queen of Peace Retreat Center—Sr. EILEEN FUCITO, C.P., Dir., 3630 Dancyville Rd., Stanton, 38069-4711. Tel: 731-548-2500.
Rites and Sacraments—Rev. BRUCE CINQUEGRANI, Dir. Tel: 901-722-4744.
Spiritual Formation—Sr. EILEEN FUCITO, C.P., Dir., 3630 Dancyville Rd., Stanton, 38069-4711. Tel: 731-548-2500.
Charismatic Renewal—Deacon WERNER ROSE, Diocesan Liaison.
Cursillo—Deacon MICHAEL HOVANEC, Diocesan Liaison.

CLERGY, PARISHES, MISSIONS AND PAROCHIAL SCHOOLS

CITY OF MEMPHIS

(SHELBY COUNTY)

1—CATHEDRAL OF THE IMMACULATE CONCEPTION (1921) Rev. Msgr. Valentine N. Handwerker, Rector; Rev. Krzysztof Rusin; Deacons Frank Williams; Bill Lifsey.
Offices: 1695 Central Ave., 38104. Tel: 901-725-2700; Fax: 901-725-2709. Web: www.iccathedral.org.
School—(Grades PreK-12), 1665 Central Ave., 38104. Tel: 901-725-2710; Fax: 901-725-2715. Web: iccathedralschool.org. Karen Gephart, Prin. (Elementary); Sally Hermsdorfer, Prin. (High School). Priests 2; Lay Teachers 42; Students 310.
Catechesis/Religious Program—Tel: 901-435-5281; 901-725-2700; Fax: 901-725-2709. Aileen G. Palmer, D.R.E. Students 65.

2—ST. ANN (Bartlett) (1950) Revs. Russell D. Harbaugh; Jacek L. Kowal; James M. Clark Jr.; Deacons Chip Jones; Bob Skinner.
Res.: 6529 Stage Rd., Bartlett, 38134. Tel: 901-373-6011; Fax: 901-373-9030.
School—(Grades PreK-8) Tel: 901-386-3328; Fax: 901-386-1030. Sisters 1; Lay Teachers 39; Students 479.
Catechesis/Religious Program—6529 Stage Rd., Bartlett, 38134. Tel: 901-373-6011; Fax: 901-373-9030. Students 291.

3—ST. ANNE'S (1933) Rev. J. David Graham; Deacons Jack Chitwood; David Woolley. In Res., Rev. Keith Stewart.
Res.: 706 S. Highland St., 38111. Tel: 901-323-3817; Fax: 901-323-3151.
School—(Grades PreK-8), 670 S. Highland St., 38111. Tel: 901-323-1344; Fax: 901-458-5215. Cristy Perry, Prin. Lay Teachers 8; Students 140.
Catechesis/Religious Program—Tel: 901-358-9569. Billie Rackley, D.R.E. Students 14.

4—ST. AUGUSTINE (1937), (African American), Rev. Robert M. Cary, C.S.P.; Deacon Joseph Randolph Jr.
Church: 1169 Kerr Ave., 38106. Tel: 901-774-2297; Fax: 901-774-1067. Email: staugchurch@aol.com. Web: www.staugustinememphis.org.
Catechesis/Religious Program—Tel: 901-774-2298. Students 30.

5—BLESSED SACRAMENT (1912) Rev. Edward K. Fisher.
Church: 2564 Hale Ave., 38112-3330. Tel: 901-452-1543; Fax: 901-452-1592. Web: chblessedsacrament.com.
Catechesis/Religious Program—Mrs. Lorena Ramirez, D.R.E. Students 110.

6—ST. BRIGID (1992) Rev. R. Bruce Cinquegrani.
Church: 7801 Lowrance Rd., 38125-2825. Tel: 901-758-0128; Fax: 901-758-8862. Email: hprewitt@stbrigidmemphis.org. Web: www.stbrigidmemphis.org.
Res.: 4200 Thunderstone Cir. W., 38125-3108. Tel: 901-759-9628.
Catechesis/Religious Program—Rose Anne Hembree, D.R.E. Students 117.

7—CHURCH OF THE ASCENSION (1974) Rev. Robert W. Marshall Jr.; Deacons John T. Oates; Harvey Stewart; G. Richmond Quinton; Michael Richardson.
Res.: 3680 Ramill Rd., 38128. Tel: 901-372-1364; Fax: 901-372-9411. Email: ascensionmemphis@bellsouth.net.
Catechesis/Religious Program—Lois Wilber, D.R.E. Students 178.

8—CHURCH OF THE HOLY SPIRIT (1975) Rev. Msgr. Albert E. Kirk; Revs. Mathew Joseph Panackachira, M.C.B.S. (India); Jorge A. Cespedes; Deacons Richard Griffith; Bill Nourse; Werner Rose.
Church: 2300 Hickory Crest Dr., 38119-6805. Tel: 901-754-7146; Fax: 901-754-0102. Web: www.hspirit.com.
Catechesis/Religious Program—Tel: 901-754-7146, Ext. 30. JoAnn Brockman, D.R.E. Students 168.

9—CHURCH OF THE INCARNATION (1978) Revs. William J. Parham; Benjamin P. Bradshaw; Deacons Miles Merwin; Robert Walker.
Office & Res.: 360 Bray Station Rd., Collierville, 38017. Tel: 901-853-7468; Fax: 901-854-0536. Web: www.incarnationchurch.com.
School—(Grades PreK-8) Tel: 901-853-7804; Fax: 901-850-2699. Web: www.goics.org. Connie Berman, Prin.; Ami Stockbridge, Admin. Asst.; Marlene Blake, Librarian. Students 204.
Catechesis/Religious Program—Tel: 901-853-0135. Derek Rotty, Dir. Adult Formation; Lea Weaver, Dir. Children's Faith Formation. Students 625.

10—CHURCH OF THE NATIVITY (1979) Rev. William F. Burke; Deacon Franklin O. Larker. In Res., Rev. Adam M. Rust.
Res.: 5955 St. Elmo, Barlett, 38135-1516. Tel: 901-382-2504; Fax: 901-382-3644. Email: gay.brigance@nativity.cdom.org.
Catechesis/Religious Program—Theresa Krier, D.R.E. Students 110.

11—CHURCH OF THE RESURRECTION (1973) Revs. Ernie DeBlasio; Miguel Angel Espadas.
Res.: 5475 Newberry Ave., 38115-3629. Tel: 901-794-8970; Fax: 901-794-8806. Email: cresurre@comcast.net. Web: resurrectionmemphis.com/Home_Page.html.
Catechesis/Religious Program—Tel: 901-794-8971. Email: predirector@comcast.net. Jacky Becker, D.R.E. Students 247.

12—ST. FRANCIS OF ASSISI (1985) Rev. Msgr. Peter P. Buchignani; Rev. Jolly Sebastian, M.C.B.S. (India); Deacons Chuck Lightcap; Mick Hovanec; William Davis; John Knight.
Res. & Church: 8151 Chimneyrock Blvd., Cordova, 38016. Tel: 901-753-1494 (Rectory); 901-756-1213 (Church); Fax: 901-755-2168.
School—(Grades PreK-8), 2100 N. Germantown Pkwy., Cordova, 38016. Tel: 901-388-7321; Fax: 901-388-8201. Email: beth.york@sfaschool.cdom.org. Mrs. Beth York, Prin.; Sharon Pallme, Librarian. Faculty 74; Students 870.
Catechesis/Religious Program—Web: www.cdom.org. Mrs. Terry Harvey, D.R.E. Students 380.

13—HOLY NAMES OF JESUS AND MARY (1939) Rev. Martin M. Orjianioke (Nigeria).
Res.: 697 Keel Ave., 38107-2599. Tel: 901-525-9870; Fax: 901-527-7436.
Catechesis/Religious Program—Students 10.

14—HOLY ROSARY (1955) Revs. James J. Martell; Charles A. Bauer; Deacons Kenneth McCarver; Fred Brunner, (Retired); Daniel Brown; Jeffrey Drzycimski.
Church, Res. & Office: 4851 Park Ave., 38117. Tel: 901-767-6949; Fax: 901-767-8504.
School—(Grades PreK-8), 4841 Park Ave., 38117. Tel: 901-685-1231; Fax: 901-818-0335. Darren Mullis, Prin.; Allyson Moore, Librarian. Students 408.
Catechesis/Religious Program—Students 20.

15—ST. JAMES (1956) Revs. William R. Kantner; Richard A. Cortese.
Res.: 4180 LeRoy, 38108. Tel: 901-767-8672; Fax: 901-767-8576. Email: stjamescatholic@bellsouth.net.
Catechesis/Religious Program—Students 92.

16—ST. JOHN'S (1947) Rev. Kazimierz Abrahamczyk, S.V.D.; Deacon Walt Bolton.
Res.: 2742 Lamar Ave., 38114. Tel: 901-743-4551; Fax: 901-743-5944. Email: abrahamczyk@aol.com.
Catechesis/Religious Program—Walter Bolton, D.R.E. Students 4.

17—ST. JOSEPH'S (1878) Revs. Anthony Clark, S.V.D.; Antonio Romo, S.V.D.; Deacons James Calicott; Curtiss Talley.
Res.: 3825 Neely Rd., 38109. Tel: 901-396-9996; Fax: 901-332-8691. Email: hstjosephchurc@comcast.net.
Catechesis/Religious Program—Students 39.

18—ST. LOUIS (1957) Rev. Msgr. John B. McArthur; Rev. Adam M. Rust; Deacons Ralph Donati, (Retired); Jack Conrad. In Res., Rev. Saji Ellickal, M.C.B.S.
Office:—203 S. White Station Rd., 38117. Tel: 901-682-6606; Fax: 901-680-0571. Web: www.stlouischurchmphs.org.
School—(Grades PreK-8), 5192 Shady Grove Rd., 38117. Tel: 901-682-9692; Fax: 901-328-9798. Web: www.stlouismemphis.org. Teddi Niedzwiedz, Prin. Lay Teachers 43; Aides 6; Students 515.
Catechesis/Religious Program—Libby Pretti, D.R.E. Students 103.

19—ST. MARY CHURCH (1860) Rev. Eric Peterson.
Church & Office: 155 Market St., 38105. Tel: 901-522-9420; Fax: 901-522-8314. Web: stmary-memphis.com.
Catechesis/Religious Program—Students 30.

20—ST. MICHAEL'S (1951) Rev. Msgr. Victor P. Ciaramitaro; Rev. Rito De Santiago-Carreon; Deacons Joseph Mensi; Norman Alexander.
Office: 3848 Forrest Ave., 38122. Tel: 901-323-0896; 901-324-6411; Fax: 901-323-3557.
Res.: 3867 Summer Ave., 38122. Tel: 901-452-5755.
School—(Grades PreK-8), 3880 Forrest Ave., 38122. Tel: 901-323-2162; Fax: 901-323-0481. Web: www-.stmichaelmemphis.org. Christina Ostrowski, Prin.; Lisa Petzinger, Librarian. Lay Teachers 17; Students 156.
Catechesis/Religious Program—Students 533.

21—OUR LADY OF PERPETUAL HELP (1952) Rev. Msgr. J. Edwin Creary; Rev. Johnnie B. Smith; Deacons David Lucchesi; William Herbers; John Moskal; Matt Hudson, Sr. High Youth Min.; Diana Davis-Harviel, Athletic Dir.; Carol Schaefgen, Office Mgr.; Ben Legett, Music Dir.
Res.: 8151 Poplar, Germantown, 38138. Tel: 901-754-1204; Fax: 901-754-0969. Web: www.olphgermantown.org.
School—(Grades PreK-8), 8151 Poplar, Germantown, 38138. Tel: 901-753-1181, Ext. 340; Fax: 901-754-1475. Mrs. Patricia Wyckoff, Prin.; Mrs. Lynn Lifsey, Asst. Prin.; Mrs. Angela Saba, Sec.; Carolyn Fore, Librarian; Barbara Moranville, Librarian. Faculty 25; Students 209.
Catechesis/Religious Program—Mr. Craig DeMille, D.R.E. Students 318.

22—OUR LADY OF SORROWS (1926) Rev. Bryan P. Timby; Deacons Donald A. Bennis; Henry P. Littleton.
Res.: 3700 Thomas St., 38127. Tel: 901-353-1530; Fax: 901-353-1052. Email: olsmemphis@aol.com. Web: www.ourladyofsorrowschurch.org.
School—(Grades PreK-8), 3690 Thomas St., 38127. Tel: 901-358-7431; Fax: 901-353-1153. Email: bryan.timby@ols.cdom.org. Web: olos.schoolfusion.us. Rev. Bryan P. Timby, Headmaster. Lay Teachers 11; Students 75.
Catechesis/Religious Program—Brenda Plessinger, D.R.E. Students 35.

23—ST. PATRICK'S (1866) Revs. Timothy F. Sullivan, C.S.P.; Bruce Nieli, C.S.P.; Deacon Eugene Champion.
Res.: 277 S. Fourth St., 38126. Tel: 901-527-2542; Fax: 901-525-1147. Web: www.stpatsmemphis.org.
Catechesis/Religious Program—Students 20.

24—ST. PAUL THE APOSTLE (1944) Revs. James L. Pugh; Herbert Ene (Nigeria).
Res.: 1425 E. Shelby Dr., 38116. Tel: 901-346-2380; Fax: 901-346-2385. Email: info@stpaulmemphis.org. Web: www.stpaulmemphis.org.
School—(Grades PreK-6) Tel: 901-346-0862; Fax: 901-396-2677. Sr. Mary Raymond, O.P., Prin. Sisters 4; Lay Teachers 13; Students 190.
Catechesis/Religious Program— Ellen Austin, D.R.E.; Maria Smith, D.R.E. Students 121.

25—ST. PETER CHURCH (1840) Revs. Thomas M. Condon, O.P.; Paul D. Watkins, O.P.; Eduardo Logiste Felix, O.P.; Deacon Eddie Ramsey.
Res.: 190 Adams Ave., 38103. Tel: 901-527-8282; Fax: 901-526-6882.
Catechesis/Religious Program—Christina Klyce, D.R.E. Students 180.

26—SACRED HEART CHURCH (1899) Revs. Joseph Dao Vu, S.V.D.; Antonio Romo, S.V.D.
1324 Jefferson Ave., 38104.
Res.: 1254 S. Lauderdale, 38106. Tel: 901-726-1891; Fax: 901-726-9272. Email: sacredheartmemphis@hotmail.com. Web: www.sacredheartmemphis.blogspot.com.
Catechesis/Religious Program—Students 105.

27—ST. THERESE THE LITTLE FLOWER (1930) Rev. Carl J. Hood; Deacon James P. Schmall.
Res.: 1644 Jackson Ave., 38107. Tel: 901-276-1412; Fax: 901-274-4476. Email: sttherese@stlfchurch.cdom.org.
Catechesis/Religious Program—Mrs. Burma Schmall, D.R.E. Students 23.

28—ST. WILLIAM (1951) Rev. Kevin W. Bravata.
Res.: 4932 Easley Ave., Millington, 38053. Tel: 901-872-4099 (Parish Office); 901-872-2279 (Religious Education); Fax: 901-872-8920. Web: www.cdom.org/web_sites/stwilliam/default.html.
Catechesis/Religious Program—Judy Longoria, D.R.E. Students 96.

OUTSIDE SHELBY COUNTY

BOLIVAR, HARDEMAN CO., ST. MARY CHURCH (1950) Rev. Wayne H. Arnold.
Res.: 223 Mecklenburg Dr., 38008-1736. Tel: 731-658-4627; Fax: 731-658-4627.
Catechesis/Religious Program—Students 9.

BROWNSVILLE, HAYWOOD CO., ST. JOHN CHURCH (1949) Rev. Msgr. Thomas D. Kirk; Rev. Robert D. Favazza.
Church: 910 N. Washington Ave., P.O. Box 872, 38012. Tel: 731-668-2596; 731-772-3514.
Catechesis/Religious Program—Tommy Sellari, D.R.E. Students 55.

CAMDEN, BENTON CO., ST. MARY CHURCH (1981) Rev. Richard J. Kaump Jr.
Res.: 220 W. Main St., 38320. Tel: 731-584-6459; Fax: 731-584-6446. Email: smchfhcatholicc@gmail.com.
Catechesis/Religious Program—Sandra Simpson, D.R.E. Students 48.
Mission—Holy Family Church 265 Cotham Dr., Huntingdon, Carroll Co. 38344. Tel: 731-986-2817.

COVINGTON, TIPTON CO., ST. ALPHONSUS CHURCH (1952) Rev. John J. Hourican.
Res.: 1512 Evergreen, 38019. Tel: 901-476-0374; Fax: 901-476-9650. Email: stalphonsus27923@bellsouth.net. Web: www.saintalphonsuschurch.org.
Church: 1225 Hwy. 51 S., P.O. Box 430, 38019-3236. Tel: 901-476-8140.
Catechesis/Religious Program—Maureen Stephens, D.R.E. Students 34.
Mission—Ave Maria 664 S. Washington, Ripley, Lauderdale Co. 38063.

DYERSBURG, DYER CO., HOLY ANGELS CHURCH (1938) Rev. Robert J. Stellini.
Mailing Address: 535 Tucker St., 38024.
Res.: 527 Tucker St., 38024. Tel: 731-287-8000; Fax: 731-287-7632. Email: hachurch@cableone.net. Web: www.holyangelscatholicchurch.net.
Catechesis/Religious Program—Ann Dedmon, D.R.E. (K-5). Tel: 731-285-9189; John McGrail, D.R.E. 7th-12h Grades. Tel: 731-286-6469. Students 109.

HUMBOLDT, GIBSON CO., SACRED HEART (1872) Rev. Michael E. Werkhoven; Deacon Ed Kutz.
Res.: 2881 E. Main St., P.O. Box 660, 38343. Tel: 731-784-3904; Fax: 731-784-5048. Email: sacredheart@aeneas.com.
Catechesis/Religious Program—2887 E. Main St., 38343. Students 39.
Mission— 9060 Telecom, Milan, Northern Gibson Co. 38358. Tel: 731-686-8686.

JACKSON, MADISON CO., ST. MARY CHURCH (1867) Rev. Msgr. Thomas D. Kirk; Revs. Robert D. Favazza; Enrique Granados Garcia; Deacons Dr. William Lafont, (Retired); Jim Moss; Dale Brown.
Res.: 1665 Hwy. 45 Byp., 38305. Tel: 731-668-2596; Fax: 731-668-9809.
School—(Grades PreK-8) Tel: 731-668-2525; Fax: 731-668-1164. Web: www.stmarysschool.tn.org. Sr. Mary Frasetti, O.P., Prin.; Ellen Watt, Librarian. Sisters 4; Lay Teachers 24; Students 321.
Catechesis/Religious Program—Email: kathleen.hicks@stmarys.tn.org. Kathleen Hicks, D.R.E. Students 201.
Mission—St. John Church P.O. Box 872, Brownsville, Haywood Co. 38012. Tel: 731-772-3514.

LEXINGTON, HENDERSON CO., ST. ANDREW THE APOSTLE (1981) Rev. Gary E. Lamb.
Church: 895 N. Broad St., 38351. Tel: 731-968-6393; Fax: 731-968-2933. Email: standrewtheapost@bellsouth.net.
Res.: 901 N. Broad St., 38351. Tel: 731-968-7944.
Catechesis/Religious Program—Tel: 731-847-2054; Fax: 731-847-2054. Students 33.
Mission—St. Regina 108 Skyline Ln., P.O. Box 92, Parsons, Decatur Co. 38363. Tel: 731-847-2054. Email: streginas@tds.net.
Catechesis/Religious Program—Students 31.

MARTIN, WEAKLEY CO., ST. JUDE'S CATHOLIC CHURCH (1962) Rev. Dennis L. Schenkel; Deacon Rodney Freed.
Church & Res.: 435 Moody Ave., 38237. Tel: 731-588-5675 (Res.); 731-587-9777 (Church); Fax: 731-587-9778. Email: office@stjudemartin.org.
Catechesis/Religious Program—Students 57.

MILAN, GIBSON CO., ST. MATTHEW MISSION (1977) Rev. Michael E. Werkhoven; Deacon Ed Kutz.
Mailing Address: *c/o Sacred Heart Church*, P.O. Box 660, Humboldt, 38343. Tel: 731-784-3904; Fax: 731-784-5048. Email: sacredheart@aeneas.com.
Catechesis/Religious Program—Students 64.

PARIS, HENRY CO., HOLY CROSS (1921) Rev. Michael A. Morgera; Deacons Michael Gore; Rodney Seyller.
Res.: 1210 E. Wood St., 38242. Tel: 731-642-4681; Fax: 731-644-9668. Email: leila.kackley@holycross.cdom.org. Web: www.holycrossparis.org.
School—(Grades PreK) Angie Taylor, Dir. Students 26.
Catechesis/Religious Program—Students 125.

SAVANNAH, HARDIN CO., ST. MARY CHURCH (1948) Rev. Anthony Azuwike (Nigeria).
Church & Res.: 2315 Pickwick St., 38372. Tel: 731-925-4852; Fax: 731-925-9612. Email: smccsavannah1@gmail.com. Web: www.stmary-savannah.org.
Catechesis/Religious Program—Patti Erisman, D.R.E. Students 48.
Mission—Our Lady of the Lake Pickwick Dam, Hardin Co.

SELMER, MCNAIRY CO., ST. JUDE THE APOSTLE CATHOLIC CHURCH (1982) Rev. Wayne H. Arnold; Deacon Jim Gray.
Res.: 1318 Poplar Ave., 38375-1913. Tel: 731-645-4188; Fax: 731-645-4188. Email: stjude9@bellsouth.net.
Catechesis/Religious Program—Students 24.

SOMERVILLE, FAYETTE CO., ST. PHILIP THE APOSTLE (1981) Rev. Stephen K. Kenny; Deacon Michael Blome.
Church: 11710 Hwy. 64, 38068. Tel: 901-465-8685; Fax: 901-466-1645. Email: spacc@saintphilipcc.org.
Catechesis/Religious Program—Ginny Modlin, D.R.E. Students 65.

UNION CITY, OBION CO., IMMACULATE CONCEPTION (1891) Rev. Robert D. Ponticello.
Res.: 1303 E. Reelfoot Ave., 38261. Tel: 731-885-0963; Fax: 731-885-9960. Email: nina.pierce@icuc.cdom.org. Web: www.icuctn.com.

School—Immaculate Conception School, (Grades PreSchool) Dawn Black, Dir.
Catechesis/Religious Program—Teresa Vallee, D.R.E. Students 144.

Chaplains of Public Institutions

MEMPHIS. *Federal Correctional Institute at Memphis*. Rev. Faustino Maramot, Chap.

Graduate Studies:
Rev.—
Cespedes-Segura, Jorge A.

Absent on Leave:
Rev.—
Schultz, Joel P.

Retired:
Revs.—
Atkinson, John V., Villa Vianney, 10599 Bishop Dozier Dr., Apt. 3, Cordova, 38016. Tel: 901-752-0766
Callis, Elbert, Villa Vianney, 10611 Bishop Dozier Dr., Apt. 4, Cordova, 38016-5559.
Coy, Richard D., 2953 Dunedin Cove, Germantown, 38138-7010.
Danner, James L., 5813 S. Gordon Ave., Tampa, FL 33611.
Foley, David M., 995 Anglers Cove, #502, Marco Island, FL 34145.
Kelly, Edward E., 8740 Delmar, #2 E., St. Louis, MO 63124.
Knight, David B., c/o His Way Spiritual Growth Ctr., 1306 Dellwood Ave., 38127. Tel: 901-357-6662
Murphy, James W., Villa Vianney, 10599 Bishop Dozier Dr., Cordova, 38016. Tel: 901-752-0766
Nobile, Angelo
Paolozzi, Joseph L., 104 B Hawks Rd., Martin, 38237.
Stewart, Michael L., 1980 S. Bailey Woods, Apt. 103, Collierville, 38017.
Thomas, Thomas P., 1026 E. Rainbow Dr., 38107-3110.

Permanent Deacons:
Bennis, Donald
Bonaiuto, Nick
Brunner, Fred
Calicott, James
Champion, Eugene
Champion, James, (Retired)
Chitwood, Jack
Conrad, Jack
Cooley, Jim
Cranford, William R.
Davis, William
Donati, Ralph, (Retired)
Gore, Michael
Gray, Jim
Griffith, Richard
Herbers, Bill
Herbers, Jerome E., (Inactive)
Hicks, Joseph, (Inactive)
Hivner, John, (Retired)
Hovanec, Mick
Howell, Larry, (Retired)
Johnson, Eldon
Jones, Chip
Kang, John
Lafont, Bill
Larker, Frank
Lightcap, Charles
McCarver, Kenneth
Mensi, Joseph
Merwin, Miles
Miller, James, (Inactive)
Nourse, Bill
Oates, John
Ramsey, Eddie
Rose, Werner
Schmall, James
Seyller, Rod
Steele, Mike
Stewart, Harvey
Talley, Curtiss
Terry, Andrew, Jr.
Tucker, Jim
Turner, Ned, (Retired)
Wells, Charles, (Inactive)
Williams, Frank
Yarbrough, Harold

INSTITUTIONS LOCATED IN THE DIOCESE

[A] COLLEGES AND UNIVERSITIES

MEMPHIS. **Christian Brothers University* (1871) (Coed), 650 E. Parkway S., 38104. Tel: 901-321-3000; Fax: 901-321-3290. Web: www.cbu.edu. Dr. John Smarrelli Jr., Ph.D., Pres.; Bro. Louis Althaus, F.S.C., Asst. to Pres.; Mr. Robert Arnold, Dir., Grants & Research; Dr. Frank Buscher, Academic Vice Pres.; Mr. Thomas Cochran, Controller; Ms. Kay Cunningham, Dir., Plough Library; Margretta daLomba Dobbs, Dir., Campus Ministry; Bro. Dominic Ehrmantraut, F.S.C., Vice Pres., Student Life; Ms. Melissa Hanson, Dir., Inst. Research & Effectiveness; Dr. Evelyn McDonald, Vice Pres. for Missions & Identity; Ms. Betty McWillie, Dir. Career Devel. & Placement; Wilson Phillips, Dir., Campus Ministry; Mr. Andrew Prislovsky, Vice Pres. for Advancement; Bro. Tom Sullivan, F.S.C., Dir., Campus Ministry; Mr. Dan Wortham, Vice Pres. Admin. & Finance.
Christian Brothers Univ. (of Memphis, Tenn.), Four-Year University with Schools of Business, Engineering, Arts, and Sciences. Graduate programs in Business, Catholic Studies, Engineering and Education. Brothers 17; Lay Teachers 227; Students 2,236.

[B] DIOCESAN SCHOOLS

MEMPHIS. *St. Augustine School*, (Grades PreK-6), 1169 Kerr Ave., 38106. Tel: 901-942-8002; Fax: 901-942-4564. Email: staugustinememphis@gmail.com. LaTonya White, Prin.; Sara O'Dell, Librarian. Lay Teachers 13; Students 141.
Bishop Byrne Middle/High School (1965) (Grades 9-12), 1475 E. Shelby Dr., 38116. Tel: 901-346-3060; Fax: 901-346-9488. Web: www.bishopbyrne.org. Mr. Clyde Israel, Pres. & Prin.; Carole Viglietti, Librarian. Lay Teachers 19; Students 192.
De La Salle Elementary at Blessed Sacrament (2000) (Grades K-8), 2540 Hale Ave., 38112. Tel: 901-866-9084; Fax: 901-866-9086. Email: principal@delasallememphis.org. Web: www.jubileeschools.org/delasalle.html. Bro. Robert Veselsky, F.S.C., Prin.; Erin Mullins, Dean, Academics. Brothers 1; Lay Teachers 17; Lay Staff 8; Students 169.
Holy Names of Jesus and Mary School, (Grades 3-8), 709 Keel Ave., 38107. Tel: 901-507-1503; Fax: 901-507-1507. Web: www.holynamesmemphis.org. Halsey Mabry, Prin.; Debra Harris, Sec.; Lisa Petzinger, Librarian. Lay Teachers 8; Students 65.
St. John Catholic School, (Grades PreK-6), 2718 Lamar Ave., 38114. Tel: 901-743-6700; Fax: 901-743-6720. Email: kristi.baird@stjohn.cdom.org. Kristi Baird, Prin.; Susan MacArthur, Librarian. (Reopened 2000) Lay Teachers 16; Students 212.
St. Joseph School, (Grades PreK-6), 3851 Neely Rd., 38109. Tel: 901-344-0021; Fax: 901-348-0787. Email: phil.amido@stjoseph.cdom.org. Mr. Dorian P. Amido, Prin.; Lynn Ward, Librarian. Priests 1; Lay Teachers 16; Students 187.
Little Flower School, (Grades PreK-2), 1666 Jackson Ave., 38107. Tel: 901-725-9900; Fax: 901-725-5779. Email: leslie.harden@stlfschool.cdom.org. Leslie Harden, Prin. Lay Teachers 14; Lay Staff 7; Students 72.
Memphis Catholic High School and Middle School, (Grades 7-12), 61 N. McLean Blvd., 38104. Tel: 901-276-1221; Fax: 901-725-1447. Email: jpohlman@memphiscatholic.org. Web: www.memphiscatholic.org. Mr. Jim Pohlman, Pres. & Prin.; Christopher Robbins, Dean, Academics. Lay Teachers 16; Students 177.
See Education That Works, LLC in the Institution Section under Miscellaneous.
St. Patrick School (1867) (Grades PreK-6), 287 S. Fourth St., 38126. Tel: 901-521-3252; Fax: 901-521-8265. Email: halsey.mabry@stpat.cdom.org. Halsey Mabry, Prin.; Lisa Petzinger, Librarian. (closed 1950; reopened 2003). Lay Teachers 18; Lay Staff 10; Students 131.
Resurrection Catholic School, (Grades PreK-5), 3572 Emerald St., 38115. Tel: 901-546-9926; Fax: 901-546-9928. Email: stephanie.anderson@resurrectionschool.cdom.org. Web: www.cdom.org; www.jubileeschools.org. Mrs. Stephanie Anderson, Prin. Brothers 1; Lay Teachers 15; Students 183.

CORDOVA. *St. Benedict at Auburndale High School*, (Grades 9-12), 8250 Varnavas Dr., 38016. Tel: 901-260-2840; Fax: 901-260-2850. Email: valadieg@sbaeagles.org. Web: www.sbaeagles.org. Mr. George Valadie, Pres. of Campus & Prin. (Grades 9-12); Rebecca Hall, Librarian. Special programs for gifted and learning disabled. Lay Teachers 86; Students 1,006.

[C] HIGH SCHOOLS, PRIVATE AND PAROCHIAL

MEMPHIS. *St. Agnes Academy* (1851) (Grades 9-12), 4830 Walnut Grove Rd., 38117. Tel: 901-767-1356; Fax: 901-435-5866. Email: jmaness@saa-sds.org. Web: www.saa-sds.org. Barbara Daush, Pres.; Mrs. Gretchen K. Kirk, D.R.E.; Mrs. Joy Maness, Dean of Upper School. Dominican Sisters of Peace., Title of Incorporation: St. Agnes Academy Lay Teachers 41; Students 352.
**Christian Brothers High School* (1871) (Grades 9-12), 5900 Walnut Grove Rd., 38120-2174. Tel: 901-261-4900; Fax: 901-261-4909. Email: info@cbhs.org. Web: www.cbhs.org. Bros. Christopher Englert, F.S.C., Pres.; Michael Fugger, F.S.C., Dir. Brothers' Community; Chris Fay, Prin.; Aislinn McEwen, Librarian. Title of Incorporation: Christian Brothers (LaSalle) High School. Brothers 5; Lay Teachers 68; Students 858.
Immaculate Conception Cathedral School (1950) (Grades PreK-12), 1725 Central Ave., 38104. Tel: 901-725-2705 High School; Fax: 901-725-2701 High School. Email: cathy.mcdonald@ic.cdom.org. Web: www.myiccs.org. Elementary: 1669 Central Ave., 38104. Tel: 901-725-2710; Fax: 901-725-2715. Karen Gephart, Prin. (Elementary); Diane Allen, Vice Prin. (Elementary); Sally Hermsdorfer, Prin. (High School); Rev. Msgr. Valentine N. Handwerker; Kate Hall, Librarian. Priests 1; Lay Teachers 40; Students 307.

JACKSON. *Sacred Heart of Jesus High School*, (Grades 9-12), 185 Greenfield Dr., 38305. Tel: 731-660-4774; Fax: 731-984-7200. Email: fran.herdlein@shjhs.org. Web: www.shjhs.org. Mr. Francis Herdlein, Prin. Lay Teachers 10; Students 59.

[D] ELEMENTARY SCHOOLS, PRIVATE

MEMPHIS. *St. Agnes Academy*, (Grades PreK-8), 4830 Walnut Grove Rd., 38117. Tel: 901-767-1377; Fax: 901-684-5316. Email: kboccia@saa-sds.org. Web: www.saa-sds.org. Barbara Daush, Pres.; Mrs. Gretchen K. Kirk, D.R.E.; Mrs. Kathleen Toes-Boccia, Dean of Lower School. Dominican Sisters of Peace. Lay Teachers 21; Students 287.
St. Dominic Boys School, (Grades PreK-8), 30 Avon Rd., 38117. Tel: 901-682-3011; Fax: 901-681-0047. Email: jmurphy@saa-sds.org. Web: www.saa.sds.org. Barbara Daush, Pres.; Mrs. Gretchen K. Kirk, D.R.E.; Mr. John Murphy, Dean. Dominican Sisters of Peace. Lay Teachers 22; Students 275.

[E] ADULT RESIDENCES & HOMES FOR AGED

MEMPHIS. *Diocese of Memphis Housing Corp.*, 1325 Jefferson Ave., 38104. Tel: 901-722-4772; 901-722-4795; Fax: 901-722-4732. Web: www.dmhcorp.org. Ms. Cherry Brooks, Dir. Bed Capacity 654; Total Assisted Annually 800; Total Staff 41.
St. Peter Manor, LLC, 108 N. Auburndale, 38104. Tel: 901-278-8200; Fax: 901-278-8210. Mary Dowling, Mgr. Staff 24; Independent-Living Apartments 283.
St. Peter Chapel & Activity Center Tel: 901-278-8200; Fax: 901-278-8210. Email: mkdowling14@msn.com.

CAMDEN. *Good Samaritan Village*, 192A Post Oak Ave., 38320. Tel: 731-584-1300; Fax: 731-584-1344. Email: gsvff@bellsouth.net. Frances Shaffer, Mgr.

DYERSBURG. *St. Joseph Village, Inc.*, 885 Hwy. 51 Byp. W., 38024. Tel: 731-285-8560; Fax: 731-285-8562. Email: kelleheathcott@yahoo.com. Kelle Heathcott, Property Mgr. Total Assisted Annually 112; Total Staff 5.

HUMBOLDT. *St. Matthew Manor*, 2575 Viking Dr., 38343. Tel: 731-784-7229; Fax: 731-784-9309; Fax: 731-784-9309. Email: boazcarol@yahoo.com. Carol Boaz, Mgr. Total Staff 2; Bed Capacity 40; Total Assisted 41.
St. Matthew Manor - West, 2575 Viking Dr., 38343. Tel: 731-824-3793; Fax: 731-784-3793 303. Email: carolboaz@yahoo.com. Carol Boaz, Mgr. Total Staff 2; Bed Capacity 27; Total Assisted 27.

JACKSON. *St. Mary Manor, LLC*, 1771 Hwy. 45 Byp., 38305. Tel: 731-668-5633; Fax: 731-668-9252. Email: stmary1@aeneas.net. Mrs. Amber Kee, Mgr. Total Staff 10; Independent Living Apartments 149.

MOSCOW. *St. Mark Village Apartments*, 85 St. Mark Cove, 38057. Tel: 901-877-3456; Fax: 901-877-3457. Email: saintmarkvillage@bellsouth.net. Mary Gordon, Mgr. Bed Capacity 24; Total Staff 3.

[F] RESIDENCES OF PRIESTS AND BROTHERS

MEMPHIS. *Brothers of the Christian Schools (Mid-West Prov.), F.S.C.*, Christian Brothers University, 650 E. Parkway S., 38104. Tel: 901-321-3251; Fax: 901-321-3290. Email: ibrown@cbu.edu. Bro. Dominic Ehrmantraut, F.S.C., Dir. Brothers 19. Christian Brothers High School, 5900 Walnut

Grove Rd., 38119. Tel: 901-261-4900; Fax: 901-261-4909. Web: www.cbhs.org. Bro. Michael Fugger, F.S.C., Dir. Brothers 6.

The Dominican Friars of Memphis, Inc., 190 Adams Ave., 38103. Tel: 901-527-8282; Fax: 901-526-6882. Revs. Thomas M. Condon, O.P.; Eduardo Logiste Felix, O.P.

Society of the Divine Word (Chicago Province), 1254 S. Lauderdale, 38106. Tel: 901-774-8191; Fax: 901-774-8192. Email: dominicnsvd@hotmail.com. Revs. Joseph Dao Vu, S.V.D.; Anthony Clark, S.V.D.; Kazimierz Abrahamczyk, S.V.D.; Tan Viet Nguyen, S.V.D.; Hien Xuan Pham, S.V.D.; Antonio Romo-Romo, S.V.D. Priests 6.

Villa Vianney Senior Priests Residence, 10605 Bishop Dozier Dr., Cordova, 38016-5558. Tel: 901-752-0766; Fax: 901-752-0633. Rev. Richard L. Mickey, M.Ed., Dir. In Residence (Retired) 3; Total Staff 2.

[G] CONVENTS AND RESIDENCES FOR SISTERS

MEMPHIS. *Missionaries of Charity*, 700 N. 7th St., 38107. Tel: 901-527-4947. Sisters 4. *Shelter* Tel: 901-526-5456. Sr. Drita Maris, M.C., Supr. Sisters 4; Total Assisted 464.

Missionary Sisters Servants of the Holy Spirit, S.Sp.S., 5280 Brenton, 38120. Tel: 901-685-3649; Fax: 901-685-3649. Sr. Maria Joseph Nguyen, S.Sp.S., Social Worker. Sisters 3.

Monastery Of St. Clare O.S.C. (1932) 1310 Dellwood Ave., 38127. Tel: 901-357-6662. Email: memphisclares@gmail.com. Web: www.poorclare.org/memphis. Sr. Mary Marguerite, O.S.C., Abbess. Sisters 5; Huehuetenango, Guatemala 6.

Sisters of St. Charles Borromeo, C.B., 4778 Normandy Ave., 38117. Tel: 901-818-9180. Email: csusindr@hotmail.com. Web: www.cbsisters.org. Sisters 3.

[H] CATHOLIC CAMPUS & YOUNG-ADULT MINISTRY

MEMPHIS. *Catholic Campus Ministry* 3625 Mynders Ave., 38111. Tel: 901-323-3051; Fax: 901-323-0925. Email: info@ccm.cdom.org. Sam Mauck, Dir., Campus & Young-Adult Ministry; Kathleen Glackin, Asst. Catholic Campus Min. & Admin. Asst.; Sr. Sharon Glumb, S.L.W., Campus Min., Univ. of Memphis & Rhodes College, UT Health Science Center (UTHSC).

MARTIN. *Interfaith Student Center* 110 Hannings Ln., 38237. Tel: 731-587-2603. Email: deacon@stjudemartin.org. Rev. Dennis L. Schenkel; Deacon Rodney Freed.

[I] MISCELLANEOUS

MEMPHIS. *St. Anne Lay Carmelite Community, c/o St. Anne Church*, 706 S. Highland, 38111. Tel: 901-937-1073 (Dir.). Email: georgiamurphy@decosimo.com.

The Catholic Cafe, Inc., c/o Glankler Brown, PLLC, 6000 Poplar Ave., Ste. 400, 38119. Tel: 901-576-1714; Fax: 901-525-2389. Email: rhutton@glankler.com. Web: www.thecatholiccafe.com. Robert Hutton, Pres.

Catholic Charities of West Tennessee, 1325 Jefferson Ave., 38104-2097. Tel: 901-722-4700; Fax: 901-722-4791. Web: www.accinwesttn.org. P.O. Box 41705, 38174-1705. Tel: 901-722-4700; Fax: 901-722-4791. Mr. Michael D. Allen, Pres. & CEO.

Education That Works, LLC, 61 N. McLean Blvd., 38104. Tel: 901-276-1221; Fax: 901-725-1447. Mr. Ted Schreck, Dir. Work Study Program.

House of the Good Shepherd of Memphis DeNeuville Learning Center (1825) 190 S. Cooper St., 38104. Tel: 901-726-5902; Fax: 901-726-1960. Email: deneuville@deneuvillecenter.org. Web: www.deneuvillecenter.org. Sr. Lakshmie Napagoda, R.G.S., Exec. Dir.

Knights of St. Peter Claver (3rd Degree St. Benedict the Black Council No. 188) and Assembly 26 Bishop James P. Lyke 4th Degree), 2744 Gerald Ford Dr. W, Cordova, 38018. Tel: 901-377-1201; Fax: 901-396-8315. William Thompson, Grand Knight.

Ladies of Charity of Memphis (1937) P.O. Box 17699, 38187-0699. Tel: 901-767-1143. Email: kmlloyd_clay@att.net. Web: www.famvin.org/lcusa. Kathy Lloyd, Pres., 1703 Dorrie Ln., 38117.

**Madonna Circle, Inc.* (Catholic Women's Service Organization), P.O. Box 172174, 38187-2174. Tel: 901-756-6430. Pat Young, Pres.

St. Martin de Porres Shrine & Institute, 190 Adams Ave., 38103. Tel: 901-578-2643; Fax: 901-578-3735. Email: stmartinshrine@bellsouth.net. Web: www.stmartinshrine.org.

St. Patrick's Center, 277 S. Fourth St., 38126. Tel: 901-543-9924; Fax: 901-529-8304. Email: tim.sullivan@stpat.cdom.org. Web: www.stpatsmemphis.org. Rev. Timothy F. Sullivan, C.S.P., Dir.; Deacon Eugene Champion, Exec. Dir.

Serra Club of Memphis, c/o The Catholic Center, 5825 Shelby Oaks Dr., 38134. David Himelright, Pres., 11550 Amos St., Eads, 38028-9336. Tel: 901-853-3822; Rev. Msgr. John B. McArthur, Chap.

Society of St. Vincent DePaul, 3522 Carnes Ave., 38111. Tel: 901-634-3522. Email: ghyden@mercuryprtg.com. Web: www.svdpmemphis.org. Gloria Hyden, Pres.; Rev. Michael A. Morgera, Spiritual Advisor.

BARTLETT. *Diocesan Council of Catholic Women*, 6161 Acorn Dr., 38134-4601. Tel: 901-213-4778. Email: presbred@aol.com.

STANTON. *Our Lady Queen of Peace Retreat Center*, 3630 Dancyville Rd., 38069-4711. Tel: 731-548-2500; Fax: 731-548-2520. Email: debbie.voyles@olqp.cdom.org. Web: www.cdom.org (Our Lady Queen of Peace Retreat Center). Sisters Eileen Fucito, C.P., Dir.; Ellen Buchignani, R.S.M., Assoc. Dir.

RELIGIOUS INSTITUTES OF MEN REPRESENTED IN THE DIOCESE

For further details refer to the corresponding bracketed number in the Religious Institutes of Men or Women section.

[0330]—*Brothers of the Christian Schools* (Midwest Prov.)—F.S.C.

[1330]—*Congregation of the Mission Western Province*—C.M.

[]—*Missionary Congregation of the Blessed Sacrament*—M.C.B.S.

[0430]—*Order of Preachers (Dominicans)*—O.P.

[1030]—*Paulist Fathers*—C.S.P.

[0420]—*Society of Divine Word*—S.V.D.

RELIGIOUS INSTITUTES OF WOMEN REPRESENTED IN THE DIOCESE

[1070-07]—*Dominican Sisters*—O.P.

[1115]—*Dominican Sisters of Peace* (Columbus, OH)—O.P.

[2420]—*Marist Missionary Sisters*—S.M.S.M.

[2710]—*Missionaries of Charity*—M.C.

[3530]—*Missionary Sisters Servants of the Holy Spirit*—S.Sp.S.

[3760]—*Order of St. Clare* (Memphis, TN)—O.S.C.

[0500]—*Sisters of Charity of Nazareth*—S.C.N.

[]—*Sisters of Charity of St. Charles Borromeo*—C.B.

[0430]—*Sisters of Charity of the Blessed Virgin Mary*—B.V.M.

[]—*Sisters of Mercy* (Ireland)—R.S.M.

[2575]—*Sisters of Mercy of the Americas*—R.S.M.

[0260]—*Sisters of the Blessed Sacrament*—S.B.S.

[3180]—*Sisters of the Cross and Passion*—C.P.

[1830]—*Sisters of the Good Shepherd* (St. Louis Prov.)—R.G.S.

[2350]—*Sisters of the Living Word*—S.L.W.

[4120-05]—*Ursuline Nuns of the Congregation of Paris* (Owensboro, KY)—O.S.U.

DIOCESAN CEMETERIES

MEMPHIS. *All Saints*, c/o Calvary Cemetery, 1663 Elvis Presley Blvd., 38106. Tel: 901-948-1529; Fax: 901-948-1511. Email: pat.posey@cemeteries.cdom.org. Web: www.cdom.org.

Calvary, 1663 Elvis Presley Blvd., 38106. Tel: 901-948-1529; Fax: 901-948-1511.

JACKSON. *Mount Calvary*, c/o 1663 Elvis Presley Blvd., 38106. Tel: 901-948-1592; Fax: 901-948-1511.

NECROLOGY

† Davis, Rev. Msgr. William F., (Retired)—Died Oct. 26, 2011

† Tagg, Joseph L. III, (Retired)—Died March 19, 2011

An asterisk (*) denotes an organization that has established tax-exempt status directly with the IRS and is not covered by the USCCB Group Ruling.

Diocese of Metuchen

Most Reverend

PAUL G. BOOTKOSKI, D.D.

Bishop of Metuchen; ordained May 28, 1966; appointed Titular Bishop of Zarna and Auxiliary Bishop of Newark July 8, 1997; ordained September 5, 1997; appointed Fourth Bishop of Metuchen January 4, 2002; installed March 19, 2002. *Res.: 10 Library Pl., Metuchen, NJ 08840.*

Most Reverend

EDWARD T. HUGHES, D.D.

Bishop Emeritus of Metuchen; ordained May 31, 1947; appointed Auxiliary to Archbishop of Philadelphia and Titular Bishop of Segia June 14, 1976; consecrated July 21, 1976; appointed Second Bishop of Metuchen December 16, 1986; installed February 5, 1987; retired September 8, 1997. *Res.: Bethany Ridge, 914 Milford-Warren Glen Rd., Milford, NJ 08848.*

146 Metlars Lane, Piscataway, NJ 08854. Tel: 732-562-1990; Fax: 732-562-1399. *Mailing Address: The Diocesan Center, P.O. Box 191, Metuchen, NJ 08840*

Web: www.diometuchen.org

ESTABLISHED NOVEMBER 19, 1981.

Square Miles 1,425.

Legal Corporate Title: The Diocese of Metuchen.

Comprises the Counties of Warren, Hunterdon, Somerset and Middlesex in the State of New Jersey.

STATISTICAL OVERVIEW

Personnel	
Bishop	1
Retired Bishops	1
Priests: Diocesan Active in Diocese	131
Priests: Diocesan Active Outside Diocese	9
Priests: Diocesan in Foreign Missions	3
Priests: Retired, Sick or Absent	47
Number of Diocesan Priests	190
Religious Priests in Diocese	36
Total Priests in Diocese	226
Extern Priests in Diocese	21
Ordinations:	
Diocesan Priests	3
Transitional Deacons	3
Permanent Deacons in Diocese	170
Total Brothers	19
Total Sisters	286
Parishes	
Parishes	100
With Resident Pastor:	
Resident Diocesan Priests	81
Resident Religious Priests	11
Without Resident Pastor:	
Administered by Priests	8
Pastoral Centers	3
New Parishes Created	1
Closed Parishes	2
Professional Ministry Personnel:	

Brothers	2
Sisters	30
Lay Ministers	115
Welfare	
Catholic Hospitals	1
Total Assisted	348,500
Health Care Centers	4
Total Assisted	27,408
Homes for the Aged	5
Total Assisted	2,047
Day Care Centers	2
Total Assisted	307
Specialized Homes	4
Total Assisted	86
Special Centers for Social Services	9
Total Assisted	29,356
Residential Care of Disabled	1
Total Assisted	6
Educational	
Diocesan Students in Other Seminaries	11
Total Seminarians	11
High Schools, Diocesan and Parish	3
Total Students	1,904
High Schools, Private	2
Total Students	1,117
Elementary Schools, Diocesan and Parish	28

Total Students	8,555
Non-residential Schools for the Disabled	1
Total Students	45
Catechesis/Religious Education:	
High School Students	1,773
Elementary Students	39,234
Total Students under Catholic Instruction	52,639
Teachers in the Diocese:	
Brothers	11
Sisters	45
Lay Teachers	795
Vital Statistics	
Receptions into the Church:	
Infant Baptism Totals	4,430
Minor Baptism Totals	231
Adult Baptism Totals	117
Received into Full Communion	228
First Communions	5,966
Confirmations	5,558
Marriages:	
Catholic	788
Interfaith	204
Total Marriages	992
Deaths	3,656
Total Catholic Population	631,946
Total Population	1,373,796

Former Bishops—Most Revs. THEODORE E. MCCARRICK, ord. May 31, 1958; appt. Titular Bishop of Rusibisir and Auxiliary to the Archbishop of New York, May 24, 1977; cons. June 29, 1977; appt. first Bishop of Metuchen, Nov. 19, 1981; installed Jan. 31, 1982; promoted to the Archdiocese of Newark, June 3, 1986; installed July 25, 1986; EDWARD T. HUGHES (Retired), ord. May 31, 1947; appt. Titular Bishop of Segia and Auxiliary to the Archbishop of Philadelphia, June 14, 1976; cons. July 21, 1976; appt. second Bishop of Metuchen, Dec. 16, 1986; installed Feb. 5, 1987; retired Sept. 8, 1997; VINCENT DEPAUL BREEN, D.D., ord. July 15, 1962; appt. Third Bishop of Metuchen July 8, 1997; cons. and installed Sept. 8, 1997; retired Jan. 4, 2002; died March 30, 2003.

The Diocesan Center—Mailing Address: P.O. Box 191, Metuchen, 08840. Tel: 732-562-1990; Fax: 732-562-1399.

Vicars General—Rev. Msgrs. WILLIAM BENWELL, J.C.L., V.G.; JOHN B. SZYMANSKI, P.A., V.G., Emeritus (Retired).

Episcopal Vicars—Rev. Msgrs. DANIEL J. HERLIHY; JOSEPH G. CELANO; Very Revs. RICHARD M. RUSK; J. WILLIAM MICKIEWICZ; Rev. Msgrs. JOHN N. FELL, S.T.D.; ROBERT J. ZAMORSKI.

The Diocesan Curia

Moderator—Rev. Msgr. WILLIAM BENWELL, J.C.L., V.G.

The Chancery

Office of the Chancellor—LORI ALBANESE, J.C.L. *Vice Chancellor*—CAROL M. MACDERMOTT.

Office of Legal and Mediation Services— St. Thomas More Society.

Commission for Ecumenical and Interreligious Initiatives—

The Tribunal

The Diocesan Center—Mailing Address: P.O. Box 191, Metuchen, 08840. Tel: 732-562-1990; Fax: 732-562-1193.

Judicial Vicar—Very Rev. RICHARD J. LYONS, J.C.L.

Associate Judicial Vicar—Rev. ROBERT B. KOLAKOWSKI, J.C.L.; MARGARET MANZA, Admin. Coord.

Canonical Staff—Rev. Msgr. WILLIAM BENWELL, J.C.L., V.G.; LORI ALBANESE, J.C.L.; Revs. NEIL W. DAVIN, C.P., J.C.L.; CHRISTOPHER FUSCO, J.C.L., J.D.; ROBERT B. KOLAKOWSKI, J.C.L.; MATTHEW R. PARATORE, J.C.L.

Auditors—SARA T. ACEVEDO; CAROL M. MACDERMOTT.

Psychological Consultants—Rev. RICHARD MUCOWSKI, O.F.M., Ed.D., Ph.D.; JEROME TRAVERS, Ph.D.; MARY BERTANI, Ed.S., L.M.F.T.

Notaries—SARA T. ACEVEDO; CAROL M. MACDERMOTT; MARGARET MANZA.

Office of Child and Youth Protection—LAWRENCE V. NAGLE, Dir.

Victim Assistance Coordinator—GINA CRISCUOLO, L.C.S.W. Tel: 908-722-1881. Email: gcriscuolo@ccdom.org.

Office of Communications and Public Relations—JOANNE WARD, Dir.; ERIN FRIEDLANDER, Assoc. Dir.

"The Catholic Spirit"—JOANNE WARD, Assoc. Publisher.

Office of Internal Audit—MARIE ZISSLER, Dir.

Department of Administrative Services

Department of Administrative Services—THOMAS G. TOOLAN, Exec. Dir.; LEONARDO G. CORTELEZZI, Assoc. Exec. Dir.

Office of Finance—THOMAS G. TOOLAN, Dir.; PATRICIA

MURTHA, Controller.

Office of Cemeteries—899 Lincoln Ave., Piscataway, 08854. Tel: 732-463-1424; Fax: 732-463-8807. MARY ELLEN GERITY, Dir.

Office of Information Systems—LEONARDO G. CORTELEZZI, Dir.; DAVID G. TORRES, Asst. Dir.

Office of Property and Facilities Management—MONICA P. DEMKOVITZ, Dir.

Office of Human Resources—ERIC DILL, Dir.; MELISSA GARCIA, Asst. Dir.

Department of Education

Department of Education—Rev. Msgr. MICHAEL J. CORONA, P.A., Exec. Dir.

Office of the Schools—ELLEN AYOUB, Supt. Assistant Superintendents: Mrs. DONNA KANOWITZ; Mrs. IRENE D. SENA; JAMES MASUCCI, Coord. School Technology; TAMARA HEMINGWAY, Coord. Institutional Advancement.

Office of Pontifical Mission Societies—Rev. Msgr. RICHARD A. BEHL, Dir.; MELISSA LEGACKI, Asst. Dir.

Catholic Scouting Apostolate—Rev. Msgr. MICHAEL J. CORONA, P.A., Moderator.

Diocesan Coordinating Committee for Home School Associations—ELLEN AYOUB, Moderator.

Department of Clergy and Religious Personnel

Department of Clergy and Religious Personnel—Rev. Msgr. EDWARD C. PULEO, Exec. Dir.

Office of Ministry to Priests—Rev. Msgr. JOSEPH M. CURRY, Dir.

Office for Priest Personnel—Rev. Msgr. EDWARD C. PULEO, Dir.

Office of the Diaconate—Deacon SAMUEL J. COSTANTINO, Dir.

Office for Religious—Sr. ASCENZA TIZZANO, M.P.F., Delegate for Relg.

Office of Vocations—Rev. Msgr. RANDALL J. VASHON, Dir.; Rev. KEITH CERVINE, Assoc. Dir.

Board for Seminary Education—Rev. Msgr. RANDALL J. VASHON, Chm.

Office of Hospital Chaplaincy—Rev. SEAN G. WINTERS, Coord.

Office of Prison Ministry—

Department of Diocesan Planning—JEFFRY KORGEN, Exec. Dir.

Department of Stewardship and Development

Department of Stewardship and Development—Rev. Msgr. SYLVESTER J. CRONIN, Exec. Dir.; SUE MANTARRO, Assoc. Dir., Office of Stewardship.

Office of Worship and Episcopal Ceremonies—Rev. Msgr. ROBERT W. MEDLEY, Dir.

Office of Liturgical Music—THOMAS A. DELESSIO, Diocesan Dir.

Office of Liturgical Formation—CLARE GIANGRECO, Dir.

Diocesan Eucharistic League—Rev. GUY W. SELVESTER, Dir.

Holy Name Society—Rev. CHESTER H. CARINA, J.C.L., Moderator.

Department of Pastoral Life

Pastoral Life—JUDITH A. PSOTA, Exec. Dir.

Office of Family Life Ministry—JUDITH A. PSOTA, Dir.

Office for Multicultural Ministries—MARILYN SANTOS, Dir.

Black Catholic Apostolate—JOSEPH L. POWELL, Coord.

Filipino Apostolate—Rev. ROBERTO CORUNA, Coord.

Commission for Hispanic Ministry—Revs. RONALD BONNEAU, C.Ss.R., Co Chm.; JAMES GILMOUR, C.Ss.R., Co Chm.

Chinese Apostolate—Rev. ABRAHAM BIT-SHING CHIU, O.F.M., Coord.

Indian Apostolate—Rev. ARULRAJ S. SINGARAYER, Coord.

Portuguese Apostolate—Rev. STANISLAW WILCZEK, C.Ss.R., Coord.

Vietnamese Apostolate—Rev. PETER TRAN, Coord.

Commission for Pro-Life Action—Rev. Msgr. RICHARD A. BEHL, Chm.

Office of Respect for Life—JENNIFER A. RUGGIERO, Dir.

Commission for Ministry for People with Disabilities—VACANT.

Office of Hispanic Ministry—Co Directors: Revs. RONALD BONNEAU, C.Ss.R.; JAMES GILMOUR, C.Ss.R.

Department of Formation and Leadership

Formation and Leadership—CECELIA REGAN, Exec. Dir.

Office for Catechesis—CECELIA REGAN, Dir.; CAROL MASCOLA, Assoc. Dir.; PATRICIA MARTIN, Prog. Coord.

Office of Parish Leadership Formation—JENNIFER HINTON, Prog. Dir.

Office of Youth and Young Adult Ministry—JAVIER BUSTAMENTE, Dir.; ANGELICA BARRERA-CRUZ, Assoc. Dir.

Office of Evangelization—JODIE D'ANGIOLILLO, Dir.

Legion of Mary—Rev. A. PAUL DA SILVA, Mod.

Charismatic Movement—Rev. ROBERT G. GORMAN, Moderator.

Diocesan Council of Catholic Women—Rev. Msgr. EDWARD M. O'NEILL, Moderator.

Office of RCIA—SARA SHARLOW, Dir.

Department of Catholic Social Services

Department of Catholic Social Services—MARIANNE MAJEWSKI, L.C.S.W., Exec. Dir., (See category for Catholic Charities under Institutions located in the Diocese for the full listing).

Catholic Relief Services—Rev. Msgr. JOSEPH J. KERRIGAN, Dir.

Office of Social Justice—24 Abeel St., New Brunswick, 08901. Tel: 732-745-9800. ERNEST C. REVOIR, Dir.

Consultative Bodies

College of Consultors—Rev. Msgrs. ROBERT J. ZAMORSKI; WILLIAM BENWELL, J.C.L., V.G.; SEAMUS F. BRENNAN; MICHAEL J. CORONA, P.A.; CHARLES W. CICERALE; SYLVESTER J. CRONIN; Very Rev. RONALD L. JANDERNOA; Rev. Msgr. EDWARD C. PULEO; Revs. DANIEL SLOAN; THOMAS J. WALSH. Liturgical Advisor: Rev. Msgr. ROBERT W. MEDLEY.

Deans—Rev. Msgr. CHARLES W. CICERALE, Cathedral Deanery; Very Revs. ROBERT G. LYNAM, Forsgate Deanery; RONALD L. JANDERNOA, Morris Canal Deanery; JONATHAN S. TOBOROWSKY, Raritan Bay Deanery; Rev. Msgr. SEAMUS F. BRENNAN, County Seat Deanery; Very Revs. BRIAN J. NOLAN, Somerset Hills Deanery; LEONARD F.A. RUSAY, Round Valley Deanery; MARCO A. CACERES, New Brunswick Deanery; Rev. Msgr. JOHN B. GORDON, Perth Amboy Deanery; Very Rev. PATRICK J. KUFFNER, Middlebrook Deanery.

Presbyteral Council—Most Rev. PAUL G. BOOTKOSKI, D.D., Pres.

Theological Commission—Rev. GLENN J. COMANDINI, S.T.D., Chm.

Diocesan Pastoral Council—Most Rev. PAUL G. BOOTKOSKI, D.D.

CLERGY, PARISHES, MISSIONS AND PAROCHIAL SCHOOLS

BOROUGH OF METUCHEN

(MIDDLESEX COUNTY), CATHEDRAL OF ST. FRANCIS OF ASSISI (1871) Rev. Msgr. Robert J. Zamorski, Rector; Revs. Gerardo B. Paderon, Parochial Vicar; Lukasz Blicharski, Parochial Vicar; Deacons Guido J. Brossoni; Frank J. Cammarano; Kenneth Hamilton; Eduardo Olegario; Joseph P. Saggese. In Res., Rev. Msgr. Sylvester J. Cronin.

Res.: 32 Elm Ave., 08840. Tel: 732-548-0100; Fax: 732-549-1033. Web: www.stfranciscathedral.org.

School—St. Francis Cathedral School, (Grades PreSchool-8), 528 Main St., 08840. Tel: 732-548-3107; Fax: 732-548-5760. Web: www.stfranciscathedralschool.org. Mrs. Barbara Stevens, Prin.; Mrs. Patricia Guidi, Librarian. Sisters of Christian Charity 1; Lay Teachers 28; Preschool 65; Students 547.

OUTSIDE THE BOROUGH OF METUCHEN

ALPHA, WARREN CO., ST. MARY (1902) [CEM] Rev. Msgr. Terrance M. Lawler; Rev. Leopoldo S. Salvania, Parochial Vicar; Deacons Keith B. McCarthy; George L. Bolash; John B. Van Haute.

Res.: 830 Fifth Ave., P.O. Box 1133, 08865. Tel: 908-454-0444; Fax: 908-454-7745. Web: www.stmaryrc.org.

ANNANDALE, HUNTERDON CO., IMMACULATE CONCEPTION (1864) [CEM 2] Rev. Msgr. Randall J. Vashon; Rev. Michael Gromadzki, Parochial Vicar; Deacons William R. Bauer; Joseph P. Campbell; Michael R. Martini; Michael A. Meyer.

Res.: 316 Old Allerton Rd., 08801. Tel: 908-735-7319; Fax: 908-735-4552. Web: www.icc-clintonnj.org.

School—Immaculate Conception School, (Grades PreK-8), 314 Old Allerton Rd., 08801. Tel: 908-735-6334; Fax: 908-238-0724. Web: www.icsclinton.org. Annamarie C. Reilly, Prin.; Kathryn Puleo, Librarian. Lay Teachers 31; Students 536.

Station—Country Arch Nursing Home Pittstown. Tel: 908-735-6600.

Station—Edna Mahan Correctional Facility for Women Clinton. Tel: 908-735-7111; Fax: 908-735-5246.

Station—Hunterdon Developmental Center Clinton. Tel: 908-735-4031; Fax: 908-730-1311.

Station—Rolling Hills Nursing Home Lebanon. Tel: 908-236-2011.

AVENEL, MIDDLESEX CO., ST. ANDREW (1920) Rev. David B. Kosmoski; Deacon Walter S. Maksimik.

Res.: 244 Avenel St., 07001. Tel: 732-634-4355; Fax: 732-750-5905. Email: our.church@standrewparish.com. Web: www.standrewparish.com.

Station—Woodbridge State School

Station—Woodbridge Emergency Reception Center 07001. Tel: 732-636-4261.

BAPTISTOWN, HUNTERDON CO., OUR LADY OF VICTORIES (1973) Rev. Msgr. David I. Fulton; Rev. Kulandairaj Madalaimuthu, Parochial Vicar; Deacon John T. Monahan.

Res.: 1005 Rte. 519, P.O. Box 127, 08803. Tel: 908-996-2068; Fax: 908-996-3525.

BASKING RIDGE, SOMERSET CO., ST. JAMES (1864) Revs. Glenn J. Comandini; Carmelo Villocillo, Parochial Vicar; Deacons Peter J. DePrima Jr.; Luke J. Hally; Thomas H. Klaas.

Res.: 184 S. Finley Ave., P.O. Box 310, 07920. Tel: 908-766-0888; Fax: 908-766-1815. Web: www.saintjamesbr.org.

School—(Grades PreSchool-8), 200 S. Finley Ave., P.O. Box 310, 07920. Tel: 908-766-4774; Fax: 908-766-4432. Web: www.sjsbr.org. Mr. Jeremiah Kenny, Prin.; Beth Albanese, Librarian. Lay Teachers 29; Students 390.

BELVIDERE, WARREN CO., ST. PATRICK (1892) Very Rev. Richard M. Rusk; Rev. Dominic Perunilam, Parochial Vicar; Deacons John F. Dumschat; William Kintis.

Res.: 327 Greenwich St., 07823. Tel: 908-475-2559; Fax: 908-475-1943. Web: www.stpatrickbelvidere.parishesonline.com.

BERNARDSVILLE, SOMERSET CO., OUR LADY OF PERPETUAL HELP (1898) [CEM] Rev. Msgrs. John N. Fell; John R. Torney, Pastor Emeritus (Retired); Rev. Antonio M. Alvarez, Parochial Vicar; Deacons John Deitchman; Joel R. Livingston; Benigno Ruiz-Diaz.

Res.: 111 Claremont Rd., 07924. Tel: 908-766-0079; Fax: 908-766-1185. Email: olphemail@aol.com. Web: www.olphbernardsville.org.

School—School of St. Elizabeth, (Grades PreK-8), Seney Dr., 07924. Tel: 908-766-0244; Fax: 908-766-5372. Web: www.steschool.org. Mr. William Venezia, Prin. Lay Teachers 15; Students 180.

Chapel—Bernardsville, Sacred Heart (Chapel of Convenience)

BLAIRSTOWN, WARREN CO., ST. JUDE (1945) Very Rev. Ronald L. Jandernoa; Deacon Michael J. Sullivan Jr.

Res.: 7 Eisenhower Rd., P.O. Box N, 07825. Tel: 908-362-6444; Fax: 908-362-6862. Email: stjudech@ptd.net. Web: www.stjudeblairstown.parishesonline.com.

BLOOMSBURY, HUNTERDON CO., CHURCH OF THE ANNUNCIATION (1948) Rev. Roberto Coruna.

Res.: 80 Main St., P.O. Box 136, 08804-0136. Tel: 908-479-4905; Fax: 908-479-4453. Email: annunciationrcc@earthlink.net.

BOUND BROOK, SOMERSET CO.

1—ST. JOSEPH (1876) [CEM] Revs. Charles T. O'Connor; Jose M. Marcelo, Parochial Vicar; Deacons George D. Coleman; Gary Newton; Gustavo Sandoval.

Office: 124 E. Second St., P.O. Box 72, 08805. Tel: 732-356-0027; Fax: 732-356-8092.

Res.: 304 John St., 08805. Tel: 732-356-8936.

2—ST. MARY OF CZESTOCHOWA (1914), (Polish), Rev. Leon S. Aniszczyk.

Res.: 193 W. High St., 08805. Tel: 732-667-3660. Email: stmarybb@optimum.net. Web: www.stmarys-boundbrook.org.

Church: 201 Vosseller Ave., 08805. Tel: 732-356-0358; Fax: 732-356-1338.

BRIDGEWATER, SOMERSET CO.

1—ST. BERNARD OF CLAIRVAUX (1843) [CEM] Rev. Msgr. Joseph G. Celano; Rev. Damian Breen, Parochial Vicar; Deacons Paul L. Anderson; Patrick J. Cline; Gerard C. Sims; Michael Wojcik.

Res.: 500 Rte. 22, 08807. Tel: 908-725-0552 (Office); Fax: 908-725-4524. Web: www.stbernardbridgewater.org.

School—St. Bernard Pre-School & Kindergarten, Tel: 908-725-0552, Ext. 813; Fax: 908-237-9789. Barbara Turse, Dir. Lay Teachers 8; Students 72.

2—HOLY TRINITY (1948) Revs. John R. Pringle; Thomas Myladil, O.C.D.; Deacon Michael A. Forrestall.

Res.: 60 Maple St., 08807. Tel: 908-526-2394; Fax: 908-526-5837. Email: htchurch08807@yahoo.com. Web: www.holytrinitynj.org.

CALIFON, HUNTERDON CO., ST. JOHN NEUMANN (1982) Very Rev. J. William Mickiewicz; Deacon Earl J. Roberts III.

Res.: 398 County Rd. 513, P.O. Box 455, 07830. Tel: 908-832-2513; Fax: 908-832-7618. Email: sjn@ccsjn.org. Web: www.ccsjn.org.

CARTERET, MIDDLESEX CO.

1—DIVINE MERCY (2010) Revs. Edmund J. Shallow; John Stec, Parochial Vicar.

Office & Holy Family Church: 213 Pershing Ave.,

07008. Tel: 732-541-5768; Fax: 732-541-5871. Email: dmpcarteret@aol.com.
Sacred Heart—67 Fitch St., 07008.
St. Elizabeth of Hungary—119 Washington Ave., 07008.
2—ST. JOSEPH (1893) Rev. James W. McGuffey; Deacons George F. Kimball; Ramon L. Torres.
Church: 55 High St., 07008. Tel: 732-541-8946; Fax: 732-541-0500. Web: www.stjosephparishfamily.com.
Res.: 7 Locust St., 07008.
School—(Grades PreK-8), 865 Roosevelt Ave., 07008. Tel: 732-541-7111; Fax: 732-541-0676. Web: www.sjps.net. Mrs. Roseann Johnson, Prin. Lay Teachers 15; Students 240.

COLONIA, MIDDLESEX CO., ST. JOHN VIANNEY (1959) Rev. Msgr. Edward M. O'Neill; Revs. Joseph Kubiak, O.F.M.Cap.; John C. Gloss, Parochial Vicar; Deacons Joseph D. Ragucci; Thomas S. Michnewicz.
Res.: 420 Inman Ave., 07067. Tel: 732-574-0150; Fax: 732-574-0050. Web: www.sjvianney.com.
School—(Grades PreK-8), 420 Inman Ave., 07067. Tel: 732-388-1662; Fax: 732-388-1003. Web: www.sjv-.net. Mrs. Carol Woodburn, Prin. Bernardine Sisters 2; Lay Teachers 22; Students 431.

DUNELLEN, MIDDLESEX CO., ST. JOHN THE EVANGELIST (1879) Rev. John C. Siceloff; Deacons Michael P. Gleason; Phillip Gonzalez.
Res.: 317 First St., 08812. Tel: 732-968-2621; Fax: 732-968-3709.

EAST BRUNSWICK, MIDDLESEX CO., ST. BARTHOLOMEW (1959) Revs. Thomas J. Walsh; Abraham Orapankal, Parochial Vicar; Deacons John H. Broehl; Anthony J. Gostkowski; John F. Kenny; Filippo Tartara.
Res.: 470 Ryders Ln., 08816. Tel: 732-257-7722; Fax: 732-257-7723.
School—(Grades PreK-8) John M. Donza, Prin. Lay Teachers 17; Students 278.

EDISON, MIDDLESEX CO.
1—GUARDIAN ANGELS (1959) Merged with St. Paul the Apostle, Highland Park and Our Lady of Korea, Quasi-Parish, Woodbridge to form Transfiguration of the Lord Parish, Highland Park.
2—ST. HELENA (1965) Revs. Anthony M. Sirianni; Antony Arockiadoss, M.S.C.; Deacon Danilo C. San Jose.
Res.: 950 Grove Ave., 08820. Tel: 732-494-3399; Fax: 732-494-2076.
School—(Grades PreK-8), 930 Grove Ave., 08820. Tel: 732-549-6234; Fax: 732-549-6205. Web: www-.sthelenaedison.org. Sr. Mary Charles Wienckoski, C.S.S.F., Prin. Felician Sisters 1; Lay Teachers 25; Students 290.
3—ST. MATTHEW THE APOSTLE (1952) Revs. George Targonski; Alphonsus Kariuki, Parochial Vicar; Deacons Barry C. Demarest; Frank Yuhas.
Res.: 81 Seymour Ave., 08817. Tel: 732-985-5063; Fax: 732-985-9104. Web: www.stmatthewtheapostle.com.
School—St. Matthew School, (Grades PreK-8), 100 Seymour Ave., 08817. Tel: 732-985-6633; Fax: 732-985-7748. Web: www.stmatthewtheapostle.com/school. Eileen Sullivan, Prin. Lay Teachers 16; Students 202.

FLEMINGTON, HUNTERDON CO., ST. MAGDALEN DE PAZZI (1864) [CEM] Revs. Timothy Christy; Joseph Kabali, Parochial Vicar; John J. O'Kane, Parochial Vicar; Deacons Michael J. Bachynsky; Stephen F. Kern; Thaddeus Wislinski.
Res.: 105 Mine St., 08822. Tel: 908-782-2922; Fax: 908-782-0952. Web: www.stmagdalen.org.
School—St. Magdalen Nursery School, (Grades N) Amy Weckesser, Dir. Lay Teachers 3; Students 33.

FORDS, MIDDLESEX CO., OUR LADY OF PEACE (1919) Rev. Msgr. Andrew L. Szaroleta; Rev. Frank W. Fellrath, Parochial Vicar; Deacons James A. Kelly Jr.; John A. Raychel. In Res., Rev. Pauly Thekkan, C.M.I.
Res.: 26 Maple Ave., Edison, 08837. Tel: 732-738-7940; Fax: 732-738-3848. Web: www.olpfords.org.
School—(Grades PreK-8), Amboy Ave., 08863. Tel: 732-738-7464; Fax: 732-738-0026. Mrs. Frances Comiskey, Prin. Lay Teachers 14; Students 204.

GREAT MEADOWS, WARREN CO., SS. PETER AND PAUL (1921) Revs. Pawel Dolinksi, S.D.S.; Dawid Adamczak, S.D.S., Parochial Vicar; Deacon Stephen Gunther.
Res.: 360 U.S. Hwy. 46, P.O. Box 156, 07838. Tel: 908-637-4269; Fax: 908-637-6896. Email: stpeterandpaul@comcast.net. Web: www.parishesonline.com/sspeterpaulgreatmeadows.

HACKETTSTOWN, WARREN CO., ASSUMPTION OF THE BLESSED VIRGIN MARY (1864) Rev. David J. Pekola; Deacon Walter H. Pidgeon.
Res.: 302 High St., P.O. Box 547, 07840-0547. Tel: 908-852-3320; Fax: 908-852-2361.
School—St. Mary of the Assumption School, (Grades PreK-8), Cook & Liberty Sts., 07840. Tel: 908-852-4791; Fax: 908-852-4180. Marilyn Walsh, Prin.; Susan Fenimore, Librarian. Lay Teachers 11; Students 163.

HAMPTON, HUNTERDON CO., ST. ANN (1859) [CEM] Rev. Michael C. Saharic.
Res.: P.O. Box 405, 08827. Tel: 908-537-2221; Fax: 908-537-9465. Web: www.saintann1859.org.
Church: 6 Church St., 08827.
Station—NJ State Hospital for Geriatrics Glen Gardner.

HELMETTA, MIDDLESEX CO., HOLY TRINITY (1911), (Polish), [CEM] Rev. Stanley Jarosz; Deacon Gregory R. D'Angelo.
Res.: 100 Main St., 08828. Tel: 732-521-0172; Fax: 732-521-0824.

HIGH BRIDGE, HUNTERDON CO., ST. JOSEPH (1880) Rev. Maurice T. Carlton.
Res.: 59 Main St., 08829. Tel: 908-638-6211; Fax: 908-638-5802.

HIGHLAND PARK, MIDDLESEX CO.
1—ST. PAUL THE APOSTLE (1912) Merged with Guardian Angels, Edison and Our Lady of Korea, Quasi-Parish, Woodbridge to form Transfiguration of the Lord Parish, Highland Park.
2—TRANSFIGURATION OF THE LORD PARISH Rev. Msgr. Daniel J. Herlihy; Rev. Bede Kim; Deacons Donald J. DeLorenzo; Seock Ro Youn. In Res., Rev. Michael Onyekwere, S.D.V.
Parish Center, 23 S. Fifth St., 08904. Tel: 732-572-0977; Fax: 732-572-7497.
Res.: 37 Plainfield Ave., Edison, 08818-1216.
Worship Sites—
Guardian Angels—
St. Paul the Apostle—502 Raritan Ave., 08904.

HILLSBOROUGH, SOMERSET CO.
1—ST. JOSEPH (Millstone Borough) (1883) Rev. Msgr. Raymond L. Cole; Deacons Joseph C. Moscinski; John Craig; Timothy A. Lawless.
Church: 34 Yorktown Rd., 08844. Tel: 908-874-3141; Fax: 908-874-7040.
Res.: 41 Yorktown Rd., 08844. Tel: 908-874-3141; Fax: 908-874-7040. Web: www.stjosephsparish.com.
2—MARY, MOTHER OF GOD (1948) Revs. Sean A. Broderick, C.S.Sp., Admin.; Michael E. Crummy, Parochial Vicar; Deacons Christopher Conroy; James N. McCormick.
Res.: 157 S. Triangle Rd., 08844. Tel: 908-874-8220; Fax: 908-874-4183. Web: www.marymotherofgod.org.
School—(Grades PreSchool) Teachers 3; Preschool 94.

HOPELAWN, MIDDLESEX CO., OUR LADY OF THE MOST HOLY ROSARY (1904) [CEM] Rev. Michael G. Krull; Deacon Edward G. Rodes.
Res.: 625 Florida Grove Rd., 08861. Tel: 732-826-2771; Fax: 732-826-0320. Web: www.holyrosarychurchnj.org. Rev. Keith Cervine, Dir.

ISELIN, MIDDLESEX CO., ST. CECELIA (1923) Revs. Jerome A. Johnson; Alfonso R. Condorson; Deacon Richard Lutomski.
Res.: 45 Wilus Way, 08830. Tel: 732-283-2300; Fax: 732-283-3326. Web: www.stcecelia.com.
School—(Grades PreK-8) Tel: 732-283-2824; Fax: 732-283-5023. Web: www.stceceliaschool.org. Sr. Margaret Mary Hanlon, M.P.F., Prin. Religious Teachers Filippini 3; Lay Teachers 15; Students 202.
Station—NJ State Home for Disabled Veterans 132 Evergreed Rd., Edison, 08818.
Station—Roosevelt Care Center 1 Roosevelt Dr., Edison, 08837.

JAMESBURG, MIDDLESEX CO., ST. JAMES THE LESS (1878) [CEM] Rev. Kevin P. Duggan, Admin.
Res.: 36 Lincoln Ave., 08831. Tel: 732-521-0100; Fax: 732-521-8287. Email: jamestheless@comcast.net.
Station—State Home for Boys Monroe Township. Tel: 732-521-0030.

KENDALL PARK, MIDDLESEX CO., ST. AUGUSTINE OF CANTERBURY (1952) Very Rev. Robert G. Lynam; Deacons Richard McCarron; Denis Mayer; James A. Tesoriero.
Res.: 45 Henderson Rd., 08824. Tel: 732-297-3000; Fax: 732-940-1746. Web: www.staugustinenj.org.
School—(Grades PreSchool-8) Tel: 732-297-6042; Fax: 732-297-7062. Sisters Mary Louise Shulas, M.P.F., Prin.; Lucy Zanoni, M.P.F., Librarian. Brothers of Sacred Heart 1; Religious Teachers Filippini 5; Lay Teachers 32; Students 525; Preschool 91.

LAMBERTVILLE, HUNTERDON CO., ST. JOHN THE EVANGELIST (1843) [CEM] Rev. Robert B. Kolakowski; Deacon Michael Semko.
Res.: 44 Bridge St., 08530. Tel: 609-397-3350; Fax: 609-397-8713. Email: info_stjohnschurch@yahoo.com. Web: www.stjohnlambertville.parishesonline.com.
School—The Jesus School, (Grades PreK-K) Tel: 609-397-0593. Email: mconaughton@diometuchen.org. Sr. Marie Conaughton, T.R.H., Prin. Teachers 4; Students 52.

LAURENCE HARBOR, MIDDLESEX CO., ST. LAWRENCE (1943) Very Rev. Jonathan S. Toborowsky; Rev. Robert V. Meyers; Deacons Stephen J. Gajewski; Gregory Ris.
Res.: 109 Laurence Pkwy., 08879. Tel: 732-566-1093; Fax: 732-765-9311.

MANVILLE, SOMERSET CO.
1—CHRIST THE KING (1948) Revs. Stanislaw Slaby, C.Ss.R.; Slawomir Romanowski, C.Ss.R., Parochial Vicar; Deacon Thomas J. Giacobbe.
211 Louis St., 08835.
Office: 98 S. 2nd Ave., P.O. Box 127, 08835.
Res.: 136 S. Main St., 08835.
School—(Grades PreSchool-8), 99 N. 13th Ave., 08835. Tel: 908-526-1339; Fax: 908-526-3541. Web: www.ctkmanville.com. Mrs. Christine N. Benson, Prin. Lay Teachers 15; Preschool 25; Students 175.
2—SACRED HEART OF JESUS (1919), (Polish), [CEM] Revs. Stanislaw Slaby, C.Ss.R.; Wojciech Kusek, C.Ss.R., Parochial Vicar; Deacon William G. Stefany.
Res.: 136 S. Main St., 08835.
Church: Filak St., P.O. Box 924, 08835. Tel: 908-725-0072; Fax: 908-685-3029. Web: www.sacred-heart-church.org.

MARTINSVILLE, SOMERSET CO., BLESSED SACRAMENT (1968) Rev. Msgr. Eugene Prus; Rev. Rico Paril; Deacon Louis Pizzigoni III.
Res.: 852 Newmans Ln., P.O. Box 563, 08836. Tel: 732-356-4442; Fax: 732-356-5172.

MIDDLESEX, MIDDLESEX CO., OUR LADY OF MOUNT VIRGIN (1943) Very Rev. Patrick J. Kuffner; Rev. Matthew R. Paratore, Parochial Vicar; Deacons John R. Czekaj; John R. Tietjen.
Res.: 600 Harris Ave., 08846. Tel: 732-356-2149; Fax: 732-356-1302. Web: www.olmv.net.

MILFORD, HUNTERDON CO., ST. EDWARD THE CONFESSOR (1944) Rev. Krzysztof Kaczynski; Deacon William J. Barr.
Res.: 61 Mill St., P.O. Box 522, 08848. Tel: 908-995-4723; Fax: 908-995-9353. Web: www.stedwardmilford.parishesonline.com.

MILLTOWN, MIDDLESEX CO., OUR LADY OF LOURDES (1921) Revs. Edward A. Czarcinski; Dario Endiape; Deacon Robert Gerling.
Res.: 233 N. Main St., 08850. Tel: 732-828-0011; Fax: 732-828-3133. Email: olol678@aol.com. Web: www.ololchurchnj.org.
School—(Grades PreK-8), 43 Cleveland Ave., 08850. Tel: 732-828-1951; Fax: 732-828-7871. Web: www.ololschoolnj.org. Sr. Elizabeth Halaj, L.S.I.C., Prin. Little Servant Sisters of the Immaculate Conception 4; Lay Teachers 11; Students 172.

MONMOUTH JUNCTION, MIDDLESEX CO., ST. CECILIA (1914) Rev. Daniel Sloan; Deacon Michael P. Murtha.
Office: 10 Kingston Ln., 08852. Tel: 732-329-2893; Fax: 732-329-4693. Web: www.stceciliaparish.net.
Res.: 46 Kingston Ln., 08852.

MONROE TOWNSHIP, MIDDLESEX CO., NATIVITY OF OUR LORD (1992) Rev. Edward R. Flanagan; Deacons Robert E. Gatto; John H. Shelton.
Res.: 185 Applegarth Rd., 08831. Tel: 609-371-0499; Fax: 609-371-0677. Web: www.nativitymonroe.org.

NEW BRUNSWICK, MIDDLESEX CO.
1—ST. JOHN THE BAPTIST (1867), (German), [CEM] Very Rev. Marco A. Caceres; Deacon Luis F. Moral.
Res.: 29 Abeel St., 08901. Tel: 732-545-5267; Fax: 732-545-0446.
Church: Neilson and Carman Sts., 08901.
2—ST. JOSEPH (1924), (Polish), Revs. Joseph A. Krajewski; Kevin Kelly, C.O., Parochial Vicar.
Res.: 15 Maple St., 08901. Tel: 732-545-2195; Fax: 732-545-8778.
3—ST. LADISLAUS (1904), (Hungarian), Rev. Capistran L. Polgar, O.F.M. In Res., Rev. Abraham Bit-shing Chiu, O.F.M.
Parish Office: 40 Plum St., 08901.
Church: 215 Somerset St., 08901. Tel: 732-545-1427; Fax: 732-545-8501. Email: stladislaus@optonline.net.
4—ST. MARY OF MOUNT VIRGIN (1904), (Italian), Unassigned.
Res.: 190 Sandford St., 08901. Tel: 732-545-5090; Fax: 732-937-9290.
Mission—St. Theresa of the Infant Jesus 15 Fox Rd., Edison, 08817.
5—OUR LADY OF MT. CARMEL (1977), (Hispanic), Revs. Raymond L. Nacarino; Jose Lorente, Parochial Vicar; Manuel Lorente, Parochial Vicar.
Res. & Church: 75 Morris St., 08901. Tel: 732-846-5873; Fax: 732-846-5397.
6—ST. PETER THE APOSTLE (1829) [CEM] Revs. Thomas A. Odorizzi, C.O.; Jeffrey Calia, C.O., Parochial Vicar; Deacon Helmut Wittreich. In Res., Very Rev. Peter Cebulka, C.O.; Rev. Kevin Kelly, C.O.
Res.: 94 Somerset St., 08901. Tel: 732-545-6820; Fax: 732-545-4069. Web: www.stpetertheapostle-.org.
7—SACRED HEART (1883) Rev. Msgr. Joseph J. Kerrigan; Deacon Nelson Torres.
Res.: 56 Throop Ave., 08901. Tel: 732-545-1681; Fax: 732-545-5059. Web: www.hub4sacredheart.org.

NORTH BRUNSWICK, MIDDLESEX CO., OUR LADY OF PEACE (1969) Rev. John V. Polyak; Deacons Francis D'Mello; David A. DeFrange.
Res.: 277 Washington Pl., 08902. Tel: 732-297-9680;

Fax: 732-297-1024.
NORTH PLAINFIELD, SOMERSET CO.
1—ST. JOSEPH (1882) Revs. George A. Farrell; Krystian Burdzy, Parochial Vicar. In Res., Very Rev. Richard J. Lyons.
Office: 99 Westervelt Ave., 07060.
Res.: 41 Manning Ave., 07060. Tel: 908-756-3383; Fax: 908-756-1155.
2—ST. LUKE (1965) Rev. Lancelot McGrath, Admin.
Res.: 300 Clinton Ave., 07063. Tel: 908-754-8811; Fax: 908-754-0120. Email: stlukesinfo@gmail.com.
OLD BRIDGE, MIDDLESEX CO.
1—ST. AMBROSE (1961) Revs. Robert G. Gorman; John C. Grimes, Parochial Vicar; John J. Werner, Parochial Vicar; Deacons Charles J. Damian; Andrew J. Strus.
Res.: 96 Throckmorton Ln., 08857. Tel: 732-679-5666; Fax: 732-679-0853. Web: www.saintambroseparish.com.
School—(Grades K-8) Tel: 732-679-4700; Fax: 732-679-6062. Web: www.stambroseschool.net. Mr. Joseph W. Norris, Prin.; Mrs. Linda Negraval, Librarian. Lay Teachers 32; Students 387.
2—MOST HOLY REDEEMER (1983) Rev. Chester H. Carina; Deacons Robert T. McGovern; A. Keith Berg; Frank C. D'Auguste.
Res.: 133 Amboy Rd., Matawan, 07747. Tel: 732-566-9334; Fax: 732-566-2245. Web: www.mostholyredeemerchurch.org.
3—ST. THOMAS THE APOSTLE (1921) Rev. Msgr. Richard A. Behl; Rev. Danilo A. Canceran; Deacons John J. Fitzsimmons; Robert Bonfante Sr.; Patrick W. Hearty. In Res., Rev. Peter Suhaka.
Res.: One St. Thomas Plaza, 08857. Tel: 732-251-4000; Fax: 732-251-4946. Web: www.saintthomasob.com.
School—(Grades PreK-8), 333 Hwy. 18, 08857. Tel: 732-251-4812; Fax: 732-251-5315. Miss Thomasina Wyatt, Prin.; Maria Krumme, Librarian. Lay Teachers 24; Students 413.
OXFORD, WARREN CO., ST. ROSE OF LIMA (1864) [CEM] Very Rev. Richard M. Rusk; Deacon Lawrence V. D'Andrea.
Res.: Academy St., P.O. Box 88, 07863. Tel: 908-453-2034. Web: www.stroseoflimaoxford.parishesonline.com.
PARLIN, MIDDLESEX CO., ST. BERNADETTE (1956) Revs. James W. Hagerman; Arulraj S. Singarayer, Parochial Vicar; Deacon Donald Zampella.
Res.: 20 Villanova Rd., 08859. Tel: 732-721-2772; Fax: 732-727-5188.
FAR HILLS-PEAPACK, SOMERSET CO., ST. ELIZABETH - ST. BRIGID Rev. Msgr. Edward C. Puleo; Deacon Lawrence J. Duffy.
Mailing Address: P.O. Box 33, Peapack, 07977. Tel: 908-234-1265; 908-234-0079; Fax: 908-234-2923.
St. Elizabeth—34 Peapack Rd., 07931.
St. Brigid—129 Main St., Peapack, 07977.
PERTH AMBOY, MIDDLESEX CO.
1—HOLY SPIRIT (1944) Rev. Michael G. Krull; Deacon Sam Costantino. In Res., Revs. Sean G. Winters; John J. Morley.
Res.: 580 Hazel Ave., 08861. Tel: 732-826-4859; Fax: 732-826-6078. Web: www.holyspiritrcc.com.
2—HOLY TRINITY (1899), (Slovak), [CEM] Rev. Wladyslaw Wiktorek, Admin.
Mailing Address: 474 Penn St., 08861. Tel: 732-826-0439; Fax: 732-826-1679.
Church: 315 Lawrie St., 08861.
3—LA ASUNCION (1981), (Hispanic), Rev. Msgr. John B. Gordon; Rev. Nicholas Norena; Deacons Enrique Garcia; Corpus V. Perez; Noe Cortez.
Mailing Address: 697 Cortlandt St., 08861. Tel: 732-442-0512; Fax: 732-442-3037. Email: asuncionchurch@aol.com.
4—ST. MARY (1845) Rev. Waldemar Latkowski, C.Ss.R.; Deacon Basilio A. Perez.
Res.: 104 Center St., 08861. Tel: 732-442-0039; Fax: 732-324-4383. Web: www.stmaryperth.com.
5—OUR LADY OF FATIMA (1960), (Hispanic), Revs. Joshy T. Nirappel, C.M.F.; Edmundo Andres, C.M.F., Parochial Vicar; Heherson Balabbo, C.M.F., Parochial Vicar; Deacons Herminio Rivera; Pablo Bencosme. In Res., Rev. Richard Todd, C.M.F.
Res.: 380 Smith St., 08861. Tel: 732-442-6634; Fax: 732-293-2544.
6—OUR LADY OF HUNGARY (1902), (Hungarian), [CEM] Rev. Msgr. John B. Gordon.
Res.: 697 Cortlandt St., 08861. Tel: 732-442-0512; Fax: 732-442-3037.
7—OUR LADY OF THE ROSARY OF FATIMA (1981), (Portuguese), Revs. Waldemar Latkowski, C.Ss.R., Admin.; Stanislaw Wilczek, C.Ss.R., Parochial Vicar.
Church: 188 Wayne St., 08861. Tel: 732-826-4360; Fax: 732-826-5167.
8—ST. STEPHEN (1892), (Polish), [CEM] Revs. Waldemar Latkowski, C.Ss.R.; Lukasz Drozak, C.Ss.R., Parochial Vicar; Wieslaw Bajor, C.Ss.R., Parochial Vicar.
Res.: 490 State St., 08861. Tel: 732-826-1395; Fax: 732-826-4217. Web: www.st-stephens-church.com.
PHILLIPSBURG, WARREN CO.
1—SS. PETER AND PAUL (1913), (Slovak), Closed. Records at St. Philip & St. James, Phillipsburg.
2—ST. PHILIP & ST. JAMES (1860) [CEM] Revs. John J. Barbella; James A. Kyrpczak, Parochial Vicar; Mark Kehoe, Parochial Vicar; Deacons John T. Flynn; Enock Berluche Sr.; George Frank. In Res., Rev. Vincent P. Chen.
Res.: 430 S. Main St., 08865-3094. Tel: 908-454-0112; Fax: 908-454-0125. Web: www.spsj.org.
School—(Grades PreK-8), 137 Roseberry St., 08865. Tel: 908-859-1244; Fax: 908-859-1202. Mrs. Judith W. Francisco, Prin.; Ms. Barbara Opdycke, Librarian. Lay Teachers 17; Students 217.
PISCATAWAY, MIDDLESEX CO.
1—ST. FRANCES CABRINI (1961) Rev. James F. Considine; Deacon Roger Ladao.
Res.: 208 Bound Brook Ave., 08854-4097. Tel: 732-885-5313; Fax: 732-885-9031. Email: sfc208@yahoo.com.
2—OUR LADY OF FATIMA (1948) Revs. Arlindo Paul DaSilva; Herbert J. Stab, Pastor Emeritus (Retired); Deacons Stanley J. Lorenc; Lawrence P. Reilly; William P. Rider. In Res., Revs. A. David Chalackal, C.M.I.; Louis A. Mattina.
Parish Office: 50 Van Winkle Pl., 08854. Tel: 732-968-5555; Fax: 732-968-5959. Web: www.olfparish.org.
Res.: 501 New Market Rd., 08854. Tel: 732-968-5556.
PITTSTOWN, HUNTERDON CO., ST. CATHERINE OF SIENA (1992) Rev. Czeslaw Zalubski, S.D.B., Admin.; Deacons Anthony Russo; Dennis K. Webster.
Res.: 2 Whitebridge Rd., P.O. Box 245, 08867-0245. Tel: 908-735-4024; Fax: 908-735-0355. Email: stcofs@embarqmail.com.
St. Catherine of Siena Pastoral Center—142 Perryville Rd., Hampton, 08827.
PLAINSBORO, MIDDLESEX CO., QUEENSHIP OF MARY (1982) Rev. Msgr. Robert W. Medley; Deacon Hugo Simao.
Res.: 16 Dey Rd., 08536. Tel: 609-799-7511; Fax: 609-799-8904. Web: www.qomchurch.org.
PORT MURRAY, WARREN CO., ST. THEODORE (1983) Rev. Zenon Boczek, S.D.S.
Res.: 855 Route 57, P.O. Box 146, 07865. Tel: 908-689-8318; 908-689-8393 (Rel. Educ. Office); Fax: 908-689-9242. Email: sttheodorenj@comcast.net. Web: www.sttheodorenj.org.
PORT READING, MIDDLESEX CO., ST. ANTHONY OF PADUA (1906) Revs. William J. Smith; Lauro Colen Sedlmayer; Deacon Michael Brucato.
Res.: 436 Port Reading Ave., 07064. Tel: 732-634-1403; Fax: 732-602-0119. Email: info_stanthony@verizon.net. Web: www.saintanthonypadua.org.
RARITAN, SOMERSET CO.
1—THE CATHOLIC CHURCH OF ST. ANN (1903), (Italian), Rev. Msgr. Michael J. Corona; Rev. Edmund A. Luciano III, Parochial Vicar; Deacons John R. Pacifico; Conrad Paulus.
Res.: 45 Anderson St., 08869. Tel: 908-725-1008; Fax: 908-707-1915. Web: www.stannparish.com.
School—(Grades PreK-8), 29 Second Ave., 08869. Tel: 908-725-7787; Fax: 908-541-9335. Sr. Gloria Caglioti, M.P.F., Prin. Religious Teachers Filippini 1; Lay Teachers 9; Students 204.
2—ST. JOSEPH (1912), (Slovak), Rev. Kenneth R. Kolibas; Deacon Roy Rabinowitz. In Res., Rev. Andrzej Wieliczko.
Res.: 16 E. Somerset St., 08869. Tel: 908-725-0163; Fax: 908-725-2333. Web: www.stjosephraritan.4LPI.com. Email: parishoffice@sjraritan.org.
SAYREVILLE, MIDDLESEX CO.
1—OUR LADY OF VICTORIES (1885) [CEM] Revs. Thomas F. Ryan; Virgilio T. Tolentino, Parochial Vicar; Deacons Edward J. Majkowski; Thomas C. Yondolino.
Mailing Address: 42 Main St., 08872.
Res.: 24 Main St., 08872. Tel: 732-257-0077; Fax: 732-651-1898. Web: olvsayrenj.com.
School—(Grades PreK-8), 36 Main St., 08872. Tel: 732-254-1676; Fax: 732-254-5066. Mrs. Rosalind M. Esemplare, Prin.; Ms. Mary Ann Jones, Librarian. Lay Teachers 13; Students 215.
2—ST. STANISLAUS KOSTKA (1914), (Polish), [CEM] Rev. Kenneth R. Murphy; Deacons David Mikolai; Andrew Ozga.
Res.: 225 MacArthur Ave., 08872. Tel: 732-254-0212; Fax: 732-390-2989.
School—(Grades K-8), 221 MacArthur Ave., 08872. Tel: 732-254-5819; Fax: 732-254-7220. Mrs. Harriet Samim, Prin. Lay Teachers 14; Students 215.
SKILLMAN, SOMERSET CO., ST. CHARLES BORROMEO (1982) Rev. Msgr. Gregory E. S. Malovetz.
Res.: 376 Burnt Hill Rd., 08558. Tel: 609-466-0300; Fax: 609-466-0062. Web: www.borromeo.org.
SOMERSET, SOMERSET CO., ST. MATTHIAS (1962) Rev. Douglas J. Haefner; Deacons John M. Radvanski; Russell B. Demkovitz.
Mailing Address: 168 J.F. Kennedy Blvd., 08873. Tel: 732-828-1400; Fax: 732-828-0866. Web: www.stmatthias.net.
Res.: 166 J.F. Kennedy Blvd., 08873.
School—(Grades PreK-8), 170 J.F. Kennedy Blvd., 08873. Tel: 732-828-1402; Fax: 732-946-3099. Web: www.stmatthias.info. Steven Rizzoli, Prin.; Sr. Jean Laurich, S.S.J., Vice Prin.; Stephanie Lanzalotto, Librarian. Lay Teachers 29; PreK Students 59; K-8 Students 503.
SOMERVILLE, SOMERSET CO., IMMACULATE CONCEPTION (1882) [CEM] Rev. Msgr. Seamus F. Brennan; Revs. Alexander J. Carles, Parochial Vicar; Charles A. Sabella, Parochial Vicar; Deacons John B. Ivers; Arnold J. DeMarco; Anthony Hancock; Frank J. Quinn; Luis E. Vindas.
Res.: 35 Mountain Ave., 08876. Tel: 908-725-1112; Fax: 908-725-6269. Web: www.immaculateconception.org.
School—(Grades PreK-8), 41 Mountain Ave., 08876. Tel: 908-725-6516; Fax: 908-725-3172. Sr. Mary John Magdalen, I.H.M., Prin. Sisters 3; Lay Teachers 29; Preschool 15; Students 435.
High School—Immaculata High School, 240 Mountain Ave., 08876. Tel: 908-722-0200; Fax: 908-218-7765. Sr. Regina Havens, I.H.M., Prin. Sisters 7; Lay Teachers 69; Students 769.
Convent—Sisters, Servants of the Immaculate Heart of Mary, 230 Mountain Ave., 08876. Tel: 908-722-6894.
SOUTH AMBOY, MIDDLESEX CO.
1—ST. MARY (1864) [CEM 2] Rev. Dennis R. Wezorak; Deacons Stephen N. Laikowski; Richard O'Brien.
Res.: 256 Augusta St., 08879. Tel: 732-721-0179; Fax: 732-721-0360.
2—SACRED HEART (1895), (Polish), [CEM] Revs. Joseph V. Romanoski; Marian Drozd, Parochial Vicar; Deacon Serge Bernatchez.
Res.: 531 Washington Ave., 08879. Tel: 732-721-0040; Fax: 732-721-4448.
School—Sacred Heart School, (Grades PreSchool-8), 229 Cedar St., 08879. Tel: 732-721-0834; Fax: 732-316-0326. Sisters Marie Connolly, O.S.F., Prin.; Kathleen Curnyn, R.S.M., Librarian. Religious 4; Lay Teachers 14; Students 211.
School—Sacred Heart Creative Kids Center Pre School, (Grades PreSchool), 529 Washington St., 08879. Tel: 732-721-1446. Paula Ryan, Dir. Students 40.
Convent—Sacred Heart Convent, 229 Walnut Ave., 08879.
SOUTH BOUND BROOK, SOMERSET CO., OUR LADY OF MERCY (1949) Rev. Msgr. James P. Moran.
Res.: 122 High St., 08880. Tel: 732-356-1037; Fax: 732-356-1318. Web: www.olmsbb.org.
SOUTH PLAINFIELD, MIDDLESEX CO.
1—OUR LADY OF CZESTOCHOWA (1943), (Polish), Rev. J. Maciej Melaniuk; Deacon Richard A. Kenton.
Res.: 120 Kosciusko Ave., 07080. Tel: 908-756-1333; Fax: 908-756-8557. Email: olcchurch@verizon.net.
2—SACRED HEART (1906) [CEM 2] Revs. John Paul Alvarado; Juan S. Salonga, Parochial Vicar; Deacons John Bertrand; Gregory Caruso; Wayne Otlowski; Joseph J. Stanczak, (Retired).
Res.: 149 S. Plainfield Ave., 07080. Tel: 908-756-0633; Fax: 908-757-5655. Web: www.churchofthesacredheart.net.
Convent—200 Randolph Ave., 07080. Tel: 908-756-0631. Sisters 2.
SOUTH RIVER, MIDDLESEX CO.
1—CORPUS CHRISTI (1944) Rev. John L. Brundage.
Rectory—100 James St., 08882. Tel: 732-254-1800; Fax: 732-254-8063. Web: www.corpuschristisouthriver.parishesonline.com.
2—ST. MARY OF OSTRABRAMA (1903), (Polish), [CEM] Revs. Stanley G. Gromadzki; Pafnouti Wassef; Deacon Thomas F. Dominiecki.
Res.: 30 Jackson St., 08882. Tel: 732-254-2220; Fax: 732-651-8182.
3—ST. STEPHEN PROTOMARTYR (1907), (Hungarian), Rev. John Szczepanik.
Res.: 20 William St., 08882. Tel: 732-257-0100; Fax: 732-257-4646.
SPOTSWOOD, MIDDLESEX CO., IMMACULATE CONCEPTION (1946) Rev. Msgr. Joseph M. Curry; Rev. Martin Espinoza, Parochial Vicar; Deacon John H. McGuire. In Res., Rev. Lazaro Perez.
Res.: 18 South St., 08884. Tel: 732-251-3110; Fax: 732-251-2407. Email: office@icspotswood.com. Web: www.chicspotswood.com.
School—(Grades PreK-8), 23 Manalapan Rd., 08884. Tel: 732-251-3090; Fax: 732-251-8270. Web: www.icsspotswood.org. Mrs. Mary Hamm, Prin.; Kathleen Gately, Librarian. Felician Sisters 1; Lay Teachers 26; Students 454.
Convent—21 Manalapan Rd., 08884. Tel: 732-251-3446.
THREE BRIDGES, HUNTERDON CO., ST. ELIZABETH ANN SETON (1984) Rev. Thomas J. Serafin; Deacon Paul

Santella.
Res.: 105 Summer Rd., 08887. Tel: 908-782-1475; Fax: 908-782-6230. Email: parishoffice@easton.net. Web: www.parishesonline.com/seasthreebridges.

WARREN, SOMERSET CO., OUR LADY OF THE MOUNT (1911) Rev. Sean W. Kenney; Deacon Thomas Sicola.
Res.: 167 Mount Bethel Rd., 07059. Tel: 908-647-1075; Fax: 908-647-7885. Web: www.olmwarren.org.

WASHINGTON, WARREN CO., ST. JOSEPH (1872) [CEM] Rev. Blaise R. Baran; Deacons Edmund Hartmann Jr.; Sylvan Webb.
Res.: 200 Carlton Ave., 07882. Tel: 908-689-0058; Fax: 908-689-3436. Web: www.stjosephwashington-.parishesonline.com.

WATCHUNG, SOMERSET CO., ST. MARY-STONY HILL (1847) [CEM] Very Rev. Brian J. Nolan.
Res.: 225 Mountain Blvd., 07069. Tel: 908-756-6524; Fax: 908-756-2111. Email: stmarywatchung@aol.com. Web: www.stmaryswatchung.org.

WHITEHOUSE STATION, HUNTERDON CO., OUR LADY OF LOURDES (1923) Very Rev. Leonard F.A. Rusay; Deacon Charles Paolino. In Res., Rev. John Primich.
Res.: 390 County Rd. 523, 08889. Tel: 908-534-2319; Fax: 908-534-5670. Email: ollparish@embarqmail.com. Web: www.ollwhs.org.

WOODBRIDGE, MIDDLESEX CO.

1—ST. JAMES (1860) [CEM 2] Rev. Msgr. Charles W. Cicerale; Rev. Peter Tran; Deacons Michael Choi; John DiJoseph; Carl E. Psota; William F. Lange. In Res., Rev. Sebastian D. Kaithackal, C.M.I.
Parish Office: 148 Grenville St., 07095. Tel: 732-634-0500; Fax: 732-602-1487. Web: www.stjamesinfo.org.
Rectory—145 Grove St., 07095.
School—(Grades PreK-8), 341 Amboy Ave., 07095. Tel: 732-634-2090. Miss Mary Erath, Prin.; Mrs. Lori Jensen, Librarian. Lay Teachers 19; Students 290.
Convent—149 Grove St., 07095. Tel: 732-634-0176.

2—OUR LADY OF KOREA, Merged with St. Paul the Apostle, Highland Park and Guardian Angels, Edison to form Transfiguration of the Lord Parish, Highland Park.

3—OUR LADY OF MOUNT CARMEL (1921) Revs. William J. Smith; Lauro Colen Sedlmayer.
Res.: 267 E. Smith St., 07095. Tel: 732-634-1438; Fax: 732-634-5368. Web: www.geocities.com/olmcwnj.

Chaplains of Public Institutions

ANNANDALE. *Mountainview Youth Correctional Facility* 08801. Tel: 732-741-6208. Attended by Immaculate Conception, Annandale.

AVENEL. *Woodbridge Developmental Center*. Attended by St. Andrew.

BELLE MEAD. *Carrier Clinic*. Deacon Joseph Moscinski, Chap.

BELVIDERE. *Warren Correctional Center*. Attended by St. Patrick, Belvidere.

CLINTON. *Edna Mahan Correctional Facility for Women*, Tel: 908-735-7111. Attended by Immaculate Conception, Annandale.
Hunterdon Developmental Center. Attended by Immaculate Conception, Annandale. (908) 735-4031

EDISON. *John F. Kennedy Medical Center*. Revs. Pauly Thekkan, C.M.I., Sebastian D. Kaithackal, C.M.I., Chap., Deacon Paul J. Sheptuck.

FLEMINGTON. *Hunterdon Medical Center*. Revs. Joseph Kabali, Chap., John Primich, Chap. Attended by St. Magdalen de Pazzi.

GLEN GARDNER. *N.J. State Hospital for Geriatrics*. Attended by St. Ann, Hampton.

HACKETTSTOWN. *Hackettstown Community Hospital*. Attended by Assumption of the Blessed Virgin Mary.

JAMESBURG. *N.J. State Training School for Boys*. Attended by St. James the Less.

LYONS. *U.S. Veterans Medical Center*. Revs. Joseph C. Chacko, William C. Warman (BAL).

MENLO PARK. *Roosevelt State Hospital*. Attended by St. Cecelia, Iselin.

NEW BRUNSWICK. *Robert Wood Johnson University Hospital*. Revs. Thomas P. Ganley, Chap., Michael Onyekwere, S.D.V.

NORTH BRUNSWICK. *Middlesex County Adult Detention Center*. Attended by Our Lady of Peace.

OLD BRIDGE. *Raritan Bay Medical Center-Old Bridge*. Rev. Danilo A. Canceran, Chap.

PERTH AMBOY. *Raritan Bay Medical Center*, Tel: 732-826-2771. Revs. Sean G. Winters, John J. Morley, Chap.

PHILLIPSBURG. *Warren Hospital*, Tel: 908-454-0112. Rev. Mark Kehoe, Chap.

RAHWAY. *East Jersey State Prison*, Tel: 732-634-4355. Attended from St. Andrew Church, Avenel.

SKILLMAN. *NJ State Neuropsychiatric Institute*. Attended by St. Charles Borromeo.

SOMERVILLE. *Somerset Medical Center*, Tel: 908-526-2394. Rev. Andrzej Wieliczko.

SOUTH AMBOY. *South Amboy Memorial Hospital*. Attended by St. Mary and Sacred Heart.

Absent on Sick Leave:
Revs.—
Bihuniak, Michael J.
Desmond, Joseph L.

On Duty Outside the Diocese:
Revs.—
Albaladejo, Juan A., Society of Jesus Christ the Priest
Bochnak, Zenon A., Military Archdiocese
Brighenti, Kenneth D., Mount St. Mary Seminary, Emmitsburg, MD.
Haddad, Wayne M., Military Archdiocese
Lambert, Timothy J., Diocese of Brooklyn
Leonard, Raymond J.
Marin, John L., Society of Jesus Christ the Priest, Guayaquil, Ecuador
Marincioni, Raniero A., Society of Jesus Christ the Priest, Ecuador
McCord, Kent G., Military Archdiocese
Rozembajgier, John M., Pontifical College Josephinum, Columbus, OH
Venditti, J. Michael, Eparchy of Passaic, NJ

Retired:
Rev. Msgrs.—
Capik, William J.
Haughney, William J.
Kasprzyk, Leon J.
Kennedy, J. Nevin
Perini, Armando J.
Szymanski, John B., P.A., V.G.
Torney, John R., P.A.
Revs.—
Attanasio, Raymond V.
Browne, Gerald
Cornejo, Vincent C.
Crowley, R. Kevin
Driscoll, Michael A.
Giordano, John C.
Hemmerling, Henry L.
Hogan, Joseph F.
Kearns, Edward A.
Kelly, Charles F.
McLaughlin, James W.
Muccilli, Sebastian
Perunilam, Thomas V.
Roca, Albert L.
Schellberg, Eugene
Scillieri, Charles P.
Stab, Herbert J.
Stingel, Louis F.
Struzik, Edward J.
Vadakkekara, J. Philip
Walega, Stanley J.

Permanent Deacons:
Abatemarco, Michael, (On Leave)
Albert, Henry F., (On Leave)
Alexander, Russell C., (Retired)
Anderson, Paul L.
Bachynsky, Michael J.
Barr, William J.
Bauer, William R.
Bencosme, Pablo
Berg, Albert K.
Berluche, Enock, Sr.
Bernatchez, Serge
Bertrand, John
Bolash, George L.
Bonfante, Robert, Sr.
Broehl, John H.
Brossoni, Guido J.
Brucato, Michael
Caimi, Ronald J., (Retired)
Cammarano, Frank J.
Campbell, Joseph P.
Caruso, Gregory
Choi, Michael
Cline, Patrick J.
Coleman, George D.
Conroy, Christopher
Coppola, Albert, (On Leave)
Cortez, Noe
Costantino, Samuel J.
Craig, John
Czekaj, John R.
D'Andrea, Lawrence V.
D'Angelo, Gregory R., (Retired)
D'Auguste, Frank C.
D'Mello, Francis
Daley, James M., (Retired)
Damian, Charles J.
Damiano, Samuel J., (Retired)
DeFrange, David A.
Deitchman, John
DeLorenzo, Donald J.
DeMarco, Arnold J.
Demarest, Barry C.
Demkovitz, Russell B.
DePrima, Peter J., Jr.
Di Joseph, John
Dominiecki, Thomas F.
Duffy, Lawrence J.
Dumschat, John F.
Fiore, Philip, (On Leave)
Fitzsimmons, John J., (Retired)
Flynn, John T.
Foldvary, Joseph J., (Retired)
Forrestall, Michael J.
Frank, George A.
Gagliano, Salvatore J., (On Leave)
Gajewski, Stephen J.
Garcia, Enrique
Gatto, Robert E.
Gerling, Robert
Giacobbe, Thomas J.
Gilheany, Thomas J., (Retired)
Gimblett, John, (On Leave)
Gleason, Michael P.
Gonzalez, Phillip
Gostkowski, Anthony J.
Gunther, Stephen
Hally, Luke J.
Hamilton, Kenneth
Hancock, Anthony
Hartmann, Edmund, Jr.
Hearty, Patrick W.
Heissenbuttel, Thomas A., (Retired)
Hendrix, James W., (On Leave)
Holowienka, Edward, (On Leave)
Holzinger, Stephen J., II, (On Leave)
Ibern, Jose, (On Leave)
Ivers, John B., (Retired)
Kaseta, Richard R., (On Leave)
Kelly, James A., Jr.
Kenny, John F.
Kenton, Richard A.
Kern, Stephen F.
Kimball, George F.
Kintis, William
Klaas, Thomas H.
Koy, Martin L., (Retired)
Krupa, Edward, (On Leave)
La Police, George D., (Retired)
Ladao, Rogelio
Laikowski, Stephen N.
Lange, William F.
Lawless, Timothy A.
Licameli, Paul G., (Retired)
Livingston, Joel R.
Long, James A., (On Leave)
Lorenc, Stanley J.
Lupini, Belardino A., (Retired)
Lutomski, Richard
Majkowski, Edward J.
Maksimik, Walter S.
Marano, Francis J., (Retired)
Martinez, Jose M., (On Leave)
Martini, Michael R.
Massimei, Eric S., (Retired)
Maurer, Joseph S., (Retired)
Mayer, Denis
McCarron, Richard
McCarthy, Keith B.
McCormick, James N.
McGann, William B., (On Leave)
McGovern, Robert T.
McGuire, John H.
McShane, John P., (Retired)
Mendoza, Alexander, (On Leave)
Meyer, Michael A.
Michnewicz, Thomas S.
Mikolai, David
Monahan, John T.
Moral, Luis S.
Moscinski, Joseph C.
Mulroy, Martin B., (Retired)
Murtha, Michael P.
Nardi, Samuel, (Retired)
Newton, Gary
O'Brien, Richard
Olegario, Eduardo
Otlowski, Wayne
Ozga, Andrew
Pacifico, John R.
Paolino, Charles
Paulus, Conrad
Payne, Alfred C., Jr., (On Leave)
Perez, Angel P., (Retired)
Perez, Basilio A.
Perez, Corpus V.
Pidgeon, Walter H.
Pizzigoni, Louis, III
Psota, Carl E.
Quinn, Frank J.

Rabinowitz, Roy
Radvanski, John M.
Ragucci, Joseph D.
Raychel, John A.
Reilly, Lawrence P.
Rider, William P.
Ris, Gregory
Rivera, Herminio
Roberts, Earl J., III
Rodes, Edward G.
Ruiz-Diaz, Benigno I.
Russo, Anthony
Rutch, Samuel, (Retired)
Saggese, Joseph P.
San Jose, Danilo C.
Sandoval, Gustavo
Santella, Paul
Semko, Michael
Shelton, John H.
Sheptuck, Paul J.
Sheridan, John T., (Retired)
Sicola, Thomas
Simao, Hugo
Sims, Gerard C.
Stanczak, Joseph J., (Retired)
Stefany, William G.
Strus, Andrew J.
Sullivan, Michael J., Jr.
Tartara, Filippo
Tesoriero, James A.
Tietjen, John R.
Torres, Nelson
Torres, Ramon L.
Van Haute, John B.
Vindas, Luis E.
Webb, Sylvan
Webster, Dennis K., (Retired)
Wislinski, Thaddeus
Wittreich, Helmut
Wojcik, Michael
Yondolino, Thomas C.
Youn, Seock Ro
Yuhas, Frank
Zampella, Donald

INSTITUTIONS LOCATED IN THE DIOCESE

[A] HIGH SCHOOLS, DIOCESAN

EDISON. *Bishop Ahr High School* (1969) One Tingley Ln., 08820. Tel: 732-549-1108; Fax: 732-494-2229. Email: dtrukowski@diometuchen.org. Web: www.bgahs.org. Sr. Donna Marie Trukowski, C.S.S.F., Prin.; Ms. Sharon Taub, Librarian. Felician Sisters 2; Lay Teachers 58; Students 850.

SOUTH AMBOY. *Cardinal McCarrick High School* (1885) 310 Augusta St., 08879. Tel: 732-721-0748; Fax: 732-727-7018. Web: www.cardinalmccarrick.com. Dr. Karen M. Juliano, Ed.D., Prin.; Rev. Msgr. John B. Gordon, Chap. Sisters 3; Lay Teachers 20; Students 285.

[B] HIGH SCHOOLS, PRIVATE

METUCHEN. *St. Joseph High School*, 145 Plainfield Ave., 08840-1099. Tel: 732-549-7600; Fax: 732-549-0664. Web: www.stjoes.org. Mr. Lawrence N. Walsh, Pres.; Bro. Matthew Scanlon, S.C., Religion Chm.; Deacon Richard McCarron, Campus Ministry; Mr. John A. Anderson, Prin.; Mrs. Patricia Brennan, Librarian. Brothers of the Sacred Heart 9; Sisters of St. Joseph (Philadelphia) 2; Lay Teachers 47; Boys 800.

WATCHUNG. *Mount St. Mary Academy* (1908) 07069. Tel: 908-757-0108; Fax: 908-756-5751. Email: lgambacorto@mountsaintmary.org. Web: www.mountsaintmary.org. Sr. Lisa D. Gambacorto, R.S.M., E.D.S., Directress & Prin.; Rev. William T. Morris, Chap.; Joan M. Ruk, Librarian. Day school for girls. College preparatory only. Sisters of Mercy 1; Lay Teachers 33; Girls 317.

[C] INTER-PAROCHIAL ELEMENTARY SCHOOLS

PERTH AMBOY. *Perth Amboy Catholic Primary School*, (Grades PreK-3), 613 Carlock Ave., 08861. Tel: 732-826-5747; Fax: 732-826-6096. Web: www.pacatholic.org. Sisters Beverly Policastro, S.C., Prin.; Dorothy Mary Sajczuk, Librarian. Lay Teachers 7; Students 115.

Perth Amboy Catholic School, (Grades 4-8), 500 State St., 08861. Tel: 732-826-1598; Fax: 732-826-7063. Email: rpiatek@diometuchen.org. Web: www.pacatholicschool.org. Sisters M. Rebecca Piatek, C.S.S.F., Prin.; Dorothy M. Sajczuk, C.S.S.F., Librarian. Lay Teachers 18; Students 124.

SOUTH PLAINFIELD. *Holy Savior Academy*, (Grades PreK-8), 1 Sacred Heart Dr., P.O. Box 1179, 07080-1179. Tel: 908-822-5890; Fax: 908-822-5891. Web: www.holysavioracademy.com. Melinda Hanlon, Prin. Lay Teachers 18; Students 275.

[D] PRE-SCHOOLS

MARTINSVILLE. *Little Friends of Jesus Nursery School*, (Grades N), 1881 Washington Valley Rd., 08836. Tel: 732-667-5272; Fax: 732-667-5277. Sr. Romilda Borges, S.D.V., Prin. Students 45.

[E] SPECIAL SCHOOLS, PRIVATE

NORTH PLAINFIELD. *McAuley School for Exceptional Children* (1966) 107 Westervelt Ave., 07060. Tel: 908-754-4114; Fax: 908-754-3312. Email: mcaschool@aol.com. Web: www.mcauleyschool.org. Sr. Lee Ann Amico, R.S.M., Dir. & Prin. Sisters 2; Lay Teachers 22; Students 35.

[F] CATHOLIC CHARITIES

PERTH AMBOY. *Catholic Charities Central Office*, 319 Maple St., 08861. Tel: 732-324-8200; Fax: 732-826-3549. Web: www.ccdom.org. Marianne Majewski, L.C.S.W., Exec. Dir.; Julio Coto, Asst. Exec. Dir.; Joan Lorah, L.C.S.W., Asst. Exec. Dir.; Christine Benitez, M.B.A., CPA, CFO; Douglas J. Susan, J.D., Dir. Compliance.

Bridgewater Family Service Center, 540 U.S. Rte. 22 E., Bridgewater, 08807. Tel: 908-722-1881; Fax: 908-704-0215. Web: ccdom.org. LuAnn Dias, Svc. Area Dir.

East Brunswick Family Service Center, 288 Rues Ln., East Brunswick, 08816. Tel: 732-257-6100; Fax: 732-651-9834. Web: www.ccdom.org. Ann Basil, L.C.S.W., Svc. Area Dir.

Catholic Charities, Edison Family Service Center, 26 Safran Ave., Edison, 08837. Tel: 732-738-1323; Fax: 732-738-3896. Web: www.ccdom.org. Wesley R. Moore, M.Div., B.S., C.S.W., Svc. Area Dir.

Flemington Family Service Center, 6 Park Ave., Flemington, 08822. Tel: 908-782-7905; Fax: 908-782-5934. Web: www.ccdom.org. Martha Rezeli, M.A., C.S.W., Svc. Area Dir.

Trinity Family Services of Catholic Charities, 271 Smith St., 08861. Tel: 732-826-9160; Fax: 732-826-8342. Web: www.ccdom.org. Ernest C. Revoir, Svc. Area Dir.

Phillipsburg Family Service Center, 700 Sayre Ave., Phillipsburg, 08865. Tel: 908-454-2074; Fax: 908-454-9871. Web: www.ccdom.org. Marci Booth, Svc. Area Dir.

Social Service Center (1982) 372 S. Main St., Phillipsburg, 08865. Tel: 908-859-5447; Fax: 908-859-6375. Email: mpopovice@ccdom.org. Sr. M. Michaelita Popovice, R.S.M., Prog. Dir.

The Ozanam Shelter for Families and Single Women, 89 Truman Dr., Edison, 08817. Tel: 732-985-0327; Fax: 732-985-2449. Web: www.ccdom.org. Wesley R. Moore, M.Div., B.S., C.S.W., Svc. Area Dir.

Catholic Charities Ozanam Inn, 20-22 Abeel St., New Brunswick, 08901. Tel: 732-729-0850; Fax: 732-729-0794. Web: www.ccdom.org. Wesley R. Moore, M.Div., B.S., C.S.W., Svc. Area Dir.

St. John's Health & Family Service Center, 24 Abeel St., New Brunswick, 08901. Tel: 732-745-9800; Fax: 732-745-9107. Web: www.ccdom.org. Ernest C. Revoir, Svc. Area Dir.

Community House at St. Thomas, 124 Bentley Ave., Old Bridge, 08857. Tel: 732-251-0022; Fax: 732-251-3482. Web: www.ccdom.org. Susan Kuzma, Case Mgr.; Joan Lorah, L.C.S.W., L.C.S.W. Exec. Dir.

Metuchen Community Services Corporation, 319 Maple St., 08861. Tel: 732-324-8200; Fax: 732-826-3549. Email: jlorah@ccdom.org. Joan Lorah, Exec. Dir.

Bakhita House, 702 Sayre Ave., Phillipsburg, 08865. Tel: 908-454-0912; Fax: 908-454-3085. Web: www.c-cdom.org. Marci Booth, Svc. Area Dir.

Community Child Care Solutions, 103 Center St., 08861. Tel: 732-324-4357; Fax: 732-826-4136.

[G] GENERAL HOSPITALS

NEW BRUNSWICK. *Saint Peter's Healthcare System, Inc.*, 254 Easton Ave., 08901. Tel: 732-745-8588; Fax: 732-745-9099.

Saint Peter's Foundation, 254 Easton Ave., 08901. Tel: 732-745-8542; Fax: 732-745-7573.

Saint Peter's Health & Management Services Corporation, 254 Easton Ave., 08901. Tel: 732-745-8556; Fax: 732-745-9099.

Saint Peter's Properties Corporation, Inc., 254 Easton Ave., 08901. Tel: 732-745-8588; Fax: 732-745-9099.

Saint Peter's University Hospital (1907) 254 Easton Ave., P.O. Box 591, 08903-0591. Tel: 732-745-8600; Fax: 732-745-9099. Email: kkillion@saintpetersuh.com. Web: www.saintpetersuh.com. Revs. A. David Chalackal, C.M.I., Chap.; Lazaro Perez, Chap.; Sisters Barbara Ortmann, O.P.; Mary Jane Bransfield, I.H.M.; James Jones. Bed Capacity 478; Bassinets 81; Neonatal Intensive Care Bassinetts 35; Intermediate Care Bassinetts 19; Patients Assisted Annually 348,500; Total Staff 2,927.

[H] HOMES FOR AGED

SOMERSET. *McCarrick Care Center*, 15 Dellwood Ln., 08873. Tel: 732-545-4200; Fax: 732-846-1089. James F. Caron, Admin.; Rev. Thomas P. Ganley, Chap.; Peg Bradley, Dir. Admissions. Patients Assisted Annually 1,875. In Res. Rev. Msgr. Leon J. Kasprzyk (Retired); Rev. Gerald Browne (Retired).

WOODBRIDGE. *St. Joseph Assisted Living*, One St. Joseph Terr., 07095. Tel: 732-634-0004; Fax: 732-634-4586. Sr. Jadwiga Zaremba, L.S.I.C., Admin.

St. Joseph Home, Assisted Living and Nursing Center Little Servant Sisters 8; Residents 56; Staff 32.

St. Joseph Nursing Home, 3 St. Joseph Ter., 07095. Little Servant Sisters 4; Bed Capacity 51; Staff 58.

[I] MONASTERIES AND RESIDENCES FOR PRIESTS AND BROTHERS

METUCHEN. *Brothers of the Sacred Heart* (1901) 145 Plainfield Ave., 08840. Tel: 732-548-2292; Fax: 732-548-3101. Bros. Ron Travers, S.C., Supr.; Ronald Cairns, S.C.; Kevin Finnegan, S.C.; Paul LaFonte, S.C.; Richard Leven, S.C.; Julian Przytulski, S.C.; Matthew Scanlon, S.C.; Aldric Smith, S.C.; John Spalding, S.C.; Michael Yerkes, S.C. Brothers 10.

NEW BRUNSWICK. *The New Brunswick Congregation of the Oratory of St. Philip Neri*, 94 Somerset St., 08901. Tel: 732-545-6820; Fax: 732-545-4069. Email: oratorians@nboratory.org. Web: www.nboratory.org. Very Rev. Peter Cebulka, C.O., Provost; Revs. Thomas A. Odorizzi, C.O., Vicar & Treas.; Kevin Kelly, C.O.; Jeffrey Calia, C.O., Sec. Priests 4.

RARITAN. *Clairvaux House*, 52 W. Somerset St., 08869. Tel: 908-722-1489; Fax: 908-393-4978. Web: shrine.cnjnet.com. Rev. Guy W. Selvester.

SAYREVILLE. *Federation of the Brothers of the Sacred Heart*, 219 MacArthur Ave., 08872. Tel: 718-522-3309.

SOMERSET. *Consolata Society for Foreign Missions* (1901) *Provincial Headquarters*, 2301 Rt. 27, P.O. Box 5550, 08875-5550. Tel: 732-297-9191; Fax: 732-940-3121. Email: supreus@consolata.net. Web: www.consolata.org. Revs. Robert Rezac, I.M.C., Prov. Supr.; David Kamau Gikonyo, I.M.C.; Van Allen Hager, I.M.C.; Paul Stefanowich, I.M.C.

Maria Regina Residence, 5 Dellwood Ln., 08873. Tel: 732-828-6800; Fax: 732-828-7206. Rev. Msgrs. John B. Szymanski, P.A., V.G., Dir. (Retired); William J. Haughney (Retired); J. Nevin Kennedy (Retired); Revs. Neil W. Davin, C.P., J.C.L.; Joseph L. Desmond; Thomas P. Ganley; Charles F. Kelly (Retired); Herbert J. Stab (Retired); Louis F. Stingel (Retired); Edward J. Struzik (Retired); A. Gregory Uhrig; Sisters M. Paula Tobben, F.S.G.M., Mgr.; M. Jessica Herbold, F.S.G.M. Retirement home for Diocesan priests.

[J] CONVENTS AND RESIDENCES FOR SISTERS

METUCHEN. *St. Clare Convent*, 52 Elm Ave., 08840. Tel: 732-549-7598. Felician Sisters 2.

St. Francis Convent, 44 Elm Ave., 08840. Tel: 732-549-3050. Sisters of Christian Charity 2.

BELVIDERE. *Augustinian Recollect Sisters*, 743 Water St., 07823. Tel: 973-757-2432. Sr. Beatriz Garcia Sanchez, Contact Person. Sisters 10.

EAST BRUNSWICK. *DePaul House - Daughters of Charity of St. Vincent de Paul*, 528 Ryders Ln., 08816. Tel: 732-238-3638. Email: dcebnj@comcast.net. Web: www.dc-northeast.org. Sisters 4.

EDISON. *St. Thomas Aquinas Convent* (1969) 15 Wren Ct., 08820. Tel: 732-321-0137; Fax: 732-549-9050. Email: srcynthia@bgahs.org. Sisters Cynthia Marie Babyak, C.S.S.F., Local Min.; Donna Marie Trukowski, C.S.S.F.; Mary Charles Wienckoski, C.S.S.F. Sisters 3.

FLEMINGTON. *The Carmel of Mary Immaculate and St. Mary Magdalen*, 26 Harmony School Rd., 08822. Tel: 908-782-4802. Web: www.flemingtoncarmel.org. Rev. Dominic Nattunilam, C.M.I., Chap. Nuns Professed with Solemn Vows 15; Novices 2.

MARTINSVILLE. *Blessed Sacrament Convent*, 1881 Washington Valley Rd., 08836. Tel: 732-667-5275; Fax: 732-667-5277. Sr. Romilda Borges, S.D.V., Local Supr. Vocationist Sisters 6.

NEW BRUNSWICK. *Sisters of St. Joseph of Peace* (1884) 61 Jefferson Ave., 08901. Tel: 732-249-5644. Email: jrusch@saintpetersuh.com. Sisters 2.

PISCATAWAY. *St. Joseph of Chestnut Hill*, 137 Metlars Ln., 08854. Tel: 732-393-9640. Email: metlarslane@yahoo.com. Sisters 3.

SOMERSET. *St. Elizabeth Convent*, 13 Renfro Rd., 08873. Tel: 732-247-3697. Email: vocations@altonfranciscans.org. Sr. M. Paula Tobben, F.S.G.M., Supr. Sisters 5.

WATCHUNG. *McAuley Hall Inc.*, 1633 U.S. Hwy 22, 07069-6505. Tel: 908-754-3663; Fax: 908-754-3502. Retired Sisters 50.

Mount St. Mary, 1645 U.S. Hwy. 22 W., 07069-6587. Tel: 908-756-0994; Fax: 908-754-0164. Web: www.mercymidatlantic.org. Sr. Patricia Vetrano, R.S.M. Professed Sisters in Residence 16.

WOODBRIDGE. *St. Joseph Convent*, 184 Amboy Ave., 07095. Tel: 732-634-0807; Fax: 732-634-7888. Email: lsicmaria@aol.com. Sr. Maria Pietrzyk, L.S.I.C., Supr. Sisters 8.

St. Joseph Home Convent, 3 Woodbridge Ter., 07095. Tel: 732-634-0004; Fax: 732-634-4586. Sr. Elizbieta Lopatka, L.S.I.C., Supr. Little Servant Sisters 14.

[K] RETREAT HOUSES

BELVIDERE. *Augustinian Recollect Sisters*, 743 Water St., 07823. Tel: 973-757-2432. Sr. Beatriz Garcia Sanchez, Contact Person. Sisters 5.

FLEMINGTON. *Our Lady of Providence*, 31 Britton Dr., 08822. Tel: 908-782-4495. Sr. Jean, L.S.P., Dir. Little Sisters of the Poor.

MILFORD. *Bethany Ridge*, 914 Milford-Warren Glen Rd., 08848. Tel: 908-995-9758; Fax: 908-995-7299. Rev. Czeslaw Zalubski, S.D.B., Dir. Spirituality Center for Priests.

WATCHUNG. *Mt. St. Mary House of Prayer* (1976) 1651 U.S. Hwy. 22, 07069-6587. Tel: 908-753-2091; Fax: 908-757-0792. Email: msmhope@msmhope.org. Web: www.msmhope.org. Sisters Theresina Flannery, R.S.M., Co-Dir.; Eileen P. Smith, R.S.M., Co-Dir.; Mary Jo Kearns, R.S.M., Co-Dir. Sisters 3.

[L] SHRINES AND PUBLIC ORATORIES

BERNARDSVILLE. *Sacred Heart Chapel* , (Chapel of Convenience), Bernards Ave., 07924. Tel: 908-766-0079; Fax: 908-766-1185. *Our Lady of Perpetual Help*, 111 Claremont Ave., 07924. Rev. Msgr. John N. Fell, S.T.D., Pastor.

RARITAN. *Shrine Chapel of the Blessed Sacrament* 50 W. Somerset St., 08869. Tel: 908-722-1489; Fax: 908-393-4978. Email: shrinechapel@yahoo.com. Web: http://shrine.cnjnet.com. Rev. Guy W. Selvester, Rector.

WASHINGTON. *National World Apostolate of Fatima, USA, Inc. Blue Army Shrine of the Immaculate Heart of Mary* P.O. Box 976, 07882. Tel: 908-689-1700; Fax: 908-689-0721. Email: service@bluearmy.com. Web: www.wafusa.org.

[M] PUBLIC ASSOCIATIONS OF THE FAITHFUL

BLOOMSBURY. *Sisters of Jesus Our Hope* (1992) 376 Bellis Rd., 08804. Tel: 908-995-7261; Fax: 908-995-7262. Web: www.sistersofjesusourhope.org. Sr. Claire Marie Lessard, S.J.H., Community Sister Servant. Sisters 8.

BOUND BROOK. *Sisters of Jesus Our Hope* (1992) 514 Church St., 08805. Tel: 732-271-5777. Web: www.sistersofjesusourhope.org. Sr. Ellen Kraft, S.J.H., Sister Servant. Sisters 3.

FLEMINGTON. *Dominican Sisters of Divine Providence* (1982) 25 Harmony School Rd., 08822. Tel: 908-782-1504; Fax: 908-788-7394. Email: smtolp@yahoo.com. Sr. M. Trinitas Sullivan, O.P., Supr. Sisters 3.

Sisters of Jesus Our Hope, 83 Bonnell St., 08822. Tel: 908-806-3332. Web: www.sistersofjesusourhope.org. Sr. Christine Quense, S.J.H., Sister Servant. Sisters 3.

OXFORD. *The Anawim Community* (1975) 354 Jonestown Rd., P.O. Box 207, 07863. Tel: 908-453-3886; 908-916-5202; Fax: 908-453-3786. Email: oxford@anawim.com. Web: www.anawim.com. Rev. Daniel H. Healy, Dir.; Very Rev. Richard M. Rusk, Missions Dir. & Vocations Dir. Priests 2; Staff 15.

STEWARTSVILLE. *Society of Jesus Christ the Priest*, 70 Edison Rd., P.O. Box 157, 08886. Tel: 908-213-1447; Fax: 908-859-5210. Email: meadwater@verizon.net. Revs. Lope D. Pascual, Nat. Dir.; Jose Lorente; Manuel Lorente; Raymond L. Nacarino, Treas.

[N] CAMPUS MINISTRY

NEW BRUNSWICK. *Catholic Center at Rutgers University* 84 Somerset St., 08901. Tel: 732-545-6663; Fax: 732-545-3495. Email: coldon@rci.rutgers.edu. Web: www.catholic-center.rutgers.edu. Very Rev. Peter Cebulka, C.O., Chap.; Rev. Keith Cervine, Chap.; Bros. Ken Apuzzo, B.H., Dir.; Patrick Reilly, B.H.; Sr. Ellen Kraft, S.J.H.

[O] MISCELLANEOUS LISTINGS

METUCHEN. *The Foundation for Catholic Education*, P.O. Box 191, 08840. Most Rev. Paul G. Bootkoski, D.D.

The Fund for the Future, Inc., P.O. Box 191, 08840. Most Rev. Paul G. Bootkoski, D.D.

The Priestly Education Fund, Inc., P.O. Box 191, 08840. Most Rev. Paul G. Bootkoski, D.D.

The Retirement Plan for the Priests of the Diocese of Metuchen, P.O. Box 191, 08840.

SOMERSET. *The Center for Great Expectations, Inc.*, 19 B Dellwood Ln., 08873. Tel: 732-247-7003, Ext. 27; Fax: 732-247-7043. Web: www.thecenterforgreatexpectations.org. Mrs. Peg Wright, Pres.

WOODBRIDGE. *Mt. Carmel Home Nursing Service*, 184 Amboy Ave., 07095. Tel: 732-634-0807; Fax: 732-634-7888. Sr. Maria Wojcik, L.S.I.C., Dir.

RELIGIOUS INSTITUTES OF MEN REPRESENTED IN THE DIOCESE

For further details refer to the corresponding bracketed number in the Religious Institutes of Men or Women section.

[]—*Brotherhood of Hope*—B.H.
[1100]—*Brothers of the Sacred Heart*—S.C.
[0470]—*The Capuchin Friars*—O.F.M.Cap.
[0275]—*Carmelites of Mary Immaculate*—C.M.I.
[0360]—*Claretian Missionaries* (Eastern Prov.)—C.M.F.
[0390]—*Consolata Missionaries*—I.M.C.
[0520]—*Franciscan Friars* (Custody of St. John Capistran)—O.F.M.
[0950]—*Oratorians*—C.O.
[]—*Order of Discaleed Carmelites*—O.C.D.
[]—*Order of Friars Minor Capachin*—O.F.M.Cap.
[1070]—*Redemptorist Fathers*—C.Ss.R.
[1190]—*Salesians of Don Bosco*—S.D.B.
[1340]—*Society of Divine Vocations*—S.D.V.
[1200]—*Society of the Divine Savior*—S.D.S.
[1335]—*Vincentian Retreat Master*—V.C.

RELIGIOUS INSTITUTES OF WOMEN REPRESENTED IN THE DIOCESE

[]—*Augustinian Recollects*—O.A.R.
[1810]—*Bernardine Sisters of the Third Order of St. Francis*—O.S.F.
[3820]—*Congregation of St. John the Baptist*—C.S.J.B.
[0760]—*Daughters of Charity of St. Vincent De Paul* (Albany Prov.)—D.C.
[0420]—*Discalced Carmelite Nuns*—O.C.D.
[1070-18]—*Dominican Sisters* (Caldwell)—O.P.
[]—*Dominican Sisters of Divine Providence*—O.P.
[1070-06]—*Dominican Sisters of Hope* (Ossining, N.Y.)—O.P.
[1170]—*Felician Sisters* (Our Lady of Hope Prov.)—C.S.S.F.
[1180]—*Franciscan Sisters of Allegany* (St. Bonaventure, NY)—O.S.F.
[]—*Franciscan Sisters of Atonement*
[2575]—*Institute of the Sisters of Mercy of the Americas*—R.S.M.
[2300]—*Little Servant Sisters of the Immaculate Conception*—L.S.I.C.
[2340]—*Little Sisters of the Poor* (Brooklyn Prov.)—L.S.P.
[]—*Marionite of the Holy Cross*—M.S.C.
[2700]—*Missionary Catechists of the Sacred Hearts of Jesus and Mary*—M.C.S.H.
[]—*Missionary Sisters of the Immaculate Conception*—S.M.I.C.
[2810]—*Missionary Sisters of the Mother of God* (Byzantine-Ukrainian)—M.S.M.G.
[3320]—*Presentation of the Blessed Virgin Mary* (New Windsor, NY)—P.B.V.M.
[3430]—*Religious Teachers Filippini* (St. Lucy Prov.)—M.P.F.
[1700]—*School Sisters of the Third Order of St. Francis*—O.S.F.
[0590]—*Sisters of Charity of Saint Elizabeth, Convent Station*—S.C.
[0660]—*Sisters of Christian Charity* (North American Eastern Prov.)—S.C.C.
[]—*Sisters of Jesus Our Hope*—S.J.H.
[3893]—*Sisters of Saint Joseph of Chestnut Hill, Philadelphia*—S.S.J.
[]—*Sisters of St. Francis of Philadelphia*
[1600]—*Sisters of St. Francis of the Martyr St. George*—F.S.G.M.
[2170]—*Sisters Servants of the Immaculate Heart of Mary*—I.H.M.
[]—*Trinitarium Sisters of Redemptor Homini*—T.R.H.
[4210]—*Vocationist Sisters*—S.V.D.

DIOCESAN CEMETERIES

EAST BRUNSWICK. *The Crematory at Holy Cross Burial Park*, 840 Cranbury Rd., 08816.

JAMESBURG. *Holy Cross Burial Park, Diocese of Metuchen Office of Cemeteries Resurrection Cemetery & Mausoleum*, 899 Lincoln Ave., Piscataway, 08854. Tel: 732-463-1424; Fax: 732-463-8807. Mary Ellen Gerity, Dir.

PISCATAWAY. *Resurrection Burial Park, Diocese of Metuchen Office of Cemeteries Resurrection Cemetery & Mausoleum*, 899 Lincoln Ave., 08854. Tel: 732-463-1424; Fax: 732-463-8807. Mary Ellen Gerity, Dir.

NECROLOGY

† Endebrock, Rev. Msgr. Donald M., Carteret, NJ St. Joseph.—Died Oct. 8, 2011

† Santa Barbara, Robert L., New Brunswick, NJ St. Mary of Mt. Virgin.—Died Nov. 30, 2011

An asterisk (*) denotes an organization that has established tax-exempt status directly with the IRS and is not covered by the USCCB Group Ruling.

Archdiocese of Miami

(Archidioecesis Miamiensis)

Most Reverend

THOMAS G. WENSKI

Archbishop of Miami; ordained May 15, 1976; appointed Titular Bishop of Kearney and Auxiliary Bishop of Miami June 24, 1997; consecrated September 3, 1997; appointed Coadjutor Bishop of Orlando July 1, 2003; installed August 22, 2003; appointed Fourth Bishop of Orlando November 13, 2004; appointed Archbishop of Miami April 20, 2010; installed June 1, 2010.

Most Reverend

JOHN C. FAVALORA, D.D.

Retired Archbishop of Miami; ordained December 20, 1961; appointed Bishop of Alexandria June 16, 1986; ordained and installed July 29, 1986; appointed Third Bishop of St. Petersburg March 7, 1989; installed May 16, 1989; appointed Third Archbishop of Miami November 3, 1994; installed December 20, 1994; retired April 20, 2010. *Office: 9401 Biscayne Blvd., Miami Shores, FL 33138.*

Pastoral Center: 9401 Biscayne Blvd., Miami Shores, FL 33138. Tel: 305-757-6241; Fax: 305-754-1897.

Web: www.archdioceseofmiami.org

Email: information@theadom.org

ESTABLISHED AUGUST 13, 1958.

Square Miles 4,958.

Created an Archbishopric, June 13, 1968.

Comprises the Counties in the southern part of the State of Florida, namely, Broward, Miami-Dade and Monroe.

For legal titles of Parishes and Archdiocesan institutions, consult the Pastoral Center.

STATISTICAL OVERVIEW

Personnel	
Archbishops	1
Retired Archbishops	1
Retired Bishops	1
Priests: Diocesan Active in Diocese	154
Priests: Diocesan Active Outside Diocese	8
Priests: Diocesan in Foreign Missions	1
Priests: Retired, Sick or Absent	72
Number of Diocesan Priests	235
Religious Priests in Diocese	61
Total Priests in Diocese	296
Extern Priests in Diocese	31
Ordinations:	
Religious Priests	2
Transitional Deacons	1
Permanent Deacons	10
Permanent Deacons in Diocese	161
Total Brothers	48
Total Sisters	277
Parishes	
Parishes	102
With Resident Pastor:	
Resident Diocesan Priests	94
Resident Religious Priests	8
Missions	4
Pastoral Centers	1
New Parishes Created	2
Professional Ministry Personnel:	
Brothers	1
Sisters	34
Lay Ministers	105
Welfare	
Catholic Hospitals	4
Total Assisted	871,781
Health Care Centers	9
Total Assisted	19,675
Homes for the Aged	3
Total Assisted	2,886
Residential Care of Children	2
Total Assisted	283
Day Care Centers	11
Total Assisted	3,233
Specialized Homes	7
Total Assisted	15,352
Special Centers for Social Services	26
Total Assisted	111,059
Residential Care of Disabled	1
Total Assisted	112
Other Institutions	4
Total Assisted	1,874
Educational	
Seminaries, Diocesan	2
Students from This Diocese	32
Students from Other Diocese	46
Diocesan Students in Other Seminaries	15
Students Religious	3
Total Seminarians	50
Colleges and Universities	3
Total Students	11,519
High Schools, Diocesan and Parish	9
Total Students	9,309
High Schools, Private	4
Total Students	3,153
Elementary Schools, Diocesan and Parish	50
Total Students	20,376
Elementary Schools, Private	2
Total Students	1,068
Non-residential Schools for the Disabled	1
Total Students	1,000
Catechesis/Religious Education:	
High School Students	4,077
Elementary Students	29,784
Total Students under Catholic Instruction	80,336
Teachers in the Diocese:	
Priests	25
Brothers	19
Sisters	45
Lay Teachers	3,324
Vital Statistics	
Receptions into the Church:	
Infant Baptism Totals	12,173
Minor Baptism Totals	912
Adult Baptism Totals	547
Received into Full Communion	880
First Communions	11,215
Confirmations	8,503
Marriages:	
Catholic	1,709
Interfaith	190
Total Marriages	1,899
Deaths	4,195
Total Catholic Population	733,876
Total Population	4,317,591

Former Archbishops—Most Revs. COLEMAN F. CARROLL, D.D., ord. June 15, 1930; appt. Titular Bishop of Pitanae and Auxiliary Bishop of Pittsburgh, Aug. 25, 1953; cons. Nov. 10, 1953; appt. first Bishop of Miami, Aug. 13, 1958; installed Oct. 7, 1958; appt. Archbishop of Miami, March 13, 1968; died July 26, 1977; EDWARD A. MCCARTHY, D.D., S.T.D., J.C.D., ord. May 29, 1943; appt. Coadjutor Archbishop of Miami "cum jure successionis," Sept. 17, 1976; appt. Archbishop of Miami, July 26, 1977; retired Nov. 3, 1994; died June 7, 2005; JOHN C. FAVALORA, D.D., S.T.L., M.Ed. (Retired), ord. Dec. 20, 1961; appt. Bishop of Alexandria June 16, 1986; ord. and installed July 29, 1986; appt. Third Bishop of St. Petersburg March 7, 1989; installed May 16, 1989; appt. Third Bishop of Miami Nov. 3, 1994; installed Dec. 20, 1994; retired April 20, 2010.

Pastoral Center—9401 Biscayne Blvd., Miami Shores, 33138. Tel: 305-757-6241; Fax: 305-754-1897.

Vicar General—Very Rev. CHANEL JEANTY, J.C.L., V.G.

Chancellors—Sr. ELIZABETH ANNE WORLEY, S.S.J., Chancellor for Admin. & COO. Tel: 305-762-1284. Email: eworley@theadom.org; Very Rev. CHANEL JEANTY, J.C.L., V.G., Chancellor Canonical Affairs. Tel: 305-762-1262. Email: cjeanty@theadom.org.

Priest Secretary to the Archbishop—Rev. RICHARD J. VIGOA. Tel: 305-762-1232. Email: rvigoa@theadom.org.

Metropolitan Tribunal— Address all Rogatory commissions and matrimonial matters to the Tribunal, *9401 Biscayne Blvd., Miami Shores, 33138.* Tel: 305-762-1161; Fax: 305-762-1178. Email: tribunal@theadom.org.

Judicial Vicar—Very Rev. GEORGE PUTHUSSERIL, V.F., J.C.D.

Adjutant Judicial Vicar—Rev. Msgr. KENNETH K. SCHWANGER, J.C.D.

Judges—Rev. Msgrs. ANDREW ANDERSON, J.C.D.; TOMAS M. MARIN, J.C.L.; Very Rev. CHANEL JEANTY, J.C.L., V.G.; Revs. FERNANDO HERIA, J.C.L.; MARK THOMAS REEVES, J.C.L. (Retired); JUDE EZEANOKWASA, J.C.D.; ALVARO PINZON, J.C.D.; FRANCIS CANCRO, J.C.D.; PHILLIP SCARCELLA, J.C.D.; JOSE BIAIN, O.F.M.; Sr. JEANNE-MARGARET MCNALLY, J.C.L., Ph.D.; Dr. STEFANO BENIGNI, J.C.D.; Dr. LUIGI SALVANESCHI, J.C.D.

Promoter of Justice—Rev. Msgr. KENNETH K. SCHWANGER, J.C.D., (non-matrimonial cases).

Defenders of the Bond—Revs. KENNETH D. WHITTAKER, J.C.L.; ALVARO PINZON, J.C.D.; MATHEW THUNDATHIL, J.C.D.; RONALD PUSAK, J.C.L. (Retired).

Notaries—Ms. GORETTI ANTHONY; Ms. KATIA ARRIAZA; Ms. MAITE LENOZ.

Assessors—Mrs. DEE DUGGAN; Mr. ROBERTO AGUIRRE.

Advocates—Deacon ANTONIO MACEO; Mrs. PAULETTE VITALE; Mrs. LOURDES CHAVEZ.

Counsel-Assistant to the Tribunal—Mr. J. PATRICK FITZGERALD, Esq.

Consultors—Rev. Msgr. PABLO A. NAVARRO, V.F.; Very Revs. CHANEL JEANTY, J.C.L., V.G.; THOMAS O'DWYER, V.F.; GEORGE PUTHUSSERIL, V.F., J.C.D.; ROBERTO GARZA; Revs. DANIEL I. KUBALA; PAUL VUTURO; JUAN CARLOS PAGUAGA.

Deans and Deaneries—Very Revs. MICHAEL GREER, V.F., (Northeast Broward); ABEL BARAJAS, V.F., (Northwest Broward); THOMAS O'DWYER, V.F., (South Broward); CHRISTOPHER MARINO, V.F., (East Dade); FEDERICO CAPDEPON, V.F., (Northeast Dade); JESUS J. ARIAS, V.F., (West Dade); GERALD R. MORRIS, V.F., (Monroe); Very Rev. Msgrs. PABLO NAVARRO, V.F., (South Dade); OSCAR CASTANEDA, V.F., (Northwest Dade).

Presbyteral Council—

President—Most Rev. THOMAS G. WENSKI, D.D.

Chairman—Rev. DANIEL I. KUBALA.

Secretary—Rev. ROBERTO M. CID.

Ex Officio—Rev. Msgr. TERENCE HOGAN, S.L.D.; Very Revs. CHANEL JEANTY, J.C.L., V.G.; ROBERTO GARZA.

Northwest Broward Deanery—Very Rev. GEORGE PUTHUSSERIL, V.F., J.C.D.

Northeast Broward Deanery—Rev. THOMAS F. FOUDY.

South Broward Deanery—Very Rev. THOMAS O'DWYER, V.F.

Northwest Dade Deanery—Rev. JOSE ESPINO.

Northeast Dade Deanery—Very Rev. FEDERICO CAPDEPON, V.F.

West Dade Deanery—Rev. DANIEL I. KUBALA.

East Dade Deanery—Very Rev. CHRISTOPHER MARINO, V.F.

South Dade Deanery—Rev. ALEJANDRO J. RODRIGUEZ.

Monroe Deanery—Very Rev. GERALD R. MORRIS, V.F.

Age Group I—Rev. JUAN CARLOS PAGUAGA.

Age Group II—Rev. PAUL VUTURO.

Age Group III—Rev. MICHAEL HOURIGAN.

Incardinated Priests—Rev. Msgr. PABLO A. NAVARRO, V.F.

Religious Priests—Rev. ALEJANDRO ROQUE, O.M.I.

Non-Incardinated Priests—Rev. ERNEST BIRIRUKA.

Incardinated Retired Priests—Rev. DAVID RUSSELL (Retired).

Appointed by the Archbishop—Very Revs. MICHAEL GREER, V.F.; ABEL BARAJAS, V.F.; JESUS J. ARIAS, V.F.; Revs. JAMES F. FETSCHER; ROBERTO M. CID; LESLY JEAN; KLEMENS DABROWSKI, S.Ch.

Ministry of General Services

Chancellor for Administration and COO—Sr. ELIZABETH ANNE WORLEY, S.S.J. Tel: 305-762-1284; Cell: 305-450-6420. Email: eworley@theadom.org.

Catholic Legal Services, Archdiocese of Miami, Inc.—RANDOLPH P. MCGRORTY, CEO; MYRIAM MEZADIEU, Chief Admin., Main Office: Ingraham Bldg., 25 S.E. Second Ave., Ste. 220, Miami, 33131. Tel: 305-373-1073; Fax: 305-373-1173. Web: cclsmiami.org; Miami Springs Office: 700 S. Royal Poinciana Blvd., Ste. 800, Miami Springs, 33166. Tel: 305-887-8333; Fax: 305-883-4498. Broward Office: 3661 W. Oakland Park Blvd., Ste. 305, Lauderdale Lakes, 33311. Tel: 800-691-7530; Fax: 800-691-5230.

Legal Services—Mr. PATRICK FITZGERALD, 110 Merrick Way, Ste. 3-B, Coral Gables, 33134. Tel: 305-443-9162; Fax: 305-443-6613.

Archdiocesan Safe Environment Program—MARY ROSS AGOSTA, Dir. Tel: 305-762-1043; Deacon RICHARD A. TURCOTTE, Ph.D., Victim Asst. Coord. Tel: 866-802-2873.

Communications - Media Relations—MARY ROSS AGOSTA, Dir.; ROSA QUIROZ, Media Coord. & Digital Specialist.

"The Florida Catholic"—ANA RODRIGUEZ-SOTO, Editor (English). Tel: 305-762-1131; Fax: 305-762-1132.

Pax Catholic Communications—1779 N.W. 28th St., Miami, 33142. Tel: 305-638-9729; Fax: 305-636-4571. Web: www.paxcc.org. Rev. ROBERTO M. CID, Gen. Mgr. Tel: 305-635-1331; Fax: 305-635-2031. Email: rmcid@paxcc.org.

Radio Paz - WACC 830 AM— 24-hour Spanish satellite radio.

Spirit Online Radio— 24-hour English Internet radio.

Radio Paz Musical— 24-hour Spanish Religious Music service - Internet.

Office of Ecumenical and Inter-Faith Relations—Rev. PATRICK H. O'NEILL, Dir.; Rev. Msgr. TERENCE HOGAN, S.L.D., Assoc. Ecumenical Officer, (Miami-Dade County); Rev. RICHARD MULLEN, O.S.A., Assoc. Ecumenical Officer, (Broward County), 9401 Biscayne Blvd., Miami Shores, 33138. Tel: 305-762-1254; Fax: 305-754-1897.

Ministry of Faith Formation

Senior Director of Faith Formation and Superintendent of Schools—KIM PRYZBYLSKI, Ph.D. Tel: 305-762-1078. Email: kpryzbylski@theadom.org.

Associate Superintendent of Schools—DONALD EDWARDS, Ph.D. Tel: 305-762-1018. Email: dedwards@theadom.org.

Office of Schools—KRISTEN HUGHES, Assoc. Supt. Schools. Tel: 305-762-1074. Email: khughes@theadom.org; ADINA VICTOR, Coord. Curriculum & Assessment. Tel: 305-762-1040. Email: avictor@theadom.org.

Office of Catechesis—PETER J. DUCTRAM, Dir. Tel: 305-762-1090. Email: pductram@theadom.org.

Office of Lay Ministry and Adult Faith Formation—CHERYL J. ORWIG WHAPHAM, Dir. Tel: 305-762-1084. Email: cwhapham@theadom.org; Mr. ROGELIO ZELADA, Assoc. Dir. Tel: 305-762-1187. Email: rzelada@theadom.org.

Archdiocese of Miami Endowment Fund, Inc.—

Archdiocese of Miami Endowment Fund, Inc.—Mrs. KATIE BLANCO CROCQUET, Pres. Tel: 305-762-1053. Email: kblanco@theadom.org.

Development and Stewardship Office—Tel: 305-762-1243.

**Catholic Community Foundation in the Archdiocese of Miami, Inc.* Mr. THOMAS BEIER, Chm.

Ministry of Catholic Charities—

Catholic Charities of the Archdiocese of Miami, Inc.—1505 N.E. 26th St., Wilton Manors, 33305. Tel: 305-754-2444; Fax: 305-754-6669. Web: www.ccadm.org. Deacon RICHARD A. TURCOTTE, Ph.D., CEO; Very Rev. ROBERTO GARZA, Dir. Mission Effectiveness; LIZETH CAMARENA, CAO. Email: lcamarena@ccadom.org; JULES JONES, CFO. Email: jjones@ccadom.org.

Social Advocacy—Deacon RICHARD A. TURCOTTE, Ph.D.

Catholic Campaign for Human Development—1505 N.E. 26th St., Wilton Manors, 33305. Tel: 305-754-2444; Fax: 305-754-6649.

Miami-Dade Region—

Elderly Services Congregate Meals—9900 N.E. 2nd Ave., Miami, 33138. Tel: 305-751-5203. Email: congregatemeals@ccadm.org.

Refugee Resettlement and Employment Services—700 S. Royal Poinciana, Ste. 800, Miami Springs, 33166. Tel: 305-883-4555; Fax: 305-883-4498. Email: refugee@ccadm.org.

Pierre Toussaint Haitian Center—9920 N.E. 2nd Ave., Miami, 33138. Tel: 305-759-3050; Fax: 305-754-7423. Email: pierretoussaint@ccadm.org.

Unaccompanied Refugee Minors Program—700 S. Royal Poinciana Bldg. #806, Miami, 33166. Tel: 305-883-3383. Email: urmp@ccadm.org.

Unaccompanied Minors—Mailing Address: P.O. Box 971580, Miami, 33157. Tel: 305-380-0141. Email: ump@ccadm.org.

Boystown of Florida, Inc.—1505 N.E. 26 St., Wilton Manors, 33305. Tel: 305-762-1332; Fax: 305-754-6649.

Emergency Services—3620 N.W. First Ave., Miami, 33127. Tel: 305-573-3333; Fax: 305-576-5111.

Family and Individual Counseling—7707 N.W. 2nd Ave., Miami, 33150. Tel: 866-758-0025.

New Life Family Center—Tel: 305-573-3333; Fax: 305-576-5111. Email: newlife@ccadm.org.

Substance Abuse—

St. Luke's Center, Inc.—Addiction Recovery Center.

St. Luke's Prevention—7707 N.W. 2nd Ave., Miami, 33150. Tel: 305-795-0077; Fax: 305-795-0030. Email: stlukes@catholiccharitiesadm.org. Web: www.catholiccharitiesadm.org/stluke. Dr. MARK L. SZUREK, Ph.D., Dir. Email: mszurek@ccadm.org.

Monroe Region—RICHARD MCGILL. Tel: 305-292-9790; Fax: 305-292-5257. Email: monroe@ccadm.org.

Theresa House—1621 Spaulding Ct., Key West, 33040. Tel: 305-292-9790.

Workforce Housing—2700 Flagler Ave., Key West, 33040. Tel: 305-292-9790.

St. Bede Permanent Housing—2700 Flagler Ave., Key West, 33040. Tel: 305-292-9790.

Child Development Services/Miami-Dade—

Centro Hispano Catolico—Child Development Center, 125 N.W. 25th St., Miami, 33127. Tel: 305-573-9093; Fax: 305-576-6446. Email: centrohispano@ccadm.org.

Good Shepherd Child Development Center—18601 S.W. 97th Ave., Perrine, 33157. Tel: 305-235-1756; Fax: 305-255-2788. Email: goodshepherd@ccadm.org.

Notre Dame Child Development Center—130 N.E. 62nd St., Miami, 33138. Tel: 305-751-6778; Fax: 305-751-6959. Email: notredame@ccadm.org.

Holy Redeemer Child Development Center—1325 N.W. 71 St., Miami, 33147. Tel: 305-836-4971; Fax: 305-836-3323.

Sagrada Familia Child Development Center—970 S.W. 1st St., Miami, 33130. Tel: 305-324-5424; Fax: 305-325-0642. Email: sagradafamilia@ccadm.org.

South Dade Child Development Center—28520 S.W. 148th Ave., Leisure City, 33033. Tel: 305-245-0979; Fax: 305-242-8796. Email: southdade@ccadm.org.

Broward Region—

Counseling—1503 N.E. 26th St., Wilton Manors, 33305. Tel: 954-332-7070.

Providence Place—1079 S.E. 22nd Ave., Pompano Beach, 33062. Tel: 954-568-6610. Email: providenceplace@ccadm.org.

Adult Day Care Programs—

Central West—6915 Stirling Rd., Davie, 33314. Tel: 954-583-6446. Email: centralwest@ccadm.org.

Centro Oeste—6915 Stirling Rd., Davie, 33314. Tel: 954-581-9719. Email: centrooeste@ccadm.org.

Wilton Manors—1503 N.E. 26th St., Wilton Manors, 33305. Tel: 954-630-9501; Fax: 954-566-6026. Email: browardelderly@ccadm.org.

Ministry of Catholic Health Services

Catholic Health Services, Inc.—4790 N. State Rd. 7, Lauderdale Lakes, 33319. Tel: 954-484-1525. Mr. RALPH LAWSON, Chm. Bd.; Sr. ELIZABETH ANNE WORLEY, S.S.J., Vice Chair & Sec.; Rev. Msgr. TOMAS M. MARIN, J.C.L., Archdiocesan Dir. Catholic Identity, 4790 N. State Rd. 7, Lauderdale Lakes, 33319. Tel: 954-484-1515; Mr. JOSEPH M. CATANIA, CPA, M.H.A., Pres. & CEO; Mr. JAMES A. BALL, COO.

Catholic Health Care Transitions Services, Inc.—4790 N. State Rd. 7, Fort Lauderdale, 33319.

Catholic Housing for the Elderly and Handicapped, Inc.—

Catholic Housing Management—JUANA MEJIA, Dir. Elderly Housing Svcs., 11410 N. Kendall Dr., Ste. 201, Miami, 33176. Tel: 305-757-2824.

Archbishop Carroll Manor—MARIO YANES, Mgr., 3667 S. Miami Ave., Miami, 33133. Tel: 305-854-8953.

Archbishop Hurley Hall—Mrs. ALEXANDRA PEREZ, Mgr., 632 N.W. 1st St., Hallandale, 33009. Tel: 954-454-0855.

Marian Towers—ADA G. HERNANDEZ, Mgr., 17505 N. Bay Rd., Miami Beach, 33160. Tel: 305-932-1300.

Archbishop McCarthy Residence—ROSLYN WILLIAMS, Mgr., 13201 N.W. 28th Ave., Opa Locka, 33054. Tel: 305-688-2700.

Palmer House—MERCEDES PUJALS, Mgr., 1225 S.W. 107th Ave., Miami, 33174. Tel: 305-221-9566.

St. Andrew Towers—CAROL NICHOLS, Mgr., 2700 N.W. 99th Ave., Coral Springs, 33065. Tel: 954-752-3960.

St. Dominic Gardens—MARIO YANES, Mgr., 5849 N.W. 7th St., Miami, 33126. Tel: 305-262-0962.

St. Elizabeth Gardens—JOHN CAMERON, Mgr., 801 N.E. 33rd St., Pompano Beach, 33064. Tel: 954-941-4597.

St. Joseph Towers—DEBRA HAMELRATH, Mgr., 3475 N.W. 30th St., Lauderdale Lakes, 33311. Tel: 954-485-5150.

St. Mary Towers—ARIESKY VAZQUEZ, Mgr., 7615 N.W. 2nd Ave., Miami, 33150. Tel: 305-757-3190.

Stella Maris House—SELMA CUNNINGHAM, Mgr., 8638 Harding Ave., Miami Beach, 33141. Tel: 305-865-6841.

St. Anne's Gardens—MERCEDES PUJALS, Mgr., 11800 Quail Roost Dr., Miami, 33177. Tel: 305-234-1994.

St. Boniface Gardens—8200 Johnson St., Pembroke Pines, 33024. Tel: 305-433-3899. Mr. VICTOR CORDERO, Mgr.

St. Vincent de Paul Gardens—BLANCA AIBELO, 10160 N.W. 19th Ave., Miami, 33147. Tel: 305-639-1590.

St. Monica Gardens, Inc.—3425 N.W. 189th St., Miami Gardens, 33056. Tel: 305-628-2500; Fax: 305-628-2600. ISABEL SOTO NORIEGA, Mgr.

Miramar Senior Housing Project, Inc.—4790 N. State Rd. 7, Lauderdale Lakes, 33319. Tel: 954-484-1515; Fax: 954-484-5416.

Nursing and Retirement Centers—

BROWARD:

St. Joseph Residence, Inc., RON BONAVITA, Admin., 3485 N.W. 30th St., Lauderdale Lakes, 33311. Tel: 954-739-1483. *St. John's Rehabilitation Hospital and Nursing Center, Inc.*, dba St. John's Nursing Center DIANE STONE, Exec. Dir., 3075 N.W. 35th Ave., Lauderdale Lakes, 33311. Tel: 954-739-6233. *St. John's Rehabilitation Hospital and Nursing Center, Inc.*, dba St. Anthony's Rehabilitation Hospital LINDA MOTTE, Admin., 3487 N.W. 30th St., Fort Lauderdale, 33311. Tel: 954-739-6233. *Catholic Hospice of Broward, Inc., 4790 N. State Rd. 7,*

Lauderdale Lakes, 33319. Tel: 954-484-1515. *Catholic Home Health Medicare Services, Inc., 4790 N. State Rd. 7, Lauderdale Lakes, 33319*. Tel: 954-484-1515. *Catholic Home Health Services, Inc., 4790 N. State Rd. 7, Lauderdale Lakes, 33319*. Tel: 954-484-1515. *Catholic Home Health Services of Broward, Inc.*, CAROL HYLTON, Admin., 3075 N.W. 35th Ave., Lauderdale Lakes, 33311. Tel: 954-486-3660.

DADE:

**St. Anne's Nursing Center, St. Anne's Residence, Inc.*, TONY FARINELLA, Exec. Dir., 11855 Quail Roost Dr., Miami, 33177. Tel: 305-252-4000. *Miami-Dade Nursing Center, Inc., c/o 4790 N. State Rd. 7, Lauderdale Lakes, 33319*. Tel: 954-484-1515. *Villa Maria Nursing and Rehabilitation Center, Inc.*, dba Villa Maria Nursing Center Mr. JAMES REISS, Exec. Dir., 1050 N.E. 125 St., North Miami, 33161. Tel: 305-891-8850. *Villa Maria Nursing and Rehabilitation Center, Inc.*, dba Villa Maria West Skilled Nursing Facility Mr. NATHANIEL JOHNSON, Admin., 8850 N.W. 122nd St., Hialeah Gardens, 33018. Tel: 305-351-7181. *Villa Maria Nursing and Rehabilitation Center, Inc.*, dba St. Catherine's Rehabilitation Hospital Mr. JAIME GONZALEZ, Admin., 1050 N.E. 125th St., North Miami, 33161. Tel: 305-357-1735. *Villa Maria Nursing and Rehabilitation Center, Inc.*, dba St. Catherine's West Rehabilitation Hospital Mr. JAIME GONZALEZ, Admin., 8850 N.W. 122nd St., Hialeah Gardens, 33018. Tel: 305-351-7181. *Villa Maria Health Care Services, Inc.*, dba Catholic Home Health Services of Miami Dade County CAROL HYLTON, Admin., 1050 N.E. 125th St., North Miami, 33161. Tel: 305-899-0400. *Miami Lakes - Catholic Hospice, Inc.*, BONNIE ALKEMA, Exec. Dir., 14875 N.W. 77 Ave., Ste. 100, Miami Lakes, 33014. Tel: 305-822-2380; Fax: 305-824-0665. Web: www.catholichospice.org. *Villa Maria Foundation, Inc., 1050 N.E. 125th St., North Miami, 33161*. Tel: 305-891-8850.

Catholic Cemeteries of the Archdiocese of Miami, Inc.—MARY JO FRICK, Exec. Dir., 11411 N.W. 25th St., Miami, 33172. Tel: 305-592-0521.

Archdiocesan Cemeteries—Administrative Managers: MARIA TRUJILLO, Our Lady of Mercy Cemetery, 11411 N.W. 25th St., Miami, 33172. Tel: 305-592-0521; OFELIA SPARDY, Our Lady Queen of Heaven Cemetery, 1500 S. State Rd. 7, North Lauderdale, 33068. Tel: 954-972-1234.

Catholic Elderly Services, Inc.— dba Catholic Health Services Foundation *4790 N. State Rd. 7, Lauderdale Lakes, 33319*. Tel: 954-484-1515.

Centro Mater Child Care Services, Inc.—Mr. JOSEPH M. CATANIA, CPA, M.H.A., Pres. & CEO; MIRIAM ROMAN, Exec. Dir., 4790 N. State Rd. 7, Lauderdale Lakes, 33319. Tel: 954-484-1515; Fax: 954-484-5416.

Centro Mater Child Care Center—418 S.W. 4th Ave., Miami, 33130. Tel: 305-545-0760; Fax: 305-324-6162.

Centro Mater Child Care Center II—421 S.W. 4th St., Miami, 33130. Tel: 305-545-6049; Fax: 305-324-6162.

Centro Mater West Child Care Center—8298 N.W. 103rd St., Hialeah Gardens, 33016. Tel: 305-357-4395; Fax: 305-357-4674.

Centro Mater West II Child Care Center—7700 N.W. 98th St., Hialeah Gardens, 33016. Tel: 305-362-9701; Fax: 305-324-6162.

Centro Mater Walker Park—800 W. 29th St., Hialeah, 33010. Tel: 305-887-1140.

Ministry of Pastoral Services

Ministry of Pastoral Services—

Apostleship of the Sea (Archdiocese of Miami)—Port Everglades: Seafarer's House/Casa del Marino, Port Everglades, 33316. Deacons RANDY MILLIKIN; GERALD MCGUINN. Port of Miami: Deacon EDGAR KELLY.

Stella Maris Seamen Center, Inc.—Mailing Address: 9401 Biscayne Blvd., Miami Shores, 33138. Tel: 954-734-1580; Fax: 954-766-2699. VACANT, Archdiocesan Dir.

Campus Ministry—Rev. HARRY LOUBRIEL, St. Thomas University, 16401 N.W. 37th Ave., Miami Gardens, 33054. Tel: 305-628-6525. Email: hloubriel@stu.edu.

Barry University—Rev. SCOTT O'BRIEN, O.P., D.Min., Chap. Tel: 305-899-3681. Email: sobrien@mail.barry.edu; Bro. FERNANDO SOROLLA-DELGADO, O.P., Campus Min. Email: fsorolla-delgado@mail.barry.edu; MICHELLE BROWN, Admin. Asst., 11300 N.E. 2nd Ave., Miami Shores, 33161. Tel: 305-899-3650. Email: mbrown@mail.barry.edu; Sr. MARY FLEISCHAKER, O.P., Liturgy & Music. Tel: 305-899-3650. Email: mfleischaker@mail.barry.edu; ALEX SCHLICH, Svc. Learning. Tel: 305-899-3650. Email: hschlich@mail.barry.edu.

FIU-University Park—Revs. ROLANDO G. GARCIA, Dir. Email: frgarcia@stagathaonline.org; ALEXANDER EKECHUKWU, C.S.Sp., Chap. Email: fralex@stagathaonline.org; BRIAN GERMAN, Campus Min., St. Agatha Church, 1111 S.W. 107th Ave., Miami, 33174. Tel: 305-934-6229. Email: bgerm002@fiu.edu.

St. Thomas University—Rev. HARRY LOUBRIEL, Dir. Campus Ministry. Tel: 305-628-6525. Email: hloubriel@stu.edu; MARY ROJAS, Graduate Asst., Campus Min. Email: mrojas@stu.edu; MARIA THOMPSON, Administrative Asst., 16400 N.W. 32nd Ave., Miami, 33054. Tel: 305-628-6525. Email: msthompson@stu.edu.

Campus Minister—EBY KURIAN, Nova Southeastern Univ., St. Thomas Univ., 16401 N.W. 37 Ave., Miami Gardens, 33054. Tel: 305-628-6721. Email: ekurian@stu.edu; CLAUDIA H. HERRERA, FIU - Biscayne Bay Campus, St. Thomas Univ., 16401 N. W. 37 Ave., Miami Gardens, 33054. Tel: 305-628-6515. Email: cherrera7@stu.edu.

University of Miami—Rev. Msgr. MICHAEL CARRUTHERS, University Chap.; RIGOBERTO VEGA, Dir. & Campus Min., St. Augustine Church, 1400 Miller Rd., Coral Gables, 33146. Tel: 305-661-1648. Email: campus@saintaugustinechurch.org.

Miami Dade College-Kendall Campus—Rev. MICHAEL A. KISH, Chap., 7270 S.W. 120th St., Miami, 33156. Tel: 305-238-7562. Email: frkish@catholic.org; ELIZABETH DE ARAZOZA, Faculty Advisor. Tel: 305-237-2976. Email: edearazo@mdc.edu.

Miami Dade College-Wolfson Campus—Rev. EDUARDO ALVAREZ, S.J., Chap., Gesu Church, 118 N.E. 2nd St., Miami, 33132. Tel: 305-379-1424. Email: gesumiami@yahoo.com.

Miami Dade College - North Campus—Prof. JULIO BORGES, Faculty Advisor. Tel: 305-237-1236. Email: jborges@mdc.edu; ANA CAROLINA CORRALES, Faculty Advisor. Tel: 305-237-1239. Email: acorrale@mdc.edu.

Catholic Daughters of America—Court 634, Regent: LANA JABOUR, St. Mary Star of the Sea Parish, 1010 Windsor Ln., Key West, 33040. Tel: 305-942-6905. Vice-Regent: JEAN MAUM. Local Chaplain: Rev. JOHN C. BAKER.

Confraternity of Our Lady of Chiquinquira—Revs. ALVARO PINZON, J.C.D., Spiritual Dir. Tel: 800-516-0638. Email: rev.pinzon@virgendechiquinquira.org. Web: www.virgendechiquinquira.org; ISRAEL E. MAGO, Vice Pres. Tel: 305-593-6123. Email: info@ologfl.org.

Family Life Ministry—LUCIA BAEZ LUZONDO, Dir. Office of Family Life. Tel: 305-762-1157. Email: lluzondo@theadom.org. Web: www.miamiarch.org/familylife.

Camino Al Matrimonio (Spanish)—Deacon JORGE GONZALEZ, Spiritual Dir., Mailing Address: P.O. Box 524160, Miami, 33152-4160. Tel: 305-226-4664.

Lay Apostolic Movements and Associations—

Agrupacion Catolica Universitaria (ACU)—Rev. NELSON GARCIA-ROSALES, Spiritual Dir., 720 N.E. 27th St., Miami, 33137. Tel: 305-576-2748. Web: acu-adsum.org; estovir.org.

St. Martin de Porres Assoc.—LEONA H. COOPER, Pres., Mailing Address: P.O. Box 330102, Miami, 33133. Tel: 305-443-9466; Fax: 305-461-8669. Email: cooperleona@yahoo.com.

Archdiocesan Council of Catholic Women—Very Rev. MICHAEL GREER, V.F., Mod., 2001 S. Ocean Blvd., Lauderdale-By-The-Sea, 33062. Tel: 954-941-7647; Mrs. BARBARA ASFENDIS, Pres., Miami Archdiocesan Council of Catholic Women (MACCW). Email: galagirlb@aol.com. Web: www.maccw.org. Spiritual Moderators: Rev. HENRYK PAWELEC, (Monroe District); VACANT, (Broward District); Rev. Msgr. KENNETH K. SCHWANGER, J.C.D., (South Dade District); Rev. WILLIAM ELBERT, (North Dade District).

Catholic Charismatic Services--Archdiocese of Miami—Rev. JOHN FINK, Spiritual Dir. & Treas. (Retired), Charismatic Services: P.O. Box 816128, Hollywood, 33081-0128. Tel: 954-961-1856; Fax: 954-961-3662. Web: www.miamiccr.com. Email: crob1@att.net; Mr. EMERY HORVATH, Dir. Spanish: Deacon MANUEL CANOVACA, Spiritual Dir.; CONCEPCION GONZALEZ, Coord., Centro Carismatico Catolico: 500 N.W. 22 Ave., Miami, 33125. Tel: 305-631-1007; Fax: 305-642-0006. Email: rcch@bellsouth.net. Web: www.rcchmiami.us.

Ministry to Cultural Groups (Non-Hispanic Ethnicities)—Rev. Msgr. JEAN PIERRE, Dir. Tel: 305-762-1236; Fax: 305-762-1348.

Nigerian Apostolate—Rev. ALEXANDER EKECHUKWU, C.S.Sp., Asst., St. Agatha, 1111 S.W. 107th Ave., Miami, 33174. Tel: 305-222-1500; Fax: 305-222-1505.

Brazilian and Portuguese Apostolate—Revs. JOSEPH F. PRANZO, C.S., Dir., St. Vincent, 6350 N.W. 18th St., Margate, 33063-2320. Tel: 954-972-0434; Fax: 954-971-9411; JEFFERSON O. BARIVIERA, C.S., Assoc. Dir.; ALEX DALPIAZ, C.S., Pastoral Asst.

Chinese Apostolate—Deacon ALEX LAM, St. Louis Catholic Church, 7270 S.W. 120 St., Miami, 33156. Tel: 350-238-7562, Ext. 105; BERNADETTE CHIK, St. Jerome Parish. Tel: 954-525-4133.

Filipino Apostolate—Ms. JANET MACASERO, Asst., 6320 Plunkett St., Hollywood, 33023. Tel: 954-981-7843.

Haitians—Rev. Msgr. JEAN PIERRE, Apostolate Dir., St. James Parish. Tel: 305-681-7428; Rev. REGINALD JEAN-MARY, 110 N.E. 62 St., Miami, 33138. Tel: 305-751-6289 Notre Dame D'Haiti Mission.

Hungarians—Deacon MIKLOS A. BEREGSZASZI, St. Catherine of Siena Parish, 9200 S.W. 107th Ave., Miami, 33176. Tel: 305-274-6333; Fax: 305-274-6337.

Indians—Rev. ZACHARIAS THOTTUVELIL, Our Lady of Health (Syro-Malabar Church), 201 N. University Dr., Coral Springs, 33071. Tel: 954-227-6985.

Italian—Very Rev. CHRISTOPHER MARINO, V.F., St. Michael the Archangel, 2987 W. Flagler St., Miami, 33135. Tel: 305-649-1811.

Caribbean Apostolate—Dr. PRINCE SMITH, 755 N.W. 184th Dr., Miami Gardens, 33169. Tel: 305-653-8492.

Native Americans—Rev. Msgr. JEAN PIERRE, Dir. Tel: 305-762-1236.

Korean—Rev. BONGMOON LEE, 14344 S. Royal Cove Cir., Davie, 33325. Tel: 954-474-9091.

Polish - (Our Lady of Czestochowa Polish Mission)—Rev. KLEMENS DABROWSKI, S.Ch., Dir., 2400 N.E. 12th St., Pompano Beach, 33062. Tel: 954-946-6347; Fax: 954-946-0512.

Vietnamese—Rev. ISIDORE BAKY, Coord., St. Helen Church, 3033 N.W. 33rd Ave., Lauderdale Lakes, 33311. Tel: 954-714-9860; Fax: 954-739-9632.

Christian Family Movement— Spanish: Movimiento Familiar Cristiano Rev. JESUS ALBERTO BOHORQUEZ, Spiritual Dir., Casa Cana, 480 E. 8th St., Hialeah, 33010. Tel: 305-888-4819; Mr. MANUEL REYES, Pres. Tel: 786-229-0708. Web: www.casacana.org. Email: casacana2011@comcast.net.

Archicofradia Nuestra Senora de la Caridad (Spanish)—Very Rev. JUAN RUMIN DOMINGUEZ, O.F.M., Rector. Email: ermita@ermitadelacaridad.org. Web: ermitadelacaridad.org.

Ministry to the Deaf or Disabled—6591 S. Flamingo Rd., Cooper City, 33330-3915. Tel: 954-434-3624; Fax: 954-434-3307. Mr. FRANK CASALE, Exec. Dir.; DENNIS ROHAN, Dir. Rel. Formation; NANCY VIDAURRE, Dir. Grants & Planning; MARY ROUKAS, Dir. Residences & Counselor; KAREN DRUMHELLER, Dir. Devel.; LIZ DISNEY, Dir. Progs.; AUDREY BROWN, Dir. Human Resources, Schott Memorial Center, Inc., 6591 S. Flamingo Rd., Cooper City, 33330. Tel: 954-434-3306; Fax: 954-434-3307.

Schott Memorial Center, Inc.—6591 S. Flamingo Rd., Cooper City, 33330. Tel: 954-434-3306; Fax: 954-434-3307. Mr. FRANK CASALE, Exec. Dir. & Contact.

Comunidad de Vida Cristiana, Regina Mundi, South Florida Region—Rev. MARCELINO GARCIA, S.J., Spiritual Dir., Casa Manresa, 12190 S.W. 56 St., Miami, 33175. Tel: 305-596-0001.

Cursillo Movement—

Cursillos de Cristiandad (Spanish)—Rev. SANTIAGO MATHEU, Spiritual Dir. Email: jmatheu41@aol.com; EDUARDO DE VARONA, Lay Coord., Casa Emaus, 16250 S.W. 112th Ave., Miami, 33157. Tel: 305-235-7160. Email: directorlaico@cursillos.org. Web: www.cursillos.org.

Cursillo (English)—LOUIS CONFESSORE, Lay Coord. Email: ces2000@bellsouth.net. Web: www.cursillomiami.org; Deacon ROBERT BINDER, Spiritual Dir., St. John Neumann. Tel: 305-255-6642. Email: margedun@bellsouth.net.

Emmaus Experience Parish Retreats—MYRNA GALLAGHER, Contact. Tel: 305-273-7650; JUDITH PASOS, Spanish Contact. Tel: 305-279-7759. Email: pasos_bravo@bellsouth.net.

Encuentros Familiares y Casa Manresa (Spanish)—Casa Manresa, P.O. Box 651512, Miami, 33265. Tel: 305-596-0001; Fax: 305-596-9655. Email: manresamiami@yahoo.com. Web: www.encuentrosfamiliares.org. Rev. MARCELINO GARCIA, S.J., Dir.

Encuentros Juveniles (Spanish and English)—Sr. CLAUDIA ORTEGA, R.M.I., Spiritual Dir., Miami Youth Center, 3333 S. Miami Ave., Miami, 33133. Tel: 305-856-3404; Fax: 305-854-8888. Web: www.encuentrosjuveniles.org.

Impactos de Cristiandad (Spanish)—Deacon ISIDORO

VILLA, Spiritual Dir., Mailing Address: P.O. Box 440967, Miami, 33144. Tel: 305-571-7111; Fax: 305-222-8769. Email: impactos@impactos.org. Web: www.impactos.org.

Knights of Columbus (English and Spanish)—Rev. LUIS R. RIVERA, Archdiocesan Chap., St. Pius X, 2500 N.E. 33 Ave., Fort Lauderdale, 33305. Tel: 954-564-1763. Web: www.floridastatecouncil.com; Mr. OSCAR LAY, Contact. Tel: 305-258-7336.

La Nueva Jerusalen Community - Comunidad de Alianza—WILLIAM F. BROWN JR., Liaison with Archdiocese of Miami. Tel: 305-273-7460. Email: wfbrownjr@gmail.com; NESTOR ARGUELLO, Coord. Tel: 305-385-7281. Email: contacto@comunidadlnj.org.

Legion of Mary— (English Speaking) Rev. RICHARD SOULLIERE, Spiritual Dir. (Retired). Lay Contacts: JUDITH PADRON (Spanish) Tel: 305-821-3673. Email: jtp1227@aol.com; MARGARET ANNIS (English) Tel: 305-895-0003. Email: mzannis@mac.com.

Marian Movements & Devotions—Rev. RICHARD SOULLIERE, Coord. (Retired), Mailing Address: P.O. Box 221937, Hollywood, 33022-1937. Tel: 954-961-6740.

Neocatechumenal Way—Archdiocesan Team: Dr. STEFANO BENIGNI, J.C.D.; LUCIA BENIGNI. Tel: 305-898-0643. Email: benigni-florida@earthlink.net. Web: www.neocatechumenalway.us.

Prison Ministry—Deacons EDGARDO FARIAS, Dir. Tel: 305-762-1093. Email: efarias@theadom.org; RAFAEL CRUZ, Assoc. Tel: 305-762-1176.

Respect Life Ministry—Mrs. JOAN CROWN, Dir., 3600 S.W. 32nd Blvd., West Park, 33023. Tel: 954-981-2922; Fax: 954-981-2901. Email: ilovelife@bellsouth.net. Web: www.respectlifemiami.org.

Project Rachel—Tel: 888-456-4673.

Respect Life Branch Offices-Emergency Pregnancy Services—

North Dade Central Office, 3268 S. University Dr., Miramar, 33025. Tel: 305-653-2921.

North Broward Office, 5115 Coconut Creek Pkwy., Margate, 33063. Tel: 954-977-7769.

Hollywood Office (S. Broward), 5600 Hollywood Blvd., Hollywood, 33021. Tel: 954-963-2229.

Ft. Lauderdale Office, 2909 N. Andrews Ave., Wilton Manors, 33311. Tel: 954-565-8506.

South Miami Office, 9360 S.W. 72nd St., Ste. 238, Miami, 33173. Tel: 305-273-8507.

Rural Life Ministry—Rev. JESUS BOHORQUEZ, Dir.

Chapels—Everglades Villages, 193 S.W. 6 Ave., Florida City, 33034. South Dade Camp, 31248 S.W. 134th Ave., Homestead, 33033. Redlands Camp, 29200 S.W. 158th Ave., Homestead, 33033. Tel: 305-258-0834; 305-258-6998.

St. Ann Mission—

Naranja and Migrant Ministry—13875 SW 264th St., Naranja, 33032. Mailing Address: P.O. Box 924884, Princeton, 33092. Tel: 305-258-6998. Rev. JESUS BOHORQUEZ.

Youth and Young Adult Ministry—Very Rev. CHANEL JEANTY, J.C.L., V.G., Pastoral Center, 9401 Biscayne Blvd., Miami Shores, 33138. Tel: 305-762-1262.

Scouting—Deacon EMILIO BLANCO, Chap., 9401 Biscayne Blvd., Miami, 33138. Tel: 305-762-1245. Email: catholicscouts@theadom.org.

Ministry of Temporalities

Finance Office—Mr. MICHAEL A. CASCIATO, CPA, CFO; Mr. JOSEPH M. CATANIA, CPA, M.H.A., Treas.

Finance Council—Members: Most Rev. THOMAS G. WENSKI, D.D.; Mr. THOMAS BEIER, Chm.; Sr. ELIZABETH ANNE WORLEY, S.S.J.; Rev. Msgrs. NOEL FOGARTY, P.A., V.F. (Retired); TOMAS M. MARIN, J.C.L.; JUDE O'DOHERTY; Revs. GABRIEL O'REILLY; PAUL V. VUTURO; Mr. ALBERT DEL CASTILLO; Mr. PEDRO GARCIA; Mr. SEAN CLANCY; Mr. THOMAS CORNISH; Mr. THOMAS G. BENSON; Mrs. CHRISTINA BROCHIN.

Building and Property Office—Mr. ORLANDO SHARPE, Interim Dir. Tel: 305-762-1035. Email: osharpe@theadom.org; Mr. JAMES DETRICK, Project Mgr. Tel: 305-762-1034. Email: jdetrick@theadom.org.

Plant Operations—Mr. ORLANDO SHARPE, Interim Dir.

Archdiocese of Miami Health Plan Trust—Rev. Msgr. TOMAS M. MARIN, J.C.L., Chm.; Ms. SUSAN WADDELL, Dir.

Pension—Most Rev. THOMAS G. WENSKI, D.D.; Rev. Msgrs. JUDE O'DOHERTY, Chm.; TOMAS M. MARIN, J.C.L., Vice Chm.

Ministry of Worship and Spiritual Life

Director—Rev. Msgr. TERENCE HOGAN, S.L.D.; Sr. CARMEN ORS, S.C.T.J.M., Admin. Asst.

Worship & Spiritual Life Commission—Very Rev. MICHAEL GREER, V.F., Chm.

Celebration and Rite Committee—Rev. Msgr. TERENCE HOGAN, S.L.D., Chm.

Spiritual Life Committee—SUSAN LORETTA.

Sacred Art & Architecture—Rev. PAUL V. VUTURO.

Liturgical Music—SUZANNE ARSENAULT.

Committee on Popular Piety—Rev. JUAN J. SOSA.

Ministry of Persons

Ministry of Persons—Very Rev. THOMAS O'DWYER, V.F., Vicar Priests. Tel: 305-762-1197; Sr. ANA MARGARITA LANZAS, S.C.T.J.M., Vicar for Rel. Tel: 305-762-1082. Email: vicarrel@theadom.org.

Vocations—Rev. DAVID A. ZIRILLI, Dir., 9401 Biscayne Blvd., Miami, 33138. Tel: 305-762-1137.

Archdiocesan Vocations Review Board—Very Revs. CHANEL JEANTY, J.C.L., V.G.; THOMAS O'DWYER, V.F.; Revs. JUAN CARLOS PAGUAGA; JUAN J. SOSA; Rev. Msgrs. KENNETH K. SCHWANGER, J.C.D.; JEAN PIERRE; Deacon EDUARDO BLANCO; Sisters CARMEN ORS, S.C.T.J.M.; YAMILE SAIEH, F.M.A.; Very Rev. JEREMIAH SINGLETON; Mrs. ROSE LITWIN; Mr. CURT NICHOLS; Dr. IAN ROBERTSON.

Permanent Diaconate—Most Rev. THOMAS G. WENSKI, D.D.; Rev. Msgr. KENNETH K. SCHWANGER, J.C.D., Chm. Advisory Board; Deacon VICTOR M. PIMENTEL, Exec. Dir.

Retired Priests' Committee—Rev. JOHN MCLAUGHLIN (Retired); Rev. Msgr. XAVIER MORRAS (Retired).

Ministry to Professional Groups—

Catholic Educators' Guild—Very Rev. CHRISTOPHER MARINO, V.F., Chap.

Catholic Funeral Directors' Guild—Rev. Msgr. ANDREW L. ANDERSON, Chap.

Catholic Lawyers' Guild—Rev. Msgr. ANDREW L. ANDERSON, Chap.

Catholic Physicians' and Dentists' Guild—Rev. Msgr. TOMAS M. MARIN, J.C.L., Chap., Dade & Broward.

Catholic Law Enforcement Ministry—VACANT, Voluntary Chap., Hollywood Police Dept. Police Chaplains: Revs. MANUEL A. SOLER, (Miami Beach & Key Biscayne Police); MICHAEL A. KISH, (City of Miami Police); VACANT, (Florida Highway Patrol, Troop K).

Catholic Fire Service Ministry—Rev. Msgr. TOMAS M. MARIN, J.C.L., Chap., Miami-Dade Fire Rescue; Revs. MICHAEL LYNCH, Fire Chap., City of Coral Gables; JAMES A. QUINN, Chap. Miami Office of the Federal Bureau of Investigations & Hallandale Beach Police Dept.

Special Apostolates

Amor en Accion (Love in Action)—Mailing Address: P.O. Box 141523, Coral Gables, 33114. Tel: 305-762-1226. ALICIA MARRILL, Pres.; TERESITA GONZALEZ, Dir. & Contact, 9401 Biscayne Blvd., Miami Shores, 33138. Email: tgonzalez@theadom.org.

Downtown Senior Citizens' Community Center at Gesu Church—Sisters MARIA ISABEL RINCON, O.P.; CECILIA ALONSO, O.P.; JULIA BARRETO, O.P., 118 N.E. 2nd St., Miami, 33132. Tel: 305-374-6099.

Pontifical Mission Societies—Rev. DAVID A. ZIRILLI, Dir.

Society for the Propagation of the Faith—Rev. DAVID A. ZIRILLI.

Holy Childhood Association—Rev. DAVID A. ZIRILLI.

The Society of St. Peter Apostle—Rev. DAVID A. ZIRILLI.

Missionary Union of Priests and Religious—Rev. DAVID A. ZIRILLI.

Priests Purgatorial Society—Rev. DAVID A. ZIRILLI.

Serra Club—

Miami—SALLY JUDE, Pres., 200 Edgewater Dr., Coral Gables, 33133. Tel: 305-325-0045; 305-667-3233.

Broward—Mr. MALCOLM MEIKLE, Pres., 111 N. Pompano Beach Blvd., #914, Pompano Beach, 33062. Tel: 954-946-2551. Email: malcolm@meikle.com.

Chaplain--Dade County - Serra Club—Rev. DAVID A. ZIRILLI.

Chaplain--Broward County - Serra Club—Rev. ANTHONY MULDERRY.

CLERGY, PARISHES, MISSIONS AND PAROCHIAL SCHOOLS

CITY OF MIAMI

(DADE COUNTY)

1—ST. MARY'S CATHEDRAL (1930) Rev. Msgr. Terence Hogan, Rector; Rev. Esteker Elyse, S.M.M. (Haiti); Deacon Ian Taylor. In Res., Revs. Alvaro Pinzon (Colombia); David A. Zirilli.

Res.: 7525 N.W. Second Ave., Miami, 33150. Tel: 305-759-4531; 305-759-4532; Fax: 305-757-7456. Web: www.cathedralofsaintmary.com.

School—7485 N.W. Second Ave., Miami, 33150. Tel: 305-795-2000; Fax: 305-795-2013. Mr. Jorge L. Rodriguez, Prin. Servants of the Pierced Heart of Jesus & Mary 5; Lay Teachers 16; Students 425.

Catechesis/Religious Program—Tel: 305-795-2016; Fax: 305-757-6870. Students 505.

St. Mary's Cathedral Foundation Trust—9401 Biscayne Blvd., 33138. Mike Casciato, Contact Person.

2—ST. AGATHA (1971) Revs. Rolando G. Garcia; Raul S. Soutuyo; Alexander Ekechukwu, C.S.Sp.; Juan A. Aviles; Deacon Angel Pintado.

Res.: 1111 S.W. 107th Ave., Miami, 33174. Tel: 305-222-1500; Fax: 305-222-1505. Email: rectory@stagathaonline.org. Web: www.stagathaonline.org.

School—1125 S.W. 107th Ave., Miami, 33174. Tel: 305-222-8751; Fax: 305-222-1517. Email: office@stagathaonline.com. Mrs. Maria P. Glass, Prin.; Patricia Hernandez, Asst. Prin. Lay Teachers 33; Students 518.

Catechesis/Religious Program—Tel: 305-222-8067; Fax: 305-222-8078. Email: reledu@stagathaonline.org. Sisters Martha Maria Gomez-Chow, S.C.T.J.M., D.R.E.; Elena A. Castillo, S.C.T.J.M., Asst. D.R.E. Students 432.

3—ST. BRENDAN (1954) Revs. Fernando Heria; Miguel A. Blanco, Parochial Vicar; Deacons Billy Lannon Jr.; Edward Blanco; Rafael Calvo-Forte; Manuel Jimenez; Edgar Kelly.

Res.: 8725 S.W. 32nd St., Miami, 33165. Tel: 305-221-0881; Fax: 305-226-6249.

School—8755 S.W. 32 St., Miami, 33165. Tel: 305-221-2722; Fax: 305-554-6726. Elizabeth Furmanick, Prin. Lay Teachers 50; Students 567.

Catechesis/Religious Program—Tel: 305-226-2628; 305-221-2861. Students 301.

4—ST. CATHERINE OF SIENA (1968) Rev. Alejandro J. Rodriguez; Deacons Miklos A. Beregszaszi; Vicente Moreno.

Res.: 9200 S.W. 107th Ave., Miami, 33176. Tel: 305-274-6333; Fax: 305-274-6337. Web: www.scsmiami.org.

Catechesis/Religious Program—Tel: 305-274-6333, Ext. 226. Lydia Mayorga, D.R.E. Students 215.

5—CHRIST THE KING (1961) Rev. William Mason, O.M.I.; Deacon George Gibson. In Res., Revs. Lucien Bouchard, O.M.I.; Antonyra Arumainathan, O.M.I. (India).

Res.: 16000 S.W. 112th Ave., Miami, 33157. Tel: 305-238-2485; Fax: 305-254-0330.

Catechesis/Religious Program—Tel: 305-235-0293. Students 97.

6—CORPUS CHRISTI (1941) Revs. Jose L. Menendez; Roberto M. Cid; Anibal Morales; Deacons Luis Benavides, Pastoral Assoc.; Antonio Perez; Alvaro Velasco.

Res.: 3220 N.W. 7th Ave., Miami, 33127. Tel: 305-635-1331; Fax: 305-635-2031.

Catechesis/Religious Program—Sr. Carmen Alvarez, R.M.I. Tel: 305-633-5824. Students 519.

Mission—San Francisco y Santa Clara 402 N.E. 29th St., Miami, 33137.

Mission—San Juan Bautista 3116 N.W. 2nd Ave., Miami, 33127.

Mission—Nuestra Senora de Altagracia 1779 N.W. 28th St., Miami, 33142.

Mission—La Milagrosa 1860 N.W. 18th Ter., Miami, 33125.

Mission—St. Robert Bellarmine 3405 N.W. 27 Ave., Miami, 33142.

7—ST. DOMINIC (1962) Revs. Alberto Rodriguez, O.P.; Restituto Perez, O.P.; Desiderio Eguino, O.P.

Res.: 5909 N.W. 7th St., Miami, 33126. Tel: 305-264-0181; Fax: 305-262-4685.

Catechesis/Religious Program—Tel: 305-264-3372. Students 206.

8—EPIPHANY (1951) Rev. Msgr. Jude O'Doherty; Rev. Cesar E. Pena; Deacons Jose Carrion; Donald Livingstone; Paul H. Munter; Norman Ruiz-Castaneda; Thomas V. Eagan; Marcos Perez.

Res.: 8081 S.W. 54 Ct., Miami, 33143. Tel: 305-667-4911; Fax: 305-667-8067.

School—5557 S.W. 84th St., Miami, 33143. Tel: 305-667-5251; Fax: 305-667-6828. Sr. Margaret Fagan, I.H.M., Prin. Sisters Servants of the Immaculate Heart of Mary 2; Lay Teachers 73; Students 973.

Catechesis/Religious Program—Tel: 305-665-0037. Students 274.

Church of the Epiphany Parish Endowment Trust—9401 Biscayne Blvd., 33138. Mike Casciato, Contact Person.

9—ST. FRANCIS XAVIER (1927) Merged with and sacramental records at Gesu Parish, Miami.

10—GESU (1896) Revs. Eduardo Alvarez, S.J.; Sergio Figueredo, S.J.; Francisco J. Permuy, S.J.; Aaron Pidel.

Res.: 118 N.E. 2nd St., Miami, 33132. Tel: 305-379-1424; Fax: 305-372-9544. Email: gesumiami@yahoo.com. Web: www.gesumiami.org.

Catechesis/Religious Program—Tel: 305-374-6099. Students 60.

11—GOOD SHEPHERD (1977) Very Rev. Jesus J. Arias; Deacons Santos Rodriguez; Julio Zayas; Arthur Merkel.
Res. & Church: 14187 S.W. 72nd St., Miami, 33183. Tel: 305-385-4320; Fax: 305-386-2407. Email: info@gscatholic.org. Web: www.gscatholic.org.
School—(Grades PreK-8) Tel: 305-385-7002; Fax: 305-385-7026. Email: office@good-shepherd-school.org. Web: www.good-shepherd-school.org. Mrs. Clara Cabrera, Prin.; Mrs. Frances Valladares, Librarian. Lay Teachers 22; Students 208.
Catechesis/Religious Program—Tel: 305-385-4320, Ext. 202. Students 649.

12—HOLY REDEEMER (1950), (African American), Rev. John T. Cox, O.M.I. In Res., Rev. Fidelis Nwankwo, C.S.Sp.
Church: 1301 N.W. 71st St., Miami, 33147. Tel: 305-691-1701; Fax: 305-691-7074. Email: hredeemr@bellsouth.net. Web: www.holyredeemerrcmiami.org.
Catechesis/Religious Program—Students 65.

13—ST. JAMES (1952) Rev. Msgr. Jean Pierre; Rev. Hector A. Perez. In Res., Rev. Martin K. Adu.
Res.: 540 N.W. 132nd St., Miami, 33168. Tel: 305-681-7428; Fax: 305-685-0631. Web: www.stjames-miami.com.
School—601 N.W. 131st St., North Miami, 33168. Tel: 305-681-3822; Fax: 305-681-6435. Religious 2; Lay Teachers 18; Students 379.
St. James Early Learning Center—565 N.W. 131st St., Miami, 33168. Tel: 305-403-0626. Mrs. Doreen Roberts, Dir. & Contact.
Catechesis/Religious Program—Tel: 305-681-2676. Students 115.

14—ST. JOACHIM (1972) Rev. Christobal DePaula.
Rectory—11740 S.W. 192nd St., Miami, 33177. Tel: 305-233-1278; Fax: 305-233-2573.
Church: 19150 S.W. 117th Ave., Miami, 33177.
Catechesis/Religious Program—Students 362.

15—ST. JOHN BOSCO (1962) Revs. Juan Carlos Paguaga; Jorge Noda; Deacon Diego Chavez.
Res. & Rectory: 1358 N.W. First St., Miami, 33125. Tel: 305-649-5464; 305-649-5465; Fax: 305-541-0988. Email: stjohnboscochurch@sjbmiami.org.
Catechesis/Religious Program—Elisa P. de Gomez, D.R.E. Students 508.

16—ST. JOHN NEUMANN (1980) Rev. Msgr. Pablo A. Navarro; Rev. Jesus S. Medina, Parochial Vicar; Deacons Thomas Aguilu; Robert Binder; Ralph Gazitua; Henri Gonzalez; Louis Phang Sang; Marco Fernandez.
Res.: 12125 S.W. 107th Ave., Miami, 33176. Tel: 305-255-6642; Fax: 305-233-3742. Email: rejoiceinthelordsjn@yahoo.com. Web: www.sjn-miami.org.
School—12115 S.W. 107th Ave., Miami, 33176. Tel: 305-255-7315; 786-242-1514; Fax: 305-255-7316. Mrs. Maria Elena Vilas, Prin. Lay Teachers 16; Aides 7; Students 339.
Catechesis/Religious Program—Tel: 305-253-3081. John Fernandez, D.R.E. Students 988.

17—ST. KEVIN (1963) Revs. Jesus Saldana; Ferry Brutus (Haiti); Jorge Luis Bello; Deacons Robert B. Dinsmore; Michael Fresneda; Esteban Ortiz.
Res.: 12525 S.W. 42nd St., Miami, 33175. Tel: 305-223-0633; Fax: 305-554-9950. Email: stkev@bellsouth.net.
School—4001 S.W. 127 Ave., Miami, 33175. Tel: 305-227-7571; Fax: 305-227-7574. Email: kevsch@miamiarch.org. Web: www.stks.org. Dr. Mayra R. Constantino, Prin.; Dr. Sharyn D. Henderson, Asst. Prin. Lay Teachers 43; Students 733.
Catechesis/Religious Program—Tel: 305-223-2469. Mrs. Amparo Martinez, D.R.E. Students 501.

18—ST. KIERAN (1967) Rev. Marcos A. Somarriba.
Res.: 3605 S. Miami Ave., Miami, 33133. Tel: 305-854-1521. Email: stkieranchurch@aol.com.
Catechesis/Religious Program—Tel: 305-854-7166. Students 100.

19—ST. LOUIS (1963) Revs. Paul Vuturo; Michael A. Kish; Armando Tolosa Pita; Deacons John Green; Thomas Hanlon; Alex Lam; Vincent McInerney; John Peremenis; Jeffrey J. Reyes; Robert Yglesias.
Res.: 7270 S.W. 120th St., Pinecrest, 33156. Tel: 305-238-7562; Fax: 305-238-6844.
School—Tel: 305-238-7562, Ext. 200; Fax: 305-238-4296. Christine Mathisen, Prin. Lay Teachers 58; Students 500.
Catechesis/Religious Program—Tel: 305-238-7562. Maria Teresa Lopez, D.R.E. Students 740.

20—ST. MICHAEL THE ARCHANGEL (1947) Very Rev. Christopher Marino; Rev. Giovanni de Jesus Pena, Parochial Vicar; Deacon Ernesto Rodriguez.
Res.: 2987 W. Flagler St., Miami, 33135. Tel: 305-649-1811; Fax: 305-642-6815. Web: www.stmichaelmiami.org.
School—300 N.W. 28th Ave., Miami, 33125. Tel: 305-642-6732; Fax: 305-649-5867. Web: stmichaelmiami.com. Carmen Alfonso, Prin. Lay Teachers 35; Students 371.
Catechesis/Religious Program—Tel: 305-643-4661; Fax: 305-642-8574. Yolanda Del Rivero, D.R.E. Students 194.

21—MOTHER OF CHRIST (1983) Revs. Raul Angulo; Julio R. Solano; Deacons Jose Leroy Martinez; Manuel Saavedra; Lazaro Ulloa; Jose F. Rosado.
Rectory—2390 S.W. 139th Pl., Miami, 33175. Tel: 305-551-7046.
Church: 14141 S.W. 26th St., Miami, 33175. Tel: 305-559-6111; Fax: 305-551-7047.
School—(Grades PreK-8) Tel: 786-497-6111; Fax: 786-497-6113. Web: www.motherofchristcatholicschool.net. Lay Teachers 16; Students 215.
Catechesis/Religious Program—Tel: 305-559-0163. Students 966.

22—NOTRE DAME D'HAITI (1981) Revs. Reginald Jean-Mary; Emmanuel Bastien, Parochial Vicar.
Mailing Address: 110 N.E. 62nd St., Miami, 33138. Tel: 305-751-6289.
Catechesis/Religious Program—Tel: 305-758-5560; Fax: 305-895-1851; 305-751-6234. Rosel Lebreton, D.R.E. Students 236.

23—OUR LADY OF DIVINE PROVIDENCE (1973) Revs. Manuel A. Soler; Fermin Solana (Cuba); Deacon Eduardo Panellas.
Church & Mailing Address: 10205 W. Flagler St., Miami, 33174. Tel: 305-551-8113; 305-551-8114; Fax: 305-220-3164. Web: www.oldpcatholicchurch.com.
Res.: 10420 S.W. 4th St., Miami, 33174. Tel: 305-226-5058.
Catechesis/Religious Program—Tel: 305-551-8113, Ext. 2013. Students 221.

24—OUR LADY OF GUADALUPE (2001) Rev. Israel E. Mago.
Mailing Address: 11402 N.W. 41st St., Ste. 221, Doral, 33178. Tel: 305-593-6123; Fax: 305-593-6130.
Catechesis/Religious Program—Students 535.

25—OUR LADY OF LOURDES (1985) Rev. Msgr. Kenneth K. Schwanger; Revs. Patrick Charles, Parochial Vicar; Luis Roger Largaespada; Deacons Michael Plummer; Jose Naranjo. In Res., Rev. Andrzej Pietraszko.
Res.: 10452 S.W. 134th Pl., Miami, 33186. Tel: 305-380-7673.
Church: 11291 S.W. 142nd Ave., Miami, 33186. Tel: 305-386-4121; Fax: 305-386-6881. Web: www.ololourdes.org.
School—14000 S.W. 112th St., Miami, 33186. Tel: 305-386-8446; Fax: 305-386-6694. Web: www.ololjaguars.org. Thomas Halfaker, Prin.; Laura G. Sanchez, Asst. Prin. Lay Teachers 27; Students 608.
Catechesis/Religious Program—Tel: 305-386-4894; Fax: 305-386-6670. Students 1,020.

26—OUR LADY OF THE HOLY ROSARY (1959) Merged with St. Richard, Miami to form Our Lady of the Holy Rosary-St. Richard Church, Miami.

27—OUR LADY OF THE HOLY ROSARY - ST. RICHARD CHURCH (2010) Revs. Luis A. Perez; Adelson Moreira, O.S.S.T.; Deacon Robert F. O'Malley Jr.
Holy Rosary-St. Richard Church—Church: 9500 S.W. 184 St., Cutler Bay, 33157. Tel: 305-233-8711; Fax: 305-254-2756.
School—18455 Franjo Rd., Cutler Bay, 33157. Tel: 305-235-5442; Fax: 305-235-5670. Carlos Naumann, Prin. Lay Teachers 26; Students 389.
Catechesis/Religious Program—Tel: 305-233-8755. Paul Otero, D.R.E. Students 391.

28—SS. PETER AND PAUL (1938) Revs. Juan M. Lopez; Juan Luis Sanchez.
Res.: 900 S.W. 26th Rd., Miami, 33129. Tel: 305-858-2621; Fax: 305-858-8073.
School—1435 S.W. 12th Ave., Miami, 33129. Tel: 305-858-3722; Fax: 305-856-4322. Lay Teachers 34; Students 492.
Catechesis/Religious Program—Students 225.

29—PRINCE OF PEACE (1987) Rev. Francisco G. Diaz; Deacon Manuel Castellanos.
Church & Res.: 12800 N.W. 6th St., Miami, 33182. Tel: 305-559-3171; Fax: 305-559-3172.
Catechesis/Religious Program—Vivian Lorenzo, D.R.E. Students 410.

30—ST. RAYMOND (1969) Rev. Enrique J. Estrada.
Res.: 3475 S.W. 17th St., Miami, 33145. Tel: 305-446-2427; Fax: 305-445-7448. Web: www.straymond.info.
Catechesis/Religious Program—Students 175.

31—ST. RICHARD (1969) Merged with Our Lady of the Holy Rosary, Miami to form Our Lady of the Holy Rosary-St. Richard, Miami.

32—ST. ROBERT BELLARMINE (1968) Merged with and sacramental records at Corpus Christi Parish, Miami.

33—ST. THOMAS THE APOSTLE (1959) Revs. Daniel I. Kubala; Alvaro Huertas (Colombia); Lesly Jean (Haiti); Deacon Carlos Pulido.
Res.: 7377 S.W. 64th St., Miami, 33143. Tel: 305-665-5600; Fax: 305-662-9034. Email: info@stamiami.org. Web: www.stamiami.org.
School—Tel: 305-661-8591; Fax: 305-661-2181. Email: school@stamiami.org. Lisa Figueredo, Prin. Lay Teachers 49; Students 532.
Catechesis/Religious Program—Tel: 305-665-6862. Email: religioused@stamiami.org. Students 220.

34—ST. TIMOTHY (1960) Rev. Msgr. Tomas M. Marin; Revs. Miguel A. Sepulveda; Pedro M. Corces; Deacons Nelson Diaz; Fernando Bestard; Manuel Buigas; Manuel Canovaca; Benito Loyola; Roberto Ochoa.
Office: 5400 S.W. 102nd Ave., Miami, 33165. Tel: 305-274-8224; Fax: 305-598-1159. Web: www.sainttimothycatholic.org.
School—Tel: 305-274-8229; Fax: 305-598-7107. Maria Isabel de Leon, Prin. Lay Teachers 40; Students 630.
Sister Carolyn Learning Center—Tel: 305-598-3184; Fax: 305-412-6650. Mrs. Rosa I. Gonzalez, Dir. Learning Ctr. (PreK & 2-3) Lay Teachers 10; Students 90.
Catechesis/Religious Program—Tel: 305-274-8225; Fax: 305-412-6608. Sr. Karen Muniz, S.C.T.J.M., D.R.E. Students 465.

35—ST. VINCENT DE PAUL (1962) Merged with and sacramental records at Saint Rose of Lima Parish, Miami Shores.

36—VISITATION (1956) Rev. Curtis A. Kiddy. In Res., Rev. Harry Loubriel.
Res.: 19100 N. Miami Ave., Miami Gardens, FL 33169. Tel: 305-652-3624; Fax: 305-652-5207. Email: visitationparish@bellsouth.net. Web: www.visitationmiami.parishesonline.com.
Catechesis/Religious Program—100 N.E. 191st St., Miami, 33169. Tel: 305-651-7044. Email: ccddre@bellsouth.net. Students 153.

METROPOLITAN DADE COUNTY

COCONUT GROVE, ST. HUGH (1959), (Hispanic), Revs. George A. Garcia; Juan R. Torres.
Res.: 3455 Royal Rd., 33133. Email: sthugh@bellsouth.net. Web: www.st-hugh.org.
Office: 3460 Royal Rd., 33133. Tel: 305-444-8363; Fax: 305-444-4312.
School—Tel: 305-448-5602; Fax: 305-444-4299. Mr. Antonio R. Cejas, Prin. Lay Teachers 20; Students 303.
Catechesis/Religious Program—Students 210.

CORAL GABLES

1—ST. AUGUSTINE (1969) [CEM] Rev. Msgr. Michael Carruthers; Rev. Eric D. Zegeer.
Office & Church: 1400 Miller Rd., 33146. Tel: 305-661-1648; Fax: 305-661-6392. Web: www.saintaugustinechurch.org.
Catechesis/Religious Program—Students 281.

2—LITTLE FLOWER (1926) Revs. Michael W. Davis; Alfredo Rolon; Damian Flanagan; Deacons Miguel Parlade; Raul Flores; Roberto Fleitas.
Office: 2711 Indian Mound Tr., 33134. Tel: 305-446-9950; Fax: 305-446-7624. Web: www.churchofthelittleflower.com.
Res.: 1270 Anastasia Ave., 33134. Tel: 305-529-5475.
School—2701 Indian Mound Tr., 33134. Tel: 305-446-1738; Fax: 305-446-2877. Email: srrosalie@stscg.org. Sisters 3; Lay Teachers 45; Students 884.
Catechesis/Religious Program—Tel: 305-446-5540; Fax: 305-446-3784. Students 316.

HIALEAH

1—ST. BENEDICT (1973) Rev. Jose L. Paniagua (Spain).
Res.: 650 W. 80th St., 33014-4125. Tel: 305-558-2150.
Church: 701 W. 77th St., 33014-4125. Tel: 305-558-2150; Fax: 305-558-3705. Email: stbenedictcathol@bellsouth.net.
Catechesis/Religious Program—Tel: 305-557-2511. Maria de la Fe, D.R.E. Students 283.

2—ST. CECILIA (1971) Unassigned.1040 W. 29th St., 33012.

3—IMMACULATE CONCEPTION (1954) Rev. Francisco J. Hernandez. In Res., Rev. Alfred Cioffi; Deacons Abelardo DeGuzman; Manuel Alfonso.
Res.: 4497 W. First Ave., 33012. Tel: 305-822-2011; Fax: 305-821-3481. Web: www.icsmiami.org.
School—125 W. 45th St., 33012. Tel: 305-822-6461; Fax: 305-822-0289. Email: icschool@miamiarch.org. Mr. Eddy Garcia, Prin. Lay Teachers 47; Students 725.
Catechesis/Religious Program—Tel: 305-823-9563; Fax: 305-822-7868. Nubia Stanley, D.R.E. Students 396.

4—ST. JOHN THE APOSTLE (1945) Rev. Msgr. Oscar F. Castaneda; Rev. Rafael Cos; Deacon Julke Llorens.
Res.: 475 E. 4th St., 33010. Tel: 305-888-9769; Fax: 305-888-9341.
School—Tel: 305-888-6819; Fax: 305-887-1256. Web: www.stjohntheapostleschool.com. Mrs. Marilyn S. Bimonte, Prin. Lay Teachers 10; Students 270.
Catechesis/Religious Program—Angelica Millan, D.R.E. Students 240.

5—MOTHER OF OUR REDEEMER (1988) Rev. Jaime H. Acevedo.
Church: 8445 N.W. 186th St., Miami, 33015. Tel: 305-829-6141; Fax: 305-829-3059. Email: info@motherofourredeemer.org.

School—Tel: 306-829-3088. Mrs. Evelyn Salinas, Prin. Lay Teachers 15; Students 201.
Catechesis/Religious Program—Tel: 305-829-3988, Ext. 1102; Fax: 305-829-3019. Students 510.

6—SAN LAZARO (1982) Rev. Jose Espino. In Res., Rev. David Smith.
Res.: 4291 W. 18 Ln., 33012. Tel: 305-556-4045; Fax: 305-556-8918.
Catechesis/Religious Program—Tel: 305-558-4078. Sr. Olga Villar, D.R.E. Students 243.

7—SANTA BARBARA (1987) Rev. Miguel Gomez.
Mailing Address: 6801 W. 30th Ave., 33018. Tel: 305-556-4442; Fax: 305-558-7256.
Res.: 3004 W. 68th Pl., 33018. Tel: 305-827-1110.
Catechesis/Religious Program—Tel: 305-556-4442, Ext. 106. Students 536.

HOMESTEAD, SACRED HEART (1929) Revs. James McCreanor; Christian E. Plancher, S.M.M.
Church & Res.: 106 S.E. First Dr., 33030-7322. Tel: 305-247-4405; Fax: 305-245-3002. Web: sacredhearthomestead.com.
Catechesis/Religious Program—Tel: 305-247-0760. Students 426.

KEY BISCAYNE, ST. AGNES (1954) Very Rev. Jose L. Hernando; Rev. Luis Ardiel Rivero.
Res.: 100 Harbor Dr., 33149. Tel: 305-361-2351; 305-361-2451; Fax: 305-361-8514. Email: stagneschurch@bellsouth.net. Web: www.stagneschurchkb.org.
School—122 Harbor Dr., 33149. Tel: 305-361-3245; Fax: 305-361-6329. Mrs. Susana T. Rivera, Prin. Lay Teachers 32; Students 477.
Catechesis/Religious Program—Tel: 305-361-1378. Nery Quintela, D.R.E. Students 495.

LEISURE CITY, ST. MARTIN DE PORRES CATHOLIC CHURCH (1990), (Hispanic), Rev. Joaquin Rodriguez.
Mailing Address: 14881 S.W. 288th St., 33033. Tel: 305-248-5355; Fax: 305-245-3047.
Catechesis/Religious Program—Students 270.

MIAMI BEACH

1—ST. FRANCIS DE SALES (1964) Rev. Gabriel Vigues; Deacon Jose Irrizarry.
Res.: 621 Alton Rd., 33139. Tel: 305-672-0093; Fax: 305-673-8559. Web: www.saintfrancisonthebeach.com.
Catechesis/Religious Program—Students 75.

2—ST. JOSEPH (1942) Rev. Juan J. Sosa.
Res.: 8670 Byron Ave., 33141. Tel: 305-866-6567; Fax: 305-864-1069. Web: wwww.stjosephmiamibeach.com.
Catechesis/Religious Program—Fax: 305-864-1049. Students 140.

3—ST. PATRICK (1926) Rev. Msgr. John J. Vaughan; Revs. Wilfredo Contreras; Mathew Thundathil (India).
Office: 3716 Garden Ave., 33140. Tel: 305-531-1124; Fax: 305-538-3203.
Res.: 3700 Meridian Ave., 33140.
School—Tel: 305-534-4616; Fax: 305-538-5463. Bertha Moro, Prin. Lay Teachers 18; Students 238.
Catechesis/Religious Program—Students 195.

MIAMI GARDENS

1—ST. MONICA (1959) Rev. Samuel Muodiaju, C.S.Sp. (Nigeria); Deacon Marco Rosales.
Res.: 3490 N.W. 191st St., 33056. Tel: 305-621-9846; Fax: 305-621-5608. Email: pastor@saintmonica.org. Web: www.saintmonica.org.
Catechesis/Religious Program—Students 132.

2—ST. PHILIP NERI CATHOLIC CHURCH, Unassigned.15700 N.W. 20th Avenue Rd., 33054. Tel: 305-705-2010; Fax: 786-320-6055. Email: cjeanty@theadom.org.

MIAMI LAKES, OUR LADY OF THE LAKES (1967) Revs. Jose Alvarez; Peter Lambert; Deacons Roger Currier; Pablo A. Fernandez; Albert Mindel; Carlos Ramirez.
Res.: 15801 N.W. 67 Ave., 33014. Tel: 305-558-2202; Fax: 305-558-2631. Email: jalvarez@ollnet.com. 16020 Kingsmoor Way.
School—6600 Miami Lakeway N., 33014. Tel: 305-362-5315; Fax: 305-362-4573. Ricardo Briz, Prin. Lay Teachers 28; Students 510.
Catechesis/Religious Program—Anita Brown, D.R.E.; Rosa Diaz, C.R.E. Students 632.

MIAMI SHORES

1—ST. MARTHA (1970) Very Rev. Federico Capdepon.
Res.: 9221 Biscayne Blvd., 33138. Tel: 305-751-0005; Fax: 305-754-6930. Web: www.saintmartha.com.
Catechesis/Religious Program—Tel: 305-751-8759. Students 180.

2—ST. ROSE OF LIMA (1946) Rev. Msgr. Seamus Doyle; Rev. Yader F. Centeno, Sch.P. (Nicaragua).
Res.: 418 N.E. 105th St., 33138. Tel: 305-758-0539; Fax: 305-751-8398. Web: www.stroseoflimamiamishores.org.
School—425 N.E. 105th St., 33138. Tel: 305-751-4257; Fax: 305-751-5034. Sr. Bernadette Keane, I.H.M., Prin. Sisters 5; Lay Teachers 31; Students 540.
Catechesis/Religious Program—Tel: 305-757-6434. Students 167.

MIAMI SPRINGS, BLESSED TRINITY (1952) Revs. Joseph T. Carney; Isidro Perez (Cuba); Deacon Dennis E. Jordan.
Res.: 4020 Curtiss Pkwy., 33166. Tel: 305-871-5780; Fax: 305-871-5781. Web: www.blessed-trinity.org.
School—Tel: 305-871-5766; Fax: 305-876-1755. Mrs. Maria Teresa Perez, Prin. Lay Teachers 22; Students 273.
Catechesis/Religious Program—Tel: 305-876-1749. Students 195.

NORTH MIAMI, HOLY FAMILY (1950) Rev. Franky Jean.
Res.: 14500 N.E. 11 Ave., 33161. Tel: 305-947-5043; 305-947-1471; Fax: 305-949-5591.
School—14650 N.E. 12th Ave., 33161. Tel: 305-947-6535; Fax: 305-947-1826. Ms. Mary Ellen McKinney, Prin. Lay Teachers 15; Students 205.
Catechesis/Religious Program—Tel: 305-947-7739; Fax: 305-947-1417. Students 104.

NORTH MIAMI BEACH, ST. LAWRENCE (1956) Rev. William Elbert; Deacon Clyde McFarland.
Res.: 2200 N.E. 191st St., 33180. Tel: 305-932-3560; Fax: 305-936-8050.
School—Tel: 305-932-4912; Fax: 305-932-7898. Email: stlawschool@gmail.com. Web: www.stlaw.org. Mrs. Dian Hyatt, Prin. Lay Teachers 13; Students 153.
Child Care Center—Tel: 305-932-5366; Fax: 305-932-2346. Email: stlawrenceccc@aol.com. Lay Teachers 10; Students 75.
Catechesis/Religious Program—Tel: 305-931-6650. Email: stlawrence@gmail.com. Web: sites.google.com/site/stlawrencereled. Kelly Lee, D.R.E.; Joanne Lambert, D.R.E. Students 235.

OPA LOCKA

1—OUR LADY OF PERPETUAL HELP CHURCH (1954) Merged with and sacramental records at Saint James Parish, North Miami.

2—ST. PHILIP (1953) Merged with and sacramental records at Saint Monica Parish, Miami Gardens.

PRINCETON, ST. ANN MISSION (1961) Rev. Jesus Alberto Bohorquez.
Mailing Address: P.O. Box 924884, 33092-4884. Tel: 305-258-6998; 305-258-0834. Email: missionsantaananarauja@gmail.com. 13875 S.W. 264 St., Naranja, 33032.
Catechesis/Religious Program—Tel: 305-248-5418. Students 800.

SUNNY ISLES BEACH, ST. MARY MAGDALEN (1955) Very Rev. Bernard G. Kirlin. In Res., Rev. Armando Alonso.
Res.: 17775 N. Bay Rd., 33160. Tel: 305-931-0600; Fax: 305-931-0601. Email: parishoffice@stmmsib.org. Web: www.stmmsib.org.
Catechesis/Religious Program—Students 144.

OUTSIDE METROPOLITAN DADE COUNTY

BIG PINE KEY, MONROE CO., ST. PETER (1962) Rev. Thomas Mullane.
Res.: 31300 Overseas Hwy., P.O. Box 430657, 33043. Tel: 305-872-2537; Fax: 305-872-0122. Email: info@stpeterbpk.com. Web: www.stpeterbpk.com.
Catechesis/Religious Program—Students 103.
Mission—Sugarloaf Firehouse Sugarloaf Shores, 33042.

COCONUT CREEK, BROWARD CO., ST. LUKE (1985) Merged with and sacramental records at Saint Vincent Parish, Margate.

CORAL SPRINGS, BROWARD CO.

1—ST. ANDREW (1969) Very Rev. George Puthusseril; Revs. Flavio Montes-Colon; Craig S. Malzacher, Parochial Vicar; Deacon Denis Mieyal.
Res.: 9950 N.W. 29th St., 33065-6103. Tel: 954-752-3950; Fax: 954-752-3986. Email: parish@sacccs.org. Web: www.standrewparish.org.
School—9990 N.W. 29th St., 33065. Tel: 954-753-1280; Fax: 954-753-1933. Email: principal@sacccs.org. Darrell Fulford, Prin. Lay Teachers 24; Students 206.
Early Childhood Enrichment Center—Tel: 954-905-6374; Fax: 954-905-6345. Mrs. Lydia Vargas, Dir. Lay Teachers 16; Students 125.
Catechesis/Religious Program—Tel: 954-905-6323. Mary Dorris, D.R.E. Students 652.

2—ST. ELIZABETH ANN SETON (1985) Revs. Edward M. Kelly; John M. Paszko; Deacons John Friel; Frank Gonzalez.
Res.: 1401 Coral Ridge Dr., 33071. Tel: 954-753-3330; Fax: 954-753-8442. Email: setonoffice@aol.com. Web: www.stelizabethcsfl.org.
Catechesis/Religious Program—Tel: 954-345-7071. Students 899.

DANIA BEACH, BROWARD CO., CHURCH OF THE RESURRECTION (1958) Merged with and sacramental records at Saint Maurice Parish, Dania Beach.

DAVIE, BROWARD CO., SAINT DAVID (1974) Revs. Gabriel O'Reilly; George Packuvettithara (India).
Res.: 3900 S. University Dr., 33328. Tel: 954-475-8046; Fax: 954-370-0819.
School—Tel: 954-472-7086; Fax: 954-452-8243. Mrs. Jane Broder, Prin. Lay Teachers 45; Students 494.
Catechesis/Religious Program—Tel: 954-475-1521. Katherine Bambenek, D.R.E. Students 400.

DEERFIELD BEACH, BROWARD CO.

1—ST. AMBROSE (1962) Revs. John Bryan Dalton; Michael Lynch.
Res. & Office: 380 S. Federal Hwy., 33441. Tel: 954-427-2225; Fax: 954-421-1638. Email: stambrosedeerfield@yahoo.com. Web: www.stambrosechurch.catholicweb.com.
School—Tel: 954-427-2226; Fax: 954-427-4293. Email: ambsch@miamiarch.org. Web: www.stambroseschooldeerfield.catholicweb.com. Ms. Anita Gentile, Prin. Lay Teachers 20; Students 200.
Catechesis/Religious Program—Students 131.

2—OUR LADY OF MERCY (1974) Rev. Kenneth D. Whittaker.
Church & Office: 5201 N. Military Tr., 33064. Tel: 954-421-3246; Fax: 954-421-1973.
Catechesis/Religious Program—Students 30.

FORT LAUDERDALE, BROWARD CO.

1—ST. ANTHONY (1921) Very Rev. Jeremiah Singleton.
Res.: 901 N.E. 2nd St., 33301. Tel: 954-463-4614; Fax: 954-527-5411. Email: stanthony@bellsouth.net. Web: www.saintanthonyfl.org.
School—820 N.E. Third St., 33301. Tel: 954-467-7747; Fax: 954-467-9908. Mrs. Lizette Hoelzel, Prin. Lay Teachers 25; Students 413.
Catechesis/Religious Program—Tel: 954-467-7749. Email: sasreligioused@yahoo.com. Students 240.

2—ST. BONAVENTURE (1985) Rev. Edmond Prendergast; Deacons Arthur DeNunzio; Joseph M. Pearce; Thomas Malinoski; Domingo Vasquez; Peter Trahan.
Res.: 1301 S.W. 136th Ave., Davie, 33325-4300. Tel: 954-424-9504; 954-424-9505; Fax: 954-424-9505. Email: info@stbonaventurechurch.com. Web: www.stbonaventurechurch.com.
Catechesis/Religious Program—Tel: 954-476-5204; Fax: 954-236-7983. Susan McCrea, D.R.E. Students 1,177.

3—ST. CLEMENT (1954) Revs. Robes C. Charles; Lazarus J. Govin.
Res.: 2975 N. Andrews Ave., 33311. Tel: 954-563-1183; Fax: 954-564-6628.
Catechesis/Religious Program—Tel: 954-563-2838. Sr. Anne Stinfil, D.R.E. Students 152.

4—DIVINE MERCY MISSION (1980) Merged with and sacramental records at Saint Clement Parish, Fort Lauderdale.

5—ST. HELEN (1968) Rev. Msgr. William Dever; Revs. Isidore Baky; Robert M. Ayala.
Res.: 3033 N.W. 33rd Ave., 33311. Tel: 954-731-7314; Fax: 954-739-9632.
School—3340 W. Oakland Park Blvd., 33311. Tel: 954-739-7094; Fax: 954-739-0797. Terry Maus, Prin. Lay Teachers 23; Students 218.
Catechesis/Religious Program—Tel: 954-484-3036. Students 180.

6—ST. JEROME (1960) Rev. Michael Grady; Deacon Frank B. O'Gorman.
Res.: 2533 S.W. 9th Ave., 33315. Tel: 954-525-4133; Fax: 954-525-0964. Web: stjeromecatholicchurch.com.
School—Tel: 954-524-1990; Fax: 954-524-7439. Sr. Vivian Gomez, R.F., Prin. Sisters of St. Philip Neri 4; Lay Teachers 19; Students 351.
Catechesis/Religious Program—2601 S.W. 9th Ave., 33315. Students 75.

7—ST. JOHN THE BAPTIST (1969) Rev. Msgr. Vincent T. Kelly; Rev. William H. Bowles. In Res., Rev. William J. Sullivan, O.S.S.T.
Res.: 4595 Bayview Dr., 33308. Tel: 954-771-8950; Fax: 954-771-4178. Email: church@stjohncc.org.
Catechesis/Religious Program—Students 230.

8—ST. MARK (1985) Revs. Edmond F. Whyte; Rolando Cabrera (Cuba), Parochial Vicar; Deacons Vincent Farinato; John Lorenzo.
Office: 5601 S. Flamingo Rd., Southwest Ranches, 33330. Tel: 954-434-3777; Fax: 954-434-3125. Email: stmark5601@aol.com.
Res.: 5551 S.W. 127th Ave., Southwest Ranches, 33330. Tel: 954-689-0519.
School—Tel: 954-434-3887; Fax: 954-434-3595. Shirley Sandusky, Prin. Students 680.
Catechesis/Religious Program—Tel: 954-252-9899; Fax: 954-434-0621. Susan Mikluscak, D.R.E. Students 985.

9—ST. MAURICE (1970) Rev. Roger Holoubek; Deacon Norman Carroll.
Res.: 2851 Stirling Rd., Dania Beach, 33312. Tel: 954-961-7777; Fax: 954-961-4358. Web: www.stmaurice.org.
Day Care Center: Tel: 954-961-5585; Fax: 954-961-5510.
Catechesis/Religious Program—Students 117.

10—OUR LADY QUEEN OF MARTYRS (1956) Rev. Jorge L. Rodriguez.
Res.: 2731 S.W. 11 Ct. (Happy Hoyer St.), 33312. Tel: 954-583-8725; Fax: 954-583-9315.

School—2785 Happy Hoyer St., 33312. Tel: 954-583-8112; Fax: 954-797-4984. Web: olqmfl.com. Mrs. Althea Mossop, Prin. Lay Teachers 18; Students 202.
Catechesis / Religious Program—Students 307.

11—ST. PIUS X (1959) Revs. Luis R. Rivera; Harry Ringenberger; Deacon George P. Sutcavage.
Res.: 2500 N.E. 33rd Ave., 33305. Tel: 954-564-1763; Fax: 954-568-2212. Web: www.saintpiusthetenth.org.
Church: 2511 N. Ocean Blvd. (A1A), 33308.
Catechesis / Religious Program—Students 30.

12—ST. SEBASTIAN (1959) Rev. James F. Fetscher.
Parish Office: 2000 S.E. 25th Ave., 33316. Tel: 954-524-9344; Fax: 954-524-9347. Email: stsebastia@aol.com.
Rectory—2518 Barbara Dr., 33316.
Catechesis / Religious Program—Students 45.

HALLANDALE, BROWARD CO.

1—ST. CHARLES BORROMEO (1968) Merged with and sacramental records at Saint Matthew Parish, Hallandale Beach.

2—ST. MATTHEW (1959) [CEM] Rev. James A. Quinn.
Res.: 542 Blue Heron Dr., Hallandale Beach, 33009. Tel: 954-458-1590; Fax: 954-458-0612. Web: www.saintmatthewcc.com.
Catechesis / Religious Program—Tel: 954-458-3600. Students 45.

HOLLYWOOD, BROWARD CO.

1—ST. BERNADETTE (1959) Rev. Brendan Dalton.
Res.: 7450 Stirling Rd., 33024. Tel: 954-432-5313; Fax: 954-432-5344. Web: www.stbernadette-fl.com.
School—Tel: 954-432-7022; Fax: 954-443-8030. Mrs. Michele Sanders, Prin.Web: www.stbernadettefl.com. Lay Teachers 16; Students 259.
Catechesis / Religious Program—Tel: 954-432-6300. Students 100.

2—LITTLE FLOWER (1924) Very Rev. Thomas O'Dwyer; Rev. Richard Mullen, O.S.A.; Deacons Walter Keough; William A. Watkins.
Res.: 1805 Pierce St., 33020. Tel: 954-922-3517; Fax: 954-922-6634. Email: littleflower_hwd@hotmail.com. Web: www.littleflowerhwd.org.
School—1843 Pierce St., 33020. Tel: 954-922-1217; Fax: 954-927-8962. Web: www.littleflowerleopards.org. Mrs. Maureen McNulty, Prin. Lay Teachers 19; Students 286.
Catechesis / Religious Program—Tel: 954-923-7634. Students 101.

3—NATIVITY (1960) [CEM] Revs. Patrick J. Murnane; Victor Babin; Jean Claude Jean-Philippe; Randall Musselman; Deacons Chandy Luka; Richard A. Turcotte.
Res.: 5220 Johnson St., 33021. Tel: 954-987-3300; Fax: 954-987-3044.
School—Tel: 954-987-3300, Ext. 221; Fax: 954-987-6368. Mrs. Elena Ortiz, Prin.; Ms. Judy Skehan, Vice Prin. Lay Teachers 44; Students 865.
Catechesis / Religious Program—Tel: 954-987-3300, Ext. 214. Students 400.

4—OUR LADY APARECIDA MISSION (1996) Merged with and sacramental records at Saint Vincent Parish, Margate.

KEY LARGO, MONROE CO., ST. JUSTIN MARTYR (1973) Rev. Stephen J. Hilley.
Res.: 105500 Overseas Hwy., 33037. Tel: 305-451-1316; Fax: 305-451-4633. Web: www.st-justinthemartyr.org.
Catechesis / Religious Program—Donna Roberts, D.R.E. Students 90.

KEY WEST, MONROE CO., ST. MARY STAR OF THE SEA (1846) Revs. John C. Baker; John R. Valega; Deacon Peter H. Batty.
Res.: 1010 Windsor Ln., 33040. Tel: 305-294-1018; Fax: 305-292-8096. Email: stmarystar@bellsouth.net. Web: www.keywestcatholicparish.org.
School—Mary Immaculate, Star of the Sea School, 700 Truman Ave., 33040. Tel: 305-294-1031; Fax: 305-294-2095. Web: maryimmaculatestarofthesea.com. Beth Harris, Prin. Brothers 1; Sisters 3; Lay Teachers 10; Students 175.
Catechesis / Religious Program—Tel: 305-295-0306. Students 150.
Mission—St. Mary, Star of the Sea Outreach Mission 5640 Mac Donald Ave., Monroe Co. 33040. Tel: 305-292-3013; Fax: 305-292-3014.
St. Mary Soup Kitchen—2700 Flagler Ave., 33040. Tel: 305-294-2772.

LAUDERDALE-BY-THE-SEA, BROWARD CO., ASSUMPTION CHURCH (1959) Very Rev. Michael Greer.
Res.: 2001 S. Ocean Blvd., 33062. Tel: 954-941-7647; Fax: 954-941-9620.
Catechesis / Religious Program—

LAUDERHILL, BROWARD CO., ST. GEORGE (1964) Merged with and sacramental records at Our Lady Queen of Martyrs Parish, Fort Lauderdale.

LIGHTHOUSE POINT, BROWARD CO., ST. PAUL THE APOSTLE (1968) Revs. Michael Hourigan; Joseph Maroor (India).
Res.: 2700 N.E. 36th St., 33064. Tel: 954-943-9154; 954-943-9155; Fax: 954-943-1954.
Catechesis / Religious Program—Students 106.

MARATHON, MONROE CO., SAN PABLO (1958) Very Rev. Gerald R. Morris.
Res.: 550 122nd St. Ocean, 33050. Tel: 305-289-0636; Fax: 305-743-8192. Email: sanpablo1@aol.com. Web: www.sanpablochurch.com.
Catechesis / Religious Program—Students 30.

MARGATE, BROWARD CO., ST. VINCENT (1960) Revs. Joseph F. Pranzo, C.S.; Alexander P. Dalpiaz, C.S.; Jefferson O. Bariviera, C.S.
Parish Office: 6350 N.W. 18th St., 33063-2320. Tel: 954-972-0434; Fax: 954-971-9411. Email: stvincent7@aol.com. Web: stvincentcatholicchurchmargate.org.
Res.: 6280 N.W. 18th St., 33063-2320. Tel: 954-586-4359.
Catechesis / Religious Program—Tel: 954-972-9907. Students 440.

MIRAMAR, BROWARD CO.

1—ST. BARTHOLOMEW (1962) Revs. Andrew Chan-A-Sue, Admin.; Jean Jadotte, Parochial Vicar; Deacons David Smith; Michel du Chaussee; Montas Onelien.
Res.: 8005 Miramar Pkwy., 33025. Tel: 954-431-3600; Fax: 954-435-9591.
School—8003 Miramar Pkwy., 33025. Tel: 954-431-5253; Fax: 954-431-3385. Christine M. Gonzalez, Prin. Lay Teachers 17; Students 224.
Catechesis / Religious Program—Students 335.

2—BLESSED JOHN XXIII CHURCH (2002) Revs. Ernest Biriruka (Burundi); Vivian Loughrey (Ireland); Deacon Victor Lopez.
Office: 16800 Miramar Pkwy., 33027. Tel: 954-392-5062; Fax: 954-392-5063. Email: blessedjohn23@hotmail.com.
Res.: 3638 S.W. 166th Ave., 33027.
Catechesis / Religious Program—Students 579.

3—ST. STEPHEN (1956) Revs. Alejandro Roque, O.M.I.; George Roy, O.M.I.; Paul Dass Selvaraj, O.M.I.
Mailing Address: 6044 S.W. 19th St., 33023. Tel: 954-987-1100; Fax: 954-966-9881.
Church: 2000 S. State Rd. 7, 33023.
Catechesis / Religious Program—Tel: 954-962-8801. Students 329.

NORTH LAUDERDALE, BROWARD CO., OUR LADY QUEEN OF HEAVEN (1974) Rev. Kidney M. Saint Jean.
Res. & Church: 1032 S.W. 49th Terr., Margate, 33068. Tel: 954-974-1178; Fax: 954-972-4008.
Catechesis / Religious Program—Students 170.

OAKLAND PARK, BROWARD CO., BLESSED SACRAMENT (1961) Rev. Robert F. Tywoniak; Deacon Dan Blaha.
Res.: 1701 E. Oakland Park Blvd., 33334. Tel: 954-564-1010; Fax: 954-566-0301. Email: bscc1701@bellsouth.net.
Catechesis / Religious Program—Students 25.

PARKLAND, BROWARD CO., MARY HELP OF CHRISTIANS CHURCH (1989) Revs. Thomas Wisniewski; Jorge I. Puerta; Deacons Vincent Eberling Jr.; Mario Lopez.
Church: 5980 University Dr., 33067. Tel: 954-323-8012; Fax: 954-323-8011. Email: parish@mhoc.org. Web: www.mhocrc.org.
School—6000 University Dr., 33067. Tel: 954-323-8006; Fax: 954-323-8010. Web: mhocschool.org. Dr. Stephen Brown, Prin. Lay Teachers 26; Students 485.
Catechesis / Religious Program—Tel: 954-323-8025. Students 642.

PEMBROKE PINES, BROWARD CO.

1—ST. BONIFACE (1971) Rev. Antonio R. Silio; Deacons Khatchig Chirinian; Jesus Tosco. In Res., Rev. Kris Bartos.
Res.: 8330 Johnson St., 33024. Tel: 954-432-2750; Fax: 954-432-2756. Web: www.stbonifacefl.com.
Catechesis / Religious Program—Students 174.

2—ST. EDWARD (1995) Revs. John P. Peloso; Albert Lahens Jr.; Deacons Carl R. Cramer; Mario Ganuza.
Res. & Church Address: 19000 Pines Blvd., 33029. Tel: 954-436-7944; Fax: 954-436-7506.
Catechesis / Religious Program—Tel: 954-430-4107. Students 2,000.

3—ST. MAXIMILIAN KOLBE (1983) Revs. Jeffrey McCormick; Alberto Rodriguez, D.SS.T.; Deacons Carl Carrieri; Jose Bermudez; Scott Joiner; Pierre Douyon.
Res.: 11051 N.W. 16th St., 33026-4034. Tel: 954-432-8289. Email: office@stmax.cc. Web: www.stmax.cc.
Church: 701 N. Hiatus Rd., 33026. Tel: 954-432-0206; Fax: 954-432-0775.
School—St. Maximilian Kolbe Education Center, Pre School (2.5 - 4 years old), 601 N. Hiatus Rd., 33026. Tel: 954-885-7250; Fax: 954-885-7252. Email: pre-school@stmax.cc. Mrs. Bernadette Viscomi, Dir. Students 95.
Catechesis / Religious Program—Tel: 954-885-7260; Fax: 954-885-7261. Students 640.

PLANTATION, BROWARD CO., ST. GREGORY (1959) Revs. Michael Hoyer; Patrick J. Naughton; Manuel Alvarez.
Res.: 200 N. University Dr., 33324. Tel: 954-473-6261; Fax: 954-473-4599. Web: www.saintgeorge.org.
School—Tel: 954-473-8169; Fax: 954-472-1638. Mrs. Cari Canino, Prin.; Mr. James Harrington, Asst. Prin. Lay Teachers 52; Students 811.
Catechesis / Religious Program—Tel: 954-473-8321. Students 340.

POMPANO BEACH, BROWARD CO.

1—ST. COLEMAN (1959) Revs. Thomas F. Foudy; Luis Garcia.
Res.: 1200 S. Federal Hwy., 33062. Tel: 954-942-3533; Fax: 954-942-7869.
School—Tel: 954-942-3500; Fax: 954-785-0603. Lay Teachers 39; Aides 9; Students 625.
Catechesis / Religious Program—1285 S.E. 22nd Ave., 33062. Tel: 954-782-1461. Students 230.

2—ST. ELIZABETH OF HUNGARY CATHOLIC CHURCH (1959) Revs. Steven O'Hala; Fritzner Bellonce; Deacons Willie Harris Sr.; Daniel Moretti.
Res.: 3331 N.E. 10th Ter., 33064-5298. Tel: 954-941-8117; Fax: 954-941-0999.
Catechesis / Religious Program—Tel: 954-943-6801; Fax: 954-941-0999. Mrs. Deborah Andra, D.R.E. Students 414.

3—ST. GABRIEL (1967) Rev. Anthony Mulderry; Deacon Joseph O. Soucy.
Res.: 731 N. Ocean Blvd., 33062. Tel: 954-943-3684; Fax: 954-943-3656.
Catechesis / Religious Program—Students 10.

4—ST. HENRY (1969) [CEM] Rev. Francis Akwue, C.S.Sp.
Res.: 1500 S. Andrews Ave., 33069. Tel: 954-785-2450; Fax: 954-785-6958. Email: pastor@sainthenrys.org. Web: www.sainthenrys.org.
Catechesis / Religious Program—Students 25.

5—ST. JOSEPH MISSION (1981) Merged with and sacramental records at Saint Elizabeth of Hungary Parish, Pompano Beach.

6—OUR LADY OF CZESTOCHOWA MISSION (1997), (Polish), Rev. Klemens Dabrowski, S.Ch.
2400 N.E. 12th St., 33062. Tel: 954-545-3861; Fax: 954-946-0512. Web: www.polishchurch.com.
Catechesis / Religious Program—Students 65.

7—SAN ISIDRO (1970) Very Rev. Abel Barajas; Rev. Philip Scheiding.
Res.: 2310 Martin Luther King Blvd., 33069-1591. Tel: 954-971-8780; Fax: 954-972-3607. Web: www.sanisidro.org.
Catechesis / Religious Program—Students 157.

SUNRISE, BROWARD CO.

1—ALL SAINTS (1982) Revs. Liam T. Quinn; Andy Lorenzo-Puga; Deacons Vincent Tola; Giuseppe Tollis.
Office: 10900 W. Oakland Park Blvd., 33351. Tel: 954-742-2666; Fax: 954-741-7238. Web: www.allsaintsvillage.com.
School—Tel: 954-742-4842; Fax: 954-742-4870. Mrs. Antoinette McNamara, Prin. Students 285.
Catechesis / Religious Program—Tel: 954-742-7742. Students 450.

2—ST. BERNARD (1971) Revs. Carlos Vega; Ivan Toledo (Cuba).
Office: 8279 Sunset Strip, 33322. Tel: 954-741-7800; Fax: 954-742-4558.
Res.: 2370 N.W. 83rd Ave., 33322.
Catechesis / Religious Program—Tel: 954-741-0275. Students 127.

TAMARAC, BROWARD CO., ST. MALACHY (1973) Revs. Dominick O'Dwyer; Anthony O'Brien; Deacons Nicholas Costea; Joseph Sommovigo; Bernard Bonnick (Jamaica).
Res.: 6200 John Horan Terr., 33321. Tel: 954-726-1237; Fax: 954-726-0822. Email: stmalachy@comcast.net.
Catechesis / Religious Program—Tel: 954-721-5337. Concetta Sobkowski, D.R.E. Students 126.

TAVERNIER, MONROE CO., SAN PEDRO (1954) Rev. Henryk Pawelec.
Res.: 89500 Overseas Hwy., Plantation Key, 33070. Tel: 305-852-5372; Fax: 305-852-3315. Web: www.sanpedroparish.org.
Catechesis / Religious Program—Students 109.

WEST HOLLYWOOD, BROWARD CO., ANNUNCIATION (1959) Rev. Michael Quilligan; Deacon Mitchell C. Abdallah.
Res.: 3781 S.W. 39th St., 33023. Tel: 954-989-0606; Fax: 954-989-0660.
School—3751 S.W. 39th St., 33023. Tel: 954-989-8287. Web: www.annum.org. Mrs. Alexandra Fernandez, Prin. Lay Teachers 18; Students 288.
Catechesis / Religious Program—Students 65.

WESTON, BROWARD CO., ST. KATHARINE DREXEL (2001) Rev. Enrique Delgado; Deacon Paul Brancheau.
Office: 2700 Glades Cir., Ste. 200, 33327. Tel: 954-389-5003; Fax: 954-389-1228. Email: stkatdrx@bellsouth.net. Web: www.st-katharinedrexel.org.
Catechesis / Religious Program—Tel: 954-389-1219. Students 731.

Special Assignment:
Rev. Msgr.—
Souckar, Michael A., Doctoral Studies, Rome, Italy
Revs.—
Adu, Martin K., Chap., Jackson Memorial Hospital
Nwankwo, Fidelis, C.S.Sp., Chap., Jackson Memorial Hospital

On Duty Outside the Archdiocese:
Rev. Msgr.—
Anderson, Andrew L., J.C.D., St. Vincent de Paul Regional Seminary, Boynton Beach
Revs.—
Alfaro, Jose N., St. Vincent de Paul Regional Seminary, Boynton Beach
O'Leary, John, Mission work, Peru
Quijano, Jose Juan, St. Vincent de Paul Regional Seminary, Boynton Beach

On Leave:
Revs.—
Colominas, Octavio
Garcia, Michel
Perales, Jorge
Rivero, Jordi
Romanello, Carmelo
Saenz, Jorge L.

Retired:
Most Rev.—
Favalora, John C., D.D., S.T.L., M.Ed.
Rev. Msgrs.—
Brice, Frederick J.
Cassidy, Martin J.
Delaney, John W.
Eivers, Michael J.
Fogarty, Noel, P.A., V.F.
Garcia, Pedro F.
Glorie, John W.
Hennessey, William J., S.T.L., M.S., V.G., P.A.
Martin, Emilio
Morras, Xavier
Ordax, Emiliano
Parappally, James (India)
Perez, Pedro Luis
Reynolds, James B.
Vallina, Emilio
Revs.—
Acevedo, Antonio
Angelini, Joseph
Bennett, Noel I.
Blasco, Ignacio
Boned, Enrique
Brohammer, Ronald
Cabrera, Sergio
Carbajales, Ignacio
Cardona, George
Carrillo, Sergio
Casabon, Luis
Clements, Charles
Connaughton, James
Coucelo, Andres
Dennison, Arthur
Duffy, George
Fenger, Guy
Fink, John
Fishwick, Joseph
Garcia, Jose
Garcia-Miro, Sergio
Gubbins, John
Honold, Thomas G.
Huesca, Omar A.
Kent, Daniel
Lleo, Pedro
Lyons, Lawrence
Massi, Anthony
McGrath, John
McLaughlin, John
Medina, Rolando
Melley, James J.
Mitchell, Walter
Miyares, Carlos
Molano, Ernesto, J.C.L.
Morras, Ignacio
Mulcahy, Sean
Murphy, James
Noguera, Ronald
O'Neill, Patrick
O'Sullivan, Sean
Pedroso, Rafael
Perez, Armando
Planas, Salvador
Puisis, Leonard
Pusak, Ronald, J.C.L.
Rausch, Dennis
Reeves, Mark Thomas, J.C.L.
Russell, David
Shannon, Brendan
Slevin, Patrick C.
Soulliere, Richard
Sullivan, Michael P.
Valoret, Joseph
Villegas, Hernando

Permanent Deacons:
Abdallah, Mitchell C., Annunciation, West Hollywood
Aguayo, Orlando, Our Lady of the Lakes, Miami Lakes
Aguilu, Thomas, St. John Neumann, Miami
Alfonso, Manuel, Immaculate Conception, Hialeah
Baez, Rodolfo, St. John Bosco, Miami
Batty, Peter H., St. Mary Star of the Sea, Key West
Benavides, Luis, Corpus Christi, Miami
Beregszaszi, Miklos A., St. Catherine of Siena, Miami
Bermudez, Jose, St. Maximilian Kolbe, Pembroke Pines
Bestard, Fernando, Bereavement Ministry
Binder, Robert, St. John Neumann, Miami
Blanco, Eduardo, St. Brendan, Miami
Blanco, Emilio, St. Benedict, Hialeah
Bonnick, Bernard (Jamaica), St. Malachy, Tamarac
Brancheau, Paul, St. Katharine Drexel, Weston
Buigas, Manuel, St. Timothy, Miami
Calvo-Forte, Rafael, St. Brendan, Miami
Canovaca, Manuel, Renovacion Catolica Carismatica
Carrieri, Carl, St. Maximilian Kolbe, Pembroke Pines
Carrion, Jose, Epiphany, Miami
Carroll, Norman, St. Maurice, Dania Beach
Castellanos, Manuel, Prince of Peace, Miami
Chavez, Diego, St. John Bosco, Miami
Chirinian, Khatchig, St. Boniface, Pembroke Pines
Chirinos, Jose, St. Augustine, Coral Gables
Costea, Nicholas, St. Malachy, Tamarac
Cramer, Carl R., St. Edward, Pembroke Pines
Cruz, Rafael, Detention Ministry
Currier, Roger, Our Lady of the Lakes, Miami Lakes
Dawson, Thomas, Holy Redeemer, Miami
de los Reyes, Rafael, Apostolate of the Divine Mercy
DeGuzman, Abelardo, Immaculate Conception, Hialeah
DeLuca, Arnold J., St. Edward, Pembroke Pines
DeNunzio, Arthur, St. Bonaventure, Davie
Desmornes, Jean E., St. Clement, Fort Lauderdale
Diaz, Nelson, St. Timothy, Miami
Dinsmore, Robert B., St. Kevin, Miami
Douyon, Pierre, St. Maximilian Kolbe, Pembroke Pines
Du-Chaussee, Michel, St. Bartholomew, Miramar
Eagan, Thomas V., Epiphany, Miami
Eberling, Vincent, Jr., Mary Help of Christians, Parkland
Edel, Charles, St. Ambrose, Deerfield Beach
Farias, Edgardo, Detention Ministry
Farinato, Vincent, St. Mark, Southwest Ranches
Fernandez, Marco, St. John Neumann, Miami
Fernandez, Pablo A., Our Lady of the Lakes, Miami Lakes
Fleitas, Roberto, Little Flower, Coral Gables
Fleurimond, Alpha, Sacred Heart, Homestead
Flores, Raul, Little Flower, Coral Gables
Franklin, Thomas, Holy Redeemer, Miami
Fresneda, Michael, St. Kevin, Miami
Friel, John, St. Elizabeth Ann Seton, Coral Springs
Galvez, Rene, Annunciation, West Hollywood
Ganuza, Mario, St. Edward, Pembroke Pines
Gazitua, Ralph, St. John Neumann, Miami
Gervasi, Angelo, St. Elizabeth Ann Seton, Coral Springs
Gibson, George, Christ the King, Miami
Gonzalez, Frank, St. Elizabeth Ann Seton, Coral Springs
Gonzalez, Henri, St. John Neumann, Miami
Gonzalez, Jorge G., Camino del Matrimonio
Gordillo, Jose Manuel, Mother of Our Redeemer, Miami
Green, John F., St. Louis, Pinecrest
Guritza, Albert, St. Peter, Big Pine Key
Hanlon, Thomas F., St. Louis, Pinecrest
Harris, Willie, Sr., St. Elizabeth of Hungary, Pompano Beach
Horton, William, St. Gregory, Plantation
Irrizarry, Jose, St. Francis de Sales, Miami Beach
Jimenez, Manuel, St. Brendan, Miami
Joiner, Scott, St. Maximilian Kolbe, Pembroke Pines
Jordan, Dennis E., C.A.C., Blessed Trinity, Miami Springs
Kelly, Edgar, St. Brendan, Miami
Keough, Walter, Little Flower, Hollywood
Kirk, John, San Pablo, Marathon
Lam, Alex S., St. Louis, Pinecrest
Lannon, Billy, Jr., St. Brendan, Miami
Lee, Steven, Gesu, Miami
Leon, Michael, Blessed Sacrament, Oakland Park
Livingstone, Donald, Epiphany, Miami
Llorens, Julke, St. John the Apostle, Hialeah
Lopez, Mario, Mary Help of Christians, Parkland
Lorenzo, John, St. Mark, Southwest Ranches
Loyola, Benito, St. Timothy, Miami
Luka, Chandy, Nativity, Hollywood
Maalouf, Joseph, Visitation, Miami Gardens
Malinoski, Thomas, B.A., St. Bonaventure, Davie
Martinez, Jose, Mother of Christ, Miami
McFarland, Clyde, St. Lawrence, North Miami
McGuinn, Gerald, Our Lady of Mercy, Deerfield Beach
McInerney, Vincent, St. Louis, Pinecrest
Merkel, Arthur, Good Shepherd, Miami
Mieyal, Denis, St. Andrew, Coral Springs
Millikin, Randy, St. Elizabeth of Hungary, Pompano Beach
Mindel, Albert, Our Lady of the Lakes, Miami Lakes
Moreno, Vicente, St. Catherine of Siena, Miami
Moretti, Daniel, St. Elizabeth of Hungary, Pompano Beach
Munter, Paul H., Epiphany, Miami
Naranjo, Jose, Our Lady of Lourdes, Miami
O'Gorman, Frank B., St. Jerome, Fort Lauderdale
O'Malley, Robert F., Jr., St. Richard, Village of Palmetto Bay
Ochoa, Roberto, St. Timothy, Miami
Okragleski, John, St. Jerome, Fort Lauderdale
Onelien, Montas, St. Bartholomew, Miramar
Ortiz, Esteban, St. Kevin, Miami
Panellas, Eduardo, Our Lady of Divine Providence, Miami
Parlade, Miguel, Little Flower, Coral Gables
Pearce, Joseph M., St. Bonaventure, Davie
Peremenis, John, St. Louis, Pinecrest
Perez, Antonio, Corpus Christi, Miami
Perez, Manuel, Our Lady of Charity Shrine, Miami
Perez, Marcos, Epiphany, Miami
Phang Sang, Louis, St. John Neumann, Miami
Pierce, John (Jack), St. Peter, Big Pine Key
Pimentel, Victor M., Diaconate Office
Pineda, Roberto, St. Joseph, Miami Beach
Pintado, Angel, St. Agatha, Miami
Plummer, Michael, Our Lady of Lourdes, Miami
Prieto, Jorge, Good Shepherd, Miami
Pulido, Carlos, St. Thomas the Apostle, Miami
Ramirez, Carlos, Our Lady of the Lakes, Miami Lakes
Reyes, Jeffrey J., St. Louis, Pinecrest
Rich, William, St. Peter, Big Pine Key
Roa, Benjamin, St. Helen, Fort Lauderdale
Rodriguez, Ernesto, St. Michael the Archangel, Miami
Rodriguez, Santos, Good Shepherd, Miami
Rojo, Orlando, Mother of Our Redeemer, Miami
Rosado, Jose, Mother of Christ, Miami
Rosales, Marco, St. Monica, Miami Gardens
Ruiz-Castaneda, Norman, Epiphany, Miami
Saavedra, Manuel, Mother of Christ, Miami
Smith, David, St. Bartholomew, Miramar
Smith, Eduardo, St. Augustine, Coral Gables
Sommovigo, Joseph, St. Malachy, Tamarac
Soucy, Joseph O., Our Lady Queen of Heaven, North Lauderdale
Starzinski, Louis, St. Bernadette, Hollywood
Sutcavage, George P., St. Pius X, Fort Lauderdale
Taylor, Ian, Cathedral of St. Mary, Miami
Thesing, John, St. John the Baptist, Fort Lauderdale
Tola, Vincent, All Saints, Sunrise
Tollis, Giuseppe, All Saints, Sunrise
Tosco, Jesus, St. Boniface, Pembroke Pines
Trahan, Peter, St. Bonaventure, Davie
Turcotte, Richard A., Ph.D., Nativity, Hollywood
Ulloa, Lazaro, Mother of Christ, Miami
Valdes, Melanio, Corpus Christi, Miami
Vasquez, Domingo, St. Bonaventure, Davie
Velasco, Alvaro, Corpus Christi, Miami
Villa, Isidoro, Spiritual Director for Impactos
Watkins, William A., Little Flower, Hollywood
Yglesias, Robert, St. Louis, Pinecrest
Zayas, Julio, Good Shepard, Miami

INSTITUTIONS LOCATED IN THE ARCHDIOCESE

[A] SEMINARIES, ARCHDIOCESAN

MIAMI. *St. John Vianney College Seminary*, 2900 S.W. 87th Ave., 33165. Tel: 305-223-4561; 305-223-4562; Fax: 305-223-0650. Email: rgarza@sjvcs.edu. Web: www.sjvcs.edu. Rev. Lucien Pierre, Dean, Men; Very Rev. Roberto Garza, Rector; Dr. Ramon J. Santos, Academic Dean; Maria Rodriguez, Librarian; Revs. Robert Vallee, Assoc. Prof. Philosophy & Liturgy Dir.; Juan Carlos Rios,

Spiritual Dir.; Joseph Kottayil, Spiritual Dir.; Ferdinand Santos (Philippines), Philosophy Prof. Priests 7; Lay Teachers 5; Total Staff 20; Students 72.

[B] SEMINARIES, ARCHDIOCESAN MISSIONARY

HIALEAH. *Redemptoris Mater Seminary*, 1040 W. 29th St., 33010. Rev. Emmanuelle DiNigris, Rector. Seminarians 11.

[C] COLLEGES AND UNIVERSITIES

MIAMI. *Barry University* (1940) President's Office, 11300 N.E. 2nd Ave., 33161. Tel: 305-899-3010; Fax: 305-899-3018. Email: lbevilacqua@mail.barry.edu. Web: www.barry.edu. Sisters Linda Bevilacqua, O.P., Ph.D., Pres.; Jeanne O'Laughlin, O.P., Ph.D., Chancellor; Mr. Bruce Edwards, Vice Pres. Business & Finance; Dr. Michael Griffin, Ed.D., Vice Pres., Opers. & Business Devel.; Dr. Linda Peterson, Provost; Dr. Carol-Rae Sodano, Dean School of Adult & Continuing Education; Angela M. Scott, Asst. Vice Provost Enrollment Svcs.; Dr. Eileen McDonough, Assoc. Vice Pres. Student Affairs; Dr. Maria Luisa Alvarez, Assoc. Vice Pres. Student Affairs & Dean of Students; Revs. Marcelo Solorzano, O.P., Univ. Chap.; Mark Wedig, O.P., Ph.D.; Jorge L. Presmanes, O.P., D.Min.; Yvette Brown, Chief Information Officer; Dr. Terry Piper, Dean School of Education; Jeffery Jensen, D.P.M., Dean School of Pediatric Medicine; Dr. Tomislav Mandakovic, Dean School of Business; Thomas C. Messner, Dir. Library Svcs.; Dr. Pegge Bell, Ph.D., Dean College of Health Sciences; Dr. Phyllis Scott, Interim Dean School of Social Work; Dr. Karen A. Callaghan, Dean, College of Arts & Sciences; Dr. Darlene A. Kluka, Interim Dean, School, Human Performance & Leisure Science; Ms. Leticia M. Diaz, Dean, School of Law; Dr. Scott F. Smith, Vice Pres., Student Affairs; Dr. Christopher Starratt, Vice Pres., Mission & Inst. Effectiveness. Sisters of St. Dominic (Adrian, MI). Priests 3; Sisters 9; Lay Teachers 791; Students 8,995.

MIAMI GARDENS. *St. Thomas University* (1961) (Coed), 16401 N.W. 37th Ave., 33054. Tel: 305-628-6000; Fax: 305-628-6703. Email: signup@stu.edu. Web: www.stu.edu. Susan Angulo, Librarian. Priests 1; Sisters 1; Lay Teachers 106; Students 2,452.

Board of Trustees: Rudy Cecchi; Bob Dickinson; Constance Fernandez; Paul Garcia; Gary Goldbloom; Betty Goosens; Ervin Gonzalez; Ray Gonzalez; Cyrus M. Jollivette; Joseph P. Lacher; Victor H. Mendelson; Dominick Miniaci; Mario Murgado; Jose Navarro; Peter Prieto; Rodger Shay; Dr. P. Alan Smurfit, Trustee Emeritus; Gregory T. Swienton.

The Member: Most Rev. Thomas G. Wenski, D.D.; Stanley G. Tate; Mario Trueba; Wini Amaturo; John J. Dooner.

Of Counsel: Mr. J. Patrick Fitzgerald, Esq.

Administration: Rev. Msgr. Franklyn M. Casale, Pres.; Rev. Edward A. Blackwell, Dir. of Campus Ministry; Beverly Bachrach, Vice Pres. Univ. Advancement; Terry O'Connor, Vice Pres. for Admin. & Treas. & CFO; Douglas Ray, Dean of the School of Law; Gregory Chan, Provost of the Univeristy, Chief Academic Officer; Dr. Joseph Iannone, Dean of the School of Graduate Studies; Dr. Breatriz Robinson, Vice Pres. Planning & Enrollment; Marivi Prado, Dir. of Mktg. & Communications, 16401 N.W. 37th Ave., 33054. Tel: 305-474-6880.

Clergy and Religious Full-Time Faculty: Revs. Harry Loubriel; James L. MacDougall, O.S.A.

[D] HIGH SCHOOLS, ARCHDIOCESAN

MIAMI. *Archbishop Coleman Carroll High School*, 10300 S.W. 167th Ave., 33196. Tel: 305-388-6700; Fax: 305-388-4371. Email: colemancarroll@colemancarroll.org. Web: www.colemancarroll.org. Sr. Maureen Cochrane, Prin.; Rev. Msgr. Kenneth K. Schwanger, J.C.D., Pres. Priests 1; Carmelite Sisters of the Most Sacred Heart 4; Deacons 1; Lay Teachers 31; Total Staff 53; Students 481.

Archbishop Curley-Notre Dame High School (1953) 4949 N.E. 2nd Ave., 33137-3199. Tel: 305-751-8367; Fax: 305-751-3517. Email: officeoftheprincipal@acnd.net. Web: www.acnd.net. Bros. Patrick Sean Moffett, C.F.C., Prin.; James DePiro, C.F.C., Vice Prin. for Academics; Mr. Douglas Romanik, Vice Prin. Advancement. Priests 1; Brothers 6; Lay Teachers 25; Students 324.

St. Brendan High School (1975) 2950 S.W. 87th Ave., 33165. Tel: 305-223-5181; Fax: 305-220-7434. Email: sabres@stbhs.org. Web: www.stbhs.org. Bro. Felix A. Elardo, F.M.S., Prin.; Rev. Jose Alvarez, Supervising Prin.; Mia Suarez, Asst. Prin.; Mrs. Isabel Lopez-Healy, Asst. Prin.; Belkis Llontop, Dean of Students; Mildred A. Copeland, Librarian; Alicia A. Rivero, Librarian. Brothers 4; Lay Teachers 72; Counselors 5; Students 1,148.

Immaculata La Salle High School (1958) 3601 S. Miami Ave., 33133. Tel: 305-854-2334; Fax: 305-858-5971. Email: principal@ilsroyals.com. Web: www.ilsroyals.com. Sr. Kim Keraitis, F.M.A., Prin.; Dr. Erik Shane, Asst. Prin. for Student Affairs; Mrs. Luisa Serratore, Asst. Prin. for Curriculum; Mrs. Maria Haugland, Financial Admin.; Mr. Christopher Crotty, Athletic Dir.; Ms. Carmen Hoyos, Activities Dir.; Mr. Jose Naranjo, Librarian & Media Specialist. Sisters 3; Lay Teachers 61; Students 761.

Msgr. Edward Pace High School (1961) 15600 Spartan Blvd., N.W. 32nd Ave., 33054. Tel: 305-624-8534; Fax: 305-521-0185. Email: agarcia@pacehs.com. Web: www.pacehs.com. Mrs. Ana Garcia, Prin.; Rebeca Bautista, Dean of Academics; Mr. Samuel Lilly, Dean of Students (Grades 10-11); Valarie Lloyd, Dean of Students (Grades 9-12); Les Brown, Dean of Students; Theresa Gula, Librarian. Email: tgula@pacehs.com. Priests 1; Lay Teachers 54; Students 918.

Our Lady of Lourdes Academy (1963) 5525 S.W. 84th St., 33143. Tel: 305-667-1623; Fax: 305-663-3121. Email: skathryn@olla.org. Web: www.olla.org. Sr. Kathryn Donze, I.H.M., Prin.; Ileana Armengol, Librarian. Priests 1; Sisters (Servants of the Immaculate Heart of Mary) 4; Lay Teachers 66; Students 818.

FORT LAUDERDALE. *Cardinal Gibbons High School* (1961) 2900 N.E. 47th St., 33308. Tel: 954-491-2900; Fax: 954-772-1025. Email: cghs@cghsfl.org. Web: www.cghsfl.org. Sr. Marie Schramko, O.S.F., Asst. Prin.; Mr. Paul D. Ott, Prin.; Revs. Oscar Alonso, Sch.P.; Charles Newburn, Sch.P.; John Callan, Sch.P.; Bros. Grant R. Ferris, O.S.F.S.; Michael Brickmann, C.S.C., Spec. Projects; Kathleen Tavernia, Librarian. Priests 3; Brothers 2; Sisters of St. Francis 2; Lay Teachers 59; Students 1,128.

St. Thomas Aquinas High School (1936) 2801 S.W. 12th St., 33312. Tel: 954-581-2127; 954-581-0700; Fax: 954-581-8263. Email: tina.jones@aquinas-sta.org. Web: www.aquinas-sta.org. Rev. Msgr. Vincent T. Kelly, Supervising Prin.; Mrs. Tina Jones, Prin.; Rev. William J. Sullivan, O.S.S.T., Asst. Supervising Prin.; Dr. Robert Mulder, Asst. Prin.; Dr. Denise Aloma, Asst. Prin.; Dr. Ian Robertson, Dept. Chair, Theology; Mrs. Kathy Myrick, Campus Min.; Mr. Rob Biasotti, Dean of Students; Mr. George Smith, Dir. of Athletics; Mrs. Alane Klink, Guidance Dir.; Mrs. Mary Lynn McAloon, Librarian. Priests 2; Sisters 1; Lay Teachers 119; Students 2,190.

SOUTHWEST RANCHES. *Archbishop Edward A. McCarthy High School* (1998) 5451 S. Flamingo Rd., 33330. Tel: 954-434-8820; Fax: 954-680-4835. Email: maverick@mccarthyhigh.org. Web: www.mccarthyhigh.org. Rev. Brendan Dalton, Supervising Prin.; Mr. Richard P. Jean, Prin.; Mrs. Camille Henderson, Librarian. Priests 2; Lay Teachers 80; Students 1,545.

[E] HIGH SCHOOLS, PRIVATE

MIAMI. *Belen Jesuit Preparatory School* (1854) 500 S.W. 127th Ave., 33184. Tel: 305-223-8600; Fax: 305-227-2565. Email: webmaster@belenjesuit.org. Web: www.belenjesuit.org. Revs. Pedro A. Suarez, S.J., Pres & Contact. Tel: 305-205-1017; Guillermo Garcia-Tunon, S.J., Prin.; Juan Manuel Dorta, S.J.; Francisco Perez-Lerena, S.J.; Pedro Cartaya, S.J.; Nelson Garcia, S.J.; Lionel Lopez; Ernesto Fernandez Travieso, S.J.; Eduardo Barrios, S.J.; Michael Chesney, S.J.; Marcelino Garcia, S.J.; Guillermo Arias, Counselor; Marta Cosculluella, Librarian. Priests 7; Sisters 1; Lay Teachers 111; Students 1,480; Brothers 3; Teachers 122.

Our Lady of Belen Jesuit Foundation, Inc., 12725 S.W. 6th St. #204, 33184. Tel: 786-621-4043; Fax: 786-621-4044.

Carrollton School of the Sacred Heart (1962) 3747 Main Hwy., 33133. Tel: 305-446-5673; Fax: 305-529-6533. Email: scooke@carrollton.org. Web: www.carrollton.org. Sr. Suzanne Cooke, R.S.C.J., Headmistress; Dr. Susan Dempf, Prin.; Roberta Rand, Librarian. Religious of the Sacred Heart 3; Lay Teachers 93; Students 800.

Christopher Columbus High School, 3000 S.W. 87 Ave., 33165. Tel: 305-223-5650; Fax: 305-559-4306. Web: www.columbushs.com. Bros. Michael Brady, F.M.S., Prin.; Edmund Sheehan, F.M.S., Librarian; Kenneth Curtin, F.M.S., Admissions Dir.; Kevin Handibode, F.M.S., Pres.; Mrs. Patricia Call, Asst. Prin. (Academic Dean); Mr. Pedro Garcia-Casals, Asst. Prin. & Academic Dean; Mr. Gerardo Gonzalez, Campus Min.; Mrs. Eyda Alegret, Dept. Leader, Religion; Mr. David Pugh, Dean of Students; Mr. Christopher McKeon, Dean of Students. Christopher Columbus High School Endowment Trust. Priests 2; Marist Brothers 15; Lay Teachers 74; Students 1,380.

HOLLYWOOD. *Chaminade-Madonna College Preparatory* (1960) 500 Chaminade Dr., 33021-5800. Tel: 954-989-5150; Fax: 954-983-4663. Email: info@chaminade-madonna.org. Web: www.chaminade-madonna.org. Rev. Lawrence Doersching, S.M., Pres.; Teresita Wardlow, Prin.; Ron Belanger, Librarian; Rev. Joseph Tedesco, S.M. Marianist Priests 2; Marianist Brothers 1; Lay Teachers 50; Students 570.

[F] SHELTERS

MIAMI. *Camillus House, Inc.* (1960) 336 N.W. 5th St., 33128. Tel: 305-374-1065, Ext. 308; Fax: 305-372-1402. Email: dr.paul@camillus.org. Web: www.camillus.org. Dr. Paul R. Ahr, Ph.D., Pres. & CEO. Provides services to the homeless: emergency services, substance abuse rehabilitation, transitional and permanent housing. Bed Capacity 800; Total Assisted Annually 11,384; Total Staff 160.

Brother Keily Place, Inc., 336 N.W. 5th St., 33128.

Brothers of the Good Shepherd of Florida, Inc. (1960) Tel: 305-759-8206; Fax: 305-756-9014. Web: www.lbgs.org. Rev. Raphael Mieszala, B.G.S., Mission Integration Dir. A Religious Congregation. Brothers 5.

Brother Mathias Barrett, Inc., 680 N.E. 52nd St., 33137.

Brownsville Housing, Inc., 336 N.W. 5th St., 33128.

Camillus Health Concern, Inc. (1984) P.O. Box 012408, 33101-2408. Tel: 305-374-1065; Fax: 305-373-7431. Web: www.camillus.org. Provides medical, dental, mental health and social services to the homeless and indigent. Total Assisted Annually 4,498; Total Staff 48.

Charity Unlimited Foundation, Inc., 336 N.W. 5th St., 33128.

Charity Unlimited Holding, Inc., 336 N.W. 5th St., 33128.

Charity Unlimited Leasing, Inc., 336 N.W. 5th St., 33128.

Charity Unlimited of Florida, Inc. (1995) Tel: 305-758-7439; Fax: 305-372-1402. Provides buildings and grounds for charitable works.

Emmaus Place, Inc., 336 N.W. 5th St., 33128.

Good Shepherd Villas, Inc., 336 N.W. 5th St., 33128.

Labre Place, Inc., 336 N.W. 5th St., 33128.

Matt Talbot House, Inc., 336 N.W. 5th St., 33128.

New Camillus House Campus, Inc., 336 N.W. 5th St., 33128.

Somerville Residence, Inc., 336 N.W. 5th St., 33128.

Gift of Hope, Missionaries of Charity (1981) 724 N.W. 17th St., 33136. Tel: 305-326-0032. Sisters M. Prema, M.C., Supr. Gen.; M. Maria Goretti, M.C.; M. Lima Marie, M.C.; M. Margaret Joseph, M.C. Total Staff 6; Bed Capacity 24; Total Assisted Annually 295.

Women's and Children's Shelter, 33136. Tel: 305-326-0032. Bed Capacity 24; Total Women Assisted 295; Total Children Assisted 43.

Soup Kitchen (1981) Tel: 305-326-0032. Total Assisted 76,867; Total Staff 6.

[G] GENERAL HOSPITALS

MIAMI. *Mercy Hospital* (1950) 3663 S. Miami Ave., 33133. Tel: 305-854-4400; Fax: 305-285-2114. Web: www.mercymiami.org. Sisters Stephanie Flynn, Trustee; Edith Gonzalez, S.S.J., Trustee & Vice Pres. Mission Integration & Contact; Elizabeth Anne Worley, S.S.J., Trustee; Revs. Fabio Arango (Colombia), Chap.; Julio Estada, Chap.; Jean Sterling Laurent, Chap.; Jairo Tellez, Chap. Sponsored by the Sisters of St. Joseph of St. Augustine, FL., Mercy Hospital and Sister Emmanuel Hospital for Continuing Care are owned and operated by HCA in a manner compliant with the Ethical and Religious Directives and requirements of the Archbishop of Miami to fulfill the essential elements of a Catholic hospital. The Sisters of St. Joseph, who serve on the hospital's governing board, hold responsibility to maintain compliance with these requirements. Sisters 1; Bed Capacity 473; Patients Assisted Annually 366,689; Total Staff 1,579.

Mercy Mission Services, Inc. dba Sister Emmanuel Hospital

Mercy Hospital, Inc.

Mercy Hospital Foundation, Inc.

FORT LAUDERDALE. *Holy Cross Hospital* (1955) 4725 N. Federal Hwy., 33308. Tel: 954-771-8000; Fax: 954-492-5741. Email: patrick.taylor@holy-cross.com. Web: www.holy-cross.com. Dr. Patrick Taylor, Pres. & CEO; Sr. Rita Levasseur, R.S.M., Vice Pres. of Mission; Ms. Barbara Ouellette, Dir. of Spiritual Care; Revs. William Muniz, Chap.; Robert Monti, Chap.; James Nero, O.F.M., Chap.; Gary Wiesmann, (Jamaica); Sr. Claudia Steger, O.S.F., Mgr., Spiritual Care; Rev. Joanne M. Afshar, Chap.; Rev. Tabatha Lennon, Chap.; Margaret Kimber, Chap.; Sr. Marilyn Canning, R.S.M., Pastoral Assoc. Sisters of Mercy 6; Sisters of St. Francis 1; Total Staff 2,800; Bed Capacity 563; Patients Assisted Annually 501,762.

Holy Cross Hospital, Inc. Tel: 954-492-5796; Fax: 954-351-5947.

Holy Cross Long Term Care, Inc. Tel: 954-492-5796; Fax: 954-351-5947.

[H] MONASTERIES AND RESIDENCES OF PRIESTS AND BROTHERS

MIAMI. *Casa San Lorenzo*, 16401 N.W. 37th Ave., Miami Gardens, 33054. Tel: 305-474-0576; 305-624-0775; Fax: 305-625-4529. Revs. Maximo J. Ortiz, O.S.A., Prior & Treas. & Regent of Studies; James L. MacDougall, O.S.A.; Jorge L. Cleto, O.S.A., Vocational Dir., Hispanic Vocations. Augustinian Fathers. Total in Residence 3.

Dominican Fathers of Miami, Inc., 5909 N.W. 7th St., 33126. Tel: 305-264-0181, Ext. 25; Fax: 305-262-4685. Web: www.opsouth.org. Revs. Restituto Perez, O.P.; Desiderio Eguino, O.P.; Mark Wedig, O.P., Ph.D.; Jorge L. Presmanes, O.P., D.Min.; Alberto Rodriguez, O.P.; Marcelo Solorzano, O.P. House of Religious Men 1; Total in Residence 6.

Marist Brothers of the Schools, Inc., 3000 S.W. 87th Ave., 33165. Tel: 305-221-0824, Ext. 22.

Marist Residences Community #1: 3000 S.W. 87th Ave., 33165. Tel: 305-221-0834. Bros. Edmund Sheehan, F.M.S., Dir.; Herbert Baker, F.M.S.; Felix Anthony, F.M.S.; Edward Breslin, F.M.S.; Eladio Gonzalez, F.M.S.; Peter Guadalupe, F.M.S.; John Healy, F.M.S.; Stephen Kappes, F.M.S.; Marcos Longoria, F.M.S.; Rafael Martin, F.M.S.; Joseph Maura, F.M.S.; Vincent Moriarty, F.M.S.; Patrick McNulty, F.M.S.; Angelo Palmieri, F.M.S.; Eugene Trzecieski, F.M.S.; Julio Vitores, F.M.S. Community #2: 8230 S.W. 136th St., Palmetto Bay, 33158. Tel: 305-251-6484; Fax: 305-378-2081. Bros. Richard Carey; Daniel J. Grogan, F.M.S.; Chanel Lambert, F.M.S.; Norbert Rodrique. Community #3: 2790 S.W. 89th Ave., 33165. Tel: 305-223-5570. Bros. Charles Filiatrault, F.M.S., Dir.; Ronald D. Barabino, F.M.S.; Fabian Mayor, F.M.S.; Bernard Nolan, F.M.S.; Joseph Teston, F.M.S.; Vincent J. Dougherty, F.M.S. Community #4: 8415 S.W. 81st Ter., 33143. Tel: 305-274-5946. Bros. Kenneth Curtin, F.M.S., Dir.; Michael Brady, F.M.S.; Albert Rivera, F.M.S.; Kevin Handibode, F.M.S.

Villa Javier Belen Jesuit Fathers, Inc., 12725 S.W. 6th St., 33184-1305. Tel: 786-621-4593; Fax: 305-222-1256. Email: belensj@aol.com. Web: www.belenjesuit.org. Revs. Guillermo Arias, S.J., Counselor & Prof.; Marcelino Garcia, S.J., Retreat Ministry; Guillermo Garcia-Tunon, S.J., Prin.; Francisco Perez-Lerena, S.J., Spiritual Dir.; Juan Manuel Dorta, S.J., Spirtual Dir.; Pedro Cartaya, S.J., Spiritual Dir.; Pedro A. Suarez, S.J., Pres. Belen Jesuit Preparatory School; Oscar Mendez, S.J. (Retired); Nelson Garcia, S.J., Counselor, Retreats; Ernesto Fernandez Travieso, S.J.; Michael Chesney, S.J., Theology Teacher & Counselor; Lionel Lopez, Spiritual Counselor. *Belen Jesuit Alumni Association* Tel: 305-661-6180; Fax: 305-661-9639. Rev. Juan Manuel Dorta, S.J., Spiritual Dir.

MIAMI GARDENS. *Discalced Carmelite Friars of Miami, Inc.*, 15710 N.W. 44 Ct., 33054. Tel: 305-816-6468. Email: casadeoracionocd@gmail.com. Web: www.carmelitasdescalzosmiami.org. Rev. P. Lazaro de La Fe, O.C.D., Supr. Total in Residence 3.

[I] CONVENTS AND RESIDENCES FOR SISTERS

MIAMI. *Claretian Missionary Sisters of Florida, Inc.*, 7080 S.W. 99th Ave., 33173. Tel: 305-274-6148; Fax: 305-274-5695. Email: usdelegation@claretiansisters.org. Web: www.claretiansisters.org. Sr. Ondina Cortes, R.M.I., Pres. Sisters 13.

Daughters of Charity of St. Vincent de Paul (1971) (Santurce, P.R.), Mision San Vicente de Paul., 500 N.W. 63rd Ave., 33126. Tel: 305-266-6485; Fax: 305-265-9671. Email: caridad@gate.net; eperezpuelles@yahoo.com. Web: www.gate.net/~caridad. Asociacion Hijas de la Caridad de San Vicente de Paul del Estado de la Florida, Inc.

Ermita Nacional de Nuestra Senora de la Caridad (1973) 3609 S. Miami Ave., P.O. Box 330555, 33133. Tel: 305-854-2404; Fax: 305-854-8022. Sr. Eva Perez-Puelles, Contact.

Daughters of St. Paul Convent (1959) 11117 S.W. 2nd St., 33174. Tel: 305-554-0175; Fax: 305-220-1639. Email: miami@paulinemedia.com. Web: www.pauline.org. Sr. Susan Miriam Wolf, F.S.P., Supr., Contact. Houses of Religious Women 1; Total in Residence 9.

Pauline Books & Media, Office: 145 S.W. 107th Ave., 33174. Tel: 305-559-6715; Fax: 305-225-4189. Web: www.pauline.org.

Handmaids of the Sacred Heart of Jesus A.C.J. (1975) St. Rafaela's Faith Community, 1615 N.E. 108th St., 33161. Tel: 305-891-9161; Fax: 305-891-9161. Email: mjsagaseta@gmail.com. Web: www.acjusa.org. Sisters 4.

Missionaries of Charity (1980) 727 N.W. 17th St., 33136. Tel: 305-545-5699. Sr. M. Ajaya, M.C., Supr. Houses of Religious Women 1; Total in Residence 6; Total Assisted 2,612.

Religious of the Apostolate of Florida, Inc., 2160 S.W. 16th Ave. Apt. #318, 33145-2871. Tel: 305-857-9980. Email: apostolatesister@bellsouth.net; aliciara2003@yahoo.com. Sisters Alicia Velazquez, R.A., Contact Person; Maria del Rosario Delgado, R.A., Admin.

**Siervas de los Corazones Traspasados de Jesus y Maria, Inc. (Servants of the Pierced Hearts of Jesus and Mary), Two Hearts Convent (Mother House)*, 3098 S.W. 14th St., 33145. Tel: 305-444-7437. Email: sisterana@piercedhearts.org. Sr. Ana M. Lanzas, S.P.H.J.M., Contact Person. Professed Sisters 25.

St. Therese Convent, 2996 S.W. 14th St., 33145.

Saint Pio's Convent, 3046 S.W. 14th St., 33145.

Immaculate Convent, 1420 S.W. 31st Ave., 33145.

FLORIDA CITY. *Guadalupan Missionaries of the Holy Spirit* (1930) 869 S.W. 3rd St., 33034. Tel: 305-248-3735. Web: misionerasguadalupanas.com. Sr. M. Isabel Saldana, Supr.

Missionary Guadalupanas of the Holy Spirit, Inc. In Residence 3.

HIALEAH. *Discalced Carmelite Nuns, Inc.*, 4525 W. 2nd Ave., 33012. Tel: 305-558-7122; Fax: 305-558-1190. Sr. Blanca Flor Caracheo, O.C.D., Pres.

Dominicas de la Inmaculada Concepcion, 571 W. 33rd Pl., 33012. Tel: 305-823-3282. Sisters Enith Montero, O.P.; Maria Teresa Flores, O.P.; Blanca Hernandez, O.P., Supr. Houses of Religous Women 1; Total in Residence 3.

Monastery of the Most Holy Trinity, (Discalced Carmelite Nuns) (2001) 4525 W. Second Ave., 33012. Tel: 305-558-7122; Fax: 305-558-1190. Sr. Blanca Flor Caracheo, O.C.D., Prioress.

Servants of Jesus of Charity, Inc., 126 W. 45th St., 33012. Tel: 305-231-2063; Fax: 305-231-2063.

HOMESTEAD. *Daughters of Mary, Mothers of Mercy (Nigeria), Inc.*, 18444 S.W. 293rd Ter., 33030. Tel: 786-429-4136. Sr. Chidi Nwanya, D.M.M.M., Supr. Tel: 305-846-1459. Email: egoigboagwula@yahoo.com. Sisters 3.

Mercy Convent, 1618 Polk St., Hollywood, 33020. Tel: 954-895-3005. Sisters 3.

MIAMI SHORES. *Franciscan Sisters of Allegany* 124 N.E. 111 St., 33161. Tel: 305-751-3093; Fax: 305-751-3093. Total in Residence 2.

St. Francis Hospital, Inc. dba Franciscan Sisters of Allegany Ministries (1966) Tel: 305-751-3093; Fax: 305-751-3093.

WESTCHESTER. *Congregation of the French-Cuban Dominican Sisters of Holy Rosary, Inc.*, 7920 S.W. 23rd St., Miami, 33155. Tel: 305-265-9759. Sr. Mary Cecilia Alonso, O.P., Pres., Treas. & Contact. Houses of Religious Women 1; Total in Residence 4.

[J] RETREAT HOUSES

MIAMI. *John Paul II Retreat House*, 720 N.E. 27th St., 33137-4697. Tel: 305-576-2748; 305-573-1418; Fax: 305-576-2748. Email: admin@estovir.org. Web: www.estovir.org. Rev. Nelson Garcia, S.J., Spiritual Dir., Contact. Total in Residence 2; Total Staff 5.

Agrupacion Catolica Universitaria, Inc. Tel: 305-576-2748; Fax: 305-576-2748.

ACU Holdings, Inc., Jesus Maestro Inc., 720 N.E. 27th St., 33137. Tel: 305-576-2748; Fax: 305-576-2748.

Jesuit Fathers of the Province of the Antilles, Inc.

PINECREST. *MorningStar Renewal Center, Inc.*, 7275 S.W. 124th St., 33156-4649. Tel: 305-238-4367; Fax: 305-238-4766. Email: info@morningstarrenewal.org. Web: www.morningstarrenewal.org. Very Rev. James Fetscher, V.F., Spiritual Dir.; Sue S. DeFerrari, Dir.

[K] SHRINES

MIAMI. *National Shrine of Our Lady of Charity* 3609 S. Miami Ave., 33133. Tel: 305-854-2404; Fax: 305-854-8022. Web: www.ermitadelacaridad.org. Very Rev. Juan Rumin Dominguez, O.F.M., Rector; Rev. Carlos J. Cespedes (Cuba). Sisters 3; Houses of Religious Women 1; Total in Residence 3.

[L] CENTERS

MIAMI. *Pauline Book & Media Center* (1959) 145 S.W. 107th Ave., 33174. Tel: 305-559-6715; Fax: 305-225-4189. Email: miami@paulinemedia.com. Web: www.pauline.org. Sr. Susan Miriam Wolf, F.S.P., Supr. Daughters of St. Paul 9; Houses of Religious Women 1; Total in Residence 9; Pauline Book & Media Center 3; Total Staff 5.

Paulinas Spanish Distribution Center (1996) Tel: 305-225-2513; 800-872-5852; Fax: 305-225-4189. Web: www.pauline.org (Spanish). Sr. Susan Miriam Wolf, F.S.P., Manager. Religious 3; Lay Staff 2.

SEPI Evangelization and Education Foundation, Inc., 7700 S.W. 56th St., 33155. Tel: 305-279-2333; Fax: 305-279-0925. Email: sepimiami@aol.com. Revs. Mario B. Vizcaino, Sch.P., Devel. Dir. Asst.; Rafael Capo, Sch.P., Dir., Contact.

Southeast Pastoral Institute, 7700 S.W. 56th St., 33155. Tel: 305-279-2333; Fax: 305-279-0925. Email: sepimiami@aol.com. Web: www.sepimiami.org. Revs. Mario B. Vizcaino, Sch.P., Devel. Dir. Asst.; Rafael Capo, Sch.P., Dir.; Olga Fernandez, Admin. Asst. & Office Mgr.

Southeast Regional Office for Hispanic Ministry, Inc., 7700 S.W. 56th St., 33155. Tel: 305-279-2333; Fax: 305-279-0925. Email: sepimiami@aol.com. Web: www.sepimiami.org. Revs. Mario B. Vizcaino, Sch.P., Devel. Dir. Asst.; Rafael Capo, Sch.P., Dir.; Olga Fernandez, Admin. Asst. & Office Mgr.

[M] PERSONAL PRELATURE

MIAMI. *Prelature of the Holy Cross and Opus Dei*, 4415 S.W. 88th Ave., 33165. Tel: 305-551-7956; Fax: 305-551-7957. Email: vacortes@earthlink.net. Revs. Victor Cortes, Contact Person; Eduardo Castillo; Christopher Schmitt.

[N] MISCELLANEOUS LISTINGS

MIAMI. *Alumni Association of the Apostolate of Cuba (in Exile), Inc.*, P.O. Box 565462, 33256-5462. Tel: 305-255-0303. Margarita M. Cuervo, Pres.; Alicia Otazo-Reyes, Sec.

Claretian Missions, Inc., 7080 S.W. 99th Ave., 33173. Tel: 305-274-6148; Fax: 305-274-5695. Email: ondina@claretiansisters.org. Web: www.claretiansisters.org. Sr. Ondina Cortes, R.M.I., Pres.

Father Tino Foundation, 12190 S.W. 57th St., 33175.

Federacion de Institutos Pastorales, Inc., 7700 S.W. 56th St., 33155. Tel: 305-279-2333; Fax: 305-279-0925. Sr. Ruth Bolarte, I.H.M., Pres. Email: srruthbolarte@aol.com.

Foundation of the Cuban Association of the S.M.O. of Malta, Inc. (1993) 2950 S.W. 27th Ave., #120, 33133. Tel: 305-285-0800; Fax: 305-285-0837. Email: juan.t.onaghten@ondlaw.com. Fernando Garcia-Chacon, Pres.; Juan T. O'Naghten, Vice Pres.; Luis F. Parajon, Treas.; Jose Joaquin Centurion, Dir.; Juan Jose Calvo, Sec.

St. Joseph Haitian Mission Manor, Inc., 11410 N. Kendall Dr., Ste. 201, 33176.

Leadership Learning Center at St. John Bosco, Inc., 1366 N.W. First St., 33125. Tel: 305-649-4730; Fax: 305-649-4733. Students 104.

Magnificat, Inc., 14130 S.W. 151 Ct., 33196. Tel: 305-253-8764; Fax: 305-205-5599. Floredenis Brown, Coord.; Valli Leoni, Asst. Coord.; Cecilia Quevedo, Treas.; Ana Sosa, Sec.; Barbara Seraphin, Historian.

New Encounter Corporation, 8670 S.W. 27th Ln., 33155. Tel: 786-390-3047. Email: clflorida1@gmail.com.

Peruvian Mission, Inc. (1994) (A Florida Not-for-Profit Corporation), P.O. Box 432745, 33143. Tel: 305-542-1589; Fax: 305-596-6738. Email: perumision@aol.com. Most Revs. Miguel Irizar, C.P., Bishop of Callao, Pres.; Luis Bambaren, S.J., Bishop of Chimbote (Retired); Very Rev. Mario Busquets Jorda, Bishop Prelature of Chuquibamba; Maria Delia Salazar, Dir., Sec. & Contact Person Board Members Most Revs. Luis Abilio Sebastiani Aguirre, S.M., Archbishop of Ayacucho; Pedro Barreto, S.J., Archbishop of Huancayo; Jose L. Astigarraga, C.P., Bishop of the Vicariate of Yurimaguas; Jorge Carrion, Bishop of Puno; Isidro Sala, Bishop of Abancay (Retired).

Teresian Institute, (Rome, Italy), Teresian Institute of Florida, Inc. (1911) An International Association of the Faithful., 3400 S.W. 99 Ave., 33165. Tel: 305-554-0035; 305-764-8222. Email: garmendia@bellsouth.net. Web: www.institucionteresiana.org. Ela Alvarado, Contact; Maria J. Garmendia, U.S. Delegate. Total in Residence 2; Total Staff 4.

Center of Activities, National Headquarters Web: www.institucionteresiana.org.

Theatine Sisters of the Immaculate Conception, Co. aka Religiosas Teatinas de la Immaculada Concepcion 12261 S.W. 6th St., 33184. Tel: 305-223-2512; Fax: 305-227-6951. Email: teatinasmia@att.net. Sr. Nilsa Castillo, R.T., Supr.

Vida Humana Internacional (Hispanic Division of Human Life International), 45 S.W. 71st Ave., 33144. Tel: 305-260-0525; Fax: 305-260-0595. Email: vhi@vidahumana.org. Web: www.vidahumana.org. Magaly Llaguno, Dir., Human Life Intl. U.S. Hispanic Outreach.

CORAL GABLES. *House of the Divine Will, Inc. dba*

Casa de la Divina Voluntad (1996) 5900 Leonardo St., 33146-3332. Tel: 305-667-5714; Fax: 305-667-7173. Email: casadivinavoluntad@msn.com. Web: www.casadivinavoluntad.org. Rev. Carlos Antonio Massieu Avila, Pres. & Chm.; Marianela Perez, Treas. & Contact Person.

CORAL SPRINGS. *Catholic Schools K12 Virtual, Inc.*, 9990 N.W. 29th St., 33065. Tel: 954-607-7772; Fax: 954-753-1933.

HIALEAH. **Opus Caritatis Corp.*, 475 E. 4th St., 33010. Tel: 305-888-9769; Fax: 305-888-9341. Rev. Msgr. Oscar F. Castaneda, Dir.

HOMESTEAD. **Centro de Artes y Oficios De La Salle, Inc., Vocational Center*, 31250 S.W. 134th Ave., 33033-5617. Tel: 305-245-5810; Fax: 305-553-3032. Web: www.celosolleh.org. Mailing Address: P.O. Box 653836, Miami, 33265-3836. Salvador Romo, Pres.; Julio Gonzalez-Portuondo, Sec.; Jose M. Dorado, Treas. Vocational Center for adults. Classes are free of charge. Also after school for children K-9. Staff 9; Total Assisted 129.

MIAMI SHORES. *Archdiocese of Miami Development Corporation*, 9401 Biscayne Blvd., 33138. Tel: 305-762-1053. Katie Blanco-Crocquet, Pres.

Archdiocese of Miami Millennium Appeal, Inc., 9401 Biscayne Blvd., 33138. Tel: 305-757-6241; Fax: 305-758-5261.

Archdiocese of Miami, Inc. (1958) 9401 Biscayne Blvd., 33138. Tel: 305-757-6241; Fax: 305-758-5261.

Asociacion Nacional de Diaconos Hispanos, Inc., 9401 Biscayne Blvd., 33138. Tel: 305-223-2065. Deacons George Benavente, Pres.; Fernando Bestard, Vice Pres. Tel: 305-762-6510; 305-271-9586.

Bahamas Mission of Florida, Inc., Archdiocese of Miami, 9401 Biscayne Blvd., 33138. Tel: 305-762-1220. Email: tmarin@adom.us. Rev. Msgr. Tomas M. Marin, J.C.L., Vice Pres.

Catholic Community Foundation in the Archdiocese of Miami, Inc. (1999) 9401 Biscayne Blvd., 33138-2998. Tel: 305-762-1080; Fax: 305-762-1020. Email: info@the-ccf.org. Web: www.the-ccf.org. Mr. Thomas Beier, Chm.; Mr. Sean Clancy, Sec.

DOM, Inc., 9401 Biscayne Blvd., 33138. Tel: 305-762-1098; Fax: 305-758-5261.

Ecclesiastical Province of Miami, Inc., 9401 Biscayne Blvd., 33138. Tel: 305-762-1098.

Francis Realty Corporation, 9401 Biscayne Blvd., 33138. Tel: 305-762-1098; Fax: 305-758-5261.

P.O.M., Inc., 9401 Biscayne Blvd., 33138. Tel: 305-762-1098; Fax: 305-758-5261.

Provincial Realty Associates, Inc. (A Florida Not-for-Profit Corporation), 9401 Biscayne Blvd., 33138. Tel: 305-762-1098; Fax: 305-758-5261. Land Holding Corporation.

**Roman Catholic Archdiocese of Nassau Foundation, Inc.*, 110 Merrick Way, Ste. 3-B, Coral Gables, 33134.

**The St. Vincent De Paul Society, Archdiocesan Council of Miami, Inc.*, Mailing Address: 9401 Biscayne Blvd., 33138. Tel: 305-762-1125. Mr. Frank Voehl, Pres.

St. Vincent De Paul Food Pantry, 29355 S. Federal Hwy., Homestead, 33030.

POMPANO BEACH. *Ministerio Catolico Verbo y Vida, Inc.*, 2310 Martin Luther King Blvd., 33069. Tel: 954-971-8780; Fax: 954-972-3607. Email: verboyvida@sanisidro.org. Web: www.verboyvida.org. Very Rev. Abel Barajas, V.F., Pres.

Word & Life Catholic Ministry, Inc. (1986) 2310 Martin Luther King Blvd., 33069. Tel: 954-971-7766; Fax: 954-970-7277. Email: wordandlife@sanisidro.org. Very Rev. Abel Barajas, V.F., Pres.

RELIGIOUS INSTITUTES OF MEN REPRESENTED IN THE ARCHDIOCESE

For further details refer to the corresponding bracketed number in the Religious Institutes of Men or Women section.

[0140]—*The Augustinians* (St. Thomas of Villanova Prov.)—O.S.A.
[0580]—*Brothers of the Good Shepherd*—B.G.S.
[0470]—*Capuchin Friars* (Detroit, MI)—O.F.M.Cap.
[0310]—*Congregation of Christian Brothers* (Eastern Prov.)—C.F.C.
[0260]—*Discalced Carmelite Friars*—O.C.D.
[0650]—*Holy Ghost Fathers*—C.S.Sp.
[0690]—*Jesuit Fathers and Brothers* (Antilles)—S.J.
[0770]—*The Marist Brothers* (Bayonne, N.J. & Poughkeepsie Provs.)—F.M.S.
[1210]—*Missionaries of St. Charles-Scalabrinians*—C.S.
[]—*Missionaries of the Company of Mary* (U.S. Prov.)—S.M.M.
[0910]—*Oblates of Mary Immaculate*—O.M.I.
[0920]—*Oblates of St. Francis de Sales*—O.S.F.S.
[]—*Order of Carmelites* (North American Prov. of St. Elias)
[0430]—*Order of Preachers (Dominican)* (St. Joseph & Southern Provs.)—O.P.
[1310]—*Order of the Holy Trinity*—O.SS.T.
[]—*Order of the Imitation of Christ*—O.I.C.
[1020]—*Pauline Fathers & Brothers*—S.S.P.
[1040]—*Piarist Fathers*—Sch.P.
[1260]—*Society of Christ*—S.Ch.R.
[0760]—*Society of Mary (Marianists)*—S.M.
[0370]—*Society of St. Columban*—S.S.C.

RELIGIOUS INSTITUTES OF WOMEN REPRESENTED IN THE ARCHDIOCESE

[]—*Assumption Sisters of Eldoret* (Kenya, Africa)—A.S.E.
[0370]—*Carmelite Sisters of the Most Sacred Heart of Los Angeles*—O.C.D.
[0685]—*Claretian Missionary Sisters*—R.M.I.
[0270]—*Congregation of Bon Secours*—C.B.S.
[1710]—*Congregation of the Third Order of St. Francis of Mary Immaculate, Joliet, IL*—O.S.F.
[0760]—*Daughters of Charity of St. Vincent de Paul*—D.C.
[0850]—*Daughters of Mary Help of Christians*—F.M.A.
[]—*Daughters of Mary, Mother of Mercy (Nigeria)*—D.M.M.M.
[0420]—*Discalced Carmelite Nuns*—O.C.D.
[1070-13]—*Dominican Sisters (Adrian)*—O.P.
[1070-06]—*Dominican Sisters (Newburgh)*—O.P.
[]—*Dominican Sisters of Our Lady of the Most Holy Rosary (Colombia)*—O.P.
[]—*Dominicas de la Inmaculada Concepcion (Ecuador)*
[1180]—*Franciscan Sisters of Allegany, New York*—O.S.F.
[1845]—*Guadalupan Missionaries of the Holy Spirit* (Mexico)—M.G.Sp.S.
[1870]—*Handmaids of the Sacred Heart of Jesus*—A.C.J.
[2575]—*Institute of the Sisters of Mercy of the Americas* (Pittsburgh, PA; Rochester, NY; Clogher, Ireland; Newfoundland, Canada)—R.S.M.
[]—*Marianitas* (Santa Mariana de Jesus Institute, Inc.)—R.M.
[2710]—*Missionaries of Charity*—M.C.
[3040]—*Oblate Sisters of Providence*—O.S.P.
[]—*Our Lady of Good Counsel* (Canada), S.B.C.
[3130]—*Our Lady of Victory Missionary Sisters*—O.L.V.M.
[0950]—*Pious Society Daughters of St. Paul*—F.S.P.
[3380]—*Religious of the Apostolate of the Sacred Heart*—R.A.
[3390]—*Religious of the Assumption*—R.A.
[2970]—*School Sisters of Notre Dame* (Baltimore, MD; Chicago, IL)—S.S.N.D.
[]—*Servants of Jesus of Charity*—S.de.J.
[]—*Servants of the Pierced Hearts of Jesus and Mary*—S.P.H.J.M.
[]—*Sisters of Charity* Cincinnati, Ohio—S.C.
[]—*Sisters of Jesus the Saviour* (Nigeria)—S.J.S.
[]—*Sisters of Notre Dame* Chardon, Ohio—S.N.D.
[3000]—*Sisters of Notre Dame de Namur (Baltimore, MA)*—S.N.D.deN.
[]—*Sisters of Our Lady of LaSalette*—S.N.D.S.
[3350]—*Sisters of Providence*—S.P.
[4090]—*Sisters of Social Service*—S.S.S.
[1620]—*Sisters of St. Francis of Millvale, Pennsylvania*—O.S.F.
[1630]—*Sisters of St. Francis of Penance and Christian Charity*—O.S.F.
[3830-13]—*Sisters of St. Joseph (Baden, PA)*—C.S.J.
[]—*Sisters of St. Joseph Benedict Cottolengo*—S.S.J.C.
[3830-09]—*Sisters of St. Joseph (Erie, PA)*—S.S.J.
[3850]—*Sisters of St. Joseph of Chambery* (Hartford, CT)—C.S.J.
[3900]—*Sisters of St. Joseph of St. Augustine, Florida*—S.S.J.
[]—*Sisters of St. Philip Neri Missionary Teachers*—R.F.
[2180]—*Sisters of the Immaculate Heart of Mary*—I.H.M.
[1490]—*Sisters of the Third Franciscan Order*—O.S.F.
[2160]—*Sisters, Servants of the Immaculate Heart of Mary* (Spain)—I.H.M.
[2180]—*Sisters, Servants of the Immaculate Heart of Mary* (Miami, FL)—I.H.M.
[2170]—*Sisters, Servants of the Immaculate Heart of Mary* (Immaculata, PA)—I.H.M.
[4020]—*Society of St. Teresa of Jesus*—S.T.J.
[4070]—*Society of the Sacred Heart*—R.S.C.J.
[]—*Theatine Sisters of the Immaculate Conception (Religiosas Teatinas de la Inmaculada Concepcion)*—R.T.

NECROLOGY

✠ Fernandez, Most Rev. Gilberto, Retired Auxiliary Bishop of Miami.—Died Sept. 30, 2011
✠ Roman, Most Rev. Agustin A., Retired Auxiliary Bishop of Miami.—Died April 11, 2012
† Conway, Laurence, (Retired)—Died May 13, 2011

An asterisk (*) denotes an organization that has established tax-exempt status directly with the IRS and is not covered by the USCCB Group Ruling.

Archdiocese for the Military Services, U.S.A.

Ordinariatus Castrensis

Most Reverend

JOSEPH T. DIMINO, D.D.

Former Archbishop for the Military Services; ordained June 4, 1949; appointed Titular Bishop of Carini and Auxiliary Bishop to the Military Ordinariate March 29, 1983; consecrated May 10, 1983; appointed Ordinary for the Military Services May 13, 1991; retired August 12, 1997.

Most Reverend

FRANCIS X. ROQUE, D.D.

Retired Auxiliary Bishop for the Military Services; ordained September 19, 1953; appointed Titular Bishop of Bagai and Auxiliary Bishop to the Military Ordinariate March 29, 1983; consecrated May 10, 1983; retired August 15, 2004.

Most Reverend

JOSEPH J. MADERA, M.SP.S., D.D.

Retired Auxiliary Bishop for the Military Services; ordained June 15, 1957; appointed Coadjutor Bishop of Fresno with the right of succession December 18, 1979; consecrated March 4, 1980; succeeded to See July 1, 1980; appointed Titular Bishop of Orte and Auxiliary Bishop of the Archdiocese for the Military Services May 28, 1991; retired August 15, 2004.

Most Reverend

TIMOTHY P. BROGLIO, J.C.D., S.T.B., M.A.

Archbishop for the Military Services; ordained May 19, 1977; appointed Titular Archbishop of Amiternum & Apostolic Nuncio to the Dominican Republic February 27, 2001; ordained a bishop March 19, 2001; appointed Archbishop for the Military Services November 17, 2007; installed January 25, 2008.

Chancery: 1025 Michigan Ave., N.E., P.O. Box 4469, Washington, DC 20017-0469. Tel: 202-719-3600; Fax: 202-269-9022.

Web: www.milarch.org

Email: info@milarch.org

Most Reverend

RICHARD B. HIGGINS, S.T.L., D.D.

Auxiliary Bishop for the Military Services; ordained March 9, 1968; appointed Titular Bishop of Casae Calanae and Auxiliary Bishop of the Archdiocese for the Military Services May 7, 2004; ordained July 3, 2004.

Most Reverend

F. RICHARD SPENCER, M.A., D.D.

Auxiliary Bishop for the Military Services; ordained May 14, 1988; appointed Titular Bishop of Auzia and Auxiliary Bishop of the Archdiocese for the Military Services May 22, 2010; ordained September 8, 2010.

Most Reverend

NEAL J. BUCKON

Auxiliary Bishop for the Military Services; ordained May 25, 1995; appointed Titular Bishop of Vissalsa and Auxiliary Bishop of the Archdiocese for the Military Services January 3, 2011; ordained February 22, 1011.

Established as the Archdiocese For The Military Services, U.S.A. (Ordinariatus Castrensis) March 25, 1985.

Serving U.S. Catholics of the Army, Navy, Air Force, Marine Corps, Coast Guard, Department of Veterans Affairs and those in Government Service overseas.

STATISTICAL OVERVIEW

Personnel	
Archbishops	1
Retired Archbishops	1
Auxiliary Bishops	3
Retired Bishops	2
Vital Statistics	
Receptions into the Church:	
Infant Baptism Totals	4,155
Minor Baptism Totals	1,119
Adult Baptism Totals	844
Received into Full Communion	335
First Communions	3,149
Confirmations	3,253
Marriages:	
Catholic	554
Interfaith	329
Total Marriages	883

Former Military Vicars—His Eminence PATRICK CARDINAL HAYES, cons. Titular Bishop of Tagaste, Oct. 28, 1914; appt. "Bishop Ordinary of U.S. Army and Navy Chaplains," Nov. 24, 1917; appt. Archbishop of New York, March 10, 1919; created Cardinal, March 24, 1924; died Sept. 4, 1938; FRANCIS CARDINAL SPELLMAN, cons. Auxiliary Bishop of Boston, Sept. 8, 1932; appt. Archbishop of New York, April 15, 1939; appt. "Military Vicar for the Armed Forces of U.S.," Dec. 11, 1939; created Cardinal, Feb. 18, 1946; died Dec. 2, 1967; TERENCE CARDINAL COOKE, cons. Auxiliary Bishop of New York, Dec. 13, 1965; appt. Archbishop of New York, March 2, 1968; appt. "Military Vicar of U.S. Armed Forces," April 4, 1968; created Cardinal, April 28, 1969; died Oct. 6, 1983; Most Revs. JOSEPH T. RYAN, appt. first Archbishop of Anchorage, Feb. 7, 1966; cons. March 25, 1966; appt. Titular Archbishop of Gabi and Coadjutor (Archbishop) of the Military Ordinariate, Oct. 24, 1975; installed first Ordinary of the Archdiocese for the Military Services March, 25, 1985; retired May 13, 1991; died Oct. 9, 2000; JOSEPH T. DIMINO, D.D. (Retired), appt. Auxiliary Bishop of Military Odinariate and Titular Bishop of Carini, March 29, 1983; cons. May 10, 1983; appt. second Ordinary for the Military Services, May 13, 1991; retired Aug. 12, 1997; His Eminence EDWIN F. O'BRIEN, ord. May 29, 1965; appt. Titular Bishop of Tizica and Auxiliary Bishop of New York Feb. 6, 1996; cons. March 25, 1996; appt. Coadjutor April 8, 1997; succeeded as Ordinary to the Military Services Aug. 12, 1997; appt. Archbishop of Baltimore July 12, 2007.

Vicar General & Moderator of the Curia—Rev. Msgr. FRANK A. PUGLIESE, M.Div., M.A., M.S. (Ed).

Episcopal Vicars—

Episcopal Vicar for Installations in Europe and Asia—Most Rev. F. RICHARD SPENCER, M.A., D.D.

Episcopal Vicar for Installations in the Eastern United States Region—VACANT.

Episcopal Vicar for Installation in Western United States Region—Most Rev. NEAL J. BUCKON, D.D.

Episcopal Vicar for Veteran Concerns—Most Rev. RICHARD B. HIGGINS, S.T.L., D.D.

Archdiocese Offices

Chancery—Mailing Address: P.O. Box 4469, Washington, 20017. Tel: 202-719-3600; Fax: 202-269-9022. Email: info@milarch.org. Web: www.milarch.org.

Chancellor—Deacon MICHAEL D. YAKIR, M.B.A.

Vice Chancellor—Sr. HELEN SUMANDER, M.C.S.T.

Office of Evangelization—

Vice Chancellor for Evangelization—Dr. MARK MOITOZA.

Office of Vocations—

Director of Vocations—Rev. KERRY M. ABBOT, O.F.M.Conv.

Assistant to the Archbishop—Sr. LISA MARIE DROVER, O.S.F.

Chief Financial Officer—Mr. WILLIAM BIGGS.

Director of Development—Ms. DAWN MARIE JONES.

Archivist—Sr. HELEN SUMANDER, M.C.S.T.

Tribunal—

Judicial Vicar—Rev. Msgr. THOMAS P. OLSZYK, J.C.L., Th.M.

Judges—Revs. JAMES E. BAKER, J.C.L.; G. PAUL HERBERT, J.C.L.; JOHN B. WARD, J.C.L.; Ms. LINDA E. PRICE, J.C.L.; Ms. DEBORAH BARTON, J.C.L.

Defenders of the Bond—Revs. G. PAUL HERBERT, J.C.L.; JORDAN F. HITE, T.O.R., J.C.L.; RICHARD H. HUGLI; JOSEPH A. GRIMALDI, J.C.L.; VINCENT RIGDON, J.C.L.; Ms. ZABRINA DECKER, J.C.L.

Assessors—JOHN L. SCHLAGETER, Esq., J.D.; Rev. JOHN C. KOZLOWSKI, O.P.

Notary—Miss PATRICIA HUTCHISON, T.O. Carmelite.

General Counsel—JOHN L. SCHLAGETER, Esq., J.D.

Presbyteral Council—Most Revs. NEAL J. BUCKON, D.D.; RICHARD B. HIGGINS, S.T.L., D.D.; F. RICHARD SPENCER, M.A., D.D.; Rev. Msgrs. FRANK A. PUGLIESE, M.Div., M.A., M.S. (Ed); THOMAS P. OLSZYK, J.C.L., Th.M.; DONALD L. RUTHERFORD; Revs. JAMES JOSLYN; KERRY M. ABBOT, O.F.M.Conv.; ALPHONSE J. STEPHENSON; JOHN A. MILEWSKI; JAMES E. BURNETT; TIMOTHY L. HUBBS; WILLIAM M. MUHM; MICHAEL PARISI; REDMOND P. RAUX.

Military Council of Catholic Women—Most Rev. NEAL J. BUCKON, D.D., Episcopal Moderator.

Areas of Service

Armed Forces, Active Duty: The Archdiocese for the Military Services is responsible for the pastoral care of the Catholic men and women who serve on active duty in the U.S. Armed Forces. It is also responsible for the dependents of these persons. Included also are the cadets and resident personnel of the three military academies (West Point--the U.S. Military Academy, the U.S. Air Force Academy at Colorado Springs, the U.S. Naval Academy at Annapolis) and the U.S. Coast Guard Academy at New London. Pastoral care is provided by priest-chaplains on loan from their dioceses or religious communities to serve as chaplains for the Military and Department of Veterans Affairs. Members of the Marines and Coast Guard are served by Navy Chaplains; Armed Forces, Reserves, National Guard: In addition to the personnel on active duty in the Armed Forces, there is a considerable reserve component. Some of these personnel serve a number of days each year on active duty with a branch of the service; some serve on extended tours of active duty; all are subject to recall to active duty in a national emergency. In addition to the reserve components of the Army, Air Force, Navy and Coast Guard, there are also the Air National Guard and the Army National Guard, which are organized on a state-by-state basis; Department of Veterans Affairs: The Archdiocese for the Military Services is responsible for the spiritual care of Catholics at V.A. medical facilities. Chaplaincy services are provided by full- and part-time priests, many of whom are retired military chaplains; U.S. Government Civilian

Employees Abroad: U.S. citizens in government service abroad (and their family members living with them) are subjects of the Archdiocese for the Military Services; Civil Air Patrol: The Civil Air Patrol, as an auxiliary of the Air Force, is under the jurisdiction of the Archdiocese for the Military Services. The jurisdiction applies to its chaplains and members only when participating in exercises on a military installation.

UNITED STATES ARMY CHAPLAINS

Army Chaplains:
Rev. Msgrs.—
Hill, Philip W. (NY)
Rutherford, Donald L.
Revs.—
Adunchezor, Christopher (Nigeria)
Albano, Alwyn M. (Philippines)
Albertson, Eric J. (ARL)
Anumata, Christopher C. (Nigeria)
Barkemeyer, John F. (CHI)
Besinga, Dino J. (Philippines)
Betz, James F. (CAM)
Blick, Ned (WCH)
Brocato, John K. (ALX)
Butera, Christopher S., M.Div., M.A. (ALN)
Carlson, Kenneth F., M.Div. (CHI)
D'Emma, Gregory J. (NEW)
Doering, Christopher E. (CHI)
Dynek, Wieslaw A. (Poland)
Eke, Rafael E. (Nigeria) (SAT)
Fleury, Joseph M., S.M.
Foley, Matthew E. (CHI)
Fukes, Gary M. (SY)
Fuller, Orlando R. (Philippines)
Gabriel, John B. (India)
Gaskin, Grantley DaCosta (WDC)
Glasgow, Robert K. (WIL)
Goulet, Daniel R. (BAL)
Greschel, Mark (CHI), Chap.
Gross, Gary L. (LIN)
Ha, Hieu Minh (ATL)
Halka, Frantisek A. (ALT)
Halladay, Paul A. (MOB)
Hernandez, Anselmo, L.C.
Herrera, Jose G. (STV)
Herron, John B. (FAR)
Hesseling, Jason E. (MAD)
Honor, Michael P. (Philippines)
Hubbs, Timothy L. (CAM)
Hurley, Paul K. (BO)
Iheke, Uche G., S.M.M.M.
Ijeoma, John Vianney (Nigeria) (LKC)
Ilokaba, Damian O. (Nigeria)
Irizarry, Alan M. (ARE)
Jong, Lyndon A. (Philippines)
Kalinowski, Joseph J. (E)
Kazarnowicz, Anthony S. (WOR)
Kelley, Edward J. (PRO)
Kenehan, David A., O.S.F.S.
Kilumbu, Claudes (Congo)
Kirchhoefer, Thomas A. (STL)
Kirk, David R. (TOL)
Kokeram, Sudash J. (NEW)
Kondik, Curtis L. (CLV)
Kopec, Krzysztof A. (WIL)
Kopec, Rajmund (NEW)
Kumai, Felix K. (Nigeria) (NY)
Lachica, Jose P. (Philippines)
Lanuevo, Victor (HON)
Lawrence, Andrew F. (DUB)
Lea, Joseph P. (PH)
Lorenc, Henryk (Poland)
Lorimer, Daniel S. (WCH)
LosBanes, Hermes (Philippines)
Madej, Paul D. (SY)
Madu, Ferdinand E. (Nigeria)
Magnuson, Sean R. (STP)
Manuel, Vincent (Nigeria) (ALX)
Martin, Edward (VEN)
Mastin, Mark, S.C.J., Chap.
Moras, Leo (India) (LUB)
Napieralski, Maciej (FBK)
Nielson, Kenneth W. (AUS)
O'Grady, J. Frank (PAT)
O'Neal, James E. (STA)
Obeng-Kyeremeh, Simon (STV)
Obiatuegwu, Thomas (Nigeria)
Ohm, Edward U. (PEO)
Okoth, George (Kenya)
Opara, Christopher (Nigeria) (NY)
Opara, Isaac (Nigeria) (LAF)
Pajarillo, Cesar C. (RCK)
Panzer, Joel (LIN)
Passamonti, Paul G. (WDC)
Pawlikowski, Matthew (NEW)
Peak, James (SPK)
Peek, Kevin T., B.A., M.Div. (ATL)
Rendon, Matthias, O.F.M.
Rzasowski, Jerzy (Poland)
Stanley, Brian L. (KAL)
Studniewski, Gary R. (WDC)
Subler, Carl A. (COL)
Travaglione, Michael, O.F.M.
Ugwuanya, Valentine C. (NEW)
Uhde, Peter M. (NEW)
Uwakwe, Uzoma E. (Nigeria)
Valentine, Timothy S., S.J.
Van Alstyne, Donald J., M.I.C.
Van Durme, Patrick, S.T.L. (ROC)
Villanueva, Edgar (HON)
Wendel, Alfred W. (ATL)
Wood, Tyson J. (BAL)
Yoakam, Lee R., O.S.B.

Army National Guard Chaplains:
Rev. Msgrs.—
Coyle, Edward J., M.A., Th.M. (ALN)
Thomas, Royce R., J.C.L., J.V. (LR)
Revs.—
Allen, Richard J. (E)
Alvarado de Jesus, Jose (PCE)
Amande, Lito D. (Philippines)
Austin, Walter J. (NO)
Brownell, Patrick P. (KNX)
Cavanaugh, Kevin P. (HRT)
Collins, James B. (NY)
Constant, Van (HT)
Converse, Brian J. (NOR)
Corneille, Cecil C. (STV)
Dolan, Patrick J., Ph.D., S.T.D. (L)
Farley, Daniel H. (LC)
Fehn, Jerome W. (STP)
Feltz, John G. (BUR)
Figueroa, Honecimo (BWN)
Giese, Samuel C. (WDC)
Gonzalez, Julio Angel (MGZ)
Holzhauser, John J. (SFS)
Jaramillo, Peter (AMA)
Kaminski, Louis T. (SCR)
Kane, Brian P. (LIN)
Kilmurray, Fintan J. (BLX)
Kozen, Bert S. (SCR)
LaVoie, Raymond J. (HBG)
Lemoi, Paul R. (PRO)
Lindsay, Michael P. (LSC)
Lippstock, Paul Eldon (DUB)
Meier, Timothy, S.J.
Murphy, David F. (WIL)
Nambatac, Alner U. (Philippines)
Russo, Ricardo, O.F.M.
Sanchez-Munoz, Alejandro (STV)
Skufca, Ronald J. (MAR)
Stang, William J., C.PP.S., M.D.
Stodola, Francis (LAR)
Weberg, Paul, O.S.B.
Whorton, Jeffrey T. (SFE)
Worster, John R. (B)

Army Reserve Chaplains:
Revs.—
Adams, Joseph M., O.S.B.
Aniekwe, Samuel O. (Nigeria)
Augustyn, Boguslaw Adam, C.Ss.R.
Axalan, Romeo J. (Philippines)
Bleboo, Lawrence T. (Ghana)
Bucon, Raymond H. (DET)
Caballejo, Yuen (ATL)
Coe, Austin J. (Korea, South)
Denemark, Emil J., S.J.
Dinello, John E. (PIT)
Dominic, Michael M. (Kenya)
Donahue, Brian G. (FAR)
Farley, Daniel H. (LC)
Fitzgibbons, Peter L. (CHL)
Grice, Edward M. (NO)
Kanai, Charles (Kenya)
Kneemiller, William C. (DAV)
Krische, James J. (BRK)
Mahalic, Philip A. (LFT)
McCabe, Edward D. (BO)
McDermott, Stephen C. (PH)
Morse, Jonathan K.
Munoz-Lasalle, Jesus M. (ARE)
Nolan, Kevin L., V.F. (LA)
Ochalek, Arkadiusz (BAL)
Onuoha, Gerald U. (Nigeria)
Pamula, Robert (Poland)
Piekarczyk, Marian A., S.D.S.
Piontkowski, Richard L., Jr., S.T.L., J.C.D. (GI)
Plaushin, Mark, O.S.F.S.
Sousa, Peter E., C.Ss.R.
Tyhovych, Ivan (STF)
Vigilanti, John A., J.C.L., Ph.D. (NY)
Yebra, Bernardino S. (Philippines) (CHR)

UNITED STATES AIR FORCE CHAPLAINS

Air Force Chaplains:
Rev. Msgrs.—
Butler, Michael T. (STL)
McManus, Gerald D. (PH)
Very Rev.—
Cannon, Col. Robert R., J.C.L. (VEN)
Revs.—
Adversario, Efren F. (AGN)
Angelo, Thomas M. (NOR)
Bartoul, William (SAM)
Beale, Kenneth R. (NEW)
Beck, R. Patrick (BEA)
Bochnak, Zenon A. (MET)
Breig, Gary R. (STL)
Bruno, Robert A., O.F.M.
Butler, Timothy A. (BO)
Catungal, Mario T., O.C.D.
Clemens, Neal C. (OAK)
Cody, Kevin W. (MAN)
Covos, Ruben (SAN)
De Guzman, Dennis (OM)
Deichert, Joseph (BIS)
Del Toro, Jose L., T.O.R.
Dinh, Van (OAK)
Fadallan, Elbert A. (LUB)
Fitz-Patrick, David M. (WDC)
Fitzgerald, R. Martin (R)
Gajda, Piotr J. (CC)
Gills, Thomas (BAL)
Glaros, Matthew J. (CLV)
Hamel, James A. (NEW)
Hirten, Timothy J. (BRK)
Juszczak, John W., C.Ss.R.
Kaim, Phillip (RCK)
King, Martin (P)
Kinney, John M. (LFT)
Knox, Sean Vincent (PT)
Kruse, David B. (BAL)
Linsky, Gary S. (CHR)
Lowe, Frank E. (SB)
McGregor, Mark D., S.J.
McGuire, David V. (RIC)
Monagle, Robert J. (BO)
Morris, Michael J. (SP)
Navarrete, Jesus (Spain)
Nguyen, Hoang Peter (CHI)
Nguyen, Son, S.V.D.
Novotny, Richard (RC)
Nwoga, Laserian (CAM)
Okorie, Onyema (FRS)
Omana, Max B. (Philippines)
Onyejegbu, Cyriacus N. (GAL)
Poole, Richard (SPK)
Raux, Redmond P. (BO)
Reinhart, David A. (TOL)
Rigonan, Antonio R. (Philippines)
Romero, Donald (DEN)
Rowan, Mark P. (RVC)
Salditos, Ricardito P. (Philippines)
Sohm, Andrew L. (OM)
Srode, John S., C.PP.S.
Tenorio, Michael C., O.F.M.Cap.
Theisen, Eugene J. (STP)
Tran, Thienan (SY)
Vitaliano, Dominic J. (PEO)
Voyt, Stephen A. (PT)
Wedeking, Patrick (GLP)
Zielinski, Chad W. (GLD)
Zygadlo, Mitchell (ROC)

Air National Guard Chaplains:
Very Rev.—
Bateman, John B., V.F. (HBG)
Revs.—
Barnhill, Robert K. (LIN)
Barry, Robert L., O.P.
Bergbower, Daniel J. (SFD)
Bohorquez, Carlos M. (SFD)
Bolger, Jesse L. (BAL)
Cheney, James W. (FAR)
Cooney, Patrick, O.S.B.
Crowley, Edmund G. (MAN)
Cunningham, Douglas D. (SY)
Decker, Douglas A. (OG)
Donovan, Bernard Thomas (SFD)
Echert, John P., S.S.L. (STP)
Fitzgerald, John P., C.A.C. (PIT)
Foster, Thomas J. (DUL)
Fuller, Timothy M. (OKL)
Giamello, Anthony (WIL)
Gomez, Walter (SJN)
Heiar, Donald Joseph, Jr. (MAD)
Humenay, Robert L. (E)
Jaeger, James P. (ROC)
Laible, Jeffrey G. (PEO)
LaMorte, Joseph P. (NY)
Love, John W. (LA)
Ludwig, Thomas (KC)
Martinez, Michael (TUC)
McKenna, Timothy J. (SEA)
Mink, John J. (WIL)
Mizeur, Thomas R. (PEO)
Moenkedick, Leo (SCL)
Myers, Christopher P., S.O.L.T.

Pitstick, Rory K.
Ramatowski, Edward F. (STL)
Rogers, Patrick W. (COL)
Silva, Caesar (HT)
Sirianni, Richard D. (P)
Stephenson, Alfonse J. (PAT)
Stevens, David E. (SFS)
Tirado, Ramon Orlando (SJN)
Vit, William J., Jr. (SC)
Weber, Joseph A. (STL)
Winters, Darvin E. (IND)

Air Force Reserve Chaplains:
Rev. Msgrs.—
Moore, William C. (STO)
Randall, Kevin S. (NOR)
Very Revs.—
Erickson, Richard M. (BO)
Fischer, Richard O. (BAK)
Hoffmann, Christopher (ORL)
Lilly, Thomas C., V.G. (ANC)
Osinski, Ronald V., V.F. (ALT)
Zalewski, Peter Lawrence (PT)
Revs.—
Amaliri, Paul Obi (TLS)
Ballou, Jeffrey A. (SPR)
Baratelli, David J., Ed.D. (NEW)
Bastian, James R. (BUF)
Beers, John Michael, Ph.D. (ALN)
Blake, Lawrence R. (STP)
Brosk, Steven J. (NEW)
Caggianelli, Gregg (VEN)
Cordery, Robert J.
Dowling, Joseph K. (NSH)
Drabek, Howard E. (GAL)
Fonseca, Oscar D. (NEW)
Fredericks, Michael (SB)
Freihofer, Michael A. (DEN)
Gaglione, John R. (BUF)
Herbert, G. Paul, J.C.L. (WDC)
Hewes, Robert S. (RVC)
Johnson, James B., V.F. (SP)
Jones, Michael T. (WDC)
Kadera, Thomas R., J.C.L. (CHY)
Kayatta, Francis P. (PRO)
Keller, Robert J. (DET)
Kelly, Thomas D. (DEN)
Kowalik, Jacek (VEN)
LaBranch, Derek R. P., M.Ed., M.A., M.Div. (SAC)
Laroche, Christopher J. (PRT)
Lillpopp, Michael (SPR)
Loseke, Jeffery S. (OM)
Mack, John P. (BUF)
Maikowski, Thomas R., Ph.D., Ed.D. (GLP)
Malloy, Francis X. (MIL)
Mattina, Louis A. (MET)
McDowell, Leo G. (GF)
McGrade, Kevin M. (BO)
McGuill, Martin F. (ARL)
McGuine, Peter M. (SD)
McNamara, Brian J. (RVC)
Medas, Michael B., M.S.W. (BO)
Mockler, Patrick J. (BLX)
Morrow, Michael J. (NY)
Nguyen, Hung Van, S.O.L.T.
O'Hara, Daniel J. (SY)
Padazinski, Michael C., J.C.D. (SFR)
Phan, John (JOL)
Richtsteig, Erik J. (SLC)
Robbins, Thomas P. (COV)
Safraniec, Joseph N. (STU) (Retired)
Schuetze, John W. (GB)
Sewell, Jack, J.C.L. (ORG)
Stakem, Ward G., O.F.M.Cap.
Stewart, Paul (PT)
Sweeney, Daniel, S.J.
Tero, Richard D. (ANC)
Tomasiewicz, Mark A. (OM)
Tran, Joseph (OAK)
Tran, Luan Quach (P)
Travers, Patrick J., J.C.L., J.D. (JUN)
Vaverek, Hayden J. (CHR)
Vu, Joseph Dang-Hai, S.D.D.
Willette, Donald C. (DEN)
Wulinski, Stanley F. (BRK)
Yanju, Henry M. (BO)
Zimmer, Eric A., S.J.
Very Rev. Archpriest—
Kaszczak, Ivan, Ph.D., M.A., B.A. (STF)

UNITED STATES NAVY CHAPLAINS

Navy Chaplains:
Revs.—
Aguilera, Salvador (ELP)
Bargola, Cerino O. (Philippines)
Barrett, Miles J. (SC)
Bautista, Jose A. (LA)
Borzych, Alexander J. (GI)
Brown, Shaun S. (NTN)
Brzek, Jon J. (PIT)
Chapa, Robert J., S.O.L.T.
Coffey, Joseph L. (PH)
Colvin, Andrew (BAK)
Creider, Philip B. (OKL)
Daigle, David A. (BGP)
Dang, Chin Van (RIC)
Delis, Robert, S.D.B.
Dermott, William R. (ALN)
Dillon, Jerome V. (OM)
Dorwart, William D., C.S.C.
Enriquez, Rean F. (Philippines)
Foley, Francis P. (PH)
Fronk, Christopher S., S.J.
Fullerton, Daniel J. (SCR)
Garrett, Benton Lee (WDC)
Gegotek, Tadeusz (BEL)
Gelinas, Robert James (NEW)
Haddad, Wayne M. (MET)
Hannigan, John T. (CHI)
Hellwig, Lee W. (HRT)
Hicks, Steven (SAN)
Hoke, John R. (HBG)
Ianucci, Thomas (RIC)
Johnson, Charles W. (AUS)
Johnson, Lawrence P. (DUL)
Kanicki, Philip A. (RIC)
Karava, Norbert, O.F.M.Cap.
Keane, Robert L., S.J.
Keener, Robert J. (CHI)
Kelly, John E. (BUF)
Kennedy, William M. (BO)
Kersten, Jay J. (LAN)
Kloak, David G. (CHI)
Koch, Joseph A., C.V.
Koester, Timothy J. (BUF)
Lindblad, Karl-Albert (NY)
Lyle, John W., O.S.F.S.
Mandato, Kieran (NY)
McClanahan, Robert P., Jr. (PT)
Mensah, Gabriel Justus (VIC)
Merris, Christopher (SD)
Mikstay, Michael (Y)
Mode, Daniel L. (ARL)
Monahan, John C., S.J.
Mudd, David A. (WDC) (Retired)
Mueller, Michael (ORL)
Muhm, William M. (NY)
O'Flanagan, Thomas P. (PMB)
Parisi, Michael (PAT)
Reardon, Joseph D. (KC)
Romanello, Carmelo (MIA)
Shaughnessy, Paul J., S.J.
Sheehan, Peter J. (PRO)
Shimotsu, John M. (ORG)
Shuley, Keith J. (CC)
Sikorski, Leszek (NY)
Simpson, Brian L. (CHI)
Spencer, Robert A. (CHR)
Sweeney, Kevin (ORG)
Thevenin, Donelson (BRK)
Tiongson, Joselito S. (Philippines)
Tran, Tung (CC)
Ubalde, Ulysses L. (NEW)

Navy Reserve Chaplains:
Rev. Msgrs.—
Coyle, Robert J. (RVC)
Hendrickson, Michael D. (SJ)
Very Rev.—
Donohue, Michael T. (NOR)
Revs.—
Arnone, Leo (ALT)
Barber, Michael C., S.J.
Barch, Howard C. (PEO)
Bergner, David J., S.D.S.
Bishop, Marc J. (BO)
Bower, Lawrence C. (BAK) (Retired)
Brighenti, Kenneth D. (MET)
Cain, Robert K.C. (TLS)
Calderone, Joseph D., O.S.A.
Cannon, Richard E. (BO)
Clark, Robert J., O.S.B.
Close, John L. (ALB)
Clovis, Stephen M. (P)
Condon, William G., C.S.C.
Cricchio, Santo, O.F.M.Conv.
Cunha, Egionor (NEW)
D'Aurora, Joseph A. (RIC)
Davantes, Carlo B.
DeSocio, John A. (ROC)
Dhein, William A. (LC)
Donohoe, Stephen S., M.Div. (BO)
Doyle, Michael J. (BO)
Duesterhaus, Michael R. (ARL)
Emechete, Innocent (Nigeria) (SAC)
Ethen, Jeffrey D. (SCL)
Foote, Job, O.S.B.
Gardocki, Patrick M., O.F.M.
Gayton, John J., M.I.C.
Gorman, Edward M., O.P.
Griffin, Thomas, O.S.A.
Hamaday, Ronald A., O.S.A.
Hoak, Jack W., O.F.M.
Johnson, Patrick D., C.S.P.
Judge, Timothy M., M.Div. (PH)
Kantor, Robert Joseph (VEN)
Kehoe, James P. (CHI)
Kilian, Waldemar A. (CHI)
Klarer, Michael E. (MAD)
Kucharczyk, Dennis H. (SAG)
Langan, William J.P., V.F. (SCR)
Legaspi, Alex L. (SFR)
Legaspi, Fulgencio Paul (Philippines)
Madey, Louis (LAN)
McCandless, William T., O.S.F.S.
Neitzke, Ron P. (JOL)
Nguyen, Van T. (NO)
O'Brien, Sean Patrick (SY)
O'Connell, Terry J. (P)
O'Neill, John J. (SFR) (Retired)
Parenti, Thomas M. (SFR)
Pimentel, Jose W., O.P.
Porpiglia, Joseph D. (BUF)
Reamer, Mark G., O.F.M.
Reilly, Mark R. (OG)
Robichaud, Paul G., C.S.P.
Sera, Enrique J. (ORG)
Slowinski, Thomas F. (DET)
Stavoy, Stephen J. (SCR)
Sullivan, Robert J. (BIR)
Thorne, Thomas P. (BGP)
Thottankara, Raju (India) (CC)
Wallace, Richard (P)
Westcott, Matthew J. (BO)

DEPARTMENT OF VETERANS AFFAIRS HOSPITALS AND CHAPLAINS:
Rev. Msgrs.—
Callahan, Kevin G. (STL)
Chacko, Joseph C. (Philippines)
Revs.—
Aban, Adolfo Aristotle (Philippines)
Adejoh, Patrick O. (Nigeria)
Anthony, Joseph (RNO)
Anyaeche, Jude (Nigeria)
Archibong, Cosmas P. (Nigeria)
Bain, Richard C. (SFR) (Retired)
Bartsch, Kenneth W., O.F.M.Conv.
Blas, Mario W. (Philippines)
Boateng-Mensah, Samanhyia (Ghana)
Brandow, Stephen J. (ALX)
Brennan, George P. (STL) (Retired)
Brioso-Texidor, Luis (SJN)
Burnett, James E. (DAV)
Butler, John J. (HON)
Bwayo, Peter K., A.J.
Byaruhanga, Frederick K. (Uganda)
Caffrey, Gerald, C.M.F.
Castillo, Rene R. (RIC)
Cavanaugh, Michael T., O.S.F.S
Cavey, Donald J. (RIC)
Chinnappan, Benjamin (India)
Clapham, Bruce (SYM)
Connery, Sean P., O.S.F.S.
Craig, Robert N., O.F.M.Cap.
Crehan, Matthias J., O.F.M.
Czartorynski, David F. (ALN)
D'Silva, Joseph R. (India)
Dagle, Harold F., M.A. (ALN) (Retired)
Dahms, Paul G. (RC)
Damian, Rinaldo (WOR)
David, Craig (ATL)
De la Pena, Uldarico (Philippines)
De La Riva, John, O.F.M.Cap.
Devore, Daniel B. (BGP)
DeWane, E. Thomas, O.Praem.
Diaz, Hector (SJN)
Diemand, James E. (SPR) (Retired)
Dieter, Thomas M. (JOL)
Dionne, Francis (SP) (Retired)
Dumas, Terrence J. (LAN) (Retired)
Eneh, Barry C. (Nigeria)
Eraly, Mathew (India)
Erestain, Alfonso E. (Philippines)
Everett, Willis E. (COL)
Ezeh, Christopher O. (Nigeria)
Florido, Robert (CHI)
Francis, R. Peter (RVC)
Franco, Joseph E. (NY)
Gardocki, Patrick M., O.F.M.
George, George C. (AUS)
Gould, Lawrence, S.A.C.
Grace, Joseph W. (LFT) (Retired)
Grasso, Joseph A., C.PP.S.
Heck, Quintin T. (MIL)
Henry, Paul J. (BAL)
Hickey, Joseph W. (NY) (Retired)
Hyde, Robert P., Jr., J.C.L. (SY)
Iheaka, Emmanuel K. (Nigeria)
Iwuchukwu, Azuka (Nigeria)
James, David John (SY)
Johnson, William B. (OAK)

Jordan, Maryon C., O.S.B.
Joseph, Vio O., S.A.C.
Kauffman, William B. (WIL)
Kiene, Joseph, O.F.M.Conv.
Kleiber, Kenneth R. (CHI)
Klein, David O., C.S.B.
Kurtenbach, Harold R. (GI) (Retired)
Lacroix, Maurice R. (MAN) (Retired)
Lagace, Raymond R., O.F.M.
Lankford, Michael G. (TR)
Leeuw, Daniel R. (ALT)
Leonard, Matthew (CHL)
Leonhardt, Louis J. (DAV) (Retired)
Lipareli, Michael A. (NY)
Lopes, Richard A., O.F.M.Cap
Maher, Raymond V., O.Carm.
Malloy, Francis X. (MIL)
Malone, H. Patrick (WCH) (Retired)
Malone, John S., C.S.Sp.
Mani, L. David (India)
McCord, Kent G. (MET)
Meier, Denis E. (SFS)
Mensah, Tony Kyere (Ghana)
Mestas, Leonard J. (BWN)
Michiels, Philip F. (SHP)
Milewski, John A. (KNX), Assoc. Dir., VA National Chap. Center
Miller, James Norman (NSH)
Moster, James, O.F.M.Cap.
Murphy, Patrick E. (MAR)
Myers, Christopher P., S.O.L.T.
Neuizil, Lowell Greg (KNX)
Njoku, Innocent E., C.S.Sp
Ntsiful-Amissah, Dominic Kofi (ALB)
O'Keeffe, Joseph (ALB)
Ochu, Austin Charles, S.M.A.
Odemokpa, Paschal (Nigeria)
Odor, Luke U. (Nigeria)
Onuwmere, Leonard, J.P. (Nigeria)
Oswald, Norman R. (MIL)
Palatucci, John F. (NY)
Paulish, W. Jeffrey (SCR)
Pavlick, Raymond A. (PAT)
Pesaresi, Thomas, M.M.
Piekarczyk, Marian A., S.D.S.
Putich, Michael J., O.F.M.
Reinders, David H. (TUC)
Repko, Joseph, M.Div. (PRM)
Rich, John A., M.M.
Rimmele, Leo R., O.S.B.
Roesch, David H. (ALT)
Roof, Francis M. (OWN)
Rowgh, Matthew T. (WH)
Saavedra, Ramon (Philippines)
Saldua, Max Ernesto M. (Philippines)
Salois, Philip G., M.S.
Santiago, Leoncio S. (CHI)
Sarnecki, Thomas G. (SCR)
Schill, Gerald F. (Damien) (FAR)
Schneider, John H. (STL)
Schuler, Emett J., O.F.M.Cap.
Shepley, Brian J. (DAV)
Sioleti, Andrew, i.v.dei.
Smith, Charles F., S.V.D.
Smith-Soucier, Martin D. (STU)
Soto, Charles, O.F.M. (Retired)
Steinmetz, Thomas P. (NTN)
Striegel, Robert M. (DAV)
Stump, James M., O.F.M.Cap.
Timoney, Conan H., C.P.
Torres, Ivan J. (SJN)
Tran, Quang Mihn
Trujillo, Ivan R. (BUF)
Tufail, Augustine (Pakistan)
Ubanii, Angelo B., S.M.M.M.
Ugobueze, John (Nigeria)
Ugochukwu, Sebastian A. (Nigeria)
Uralikunnel, George V. (India)
Uwandu, Marcellinus U. (Nigeria)
Vander Heyden, William F. (GB)
VanDoan, Vincent (LAN)
Vennetti, Robert C., M.I.C.
Vistal, Felix (DAL)
Vu, Joseph Duc (Vietnam)
Warman, William C. (BAL)
Westfall, Joseph B. (LFT)
Wright, Gerald, O.M.V.
Wydeven, John L. (OAK)
Young, Dennis M. (STA)
Youssef, Clement, C.S.B.
Zatalava, James D. (ALT)

CIVIL AIR PATROL:
Revs.—
Juroszek, Robert S. (TOR)
O'Connor, Michael P. (BLX)

DIOCESES WITH PRIESTS SERVING IN UNIFORM IN THE ARCHDIOCESE FOR THE MILITARY SERVICES

Agana, Guam.
Albany.
Alexandria.
Allentown.
Altoona-Johnstown.
Arecibo, Puerto Rico.
Arlington.
Atlanta.
Austin.
Baker.
Baltimore.
Beaumont.
Belleville.
Bismarck.
Boston.
Bridgeport.
Brooklyn.
Buffalo.
Camden.
Charleston.
Chicago.
Cleveland.
Columbus.
Corpus Christi.
Denver.
Detroit.
Dubuque.
Duluth.
El Paso.
Eparchy of St. Maron.
Eparchy of St. Nicholas.
Erie.
Fresno.
Gallup.
Galveston-Houston.
Gaylord.
Grand Island.
Green Bay.
Harrisburg.
Hartford.
Honolulu.
Houma-Thibodaux.
Kalamazoo.
Kansas City-St. Joseph.
LaCrosse.
Lafayette, IN.
Lansing.
Lincoln.
Los Angeles.
Lubbock.
Madison.
Manchester.
Marquette.
Memphis.
Metuchen.
Miami.
Mobile.
Newark.
Newton (Melkite Rite).
New York.
Norwich.
Oakland.
Oklahoma City.
Omaha.
Orange.
Orlando.
Palm Beach.
Paterson.
Pensacola-Tallahassee.
Peoria.
Philadelphia.
Pittsburgh.
Ponce, Puerto Rico.
Portland, OR.
Providence.
Raleigh.
Rapid City.
Reno.
Richmond.
Rochester.
Rockford.
Rockville Centre.
Sacramento.
St. Augustine.
St. Louis.
St. Paul-Minneapolis.
St. Petersburg.
St. Thomas, Virgin Islands.
San Angelo.
San Antonio.
San Bernardino.
San Diego.
San Jose in California.
San Juan, Puerto Rico.
Santa Fe.
Scranton.
Seattle.
Sioux City.
Spokane.
Springfield in Illinois.
Syracuse.
Toledo.
Trenton.
Tulsa.
Venice.
Victoria.
Washington, D.C.
Wichita.
Wilmington.
Worcester.
Yakima.
Youngstown.

RELIGIOUS INSTITUTES WITH PRIESTS SERVING IN UNIFORM IN THE ARCHDIOCESE FOR THE MILITARY SERVICES

[]—*Vincentian Fathers*—C.M.
[]—*Society of the Precious Blood*—C.PP.S.
[]—*Congregation of the Holy Cross*—C.S.C.
[]—*Paulist Fathers*—C.S.P.
[]—*Redemptorist Fathers*—C.SS.R.
[]—*Congregation of Marians of the Immaculate Conception*—M.I.C.
[]—*Missionaries of the Holy Apostles*—M.S.A.
[]—*Carmelite Fathers*—O.Carm.
[]—*Cistercians of the Strict Observance*—O.C.S.O.
[]—*Franciscan Fathers*—O.F.M.
[]—*Cap. Capuchins*—O.F.M.
[]—*Conventual Franciscans*—O.F.M.Conv.
[]—*Dominican Fathers*—O.P.
[]—*Norbertines*
[]—*Order of St. Benedict*—O.S.B.
[]—*Oblates of St. Francis de Sales*—O.S.F.S.
[]—*Salesian Fathers*—S.D.B.
[]—*Jesuit Fathers*—S.J.
[]—*Society of Mary*—S.M.
[]—*Society of Our Lady of the Most Holy Trinity*—S.O.L.T.
[]—*Society of the Divine World*
[]—*Third Order Regular of St. Francis*—T.O.R.
[]—*Legionaries of Christ*—L.C.
[]—*Sons of Mary Mother of Mercy*—S.M.M.M.

ASSOCIATIONS SUPPORTING THE MISSION OF THE ARCHDIOCESE

21st Century Centurions.
The Chaplains Aid Association.
National Conference of Veterans Affairs Catholic Chaplains, Inc. Most Rev. Richard B. Higgins, (Episcopal Advisor), Rev. James E. Burnett, Pres.
Catholic War Veterans, USA, Inc., 441 N. Lee St., Alexandria, VA 22314-2301. Tel: 703-549-3622.

Archdiocese of Milwaukee

(Archidioecesis Milvauchiensis)

Most Reverend

JEROME E. LISTECKI

Archbishop of Milwaukee; ordained May 14, 1975; appointed Auxiliary Bishop of Chicago and Titular Bishop of Nara November 7, 2000; consecrated January 8, 2001; appointed Bishop of La Crosse December 29, 2004; installed March 1, 2005; appointed Archbishop of Milwaukee November 14, 2009; installed January 4, 2010. *Chancery Office: Archbishop Cousins Catholic Center, 3501 S. Lake Dr., P.O. Box 070912, Milwaukee, WI 53207-0912.*

Chancery Office: Archbishop Cousins Catholic Center, 3501 S. Lake Dr., P.O. Box 070912, Milwaukee, WI 53207-0912. Tel: 414-769-3340; Fax: 414-769-3408.

Web: www.archmil.org

Email: information@archmil.org

Most Reverend

REMBERT G. WEAKLAND, O.S.B., D.D.

Archbishop Emeritus of Milwaukee; ordained June 24, 1951; appointed Archbishop of Milwaukee September 20, 1977; consecrated and installed as Ninth Archbishop November 8, 1977; retired May 24, 2002. *Res.: Wilson Commons, 1400 W. Sonata Dr., #218, Milwaukee, WI 53221.*

Most Reverend

DONALD J. HYING

Auxiliary Bishop of Milwaukee; ordained May 20, 1989; appointed Auxiliary Bishop of Milwaukee and Titular Bishop of Regiae May 26, 2011; installed July 20, 2011. *Chancery Office: Archbishop Cousins Catholic Center, 3501 S. Lake Dr., P.O. Box 070912, Milwaukee, WI 53207.*

Most Reverend

RICHARD J. SKLBA, D.D.

Retired Auxiliary Bishop of Milwaukee; ordained December 20, 1959; appointed Auxiliary Bishop of Milwaukee and Titular Bishop of Castro November 6, 1979; consecrated December 19, 1979; retired October 18, 2010. *Res.: 836 N. Broadway, Milwaukee, WI 53202-3608.* Tel: 414-962-3941. *All official communications should be addressed to: Archbishop Cousins Catholic Center, 3501 S. Lake Dr., P.O. Box 070912, Milwaukee, WI 53207-0912.* Tel: 414-769-3486.

Square Miles 4,758.

Established November 28, 1843; Created Archbishopric February 12, 1875.

Corporate Title: Archdiocese of Milwaukee.

Comprises the Counties of Dodge, Fond du Lac, Kenosha, Milwaukee, Ozaukee, Racine, Sheboygan, Walworth, Washington and Waukesha in the State of Wisconsin.

For legal titles of parishes and archdiocesan institutions, consult the Chancery Office.

STATISTICAL OVERVIEW

Personnel	
Archbishops	1
Retired Archbishops	1
Auxiliary Bishops	1
Retired Bishops	1
Abbots	1
Retired Abbots	3
Priests: Diocesan Active in Diocese	171
Priests: Diocesan Active Outside Diocese	10
Priests: Diocesan in Foreign Missions	3
Priests: Retired, Sick or Absent	155
Number of Diocesan Priests	339
Religious Priests in Diocese	345
Total Priests in Diocese	684
Extern Priests in Diocese	27
Ordinations:	
Diocesan Priests	6
Transitional Deacons	4
Permanent Deacons in Diocese	177
Total Brothers	71
Total Sisters	1,252
Parishes	
Parishes	205
With Resident Pastor:	
Resident Diocesan Priests	169
Resident Religious Priests	27
Without Resident Pastor:	
Administered by Deacons	4
Administered by Lay People	5
Welfare	
Catholic Hospitals	10
Total Assisted	1,891,652
Health Care Centers	1
Total Assisted	11,071
Homes for the Aged	18
Total Assisted	32,346
Day Care Centers	4
Total Assisted	601
Specialized Homes	4
Total Assisted	3,044
Special Centers for Social Services	11
Total Assisted	169,789
Residential Care of Disabled	3
Total Assisted	164
Other Institutions	19
Total Assisted	23,985
Educational	
Seminaries, Diocesan	1
Students from This Diocese	32
Diocesan Students in Other Seminaries	11
Seminaries, Religious	3
Students Religious	149
Total Seminarians	192
Colleges and Universities	5
Total Students	24,906
High Schools, Diocesan and Parish	6
Total Students	2,939
High Schools, Private	7
Total Students	3,646
Elementary Schools, Diocesan and Parish	93
Total Students	23,883
Elementary Schools, Private	4
Total Students	1,118
Non-residential Schools for the Disabled	1
Total Students	20
Catechesis/Religious Education:	
High School Students	12,958
Elementary Students	27,390
Total Students under Catholic Instruction	97,052
Teachers in the Diocese:	
Priests	26
Sisters	99
Lay Teachers	4,037
Vital Statistics	
Receptions into the Church:	
Infant Baptism Totals	6,726
Minor Baptism Totals	322
Adult Baptism Totals	223
Received into Full Communion	404
First Communions	7,374
Confirmations	5,377
Marriages:	
Catholic	1,250
Interfaith	512
Total Marriages	1,762
Deaths	4,913
Total Catholic Population	625,765
Total Population	2,327,812

Former Bishops—Most Revs. JOHN MARTIN HENNI, D.D., cons. March 19, 1844; created Archbishop, Feb. 11, 1875; died Sept. 7, 1881; MICHAEL HEISS, D.D., cons. Bishop of La Crosse, Sept. 6, 1868; appt. Coadjutor of Milwaukee and Titular Archbishop of Adrianople, March 14, 1880; succeeded to Archbishop Henni in 1881; died March 26, 1890; FREDERICK XAVIER KATZER, D.D., cons. Sept. 21, 1886; Bishop of Green Bay; transferred to Milwaukee and raised to the Archiepiscopal Dignity, Jan. 30, 1891; died July 20, 1903; SEBASTIAN GEBHARD MESSMER, D.D., D.C.L., ord. July 23, 1871; cons. March 27, 1892; Bishop of Green Bay; transferred to Milwaukee and raised to the Archiepiscopal dignity Dec. 10, 1903; made assistant at the Pontifical Throne, Nov. 16, 1906; died Aug. 4, 1930; His Eminence SAMUEL ALPHONSUS STRITCH, D.D., ord. May 21, 1910; cons. Nov. 30, 1921; Bishop of Toledo; transferred to Milwaukee and raised to the Archiepiscopal dignity, Aug. 26, 1930; transferred to Chicago, Dec. 27, 1939; created Cardinal, Feb. 18, 1946; died May 27, 1958; Most Rev. MOSES E. KILEY, S.T.D., appt. Bishop of Trenton, Feb. 10, 1934; cons. March 17, 1934; appt. Archbishop of Milwaukee, Jan. 1, 1940; died April 15, 1953; His Eminence ALBERT G. MEYER, S.T.D., S.S.L., ord. July 11, 1926; cons. Bishop of Superior, April 11, 1946; appt. Archbishop of Milwaukee, July 21, 1953; transferred to Chicago, Sept. 24, 1958; created Cardinal, Dec. 14, 1959; died April 9, 1965; Most Revs. WILLIAM E. COUSINS, D.D., ord. April 23, 1927; appt. Titular Bishop of Forma and Auxiliary Bishop of Chicago Dec. 17, 1948; cons. March 7, 1949; appt. Bishop of Peoria, May 19, 1952; installed July 2, 1952; appt. Archbishop of Milwaukee, Dec. 18, 1958; installed Jan. 27, 1959; retired Sept. 20, 1977; died Sept. 14, 1988; REMBERT G. WEAKLAND, O.S.B. (Retired), ord. June 24, 1951; appt. Archbishop of Milwaukee, Sept. 20, 1977; cons. and installed as Ninth Archbishop, Nov. 8, 1977; retired May 24, 2002; His Eminence TIMOTHY M. DOLAN, ord. June 19, 1976; appt. Auxiliary Bishop of St. Louis June 19, 2001; installed Aug. 15, 2001; appt. Archbishop of Milwaukee June 25, 2002; installed as Tenth Archbishop Aug. 28, 2002; appt. Archbishop of New York Feb. 23, 2009; elevated to Cardinal Feb. 18, 2012.

Archbishop Cousins Catholic Center—3501 S. Lake Dr., P.O. Box 070912, Milwaukee, 53207-0912. Tel:

414-769-3300; Fax: 414-769-3408.
Vicars General—Most Rev. DONALD J. HYING; Very Revs. PATRICK E. HEPPE; WILLIAM J. KOHLER.
Moderator of the Curia—Very Rev. WILLIAM J. KOHLER.
Chief of Staff—JEROME T. TOPCZEWSKI. Tel: 414-769-3590; Fax: 414-769-3430. Email: topczewskij@archmil.org.
Archdiocesan Consultors—Most Revs. DONALD J. HYING; RICHARD J. SKLBA, S.S.L., S.T.D.; Very Revs. CURT J. FREDERICK, J.C.L., M.Div.; RALPH C. GROSS, J.C.L.; JEFFREY R. HAINES; JOHN D. HEMSING; PATRICK E. HEPPE; Rev. Msgr. T. GEORGE GAJDOS; Revs. DENNIS ACKERET; MICHAEL BERTRAM, O.F.M.Cap.; JOSEPH F. HORNACEK (Retired); JEROME M. HUDZIAK, Ph.D. (Retired); JOHN G. YOCKEY.
Archdiocesan Council of Priests—Most Rev. DONALD J. HYING; Very Revs. CURT J. FREDERICK, J.C.L., M.Div.; RALPH C. GROSS, J.C.L.; JEFFREY R. HAINES; JOHN D. HEMSING; PATRICK E. HEPPE; WILLIAM E. KOHLER; Rev. Msgr. T. GEORGE GAJDOS; Revs. DENNIS ACKERET; MICHAEL BERTRAM, O.F.M.Cap.; ALLEN J. BRATKOWSKI; AARON J. ESCH; JOSEPH F. HORNACEK (Retired); JEROME M. HUDZIAK, Ph.D. (Retired); ALAN F. JURKUS; EDWIN M. KORNATH; STEVEN KROPP, O.F.M.Cap.; ROBERT J. LOTZ, Ed.D.; BRIAN G. MASON; ROMANUS N. NWARU; LUIS PACHECO-SANCHEZ; MICHAEL J. PETRIE; DAVID H. REITH; RAFAEL G. RODRIGUEZ; JAMES T. VOLKERT; ROBERT J. WEIGHNER; JOHN G. YOCKEY; CHARLES G. ZABLER.
Archdiocesan Pastoral Council—CAROL ABRAHAM; ROBERT ALEXANDER; DAVE BAUDRY; Sr. DIANE BAUKNECHT, C.S.A.; GENE BRAH; MICHAEL CHMIELEWSKI; JOHN ELLGAS; DIANE FOX; Sr. PHYLLIS MARIE GRZECZKA, S.S.N.D.; JANE JONITETZ; BOB LYNCH; MARI MALDONADO; MARY MERZ; ANTHONY MONTEMURRO; PETER DOAN NGUYEN; MARK OTHMER; KURT PIERNOT; Rev. DAVID H. REITH; KEN RISTOW; DAVE SALKOWSKI; KEVIN SULLIVAN; PAUL ZARLING.
Archbishop's Executive Council—Most Rev. DONALD J. HYING; Very Revs. PATRICK E. HEPPE; WILLIAM E. KOHLER; BARBARA ANNE CUSACK, J.C.D.; JOHN J. MAREK; JEROME T. TOPCZEWSKI.
Archives—
Archivist—SHELLY TAYLOR. Tel: 414-769-3407. Email: taylors@archmil.org.
Building Services—
Maintenance Coordinator—STEVE JUPP. Tel: 414-769-3566. Email: jupps@archmil.org.
Cemeteries and Mausoleums—7301 W. Nash St., Milwaukee, 53216.
Director—THOMAS G. CHAMPA. Tel: 414-438-4420. Email: champat@archmil.org.
Spiritual Director—Rev. MARVIN I. LAZARSKI, 3801 W. Morgan Ave., Milwaukee, 53221. Tel: 414-645-0611.
Chancery Office—Email: chancery@archmil.org.
Chancellor—BARBARA ANNE CUSACK, J.C.D. Tel: 414-769-3341. Email: cusackb@archmil.org.
Vice Chancellor—Rev. JAMES C. CONNELL, J.C.D.
Communications Office—Email: communication@archmil.org.
Director—JULIE WOLF. Tel: 414-769-3494. Email: wolfj@archmil.org.
Schools Marketing Coordinator—KATHRYN HEINO. Tel: 414-769-3453. Email: heinok@archmil.org.
Hispanic Communications Coordinator—MARIA PRADO. Tel: 414-769-3504. Email: pradom@archmil.org.
Communications Coordinator—AMY TAYLOR. Tel: 414-769-3435. Email: taylora@archmil.org.
Ecumenical and Interfaith Concerns—
Director—JUDI A. LONGDIN. Tel: 414-769-3483. Email: longdinj@archmil.org.
Financial Services—
Archdiocesan Treasurer and Finance Officer—JOHN J. MAREK. Tel: 414-769-3334. Email: marekj@archmil.org.
Diocesan Fiscal Services Director—MICHAEL FRIES. Tel: 414-769-3347. Email: friesm@archmil.org.
Parish and School Financial Services Director—JAY FRYMARK. Tel: 414-769-3336. Email: frymarkj@archmil.org.
Parish and School Financial Services Associate Director—DOUG MILLER. Tel: 414-769-3377. Email: millerdb@archmil.org.
Staff Accountants—JANICE O'CONNOR. Tel: 414-769-3314. Email: oconnorj@archmil.org; CAROL ABUYA. Tel: 414-769-3315. Email: abuyac@archmil.org.
Payroll Bookkeeper—BARBARA KISSH. Tel: 414-769-3318. Email: kisshb@archmil.org.
Accounts Payable Bookkeeper—DAVID WILLSHER. Tel: 414-769-3316. Email: willsherd@archmil.org.
Lay Pension and Life Insurance Coordinator—BRIDGET FISCHER. Tel: 414-769-3317. Email: fischerb@archmil.org.
Financial Services Support Coordinator—KIM KASTEN. Tel: 414-769-3326. Email: kastenk@archmil.org.
Corporate Legal Counsel—DENNIS PURTELL. Tel: 414-769-3376.
Archdiocesan Marian Shrine—Tel: 414-257-0155.
Campus Ministry—
Coordinator—RANDY NOHL. Tel: 414-769-2216. Email: nohlr@archmil.org.
Directors—Rev. MICHAEL LIGHTNER, St. Catherine of Alexandria Catholic Campus Ministry Center, Inc., 3001 N. Downer Ave., Milwaukee, 53211. Tel: 414-964-6640. Email: lightnerm@archmil.org; BRIAN ZANIN, Blessed John Henry Newman Catholic Campus Ministry Center, Inc., 344 N. Prairie St., Whitewater, 53190. Tel: 262-473-5555. Email: zaninb@uww.edu.
Catechesis and Youth Ministry Office—
Director—GARY POKORNY, M.Div., D.Min. (Cand.). Tel: 414-769-2242. Email: pokornyg@archmil.org.
Catholic Charities—
Executive Director—JAMES M. BRENNAN. Tel: 414-769-3330. Email: jbrennan@ccmke.org.
Operations Service Director—Sr. TONI ANNE GRADISNIK. Tel: 414-769-3402. Email: tgradisnik@ccmke.org.
Finance Director—JACQUELINE BEIER. Tel: 414-769-3420. Email: jbeier@ccmke.org.
Advancement Director—SANDY LESKE. Tel: 414-769-3524. Email: sleske@ccmke.org.
Adult Care Ministries Director—JANE DEGEORGE. Tel: 262-547-2463. Email: jdegeorge@ccmke.org.
Family and Children's Ministries Director—RICARDO CISNEROS. Tel: 414-771-2881. Email: rcisneros@ccmke.org.
Social Justice Ministries Director—SUSAN HOWLAND. Tel: 414-771-2881. Email: showland@ccmke.org.
Legal Services for Immigrants Director—BARBARA GRAHAM. Tel: 414-643-8570. Email: bgraham@ccmke.org.
Human Resource Coordinator—SHELBY MILCZARSKI. Tel: 414-769-3415. Email: smilczarski@ccmke.org.
Communications Director—SHARON BRUMER. Tel: 414-769-3543. Email: sbrumer@ccmke.org.
Grant Writer—WANDA WOODS. Tel: 414-769-3413. Email: wwoods@ccmke.org.
Information & Telecommunications Systems Director—RICK BERG. Tel: 414-769-3534. Email: rberg@ccmke.org.
Volunteer Coordinator—SUSI KUREK. Tel: 414-769-3401. Email: skurek@ccmke.org.
Catholic Herald—
Publisher—Most Rev. JEROME E. LISTECKI. Tel: 414-769-3497. Email: archbishoplistecki@archmil.org.
Executive Editor and General Manager—BRIAN T. OLSZEWSKI. Tel: 414-769-3466. Email: olszewskib@archmil.org.
Managing Editor—MARYANGELA LAYMAN ROMAN. Tel: 414-769-3476. Email: laymanromanm@archmil.org.
Human Resource Services—
Director of Personnel Services—RICHARD J. TANK. Tel: 414-769-3458. Email: tankr@archmil.org.
Central Offices and Agencies Director—SUSAN GORSKI. Tel: 414-769-3328. Email: gorskis@archmil.org.
Parish and School Personnel Director—JANE BUDNEY. Tel: 414-769-3370. Email: budneyj@archmil.org.
Human Resources & Benefits Administrator—MARY ANNE ZERA. Tel: 414-769-3540. Email: zeram@archmil.org.
Information Services—
Director and System Administrator—ALLAN RIES. Tel: 414-769-3332. Email: riesa@archmil.org.
Webmaster and Coordinator of Electronic Communications—MARK BARTHEL. Tel: 414-769-3454. Email: barthelm@archmil.org.
Computer Systems Trainer and Help Desk—MARGARET ERHART. Tel: 414-769-3335. Email: erhartm@archmil.org.
Intercultural Ministries Office—
Coordinator—EVA J. DIAZ, M.A.P.S. Tel: 414-769-3397. Email: diaze@archmil.org.
Associate for Hispanic Ministry—JORGE BENAVENTE. Tel: 414-769-3393. Email: benaventej@archmil.org.
Ministry to the Deaf and Hard of Hearing—Rev. CHRISTOPHER L. KLUSMAN. Email: cklusman@stromans.com.
John Paul II Center—
Coordinator—RANDY NOHL. Tel: 414-758-2215. Email: nohlr@archmil.org.
Ministry Formation Institute Director—Deacon JOHN A. EBEL. Tel: 414-758-2212. Email: ebelj@archmil.org.
Ministry Formation Institute Associate Director—MANUEL MALDONADO. Tel: 414-758-2207. Email: maldonadom@archmil.org.
Nazareth Project Director—LYDIA LOCOCO. Tel: 414-758-2213. Email: lococol@archmil.org.
Nazareth Project Associate Director—JENNIFER OLIVA. Tel: 414-758-2211. Email: olivaj@archmil.org.
Metropolitan Tribunal—
Judicial Vicar—Very Rev. PAUL B.R. HARTMANN, M.Div., J.C.L. Tel: 414-769-3304. Email: hartmannp@archmil.org.
Tribunal Chancellor—Ms. ZABRINA R. DECKER, J.C.L. Tel: 414-769-3302. Email: deckerz@archmil.org.
Office Manager—Mr. MAURICE C. THOMPSON, B.S. Tel: 414-769-3301. Email: thompsonm@archmil.org.
Judges for First Instance—Very Rev. PAUL B.R. HARTMANN, M.Div., J.C.L.; JESUS CABRERA, J.C.L.; Rev. BERNARD S. SIPPEL, M.Div. (Retired).
Judges for Second Instance—Revs. JOHN CELLA, O.F.M., J.C.D., M.Div., M.B.A.; JAMES E. CONNELL, J.C.D.; BARBARA ANNE CUSACK, J.C.D.; JESUS CABRERA, J.C.L.; Very Revs. CURT J. FREDERICK, J.C.L., M.Div.; PAUL B.R. HARTMANN, M.Div., J.C.L.; Revs. DENNIS C. KLEMME, J.C.D. (Retired); MICHAEL T. NEWMAN, J.C.L.; PHILIP D. REIFENBERG, J.C.L.; BERNARD S. SIPPEL, M.Div. (Retired).
Defenders of the Bond—Ms. ZABRINA R. DECKER, J.C.L.; Sr. AUDREY STRAUB, S.S.N.D., J.C.L.
Procurators and Advocates—STEPHEN J. HARVEY, M.Div.; Mr. MAURICE C. THOMPSON, B.S.; ANDREW R.J. VAUGHN, M.A.
Promoter of Justice—Rev. PHILIP D. REIFENBERG, J.C.L.
Office for Marital Reconciliation-Separation—Very Rev. PAUL B.R. HARTMANN, M.Div., J.C.L.
Archdiocesan Court of Equity—Very Rev. PAUL B.R. HARTMANN, M.Div., J.C.L.; Ms. ZABRINA R. DECKER, J.C.L.
Notaries—MARY CHRISTINE ELLISON; KAREY GAWRYCH; Mr. MAURICE C. THOMPSON, B.S.
Ordained and Lay Ecclesial Ministry—
Vicar for Ordained and Lay Ecclesial Ministry—Very Rev. PATRICK E. HEPPE. Tel: 414-769-3490. Email: heppep@archmil.org.
Director of Priest and Lay Ecclesial Personnel, Placement—RICHARD J. TANK. Tel: 414-769-3458. Email: tankr@archmil.org.
Minister to Priests—Rev. MARTIN PABLE, O.F.M.Cap., Ph.D. Tel: 414-372-3620, Ext. 22. Email: mpable@thecapuchins.org.
Associate Director for Deacon Services and Clergy Advocacy and Oversight—Deacon DAVID L. ZIMPRICH. Tel: 414-769-3409. Email: zimprichd@archmil.org.
Parish Mission—
Coordinator—MARK KEMMETER. Tel: 414-769-3352. Email: kemmeterm@archmil.org.
Schools Office—
Superintendent—KATHLEEN A. CEPELKA, Ph.D., Supt. Tel: 414-758-2251. Email: cepelkak@archmil.org.
Director, Academics and Faith Center of Excellence—SUSAN NELSON. Tel: 414-758-2263. Email: nelsons@archmil.org.
Associate Superintendents—PATRICK LOFTON. Tel: 414-758-2262. Email: loftonp@archmil.org; BRENDA WHITE. Tel: 414-758-2252. Email: whiteb@archmil.org.
Special Assistant—Bro. NIVARD SCHEEL, C.F.X. Tel: 414-758-2257. Email: scheeln@archmil.org.
Sexual Abuse Prevention and Response Services—
Victim Assistance Coordinator—VACANT. Tel: 414-758-2232.
Safe Environment Coordinator—PATTI LOEHRER. Tel: 414-769-3449. Email: loehrerp@archmil.org.
Social Justice Ministry—
Coordinator—ROBERT SHELLEDY. Tel: 414-758-2286. Email: shelledyr@archmil.org.
Stewardship and Development—
Development Director—DEBRA LETHLEAN. Tel: 414-769-3322. Email: lethleand@archmil.org.
Catholic Stewardship Appeal Director—ROBERT BOHLMANN. Tel: 414-769-3320. Email: bohlmannr@archmil.org.
Major and Planned Giving Director—MICHELE WEINSCHROTT. Tel: 414-769-3583. Email: weinschrottm@archmil.org.
Parish Stewardship Director—BARBARA VITE. Tel: 414-769-3485. Email: viteb@archmil.org.
Systems and Operations Director—LORETTA O'KELLY. Tel: 414-769-3323. Email: okellyl@archmil.org.
World Mission Ministries—
Director—FRAN CUNNINGHAM, O.S.F. Tel: 414-758-2282. Email: cunninghamf@archmil.org.
Associate Director—ELIZABETH C. HOWAYECK. Tel: 414-758-2283. Email: howayecke@archmil.org.
Worship—
Coordinator—DEAN DANIELS. Tel: 414-769-3359. Email: danielsd@archmil.org.

CLERGY, PARISHES, MISSIONS AND PAROCHIAL SCHOOLS

CITY OF MILWAUKEE

(MILWAUKEE COUNTY)

1—CATHEDRAL OF ST. JOHN THE EVANGELIST (1847) Very Rev. Jeffrey R. Haines, Rector; Deacon Thomas N. Hunt.
Mailing Address: 831 N. Van Buren St., 53202. In Res., Rev. R. Thomas Venne (Retired).
Res.: 802 N. Jackson St., 53202. Tel: 414-276-9814; Fax: 414-276-8285. Email: cathedral@stjohncathedral.org. Web: stjohncathedral.org.
Catechesis/Religious Program—East Side Child & Youth Ministry, 2480 N. Cramer St., 53211. Tel: 414-263-8230; Fax: 414-962-3829. Students 21.

2—ST. ADALBERT (1908), (Polish—Hispanic), Revs. Luis Pacheco-Sanchez; Jose Gonzalez.
Office: 1923 W. Becher St., 53215. Tel: 414-645-0413; Fax: 414-645-0166. Email: stadalberto@hotmail.com.
School—1913 W. Becher St., 53215-2688. Tel: 414-645-5450; Fax: 414-645-5510. Ms. Julia Hutchinson, Prin. Lay Teachers 25; Students 477.
Catechesis/Religious Program—Students 445.

3—ST. AGNES, Closed. For sacramental records, contact Archdiocese of Milwaukee Archives Office, Tel: 414-769-3407.

4—ST. ALBERT, Closed. For sacramental records, contact Archdiocese of Milwaukee Archives Office, Tel: 414-769-3407.

5—ST. ALEXANDER (1926), (Polish), Merged with St. Helen & St. John Kanty, Milwaukee to form Blessed John Paul II Parish, 3307 S. 10th St., Milwaukee, WI 53215-5116, 414-744-3695, Fax: 414-744-2874

6—ALL SAINTS (1994) Rev. Carl E. Diederichs; Deacon Edward Blaze.
Office: 4060 N. 26th St., 53209-6695. Tel: 414-444-5610; Fax: 414-444-5709.
Catechesis/Religious Program—Students 54.
Mission—St. John's Chapel 3717 W. Keefe, Milwaukee Co. 53216.

7—ST. ANNE, Closed. For sacramental records, contact Archdiocese of Milwaukee Archives Office, Tel: 414-769-3407.

8—ST. ANTHONY OF PADUA (1872) Revs. Cliff O. Ermatinger; Josegerman Zapata-Ramirez.
Church & Res.: 1711 S. 9th St., 53204. Tel: 414-645-1455; Fax: 414-645-1456. Email: antonius@archmil.org. Web: stanthonyofpaduaparish.org.
School—1727 S. 9th St., 53204. Tel: 414-384-6612; Fax: 414-384-6613. Email: zeus@stanthonyschools.com. Web: www.stanthonysschool.org. Jesus Rodriguez, Pres.; Ramon Cruz, Prin.; Mrs. Claire Brefka, Dir., Opers. Lay Teachers 70; Students 1,575.
Catechesis/Religious Program—Tel: 414-839-6709. Email: melendeze@archmil.org. Students 242.

9—ST. ANTHONY OF PADUA (1923) Closed. For sacramental records, contact St. Vincent Pallotti Parish, Milwaukee, Tel: 414-453-4225.

10—ST. AUGUSTINE OF HIPPO (1888) Rev. Jan M. Kieliszewski; Paul Weisenberger, Dir. Worship; Debbi Barycki, Dir. Youth Min.
Res.: 2530 S. Howell Ave., 53207. Tel: 414-744-0808; Fax: 414-744-1231. Email: staugy1@wi.rr.com. Web: www.staugustine.4lpi.com.
See St. Thomas Aquinas Academy located in the institution section under Consolidated Elementary Schools.
Catechesis/Religious Program—Karen Bushman, D.R.E. (Elementary). Students 35.

11—ST. BARBARA, Closed. For sacramental records, contact Archdiocese of Milwaukee Archives Office, Tel: 414-769-3407.

12—BASILICA OF ST. JOSAPHAT (1888), (Polish), Very Rev. Michael J. Glastetter, O.F.M.Conv., Rector & Pastor; Rev. Alejandro Lopez, O.F.M.Conv., Parochial Vicar.
Res.: 2333 S. 6th St., 53215. Tel: 414-645-5623; Fax: 414-645-2216. Email: sjbdome@archmil.org. Web: www.thebasilica.org.
School—801 W. Lincoln Ave., 53215. Tel: 414-645-4378; Fax: 414-645-1978. Ms. Carolyn Trawitzki. Lay Teachers 15; Students 223; School Sisters of St. Francis 2; School Sisters of Notre Dame 1.
Basilica of Saint Josaphat Endowment Fund—Mailing Address: 2333 S. 6th St., 53215. Tel: 414-645-5623. Email: sjbdome@archmil.org.
Saint Josaphat Parish School Endowment Fund—Mailing Address: 2333 S. 6th St., 53215. Tel: 414-645-5623. Email: sjbdome@archmil.org.
Catechesis/Religious Program—Parish Center, 2322 S. 7th St., 53215. Tel: 414-671-3938. Students 105.

13—ST. BENEDICT THE MOOR (1908) Rev. Jerome Schroeder, O.F.M.Cap.; Deacon John I. Champagne. In Res., Revs. Michael Crosby, O.F.M.Cap.; James Zelinski, O.F.M.Cap.; Bro. David Schwab, O.F.M.Cap.
Res.: 1015 N. 9th St., 53233. Tel: 414-271-0135; Fax: 414-271-0637. Email: stbens@sbcglobal.net. Web: www.stbensmilwaukee.org.
Catechesis/Religious Program—Students 16.

14—ST. BERNADETTE (1958) Rev. Gregory J. Greiten.
Res.: 8200 W. Denver Ave., 53223. Tel: 414-358-4600; Fax: 414-358-1478. Email: stbernadette@archmil.org. Web: www.stbweb.com.
School—Northwest Catholic School - West Campus formerly St. Bernadette School , (Combined schools from St. Bernadette, St. Catherine of Alexandria, and Our Lady of Good Hope), 8202 W. Denver Ave., 53223. Tel: 414-352-6927; Fax: 414-760-1037.
See Northwest Catholic School Association, Milwaukee under Consolidated Elementary Schools in the Institution section.
Catechesis/Religious Program—Tel: 414-365-2020. Twinned with St. Catherine of Alexandria. Students 17.

15—BLESSED JOHN PAUL II PARISH (2011) Revs. Michael A. Ignaszak; Javier Guatiua.
3307 S. 10th St., 53215. Tel: 414-744-3695.
School—St. John Kanty School, 2840 S. 10th St., 53215. Tel: 414-483-8780; Fax: 414-744-1846. Beth Eichman, Prin. Lay Teachers 10; Students 173.
Catechesis/Religious Program—Roy Salinas, D.R.E. Students 175.

16—BLESSED SACRAMENT (1927), (Polish), Rev. Robert D. Turner; Deacon Paul Klingseisen.
Res.: 3100 S. 41st St., 53215. Tel: 414-649-4720; Fax: 414-649-4727. Email: blsacrament@wi.rr.com. Church: S. 41st St. and W. Oklahoma Ave., 53215.
School—3126 S. 41st St., 53215. Tel: 414-649-4730; Fax: 414-649-4726. Email: blschool@archmil.org. Web: www.blsacrament.com. Mrs. Carol Degen, Prin. Lay Teachers 16; Students 160.
Catechesis/Religious Program—Students 54.

17—BLESSED SAVIOR PARISH (2007) Rev. Gregory A. Chycinski; Judy Adrian, Pastoral Assoc.
8607 W. Villard Ave., 53225. Tel: 414-464-5033. Email: blessedsavior@archmil.org. (A merger of the following parishes: Corpus Christi, Mary Queen of Martyrs, Our Lady of Sorrows and St. Philip Neri).
School—Blessed Savior Catholic School Lay Teachers 51; Students 717.
School—West Campus, 8545 W. Villard Ave., 53225. Tel: 414-464-5775; Fax: 414-464-5737. Mr. Michael Brown, Prin.
School—East Campus, 5140 N. 55th St., 53218. Tel: 414-438-2745; Fax: 414-438-9330. Barbara O'Donnell, Prin.
School—North Campus, 5501 N. 68th St., 53218. Tel: 414-466-0470; Fax: 414-466-3740. Thomas Hage, Prin.
School—South Campus, 4059 N. 64th St., 53216. Tel: 414-463-3878; Fax: 414-535-9265. Patricia Wilkum, Prin.
Catechesis/Religious Program—Sr. Judene Studer, S.S.N.D., Dir. Faith Formation. Students 39.

18—BLESSED VIRGIN OF POMPEI, Closed. For sacramental records, contact Archdiocese of Milwaukee Archives Office, Tel: 414-769-3407.

19—ST. BONIFACE, Closed. For sacramental records, contact Archdiocese of Milwaukee Archives Office, Tel: 414-769-3407.

20—ST. CASIMIR (1894), (Polish—Spanish), Closed. For sacramental records, contact Our Lady of Divine Providence, Milwaukee, Tel: 414-264-0049.

21—ST. CATHERINE (1922) Very Rev. John R. Kern; Deacon Ralph W. Kornburger Jr. In Res., Rev. Thomas Suriano (Retired).
Res.: 5101 W. Center St., 53210. Tel: 414-445-5115; Fax: 414-445-5198.
School—2647 N. 51st St., 53210. Tel: 414-445-2846; Fax: 414-445-0448. Deborah Zabinski, Prin. Lay Teachers 20; Students 209.
Catechesis/Religious Program—Cindy Lieb, D.R.E. Students 45.

22—ST. CATHERINE (Granville) (1855) [CEM] Debra A. Hintz, Parish Dir.
Res.: 8661 N. 76th Pl., 53223. Tel: 414-365-2020; Fax: 414-365-2021 (Office). Email: stc_alex@execpc.com. Web: www.saintcatherinealexandria.org.
See Northwest Catholic School Association, Milwaukee in the Institution Section under Consolidated Elementary Schools.
Catechesis/Religious Program—Nicole Fastabend, Dir. Christian Formation. Students 61.

23—ST. CHARLES BORROMEO (1960) Rev. Carmelo Giuffre.
Res.: 5571 S. Marilyn Ave., 53221. Tel: 414-281-8115; Fax: 414-281-8150. Email: info@scbmil.org. Web: www.scbmil.org.
School—3100 W. Parnell Ave., 53221. Tel: 414-282-0767; Fax: 414-817-9605. Email: eknippel@scbmil.org. Lay Teachers 16; Students 182.
Catechesis/Religious Program—Tel: 414-281-8115, Ext. 24. Email: ckrol@scbmil.org. Web: www.scbmil.org. Students 238.

24—CONGREGATION OF THE BLESSED TRINITY (1991) Merged with St. Catherine

25—CONGREGATION OF THE GREAT SPIRIT (1989), (Native American), Rev. Edward J. Cook.
Res. & Mailing Address: 1050 W. Lapham Blvd., 53204. Tel: 414-672-6989; Fax: 414-671-6990. Email: siggenauk@sbcglobal.net. Web: www.congregationofthegreatspirit.org.
Catechesis/Religious Program—

26—CORPUS CHRISTI (1958) Closed. For sacramental records, contact Blessed Savior, Milwaukee, Tel: 414-464-5033

27—SS. CYRIL AND METHODIUS (1893) Rev. Andrzej Galant, S.Ch.
Office: 2427 S. 15th St., 53215. Tel: 414-383-3973; Fax: 414-383-3974.

28—ST. ELIZABETH, Closed. For sacramental records, contact Archdiocese of Milwaukee Archives Office, Tel: 414-769-3407.

29—ST. EMERIC (1919) Closed. For sacramental records, contact Sacred Heart, Milwaukee, Tel: 414-774-9418.

30—ST. FLORIAN (1911), (German—Austrian), Rev. David J. Centner, O.C.D. In Res., Rev. Ralph Elias-Haddix, O.C.D.
Res.: 1210 S. 45th St., 53214. Tel: 414-383-3565; Fax: 414-383-2708. Email: stflorian@archmil.org. Web: www.stflorian.org.
See Mary Queen of Saints Catholic Academy, West Allis under Consolidated Elementary Schools located in the Institution Section.
Catechesis/Religious Program—Students 67.

31—ST. FRANCIS OF ASSISI (1871), (Hispanic—African American), Rev. Michael Bertram, O.F.M.Cap.
Mailing Address: 1927 N. 4th St., 53212. In Res., Revs. Perry McDonald, O.F.M.Cap.; Michael Bertram, O.F.M.Cap.
Res.: 327 W. Brown St., 53212. Tel: 414-374-5752.
St. Francis Institute Milwaukee—1927 N. 4th St., 53212. Tel: 414-374-8841, Ext. 438. Email: jschroeder2345@gmail.com. Rev. Jerome Schroeder, O.F.M.Cap., Dir. & Contact Person.
Catechesis/Religious Program—1927 N. 4th St., 53212. Tel: 414-374-5750; Fax: 414-374-5553. Students 40.

32—ST. GABRIEL (1913), (Lithuanian), Closed. For sacramental records, contact Archdiocese of Milwaukee Archives Office, Tel: 414-769-3407.

33—ST. GALL, Closed. For sacramental records, contact Archdiocese of Milwaukee Archives Office, Tel: 414-769-3407.

34—ST. GERARD (1925) Closed. For sacramental records, contact Archdiocese of Milwaukee Archives Office, Tel: 414-769-3407.

35—GESU PARISH (1893) Revs. Karl J. Voelker, S.J.; Kenneth J. Herian, S.J.; Lawrence A. Jonas, S.J.; Joseph B. Kappes, S.J.
Res.: 1210 W. Michigan St., P.O. Box 495, 53201-0495. Tel: 414-288-7101; Fax: 414-288-5339. Email: gesuparish@gmail.com. Web: www.gesuparish.org.
Catechesis/Religious Program—Students 110.

36—ST. GREGORY THE GREAT (1955) Rev. Thomas P. Demse.
Office: 3160 S. 63rd St., 53219. Tel: 414-543-8292; Fax: 414-328-3881.
Res.: 3129 S. 63rd St., 53219.
School—3132 S. 63rd St., 53219. Tel: 414-321-1350. Lay Teachers 20; Students 293.
Catechesis/Religious Program—Tel: 414-543-8292. Students 129.

37—ST. HEDWIG (1871), (Polish), Closed. For sacramental records, contact Archdiocese of Milwaukee Archives Office, Tel: 414-769-3407.

38—ST. HELEN (1925), (Polish), Merged with St. Alexander & St. John Kanty, Milwaukee to form Blessed John Paul II Parish, 3307 S. 10th St., Milwaukee, WI 53215-5116, 414-744-3695, Fax: 414-744-2874

39—HOLY ANGELS, Closed. For sacramental records, contact Archdiocese of Milwaukee Archives Office, Tel: 414-769-3407.

40—HOLY CROSS (1879) Closed. For sacramental records, contact St. Vincent Pallotti, Milwaukee, Tel: 414-453-4225.

41—HOLY REDEEMER, Closed. For sacramental records, contact Archdiocese of Milwaukee Archives Office, Tel: 414-769-3407.

42—HOLY ROSARY (1885), (Irish), Closed. For sacramental records, contact Archdiocese of Milwaukee Archives Office, Tel: 414-769-3407.

43—HOLY SPIRIT (1902), (German), Closed. For sacramental records, contact Archdiocese of Milwaukee Archives Office, Tel: 414-769-3407.

44—HOLY TRINITY-OUR LADY OF GUADALUPE (1849),

(Hispanic), Closed. For sacramental records, contact Our Lady of Guadalupe, Milwaukee, Tel: 414-271-6181.

45—ST. HYACINTH (1883), (Polish—Hispanic), Revs. Carlos Florez-Ardilla; Hugo Londono; Martha Andrade, Dir. Admin. Svcs.; Deacons Rogelio Macias; Luis Pena.
Tri-Parish Office & Mailing Address: 1138 S. 25th St., 53204-1940.
Church: 1414 W. Becher St., 53215. Tel: 414-645-8786; Fax: 414-645-8918. Email: sthy@archmil.org.
Catechesis/Religious Program—Students 136.

46—ST. IGNATIUS LOYOLA, Closed. For sacramental records, contact Archdiocese of Milwaukee Archives Office, Tel: 414-769-3407.

47—IMMACULATE CONCEPTION (1870) Rev. Ronald E. Kotecki.
Res.: 1023 E. Russell Ave., 53207. Tel: 414-769-2480; Fax: 414-769-2492. Email: icbayview@voyager.net.
See St. Thomas Aquinas Academy located in the Institution Section under Consolidated Elementary Schools
Catechesis/Religious Program—Fax: 414-769-2492. Students 18.

48—ST. JOHN DE NEPOMUC, Closed. For sacramental records, contact Archdiocese of Milwaukee Archives Office, Tel: 414-769-3407.

49—ST. JOHN KANTY (1907), (Polish), Merged with St. Alexander & St. Helen, Milwaukee to form Blessed John Paul II Parish, 3307 S. 10th St., Milwaukee, WI 53215-5116, 414-744-3695, Fax: 414-744-2874

50—ST. JOSEPH, Closed. For sacramental records, contact St. Joseph, Wauwatosa, Tel: 414-771-4626.

51—ST. LAWRENCE (1888) Closed. For sacramental records, contact Archdiocese of Milwaukee Archives Office, Tel: 414-769-3407.

52—ST. LEO, Closed. For sacramental records, contact Archdiocese of Milwaukee Archives Office, Tel: 414-769-3407.

53—ST. MARGARET MARY (1955) Rev. Vincent F. Kobida. Tel: 414-502-0280.
Rectory, Office & Parish Ctr.: 3970 N. 92nd St., 53222-2506. Tel: 414-461-6073. Email: ladams@stmmp.org. Web: www.stmmp.org.
School—3950 N. 92nd St., 53222-2587. Tel: 414-463-8760; Fax: 414-463-2373. Ryan Krienke, Prin. Lay Teachers 15; Students 212.
Catechesis/Religious Program—3970 N. 92nd St., 53222. Tel: 414-461-6073; Fax: 414-462-8419. Students 59.

54—ST. MARTIN DE PORRES (1994), (African American), Rev. David Preuss, O.F.M.Cap.
Office: 128 W. Burleigh St., 53212-2046. Tel: 414-372-3090; Fax: 414-372-0356. Email: smdp@smdpmilw.com.
Catechesis/Religious Program—Mary Heyn, D.R.E. Students 45.

55—ST. MARY MAGDALEN (1925), (Polish—Korean), Rev. Benedict Ko, M.S.C.
Res.: 1854 W. Windlake Ave., 53215. Tel: 414-645-4773; Fax: 414-645-5622. Email: stmarymagd@yahoo.com.
Catechesis/Religious Program—Students 4.

56—ST. MARY OF CZESTOCHOWA (1907), (Polish), Closed. For sacramental records, contact Our Lady of Divine Providence, Milwaukee, Tel: 414-264-0049.

57—MARY, QUEEN OF MARTYRS (2001) Closed. For sacramental records, contact Blessed Savior, Milwaukee, Tel: 414-464-5033.

58—ST. MATTHEW (1892) Closed. For sacramental records, contact Archdiocese of Milwaukee Archives Office, Tel: 414-769-3407.

59—ST. MATTHIAS (1850) [CEM] Revs. David E. Cooper; Paul A. Stanosz; Deacon David W. Sommers.
9306 W. Beloit Rd., 53227. Tel: 414-321-0893; Fax: 414-321-1330. Email: info@stmatthias-milw.org. Web: www.stmatthias-milw.org.
School—9300 W. Beloit Rd., 53227. Tel: 414-321-0894; Fax: 414-321-9228. Lay Teachers 30; Students 430.
Catechesis/Religious Program—Students 377.

60—ST. MAXIMILIAN KOLBE, (Polish), Rev. Andrzej Galant, S.Ch.
Res.: 2427 S. 15th St., 53215. Tel: 414-383-3973; Fax: 414-383-3974. Email: pastor@sscmmkparish.org. Web: www.sscmmkparish.org.
School—(Polish Saturday School for Children) (ages 5-13) 47.

61—ST. MICHAEL (1883) Rev. Dennis J. Lewis, Admin.; Deacon Salvador Rosado; Sr. Alice Thepouthay, Laotian Pastoral Ministry & Pastoral Assoc.; Shanedra Johnson, Youth Dir. & Pastoral Assoc.
Res.: 1445 N. 24th St., 53205. Tel: 414-933-3143; Fax: 414-933-1915. Email: st.michaelsrectory@sbcglobal.net.
Catechesis/Religious Program— Margaret M. Rauh, D.R.E. Students 111.

62—MOTHER OF GOOD COUNSEL (1925) Rev. Robert Marsicek, S.D.S.; Deacons Dean J. Collins; Andrew Meuler.
Church: 6924 W. Lisbon Ave., 53210-1259. Tel: 414-442-7600; Fax: 414-444-0408. Email: mgc@mgcparish.org. Web: www.mgcparish.org.
School—3001 N. 68th St., 53210-1299. Tel: 414-442-7600, Ext. 118. Regina Shaw, Prin. Lay Teachers 18; Students 215.
Catechesis/Religious Program—Tel: 414-442-7600, Ext. 107. Email: ehrmann@mgcparish.org. Students 45.

63—MOTHER OF PERPETUAL HELP (1941) Closed. For sacramental records, contact Archdiocese of Milwaukee Archives Office, Tel: 414-769-3407.

64—ST. NICHOLAS, Closed. For sacramental records, contact Archdiocese of Milwaukee Archives Office, Tel: 414-769-3407.

65—OLD ST. MARY (1846), (Bavarian—German), Very Rev. Timothy L. Kitzke; Revs. Brian G. Mason; Michael F. Michalski; Terri Balash, Dir. Pastoral Care; Dan Peter, Dir. Fin. & Property. Email: dpeter@oldsaintmary.org; Joseph P. Wittmann, Dir. Liturgy & Music. In Res., Most Rev. Richard J. Sklba (Retired).
Res.: 836 N. Broadway, 53202. Tel: 414-271-6180; Fax: 414-271-7782. Email: info@oldsaintmary.org.
Catechesis/Religious Program—835 N. Milwaukee St., 53202-3605. Ken Gardinier, D.R.E. Students 41.

66—OUR LADY OF DIVINE PROVIDENCE (2003) Very Rev. Timothy L. Kitzke; Revs. Brian G. Mason; Michael F. Michalski.
Res.: 919 E. Clarke St., #2, 53212. Tel: 414-264-0049; Fax: 414-264-7177. Email: oldp3055@tds.net. Web: www.oldp.4lpi.com.
Catechesis/Religious Program—2480 N. Cramer St., 53211. Tel: 414-962-3776; Fax: 414-962-3829. Email: escym@sbcglobal.net. Students 6.

67—OUR LADY OF GOOD HOPE (1952) Rev. Charles G. Zabler, Admin.; Barbara Krieger, Pastoral Assoc.; Beth Hoegger, Pastoral Musician.
Office: 7152 N. 41st St., 53209. Tel: 414-352-1148; Fax: 414-352-3042. Email: parish.office@olghparish.org. Web: www.olghparish.org.
School—Northwest Catholic - East Campus, 7140 N. 41st St., 53209. Tel: 414-352-6927; Fax: 414-352-7358. Michelle Paris, Prin.; Diana Erlandson, Prin. Lay Teachers 19; Students 209.
Catechesis/Religious Program—Tel: 414-352-8140. Students 62.

68—OUR LADY OF GUADALUPE PARISH (2000), (Hispanic), Very Rev. Jose Luis Moreno, S.J.; Deacon Juan A. Molina Sr., (Retired).
Mailing Address: 723 W. Washington St., 53204.
Res.: 613 S. 4th St., 53204. Tel: 414-645-7624; Fax: 414-645-3733. Email: guadalupe@archmil.org.
Catechesis/Religious Program—Total combined with St. Patrick, Milwaukee 153.

69—OUR LADY OF LOURDES (1958) Rev. William C. Burkert; Deacon John P. Monday; Mrs. Judith Bialk, Pastoral Assoc.
3722 S. 58th St., 53220. Tel: 414-545-4316; Fax: 414-541-2251. Email: olol@archmil.org. Web: www.olol.4lpi.com.
Catechesis/Religious Program—Tel: 414-541-9470. Students 221.

70—OUR LADY OF SORROWS (1955) Closed. For Sacramental records, contact Blessed Savior, Milwaukee, Tel: 414-464-5033.

71—OUR LADY QUEEN OF PEACE (1948) Rev. Gregory M. Spitz.
Res.: 3222 S. 29th St., 53215. Tel: 414-672-0313; Fax: 414-672-0441. Email: parish@olqpmke.org. Web: www.olqpmke.org.
School—2733 W. Euclid Ave., 53215. Tel: 414-672-6660; Fax: 414-672-2739. Email: school@olqpmke.org. Janet Orlowski, Prin. Lay Teachers 18; Students 196.
Catechesis/Religious Program—Students 18.

72—ST. PATRICK (1876) [CEM] Very Rev. Jose Luis Moreno, S.J.
Res.: 723 W. Washington St., 53204. Tel: 414-645-7624; Fax: 414-645-3733. Email: stpats@archmil.org.
Catechesis/Religious Program—Total combined with Our Lady of Guadalupe, Milwaukee 153.

73—ST. PAUL (1920) Rev. Romanus N. Nwaru.
Res.: 1720 E. Norwich Ave., 53207. Tel: 414-482-3510; Fax: 414-482-1031.
See St. Thomas Aquinas Academy located in the Institution Section under Consolidated Elementary Schools.
Catechesis/Religious Program—Tel: 414-481-0777; Fax: 414-482-3025. Students 29.

74—SS. PETER AND PAUL (1889), (German), Very Rev. Timothy L. Kitzke, In Solidum Team Mem.; Revs. Brian G. Mason, In Solidum Team Mem.; Michael F. Michalski, In Solidum Team Mem. & Mod.
Res.: 2491 N. Murray Ave., 53211. Tel: 414-962-2443; Fax: 414-962-8183. Email: sspp@execpc.com. Web: www.ssppmilw.org.
See Catholic East Elementary, Milwaukee under Consolidated Elementary Schools located in the Institution section.
Catechesis/Religious Program—East Side Child & Youth Ministry, Consolidated from the following parishes: SS. Peter & Paul, Our Lady of Divine Providence, Cathedral of St. John the Evangelist, and Three Holy Women., 2480 N. Cramer St., 53211. Tel: 414-962-3776; Fax: 414-962-3839. Email: escym@sbcglobal.net. Students 82.

75—ST. PHILIP NERI (1956) Closed. For sacramental records, contact Blessed Savior, Milwaukee, Tel: 414-464-5033.

76—PRINCE OF PEACE/PRINCIPE DE PAZ (1999) Revs. Carlos Florez-Ardilla; Hugo Londono; Martha Andrade, Dir. Admin. Svcs.; Deacons Rogelio Macias; Luis Pena.
Tri-Parish Office: 1138 S. 25th St., 53204-1940. Tel: 414-645-8786; Fax: 414-645-8918. Email: poppdp@archmil.org.
Church: 1126 S. 25th St., 53204.
School—(25th St. Campus), 1114 S. 25th St., 53204. Tel: 414-383-2157; Fax: 414-383-7645.
School—(22nd St. Campus), 1646 S. 22nd St., 53204. Tel: 414-645-4922; Fax: 414-645-4940. Ms. Judith Birlem, Prin. Religious 2; Lay Teachers 32; Students 510.
Catechesis/Religious Program—Sr. Carmelita De Anda, D.R.E. Students 213.

77—ST. RAFAEL THE ARCHANGEL (1999), (Hispanic), Revs. Luis Pacheco-Sanchez; Jose Gonzalez; Bob PerciField, Business Mgr.
Res.: 2059 S. 33rd St., 53215. Tel: 414-645-9172; Fax: 414-645-4732.
School—Tel: 414-645-1300; Fax: 414-645-1415. Mrs. Carolyn Ettlie, Prin. Lay Teachers 14; Students 365.
Catechesis/Religious Program—Students 179.

78—ST. RITA (1936), (Italian), Closed. For sacramental records, contact Archdiocese of Milwaukee Archives Office, Tel: 414-769-3407.

79—ST. ROMAN (1956), (Polish), Revs. Brian T. Holbus; John J. Pulice (Retired); Christopher L. Klusman.
Res.: 1710 W. Bolivar Ave., 53221. Tel: 414-282-9063; Fax: 414-282-6464. Email: stroman@stromans.com. Web: www.stromans.com.
School—1810 W. Bolivar Ave., 53221. Tel: 414-282-7970; Fax: 414-282-5140. Email: stromanschool@stromans.com. Lay Teachers 25; Students 264.
Catechesis/Religious Program—Students 225.

80—ST. ROSE (1888) Rev. Dennis J. Lewis; Deacon Julio Lopez.
Res.: 528 N. 31st St., 53208. Tel: 414-342-1778; Fax: 414-342-7510. Email: stroseco@sbcglobal.net.
See St. Rose Catholic Urban Academy, Milwaukee under Elementary Schools, Archdiocesan located in the Institution section.
Catechesis/Religious Program—Students 24.

81—SACRED HEART (1917), (Croatian), Rev. Paul Maslach, O.F.M. (Croatia).
Res.: 917 N. 49th St., 53208. Tel: 414-774-9418; Fax: 414-774-7406. Email: sh.croatian@yahoo.com.
Catechesis/Religious Program—Students 27.

82—ST. SEBASTIAN (1911) Rev. Richard J. Aiken; Deacons Warren D. Braun, (Retired); James J. Peterson.
Res.: 5400 W. Washington Blvd., 53208. Tel: 414-453-1061; Fax: 414-453-9449. Email: saintsebs@saintsebs.org. Web: www.saintsebsonline.net.
School—1747 N. 54th St., 53208. Tel: 414-453-5830. Web: www.saintsebastianonline.net/school/. Lay Teachers 24; Students 321.
St. Sebastian School Foundation, Inc.—
Catechesis/Religious Program—Tel: 414-453-7150. Students 175.

83—ST. STANISLAUS (1866) Rev. Canon Benoit Jayr. In Res., Rev. Canon Denis Buchholz.
Church & Bus. Office: 524 W. Historic Mitchell St., 53204. Tel: 414-226-5490; Fax: 414-226-5534. Email: ststanislaus@institute-christ-king.org.

84—ST. STEPHEN, MARTYR (1907), (Slovak), Closed. For sacramental records, contact Archdiocese of Milwaukee Archives Office, Tel: 414-769-3407.

85—ST. THERESE (1956) Dr. Alexandra Guliano, Parish Dir.; Heather Goeden, Pastoral Assoc.; Elterine Jankowski-Biggers, Pastoral Musician.
Mailing Address: 9525 W. Bluemound Rd., 53226.
Res.: 9427 W. Bluemound Rd., 53226. Tel: 414-771-2500; Fax: 414-771-2410. Email: info@sainttheresemilwaukee.org. Web: www.sainttheresemilwaukee.org.
Catechesis/Religious Program—Students 65.

86—ST. THOMAS AQUINAS, Closed. For sacramental records, contact Archdiocese of Milwaukee Archives Office, Tel: 414-769-3407.

87—THREE HOLY WOMEN CATHOLIC PARISH (2000) Very Rev. Timothy L. Kitzke; Revs. Brian G.

Mason; Michael F. Michalski.
Res.: 2003 N. Oakland Ave., 53202. Email: kitzket@archmil.org.
Church Office: 1716 N. Humboldt Ave., 53202. Tel: 414-271-6577; Fax: 414-271-7988. Email: mbergemann@threeholywomen.org. Web: www.threeholywomen.org.
Catechesis/Religious Program—(Collaborative), 2480 N. Cramer St., 53211. Tel: 414-962-3776; Fax: 414-962-3829. Email: escym@sbcglobal.net. Students 43.

88—ST. VERONICA (1925) Very Rev. Mark Payne.
Mailing Address: 353 E. Norwich St., 53207. Tel: 414-482-2920. Email: parishoffice@saintveronica.org. Web: saintveronica.org.
See St. Thomas Aquinas Academy located in the Institution Section under Consolidated Elementary Schools.
Catechesis/Religious Program—Tel: 414-481-0777; Fax: 414-482-3025. Karen Bushman, D.R.E.; Debbi Barycki, Youth Min. Students 245.

89—ST. VINCENT DE PAUL (1888), (Polish), [CEM] Revs. Carlos Florez-Ardilla; Hugo Londono; Deacons Rogelio Macias; Luis Pena; Martha Andrade, Dir. Admin. Svcs.
Tri-Parish Office & Mailing Address: 1138 S. 25th St., 53204.
Church: 2114 W. Michell St., 53204. Tel: 414-645-8786; Fax: 414-645-8918. Email: stvincent@archmil.org.
Catechesis/Religious Program—Students 64.

90—ST. VINCENT PALLOTTI (1998) Rev. John R. Scheer, S.A.C.
Res.: 145 S. 76th St., 53213. Tel: 414-453-5344, Ext. 102; Fax: 414-453-4225. Web: www.stvincentpallotti.org.
School—St. Vincent Pallotti Catholic School, 201 N. 76th St., 53213. Tel: 414-258-4165; Fax: 414-258-9844. Mr. Jeffrey Johnson, Prin. Lay Teachers 15; Students 186.
Catechesis/Religious Program—Tel: 414-453-5344, Ext. 116. Students 29.

91—ST. WENCESLAUS (1883), (Hispanic), Closed. For sacramental records, contact Archdiocese of Milwaukee Archives Office, Tel: 414-769-3407.

OUTSIDE THE CITY OF MILWAUKEE

ADELL, SHEBOYGAN CO., ST. PATRICK (1853), (Irish), Closed. For sacramental records, contact Archdiocese of Milwaukee Archives Office, Tel: 414-769-3407.

ALLENTON, WASHINGTON CO.

1—ST. ANTHONY (1851) Closed. For sacramental records, contact Resurrection, Allenton, Tel: 262-629-5240.

2—RESURRECTION (1997) [CEM 3], Consolidation of Sacred Heart, Allenton; St. Anthony, Allenton and Ss. Peter and Paul, Nenno. Very Rev. Richard J. Stoffel, Team Mod.; Rev. Joseph Dominic, S.A.C. (India), Team Member.
Parish Office—215 Main St., P.O. Box 96, 53002. Tel: 262-629-5240. Email: alleluia@nconnect.net.
Church: 215 Main St., 53002.
Catechesis/Religious Program—Tel: 262-629-1500. Email: reled@nconnect.net. Students 107.

3—SACRED HEART (1917) Closed. For sacramental records, contact Resurrection, Allenton, Tel: 262-629-5240.

ARMSTRONG, FOND DU LAC CO., OUR LADY OF ANGELS (1856), (Irish), Closed. For sacramental records, contact Good Shepherd, Eden, Tel: 920-477-3201.

ASHFORD, FOND DU LAC CO., ST. MARTIN (1847) [CEM] Rev. Neil G. Zinthefer; Jane M. Osypowski, Business Mgr.
Mailing Address: P.O. Box 740, Campbellsport, 53010. Tel: 920-533-4441; Fax: 920-533-5280. Email: stmatts@archmil.org. N1271 Minnie Ln., Campbellsport, 53010.
Catechesis/Religious Program—Included with St. Matthew, Campbellsport., 419 Mill St., P.O. Box 740, Campbellsport, 53010. Email: stmatts@archmil.org. Beth Schmidt, D.R.E. Tel: 920-533-8060.

AUBURN, FOND DU LAC CO., ST. MATTHIAS (1863), (German), Closed. For sacramental records, contact Holy Trinity, Kewaskum, Tel: 262-626-2860.

BEAVER DAM, DODGE CO.

1—ST. KATHARINE DREXEL (2003) [CEM] Revs. Michael J. Erwin; Selvin Garcia, F.M.M.
Mailing Address: 131 W. Maple Ave., 53916.
Church: 511 S. Spring St., 53916. Fax: 920-885-7602. Web: stkatharinedrexelbd.org.
School—(Grades PreSchool-8), 503 S. Spring St., 53916. Tel: 920-885-5558; Fax: 920-885-7610. Web: www.skds.org. Barbara M. Haase, Prin.; Ruth Kaiser, Librarian. Lay Teachers 17; Students 274.
Catechesis/Religious Program—Combined program (PreK - 11). Students 196.

2—ST. MICHAEL (1893) Closed. For sacramental records, contact St. Katharine Drexel, Beaver Dam, Tel: 920-887-2082.

3—ST. PATRICK (1860) Closed. For sacramental records, contact St. Katharine Drexel, Beaver Dam, Tel: 920-887-2082.

4—ST. PETER (1855) Closed. For sacramental records, contact St. Katharine Drexel, Beaver Dam, Tel: 920-887-2082.

BELGIUM, OZAUKEE CO., ST. MARY (1848), (German—Luxembourg), [CEM] Rev. Richard J. Fleischman, Admin.
Church: 675 Co. Rd. D, 53004-9799. Tel: 262-285-3040 (Parish Office); Fax: 262-285-4104.
Catechesis/Religious Program—Tel: 262-285-4361. Terri Riesselmann, D.R.E. Students 204.

BIG BEND, WAUKESHA CO., ST. JOSEPH (1920) Rev. Richard J. Robinson.
Res.: S89 W22650 Milwaukee Ave., 53103. Tel: 262-662-2832; Fax: 262-662-0783. Email: parish@stjoesbb.com. Web: www.stjoesbb.com.
School—Tel: 262-662-2737; Fax: 262-662-2684. Email: school@stjoesbb.com. Susan Shawver, Prin. Lay Teachers 15; Students 131.
Catechesis/Religious Program—Tel: 262-662-3317. Email: cfm@stjoesbb.com. Mary L. Kozlik, D.R.E.; Lorraine Labadie, D.R.E. Students 486.

BRANDON, FOND DU LAC CO., ST. BRENDAN (1921), (German), [CEM], Also serves St. Joseph, Waupun and St. Mary, Springvale. Very Rev. Michael L. Wild.
Mailing Address: 118 W. Main St., Waupun, 53963. Tel: 920-324-5400; Fax: 920-324-1040. Email: pastor@saintjoes.com.
Catechesis/Religious Program—Tel: 920-346-5110. Students 17.

BRIGHTON, KENOSHA CO., ST. FRANCIS XAVIER (1838), (German), [CEM] Rev. Russell L. Arnett, Admin.
Res. & Mailing Address: 1704 240th Ave., Kansasville, 53139. Tel: 262-878-2267; Fax: 262-878-3683. Email: sfxsjb@archmil.org.
School—Providence Catholic School, 1481-172nd Ave., Union Grove, 53182. Tel: 262-859-2007; Fax: 262-859-2604. Email: eastcampus@providencecatholicschool.org. Web: www.providencecatholicschool.org. Mrs. Suzanne Meyer, Prin. Lay Teachers 5; Students 67.
Catechesis/Religious Program—Combined with St. John the Baptist, Paris. Sr. Kathryn Dean Strandell, O.S.F., D.R.E. (Gr. K-8). Students 57.

BRISTOL, KENOSHA CO.

1—HOLY CROSS (2009) Rev. Roger A. Savage.
Res.: 18700 116th St., 53104. Tel: 262-857-2068.
Catechesis/Religious Program—Tel: 262-857-9032. Students 160.

2—ST. SCHOLASTICA (1945) [CEM] Closed. For sacramental records, contact Holy Cross, Bristol, Tel: 262-857-2068.

BROOKFIELD, WAUKESHA CO.

1—ST. DOMINIC (1866) Revs. David H. Reith; Sean T. O'Connell; Deacons Gregory H. Diciaula; Larry LaFond; Rich Harter, Pastoral Assoc. for Admin Svcs & Adult & Family Min.; Susan Petersen McNeil, Pastoral Assoc. for Human Concerns; Julie Cucunato, Liturgy & Music Dir.; Karen Chaffee, Dir. Finance Admin. & Technology; Meg Picciolo, Dir. Mktg. & Communication.
18255 W. Capitol Dr., 53045-1422. Tel: 262-781-3480; Fax: 262-781-3283. Email: parish@stdominic.net. Web: www.stdominic.net.
Rectory—3760 Arroyo Rd., 53045-1422. Tel: 262-781-2002.
School—18105 W. Capitol Dr., 53045-1425. Tel: 262-783-7565; Fax: 262-783-5947. Email: john.chovanec@stdominic.net. Mr. John Chovanec, Prin. Lay Teachers 27; Students 461.
Catechesis/Religious Program—Kathleen Beuscher, Dir. Child Ministry; Debbie Olla, Dir. Youth & Young Adult Ministry. Students 691.

2—ST. JOHN VIANNEY (1956) Revs. Kenneth P. Knippel; Phillip A. Bogacki; Deacon John A. Ebel; David Sanders, Dir. Liturgy & Music; Mary Janowak, Dir. Adult & Family Ministry & Human Concerns; Mike Schaumann, Dir. Admin. Svcs.
1755 N. Calhoun Rd., 53005-5036. Tel: 262-796-3940; Fax: 262-796-3958. Web: www.stjohnv.org.
School—17500 W. Gebhardt Rd., 53045-5096. Tel: 262-796-3942; Fax: 262-796-3953. Pamela Pyzyk, Prin. Lay Teachers 26; Students 465.
Catechesis/Religious Program—Tel: 262-796-3944. Email: dawnv@stjohnv.org. John Thompson, Youth Min.; Claire Hoffmeyer, Assoc. Dir., Youth Min.; Dawn Van Dorf, Dir. Child Ministry. Students 699.

3—ST. LUKE (1956) Rev. Kenneth J. Augustine.
Res.: 18000 W. Greenfield Ave., 53045. Tel: 262-782-0032; Fax: 262-782-6057. Email: stluke@stlukebrookfield.org. Web: www.stlukebrookfield.org.
Catechesis/Religious Program—Marian Lamoureux, D.R.E. Students 95.
Convent—

BURLINGTON, RACINE CO.

1—ST. CHARLES (1908) [CEM] Revs. Steven J. Amann; Sergio Lizama, S.A.C.
Res.: 440 Kendall St., 53105. Tel: 262-763-2260; Fax: 262-763-9171. Email: jmorrow@mystcharles.org. Web: www.mystcharles.org.
School—449 Conkey St., 53105. Tel: 262-763-2848; 262-762-2637 (Grade School); Fax: 262-763-3818. Email: principalstcharles@wi.rr.com. Sr. Margaret Pietsch, Prin. Lay Teachers 16; Students 208.
Catechesis/Religious Program—Tel: 262-763-6002 (Grade School Rep.). Email: jimandkathymartin@gmail.com (High School Rep.). Students 239.

2—IMMACULATE CONCEPTION (1838), (German), [CEM] Rev. James T. Volkert.
Res.: 108 McHenry St., 53105. Tel: 262-763-1500; Fax: 262-763-1680. Email: parishoffice@stmb.org.
School—225 W. State St., 53105. Tel: 262-763-1515; Fax: 262-763-1508. Web: www.stmb.org. Priests 1; Lay Teachers 23; Students 342.
Catechesis/Religious Program—Students 126.
Chapel—

BUTLER, WAUKESHA CO., ST. AGNES (1915) Rev. Timothy C. Bickel; Deacon Raymond Waitrovich.
Office: 12801 W. Fairmount Ave., 53007. Tel: 262-781-9521; Fax: 262-781-3512. Email: stagnes007@archmil.org.
School—Tel: 262-781-4996. Kay Bobb, Prin. Lay Teachers 14; Students 156.
Catechesis/Religious Program—Tel: 262-781-6998. Gerry Wolf, D.R.E. Students 128.

BYRON, FOND DU LAC CO.

1—ST. JOHN (1847) Closed. For sacramental records, contact Sons of Zebedee: Saints James and John, Byron, Tel: 920-922-1167.

2—SONS OF ZEBEDEE: SAINTS JAMES AND JOHN (2000) [CEM] Rev. Michael C. Petersen.
Mailing Address: W5882 Church Rd., Fond du Lac, 54937-8602. Tel: 920-922-1167; Fax: 920-922-1924.
Catechesis/Religious Program—Students 78.

CALEDONIA, RACINE CO., ST. LOUIS (1846) [CEM] Rev. Mark J. Danczyk; Deacon Jim Zdeb.
Parish Office—13207 Hwy. G, 53108-9531. Tel: 262-835-4533; Fax: 262-835-0421. Email: stlouis@wi.rr.com. Web: stlouis4lpi.com.
Catechesis/Religious Program— Michael Riedl, Dir., Child Formation; Colleen Rooney, Dir., Youth Formation. Students 194.
Mission—Tel: 262-835-4533.

CAMPBELLSPORT, FOND DU LAC CO., ST. MATTHEW (1864) [CEM] Rev. Neil G. Zinthefer; Jane M. Osypowski, Business Mgr.
Parish Center—419 Mill St., P.O. Box 740, 53010. Tel: 920-533-4441; Fax: 920-533-5280. Email: stmatts@archmil.org.
School—P.O. Box 639, 53010. Tel: 920-533-4103; Fax: 920-533-8078. Email: smslions@charter.net. Joan Schlaefer, Prin. Lay Teachers 11; Students 111.
Catechesis/Religious Program—Beth Schmidt, D.R.E. Tel: 920-533-8060. Students 209.

CASCADE, SHEBOYGAN CO., ST. MARY-CASCADE (1852) Closed. For sacramental records, contact Archdiocese of Milwaukee Archives Office, Tel: 414-769-3407.

CEDARBURG, OZAUKEE CO.

1—DIVINE WORD (1970) Closed. For sacramental records, contact St. Francis Borgia, Cedarburg, Tel: 262-377-1070.

2—ST. FRANCIS BORGIA (1844) [CEM] Very Rev. Thomas P. Eichenberger; Rev. Daniel R. Janasik.
Cemetery: Pioneer Rd., Mequon, 53092.
Res.: 1375 Covered Bridge Rd., 53012. Tel: 262-377-1070. Email: office@saintfrancisborgia.org. Web: www.saintfrancisborgia.org.
School—N43 W6005 Hamilton Rd., 53012. Tel: 262-377-2050; Fax: 262-377-4099. Email: office@sfbschool.org. Kelly Swietlik, Prin. Lay Teachers 34; Students 366.
Catechesis/Religious Program—Students 591.

CLYMAN, DODGE CO., ST. JOHN (1900), (German—Irish), [CEM 2], Also serves Holy Family, Reeseville & St. Columbkille, Elba. Rev. Richard Wendell.
Mailing Address: 302 Prairie St., P.O. Box 277, Reeseville, 53579-0277. Tel: 920-927-3102.
Catechesis/Religious Program—Connie Caine, D.R.E. Tel: 920-210-1865. Students 10.

CUDAHY, MILWAUKEE CO.

1—ST. FREDERICK (1896) Closed. For sacramental records, contact Nativity of the Lord, Cudahy, Tel: 414-744-6622.

2—HOLY FAMILY (1900) Closed. For sacramental records, contact Nativity of the Lord, Cudahy, Tel: 414-744-6622.

3—ST. JOSEPH (1909), (Slovak—Moravian), Closed. For sacramental records, contact Nativity of the Lord, Cudahy, Tel: 414-744-6622.

4—NATIVITY OF THE LORD PARISH (2000) [JC] Rev. Philip D. Reifenberg; Bryan Martin, Dir. Admin. Svcs.
Res. & Office: 4611 S. Kirkwood Ave., 53110. Tel: 414-744-6622; Fax: 414-483-4599. Email: nativityofthelord@yahoo.com.

Church: 3672 E. Plankinton Ave., 53110.
See St. Thomas Aquinas Academy located in the Institution Section under Consolidated Elementary Schools.
Catechesis/Religious Program—3658 E. Plankinton Ave., 53110. Tel: 414-481-0777, Ext. 117. Email: karenbushman@saintveronica.org. Students 56.

DACADA, SHEBOYGAN CO., ST. NICHOLAS (1848), (Luxembourgian), Closed. For sacramental records, contact Archdiocese of Milwaukee Archives Office, Tel: 414-769-3407.

DELAFIELD, WAUKESHA CO., ST. JOAN OF ARC (1923) [CEM] Rev. Michael D. Strachota.
Res.: 120 Nashotah Rd., Nashotah, 53058. Tel: 262-646-8078; Fax: 262-646-8079. Email: parish@sjarc.org. Web: www.sjarc.org.
School—Tel: 262-646-5821; Fax: 262-646-5861. Email: school@sjarc.org. Mrs. Holly Cerveny, Prin. Lay Teachers 9; Students 118.
Catechesis/Religious Program—Tel: 262-646-5979. Email: re@sjarc.org. Students 290.

DELAVAN, WALWORTH CO., ST. ANDREW (1848) [CEM] Revs. James T. Schuerman; Oriol Regales; Deacon Philip O. Kilkenny.
Res.: 714 E. Walworth Ave., 53115. Tel: 262-728-5922; Fax: 262-728-5878. Email: standrewsdelavan@sbcglobal.net.
School—115 S. 17th St., 53115. Tel: 262-728-6211; Fax: 262-728-3683. Web: standrews-delavan.org. Julie Kadrich, Prin. Lay Teachers 13; Students 134.
Catechesis/Religious Program—Tel: 262-728-2792. Joan Zomer, C.R.E. (English Students); Sr. Graciela Peredes, C.R.E. (Hispanic Students); Patty Kostechka, C.R.E. (Deaf Students). Students 210.

DOTYVILLE, FOND DU LAC CO., ST. MICHAEL (1853), (German), Closed. For sacramental records, contact Good Shepherd, Eden, Tel: 920-477-3201.

DOUSMAN, WAUKESHA CO., ST. BRUNO (1852) [CEM] Very Rev. Ralph C. Gross; Deacons Tom Filipiak; Gordon J. Snyder; Karen Warnes, Pastoral Assoc.
Office: 226 W. Ottawa Ave., 53118. Tel: 262-965-2332; Fax: 262-965-4749. Email: stbruno@wi.rr.com. Web: www.stbrunoparish.com.
Res.: 266 W. Ottawa Ave., 53118.
School—246 W. Ottawa Ave., 53118. Tel: 262-965-2291; Fax: 262-965-2249. Email: mrralphlynch@hotmail.com. Mr. Ralph Lynch, Prin. Lay Teachers 13; Students 109.
Catechesis/Religious Program—Tel: 262-965-4200. Students 233.

EAGLE, WAUKESHA CO., ST. THERESA (1852) [CEM 2] Rev. Dennis Ackeret.
Office: 136 W. Waukesha Rd., 53119-2026. Tel: 262-594-5200; Fax: 262-594-5201. Email: parishoffice@sttheresaeagle.com. Web: www.sttheresaeagle.com.
Catechesis/Religious Program—Tel: 262-592-3075. Students 194.

EAST TROY, WALWORTH CO., ST. PETER (1854), (Irish—German), [CEM] Rev. Lawrence J. Chapman; Deacon Donald Kuban.
Res. & Mailing Address: 1975 Beulah Ave., 53120. Tel: 262-642-7225, Ext. 3. Email: stpeterset@centurytel.net. Web: steepleconnection.com.
School—3001 Elm St., 53120. Tel: 262-642-5533; Fax: 262-642-5897. Sarah Halbesma, Prin.; Ashley Schmidt, Co-Prin. Lay Teachers 13; Students 119.
Catechesis/Religious Program—Tel: 262-642-7225, Ext. 5. Students 287.

EDEN, FOND DU LAC CO.
1—ST. MARY (1888), (Irish), Closed. For sacramental records, contact Good Shepherd, Eden, Tel: 920-477-3201.
2—SHEPHERD OF THE HILLS (GOOD SHEPHERD) (2001) [JC 6] Very Rev. Joseph J. Juknialis. In Res., Rev. Charles H. Wester (Retired).
Res.: N4348 Mercury Ln., 53019. Tel: 920-477-2079; Fax: 920-477-3030. Email: jjj@sothparish.org. Web: www.sothparish.org.
School—W1562 Cty. Rd. B, 53019. Tel: 920-477-3551. Email: jhively@sothparish.org. Patrick Seghers, Prin. Lay Teachers 13; Students 125.
Catechesis/Religious Program—Brad Mintie, D.R.E. Students 211.
Mission—St. Michael Chapel N3604 Scenic Dr., Cascade, Sheboygan Co. 53011. Tel: 920-477-3201; Fax: 920-477-3030.

ELBA, DODGE CO., ST. COLUMBKILLE (1856), (Irish), [CEM], Also serves Holy Family, Reeseville and St. John the Baptist, Clyman. Rev. Richard Wendell.
Mailing Address: 302 Prairie St., P.O. Box 277, Reeseville, 53579-0277. Tel: 920-623-3989; 920-927-3102.
Catechesis/Religious Program—Fax: 920-927-1970. Students 3.

ELDORADO, FOND DU LAC CO.
1—ST. MARY, Closed. For sacramental records, contact Our Risen Savior, Eldorado, Tel: 920-922-2412.
2—OUR RISEN SAVIOR (1998), (Irish—German), [CEM 2] Rev. John L. Simon.
Church: W8272 Forest Avenue Rd., 54932. Tel: 920-922-2412; Fax: 920-921-1309. Email: motherandsonoffice@att.net.
Catechesis/Religious Program—Students 58.

ELKHART LAKE, SHEBOYGAN CO.
1—ST. GEORGE (1896) Closed. For sacramental records, contact St. Thomas Aquinas, Elkhart Lake, Tel: 920-876-2457.
2—ST. THOMAS AQUINAS (2001) [CEM 2], (Merger of St. George, Elkhart Lake and St. Fridolin, Glenbeulah.) Very Rev. Dennis E. Van Beek.
Res.: 94 N. Lincoln St., P.O. Box T, 53020-0396. Tel: 920-876-2457; Fax: 920-876-2036. Email: st.thomas.aquinas@frontier.com.
Catechesis/Religious Program—Students 165.

ELKHORN, WALWORTH CO., ST. PATRICK (1878), (Irish—German), [CEM] Revs. James T. Schuerman, Temp. Admin.; Oriol Regales.
Res.: 107 W. Walworth St., 53121. Tel: 262-723-5565; Fax: 262-723-7856. Email: stpatelkhorn@charter.net. Web: www.stpatrickselkhorn.org.
School—534 Sunset Dr., 53121. Tel: 262-723-4258; Fax: 262-723-1577. Email: stpatrickschool@charter.net. Miss Julie Muellenbach, Prin. Lay Teachers 6; Students 87.
Catechesis/Religious Program—Tel: 262-723-5565. Students 370.

ELM GROVE, WAUKESHA CO., ST. MARY'S VISITATION (1848) [CEM] Rev. Laurin J. Wenig; Deacons Charles J. Kustner; Richard T. Piontek.
Res.: 1260 Church St., 53122. Tel: 262-782-4575; Fax: 262-782-0677. Email: stmary@stmaryeg.org. Web: www.stmaryeg.org.
School—13000 Juneau Blvd., 53122. Tel: 262-782-7057; Fax: 262-782-3035. Mary Tretow, Prin. Lay Teachers 22; Students 281.
Catechesis/Religious Program—Tel: 414-771-4626; Fax: 262-782-0677. Email: stmaryeg@stmaryeg.org. Students 230.

FARMINGTON, WASHINGTON CO., ST. JOHN OF GOD (1859), (Irish), Closed. For sacramental records, contact St. Michael, St. Michael, 53040, Tel: 262-334-5270.

FOND DU LAC, FOND DU LAC CO.
1—HOLY FAMILY (2000) Rev. Victor R. Capriolo, Team Mod.; Very Rev. Robert X. Stiefvater, Team; Revs. Luke N. Strand, Team; Max Tzul, Team.
Church: 271 Fourth Street Way, 54937. Tel: 920-921-0580; Fax: 920-922-4866. Email: holyfam@hffdl.org. Web: www.hffdl.org.
Catechesis/Religious Program—Fax: 920-922-4866. Students 1,041.
2—ST. JOSEPH (1871) Closed. For sacramental records through June 12, 1967, contact Archdiocese of Milwaukee Archives Office, Tel: 414-769-3407. For records after June 12, 1967, contact Holy Family, Fond du Lac, Tel: 920-921-0580.
3—ST. LOUIS (1847), (French), Closed. For sacramental records through September 19, 1959, contact Archdiocese of Milwaukee Archives Office, Tel: 414-769-3407. For records after September 19, 1959, contact Holy Family, Fond du Lac, Tel: 920-921-0580.
4—ST. MARY (1866), (German), Closed. For sacramental records through 1975, contact Archdiocese of Milwaukee Archives Office, Tel: 414-769-3407. For records after 1975, contact Holy Family, Fond du Lac, Tel: 920-921-0580.
5—ST. PATRICK (1855) Closed. For sacramental records through September 18, 1960, contact Archdiocese of Milwaukee Archives Office, Tel: 414-769-3407. For records after September 18, 1960, contact Holy Family, Fond du Lac, Tel: 920-921-0580.
6—SACRED HEART (1957), (German), Closed. For sacramental records through November 1970, contact Archdiocese of Milwaukee Archives Office, Tel: 414-769-3407. For records after November 1970, contact Holy Family, Fond du Lac, Tel: 920-921-0580.

FONTANA, WALWORTH CO., ST. BENEDICT (1912) [JC] Rev. Norberto Sandoval; Deacon Henry F. Iwan.
Res.: 137 Dewey Ave., 53125-1239. Tel: 262-275-2480; Fax: 262-275-6426. Email: office@stbensparish.org. Web: www.stbensparish.org.
Catechesis/Religious Program—Tel: 262-275-2993. Michael Dowling, Dir. Faith Formation; Beth Peyer, C.R.E. (Gr. K-11); Roberto Cortes, C.R.E. (Hispanic Min.). Students 251.

FOX LAKE, DODGE CO.
1—ANNUNCIATION (1998) [CEM 3] Very Rev. Michael L. Wild.
Res.: 305 W. Green St., 53933-9472. Tel: 920-928-3513.
Catechesis/Religious Program—Tel: 920-928-6022. Jennifer Tallman, D.R.E. Students 62.
2—ST. MARY (1850), (Irish), Closed. For sacramental records, contact Annunciation, Fox Lake, Tel: 920-928-3513.

FOX POINT, MILWAUKEE CO., ST. EUGENE (1957) Revs. Jerome Herda; Paul J. Fliss; Joseph J. Shimek; Colleen Hutt, Pastoral Assoc.; William Lieven, Dir. Music & Liturgy; Douglas Byers, Dir. Admin. Svcs.; Monica Cardenas, Dir. Parish Stewardship Devel. & Office Mgr. In Res., Rev. Charles Mbuyi Banduku (Congo).
Res.: 7600 N. Port Washington Rd., 53217. Tel: 414-918-1100; Fax: 414-918-1111. Email: sainteugene@archmil.org. Web: www.steugenecongregation.org.
School—Tel: 414-918-1120; Fax: 414-918-1122. Rebecca Jones, Prin. Lay Teachers 18; Students 188.
Catechesis/Religious Program—Tel: 414-918-1130. Ms. Jeanette Lambrecht, D.R.E. (Child Ministry); Rita Capriolo, D.R.E. (Youth Ministry). Students 257.

FRANKLIN, MILWAUKEE CO.
1—ST. JAMES (1857) [CEM] Daniel L. Hull, Parish Dir.; Rev. Bernard S. Sippel (Retired); Deacon Claude V. Kennedy.
Office: 7219 S. 27th St., 53132. Tel: 414-761-0480; Fax: 414-761-2208.
Catechesis/Religious Program—Students 116.
2—ST. MARTIN OF TOURS (1998) [CEM] Revs. Yvon Sheehy, S.C.J.; Thi Pham, S.C.J.; Robert Naglich, S.C.J.
Res.: 7963 S. 116th St., 53132. Tel: 414-425-1114; Fax: 414-425-2527. Email: parish@stmoftours.org. Web: www.stmoftours.org.
School—7933 S. 116th St., 53132. Tel: 414-425-9200. Jeanne Johnson, Prin. Lay Teachers 15; Students 90.
Catechesis/Religious Program—Students 218.
3—SACRED HEARTS OF JESUS AND MARY (1858) Closed. For sacramental records, contact St. Martin of Tours, Franklin, Tel: 414-425-1114.

FREDONIA, OZAUKEE CO.
1—HOLY ROSARY (2001) [CEM 4], (Merger of St. Rose of Lima, Fredonia; Mother of Sorrows, Little Kohler and Holy Cross, Holy Cross.) Revs. Richard J. Fleischman, Team Mod.; Todd Budde, Team Member.
Res.: 305 Fredonia Ave., P.O. Box 250, 53021-0250. Tel: 262-692-9994; Fax: 262-692-3085.
School—Rosemary Catholic 53021. Tel: 262-692-2141. Lay Teachers 8; Students 74.
Catechesis/Religious Program—Tel: 262-692-9994, Ext. 315. Students 106.
2—ST. ROSE OF LIMA (1909) Closed. For sacramental records, contact Holy Rosary, Fredonia, Tel: 262-692-9994.

GENESEE DEPOT, WAUKESHA CO., ST. PAUL (1863) [CEM] Rev. Mark Molling; Deacon Larry E. Normann, Liturgy Dir. & Biblical Stewardship; Len Grassmann, Pastoral Assoc.; Rosemarie Etzel, Dir. Admin. Svcs.; Peggy Kolonko, Music Dir.
Mailing Address: S38 W31602 Hwy. D, P.O. Box 95, 53127. Tel: 262-968-3865; Fax: 262-968-5546. Email: office@stpaulgenesee.net. Web: www.stpaulgenesee.net.
School—Tel: 262-968-3175. Cheryl Sanford, Prin. Lay Teachers 15; Students 137.
Catechesis/Religious Program—Tel: 262-968-2276. Janet Shanahan, D.R.E. (Grades K-8); Amy Golden, Youth Min. (Grades 9-12); Bridget Klawitter, D.R.E. (Adult). Students 575.

GERMANTOWN, WASHINGTON CO., ST. BONIFACE (1845) [CEM] Rev. Loyola Amalraj.
Res.: W204 N11940 Goldendale Rd., 53022. Tel: 262-628-2040; Fax: 262-628-2076. Email: dplastine@stbonifacewi.org. Web: www.stbonifacewi.org.
School—W204 N11968 Goldendale Rd., 53022. Tel: 262-628-1955; Fax: 262-628-1689. Lay Teachers 16; Students 243.
Catechesis/Religious Program—Tel: 262-628-8143. Students 509.

GLENBEULAH, SHEBOYGAN CO., ST. FRIDOLIN (1878) Closed. For sacramental records, contact St. Thomas Aquinas, Elkhart Lake, Tel: 920-876-2457.

GRAFTON, OZAUKEE CO., ST. JOSEPH (1849) [CEM] Brenda Cline, Parish Dir.; Deacon Alfred C. Lazaga.
Pastoral Center—1619 Washington St., 53024. Tel: 262-375-6500; Fax: 262-375-6509. Email: stjosephs@wi.rr.com. Web: www.stjosephgrafton.org.
School—Tel: 262-375-6505. Lay Teachers 17; Students 203.
Catechesis/Religious Program—Students 498.

GREENDALE, MILWAUKEE CO., ST. ALPHONSUS (1938) Revs. Alan F. Jurkus; Mark J. Brandl; Deacons Theodore A. Gurzynski; James Leggett.
Parish Ministry Center: 5960 W. Loomis Rd., 53129. Tel: 414-421-2442; Fax: 414-421-8744. Email: stals@st-alphonsus.org. Web: www.st-alphonsus.org.
School—6000 W. Loomis Rd., 53129. Tel: 414-421-1760; Fax: 414-433-0709. Patrice Wadzinski, Prin. Lay Teachers 26; Students 372.
Catechesis/Religious Program—Tel: 414-421-0690. Students 743.

GREENFIELD, MILWAUKEE CO., ST. JOHN THE EVANGELIST (1916) Rev. Daniel P. Volkert.
Res.: 8500 W. Cold Spring Rd., 53228. Tel: 414-321-1965; Fax: 414-321-4407. Email: rectory@stjohns-grfd.org. Web: www.stjohns-grfd.org.
School— 53228. Tel: 414-321-8540; Fax: 414-321-4450. Email: principal@stjohns-grfd.org. Mary Laidlaw Otto, Prin. Lay Teachers 16; Students 169.
Catechesis/Religious Program—Tel: 414-321-8922. Students 145.

HALES CORNERS, MILWAUKEE CO., ST. MARY (1842) [CEM] Very Rev. Charles H. Schramm; Rev. Matthew Widder; Deacons John R. Burns; William Goulding; Ms. Brigid O'Donnell, Pastoral Assoc.
9520 W. Forest Home Ave., 53130.
School—9553 W. Edgerton Ave., 53130. Tel: 414-425-3100; Fax: 414-425-6270. Email: school@stmaryhc.org. Gina Brown, Prin. Lay Teachers 32; Students 466.
Catechesis/Religious Program—Tel: 414-425-3101; Fax: 414-425-9432. James Beuscher, D.R.E. (Child/ Middle School); Tim Winters, Youth & Young Adult Min. Students 537.

HARTFORD, WASHINGTON CO., ST. KILIAN (1863) [CEM 4] Rev. David W. La Plante; Sr. Eileen Brynda, O.P., Pastoral Assoc.
Office & Mailing Address: 428 Forest St., 53027. Tel: 262-673-4831; Fax: 262-673-4872. Web: stkiliancong.org.
School—245 High St., 53027. Tel: 262-673-3081; Fax: 262-673-0412. Mort Zaydel, Prin. Tel: 262-673-3081, Ext. 116. Lay Teachers 14; Students 174.
Catechesis/Religious Program—Tel: 262-673-4831, Ext. 406. June Strobel, D.R.E. Tel: 262-673-4831, Ext. 406. Students 317.

HARTLAND, WAUKESHA CO., ST. CHARLES (1906) [CEM] Rev. Kenneth E. Omernick.
Office: 313 Circle Dr., 53029-1824. Tel: 262-367-0800; Fax: 262-367-6960. Email: parish@stcharleshartland.com. Web: www.stcharleshartland.com.
Res.: 521 Renson Rd., 53029. Tel: 262-367-9936.
School—526 Renson Rd., 53029. Tel: 262-367-2040. Web: www.stcharleshartland.com. Michael Halstead, Prin. Lay Teachers 15; Students 199.
Catechesis/Religious Program—Tel: 262-367-3277. Students 820.

HOLY CROSS, OZAUKEE CO., HOLY CROSS (1845), (Luxembourgian), Closed. For sacramental records, contact Holy Rosary, Fredonia, Tel: 262-692-9994.

HORICON, DODGE CO.
1—ST. MALACHY (1856) Closed. For sacramental records, contact Sacred Heart, Horicon, Tel: 920-485-0694.
2—SACRED HEART (2001) [CEM 2], (Merger of St. Malachy, Horicon and Immaculate Conception, Juneau.) Rev. Michael J. Petrie.
Mailing Address: 950 Washington St., P.O. Box 27, 53032. Email: sheartchurch@sbcglobal.net. Web: www.sheart.org.
Catechesis/Religious Program—Tel: 920-485-0694; Fax: 920-485-0906. Students 293.

HUBERTUS, WASHINGTON CO.
1—ST. GABRIEL (2002) [CEM] [JC 3] Rev. Charles T. Hanel; Deacon Steven J. Przedpelski.
Res.: 1200 St. Gabriel Way, 53033. Tel: 262-628-1141; Fax: 262-628-1911. Email: sgabriel@sgabrielp.org. Web: www.stgabrielparish.4lpi.com.
School—3733 Hubertus Rd., 53033. Tel: 262-628-1711; Fax: 262-628-0280. Web: www.sgabriel.org. Lay Teachers 10; Students 128.
Catechesis/Religious Program—Students 326.
2—ST. HUBERT (1846) Closed. For sacramental records before 1961, contact the Archdiocese of Milwaukee Archives, Tel: 414-769-3407. For sacramental records after 1960, contact St. Gabriel, Hubertus, Tel: 262-628-1141.
3—ST. MARY OF THE HILL (1924), (German—Irish), [CEM] [JC] Rev. Fred Alexander, O.C.D.
Mailing Address: 1515 Carmel Rd, 53033-9770. Tel: 262-628-3606; Fax: 262-673-7505. Email: secretary@stmaryhh.org. Web: www.stmaryhh.org.
Res.: 1525 Carmel Rd., 53033. Tel: 262-628-1838; Fax: 262-673-7568.
Catechesis/Religious Program—Tel: 262-628-3606, Ext. 4. Email: dre@stmaryhh.org. Tammy Streitmatter, D.R.E. Students 100.

JOHNSBURG, FOND DU LAC CO., ST. JOHN THE BAPTIST (1840) [CEM] Rev. Joseph H. Coerber.
Res.: N9288 County W, Fond du Lac, 54937. Tel: 920-795-4316; Fax: 920-898-9002.
School— Consolidated Parochial Elementary School (CPES): St. John the Baptist, Johnsburg; St. Mary, Marytown; Holy Cross, Mount Calvary; St. Cloud, St. Cloud. Lay Teachers 13; Students 103.
Catechesis/Religious Program—Tel: 920-898-4040. Students 83.

JUNEAU, DODGE CO., IMMACULATE CONCEPTION (1875) Closed. For sacramental records, contact Sacred Heart, Horicon, Tel: 920-485-0694.

KANSASVILLE, RACINE CO., ST. MARY-DOVER (1869) [CEM] Rev. Robert C. Kacalo.
23211 Church Rd., 53139.
Res.: 3320 S. Colony, Union Grove, 53182. Email: gagnonj@foursaints.org. Web: www.stmary-strobert.org.
Catechesis/Religious Program—Tel: 262-878-3476; Fax: 262-878-0194. Email: dillonc@foursaints.org. Students 57.

KENOSHA, KENOSHA CO.
1—ST. ANTHONY (1910), (Slovak), [JC] Rev. Paul L. Raczynski.
Mailing Address: 2223 51st St., 53140. Tel: 262-652-1844; Fax: 262-605-8262.
Catechesis/Religious Program—Students 7.
2—ST. CASIMIR (1901) Closed. For sacramental records, contact Archdiocese of Milwaukee Archives Office, Tel: 414-769-3407.
3—ST. ELIZABETH (2000), (Polish—German), [CEM 2] Rev. Roman Stikel.
Mailing Address: 4816 7th Ave., 53140.
Res.: 4804 7th Ave., 53140. Tel: 262-657-6875.
Catechesis/Religious Program—Students 70.
4—ST. GEORGE (1851), (German), Closed. For sacramental records, contact Archdiocese of Milwaukee Archives Office, Tel: 414-769-3407.
5—ST. JAMES (1845), (Irish), [CEM] Rev. Dominic Thomas, M.C.B.S. (India).
Res.: 5804 Sheridan Rd., 53140. Tel: 262-658-8071; Fax: 262-658-2490. Email: stjames@wi.rr.com. Web: www.stjameskenosha.4lpi.com.
Catechesis/Religious Program—Students 54.
6—ST. MARK (1924) Rev. Stephen Forrest; Deacon Alvaro Dominguez; Karen Metallo, Pastoral Assoc.
Res.: 7117 14th Ave., 53143. Tel: 262-656-7373; Fax: 262-656-7375. Email: stmark@archmil.org. Web: www.stmark-kenosha.org.
See St. Joseph Catholic Academy, Inc., Kenosha under School Systems located in the Institution section.
Catechesis/Religious Program—1320 73rd St., 53143. Tel: 262-656-7362. Students 487.
Latin American Center—7101 13th Ave., 53143-5459. Tel: 262-656-7370.
7—ST. MARY (1929) Revs. Michael T. Newman; Todd Belardi; Deacons Ronald F. Lesjak; James S. Francois; Wilson A. Shierk.
Res.: 7307 40th Ave., 53142. Tel: 262-694-6018; Fax: 262-694-6048.
School—7400 39th Ave., 53142. Tel: 262-694-6018, Ext. 130; Fax: 262-694-6740. Dr. Jacqueline Lichter, Prin. Lay Teachers 19; Students 267.
Catechesis/Religious Program—7401-40th Ave., 53142. Tel: 262-694-6018, Ext. 134; Fax: 262-842-0379. Jane Delfield, Dir. Adult & Family Min.; Sandy Slivon, Dir. Child & Early Adolescent Min.; Elizabeth Ann Dillon, Dir., Youth Min. Students 465.
8—OUR LADY OF MOUNT CARMEL (1904), (Italian), Unassigned. In Res., Revs. Dwight Campbell (PEO); Benjamin Reese (PEO).
Res.: 1919 54th St., 53140. Tel: 262-652-7660; Fax: 262-652-2542. Email: parishoffice@olmckenosha.org.
School—Mt. Carmel Preschool, 5400 19th Ave., 53140. Tel: 262-653-1464. Students 62.
Catechesis/Religious Program—Tel: 262-652-5057. Twinned with St. Elizabeth and Our Lady of the Holy Rosary, St. Therese & St. Anthony, Kenosha. Students 225.
9—OUR LADY OF THE HOLY ROSARY (1904) Very Rev. William Hayward, M.I.C.
Res.: 2224 45th St., 53140. Tel: 262-652-2771; Fax: 262-652-0183. Email: rectory@hrosary.org. Web: www.hrosary.org.
School—All Saints Catholic School North Campus, 4400 22nd Ave., 53140. Tel: 262-652-2771, Ext. 25; Fax: 262-652-6179. Web: www.allsaintskenosha-.org. Dr. Jacqueline Lichter, Lead Prin.; Bruce Varick, Assoc. Prin. Lay Teachers 12; Students 178.
Catechesis/Religious Program—Corinne Dillon, Co-ord. Christian Formation. Collaborative program with St. Elizabeth and Our Lady of Mt. Carmel, Kenosha. Holy Rosary Students 217.
10—ST. PETER (1903) Revs. Ireneusz Chodakowski, M.I.C.; Angelo Casimiro, M.I.C.; Deacon Terrance A. Maack.
Res.: 2224 30th Ave., 53144. Tel: 262-551-9004; Fax: 262-552-7004. Web: www.stpeterskenosha.com.
Catechesis/Religious Program—Students 229.
11—ST. THERESE (1953) Rev. Pradeep Joseph Sebastian, M.C.B.S. Email: kaippallymcbs@gmail.com.
Res.: 9005 22nd Ave., 53143-6699. Tel: 262-694-4695; Fax: 262-694-7284. Email: valang@tds.net. Web: www.st-therese-kenosha.org.
Catechesis/Religious Program—Tel: 262-694-0118. Students 96.
12—ST. THOMAS AQUINAS (1911) Closed. For sacramental records, contact Archdiocese of Milwaukee Archives Office, Tel: 414-769-3407.

KEWASKUM, WASHINGTON CO., HOLY TRINITY (1861) [CEM 2] [JC 3] Rev. Edwin M. Kornath; Deacon Ralph E. Horner.
Res.: 331 Main St., P.O. Box 461, 53040. Tel: 262-626-2860; Fax: 262-626-2301. Email: htkewaskum@alexssa.net.
School—305 Main St., 53040. Tel: 262-626-2603; Fax: 262-626-8863. Web: www.htschool.net. Ms. JoAnn Karpin, Prin. Lay Teachers 15; Students 151.
Catechesis/Religious Program—Combined program with St. Michaels, St. Michael., Tel: 262-626-2650. Mary Straub, D.R.E. Students 206.

KOHLER, SHEBOYGAN CO., ST. JOHN EVANGELIST (1927) Rev. Robert J. Lotz.
Res.: 600 Green Tree Rd., 53044. Tel: 920-452-9623; Fax: 920-452-9633.
Catechesis/Religious Program—Tel: 920-458-9931. Students 160.

LAKE FIVE, WASHINGTON CO., ST. COLUMBA (1843) Closed. For sacramental records, contact St. Gabriel, Hubertus, Tel: 262-628-1141.

LAKE GENEVA, WALWORTH CO., ST. FRANCIS DE SALES (1842) [CEM] Rev. Msgr. David J. Malloy; Rev. Jose-Angel Anaya-Estrada (Colombia).
Res.: 148 W. Main St., 53147. Tel: 262-248-8524; Fax: 262-248-5302. Email: parish@sfdslg.org. Web: www.sfdslg.org.
School—130 W. Main St., 53147. Tel: 262-248-2778; Fax: 262-248-7860. Lay Teachers 10; Students 161.
Catechesis/Religious Program—Tel: 262-248-8526. Email: rep@sfdslg.org. Mrs. Anne Trautner, D.R.E. Students 308.

LE ROY, DODGE CO., ST. ANDREW (1849) [CEM], Also serves St. Mary, Mayville. Rev. Thomas E. Biersack.
Res.: W3081 County Tr. Y, Lomira, 53048. Tel: 920-583-4125; 920-387-3130, Ext. 335; Fax: 920-387-1121.
Catechesis/Religious Program—Students 62.

LIMA, SHEBOYGAN CO., ST. ROSE (1860) Closed. For sacramental records, contact Blessed Trinity, Sheboygan Falls, Tel: 920-467-4616.

LITTLE KOHLER, OZAUKEE CO., MOTHER OF SORROWS, Closed. For sacramental records, contact Holy Rosary, Fredonia, Tel: 262-692-9994.

LOMIRA, DODGE CO., ST. MARY (1870), (German), [CEM] Rev. Dennis G. Budka.
Res.: 699 Milwaukee St., 53048. Tel: 920-269-4429; Fax: 920-269-7359. Email: stmarytheresa@gmail.com.
Catechesis/Religious Program—Tel: 920-269-4326. Stephen C. Martin, D.R.E. Students 142.

LOST LAKE, DODGE CO., ST. MARY (1893) Closed. For sacramental records, contact Annunciation, Fox Lake, Tel: 920-928-3513.

LYONS, WALWORTH CO.
1—ST. JOSEPH (1870), (German), [CEM 2] Rev. John H. Baumgartner.
Res.: 1540 Mill St., Box 60, 53148-0060. Tel: 262-763-2050; Fax: 262-763-9377. Email: saintjoe@bizwi.rr.com.
Catechesis/Religious Program—Students 79.
2—ST. KILIAN, Closed. For sacramental records, contact St. Joseph, Lyons, Tel: 262-763-2050.

MAPLETON, WAUKESHA CO., ST. CATHERINE (1847), (Irish), [CEM] Rev. Michael D. Strachota, Temp. Admin.
Res.: W359 N8512 Brown St., Oconomowoc, 53066. Tel: 920-474-7000; 877-871-8489 (Toll Free); Fax: 920-474-4661.
Catechesis/Religious Program—Fax: 920-474-4461. Students 346.

MARYTOWN, FOND DU LAC CO., ST. MARY (1849) [CEM] Rev. Joseph H. Coerber.
Res.: N10232 Hwy. G, New Holstein, 53061. Tel: 920-898-4040; Fax: 920-898-9002. Email: vsitbvm@tcei.com.
Catechesis/Religious Program—Students 55.

MAYVILLE, DODGE CO., ST. MARY (1856) [CEM], Also serves St. Andrew, LeRoy. Rev. Thomas E. Biersack; Deacon Willis Heideman.
Res.: W3081 Hwy. Y, Lomira, 53048. Tel: 920-583-4125.
Church: 302 S. German St., P.O. Box 22, 53050-0022. Tel: 920-387-2470; 920-387-3130 (Parish Center); Fax: 920-387-1121. Web: www.stmary-standrew.org.
School—(Grades K-8), 28 Naber St., 53050. Tel: 920-387-2920. Lay Teachers 6; Students 62.
Catechesis/Religious Program—Fax: 920-387-0362. Students 171.

MENOMONEE FALLS, WAUKESHA CO.
1—ST. ANTHONY (1846) [CEM] Rev. Dennis J. Wieland.
Res.: N74 W13604 Appleton Ave., 53051. Tel: 262-251-5910; Fax: 262-251-6564. Web: www.stanthony-parish.org.
School—N74 W13646 Appleton Ave., 53051. Tel: 262-251-4390; Fax: 262-251-2412. Email: aschram@bizwi.rr.com. Anne Schramka, Prin. Lay Teachers 17; Students 192.
Catechesis/Religious Program—Tel: 262-251-8868. John Hying, Dir. Child Min. Students 468.
2—GOOD SHEPHERD (1957) Rev. Kenneth A. Mich;

Deacon Sanford Sites; Mark Steimle, Dir. of Admin. Svcs.; Jane Clare Ishiguro, Pastoral Assoc.
Church & Office: N88 W17658 Christman Rd., 53051-2630. Tel: 262-255-2035; Fax: 262-255-2020. Email: goodshepherd@gdinet.com. Web: www.mygoodshepherd.org.
Catechesis / Religious Program—Suzanne Foster, Dir. Youth Ministry; Lorrie Maples, Dir. Child Ministry. Students 232.

3—ST. JAMES (1847) [CEM] Rev. Michael F. Moran; Daryl Olszewski, Pastoral Assoc.
Res.: W 220-N 6588 Town Line Rd., 53051. Tel: 262-251-3944; Fax: 262-250-2679. Web: www.stjames-parish.com.
Catechesis / Religious Program—Tel: 262-251-0897. Tracy Derezynski, D.R.E. (Youth Min.); Sue Devine-Simon, D.R.E. (Child Min.). Students 745.

4—ST. MARY (1905) [CEM] Rev. Michael F. Merkt; Sr. Jane Mary Lorbiecki, S.S.N.D., Pastoral Assoc.; Deacons Robert H. Buth, (Retired); Thomas C. Monday.
Church: N89 W16297 Cleveland Ave., 53051. Tel: 262-251-0220; Fax: 262-251-6948. Email: info@stmarymf.org. Web: stmarymf.org.
School—N89 W16215 Cleveland Ave., 53051. Tel: 262-251-1050; Fax: 262-502-1671. Mrs. Linda Joyner, Prin. Lay Teachers 25; Students 357.
Catechesis / Religious Program—Tel: 262-251-1154. Students 232.

MEQUON, OZAUKEE CO.

1—ST. JAMES (1851), (German), Closed. For sacramental records, contact Lumen Christi, Mequon, Tel: 262-242-7967.

2—LUMEN CHRISTI (2005) [CEM] Revs. Daniel J. Sanders; Aaron J. Esch; Deacons Anthony Monfre; Joseph P. Wenzler.
11300 N. St. James Ln., 28W, 53092. Tel: 262-242-7967; Fax: 262-242-7970. Email: lcmail@lumenchristiparish.org. Web: www.lumenchristiparish.org.
School—(2005)Tel: 262-242-7960; Fax: 262-512-8986. Email: schumacherg@lumenchristiparish.org. Web: www.lumenchristiparish.org/school/. Mrs. Gloria Schumacher, Prin. Lay Teachers 31; Students 370.
Catechesis / Religious Program—Tel: 262-512-8985; Fax: 262-242-7977. Web: www.lumenchristiparish.org/cf/. Michelle Zakula, Dir. Formation. Students 535.

MITCHELL, SHEBOYGAN CO., ST. MICHAEL (1852) Closed. For sacramental records, contact Archdiocese of Milwaukee Archives Office, Tel: 414-769-3407.

MONCHES, WAUKESHA CO., ST. JOHN (1843) [CEM] Closed. For sacramental records, contact Blessed Teresa of Calcutta, North Lake, Tel: 262-966-3191.

MOUNT CALVARY, FOND DU LAC CO.

1—HOLY CROSS (1849) [CEM] Closed. For sacramental records contact St. Isidore, Mount Cavalry, Tel: 920-753-3311.

2—ST. ISIDORE CONGREGATION (2010) [CEM 3] Rev. Steven Kropp, O.F.M.Cap.
P.O. Box 176, 53057-0716. Tel: 920-753-3311.
308 S. Cty. Rd. W, 53057.
Catechesis / Religious Program—Danelle Kegley, D.R.E. Students 121.

MUKWONAGO, WAUKESHA CO., ST. JAMES (1896) Rev. Michael G. Savio.
Res.: 830 Cty. Rd. NN East, 53149. Tel: 262-363-7615; Fax: 262-363-2416. Email: parish@stjmuk.org. Web: www.stjamesmukwonago.org.
Catechesis / Religious Program—Tel: 262-363-7615, Ext. 121. Suzanne Foster, D.R.E. Students 394.

MUSKEGO, WAUKESHA CO., ST. LEONARD CONGREGATION (1957) Very Rev. William E. Kohler; Deacons Rick J. Wirch; Ralph Wisniewski; Bridget Klawitter, Pastoral Assoc.
Res.: W173 S7743 Westwood Dr., 53150. Tel: 262-679-1773; Fax: 262-679-4210. Email: parish@stleonards.org. Web: www.stleonards.org.
School—Sue Watkinson, Prin. Lay Teachers 20; Students 223.
Catechesis / Religious Program—Tel: 262-679-0880; Fax: 262-679-8502. Web: www.stleonard-reled.com. Lisa Jachimiec, D.R.E. Students 724.

NABOB, WASHINGTON CO., ST. MATTHIAS (1848) Closed. For sacramental records, contact St. Lawrence, St. Lawrence, Tel: 262-644-5701.

NENNO, WASHINGTON CO.

1—ST. ANTHONY, Closed. For sacramental records, contact Resurrection, Allenton, Tel: 262-629-5240.

2—SS. PETER AND PAUL (1848) Closed. For sacramental records, contact Resurrection, Allenton, Tel: 262-629-5240.

NEOSHO, DODGE CO., ST. MATTHEW (1857), (German), [CEM], Also serves St. Mary, Woodland & St. John, Rubicon. Rev. Alois Van Beek.
Res.: 148 W. Lehman St., P.O. Box 45, 53059. Tel: 920-625-3144. Email: mattneo3@nconnect.net. Web: mjmtriparish.org.
Catechesis / Religious Program—Tel: 920-625-3092. Combined with St. Mary, Woodland. Students 47.
Mission—St. Mary Woodland, Dodge Co. 53099.

NEW BERLIN, WAUKESHA CO.

1—ST. ELIZABETH ANN SETON (1981) Rev. Joseph A. Aufdermauer; Deacon Jeffrey J. Copson; Liz Hanna, Pastoral Assoc.; Dennis Wisialowski, Dir. Admin. Svcs.; Linda Noel Halverson, Dir. Music & Liturgy; Mickey Holtz, Dir. Youth Ministry.
Church & Office: 12700 W. Howard Ave., 53151. Tel: 262-782-6760; Fax: 262-782-4763. Email: seaseton@tds.net. Web: mystelizabeth.com.
Catechesis / Religious Program—Tel: 262-782-8982. Ann Hepp, Dir. Christian Formation. Students 390.

2—HOLY APOSTLES (1855) [CEM] Revs. Donald H. Thimm; Charles Wrobel; Deacon Michael J. Chmielewski.
16000 W. National Ave., 53151. Tel: 262-786-7330; Fax: 262-786-0425. Web: www.hanb.org. In Res., Revs. Matthew Widder; Charles Wrobel.
School—3875 S. 159 St., 53151. Tel: 262-786-7331. Gregory Young, Prin. Sisters 1; Lay Teachers 25; Students 410.
Catechesis / Religious Program—Tel: 262-786-2035. Students 710.

NEW MUNSTER, KENOSHA CO., ST. ALPHONSUS (1849), (German), [CEM] Deacon Stanley J. Lowe, Parish Dir.; Revs. Anthony J. Russo; Lawrence J. Chapman.
Res.: 6301 344th Ave., P.O. Box 767, 53152. Tel: 262-537-4370; Fax: 262-537-3527. Email: rectory@st-alphonsus.com.
School—6211 344th Ave., P.O. Box 922, 53152. Tel: 262-537-4379. Lay Teachers 12; Students 84.
Catechesis / Religious Program—Tel: 262-537-4370, Ext. 239. Students 145.

NEWBURG, WASHINGTON CO., HOLY TRINITY (1859), (German), [CEM 3] Rev. Kevin J. Kowalske; Deacon Michael S. Koebel.
521 Congress St., Box 16, 53060-0016.
Res.: Box 16, 53060-0016. Tel: 262-675-6256. Email: htrinity@archmil.org.
Catechesis / Religious Program—Students 39.
Station—St. Augustine (1857) Trenton.
Station—St. Peter (1855) Farmington.

NORTH FOND DU LAC, FOND DU LAC CO., PRESENTATION OF THE BLESSED VIRGIN MARY (1902), (Irish—German), [JC] Rev. John L. Simon.
Rectory—706 Minnesota Ave., 54937-1326. Tel: 920-921-9383; Fax: 920-921-1309. Email: motherandsonoffice@att.net.
Catechesis / Religious Program—Tel: 920-921-5873. Email: motherandsonre@att.net. Students 110.

NORTH LAKE, WAUKESHA CO.

1—BLESSED TERESA OF CALCUTTA (2006) [JC 2] Rev. Anthony T. McCarthy.
P.O. Box 68, 53064-0068. Tel: 262-966-2191. Email: office@blteresaparish.org. Web: www.blteresaparish.org.
Catechesis / Religious Program—Karin Frederickson, D.R.E. Students 320.

2—ST. CLARE (1916) [CEM] Closed. For sacramental records, contact Blessed Teresa of Calcutta, North Lake.

OAK CREEK, MILWAUKEE CO.

1—ST. MATTHEW (1841) [CEM] Rev. Patrick J. O'Loughlin.
Res.: 9303 S. Chicago Rd., 53154. Tel: 414-762-4200. Email: parish@stmattoc.org. Web: www.stmattoc.org.
School—9329 S. Chicago Rd., 53154. Tel: 414-762-6820; Fax: 414-762-3686. Email: school@stmattoc.org. Lay Teachers 12; Students 195.
Catechesis / Religious Program— Shelly Madden, Dir. Youth Ministry; Carol Daun, Dir. Family & Child. Students 381.

2—ST. STEPHEN (1847), (German), [CEM 2] Rev. Richard A. Liska; Deacon Leon J. Zalewski.
Mailing Address: 1441 W. Oakland Rd., 53154. Tel: 414-762-0552; Fax: 414-762-0583.
Catechesis / Religious Program—Sr. Mary Alice Walters, C.S.A., C.R.E. Religious 1; Lay Teachers 9; Students 264.

OAKFIELD, FOND DU LAC CO., ST. JAMES (1909) Closed. For sacramental records, contact Sons of Zebedee: Saints James and John, Byron, Tel: 920-583-4376.

OCONOMOWOC, WAUKESHA CO., ST. JEROME (1860) [CEM] Revs. John G. Yockey; Erich Weiss.
Res.: 995 S. Silver Lake St., 53066. Tel: 262-569-3020; Fax: 262-569-3022. Email: parish@stjerome.org. Web: www.stjerome.org.
School—1001 S. Silver Lake St., 53066. Tel: 262-569-3030; Fax: 262-569-3023. Email: school@stjerome.org. Third Order Schoenstatt 1; Lay Teachers 23; Students 289.
Catechesis / Religious Program—Tel: 262-569-3025. Email: prep@stjerome.org. Students 266.

PARIS, KENOSHA CO., ST. JOHN THE BAPTIST (1859) [CEM] Rev. Russell L. Arnett, Admin.
Parish Office—1704 240th Ave., Kansasville, 53139. Tel: 262-859-2484. Email: sfxsjb@archmil.org.
School—Providence Catholic School, Consolidated with St. Francis Xavier, Brighton, 1481 172nd Ave., Union Grove, 53182. Tel: 262-859-2007; 262-878-2713; Fax: 262-859-2604. Email: eastcampus@providencecatholicschool.org. Web: www.providencecatholicschool.org. Mrs. Suzanne Meyer, Prin. Lay Teachers 5; Students 67.
Catechesis / Religious Program—Tel: 262-878-2267; Fax: 262-878-3683. Sr. Kathryn Dean Strandell, O.S.F., D.R.E. (Grades K-8). Students 57.

PELL LAKE, WALWORTH CO., ST. MARY (1928) [JC] Closed. For sacramental records, contact St. Francis de Sales, Lake Geneva, Tel: 262-248-8524/ 8525.

PEWAUKEE, WAUKESHA CO.

1—ST. ANTHONY ON THE LAKE (1918) Rev. Anthony J. Zimmer; Kathie Amidei, Pastoral Assoc.; Michael Witte, Pastoral Assoc.
Res.: W 280 N. 2101 Hwy. SS., 53072. Tel: 262-691-2326; Fax: 262-691-2063. Email: parish@stanthony.cc. Web: www.stanthony.cc.
School—Tel: 262-691-0460; 262-691-1173 (Parish Center); Fax: 262-691-7376. Email: principal@stanthony.cc. Lay Teachers 14; Students 203.
Catechesis / Religious Program—Tel: 262-691-9170. Email: parish@stanthony.cc. Ann Fons, D.R.E.; Debbie Kusch, D.R.E.; Cindi Petre, D.R.E. Students 773.

2—ST. MARY (1858) Closed. For sacramental records, contact Queen of Apostles, Pewaukee, Tel: 262-691-1535.

3—SS. PETER AND PAUL (1848) Closed. For sacramental records, contact Queen of Apostles, Pewaukee, Tel: 262-691-1535.

4—QUEEN OF APOSTLES (1997) [CEM 2], Consolidation of St. Mary's, Pewaukee and Ss. Peter and Paul, Pewaukee. Rev. Robert J. Drutowski; Deacons Eugene A. Kempka; Gregory R. Price.
Mailing Address: P.O. Box 220, 53072-0220. N35 W23360 Capitol Dr., 53072. Tel: 262-691-1535; Fax: 262-691-9219. Email: qoapar@execpc.com. Web: www.queenofapostles.net.
School—449 W. Wisconsin Ave. Tel: 262-691-2120; Fax: 262-691-8606. Email: qoaschool@wi.rr.com. Web: queenofapostlesschool.net. Mr. Laurence Patterson, Prin. Tel: 262-691-2120. Lay Teachers 15; Students 146.
Catechesis / Religious Program—Tel: 262-691-2878. Lynn Famularo, D.R.E.; Bill Eder, Youth Min. Students 300.

PLEASANT PRAIRIE, KENOSHA CO., ST. ANNE (1998) Rev. Robert J. Weighner; Deacon William Clark.
Church: 9091 Prairie Ridge Blvd., 53158. Tel: 262-942-8300; Fax: 262-942-8472. Email: info@saint-anne.org. Web: www.saint-anne.org.
Catechesis / Religious Program—Tel: 262-694-0026; Fax: 262-942-8472. Email: info@saint-anne.org. Students 306.

PLYMOUTH, SHEBOYGAN CO., ST. JOHN THE BAPTIST (1861) [CEM] Very Rev. Dennis E. Van Beek.
Res.: 115 Plymouth St., 53073. Tel: 920-892-4006; Fax: 920-893-8444. Email: sjparish@sjbplymouth.org. Web: www.sjbplymouth.org.
School—116 Pleasant St., 53073. Tel: 920-893-5961; Fax: 920-893-3160. Email: school@sjbplymouth.org. Mrs. Lisa Oldenburg, Prin. Lay Teachers 19; Students 242.
Catechesis / Religious Program—Tel: 920-892-6015. Email: sjbreled@hotmail.com. Students 383.

PORT WASHINGTON, OZAUKEE CO.

1—ST. MARY (1853) [CEM] Revs. Patrick Wendt, In Solidum Team Mod.; Thomas F. Lijewski, In Solidum Team Mem.
Office: 430 N. Johnson St., 53074. Tel: 262-284-5771; Fax: 262-284-4112. Email: maryport@archmil.org. Web: stmaryport.org.
School—Consolidated with St. Peter of Alcantara to form Port Washington Catholic School, Inc., 1802 N. Wisconsin St., 53074. Tel: 262-284-2682 (Grades 5-8); Fax: 262-284-4216. Email: ptcath2@execpc.com. Web: www.portcatholic.org. 446 N. Johnson St., 53074. Tel: 262-284-2441 (PreK-4). School Sisters of Notre Dame 1; Lay Teachers 17; Students 254.
Catechesis / Religious Program—Consolidated with St. Peter of Alcantara, Port Washington and Immaculate Conception, Saukille., Tel: 262-284-6472. Email: portchild@archmil.org. Denise Murre, D.R.E. (Grades K-6); Maureen Kavanaugh, D.R.E. (Grades 7-11). Tel: 262-284-2102. Students 596.

2—ST. PETER OF ALCANTARA (1966) Revs. Patrick Wendt, In Solidum Team Mod.; Thomas F. Lijewski, In Solidum Team Mem.; Deacon Thomas J. Surges; Mary McHugh, Pastoral Assoc.; Mr. Timothy Charek, Dir. Admin. Svcs.
Res.: 1800 N. Wisconsin St., 53074. Tel: 262-284-4266; Fax: 262-284-4216. Email: stpeterport@archmil.org. Web: www.stpeterport.org.
See school listing under St. Mary, Port Washington for details.

Catechesis/Religious Program—Consolidated with St. Mary, Port Washington and Immaculate Conception, Saukille., Tel: 262-284-6472 (Child Ministry); 262-284-2102 (Youth Ministry). Web: www.portyouth.org (Youth Ministry); www.stmary-stpeter-kids.com (Child Ministry). Denise Murre, D.R.E. (Grades K-6); Maureen Rotramel, D.R.E. (Grades 7-12). Students 176.

RACINE, RACINE CO.

1—ST. CASIMIR (1913), (Lithuanian), Closed. For sacramental records, contact Archdiocese of Milwaukee Archives Office, Tel: 414-769-3407.

2—CRISTO REY (1980), (Hispanic), Revs. Esteban Redolad, In Solidum Team Mod.; Antony Primal Thomas, In Solidum Team Mem.
Res.: 800 Wisconsin Ave., 53403. Tel: 262-632-3151; Fax: 262-637-1536. Email: cristorey@archmil.org.
Catechesis/Religious Program—Students 125.

3—ST. EDWARD (1919) Rev. Allen J. Bratkowski.
Office and Res.: 1401 Grove Ave., 53405. Tel: 262-636-8040; Fax: 262-636-8052. Email: parish@saintedwardracine.org. Web: www.stedwardracine.org.
School—St. Edward-Our Lady of Grace Academy, 1435 Grove Ave., 53405. Fax: 262-636-8045. Email: steds@wi.rr.com. Pierre N. Antoine, Prin. Lay Teachers 11; Students 144.
Catechesis/Religious Program—Tel: 262-636-8040, Ext. 4. Students 65.

4—HOLY NAME (1884), (German), Closed. For sacramental records, contact Archdiocese of Milwaukee Archives Office, Tel: 414-769-3407.

5—HOLY TRINITY (1914) Closed. For sacramental records, contact Archdiocese of Milwaukee Archives Office, Tel: 414-769-3407.

6—ST. JOHN NEPOMUK (1896) [JC] Janet M. Ruidl, Parish Dir.; Rev. Donald F. Zerkel (Retired).
Res.: 700 English St., 53402. Tel: 262-634-5647; Fax: 262-637-1436. Email: stjohnnepomuk@wi.rr.com.
See John Paul II Academy at Sacred Heart Congregation, Racine.
Catechesis/Religious Program—1911 Green St., 53402. Tel: 262-634-5647; Fax: 262-634-1436. Students 43.

7—ST. JOSEPH (1875) [JC 4] Revs. Ronald O. Crewe; Sean Granger.
Office: 1532 N. Wisconsin St., 53402. Tel: 262-633-8284; Fax: 262-633-8285. Email: info@st-joes.org. Web: st-joes.org.
Res.: 1526 Erie St., 53402. Tel: 262-632-6487.
School—1525 Erie St., 53402. Tel: 262-633-2403. Joseph Majowski, Prin. Lay Teachers 16; Students 161.
Catechesis/Religious Program—Tel: 262-633-9005. Susan Gehrig, D.R.E. Students 146.

8—ST. LUCY (1958) Revs. Mark R. Jones; Sean Granger; Sandra Gottfredsen, Pastoral Assoc.
Res.: 3101 Drexel Ave., 53403. Tel: 262-554-1801; Fax: 262-554-2009. Email: stlucy@archmil.org. Web: www.stlucychurch.org.
Rectory—2337 Mitchell, 53403.
School—3035 Drexel Ave., 53403. Fax: 262-554-7618. Email: stlucyschool@archmil.org. Web: www-.stlucysschool.com. Lay Teachers 15; Students 264.
Catechesis/Religious Program—Tel: 262-554-1801, Ext. 208; Fax: 262-554-2009. Students 295.

9—ST. MARY BY THE LAKE (1852) [JC] Rev. Stephen J. Stradinger.
Mailing Address: P.O. Box 044200, 53404-7004. Tel: 262-639-3616; Fax: 262-639-1999. Email: stmarybl@wi.twcbc.com. Web: www.stmarybythelake.org.
Church: 7605 Lakeshore Dr., 53402. Tel: 262-321-0989.
Catechesis/Religious Program—Tel: 262-639-4493; Fax: 262-639-1999. Students 74.

10—ST. PATRICK (1856) [JC 4] Revs. Esteban Redolad, In Solidum Team Mod.; Antony Primal Thomas, In Solidum Team Mem.; Deacon Leonides Rocha.
Res.: 1100 Erie St., 53402. Tel: 262-632-8808; Fax: 262-637-1536. Email: church@stpatrickracine.com. Web: stpatrickracine.com.
Catechesis/Religious Program—Email: church@stpatrick.com. Laura Gabriela Cabrera, C.R.E. Students 202.

11—ST. PAUL THE APOSTLE (1965) [JC] Rev. Terrance J. Huebner; Deacons Patrick H. Frye; Keith A. Hansen; Dale T. Nees; Willard M. Widmar; Ronnie Quella, Music Dir.; Colleen Kechter, Dir. Admin. Svcs.
Res.: 6400 Spring St., 53406. Tel: 262-886-0530; Fax: 262-886-0737. Web: www.stpaulracine.org.
Catechesis/Religious Program—Tel: 262-886-0531. Leticia Gutierrez-Kenny, Dir. Child Ministry; Johnathan Bator, Dir. Youth & Young Adult Ministry. Students 217.

12—ST. RICHARD OF CHICHESTER (1998) [JC] Very Rev. Ronald J. Gramza; Deacons Howard J. Wirtz; David J. BackesWeb: new-wood.blogspot.com.
Res.: 1509 Grand Ave., 53403. Tel: 262-637-8374; Fax: 262-635-2426. Email: strichard@archmil.org. Web: www.strichardparish.org.
Catechesis/Religious Program—Students 37.

13—ST. RITA (1926) [CEM] Rev. Kevin C. Mullins, O.S.A. In Res., Revs. John R. Flynn, O.S.A.; Jerome G. Knies, O.S.A.; Henry Maibusch, O.S.A.; Bro. Robert J. Schurman, O.S.A.
Res.: 4339 Douglas Ave., 53402. Tel: 262-681-3221; Fax: 262-639-3602. Email: sritarac@archmil.org. Web: www.st-ritas.org.
School—4433 Douglas Ave., 53402. Tel: 262-639-3333. Email: principal@st-ritas.org. Lay Teachers 18; Students 267.
Catechesis/Religious Program—Tel: 262-639-6280; Fax: 262-639-3370. Leticia Gutierrez-Kenny, D.R.E. Students 230.

14—ST. ROSE (1886) Closed. For sacramental records, contact Archdiocese of Milwaukee Archives Office, Tel: 414-769-3407.

15—SACRED HEART CONGREGATION (1916) [CEM 4] [JC 12] Rev. Ronald O. Crewe.
Res.: 2201 Northwestern Ave., 53404. Tel: 262-634-5526; Fax: 262-634-5767. Email: shracine@archmil.org. Web: www.sacredheartracine.com.
School—John Paul II Academy, 2023 Northwestern Ave., 53404. Tel: 262-637-2012; Fax: 262-637-5130. Pierre N. Antoine, Prin. Sacred Heart & St. John Nepomuk schools merged. Lay Teachers 15; Students 185.
Catechesis/Religious Program—Tel: 262-634-3607. Mr. Mark Lyons, D.R.E. Students 85.

16—ST. STANISLAUS (1904), (Polish), Closed. For sacramental records, contact Archdiocese of Milwaukee Archives Office, Tel: 414-769-3407.

RANDOLPH, COLUMBIA CO., ST. GABRIEL, Closed. For sacramental records, contact Annunciation, Fox Lake, Tel: 920-928-3513.

RANDOM LAKE, SHEBOYGAN CO.

1—ST. MARY (1855) Closed. For sacramental records, contact Archdiocese of Milwaukee Archives Office, Tel: 414-769-3407.

2—OUR LADY OF THE LAKES (1998) [CEM 4] Revs. Richard J. Fleischman, Team Mod.; Todd Budde, Team Member; Debbie Hamm, Pastoral Assoc.
Mailing Address: 230 Butler St., 53075-1710. Tel: 920-994-4380; Fax: 920-994-2605. Email: ourladyrlp@archmil.org. Web: www.ourladylakes.org.
School—(Grades PreK-6), 306 Butler St., 53075-1712. Tel: 920-994-9962; Fax: 920-994-2499. Email: ourladyrls@archmil.org. James Rick Erickson, Prin. Lay Teachers 4; Students 32.
Catechesis/Religious Program—Tel: 920-994-8033. Teresa Mahler, D.R.E. Students 120.
Chapel—St. Mary 300 Butler St., 53075.
Chapel—St. Nicholas W4274 Hwy. K, 53075.
Chapel—St. Patrick W4690 Hwy. A, Adell, 53001.

REESEVILLE, DODGE CO., HOLY FAMILY (1901), (German—Irish), [CEM], Also serves St. Columbkille, Elba and St. John the Baptist, Clyman. Rev. Richard Wendell.
302 Prairie St., P.O. Box 277, 53579-0277. Tel: 920-927-3102; Fax: 920-927-1970.
Res.: 714 Church St., Box 190, Clyman, 53016. Tel: 920-386-8039; Fax: 920-927-1970. Email: triparish@charter.net.
Catechesis/Religious Program—Students 38.

RICHFIELD, WASHINGTON CO., ST. MARY (1854), (German), Closed. For sacramental records before 1967, contact Archdiocese of Milwaukee Archives Office, Tel: 414-769-3407. For sacramental records after 1966, contact St. Gabriel, Hubertus, Tel: 262-628-1141.

RIPON, FOND DU LAC CO.

1—ST. CATHERINE OF SIENA (2005) [CEM] Rev. Robert A. Fictum.
218 Blossom St., 54971-1526. Tel: 920-748-2325. Email: ccofripon@centurytel.net. Web: www.stcatofsiena.org.
Catechesis/Religious Program—Fax: 920-748-3760. Email: karenmiller@centurytel.net. Students 204.

2—ST. PATRICK (1858) Closed. For sacramental records, contact St. Catherine of Siena, Ripon, Tel: 920-748-2345.

3—ST. WENCESLAUS (1896), (Polish), Closed. For sacramental records, contact St. Catherine of Siena, Ripon, Tel: 920-748-2345.

RUBICON, DODGE CO., ST. JOHN (1870), (German), [CEM] [JC], Also serves St. Matthew, Neosho and St. Mary, Woodland. Rev. Alois VanBeek.
Mailing Address: W1170 Rome Rd., 53078. Tel: 262-673-3380.
Res.: 148 W. Lehman, Neosho, 53059. Tel: 920-625-3144.
Church: W1170 Rome Rd., P.O. Box 17, 53078. Tel: 262-673-3380.
Catechesis/Religious Program—Tel: 262-673-4397. Students 137.

ST. CLOUD, FOND DU LAC CO., ST. CLOUD (1870), (German), [CEM] Closed. For sacramental records, contact St. Isidore, Mount Calvary, Tel: 920-753-3311.

ST. FRANCIS, MILWAUKEE CO., SACRED HEART OF JESUS (1868) [CEM] Unassigned.
Office: 3635 S. Kinnickinnic Ave., 53235-3741. Tel: 414-481-2330; Fax: 414-744-7222. Email: shjsf@execpc.com. Web: sacredheartofjesus.4lpi.com. See St. Thomas Aquinas Academy located in the Institution Section under Consolidated Elementary Schools.
Catechesis/Religious Program—Combined program with Immaculate Conception, St. Augustine, St. Veronica, and St. Paul, Milwaukee and Nativity of the Lord, Cudahy., Tel: 414-481-0777, Ext. 117. Email: karenbushman@saintveronica.org. Sacred Heart Students 32; Combined Students 332.

ST. GEORGE, SHEBOYGAN CO., ST. GEORGE (1860) Closed. For sacramental records, contact Blessed Trinity, Sheboygan Falls, Tel: 920-467-4616.

ST. JOE, FOND DU LAC CO., ST. JOSEPH (1858), (German), [CEM] Closed. For sacramental records, contact St. Isidore, Mount Calvary, Tel: 920-753-3311.

ST. KILIAN, FOND DU LAC CO., ST. KILIAN (1848) [CEM] Rev. Neil G. Zinthefer; Jane M. Osypowski, Business Mgr.
N189 County Rd. W., P.O. Box 740, Campbellsport, 53010. Tel: 920-533-4441; Fax: 920-533-5280. Email: stmatts@archmil.org.
Catechesis/Religious Program—419 Mill St., P.O. Box 740, Campbellsport, 53010. Tel: 920-533-4441; Fax: 920-533-5280. Beth Schmidt, D.R.E. Tel: 920-533-8060. (Twinned with St. Matthew)

ST. LAWRENCE, WASHINGTON CO., ST. LAWRENCE (1846), (German), [CEM] Rev. Joseph Dominic, S.A.C. (India).
Res.: 4886 Hwy. 175, Hartford, 53027. Tel: 262-644-5701; Fax: 262-644-5701. Email: stlawrenceoffice@gmail.com.
Catechesis/Religious Program—Tel: 262-644-0011. Email: stlawreled@gmail.com. Students 131.

ST. MARTIN, MILWAUKEE CO., HOLY ASSUMPTION, Closed. For sacramental records through 1990, contact St. Mary, Hales Corners, Tel: 414-425-2174. For sacramental records after 1990, contact St. Martin of Tours, Franklin, Tel: 414-425-1114.

ST. MICHAEL, WASHINGTON CO., ST. MICHAEL (1846), (German—Irish), [CEM] [JC 2] Rev. Edwin M. Kornath; Deacon Ralph E. Horner.
8883 Forestview Rd., Kewaskum, 53040. Email: stmickew@kmoraine.com.
Res.: 331 Main St., Kewaskum, 53040. Tel: 262-334-5270; Fax: 262-334-5233. Email: htkewaskum@alexssa.net.
Catechesis/Religious Program—Tel: 262-626-2650. Email: straubm@archmil.org. Mary Straub, D.R.E. Twinned with Holy Trinity. Students 49.

ST. PETER, FOND DU LAC CO., ST. PETER (1867), (German), Closed. For sacramental records through 1952, contact Archdiocese of Milwaukee Archives Office, Tel: 414-769-3407. For records after 1952, contact Holy Family, Fond du Lac, Tel: 920-921-0580.

SAUKVILLE, OZAUKEE CO., IMMACULATE CONCEPTION (1858) [CEM] Revs. Patrick Wendt, In Solidum Team Mod.; Thomas F. Lijewski, In Solidum Team Mem.; Mr. Timothy Charek, Dir. Admin. Svcs.
Res.: 145 W. Church St., 53080. Tel: 262-284-0276; Fax: 262-284-3090.
Catechesis/Religious Program—Tel: 262-284-0277. Students 92.

SHARON, WALWORTH CO., ST. CATHERINE (1854) [CEM] Mr. Thomas McKenna, Parish Dir.
Mailing Address: P.O. Box 502, 53585. Tel: 262-736-4615.
Res.: Tel: 815-520-3190.
Catechesis/Religious Program—Students 30.

SHEBOYGAN, SHEBOYGAN CO.

1—ST. CLEMENT (1914) [JC] Rev. James E. Connell; Deacon Baleriano O. Gonzalez.
Res.: 522 New York Ave., 53081. Tel: 920-457-4629; Fax: 920-452-2417. Email: parishoffice@stclementsheboygan.org.
Catechesis/Religious Program—824 Superior Ave., 53081. Tel: 920-452-0129. Collaborated with Holy Name of Jesus. Students 48.

2—SS. CYRIL AND METHODIUS (1910), (Slovenian), [CEM] Rev. Glenn E. Powers.
Office & Mailing Address: 2720 Henry St., 53081. Tel: 920-457-7110; Fax: 920-457-5885. Email: sscm@charter.net.
Church: 822 New Jersey Ave., 53081.
Catechesis/Religious Program—828 New Jersey Ave., 53081. Tel: 920-457-8422; Fax: 920-457-4001. 834 New Jersey Ave., 53081. Students 70.

3—ST. DOMINIC (1927), (German—Dutch), [JC] Rev. Alan D. Veik, O.F.M.Cap.; Deacon Donald J. Lydolph.
Res.: 2133 N. 22nd St., 53081. Tel: 920-458-7070; Fax: 920-458-3280. Email: dominic@stdominic.us. Web: www.stdominic.us.
School—2108 N. 21st St., 53081. Tel: 920-452-8747;

Fax: 920-458-4809. Peggy Henseler, Prin. Lay Teachers 13; Students 125.
Catechesis/Religious Program—Tel: 920-458-5390. Students 218.

4—HOLY NAME (1845), (German), [JC] Rev. James E. Connell.
Res.: 807 Superior Ave., 53081-3442. Tel: 920-458-7721; Fax: 920-459-9108. Email: holyname1@charter.net. Web: www.holynamesheboygan.org.
School—814 Superior Ave., 53081. Tel: 920-452-1571; Fax: 920-208-4371. Web: webpages.charter.net/hfs_school. Kay Miller, Prin. Lay Teachers 15; Students 180.
Catechesis/Religious Program—824 Superior Ave., 53081. Tel: 920-452-0129. Betty Macknick, C.R.E. (Gr. K-8); Dianne Marshall, Youth Min. (Gr. 9-12). Students 118.

5—IMMACULATE CONCEPTION (1903), (Lithuanian), [CEM] Rev. Glenn E. Powers.
Office: 2720 Henry St., 53081. Tel: 920-457-3967; Fax: 920-457-5885. Email: icparish@charter.net.
Res.: 2705 S. 14th St, 53081.
Christ Child Academy—2722 Henry St., 53081. Tel: 920-459-2660. Mark Ruedinger, Prin. Lay Teachers 14; Students 179.
Catechesis/Religious Program—834 New Jersey Ave., 53081. Tel: 920-457-8422. Email: sscmdre@archmil.org. Charles Yurk, D.R.E. Students 78.
Mission—St. Mary Assumption 2030 Assumption St., New Orleans, LA 70195.

6—ST. PETER CLAVER (1888), (German), [CEM] Rev. Richard J. Cerpich (Retired); Deacon Michael F. Burch, Parish Dir.; Sr. Marilyn Brodd, O.S.F., Pastoral Assoc.
Res.: 1444 S. Eleventh St., 53081. Tel: 920-457-9408; Fax: 920-803-2470. Email: spcparish@archmil.org. Web: www.spcparish.com.
Christ Child Academy—(Grades PreK-5), See Immaculate Conception for Details., Tel: 920-459-2663; Fax: 920-457-5885. Email: christ-child-academy@archmil.org.
Catechesis/Religious Program—822 New Jersey Ave., 53081. Tel: 920-452-2759. Barbara Leonhardt, D.R.E. Students 103.

SHEBOYGAN FALLS, SHEBOYGAN CO.

1—BLESSED TRINITY (2001), (German), [CEM] [JC 3], (Merger of St. Mary, Sheboygan Falls; St. Rose, Lima; and St. George, St. George.) Rev. Robert J. Lotz.
Rectory—327 Giddings Ave., 53085-1598. Tel: 920-467-4616; Fax: 920-467-4290. Email: sandy@blessedtrinityparish.org. Web: www.blessedtrinityparish.org.
Catechesis/Religious Program—Tel: 920-467-6282. Students 252.

2—ST. MARY (1896), (German), Closed. For sacramental records, contact Blessed Trinity, Sheboygan Falls, Tel: 920-467-4616.

SHOREWOOD, MILWAUKEE CO., ST. ROBERT (1912) Revs. Dennis A. Dirkx; Kevin McManaman; Elizabeth Cleveland, Business Mgr.; Lisa Lesjak, Dir. School Advancement.
Res.: 4019 N. Farwell Ave., 53211. Tel: 414-332-1164; Fax: 414-332-2599. Web: www.strobert.org.
School—2200 E. Capitol Dr., 53211. Tel: 414-332-1164, Ext. 3018; Fax: 414-332-7355. Lauren Beckmann, Prin. Lay Teachers 26; Students 316.
Catechesis/Religious Program—Tel: 414-332-1164, Ext. 3012. Gail DeFrancisco, D.R.E. Students 177.

SLINGER, WASHINGTON CO., ST. PETER (1856), (German), [CEM 2] Very Rev. Richard J. Stoffel.
Mailing Address: 208 E. Washington St., 53086.
Res.: 214 E. Washington St., 53086. Tel: 262-644-8083; Fax: 262-644-7951. Email: stpeter@nconnect.net. Web: www.stpeterslinger.com.
School—206 E. Washington St., 53086. Web: www-.stpeterslinger.com. Cheryl Jaeger, Prin. & Marketing Dir. Lay Teachers 6; Students 65.
Catechesis/Religious Program—Paul Rogers, D.R.E.; Joshua Dieterich, D.R.E. Students 428.

SOUTH MILWAUKEE, MILWAUKEE CO.

1—ST. ADALBERT (1898) Closed. For sacramental records, contact Divine Mercy, South Milwaukee, Tel: 414-762-6810.

2—DIVINE MERCY (2003) [JC] Revs. Robert Betz, Team Mod.; Thunkuchan Steve Varghese, S.A.C. (India), Team Mem.
Office: 695 College Ave., 53172. Tel: 414-762-6810; Fax: 414-762-2440. Email: dmparish@archmil.org. Web: www.divinemercysm.org.
Church: 800 Marquette Ave., 53172.
School—College Ave., 695 College Ave., 53172. Tel: 414-764-4360; Fax: 414-764-6740. Email: divinemercy@archmil.org. Judy Kalinowski, Prin. Tutors 1; Lay Teachers 15; Students 147.
Catechesis/Religious Program—Students 342.

3—ST. JOHN (1893), (Irish), Closed. For sacramental records, contact Divine Mercy, South Milwaukee, Tel: 414-762-6810.

4—ST. MARY (1893) Closed. For sacramental records, contact Divine Mercy, South Milwaukee, Tel: 414-762-6810.

5—ST. SYLVESTER (1962), (Polish—Irish), Closed. For sacramental records, contact Divine Mercy, South Milwaukee, Tel: 414-762-6810.

SPRINGVALE, COLUMBIA CO., ST. MARY (1858), (Irish), [CEM], See Immaculate Conception for Details. Very Rev. Michael L. Wild.
Mailing Address: 118 W. Main St., Waupun, 53963-1453. Tel: 920-324-5400; Fax: 920-324-1040.
Catechesis/Religious Program—Tel: 920-346-5110.

STURTEVANT, RACINE CO., ST. SEBASTIAN (1905) Rev. Paul L. Raczynski.
Res.: 3126 95th St., 53177. Tel: 262-886-4398.
Catechesis/Religious Program—Tel: 262-886-4420. Students 8.

THERESA, DODGE CO., ST. THERESA (1849) [CEM] Rev. Dennis G. Budka.
102 Church St., St. Theresa, 53091. Tel: 920-269-4429. Email: stmarytheresa@gmail.com. Mailing Address: 699 Milwaukee St., Lomira, 53048. Email: natheres@charter.net.
School—Consolidated Catholic School of Lomira-Theresa, Day care, before and after school care and pre-school., 105 W. Rock River St., 53091. Tel: 920-488-4543.
Catechesis/Religious Program—Tel: 920-269-7273; Fax: 920-269-7359. Stephen C. Martin, D.R.E. Students 41.

THIENSVILLE, OZAUKEE CO., ST. CECILIA (1919) Closed. For sacramental records, contact Lumen Christi, Mequon, Tel: 262-242-7967.

THOMPSON, WASHINGTON CO., ST. PATRICK (Tn. Erin) (1855), (Irish), Closed. For sacramental records, contact St. Kilian, Hartford, Tel: 262-673-4831.

TWIN LAKES, KENOSHA CO., ST. JOHN THE EVANGELIST (1932) [CEM] Deacon Stanley J. Lowe, Parish Dir.; Revs. Lawrence J. Chapman; Anthony J. Russo.
Res.: 701 N. Lake Ave., 53181. Tel: 262-877-2557; Fax: 262-877-2431.
Catechesis/Religious Program—Tel: 262-877-2557, Ext. 223. Students 179.

UNION GROVE, RACINE CO., ST. ROBERT BELLARMINE (1965) Rev. Robert C. Kacalo.
Res.: 3320 S. Colony Ave., 53182. Tel: 262-878-3476; Fax: 262-878-0194. Email: rstrobertbella@wi.rr.com. Web: www.stmary-strobert.org.
Catechesis/Religious Program—Kevin Phillips, Dir. Christian Formation. Students 294.

WATERFORD, RACINE CO., ST. THOMAS AQUINAS (1851) [CEM] Rev. Eugene J. Doda Jr.; Deacons Carl A. Mahnke, (Retired); Jim Nickel; Joseph H. Hying, (Retired).
Res.: 305 S. First St., 53185. Tel: 262-534-2255; Fax: 262-534-2929. Email: rectory@stthomas.pvt.k12.wi.us.
School—Tel: 262-534-2265; Fax: 262-534-5549. Web: www.stthomaswaterford.org. Lay Teachers 17; Students 199.
Catechesis/Religious Program—Students 450.

WAUKESHA, WAUKESHA CO.

1—ST. JOHN NEUMANN (1981) Rev. John P. Schreiter; Ray Ellingen, Dir., Admin. Svcs.
Mailing Address: 2400 W. State Hwy. 59, 53189-6323. Tel: 262-549-0223; Fax: 262-549-0444.
School—Waukesha Catholic School System, (Grades PreK-8) Tel: 262-896-2920 (St. William); 262-896-2930 (St. Joseph); 262-896-2932 (St. Mary); Fax: 262-896-2925.
Catechesis/Religious Program—Jeanne Nelson, Lifelong Faith Formation Dir. Students 85.

2—ST. JOSEPH (1844), (Hispanic), Rev. William W. Key; Deacons Aristeo Ortiz; Antonio Palacios; Jorge Benavente.
Parish Office—818 N. East Ave., 53186. Tel: 262-542-2589; Fax: 262-542-2570.
School—Waukesha Catholic School System, (Grades 6-8), 841 Martin St., 53186. Tel: 262-896-2930; Fax: 262-896-2935. Mrs. Kathleen Rempe, Prin.
Catechesis/Religious Program—Tel: 262-542-2589, Ext. 110. Juana Avila Palacios, D.R.E. Students 250.

3—ST. MARY (1950) Rev. Howard G. Haase.
Res.: 225 S. Hartwell Ave., 53186-6400. Tel: 262-547-6555; Fax: 262-547-6714. Email: office@stmarywk.org. Web: www.stmarywaukesha.4lpi.com.
School—School is a campus of the Waukesha Catholic School System., 520 E. Newhall Ave., 53186. Tel: 262-896-2932; Fax: 262-896-2931. Web: www.waukeshacatholicschoolsystem.org.
Catechesis/Religious Program—Mr. Jim Gill, D.R.E. Students 320.

4—ST. WILLIAM (1957) [JC] Very Rev. Curt J. Frederick; Rev. Kevin Barnekow; Charlotte Villwock, Liturgy/Music Min.
Res.: 440 N. Moreland Blvd., 53188. Tel: 262-349-9585; Fax: 262-547-3616. Email: frederick@archmil.org. Web: swparish.org.
School—Waukesha Catholic, (Grades PreK-5), 444 N. Moreland Blvd., 53188. Tel: 262-896-2920; Fax: 262-896-2925. Robert Radomski, Campus Prin.
Catechesis/Religious Program—Tel: 262-547-2763, Ext. 206. Kay Hokans, D.R.E. (Child Min.); Barb Gawlik, D.R.E. (Youth Min.); Cindy Bergland, D.R.E. (Adult & Family Min.). Students 698.

WAUPUN, FOND DU LAC CO., ST. JOSEPH (1866), (Irish), [CEM], Also serves St. Brendan, Brandon & St. Mary, Springvale. Very Rev. Michael L. Wild.
Office: 118 W. Main St., 53963. Tel: 920-324-5400. Email: office@stjoeschurch.org. Web: www.stjoeschurch.org.
Catechesis/Religious Program—Tel: 920-324-3891. Email: childfam@stjoeschurch.org. Students 113.

WAUWATOSA, MILWAUKEE CO.

1—ST. BERNARD (1911), (Irish), Rev. Michael Barrett.
Res.: 7474 Harwood Ave., 53213. Tel: 414-258-4320; Fax: 414-258-9972. Email: admin@stbernardparish.org. Web: www.stbernardparish.org.
School—Wauwatosa Catholic School, 1500 Wauwatosa Ave., 53213. Tel: 414-258-9977. Julia D'Amato, Prin. Religious 1; Lay Teachers 15; Students 200.
Catechesis/Religious Program—Students 98.

2—CHRIST KING (1939) Rev. Msgr. T. George Gajdos; Rev. John Burns; Deacon Arthur C. Dallman.
Res.: 2604 N. Swan Blvd., 53226. Tel: 414-258-2604; Fax: 414-258-1993. Email: parish@christkingparish.org. Web: www.christkingparish.
School—2646 N. Swan Blvd., 53226. Tel: 414-258-4160; Fax: 414-258-0916. Gregory Meuler, Prin. Lay Teachers 28; Students 421.
Catechesis/Religious Program—Liz Kuhn, D.R.E. Students 238.

3—ST. JOSEPH CONGREGATION (1855) Rev. James E. Kimla.
Mailing Address: 12130 W. Center St., 53222-4096. Email: brenda@stjoetosa.archmil.org. Web: www.stjoetosa.com.
School—2750 N. 122nd St., 53222. Fax: 414-771-9826. Linda Cooney, Prin. Lay Teachers 16; Students 218.
Catechesis/Religious Program—Students 267.

4—ST. JUDE THE APOSTLE (1928) Rev. Charles Conley; Deacon Donald A. Borkowski; James Pluer, Liturgy/Music Dir.; Lynn Musolf, Dir. Admin. Svcs. In Res., Rev. Juvenalis Asantemungu (Tanzania).
Res.: 734 Glenview Ave., 53213. Tel: 414-258-8821; Fax: 414-258-7371. Web: www.stjudewauwatosa.org.
School—800 Glenview Ave., 53213. Tel: 414-771-1520; Fax: 414-771-3748. Catherine LaDien, Prin. Sisters 1; Lay Teachers 32; Students 486.
Catechesis/Religious Program—Tel: 414-259-0950. Gary Heun, D.R.E. Students 179.

5—ST. PIUS X (1952) Rev. Robert Marsicek, S.D.S.
Res.: 2506 Wauwatosa Ave., 53213. Tel: 414-453-3875; Fax: 414-453-7570. Email: stpiusx@mcleodusa.net. Web: st.piusparish.org.
School—7474 Harwood Ave., 53213. Tel: 414-258-4320; Fax: 414-258-9972. Lay Teachers 20; Students 204.
Catechesis/Religious Program—Students 194.

WAYNE, WASHINGTON CO., ST. BRIDGET, Closed. For sacramental records, contact Holy Trinity, Kewaskum, Tel: 262-626-2860.

WEST ALLIS, MILWAUKEE CO.

1—ST. ALOYSIUS GONZAGA (1920) Revs. Jeffery A. Prasser; Thomas Vathappallil, M.C.B.S.
Rectory—1414 S. 93rd St., 53214. Tel: 414-476-3803; Fax: 414-774-7727. Email: staloysius@archmil.org. Web: www.staloysius.41pi.com.
Catechesis/Religious Program—Tel: 414-727-4451. Jan Grosshadl, D.R.E. Students 82.

2—ST. AUGUSTINE (1928), (Croatian), [CEM] Rev. Lawrence Frankovich, O.F.M.
Res.: 6762 W. Rogers St., 53219. Tel: 414-541-5207; Fax: 414-541-0273. Email: staugwa@att.net.
See Mary Queen of Saints Catholic Academy under Consolidated Elementary Schools located in the Institution section.
Catechesis/Religious Program—6753 W. Rogers St., 53219. Students 35.

3—HOLY ASSUMPTION (1902) Rev. Leonard R. Copeland, O.C.D.; Deacon George P. Sherman. In Res., Rev. Robert E. Massey (Retired).
Res.: 1525 S. 71st St., 53214. Tel: 414-774-3010; Fax: 414-774-3735. Email: haparish@archmil.org. Web: www.haparish.org.
Catechesis/Religious Program—Students 31.

4—IMMACULATE HEART OF MARY (1948) Revs. Jeffery A. Prasser; Thomas Vathappallil, M.C.B.S.; Deacons Dennis E. Fietz; Walter Henry; Keith R. Marx.
Res.: 1121 S. 116th St., 53214. Tel: 414-453-5192; Fax: 414-453-0137. Email: info@ihmwestallis.com. Web: ihmwestallis.com.
Catechesis/Religious Program—Tel: 414-453-0300. Web: ihmwestallis.com. Students 65.

5—ST. JOSEPH (1909), (Polish), Closed. For sacramental records, contact Archdiocese of Milwaukee Archives Office, Tel: 414-769-3407.

6—ST. MARY, HELP OF CHRISTIANS (1907), (Slovenian), [CEM] Closed. For sacramental records, contact Archdiocese of Milwaukee Archives Office, Tel: 414-769-3407.

7—MARY, QUEEN OF HEAVEN (1958) Revs. Jeffery A. Prasser; Thomas Vathappallil, M.C.B.S.
Office: 2322 S. 106th St., 53227. Tel: 414-328-5566; Fax: 414-328-5561.
See Mary Queen of Saints Academy in the Institution Section listed under Consolidated Elementary schools.
Catechesis/Religious Program—Tel: 414-328-5560. Linda Koch, D.R.E. Students 98.

8—OUR LADY OF MT. CARMEL (1938), (Italian), Closed. For sacramental records, contact Archdiocese of Milwaukee Archives Office, Tel: 414-769-3407.

9—ST. RITA (1924) Rev. Dennis M. Witz.
Res.: 2318 S. 61st St., 53219. Tel: 414-541-7515; Fax: 414-541-7568. Email: stritaparishwa@wi.rr.com. Web: stritaparish-westallis.4lpi.com.
See Mary Queen of Saints Catholic Academy Association under Consolidated Elementary Schools located in the Institution section.
Catechesis/Religious Program—Tel: 414-541-7515. Karen Barczak, D.R.E. Students 116.

WEST BEND, WASHINGTON CO.

1—ST. FRANCES CABRINI (1955) Rev. Nathan D. Reesman, Admin.; Deacons Michael S. Koebel; Ronald Schneider.
Parish Office—1025 S. 7th Ave., 53095. Tel: 262-338-2366, Ext. 13; Fax: 262-338-2348. Web: www.saintfrancescabrini.com.
School—529 Hawthorn Dr., 53095. Tel: 262-334-7142; Fax: 262-334-8168. Web: stfcabrini.com. Mark Quinn, Prin. Lay Teachers 31; Students 407.
Catechesis/Religious Program—Tel: 262-334-9511. Judy Schroeder, D.R.E. Students 405.

2—HOLY ANGELS (1852) [CEM] Rev. Gerald W. Brittain; Deacon Mark Jansen.
Res.: 138 N. 8th Ave., 53095. Tel: 262-334-3038; Fax: 262-334-3088. Email: parish@hawb.org. Web: hawb.org.
School—230 N. 8th Ave., 53095. Tel: 262-338-1148. Email: has@has.pvt.k12.wi.us. Web: www.has.pvt.k12.wi.us. Mike Sternig, Prin. Lay Teachers 21; Students 327.
Catechesis/Religious Program—Tel: 414-334-9393. Email: dre@hawb.org. Joseph Heit, D.R.E. Students 363.

3—IMMACULATE CONCEPTION (1857) [CEM 2] Rev. John J. Radetski; Dan Schroeder, Pastoral Assoc.; Deacon James Chrisien; Marilyn Muraski, Music Coord.
Res.: 406 Jefferson St., 53090. Tel: 262-338-5600; Fax: 262-335-2475. Email: stmy@stmaryparishwb.org. Web: www.stmaryparishwb.org.
School—415 Roosevelt St., 53090. Tel: 262-338-5602. Sue Nygaard, Prin. Lay Teachers 5; Students 106.
Catechesis/Religious Program—Tel: 262-338-5605. Mary Abel, D.R.E. Students 190.

WHITEFISH BAY, MILWAUKEE CO.

1—HOLY FAMILY (1949) Revs. Dennis A. Dirkx; Kevin McManaman. In Res., Rev. James E. Kimla.
Office: 4825 N. Wildwood Ave., 53217. Tel: 414-332-9220; Fax: 414-961-7396. Email: holyfam@hfparish.org. Web: www.hfparish.org.
School—4849 N. Wildwood Ave., 53217. Tel: 414-332-8175; Fax: 414-961-7196. Email: hfpschool@hfparish.org. Angela Little, Prin. Lay Teachers 20; Students 201.
Catechesis/Religious Program—Tel: 414-332-8156; Fax: 414-961-7396. Email: hfreled@hfparish.org. Gail DeFrancisco, D.R.E. Students 313.

2—ST. MONICA (1923) Revs. Jerome Herda; Joseph J. Shimek; Paul J. Fliss; Deacon Eugene E. Van Garsse. In Res., Rev. John R. Paczesny (Retired).
Res.: 160 E. Silver Spring Dr., 53217. Tel: 414-332-1576; 414-332-1577; Fax: 414-332-2462. Email: office@st-monica.org. Web: www.st-monica.org.
School—5635 N. Santa Monica Blvd., 53217. Tel: 414-332-3660; Fax: 414-332-8649. Web: www.st-monicaschool.org. Julie Robinson, Prin. Lay Teachers 31; Students 421.
Catechesis/Religious Program—Tel: 414-964-8780; Fax: 414-964-2493. Colleen Hutt, D.R.E. Students 404.

WHITEWATER, WALWORTH CO., ST. PATRICK (1853) [CEM] Rev. Thomas Perrin, S.D.S.
Office: 1235 W. Main St., 53190-1620. Tel: 262-473-3143; Fax: 262-473-3052.
Catechesis/Religious Program—Tel: 262-473-8834. Mary Sue Reutebuch, Dir Faith Formation. Students 139.

WILMOT, KENOSHA CO., HOLY NAME OF JESUS (1856) [CEM] Closed. For sacramental records, contact Holy Cross, Bristol, Tel: 262-857-2068.

WIND LAKE, RACINE CO., ST. CLARE (1965) Rev. Aurelio H. Perez.
Res. & Mailing Address: Parish Office, 7616 Fritz St., 53185. Tel: 262-895-2729; Fax: 262-895-3601. Email: clarewl@tds.net.
Catechesis/Religious Program—Tel: 262-895-2797. Judee Weber, Dir., Christian Formation. Students 222.

WOODHULL, FOND DU LAC CO., ST. JOHN THE BAPTIST, Closed. For sacramental records, contact Our Risen Savior, Eldorado, Tel: 920-922-2412.

WOODLAND, DODGE N CO., ST. MARY, (German), [CEM], Also serves St. Matthew, Neosho & St. John, Rubicon. Rev. Alois VanBeek.
Mailing Address: 148 W. Lehman St, P.O. Box 45, Neosho, 53059. Tel: 920-625-3144; Fax: 920-625-2143. Email: mattneo3@nconnect.net. Web: mjmtriparish.org.
Catechesis/Religious Program—Combined with St. Matthew, Neosho., Tel: 920-625-3092. Students 37.

Chaplains of Public Institutions

MILWAUKEE. *St. Luke's Medical Center*, 2900 W. Oklahoma Ave., 53215.
Milwaukee County House of Correction. Attended by St. James, Franklin.
Milwaukee County Jail. Bro. Jerome Smith, O.F.M.Cap., Chap.

JUNEAU. *Dodge County Center*. Attended by Sacred Heart, Horicon.

KENOSHA. *Kenosha Hospital and Medical Center*, 6308 8th Ave., 53143-5082. Vacant.

WALES. *Ethan Allen School for Boys*, P.O. Box 900, 53183-0900. Tel: 414-646-3341. Vacant.

WAUWATOSA. *Froedtert Memorial Lutheran Hospital*, 9200 W. Wisconsin Ave., 53226.

WEST ALLIS. *West Allis Memorial Hospital*, 8901 W. Lincoln Ave., 53227. Tel: 414-328-6000.

WOOD. *Veterans Administration Medical Center* 53193. Tel: 414-384-2000. Rev. Norman R. Oswald, Chief, Chap. Svc.

Special Assignment:
Very Revs.—
Hartmann, Paul B.R., M.Div., J.C.L., Metropolitan Tribunal, 3501 S. Lake Dr., P.O. Box 070912, 53207-0912. Pres., Catholic Memorial High School, 601 E. College Ave., Waukesha, 53186-5538. Tel: 262-542-7101, Ext. 243
Hemsing, John D., Rector, St. Francis de Sales Seminary, 3257 S. Lake Dr., St. Francis, 53235.
Heppe, Patrick E., Dir. Ordained & Lay Ecclesiastical Min., 3501 S. Lake Dr., P.O. Box 070912, 53207-0912. Tel: 414-769-3490
Revs.—
Avella, Steven M., Faculty, Marquette University, 3222 S. 29th St., 53215.
Berger, Peter, Dir., Vocations Office, 3257 S. Lake Dr., St. Francis, 53235.
Bustos, Javier, S.T.D., Dir., Sacred Heart School of Theology Faculty, P.O. Box 429, Hales Corners, 53130-0429.
Cane-Gombau, Pere, Missionary Community of St. Paul, 1505 Howard St., Racine, 53404.
Cirujeda, Pablo, Missionary Community of St. Paul, 1505 Howard St., Racine, 53404.
Connell, James E., J.C.D., Vice Chancellor, Archdiocese of Milwaukee, 3501 S. Lake Dr., P.O. Box 07912, 53207-0912. Tel: 414-769-3338
DeVries, Thomas D., Faculty, St. Francis de Sales Seminary, 3257 S. Lake Dr., St. Francis, 53235.
Duffy, James H., Madonna House, Combermere ON KOJ 1LO Canada.
Gaberle, Jiri, Ministry to Healthcare Facilities, 4800 Coldspring Rd. #28, Greenfield, 53220.
Heck, Quintin T., Clement Zablocki VA Medical Center, 5000 W. National Ave., 53295. Tel: 414-384-2000, Ext. 42159
Keefe, Charles R., Pastoral Care Dir., Milwaukee Catholic Home, 2462 N. Prospect Ave., 53211-4462.
Lampe, Stephen J., M.Div., S.S.L., S.T.D., Faculty, Cardinal Stritch Univ., 6801 N. Yates Rd., 53217-3985. Tel: 414-410-4000, Ext. 4830
Lazarski, Marvin I., Arch. Cemetery System, 3801 W. Morgan Ave., 53321. Tel: 414-645-0611
Lightner, Michael, Chap., St. Catherine of Alexandria Catholic Campus Ministry Center, Inc., 3001 N. Downer Ave., 53211.
Lobacz, James E., Dir., Archbishop's Office and Vicar for Senior Priests, P.O. Box 070912, 53207-0912.
Massingale, Bryan N., Marquette University, P.O.Box 1881, 53202-1881. (Faculty)
O'Brien, Timothy J., Faculty, Marquette University, 8521 Kenyon Ave., Wauwatosa, 53226.
Oswald, Norman R., Chief Chap., Veterans Administrative Medical Center, 5000 W. National Ave., 53295.
Rodriguez, Rafael G., Dir. Formation & Dean Students, St. Francis de Sales Seminary, 3257 S. Lake Dr., St. Francis, 53235.
Stanfield, William L., Dir., Vice Rector & Dean Formation, St. Francis Seminary, Continuing Formation of Clergy, 3257 S. Lake Dr., St. Francis, 53235. Tel: 414-747-6410

On Duty Outside the Archdiocese:
Revs.—
Brundage, Thomas T., M.Div., J.C.L., Tribunal, Archdiocese Anchorage, Pastoral Center, 225 Cordova St., Anchorage, AK 99501.
Colom, Marti, La Sagrada Familia, Apartado 53, Azua, Dominican Republic.
Kinney, M. Eugene, St. Anthony of Padua, 5081 N. Rainbow Blvd., #107, Las Vegas, NV 89130.
Lamb, Matthew L., Faculty, Ave Maria University, 5050 Ave Maria Blvd., Immokalee, FL 34142-9505.
Malloy, Francis X., Bay Pines VA Medical Center, Bay Pines FL, 33744
McDermott, Robert T., St. Roch Parish, 6052 Waterman Blvd., St. Louis, MO 63112.
Mikalofsky, Hilarion A., Ch. Lt. Col. (Retired), 82 Edgewater Dr., Lakeside City, TX 76308.
Olszyk, Thomas P., J.C.L., Tribunal, Military Archdiocese, P.O. Box 4469, Washington, DC 20017-0469.
Pocernich, Eugene, Resurrection Medical Center, 7435 Talcott Ave., Chicago, IL 60631.
Witczak, Michael G., M.Div., S.L.D., Faculty, Catholic University of America, 620 Michigan Ave, NE, Washington, DC 20064.

On Leave:
Rev.—
Dulek, Lawrence V.

Study Leave:
Rev.—
Martin Pinillos, Ricardo, Catholic University of America, Washington, DC 20064.

Personal Leave:
Revs.—
Fait, Thomas G.
Lavann, Jason
Lee, Roy
Richter, Robert J.

Sick Leave:
Rev.—
Kienzle, Jerome C.

Awaiting Assignment:
Rev. Msgr.—
Shecterle, Ross A.
Rev.—
Nowicki, Gary D.

Retired:
Most Revs.—
Sklba, Richard J., S.S.L., S.T.D.
Weakland, Rembert G., O.S.B.
Very Rev.—
Last, Carl A., 21452 Keating Way, Lutz, FL 33549.
Revs.—
Acker, Karl H., Wilson Commons, 1400 W. Sonata Dr., #140, 53221.
Anderson, Joseph G., 17452 W. Lincoln Ave., New Berlin, 53146.
Andre, Leonard J., Alexian Village, 7979 Glenbrook Rd., #4021, 53223.
Arciszewski, Gilbert, 9151 S. Aspen Dr., #9, Oak Creek, 53154.
Artmann, Robert J., 523 Kennedy Dr., Northglenn, CO 80234.
Bales, Robert, St. Albert the Great, 2420 St. Albert Dr., Sun Prairie, 53590-9336.
Baran, Joseph L., 2022 N. 86th St., Wauwatosa, 53226-2745.
Baranowski, Stanley A., W782 County Rd. A, Randolph, 53956.
Barbian, Leonard M., 6750 Parkedge Cir., Franklin, 53132.
Berghammer, Robert J., 201 A-J Ct., Theresa, 53091.
Bittner, Wayne W., 306 N. Highland Ave., #327, Plymouth, 53073.
Brady, James J., Clement Manor, 9339 W. Howard Ave., #212, Greenfield, 53228.
Brahm, Harvey, San Camillo #725, 10200 W. Bluemound Rd., Wauwatosa, 53226.
Breitbach, Richard C., 14140 Regis St., Brookfield, 53005.
Brophy, John L., 18450 Emerald Dr., Unit A, Brookfield, 53045.
Carek, Peter P., St. Anne Salvatorian Campus, 3800 N. 92nd St., #123A, 53222.
Carroll, Edward E., 3524 7th Ave. Apt. 127, Kenosha, 53140.

Cera, James B., Alexian Village #116, 9301 N. 76th St., 53223.
Cerpich, Richard J., 2532 S. 7th St., Sheboygan, 53081.
Cunningham, Joseph L., W 369 S10450 Shearer Rd., Eagle, 53119.
Dammeir, James L., 4208 N. 16th St., 53209-6923.
Daniels, Paul A., 2602 S. 94th St., 53227.
Debski, Joseph E., 2209 Browns Lake Dr. #105, Burlington, 53105.
DeLeers, Stephen V., 1742 N. Prospect Ave., #313, 53202.
Derfus, Kenneth J., Camillus Court East #205, 10100 W. Bluemound Rd., Wauwatosa, 53226.
Dietzler, William J., 4127 81st Pl., Kenosha, 53142.
Dineen, Michael P., 1016 North Ave., Sheboygan, 53083.
Dolezal, Richard R., 5053 N. Ridgeway, Chicago, IL 60625-6021.
Drenzek, Peter C., S70 W17635 Muskego Dr., Muskego, 53150.
Endejan, John, 9410 W. Loomis Rd., #5, Franklin, 53132.
Ernster, James M., 570 Hwy. D, Belgium, 53004.
Eschweiler, Edward R., Clement Manor, 9405 W. Howard Ave., #369, Greenfield, 53228.
Esser, Paul M., P.O. Box 148, Nashotah, 53058.
Filut, David C., W157 S7275 Quitewood Dr., Muskego, 53150.
Fleischmann, George R., High Grove, 3940 S. Prairie Hill Ln., #215, Greenfield, 53228.
Frederick, Joseph B., 237 Southtowne Pl., #BB212, South Milwaukee, 53172.
Gloudeman, Robert J., 10020 Whitnall Edge Dr. # D, Franklin, 53132.
Gosma, Robert D., W379 S4988 W. Pretty Lake Rd., Dousman, 53118.
Grellinger, R. Michael, 250 Meadow Ln., Hartland, 53029-1832.
Gurath, Guy G., 211 Fredonia Ave., Fredonia, 53021.
Haas, Joseph H., P.O. Box 14363, West Allis, 53214-0363.
Hammer, Michael J., 709 E. Juneau Ave., #704, 53202.
Hauser, Gerald B., 21025 George Hunt Circle, #1203, Waukesha, 53186.
Heinze, Arthur G., 9032 W. Elm Ct., Unit D, Franklin, 53132.
Hentzner, John T., San Camillo, 10200 W. Bluemound Rd., #1021, Wauwatosa, 53226.
Hessel, Gerald J., 2001 41st St., Kenosha, 53140-5615.
Hmircik, Donald A., 237 Winnebago St., #214, North Fond Du Lac, 54937.
Hornacek, Joseph F., 1355 Hillwood Blvd., Unit C, Pewaukee, 53072.
Hudziak, Jerome M., Ph.D., 10020 Whitnall Edge Dr., Unit C, Franklin, 53132.
Hussli, Edward J., HCR1, Box 81, Clam Lake, 54517.
Janette, Paul, San Camillo, 10200 W. Bluemound Rd., #402, Wauwatosa, 53226.
Johnson, Howard J., W6332 Lake Ellen Dr., Cascade, 53011.
Kasten, Edward F., Alexian Village, 7979 W. Glenbrook Rd., #6002, 53223.
Kazmierczak, Carl M., 8051 W. Leroy Ave., 53220.
Klauck, Stanley B., Alexian Village, 9301 N. 76th St. #343, 53223.
Klemme, Dennis C., J.C.D., W267 N2515 Meadowbrook Rd., Pewaukee, 53072.
Klink, Anthony G., P.O. Box 93, Berlin, 54923.
Knoebel, Thomas L., Ph.D., M.Div., 7569 W. Tuckaway Pines Cir., Franklin, 53132.
Konkel, Eugene J., S.S., St. Patrick's Seminary & Univ., 320 Middlefield Rd., Menlo Park, CA 94025-3563.
Lasecki, Daniel J., 1601 Division Ave., Sheboygan, 53083.
Le Mieux, Thomas A., P.O. Box 210048, 53221-8001.
Lippert, Paul R., Box 238, Plainfield, 54966-0238.
Lisowski, Edward E., P.O. Box 210182, 53221.
Loehr, Charles D., St. Francis Home, 345 E. 1st St., #231, Fond Du Lac, 54935.
Loehr, James P., 739 Roosevelt Ave., Oconomowoc, 53066.
Luljak, Louis P., 120 Hibiscus Wood Ct., #130, Deltona, FL 32725.
Macoskie, Melvin H., 280 Birch Rock Way, C-9, Mukwonago, 53149.
Maney, Robert L., 3301 S. 93rd St., #107, 53227.
Marek, Dean V., 1965 Tiffany Cove Ln., S.W., Rochester, MN 55902-1125.
Massey, Robert E., 1525 S. 71st St., West Allis, 53214-4893.
Mateljan, Roy A., 868 Americana Dr., Fond Du Lac, 54935-2954.
Matt, Erwin H., Juniper Court #103, 3209 S. Lake Dr., St. Francis, 53235.
Metz, Kenneth J., All Souls Catholic Church, 301 W. 8th St., Sanford, FL 32771.
Michalski, Melvin E., Ph.L., Th.D., 3257 S. Lake Dr., St. Francis, 53235.
Miralbes-Drago, Julio E., P.O. Box 070912, 53207-0912.
Mirsberger, Richard E., 9995 W. North Ave. #353, Wauwatosa, 53226.
Molter, Richard J., 6545 Mariner Dr., #6, Racine, 53406.
Mueller, Robert F., Camillus Court E. #301, 10100 W. Bluemond Rd., Wauwatosa, 53226.
Murphy, Daniel T., 4260 S. 94th St., Greenfield, 53228.
Murray, William F., Archdiocese of Milwaukee, P.O. Box 070912, 53207-0912.
Nawrocki, Robert W., 3589A S. 14th St., 53221.
Nelson, Andrew L., 2525 S. Shore Dr., #21F, 53207.
Novotny, Robert J., Wilson Commons, 1400 Sonata Dr., #223, 53221.
Orzechowski, Walter B., N8180 Lakeview Rd., Fond du Lac, 54935.
Paczesny, John R., 160 E. Silver Spring Dr., Whitefish Bay, 53217.
Pulice, John J., 2325 W. Jonathan Dr., Oak Creek, 53154.
Rausch, John W., Box 475, Eagle, 53119.
Rebatzki, George M., 17330 W. Birch Dr. #102, Brookfield, 53045.
Repenshek, Jerome V., 2060 Rainbow Lakes, Unit 216, West Bend, 53090.
Richetta, John J., 4014 81st St., Kenosha, 53142.
Rinzel, Jerome A., 121 River Ct., Theresa, 53091-9548.
Rodriguez, Robert, 502 Amber Horizon St., Henderson, NV 89015.
Roensch, Frederick J., P.O. Box 210, Nashotah, 53058.
Roscioli, Dominic J., 5412 23rd Ave., Kenosha, 53140-3505.
Safiejko, Edward M., 10420 Plum Tree Cir., #102, Hales Corners, 53130.
Sanfelippo, Frank J., Alexian Village, 7979 W. Glenbrook Rd., #6017, 53223.
Scheuerell, Charles A., P.O. Box 211, Nashotah, 53058.
Schlenker, Richard J., Wilson Commons #223, 1400 Sonata Dr., 53221.
Schmidt, Donald, Marquette Manor, 2409 10th Ave., Unit 10, South Milwaukee, 53172.
Schmitz, John A., 1011 Berlin Rd., Ripon, 54971.
Schneider, Karl J., 8523 W. Hawthorne Ave., Wauwatosa, 53226.
Schubert, Herbert, 5104 S. Hidden Dr., # 21, Greenfield, 53221.
Schwartz, Norman R., 3209 S. Lake Dr., #412, St. Francis, 53235.
Sepich, Lawrence, 8638 Westlake Dr., Greendale, 53129.
Sippel, Bernard S., M.Div., 10300 W. Bluemound Rd., #220, Wauwatosa, 53226.
Sippel, Edward F., 519 W. 11th St., Fond du Lac, 54935.
Skeris, Robert A., 722 Dillingham Ave., Sheboygan, 53081.
Slodowski, Bruno, 5116 22nd Ave., Kenosha, 53140.
Sommer, Allan J., 8036 W. Manor Cir., 53223.
Stangel, Mark J., Clement Manor, 9405 W. Howard Ave., #358, Greenfield, 53228.
Strupp, James A., 580 S. 18th Ave., West Bend, 53095-3755.
Sturm, Michael O., W192 N16330 Lea Fon Cir., Jackson, 53037-9569.
Surges, Robert F., S76 W16851 Gregory Dr., Unit C, Muskego, 53150.
Suriano, Thomas, 5101 W. Center St., 53210-2361.
Talaska, Richard J., 8891 Woodbridge Dr., Greendale, 53129.
Theisen, John J., 536 Lake Dr., Random Lake, 53075.
Thielen, Jeffrey M., 3134 Wood Rd., Unit 3, Racine, 53406-6202.
Tikalsky, Russell F., 2318 S. 61st St., West Allis, 53219.
Tino, Robert F., 6817 Canterwood Dr., S.E., Olympia, WA 98513-6510.
Twomey, John E., The Heritage #318, 3223 North St., East Troy, 53120.
Uhen, Cletus V., St. Monica's Home, 3920 N. Green Bay Rd., Racine, 53404.
Van Abel, John W., 235 Tamarack Dr., #8, Lake Mills, 53551.
Van Vlaenderen, Leonard S., P.O. Box 100522, Cudahy, 53110.
Venne, R. Thomas, 802 N. Jackson Ave., 53202.
Verberg, Richard R., 8565 W. Waterford Ave., #4, Greenfield, 53228.
Verhalen, Charles J., Camillus Health Center, 10101 W. Wisconsin Ave., #1124, Wauwatosa, 53226.
Vogel, Walter J., 6845 S. 68th St., #104, Franklin, 53132-8239.
Vojtik, James P., W228 S2376 Oriole Dr., Waukesha, 53186.
Walker, Thomas J., 17197 S.W. Smith Ave., #13, Sherwood, OR 97140.
Wawrzyniakowski, Edward J., N7594 Sandy Beach Rd., Fond du Lac, 54937.
Weis, Denis P., 322 N. 90th St., 53226.
Weishar, Paul M., The Gables at Germantown, N109 W17110 Ava Cir. #315, Germantown, 53022.
Wester, Charles H., N4346 Mercury Ln., Eden, 53019.
Whalen, William, W3327 Orchard Ave., Green Lake, 54941.
Wheatley, Charles, 210 Glen Este Blvd., Haines City, FL 33844.
Wilimek, Louis, 1833 Northwood Ct., Sheboygan, 53081.
Winkler, Eugene, Clement Manor, 3939 S. 92nd St., #120, Greenfield, 53228.
Witon, Russell F., 11515 W. Cleveland Ave., # 303A, West Allis, 53227.
Wittliff, Thomas F., 2260 S. 4th St., 53207.
Wolf, Joseph A., N84 W13920 Fond du Lac Ave., Menomonee Falls, 53051.
Zerkel, Donald F., P.O. Box 74, Newburg, 53060.
Zwaska, Victor L., Westwood, 925 Kenwood Dr., #3172, Duluth, MN 55811.

Permanent Deacons:
Acosta, Carlos R., (Retired)
Aird, Gordon, St. Francis Borgia, Cedarburg; (Diocese of Phoenix)
Aschenbrener, James L., (Retired)
Backes, David J., Divine Mercy, South Milwaukee
Banach, James D., St. Gregory the Great, Milwaukee
Banach, William A., Basilica of St. Josaphat, Milwaukee
Benavente, Jorge, St. Joseph, Waukesha
Blas, Franciso, Cristo Rey, Racine
Blaze, Edward, All Saints, Milwaukee
Borkowski, Donald A., St. Jude the Apostle, Wauwatosa
Brah, Eugene D., Mary Queen of Heaven, West Allis
Braun, Warren D., (Retired)
Brousseau, Gerald A., (Retired)
Brown, Richard J., St. Joseph, Big Bend
Burch, Michael F., St. Peter Claver, Sheboygan
Burmeister, Dan, St. Lucy, Racine
Burns, John R., St. Mary, Hales Corners
Buth, Robert H., St. Mary's, Menomonee Falls
Buyck, Gerald W., (Out of Archdiocese)
Campbell, Scott, St. William, Waukesha
Cebrzynski, Stanley, (Retired)
Cesarec, Michael E., (Retired)
Chalhoub, Robert, (Retired)
Champagne, John I., St. Benedict the Moor, Milwaukee
Chmielewski, Michael J., Holy Apostles, New Berlin
Chrisien, James, (Personal Leave)
Clark, William, St. Anne, Pleasant Prairie; (Archdiocese of Chicago)
Coca, Emilio, (Retired), St. Patrick, Racine
Cody, Edward F., St. Katharine Drexel, Beaver Dam
Collins, Dean J., Mother of Good Counsel, Milwaukee
Connors, Joseph, (Retired)
Copson, Jeffrey J., St. Elizabeth Ann Seton, New Berlin
Cornejo, Carlos, St. Anthony, Milwaukee
D'Alessio, John, St. Elizabeth Ann Seton, New Berlin
Dahlen, Clarence J., (Retired)
Dallman, Arthur C., (Retired)
Diciaula, Gregory H., St. Dominic, Brookfield
Dominguez, Alvaro, St. Mark, Kenosha
Doyle, James B., (Out of Archdiocese)
Dunn, William, (Retired), (Archdiocese of Chicago)
Ebel, John A., St. John Vianney, Brookfield
Fazen, Robert J., St. Matthew, Campbellsport
Ference, Dennis H., (Retired)
Fietz, Dennis E., Immaculate Heart of Mary, West Allis
Filipiak, Thomas P., St. Bruno, Dousman
Finley, Michael J., St. John Neumann, Waukesha
Foeckler, Allan J., St. Charles Borromeo, Milwaukee
Fogarty, Thomas
Francois, James S., St. Mary, Kenosha
Frye, Patrick H., Paul the Apostle, Racine
Fuentes, Roberto, Cristo Rey, Racine
Gaudioso, Carmelo, (Out of Archdiocese)
Gavin, John R., Immaculate Conception, Sheboygan
Gonzales, Jose U., St. Joseph, Wauwatosa
Gonzalez, Baleriano O., St. Clement, Sheboygan
Goodman, Robert E., Three Holy Women, Milwaukee

Goulding, William, St. Mary, Hales Corners
Govek, Richard J., (Retired)
Griffiths, Joseph J., (Out of Archdiocese)
Gulig, Richard P., St. Peter Claver, Sheboygan
Gurzynski, Theodore A., St. Alphonsus, Greendale
Guzman, Armindo, (Out of Archdiocese)
Hansen, Keith A., St. Paul the Apostle, Racine
Heideman, Willis, St. Mary, Mayville; St. Andrew, LeRoy
Henry, Walter, Immaculate Heart of Mary, West Allis
Hiller, Richard D., (Retired)
Horner, Ralph E., Holy Trinity, Kewaskm, St. Michael, St. Michaels
Huber, Paul, (Personal Leave)
Hughes, Larry L., Holy Family, Fond du Lac
Hunt, Thomas N., Cathedral of St. John the Evangelist, Milwaukee
Hying, Joseph H., (Retired)
Iwan, Henry F., St. Benedict, Fontana
Jansen, Mark, Holy Angels, West Bend
Jens, William T., Blessed Trinity, Sheboygan Falls
Kabara, Donald F., (Retired)
Kaczmarek, Raymond J., (Retired)
Kastenholz, Joseph H., (Retired)
Kehrer, Daniel F., St. Elizabeth, Kenosha
Kempka, Eugene A., St. Joseph, Waukesha
Kennedy, Claude V., (Retired)
Kennedy, David L., (Out of Archdiocese)
Kilkenny, Philip O., St. Andrew, Delavan
Klingseisen, Paul, Blessed Sacrament, Milwaukee
Klinkhammer, Phillip H., (Retired)
Koebel, Michael S., St. Frances Cabrini, West Bend
Kornburger, Ralph W., Jr., St. Catherine, Milwaukee
Kuban, Donald J., St. Peter, East Troy, (Diocese of Phoenix)
Kustner, Charles J., St. Mary, Elm Grove
La Fond, M. Larry, Jr., St. Dominic, Brookfield
Lauer, David A., (Personal Leave)
Lazaga, Alfred C., St. Joseph, Grafton
Lebron, Gregorio M., (Retired)
Leggett, A. James, Divine Mercy, South Milwaukee
Lesjak, Ronald F., St. Mary, Kenosha
Libecki, John K., (Retired)
Lopez, Julio, Sts. Rose and Michael, Milwaukee
Losiniecki, Thomas, (Retired)
Lowe, Stanley J., St. Alphonsus, New Munster; St. John the Evangelist, Twin Lakes
Lydolph, Donald J., St. Dominic, Sheboygan
Maack, Terrance A., St. Peter, Kenosha
Macias, Rogelio, St. Patrick and St. Rafael the Archangel, Milwaukee
Mahnke, Carl A., (Retired), St. Thomas Aquinas, Waterford; St. Clare, Wind Lake
Majewski, Edward H., (Retired)
Major, Troy, St. Francis of Assisi, Milwaukee
Malueg, Gerald D., Holy Rosary, Fredonia
Martino, Anthony, (On Duty Outside of the Archdiocese)
Marx, Keith R., Immaculate Heart of Mary, West Allis
McGuine, Thomas W., (On Duty Outside of the Archdiocese)
Mensah, Anthony J., (Retired)
Meuler, Andrew, Mother of Good Counsel, Milwaukee
Miller, Kenneth J., (Retired)
Missureli, Russell A., St. Edward, Racine
Moczydlowski, Chester A., (Retired)
Molina, Juan A., Sr., (Retired)
Monday, John P., Our Lady of Lourdes, Milwaukee
Monday, Thomas C., St. Mary, Menomonee Falls
Monfre, Anthony, Lumen Christi, Mequon
Monzel, Paul S., Presentation, North Fond du Lac; Our Risen Savior, Eldorado
Munoz, Ricardo, Holy Family, Fond du Lac
Nawrocik, Zenon L., (Out of Archdiocese)
Nees, Dale T., St. Paul the Apostle, Racine
Nguyen, Bruno Long H., St. Martin of Tours, Franklin
Nickel, James, St. Thomas Aquinas, Waterford
Niggemann, Richard D., Waukesha County Jail, Waukesha
Normann, Larry E., St. Paul, Genesee Depot
Nowicki, Edward J., (Retired)
Ode, LeRoy, Sacred Heart of Jesus, St. Francis
Ortiz, Aristeo, St. Joseph, Waukesha
Palacios, Antonio, St. Joseph, Waukesha
Pemper, Frank, (Out of Archdiocese)
Pena, Luis, Sts. Hyacinth and Vincent de Paul, Milwaukee
Peterson, James J., St. Sebastian, Milwaukee
Pettey, Lawrence C., (Retired)
Piontek, Richard T., St. Mary, Elm Grove; (Archdiocese of Chicago)
Pollak, David R., St. Charles Borromeo, Milwaukee
Ponec, Gerald R., Nativity of the Lord, Cudahy
Price, Gregory R., Queen of Apostles, Pewaukee
Przedpelski, Steven J., Holy Trinity, Newburg
Ramirez-Murphy, Eugenio, Our Lady of Divine Providence, Milwaukee
Regan, Sylvester R., (Retired)
Reyes, Edwin, St. Alexander, Helen; St. John Kanty, Milwaukee
Rocha, Leonides, St. Patrick, Racine
Rodriguez, Virgilio, (Out of Archdiocese)
Rooney, Michael R., St. James, Menomonee Falls
Rosado, Salvador, St. Francis of Assisi, Milwaukee
Salazar, Roberto, (On Duty Outside of the Archdiocese)
Schieffer, Robert M., (Retired)
Schimmels, Thomas J., (Retired)
Schneider, Ronald W., St. Francis Cabrini, West Bend; (Archdiocese of Washington, D.C.)
Schopper, Eugene E., (Retired)
Sherman, George P., (Retired)
Shierk, Wilson A., St. Mary, Kenosha
Sites, Sanford, Good Shepherd, Menomonee Falls
Smallhoover, James A., St. James, Mukwonago
Snyder, Gordon J., St. Bruno, Dousman
Sommers, David W., St. Matthias, Milwaukee
Starns, Terry, St. Mary, Waukesha
Starr, Robert G., St. Mary of the Lake, Racine; (Archdiocese of Chicago)
Stodola, John, St. Matthew, Oak Creek
Surges, Thomas J., St. Peter of Alcantara, Port Washington
Van Garsse, Eugene E., St. Monica, Whitefish Bay
Villarreal, Hector, St. Patrick, Whitewater
Waitrovich, Raymond, (Retired)
Weber, C. Edward, (Retired)
Wells, Randal S., St. Katharine Drexel, Beaver Dam
Wendt, Bernard J., (Retired)
Wenzler, Joseph P., Lumen Christi, Mequon
Widmar, Willard M., St. Paul the Apostle, Racine
Winkowski, Richard, (Personal Leave)
Wirch, Rick J., St. Leonard, Muskego
Wirtz, Howard J., (Retired)
Wisniewski, Ralph, St. Leonard, Muskego
Wittak, Jay W., St. Robert Bellarmine, Union Grove; (Diocese of Marquette)
Wodushek, Robert A., (Retired)
Zalewski, Leon J., St. Stephen, Milwaukee
Zdeb, James, St. Louis, Caledonia; (Archdiocese of Chicago)
Zimprich, David L., St. William, Waukesha
Zozakiewicz, Daniel T., (Retired)
Zuniga, Jorge, Prince of Peace-Principe de Paz, Milwaukee

INSTITUTIONS LOCATED IN THE DIOCESE

[A] SEMINARIES, ARCHDIOCESAN

ST. FRANCIS. *Saint Francis de Sales Seminary*, 3257 S. Lake Dr., 53235. Tel: 414-747-6400; Fax: 414-747-6442. Email: dbrotz@sfs.edu. Web: www.sfs.edu. Very Rev. John D. Hemsing, Pres. & Rector; Revs. William L. Stanfield, Vice Rector & Dir. Pastoral Formation; Thomas D. DeVries, Spiritual Dir.; Rafael G. Rodriguez, Dean Formation & Students; Kathleen Frymark, Co-Dir. Salzmann Library; Rev. David E. Windsor, C.M., Psy.D., Dir. Admissions. Priests 5; Administration & Faculty 10; Seminarians 32.

[B] SEMINARIES, RELIGIOUS OR SCHOLASTICATES

FRANKLIN. *Xaverian Missionary Fathers College Seminary*, 4500 Xavier Dr., 53132. Tel: 414-421-0831; Fax: 414-421-9108. Email: xavmissionswi@hotmail.com. Web: www.xaviermissionaries.org. Very Rev. Alfredo Turco, S.X. (Italy), Supr./Rector; Revs. Lawrence Crosara, S.X.; Victor Mosele, S.X. (Italy); Dominic Caldognetto, S.X. (Italy); Aniello Salicone, S.X. (Italy). Priests 6.

HALES CORNERS. *Sacred Heart School of Theology*, 7335 S. Hwy. 100, P.O. Box 429, 53130-0429. Tel: 414-425-8300; Fax: 414-529-6999. Email: tknoebel@shst.edu. Web: www.shst.edu. Revs. Jan de Jong, S.C.J., S.T.D., S.T.L., Pres. Rector; Thomas L. Knoebel, Ph.D., M.Div., Vice Rector; Vice Pres. External Affairs; Dir., Recruitment & Admissions (Retired); Raul Gomez Ruiz, S.D.S., Ph.D., Vice Pres. Academic Affairs; Dir. Intellectual Formation; James Walters, S.C.J., M.S., M.Div., Dir. Hispanic Studies; Robert W. Schiavone, M.A., Vice Pres. Pastoral Formation; Peter Schuessler, S.D.S., M.A., Vice Pres. Human & Spiritual Formation; C. Michael Weldon, O.F.M., M.Div., Dir. Spiritual Formation; Mr. Jonathan Drayna, Dir. Communications; Mr. Michael Erato, Dir. Plant Opers.; Mr. Eugene Engeldinger, M.A., M.L.S., Dir. Library & Information Svcs.; Ms. Rose Kopenec, M.A., Registrar & Asst. to Vice Pres. Academic Affairs; Dir. Pre-Theology Academics; Ms. Sally Smits, M.B.A., Vice Pres. Finance & Personnel; Revs. Otto N. Bucher, O.F.M.Cap., S.S.L., S.T.L., Prof. Emeritus; Joseph Gole, S.T.D. (Slovenia), Prof. Emeritus; Sisters Martine Hundelt, S.S.S.F., Ph.D., Prof. Emerita; Joan Koehler, S.S.S.F., M.Ed., M.A., Prof. Emerita; Dr. Bruce Malchow, Ph.D., Prof. Emeritus; Rev. Hugh G. Birdsall, S.D.S., M.A., M.S., Prof. Emeritus. Priests 23; Sisters 6; Lay Teachers 14; Lay Staff 18; Total Enrollment 149.

Full-Time Faculty: Revs. Charles Brown, S.C.J., Ph.D.; Javier Bustos, S.T.D.; Jerome M. Hudziak, Ph.D. (Retired); Scott Jones, S.D.S., Ph.D., Asst. Prof. Church History; Melvin E. Michalski, Ph.L., Th.D., Prof. Emeritus (Retired); Andre Papineau, S.D.S., M.A.; Joseph Toan Do, S.T.L., Asst Prof. Scripture; George Mangiaracina, O.C.D., S.L.D., Asst. Prof. Systematic Theology; Stephen E. Malkiewicz, O.F.M., M.A., Assoc Dir. Human & Spiritual Formation; Michael Udoekpo, S.T.L., Asst. Prof. Scripture; Sisters Mary C. Carroll, S.S.S.F., M.A., D.Min.; Marilyn Cowser, O.S.F., M.A.; Dr. John Gallam, Ph.D.; Dr. Richard Lux, Ph.D., Prof. Emeritus; Dr. Patrick J. Russell, Ph.D.; Dr. Steven Shippee, Ph.D., Prof.; Mr. C. Christian Rich, B.A., M.M.; Ms. Kathleen M. Harty, M.R., M.A.L.S., Librarian.

Part-Time Faculty: Revs. Daniel Pekarske, S.D.S., Ph.D.; John Cella, O.F.M., J.C.D., M.Div., M.B.A., Adjunct Prof. Common Law; James T. Schuerman, Adunct Prof. Systematics; Dr. Sherry Blumberg, Ph.D.; Dr. Joseph Cannon, Adjunct Prof. Philosophy; Ms. Brigid O'Donnell, M.A.; Eva J. Diaz, M.A.P.S.; Sisters Susan Klein, O.P.; Bea Dorsey, S.S.S.F., Adjunct Lecturer, Scripture.

MOUNT CALVARY. *St. Lawrence Seminary*, 301 Church St., 53057. Tel: 920-753-7500; Fax: 920-753-7507. Web: www.stlawrence.edu. Revs. Dennis Druggan, O.F.M.Cap., Rector & Pres.; Campion Baer, O.F.M.Cap.; Oliver Bambenek, O.F.M.Cap., Librarian; Jerome Higgins, O.F.M.Cap., M.Ed., M.A.S., D.Min. (Retired); Ronald Smith, O.F.M.Cap.; Gary Wegner, O.F.M.Cap., Dean Students; John Holly, O.F.M.Cap, Local Min.; Bros. Jerome Campbell, O.F.M.Cap.; Lawrence Groeschel, O.F.M.Cap; Neal Plale, O.F.M.Cap.; Carl Schaefer, O.F.M.Cap.; John Scherer, O.F.M.Cap.; John Willger, O.F.M.Cap.; Mr. David Bartel, Academic Dean; Mr. Timothy Schroeder, Business Mgr. High School Seminary and Ministry Program Priests 7; Brothers 5; Sisters 2; Lay Teachers 17; Non-Teaching Lay Staff 44; Students 205; Total Staff 75.

[C] COLLEGES AND UNIVERSITIES

MILWAUKEE. *Alverno College*, 3400 S. 43rd St., P.O. Box 343922, 53234-3922. Tel: 414-382-6000; Fax: 414-382-6354. Web: www.alverno.edu. Marc McSweeney, Chm., Bd. of Trustees; Mary J. Meehan, Pres.; Sr. Kathleen O'Brien, O.S.F., Sr. Vice Pres. Academic Affairs; Mr. James Oppermann, Sr. Vice Pres. Finance & Mgmt. Svcs.; Carol Brill, Library Dir. Sisters 14; Faculty 120; Students 2,605; Total Staff 247.

Cardinal Stritch University (1937) 6801 N. Yates Rd., 53217. Tel: 414-410-4000; Fax: 414-410-4239. Email: admityou@stritch.edu. Web: www.stritch.edu. Dr. James Loftus, Ph.D., Pres.; Dr. Anthea L. Bojar, Exec. Vice Pres. Academic Affairs; Revs. James Gannon, O.F.M., Office of Campus Ministry; Trinette McCray, Office of Campus Ministry. Conducted by Sisters of St. Francis of Assisi. Priests 1; Sisters 8; Lay Teachers 128; Students 5,842; Total Staff 333.

**Marquette University* (1881) *Office of Institutional Research*, P.O. Box 1881, 53201-1881. Tel: 414-288-1906; Fax: 414-288-6318. Email: webquestions@marquette.edu; ir.surveys@marquette.edu. Web: www.marquette.edu.

Marquette University, Conducted under the auspices of the Society of Jesus. Jesuit Priests 15; Women Religious 5; Total Faculty 1,166; Students 11,806.

Major University Officers: Rev. Scott R. Pilarz, S.J., Pres.; Mr. John C. Lamb, Vice Pres. Finance; Ms. Cynthia M. Bauer, Vice Pres. & Gen. Counsel; Ms. Rana Altenburg, Vice Pres. Public Affairs; Dr. L. Christopher Miller, Vice Pres. Student Affairs; Ms. Julie Tolan, Vice Pres. Univ. Advancement; Dr. John Pauly, Provost; Dr. Gary Meyer, Vice Provost Undergraduate Programs & Teaching; Dr. Jeanne M. Hossenlopp, Vice Provost Research & Dean Graduate School; Ms. Stephanie Russell, Vice Pres. Mission & Ministry; Mr. Arthur F. Scheuber, Vice Pres. Admin.; Ms. Patricia L. Geraghty, Vice Pres. Office of Mktg.

Deans: Rev. Philip J. Rossi, S.J., Interim Dean Helen Way Klinger College of Arts & Sciences; Dr. Linda Salchenberger, Dean College of Business

Admin.; Dr. Lori Bergen, Dean J. William and Mary Diederich College of Communication; Dr. William K. Lobb, Dean School of Dentistry; Dr. William Henk, Dean College of Educ.; Dr. Robert H. Bishop, Opus Dean, College of Engineering; Dr. William Cullinan, Dean College of Health Sciences; Mrs. Janice Welburn, Dean Univ. Libraries; Dr. Margaret Callahan, Dean College of Nursing; Dr. Robert J. Deahl, Dean College of Professional Studies; Mr. Joseph D. Kearney, Dean Law School. Additional Department Heads: Rev. D. Edward Mathie, S.J., Dir. Campus Min.; Dr. Susan Wood, Chair Dept. of Theology.

Mount Mary College (1913) 2900 N. Menomonee River Pkwy., 53222-4545. Tel: 414-258-4810; Fax: 414-256-1224. Web: www.mtmary.edu. Eileen Schwalbach, Pres.; Julie Kamikawa, Asst. Dir. Library. School Sisters of Notre Dame. Sisters 5; Lay Teachers 73; Students 1,772; Total Staff 398.

FOND DU LAC. *Marian University, Inc.* (1936) 45 S. National Ave., 54935. Tel: 920-923-7617; Fax: 920-923-8087. Email: admissions@marianuniversity.edu. Web: www.marianuniversity.edu. Dr. Steven Disalvo, Pres.; Dr. Edward H. Ogle, Exec. Vice Pres. Academic & Student Affairs; Sr. Marie Scott, C.S.A., Campus Min.; Mary Ellen Gormican, Librarian. Sisters of the Congregation of St. Agnes 4; Lay Teachers 90; Students 2,881; (incl. all part-time & adjunct) 309.

[D] HIGH SCHOOLS, ARCHDIOCESAN AND PAROCHIAL

MILWAUKEE. *Pius XI High School* (1929) 135 N. 76th St., 53213. Tel: 414-290-7000; Fax: 414-290-7001. Email: piusxi@piusxi.org. Web: www.piusxi.org. Dr. Melinda Skrade, Chief Admin.; Betty Hunt, Dir. Academic Operations; Rebecca White, Librarian; Rev. Peter Berger. Priests 1; School Sisters of St. Francis 3; Lay Teachers 75; Students 900.

St. Thomas More High School, 2601 E. Morgan Ave., 53207. Tel: 414-481-8370; Fax: 414-481-3382. Email: ljanick@tmore.org. Web: www.tmore.org. Mr. Terry Benter, Prin. (Coed) Lay Teachers 30; Students 438; Total Staff 50.

BURLINGTON. *Catholic Central High School* (1925) 148 McHenry St., 53105. Tel: 262-763-1510; Fax: 262-763-1509. Email: ggroth@cchsnet.org. Web: www.cchsnet.org. Gregory Groth, Prin.; Mark Sheldon, Dean of Students; Eric Henderson, Dean of Students. Lay Teachers 19; Students 151.

WAUKESHA. *Catholic Memorial High School* (1949) 601 E. College Ave., 53186-5538. Tel: 262-542-7101; Fax: 262-542-1633. Email: fr.hartmann@catholicmemorial.net. Web: www.catholicmemorial.net. Very Rev. Paul B.R. Hartmann, M.Div., J.C.L., Pres. Tel: 262-542-7101, Ext. 243; Fax: 262-521-4444; Mr. Bob Hall, Prin. Clergy 1; Lay Teachers 50; Students 705; Total Staff 72.

[E] HIGH SCHOOLS, PRIVATE

MILWAUKEE. *Divine Savior Holy Angels High School, Inc.* (Girls), 4257 N. 100th St., 53222. Tel: 414-462-3742; Fax: 414-466-0590. Web: www.dsha.info. Ellen Bartel, Pres.; Dan Quesnell, Prin.; Maria-Christina Thiele, Librarian. Sponsored by the Sisters of the Divine Savior. Sisters 2; Lay Teachers 60; Students 676; Total Staff 97.

St. Joan Antida High School, Inc. (Girls), 1341 N. Cass St., 53202. Tel: 414-272-8423; Fax: 414-272-3135. Email: cmarino@saintjoanantida.org. Web: www.saintjoanantida.org. Cynthia A. Marino, Head of School; Maria Schram, Prin.; Roberta Szabo, Librarian. Sisters of Charity of St. Joan Antida 2; Lay Teachers 16; Students 276; Total Staff 34.

Marquette University High School (Boys)., 3401 W. Wisconsin Ave., 53208. Tel: 414-933-7220; Fax: 414-937-8588. Web: www.muhs.edu. Jeff Monday, Prin.; Revs. Terrence M. Brennan, S.J.; Mark A. Carr, S.J.; Thomas C. Manahan, S.J.; Warren J. Sazama, S.J., Pres.; Charles L. Stang, S.J.; Ms. Ann O'Hara, Librarian. (See separate listing for resident information). Priests 5; Religious 2; Lay Teachers 80; Students 1,067; Total Staff 125.

**Messmer High School* (1926) 742 W. Capitol Dr., 53206. Tel: 414-264-5440; Fax: 414-264-0672. Email: generalinfo@messmerschools.org. Web: www.messmerschools.org. Bro. Bob Smith, Pres., CEO & Prin.; Mike Bartels, Vice Pres.; Ivma Espovza, Dir. Admin. Svcs. Brothers 1; Teachers 52; Part-Time Teachers 5; Students 696.

Messmer Preparatory Catholic School (1999) 3027 N. Fratney St., 53212. Tel: 414-264-6070; Fax: 414-264-6430. Email: generalinfo@messmerschools.org. Web: www.messmerschools.org. Bro. Bob Smith, Pres., CEO & Prin.; Anne Aroh, Prin.; Mike Bartels, Vice Pres.; Ivma Espovza, Dir. Admin. Svcs. Brothers 1; Lay Teachers 26; Students 455.

RACINE. *St. Catherine's High School* (1864) 1200 Park Ave., 53403. Tel: 262-632-2785; Fax: 262-632-5144. Web: www.saintcats.org. Mr. Christopher Olley, Pres.; Mr. Andrew Meuler, Prin.; Sr. Jane Weiss, Asst. Prin. Dominican Sisters (Racine) 3; Lay Teachers 32; Students 441.

WHITEFISH BAY. *Dominican High School* (1956) 120 E. Silver Spring Dr., 53217. Tel: 414-332-1170; Fax: 414-332-4101. Email: dhs@dominicanhighschool.com. Web: dominicanhighschool.com. Edward Foy, Dean Academics & Campus Min.; Brian Geittmann, Dean Students; Amy Krzykowski, Librarian; Colleen K. Brady, Head of School. Sponsored by Sinsinawa Dominicans. Dominican Sisters of the Congregation of the Most Holy Rosary, Sinsinawa, WI 1; Administrators 3; Lay Teachers 30; Students 285.

[F] ELEMENTARY SCHOOLS, ARCHDIOCESAN

MILWAUKEE. *St. Rose and St. Leo Catholic School*, 514 N. 31st St., 53208. Tel: 414-933-6070; Fax: 414-933-3071. Email: generalinfo@messmerschools.org. Web: www.messmerschools.org. Bro. Bob Smith, Pres., CEO & Prin.; Lewis Lea, Prin.; Mike Bartels, Vice Pres.; Ivma Espovza, Dir. Admin. Svcs. In partnership with Messmer Catholic Schools. Brothers 1; Lay Teachers 26; Students 445.

[G] ELEMENTARY SCHOOLS, PRIVATE

MILWAUKEE. *St. Coletta Day School of Milwaukee* (1956) 1740 N. 55th St., 53208. Tel: 414-453-1850; Fax: 414-453-9449. Email: info@scdsmke.org. Web: www.scdsmke.org. William A. Koehn, Prin. & Admin. For Exceptional Children. Lay Teachers 3; Students 20.

Nativity Jesuit Middle School, Inc. (Boys), 1515 S. 29th St., 53215-1912. Tel: 414-645-1060. Email: nativity@njms.org. Web: www.njms.org. Rev. James P. Flaherty, S.J., Pres.; Jim Wilkinson, Prin. Wisconsin Province of the Society of Jesus. Priests 1; Religious 1; Lay Teachers 11; Students 79; Total Staff 8.

Notre Dame Middle School, Inc. (1996) 1420 W. Scott St., 53204. Tel: 414-671-3000; Fax: 414-671-6138. Email: info@ndmswi.org. Web: ndmswi.org. Mary McIntosh, Pres.; Sisters Jean Ellman, S.S.N.D., Prin.; Doris Jean LeBrun, S.S.N.D., Librarian. Sponsored by: School Sisters of Notre Dame. Sisters 6; Lay Teachers 10; Volunteers 1; Students 139.

[H] CONSOLIDATED ELEMENTARY SCHOOLS

MILWAUKEE. *All Saints Catholic East School System, Inc.*, 2461 N. Murray Ave., 53211. Tel: 414-964-1770; Fax: 414-964-6578. Email: gailkraig@archmil.org. Rev. Brian G. Mason, Bd. Chm.; Gail Kraig, Prin. Sponsored by the following Milwaukee parishes: Cathedral of St. John the Evangelist; Our Lady of Divine Providence; Old St. Mary's; Ss. Peter and Paul; Three Holy Women Catholic Parish. Lay Teachers 20; Students 205.

Holy Wisdom Academy (2002) *c/o Blessed John Paul II Congregation*, 3307 S. 10th, 53215-5039. Tel: 414-744-3695; Fax: 414-744-2874. Revs. Michael A. Ignaszak, Contact; Javier Guatiua; Mr. Richard Mason, Prin. Sponsored by Blessed John Paul II, Milwaukee. Sisters 5; Lay Teachers 16; Total Enrollment 287.

Northwest Catholic School Association Formerly St. Bernadette, St. Catherine of Alexandria, and Our Lady of Good Hope Schools., West Campus: 8202 W. Denver Ave., 53223. Tel: 414-352-6927. East Campus: 7140 N. 41st St., 53209. Tel: 414-352-6927. Debra A. Hintz, Pastor/Parish Dir.; Diana Erlandson, Prin. (West Campus); Michelle Paris, Prin. (East Campus); Grace Stroik, Librarian (West Campus); Jane Schindler, Librarian (East Campus). Lay Teachers 27; Students 403.

St. Thomas Aquinas Academy, 341 E. Norwich St., 53207. Tel: 414-744-1214; Fax: 414-744-8340. Web: thomasaquinasacademy.com. Rev. Romanus N. Nwaru, Contact Person; Rhonda Friday, Prin.; Mrs. Diane Karabon, Librarian. Sponsored by St. Augustine, St. Paul, St. Veronica & Immaculate Conception, Milwaukee; Nativity of the Lord, Cudahy, and Sacred Heart of Jesus, St. Francis. Lay Teachers 19; Students 208.

JOHNSBURG. *Consolidated Parochial Elementary School* (1969) N9290 County Rd. W, Fond du Lac, 54937. Tel: 920-795-4222; Fax: 920-795-4126. Email: cpes@ppcws.net. Web: cpesonline.com. Gerard Stepanek, Prin. Members: St. John the Baptist, Johnsburg; St. Mary, Marytown; Holy Cross, Mount Calvary; St. Cloud, St. Cloud. Priests 2; Lay Teachers 13; Students 96.

KENOSHA. *All Saints Catholic School of Kenosha, Inc.*, (Grades K-8), 7400-39 Ave., 53142. Tel: 262-694-6740. Web: www.allsaintskenosha.org. Dr. Jacqueline Lichter, Ph.D., Lead Prin.; Bruce Varick, Assoc. Prin. Students 455.

WAUKESHA. *Waukesha Catholic School System, Inc.* (1990) 221 S. Hartwell Ave., 53186. Tel: 262-896-2929; Fax: 262-896-2934. Email: business@waukeshacatholicschoolsystem.org. Rev. Howard G. Haase, Pastor Liaison. Tel: 262-542-2589. Members: St. Joseph, St. Mary, St. John Neumann, St. William.

St. Joseph Campus, 818 N. East Ave., 53186. Tel: 262-896-2930; Fax: 262-896-2935. Email: stjoe@wcssonline.org. Mrs. Kathleen Rempe, Prin. Lay Teachers 18; Students 227.

St. Mary Campus, 520 E. Newhall Ave., 53186. Tel: 262-896-2932; Fax: 262-896-2931. Email: stmary@wcssonline.org. Ms. Lisa Kovaleski, Prin. Lay Teachers 18; Students 284.

St. William Campus, 444 N. Moreland Blvd., 53188. Tel: 262-896-2920; Fax: 262-896-2925. Email: stwm@wcssonline.org. Robert Radomski, Prin. Lay Teachers 11; Students 161.

WEST ALLIS. *Mary Queen of Saints Catholic Academy* (2004) 1435 S. 92nd St., 53214. Tel: 414-476-0751; Fax: 414-259-9285. Web: mqsca.org. Rev. Leonard R. Copeland, O.C.D., Priest Designate; Donna Larson, Prin.; Beverley Walloch, Librarian. Sponsored by St. Florian, West Milwaukee; Holy Assumption, Immaculate Heart of Mary, Mary Queen of Heaven, St. Aloysius, St. Augustine & St. Rita, West Allis. Religious 1; Lay Teachers (Full-Time) 11; Lay Teachers (Part-Time) 5; Students 202; Sisters 1.

[I] SCHOOL SYSTEMS

FOND DU LAC. *St. Mary's Springs Academy of Fond du Lac, WI*, (Grades K-12), Admin. Office: 114 Amory St., 54935. Tel: 920-924-0993; 920-921-4870, Ext. 8009 (Business Office); Fax: 920-922-7849. Web: www.smsacademy.org. Kevin J. Shaw, Pres. Tel: 920-924-0993; Joanne Michaels, Librarian. Lay Teachers 56; Students 701; Total Staff 104; Religious Order 1.

Pre-School & Elementary (Grades PreK-2), 95 E. 2nd St., 54935. Tel: 920-921-5300; Fax: 920-921-5908. Doug Olig, Lead Prin.

Elementary & Middle School (Grades 3-8), 63 E. Merrill Ave., 54935. Tel: 920-921-9610; Fax: 920-921-0457. Email: eflood@smsacademy.org. Erin Flood, Asst. Prin.

High School, 255 County Rd. K, 54937. Tel: 920-921-4870; Fax: 920-921-2786. Email: dolig@smsacademy.org. Web: www.smsacademy.org.

KENOSHA. *St. Joseph Catholic Academy, Inc.*, (Grades PreK-12), 2401 69th St., 53143. Tel: 262-654-8651; Fax: 262-654-1615. Email: rfreund@kenoshastjoseph.com. Web: www.kenoshastjoseph.com. Mr. Robert Freund, Pres.; Edward G. Kovochich, Admin. (K-12); Ms. Kerstin Santarelli, Prin. (K-5). Sisters 1; Lay Teachers 50; Students 770; Total Staff 75.

[J] CHILD CARE CENTERS

MILWAUKEE. *Child Development Center of St. Joseph* (1999) 1600 W. Oklahoma Ave., 53215. Tel: 414-645-5337; Fax: 414-645-5329. Email: jvasquez@cdcsj.org. Web: www.cdcsj.org. Jose Vasquez, Pres. & CEO. Sponsored by the Congregation of the Sisters of St. Felix of Cantalice of the United States of America, Inc. (Felician Sisters). Felician Sisters 3; Religious 1; Lay Teachers 41; Children 230; Total Staff 52; Other Staff 8.

Guardian Angel Learning Center, Inc., 1540 N. Jefferson, 53202. Tel: 414-277-9474; Fax: 414-277-9482. Email: gschool1@wi.rr.com. Web: www.scsja.org. Sr. Marie Louise Balistrieri, S.C.S.J.A., Admin. Sisters of Charity of St. Joan Antida, The center is licensed for ages 6 weeks to 12 years. Sisters of Charity of St. Joan Antida 1; Sisters of Charity B.V.M. 1; Lay Teachers 23; Students 85.

SOUTH MILWAUKEE. *Franciscan Villa Child Day Center*, 3601 S. Chicago Ave., 53172. Tel: 414-570-5410; Fax: 414-764-0706. Email: stacysuehring@catholichealth.net. Web: www.franciscanvilla.org. Affiliate of Catholic Health Initiatives. Lay Teachers 8; Children 50.

[K] GENERAL HOSPITALS

MILWAUKEE. *Columbia St. Mary's Hospital Milwaukee, Inc.* (1859) 2320 N. Lake Dr., P.O. Box 503, 53201-0503. Fax: 414-270-4869. Web: www.columbia-stmarys.org. Deborah Friberg, Pres.; Revs. Paul Schwan, Mgr. Special Care Svcs.; Charles R. Keefe; Rev. Vicki Watkins; Cindy Wagner, Chap.; Pedro Acosta Zapata, Chap.; Alex Chamtcheu, Chap.; Sr. Mary Elizabeth Cullen, Chap. Corporate Title: Columbia St. Mary's

Hospital Milwaukee, Inc.; Ascension Health System. Bed Capacity 422; Patients Assisted Annually 230,160; Total Staff 2,284.

Ministry Health Care, Inc. (1984) 11925 W. Lake Park Dr., 53224. Tel: 414-359-1060; Fax: 414-359-1033. Email: info@ministryhealth.org. Web: www.ministryhealth.org. Nicholas Desien, Pres. & CEO.

Subsidiaries and Affiliated Hospitals located throughout Wisconsin:

Door County Memorial Hospital (1942) Sturgeon Bay. Tel: 920-743-5566; Fax: 920-743-8165.

Mercy Medical Center of Oshkosh, Inc. (1891) Oshkosh. Tel: 920-223-0504; Fax: 920-223-0508.

Ministry Home Care, Inc. (1998) Marshfield. Tel: 715-389-3802; Fax: 715-387-9950.

Ministry Weight Management, Inc. (1995) Rhinelander. Tel: 715-361-2000; Fax: 715-361-2011.

Sacred Heart-Saint Mary's Hospitals, Inc. (1981) Tomahawk and Rhinelander, WI, Tel: 715-369-6600; Fax: 715-369-6441.

Saint Elizabeth's Hospital of Wabasha, Inc. (1898) Wabasha, MN. Tel: 651-565-4531; Fax: 651-565-2482.

Saint Joseph's Hospital of Marshfield, Inc. (1955) Marshfield. Tel: 715-387-1713; Fax: 715-387-8601.

Saint Clare's Hospital of Weston, Inc. (2002) Weston. Tel: 715-393-2501; Fax: 715-359-1087.

St. Michael's Hospital of Stevens Point, Inc. (1913) Stevens Point. Tel: 715-346-5000; Fax: 715-346-5088.

Our Lady of Victory Hospital, Inc., Stanley. Tel: 715-644-5571; Fax: 715-644-6221.

Dr. Kate Newcomb Convalescent Center, Inc. (1980) Woodruff. Tel: 715-356-8560; Fax: 715-356-6097.

Eagle River Memorial Hospital, Incorporated (1941) Eagle River. Tel: 715-479-7411; Fax: 715-479-0395.

The Howard Young Medical Center, Inc. (1954) Woodruff. Tel: 715-356-8000; Fax: 715-356-6097.

Howard Young Health Care, Inc. (1984) Woodruff. Tel: 715-356-8000; Fax: 715-356-6097.

Affinity Health System (1999) Menasha, 54952. Tel: 920-720-1713; Fax: 920-720-1720.

Agape Community Center of Milwaukee, Inc. (1989) Tel: 414-464-4440; Fax: 414-464-9420.

Ministry Medical Group, Inc. Tel: 414-359-1060; Fax: 414-359-1033.

Wheaton Franciscan Healthcare - St. Francis, Inc. (1946) 3237 S. 16th St., 53215. Tel: 414-647-5000; Fax: 414-647-5565. Web: www.mywheaton.org. Mr. Daniel Mattes, Pres.; Rev. Kevin Ori, Chap. Sponsored by the Congregation of the Sisters of St. Felix of Cantalice of the United States of America, Chicago Province (Felician Sisters). Sisters 6; Bed Capacity 260; Patients Assisted Annually 151,178; Total Staff 948.

Wheaton Franciscan, Inc. (1927) St. Joseph Campus: 5000 W. Chambers St., 53210. Tel: 414-447-2000; Fax: 414-874-4393. Web: www.mywheaton.org. The Wisconsin Heart Hospital Campus: 10000 W. Bluemound Rd., Wauwatosa, 53226. Fax: 414-778-7811. Debra K. Standridge, Pres.; Trisha Crissman, Interim Regl. Dir. Franciscan Sisters, Daughters of the Sacred Hearts of Jesus and Mary (Wheaton, IL) 8; Bed Capacity 744; Patients Assisted Annually 404,858; Total Staff 2,942.

Elmbrook Memorial Campus, 19333 W. North Ave., Brookfield, 53045. Tel: 262-785-2000; Fax: 262-785-2485.

FOND DU LAC. *Agnesian Health Care, Inc. dba St. Agnes Hospital* 430 E. Division St., 54935. Tel: 920-929-2300; Fax: 920-926-4866. Email: littles@agnesian.com. Web: www.agnesian.com. Mr. Robert A. Fale, Pres. & CEO. Sisters 6; Bed Capacity 158; (TCU) 9; Patients Assisted Annually 669,017; Total Staff 1,951.

FRANKLIN. *Wheaton Franciscan Healthcare-Franklin, Inc.*, 10101 S. 27th St., 53132. Tel: 414-325-8640; Fax: 414-325-4511. Mr. Daniel Mattes, Pres.

KENOSHA. *St. Catherine's Hospital Inc.* (1917) 6308 Eighth Ave., 53143. Tel: 262-656-2112; Fax: 262-654-2624. Richard O. Schmidt Jr., Pres. & CEO. Sponsored by Wheaton Franciscan Healthcare

MEQUON. *Columbia St. Mary's Hospital Ozaukee, Inc.* (1995) *The Heritage Center*, 2320 N. Lake Dr., Ste. 1700A, 53211. Tel: 414-243-7300; Fax: 414-243-7416. Web: www.columbia-stmarys.org. Deborah Friberg, Pres.; Revs. Paul Schwan, Chap.; John R. Paczesny, Chap. (Retired); Sr. Angela Spence, Chap. Ascension Health System Bed Capacity 172; Patients Assisted Annually 138,082; Total Staff 861.

RACINE. *Wheaton Franciscan Healthcare - All Saints, Inc.* (1974) 3801 Spring St., 53405. Tel: 262-687-4011; Fax: 262-687-8039. Web: www.mywheaton.org. Kenneth R. Buser, Pres. Bed Capacity 355; Total Patients Assisted 146,956; Total Staff 2,472.

SHEBOYGAN. *St. Nicholas Hospital* (1890) 3100 Superior Ave., 53081. Tel: 920-459-8300; Fax: 920-452-8336. Email: aliebelt@sns.hshs.org. Web: www.stnicholashospital.org. Andrew J. Bagnall, Pres. & CEO; Martin Folan, Dir. Spiritual & Pastoral Support Svcs. Bed Capacity 185; Total Assisted Annually 91,640; Total Staff 472.

WAUPUN. *Waupun Memorial Hospital, Inc.*, 620 W. Brown St., 53963. Tel: 920-324-5581; Fax: 920-324-2085. Web: www.agnesian.com. Deann Thurmer, COO. Corporate Title: Waupun Memorial Hospital, Inc. Bed Capacity 25; Patients Assisted Annually 53,154; Total Staff 267.

[L] SPECIAL HOSPITALS AND SANATORIA

MILWAUKEE. *Sacred Heart Rehabilitation Institute, Inc.* (1955) *The Heritage Center*, 2320 N. Lake Dr., Ste. 1700A, 53211. 2301 N. Lake Dr., 53211. Fax: 414-270-4869. Deborah Friberg, Pres.; Cindy Wagner, Chap.; Rev. Paul Schwan, Chap. Ascension Health System. Bed Capacity 31; Patients Assisted Annually 11,071; Total Staff 117.

[M] PROTECTIVE INSTITUTIONS

MILWAUKEE. *St. Charles Youth and Family Services, Inc.* (1920) 151 S. 84th St., 53214. Tel: 414-476-3710; Fax: 414-778-5985. Email: scarpenter@stcharlesinc.org. Web: www.stcharlesinc.org. Ms. Cathy Connolly, Pres. Bed Capacity 118; Residents 136; Total Assisted Annually 3,000; Total Staff 250.

Daystar, Inc., P.O. Box 2130, 53201-2130. Tel: 414-385-0334; Fax: 414-385-0336. Email: daystar@daystarinc.org. Web: www.daystarinc.org. Transitional living program for formerly battered women without children, for up to two years. Bed Capacity 10; Residents 10; Total Assisted Annually 25; Total Staff 8.

MOUNT CALVARY. *Cristo Rey Ranch, Inc.*, 998 Calvary St., 53057. Tel: 920-753-2026; 920-753-3211; Fax: 920-753-3100. Email: wbodden@villalorettonh.org; nunbetterfarm@hotmail.com. Sister Servants of Christ the King, Provides weekend respite services to families caring for emotionally/behaviorally challenged children and adolescents. Program emphasis on pet therapy. Some day and evening programs thru County Social Services Department. Bed Capacity 4; Total Assisted Annually 9; Total Staff 3.

WAUWATOSA. *Carmelite Home, Inc.* (1917) 1214 Kavanaugh Pl., 53213. Tel: 414-258-4791; Fax: 414-258-8464. Email: carmelitedcl@sbcglobal.net. Peter Wellsmith, Prin.; Sr. Maria Goretti, D.C.J., Admin.; James E. Lewis, M.S.W., Treatment Dir. MSW & ICSW. Residential Treatment Center for Adolescent Boys. Carmelite Sisters D.C.J. 3; Residents 10; Lay Teachers 2; Total Staff 26.

[N] HOMES FOR AGED AND NURSING HOMES

MILWAUKEE. *Alexian Village of Milwaukee, Inc.* (1980) 9301 N. 76th St., 53223. Tel: 414-355-9300; Fax: 414-357-5106. Email: gmohn@alexianbrothers.net. Web: www.alexianvillage.net. Gary Mohn, CEO; Rev. Joe Jagodensky, S.D.S., Chap. Congregation of Alexian Brothers, Immaculate Conception Province, Continuing Care Retirement Community. Units 457; Residents 491; Brothers 3; Total Assisted Annually 79; Total Staff 302.

St. Ann Rest Home, 2020 S. Muskego Ave., 53204-3522. Tel: 414-383-2630; Fax: 414-383-0305. Web: www.stannresthome.org. Rev. Linus E. Kopczewski, O.F.M., Pastoral Care Min.; Sr. Andrea K. Andrzejewska, Admin. Conducted by the Dominican Sisters (Congregation of the Immaculate Conception). Sisters 8; Bed Capacity 50; Residents 50; Total Staff 47.

St. Anne's Salvatorian Campus, 3800 N. 92nd St., 53222. Tel: 414-463-7570; Fax: 414-463-2311. Email: lvogt@wi.rr.com. Web: www.stannessc.org. Ms. Lynn Vogt, Admin.; Rev. Michael Burns, S.D.S., Chap. Sisters of the Divine Savior. Assisted Living Apartments 43; Studio Apts. 48; Residents 106; Total Staff 247.

**Milwaukee Catholic Home*, 2462 N. Prospect Ave., 53211-4462. Tel: 414-224-9700; Fax: 414-224-1666. Email: info@milwaukeecatholichome.org. Web: milwaukeecatholichome.org. David Fulcher, Exec. Dir.; Rev. Charles R. Keefe, Dir. Pastoral Care. Corporate Title: Milwaukee Catholic Home, Inc. Retirement Home Residents 120; Retirement Home Total Staff 67; Nursing Home Residents 122; Nursing Home Total Staff 200; Day Care (Adult) 20; Assisted Living 29.

Villa St. Francis, Inc. (1990) 1910 W. Ohio Ave., 53215. Tel: 414-649-2888; Fax: 414-649-2880. Email: jvasquez@villastfrancis.org. Web: www.villastfrancis.org. Jose Vasquez, Pres. & CEO. Sponsored by the Congregation of the Sisters of St. Felix of Cantalice of the United States of America, Inc. (Felician Sisters), Assisted Living Facility for the Elderly Felician Sisters 2; Resident Apartments 129; Total Assisted Annually 160; Total Staff 70.

**Wheaton Franciscan Healthcare-Terrace at St. Francis, Inc.* (1994) 3200 S. 20th St., 53215. Tel: 414-389-3200; Fax: 414-389-3300. James D. Gresham, Pres. Member of Wheaton Franciscan Healthcare. Sponsored by the Felician Sisters and the Wheaton Franciscan Sisters., Skilled Nursing Facility for Transitional & Extended Subacute Care. Bed Capacity 81; Patients Assisted Annually 528; Total Staff 82.

BROOKFIELD. *Wheaton Franciscan Healthcare - Pharmacy Enterprises, and Franciscan Woods, Inc. dba Wheaton Franciscan Healthcare - Pharmacy Enterprises and Franciscan Woods, Inc.* (1987) 19525 W. North Ave., 53045. Tel: 262-780-3100. Web: www.mywheaton.org. James D. Gresham, Pres. Franciscan Sisters, Daughters of the Sacred Hearts of Jesus and Mary, Wheaton, IL. Bed Capacity 120; Total Assisted Annually 789; Total Staff 117.

FOND DU LAC. *St. Francis Home* (1978) 33 Everett St., 54935. Tel: 920-923-7980; Fax: 920-923-7995. Douglas Trost, CEO. Sisters of St. Agnes, C.S.A. Sisters 2; Bed Capacity 107; Total Staff 229.

St. Clare Terrace (1991) Tel: 920-923-7996; Fax: 920-923-7995. Residents 30; Independent Elderly Apartments 30; Total Staff 3.

St. Francis Terrace (1998) Tel: 920-923-7980; Fax: 920-923-7995. Residents 52; Assisted Living Units 55; Total Staff 46.

GREENFIELD. *Clement Manor Health Center*, 3939 S. 92nd St., 53228. Tel: 414-321-1800; Fax: 414-546-7357. Web: www.clementmanor.com. Richard Rau, Pres. & CEO; Mr. Dennis Ferger, Admin.; Rev. Albert Lis, O.F.M., Chap. Sponsored by School Sisters of St. Francis., Corporate Title: Clement Manor, Inc. Residents 166; Adult Day Care 35.

KENOSHA. *St. Joseph's Home and Rehabilitation Center*, 9244 29th Ave., 53143. Tel: 262-694-0080; Fax: 262-694-7325. Email: asi@tds.net. Web: stjosephshome.com. Sisters Mary Emmanuel Apanites, D.C.J., Admin.; M. Jacinta Cusumano, D.C.J.; Rev. Anthony Jelinek. Corporate Title: Carmelite Sisters of the Divine Heart of Jesus; St. Joseph's Villa, Independent living Apts. Sisters 7; Bed Capacity 90; Residents 90; Apartments 44; Total Staff 125.

MOUNT CALVARY. *Villa Loretto Nursing Home*, N8114 County WW, 53057. Tel: 920-753-3211; Fax: 920-753-3100. Email: srandall@villalorettonh.org. Web: villalorettonh.org. Sr. Stephen Bloesl, Supr. Corporate Title: Sister Servants of Christ the King, Inc. dba Villa Loretto. Sisters 5; Bed Capacity 52; Total Assisted Annually 78; Total Staff 133.

Villa Rosa, Inc., N8120 County WW, 53057. Tel: 920-753-3015; Fax: 920-753-2508. Email: lschmitz@villalorettonh.org. Web: villalorettonh.org. Sr. Stephen Bloesl, Pres.; Lynn Schmitz, Mgr. Bed Capacity 20; Total Assisted Annually 25; Total Staff 13.

RACINE. *Marian Housing Center, Inc.* (1985) 4105 Spring St., 53405. Tel: 262-633-5807; Fax: 262-633-9780. Web: www.fm-inc.org. Units 40; Total Staff 3; Residents 43.

St. Monica's Senior Citizens Home, Inc., 3920 N. Green Bay Rd., 53404. Tel: 262-639-5050; Fax: 262-639-5673. Email: sr.irene@tds.net. Sr. Irene Hanika, O.S.A., Supr. & Admin. Nonprofit Corp. Sisters of St. Rita 5; Bed Capacity 110; Residents 110; Total Assisted Annually 29,200; Total Staff 49.

SOUTH MILWAUKEE. *Franciscan Villa of South Milwaukee, Inc.* (1966) Residential Care Apartment Complex., 3601 S. Chicago Ave., 53172. Tel: 414-764-4100; Fax: 414-764-0706. Email: daninecasper@catholichealth.net. Web: www.franciscanvilla.org. Jamie Weibeler, Admin. & CEO. Catholic Health Initiatives Residents 150; Alzheimer's Assisted Living 64; Child Day Care 36; Franciscan Courts (Apartments) 39; Franciscan Garden (Apartments) 48; Total Staff 360.

WAUWATOSA. *St. Camillus Health Center, Inc.*, 10101 W. Wisconsin Ave., 53226. Tel: 414-258-1814; Fax: 414-259-4987. Email: rljohnson@stcam.com. Web: www.stcam.com. Very Rev. Richard O'Donnell, M.I.; Revs. Augustin Orosa, M.I., Dir. Pastoral Care; Davies Edassery, S.A.C. (India), Chap.; Bro. Mario Crivello, M.I., Chap.; Rick Johnson, Pres. & CEO; Samantha Erschen, Chap.; Christine Winkowski, Chap. Order of the Servants of the Sick (Order of St. Camillus), Skilled Nursing Home and Assisted Living. Bed Capacity 67; Patients Assisted Annually 250; Total Staff 500.

[O] PERSONAL PRELATURES

BROOKFIELD. *Prelature of the Holy Cross and Opus Dei Layton Study Center*, 12900 W. North Ave., 53005. Tel: 262-784-1523; Fax: 262-782-5183. Email:

info@opusdei.org. Revs. Timothy J. Uhen; John C. Kubeck.

[P] MONASTERIES AND RESIDENCES FOR PRIESTS AND BROTHERS

MILWAUKEE. *Alexian Brothers Community* (1980) Immaculate Conception Province, 9301 N. 76th St., 53223-1072. Tel: 414-507-9157; Fax: 414-357-5290. Email: dmccormick@alexianbrothers.net. Web: www.alexianbrothers.net. Bros. John Grider, C.F.A.; Daniel McCormick, C.F.A.; Robert Petersen, C.F.A. Brothers 3.

Arrupe House Jesuit Community, 831 N. 13th St., 53233-1706. Tel: 414-288-5855; Fax: 414-288-5852. Revs. John L. Treloar, S.J., Supr.; Walter E. Boehme, S.J.; Christopher M. Hadley, S.J.; D. Thomas Hughson, S.J.; Michael R. Kolb, S.J.; G. Thomas Krettek, S.J.; Very Rev. Thomas A. Lawler, S.J.; Revs. Eugene F. Merz, S.J.; Sang-Hun Pak, S.J. (Korea, South); John M. Paul, S.J., Min.; Philip J. Rossi, S.J.; Warren J. Sazama, S.J.; Thomas P. Sweetser, S.J.; Matthew S. Walsh, S.J.; Patrick J. Burns, S.J.; Frederick E. Brenk, S.J. Society of Jesus, Wisconsin Prov. Priests 16.

St. Camillus Delegate House, 3345 S. 10th St., 53215. Tel: 414-481-3696; Fax: 414-481-8044. Very Rev. Richard O'Donnell, M.I., Delegate; Revs. Bernard Blasich; Scott Binet, M.I., M.D.; Stephen Braddock; John Gallagher; Louis Lussier, M.I.; Carlo Notaro, M.I.; Albert Schempp, M.I., Chap. & Prov. Counselor. Delegate offices for the U.S.A. Camillians of the Order of the Servants of the Sick (Order of Saint Camillus) Priests 6.

St. Conrad Friary, 3138 N. 2nd St., 53212. Tel: 414-372-3620. Revs. Richard Hart, O.F.M.Cap., M.A.; Randall Knauf, O.F.M.Cap; Niles J. Kauffman, O.F.M.Cap., M.A.; Martin Pable, O.F.M.Cap., Ph.D.; David Preuss, O.F.M.Cap.; Bros. Kent Bauer, O.F.M.Cap, Local Min.; Nick Blatter, Postulant; Fred Cabras, Postulant; Jason Graves, Postulant; Michael Mascarenhas, Postulant; Fadi Touma, Postulant. Capuchin Friars, Province of St. Joseph. Priests 5; Brothers 6; Total in Residence 11.

Jesuit Community at Marquette University, 1404 W. Wisconsin Ave., 53233-2238. Tel: 414-288-5000; Fax: 414-288-1758. Revs. James P. Flaherty, S.J.; Thomas S. Anderson, S.J.; Ronald Bieganowski, S.J.; Thaddeus J. Burch, S.J.; Thomas A. Caldwell, S.J.; Michael D. Class, S.J.; Martin-Claude Domfang, S.J.; J. Patrick Donnelly, S.J.; Robert M. Doran, S.J.; Eugene M. Dutkiewicz, S.J.; Robert L. Faricy, S.J.; John P. Fitzgibbons, S.J.; Grant S. Garinger, S.J.; James J. Gladstone, S.J.; Gerald E. Goetz, S.J., Min.; Michael A. Guzik; G. Simon Harak, S.J.; Kenneth J. Herian, S.J.; Phillip R. Hurley, S.J.; Robert J. Joda, S.J.; Joseph B. Kappes, S.J.; William J. Kelly, S.J.; William J. Kidd, S.J.; James M. Kubicki, S.J.; William S. Kurz, S.J.; Jeffrey T. LaBelle, S.J., Rector; John D. Laurance, S.J.; Douglas J. Leonhardt, S.J.; Frank A. Majka, S.J.; Thomas C. Manahan, S.J.; D. Edward Mathie, S.J.; Donald R. Matthys, S.J.; Jose Moreno, S.J.; Charles L. Mnubi; Joseph G. Mueller, S.J.; James J. O'Leary, S.J.; Gregory J. O'Meara, S.J.; Scott R. Pilarz, S.J.; Nicholas F. Pope, S.J.; Luis Rodriguez, S.J.; David G. Schultenover, S.J.; David M. Shields, S.J.; Walter J. Stohrer, S.J.; Roland J. Teske, S.J.; Andrew J. Thon, S.J.; Karl J. Voelker, S.J.; James B. Warosh, S.J.; Robert A. Wild, S.J.; Frederick P. Zagone, S.J.; Michael J. Zeps, S.J.; Mr. Privilege Haang'andu, S.J. Marquette Jesuit Associates, Inc. Priests 50; Scholastics 2.

Jesuit Provincial Office, Wisconsin Province, P.O. Box 080288, 53208-8004. Tel: 414-937-6949; Fax: 414-937-6950. Email: wisprov@jesuitswisprov.org. Web: www.jesuitswisprov.org. Revs. Paul Coelho, S.J., Vocation Dir.; James S. Prehn, S.J., Asst. Secondary Educ.; Patrick J. Burns, S.J., Prov. Asst.; Eugene M. Dutkiewicz, S.J., Asst. Pastoral Min. & Retreat Min.; Very Rev. Thomas A. Lawler, S.J., Prov.; Revs. Theodore G. Munz, S.J., Treas.; John M. Paul, S.J., Dir. Formation; John L. Treloar, S.J., Asst. for Higher Educ. & Prov. Delegate for Conduct in Ministry. Corporate Title: Wisconsin Province of the Society of Jesus. Priests 8.

Priests of the Province Serving Abroad: Revs. James E. Grummer, S.J., Rome, Italy; John D. Mace, S.J., Phnom Penh, Cambodia; Daniel C. McDonald, S.J., Rome, Italy; John R. Schak, S.J., Salta, Argentina; Nicholas E. Schiel, S.J., Olancho, Honduras; James J. Strzok, S.J., Karen, Kenya; Anthony J. Wach, S.J., Gulu, Uganda.

Members of the Province Not Otherwise Listed: Revs. Joseph A. Brown, S.J.; Charles F. Burns, S.J., San Diego, CA; William J. Ellos, S.J., San Antonio, TX; John F. Montag; Patrick L. Murphy, S.J., Cape Canaveral, FL; James M. Radde, S.J., St. Paul, MN; Gregory A. Schissel, S.J., Dittmer, MO.

Pallotti House, 5424 W. Bluemound Rd., 53208. Tel: 414-258-0653; Fax: 414-258-9314. Email: pallotti_milw@yahoo.com. Web: www.pallottines.org. Revs. Joseph Dominic, S.A.C. (India); Davies Edassery, S.A.C. (India); Joseph Dominic Elukunnel, S.A.C. (India); Jose Eluvathingal, S.A.C. (India); Jerome A. Hapka, S.A.C.; Stephen Kaichiramattathil, S.A.C. (India); Florent Kanga, S.A.C., Cameroon; Joseph Koyickal, S.A.C. (India); Thomas Kuttiyanickal, S.A.C. (India); Sergio Lizama, S.A.C.; Very Rev. Leon J. Martin, S.A.C., Prov. Supr.; Revs. James Palakudy, S.A.C. (India); John R. Scheer, S.A.C.; Bruce J. Schute, S.A.C.; Gregory P. Serwa, S.A.C.; Thunkuchan Steve Varghese, S.A.C. (India); Bro. James Scarpace, S.A.C., Coord. Residence of Fathers and Brothers and Offices of Mother of God Province of the Society of the Catholic Apostolate also, Formation House: Novitiate. Priests 12; Brothers 1.

Pere Marquette Jesuit Community, 726 N. 34th. St., 53208-3301. Tel: 414-342-7503; Fax: 414-937-8588. Revs. Mark A. Carr, S.J., Supr.; Terrence M. Brennan, S.J.; Charles L. Stang, S.J.; Christopher J. Krall, S.J.; Mr. Brian J. Taber. Society of Jesus, Wisconsin Province. Priests 3; Scholastics 2.

Provincial Offices - Discalced Carmelites (1947) 1233 S. 45th St., 53214-3693. Tel: 414-672-7212; Fax: 414-672-3138. Email: projjs@gmail.com. Web: www.ocdwashprov.com. Very Rev. John Sullivan, O.C.D., Prov.; Sr. Beth Lyman, S.S.S.F., Prov. Admin. Asst. Priests 19; Brothers 4.

Serving Abroad: Revs. Arnold Boehme, O.C.D., Haifa, Isreal; Dennis Geng, O.C.D., Treas., Nairobi, Kenya; Thomas Martin, O.C.D., Formation Team, Retreats, Quezon City, Philippines; Ignacio Read, O.C.D., Novice Formation Team, Davao City, Philippines; Alan J. Rieger, O.C.D., Local Supr. & Spirituality Ctr., Quezon City, Philippines; Eugene C. Wehner, O.C.D., Community Svc. Librarian & Formation Team, Nairobi, Kenya.

Priests of the Province Not Otherwise Listed: Most Rev. Julio Labayen, O.C.D. (Philippines) (Retired), Paranaque, Metro Manila, Philippines; Revs. Joseph Okanda Abwanda, O.C.D. (Kenya), Seminary Spiritual Direction, Formation Team & Dir. Philosophy, Nairobi, Kenya; Nicholas Olonde Adongo, O.C.D. (Kenya), Delegate of Very Rev. Fr. Provincial, Nairobi, Kenya; Joseph Uri Baru, O.C.D. (Uganda), Graduate Studies, Rome, Italy.; Lawrence Daniels, O.C.D., Jinga, Uganda; Santulino Ekada, O.C.D. (Kenya), Rector, Nairobi, Kenya; Reginald Foster, O.C.D., Latinist, 3553 S. 41st St., #403, 53221. Milwaukee, WI; William Healy, O.C.D. (Retired), Milwaukee, WI; Jose Maria Lopez, O.C.D. (Philippines), Davao City, Philippines; Jacob Mugo Mbiti, O.C.D. (Kenya), (Tindinyo); Timothy McGough, O.C.D. (Retired), Kenosha, WI; Raymond Achuka Onsongo, O.C.D. (Kenya), (Tindinyo); Richard Opendi, O.C.D. (Uganda), (Uganda); Steven Payne, O.C.D., Dir. ISRF, Nairobi, Kenya; Abednecco Wambua Peter, O.C.D. (Kenya), Upper Kabete; Bernard Ybiernas, O.C.D. (Philippines), Bacolod City, Philippines; Daniel Mutuku Ngwili, O.C.D. (Kenya), Upper Kabete; Titus Waita Kimeu, O.C.D., Nairobi, Kenya; Elijah Martin, O.C.D., Graduate Studies, Ottawa, Canada; Stephen Nyakundi Mose, O.C.D. (Kisii); Felix Kalila Mukeya, O.C.D. (Kenya) Kisii; Deacon Samson Ongaki Gwaro, O.C.D. (Kenya) Tindinyo; Bros. Bonaventure Potter, O.C.D., (Retired), Milwaukee, WI; Sebastian Reale, O.C.D., Biddeford, ME.

Salvatorian Provincial Offices, 1735 N. Hi-Mount Blvd., 53208-1720. Tel: 414-258-1735; Fax: 414-258-1934. Email: sds@salvatorians.com. Web: salvatorians.com. Rev. Thomas Tureman, S.D.S., Dir. Missions. Society of the Divine Savior.

Provincial Council: Very Rev. David Bergner, S.D.S., M.S.W., Ph.D., Prov.; Revs. Jeffrey Wocken, S.D.S., M.A., Vicar Prov.; Robert Marsicek, S.D.S., Consultor; Scott Jones, S.D.S., Ph.D., Consultor; Scott Wallenfelsz, S.D.S., M.B.A., International Dir. Finance; Bro. Sean McLaughlin, S.D.S., M.A., Consultor.

Priests in Residence: Rev. Daniel Pekarske, S.D.S., Ph.D.

Priests/Brothers at Residences Not Listed Elsewhere: Revs. Michael Burns, S.D.S.; Bruce Clanton, S.D.S., P.O. Box 574, Racine, 53401-0574. Tel: 262-880-5047; Michael Hoffman, S.D.S., Archivist, 7811 W. Center St., 53222-4920; Joe Jagodensky, S.D.S.; Carey T. Lahrs, S.D.S.; Karl LeClaire, S.D.S.; John Vianney Muweesi, S.D.S.; Thomas Perrin, S.D.S.; Peter Schuessler, S.D.S., M.A.; Bros. Omar Oyangoran, S.D.S.; Arturo Ysmael, S.D.S.

7100 Old Loomis Rd., Greendale, 53129-2761. Tel: 414-427-8352. Revs. Michael Bigley, S.D.S.; Hugh G. Birdsall, S.D.S., M.A., M.S., 7100 W. Old Loomis Rd., Greendale, 53129-2761. Tel: 414-427-8352; Joseph Lubrano, S.D.S.; Andre Papineau, S.D.S., M.A. Society of the Divine Savior. Priests 4.

Priests of the USA Province serving at the Generalate in Rome, Italy: Very Rev. Paul Portland, S.D.S., Gen. Sec. *St. Joseph's Salvatorian Community (Novitiate)*, 3221-C S. Lake Dr., St. Francis, 53235-3702. Tel: 414-744-2402. Revs. Reed Mungovan, S.D.S. Email: reedcmungovan@hotmail.com; Joseph Rodrigues, S.D.S., Dir. Candidates and Vocations. *Salvatorian Formation House*, 9077 S. 49 St., Franklin, 53132-7606. Tel: 414-235-4395. Rev. Raul Gomez Ruiz, S.D.S., Ph.D.; Bro. Benjamin Babb, S.D.S., Student.

Priests and Brothers Residing Outside the Archdiocese of Milwaukee: Revs. Thomas Bielawa, S.D.S., Venice; Keith Brennan, S.D.S. (Retired), Tucson; Peter Coffey, S.D.S. (Retired), Brooklyn; Richard Driscoll, S.D.S., Venice; John E. Gorman, S.D.S., Wilm; Lloyd Kramlich, S.D.S., Phoenix; Michael Newman, S.D.S. (Retired), Sacramento; Joseph Wambach, S.D.S., Phoenix; Robert Wicht, S.D.S., Santa Rosa; Bros. Robert Broeg, S.D.S., Portland; Ervan Digman, S.D.S., Madison; Peter Farnesi, S.D.S., Venice; Regis Fust, S.D.S., Green Bay; Kilian Harrington, S.D.S., St. Cloud; William Hoefgen, S.D.S., Green Bay; Marvin Kluesner, S.D.S., WDC; Joseph Kreutzer, S.D.S., Birmingham; Samuel Larson, S.D.S., Bismark; George Maufort, S.D.S., Bismark; Most Rev. Thomas Meyer, S.D.S., Green Bay; Bros. Roger Nelson, S.D.S., WDC; Jeffrey St. George, S.D.S., Birmingham; Van Todd, S.D.S., Nashville; Matthew Wood, S.D.S., Green Bay.

Salvatorians - Jordan Hall, 7979 W. Glenbrook Rd., 53223-1055. Bro. John Hauenstein, S.D.S., Coord.; Revs. David Brusky, S.D.S. (Retired); Neil Durham, S.D.S. (Retired); Carl Gleason, S.D.S. (Retired); Cletus LaMere, S.D.S. (Retired); Thomas Novak, S.D.S. (Retired); Bros. George Armstrong, S.D.S., (Retired); Paul Bauer, S.D.S., (Retired); Nicholas Crosby, S.D.S., (Retired); Andre Duhaime, S.D.S., (Retired); Edward Havlovic, S.D.S., (Retired); Bertrand Hanf, S.D.S., (Retired); John Rice, S.D.S.; David Souzer, S.D.S., (Retired); Most Rev. Benedict Stoegbauer, S.D.S., (Retired); Rev. Jude Weisenbeck, S.D.S. (Retired). Fathers & Brothers of the Society of the Divine Savior. Priests 8; Brothers 8.

St. Vincent Community, 145 S. 76th St., 53214. Tel: 414-476-2447. Email: pallotti_milw@yahoo.com. Web: www.pallottines.org. Revs. John R. Scheer, S.A.C., Rector; Eugene H. Jarosch, S.A.C.; Richard J. Lorenz, S.A.C. Priests 3.

BENET LAKE. *St. Benedict's Abbey* (1945) 12605 224th Ave., 53102-1000. Tel: 262-396-4311; Fax: 262-396-4365. Email: benedictines@msn.com. Web: www.BenetLake.org. Rt. Revs. Edmund J. Boyce, O.S.B., Abbot; Andrew V. Garber, O.S.B., Resigned Abbot, Prior; Robert C. Schoofs, O.S.B., Resigned Abbot; Leo M. Ryska, O.S.B., Resigned Abbot; Very Rev. Henry V. Nurre, O.S.B., Sub-Prior; Revs. Lawrence L. Fedor, O.S.B.; Donald J. Gibbs, O.S.B.; Kevin J. Murphy, O.S.B.; Stephen E. Lattner, O.S.B., Prior. Priests 9; Brothers 10.

BURLINGTON. *Queen of Peace Friary*, 2281 Browns Lake Dr., 53105. Tel: 262-763-3241; Fax: 262-763-3326. Revs. Thomas Wojciechowski, O.F.M., Guardian; Sereno Baiardi, O.F.M.; Sante DeAngelis, O.F.M.; Bede Hepnar, O.F.M.; Stan Janowski, O.F.M.; Bronislaus Jaskulski, O.F.M.; James Krasman, O.F.M.; Ponciano Macabalo, O.F.M.; Felix Reczek, O.F.M.; Vianney Sipulski, O.F.M.; DePaul Sobotka, O.F.M.; Howard Stunek, O.F.M.; Noel Wall, O.F.M.; Raymond Zsolczai; Bros. David Dodge, O.F.M.; Gregory Havel, O.F.M.; Joseph Krymkowski, O.F.M.; Michael Kulan, O.F.M.; Jude Lustyk, O.F.M.; Edward Makowiecki, O.F.M.; Michael May, O.F.M.; Roger Srednicki, O.F.M.; Theodore Tokarz, O.F.M.; Most Rev. Didacus Weber, O.F.M. Franciscan Friars of the Assumption B.V.M. Province., Retirement Home for Franciscan Friars Priests 15; Brothers 10.

EAST TROY. *Divine Word Missionaries* (1875) Box 107, 53120-0107. Tel: 262-642-3300; Fax: 262-642-7754. Email: edpeklo@aol.com. Revs. Andrew Biller, S.V.D. (Retired); John F. Fincutter, S.V.D. (Retired); Patrick Fincutter, S.V.D. (Retired); Lucien Gaudreault, S.V.D.; Vincent Ohlinger, S.V.D.; Edward Peklo, S.V.D., Rector; Bro. Bernard Scherger, S.V.D. Society of the Divine Word. Priests 6; Brothers 1; Total in Residence 7.

FRANKLIN. *Dehon Study Center* (1993) 10731 W. Rawson Ave., 53132. Tel: 414-425-3768; Fax: 414-425-8768. Web: www.sacredheartusa.org. Rev. Paul J. McGuire, S.C.J. Priests of the Sacred Heart.

Francis and Clare Friary (2002) 9230 W. Highland Park Ave., 53132. Tel: 414-525-9253; Fax: 414-525-9289. Email: province@ofm-abvm.org. Web: www.franciscan-friars.org. *Provincial Offices of the Franciscan Friars, Assumption BVM Province, Inc.* (2002) Tel: 414-525-9253; Fax: 414-525-9289.

Email: province@ofm-abvm.org. Revs. John Cella, O.F.M., J.C.D., M.Div., M.B.A., Dir., Franciscan Pilgrimage Programs, Inc. & Guardian; James Gannon, O.F.M., Dir. Franciscan Mission - Cardinal Stritch Univ., Milwaukee & Provinical Vicar; Leslie Hoppe, O.F.M., Prof. Chicago Theological Union; Albert Lis, O.F.M., Chap. Clement Manor, Greenfield, WI; John Puodziunas, O.F.M., Prov. Min.; Paul Reczek, O.F.M., Communications Dir.; Stephen E. Malkiewicz, O.F.M., M.A., Faculty, Sacred Heart Seminary, Hales Corner; Michael Weldon, O.F.M., Faculty, Sacred Heart Seminary, Hales Corners; Bros. Andrew J. Brophy, O.F.M., Sec. of the Province & Prov. Brusar; Regis Howitz, O.F.M.; Patrick McCormack, O.F.M., Devel. Office. Priests 8; Brothers 3.

St. Francis Residence (1985) 12001 W. Woods Rd., 53132. Tel: 414-529-0332; Fax: 414-529-8777. Revs. Charles Brown, S.C.J., Ph.D.; Paul J. McGuire, S.C.J.; Dominic Peluse, S.C.J.; Bros. Andrew Lewandowski, S.C.J.; John Monek, S.C.J. Priests 2; Brothers 2.

St. Joseph's at Monastery Lake (1979) 7330 S. Lovers Lane Rd., 53132-1849. Tel: 414-525-2457. Revs. Yvon Sheehy, S.C.J., Local Supr.; Byron Haaland, S.C.J.; Paul Kelly, S.C.J.; Robert Naglich, S.C.J.; Thi Pham, S.C.J.; Bros. Raymond Kozuch, S.C.J.; Long Nguyen, S.C.J.; Frank Presto, S.C.J. Priests of the Sacred Heart. Priests 5; Brothers 3.

Sacred Heart at Monastery Lake (1989) 7330 S. Lovers Lane Rd., 53132. Tel: 414-425-5968; 414-425-5981; Fax: 414-425-0268. Web: www.scj.org. Revs. James D. Brackin, S.C.J., M.Div., J.D., Local Coord.; Michael Burke, S.C.J.; Paul Casper, S.C.J.; Thomas Cassidy, S.C.J.; Mark Fortner, S.C.J.; Edward Griesemer, S.C.J.; John Klingler, S.C.J.; William Pitcavage, S.C.J.; Lawrence Rucker, S.C.J.; Anthony P. Russo, S.C.J.; James Schifano, S.C.J; David Szatkowski, S.C.J.; Thomas Westhoven, S.C.J.; Stephen Wiese, S.C.J.; Charles Wonch, S.C.J.; Bros. Peter Mankins, S.C.J.; Matthew Miles, S.C.J.; Timothy Murphy, S.C.J.; Leonard Zaworki, S.C.J.; Deacon David Nagel. Priests 19; Brothers 4; Deacons 1.

Attached to the Community But Living Elsewhere: Revs. Donald Barnd, S.C.J.; Joseph Gole, S.T.D. (Slovenia); Vincent MacDonald, S.C.J., The Congregational Home, 3150 Lilly Rd., Brookfield, 53005; Lawrence Rucker, S.C.J.; James Schifano, S.C.J; Leonard Tadyszak, S.C.J.; Stephen Wiese, S.C.J.; Bro. Timothy Murphy, S.C.J.

HALES CORNERS. *Priests of the Sacred Heart* (1933) 7373 S. Lovers Lane Rd., P.O. Box 289, 53130-0289. Tel: 414-425-6910; Fax: 414-425-2938. Email: provsec@poshusa.org. Web: www.sacredheartusa.org. Revs. Thomas Cassidy, S.C.J., Prov. Supr.; Joseph Dean, S.C.J., Dir. Admissions; Edward Kilianski, S.C.J., Dir. Justice & Peace; Bros. Raymond Kozuch, S.C.J., Dir. Vocations; Duane Lemke, S.C.J., Dir. Formation; Deacon David Nagel, Dir. Missions; Bro. Frank Presto, S.C.J., Prov. Sec.

Priests of the Province Serving Abroad: Most Rev. Evert Baaij, S.C.J., Upper Dickens Nazareth, N. Mandela Metlo 6001 South Africa. Tel: 27-41-373-4734; Fax: 27-41-373-6141.

Attached to the Province but Living Elsewhere: Revs. Bryan Benoit, S.C.J., P.O. Box 220, Dittmer, MO 63023. Tel: 636-285-1733; Jerome Clifford, S.C.J., 5463 Dempsey, Saint Louis, MO 63110. Tel: 314-771-5867; Mark Mastin, S.C.J., Serving with Military Ordinariate as a Chaplain; Michael McMillen, S.C.J., 5728 N. Talman, Chicago, IL 60659. Tel: 773-944-5448; James Schroeder, S.C.J., 5375 Kenrick Parke Dr. N. #305, St. Louis, MO 63119. Tel: 314-968-3765; Fax: 314-647-3688; Francis Vu Tran, S.C.J.; Bro. Bernard Taube, S.C.J., 2833 Moland St., #3, Madison, 53704.

Sacred Heart Monastery (1929) 7335 S. Lovers Ln. Rd., P.O. Box 566, 53130. Tel: 414-425-8300; Fax: 414-529-6988. Web: www.sacredheartusa.org.

Priests of the Sacred Heart, 7335 S. Lovers Ln. Rd., P.O. Box 566, 53130-0566. Tel: 414-425-5323; Fax: 414-529-6988. Revs. Jan de Jong, S.C.J., S.T.D., S.T.L.; Paul Grizzelle-Reid, S.C.J., M.S., M.Div.; Wayne Jenkins, S.C.J.; James Walters, S.C.J., M.S., M.Div. Priests 3.

HOLY HILL. *Discalced Carmelite Monastery - Holy Hill Basilica of the National Shrine of Mary, Help of Christians, Holy Hill* (Shrine 1863) (Carmelite Friars 1906) Mailing Address: 1525 Carmel Rd., Hubertus, 53033. Tel: 262-628-1838; Fax: 262-628-0170. Email: juderj@juno.com. Web: www.holyhill.com. Revs. Fred Alexander, O.C.D., Pastor, St. Mary of the Hill; Michael Berry, O.C.D., Vocations Dir.; Donald Brick, O.C.D., Rector; Patrick J. Farrell, O.C.D.; Michael Griffin, O.C.D.; Cyril Guise, O.C.D., Dir. Devel.; Jude Peters, O.C.D., Prior; Phillip Thomas, O.C.D., Novice Master; Ernest Unverdorben, O.C.D.; Bros. Martin Murphy, O.C.D.; Frank Salamone, O.C.D. Priests 11; Brothers 2. *Retreat Center*, 1525 Carmel Rd., Hubertus, 53033. Tel: 262-628-1838, Ext. 127; Fax: 262-628-4294. Email: karengirard@holyhill.com. Web: www.holyhill.com. Revs. John Grennon, O.C.D., Provincial Delegate to O.C.D's; Daniel Chowning, O.C.D., First Councilor.

KENOSHA. *Missionary Congregation of the Blessed Sacrament, Inc., Zion Province*, 5804 Sheridan Rd., 53140. Tel: 262-658-8071; Fax: 262-658-2490. Email: thomasd@archmil.org. Revs. Abraham Karott George, M.C.B.S., Member; Sebastian Madathummuriyil, M.C.B.S., Member; Joseph Mulangattil, M.C.B.S., Member; Joseph Pottenparambil, Member; Pradeep Joseph Sebastian, M.C.B.S., Member; Dominic Thomas, M.C.B.S. (India), Contact Person; Thomas Vathappallil, M.C.B.S., Member.

MOUNT CALVARY. *St. Felix Friary*, N8477 County Rd. WW, 53057. Tel: 920-753-3111; Fax: 920-753-2306. Email: froliver@stlawrence.edu. Revs. Oliver Bambenek, O.F.M.Cap.; Brian Braun, O.F.M.Cap.; Steven Kropp, O.F.M.Cap.; Ken Smits, O.F.M.Cap.; Robert Wheelock, O.F.M.Cap.; Michael Zuelke, O.F.M.Cap. Priests 6.

St. Lawrence Friary (1856) 301 Church St., 53057. Tel: 920-753-7500; Fax: 920-753-7507. Email: frjohn@stlawrence.edu. Web: stlawrence.edu. Revs. John Holly, O.F.M.Cap, Campus Min. & Local Min.; Campion Baer, O.F.M.Cap., Teacher; Dennis Druggan, O.F.M.Cap., Rector & Teacher; Jerome Higgins, O.F.M.Cap., M.Ed., M.A.S., D.Min., Sisters Chap. & Spiritual Dir. (Retired); Ronald Jansch, O.F.M.Cap. (Retired); Elroy Pesch, O.F.M.Cap. (Retired); Kenan Siegel, O.F.M.Cap. (Retired); Ronald Smith, O.F.M.Cap., Spiritual Dir. & Supvr.; Ken Smits, O.F.M.Cap., Chap.; Joachim Strupp, O.F.M.Cap., Sisters' Chap. (Retired); Vernon Wagner, O.F.M.Cap. (Retired); Gary Wegner, O.F.M.Cap., Teacher & Dean of Students; Paul Yaroch, O.F.M.Cap., Chap. St. Joseph Convent, Campbellsport (Retired); Bros. Jerome Campbell, O.F.M.Cap., Maintenance Personnel; Lawrence Groeschel, O.F.M.Cap, Supvr. Priests 12; Brothers 5. Supervisory Seminary Staff: Bros. Neal Plale, O.F.M.Cap., Teacher; John Scherer, O.F.M.Cap., Vicar, Teacher; John Willger, O.F.M.Cap., Teacher.

RACINE. *Augustinian Novitiate*, 4339 Douglas Ave., 53402-2956. Tel: 262-681-3221; Fax: 262-639-3602. Revs. Jerome G. Knies, O.S.A., Prior; John R. Flynn, O.S.A., Novice Dir. Priests 2; Novices 3.

TWIN LAKES. *La Salette Missionaries* (1967) 10330-336th Ave., Box 777, 53181. Tel: 262-877-3111. Web: www.lasaletteshrine.org. Revs. Gerald Lebanowski, M.S., Dir.; James Stajkowski, M.S.; Bros. Adam Mateja, M.S.; Anthony Sepanik, M.S. Priests 2; Brothers 2.

WAUWATOSA. *Jesuit Community at St. Camillus*, 10100 W. Bluemound Rd., 53226-4377. Tel: 414-259-3731 (nurse manager); Fax: 414-259-4950. Revs. Anthony L. Dagelen, S.J.; William J. Brennan, S.J.; Robert E. Brodzeller, S.J.; John P. Daly, S.J.; Joseph F. Eagan, S.J.; Robert H. Fitzgerald, S.J.; James E. Fitzgerald, S.J.; Davind H. Gau, S.J.; Joseph C. Gill, S.J.; Jonathan Haschka, S.J., Supr.; J. Cletus Healy, S.J.; John A. Hennessy, S.J.; J. Robert Hilbert, S.J.; Robert E. Hoene, S.J.; Lawrence A. Jonas, S.J.; William T. Kolarec, S.J.; Michael D. Kurimay, S.J.; Robert W. Leiweke, S.J.; Jeffrey R. Loebl, S.J.; James E. Mauel, S.J.; Richard McCaslin, S.J.; Michael G. Morrison, S.J.; William L. Mugan, S.J.; John E. Naus, S.J.; William F. O'Leary, S.J.; Joseph N. Pershe, S.J.; Francis Paul Prucha, S.J.; John H. Rainaldo, S.J.; Leon S. Rausch, S.J.; Gerald T. Regan, S.J.; Aloysius F. Schmitz, S.J.; Richard F. Sherburne, S.J.; Paul B. Steinmetz, S.J.; William J. Sullivan, S.J.; Kenneth T. Walleman, S.J.; Patrick E. Walsh, S.J.; John W. Wambach, S.J.; Bros. James F. Becwar, S.J.; William E. Biernatzki, S.J.; Mr. Jacob J. Boddicker, S.J., Min. Society of Jesus, Wisconsin Province. Priests 37; Brothers 2; Scholastics 1.

[Q] CONVENTS AND RESIDENCES FOR SISTERS

MILWAUKEE. *Ancilla Convent* Inter-Community living for religious women.

3601 S. 41st St., 53221. Tel: 414-384-6535. Sr. Barbarina Jantsch, S.S.S.F., Dir. Sisters 20.

St. Clare Convent, 3276 S. 16th St., 53215. Tel: 414-647-2437. Email: smverona@wi.rr.com. Sisters M. Verona Schultz, Local Min.; Susan Holbach, C.S.S.F.; M. Presentia Nitecke, C.S.S.F. Felician Sisters. Sisters 4.

Dominican Sisters of the Perpetual Rosary (1897) 217 N. 68th St., 53213. Tel: 414-258-0579; Fax: 414-258-8831. Email: frannl@wi.rr.com; domsisters@wi.rr.com. Web: www.dsopr.org. Sr. Miriam Leonard, O.P., Prioress. Cloistered Dominican Sisters of the Perpetual Rosary. Professed Sisters 9.

St. Francis Convent, 3170 S. 17th St., 53215. Tel: 414-643-6387; Fax: 414-647-5372. Email: beatricecssf@hotmail.com. Sr. M. Beatrice Knipple, Local Min. Felician Sisters. Sisters 5.

St. Joseph Convent, General Motherhouse of the School Sisters of St. Francis (1874) 1501 S. Layton Blvd., 53215. Tel: 414-384-4105; Fax: 414-944-6060. Email: generalate@sssf.org. Web: www.sssf.org. Sisters Kathleen Kluthe, O.S.F., Pres.; Rita Eble, O.S.F, 1st Vice Pres.; Elsa Paul Chiriyankandath, O.S.F., Vice Pres.; Francitta Pazhukkathara, O.S.F., Vice Pres.; Carol Rigali, O.S.F., Prov.

School Sisters of St. Francis, Inc. Sisters 42; Total in Congregation 956.

Mercedes Molina - Instituto Santa Mariana de Jesus, 1234 N. 24th Pl., 53205. Tel: 414-931-7163. Email: cardeanda@hotmail.com. Sr. Maria del Carmen de Anda, R.M., Supr. Corporate Title: Mercedes Molina, Inc. Sisters 4.

Sacred Heart Center, 1545 S. Layton Blvd., 53215. Tel: 414-383-9038; Fax: 414-647-4889. S. Joann Riesterer, O.S.F., Coord. of Health & Housing Svcs.; Sisters Carol Ann Jaeger, O.S.F., Coord. Sisters Living Group; Marcian Swanson, Facility Dir. Home for retired and infirm School Sisters of St. Francis Sisters 35.

San Damiano Convent (2000) 2008 E. Euclid Ave., 53207. Tel: 414-489-9195; Fax: 414-483-5861. Email: smramona@fs-inc.net. Sr. Mary Ramona Dombrowski, C.S.S.F., Local Min. Felician Sisters 3.

Sisters of Charity of St. Joan Antida Convent (Presentation), 1329 N. Cass St., 53202. Tel: 414-276-4173. Email: present@scsja.org. Sr. Elizabeth A. Weber, S.C.S.J.A., Supr. Sisters 7.

Sisters of Charity of St. Joan Antida Convent (St. Charles Community), 3214 W. Parnell Ave., 53221. Tel: 414-282-9627. Email: stchas@scsja.org. Sr. Monica Fumo, S.C.S.J.A., Supr. Sisters 8.

Sisters of Charity of St. Joan Antida Regina Mundi Provincial House and Novitiate, 8560 N. 76th Pl., 53223. Tel: 414-354-9233; Fax: 414-355-6463. Email: sisters@scsja.org. Web: www.scsja.org. Sr. Anne Marie Baemmert, S.C.S.J.A., Prov. Sisters 5; Total in Community 35.

Sisters of the Divine Savior (1888) 4311 N. 100th St., 53222-1393. Tel: 414-466-0810; Fax: 414-466-4335. Email: smithb@salvatoriansisters.org. Web: www.sdssisters.org. Provincial Administration

Provincial Team: Corporate Title: Sisters of the Divine Savior, Inc. Sisters Carol Thresher, S.D.S., Prov. Leader; Patrice M. Colletti, S.D.S., Vicaress; Ellen Sinclair, S.D.S., Treas.

Salvatorian Sisters Residence (2001) 3810 N. 92nd St., 53222-2504. Tel: 414-760-7900; Fax: 414-358-9906. Sr. Virginia Honish, S.D.S., Coord. Sisters 20.

United States Province, 1515 S. Layton Blvd., 53215. Tel: 414-384-1515; Fax: 414-384-1950. Email: info@sssf.org. Web: www.sssf.org. Sisters Carol Rigali, O.S.F., Prov. Team; Marilyn Ketteler, O.S.F., Prov. Team; Deborah Fumagalli, O.S.F., Prov. Team. School Sisters of St. Francis, Corporate Title: The School Sisters of St. Francis of St. Joseph's Convent, Milwaukee, Wisconsin, Inc.; Corporate Title: Congregational Support Charitable Trust. Total in U.S. Province 564.

BURLINGTON. *Misioneras Franciscanas de la Juventud, Inc.*, 456 Kendall St., 53105. Tel: 262-767-0796. Email: emtenu@yahoo.com. Sr. Emma Teresa, M.F.J., Contact Person.

Missionary Sisters of the Holy Family, 31144 Hunters Tr., 53105. Tel: 262-514-2076. Email: misifab@wi.rr.com. Sr. Joanna Barbara Kacka, M.S.F., Supr. Total in Community 5.

CAMPBELLSPORT. *St. Joseph Convent*, 526 Mill St., 53010. Tel: 920-533-1100; Fax: 920-533-1145. Michael Kurtz, Facility Dir.; Sisters Marilita Lorenz, Living Group Coord.; Charlotte Schuele, O.S.F., Dir. Pastoral Svcs. School Sisters of St. Francis, Retirement Home/Health Care Center. Sisters 115.

CEDAR GROVE. *Sacred Heart of the Lake Chalet*, Box 46A, 53013. Tel: 262-285-3084. *Felician Sisters*, 1635 S. 21st St., Manitowoc, 54220. Tel: 920-652-0653. Sisters Mary Christopher Moore, C.S.S.F., Provincial Min.; M. Odelle Siskoski, 1635 S. 21st St., Manitowoc, 54220. Tel: 920-652-0653. Recreation Home for Felician Sisters of the Mother of Good Counsel.

DELAVAN. *Villa Celine*, 3127 S. Shore Dr., 53115. Tel: 773-792-6363; Fax: 773-792-9590. Sr. Virginia Ann Wanzek, C.R., Prov. Supr. & Contact Person. Summer Rest Home for Sisters of the Resurrection.

ELM GROVE. *Notre Dame of Elm Grove*, 13105

Watertown Plank Rd., 53122-2291. Tel: 262-782-1450; Fax: 262-782-2349. Email: jarmatowski@ssnd-milw.org. Web: www.ssnd-milw.org. Sisters Marie Estelle Kuczynski, S.S.N.D., Admin. Leader; Joanne Armatowski, S.S.N.D., Admin. The School Sisters of Notre Dame, Milwaukee Province, Inc., S.S.N.D. Assisted Care, Independent Living. Total in Residence 145; Total Staff 120.

School Sisters of Notre Dame, Provincial Offices, 13105 Watertown Plank Rd., 53122-2291. Tel: 262-782-9850; Fax: 262-782-5725. Email: finance@ssnd-milw.org. Web: www.ssnd-milw.org. Mary Anne Owens, S.S.N.D., Prov. Leader.

School Sisters of Notre Dame, Milwaukee Province, Inc.

School Sisters of Notre Dame at Milwaukee, Wisconsin, Inc. Charitable Trust Total in Milwaukee Province 349; Total Staff 32.

School Sisters of Notre Dame of North America, Inc., c/o NAMA Coordinating Center, 13105 Watertown Plank Rd., 53122-2291. Tel: 262-207-0047; Fax: 262-754-4878. Email: pmurphy@ssnd.org. Sr. Patricia Murphy, S.S.N.D., Dir.

FOND DU LAC. *Nazareth Center-Nazareth Court* (1998) 375 Gillett St., 54935. Tel: 920-923-7993; Fax: 920-926-6200. Email: probinsoncsa@gmail.com. Douglas Trost, Admin. Retirement Home of the Congregation of Sisters of St. Agnes., Retirement Home of the Congregation of Sisters of St. Agnes Sisters 53.

St. Agnes Convent (1858) Motherhouse, 320 County Rd. K, 54937-8158. Tel: 920-907-2300; Fax: 920-923-3194. Web: www.csasisters.org. Sr. Joann Sambs, C.S.A., Gen. Supr.

Congregation of Sisters of St. Agnes of Fond du Lac, Wisconsin, Inc. Sisters 26; Total in Community 253.

MEQUON. *Sisters of the Sorrowful Mother, Novitiate House*, 4823 W. Bonniwell Rd., 53097-2202. Tel: 262-242-5770; Fax: 262-236-0174. Email: ssmvoc@aol.com. Web: ssmfranciscans.org. Sisters 3.

MOUNT CALVARY. *Loretto Convent*, N8114 County WW, 53057. Tel: 920-753-3211; Fax: 920-753-3100. Email: sistertheresa@villalorettonh.org. Web: villalorettonh.org. General Motherhouse of Sister-Servants of Christ the King; Corporate Title: Congregation of Sister Servants of Christ the King, Inc. Sisters 7.

Our Lady of Mt. Carmel Convent 53057. Tel: 920-753-2131; 920-753-2036; Fax: 920-753-2116. Email: mbauer@ssnd-milw.org. Sr. Maxine Bauer, S.S.N.D., Leadership. Home for Retired Sisters. School Sisters of Notre Dame 25.

OCONOMOWOC. *St. Joseph Convent*, 2653 Mill Rd., 53066. Tel: 414-646-2707. Sr. M. Carolita Turzinski, C.S.S.F., Local Min. Sponsored by the Congregation of the Sisters of St. Felix of Cantalice of the United States of America, Inc. Sisters 3.

PEWAUKEE. *Carmel of the Mother of God* (1940) W267 N2517 Carmelite Rd., 53072-4528. Tel: 262-691-0336; Fax: 262-695-0143. Email: pewaukeecarmel@aol.com. Web: www.pewaukeecarmel.com. Sr. Mary Agnes Kramer, O.C.D., Prioress; Rev. Dennis C. Klemme, J.C.D., Chap. (Retired). Discalced Carmelite Nuns. Professed Sisters 8.

RACINE. *Convent of St. Catherine of Siena* (1862) Tel: 262-639-4100; Fax: 262-639-9702. Email: sienactr3@racinedominicans.org. Web: www.racinedominicans.org. Motherhouse of the Sisters of St. Dominic (Congregation of St. Catherine of Siena)., Corporate Title: Sisters of St. Dominic.; Corporation Founded 1903.

Siena Center, 5635 Erie St., 53402-1900. Tel: 262-639-4100; Fax: 262-639-9702. Web: www.racinedominicans.org. Sr. Sharon Simon, O.P., Pres. Sisters in Archdiocese 139; Total Religious in Community 159.

St. Rita's Convent, 4014 N. Green Bay Rd., 53404. Tel: 262-639-1766; Fax: 262-639-5673. Email: sr.irene@sbcglobal.net. Web: sistersofstrita.org. Sr. Irene Hanika, O.S.A., Supr. & Contact Person. Sisters 4.

ST. FRANCIS. *St. Francis Convent, Motherhouse of the Sisters of St. Francis of Assisi* (1849) 3221 S. Lake Dr., 53235-3799. Tel: 414-744-1160; Fax: 414-744-7193. Email: lakeosfs@lakeosfs.org. Web: www.lakeosfs.org. Sisters Florence Deacon, O.S.F., Dir. of the Congregation; Diana De Bruin, O.S.F., Assoc. Dir.; Margaret Kruse, O.S.F., Assoc. Dir.

The Sisters of St. Francis of Assisi, Inc.

The Ongoing Community Support Trust of the Sisters of St. Francis of Assisi, Corporate Title: The Sisters of St. Francis of Assisi, Milwaukee, Wis. Total in Community 237; Sisters in Archdiocese 168.

WAUWATOSA. *Provincial Motherhouse of the Carmelite Sisters of the Divine Heart of Jesus* (1891) 1230 Kavanaugh Pl., 53213. Tel: 414-453-4040; Fax: 414-453-5603. Email: simmaculatao@gmail.com. Web: carmelitedejnorth.org. Sr. Maria Giuseppe, Prov. Supr. Corporate Title: Carmelite Sisters of the Divine Heart of Jesus, Milwaukee, Wisconsin. Sisters 6; Novices 3; Total Religious in Province 27; Total Assisted 185; Total Staff 93.

WEST ALLIS. *Missionary Sisters of the Holy Family* (1905) 1665 S. 64th St., 53214. Tel: 414-327-4068; Fax: 414-327-4068. Email: misifa@wi.rr.com. Sr. Danuta Kujalowicz, M.S.F., Supr. Total in Community 6.

Sisters of Charity of St. Joan Antida Convent (Regina Coeli), 2716 Root River Pkwy., 53227. Tel: 414-545-2917. Email: rcoeli@scsja.org. Sr. Kathleen M. Lundwall, S.C.S.J.A., Supr. Sisters 2.

[R] HERMITAGES

SLINGER. *Carmelite Hermit of the Trinity - CHT* (1982) *Mount Carmel Hermitage*, 4270 Cedar Creek Rd., 53086-9372. Email: jmjose@catholic.org. Web: http://carmelitehermit.homestead.com. Rev. James M. Tambornino, S.O.L.T.; Sr. Joseph Marie, C.H.T., Foundress & Admin. Priests 1; Hermit Sisters (Professed) 1.

[S] RETREAT HOUSES

MILWAUKEE. *The Dwelling Place* (1986) 1611 Manitoba, South Milwaukee, 53172. Tel: 414-571-1027. Email: jschroeder23@wi.rr.com. Revs. Francis Dombrowski, O.F.M.Cap.; Jerome Schroeder, O.F.M.Cap.; Mary Klotz, Team Member. Priests 2; Total in Residence 3; Total Staff 3.

BENET LAKE. *St. Benedict's Retreat Center* (1945) 12605 224th Ave., 53102-1000. Tel: 262-396-4311; Fax: 262-396-4365. Email: benetlakeretreatcenter@gmail.com. Web: www.benetlake.org. Rt. Rev. Leo M. Ryska, O.S.B., Dir.; Denise R. Moczulewski, Co-Dir.

BRISTOL. *Mercy Retreat Center*, 12009 221st Ave., 53104. Tel: 262-862-6648. Sr. Timothy Matthews, R.S.M., Contact Person. Tel: 630-365-0828. Sisters of Mercy of the Americas West Midwest Community.

ELKHORN. *St. Vincent Pallotti Center* Pallottine Fathers, N. 6409 Bowers Rd., 53121. Tel: 262-723-2108; Fax: 262-723-8608. Email: vpallelk@elknet.net; pallotti_milw@yahoo.com. Web: www.pallottines.org. Retreat and Christian Formation Center Lay Staff 3.

OCONOMOWOC. *The Redemptorist Retreat Center*, 1800 N. Timber Trail Ln., 53066-4897. Tel: 262-567-6900; Fax: 262-567-0134. Email: rrc@redemptoristretreat.org. Web: www.redemptoristretreat.org. Revs. Charles Beierwaltes, C.Ss.R.; Richard Mevissen, C.Ss.R.; Edward F. Monroe, C.Ss.R.; Edward Vezla, C.Ss.R.; James White, C.Ss.R.; Bro. Gerard Patin, C.Ss.R. Priests 5; Total in Residence 6; Brothers 1.

RACINE. *Siena Retreat Center, Inc.*, 5635 Erie St., 53402-1900. Tel: 262-639-4100; Fax: 262-898-7332. Claire Anderson, Contact Person.

WAUKESHA. *Schoenstatt Retreat Center*, W284 N698 Cherry Ln., 53188-9402. Tel: 262-522-4300; Fax: 262-522-4301. Email: intlcenter@schsrsmary.org. Web: www.schoenstattwisconsin.org. Sisters M. Taqui Perez, Supr.; M. Jacinta Brunner, Dir. Sisters 12; Total Staff 2.

[T] SECULAR INSTITUTES

MILWAUKEE. *Secular Institute of the Schoenstatt Sisters of Mary* (1926) 5310 W. Wisconsin Ave., 53208-3061. Tel: 414-774-3536; Fax: 414-774-0520. Sr. M. Virginia Riedl, Supr. Sisters 5.

Secular Institute of the Schoenstatt Sisters of Mary - Adoration House, 5522 Bluemound Rd., 53208-3012. Tel: 414-453-5492. Sr. M. Gloriana Rivera, Supr. Sisters 3.

WAUKESHA. *Secular Institute of Schoenstatt Fathers* (1965)Tel: 262-548-9061; Fax: 262-548-9593. Email: frgerold@hotmail.com. Web: www.schoenstatt-wisconsin.org.

Schoenstatt Fathers (1965) W284 N746 Cherry Ln., 53188. Tel: 262-548-9061; Fax: 262-548-9593. Revs. Dietrich A. Haas; Gerold M. Langsch; Johnson Nellissery; Jonathan J. Niehaus; Mark J. Niehaus; Francisco Rojas. Priests 8; Total in Residence 5. Attached to the house but living elsewhere: Revs. Christian Christensen, I.S.S.S., Supr. (Austin, TX); Marcelo Aravena; Jesus Ferras (Austin, TX); Hector R. Vega, C.C., (Corpus Christi, TX).

Secular Institute of the Schoenstatt Sisters of Mary (1926) W284 N404 Cherry Ln., 53188-9416. Tel: 262-522-4200; Fax: 262-522-4201. Email: schoenstattsisters@schsrsmary.org. Web: www.schsrsmary.org. Sisters M. Joanna Buckley, Prov. Supr.; M. Cynthia Day, Supr. Sisters 30.

[U] ASSOCIATIONS OF THE FAITHFUL

BELOIT. *Franciscan Sisters of Our Lady* (1981) 2110 Bootmaker Dr., 53511-2318. Tel: 608-365-7257. Sr. Mary James Geenen, F.S.O.L., Supr. Sisters 3.

FRANKLIN. *Franciscan Sisters of Saint Clare, Inc.* (1977) 7732 S. 51st St., 53132. Tel: 414-423-5277; Fax: 414-421-7869. Email: smcs@wi.rr.com. Web: fssclare.org. Sr. Mary Celine Stein, F.S.S.C., Supr. Gen. Non-Cloistered Contemplative Community. Professed Sisters 2; Lay Affiliates 27; Postulants 1.

[V] MISSIONARY ACTIVITIES

MILWAUKEE. *Milwaukee Archdiocesan Office for World Mission* (1966) (Formerly Latin American Office), 3501 S. Lake Dr., P.O. Box 070912, 53207-0912. Tel: 414-758-2281; Fax: 414-769-3408. Email: wmo@archmil.org. Web: www.archmil.org/offices/world-mission.htm. Sr. Frances P. Cunningham, O.S.F., Dir.; Elizabeth C. Howayeck, Intl. Mission Coord. Sends priests and supports laity in overseas mission. Educates and raises funds for worldwide mission. Promotes parish twinning between archdiocese and other countries.

Our Blessed Lady of Victory Mission, Inc. (1933) 5422 W. Vliet St., 53208. Tel: 414-774-3128. Email: oblvmission@yahoo.com. Lisa Hutchinson, Pres.

Society for the Propagation of the Faith, Archdiocese of Milwaukee (1822) (Pontifical Mission Aid Societies), 3501 S. Lake Dr., P.O. Box 070912, 53207-0912. Tel: 414-758-2281; Fax: 414-769-3408. Email: wmo@archmil.org. Web: www.archmil.org/offices/world-mission.htm. Sr. Frances P. Cunningham, O.S.F., Dir.; Elizabeth C. Howayeck, Intl. Mission Coord.

Society for the Propagation of the Faith, Holy Childhood Association dba Society for the Propagation of the Faith, Archdiocese of Milwaukee (1822) (Pontifical Mission Aid Societies), 3501 S. Lake Dr., P.O. Box 070912, 53207-0912. Tel: 414-758-2281; Fax: 414-769-3408. Email: wmo@archmil.org. Web: www.archmil.org/offices/world-mission.htm. Sr. Frances P. Cunningham, O.S.F., Dir.; Elizabeth C. Howayeck, Intl. Mission Coord.

ELM GROVE. *Family Unity International, Inc.*, 12750 Stephen Pl., 53122-1964. Tel: 262-797-8988; Fax: 262-797-0637. Email: jparks@wi.rr.com. Web: www.workingboyscenter.org. Patricia J. Parks, Pres. Organization operates with the corporate participation of the director of the Milwaukee Archdiocesan Office for World Mission.

GREENDALE. *Volunteer Missionary Movement (VMM)*, 5980 W. Loomis Rd., 53129-1824. Tel: 414-423-8660; Fax: 414-423-8964. Email: vmm@vmmusa.org. Web: www.vmmusa.org. Victor J. Doucette, Exec. Dir. Recruits, trains, and sends Christian men and women to serve for two years in areas of need in the world.

RACINE. *Community of St. Paul, Inc.* (1994) 1505 Howard St., 53404. Tel: 262-634-2666; Fax: 262-635-1910. Email: racine@comsp.org. Rev. Pere Cane-Gombau, Pres.; Ms. Angels Fornaguerra, Vice Pres.; Revs. Pablo Cirujeda, Treas.; Marti Colom, Sec.; Ms. Maria Jose Morales, Sec.; Rev. Javier Guatiua, Bd. Member; Ms. Montserrat Madrid, Bd. Member. Public Association of Christian Faithful, comprised of clergy and laity. It is present in North and South America. It fosters pastoral activities and human development initiatives, while promoting mission awareness internationally.

[W] SOCIETIES

MILWAUKEE. **Christ Child Society, Inc. - Milwaukee Chapter*, 4033 W. Good Hope Rd., 53209-2268. Tel: 414-540-0489; Fax: 414-540-0549. Email: mkeccs@sbcglobal.net. Web: www.christchildsociety.com. Alice Bradee, Pres.

Priests' Purgatorial Society, 3501 S. Lake Dr., P.O. Box 070912, 53207-0912. Tel: 414-769-3340; Fax: 414-769-3908. Email: cusackb@archmil.org. Web: archmil.org. Barbara Anne Cusack, J.C.D., Sec.

**St. Vincent de Paul Society of Milwaukee*, 9601 W. Silver Spring Dr., 53225-3301. Tel: 414-462-7837; Fax: 414-462-5458. Deborah Duskey, Exec. Dir.

FOND DU LAC. **Christ Child Society - Fond du Lac Chapter*, 941 Mequon Ave., 54935. Tel: 920-921-7009. Mary Lloyd, Pres.

LOMIRA. *Legion of Mary*, W1474 County Hwy. H, 53048. Tel: 920-269-4009. Rev. Charles J. Verhalen, Spiritual Dir. (Retired), 10100 W. Blue Mound Rd., #216, Wauwatosa, 53226; Anthony Hesprich, Pres.

WEST ALLIS. *Milwaukee Archdiocesan Holy Name Union*, P.O. Box 270562, 53227. Tel: 414-327-2199; Fax: 414-546-4650. Email: stevenandbecky@sbcglobal.net. Mr. Steven R. Lazarczyk, Pres.; Rev. Edward Griesemer, S.C.J.

WHITEWATER. *Cursillos in Christianity*, 236 S. Elizabeth St., 53190. Tel: 262-473-3130. Email:

james.carlson@wicourts.gov. Web: www.cursillo.org/milwaukee. Rev. William W. Key, Spiritual Dir., English Speaking Secretariat; James Carlson, Lay Dir. Tel: 262-639-6576. Total Staff 7.

[X] NEWMAN CENTERS

MILWAUKEE. *Marquette University/Campus Ministry* P.O. Box 1881 - AMU236, 53201-1881. Tel: 414-288-6873; Fax: 414-288-3696. Email: susan.niemi@marquette.edu. Web: www.marquette.edu/cm. Rev. D. Edward Mathie, S.J., Dir.; Gerald Fischer, Assoc. Dir.

Milwaukee Archdiocesan Campus Ministry 3501 S. Lake Dr., P.O. Box 070912, 53207-0912. Tel: 414-758-2216; Fax: 414-769-3408. Email: nohlr@archmil.org. Web: www.johnpaul2center.org.

Campus Ministry of the Archdiocese of Milwaukee

Blessed John Henry Newman Catholic Campus Ministry Center, Inc. 344 N. Prairie St., Whitewater, 53190. Tel: 262-473-5555; Fax: 262-473-5855. Email: zaninb@uww.edu. Brian Zanin, Dir. Campus Ministry.

St. Catherine of Alexandria Catholic Campus Ministry Center, Inc. 3001 N. Downer Ave., 53211. Tel: 414-964-6640; Fax: 414-964-3608. Email: dawn.kinsman@yahoo.com. Rev. Michael Lightner, Dir. Campus Ministry.

[Y] MISCELLANEOUS

MILWAUKEE. *Adult Learning Center, Inc.*, 1916 N. 4th St., 53212. Tel: 414-263-5874; Fax: 414-431-2031. Email: herb@alcmke.org. Herb Hayden, Exec. Dir.; Sr. Callista Robinson, Asst. Admin.

Agape Community Center of Milwaukee, Inc. (1989) 6100 N. 42nd St., 53209. Tel: 414-464-4440; Fax: 414-464-9420. Email: abachrach@agape-center.org. Web: www.ministryhealth.org. Ann Bachrach, Exec. Dir. Corporate Sponsor: Ministry Health Care, Inc. (Milwaukee, WI); Sponsored by Sisters of the Sorrowful Mother. Total Staff 13; Total Assisted 1,547.

Alexian Elderly Services, Inc., 9301 N. 76th St., 53223. Tel: 414-355-9300; Fax: 414-357-5106. Email: gmohn@alexianbrothers.net. Gary Mohn, Contact Person.

Alternative Residential Arrangements, Inc., P.O. Box 070912, 53207-0912. Tel: 414-358-0852; Fax: 414-358-0669. Group Homes for Developmentally disabled adults.
Other Locations:
6609 N. 53rd St., 53223. Tel: 414-358-0852; Fax: 414-358-0669.
5255 S. 18th St., 53221. Tel: 414-282-6366; Fax: 414-282-3205.

St. Ann Center for Intergenerational Care, Inc., 2801 E. Morgan Ave., 53207. Tel: 414-977-5000; Fax: 414-977-5050. Email: jpglaser@stanncenter.org. Web: www.stanncenter.org. John P. Glaser, CFO.

Apostleship of Prayer, 3211 S. Lake Dr., Ste. 216, 53235. Tel: 414-486-1152; Fax: 414-486-1159. Email: info@apostleshipofprayer.org. Web: www.apostleshipofprayer.org. Revs. Phillip R. Hurley, S.J., Dir. Youth & Young Adults; James M. Kubicki, S.J., Natl. Dir.

Archdiocesan Marian Shrine, P.O. Box 070912, 53207-0912.

**Archdiocese of Milwaukee Catholic Community Foundation, Inc.*, 637 E. Erie St., 53202. Tel: 414-431-6402; Fax: 414-431-6407. Email: info@legaciesoffaith.org. Web: legaciesoffaith.org. Ms. Mary Ellen Markowski, Pres.

Assisi Homes - Jefferson Court, Inc. (1993) 415 E. Knapp St., 53202. Tel: 414-271-5370; Fax: 414-271-5988. Web: www.fm-inc.org. Housing Units 222; Residents 247; Total Staff 11.

St. Benedict Community Meal (1970) (Province of St. Joseph of the Capuchin Order, Inc.)., 1015 N. 9th St., 53233. Tel: 414-271-0135; Fax: 414-502-0494. Email: stbens@sbcglobal.net. Web: stbensmilwaukee.org. Bro. David Schwab, O.F.M.Cap., Meal Dir. Provides a free evening meal Sunday through Friday to those in need. Total Assisted 100,000; Total Staff 8.

St. Camillus Communities, Inc. - House I, 3345 S. 10th St., 53215. Tel: 414-481-3696; Fax: 414-481-8044. Very Rev. Richard O'Donnell, M.I., Pres.; Revs. Peter C. Opara, M.I.; Pedro Tramontin; Leandro Blanco. Total in Residence 4.

St. Camillus Communities, Inc. - House II, 10213 W. Wisconsin Ave., Wauwatosa, 53226. Tel: 414-443-1802. Revs. Joseph L. Bisoffi, M.I.; William Cronin, M.I.; Augustin Orosa, M.I. Total in Residence 3.

Capuchin Franciscan Volunteer Corps, 1927 N. 4th St., 53212. Tel: 414-374-8841, Ext. 29; Fax: 414-374-5553. Email: capcorps@thecapuchins.org. Web: www.capcorps.org. Shelly Roder, Dir.; Marcia Lee, Assoc. Dir. Purpose: The Capuchin Franciscan Volunteer Corps Midwest is an intentional community of full-time volunteers who live simply, practice Franciscan spirituality, and examine issues of social justice through reflection and action. Total Assisted 10,000; Total Staff 2.

Casa Romero Renewal Center, Inc. (2001) 423 W. Bruce St., 53204. Tel: 414-224-7564; Fax: 414-270-9817. Email: casaromero@wi.rr.com. Web: www.casaromerocenter.org. Rev. David M. Shields, S.J., Exec. Dir.

St. Catherine Residence, Inc. (1913) 1032 E. Knapp St., 53202. Tel: 414-272-8470; Fax: 414-272-7579. Web: www.stcatherineresidence.org. Lynne J. Oehlke, Pres.

St. Catherine Residence, Inc., Affordable housing serving women in transition and those who will benefit from an environment where women support, encourage, and network with each other. Includes a Right Start Program for first-time, single, pregnant women over the age of 17. Residents 150.

The Catholic Charismatic Renewal Office of Southeastern Wisconsin, Inc. (1980) P.O. Box 070637, 53207-0637. Tel: 414-482-1727; Fax: 414-482-3616. Email: ccr@archmil.org. Web: www.ccrmilwaukee.com. Deacon Patrick H. Frye, Liaison; Rosalita Villa, Office Mgr.

Magnificat-West Bend Chapter: Mary Mother of All Hearts, 3351 Town Line Rd., West Bend, 53095. Tel: 262-677-1192. Terri Biertzer, Pres. & Coord.

Catholic Charities Foundation, Inc., 3501 S. Lake Dr., P.O. Box 070912, 53207-0912. Tel: 414-769-3400; Fax: 414-769-3428. Email: Catholiccharities@ccmke.org. Web: www.ccmke.org. James M. Brennan, Exec. Dir.; Jacqueline Beier, Fin. Dir.

Catholic Charities of the Archdiocese of Milwaukee, Inc. (1920) 3501 S. Lake Dr., P.O. Box 070912, 53207-0912. Tel: 414-769-3400; Fax: 414-769-3428. Email: catholiccharities@ccmke.org. Web: www.ccmke.org. James M. Brennan, Exec. Dir.; Sr. Toni Anne Gradisnik, Opers. Svcs. Dir. Tel: 414-769-3402; Jacqueline Beier, Fin. Dir. Tel: 414-769-3420; Sandy Leske, Advancement Dir. Tel: 414-769-3524; Jane DeGeorge, Adult Care Ministries Dir. Tel: 262-547-2463; Ricardo Cisneros, Family & Children's Ministries Dir. Tel: 414-771-2881; Susan Howland, Social Justice Ministries Dir. Tel: 414-771-2881; Barbara Graham, Legal Svcs., Immigrants Dir. Tel: 414-643-8570; Shelby Milczarski, Human Resources Coord. Tel: 414-769-3415; Sharon Brumer, Communications Dir. Tel: 414-769-3543; Wanda Woods, Grant Writer. Tel: 414-769-3413; Rick Berg, Information & Telecommunications Systems Dir. Tel: 414-769-3534; Susi Kurek, Volunteer Coord. Tel: 414-769-3401.

St. Clare Management, Inc., 1545 S. Layton Blvd., 53215. Tel: 414-385-5330; Fax: 414-385-5333. Web: www.stclaremgt.org. Margaret E. Kidder, Exec. Dir. Sponsored by the School Sisters of St. Francis, Housing Management organization committed to providing quality residential services to low income elderly and/or persons with disabilities.

Clare Towers, Inc. dba Clare Towers, Clare Woods, Clare Heights, Clare Meadows, Clare Court, & Clare Lakes 1545 S. Layton Blvd., 53215. Tel: 414-385-5330; Fax: 414-385-5333. Web: www.stclaremgt.org. Sponsored by School Sisters of St. Francis, Housing facilities for physically disabled to live independently. Apartments 140.

**Columbia St. Mary's Foundation, The Heritage Center*, 2320 N. Lake Dr., 53211. Tel: 414-270-4900; Fax: 414-270-4901. Randall Perry, Chm. Bd. Dirs.; Lisa A. Froemming, Pres. & CEO.

Dismas Ministry (2000) P.O. Box 070363, 53207. Tel: 414-977-5064; Fax: 414-481-6764. Email: dismas@dismasministry.org. Web: www.dismasministry.org. Ronald Zeilinger, Exec. Dir. A national Catholic outreach to inmates, victims, their families, those released from prison, and the community.

Dominican Center for Women, Inc., 2470 W. Locust St., 53206-1134. Tel: 414-444-9930; Fax: 414-444-4041. Email: kierzek.sara@gmail.com. Sr. Patricia Rogers, Dir. & Contact Person.

Eastside Senior Services (1974) 2618 N. Hackett Ave., 53211. Tel: 414-961-0661; Fax: 414-961-0661. Email: eastside@interfaithmilw.org. Jane Raymer, Dir. Sponsored by SS. Peter and Paul, Lake Park Lutheran Church, ELCA, St. Mark's Episcopal Church, Plymouth Church, United Church of Christ, Our Lady of Divine Providence, Three Holy Women, Immanuel Presbyterian, Cathedral of St. John the Evangelist and Old St. Mary's, Milwaukee., Corporate Title: Eastside Senior Services, Inc. - an Interfaith Outreach Program Total Assisted 350; Total Staff 2.

**Erica P. John Fund, Inc.*, 330 E. Kilbourn Ave., Ste. 1454, 53202-3144. Tel: 414-607-6040; Fax: 414-607-6045. Paula N. John, Pres.

Faith in Our Future Trust, P.O. Box 070504, 53207-0504. Tel: 414-769-3300. Most Rev. Jerome E. Listecki, Trustee.

Felician Services, Inc., 2008 E. Euclid Ave., 53206. Tel: 414-489-9195. Sr. Clarette Stryzewski, Pres. & CEO. Felician Sisters. Sisters 3.

**St. Francis Foundation of Milwaukee, Inc.* (1968) 1600 W. Oklahoma Ave., 53215. Tel: 414-645-5337, Ext. 270; Fax: 414-645-9002. Email: dmccauley@cdcsj.org. Web: www.touchingliveseveryday.org. Sponsored by the Congregation of the Sisters of St. Felix of Cantalice of the United States of America, Inc. (Felician Sisters)., Fund development for Villa St. Francis, Child Development Center of St. Joseph and other ministries of the Felician Sisters.

Franciscan Peacemakers, Inc., Milwaukee (1995) 128 W. Burleigh St., 53212. Tel: 414-559-5761; 414-562-4780. Email: przedpel@yahoo.com. Web: www.franpax.com. Deacon Steven J. Przedpelski, Exec. Dir.; Carmen Mojica, A.P.S.W., M.S.W., Social Worker & Therapist. Total Assisted Annually 37,000; Total Staff 2.

House of Peace (1968) 1702 W. Walnut St., 53205-1616. Tel: 414-933-1300; Fax: 414-933-0395. Email: ghoward@thecapuchins.org. Web: www.houseofpeacemilwaukee.org. Gerri Sheets-Howard, M.A., Dir.; Rev. Matthew Gottschalk, O.F.M.Cap., Spiritual Dir. In Res. Rev. Alan D. Veik, O.F.M.Cap.
Affiliates: Rev. Michael Fountain, O.F.M.Cap.; Bros. T.L. Michael Auman, O.F.M.Cap.; Isidore Herriges, O.F.M.Cap.

The Jesuit Partnership, 3400 W. Wisconsin Ave., 53208-3841. Tel: 414-937-6955; Fax: 414-937-6950. Very Rev. Thomas A. Lawler, S.J., Pres.; Revs. Patrick J. Burns, S.J., Vice Pres.; Theodore G. Munz, S.J., Treas.

**St. Joan Antida High School Foundation, Ltd.*, 1341 N. Cass St., 53202. Tel: 414-354-9233; Fax: 414-355-6463. 8560 N. 76th Pl., 53223. Sr. Kathleen M. Lundwall, S.C.S.J.A., Contact Person.

The Korean Catholic Community of Milwaukee, 1854 W. Windlake Ave., 53215. Tel: 414-645-4773; Fax: 414-645-5622. Email: st.marymagd@yahoo.com. Rev. Benedict Ko, M.S.C.

**LaFarge Lifelong Learning Institute, Inc.* (1969) 1501 S. Layton Blvd., 53215. Tel: 414-944-6023; Fax: 414-944-6060. Email: cfoxho@sssf.org. Sr. Charlita Foxhoven, Corp. Sec. Continuing Education Program for older adults.

Lay Salvatorians, Inc. (2003) 1735 N. Hi-Mount Blvd., 53208-1720. Tel: 414-744-1160. Rev. Scott Wallenfelsz, S.D.S., M.B.A., Dir. Finance & Contact Person.

Layton Blvd. West Neighbors, Inc., 1545 S. Layton Blvd., 53215. Tel: 414-383-9038; Fax: 414-647-4886. Email: lbwn@execpc.com. Web: www.lbwn.org. Charlotte John-Gomez, Exec. Dir. Sponsored by School Sisters of St. Francis, Purpose: To stabilize and revitalize the area of the city known as Layton Blvd. West Neighbors by building partnerships which achieve shared responsibility for the Neighborhood.

MAREDA, 3501 S. Lake Dr., P.O. Box 070912, 53207-0912. Tel: 414-758-2242; Fax: 414-769-3408. Email: pokornyg@archmil.org. Web: www.archmil.org. James Beuscher, Chm. Archdiocese of Milwaukee, Office of Catechesis and Youth Ministry

Milwaukee Achiever Literacy Services, Inc. (1983) 5566 N. 69th t., 53218. Tel: 414-463-8820; Fax: 414-463-9484. Email: tweber@milwaukeeachiever.org. Web: www.milwaukeeachiever.org. Dennis J. Purtell, Esq., Legal Counsel. Founded by the School Sisters of St. Francis; Sisters of St. Francis of Assisi; School Sisters of Notre Dame, Purpose: To provide adult literacy education and workforce development to economically and educationally disadvantaged adults in the Greater Milwaukee area. Total Assisted Annually 1,900; Total Staff 25.

Milwaukee Archdiocesan Council of Deacons (1975)Tel: 414-769-3409; Fax: 414-769-3408. Email: zimprichd@archmil.org. Advisory/Governing Board of Deacons.
P.O. Box 070912, 53207-0912. Tel: 414-769-3409; Fax: 414-769-3408. Deacon Michael J. Finley.

Milwaukee Archdiocesan Principals' Association (MAPA), P.O. Box 070912, 53201-3087. Tel: 414-758-2251; Fax: 414-769-3408. Email: cepelkak@archmil.org. Kathleen A. Cepelka, Ph.D., Supt. Catholic Schools. Archdiocese of Milwaukee, Office for Schools.

Milwaukee Catholic Press Apostolate (1869) 3501 S. Lake Dr., P.O. Box 070913, 53207-0913. Tel: 414-769-3500; Fax: 414-769-3468. Email: chnonline@archmil.org. Web: www.chnonline.org. Brian T. Olszewski, Exec. Editor & Gen. Mgr.

**Ministry Medical Group, Inc.* (1999) 11925 W. Lake

Park Dr., 53224. Tel: 414-359-1060; Fax: 414-359-1033. Email: info@ministryhealth.org. Web: www.ministrymedicalgroup.org. Stewart Watson, M.D., Pres. & CEO.

National Association of Catholic Chaplains, 4915 S. Howell Ave., Ste. 501, 53207. Tel: 414-483-4898; Fax: 414-483-6712. Mr. David A. Lichter, Exec. Dir.

National Office of Post-Abortion Reconciliation and Healing, Inc. (1991) 3501 S. Lake Dr., P.O. Box 070477, 53207-0477. Tel: 414-483-4141; 800-593-2273; Fax: 414-483-7376. Email: noparh@juno.com. Web: www.noparh.org. Victoria M. Thorn, Exec. Dir. Total Assisted 4,500; Total Staff 3.

O.S.F. Services, Inc. (1983) 400 W. River Woods Pkwy., 53212. Tel: 414-465-3111; Fax: 414-465-3001. John D. Oliverio, Pres. Sponsored by Franciscan Sisters, Daughters of the Sacred Hearts of Jesus and Mary, Wheaton, IL.

Pallottine Fathers and Brothers, Inc., Disability Trust, 5424 W. Bluemound Rd., 53208. Tel: 414-259-0688; Fax: 414-258-9314. Email: pallotti_milw@yahoo.com. Web: www.pallottines.org. Very Rev. Leon J. Martin, S.A.C., Pres. & Treas.

Pallottine Fathers and Brothers, Inc., Educational and Apostolic Ministry Trust, 5424 W. Bluemound Rd., 53208. Tel: 414-259-0688; Fax: 414-258-9314. Email: pallotti_milw@yahoo.com. Web: www.pallottines.org. Very Rev. Leon J. Martin, S.A.C., Prov. & Treas.

Priests of the Sacred Heart Christ the King Parish Building Trust, Priests of the Sacred Heart, P.O. Box 289, Hales Corners, 53130. Tel: 414-425-6910; Fax: 414-425-2938. Deacon David Nagel, Contact Person.

S.E.T. Ministry, Inc., 2977 N. 50th St., 53210. Tel: 414-449-2680; Fax: 414-442-1770. Laurene Gramling Laehn, Pres. & CEO. Wheaton Franciscan Services, Inc., Corporate Sponsor, Joint Sponsored by 18 Religious Congregations, Health and Human Services Outreach Programs. Total Assisted 5,000.

Salvatorian Institute of Philosophy and Theology, Inc. (1993) 1735 N. Hi-Mount Blvd., 53208-1720. Tel: 414-258-1735. Rev. Scott Wallenfelsz, S.D.S., M.B.A., Dir. Finance.

**Santa Fe Communications, Inc.*, 1126 S. 70th St., Ste. N601, 53214-3155. Tel: 414-475-4444; Fax: 414-475-3621. Bruno John, Pres.

SASC, Inc., 3800 N. 92nd St., 53222-2589. Tel: 414-463-7570; Fax: 414-463-2311. Ms. Lynn Vogt, Admin. & Contact Person.

SDS Hope House, Inc., 4311 N. 100th St., 53222-1393. Tel: 414-466-0810; Fax: 414-466-4335. Sr. Carol Thresher, S.D.S., Contact Person.

Servants of Saint Camillus Disaster Relief Services, Inc., 1039 E. Russell Ave., 53207. Tel: 414-731-7318. Rev. Scott Binet, M.I., M.D., Contact Person.

Seton Health Corporation of Wisconsin (1984) *The Heritage Center*, 2320 N. Lake Dr., Ste. 1700A, 53211. Fax: 414-270-4869. Bruce McDonald, Bd. Chm. Operated by Ascension Health System.

Society of the Divine Savior Ongoing Community Support Trust, 1735 N. Hi Mount Blvd., 53208-1720. Tel: 414-258-1735; Fax: 414-258-1934. Email: sds@salvatorians.com. Web: salvatorians.com.

Ongoing Community Support Trust

St. Stephen's League (of the Archdiocesan Council of Deacons), P.O. Box 070912, 53207-0912. Tel: 414-769-3409; Fax: 414-769-3408. Email: zimprichd@archmil.org. Deacon David L. Zimprich.

Telos, Inc Clare Place and Clare Central., 1545 S. Layton Blvd., 53215. Tel: 414-385-5330; Fax: 414-385-5333. Web: www.stclaremgt.org. Sponsored by the School Sisters of St. Francis., Housing for physically disabled to live independently.

1545 S. Layton Blvd., 53215. Tel: 414-385-5330; Fax: 414-385-5333. Apartments 24.

Theological Studies, Inc., Marquette University, 100 Coughlin Hall, P.O. Box 1881, 53201-1881. Tel: 414-288-3165; Fax: 414-288-1413. Email: tseditor@marquette.edu. Web: www.ts.mu.edu. Revs. David G. Schultenover, S.J., Editor; R. Daniel Kendall, S.J., Book Review Editor. Tel: 202-687-4250; Fax: 202-687-5835; John L. Treloar, S.J., Business Mgr. Publisher of the quarterly Theological Studies.

**Wheaton Franciscan Healthcare-Southeast Wisconsin, Inc.* (1986) 400 W. River Woods Pkwy., 53212. Tel: 414-465-3111; Fax: 414-465-3001. Web: www.mywheaton.org. John D. Oliverio, Pres. & CEO. Franciscan Sisters, Daughters of the Sacred Hearts of Jesus and Mary, Wheaton, IL.

**Wheaton Franciscan Healthcare-Foundation for St. Francis and Franklin, Inc.*, 3237 S. 16th St., 53215. Tel: 414-647-5000. Mr. Daniel Mattes, Chm.

Wheaton Franciscan Home Health and Hospice, Inc. (1986) 3070 N. 51st St., Ste. 406, 53210-1661. Tel: 414-874-6161. Web: www.mywheaton.org. James D. Gresham, Pres. Franciscan Sisters, Daughters of the Sacred Hearts of Jesus and Mary, Wheaton, IL. Total Assisted Annually 5,881; Total Staff 153.

**Wheaton Franciscan Medical Group, Inc.* (1933) 400 W. River Woods Pkwy., 53212. Tel: 414-465-3000; Fax: 414-465-3001. Web: www.mywheaton.org. John D. Oliverio, Pres. & C.E.O.

Wheaton Franciscan-St. Joseph Foundation, Inc. (1984) 5000 W. Chambers St., 53210. Tel: 414-447-2844; Fax: 414-874-4399. Web: www.mywheaton.org. Rachelle Marquardt, Exec. Dir. Sponsored by Franciscan Sisters, Daughters of the Sacred Hearts of Jesus and Mary, Wheaton, IL.

BROOKFIELD. **Wheaton Franciscan Healthcare-Circle of Life Foundation, Inc.*, 13950 W. Capitol Dr., 53005. Tel: 414-535-6829. Web: www.mywheaton.org. James D. Gresham, Exec. Dir.

**Wheaton Franciscan-Elmbrook Memorial Foundation, Inc.* (2001) 19333 W. North Ave., 53045-4198. Tel: 262-785-2000. Email: shelli.marquardt@wfhc.org. Web: www.mywheaton.org. Rachelle Marquardt, Exec. Dir.

BROWN DEER. *Sisters of the Sorrowful Mother Charitable Trust* (1990) 9056 N. Deerbrook Tr., 53223-2474. Tel: 414-357-8940; Fax: 414-357-8950. Sr. M. Teresina Marra, Trustee. To help provide for the needs of the aged and infirm members of the Sisters of the Sorrowful Mother.

Sisters of the Sorrowful Mother International Finance, Inc. (1976) 9056 N. Deerbrook Tr., 53223-2474. Tel: 414-357-8940; Fax: 414-357-8950. Web: ssmgen.org. Sr. M. Teresina Marra, Chairperson.

Sisters of the Sorrowful Mother-Generalate, Inc. (1980) 9056 N. Deerbrook Tr., 53223-2474. Tel: 414-357-8940; Fax: 414-357-8950. Web: www.ssmgen.org. Sr. M. Teresina Marra, Gen. Supr.

BURLINGTON. *General Secretariat of the Franciscan Missions, Inc.*, P.O. Box 130, Waterford, 53185. Tel: 262-534-5470; Fax: 262-534-4342. Email: framis@wi.net. Web: franciscanmissions.org. Revs. Sereno Baiardi, O.F.M., Dir.; Sante De Angelis, O.F.M., Assoc. Dir.; Ponciano Macabalo, O.F.M. General Secretariat of the Franciscan Missions, Inc. Missionaries 5,400.

FOND DU LAC. **Agnesian HealthCare Foundation, Inc.*, 430 E. Division St., 54935. Tel: 920-926-4997. Rita Meidam, Contact Person.

Hazotte Ministries, Inc., 320 County Rd. K, 54937-8158. Tel: 920-907-2300; Fax: 920-923-3194. Sr. Hertha Longo, C.S.A., Pres. Sponsored by the Congregation of Sisters of St. Agnes.

FRANKLIN. *Franciscan Pilgrimage Programs, Inc.* (1974) P.O. Box 321490, 53132-6231. Tel: 414-427-0570; Fax: 414-427-0590. Email: linda@franciscanpilgrimages.com. Web: www.franciscanpilgrimages.com. Rev. John Cella, O.F.M., J.C.D., M.Div., M.B.A., Dir. & CEO. Catholic Franciscan Pilgrimages for religious men and women, leaders in Franciscan based institutions, members of the Secular Franciscan Order and any others who desire to deepen or discover Franciscan values and spirituality.

GLENDALE. *Metro Physicians, Inc.*, 400 W. River Woods Pkwy, 53212. Tel: 414-465-3000; Fax: 414-465-3582. Mark Meier, M.D., Pres.

GREENFIELD. *Clement Manor Retirement Community*, 9339 W. Howard, 53228. Tel: 414-546-7374; Fax: 414-546-7357. Web: www.clementmanor.com. Mr. Greg Szpak, Dir. Res. Svcs.; Rev. Albert Lis, O.F.M., Chap. Sponsored by the School Sisters of St. Francis, Corporate Title: Clement Manor, Inc. Residents 235; Apartments 129; Assisted Living Apartments 85.

Our Lady of the Angels, Inc., 3995 S. 92nd St., 53228. Tel: 414-810-0950; Fax: 414-810-1141.

HALES CORNERS. *Congregation of the Priests of the Sacred Heart Support and Maintenance Trust* (1991) 7373 S. Lovers Lane Rd., P.O. Box 289, 53130. Tel: 414-425-6910; Fax: 414-425-2938. Email: provsec@poshusa.org. Web: www.sacredheartusa.org. Revs. Paul J. McGuire, S.C.J., Trustee; James Walters, S.C.J., M.S., M.Div., Trustee; Bro. Raymond Kozuch, S.C.J., Trustee.

Development Office (1929) Sacred Heart Monastery-Priests of the Sacred Heart-Reign of the Sacred Heart, Inc., 6889 S. Lovers Lane Rd., P.O. Box 900, 53130. Tel: 414-425-3383; Fax: 414-425-5719. Web: www.sacredheartusa.org. Bro. Frank Presto, S.C.J., Exec. Dir. U.S. Province of the Priests of the Sacred Heart.

KENOSHA. *Assisi Homes - Kenosha, Inc.* (1994) Independent Housing for Low Income Elderly, 1860 27th Ave., 53140. Tel: 262-551-9821; Fax: 262-551-9843. Web: www.fm-inc.org. Units 60; Residents 60; Staff 3.

Assisi Homes - Saxony, Inc. (1994) Independent Housing for Low Income Elderly, 1876 22nd Ave., 53140. Tel: 262-551-9005; Fax: 262-551-7586. Web: www.fm-inc.org. Housing Units 224; Residents 221; Total Staff 8.

Catholic Woman's Club, c/o PPG Partners, LLC, 5525 Green Bay Rd., 53144. Tel: 262-657-2060; Fax: 262-657-2080. Email: osterj@ppgpartners.net. Michael DeFazio, Pres. & Contact Person.

Franciscan Seniors, Kenosha, Inc. (1994) 1920 27th Ave., 53140. Tel: 630-462-9271; 262-551-0989; Fax: 262-551-8683. Web: www.fm-inc.org.

St. Mark Latin American Center, 7101 13th Ave., 53143. Tel: 262-656-7370; Fax: 262-656-7375. Email: stmark@archmil.org. Web: www.stmark-kenosha.org. Rev. Stephen Forrest; Deacon Alvaro Dominquez; Betty Regalado, Coord. of Human Resources; Martha Sanchez, Sec. Total Assisted 2,500; Total Staff 2.

RACINE. *Catherine Marian Housing, Inc.* (1989) 5635 Erie St., 53402. Tel: 262-639-4100; Fax: 262-639-9702. Web: www.racinedominicans.org. Congregation of St. Catherine of Siena and Franciscan Ministries, Inc.

St. Catherine's High School Corporation (1972) 1200 Park Ave., 53403. Fax: 262-632-5144. Tom Leuenberger, Chm.

St. Catherine's High School of Racine, Inc. (1957) 5635 Erie St., 53402-1900. Tel: 262-639-4100; Fax: 262-639-9702. Sr. Sharon Simon, O.P., Pres.

St. Catherine's Infirmary, Inc. (1966) 5635 Erie St., 53402-1900. Tel: 262-639-4100; Fax: 262-639-9702. Sr. Sharon Simon, O.P., Pres.

Dominican College of Racine, Inc. (1957) 5635 Erie St., 53402-1900. Tel: 262-639-4100; Fax: 262-639-9702. Sr. Sharon Simon, O.P., Pres.

HOPES Center of Racine, Inc., 506 7th St., 53403. Tel: 262-898-2940; Fax: 262-898-1772. Email: mmcmahin@racinedominicans.org. Sr. Maryann McMahon, Exec. Dir.

NewBridges, Ltd., 1510 Villa St., 53403. Tel: 262-637-8374; Fax: 262-635-2426. Very Rev. Ronald J. Gramza, Chm.

Racine Dominican Ministries, Inc. (1989) 5635 Erie St., 53402-1900. Tel: 262-639-4100; Fax: 262-639-9702. Web: www.racinedominicans.org. Sr. Sharon Simon, O.P., Pres.

Racine Dominican Ministries, Inc.-Eco-Justice Center, 7133 Michna Rd., 53402. Tel: 262-681-8527. Email: eco-justice@racinedominicans.org. Web: www.racinedominicans.org. Sr. Janet Weyker, O.P., Dir. & Contact Person.

Racine Dominican Ministries, Inc.-Senior Companion Program (1978) 5635 Erie St., 53402. Tel: 262-639-4100; Fax: 262-639-9702. Email: scp@racinedominicans.org. Web: www.racinedominicans.org. Sr. Joyce Ballweg, O.P., Dir.

Wheaton Franciscan Healthcare-All Saints Foundation, Inc. (1986) 1320 Wisconsin Ave., 53403. Tel: 262-687-2239; Fax: 262-687-2674. Web: www.mywheaton.org. Christopher Krizek, Exec. Dir. Franciscan Sisters, Daughters of the Sacred Hearts of Jesus and Mary, Wheaton, IL.

ST. FRANCIS. *Archdiocese of Milwaukee Cemeteries Perpetual Care Trust*, 3501 S. Lake Dr., 53235. Tel: 414-769-3300. Most Rev. Jerome E. Listecki, Trustee.

Canticle and Juniper Courts Foundation, Inc., 3221 S. Lake Dr., 53235. Tel: 414-294-7337; Fax: 414-744-7190. Rev. Scott Wallenfelsz, S.D.S., M.B.A., Contact Person.

Canticle Court, Inc. (1987) 3201 S. Lake Dr., 53235-3708. Tel: 414-744-5878; Fax: 414-744-7636. Email: jschmitt@lakeosfs.org. Mr. John Schmitt, Pres. & CEO. Sponsored by the Sisters of St. Francis of Assisi., An Apartment building sponsored by the Sisters of St. Francis of Assisi funded by HUD for low income elderly persons who can live independently. Units 48; Total in Residence 46; Total Assisted Annually 46; Total Staff 3.

Foundation for Religious Retirement, Inc. (1987) 3221 S. Lake Dr., 53235. Tel: 414-294-7324; Fax: 414-744-7193. Email: jparrott@thefrr.org. Web: www.thefrr.org. Jan Parrott, Exec. Dir. To raise funds to assist in supporting retired women religious in the Milwaukee Archdiocese.

Juniper Court, Inc. (1993) 3209 S. Lake Dr., 53235-3712. Tel: 414-744-5878; Fax: 414-744-7636. Email: jschmitt@lakeosfs.org. Mr. John Schmitt, Pres. & CEO. Sponsored by the Sisters of St. Francis of Assisi, St. Francis, WI., An apartment building for persons of low to moderate income who can live independently. Total in Residence

52; Total Units 52; Total Assisted Annually 52; Total Staff 3.

Southeastern Wisconsin Catholic Parish Investment Management Trust, 3501 S. Lake Dr., 53235. Tel: 414-769-3334. Most Rev. Jerome E. Listecki, Trustee.

SHEBOYGAN. *The Sheboygan County Catholic Fund, Inc.*, 522 New York Ave., 53081. Tel: 920-457-4629. A fund to provide youth and adult religious education programs within the county.

STONE BANK. **Tyme Out Youth Ministry Center, Inc.* (1980) W332 N6786 County Rd. C, Nashotah, 53058-9737. Tel: 262-966-1800; Fax: 262-966-1815. Email: youth@tymeout.org. Web: www.tymeout.org. Joseph Nettesheim, Exec. Dir. Total Staff 10.

WAUKESHA. *St. Thomas More Lawyers Society of Wisconsin*, 601 E. College Ave., 53186. Tel: 262-542-7101; Fax: 262-521-4444. Email: webmaster@stthomasmorewi.org. Web: www.stthomasmorewi.org. Very Rev. Paul B.R. Hartmann, M.Div., J.C.L., Chap.

WAUWATOSA. *St. Camillus Health System, Inc.*, 10101 W. Wisconsin Ave., 53226. Tel: 414-258-1814. Very Rev. Richard O'Donnell, M.I., Pres.; Rev. Louis Lussier, M.I., Counselor; Bro. Mario Crivello, M.I., Counselor. Management Corporation. Order of the Servants of the Sick (Order of St. Camillus). Total Assisted 596.

St. Camillus Ministries, Inc., 10101 W. Wisconsin Ave., 53226. Tel: 414-258-1814. Very Rev. Richard O'Donnell, M.I., Pres.; Rev. Louis Lussier, M.I., Counselor; Bro. Mario Crivello, M.I., Counselor. St. Camillus Ministries, Inc. operates under the auspices of the Order of St. Camillus and sponsors all social concerns ministry of the Order. Total Served 596; Total Staff 3.

Friends of Calvary Cemetery, Inc., 2515 N. 66th St., 53213. Tel: 414-778-1187; Fax: 414-778-1187. Email: swerk@juno.com. Mr. Keith Schultz, Pres. Purpose: To raise funds in connection with the restoration of Calvary Chapel located at Calvary Cemetery, 5503 West Bluemound Rd., Milwaukee, WI and overseeing such restoration.

The Milwaukee Guild of the Catholic Medical Association, 737 N. Robertson St., 53213-3337. Tel: 414-771-7962; Fax: 414-771-7962. Email: milwaukee@wisconsincma.org. Web: www.wisconsincma.org. Michael Phillips, Pres.

Order of St. Camillus Foundation, Inc., 10200 W. Bluemound Rd., 53226. Tel: 414-259-8335; Fax: 414-259-4590. David Kremer, Exec. Dir. & Contact Person; Very Rev. Richard O'Donnell, M.I., Pres.; Rev. Louis Lussier, M.I.; Bro. Mario Crivello, M.I., Counselor.

San Camillo, Inc., 10200 W. Blue Mound Rd., 53226. Tel: 414-259-6300. Rick Johnson, Pres. & CEO; Very Rev. Richard O'Donnell, M.I.; Rev. Louis Lussier, M.I.; Bro. Mario Crivello, M.I., Counselor; Marie D'Amico, Vice Pres. Housing. Order of the Servants of the Sick (Order of St. Camillus), Independent living facilities for older adults. Residents 340; Total Assisted 200; Total Staff 500.

Wheaton Franciscan Laboratories, Inc., 11020 W. Plank Ct., #100, 53226. Tel: 414-256-5565; Fax: 414-256-5566. Mr. Mark Charbogian, Vice Pres. Laboratory Svcs.

WEST ALLIS. **Catholic Schools Staff Development Association* (1961) 1435 S. 92nd St., 53214. Tel: 414-476-0751; Fax: 414-259-9285. Email: larsond@archmil.org. Donna Larson, Prin. Purpose: To build a community of educators in Catholic education, emphasizing the critical importance of on-going professional development.

WEST BEND. **Casa Guadalupe Education Center, Inc.*, 479 N. Main St., 53090. Tel: 262-306-2900; Fax: 262-306-2901. Email: mlbcasaguadalupe@sbcglobal.net. Web: www.casaguadalupeonline.org. Mary Lynn Bennett, Contact Person.

WILLIAMS BAY. **The National Communicators Network for Women Religious (NCNWR)*, P.O. Box 1049, 53191. Email: coordinator@ncnwr.org. Web: www.ncnwr.org. Susan Oxley, Coord.

[Z] CLOSED PARISHES

MILWAUKEE. *St. Agnes* For sacramental records, contact Archives, Archdiocese of Milwaukee, P.O. Box 070912, Milwaukee, 53207-0912. Tel: 414-769-3407; Fax: 414-769-3408

St. Albert For sacramental records, contact Archives, Archdiocese of Milwaukee, P.O. Box 070912, Milwaukee, 53207-0912. Tel: 414-769-3407; Fax: 414-769-3408

St. Alexander Closed. For sacramental records, contact Blessed John Paul II Parish, 3307 S. 10th St., Milwaukee, 53215-5116, Tel: 414-744-3695, Fax: 414-744-2874.

St. Anne For sacramental records, contact Archives, Archdiocese of Milwaukee, P.O. Box 070912, Milwaukee, 53207-0912. Tel: 414-769-3407; Fax: 414-769-3408

St. Anthony of Padua For sacramental records, contact St. Vincent Pallotti, 7622 W. Stevenson St., Milwaukee, 53223. Tel: 414-453-5344; Fax: 414-453-4225

St. Barbara For sacramental records, contact Archives, Archdiocese of Milwaukee, P.O. Box 070912, Milwaukee, 53207-0912. Tel: 414-769-3407; Fax: 414-769-3408

Blessed Trinity Closed. For sacramental records, contact St. Catherine Parish, 5102 W. Center St., Milwaukee, 53210-2361, Tele: 414-445-5115, Fax: 414-445-5198.

Blessed Virgin of Pompei For sacramental records, contact Archives, Archdiocese of Milwaukee, P.O. Box 070912, Milwaukee, 53207-0912 Tel: 414-769-3407; Fax: 414-769-3408.

St. Boniface For sacramental records, contact Archives, Archdiocese of Milwaukee, P.O. Box 070912, Milwaukee, 53207-0912. Tel: 414-769-3407; Fax: 414-769-3408

St. Casimir For sacramental records, contact Our Lady of Divine Providence, 3055 N. Fratney St., Milwaukee, 53212, Tel: 414-264-0049, Fax: 414-264-7177.

Corpus Christi For sacramental records, contact Blessed Savior, 8607 W. Villard Ave., Milwaukee, 53225, Tel: 414-464-5033; Fax: 414-464-0079

St. Elizabeth For sacramental records, contact Archives, Archdiocese of Milwaukee, P.O. Box 070912, Milwaukee, 53207-0912. Tel: 414-769-3407; Fax: 414-769-3408

St. Emeric For sacramental records, contact Sacred Heart, 917 N. 49th St., Milwaukee, 53208. Tel: 414-774-9418; Fax: 414-774-7406

St. Gabriel For sacramental records, contact Archives, Archdiocese of Milwaukee, P.O. Box 070912, Milwaukee, 53207-0912. Tel: 414-769-3407; Fax: 414-769-3408

St. Gall For sacramental records, contact Archives, Archdiocese of Milwaukee, P.O. Box 070912, Milwaukee, 53207-0912. Tel: 414-769-3407; Fax: 414-769-3408

St. Gerard For sacramental records, contact Archives, Archdiocese of Milwaukee, P.O. Box 070912, Milwaukee, 53207-0912. Tel: 414-769-3407; Fax: 414-769-3408

St. Hedwig For sacramental records, contact Archives, Archdiocese of Milwaukee, P.O. Box 070912, Milwaukee, 53207-0912. Tel: 414-769-3407, Fax: 414-769-3408

St. Helen Closed. For sacramental records, contact Blessed John Paul II Parish, 3307 S. 10th St., Milwaukee, 53215-5116, Tel: 414-744-3695, Fax: 414744-2874.

Holy Angels For sacramental records, contact Archives, Archdiocese of Milwaukee, P.O. Box 070912, Milwaukee, 53207-0912. Tel: 414-769-3407; Fax: 414-769-3408

Holy Cross For sacramental records, contact St. Vincent Pallotti, 7622 W. Stevenson St., Milwaukee. Tel: 414-453-5344; Fax: 414-453-4225

Holy Redeemer For sacramental records, contact Archives, Archdiocese of Milwaukee, P.O. Box 070912, Milwaukee, 53207-0912. Tel: 414-769-3407; Fax: 414-769-3408

Holy Rosary For sacramental records, contact Archives, Archdiocese of Milwaukee, P.O. Box 070912, Milwaukee, 5307-0912. Tel: 414-769-3407, Fax: 414-769-3408

Holy Spirit For sacramental records, contact Archives, Archdiocese of Milwaukee, P.O. Box 070912, Milwaukee, 53207-0912. Tel: 414-769-3407; Fax: 414-769-3408

Holy Trinity-Our Lady of Guadalupe For sacramental records, contact Our Lady of Guadalupe, 613 S. 4th St., Milwaukee, 53204. Tel: 414-271-6181; Fax: 414-278-6090

St. Ignatius For sacramental records, contact Archives, Archdiocese of Milwaukee, P.O. Box 070912, Milwaukee, 53207-0912. Tel: 414-769-3407; Fax: 414-769-3408

St. John de Nepomuc For sacramental records, contact Archives, Archdiocese of Milwaukee, P.O. Box 070912, Milwaukee, 53207-0912. Tel: 414-769-3407; Fax: 414-769-3408

St. John Kanty Closed. For sacramental records, contact Blessed John Paul II Parish, 3307 S. 10th St., Milwaukee, 53215-5116, Tel: 414-744-3695, Fax: 414-744-2874.

St. Joseph For sacramental records, contact St. Joseph, 12130 Center St., Wauwatosa, 53222-4096. Tel: 414-771-4626; Fax: 414-771-4311

St. Lawrence For sacramental records, contact Archives, Archdiocese of Milwaukee, P.O. Box 070912, Milwaukee, 53207-0912. Tel: 414-769-3407; Fax: 414-769-3408

St. Leo For sacramental records, contact Archives, Archdiocese of Milwaukee, P.O. Box 070912, Milwaukee, 53207-0912. Tel: 414-769-3407; Fax: 414-769-3408

St. Mary of Czestochowa For sacramental records, contact Our Lady of Divine Providence, 3055 N. Fratney St., Milwaukee, 53212. Tel: 414-264-0049, Fax: 414-264-7177

Mary Queen of Martyrs For sacramental records, contact Blessed Savior, 8607 W. Villard Ave., Milwaukee, 53225. Tel: 414-464-5033; Fax: 414-464-0079

St. Matthew For sacramental records, contact Archives, Archdiocese of Milwaukee, P.O. Box 070912, Milwaukee, 53207-0912. Tel: 414-769-3407; Fax: 414-769-3408

St. Michael For sacramental records, contact Good Shepherd, W762 Armstrong Rd., Campbellsport, 53010-1400. Tel: 920-477-3201 Fax: 920-477-3030

Mother of Perpetual Help For sacramental records, contact Archives, Archdiocese of Milwaukee, P.O. Box 070912, Milwaukee, 53207-0912. Tel: 414-769-3407; Fax: 414-769-3408

St. Nicholas For sacramental records, contact Archives, Archdiocese of Milwaukee, P.O. Box 070912, Milwaukee, 53207-0912. Tel: 414-769-3407; Fax: 414-769-3408

Our Lady of Sorrows For sacramental records, contact Blessed Savior, 8607 W. Villard Ave., Milwaukee, 53225. Tel: 414-464-5033, Fax: 414-464-0079

St. Philip Neri For sacramental records, contact Blessed Savior, 8607 W. Villard Ave., Milwaukee, 53225. Tel: 414-464-5033; Fax: 414-464-0079

St. Rita For sacramental records, contact Archives, Archdiocese of Milwaukee, P.O. Box 070912, Milwaukee, 53207-0912. Tel: 414-769-3407, Fax: 414-769-3408

St. Stephen Martyr For sacramental records, contact Archives, Archdiocese of Milwaukee, P.O. Box 070912, Milwaukee, 53207-0912. Tel: 414-769-3407; Fax: 414-769-3408

St. Thomas Aquinas For sacramental records, contact Archives, Archdiocese of Milwaukee, P.O. Box 070912, Milwaukee, 53207-0912. Tel: 414-769-3407; Fax: 414-769-3408

St. Wenceslaus For sacramental records, contact Archives, Archdiocese of Milwaukee, P.O. Box 070912, Milwaukee, 53207-0912. Tel: 414-769-3407, Fax: 414-769-3408

ADELL. *St. Patrick* For sacramental records, contact Archives, Archdiocese of Milwaukee, P.O. Box 070912, Milwaukee, 53207-0912. Tel: 414-769-3407; Fax: 414-769-3408

ALLENTON. *Sacred Heart* For sacramental records, contact Resurrection, P.O. Box 96, Allenton, 53002-0096. Tel: 262-629-5240

ARMSTRONG. *Our Lady of Angels* For sacramental records, contact Good Shepherd, W1562 Cty. Rd. B, Eden, 53019. Tel: 920-477-3201; Fax: 920-477-3030

AUBURN. *St. Matthias* For sacramental records, contact Holy Trinity, 331 Main St., P.O. Box 461, Kewaskum, 53040. Tel: 262-626-2860, Fax: 262-626-2301

BEAVER DAM. *St Michael* For sacramental records, contact St. Katharine Drexel, 131 W. Maple Ave., Beaver Dam, 53916. Tel: 920-887-2082, Fax: 920-885-7602

St. Patrick For sacramental records, contact St. Katharine Drexel, 131 W. Maple Ave., Beaver Dam, 53916. Tel: 920-887-2082, Fax: 920-885-7602

St. Peter For sacramental records, contact St. Katharine Drexel, 131 W. Maple Ave., Beaver Dam, 53916. Tel: 920-887-2082, Fax: 920-885-7602

BRISTOL. *St. Scholastica* For sacramental records, contact Holy Cross, 18700 116th St., Bristol, 53104. Tel: 262-857-2068

BYRON. *St. John* For sacramental records, contact Sons of Zebedee: Saints James and John, W5882 Church Rd., Fond du Lac, 54937-8602. Tel: 920-922-1167

CASCADE. *St. Mary* For sacramental records, contact Archives, Archdiocese of Milwaukee, P.O. Box 070912, Milwaukee, 53207-0912. Tel: 414-769-3407, Fax: 414-769-3408

CEDARBURG. *Divine Word* For sacramental records, contact St. Francis Borgia, 1375 Covered Bridge Rd., Cedarburg, 53012. Tel: 262-377-1070; Fax: 262-377-6898

COLGATE. *St. Columba* For sacramental records, contact St. Francis Borgia Parish, 1375 Covered Bridge Rd., Cedarburg, 53012. Tel: 262-377-1070; Fax: 262-377-6898

CUDAHY. *St. Frederick* For sacramental records, contact Nativity of the Lord, 4611 S. Kirkwood Ave., Cudahy, 53110. Tel: 414-744-6622

Holy Family For sacramental records, contact Nativity of the Lord, 4611 S. Kirkwood Ave., Cudahy, 53110. Tel: 414-744-6622

St. Joseph For sacramental records, contact Nativity of the Lord, 4611 S. Kirkwood Ave.,

Cudahy, 53110. Tel: 414-744-6622

DACADA. *St. Nicholas* For sacramental records, contact Archives, Archdiocese of Milwaukee, P.O. Box 070912, Milwaukee, 53207-0912. Tel: 414-769-3407, Fax: 414-769-3408

DOTYVILLE. *St. Michael* For sacramental records, contact Good Shepherd, W1562 Cty. Rd. B, Eden, 53019. Tel: 920-477-3201; Fax: 920-477-3030

EDEN. *St. Mary* For sacramental records, contact Good Shepherd, W1562 Cty. Rd. B, Eden, 53019. Tel: 920-477-3201; Fax: 920-477-3030

ELDORADO. *St. Mary* For sacramental records, contact Our Risen Savior, W8272 Forest Ave. Rd., Eldorado, 54932-9801. Tel: 920-922-2412

ELKHART LAKE. *St. George* For sacramental records, contact St. Thomas Aquinas, P.O. Box T, Elkhart Lake, 53020-0396. Tel: 920-876-2457

FARMINGTON. *St. John of God* For sacramental records, contact St. Michael, 8877 Forestview Rd., Kewaskum, 53040. Tel: 262-334-5270; Fax: 262-334-5233

FOND DU LAC. *St. Joseph* For sacramental records prior to June 12, 1967, contact Archdiocese of Milwaukee Archives, Tel: 414-769-3407. For records after June 12, 1967, contact Holy Family, 271 Fourth St. Way, Fond du Lac, 54935. Tel: 920-921-0580

St. Louis For sacramental records prior to Sept. 20, 1959, contact Archdiocese of Milwaukee Archives, Tel: 414-769-3407. For records after Sept. 20, 1959, contact Holy Family, 271 Fourth St. Way, Fond du Lac, 54935. Tel: 920-921-0580

St. Mary For sacramental records through 1975, contact Archdiocese of Milwaukee Archives, Tel: 414-769-3407. For records after 1975, contact Holy Family, 271 Fourth St. Way, Fond du Lac, 54935. Tel: 920-921-0580.

St. Patrick For sacramental records prior to September 19, 1960, contact Archdiocese of Milwaukee Archives, Tel: 414-769-3407. For records after September 19, 1960, contact Holy Family, 271 Fourth St. Way, Fond du Lac, 54935. Tel: 920-921-0580

Sacred Heart For sacramental records prior to December, 1970, contact Archdiocese of Milwaukee Archives, Tel: 414-769-3407. For records after November, 1970, contact Holy Family, 271 Fourth St. Way, Fond du Lac, 54935. Tel: 920-921-0580

FOX LAKE. *St. Mary* For sacramental records, contact Annunciation, 305 Green St., P.O. Box 85, Fox Lake, 53933-0085. Tel: 920-928-3513; Fax: 920-928-6334

FRANKLIN. *Sacred Hearts of Jesus and Mary* For sacramental records, contact St. Martin of Tours, 7963 S. 116th St., Franklin, 53132. Tel: 414-425-1114; Fax: 414-425-2527

FREDONIA. *St. Rose of Lima* For sacramental records, contact Holy Rosary, 305 Fredonia Ave., P.O. Box 250, Fredonia, 53021-0250. Tel: 262-692-9994; Fax: 262-692-3085

GLENBEULAH. *St. Fridolin* For sacramental records, contact St. Thomas Aquinas, P.O. Box T, Elkhart Lake, 53020-0396. Tel: 920-876-2457

HOLY CROSS. *Holy Cross* For sacramental records, contact Holy Rosary, 305 Fredonia Ave., P.O. Box 250, Fredonia, 53021-0250. Tel: 262-692-9994; Fax: 262-692-3085

HORICON. *St. Malachy* For sacramental records, contact Sacred Heart, 113 Valley St., Horicon, 53032. Tel: 920-485-0694

HUBERTUS. *St. Hubert* For sacramental records after 1960, contact St. Gabriel, 1200 St. Gabriel Way, Hubertus, 53033-9794, Tel: 262-628-1141, Fax: 262-628-1911. For sacramental records prior to 1961, contact the Archdiocese of Milwaukee Archives, Tel: 414-769-3407.

JUNEAU. *Immaculate Conception* For sacramental records, contact Sacred Heart, 113 Valley St., Horicon, 53032. Tel: 920-485-0694

KENOSHA. *St. Casmir* For sacramental records, contact the Archdiocese of Milwaukee Archives. Tel: 414-769-3407

St. George For sacramental records, contact the Archdiocese of Milwaukee Archives. Tel: 414-769-3407

St. Thomas Aquinas For sacramental records, contact Archdiocese of Milwaukee Archives, Tel: 414-769-3407.

LAKE FIVE. *St. Columba* For sacramental records, contact St. Gabriel, 1200 St. Gabriel Way, Hubertus 53033-9794. Tel: 262-628-1141, Fax: 262-628-1911

LIMA. *St. Rose of Lima* For sacramental records, contact Blessed Trinity, 327 Giddings Ave., Sheboygan Falls, 53085. Tel: 920-467-4616; Fax: 920-467-4290

LITTLE KOHLER. *Mother of Sorrows* For sacramental records, contact Holy Rosary, 305 Fredonia Ave., P.O. Box 250, Fredonia, 53021-0250. Tel: 262-692-9994; Fax: 262-692-3085

LOST LAKE. *St. Mary* For sacramental records, contact Annunciation, 305 Green St., P.O. Box 85, Fox Lake, 53933-0085. Tel: 920-928-3513; Fax: 920-928-6334

LYONS. *St. Kilian* For sacramental records, contact St. Joseph, 1540 Mill St., P.O. Box 60, Lyons, 53148-0060. Tel: 262-763-2050; Fax: 262-763-9377

MEQUON. *St. James* For sacramental records, contact Lumen Christi, 11300 N. St. James Ln., 28W. Mequon, 53092, Tel: 262-242-7967; Fax: 262-242-7970.

MITCHELL. *St. Michael* For sacramental records, contact Archives, Archdiocese of Milwaukee, P.O. Box 070912, Milwaukee, 53207-0912. Tel: 414-769-3407, Fax: 414-769-3408

MONCHES. *St. John* (1843) For sacramental records, contact Blessed Teresa of Calcutta, P.O. Box 68, North Lake, 53064-0068, Tel: 262-966-2191, Fax: 262-966-1829.

MOUNT CALVARY. *Holy Cross* For sacramental records, contact St. Isidore, Mount Calvary. Tel: 920-753-3311, Fax: 920-753-2130

NABOB. *St. Matthias* For sacramental records, contact St. Lawrence, 4886 Hwy. 175, Hartford, 53027. Tel: 262-644-5701

NENNO. *St. Anthony* For sacramental records, contact Resurrection, P.O. Box 96, Allenton, 53002-0096. Tel: 262-629-5240

SS. Peter and Paul For sacramental records, contact Resurrection, P.O. Box 96, Allenton, 53002-0096. Tel: 262-629-5240

NORTH LAKE. *St. Clare* Closed. For sacramental records, contact Blessed Teresa of Calcutta, P.O. Box 68, North Lake, 53064-0068, Tel: 262-966-2191, Fax: 262-966-1829.

OAKFIELD. *St. James* For sacramental records, contact Sons of Zebedee: Saints James and John, W5882 Church Rd., Fond du Lac, 54937-8602. Tel: 920-922-1167

PELL LAKE. *St. Mary* For sacramental records, contact St. Francis de Sales, 148 W. Main St., Lake Geneva, 53147. Tel: 262-248-8524/8525; Fax: 262-248-5302

PEWAUKEE. *St. Mary* For sacramental records, contact Queen of Apostles, W280 N2101 Hwy. SS, Pewaukee, 53072. Tel: 262-691-1535; Fax: 262-691-7376

SS. Peter and Paul For sacramental records, contact Queen of Apostles, W280 N2101 Hwy. SS, Pewaukee, 53072. Tel: 262-691-1535; Fax: 262-691-7376

RACINE. *St. Casimir* For sacramental records, contact Archives, Archdiocese of Milwaukee, P.O. Box 070912, Milwaukee, 53207-0912. Tel: 262-769-3407; Fax: 262-769-3408

Holy Name For sacramental records, contact Archives, Archdiocese of Milwaukee, P.O. Box 070912, Milwaukee, 53207-0912. Tel: 262-769-3407; Fax: 262-769-3408

Holy Trinity For sacramental records, contact Archives, Archdiocese of Milwaukee, P.O. Box 070912, Milwaukee, 53207-0912. Tel: 262-769-3407; Fax: 262-769-3408

St. Rose For sacramental records, contact Archives, Archdiocese of Milwaukee, P.O. Box 070912, Milwaukee, 53207-0912. Tel: 262-769-3407; Fax: 262-769-3408

St. Stanislaus For sacramental records, contact Archives, Archdiocese of Milwaukee, P.O. Box 070912, Milwaukee, 53207-0912. Tel: 262-769-3407; Fax: 262-769-3408

RANDOLPH. *St. Gabriel* For sacramental records, contact Annunciation, 305 Green St., P.O. Box 85, Fox Lake, 53933-0085. Tel: 920-928-3513; Fax: 920-928-6334

St. Mary For sacramental records, contact Annunciation, 305 Green St., P.O. Box 85, Fox Lake, 53933-0085. Tel: 920-928-3513, Fax: 920-928-6334

RANDOM LAKE. *St. Mary* For sacramental records, contact Archives, Archdiocese of Milwaukee, P.O. Box 070912, Milwaukee, 53207-0912. Tel: 262-769-3407; Fax: 262-769-3408

RICHFIELD. *St. Mary* For sacramental records after 1966, contact St. Gabriel, Hubertus. For sacramental records before 1967, contact Archives, Archdiocese of Milwaukee, P.O. Box 070912, Milwaukee, 53207-0912. Tel: 414-769-3707; Fax: 414-769-3408

RIPON. *St. Patrick* For sacramental records, contact St. Catherine of Siena, 218 Blossom St., Ripon, 54971-1560. Tel: 920-748-2345; Fax: 920-748-3760

St. Wenceslaus For sacramental records, contact St. Catherine of Siena, 218 Blossom St., Ripon, 54971-1560, Tel: 920-748-2345; Fax: 920-748-3760

ST. CLOUD. *St. Cloud* For sacramental records, contact St. Isidore, Mount Calvary. Tel: 920-753-3311; Fax: 920-753-2130

ST. GEORGE. *St. George* For sacramental records, contact Blessed Trinity, 327 Giddings Ave., Sheboygan Falls, 53085. Tel: 920-467-4616; Fax: 920-467-4290

ST. JOE. *St. Joseph* For sacramental records, contact St. Isidore, Mount Calvary. Tel: 920-753-3311; Fax: 920-753-2130

ST. MARTIN. *Holy Assumption* For sacramental records through 1990, contact St. Mary, 9520 W. Forest Home Ave., Hales Corners, 53130. Tel: 414-425-2174; Fax: 414-425-9432. For records after 1990, contact St. Martin of Tours, 7963 S. 116th St., Franklin, 53132. Tel: 414-425-1114; Fax: 414-425-1114

ST. PETER. *St. Peter* For sacramental records prior to 1953, contact Archdiocese of Milwaukee Archives; Tel: 414-769-3407. For records after 1952, contact Holy Family, 271 Fourth St. Way, Fond du Lac, 54935, Tel: 920-921-0580.

SOUTH MILWAUKEE. *St. Adalbert* For sacramental records, contact Divine Mercy, 1304 Manitoba Ave., South Milwaukee, 53172. Tel: 414-762-6810

St. John For sacramental records, contact Divine Mercy, 1304 Manitoba Ave., South Milwaukee, 53172. Tel: 414-762-6810

St. Mary For sacramental records, contact Divine Mercy, 1304 Manitoba Ave., South Milwaukee, 53172. Tel: 414-762-6810

St. Sylvester For sacramental records, contact Divine Mercy, 1304 Manitoba Ave., South Milwaukee, 53172. Tel: 414-762-6810

THIENSVILLE. *St. Cecilia* For sacramental records, contact Lumen Christi, 11300 N. St. James Ln., 28W, Mequon, 53092, Tel: 262-242-7967, Fax: 262-242-7970.

THOMPSON. *St. Patrick* For sacramental records, contact St. Kilian, 264 W. State St., Hartford, 53027. Tel: 262-673-4831

WAYNE. *St. Bridget* For sacramental records, contact Holy Trinity, 331 Main St., P.O. Box 461, Kewaskum, 53040. Tel: 262-626-2860; Fax: 262-626-2301

WEST ALLIS. *St. Joseph* For sacramental records, contact Archives, Archdiocese of Milwaukee, P.O. Box 070912, Milwaukee, 53207-0912. Tel: 414-769-3407; Fax: 414-769-3408

Our Lady of Mount Carmel For sacramental records, contact Archives, Archdiocese of Milwaukee, P.O. Box 070912, Milwaukee, 53207-0912. Tel: 414-769-3407; Fax: 414-769-3408

St. Mary Help of Christians For sacramental records, contact Archives, Archdiocese of Milwaukee, P.O. Box 070912, Milwaukee, 53207-0912. Tel: 414-769-3407; Fax: 414-769-3408

WILMOT. *Holy Name of Jesus* For sacramental records, contact Holy Cross, 18700 116th St., Bristol, 53104. Tel: 262-857-2068

WOODHULL. *St. John the Baptist* For sacramental records, contact Our Risen Savior, W8272 Forest Ave. Rd., Eldorado, 54932-9801. Tel: 920-922-2412

RELIGIOUS INSTITUTES OF MEN REPRESENTED IN THE ARCHDIOCESE

For further details refer to the corresponding bracketed number in the Religious Institutes of Men or Women section.

[0120]—*Alexian Brothers* (Immaculate Conception Prov.)—C.F.A.

[0140]—*The Augustinians* (Mother of Good Counsel Prov.)—O.S.A.

[0200]—*Benedictine Monks*—O.S.B.

[0600]—*Brothers of the Congregation of Holy Cross* (Midwest Prov.)—C.S.C.

[0470]—*The Capuchin Friars* (Prov. of St. Joseph)—O.F.M.Cap.

[0740]—*Congregation of Marians of the Immaculate Conception*—M.I.C.

[1130]—*Congregation of the Priests of the Sacred Heart*—S.C.J.

[0480]—*Conventual Franciscans* (St. Bonaventure, Prov. of Our Lady of Consolation)—O.F.M.Conv

[0260]—*Discalced Carmelite Friars* (Prov. of the Immaculate Heart of Mary)—O.C.D.

[0520]—*Franciscan Friars*—O.F.M.

[0690]—*Jesuit Fathers and Brothers*—S.J.

[0720]—*The Missionaries of Our Lady of La Salette* (Prov. of Mary, Queen of Peace)—M.S.

[0430]—*Order of Preachers* (Province of St. Albert the Great)—O.P.

[0240]—*Order of St. Camillus-Camillian Fathers and Brothers*—M.I.

[1070]—*Redemptorist Fathers* (St. Louis Prov.)—C.Ss.R.

[0990]—*Society of the Catholic Apostolate* (Mater Dei Prov.)—S.A.C.

[1200]—*Society of the Divine Savior* (American Prov.)—S.D.S.

[0420]—*Society of the Divine Word* (Northern Prov.)—S.V.D.

[1360]—*Xaverian Missionary Fathers*—S.X.

RELIGIOUS INSTITUTES OF WOMEN REPRESENTED IN THE ARCHDIOCESE

[0230]—*Benedictine Sisters of Pontifical Jurisdiction* (Erie, PA)—O.S.B.

[0360]—*Carmelite Sisters of the Divine Heart of Jesus*—Carmel.D.C.J.

[]—*The Christian Sisters (Pious Union)*—C.S.

[]—*Congregation of Institutio Santa Mariana de Jesus*

[3710]—*Congregation of the Sisters of Saint Agnes*—C.S.A.

[1780]—*Congregation of the Sisters of the Third Order of St. Francis of Perpetual Adoration* (Eastern Region)—F.S.P.A.

[0760]—*Daughters of Charity of St. Vincent De Paul*—D.C.

[0790]—*Daughters of Divine Charity*—F.D.C.

[0420]—*Discalced Carmelite Nuns*—O.C.D.

[1060]—*Dominican Contemplative Sisters*—O.P.

[1070-03]—*Dominican Sisters*—O.P.

[]—*Dominican Sisters* (Vietnam)

[1070-09]—*Dominican Sisters*—O.P.

[1070-27]—*Dominican Sisters*—O.P.

[1070-25]—*Dominican Sisters*—O.P.

[1115]—*Dominican Sisters of Peace*—O.P.

[1170]—*Felician Sisters*—C.S.S.F.

[1230]—*Franciscan Sisters of Christian Charity*—O.S.F.

[1310]—*Franciscan Sisters of Little Falls, MN*—O.S.F.

[1415]—*Franciscan Sisters of Mary*—F.S.M.

[1430]—*Franciscan Sisters of Our Lady of Perpetual Help*—O.S.F.

[]—*Franciscan Sisters of Our Lady (Pious Union)*—F.S.O.L.

[]—*Franciscan Sisters of St. Clare (Pious Union)*—F.S.S.C.

[1470]—*Franciscan Sisters of St. Joseph*—F.S.S.J.

[1240]—*Franciscan Sisters, Daughters of the Sacred Hearts of Jesus and Mary*—O.S.F.

[]—*Hermitage of the Trinity*

[1820]—*Hospital Sisters of the Third Order of St. Francis*—O.S.F.

[]—*Missionary Sisters of the Holy Family*—M.S.F.

[3230]—*Poor Handmaids of Jesus Christ*—P.H.J.C.

[2970]—*School Sisters of Notre Dame*—S.S.N.D.

[1680]—*School Sisters of St. Francis*—O.S.F.

[]—*Secular Institute of Schoenstatt Sisters of Mary*—I.S.S.M.

[0600]—*Sisters of Charity of St. Joan Antida*—S.C.S.J.A.

[0430]—*Sisters of Charity of the Blessed Virgin Mary*—B.V.M.

[2575]—*Sisters of Mercy of the Americas*—R.S.M.

[3800]—*Sisters of St. Elizabeth*—S.S.E.

[1705]—*The Sisters of St. Francis of Assisi*—O.S.F.

[1520]—*Sisters of St. Francis of Christ the King*—O.S.F.

[3930]—*Sisters of St. Joseph of the Third Order of St. Francis*—S.S.J.-T.O.S.F.

[4020]—*Sisters of St. Rita*—O.S.A.

[1030]—*Sisters of the Divine Savior*—S.D.S.

[4100]—*Sisters of the Sorrowful Mother (Third Order of St. Francis)*—S.S.M.

[3510]—*Sisters Servants of Christ the King*—S.S.C.K.

ARCHDIOCESAN CEMETERIES

MILWAUKEE. *St. Adalbert*
Calvary
Holy Cross
Holy Trinity
Mount Olivet

FRANKLIN. *All Souls*

KENOSHA. *All Saints*

MEQUON. *Resurrection*

SHEBOYGAN. *Calvary Cemetery, Sheboygan, Wisconsin*, 902 North Ave., 53083. Tel: 920-458-7721. Mr. Vern Baus, Coord. Svcs. & Contact Person.

SOUTH MILWAUKEE. *Holy Sepulcher*, 675 College Ave., 53172-1252. Tel: 414-762-6800. Gregg F. Apostoloff, Archdiocesan Dir.

TAYCHEEDAH. *St. Charles Cemetery* 54935. Tel: 920-921-0347. (See St. Patrick Parish, Fond du Lac)

WAUKESHA. *St. Joseph*

NECROLOGY

† Schmit, Rev. Msgr. Ralph R., (Retired)—Died Nov. 10, 2011

† Aiello, John D., (Retired)—Died July 15, 2011

† Beck, Richard P., (Retired)—Died April 23, 2011

† Bryl, Thaddeus J., (Retired)—Died Dec. 2, 2010

† Myszel, George G., (Retired)—Died Sept. 14, 2011

† Neuman, Eugene C., (Retired)—Died Aug. 19, 2011

† Quartana, Donald F., (Retired)—Died Sept. 25, 2011

† Roetzer, Russell G., (Retired)—Died April 28, 2011

† Wawiorka, Raymond W., (Retired)—Died Oct. 28, 2011

An asterisk (*) denotes an organization that has established tax-exempt status directly with the IRS and is not covered by the USCCB Group Ruling.

Archdiocese of Mobile

(Archidioecesis Mobiliensis)

Most Reverend

THOMAS J. RODI

Archbishop of Mobile; ordained May 20, 1978; appointed Bishop of Biloxi May 15, 2001; ordained and installed July 2, 2001; appointed Archbishop of Mobile April 2, 2008; installed June 6, 2008. *400 Government St., Mobile, AL 36602.* Tel: 251-434-1585. Email: archbishop@mobilearchdiocese.org.

Most Reverend

OSCAR H. LIPSCOMB, D.D., PH.D.

Archbishop Emeritus of Mobile; ordained July 15, 1956; appointed July 29, 1980; consecrated November 16, 1980; retired April 2, 2008. *Res.: 400 Government St., Mobile, AL 36602.* Tel: 251-434-1585. Email: olipscomb@mobilearchdiocese.org.

CARITAS CHRISTI URGET NOS

Chancery Office: 400 Government St., Mobile, AL 36602. Tel: 251-434-1585; Fax: 251-434-1588.

Email: chancery@mobilearchdiocese.org

Square Miles 22,969.

Established as Vicariate-Apostolic of Alabama and the Floridas, 1825; Diocese of Mobile, May 15, 1829; Name changed to Diocese of Mobile-Birmingham, July 9, 1954; Redesignated, June 28, 1969. Raised to rank of Archdiocese November 16, 1980.

Comprises the lower 28 Counties of the State of Alabama, namely: Choctaw, Clarke, Wilcox, Dallas, Autauga, Elmore, Lee, Russell, Macon, Montgomery, Lowndes, Barbour, Bullock, Pike, Crenshaw, Butler, Monroe, Conecuh, Escambia, Covington, Coffee, Geneva, Dale, Henry, Houston, Washington, Baldwin and Mobile.

For legal titles of parishes and archdiocesan institutions consult the Chancery Office.

STATISTICAL OVERVIEW

Personnel	
Archbishops	1
Retired Archbishops	1
Priests: Diocesan Active in Diocese	60
Priests: Diocesan Active Outside Diocese	5
Priests: Retired, Sick or Absent	30
Number of Diocesan Priests	95
Religious Priests in Diocese	29
Total Priests in Diocese	124
Extern Priests in Diocese	4
Ordinations:	
Diocesan Priests	2
Transitional Deacons	3
Permanent Deacons in Diocese	54
Total Brothers	10
Total Sisters	116
Parishes	
Parishes	76
With Resident Pastor:	
Resident Diocesan Priests	48
Resident Religious Priests	14
Without Resident Pastor:	
Administered by Priests	14
Missions	10
Pastoral Centers	3
Professional Ministry Personnel:	
Brothers	1
Sisters	3
Lay Ministers	24
Welfare	
Catholic Hospitals	1
Total Assisted	173,104
Health Care Centers	3
Total Assisted	5,462
Homes for the Aged	5
Total Assisted	1,151
Residential Care of Children	1
Total Assisted	65
Day Care Centers	6
Total Assisted	429
Special Centers for Social Services	10
Total Assisted	48,608
Residential Care of Disabled	1
Total Assisted	58
Educational	
Diocesan Students in Other Seminaries	22
Total Seminarians	22
Colleges and Universities	1
Total Students	1,867
High Schools, Diocesan and Parish	3
Total Students	1,552
Elementary Schools, Diocesan and Parish	17
Total Students	4,637
Catechesis/Religious Education:	
High School Students	690
Elementary Students	3,746
Total Students under Catholic Instruction	12,514
Teachers in the Diocese:	
Priests	3
Brothers	2
Sisters	14
Lay Teachers	535
Vital Statistics	
Receptions into the Church:	
Infant Baptism Totals	1,182
Adult Baptism Totals	107
Received into Full Communion	245
First Communions	694
Confirmations	1,193
Marriages:	
Catholic	202
Interfaith	139
Total Marriages	341
Deaths	658
Total Catholic Population	68,662
Total Population	1,761,543

Former Prelates—Rt. Revs. MICHAEL PORTIER, D.D., ord. May 16, 1818; First Bishop; cons. Nov. 5, 1826; died May 14, 1859; JOHN QUINLAN, D.D., ord. Aug. 30, 1852; cons. Dec. 4, 1859; died March 9, 1883; DOMINIC MANUCY, D.D., ord. Aug. 15, 1850; appt. Vicar Apostolic of Brownsville and cons. Bishop of Dulma Dec. 8, 1874; transferred to Mobile March 9, 1884, but resigned in the same year; died at Mobile, Dec. 4, 1885; JEREMIAH O'SULLIVAN, D.D., ord. June 30, 1868; cons. Sept. 20, 1885; died Aug. 10, 1896; E. P. ALLEN, ord. Dec. 17, 1881; cons. May 16, 1897; died Oct. 21, 1926; Most Revs. THOMAS J. TOOLEN, D.D., ord. Sept. 27, 1910; cons. May 4, 1927; appt. Archbishop "ad personam," May 27, 1954; resigned Oct. 8, 1969; died Dec. 4, 1976; JOHN L. MAY, D.D., ord. May 3, 1947; appt. Titular Bishop of Tagarbala and Auxiliary Bishop of Chicago, June 21, 1967; cons. Aug. 24, 1967; transferred to Mobile, Oct. 8, 1969; installed Dec. 10, 1969; appt. to Saint Louis, Jan. 29, 1980; died March 24, 1994; OSCAR H. LIPSCOMB, D.D., Ph.D. (Retired), ord. July 15, 1956; appt. July 29, 1980; cons. Nov. 16, 1980; retired April 2, 2008.

Vicar General and Moderator of the Curia—Rev. Msgr. STEPHEN E. MARTIN, V.G., 400 Government St., Mobile, 36602. Tel: 251-434-1585; Fax: 251-434-1588. Email: vicargeneral@mobilearchdiocese.org.

Vicars Forane—Very Rev. JAMES F. ZOGHBY, V.F., Mobile Deanery, 6300 McKenna Dr., Mobile, 36608. Tel: 251-342-1852; Fax: 251-342-6313; Rev. Msgrs. F. CHARLES TRONCALE, V.F., Montgomery Deanery, 620 Gilmer Ave., Tallassee, 36078. Tel: 334-283-2169; PATRICK J. GALLAGHER, Dothan Deanery, 2700 W. Main St., Dothan, 36301. Tel: 334-793-5802; Fax: 334-792-2816; Very Rev. PAUL G. ZOGHBY, Baldwin/Escambia Deanery, 601 W. Laurel, Foley, 36535. Tel: 251-943-4009; Fax: 251-943-4010.

Chancellor—Deacon WALTER J. CRIMMINS. Email: wcrimmins@mobilearchdiocese.org.

Archivist—Mrs. KAREN J. HORTON.

Archives Office—14 S. Franklin St., Mobile, 36633. Tel: 251-415-3850; Fax: 251-434-1588. *Mailing Address: 400 Government St., Mobile, 36602.*

Metropolitan Tribunal—14 S. Franklin St., P.O. Box 2405, Mobile, 36652-2405. Tel: 251-432-4609; Fax: 251-432-4647. Please address all rogatory commissions and matrimonial matters to the Office of the Tribunal.

Judicial Vicar—Rev. Msgr. JAMES S. KEE, S.T.L., J.C.L., J.V.

Associate Judges—Rev. Msgr. KENNETH J. KLEPAC, J.C.L.; Deacon J. DOUGLAS SINCHAK, M.S., J.C.L.

Defenders of the Bond—Mrs. KATHERINE S. WEBER, M.S. (Th), J.C.L.; Deacon RICK CONASON, J.D., J.C.L.

Advocate—Rev. JOHNNY S. SAVOIE.

Auditor—Rev. J. FRANCIS SOFIE JR.

Notaries and Secretaries—Mrs. SHARON B. CUSIMANO; Mrs. PATRICIA K. CONNER.

Archdiocesan Consultors—Rev. Msgrs. STEPHEN E. MARTIN, V.G.; JAMES S. KEE, S.T.L., J.C.L., J.V.; Rev. JAMES J. CINK; Rev. Msgr. WILLIAM J. SKONEKI; Revs. PATRICK R. DRISCOLL; MARK I. NESKE; Very Rev. JAMES F. ZOGHBY, V.F.

Vicars for Religious—Rev. ROBERT B. RIMES, S.J., Spring Hill College, 4000 Dauphin St., Mobile, 36608. Tel: 251-460-2175.

Archdiocesan Finance Council—356 Government St., P.O. Box 230, Mobile, 36601. Tel: 251-432-2737; Fax: 251-434-1547. Email: wpuckett@mobilearchdiocese.org.

Presbyteral Council—Most Rev. THOMAS J. RODI, Pres. Officers: Very Rev. PAUL G. ZOGHBY, Chm.; Rev. Msgr. STEPHEN E. MARTIN, V.G., Sec.

Elected Members—Group I: Rev. Msgr. F. CHARLES TRONCALE, V.F. Group II: Rev. STEVEN T. WILLIAMS. Group III: Rev. PATRICK R. DRISCOLL.

Religious—Rev. PATRICK HEALY, S.S.J.
Jesuit—Very Rev. EDWARD B. ARROYO, S.J.

Priests' Personnel Committee—400 Government St., Mobile, 36602. Tel: 251-434-1585.

Priests' Retirement Board/Clergy Retirement Association—Mr. WALTER C. PUCKETT, Mailing Address: P.O. Box 230, Mobile, 36601. Tel: 251-432-2737. Email: wpuckett@mobilearchdiocese.org.

Archdiocesan Offices and Directors

Catholic Education—Mailing Address: P.O. Box 129, Mobile, 36601. Tel: 251-438-4611.
Executive Director—Miss GWENDOLYN P. BYRD. Email: gbyrd@mobilearchdiocese.org.
Schools Office—Miss GWENDOLYN P. BYRD, Supt., Mailing Address: P.O. Box 129, Mobile, 36601. Tel: 251-438-4611.
Catholic Youth Organization—Mr. PAUL CRANE, Exec. Dir., Mailing Address: P.O. Box 6955, Mobile, 36660. Tel: 251-471-0062.
Catholic Youth Ministry—Mrs. JANET MASLINE, Dir., Mailing Address: P.O. Box 129, Mobile, 36601. Tel: 251-433-4138. Email: jmasline@mobilearchdiocese.org.

Office of Religious Education—Mr. PATRICK ARENSBERG, Dir. Email: parensberg@mobilearchdiocese.org; Mr. DAVID M. O'BRIEN, Assoc. Dir. Adult Faith Formation.

Catholic Foundation of the Archdiocese of Mobile—356 Government St., P.O. Box 230, Mobile, 36601. Tel: 251-434-1556; Fax: 251-434-1547. Email: catholicfoundation@mobilearchdiocese.org. Ms. D. SUSAN WALLACE, Exec. Dir.

Catholic Publishing Co., Inc.— Publisher of the Archdiocesan Newspaper "The Catholic Week" LARRY WAHL, Editor, Mailing Address: P.O. Box 349, Mobile, 36601. Tel: 251-432-3529.

Catholic Social Services—400 Government St., Mobile, 36602. Mailing Address: P.O. Box 759, Mobile, 36601. Tel: 251-434-1550; Fax: 251-431-1549. Mrs. MARILYN D. KING, Exec. Dir. Email: mdking@cssmobile.org. Total Assisted Annually 42,051.
Apostolate for Persons with Disabilities—Mrs. RUTH P. BRELAND, Dir., 400 Government St., Mobile, 36602. Tel: 251-342-6449. Email: rbreland@cssmobile.org.
Catholic Deaf Ministry—Mr. WILLIAM F. JONES. Tel: 251-340-0990.
Mass for Shut-Ins—Mr. TOM STOUT. Tel: 251-433-0013.
Pregnancy Services—
2-B Choices for Women—100 S. University Blvd., Mobile, 36608. Tel: 251-343-4636; Fax: 251-343-6176. Mrs. JERRY ANN BODDEN, Dir. Total Assisted 1,215.
To Be Help for Pregnant Women—399 S. Section St., P.O. Box 783, Fairhope, 36532. Tel: 251-928-8661; Fax: 251-928-8871. Mrs. SONJA G. BRUECK, Dir. Total Assisted 168.
Refugee Resettlement—406 Government St., Mobile, 36602. Tel: 251-432-2727; Fax: 251-432-2927. Mrs. JANA J. CURRAN, Dir. Total Assisted 484.
Respect Life Office—400 Government St., Mobile, 36602. Tel: 251-434-1550; Fax: 251-434-1549. Mrs. ELIZABETH B. CORNELSON, Dir. Email: bcornelson@cssmobile.org.
Service Center of Catholic Social Services—555 Dauphin St., Mobile, 36602. Tel: 251-434-1500; Fax: 251-434-1509. Email: cscadmin@mobilecss.org. Web: www.mobilecss.org. Sr. MARY ANN PLASKON, R.S.M., L.C.S.W., Dir. Total Assisted 34,423. Total Staff 18.
Bay Minette Office—610 Railroad Ave., Bay Minette, 36507. Tel: 251-937-7858. Mrs. BUFFY L. MARSTON, Dir. Email: fscbm@aol.com. Total Assisted 956.
Robertsdale Baldwin Office—23010 Hwy. 59 N., P.O. Box 870, Robertsdale, 36567. Tel: 251-947-2293; Fax: 251-947-4058. Ms. MICHELE J. PROCKUP, Dir. Email: michelecssbald@gulftel.com. Total Assisted Annually 4,341.
Clarke County Office—3309 College Ave., P.O. Box 85, Jackson, 36545. Tel: 251-246-0131; Fax: 251-246-4414. Mrs. SHIELA L. SMITH, Dir. Email: cssclarke@mindspring.com. Total Assisted 1,845.
Dothan Office—557 W. Main St., Dothan, 36302. Tel: 334-793-3601; Fax: 334-702-0825. Ms. VICKIE A. ALLEMAN, Dir. Email: vaua@aol.com. Total Assisted Annually 3,118.
Montgomery Office—4455 Narrow Lane Rd., Montgomery, 36116. Tel: 334-288-8890; Fax: 334-288-9322. Mr. BARRY F. CAVAN, Dir. Email: cavan@cssalabama.org. Total Assisted 3,000.
St. Margaret's Services—Mrs. CAROL B. HERRON, Supvr. Email: herron@cssalabama.org.
Other Social Service Ministries—
Allen Memorial Home—Ms. CHERYL ROBINSON, Admin. Bed Capacity 119; Patients Assisted Annually 500; Total Staff 165. 735 S. Washington Ave., Mobile, 36603. Tel: 251-433-2642; Fax: 251-433-5502. Email: allenmhome@aol.com.
Campaign for Human Development—Mrs. MARILYN D. KING, Dir. Funding Office for charitable and other works of Archdiocese. 400 Government St., Mobile, 36602. Tel: 251-434-1550; Fax: 251-431-1549. Mailing Address: P.O. Box 759, Mobile, 36601.
Ladies of Charity—Baldwin-Escambia Deanery, 22524 Hightower Dr., Foley, 36535. Mobile Deanery, P.O. Box 6987, Mobile, 36660. Tel: 251-661-9448. *St. Jude, 3300 S. Boone St., Montgomery, 36108.*
St. Mary's Home, Mobile—4350 Moffat Rd., Mobile, 36618. Tel: 251-344-7733; Fax: 251-344-9753. Mr. PHILLIP A. WYNNE, Admin. Dependent Children 65. Email: awynne@stmaryshomemobile.org.

Censor Librorum—Rev. Msgr. STEPHEN E. MARTIN, V.G., Mailing Address: 400 Government St., Mobile, 36602. Tel: 251-434-1585; Fax: 251-434-1588.

Development Office—356 Government St., P.O. Box 230, Mobile, 36601. Tel: 251-438-9668; Fax: 251-434-1547. Ms. D. SUSAN WALLACE, Dir. Funding Office for charitable and other works of Archdiocese.Email: swallace@mobilearchdiocese.org. Encompasses: Catholic Charities Appeal Office and Planned Giving.

Financial Services—356 Government St., P.O. Box 230, Mobile, 36601. Tel: 251-432-2737; Fax: 251-434-1547.
Executive Director—Mr. WALTER C. PUCKETT. Email: wpuckett@mobilearchdiocese.org.
Accounting Department—Mrs. CINDY S. LARRY, CPA, Comptroller. Email: clarry@mobilearchdiocese.org.
Administration—Mr. DAVID V. WILTON, Dir. Email: dwitton@mobilearchdiocese.org.
Human Resources and Payroll—Mrs. VICKI A. STRICKLIN, Dir. Email: vstricklin@mobilearchdiocese.org.
Information Technology—Mr. JOSEPH E. ROBERTSON, Dir. Email: oit@mobilearchdiocese.org.
Real Estate, Property/Liability Insurance & Risk Management—Mr. JAMES D. WEISSER. Email: jweisser@mobilearchdiocese.org.
Catholic Cemetery—1700 Dr. Martin Luther King, Jr. Ave., Mobile, 36601. Tel: 251-479-5305. *Mailing Address: P.O. Box 230, Mobile, 36601.* Mr. ROBERT OVERMEYER, Mgr.
Friends of Catholic Cemetery—Mailing Address: 1400 Joyce Rd., Mobile, 36618. Mrs. MICHELLE ROGERS, Pres. Tel: 251-583-2187.
Catholic Housing of Mobile, Inc.—Most Rev. THOMAS J. RODI, Pres.; Rev. Msgr. STEPHEN E. MARTIN, V.G., Vice Pres., Mailing Address: P.O. Box 230, Mobile, 36601. Nonprofit Corp. of the State of Alabama; Encompasses Cathedral Place Apartments.
Catholic Housing Authority of Montgomery, Inc.— Most Rev. THOMAS J. RODI, Pres., 3721 Wares Ferry Rd., Montgomery, 36109. Nonprofit Corp. of the State of Alabama; Encompasses Seton Haven Apartments.
Holy Childhood Association—Rev. JAMES E. DANE, Dir., Mailing Address: P.O. Box 13357, Eight Mile, 36613. Tel: 251-981-8132.
McGill Institute, A Corporation—Mailing Address: P.O. Box 230, Mobile, 36601.
McGill-Toolen Foundation—Mailing Address: 1501 Old Shell Rd., Mobile, 36604. Tel: 251-441-0809; Fax: 251-433-8356.
Pontifical Mission Societies of the United States—Rev. JAMES E. DANE, Dir., Mailing Address: St. Bridget, P.O. Box 13357, Eight Mile, 36613. Tel: 251-981-8132 Encompasses: Propagation of the Faith, Holy Childhood Assoc., Missionary Co-op.

Liturgical Commission—Rev. Msgr. STEPHEN E. MARTIN, V.G., Mailing Address: 400 Government St., Mobile, 36602. Tel: 251-434-1585; Fax: 251-434-1588. Email: vicargeneral@mobilearchdiocese.org.

Pastoral Services—Mailing Address: 400 Government St., Mobile, 36602. Tel: 251-434-2606; Fax: 251-434-1588. Deacon WALTER J. CRIMMINS, Exec. Dir. Email: pastoralservices@mobilearchdiocese.org.
Apostleship of Prayer—Deacon WALTER J. CRIMMINS, Mailing Address: 400 Government St., Mobile, 36602. Tel: 251-434-2606. Email: pastoralservices@mobilearchdiocese.org.
Apostleship of the Sea—Rev. LITO J. CAPEDING, Chap., 400 Government St., Mobile, 36602. Tel: 251-432-7339. Email: lcapeding@mobilearchdiocese.org.
Apostolate for Aging—Deacon STEPHEN R. SEYMOUR, 5644 Bayou St. John Ave., Orange Beach, 36561.
Archdiocesan Council of Catholic Women (ACCW)—Mrs. MARY ELIZABETH DURYEA, Pres., Mailing Address: P.O. Box 340, Bay Minette, 36507; Ms. GINNY WILKINS, Pres., 3914 Cypress Shores Dr. N., Mobile, 36619.
Charismatic Movement—Deacon JAMES LABADIE, Our Lady Queen of Mercy, 4421 Narrow Lane Rd., Montgomery, 36116. Tel: 334-284-3463; Fax: 334-281-7884.
Ecumenical Commission—Rev. DAVID J. TOKARZ, Dir., 1801 Cody Rd. S., Mobile, 36695. Tel: 251-633-6762; Fax: 251-633-7790. Email: dtokarz@mobilearchdiocese.org.
Family Life Office—Mr. TOM MCDONALD; Mrs. CAROLINE MCDONALD, Mailing Address: 1413 Old Shell Rd., Mobile, 36604. Tel: 251-490-1027.
Hispanic Apostolate—Rev. JOHN E. KANE, C.M., Archdiocesan Dir., 1000 Fourth Ave., Opelika, 36801. Tel: 334-749-8359; Fax: 334-749-6312.
Mobile & Baldwin/Escambia Deaneries—Ms. RHINA GUILLEN-GOMEZ, Co Dir.; Ms. VICTORIA P. ROBERTSON, Co Dir., 400 Government St., Mobile, 36602. Tel: 251-690-6907; Fax: 251-690-6909. Email: hispanicaom@bellsouth.net. Sacramental Ministers: Revs. CHRISTOPHER J. VISCARDI, S.J.; FRANCISCO J. SAN MARTIN, S.J.
Montgomery Deanery—Co Directors: Sisters VERONICA RYAN, O.S.B., 1000 Fourth Ave., Opelika, 36801. Tel: 334-749-8359; Fax: 334-749-6312; JANET SANTIBANEZ, M.S.B.T., St. Peter, 219 Adams Ave., Montgomery, 36101. Tel: 334-202-7626. Email: vryan@mobilearchdiocese.org. Sacramental Ministers: Revs. JOSE J. PAILLACHO; PHILIP A. MCKENNA.
Dothan Deanery—Mr. CLAUDIO SAMPER, Dir., 2700 W. Main St., Dothan, 36301. Tel: 334-805-4570; Fax: 334-792-2816. Sacramental Ministers: Rev. LUIS FERNANDO-DIAZ, S.T.; Deacon ALFONSO DIAZ-RIVERA.
Holy Name Society—Deacon JOSEPH V. CONNICK, 400 Government St., Mobile, 36602. Tel: 251-432-7339.
Prison Ministry—Deacon JOHN F. ROSS, Archdiocesan Dir., 900 A.B. Stubbs Rd., Ozark, 36360. Tel: 334-774-7280. Email: jross@mobilearchdiocese.org.
Vicar for Vietnamese Affairs—Rev. CU MINH DUONG, Archdiocesan Dir., St. Monica, 1131 Dauphin Island Pkwy., Mobile, 36605. Tel: 251-479-7360.

Permanent Diaconate Program—Deacon STEPHEN R. SEYMOUR, Dir., 5644 Bayou St. John Ave., Orange Beach, 36561. Tel: 251-490-8062.

Priests' Eucharistic League—Rev. MICHAEL DEN IRWIN JR., Chm., 725 Elba Hwy., Troy, 36079. Tel: 334-566-2630. Email: dirwin@mobilearchdiocese.org.

Victim Assistance Coordinator—Rev. JAMES J. CINK, Dir., P.O. Box 230, Mobile, 36601. Tel: 251-434-1559 (Office). Email: childprotection@bellsouth.net.

Vocations—Revs. ALEJANDRO E. VALLADARES, S.T.L., Dir., 6051 Old Shell Rd., Mobile, 36608. Tel: 251-343-3662. Email: avalladares@mobilearchdiocese.org; DAVID M. SHOEMAKER, Asst. Dir., Holy Redeemer, 515 W. Broad St., Eufaula, 36027. Tel: 334-687-3716. Email: dshoemaker@mobilearchdiocese.org.

CLERGY, PARISHES, MISSIONS AND PAROCHIAL SCHOOLS

CITY OF MOBILE

(MOBILE COUNTY)

1—CATHEDRAL OF THE IMMACULATE CONCEPTION (1704) Most Rev. Thomas J. Rodi; Rev. Msgr. Stephen E. Martin, Rector; Deacons John T. Cretaro; Joseph V. Connick. In Res., Most Rev. Oscar H. Lipscomb (Retired).
Cathedral & Rectory—400 Government St., 36602. Tel: 251-434-1565; Fax: 251-434-1597.

2—ST. CATHERINE OF SIENA (1913) Rev. Msgr. James S. Kee.
Res.: 2605 Springhill Ave., 36607. Tel: 251-473-1415; 251-473-1427; Fax: 251-473-6307.
Catechesis/Religious Program—Students 13.

3—CORPUS CHRISTI PARISH, MOBILE (1958) Very Rev. James F. Zoghby; Rev. John S. Boudreaux; Deacon Arthur W. Robbins.
Res.: 6300 McKenna Dr., 36608. Tel: 251-342-1852; Fax: 251-342-6313. Email: church@corpuschristiparish.com. Web: corpuschristiparish.com.
School—(Grades K-8) Tel: 251-342-5474; Fax: 251-380-0325. Mrs. Joan T. McMullen, Prin.; Barbara Lenaghan, Librarian. Lay Teachers 27; Students 545; Aides 14.
Catechesis/Religious Program—Tel: 251-342-5474, Ext. 2; Fax: 251-380-0325. Students 159.

4—ST. DOMINIC PARISH, MOBILE (1958) Revs. James J. Cink; Frederick G. Boni, Parochial Vicar; Deacons Edward Connick; Robert Kirby. In Res., Rev. Msgr.

Francis C. Murphy (Ireland) (Retired).
Res.: 4156 Burma Rd., 36693. Tel: 251-661-5130; Fax: 251-661-0469. Web: www.stdominicmobile.org.
School—(Grades PreK-8), 4160 Burma Rd., 36693. Tel: 251-661-5226; Fax: 251-660-2242. Mrs. Linda Mathis, Prin. Lay Teachers 32; Students 504.
Catechesis/Religious Program—Students 95.
Convent—Tel: 251-661-3229.

5—ST. FRANCIS XAVIER (1867), (African American), Rev. Akama Ukanide, M.S.P.; Deacon Alexander Moore, Pastoral Assoc.
Res.: 2034 St. Stephens Rd., 36617. Tel: 251-473-4975; Fax: 251-473-4940.
Catechesis/Religious Program—Students 17.

6—HOLY FAMILY (1959) Rev. Mark I. Neske.
Res.: 1400 Joyce Rd., 36618. Tel: 251-344-0271; Fax: 251-344-0296. Email: holyfamilychu637@bellsouth.net.

7—ST. IGNATIUS PARISH, MOBILE (Spring Hill) (1947) Rev. W. Bry Shields; Deacons Charles J. Fontana; Marvin C. Johns. In Res., Rev. Cecil R. Spotswood.
Res.: 3704 Springhill Ave., 36608. Tel: 251-342-9221; Fax: 251-341-1481.
School—(Grades PreK-8), 3650 Springhill Ave., 36608. Tel: 251-342-5442; Fax: 251-344-0944. Mr. Gary Blackburn, Prin.; Maureen Goodwin, Vice Prin.; Mrs. Dorothy Beattie, Librarian. Lay Teachers 32; Students 530.
Mother's Day Out—Tel: 251-445-6750; Fax: 251-345-1064. Lay Teachers 5; Students 37.
Catechesis/Religious Program—Students 150.

8—ST. JOAN OF ARC (1920) Rev. Msgr. Kenneth J. Klepac.
Res.: 1260 Elmira St., 36604. Tel: 251-432-3505.

9—ST. JOSEPH (1857) Rev. Msgr. Stephen E. Martin. Mailing Address: 400 Government St., 36602. 808 Springhill Ave., 36602. Tel: 251-434-1565.

10—ST. JOSEPH (Maysville) (1944), (African American), Rev. Jeremiah A. Brady, S.S.J.; Deacon Ronnie A. Hathorne.
Res.: 1703 Dublin St., 36605. Tel: 251-473-3761.
Convent—1701 Dublin St., 36605. Tel: 251-478-3292.

11—LITTLE FLOWER (1928) Rev. John G. Lynes.
Res.: 2053 Government St., 36606. Tel: 251-478-3381; Fax: 251-476-4064.
School—(Grades K-8), 2103 Government St., 36606. Tel: 251-479-5761; Fax: 251-450-3696. Clara Brunk, Prin. Lay Teachers 10; Students 151.
Catechesis/Religious Program—Students 63.
Convent—359 Pinehill Dr., 36606. Tel: 251-479-9116.

12—ST. MARY (1867) Rev. Msgr. G. Warren Wall; Rev. Daniel F. Good, Parochial Vicar; Sr. M. Magdalena Langlois, C.S.A., Pastoral Assoc.; Deacons Ernest J. Johnson; Holcombe Pryor.
Mailing Address: 106 Providence St., 36604. In Res., Rev. Msgr. Maurice L. Shields (Retired).
Res.: 1453 Old Shell Rd., 36604. Tel: 251-432-8679; Fax: 251-432-1009.
School—(Grades PreK-8) Tel: 251-433-9904; Fax: 251-438-9069. Mrs. Debbie Ollis, Prin.; Sue Lyon, Librarian. Lay Teachers 41; Students 501.
Catechesis/Religious Program—Students 31.

13—ST. MATTHEW (1904) Rev. Joseph M. Bolling.
Res.: 906 Garrity St., 36605-4699. Tel: 251-432-4784.

14—ST. MONICA (1950) Rev. Cu Minh Duong; Deacon Truat Van Nguyen.
Res.: 1131 Dauphin Island Pkwy., 36605. Tel: 251-479-7360.

15—MOST PURE HEART OF MARY (1899), (African American), Rev. Patrick Healy, S.S.J.; Deacon James D. Bryant.
Res. & Mailing Address: 304 Sengstak St., 36603. Tel: 251-432-3344; Fax: 251-432-1192. Email: mphm@josephite.com. Web: www.josephite.com/parish/al/mphm.
School—Most Pure Heart of Mary, (Grades K-8) Tel: 251-432-5270; Fax: 251-432-5271. Sr. Nancy Crossen, O.S.F., Prin.; Sheila Mahoney, Librarian. Students 170.
Catechesis/Religious Program—Students 26.
Convent—310 Sengstak St., 36603. Tel: 251-433-6519.

16—OUR LADY OF LOURDES (1941) Rev. J. Francis Sofie Jr.; Deacon Gordon Kenny.
Res.: 1621 Boykin Blvd., 36605. Tel: 251-479-9885; Fax: 251-479-9892.
Catechesis/Religious Program—Students 20.

17—OUR SAVIOR (1977) Rev. David J. Tokarz; Deacon Charles H. Kenny.
Office:—1801 Cody Rd. S., 36695. Tel: 251-633-6762; Fax: 251-633-7790.
Catechesis/Religious Program—Students 141.

18—ST. PIUS X (1954) Revs. Johnny S. Savoie; Stephen G. Vrazel, Parochial Vicar; Deacon William L. Tew.
Res.: 217 S. Sage Ave., 36606. Tel: 251-471-2449; Fax: 251-471-2441.
School—(Grades K-8) Tel: 251-473-5004; Fax: 251-473-5008. Mrs. Lauren Alvarez, Prin.; Diane Roberts, Librarian. Sisters 1; Lay Teachers 27; Students 369.
Catechesis/Religious Program—Tel: 251-473-4381. Students 25.

19—PRINCE OF PEACE (1970), (African American), Rev. John R. Basiimwa, F.M.H.
Res.: 454 Charleston St., 36603. Tel: 251-432-2364; Fax: 251-432-2372.
Catechesis/Religious Program—Tel: 251-433-1494. Students 20.

OUTSIDE THE CITY OF MOBILE

ANDALUSIA, COVINGTON CO., CHRIST THE KING (1933) Rev. Antony Pullukattu Xavier.
Res.: 504 Sanford Rd., P.O. Drawer 1546, 36420. Tel: 334-222-4808. Email: ctk@centurytel.net.
Catechesis/Religious Program—Students 36.

ATMORE, ESCAMBIA CO., ST. ROBERT BELLARMINE (1943) Rev. Gordon N. Milsted.
Res.: 600 S. Main St., 36502-2825. Tel: 251-368-3615; Fax: 251-368-1801.
Catechesis/Religious Program—Students 30.

AUBURN, LEE CO., ST. MICHAEL (1912) Rev. Msgr. William J. Skoneki; Rev. James N. Morrison, Parochial Vicar; Deacons John Read Haughery; Paul W. Brown.
Res.: 1100 N. College St., 36830. Tel: 334-887-5540; 334-887-5573; Fax: 334-887-5572. Email: stmichaels@charter.net. Web: www.stmichaelsauburn.com.
Catechesis/Religious Program—Students 397.
Chaplaincy—Tel: 334-209-1711. Email: cdm.auburn@gmail.com. Web: www.aucatholic.org. Auburn Catholic Campus Ministry.

BAY MINETTE, BALDWIN CO., ST. AGATHA CHURCH (1951) Rev. Gordon N. Milsted, Parochial Admin. Church: 1001 Hand Ave., 36507. Tel: 251-937-2026. Web: stagathaparish.org.

BAYOU LABATRE, MOBILE CO., ST. MARGARET (1880) [CEM] Rev. Bieu Van Nguyen.
Res.: P.O. Box 365, Bayou La Batre, 36509. Tel: 251-824-2415; Fax: 251-824-2415.

BELLE FONTAINE, MOBILE CO., ST. PHILIP NERI (1908) Rev. James F. Carlsen; Deacon James L. Scott.
Res.: 9101 Dauphin Island Pkwy., 36582. Tel: 251-973-2096.
Catechesis/Religious Program—Students 41.

BREWTON, ESCAMBIA CO., ST. MAURICE (1948) Rev. Adrian L. Cook.
Res.: 202 E. Jackson St., P.O. Box 206, 36427-0206. Tel: 251-867-5189.

BUTLER, CHOCTAW CO., ST. JOHN THE EVANGELIST (1958) Rev. Wayne M. Youngman.
Res.: 401 E. Pushmataha St., P.O. Box 456, 36904. Tel: 205-459-3129.
Mission—St. Paul Chatom, 36518. P.O. Box 456, Washington Co. 36904.

CAMDEN, WILCOX CO., ST. JOSEPH Rev. Vincent Huu Phan.
Res.: 490 Whiskey Run Rd., 36767.
Mission—Mission of Annunciation Parish 565 Whetstone ST., Monroeville, Wilcox Co. 36460. Tel: 251-575-2644.

CHASTANG, MOBILE CO., ST. PETER THE APOSTLE (1860) [CEM] Rev. Andrew Toyinbo, M.S.P.
Mailing Address: P.O. Box 456, Mount Vernon, 36560. Tel: 251-829-5134; Fax: 251-829-6874.
Catechesis/Religious Program—Students 16.
Mission—Our Lady of Sorrows Fairford, Washington Co.

CHICKASAW, MOBILE CO., ST. THOMAS THE APOSTLE (1947) Rev. William Patrick Saucier; Deacon Tony LePiane.
Res.: 251 N. Craft Hwy., 36611. Tel: 251-456-7931; Fax: 251-452-9837.
Parish Center—253 N. Craft Hwy., 36611. Tel: 251-452-9837.

CITRONELLE, MOBILE CO., ST. THOMAS (1913) [CEM] Rev. John Coghlan.
Res.: 8025 State St., P.O. Box 61, 36522. Tel: 251-866-7505.
Mission—St. Theresa Mount Vernon, Mobile Co. 36560. Tel: 251-829-6900.

DAPHNE, BALDWIN CO.

1—CHRIST THE KING PARISH, DAPHNE (1896) [CEM] Revs. Matthew O'Connor; Travis J. Burnett, Parochial Vicar; Deacons Malcolm Zellner; Walter Crimmins; William Pearson.
Res.: 711 College Ave., 36526. Tel: 251-626-2343; 251-626-3740; Fax: 251-621-1640. Email: ctk@zebra.net. Web: ctk-daphne.org.
School—(Grades K-8), 1503 Main St., P.O. Box 1890, 36526. Tel: 251-626-1692; Fax: 251-626-9976. Email: cksdaphne@aol.com. Web: ctheking.org. Mr. Maxwell Crain, Prin. Lay Teachers 30; Students 465.
Catechesis/Religious Program—Tel: 251-626-5963. Terry Abeln, D.R.E. Students 397.

2—SHRINE OF THE HOLY CROSS (1948) Rev. Lito J. Capeding (Philippines); Deacon Joseph G. Gottstine.
Res.: 612 Main St., 36526. Tel: 251-621-9793; Fax: 251-621-9315.

DAUPHIN ISLAND, MOBILE CO., ST. EDMUND-BY-THE-SEA, [CEM] Rev. William N. Gorman.
Res.: P.O. Box 6, 36528. Tel: 251-861-2352.
Church: Cadillac Ave., 36528.

DOTHAN, HOUSTON CO., ST. COLUMBA (1943) Rev. Msgr. Patrick J. Gallagher; Deacon Rick Risher. In Res., Rev. Patrick Maher (Retired).
Res.: 2700 W. Main St., 36301. Tel: 334-793-5802; Fax: 334-792-2816. Web: stcolumbacatholic.com.
Rectory—109 Pinetree Dr., 36301.
Catechesis/Religious Program—Tel: 334-792-3065. Students 278.

ELBERTA, BALDWIN CO., ST. BARTHOLOMEW (1911), (German), [CEM] Rev. Jesu Alangaram Ronald Gajettan; Deacon Kenneth J. Kaiser.
Res.: P.O. Drawer 280, 36530. Tel: 251-986-8142; Fax: 251-987-5251.
School—St. Benedict's, (Grades K-8), P.O. Box 819, 36530. Tel: 251-986-8143; Fax: 251-986-8144. Jaivi Howell, Prin. Lay Teachers 15; Students 230; Aides 4.
Catechesis/Religious Program—Students 40.

ENTERPRISE, COFFEE CO., ST. JOHN (1959) Rev. Gregory Okorobia; Deacon Karl Lukas.
Res.: 614 Alberta, 36330. Tel: 334-347-7345.
Church: 123 Heath St., 36330-1915. Tel: 334-347-6751; Fax: 334-347-0849. Email: stjohn007@centurytel.net. Web: www.stjohnenterprise.org.
Mission—St. Mary 100 S. Commerce, Geneva, Geneva Co. 36340.

EUFAULA, BARBOUR CO., HOLY REDEEMER (1859) Rev. David M. Shoemaker.
Res.: 515 W. Broad St., 36027. Tel: 334-687-3716; Fax: 334-687-3766. Email: holyredeemer@eufaula.rr.com. Web: www.holyredeemeronline.com.
Catechesis/Religious Program—Students 14.
Mission—St. Pius X 308 Kennon St., Union Springs, Bullock Co. 36089.
Mission—Bullock County Correctional Facility P.O. Box 5107, Union Springs, Bullock Co. 36089. Tel: 334-738-5625.
Mission—Ventress Correctional Facility P.O. Box 769, Clayton, Barbour Co. 36016. Tel: 334-775-3331.

FAIRHOPE, BALDWIN CO., ST. LAWRENCE (1961) Revs. Steven T. Williams; Babu Arul Raj Jesu Raj, Parochial Vicar; Deacon George W. Yeend Jr.
Res.: 370 S. Section St., 36532. Tel: 251-928-5931; Fax: 251-928-5938.
Catechesis/Religious Program—Students 325.
Chapel—Battles Wharf, Baldwin Co., Sacred Heart

FOLEY, BALDWIN CO., ST. MARGARET QUEEN OF SCOTLAND (1951) [CEM] Very Rev. Paul G. Zoghby; Deacon William Scarboro Jr.
Res.: 601 W. Laurel Ave., 36535. Tel: 251-943-4009; 251-943-3528 (Rectory); Fax: 251-943-4010.

GRAND BAY, MOBILE CO., ST. JOHN BAPTIST (1924) Rev. Antony Kadavil.
Res.: P.O. Box 417, 36541. Tel: 251-865-6902; Fax: 251-865-1412.
Church: 12450 Hwy. 188, Shell Rd., 36541.

GREENVILLE, BUTLER CO., ST. ELIZABETH (1894) Rev. Antony Pullukattu Xavier.
Res.: 407 E. Walnut St., 36037. Tel: 334-382-6203.

GROVE HILL, CLARKE CO., SACRED HEART (1944) Rev. Wayne M. Youngman.
Res.: Hwy. 43 N., P.O. Box 70, 36451. Tel: 251-275-3665.
Mission—Visitation 135 W. Clinton St., Jackson, Clarke Co. 36545.
Mission—St. Joseph W. Front St., Thomasville, Clarke Co. 36784.

GULF SHORES, BALDWIN CO., OUR LADY OF THE GULF (1952) Rev. Msgr. Robert W. Fulton.
Res.: 308 E. 22nd Ave., P.O. Box 515, 36547-0515. Tel: 251-968-7062.
Catechesis/Religious Program—Tel: 251-967-2537. Suzette Taylor, D.R.E. Students 37.

HERON BAY, MOBILE CO., ST. MICHAEL THE ARCHANGEL (1880) Revs. Bieu Van Nguyen; James F. Carlsen, Parochial Vicar.
Mailing Address: 15872 Heron Bay Loop Rd. E., Coden, 36523. Tel: 251-873-4719.

HOLY TRINITY, RUSSELL CO., ST. JOSEPH (1925) Revs. Guy Wilson, S.T.; Luis Fernando-Diaz, S.T., Parochial Vicar; Bro. David Sommer, S.T., Pastoral Assoc. In Res., Rev. Thaddeus Searles, S.T.
Church: 1444 Hwy. 165, Fort Mitchell, 36856. Tel: 334-855-3148; Fax: 334-855-3115. Email: stjosephcathch@yahoo.com. Web: www.way.to/stjoseph.
St. Joseph Child Development Center—Tel: 334-855-4675. Teachers 6; Students 46.
Mission—John XXIII Center 16 Sussex St., Hurtsboro, Russell Co. 36860. Tel: 334-667-7770; Fax: 334-667-0708.

LILLIAN, BALDWIN CO., ST. JOSEPH (1941) [JC] Rev.

Joseph Mudavankunnel, M.S.F.S.; Deacons Richard M. Sullivan; Eugene Geri.
Res.: 34290 U.S. Hwy. 98, 36549. Tel: 251-962-2049; Fax: 251-962-3649.

MAGNOLIA SPRINGS, BALDWIN CO., ST. JOHN THE BAPTIST (1881) [CEM] [JC 2] Rev. Msgr. Guido Calleja.
Res.: 10800 St. John's Ln., P.O. Box 206, 36555. Tel: 251-965-7719.
Mission—Our Lady of Bon Secour Bon Secour, Baldwin Co.

MILLBROOK, ELMORE CO., ST. ELIZABETH ANN SETON (1978) Merged with St. Mark's Mission, Wetumpka to form Our lady of Guadalupe, Wetumpka.

MON LUIS ISLAND, MOBILE CO., ST. ROSE OF LIMA (1853) [CEM] Rev. Austin Conry.
Res.: 2951 Durette Ave. (Mon Luis Island), Coden, 36523. Tel: 251-973-2592.

MONROEVILLE, MONROE CO., ANNUNCIATION (1982) Rev. Vincent Huu Phan.
Res.: 565 Whetstone St., 36460. Tel: 251-575-2644.
Catechesis/Religious Program—Students 18.
Mission—St. Joseph 490 Whiskey Run Rd., Camden, Wilcox Co. 36767.

MONTGOMERY, MONTGOMERY CO.

1—ST. ANDREW KIM TAEGON (1910) Rev. Peter Yong Mo Yeon (BIR), Parochial Admin.
Mailing Address: P.O. Box 241303, 36124.
Res.: 433 Clayton St., 36124. Tel: 334-262-3241.

2—ST. BEDE THE VENERABLE CATHOLIC CHURCH (1925) Revs. David P. Carucci; Jose J. Paillacho; Deacons Charles Gulley; Arnold Brewer; Joseph Phung.
Office: 3870 Atlanta Hwy., 36109. Tel: 334-272-3463. Web: www.stbede.org.
School—Montgomery Catholic Preparatory School - St. Bede Campus, (Grades K-6), 3850 Atlanta Hwy., 36109. Tel: 334-272-3033; Fax: 334-272-9394. Web: montgomerycatholic.org. Ms. Laurie Gulley, Prin. Lay Teachers 23; Students 381.
Catechesis/Religious Program—Generations of Faith Program Students 128.
St. Bede Child Development Center—3840 Atlanta Hwy., 36109. Tel: 334-277-8551; Fax: 334-213-2347.

3—CHURCH OF THE HOLY SPIRIT (1977) Revs. Patrick R. Driscoll; Philip A. McKenna; Deacon Eugene Wadas.
Res.: 8570 Vaughn Rd., 36117. Tel: 334-277-5631; Fax: 334-272-1008. Email: office@holy-spirit-church.com. Web: www.holy-spirit-church.com.
Catechesis/Religious Program—Tel: 334-277-3428. Email: ktryan@holy-spirit-church.com. Students 492.

4—ST. JOHN THE BAPTIST (1908) Rev. David P. Carucci, Admin.
Res.: 543 S. Union St., 36104. Tel: 334-264-6274; Fax: 334-262-3012.

5—ST. JUDE PARISH (1934), (African American), Rev. Paul McQuillen, S.S.E.; Deacon Fred J. Briers. In Res., Rev. Matthew A. Sindik (Retired).
Res.: 2048 W. Fairview Ave., 36108. Tel: 334-265-1390; Fax: 334-265-1399. Web: www.csjchurch.blogspot.com.
High School—(Grades 7-12) Tel: 334-264-5376; Fax: 334-264-6669. Web: www.stjudeei.org. Mrs. Wanda Twitty, Prin. Lay Teachers 14; Students 120.
Catechesis/Religious Program—Students 30.

6—OUR LADY QUEEN OF MERCY (1954) Rev. Michael R. Sreboth.
Res.: 4421 Narrow Lane Rd., 36116. Tel: 334-288-2850; Fax: 334-281-7884.
Catechesis/Religious Program—Students 33.
Child Development Center—Tel: 334-613-0340.

7—ST. PETER (1834) [CEM] Rev. David P. Carucci, Admin.
Res.: 219 Adams Ave., P.O. Box 114, 36101. Tel: 334-262-7304; Fax: 334-262-9735. Web: stpetersof-montgomery.com. In Res., Rev. Charles J. McCabe.

8—RESURRECTION CATHOLIC CHURCH (1943) Revs. Manuel Williams, C.R.; Fred Briers, C.R.
Res.: 2815 Forbes Rd., 36110. Tel: 334-269-1770; Fax: 334-265-8081. Email: parish@rcmsouth.org. Web: www.rcmsouth.org.
School—Resurrection Catholic School, (Grades PreK-8) Tel: 334-265-4615; Fax: 334-265-4568. Sr. Gail Trippett, C.S.J., Prin.; Brenda Overby, Librarian. Lay Teachers 14; Students 125.
Mission—Resurrection Catholic Mission 2815 Forbes Rd., Montgomery Co. 36110. Tel: 334-263-4221; Fax: 334-263-4999. Rev. Manuel Williams, C.R., Dir.

MOUNT VERNON, MOBILE CO., ST. CECILIA (1929) [CEM] Rev. John Coghlan.
Res.: 1305 Military Rd., P.O. Box 847, 36560. Tel: 251-866-7505.

OPELIKA, LEE CO., ST. MARY CHURCH (1910) Rev. John E. Kane, C.M.
Res.: 1000 4th Ave., 36801. Tel: 334-749-8359; Fax: 334-749-6312.
Catechesis/Religious Program—Tel: 334-745-3432. Students 43.

ORANGE BEACH, BALDWIN CO., ST. THOMAS BY THE SEA (1991) Rev. James E. Dane; Deacons Henry Pouliot; Patrick J. Clemens; Stephen R. Seymour.
Mailing Address: 26547 Perdido Beach Blvd., P.O. Box 1190, 36561. Tel: 251-981-8132; Fax: 251-981-1981. Email: stthomas@gulftel.com. Web: www.st-thomasbythesea.org.

ORRVILLE, DALLAS CO., IMMACULATE CONCEPTION Rev. Stephen Hornat, S.S.E.
Church: 13663 Alabama Hwy. 22 W., 36767.
Res.: 309 Washington St., Selma, 36703. Tel: 334-874-8931; Fax: 334-874-8976.

OZARK, DALE CO., ST. JOHN (1958) [JC] Rev. Paul Egbe, Admin.; Deacon John Ross Jr.
Res.: 475 Camilla Ave., P.O. Box 1008, 36361-1008. Tel: 334-774-6826; Fax: 334-774-8675.
Catechesis/Religious Program—Students 45.

PHENIX CITY, RUSSELL CO.

1—MOTHER MARY PARISH (1940) Rev. Thomas D. Weise, Admin.
Res.: 1502 Broad St., 36867. Tel: 334-298-9025; Fax: 334-298-9233.
School—(Grades K-8) Tel: 334-298-6371; Fax: 334-298-7934. Sr. M. Cecelia Harrison, F.M.S., Prin. Sisters 2; Lay Teachers 12; Students 88.
Catechesis/Religious Program—Students 15.
Convent—Franciscan Missionary Sisters of Our Lady of Perpetual Help of Jamaica, Tel: 334-291-0122.

2—ST. PATRICK (1911) Rev. Thomas D. Weise.
Res.: 1502 Broad St., P.O. Box 147, 36868-0147. Tel: 334-298-9025; Fax: 334-298-9233. Email: stpats123@gmail.com. Web: home.etvea.net/~stpats/index.
School—(Grades PreK-8), 3910 Lakewood Dr., P.O. Box 1614, 36868. Tel: 334-298-3408; Fax: 334-298-3352. Mr. Dom Manio, Prin. Lay Teachers 12; Students 76; Aides 3.
Catechesis/Religious Program—Students 112.

PLATEAU, MOBILE CO., OUR MOTHER OF MERCY (1926), (African American), Rev. Akama Ukanide, M.S.P.
Mailing Address: P.O. Box 10306, Prichard, 36610. Tel: 251-473-4975; Fax: 251-473-4940.
Res.: 805 East St., 36610.

PRATTVILLE, AUTAUGA CO., ST. JOSEPH CHURCH (1962) Rev. Jan Zagorski.
Res.: 511 N. Memorial Dr., 36067-2133. Tel: 334-365-8680; Fax: 334-365-2267. Email: office@stjosephprattville.org.
Catechesis/Religious Program—Tel: 334-365-8680, Ext. 212. Students 263.

PRICHARD, MOBILE CO.

1—ST. JAMES MAJOR (1925), (African American), Rev. Godwin Ani, S.S.J.
Res.: 714 S. College St., 36610. Tel: 251-456-6842; Fax: 251-456-6843.
Catechesis/Religious Program—Students 69.

2—OUR LADY OF FATIMA (1949) Closed. For inquiries for parish records contact the chancery.

ROBERTSDALE, BALDWIN CO., ST. PATRICK (1974) Rev. Patrick J. Madden.
Res.: P.O. Box 1367, 36567. Tel: 251-947-5054; Fax: 251-947-3860.
School—(Grades K-8), P.O. Drawer 609, 36567. Tel: 251-947-7395. Sr. Margaret Harte, P.B.V.M., Prin. Presentation Sisters 1; Lay Teachers 13; Students 210.
Catechesis/Religious Program—Students 35.
Convent—P.O. Box 609, 36567. Tel: 251-947-7396.

SELMA, DALLAS CO., OUR LADY QUEEN OF PEACE (1850) Rev. Stephen Hornat, S.S.E.
Res.: 2511 Summerfield Rd., 36701. Email: gofpchurchselma@yahoo.com.
Office: 309 Washington St., 36703. Tel: 334-874-8931 (Office & Res.); Fax: 334-874-8976.
Catechesis/Religious Program—Students 32.

SEMMES, MOBILE CO., HOLY NAME OF JESUS (1977) Rev. John L. Holleman; Deacon Frank Lee.
Res.: 2275 Snow Rd. N., P.O. Box 557, 36575. Tel: 251-649-4794; Fax: 251-649-7660.
Catechesis/Religious Program—Students 70.

TALLASSEE, ELMORE CO., ST. VINCENT DE PAUL (1955) [JC] Rev. Msgr. F. Charles Troncale; Deacon Frank May.
Res.: 620 Gilmer Ave., P.O. Box 780487, 36078-0487. Tel: 334-283-2169; Fax: 334-283-8500.

TILLMAN'S CORNER, MOBILE CO., ST. VINCENT DE PAUL (1971) Rev. James A. Havens; Deacon Robert Nouwen.
Res.: 5023 Camelot Dr., 36619. Tel: 251-661-3908; Fax: 251-665-4956. Web: svsparish.com.
School—6571 Larkspur Dr., 36619. Tel: 251-666-8022; Fax: 251-666-1296. Mary McLendon, Prin. Lay Teachers 10; Students 181.
Catechesis/Religious Program—Tel: 251-661-3908. Students 50.

TROY, PIKE CO., ST. MARTIN OF TOURS (1915) Rev. Michael Den Irwin Jr.
Res.: 725 Elba Hwy., 36079. Tel: 334-566-2630. Email: stmartin@troycable.net.
Catechesis/Religious Program—Students 45.

TUSKEGEE INSTITUTE, MACON CO., ST. JOSEPH (1940) Rev. Romanus Ezeugwa, M.S.P.; Deacon Stanley B. Maxwell.
Res.: 2007 Montgomery Rd., 36088. Tel: 334-727-2710.
School—(Grades K-8), 2009 Montgomery Rd., 36088. Tel: 334-727-0620; 334-727-0642. Mr. Clima White, Interim Prin. Lay Teachers 8; Students 100.

WETUMPKA, ELMORE CO., OUR LADY OF GUADALUPE (2006) Rev. Albert P. Kelly.
Mailing Address: P.O. Box 479, Elmore, 36025.
Res. & Church: 545 White Rd., 36092. Tel: 334-567-0047; Fax: 334-567-0311.

WHISTLER, MOBILE CO., ST. BRIDGET (1864) Rev. William Patrick Saucier. In Res., Rev. Eamon Miley.
Res.: 3625 W. Main St., 36613. Tel: 251-457-6847.

Chaplains of Public Institutions

CLAYTON. *Ventress Correctional Institution*. Rev. David M. Shoemaker.
515 W. Broad St., Eufaula, 36027. Tel: 334-687-3716; Fax: 334-687-3766.

UNION SPRINGS. *Bullock County Correctional Facility*. Rev. David M. Shoemaker.
515 W. Broad St., Eufaula, 36027. Tel: 334-687-3716; Fax: 334-687-3766.

On Leave from the Archdiocese:
Rev. Msgr.—
Farmer, Michael L., V.G., S.T.L., Pontifical North American College, Vatican City 00120 Vatican City State.
Revs.—
Dean, Justin Damian, St. Benedict's Abbey, 1020 N. 2nd St., Atchison, KS 66002.
McManus, Dennis Douglas, Georgetown University, P.O. Box 571250, Washington, DC 20057.
Prendergast, Fergus J.
Robinson, Jerome
Walters, Erik T.A.

On Leave for Military:
Revs.—
Halladay, Paul A.
Harbour, Linn S.

Special Assignment:
Revs.—
Miley, Eamon, Chap., Convent of Mercy Sisters, 3625 W. Main St., Whistler, 36612.
Spotswood, Cecil R., Chap., Carmelite Monastery and Visitation Monastery, 3704 Springhill Ave., 36608.
Weishaar, Leo G., Chap., Providence Hospital, P.O. Box 850429, 36685. Tel: 251-633-1341

Retired:
Rev. Msgrs.—
Cunningham, Peter J.
Cusack, Francis V., V.G.
Deasy, Timothy J.
Dorrill, James F., Ph.D.
Hay, Theodore H., S.T.L.
James, William R.
Jennings, Joseph
Murphy, Francis
Shields, Maurice L.
Revs.—
Becherer, David A.
Biven, Louis Russell
Blanchet, Leo
Bolling, Francis Joseph
Coleman, James Montini
Folsom, William P., Jr.
Holden, James T.
Keller, Brendan
Kieltyka, Robert
Maher, Patrick
Moreno, Antonio O.
Reskey, George A.
Robinson, John C.
Schrenger, Arthur C.
Sindik, Matthew A.
Stauter, Andrew
Trosch, David

Permanent Deacons:
Bosarge, Vincent
Brewer, Arnold L., (Retired)
Briers, Fred J.
Brown, Paul W.
Bryant, James D.
Clemens, Patrick J.
Connick, Edward G.
Connick, Joseph V.
Cretaro, John T.
Crimmins, Walter J.
Diaz-Rivera, Alfonso

Dolan, William R., (Retired)
Fontana, Charles J., (Retired)
Geri, Eugene
Gottstine, Joseph G.
Gulley, Charles, (Retired)
Hamilton, John B., (On Leave)
Hathorne, Ronnie A.
Haughery, John Read
Johns, Marvin C., (Retired)
Johnson, Ernest
Kaiser, Kenneth J.
Kenny, Charles H.
Kenny, Gordon
King, A. B., (On Leave)
Kirby, Robert E.
Labadie, James
Lee, Frank A., (Retired)
LePiane, Tony
Lopez, Abraham, (Retired)
Lukas, Karl L.
Maxwell, Stanley B.
May, Frank J.
McGonagle, Joseph P., (Retired)
Mears, Clarence L.
Moore, Alexander, (Retired)
Nguyen, Truat Van
Nouwen, Robert
Pearson, William
Phung, Joseph H.
Pouliot, Henry, (Retired)
Pryor, William Holcombe
Quintero, Mario
Risher, Rick
Robbins, Arthur
Ross, John F.
Scarboro, William, Jr.
Scott, James L.
Seymour, Stephen R.
Sheldon, Paul, (On Leave)
Shippen, Samuel, (Retired)
Sinchak, J. Douglas, M.S., J.C.L.
Sullivan, Richard M., (Retired)
Tew, William L.
Wadas, Eugene, (Retired)
Yeend, George W., Jr.
Zellner, Malcolm

INSTITUTIONS LOCATED IN THE ARCHDIOCESE

[A] COLLEGES AND UNIVERSITIES

MOBILE. *Spring Hill College* (1830) 4000 Dauphin St., 36608. Tel: 251-380-4000; Fax: 251-460-2195. Web: www.shc.edu. Rev. Richard P. Salmi, S.J., Pres.; Very Rev. Edward B. Arroyo, S.J., Rector; Revs. Rafael Baylon, S.J.; David Borbridge, S.J.; Stephen Campbell, S.J.; Marvin Kitten, S.J.; Robert B. Rimes, S.J.; Javier San Martin, S.J.; Michael A. Williams, S.J.; Christopher J. Viscardi, S.J.; Bro. Ferrell Blank. Priests 10; Brothers 1; Lay Teachers 75; Students 1,867.

[B] HIGH SCHOOLS, ARCHDIOCESAN

MOBILE. *McGill-Toolen Catholic High School*, 1501 Old Shell Rd., 36604. Tel: 251-432-0784; Fax: 251-433-8356. Email: shieldsb@mcgill-toolen.org. Web: www.mcgill-toolen.org. Rev. W. Bry Shields, Pres.; Deacon Holcombe Pryor; Mrs. Michelle Haas, Prin. Priests 1; Brothers of the Sacred Heart 3; Sisters of Loretto 1; Lay Teachers 84; Students 1,078.

MONTGOMERY. *St. Jude Educational Institute*, 2048 W. Fairview Ave., 36108. Tel: 334-263-6121; Fax: 334-264-6669. Web: www.stjudeei.org. Mrs. Wanda Twitty, Prin.; Marilyn Bibbins, Librarian. Lay Teachers 20; Students 206.

Montgomery Catholic Preparatory School (1873) (Grades K-12), 5350 Vaughn Rd., 36116. Tel: 334-272-7220; Fax: 334-272-2440. Email: aceasar@montgomerycatholic.org. Web: montgomerycatholic.org. Mrs. Anne O. Ceasar, Pres.; Anna Lee Ingalls, Dir., Devel. (K-12). Lay Teachers 63; Total Enrollment 795.

St. Bede Campus (1958) (Grades K-6), 3850 Atlanta Hwy., 36109. Tel: 334-272-3033; Fax: 334-272-9394. Ms. Laurie Gulley, Prin. Teachers 29; Students 345.

High School Campus (1873) Mrs. Fran Taylor, Prin. Teachers 23; Students 301.

Middle School Campus (2004) (Grades 7-8), 5350 Vaughn Rd., 36116. Tel: 334-272-2465; Fax: 334-272-2330. Email: mnolen@montgomerycatholic.org. Ms. Maria Nolen, Prin.; Lee Ann Barranco, Librarian (K-6); Amy Johnson, Librarian (7-12). Teachers 11; Students 149.

[C] CHILDREN'S HOMES

MOBILE. *St. Mary's Home, Mobile*, 4350 Moffat Rd., 36618. Tel: 251-344-7733; Fax: 251-344-9753. Mr. Phillip A. Wynne, Admin. Dependent Children 65.

[D] GENERAL HOSPITALS

MOBILE. *Providence Foundation* (1985) 6701 Airport Blvd. B 227, P.O. Box 850429, 36608. Tel: 251-639-2050; Fax: 251-639-2052. Robert B. Doyle III, Chm. of the Bd.; Jean Wilkins, Sec.; G. Timothy Gaston, Treas.

Providence Healthcare Services (1986) 6801 Airport Blvd., P.O. Box 850429, 36685. Tel: 251-633-1600; Fax: 251-633-1679. Thomas A. Gangle, Chm.; Ijaz Iqbal, M.D., Vice Chm.; Clark P. Christianson, Pres. Total Staff 51.

Providence Hospital (1854) 6801 Airport Blvd., P.O. Box 850429, 36685. Tel: 251-633-1600; Fax: 251-633-1679. Web: www.providencehospital.org. Clark P. Christianson, Pres. & CEO; Ms. Beth McFadden Rouse, Chm.; Rev. Leo G. Weishaar, Chap. Daughters of Charity of St. Vincent de Paul 5; Bed Capacity 349; Patients Assisted Annually 173,104; Nurses 635; Total Staff 1,953.

Seton Health Corp. of South Alabama (1986) 6801 Airport Blvd., P.O. Box 850429, 36608. Tel: 251-633-1660; Fax: 251-633-1679. Web: providencehospital.org. Clark P. Christianson, Pres.; Thomas A. Gangle, Sec. & Treas.; Ms. Beth McFadden Rouse, Chm.

Seton Medical Management, Inc. (1986) 6701 Airport Blvd., Ste. D-241, 36608. Tel: 251-639-2661; Fax: 251-639-2664. Thomas A. Gangle, Chm.; Dr. James L. Walker, Pres. & Vice Chair; C. Susan Cornejo, Sec. & Treas. Patients Assisted Annually 171,499; Nurses 58; Total Staff 317.

[E] SPECIAL HOSPITALS, SCHOOLS AND HOMES FOR THE AGED

MOBILE. *Allen Memorial Home Skilled Nursing Facility*, 735 S. Washington Ave., 36603. Tel: 251-433-2642; Fax: 251-433-5502. Email: crobinson@allenmemorial.net. Ms. Cheryl Robinson, Admin. Bed Capacity 119; Patients Assisted Annually 1,154; Total Staff 175.

Corpus Christi Preschool (Full Day Infant-PK4), 6300 McKenna Dr., 36608. Tel: 251-342-2424; Fax: 251-343-3119. Email: preschool@corpuschristiparish.com. Mrs. Linda M. Hawkins, Dir.

Little Sisters of the Poor, Home For the Aged, Inc. (1901) Sacred Heart Residence, 1655 McGill Ave., 36604. Tel: 251-476-6335; Fax: 251-478-6519. Email: msmobile@littlesistersofthepoor.org. Web: www.littlesistersofthepoormobile.org. Sr. Marcel Joseph McCanless, L.S.P., Supr. Sisters 9; Residents 87. In Res. Rev. Msgr. Peter J. Cunningham, Chap. (Retired); Revs. David A. Becherer (Retired); L. Russell Biven (Retired); Francis Joseph Bolling (Retired); Andrew Stauter (Retired).

DAPHNE. *Mercy Medical* (1949) P.O. Box 1090, 36526. Tel: 251-621-4200; Fax: 251-621-4845. Email: donnaw@mercymedical.com. Web: www.mercymedical.com. Mr. Jack Bell, Pres. & CEO. Acute Rehabilitation Hospital, Hospice, Home Health, Long Term Care, Skilled Nursing Facility, Alzheimer's Care, Assisted Living, Lifecare Retirement. Sisters of Mercy 3; Professional Nurses 196; Bed Capacity 142; Patients/Residents Assisted Annually 4,875; Residential Care Units 308; Total Staff 419.

Carroll Place, Fairhope, 36532. Tel: 251-928-5555; Fax: 251-990-2620. (Assisted living community.)

Catherine Place, 36526. Tel: 251-626-9000; Fax: 251-626-7981. (Assisted living community.)

The Hamlet, Fairhope, 36532. Tel: 251-928-5413; Fax: 251-990-3035. (Retirement community.)

Mercy Life of Alabama, 101 Villa Dr., 36526. Tel: 251-621-4452; Fax: 251-621-4324. Web: www.mercymedical.com. Necie Borroni, CFO. (A component corporation of Mercy Medical)

Portier Place, 36608. Tel: 251-343-4449; Fax: 251-304-3143. (Retirement community.)

John McClure Snook Regional Center, 27296 County Rd. 13, 36526. Tel: 251-625-2555; Fax: 251-625-2556. (Assisted living Alzheimer community.)

DOTHAN. *St. Columba Preschool*, 2700 W. Main St., 36301. Tel: 334-793-6742; Fax: 334-792-2816. Email: cdstc@alanet.com. Mrs. Cathy Dedmon, Dir.

MONTGOMERY. *St. Bede Child Development Center*, 3870 Atlanta Hwy., 36109. Tel: 334-277-8551. Email: cjones@school.stbede.org. Cathy Jones, Dir. Students 125; Total Staff 28.

[F] HOUSING FOR THE ELDERLY

MOBILE. *Cathedral Place*, 351 Conti St., 36602. Tel: 251-434-1590; Fax: 251-434-1592. Email: marie.dismukes@royalmgmt.com. Web: www.royalmgmt.com. Marie Dismukes, Managing Agent; Marvin Dismukes, Mgr. Residents 156; Total Staff 5.

Rendu Terrace West, Inc., c/o 6801 Airport Blvd., P.O. Box 850429, 36685. Porter Sue Simpson, Mgr.

MONTGOMERY. *Seton Haven*, 3721 Wares Ferry Rd., 36109. Tel: 334-272-4000; Fax: 334-272-1788. Email: setonhaven@bellsouth.net. Ms. A. Ann Alosi, Admin. Residents 100; Total Staff 12.

[G] MONASTERIES AND RESIDENCES OF PRIESTS AND BROTHERS

MOBILE. *Brothers of the Sacred Heart* (1821) 2609 Springhill Ave., 36607. Tel: 251-438-3812. Bros. Joseph Donovan, S.C.; Matthias Amos, S.C.; Lee Barker, S.C., M.Ed.; Celestine Algero, S.C., Ph.D.; Paul Mulligan, S.C., M.R.E.; Virgil Harris, S.C. Brothers 6.

SELMA. *Edmundite Fathers*, Edmundite Missions House, 1401 Broad St., 36701. Tel: 334-872-6221; Fax: 334-872-8123. Email: myhalyk@aol.com. Web: www.edmunditemissions.com. Revs. Paul McQuillen, S.S.E.; Richard Myhalyk, S.S.E., Mission Dir. & CEO; Stephen Hornat, S.S.E.; Bro. Peter J. Stanfield, S.S.E., Pastoral Assoc.; Rev. Stanley Deresienski, S.S.E.

Fathers of St. Edmund Southern Missions, Inc. Priests 4; Brothers 1; Total Assisted 155,520; Total Staff 48.

[H] CONVENTS AND RESIDENCES OF SISTERS

MOBILE. *Blessed Trinity Missionary Cenacle*, 604 Barksdale Dr. W., 36606. Tel: 251-476-4803. Missionary Servants 4.

Convent of the Sisters of Mercy of the Americas South Central Community, 101 Wimbledon Dr. W., 36608. Tel: 251-344-1377; Fax: 251-344-1617. Email: scoberkirch@bellsouth.net. Web: www.mercysistersbalt.com. Sr. Carolyn Oberkirch, R.S.M., Admin. Sisters 18; Total Staff 17.

Other Residences: *Convent of the Sisters of Mercy of the Americas South Central Community*, 4301 Bit & Spur Rd., 36608. Tel: 251-343-3674. *Convent of the Sisters of Mercy of the Americas South Central Community*, 2902 Brierwood Dr., 36606. Tel: 251-476-4605. *Convent of the Sisters of Mercy of the Americas South Central Community*, 172 N. Lafayette St., 36604. Tel: 251-432-3178.

Convent of the Sisters of St. Agnes, 1701 Dublin St., 36605. Tel: 251-478-3292. Email: smitscsa@bellsouth.net. Web: www.csasisters.org. Sisters 4.

Monastery of Discalced Carmelite Nuns (1943) 716 Dauphin Island Pkwy., 36606. Sr. Mary Josepha, O.C.D., Prioress. Solemnly Professed 7.

101 Wimbledon Dr., W., 36608. Tel: 251-344-1377. Sr. Marie Therese Casey, O.C.D., Prioress. Solemnly Professed 4.

Sisters of Loretto (1926) 1408 Old Shell Rd., 36604-2244. Tel: 251-454-9898. Email: sandyardoyno@att.net. Sr. Sandra Ardoyno, S.L.

Visitation Monastery and Retreat House (1833) 2300 Spring Hill Ave., 36607. Tel: 251-473-2321; Fax: 251-476-9761. Web: www.VisitationMonasteryMobile.org. Sr. Margaret Mary Rumpf, V.H.M., Supr. Sisters 9; Total Staff 3.

CAMDEN. *Sisters of St. Joseph*, 112 Bridgeport Rd., 36726. Tel: 334-682-4144; Fax: 251-746-2467. Email: roseannecook@yahoo.com.

HOLY TRINITY. *Blessed Trinity Shrine Retreat and Cenacle*, 107 Holy Trinity Rd., Fort Mitchell, 36856. Tel: 334-855-4474; Fax: 334-855-4525. Web: www.msbt.org/mis_btsr.htm. Sisters Theresa Mary Finan, M.S.B.T., Co-Dir.; Barbara De Moranville, M.S.B.T., Co-Dir. Missionary Servants of the Most Blessed Trinity 6; Retreat House Capacity 40.

MARBURY. *Dominican Monastery of St. Jude (St. Jude Monastery)*, P.O. Box 170, 36051. Tel: 205-755-1322; Fax: 205-755-9847. Email: stjudemonastery@aol.com. Web: www.stjudemonastery.org. Sr. Mary Joseph, O.P., Prioress. Cloistered Dominican Nuns of Perpetual Adoration and Rosary. Professed Sisters 5; Novices 2.

MONTGOMERY. *Mater Dei Missionary Cenacle*, 784 Spring Valley Rd., 36116. Tel: 334-288-4544; Fax: 334-288-9322. Email: nagle@cssalabama.org. Web: cssalabama.org. Missionary Servants of the Most Blessed Trinity 3.

OZARK. *Sinsinawa Dominican Sisters*, 375 County Rd. 404, 36360. Tel: 334-299-6671. Email: psmithop@troycable.net. Sr. Penny Smith, O.P.

PINE APPLE. *Sisters of St. Joseph of Rochester*, 702 County Rd. 59, 36768. Tel: 251-746-2584; Fax: 251-746-2584. Web: www.ssjrochester.org. Sisters 2.

[I] NEWMAN CENTERS

MOBILE. *Sacred Heart of Jesus Catholic Student Center at University of South Alabama* (2003) Catholic Student Center, 6051 Old Shell Rd., 36608. Tel: 251-343-3662; Fax: 251-460-4687. Email: sacredhrtfralex@mindspring.com. Rev. Alejandro E. Valladares, S.T.L., Campus Min. & Vocations Dir.

Spring Hill College Campus Ministry 4000 Dauphin St., 36608-1791. Tel: 251-380-3495; Fax: 251-460-2174. Web: www.shc.edu. Very Rev. Edward B. Arroyo, S.J., Rector; Rev. Marvin Kitten, S.J.; Maureen Bergan, Dir., Campus Ministry.

AUBURN. *Auburn University Newman Center* 115 Mitcham Ave., 36830. Tel: 334-887-5380; Fax: 334-887-5572. Web: www.aucatholic.org. Rev. Msgr. William J. Skoneki.

DOTHAN. *George C. Wallace Jr. Community College Newman Center* 2700 W. Main St., 36301. Tel: 334-793-5802; Fax: 334-792-2816. Email: saintcolumba@ala.net. Rev. Msgr. Patrick J. Gallagher.

MONROEVILLE. *Alabama Southern Community College Newman Center* 565 Whetstone St., 36460. Tel: 251-575-2644. Email: annuneat@frontiernet.net. Rev. Vincent Huu Pham.

MONTGOMERY. *Alabama State University Newman Center* 553 S. Union St., 36104. Tel: 334-264-6274. Rev. David P. Carucci.

Huntington College Newman Center 4421 Narrow Lane Rd., 36116. Tel: 334-288-2850. Email: frsreboth@olam.org. Web: www.olqm.org. Rev. Michael R. Sreboth.

SELMA. *Marion Institute Newman Center* 309 Washington St., 36703. Tel: 334-874-8931; Fax: 334-874-8976. Rev. Stephen Hornat, S.S.E. Students 52.

TROY. *St. Martin Catholic Newman Center* 725 Elba Hwy., 36079. Tel: 334-566-2630. Rev. Den Irwin.

TUSKEGEE INSTITUTE. *Tuskegee University Newman Center* 2007 Montgomery Rd., 36088. Tel: 334-727-2710; Fax: 334-727-5767. Rev. Romanus Ezeugwa, M.S.P. Total Staff 1.

[J] MISCELLANEOUS LISTINGS

MOBILE. *Apostleship of Prayer*, 400 Government St., 36602. Tel: 251-434-1585. Deacon Walter J. Crimmins, Exec. Dir., Pastoral Svcs.

Catholic High Schools Alumni Association of Mobile (1979) 1501 Old Shell Rd., 36604. Tel: 251-445-2913; Fax: 251-433-8356. Email: wattsm@mcgill-toolen.org. Web: www.mcgill-toolen.org. Marian Watts, Alumni Dir.

Catholic University, Friends of, Sacred Heart Residence, 1655 McGill Ave., 36604. Tel: 251-476-6335. Rev. Louis Russell Biven (Retired).

Cursillo, Our Savior Parish, 1801 Cody Rd. S., 36695. Tel: 251-633-6762; Fax: 251-633-7790. Rev. David J. Tokarz, Spiritual Dir.; Sr. Margaret Cosgrove, M.S.B.T., Asst. Dir. Tel: 251-471-3449; Mr. Woody H. Perkins, Lay Dir. Tel: 251-343-7088.

L'Arche, 151 S. Ann St., 36604. Tel: 251-438-2094; Fax: 251-438-2094. Email: larchmob@hotmail.com. Web: larchemobile.org. Christian nonprofit organization-community where persons with intellectual disabilities share their lives together in a home. Disabled People 22; Team Members 40.

Ladies of Charity, P.O. Box 6987, 36660-0987. Tel: 251-661-9448.

Men of St. Joseph, 14 Midtown Park E., 36606. Tel: 251-445-1569; Fax: 251-450-2788. Web: www.menofstjoseph.com. Todd Martin, Chm.

Mobile Provincial Conference of Bishops and Priests' Councils, Mailing Address: 400 Government St., 36602. Tel: 251-434-1585.

**Providence Building Corporation* (1985) P.O. Box 850429, 36685. Tel: 251-633-1600; Fax: 251-633-1679. Web: providencehospital.org. 6801 Airport Blvd., 36608. Tel: 251-633-1600; Fax: 251-633-1679. James Hirs, Sec. & Treas.

Serra Club of Mobile, 711 Dauphin St., 36602. Mr. Jon Green, Pres.

DOTHAN. *Serra Club of Dothan*, 41 Georgian Ter., Midland City, 36350-3223. Dr. Nicholas E. Barreca, Pres.

ELBERTA. *Mary's Shelter*, 14001 Boros Rd., P.O. Box 18, 36530. Tel: 251-986-6200; Fax: 251-986-6357. Email: marysshelter@gulftel.com. Web: maryshelter.org. Ms. Donna McCarley, M.S.W., Exec. Dir.

FAIRHOPE. **Archangel Communications*, 399 S. Section St., P.O. Box 1526, 36533. Tel: 251-928-2111; Fax: 251-929-2660. Email: office@archangelradio.org. Joseph Roszkowski, Pres.; Daniel di Silva, Station Mgr.

Boy Scouts, 370 S. Section St., 36532. Tel: 251-928-5931. Rev. Steven T. Williams, Chap.

HURTSBORO. *Blessed John XXIII Center* (1964) P.O. Box 117, 36860. Tel: 334-667-7770; Fax: 334-667-0708. Email: blessedjohnXXIIIcenter@earthlink.net. Rev. Dennis M. Berry, S.T., Admin.; Mr. Lewis H. Smith, Dir.

MONTGOMERY. *City of St. Jude, Inc., The* (1934) Mailing Address: 2048 W. Fairview Ave., 36108. Tel: 334-265-6791; Fax: 334-269-6750. Email: pmcquillen@cityofstjude.org. Web: www.cityofstjude.org. Rev. Paul McQuillen, S.S.E., Dir.; Mr. Douglas H. Watson, Exec. Dir.

St. Jude Church & Rectory Tel: 334-265-1390; Fax: 334-265-1399.

City of St. Jude Apartments (1992) Tel: 334-265-8356; Fax: 334-265-1908. Barbara J. Peters, Mgr. Units 96; Total Staff 2.

Father Purcell Memorial Exceptional Children's Center (1958) Tel: 334-834-5590; Fax: 334-834-5602. Ms. Brenda Withers, Admin. Patients Assisted Annually 58; Total Staff 103.

St. Jude Social Services Center Tel: 334-269-1983; Fax: 334-269-1988. Sr. Barbara Ann Lengvarsky, V.S.C., Dir. Total Assisted Annually 1,475; Total Staff 1.

St. Jude Educational Institute (1938) Tel: 334-264-5376 (H.S.); Fax: 334-264-6669 (H.S.). Students 214; Total Staff 25.

Montgomery Deanery Respect Life Committee, 620 Gilmer Ave., Tallassee, 36078.

Resurrection Catholic Missions, 2815 Forbes Rd., 36110. Tel: 334-263-4221; Fax: 334-263-4999. Rev. Manuel Williams, C.R., Missions Dir.

Resurrection Catholic Nursing Home, 2815 Forbes Rd., 36110. Tel: 334-269-1770; Fax: 334-265-8081. Kenneth Owens, Admin. Skilled Nursing Facility and Assisted Living Facility. Registered Nurses 4; Licensed Practical Nurses 10; Bed Capacity 65; Inpatients 61.

Father Walter Memorial Center for Handicapped Children Tel: 334-262-6421; Fax: 334-262-2265. Kim K. Johnson, Admin. A skilled nursing facility for the mentally and physically handicapped child. Operated by The Resurrection Catholic Missions. RN's 8; LPN's 13; Bed Capacity 54; Patients Assisted Annually 54; Total Staff 82.

Resurrection Early Childhood Center Tel: 334-265-4615; Fax: 334-265-4568. Sr. Gail Trippett, C.S.J., Prin. Licensed by Alabama State Dept. of Human Resources for 45 Students, Ages 2 1/2 to 5.

School That Works, 2048 W. Fairview Ave., 36108. Tel: 334-264-5376; Fax: 334-264-6669. Web: www.stjudeei.org. Mrs. Wanda Twitty, Pres.

Serra Club of Montgomery, 409 Apache Ct., 36117. Mr. Lawrence Russo.

Seton Haven Management Corporation, 3721 Wares Ferry Rd., 36109. Tel: 334-272-4000. Rick Courson, Pres.

SELMA. *Edmundite Guild* Society of St. Edmund, Inc., P.O. Drawer 490, 36701. Tel: 888-540-7722; Fax: 334-875-8189. Email: myhalyk@aol.com. Rev. Richard Myhalyk, S.S.E., Mission Dir. & CEO. Priests 5; Brothers 1.

RELIGIOUS INSTITUTES OF MEN REPRESENTED IN THE ARCHDIOCESE

For further details refer to the corresponding bracketed number in the Religious Institutes of Men or Women section.

[0200]—*Benedictine Monks*—O.S.B.

[1100]—*Brothers of the Sacred Heart* (New Orleans Prov.)—S.C.

[1330]—*Congregation of the Mission* (Eastern Prov.)—C.M.

[1080]—*Congregation of the Resurrection* (Chicago Prov.)—C.R.

[0690]—*Jesuit Fathers and Brothers* (New Orleans Prov.)—S.J.

[]—*Missionaries of St. Francis de Sales*—M.S.F.S.

[0840]—*Missionary Servants of the Most Holy Trinity*—S.T.

[0854]—*Missionary Society of St. Paul of Nigeria*—M.S.P.

[0440]—*Society of Saint Edmund* (Selma, AL)—S.S.E.

[0700]—*St. Joseph's Society of the Sacred Heart* (Baltimore, MD)—S.S.J.

RELIGIOUS INSTITUTES OF WOMEN REPRESENTED IN THE ARCHDIOCESE

[3710]—*Congregation of the Sisters of Saint Agnes*—C.S.A.

[0760]—*Daughters of Charity of St. Vincent de Paul*—D.C.

[0820]—*Daughters of the Holy Spirit*—D.H.S.

[0420]—*Discalced Carmelite Nuns*—O.C.D.

[1050]—*Dominican Contemplative Nuns*—O.P.

[1070-03]—*Dominican Sisters*—O.P.

[1070-13]—*Dominican Sisters*—O.P.

[1070-18]—*Dominican Sisters*—O.P.

[]—*Franciscan Missionary Sisters* (Jamaica)—F.M.S.

[]—*Handmaids of the Holy Child Jesus*—H.H.C.J.

[2575]—*Institute of the Sisters of Mercy of the Americas*—R.S.M.

[2340]—*Little Sisters of the Poor*—L.S.P.

[2790]—*Missionary Servants of the Most Blessed Trinity*—M.S.B.T.

[]—*Order of St. Benedict*—O.S.B.

[]—*Sisters for Christian Community*—S.F.C.C

[]—*Sisters of Charity of Nazareth* (Nazareth, KY)—S.C.N.

[2360]—*Sisters of Loretto At the Foot of the Cross*—S.L.

[2550]—*Sisters of Mercy*—R.S.M.

[1650]—*Sisters of St. Francis of Philadelphia*—O.S.F.

[3830-14]—*Sisters of St. Joseph*—S.S.J.

[3830-15]—*Sisters of St. Joseph*—C.S.J.

[3840]—*Sisters of St. Joseph of Carondelet*—C.S.J.

[3850]—*Sisters of St. Joseph of Chambery*—C.S.J.

[3480]—*Sisters of the Resurrection*—C.R.

[2150]—*Sisters, Servants of the Immaculate Heart of Mary*—I.H.M.

[3330]—*Union of the Sisters of the Presentation of the Blessed Virgin Mary*—P.B.V.M.

[4170]—*Vincentian Sisters of Charity* (Perryville, PA)—V.S.C.

[4190]—*Visitation Nuns*—V.H.M.

NECROLOGY

† Hyndman, Ernest R., Bay Minette, AL St. Agatha Parish—Died Aug. 2, 2011

† Kissell, Wilbur T., Montgomery, AL St. Andrew Kim Taegon—Died March 14, 2011

An asterisk (*) denotes an organization that has established tax-exempt status directly with the IRS and is not covered by the USCCB Group Ruling.

Diocese of Monterey in California

(Montereyensis in California)

Most Reverend

RICHARD J. GARCIA, D.D.

Bishop of Monterey; ordained June 15, 1973; appointed Titular Bishop of Bapara and Auxiliary Bishop of Sacramento November 25, 1997; ordained January 28, 1998; appointed Fourth Bishop of Monterey December 19, 2006; installed January 30, 2007. Email: rjgb@dioceseofmonterey.org.

Pastoral Office: 425 Church St., Monterey, CA 93940. Tel: 831-373-4345; Fax: 831-373-1175. *Mailing Address: P.O. Box 2048, Monterey, CA 93942-2048*

Web: www.dioceseofmonterey.org

Email: diocese@dioceseofmonterey.org

ESTABLISHED DECEMBER 14, 1967.

Square Miles 21,916.

Comprises the Counties of Monterey, San Benito, San Luis Obispo and Santa Cruz in the State of California.

Legal Titles:
Diocese of Monterey in California.
The Roman Catholic Bishop of Monterey, California, a Corporation Sole.
The Diocese of Monterey Education & Welfare Corporation.
The Bishop Harry A. Clinch Endowment Fund of the Diocese of Monterey.
Catholic Charities of the Diocese of Monterey (Corporation).
Villa Serra Corporation.
Ave Maria Convalescent Hospital, Inc.
St. Francis Central Coast Catholic High School, Inc.
Bishop Harry A. Clinch Trust Fund.
For legal titles of parishes and diocesan institutions, consult the Pastoral Office.

STATISTICAL OVERVIEW

Personnel	
Bishop	1
Retired Bishops	1
Priests: Diocesan Active in Diocese	53
Priests: Diocesan Active Outside Diocese	3
Priests: Retired, Sick or Absent	23
Number of Diocesan Priests	79
Religious Priests in Diocese	32
Total Priests in Diocese	111
Extern Priests in Diocese	11
Ordinations:	
Transitional Deacons	2
Permanent Deacons in Diocese	21
Parishes	
Parishes	46
With Resident Pastor:	
Resident Diocesan Priests	42
Resident Religious Priests	3
Without Resident Pastor:	
Administered by Lay People	1
Missions	9
Welfare	
Catholic Hospitals	1
Total Assisted	198,890
Homes for the Aged	1
Total Assisted	50
Special Centers for Social Services	4
Total Assisted	23,984
Educational	
Diocesan Students in Other Seminaries	13
Total Seminarians	13
High Schools, Diocesan and Parish	2
Total Students	541
High Schools, Private	3
Total Students	992
Elementary Schools, Diocesan and Parish	11
Total Students	2,737
Elementary Schools, Private	3
Total Students	647
Catechesis/Religious Education:	
High School Students	1,549
Elementary Students	6,492
Total Students under Catholic Instruction	12,971
Teachers in the Diocese:	
Sisters	13
Lay Teachers	311
Vital Statistics	
Receptions into the Church:	
Infant Baptism Totals	6,573
Minor Baptism Totals	443
Adult Baptism Totals	190
Received into Full Communion	1,182
First Communions	4,410
Confirmations	1,703
Marriages:	
Catholic	749
Interfaith	109
Total Marriages	858
Deaths	1,223
Total Catholic Population	200,469
Total Population	1,002,345

Former Prelates of the Diocese of Monterey—Most Revs. HARRY ANSELM CLINCH, D.D., ord. June 6, 1936; appt. Titular Bishop of Badiae and Auxiliary to the Bishop of Monterey-Fresno, Dec. 5, 1956; cons. Feb. 27, 1957; installed as first Bishop of Monterey in California, Dec. 14, 1967; retired Jan. 19, 1982; died March 8, 2003; THADDEUS SHUBSDA, D.D., ord. April 26, 1950; Titular Bishop of Trau and Auxiliary Bishop of Los Angeles; Episcopal Ordination; appt. Feb. 19, 1977; named Bishop of Monterey in California, June 1, 1982; installed as second Bishop of Monterey, July 1, 1982; died April 26, 1991; SYLVESTER D. RYAN, D.D. (Retired), ord. May 3, 1957; appt. Auxiliary Bishop of Los Angeles and Titular Bishop of Remesiana Feb. 17, 1990; ord. Bishop on May 31, 1990; appt. Third Bishop of Monterey Jan. 28, 1992; installed March 19, 1992; retired Dec. 19, 2006.

Vicar General—Very Rev. PETER A. CRIVELLO, V.G., 425 Church St., Monterey, 93940. Mailing Address: P.O. Box 2048, Monterey, 93942-2048. Tel: 831-373-4345; Fax: 831-373-1175. Email: frpeter@sancarloscathedral.org.

Chancellor—Sr. PATRICIA M. MURTAGH, I.M., Chancellor & Dir. Protection of Children & Young People, 425 Church St., Monterey, 93940. Mailing Address: P.O. Box 2048, Monterey, 93942-2048. Tel: 831-373-4345; Fax: 831-373-1175. Email: srpmurtagh@dioceseofmonterey.org.

Vicar for Clergy—Rev. PAUL P. MURPHY, St. Angela Merici, 146 8th St., Pacific Grove, 93950. Tel: 831-372-0338; Fax: 831-372-0338; Cell: 831-254-9294. Email: montereypriest@yahoo.com.

Vicar for Hispanic Clergy—Rev. MIGUEL ANGEL GRAJEDA, St. Patrick's Church, 721 Main St., Watsonville, 95076. Tel: 831-724-1317; Fax: 831-724-1627. Email: saintpatricks@sbcglobal.net.

Vicar for Religious—Sr. JEAN FITZGERALD, O.P., Mailing Address: P.O. Box 995, Soquel, 95073-0995. Tel: 831-464-6840. Email: srjfitzgerald@dioceseofmonterey.org.

Vicar for Retired Priests—Rev. PAUL R. VALDEZ, J.C.L., KCHS, St. Jude, 303 Hillcrest Ave., Marina, 93933. Tel: 831-384-5434.

Vicar for Temporalities & Administration—THOMAS H. RIORDAN, 425 Church St., Monterey, 93940. Tel: 831-373-4345; Fax: 831-373-1175. Mailing Address: P.O. Box 2048, Monterey, 93942-2048. Email: triordan@dioceseofmonterey.org.

Pastoral Office—Administrative Assistants: DONA LOGEMAN ACUFF. Email: dacuff@dioceseofmonterey.org; LETICIA FLORES-MCPHERSON. Email: lmcpherson@dioceseofmonterey.org; ANALUISA GONZALEZ. Email: agonzalez@dioceseofmonterey.org; AIKO SOKOLOWSKI. Email: asokolowski@dioceseofmonterey.org; 425 Church St., Monterey, 93940. Mailing Address: P.O. Box 2048, Monterey, 93942-2048. Tel: 831-373-4345; Fax: 831-373-1175. Email: diocese@dioceseofmonterey.org.

Pastoral Office, Ecclesiastical Notaries—DONA LOGEMAN ACUFF. Email: dacuff@dioceseofmonterey.org; ANALUISA GONZALEZ. Email: agonzalez@dioceseofmonterey.org.

Vicars Forane—Rev. JAMES R. HENRY, V.F., Salinas and Monterey; Very Revs. MATTHEW PENNINGTON, V.F., Santa Cruz; RUDY RUIZ, V.F., San Benito; CLAUDIO CABRERA-CARRANZA, V.F., Salinas Valley; KENNETH J. BROWN, V.F., San Luis Obispo.

Diocesan Consultors—Very Revs. KENNETH J. BROWN, V.F.; PETER A. CRIVELLO, V.G.; Revs. JAMES R. HENRY, V.F.; PAUL P. MURPHY; Very Rev. MATTHEW PENNINGTON, V.F.; Revs. ROY SHELLY, M.A., Ph.D.; ROBERTO VERA.

Diocesan Departments, Directors and Offices

Archives—Rev. CARL M.D. FARIA, 580 Fremont St., Monterey, 93940. Tel: 831-373-2127; Fax: 831-655-4809. Email: archives@dioceseofmonterey.org; Mailing Address: P.O. Box 2048, Monterey, 93942-2048.

Office of Legal Counsel—SUSAN A. MAYER, Esq., 425 Church St., Monterey, 93940. Email: smayer@dioceseofmonterey.org; Mailing Address: P.O. Box 2048, Monterey, 93942-2048. Tel: 831-373-4345; Fax: 831-373-5765.

Finance Officer—THOMAS H. RIORDAN, 425 Church St., Monterey, 93940. Tel: 831-373-4345; Fax: 831-373-1175. Email: triordan@dioceseofmonterey.org; Mailing Address: P.O. Box 2048, Monterey, 93942-2048.

Communication— "Vistas" Monterey Office - Spokesman: Deacon WARREN HOY, Mailing Address: P.O. Box 2048, Monterey, 93942. Tel: 831-373-4345; Fax: 831-373-5765. Email: observer@dioceseofmonterey.org.

Communications Coordinator—PETER STEMP, 485 Church St., Monterey, 93940. Tel: 831-373-4345; Fax: 831-373-5765. Email: pstemp@dioceseofmonterey.org.

Accounting Office—STEPHANIE MAYER, Controller The Roman Catholic Bishop of MontereyEmail: stephanie.mayer@dioceseofmonterey.org; ANNE M. MCGUIRE, Dir. Business Support. Email: amcguire@dioceseofmonterey.org; STEVE HAWTHORNE, Information Systems Mgr. Email: shawthorne@dioceseofmonterey.org; KATHY SINGH, Controller, Bishop Clinch Endowment & Catholic

Charities. Email: ksingh@dioceseofmonterey.org; TERI DAWN, Payroll Specialist. Email: tdawn@dioceseofmonterey.org; ROSE GRAHAM, Annual Ministries Appeal. Email: rgraham@dioceseofmonterey.org; KAREN PRESTIGIACOMO, Accounts Payable. Email: kprestigiacomo@dioceseofmonterey.org; 425 Church St., Monterey, 93940. Tel: 831-373-4346; Fax: 831-373-2831. Mailing Address: P.O. Box 2048, Monterey, 93942-2048.

Human Resources—SUSAN A. MAYER, Esq., Dir.; STEFANIE OLSEN, Human Resources Assoc. Dir., 425 Church St., Monterey, 93940. Tel: 831-373-4345; Fax: 831-373-5765. Email: humanres@dioceseofmonterey.org; Mailing Address: P.O. Box 2048, Monterey, 93942-2048.

Catholic Schools Department—485 Church St., Monterey, 93940. Mailing Address: P.O. Box 350, Monterey, 93942-0350. Tel: 831-373-1608; Fax: 831-373-0173. KATHLEEN RADECKE, Supt. Email: kradecke@dioceseofmonterey.org; MIRIAM "MIMI" SCHWERTFEGER, Asst. Dir. Email: mschwertfeger@dioceseofmonterey.org.

Cemeteries—TIM BENNETT, Dir., Administrative Office, 792 Fremont Blvd., Monterey, 93940. Mailing Address: P.O. Box 2048, Monterey, 93942-2048. Tel: 831-372-0327; Fax: 831-372-8726. Email: tbennett@dioceseofmonterey.org.

Diocesan Tribunal—425 Church St., Monterey, 93940. Mailing Address: P.O. Box 350, Monterey, 93942-0350. Tel: 831-373-1833; Fax: 831-373-6761. Email: fsanfilippo@dioceseofmonterey.org.

Judicial Vicar—Rev. KENNETH J. LAVERONE, O.F.M., M.A., J.C.L.; FRAYLNE SAN FILIPPO, Dir.

Judges—Revs. KENNETH J. LAVERONE, O.F.M., M.A., J.C.L.; DAVID SCHUYLER, S.M., J.C.D.; Sr. ELIZABETH MCDONOUGH, O.P., J.C.D., S.T.L.

Defenders of the Bond—Sr. LILIANA BONELLO, I.M., J.C.L.; Revs. PEDRO ESPINOZA, J.C.L.; ROBERT HAYES, J.C.L.; PAUL R. VALDEZ, J.C.L., KCHS.

Advocates—Revs. JOHN C. GRIFFIN; MICHAEL MARINI (Retired).

Promoter of Justice—Rev. PAUL R. VALDEZ, J.C.L., KCHS.

Notary—FRAYLNE SAN FILIPPO.

Divine Worship Department—Sr. BARBARA ANN LONG, O.P., Dir.; KAREN BENNETT, Administrative Asst., 126 High St., Santa Cruz, 95060. Tel: 831-423-4973; Fax: 831-423-2170. Email: worship@dioceseofmonterey.org.

Pastoral Response Coordinator—CAROL KAPLAN, Dir. MFT, 425 Church St., Monterey, 93940. Tel: 800-321-5220; Fax: 831-373-5765. Mailing Address: P.O. Box 2048, Monterey, 93942-2048.

Pastoral Support & Planning—Deacon WILLIAM T. (BILL) DITEWIG, Ph.D., Dir., 485 Church St., Monterey, 93940. Tel: 831-373-1335, Ext. 263; Fax: 831-373-3351. Email: wditewig@dioceseofmonterey.org.

Protection of Children and Young People—Sr. PATRICIA M. MURTAGH, I.M., Dir., 425 Church St., Monterey, 93940. Tel: 831-373-4345, Ext. 221; Fax: 831-373-1175. Email: srpmurtagh@dioceseofmonterey.org; Mailing Address: P.O. Box 2048, Monterey, 93942-2048.

Clergy Life & Ministry—Rev. PAUL P. MURPHY, St. Angela Merici, 146 8th St., Pacific Grove, 93950. Tel: 831-372-0338; Cell: 831-254-9294; Fax: 831-372-0338. Email: montereypriest@yahoo.com.

Office of Stewardship—Mailing Address: P.O. Box 2048, Monterey, 93942-2048. 485 Church St., Monterey, 93940. Tel: 831-373-1834; Fax: 831-373-3534. Email: stewardship@dioceseofmonterey.org. THERESA ALLION, Administrative Asst. Tel: 831-645-2812. Email: tallion@dioceseofmonterey.org.

Office of Faith Formation—Deacon WILLIAM T. (BILL) DITEWIG, Ph.D., Dir., 485 Church St., Monterey, 93940. Tel: 831-373-1335, Ext. 263; Fax: 831-373-3351. Email: wditewig@dioceseofmonterey.org.

Campus Ministry Department—Deacon WILLIAM T. (BILL) DITEWIG, Ph.D., Dir., 485 Church St., Monterey, 93940. Tel: 831-373-1335, Ext. 263; Fax: 831-373-3351. Email: wditewig@dioceseofmonterey.org; Revs. JERRY MAHER, University of California - Santa Cruz, 285 Meder St., Santa Cruz, 95060. Tel: 831-423-9400; Fax: 831-423-8163. Email: newman.ucsc@dioceseofmonterey.org. Web: www.newmanite.org; MANUEL RECERA, Dir. Campus Ministry, California State University at Monterey Bay (CSUMB), 485 Church St., Monterey, 93940. Tel: 831-373-1335, Ext. 248; Fax: 831-373-3351. Email: newman.csumb@dioceseofmonterey.org; JOHN ULRICH, S.M, M.A., Dir. Campus Ministry, California State Polytechnic University, San Luis Obispo. Email: frjohn@slonewman.org; KEVIN DUGGAN, S.M., M.Div., Assoc. Dir. Campus Ministry, California State Polytechnic University, San Luis Obispo, 1472 Foothill Blvd., San Luis Obispo, 93401. Tel: 805-543-4105; Fax: 831-543-5671.

Catechetical Ministries Department—485 Church St., Monterey, 93940. Tel: 831-373-1335; Fax: 831-373-3351. TISH SCARGILL, Dir. Email: tscargill@dioceseofmonterey.org; OLGA FLORES, Administrative Asst. Tel: 831-373-1335; Fax: 831-373-3351. Email: oflores@dioceseofmonterey.org; TERRY BURROWS, Consultant, San Luis Obispo Deanery, 751 Palm St., San Luis Obispo, 93401. Tel: 805-781-8220, Ext. 15; Fax: 805-781-8214. Email: tburrows@dioceseofmonterey.org.

Hispanic Ministry Department—Sr. LYDIA SCHNEIDER, I.M., Dir., 485 Church St., Monterey, 93940. Tel: 831-373-1335; Fax: 831-373-3351. Email: hispanic@dioceseofmonterey.org.

Migrant Ministry Coordinator—MARINA OCAMPO, 405 Palma Dr., Salinas, 93901-1822. Tel: 831-796-0136; Fax: 831-796-0138.

Permanent Diaconate—Deacons WILLIAM T. (BILL) DITEWIG, Ph.D., Dir., 485 Church St., Monterey, 93940. Tel: 831-373-1335, Ext. 263; Fax: 831-373-3351. Email: wditewig@dioceseofmonterey.org; ANDRES LARRAZA, Ph.D., Assoc. Dir. Deacon Formation for Hispanics. Tel: 831-402-0472. Email: alarraza@dioceseofmonterey.org; Mrs. CLAUDIA LARRAZA, Administrative Asst., 485 Church St., Monterey, 93940. Tel: 831-373-1335; Fax: 831-373-3351. Email: formation@dioceseofmonterey.org.

Family Life and Social Concerns—Ms. SHEILAH LYNCH, Dir. Email: slynch@dioceseofmonterey.org; 485 Church St., Monterey, 93940. Tel: 831-373-1335; Fax: 831-373-3351.

Respect Life—Rev. DEREK HUGHES, Dir. Email: dhughes@dioceseofmonterey.org; 485 Church St., Monterey, 93940. Tel: 831-373-1335; Fax: 831-373-3351.

Spiritual Direction Ministry—Mrs. BARBARA WINSTON, Coord., 485 Church St., Monterey, 93940. Tel: 831-373-1335; Fax: 831-373-3351. Email: bwinston@dioceseofmonterey.org.

Youth and Young Adult Ministry—Rev. EDWIN LIMPIADO, C.S.S., Dir. Email: elimpiado@dioceseofmonterey.org; PETRA ROBLES, Administrative Asst., 485 Church St., Monterey, 93940. Tel: 831-373-1335; Fax: 831-373-3351. Email: youth@dioceseofmonterey.org.

Scouting—485 Church St., Monterey, 93940. Tel: 831-373-1335; Fax: 831-373-3351. Email: scouting@dioceseofmonterey.org. ED CALLAHAN, Chap., 247 Via Promesa, Paso Robles, 93446. Tel: 831-373-1335; Fax: 831-373-3351. Email: scouting@dioceseofmonterey.org.

Vocations Director—Rev. ROY SHELLY, M.A., Ph.D., Dir.; Mrs. CLAUDIA LARRAZA, Administrative Asst., 485 Church St., Monterey, 93940. Tel: 831-373-1335; Fax: 831-373-3351. Email: vocations@dioceseofmonterey.org.

Holy Childhood Association—Sr. PATRICIA M. MURTAGH, I.M., Coord., Diocese of Monterey, 425 Church St., Monterey, 93940. Tel: 831-373-2628; Fax: 831-373-1175. Mailing Address: P.O. Box 2048, Monterey, 93942-2048. Email: srpmurtagh@dioceseofmonterey.org.

Pontifical Mission Societies—Sr. PATRICIA M. MURTAGH, I.M., Coord., Diocese of Monterey, 425 Church St., Monterey, 93940. Tel: 831-373-2628; Fax: 831-373-1175. Email: srpmurtagh@dioceseofmonterey.org; Mailing Address: P.O. Box 2048, Monterey, 93942-2048.

St. Joseph's Conference Center—485 Church St., Monterey, 93940.

Catholic Charities of the Diocese of Monterey—TERRIE IACINO, Interim Exec. Dir. Email: tlacino@dioceseofmonterey.org; ELENA PRAKASH, Administrative Asst. Email: eprakash@dioceseofmonterey.org.

Administrative Offices—922 Hilby Ave., Ste. C, Seaside, 93955-5357. Tel: 831-393-3110; Fax: 831-393-3115.

Catholic Charities - Salinas Office—Buckley Hall, St. Mary of the Nativity, 1705 2nd Ave., Salinas, 93905. Immigration & Citizenship. Tel: 831-422-0602; Fax: 831-422-0759. *Family Supportive Services.* Tel: 831-753-5314; Fax: 831-422-0759.

Catholic Charities - San Luis Obispo Office—Mission San Luis Obispo, 751 Palm Ave., San Luis Obispo, 93401. Tel: 805-541-9110; Fax: 805-541-9121. (Immigration & Citizenship Svcs.; Family Supportive Svcs.)

Catholic Charities - Watsonville Office—217 E. Lake St., Watsonville, 95076. Tel: 831-722-2675; Fax: 831-722-9921. (Family Supportive Svcs.; Immigration & Citizenship Svcs. & Mental Health Counseling)

Campaign for Human Development—Ms. SHEILAH LYNCH, Dir., 485 Church St., Monterey, 93940. Tel: 831-373-1335; Fax: 831-373-3351. Email: slynch@dioceseofmonterey.org.

Catholic Relief Service—Ms. SHEILAH LYNCH, Dir., 485 Church St., Monterey, 93940. Tel: 831-373-1335; Fax: 831-373-3351. Email: slynch@dioceseofmonterey.org.

Committees and Councils

Administrative Committee Priests' Pension Plan—Most Rev. RICHARD J. GARCIA, D.D.; Revs. EUGENIO ARAMBURO; JOSEPH L. OCCHIUTO; GREGORY SANDMAN; MICHAEL L. CROSS, (Pro Tem); PAUL R. VALDEZ, J.C.L., KCHS, Chm.

Ave Maria Board—Most Rev. RICHARD J. GARCIA, D.D., Chm.; THOMAS H. RIORDAN, Pres./Finance Officer; CLANCY D'ANGELO, Vice Pres.; Sr. THERESA MCSHANE, Sec.; DONA LOGEMAN ACUFF, Recording Sec.; Mrs. LOU LANGLEY.

Bishop Harry A. Clinch Endowment Fund, The Bishop Sylvester D. Ryan Continuing Education Fund— The Bishop Shubsda Memorial Seminary Endowment Burse and The Cemetery Endowment Burse Most Rev. RICHARD J. GARCIA, D.D.; JAMES D. CHILDS; LEAH DUNCAN; MARK FAYLOR; JAMES HARRISON; ELIZABETH HELFRICH; SUSAN A. MAYER, Esq., Ex Official; MICHAEL MORRIS; RONALD PASQUINELLI; JOSEPH PEZZINI; THOMAS H. RIORDAN, Vicar for Temporalities & Admin./Finance Officer, (Staff); LARRY SAGE; ROBERT SEMAS; KATHY SINGH, Controller, (Staff).

Building Commission—Contact Persons: Rev. JOHN C. GRIFFIN, Carmel Mission, P.O. Box 2235, Carmel, 93921-2235. Tel: 831-624-1271; Fax: 831-624-8050; THOMAS H. RIORDAN, Diocese of Monterey, 425 Church St., P.O. Box 2048, Monterey, 93942-2048. Tel: 831-373-4345; Fax: 831-373-1175. Email: triordan@dioceseofmonterey.org.

Catholic Charities Board—Most Rev. RICHARD J. GARCIA, D.D., Chm.; CYNTHIA ZOLLER-SILVER, Pres.; MARIA ANDERSON; JIM COOK; RON FREDRICKSON; CHRIS HAUPT; SUSAN A. MAYER, Esq., Gen. Counsel & Bd. Member; Rev. JERRY MCCORMICK, Sec. (Retired); ALBERT NICORA; MARTINA O'SULLIVAN, M.S.W.; CAMERINO PADILLA; CHRISTOPHER PANETTA; ANA VENTURA-PHARAS; LARRY SAGE, Treas. Staff: THOMAS H. RIORDAN, Vicar for Temporalities & Admin./Finance Officer; KATHY SINGH, Controller, Catholic Charities; TERRIE IACINO, Interim Exec. Dir.

Diocesan Consultors—Very Revs. KENNETH J. BROWN, V.F.; PETER A. CRIVELLO, V.G.; Revs. JAMES R. HENRY, V.F.; PAUL P. MURPHY; Very Rev. MATTHEW PENNINGTON, V.F.; Revs. ROY SHELLY, M.A., Ph.D.; ROBERTO VERA.

Finance Council—Most Rev. RICHARD J. GARCIA, D.D.; RONALD PASQUINELLI, Chm.; ROSEMARY ANDERSON; RICHARD FALGE; HARRY HOW; GARY PLUMMER; JIM ROTTER; TOD SANCHEZ; MOSE THOMAS; Rev. PAUL R. VALDEZ, J.C.L., KCHS. Ex Officio: THOMAS H. RIORDAN, Vicar for Temporalities & Admin./Finance Officer; STEPHANIE MAYER, Controller; SUSAN A. MAYER, Esq., Gen. Counsel; DONA LOGEMAN ACUFF, Recording Sec.

Insurance Committee—SUSAN A. MAYER, Esq.; THOMAS H. RIORDAN; Rev. PAUL R. VALDEZ, J.C.L., KCHS.

Lay Employees Non-Qualified Pension Committee—THOMAS H. RIORDAN, Chm.; TONY KARACHALE, Consultant.

Lay Employee Pension Plan Committee—CLANCY D'ANGELO; TONY KARACHALE, Consultant; SUSAN A. MAYER, Esq.; RONALD PASQUINELLI; THOMAS H. RIORDAN, Ex Officio; TOD D. SANCHEZ; DAVID J. SULLIVAN.

Permanent Diaconate Advisory Board—Deacon ANDRES LARRAZA, Ph.D.; Mrs. CLAUDIA LARRAZA; Deacon MANUEL ESPINOZA; Mrs. FRANCISCA ESPINOZA; Deacon DOUGLAS WINSTON; Mrs. BARBARA WINSTON.

Presbyteral Council—Most Rev. RICHARD J. GARCIA, D.D.; Very Revs. KENNETH J. BROWN, V.F.; PETER A. CRIVELLO, V.G.; Revs. PATRICK DOOLING; JAMES R. HENRY, V.F.; ENRIQUE HERRERA; EDWIN LIMPIADO, C.S.S.; MICHAEL MARINI (Retired); PAUL P. MURPHY, Vicar for Clergy; Very Rev. MATTHEW PENNINGTON, V.F.; Revs. RAYMOND TINTLE, O.F.M.; ROBERTO VERA; Very Rev. RUDY RUIZ, V.F.; DONA LOGEMAN ACUFF, Recording Sec.

Clergy Life and Ministry Board—Most Rev. RICHARD J. GARCIA, D.D.; Revs. PAUL P. MURPHY, Dir.; PATRICK DOOLING; ANALUISA GONZALEZ, Recording Sec.; Rev. ALBERTO CABRERA; Deacon ANDRES LARRAZA, Ph.D.; BARBARA MORRISON; Rev. LUCAS PANTOJA.

Clergy Personnel Board—Most Rev. RICHARD J. GARCIA, D.D.; Rev. MIGUEL ANGEL GRAJEDA; Deacon ANDRES LARRAZA, Ph.D.; Revs. EFRAIN MEDINA; PAUL P. MURPHY, Vicar for Clergy; Sr. PATRICIA M. MURTAGH, I.M., Chancellor; Mrs. NICKI PASCULLI; Revs. GREGORY SANDMAN; ROY SHELLY, M.A., Ph.D., Moderator of the Curia.

Safety Committee—TIM BENNETT; SUSAN A. MAYER, Esq.; ANNE MCGUIRE; THOMAS H. RIORDAN; KATHLEEN RADECKE; KAREN VICTORINO; MIRIAM "MIMI" SCHWERTFEGER, Recording Sec.; Sr.

PATRICIA M. MURTAGH, I.M.; TISH SCARGILL; SUZY BROWN.

St. Francis Central Coast Catholic High School, Inc.—Most Rev. RICHARD J. GARCIA, D.D.; Very Rev. TIMOTHY PLOCH, S.D.B.; Most Rev. SYLVESTER D. RYAN, D.D., Retired Bishop of Monterey (Retired); Mr. WILLIAM GOODMAN; THOMAS H. RIORDAN; Rev. ALBERT MENGON, S.D.B.; MARIE MARHEINEKE, Recording Sec.

Vocations Board—Most Rev. RICHARD J. GARCIA, D.D.; Sr. CARMEN BOTELLO, F.M.A.; Mrs. SALLY GRIEG; Rev. LUCAS PANTOJA; Sr. MARIA ROMERO; Revs. ROY SHELLY, M.A., Ph.D.; ROBERTO VERA.

CLERGY, PARISHES, MISSIONS AND PAROCHIAL SCHOOLS

CITY OF MONTEREY

(MONTEREY COUNTY), CATHEDRAL OF SAN CARLOS BORROMEO (1770) Very Rev. Peter A. Crivello, Rector; Rev. Patrick Dooling, Parochial Vicar; Deacon Andres Larraza; Sr. Maria Romero, Pastoral Assoc.
Mailing Address: 500 Church St., 93940. Tel: 831-373-2628; Fax: 831-373-0518. Web: www.sancarloscathedral.net.
Res.: 550 Church St., 93940.
School—(1898), (Grades K-8), 450 Church St., 93940. Tel: 831-375-1324; Fax: 831-375-9736. Email: principal@sancarlosschool.org. Web: www.sancarlosschool.org. Teresa Bennett, Prin.; Mr. Timothy Krislyn, Asst. Prin. Lay Teachers 16; Total Staff 29; Students 294.
Catechesis/Religious Program—Tel: 831-373-2628; Fax: 831-373-0516. Cynthia Friesen, D.R.E. Students 207.

OUTSIDE THE CITY OF MONTEREY

APTOS, SANTA CRUZ CO., RESURRECTION (1968) Rev. Ronald Shirley; Deacon Patrick Conway, Pastoral Assoc.
Res.: 7600 Soquel Dr., P.O. Box 87, 95001. Tel: 831-688-4300; Fax: 831-688-6921. Email: resurrectionparish@sbcglobal.net. Web: www.resurrection-aptos.org.
School—Good Shepherd School (Inter-Parish), (Grades PreK-8), 2727 Mattison Ln., Santa Cruz, 95065. Tel: 831-476-4000; Fax: 831-476-0948. Email: achavarria@gsschool.org. Web: www.gsschool.org. Daniel Anderson, Prin. Lay Teachers 12; Students 209.
Catechesis/Religious Program—Tel: 831-688-4300; Fax: 831-688-6921. Students 170.

ARROYO GRANDE, SAN LUIS OBISPO CO., ST. PATRICK (1886) Very Rev. Kenneth J. Brown.
Res.: 501 Fair Oaks Ave., P.O. Box 860, 93421. Tel: 805-489-2680; Fax: 805-489-1316. Email: info@stpatsag.org. Web: www.stpatsag.org.
School—(1963), (Grades PreSchool-8), 900 W. Branch St., 93420. Tel: 805-489-1210; Fax: 805-489-7662. Email: mhalderman@stpatricksschool.net. Web: www.stpatschoolag.com. Maureen Halderman, Prin. Sisters of Mercy 1; Lay Teachers 9; Total Staff 38; Students 336.
Catechesis/Religious Program—Tel: 805-481-2990. Students 324.
Mission—St. Francis of Assisi 17th & Beach, Oceano, San Luis Obispo Co. 93445.
Shamrock Thrift Shop—924 Grand Ave., Grover City, 93433. Tel: 805-481-0612. Alanna Owen, Mgr.

ATASCADERO, SAN LUIS OBISPO CO., ST. WILLIAM'S (1948) [JC] Rev. George Batchelder.
Res.: 6410 Santa Lucia Rd., 93422. Tel: 805-466-0849; Fax: 805-461-0743. Email: office@st-williams.org. Web: www.st-williams.org.
Catechesis/Religious Program—Troylyn Lindsay, Parish Catechetical Leader. Students 219.

BOULDER CREEK, SANTA CRUZ CO., ST. MICHAEL (1921) Rev. Robert Murrin.
Res.: 13005 Pine St., 95006. Tel: 831-338-6112; Fax: 831-338-7522. Email: st.michaelschurch@sbcglobal.net.
Catechesis/Religious Program—Debbie Esteban-Moyer, C.R.E. Students 14.

CAMBRIA, SAN LUIS OBISPO CO., SANTA ROSA (1961) [CEM] Rev. Mark Stetz.
Res.: 1174 Main St., 93428. Tel: 805-927-4816; Fax: 805-927-2880. Email: admin@santarosaparish.org. Web: www.santarosaparish.org.
Catechesis/Religious Program—Tel: 805-924-1728. Students 62.

CAPITOLA, SANTA CRUZ CO., ST. JOSEPH (1904) [JC] Very Rev. Matthew Pennington; Barbara Day, Business Mgr. & Parish Admin.
Res.: 435 Monterey Ave., 95010. Tel: 831-475-8211; Fax: 831-475-2601. Email: stjosephs@stjoscap.org. Web: www.stjoscap.org.
School—Good Shepherd School (Inter-Parish), (Grades K-8), 2727 Mattison Ln., Santa Cruz, 95065. Tel: 831-476-4000; Fax: 831-476-0948. Email: snelson@gsschool.org. Web: www.gsschool.org. Daniel Anderson, Prin. Lay Teachers 18; Students 202.
Catechesis/Religious Program—Tel: 831-475-9510; Fax: 831-475-2601. David Suddjian, D.R.E. & Liturgy Dir. Students 157.

CARMEL VALLEY, MONTEREY CO., OUR LADY OF MT. CARMEL (1953) Rev. Emil Robu.
Res.: 9 El Caminito Rd., 93924. Tel: 831-659-2224; Fax: 831-659-9186. Email: olmc@ourladycarmelvalley.org. Web: www.ourladycarmelvalley.org.
Catechesis/Religious Program—Students 33.

CARMEL, MONTEREY CO., SAN CARLOS BORROMEO BASILICA (1771) [CEM], (Carmel Mission) Rev. John C. Griffin. In Res., Rev. Edwin Limpiado, C.S.S.
Res.: 3080 Rio Rd., 93923. Tel: 831-624-1271; Fax: 831-624-8050. Email: info@carmelmission.org. Web: www.carmelmission.org.
School—Junipero Serra School, (Grades K-8), 2992 Lasuen Dr., 93923. Tel: 831-624-8322; Fax: 831-624-8311. Margaret A. Burger, Prin. Lay Teachers 16; Students 174.
Catechesis/Religious Program—Tel: 831-624-1271, Ext. 216; Fax: 831-624-6840. Students 165.
Mission—St. Francis of the Redwoods Hwy. 1, Big Sur, Monterey Co. 93920.
Chapel—Blessed Sacrament

CASTROVILLE, MONTEREY CO., OUR LADY OF REFUGE (1869) [JC] Revs. Pedro Espinoza; Jose Aurelio Ortiz Matiz.
11140 Preston St., 95012. Tel: 831-633-4015; Fax: 831-633-4653. Email: olorcchurch@olorc.org.
Res.: 14931 Charter Oak Blvd., Salinas, 93907.
Catechesis/Religious Program—Tel: 831-633-4016. Sr. Christina Bortolotti, D.R.E. Students 574.

CAYUCOS , SAN LUIS OBISPO CO., ST. JOSEPH (1905) Rev. Edward J. Holterhoff, Admin.; Rev. Msgr. Charles G. Fatooh, Sacramental Min.
Res.: 360 Park Ave., P.O. Box 437, 93430. Tel: 805-995-3243; Fax: 805-995-2838. Email: stjosephcayucos@charter.net.
Catechesis/Religious Program—

CORRALITOS, SANTA CRUZ CO., HOLY EUCHARIST (1969) Rev. Derek Hughes (Ireland), Admin.
Res.: 527 Corralitos Rd., 95076. Tel: 831-722-5490; Fax: 831-722-5421. Email: office.holyeucharistca@yahoo.com. Web: www.holyeucharistca.com.
Catechesis/Religious Program—Email: stmahan@yahoo.com. Students 71.

DAVENPORT, SANTA CRUZ CO., ST. VINCENT DE PAUL (1915) Rev. James Catalano, O.S.J., Parochial Admin.
123 Marine View Ave., P.O. Box 284, 95017. Tel: 831-471-1702.
Res.: 544 W. Cliff Dr., Santa Cruz, 95060. Tel: 831-457-1868; Fax: 831-457-1317.
Catechesis/Religious Program—123 Marine View Ave., 95017. Tel: 831-471-1702, Ext. 27. Students 10.

FELTON, SANTA CRUZ CO., ST. JOHN'S (1952) Rev. Michael L. Cross.
Res.: 120 Russell Ave., P.O. Box M-1, 95018. Tel: 831-335-4657; Fax: 831-335-4648. Email: st.johns.ch@sbcglobal.net.
Catechesis/Religious Program—Noli Farwell, D.R.E. Students 24.

GONZALES, MONTEREY CO., ST. THEODORE (1892) [JC] Rev. Efrain Medina, Admin.
Office: 125 S. Center St., P.O. Box B, 93926.
Res.: 120 First St., P.O. Drawer B, 93926. Tel: 831-675-3648; Fax: 831-675-8360.
Catechesis/Religious Program—Tel: 831-675-3668, Ext. 7; Fax: 831-675-2974. Students 732.
Mission—Chualar Mission Scott & Grant Sts., Chualar, Monterey Co. 93925. Tel: 831-676-6220.

GREENFIELD, MONTEREY CO., HOLY TRINITY (1951), (Mexican—Italian), Rev. Enrique Herrera.
Res.: 27 S. El Camino Real, Box 276, 93927. Tel: 831-674-5428; Fax: 831-674-5285. Web: holytrinitygreenfield.org.
Catechesis/Religious Program—Tel: 831-674-3695. Gloria Aguilar, D.R.E. Students 412.

HOLLISTER, SAN BENITO CO
1—ST. BENEDICT, Merged with Sacred Heart, Hollister to form Sacred Heart/St. Benedict Catholic Community, Hollister.
2—SACRED HEART (1877) Merged with St. Benedict, Hollister to form Sacred Heart/St. Benedict Catholic Community, Hollister.
3—SACRED HEART/ST. BENEDICT CATHOLIC COMMUNITY (1877) [CEM] Very Rev. Rudy Ruiz; Rev. Heibar Castanada, Parochial Vicar Pro Tem.
Res.: 540 College St., 95023. Tel: 831-637-9212; Fax: 831-637-7299. Email: shparish@sacredheart-stbenedict.org.
St. Benedict Church: 1200 Fairview Rd., 95023.
Pastoral Center—680 College St., 95023. Fax: 831-637-7299.
School—(Grades PreSchool-8), 670 College St., 95023. Tel: 831-637-4157; Fax: 831-637-4164. Email: gjurevich@sacredheartschool.org. Web: sacredheartschool.org. Gayla Jurevich, Prin. Lay Teachers 17; Students 263.
Catechesis/Religious Program—Tel: 831-637-8291. Jeanmarie Centeno, D.R.E.; Dolores Fenzel, S.A., Dir. Adult Faith Formation. Students 800.

JOLON, MONTEREY CO., SAN ANTONIO MISSION (1771) Deacon Dustin Miller.
Res.: Box 803, 93928. Tel: 831-385-4478; Fax: 831-386-9332. Email: office@missionsanantonio.net. Web: missionsanantonio.net.
Catechesis/Religious Program—Joan Steele, D.R.E. & Mission Admin.; Victoria Villegas, Catechist. Students 7.

KING CITY, MONTEREY CO., ST. JOHN THE BAPTIST (1891), (Hispanic), Very Rev. Claudio Cabrera-Carranza; Rev. Dennis M. Peterson.
Res.: 504 N. Third St., 93930. Tel: 831-385-3377; Fax: 831-385-3317. Email: stjohnscc@att.net.
Catechesis/Religious Program—Tel: 831-385-3464. Students 309.
Mission—St. Luke Main St., San Lucas, Monterey Co. 93954.

LOS GATOS, SANTA CRUZ CO., CHRIST CHILD (1983) Rev. Eugenio Aramburo.
Res.: 23230 Summit Rd., 95033. Tel: 408-353-2210; Fax: 408-353-8680.
Catechesis/Religious Program—Kim Avoy, D.R.E. Students 37.

LOS OSOS, SAN LUIS OBISPO CO., ST. ELIZABETH ANN SETON (1984) Rev. Lucas Pantoja, Parochial Admin.
Res. & Mailing Address: 2050 Palisades Ave., 93402. Tel: 805-528-5319; Fax: 805-528-8893.
Catechesis/Religious Program—Students 71.

MARINA, MONTEREY CO., ST. JUDE PARISH COMMUNITY (1963) Rev. Paul R. Valdez.
Res.: 303 Hillcrest Ave., 93933. Tel: 831-384-5434; Fax: 831-384-7011. Email: st_jude_marina_amy@sbcglobal.net.
Catechesis/Religious Program—Tel: 831-384-8268. Annie F. Punzalan, D.R.E. Students 188.

MORRO BAY, SAN LUIS OBISPO CO., ST. TIMOTHY (1950) Rev. Edward J. Holterhoff, Parochial Admin.
Mailing Address: 962 Piney Way, 93442. Tel: 805-772-2840; Fax: 805-772-3184. Email: osainttims@sbcglobal.net. Web: www.sttimothymorrobay.org.
Catechesis/Religious Program—Students 65.

NIPOMO, SAN LUIS OBISPO CO., ST. JOSEPH (1968) Rev. Alberto Cabrera; Most Rev. Sylvester D. Ryan, Retired Bishop of Monterey (Retired); Deacon Gregory Dutra.
Res.: 298 S. Thompson, 93444. Tel: 805-929-1922; Fax: 805-929-2662.
Catechesis/Religious Program—Tel: 805-929-1921. Students 260.

PACIFIC GROVE, MONTEREY CO., ST. ANGELA MERICI CHURCH (1928) [CEM] Revs. Paul P. Murphy; Romeo Evangelista.
Res.: 161 9th St., 93950. Tel: 831-655-4160; Fax: 831-372-5026. Email: stangelachurch@gmail.com. Web: www.stangelapacificgrove.org.
Church: 362 Lighthouse Ave., 93950.
Office:—146 Eighth St., 93950.
Preschool - Children's Center—136 Eighth St., 93950. Tel: 831-372-3555; Fax: 831-372-1965. Email: stangelas@redshift.com. Virginia Ziomek, Prin. Lay Teachers 8; Students 62.
Catechesis/Religious Program—Students 35.

PAJARO, MONTEREY CO., OUR LADY OF THE ASSUMPTION (1953), (Hispanic), [CEM] Revs. Victor M. Prado; Francisco J. Montes.
Res.: 100 Salinas Rd., 95076. Tel: 831-722-1104; Fax: 831-722-1931.
Catechesis/Religious Program—Tel: 831-722-9938. Marielena Curiel, D.R.E. Students 483.

PASO ROBLES, SAN LUIS OBISPO CO., ST. ROSE (1922) [CEM] [JC] Rev. Roberto Vera.
Office: 642 Trigo Ln., P.O. Box 790, 93447. Tel: 805-238-2218; Fax: 805-238-2762. Email: info@saintrosechurch.org. Web: www.saintrosechurch.org.
Res.: 641 Trigo Ln., P.O. Box 790, 93447. Tel: 805-238-2218; Fax: 805-238-2762.
School—(Grades PreK-8), 900 Tucker Ave., 93446. Tel: 805-238-0304; Fax: 805-238-7393. Email: srsoffice@saintrosecatholicschool.org. Web: www.saintrosecatholicschool.org. Sr. Rebeca Munoz, S.J.S., Prin. Lay Teachers 16; Students 218.
Catechesis/Religious Program—Students 420.

PISMO BEACH, SAN LUIS OBISPO CO., ST. PAUL THE APOSTLE (1929) [JC] Revs. Victor P. Abegg, O.F.M.Conv.; Alphonse Van Guilder, O.F.M.Conv., Parochial Vicar; Bro. Robert Ouellette, O.F.M.Conv., Pastoral Assoc. In Res., Revs. Peter Parchem, O.F.M.Conv., Pastor Emeritus; John Farao,

O.F.M.Conv., Prison Chap. (CA Men's Colony).
Res.: 800 Bello St., 93449. Tel: 805-773-2219; Fax: 805-773-8617. Email: stpaulspismobeach@charter.net. Web: www.stpaulspismobeach.com.
Catechesis/Religious Program—Tel: 805-773-3185. Students 61.

SALINAS

1—CHRIST THE KING (1995), (Hispanic), Rev. Antonio Sanchez.
Res.: 240 Calle Cebu, 93901. Tel: 831-422-6543; Fax: 831-422-7218.
Religious Education Office—Tel: 831-422-6722.
Catechesis/Religious Program—Students 620.

2—MADONNA DEL SASSO (1960) Revs. Gregory Sandman; James R. Henry, Senior Priest; Joey R. Buena, C.S.S., Parochial Vicar; Wayne Dawson, Parochial Vicar.
Res.: 320 E. Laurel Dr., 93906. Tel: 831-422-5323; Fax: 831-422-0536.
School—(Grades PreK-8), 20 Santa Teresa Way, 93906. Tel: 831-424-7813; Fax: 831-424-3359. Web: madonnadelsasso.com. Dr. Charles E. White, Prin. Sisters of Notre Dame 1; Lay Teachers 14; Students 307.
Catechesis/Religious Program—Students 913.

3—ST. MARY OF THE NATIVITY (1947), (Hispanic), Rev. Jose Alberto Vazquez-Martinez.
Res.: 1702 Second Ave., 93905. Tel: 831-758-1669; Fax: 831-758-4715. Web: www.stmarysalinas.org.
Catechesis/Religious Program—Tel: 831-422-9964; Fax: 831-422-1217. Web: www.stmarysalinas.org/ingles/religiouseducation.html. Ms. Edith Sanchez, D.R.E. Students 900.

4—SACRED HEART (1877) [JC] Very Rev. Ignacio Martinez; Rev. Roy Margallo, Parochial Vicar; Deacons Rick Gutierrez; Douglas Winston.
Res.: 22 Stone St., 93901-2643. Tel: 831-424-1959; Fax: 831-424-0788. Email: scrhrtchurch@sbcglobal.net. Web: www.shsalinas.org.
School—(Grades K-8), 123 W. Market St., 93901. Tel: 831-771-1310; Fax: 831-771-1314. Email: shs1906@yahoo.com. Ms. Jennifer Dean, Prin. Sisters 1; Lay Teachers 14; Total Staff 32; Students 277.
Catechesis/Religious Program—Tel: 831-772-8223. Mary Scattini, D.R.E.; Jose Luis Medina, D.R.E. Students 465.

SAN JUAN BAUTISTA, SAN BENITO CO., SAN JUAN BAUTISTA (1797), (Hispanic), [CEM], (Old Mission) Very Rev. James Henry, Pastoral Admin.
Res.: 406 Second St., P.O. Box 400, 95045. Tel: 831-623-2127; Fax: 831-623-2433. Web: www.oldmissionsjb.org.
Catechesis/Religious Program—Tel: 831-623-4178. Email: faithformation@oldmissionsjb.org. Students 113.

SAN LUIS OBISPO, SAN LUIS OBISPO CO.

1—NATIVITY OF OUR LADY (1964) Rev. Michael Cicinato; Deacon Greg Wilhelm.
Res.: 221 Daly Ave., 93405-1099. Tel: 805-544-2357; Fax: 805-544-6756. Email: parish@nativityslo.org. Web: www.nativityslo.org.
Catechesis/Religious Program—Anne Lorenzen, D.R.E. Students 109.

2—SAN LUIS OBISPO (1772), (Old Mission) Revs. Russell D. Brown; Braulio Valencia, Parochial Vicar; Deacon Charles M. Roeder.
Res.: 751 Palm St., 93401. Tel: 805-781-8220; Fax: 805-781-8214. Email: office@oldmissionslo.org. Web: www.missionsanluisobispo.org.
Preschool—221 Daly St., 93401. Tel: 805-549-8819. Teri Stegman, Prin.
School—(Grades PreK-8), 761 Broad St., 93401. Tel: 805-543-6019; Fax: 805-543-6246. Teri Stegman, Prin. Lay Teachers 18; Students 328.
Catechesis/Religious Program—Tel: 805-781-8220, Ext. 18. Students 189.

SAN MIGUEL, SAN LUIS OBISPO CO., SAN MIGUEL (1797), (Hispanic—Filipino), [CEM], (Old Mission) Rev. Raymond Tintle, O.F.M. In Res., Revs. Thomas Frost, O.F.M.; Larry Gosselin, O.F.M.; Joseph Zermeno, O.F.M.
Res.: 775 Mission St., P.O. Box 69, 93451. Tel: 805-467-2131; Fax: 805-467-2141. Email: info@missionsanmiguel.org. Web: www.missionsanmiguel.org.
Catechesis/Religious Program—Tel: 805-467-2325. Students 104.
Mission—Our Lady of Ransom San Ardo, Monterey Co.
Mission—Our Lady of Guadalupe Bradley, Monterey Co.
Station—Heritage Ranch Paso Robles.

SANTA CRUZ, SANTA CRUZ CO.

1—HOLY CROSS (1791) [CEM 3] [JC 2] Rev. Joseph L. Occhiuto. In Res., Rev. Jerry Maher.
Res.: 126 High St., 95060. Tel: 831-423-4182; Fax: 831-423-1043. Email: office@holycrosssantacruz.com. Web: www.holycrosssantacruz.com.
School—Holy Cross School (1862), (Grades PreSchool-8), 150 Emmet St., 95060. Tel: 831-423-4447; Fax: 831-423-0752. Email: admin@holycsc.org. Web: www.holycsc.org. Sr. Adrienne Pinnette, O.P., Prin. Adrian Dominican Sisters 2; Lay Teachers 18; Total Staff 33; Students 211.
Catechesis/Religious Program—Tel: 831-458-3041; Fax: 831-458-1043. Email: faith@holycrosssantacruz.com. Students 170.
Mission—Mision Galeria 130 Emmet St., Santa Cruz Co. 95060. Tel: 831-426-5686. Web: www.geocities.com/missionbell.

2—STAR OF THE SEA (1947) [CEM] Rev. Ronald L. Green, Sacramental Min.
Res.: 515 Frederick St., 95062. Tel: 831-429-1018; Fax: 831-429-5832. Web: www.ourladystar.org.
School—Good Shepherd School, 2727 Mattison Ln., 95062. Tel: 831-476-4000; Fax: 831-476-0948. Web: www.gsschool.org. Daniel Anderson, Prin. (Inter-Parish) Lay Teachers 18; Students 209.
Catechesis/Religious Program—Students 352.
Chapel—Villa Maria del Mar, Tel: 831-475-1236; Fax: 831-475-8867.

SANTA MARGARITA, SAN LUIS OBISPO CO., SANTA MARGARITA DE CORTONA (1934) [JC] Rev. Robert Travis.
Res.: 22515 "H" St., P.O. Box 350, 93453. Tel: 805-438-5383; Fax: 805-438-4313. Email: decortona@aol.com.
Catechesis/Religious Program—Tel: 805-239-1597. Cathy Solkshinitz, D.R.E. Students 50.
Mission—St. James Mission P.O. Box 3055, Carrissa Plains, San Luis Obispo Co. 93453. Tel: 805-475-2222.

SCOTTS VALLEY, SANTA CRUZ CO., SAN AGUSTIN (1969) Rev. Seamus O'Brien.
Res.: 257 Glenwood Dr., 95066. Tel: 831-438-3633; Fax: 831-438-0973. Email: sanagustin@sbcglobal.net.
Catechesis/Religious Program—Students 290.

SEASIDE, MONTEREY CO., ST. FRANCIS XAVIER (1950) Rev. Michael Volk.
Res.: 1475 LaSalle Ave., 93955. Tel: 831-394-8546; Fax: 831-394-5414.
Catechesis/Religious Program—Sr. Carmelita Heredia, S.A., D.R.E. Students 485.
Mission—, Seaside, Monterey Co. 93955. Tel: 831-394-3759. Email: gsfrparish@aol.com.

SOLEDAD, MONTEREY CO., OUR LADY OF SOLITUDE (1933), (Spanish), [CEM] [JC] Rev. Dennis Gallo.
235 Main St., 93960. Tel: 831-678-2731; Fax: 831-678-2968.
Catechesis/Religious Program—Tel: 831-678-1277; Fax: 831-678-0111. Sr. Theresita Crasta, I.M., D.R.E. Students 804.
Mission—Nuestra Senora de la Soledad Rte. 1, Box 72, Monterey Co. 93960. Tel: 408-678-2586.

SPRECKELS, MONTEREY CO., ST. JOSEPH (1969) Rev. Roy Shelly; Deacon William T. (Bill) Ditewig.
Mailing Address: Spreckels Blvd. & Railroad Ave., P.O. Box 7158, 93962. Email: office@stjchurch.org. Web: stjchurch.org.
Catechesis/Religious Program—Religious Education Center, 15 First St., P.O. Box 7158, 93962. Tel: 831-455-8720; Fax: 831-455-9357. Carrie Aragon, D.R.E. Students 205.

TRES PINOS, SAN BENITO CO., IMMACULATE CONCEPTION (1892) Very Rev. Larry Kambitsch.
Mailing Address: P.O. Box 247, 95075.
Res.: 7290 Airline Hwy., 95075. Tel: 831-628-3216; Fax: 831-628-3602. Email: secretary@icctp.org.
Catechesis/Religious Program—Email: religioused@icctp.org. Ann Ventura, D.R.E. Students 85.

WATSONVILLE, SANTA CRUZ CO.

1—OUR LADY HELP OF CHRISTIANS (1854), (Portuguese—Spanish), Revs. David Purdy, S.D.B.; Luis A. Oyarzo, S.D.B.; Albert Mengon, S.D.B. In Res., Bro. Abel Zanella, S.D.B., (Retired).
Res.: 2401 E. Lake Ave., 95076. Tel: 831-722-2665; Fax: 831-722-8305. Email: olhcchurch@yahoo.com.
Catechesis/Religious Program—Tel: 831-722-2392. Sr. Silva Castillo, F.M.A., D.R.E. Students 364.

2—ST. PATRICK (1861) Revs. Miguel Angel Grajeda; Marc Rene Dauphine.
Res.: 721 Main St., 95076. Tel: 831-724-1317; Fax: 831-724-1627. Email: saintpatricks@sbcglobal.net.
Catechesis/Religious Program—Tel: 831-724-2141. Sylvia Pineda, D.R.E. (English & Spanish); Veronica Ruiz, C.R.E. Students 1,166.

Shrines

SANTA CRUZ, SANTA CRUZ CO., SHRINE OF ST. JOSEPH GUARDIAN OF THE REDEEMER (1952) Rev. Rafael Lavilla, O.S.J., Dir.
Res.: 544 W. Cliff Dr., 95060-6147. Tel: 831-471-0442; Fax: 831-457-1317. Email: guardian@osjoseph.org. Web: www.osjoseph.org.
Guardian of the Redeemer Bookstore—Tel: 831-471-1700.

Chaplains of Public Institutions

ATASCADERO. *Atascadero State Hospital*. Deacon Daniel Weber.

PASO ROBLES. *El Paso de Robles School*. Mr. Jose Domingo Ojeyda. Dept. of the Youth Authority.

SAN LUIS OBISPO. *California Men's Colony East*. Rev. John Farao, O.F.M.Conv., Chap.
California Men's Colony West. Rev. John Farao, O.F.M.Conv.

SOLEDAD. *Correctional Training Facility*. Christina McNamara, Chap. Christina McNamara, Chaplain
Salinas Valley State Prison. Rev. Joel J. Almendras, Chap.

Special Assignment:
Very Rev.—
Crivello, Peter A., V.G., Pastoral Office, 631 Abrego St., P.O. Box 2048, 93942-2048. Tel: 831-373-4345; Fax: 831-373-1175
Revs.—
Castro, Dominic Joseph, M.Div., Chap., 1130 Fremont Blvd., #105-270, Seaside, 93955. Naval Postgraduate School, Monterey, CA
Deibel, David, 4403 Redwood Rd., Napa, 94558. Tel: 707-252-3745
Kelly, Tom, Vandenberg Airforce Base, 30 SW/HC, Vandenberg Afb, 93437. Tel: 805-606-5773
Laverone, Kenneth J., O.F.M., M.A., J.C.L., Judicial Vicar, Diocesan Tribunal, 435 Church St., 93940. Tel: 831-373-1833; Fax: 831-373-6761
McCarthy, Scott, Catholic Chap., 20 Hitchcock Rd., Salinas, 93908. Tel: 831-601-4679
Miller, Michael J., St. Patrick's Seminary, 320 Middlefield Rd., Menlo Park, 94025. Tel: 650-633-4015
Shelly, Roy, M.A., Ph.D., Dir. Vocations, 435 Church St., 93940. Tel: 831-645-2813; Fax: 831-373-6761

On Leave:
Revs.—
Calvario, Fredy
Chavez, Jose
Cortes, Antonio
Fitz-Henry, Edward
Gilbert, Dennis M., Church of the Resurrection, 725 Cascade Dr., Sunnyvale, 94087.
Gomez, Miguel
Rivera, Walter Espinoza

Retired:
Rev. Msgrs.—
MacMahon, Eamon, 24631 Guadalupe St., Carmel, 93923. Tel: 831-624-2275
Murphy, D. Declan, P.A., Ceann Mhara, Myrtleville, County Cork, Ireland. Tel: 011-353-4831-566
Stieger, Joseph, c/o 161 Broad St., San Luis Obispo, 93405. Tel: 805-543-3284
Revs.—
Adams, Michael T., Mary Star of the Sea Church, 870 8th St., San Pedro, 90731. Tel: 310-833-3541
Arul, John
Betrozoff, Larry, 528-B Sixth St., Hollister, 95023-3818. Tel: 831-636-7844. P.O. Box 1136, Tres Pinos, 95075-1136.
Canal, Manuel, 670 Edwards Ave., Salinas, 93901. Tel: 831-754-6304
Carvajal, Raul H.
Clark, Richard, 155 Boulder St., Boulder Creek, 95006.
Freiermuth, Harry, 41 Tharp Ave., Watsonville, 95076. Tel: 831-724-4460
Hercek, Joseph R., V.F., P.O. Box 2230, Atascadero, 93423.
Marini, Michael, 518 King St., Santa Cruz, 95060. Tel: 831-457-8628
Matz, Leo, 2609 San Martin Ct., Mission Viejo, 92692.
McCormick, Jerry, P.O. Box 51338, Pacific Grove, 93950. Tel: 831-372-8644
McDonald, Martin, 2 Huband Meys, Stephens Ln., Dublin 2, Ireland. Cell: 011-35-387-969-0117. Email: martinjmcdonald@hotmail.com
Santamaria, Max, Ctra. De Arizala #5, Abarzuza, Navarra 31178 Spain. Tel: 011-344-452-0021
Schwarz, Robert, 651 Sinex Ave., L-118, Pacific Grove, 93950. Tel: 831-372-8848
Vela, Fabian, EGI-Bldg 1, Room 414, Looc. Maribago, Lupu City, Cebu 6015 Philippines.

Permanent Deacons:
Conway, Patrick, 88 Mar Monte Ave., La Selva Beach, 95076. Tel: 831-840-3750 (Home) (Resurrection, Aptos)
Cooper, Jim, (Retired), 633 Ramona Ave #49, Los Osos, 93402. Tel: 805-439-1775
Ditewig, William T. (Bill), Ph.D., Dir. of Faith Formation, Diaconate & Planning, "Ther Villa's", 23799 Monterey-Salinas Hwy., Unit 8, Corral De Tierra, 93908. (St. Joseph's - Spreckels)

Dutra, Greg, 210 LaJoya Dr., Nipomo, 93444. Tel: 805-929-1235 (Home) (St. Joseph's, Nipomo)
Espinoza, Manuel, 1813 Driftwood Dr., Paso Robles, 93447. Tel: 805-238-5588 (St. Rose of Lima, Paso Robles)
Figenshow, Carl, 22551 Murietta Rd., Salinas, 93908. Tel: 831-455-0377 (Home); Cell: 831-676-8169 (Madonna del Sasso, Salinas)
Gutierrez, Richard, P.O. Box 7254, Spreckels, 93962. Tel: 831-455-1640 (Home); Cell: 831-594-1836 (Sacred Heart Salinas & Prison Youth Ministry, Salinas)
Hoy, Warren, 1168 Roosevelt St., 93940. Tel: 831-642-9821 (Carmel Mission, Carmel)
Larraza, Andres, Ph.D., P.O. Box 1568, 93942. Tel: 831-402-0472 (San Carlos Cathedral, Monterey)
Michaelson, Steve, 2489 Deer Springs Dr., Paso Robles, 93446. Tel: 805-237-0460
Miller, Dustin, 49397 Sapaque Rd., Bradley, 93426. Tel: 805-472-2749 (Mission San Antonio, Jolon)
Miller, Harold, (Retired), 341 Pheasant Ridge Rd., Del Rey Oaks, 93940. Tel: 831-883-2601
Pasculli, Nicholas, 25385 Markham Ln., Salinas, 93908. Tel: 831-758-6425 (Home); Cell: 831-905-9632 (Carmel Mission Basilica, Carmel)
Patino, Hugo, 903 Jefferson St., 93940. Tel: 831-324-4725 (Holy Cross - Santa Cruz)
Reichmuth, William (Bill), 1135 Mestres Dr., Pebble Beach, 93953. Tel: 831-646-0358 (Home); Cell: 831-233-9551 (Carmel Mission, Carmel)
Roeder, Chuck, 6082 Pebble Beach Way, San Luis Obispo, 93401. Tel: 805-544-2707 (Home); Cell: 805-745-1718 (Old Mission, San Luis Obispo)
Rutledge, Clark, P.O. Box 1232, Morro Bay, 93443. Tel: 805-772-2993 (Home) (St. Timothy's, Morro Bay)
Weber, Dan, Office of the Catholic Chaplain, P.O. Box 7001, Atascadero, 93423-7001. Tel: 805-468-2489 (Atascadero State Hospital, Cambria)
Wilhelm, Greg, 779 Mutsuhito Ave., San Luis Obispo, 93401. Tel: 805-544-0431 (Home Office); Cell: 805-550-0739 (Nativity of Our Lady, San Luis Obispo)
Winston, Douglas, 235 Montclair Ln., Salinas, 93906. Tel: 831-449-5636 (Home); Cell: 831-595-1939 (Sacred Heart, Salinas)
Wolverton, Van, 1057 Carr Ave., Aromas, 95004. Tel: 831-726-9145 (Christ the King, Salinas)

INSTITUTIONS LOCATED IN THE DIOCESE

[A] HIGH SCHOOLS, PRIVATE

MONTEREY. *Santa Catalina Upper School* (1950) (Girls), 1500 Mark Thomas Dr., 93940-5291. Tel: 831-655-9300; Fax: 831-649-3056. Email: sister.claire@santacatalina.org. Web: www.santacatalina.org. Sr. Claire Barone, Head of School; Dr. John Murphy, Head of Upper School; Diane Kabat, Librarian. Lay Teachers 41; Total Enrollment 252.

SALINAS. *Christian Brothers Institute of California, Inc. dba Palma School* (1951) (Boys), 919 Iverson St., 93901-1816. Tel: 831-422-6391; Fax: 831-422-5065. Email: dunne@palmaschool.org. Web: www.palmaschool.org. Bro. Patrick D. Dunne, C.F.C., Pres. & Community Leader; David J. Sullivan, Prin.; Mrs. Carla McDowell, Librarian. Congregation of Christian Brothers. Brothers 1; Lay Teachers 31; Boys (Jr. High) 132; Boys (Total) 533; Total Staff 44.

Congregation of Christian Brothers Residence, 919 Iverson St., 93901. Tel: 831-422-6391; Fax: 831-422-5065. Bro. W. Christian Vollmer, C.F.C., Community Leader. Brothers 1.

[B] HIGH SCHOOLS, DIOCESAN

SALINAS. *Notre Dame High School*, 455 Palma Dr., 93901. Tel: 831-751-1850; Fax: 831-757-5749. Email: info@notredamesalinas.org. Web: www.notredamesalinas.org. Andrew Bedell, Prin. Lay Teachers 25; Girls 251.

SAN LUIS OBISPO. *Mission College Preparatory Catholic High School*, 682 Palm St., 93401. Tel: 805-543-2131; Fax: 805-543-4359. Email: info@missionprep.org. Web: www.missionprep.org. James D. Childs, Prin. Lay Teachers 23; Students 290; Total Staff 39.

WATSONVILLE. *St. Francis Central Coast Catholic High School* (2001) 2400 E. Lake Ave., 95076. Tel: 831-724-5933; Fax: 831-724-5995. Email: principal@stfrancishigh.net. Web: www.stfrancishigh.net. Mr. Keith B. Mathews, Prin. & Pres.; Rev. David Purdy, S.D.B., Campus Min. Joint High School between Diocese of Monterey and Salesians of St. John Bosco. Priests 1; Lay Teachers 19; Total Enrollment 216; Total Staff 20.

Moreland Notre Dame School (1899) 133 Brennan St., 95076. Tel: 831-728-2051; Fax: 831-728-2052. Email: cgrul@mndschool.org. Web: www.mndschool.org.

Sisters of Notre Dame de Namur (1899) Tel: 831-728-2051; Fax: 831-728-2052. Email: leahy@sndden.org. Web: sndden.org. Christine Grul, Prin.; Carrie Mann Salady, Librarian. Sisters 4; Lay Teachers 10; Students 225.

[C] ELEMENTARY SCHOOLS, PRIVATE

MONTEREY. *Santa Catalina Lower School* (1950) (Grades PreK-8), (Coed), 1500 Mark Thomas Dr., 93940-5291. Tel: 831-655-9324; Fax: 831-655-9303. Email: christy.pollacci@santacatalina.org. Web: www.santacatalina.org. Sr. Claire Barone, Head of School; Mrs. Linda Mutty, Div. Head, Grades 6-8; Christy Pollacci, Div. Head, PreK-5 & Dir. of Admission; Linda Hughes, Admin. Assist.; Diane Kabat, Librarian. Lay Teachers 30; Total Enrollment 262.

CORRALITOS. *Salesian Elementary & Jr. High School: Mary Help of Christians Youth Center* (1978) (Grades K-8), 605 Enos Ln., 95076. Tel: 831-728-5518; Fax: 831-728-0273. Web: salesianschool.org. Sr. Carmen Botello, F.M.A., Prin.; Mrs. Katie Davis, Vice Prin. Sisters 6; Lay Teachers 14; Students 162.

WATSONVILLE. *St. Francis Youth Center*, 2401 E. Lake Ave., 95076. Tel: 831-722-2665; Fax: 831-722-8305. Rev. Albert Mengon, S.D.B., Dir. St. Francis Youth Center supports youth activities at parish summer camp and school level. Priests 3; Brothers 2; Total Staff 5.

[D] GENERAL HOSPITALS

SANTA CRUZ. *Dominican Hospital dba of Catholic Healthcare West* 1555 Soquel Dr., 95065. Tel: 831-462-7700; Fax: 831-462-7555. Web: www.dominicanhospital.org. Dr. Nanette Mickiewicz, M.D., Pres. Sponsored by Sisters of St. Dominic, Congregation of the Most Holy Rosary, Adrian, MI. Sisters 10; Bed Capacity 325; Total Assisted 198,892; Total Staff 1,688.

[E] SPECIAL HOSPITALS AND SANATORIA ACUTE CARE HOSPITAL

MONTEREY. *Ave Maria Convalescent Hospital* (1954) 1249 Josselyn Canyon Rd., 93940. Tel: 831-373-1216; Fax: 831-373-2238. Email: gjamch@comcast.net. Franciscan Sisters of the Immaculate Conception 1; Bed Capacity 31; Patients Assisted Annually 50; Total Staff 56.

[F] MONASTERIES AND RESIDENCES OF PRIESTS AND BROTHERS

MONTEREY. *Oratorian Community-Congregation of the Oratory of Pontifical Right*, 302 High St., P.O. Box 1688, 93942-1688. Tel: 831-373-0476; Fax: 831-373-1718. Very Rev. Peter C. Sanders, Provost. Tel: 831-375-9769; Rev. Thomas A. Kieffer, Orat., Vicar & Sec. Tel: 831-372-1325. Priests 2.

ARROYO GRANDE. *St. Joseph Cupertino Friary*, 1352 Dale Ave., P.O. Box 820, 93421-0820. Tel: 805-473-2256; Fax: 805-489-8303. Very Rev. Christopher Deitz, O.F.M.Conv., Guardian; Rev. Charles Shelton, O.F.M.Conv.; Bros. Michael Paul, O.F.M.Conv.; John Fleming, O.F.M. Conv. Priests 2; Brothers 2.

St. Joseph Cupertino Province, Provincial Center, P.O. Box 820, 93421. Tel: 805-489-1012; Fax: 805-489-8303. Email: cldeitz@earthlink.net. Very Revs. Christopher Deitz, O.F.M.Conv., Min. Prov.; Gary Klauer, O.F.M.Conv., Vicar Prov.; Rev. Stephen Gross, O.F.M.Conv. Delegate to Secular Franciscan Order; Bro. George Cherrie, O.F.M.Conv., Prov. Econom. Priests 5; Brothers 1. Attached to the Province but outside friaries: Revs. Kerry Abbott, O.F.M.Conv., Vocation Dir., (Archdiocese for the Military Services); Anthony Howard, O.F.M. Conv., Chap.

BIG SUR. *New Camaldoli Hermitage* (1958) 62475 Coast Hwy. # 1, 93920-9533. Tel: 831-667-2456; Fax: 831-667-0209. Email: monks@contemplation.com. Web: www.contemplation.com. Very Rev. Raniero Hoffman, O.S.B.Cam., Prior; Revs. Bruno Barnhardt, O.S.B.Cam.; Cyprian Consiglio, O.S.B.Cam.; Michael Fish, O.S.B.Cam.; Daniel Manger, O.S.B.Cam.; Bernard Massicotte, O.S.B.Cam.; Zacchaeus Maria Naegele, O.S.B.Cam.; Isaiah Teichert, O.S.B.Cam.; Robert Hale, O.S.B.Cam., Incarnation Monastery, 1369 La Loma Ave., Berkeley, 94708. Tel: 510-845-0601; Fax: 510-548-6439. Professed Monks (including 12 Priests) 20; Brothers 8.

On Special Assignment: Revs. Andrew Colnaghi, O.S.B.Cam., Supr., Incarnation, Incarnation Monastery, 1369 La Loma Ave., Berkeley, 94708. Tel: 510-845-0601; Fax: 510-548-6439; Thomas Matus, O.S.B.Conv.; Arthur Poulin, O.S.B.Cam., Incarnation Monastery, 1369 La Loma Ave., Berkeley, 94708. Tel: 510-845-0601; Fax: 510-548-6439; Joseph Wong, O.S.B.Cam.

SALINAS. *Palma Community of Edmund Rice Christian Brothers* (1951) 263 W. Acacia St., 93901. Tel: 831-229-1101; Fax: 831-422-5065. Email: dunne@palmaschool.org. Web: palmaschool.org. Bros. Patrick D. Dunne, C.F.C., Pres. & Community Leader; Gerard F. Murray, C.F.C. Congregation of Christian Brothers. Brothers 2.

SAN JUAN BAUTISTA. *Franciscan Friars*, P.O. Box 970, 95045-0970. Tel: 831-623-4234; Fax: 831-623-9046. Email: info@stfrancisretreat.com. Web: www.stfrancisretreat.com. Revs. Philip Garcia, O.F.M.; William Haney, O.F.M.; Armando Lopez, O.F.M.; Bros. Mateo Guerrero, O.F.M.; Bill Short, O.F.M., Dir.; Keith Warner, O.F.M., Guardian. Priests 3; Brothers 3; Total Staff 24.

SAN LUIS OBISPO. *Monastery of the Risen Christ*, P.O. Box 3931, 93403. Tel: 805-544-1810; Fax: 805-544-1810. Email: monrc87@aol.com. Web: www.daily-word-of-life.com/monastery.htm. Priests 5; Brothers 2. *Men's Residence*, 2308 O'Connor Way, 93405. Tel: 805-544-1810; Fax: 805-544-1810. Email: monrc87@aol.com. Web: www.daily-word-of-life.com/monastery.htm. Rt. Rev. David Geraets, O.S.B., Prior; Revs. Raymond V. Roh, O.S.B., Subprior; Stephen Odenbrett, O.S.B.; Albert Meyer, O.S.B.; Raymond Greco, O.S.B. (Retired); Stephen G. Coffey, O.S.B.; Bros. Alfonso Daniel, O.S.B.; Michael Rodgers, O.S.B., Junior Monk. Junior Monk (Simple Profession) 2; Total Staff 7.

Society of Mary (Marists)-S.M. (1816) 695 Cerro Romauldo Ave., 93405. Tel: 805-541-4954. Revs. John Ulrich, S.M, M.A., Contact; Kevin Duggan, S.M., M.Div., Supr. Community. Priests 2.

SAN MIGUEL. *Franciscan Friars, O.F.M.* (Province of St. Barbara, Old Mission), P.O. Box 69, 93451. Tel: 805-467-3256; Fax: 805-467-2141. Revs. Thomas Frost, O.F.M., Asst. Novicemaster & Vicar; Larry Gosselin, O.F.M., Guardian; Joe Lu, O.F.M.; Raymond Tintle, O.F.M.; Joseph Zermeno, O.F.M.; Bros. Regan Chapman, O.F.M, Novicemaster; Antonio Gregory, O.F.M.; Victor Hunter, O.F.M.; Zeno Im, O.F.M.; Anthony Lavorin, O.F.M.; Arturo Noyes, O.F.M.; Dick Tandy, O.F.M. Priests 5; Brothers 7; Total in Residence 12; Total Staff 7.

Novitiate House for the Franciscan Friars, O.F.M. (Province of St. Barbara), P.O. Box 69, 93451. Tel: 805-467-2801; Fax: 805-467-2141. Revs. Thomas Frost, O.F.M., Asst. Novicemaster & Vicar; Larry Gosselin, O.F.M., Guardian; Bros. Regan Chapman, O.F.M, Master of Novices; Richard Tandy, O.F.M., Novice; Antonio Gregory, O.F.M., Novice; Joseph Lu, O.F.M., Novice, (Province of Holy Spirit, Australia); Zeno Im, O.F.M., Novice. Novices 4; Total in Residence 6.

SANTA CRUZ. *Oblates of St. Joseph Provincial House and Shrine*, 544 W. Cliff Dr., 95060. Tel: 831-457-1868; Fax: 831-457-1317. Email: provincial@osjoseph.org. Web: www.osjoseph.org.

Oblates of St. Joseph, Provincial House and Shrine of St. Joseph, Guardian of the Redeemer Religious Community Tel: 831-471-1702; Fax: 831-457-1317. Email: guardian@osjoseph.org. Web: www.osjoseph.org. Brothers 1. *Provincial* Tel: 831-457-1868; Fax: 831-457-1317. Email: provincial@osjoseph.org. Web: www.osjoseph.org. *Shrine of St. Joseph* Tel: 831-471-0442; Fax: 831-457-1317. Email: guardian@osjoseph.org. Web: www.osjoseph.org. Revs. Rafael Lavilla, O.S.J., Shrine Dir.; John Warburton, O.S.J., Prov. Supr. & Rector; James Catalano, O.S.J.; Bro. Duain O'Mara, O.S.J. Priests 4; Brothers 1; Total in Residence 5. In Res. Rev. Aldo Grasso, O.S.J. (Italy). *Religious Community* Tel: 831-471-1702; Fax: 831-457-1317. Web: www.osjoseph.org.

WATSONVILLE. *Salesians of St. John Bosco Saint Francis Salesian Community*, 2401 East Lake Ave., 95076-2670. Tel: 831-722-2665; Fax: 831-722-8305. Web: www.donboscowest.org. Revs. Albert Mengon, S.D.B., Dir.; David Purdy, S.D.B.; Luis A. Oyarzo Vargas, S.D.B.; Bro. Michael Herbers, S.D.B., Camp Dir. Priests 3; Brothers 2. In Res. Bro. Abel Zanella, S.D.B., (Retired).

[G] CONVENTS AND RESIDENCES FOR SISTERS

MONTEREY. *Franciscan Sisters Ave Maria Convent*, 1249 Josselyn Canyon Rd., 93942-1977. Tel: 831-373-1216; Fax: 831-373-2238. Motherhouse of the Franciscan Sisters of the Immaculate Conception and St. Joseph for the Dying.

APTOS. *St. Joseph's Monastery of the Poor Clares (Colettines)* (1921) 1671 Pleasant Valley Rd., P.O.

Box 160, 95001-0160. Tel: 831-761-9659; 831-761-9481; Fax: 831-761-9481. Sr. Francis Maria, P.C.C., Abbess. Poor Clares of California, Inc. Professed Sisters Cloistered 9; Extern Sisters 2.

ARROYO GRANDE. *Sisters of Mercy*, 451 Woodland, 93420. Tel: 805-489-8788; Fax: 805-489-4367. Sisters 1.

CARMEL. *Carmelite Monastery of Our Lady and St. Therese* (1925) 27601 Hwy. 1, 93923-9612. Tel: 831-624-3043; Fax: 831-624-5495. Email: carmelitesofcarmelca@catholic.org. Web: www.carmelitesistersbythesea.net. Sr. Mercedes Martinez, Prioress. Professed Nuns 9.

Sisters of Notre Dame de Namur (1930) 27951 Hwy. 1, 93923. Tel: 831-624-9416; Fax: 831-624-4865. Email: carmelhop@sndden.org.

CORRALITOS. *Daughters of Mary Help of Christians* (1872) 605 Enos Ln., 95076. Tel: 831-728-4700; Fax: 831-728-5802. Email: fmasuocor@gmail.com. Sr. Carmen Botello, F.M.A., Supr. & Prin. Sisters 6.

GONZALES. *Sisters of Charity of the Infant Mary Capitanio Convent*, 512 Fairview Dr., P.O. Box 178, 93926. Tel: 831-675-2975; Fax: 831-675-2974. Email: sistersmb@att.net. Sr. Rosangela Filippini, I.M., Supr. Residents 6.

SALINAS. *Sisters of Charity of the Infant Mary*, 15785 Alto Way, 93907-9148. Tel: 831-663-3675; Fax: 831-663-3749. Email: virgennina@aol.com. Sr. Patricia M. Murtagh, I.M., Supr. Sisters of Charity of the Infant Mary. Residents 5.

Sisters of Notre Dame, 56 Talbot St., 93901. Tel: 831-424-4370. Email: bmatasci@aol.com. Residents 2.

Sisters of St. Joseph of Carondolet (1950) 1335 Byron Dr., 93901. Tel: 831-758-0931; Fax: 831-758-1318. Email: srroberta@catholic.org. Madonna Manor.

SAN JUAN BAUTISTA. *Franciscan Sisters of the Atonement*, 408 Second St., P.O. Box 1094, 95045. Tel: 831-623-4267; Fax: 831-623-4359. Franciscan Sisters of the Atonement 4.

SAN LUIS OBISPO. *Monastery of the Risen Christ* (Women's Residence), P.O. Box 3931, 93403-3931. Tel: 805-544-7808; Fax: 805-544-1810. Email: monrc87@aol.com. Web: www.daily-word-of-life.com/monastery.htm. 2304 O'Connor Way, 93405. Tel: 805-544-7808; Fax: 805-554-1810. Connie Mayrhofer, O.B.L., O.S.B.

SAN MIGUEL. *Franciscan Sisters of the Atonement (Graymoor)* (1909) 1075 Mission St., P.O. Box 238, 93451. Tel: 805-467-0022.

SOQUEL. *St. Clare's Retreat* (1950) 2381 Laurel Glen Rd., 95073. Tel: 831-423-8093. Email: stclares@sbcglobal.net. Web: www.nonprofitpages.com/stclaresretreat/. Sr. Maureen Theresa, O.S.F., Supr. Total in Residence 3.

WATSONVILLE. *Moreland Notre Dame Convent*, 656 Main St., 95076. Tel: 831-724-7696; Fax: 831-728-2052. Email: taleahysnd@aol.com. Web: sndden-ca.org. Sr. Teresa Ann Leahy, Coord. Sisters of Notre Dame de Namur. Residents 4.

[H] RETREAT HOUSES

APTOS. *Camp St. Francis*, 2320 Sumner Ave., 95003. Tel: 831-684-1439; Fax: 831-662-2454. Bro. Michael Herbers, S.D.B., Dir. Conducted by Salesians of St. John Bosco.; Summer Camp for Boys 8-13, Meeting Center for large groups and Retreat Center for large groups of youth and adults.

SAN JUAN BAUTISTA. *St. Francis Retreat Center* Conducted by Franciscan Friars. Province of St. Barbara., Dir., P.O. Box 970, 95045. Tel: 831-623-4234; Fax: 831-623-9046. Email: info@stfrancisretreat.com. Web: www.stfrancisretreat.com. Revs. Barry Brunsman, O.F.M., Chap.; Philip Garcia, O.F.M., Retreat Ministry; William Haney, O.F.M., Retreat Ministry; Bros. William Short, O.F.M., Dir.; Keith Warner, O.F.M., Guardian. Retreats for men, women, singles, married couples, A.A. and 12-step. Programs include Spiritual Growth, Ecumenical, Spanish. Priests 3; Brothers 3; Total in Residence 6; Total Staff 20. In Res. Bro. Mateo Guerrero, O.F.M.

SAN MIGUEL. *San Miguel Retreat House*, P.O. Box 69, 93451. Tel: 805-467-3256; Fax: 805-467-3399. Rev. Larry Gosselin, O.F.M., Guardian & Retreat Dir. Staff 2.

SANTA CRUZ. *Villa Maria del Mar Retreat Center*, 21918 E. Cliff Dr., 95062. Tel: 831-475-1236; Fax: 831-475-8867. Email: villamaria@snjmuson.org. Web: www.villamariadelmar.org. Sr. Patricia Doyle, S.N.J.M., Admin. Sisters of the Holy Names of Jesus and Mary, U.S.-Ontario Province Corp. Sisters 4; Lay Staff 15; Total Staff 20.

SOQUEL. *St. Clare's Retreat House* (1950) 2381 Laurel Glen Rd., 95073. Tel: 831-423-8093. Email: stclares@sbcglobal.net. Web: www.nonprofitpages.com/stclaresretreat. Sr. Maureen Theresa, O.S.F, Retreat Dir. Franciscan Missionary Sisters of Our Lady of Sorrows 3; Total Staff 8.

[I] NEWMAN CHAPLAINS AND CENTERS

MONTEREY. *Department of Campus Ministry* (1970) 485 Church St., 93940. Tel: 831-373-1335; Fax: 831-373-3351. Web: www.dioceseofmonterey.org. Total Staff 9.

California State Polytechnic Institute / Cuesta College Newman Catholic Center, 1472 Foothill Blvd., San Luis Obispo, 93405-1416. Tel: 805-543-4105; Fax: 805-543-5671. Email: ncc@slonewman.org. Web: www.slonewman.org. Revs. John Ulrich, S.M, M.A., Dir.; Kevin Duggan, S.M., M.Div., Assoc. Dir.; Linda Garcia-Inchausti, Dir. of Admin.

Cabrillo College Santa Cruz, 95064. Tel: 831-479-6100; Fax: 831-423-8163. Rev. Jerry Maher, Dir.

University of California at Santa Cruz 285 Meder St., Santa Cruz, 95060. Tel: 831-423-9400; Fax: 831-423-8163. Email: newmanslug@aol.com. Web: www.newmanite.org. Rev. Jerry Maher, Dir.

California State University of Monterey Bay 485 Church St., 93940. Tel: 831-373-1335; Fax: 831-373-3315.

485 Church St., 93940. Tel: 831-373-1335; Fax: 831-373-3315. Rev. Dominic Joseph Castro, M.Div., Dir.

[J] SENIOR RESIDENCES

SANTA CRUZ. *Dominican Oaks Corporation* (1988) 3400 Paul Sweet Rd., 95065. Tel: 831-462-6257; Fax: 831-462-6742. Web: www.dominicanoaks.com. Sponsored by Dominican Hospital, a dba of Catholic Healthcare West. Total in Residence 230; Total Staff 90.

[K] MISCELLANEOUS

MONTEREY. *Newman Institute for Historical and Religious Studies, Domus Patris Foundation*, P.O. Box 748, 93942. Tel: 831-373-0477. Rev. Thomas A. Kieffer, Orat., Admin.

SALINAS. *Magnificat the Monterey Bay Chapter*, 302 San Juan Grade Rd., 93906. Tel: 831-449-1069; Fax: 831-449-1069. Email: dlraras@pacbell.net. Dora Lee Raras, Coord.; Stella Marquez, Treas.; Josee Henrard, Asst. Coord.; Diosefe Lantaca, Sec. A Ministry to Catholic Women.

WATSONVILLE. *St. Thomas More Society*, c/o 262 E. Lake Ave., 95076. Tel: 831-722-2456; Fax: 831-722-0414.

RELIGIOUS INSTITUTES OF MEN REPRESENTED IN THE DIOCESE

For further details refer to the corresponding bracketed number in the Religious Institutes of Men or Women section.

[]—*Camaldolese Hermits*—O.S.B.Cam.

[0310]—*Congregation of Christian Brothers* (Western U.S. Prov., Joliet, IL)—C.F.C.

[0480]—*Conventual Franciscans*—O.F.M.Conv.

[0520]—*Franciscan Friars* (Santa Barbara Prov.)—O.F.M.

[0930]—*Oblates of St. Joseph* (Asti, Italy)—O.S.J.

[0950]—*Oratorians*—Orat.

[0200]—*Order of St. Benedict* (Monastery of the Risen Christ)—O.S.B.

[1190]—*Salesians of Don Bosco (Turin, Italy)*—S.D.B.

[]—*Society of Jesus*—S.J.

[0780]—*Society of Mary - Marists Fathers*—S.M.

RELIGIOUS INSTITUTES OF WOMEN REPRESENTED IN THE DIOCESE

[1070-13]—*Congregation of the Most Holy Rosary - Adrian Dominican Sisters*—O.P.

[0880]—*Daughters of Mary & Joseph*—D.M.J.

[0850]—*Daughters of Mary of Help of Christians - Salesian Sisters*—F.M.A.

[0420]—*Discalced Carmelite Nuns*—O.C.D.

[1070-04]—*Dominican Sisters of San Rafael*—O.P.

[1390]—*Franciscan Missionary Sisters of Our Lady of Sorrows*—O.S.F.

[1190]—*Franciscan Sisters of the Atonement*—S.A.

[1300]—*Franciscan Sisters of the Immaculate Conception and St. Joseph for the Dying*—O.S.F.

[]—*Immaculate Heart of Mary*—I.H.M.

[]—*Immaculate Heart Sisters of Africa*—I.H.S.A.

[3760]—*Order of St. Clare* (Poor Clares Colettines P.C.C.)—P.C.C.

[]—*Redwood Franciscans*—O.S.F.

[]—*Schools Sisters of Notre Dame*—S.S.N.D.

[]—*Sister Servants of the Blessed Sacrament*—S.V.S.

[]—*Sisters of Charity of the Infant Mary*—I.M.

[2549]—*Sisters of Mercy* (Irish American Prov.)—R.S.M.

[]—*Sisters of Mercy of the Americas, West, Midwest Community*—R.S.M.

[3000]—*Sisters of Notre Dame de Namur*—S.N.D.deN.

[3840]—*Sisters of St. Joseph of Carondelet*—C.S.J.

[]—*Sisters of the Holy Family*—S.H.F.

[1990]—*Sisters of the Holy Name of Jesus and Mary*—S.N.J.M.

DIOCESAN CEMETERIES

MONTEREY. *Diocesan Cemeteries Office*, Mailing Address: P.O. Box 2048, 93942-2048. 792 Fremont Blvd., 93940. Tel: 831-372-0327; Fax: 831-372-8726. Email: cemeteries@dioceseofmonterey.org. Tim Bennett, Dir.

San Carlos (Monterey), 792 Fremont Blvd., 93940. Tel: 831-372-0327; Fax: 831-372-8726.

CAMBRIA. *Old Santa Rosa (Cambria)*, P.O. Box 13428, San Luis Obispo, 93401. Tel: 805-541-0584; Fax: 805-541-2127.

HOLLISTER. *Sacred Heart / Calvary Cemetery*, 1100 Hillcrest Rd., 95023. Tel: 831-637-0131; Fax: 831-637-2980.

SALINAS. *Queen of Heaven Salinas*, 18200 Damian Way, 93907. Tel: 831-449-5890; Fax: 831-449-6928.

SAN LUIS OBISPO. *Old Mission San Luis Obispo*, P.O. Box 13428, 93401. Tel: 805-541-0584; Fax: 805-541-2127.

SANTA CRUZ. *Holy Cross Cemetery Santa Cruz*, 2271 7th Ave., 95062. Tel: 831-475-3222; Fax: 831-475-6132.

NECROLOGY

† Frerkes, James, (Retired)—Died Sept. 8, 2011
† O'Halloran, Richard, (Retired)—Died Nov. 6, 2011
† Plastino, James L., (Retired)—Died July 20, 2011

An asterisk (*) denotes an organization that has established tax-exempt status directly with the IRS and is not covered by the USCCB Group Ruling.

Diocese of Nashville

(Dioecesis Nashvillensis)

Most Reverend

DAVID R. CHOBY

Bishop of Nashville; ordained September 6, 1974; appointed Bishop of Nashville December 20, 2005; ordained February 27, 2006. *Office: 2400 21st Ave., S., Nashville, TN 37212.*

Chancery Office: 2400 21st Ave., S., Nashville, TN 37212. Tel: 615-383-6393; Fax: 615-292-8411.

Web: www.dioceseofnashville.com

ESTABLISHED JULY 28, 1837.

Square Miles 16,302.

Comprises the Counties of Bedford, Cannon, Cheatham, Clay, Coffee, Davidson, DeKalb, Dickson, Franklin, Giles, Grundy, Hickman, Houston, Humphreys, Jackson, Lawrence, Lewis, Lincoln, Macon, Marshall, Maury, Montgomery, Moore, Overton, Perry, Putnam, Robertson, Rutherford, Smith, Stewart, Sumner, Trousdale, VanBuren, Warren, Wayne, White, Williamson and Wilson in the State of Tennessee.

For legal titles of parishes and diocesan institutions, consult the Chancery Office.

STATISTICAL OVERVIEW

Personnel	
Bishop	1
Priests: Diocesan Active in Diocese	31
Priests: Diocesan Active Outside Diocese	1
Priests: Retired, Sick or Absent	11
Number of Diocesan Priests	43
Religious Priests in Diocese	24
Total Priests in Diocese	67
Extern Priests in Diocese	16
Ordinations:	
Diocesan Priests	1
Permanent Deacons in Diocese	69
Total Brothers	1
Total Sisters	2
Parishes	
Parishes	53
With Resident Pastor:	
Resident Diocesan Priests	30
Resident Religious Priests	13
Without Resident Pastor:	
Administered by Priests	9
Administered by Deacons	1
Missions	3
Pastoral Centers	2
Professional Ministry Personnel:	
Brothers	1
Sisters	3
Lay Ministers	26
Welfare	
Catholic Hospitals	3
Total Assisted	614,000
Homes for the Aged	2
Total Assisted	320
Day Care Centers	3
Total Assisted	580
Special Centers for Social Services	8
Total Assisted	55,800
Educational	
Diocesan Students in Other Seminaries	26
Total Seminarians	26
Colleges and Universities	1
Total Students	1,080
High Schools, Diocesan and Parish	2
Total Students	1,536
High Schools, Private	1
Total Students	256
Elementary Schools, Diocesan and Parish	16
Total Students	3,774
Elementary Schools, Private	2
Total Students	628
Catechesis/Religious Education:	
High School Students	988
Elementary Students	6,763
Total Students under Catholic Instruction	15,051
Teachers in the Diocese:	
Brothers	1
Sisters	9
Lay Teachers	293
Vital Statistics	
Receptions into the Church:	
Infant Baptism Totals	1,849
Minor Baptism Totals	206
Adult Baptism Totals	195
Received into Full Communion	303
First Communions	1,802
Confirmations	1,597
Marriages:	
Catholic	208
Interfaith	191
Total Marriages	399
Deaths	473
Total Catholic Population	77,736
Total Population	2,418,763

Former Bishops—Rt. Revs. RICHARD PIUS MILES, O.P., D.D., cons. Sept. 16, 1838; died Feb. 21, 1860; JAMES WHELAN, O.P., D.D., cons. May 8, 1859; resigned May, 1863; died Feb. 18, 1878; P. A. FEEHAN, cons. Nov. 1, 1865; created first Archbishop of Chicago, Sept. 10, 1880; died July 12, 1902; JOSEPH RADEMACHER, D.D., cons. June 24, 1883; transferred to Ft. Wayne, July 13, 1893; died Jan. 12, 1900; THOMAS S. BYRNE, D.D., cons. July 25, 1894; died Sept. 4, 1923; Most Revs. ALPHONSE J. SMITH, D.D., cons. March 25, 1924; died Dec. 16, 1935; WILLIAM L. ADRIAN, D.D., cons. April 16, 1936; died Feb. 13, 1972; JOSEPH A. DURICK, D.D., cons. March 24, 1955; retired April 8, 1975; died June 26, 1994; JAMES D. NIEDERGESES, D.D., cons. May 20, 1975; retired Oct. 13, 1992; died Nov. 16, 2007; EDWARD U. KMIEC, D.D., S.T.L. ord. Dec. 20, 1961; appt. Titular Bishop of Simidicca and Auxiliary Bishop of Trenton Aug. 26, 1982; cons. Nov. 3, 1982; appt. Bishop of Nashville Oct. 13, 1992; installed Dec. 3, 1992; appt. Bishop of Buffalo Aug. 12, 2004.

Vicars General—Very Revs. DAVID R. PERKIN, J.C.L., V.G., 2400 21st Ave., S., Nashville, 37212; DEXTER S. BREWER, J.C.L., J.V.

Moderator of the Curia and Vicar General—Very Rev. DAVID R. PERKIN, J.C.L., V.G., The Catholic Center, 2400 21st Ave., S., Nashville, 37212.

Deans—Revs. PHILIP M. BREEN, Central Deanery; MICHAEL O'BRYAN, Northeast Deanery; DAVID GAFFNY, Northwest Deanery; JOSE KARIAMADAM, C.M.I., Southeast Deanery; EDWARD T. ALBERTS, Southwest Deanery.

Chancery Office—2400 21st Ave. S., Nashville, 37212. Tel: 615-383-6393; Fax: 615-292-8411. Office Hours: Mon.-Fri. 8-4:30; All Official business should be directed to this office.

Chancellor—Deacon HANS M. TOECKER.

Executive Assistant to the Bishop—Ms. ELIZABETH CLAY.

Accounting Systems—Mr. WILLIAM J. WHALEN, CFO; Mr. DOUG ANDERSON, Controller; TERESA OSBORNE, Asst. Controller, Catholic Community Investment and Loan.

General Counsel—Rev. JAMES K. MALLETT (Retired).

Diocesan Tribunal—2400 21st Ave. S., Nashville, 37212. Tel: 615-783-0273; Fax: 615-783-0779.

Judicial Vicar—Very Rev. DEXTER S. BREWER, J.C.L., J.V.

Adjutant Judicial Vicar—Very Rev. DAVID R. PERKIN, J.C.L., V.G.

Director of Tribunal—Ms. JANETTE BUCHANAN, J.C.L.

Defenders of the Bond—Revs. JOHN C. HENRICK; JOHN SIMS BAKER; STEPHEN A. KLASEK.

Advocate—Mrs. PATRICIA STORY.

Judges—Most Rev. DAVID R. CHOBY, D.D., J.C.L.; Very Rev. DEXTER S. BREWER, J.C.L., J.V.; Revs. RICHARD G. BUCHIGNANI, J.C.L. (Retired); WILLIAM S. BEVINGTON (Retired); JAMES K. MALLETT (Retired); Very Rev. DAVID R. PERKIN, J.C.L., V.G.; Ms. JANETTE BUCHANAN, J.C.L.

Formal Case Instructor—Mrs. PATRICIA STORY.

Documentary Case Instructor—Mrs. ANN H. KANENGIETER.

Auditors— All priests and deacons assigned in the Nashville and Knoxville dioceses.

Secretary-Notaries—Mrs. PATRICIA STORY; Mrs. JULIE CONNOLLY; Mrs. ANN H. KANENGIETER; Ms. ERIN STRACENER.

Presbyteral Council—Very Rev. DEXTER S. BREWER, J.C.L., J.V.; Revs. JOHN SIMS BAKER; JOHN C. HENRICK; THOMAS KALAM, C.M.I.; MARK BECKMAN; PHILIP M. BREEN; EDWARD F. STEINER III; J. PATRICK CONNOR, V.G. (Retired); PATRICK J. KIBBY; Very Rev. DAVID R. PERKIN, J.C.L., V.G.; Revs. JOSEPH MCMAHON; DAVID RAMIREZ.

Diocesan Finance Board—Most Rev. DAVID R. CHOBY, D.D., J.C.L.; Very Revs. DAVID R. PERKIN, J.C.L., V.G.; DEXTER S. BREWER, J.C.L., J.V.; Rev. MARK HUNT; Mr. DENNIS DONOVAN; Mr. MICHAEL J. KANE; Mr. JOHN SCHNEIDER; Mr. WILLIAM HILL; Mr. KEVIN MARCHETTI; Mr. EDWARD STACK; Mr. WILLIAM P. VARLEY; Mr. GEORGE SMITH; Mr. WILLIAM J. WHALEN; Mr. PAT WATSON, Chair; DON WILLIAMSON.

DIONASH— A Partnership acting as Nominee for marketable securities for the Diocese of Nashville.

Diocesan Offices and Directors

The following offices and agencies are located at the Chancery unless otherwise indicated.

Archives and Records—Deacon HANS M. TOECKER; Ms. BARBARA BALTZ, Archives Coord.

Campaign for Human Development—Mr. WILLIAM P. SINCLAIR, A.C.S.W., Dir., St. Mary Villa, 30 White Bridge Rd., Nashville, 37205.

Campus Ministries—VACANT.

Vanderbilt—Rev. JOHN SIMS BAKER, 2417 W. End Ave., Nashville, 37240. Tel: 615-322-0104.

MTSU-Murfreesboro—Rev. MARK SAPPENFIELD, St. Rose of Lima Church, 1601 N. Tennessee Blvd., Murfreesboro, 37130. Tel: 615-893-1843.

Austin Peay-Clarksville—Deacon TIMOTHY F. WINTERS, Immaculate Conception, 709 Franklin St., Clarksville, 37040. Tel: 931-645-6275.

Tenn. Tech-Cookeville—Mr. CLARK JAMESON; Mrs. MARY JAMESON, St. Thomas Aquinas Church, 421 N. Washington Ave., Cookeville, 38501. Tel: 931-526-2575.

Fisk-Meharry-Tennessee State University Campus Ministries—Deacon HENRY HARRINGTON JR., St. Vincent de Paul Church, 1700 Heiman St., Nashville, 37208. Tel: 615-320-0695.

Univ. of South-Sewanee—Rev. JEAN BAPTISTE KYABUTA, Good Shepherd Church, 2021 Decherd Blvd., Decherd, 37324. Tel: 931-967-0961.

Catholic Charismatic Renewal—Rev. JOHN L. KIRK, Bishop's Liaison; Mrs. TERESA SEIBERT, Assoc. Liaison.

Catholic Charities of Tennessee, Inc.—Mr. WILLIAM P. SINCLAIR, A.C.S.W., Dir., St. Mary Villa, 30 White Bridge Rd., Nashville, 37205. Tel: 615-352-3087; Fax: 615-352-8591.

Catholic Medical Association, Nashville Chapter—RACHEL KAISER, M.D., Pres. Email: rtkaiser@bellsouth.net. Web: www.cathmed.org.

Catholic Public Policy Commission of TN—JENNFIER MURPHY, Exec. Sec.

Catholic Relief Services—Deacon HANS M. TOECKER, Dir.

Catholic Social Services of Nashville—Ms. EILEEN BEEHAN, Dept. Dir., St. Mary Villa, 30 White Bridge Rd., Nashville, 37205. Tel: 615-352-3087.

Catholic Youth Office and Search Program—Rev. NICHOLAS ALLEN, 2011 W. End Ave., Nashville, 37203. Tel: 615-327-0674.

Cemeteries—Mr. WILLIAM J. WHALEN, CFO.

Censor Librorum—Rev. JAMES K. MALLETT (Retired).

Priest Benefit Foundation—Revs. JOHN C. HENRICK; MARK HUNT; MICHAEL BALTRUS; Very Revs. DAVID R. PERKIN, J.C.L., V.G.; DEXTER S. BREWER, J.C.L., J.V.; Revs. STEPHEN A. KLASEK; JOHN SIMS BAKER; Mr. WILLIAM J. WHALEN; TERRY ROBINSON, P.H.R.

Clergy Personnel Board—Revs. STEPHEN A. KLASEK; MARK BECKMAN; Very Rev. DAVID R. PERKIN, J.C.L., V.G.; Rev. PHILIP M. BREEN.

Continuing Education of Clergy—Rev. EDWARD F. STEINER III, Dir.

Cursillo—JOE MCLAUGHLIN, Lay Dir.; Deacon MARTIN DESCHENES, Assoc. Spiritual Advisor.

Permanent Diaconate Office—Deacon RONALD B. DEAL JR., Dir.

Diocesan Communications Director—RICK MUSSACHIO.

Diocesan Planning—Rev. STEPHEN A. KLASEK, Dir.

Hispanic Ministry—Rev. DAVID RAMIREZ, Dir.; Mrs. ANABELL C. TREVINO, Asst. Dir.

Korean Catholic Community of St. Joseph—Rev. JAE SANG HAN, 5565 Pettus Rd., Antioch, 37013. Tel: 615-727-1225. Email: koreancc@comcast.net.

Holy Childhood Association—Deacon HANS M. TOECKER, Dir.

Human Resources—TERRY ROBINSON, P.H.R., Dir.

Lay Retirement Administrative Board—Mr. WILLIAM J. WHALEN; D. SCOTT DONNELLAN; TED SAUNDERS; RITA RAYMER; CHRISTOPHER P. KELLY; Mr. JOHN SCHNEIDER; Very Rev. DEXTER S. BREWER, J.C.L., J.V.; TERRY ROBINSON, P.H.R.

Liturgical Life—VACANT.

Ministry Formation—SHERI ISHAM, Office of Catechetical Formation, Catechetical Coord.; Mr. THOMAS SAMORAY, Engaged Couple Formation, Prog. Coord.

Newspaper— "The Tennessee Register" RICK MUSACCHIO, Editor in Chief.

Prison Ministry—TERRANCE HORGAN, Ph.D., Criminal Justice Advocacy.

Pontifical Mission Societies—Deacon HANS M. TOECKER, Dir.

Catholic Charities Refugee Services—KELLYE BRANSON, Dir., 10 S. 6th St., Nashville, 37206. Tel: 615-259-3567; Fax: 615-259-2851.

Schools Office—THERESE WILLIAMS, Supt., 30 White Bridge Rd., Nashville, 37205. Tel: 615-352-3087.

Stewardship and Development—Mr. RONALD SZEJNER.

Victim Assistance Coordinator—Deacon HANS M. TOECKER, 2400 21st Ave., S., Nashville, 37212. Tel: 615-783-0765; Fax: 615-292-8411. Email: hans.toecker@dioceseofnashville.com.

Vietnamese Ministry—Rev. PETER DO QUANG CHAU, P.O. Box 55, Ashland City, 37015. Tel: 615-792-4255.

Vocations—Most Rev. DAVID R. CHOBY, D.D., J.C.L., 2400 21st Ave. S., Nashville, 37212; Mr. THOMAS SAMORAY, Dir. Vocations Awareness. Tel: 615-783-0754.

CLERGY, PARISHES, MISSIONS AND PAROCHIAL SCHOOLS

CITY OF NASHVILLE

(DAVIDSON COUNTY)

1—CATHEDRAL OF THE INCARNATION (1909) Rev. Edward F. Steiner III; Deacons Mark Faulkner; Thales Finchum; John G. Krenson; James W. McKenzie; Jayd Neely.
Church: 2015 W. End Ave., 37203. Tel: 615-327-2330; Fax: 615-320-5650.
Catechesis/Religious Program—Robin Baskins, D.R.E. Students 181.

2—ST. ANN (1921) Rev. Philip M. Breen; Deacons John P. Casey; William J. Dickson; James Walsh; Martin Mulloy, Pastoral Assoc.
Church: 5101 Charlotte Ave., 37209. Tel: 615-298-1782; Fax: 615-297-4326.
School—(Grades K-8) Tel: 615-269-0568; Fax: 615-297-1383. Mr. John Foreman, Prin.; Judy Graham, Librarian. Lay Teachers 14; Students 175.
Catechesis/Religious Program—Students 80.

3—ASSUMPTION (1859) Attended by St. Pius X Church, Nashville. Rev. Michael D'Souza. In Res., Rev. Athanasius Abanulo.
Church: 1227 Seventh Ave. N., 37208. Tel: 615-256-2729.
Catechesis/Religious Program—Students 98.

4—CHRIST THE KING (1937) Very Rev. Dexter S. Brewer; Rev. Joseph V. McMahon; Deacons Andrew D. McKenzie; Robert H. True; David Lybarger. In Res., Rev. Francis G. Appreh.
Church: 3001 Belmont Blvd., 37212. Tel: 615-292-2884; Fax: 615-383-0026.
School—(Grades K-8), 3105 Belmont Blvd., 37212. Tel: 615-292-9465; Fax: 615-292-2477. Dr. Christine Caron Gebhardt, Prin.; Rhonda Keckley, Librarian. Lay Teachers 24; Students 260.
Catechesis/Religious Program—Students 144.

5—CHURCH OF THE MOST HOLY NAME (1857) Rev. Joseph P. Edwidge Carre; Deacon Robert L. Mahoney.
Church: 521 Woodland St., 37206. Tel: 615-254-8847; Fax: 615-730-8352.
Catechesis/Religious Program—Mary Catherine Dean, D.R.E. Students 20.

6—ST. EDWARD (1952) Rev. Joseph P. Breen; Deacons Brian Edwards; John Calzavara; Edgardo Jayme.
Church: 188 Thompson Ln., 37211. Tel: 615-833-5520; Fax: 615-833-3738.
School—(Grades K-8), 190 Thompson Ln., 37211. Tel: 615-833-5770; Fax: 615-833-9739. Dr. Sue Baumgartner, Prin. Lay Teachers 25; Students 413.
Catechesis/Religious Program—Students 155.

7—ST. HENRY (1955) Revs. Michael O. Johnston; Stephen J. Wolf; Deacons Jack Srouji; Martin Deschenes; Gregory Meinhart.
Church: 6401 Harding Pike., 37205. Tel: 615-352-2259; Fax: 615-356-6321.
School—(Grades K-8) Tel: 615-352-1328; Fax: 615-356-9293. Sr. Ann Hyacinth Genow, O.P., Prin.; Mrs. Kerry Connor, Librarian. Dominican Sisters of St. Cecilia Congregation 4; Lay Teachers 44; Students 650.
Catechesis/Religious Program—Tel: 615-353-0668. Betsy Gromos, D.R.E.; Kristin Hoback, D.R.E. Students 219.

8—HOLY ROSARY (1954) Revs. Mark Hunt; James Panackal, C.M.I.; Deacons Gilbert P. Huhlein; Kenneth Steinbrecher; Wayne Gregory.
Church: 192 Graylynn Dr., 37214. Tel: 615-889-4065; Fax: 615-889-3421.
School—(Grades PreK-8), 190 Graylynn Dr., 37214. Tel: 615-883-1108; Fax: 615-885-5100. Mrs. Mary Hart, Prin. Lay Teachers 30; Students 386.
Catechesis/Religious Program—Students 80.

9—ST. MARY OF THE SEVEN SORROWS (1847) Rev. James Norman Miller.
Mailing Address: P.O. Box 190606, 37219.
Res.: 301 Criddle St., #401, 37219. Tel: 615-252-6414.
Church: 330 Fifth Ave. N., 37219. Tel: 615-256-1704; Fax: 615-256-7307.

10—ST. MARY VILLA PARISH COMMUNITY (1982) Rev. Paul Hostettler; Deacon Harold McBrayer.
Church: 34 White Bridge Rd., 37205. Tel: 615-352-3087; Fax: 615-352-8591.

11—ST. PATRICK (1890) Very Rev. David R. Perkin; Deacon Thomas H. Cook.
Church: 1219 2nd Ave. S., 37210. Tel: 615-256-6498; Fax: 615-256-6476.
Catechesis/Religious Program—Students 10.

12—ST. PIUS X (1958) Rev. Michael D'Souza.
Church: 2800 Tucker Rd., 37218. Tel: 615-244-4093; Fax: 615-244-4093.
School—St. Pius X Classical Academy, (Grades PreK-8), 2750 Tucker Rd., 37218. Tel: 615-255-2049; Fax: 615-255-2049. David Carey, Prin.; Bro. Tom Eaton, Librarian. Dominican Sisters of St. Cecilia Congregation 2; Lay Teachers 10; Students 94.
Catechesis/Religious Program—Allison Bernhardt-Gafford, D.R.E.

13—ST. VINCENT DE PAUL (1932) Rev. John Eaton, O.F.M.; Deacons Henry Harrington Jr.; William Hill.
Church: 1700 Heiman St., 37208. Tel: 615-320-0695; Fax: 615-320-0698.
Catechesis/Religious Program—Mary Hernandez, D.R.E. Students 60.

OUTSIDE THE CITY OF NASHVILLE

ANTIOCH, DAVIDSON CO.

1—ST. IGNATIUS OF ANTIOCH (1976) Rev. John C. Henrick; Deacons Doug Shafer; John Downey.
Church: 601 Bell Rd., 37013. Tel: 615-367-0085; Fax: 615-367-1712.
Catechesis/Religious Program—Jan Trahan, D.R.E. Students 212.

2—OUR LADY OF GUADALUPE (2007) Rev. Anthony Lopez, Admin.
3112 Nolensville Rd., 37211. Tel: 615-333-8660.

ASHLAND CITY, CHEATHAM CO., ST. MARTHA (1975) Rev. Peter Do Quang Chau.
Mailing Address: P.O. Box 55, 37015.
Church: 3331 Bell St., 37015. Tel: 615-792-4255; Fax: 615-792-4255.
Catechesis/Religious Program—Teresa Fraim, D.R.E. Students 99.

BRENTWOOD, WILLIAMSON CO., HOLY FAMILY (1989) Revs. Edward T. Alberts; Titus Augustine, C.M.I.; Deacon Ronald B. Deal Jr.
Church & Mailing Address: 9100 Crockett Rd., 37027. Tel: 615-373-4696; Fax: 615-377-3823.
Catechesis/Religious Program—Tel: 615-373-4351. Catherine Birdwell, D.R.E. Students 1,230.

CENTERVILLE, HICKMAN CO., CHRIST THE REDEEMER (1983) Attended by Holy Trinity, Hohenwald. Rev. Joseph K. Dowling.
Mailing Address: P.O. Box 323, 37033. Tel: 931-796-3738.
Church: 1515 Woodland Dr., 37033. Tel: 931-729-4669.
Catechesis/Religious Program—Melanie Harris, D.R.E. Students 21.

CLARKSVILLE, MONTGOMERY CO., IMMACULATE CONCEPTION (1845) Revs. David J. Gaffny; Theophilus Ebulueme; Charles Mathew, O.F.M.; Deacons Dominick Azzara; Robert Berberich; Timothy Winters.
Res.: 709 Franklin St., 37040. Tel: 931-645-6275; Fax: 931-552-0331.
School—Immaculate Conception School, (Grades K-8), 1901 Madison St., 37043. Tel: 931-645-1865; Fax: 931-645-1160. Denise Tucker, Prin. Lay Teachers 14; Students 134.
Catechesis/Religious Program—Students 410.

COLUMBIA, MAURY CO., ST. CATHERINE (1843) Rev. Davis Chackaleckel, M.S.F.S.; Deacon Price Keller. In Res., Rev. Louis E. Rojas, S.A.C., Hispanic Ministry.
Church & Mailing Address: 3019 Cayce Ln., 38401. Tel: 931-388-3803; Fax: 931-381-8837.
Catechesis/Religious Program—Tel: 931-381-6784. Jeanette Sparkman, D.R.E. Students 239.

COOKEVILLE, PUTNAM CO., ST. THOMAS AQUINAS (1951) Rev. Chad Puthoff, S.D.S.
Church: 421 N. Washington Ave., 38501. Tel: 931-526-2575; Fax: 931-526-5869.
Catechesis/Religious Program—Tel: 931-526-4411. Valerie Richardson, D.R.E. Students 204.
Mission—Divine Savior Celina, Clay Co.

DECHERD, FRANKLIN CO., GOOD SHEPHERD (1900) Rev. Jean Baptiste Kyabuta.
Church: 2021 Decherd Blvd., 37324. Tel: 931-967-0961; Fax: 931-967-3569.
School—(Grades PreK-8), 2037 Decherd Blvd., 37324. Tel: 931-967-5673. Kelly Doyle, Prin. Lay Teachers 8; Students 82.
Catechesis/Religious Program—Brigid Stewart, D.R.E. Students 32.
Mission—St. Margaret Mary 9458 Old Alto Hwy., Alto, Franklin Co. 37324.

DICKSON, DICKSON CO., ST. CHRISTOPHER (1951) Rev. Mathew Perumpally; Deacon James Tucker.
Church: 713 W. College St., 37055. Tel: 615-446-3927; Fax: 615-446-7339.
Catechesis/Religious Program—Michelle Brenner, D.R.E.; Amber Gonzales, D.R.E. Students 135.

DOVER, STEWART CO., ST. FRANCIS OF ASSISI (1982) Rev. David J. Gaffny.
Mailing Address: P.O. Box 307, 37058-0307.
Church: 1489 Donelson Pkwy. Tel: 931-232-9422.
Catechesis/Religious Program—Tel: 931-232-1924. Linda Allen, D.R.E. Students 26.

FAYETTEVILLE, LINCOLN CO., ST. ANTHONY (1983) Rev. Jose Kariamadam, C.M.I.
Church: 1900 Huntsville Hwy., 37334. Tel: 931-433-6525; Fax: 931-433-6283.
Catechesis/Religious Program—Students 101.

FRANKLIN, WILLIAMSON CO.

1—ST. MATTHEW (1979) Revs. Mark Beckman; Nicholas Allen; Deacon John W. Myers.
Church: 535 Sneed Rd. W., 37069. Tel: 615-646-0378; Fax: 615-646-5230.
School—(Grades K-8), 533 Sneed Rd. W., 37069. Tel: 615-662-4044; Fax: 615-662-6822. Barby Magness, Prin.; Marcia Newman, Librarian. Lay

Teachers 33; Students 438.
Catechesis/Religious Program—Sr. Lauren Cole, R.S.M., D.R.E. Students 249.

2—ST. PHILIP (1843) Revs. Marneni Showraiah, O.F.M., Admin.; Tien Tran, Pastoral Assoc.
Church: 113 2nd Ave. S., 37064. Tel: 615-794-4236; Fax: 615-794-3083.
Catechesis/Religious Program—Tel: 615-794-8588. Kimberlie Leisinger, D.R.E. Students 610.

GALLATIN, SUMNER CO., ST. JOHN VIANNEY (1929) Rev. Stephen G. Gideon.
Church: 449 N. Water St., 37066. Tel: 615-452-2977; Fax: 615-452-0323.
School—(Grades PreK-8) Tel: 615-230-7048; Fax: 615-206-9839. Jennifer McCormick, Prin. Lay Teachers 10; Students 127.
Catechesis/Religious Program—Students 104.

HENDERSONVILLE, SUMNER CO., OUR LADY OF THE LAKE (1969) Revs. Eric L. Fowlkes; Leon Gerald Strange; Sr. Maria Edwards, R.S.M., Pastoral Assoc.; Deacon James F. Carr.
Church & Mailing Address: 1729 Stop Thirty Road, 37075. Tel: 615-824-3276; Fax: 615-824-7989.
Catechesis/Religious Program—Cyndi Sabatino, D.R.E. Students 669.

HOHENWALD, LEWIS CO., HOLY TRINITY (1983) Rev. Joseph K. Dowling.
Church: 610 Kimmins St., 38462. Tel: 931-796-3738; Fax: 931-796-3738.
Catechesis/Religious Program—Darie McCarthy, D.R.E. Students 18.

JOELTON, DAVIDSON CO., ST. LAWRENCE (1885) [CEM] Rev. Abraham M. Panthalanickal.
Church: 5655 Clarksville Hwy., 37080. Tel: 615-876-2127; Fax: 615-876-7923.
Catechesis/Religious Program—Students 27.

LAFAYETTE, MACON CO., HOLY FAMILY (1982) Rev. Dennis Holly, G.H.M.
Tel: 615-688-4104.
Church: 901 Vinson Rd., 37083. Tel: 615-666-6466.
Catechesis/Religious Program—Edith Kanyock, D.R.E. Students 37.

LAWRENCEBURG, LAWRENCE CO., SACRED HEART (1870) [CEM] Rev. Joseph Mundakal, C.M.I.
Mailing Address: P.O. Box 708, 38464.
Church: 222 Berger St., 38464. Tel: 931-762-3183; Fax: 931-762-5128.
School—(Grades K-8), 220 Berger St., 38464. Tel: 931-762-6125; Fax: 931-762-6125. Rosemary Harris, Prin. Lay Teachers 6; Students 83.
Catechesis/Religious Program—Students 81.

LEBANON, WILSON CO., ST. FRANCES CABRINI (1953) Rev. Michael O'Bryan; Deacon James A. Dixon.
Church: 300 S. Tarver Ave., 37087. Tel: 615-444-0524; Fax: 615-444-3704.
Catechesis/Religious Program—Students 158.

LEWISBURG, MARSHALL CO., ST. JOHN THE EVANGELIST (1982) Rev. William Kelly, S.D.S.
Church: 1061 S. Ellington, 37091. Tel: 931-359-5017; Fax: 931-359-5281.
Catechesis/Religious Program—Students 63.

LORETTO, LAWRENCE CO., SACRED HEART (1872) [CEM] Rev. Luckas Arulappa, M.S.F.S.; Deacon Samuel Beckman.
Mailing Address: P.O. Box 86, 38469.
Church: 305 Church St., 38469. Tel: 931-853-4370; Fax: 931-853-4373.
School—(Grades K-8), 307 Church St., 38469. Tel: 931-853-4388. Mrs. Catherine N. Bradley, Prin. Lay Teachers 6; Students 79.
Catechesis/Religious Program—Dotty Thomas, D.R.E. Students 41.

MADISON, DAVIDSON CO., ST. JOSEPH (1953) Rev. Tomy P. Joseph, M.S.F.S.; Deacons Gordon W. McBride Sr.; Theodore B. Welsh; Don Craighead.
Church: 1225 Gallatin Pike S., 37115-4698. Tel: 615-865-1071; Fax: 615-868-4900.
School—(Grades K-8) Tel: 615-865-1491; Fax: 615-612-0228. Sr. Martha Ann Titus, O.P., Prin.; Susan Guyton, Librarian. Dominican Sisters of St. Cecilia Congregation 3; Lay Teachers 27; Students 381.
Catechesis/Religious Program—Jacqueline Beals, D.R.E. Students 63.

MANCHESTER, COFFEE CO., ST. MARK (2000) Rev. Stephen A. Klasek; Deacon Ronald F. Munn.
Res.: 304 W. Gizzard St., Tullahoma, 37388. Tel: 931-455-3060; Fax: 931-461-9652.
Church & Mailing: 2941 McMinnville Hwy., 37349. Tel: 931-723-4107; Fax: 931-723-4123.
Catechesis/Religious Program—Students 96.

MCEWEN, HUMPHREYS CO., ST. PATRICK'S (1855) [CEM] Rev. Michael Baltrus.
Mailing Address: 175 St. Patrick's St., 37101.
Church: 175 St. Patrick's St., 37101. Tel: 931-582-3493; Fax: 931-582-6386.
School—(Grades PreK-8) Tel: 931-582-3493. Sr. Francine, O.P., Prin. Dominican Sisters of St. Cecilia Congregation 3; Lay Teachers 7; Students 82.
Catechesis/Religious Program—Alyssa Ginter, D.R.E. Students 25.

MCMINNVILLE, WARREN CO., ST. CATHERINE (1958) Rev. David Cooney, S.D.S.
Church: 1024 Faulkner Spring Rd., 37110. Tel: 931-473-4932; Fax: 931-473-0799.
Catechesis/Religious Program—Judy Davis, D.R.E.; Janice Saylors, D.R.E. Students 90.

MURFREESBORO, RUTHERFORD CO., ST. ROSE OF LIMA (1929) Revs. Mark Sappenfield, Admin.; Jacob Dio, M.S.F.S.; Deacons Thomas McGrane; Roger F. Huber; Peter Semich.
Church & Res.: 1601 N. Tennessee Blvd., 37130. Tel: 615-893-1843; Fax: 615-895-1150.
School—(Grades K-8) Tel: 615-898-0555; Fax: 615-898-0497. Sr. Marie Hannah, O.P., Prin.; Holly Bruser, Librarian. Sisters 4; Teachers 22; Students 316.
Catechesis/Religious Program—Mary Parod, D.R.E. Students 500.

OLD HICKORY, WILSON CO., ST. STEPHEN (1942) Rev. Patrick J. Kibby; Deacons Gordon S. Rose; Hans Toecker; Fred Bourland.
Church: 14544 Lebanon Rd., 37138. Tel: 615-758-2424; Fax: 615-754-0043.
Catechesis/Religious Program—Scott Goudeau, D.R.E.; Greg Karn, D.R.E. Students 463.

PULASKI, GILES CO., IMMACULATE CONCEPTION (1941) Rev. Jose Karimadam, C.M.I.; Deacon W. Michael Hume, Parish Coord.
Mailing Address: 100 Chapel Rd., 38478. Tel: 931-363-5776.
Catechesis/Religious Program—Jewel Dobry, D.R.E. Students 10.

SAINT JOSEPH, LAWRENCE CO., ST. JOSEPH (1872) Attended by Sacred Heart, Loretto. Rev. Luckas Arulappa, M.S.F.S.
Mailing Address: P.O. Box 86, Loretto, 38469. Tel: 931-853-4370; Fax: 931-853-4373.
Church: American Blvd., St. Joseph, 38481.

SHELBYVILLE, BEDFORD CO., ST. WILLIAM (1941) Rev. Thomas Kalam, C.M.I. In Res., Rev. Alejandro Godinez, Hispanic Ministry.
Church: 719 N. Main St., 37160. Tel: 931-684-8745; Fax: 931-684-6154.
Catechesis/Religious Program—Mr. Dan Strasser, D.R.E.; Mrs. Dan Strasser, D.R.E. Students 51.

SMITHVILLE, DEKALB CO., ST. GREGORY (1982) Attended by St. Catherine, McMinnville. Rev. David Cooney, S.D.S.
Mailing Address: P.O. Box 712, 37166.
Church: 712 Main St. Tel: 931-473-4932; Fax: 931-473-0799.
Catechesis/Religious Program—Maureen Nokes, D.R.E. Students 21.

SMYRNA, RUTHERFORD CO., ST. LUKE (1982) Rev. Richard Gagnon, S.D.S.; Deacons Ken Levinson; Simeon Panagatos; Jose G. Pineda.
Mailing Address: P.O. Box 907, 37167-0907.
Church: 10682 Old Nashville Hwy., 37167. Tel: 615-459-9672; Fax: 615-459-3989.
Catechesis/Religious Program—Denise M. Leaver, D.R.E. Students 188.

SPARTA, WHITE CO., ST. ANDREW (1982) Rev. John Pantuso, S.D.S.
Church: 829 Valley View Dr., 38583. Tel: 931-738-2140; Fax: 931-738-2592.
Catechesis/Religious Program—Students 38.

SPRING HILL, MAURY CO., CHURCH OF THE NATIVITY Rev. John L. Kirk.
2001 Campbell Station Pkwy., Ste. C-7, 37174. Tel: 615-302-4004. Web: www.nativitycatholic.net.
Catechesis/Religious Program—Students 268.

SPRINGFIELD, ROBERTSON CO., OUR LADY OF LOURDES (1946) [CEM] Rev. Prentice C. Dean, Admin.
Church: 103 Golf Club Ln., 37172. Tel: 615-384-6200; Fax: 615-384-5837.
Catechesis/Religious Program—Carol Twork, D.R.E. Students 120.
Mission—*St. Michael* [CEM] Cedar Hill, Robertson Co.

TENNESSEE RIDGE, HOUSTON CO., ST. ELIZABETH ANN SETON (1977) Attended by St. Patrick, McEwen.
Church & Mailing Address: 755 State Rte. 49, 37178. Tel: 931-721-3769; Fax: 931-721-3775.
Catechesis/Religious Program—

TULLAHOMA, COFFEE CO., ST. PAUL THE APOSTLE (1954) Rev. Stephen A. Klasek; Deacon Ronald F. Munn.
Church: 304 W. Grizzard St., 37388. Tel: 931-455-3050; Fax: 931-461-9652.
School—(Grades K-8) Tel: 931-455-4221; Fax: 931-455-8298. Susan Molvik, Prin.; Brenda Goethals, Librarian. Lay Teachers 13; Students 74.
Catechesis/Religious Program—Students 60.

WAYNESBORO, WAYNE CO., ST. CECILIA (1982) Attended by Holy Trinity, Hohenwald. Rev. Joseph K. Dowling.
Mailing Address: *Holy Trinity Church*, 610 Kimmins St., Hohenwald, 38462.
Church: 526 Hwy. 64 E., 38485. Tel: 931-796-3738; Fax: 931-796-3738.
Catechesis/Religious Program—Jennifer Ostrowski, D.R.E. Students 10.

On Special Assignment:
Very Rev.—
Perkin, David R., J.C.L., V.G., Moderator of the Curia & Vicar Gen.

On Duty Outside the Diocese:
Rev.—
Campion, Owen F., Our Sunday Visitor, 200 Noll Plaza, Huntington, IN 46750.

Unassigned:
Rev.—
Sappenfield, John P.

Retired:
Revs.—
Bevington, William S.
Buchignani, Richard G., J.C.L.
Burakowski, Wieslaw
Clements, Daniel A., P.O. Box 26122, Knoxville, 37912.
Connor, J. Patrick, V.G., 9126 Sawyer Brown Rd., 37221.
Mallett, James K., 728 Bacon Tr., #61, Chattanooga, 37412.
McMurry, John E., S.S.
McMurry, Vincent deP., S.S.
Murray, James B., 10605 Bishop Dozier Dr., Cordova, 38016.
Niedergeses, Bernard

Permanent Deacons:
Azzara, Dominic D., Immaculate Conception, Clarksville
Bainbridge, Frank, (Retired)
Batcheldor, James M., Jr., (Retired)
Beckman, Samuel C., Sacred Heart, Loretto
Berberich, Robert R., Immaculate Conception, Clarksville
Bourland, Fred, St. Stephen, Old Hickory
Calzavara, John, St. Edward, Nashville
Carr, James F., Our Lady of the Lake, Hendersonville
Carroll, John B., (Retired)
Casey, Bernard J., (On Duty Outside the Diocese)
Casey, John P., St. Ann, Nashville
Cheasty, John C., (On Duty Outside the Diocese)
Coen, Joseph, Sr., (Retired)
Cook, Thomas H., St. Patrick, Nashville
Craighead, Don, St. Joseph, Madison
Deal, Ronald B., Jr., Holy Family, Brentwood
Deschenes, Martin, St. Henry, Cursillo, Nashville
Desmond, Mark, (On Duty Outside the Diocese)
Dickson, William J., (Retired)
Dixon, James A., St. Francis Cabrini, Lebanon
Downey, John, St. Ignatius of Antioch
Edwards, Brian, John Paul II High School, Hendersonville
Faulkner, Mark C., Cathedral of the Incarnation, Nashville
Finchum, Thales, Cathedral of the Incarnation, Nashville
Francescon, Samuel A., (Retired)
Graham, Robert L., (Retired)
Gregory, L. Wayne, Holy Rosary, Nashville
Harrington, Henry, Jr., St. Vincent de Paul, Nashville
Henry, James R., (Retired)
Hill, William, St. Vincent de Paul, Nashville
Huber, Roger F., St. Rose of Lima, Murfreesboro
Huhlein, Gilbert P., Holy Rosary, Nashville
Hume, W. Michael, Immaculate Conception, Springfield
Jayme, Edgardo, St. Edward, Nashville
Keany, James, St. Thomas Aquinas, Cookeville
Keller, I. Price, St. Catherine, Columbia
Kopczynski, Michael R., (Unassigned)
Krenson, John G., Cathedral of the Incarnation, Nashville
Levinson, Ken, St. Luke, Smyrna
Lovell, David, (Unassigned)
Lybarger, David, Christ the King, Nashville
Mahoney, Robert L., Holy Name, Nashville
McBrayer, J. Harold, Jr., St. Mary Villa Parish Community, Nashville
McBride, Gordon W., Sr., St. Joseph, Madison
McGrane, Thomas J., St. Rose Lima, Murfreesboro
McKenzie, Andrew D., Christ the King, Nashville
McKenzie, James W., Cathedral of the Incarnation, Nashville
Meinhart, Gregory, St. Henry, Nashville
Melchior, Daniel, St. Anthony, Fayetteville
Miller, Thomas, (Unassigned)
Montini, Robert A., (On duty outside of Diocese)
Mulloy, Martin, St. Ann, Nashville
Munn, Ronald F., St. Mark, Manchester; St. Paul the Apostle, Tullahoma

Myers, John W., St. Matthew, Franklin
Neely, Jayd, Cathedral of the Incarnation, Nashville
Panagatos, Simeon W., St. Luke, Smyrna
Pineda, Jose G., St. Luke, Smyrna
Randall, Ralph, (Retired)
Rose, Gordon, St. Stephen, Old Hickory
Semich, Peter, St. Rose of Lima, Murfreesboro
Shafer, L. Douglas, St. Ignatius of Antioch, Antioch
Srouji, Jack, St. Henry, Nashville
Stanford, James E., (Retired)
Steinbrecher, Kenneth, Holy Rosary, Nashville
Toecker, Hans M., St. Stephen, Old Hickory; Chancellor
True, Robert H., Christ the King, Nashville
Tucker, James, St. Christopher, Dickson
Walsh, James, (Retired)
Walter, James, (On Duty Outside of Diocese)
Weaver, Matthew, (On Duty Outside of Diocese)
Weller, Richard, (Retired)
Welsh, Theodore B., St. Joseph, Madison
Winters, Timothy F., Immaculate Conception, Clarksville

INSTITUTIONS LOCATED IN THE DIOCESE

[A] COLLEGES

NASHVILLE. *Aquinas College*, 4210 Harding Pike, 37205. Tel: 615-297-7545; Fax: 615-279-3891. Email: admissions@aquinascollege.edu. Web: www.aquinascollege.edu. Sisters Ann Marie Karlovic, O.P., Chm., Bd Directors; Mary Peter Muehlenkamp, O.P., Pres.; Elizabeth Anne Allen, O.P., Vice Pres., Academic Affairs; Rev. John O'Neill; Mark Hall, Librarian. Dominican Sisters of St. Cecilia Congregation. Priests 1; Sisters 13; Lay Teachers 112; Students 873.

[B] HIGH SCHOOLS, DIOCESAN

NASHVILLE. *Father Ryan High School* (1925) Corporate Title: Father Ryan High School, Inc., 700 Norwood Dr., 37204. Tel: 615-383-4200; Fax: 615-383-9056. Email: mcintyrej@fatherryan.org. Web: www.fatherryan.org. Mr. James McIntyre, Pres.; Rev. Nicholas Allen, Part-Time Chap.; Mr. Paul Davis, Prin.; Christi Foreman, Librarian. Priests 1; Lay Teachers 85; Students 890.

Father Ryan Board of Trust, Devel. & Alumni Office, 770 Norwood Dr., 37204. Tel: 615-269-7926.

HENDERSONVILLE. *Pope John Paul II High School, Inc.* (2002) 117 Caldwell Ln., 37075. Tel: 615-822-2375; Fax: 615-822-6226. Email: info@jp2hs.org. Web: www.jp2hs.org. Faustin N. Weber, Headmaster. Lay Teachers 65; Students 614.

[C] HIGH SCHOOLS, PRIVATE

NASHVILLE. *St. Cecilia Academy* (1860) The Dominican Campus, 4210 Harding Rd., 37205. Tel: 615-298-4525; Fax: 615-783-0561. Email: hayesd1@stcecilia.edu. Web: www.stcecilia.edu. Sr. Mary Thomas Huffman, O.P., Prin.; Linda Braddock, Librarian.

St. Cecilia Academy. Conducted by the St. Cecilia Congregation of Dominican Sisters. Sisters 7; Lay Teachers 25; Students 265.

[D] ELEMENTARY SCHOOLS, PRIVATE

NASHVILLE. **St. Bernard Academy*, (Grades PreK-8), 2020 24th Ave. S., 37212-4202. Tel: 615-385-0440; Fax: 615-783-0241. Web: www.stbernardacademy.org. Carl Sabo, Head of School; Jennifer Kitchell, Librarian.

Saint Bernard Academy Corporation. Sisters 1; Lay Teachers 27; Students 300.

Overbrook School (1936) (Grades PreK-8), 4210 Harding Rd., 37205. Tel: 615-292-5134; Fax: 615-783-0560. Web: www.overbrook.edu. Sr. Mary Gertrude, O.P., Prin.; Margaret Lang, Office Mgr.; Erin Griffin, Librarian. The St. Cecilia Congregation of Dominican Sisters. Sisters 5; Lay Teachers 25; Students 333.

[E] CHILD-CARING INSTITUTIONS

NASHVILLE. **St. Bernard After School Program*, 2020 24th Ave. S., 37212. Tel: 615-298-1298; Fax: 615-783-0241. Suzanne Southworth, Dir. Lay Staff 6; Students 60.

St. Mary Villa Child Development Center, 30 White Bridge Rd., 37205. Tel: 615-356-6336; Fax: 615-356-6421. Email: mmiller@stmaryvilla.org. Michael Miller, Exec. Dir. Total Staff 52; Children 210.

St. Mary Villa, Inc., 30 White Bridge Rd., 37205. Tel: 615-356-6336; Fax: 615-356-6421.

[F] GENERAL HOSPITALS

NASHVILLE. *Baptist Hospital*, 2000 Church St., 37236. Tel: 615-284-5555; Fax: 615-284-1592. Web: www.baptisthospital.com. Bernard J. Sherry, Pres. & CEO.

Seton Corporation dba Baptist Hospital Chaplains 3; Bed Capacity 683; Patients Assisted Annually 96,327; Lay Staff 3,144.

Baptist Hospital Foundation (1978) 4220 Harding Rd., 37205. Tel: 615-222-6800; Fax: 615-222-6159. Web: sths.com/foundation.php.

Saint Thomas Health Services Fund dba Baptist Hospital Foundation (fka Saint Thomas Foundation)

St. Thomas Hospital (1898) 4220 Harding Rd., 37205. Tel: 615-222-2111; Fax: 615-222-6502. Email: nshlsthl@stthomas.org. Web: www.saintthomas.org. Dawn Rudolph, Pres. & CEO; Rev. Francis G. Appreh, Chap.; Jerry Kearney, Vice Pres. Mission.

St. Thomas Hospital. Ascension Health, St. Louis, MO. Sisters 1; Chaplains 12; Lay Staff 2,613; Bed Capacity 541; Patients Assisted Annually 166,358.

Saint Thomas Foundation Tel: 615-222-6800; Fax: 615-222-6159.

St. Thomas Network aka St. Thomas Health Services (1986) 4220 Harding Rd., 37205. Tel: 615-222-2111; Fax: 615-222-6502.

Saint Thomas Network (fka Saint Thomas Health Services

Covenant Care, Inc. Tel: 615-222-2111; Fax: 615-222-6502.

Seton Corporation (2001) 4220 Harding Rd., 37205. Tel: 615-252-3286; Fax: 615-252-6386. Email: jhardcastle@boultcummings.com. Web: www.stthomas.org. Jay Hardcastle, Attorney.

CENTERVILLE. *Hickman Community Hospital aka Baptist Hickman Community Hospital* 135 E. Swan St., 37033-1466. Tel: 931-729-4271; Fax: 931-729-4612. Email: jack.keller@baptisthospital.com. Web: www.hickmanhospital.com. Jack Keller, CEO/Admin.

Hickman Community Health Care Services, Inc. dba Hickman Community Hospital (fka Baptist Hickman Community Health Care Services, Inc. dba Baptist Hickman Community Hospital) Bed Capacity 25; Patients Assisted Annually 36,759; Lay Staff 156.

MURFREESBORO. *Middle Tennessee Medical Center*, 1700 Medical Center Pkwy., 37129. Tel: 615-396-4101; Fax: 615-396-4119. Web: www.mtmc.net. Gordon Ferguson, Pres. & CEO.

Middle Tennessee Medical Center, Inc. Chaplains 2; Bed Capacity 286; Patients Assisted Annually 16,451; Lay Staff 1,122.

Middle Tennessee Medical Center Foundation, 400 N. Highland Ave., 37130. Tel: 615-396-4693; Fax: 615-396-4997. Web: www.mtmc.org.

Middle Tennessee Medical Center Foundation

[G] HOMES FOR THE AGED

NASHVILLE. *Villa Maria Manor, Inc. dba Villa Maria Manor* 32 White Bridge Rd., 37205. Tel: 615-352-3084; Fax: 615-352-0553. Email: sclinton@VillaMariaManor.org. Mr. David Glascoe, Mng. Agent. Residents 230.

[H] MONASTERIES AND RESIDENCES OF PRIESTS AND BROTHERS

NASHVILLE. *Franciscan Friars*, 1700 Heiman St., 37208. Tel: 615-665-7313; Fax: 615-320-0698. Email: shadeaura@aol.com. Revs. John Eaton, O.F.M.; Albert Merz, O.F.M.

[I] CONVENTS AND RESIDENCES FOR SISTERS

NASHVILLE. *St. Cecilia Convent* Motherhouse and Novitiate of St. Cecilia Congregation of Dominican Sisters., 801 Dominican Dr., 37228-1905. Tel: 615-256-5486; Fax: 615-687-3512. Web: www.nashvilledominican.org. Sisters Ann Marie Karlovic, O.P., Prioress Gen.; Ignatius Connolly, O.P., Prioress. Sisters in Residence 152; Novices 24; Postulants 16.

Mercy Convent, 2629 Pennington Bend Rd., 37214. Tel: 615-885-1863; Fax: 615-885-4304. Sr. Mary Judith Coode, R.S.M., Coord.; Rev. James Panackal, C.M.I.

Sisters of Mercy of Nashville, TN, Inc. Sisters 19.

[J] CAMPS AND COMMUNITY CENTERS

FAIRVIEW. *Camp Marymount* Catholic summer camp for boys and girls., 1318 Fairview Blvd., 37062. Tel: 615-799-0410; Fax: 615-799-2261. Email: info@campmarymount.com. Web: www.campmarymount.com. Tommy Hagey, Dir.

[K] RENEWAL CENTERS

LIBERTY. *Carmel Center of Spirituality*, P.O. Box 117, 37095. Tel: 615-536-5177. Email: carmliberty@yahoo.com. P.O. Box 117, 37095. Revs. Thomas Kalam, C.M.I.; Jose Kariamadam, C.M.I.; James Panackal, C.M.I.

[L] MISCELLANEOUS

NASHVILLE. *Catholic Community Foundation of Middle Tennessee, Inc.* (2011) 2400 21st Ave. S., 37212. Tel: 615-783-0278; Fax: 615-292-8411. Web: www.ccfmtn.org.

Catholic Community Investment and Loan, Inc., 2400 21st Ave. S., 37212.

Catholic Foundation of Tennessee, Inc., 2400 21st Ave. S., 37212. Tel: 615-783-0774; Fax: 615-292-8411.

**Catholic Media Productions*, 700 Harpeth Knoll Ct., 37221. Tel: 615-646-4041; Fax: 615-662-7454. Email: JimWalsh@webelieveshow.org. Web: www.webelieveshow.org. James F. Walsh Jr., Chm. & CEO.

Diocesan Council of Catholic Women, 2400 21st Ave. S., 37212. Tel: 615-889-4065; Fax: 615-889-3421. Email: merve8371@aol.com. Rev. Kevin Dowling, Dir.

Diocesan Properties, Inc. dba Marina Manor East Apartments 2400 21st Ave. S., 37212. Tel: 615-383-6393; Fax: 615-292-8411. Mr. William J. Whalen, Sec. & Treas.

Dominican Campus, 4210 Harding Rd., 37205. Tel: 615-383-3230; Fax: 615-383-3196. Email: muehe@dominicancampus.org. Roger Muehe, CFO; Rev. John O'Neill.

Endowment for the Advancement of Catholic Schools, Trust, 2400 21st Ave. S., 37212. Tel: 615-383-6393; Fax: 615-292-8411. Most Rev. David R. Choby, D.D., J.C.L.

FrassatiUSA Inc., P.O. Box 50571, 37205.

**St. Henry Property Development, Inc. dba The Cloister* 30 White Bridge Rd., 37205. Tel: 615-760-4424; Fax: 615-352-8591. Email: david@maryqueenofangels.com. David Glacoe, Admin.

Ladies of Charity of Nashville, Inc., 2216 State St., 37203. Tel: 615-327-3453; 615-327-3430; Fax: 615-321-3312. Affiliated with the Ladies of Charity of the United States of America, LCUSA, and the Association of International Charities, AIC.

Ladies of Charity Welfare Agency, Inc. (1617) 2212 State St., 37203. Tel: 615-327-3430; Fax: 615-321-3312. Email: locwelfare@bellsouth.net. Mrs. Terri Puma, Exec. Dir.; Rev. Philip M. Breen, Moderator.

Mary, Queen of Angels. Inc. (1999) 30 White Bridge Rd., 37205. Tel: 615-760-4424; Fax: 615-352-8591. Email: david@maryqueenofangels.com. Web: www.maryqueenofangels.com. Mr. David Glascoe, CEO.

Mid-Tennessee Rural Outreach Association, 30 White Bridge Rd., 37205. Tel: 615-352-3087.

Mid-Tennessee Rural Outreach Association; Assumption-St. Vincent North Nashville Outreach Association.

Parish Twinning Program of the Americas, 309 Windemere Woods Dr., 37215. Tel: 615-298-3002; Fax: 615-298-2253. Email: parishprogram@aol.com. Web: www.parishprogram.org. Theresa Patterson, Exec. Dir.

**Visitation Hospital Foundation*, 237 Old Hickory Blvd., Ste. 201, 37221. Tel: 615-673-3501; Fax: 615-673-3503. Email: visitationHF@aol.com. Theresa Patterson, Exec. Dir.; Jeff Patterson, Assoc. Dir.; Fran Rajotte, Dir. Devel. & Communications.

HENDERSONVILLE. *Priests Eucharistic League*, 200 Sanders Ferry Rd., Apt. 2412, 37075. Tel: 615-431-0472. Email: wsbev@aol.com. Rev. William S. Bevington, Dir. (Retired).

RELIGIOUS INSTITUTES OF MEN REPRESENTED IN THE DIOCESE

For further details refer to the corresponding bracketed number in the Religious Institutes of Men or Women section.

[0275]—*Carmelites of Mary Immaculate*—C.M.I.
[0520]—*Franciscan Friars* (Prov. of Sacred Heart)—O.F.M.
[0570]—*Glenmary Home Missioners*—G.H.M.
[0690]—*Jesuit Fathers and Brothers*—S.J.
[]—*Missionaries of St. Francis de Sales* (Annecy, France)—M.S.F.S.
[1200]—*Society of the Divine Savior* (Milwaukee, WI)—S.D.S.

RELIGIOUS INSTITUTES OF WOMEN REPRESENTED IN THE DIOCESE

[0760]—*Daughters of Charity of St. Vincent de Paul* (East Central Prov., Evansville, IN)—D.C.
[1070-03]—*Dominican Sisters*—O.P.
[1070-07]—*Dominican Sisters*—O.P.

[1070-09]—*Dominican Sisters*—O.P.
[2575]—*Institute of the Sisters of Mercy of the Americas* (Baltimore, MD; Cincinnati, OH)—R.S.M.
[]—*Sacred Heart Congregation* (Mexico)
[]—*Sacred Heart Congregation (India)*—S.H.
[1680]—*School Sisters of St. Francis*—O.S.F.
[]—*Sisters for Christian Community* (St. Louis)—S.F.C.C.
[0990]—*Sisters of Divine Providence* (St. Louis Prov.)—C.D.P.
[1705]—*Sisters of St. Francis of Assisi*—O.S.F.
[3270]—*Sisters of the Most Precious Blood*—C.PP.S.

DIOCESAN CEMETERIES

NASHVILLE. *Calvary Cemetery*, 1001 Lebanon Rd., 37210.

NECROLOGY

(No Deaths)

An asterisk (*) denotes an organization that has established tax-exempt status directly with the IRS and is not covered by the USCCB Group Ruling.

Archdiocese of Newark

(Archidioecesis Novarcensis)

Most Reverend

PETER LEO GERETY, D.D.

Archbishop Emeritus of Newark; ordained June 29, 1939; appointed Coadjutor Bishop of Portland March 4, 1966; Episcopal ordination June 1, 1966; appointed Apostolic Administrator February 18, 1967; succeeded to See September 15, 1969; appointed Archbishop of Newark April 2, 1974; installed June 28, 1974; Pallium conferred December 12, 1974; retired June 1, 1986. *Res.: 60 Home Ave., Rutherford, NJ 07070.* Tel: 201-460-1369; Fax: 201-842-0724.

Most Reverend

DOMINIC A. MARCONI, D.D.

Retired Auxiliary Bishop of Newark; ordained May 30, 1953; appointed Titular Bishop of Bure and Auxiliary Bishop of Newark May 3, 1976; Episcopal ordination June 25, 1976; retired July 1, 2002. *Res.: 71 Washington Ave., Chatham, NJ 07928-2014.* Tel: 973-635-8777; Fax: 973-635-8647.

Most Reverend

DAVID ARIAS, O.A.R.

Retired Auxiliary Bishop of Newark; ordained May 31, 1952; appointed Titular Bishop of Badie and Auxiliary Bishop of Newark January 25, 1983; Episcopal ordination April 7, 1983; retired May 21, 2004. *Res.: St. Joseph of the Palisades Rectory, 6401 Palisade Ave., West New York, NJ 07093.* Tel: 201-854-7006. *Office:* . Tel: 201-861-6644; Fax: 201-861-7744.

Most Reverend

CHARLES J. McDONNELL

Retired Auxiliary Bishop of Newark; ordained May 29, 1954; appointed Titular Bishop of Pocofelto and Auxiliary Bishop of Newark March 15, 1994; Episcopal ordination May 12, 1994; retired May 21, 2004. *Res.: Holy Trinity Rectory, 34 Maple Ave., Hackensack, NJ 07601.* Tel: 201-343-5170; Fax: 201-343-5067.

Most Reverend

JOHN J. MYERS, J.C.D., D.D.

Archbishop of Newark; ordained December 17, 1966; appointed Coadjutor Bishop of Peoria July 14, 1987; Episcopal ordination September 3, 1987; succeeded to See of Peoria January 23, 1990; appointed Fifth Archbishop of Newark July 24, 2001; installed October 9, 2001; Pallium conferred June 29, 2002. *Res.: Cathedral Basilica of the Sacred Heart, 89 Ridge St., Newark, NJ 07104.* Tel: 973-484-4600; Fax: 973-497-4018.

MYSTERIUM ECCLESIAE LUCEAT

Archdiocesan Center: 171 Clifton Ave., P.O. Box 9500, Newark, NJ 07104-9500. Tel: 973-497-4000; Fax: 973-497-4033.

Web: www.rcan.org

Email: webmaster@rcan.org

Most Reverend

EDGAR M. DA CUNHA, S.D.V.

Auxiliary Bishop of Newark; ordained March 27, 1982; appointed Titular See of Ucres and Auxiliary Bishop of Newark June 27, 2003; Episcopal ordination September 3, 2003. *Res.: 170 Broad St., Newark, NJ 07104.* Tel: 973-482-8619; Fax: 973-497-4555.

Most Reverend

THOMAS A. DONATO, D.D.

Auxiliary Bishop of Newark; ordained May 29, 1965; appointed Titular Bishop of Jamestown and Auxiliary Bishop of Newark May 21, 2004; Episcopal ordination August 4, 2004. *Res.: St. Henry's Parish, 82 W. 29th St., Bayonne, NJ 07002.* Tel: 201-436-0857; Fax: 201-823-4611.

Most Reverend

JOHN W. FLESEY, S.T.D., D.D.

Auxiliary Bishop of Newark; ordained May 31, 1969; appointed Titular Bishop of Allegheny and Auxiliary Bishop of Newark May 21, 2004; Episcopal ordination August 4, 2004. *Res.: Most Blessed Sacrament, 787 Franklin Lake Rd., Franklin Lakes, NJ 07417.* Tel: 201-891-4200; Fax: 201-891-4243.

Most Reverend

MANUEL A. CRUZ

Auxiliary Bishop of Newark; ordained May 31, 1980; appointed Titular Bishop of Gaguari and Auxiliary Bishop of Newark May 19, 2008; Episcopal ordination September 8, 2008; installed September 8, 2008. *Res.: 306 Martin Luther King Blvd., Newark, NJ 07102.* Tel: 973-497-4009; Fax: 973-497-4525.

Square Miles 513.

Diocese Established, 1853; Erected an Archdiocese, December 10, 1937.

Comprises Four Counties in the State of New Jersey, viz.: Bergen, Hudson, Essex and Union.

For legal titles of parishes and archdiocesan institutions, consult the Chancery Office.

STATISTICAL OVERVIEW

Personnel	
Archbishops	1
Retired Archbishops	1
Auxiliary Bishops	4
Retired Bishops	3
Abbots	1
Priests: Diocesan Active in Diocese	427
Priests: Diocesan Active Outside Diocese	52
Priests: Diocesan in Foreign Missions	18
Priests: Retired, Sick or Absent	227
Number of Diocesan Priests	724
Religious Priests in Diocese	167
Total Priests in Diocese	891
Extern Priests in Diocese	70
Ordinations:	
Diocesan Priests	18
Permanent Deacons	35
Permanent Deacons in Diocese	184
Total Brothers	78
Total Sisters	809
Parishes	
Parishes	219
With Resident Pastor:	
Resident Diocesan Priests	177
Resident Religious Priests	25
Without Resident Pastor:	
Administered by Priests	18
Closed Parishes	1
Professional Ministry Personnel:	
Brothers	7
Sisters	68
Lay Ministers	534
Welfare	
Catholic Hospitals	3
Total Assisted	916,533
Health Care Centers	1
Total Assisted	11,077
Homes for the Aged	4
Total Assisted	666
Day Care Centers	4
Total Assisted	563
Specialized Homes	5
Total Assisted	905
Special Centers for Social Services	23
Total Assisted	72,104
Educational	
Seminaries, Diocesan	3
Students from This Diocese	88
Students from Other Diocese	50
Diocesan Students in Other Seminaries	4
Students Religious	51
Total Seminarians	143
Colleges and Universities	4
Total Students	17,093
High Schools, Diocesan and Parish	10
Total Students	5,651
High Schools, Private	21
Total Students	7,869
Elementary Schools, Diocesan and Parish	76
Total Students	16,464
Elementary Schools, Private	5
Total Students	903
Catechesis/Religious Education:	
High School Students	4,000
Elementary Students	65,115
Total Students under Catholic Instruction	117,238
Teachers in the Diocese:	
Priests	25
Brothers	11
Sisters	107
Lay Teachers	2,489
Vital Statistics	
Receptions into the Church:	
Infant Baptism Totals	13,362
Minor Baptism Totals	174
Adult Baptism Totals	331
Received into Full Communion	126
First Communions	11,571
Confirmations	9,421
Marriages:	
Catholic	2,051
Interfaith	338
Total Marriages	2,389
Deaths	9,260
Total Catholic Population	1,318,557
Total Population	2,859,850

Former Bishops—Most Revs. JAMES ROOSEVELT BAYLEY, D.D., cons. Oct. 30, 1853; promoted to the Archiepiscopal See of Baltimore, July 30, 1872; died Oct. 3, 1877; MICHAEL AUGUSTINE CORRIGAN, D.D., cons. May 4, 1873; promoted to the Archiepiscopal See of Petra, Oct. 1, 1880; succeeded to the Archiepiscopal See of New York, Oct. 10, 1885; died May 5, 1902; WINAND MICHAEL WIGGER, D.D., cons. Oct. 18, 1881; died Jan. 5, 1901; JOHN JOSEPH O'CONNOR, D.D., ord. Dec. 22, 1877; cons. July 25, 1901; died May 20, 1927; THOMAS J. WALSH, S.T.D., J.C.D., ord. Jan. 27, 1900; appt. Bishop of Trenton, May 10, 1918; cons. July 25, 1918; made Assistant at the Pontifical Throne March 13, 1922; transferred to the See of Newark, March 2, 1928; appt. First Archbishop of Newark, Dec. 10, 1937; Pallium conferred, Dec. 18, 1937; installed April 27, 1938; died June 6, 1952; THOMAS A. BOLAND, S.T.D., LL.D., ord. Dec. 23, 1922; appt. Titular Bishop of Hirina and Auxiliary to the Archbishop of Newark, May 21, 1940; cons. July 25, 1940; transferred to Paterson, June 21, 1947; appt. Second Archbishop of Newark, Nov. 15, 1952;

installed Jan. 14, 1953; Assistant at the Pontifical Throne, May 6, 1965; retired April 2, 1974; died March 16, 1979; PETER LEO GERETY, D.D. (Retired), ord. June 29, 1939; appt. Coadjutor Bishop of Portland, March 4, 1966; cons. June 1, 1966; succeeded to See, Sept. 15, 1969; appt. Third Archbishop of Newark, April 2, 1974; installed June 28, 1974; retired June 1, 1986; THEODORE E. MCCARRICK, Ph.D., ord. May 31, 1958; appt. Auxiliary Bishop of New York and Titular Bishop of Rusibisir, May 24, 1977; Episcopal ordination June 29, 1977; appt. First Bishop of Metuchen, Nov. 19, 1981; appt. Fourth Archbishop of Newark, May 30, 1986; Pallium conferred June 29, 1986; installed July 25, 1986; appt. to See of Washington, D.C., Nov. 21, 2000; installed Jan. 3, 2001.

Archdiocesan Officials

Archdiocesan Officials—Web: www.rcan.org.

Archdiocesan Bishop—Most Rev. JOHN J. MYERS, D.D., J.C.D.

Archbishop Emeritus of Newark—Most Rev. PETER L. GERETY, D.D. (Retired).

Vicar General, Moderator of the Curia and Chancellor—Rev. Msgr. JOHN E. DORAN, V.G. Tel: 973-497-4002.

Auxiliary Bishop of Newark and Regional Bishop for Essex County—Most Rev. EDGAR M. DA CUNHA, S.D.V., D.D.

Auxiliary Bishop of Newark and Regional Bishop for Hudson County—Most Rev. THOMAS A. DONATO, D.D.

Auxiliary Bishop of Newark and Regional Bishop for Bergen County—Most Rev. JOHN W. FLESEY, S.T.D., D.D.

Auxiliary Bishop of Newark, Regional Bishop for Union County and Rector of the Cathedral Basilica of the Sacred Heart—Most Rev. MANUEL A. CRUZ, D.D.

Vice Chancellor & Secretary to the Archbishop and Director/Master of Ceremonies for Pontifical Liturgies—Rev. Msgr. MICHAEL A. ANDREANO, M.B.A. Tel: 973-497-4005.

Delegate for Religious—Sr. JOANNE BEDNAR, S.C.C. Tel: 973-497-4582.

Metropolitan Judicial Vicar—Very Rev. ROBERT G. MCBRIDE, J.C.L., V.F. Tel: 973-497-4145.

Adjutant Judicial Vicar—Rev. Msgr. ROBERT E. EMERY, J.C.L., M.A., V.G. Tel: 973-497-4151.

Episcopal Vicar for Healthcare and Social Concerns—Rev. Msgr. RONALD J. ROZNIAK, V.E., P.A. Tel: 201-444-2000.

Vicar for Education and Superintendent of Schools—Rev. Msgr. KEVIN M. HANBURY, Ed.D. Tel: 973-497-4260.

Vicar for Family Life—Rev. MARC A. VICARI, M.Div. Tel: 973-497-4324.

Vicar for Pastoral Life—Rev. Msgr. RICHARD J. ARNHOLS, M.Div. Tel: 973-497-4321.

Fiscal Officer—Mr. JOSEPH PESCATORE. Tel: 973-497-4560.

Minister for Priests—Rev. GABRIEL B. COSTA, Ph.D. Tel: 845-938-5625; 862-215-2333.

Director of Selection & Formation of Permanent Deacons—Rev. JAMES V. TETI, J.C.L., S.T.B. Tel: 201-261-6322.

Director of Vocations—Rev. JOHN D. GABRIEL, M.Div. Tel: 973-497-4365.

Director of Communications and Public Relations—Mr. JAMES GOODNESS, M.A. Tel: 973-497-4186.

Regional Bishops & Deans

Regional Bishops & Deans—Most Revs. JOHN W. FLESEY, S.T.D., D.D., Regl. Bishop for Bergen County; EDGAR M. DA CUNHA, S.D.V., D.D., Regl. Bishop for Essex County; THOMAS A. DONATO, D.D., Regl. Bishop for Hudson County; MANUEL A. CRUZ, D.D., Regl. Bishop for Union County.

BERGEN COUNTY

Northwest Bergen Region Deanery 1: Very Rev. THOMAS P. LIPNICKI, V.F., Our Lady of Perpetual Help, 25 Purdue Ave., Oakland, 07436. Tel: 201-337-7596; Fax: 201-337-7810. Northern Valley Bergen Deanery 2N: Very Rev. PAUL A. CANNARIATO, V.F., St. Anthony, 199 Walnut St., Northvale, 07647-2122. Tel: 201-768-1177; Fax: 201-768-2522. St. Mary, 20 Legion Place, Closter, 07624. Tel: 201-768-7565; Fax: 201-784-5814. Bergen Pascack Valley Deanery 2P: Very Rev. CHARLES P. GRANDSTRAND, V.F., Our Lady of Mercy, 2 Fremont Ave., Park Ridge, 07656. Tel: 201-391-5315; Fax: 201-391-5614. Central Bergen Region Deanery 3: Very Rev. DAVID W. MILLIKEN, V.F., Ascension, 256 Azalea Dr., New Milford, 07646. Tel: 201-836-8961; Fax: 201-836-5896. Southwest Bergen Region Deanery 4: Rev. Msgr. WILLIAM J. REILLY, V.F., Most Holy Name Parish, 99 Marsellus Pl., Garfield, 07026. Tel: 973-340-0032; Fax: 973-340-1618. South Central Bergen Deanery 5: Very Rev. ARTHUR F. HUMPHREY, V.F., St. Margaret of Cortona, 31 Chamberlain Ave., Little Ferry, 07643. Tel: 201-641-2988; Fax: 201-641-0664. Southeast Bergen Region Deanery 6: Very Rev. STEVEN CONNER, V.F., Holy Trinity, 2367 Lemoine Ave., Fort Lee, 07024. Tel: 201-947-1216. South Bergen Region Deanery 7: Rev. Msgr. LEWIS V. PAPERA, V.F., Corpus Christi Parish, 218 Washington Pl., Hasbrouck Heights, 07604. Tel: 201-288-4844; Fax: 201-288-0237.

HUDSON COUNTY

North Hudson Deanery 8: Very Rev. CARLO FORTUNIO, V.F., Holy Redeemer Parish, 6502 Jackson Ave., West New York, 07093. Tel: 201-868-9444; Fax: 201-868-5944. Central Hudson Region Deanery 9: Very Rev. JAMES P. WHELAN, V.F., St. Lawrence Parish, 22 Hackensack Ave., Weehawken, 07086. Tel: 201-863-6464; Fax: 201-863-6656. Jersey City North Region Deanery 10: Very Rev. ANDRES J. REYES, V.F., St. Paul of the Cross, 156 Hancock Ave., Jersey City, 07307. Tel: 201-798-7900; Fax: 201-798-7902. Jersey City Downtown Deanery 11: Very Rev. VICTOR P. KENNEDY, V.F., Parish of the Resurrection, 209 Third St., Jersey City, 07302-0407. Tel: 201-434-8500; Fax: 201-333-1816. Jersey City South Deanery 12: Very Rev. JOHN J. CRYAN, V.F., M.Div., Our Lady of Mercy & Our Lady of Sorrows, 40 Sullivan Dr., Jersey City, 07302. Tel: 201-434-0798; Fax: 201-432-2885. Bayonne Deanery 13: Rev. Msgr. PAUL D. SCHETELICK, V.F., St. Andrew Parish, 125 Broadway, Bayonne, 07002. Tel: 201-437-0833; Fax: 201-858-3477. West Hudson Region Deanery 14: Very Rev. MICHAEL G. WARD, V.F., St. Cecilia Parish, 120 Kearny Ave., Kearny, 07032-2316. Tel: 201-991-1116; Fax: 201-998-4437.

ESSEX COUNTY

West Essex Deanery 15: Very Rev. ANTHONY J. RANDAZZO, V.F., Notre Dame, 359 Central Ave., North Caldwell, 07006. Tel: 973-226-0979; Fax: 973-226-4118. North Essex Deanery 16: Very Rev. JUANCHO G. DELEON, V.F., St. Valentine Church, 125 N. Spring St., Bloomfield, 07003. Tel: 973-743-0220; Fax: 973-743-2041. Central Essex Deanery 17: Very Rev. GEORGE FAOUR, V.F., St. John, 94 Ridge St., Orange, 07050. Tel: 973-674-0110; Fax: 973-674-3965. South Essex Deanery 18: Very Rev. MICHAEL M. WALTERS, M.A., J.C.L., V.F., Our Lady of Sorrows, 217 Prospect St., South Orange, 07079. Tel: 973-763-5454; Fax: 973-763-9506. North Newark Essex Deanery 19: Very Rev. JAN SASIN, V.F., St. Francis Xavier, 243 Abington Ave., W., Newark, 07107. Tel: 973-482-8410; Fax: 973-485-7471. Central Newark Deanery 20: Very Rev. PHILIP J. WATERS, O.S.B., V.F., St. Mary of the Immaculate Conception, 528 Martin Luther King Blvd., Newark, 07102-1314. Tel: 973-792-5793; Fax: 973-643-6922. Ironbound Deanery 21: Rev. Msgr. JOSEPH F. AMBROSIO, V.F., Our Lady of Mt. Carmel, 259 Oliver St., Newark, 07105. Tel: 973-589-2090; Fax: 973-589-2662.

UNION COUNTY

Union Northwest Deanery 22: Very Rev. JOHN M. MCCRONE, V.F., Our Lady of Lourdes, 300 Central Ave., Mountainside, 07092. Tel: 908-232-1162; Fax: 908-232-0776. Union North Deanery 23: Very Rev. JOSEPH J. BEJGROWICZ, V.F., St. Theresa, 541 Washington Ave., Kenilworth, 07033. Tel: 908-272-4444; Fax: 908-272-4424. Union County Southeast Deanery 24: Very Rev. ROBERT G. MCBRIDE, J.C.L., V.F., Saint John the Apostle, 1805 Penbrook Ter., Linden, 07036. Tel: 908-486-6363; Fax: 908-486-5345. Elizabeth Deanery 25: Very Rev. JOHN E. WASSELL, V.F., Holy Rosary/St. Michael, 52 Smith St., Elizabeth, 07201. Tel: 908-354-2454; Fax: 908-354-3207. Union County Southwest Deanery 26: Very Rev. JOHN J. PALADINO, V.F., St. Bartholomew, 2032 Westfield Ave., Scotch Plains, 07076.

Advisory Bodies

College of Consultors—Members: Most Revs. EDGAR M. DA CUNHA, S.D.V., D.D.; THOMAS A. DONATO, D.D.; JOHN W. FLESEY, S.T.D., D.D.; MANUEL A. CRUZ, D.D.; Rev. Msgrs. JOHN E. DORAN, V.G.; RONALD J. ROZNIAK, V.E., P.A., Sec.; RICHARD J. ARNHOLS, M.Div.; Very Rev. JOSEPH J. BEJGROWICZ, V.F.; Revs. JOSEPH A. FERRARO; JOHN D. GABRIEL, M.Div.; Rev. Msgr. RENATO GRASSELLI, S.T.L.

Presbyteral Council—Most Revs. JOHN J. MYERS, D.D., J.C.D.; EDGAR M. DA CUNHA, S.D.V., D.D.; JOHN W. FLESEY, S.T.D., D.D.; THOMAS A. DONATO, D.D.; MANUEL A. CRUZ, D.D.; Rev. Msgrs. JOHN E. DORAN, V.G.; ROBERT E. EMERY, J.C.L., M.A., V.G.; JOSEPH F. AMBROSIO, V.F.; MICHAEL A. ANDREANO, M.B.A.; RICHARD J. ARNHOLS, M.Div.; PAUL L. BOCHICCHIO, V.F.; EDWARD G. BRADLEY, S.T.L., M.A.; KEVIN M. HANBURY, Ed.D.; DAVID C. HUBBA; JOHN J. LAFERRERA; LEWIS V. PAPERA, V.F.; RONALD J. ROZNIAK, V.E., P.A.; Very Revs. JOHN J. PALADINO, V.F.; MICHAEL G. WARD, V.F.; JOHN E. WASSELL, V.F.; Revs. JOSEPH A. D'AMICO; JOSEPH C. DOYLE; MICHAEL A. SAPORITO; JOSEPH A. FERRARO; JOHN D. GABRIEL, M.Div.; GEORGE D. GILLEN; JAMES M. MANOS; ROBERT B. STAGG; MARC A. VICARI, M.Div.

Archdiocesan Finance Council—LESLIE A. HYNES, Esq., Chm. Members: HENRY J. AMOROSO, Esq., Vice Chm.; ROBERT C. BUTLER; CHARLES C. CARELLA, Esq.; ANTHONY J. DENICOLA; Rev. Msgr. JOHN E. DORAN, V.G.; GEORGE FIORE, M.C.R.; WILLIAM C. FREDA, CPA; LINDA GRAVES; BRIAN D. MCAULEY; W. PETER MCBRIDE; JOSEPH MCSWEENEY; WILLIAM MUMMA; GERALD NOLAN; Ms. DENISE ROVER; Rev. Msgr. RONALD J. ROZNIAK, V.E., P.A.; GARRY J. SCHEURING; Ms. LIZA M. WALSH, Esq.

Priest Personnel Policy Board—Rev. Msgrs. JOSEPH A. PETRILLO, Archbishop's Liaison; WILLIAM J. FADROWSKI, Archbishop's Delegate. Ex Officio Members: Rev. Msgr. EDWARD G. BRADLEY, S.T.L., M.A.; Rev. STANLEY GOMES. Elected Members: Rev. Msgrs. JAMES A. BURKE (Retired); MICHAEL J. DESMOND; TIMOTHY J. SHUGRUE; DONALD E. GUENTHER (Retired); JOSEPH A. PETRILLO; JAMES M. CAFONE, S.T.D.; Revs. TIMOTHY G. GRAFF; BRYAN E. PAGE; CHARLES PINYAN; MICHAEL A. SAPORITO.

Diaconate Executive Committee—Deacon JOSEPH YANDOLI, Chm.

Archdiocesan Stewardship Advisory Committee—Deacon KENNETH DIPAOLA. Tel: 973-497-4332; Revs. LARRY EVANS; MICHAEL J. KREDER; JOHN J. GALEANO; Very Rev. JOHN M. MCCRONE, V.F.; Rev. Msgr. LAWRENCE J. MILLER; Rev. CHARLES PINYAN; Deacon NICHOLAS J. DELUCCA; Ms. EVEY JOHNSON; Ms. LYNN GULLY, Chair; Ms. CARLA REPOLLET; TROY JOSEPH SIMMONS, M.A., C.C.

New Energies - Archdiocesan Implementation Team—Most Rev. EDGAR M. DA CUNHA, S.D.V., D.D., Chm. & Regl. Bishop; Rev. Msgrs. JOHN E. DORAN, V.G.; WILLIAM C. HARMS (Retired). Tel: 973-497-4047; Fax: 973-497-4555. Members: Rev. KEVIN E. CARTER; Very Rev. JOHN E. WASSELL, V.F.; Sr. LINDA KLAISS, S.S.J.; Mrs. JENNIFER LEITNER; Mrs. GLADYS POZZA; Mr. MARK HOWARD; Sr. JOAN KURKOSKI, S.S.J.; Very Rev. Msgr. LEWIS V. PAPERA, V.F.

Archdiocesan Offices and Agencies

Office of the Archbishop—Fax: 973-497-4018.

Vice Chancellor, Secretary to the Archbishop and Director/Master of Ceremonies for Pontifical Liturgies—Rev. Msgr. MICHAEL A. ANDREANO, M.B.A. Tel: 973-497-4005.

Executive Assistant to the Archbishop—Mrs. ROSEANN BIASI-VAZQUEZ. Tel: 973-497-4006.

Assistant to the Archbishop for Public Affairs—Rev. Msgr. CHRISTOPHER J. HYNES, Ed.S. Tel: 973-497-4107.

Office of the Vicar General, Moderator of the Curia and Chancellor—Fax: 973-497-4525.

Executive Assistant to the Vicar General—LEOCADIA MATUSZCZAK, M.B.A. Tel: 973-497-4003; AMY BARR, Administrative Asst. to Regl. Bishop of Union County. Tel: 973-497-4010.

N.B. Dispensation requests or questions regarding canonical matters can be directed to Very Rev. Robert G. McBride, 171 Clifton Ave., Newark, NJ 07104-0500.

Office of Child and Youth Protection—Mr. JAMES GOODNESS, M.A., Coord. Review Bd. Tel: 973-497-4186; KAREN CLARK, Dir. Safe Environment Prog. Tel: 973-497-4012.

Victims Assistance Coordinator—WENDY PIERSON. Tel: 201-407-3256.

Advocate Publishing Corporation— Publisher of "The Catholic Advocate" (the Archdiocesan newspaper), "New Jersey Catolico" (Spanish language monthly), and Directory & Almanac Tel: 974-497-4200 Main Office; Fax: 973-497-4192. MICHAEL GABRIELE, Editor & Assoc. Publisher. Tel: 973-497-4193. Email: gabrielma@rcan.org; WARD MIELE, Mng. Editor. Tel: 973-497-4199. Email: mielejos@rcan.org; MARGE PEARSON-MCCUE, Dir. Advertising & Oper. Tel: 973-497-4201. Email: pearsoma@rcan.org.

Office of Banking and Investments—MATTHEW PHELAN, Dir. Tel: 973-497-4069; Fax: 973-497-4320. Email: phelanma@rcan.org.

Office of Black Catholic Affairs—Sr. PATRICIA LUCAS, D.H.M., Dir.

Campus Ministry—Rev. JAMES N. CHERN, Dir. Tel: 973-746-2323; Fax: 973-783-3313. Email: cernjam@comcast.net.

Catechetical Office—Mr. RONALD L. PIHOKKER, M.A., Dir. Tel: 973-497-4285.

Office of Catholic Cemeteries—Tel: 973-497-7981; Fax:

973-497-7984.

Cemeteries Office—Tel: 973-497-7981.

Mausoleum Office—Tel: 973-497-7988. ANDREW P. SCHAFER, Exec. Dir. Tel: 973-497-7975. Email: schafean@rcan.org.

Archdiocesan Cemeteries— COLONIA: St. Gertrude; MAHWAH: Maryrest; EAST HANOVER: Gate of Heaven; EAST ORANGE: Holy Sepulchre, St. Mary; FRANKLIN LAKES: Christ the King; JERSEY CITY: Holy Name, Saint Peter; NORTH ARLINGTON: Holy Cross; RIVER VALE: St. Andrew.

Parochial Cemeteries— NEWARK: Mount Olivet; BELLEVILLE: St. Peter's; BLOOMFIELD: Mount Olivet; CLARK: St. Mary's; FORT LEE: Madonna; HACKENSACK: St. Joseph's; HOHOKUS: St. Luke's; LINDEN: Mount Calvary; LYNDHURST: St. Joseph's; ORANGE: St. John's; PLAINFIELD: St. Mary's; SHORT HILLS: St. Rose of Lima; SUMMIT: St. Teresa's; TENAFLY: Mount Carmel; UPPER MONTCLAIR: Immaculate Conception.

Centro Guadalupe—547 35th St., Union City, 07087. Tel: 201-348-8400; Fax: 201-348-1809. Rev. ENRIQUE A. EGUIARTE, O.A.R., Dir. Email: njcentroguadalupe@hotmail.com.

Office of Clergy Personnel—Fax: 973-497-4219. Rev. Msgr. JOSEPH A. PETRILLO, Exec. Dir. Tel: 973-497-4222; CRISTINA PARDO, Administrative Asst. Tel: 973-497-4220.

Adjunct Clergy Personnel—Fax: 973-497-4180. Rev. STANLEY GOMES, Dir. Tel: 973-497-4374; ANNETTE CHIRICHELLA, Administrative Asst. Tel: 973-497-4220.

Continuing Education and Formation of Priests—Fax: 973-497-4180. Rev. DONALD K. HUMMEL, D.Min., Dir. Tel: 973-497-4218; ANNETTE CHIRICHELLA, Administrative Asst. Tel: 973-497-4225.

Office of the Permanent Diaconate—Revs. JAMES V. TETI, J.C.L., S.T.B., Dir. Selection & Deacon Formation, Annunciation, 50 W. Midland Ave., Paramus, 07652-2140. Tel: 201-261-6322; DONALD K. HUMMEL, D.Min., Assoc. Dir. Formation for the Permanent Diaconate. Tel: 973-497-4218; Deacon JOHN J. MCKENNA, Dir. Deacon Personnel. Tel: 973-497-4195; ANNETTE CHIRICHELLA, Administrative Asst. Tel: 973-497-4225.

Ministry to Retired Priests—Rev. Msgr. EDWARD G. BRADLEY, S.T.L., M.A., Dir., Seton Hall Preparatory, 11 Beverly Rd., West Orange, 07052. Tel: 973-669-9561.

Office of Communications and Public Relations—Mr. JAMES GOODNESS, M.A., Dir. Tel: 973-497-4186; Fax: 973-497-4185. Email: goodneja@rcan.org.

Office of Information Technology Services—ROBERT J. KENNELLY, Chief Technology Officer. Tel: 973-497-4161; Fax: 973-497-4277. Email: kennelro@rcan.org.

Office of Archdiocesan Counsel— Carella, Byrne, Cecchi, Olstein, Brody and Agnello, P.C., Archdiocesan Counsel. *5 Becker Farm Rd., Ste. 2, Roseland, 07068-1739.* Tel: 973-994-1700; Fax: 973-994-1744. CHARLES M. CARELLA, Esq., Counsellor-at-Law.

Delegate for Religious—Sr. JOANNE BEDNAR, S.C.C. Tel: 973-497-4582; Fax: 973-497-4219.

Office of Development—Ms. CARLA REPOLLET, Exec. Dir. Tel: 973-497-4127; Fax: 973-497-4031. Email: gonzalca@rcan.org.

Archbishop's Annual Appeal/Major Gifts—Ms. CARLA REPOLLET, Dir. Tel: 973-497-4127 Gen. Inquiries; 973-497-4129 Archbishop's Annual Appeal Inquiries.

Office of Planned Giving—Ms. LYNN GULLY, Assoc. Dir. Devel. Tel: 973-497-4589. Email: gullylyn@rcan.org; THERESA LYNCH, Coord. Devel. Tel: 973-497-4042. Email: lynchthe@rcan.org.

Parish Capital Campaigns—Deacon KENNETH DIPAOLA, Assoc. Dir. Tel: 973-497-4332. Email: dipaolke@rcan.org.

Stewardship and Special Projects—Ms. LYNN GULLY, Assoc. Dir. Tel: 973-497-4589. Email: gullylyn@rcan.org; Ms. CARMEN OLIVIO. Tel: 973-497-4046. Email: olivocar@rcan.org.

Office of Evangelization—Fax: 973-497-4317. Most Rev. EDGAR M. DA CUNHA, S.D.V., D.D., Vicar for Evangelization. Tel: 973-497-4318. Email: dacunhed@rcan.org; LILIANA SOTO-CABRERA, Coord. Evangelization. Tel: 973-497-4353. Email: sotolili@rcan.org.

Family Life Ministries—Fax: 973-497-4317. Rev. MARC A. VICARI, M.Div., Vicar for Family Life. Tel: 973-497-4324; NANCY DELLISANTI, Pre-Cana Reservations. Tel: 973-497-4328. Web: www.rcan.org/famlife/precana.htm (Pre-Cana registration online).

Ministry to the Bereaved, Separated, Divorced, Retrouvaille—JANET MCCORMICK, M.A., Assoc. Dir.; VACANT, Chap., Widows, Widowers & Bereaved. Tel: 973-497-4327.

Hispanic Family Life Ministries—YAMILKA GENAO, Assoc. Dir. Tel: 973-497-4326.

Couples for Christ—Rev. PAUL J. LEHMAN, Spiritual Dir. (Retired). Tel: 973-948-4546; SONNY AGUILING, Area Dir., CFC, NJ. Tel: 908-272-3867. Email: saguiling@comcast.net.

Focolare Movement (East Coast Regional Directors)—MARIGEN LOHLA; TERRY GUNN; MARIAPOLIS LUMINOSA, 200 Cardinal Rd., Hyde Park, NY 12538. Tel: 845-229-0230. Local Coordinators: JIM MILWAY; MARY JANE MILWAY. Tel: 973-726-6224. Web: www.rc.net/focolare.

Engaged Encounter Registration—LINDA ALEXANDER, Sec. Tel: 973-497-4323.

Worldwide Marriage Encounter—Tel: 800-823-5683. Newark Ecclesial Team: Very Rev. MICHAEL M. WALTERS, M.A., J.C.L., V.F.

Registration Couple—Tel: 800-823-LOVE. SYLVIA VASSALO; SAL VASSALO. Tel: 800-823-5683. Web: www.wwme.org.

Natural Family Planning—Chaircouple: DAMON OWENS; MELANIE OWENS. Tel: 973-497-4325. Email: nfp@rcan.org.

Office of Divine Worship—Fax: 973-497-4314. Revs. THOMAS A. DENTE, Dir. Tel: 973-497-4347; THOMAS B. IWANOWSKI, Assoc Dir. Parish Life. Tel: 973-497-4344; JOHN J. CHADWICK, S.T.D., Dir. R.C.I.A. Tel: 973-497-4346; JOAN M. CONROY, Coord. Tel: 973-497-4343; 973-497-4361 Book Orders; Rev. Msgr. CHARLES W. GUSMER, S.T.D., V.E., Liturgical Consultant (Retired). Tel: 973-239-7960; JOHN J. MILLER, Music Ministry. Tel: 973-497-4346; REGINA CHAMBERLAIN, Administrative Asst. Tel: 973-497-4345.

Office of Finance—Fax: 973-497-4033. Mr. JOSEPH PESCATORE, Fiscal Officer. Tel: 973-497-4560. Email: pescatjo@rcan.org; BEN CARADANG, Dir. Tel: 973-497-4054.

Hispanic Apostolate—Most Rev. MANUEL A. CRUZ, D.D., Vicar. Tel: 973-497-4009; Fax: 973-497-4525; Rev. JOSE I. GAMBA, Coord. Tel: 973-497-4335. Email: hisp_apost@rcan.org. Web: www.rcan.org/hispanic/.

Department of Human Concerns—Rev. TIMOTHY G. GRAFF, Dir. Tel: 973-497-4341; Fax: 973-497-4317. Email: grafftim@rcan.org.

Public Policy Committee of the New Jersey Catholic Conference—Rev. TIMOTHY G. GRAFF, Social Concerns Rep.

Office of Human Resources—Fax: 973-497-4103. Deacon JOHN J. MCKENNA, Exec. Dir. Tel: 973-497-4125. Email: mckennjo@rcan.org; DOUG MCGUIRK, Dir. Pensions & Benefits. Tel: 973-497-4095. Email: mcguirdo@rcan.org; RAMONA FLORES, Dir. Human Resources. Tel: 973-497-4026. Email: floresra@rcan.org; SERENA JOHNSON, Benefits Admin. Tel: 973-497-4092. Email: johnsosr@rcan.org; MARIA DEPAULA, Admin. & Technical Supvr. Tel: 973-497-4089. Email: depaulma@rcan.org.

Office Services/Mailroom—Tel: 973-497-4035 Mailroom. LUCIA LOPEZ, Oper. Supvr. Tel: 973-497-4045. Email: lopezluc@rcan.org; ELIZABETH MATOS, Supvr. Mailroom. Tel: 973-497-4035. Email: matoseli@rcan.org.

Metropolitan Tribunal— N.B. Dispensation requests or questions regarding canonical matters can be directed to Very Rev. Robert G. McBride, J.C.L. at 973-497-4145 or 171 Clifton Ave., Newark, NJ 07104. Very Rev. ROBERT G. MCBRIDE, J.C.L., V.F., Judicial Vicar; Rev. Msgrs. ROBERT E. EMERY, J.C.L., M.A., V.G., Adjutant Judicial Vicar. Tel: 973-497-4145; FRANK G. DEL PRETE, J.C.D., Special Del. of the Archbishop for Nuptial Matters.

Full-time Staff—Sr. CATHERINE MARY RAYMOND, F.S.P., J.C.L., Dir. Admin.

Archdiocesan Judges—Very Rev. JOHN J. CRYAN, V.F., M.Div.; Rev. JOSEPH A. D'AMICO; Rev. Msgrs. FRANK G. DEL PRETE, J.C.D.; ROBERT E. EMERY, J.C.L., M.A., V.G., Adjutant Judicial Vicar; ROBERT J. HARRINGTON, M.Div.; Very Rev. ROBERT G. MCBRIDE, J.C.L., V.F.; Revs. BERNARD N. MOHAN, B.S. (Retired); FRANK ROSE, M.Div.; ROBERT WOLFEE, M.Div.

Defenders of the Bond—Rev. Msgr. ROBERT S. MEYER ESQ., S.T.L., J.D., J.C.L.; Very Rev. MICHAEL M. WALTERS, M.A., J.C.L., V.F.; Rev. Msgr. DESMOND VELLA, J.C.D.; Sr. CATHERINE MARY RAYMOND, F.S.P., J.C.L.

Part-time Staff/Advocates/Procurators—Rev. BRYAN F.J. ADAMCIK; Very Rev. PAUL A. CANNARIATO, V.F.; Revs. MICHAEL FUGEE; GERALD F. GREAVES; RAPHAEL JOON YOUNG LEE; Deacons ANTHONY A. BALESTRIERI; WILLIAM A. BENEDETTO; MICHAEL J. KEARY; PAUL KLIAUGA; LUIS LORZA; DANIEL O'NEILL; JAMES P. TOBIN; NICHOLAS VALDEZ.

Notaries—SANDRA PERRINI; JOHN WALSH. Fax: 973-497-4138.

Secretarial Staff—ROSE MARIE FITZGERALD; NANCY I. NEGRON.

N.B. Dispensation requests or questions regarding canonical matters can be directed to Very Rev. Robert G. McBride, J.C.L. at 171 Clifton Ave., Newark, NJ 07104.

Ministerial Development Center—Very Rev. MICHAEL M. WALTERS, M.A., J.C.L., V.F., Dir. Tel: 973-497-4350; Fax: 973-497-4317. Email: waltermi@rcan.org.

Multicultural Affairs—Fax: 973-497-4555. Rev. Msgr. WILLIAM J. REILLY, V.F., Coord.

Brazilian Apostolate—Saint James, 143 Madison St., Newark, 07105. Tel: 973-344-8322. Rev. CLEMENT M. KRUG, C.Ss.R., Coord.

Chinese Apostolate—St. Peter College, 50 Glenwood Ave., Jersey City, 07306. Tel: 201-432-7399. Rev. MICHEL MARCIL, S.J., Coord.

Filipino Apostolate—St. John the Evangelist, 29 N. Washington Ave., Bergenfield, 07621. Tel: 201-384-0101. Rev. ERNESTO C. TIBAY, Coord.

Haitian Apostolate—Saint Leo, 103 Myrtle Ave., Irvington, 07111. Tel: 973-372-1272. Rev. Msgr. BEAUBRUN ARDOUIN, Coord.

Asian-Indian Apostolate—Saint Aloysius, 691 West Side Ave., Jersey City, 07304. Tel: 201-433-6365. Rev. THOMAS THOTTUNGAL, Coord.

Chaplain to the India Catholic Association (Syro-Malabar Rite)—Our Lady of Sorrows, 30 Madonna Pl., Garfield, 07026. Tel: 973-772-7889. Rev. JOY ALAPPATT, Coord.

Liaison to the Irish Community—Seton Hall Prep, 120 Northfield Ave., West Orange, 07052. Tel: 973-325-6624. Rev. Msgr. MICHAEL E. KELLY, M.A.

Italian Apostolate—Our Lady of Mount Carmel Rectory, 259 Oliver St., Newark, 07105. Tel: 973-589-2090. Rev. Msgr. JOSEPH F. AMBROSIO, V.F., Coord.

Korean Apostolate—St. Andrew Kim (Korean), 280 Parker Ave., Maplewood, 07040. Tel: 973-763-1170. Rev. MINHYUN CHO, Coord.

Nigerian IBO Catholic Community—Blessed Sacrament/Saint Charles Borromeo, 15 Van Ness Pl., Newark, 07108. Tel: 973-824-6548. Rev. Msgr. ANSELM I. NWAORGU, Ph.D., Coord.

Polish Apostolate—Rev. ANDRZEJ OSTASZEWSKI, Ph.D., Coord., St. Casimir, 164 Nichols St., Newark, 07105-2596. Tel: 973-344-2743.

Portugese Apostolate—Our Lady of Fatima, 403 Spring St., Elizabeth, 07201. Tel: 908-355-3810. Rev. JOSEPH E.S. DOS SANTOS, Coord.

Vietnamese Apostolate—Saint Michael Rectory, 252 Ninth St., Jersey City, 07302. Tel: 201-434-8500. Rev. JOSEPH MINH TRI NGUYEN, Coord.

Parish Business Services—NANCY F. LYSTASH, Exec. Dir. Tel: 973-497-4074; Fax: 973-497-4320. Email: lystasna@rcan.org.

Office of Parish Internal Audit—Fax: 973-497-4320. THERESE A. KROPP, Asst. Dir. Tel: 973-497-4073. Email: kroppter@rcan.org.

Office of Research and Planning—Mr. MARK HOWARD, Dir. Tel: 973-497-4024. Email: howard@rcan.org; PATRICIA RUSSILLO, Coord. Tel: 973-497-4027. Email: russilpa@rcan.org.

Pastoral Ministry with the Deaf—Fax: 973-497-4317. Deacon THOMAS SMITH, B.A., C.S.W., Dir. Tel: 973-497-4312; Teletype: 973-497-4311.

Pastoral Ministry with Persons with Disabilities—ANNE MASTERS, M.A., Dir. Tel: 973-497-4309; Fax: 973-497-4317.

Ministry to People on the Move—

Apostleship of the Air—Newark International Airport Chaplaincy, P.O. Box 2220, Newark, 07114. Tel: 973-961-0260. Rev. DAVID J. BARATELLI, Ed.D., Chap.

Apostleship of the Sea—Newark International Airport Chaplaincy, Stella Maris Chapel, 114 Corbin St., Port Newark, 07101. Tel: 973-589-7946. Revs. JOHN F. CORBETT, Dir.; ROBERT J. CIO, Chap.

Office of Property Management Administration—Fax: 973-497-4362. Mr. STEVEN BELLOISE, Exec. Dir. Tel: 973-497-4118.

The Heritage Tour—TROY JOSEPH SIMMONS, M.A., C.C., Patrimony Project Mgr. Tel: 973-497-4116.

Respect Life Office—1805 Penbrook Terr., Linden, 07036. Tel: 732-388-8211; Fax: 908-486-5345. Email: arnewrespect@sjanj.net. Rev. JOSEPH A. MEAGHER, Dir.; MICHELLE KRYSTOFIK, Assoc. Dir.

Risk Management, Insurance Services and Business Administration—Fax: 973-497-4313. JOSEPH A. FRANK, Exec. Dir. Tel: 973-497-4041. Email: frankjoe@rcan.org; DONNA M. WROBEL, Asst. Dir. Tel: 973-497-4044. Email: wrobeldo@rcan.org.

Office of the Superintendent of Schools/Vicariate for Education—Tel: 973-497-4260; Fax: 973-497-4249. Rev. Msgr. KEVIN M. HANBURY, Ed.D., Vicar for Educ. & Supt. Schools; Bro. RALPH DARMENTO, F.S.C., Deputy Supt. Schools; Sr. PATRICIA BUTLER,

S.C., M.A., Assoc. Supt. Elementary School Admin. Assistant Superintendents for Elementary Schools: Sisters PATRICIA BUTLER, S.C., M.A., Assoc. Supt. Elementary Admin. (Essex and Union Counties); MARIE GAGLIANO, M.P.F., M.A., Asst. Supt. (Hudson and Bergen).

Assistant Superintendent of Curriculum, Instruction and Assessment—Ms. BARBARA DOLAN. Directors: GLORIA CASTUCCI, M.A., Early Childhood; THOMAS HART, Ph.D., Educational Technology; Sr. LORETTA HOGAN, S.S.J., M.A., Elementary School Finance; Mrs. GRACE PIETROPINTO, B.S., Regl. High School Finance; MARY MCELROY, Esq., NJ Network of Catholic School Families; LAURA CRISTIANO, School Mktg.; Sr. ANNE KAVANAGH, R.D.C., Govt. Programs, Personnel & Events.

Child Nutrition Program—Fax: 973-497-4174. EVERETTE GEORGE, Child Nutrition Coord. Tel: 973-497-4164.

Vicar for Pastoral Life—Fax: 973-497-4317. Rev. Msgr. RICHARD J. ARNHOLS, M.Div. Tel: 973-497-4321; MARISA ACOSTA, Administrative Asst. Tel: 973-497-4013.

Vocations Office—Rev. JOHN D. GABRIEL, M.Div., Dir. Assistant Directors: Revs. JUAN CARLOS VARGAS; JOSE H. VICTORIA; Sr. THERESIA MARIA HOLTSCHLAG; BARBARA KELLY, Exec. Asst. Tel: 973-497-4365; Fax: 973-497-4369.

Emmaus House of Discernment—91 Washington St., Newark, 07102. Tel: 973-624-1301. Rev. JOHN D. GABRIEL, M.Div., Dir.

Youth and Young Adult Ministries—499 Belgrove Ave., Kearny, 07032. Tel: 201-998-0088; Fax: 201-299-0801. Web: www.newarkoym.com. Rev. TIMOTHY G. GRAFF, Pastoral Mod. Tel: 201-998-0088, Ext. 4142. Email: grafftim@rcan.org; THOMAS G. CONBOY, Dir. Youth & Young Adult Svcs. Tel: 201-998-0088, Ext. 4146. Email: conboyth@rcan.org; TRACEY VIEIRA, Assoc. Dir. AYRC Retreats & Spirituality. Tel: 201-998-0088, Ext. 4153; Sr. MARILYN MINTER, C.S.S.F., Assoc. Dir. Parish Outreach & Training.

CYO Retreat Center—499 Belgrove Dr., Kearny, 07032. Tel: 201-998-0088; Fax: 201-299-0801. JUDY FURKA, Facility Coord. Tel: 201-998-0088, Ext. 4148. Email: furkajud@rcan.org; LEANNE CHRISTMANN, Reservation Coord. Tel: 201-998-0088, Ext. 4145. Email: christle@rcan.org; DULCE BAUSA, Dir. Food Svcs. Tel: 201-998-0088, Ext. 4152. Email: dulcembausausa@aol.com; Mr. RICH DONOVAN, Coord. Special Events & Summer Camp Prog. (June-Aug.). Tel: 201-998-0088, Ext. 4155 (Special Events); 201-998-0088, Ext. 4150 (Summer Camp Prog.). Email: donovari@rcan.org.

Boy Scouts of America/Catholic Committee on Scouting—499 Belgrove Dr., Kearny, 07032. Tel: 201-998-0088; Fax: 201-299-0801. Web: www.newarkoym.com. Rev. EUGENE J. FIELD, Chap. Tel: 201-641-6464; Mr. RICH DONOVAN, Assoc. Dir. Tel: 201-998-0088, Ext. 4150. Email: donovari@rcan.org.

Archdiocesan Girl Scouts—Rev. TIMOTHY G. GRAFF, Chap. Tel: 973-497-4341; 201-998-0088, Ext. 4142. Email: grafftim@rcan.org; JUDY FURKA, Coord. Tel: 201-998-0088, Ext. 4148. Email: furkajud@rcan.org.

Catholic Health and Human Services

Catholic Health and Human Services Corporation—One Passaic St., Ridgewood, 07450. Tel: 201-444-2000.

Administration—Rev. Msgr. RONALD J. ROZNIAK, V.E., P.A., Chm. & CEO.

Catholic Charities of the Archdiocese of Newark—

Administration—590 N. 7th St., Newark, 07107. Tel: 973-266-4100; Fax: 973-596-4057. HENRY J. AMOROSO, Esq., Chm. Bd. of Trustees, HJA Strategies, LLC, 155 Polifly Rd., Hackensack, 07601. Tel: 201-487-6705; Fax: 201-343-5181; PHILLIP FRESE, Ph.D., CPA, Pres. & CEO, 590 N. 7th St., Newark, 07107. Tel: 973-596-4052; Ms. DEBRA A. GIARRAFFA, Exec. Asst. to CEO, 590 N. 7th St., Newark, 07107. Tel: 973-596-4052; Fax: 973-596-4057.

Catholic Charities of the Archdiocese of Newark—Main automated attendant number Tel: 973-596-4100. ALLAN J. DAUL, M.S.W., Exec. Dir. Tel: 973-596-4050; JOYCELYNN JORDAN, Asst. to Exec. Dir., 590 N. 7th St., Newark, 07107. Tel: 973-266-7989; Fax: 973-266-7950.

Mount Carmel Guild Behavioral Health System—PHILLIP FRESE, Ph.D., CPA, CEO. Tel: 973-596-4052; Fax: 973-596-4057; Ms. ELIZABETH A. MCCLENDON, L.C.S.W., A.C.S.W., Assoc. Exec. Dir. Tel: 973-266-7992; Fax: 973-596-4057; Ms. DEBRA A. GIARRAFFA, Asst. to Assoc. Exec. Dir., 590 N. 7th St., Newark, 07107. Tel: 973-596-4052; Fax: 973-596-4057.

Catholic Charities - Programs—

Children and Family Services Division—LESLEY MOORE, L.C.S.W., Dir., 249 Virginia Ave., Jersey City, 07304. Tel: 201-798-9957; Fax: 201-333-4425. *Children & Family Services Division Office*, RUTH CAPELLAN, 249 Virginia Ave., Jersey City, 07304. Tel: 201-798-9956; Fax: 201-333-4425. *Hudson YB*, D. KHALIL ODOM, 591 Summit Ave., Jersey City, 07306. Tel: 201-656-5101. Email: hudsonyb@gmail.com. *West Side Children's Counseling Center*, LESLEY MOORE, L.C.S.W., 249 Virginia Ave., Jersey City, 07304. Fax: 201-333-4425. *Intensive Family Support Services*, ISKRA GOMEZ, L.C.S.W., 249 Virginia Ave., Jersey City, 07304. Tel: 201-798-9925; Cell: 973-432-7346; Fax: 201-333-4211. *Intensive In-Community Family Services (PFC)*, SHELLEY STEINBERG, L.C.S.W., 249 Virginia Ave., Jersey City, 07304. Tel: 201-798-9921; Fax: 201-333-4211. *Intensive In-Home Family Counseling*, SHELLEY STEINBERG, L.C.S.W., 249 Virginia Ave., Jersey City, 07304. Tel: 201-798-9921; Fax: 201-333-4211. *Family and Adoption Services*, PATRICIA CHIARELLO, M.S.W., 499 Belgrove Dr., Kearny, 07032. Tel: 201-246-7378; Fax: 201-991-3771. *Hudson Mobile Response and Stabilization Services (MRSS)*, PATRICIA VALDIVIA, Prog. Mgr., 249 Virginia Ave., Jersey City, 07304. Tel: 201-798-7452; Cell: 973-418-1679; Fax: 201-333-4099. *Family Resource Center*, GILMA GARCIA, M.S.W., 249 Virginia Ave., Jersey City, 07304. Tel: 201-798-9904; 201-798-9900; Cell: 973-204-1109; Fax: 201-333-4211. *In-Home Hispanic Family Services, Child Protective Services*, DAWN GRAYER, L.S.W., 505 South Ave. E., Cranford, 07016. Tel: 908-497-3946; Fax: 908-276-1067. *School Social Services*, SHELLEY STEINBERG, L.C.S.W., 37 Evergreen Place, East Orange, 07018. Tel: 201-266-7983; Cell: 973-222-3159; Fax: 973-266-7970. *Strong Futures*, KATHY ELIAS, 511 Monastery Place, Union City, 07087. Tel: 201-864-2290; Cell: 973-868-7824; Fax: 201-770-1692. *Strong Futures Essex*, KATHY ELIAS, 481 Sanford Ave., Newark, 07106. Cell: 973-868-7824.

Workforce Development Division—KRISTIN RETLIN, Dir. Tel: 973-268-3162; VACANT, Office Mgr., 321 Central Ave., Newark, 07103. Tel: 973-268-3161; Fax: 973-350-0792.

Workforce Development - SAIF—JANICE STUBBS, 37 Evergreen Place, East Orange, 07018. Tel: 973-266-7984; Fax: 973-266-7990.

Workforce Development - Boland Training Center—MICHAEL MYERS, M.A., 321 Central Ave., Newark, 07103. Tel: 973-268-3163; Fax: 973-350-0790.

Workforce Development - Workshop—MADELINE DIEHL, 321 Central Ave., Newark, 07103. Tel: 973-268-3176; Fax: 973-350-0790.

Workforce Development - Cleaning Services—ELOISE WIGGS, 321 Central Ave., Newark, 07103. Tel: 973-268-3179; Fax: 973-350-0790; Cell: 973-204-7552.

Workforce Development - Hudson County—MARIA V. RODRIGUEZ, 2201 Bergenline Ave., Union City, 07087. Tel: 201-325-4800; Fax: 201-601-0490.

Displaced Homemaker - Hudson County—MARIA V. RODRIGUEZ, 2201 Bergenline Ave., Union City, 07087. Tel: 201-325-4800; Fax: 201-601-0490.

Supported Employment - Hudson County—HARRY FRAZIER, M.S.W., 2201 Bergenline Ave., Union City, 07087. Tel: 201-558-3789; Fax: 201-902-0656.

Housing Division—

St. Lucy's Single Person Shelter— (Men and Women). TOM JOHNSON, Prog. Coord. Tel: 201-653-3366, Ext. 222; Fax: 201-656-0412; THERESA M. CELESTE, Administrative Asst. to Div. Dir., 619 Grove St., Jersey City, 07310. Tel: 201-653-3366, Ext. 304; Fax: 201-653-3070.

Canaan House— (HIV/AIDS). LANCE KEARNY, Prog. Mgr., 389 Bergen Ave., Jersey City, 07304. Tel: 201-434-3967; Fax: 201-432-4223.

Franciska Residence— (HIV/AIDS). JAMES SMITH, Prog. Mgr., 615 Grove St., Jersey City, 07310. Tel: 201-653-3366, Ext. 302; Fax: 201-653-3070.

Hope House— (Women and Children). NANCY GONZALEZ, Prog. Mgr., 246 Second St., Jersey City, 07302. Tel: 201-420-1070; Fax: 201-420-1825.

St. Jude's Oasis—LAURIE CHERRY, Prog. Mgr., 612, 614, 616, 618 & 620 Grove St., Jersey City, 07310. Tel: 201-653-3366, Ext. 205; Fax: 201-418-8790; 201-656-0412.

St. Rocco's Family Residence— (Women and Children). GERALDINE COOLEY, Prog. Mgr., 368 S. 7th St., Newark, 07103. Tel: 973-286-4175; Fax: 973-242-4864.

Good Shepherd— (HIV/AIDS support services). ERNEST MCCULLOUGH, Prog. Mgr., 404 University Ave., Newark, 07102. Tel: 973-799-0484; Fax: 973-799-0486.

St. Bridget's Residence— (AIDS/HIV Support/ Outreach Center). ERNEST MCCULLOUGH, Prog. Mgr., 404 University Ave., Newark, 07102. Tel: 973-799-0484; Fax: 973-799-0486.

Adult Services Division—CLARE ELTON, L.S.W., C.A.L.A., Dir. Tel: 908-497-3938; JACKLYN MILONAS, Administrative Asst., 505 South Ave. E., Cranford, 07016. Tel: 908-497-4002; Fax: 908-709-9580.

Adult Protective Services—SUSAN HARRIGAN FOWLES, L.C.S.W., 505 South Ave. E., Cranford, 07016. Tel: 908-497-3932; Fax: 908-709-9580.

Bergen Care Management Program, Veteran's Assessment—TAMAR AULET, M.S., 415 Fifth Ave., River Edge, 07661. Tel: 201-265-3840, Ext. 226; Fax: 201-265-3809.

River Edge Social Day Care Center—KATARZYNA DEWARA, M.S.W., 415 Fifth Ave., River Edge, 07661. Tel: 201-265-3840, Ext. 224; Fax: 201-265-3809.

Engel Center— (Adult Social Day Care). LAGRETTA STEPHENS, 505 South Ave. E, Cranford, 07016. Tel: 908-497-3945; Fax: 908-709-9580.

Telephone Reassurance, Home Shopping Services, Hispanic Translation Services, Information and Referral, Visually Impaired Seniors Program—GABRIELA RICHTER, 505 South Ave. E., Cranford, 07016. Tel: 908-497-3950; Fax: 908-709-9580.

Hudson County, Visually Impaired Seniors Program—IVIS L. ALVAREZ, M.A., 2201 Bergenline Ave., Union City, 07087. Tel: 201-325-4811.

Hudson County Prevention, Information, and Education Services for Seniors (P.I.E.S. for Seniors)—KELLEY ROONEY, 505 South Ave. E., Cranford, 07016. Tel: 908-497-3953; Fax: 908-709-9580.

Hudson County Jail Substance Abuse Program—KELLEY ROONEY, 505 South Ave. E., Cranford, 07016. Tel: 908-497-3953; Fax: 908-709-9580.

Union County Jail— (Women's Substance Abuse Program, Ryan White HIV Discharge Planning Program & HIV Rapid Testing Program). KELLEY ROONEY, 505 South Ave. E., Cranford, 07016. Tel: 908-497-3953; Fax: 908-709-9580.

Immigration Assistance— Bishop Francis Center. REX CHEN, Mng. Attorney, 976 Broad St., Newark, 07102. Tel: 973-733-3516, Ext. 207; Fax: 973-733-9631; ALEXIA SCHAPIRA, Mng. Attorney. Tel: 973-733-3516, Ext. 229; Fax: 973-733-9631.

Community Access and Volunteer Services Division—CATHERINE L'INSALATA, M.S., C.S.W., Dir. Tel: 973-266-7978; PAMELA GRAHAM, Asst. to Dir., 37 Evergreen Place, East Orange, 07018. Tel: 973-266-7967; Fax: 973-676-0172.

Emergency Food and Nutrition Network—SHARON REILLY-TOBIN, B.A., C.S.W., Dir., 37 Evergreen Place, East Orange, 07018. Tel: 973-266-7966; Fax: 973-675-6935.

New Day Community—VINCENT MCMAHON, Ed.D., Dir. Tel: 201-998-8235; 973-763-6430.

Parish Access Centers— Information and Referral Tel: 800-227-7413.

Parish Access Center - Essex/Union County—ANDREW SMOLIN, 37 Evergreen Place, East Orange, 07018. Tel: 973-266-7991; Fax: 973-676-0172.

Parish Access Center - Hudson/Bergen County—CHAQUIRA VASQUEZ, 249 Virginia Ave., Jersey City, 07304. Tel: 201-798-9958; Fax: 201-333-4412.

Parish Access Center - Union County—GLORIA WIERZALIS, 505 South Ave. E., Cranford, 07016. Tel: 908-497-3966; Fax: 908-276-7185.

Catholic Campaign for Human Development—CATHERINE L'INSALATA, M.S., C.S.W., 37 Evergreen Place, East Orange, 07018. Tel: 973-266-7978; Fax: 973-676-0172.

Mount Carmel Guild Behavior Health System—590 N. Seventh St., Newark, 07107. PHILLIP FRESE, Ph.D., CPA, CEO. Tel: 973-596-4052; Fax: 973-596-4057; Ms. ELIZABETH A. MCCLENDON, L.C.S.W., A.C.S.W., Assoc. Exec. Dir. Tel: 973-266-7992; Fax: 973-596-4057; Ms. DEBRA A. GIARRAFFA. Tel: 973-596-4052; Fax: 973-596-4057; Mr. JOHN WESTERVELT, B.A., CFO. Tel: 973-596-3984; Fax: 973-412-7710; ELENA TORRES, Spanish Speaking. Tel: 973-266-7942.

Behavioral Health Services—SHEYLA MEJIAS, Essex County, 58 Freeman St., Newark, 07105. Tel: 973-596-3857; Fax: 973-596-3701; MARGERY A. GRIMM-DEFRANCO, L.R.C., Dir. Partial Care Svcs., 58 Freeman St., Newark, 07105. Tel: 973-596-3971; TOLA ASHIANOR, Hudson County, 2201 Bergenline Ave., Union City, 07087. Tel: 201-558-3726; AHYLAZBETH GIANNANTONIO, Hudson County, 2201 Bergenline Ave., Union City, 07087. Tel: 201-558-3726; JEANETTE VELLA, Union County, 108 Alden St., Cranford, 07016. Tel: 908-497-3982. *PACT (Program for Assertive Community Treatment)*, THOMAS RITTER, Dir. PACT/ICMS, 269 Oliver St., Newark, 07107.

Tel: 973-466-1348; Fax: 973-466-2715. *ICMS-Essex (Integrated Case Management Services-Essex County)*, DORIS BOYD, Ph.D., 269 Oliver St., Newark, 07105. Tel: 973-522-2125. *ICMS-Union (Integrated Case Management Services-Union County)*, ANGELA ROMANO-LUCKY, L.C.S.W., Mgr., 505 South Ave., E, Cranford, 07016. Tel: 908-497-2923; Fax: 908-709-9812. *Therapeutic Nursery Program - Bloomfield*, VACANT, Dir., 236 Hoover Ave., Bloomfield, 07003. Tel: 973-639-6501. *Therapeutic Nursery Program - Cranford*, VACANT, Dir., 505 South Ave., E., Cranford, 07016. Tel: 973-497-3916; Fax: 908-709-9612.

Mount Carmel Guild Schools Corporation—PHILLIP FRESE, Ph.D., CPA, CEO. Tel: 973-596-4052; ALLAN J. DAUL, M.S.W., Exec. Dir. Tel: 973-596-4050; 973-596-4100 (Main Office); JOYCELYNN JORDAN, Asst. to Mr. Daul, 590 N. 7th St., Newark, 07107. Tel: 973-266-7989; Fax: 973-266-7950.

Mount Carmel Guild Academy—JAMES BADAVAS, Prin., 100 Valley Way, West Orange, 07052. Tel: 973-325-4400, Ext. 106; Fax: 973-669-8450; SARA RIVERA, Administrative Asst. Tel: 973-325-4400, Ext. 100; CALLIE JOHNSON, Sec. Tel: 973-325-4400, Ext. 101. Program Coordinators: CATHERINE CRUZ. Tel: 973-325-4400, Ext. 135 (Autistic Prog.); ROUSSEL SIMON. Tel: 973-325-4400, Ext. 201.

Mount Carmel Guild School and Preschool—KATHARINE THORNTON, M.P.A., Prin., 236 Hoover Ave., Bloomfield, 07003. Tel: 973-639-6622; 973-639-6624; Fax: 973-639-6626; Cell: 201-913-0265; JOANIE D'ORSI, Sec.

Education Division—

Early Childhood Programs— (Child Study Services). LIZ DRISCOLL, Dir., 37 Evergreen Place, East Orange, 07018. Tel: 973-266-7951; Fax: 973-677-2572.

Mount Carmel Guild Little Schoolhouse—SHOMONE WHEELER, Prog. Mgr., 103-110 Third St., Elizabeth, 07206. Tel: 908-282-4610; 908-282-4611; Fax: 908-353-0437.

Mount Carmel Guild Cares—LAUREN PANETTA, Prog. Mgr., 594 N. 7th St., Newark, 07104. Tel: 973-497-7714; 973-497-7715; Fax: 973-497-0891.

Mount Carmel Guild Child Study Services—ADRIA GOLDENKRANTZ, Case Mgr. Tel: 973-266-7953; IVY ABRAHAM-HALL, Sec., 37 Evergreen Place, East Orange, 07018. Tel: 973-266-7952; Fax: 973-675-7389.

St. Valentine's Preschool—LIZ DRISCOLL, Dir. Tel: 973-266-7951; THERESA SMITH, 236 Hoover Ave., Bloomfield, 07003. Tel: 973-639-6622; Fax: 973-639-6626.

Commissions and Organizations

Bukas-Loob Sa Diyos Community (BLD) (Open to the Spirit of God)—Divine Mercy Parish, 232 Central Ave., Rahway, 07065. Tel: 973-856-8222. Rev. PAUL J. LEHMAN, Spiritual Dir. (Retired). District Servant Leaders: RICHARD DE LA FUENTE; LEE DE LA FUENTE. District Council of Stewards: RICHARD SANTIAGO; IRMA SANTIAGO; NOEL TRILLANA; LETTY TRILLANA; MON CHAN; BINGLE CHAN; MANNY SAN LUIS; JUDY SAN LUIS; OLLIE FELIBRICO; ANNIE FELIBRICO; FIL FLORES, Secretariat; HUM FLORES, Secretariat.

Charismatic Renewal—5808 Kennedy Blvd., West New York, 07093. Tel: 201-867-5535. Rev. PHILIP J. ROTUNNO, Coord. English & Multicultural Prayer Groups (Retired).

Archdiocesan Commission of Christian Unity—Revs. LUKE A. EDELEN, O.S.B., Chm. Tel: 973-643-4800; PHILIP F.A. LATRONICO, M.A., M.Div., Exec. Sec. Tel: 201-935-6492; Fax: 973-497-4317.

The Community of God's Love—70 W. Passaic Ave., Rutherford, 07070. ANDREW J. CEVASCO, Dir. Tel: 201-342-6000; Rev. PHILIP F.A. LATRONICO, M.A., M.Div., Chap. Tel: 201-935-6492.

Cursillo Movement—25 Perdue Ave., Oakland, 07436. Very Rev. THOMAS P. LIPNICKI, V.F., Spiritual Dir. Tel: 201-337-7596; PATRICK CARR, Lay Dir. Tel: 973-228-4493; JOANNE RINKUS, Cursillo Sec., 504 River Renaissance, East Rutherford, 07073. Tel: 973-249-0049.

Archdiocesan Commission for Interreligious Affairs—Revs. EUGENE P. SQUEO, J.D., Chm. Tel: 201-332-8600; PHILIP F.A. LATRONICO, M.A., M.Div., Exec. Sec. Tel: 201-935-6492.

Archdiocesan Commission on Justice and Peace—Rev. TIMOTHY G. GRAFF, Exec. Sec. Tel: 973-497-4341.

Archdiocesan Liturgical Commission—Rev. Msgr. GERARD H. MCCARREN, S.T.D., Chm. Tel: 973-497-4345. Members: Most Rev. MANUEL A. CRUZ, D.D.; Rev. Msgrs. BEAUBRUN ARDOUIN; KEVIN M. HANBURY, Ed.D.; RICHARD F. GRONCKI; CHARLES W. GUSMER, S.T.D., V.E. (Retired); JOSEPH P. MASIELLO, V.F.; Revs. THOMAS A. DENTE; JOSEPH A. MANCINI; MARC A. VICARI, M.Div.; CHARLES MILLER; CHARLES PINYAN; NEIL XAVIER O'DONOGHUE, Ph.D.; Deacon JOHN J. MCKENNA; Mr. RONALD L. PIHOKKER, M.A.; FRANK VALLICIERGO; MARY CLINTON; ANITA FOLEY; HOLLY LAWMASTER; JOHN J. MILLER; LILIANA SOTO-CABRERA.

Archdiocesan Liturgies for the Archdiocese of Newark—Rev. JOSEPH A. SCARANGELLA, Coord./ Master of Ceremonies.

Magnificat, A Ministry to Catholic Women—160 Jefferson Ave., Emerson, 07630. Tel: 201-262-1122. Email: grand174@aol.com. Very Rev. PAUL A. CANNARIATO, V.F., Spiritual Advisor; ELIZABETH TOBIN, Coord.; MELANIE SUTER, Asst. Coord.; PATRICIA PATTERMAN, Treas.; GAIL ARTOLA, Sec.

Commission for the Men's Apostolate—45 S. Springfield Ave., Springfield, 07081. Tel: 973-376-3044. Rev. Msgr. WILLIAM C. HATCHER, Chm.

Pontifical Mission Societies—

Propagation of the Faith; Society of St. Peter the Apostle; Holy Childhood Association; Missionary Union of Priests & Religious—Fax: 973-497-4371. Rev. MICHAEL FUGEE, Dir. Tel: 973-497-4375; Sr. ARLINE ZURICH, O.S.B., Mission Mod. for Holy Childhood Assoc. Tel: 973-497-4376.

Archdiocesan Pro-Life Commission—1805 Penbrook Terr., Linden, 07036. Tel: 732-388-8211. JAMES SONDEY, Chm.

Renew International—1232 George St., Plainfield, 07062-1717. Tel: 908-769-5400; Fax: 908-769-5660. Email: renew@renewintl.org. Web: www.renewintl.org; www.parishlife.com; www.whycatholic.org; www.campusrenew.org; www.renewtot.org. Rev. Msgr. THOMAS A. KLEISSLER, Pres. Emeritus (Retired); Sisters THERESA RICKARD, O.P., D.Min., Pres. & Exec. Dir.; KATHLEEN (KASS) COLLINS, S.F.C.C., Pastoral Svc. Team; HONORA NOLTY, O.P., Dir. Pastoral Svcs. & Asst. Dir.; EILEEN CARMODY, P.B.V.M., Human Resources Admin.; Dr. LAURA ZANE KOLMAR, Asst. Dir. Pastoral Svcs.; MARY BETH ORIA, Dir. Business Oper.; DEIRDRE TRABERT MALACREA, Dir. Mktg. & Communications; Sr. MARY MCGUINNESS, O.P., Special Projects Coord.; RICHARD MICHALOWSKI, Finance Controller; Mr. PETER DENIO, New Project Coord.; Mr. GREG KREMER, Special Asst. to Exec. Dir.; Ms. KATHLEEN OGLE, Mng. Editor.

Pastoral Services Team—Sisters MAUREEN COLLEARY, F.S.P.; KATHLEEN (KASS) COLLINS, S.F.C.C.; MARIE COOPER, S.J.C.; JUAN RAMON CORDOVA; Sr. MARENID FABRE, O.P.; ALMA GARCIA; MANUEL HERNANDEZ; Rev. ALEJANDRO LOPEZ-CARDINALE; Sr. VERONICA MENDEZ, R.C.D.; ANNE SCANLAN; Sr. PAT THOMAS, O.P.

Archdiocesan Council of Catholic Women (N.C.C.W.)—Tel: 973-497-4356; Fax: 973-497-4317. D. JEAN SCHNEIDER, Pres. Email: d.jeansch@juno.com; MARY R. LOFTUS, Immediate Past Pres. & Recording Sec., 263 Concord Dr., Paramus, 07652. Tel: 201-265-2048; BEATRICE MAHR, First Vice Pres.; MARGARET HENDERSON, Second Vice Pres. Tel: 908-688-2228; ADELE CICCONE, Treas. Tel: 201-939-7639.

District Moderators and Officers—CLARINDA BRUECK, Pres. Bergen-Hackensack. Tel: 201-939-3855; MARY R. LOFTUS, Pres. Bergen-Paramus. Tel: 201-967-7614; ETTA MARIE RIZZUTO, Pres. Essex-Suburban. Tel: 973-676-4725; FRANCES DONNELLY, Contact-Union County. Tel: 908-688-1032.

Archdiocesan Women's Commission—PAMELA MUELLER-SWARTZEBERG, Chm.; LORETTA LOVELL, Administrative Asst. Tel: 973-497-4010. Members: ANN BURGMEYER; MARTA CABRERA; MARY ELAINE CONNELL; ANNA GROVES; CATHERINE L'INSALATA, M.S., C.S.W.; Sr. MARGARET T. MCGOVERN, O.P.; CHRISTINE FLAHERTY; HOLLY LAWMASTER; LILIANA SOTO-CABRERA; NIVEDITA SRINIVAS.

Miscellaneous Organizations in the Archdiocese

Affirmative Action—5 Becker Farm Rd., Roseland, 07068. Tel: 973-994-1700. CHARLES M. CARELLA, Esq., Counselor at Law, Officer.

Archdiocesan/University Archives—Seton Hall University, Walsh Library, 400 S. Orange Ave., South Orange, 07079. Tel: 973-761-9476; Fax: 973-761-9550. Rev. Msgr. FRANCIS R. SEYMOUR, Archdiocesan Archivist. Tel: 973-761-9126. Email: seymoufr@shu.edu; ALAN DELOZIER, University Archivist. Tel: 973-275-2378. Email: delozial@shu.edu; Dr. KATHLEEN DODDS, Archival Asst. Tel: 973-761-9476. Email: doddskat@shu.edu.

Censores Librorum—Rev. Msgrs. JAMES M. CAFONE, S.T.D., Chm.; EDWARD J. CIUBA (Retired); CHARLES W. GUSMER, S.T.D.; GERARD H. MCCARREN, S.T.D.; JOSEPH R. REILLY, S.T.L., Ph.D.; C. ANTHONY ZICCARDI, S.T.L., S.S.L.; Revs. DONALD E. BLUMENFELD, Ph.D.; JOHN S. GRIMM, S.T.L., J.D.; THOMAS G. GUARINO, S.T.D., K.H.S.; MARK FRANCIS O'MALLEY, Hist.Eccl.D.; LAWRENCE B. PORTER, Ph.D., K.H.S.

Holy Name Federation—1805 Penbrook Terr., Linden, 07036. Tel: 908-486-6363. Rev. Msgr. JOHN J. LAFERRERA, Essex-West Hudson County Dir.; Revs. RICHARD J. CARRINGTON, Hudson County Dir.; JOSEPH G. SHEEHAN, Union County Dir. (Retired).

Legion of Mary—

Archdiocese of Newark Commitium—St. Michael's Church, 172 Broadway, Newark, 07104. Tel: 973-484-7100.

Bergen County Curia—Our Lady of the Most Holy Eucharist Curia of Bergen County. VACANT, Spiritual Dir.

Hispanic Curia of Essex and Union Counties—St. John Church, 94 Ridge St., Orange, 07050. Rev. CARLOS M. VIEGO, Spiritual Dir.

Hispanic Curia of Hudson County—Rev. FELIPE LOPEZ, Dir. (Retired), St. Paul the Apostle, 14 Greenville Ave., Jersey City, 07305. Tel: 201-433-8500, Ext. 22; Fax: 201-433-9886.

Maria Immaculata Curia of Hudson County—St. John Vianney Residence, 60 Home Ave., Rutherford, 07070. Tel: 201-933-5155. VACANT, Spiritual Dir.

Our Lady, Gate of Heaven Curia (Korean)—257 Central Ave., Orange, 07050. Tel: 973-672-6650. Rev. Msgr. AUGUSTIN C. PARK, Spiritual Dir. (Retired).

Mary Most Humble Curia (Korean)—VACANT, Spiritual Dir.

Our Lady Mother of God Curia (Korean)—Church of Korean Martyrs, 595 Saddle River Rd., Saddle Brook, 07663. Tel: 201-703-0080. Rev. Msgr. AUGUSTIN C. PARK, Spiritual Dir. (Retired).

New Jersey Historical Records Commission—Most Rev. DOMINIC A. MARCONI, D.D., Chm. (Retired); JOSEPH F. MAHONEY, Ph.D., Dir., Seton Hall University, Fahy Hall, 400 South Orange Ave., South Orange, 07079. Tel: 973-275-2773.

Our Lady of Fatima First Saturday Family—(Ministry to the Disabled) Revs. PETER J. PALMISANO, Chap., Our Lady of Mount Virgin Rectory, 188 MacArthur Ave., Garfield, 07026. Tel: 973-772-2295; KEVIN E. CARTER, Chap., Saint Nicholas Rectory, 122 Ferry St., Jersey City, 07307. Tel: 201-659-5354.

Pastoral Association for Music & Liturgy—Mr. ANDREW CYR.

Serra Clubs—GEORGE KINGSTON, Regl. Representative, 12 Stonegate Dr., Mount Holly, 08060; ANTHONY ORTWEIN, Deputy Regl. Representative, 755 Johnston Dr., Bethlehem, PA 18017; JOSEPH PAGANO, Governor, District 22, 469 Teal Pl., Secaucus, 07094.

Serra Club of Bergen County—Dr. MARY NORTON, 116 Boston Ave., North Arlington, 07031; Rev. JOSEPH M. QUINLAN, Chap. (Retired).

Serra Club of the Oranges—ROSE MARIE DEEHAN, 331 S. Ridgewood Rd., South Orange, 07079; Rev. THOMAS P. NYDEGGER, Ed.D., M.Div., Chap.

Serra Club of Union County West—Co Presidents: JOSEPH DUNA, 139 Stoneridge Rd., New Providence, 07974. Tel: 908-289-7979; JOHN SALVO, 139 Stoneridge Rd., New Providence, 07974. Tel: 908-289-7979; Rev. ALEX PINTO, Chap.

Serra Club of West Essex—DAVID O'BOYLE, 45 Musano Ct., West Orange, 07052. Tel: 973-669-8007; Rev. DANIEL A. DANIK, Chap. (Retired).

Serra Club of North Essex—Rev. WARD P. MOORE (Retired), St. Thomas More Parish, Fairfield, 07004; NEIL PAGANO, Pres. Tel: 973-227-4689.

Serra Club of Hudson County—ROBERT P. HAGGERTY, Esq. Tel: 201-437-6674; Rev. Msgr. LAWRENCE J. MILLER, Chap.

The Scholarship Fund for Inner City Children—Fax: 973-497-4282. GERARD O'CONNOR, Exec. Dir. Tel: 973-497-4579. Email: oconnoge@rcan.org; NANCY LOZANO, Database Mgr. Email: lozanono@rcan.org; MARY FLANNERY, Finance Asst. Tel: 973-497-4281; SYLVIA MORGADO, C.S.F., Prog. Admin. Tel: 973-497-4581.

Archdiocesan School Council Membership Roster—Mrs. DONNA J. BABOULIS, Esq., Pres.; Mrs. ELLEN SHORT, Vice Pres.; Bro. RALPH DARMENTO, F.S.C., Deputy Supt. of Schools Liaison to Council; Mrs. KAY GRUSENSKI, Sec. Members: Mrs. ROSE BRIZAN; Mrs. PATRICIA DRIMONES; Dr. MADELYN M. HEALY; Mr. JAMES MCKENNA; Mr. KEVIN LYONS; Ms. AGATHA NIEMIEC; Mr. LOUIS PANICO; Ms. PAULA FRANZESE ROSELLA ESQ.; Mr. STEPHEN BROWN; Mr. MARK DEMO; Ms. SUSAN HUGHES; Mr. MICHAEL CORCORAN; Mrs. ADRIANA MYSLIWIEC, Esq.; Mrs. LAURIE GIBNEY; Mrs. ALICEA SKINNER.

University Heights Property Co., Inc.—Tel: 973-690-3606; Fax: 973-690-3601.

Cathedral Affiliated Group at Orange, Inc.—Tel: 973-690-3606; Fax: 973-690-3601.

CLERGY, PARISHES, MISSIONS AND PAROCHIAL SCHOOLS

CITY OF NEWARK

1—CATHEDRAL BASILICA OF THE SACRED HEART (1898) Most Rev. Manuel A. Cruz, Rector; Revs. Yunior Almonte-Mendez, Parochial Vicar; Joseph A. Mancini, Coord. & Master of Ceremonies for Archdiocesan Liturgies; Joseph A. Scarangella, Assoc. Coord. & Master of Ceremonies for Archdiocesan Liturgies; Deacons Thomas DeBenedictis; Michael J. Keary; Guy W. Mier; Eduardo Pons; Craig Stewart; John J. Miller, Dir. Music. In Res., Most Rev. John J. Myers; Rev. Msgrs. John E. Doran; Michael A. Andreano.
Res.: 89 Ridge St., 07104. Tel: 973-484-4600; Fax: 973-483-8253. Web: www.cathedralbasilica.org.
Catechesis/Religious Program—Sr. Ana Josefa Fa jardo, D.R.E.
Convent—Sacred Heart Convent, 109 Parker St., 07104. Tel: 973-484-1516.

2—ST. ALOYSIUS (1877) Revs. Paulo Frade; Elky Reyes Pichardo.
Res.: 66 Fleming Ave., 07105. Tel: 973-344-4736; Fax: 973-522-1169.
Catechesis/Religious Program—Students 168.

3—ST. ANN (1886) Merged with St. Rocco's, Newark to form The Parish of the Transfiguration, Newark.

4—ST. ANTONINUS (1875) Rev. William J. Halbing; Deacon Rajgopal K. Srinivasa; Gerard Cleffi, Pastoral Assoc. In Res., Rev. Paul J. Lehman, Pastor Emeritus (Retired).
Res.: 337 South Orange Ave., 07103. Tel: 973-623-0258; Fax: 973-623-0694. Email: st_antoninus@msn.com.
Catechesis/Religious Program—Students 16.

5—ST. AUGUSTINE'S (1874), (German), Rev. Luis O. Gonzalez, Admin.
Church Office: P.O. Box 7126, 07107. Tel: 973-482-1817; Fax: 973-482-1817.
Convent—Sisters Missionaries of Charity, 168 Sussex Ave., 07103. Tel: 973-483-0165. Sr. M. Regi Paul, M.C., Local Supr.
Soup Kitchen and Women's Shelter Queen of Peace—170 Sussex Ave., 07103. Tel: 973-481-9056.
Catechesis/Religious Program—Students 60.

6—ST. BENEDICT'S (1854) Revs. Manoel J. Oliveira; Mate Skublics. In Res., Rev. Javier Losarcos (Retired).
Res.: 65 Barbara St., 07105. Tel: 973-589-7930; Fax: 973-589-3665. Web: www.saintbenedictnewark.org.
See Ironbound Catholic Academy, Newark under St. Casimir's, Newark for details.
Catechesis/Religious Program—Students 125.

7—BLESSED SACRAMENT-ST. CHARLES BORROMEO (1905), (African American), Rev. Msgr. Anselm I. Nwaorgu; Rev. Longinus N. Ugwuegbulem; Deacon Emeruwa Anyanwu.
Res.: 15 Van Ness Pl., 07108. Tel: 973-824-6548; Fax: 973-624-6030. Web: www.bssc.fatcow.com.
Catechesis/Religious Program—Email: bsscbchurch@yahoo.com. Web: www.bsscbchurch.com. Students 25.

8—ST. BRIDGET'S (1887) Merged with St. Patrick's Pro-Cathedral. Records located at St. Patrick's, Newark. Tel: 973-623-0497.

9—ST. CASIMIR'S (1908), (Polish), Rev. Andrzej Ostaszewski.
Res.: 164 Nichols St., 07105-2596. Tel: 973-344-2743; Fax: 973-344-8182. Email: stcrectory@stcasimirrcc.com.
School—Ironbound Catholic Academy (1910), Serves St. Benedict's, St. Casimir's, Immaculate Heart of Mary, St. James, and Our Lady of Mt. Carmel, Newark., 380 E. Kinney St., 07105. Tel: 973-589-0108; Fax: 973-589-0239. Mrs. Elge Sausaitiene, Prin. Lay Teachers 13; Students 184.
Catechesis/Religious Program—Tel: 973-743-6285. Maria Murano, D.R.E. Students 20.

10—ST. CHARLES BORROMEO'S (1910) Merged with Blessed Sacrament. Records located at Blessed Sacrament, Newark. Tel: 973-824-6548.

11—ST. COLUMBA'S (1869), (Hispanic), Revs. Luis O. Gonzalez; Andres Codoner Contell, Parochial Vicar.
Res.: 25 Thomas St., 07114. Tel: 973-622-7712; Fax: 973-504-8075. Email: scolumba@verizon.net. Web: www.stcolumbanewark.com.
Catechesis/Religious Program—Dr. Mercedes Valle, D.R.E. Students 190.
Convent—Sisters of Charity, 7 South St., 07102. Tel: 973-622-7325.

12—ST. FRANCIS XAVIER (1914) [JC] Very Rev. Jan Sasin; Revs. Cayetano Moncada Laguado; Dieuseul Adain (Haiti).
Res.: 243 Abington Ave., 07107-2598. Tel: 973-482-8410; Fax: 973-485-7471. Email: xavier571@hotmail.com.
School—(1924), (Grades PreK-8), 594 N. Seventh St., 07107. Tel: 973-482-9410; Fax: 973-482-2466. Sr. Clare Ricciardelli, M.P.F., Prin. Maestre Pie Filippini (Religious Teachers Filippini) 1; Lay Teachers 12; Students 200.
Catechesis/Religious Program—Sr. Clare Ricciardelli, M.P.F., D.R.E. Students 227.
Convent—Tel: 973-484-5200.

13—HOLY TRINITY (1901), (Lithuanian), Merged with Epiphany, Newark. Sacramental records located at Holy Trinity - Epiphany, Newark.

14—HOLY TRINITY - EPIPHANY (1992), (Portuguese), Rev. Msgr. Joseph F. Ambrosio, Admin.
Rectory—Holy Trinity - Epiphany, 207 Adams St., 07105. Tel: 973-491-9761; Fax: 973-344-5641.
Catechesis/Religious Program—Students 120.

15—IMMACULATE CONCEPTION (1925), (Italian), Revs. Juan Carlos Zapata; Marco Pacciana.
Office & Res.: 654 Summer Ave., 07104. Tel: 973-482-0619; Fax: 973-482-8257. Web: olgc-ic.org.
Catechesis/Religious Program—Mariana Villegas, D.R.E. Students 87.

16—IMMACULATE HEART OF MARY (1926), (Spanish), Revs. Luis A. Vargas, T.O.R. (Peru); Lucio M. Nontol, T.O.R. (Peru), Parochial Vicar; Deacon Miguel Loperena.
Res.: 202 Lafayette St., 07105. Tel: 973-589-8249; Fax: 973-589-1858. Email: heart.of.mary@verizon.net.
See Ironbound Catholic Academy, Newark under St. Casimir's, Newark for details.
Catechesis/Religious Program—Students 125.

17—ST. JAMES (1854), (Brazilian—Portuguese), Revs. Clement M. Krug, C.Ss.R.; Gerard Oberle, C.Ss.R.; Celso Martins Jr., C.Ss.R.; Karl Esker, C.Ss.R.
Parish Center & Mailing Address: 142 Jefferson St., 07105. Tel: 973-344-8322; Fax: 973-344-6158. Email: saintjamesrc@optonline.net. Web: www.stjameschurchrc.com.
See Ironbound Catholic Academy, Newark under St. Casimir's, Newark for details.
Rectory—143 Madison St., 07105.
Catechesis/Religious Program—Sr. Hilaria de Oliveira, O.S.F., D.R.E. Students 53.

18—ST. JOHN'S (1826) Rev. Msgr. Neil J. Mahoney; Barbara Maran, Pastoral Assoc.; Vincent Smith, Parish Mgr. In Res., Revs. Clement Kagoma; Thomas A. Orians, S.A.
Res.: 22 Mulberry St., P.O. Box 200147, 07102. Tel: 973-623-0822; Fax: 973-623-6804. Email: info@njsoupkitchen.org. Web: www.njsoupkitchen.org.
Chapel—St. John's Chapel Gateway I, 07102.

19—ST. JOSEPH'S (1850) Closed. Sacramental records located at the Archives, Walsh Library, Seton Hall University, South Orange. Tel: 973-761-9476; Fax: 973-761-9550.

20—ST. LUCY'S (1891), (Italian), Rev. Luigi Zanotto, M.C.C.J.; Rev. Msgr. Joseph J. Granato, Pastor Emeritus (Retired); Revs. Provvido Crozzoletto, M.C.C.J.; Paul Donohue, M.C.C.J.; John Michael Converset, M.C.C.J.; Deacon Simplice Ahoua.
Res.: 118 Seventh Ave., 07104. Tel: 973-482-6663; Fax: 973-482-6575. Email: stlucysnwk@yahoo.com. Web: www.saintlucy.net.
Catechesis/Religious Program—Tel: 973-482-6663; Fax: 973-482-6575. Alba Rose Colucci, D.R.E. Students 196.
Comboni Missionaries of the Heart of Jesus (Verona Fathers)—

21—ST. MARY MAGDALENE (1893) Closed. Sacramental records located at the Archives, Walsh Library, Seton Hall University, South Orange. Tel: 973-761-9476; Fax: 973-761-9550.

22—ST. MARY'S (1842), (Newark Abbey Church) Very Rev. Philip J. Waters, O.S.B.; Rev. Linus V. Edogwo (Nigeria); Sr. Linda Klaiss, S.S.J., Pastoral Assoc.; Mr. Ambrose Amoakoh, Pastoral Min.
Res.: 528 Martin Luther King, Jr. Blvd., 07102. Tel: 973-792-5793; Fax: 973-643-6922. Email: pwaters@sbp.org. Web: www.smpnewark.org.
School—Tel: 973-792-5749; Fax: 973-286-3873. Sr. Teresa Shaw, S.S.J., Prin. Sisters of St. Joseph of Chestnut Hill 3; Lay Teachers 16; Students 200.
Catechesis/Religious Program— Sr. Linda Klaiss, S.S.J., D.R.E. Students 80.

23—ST. MICHAEL'S (1878) Revs. Antonio L. da Silva, S.D.V. (Brazil); Javier Flores, S.D.V. (Venezuela); Babu Thelappilly, S.D.V. (India); Deacons Daniel Ravelo; Restituto Quintana; Cecilio S. Polanco; Miguel Figueroa; Jose A. Negron.
Res.: 25 Crittenden St., 07104. Tel: 973-484-7100; Fax: 973-482-7209. Email: smc172broadway@yahoo.com. Web: www.saintmichaelparish.com.
School—(1881) 27 Crittenden St., 07104. Tel: 973-482-7400; Fax: 973-482-1833. Web: www.stmichaelnwkpenguins.com. Linda C. Cerino, Prin. Sisters of St. Martha 4; Lay Teachers 24; Students 475.
Perpetual Help Day Nursery—170 Broad St., 07104. Tel: 973-484-3535; Fax: 973-484-2526. Vocationist Sisters 7; Lay Teachers 13; Children 140.
Catechesis/Religious Program—Tel: 973-482-1109; Fax: 973-482-7209. Sr. Joy Sabesaje, S.D.V., D.R.E. Students 300.
Convent—Tel: 973-484-5261 (Sisters of St. Martha); 973-484-3535 (Vocationist Sisters).

24—OUR LADY OF FATIMA (1956), (Portuguese), Revs. Antonio F. DaSilva; Antonio Nuno Rocha; Deacon Albino P. Marques.
Res.: 82 Congress St., 07105. Tel: 973-589-8433; Fax: 973-589-2611.
See Ironbound Catholic Academy, Newark under St. Casimir's, Newark for details.
Day Nursery—79 Jefferson St., 07105. Tel: 973-589-1639.
Catechesis/Religious Program—Mary Jo Branco, D.R.E. Students 4.

25—OUR LADY OF GOOD COUNSEL (1902) Revs. Juan Carlos Zapata; Marco Pacciana; Deacon Jose Rodriguez. In Res., Rev. Owen F. Ince; Very Rev. John F. Connor (Retired).
Res.: 654 Summer Ave., 07104. Tel: 973-482-1274; Fax: 973-482-8257. Web: olgc-ic.org.
See Christ the King Preparatory School of Newark, N.J., Corp. in the Institution Section under High Schools, Private for details.
Catechesis/Religious Program—Mariana Villegas, D.R.E. Students 215.

26—OUR LADY OF MT. CARMEL (1889), (Italian), Rev. Msgr. Joseph F. Ambrosio; Rev. Anthony Forte, Parochial Vicar.
Res.: 259 Oliver St., 07105. Tel: 973-589-2090; Fax: 973-589-2662. Email: mtcarmel259@optonline.net. Web: www.ourladyofmtcarmelnewark.e-paluch.com.
See Ironbound Catholic Academy, Newark under St. Casimir's, Newark for details.
Catechesis/Religious Program—Regina Oliveira, D.R.E. Students 30.

27—OUR LADY OF THE ROSARY (1918), (Italian), Closed. For inquiries for parish records contact Our Lady of Mt. Carmel, Newark. Tel: 973-589-2090.

28—THE PARISH OF THE TRANSFIGURATION (2005) Rev. Josephat Kato Kalema (Uganda), Admin.; Deacons Justo Rodriguez; Cesar A. Ortega-Escobar.
103 16th Ave., 07103. Tel: 973-642-4217; 973-824-1652; Fax: 973-824-4944. In Res., Revs. Patrick Nsionu; Augustine Odimmeywua.
Catechesis/Religious Program—Rev. Patrick Nsionu, D.R.E. Students 60.

29—ST. PATRICK'S PRO-CATHEDRAL (1848) Rev. Msgr. Neil J. Mahoney; Deacon Leonides Aponte; Vincent Smith, Parish Mgr.
Mailing Address: 91 Washington St., 07102.
Res.: 39 Bleeker St., 07102. Tel: 973-623-0497; Fax: 973-623-2030. Email: evelydjss@aol.com.
Catechesis/Religious Program—Students 28.

30—ST. PETER'S (1864) Closed. Sacramental records located at the Archives, Walsh Library, Seton Hall University, South Orange. Tel: 973-761-9476; Fax 973-761-9550.

31—ST. PHILIP NERI (1887) Closed. Sacramental records located at the Archives, Walsh Library, Seton Hall University, South Orange. Tel: 973-761-9476; Fax 973-761-9550.

32—QUEEN OF ANGELS (1930), (African American), Close. Sacramental records are located at St. Augustine parish, P.O. Box 7126, Newark, Tel: 973-482-1817., 40 Irvine Turner Blvd., 07103.
School—40 Irvine Turner Blvd., 07103. Tel: 973-642-1531; Fax: 973-622-0472. Everlyn V. Hay, Prin. Lay Teachers 11; Students 150.
Catechesis/Religious Program—Tel: 973-372-4992; Fax: 973-642-1610. Students 15.

33—ST. ROCCO'S (1899) Merged with St. Ann, Newark to form The Parish of the Transfiguration, Newark.

34—ST. ROSE OF LIMA (1888) Rev. Msgr. William J. Linder; Rev. Robert J. Cormier, Parochial Vicar; Sr. Angela Mercedez, Pastoral Assoc.; Ms. Madge Wilson, Pastoral Outreach.
Res.: 11 Gray St., 07107. Tel: 973-482-0682; Fax: 973-482-2137. Email: linder@newcommunity.org.
Catechesis/Religious Program—Sr. Pauline Echebiri, D.R.E. Students 217.
Convent—Tel: 973-268-9782; 973-481-6717.

35—SACRED HEART (Vailsburg) (1892) Closed. For inquiries for parish records contact the chancery.

36—ST. STANISLAUS (1889), (Polish), Rev. Bogumil Chrusciel.
Res.: 146 Irvine Turner Blvd., 07103. Tel: 973-642-7961; Fax: 973-642-2295. Email: ststannk@optonline.net.
Catechesis/Religious Program—

37—ST. STEPHEN'S (1902) Closed. Sacramental records located at the Archives, Walsh Library, Seton Hall University Archives, South Orange. Tel: 973-761-9476; Fax: 973-761-9550.

38—ST. THOMAS AQUINAS (1957), (Hispanic), Rev. Raul E.L. Comesanas; Deacon Mario Eschavarria.
Res.: 40 Ludlow St., 07114. Tel: 973-242-6703; Fax:

973-242-7143.
Catechesis/Religious Program—Ms. Madeline Santiago, D.R.E. Students 65.

OUTSIDE THE CITY OF NEWARK

ALLENDALE, BERGEN CO., GUARDIAN ANGEL (1954) Rev. Charles Pinyan. In Res., Rev. Donald P. Sheehan (Retired).
Res.: 320 Franklin Turnpike, 07401. Tel: 201-327-4359; Fax: 201-327-6478. Email: gachurch@guardianangelchurch.org. Web: www.guardianangelallendale.parishesonline.com.
Catechesis/Religious Program—Tel: 201-327-0352. Email: inayden@guardianangelchurch.org. Irene Nayden, D.R.E. Students 366.

BAYONNE, HUDSON CO.

1—ST. ANDREW'S (1914) Rev. Msgr. Paul D. Schetelick; Rev. John R. Doherty, Pastor Emeritus (Retired). In Res., Revs. Thomas M. Foye (Retired); John R. Barno.
Res.: 125 Broadway, 07002. Tel: 201-437-0833; Fax: 201-858-3477. Email: andrew3513@aol.com. Web: www.saintandrewsparish.com.
See All Saints Catholic Academy, Bayonne under St. Mary Star of the Sea
Catechesis/Religious Program—Students 235.

2—ST. HENRY'S (1889) Most Rev. Thomas A. Donato; Revs. Richard J. Berbary; Maciej J. Zajac.
Res.: 82 W. 29th St., 07002. Tel: 201-436-0857; Fax: 201-823-4611. Email: sthenryrc@verizon.net. Web: www.sthenry.net.
See All Saints Catholic Academy, Bayonne under St. Mary Star of the Sea
Catechesis/Religious Program—Avenue C & 28 St., 07002. Tel: 201-339-0319. Marie Pope, C.R.E. Students 440.

3—ST. JOSEPH'S (1888), (Slovak), Merged with St. Michael's, Bayonne to form Saint Michael/Saint Joseph Parish, Bayonne.

4—ST. MARY STAR OF THE SEA (1861) Rev. Msgr. Lawrence J. Miller; Revs. Thomas P. Conheeney (Retired); Jose Manuel De la Pena; Edison Escario.
Res.: 326 Avenue C, 07002. Tel: 201-437-4090; Fax: 201-437-0388. Email: stmaryss@optonline.net.
School—All Saints Catholic Academy (2008), (Grades PreK-8), 19 W. 13th St., 07002. Tel: 201-443-8384; Fax: 201-437-6084. Mr. Joseph Moran, Prin. Lay Teachers 21; Students 481.
Catechesis/Religious Program—Tel: 201-437-0010. Ms. Philomena Coco, D.R.E. Students 100.

5—SAINT MICHAEL AND SAINT JOSEPH Revs. Gerard Michael Lombardo; John J. Gibbons, Pastor Emeritus (Retired). In Res., Rev. George Joseph.
Res.: 15-21 E. 23rd St., 07002-3737. Tel: 201-436-1412; Fax: 201-436-5979.
School: See All Saints Catholic Academy, Bayonne under St. Mary Star of the Sea
Catechesis/Religious Program—Barbara Godfrey, D.R.E. Students 115.

6—ST. MICHAEL'S (1907), (Lithuanian), Merged with St. Joseph, Bayonne to form Saint Michael/Saint Joseph Parish, Bayonne.

7—MT. CARMEL (1898), (Polish), [CEM] Rev. Msgr. Ronald J. Marczewski; Revs. Robert A. Pachana; Grzegorz Podsiadlo, S.D.S.
Res.: 39 E. 22nd St., 07002. Tel: 201-339-2070; Fax: 201-339-3676. Web: www.olmcparish.com.
See All Saints Catholic Academy, Bayonne under St. Mary Star of the Sea
Catechesis/Religious Program—Students 117.

8—OUR LADY OF THE ASSUMPTION (1902), (Italian), Rev. Joseph F. Barbone. In Res., Rev. Thomas C. Roberts.
Res.: 93 W. 23rd St., 07002-2621. Tel: 201-436-8160; Fax: 201-436-4135. Email: olassumption@hotmail.com. Web: www.olassumption.org.
Church: 91 W. 23rd St., 07002-2621. Fax: 201-436-3145.
See All Saints Catholic Academy, Bayonne under St. Mary Star of the Sea
Catechesis/Religious Program—Tel: 201-437-1867; Fax: 201-436-4897. Marco Guerrero, D.R.E. Students 351.

9—ST. VINCENT DE PAUL (1894) Revs. Vinh Quang Nguyen; Eric W. Fuchs, Parochial Vicar; Jacek J. Napora, Parochial Vicar; Deacon Michael P. Missaggia. In Res., Rev. Carl J. Arico (Retired).
Res.: 979 Ave. C, 07002. Tel: 201-436-2222; Fax: 201-437-5235.
See All Saints Catholic Academy, Bayonne under St. Mary Star of the Sea
Catechesis/Religious Program—Tel: 201-823-0184. Sr. Claudette Marie Jaszczynski, C.S.JB., D.R.E. Students 222.

BELLEVILLE, ESSEX CO.

1—ST. ANTHONY'S (1901), (Italian), Revs. Joseph A. Ferraro; Edito Gamallo; Dave Thomas N. Sison; Deacon Louis Acocella.
Res.: 750 N. Seventh St., 07107. Tel: 973-481-1991; Fax: 973-481-1993.
Church: 63 Franklin St., 07109.
Catechesis/Religious Program—25 N. 7th St., 07109. Tel: 973-751-0549. Students 179.

2—ST. PETER'S (1837) [CEM] Revs. Ivan Sciberras; Mayhel A. Velasquez, Parochial Vicar; Deacons William Valladares; Julio Roig, (Retired). In Res., Rev. Mark A. O'Connell (Retired).
Res.: 155 William St., 07109. Tel: 973-751-2002; Fax: 973-751-6201.
School—(1854), (Grades PreK-8), 152 William St., 07109. Tel: 973-759-3143; Fax: 973-759-4160. Phyllis A. Sisco, Prin. Lay Teachers 17; Students 186.
Catechesis/Religious Program—Tel: 973-751-4290. Students 275.
Retreat Center—149 Williams St., 07109. Tel: 973-751-2002, Ext. 121.

BERGENFIELD, BERGEN CO., ST. JOHN THE EVANGELIST (1905) Rev. Msgr. Richard J. Arnhols; Revs. Raymond R. Filipski; Manuel Dueñas; Gustavo A. Alfaro; Arcadio B. Munoz (Philippines); Deacon James Detura.
Res.: 29 N. Washington Ave., 07621. Tel: 201-384-0101; Fax: 201-384-2055. Email: pastor@sjrc.org. Web: www.sjrc.org.
School—Transfiguration Academy (2006), (Grades PreK-8), 10 Bradley Ave., 07621. Tel: 201-384-3627; Fax: 201-384-0293. Email: principal@transfigurationacademy.org. Web: www.transfigurationacademy.org. Sr. Madeline Hanson, S.S.N.D., Dir. Devel.; Salvatore Tralongo, Prin. Sisters of Notre Dame 1; Lay Teachers 25; Students 300.
Catechesis/Religious Program—15 N. Washington Ave., 07621. Tel: 201-384-3601; Fax: 201-384-9306. Web: www.sjrc.org. Rosemarie Flood, D.R.E. Students 622.

BERKELEY HEIGHTS, UNION CO., CHURCH OF THE LITTLE FLOWER (1955) Revs. Andrew M. Prachar; Marek Chachlowski (Poland); Deacons James P. Stumbar; Michael V. Montemurro. In Res., Rev. Msgr. William C. Harms (Retired).
Res. & Church: 110 Roosevelt Ave., 07922. Tel: 908-464-1585; Fax: 908-464-6342. Email: ebonacci@lfbhnj.org. Web: www.lfbhnj.org.
Catechesis/Religious Program—Tel: 908-464-7444. Students 761.

BLOOMFIELD, ESSEX CO.

1—CHURCH OF ST. THOMAS THE APOSTLE (1939) Revs. Charles J. Miller, O.F.M.; Nnaemeka A. Onyemaobi; Marek B. Wysocki; Deacons Thomas J. Coyle; Albert H. Tizzano; Brian Murphy; Mr. Robert Miller, Pastoral Assoc.; Timothy Dennin, Youth Min. In Res., Rev. Thomas F. Blind.
Res.: 60 Byrd Ave., 07003. Tel: 973-338-9190; Fax: 973-338-4224.
School—(1939), (Grades PreK-8), 50 Byrd Ave., 07003. Tel: 973-338-8505; Fax: 973-338-9565. Joan Ferraer, Prin.; Ann Bialkowski, Librarian. Sisters 1; Lay Teachers 18; Students 246.
Catechesis/Religious Program—Tel: 973-338-7400. Students 694.
Convent—55 Day St., 07003. Tel: 973-338-9118; Fax: 973-338-6495.

2—SACRED HEART (1878) [CEM] Revs. James T. Brown; Daniel A. Danik, Pastor Emeritus (Retired); Andrew J. Park; Peter O. Iwuala; Deacon Jerry S. Rossi; Dr. Ryan Malone, Music Dir.
Res.: 76 Broad St., 07003. Tel: 973-748-1800; Fax: 973-748-2028. Email: sacredheart10@comcast.net. Web: sacredheartbloomfield.4lpi.com.
Catechesis/Religious Program—Tel: 973-743-4061. Nancy Plate, D.R.E. Students 151.

3—ST. VALENTINE (1899), (Polish), Very Rev. Juancho G. DeLeon; Deacons Joseph J. Malanga; Louis Rusignuolo. In Res., Rev. John J. Donohue.
Res.: 125 N. Spring St., 07003. Tel: 973-743-0220; Fax: 973-743-2041.
Catechesis/Religious Program—Tel: 973-743-6122. Josephine Sarno, D.R.E. Students 173.

BOGOTA, BERGEN CO., ST. JOSEPH'S (1929) Rev. Richard Supple, O.Carm.; Ms. Mary Sause, Pastoral Assoc.; Deacons Walter Lynn; Michael Fitzgerald. In Res., Rev. Gregory Battafarano, O.Carm.
Res.: 115 E. Fort Lee Rd., 07603-1301. Tel: 201-342-6300; Fax: 201-883-9392.
School—(1925) 131 E. Fort Lee Rd., 07603-1301. Tel: 201-487-8641; Fax: 201-487-7405. James Newman, Prin. Lay Teachers 12; Preschool 35; Students 255; Total Enrollment 290.
Catechesis/Religious Program—Tel: 201-343-4316; Fax: 201-883-9302. Patricia Rodriguez, D.R.E. Students 315.
Convent—Tel: 201-342-4684.

CALDWELL, ESSEX CO., ST. ALOYSIUS (1892) Rev. Msgr. Michael J. Desmond; Revs. Patrick R. Flannery; Juan Carlos Vargas; Joseph T. Wozniak, Music Min. In Res., Rev. Msgr. Benjamin A. Piazza (Retired).
Res.: 219 Bloomfield Ave., 07006. Tel: 973-226-0221; Fax: 973-226-2204. Email: stalscaldwell@verizon.net. Web: www.rc.net/newark/st_aloysius.
School—Trinity Academy (1991), (Grades PreK-8), 235 Bloomfield Ave., 07006. Tel: 973-226-3386; Fax: 973-226-6548. Mrs. Dorothy McMahon, Prin. (Co-Sponsored) Trinity Academy. Inter-Parochial Lay Teachers 20.
Catechesis/Religious Program—Tel: 973-226-0209; Fax: 973-226-0923. Edward Karpinski, D.R.E. (Jr. High); Agnes Egan, D.R.E. (Elementary); Sr. Justine Pinto, O.P., Adult Educ. & Social Concerns; Jacqueline A. Alworth, Youth Min. Students 673.

CEDAR GROVE, ESSEX CO., ST. CATHERINE OF SIENA (1949) Rev. Msgrs. Robert H. Slipe; Charles W. Gusmer, Pastor Emeritus (Retired); Revs. Stephen A. Kopacz; Robert P. McLaughlin; Mrs. Carol Orlando, Pastoral Assoc.
Res.: 339 Pompton Ave., 07009. Tel: 973-239-7960; Fax: 973-239-1008. Email: stcatherine@scscedargrove.org.
School—(1958) 39 E. Bradford Ave., 07009. Tel: 973-239-6968. Celine Kerwin, Prin. Sisters of St. Dominic 1; Lay Teachers 20; Students 270.
Catechesis/Religious Program—Tel: 973-239-3332. Rosemary Couillou, D.R.E. Students 570.

CLARK, UNION CO., ST. AGNES (1961) Revs. Dennis J. Cohan; Denis S. Surban. In Res., Rev. Donald K. Hummel.
Res.: 332 Madison Hill Rd., 07066. Tel: 732-388-7852; Fax: 732-388-7064. Email: stagneschurch@comcast.net. Web: www.stagnesparish.com.
School—(1963), (Grades PreK-8), 342 Madison Hill Rd., 07066. Tel: 732-381-0850; Fax: 732-381-1745. Web: stagnesschool.com. Mrs. Heather Muller-Schnaars, Prin. Lay Teachers 16; Students 109.
Catechesis/Religious Program—Tel: 732-388-2560. Email: cff@stagnesparish.com. Sr. Margaret McDermott, S.S.J., D.R.E. Students 563.

CLIFFSIDE PARK, BERGEN CO., EPIPHANY (1916) Revs. Ken Evans, Admin.; James G. Tucker; Miroslaw Kusibab, C.S.M.A. (Poland); Deacon John C. Holoduek.
Res.: 247 Knox Ave., 07010. Tel: 201-943-7320; Fax: 201-943-1779. Email: epiphanycp@juno.com.
Catechesis/Religious Program—263 Lafayette Ave., 07010. Students 120.

CLOSTER, BERGEN CO., ST. MARY (1911) Very Rev. Paul A. Cannariato; Deacon James P. Tobin. In Res., Rev. Richard J. Mroz.
Res.: 20 Legion Pl., 07624. Tel: 201-768-7565; Fax: 201-784-5814.
Catechesis/Religious Program—Tel: 201-767-8247. Ms. Mary Lowe, D.R.E. Students 160.

CRANFORD, UNION CO., ST. MICHAEL'S (1872) Rev. Msgr. Timothy J. Shugrue; Revs. John P. McGovern, Pastor Emeritus (Retired); Edgardo P. Jocson, Parochial Vicar; Robert S. Gajewski, Parochial Vicar; Deacon Daniel Wilverding; Joan F. Genova, Bus. Admin.
Res.: 40 Alden St., 07016. Tel: 908-276-0360; Fax: 908-272-0273.
School—(1929), (Grades PreK-8), 100 Alden St., 07016. Tel: 908-276-9425; Fax: 908-276-4371. Sandy Miragliotta, Prin.; Maria Singer, Librarian. Lay Teachers 25; Students 340.
Catechesis/Religious Program—100 Alden St., 07016. Tel: 908-276-2050. Jacqueline Karmol, D.R.E. Students 1,486.

CRESSKILL, BERGEN CO., ST. THERESE OF LISIEUX (1925) Revs. Samuel Citero, O.Carm.; Joseph P. O'Brien, O.Carm., Pastor Emeritus; Deacon Anthony Porcaro. In Res., Rev. Joseph F. McGowan, O.Carm.
Res.: 120 Monroe Ave., 07626. Tel: 201-567-2528; Fax: 201-567-6759. Email: therese1@optonline.net. Web: www.4sttherese.org.
School—(Grades PreK-8), 220 Jefferson Ave., 07626. Tel: 201-568-4296; Fax: 201-568-3179. Sisters Helene Byrne, M.F.I.C., Prin.; Agnes Regan, M.F.I.C., Vice Prin. Lay Teachers 25; Students 245.
Catechesis/Religious Program—200 Jefferson Ave., 07626. Tel: 201-567-4781; Fax: 201-541-1269. Lois Pagnozzi, D.R.E. Students 556.
Convent—Tel: 201-568-0100.

DEMAREST, BERGEN CO.

1—ST. JOSEPH (1989), (Korean), Merged with St. Joseph's, Demarest to form the Parish of St. Joseph, Demarest.

2—ST. JOSEPH'S (1931), (Korean), Merged with St. Joseph, Demarest to form the Parish of St. Joseph, Demarest.

3—PARISH OF ST. JOSEPH (2008) Revs. Jungsoo Kim; Dong Kyum Kim; Donato Cabardo.
Res. & Mailing Address: 573 Piermont Rd., 07627. Tel: 201-768-2371; Fax: 201-767-8874. Email: stjosephdemarest@gmail.com. Web: www.stjosephdemarest.com.
Catechesis/Religious Program—Students 360.

DUMONT, BERGEN CO., ST. MARY'S (1914) Revs. Dominic G. Ciriaco; Raul R. Gaviola; Deacon John Sylvester. In Res., Rev. Onyedika Michael

Otuwurunne.
Res.: 280 Washington Ave., 07628. Tel: 201-384-0557; Fax: 201-384-4986.
Catechesis/Religious Program—Tel: 201-384-3062; Fax: 201-384-2852. William J. Mascitello, D.R.E. Students 585.

EAST NEWARK, HUDSON CO., ST. ANTHONY'S (1901), (Italian), Revs. Joseph D. Girone; Francisco J. Rodriguez, Parochial Vicar.
Res.: 409 N. Second St., 07029. Tel: 973-483-4680; Fax: 973-483-2396. Email: stanthony4@verizon.net.
Catechesis/Religious Program—Margaret A. Sanzo, D.R.E. Students 150.

EAST ORANGE, ESSEX CO.

1—HOLY NAME OF JESUS (1910) Revs. William G. Cook; Jude Caliba; Deacon Leo Woodruff.
Res.: 184 Midland Ave., 07017. Tel: 973-675-5901; Fax: 973-674-1767. Email: holynameeo@verizon.net.
Parish Center—200 Midland Ave., 07017-1855. Tel: 973-675-4444; Fax: 973-674-1767.
Catechesis/Religious Program—Students 35.

2—HOLY SPIRIT-OUR LADY HELP OF CHRISTIANS (1882), (African American—Haitian), Rev. Jean Max Osias, Admin.; Deacon Pierre J. Merceus.
17 N. Clinton St., 07017.
Res.: 190 Columbia Ave., North Plainfield, 07060. Tel: 973-673-1077; Fax: 973-676-6494.
School—(1883), (Grades PreK-8), 23 N. Clinton St., 07017. Tel: 973-677-1546; Fax: 973-677-3939. Web: www.njolhc.org. Sr. Patricia Hogan, O.P., Prin. Lay Teachers 11; Students 225.
Catechesis/Religious Program—Anita Hernandez, D.R.E. Students 50.

3—SAINT JOSEPH PARISH (1916) Rev. Frederick A. Pfeifer; Deacon Carlos Valentin; Cynthia Williams, Business Mgr.
110 Telford St., 07018. Tel: 973-678-4030; Fax: 973-677-7875. Email: st.josepheo@verizon.net. In Res., Rev. George F. Sharp (Retired).
School—Saint Joseph School, 115 Telford St., 07018. Tel: 973-674-2326; Fax: 973-674-7718. Ms. Karen Cavaness, Prin. Religious Teachers Filippini 1; Daughters of Mary, Mother of Mercy, D.M.M.M. 1; Lay Teachers 22; Students 360.
Catechesis/Religious Program—Sr. Theresia Maria, D.R.E. Students 70.

4—OUR LADY OF ALL SOULS (1914) Closed. Sacramental records located at the Archives, Walsh Library, Seton Hall University, South Orange, Tel: 973-761-9476; Fax: 973-761-9550.

5—OUR LADY OF THE MOST BLESSED SACRAMENT (1916) Closed. Sacramental records located at the Archives, Walsh Library, Seton Hall University, South Orange. Tel: 973-761-9476; Fax: 973-761-9550.

EAST RUTHERFORD, BERGEN CO., ST. JOSEPH'S (1872) [CEM] Revs. Joseph J. Astarita; Arokiadoss Raji; Sr. Marigene Kennedy, O.S.F., Pastoral Min. Tel: 201-939-0457.
Res.: 120 Hoboken Rd., 07073. Tel: 201-939-0457; Fax: 201-939-4196.
Catechesis/Religious Program—Tel: 201-939-3441. Verna Paiotti, D.R.E. Students 506.

EDGEWATER, BERGEN CO., HOLY ROSARY (1906) Rev. George Ruane; Deacons Robert E. Thomson; Michael A. Lydon.
Res.: 365 Undercliff Ave., 07020. Tel: 201-945-6329 (Parish Center); Fax: 201-945-6599. Email: holyrosary@aol.com. Web: www.edgewateronlin.com/holyrosarychurch.
See Christ the Teacher Interparochial School, under Madonna, Fort Lee.
Catechesis/Religious Program—Linda Corona, D.R.E. Students 88.

ELIZABETH, UNION CO.

1—SAINT ADALBERT AND SAINTS PETER & PAUL, [CEM] Revs. Krzysztof Szczotka (Poland); Marian Spanier; Deacon Philip Rejrat. In Res., Rev. Msgr. Bronislaw Wielgus (Retired).
Res.: 250 E. Jersey St., 07206. Tel: 908-352-2791; Fax: 908-354-2828. Email: office@stadalbert.us; pastor@stadalbert.us.
Catechesis/Religious Program—Students 43.

2—ST. ADALBERT'S (1905), (Polish), Merged with SS. Peter & Paul, Elizabeth to form Saint Adalbert/Saints Peter & Paul Parish, Elizabeth.

3—ST. ANTHONY'S (1895), (Italian), Revs. Patrick Diver, S.D.B.; Gennaro J. Sesto, S.D.B.; Richard Crager; Javier Aracil; George Atok, S.D.B.
Res.: 853 Third Ave., 07202. Tel: 908-351-3300; Fax: 908-351-3609. Email: elizsdb@aol.com.
School—Our Lady of Guadalupe Academy, (Grades PreK-8), 227 Centre St., 07202. Tel: 908-352-7419; Fax: 908-352-7062. Deacon Joseph Caporaso, Prin. Sisters of Charity of Convent Station 1; Benedictine Sisters 4; Lay Teachers 18; Students 220.
Catechesis/Religious Program—Sr. M. Charitina Frabizio, S.C., D.R.E. Students 350.
Convent—Tel: 908-354-0825; Fax: 908-354-4451.

4—BLESSED SACRAMENT (1922) Rev. Gerardo D. Gallo; Deacon Eliut Casanova; Lucia Solis, Pastoral Assoc. In Res., Rev. Alejandro Lopez-Cardinale.
Res.: 1096 North Ave., 07201. Tel: 908-352-0338; Fax: 908-352-4553.
See Our Lady of Guadalupe Academy under St. Anthony, Elizabeth.
Catechesis/Religious Program—Ms. Marylou Podolski, D.R.E. (English); Lucia Solis, D.R.E. (Spanish). Students 200.

5—ST. GENEVIEVE'S (1920) Revs. George D. Gillen; Roy James DeLeo (Retired); Ronnie Nombre (Philippines); Joseph Khai Vu (Vietnam).
Res.: 200 Monmouth Rd., 07208. Tel: 908-351-4444; Fax: 908-351-5454. Email: stgens@optonline.net.
School—(1929), (Grades PreK-8), 209 Princeton Rd., 07208. Tel: 908-355-3355; Fax: 908-355-1460. Catherine Coyle, Prin. Lay Teachers 14; Students 227.
Catechesis/Religious Program—Tel: 908-355-1584. Students 188.
Convent—

6—ST. HEDWIG'S (1925), (Polish), Revs. Andrzej Zmarlicki; Piotr J. Maslanka.
Parish Office: 717 Polonia Ave., 07202. Tel: 908-352-1448; Fax: 908-352-8389.
Res.: 716 Clarkson Ave., 07202.
Church: 600 Myrtle St., 07202.
Religious Education Center—717 Polonia Ave., 07202. Michele Yamakaitis, D.R.E. Students 48.

7—HOLY ROSARY (1886) Merged Records at Our Lady of Most Holy Rosary/St. Michael, Elizabeth. Tel: 908-354-2454; Fax: 908-354-3207.

8—IMMACULATE CONCEPTION (1907) Revs. Jorge Chacon; Wilson Bello. In Res., Rev. Brendan Quinn.
Pastoral Center: 417 Union Ave., 07208. Tel: 908-352-6662; Fax: 908-352-8484. Web: iconceptionparish.org.
Res.: 425 Union Ave., 07208. Tel: 908-352-6662.
Catechesis/Religious Program—417 Union Ave., 07208. Students 181.

9—IMMACULATE HEART OF MARY (1947), (Hispanic), Merged with St. Patrick's, Elizabeth to form Immaculate Heart of Mary and Saint Patrick, Elizabeth.

10—IMMACULATE HEART OF MARY AND SAINT PATRICK (1858), (Hispanic), [CEM] Revs. Fabio Roy De Jesus Brenes-Chaves; Wellington Manuel Munoz, Parochial Vicar; Deacon Nestor Charriez.
Res.: 215 Court St., 07206. Tel: 908-354-0023; 908-355-0807; Fax: 908-355-0526.
School—St. Patrick High School/Academy, (Grades 5-12), 221-227 Court St., 07206. Tel: 908-353-5220; Fax: 908-351-6086; 908-629-1123. Joseph Picaro, Prin. Sisters 1; Lay Teachers 15; Students 200.
Catechesis/Religious Program—Students 131.

11—ST. JOSEPH'S (1911), (Slovak), Closed. Records at Holy Family, Linden. Tel: 908-862-1060.

12—ST. MARY OF THE ASSUMPTION (1844) [CEM] Rev. Msgr. Robert J. Harrington; Revs. John Martin; Esterminio Chica; Deacons Luis Carlos Lorza; Pedro Herrera; Jorge A. Montalvo; Sr. Elaine Maguire, F.S.P., Pastoral Assoc.; Maria Castillo-Lorza, Pastoral Assoc. In Res., Rev. Msgr. Jeremias R. Rebanal (Retired).
Res.: 155 Washington Ave., 07202. Tel: 908-352-5154; Fax: 908-352-0350.
See Our Lady of Guadalupe Academy, Elizabeth under St. Anthony
High School—237 S. Broad St., 07202. Tel: 908-352-4350; Fax: 908-352-2359. Janet Malko, Prin.; Anna Rojas, Dir. Lay Teachers 18; Students 200.
Child Care Center—Tel: 908-355-8723. Students 39.
Catechesis/Religious Program—Tel: 908-352-0926. Deacon Jorge A. Montalvo, D.R.E. Students 264.
Convent—Tel: 908-352-1455.

13—OUR LADY OF FATIMA (1973), (Portuguese), Revs. Jose Manuel Fernandes (Portugal); Joseph E.S. Dos Santos, Parochial Vicar; Deacons Manuel Almeida; Jose Homen; Margaret De Jesus, Music Min. In Res., Rev. John F. Corbett.
Res.: 403 Spring St., 07201. Tel: 908-355-3810; Fax: 908-355-4791. Email: olfatimachurch-elizabeth@live.com.
Catechesis/Religious Program—Tel: 908-352-9713. Pedro da Costa, D.R.E. Students 701.

14—OUR LADY OF MOST HOLY ROSARY/ST. MICHAEL (1886/1852) [JC] Very Rev. John E. Wassell; Revs. Geto Jacques (Haiti); Zephyrin Kabengele Katompa; Deacons Orlando Sanchez; Wilbert Alexandre.
Res.: 52 Smith St., 07201. Tel: 908-354-2454; Fax: 908-354-3207. Email: secretary@holyrosarystmichael.com. Web: www.holyrosarystmichael.com.
Catechesis/Religious Program—Students 236.

15—ST. PATRICK, Merged with Immaculate Heart of Mary, Elizabeth to form Immaculate Heart of Mary and Saint Patrick, Elizabeth.

16—SS. PETER AND PAUL'S (1895), (Lithuanian), Merged with St. Adalbert, Elizabeth to form Saint Adalbert/Saints Peter & Paul Parish, Elizabeth.

17—SACRED HEART (1871) Merged All records at Our Lady of Fatima Parish, Elizabeth. Tel: 908-355-3810.

ELMWOOD PARK, BERGEN CO., ST. LEO'S (1910) Revs. Bartley Baker; Reinerio Agaloos.
Res.: 324 Market St., 07407. Tel: 201-796-3521; Fax: 201-703-8408. Email: stleoschurch2001@yahoo.com. Web: www.stleosep.net.
School—(1912), (Grades PreK-8), 300 Market St., 07407. Tel: 201-796-5156; Fax: 201-796-2092. Web: www.stleonj.org. Elizabeth Pinto, Prin. Franciscan Sisters of Peace 1; Lay Teachers 15; Students 280.
Catechesis/Religious Program—William Schulenburg, Pastoral Assoc./Faith Formation. Students 160.
Convent—305 Miller Ave., 07407. Tel: 201-797-6993.

EMERSON, BERGEN CO., CHURCH OF THE ASSUMPTION (1947) Revs. Dominick J. Lenoci; Camilo Lopez; Deacons John E. Hogan; Joseph J. Paulillo.
Res.: 29 Jefferson Ave., 07630. Tel: 201-262-1122; Fax: 201-262-7855. Email: church@assumptionacad.org. Web: www.geocities.com/assumption07630/church.
School—(Grades PreK-8), 35 Jefferson Ave., 07630. Tel: 201-262-0300; Fax: 201-262-5910. Ms. Susan Jurevich, Prin.; Ms. Eleni Mylonas, Dir. Early Childhood Prog. Sisters 1; Lay Teachers 19; Students 260.
Catechesis/Religious Program—Tel: 201-986-0970. Sr. Dominic Marie McDonnell, O.P., D.R.E. Students 500.

ENGLEWOOD, BERGEN CO., ST. CECILIA'S (1866) [JC] Revs. Hilary Milton, O.Carm.; Herman Kinzler, O.Carm., Parochial Vicar; Paul Schweizer, O.Carm.; Sr. Thomas Marie, O.P., Pastoral Assoc. In Res., Rev. Anthony Palo, O.Carm.
Res.: 55 W. Demarest Ave., 07631. Tel: 201-568-0364; Fax: 201-568-0654.
Catechesis/Religious Program—Tel: 201-568-7882. Esther Lara, D.R.E. Students 160.

FAIR LAWN, BERGEN CO., ST. ANNE'S (1909) Revs. Joseph C. Doyle; Colin Adrian Kay; Deacons Walter J. Maher; Richard M. McGarry. In Res., Rev. Msgr. Joseph T. Slinger (Retired).
Res.: 15-05 Saint Anne St., 07410. Tel: 201-791-1616; Fax: 201-791-1871.
School—(1949) 1-30 Summit Ave., 07410. Tel: 201-796-3353; Fax: 201-796-9058. Loretta Stachiotti, Prin. Lay Teachers 25; Students 321.
Catechesis/Religious Program—Donna Stickna, D.R.E. Students 735.

FAIRFIELD, ESSEX CO., ST. THOMAS MORE (1962) Revs. James M. Manos; Ward P. Moore, Pastor Emeritus (Retired); Eugene Gniewyk; Deacons P. Aidan King; Dominic S. Messina.
Res.: 210 Horseneck Rd., 07004. Tel: 973-227-0055; Fax: 973-227-2495. Email: stmparish@verizon.net. Web: www.stmchurch.net.
Catechesis/Religious Program—12 Hollywood Ave., 07004. Tel: 973-227-3607; Fax: 973-808-9032. Cabrina Kinslow, D.R.E.; Mr. Craig Jandoli, Coord. Youth Min. (Jr. & Sr. High). Students 765.

FAIRVIEW, BERGEN CO.

1—ST. JOHN THE BAPTIST (1873) Revs. Jose I. Gamba; Giordano Belanich; Melvin Oseguera; Deacon Anton Tarabokija. In Res., Rev. Felipe Lopez (Retired).
Res.: 239 Anderson Ave., 07022. Tel: 201-945-4865; Fax: 201-945-8171. Email: sjbhope@verizon.net.
Catechesis/Religious Program—Students 173.

2—OUR LADY OF GRACE (1913), (Italian), Very Rev. Peter T. Sticco, S.A.C.; Rev. Francis M. Gaetano, S.A.C.
Res.: 395 Delano Pl., 07022. Tel: 201-943-0904; Fax: 201-313-5616. Email: frpeter@nj.rr.com. Web: www.olgrc.org.
School—(Grades PreSchool-8), (plus 2 & 3 yr. old program), 400 Kamena St., 07022. Tel: 201-945-8300; Fax: 201-945-4580. Email: olgschool@olgfairview.org. Web: www.olgfairview.org. Sisters Alice Marie D'Onofrio, C.S.A.C., Prin.; Angela Verdi, C.S.A.C., Librarian. Lay Teachers 16; Students 330.
Catechesis/Religious Program—Tel: 201-945-1201. Students 165.
Convent—St. Vincent Pallotti, 545 Victory Ave., Ridgefield, 07657.

FORT LEE, BERGEN CO.

1—HOLY TRINITY (1906) Revs. Richard E. Cabezas; Edmundo Sombilon; Peter Baratta Jr., Music Min. In Res., Rev. Paul Hwang.
Res.: 2367 Lemoine Ave., 07024-6269. Tel: 201-947-1216; Fax: 201-947-1217.
School—Christ the Teacher Interparochial School, (Grades PreK-8) Tel: 201-944-0421; Fax: 201-994-6293. Sr. Rosemarie Bartnicki, O.S.F., Prin. Co-Sponsored. (See Madonna Parish, Fort Lee).
Catechesis/Religious Program—Tel: 201-947-1216. Sr. Rose O'Brien, C.B.S., D.R.E. Students 112.
Convent—Tel: 201-944-2911.

2—MADONNA (1858) [CEM] Revs. Stephen A. Carey;

Paul Kyung Lee; John Berchmans Antony (India).
Res.: 340 Main St., 07024. Tel: 201-944-2727; Fax: 201-944-5986. Email: madonnachurch@verizon.net.
School—Christ the Teacher Interparochial School, (Grades PreK-8), 359 Whiteman St., 07024. Tel: 201-944-0421; Fax: 201-944-6293. Sr. Rosemarie Bartnicki, O.S.F., Prin. Students 290.
Catechesis/Religious Program—Madonna Religious Education Center, Tel: 201-944-4261. Students 140.

FRANKLIN LAKES, BERGEN CO., MOST BLESSED SACRAMENT (1961) Most Rev. John W. Flesey; Rev. John R. Job; Sisters Rose Marie Kean, S.S.J., Pastoral Assoc.; Anne Lucille Coates, S.S.J., Pastoral Assoc.
Parish Center: 787 Franklin Lake Rd., 07417. Tel: 201-891-4200; Fax: 201-891-4243. Web: www.mostblessedsacrament.org. In Res., Rev. Michael Donovan.
Res.: 835 High Mountain Rd., 07417. Tel: 201-848-9717.
School—(1963), (Grades PreK-8), 785 Franklin Lake Rd., 07417. Tel: 201-891-4250; Fax: 201-847-9227. Email: jmathews@rcmbs.org. Web: www.ombs.org. Ms. JoAnn Mathews, Prin.; Mr. Chris Wild, Media Specialist; Ms. Marie Nicole Cascio, Librarian. Lay Teachers 25; Students 240.
Catechesis/Religious Program—Tel: 201-891-8390; Fax: 201-891-4243. Marcia Klink, D.R.E. Students 735.
Convent—

GARFIELD, BERGEN CO.

1—CHURCH OF OUR LADY OF SORROWS (1917) Revs. Paul Kottackal, Admin.; Michael Guba.
Res.: 69 Market St., 07026. Tel: 973-772-7889; Fax: 973-772-7806. Email: olosc@optonline.net.
Church: 30 Madonna Pl., 07026.
Catechesis/Religious Program—Tel: 973-478-4929. Kathleen Skrupskis, D.R.E. Students 256.

2—HOLY NAME (1911), (Hispanic), Rev. Msgr. William J. Reilly; Deacon Cesar Torres; Sr. Josefa Gonzalez, H.S.C.J., Pastoral Assoc.; Ms. Dalia Serrano, Pastoral Assoc.
Res.: 99 Marsellus Pl., 07026. Tel: 973-340-0032; Fax: 973-340-1618.
Catechesis/Religious Program—Students 270.

3—OUR LADY OF MT. VIRGIN (1901), (Italian), Revs. Peter J. Palmisano; Pedro Bismarck Chau; Bro. James Konchalski, O.S.B. In Res., Rev. George M. Reilly (Retired).
Res.: 188 MacArthur Ave., 07026. Tel: 973-772-2295; Fax: 973-478-4389.
Catechesis/Religious Program— Mrs. Rose Todaro, D.R.E. Students 150.

4—ST. STANISLAUS KOSTKA (1917), (Polish), Revs. Edward P. Szpiech; Mariusz G. Luksza; Piotr Haldas, S.D.S.
Res.: 184 Ray St., 07026. Tel: 973-772-7922; Fax: 973-772-4178. Email: ststankostka@optonline.net.
Catechesis/Religious Program—Tel: 973-772-7222. Ethel Kordosky, D.R.E. Students 265.
Convent—210 Lanza Ave., 07026. Tel: 973-772-4644.

GARWOOD, UNION CO., CHURCH OF ST. ANNE (1925) Rev. Richard A. Villanova; Sr. Maria James Riedel, O.S.F., Pastoral Assoc. for Catechetics.
Res.: 325 Second Ave., 07027. Tel: 908-789-0280; Fax: 908-789-3099. Email: stannesec@comcast.net. Web: www.parishofstannegarwood.org.
Catechesis/Religious Program—Tel: 908-789-4745. Email: stannereled@comcast.net. Students 93.

GLEN ROCK, BERGEN CO., ST. CATHARINE (1953) Revs. Thomas S. Wisniewski; William F. Benedetto; Joseph Kwiatkowski; Annette Gallagher, Pastoral Assoc.; Sally Trahan, Pastoral Assoc.; Rosemary Miller, Pastoral Assoc.; Deacons Leonard A. Minichino, Pastoral Assoc.; James A. Mueller, Pastoral Assoc.; John A. Sarno, Pastoral Assoc.; Joseph Castoro.
Res.: 905 S. Maple Ave., 07452. Tel: 201-445-3703; Fax: 201-670-7149. Email: parishoffice@stcatharinechurch.org. Web: www.stcatharinechurch.org.
School—Academy of Our Lady, (Grades PreK-8), 180 Rodney St., 07452. Tel: 201-445-0622; Fax: 201-445-8345. Email: principal@academyofourlady.org. Web: www.academyofourlady.org. Patricia Keenaghan, Prin. Lay Teachers 38; Students 460.
Catechesis/Religious Program—Tel: 201-444-5690; Fax: 201-445-8345. Email: religiouseducation@stcatharinechurch.org. Roberta Maguire, D.R.E. Students 723.

GUTTENBERG, HUDSON CO., ST. JOHN NEPOMUCENE (1910), (Slovak), Merged with Our Lady Help of Christians, West New York to form Holy Redeemer, West New York.

HACKENSACK, BERGEN CO.

1—CHURCH OF ST. FRANCIS OF ASSISI (1917), (Italian—Hispanic), Revs. Brian Tomlinson, O.F.M.Cap.; Pius Caccavalle, O.F.M.Cap.; Francisco Arredondo, O.F.M.Cap., Parochial Vicar; Deacons Alejandro Polanco; Joseph G. Vrindten; Angel Hernandez.
Res.: 50 Lodi St., 07601. Tel: 201-343-6243; Fax: 201-343-0854.
School—Padre Pio Academy, (Grades PreK-8), 100 S. Main St., 07601. Tel: 201-488-8862; Fax: 201-525-0498. Patricia Vrindten, Prin. Lay Teachers 25; Students 230.
Catechesis/Religious Program—Tel: 201-488-2614. Mr. Alex Collantes, D.R.E. Students 250.

2—HOLY TRINITY (1861) [CEM] Revs. Paul Prevosto; Jorge E. Acosta; John Thottukulappananiyil; Deacon Gregory Quinn; Sr. Emily Marie Walsh, S.C., Pastoral Assoc. In Res., Revs. Robert J. Cio; David S. McLaughlin.
Res.: 34 Maple Ave., 07601. Tel: 201-343-5170; Fax: 201-343-5067. Email: churchholytrinity@yahoo.com. Web: www.holytrinitysite.org.
See Padre Pio Academy, Hackensack under Church of St. Francis of Assisi
Catechesis/Religious Program—Students 330.
Convent—Tel: 201-342-1996; Fax: 201-968-0035.

3—IMMACULATE CONCEPTION (1891) Rev. Gerard J. Graziano.
Res.: 49 Vreeland Ave., 07601. Tel: 201-440-2798; Fax: 201-440-6756. Email: immcon@verizon.net. Web: www.icchackensack.org.
School: See Padre Pio Academy under Church of St. Francis of Assisi, Hackensack.
Catechesis/Religious Program—Students 55.

4—ST. JOSEPH'S (1909), (Polish), Rev. Wieslaw P. Strzadala, S.D.S.
Res.: 460 Hudson St., 07601. Tel: 201-440-3224; Fax: 201-641-8685.
School: See Padre Pio Academy under Church of St. Francis of Assisi, Hackensack.
Catechesis/Religious Program—Agnieszka Barowicz, D.R.E. (Polish).

HARRINGTON PARK, BERGEN CO., OUR LADY OF VICTORIES (1910) Revs. Bryan F.J. Adamcik; Nicholas V. Bellotti; Deacons Al McLaughlin; Tom Lagatol.
Res.: 81 Lynn St., 07640-1831. Tel: 201-768-1706; Fax: 201-768-3962. Email: olvch@juno.com. Web: www.ourchurch.com/member/o/olvparish/.
Catechesis/Religious Program—155 The Parkway, 07640-1820. Tel: 201-768-1400. Susan Evanella, C.R.E. & Youth Min. Students 330.
Convent—145 The Parkway, 07640-1820. Tel: 201-768-1705.

HARRISON, HUDSON CO.

1—HOLY CROSS (1865) Rev. Joseph D. Girone; Rev. Msgr. John J. Gilchrist, Pastor Emeritus (Retired); Rev. Francisco J. Rodriguez, Parochial Vicar. In Res., Rev. Timothy G. Graff.
Res.: 16 Church Sq., 07029. Tel: 973-484-5678; Fax: 973-484-0906. Email: hcsecretary@comcast.net.
See Mater Dei Academy, Kearny under St. Stephen
Catechesis/Religious Program—Students 182.
Convent—Carmelite Friars, 324 Jersey St., 07029. Tel: 973-485-7233.

2—OUR LADY OF CZESTOCHOWA (1908), (Polish), Rev. Pawel Molewski. In Res., Rev. Msgr. Joseph P. Plunkett (Retired).
Res.: 115 S. Third St., 07029. Tel: 973-483-2255; Fax: 973-483-4688. Email: rectory@olczestochowa.com. Web: www.olczestochowa.com.
Catechesis/Religious Program—Marzena Zmude-Dudek, D.R.E. Students 56.

HASBROUCK HEIGHTS, BERGEN CO., CORPUS CHRISTI (1897) Rev. Msgr. Lewis V. Papera; Rev. Raymond M. Holmes; Deacons Vincent J. DeFedele; Paul Carris; Joanna Kowalska, Music Min.
Parish Offices & Center—218 Washington Pl., 07604. Tel: 201-288-4844; Fax: 201-288-0237. Email: corchris@optonline.net.
School—(1928), (Grades PreK-8), 215 Kipp Ave., 07604. Tel: 201-288-0614; Fax: 201-288-5956. Michelle Murillo, Prin. Lay Teachers 31; Students 467.
Catechesis/Religious Program—Tel: 201-288-4844, Ext. 141; Fax: 201-288-0137. Josephine Nese, D.R.E. Students 562.

HAWORTH, BERGEN CO., SACRED HEART (1914) Revs. Stephen J. Fichter; Antonio L. Ricarte; Sr. Joanne Picciurro, Pastoral Assoc.
123 Maple St., P.O. Box S, 07641.
Res.: 102 Maple St., 07641. Tel: 201-387-0080; Fax: 201-439-1395.
Catechesis/Religious Program—102 Park St., 07641. Students 482.

HILLSDALE, BERGEN CO., ST. JOHN THE BAPTIST (1925) Rev. John J. Korbelak; Rev. Msgr. Philip D. Morris, Pastor Emeritus (Retired); Rev. Bruce E. Harger; Sr. Mary McFarland, O.P., Pastoral Assoc.; Jennifer Cannon, Business Mgr.; Catherine Wollyung, Pastoral Assoc. for Catechetics; Deacons Albert J. Ganter; John A. Gray. In Res., Rev. Msgr. Thomas M. O'Leary (Retired).
Res.: 69 Valley St., 07642. Tel: 201-664-3131; Fax: 201-664-0772.
School—St. John's Academy Interparochial (1955), (Grades PreK-8), 460 Hillsdale Ave., 07642. Tel: 201-664-6364; Fax: 201-664-8096. Elizabeth Viola, Prin.; Sharon Gallagher, Asst. Prin. Sisters 1; Lay Teachers 31; Students 435.
Catechesis/Religious Program—Faith Formation Center, 1 Valley St., 07642. Tel: 201-666-2707. Melissa Wing, Youth Min. Students 1,076.

HILLSIDE, UNION CO.

1—ST. CATHERINE OF SIENA (1912) Rev. Aurelio Yanez Gomez (Colombia).
Res.: 19 King St., 07205. Tel: 908-351-1515; Fax: 908-351-2139. Email: scatherineparish@aim.com. Web: stcathshillside.rcan.org.
School: See Hillside Catholic Academy, Hillside under Christ the King, Hillside for details.
Catechesis/Religious Program—Elizabeth. Diana Kelly, D.R.E. Students 205.

2—CHRIST THE KING (1948) Rev. Msgr. Venantius M. Fernando; Rev. Sergio O. Nadres (Philippines).
Res.: 411 Rutgers Ave., 07205. Tel: 908-686-0722; Fax: 908-686-2504. Email: christthekinghillside@yahoo.com. Web: www.christtheking-hillsidenj.com.
School—Hillside Catholic Academy, Hillside (2004), (Grades K-8), 397 Columbia Ave., 07205. Tel: 908-686-6740; Fax: 908-686-3819. Email: admin@hillsidecatholicacademy.org. Web: hillsidecatholicacademy.org. Michael Butchko, Prin. Lay Teachers 17; Students 180.
Catechesis/Religious Program—Tel: 908-686-0234. Web: www.ctkre.org. Gloria Ferro, D.R.E. Students 78; R.C.I.A. program for children 7.

HOBOKEN, HUDSON CO.

1—ST. ANN'S (1900) Very Rev. Vincent Fortunato, O.F.M.Cap.; Rev. Dominic Dellaporte, Parochial Vicar; Bro. Robert J. Reinke, C.F.P., Pastoral Assoc.
Res.: 704 Jefferson St., 07030. Tel: 201-659-1114; Fax: 201-659-1416.
School—Hoboken Catholic Academy, (Grades PreK-8), 555 Seventh St., 07030. Tel: 201-963-9535; Fax: 201-963-1256. Mrs. Rose Perry, Prin.
Catechesis/Religious Program—Students 36.

2—ST. FRANCIS (1888), (Italian), Rev. Michael V. Guglielmelli.
Res.: 308 Jefferson St., 07030. Tel: 201-659-1772; Fax: 201-222-7975. Email: 3rdjeff@gmail.com. Web: stfrancishoboken.com.
See Hoboken Catholic Academy, Hoboken under St. Ann's, Hoboken for details.
Catechesis/Religious Program—Email: dre@stfrancishoboken.com. Ms. Frances Fitzgerald, D.R.E. Students 150.

3—ST. JOSEPH'S (1871) Merged with Our Lady of Grace, Hoboken to form Our Lady of Grace and Saint Joseph Parish, Hoboken. For inquiries for parish records, contact Our Lady of Grace and Saint Joseph Parish.

4—OUR LADY OF GRACE (1851) Merged with St. Joseph's, Hoboken to form Our Lady of Grace and Saint Joseph Parish, Hoboken.

5—OUR LADY OF GRACE AND SAINT JOSEPH PARISH (1851) Revs. Alexander M. Santora; Ordanico De La Pena, Parochial Vicar; Megan Moffit, Pastoral Assoc. In Res., Rev. Martin Okoro, C.M.F.
Rectory—400 Willow Ave., 07030. Tel: 201-659-0369; Fax: 201-659-5833. Email: olgrace@optonline.com. Web: www.olghoboken.com.
See Hoboken Catholic Academy, Hoboken under St. Ann's, Hoboken for details.
Catechesis/Religious Program—Students 75.

6—SS. PETER AND PAUL CHURCH (1889) Rev. Msgr. Robert S. Meyer Esq.; Rev. A. Benito Prado.
Res.: 404 Hudson St., 07030. Tel: 201-659-2276; Fax: 201-659-5062. Email: secretary@spphoboken.com. Web: www.spphoboken.com.
See Hoboken Catholic Academy, Hoboken under St. Ann's, Hoboken for details.
Catechesis/Religious Program—Students 146.

HO HO KUS, BERGEN CO., ST. LUKE'S (1864) [CEM] Revs. James J. Weiner; Duverney Bermudez; Deacons John McKeon; Andrew E. Saunders; Ann McClelland, Business Mgr. In Res., Rev. Paschal B. Tsiquaye.
Res.: 340 N. Franklin Tpke., 07423. Tel: 201-444-0272; Fax: 201-652-7044. Web: www.churchofstluke.org. Email: admin@churchofstluke.org.
Catechesis/Religious Program—Tel: 201-447-2779. Email: ccd@churchofstluke.org. Ms. Bridget Sarkowicz, D.R.E. Students 673.

IRVINGTON, ESSEX CO.

1—ASSUMPTION OF THE BLESSED VIRGIN MARY (1907), (Hungarian), Closed. Sacramental records located at the Archives, Walsh Library, Seton Hall University, South Orange. Tel: 973-596-9476; Fax: 973-761-9550.

2—GOOD SHEPHERD (2005) Rev. Frank J. Rocchi.
Res.: 954 Stuyvesant Ave., 07111. Tel: 973-375-8568; Fax: 973-375-7040. Email:

gsirvington@comcast.net. Web: goodshepherd.150m.com.
School—Good Shepherd Academy (2005) 285 Nesbit Ter., 07111. Tel: 973-375-0659; Fax: 973-375-0766. Thomas Scalea, Prin. Students 216.
Catechesis / Religious Program—Tel: 973-375-2688. Students 35.

3—ST. LEO'S (1878) Rev. Msgr. Beaubrun Ardouin; Deacon Nelson Ramirez.
Res.: 103 Myrtle Ave., 07111. Tel: 973-372-1272; Fax: 973-416-8819. Email: saintleochurch@comcast.net.
See St. Leo's/Sacred Heart School, Irvington for details.
Catechesis / Religious Program—Sr. Regina Maraizu, D.M.M.M., D.R.E. Students 80.
Convent—Tel: 973-757-2432.

4—ST. PAUL THE APOSTLE (1948) Merged with Immaculate Heart of Mary, Maplewood to form Good Shepherd, Irvington.

5—SACRED HEART OF JESUS (1925), (Polish), Rev. Tadeusz Trela.
Res.: 537 Grove St., 07111. Tel: 973-373-2232; Fax: 973-373-5935. Email: sacredheart07111@gmail.com.
School—St. Leo's / Sacred Heart School, (Grades PreK-8), 123 Myrtle Ave., 07111. Tel: 973-372-7555; Fax: 973-416-8819. Sr. Carina Okeke, D.M.M.M., Prin.
Catechesis / Religious Program—Marek Sasko, Youth Min. Students 68.

JERSEY CITY, HUDSON CO.

1—ST. AEDAN'S (1912) Unassigned.
Res.: 800 Bergen Ave., 07306. Tel: 201-433-6800; Fax: 201-433-1222. Web: www.staedanparish.org.
Catechesis / Religious Program—Reina Osi, D.R.E. Students 40.

2—ST. ALOYSIUS (1897) Revs. Joseph A. D'Amico; Eduardo A. Bustamante; Ralph C. Siendo; Deacon Alfredo Zapata. In Res., Rev. James Delaney, C.S.Sp.
Res.: 691 West Side Ave., 07304. Tel: 201-433-6365; Fax: 201-451-6438. Email: saintaloysius@verizon.net. Web: www.staloysiuschurch.net.
School—(1897), (Grades PreK-8), 721 West Side Ave., 07306. Tel: 201-433-4270; Fax: 201-433-6916. Helen O'Connell, Prin.; Michelle Bernatowicz, Vice Prin. Lay Teachers 12; Students 306.
Catechesis / Religious Program—Sr. Georgette A. Gavioli, S.S.J., D.R.E. Students 217.

3—ST. ANN'S (1910), (Lithuanian), Closed. Sacramental records located at the Archives, Walsh Library, Seton Hall University, South Orange. Tel: 201-761-9476; Fax: 201-761-9550.

4—ST. ANN'S (1911), (Polish), Rev. Kazimierz Kuczynski; Deacon John J. Karal.
Res.: 291 St. Paul's Ave., 07306-5008. Tel: 201-656-4018; Fax: 201-656-0741.
Catechesis / Religious Program—Students 35.
Mission—, Hudson Co. Tel: 201-656-0405.

5—ST. ANNE'S (1903) Revs. Nigel R. Mohammed, Admin.; Titus C. Njoku, Parochial Vicar; Edward T. Veluz, Parochial Vicar.
Res.: 3545 John F. Kennedy Blvd., 07307. Tel: 201-360-0838; Fax: 201-721-5996. Email: sarc2000@verizon.net. Web: stannesjc.com.
School—(1904), (Grades PreK-8), 255 Congress St., 07307. Tel: 201-659-0450. Web: mysite.verizon.net/gerrity/. Ms. Gina Marie Iacona, Prin. Lay Teachers 11; Students 185.
Catechesis / Religious Program—Tel: 201-659-1794. Sr. Alberta Manzo, O.S.F., D.R.E. Students 115.
Convent—246 Congress St., 07307. Tel: 201-963-0998.

6—ST. ANTHONY OF PADUA (1884), (Polish), Rev. Joseph Urban.
Res.: 330 Sixth St., 07302. Tel: 201-653-0343; Fax: 201-653-0005. Email: pastor433@verizon.net. Web: www.stanthonyjc.com.
Catechesis / Religious Program—Students 54.

7—ASSUMPTION/ALL SAINTS (1896) Merged with St. Patrick's, Jersey City to form St. Patrick and Assumption/All Saints Church, Jersey City.

8—ST. BONIFACE'S (1863) Merged with St. Bridget, St. Mary, St. Michael and St. Peter to form Parish of the Resurrection, June 1997. For inquiries for parish records call Tel: 201-434-8500.

9—ST. BRIDGET'S (1869) Merged with St. Boniface, St. Mary, St. Michael and St. Peter to form Parish of the Resurrection, June 1997. For inquiries for parish records call Tel: 201-434-8500.

10—CHRIST, THE KING (1930), (African American), Rev. Stephen J. Giorno, S.T.; Deacon Keith McKnight.
Res.: 768 Ocean Ave., 07304. Tel: 201-333-4862; Fax: 201-433-6352.
Catechesis / Religious Program—Valerie Lewis-Mosley, D.R.E. Students 29.

11—CHURCH OF OUR LADY OF SORROWS (1914) Very Rev. John J. Cryan; Sisters Alice McCoy, O.P., Pastoral Assoc.; Elise Redmerski, O.P., Pastoral Assoc.
93-95 Clerk St., 07305. Tel: 201-433-0626; Fax: 201-433-2928. Email: ols9395@comcast.net. Web: olsjc.com.
Res.: *Our Lady of Mercy*, 340 Winfield Ave., 07305.
Mary House Peace Center and Food Pantry—Tel: 201-434-3175.
Catechesis / Religious Program—Students 51.

12—HOLY ROSARY (1885), (Italian), Rev. Jerzy R. Zaslona, Admin. In Res., Rev. Jaroslaw Zaniewski.
Res.: 344 Sixth St., 07302. Tel: 201-795-0120; Fax: 201-610-1389.
Catechesis / Religious Program—Sr. Paula Rodrigo.

13—ST. JOHN THE BAPTIST (1884) Revs. Michael C. Santoro; Joseph A. Meagher; Edinson E. Ramirez. In Res., Rev. Gregory V. Gebbia, O.F.M.
Res.: 3026 John F. Kennedy Blvd., 07306. Tel: 201-653-8814; Fax: 201-653-3771. Email: johns3026@comcast.net.
Catechesis / Religious Program—Twinned with Our Lady of Mt. Carmel, Jersey City. JoAnne Oziemblo, D.R.E. Students 10.

14—ST. JOSEPH (1856) Revs. James V. Pagnotta; Armando S. Crisostomo Jr.
Res.: 511 Pavonia Ave., 07306-1303. Tel: 201-653-0392; Fax: 201-222-6481. Email: stjosephjc@yahoo.com. Web: www.stjosephjc.com.
Church: Baldwin Ave., 07306.
School—(1876), (Grades PreK-8), 509 Pavonia Ave., 07306. Tel: 201-653-0128; Fax: 201-222-5324. John Richards, Prin. Lay Teachers 11; Students 200.
Catechesis / Religious Program—Tel: 201-659-5929. Ms. Maria C. Pellecchia, D.R.E. Students 90.

15—ST. LUCY'S (1884) Closed. For inquiries for parish records contact Parish of the Resurrection. Tel: 201-434-8500.

16—ST. MARY'S (1854), (Hispanic—Filipino), Merged with St. Boniface, St. Bridget, St. Michael, and St. Peter, to form Parish of the Resurrection, June 1997. For inquiries for parish records call Tel: 201-434-8500.

17—ST. MICHAEL'S (1867) Merged with St. Boniface, St. Bridget, St. Mary and St. Peter to form Parish of the Resurrection, June 1997. For inquiries for parish records call Tel: 201-434-8500.

18—ST. NICHOLAS (1886), (German), Revs. Kevin E. Carter; Alex Ver (Philippines); Deacons Robert A. Baker Sr.; Wilson Cordero; Clodualdo M. Leonida.
Res.: 122 Ferry St., 07307. Tel: 201-659-5354; Fax: 201-798-6868. Web: www.saintnicholasparishjcnj.org.
School—(1886), (Grades PreK-8), 118 Ferry St., 07307. Tel: 201-659-5948. Sr. Ellen Fischer, S.C.C., Prin. Sisters of Christian Charity 3; Lay Teachers 11; Students 230.
Catechesis / Religious Program—Tel: 201-659-5354. Lorraine Glasser, D.R.E.; Julia Cordero, D.R.E. (Spanish). Students 160.
Convent—Tel: 201-659-5644.

19—OUR LADY OF CZESTOCHOWA (1911) Rev. Thomas J. Ciba; Mr. Dana Callan-Farley, Pastoral Assoc.; Mr. Jonathan Tessero, Music Min.
Res.: 120 Sussex St., 07302. Tel: 201-434-0798; Fax: 201-985-0918. Email: olcjc@olcjc.org. Web: www.olcjc.org.
School—(1911), (Grades PreK-8), 248 Marin Blvd., 07302. Tel: 201-434-2405; Fax: 201-434-6068. Email: stefanellia@olcschool.org. Web: www.olcschool.org. Mrs. Anne Stefanelli, Prin. Lay Teachers 40; Students 358.
Catechesis / Religious Program—Students 370.

20—OUR LADY OF MERCY (1963), (Filipino), Very Rev. John J. Cryan; Revs. Marty Borbon Jacinto; Joseph Udeze, C.M.F.; Deacon Nicholas Fargo.
Res.: 40 Sullivan Dr., 07305. Tel: 201-434-7500; Fax: 201-432-2885. Email: olmjcnj@aol.com. Web: www.olmnj.org.
School—(Grades PreK-8), 254 Bartholdi Ave., 07305. Tel: 201-434-4091; Fax: 201-434-8405. Email: principalolm@aol.com. Victoria Hayes, Prin. Lay Teachers 25; Students 250.
Catechesis / Religious Program—Email: religioused@aol.com. Regina Matias-Villa, Coord. Faith Formation. Students 190.

21—OUR LADY OF MT. CARMEL (1905), (Italian), Rev. Michael C. Santoro.
Res.: 99 Broadway, 07306. Tel: 201-435-7080; Fax: 201-432-4476. Email: mtcarmelschool@comcast.net.
Catechesis / Religious Program—JoAnne Oziemblo, D.R.E. Students 76.

22—OUR LADY OF VICTORIES (1917) Revs. Victor E. Paloma; Christopher Panlilio. In Res., Rev. James Tortora.
Res.: 2217 John F. Kennedy Blvd., 07304-1416. Tel: 201-433-4152; Fax: 201-433-0705. Email: olvictories1@aol.com. Web: www.olvjc.com.
Catechesis / Religious Program—Students 85.

23—PARISH OF THE RESURRECTION (1997), (Formerly Parishes of St. Boniface, St. Bridget, St. Mary, St. Michael and St. Peter) Very Rev. Victor P. Kennedy; Revs. Marcos Sequiera-Ruiz; Jose Maria M. Parcon (Philippines); Robert E. Tooman; Bro. Louis N. Mauro, S.J., Business Mgr.; Deacons Marcelo David; Pedro Gonzalez; Cesar C. Sarmiento; Leopoldo Polanco; Ralph M. Savo; Ms. Roxanne Clark, Pastoral Assoc.; Ms. Elizabeth Hopf, Pastoral Assoc. In Res., Rev. Joseph Minh Tri Nguyen.
Mailing Address & Parish Office: 209 Third St., 07302. Tel: 201-434-8500; Fax: 201-333-1816. Email: resjc@aol.com.
School—Resurrection, Brunswick Campus (1873), (Grades PreK-8), 189 Brunswick St., 07302. Tel: 201-653-1699; Fax: 201-418-9019. Email: rs.office@yahoo.com. Sr. Eleanor Uhl, Co-Prin. (Grades 4-8).
Catechesis / Religious Program—Tel: 201-795-3426; Fax: 201-333-1816. Sr. Mary Lynch, S.S.N.D., D.R.E. Students 137.
St. Boniface—, Merged with St. Bridget, St. Michael, St. Mary, & St. Peter, Jersey City to form Parish of the Resurrection, Jersey City.
St. Bridget—, Merged with St. Boniface, St. Michael, St. Mary & St. Peter, Jersey City to form Parish of the Resurrection, Jersey City.
St. Michael—, Merged with St. Boniface, St. Bridget, St. Mary & St. Peter, Jersey City to form Parish of the Resurrection, Jersey City. (Shrine of St. Jude Perpetual Novena)
St. Mary—, Merged with St. Boniface, St. Bridget, St. Michael & St. Peter, Jersey City to form Parish of the Resurrection, Jersey City.
St. Peter—, Merged with St. Boniface, St. Bridget, St. Michael & St. Mary, Jersey City to form Parish of the Resurrection, Jersey City., 144 Grand St., 07302.

24—ST. PATRICK AND ASSUMPTION/ALL SAINTS CHURCH Revs. Eugene P. Squeo; Marc Arthur Francois (Haiti); Francis E. Schiller; Anthony Aracich, S.J.; Deacon Jesus Reyes.
Res.: 492 Bramhall Ave., 07304. Tel: 201-332-8600; Fax: 201-324-3919.
Convent—345 Pacific Ave., 07304. Tel: 201-451-2765.
Catechesis / Religious Program—Ann Marie Padilla, D.R.E. Students 77.

25—ST. PATRICK'S (1869) Merged with Assumption/All Saints, Jersey City to form St. Patrick and Assumption/All Saints Church, Jersey City.

26—ST. PAUL OF THE CROSS (1868) Very Rev. Andres J. Reyes; Rev. Alfie A. Pangilinan; Deacon Arnulfo Cuesta.
Res.: 156 Hancock Ave., 07307. Tel: 201-798-7900; Fax: 201-798-7902. Email: stpaulcros@aol.com. Web: www.stpaulcrossjc.com.
Catechesis / Religious Program—Ela Ramirez, C.R.E. Students 189.

27—ST. PAUL'S (1861) Revs. Thomas Thottungal; Juan P. Morales; Deacon Frank Gonzalez. In Res., Rev. Raymond T. McKeon (Retired); Rev. Msgr. James J. Finnerty (Retired).
Res.: 14 Greenville Ave., 07305. Tel: 201-433-8500; Fax: 201-433-9886. Email: stpauljc@aol.com.
Catechesis / Religious Program—Virginia San Lorenzo, D.R.E. Students 110.
Convent—Dominican Sisters of Hope, 20 Greenville Ave., 07305. Tel: 201-434-2962.

28—ST. PETER'S (1831), (Hispanic), Merged with St. Boniface, St. Bridget, St. Mary and St. Michael to form Parish of the Resurrection, June 1997. For parish inquiries call Tel: 201-434-8500.

29—SACRED HEART (1905) Closed. Sacramental records located at the Archives, Walsh Library, Seton Hall University, South Orange. Tel: 973-761-9476; Fax: 973-761-9550.
School—Sacred Heart, (Grades K-8), 183 Bayview Ave., 07307. Tel: 201-332-7111; Fax: 201-332-7160. Sr. Frances Salemi, S.C., Prin. Lay Teachers 14; Students 247.

KEARNY, HUDSON CO.

1—ST. CECILIA'S (1893) Very Rev. Michael G. Ward; Revs. Yuvan Arbey Alvarez; Janusz Pigan; Deacon Justo Aliaga. In Res., Rev. Msgr. Francis R. Seymour.
Res.: 120 Kearny Ave., 07032. Tel: 201-991-1116; Fax: 201-998-4437. Email: stcecilia@stceciliakearny.org. Web: www.stceciliakearny.org.
Catechesis / Religious Program—Cristine Pardo, C.R.E. Students 325.

2—OUR LADY OF SORROWS (1915), (Lithuanian), Very Rev. Michael G. Ward, Admin.; Deacons Leonard J. Mackesy; John P. Sarnas. In Res., Rev. Patrick R.C. Wilhelm (Retired).
Res.: 136 Davis Ave., 07032. Tel: 201-998-4616; Fax: 201-997-8659. Email: olskrny@verizon.net.
Catechesis / Religious Program—Lucille Muldoon, C.R.E. Students 31.

3—ST. STEPHEN (1904) Revs. Joseph A. Mancini; Paciano A. Barbieto; Deacons Herbert R. Gimbel; Earl W. White; Robert Maidhof, Music Min.; Deacon Robert C. Millea.

Res.: 141 Washington Ave., 07032. Tel: 201-998-3314; Fax: 201-998-4924.
School—Mater Dei Academy (1904) 131 Midland Ave., 07032. Tel: 201-991-2371; Fax: 201-991-7829. Mrs. Deborah DeMattia, Prin. Lay Teachers 12; Students 256.
Catechesis/Religious Program—Tel: 201-991-0236. Mrs. Margaret Kelly, D.R.E. Students 154.

KENILWORTH, UNION CO., ST. THERESA'S (1949) Very Rev. Joseph J. Bejgrowicz; Revs. Jose Erlito Ebron (Philippines); Hong-Ray Peter Cho; Richard Donovan, Youth Min. Tel: 908-709-1930. In Res., Rev. Alfred J. Kowalski (Retired).
Res.: 541 Washington Ave., 07033. Tel: 908-272-4444; Fax: 908-272-4424. Email: sainttheresa@icatholiczone.com.
School—(Grades PreK-8), 540 Washington Ave., 07033. Tel: 908-276-7220; Fax: 908-709-1103. Sr. Emy DeFilippi, F.M.A., Prin. Salesian Sisters 4; Lay Teachers 17; Students 316.
Catechesis/Religious Program—Tel: 908-276-4881. Sr. Monique Huarte, F.M.A., Pastoral Min. Catechesis. Students 675.
Convent—Tel: 908-276-5028.

LEONIA, BERGEN CO., ST. JOHN THE EVANGELIST'S (1912) Revs. Richard P. Kwiatkowski; Arlou Buslon (Philippines); Sr. Patricia McDermott, F.S.P., Pastoral Assoc.; Deacon Joseph Yandoli, Business Mgr.
Res.: 235 Harrison St., 07605. Tel: 201-947-4545; Fax: 201-947-3891.
School—(Grades PreK-8), 260 Harrison St., 07605. Tel: 201-944-4361; Fax: 201-944-2195. Ana M. Castaneda, Prin. School Sisters of Notre Dame 1; Franciscan Sisters of Peace 1; Lay Teachers 16; Students 169.
Catechesis/Religious Program—Tel: 201-944-4346. Gerri Bianchi, D.R.E. Students 233.
Convent—Tel: 201-944-4362.

LINDEN, UNION CO.

1—ST. ELIZABETH OF HUNGARY (1909) Very Rev. Benedict M. Worry, O.S.B.; Revs. Vincent Liem, O.Cist.; Alberto Cap, O.Cist.; Deacon John P. Bejgrowicz.
Res.: 179 Hussa St., 07036. Tel: 908-486-2514; Fax: 908-486-1757. Web: www.sainteonline.org.
School—Saints Mary and Elizabeth Academy, (Grades PreK-8), 170 Hussa St., 07036. Tel: 908-486-2507; Fax: 908-486-4032. Web: www.s-meacademy.org. Ms. Patricia Reid, Prin. Students 209.
Catechesis/Religious Program—170 Hussa St., 07036. Mrs. Florence Manguiat, D.R.E. Students 126.

2—HOLY FAMILY (Tremley Point) (1955), (Slovak), [CEM] Rev. Eugene Diurczak.
Res.: 210 Monroe St., 07036. Tel: 908-862-1060; Fax: 908-862-9483.
Church: 2709 Parkway Ave., 07036. Fax: 908-862-1060.
Catechesis/Religious Program—Marybeth Strano, D.R.E. Students 24.

3—ST. JOHN THE APOSTLE (1948) Very Rev. Robert G. McBride; Revs. Luke Tran; Zbigniew Kukielka; Deacons Michael D. York; Edward A. Campanella; Guy Paredes, (Retired); Timothy A. Kennedy.
Res.: 1805 Penbrook Ter., 07036. Tel: 908-486-6363; Fax: 908-486-5345. Email: parish@sjanj.net. Web: www.sjanj.net.
School—(1950), (Grades PreK-8), Valley Rd., Clark, 07066. Tel: 732-388-1360; Fax: 732-388-0775. Web: www.sjanj.org. Sr. Donna Marie O'Brien, O.P., Prin. Sisters of St. Dominic 1; Lay Teachers 23; Students 381.
Catechesis/Religious Program—Tel: 732-388-1253. Students 619.
Convent—1731 Valley Rd., 07036. Tel: 908-486-3701.

4—ST. THERESA OF THE CHILD JESUS (1925), (Polish), Revs. Miroslaw K. Kroll; Tadeusz Jank; Ireneusz Pierzchala.
Res.: 122 Liberty St., 07036. Tel: 908-862-1116; Fax: 908-862-2930.
Church: 131 E. Edgar Rd., 07036.
School: See Sts. Mary and Elizabeth Academy under St. Elizabeth of Hungary, Linden
Catechesis/Religious Program—Sr. Irene Lisowska, D.R.E. Students 410.

LITTLE FERRY, BERGEN CO., ST. MARGARET OF CORTONA (1912) Very Rev. Arthur F. Humphrey; Sr. Dorothy A. Donovan, S.S.J., Pastoral Assoc.
Res.: 31 Chamberlain Ave., 07643-1898. Tel: 201-641-2988; Fax: 201-641-0664. Email: smcortona1912@aol.com.
Catechesis/Religious Program—Tel: 201-641-3937. Students 225.

LIVINGSTON, ESSEX CO.

1—ST. PHILOMENA (1927) Rev. Msgr. Kevin M. Hanbury, Admin.; Rev. Brian X. Needles; Deacons Fred Smith; Joseph Francione. In Res., Rev. Matthew Eraly (India).
Res.: 386 S. Livingston Ave., 07039. Tel: 973-992-0994; Fax: 973-992-0970. Email: staff@stphilomena.org. Web: www.stphilomena.org.
School—Aquinas Academy (1952), (Grades PreK-8), 388 S. Livingston Ave., 07039. Tel: 973-992-1587; Fax: 973-992-1742. Sr. Lena Picillo, O.P., Prin. Dominican Sisters of Caldwell 2; Lay Teachers 12; Students 150.
Early Childhood Center—Tel: 973-992-5181; Fax: 973-992-2652. Gloria Castucci, Dir. Lay Teachers 4; Aides 9; Students 120.
Catechesis/Religious Program—Tel: 973-992-4466. Email: gruth2@verizon.net. Gary Ruth, D.R.E. Students 758.
Convent—392 S. Livingston Ave., 07039. Tel: 973-992-1581.

2—ST. RAPHAEL (1961) Revs. Gerald F. Greaves; Peter M. Aquino; Yolanda Cifarelli, Pastoral Assoc.
Res.: 346 E. Mt. Pleasant Ave., 07039. Tel: 973-992-9490; Fax: 973-740-0236. Email: straphaelrcc@comcast.net. Web: www.straphaels.net.
Catechesis/Religious Program—Ann Marie Gesualdo, Youth Min. Students 510.

LODI, BERGEN CO.

1—ST. FRANCIS DE SALES (1854) [CEM] Revs. John J. Galeano; John C. DeSousa.
Res.: 125 Union St., 07644. Tel: 973-779-4330; Fax: 973-779-8842. Email: francisdesales@optonline.net.
Catechesis/Religious Program—Tel: 973-779-3949. Students 130.
Convent—Tel: 973-773-4366.

2—ST. JOSEPH'S (1917) Revs. Michael Marotta, C.R.M.; Americo Salvi, C.R.M.; Anastacio Villaluz, C.R.M., Parochial Vicar; Deacons Stephen Marchese; Jorge E. Ochoa.
Res.: 40 Spring St., 07644. Tel: 973-779-0643; Fax: 973-471-1442. Email: stjoelodi@aol.com.
Catechesis/Religious Program—Tel: 973-779-8275; Fax: 973-779-0490. Email: sjreolodi@aol.com. Maria Linda De Los Santos, D.R.E. Students 181.

LYNDHURST, BERGEN CO.

1—ST. MICHAEL'S (1912), (Polish), Revs. Stanley Kostrzomb; Joseph Szklarski. In Res., Revs. George F. Sharp (Retired); John A. Quill.
Res.: 624 Page Ave., 07071. Tel: 201-939-1161; Fax: 201-939-7571. Email: stmichaelparish@comcast.net. Web: www.st-michael.org.
Catechesis/Religious Program—Mr. Gene DeHaven, D.R.E.; Mr. Michael Mages, Youth Min. Students 119.

2—OUR LADY OF MOUNT CARMEL (1966), (Italian), Rev. Nazareno Orlandi.
Res.: 197 Kingsland Ave., 07071. Tel: 201-935-1177; Fax: 201-935-5675. Email: olmc1177@verizon.net.
Catechesis/Religious Program—146 Copeland Ave., 07071. Tel: 201-935-5467. Patricia Hirsch, D.R.E. Students 260.

3—SACRED HEART (1902) [CEM] Revs. James E. Starasinich; Pedro E. Vilchez; Deacon Stephen Rodack, (Retired). In Res., Rev. Joseph A. Barrow (Retired).
Res.: 324 Ridge Rd., 07071. Tel: 201-438-1147; Fax: 201-507-5861. Email: sacredheart@comcast.net.
School—(Grades PreK-8), 620 Valley Brook Ave., 07071. Tel: 201-939-4277; Fax: 201-939-0534. Email: sacredheartlynd@hotmail.com. Web: sacredheartlynd.org. Margaret Smiriga, Prin.; Joann Hessian, Librarian. Sisters 2; Lay Teachers 15; Students 270.
Catechesis/Religious Program—Tel: 201-935-3094. Email: sacredheartchurch@comcast.net. Mrs. Margaret Dacchille, P.C.L. Students 220.

MAHWAH, BERGEN CO.

1—IMMACULATE CONCEPTION (1930) Rev. William P. Sheridan; Jennifer Edwards, Pastoral Assoc. In Res., Rev. John J. Chadwick.
Res.: 900 Darlington Ave., 07430. Tel: 201-327-1276; Fax: 201-327-0185. Email: churchimmaculateconception@yahoo.com. Web: www.immaculateconceptionmahwah.org.
See St. Paul's Interparochial School, Ramsey under St. Paul's, Ramsey for details.
Catechesis/Religious Program—Tel: 201-825-0333. Michele Hans, Catechetical Associate. Students 276.

2—IMMACULATE HEART OF MARY (1915), (Polish), Revs. Floyd Rotunno; Marek Bokota.
Res.: 47 Island Rd., 07430. Tel: 201-529-3517; Fax: 201-529-4401. Email: ihmpastor@optonline.net.
See St. Paul's Interparochial School, Ramsey under St. Paul's, Ramsey for details.
Catechesis/Religious Program—Tel: 201-529-2294. Barbara A. Dillon, D.R.E. Students 272.

MAPLEWOOD, ESSEX CO.

1—ST. ANDREW KIM (1972), (Korean), Revs. Minhyun Cho; James Hooyeon Cho, Parochial Vicar; Jae Chun Lee, Pastoral Assoc. In Res., Rev. Msgr. Augustin C. Park, Pastor Emeritus (Retired), Co-ord. Korean Apostolate.
Res.: 280 Parker Ave., 07040. Tel: 973-763-1170; Fax: 973-763-1169. Email: catholicmaplewood@yahoo.com. Web: www.ilovesak.org.
Catechesis/Religious Program—Deacon Thomas Bulgia, Youth Min.; Kwang Ho Chi, D.R.E.; Kenny Lee, D.R.E. Students 160.
Convent—Tel: 973-762-1297; Fax: 973-763-1169. Email: orangsr@hanmail.net.

2—IMMACULATE HEART OF MARY (1954) Merged with St. Paul the Apostle, Irvington to form Good Shepherd, Irvington. For inquiries for sacramental records, contact Good Shepherd, Irvington; Tel: 973-375-8568.

3—ST. JOSEPH'S (1914) Revs. Eustace Edomobi (Nigeria); Manolo Punzalan; Deacon John J. Florio; Mrs. Jennifer Leitner, Pastoral Assoc.; Ms. Diane Pew, Pastoral Assoc.; Mr. Dugan McGinley, Dir. Music & Liturgy. In Res., Rev. Thomas A. Dente.
Res.: 767 Prospect St., 07040. Tel: 973-761-5933; Fax: 973-761-6705. Email: info@stjosephmaplewood.org. Web: www.stjosephmaplewood.org.
Catechesis/Religious Program—Thomas C. Berrios, Youth Min. Students 240.

MAYWOOD, BERGEN CO., OUR LADY QUEEN OF PEACE (1950) Revs. Lawrence J. Fama; Kevin J. Schott; Deacons Anthony Balistieri; Joseph L. Mantineo; Steven Taylor, Music Min.
Res.: 400 Maywood Ave., 07607. Tel: 201-845-9566; Fax: 201-845-3742. Email: admin@olqp.org. Web: www.olqp-maywood.org.
School: See St. Peter Academy, River Edge under St. Peter the Apostle, River Edge for details.
Catechesis/Religious Program—Tel: 201-845-9545. Angela Connelly, D.R.E. Students 278.

MIDLAND PARK, BERGEN CO., NATIVITY (1955) Revs. Peter K. Funesti; Raymond E. Rodrigue. In Res., Rev. Msgr. James A. Burke (Retired); Rev. Ron Stanley.
Res.: 315 Prospect St., 07432. Tel: 201-444-6362; Fax: 201-444-5056.
Catechesis/Religious Program—Tel: 201-447-1776. Ms. Olivia Harrington, D.R.E. Students 478.

MONTCLAIR, ESSEX CO.

1—IMMACULATE CONCEPTION (1864) [CEM] Revs. Joseph A. Scarangella; Aro Nathan; Preston L. Dibble, Music Min. In Res., Revs. Frank J. Burla (Retired); Louis M. Pambello.
Res.: 30 N. Fullerton Ave., 07042. Tel: 973-744-1005; Fax: 973-744-7936.
Parish Center—1 Munn St., 07042. Tel: 973-744-5650; Fax: 973-744-7936. Email: parishoffice@mtcimmaculate.org. Web: www.mtcimmaculate.org.
See Immaculate Conception High School (Coed), Montclair in the Institution Section under High Schools, Private for details.
Catechesis/Religious Program—Mary Clinton, D.R.E. Students 380.
Cemetery & Mausoleum—712 Grove St., Upper Montclair, 07043.

2—OUR LADY OF MT. CARMEL (1907), (Italian), Rev. Anthony J. Lionelli. In Res., Rev. Thomas M. Cembor.
Res.: 94 Pine St., 07042. Tel: 973-744-1074; Fax: 973-744-0205. Email: olmc_mont@verizon.net. Web: www.olmc-montclair.org.
Catechesis/Religious Program—Bruno Suria, D.R.E. Students 70.

3—ST. PETER CLAVER (1931), (African American), Rev. Richard D. Carlson; Deacon Wilfrid Leconte.
Res.: 56 Elmwood Ave., 07042. Tel: 973-783-4852; Fax: 973-783-3261. Email: peterclave@aol.com. Web: www.saintpeterclaverchurch.org.
Catechesis/Religious Program—Sharon Huebner, D.R.E. Students 84.

MOONACHIE, BERGEN CO., ST. ANTHONY (1931) Closed. Sacramental records located at the Archives, Walsh Library, Seton Hall University, South Orange. Tel: 973-761-9476; Fax: 973-761-9550.

MOUNTAINSIDE, UNION CO., CHURCH OF OUR LADY OF LOURDES (1958) Very Rev. John M. McCrone; Rev. Grace G. Arachi; Deacons John J. Wedemeyer; Michael DeRoberts. In Res., Rev. Msgr. Thomas J. McDade.
Res.: 300 Central Ave., 07092. Tel: 908-232-1162; Fax: 908-232-0776. Email: office@ollmountainside.org. Web: www.ollmountainside.org.
School—Holy Trinity Interparochial School (Westfield Campus) (1991), (Grades PreK-8), 336 First St., Westfield, 07090. Tel: 908-233-0484; Fax: 908-233-6204. Email: office-wc@htisnj.com. Web: www.htisnj.com. Sr. Maureen Fichner, S.S.J., Prin. Lay Teachers 15; Students 131.
School—Holy Trinity Interparochial School (Mountainside Campus), 200 Central Ave., 07092. Tel: 908-233-1899; Fax: 908-233-2109.
Catechesis/Religious Program—Tel: 908-233-1777. Christina Nixon, D.R.E.; Kevin Donahue, Youth Min. Students 378.

NEW MILFORD, BERGEN CO., ASCENSION (1953) Very Rev. David W. Milliken; Rev. Ernesto C. Tibay;

Deacon Paul Kliauga.
Res.: 256 Azalea Dr., 07646. Tel: 201-836-8961; Fax: 201-836-5896.
School—Transfiguration Academy, 10 Bradley Ave., Bergenfield, 07621. Tel: 201-834-3627; Fax: 201-834-0293. Salvatore Tralongo, Prin. Students 115.
Catechesis/Religious Program—1092 Carnation Dr., 07646. Tel: 201-836-3085; Fax: 201-836-3130. Theresa Carbone, C.R.E. Students 300.

NEW PROVIDENCE, UNION CO., OUR LADY OF PEACE (1942) Rev. William A. Mahon; Rev. Msgrs. Paul J. Hayes, Pastor Emeritus (Retired); Charles W. Gusmer (Retired); Rev. Philip A. Sanders; Deacons Charlie Boucher II; Kenneth DiPaola.
Res.: 111 South St., 07974. Tel: 908-464-7600; Fax: 908-508-1845. Email: new-secretary@olpnp.com. Web: www.ourladyofpeaceparish.org.
School—The Academy of Our Lady of Peace, (Grades PreK-8), 99 South St., 07974. Tel: 908-464-8657; Fax: 908-464-3377. Thomas C. Berrios, Prin. Lay Teachers 20; Librarian 1; Students 233.
Catechesis/Religious Program—Tel: 908-464-8156. Email: catoff@olpnp.com. Students 412.
Convent—Tel: 908-464-8223.

NORTH ARLINGTON, BERGEN CO., QUEEN OF PEACE (1922) Rev. Msgrs. William J. Fadrowski; Thomas G. Madden, Pastor Emeritus (Retired); Revs. Scott Attanasio; Charles M. Kelly; Bro. Francis M. Farrell, F.M.S., Pastoral Assoc.; Sr. Anita Maria O'Dwyer, S.S.J., Pastoral Assoc.; Deacons William R. Benedetto; William H. Myers.
Res.: 10 Franklin Pl., 07031. Tel: 201-997-0700; Fax: 201-997-6214. Email: qpchurch@comcast.net. Web: www.qpgs.org/church.htm.
School—(1925), (Grades PreK-8), 21 Church Pl., 07031. Tel: 201-998-8222; Fax: 201-997-7930. Email: info@qpgs.org. Web: www.qpgs.org. Ms. Terri Suchocki, Prin. Lay Teachers 16; Students 288.
High School—(1930) 191 Rutherford Pl., 07031. Tel: 201-998-8227; Fax: 201-998-3040. Email: qphs@qphs.org. Web: www.qphs.org. Bro. Lawrence Lavallee, F.M.S., Prin.; Charles Syby, Asst. Prin. Sisters 3; Brothers 1; Lay Teachers 32; Students 380.
Catechesis/Religious Program— Mary Fleischbein, D.R.E. Students 453.
Convent—Tel: 201-997-2141; 201-991-0235 (La Salle Parish Center).

NORTH BERGEN, HUDSON CO.
1—ST. BRIGID (1900) Merged with St. Rocco's, Union City to form Saint Rocco/Saint Brigid, Union City. For inquiries see Saint Rocco/Saint Bridgid, Union City listing.
2—OUR LADY OF FATIMA (1963) Rev. Peter G. Wehrle.
Res.: 8016 Kennedy Blvd., 07047. Tel: 201-869-7244; Fax: 201-869-0940. Email: office@ourladyoffatimanj.org. Web: www.ourladyoffatimanj.org.
Catechesis/Religious Program—Tel: 201-869-0506. Robert Burkot, D.R.E. Students 176.
3—SACRED HEART (1917), (Polish), Rev. Anthony G. Robak.
Mailing Address: Box 9007, 07047. Email: att33940@attglobal.net.
Res.: 246 Hudson Pl., Cliffside Park, 07010. Tel: 201-943-0305; Fax: 201-943-2676. Email: att33940@attglobal.net.
Catechesis/Religious Program—Mr. Robert Francin Jr., D.R.E. Students 65.

NORTH CALDWELL, ESSEX CO., NOTRE DAME (1962) Very Rev. Anthony J. Randazzo; Sr. Carol Jaruszewski, R.S.M., Pastoral Assoc. In Res., Rev. Msgrs. Kenneth J. Herbster (Retired); Owen J. Hendry (Retired).
Res.: 359 Central Ave., 07006. Tel: 973-226-0979; Fax: 973-226-4118. Email: ndparish@aol.com. Web: www.notredameparish.com.
See Trinity Academy under St. Aloysius, Caldwell for details.
Catechesis/Religious Program—Tel: 973-228-3338. Students 480.

NORTHVALE, BERGEN CO., ST. ANTHONY'S (1890) Very Rev. Gerald T. Hahn; Deacon Joseph S. Romano.
Res.: 199 Walnut St., 07647. Tel: 201-768-1177; Fax: 201-768-2522. Email: stanthonychurch@optonline.net.
Catechesis/Religious Program—Tel: 201-768-5945. Leslie Cooke, D.R.E.; Lu Ann Weis, Youth Min. Students 349.

NORWOOD, BERGEN CO., IMMACULATE CONCEPTION (1921) Rev. Leo J. Butler; Sr. Elizabeth Holler, S.C., Pastoral Assoc.; Deacon James J. Puliatte.
Res.: 211 Summit St., 07648. Tel: 201-768-1600; Fax: 201-768-8006. Email: iccnorwood@verizon.net. Web: www.iccnorwood.org.
Catechesis/Religious Program—Tel: 201-768-1771. Sr. Susanne Reynolds, S.S.J., D.R.E.; Eileen Leocata, Coord. Youth Min. Students 200.

NUTLEY, ESSEX CO.
1—HOLY FAMILY (1909), (Italian), Rev. Msgr. Paul L. Bochicchio; Revs. John F. Gordon; Mauro Primavera; Sr. Eileen Hubbert, S.S.J., Pastoral Assoc.
Res.: 28 Brookline Ave., 07110. Tel: 973-667-0026; Fax: 973-661-1714.
School—Good Shepherd Academy, Elementary, 24 Brookline Ave., 07110. Tel: 973-667-2049; Fax: 973-661-9259. Sr. Jane Feltz, Prin.
Catechesis/Religious Program—Tel: 973-667-6018. Sr. Angelina DelVecchio, M.P.F., D.R.E. Students 663.
Convent—60 Harrison St., 07110. Tel: 973-667-2050.
2—ST. MARY'S (1876) Revs. Ernest G. Rush; Michael E. Gubernat, Parochial Vicar; Thomas D. Nicastro Jr., Parochial Vicar; Deacon Reynaldo M. Trinidad; Karen E. Moore, Business Admin. In Res., Rev. Matthew Kunnath (Retired); Most Rev. Charles J. McDonnell (Retired).
Res.: 17 Msgr. Owens Pl., 07110. Tel: 973-235-1100; Fax: 973-661-0233. Email: info@stmarysnutley.org. Web: www.stmarysnutley.org.
See Good Shepherd Academy, Nutley under Holy Family, Nutley for details.
Catechesis/Religious Program—Tel: 973-667-8239; Fax: 973-661-0233. Brian Lynch, D.R.E. Students 600.
3—OUR LADY OF MOUNT CARMEL (1925), (Polish), Revs. Dennis E. Reiff; Malachy E. Odoh, Parochial Vicar; Deacon Aldo P. Antola.
Res.: 120 Prospect St., 07110. Tel: 973-667-2580; Fax: 973-667-0648. Email: olmcnutley@optimum.net. Web: www.olmc-nutley.org.
See Good Shepherd Academy, Nutley under Holy Family, Nutley for details.
Catechesis/Religious Program—Email: olmc.religion@optimum.net. Sr. Mary Rose Conforto, M.P.F., D.R.E.; Denise Roman, Youth Min. Students 110.
Convent—60 Harrison St., 07110. Tel: 973-667-2050.

OAKLAND, BERGEN CO., OUR LADY OF PERPETUAL HELP (1960) Very Rev. Thomas P. Lipnicki; Carol Willis, Pastoral Assoc.; Mrs. Kate Unger, Parish Nurse.
25 Purdue Ave., 07436. Tel: 201-337-7596; Fax: 201-337-7810. Email: parish@olphoakland.org. Web: www.olphoakland.org.
Catechesis/Religious Program—Tel: 201-337-5537. Email: reled@olphoakland.org. Mrs. Colleen Jagde, P.C.L.; Brian Salvatore, Youth Min. Students 500.

OLD TAPPAN, BERGEN CO., ST. PIUS X (1954) Rev. Patrick M. Mulewski; Deacons John J. McKenna; Richard G. Hodges; Ron Binaghi, Youth Min.; Jeanine Binaghi, Youth Min.; Fred Golz, Music Min.
Res.: 268 Old Tappan Rd., 07675. Tel: 201-664-0913; Fax: 201-664-1013. Email: stpiusot@optonline.net. Web: www.saintpiuschurch.com; www.saintpiusmusic.com.
Catechesis/Religious Program—Tel: 201-664-0927. Maria C. Charowsky, D.R.E. Students 402.

ORADELL, BERGEN CO., ST. JOSEPH'S (1903) Revs. Thomas B. Iwanowski; George M. Reilly, Pastor Emeritus (Retired); Raul Silva; Roy B. Regaspi; Heath Winborn, Dir. Opers.
Res.: 105 Harrison St., New Milford, 07646. Tel: 201-261-0148; Fax: 201-261-0369. Email: office@sjcnj.org. Web: www.sjcnj.org.
School—(1939), (Grades PreK-8), 305 Elm St., 07649. Tel: 201-261-2388; Fax: 201-261-0830. Colette Vail, Prin.; Maria Rose Contini, Librarian. Lay Teachers 27; Students 285.
Catechesis/Religious Program—300 Elm St., 07649. Tel: 201-261-1144; Fax: 201-634-0640. Anthony Armando, C.R.E. & Youth Min. Students 925.

ORANGE, ESSEX CO.
1—HOLY SPIRIT (1931) Merged For inquiries for parish records contact Holy Spirit-Our Lady Help of Christians, East Orange. Tel: 201-673-1077.
2—ST. JOHN'S (1862), (Hispanic), [CEM] Very Rev. George Faour; Rev. Msgr. Ricardo Gonzalez, Pastor Emeritus (Retired); Rev. Carlos M. Viego, Parochial Vicar; Deacon Jerry Romero.
Res.: 94 Ridge St., 07050. Tel: 973-674-0110; Fax: 973-674-3965. Email: stjohnora@comcast.net. Web: www.stjohnscatholicchurch.net.
School—(1862), (Grades PreK-8), 455 White St., 07050. Tel: 973-674-8951; Fax: 973-674-6126. Sr. Kieran Chidi Nduagbo, D.D.L., Prin. Sisters of Charity 2; Daughters of Divine Love 2; Lay Teachers 11; Students 205.
Catechesis/Religious Program—Students 165.
Convent—Tel: 973-673-1263; Fax: 973-731-9604.
Convent—Sisters of Charity, 70 Ridge St., 07050.
3—MT. CARMEL (1896), (Italian), Revs. Sean Britto, C.S.J.; Victor Shoemaker, C.S.J.
Res.: 103 S. Center St., 07050. Tel: 973-674-2052; Fax: 973-675-1342. Email: olmcorange@yahoo.com. Web: www.ourladyofmtcarmel.info.
Catechesis/Religious Program—Students 62.
4—OUR LADY OF THE VALLEY (1873) Revs. John Grinsell, S.D.B.; Armand Quinto, S.D.B.
Res.: 510 Valley St., 07050. Tel: 973-674-7500; Fax: 973-672-8341. Email: olvgeneral@comcast.net. Web: www.olvalley.org.
Catechesis/Religious Program—Tel: 973-674-4272. Email: margaretnovak@comcast.net. Margaret Novak, D.R.E. Students 105.
5—ST. VENANTIUS (1886) Merged Sacramental records located at the Archives, Walsh Library, Seton Hall University, South Orange. Tel: 973-761-9126; Fax: 973-761-9550.

PALISADES PARK, BERGEN CO.
1—ST. MICHAEL'S (1912) Revs. James F. Reilly; Ethiege Silva, O.M.I.; Deacon Joseph Kim; John Portscher, Music Dir. In Res., Rev. Stanley M. Lobo (Retired).
Res.: 19 E. Central Blvd., 07650-1799. Tel: 201-944-1061; Fax: 201-947-1798. Email: saintmichaelpp@aol.com.
School—Notre Dame Interparochial, Elementary Division (1991), (Grades PreK-8), 312 First St., 07650. Tel: 201-947-5262; Fax: 201-947-8319. Rita Miragliotta, Prin.
Catechesis/Religious Program—Students 88.
2—ST. NICHOLAS (1923), (Italian—Brazilian), Revs. Armando M. Palmieri, S.D.V. (Italy); Stephen Ehiahuruike, S.D.V., Parochial Vicar.
Res.: 442 E. Brinkerhoff Ave., 07650. Tel: 201-944-1154; Fax: 201-944-9510. Email: stnicholas07650@live.com. Web: www.saintnicholas-parish.info.
See Notre Dame Interparochial, Elementary Division under St. Michael's, Palisades Park for details.
Catechesis/Religious Program—Tel: 201-944-1138. Bro. Felix Mazeli, S.D.V., D.R.E. Students 69.

PARAMUS, BERGEN CO.
1—CARMELITE CHAPEL OF ST. THERESE (1970) Revs. Eugene Joseph Bettinger, O.Carm.; Guy McPartland, O.Carm.
Res.: 1095 Teaneck Rd., Teaneck, 07666. Tel: 201-837-3354.
Chapel: Bergen Town Center, 07652. Tel: 201-845-6115; Fax: 201-837-3360.
2—CHURCH OF THE ANNUNCIATION (1953) Rev. James V. Teti; Deacons Joseph Niland; William D. Joyce; Sr. Clare DeGregorio, C.S.J., Pastoral Assoc. In Res., Rev. Msgr. Richard F. Groncki.
Res.: 50 W. Midland Ave., 07652-2140. Tel: 201-261-6322; Fax: 201-261-6227. Email: info@annunciationchurch.org. Web: annunciationchurch.org.
Parish Center & Mailing Address: 49 Demarest Rd., 07652-2109.
See Visitation Academy, Paramus under Our Lady of Visitation, Paramus for details.
Catechesis/Religious Program—Tel: 201-261-4119. Mrs. Gladys Pozza, Dir. Faith Formatioin. Students 442.
3—OUR LADY OF THE VISITATION (1952) Revs. Eugene J. Field; Jose Monte De Oca; Sebastian Kunnath; Deacons Peter R. Emr; Todd Rushing. In Res., Very Rev. Matthias T. Conva (Retired).
Res.: 234 Farview Ave., 07652. Tel: 201-261-6080; Fax: 201-261-2995. Email: rectory@olvcommunity.org. Web: www.olvcommunity.org.
School—Visitation Academy (1991), (Grades PreK-8), 222 Farview Ave., 07652. Tel: 201-262-6067; Fax: 201-261-4613. Sr. Philomena Marie McCartney, O.P., Prin.; Carolyn O'Leary, Asst. Prin. Co-Sponsored. Sisters 1; Lay Teachers 20; Students 315.
Catechesis/Religious Program—Tel: 201-265-3812. Mrs. Barbara D'Arrigo, D.R.E.; Mr. Robert Leichte, Youth Min. Students 450.

PARK RIDGE, BERGEN CO., OUR LADY OF MERCY (1902) Very Rev. Charles P. Granstrand; Rev. Robert T. Ulak; Deacon George F. Rice; Mr. John Rokoszak, Pastoral Assoc. In Res., Rev. Msgr. Carl D. Hinrichsen (Retired).
Res.: 2 Fremont Ave., 07656. Tel: 201-391-5315; Fax: 201-391-5614. Email: olm.church@gmail.com. Web: www.urolm.org.
School—Our Lady of Mercy Academy (1950), (Grades PreK-8), 25 Fremont Ave., 07656. Tel: 201-391-3838; Fax: 201-391-3080. Laraine Meehan, Prin.; Karen Lawrence, Librarian. Lay Teachers 32; Students 374.
Catechesis/Religious Program—50 Pascack Rd., 07656. Tel: 201-391-3590; Fax: 201-802-1771. Amy Ballanco, D.R.E. Students 831.

PLAINFIELD, UNION CO.
1—ST. BERNARD'S (1921) Merged with St. Stanislaus Kostka to form The Parish of St. Bernard and St. Stanislaus, Plainfield.
2—ST. MARY (1851) [CEM] Revs. Luis P. Gonzalez; Kenneth Jones, Pastor Emeritus (Retired); Rafael Velazquez; Pablo A. Martinez; Deacon Pedro Nieves. In Res., Rev. Michael J. Feketie (Retired).
Res.: 516 W. Sixth St., 07060. Tel: 908-756-0085; Fax: 908-756-1658. Email: stmarysplainfield@msn.com. Web:

www.stmarysnj.com.
Catechesis/Religious Program—Students 722.
Convent—Missionaries of Charity, (Contemplative), 513 Liberty St., 07060. Tel: 908-754-1978. Sisters 14.
Cemetery—300 Berckman St., 07060.

3—THE PARISH OF ST. BERNARD AND ST. STANISLAUS (2005) Revs. Frank Rose; Jan Krzystof Lebdowicz (Poland); Beverly Cirino, Pastoral Assoc.
Office & Rectory: 368 Sumner Ave., 07062. Tel: 908-756-3393; Fax: 908-756-3059. Email: office@bestchurch.net. Web: www.bestchurch.net.
Catechesis/Religious Program—Ms. Patricia Cook, D.R.E.; Chuck Ropars, Youth Min.; Karole Lechowsk, Youth Min.; Mark Nekhay, Youth Min. Students 150.

4—ST. STANISLAUS KOSTKA (1919) Merged with St. Bernard's to form The Parish of St. Bernard and St. Stanislaus, Plainfield.

RAHWAY, UNION CO.

1—DIVINE MERCY PARISH (2010) [CEM] Revs. Dennis J. Kaelin; Peter Vo; Robert Lamirez.
232 Central Ave., 07065.
Res. & Office: 232 Central Ave., 07065. Tel: 732-388-0082; Fax: 732-388-0020. Email: stmaryschurchnj@comcast.net. Web: www.divinemercyparishnj.com.
See Sts. Mary & Elizabeth Academy, Linden under St. Elizabeth's, Linden for details.
Catechesis/Religious Program—Tel: 732-382-0004; Fax: 732-382-4784. Email: frdenniskaelin@yahoo.com. Students 217.

2—ST. MARK'S (1871), (German), Merged with St. Mary's, Rahway to form Divine Mercy Parish, Rahway.

3—ST. MARY'S (1854) [CEM] Merged with St. Mark's, Rahway to form Divine Mercy, Rahway.

RAMSEY, BERGEN CO., ST. PAUL (1939) Rev. Richard J. Kelly; Rev. Msgr. Lawrence W. Cull, Pastor Emeritus (Retired); Rev. Yeongmin Kim; Deacons Jeremiah K. Rehse; Fritz Kautz; Mr. John Nunziata, Pastoral Assoc.; Mr. Keith Guthrie, Dir. Music & Worship; Genny Latour Huss, Dir. Sr. Ministry; Mr. Robert Cestola, Business Mgr.
Res.: 200 Wyckoff Ave., 07446. Tel: 201-327-0976; Fax: 201-327-6197.
School—St. Paul's Interparochial School, 187 Wyckoff Ave., 07446. Tel: 201-327-1108; Fax: 201-236-1318. Gail Ritchie, Prin. Lay Teachers 27; Students 268.
Catechesis/Religious Program—Tel: 201-327-8010. Sr. Christine Tobin, S.F.C.C., Dir. Faith Formation; Ms. Diane Campbell, D.R.E.; Eric Erler, Youth Min. Students 1,700.

RIDGEFIELD PARK, BERGEN CO., ST. FRANCIS OF ASSISI (1890) Revs. Larry Evans II; Viktor Markovic; Guillermo Mora (Colombia).
Res.: 114 Mt. Vernon St., 07660. Tel: 201-641-6464; Fax: 201-641-2282. Email: pacosta@stfrancisrp.org. Web: www.stfrancisrp.org.
Catechesis/Religious Program—Celeste Farrell, D.R.E. Students 287.

RIDGEFIELD, BERGEN CO., ST. MATTHEW'S (1899) Very Rev. Steven Conner; Revs. Jose Manuel; Romeo Panes, O.S.J.; Deacon Joseph A. Dickson. In Res., Rev. Msgr. William J. Koplik (Retired).
Res.: 555 Prospect Ave., 07657. Tel: 201-945-3500; Fax: 201-945-3796. Email: stmatthews@nj.rr.org. Web: stmatthewridgefield.org.
School—Notre Dame Interparochial Primary Division (1991), (Grades PreK-8), 312 First St., Palisades Park, 07650. Tel: 201-947-5262; Fax: 201-947-8319. Web: www.notredameint.org. Rita Miragliotta, Prin.; Rose Ramundo, Librarian. Lay Teachers 20; Students 311.
Catechesis/Religious Program—Students 246.

RIDGEWOOD, BERGEN CO., OUR LADY OF MOUNT CARMEL (1889) Rev. Msgr. Ronald J. Rozniak; Revs. Thomas Patrick Quinn; Kevin G. Waymel; Deacons Robert V. Thomann; Nicholas De Lucca; Mrs. Linda English, Pastoral Assoc.; Mr. Peter Sicko, Music Min.; Glen McCall, Youth Min. In Res., Revs. Mert Cordero; Thomas E. Pendrick.
Res.: 1 Passaic St., 07450-4309. Tel: 201-444-2000, Ext. 205; Fax: 201-444-2002. Web: www.olmcridgewood.com. Email: pfrazza@olmcridgewood.com.
School—Academy of Our Lady, (Grades PreK-8) Tel: 201-445-0622; Fax: 201-445-8345. Patricia Keenaghan, Prin.
Catechesis/Religious Program—Tel: 201-444-0211; Fax: 201-444-4421. Ms. Cathy Hunt, D.R.E.; Sarah Kearns, Asst. D.R.E. Students 1,745.

RIVER EDGE, BERGEN CO., ST. PETER THE APOSTLE (1948) Rev. Michael J. Sheehan; Rev. Msgr. David J. Casazza, Pastor Emeritus (Retired); Revs. Michael J. German; Matthew R. Dooley; Deacons Edward Bowen; Andrew J. Golden. In Res., Rev. James P. Ferry.
Res.: 445 Fifth Ave., 07661. Tel: 201-261-3366; Fax: 201-261-0117. Email: reception@saint-peter.org. Web: www.saint-peter.org.
School—St. Peter Academy (1952), (Grades PreK-8), 431 Fifth Ave., 07661. Tel: 201-261-3468; Fax: 201-261-4316. Web: www.spare.org. Mr. James McCarthy, Prin. Lay Teachers 18; Students 194.
Catechesis/Religious Program—Tel: 201-265-6019. Email: faithformation@saint-peter.org. Eileen Hanrahan, Pastoral Min. Catechesis. Students 709.

ROCHELLE PARK, BERGEN CO., SACRED HEART (1917) Rev. Robert Wolfee. In Res., Rev. Michael Fugee.
Res.: 12 Terrace Ave., 07662. Tel: 201-843-1722; Fax: 201-843-3542.
See Visitation Academy, Paramus under Our Lady of the Visitation for details.
Catechesis/Religious Program—Tel: 201-843-1077. Karl Patterman, D.R.E. Students 258.

ROSELAND, ESSEX CO., OUR LADY OF THE BLESSED SACRAMENT (1955) Revs. Robert G. Laferrera; Christopher D. Isinta; Deacon Pat Quagliana; Sr. Rie Crowley, S.S.J., Pastoral Assoc. (Sick and Homebound Parish Outreach); Donald Pennell, Pastoral Assoc. (Liturgical Music). In Res., Rev. James B. Sullivan (Retired).
Res.: 28 Livingston Ave., 07068. Tel: 973-226-7288; Fax: 973-226-4893. Email: olbs28@verizon.net. Web: www.olbs.org.
School—Trinity Academy - PreK, Tel: 973-226-4252. Sr. Suzanne Janis, O.P., Dir.
School: See Trinity Academy under St. Aloysius in Caldwell for details (Grade K-8).
Catechesis/Religious Program—Tel: 973-226-5251; Fax: 973-403-8871. Catherine Gibbons, D.R.E. Students 498.

ROSELLE PARK, UNION CO., THE ASSUMPTION (1907) Rev. James F. Spera.
Res.: 113 Chiego Pl., 07204. Tel: 908-245-1107; Fax: 908-245-2789. Email: assumptionrp@hotmail.com.
Catechesis/Religious Program—110 Chiego Pl., 07204. Tel: 908-245-6572. Rosabel Farruggio, D.R.E. Students 330.

ROSELLE, UNION CO., CHURCH OF ST. JOSEPH THE CARPENTER (1895) Rev. Krzysztof K. Maslowski; Deacon Vincent Belluscio. Sisters of St. Joseph, Chestnut Hill.
Res.: 157 E. Fourth Ave., 07203. Tel: 908-241-1250; Fax: 908-241-6311. Email: sjr157@stjosephroselle.org. Web: www.stjosephsroselle.org.
School—(1913), (Grades PreK-8), 140 E. Third Ave., 07203. Tel: 908-245-6560; Fax: 908-245-3342. Web: www.stjosephsroselle.org. Mary Ellen Woodstock, Prin. Sisters 1; Lay Teachers 17; Students 255.
Catechesis/Religious Program—Students 150.
Convent—135 E. Fourth Ave., 07203. Tel: 908-245-1594.

RUTHERFORD, BERGEN CO., CHURCH OF ST. MARY (1908) Revs. Michael J. Kreder; Charles W. Hartling (Retired); Deacons John Di Meo; James J. Guida; Michael Matthews.
91 Home Ave., 07070. Email: rcansmr@aol.com. Web: www.stmaryrutherford.org.
Res.: 98 Home Ave., 07070. Tel: 201-438-2200; Fax: 201-438-1098. Email: rcansmr@aol.com. Web: www.stmaryrutherford.org.
School—Academy at Saint Mary (1916), (Grades PreK-8), 72 Chestnut St., 07070. Tel: 201-933-8410; Fax: 201-531-9020. Email: principal.smes@gmail.com. Web: www.academyatsmes.org. Elena Simmons, Prin. Lay Teachers 17; Students 270.
High School—(1928) 64 Chestnut St., 07070. Tel: 201-933-5220; Fax: 201-933-0834. Web: www.stmaryhs.org. Roy Corso, Prin. Lay Teachers 30; Students 333.
Catechesis/Religious Program—Tel: 201-438-2476; Fax: 201-438-1098. Betty Hatler, D.R.E. Students 435.

SADDLE BROOK, BERGEN CO.

1—CHURCH OF KOREAN MARTYRS (1986), (Korean), Revs. Hongshik Don Bosco Park, Admin.; Jinwook Han; Deacon Francis E. Noh.
Res.: 585 Saddle River Rd., 07663. Tel: 201-703-0002; Fax: 201-703-7111. Email: martyrsnj@yahoo.com. Web: www.rcckm.org.
Catechesis/Religious Program—Taek Daniel Kim, D.R.E. Students 250.

2—ST. PHILIP THE APOSTLE (1953) Revs. Theesmas Pankiraj; Matthew Fonseka; John Z. Radwan.
Res.: 488 Saddle River Rd., 07663. Tel: 201-843-1888; Fax: 201-368-9161. Email: ourparish@stphilipsb.org. Web: www.stphilipsb.org.
Catechesis/Religious Program—Tel: 201-843-2240; Fax: 201-843-3150. Email: reled@stphilipsb.org. Web: reled-stphilipsb.org. Pat Schauble, D.R.E.; Justin Aughey, Youth Min. Students 491.
Convent—426 Saddle River Rd., 07663. Tel: 201-843-1431.

SADDLE RIVER BOROUGH, BERGEN CO., ST. GABRIEL THE ARCHANGEL (1952) Rev. Msgr. Frank G. Del Prete; Rev. Raphael Lee.
Res.: 3 W. Church Rd., 07458. Tel: 201-327-5663; Fax: 201-327-7063. Email: stgabriel@optonline.net. Web: www.stgabrielchurch.com.
See St. John's Academy, Hillsdale under St. John the Baptist, Hillsdale for details.
Catechesis/Religious Program—Tel: 201-825-0275; Fax: 201-327-7063. Patricia Pula, D.R.E. Students 550.

SCOTCH PLAINS, UNION CO.

1—ST. BARTHOLOMEW (1948) Very Rev. John J. Paladino; Revs. Kevin A. Gugliotta, Parochial Vicar; Thomas A. Dente; Deacons Robert Gurske; Don Hessemer; Paul Milan, Dir. Worship. In Res., Rev. Msgr. John Philip O'Connor (Retired); Revs. John J. Lester (Retired); Kevin F. Murphy.
Res.: 2032 Westfield Ave., 07076. Tel: 908-322-5192; Fax: 908-322-2598. Email: contact@stbartholomewchurch.org. Web: www.stbartholomewchurch.org.
School—St. Bartholomew Academy (1950), (Grades PreK-8) Tel: 908-322-4265; Fax: 908-322-7065. Web: www.stbacademy.org. Sr. Elizabeth Calello, M.P.F., Prin.; Marianne Luongo, Librarian. Religious Teachers Filippini 1; Lay Teachers 16; Students 200.
Catechesis/Religious Program—Tel: 908-322-2359. Sr. Phyllis Vella, M.P.F., D.R.E.; Patricia Krema, D.R.E.; Ms. Diane McGee, D.R.E.; Linda Ann Attanasio, Dir. Adult Educ. & Formation; Angela Kobliska, Youth Min.; Paul Kobliska, Youth Min.; Elaine Coupe, Youth Min. Students 685.
Convent—Tel: 908-322-5619.

2—IMMACULATE HEART OF MARY (1964) Rev. Msgr. Sean R. Cunneen; Revs. Antonio Kuizon (Philippines); Francis A. Heinen (Retired); Felicia S. Levine, Pastoral Assoc.
Res.: 1571 S. Martine Ave., 07076. Tel: 908-889-2100; Fax: 908-889-9477. Email: ihm123@aol.com. Web: www.ihmparish.net.
Catechesis/Religious Program—Jeanne Fox, D.R.E.; Ms. Katie Wills, Music Min.; Ms. Pamela Streisel, 7th & 8th Grade Youth Min.; Mr. Matthew Butler, High School Youth Min. Students 708.

SECAUCUS, HUDSON CO., IMMACULATE CONCEPTION (1908) Revs. Joseph P. Pietropinto; John J. Prada; Deacon Earle S. Connelly Jr. In Res., Rev. Alan F. Guglielmo (Retired).
Res.: 1219 Paterson Plank Rd., 07094. Tel: 201-863-4840; Fax: 201-863-3537.
Catechesis/Religious Program—Tel: 201-863-4840, Ext. 28. Linda Meyer, D.R.E.; Faith Elizabeth Rose, Youth Min. Students 475.

SHORT HILLS, ESSEX CO., ST. ROSE OF LIMA (1852) [CEM] Rev. Msgr. George R. Trabold; Revs. M. Christen Beirne, Parochial Vicar; Michael S.P. Trainor; Deacons Anthony Scalzo; Joseph M. Persinger; David J. Hughes. In Res., Rev. Msgr. Philip D. Morris (Retired).
Res.: 50 Short Hills Ave., 07078. Tel: 973-379-3912; Fax: 973-379-6157. Email: jschultz@stroseshorthills.org. Web: www.stroseshorthills.org.
School—(1869), (Grades PreK-8), 52 Short Hills Ave., 07078. Tel: 973-379-3973; Fax: 973-379-3722. Diane L. Pollak, Prin. Lay Teachers 23; Students 200.
Catechesis/Religious Program—Tel: 973-376-1960; Fax: 973-376-3818. Michael Wojcik, D.R.E. Students 750.

SOUTH ORANGE, ESSEX CO., OUR LADY OF SORROWS (1887) Rev. Msgr. Robert E. Emery; Rev. Richard Pfannenstiel; Deacon John M. Inguaggiato; Sr. Mary Selena McHugh, S.C.C., Pastoral Assoc. In Res., Very Rev. Michael M. Walters.
Res.: 217 Prospect St., 07079. Tel: 973-763-5454; Fax: 973-763-9506. Email: ols217so@msn.com. Web: www.olschurch.com.
School—(1890), (Grades PreK-8), 172 Academy St., 07079. Tel: 973-763-5169; Fax: 973-378-9781. Web: www.ourladyofsorrowsschool.org. Sr. Judith Blair, S.C.C., Prin.; Josephine Gorgio, Librarian. Religious 2; Lay Teachers 24; Students 212.
Day Care Nursery—Tel: 973-763-4040; Fax: 973-763-5151. Email: thenurseryols@verizon.net. Bonnie Hughes, Dir. Total Staff 18; Toddler 13; Infant 12.
Catechesis/Religious Program—Tel: 973-763-5454, Ext. 235. Email: reled@olschurch.com. Joan Csedrik, D.R.E.; Christopher Kaiser, Youth Min. Students 373.

SPRINGFIELD, UNION CO., ST. JAMES THE APOSTLE (1923) Rev. Msgr. William C. Hatcher; Rev. James Worth; Deacons Jerry Bongiovanni; Daniel O'Neill.
Res.: 45 S. Springfield Ave., 07081. Tel: 973-376-3044; Fax: 973-376-0560. Web: www.saintjamesparish.org.
School—(Grades PreK-8), 41 S. Springfield Ave., 07081. Tel: 973-376-5194; Fax: 973-376-5228. Email: sjschool@saintjamesparish.org. Ms. Patricia Dolansky. Lay Teachers 18; Students 221.
Catechesis/Religious Program—Tel: 973-376-2061. Nancy Caputo, C.R.E.; Kimberly Mailley, Youth Min. Students 524.

SUMMIT, UNION CO., ST. TERESA'S (1863) [CEM] Revs.

Brian G. Plate; Marco A. Celis Quintero; Rolando Rosendo DeGracia Yadao; Piotr Koziolkiewicz; Angela Intili Stokes, Pastoral Assoc.; Greg Scime, Dir. Music.
Res.: 306 Morris Ave., 07901. Tel: 908-277-3700; Fax: 908-273-5909. Web: www.stteresachurch.org.
School—(Grades PreK) Tel: 908-277-6043; Fax: 908-273-1770. Leann Durner, Prin.
Catechesis/Religious Program—Tel: 908-273-6975; Fax: 908-273-1770. Sheila Higgins, D.R.E.; Francoise Gross, Youth Min., Middle School & Confirmation. Students 1,040; Preschool/Kindergarten 200.
Cemetery & Mausoleum—140 Passaic Ave., 07901. Tel: 908-598-9426 (Cemetery); 908-277-3741 (Mausoleum).

TEANECK, BERGEN CO., ST. ANASTASIA'S (1908) Revs. Daniel O'Neill, O.Carm.; William O'Malley, O.Carm.; Deacons Kevin J. Regan; Roland Bianchi. In Res., Revs. Emmett Gavin, O.Carm.; Eugene Joseph Bettinger, O.Carm.
Res.: 1095 Teaneck Rd., 07666. Tel: 201-837-3354; Fax: 201-837-3360. Email: secretary@saintanastasia.org. Web: www.saintanastasia.org.
Catechesis/Religious Program—Tel: 201-837-3356. Sr. Adrienne Bradley, S.S.J., D.R.E. Students 225.
Convent—Tel: 201-837-3153.

TENAFLY, BERGEN CO., OUR LADY OF MOUNT CARMEL (1873) Rev. Leonard Gilman, O.Carm.; Deacons Lex Ferrauiola; David B. Loman. In Res., Rev. John F. Russell, O.Carm.
Res.: 10 County Rd., 07670. Tel: 201-568-0545; Fax: 201-568-3215.
School—(1879), (Grades PreK-8) Tel: 201-567-6491; Fax: 201-568-1402. Sylvia Cosentino, Prin.; Mrs. Debbie Solga, Librarian. Lay Teachers 21; Students 254.
Catechesis/Religious Program—Tel: 201-871-4662. Elliot Guerra, Coord. Youth Min.; Sr. Regina Chassar, S.S.J., D.R.E. Students 447.

UNION CITY, HUDSON CO.

1—ST. ANTHONY OF PADUA (1899), (Italian), Revs. Jose E. Marquez; Ivan Zant, Parochial Vicar.
Res.: 615 Eighth St., 07087. Tel: 201-867-3818; Fax: 201-867-8859.
See Mother Seton Interparochial under Sts. Joseph and Michael, Union City.
Catechesis/Religious Program—Luis Tobar, D.R.E. Students 275.

2—ST. AUGUSTINE'S (1886) Revs. Thomas J. Devine, O.A.R.; Jose Antonio Ciordia; Blas Montenegro, O.A.R.; Deacon Edward Donosso.
Res.: 3900 New York Ave., 07087. Tel: 201-863-0233.
School—(1891), (Grades PreK-8), 3920 New York Ave., 07087. Tel: 201-865-5319; Fax: 201-865-2567. Sr. Lillian Sharrock, S.C., Prin. Sisters of Charity 4; Lay Teachers 18; Students 370.
Catechesis/Religious Program—Tel: 201-863-0233; Fax: 201-863-1341. Mr. David Pressey Waldburg, D.R.E.; Mr. Damian De Armas, D.R.E. Students 600.
Convent—342 39th St., 07087. Tel: 201-348-0527.

3—HOLY FAMILY (1857) Rev. Francisco J. Legarra, O.A.R.
Res.: 530 35th St., 07087. Tel: 201-867-6535; Fax: 201-867-1357.
Catechesis/Religious Program—Carol Stronach, D.R.E. (English); Juana Alvarado, D.R.E. (Spanish). Students 120.

4—STS. JOSEPH AND MICHAEL (1887; 1851) Revs. Richard J. Carrington; Christian Jaramillo Basquerizo; Deacons Thomas Barrett; Asterio Velasco; Ricardo L. Flores. In Res., Rev. Hector Larrea.
Res.: 1314 Central Ave., 07087. Tel: 201-865-2325; Fax: 201-348-4412. Email: stsjosephandmichael@gmail.com.
School—Mother Seton Interparochial, (Grades PreK-8), 1501 New York Ave., 07087. Tel: 201-863-8433; Fax: 201-863-8145. Mary P. McErlaine, Prin. Lay Teachers 8; Students 230.
Catechesis/Religious Program—Tel: 201-863-8145. Ms. Victoria Velasco, Dir. Youth. Students 380.

5—SAINT ROCCO/SAINT BRIGID (1912) Revs. Manuel D. Rios; Juan Luis Calderon, O.A.R. (Spain), Parochial Vicar.
Res.: 4206 Kennedy Blvd., 07087. Tel: 201-863-1427; Fax: 201-863-3877. Email: strocco@verizon.net.
Catechesis/Religious Program—Students 114.
Mission House—4214 Kennedy Blvd., 07087. Tel: 201-863-5727.

UNION, UNION CO.

1—HOLY SPIRIT (1963) Revs. Armand Mantia; Alfred Burke; Marco Hurtado-Olazo; Deacons Joseph J. Carlo; Stanley W. Kwiatek.
Res.: 984 Suburban Rd., 07083. Tel: 908-687-3327; Fax: 908-687-1312. Email: holyspiritchurch@comcast.net. Web: www.holyspiritunion.org.
School—(Grades PreK-8), 970 Suburban Rd., 07083. Tel: 908-687-8415; Fax: 908-687-3996. Barbara Prescott, Prin. Lay Teachers 14; Students 240.
Catechesis/Religious Program—984 Suburban Rd., 07083. Tel: 908-964-7533. Catherine Drake, D.R.E. Students 500.

2—ST. MICHAEL'S (1928) Revs. Charles B. McDermott; Wilson A. Paculan; Ward P. Moore (Retired); Ranulfo D. Docabo.
Res.: 1212 Kelly St., 07083. Tel: 908-688-1232; Fax: 908-810-1076. Email: stmichaelunion@comcast.net.
School—(1931), (Grades PreK-8) Tel: 908-688-1063; Fax: 908-687-7927. Antoinette Telle, Prin. Sisters of St. Dominic 1; Lay Teachers 24; Students 363.
Catechesis/Religious Program—Tel: 908-964-0965. Marilynn Dragone, C.R.E.; Philip Matrale, Youth Min. Tel: 908-686-3762. Students 645.
Convent—1211 Orange Ave., 07083. Tel: 908-686-3839.

UPPER MONTCLAIR, ESSEX CO., ST. CASSIAN (1895) Revs. Marc A. Vicari; Camilo E. Cruz, Parochial Vicar.
Res.: 187 Bellevue Ave., 07043. Tel: 973-744-2850; Fax: 973-744-6187. Email: parishoffice@stcassianchurch.org. Web: www.saintcassianchurchuppermontclair.org.
School—(Grades PreK-8), 190 Lorraine Ave., 07043. Tel: 973-746-1636; Fax: 973-746-3271. Email: info@stcassianschool.org. Mary Cassels, Prin. Lay Teachers 15; Students 225.
Catechesis/Religious Program—Regina Sammon, D.R.E. Students 585.

UPPER SADDLE RIVER, BERGEN CO., CHURCH OF THE PRESENTATION (1961) Revs. Robert B. Stagg; Lope Lesigues; Jacek Marchewka. In Res., Rev. Msgr. Edward J. Ciuba (Retired).
Office: 271 W. Saddle River Rd., 07458. Tel: 201-327-1313; Fax: 201-760-2570. Web: www.churchofpresentation.org.
Res.: 41 Riverview Ter., 07458.
See St. Paul's Interparochial School, Ramsey under St. Paul's, Ramsey for details.
Catechesis/Religious Program—Students 1,424.

VERONA, ESSEX CO., OUR LADY OF THE LAKE (1923) Revs. Michael A. Hanly; Jerome S. Arthasseril (India); Paul C. Houlis; Deacon David Strader. In Res., Very Rev. Albert J. Berner.
Res.: 32 Lakeside Ave., 07044. Tel: 973-239-5696; Fax: 973-239-7190. Email: maryjane_curran@ollverona.org. Web: www.ollverona.org.
School—(1924), (Grades PreK-8), 22 Lakeside Ave., 07044. Tel: 973-239-1160; Fax: 973-239-6496. Sr. Mary Agnes Sullivan, O.P., Prin. Sisters 1; Lay Teachers 10; Students 196.
Catechesis/Religious Program—Margaret Gardner, D.R.E.; Barbara Camp, Youth Min. Students 847.
Convent—Tel: 973-239-4767.

WALLINGTON, BERGEN CO., MOST SACRED HEART OF JESUS (1942), (Polish), [CEM] Very Rev. Canon Felix R. Marciniak; Revs. Steven D. D'Andrea; Jerzy Pikulinski; Deacons Victor J. Puzio; Domenick DiBernardo; Sr. Emilia Zdeb, S.S.N.D., Pastoral Assoc.
Res.: 127 Paterson Ave., 07057. Tel: 973-778-7405; Fax: 973-777-4982. Email: mostsacredheart@comcast.net. Web: www.mostsacredheart.org.
School—(1943), (Grades PreK-8), 6 Bond St., 07057. Tel: 973-777-4817. Email: mostsacredheartschool@comcast.net. Sr. Lisa Marie DiSabatino, C.S.S.F., Prin. Sisters 2; Lay Teachers 18; Students 257.
Catechesis/Religious Program—Tel: 973-777-9505; Fax: 973-778-7750; 973-777-4982. Sr. Marie Victoria Bartkowski, D.R.E. Students 305.
Convent—27 Dankhoff Ave., 07057. Tel: 973-777-5124.

WASHINGTON TOWNSHIP, BERGEN CO., OUR LADY OF GOOD COUNSEL (1959) Revs. Stephen J. Cinque; Stephen J. Duffe; Sr. Joseph Miriam Blackwell, M.S.B.T., Pastoral Assoc.; Deacon Robert Glasner. In Res., Rev. Stephen J. Toth.
Res.: 668 Ridgewood Rd., 07676. Tel: 201-664-6624; Fax: 201-664-0095. Email: olgcwt@aol.com. Web: www.olgcwt.org.
See Our Lady of Mercy Interparochial School, Park Ridge under Our Lady of Mercy, Park Ridge for details.
See St. John's Academy Interparochial, Hillsdale under St. John The Baptist, Hillsdale for details.
Catechesis/Religious Program—Tel: 201-664-1679. Matthew De Caux, C.R.E. Students 158.

WEEHAWKEN, HUDSON CO., ST. LAWRENCE'S (1887) Very Rev. James P. Whelan.
Res.: 1 St. Lawrence Pl., 07086. Tel: 201-863-6464; Fax: 201-863-6656. Email: stlawrencec@optonline.net. Web: www.stlawrence-church.net.
See Hoboken Catholic Academy, Hoboken under St. Ann's, Hoboken for details.
Catechesis/Religious Program—Students 91.

WEST NEW YORK, HUDSON CO.

1—HOLY REDEEMER Very Rev. Carlo Fortunio (Italy); Rev. Paolo Tanzini. In Res., Rev. Angelo Pochetti (Italy).
Res.: 6502 Jackson St., 07093. Tel: 201-868-9444; Fax: 201-868-5944. Email: holyredeemer569@verizon.net.
Office: 569 65th St., 07093.
Catechesis/Religious Program—Ed Mendoza, D.R.E.; Philip Dispensa, D.R.E.; Jaime Trelles, D.R.E.; Rosa Trelles, D.R.E. Students 320.

2—ST. JOSEPH OF THE PALISADES (1875), (Hispanic), Rev. Msgr. Gregory J. Studerus; Revs. Jozef Krajnak, S.D.B., Parochial Vicar; Jesus Orlando Rengifo, Parochial Vicar; Oscar D. Fonseca, Parochial Vicar; Alexander Cruz. In Res., Most Rev. David Arias, O.A.R., Pastor Emeritus; Rev. Juan Luis Calderon, O.A.R. (Spain).
Res.: 6401 Palisade Ave., 07093. Tel: 201-854-7006; Fax: 201-861-7799. Email: st.joseph.wny@verizon.net.
School—(1872), (Grades PreK-8), 6408 Palisade Ave., 07093. Tel: 201-861-3227; Fax: 201-861-5744. Web: www.stjosephpalisadeselem.com. Eileen Donovan-Ferrando, Prin. Franciscan Missionary Sisters of the Sacred Heart 3; Lay Teachers 10; Students 197.
Catechesis/Religious Program—Andres Melendez, C.R.E.; Janet Melendez, C.R.E. Students 600.
Chapel—Immaculate Heart of Mary 7615 Broadway, North Bergen, 07047.
Chapel—Cor Jesu 5400 Broadway, 07093.
Convent—6414 Palisade Ave., 07093. Tel: 201-861-3337.

3—ST. MARY HELP OF CHRISTIANS (1895) Merged with St. John Nepomucene, Guttenberg to form Holy Redeemer, West New York.

4—OUR LADY OF LIBERA (1902) Very Rev. Carlo Fortunio (Italy), Admin.; Rev. Philip J. Rotunno, Pastor Emeritus (Retired); Deacon Jesus D. Aristy; Edward Mendoza, Business Mgr.
Res.: 5808 John F. Kennedy Memorial Blvd., 07093. Tel: 201-867-2642.
Catechesis/Religious Program—Ana M. Castaneda, D.R.E. (English); Ana M. Zarama, D.R.E. (Spanish). Students 85.

WEST ORANGE, ESSEX CO.

1—ST. JOSEPH'S (1931) Rev. Msgr. Donald E. Guenther (Retired); Deacons Richard O'Hara; Luis Velo. In Res., Rev. Msgr. Thomas P. Ivory (Retired); Rev. James R. White.
Res.: 44 Benvenue Ave., 07052. Tel: 973-669-3221; Fax: 973-669-0385. Email: stjosephwestorange@hotmail.com. Web: stjosephwestorange.com.
School—Blessed Pope John XXIII Academy (2006), (Grades PreK-8), (Co-Sponsored with Our Lady of Lourdes, West Orange), 8 St. Cloud Pl., 07052. Tel: 973-731-3503; Fax: 973-731-2117. Web: www.bpjxxii-i.org. Lynda Wright, Prin.; Charles O'Brien, Librarian. Lay Teachers 21; Students 200.
Catechesis/Religious Program—Pauline Alger, Pastoral Assoc. & D.R.E. Students 140.

2—OUR LADY OF LOURDES (1914) Rev. Msgr. Joseph A. Petrillo; Rev. Edson Fernando Costa; Deacon Ernesto Abad. In Res., Rev. Hippolytus Duru (Nigeria) (NY).
Res.: 1 Eagle Rock Ave., 07052. Tel: 973-325-0110; Fax: 973-325-9105. Email: ollwo@comcast.net. Web: www.lourdeswestorgange.com.
See Blessed Pope John XIII Academy, West Orange under St. Joseph's, West Orange for details.
Catechesis/Religious Program—Tel: 973-325-0029. Eileen Morgan, D.R.E. Students 123.
Convent—Tel: 973-325-0318; Fax: 973-325-0691.

WESTFIELD, UNION CO.

1—ST. HELEN (1968) Rev. Michael A. Saporito; Rev. Msgr. James F. Bouffard; Rev. Frank J. Fano; Deacon John W. Lynch; Marilyn Ryan, Pastoral Assoc.; Carolyn Colonna, Business Mgr.; Cindy Brogan, Music Min.
Res.: 1600 Rahway Ave., 07090. Tel: 908-232-1214; Fax: 908-317-5459. Email: sthelen@sainthelen.org. Web: www.sainthelen.org.
See Holy Trinity Interparochial school, Westfield under Holy Trinity, Westfield for details.
Catechesis/Religious Program—Kathy Dulan, D.R.E.; Cathy Ochs, D.R.E.; Matthew T. Toriello, Youth Min.; Patricia Gardner, Youth Min. Students 1,763.

2—HOLY TRINITY (1872) Rev. Msgr. Joseph P. Masiello; Rev. James M. Moran, Parochial Vicar; Deacons Thomas A. Pluta; Keith Gibbons.
Church & Office: 315 First St., 07090. Tel: 908-232-8137; Fax: 908-654-8780. Email: donna.campa@verizon.net. Web: www.htrcc.org.
School—Holy Trinity Interparochial, (Grades PreK-8), Interparochial (co-sponsored), 336 First St., 07090. Tel: 908-233-0484; Fax: 908-233-6204. Email: office-wc@htisnj.com. Web: www.htisnj.com. Sr. Maureen Fichner, S.S.J., Prin.; Renee Rauch,

Librarian.
School—Holy Trinity Interparochial (Mountainside Campus), (Grades PreK-K), 304 Central Ave., Mountainside, 07092. Tel: 908-233-1899; Fax: 908-654-6690. Sr. Maureen Fichner, S.S.J., Prin.; Renee Rauch, Librarian. Students 360.
Catechesis/Religious Program—Tel: 908-233-7455; Fax: 908-233-0837. Email: mangelo@parishmail.com. Michelle Angelo, D.R.E.; Patricia Martin, Youth Min. Students 830.

WESTWOOD, BERGEN CO., ST. ANDREW'S (1889) [CEM] Revs. John R. O'Connell; Rafael I. Galvez-Pineda; Deacon Robert S. Pontillo; Alan Pitman, Youth Min.
Res.: 120 Washington Ave., 07675. Tel: 201-666-1100; Fax: 201-722-1432. Email: parishinfo@standrewcc.com. Web: www.standrewcc.com.
See St. John's Academy, Hillsdale under St. John the Baptist, Hillsdale for details.
Catechesis/Religious Program—Tel: 201-664-6777. Email: reled@standrewcc.com. Mary Jean Conroy, D.R.E.; Carol Stalter, Asst. D.R.E. Students 806.

WOOD RIDGE, BERGEN CO., OUR LADY OF THE ASSUMPTION (1926) Revs. Richard J. Mucowski, O.F.M.; Julian S. Jagudilla, O.F.M.; Bro. Paul Keenan, O.F.M.; Deacons Nicholas Valdez; Francis P. Materia.
Res.: 143 First St., 07075. Tel: 201-438-5555; Fax: 201-438-6747. Email: assumption143@yahoo.com. Web: www.assumption-parish.org.
Catechesis/Religious Program—Hayes Center, 142 Second St. Tel: 201-933-6118; Fax: 201-438-6747. Email: arewrnj@yahoo.com. Caroline Valdez, D.R.E.; Eileen Barroso, Youth Min.; John Calabrese, Youth Min.; Lisa Pisano, Youth Min.; Michael Pisano, Youth Min. Students 346.
Convent—450 Main Ave., 07075. Tel: 201-939-4274.

WOODCLIFF LAKE, BERGEN CO., OUR LADY MOTHER OF THE CHURCH (1967) Rev. Sean Manson; Rev. Msgr. Cajetan P. Salemi, Pastor Emeritus (Retired); Deacon Stanley F. Fedison. In Res., Rev. Robert A. Antczak (Retired).
Church: 209 Woodcliff Ave., 07677. Tel: 201-391-2826; Fax: 201-391-7101. Email: judiolmc@yahoo.com. Web: www.motherofthechurch.com.
Rectory—130 Apple Ridge, 07677.
See St. John's Academy, Hillsdale under St. John the Baptist, Hillsdale for details.
Catechesis/Religious Program—Tel: 201-391-7400; Fax: 201-391-7162. Francesca Orefice, Dir. Faith Formation; Connie Trombetta, C.R.E. Students 305.

WYCKOFF, BERGEN CO., ST. ELIZABETH (1902) Rev. Msgr. Robert E. Harahan; Revs. Roberto Ortiz; Jose Helber Victoria-Tovar; Deacon Anthony Liguori Jr.
Res.: 700 Wyckoff Ave., 07481. Tel: 201-891-1122; Fax: 201-847-8518. Email: rectory@saintelizabeths.org. Web: www.saintelizabeths.4pi.com.
School—(Grades PreK-8), Greenwood Ave., 07481. Tel: 201-891-1481; Fax: 201-891-8669. Dr. Constance McCue, Prin. Lay Teachers 30; Students 255.
Catechesis/Religious Program—Tel: 201-891-3262; Fax: 201-891-3708. Jonathan Camiolo, D.R.E. Students 1,010.

Hospital Chaplaincy

NEWARK. *Office of Health Care Personnel.* Most Rev. Manuel A. Cruz, D.D., Archdiocesan Dir., Hospital Chaplaincy, St. Michael's Medical Center, 171 Clifton Ave., 07104. Tel: 973-497-4010.

Bergen County

ENGLEWOOD. *Englewood Hospital & Medical Center*, 350 Engle St., 07631. Tel: 201-894-3000. Rev. Vinh Quang Nguyen, Chap.

HACKENSACK. *Hackensack University Medical Center*, 30 Prospect St., 07601. Tel: 201-996-2000; 201-996-2345. Revs. Bernard Duga, Chap. (Adjunct), Alex C. Nnaukwu, Chap. (Adjunct), Charles Okoye, Chap., Anthony Udogu, Chap. (Adjunct).

PARAMUS. *Bergen Regional Medical Center*, 230 E. Ridgewood Ave., 07652. Tel: 201-967-4177; Fax: 201-967-4277. Rev. John A. Quill, Chap.

RIDGEWOOD. *Valley Hospital*, 223 N. Van Dien Ave., 07450. Tel: 201-447-8150. Revs. Mert Cordero, Chap., Stephen J. Toth, Chap.

TEANECK. *Holy Name Hospital*, 718 Teaneck Rd., 07666. Tel: 201-833-3000; 201-833-3243 (Pastoral Care). Sr. Lois Jablonski, S.S.J., M.Div., Pastoral Staff, Revs. Paterno Gorospe, Chap., John T. Michalczak, Chap., Deacon Willy Malarcher, Chap.

Essex County

NEWARK. *Beth Israel Medical Center*, 201 Lyons Ave., 07112. Tel: 973-926-7000; 973-926-7178 (Pastoral Care). Vacant.
St. Michael Medical Center, 111 Central Ave., 07102. Tel: 973-877-5467. Deacons Dennis F. La Scala, Chap., Edward McFadden, Chap.
University of Medicine & Dentistry (UMDNJ), 100 Bergen St., 07103. Tel: 973-972-4300. Deacon Sixto Lopez, Hospital Min.

BELLEVILLE. *Clara Maass Medical Center*, One Clara Maass Dr., 07109. Tel: 973-450-2000. Rev. John J. Donohue, Chap. (Adjunct).

CEDAR GROVE. *Essex County Hospital Center*, 125 Fairview Ave., 07009. Tel: 973-228-8000. Vacant.
St. Vincent Nursing Home, 315 E. Lindsley Rd., 07009. Tel: 973-754-4800. Sr. Elizabeth Ann Noonan, S.C., Chap., Deborah Quinn Martone, Admin.

EAST ORANGE. *Veterans Administration Hospital*, Tremont Ave. & Center St., 07019. Tel: 973-676-1000; 973-972-5688 (Pastoral Care). Rev. Mathew Eraly.

LIVINGSTON. *St. Barnabas Medical Center*, 94 Old Short Hills Rd., 07039. Tel: 973-533-5015. Rev. Hippolytus Duru (Nigeria) (NY), Chap. (Adjunct), Sr. MaryAnn Boyle, S.S.J., Chap., Deacon William McDermott, Assoc. Chap.

MONTCLAIR. *Mountainside Hospital*, One Bay Ave., 07042. Tel: 973-429-6000; 973-429-6047 (Pastoral Care). Rev. Thomas M. Cembor, Chap.

ORANGE. *Pope John Paul II Pavilion*, 135 S. Centre St., 07050. Tel: 973-266-3000. Vacant.

WEST ORANGE. *Kessler Institute for Rehabilitation*, 1199 Pleasant Valley Way, 07052. Tel: 973-731-3600. Vacant.

Hudson County

BAYONNE. *Bayonne Medical Center*, 29 E. 29th St., 07002. Tel: 201-858-5000. Vacant.

JERSEY CITY. *Christ Hospital*, 176 Palisades Ave., 07304. Tel: 201-795-8200. Sr. Nancy Craig.
Jersey City Medical Center, 50 Baldwin Ave., 07304. Tel: 201-915-2000. Vacant.

KEARNY. *West Hudson Hospital*, 206 Bergen Ave., 07032. Tel: 201-955-7000. Vacant.

NORTH BERGEN. *Palisades Medical Center*, 7600 River Rd., 07047. Tel: 201-854-5000. Vacant.

Union County

BERKELEY HEIGHTS. *Runnells Specialized Hospital*, 40 Watchung Ave., 07922. Tel: 908-771-5700. Vacant.

ELIZABETH. *Trinitas Regional Medical Center*, 225 Williamson St., 07202. Tel: 201-418-1000. Revs. Michael C. Barone, Brendan Quinn, Sisters Mary Corrigan, S.C., Pastoral Staff, Maria Kratz, I.H.M., Pastoral Staff, Prudentia Osuji, S.C., Pastoral Staff, Marie Tansey, S.C., Pastoral Staff.

RAHWAY. *Rahway Hospital*, 865 Stone St., 07065. Tel: 732-381-4200. Vacant.

SUMMIT. *Overlook Hospital*, 99 Beauvoir Ave., 07902. Tel: 908-522-2000. Rev. Robert J. Cio, Chap., Sr. Patricia Murphy, S.S.J., Dir., Pastoral Staff.

Prison Ministry

NEWARK. *Office of Prison Ministry*, 8 Boxwood Dr., Caldwell, 07006. Cell: 973-650-2098. Email: GQuinn57@aol.com. Deacon Gregory C. Quinn, Dir. Tel: 973-650-2098.

Bergen County

HACKENSACK. *Bergen County Correctional Facility*, 160 S. River Rd., 07601. Tel: 201-527-3018. Rev. Onyedika Michael Otuwurunne, Chap.

PARAMUS. *Bergen County Juvenile Detention Center*, 296 E. Ridgewood Ave., 07652. Tel: 201-599-6185. Deacon Michael J. Cechony, Prison Minister.

Essex County

NEWARK. *Essex County Correctional Facility*, 354 Doremus Ave., 07105. Tel: 973-274-7826. Revs. Leo O. Farley, Prison Min. (Retired), Paul J. Nolan, Prison Min. (Retired), Deacon Gregory Quinn, Chap., Sisters Mary Henrietta, Mary Victor.
Essex County Juvenile Detention Center, 208 Sussex Ave., 07103. Tel: 973-497-4720. Rev. Bryan E. Page, Deacon Gregory Quinn, Chap.
Northern State Prison, 168 Frontage Rd., 07114. Tel: 973-465-0068, Ext. 4505. Revs. Thomas C. Roberts, Chap., Robert J. Cormier, Chap., Francisco Javier Cabezas, Deacon David Loman, Prison Min., Mr. Gerald Carty, Prison Min., Mr. Bob Donfield, Prison Min.

Hudson County

SECAUCUS. *Hudson County Juvenile Correctional Center*, 635 County Ave., 07094. Tel: 201-319-3750 (Promise/Outreach Ministry). Rev. Giordano Belanich, Sr. Antonelle Chunka, C.S.S.F., Pastoral Staff, Bro. Thomas Corey, B.S.C.D., Pastoral Staff.

SOUTH KEARNY. *Hudson County Correctional Center*, 35 Hackensack Ave., 07032. Tel: 973-558-7000. Revs. Paul J. Nolan, Prison Min. (Retired), John J. Galeano, Francisco Javier, Deacon David Loman, Mr. John Geelan, Pastoral Staff.
Talbot Hall Assessment Center, 100-140 Lincoln Highway. Tel: 973-589-1114. Deacons Edward J. Campanella, Herb Gimbel, Michael York, John Rennie, Prison Min.

Union County

NEWARK. *Delaney Hall Assessment Center*, 451 Doremus Ave., 07105. Tel: 973-274-0115. Rev. Paul J. Nolan (Retired), Deacon Michael York, Prison Min., Catherine Fink, Prison Min., Thomas More Fink, Prison Min., Walter Matthei, Prison Min.

ELIZABETH. *Elizabeth Federal Detention Center*, 625 Evans St., 07201. Tel: 908-352-3776. Revs. George F. Sharp (Retired), Thomas L. Sheridan, S.J.
Union County Jail, 15 Elizabethtown Plaza, 07207. Tel: 908-558-2636. Rev. Augustine Odimmeywua, Prison Min., Deacon Michael DeRoberts, Chap.

Special Assignment in the Archdiocese:
Rev. Msgr.—
Kleissler, Thomas A., Pastor Emeritus (Retired), The Parish of St. Bernard & St. Stanislaus, 1235 George St., Plainfield, 07062.
Revs.—
Dowd, William J., Chap., 724 Drum Point Rd., Brick, 08723-7548.
Sudol, Gerard J., Chap., 136 Brookline Ave., Nutley, 07110.

On Duty Outside the Archdiocese:
Rev. Msgrs.—
Baldacchino, Peter, Chancellor, Mission Sui Juris, Holy Cross Parish, Grand Turks Islands, Turks and Caicos Islands.
Casale, Franklyn M., St. Thomas University, 16400 N.W. 32nd Ave., Miami, FL 33054.
Figueiredo, Anthony J., S.T.D., Pontifical Council Cor Unum Villa Stritch Via Della Nocetta 63, Rome, Vatican City State 00164 Italy.
Fuhrman, Robert J., Pontifical Mission Societies, 70 W. 36th St., Fl. 8, New York, NY 10018-1256. Tel: 212-563-8700
Sheeran, Robert T., S.T.D. (SFR), Marin Catholic High School, Kentfield, CA
Tiboni, Vito, Veterans' Hospital, 800 Poly Pl., Apt. 15W, Brooklyn, NY 11209.
Revs.—
Abalon, Jose Amante M., Holy Cross Mission, Gran Turks & Caicos Islands, British West Indies
Abalon, Jose Manuel M., St. Patrick Parish, 335 Main St., Brockton, MA 02301.
Arata, Miguel A., Rooma Katoliku Kirik Kogudus, Veski TN 1-1A, EE2400, Tartu, Estonia.
Basile, Gioacchino, St. Gabriel Parish, 26-26 98th St., East Elmhurst, NY 11369.
Becerra, Robert L., Santa Clara Parish, P.O. Box 215, Santa Clara, NM 88026.
Busichio, Salvatore, 926 Woodway Bluff Cir., Cary, NC 27513-2029.
Carranza, Fernando, Redemptoris Master Seminary, P.O. Box 211669, Dallas, TX 75211.
Carraro, Francesco, Redemptoris Mater Seminary, 672 Passaic Ave., Kearny, 07032.
Dellagiovanna, Mariano N., Diocese of Gaylord, 611 W. North St., Gaylord, MI 49735-8349.
Donnarumma, Francesco, Parroquia San Jose, Apt. 25, Penuelas 00624 Puerto Rico.
Fedele, Giuseppe, Holy Cross Mission, P.O. Box 70, Grand Turks, Turks and Caicos Islands.
Flor, Carlos, Immaculate Conception, 22 Lowe St., Revere, MA 02151.
Flora, Giandomenico M., St. Raphael Parish, 162 Oak St., Bridgeport, CT 06604.
Francesco, Richard G., Diocese of Helena, P.O. Box 1729, Helena, MT 59624-1729.
Garcia, Sebastian J., Redemptoris Mater Archdiocesan Missionary Seminary, 672 Passaic Ave., Kearny, 07032.
Gonzalez, Octavio, Parroquia San Jose, Apartado 25, Penuelas, PR 00624.
Guberovic, Zeljko J., Diocese of Gaylord, 611 W. North St., Gaylord, MI 49735-8349.
Guillen, Randy, 334 E. Pomona St., Santa Ana, CA 92707.
Ince, Owen F., Redemptoris Mater House of Formation, 672 Passaic Ave., Kearny, 07032.
Jaskowiak, Wojciech B., Redemptoris Mater Seminary, 130 Chalan Seminariu, Yona, GU 96915.
Kimel, Alvin, 6109 Saddle Ridge Rd., Roanoke, VA 24018.
Lek, Basil L., Diocese of Fairbanks, 1316 Peger Rd., Fairbanks, AK 99709.
Martin, Oscar, Our Lady of the Assumption, 404 Sumner St., Boston, MA 02128.
Miller, Frederick L., Mt. St. Mary Seminary, 16300 Old Emmitsburg Rd., Emmitsburg, MD 21727.
Morelli, Attilio, Sacre Coeur Church, 301 Roosevelt, Creve Coeur, IL 61610.
Ortiz-Garay, Jorge, St. Joseph Parish, 856 Pacific St., Brooklyn, NY 11238.
Passant, Paul A., Redemptoris Mater House of Formation, 672 Passaic Ave., Kearny, 07032.
Picone, Alfonso (Italy), St. Raphael Parish, 162 Oak St., Bridgeport, CT 06604.
Rizzo, Giovanni, M.Div., Casa Santa Maria, Via Dell' Umilta 30, Rome, 00187 Italy.

Romerde, Manuel R., Diocese of Tagilaran, P.O. Box 18, Tagbilaran City, 6300, Bohol Philippines.
Russo, Michael A. (OAK), St. Mary College, Box 5166, Moraga, CA 94575.
Schute, Arthur B. (Retired), 276 Orlando Blvd., Port Charlotte, FL 33954.
Smutelovic, Peter, Villa Stritch, Via della Nocetta 63, Rome 00164 Italy.
Tran, Joseph M. Duykim N., Toa Giam Muc, Kim Son, Ninh Binh Vietnam.
Tran, Peter Hung Viet, Diocese of Metuchen, P.O. Box 191, Metuchen, 08840.
Trujillo-Gonzalez, Francisco de Asis, Diocese of Peoria, 607 N.E. Madison Ave., Peoria, IL 61603. Sacre Coeur Church, 301 Roosevelt, Creve Coeur, IL 61610.
Urnick, Charles B., St. John the Baptist, P.O. Box 31230, Laughlin, NV 89028.
Venturini, Fabio, Redemptoris Mater House of Formation, 672 Passaic Ave., Kearny, 07032.
West, Peter, Priests for Life, 128 Targee St., Staten Island, NY 10304.
Wilson, William P. (Retired), RR1 - Box 59, Falls, PA 18615-9726.

Military Chaplains:
Rev. Msgr.—
Newland, Ronald A. (Retired), 21 Park End Ter., P.O. Box 61, Fort Tilden, NY 11695-0061.
Revs.—
Beale, Kenneth R., Capt., 96 ABW/HC, 202 N. 8th St. Ste. 1, Eglin Afb, FL 32542-5651.
Berchmanz, Anthony, Chap., 5970-B Mission Center Rd., San Diego, CA 92123.
Brosk, Steven J., 4 Liberty Place, P.O. Box 871, Sugarloaf, PA 18249.
D'Emma, Gregory J., Catholic Chaplain-USAWC Memorial Chapelin, 452 Mara Cir., Carlisle, PA 17013.
Gelinas, Robert James, PSC 559 Box 6092, Fpo, AP 96377.
Hamel, James A., Air Force Chaplain Corps College, 10100 Lee Rd., Fort Jackson, SC 29204.
Hanrahan, William P., Chap., P.O. Box 273, Seward, AK 99664-0273.
Kokeram, Sudash J., 9462 Gooden Dr., Fayetteville, NC 28314.
Kopec, Rajmund, Capt., Zone 1 Chape HHC ASG-KU, APO, AE 09366.
Lesak, William P., 3519 Cranberry Ln., New Bern, NC 28562.
Pawlikowski, Matthew, Capt., 151 Lofton Dr., Fayetteville, NC 28311.
Ubalde, Ulysses, 2nd Battalion 10th Marines, PSC Box 20107, Camp Lejeune, NC 28542.
Ugwuanya, Valentine C., Catholic Chaplains Office, 3101 Indiana Ave., Bldg. 5875, Fort Campbell, KY 42223.
Uhde, Peter (OG), Air Force Chaplain Corps College, 10100 Lee Rd., Fort Jackson, SC 29204.

Medical Leave:
Revs.—
Guillen, Fernando E.
McFadden, Brian F.
McLaughlin, Thomas R.
Pambello, Louis

Absent on Leave:
Rev. Msgr.—
Laferrera, John J.
Revs.—
Bertiz, Santos B.
Byrne, John M.
Cheng, Jian (Joseph)
Cionca, Calin
Cocozza, Dennis E.
Dugue, Nerva W.
Figurelli, Nicholas G., B.S., M.A.
Hann, Gregory B.
Hoatson, Robert M.
Lusik, William A.
Marcantuono, Anthony L.
Michota, Peter
Mieliwocki, Richard J.
Scaramella, Renzo L.
Ward, Gary C.

Retired:
Most Revs.—
Gerety, Peter Leo, D.D.
Marconi, Dominic A., D.D.
McDonnell, Charles J., D.D.
Arias, David, O.A.R., D.D.
Rev. Msgrs.—
Agan, Jose, c/o Maria Bocanegra, 332 Belgrove Dr., Kearny, 07032.
Alba, Jose, 24 JM Basa St., Iloilo City 5000, Philippines.
Antao, John S., 65 Elmora Ave., 07202.
Burke, James A., Nativity Church, 315 Prospect St., Midland Park, 07432.
Burns, G. Thomas, 7761 Bergamo Ave., Sarasota, FL 34238.
Capozzelli, Emmanuel M., Rev. Msgr. James F. Kelley Residence, 247 Bloomfield Ave., Caldwell, 07006.
Casazza, David J., 426 Jefferson Ave., Avon-by-the-Sea, 07717.
Chabak, Robert M., V.F., 302 6th Ave., Normandy Beach, 08739.
Cheplic, Peter A., St. John Vianney Residence., 60 Home Ave., Rutherford, 07070.
Chiang, Joseph, St. John Vianney Residence, 60 Home Ave., Rutherford, 07070.
Ciuba, Edward J., Church of the Presentation, 271 W. Saddle River Rd., Saddle River, 07458.
Cull, Lawrence W., 110 E 22nd St., Ship Bottom, 08008.
Doyle, Vincent J., J.C.D., 134 Valencia Dr., Brick, 08723.
Eilert, Edward J., St. John Vianney Residence, 60 Home Ave., Apt. 21, Rutherford, 07070.
Finnerty, James J., St. Paul the Apostle Parish, 14 Greenville Ave., Jersey City, 07305.
Gilchrist, John J., 499 Belgrove Dr., Kearny, 07032.
Gonzalez, Ricardo, 78 Meridian Dr., Brick, 08724.
Granato, Joseph J., 201 Clifton Ave., 07104.
Guenther, Donald E., St. Theresa of Avila, 306 Morris Ave., Summit, 07901.
Gusmer, Charles W., S.T.D., V.E., Our Lady of Peace, 111 South St., New Providence, 07974.
Hajduk, Edward J., S.T.L., M.S.S., St. John Vianney Residence, 60 Home Ave., Rutherford, 07070.
Harms, William C., Little Flower Parish, 100 Roosevelt Ave., Berkeley Heights, 07922.
Hayes, Paul J., St. Joseph for the Elderly, 140 Shepherd Ln., Totowa, 07512.
Hendry, Owen J., 7 Dogwood Dr., Ocean, 07712.
Herbster, Kenneth J., V.F., Notre Dame Church, 359 Central Ave., North Caldwell, 07006.
Hinrichsen, Carl D., Our Lady of Mercy Rectory, 2 Fremont Ave., Park Ridge, 07656.
Houghton, Francis J., 2316 Blue Jay Tr., Point Pleasant, 08742.
Ivory, Thomas P., S.T.D., St. Joseph Church, 44 Benvenue Ave., West Orange, 07052.
Judge, John G., 603 Center St., Forked River, 08731.
Kleissler, Thomas A., 521 Ocean Ave., Apt. 24, Avon By The Sea, 07717.
Koplik, William J., St. Matthew, 555 Prospect Ave., Ridgefield, 07657.
LoBianco, Francis R., 32 Woodland Ave., Jamaica Plain, MA 02130.
Lutz, George C., 159 Franklin St., Apt. 6, Bloomfield, 07003.
Madden, Thomas G., St. John Vianney Residence, 60 Home Ave., Rutherford, 07070.
Martin, Kelly Ireland, St. Joseph Home for the Elderly, 140 Sheperd Ln., Totowa, 07512.
McCarthy, Thomas A., 521 Piermont Ave., Apt. 209, River Vale, 07675.
Morris, Philip D., S.T.D., St. Rose of Lima, 50 Short Hills Ave., Short Hills, 07078.
Naedele, William B., Winchester Gardens, 333 Elmwood Ave. Apt. 5020, Maplewood, 07040.
Newland, Ronald A., 21 Park End Ter., Rockaway Point, NY 11697-2303.
O'Connor, John Philip, St. Bartholomew, 2032 Westfield Ave., Scotch Plains, 07076.
O'Donnell, Hugh A., 503 Gallows Hill Rd., Cranford, 07016.
O'Leary, Thomas M., St. John the Baptist, 69 Valley St., Hillsdale, 07642.
Park, Augustin C., 18 Cleveland St., Orange, 07050.
Piazza, Benjamin A., St. Aloysius, 219 Bloomfield Ave., Caldwell, 07006.
Plunkett, Joseph P., Our Lady of Czestochowa Parish, 115 S. 3rd St., Harrison, 07029.
Rebanal, Jeremias R., J.C.D., Ph.D., St. Mary of Assumption, 155 Washington Ave., 07202.
Salemi, Cajetan P., 1600 16th Ave., Belmar, 07719.
Sheerin, James O., St. John Vianney Residence, 60 Home Ave., Apt. 46, Rutherford, 07070.
Slinger, Joseph T., Ph.D., St. Anne, 15-05 Saint Anne St., Fair Lawn, 07410.
Stengel, Charles G., St. John Vianney Residence, 60 Home Ave., Apt. 37, Rutherford, 07070.
Strelecki, Richard T., St. John Vianney Residence, 60 Home Ave., Apt. 32, Rutherford, 7070.
Turro, James C., Ph.D., Immaculate Conception Seminary, Seton Hall University, South Orange, 07079.
Wielgus, Bronislaw, St. Adalbert/Sts. Peter & Paul, 250 E. Jersey St., 07206.
Zaccardo, Peter J., 53 Seaview Ave., Brick, 08723.
Very Revs.—
Connor, John F., S.T.B., Our Lady of Good Counsel, 654 Summer Ave., 07104-3418.
Conva, Matthias T., Our Lady of the Visitation, 234 Fairview Ave., Paramus, 07652.
Revs.—
Antczak, Robert A., V.F., Our Lady Mother of the Church, 130 Apple Ridge Rd., Woodcliff Lake, 07677.
Arico, Carl J., St. Vincent de Paul Parish, 979 Avenue C, Bayonne, 07002.
Arvay, Alfred S., St. Joan of Arc Parish, 13485 Spring Hill Dr., Spring Hill, FL 34609.
Ashe, Kevin P., 446 Adamston Rd., Brick, 08723.
Aymanathil, Mathew, c/o Job Haines Home, 250 Bloomfield Ave., Bloomfield, 07003.
Bajek, Gerald A., St. John Vianney Residence, 60 Home Ave., Apt. 38, Rutherford, 07070.
Ballance, Harvey, 92 Edgemont Rd., Montclair, 07043.
Barrow, Joseph A., Sacred Heart Parish, 324 Ridge Rd., Lyndhurst, 07071.
Basil, John E., 295 N. 7th St., Surf City, 08008-5206.
Bauman, John, 270 Terrace Ave., Jersey City, 07307.
Benedetto, James F., Rev. Msgr. James F. Kelley Residence, 247 Bloomfield Ave., Apt. 12, Caldwell, 07006.
Bernas, Eugene (Philippines), St. Genevieve Church, 4835 W. Altgeld St., Chicago, IL 60639.
Brennan, Robert M., St. John Viannex Annex, 64 Home Ave., Rutherford, 07070.
Burla, Frank J., Immaculate Conception, 30 N. Fullerton Ave., Montclair, 07042.
Buzzerio, Joseph E., 74 Third Place, Bogota, 07603.
Carroll, James J., 3 Mary St., Warren, 07059.
Celiano, Alfred V., Ph.D., Seton Hall University, 400 South Orange Ave., South Orange, 07079.
Coda, Joseph F., St. John Vianney Residence, 60 Home Ave., Rutherford, 07070.
Collins, Neil J., St. John Vianney Residence, 60 Home Ave. Apt. 23, Rutherford, 07070.
Conheeney, Thomas P., St. Mary, Star of the Sea Parish, 326 Ave. C, Bayonne, 07002.
Cooper, Donald A., 1674 Ferro Ln., P.O. Box 3, Toms River, 08755.
Cozzini, Robert P., Msgr. James F. Kelley Residence, 247 Bloomfield Ave., Caldwell, 07006.
Daly, Robert L. (MET), Immaculate Conception Rectory, 18 South St., Spotswood, 08884.
Danik, Daniel A., 2046 Ingalls Ave., Linden, 07036.
DeLeo, Roy James, St. Genevieve, 200 Monmouth Rd., 07208.
Di Pasquale, Donald J., Rev. Msgr. James F. Kelley Residence, 247 Bloomfield Ave., Apt. 7, Caldwell, 07006.
DiGirolamo, Dante, Eucharistic Shrine of the Adorable Face of Jesus, P.O. Box 455, Kearny, 07032.
Doherty, John R., 362 Orient Way, Rutherford, 07070.
Dowling, John C., P.O. Box 641, Kenilworth, 07033.
Driscoll, William D., 51 Monterey Ave., Teaneck, 07666.
Farley, Leo O., Rev. Msgr. James F. Kelley Residence, 247 Bloomfield Ave., Caldwell, 07006.
Feehan, Stephen S., Ph.D., 49 Timerline Dr., Little Egg Harbor Twp, 08087-3060.
Feketie, Michael J., St. Mary Parish, 516 W. 6th St., Plainfield, 07060.
Fernando, Bernard, 2808 Theresa Dr., Kissimmee, FL 34744.
Ferrazoli, Henry R., 145 S. Ocean Ave., Apt 309, West Palm Beach, FL 33404-5755.
Fiorino, Dominic J., Msgr. James F. Kelley Residence, 247 Bloomfield Ave., Apt. 4, Caldwell, 07006.
Foye, Thomas M., St. Andrew, 125 Broadway, Bayonne, 07002.
French, Walter V., 26 Rogerene Way, Landing, 07850.
Fu, Joseph, Sacred Heart, 2 Welfare Rd., Wong Chuk Hang, Aberdeen, Hong Kong.
Fuccile, Dominic G., 7 Lance Dr., Brick, 08723.
Furrevig, Edward G., 1694 Tilford Boulevard, Brick, 08724.
Gibbons, John J., M.Div., 626 Aviary Way, Toms River, 08755.
Gibney, Robert G., Msgr. James F. Kelley Residence, 247 Bloomfield Ave., Caldwell, 07006.
Guglielmo, Alan F., Immaculate Conception, 1219 Paterson Plank Rd., Secaucus, 07094.
Gusmer, Charles, Our Lady of Peace, 111 South St., New Providence, 07974.
Gyure, William, P.O. Box 3325, Payson, AZ 85547.
Hansen, Michael H., c/o Judith C. Deriso, 48 Williams Ave., South Hackensack, 07606.
Hartling, Charles W., P.O. Box 608, Saylorsburg, PA 18353.
Hazewski, Eugene J., 28 Oranjestad St., Toms River, 08757.
Heinen, Francis A., Rev. Msgr. James F. Kelley Residence, 247 Bloomfield Ave., Caldwell, 07006.
Holian, John P., 10 Overlook Rd., Apt. 4-J, Summit, 07901.
Horgan, Timothy J., St. Matthew, 102 Barbuda St.,

P.O. Box 3453, Toms River, 08756-3453.
Iaquinto, Robert, 47 Vendor Ln., Mays Landing, 08330.
Idzik, George, P.O. Box 1035, Clifton, 07014.
Jacunski, Robert D., Msgr. James F. Kelley Residence, 247 Bloomfield Ave., Caldwell, 07006.
Jones, Kenneth, 985 Chapel Hill Rd., Whitingham, VT 05342.
Kennedy, John F., V.F., 25 Portsmouth St., Apt. B, Whiting, 08759-2051.
Kenny, Thomas A., 24 Chesapeake Ct., Barnegat, 08005.
Kilcarr, Stephen M., B.A., Seton House, 11 Beverly Rd., West Orange, 07052.
Kirchner, James A., P.O. Box 4142, Prescott, AZ 86302.
Komar, John E., St. John Vianney Residence, 60 Home Ave., Apt. 45, Rutherford, 07070.
Kowalski, Alfred J., St. Theresa, 541 Washington Ave., Kenilworth, 07033.
Krozser, John J., 1616 Georgetowne Blvd., Sarasota, FL 34232.
Kunnath, Matthew, St. Mary, 17 Msgr. Owens Pl., Nutley, 07110.
Kunze, Robert W., 12 Farrington Plaza, Somerset, 08873.
Langdon, Robert H., John Vianney Annex, 64 Home Ave., Rutherford, 07070.
Laskowski, Norbert F., B.A., Rev. Msgr. James F. Kelley Residence, 247 Bloomfield Ave., Caldwell, 07006.
Lavaroni, Rino, Vicolo Cooperative #6, Remanzacco, Udine Italy.
Lennon, Peter F., Seton Hall University, 400 South Orange Ave., South Orange, 07079.
Lester, John J., St. Bartholomew, 2032 Westfield Ave., Scotch Plains, 07076.
Lobo, Stanley M., St. Michael Parish, 19E Central Blvd., Palisades Park, 07650.
Looney, Mathew D., 15 Nelson Ct., Toms River, 08757.
Lopez, Felipe, St. John the Baptist, 239 Anderson Ave., Fairview, 07022.
Losarcos, Javier, St. Benedict Parish, 65 Barbara St., 07105.
Lukenda, Raymond T., 133 Liberty Ave., Linden, 07036.
Macho, George S., 1825 Buttonwood Ave., Toms River, 08755.
Mader, George L., Msgr. James F. Kelley Residence, 247 Bloomfield Ave., Caldwell, 07006.
Maione, Francis T., 78 Honeysuckle Rd., Manahawkin, 08050.
Manning, Paul R., McKeen Towers, 311 S. Flagler Dr., Apt. 1109, West Palm Beach, FL 33401.
Marchand, Gerald A., P.O. Box 3102, Point Pleasant, 08742.
Marcone, Eugene F., 67 Claudia Ln., Manahawkin, 08050.
Marotta, Robert G., Farthingville, Dromina Charleville County Cork, Ireland.
McGovern, John P., 62 Tarpon Dr., Sea Girt, 08750.
McKeon, Raymond T., St. Paul the Apostle, 14 Greenville Ave., Jersey City, 07305.
McLaughlin, Donald E., 429 Compass Ave., Beachwood, 08722.
McNulty, Francis J., Msgr. James F. Kelley Residence, 274 Bloomfield Ave., Caldwell, 07006.
Melillo, William J., M.A., M.Div., Seton House, 11 Beverly Rd., West Orange, 07052.
Mohan, Bernard N., B.S., 409 Earl Dr., Brick, 08723.
Moore, Ward P., 107 Riverview Ave., #116, Neptune City, 07753.
Moran, Michael J., M.Div., 246 Larch Lane, Mahwah, 07430.
Morel, John J., St. John Vianney Residence, 60 Home Ave., Apt. 25, Rutherford, 07070.
Morley, John M., Seton Hall University, 400 South Orange Ave., South Orange, 07079.
Morley, John F., Ph.D., 400 Seton Hall University, South Orange, 07079.
Morris, John J., 5424 Keystone Pl., Virginia Beach, VA 23464.
Mukalel, Joseph V., 2 Amherst Ct., Maplewood, 07040.
Murphy, Joseph H., 175 Mount Nebo Rd., Milford, 08848.
Myers, J. Edward, 432 Bethel Village Cir., Lehigh Acres, FL 33936.
Naddeo, Henry M., c/o Carmine Naddeo, 97 Bryant Ave., Bloomfield, 07003.
Navarro, Pedro, 12 W. Concourse, Keyport, 07735.
Nestor, Robert P., Ed.D., 400 Seton Hall University, South Orange, 07079.
Netta, John G., P.O. Box 144, West Creek, 08092.
Nolan, Paul J., 77 Lee Ct., Jersey City, 07305.
Norton, Thomas, 521 Piermont Ave., #424, River Vale, 07675.
O'Brien, William, 3436 Vicari Ave., Toms River, 08755.
O'Connell, Mark A., St. Peter, 155 William St., Belleville, 07109.
O'Leary, Robert A., 252 Genes Dr., Toms River, 08753.
Oddo, Peter A., P.O. Box 11, Swartswood, 07877.
Olszewski, John S., S.T.L., 28 Orangestad St., Toms River, 08757.
Osbahr, Theodore W., V.F., P.O. Box 417, Belvidere, 07823-0417.
Osorio, Rudolfo B., 664 Paulison Ave., Clifton, 07011.
Palasits, John A., 72B Bellhaven Ct., Whiting, 08759.
Patete, Michael A., 184 Bonaire Dr., Toms River, 08757.
Patricius, J. M., St. Michael Parish, 15 E. 23rd St., Bayonne, 07002.
Petrillo, Thomas J., 567 Garfield Ave., Toms River, 08753.
Po, Fernando R., D.S.L., Allendale Nursing Home, 85 Harreton Rd., Allendale, 07401.
Provinzano, Rocco, The Barry Fam., 25 Vermont Ave., Port Monmouth, 07758.
Quinlan, Joseph M. (TR), 18 Ellsworth Ct., Red Bank, 07701.
Ransom, Donald B., 6600 Boulevard East, Apt. 21G, West New York, 07093.
Redstone, James, 161 Briar Mills Dr., Brick, 08724.
Reed, William C., 5 Crescent Rd., East Orange, 07017.
Regula, Ronald R., P.O. Box 2281, Bloomfield, 07003.
Reilly, George M., Our Lady of Mount Virgin Parish, 188 MacArthur Ave., Garfield, 07026.
Reilly, James, St. John Vianney Residence, 60 Home Ave., Apt. 34, Rutherford, 07070.
Reinbold, Charles, Mt. St. Francis, 250 South St., Peekskill, NY 10566.
Renard, John F., 78 Seaview Ave., Brick, 08723.
Revuelto, Manuel, Calle Julio Romero de Torres, 5 Urbanizacion Casablanca Marbella, Malaga 29600 Spain.
Rice, Joseph P., St. John Vianney Residence, 60 Home Ave., Rutherford, 07070.
Rotunno, Philip J., 7004 Boulevard E., Unit 7C, Guttenberg, 07093.
Ruane, Gerald P., Ph.D., 11 Rushmore Dr., Brick, 08724.
Ryan, John P., P.O. Box 3621 Hemlock Farms, Lords Valley, PA 18428.
Saltarin, Jose C., c/o Antonia Sison, 734 Ten Eyck Ave., Lyndhurst, 07071. Tel: 201-636-2778
Schreitmueller, Henry, 8 Poinsettia Ct., Kinnelon, 07405.
Schulte, William P., Brewster's Guest House, 477 Mt. Prospect Ave., 07104.
Sharp, George F., St. Michael the Archangel Parish, 624 Page Ave., Lyndhurst, 07071. Tel: 201-939-1161
Sheehan, Donald P., Guardian Angel, 320 Franklin Tpke., Allendale, 07401.
Sheehan, Joseph G., P.O. Box 438, Island Heights, 08732-0273.
Spino, John J., 116 New Jersey Ave., Point Pleasant Beach, 08742.
St. Amand, Kenneth J., Allendale Nursing Home, 85 Harreton Rd., Allendale, 07401.
Stasik, Thaddeus, St. John Vianney Residence, 60 Home Ave., Rutherford, 07070.
Sullivan, James B., O.L. of the Blessed Sacrament, 28 Livingston Ave., Roseland, 07068.
Theobald, Charles, 602 Bloomfield Ave., Montclair, 07042.
Thompson, Edward C., 343 Manor Dr., Nazareth, PA 18064.
Wilhelm, Patrick R.C., Our Lady of Sorrows, 136 Davis Ave., Kearny, 07032.
Wilson, William P., RR1, Box 59, Falls, PA 18615-9726.
Wortmann, Joseph F., M.A., Seton Hall University, 400 South Orange Ave., South Orange, 07079.
Yeo, Wilfred, 4 Sumutka Ct., Carteret, 07008.
Zuber, Thaddeus F., St. John Vianney Residence, 60 Home Ave., Rutherford, 07070.
Zubik, Rudolf, St. John Vianney Residence, 60 Home Ave., Apt. 24, Rutherford, 07070.

Permanent Deacons:
Abad, Ernesto, Our Lady of Lourdes, West Orange
Acocella, Louis, Ed.D., St. Anthony, Newark
Ahoua, Simplice, St. Lucy, Newark
Alexandre, Wilbert, Holy Rosary & St. Michael, Elizabeth
Aliaga, Justo, St. Cecilia, Kearny
Almeida, Manuel, Our Lady of Fatima, Elizabeth
Antola, Aldo P., Our Lady of Mt. Carmel, Nutley
Anyanwu, Emeruwa, Blessed Sacrament/St. Charles, Newark
Aponte, Leonides, St. Patrick's Pro-Cathedral, Newark
Aristy, Jesus D., Our Lady of Libera, West New York
Baker, Robert A., Sr., M.B.A., C.F.E., St. Nicholas, Jersey City
Balestrieri, Anthony A., Our Lady Queen of Peace, Maywood; B.S. Pollack Hospital, Jersey City
Baltus, John M., St. Theresa, Kenilworth
Barrett, Thomas J., St. Joseph's and St. Michael's, Union City
Bates, Harold L., Ascension, New Milford
Bejgrowicz, John P., St. Elizabeth, Linden
Bellascio, Vincent, St. Joseph the Carpenter, Roselle
Benedetto, William R., Queen of Peace, North Arlington; Rahway Hospital, Rahway
Besida, Dennis J., St. Thomas, Bloomfield
Bongiovanni, Jerome C., St. James, Springfield
Boucher, Charlie, II, Our Lady of Peace, New Providence
Bowen, Edward J., St. Peter the Apostle, River Edge
Bulgia, Thomas, St. Andrew Kim, Maplewood
Campanella, Edward, St. John the Apostle, Linden
Caporaso, Joseph, St. Anthony of Padua, Elizabeth; St. Genevieve, Elizabeth
Carlo, Joseph J., Holy Spirit, Union
Carris, Paul, Corpus Christi, Hasbrouck Heights
Casanova, Eliot, Blessed Sacrament, Elizabeth
Castoro, Joseph, St. Catherine, Glen Rock
Cechony, Michael J., (Retired)
Charriez, Nestor, St. Patrick/Immaculate Heart of Mary, Elizabeth
Connelly, Earle S., Jr., Immaculate Conception, Secaucus
Cordero, Juan A., St. Nicholas, Jersey City
Coyle, Thomas J., St. Thomas, Bloomfield
Cuesta, Arnulfo, St. Paul of the Cross, Jersey City
David, Marcelo, Parish of the Resurrection, Jersey City
DeBenedictis, Thomas, Cathedral Basilica of the Sacred Heart, Newark
DeFedele, Vincent J., Corpus Christi, Hasbrouck Heights
DeLucca, Nicholas J., Our Lady of Mt. Carmel, Ridgewood
DeMaria, Joseph, Jr., (On Duty Outside the Diocese)
DeRoberts, Michael, Our Lady of Lourdes, Mountainside
Detura, James, St. John the Evangelist, Bergenfield
Di Meo, John J., St. Mary, Rutherford
DiBernardo, Domenick, Most Sacred Heart of Jesus, Wallington
DiPaola, Kenneth, Our Lady of Peace, New Providence
Donosso, Edward G., St. Augustine, Union City
Echevarria, Mario, St. Thomas Aquinas, Newark
Emr, Peter R., Our Lady of the Visitation, Paramus
Estremera, Alejandro, St. Rose of Lima, Newark
Fargo, Nicholas C., Our Lady of Mercy, Jersey City
Fedison, Stanley F., Our Lady Mother of the Church, Woodcliff Lake
Ferraiuola, Lex, Our Lady of Mt. Carmel, Tenafly
Figueroa, Miguel, St. Michael, Newark
Fitzgerald, Michael J., St. Joseph, Bogota
Flores, Ricardo L., SS. Joseph & Michael, Union City
Florio, John J., St. Joseph, Maplewood
Ganter, Albert J., St. John the Baptist, Hillsdale
Gibbons, Keith, Holy Trinity, Westfield
Gimbel, Herbert, St. Stephen, Kearny
Glasner, Robert, Our Lady of Good Counsel, Washington Township
Golden, Andrew J., St. Peter the Apostle, River Edge
Gonzalez, Frank, St. Paul the Apostle, Jersey City
Gonzalez, Pedro, Parish of the Resurrection, Jersey City
Gray, John A., St. John the Baptist, Hillsdale
Guida, James J., St. Mary, Rutherford
Gurske, Robert, St. Bartholomew, Scotch Plains
Hernandez, Angel, St. Francis of Assisi, Hackensack
Herrera, Pedro, St. Mary of the Assumption, Elizabeth
Hessemer, Don, St. Bartholomew, Scotch Plains
Hogan, John E., Church of the Assumption, Emerson
Holoduek, John C., Epiphany, Cliffside Park
Homen, Jose, Our Lady of Fatima, Elizabeth
Hughes, David J., St. Rose of Lima, Short Hills
Inguaggiato, John M., Our Lady of Sorrows, South Orange
Karal, John J., St. Ann, Jersey City
Kautz, Frederick, St. Paul, Ramsey
Keary, Michael J., Cathedral Basilica of the Sacred Heart, Newark
Kennedy, Timothy A., St. John the Apostle, Linden
Kim, Joseph, St. Michael, Palisades Park
King, Patrick A., St. Thomas More, Fairfield
Kliauga, Paul, Ascension, New Milford

Kwiatek, Stanley W., Holy Spirit, Union
La Scala, Dennis F., St. Michael Med. Ctr., Newark; St. Lucy, Newark
Lagatol, Tom, Our Lady of Victory, Harrington Park
Leary, Gerald, (Retired)
LeConte, Wilfrid, St. Peter Claver, Montclair
Leonida, Clodualdo M., St. Nicholas, Jersey City
Liguori, Anthony, Jr., St. Elizabeth, Wyckoff
Liptak, Stephen J., (Retired)
Loman, David B., Our Lady of Mt. Carmel, Tenafly
Loperena, Miguel A., Immaculate Heart of Mary, Newark
Lopez, Sixto, University Hospital, Newark
Lorza, Louis C., St. Mary of the Assumption, Elizabeth
Lydon, Michael A., Holy Rosary, Edgewater
Lynch, John W., St. Helen, Westfield
Lynn, Walter, St. Joseph, Bogota
Mackesy, Leonard J., Our Lady of Sorrows, Kearny
Maione, Michael, (On Duty Outside the Diocese)
Malanga, Joseph J., St. Valentine, Bloomfield
Malarcher, Willy J., Holy Name Hospital, Teaneck
Mantineo, Joseph L., Our Lady Queen of Peace, Maywood
Marchese, Stephen, St. Joseph, Lodi
Marques, Albino P., Our Lady of Fatima, Newark
Materia, Francis P., Our Lady of the Assumption, Wood Ridge
McDermott, William, (On Duty Outside the Diocese)
McFadden, Edward, St. Michael's Hospital, Newark
McGarry, Richard M., (Retired)
McKenna, John J., St. Pius X, Old Tappan
McKeon, John W., St. Luke, Hohokus
McKnight, Keith, Christ the King, Jersey City
McLaughlin, Albert, Our Lady of Victory, Harrington Park
McQuade, Francis, Our Lady of Sorrows, South Orange
Merceus, Pierre J., Holy Spirit/OLHC, East Orange
Messina, Dominic S., St. Thomas More, Fairfield
Meyers, Patrick, (Retired)
Mier, Guy W., Cathedral Basilica of the Sacred Heart, Newark
Millea, Robert C., St. Stephen, Kearny
Minichino, Leonard A., St. Catharine's, Glen Rock
Missaggia, Michael P., St. Vincent de Paul, Bayonne
Montalvo, Jorge A., St. Mary of the Assumption, Elizabeth
Montemurro, Michael V., Little Flower, Berkeley Heights
Moore, Brett O., (Retired)
Moore, Willie, Blessed Sacrament/St. Charles Borromeo
Mueller, James A., St. Catherine, Glen Rock
Murphy, Brian, St. Thomas the Apostle, Bloomfield
Myers, William, Queen of Peace, North Arlington
Negron, Jose A., St. Michael, Newark
Nieves, Pedro, St. Mary, Plainfield
Niland, Joseph, Annunciation, Paramus
Noh, Francis E., Korean Martyrs, Saddle Brook
O'Connell, Brian, (On Duty Outside the Archdiocese)
O'Hara, Richard, Seton Hall Prep; St. Joseph, West Orange
O'Neill, Daniel, St. James, Springfield
Ochoa, Jorge E., St. Joseph, Lodi
Ortega-Escobar, Cesar, Parish of the Transfiguration, Newark
Ortiz, Jaime, (On Duty Outside the Diocese)
Osborne, Charles E., (Retired), (On Duty Outside the Diocese)
Paredes, Guy, (Retired)
Paulillo, Joseph J., St. Andrew's, Westwood
Persinger, Joseph M., St. Rose of Lima, Short Hills
Pluta, Thomas A., Holy Trinity, Westfield
Polanco, Alejandro, St. Francis, Hackensack
Polanco, Cecilio S., St. Michael, Newark
Polanco, Leopoldo, Resurrection, Jersey City
Pons, Eduardo, Cathedral Basilica of the Sacred Heart, Newark
Pontillo, Robert, St. Andrew, Westwood
Porcaro, Anthony, St. Therese of Lisieux, Cresskill
Puliatte, James J., Imaculate Conception, Norwood
Puzio, Victor J., Sacred Heart, Wallington
Quagliana, Pat, M.A., M.A., Our Lady of the Blessed Sacrament, Roseland
Quinn, Gregory C., Holy Trinity, Hackensack
Quintana, Restituto, St. Michael's, Newark
Ramirez, Nelson, St. Leo, Irvington
Ravelo, Daniel, St. Michael's, Newark
Raymundo, Ranulfo, (On Duty Outside the Diocese)
Regan, Kevin J., St. Anastasia, Teaneck
Rehse, Jeremiah K., St. Paul, Ramsey
Reyes, Jesus, St. Patrick and Assumption/All Saints, Jersey City
Riccio, Dominick, (On Duty Outside the Diocese)
Rivera, Oscar, Our Lady of Good Counsel, Newark
Rodack, Stephen, (Retired)
Rodriguez, Jose A., Our Lady of Good Counsel, Newark
Rodriguez, Justo, The Parish of the Transfiguration, Newark
Rodriguez, Vicente, St. Francis Xavier, Newark
Roig, Julio, (Retired)
Romano, Joseph S., St. Anthony, Northvale
Romero, Jerry, St. John, Orange
Rosado, Jose F., (On Duty Outside the Diocese)
Rossi, Jerry S., Sacred Heart, Bloomfield
Rushing, Todd, Our Lady of the Visitation, Paramus
Rusignuolo, Louis, St. Valentine, Bloomfield
Sanchez, Orlando, Holy Rosary St. Michael, Elizabeth
Sarmiento, Cesar C., Parish of the Resurrection, Jersey City
Sarnas, John P., Our Lady of Sorrows, Kearny
Sarno, John A., St. Catherine, Glen Rock
Saunders, Andrew E., St. Luke, Ho-Ho-Kus
Savo, Ralph M., Parish of the Resurrection, Jersey City
Scalzo, Anthony, St. Rose of Lima, Short Hills
Smith, John F., St. Philomena, Livingston
Smith, Thomas M., Archdiocese of Newark; St. John, Newark
Soto, Anibal, (On Duty Outside the Diocese)
Srinivasa, Rajgopal K., St. Antoninus, Newark
Stewart, Craig, Cathedral Basilica, Newark
Strader, David, Our Lady of the Lake, Verona
Stumbar, James P., Little Flower, Berkeley Heights
Sylvester, John, St. Mary, Dumont
Tarabokija, Anton, St. John the Baptist, Fairview
Thomann, Robert V., Holy Rosary, Edgewater
Thomson, Robert E., Holy Rosary, Edgewater
Tizzano, Albert H., St. Thomas, Bloomfield
Tobin, James P., St. Mary, Closter
Torres, Cesar Augusto, Most Holy Name, Garfield
Trinidad, Reynaldo M., St. Mary, Nutley
Valdez, Nicholas, Assumption, Woodridge
Valentin, Carlos, St. Joseph, East Orange
Valladares, Guillermo, St. Peter's, Belleville
Vega, Alcides, (On Duty Outside the Diocese)
Velasco, Asterio, SS. Joseph & Michael, Union City
Velo, Luis, St. Joseph, West Orange
Vrindten, Joseph G., St. Francis, Hackensack
Vuolo, Pasquale, (Retired)
Wedemeyer, John J., Our Lady of Lourdes, Mountainside
White, Earl, St. Stephen, Kearny
Yandoli, Joseph, St. John, Leonia
York, Michael D., St. John the Apostle, Linden
Zapata, Alfredo, St. Aloysius, Jersey City

INSTITUTIONS LOCATED IN THE ARCHDIOCESE

[A] SEMINARIES, ARCHDIOCESAN

KEARNY. *Redemptoris Mater Archdiocesan Missionary Seminary* (1990) 672 Passaic Ave., 07032. Tel: 201-997-3220; Fax: 201-997-5552. Email: secretary@rmnewark.org. Rev. Msgr. Renato Grasselli, S.T.L., Rector; Revs. Tobias Rodriguez, Vice Rector; Neil Xavier O'Donoghue, Ph.D., Prefect of Studies & Librarian; Roberto Santamaria, Spiritual Dir.; Justino Cornejo-Castillero. Priests 5; Students 45.

SOUTH ORANGE. *Immaculate Conception Seminary School of Theology*, 400 South Orange Ave., 07079. Tel: 973-761-9575; Fax: 973-761-9577. Email: theology@shu.edu. Web: www.shu.edu/academics/theology.

Administration Officers: Amado Gabriel Esteban, Ph.D., Pres.; Rev. Msgr. Robert F. Coleman, J.C.D., Rector & Dean; Revs. Robert K. Suszko, M.B.A., M.Div., Vice Rector & Dir. of Formation & Business Mgr.; Christopher M. Ciccarino, S.S.L., S.T.D., Assoc. Dean; Dianne M. Traflet, J.D., S.T.D., Assoc. Dean; Rev. Douglas J. Milewski, S.T.D., Assoc. Dean Undergraduate Programs; Rev. Msgrs. Gerard H. McCarren, S.T.D., Spiritual Dir.; Joseph R. Chapel, S.T.D., Asst. Spiritual Dir.; Revs. Lawrence B. Porter, Ph.D., K.H.S., Dir. Seminary Library; Renato J. Bautista, M.Div., Asst. Dir., Formation; Donald E. Blumenfeld, Ph.D., Dir. Pastoral Formation; Rev. Msgr. Anthony J. Kulig, K.H.S., M.A., Formation Faculty & Dir. Liturgy; Rev. Walter D. Lucey, M.Div., Formation Faculty; Ewa Bracko, M.B.A., Asst. Business Mgr.; Dir. of Finances, Inst. for Christian Spirituality; Diane M. Carr, M.A., Academic Svcs. & Admissions Coord.; Catherine A. Cunning, M.A., Dir. Seminary Devel.; Eilish R. Harrington, Institutional Research Specialist; Stella F. Wilkins, M.A., M.L.S., Librarian; Olivia Dinneen, L.C.S.W., Dir., Counseling Svcs.; Sr. B. Phyllis Kapuscinski, N.D.S., Ph.D., ESL Coord.; John Nowik, M.M., Music Dir. & Adjunct Prof., Liturgy; Sr. Concetta Russo, M.P.F., Librarian; Margaret T. Applin, Fin. Aid Officer.

Full-Time Faculty: Justin M. Anderson, Ph.D., Asst. Prof., Moral Theology; Revs. W. Jerome Bracken, C.P., Ph.D., Assoc. Prof. Moral Theology; John J. Chadwick, S.T.D., Asst. Prof., Systematic Theology; Rev. Msgr. Joseph R. Chapel, S.T.D., Assoc. Prof., Moral Theology; Assoc. Prof.; Dir, Perm. Diaconate Prog.; Rev. Christopher M. Ciccarino, S.S.L., S.T.D., Asst. Prof., Biblical Studies; Assoc. Dean; Timothy P. Fortin, Ph.D, Asst. Prof. Philosophical Theology; Zeni V. Fox, Ph.D., Prof. Pastoral Theology; Rev. Pablo T. Gadenz, S.S.L., S.T.D., Asst. Prof. Biblical Studies; Gregory Y. Glazov, D.Phil., Oxon, Assoc. Prof. Biblical Studies; Rev. Thomas G. Guarino, S.T.D., K.H.S., Prof. Systematic Theology; Eric M. Johnston, Ph.D., Asst. Prof. Undergraduate Theology; Rev. Msgr. Gerard H. McCarren, S.T.D., Assoc. Prof. Systematic Theology & Spiritual Dir.; Rev. Douglas J. Milewski, S.T.D., Assoc. Prof. Theology & Assoc. Dean Undergrad Progs.; Jeffrey L. Morrow, Ph.D., Asst. Prof. Undergraduate Theology; Revs. Mark Francis O'Malley, Hist.Eccl.D., Asst. Prof. Church History; Lawrence B. Porter, Ph.D., K.H.S., Prof. Systematic Theology & Dir. Seminary Library; Joseph P. Rice, Ph.D., Asst. Prof. Philosophical Theology; Ellen R. Scully, Ph.D., Asst. Prof., Undergraduate Theology; Dianne M. Traflet, J.D., S.T.D., Asst. Prof. Pastoral Theology & Assoc. Dean; Víctor Velarde-Mayol, Ph.D., M.D., Asst. Prof., Philosophical Theology; Rev. Msgr. Robert J. Wister, Hist.Eccl.D., Prof., Church History.

Darlington Fund Tel: 973-761-9552; Fax: 973-761-9577. Development Agency for Immaculate Conception Seminary. Priests 17; Lay Teachers 10; Total Staff 23; Total Enrollment 326.

Seton Hall University College Seminary (1856) Saint Andrew's Hall, 07079. Tel: 973-761-9420; Fax: 973-761-9421. Email: joseph.reilly@shu.edu. Web: collegeseminary.shu.edu. Rev. Msgrs. Joseph R. Reilly, S.T.L., Ph.D., Rector; David C. Hubba, Spiritual Dir.; Deacon Pat Quagliana, M.A., M.A., Asst. to Rector. Priests 2; Deacons 1; Seminarians 33; Total Enrollment 36.

[B] COLLEGES AND UNIVERSITIES

CALDWELL. *Caldwell College, Inst. Research Office*, 120 Bloomfield Ave., 07006. Tel: 973-618-3000; Fax: 973-618-3847. Email: admissions@caldwell.edu. Web: www.caldwell.edu. Incorporated under the laws of the State of New Jersey with full power to confer degrees. Priests 1; Sisters 1; Sisters of St. Dominic of Caldwell 5; Lay Teachers 221; Students 2,793.

College Faculty: Nancy H. Blattner, Ph.D., Pres.; Dr. Patrick Progar, Vice Pres., Academic Affairs; Dr. Peter Panos, Dir. Jennings Library.

JERSEY CITY. *Saint Peter's College*, 2641 Kennedy Blvd., 07306-5997. Tel: 201-761-6000; Fax: 201-761-6011. Email: lnieves@spc.edu. Web: www.spc.edu. Eugene Cornacchia, Ph.D., Pres.; Mr. Kenneth Payne, Vice Pres. Office of Finance & Business; Dr. Marylou Yam, Vice Pres. Academic Affairs; Dr. Anna Cicirelli, Dean of Upper Classmen; Mr. Joe Giglio, Dir. Admissions & Enrollment Mktg.; Dr. Velda Goldberg, Academic Dean; Mr. Ben Scholz, Dir. Enrollment, Research, & Technology; Ms. Irma Williams, Registrar & Exec. Dir. Enrollment Svcs.; Mary Sue Callan-Farley, Dir. Campus Ministry. Priests 22.

St. Aedan's: St. Peter's College Church, 800 Bergen Ave., 07306. Tel: 201-433-6800. Revs. Vincent B. Sullivan, S.J., Admin.; Peter W. Gyves, S.J.

St. Peter's College Jesuit Community, Gothic Towers, 50 Glenwood Ave., 07306-4606. Fax: 201-432-7397. Priests 7; Lay Teachers 106; Students 3,010.

Jesuit Center, St. Peter Hall, 2652 Kennedy Blvd., 07306. Revs. Anthony Aracich, S.J.; Anthony J. Azzarto, S.J.; Michael Braden, S.J.; Rocco C. Danzi, S.J.; Mark T. DeStephano, S.J.; Juan Diaz Vilar; Charles A. Gallagher, S.J.; Peter W. Gyves, S.J.; Stephen Hess, S.J.; Robert E. Kennedy, S.J.; Donal T. MacVeigh, S.J.; Oscar G. Magnan; Edmund W. Majewski, S.J.; Michel Marcil, S.J.; Robert E. McCarty, S.J.; William A. McKenna, S.J.; John A. Mullin, S.J.; Peter O'Brien, S.J.; Robert V. O'Hare, S.J.; Joseph J. Papaj, S.J.; John P. Ruane, S.J.; Jose Luis S. Salazar, S.J.; Thomas L. Sheridan, S.J.; David X. Stump, S.J.; Vincent B. Sullivan, S.J.; John P. Wrynn; Bro. Louis N. Mauro, S.J.

LODI. *Felician College* 07644. Tel: 201-559-6000; Fax: 201-559-6188. Email: martink@felician.edu. Web: www.felician.edu. Priests 3; Brothers 1; Sisters 18; Full-time faculty 123; Part-time faculty 119; Total Enrollment 2,301.

Lodi Campus, 262 Main St., 07644. Tel: 201-559-6000; Fax: 201-559-6188. Sr. Theresa Mary Martin, C.S.S.F., Pres.; Dr. Charles J. Rooney, Sr. Vice

Pres. for Admin. & Finance; Susan M. Chalfin, Vice Pres. Student Svcs. & Admin., Rutherford Campus; Sisters Mary Rosita Brennan, C.S.S.F., Provost & Vice. Pres. for Academic Affairs; Mary Tarcilia Juchniewicz, C.S.S.F., Vice Pres. for Student Affairs; Marc J. Chalfin, Exec. Vice Pres. for Admin. & Finance; Arthur D. Goon, Vice Pres. Enrollment Mgmt.; Jerry Trombella, Asst. Vice Pres. Institutional Research; Dr. Beth M. Castiglia, Dean Dept. of Business; Dr. Maureen Murphy-Ruocco, Assoc. Dean, Div. of Health Education; Dr. Muriel M. Shore, Dean Div. of Health Sciences; Rev. Damian Colicchio, Dir. Campus Ministry; Celeste A. Oranchak, Vice Pres. Inst. Advancement; Dr. Edward S. Kubersky, Dean, Dept. Arts & Sciences; Paul Glassman, Dir. Library; Robert W. Decker, Vice Pres. College Svcs.

SOUTH ORANGE. *Seton Hall University* (1856) 400 South Orange Ave., 07079. Tel: 973-761-9000; Fax: 973-275-2361. Web: www.shu.edu. Amado Gabriel Esteban, Ph.D., Pres. Priests 44; Lay Teachers 463; Students 9,579.

Officers of University: Rev. Paul A. Holmes, S.T.D.; Laura A. Wankel, Ed.D., Vice Pres. Student Affairs; Dennis Garbini, M.B.A., Vice Pres. Finance & Technology; Catherine Kiernan, J.D., Vice Pres. & General Counsel; G. Gregory Tobin, Interim Vice Pres. for Univ. Advancement; Kathleen M. Boozang, J.D., L.L.M., Interim Vice Provost for Academic Affairs.

Administrators: Gregory A. Burton, Ph.D., Assoc. Provost; Dean, Research & Graduate Studies; Tracy Gottlieb, Dean Enrollment Mgmt.; Dr. Chrysanthy Grieco, Dean Univ. Libraries; Robert DeMartino, Ph.D., Dir. Grants & Research; Patrick Lyons, Dir. University Athletics & Recreational Svcs.; Rev. Msgr. James M. Cafone, S.T.D., Min. to Priest Community; Revs. Stanley Gomes, Dir. Campus Ministry; Thomas P. Nydegger, Ed.D., M.Div., Assoc. Vice Pres., Student Affairs; Ms. Pamela Ferguson, Assoc. Vice Pres., Devel.; Mr. Tom White, M.A., Asst. Vice Pres., Public Rels. & Mktg.; Mr. Matthew Borowick, M.B.A., Assoc. Vice Pres., Alumni & Govt. Rels.; Mr. Craig Becker, M.S., M.P.A., Asst. Vice Pres., Finance; Karen Van Norman, M.Ed., Assoc. Vice Pres. & Dean of Students.

College of Arts and Sciences Dr. Joan Guetti, Dean. Tel: 973-761-9022.

School of Business Dr. Joyce Strawser, Acting Dean. Tel: 973-761-9013.

College of Education and Human Services Joseph De Pierro, Dean. Tel: 973-761-9025.

College of Nursing Phyllis Hansell, Ed.D., Dean. Tel: 973-761-9014.

School of Law Patrick E. Hobbs, J.D., L.L.M., Dean. One Newark Center, 07102. Tel: 973-642-8750.

School of Theology Rev. Msgr. Robert F. Coleman, J.C.D., Rector & Dean. Tel: 973-761-9016.

School of Health and Medical Science Brian B. Shulman, Ph.D., Dean.

School of Diplomacy and Intl. Rels. Ambassador John K. Menzies, Ph.D., Dean.

Priest Community: Rev. John F. Morley, Ph.D. (Retired); Rev. Msgrs. Robert F. Coleman, J.C.D.; David C. Hubba; Richard M. Liddy, Ph.D.; Dennis Mahon; Robert T. Sheeran, S.T.D. (SFR); James C. Turro, Ph.D. (Retired); Robert J. Wister, Hist.Eccl.D.; Revs. Renato J. Bautista, M.Div.; Donald E. Blumenfeld, Ph.D.; Ian Boyd; Gerald Buonopane; W. Jerome Bracken, C.P., Ph.D.; Alfred V. Celiano, Ph.D. (Retired); Christopher M. Ciccarino, S.S.L., S.T.D.; Rev. Msgr. James M. Cafone, S.T.D.; Revs. John J. Chadwick, S.T.D.; Gabriel B. Costa, Ph.D.; John D. Dennehy; Nicholas G. Figurelli, B.S., M.A.; Lawrence E. Frizzell, D.Phil.; Pablo T. Gadenz, S.S.L., S.T.D.; Nicholas S. Gengaro, S.T.D.; Stanley Gomes; Thomas G. Guarino, S.T.D., K.H.S.; Warren R. Hall; Rev. Msgr. Kevin M. Hanbury, Ed.D.; Rev. Paul A. Holmes, S.T.D., Vice Pres. & Interim Dean; Rev. Msgrs. Christopher J. Hynes, Ed.S., Adjunct Prof.; Anthony J. Kulig, K.H.S., M.A.; Revs. Peter F. Lennon (Retired); Walter D. Lucey, M.Div.; Rev. Msgr. Gerard H. McCarren, S.T.D.; Revs. John F. Morley, Ph.D. (Retired); Brian Keenan Muzas; Robert P. Nestor, Ed.D. (Retired); Mark O'Malley; Lawrence B. Porter, Ph.D., K.H.S.; Rev. Msgr. John A. Radano; Rev. John J. Ranieri, Ph.D.; Rev. Msgrs. Joseph R. Reilly, S.T.L., Ph.D.; Francis R. Seymour; Rev. Robert K. Suszko, M.B.A., M.Div.; Rev. Msgr. C. Anthony Ziccardi, S.T.L., S.S.L. In Res. Rev. Msgr. Joseph R. Chapel, S.T.D.; Revs. Douglas J. Milewski, S.T.D.; Thomas P. Nydegger, Ed.D., M.Div.; Joseph F. Wortmann, M.A. (Retired).

[C] HIGH SCHOOLS, PRIVATE

NEWARK. *Saint Benedict's Preparatory School* (1868) (Grades 7-12), 520 Dr. Martin Luther King Blvd., 07102-1314. Tel: 973-792-5700; Fax: 973-643-6922. Email: graybee@sbp.org. Web: www.sbp.org. Rev. Edwin D. Leahy, O.S.B., Headmaster; Paul E. Thornton, Vice Pres. Devel.; Revs. Ivan Lamourt, Asst. Headmaster; Edwin D. Leahy, O.S.B., Prin. Benedictine Monks of Newark Abbey 14; Priests 10; Brothers 4; Lay Teachers 53; Total Enrollment 571.

Christ the King Preparatory School of Newark, N.J., Corp., 239 Woodside Ave., 07104. Tel: 973-483-0033; Fax: 973-481-0693. Email: smsullivan@ctleprep.org. Web: www.ctkprep.org. Revs. Robert J. Sandoz, O.F.M., Pres.; Gregory V. Gebbia, O.F.M., Dean Student Life; Ms. Cynthia Bielskie, Prin. Priests 2; Sisters 3; Lay Teachers 18.

Christ the King Work Study Program, 239 Woodside Ave., 07104. Tel: 973-483-0033; Fax: 973-481-0693. Email: smsullivan@ctkprep.org. Web: www.ctkprep.org. Rev. Robert J. Sandoz, O.F.M., Pres.; Ms. Cynthia Bielskie, Prin. Priests 2; Sisters 3; Lay Teachers 18.

St. Vincent Academy (1869) (Girls), 228 W. Market St., 07103. Tel: 973-622-1613; Fax: 973-622-1128. Email: jfavata@svanj.org. Web: www.svanewark.org. Sisters June Favata, Admin. Dir.; Margaret Killough, Fin. Dir.; Mary F. Nolan, Student Svcs. Dir.; Sr. Monica Donohoe, Librarian. Sisters 6; Lay Teachers 20; Students 305.

BAYONNE. *Holy Family Academy* (1925) 239 Ave. A, 07002. Tel: 201-339-7341; Fax: 201-339-9295. Email: hfa@bayonne.net. Web: www.hfa.bayonne.net. Mrs. Mary Tremitiedi, Prin.; Mrs. Jean Stroud, Dean of Studies. Sisters 2; Lay Teachers 20; Girls 145.

Marist High School (1954) (Coed), 1241 Kennedy Blvd., 07002. Tel: 201-437-4545; Fax: 201-437-6013. Email: rslaski@marist.org. Web: www.marist.org. Ms. Alice Miesnik, Prin.; Bros. Luke Reddington, F.M.S., Volunteer; James Devine, Teacher; Robert Warren, F.M.S., Teacher; William Maske, F.M.S., Teacher; Sisters Mary Fallon, S.C., Guidance Dir.; Helen Moores, S.C., Focus Educ. Teacher; Mary Agnes Gore, O.P., Guidance Office Asst.; Daniel Short, Librarian. Marist Brothers. Brothers 4; Sisters 3; Lay Teachers 26; Students 414.

CALDWELL. *Mount St. Dominic Academy* (Girls), 3 Ryerson Ave., 07006-6196. Tel: 973-226-0660; Fax: 973-226-2693. Email: mainoffice@msdacademy.org. Web: www.msdacademy.org. Sr. Frances Sullivan, O.P., Head of School; Irena Telyan, Librarian. Sisters of St. Dominic of Caldwell. Sisters 4; Lay Teachers 38; Girls 345.

DEMAREST. *Academy of the Holy Angels* (Girls), 315 Hillside Ave., 07627. Tel: 201-768-7822; Fax: 201-768-6933. Web: www.holyangels.org. Sr. Virginia Bobrowski, Pres.; Jennifer Moran, Prin.; Catherine Korvin, Librarian. Conducted by School Sisters of Notre Dame. Sisters 9; Lay Teachers 51; (Girls) 568.

ELIZABETH. *Benedictine Academy*, 840 N. Broad St., 07208-2508. Tel: 908-352-0670; Fax: 908-352-0698; 908-352-9424. Web: www.benedictineacad.org. Email: principal@benedictineacad.org. Sr. Germaine Fritz, O.S.B., Pres.; Kenneth Jennings, Prin.; Sisters Martin Elizabeth Duffy, O.S.B., Librarian; Donna Jo Repetti, Guidance Counselor. Benedictine Sisters of Elizabeth, NJ., College Preparatory High School (Girls) Sisters 8; Lay Teachers 21; Total Staff 37; Girls 168.

St. Patrick High School (Coed), 221 Court St., 07206. Tel: 908-353-5220; Fax: 908-629-1123. Web: www.stpatrickhs.org. Joseph L. Picaro, Prin.; Barbara McElroy, Librarian. Students 239.

JERSEY CITY. *St. Anthony High School*, 175 Eighth St., 07302. Tel: 201-653-5143; Fax: 201-653-8120. Email: stanthony@stanthonyhighschool.org. Web: www.stanthonyhighschool.org. Sr. Mary Felicia Brodowski, C.S.S.F., Pres.; Charles Alexander Tortorella, Prin. Conducted by Felician Sisters. Sisters 1; Lay Teachers 22; Total Staff 10; Students 250.

St. Dominic Academy (Girls), 2572 John F. Kennedy Memorial Blvd., 07304. Tel: 201-434-5938; Fax: 201-434-2603. Email: tcorbo@stdominicacad.com. Web: www.stdominicacad.com. Ms. Barbara Griffin, Head of School; Mr. Thomas Corbo, Prin.; Sr. MaryLou Bauman, Vice Prin.; Sharon Buge, Dir. Fin.; Ms. Marilyn French, Librarian. Dominican Sisters of Caldwell. Sisters 11; Lay Teachers 28; Total Staff 35; Students 354.

St. Peter's Preparatory School (1872) 144 Grand St., 07302. Tel: 201-547-6400; Fax: 201-547-2341. Web: www.stpetersprep.org. Mr. William Ahearn, Chm. Bd.; Rev. Robert E. Reiser, S.J., Pres.; Mr. James C. DeAngelo, Prin.; Ms. Mary Durante, Vice Prin.; Mr. John Morris, Dean, Students; Robert Nodine, Vice Pres. Fin.; Mr. James Horan, Vice Pres. Planning & Principal Giving. Priests 6; Seminarians 2; Religious Sisters 2; Lay Teachers 72; Students 960.

Jesuit Community, 50 Glenwood Ave., 07302. Revs. Anthony J. Azzarto, S.J., Guidance & Religion Teacher; John A. Mullin, S.J., Supr. & Guidance Counselor; Robert V. O'Hare, S.J., Mathematics Teacher; Robert E. Reiser, S.J., Pres.; Mr. Benjamin J. Brenkert, S.J., Guidance Counselor & Religion Teacher; Mr. Matthew Prochilo, S.J., Religion Teacher In Res. Revs. James J. Dinneen, S.J., Spiritual Dir.; Enrico Raulli, S.J., English Teacher.

LODI. *Immaculate Conception High School* (1915) 258 S. Main St., 07644. Tel: 973-773-2400; Fax: 973-614-0893. Email: jazzolino@ichslodi.org. Web: www.ichslodi.org. Mr. Joseph R. Azzolino, Pres. & Prin.; Deborah Ebbinghousen, Librarian; Maria Grieco, Librarian. Sisters 1; Lay Teachers 15; Lay Staff 14; Girls 160.

MONTCLAIR. *Immaculate Conception High School* (Coed), 33 Cottage Pl., 07042. Tel: 973-744-7445; Fax: 973-744-3926. Email: ichsmont@yahoo.com. Web: www.ichspride.org. Sr. Maureen Crowley, S.C., Pres.; Jo Ann Degnan, Prin.; Sr. Ann Fay, S.C., Librarian. Sisters 4; Lay Teachers 16; Students 180.

ORADELL. *Bergen Catholic* (1955) (Boys), 1040 Oradell Ave., 07649. Tel: 201-261-1844; Fax: 201-599-9507. Email: president@bergencatholic.org. Web: www.bergencatholic.org. Bro. Brian M. Walsh, C.F.C., Pres.; Timothy J. McElhinney, Prin.; Rev. Antonio L. Ricarte, Chap., (part-time); John Puzio, Librarian. Congregation of Christian Brothers. Brothers 4; Lay Teachers 55; Total Staff 59; Boys 769; Staff 28.

RAMSEY. *Don Bosco Preparatory High School* (1915) 492 N. Franklin Tpke., 07446. Tel: 201-327-8003; Fax: 201-327-3397. Web: www.donboscoprep.org. Rev. James Heuser, S.D.B., Dir./Pres.; John F. Stanczak, Prin.; Albert Del Principio, Asst. Prin., Academics; Mr. Edward Nekel, Asst. Prin., Student Affairs; Revs. James Cerbone, S.D.B.; Manuel Gallo, S.D.B., Coord. Youth Min.; John Janko, S.D.B., Facilities Mgr.; Brendan K. Kilroy, S.P.S., Senior Guidance Counselor; James Marra, S.D.B., Dir. of Advancement & Finance Admin.; Eugene Palumbo, S.D.B.; Philip Pascucci, S.D.B. (Retired); Jerzy Schneider, S.D.B. (Retired); Alfred Flatoff, S.D.B.; Bro. James Wiegand, S.D.B., Asst. Athletic Dir.; Thomas DeLucci, Guidance Dir.; Christine Green, Librarian. Salesians of St. John Bosco. Priests 4; Brothers 2; Sisters 2; Lay Teachers 75; Students 915.

SOUTH ORANGE. *Marylawn of the Oranges*, 445 Scotland Rd., 07079. Tel: 973-762-9222; Fax: 973-378-7975. Email: clopez@marylawn.us. Web: www.marylawn.net. Christine Lopez, Prin.; Sr. Joan Digan, S.C., Librarian. Sisters 3; Lay Teachers 20; Girls 200.

SUMMIT. *Oak Knoll School of the Holy Child Upper School* (1924) (Grades 7-12), (Girls), 44 Blackburn Rd., 07901. Tel: 908-522-8100 (Main); 908-522-8130; Fax: 908-273-4616. Email: timothy.saburn@oakknoll.org. Web: www.oakknoll.org. Mr. Timothy J. Saburn, Head of School; Mrs. Mary Sciarrillo, Prin.; Mary Hoskins-Clark, Librarian; Marianne Corrado, Asst. Librarian. Conducted by the Sisters of the Holy Child Jesus. Lay Teachers 50; Total Staff 30; Students 314.

UPPER MONTCLAIR. *Lacordaire Academy (Upper School)*, 155 Lorraine Ave., 07043. Tel: 973-744-1156; Fax: 973-783-9521. Web: www.lacordaire.net. Brian F. Morgan, Head of School. Sisters of St. Dominic. Sisters 1; Lay Teachers 17; Total Staff 28; Girls 62.

WEST ORANGE. *Seton Hall Preparatory School*, 120 Northfield Ave., 07052. Tel: 973-325-6624; Fax: 973-736-2930. Email: mkelly@shp.org. Web: www.shp.org. Rev. Msgr. Michael E. Kelly, M.A., Headmaster; Michael Gallo, Asst. Headmaster; Kevin McNulty, Dean Faculty; Carole Marazzi, Librarian; Rev. James R. White, Chap. Priests 6; Lay Instructors 90; Students 970.

Resident Faculty: Rev. Msgr. Edward G. Bradley, S.T.L., M.A.; Revs. Bruce G. Janiga, M.A.; Stephen M. Kilcarr, B.A. (Retired); William J. Melillo, M.A., M.Div. (Retired).

[D] HIGH SCHOOLS, ARCHDIOCESAN

CLARK. *Mother Seton (Girls) Regional High School*, One Valley Rd., 07066. Tel: 732-382-1952; Fax: 732-382-4725. Email: srreginamartin@motherseton.org. Web: www.motherseton.org. Sr. Regina Martin, S.C., Prin.; Joan Barron, Asst. Prin.; Sr. Jacquelyn Balasia, S.C., Asst. Prin.; Maureen Connell, Dir. Administrative Services; Sr. Mary Anne Katlack, S.C., Campus Minister; Rev. Kevin F. Murphy, Chap.; Marge Barkan, Librarian. Sisters of Charity of St. Elizabeth. Sisters 6; Lay Teachers 35; Girls 400.

JERSEY CITY. *Hudson Catholic Regional High School*, 790 Bergen Ave., 07306. Tel: 201-332-5970; Fax: 201-332-6373. Email: contact@hudsoncatholic.org. Web: www.hudsoncatholic.org. Rev. Warren R.

Hall, Pres.; Sr. Joann Marie Aumand, S.C.C., Prin. Priests 1; Sisters 1; Brothers 4; Lay Teachers 21; Total Staff 32; Boys 291; Girls 91.

MONTVALE. *St. Joseph Regional High School* (1962) (Boys), 40 Chestnut Ridge Rd., 07645. Tel: 201-391-3300; Fax: 201-391-8073. Web: www.saintjosephregional.org. Barry Donnelly, Prin. Brothers 1; Lay Teachers 35; Boys 500.

PARAMUS. *Paramus Catholic High School* (Coed), 425 Paramus Rd., 07652. Tel: 201-445-4466; Fax: 201-445-6440. Email: jvail@paramus-catholic.org. Web: www.paramuscatholic.org. James P. Vail, Pres.; Declan Lynch, Vice Pres., Finance; Ryan Casey, Vice Pres., Advancement; Joseph P. Agostino, Prin.; Leonard Lewandoski, Vice Prin.; Stephanie Macaluso, Vice Prin.; Vincent Sausto, Vice Prin., Academics; Oksana Korduba, Librarian; Rev. Thomas E. Pendrick, Chap.; Mary Ann Lemieux, Dean Student Svcs.; Scott Langan, Dean Student Activities; Stella Scarano, Dean Students; Joseph F. Wilson, Dean Campus Ministry; Ralph M. Manno, Dean Students; Christopher Partridge, Dir., Opers. & Alumni Rels.; Brian Niland, Dir., School Safety; Michael Shea, Dir., Transportation; Matthew Liddle, Dir., Technology. Priests 1; Sisters 1; Lay Teachers 104; Total Staff 115; Students 1,517.

ROSELLE. *Roselle Catholic High School* (Coed), 350 Raritan Rd., 07203. Tel: 908-245-2350; Fax: 908-241-3869. Email: info@rosellecatholic.org. Web: www.rosellecatholic.org. Bro. Owen Ormsby, F.M.S., Pres.; Dr. Robert J. Stickles, Ed.D., J.D., Prin.; Sally Hanford, Librarian. Marist Brothers. Brothers 4; Lay Teachers 33; Total Staff 58; Students 560.

SCOTCH PLAINS. *Union Catholic Regional High School* (Coed), 1600 Martine Ave., 07076. Tel: 908-889-1600; Fax: 908-889-7867. Email: mainoffice@unioncatholic.org. Web: www.unioncatholic.org. Sr. Percylee Hart, R.S.M., Prin.; James Reagan Sr., Librarian. Lay Teachers 45; Total Staff 77; Students 725.

SUMMIT. *The Oratory Catholic Preparatory School* (1907) (Grades 7-12), 1 Beverly Rd., 07901. Tel: 908-273-1084; Fax: 908-273-5505. Email: mainoffice@oratoryprep.org. Web: www.oratoryprep.org. Mr. Robert Costello, Head of School; Mr. John Horan, Asst. Headmaster; Sherry Mahan, Admin. Asst. to Head of School, 1 Beverly Rd., 07901; Rev. Salvatore DiStefano, Chap.; Mr. Owen McGowan, Dean Academics. Priests 1; Brothers 1; Lay Teachers 32; Total Staff 15; Students 292.

WASHINGTON TOWNSHIP. *Immaculate Heart Academy* (Girls), 500 Van Emburgh Ave., 07676. Tel: 201-445-6800; Fax: 201-445-7416. Email: pmolloy@ihahs.com. Web: www.ihahs.com. Ms. Patricia Molloy, Prin. Sisters 1; Lay Teachers 74; Total Staff 92; Girls 844.

[E] ELEMENTARY SCHOOLS, PRIVATE

NEWARK. *Link Community School, Inc.*, 120 Livingston St., 07103. Tel: 973-642-0529; 973-642-8510; Fax: 973-642-1978. Email: leslie.baynes@linkschool.org. Web: www.linkschool.org. Maria Paradiso, Head of School. Dominican Sisters of Caldwell. Lay Teachers 15; Jesuit Volunteer 1; Students 128.

ELIZABETH. *St. Patrick Academy*, (Grades 5-8), 227 Court St., 07206. Tel: 908-351-2188; Fax: 908-629-1123. Web: www.stpatrickhs.org. Bro. Daniel McCulloch, C.F.C., Dir.; Joseph Picaro, Prin. Lay Teachers 3; Total Staff 4; Total Enrollment 45.

JERSEY CITY. *Concordia Learning Center at St. Joseph's School for the Blind*, 761 Summit Ave., 07307. Tel: 201-876-5432; Fax: 201-876-5431 (Admin.); 201-876-5430 (Ed.). Email: info@sjsnj.org. Web: www.sjsnj.org. Judy Ortman, Exec. Dir. Non-graded and graded school for blind, visually impaired, multi-disabled children; early intervention program, 5-day residential program, outreach services. Lay Teachers 23; Students 136; Total Staff 95.

St. Joseph's School for the Blind, 761 Summit Ave., 07307. Tel: 201-876-5432; Fax: 201-876-5431. Email: info@sjsnj.org. Web: www.sjsnj.org. Judy Ortman, Exec. Dir. Non-graded and graded school for blind, visually impaired, multi-disabled children; early intervention program, 5-day residential program, outreach services. Lay Teachers 23; Students 136; Total Staff 95.

LODI. *The Felician School for Exceptional Children* (1971) 260 S. Main St., 07644. Tel: 973-777-5355; Fax: 973-777-0725. Email: fsecinlodi@aol.com. Web: www.fsec.org. Sr. Mary Ramona, C.S.S.F., Dir. Sisters 6; Lay Teachers 18; Total Staff 49; Children 90.

Day Program Tel: 973-777-5355, Ext. 12; Fax: 973-777-0725. Capacity 150.

SUMMIT. *Oak Knoll School of The Holy Child, Lower School* (1924) (Grades K-6), (Coed), 44 Blackburn Rd., 07901. Tel: 908-522-8120; 908-522-8100 (Main); Fax: 908-598-9757. Email: timothy.saburn@oakknoll.org. Web: www.oakknoll.org. Mr. Timothy J. Saburn, Head of School; Mrs. Joanne L. Ainsworth, Prin.; Megan Watkins, Dir. Student Svcs.; Elinor Takenaga, Librarian. Conducted by the Sisters of the Holy Child of Jesus. Lay Teachers 28; Total Staff 30; Students 223.

UNION CITY. *St. Francis Academy*, 1601 Central Ave., 07087. Tel: 201-863-4112; Fax: 201-601-5905. Email: lucy@stfrancisacademy.com. Web: www.stfrancisacademy.com. Sr. Mary Dora Sartino, O.S.F., Pres.; Ms. Deborah Savage, Prin.; Louise Levendusky, Librarian. Missionary Franciscan Sisters of the Immaculate Conception. Sisters 11; Lay Teachers 29; Students 277.

UPPER MONTCLAIR. *Lacordaire Academy-Elementary Division*, (Grades PreK-8), 153 Lorraine Ave., 07043. Tel: 973-746-2660; Fax: 973-783-6804. Email: lmazzari@lacordaire.net. Web: www.lacordaire.net. Lauren Mazzari, Head, Lower & Middle School; Joan Hearst, Dir., Admissions. Dominican Sisters of Caldwell. Lay Teachers 16; Total Staff 3; Students 140.

[F] GENERAL HOSPITALS

NEWARK. *Columbus Campus of Saint Michael's Medical Center, Newark* A member of Catholic Health East., 495 N. 13th St., 07107. Tel: 973-268-1475; Fax: 973-268-1523. Parent Corporation: Saint Michael's Medical Center, Inc.

St. James Campus of Saint Michael's Medical Center, Newark A member of Catholic Health East., 155 Jefferson St., 07105. Tel: 973-589-1300; Fax: 973-465-2861. Web: www.cathedralhealth.org. Parent Corporation: Saint Michael's Medical Center, Inc. Bed Capacity 40.

Life at Saint Michael's, Inc., 111 Central Ave., 07102-9880. Tel: 973-877-5350; Fax: 973-877-5672. Mr. David A. Ricci, Pres. & CEO.

Saint Michael's Medical Center A member of Catholic Health East., 111 Central Ave., 07102-9880. Tel: 973-877-5350; Fax: 973-877-5593. Mr. David A. Ricci, Pres. & CEO; Corrine Francis, Vice Pres. Mission Integration; Dr. Claudia Komer, Pres. Medical Staff; Dr. Catherine B. Polera, Vice Pres., Medical Affairs & Chief Medical Officer. Parent Corporation: Catholic Health East. Bed Capacity 358; Inpatient 14,000; Outpatient 58,000; Total Staff 1,580.

Mount Carmel Guild Behavioral Health System, Inc., 590 N. 7th St., 07107. Tel: 973-266-7992; Fax: 973-596-4057. Web: www.ccannj.org. Ms. Elizabeth A. McClendon, L.C.S.W., A.C.S.W., Assoc Exec. Dir.; Phillip Frese, Ph.D., CPA, CEO. Behavioral Health Services in 3 counties. Total Staff 200; Patients Assisted Annually 11,077; Bed Capacity 290.

ELIZABETH. *Trinitas Regional Medical Center*, 225 Williamson St., 07207. Tel: 908-994-5000; Fax: 908-994-5756. Web: www.trinitasrmc.com. Gary S. Horan, Pres. & CEO; Sr. Mary Corrigan, S.C., Vice Pres. Mission Effectiveness. Sisters of Charity of Saint Elizabeth and Elizabethtown Healthcare Foundation. Sisters 9; Total Staff 2,711; Bed Capacity 531; Bassinets 11; Patients Assisted Annually 443,303; Long-Term Care Center Beds 120.

Trinitas Regional Medical Center, Williamson Street Campus, 225 Williamson St., 07207.

Trinitas Regional Medical Center, New Point Campus, 655 E. Jersey St., 07206.

**Marillac Corp.*, 240 Williamson St., 07207. Tel: 908-994-5756; Fax: 908-994-5520. Gary S. Horan, Pres. & CEO.

TEANECK. *Holy Name Hospital*, 718 Teaneck Rd., 07666. Tel: 201-833-3000; Fax: 201-833-3230. Web: www.holyname.org. Michael Maron, Pres. & CEO; Maureen Morosco, Chap.; Sisters Beatriz Duque, P.B.V.M., Chap.; Breda Boyle, C.S.J.P., Dir., Pastoral Care. Sisters of St. Joseph of Peace. Bed Capacity 361; Bassinets 11; Total Staff 2,504; Total Assisted 389,487.

Holy Name EMS, 718 Teaneck Rd., 07666. Tel: 201-833-3248; Fax: 201-833-7213.

School of Nursing Tel: 201-833-3002. Sisters 4. Pastoral Care: Sisters Regina O'Connell, C.S.J.P., Hospice/Palliative Care; Beatriz Duque, P.B.V.M., Chap.; Nora Molyneux, C.S.J.P., Vice Pres. Mission; Revs. Paterno Gorospe; John T. Michalczak.

[G] HOMES FOR AGED

CALDWELL. *St. Catherine of Siena, Inc.*, 7 Ryerson Ave., 07006. Tel: 973-226-1577; Fax: 973-226-5058. Email: lramm@caldwellop.org. Web: www.caldwellop.org. Sisters Arlene Antczak, O.P., Prioress; Luella Ramm, O.P., Vicaress & Treas.; Patricia Stringer, O.P., Sec.; Elsie Bernauer, O.P., Councilor; Ms. Deirdre Radtke, Admin. Bed Capacity 30; Total of Sisters in Convent Living with Support Services 35; Total Staff 50.

CEDAR GROVE. *St. Vincent's Nursing Home* (Div. of St. Joseph's Regional Medical Center), 315 E. Lindsley Rd., 07009. Tel: 973-754-4800; Fax: 973-812-4491. Deborah Quinn Martone, Admin.; Sr. Elizabeth Noonan, Chap. Conducted by Sisters of Charity of St. Elizabeth. Sisters 2; Capacity: Long term care beds 151; Patients Assisted Annually 186; Total Staff 190.

JERSEY CITY. *St. Ann's Home for the Aged*, 198 Old Bergen Rd., 07305. Tel: 201-433-0950; Fax: 201-433-6554. Email: first_choice_home@yahoo.com. Web: www.saintannshome.com. Sr. Norah Clarke, C.S.J.P., LNHA CEO; Janet Merly-Liranzo, LNA Admin.; Sr. Josephine Pate, C.S.J.P., Admissions Coord.; James Barry, Pastoral Care. Sisters of St. Joseph of Peace 7; Bed Capacity 120; Total Staff 204; Under Care (Male & Female) 120; Adult Medical Day Care Clients 50.

Margaret Anna Cusack Care Center, Inc., 537 Pavonia Ave., 07306. Tel: 201-653-8300, Ext. 2152; Fax: 201-653-7705. Email: info@cusackcarecenter.org. Web: www.cusackcarecenter.org. Thomas P. Sheehy, Admin. Sponsored by the Sisters of St. Joseph of Peace., Skilled Nursing Facility for Men & Women. Sisters 2; Bed Capacity 139; Total Assisted Annually 275; Total Staff 220.

[H] HOMES FOR THE BLIND

JERSEY CITY. *St. Joseph's Home for the Blind* (1886) (Skilled nursing facility for men and women), 537 Pavonia Ave., 07306. Tel: 201-653-8300, Ext. 2152; Fax: 201-653-7705. Email: info@cusackcarecenter.org. Web: www.cusackcarecenter.org. Thomas P. Sheehy, Admin. Sisters of St. Joseph of Peace. Sisters 2; Bed Capacity 139; Total Staff 200; Nursing Home Patients 275; Total Assisted Annually 220.

[I] DAY NURSERIES

NEWARK. *Perpetual Help Day Nursery* (1967) 170 Broad St., 07104. Tel: 973-484-3535; Fax: 973-497-2526. Email: perhelp@yahoo.com; srmcriscina@yahoo.com. Sr. Christina Peteros, Prin. Vocationist Sisters. Sisters 6; Lay Teachers 15; Total Staff 22; Children 136.

JERSEY CITY. *St. Elizabeth's Child Care Center*, 129 Garrison Ave., 07306. Tel: 201-795-1443; Fax: 201-795-4121. Email: st.stelizabethfsse@yahoo.com School E-mail. Sisters Rosita Chirayath, Supr.; Shelcy Catherine Kulangara, Prin. Franciscan Sisters of St. Elizabeth. Sisters 9; Total Staff 36; Children 300.

NUTLEY. *Holy Family Day Nursery and Convent*, 174 Franklin Ave., 07110. Tel: 973-235-1170; Fax: 973-235-1940. Sr. Romilda Chiga, F.S.S.E., Supr. Franciscan Sisters of St. Elizabeth. Sisters 9; Children 70.

RAMSEY. *St. Joseph Pre-School*, 372 Wyckoff Ave., 07446. Tel: 201-825-8386. Sr. Marie Elise Kurikombil, Prin. Franciscan Sisters of St. Elizabeth. Sisters 4; Children 60.

[J] PROTECTIVE INSTITUTIONS

NEWARK. *Missionaries of Charity, Queen of Peace Women's Shelter & Soup Kitchen* (1982) 168 Sussex Ave., 07103. Tel: 973-481-9056; 973-483-0165. Missionaries of Charity. Total Staff 8; Total Assisted (Shelter) 300; Total Assisted (Soup Kitchen) 34,200.

HOBOKEN. *Good Counsel, Inc. (St. Francis Home)*, 411 Clinton St., 07030. Tel: 201-798-9059; 201-795-0637; 800-723-8331 (Hotline); Fax: 201-795-0809. Email: cbell@goodcounselhomes.org. Web: www.goodcounselhomes.org; www.postabortionhelp.org. Rev. Benedict J. Groeschel, C.F.R., Chm.; Christopher R. Bell, Pres. & Exec. Dir. Housing, counseling and referrals for single women who are pregnant or single mothers with children. Counseling for men and women experiencing post abortion stress.

Good Counsel, Inc., P.O. Box 6068, 07030. Rev. Benedict J. Groeschel, C.F.R., Chm.; Christopher R. Bell, Exec. Dir. Residences for single mothers and children. Post abortion counseling and referrals. Women & Children Assisted Annually 315; Total Staff 50; Total Assisted Annually 4,000; Total Hotline Assistance 2,800; Bed Capacity 45.

JERSEY CITY. *St. Joseph's Home*, 81 York St., 07302. Tel: 201-413-9280; Fax: 201-451-0952. Sr. Rosemary Coffey, Dir. Transitional housing for homeless women and children. Total Staff 13; Total Assisted 130; Bed Capacity 60.

The Nurturing Place Tel: 201-413-1982; Fax: 201-413-1223. Sr. Barbara Moran, C.S.J.P., Dir. Tel: 201-413-1982. A developmental child care center for disadvantaged youngsters. Total Staff 14; Total

Assisted 110.

[K] HOMES FOR WOMEN

JERSEY CITY. *St. Mary's Residence*, 240 Washington St., 07302-3806. Tel: 201-432-6289; Fax: 201-451-0952. Sr. Harriet Hamilton, O.S.F., Admin. Sisters of St. Joseph of Peace., (Single working women of low income assisted; no children). Bed Capacity 40; Total Staff 9; Total Assisted 50.

[L] MONASTERIES AND RESIDENCES OF PRIESTS AND BROTHERS

NEWARK. *Franciscan Friars of the Renewal, Most Blessed Sacrament Friary*, 375 13th Ave., 07103. Tel: 973-622-6622; Fax: 973-624-8998. Revs. Anthony Baetzold, Local Servant; Glenn Sudano, C.F.R.; Mariusz Koch, C.F.R., Community Servant; Bros. Nicholas Maria White, C.F.R.; Mariano Joseph Demma, C.F.R. Novices 5.

Newark Abbey (1857) 528 Dr. Martin Luther King, Jr. Blvd., 07102. Tel: 973-792-5800; Fax: 973-643-6922. Email: newarkabbey@sbp.org. Web: www.newarkabbey.org. Rt. Rev. Melvin J. Valvano, O.S.B., Abbot; Very Revs. Augustine J. Curley, O.S.B., Prior; Matthew S. Wotelko, O.S.B., Subprior; Revs. Albert T. Holtz, O.S.B., Novice Master; Luke A. Edelen, O.S.B.; Francis Flood, O.S.B.; Charles Hayden; Charles W. Henry, O.S.B.; Edwin D. Leahy, O.S.B.; Maynard G. Nagengast, O.S.B.; Boniface J. Treanor, O.S.B.; Very Rev. Philip J. Waters, O.S.B., V.F.; Bros. Maximillian Buonocore, O.S.B.; Mark Hayden, O.S.B.; Gereon J. Reuter, O.S.B.; Anthony Streit, O.S.B.; Patrick Winbush, O.S.B.

BAYONNE. *Marist Brothers*, Champagnat Residence, 1241 Kennedy Blvd., 07002. Tel: 201-437-4115. Web: www.maristbr.com. Bro. James Devine, F.M.S., Dir. Brothers 7.

Marist Brothers of the Schools, Inc. The Marist Brothers, The Marist Brothers, Provincial Office, 1241 Kennedy Blvd., 07002. Tel: 201-823-1115; Fax: 201-823-2232. Email: maristbrothersus@aol.com. Web: www.maristbr.com. Bro. Ben Consigli, F.M.S., Provincial.

CALDWELL. *The Rev. Msgr. James F. Kelley Residence for Retired Priests*, 247 Bloomfield Ave., 07006. Tel: 973-364-1121; Fax: 973-364-9873. Mrs. Joan Stevens, Admin.; Rev. Msgr. Emmanuel M. Capozzelli (Retired); Revs. James F. Benedetto, Dir. (Retired); Robert P. Cozzini (Retired); Donald J. Di Pasquale (Retired); Leo O. Farley (Retired); Dominic J. Fiorino (Retired); Robert G. Gibney (Retired); Francis A. Heinen (Retired); Robert D. Jacunski (Retired); Norbert F. Laskowski, B.A. (Retired); George L. Mader (Retired); Francis J. McNulty (Retired).

CLIFFSIDE PARK. *St. Patrick's Missionary Society*, 70 Edgewater Rd., P.O. Box 3080, 07010-4080. Tel: 201-943-6575; Fax: 201-943-2946. Email: spsnj@spms.org. Web: www.spms.org. Revs. Patrick Cullen, S.P.S. (Retired); Brendan K. Kilroy, S.P.S.; Michael E. Morris, S.P.S.

JERSEY CITY. *Brothers of the Christian Schools* Hudson Catholic Brothers' Residence, 790 Bergen Ave., 07306-4535. Tel: 201-332-5970; 201-332-0971 (House); Fax: 201-332-6373. Bro. Patrick King, F.S.C., Dir. Brothers 6.

Jesuit Community of St. Peter's Prep, Inc., 50 Glenwood Ave., 07302-4433. Tel: 201-432-7397; Fax: 201-432-7399. Revs. Anthony J. Azzarto, S.J., Alumni Chap. & Guidance Counselor; John A. Mullin, S.J., Supr., Guidance Counselor; Robert V. O'Hare, S.J.; Bro. Louis N. Mauro, S.J., Business Mgr. (Resurrection Parish). Total in Residence 8; Priests 5; Brothers 2; Scholastics 1.

Jesuits of Saint Peter's College, Inc., 50 Glenwood Ave., 07306-4606. Tel: 201-432-7399; Fax: 201-432-7397. Email: vsullivansj@juno.com. Revs. Vincent B. Sullivan, S.J., Rector; Anthony Aracich, S.J.; Anthony J. Azzarto, S.J.; Michael Braden, S.J.; Rocco C. Danzi, S.J.; Mark T. DeStephano, S.J.; J. Juan Diaz Vilar, S.J. (Spain); Charles A. Gallagher, S.J.; Peter W. Gyves, S.J.; Stephen Hess, S.J.; Robert E. Kennedy, S.J.; Donal T. MacVeigh, S.J.; Oscar G. Magnan; Edmund W. Majewski, S.J.; Michel Marcil, S.J., Exec. Dir. U.S. Catholic China Bureau; Robert E. McCarty, S.J.; William A. McKenna, S.J.; John A. Mullin, S.J.; Peter O'Brien, S.J.; Robert V. O'Hare, S.J.; Joseph J. Papaj, S.J.; John P. Ruane, S.J.; Jose Luis S. Salazar, S.J., Prof. Theology; Thomas L. Sheridan, S.J.; David X. Stump, S.J.; John F. Wrynn, S.J.; Bro. Louis N. Mauro, S.J. Total Staff 27; Total in Residence 27.

MAHWAH. *Paulist Fathers - Paulist Press*, 997 MacArthur Blvd., 07430. Tel: 201-825-7300; Fax: 201-825-8345. Email: info@paulistpress.com. Web: www.paulistpress.com. Revs. Mark-David Janus, C.S.P., Pres. & Publisher; Kevin A. Lynch, C.S.P., Publisher Emeritus & Senior Editor.

MONTCLAIR. *Comboni Missionaries of the Heart of Jesus (Verona Fathers)*, P.O. Box 138, 07042-0138. Tel: 973-744-8080; Fax: 973-744-8919. Email: luigizb@yahoo.com. 118 7th Ave., 07104. Revs. Luigi Zanotto, M.C.C.J., Supr.; Provvido Crozzoletto, M.C.C.J.; John Michael Converset, M.C.C.J., Office of Justice and Peace; Paul Donohue, M.C.C.J. Total Staff 1; Total in Residence 1.

MONTVALE. *Xaverian Brothers*, Xaverian Brothers' Residence, 40 Chestnut Ridge Rd., 07645. Tel: 201-391-8071; Fax: 201-391-8073. Brothers 1.

ORADELL. *Congregation of Christian Brothers*, Bergen Catholic Brothers' Residence, 1040 Oradell Ave., 07649. Tel: 201-261-1816; Fax: 201-599-9507. Brothers 8.

ORANGE. *The Salesian Community* (1998) Don Bosco Residence, 518-B Valley St., 07050. Tel: 973-674-2400; Fax: 973-674-7051. Revs. Stephen Leake, S.D.B., M.A., Dir.; James Mulloy, S.D.B., Dean, Pre Novices; David Moreno, S.D.B.; Bros. Jared Anderson, S.D.B.; Eduardo Chincha, S.D.B.; Adam Dupre, S.D.B.; Michael Eguino, S.D.B.; John Rasor, S.D.B.; Juan Pablo Rubio, S.D.B.; Marc Stockhausen, S.D.B.; Miguel Suarez, S.D.B. Total Staff 4; Total in Residence 26; Candidates 15. *Don Bosco Vocation Office*, 315 Self Pl., South Orange, 07079. Tel: 973-761-0201. Revs. Steve Ryan, S.D.B., Prov. Youth Min.; Dominic Tran, S.D.B., M.A., Vocation Dir.

RAMSEY. *Don Bosco Prep Salesian Residence* (1915) 492 N. Franklin Tpke., 07446-2811. Tel: 201-327-8100; Fax: 201-327-3397. Revs. James Heuser, S.D.B., Director & Pres.; James Cerbone, S.D.B.; Alfred Flatoff, S.D.B.; Manuel Gallo, S.D.B., Coord. Youth Ministry; John Janko, S.D.B., Facilities Mgr.; James Marra, S.D.B., Dir. of Advancement; Matthew Marshack; Eugene Palumbo, S.D.B.; Philip Pascucci, S.D.B. (Retired); Franco Pinto, S.D.B.; Jerzy Schneider, S.D.B. (Retired); Bros. Minh Dang, S.D.B., Teacher; James Wiegand, S.D.B., Asst. Athletic Dir. Total in Residence 12.

ROSELLE. *Marist Brothers Residence, Roselle Catholic High School*, 376 Raritan Rd., 07203. Tel: 908-245-3574; Fax: 908-620-9507. Brothers 11.

RUTHERFORD. *St. John Vianney Residence for Priests*, 60 Home Ave., 07070. Tel: 201-933-5155. Carol Hubba, Admin.; Rev. Msgr. Edward J. Hajduk, S.T.L., M.S.S., Dir. (Retired). Tel: 201-933-5155. Total in Residence 23; Total Staff 16. In Res. Most Rev. Peter L. Gerety, D.D., Archbishop Emeritus (Retired); Rev. Msgrs. Peter A. Cheplic (Retired); Joseph Chiang (Retired); Edward J. Eilert (Retired); Thomas G. Madden (Retired); James O. Sheerin (Retired); Charles G. Stengel (Retired); Richard T. Strelecki (Retired); Revs. Gerald A. Bajek (Retired); Robert M. Brennan (Retired); Joseph F. Coda (Retired); Neil J. Collins (Retired); Eugene J. Hazewski (Retired); John E. Komar (Retired); Robert H. Langdon (Retired); Felipe Lopez (Retired); John J. Morel (Retired); James J. Reilly, S.T.L.; Joseph P. Rice (Retired); Thaddeus Stasik (Retired); Thaddeus F. Zuber (Retired); Rudolf Zubik (Retired).

SOUTH ORANGE. *Pallottine Fathers & Brothers*, 204 Raymond Ave., P.O. Box 979, 07079-0979. Tel: 973-762-2926; Fax: 973-762-2939. Very Rev. Peter T. Sticco, S.A.C., Prov.; Bro. Francis Meo, S.A.C., Admin.

Salesian Office of Youth Ministry & Vocations, 315 Self Pl., 07079. Tel: 973-761-0201; Fax: 973-763-9330. Email: ym@salesianym.com. Web: www.salesianym.com. Revs. Steve Ryan, S.D.B.; Dominic Tran, S.D.B., M.A.

TENAFLY. *Society of African Missions, Provincialate, S.M.A. Fathers*, 23 Bliss Ave., 07670. Tel: 201-567-0450; 201-567-9085; Fax: 201-541-1280; 800-670-8328. Email: smausa-c@smafathers.org. Web: www.smafathers.org. Very Rev. Michael P. Moran, S.M.A., Prov. Supr.; Revs. Brendan Darcy, S.M.A., Local Supr. & Vice Prov.; Herve Yepie Abou, S.M.A.; Edward J. Biggane, S.M.A.; Gustavo Buccilli; Daniel Cullen, S.M.A.; Thomas E. Hayden, S.M.A., Serving Outside Archdiocese.; Patrick Kelly, S.M.A.; James J. McConnell, S.M.A., Queen of Angels.; John Francis Murray, S.M.A.; Simon Thomas, S.M.A.; Clark Yates, S.M.A.

UNION CITY. *Augustinian Recollects, St. Nicholas of Tolentine Monastery* Prov. of St. Nicholas of Tolentine. , 3201 Central Ave., 07087. Tel: 201-433-7550; Fax: 201-422-7570. Email: nicholas@agustinosrecoletos.org. Rev. Francisco J. Legarra, O.A.R., Supr.

Capuchin Friars - Province of the Sacred Stigmata of St. Francis, Office of the Provincial Min., 319 36th St., P.O. Box 809, 07087. Tel: 201-865-0611; Fax: 201-866-7035. Email: stigmatanj@aol.com. Revs. Nicholas A. Mormando, O.F.M.Cap., Provincial Min.; Ronald Giannone, O.F.M.Cap., Vicar Prov.; Remo DiSalvatore, O.F.M.Cap., Councilor; Bros. Rudolph Pieretti, O.F.M. Cap., Councilor; John Russo, O.F.M.Cap., Councillor; Margaret Milizzo, Admin. Asst. Priests 30; Brothers 13.

Congregation of the Passion (Passionists)-St. Michael's Residence, 526 Monastery Pl., 07087. Tel: 201-864-0018; Fax: 201-867-8651. Email: thepassionists@cpprov.org. Web: www.thepassionists.org. Revs. Victor Hoagland, C.P., Dir.; Lucian Clark, C.P.; Kevin Dance, C.P.; Xavier Vitacolonna, C.P.; Bros. James Fitzgerald; Andre Mathieu, C.P. *The Passionist Missionaries* Tel: 201-867-6400; Fax: 201-867-7596. Anne Marie Gardiner, Dir. *Passionist Press, Inc.* Tel: 201-867-6400; Fax: 201-867-8651. Email: crossplace@cpprov.org. Rev. Victor Hoagland, C.P. *Passionist Volunteers, International* Tel: 201-867-6400. Rev. Lucian Clark, C.P., Contact Person. *"Compassion" Magazine* Tel: 201-867-6400; Fax: 201-864-1337. Revs. Paul Zilonka, C.P., Dir. Tel: 201-864-0018; Xavier Vitacolonna, C.P. Tel: 201-864-0018; Lucian Clark, C.P.; Bros. James Fitzgerald, Editor. Tel: 201-864-0018; Andre Mathieu, C.P. *Passionist Archives* Tel: 201-867-6400; Fax: 201-617-7011. Rev. Robert Carbonneau, C.P., Dir. Archives & Province Historian; Mr. Sean Pelagrine, Archivist. Tel: 201-867-6400.

VERONA. *The Salvatorian Fathers* (1881) (Polish Mission House), 23 Crestmont Rd., 07044. Tel: 973-746-8770; Fax: 973-857-7789. Email: wmarek@verizon.net. Web: www.salvator.org. Revs. Marek Wiorkiewicz, S.D.S., Supr.; Zenon Boczek, S.D.S., Vice Supr.; Palka Bogdan, S.D.S.; Pawel Dolinski, S.D.S.; Andrzej Kielkowski, S.D.S.; Ludwik Kolodziej, S.D.S.; Jan J. Mysliwiec, S.D.S.; Damian Tomiczek, S.D.S.; Strzadala Wieslaw, S.D.S.; Bro. Piotr Bogawski, S.D.S.

WEST ORANGE. *Augustinian Recollects* Prov. Res., Monastery of St. Cloud, 29 Ridgeway Ave., 07052. Tel: 973-731-0616, Ext. 12; Fax: 973-731-1033. Email: SAprovince@oar.cc. Web: www.augustinianrecollects.us. Very Rev. Joseph Gallardo, O.A.R., Prior Prov.; Rev. Charles F. Huse, O.A.R., Prov. Sec.; Bro. Anthony Torretti, O.A.R., Prov. Procurator. Priests 2; Brothers 1.

[M] CONVENTS AND RESIDENCES FOR SISTERS

NEWARK. *Daughters of Mary Mother of Mercy (DMMM)*, 44 Monticello Ave., 07106. Tel: 862-902-7029.

Hermanas Misioneras del Corazon de Jesus (HMCJ), Sacred Heart Convent, 109 Parker St., 07104. Tel: 973-484-1516; Fax: 973-484-9701. Email: misionerascj@aol.com. Sr. Ana Josefa Fa jardo, Supr. Parish Ministry. Sisters 4.

Holy Family Sisters of the Needy, St. Rose of Lima Convent, 526 Orange St., 07107. Tel: 973-481-6717. Email: srmavit@yahoo.com. Sr. Mary Francis Okoroji, Local Supr. Sisters 5.

Missionaries of Charity - St. Augustine Convent (1981) 168 Sussex Ave., 07103. Tel: 973-483-0165. Sisters 8.

Missionary Sisters of the Most Blessed Sacrament and Mary Immaculate Day Care Center., 121 Congress St., 07105. Tel: 973-589-5794; Fax: 973-589-2474. Email: grande815@msn.com; nepo867@msn.com. Rev. Lucio M. Nontol, T.O.R. (Peru), Dir.

Sisters of St. Joseph of Chestnut Hill, Thea House (1992) 39 Bleeker St., 07102. Tel: 973-622-7056. Email: ssjthea@gmail.com. Total in Residence 4.

Vocationist Sisters (1921) (Our Lady of Perpetual Help Center). Perpetual Help Day Nursery., 170 Broad St., 07104. Tel: 973-484-3535; Fax: 973-484-2526. Email: perhelp@yahoo.com. Sisters 6; Total Assisted 145; Total Staff 22.

CALDWELL. *Motherhouse of Sisters of St. Dominic*, 1 Ryerson Ave., 07006. Tel: 973-403-3331; Fax: 973-228-9611. Email: pstringer@caldwellop.org. Web: www.caldwellop.org. Sr. Arlene Antczak, O.P., Prioress. Sisters in Community 149; Sisters in Diocese 131.

DEMAREST. *Missionary Benedictine Sisters of Tutzing* (1997) 274 County Rd., 07627. Tel: 201-767-3114; Fax: 201-767-8874. Sr. Asella Kim, O.S.B., Supr. Sisters 4.

ELIZABETH. *St. Walburga Monastery*, 851 N. Broad St., 07208-2593. Tel: 908-352-4278; Fax: 908-352-6331. Email: Bensisnj@aol.com. Web: www.catholic-forum.com/bensisnj. Benedictine Sisters of Elizabeth, NJ. Sisters in Archdiocese 36; Professed Sisters 43.

ENGLEWOOD CLIFFS. *St. Michael Villa*, 399 Hudson Ter., 07632. Tel: 201-871-1620; Fax: 201-871-7313. Sr. Ann Rutan, C.S.J.P., Admin.; Rev. William T. Morris, Chap. Sisters of St. Joseph of Peace., Senior Sisters Residence and Infirmary for Eastern Region. Sisters 40; Total Staff 52; Total in Residence 39.

Sisters of St. Joseph of Peace, 399 Hudson Ter.,

07632. Tel: 201-568-6348; Fax: 201-568-9880. Web: www.csjp.org/sjp. Sisters Margaret Byrne, C.S.J.P., Congregation Leader; Teresa Donohue, C.S.J.P., Asst. Congregation Leader; Kristin Funari, C.S.J.P; Anne Hayes, C.S.J.P.; Coralie Muzzy, C.S.J.P.; Ann Taylor, C.S.J.P., Congregation Archivist. Congregation of Sisters of St. Joseph of Peace., Eastern U.S. Offices for Sisters of St. Joesph of Peace. Sisters in Community 94.

Congregation Leadership Team:

St. Ann's Home for the Aged Tel: 201-433-0950; Fax: 201-433-6554. Total Staff 215; Total in Residence 120.

St. Ann's Day Care Tel: 201-433-0950; Fax: 201-985-9638. Staff 10; Adults 50.

Cusack Care Center at St. Joseph Home for the Blind Tel: 201-653-8300; Fax: 201-963-4346. Total Staff 220; Total in Residence 275; Bed Capacity 139.

Concordia Learning Center at St. Joseph School for the Blind: A New Jersey Non-profit Corp. Tel: 201-876-5432; Fax: 201-876-5431. Total Staff 95; Students 246; Lay Teachers 16.

Holy Name Medical Center Tel: 201-833-3000; Fax: 201-833-3230.

St. Joseph Home Tel: 201-413-9280. Bed Capacity 60; Total Staff 13; Total Assisted 106.

Kenmare High School Tel: 201-451-1177; Fax: 201-451-0952.

St. Mary's Residence Tel: 201-432-6289. Total Staff 10; Total Assisted 47.

St. Michael Villa Tel: 201-871-1620; Fax: 201-871-7313.

Nurturing Place Day Care Tel: 201-413-1982. Child Development Center Total Staff 15; Total Assisted 110.

The York Street Project Tel: 201-451-9838; Fax: 201-451-0952. Total Staff 9.

Stella Maris Retreat Center Tel: 732-229-0602; Fax: 732-229-8960. Total Staff 10; Total in Residence 3.

WATERSPIRIT Ministry Tel: 732-923-9788; Fax: 732-229-8960. Total Staff 3.

FORT LEE. *Holy Trinity Convent (Inter Community)*, 199 Myrtle Ave., 07024. Tel: 201-944-2911. Dominican Sisters of Hope 1; Franciscan Sisters of St. Francis 2; Sisters of Charity 1.

IRVINGTON. *Immaculate Conception Convent, St. Leo*, 121 Myrtle Ave., 07111. Tel: 973-757-2432. Augustinian Recollect Sisters (Cloistered) 11.

JERSEY CITY. *St. Nicholas Convent*, 115 Ferry St., 07307. Tel: 201-659-5644; Fax: 201-798-6868. Email: sjmaumand@yahoo.com. Sr. Joann Marie Aumand, S.C.C., Supr.

LODI. *Immaculate Conception Convent* (1913) 260 S. Main St., 07644-2196. Tel: 973-473-7447; Fax: 973-473-7126. Email: sconniet@feliciansisters.org. Web: www.feliciansisters.org. Sr. Constance Marie Tomyl, Prov. Sec.

The Order of the Felician Sisters of St. Francis., Convent and Infirmary of the Felician Sisters. Sisters in New Jersey 135; Sisters in Province 776.

PLAINFIELD. *Contemplative Convent of the Missionaries of Charity*, 513 Liberty St., 07060. Tel: 908-754-1978. Sr. Mary Nieves, M.C., Supr. Total in Residence 14.

RIDGEFIELD. *Pallottine Sisters - St. Vincent Pallotti Convent*, 545 Victory Ave., 07567. Tel: 201-941-4552. Email: sralicemarie@gmail.com. Sisters 2.

SADDLE BROOK. *Miyazaki Caritas Sisters (Korea) - Caritas Sisters Convent*, 9 Jamros Terr., 07663. Tel: 201-398-0199; Fax: 201-703-7111.

SCOTCH PLAINS. *Union Catholic Convent* (1962) 1600 Martine Ave., 07076. Tel: 908-889-1600. Sisters of Mercy of New Jersey (R.S.M.) and Sisters of St. Joseph (S.S.J.). Total in Residence 5.

SUMMIT. *Monastery of Our Lady of the Rosary* (1919) 543 Springfield Ave., 07901. Tel: 908-273-1228; Fax: 908-273-6511. Email: nunsopsummit@op.org. Web: www.nunsopsummit.org. Sr. Denise Marie Atkins, O.P., Prioress; Rev. Gregory Salomone, O.P., Chap.

Monastery of Our Lady of the Rosary, Dominican Nuns of the Perpetual Rosary Professed Sisters 13; Novices 6; Temporary Professed Sisters 2; Postulants 1.

TENAFLY. *Convent of Our Lady of the Angels*, 253 Knickerbocker Rd., 07670. Tel: 201-568-2171; Fax: 201-568-2352. Email: franciscans253@yahoo.com. Web: www.mficusa.org. Sr. Alphonsina Molloy, M.F.I.C., Local Min. Missionary Franciscan Sisters of the Immaculate Conception. Sisters 42.

UNION. *Sisters of St. Francis of the Providence of God*, 1137 Burnet Ave., 07083. Tel: 908-206-1136. Sisters 2.

UNION CITY. *Holy Rosary Convent* (1904) 1514 Central Ave., 07087. Tel: 201-617-4638; Fax: 201-601-2301. Email: holyrosaryconvent@verizon.net. Sisters of the Catholic Apostolate (Pallottines). Sisters 3.

[N] RETREAT HOUSES

KEARNY. *Archdiocesan Youth Retreat Center* Archdiocesan Youth Center and Retreat House. Retreats for groups, parishes, days of prayer recollection, workshops, seminars for laity, priests, and religious. Rooms for overnight and food service. High and Low ropes challenge course available., 499 Belgrove Dr., 07032. Tel: 201-998-0088; Fax: 201-299-0801. Web: www.newarkoym.com. Rev. Timothy G. Graff, Pastoral Mod.

MAHWAH. *Carmel Retreat* Carmelite Community and House of Prayer. Retreats (groups, directed, private), Days of prayer, rentals, meetings, seminars. , 1071 Ramapo Valley Rd., 07430. Tel: 201-327-7090; Fax: 201-327-9133. Email: mail@carmelretreat.com. Web: www.carmelretreat.com. Sr. Eileen T. McGovern, S.S.J., Dir. Priests 1; Brothers 1; Total in Residence 2. In Res. Rev. Michael Wastag, O.Carm., M.A., M.Div.; Bro. Thomas Murphy, O.Carm.

[O] CAMPUS MINISTRY

NEWARK. *The Newman Catholic Center at University Heights (Rutgers/Newark/NJIT)* 91 Washington St., 07102. Tel: 973-624-1301; Fax: 973-623-1728. Email: NewmanCenter@optonline.net. Web: www.newmanclubnewark.org. Rev. Bryan E. Page, Dir. & Chap.; Sisters Faustine of Jesus, Campus Min.; Monika-Maria, Campus Min.; Danielle O'Sullivan, Office Mgr. Serving Essex County College, Rutgers University/Newark Campus, New Jersey Institute of Technology & UMDNJ Total Staff 5.

HOBOKEN. *Catholic Campus Ministry at Stevens Institute of Technology* Mailing Address: *Ss. Peter and Paul Parish Center*, 408 Hudson St., 07030. Web: www.ccm-nj.com. Revs. Amilcar B. Prado, Campus Min. & Chap.; Matthew R. Dooley, Chap. (Part-Time). Total Staff 1.

JERSEY CITY. *New Jersey City University, Gilligan Student Union* 2039 Kennedy Blvd., GSUB Rm. 316, 07305-1597. Tel: 201-200-2565 (Office); 973-792-5710 (Residence); Fax: 201-200-2329 (Office of Campus Life). Web: www.catholiccampusministry.org. Rev. Luke A. Edelen, O.S.B., Chap. & Campus Min. Total Staff 1.

MAHWAH. *Ramapo College* (1969) 505 Ramapo Valley Rd., Room SC207, 07430. Tel: 201-684-7251; Fax: 201-825-0276. Email: wsherida@ramapo.edu. Web: www.ramapo.edu/studentlife/ministry/catholic_Ministry/CM_index.htm. Rev. William P. Sheridan, Chap. Total Staff 1; Students 5,500.

TEANECK. *Fairleigh Dickinson Univ.-Teaneck Campus* 1000 River Rd., 07666. Tel: 201-692-2570; Fax: 201-692-2769. Rev. James P. Ferry, Campus Min. Total Staff 2.

UNION. *Kean University* Catholic Campus Ministry, 1000 Morris Ave., 07083-7131. Tel: 908-737-4835; Fax: 201-985-0918. Rev. Thomas F. Blind, Chap.

UPPER MONTCLAIR. *Newman Catholic Center at Montclair State University* 894 Valley Rd., 07043-2116. Tel: 973-746-2323; Fax: 973-783-3313. Email: chernjam@comcast.net. Web: www.msunewman.com. Rev. James N. Chern, Dir., Newman Catholic Ctr. & Chap. at Montclair State Univ.; Mary Kominsky, Office Mgr. & Pastoral Assoc. Total Staff 2.

[P] SHRINES

KEARNY. *Eucharistic Shrine of the Adorable Face of Jesus* 672 Passaic Ave., 07032-1305. Tel: 201-997-1270; Fax: 201-997-5552. Email: eushrine@juno.com. Rev. Msgr. Renato Grasselli, S.T.L., Shrine Dir.

[Q] MISCELLANEOUS LISTINGS

NEWARK. *Catholic Health and Human Services Corporation*, 1160 Raymond Blvd., 07102. Tel: 973-854-2447.

CatholiCare, Inc., 171 Clifton Ave., P.O. Box 9500, 07104-0500. Tel: 973-497-4002; Fax: 973-497-4018. Rev. Msgr. John E. Doran, V.G., Vicar Gen. & Moderator of Curia.

Columbus Acquisition Corp. A member of Catholic Health East., 495 N. 13th St., 07107. Email: hatalaa@lourdesnet.org. Alexander J. Hatala, Pres.

Deacon St. Lawrence Welfare Fund, Office of Permanent Diaconate, 171 Clifton Ave., P.O. Box 9500, 07104-9500. Tel: 973-497-4125; Fax: 973-497-4103. Email: mckennjo@rcan.org. Deacon John J. McKenna.

Diaconate Executive Committee, Archdiocesan Center, 171 Clifton Ave., P.O. Box 9500, 07104-9500. Tel: 973-497-4125; Fax: 973-497-4103. Email: mckennjo@rcan.org. Deacon John J. McKenna.

Saint James Care, Inc. A member of Catholic Health East., 155 Jefferson St., 07107. Alexander J. Hatala, Pres.

St. Mary's Senior Residence, Inc., 590 N. 7th St., 07107. Tel: 973-596-3984; Fax: 973-412-7710. Mr. John Westervelt, B.A., Vice Pres. & Treas.

St. Michael Foundation, Inc. Subsidiary of Saint Michael's Medical Center., *St. Michael's Medical Center*, 111 Central Ave., 07102. Fax: 973-690-3601. Mr. David A. Ricci, Pres.; Richard A. Boiardo M.D., Chair-Elect.

New Jersey Caritas Corporation, Inc., 171 Clifton Ave., 07104. Tel: 973-497-4002; Fax: 973-497-4018. Rev. Msgr. John E. Doran, V.G.

Domus Corporation, Inc., 590 N. 7th St., 07107. Tel: 973-596-3984; Fax: 973-424-9596.

Myers Senior Residence, Inc., 590 N. 7th St., 07107. Tel: 973-596-3984; Fax: 973-412-7710.

Canaan House, Inc., 494 Broad St., 07102. Tel: 973-596-5115; Fax: 973-424-9596.

Sunrise House, 185 Parkhurst St., 07114. Tel: 973-624-9478; Fax: 973-424-9596.

Carmel House of Jersey City, Inc., 494 Broad St., 07102. Tel: 973-596-5115; Fax: 973-424-9596.

University Heights Property Company, Inc., 1160 Raymond Blvd., 07102. Tel: 973-690-3606; Fax: 973-690-3601. Mr. Roosevel N. Nesmith Esq., Chm.; Mr. David A. Ricci, Pres.; Anita C. Holland, Sec.

BAYONNE. *The Benoit Trust*, 1241 Kennedy Blvd., 07002. Tel: 201-823-1115; Fax: 201-823-2232. Email: maristpto@aol.com. Bros. Richard Carey, F.M.S., Trustee; Benedict Lo Balbo, F.M.S., Trustee. Congregation of the Marist Brothers.

The Gregoire Trust, 1241 Kennedy Blvd., 07002. Tel: 201-823-1115; Fax: 201-823-2232. Email: maristpto@aol.com. Bros. Benedict LoBalbo, F.M.S., Trustee; Edward Breslin, Trustee; Lawrence Lavallee, F.M.S., Trustee; Ken Hogan, F.M.S., Trustee; Richard Carey, F.M.S., Trustee.

Lewiston Mission Trust, 1241 Kennedy Blvd., 07002. Tel: 201-823-1115; Fax: 201-823-2232. Bros. Edward J. O'Neill, F.M.S., Trustee; Benedict Lo Balbo, F.M.S., Trustee & Contact Person.

ELIZABETH. *St. Joseph's Social Service Center* (1986) 118 Division St., 07201. Tel: 908-352-2989; 908-354-5456; Fax: 908-354-1433. Sr. Jacinta Fernandes, O.S.B., Dir. Total Staff 12; Total Assisted 8,500.

FAIRVIEW. *Pallottine Intra-Community Operating Corporation*, Mailing Address: P.O. Box 979, South Orange, 07079. Tel: 973-762-2926; Fax: 973-762-2939. 395 Delano Pl., 07022. Tel: 201-943-0972; Fax: 201-313-5616. Very Rev. Peter T. Sticco, S.A.C.

JERSEY CITY. *St. Patrick and Assumption All Saints Foundation*, 492 Bramhall Ave., 07304. Tel: 201-332-8600; Fax: 201-324-3919. Email: jcfran@bellatlantic.net. Rev. Francis E. Schiller, B.A., J.D., Contact Person.

St. Patrick's Housing Corp., 492 Bramhall Ave., 07304. Tel: 201-332-8600; Fax: 201-324-3919. Rev. Eugene P. Squeo, J.D., Pres.

Trinity Child Care Center, 492 Bramhall Ave., 07304. Tel: 201-332-8600. Sr. Maeve McDermott, S.C., Prin.; Rev. Francis E. Schiller, B.A., J.D., Contact Person.

KEARNY. *Family of Nazareth, Inc.* (1991) 672 Passaic Ave., 07032. Tel: 201-997-3220; Fax: 201-997-5552. Email: fnazareth@rmnewark.org. Fred Canlas, Pres.; Luis Abarca, Trustee. A foundation to support the work of the Redemptoris Mater Missionary Seminary and for the new evangelization.

LODI. **The Promise Outreach, Inc.* (1982) Volunteers visit, correspond with, and provide opportunity for spirituality and other basic needs to teens in programs, correctional institutions and centers of rehabilitation., 260 S. Main St., 07644. Tel: 973-460-3229; Fax: 973-473-7126. Email: vimsters@aol.com. Web: home.catholicweb.com/thepromiseoutreachinc. Sisters Antonelle Chunka, C.S.S.F., Dir.; Clare Marie Klein, C.S.S.F., Volunteer Coord.; Bro. Thomas Corey, B.S.C.D., Co-Dir.; Sr. Lois Marie Parenti, C.S.S.F., Treas. Total Staff 20; Total Assisted Annually 800.

MAHWAH. *Paulist Press*, 997 MacArthur Blvd., 07430. Tel: 201-825-7300; Fax: 201-825-8345. Email: info@paulistpress.com. Web: www.paulistpress.com. Revs. Kevin A. Lynch, C.S.P., Senior Editor; Mark-David Janus, C.S.P., Pres. & Publisher. Priests 2; Total Staff 50.

MONTCLAIR. *Tri-State Coalition for Responsible Investment*, 40 S. Fullerton Ave., 07042. Tel: 973-509-8800; Fax: 973-509-8808. Email: Pdaly@tricri.org. Web: www.tricri.org. Sr. Patricia A. Daly, O.P., Exec. Dir.

ORANGE. *Mee Joo Catholic Inc.*, 18 Cleveland St., 07050. Tel: 973-672-6335; Fax: 973-672-0509. Email: augpark@yahoo.com. Rev. Msgr. Augustin C. Park, Coord. (Retired).

PLAINFIELD. **The People of Hope* (1977) 1040 Plainfield Ave., St. Francis Bldg., 07060. Tel: 908-222-9722; Fax: 908-222-9755. David Touhill, Senior Coord. The People of Hope is a Catholic Charismatic Covenant community of prayer, family life, and evangelization. Officially recognized as a private association of the faithful in 2006 by Archbishop Myers, the People of Hope sponsors marriage and family retreats, youth, university, and young adult programs, Christian business seminars, and other evangelistic events. Its largest outreach is Koinonia Academy, a K-12 school, founded in 1984. The Community is organized to encourage individuals and families to dedicate their lives to God under the Lordship of Jesus Christ, to help in the renewal of the Catholic Church and to assist the spreading of the Gospel message of Jesus Christ locally and throughout the world. To be "a witness of an authentically Christian life, given over to God." (Pope Paul VI, Evangelii Nuntiandi, 1975).

RENEW International, 1232 George St., 07062-1717. Tel: 908-769-5400; Fax: 908-769-5660. Email: renew@renewintl.org. Web: www.renewintl.org. Sr. Theresa Rickard, O.P., D.Min., Pres. & Exec. Dir.; Rev. Msgr. Thomas A. Kleissler, Pres. Emeritus (Retired); Sisters Honora Nolty, O.P., Asst. Dir., Pastoral Svcs.; Eileen Carmody, P.B.V.M., Human Resources Admin.; John Carney, Dir., Devel.; Dr. Laura Zane Kolmar, Asst. Dir., Pastoral Svcs.; Mr. Greg Kremer, Spec. Asst. to Exec. Dir.; Deirdre Trabert Malacrea, Dir., Mktg. & Communications; Richard Michalowski, Fin. Controller; Ms. Kathleen Ogle, Mng. Editor; Mary Beth Oria, Dir., Business Opers.

Pastoral Services Team: Sisters Maureen Colleary, F.S.P.; Marie Cooper, S.J.C.; Juan Ramon Cordova; Sr. Marenid Fabre, O.P.; Alma Garcia; Manuel Hernandez; Rev. Alejandro Lopez-Cardinale; Sr. Veronica Mendez, R.C.D.; Anne Scanlan; Sr. Pat Thomas, O.P.

Operations, Resources and Administrative Staff: Christopher Burns; Susan Capurso; Regina Crowley; Christina Garzon; Marty Hagedorn; Lynn Hull; Yvette Hutchins; Sarah Iles; Eartha Johnson; Margarita Morales; Carolyn Newkirk; Deacon Charles Paolino; Amy Reed.

RIDGEWOOD. *Trinity Management & Technology Corp.*, 1 Passaic St., 07450. Tel: 973-596-3602; Fax: 973-690-3601. Rev. Msgr. Ronald J. Rozniak, V.E., P.A., Chm.; Bro. Benedict Lo Balbo, F.M.S., Sec. & Contact Person.

RUTHERFORD. *The Community of God's Love* Catholic Charismatic Community, 70 W. Passaic Ave., 07070. Tel: 201-935-0344; Fax: 201-935-0111. Email: theCGL@aol.com. Web: thecgl.org. Rev. Philip F.A. Latronico, M.A., M.Div., Chap.; Andrew J. Cevasco, Community Dir.

SHORT HILLS. *Friends of the Newark Monastery, Inc.*, 9 Grosvenor Rd., 07078. Email: aluzarraga@shearman.com. Alberto Luzarraga, Pres. & Contact Person.

SOUTH ORANGE. *The Pallottines of South Orange, Inc.*, 204 Raymond Ave., 07079-2305. Tel: 973-763-5591; Fax: 973-762-2939. Bro. Francis Meo, S.A.C., Supr.

Salesians of Don Bosco, Salesians House, 315 Self Pl., 07079. Tel: 973-761-0201; Fax: 973-763-9330. Email: ym@salesianym.com. Web: www.salesianym.com.

Offices of Vocation and Youth Ministry Tel: 973-761-0102; Fax: 973-763-9330. Email: salvoc@aol.com. Web: www.salesianvocation.com. Revs. Steve Ryan, S.D.B., Vocation Dir. & Prov. Councillor for Youth Ministry; P. Francis Pinto, S.D.B. Total in Residence 2.

U.S. Catholic China Bureau (1989) Seton Hall University, 07079-2689. Tel: 973-763-1131; Fax: 973-774-7084. Email: chinabur@shu.edu. Web: www.usccb.net. Revs. Mark T. DeStephano, S.J., Chair, Bd. of Directors; Michel Marcil, S.J., Exec. Dir.; Mengpin Hsiao, Admin. Asst. Exists to foster communication and friendship with the people of China through sharing the values of the Gospel of Jesus Christ. It promotes understanding among American Catholics about the Catholic Church and the situation of Catholic communities in China. It fosters re-engagement of the U.S. Catholic Church in a new missionary partnership with the Catholic Church in China. USCCB publishes the "China Church Quarterly", sponsors National Catholic China Conference, religious study tours to China and other activities to sustain a shared commitment to mission with the Catholic Church in China. Total Staff 2.

SUMMIT. *Association of the Monasteries of Nuns of the Order of Preachers in the United States of America*, 543 Springfield Ave., 07901-4400. Tel: 650-322-1801, Ext. 25; Fax: 650-322-6816. Sisters Mary John Molesworth, O.P., Pres.; Miriam Scheel, O.P., Vice Pres.; Mary Desmond, O.P., Sec. & First Counselor; Maria Christine Behlow, O.P., Treas.

Christ Child Society of Summit, N.J., P.O. Box 125, 07902-0125. Tel: 908-598-1377. Email: lambinewsham@msn.com. Lambi Newsham, Pres.

TEANECK. *Holy Name Health Care Foundation*, 718 Teaneck Rd., 07666. Tel: 201-833-3187; Fax: 201-833-3708. Email: foundation@mail.holyname.org. Web: www.holyname.org. Michael Maron, Pres. & CEO. Sisters of St. Joseph of Peace.

UNION. *Association of St. Philomena's Helpers and Servants to the Suffering & the Poor* (1996) P.O. Box 393, 07083-0393. Tel: 908-964-7653; Fax: 908-687-4209.

UNION CITY. *Cofradia Arquidiocesana de la Virgen de la Caridad del Cobre, Inc.*, 3333 Hudson Ave., P.O. Box 682, 07087. Tel: 201-941-0530. Manuel Sanchez, Treas.

**New Jersey Friends of Mandeville, Inc.*, 526 Monastery Pl., 07087. Tel: 201-867-6400. Mr. Greg Hapson, CFO.

RELIGIOUS INSTITUTES OF MEN REPRESENTED IN THE ARCHDIOCESE

For further details refer to the corresponding bracketed number in the Religious Institutes of Men or Women section.

[0100]—*Adorno Fathers*—C.R.M.
[0200]—*Benedictine Monks* (Newark Abbey; St. Mary Abbey)—O.S.B.
[0330]—*Brothers of Christian Schools* (Baltimore Prov.; Long Island/New England Prov.; New York Prov.)—F.S.C.
[0470]—*The Capuchin Friars* (Prov. of the Stigmata)—O.F.M.Cap.
[0270]—*Carmelite Fathers & Brothers* (American Prov.)—O.Carm.
[0380]—*Comboni Missionaries of the Heart of Jesus (Verona)*—M.C.C.J.
[0310]—*Congregation of Christian Brothers*—C.F.C.
[]—*Congregation of Saint John*
[1000]—*Congregation of the Passion* (Eastern Prov.)—C.P.
[0520]—*Franciscan Friars* (Prov. of Most Holy Name; Prov. of the Assumption)—O.F.M.
[0530]—*Franciscan Friars of the Atonement*—S.A.
[0535]—*Franciscan Friars of the Renewal*—C.F.R.
[0690]—*Jesuit Fathers and Brothers* (Prov. of New York)—S.J.
[0770]—*The Marist Brothers*—F.M.S.
[0840]—*Missionary Servants of the Most Holy Trinity*—S.T.
[0150]—*Order of the Augustinian Recollects* (Prov. of St. Augustine)—O.A.R.
[0150]—*Order of the Augustinian Recollects* (Prov. of St. Nicholas of Tolentine)—O.A.R.
[1030]—*Paulist Fathers*—C.S.P.
[]—*Province of the Immaculate Conception*
[1070]—*Redemptorist Fathers* (Byzantine Ukrainians)—C.Ss.R.
[1070]—*Redemptorist Fathers* (Prov. of Campo Grande, Brazil)—C.Ss.R.
[1190]—*Salesians of Don Bosco*—S.D.B.
[0110]—*Society of African Missions*—S.M.A.
[0990]—*Society of the Catholic Apostolate* (Prov. of the Immaculate Conception)—S.A.C.
[1200]—*Society of the Divine Savior*—S.D.S.
[1170]—*St. Patrick Missionary Society*—S.P.S.
[0560]—*Third Order Regular of Saint Francis* (U.S.A. Commissarate of the Spanish Prov.)—T.O.R.
[]—*Union Lumen Dei*—L.D.
[1340]—*Vocationist Fathers*—S.D.V.

RELIGIOUS INSTITUTES OF WOMEN REPRESENTED IN THE ARCHDIOCESE

[]—*Augustinian Recollect Sisters* (Mexico)—O.A.R.
[0230]—*Benedictine Sisters of Pontifical Jurisdiction-Newark* (Benedictine Sisters of Baltimore; Benedictine Sisters of Elizabeth)—O.S.B.
[]—*Congregation of Caritas Sisters of Miyazaki* Korean Province
[]—*Congregation of Kkottongnae Sisters of Jesus*—C.S.K.J.
[]—*Congregation of the Apostolic Sisters of Saint John*—C.S.J.
[]—*Congregation of the Immaculate Heart of Mary*
[]—*Daughters of Divine Love*—D.D.L.
[]—*Daughters of Mary*—D.M.
[0850]—*Daughters of Mary Help of Christians*—F.M.A.
[]—*Daughters of Mary, Mothers of Mercy* (Nigeria)—D.M.M.M.
[]—*Daughters of the Heart of Mary*—D.H.M.
[1070-11]—*Dominican Sisters* (Sparkill, NY)—O.P.
[1070-15]—*Dominican Sisters* (Blauvelt, NY)—O.P.
[1070-18]—*Dominican Sisters* (Caldwell, NJ)—O.P.
[1070-06]—*Dominican Sisters of Hope* (Newburgh, NY)—O.P.
[1170]—*Felician Sisters*—C.S.S.F.
[1400]—*Franciscan Missionary Sister of the Sacred Heart*—F.M.S.C.
[1180]—*Franciscan Sisters of Allegany, New York*—O.S.F.
[1425]—*Franciscan Sisters of Peace*—F.S.P.
[1460]—*Franciscan Sisters of St. Elizabeth*—F.S.S.E.
[]—*Hermanas Missionaras del Corazon de Jesus* (Dominican Republic)—H.M.C.J.
[]—*Holy Family Sisters of the Needy*—H.F.S.N.
[3790]—*Institute of the Sisters of St. Dorothy*—S.S.D.
[2710]—*Missionaries of Charity* (Active and Contemplative)—M.C.
[0210]—*Missionary Benedictine Sisters of Tutzing* (Korean Mission)—O.S.B.
[1360]—*Missionary Franciscan Sisters of the Immaculate Conception*—M.F.I.C.
[2790]—*Missionary Servants of the Most Blessed Trinity*—M.S.B.T.
[2780]—*Missionary Sisters of the Most Blessed Sacrament and Mary Immaculate*—M.SS.M.I.
[]—*Miyazaki Caritas Sisters* (Japan/Korea)—C.S.M.
[3430]—*Religious Teachers Filippini*—M.P.F.
[2970]—*School Sisters of Notre Dame*—S.S.N.D.
[1700]—*School Sisters of the Third Order of St. Francis* (Bethlehem, PA)—O.S.F.
[]—*Sisters of Charity (Halifax)*
[0590]—*Sisters of Charity of Saint Elizabeth, Convent Station*—S.C.
[0650]—*Sisters of Charity of St. Vincent de Paul of New York*—S.C.
[0660]—*Sisters of Christian Charity*—S.C.C.
[2575]—*Sisters of Mercy of the Americas* (New Jersey)—R.S.M.
[]—*Sisters of Peace Pentecost*
[3893]—*Sisters of Saint Joseph of Chestnut Hill, Philadelphia*—S.S.J.
[1650]—*Sisters of St. Francis of Philadelphia*—O.S.F.
[1660]—*Sisters of St. Francis of Providence of God*—O.S.F.
[]—*Sisters of St. Francis of the Neumann Communities*—O.S.F.
[3820]—*Sisters of St. John the Baptist*—C.S.J.B.
[3890]—*Sisters of St. Joseph of Peace*—C.S.J.P.
[3937]—*Sisters of St. Martha of Antigonish, N.S.*—C.S.M.
[3140]—*Sisters of the Catholic Apostolate (Pallottine)*—C.S.A.C.
[0970]—*Sisters of the Divine Compassion*—R.D.C.
[]—*Sisters of the Holy Name of Jesus and Mary*—S.N.J.M.
[]—*Sisters of the Immaculate Heart of Mary of Mirinae*—I.H.M.M.
[3610]—*Sisters Servants of Mary Immaculate*—S.S.M.I.
[2160]—*Sisters, Servants of the Immaculate Heart of Mary (Scranton)*—I.H.M.
[4060]—*Society of the Holy Child Jesus*—S.H.C.J.
[]—*Union Lumen Dei*—L.D.
[4210]—*Vocationist Sisters*—S.D.V.

ARCHDIOCESAN CEMETERIES

Office of Catholic Cemeteries, Tel: 973-497-7981; Fax: 973-497-7984; Tel: 973-497-7981 (Cemeteries Office); 973-497-7988 (Mausoleum Office). Rev. Msgr. William B. Naedele, Dir. (Retired); Andrew P. Schafer, Exec. Dir. Tel: 973-497-7975.

COLONIA
St. Gertrude

MAHWAH
Maryrest

EAST HANOVER
Gate of Heaven

EAST ORANGE
Holy Sepulchre
St. Mary

FRANKLIN LAKES
Christ the King

JERSEY CITY
Holy Name
Saint Peter

NORTH ARLINGTON
Holy Cross

RIVER VALE
St. Andrew

PAROCHIAL CEMETERIES

NEWARK. *Mount Olivet*
BELLEVILLE. *St. Peter's*
BLOOMFIELD. *Mount Olivet*
CLARK. *St. Mary's*
FORT LEE. *Madonna*

HACKENSACK. *St. Joseph's*
HOHOKUS. *St. Luke's*
LINDEN. *Mount Calvary*
LYNDHURST. *St. Joseph's*
ORANGE. *St. John's*
PLAINFIELD. *St. Mary's*
SHORT HILLS. *St. Rose of Lima*
SUMMIT. *St. Teresa's*
TENAFLY. *Mount Carmel*
UPPER MONTCLAIR. *Immaculate Conception*

NECROLOGY

† Daly, Rev. Msgr. Thomas J., (Retired)—Died April 4, 2011
† Flusk, Rev. Msgr. Joseph F., (Retired)—Died July 9, 2011
† Kelly, Rev. Msgr. Martin, (Retired)—Died Feb. 2, 2011
† Matash, Rev. Msgr. Edward M., (Retired)—Died Feb. 15, 2011
† O'Brien, Rev. Msgr. Martin F., (Retired)—Died Oct. 26, 2011
† Sheehan, Rev. Msgr. James M., Newark, NJ Cathedral Basilica of the Sacred Heart.—Died Aug. 28, 2011
† Cialone, Donald F., Westfield, NJ Holy Trinity.—Died Feb. 9, 2011
† Galdon, Peter P., (Retired)—Died Nov. 9, 2011
† Galvis Rios, Hector F., Jersey City, NJ Our Lady of Mount Carmel.—Died Jan. 31, 2011
† Garoffolo, Vincent, (Retired)—Died July 11, 2011
† Giblin, William M., (Retired)—Died May 13, 2011
† Leonard, Patrick J., (Retired)—Died Feb. 7, 2011
† Miodowski, Leonard A., (Retired)—Died Aug. 2, 2011
† Mulvey, John J., (Retired)—Died Sept. 8, 2011
† Nardone, Richard M., (Retired)—Died March 27, 2011
† Ponce, Francisco, Jersey City, NJ St. Joseph.—Died June 28, 2011
† Rischmann, Edward J., (Retired)—Died June 7, 2011
† Sapeta, Joseph S., (Retired)—Died Jan. 24, 2011
† Scherer, Donald R., (Retired)—Died Dec. 3, 2010
† Waldron, John R., (Retired)—Died March 27, 2011

An asterisk (*) denotes an organization that has established tax-exempt status directly with the IRS and is not covered by the USCCB Group Ruling.

Archdiocese of New Orleans

(Archidioecesis Novae Aureliae)

Most Reverend

GREGORY M. AYMOND, D.D.

Archbishop of New Orleans; ordained May 10, 1975; ordained Auxiliary Bishop of New Orleans January 10, 1997; appointed Coadjutor Bishop of Austin June 2, 2000; installed Bishop of Austin August 3, 2000; appointed Archbishop of New Orleans June 12, 2009; Pallium conferred by Pope Benedict XVI at the Vatican June 29, 2009; installed Archbishop of New Orleans August 20, 2009. *Archdiocesan Administration Building: 7887 Walmsley Ave., New Orleans, LA 70125-3496.* Tel: 504-861-9521.

Most Reverend

ALFRED C. HUGHES, S.T.D.

Former Archbishop of New Orleans; ordained December 15, 1957; appointed Auxiliary Bishop of Boston July 21, 1981; ordained Auxiliary Bishop of Boston September 14, 1981; appointed Bishop of Baton Rouge September 7, 1993; installed Bishop of Baton Rouge November 4, 1993; appointed Coadjutor Archbishop of New Orleans February 16, 2001; appointed Archbishop of New Orleans January 3, 2002; retired August 20, 2009. *Office: 7887 Walmsley Ave., New Orleans, LA 70125.* Tel: 504-861-9521.

Most Reverend

FRANCIS B. SCHULTE, D.D.

Former Archbishop of New Orleans; ordained May 10, 1952; appointed Titular Bishop of Afufenia and Auxiliary Bishop of Philadelphia June 27, 1981; ordained to the episcopacy August 12, 1981; appointed Sixth Bishop of Wheeling-Charleston June 4, 1985; promoted to Metropolitan See of New Orleans December 13, 1988; installed February 14, 1989; retired January 3, 2002. *Office: 7887 Walmsley Ave., New Orleans, LA 70125.*

Archdiocesan Administration Building: 7887 Walmsley Ave., New Orleans, LA 70125-3496. Tel: 504-861-9521; Fax: 504-866-2906.

Web: www.archdiocese-no.org

Most Reverend

SHELTON J. FABRE, V.G.

Auxiliary Bishop of New Orleans; ordained August 5, 1989; appointed Auxiliary Bishop of New Orleans and Titular Bishop of Prudenziana December 13, 2006; ordained February 28, 2007. *Office: 7887 Walmsley Ave., New Orleans, LA 70125-3496.*

Most Reverend

DOMINIC CARMON, S.V.D., D.D.

Retired Auxiliary Bishop of New Orleans; ordained February 2, 1960; appointed Auxiliary Bishop of New Orleans and Titular Bishop of Rusicade December 16, 1992; consecrated February 11, 1993; retired December 13, 2006. *Res.: 3270 Continental Dr., Kenner, LA 70065-2663.* Tel: 504-273-5863; Fax: 504-273-5747.

Square Miles 4,208.

Established April 25, 1793; Archdiocese July 19, 1850.

Comprises the following Parishes of Louisiana: Orleans, St. Bernard, Plaquemines, Jefferson, St. Charles, St. John the Baptist, St. Tammany and Washington.

For legal titles of parishes and archdiocesan institutions, consult the Chancery Office.

STATISTICAL OVERVIEW

Personnel	
Archbishops	1
Retired Archbishops	2
Auxiliary Bishops	1
Retired Bishops	1
Abbots	1
Priests: Diocesan Active in Diocese	130
Priests: Diocesan Active Outside Diocese	10
Priests: Retired, Sick or Absent	62
Number of Diocesan Priests	202
Religious Priests in Diocese	162
Total Priests in Diocese	364
Extern Priests in Diocese	17
Ordinations:	
Diocesan Priests	2
Religious Priests	4
Transitional Deacons	4
Permanent Deacons in Diocese	217
Total Brothers	77
Total Sisters	429
Parishes	
Parishes	108
With Resident Pastor:	
Resident Diocesan Priests	82
Resident Religious Priests	22
Without Resident Pastor:	
Administered by Priests	4
Missions	10
Pastoral Centers	2
Welfare	
Health Care Centers	9
Total Assisted	124,078
Homes for the Aged	25
Total Assisted	2,471
Residential Care of Children	1
Total Assisted	25
Day Care Centers	8
Total Assisted	968
Specialized Homes	3
Total Assisted	1,439
Special Centers for Social Services	264
Total Assisted	353,797
Residential Care of Disabled	8
Total Assisted	119
Other Institutions	4
Total Assisted	199
Educational	
Seminaries, Diocesan	2
Students from This Diocese	35
Students from Other Diocese	138
Seminaries, Religious	2
Students Religious	13
Total Seminarians	48
Colleges and Universities	3
Total Students	9,781
High Schools, Diocesan and Parish	10
Total Students	4,469
High Schools, Private	13
Total Students	8,738
Elementary Schools, Diocesan and Parish	53
Total Students	22,298
Elementary Schools, Private	8
Total Students	2,173
Non-residential Schools for the Disabled	1
Total Students	190
Catechesis/Religious Education:	
High School Students	3,691
Elementary Students	10,424
Total Students under Catholic Instruction	61,812
Teachers in the Diocese:	
Priests	42
Scholastics	2
Brothers	31
Sisters	46
Lay Teachers	3,544
Vital Statistics	
Receptions into the Church:	
Infant Baptism Totals	4,023
Minor Baptism Totals	303
Adult Baptism Totals	216
Received into Full Communion	202
First Communions	4,155
Confirmations	3,555
Marriages:	
Catholic	1,071
Interfaith	340
Total Marriages	1,411
Deaths	3,514
Total Catholic Population	485,973
Total Population	1,214,932

Former Bishops and Archbishops—Rt. Revs. LUIS PENALVER Y CARDENAS, D.D., cons. in 1793; transferred to Guatemala, in 1801; resigned in 1806; retired to Havana, Cuba; died in Havana, July 17, 1810; Under the administration of the Archbishop of Baltimore from 1805-1815.; FRANCIS PORRO Bishop-elect; LOUIS WILLIAM DUBOURG, S.S., D.D., cons. Sept. 24, 1815; died Archbishop of Besancon, Dec. 1833; JOSEPH ROSATI, C.M., D.D., cons. March 25, 1824; Bishop of Tanagre and coadjutor; transferred to St. Louis, March 20, 1827; died Sept. 25, 1843; LEO DE NECKERE, C.M., D.D., cons. Aug. 4, 1829; died Sept. 4, 1833; Most Revs. ANTOINE BLANC, first Archbishop; cons. Nov. 22, 1835; Archbishop, July 19, 1850; died June 20, 1860; JEAN MARIE ODIN, C.M., D.D., cons. Bishop of Claudiopolis and Vicar-Apostolic of Texas, March 6, 1842; transferred to Galveston, 1847; promoted to New Orleans in 1861; died at Ambierle, France, May 25, 1870; NAPOLEON J. PERCHE, cons. Bishop of Abdera and coadjutor, March 21, 1870; promoted to the See of New Orleans, May 25, 1870; died Dec. 1883; F. X. LERAY, D.D., cons. Bishop of Natchitoches, April 22, 1877; appt. coadjutor of New Orleans, and Bishop of Janopolis, Oct. 23, 1879; promoted to the See of New Orleans, Dec., 1883; died at Chateaugiron, France, Sept. 23, 1887; FRANCIS JANSSENS, D.D., cons. Bishop of Natchez, MS, May 1, 1881; promoted to the Archiepiscopal See of New Orleans, Aug. 7, 1888; died June 9, 1897; PLACIDE LOUIS CHAPELLE, D.D., Apostolic Delegate Extraordinary for Cuba and Puerto Rico; Archbishop of New Orleans; appt. Bishop of Arabissus and Coadjutor of Santa Fe cum jure successionis, Aug. 21, 1891; cons. Nov. 1, 1891; promoted to the Titular Archiepiscopal See of Sebaste May 10, 1893; Archbishop of Santa Fe, Jan. 9, 1894; appt. to New Orleans, Dec. 1, 1897; died Aug. 9, 1905; JAMES H. BLENK, S.M., D.D., appt. Bishop of Puerto Rico, June 12, 1899; cons. July 2, 1899; promoted to the See of New Orleans, April 20, 1906; died April 20, 1917; JOHN W. SHAW, D.D., appt. Coadjutor Bishop of San Antonio, Feb. 7, 1910; cons. Titular Bishop of Castabala, April 14, 1910; succeeded to the See of San Antonio, March 11, 1911; made assistant at the Pontifical Throne, Sept., 1916; promoted to the See of New Orleans, Jan. 25, 1918; died Nov. 2, 1934; JOSEPH FRANCIS RUMMEL, D.D., ord. May 24, 1902; appt. Bishop of Omaha, March 30, 1928; cons. May 29, 1928; appt. Archbishop of New Orleans, March 9, 1935; died Nov. 8, 1964; His Eminence JOHN CARDINAL CODY, D.D., S.T.D., cons. July 2, 1947; promoted to Coadjutor cum jure successionis of New Orleans, Aug. 10, 1961; acceded to the See, Nov. 8, 1964; transferred to Chicago, June 16, 1965; created Cardinal, June 26, 1967; died April 25, 1982; Most Revs. PHILIP M. HANNAN, D.D., J.C.D., S.T.L. (Retired), Archbishop of New Orleans; ord. Dec. 8, 1939; appt. Titular Bishop of Hieropolis and Auxiliary Bishop of Washington, June 16, 1956; cons. Aug. 28, 1956; promoted to Archbishop of New Orleans, Sept. 29, 1965; retired Feb. 14, 1989; died Sept. 29, 2011.; FRANCIS B. SCHULTE, D.D. (Retired), Archbishop of New Orleans; ord. May 10, 1952; appt. Titular Bishop of Afufenia and Auxiliary Bishop of Philadelphia, June 27, 1981; appt. Sixth Bishop of Wheeling-Charleston, June 4, 1985; appt. Archbishop of New Orleans, Dec. 13, 1988; installed Feb. 14, 1989; Pallium conferred by Pope John Paul II at the Vatican, June 29, 1989; retired Jan. 3, 2002; ALFRED C. HUGHES, S.T.D. (Retired), ord. Dec. 15, 1957; appt. Auxiliary Bishop of Boston July 21, 1981; ord. Auxiliary Bishop of Boston Sept. 14, 1981; appt. Bishop of Baton Rouge Sept. 7, 1993; installed Bishop of Baton Rouge Nov. 4, 1993; appt. Coadjutor Archbishop of New Orleans Feb. 16, 2001; appt. Archbishop of New Orleans Jan. 3, 2002; retired June 12, 2009.

Vicar General—Most Rev. SHELTON J. FABRE, V.G.

Moderator of the Curia—Most Rev. SHELTON J. FABRE, V.G.

Chancellor—Very Rev. GERALD L. SEILER JR., M.Div., J.C.L., 7887 Walmsley Ave., New Orleans, 70125-3496. Tel: 504-861-6256; 504-861-9521; Fax: 504-866-2906.

Vice Chancellor and Special Delegate for Dispensations and Permissions—Deacon A. DAVID WARRINER JR.

Financial and Administrative Services—Mr. JOHN L. ECKHOLDT.

Archdiocesan Administration Building—7887 Walmsley Ave., New Orleans, 70125-3496. Tel: 504-861-9521; Fax: 504-866-2906. Office Hours: Mon.-Fri. 9-5.

Metropolitan Tribunal—Rev. PETER O. AKPOGHIRAN, Judicial Vicar All rogatorial commissions should be sent to this address c/o: 7887 Walmsley Ave., New Orleans, 70125-3496. Tel: 504-861-6291; Fax: 504-866-2906. Email: tribunal@archdiocese-no.org.

Court of First Instance—

Adjutant Judicial Vicars—Rev. Msgr. CLINTON J. DOSKEY, J.C.L. (Retired); Rev. VIEN THE NGUYEN, J.C.L., M.Div.

Court of Second Instance— Reviews all marriage cases from the six dioceses of Louisiana.

Adjutant Judicial Vicar—Very Rev. GERALD L. SEILER JR., M.Div., J.C.L., 7887 Walmsley Ave., New Orleans, 70125-3496. Tel: 504-861-6256; Fax: 504-866-2906.

Coordinator (Court of Second Instance)—Deacon A. DAVID WARRINER JR.

Judges—Rev. Msgr. L. EARL GAUTHREAUX, J.C.L.; Revs. VIEN THE NGUYEN, J.C.L., M.Div.; JOHN J. PAYNE JR., J.C.L.; Rev. Msgr. ANDREW C. TAORMINA, J.D., V.F.

Associate Judges—Deacons PETER E. DUFFY, J.D.; FRANS LABRANCHE JR., J.D.

Defenders of the Bond—Revs. WILLIAM J. O'DONNELL, J.C.L. (Retired); NICHOLAS P. PERICONE; Deacon A. DAVID WARRINER JR.

Approved Advocates— Priests and Deacons of the Archdiocese.

Appointed Special Advocates—Deacons ANDREA CAPACI; ARTHUR KINGSMILL, J.D.; KEVIN M. STEEL; MICHAEL G. ZAIONTZ.

Secretaries/Ecclesiastical Notaries (Court of First Instance)—Ms. LOUANN HOOD; Ms. GERI WOODWARD.

Secretary/Ecclesiastical Notary (Court of Second Instance)—Ms. JANET URRUTIA.

Archdiocesan Consultors—Most Rev. SHELTON J. FABRE, V.G.; Rev. Msgr. CLINTON J. DOSKEY, J.C.L. (Retired); Very Revs. NEAL W. MCDERMOTT, O.P.; MICHAEL P. JACQUES, S.S.E., V.F.; Rev. JOSEPH S. PALERMO JR., J.D.

Canonical Consultant to the Archbishop—Rev. VIEN THE NGUYEN, J.C.L., M.Div.

Deans—Very Revs. MICHAEL P. JACQUES, S.S.E., V.F., Cathedral Deanery I; DAVID J. ROBICHEAUX, V.F., City Park-Gentilly Deanery II; PHILIP G. LANDRY, V.F., Uptown Deanery III; Rev. Msgr. ANDREW C. TAORMINA, J.D., V.F., East Jefferson Deanery IV; Very Rev. JOHN-NHAN TRAN, V.F., St. John-St. Charles Deanery V; Rev. WARREN L. COOPER, West Bank Deanery VI; Very Revs. WILLIAM O'RIORDAN, V.F., Algiers-Plaquemines Deanery VII; DANILO C. DIGAL, V.F., St. Bernard Deanery VIII; RODNEY P. BOURG, V.F., West St. Tammany-Washington Deanery IX; MARK LOMAX, V.F., East St. Tammany-Washington Deanery X.

Archdiocesan Administrative Council—Most Revs. GREGORY M. AYMOND, Chm.; SHELTON J. FABRE, V.G., Vice Chm.; Deacon JESSE A. WATLEY, Sec. Members of the Board: Very Revs. GERALD L. SEILER JR., M.Div., J.C.L.; PATRICK J. WILLIAMS, M.Div., M.S.; Deacon A. DAVID WARRINER JR.; Sisters ANTHONY BARCZYKOWSKI, D.C.; SYLVIA THIBODEAUX, S.S.F.; Mrs. SARAH COMISKEY MCDONALD; Mr. JOHN L. ECKHOLDT; Dr. JAN DANIEL LANCASTER.

Presbyteral Council of the Archdiocese of New Orleans—Most Rev. GREGORY M. AYMOND, Pres.

Archdiocesan Finance Council—Most Revs. GREGORY M. AYMOND, Chm.; SHELTON J. FABRE, V.G., Vice Chm.

Ministerial Council—

Archbishop—Most Rev. GREGORY M. AYMOND, D.D.

Vicar General—Most Rev. SHELTON J. FABRE, V.G.

Members— Directors of archdiocesan ministries.

Censores Librorum—Very Rev. GERALD L. SEILER JR., M.Div., J.C.L., Coord.

Louisiana Conference of Catholic Bishops—Mr. DANIEL J. LOAR, Dir., 3423 Hundred Oaks Ave., Baton Rouge, 70808-1548. Tel: 225-344-7120; Fax: 225-383-9591. Email: lccb@cox.net. Web: www.laccb.org.

Office of the Vicar General and Moderator of the Curia

Moderator of the Curia—Most Rev. SHELTON J. FABRE, V.G., 7887 Walmsley Ave., New Orleans, 70125-3496. Tel: 504-861-6262; Fax: 504-861-6312; 504-866-2906.

Vicar General—Most Rev. SHELTON J. FABRE, V.G., 7887 Walmsley Ave., New Orleans, 70125. Tel: 504-861-6262; Fax: 504-861-6312.

Archives and Records (Archdiocesan)—Dr. EMILIE G. LEUMAS, C.A., 7887 Walmsley Ave., New Orleans, 70125-3496. Tel: 504-861-6241; Fax: 504-866-2906. Email: archives@archdiocese-no.org; Rev. WILLIAM F. MAESTRI, M.Div., M.A., Biomedical Liaison.

Canonical Permissions and Dispensations—Very Rev. GERALD L. SEILER JR., M.Div., J.C.L., 7887 Walmsley Ave., New Orleans, 70125-3496. Tel: 504-861-6256; 504-861-9521; Fax: 504-866-2906. Email: chancellor@archdiocese-no.org.

Catholic Foundation for the Archdiocese of New Orleans, Inc.—Mr. PETER R. QUIRK, Exec. Dir., 1000 Howard Ave., Ste. 700, New Orleans, 70113-1903. Tel: 504-596-3045; Fax: 504-596-3068. Email: catholicfoundation@archdiocese-no.org.

Communications, Office of—Mrs. SARAH COMISKEY MCDONALD, Dir., 1000 Howard Ave., Ste. 400, New Orleans, 70113. Tel: 504-596-3023; Fax: 504-596-3020. Email: communications@archdiocese-no.org.

Cultural Heritage Office—Dr. EMILIE G. LEUMAS, C.A., Dir., 7887 Walmsley Ave., New Orleans, 70125-3496. Tel: 504-527-5781; Fax: 504-527-5797. Email: archives@archdiocese-no.org.

Stewardship & Development Office—Mr. PETER R. QUIRK, Exec. Dir., 1000 Howard Ave., Ste. 700, New Orleans, 70113-1903. Tel: 504-596-3045; Fax: 504-596-3068. Email: development@archdiocese-no.org.

Legal Services—CHARLES I. DENECHAUD III; OTTO SCHOENFELD; RICHARD BORDELON; TODD R. GENNARDO; RALPH J. AUCOIN, 1010 Common St., Ste. 3010, New Orleans, 70112. Tel: 504-522-4756; Fax: 504-568-0783.

Newspaper— Newspaper of the Archdiocese of New Orleans. Published by Clarion Herald Publishing Co., Inc., "Clarion Herald" Rev. Msgr. CROSBY W. KERN, Moderator; PETER P. FINNEY JR., Gen. Mgr. & Exec. Editor, 1000 Howard Ave., Ste. 400, New Orleans, 70113-1903. Tel: 504-596-3035; Fax: 504-596-3020. Email: clarionherald@clarionherald.org.

Old Ursuline Convent—Rev. Msgr. CROSBY W. KERN, Admin., 1100 Chartres St., New Orleans, 70116. Mailing Address: 615 Pere Antoine Alley, New Orleans, 70116. Tel: 504-525-9585, Ext. 135. Email: saintlouiscathedral-no@archdiocese-no.org.

Safe Environment Coordinator—Sr. MARY ELLEN WHEELAHAN, O.Carm., Coord., 7887 Walmsley Ave., New Orleans, 70125. Tel: 504-861-6278; Fax: 504-866-2906. Email: srmwheelahan@archdiocese-no.org.

Special Projects for the Archbishop and Vicar General—Very Rev. NEAL W. MCDERMOTT, O.P., Dir.

Victims Assistance Coordinator—Sr. CARMELITA CENTANNI, M.S.C., Ph.D., 7887 Walmsley Ave., New Orleans, 70125-3496. Tel: 504-861-6253; 866-792-2873 (Toll Free); Fax: 504-866-2906. Email: srcarmelita@archdiocese-no.org.

Department of Christian Formation

Executive Director—Most Rev. SHELTON J. FABRE, V.G., Interim Exec. Dir., 7887 Walmsley Ave., New Orleans, 70125-3496. Tel: 504-861-6262; Fax: 504-861-6312. Email: bishopfabre@archdiocese-no.org.

Campus Ministry—Ms. RACHEL LONGEST, Archdiocesan Coord.

Catholic Schools Office—Dr. JAN DANIEL LANCASTER, Supt., 7887 Walmsley Ave., New Orleans, 70125-3496. Tel: 504-866-7916; Fax: 504-861-6260. Email: superintendent@archdiocese.no.org. Assoc. Superintendents, Elementary Schools: Sr. LEONA BRUNER, S.S.F., Curriculum/Early Childhood; Ms. CAROLE ELLIOT, Early Childhood/Public Rels./ Testing; Mrs. CAROLYN MORVANT, Govt. Programs/ Special Needs; Mr. JOSEPH R. ROSOLINO, Catholic Identity/School Personnel; Mr. VINCENT SCOZZARI, Catholic Identity/Crisis Team; Dr. LISA TAYLOR, Assoc. Supt. High Schools, Secondary School Technology; Sr. MARY HILARY SIMPSON, O.P., Dir. Instrumental Music, 7887 Walmsley Ave., New Orleans, 70125-3496. Tel: 225-294-5794; Fax: 504-861-6260.

Office of Eucharistic Renewal—Mr. TODD AMICK, Dir., 1007 Airline Park Blvd., Metairie, 70003. Tel: 504-482-8010; Fax: 504-836-0552.

Catholic Youth Organization - Youth and Young Adult Ministry Office—Mr. JOHN SMESTAD JR., Dir., 1007 Airline Park Blvd., Metairie, 70003. Tel: 504-836-0551; Fax: 504-836-0552.

Youth Retreats— Youth Retreats: Contact CYO-Youth and Adult Ministry Office. *1007 Airline Park Blvd., Metairie, 70003.* Tel: 504-836-0551.

Religious Education—Mrs. ALICE HUGHES, Dir., 7887 Walmsley Ave., New Orleans, 70125. Tel: 504-861-6270; Fax: 504-861-6276.

Pontifical Mission Societies—

Pontifical Mission Societies/Holy Childhood Association/Propagation of the Faith—Propagation of the Faith, St. Peter the Apostle, Missionary Union, Mission Outreach Programs; Acompano, Sotuta Mission, Bridge Builders, Christ the Healer and Christ the Builder. Rev. JAMES J. JEANFREAU JR., Dir., 7887 Walmsley Dr., New Orleans, 70125. Tel: 504-527-5771; Fax: 504-527-5798. Email: pof@archdiocese-no.org.

Department of Clergy

Executive Director—Very Rev. PATRICK J. WILLIAMS, M.Div., M.S., 7887 Walmsley Ave., New Orleans, 70125-3496. Tel: 504-861-6268; Fax: 504-866-2906. Email: frpatwilliams@archdiocese-no.org.

Continuing Formation for Priests—Rev. MARK S. RAPHAEL, Dir. Tel: 504-861-6269; Fax: 504-866-2906.

Permanent Diaconate—Deacon RAPHAEL DUPLECHAIN JR., Dir., 7887 Walmsley Ave., New Orleans, 70125-3496. Tel: 504-861-6329; 504-861-9521; Fax: 504-866-2906.

Priest Personnel Office—Very Rev. PATRICK J. WILLIAMS, M.Div., M.S.

Ministry to Retired Priests—Liaisons: Rev. LEO A. MEYER (Retired). Tel: 504-835-9605; Rev. Msgr. LANAUX J. RARESHIDE. Tel: 985-643-6124.

Ministry to Sick Priests—Rev. WARREN L. COOPER, Coord. Tel: 504-737-4537.

Psychological Services—Mr. GLENN LEBOEUF, L.C.S.W., B.C.D., Coord. Tel: 504-861-6222; 504-885-4611.

Vocation Office—Rev. STEVEN V. BRUNO, Dir., 7887 Walmsley Ave., New Orleans, 70125-3496. Tel: 504-861-6298; 504-861-9521; Fax: 504-866-2906.

Department of Community Services

Executive Director—Sr. ANTHONY BARCZYKOWSKI, D.C., 1000 Howard Ave., Ste. 100, New Orleans, 70113-1900. Tel: 504-596-3092; Fax: 504-596-3466. Email: sranthony@archdiocese-no.org.

Apostleship of the Sea—Deacon PATRICK L. DEMPSEY, Dir. & Port Min., Stella Maris Maritime Center, 14538 River Rd., Destrehan, 70047. Tel: 985-307-0601.

Christopher Homes, Inc.—Deacon DENNIS F. ADAMS, Dir., 1000 Howard Ave., Ste. 100, New Orleans, 70113-1903. Tel: 504-596-3460; Fax: 504-596-3466. Web: www.christopherhomes.org. Email: dfadams@chi-no.org.

Disaster Relief—Sr. ANTHONY BARCZYKOWSKI, D.C., Dir., 1000 Howard Ave., Ste. 100, New Orleans, 70113-1900. Tel: 504-596-3092; Fax: 504-596-3466.

Catholic Charities

Catholic Charities Archdiocese of New Orleans—1000 Howard Ave., Ste. 1000, New Orleans, 70113. Tel: 504-523-3755; Fax: 504-523-2789; Tel: 866-891-2210 Care Line. Email: ccano@ccano.org. Web: www.ccano.org. Mr. GORDON R. WADGE, Pres. & CEO; Mrs. CHERYL D. LABORDE, CFO; Mr. ORVILLE DUGGAN, Chief Admin. Officer; Deacon STEVEN L. FERRAN, Vice Pres. Catholic Identity & Mission; Mr. MARTIN GUTIERREZ, Vice Pres. Community Svcs. Ministry; Ms. SAMANTHA PICHON, Vice Pres. Health Ministry; Dr. ELMORE RIGAMER, Medical Dir. If additional information is needed, please contact the main office at 504-523-3755.

Cafe Hope— (An Affiliated Ministry) Mr. LUIS AROCHA JR., Exec. Dir., 1101 Barataria Blvd., Marrero,

70072. Tel: 504-756-HOPE (4673).

Communications Department—Mrs. MARGARET DUBUISSON, Dir. Tel: 504-592-5691.

Community Services Ministry—Mr. MARTIN GUTIERREZ, Vice Pres. Tel: 504-310-6914.

Community Outreach Ministries—Ms. MARIA CARCACHE, Dir. Tel: 504-457-3462.

Hispanic Apostolate Community Services— Emergency Assistance, Health Services, Housing Counseling, Job Services, Tax Preparation Advocacy, Workers Rights/Public Safety Initiative.

Immigration Services— (Provides assistance with citizenship, work authorization and translation of legal documents.) Community Relations & Liaison, Immigration Services, Immigration Legal Services.

Parish & Community Ministries— (Case Management Services offered by appointment in various areas of the Archdiocese of New Orleans). Tel: 504-523-3755.

Refugee Services—

Community Staffing Services—Mr. GREG FAVRET, Prog. Dir., 1920 Clio St., New Orleans, 70113. Tel: 504-581-4987; Fax: 504-581-2028.

Domestic Violence/Sexual Assault Services—Ms. MARY CLAIRE LANDRY, Dir. Tel: 504-310-6885; 504-866-9554 Crisis Line; Fax: 504-310-6876.

Crescent House—

New Orleans Family Justice Center—

Project S.A.V.E.— (Stopping Abuse through Victim Empowerment).

Sexual Assault Program—

Education Services—Ms. ARLEEN LANDRY, Dir., 8326 Apricot St., 2nd Fl., New Orleans, 70118. Tel: 504-861-6360; Fax: 504-861-6361.

Adult Education— (GED & Computer Literacy, ESL & Citizenship Classes)

After School Assembly— Cathedral Academy, Independence Elementary, Middle & High Schools.

Head Start Centers— El Yo Yo Head Start/Early Head Start, Incarnate Word Head Start/Early Head Start, Leslie Early Head Start, Louise Head Start, St. John the Baptist Head Start.

Summer Witness Program—

Homeless Services—Ms. CONNIE ANDRY, Dir. Tel: 504-310-8738; Fax: 504-596-3098.

Baronne Street Transitional Housing—

Beyond Shelter—

Bridges to Self-Sufficiency—

CARE Center— (Orleans Parish).

Jefferson CARE Center—

Oil Spill Case Management—Ms. SHIRLEY LACHMANN, Dir. Our Lady of Lourdes Church (serving St. Bernard Parish), St. Anthony Catholic Church (serving Jefferson Parish), St. Patrick Catholic Church (serving West Bank of Plaquemines Parish), St Thomas Catholic Church (serving East Bank of Plaquemines Parish).Tel: 866-891-2210 (CCANO Care Line).

Operation Helping Hands—Mr. KEVIN FITZPATRICK, Dir., 3738 Paris Ave., New Orleans, 70122. Tel: 504-324-4318; Fax: 504-324-9643.

Sojourner Truth Neighborhood Center—2200 Lafitte St., New Orleans, 70119. Tel: 504-827-9963.

Deaf Action Center of Greater New Orleans—

Development Department—Ms. HELEN READ SMITH, Dir.

Archbishop's Community Appeal (ACA)—1000 Howard Ave., Ste. 1000, New Orleans, 70113-1903. Tel: 504-592-5688; Fax: 504-581-2255.

Food for Families/Food for Seniors—Mr. TIMOTHY ROBERTSON, Exec. Dir. Tel: 504-245-7207; Fax: 504-248-2664.

Foster Grandparents—Mr. SHELLI TARVER, Prog. Dir. Tel: 504-310-6882.

Health Ministry—Ms. SAMANTHA PICHON, Vice Pres. Tel: 504-310-8770.

Adult Day Health Care Centers—Ms. PASHENA CASIMIRE, Div. Dir., 200 Beta St., Belle Chasse, 70037. Tel: 504-392-0502 Alpha House, Greenwalt, New Directions.

Ciara Permanent Housing—Mr. MICHAEL LOMAX, Prog. Dir. Tel: 504-861-0643.

Counseling Solutions— (Counseling Services by appointment). Tel: 504-523-3755.

Catholic Charities School-Based Counseling (CCSBC)—

Family Behavioral Health & Supporting Housing—Ms. MAMIE HALL-LANDRY, Admin. Tel: 504-310-6944; Fax: 504-569-9676.

Independent Living Skills Program—Ms. JUDY POTTER, Admin. Tel: 504-340-5100.

Therapeutic Family Services—Ms. MAMIE HALL-LANDRY, Admin. Tel: 504-310-6944.

Padua Community Services—Ms. PASHENA CASIMIRE, Div. Dir., 200 Beta St., Belle Chasse, 70037-1499. Tel: 504-392-0502; Fax: 504-392-5411.

Home & Community-Based Waiver Program—

Padua Community Homes— Ocean Avenue (Lac Couture, Harvey), St. Jude the Apostle (Claire St., Gretna), Sts. Mary & Elizabeth (N. Elm St., Metairie), St. Peter the Fisherman (Airport Rd., Slidell), St. Rosalie (Kass St., Gretna).

Padua Pediatric Program—

Pro-Life Services—Ms. MICHELLE BLACK, Dir., 3019 N. Arnoult Rd., Metairie, 70002-4714. Tel: 504-885-1141; 866-566-1399 (Toll Free); Fax: 504-885-1519.

ACCESS Pregnancy & Referral Centers—Ms. KAY B. BONGARD, Administrative Dir., 24-Hour Hotline: 504-581-LIFE. Metairie, New Orleans (Bywater and Mid-City), West Bank.

Adoption Services—Ms. DANNA P. COUSINS, M.S.W., G.S.W., Prog. Dir. Tel: 504-885-1141.

St. Vincent Maternity Clinic—Ms. DARLEEN CRANE, R.N., Dir. Tel: 504-837-6346.

St. Louise de Marillac Ministry—Ms. MEGAN THIEL, Admin. Tel: 504-861-6343.

Voyage House—c/o Catholic Charities, 1000 Howard Ave., Ste. 1000, New Orleans, 70113-1942. Ms. ALECIA BLANCHARD, Admin. & Prog. Dir. Tel: 504-269-3969. Residential facility for women who experience substance abuse &/or mental health issues.

North Shore Region—Mr. CRAIG MARINELLO, Regl. Dir., 19266 Slemmer Rd., Covington, 70433.

Office of Justice and Peace—Mr. THOMAS M. COSTANZA, Dir. Tel: 504-596-3097; Fax: 504-596-3098; Mr. NICHOLAS ALBARES, Parish Social Ministry Coord. Tel: 504-592-5692.

Catholic Campaign for Human Development (CCHD)—

Catholic Relief Services (CRS)—

Cornerstone Builders—Mr. RONNIE MOORE, Prog. Dir. Tel: 504-310-8769.

PACE Greater New Orleans— (Program of All-inclusive Care for the Elderly) (An Affiliated Ministry) Ms. STEPHANIE SMITH, Exec. Dir., 4201 N. Rampart St., New Orleans, 70117. Tel: 504-945-1531; Fax: 504-945-1537; Ms. YVETTE WILLIAMS-JONES, Center Dir.

Parenting and Mentoring— (Isaiah 43). Deacon STEVE FERRAN, Vice Pres. Catholic Identity & Mission. Tel: 504-310-6920; Fax: 504-596-3098.

PHILMAT, Inc.—Mr. GORDON R. WADGE, Pres., 1000 Howard Ave., Ste. 1000, New Orleans, 70113. Tel: 504-596-3099; Fax: 504-596-3099.

Spirit of Hope—Ms. SHAULA LOVERA, Prog. Dir. Tel: 504-310-8743.

Volunteer Department—Ms. SHANNON MURPHY, Dir. Tel: 504-310-6962; Fax: 504-523-2789.

Department of Financial and Administrative Services

Officers—Mr. JOHN L. ECKHOLDT, CFO; Mr. JEFFREY J. ENTWISLE, COO, 7887 Walmsley Ave., New Orleans, 70125-3496. Tel: 504-861-6252; 504-861-9521; Fax: 504-866-2906. Email: amyers@archdiocese-no.org.

Accounting Office—Mr. KENNETH JAYROE, Chief Accounting & Budget Officer, 7887 Walmsley Ave., New Orleans, 70125-3496. Tel: 504-861-6236; 504-861-9521; Fax: 504-866-2906. Email: kjayroe@archdiocese-no.org.

Building Office—Mr. ANDRE L. VILLERE JR., Dir., 7887 Walmsley Ave., New Orleans, 70125-3496. Tel: 504-861-6210; 504-861-9521; Fax: 504-861-7652. Email: avillere@archdiocese-no.org.

Human Resources—Ms. BETH TINTO, Dir., 1000 Howard Ave., Ste. 1200, New Orleans, 70113. Tel: 504-310-8792; Fax: 504-568-1699. Email: etinto@archdiocese-no.org.

Insurance Office—Ms. CHERYL HARPER, Oper. Mgr., 1000 Howard Ave., Ste. 1202, New Orleans, 70113. Tel: 504-527-5760; Fax: 504-527-5799. Email: charper@catholicmutual.org; Ms. SUE FOSTER, Contracts/Risk Mgmt. Email: sfoster@catholicmutual.org.

Internal Audit/Special Assignments—Mrs. ANGELA WILCOX, Sr. Internal Auditor. Tel: 504-861-6231; Ms. CORINNE CADIS-MARCH, Financial Review Officer, 7887 Walmsley Ave., New Orleans, 70125-3496. Tel: 504-861-6203; Fax: 504-355-0077.

Information Technology—Mr. JUSTIN GIBSON, Dir., 1000 Howard Ave., Ste. 700, New Orleans, 70113-1903. Tel: 504-596-3064; Fax: 504-566-9718. Email: isd@archdiocese-no.org.

New Orleans Archdiocesan Cemeteries and New Orleans Cemeteries Trust—Mr. JODY C. ROME, Dir., 1000 Howard Ave., Ste. 500, New Orleans, 70113-1903. Tel: 504-596-3050; Fax: 504-596-3055. Email: jrome@archdiocese-no.org.

Property and Building Management—Ms. ELIZABETH LACOMBE, Dir., 1000 Howard Ave., Ste. 107, New Orleans, 70113-1903. Tel: 504-596-3070; Fax: 504-596-3073. Email: llacombe@archdiocese-no.org.

Parish Sites & Boundaries Committee—Rev. Msgr. FRANK J. GIROIR, Chm.

Property Records Office—Mrs. EMILY MORRIS, 7887 Walmsley Ave., New Orleans, 70125-3496. Tel: 504-861-6323; Fax: 504-866-2906.

School Food and Nutrition Services of New Orleans Inc.—Ms. JANET SANDERSON, COO, 1000 Howard Ave., Ste. 300, New Orleans, 70113-1925. Tel: 504-596-3434; Fax: 504-596-3459; 504-596-6901. Email: jsanderson@schoolcafe.org.

Department of Pastoral Services

Executive Director—Deacon JESSE A. WATLEY, 7887 Walmsley Ave., New Orleans, 70125-3496. Tel: 504-861-6294; 504-861-9521; Fax: 504-866-2906. Email: pservices@archdiocese-no.org.

Black Catholic Ministries—Dr. JOYCE F. GILLIE CRUSE, Dir., 7887 Walmsley Ave., New Orleans, 70125-3496. Tel: 504-861-6207; 504-861-9521; Fax: 504-866-2906.

Center of Jesus the Lord—Rev. LANCE J. CAMPO, S.T.L., Dir., 1236 N. Rampart St., New Orleans, 70116-2497. Tel: 504-529-1636; Fax: 504-529-5003.

Charismatic Renewal—Liaisons: Mr. AL MANSFIELD; Mrs. PATTI MANSFIELD, 1901 Division St., Metairie, 70001-2716. Tel: 504-828-1368; Fax: 504-831-5810. Email: info@ccrno.org; Mailing Address: P.O. Box 7515, Metairie, 70010-7515.

Ecumenical Officer—Rev. DONALD A. HAWKINS, S.J., 6220 LaSalle Pl., New Orleans, 70118-6236. Tel: 504-865-7420, Ext. 255; Fax: 504-866-3391. Email: dhawkins@hnjchurch.org.

Family Life Apostolate—Deacon ANDREA CAPACI, Dir., 7887 Walmsley Ave., New Orleans, 70125-3496. Tel: 504-861-6243; 504-861-9521; Fax: 504-866-2906. Email: familylife@archdiocese-no.org.

Catholic Counseling Service—Tel: 504-861-6245.

Commission for Persons with Disabilities—Mrs. JANET PESCE, 7887 Walmsley Ave., New Orleans, 70125-3496. Tel: 504-861-6243; Fax: 504-866-2906. Email: familylife@archdiocese-no.org.

Filipino Catholic Ministry—Dr. ADLAI DEPANO, Coord.; Rev. ROBUSTIANO D. MORGIA, Spiritual Advisor, 7411 Sussex Pl., New Orleans, 70126. Tel: 504-280-7370.

Hanmaum Korean Catholic Chapel—Rev. JUNG YEON KIM, Chap., 4812 W. Napoleon Ave., Metairie, 70001-2364. Tel: 504-888-8772; Fax: 504-888-2366.

Hispanic Apostolate Pastoral Services—Rev. LANCE J. CAMPO, S.T.L., Coord., 4309 Williams Blvd., Kenner, 70063. Mailing Address: P.O. Box 640577, Kenner, 70064. Tel: 504-467-2550; Fax: 504-467-2552.

Prisons Apostolate—Deacon WILLIAM B. JARRELL, Archdiocesan Dir., Mailing Address: P.O. Box 388, Gretna, 70054-0388. Tel: 504-374-7709, Ext. 3109. Email: dcbillctk@bellsouth.net.

Racial Harmony Liaison— Liaison to the Committee for Implementation of the Pastoral Letter on Racial Harmony. *1000 Howard Ave., Ste. 109, New Orleans, 70113*. Tel: 504-861-6272; Fax: 504-267-9759. Email: srrooney@archdiocese-no.org. Web: orh.arch-no.org. Sr. TERESA ROONEY, C.H.F.

Renovacion Carismatica Catolica Hispana—Deacon DAVID CALDERO, Dir., Mailing Address: P.O. Box 640057, Kenner, 70064. Tel: 985-764-6187.

Vietnamese Catholics Office—

Liaisons for the Vietnamese Community—Revs. MICHAEL JOSEPH VINH NGOC NGUYEN, 9701 Hammond St., New Orleans, 70127-3519. Tel: 504-242-8669; Fax: 504-242-8767; NGHIEM VAN NGUYEN, 5069 Willowbrook Dr., P.O. Box 870607, New Orleans, 70187-0607. Tel: 504-254-5660; Fax: 504-254-9250; Very Rev. JOHN-NHAN TRAN, V.F., 529 W. 5th St., La Place, 70068-3941. Tel: 985-652-3435; Fax: 985-651-2920.

Worship Office—Rev. Msgr. KENNETH J. HEDRICK, Dir., 7887 Walmsley Ave., New Orleans, 70125-3496. Tel: 504-861-6300; 504-861-9521; Fax: 504-866-2906. Email: worship@archdiocese-no.org.

Liturgical Commission—Rev. Msgr. KENNETH J. HEDRICK, Coord., 7887 Walmsley Ave., New Orleans, 70125-3496. Tel: 504-861-6300; 504-861-9521; Fax: 504-866-2906. Email: worship@archdiocese-no.org.

Department of Religious

Executive Director—Sr. SYLVIA THIBODEAUX, S.S.F. Liaison between the Archbishop and all religious congregations of sisters and brothers, with third orders and secular institutes, and with leadership conferences of women and men religious. 7887 Walmsley Ave., New Orleans, 70125-3496. Tel: 504-861-6281; 504-861-9521; Fax: 504-866-2906. Email: rpersonnel@archdiocese-no.org.

Archdiocesan Offices and Corporations

Bernard A. Grehan Trust—7887 Walmsley Ave., New Orleans, 70125-3496. Tel: 504-861-9521.

Catholic Charities Children's Day Care Centers Inc.—Registered Office, 1000 Howard Ave., Ste. 1000, New Orleans, 70113-1942.

Mental Health Association Development Corporation—7887 Walmsley Ave., New Orleans, 70125-3496. Tel: 504-861-9521.

St. Elizabeth's Home Registered Office—

St. Gertrude's Retirement Center—

St. Mary's Catholic Orphan Boys' Asylum Board—1000 Howard Ave., Ste. 1000, New Orleans, 70113-1942.

St. Michael Special School—1522 Chippewa St., New Orleans, 70130. Registered Office: 7887 Walmsley Ave., New Orleans, 70125. Tel: 504-524-7285; Fax: 504-524-5883. Web: www.archdiocese-no.org/stmichael. Mrs. JANE SILVA, Dir. & Prin.

St. Vincent's Infant and Maternity Home Registered Office—

Catholic Organizations

Archconfraternity of St. Ann—4920 Loveland St., Metairie, 70006.

*Beginning Experience—*Ms. BETH ORGERON, Pres., 7887 Walmsley Ave., New Orleans, 70125.

*Blue Army of Our Lady of Fatima—*Rev. WARREN L. COOPER, Spiritual Dir., 10021 Jefferson Hwy., River Ridge, 70123. Tel: 504-737-4537.

Catholic Charities Association Inc.—1000 Howard Ave., Ste. 1000, New Orleans, 70113-1942.

The Christ Committee of New Orleans—123 Iroquois Dr., Abita Springs, 70420. Tel: 985-893-0169. Email: kcicno@bellsouth.net.

*Chateau de Notre Dame Guild—*Rev. ALBERTO BERMUDEZ, Spiritual Dir., 2820 Burdette St., Apt. 304, New Orleans, 70125-2596. Tel: 504-655-1782.

*Community of John the Evangelist—*Ms. VIVIEN MICHALS, Contact, 2639 DeSoto St., New Orleans, 70119. Tel: 504-944-4000.

Confraternity of the Holy Face—1050 Robert Blvd., Slidell, 70458.

*Council of Catholic Men—*Mr. BEN RAPHAEL, Dir., 7887 Walmsley Ave., New Orleans, 70125-3496. Tel: 504-202-1061.

*Council of Catholic School Cooperative Clubs—*Rev. Msgr. ROBERT D. MASSETT, Spiritual Moderator, 6425 W. Metairie Ave., Metairie, 70003. Tel: 504-733-0922; Fax: 504-733-0869.

*The Cursillo Movement—*Mr. BILLY APP, Lay Dir., Mailing Address: P.O. Box 741745, New Orleans, 70174-1745. Tel: 504-464-0181, Ext. 111. Web: www.neworleanscursillo.org.

*Engaged Encounter—*Executive Couple: DERRICK SALVANT; TY SALVANT.

*Holy Name Societies—*Mr. ANTHONY SMITH, Pres. & Exec. Sec., Mailing Address: P.O. Box 6644, Metairie, 70009-6644. Tel: 504-302-2801.

*Ladies of Charity of the Archdiocese—*Sr. JULIANNE BLANCHARD, D.C., Spiritual Dir., 954 Felicity St., New Orleans, 70130. Tel: 504-371-5778.

Lay Carmelites of Our Lady of Mount Carmel—1437 Ave. C, Marrero, 70072.

Legatus of New Orleans—332 East Ave., Harahan, 70123. Tel: 504-343-2478. Web: www.legatus.org.

*Legion of Mary—*Rev. JOSEPH E. CAZENAVETTE, Spiritual Dir., New Orleans Regia, 312 Lafitte St., Mandeville, 70448-5827. Tel: 985-626-5671.

*Magnificat, Ministry to Catholic Women—*Mrs. PETER QUIRK, Pres. Central Svc. Team, 1201 Beverly Garden Dr., Metairie, 70002. Tel: 504-834-0057.

Magnificat Chapters—

*Metairie Chapter—*Mrs. DONNA MC NAMARA, Coord., 3416 Metairie Court, Metairie, 70002-1916. Tel: 504-833-3562.

*New Orleans Chapter—*Mrs. CLAUDIA MARSHALL, Coord., 2230 Soniat St., New Orleans, 70115-6426. Tel: 504-899-0390.

*Slidell Chapter—*Mrs. EDOLIA BARROS, Coord., 35300 Laurent Rd., Slidell, 70460-3644. Tel: 985-641-2585.

*West Bank Chapter—*Ms. BEVERLY TRAHAN, Coord., 2254 S. VonBraun Ct., Harvey, 70058-3083. Tel: 504-368-0869.

*West St. Tammany Chapter—*BETH MONTELEPRE, Coord., 83400 Pine Dr., Folsom, 70437-3260. Tel: 985-796-1274.

*Marians of Metairie—*Ms. BRENDA CONNOLLY, 1125 Sena Dr., Metairie, 70005-1628. Tel: 504-837-3345.

*Marians of New Orleans—*Ms. JOSEPHINE L. POCHE, Pres., 1329 Homestead Ave., Metairie, 70002-1566. Tel: 504-833-9470.

*Marriage Encounter—*Mr. GARY DAIGLE; Mrs. MARCIA DAIGLE. Tel: 985-649-0999.

*Maryknoll Mission Education Center (Promotion of Missionary Work)—*Mr. MATTHEW F. ROUSSO, Dir., 7730 Walmsley Ave., New Orleans, 70125. Tel: 504-866-8516.

*Mary's Children—*Mrs. NORA LAMBERT, Pres., 631 St. Charles Ave., New Orleans, 70130-3411. Tel: 504-218-8739.

*Mary's Helpers (Medjugorje Information)—*Mrs. GAYLE PONSETI, Admin., Mailing Address: P.O. Box 1853, Marrero, 70073-1853. Tel: 504-348-7729; 800-573-4130.

*Medjugorje Star—*Rev. CHARLES SELLARS, O.M.I., Spiritual Dir. Email: medjugorje@mindspring.com. Web: medjugorje.home.mindspring.com. Directors: HUBIE MULE; KAY MULE, 2627 David Dr., Metairie, 70003-4599. Tel: 504-889-1713; Fax: 504-889-1714.

Metairie Program— 6017 Camphor St., Metairie, 70003.

*MIR Group (Medjugorje Information Center)—*Mr. T. ROY BROUSSARD, Pres., 1 Galleria Blvd., Ste. 744, Metairie, 70001-2081. Tel: 504-849-2570; Fax: 504-849-2574. Email: themirgroup@aol.com.

*Missionaries of St. Therese—*Rev. JAMES J. JEANFREAU JR., Spiritual Moderator, 1000 Howard Ave., Ste. 1213, New Orleans, 70113. Tel: 504-527-5771.

*Naim Conference—*Ms. SYBIL JOHNSON, Pres., New Orleans Chapter, 1308 Aris Ave., Metairie, 70005. Tel: 504-837-4267. Email: familylife@archdiocese-no.org.

*National Council of Catholic Men—*Mr. BEN RAPHAEL, Dir., Mailing Address: P.O. Box 6644, Metairie, 70009-6644. Tel: 504-202-1061.

*National Council of Catholic Women—*VACANT.

*Pax Christi New Orleans—*Chairpersons: Mr. TOM EGAN; Mrs. JEANNIE EGAN, Mailing Address: P.O. Box 50304, New Orleans, 70150-0304. Tel: 504-522-3751. Email: jeanegan@tulane.edu.

People Program— 1974 *2240 Lake Shore Dr., New Orleans, 70122.* Tel: 504-284-7678; Fax: 504-284-7840. Email: info@peopleprogram.org. Web: www.peopleprogram.org. LAVERNE KAPPEL, Exec. Dir. Email: director@peopleprogram.org.

Westbank Program—6201 Stratford Pl., New Orleans, 70131. Tel: 504-394-5433.

Metairie Program—6017 Camphor St., Metairie, 70003.

*Priests for Life—*Rev. LANCE J. CAMPO, S.T.L., Coord.

*Retrouvaille/Rediscovery—*JUDI DIEDLING; MIKE DIEDLING. Tel: 985-641-3802.

*Rosary Congress Committee—*Very Rev. NEAL W. MCDERMOTT, O.P., Spiritual Dir., 4640 Canal St., New Orleans, 70119. Tel: 504-488-2651. Web: www.rosarycongress.org.

*St. Elizabeth's Guild—*Mrs. DEBORAH B. ALCIATORE, Pres., c/o 1000 Howard Ave., Ste. 1000, New Orleans, 70113-1942.

*St. Thomas More Catholic Lawyers Association—*Rev. JOSEPH S. PALERMO JR., J.D., 2901 S. Carrollton Ave., New Orleans, 70118-4391. Tel: 504-866-7426, Ext. 3335; Fax: 504-866-3119.

*St. Vincent de Paul Society—*Mr. CLAIBORNE PERRILLIAT, Pres.; Deacon RUDOLPH J. RAYFIELD SR., Exec. Dir., Mailing Address: P.O. Box 792880, New Orleans, 70179. Tel: 504-940-5031; Fax: 504-866-4731. Email: svdped@bellsouth.net. Web: www.svdnola.org.

St. Vincent's Infant and Maternity Home Guild—c/o 1000 Howard Ave., Ste. 1000, New Orleans, 70113-1942.

Scouting—

*Archdiocesan Liaison—*Mr. JOHN SMESTAD JR., Dir. CYO/Youth Ministry. Email: jsmestad@archdiocese-no.org.

*Catholic Committee on Boy Scouting—*Deacon DANIEL FLYNN, Pastoral Min., 251 Halsey Dr., Harahan, 70123-4401. Tel: 504-737-8370.

*Catholic Committee on Girl Scouting—*VACANT.

Serra Clubs—

*Serra Club of New Orleans—*Rev. STEVEN V. BRUNO, Chap., 7887 Walmsley Ave., New Orleans, 70125-3496. Tel: 504-861-6298; Fax: 504-866-2906.

*Serra Club of Downtown New Orleans—*Rev. Msgr. ANDREW C. TAORMINA, J.D., V.F., Chap., 448 Metairie Rd., Metairie, 70005-4371. Tel: 504-834-0340.

*Serra Club of East Jefferson—*Rev. Msgr. ROBERT D. MASSETT, Chap., 6425 W. Metairie Ave., Metairie, 70003-4327. Tel: 504-733-0922.

*Serra Club of West St. Tammany—*Rev. Msgr. FRANK J. GIROIR, Chap., P.O. Box 40, Madisonville, 70447-0040. Tel: 985-845-7342; Mr. LARRY BUCKLEY, Pres. Tel: 985-892-7898 Serra Club of West Bank.

*Serra Club of St. Bernard—*Ms. JACKIE PALAMA, Pres. Tel: 504-812-3923; Ms. SALLY WOLFE, District Governor. Tel: 504-861-9026.

*The Theresians International—*Mrs. ALICE RAYER, Pres., 1750 St. Charles Ave., Apt. 224, New Orleans, 70122. Tel: 504-544-6691.

*Woman's New Life Center—*Ms. SUSAN M. MIRE, M.A., Founder; Mrs. ANGELA THOMAS, Esq., CEO, 3032 Ridgelake Dr., Ste. 101, Metairie, 70002. Tel: 504-496-0212; Fax: 504-831-3155. Email: info@womansnewlife.com. Web: www.womansnewlife.com.

CLERGY, PARISHES, MISSIONS AND PAROCHIAL SCHOOLS

CITY OF NEW ORLEANS

(ORLEANS CIVIL PARISH)

1—CATHEDRAL - BASILICA OF ST. LOUIS KING OF FRANCE (1720), (A Minor Basilica) Rev. Msgr. Crosby W. Kern, Rector; Deacons Ronald Guidry, Master of Ceremonies; Richard Brady; A. David Warriner Jr.; Larry D. Oney. In Res., Rev. William F. Maestri.
Res.: 615 Pere Antoine Alley, 70116-3291. Tel: 504-525-9585; Fax: 504-525-9583. Email: saintlouiscathedral-no@archdiocese-no.org. Web: www.stlouiscathedral.org.
School—Cathedral Academy, 820 Dauphine St., 70116-3089. Tel: 504-525-3860; Fax: 504-525-3193. Web: cathedralacademyno.org. Sr. Mary Sheila Marksim, O.P., Prin. Nuns 4; Lay Teachers 10; Students 163.
Mission—Our Lady of Guadalupe, Orleans Civil Parish. Tel: 504-525-1551; Fax: 504-525-1827. Email: judeshrine@aol.com.
Shrine—International Shrine of St. Jude Rev. Anthony Rigoli, O.M.I.
Res.: 411 N. Rampart St., 70112-3594.
*St. Jude Community Center—*400 N. Rampart St., 70112-3594. Tel: 504-553-5790.

2—ALL SAINTS (1919), (African American), Rev. Michael Saah-Buckman, S.S.J.; Deacon Larry L. Calvin.
Res.: 1441 Teche St., 70114-5899. Tel: 504-361-8835; Fax: 504-361-9802.
*Catechesis/Religious Program—*Students 69.

3—ST. ALPHONSUS (1847), (Irish), Revs. Richard Thibodeau, C.Ss.R.; Eugene Harrison, C.Ss.R, Parochial Vicar; Terrence McCloskey, C.Ss.R., Parochial Vicar; Bro. Thomas Wright, C.Ss.R. In Res., Revs. Gerard B. LaPorte, C.Ss.R.; Byron J. Miller, C.Ss.R.
Res.: 2030 Constance St., 70130-5004. Tel: 504-522-6748; Fax: 504-523-3734. Email: stalphonsusoffice@parishmail.com. Web: www.stalphonsusneworleans.com.
*School—*2001 Constance St., 70130-5094. Tel: 504-523-6594. Sr. Monica Ellerbusch, R.S.M., Prin. Lay Teachers 10; Students 181.
*Catechesis/Religious Program—*Tel: 504-525-2495; Fax: 504-581-9181. Students 75.
*Blessed Seelos Center—*919 Josephine St., 70130-5071. Web: www.seelos.org. Rev. Byron J. Miller, C.Ss.R., Exec. Dir.
*Mercy Senior Activity Center—*1017 St. Andrew St., 70130-5021. Tel: 504-568-0607; Fax: 504-568-0699. Sr. Jane Briseno, R.S.M., Dir.

4—ST. ANDREW THE APOSTLE (1952) Revs. Paul S. Hart; Clayton "Beau" Charbonnet, Parochial Vicar; Deacon John J. Walker IV.
Res.: 3101 Eton St., 70131-5399. Tel: 504-393-2334; Fax: 504-392-0635.
*School—*3131 Eton St., 70131. Tel: 504-394-4171; Fax: 504-391-3627. Sisters 2; Lay Teachers 68; Students 640.
*Catechesis/Religious Program—*Tel: 504-393-0140; Fax: 504-393-0334. Students 40.

5—ANNUNCIATION (1844) Merged with St. Cecilia, St. Gerard, SS. Peter & Paul & St. Vincent de Paul to form Blessed Francis Xavier Seelos, New Orleans.

6—ST. ANTHONY OF PADUA (1915), Assumed parish territory of Sacred Heart of Jesus, New Orleans. Revs. John G. Restrepo, O.P.; David K. Seid, O.P., Parochial Vicar; Deacon Joseph M. Dardis. In Res., Revs. Michael M. Burke, O.P.; Christopher T. Eggleton, O.P.; Eduardo Gabriel, O.P.; Charles K. Johnson, O.P.; Bro. Herman D. Johnson, O.P.; Revs. Justin Kauchak, O.P.; John E. Lydon, O.P.; Very Rev. Neal W. McDermott, O.P.; Rev. John M. Pitzer, O.P.; Bro. Fernando Sorolla, O.P.
Res.: 4640 Canal St., 70119-5808. Tel: 504-488-2651; Fax: 504-488-1842. Email: stantno@archdiocese-no.org.
*School—*4601 Cleveland Ave., 70119-5813. Tel: 504-488-4426; Fax: 504-488-5373. Email: paduastars@archdiocese-no.org. Web: www.stanthonypadua.net. Sr. Ruth Angelette, O.P., Prin. Dominican Sisters of Peace 1; Lay Teachers 18; Students 186.
*Catechesis/Religious Program—*Students 18.

7—ST. AUGUSTINE (1841), (African American), Rev. Quentin E. Moody.
Res.: 1210 Gov. Nicholls St., 70116-2324. Tel: 504-525-5934; Fax: 504-523-2473.
*Catechesis/Religious Program—*Students 14.

8—BLESSED FRANCIS XAVIER SEELOS (2001) [CEM] Rev. Joseph A. Benson; Deacon Jesse A. Watley; Ms. Arthine T. Vicks, Pastoral Assoc.
Res.: 3053 Dauphine St., 70117-6724. Tel: 504-943-5566; Fax: 504-943-5501.
*Catechesis/Religious Program—*Students 64.

9—BLESSED SACRAMENT (1915), (African American),

Merged See Blessed Sacrament-St. Joan of Arc, New Orleans. For inquiries about sacramental records, contact Blessed Sacrament-St. Joan of Arc parish.

10—BLESSED SACRAMENT-ST. JOAN OF ARC (2008), Merger of Blessed Sacrament & St. Joan of Arc, New Orleans, worshipping at St. Joan of Arc Church, which was establised in 1909. Rev. Charles Andrus, S.S.J.; Deacon Irvin Stewart Sr.
8321 Burthe St., 70118-1195. Tel: 504-866-7330; Fax: 504-866-1319. Email: bssj@josephite.com. Web: www.josephite.com/parish/la/bssj.
School—St. Joan of Arc School, 919 Cambronne St., 70118-1199. Tel: 504-861-2887; Fax: 504-866-9588. Email: stjoanno@archdiocese-no.org. Ms. Dionne Frost, Prin.
Catechesis/Religious Program—Lynn Buggage, D.R.E. Students 50.

11—BLESSED TRINITY (2008), Merger of St. Matthias, Our Lady of Lourdes and St. Monica, New Orleans, worshipping at St. Matthias Church, which was established in 1920. Rev. John Asare-Dankwah (Ghana).
4230 S. Broad St., 70125-3699. Tel: 504-822-3394; Fax: 504-822-3397. In Res., Rev. Augustine Appian.

12—ST. BRIGID (1977) Closed. See Mary Queen of Vietnam, New Orleans. For inquiries regarding sacramental records, contact Archives.

13—ST. CECILIA (1897) Merged with Annunciation, St. Gerard, SS. Peter & Paul & St. Vincent de Paul to form Blessed Francis Xavier Seelos, New Orleans.

14—CORPUS CHRISTI (1916), (African American), Merged See Corpus Christi-Epiphany. For inquiries regarding sacramental records, contact Corpus Christi-Epiphany parish.

15—CORPUS CHRISTI-EPIPHANY (2008), Merger of Corpus Christi & Epiphany, New Orleans, worshipping at Corpus Christi Church, which was established in 1916. Revs. John G. Harfmann, S.S.J.; Godwin B. Akpan, S.S.J., Parochial Vicar.
2022 St. Bernard Ave., 70116-1388. Tel: 504-945-8931; Fax: 504-947-5347. Email: cce@josephite.com.
Catechesis/Religious Program—Students 46.

16—ST. DAVID (1937), (African American), Assumed territory of St. Maurice, New Orleans. Rev. Oswald P. Pierre-Jules, S.S.J. In Res., Rev. John E. O'Hallaran, S.S.J.
Res.: 5617 St. Claude Ave., 70117-2533. Tel: 504-947-2853; Fax: 504-943-0577.

17—ST. DOMINIC (1924) Very Revs. Martin J. Gleeson, O.P.; Michael O'Rourke, O.P.; David G. Caron, O.P.; Mark Edney, O.P.; Rev. Daniel Shanahan, O.P.; Bros. Roger Shondel, O.P.; Richard J. Bontempo, O.P.; Mariano D. Veliz, O.P.; Deacons John Pippenger; Lloyd E. Huck.
Res.: 775 Harrison Ave., 70124-3192. Tel: 504-482-4156; Fax: 504-488-0906. Web: www.stdominicnola.org.
School—6326 Memphis St., 70124. Tel: 504-482-4123; Fax: 504-486-3870. Sisters 2; Lay Teachers 42; Students 517.
Catechesis/Religious Program—6361 Memphis St., 70124. Tel: 504-486-9731. Students 79.

18—EPIPHANY (1948), (African American), Merged See Corpus Christi-Epiphany. For inquiries regarding sacramental records, contact Corpus Christi-Epiphany parish.

19—ST. FRANCES XAVIER CABRINI (1952) Merged with St. Raphael the Archangel & St. Thomas the Apostle, New Orleans to form Transfiguration of the Lord, New Orleans. For inquiries regarding sacramental records, contact the archives office.

20—ST. FRANCIS DE SALES (1870), (African American), Merged with Holy Ghost, New Orleans to form St. Katharine Drexel. For inquiries regarding sacramental records, contact St. Katharine Drexel parish.

21—ST. FRANCIS OF ASSISI (1890) Very Rev. Philip G. Landry; Deacon Wilbur A. Toups.
Res.: 631 State St., 70118-5899. Tel: 504-891-4479; Fax: 504-891-4470. Email: sfa@stfrancisuptown.com. Web: www.stfrancisuptown.com.
Catechesis/Religious Program—Students 142.

22—ST. GABRIEL THE ARCHANGEL (1954), (African American), Rev. Msgr. Douglas A. Doussan.
Office: 4700 Pineda St., 70126-3599. Tel: 504-282-0296; Fax: 504-288-8585. Web: www.stgabe.net.
Catechesis/Religious Program—Students 17.

23—ST. GERARD (1971) Merged with Annunciation, St. Cecilia, SS. Peter & Paul & St. Vincent de Paul to form Blessed Francis Xavier Seelos, New Orleans.

24—GOOD SHEPHERD (2008) Rev. Msgr. Christopher Nalty.
1025 Napolean Ave., 70115-2898. Tel: 504-899-1378; Fax: 504-899-0480. Email: ststephenpar@archdiocese-no.org. In Res., Revs. Douglas C. Brougher; Thomas E. Chambers, C.S.C.
School—St. Stephen Catholic School, 1027 Napoleon Ave., 70115-2899. Tel: 504-891-1927; Fax: 504-891-1928. Email: ststephen@archdiocese-no.org. Ms. Peggy LeBlanc, Prin.
Catechesis/Religious Program—Phillip Bellini, D.R.E. Students 44.

25—ST. HENRY (1856) Merged with Our Lady of Good Counsel & St. Stephen, New Orleans to form Good Shepherd. For inquiries reagrding sacramental records, contact Good Shepherd parish.

26—HOLY GHOST (1915), (African American), Merged See St. Katharine Drexel. For inquiries regarding sacramental records contact St. Katharine Drexel parish.

27—HOLY NAME OF JESUS (1892), Assumed parish territory of St. Thomas More, New Orleans. Revs. Donald A. Hawkins, S.J.; Robert A. Hagan, S.J., Parochial Vicar. In Res., Revs. George F. Lundy, S.J.; Paul Schott, S.J.; Charles Wrightington, S.J.
Office & Mailing Address: 6220 LaSalle Pl., 70118-6236. Tel: 504-865-7430; Fax: 504-866-3391. Church: 6367 St. Charles Ave., 70118.
School—6325 Cromwell Pl., 70118-6299. Tel: 504-861-1466; Fax: 504-861-1480. Courtney Wolbrette, Prin. Sisters of Mercy 5; Lay Teachers 50; Students 485.
Catechesis/Religious Program—Tel: 504-572-2469. Students 61.

28—HOLY NAME OF MARY (ALGIERS) (1848) [CEM 2] [JC 2] Rev. Michael Roberson; Deacon Dean D. Herrick.
Res.: 500 Eliza St., 70114-1098. Tel: 504-362-5511; Fax: 504-367-3504. Email: hnmary@bellsouth.net.
Catechesis/Religious Program—Students 23.

29—HOLY SPIRIT (1972) Rev. Terence Hayden (Ireland); Deacon Daniel F. Reynolds; Pam Kamphuis, Music Ministry Coord.
Res.: 6201 Stratford Pl., 70131-7397. Tel: 504-394-5492; Fax: 504-398-0901. Web: www.holyspirit-no.org.
Catechesis/Religious Program—Jane Nix, D.R.E. Students 17.

30—HOLY TRINITY, Closed. For inquiries for parish records contact the chancery.

31—IMMACULATE CONCEPTION (1851) Revs. Stephen J. Sauer, S.J.; Paul Osterle, S.J.; Jeffrey C. Johnson, S.J., Parochial Vicar. In Res., Very Rev. Mark Lewis, S.J.; Rev. Michael D. Dooley, S.J.
Res.: 130 Baronne St., 70112-2304. Tel: 504-529-1477; Fax: 504-524-0155. Email: admin@jesuitchurch.net. Web: www.jesuitchurch.net.
Catechesis/Religious Program—Valerie Robinson, D.R.E. Students 54.

32—IMMACULATE HEART OF MARY (1954) Closed. See St. Maria Goretti. For inquiries regarding sacramental records, contact Archives.

33—INCARNATE WORD (1922) Closed. See Mater Dolorosa, New Orleans. For inquiries regarding sacramental records, contact Mater Dolorosa. Also known as St. Theresa of the Little Flower.

34—ST. JAMES MAJOR (1920) Rev. Richard N. Maughan; Deacon Glenn J. Wiltz.
Res.: 3736 Gentilly Blvd., 70122-6128. Tel: 504-304-6750; Fax: 504-304-6807. Email: stjamesmajor@cox.net.
Catechesis/Religious Program—Students 44.

35—ST. JOAN OF ARC (1909) Merged with Blessed Sacrament, New Orleans to form Blessed Sacrament-St. Joan of Arc parish. For inquiries regarding sacramental records, contact Blessed Sacrament-St. Joan of Arc parish.

36—ST. JOHN THE BAPTIST (1851), (Irish), Open for weddings and funerals only. Church under care of pastor of St. Patrick, New Orleans. For inquiries regarding sacramental records, contact Archives., Mailing Address: 724 Camp St., 70130-3757. Tel: 504-525-4413; Fax: 504-568-1324.
Res.: 1139 Oretha Castle Haley Blvd., 70113-1215.

37—ST. JOSEPH (1844) Rev. Thomas J. Stehlik, C.M. 1802 Tulane Ave., 70112-2246. Tel: 504-522-3186, Ext. 141; Fax: 504-522-3171.
(Legal Title: St. Joseph Roman Catholic)
Catechesis/Religious Program—

38—ST. JULIAN EYMARD (1952) Closed. Parish territory assigned to Holy Name of Mary, New Orleans. For inquiries regarding sacramental records, contact Holy Name of Mary parish.

39—ST. KATHARINE DREXEL (2008), Merger of Holy Ghost and St. Francis de Sales, New Orleans, worshipping at Holy Ghost Church, which was established in 1915. Rev. John Cisewski.
2015 Louisiana Ave., 70115-5294. Tel: 504-891-3172; Fax: 504-891-9284.
School—Holy Ghost School, 2035 Toledano St., 70115-5295. Tel: 504-899-6782; Fax: 504-899-6782. Email: holyghost@archdiocese-no.org. Sr. M. Angela Smith, S.S.F., Prin. Sisters 6; Lay Teachers 11; Students 280.
Catechesis/Religious Program—Grace Lemieux, D.R.E. Students 36.

40—ST. LEO THE GREAT (1920), (African American), Merged with St. Raymond, New Orleans to form St. Raymond-St. Leo the Great. For inquiries regarding sacramental records, contact St. Raymond-St. Leo the Great.

41—ST. MARIA GORETTI (1965), Assumed parish territory of Immaculate Heart of Mary & St. Simon Peter, New Orleans. For inquiries about sacramental records for Immaculate Heart of Mary, St. Maria Goretti or St. Simon Peter, contact Archives tel. 504-861-6241. Rev. Msgr. L. Earl Gauthreaux; Rev. Robustiano D. Morgia; Deacons Ildefonso R. DeLeon; Oscar G. Foster III.
Mailing Address: 7300 Crowder Blvd., 70127-1599. Tel: 504-242-7554; Fax: 504-242-0755. In Res., Rev. Victor H. Cohea.
School—Tel: 504-242-1313; Fax: 504-242-4126.
Catechesis/Religious Program—Students 91.

42—ST. MARY OF THE ANGELS (1925), (African American), Rev. Dennis Bosse, O.F.M.; Bro. Mark Gehert; Jeoffre Duplessis, Music Min.
Res.: 3501 N. Miro St., 70117-5899. Tel: 504-945-3186; Fax: 504-945-9115.
Catechesis/Religious Program—Vanessa Matthews, D.R.E. & Youth Min. Students 28.

43—MARY, QUEEN OF VIETNAM (1983), (Vietnamese), [JC], Assumed St. Nicholas of Myra & St. Brigid, New Orleans. Rev. Nghiem Van Nguyen.
Mailing Address: P.O. Box 870607, 70187. In Res., Rev. Nguyen Van Nguyen.
Res.: 5069 Willowbrook Dr., 70129-1047. Tel: 504-254-5660; Fax: 504-254-9250.
Catechesis/Religious Program—Tel: 504-254-5247. Students 915.
Mission—Our Lady of La Vang 6054 Vermillion Blvd., Orleans Civil Parish 70122-4296. Tel: 504-283-0559; Fax: 504-286-1937. Rev. Dominic Huyen Duc Nguyen.
Chapel—Vietnamese Martyrs 14400 Peltier Dr., New Orleans East, 70129-1713. Tel: 504-254-5660.
Shrine—Vietnamese Martyrs Shrine of the Archdiocese of New Orleans

44—MATER DOLOROSA (1848), Assumed Incarnate Word, New Orleans & St. Theresa of the Child Jesus, also known as St. Theresa of the Little Flower. Rev. John T. Hinton. In Res., Revs. Harry J. Adams; Francis Ferrie (Retired).
Res.: 8128 Plum St., 70118-2012. Tel: 504-866-3669; Fax: 504-866-2349.
Catechesis/Religious Program—Tel: 504-866-5641. Dee Collura, D.R.E. Students 80.

45—ST. MATTHIAS (1920), (African American), Merged with Our Lady of Lourdes & St. Monica, New Orleans to form Blessed Trinity. For inquiries regarding sacramental records, contact Blessed Trinity parish.

46—ST. MAURICE (1852) Closed. Assumed by St. David, New Orleans. For inquiries regarding sacramental records, contact Archives.

47—ST. MONICA (1924) [CEM] Merged with Our Lady of Lourdes & St. Matthias to form Blessed Trinity. For inquiries regarding sacramental records, contact Blessed Trinity parish.

48—ST. NICHOLAS OF MYRA (1971) [CEM] Closed. Assigned to St. Brigid, New Orleans, which was assigned to Mary Queen of Vietnam. For inquiries regarding sacramental records, contact Archives.

49—OUR LADY OF GOOD COUNSEL (1887) Merged with St. Henry & St. Stephen. See Good Shepherd. For inquiries regarding sacramental records, contact Good Shepherd.

50—OUR LADY OF GUADALUPE /INTERNATIONAL SHRINE OF ST. JUDE (1826), (African American), Revs. Anthony Rigoli, O.M.I.; John Morin, O.M.I., Parochial Vicar; Deacon Rudolph J. Rayfield Sr.
Res.: 411 N. Rampart St., 70112. Tel: 504-525-1551; Fax: 504-525-1827.
Catechesis/Religious Program—Tel: 504-522-8546. Students 65.

51—OUR LADY OF LOURDES (1905), (African American), Merged with St. Monica & St. Matthias, New Orleans to form Blessed Trinity worshipping at St. Matthias. For inquiries regarding sacramental records, contact Blessed Trinity parish.

52—OUR LADY OF THE ROSARY (1907) Very Rev. David J. Robicheaux; Deacons James Bialas; Michael G. Zaiontz.
1322 Moss St., 70119-2998. Tel: 504-488-2659; Fax: 504-488-6741. Web: www.ourladyoftherosary-no.com. In Res., Most Rev. Shelton J. Fabre.
School—Holy Rosary Academy, Tel: 504-482-7173; Fax: 504-482-7229.
Catechesis/Religious Program—Program in conjunction with St. Dominic Church. Students 225.

53—OUR LADY STAR OF THE SEA (1911) [CEM] Rev. Rodney Anthony Ricard; Deacons Melvin C. Jones Sr.; Brian A. Gabriel; Uriel Andrew Durr.
Res.: 1835 St. Roch Ave., 70117-8199. Tel: 504-944-0166; Fax: 504-948-9555. Email: starofthecity@aol.com. Web: www.olss-no.com.
Catechesis/Religious Program—Students 47.

54—ST. PATRICK (1833), (Irish), Assumed St. John

the Baptist, New Orleans. Rev. Stanley P. Klores; Deacon Chris DiGrado.
Res.: 724 Camp St., 70130-3757. Tel: 504-525-4413; Fax: 504-568-1324. Email: stpatrick@archdiocese-no.org. Web: www.oldstpatricks.org.
Catechesis/Religious Program—Robert Ramirez, D.R.E.

55—St. Paul the Apostle (1947), (African American), [CEM] Rev. Alfred A. Ayem, S.V.D.; Deacon Graylin J. Miller.
Res.: 6828 Chef Menteur Hwy., 70126-5297. Tel: 504-242-8820; Fax: 504-242-8806.
Catechesis/Religious Program—Students 95.

56—SS. Peter and Paul (1848) Merged with Annunciation, St. Cecilia, St. Gerard & St. Vincent de Paul to form Blessed Francis Xavier Seelos, New Orleans.

57—St. Peter Claver (1920), (African American), Very Rev. Michael P. Jacques, S.S.E.; Deacons Terrel J. Broussard; Allen Stevens; Lawrence C. Houston; Pearl Dupart, Assoc. Dir. Social Apostolate; Cheryln Wheeler, Dir. Devel & Commun.; Henri Reed, Family Life Dir.; Mary Boutte, Youth Minister; Veronica Downs-Dorsey, Music Dir.
1923 St. Philip St., 70116-2199. Tel: 504-822-8059; 504-821-3146; Fax: 504-822-9251. Web: www.stpeterclaverneworleans.org.
School—St. Peter Claver School, 1020 N. Prieur St., 70116-2194. Tel: 504-822-8191; Fax: 504-822-2692. Web: spclaver.eduk12.net. Ms. Vanessa Chavis, Prin. Lay Teachers 23; Students 280.
Catechesis/Religious Program—Alena Boucree, D.R.E.; Ayanna Talbert, Asst. D.R.E. Students 217.

58—St. Philip the Apostle (1949), (African American), Closed. Assigned to St. Mary of the Angels, New Orleans, under the care of Franciscans. Buildings are under the care of the Archdiocese of New Orleans. For inquiries regarding sacramental records, contact Archives.

59—St. Pius X (1953) Very Rev. Patrick J. Williams; Deacons William A. Glennon; Christopher A. Bertucci. In Res., Rev. Msgr. Clinton J. Doskey (Retired).
Res.: 6666 Spanish Fort Blvd., 70124-4398. Tel: 504-282-3332; Fax: 504-283-8984. Email: spx-rectory@archdiocese-no.org. Web: www.stpiusxnola.org.
School—6600 Spanish Fort Blvd., 70124-4399. Tel: 504-282-2811; Fax: 504-282-3043. Email: spxsch@archdiocese-no.org. Lay Teachers 22; Students 369.
Catechesis/Religious Program—Students 57.

60—St. Raphael the Archangel (1947) Merged with St. Frances Cabrini & St. Thomas the Apostle, New Orleans to form Transfiguration of the Lord New Orleans. For inquiries regarding sacramental records, contact Archives.

61—St. Raymond (1927), (African American), Merged with St. Leo the Great, New Orleans to form St. Raymond-St. Leo the Great. For inquiries regarding sacramental records, contact St. Raymond-St. Leo the Great parish.

62—St. Raymond-St. Leo the Great (2008), Merger of St. Leo the Great & St. Raymond, New Orleans, worshipping at St. Leo the Great Church, which was established in 1920. Revs. Anthony Bozeman, S.S.J.; Robert P. Zawacki, S.S.J., Parochial Vicar; Deacons Royal C. Shelton; Dwight Alexander.
2916 Paris Ave., 70119. Tel: 504-945-8750; Fax: 504-309-1691. Email: crivera@archdiocese-no.org.
School—St. Leo the Great School, 1501 Abundance St., 70119-2098. Tel: 504-943-1482; Fax: 504-944-5895. Mrs. Carmel Mire, Prin.
Catechesis/Religious Program—Marlene Wilson, D.R.E. Students 48.

63—The Resurrection Of Our Lord (1963) Rev. MichaelJoseph Vinh Ngoc Nguyen.
Res.: 9701 Hammond St., 70127-3519. Tel: 504-242-8669; Fax: 504-242-8767.
School—Resurrection of Our Lord School, 4861 Rosalia Dr., 70127-3598. Tel: 504-243-2257; Fax: 504-241-5532. Email: resurrection@archdiocese-no.org. Dr. Si Nguyen, Prin. Lay Teachers 46; Students 485.
Catechesis/Religious Program—Students 26.

64—St. Rita Catholic Church (1921) Rev. Dennis J. Hayes III.
Res.: 2729 Lowerline St., 70125-3599. Tel: 504-866-3621; Fax: 504-861-0338. Email: stritachurchno@archdiocese-no.org.
School—St. Rita Catholic School, 65 Fontainebleau Dr., 70125-3495. Tel: 504-866-1777; Fax: 504-861-8512. Email: stritano@archdiocese-no.org. Sr. Mary Annette Baxley, M.S.C., Prin. Sisters 8; Lay Teachers 11; Students 200.
Catechesis/Religious Program—Students 13.

65—St. Rose of Lima (1857) Closed. Assigned to Our Lady of the Rosary, New Orleans. Buildings are under the care of the Archdiocese of New Orleans. For inquiries regarding sacramental records, contact Archives.

66—Sacred Heart of Jesus (1879) [CEM] Closed. Parish territory assigned to St. Anthony of Padua, New Orleans. For inquiries for sacramental records, contact the archives office.

67—St. Simon Peter (1986) Closed. Assigned to St. Maria Goretti, New Orleans. For inquiries regarding sacramental records, contact Archives.

68—St. Stephen (1849) Merged with Our Lady of Good Counsel & St. Henry, New Orleans to form Good Shepherd. For inquiries regarding sacramental records, contact Good Shepherd parish.

69—St. Theresa of Avila (1848), Special care to the Hispanic Community. Revs. Teodoro Agudo, O.F.M-.Cap. (Spain); Eutiquiano Miguel, O.F.M.Cap.
Res.: 1404 Erato St., 70130-4387. Tel: 504-525-4226; Fax: 504-525-6014.
Catechesis/Religious Program—Students 30.

70—St. Theresa of the Child Jesus (1929) Closed. Parish territory entrusted to Incarnate Word, New Orleans. For inquiries regarding sacramental records, contact the archives office.

71—St. Thomas More (1970) Closed. Became a campus ministry center (Tulane Catholic Center) serving Tulane University. For inquiries regarding sacramental records, contact Holy Name of Jesus parish.

72—St. Thomas the Apostle (1974) Merged Became a campus ministry center (UNO Newman Center) serving the University of New Orleans. For inquiries regarding sacrmental records, contact Archives.

73—Transfiguration of the Lord (2008), Merger of St. Frances Cabrini, St. Raphael the Archangel & St. Thomas the Apostle, New Orleans. Rev. Paul H. Desrosiers; Deacon Peter C. Rizzo.
Mailing Address: UNO Newman Center, 2000 Lakeshore Dr., 70148-0001. Tel: 504-288-6336; Fax: 504-288-6344. Email: newmancenter@uno.edu. 2212 Prentiss Ave., 70148.

74—St. Vincent De Paul (1838) Merged with Annunciation, St. Cecilia, St. Gerard & SS. Peter & Paul to form Blessed Francis Xavier Seelos, New Orleans.

OUTSIDE THE CITY OF NEW ORLEANS

Abita Springs, St. Tammany Parish, St. Jane de Chantal (1887) [JC] Revs. Robert C. Cavalier; Jeffery Jambon, Parochial Vicar; Deacons Frans Labranche Jr.; Donald E. Bourgeois; Mark C. Coudrain.
Res.: 22122 Main St., P.O. Box 1870, 70420-1870. Tel: 985-892-1439; Fax: 985-871-9547.
Catechesis/Religious Program—72040 Maple St., 70420-3931. Tel: 985-893-3914. Students 300.
Mission—St. Michael the Archangel Bush, St. Tammany Parish. Fax: 985-886-0302.

Ama, St. Charles Parish, St. Mark (1974) Revs. David L. Rabe; Anton Ba Phan, Parochial Vicar.
Res.: P.O. Box 556, 70031-0556. Tel: 504-431-8505; Fax: 504-431-8506. Email: stmarkama@yahoo.com.
Catechesis/Religious Program—Tel: 504-431-8507. Ms. Mary Loup, D.R.E. Students 68.

Arabi, St. Bernard Parish

1—St. Louise De Marillac (1954) Closed. Assigned to Our Lady of Prompt Succor, Chalmette. For inquiries regarding sacramental records, contact Archives.

2—St. Robert Bellarmine (1964) Closed. Assigned to Our Lady of Prompt Succor, Chalmette. For inquiries regarding sacramental records, contact Archives.
Res.: 408 Cougar Dr., 70032-2098.

Avondale, Jefferson Parish, St. Bonaventure (1965) Rev. Patrick Gannon; Deacon Brian J. Klause.
Res.: 329 S. Jamie Blvd., 70094-2821. Tel: 504-436-1279; Fax: 504-436-1300.
Catechesis/Religious Program—Tel: 504-436-0744. Tina Adams, D.R.E. Students 72.

Belle Chasse, Plaquemines Parish, Our Lady of Perpetual Help (1928) [CEM] Very Rev. William O'Riordan; Deacon Leslie D. Vincent.
Res.: 8968 Hwy. 23, 70037-2296. Tel: 504-394-0314; Fax: 504-394-0376. Email: churchoffice@olphbc.org. Web: www.olphbc.org.
School—8970 Hwy. 23. Tel: 504-394-0757; Fax: 504-394-1627. Sr. Elizabeth Hebert, S.L.W., Prin. Sisters 1; Lay Teachers 15; Students 247.
Catechesis/Religious Program—Dolly Roy, D.R.E. Students 372.

Bogalusa, Washington Parish, Annunciation Catholic Church (1906) [JC 3] Rev. Patrick Collum.
Res.: 517 Avenue B, 70427-3711. Tel: 985-732-4280; Fax: 985-735-1042. Web: www.accbogalusa.org. 202 W. 5th St., 70427-3723.
School—511 Avenue C, 70427-3797. Tel: 985-735-6643; Fax: 985-735-6119. Email: annunciationsch@archdiocese-no.org. Web: www.acs-bogalusa.org. Lay Teachers 18; Students 155.
Catechesis/Religious Program—Students 25.

Bridge City, Jefferson Parish, Holy Guardian Angels (1963) Closed. Mission of Our Lady of Prompt Succor, Westwego.

Buras, Plaquemines Parish, Our Lady of Good Harbor (1864) [CEM] Closed. Parish & mission territory assigned to St. Patrick, Port Sulphur. For inquiries regarding sacramental records, contact Archives.

Chalmette , St. Bernard Parish

1—St. Mark (1964) Closed. Assigned to Our Lady of Prompt Succor, Chalmette. For inquiries regarding sacramental records, contact Archives.

2—Our Lady of Prompt Succor (1951), Parish assumed territory of Prince of Peace, Chalmette, St. Bernard Parish; St. Louise de Marillac, Arabi, St. Bernard Parish; St. Mark, Chalmette, St. Bernard Parish; & St. Robert Bellarmine, Arabi, St. Bernard Parish. Very Rev. Danilo C. Digal; Deacon Lino G. Parulan.
Res.: 2320 Paris Rd., 70043-5098. Tel: 504-271-3441; Fax: 504-271-2927. Email: olpschal@archdiocese-no.org; ourladysuccor@bellsouth.net. Web: www.olps-chalmette.org.
School—Our Lady of Prompt Succor Central School, 2305 Fenelon St., 70043-4951. Tel: 504-271-2953; Fax: 504-271-1490. Email: scoll8312@aol.com. Web: www.olpsschool.org. Sharon Coll, Prin. Lay Teachers 24; Students 380.
Catechesis/Religious Program—Tel: 504-271-1217. Brenda Tromatore, D.R.E. Students 203.
Mission—Chapel of St. Lawrence St. Bernard Parish Prison, St. Bernard Parish 70043. Tel: 504-278-7645; Fax: 504-278-7785.

3—Prince of Peace (1977) Closed. See Our Lady of Prompt Succor, Chalmette. For inquiries regarding sacramental records, contact Archives.

Covington, St. Tammany Parish

1—St. Benedict (1970) Rev. Jonathan M. DeFrange, O.S.B.; Deacon Nelvin Luke.
Res.: 20370 Smith Rd., 70435. Tel: 985-892-5202; Fax: 985-892-4211.
Catechesis/Religious Program—Students 165.

2—Most Holy Trinity (2006) Very Rev. Rodney P. Bourg; Deacons Thomas E. Caffery Jr.; Michael J. Talbot.
4465 Hwy. 190 E. Service Rd., 70433-4957. Tel: 985-892-0642; Fax: 985-893-9287. Email: office@mostholytrinityano.org. In Res., Rev. Dean L. Robins.
Res.: 285 Ponchitolawa Dr., 70433-6203.
Catechesis/Religious Program—Patricia Hebert, D.R.E. Students 164.

3—St. Peter (1843) Revs. Paul Van Tung Nguyen; Robert T. Cooper, Parochial Vicar; Deacons James Clyde Ardoin; Dennis F. Adams.
Res.: 125 E. 19th St., 70433-3195. Tel: 985-892-2422; Fax: 985-898-1998. Email: rectory@stpeterparish.com. Web: www.stpeterparish.com.
School—Tel: 985-892-1831; Fax: 985-898-2185. Email: stpetercov@stpetercov.org. Mrs. Melody Barousse, Prin. Lay Teachers 35; Students 741.
Catechesis/Religious Program—Tel: 985-893-2446; Fax: 985-892-7567. Email: ore@stpeterparish.com. Students 337.

Crown Point, Jefferson Parish, St. Pius X (1971) Closed. Mission of St. Anthony, Lafitte.

Des Allemands , St. Charles Parish, St. Gertrude (1955) [CEM] Revs. Joseph Duc Dzien; Edward J. Lauden, Parochial Vicar.
Res.: P.O. Box 767, 70030-0767. Tel: 985-758-7542; Fax: 985-758-7591. Email: stg_office@yahoo.com.
Catechesis/Religious Program—Tel: 985-758-1332. Tina Montz, C.R.E. Students 101.

Destrehan, St. Charles Parish, St. Charles Borromeo (1723), (German), [CEM] Revs. Thomas M. McCann III; Daniel E. Brouillette, Parochial Vicar; Deacons Harry Schexnayder; Michael Stohlman; Jeffrey R. Tully.
Res.: 13396 River Rd., P.O. Box 428, 70047-0428. Tel: 985-764-6383; Fax: 985-764-3948.
School—Tel: 985-764-9232; Fax: 985-764-3726. Lay Teachers 37; Students 378; Preschool 82.
Catechesis/Religious Program—Students 409.

Diamond, Plaquemines Parish, St. Jude (1981) Closed. Parish territory entrusted to St. Patrick, Port Sulphur. For inquiries regarding sacramental records, contact Archives.

Edgard , St. John the Baptist Parish, St. John the Baptist (1770), (African American), [CEM] Rev. Joel P. Cantones; Deacon Warren R. Pierre.
Res.: 2361 Hwy. 18, 70049-9101. Tel: 985-497-3412; 985-497-8470; Fax: 985-497-3965.
Catechesis/Religious Program—Students 157.

Florissant, St. Bernard Parish, San Pedro Pescador (1966), (Islenos), Closed. Parish territory assigned to St. Bernard, St. Bernard. For inquiries regarding sacramental records, contact St. Bernard parish.

Folsom, St. Tammany Parish, St. John the Baptist (1921) Rev. Timothy J. Burnett, O.S.B.; Deacon Julius T. Zimmer.

Res.: 11345 St. John Church Rd., 70437-7155. Office: Tel: 985-796-3806; Fax: 985-796-9554.
Catechesis / Religious Program—Tel: 985-796-5507. Students 107.

FRANKLINTON, WASHINGTON PARISH, HOLY FAMILY (1982) Rev. Peter E. Hammett, O.S.B.
Res.: 1213 14th Ave., 70438. Tel: 985-839-4040; Fax: 985-839-2429.
Catechesis / Religious Program—Tel: 985-839-2428. Students 64.

GARYVILLE, ST. JOHN THE BAPTIST PARISH, ST. HUBERT (1907) Rev. William H. Blank; Deacon Garland J. Roussel Jr.
Res. & Office: 176 Anthony Monica St., P.O. Box K, 70051-0851. Tel: 985-535-3312; Fax: 985-535-1849. Email: sthubert@rtconline.com.
Catechesis / Religious Program—Students 47.

GRETNA, JEFFERSON PARISH
1—ST. ANTHONY (1920) Closed. Mission of St. Joseph, Gretna.
2—ST. CLETUS (1965) Rev. Tuan Anh Pham; Deacon Patrick L. Dempsey.
Res.: 3600 Claire Ave., 70053-7699. Tel: 504-367-7951; Fax: 504-367-7928.
School—Tel: 504-366-3538; Fax: 504-366-0011. Mrs. Jill Grabert, Prin. Lay Teachers 40; Students 581.
Catechesis / Religious Program—Tel: 504-361-4805. Students 121.
3—ST. JOSEPH (1857) Rev. James Richard Day; Deacon Herman J. Williams.
Res.: 610 Sixth St., 70053-6098. Tel: 504-368-1313; Fax: 504-368-6841.
Catechesis / Religious Program—Students 10.
Mission—St. Anthony Mission 924 Monroe St., Jefferson Parish 70053-2299. Tel: 504-368-6161.
School—St. Anthony School, 900 Franklin Ave., 70053-2224. Tel: 504-367-0689; Fax: 504-361-9054. Miss Jo Anna Russo, Prin.

HAHNVILLE , ST. CHARLES PARISH, OUR LADY OF THE HOLY ROSARY (1877) [CEM] Rev. Bernard C. Francis.
Res.: #1 Rectory Ln., 70057. Tel: 985-783-1199; Fax: 985-783-1974. Email: olrhahn@aol.com.
Catechesis / Religious Program—Jacqueline Robert, D.R.E. Students 125.

HARAHAN, JEFFERSON PARISH, ST. RITA (1950) Rev. Herbert J. Kiff Jr.; Deacons Danny Flynn; Gary J. Borne; Nolen J. LeBlanc.
Mailing Address: 7100 Jefferson Hwy., 70123-4928. Fax: 504-737-2921.
Res.: 160 Imperial Woods Dr., 70123-4998. Tel: 504-737-2915; Fax: 504-737-2921.
School—194 Ravan Ave., 70123-4999. Tel: 504-737-0744; Fax: 504-738-2184. Theresa Faucheux, Prin. Lay Teachers 32; Students 410.
Catechesis / Religious Program—Email: hhuertel@archdiocese-no.org. Students 46.

HARVEY, JEFFERSON PARISH
1—INFANT JESUS OF PRAGUE (1969) Closed. Mission of St. Martha, Harvey.
2—ST. JOHN BOSCO (1983) Revs. Donald Delaney, S.D.B.; Joseph Vien Hoang, S.D.B.; Deacon Kevin M. Steel.
Res.: 2114 Oakmere Dr., 70058-2275. Tel: 504-340-0444; Fax: 504-340-9521. Email: stjohnbosco@archdiocese-no.org. Web: www.archdiocese-no.org/sjbc.
Catechesis / Religious Program—Matthew LaGrange, Youth Min. Students 26.
3—ST. MARTHA (1973) Rev. Lich Van Nguyen; Deacons Tyrell Manieri; Larry Murphy.
Res.: 2555 Apollo Dr., 70058-5813. Tel: 504-366-1604; Fax: 504-366-1100.
Catechesis / Religious Program—Tel: 504-366-4142. Students 88.
Mission—Infant Jesus of Prague 700 Maple St., Jefferson Parish 70058-4008. Tel: 504-368-1397; Fax: 504-368-0662. Deacons Larry Murphy; Tyrell Manieri.
4—ST. ROSALIE (1949) Revs. John DiFiore, S.D.B.; Kenneth Rodes, S.D.B., Parochial Vicar.
Parish Offices—600 2nd Ave., 70058-2728. Tel: 504-340-1962; Fax: 504-340-1546.
Rectory—608 1st Ave., 70058-2799. Tel: 504-341-5656.
School—617 Second Ave., 70058-2798. Tel: 504-341-4342; Fax: 504-347-0271. Mary C. Wenzel, Prin. Lay Teachers 60; Students 800.
Catechesis / Religious Program—Students 73.

JEFFERSON, JEFFERSON PARISH, ST. AGNES (1931) Rev. Bac-Hai Viet Tran; Deacons Piero Caserta; Frank G. DiFulco.
Res.: 3310 Jefferson Hwy., 70121-2699. Tel: 504-833-3366; Fax: 504-834-1532. Email: stagneschurch@nocoxmail.com.
School—3410 Jefferson Hwy., 70121. Tel: 504-835-6486; Fax: 504-835-4295. Web: www.mystagnes.com. Lay Teachers 16; Students 187.
Catechesis / Religious Program—Students 61.

KENNER, JEFFERSON PARISH
1—DIVINE MERCY (2009), Merger of Nativity of Our Lord and St. Elizabeth Ann Seton, Kenner. Temporarily worshipping at Nativity of Our Lord and St. Elizabeth Ann Seton churches until completion of a new parish church. All sacramental records located at Divine Mercy parish office. Revs. David W. Dufour; Jeffrey A. Montz, Parochial Vicar; Deacons Andrea Capaci; Noel W. Martinsen.
Parish Office: 3325 Loyola Dr., 70065-2567. Tel: 504-466-5016; Fax: 504-467-8575. Email: office@divinemercyparish.org. Web: divinemercyparish.org.
School—St. Elizabeth Ann Seton, 4119 St. Elizabeth Dr., 70065. Tel: 504-468-3524; Fax: 504-469-6014. Web: www.seasparish.com/school. Joan Kathmann, Prin. Lay Teachers 29; Students 485.
Catechesis / Religious Program—Luke Arredonclo, D.R.E. (Elementary); Mari Pablo, Youth Min. (High School). Students 76.
2—ST. ELIZABETH ANN SETON (1981) Merged with Nativity of Our Lord, Kenner to form a new parish, Divine Mercy. For inquiries regarding sacramental records, contact Divine Mercy parish office.
3—ST. JEROME (1963) Rev. James J. Jeanfreau Jr.; Deacons Luis Campuzano Sr., Pastoral Assoc.; Daniel J. Cordes.
Res.: 2400 33rd St., 70065-3899. Tel: 504-443-3174; Fax: 504-443-5499.
Catechesis / Religious Program—Gail Bordelon, D.R.E. Students 144.
4—NATIVITY OF OUR LORD (1977) Merged with St. Elizabeth Ann Seton, Kenner to form Divine Mercy parish. For inquiries regarding sacramental records, contact Divine Mercy parish.
5—OUR LADY OF PERPETUAL HELP (1869) Revs. Richard M. Miles; Raymond J. Guillot, Parochial Vicar; Deacons Jeffrey Fariss; Greg A. Gross; Norbert Gubert; Sr. M. Michaeline Green, O.P., Pastoral Assoc.
Res.: 1908 Short St., 70062-7599. Tel: 504-464-0361; Fax: 504-465-0930.
School—Tel: 504-464-0531; Fax: 504-464-0725. Email: srglaeser@olphla.org. Web: www.olphla.org. Bro. Augustine Kozdroj, F.S.E., Prin. Franciscan Sisters 1; Lay Teachers 18; Students 218.
Catechesis / Religious Program—531 Williams Blvd., 70062. Web: www.perpetualhelp.org. Sr. Christella Emano, S.F.C.C., D.R.E. Students 70.

LA PLACE, ST. JOHN THE BAPTIST PARISH
1—ASCENSION OF OUR LORD (1979) Rev. Walter J. Austin; Deacon Thomas J. St. Pierre.
Res.: 799 Fairway Dr., 70068-2007. Tel: 985-652-2615; Fax: 985-652-7291. Email: rascension@comcast.net. Web: www.aolparish.org. 1900 Greenwood Dr., 70068.
School—1809 Greenwood Dr., 70068-2098. Tel: 985-652-4532; Fax: 985-651-5151. Email: office@aolcrusaders.org. Lay Teachers 14; Students 243.
Catechesis / Religious Program—Students 45.
2—ST. JOAN OF ARC (1947) [JC] Very Rev. John-Nhan Tran; Rev. Hoai Thanh Nguyen; Deacons Dominic J. Arcuri; Paul Cimino; Kenneth Madere.
Res.: 529 W. 5th St., 70068. Tel: 985-652-9100; Fax: 985-651-2920. Email: secretary@sjachurch.com. Web: www.sjachurch.com.
School—412 Fir St., 70068-4310. Tel: 985-652-6310; Fax: 985-652-6390. Web: www.sja-school.com. Mr. Larry J. Bourgeois Jr., Prin. Lay Teachers 40; Students 530.
Catechesis / Religious Program— Helena Cupit, D.R.E. Students 83.
Convent—Daughters of Divine Providence, 386 Fir St., 70068-3941. Tel: 985-359-3163.

LACOMBE, ST. TAMMANY PARISH
1—ST. JOHN OF THE CROSS (1984) Rev. Gilmer Martin; Deacons Ricky J. Suprean; Francis W. Drake; Steven L. Ferran; Margaret Zinser, Office Admin.
Res.: 61051 Brier Lake Dr., 70445-2911. Tel: 985-882-3779; Fax: 985-882-9282. Email: sjc1286@bellsouth.net. Web: home.catholicweb.com/stjohnofthecross/.
Community Center—61038 Brier Lake Dr., 70445-2911. Tel: 985-882-6625.
Catechesis / Religious Program—Tel: 985-882-6225. Liz Loga, D.R.E. Students 23.
2—SACRED HEART (1890) Rev. Kyle V. Dave; Deacons William P. Curry Jr.; Steven L. Ferran.
Res.: P.O. Box 1080, 70445-1080. Tel: 985-882-5229; Fax: 985-882-9034.
Catechesis / Religious Program—Tel: 985-882-8041. Students 117.

LAFITTE, JEFFERSON PARISH, ST. ANTHONY (1936) [CEM], Assumed parish territory of St. Pius X, Crown Point which became a mission of the parish. Rev. John Ryan. In Res., Rev. Donald Duffy (Retired).
Res.: 2653 Jean Lafitte Blvd., 70067. Tel: 504-689-4101; Fax: 504-689-4102.
Catechesis / Religious Program—Tel: 504-689-0069. Ms. Wendy M. Houin, D.R.E. (Elementary); Ms. Paula Martin, D.R.E. (High School). Students 320.
Mission—St. Pius X 8151 Barataria Blvd., Crown Point, 70072-9704.

LULING, ST. CHARLES PARISH
1—ST. ANTHONY OF PADUA (1961) Revs. David L. Rabe; Anton Ba Phan, Parochial Vicar.
Res.: 234 Angus Dr., 70070-4427. Tel: 985-785-8885; Fax: 985-785-8882.
Catechesis / Religious Program—Tel: 504-785-0050. Students 73.
2—HOLY FAMILY (1980) Rev. John M. Perino.
Res.: 155 Holy Family Ln., 70070-6103. Tel: 985-785-8585; Fax: 985-785-4983. Email: hlyfamilystaff@bellsouth.net.
Catechesis / Religious Program—Tel: 985-331-9100. Mrs. Andrea Alday, C.R.E. (High School); Mrs. Fran M. Petit, C.R.E. (Elementary). Students 487.

MADISONVILLE, ST. TAMMANY PARISH, ST. ANSELM (1962) Rev. Msgr. Frank J. Giroir; Deacon John Glover.
Res.: P.O. Box 40, 70447-0040. Tel: 985-845-7342; Fax: 985-845-3076.
Catechesis / Religious Program—Michael Barocco, D.R.E. Students 624.

MANDEVILLE, ST. TAMMANY PARISH
1—MARY, QUEEN OF PEACE (1988) Rev. Ronald L. Calkins; Deacons John J. Finn; George (Butch) Shartle; Edward Beckendorf.
Res.: 1501 W. Causeway Approach, 70471-3047. Tel: 985-626-6977; Fax: 985-626-6971. Email: mqop@maryqueenofpeace.org. Web: www.maryqueenofpeace.org.
School—1515 W. Causeway Approach, 70471. Tel: 985-674-2466; Fax: 985-674-1441. Email: school@maryqueenofpeace.org. Web: www.m-qop.org. Mrs. Sybil Skansi, Prin. Students 527.
Catechesis / Religious Program—Tel: 985-674-9794. Students 670.
2—OUR LADY OF THE LAKE ROMAN CATHOLIC CHURCH (1850) [JC] Revs. John Talamo; Joseph E. Cazenavette, Parochial Vicar; Deacons Ed Kelley; Jay C. Frantz; Jay J. Weil III.
Res.: 312 Lafitte St., 70448-5827. Tel: 985-626-5671; Fax: 985-626-5422. Email: oll@ollparish.info. Web: www.ollparish.info.
School—316 Lafitte St., 70448-5827. Tel: 985-626-5678; Fax: 985-626-4337. Email: pjohnson@ourladyofthelakeschool.org. Web: www.ourladyofthelakeschool.org. Frank Smith, Headmaster. Lay Teachers 44; Students 804.
Catechesis / Religious Program—Tel: 985-626-5671, Ext. 114. Email: suzanne@ollparish.info. Suzanne Blake, C.R.E. Students 673.

MARRERO, JEFFERSON PARISH
1—ST. AGNES LE THI THANH (1995), (Vietnamese), [JC], (Personal Parish for Southeast Asians) Rev. Joseph Pham Van Tue.
Mailing Address, Office & Rectory: 1000 Westwood Dr., 70072-2415. Tel: 504-347-4725; Fax: 504-340-2476.
Church: 6851 St. Le Thi Thanh St., 70072-2556.
Mission—Assumption of Mary 172 Noel Dr., Avondale, Jefferson Civil Parish 70094-2900. Rev. James Nguyen Bach, Admin.
Mission—St. Joseph 6450 Kathy Ct., Orleans Civil Parish 70131-7515. Rev. Peter Nam Van Tran, Admin.
Catechesis / Religious Program—Students 921.
2—IMMACULATE CONCEPTION (1924) Revs. Damian Hinojosa; David Nations, C.M., Parochial Vicar; Deacons Cesar C. Carillo; Gerard L. Labodot; Carmelitte Venturella, Business Mgr.; Janel Ockman, Music Dir.
Res.: 4401 7th St., 70072-2099. Tel: 504-341-9516; Fax: 504-341-9517. Email: icchurchparish@aol.com. Web: www.icchurchparish.org.
School—601 Avenue C, 70072-2098. Tel: 504-347-4409; Fax: 504-341-2766. Email: iconception@archdiocese-no.org. Web: icschargers.org. Sr. Maria Colombo, F.M.A., Prin. (Grade School). Salesian Sisters 2; Lay Teachers 53; Students 808.
Catechesis / Religious Program—Lynn Gordon, D.R.E. Students 125.
3—ST. JOACHIM (1985) Rev. G. Amaldoss.
Res.: 5505 Barataria Blvd., 70072-6660. Tel: 504-341-9226; Fax: 504-348-0093.
Catechesis / Religious Program—Mrs. Sarah Blair, D.R.E.; Donna Gagliano, D.R.E. Students 70.
4—ST. JOSEPH THE WORKER (1955) Rev. Otis W. Young Jr.
Res.: 455 Ames Blvd., 70072-1599. Tel: 504-347-8438; Fax: 504-340-9538.
Catechesis / Religious Program—Tel: 504-348-4784; Fax: 504-347-0852. Students 103.
5—THE VISITATION OF OUR LADY (1963) Revs. Michael J. Kettenring, Admin.; Bryan J. Howard, Parochial Vicar; Deacons James P. Rooney Jr.; James A. Venturella.
Res.: 3500 Ames Blvd., 70072-5699. Tel: 504-347-2203; Fax: 504-347-2223. Email: volchurch@vol.org. Web: www.vol.org.

School—3520 Ames Blvd., 70072-5698. Tel: 504-347-3377; Fax: 504-341-5378. Email: volschool@vol.org. Mrs. Carolyn Levet, Prin. Lay Teachers 39; Students 773.

Catechesis / Religious Program—Tel: 504-341-8477; Fax: 504-347-2223. Cheryl Tourelle, D.R.E. Students 151.

METAIRIE, JEFFERSON PARISH

1—ST. ANGELA MERICI (1964) Rev. Msgr. Kenneth J. Hedrick; Rev. Peter A. Tomczak, Parochial Vicar; Deacons Gilbert R. Schmidt; Nicholas Chetta; Raymond E. Heap; David P. Aaron.

Res.: 901 Beverly Garden Dr., 70002-5085. Tel: 504-835-0324; Fax: 504-834-9709. Web: www.stangela.org.

School—835 Melody Dr., 70002-5095. Tel: 504-835-8491; Fax: 504-835-4463. Web: www.stangelaschool.org. Mrs. Colleen Remont, Prin. Lay Teachers 30; Students 400.

Catechesis / Religious Program—Tel: 504-837-9347. Students 400.

2—ST. ANN CHURCH AND SHRINE (1971) Revs. Michael J. Schneller; Luke Hungdung Nguyen; Deacons Philip E. Doolen; Raymond J. Bertin; Thomas H. Fox.

4940 Meadowdale St., 70006-4040.

Res.: 4841 Meadowdale St., 70006-4037. Tel: 504-324-6028; Fax: 504-455-7076. Email: stannmet@bellsouth.net (Church Office). Web: stannchurchandshrine.org.

School—4921 Meadowdale St., 70006-4098. Tel: 504-455-8383; Fax: 504-455-9572. Email: stann@stannschool.org. Web: www.stannschool.org. Lay Teachers 53; Students 863.

Catechesis / Religious Program—Tel: 504-455-7071, Ext. 225. Email: stannreled@bellsouth.net. Students 175.

3—ST. BENILDE (1964) Rev. Patrick B. Wattigny; Deacons Clifford S. Wright; Biaggio DiGiovanni.

Res.: 1901 Division St., 70001-2798. Tel: 504-834-4980; Fax: 504-831-5810.

School—1801 Division St., 70001-2799. Tel: 504-833-9894; Fax: 504-834-4380. Web: www.stbenilde.com. Mrs. Vickie G. Helmsetter, Prin. Lay Teachers 14; Students 302.

Catechesis / Religious Program—Students 37.

4—ST. CATHERINE OF SIENA (1921) Revs. Eugene F. Jacques; Alberto Villosillo, Parochial Vicar; Deacons Michael Coney; Jere Crago, Pastoral Assoc.; Don M. Richard.

Res.: 105 Bonnabel Blvd., 70005-3736. Tel: 504-835-9343; Fax: 504-835-1525. Email: frgene@archdiocese-no.org. Web: www.stcatherineparish.com.

School—400 Codifer Blvd., 70005-3797. Tel: 504-831-1166; Fax: 504-833-8982. Web: www.stcatherine.k12.la.us. Mrs. Frances Dee Tarantino, Prin. Sisters of Charity of the Incarnate Word 2; Lay Teachers 69; Students 843.

Catechesis / Religious Program—Tel: 504-835-6648. Students 48.

5—ST. CHRISTOPHER THE MARTYR (1947) Revs. Frank Candalisa; Kevin T. DeLerno, Parochial Vicar; Deacons Charles Duke; Gerald J. Martinez; Frank Minor.

Res.: 309 Manson Ave., 70001-4898. Tel: 504-837-8214; Fax: 504-837-8303. Email: scmrectory@bellsouth.net.

School—(Grades Toddler-8), 3900 Derbigny St., 70001-4999. Tel: 504-837-6871; Fax: 504-834-0522. Email: arnochrist@archdiocese-no.org. Web: www-.stchristopherschool.org. Ruth Meche, Prin. Lay Teachers 40; Students (PreK) 141; Students (K-8) 598.

Catechesis / Religious Program—Students 97.

6—ST. CLEMENT OF ROME (1965) Revs. Luis F. Rodriguez; Peter P. Finney III, Parochial Vicar; Deacons Kenneth Boe; David Caldero.

Res.: 4317 Richland Ave., 70002-3097. Tel: 504-887-7821; Fax: 504-454-3906.

School—3978 W. Esplanade Ave., 70002-3099. Tel: 504-888-0386; Fax: 504-885-8273. Lay Teachers 40; Students 538.

Catechesis / Religious Program—Students 126.

7—ST. EDWARD THE CONFESSOR (1964) Very Rev. Gerald L. Seiler Jr.; Rev. Christian W. DeLerno, Parochial Vicar; Deacons Gerard J. Fasullo Sr.; Steven J. Koehler. In Res., Rev. Mark S. Raphael.

Parish Office:—4921 W. Metairie Ave., 70001-4466. Tel: 504-888-0703; Fax: 504-455-5443. Email: stedward@steddy.org. Web: www.steddy.org.

School—Tel: 504-888-6353; Fax: 504-456-0960. Dr. Thomas Becker, Prin. Sisters of the Living Word 2; Lay Teachers 29; Students 491.

Catechesis / Religious Program—Sr. Mary de Lourdes Charbonnet, S.L.W., D.R.E. Students 35.

Chapel—Hanmaum Korean Catholic Chapel 4812 W. Napoleon Ave., 70001-2364. Tel: 504-888-8772; Fax: 504-888-2366.

8—ST. FRANCIS XAVIER (1924) Rev. Msgr. Andrew C. Taormina; Deacons Robert D. Normand; Arthur G. Kingsmill.

Res.: 105 Vincent Ave., 70005. Tel: 504-834-0340 (Office); 504-837-4733 (Res./Rectory); Fax: 504-837-8735 (Office). Web: www.stfrancisxavier.com.

School—215 Betz Pl., 70005-4167. Tel: 504-833-1471; Fax: 504-833-1498. Barbara Martin, Prin. Lay Teachers 34; Students 440.

Catechesis / Religious Program—Tel: 504-834-0348. Students 115.

9—ST. LAWRENCE THE MARTYR (1958) Closed. Parish territory assigned to Our Lady of Divine Providence, Metairie. For inquiries regarding sacramental records, contact Our Lady of Divine Providence parish.

10—ST. LOUIS KING OF FRANCE (1947) Rev. Hoang Minh Tuong; Deacons J. Glen Casanova; Wilbur Martinez.

Res.: 1609 Carrollton Ave., 70005-1498. Tel: 504-834-9977; Fax: 504-834-9979.

School—1600 Lake Ave., 70005-1499. Tel: 504-833-8224; Fax: 504-838-9938. Pamela Schott, Prin. Lay Teachers 22; Students 260.

Catechesis / Religious Program—Students 35.

11—ST. MARY MAGDALEN (1955) Rev. Msgr. Robert D. Massett; Revs. Nicholas P. Pericone; Kenneth Allen; Deacons Angeles Robin; Henry Nuss. In Res., Rev. Nicholas P. Pericone.

Res.: 6425 W. Metairie Ave., 70003-4327. Tel: 504-733-0922; Fax: 504-733-0869. Email: magdalen@smm.nocoxmail.com. Web: www.stmarymagdalenchurch.com.

School—6421 W. Metairie Ave., 70003-4395. Tel: 504-733-1433; Fax: 504-736-0727. Email: stmarymag@archdiocese-no.org. Mrs. Kim Downes, Prin. Lay Teachers 28; Students 399.

Catechesis / Religious Program—Tel: 504-733-8980. Linda Earle, D.R.E. Students 98.

12—OUR LADY OF DIVINE PROVIDENCE (1965), Assumed parish territory of St. Lawrence the Martyr, Metairie. Revs. Michael J. Mitchell; Jose Roberto Gomez, Parochial Vicar; Deacons Fred C. Memleb Jr.; Roberto Angeli; Javier Olondo, Music Min.

Res.: 1000 N. Starrett Rd., 70003-5899. Tel: 504-466-4511; Fax: 504-466-4858. Web: www.oldp.org.

School—917 N. Atlanta St., 70003-5898. Tel: 504-466-0591; Fax: 504-466-0671. Email: oldp@archdiocese-no.org. Web: www.oldpschool.org. Mrs. Elvina DiBartolo, Prin. Lay Teachers 30; Students 251.

Catechesis / Religious Program— Mrs. Mickie Morris, D.R.E.; Willie Leonard, Youth Min. Students 160.

13—ST. PHILIP NERI (1960) Rev. Msgr. Henry J. Bugler; Deacons Paul G. Hauck; John P. LeDoux; Thomas P. Lotz; Mr. Joseph E. Murray Sr., Business Mgr.

Res.: 6500 Kawanee Ave., 70003-3298. Tel: 504-887-5535; Fax: 504-885-6259. Web: www.archdiocese-no.org/stphilipnerichurch.

School—6600 Kawanee Ave., 70003-3199. Tel: 504-887-5600; Fax: 504-456-6857. Web: www.stphilipneri.org. Dr. Carol Stack, Prin. Lay Teachers 59; Students 716.

Catechesis / Religious Program—Tel: 504-889-0089. Ruby Kirsch, Coord. Rel. Educ. Students 70.

NORCO, ST. CHARLES PARISH, SACRED HEART OF JESUS (1959) Rev. Msgr. Terry B. Becnel. In Res., Rev. John J. Marse.

Res.: 401 Spruce St., 70079-2137. Tel: 985-764-6503; Fax: 985-725-0512. Email: shn@archdiocese-no.org. Web: www.sacredheartchurchnorco.org.

School—453 Spruce St., 70079. Tel: 985-764-9958; Fax: 985-764-0041. Email: sacredhrtjesus@archdiocese-no.org. Web: sacredheartschoolnorco.org. Cheryl Orillion, Prin. Lay Teachers 14; Students 136.

Catechesis / Religious Program—Students 225.

PARADIS, ST. CHARLES PARISH, ST. JOHN THE BAPTIST (1971) Revs. Joseph Duc Dzien; Edward J. Lauden; Deacon Garland Bourgeois Jr.

Res.: P.O. Box 1498, 70080-1498. Tel: 985-758-2668; Fax: 985-758-2901. Email: stjohnch@bellsouth.net.

Catechesis / Religious Program—Tel: 985-758-1593. Students 90.

PEARL RIVER, ST. TAMMANY PARISH, SS. PETER AND PAUL (1970) Rev. Ray A. Hymel; Deacons John Patrick Downey; Richard W. Calkins; Eugene P. Templet.

Res.: 66192 St. Mary Dr., 70452-5705. Tel: 985-863-7935; Fax: 985-863-5431. Email: info@sppcprla.com. Web: www.sppcprla.com.

Catechesis / Religious Program—Students 148.

POINTE A LA HACHE, PLAQUEMINES PARISH, ST. THOMAS (1844) [CEM 2] Rev. Joseph M. Tran.

17605 Hwy. 15, 70082.

Catechesis / Religious Program—Students 55.

Mission—Assumption of Our Lady 6951 Hwy. 39, Braithwaite, Plaquemines Parish 70040-0063. Tel: 504-682-5607; Fax: 504-682-5617.

PORT SULPHUR, PLAQUEMINES PARISH, ST. PATRICK (1870) [CEM], Assumed St. Jude, Diamond and Our Lady of Good Harbor, Buras and its missions, St. Ann, Empire and St. Anthony, Boothville-Venice. Rev. Gerard P. Stapleton; Deacon Patrick R. Becnel.

Res.: 28698 Hwy. 23, 70083-9623. Tel: 504-564-6792; Fax: 504-564-9760.

Catechesis / Religious Program—Students 80.

RESERVE, ST. JOHN THE BAPTIST PARISH

1—OUR LADY OF GRACE (1937), (African American), Revs. Roderick J. D. Coates, S.S.J.; Christopher C. Amadi, S.S.J., Parochial Vicar; Deacon Larry D. Oney.

Res.: 772 Hwy. 44, P.O. Box 464, 70084-0464. Tel: 985-536-2613; Fax: 985-536-1819.

School—Tel: 985-536-4291; Fax: 985-536-4250. Stephanie Aubert, Prin. Lay Teachers 9; Students 229.

Catechesis / Religious Program—Tel: 985-536-2028. Myrtle Ann Lucas, D.R.E. Students 85.

2—ST. PETER (1864) [CEM] Rev. Martin J. Smullen; Deacon David W. Farinelli.

Res.: 1550 Hwy. 44, P.O. Box 435, 70084-0435. Tel: 985-536-2887; Fax: 985-536-7078.

School—Tel: 985-536-4296; Fax: 985-536-4305. Mrs. Paula Poche, Prin. Lay Teachers 18; Students 223.

Catechesis / Religious Program—Tel: 985-536-2886. Students 213.

RIVER RIDGE, JEFFERSON PARISH, ST. MATTHEW THE APOSTLE (1959) Rev. Burnick J. Terrebonne; Deacons Wayne A. Lobell; Nathan F. Simoneaux Jr.; Jerry B. Clark Sr. In Res., Rev. Warren L. Cooper.

Res.: 10021 Jefferson Hwy., 70123-2498. Tel: 504-737-4537; Fax: 504-737-4033.

School—Tel: 504-737-4604; Fax: 504-738-7985. Email: church@stmatthew.nocoxmail.com. Web: www.stmatthew-riverridge.4lpi.com. Lay Teachers 41; Students 554.

Catechesis / Religious Program—Students 92.

ST. BERNARD, ST. BERNARD PARISH, ST. BERNARD (1787) [CEM], Assumed parish territory of San Pedro Pescador, Florissant. Rev. John C. Arnone; Deacon Norbert P. Billiot Jr.

Mailing Address: P.O. Box 220, Saint Bernard, 70085. Tel: 504-281-2667; Fax: 504-281-2268.

Church: 2805 Bayou Rd., Saint Bernard, 70085-9748. Tel: 504-281-2267; Fax: 504-281-2268.

Catechesis / Religious Program—Rhonda Serpas, D.R.E. Students 43.

SLIDELL, ST. TAMMANY PARISH

1—ST. GENEVIEVE (1968) Rev. Jose Roel G. Lungay; Deacons Daniel Haggerty Jr.; Paul Mumme Sr.; Reginald J. Seymour; Ryan Rhodes, Music Min.

58203 Hwy. 433, 70460.

Res. and Mailing Address: 58031 St. Genevieve Ln., 70460. Tel: 985-643-0093 (Rectory); 985-643-3832 (Office); 985-641-6771 (Office); Fax: 985-649-5294 (Office). Email: stgenevieve@stgenevieve.us.

Catechesis / Religious Program—(Combined with St. Margaret Mary, Slidell) Ona New, D.R.E. Students 54.

Mission—Edolia Barros 35300 Laurent Rd., 70460. Tel: 985-641-2585. Email: edoliabarros@charter.net.

2—ST. LUKE THE EVANGELIST (1982) Very Rev. Mark Lomax; Rev. Joseph Thang Dinh Tran, Parochial Vicar; Deacons Robert Binney, (Retired); Harold Burke; Robert Trainor, (Retired); Ronald C. LeBlanc; Paul G. Augustin.

Office:—910 Cross Gates Blvd., 70461-8414. Tel: 985-641-6429; Fax: 985-847-0742. Email: office@stlukeslidell.org. Web: www.stlukeslidell.org.

Catechesis / Religious Program—Tel: 985-641-2570; Fax: 985-641-6570. Students 503.

3—ST. MARGARET MARY (1965) Rev. Msgr. Lanaux J. Rareshide; Rev. Thomas Kilasara; Deacons John C. Weber; Carlos A. Ramirez; Louis F. Bauer.

Res.: 1050 Robert Blvd., 70458-2098. Tel: 985-643-6124; Fax: 985-643-6126.

School—Tel: 985-643-4612; Fax: 985-643-4659. Mr. Bobby Ohler, Prin. Lay Teachers 36; Students 646.

Catechesis / Religious Program—Tel: 985-649-3055. Students 397.

4—OUR LADY OF LOURDES (1890) [CEM] Rev. Msgr. Frank J. Lipps; Rev. John P. Grenham, Parochial Vicar; Deacons Charles B. Faler Jr.; Robert Dunbar.

400 Westchester Blvd., 70458.

Res.: 3924 Berkley St., 70458-5143. Tel: 985-643-4137; Fax: 985-643-1675. Email: mguidry@ollourdes.org. Web: www.ollparish-slidell.com; www.ollonline.com.

School—345 Westchester Pl., 70458-5299. Tel: 985-643-3230; Fax: 985-645-0648. Mr. Robert V. Kiefer Jr., Prin. Lay Teachers 30; Students 500.

Catechesis / Religious Program—Tel: 985-643-4128. Email: pandrews@ollourdes.org. Mrs. Patricia S. Andrews, D.R.E. Students 278.

TERRYTOWN, JEFFERSON PARISH, CHRIST THE KING (1963) Rev. Michael Nam Hoang Nguyen; Deacons William B. Jarrell; Walfredo Corral; Kevin M. Steel; Cornelius Armshaw.

Res.: 535 Deerfield Rd., 70056-2899. Tel: 504-361-1500; Fax: 504-361-0632. Email: ckchurch@bellsouth.net. Web:

www.ctkterrytown.parishesonline.com.
School—2106 Deerfield Rd., 70056-2899. Tel: 504-367-3601; Fax: 504-367-3679. Email: christkingsch@archdiocese-no.org. Web: www.archdiocese-no.org/ctk. Lay Teachers 30; Students 350.
Catechesis/Religious Program—Students 123.

VIOLET, ST. BERNARD PARISH, OUR LADY OF LOURDES (1916) Rev. John C. Arnone; Deacon Norbert P. Billiot Jr.
Mailing Address: P.O. Box 462, 70092. Tel: 504-281-2667; Fax: 504-281-2268.
Church: 2621 Colonial Blvd., 70092. Tel: 504-281-2267.
Catechesis/Religious Program—Rhonda Serpas, D.R.E. Students 80.

WAGGAMAN, JEFFERSON PARISH, OUR LADY OF THE ANGELS (1978) [CEM] Rev. Patrick Gannon.
Res.: 139 Herman St., 70094-2404. Tel: 504-436-4459; Fax: 504-436-8465.
Catechesis/Religious Program—Students 71.

WESTWEGO, JEFFERSON PARISH, OUR LADY OF PROMPT SUCCOR (1920) [CEM] Rev. Edward M. Grice; Deacon Wilfred Robichaux Jr.
Res.: 146 Fourth St., 70094-4297. Tel: 504-341-9522; Fax: 504-341-5957. Email: olpschurch@olps.nocoxmail.com.
School—531 Avenue A, 70094-4294. Tel: 504-341-9505; Fax: 504-341-9508. Sr. Suzanne Miller, F.M.A., Prin. Sisters 4; Lay Teachers 15; Students 185.
Catechesis/Religious Program—Students 105.
Mission—Holy Guardian Angels Mission 1701 Bridge City Ave., Bridge City, Jefferson Parish 70094. Web: www.hgaparish.org.

Non-Parochial Churches & Chapels

NEW ORLEANS, ORLEANS PARISH

1—CHAPEL OF THE VIETNAMESE MARTYRS (1978), (Vietnamese), Rev. Nghiem Van Nguyen. In Res., Rev. Nguyen Van Nguyen.
Church: 14400 Peltier Dr., 70129-1713. Tel: 504-254-5660; Fax: 504-254-9250.
Catechesis/Religious Program—Students 545.

2—ST. JOSEPH CHAPEL (1895) Mailing Address: *c/o Archdiocesan Cemeteries Office*, 1000 Howard Ave, Ste. 500, 70113-1903. Tel: 504-596-3050; Fax: 504-596-3055. St. Joseph Cemetery, 2220 Washington Ave., 70113-2647. Tel: 504-488-4989; 504-488-5200.

3—ST. MARY CHAPEL (1845), (Shrine of St. Lazarus of Jerusalem), Mailing Address: 1100 Chartres St., 70116-2596.
Church: 1116 Chartes St., 70116-2596. Tel: 504-525-9585; Fax: 504-525-9583.

4—ST. MARY'S ASSUMPTION (1858), (German), Revs. Richard Thibodeau, C.Ss.R.; Eugene Harrison, C.Ss.R, Parochial Vicar; Terrence McCloskey, C.Ss.R., Parochial Vicar; Bro. Thomas Wright, C.Ss.R., Pastoral Assoc.
Church: 2030 Constance St., 70130-5099. Tel: 504-522-6748; Fax: 504-523-3734.
Catechesis/Religious Program—Students 75.

5—ST. MARY'S CHAPEL Revs. Richard Thibodeau, C.Ss.R.; Eugene Harrison, C.Ss.R.
1516 Jackson Ave., 70130. Tel: 504-522-6748.

6—OUR LADY OF PROMPT SUCCOR NATIONAL SHRINE (1926) Mailing Address: 2734 Nashville Ave., 70115. Church: 2701 State St., 70118-6399. Tel: 504-866-0200; Fax: 504-866-8300.

7—ST. ROCH CHAPEL, St. Roch Cemetery, St. Roch Ave. & Music St., 70117-8223. Tel: 504-304-0576; 504-482-5065. Mailing Address: *c/o Archdiocesan Cemeteries Office*, 1000 Howard Ave., Ste. 500, 70113. Tel: 504-596-3050; Fax: 504-596-3055.

MANDEVILLE, ST. TAMMANY PARISH, ST. DYMPHNA CATHOLIC CENTER AND CHAPEL (1971) Rev. Raphael Barousse, O.S.B., Chap.; Deacons Louis F. Bauer; Ronald C. LeBlanc, Dir. Pastoral Care; Ricky J. Suprean.
Southeast Louisiana Hospital, P.O. Box 3850, 70470-3850. Tel: 504-626-6317.

METAIRIE, JEFFERSON PARISH, HANMAUM KOREAN CATHOLIC CHAPEL (1990) Rev. Jung Yeon Kim (Korea, South), Chap.
4812 W. Napoleon Ave., 70001-2364. Tel: 504-888-2366; Fax: 504-888-8772.

Pilgrimage Shrines

NEW ORLEANS, ORLEANS PARISH

1—NATIONAL SHRINE OF BLESSED FRANCIS XAVIER SEELOS (2000) Rev. Byron J. Miller, C.Ss.R., Dir.
919 Josephine St., 70130-5071. Tel: 504-525-2495; Fax: 504-581-9181. Web: www.seelos.org.

2—OUR LADY OF PROMPT SUCCOR NATIONAL SHRINE (1926) Sr. Carla Dolce, O.S.U., Prioress.
Mailing Address: *Ursuline Convent*, 2734 Nashville Ave., 70115.
Res.: 2705 State St., 70118-6399. Tel: 504-866-0200; Fax: 504-866-8300.

3—SHRINE OF ST. JUDE THADDEUS (1826), (African American), Rev. Anthony Rigoli, O.M.I.
411 N. Rampart St., 70112-3594. Tel: 504-525-1551; Fax: 504-525-1827.
Catechesis/Religious Program—Tel: 504-522-8546. Students 65.

4—SHRINE OF ST. LAZARUS OF JERUSALEM Rev. Msgr. Crosby W. Kern, Rector.
Mailing Address: 1100 Chartres St., 70116-2596.
Church: 1116 Chartres St., 70116-2596. Tel: 504-525-9585; Fax: 504-525-9583.

METAIRIE, JEFFERSON PARISH, ST. ANN NATIONAL SHRINE (1971) Rev. Michael J. Schneller.
4940 Meadowdale St., 70006-4040. 3601 Transcontinental Dr., 70006.
Church: 4940 Meadowdale St., 70006-4040. Tel: 504-455-7071; Fax: 504-455-7076. Email: stannmet@bellsouth.net. Web: stannchurchandshrine.org.
Catechesis/Religious Program—Students 175.

Non-Parochial Community

NEW ORLEANS, ORLEANS PARISH, ST. NICHOLAS OF MYRA BYZANTINE CATHOLIC MISSION (1976), Ruthenian Rite Church Jurisdiction. Rev. Phillip J. Linden Jr., S.S.J.; Deacons Eric H. Gamble; Gregory Haddad, Mission Admin.
Mailing Address: P.O. Box 1359, Gray, 70359-1359. Church: 2435 S. Carrollton Ave., 70118. Tel: 504-861-0806; Fax: 985-872-9123. Email: stnicholasnola@yahoo.com.

Chaplains of Public Institutions

Hospitals

NEW ORLEANS. *Children's Hospital*, 200 Henry Clay Ave., 70118. Tel: 504-899-9511. Rev. Randy P. Roux, Chap., Deacons Thomas P. Lotz, Pastoral Min., Glenn Wiltz Sr., Pastoral Min.
Kindred Hospital, 3601 Coliseum St., 70115-3687. Tel: 504-899-1555; Fax: 504-899-1509. Deacons Frank G. DiFulco, Pastoral Min., Daniel F. Reynolds, Pastoral Min.
Ochsner Baptist Medical Center, 2700 Napoleon Ave., 70115-6996. Tel: 504-899-9311. Rev. Msgr. Henry H. Engelbrecht, Chap. Baptist Campus
Touro Infirmary, 1401 Foucher St., 70115-3593. Tel: 504-897-7011. Rev. Douglas C. Brougher, Dir., Pastoral Care & Chap. Tel: 504-897-7011; 504-899-1378.
University Hospital, 2021 Perdido St., 70112-1396. Tel: 504-903-3000. Rev. Eutiquiano Miguel, O.F.M.Cap., Chap.

COVINGTON. *Lakeview Regional Medical Center*, 95 E. Fairway Dr., 70433. Tel: 504-867-3800. Deacon Edward F. Kelley, Pastoral Min.
St. Tammany Hospital, 1202 S. Tyler St., 70433. Tel: 504-898-4000. Attended by Priests and Deacons from West St. Tammany Deanery.

GRETNA. *Ochsner Medical Center, West Bank*, 2500 Belle Chasse Hwy., 70056-7127. Tel: 504-392-3131. Rev. Terence Hayden (Ireland), Chap., Deacons James P. Rooney Jr., Pastoral Min., Leslie D. Vincent, Dir. Pastoral Care.

JEFFERSON. *Ochsner Foundation Hospital*, 1516 S. Clearview Pkwy., 70121-2484. Tel: 504-842-3000. Rev. Edmund Akordor, Chap.

MANDEVILLE. *Southeast Louisiana Hospital*, P.O. Box 3850, 70470-3850. Tel: 504-626-6317; Fax: 504-626-6658. Rev. Raphael Barousse, O.S.B., Chap., Deacons Ronald C. LeBlanc, Dir. Pastoral Ministry, Louis F. Bauer, Pastoral Min., Ricky J. Suprean, Pastoral Min.

MARRERO. *West Jefferson General Hospital*, 4500 11th St., 70072-3191. Tel: 504-347-5511. Vacant.
Wynhoven Health Care Center, 1050 Medical Center Blvd., 70072-3170. Tel: 504-347-0777. Rev. Denver B. Pentecost, Chap.

METAIRIE. *East Jefferson General Hospital*, 4200 Houma Blvd., 70002-2970. Tel: 504-454-4000. Rev. John J. Marse, Chap., Deacons Raymond E. Heap, Pastoral Min., Gary J. Borne, Pastoral Min., Joseph G. Casanova, Pastoral Min., Steven J. Koehler, Pastoral Min.
Tulane Lakeside Hospital, 4700 S.1-10 Service Rd. West, 70001. Tel: 504-780-8282. Deacon Gerard L. Labadot, Pastoral Min.

SLIDELL. *Greenbriar Nursing & Convalescent Home*, 505 Robert Rd., 70458-1699. Tel: 985-643-6900. Rev. Thomas Kilasara, Chap.
Guest House of Slidell Nursing Home, 1051 Robert Rd., 70458-2011. Tel: 985-643-5630. Rev. Thomas Kilasara, Chap.
Live Oak Village Assisted Living Community, 2200 Gause Blvd. E., 70461-8414. Tel: 985-781-4545. Chaplain: Priests and Deacons of St. Luke the Evangelist, Slidell.
North Shore Living Center, 106 Medical Center Dr., 70461-7833. Tel: 985-643-0307. Attended by St. Luke the Evangelist, Slidell.
North Shore Regional Medical Center, 100 Medical Center Dr., 70461-7833. Tel: 985-649-7070. Attended by St. Luke the Evangelist, Slidell.
Slidell Memorial Hospital, 1001 Gause Blvd., 70458-2987. Tel: 985-643-2200. Attended by St. Margaret Mary, Slidell.
Trinity Neurologic Rehabilitation Center at Slidell, 1400 W. Lindberg Dr., 70458-3193. Tel: 985-641-4985. Rev. Thomas Kilasara, Chap.

Colleges and Universities

NEW ORLEANS. *Delgado College*, 615 City Park Ave., 70119.
Delgado Community College, School of Nursing, 1450 Claiborne Ave., 70112.
Louisiana State University Medical Center.
Southern University in New Orleans, 6400 Press Dr., 70126.
Tulane Catholic Center, 1037 Audubon St., 70118-5294. Tel: 504-866-0984. Rev. Charles K. Johnson, O.P., Dir. Ministry.
University of New Orleans, UNO Newman Center, 2000 Lakeshore Dr., 70148-0001. Tel: 504-288-6336. Rev. Paul H. Desrosiers, Chap.

Prisons

NEW ORLEANS. *Orleans Parish Criminal Sheriff's Office Community Correctional Center*, 2800 Gravier St., 70119. Tel: 504-826-7050. Rev. Theodore M. Kalamaja, S.J., Chap.

ANGIE. *Rayburn Correctional Center*, 27268 Hwy. 21, 70426-3030. Tel: 985-848-5232. Deacon Michael J. Talbot, Pastoral Min. (Dedicated to Sen. Rayburn)

ANGOLA. *Louisiana State Penitentiary*.
17544 Tunica Trace, 70712. Tel: 225-655-4411.

CHALMETTE. *St. Bernard Parish Prison*, St. Bernard Courthouse, 70043-4793. Tel: 504-279-8823. (Vacant)

GRETNA. *Jefferson Parish Correctional Center*, P.O. Box 388, 70054-0388. Tel: 504-374-7700, Ext. 3109. Rev. John F. Paul, S.J., Chap., Deacons William B. Jarrell, Pastoral Min., James A. Venturella, Pastoral Min.

HARVEY. *Rivarde Juvenile Detention Home*, 1525 Manhattan Blvd., 70058-3405. Tel: 504-392-2097. Deacons Tyrell Manieri, Pastoral Min., John J. Walker IV.

MANDEVILLE. *St. Tammany Parish Prison*, Tel: 985-892-8324. Deacon Eugene P. Templet, Pastoral Min.

On Special Assignment:
Revs.—
Bermudez, Alberto, Chap., Chateau de Notre Dame Nursing Home and Apartments, New Orleans
Cooper, Warren L., Min. to Ill Priests; Hospital Chap. Coord.
Jambon, Jeffery, Northshore Hispanic Min.
Maestri, William F., M.Div., M.A., Archdiocesan Medical Ethics Liaison

---

On Duty Outside the Archdiocese:
Rev. Msgr.—
Calkins, Arthur B., Villa Stritch, Via della Nocetta, 63, 00164, Rome, Italy.
Revs.—
deWater, Joseph M., Riinsburgerweg, 4W59A 2215 RA, Voorhout, The Netherlands.
Paysse, Wayne C., Black and Indian Mission Office, 2021 H St., N.W., Washington, DC 20006.
Planea, John (Philippines), Holy Infant Mission, Santo Nino, W. Samar 6711 Philippines.

On Administrative Leave:
Revs.—
Fraser, Michael B.
Kinane, Gerard P.
Sanders, Patrick B.

On Medical Leave of Absence:
Revs.—
Berner, Francis
Mongeon, Peter M.

Retired:
Most Revs.—
Hughes, Alfred C., S.T.D., 2901 S. Carrollton Ave., 70125.
Carmon, Dominic, S.V.D., D.D., 3270 Continental Dr., Kenner, 70065-2663.
Rev. Msgrs.—
Bilinsky, William, 84031 Pine Dr., Folsom, 70437.
Byrnes, Donald M., 2832 Burdette St., Apt. 416, 70125.
Carroll, Ralph E., 3724 Whitney Pl., Metairie, 70002.
Doskey, Clinton J., J.C.L., St. Pius X, 6666 Spanish Fort Blvd., 70124-4398. Adjutant Judicial Vicar, Metropolitan Tribunal
Duke, Charles J., 3513 Lemon St., Metairie, 70006.
Glasgow, T. Gaspard, St. John Vianney Villa, 4701 Wichers Dr., Apt. B, Marrero, 70072.
Hebert, Ray P., St. John Vianney Villa, 4701 Wichers Dr., Apt. D, Marrero, 70072.

Hecker, Lawrence A., 1419 Milan St., Apt. 101, 70115.
Hotard, Howard H., 75352 River Rd., Covington, 70435.
LeBourgeois, Louis P., 70212 Nancy Rd., 70471.
Lorio, Joseph O., The Haven II, 8215 YMCA Plaza Dr., Apt. 257, Baton Rouge, 70810.
Luminais, J. Anthony, P.O. Box 344, Hanceville, AL 35077-0344.
Roeten, Winus, 9512 Kuepferle Ct., River Ridge, 70123.
Roppolo, Ignatius M., 2820 Burdette St., Apt. 707, 70125.
Roy, Allen J., St. John Vianney Villa, 4701 Wichers Dr., Apt. H, Marrero, 70072.
Schutten, Marion F., 19392 Crawford Rd., Covington, 70434.
Tomasovich, John A., 69 Lake Lynn Dr., Harvey, 70058.
Vincent, Robert G., P.O. Box 459, LaPlace, 70069-0459.

Revs.—
Barattini, John H., Casella Postale 79, 16043, Chiavari, Italy.
Braud, Ronald J., 2820 Burdette St., Apt. 604, 70125.
Brignac, H. L., 1400 Haring Rd., La Place, 70068.
Caluda, Charles J., 3205 Bayou Rd., Saint Bernard, 70085.
Carabello, Francis J., 840 Oakwood Dr., Terrytown, 70056.
Dabria, Jerry J., 1117 Melody Dr., Metairie, 70002.
Dixon, James R., St. Anthony Rectory, 901 N.E. 2nd St., Fort Lauderdale, FL 33301-1621.
Duffy, Donald, 2653 Jean Lafitte Blvd., Lafitte, 70067.
Ferlita, Ernest, S.J., 6321 Stratford Pl., 70131.
Fernandez, Luis J., VA Medical Center, 6863 S.W. 16th St., Miami, FL 33155-1709.
Ferrie, Francis, 8128 Plum St., 70118-2012.
Finn, John P., 122 Oak Ln., Luling, 70070.
Green, Austin E., O.P., 4640 Canal St., 70119.
Griffin, Thomas A., S.J., 6321 Stratford Pl., 70131.
Hall, Adrian B., 3310 Jefferson Hwy., Jefferson, 70121.
Heffner, Carroll, 3310 Jefferson Hwy., Jefferson, 70121.
Highfill, Brian H., 1271 Mound House St., Las Vegas, NV 89110-5900. (Retired Military)
Jenniskens, Thomas J., S.J., Ignatius Residence, 6321 Stratford Pl., 70131-7325.
Kennedy, Patrick J. R., 924 Monroe St., Gretna, 70053-2299.
Kennelly, Michael F., S.J., Ignatius Residence, 6321 Stratford Pl., 70131-7325.
Kissinger, Rodney T., S.J., Ignatius Residence, 6321 Stratford Pl., 70131-7325.
Lesseps, Roland J., S.J., B.S., Ph.D., Ignatius Residence, 6321 Stratford Pl., 70131.
Lobo, Raul Venust, St. John Vianney Villa, 4701 Wichers Dr., Apt. F, Marrero, 70072.
McCown, Robert M., SJ, B.A., B.S., M.A., Ignatius Residence, 6321 Stratford Pl., 70131.
McGough, William J., 309 W. 9th Ave., Covington, 70433.
Mead, James Herbert, S.J., B.A., S.T.L., Ph.D., S.T.B., Ignatius Residence, 6321 Stratford Pl., 70131-7325.
Meyer, Leo A., 805 Rue Decatur, Metairie, 70005.
Mitchell, Royce J., 2820 Burdette St., Apt. 706, 70125.
Monzillo, Oneil, 532 Indian Bluff, Apt. #104, Las Vegas, NV 89145.
Morgan, Brendan P., P.O. Box 73128, Metairie, 70033.
Nguyen, Joseph Luu, S.D.D., 13401 N. Lemans St., 70129.
O'Donnell, William J., J.C.L., 80335 Hollowhill Rd., Bush, 70431.
O'Grady, Peter, 411 Shrewsbury Rd., Jefferson, 70121.
O'Neill, Michael F., 620 Birkdale Cove, Niceville, FL 32578.
Pearce, Donald, S.J., Ignatius Residence, 6321 Stratford Pl., 70131-7325.
Perera, Denzil M., 1236 N. Rampart St., 70116.
Perkovic, Anton, 444 Adair St., 70448.
Pham, Bernardo Son, S.D.D., 13401 N. Lemans St., 70129.
Piovan, Benjamin, Mission San Miguel Archangel, Ave. Central 4649 Y Calle 44, Col Vista Hermosa, C.P. 25010, Saltillo Coahuila, Mexico.
Poche, Louis, S.J., Ignatius Residence, 6321 Stafford Pl., 70131.
Qui, Vincent, 21 Pat Dr., Avondale, 70094.
Racivitch, Herve P., S.J., B.A., L.L.B., S.T.L., Ignatius Residence, 6321 Stratford Pl., 70131-7325.
Ratchford, Robert J., S.J., B.S., S.T.L., Ph.D., Ignatius Residence, 6321 Stratford Pl., 70131-7325.
Reynolds, Fred G., S.J., 6321 Stratford Pl., 70131.
Schott, James E., 501 Lake Ave., Apt. 3A, Metairie, 70005.
Schroder, John F., S.J., Ignatius Residence, 6321 Stratford Pl., 70131.
Serio, Anthony, 3809 Hudson St., Metairie, 70006.
Texada, David Ker, 1923 Salem St., Alexandria, 71301-3840.
Thomas, Curtis R., 911 Woods Run Rd., Bardstown, KY 40004.
Tranchina, Joseph, 2820 Burdette St., Apt. 418, 70125.
Trinchard, Paul, 7117 Edgewater Dr., 70471.
Trutter, Carl B., O.P., Our Lady of Wisdom Healthcare Center, 5600 General De Gaulle Dr., 70131.
Vitte, Jules, Le Grand Angle, 9 Rue Jean Dollfus, 90.000 Belfort, France.
Vu, J.B Han, 12772 Louise St., Garden Grove, CA 92841.
Walsh, Laurence, Lyrattin, Ballinamult, Co. Waterford, Ireland.
White, Anthony J., St. John Vianney Villa, 4701 Wichers Dr. Apt. E, Marrero, 70072.

Permanent Deacons:
Aaron, David P., St. Angela Merici, Metairie
Adams, Dennis F., St. Peter, Covington
Alexander, Dwight, St. Raymond & St. Leo the Great, New Orleans
Angeli, Santiago Roberto, Pastoral Min., Ozanam Inn, New Orleans; Our Lady of Divine Providence, Metairie
Arcuri, Dominic Joseph, St. Joan of Arc, La Place
Ardoin, James Clyde, St. Peter, Covington
Armshaw, Cornelius, (Retired)
Attaway, Charles, (On Leave)
Augustin, Paul G., St. Luke the Evangelist, Slidell; Pastoral Min, Reconcile New Orleans/Cafe Reconcile
Balderas, Robert, Sr., (Retired)
Bauer, Louis F., St. Margaret Mary, Slidell; Pastoral Min., Southeast Louisiana Hospital, Mandeville
Beaumont, Robert G., Sr., Master of Ceremonies
Beckendorf, Edward, Mary Queen of Peace, Mandeville
Becnel, Patrick R., St. Patrick, Port Sulphur; Pastoral Min., Plaquemines Parish Sheriff's Office
Bertin, Raymond J., St. Ann Church and Shrine, Metairie
Bertucci, Christopher A., St. Pius X, New Orleans
Beyer, Walter L., (Retired)
Bialas, James, Diaconate Formation, Our Lady of the Rosary, New Orleans
Bienvenu, Roland, (Retired)
Billiot, Norbert P., Jr., Our Lady of Lourdes, Violet; St. Bernard, St. Bernard
Binney, Robert, (Retired)
Blanchard, John, (Retired)
Boe, Kenneth, St. Clement of Rome, Metairie
Borne, Gary J., St. Rita, Harahan; Pastoral Min, East Jefferson General Hospital
Bourgeois, Donald E., St. Jane de Chantal, Abita Springs
Bourgeois, Garland, Jr., St. John the Baptist, Paradis; St. Gertrudes, Des Allemands; Pastoral Min., St. Charles Parish Prison
Brady, Richard, Perm. Diaconate Adv. Bd., St. Louis Cathedral; Master of Ceremonies
Broussard, Terrel J., St. Peter Claver
Burke, Harold, St. Luke the Evangelist; Pastoral Min., Pope John Paul II High School; Pastoral Min., Northshore Regional Medical Center; Slidell
Caffery, Thomas E., Jr., Perm. Diaconate Adv. Bd., Most Holy Trinity, Covington
Caldero, David, Pastoral Assoc., St. Clement of Rome, Metairie
Calkins, Richard W., Chap., SS. Peter & Paul, Pearl River; Perm. Diaconate Personnel Bd.
Calvin, Larry Lee, All Saints, New Orleans
Campeaux, Barry G., (On Duty Outside the Diocese)
Campuzano, Luis A., Pastoral Assoc., St. Jerome, Kenner
Capaci, Andrea, Dir., Family Life Apostolate; Divine Mercy, Kenner; Appointed Special Advocate, Metropolitan Tribunal; Pastoral Min., Archbishop Chapelle High School
Carrillo, Cesar Cornelio, Immaculate Conception, Marrero
Casanova, Joseph Glen, Pastoral Min., East Jefferson Hospital; St. Louis King of France, Metairie
Caserta, Piero, St. Agnes, Jefferson; Pastoral Min., Covenant House
Chetta, Nicholas, St. Angela Merici, Metairie
Cimino, Paul, St. Joan of Arc, La Place
Clark, Jerry B., Sr., St. Matthew the Apostle, River Ridge
Coney, Michael, St. Catherine of Siena, Metairie
Cordes, Daniel J., St. Jerome, Kenner
Corral, Walfredo, Christ the King, Terrytown; Pastoral Min., Ozanam Inn
Coudrain, Mark C., St. Jane de Chantal, Abita Springs
Crago, Jere, Pastoral Assoc., St. Catherine of Siena, Metairie
Curry, William P., Jr., Sacred Heart, Lacombe
Daigle, Irving J., (On Duty Outside the Archdiocese)
Dardis, Joseph M., St. Anthony of Padua, New Orleans
Deichmann, Richard, (Retired)
DeLeon, Ildefonso R., St. Maria Goretti, New Orleans
Dempsey, Patrick L., St. Cletus, Gretna; Dir., Apostleship of the Sea & Stella Maris Ministry
DiFulco, Frank G., St. Agnes, Jefferson; Pastoral Min., Kindred Hospital
DiGiovanni, Biaggio, St. Benilde, Metairie; Exec. Dir., Ozanam Inn, New Orleans
DiGrado, Chris, Master of Ceremonies, St. Patrick, New Orleans
Donnaud, Paul J., (Retired)
Doolen, Philip E., Pastoral Assoc., St. Ann Church & Shrine, Metairie
Dorsey, Dan, (Retired)
Dorvin, Edwin, (Retired)
Downey, John Patrick, SS Peter and Paul, Pearl River; Pastoral Min., Southeast Louisiana State Hospital, Mandeville
Drake, Francis W., St. John of the Cross, Lacombe
Duet, Ferris J., Jr., (On Leave of Absence)
Duffy, Peter E., J.D., (Retired)
Duke, Charles, St. Christopher the Martyr, Metairie
Dunbar, Robert, Our Lady of Lourdes, Slidell
Duplechain, Raphael, Jr., Permanent Diaconate, Dir.
Durbin, Oscar A., (Retired)
Durr, Uriel Andrew, Our Lady Star of the Sea, New Orleans; Pastoral Min., Cabrini High School
Faler, Charles B., Jr. Our Lady of Lourdes, Slidell
Farinelli, David W., Coord., Marriage Preparation & Enrichment, Family Life Apostolate
Fariss, Jeffrey, Our Lady of Perpetual Help, Kenner
Fasullo, Gerard, Sr., St. Edward the Confessor, Metairie; Master of Ceremonies
Ferran, Steven L., Our Lady of the Lake, Mandeville; Asst. Dir., Perm. Diaconate; Vice Pres., Catholic Identity and Mission, Catholic Charities
Ferretti, Anthony J., (Retired)
Finn, John Joseph, Mary Queen of Peace, Mandeville
Flynn, Dan, St. Rita, Harahan; Catholic Committee on Boy Scouting
Fonseca, Rodrigo Alonso, Center of Jesus the Lord, New Orleans; Prison Apostolate
Foster, Oscar G., III, St. Maria Goretti; Pastoral Min., Ozanam Inn
Fox, Thomas H., St. Ann Church & Shrine; Pastoral Min., Holy Cross High School
Frantz, Jay C., Our Lady of the Lake Roman Catholic Church, Mandeville
Fray, Ralph, (Retired)
Frilot, George H., II, (On Leave)
Gabriel, Brian A., Our Lady Star of the Sea, New Orleans
Gamble, Eric H., (On Leave)
Garon, Henry A., (Retired)
Glapion, Lloyd St. Clair, (Retired)
Glennon, William A., Jr., (Retired), St. Pius X, New Orleans
Glover, John A., St. Anselm, Madisonville
Gross, Greg Andrew Nicholas, Our Lady of Perpetual Help, Kenner; Pastoral Min., Ozanam Inn
Gubert, Norbert, Our Lady of Perpetual Help, Kenner
Guidry, Ronald, Master of Ceremonies, St. Louis Cathedral, New Orleans
Guitterrez, Clayton J., (On Leave)
Guntherberg, Thomas James, (On Leave)
Haggerty, Daniel, Jr., Dir. Pastoral Care, F.B.I. & Slidell Police Dept.; St. Genevieve, Slidell
Hamm, John David, (Retired)
Hartman, Charles, (Retired)
Hauck, Paul G., St. Philip Neri, Metairie; Pastoral Min., Ozanam Inn
Heap, Raymond E., Pastoral Min., East Jefferson Hospital, Metairie; St. Angela Merici, Metairie
Heine, Charles, (Administrative Leave)
Herrick, Dean D., Holy Name of Mary, Algiers; Pastoral Min., Ozanam Inn
Houston, Lawrence C., St. Peter Claver, New Orleans
Howard, John, (Retired)
Huck, Lloyd E., St. Dominic, New Orleans
Insley, J. Vernon, St. Bonaventure, Avondale
Jackson, Earl D., Sr., (On Duty Outside Archdiocese)
Jarrell, William B., Christ the King, Terrytown; Dir., Archdiocese Prisons Ministry

Johnson, David L., (On Duty Outside the Diocese)
Johnson, Dwight J., (On Leave)
Jones, Melvin C., Sr., (Retired)
Kelley, Edward Francis, Our Lady of the Lake, Mandeville; Pastoral Min., Lakeview Regional Hospital
Kingsmill, Arthur George, St. Francis Xavier, Metairie & Archdiocesan Metropolitan Tribunal, New Orleans
Klause, Brian Joseph, St. Bonaventure, Avondale; Pastoral Min., Jefferson Parish Correctional Center, Gretna
Koehler, Steven J., St. Edward the Confessor, Metairie; Pastoral Min., East Jefferson General Hospital
Labadot, Gerard L., Pastoral Min., Tulane University Hosp.
Labranche, Frans, Jr., J.D., St. Jane de Chantal, Abita Springs; Assoc. Judge, Metropolitan Tribunal
Landry, Coy, (Retired)
LeBlanc, Nolen J., St. Rita, Harahan
LeBlanc, Ronald C., St. Luke the Evangelist, Slidell; Pastoral Min., Southeast Louisiana Hospital
LeDoux, John P., St. Philip Neri, Metairie
Lewis, Raymond, (Retired)
Lobell, Wayne A., St. Matthew the Apostle, River Ridge; Stella Maris Port Ministry
Lorenz, Fallon Herbert, (On Duty Outside the Archdiocese)
Lotz, Thomas P., St. Philip Neri, Metairie; Pastoral Min., Children's Hospital
Luke, Nelvin, St. Benedict Church, St. Benedict
Madere, Kenneth P., St. Joan of Arc, La Place
Mallerich, Walton J., (On Leave)
Manieri, Tyrell, St. Martha, Harvey; Infant Jesus of Prague Mission; Pastoral Min., Rivarde Juvenile Detention Center, Gretna
Martinez, Gerald J., Dir. Archdiocese Stewardship, St. Christopher the Martyr, Metairie
Martinez, Wilbur, (Retired)
Martinsen, Noel W., Divine Mercy, Kenner; Pastoral Min., St. Charles Parish Correctional Center
Matherne, Landry, (Retired)
Memleb, Fred C., Jr., (On Leave), Our Lady of Divine Providence, Metairie
Mendel, August B., (Retired)
Mendieta, Roberto, (Retired)
Miller, Graylin J., St. Paul the Apostle, New Orleans; Pastoral Min., Orleans Parish Correctional Center
Minor, Francis M., St. Christopher the Martyr, Metairie
Mire, Louis N., (Retired)
Mistretta, Nicholas L., (Retired)
Morales, G. Ernesto, (Retired)
Mumme, Paul, Sr., St. Genevieve, Slidell
Murphy, Larry, Adv. Formation Program, St. Martha, Harvey; Infant Jesus of Prague Mission, Harvey
Normand, Robert D., St. Francis Xavier, Metairie; Advocate, Metropolitan Tribunal
Nunez, Charles R., Sr., (Retired)
Nuss, Henry, St. Mary Magdalen, Metairie
Ohlmeyer, Sterling, (Retired)
Oney, Larry D., St. Louis Cathedral & Our Lady of Grace, Reserve; Perm. Diaconate Advis. Bd.
Parulan, Lino G., Our Lady of Prompt Succor, Chalmette; Pastoral Min., Stella Maris Port Ministry
Perez, Jose D., (Duty Outside)
Pierre, Warren R., St. John the Baptist, Edgard; Pastoral Min., Nelson Coleman Correctional Center, St. Charles Parish
Pippenger, John, St. Dominic, New Orleans
Ramirez, Carlos Alfredo, St. Margaret Mary, Slidell; E. Northshore Hispanic Apostolate
Rayfield, Rudolph J., Sr., Our Lady of Guadalupe, New Orleans, Exec. Dir., Society of St. Vincent de Paul
Read, Charles, Jr., (Retired)
Reynolds, Daniel F., Holy Spirit; Pastoral Min., Kindred Hospital, New Orleans
Rhodes, Frank W., Jr., (On Duty Outside the Archdiocese)
Richard, Don Michael, St. Catherine of Siena, Metairie
Richardson, Ray, (On duty Outside Archdiocese)
Rivere, Raymond H., (Retired)
Rizzo, Peter C., Transfiguration of the Lord, New Orleans
Robicheaux, Wilfred, Jr., Our Lady of Prompt Succor, Westwego; Holy Guardian Angels Mission, Bridge City
Robin, Angelas, St. Mary Magdalen, Metairie
Rooney, James P., Jr., Visitation of Our Lady; Pastoral Min., Ochsner Medical Center, Westbank
Rosato, Joseph R., Tulane Catholic Center; Pastoral Min., Christ the Healer Prog.
Rougelot, Sidney, (Retired)
Roussel, Garland Joseph, Jr., St. Hubert, Garyville; St. John Parish Correctional Facility
Roussel, Theodore J., (Retired)
Scalise, Bertrand, Jr., (On Duty Outside the Archdiocese)
Schexnayder, Harry, St. Charles Borromeo, Destrehan
Schlette, Peter B., (On Duty Outside the Archdiocese)
Schmidt, Gilbert R., St. Angela Merici, Metairie; Master of Ceremonies
Seruntine, Alex J., Jr., (Retired)
Seymour, Reginald John, St. Genevieve, Slidell
Shartle, George (Butch), Mary Queen of Peace, Mandeville
Shelton, Royal C., St. Raymond-St. Leo the Great, New Orleans
Sierra, Jose A., Blessed Francis Xavier Seelos, New Orleans; Master of Ceremonies
Simoneaux, Nathan F., Jr., St. Matthew the Apostle, River Ridge; Advocate, Metropolitan Tribunal
Smith, Charles J., (On Duty Outside Archdiocese)
Smith, Gilbert W., (Retired)
St. Pierre, Thomas Joseph, Ascension of Our Lord, La Place
Stahl, Rudolph W., (On Duty Outside the Archdiocese)
Stall, Louis W., (Retired)
Steel, Kevin M., St. John Bosco, Harvey; Christ the King, Terrytown; Advocate, Metropolitan Tribunal
Stevens, Allen, Pastoral Assoc., St. Peter Claver
Stewart, Irvin, Sr., Blessed Sacrament - St. Joan of Arc, New Orleans
Stohlman, Michael H., St. Charles Borromeo, Destrehan
Strahan, Douglas H., (Retired)
Suprean, Ricky J., St. John of the Cross, Lacombe; Pastoral Min., Southeast Louisiana Hospital
Swiler, James W., (On Duty Outside the Archdiocese)
Talbot, Michael J., Most Holy Trinity; Pastoral Min., Dir. Pastoral Care, Rayburn Correctional Center, Angie
Templet, Eugene P., SS. Peter & Paul, Pearl River; Pastoral Min., St. Tammany Parish Prison
Toups, Wilbur A., St. Francis of Assisi, New Orleans
Trainor, Robert, (Retired)
Tully, Jeffrey R., St. Charles Borromeo, Destrehan
Venturella, James A., Visitation of Our Lady; Pastoral Min., Jefferson Parish Correctional Center, Gretna
Vincent, Daniel S., (On Duty Outside Archdiocese)
Vincent, Harold A., Dir. of Pastoral Care, Xavier University of Louisiana; Perm. Diaconate Personnel Board
Vincent, Leslie D., Our Lady of Perpetual Help, Belle Chasse; Pastoral Min., Ochsner Medical Center-West Bank, Gretna
Walker, John J., IV, St. Andrew the Apostle, New Orleans; Pastoral Min., Rivarde Juvenile Detention Ctr.
Warriner, A. David, Jr., Master of Ceremonies, St. Louis Cathedral; Coord., Court of Second Instance, Metropolitan Tribunal; Vice Chancellor; Delegate, Dispensations & Permissions; Defender of the Bond
Watley, Jesse A., Exec. Dir., Dept. of Pastoral Services, Blessed Francis Xavier Seelos, New Orleans; Master of Ceremonies
Weber, John C., St. Margaret Mary, Slidell
Webre, Milton G., (On Duty Outside Archdiocese)
Weil, Jay J., III, Our Lady of the Lake Roman Catholic Church, Mandeville
White, Alfred, (On Leave)
Williams, Everett, (Retired)
Williams, Herman J., Pastoral Assoc., St. Joseph, Gretna
Wiltz, Glenn J., St. James Major, New Orleans; Pastoral Min., Children's Hospital
Wright, Clifford S., St. Benilde, Metairie
Zaiontz, Michael G., Our Lady of the Rosary, New Orleans; Advocate, Metropolitan Tribunal
Zimmer, Julius T., St. John the Baptist, Folsom

INSTITUTIONS LOCATED IN THE ARCHDIOCESE

[A] SEMINARIES, ARCHDIOCESAN

NEW ORLEANS. *Notre Dame Seminary Graduate School of Theology* (1923) 2901 S. Carrollton Ave., 70118-4391. Tel: 504-866-7426; Fax: 504-866-3119. Email: illjmb@nds.edu. Web: www.nds.edu. Priests 9; Laymen 4; Women Religious 3; Seminarians 70.

Administration: Rev. David Kelly, Dir. Pastoral Field Education; Dr. David Liberto, M.A., Ph.D., Academic Dean; Rev. Jose I. Lavastida, S.T.D., S.T.L., N.D.S., Pres. & Rector; Ms. Cynthia Garrity, Registrar; Mr. George Dansker, M.P.H., M.L.I.S., Librarian; Mr. Wayne Trosclair, B.S., Dir. of Facilities & Student Services; Ms. Michelle W. Klein, Business Mgr.; Sisters Janet Bodin, M.S.C., M.A., Ph.D., Dir. Pre-Theology/Phil.; Theresa Marie Tran, S.S.C., Assoc. Dir. Pastoral Field Educ.

Faculty: Revs. Joseph M. Krafft; Donald Martin, S.J., M.A., Ph.D.; Vien The Nguyen, J.C.L., M.Div.; Mark S. Raphael; Very Rev. Patrick J. Williams, M.Div., M.S.; Sisters Janet Bodin, M.S.C., M.A., Ph.D.; Elizabeth Fitzpatrick, O.Carm., M.A.; Rev. Joseph S. Palermo Jr., J.D.; Dr. Mark Barker; Dr. Basil Davis, M.A., Ph.D.; Dr. James M. Jacobs, M.A., Ph.D.; Dr. David Liberto, M.A., Ph.D.; Mr. Angelo Lupinetti; Mr. Kevin Redmann; Mr. George Dansker, M.P.H., M.L.I.S., Librarian; Dr. Chris Baglow, Ph.D.; Dr. Brant Pitre, Ph.D.

ST. BENEDICT. *St. Joseph Seminary College* (1890) 75376 River Rd., 70457-9999. Tel: 504-892-1800; Fax: 504-867-2295. Email: rector@sjasc.edu. Web: www.sjasc.edu. Very Rev. Gregory M. Boquet, O.S.B., M.A., Pres. & Rector; Rt. Rev. Justin Brown, O.S.B., Abbot; Friar Vincent Dufresne, S.T.L.; Revs. Scott J. Underwood, O.S.B., M.T.S., M.Ed.; Matthew R. Clark, O.S.B., M.A., Vice Rector; Vanessa Crouere, Dir. Devel.; Kit Friedrichs-Baumann, Dir. Grants & Devel. Assoc.; George J. Binder, Dir. Fin. Aid; Revs. Augustine E. Foley, O.S.B., M.A.Th.; Thomas L. Gwozdz, S.B.D., Ph.D.; Very Rev. Thomas C. Ranzino (BR); Dr. Jude Lupinetti, Ph.D., Academic Dean; Rev. Killian Tolg, B.A., M.A., Dean of Students; Bro. Simon Stubbs, O.S.B., Communications Dir.; Ms. Judith Gaubert, Dir. Finance. Benedictine Monks. Conducted by Provinces of New Orleans and Mobile and Monks of St. Joseph's Abbey. Priests 23; Brothers 13; Novices 2; Sisters 2; Lay Teachers 10; Seminarians 81; Total Enrollment 179; Lay Staff 15.

Faculty: Rev. Charles J. Benoit, O.S.B., M.A.Th.; Daniel Burns, Ph.D.; Richard Moore, B.G.E., M.S., M.A.; Rev. Josh Rodrigue; David Arbo, B.A., M.A.; Revs. Matthew R. Clark, O.S.B., M.A.; Jonathan DuFrange, B.A., M.T.S., M.A., Ph.D.; Augustine E. Foley, O.S.B., M.A.Th.; Thomas L. Gwozdz, S.B.D., Ph.D.; Sr. Jeanne d'Arc Kernion, O.S.B., B.A., M.A.; Ms. Josette Beaulieu-Grace, B.A., M.A.; Al Dranguet, B.A., M.A.; Peter M. Emerson, Ph.D.; Agnieszka Gutthy, Ph.D.; John E. Hebert, Ph.D.; Dr. Ann K. Nauman, Ph.D., Prof. Emerita; Francie Rich, B.F.A., M.F.A.; Casey Edler, B.A., M.A.; Robert Calmes, B.S., M.A.; Frances Legrand, B.A., M.A.; John Reilly, B.A.; Colby McCurdy, B.Mus., M.Musj.; Elizabeth Simmons, B.A., M.A.; Cory Hayes, B.A., M.A.

Religious Studies Institute: Jeremy Thompson, B.S., M.A., Ph.D.; Revs. Chris Decker; Vincent Dufresne, B.A., S.T.B., S.T.L.; Tom Ranzino, B.A., M.A.; Brenda Atkinson, M.A.; Rick Beben; Elizabeth Bourgeois, M.R.E., B.A.; Mr. Chris Redden; Mr. Kenneth J. Thevenet, M.Mus.; Rev. Jamin David, J.C.L., B.A., M.Div.; Francis Vanderwall, Ph.D.

Diaconate Program: Revs. Anthony Russo, Ph.D.; Gary Belsome, B.A., M.Div.; Mark Alise, Ph.D.; Ann Schneller, B.S., M.A.; Francis Vanderwall, Ph.D.

Professional Lay Staff: Todd Russell, Dir. Institute Technology; Carla Weeden, Academic Sec.; Janice Lewis, Sec. to President-Rector; Nicole D'Argeneaux, Accounting; Pamela Egan, R.N., N.P., Dir., Student Health Svcs.; Beverly Krieger, Sec.; Bonnie Wood, Librarian.

[B] SEMINARIES, RELIGIOUS OR SCHOLASTICATES

NEW ORLEANS. *Josephite House of Studies*, 2000 St. Bernard Ave., 70116-1390. Priest Candidates 1.

METAIRIE. *Congregation of the Mother Coredemptrix Formation House* (1991) 112 Lilac St., 70005-1817. Tel: 504-835-9746; Fax: 504-835-9746. Email: hvmvn@dongcong.net. Priests 1; Brothers 8.

[C] COLLEGES AND UNIVERSITIES

NEW ORLEANS. *Loyola University New Orleans* (1912) 6363 St. Charles Ave., 70118-6195. Tel: 504-865-2011 (General); 504-865-3847 (Pres. Office); Fax: 504-865-3851. Email: ghoward@loyno.edu. Web: www.loyno.edu. Revs. Kevin Wildes, S.J., Pres.; Theodore A. Dziak, S.J., Jesuit Center Dir., Vice Pres. Mission & Ministry; Dr. Edward Kvet, Provost/Vice Pres. for Academic Affairs; Revs. Michael A. Bouzigard, S.J., M.A., M.Div., M.Phil; James C. Carter, S.J., Pres. Emeritus; Gerald M. Fagin, S.J.; Lawrence Moore, S.J.; Leo A. Nicoll, S.J.; Peter S. Rogers, S.J.; Very

Rev. Alfred C. Kammer, S.J., B.A., M.A., J.D., Exec. Dir. Jesuit Social Research Institute (New Orleans Society of Jesus); Revs. William J. Farge, S.J.; Robert S. Gerlich, S.J.; Stephen C. Rowntree, S.J., B.A., M.A., M.Div., M.Th.; Bro. Gebhard R.M. Frohlich, S.J., (Retired); Rev. Kenneth P. Keulman; Jo Ann Cruz, Interim Dean College of Humanities & Natural Sciences; Donald R. Boomgaarden, Dean College of Music; William B. Locander, Dean College of Business; Maria Pabon Lopez, College, Law; Deborah L. Poole, Interim Dean Univ. Library; Dr. Luis Miron, Dean College of Social Studies Sciences; Revs. John F. Armstrong, S.J., Formation Asst. (New Orleans Province of the Society of Jesus); George F. Lundy, S.J., M.Div., Ph.D.; Charles Wrightington, S.J.; Gregg Grovenburg, S.J., Campus Min.; Deacon Sylvester Tan, S.J. Priests 18; Brothers 1; Sisters 2; Lay Teachers 522; Students 5,171.

Our Lady of Holy Cross College, 4123 Woodland Dr., 70131-7399. Tel: 504-394-7744; Fax: 504-391-2421. Email: admissions@olhcc.edu. Web: www.olhcc.edu. Myles M. Seghers, Ph.D., Interim Pres.; James Curry, Vice Pres. Academic Affairs; Sr. Marjorie Hebert, M.S.C., Vice Pres. Fin. Mgmt. & Admin.; Patricia Prechter, Ed.D., M.S.N., P.N.P., Interim Provost; Debbie Panepinto, Registrar; Sr. Helen Fontenot, M.S.C., Librarian. Priests 2; Congregation of the Sisters Marianites of Holy Cross 2; Sisters 1; Lay Teachers 49; Students 1,260; Total Staff 40.

Xavier University of Louisiana (Coed), One Drexel Dr., 70125-1098. Tel: 504-486-7411; Fax: 504-520-7904. Email: apply@xula.edu. Web: www.xula.edu. Dr. Norman C. Francis, Pres.; Dr. Loren Blanchard, Vice Pres. Academic Affairs; Rev. Giles Conwill, Dir. Office of Campus Ministry; Mr. Robert Skinner, Librarian. Priests 2; Brothers 1; Sisters 4; Lay Teachers 267; Students 3,399.

[D] HIGH SCHOOLS, ARCHDIOCESAN

COVINGTON. *Archbishop Hannan High School*, 71324 Hwy. 1077, 70433. Tel: 985-249-6363; Fax: 985-249-6370. Email: principal@hannanhigh.org. Rev. Charles L. Latour, O.P., Prin.; Mrs. Nancy Baird, Ph.D., Dir., Inst. Advancement; Dr. Donnalyn Hassenboehler, Asst. Prin.; Joe Hines, Athletic Dir.; Susan Yates, Librarian; Craig Fiedler, Dir., Admission. Priests 1; Lay Teachers 27; Students 309.

St. Scholastica Academy, P.O. Box 1210, 70434-1210. Tel: 985-892-2540; Fax: 985-893-5256. Email: mkv@ssacad.org. Web: www.ssacad.com. Mrs. Marguerite S. Celestin, Pres.; Mary Kathryn Villere, Prin.; Bobbie Landry, Librarian. Sisters 1; Lay Teachers 52; Students 693.

LA PLACE. *St. Charles Catholic High School*, 100 Dominican Dr., 70068-3499. Tel: 985-652-3809; Fax: 985-652-2609. Email: stcharlescath@archdiocese-no.org. Web: www.stcharlescatholic.org. Mr. Andrew C. Cupit, Prin.; Angie Louque, Librarian. Lay Teachers 33; Students 448.

MARRERO. *Academy of Our Lady* (2007) 537 Ave. D, 70072-2027. Tel: 504-341-6217; Fax: 504-341-6229. Email: ourlady@theacademyofourlady.org. Web: www.theacademyofourlady.org. Sr. Michelle Geiger, F.M.A., Prin.; Michelle Maher, Librarian; Linda Todd, Librarian. Merger of Archbishop Blenk High School, Gretna & Immaculata High School, Marrero. Sisters 3; Lay Teachers 39; Girls 575.

Archbishop Shaw High School, 1000 Barataria Blvd., 70072-3052. Tel: 504-340-6727; Fax: 504-347-9883. Email: arnoshaw@archdiocese.org. Web: www.archbishopshaw.org. Revs. James McKenna, S.D.B., Pres. & Dir.; Louis Konopelski, S.D.B., Prin.; Mr. John Corb, Financial Admin.; Bro. Gerald Meegan, S.D.B., Youth Min.; Revs. Thomas McGahee, S.D.B.; Emil Fardellone, S.D.B.; Bros. Joseph Tortorici; Dave Verrett; Mrs. Susan LaHaye, Librarian. Salesians of St. John Bosco. Priests 5; Brothers 2; Lay Teachers 36; Boys 353.

METAIRIE. *Archbishop Chapelle High School*, 8800 Veterans Blvd., 70003-5235. Tel: 504-467-3105; Fax: 504-466-3191. Email: achs@archbishopchapelle.org. Web: www.archbishopchapelle.org. Mrs. Jane Ann Frosch, Pres.; Ms. Cathy Yaeger, Prin.; Annette Thibodeaux, Librarian. Priests 1; Lay Teachers 72; Girls 850.

Archbishop Rummel High School, 1901 Severn Ave., 70001. Tel: 504-834-5592; Fax: 504-832-4016. Email: info@rummelraiders.com. Web: www.rummelraiders.com. Mr. Michael Scalco, Pres./Prin.; Ms. Deborah Lobrano, Librarian. Lay Teachers 70; Boys 900.

Archbishop Rummel Alumni Association Inc. Fax: 504-833-5796. Web: www.raiderpride.com. Dominick Impastato, Pres.

SLIDELL. *Pope John Paul II Catholic High School* (1980) 1901 Jaguar Dr., 70461-9098. Tel: 985-649-0914; Fax: 985-649-5494. Email: pjp@pjp.org. Web: www.pjp.org. Mr. Richard Berkowitz, M.Ed., Pres.; Ms. Martha M. Mundine, Prin. Lay Teachers 21; Students 315.

[E] HIGH SCHOOLS, RELIGIOUS COMMUNITY SPONSORED

NEW ORLEANS. *Academy of the Sacred Heart "The Rosary"* (1887) 4521 St. Charles Ave., 70115-9990. Tel: 504-891-1943; Fax: 504-891-9939. Email: ash@ashrosary.org. Web: www.ashrosary.org. Dr. Timothy Burns, Ph.D., B.A., M.A., Headmaster; Yvonne S. Adler, Ph.D., Prin.; Mrs. Josephine Schloegel, Librarian. Carmelites 1; Lay Teachers 29; Girls 201.

St. Augustine High School (1951) (Grades 6-12), 2600 A.P. Tureaud Ave., 70119-1299. Tel: 504-944-2424; Fax: 504-947-7712. Email: staughs@archdiocese-no.org. Web: purpleknights.com. Rev. Charles Andrus, S.S.J., Interim Pres.; Mr. Don Boucree, Prin.; Rev. Wilbur J. Atwood, S.S.J., Librarian. Josephite Community., (See Separate Listing for Residence.) Priests 4; Lay Teachers 65; Boys 655.

Brother Martin High School (1869) (Grades 7-12), 4401 Elysian Fields Ave., 70122-3898. Tel: 504-283-1561; Fax: 504-286-8462. Email: gmrando@cox.net. Web: brothermartin.com. Mr. John J. Devlin III, Pres.; Mr. Gregory Rando, Prin.; Keiren Aucoin, Librarian. Brothers of the Sacred Heart 3; Sisters 1; Lay Teachers 104; Boys 1,206.

Cabrini High School (1959) (Grades 8-12), 1400 Moss St., 70119-2904. Tel: 504-482-1193; Fax: 504-483-8671. Ardley Hanemann Jr., Pres.; Mrs. Yvonne L. Hrapmann, Prin.; Helene Tucker, Academic Asst. Prin.; Sandra Granier, Librarian. Missionary Sisters of the Sacred Heart 1; Marianites of the Holy Cross 1; Lay Teachers 48; Girls 450.

Cabrini High School, Inc. Tel: 504-482-1193; Fax: 504-483-8673. Web: cabrinihigh.com. Mrs. Yvonne L. Hrapmann, Prin.; Sandra Granier, Librarian.

De La Salle High School (1949) (Grades 10-12), (Coed), 5300 St. Charles Ave., 70115-4999. Tel: 504-895-5717; Fax: 504-895-1300. Email: peggys@delasallenola.com. Web: www.delasallenola.com. Mr. William Hebert, Pres.; Peggy St. John, Prin.; Hasumati Parikh, Librarian. Brothers of the Christian Schools 1; Lay Teachers 30; Students 295.

Holy Cross School (1879) (Grades 5-12), 5500 Paris Ave., 70122-2659. Tel: 504-942-3100; Fax: 504-286-5665. Email: contacthc@holycrosstigers.com. Web: www.holycrosstigers.com. Dr. Joseph H. Murry Jr., High School Prin.; Teresa Billings, Middle School Prin.; Mr. Charles DiGange, Headmaster; Very Rev. Patrick J. Williams, M.Div., M.S., Chap. Brothers of the Congregation of Holy Cross, Southwest Province 1; Lay Teachers 63; Boys 821.

Jesuit High School (1847) (Boys), 4133 Banks St., 70119-6883. Tel: 504-486-6631; Fax: 504-483-3816. Email: principal@jesuitnola.org. Web: www.jesuitnola.org. Rev. Raymond R. Fitzgerald, S.J., Pres.; Mr. Michael Giambelluca, Prin.; Revs. Norman B. O'Neal, S.J.; Nicholas T. Schiro, S.J.; Donald E. Saunders, S.J. Priests 4; Brothers 1; Lay Teachers 90; Boys 1,088.

Office: 710 Baronne St., 70113-1064. Tel: 504-571-1055; Fax: 504-571-1744. Priests 4; Brothers 1; Lay Teachers 92; Boys 1,088.

St. Mary's Academy of the Holy Family, Mailing Address: 6905 Chef Menteur Blvd., 70126-5215. Tel: 504-245-0318; Fax: 504-245-0422. Email: smaoffice@archdiocese-no.org. Web: www.smaneworleans.com. Sr. Jennie Jones, S.S.F., Prin.; Michelle Ochillo, Librarian. Sisters 12; Lay Teachers 39.

St. Mary's Dominican High School (1860) 7701 Walmsley Ave., 70125-3494. Tel: 504-865-9401; Fax: 504-866-5958. Email: president@stmarysdominican.org. Web: www.stmarysdominican.org. Dr. Cynthia A. Thomas, Ed.D., Pres.; Mrs. Carolyn Favre, Prin. Sisters 7; Brothers 1; Lay Teachers 59; Students 885; Personnel Total 108.

Mount Carmel Academy (1833) 7027 Milne Blvd., 70124-2395. Tel: 504-288-7626; Fax: 504-288-7629. Email: mca@mcacubs.org. Web: www.mtcarmelcubs.org. Sr. Camille Anne Campbell, O.Carm., Pres. & Prin.; Rev. Michael J. O'Rourke, O.P., Chap.; Mrs. Terri Rousey, Librarian. Congregation of Our Lady of Mount Carmel. Sisters 3; Lay Teachers 126; Girls 1,183.

Ursuline Academy, (Grades 8-12), Secondary Dept. Day School College Prep., 2635 State St., 70118-6399. Tel: 504-861-9150; Fax: 504-861-7392. Email: admissions@ursulineneworleans.org. Web: www.ursulineneworleans.org. Gretchen Z. Kane, B.S., M.S., Pres.; John Gabriel, Prin.; Susan Young, Librarian. Lay Teachers 40; Girls 438.

Xavier University Preparatory School, 5116 Magazine St., 70115-1899. Tel: 504-899-6061, Ext. 310; Fax: 504-891-8766. Email: xavierprep@xavierprep.com. Web: www.xavierprep.com. Joseph E. Peychaud Jr., Pres. & Prin.; Sr. Nathalee Bryant, S.B.S., Librarian. Sisters 2; Lay Teachers 22; Girls 276.

COVINGTON. *The St. Paul's School* (1911) (Grades 8-12), P.O. Box 928, 70434-0928. Tel: 985-892-3200; Fax: 985-892-4048. Email: stpauls@stpauls.com. Web: www.stpauls.com. Bro. Raymond Bulliard, F.S.C., Prin. Day School for Young Men Brothers of the Christian Schools of the New Orleans-Santa Fe Province 6; Lay Teachers 60; Boys 850.

[F] HIGH SCHOOLS, PAROCHIAL

NEW ORLEANS. *Holy Rosary High School* (1996) 3368 Esplanade Ave., 70119-3132. Tel: 504-482-7173; Fax: 504-482-7229. Email: holyrosaryaca@archdiocese-no.org. Mr. Len Enger, Prin.; Dawn Held, Librarian. Lay Teachers 18; Students 114.

[G] HIGH SCHOOLS - ALTERNATIVE

NEW ORLEANS. *St. Gerard Majella Alternative School* (1991) 1941 Dauphine St., 70116-1609. Tel: 504-309-9543; Fax: 504-309-9542. Email: majellaalt@archdiocese-no.org. Sr. Rose Elaine Kessler, S.S.N.D., Prin. Sisters 1; Lay Teachers 4; Students 25.

[H] ELEMENTARY SCHOOLS, ARCHDIOCESAN

MARRERO. *Archbishop Shaw Junior High School*, (Grades 8-9), 1000 Barataria Blvd., 70072-3052. Tel: 504-340-6727; Fax: 504-347-9883. Email: arnoshaw@archdiocese-no.org. Web: www.archbishopshaw.org. Rev. James McKenna, S.D.B., Dir. & President; Cheryl Welch, Prin., Jr. High; Rev. Louis Konopelski, S.D.B., Prin.; Mrs. Susan LaHaye, Librarian. Priests 5; Brothers 2; Lay Teachers 36; Students 153.

[I] ELEMENTARY SCHOOLS - CATHOLIC, OTHER

NEW ORLEANS. *St. Benedict the Moor School* (1998) (Grades PreK-4), 5010 Piety Dr., 70126. Tel: 504-288-2745; Fax: 504-282-9386. Email: stbenmoor@archdiocese-no.org. Drue Dumas, Prin. Sisters 1; Lay Teachers 5; Students 88.

Good Shepherd Nativity School (2001) 353 Baronne St., 70112-1628. Tel: 504-598-9399; Fax: 504-598-9346. Email: epaul@thegoodshepherdschool.org. Web: www.thegoodshepherdschool.org. Mrs. Emily Paul, Prin.; Wendy Ruckman, Librarian. Lay Teachers 12; Total Staff 21; Students 83.

Stuart Hall School for Boys, 2032 S. Carrollton Ave., 70182. Tel: 504-861-1954; Fax: 504-861-5389. Email: claforge@stuarthall.org. Web: www.stuarthall.org. Dr. Cissy LaForge, B.S., M.Ed., Ph.D., Prin.; Nancy Dunphy, Librarian. Lay Teachers 40.

[J] ELEMENTARY SCHOOLS, RELIGIOUS COMMUNITY SPONSORED

NEW ORLEANS. *Academy of the Sacred Heart* (1887) (Grades Toddler-12), 4521 St. Charles Ave., 70115-4831. Tel: 504-891-1943; Fax: 504-891-9939. Email: ash@ashrosary.org. Web: www.ashrosary.org. Dr. Timothy Burns, Ph.D., B.A., M.A., Headmaster; Yvonne S. Adler, Ph.D., U.S. Div. Head; Kay Higginbotham, P.S. & L.S. Div. Head; Kim Duckworth, M.S. Div. Head; Phina Schloegel, Librarian; Libby Adams, Librarian; Sr. Maureen Little, R.S.C.J., Dir., Formation Ministry. Religious of the Sacred Heart 1; Carmelites 1; Lay Teachers 92; Girls 801.

St. Augustine High School, (Grades 6), 2600 A.P. Tureaud Ave., 70119-1299. Tel: 504-944-2424; Fax: 504-947-7712. Email: sdavidson@purpleknights.com. Web: purpleknights.com. Revs. Charles Andrus, S.S.J., Interim Pres.; Wilbur J. Atwood, S.S.J., Librarian. Priests 5; Religious Brothers 1; Lay Teachers 55; Boys 700.

Brother Martin High School (Grade 7), 4401 Elysian Fields Ave., 70122-3898. Tel: 504-283-1561; Fax: 504-286-8462. Web: brothermartin.com. Zachary Fields, Prin.; Keiren Aucoin, Librarian; Cynthia Bellina, Librarian. Lay Teachers 14; Boys 90.

Cabrini High School (1959) (Grades 8-12), 1400 Moss St., 70119-2904. Tel: 504-482-1193; Fax: 504-483-8671. Web: cabrinihigh.com. Ardley Hanemann Jr., Pres.; Mrs. Yvonne L. Hrapmann, Prin.; Helene Tucker, Asst. Academic Prin.; Sandra Granier, Librarian. Sisters 2; Lay Teachers 48; Students 466.

Christian Brothers School, (Grades 5-7), City Park, #8 Fredericks Ave., 70124-4602. Tel: 504-486-6770; Fax: 504-486-1053. Email: school@cbs-no.org. Web: www.cbs-no.org. Bro. Laurence

Konersmann, Pres.; Mr. Joey M. Scaffidi, Prin.; Mrs. Carol Maquar, Librarian. Brothers 3; Lay Teachers 17; Boys 290.

De La Salle Junior High School, (Grades 8-9), (Coed), 5300 St. Charles Ave., 70115-4999. Tel: 504-895-5717; Fax: 504-895-1300. Email: peggys@delasallenola.com. Web: www.delasallenola.com. Mr. William Hebert, Pres.; Peggy St. John, Prin.; Hasumati Parikh, Librarian. Lay Teachers 25; Students 148.

Holy Cross School, (Grades 5-12), 5500 Paris Ave., 70122. Tel: 504-942-3100; Fax: 504-286-5665. Email: contacthc@holycrosstigers.com. Web: www.holycrosstigers.com. Dr. Joseph H. Murry Jr., High School Prin.; Teresa Billings, Middle School Prin.; Mr. Charles DiGange, Headmaster; Mrs. Pam Falgoust, Librarian; Rev. Michael J. Mitchell, Chap. Lay Teachers 62; Boys 937.

Jesuit High School, (Grades 8), 4133 Banks St., 70119-6883. Tel: 504-486-6631; Fax: 504-483-3816. Email: principal@jesuitnola.org. Web: www.jesuitnola.org. Rev. Raymond R. Fitzgerald, S.J., Pres.; Mr. Michael A. Giambelluca, Prin. Priests 1; Lay Teachers 19; Boys 260; Scholastics 1.

St. Mary's Academy, (Grades PreK-12), 6905 Chef Menteur Blvd., 70126. Tel: 504-245-0200; Fax: 504-245-0422. Email: smaoffice@archdiocese-no.org. Web: www.smaneworleans.com. Sr. Jennie Jones, S.S.F., Prin.; Michelle Ochillo, Librarian. Sisters of the Holy Family 12; Lay Teachers 42.

Ursuline Academy, (Grades Toddler-7), 2635 State St., 70118-6399. Tel: 504-861-9150; Fax: 504-866-5293. Email: admissions@ursulineneworleans.org. Web: www.ursulineneworleans.org. Gretchen Z. Kane, B.S., M.S., Pres.; Kimberly Harper, Prin.; Pat Prudhomme, Librarian. Lay Teachers 39; Students 338.

COVINGTON. *The St. Paul's School*, (Grades 8-12), P.O. Box 928, 70434-0928. Tel: 985-892-3200; Fax: 985-892-4048. Email: stpauls@stpauls.com. Web: www.stpauls.com. Bro. Raymond Bulliard, F.S.C., Prin.; Trevor Watkins, Asst. Prin. Brothers of the Christian Schools., (See St. Paul's School under High Schools, Private) Brothers 6; Lay Teachers 60; Boys 850.

[K] SPECIAL EDUCATION

NEW ORLEANS. *St. Michael Special School*, 1522 Chippewa St., 70130. Tel: 504-524-7285; Fax: 504-524-5883. Email: stmichspecial@archdiocese-no.org. Mrs. Jane Silva, Prin. Lay Teachers 23; Students 191.

[L] DAY CARE CENTERS, CAMPS AND PRESCHOOLS

NEW ORLEANS. *Cub Corner* (1975) Pre-School, 420 Robt E. Lee Blvd., 70124. Tel: 504-286-8673; Fax: 504-286-8676. Web: www.home.bellsouth.net/p/pwp-mountcarmel. Elizabeth Coe, Child Care Dir.; Sr. Gwen Grillot, O.Carm., Exec. Dir. (A Ministry of the Sisters of Mount Carmel). Religious 3; Lay Staff 30.

St. John Berchmans Child Development Center (Not open at this time. Contact the Sisters of the Holy Family for information.), Mailing Address: 6901 Chef Menteur Hwy., 70126-5290. 2710 Gentilly Blvd., 70182-8623.

Lafon Child Development Center (1965) (Not open at this time. Contact the Sisters of the Holy Family for information.), 7024 Chef Menteur Hwy., 70126-5295. Mailing Address: 6901 Chef Menteur Hwy., 70126-5290.

Leslie Early Head Start Center, 2126 Constance St., 70130-5044. Tel: 504-522-2725.

Louise Early Head Start Center, 1205 Louisiana Ave., 70115-2488. Tel: 504-891-2871.

Rosary Child Development Center (2000) 5100 Willowbrook Dr., 70129-1047. Tel: 504-254-1528; Fax: 504-254-1531. Email: rosarycdc@yahoo.com. Sr. Thien-An Nguyen, F.M.S.R., Dir. Total Staff 21; Children (Daily Average) 100.

St. John the Baptist Head Start Program, 1920 Clio St., 70113-1214. Tel: 504-529-2557 (Preschool).

El Yo Yo Head Start/Early Head Start, 735 Gen. Pershing St., 70115. Tel: 504-899-6165.

Incarnate Word Head Start/Early Head Start, 8326 Apricot St., 70115. Tel: 504-861-6360.

[M] HOMES FOR CHILDREN AND YOUTH

NEW ORLEANS. *Boys Hope Girls Hope* (1980) Group Homes for Boys and Girls., P.O. Box 19307, 70179-0307. Tel: 504-484-7744; Fax: 504-484-6120. Web: www.bhghnola.org. Chuck Roth, Executive Director. Total Staff 12; College Students 6; Boys 8; Girls 8; Total Assisted 25.

**Covenant House New Orleans* (1987) Home for Runaway, Abused & Homeless Youth aged 16-21., 611 N. Rampart St., 70112-3540. Tel: 504-584-1102; Fax: 504-584-1171. Email: jkelly@covenanthouse.org. Web: covenanthouseno.org. Mr. James R. Kelly, Exec. Dir.; Amber L. Vidal, Exec. Asst. Total Assisted 1,300; Total Staff 60.

BELLE CHASSE. *Padua Pediatric Program* A residential program for children (birth to 25 yrs) who are severely/profoundly mentally retarded and non-ambulatory., 200 Beta St., 70037-1499. Tel: 504-392-0502; Fax: 504-392-5411. Mrs. Pashina Casimire, Div. Dir.; Ms. Ronna Trager, Prog. Dir.

[N] RESIDENCES, ADULT

NEW ORLEANS. *Baronne Street Transitional Housing/CARE Center* (Crisis & Residential Emergency Center), *c/o Catholic Charities*, 1000 Howard Ave., Ste. 1000, 70113-1942. Tel: 504-269-9311. Ms. Connie Andry, Dir., Homeless Svcs.

Ozanam Inn Shelter for Homeless Men, 843 Camp St., 70130-3751. Tel: 504-523-1184; Fax: 504-523-1187. Web: www.ozanaminn.org. Deacon Biaggio DiGiovanni, Exec. Dir. Sponsored by Society of St. Vincent de Paul. Total Staff 12; Total Assisted 35,040; Bed Capacity 96.

Project Lazarus (1986) Residential Program for Persons with AIDS, P.O. Box 3906, 70177-3906. Tel: 504-949-3609; Fax: 504-944-7944. Email: info@projectlazarus.net. Web: www.projectlazarus.net. Mr. Eric Oleson, Exec. Dir. Total in Residence 24; Total Assisted Annually 95; Total Staff 25.

GRETNA. *St. Jude the Apostle*, c/o 1000 Howard Ave., Ste. 1000, 70113. Community Home for Developmentally Disabled Adults.

Ocean Avenue, c/o 1000 Howard Ave., Ste. 1000, 70113. Community Home for Developmentally Disabled Adults.

St. Rosalie, c/o 1000 Howard Ave., Ste. 1000, 70113. Community Home for Developmentally Disabled Adults.

MARRERO. *Jefferson CARE Center*, c/o 1000 Howard Ave., Ste. 1000, 70113. Ms. Patricia G. Jones, Prog. Dir. Temporary Residence for Homeless Families.

METAIRIE. *Ss. Mary & Elizabeth*, c/o 1000 Howard Ave., Ste. 1000, 70113. Community Home for Developmentally Disabled Adults.

SLIDELL. *St. Peter the Fisherman*, c/o 1000 Howard Ave., Ste. 1000, 70113. Community Home for Developmentally Disabled Adults.

[O] DAY CARE CENTERS (ADULT)

NEW ORLEANS. *New Directions Adult Day Health Care Center*, 1523 N. Dorgenois St., 70119-2419. Tel: 504-943-9418; Fax: 504-948-3633. c/o 1000 Howard Ave., Ste. 1000, 70113.

COVINGTON. *Alpha House Adult Day Health Care Center*, 20127 Hwy. 36, 70433-8658. Tel: 985-892-7074; Fax: 985-893-1962.

KENNER. *The Greenwalt Adult Day Health Care Center*, 1926 18th St., 70062-6208. Tel: 504-461-5889; Fax: 504-461-5795.

NORCO. *Norco Adult Day Care*, 425 Spruce St., 70079-8464. Tel: 985-764-9084; Fax: 985-764-8464. Maida Botts-Camp, Coord.

[P] HOMES AND RESIDENCES FOR FAMILIES AND SENIOR CITIZENS

NEW ORLEANS. *Annunciation Inn, Inc.*, Mailing Address: 1000 Howard Ave., Ste. 100, 70113. Tel: 504-944-0512; Fax: 504-944-0575. 1220 Spain St., 70117. Tel: 504-596-3460; Fax: 504-596-3466. Deacon Dennis F. Adams, Exec. Dir. Elderly Affordable Housing Units 106.

The Apartments at Mater Dolorosa, 1000 Howard Ave., Ste. 100, 70113. Tel: 504-865-7222; Fax: 504-861-9225. 1226 S. Carrollton Ave., 70118. Tel: 504-596-3460; Fax: 504-596-3466. Dagianna Pertuit, Community Mgr. Elderly Affordable Housing Total Staff 3; Residential Units 68.

Chateau de Notre Dame Residence and Nursing Home, 2832 Burdette St., 70125-2596. Tel: 504-866-2741; Fax: 504-866-2861. Email: wplaisance@archdiocese-no.org. Web: cdnd.org. Mr. Wayne Plaisance, CEO. Residential Units 100; Nursing Beds 171; Priests 1; Sisters 2; Lay Staff 210.

Christopher Inn Apts. Elderly Affordable Housing, 1000 Howard Ave., Ste. 100, 70113. Tel: 504-596-3460; Fax: 504-596-3466. *Christopher Homes, Inc.*, 2110 Royal St., 70116. Tel: 504-949-0312; Fax: 504-945-2634. Deacon Graylin Miller, Community Mgr. Residents 144; Total Staff 8.

DeLille Inn (1987) Mailing Address: 1000 Howard Ave., Ste. 100, 70113. Tel: 504-596-3460; Fax: 504-596-3466. 6924 Chef Menteur Hwy., 70126. Tel: 504-245-8660; Fax: 504-245-8677. Deacon Dennis F. Adams, Exec. Dir. Elderly Affordable Housing Total in Residence 51; Residential Units 51.

St. John Berchman's Manor, 1000 Howard Ave., Ste. 100, 70113. Tel: 504-943-9331; Fax: 504-943-9380. *St. John Berchman's Manor*, 3400 St. Anthony Ave., 70122. Tel: 504-596-3460; Fax: 504-596-3466. Deacon Dennis F. Adams, Exec. Dir. Elderly Affordable Housing Units 149; Total Staff 5.

Lafon Nursing Facility of the Holy Family, 6900 Chef Menteur Blvd., 70126. Tel: 504-241-6285. Beverly Greenwood, Admin. Sisters of the Holy Family. Sisters 5; Residents 75; Total Staff 130; Bed Capacity 155.

St. Martin's Manor Elderly Affordable Housing; Not currently open due to Hurricane Katrina; Scheduled to reopen Fall of 2012, 1000 Howard Ave., Ste. 100, 70113. Tel: 504-596-3460; Fax: 504-596-3466. Residential Units 140.

The Mental Health Association Development Corporation dba The 1540 House 1000 Howard Ave., Ste. 100, 70113. Tel: 504-596-3460; Fax: 504-596-3466. Affordable Housing for the Mentally Ill Residential Units 12.

Nazareth II, 1000 Howard Ave., Ste. 100, 70113. Tel: 504-246-9640; Fax: 504-245-4273. 9460 Hayne Blvd., 70127. Tel: 504-596-3460; Fax: 504-596-3466. Deacon Dennis F. Adams, Exec. Dir. Elderly Affordable Housing Residential Units 120; Total in Residence 120.

Nazareth Manor, 1000 Howard Ave., Ste. 100, 70113. Tel: 504-246-9630; Fax: 504-241-9631. *Nazareth Manor*, 9630 Hayne Blvd., 70127. Tel: 504-596-3460; Fax: 504-596-3466. Deacon Dennis F. Adams, Exec. Dir.

Nazareth Manor, Inc., Elderly Affordable Housing Apartments 150; Total Staff 12.

Our Lady of Wisdom Healthcare Center (Inter-Community Health Care, Inc.), 5600 Gen. de Gaulle Dr., 70131. Tel: 504-394-5991; Fax: 504-304-5421. Web: www.olwhealth.org. Bob Laster, Admin. Inter-community healthcare facility for Archdiocesan clergy and Religious Men: Order of Preachers, Society of Jesus, Society of Mary (Marists), Vincentian, Christian Brothers and Brothers of the Sacred Heart; Religious Women: Sisters of St. Joseph of Medaille, Sisters of Mercy, Sisters of the Living Word, Dominican Sisters of Peace, Sisters of the Immaculate Conception, Marianites of the Holy Cross, Sisters of Mount Carmel, Order of Saint Clare (Poor Clares) and Daughters of Charity. Total Staff 150; Bed Capacity 138; Total Assisted Annually 200.

Villa Additions Not currently open due to Hurricane Katrina, Gause Blvd. W., Slidell, 70460. Elderly Affordable Housing Residential Units 75.

Villa St. Maurice, Inc. Not currently open due to Hurricane Katrina, 500 St. Maurice Ave., 70117-1568. Elderly Affordable Housing Residential Units 110.

LA PLACE. *Dubourg Home* (1981) 201 Rue Dubourg, 70068-2433. Tel: 985-652-1981; Fax: 985-651-6147. Email: lrichard@chi-ano.org. Mrs. Lynn Williams, Community Mgr. Units 115; Total Staff 6; Total in Residence 116.

MANDEVILLE. *Rouquette III* (1998) 4300 Hwy. 22, 70448-2824. Tel: 985-626-5217; Fax: 985-626-9226. Brenda Schouest, Community Mgr. Elderly Affordable Housing Residential Units 61; Total Staff 3.

St. Tammany Manor (1979) St. Tammany Manor, Inc.; Residence for Senior Citizens, 4300 Hwy. 22, 70448-2824. Tel: 985-626-5217; Fax: 985-626-9226. Brenda Schouest, Community Mgr. Residential Units 170; Total in Residence 170; Total Staff 21.

MARRERO. *Monsignor Wynhoven Apartments, Inc.* Elderly Affordable Housing, 4600-10th St., 70072-3048. Tel: 504-347-8442; Fax: 504-340-6076. Ann Lucius, Community Mgr. Residents 351; Total Staff 15.

Wynhoven Health Care Center, 1050 Medical Center Blvd., 70072-3170. Tel: 504-347-0777; Fax: 504-341-7240. Web: www.wynhoven.org. Jane Fockler, Admin.; Mr. Wayne Plaisance, Exec. Dir. Bed Capacity 188; Total Assisted 183; Total Staff 201.

MERAUX. *St. Bernard II* Not currently open due to Hurricane Katrina, *St. Bernard II*, 4929 York St., Metairie, 70001. Tel: 545-596-3460; Fax: 504-596-3466. 1000 Howard Ave., Ste. 100, 70113. Tel: 504-596-3460; Fax: 504-596-3466. Elderly Affordable Housing

St. Bernard II, 1000 Howard Ave., Ste. 100, 70113. Tel: 504-596-3460; Fax: 504-596-3466. *St. Bernard II*, 4929 York St., Metairie, 70001.

St. Bernard III Not currently open due to Hurricane Katrina, 1000 Howard Ave., Ste. 100, 70113. Tel: 504-596-3460; Fax: 504-596-3466. 4300 Hwy. 22, Mandeville, 70471. Elderly Affordable Housing

METAIRIE. *Metairie Manor*, 4929 York St., 70001-1013. Tel: 504-456-1467; Fax: 504-887-3718. Flo Ronan, Community Mgr. Elderly Affordable Housing Residential Units 287; Total in Residence 287.

[Q] CATHOLIC HEALTH SERVICES

NEW ORLEANS. *Daughters of Charity Services of New Orleans*, 3201 S. Carrollton Ave., 70118-4307. Tel: 504-207-3060; Fax: 504-483-6016. Email:

jfirstley@dcsno.org. Michael G. Griffin, Pres. & CEO. Total Staff 60.

Health Center-Metairie, 111 N. Causeway Blvd., Metairie, 70001-4540. Tel: 504-207-3060. Email: rarnaud@dcsno.org. Mr. Vincent Sessoms.

Health Center-Uptown, 3201 S. Carrollton Ave., 70118. Tel: 504-207-3060. Email: vsessoms@dcsno.org.

Health Center-Bywater/St. Cecilia, 1030 Lesseps St., 70117-5534. Tel: 504-207-3060.

Daughters of Charity Neighborhood Health Partnership, 3201 S. Carrollton Ave., 70118. Tel: 504-207-3060; Fax: 504-483-7833. Email: alandrum@dcsno.org. Ms. Aziza Landrum, Dir. Community Care.

Daughters of Charity Services of New Orleans Foundation, 3201 S. Carrollton Ave., 70118. Tel: 504-482-2080; Fax: 504-483-6016. Michael G. Griffin, Pres. & CEO.

CHALMETTE. *St. Bernard Health Center, Inc.*, 7718 W. Judge Perez, Arabi, 70032. Tel: 504-281-2800; Fax: 504-278-4692. Frank A. Folino, Admin.

METAIRIE. *Sisters of Mercy Ministries dba Mercy Family Center* Psychological and psychiatric evaluation, counseling and tutorial services., 110 Veterans Memorial Blvd., Ste. 425, 70005. Tel: 504-838-8283; Fax: 504-838-9799. Email: sengro@mercyfamilycenter.com. Web: www.mercyfamilycenter.com.

1445 W. Causeway Approach, Mandeville, 70471. Tel: 985-727-7993; Fax: 985-727-7016. Email: dwalker1@mercyfamilycenter.com. Elaine Moore, Pres.; Stephen J. Engro, Dir. Devel.; Rex Menasco, Exec. Dir. Total Assisted 2,800; Total Staff 34.

[R] MONASTERIES AND RESIDENCES OF PRIESTS AND BROTHERS

NEW ORLEANS. *Brothers of the Sacred Heart* (1821) *Provincial Office, New Orleans Province*, 4600 Elysian Fields Ave., 70122-3826. Tel: 504-301-4758; Fax: 504-301-4843. Email: noprovince@hotmail.com. Bros. Ronald Talbot, S.C., Prov.; Ivy LeBlanc, S.C., Treas.; Ronald Hingle, S.C., Vocation Dir. *Brothers of the Sacred Heart Foundation of the New Orleans Province, Inc.* (1977) 4600 Elysian Fields Ave., 70122. Tel: 504-301-4758; Fax: 504-301-4843. Bro. Ivy LeBlanc, S.C., Exec. Dir., 1156 Park Ave., 70122. Tel: 504-488-1353. Email: bileblanc@hotmail.com.

New Orleans Residences: Bros. Carl Bouchereau, S.C., 4671 Painters St., 70122. Tel: 504-324-4508; Louis Couvillon, S.C., 4671 Painters St., 70122. Tel: 504-324-4508; Neal Golden, S.C., 4671 Painters St., 70122. Tel: 504-324-4508; William Boyles, S.C., 4671 Painters St., 70122. Tel: 504-324-4508; Bosco Faget, S.C., Our Lady of Wisdom Healthcare Center, 5600 Gen. DeGaulle Dr., 70131. Tel: 504-394-5991; Neri Falgout, S.C.; Bertrand Petit Frere (Haiti); Kevin Piper, S.C., 1156 City Park Ave., 70122. Tel: 504-301-4758. Email: lions_86@hotmail.com.

Congregation of the Mission Western Province (Vincentians), DePaul Residence, 812 Constantinople St., 70115-2726. Tel: 504-897-3976; Fax: 504-899-7603; 504-899-3603. Revs. George Weber, C.M. (Retired); Louis Arceneaux, C.M.

Congregation of the Mission Western Province, Louisiana

Dominican Friars, Southern Dominican Province of St. Martin de Porres (1979) *Provincial Headquarters*, 1421 N. Causeway Blvd., Ste. 200, Metairie, 70001-4144. Tel: 504-837-2129; Fax: 504-837-6604. Email: provincial@opsouth.org. Web: www.opsouth.org. Rev. Christopher T. Eggleton, O.P., Prov.; Very Rev. David G. Caron, O.P., Socius & Vicar Prov.; Revs. Justin Kauchak, O.P., Steward; Paul Philibert, O.P., Promoter for Permanent Formation, (Raleigh, NC); John M. Pitzer, O.P., Promoter of Vocations & Promoter, Devel. Priests in the Archdiocese 24; Brothers in the Archdiocese 3.

Assigned but working elsewhere: Rev. George Boudreau.

Working Abroad: Revs. James Linus Dolan, O.P., Provincia Dominicana de San Juan Bautista del Peru, Apartado 4169, Lima 1, Peru. Tel: 427-7426 (011-51-1); Fax: 427-6791 (011-51-1); Leobardo Almazan, O.P., (Italy); Jose D. Padilla, O.P.; Philip Neri Powell, O.P., (U.K.); Marcos Ramos, O.P., (Canada); Jaime Diaz, O.P., (Colombia); Bro. Angel Mendez (Mexico). *Dominican Vocation Sponsors*, 1421 N. Causeway Blvd., Ste. 200, Metairie, 70001-4144. Tel: 504-837-2129; Fax: 504-837-6604. *DePorres Property Corporation*, 1421 N. Causeway Blvd., Ste. 200, Metairie, 70001-4144. Tel: 504-837-2129; Fax: 504-837-6604. *Southern Dominican Foundation*, 1421 N. Causeway Blvd., Ste. 200, Metairie, 70001-4144. Tel: 504-837-2129; Fax: 504-837-6604. Rev. Christopher T. Eggleton, O.P., Pres.; Very Rev. David G. Caron, O.P., Vice Pres. & Sec.; Revs. Justin Kauchak, O.P., Treas.; John M. Pitzer, O.P., Promoter of Devel. *Southern Dominican Global Missions*, 4640 Canal St., 70119. Tel: 504-488-2652. Bro. Herman D. Johnson, O.P., Dir.

Ignatius Residence, 6321 Stratford Pl., 70131-7325. Tel: 504-394-2411; Fax: 504-433-2882. Email: ratch123@jesuits.net. Revs. James P. Bradley, S.J., B.S., M.A., S.T.L., Ph.D., Supr.; Kenneth A. Buddendorff, S.J., Asst. Dir.; Claude P. Boudreaux, S.J. (Retired); Clair M. Cazayoux, S.J. (Retired); Thomas A. Griffin, S.J. (Retired); John J. Heaney, S.J.; Ernest J. Jacques, S.J.; Thomas J. Jenniskens, S.J. (Retired); Theodore M. Kalamaja, S.J.; Rodney T. Kissinger, S.J. (Retired); Roland J. Lesseps, S.J., B.S., Ph.D. (Retired); Robert M. McCown, SJ, B.A., B.S., M.A. (Retired); James Herbert Mead, S.J., B.A., S.T.L., Ph.D., S.T.B. (Retired); Vincent A. Orlando, S.J.; Austin N. Park, S.J. (Retired); John F. Paul, S.J.; Donald Pearce, S.J. (Retired); Louis Poche, S.J. (Retired); Bro. John E. Puza, S.J., (Retired); Revs. Herve P. Racivitch, S.J., B.A., L.L.B., S.T.L. (Retired); Robert J. Ratchford, S.J., B.S., S.T.L., Ph.D. (Retired); Fred G. Reynolds, S.J. (Retired); John F. Schroder, S.J. (Retired); Bros. Anthony S. Coco, S.J.; George A. Murphy, S.J., (Retired); Joseph J. Remich, S.J., (Retired); Terence N. Todd, S.J. Priests 22; Brothers 5.

Jesuit Provincial Office (1907) New Orleans Province, 710 Baronne St., Ste. B, 70113. Tel: 504-571-1055; Fax: 504-571-1744. Email: noprovsj@norprov.org. Very Rev. Mark Lewis, S.J., Ph.D., M.Div., S.T.L., Ph.L., M.A., Prov.; Mary Baudouin, Provincial Asst. for Social Min.; Revs. Michael D. Dooley, S.J., B.A., M.Div., M.Ed., Provincial Asst. for Secondary Ed.; Warren J. Broussard, S.J., M.Div., M.S.W., Asst. for Pastoral and Retreat Min.; Bro. Lawrence J. Lundin, S.J., B.A., M.B.A., Treas.; Rev. John F. Armstrong, S.J., Prov. Asst. for Formation; Michael S. Bourg, Dir. Devel.; Revs. Paul Deutsch, S.J., Vocation Promoter; Raymond R. Fitzgerald, S.J., Socius to the Provincial; Michael A. Bouzigard, S.J., M.A., M.Div., M.Phil, Prov. Asst., Intl. Ministry.

Catholic Society of Religious and Literary Education Priests 7; Brothers 1.

Priests of the Province Abroad: Revs. Charles B. Thibodeaux, S.J., M.Div., Casa Parroquial, Santa Rosa (Misiones), Paraguay. Tel: 595-858-221; Fax: 595-858-221; Edward G. Benya, S.J., B.S., S.T.L., CP 3910, Teresina, PI 64-051-971 Brazil. Tel: 55-86-237-0666; Fax: 55-51-590-4895; A. Gerard Fineran, S.J., S.T.L., Vila Kostka C.P. 9, Indaiatuba, SP 13330-970 Brazil. Tel: 55-193-894-8555; Fax: 55-19-3894-8866; David H. Romero, S.J., B.A., M.A., CP 3937 Noviciado Ir. Vincente Canas, Manaus-AM 69085-970 Brazil. Tel: 011-55-92-682-2033; Patrick S. Madigan, S.J., B.A., M.A., S.T.L., Arrupe College, POB MP 320, Mt. Pleasant, Harare, Zimbabwe. Tel: 2634-745-411; Fax: 263-4-745-904; John R. Stacer, S.J., M.A., Ph.D., S.T.L., Arrupe College, POB MP 320, Mt. Pleasant, Harare, Zimbabwe. Tel: 2634-745-411; Fax: 2634-745-904; Joseph A. Carola, S.J., B.A., M.Div., S.T.L., S.T.D., Pontifical Gregorian Univ., Piazza della Pilotta 4, Rome 00187 Italy. Tel: 39-06-6701-5226; Fax: 39-06-6701-5419; Michael S. Gallagher, S.J., B.A., M.A., J.D., M.Div., S.T.M., Luwisha House, Plot 5880 Great East Rd., Lusaka, Zambia. Tel: 260-1-293320; Fax: 260-1-290912; David A. Brown, S.J., B.S., M.A., M.Div., Campion Hall, Oxford OX1 1QS England. Tel: 44 1865 286 135; Anthony J. Corcoran, S.J. *Jesuit Health Trust* Tel: 504-571-1055; Fax: 504-571-1744. Bro. Lawrence J. Lundin, S.J., B.A., M.B.A., Sec. *Jesuits of Pohnpei*, P.O. Box 160, Pohnpei, FM 96941-0160. Tel: 691-320-2317. Rev. David L. Andrus, S.J., B.S., M.Div. *Arrupe International Residence*, P.O. Box 216 UP 1144, Quezon City, Philippines. Tel: 632-426-5911; Fax: 632-426-5964.

Josephite Fathers and Brothers 70119. Tel: 504-944-2424. (See Separate Listing for School) *The Josephite Faculty House of St. Augustine High School*, 2600 A.P. Tureaud, 70119. Tel: 504-944-2424. Rev. Wilbur J. Atwood, S.S.J., Rector; Bro. Laurence E. Price, S.S.J., Vice Rector; Revs. Joseph M. Doyle, S.S.J.; John J. Raphael, S.S.J.; Joseph McKinley, S.S.J.

Loyola Jesuit Community, 1575 Calhoun St., 70118-6153. Tel: 504-865-3448; Fax: 504-895-0179. Rev. Peter S. Rogers, S.J., Pres.

ST. BENEDICT. *St. Joseph Abbey* (1890) 75376 River Rd., 70457. Tel: 985-892-1800; Fax: 985-867-2270. Web: www.sjasc.edu. Rt. Revs. Justin Brown, O.S.B., Abbot; Patrick Regan, O.S.B. (Retired); Revs. Raphael Barousse, O.S.B.; Adam Begnaud, O.S.B., M.S.; Charles J. Benoit, O.S.B., M.A.Th.; Very Rev. Gregory M. Boquet, O.S.B., M.A.; Revs. Basil David Burns, O.S.B.; Matthew R. Clark, O.S.B., M.A.; Cyril K. Crawford, O.S.B., B.A., M.Div.; Jonathan M. DeFrange, O.S.B.; Sean B. Duggan, O.S.B.; Augustine E. Foley, O.S.B., M.A.Th.; Peter E. Hammett, O.S.B.; Michael Jung, O.S.B.; Aelred Kavanagh, O.S.B., M.T.S., S.T.M., S.T.D.; Killian Tolg, B.A., M.A.; William J. MacCandless, O.S.B.; Paul Miranne, O.S.B.; Lawrence J. Phelps, O.S.B.; Scott J. Underwood, O.S.B., M.T.S., M.Ed.; Ambrose G. Wathen, O.S.B. Priests 23; Brothers 11.

[S] CONVENTS AND RESIDENCES FOR SISTERS

NEW ORLEANS. *Congregation of St. Joseph, C.S.J.*, 4030 Delgado Ave., 70119-3807. Web: www.csjoseph.org. Total Sisters in Archdiocese 12; Candidate 1.

Congregation of St. Joseph Ministry Against the Death Penalty, 3009 Grand Rt. St. John #6, 70122. Tel: 504-948-6557; Fax: 504-948-6558. Web: www-.prejean.org. Sr. Geraldine Riendeau, C.S.J., Sec. & Treas.

Congregation of the Marianites of the Holy Cross (1841) 1011 Gallier St., 70117-6111. Tel: 504-945-1620; Fax: 504-944-0756. Email: mscsec@marianites.org. Web: www.marianites.org. Sr. Suellen Tennyson, M.S.C., Congregational Leader. Total Sisters in Archdiocese 53.

Congregation of the Sisters of the Holy Faith, C.H.F., 1063 Moss St., 70119. Web: www.holyfaithsisters.net. Total Sisters in Archdiocese 4.

Daughters of Charity of St. Vincent de Paul, D.C., Sisters' Residence, 7817 S. Claiborne Ave., 70125. Tel: 504-861-4516. Email: sranthony@archdiocese-no.org. Sr. Anthony Barczykowski, D.C., Sister Servant. Total Sisters in Archdiocese 37.

Daughters of Our Lady of the Holy Rosary Queen of Peace Province (1967) 1492 Moss St., 70119-2904. Tel: 504-486-0039; Fax: 504-483-7910. Email: fmsrusaprovince@yahoo.com. Web: www.dongmancoi.org. Sr. Mary James Hang-Nga Thi Tran, F.M.S.R., Prov. Supr. Total Sisters in Archdiocese 55.

Dominican Sisters (Cabra, Ireland) O.P., 916 St. Andrew St., 70130. Tel: 504-522-5974. Web: www.cabraop.org. Total Sisters in Archdiocese 3.

Dominican Sisters of Peace, 5660 Bancroft Dr., 70122. Tel: 504-283-1122; Fax: 504-283-1217. Email: srsueop@aol.com. Total Sisters in House 5.

Dominican Sisters of Peace, 580 Broadway, 70118-3564. Tel: 504-865-7302; Fax: 504-865-8079. Email: srpeace@oppeace.org. Web: www.oppeace.org. 7320 St. Charles Ave., 70118. Tel: 504-861-9587. Sr. Theresa Fox, O.P., Mission Group Coord. Total Sisters in Archdiocese 33.

Franciscan Poor Clares (1885) 720 Henry Clay Ave., 70118-5891. Tel: 504-895-2019; Fax: 504-899-6218. Email: sisterct@juno.com. Web: www.poorclarenuns.com. Sr. Charlene Toups, O.S.C., Abbess. Nuns of the Order of St. Clare. Solemn Professed Nuns 8; Postulants 1.

Missionary Sisters of the Sacred Heart (Cabrini) M.S.C., 3443 Esplanade Ave., Apt. 314, 70119. Tel: 504-377-7561.

Presentation Sisters of the Blessed Virgin Mary (1968) 1802 Tulane Ave., 70112. Tel: 504-273-5573; Fax: 504-598-4297. Email: vbutler15@cox.net. Web: www.pbvmunion.org.

Union of Sisters of the Presentation of the Blessed Virgin Mary (United States Prov.)

Lantern Light, Inc. Ministry of the Union of Sisters of the Presentation of the Blessed Virgin Mary (United States Prov.), 1802 Tulane Ave., 70112. Tel: 504-273-5573; Fax: 504-598-4297. Email: vbutler7@bellsouth.net. Web: www.lanternlight-.org.

Religious of the Sacred Heart, R.S.C.J. (1800) 2545 Bayou Rd., 70119. Tel: 504-309-2828. Web: www.rscj.org. Sr. Maureen Little, R.S.C.J., Area Dir. Sisters 10. 2545 Bayou Rd., 70119. Tel: 504-309-2828. Sisters 2; Total Sisters in Archdiocese 10.

Sisters of Mercy of the Americas, R.S.M., 6024 Freret St., 70118. Tel: 504-899-4780. Email: mmouledoux@mercysc.org. Web: www.mercysc.org.

Sisters of Mercy of the Americas, South Central Community, Inc. Total Sisters in Archdiocese 20.

Sisters of the Blessed Sacrament, S.B.S., 4921 Dixon St., 70125.

Raphael House Trinity House Umoja Total Sisters in the Archdiocese 8.

Sisters of the Holy Family Motherhouse, S.S.F. (1842) 6901 Chef Menteur Hwy., 70126-5290. Tel: 504-241-3088; Fax: 504-241-9774. Email: emartinssfd@aol.com. Web: www.sistersoftheholyfamily.org. Sr. Eva Regina Martin, S.S.F., Congregational Leader; Rev. Victor H. Cohea, Chap. Total Sisters in Archdiocese 53.

Sisters, Servants of Mary, S.de.M., 5001 Perlita St., 70122-1999. Tel: 504-282-5549; Fax: 504-282-5550. Email: ssm2@cox.net. Web: sisterservantsofmary.com. Sr. Elvia Navarro,

S.de.M., Supr. Total Home Nursing Sisters in Archdiocese 13.

Tau House, 1029 Gov. Nicholls St., 70116-2432. Tel: 504-529-3569. Email: roddyssnd@aol.com; margmary27@hotmail.com. Sisters Ann Roddy, S.S.N.D, B.A., M.A., Admin.; Margaret Mary Friesenhahn, S.S.N.D., B.A., M.A. Center for the Empowerment of those infected with or affected by HIV/AIDS. Total in Residence 2; Total Staff 3.

Ursuline Sisters of the Roman Union, O.S.U. (1727) 2734 Nashville Ave., 70115. Tel: 504-861-4686; Fax: 504-866-8300. Sr. Carla Dolce, O.S.U., Prioress. Total Sisters in Archdiocese 8.

COVINGTON. *Carmelite Nuns, Discalced, O.C.D., Monastery of St. Joseph and St. Teresa* (1877) 73530 River Rd., 70435-2206. Tel: 985-898-0923; Fax: 985-871-9333. Email: covingtoncarmel@yahoo.com. Web: www.covingtoncarmel.org. Professed Nuns 7.

Daughters of Divine Providence, F.D.P. (1832) 74684 Airport Rd., 70435-5621. Tel: 985-809-8854; Fax: 985-809-8854. Email: divineprovidence@netzero.net. Total Sisters in Archdiocese 3.

Teresian Sisters (Society of St. Teresa of Jesus), S.T.J., Provincial Office, 18080 St. Joseph's Way, 70435-5623. Tel: 985-893-1470; Fax: 985-893-2476. Email: teresians@aol.com. Web: www.teresians.org. Sr. Gina Marie Geraci, S.T.J., Prov. Sisters 11.

Formation House, 18158 St. Joseph's Way, 70435-5624. Tel: 985-893-1557; Fax: 985-871-0724. Email: claricestj@excite.com. Sr. Clarice Suchy, S.T.J., Community Coord.

LACOMBE. *Congregation of Our Lady of Mount Carmel, O.Carm.* (1833) *Generalate*, P.O. Box 476, 70445-0476. Tel: 985-882-7577; 504-524-2398; Fax: 504-524-5011. Sr. Elizabeth Fitzpatrick, O.Carm., M.A., Pres. Sisters 82. *Mount Carmel Development Office*, P.O. Box 1160, 70445-1160. Tel: 985-882-7577; 504-524-2398; Fax: 504-524-5011. Email: development@sistersofmountcarmel.org.

Cub Corner Tel: 504-286-8673; Fax: 504-286-8676. Sr. Gwen Grillot, O.Carm., Exec. Dir. Total Staff 30; Total Enrollment 126.

Carmelite Spirituality Center (2004) 62292 Fish Hatchery Rd., P.O. Box 130, 70445-0130. Tel: 985-882-7579; Fax: 985-882-6563. Email: carmelcenter@bellsouth.net. Web: www.carmelite-spirituality.org.

MARRERO. *Salesian Sisters (Daughters of Mary Help of Christians) F.M.A.*, 2605 Crestwood Rd., 70072-2016. Tel: 504-347-4887. Email: fmamarrero@aol.com. Web: www.salesiansisters.org. Sisters in Archdiocese 5.

METAIRIE. *Daughters of St. Paul Convent, F.S.P.*, Pauline Book & Media Center, 4403 Veterans Memorial Blvd., 70006-5321. Tel: 504-887-7631; Fax: 504-887-1357. Email: metairie@paulinemedia.com. Total Sisters in Archdiocese 5.

Incarnate Word Sisters, C.C.V.I., 80 Metairie Ct., 70001-3032. Tel: 504-833-7972. Total Sisters in Archdiocese 4.

Religious of Our Lady of the Retreat in the Cenacle, R.C., The Cenacle Retreat House, 5500 St. Mary St., 70006. Tel: 504-887-1420; Fax: 504-887-6624. Email: cenacle2@aol.com. Web: www.cenaclesisters.org/metairie. Sr. Ann Wylder, R.C., Coord. Sisters 7; Total Staff 21.

Sisters of the Living Word, S.L.W., 4900 Park Dr., 70001-3237. Tel: 504-455-5905. Email: srstump@steddy.org. Web: www.slw.org. Sisters 2; Total Sisters in Archdiocese 9.

[T] RETREAT HOUSES

NEW ORLEANS. *Archdiocesan Spirituality Center*, 2901 S. Carrollton Ave., 70118-4391. Tel: 504-861-3254; Fax: 504-861-0584. Sr. Dorothy Trosclair, O.P., Exec. Dir.

Center of Jesus the Lord, 1236 N. Rampart St., 70116-2497. Tel: 504-529-1636; Fax: 504-529-5003. Email: office@centerofjesusthelord.org. Web: www.centerofjesusthelord.org. Rev. Lance J. Campo, S.T.L., Dir. Total Assisted 326; Total Staff 5; Total in Residence 3.

Sophie Barat House, 1719 Napoleon Ave., 70115-4809. Tel: 504-899-6027; Fax: 504-899-6210. Email: jmckinlay@rscj.org. Sisters Mary Blish, R.S.C.J.; Jane McKinlay, R.S.C.J.; Annice Callahan; Anne Sturges. Total Staff 6; Total in Residence 4.

LACOMBE. *Carmelite Spirituality Center*, 62292 Fish Hatchery Rd., P.O. Box 130, 70445-0130. Tel: 985-882-7579; Fax: 985-882-6563. Email: carmelcenter@bellsouth.net. Web: www.carmelitespirituality.org. Sisters Barbara Breaud, O.Carm., Exec. Dir.; Terry Falco, R.S.M., Program Dir.; Lena Collins, O.Carm., House Dir.

METAIRIE. *Cenacle Retreat House* (1958) 5500 St. Mary St., 70006. Tel: 504-887-1420; Fax: 504-887-6624. Email: cenacle2@aol.com. Web: www.cenaclesisters.org/metairie. Sr. Ann Wylder, R.C., Retreat House Admin. Religious 7; Total Staff 21.

PONCHATOULA. *Magnificat Center of the Holy Spirit*, 23629 Faith Rd., 70454. Tel: 985-386-5815; 800-531-9710; Fax: 504-200-7771. Total in Residence 90; Total Staff 4.

ST. BENEDICT. *Abbey Christian Life Center*, 75276 River Rd., 70457-9900. Tel: 985-892-3473; 985-892-1800; Fax: 985-892-3448. Conducted by Benedictine Monks

[U] MISCELLANEOUS

NEW ORLEANS. *Christian Brothers Foundation*, 8 Friederichs Ave., 70124-4602. Tel: 504-488-2802; Fax: 504-486-1053. Email: foundation@cbs-no.org.

Jesuit Seminary and Mission Fund, 710 Baronne St., Ste. B, 70113-1064. Tel: 504-571-1055; Fax: 504-571-1744. Email: jesuits@norprov.org. Web: www.norprov.org. Michael S. Bourg, Exec. Dir., Advancement.

**Lord, Teach Me To Pray, Inc.*, 11 Warbler St., 70124-4401.

MCA Foundation, 7027 Milne Blvd., 70124. Tel: 504-288-7626, Ext. 137; Fax: 504-288-7629. Email: mca@mcacubs.org. Web: www.mtcarmelcubs.org. Sr. Elizabeth Fitzpatrick, O.Carm., M.A., Pres.

**Pan African Roman Catholic Clergy Conference* (1999) 7300 Crowder Blvd., 70127-1599. Tel: 504-242-7554. Revs. Christopher Coleman, Ph.D., Pres.; Victor H. Cohea, Treas.

The Patrons of the Vatican Museums in the South, Inc. (1985) 775 Harrison Ave., 70124-3192. Tel: 504-482-4158; Fax: 504-485-0906. Email: vmcinnes@att.net. Dr. Rudolph H. Ehrensing, Pres.

Pierre Toussaint Foundation of New Orleans, Inc. (1995) 2600 A.P. Tureaud Ave., 70119-1299. Tel: 504-949-3113; Fax: 504-945-4134. Email: josmdoyle@netscape.net. Rev. John J. Raphael, S.S.J., Pres.

**Second Harvest Food Bank of Greater New Orleans and Acadiana* (1982) 700 Edwards Ave., 70123-2236. Tel: 504-734-1322; Fax: 504-733-8336. Web: www.no-hunger.org. Total Staff 69.

Stella Roman Foundation, Inc., 1010 Common St., Ste. 3010, 70112. Tel: 504-522-4756; Fax: 504-568-0783. Email: cidlaw@bellsouth.net.

ABITA SPRINGS. *The Christ in Christmas Committee of New Orleans*, 123 Iroquis Dr., 70420. Tel: 985-893-0169. Email: kcicno@bellsouth.net. Stephen F. Hart, Chm.

METAIRIE. *Equestrian Order of the Holy Sepulchre* (of Jerusalem, Southeastern Lieutenancy of the U.S.), 2955 Ridgelake Dr., Ste. 205, 70002. Tel: 504-832-0892; Fax: 504-832-1929. Email: office@sleohs.com. Anthony J. Capritto, Lieutenant.

International Dominican Foundation (2002) One Galleria Blvd., Ste. 710-B, 70001. Tel: 504-836-8180; Fax: 504-836-8180. Email: info@intldom.org. His Eminence Donald Cardinal Wuerl, S.T.D., Chm. Bd.; Very Rev. Mark Edney, O.P., Pres.

124 Airline Drive, Inc., 4133 Banks St., 70119-6883. Tel: 504-486-6631; Fax: 504-483-3816. Rev. Raymond R. Fitzgerald, S.J., Pres.

Southern Dominican Foundation, 1421 N. Causeway Blvd., Ste. 200, 70001-4144. Tel: 504-837-2129; Fax: 504-837-6604. Email: provincial@opsouth.org. Web: www.opsouth.org. Rev. Christopher T. Eggleton, O.P., Pres.; Very Rev. David G. Caron, O.P., Vice Pres. & Sec.; Revs. Justin Kauchak, O.P., Treas.; John M. Pitzer, O.P., Promoter Devel. & Vocations.

Southern Dominican Global Missions, 4640 Canal St., 70119. Tel: 504-488-2652. Bro. Herman D. Johnson, O.P., Dir.

**Willwoods Community* (1978) 3330 N. Causeway Blvd., Ste. 345, 70002. Tel: 504-830-3700; Fax: 504-840-9838. Email: t.chambers@willwoods.org. Web: www.willwoods.org. Rev. Thomas E. Chambers, C.S.C., Ph.D., Pres.

**WLAE-TV, Educational Broadcasting Foundation, Inc.*, 3330 N. Causeway Blvd., Ste. 345, 70002. Tel: 504-830-3700; Fax: 504-840-9838. Email: info@wlae.com. Web: www.wlae.com.

MONTZ. **Lyke Foundation*, 102 Ann Ct., 70068. Tel: 985-287-0161. P.O. Box 490, La Place, 70069-0490. Richard Cheri, Exec. Dir.; Kathleen Kennedy, Pres.; Andrew Lyke, Sec.; Rev. Fernand Cheri, O.F.M., Treas.

SECULAR INSTITUTES

ABITA SPRINGS. *Caritas (1950) Administration Center*, P.O. Box 308, 70420-0308. Tel: 985-892-4345. Email: caritas11r@aol.com.

Daraja House (1980) P.O. Box 524, Covington, 70434. Tel: 985-893-2261.

RELIGIOUS INSTITUTES OF MEN REPRESENTED IN THE ARCHDIOCESE

For further details refer to the corresponding bracketed number in the Religious Institutes of Men or Women section.

[0200]—*Benedictine Monks*—O.S.B.
[0330]—*Brothers of the Christian Schools* (New Orleans Prov.)—F.S.C.
[0470]—*The Capuchin Friars*—O.F.M.Cap.
[]—*Congregation of Christian Brothers (Edmund Rice)*—C.F.C.
[1330]—*Congregation of the Mission of St. Vincent de Paul Fathers & Brothers* (Southern Prov.)—C.M.
[]—*Congregation of the Mother Coredemptrix*—C.M.C.
[0260]—*Discalced Carmelite Friars*—O.C.D.
[0520]—*Franciscan Friars*—O.F.M.
[0690]—*Jesuit Fathers and Brothers* (New Orleans)—S.J.
[0780]—*Marist Fathers and Brothers* (USA Prov.)—S.M.
[0910]—*Oblates of Mary Immaculate* (Southern American Prov.)—O.M.I.
[0430]—*Order of Preacher-Dominicans* (St Martin de Porres/Southern Prov.)—O.P.
[1100]—*Priests and Brothers of the Sacred Heart* (Metuchen, NJ)—S.C.
[0610]—*Priests of the Congregation of Holy Cross* (Southern Prov.; Indiana Prov.)—C.S.C.
[1070]—*Redemptorist Fathers and Brothers* (New Orleans)—C.Ss.R.
[1190]—*Salesians of Don Bosco*—S.D.B.
[0440]—*Society of St. Edmund*—S.S.E.
[0420]—*Society of the Divine Word* (St. Augustine Prov.)—S.V.D.
[0700]—*St. Joseph's Society of the Sacred Heart* (Baltimore, MD)—S.S.J.

RELIGIOUS INSTITUTES OF WOMEN REPRESENTED IN THE ARCHDIOCESE

[0230]—*Benedictine Sisters of Pontifical Jurisdiction* (Colorado)—O.S.B.
[0400]—*Congregation of Our Lady of Mount Carmel*—O.Carm.
[3110]—*Congregation of Our Lady of the Retreat in the Cenacle*—R.C.
[1940]—*Congregation of Sisters of the Holy Faith*—C.H.F.
[2410]—*Congregation of the Marianites of Holy Cross*—M.S.C.
[0460]—*Congregation of the Sisters of Charity of the Incarnate Word*—C.C.V.I.
[3832]—*Congregation of the Sisters of St. Joseph*—C.S.J.
[1950]—*Congregation of the Sisters of the Holy Family*—S.S.F.
[0800]—*Daughters of Divine Providence*—F.D.P.
[0850]—*Daughters of Mary Help of Christians*—F.M.A.
[0895]—*Daughters of Our Lady of the Holy Rosary*—F.M.S.R.
[0760]—*Daughters of St. Vincent de Paul*—D.C.
[0420]—*Discalced Carmelite Nuns*—O.C.D.
[1110]—*Dominican Sisters of Our Lady of the Rosary and of Saint Catherine of Siena, Cabra, Ireland*—O.P.
[]—*Dominican Sisters of Peace*—O.P.
[1115]—*Dominican Sisters of Peace*—O.P.
[]—*Lovers of the Holy Cross Sisters at Cho Quan*—L.H.C.
[2860]—*Missionary Sisters of the Sacred Heart*—M.S.C.
[0950]—*Pious Society Daughters of St. Paul*—F.S.P.
[3760]—*Poor Clare Nuns, Order of St. Clare*—O.S.C.
[2970]—*School Sisters of Notre Dame* (Dallas & Mankato)—S.S.N.D.
[0660]—*Sisters of Christian Charity* (Wilmette, IL)—S.C.C.
[1010]—*Sisters of Divine Providence of San Antonio, Texas*—C.D.P.
[2575]—*Sisters of Mercy of the Americas* (Brooklyn; St. Louis)—R.S.M.
[2630]—*Sisters of Mercy of the Holy Cross*—S.C.S.C.
[1670]—*Sisters of St. Francis of Savannah*—O.S.F.
[1530]—*Sisters of St. Francis of the Congregation of Our Lady of Lourdes, Sylvania, Ohio*—O.S.F.
[0260]—*Sisters of the Blessed Sacrament for Indians and Colored People*—S.B.S.
[2050]—*Sisters of the Holy Spirit and Mary Immaculate*—S.H.Sp.
[2120]—*Sisters of the Immaculate Conception*—C.I.C.
[2350]—*Sisters of the Living Word*—S.L.W.
[3600]—*Sisters Servants of Mary*—S.de.M.

[4020]—*Society of St. Teresa of Jesus*—S.T.J.

[4060]—*Society of the Holy Child Jesus*—S.H.C.J.

[4070]—*Society of the Sacred Heart*—R.S.C.J.

[3330]—*Union of the Sisters of the Presentation of the Blessed Virgin Mary*—P.B.V.M.

[4110]—*Ursuline Nuns*—O.S.U.

NECROLOGY

✠ Hannan, Most Rev. Philip M., Retired Archbishop of New Orleans.—Died Sept. 29, 2011

† Reisch, Rev. Msgr. Milton L., (Retired)—Died July 18, 2011

† Van der Werff, Rev. Msgr. Martin, (Retired)—Died March 31, 2011

† Boileau, David A., (Retired)—Died Jan. 24, 2011

† Young, Bernard L., (Retired)—Died Oct. 31, 2011

An asterisk (*) denotes an organization that has established tax-exempt status directly with the IRS and is not covered by the USCCB Group Ruling.

Diocese of New Ulm

(Dioecesis Novae Ulmae)

Most Reverend

JOHN M. LEVOIR

Bishop of New Ulm; ordained May 30, 1981; appointed Bishop of New Ulm July 14, 2008; ordained September 15, 2008. *Office: 1400 6th St. N., New Ulm, MN 56073-2099.*

ESTABLISHED NOVEMBER 18, 1957.

Square Miles 9,863.

Comprises the Counties of Big Stone, Brown, Chippewa, Kandiyohi, Lac Qui Parle, Lincoln, Lyon, McLeod, Meeker, Nicollet, Redwood, Renville, Sibley, Swift, and Yellow Medicine in the State of Minnesota.

For legal titles of parishes and diocesan institutions, consult the Diocesan Pastoral Center.

Diocesan Pastoral Center: 1400 6th Street North, New Ulm, MN 56073-2099. Tel: 507-359-2966; Fax: 507-354-3667.

Web: www.dnu.org

Email: dnu@dnu.org

STATISTICAL OVERVIEW

Personnel	
Bishop	1
Priests: Diocesan Active in Diocese	43
Priests: Diocesan in Foreign Missions	2
Priests: Retired, Sick or Absent	22
Number of Diocesan Priests	67
Total Priests in Diocese	67
Extern Priests in Diocese	4
Ordinations:	
Diocesan Priests	1
Permanent Deacons in Diocese	4
Total Sisters	52
Parishes	
Parishes	76
With Resident Pastor:	
Resident Diocesan Priests	35
Without Resident Pastor:	
Administered by Priests	31
Administered by Religious Women	6
Administered by Lay People	4
Professional Ministry Personnel:	
Sisters	24
Lay Ministers	51
Welfare	
Catholic Hospitals	1
Total Assisted	9,701
Health Care Centers	1
Total Assisted	9,274
Homes for the Aged	11
Total Assisted	399
Residential Care of Disabled	1
Educational	
Diocesan Students in Other Seminaries	7
Students Religious	1
Total Seminarians	8
High Schools, Diocesan and Parish	3
Total Students	348
Elementary Schools, Diocesan and Parish	15
Total Students	1,737
Catechesis/Religious Education:	
High School Students	2,536
Elementary Students	5,139
Total Students under Catholic Instruction	9,768
Teachers in the Diocese:	
Sisters	3
Lay Teachers	189
Vital Statistics	
Receptions into the Church:	
Infant Baptism Totals	773
Minor Baptism Totals	21
Adult Baptism Totals	15
Received into Full Communion	87
First Communions	852
Confirmations	841
Marriages:	
Catholic	152
Interfaith	132
Total Marriages	284
Deaths	706
Total Catholic Population	61,917
Total Population	284,768

Former Bishops—Most Revs. ALPHONSE J. SCHLADWEILER, D.D., ord. June 9, 1929; appt. Nov. 28, 1957; cons. Jan. 29, 1958; installed Jan. 30, 1958; retired Dec. 23, 1975; died April 3, 1996; RAYMOND A. LUCKER, S.T.D., ord. June 7, 1952; appt. Titular Bishop of Meta and Auxiliary Bishop of St. Paul & Minneapolis July 12, 1971; cons. Sept. 8, 1971; appt. Bishop of New Ulm, Dec. 23, 1975; installed Feb. 19, 1976; retired Nov. 17, 2000; died Sept. 19, 2001; JOHN C. NIENSTEDT, ord. July 27, 1974; appt. Auxiliary Bishop of Detroit June 12, 1996; ord. July 9, 1996; appt. Bishop of New Ulm June 12, 2001; installed Aug. 6, 2001; appt. Coadjutor Archbishop of Saint Paul and Minneapolis April 24, 2007.

Diocesan Officials

Diocesan Pastoral Center—Most Rev. JOHN M. LEVOIR, 1400 6th Street North, New Ulm, 56073-2099. Tel: 507-359-2966; Fax: 507-354-3667.

Vicar General—Rev. Msgr. DOUGLAS L. GRAMS, J.C.L., 1400 6th St. N., New Ulm, 56073-2099. Tel: 507-359-2966; Fax: 507-354-3667.

Chancellor—Rev. Msgr. EUGENE L. LOZINSKI, J.C.L., Diocesan Pastoral Center, 1400 6th St. N., New Ulm, 56073-2099. Tel: 507-359-2966, Ext. 315; Fax: 507-354-3667.

Vice-Chancellor—Rev. JOHN G. BERGER, Church of St. Gregory the Great, 440 6th St., P.O. Box 5, Lafayette, 56054-0005. Tel: 507-228-8298.

Diocesan Tribunal—

Judicial Vicar (Officialis)—Rev. JOHN G. BERGER, Church of St. Gregory the Great, 440 6th St., P.O. Box 5, Lafayette, 56054-0005. Tel: 507-228-8298.

Moderator—VACANT, Diocesan Pastoral Center, 1400 6th St. N., New Ulm, 56073-2099. Tel: 507-359-2966; Fax: 507-354-3667.

Associate Judges—Rev. Msgr. EUGENE L. LOZINSKI, J.C.L.; Rev. PAUL L. WOLF; Rev. Msgr. DOUGLAS L. GRAMS, J.C.L.

Defender of the Bond—Rev. MARK S. MALLAK, J.C.L.

Office Manager—Mrs. JANELLE BOYUM. Tel: 507-359-2966, Ext. 319.

Notary—Mrs. JANELLE BOYUM.

Diocesan Boards and Councils

Building Committee—Revs. GEORGE V. SCHMIT JR., Chm., Church of St. Mary, 220 S. 10th St., P.O. Box 500, Bird Island, 55310-0500. Tel: 320-365-3593; Fax: 320-365-3142; MICHAEL M. DOYLE; Mrs. KAY OSBORNE; Mr. JOE EIKMEIER; Mr. RAYMOND MARTIN; Mrs. ANN PRZYBILLA; Mr. RICHARD GREENE.

College of Consultors—Rev. Msgrs. DOUGLAS L. GRAMS, J.C.L.; EUGENE L. LOZINSKI, J.C.L.; Revs. ANTHONY R. HESSE; JEROME E. PAULSON, J.C.L.; STEVEN J. VERHELST; PAUL H. VAN DE CROMMERT.

Priests' Council—Rev. Msgrs. DOUGLAS L. GRAMS, J.C.L.; EUGENE L. LOZINSKI, J.C.L.; Revs. KEITH R. SALISBURY; ANDREW J. MICHELS; ROBERT J. MRAZ; JAMES W. DEVORAK; PAUL H. VAN DE CROMMERT; ANTHONY R. HESSE; JEROME E. PAULSON, J.C.L.; STEVEN J. VERHELST; JOSEPH A. STEINBEISSER; BERNARD J. STEINER (Retired).

Committee on Parishes—Revs. PAUL D. TIMMERMAN; ANTHONY J. STUBEDA; BRIAN W. OESTREICH; Rev. Msgr. DOUGLAS L. GRAMS, J.C.L.; Revs. GEORGE V. SCHMIT JR.; RONALD V. HUBERTY, Chm.; Sr. MARY ANN KUHN, S.S.N.D.; JOANN EVJEN; Ms. MARY NORDSTROM; Mrs. SHIRLEY NOWAK; Sr. VIVIAN PETERSEN, O.S.B.; Mr. DAN J. ROSSINI, (Staff Liaison). On Call Members: Mrs. KARLA CROSS; Sr. ANNA MARIE REHA, S.S.N.D.; Mr. THOMAS P. KEAVENY.

Property Committee—Mr. ANDY RHODE, Chm.; Rev. JOHN H. BRUNNER; Mr. PHILIP LIESCH; Mr. BILL BRENNAN; Mr. MICHAEL H. BOYLE; Mr. DAN J. ROSSINI; Mr. THOMAS J. HOLZER, Staff Liaison.

Corporate Board—Most Rev. JOHN M. LEVOIR; Rev. Msgr. EUGENE L. LOZINSKI, J.C.L.; Mr. MICHAEL H. BOYLE; Mr. PAUL A. ZINS; Rev. Msgr. DOUGLAS L. GRAMS, J.C.L.

Diocesan Pastoral Council—Mrs. ROSE MARY KIRTZ, Chm., 520 2nd St. E., Hector, 55342. Tel: 320-848-2167; Mr. TOM GREEN, Vice Chm.; Ms. LINDA BUSCH, Sec.; Sr. LOIS L. BYRNE, P.B.V.M., M.S.W.-L.I.C.S.W., M.A. Members: Sr. CAROLE FREKING, O.S.F.; Mr. JERRY BROWN; Ms. CAROLYN BOERBOOM; Mr. MICHAEL BREDECK; Mr. TIMOTHY DOLAN; Mrs. JOANNE GREEN; Mrs. MARY SCHMITZ; Mr. RON SKJONG; Ms. ARLYCE ANDERSON; Mr. RON POLMAN; Ms. JAN RAUENHORST; Mr. BRUCE BOT; Rev. MARK S. MALLAK, J.C.L.; Mr. JIM HUBLEY; Ms. ARNOLDA FISCHER; Ms. DIANA KROELLS; Mr. DAVE MOLDAN; Mr. DAN J. ROSSINI, Staff Liaison.

Finance Council—Rev. JEFFREY P. HOREJSI; Mrs. CHRIS HEIDERSCHEIDT; Ms. LORI THUL; Mr. DON CLASEMANN; Mr. DAVID LYNN; Mr. STEVE SCHREIBER; Rev. MARK S. STEFFL; Mr. THOMAS J. HOLZER, Staff Liaison.

Sisters' Council—Sisters ANNA MARIE REHA, S.S.N.D., Chm.; LOIS ANNE PALKERT, O.S.F., Vice Chm.; JODELLE ZIMMERMAN, O.S.B., Sec. & Treas.; LOIS L. BYRNE, P.B.V.M., M.S.W.-L.I.C.S.W., M.A., Committee on Parishes Rep.; MARY ANN KUHN, S.S.N.D., Diocesan Pastoral Council Rep.; VACANT, E & C Rep.

Diocesan Pastoral Center

Coordinator of Diocesan Staff— Human Resources. Mr. DAN J. ROSSINI, Diocesan Pastoral Center,

1400 6th St. N., New Ulm, 56073-2099. Tel: 507-359-2966, Ext. 322; 507-233-5322; Fax: 507-354-3667. Email: drossini@dnu.org.

Office of Pastoral Planning—Mr. THOMAS P. KEAVENY, Dir., 1400 6th St. N., New Ulm, 56073-2099. Tel: 507-359-2966. Email: tkeaveny@dnu.org.

Human Resources Consultant—Mr. LARRY VANDEN PLAS. Tel: 651-788-3572.

Office of Finance and Cemeteries—Mr. THOMAS J. HOLZER, Dir., Diocesan Pastoral Center, 1400 6th St. N., New Ulm, 56073-2099. Tel: 507-359-2966, Ext. 309; 507-233-5309; Fax: 507-354-3667. Email: tomholzer@dnu.org.

Office of Development and Diocesan Foundation—Mr. WAYNE A. PELZEL, Dir., Diocesan Pastoral Center, 1400 6th St. N., New Ulm, 56073-2099. Tel: 507-359-2966, Ext. 310; 507-233-5310; Fax: 507-354-3667. Email: wpelzel@dnu.org.

Office of Evangelization and Catechesis—

Religious Education and Faith Formation—Mr. BRYAN REISING, D.R.E. Tel: 507-359-2966, Ext. 324; 507-233-5324. Email: breising@dnu.org.

Catholic Schools—Mrs. KARLA CROSS. Tel: 507-359-2966, Ext. 323; 507-233-5323. Email: kcross@dnu.org.

Lay Ecclesial Certification—Mrs. KARLA CROSS, Coord. Email: kcross@dnu.org.

Youth Ministry and Vocation Awareness—Ms. MARGARET MCHUGH, Dir., Diocesan Pastoral Center, 1400 6th St. N., New Ulm, 56073-2099. Tel: 507-359-2966, Ext. 327; 507-233-5327; Fax: 507-354-3667. Email: mmchugh@dnu.org.

Riverbend TEC (Together Encounter Christ)—Rev. DENNIS C. LABAT, Coord., Church of St. Raphael, 112 W. Van Dusen, Springfield, 56087-1396. Tel: 507-723-4141. Email: riverbendtec@newulmtel.net. Web: www.riverbendtec.org.

Committee for Evangelization & Catechesis—Mr. MICHAEL P. MCNEIL, Chm.; Ms. DIANA M. MCCARNEY; Mr. RON SKJONG; Rev. PAUL D. TIMMERMAN; Ms. SHERRY PLAETZ; Mrs. SHARON PIOTTER; Sr. BEATRIZ MARTINEZ, S.S.N.D. Ex Officio Members: Mrs. KARLA CROSS; Ms. MARGARET MCHUGH; Mr. BRYAN REISING.

Communications and Advancement—Mr. DAN J. ROSSINI, Dir. Tel: 507-359-2966, Ext. 333; 507-233-5333. Email: drossini@dnu.org.

The "Prairie Catholic"—Mr. DAN J. ROSSINI, Dir. & Editor-in-Chief. Tel: 507-359-2966, Ext. 333; 507-233-5333. Email: drossini@dnu.org; Mrs. CHRISTINE CLANCY, Editor, Diocesan Pastoral Center, 1400 6th St. N., New Ulm, 56073-2099. Tel: 507-359-2966, Ext. 332; 507-233-5332; Fax: 507-354-3667. Email: cclancy@dnu.org; Mr. SAM PATET, Reporter/Website. Tel: 507-359-2966, Ext. 333; 507-233-5333; Fax: 507-354-3667.

Office of Worship and Lay Ministry—Mrs. ANGELA J. PRZYBILLA, Dir. Tel: 507-359-2966, Ext. 320; 507-233-5320. Email: aprzybilla@dnu.org.

Worship Committee—Sr. JOANNE BACKES, O.S.B.; Mrs. SARAH JIRAK; Ms. MARY BOLEK; Ms. LESLIE BRINKMAN; Ms. JEAN SCHUELLER; Mrs. MARGE MARTIN; Sr. ELIZABETH GRUENES, O.S.B.; Rev. ANTHONY R. HESSE; Mrs. ANN PRZYBILLA, Staff Liaison.

Charismatic Renewal—VACANT, Diocesan Liaison.

Ecumenism and Interreligious Affairs—Rev. PAUL D. TIMMERMAN, 508 13th St. N., Benson, 56215-1228. Tel: 320-842-4271. Email: fatherpaultimmerman@gmail.com.

Office of Social Concerns and Family Life—Mr. CHRISTOPHER A. LOETSCHER, Dir., Diocesan Pastoral Center, 1400 6th St. N., New Ulm, 56073-2099. Tel: 507-359-2966, Ext. 338; 507-233-5338; Fax: 507-354-3667. Email: cloetscher@dnu.org.

Social Concerns Committee—Rev. JEFFREY P. HOREJSI; Mr. PAUL HAYDEN; Sr. DONNA WERMUS, S.S.N.D.; Mrs. EILEEN WALLACE; Mr. JIM HUBLEY. Ex Officio Members: Sr. ANNA MARIE REHA, S.S.N.D.; Rev. PHILIP M. SCHOTZKO; Mr. THOMAS P. KEAVENY; Mr. CHRISTOPHER A. LOETSCHER, Staff Liaison.

Office of Catholic Charities—Tel: 507-359-2617; 866-670-5163; Fax: 507-354-3667. Mr. THOMAS P. KAEVENY, M.S.W., L.I.C.S.W., Dir. Email: tkeaveny@dnu.org; Mrs. PAULETTE KRAL, Office Admin. Email: pkral@dnu.org.

New Ulm Diocesan Office—Diocesan Pastoral Center, 1400 6th St. N., New Ulm, 56073.

Hutchinson Regional Office—Suites 12 & 13: 902 Hwy. 155, Hutchinson, 55350. Mrs. SANDRA "SAM" RICKERTSEN, M.S., L.A.M.F.T., Outreach Counselor.

Marshall Regional Office—Campus Religious Center, 1418 State St., Marshall, 56258. Mrs. TAMI J. DALE, L.S.W., M.S., L.P.C.C., Outreach Counselor.

Willmar Regional Office—713 12th St., S.W., Willmar, 56201-3099. Sr. LOIS L. BYRNE, P.B.V.M., M.S.W.-L.I.C.S.W., M.A., Outreach & Pregnancy Counselor, Project Rachel and Spiritual Direction. Catholic Charities Advisory Committee: Sr. THERESE COLLISON, S.S.N.D.; Mrs. BARBARA DIETZ; Ms. MEG DWYER-LEE, L.P.; Sr. CAROLE FREKING, O.S.F.; Mr. NOEL "CHUCK" KOENIGS, M.S.W.; Ms. CINDY NELSON, L.S.W.; Rev. PAUL A. SCHUMACHER; Sr. ANNA MARIE REHA, S.S.N.D.; Mr. CHRISTOPHER A. LOETSCHER; Mr. THOMAS P. KEAVENY, Staff Liaison.

Family Life—Mr. CHRISTOPHER A. LOETSCHER, Dir., Diocesan Pastoral Center, 1400 6th St. N., New Ulm, 56073-2099. Tel: 507-359-2966, Ext. 338; 507-233-5338; Fax: 507-354-3667. Email: cloetscher@dnu.org. Marriage Preparation, Resources & Referral for Marriage & Family Concerns, Divorced/Separated.

Family Life Education—Sr. CANDACE FIER, I.S.S.M., Dir., 1400 6th St. N., New Ulm, 56073-2099. Tel: 507-359-2966; 507-233-5328. Email: cfier@dnu.org. Natural Family Planning, Chastity Education, Theology of the Body, Bioethics.

Retrouvaille—Tel: 800-470-2230.

AIDS Ministry—Rev. PAUL A. SCHUMACHER, Church of the Holy Redeemer, 503 W. Lyon St., Marshall, 56258. Tel: 507-532-5711; Fax: 507-532-3262.

Propagation of the Faith/Holy Childhood Association—Rev. PHILIP M. SCHOTZKO, Diocesan Pastoral Center, 1400 6th St. N., New Ulm, 56073-2099. Tel: 507-359-2966; Fax: 507-354-3667.

San Lucas Mission Office—Rev. Msgr. GREGORY T. SCHAFFER; KATHY HUEBERT, Administrative Asst., Diocesan Pastoral Center, 1400 6th St. N., New Ulm, 56073-2099. Tel: 507-359-2966, Ext. 304; Fax: 507-354-3667. Email: khuebert@dnu.org.

Hispanic Ministry—Sr. ANNA MARIE REHA, S.S.N.D., Diocesan Pastoral Center, 1400 6th St. N., New Ulm, 56073-2099. Tel: 507-359-2966, Ext. 321; 507-233-5321; Fax: 507-354-3667. Email: areha@dnu.org.

Office of Personnel—

Priest Personnel—Rev. Msgr. DOUGLAS L. GRAMS, J.C.L., Exec. Dir., Diocesan Pastoral Center, 1400 6th St. N., New Ulm, 56073-2099. Tel: 507-359-2966, Ext. 303; Fax: 507-354-3667.

Priest Personnel Board—Rev. Msgr. DOUGLAS L. GRAMS, J.C.L., Exec. Dir.; Rev. DENNIS C. LABAT; Rev. Msgr. EUGENE L. LOZINSKI, J.C.L.; Revs. TODD J. PETERSEN; GEORGE V. SCHMIT JR.; RONALD V. HUBERTY; Rev. Msgr. JOHN A. RICHTER.

Pastoral Administrators—Rev. DENNIS C. LABAT, Supvr., Diocesan Pastoral Center, 1400 6th St. N., New Ulm, 56073-2099. Tel: 507-359-2966, Ext. 316; Fax: 507-354-3667. Email: dlabat@newulmtel.net.

Victim Assistance Coordinator—Mr. CHRISTOPHER A. LOETSCHER. Tel: 507-359-2966, Ext. 338; 507-233-5338; Fax: 507-354-3667. Email: cloetscher@dnu.org.

Bishop's Delegate in Matters Pertaining to Sexual Misconduct—Rev. Msgr. DOUGLAS L. GRAMS, J.C.L., Diocesan Pastoral Center, 1400 6th St. N., New Ulm, 56073-2099. Tel: 507-359-2966; Fax: 507-354-3667.

Bishop's Delegate for the Permanent Diaconate—Rev. Msgr. EUGENE L. LOZINSKI, J.C.L. Tel: 320-864-5162; 320-864-2963 (Rectory); Fax: 320-864-5163.

Safe Environment Coordinator—Sr. CANDACE FIER, I.S.S.M., 1400 6th St. N., New Ulm, 56073. Tel: 507-359-2966; Fax: 507-354-3667. Email: cfier@dnu.org.

Office of Conciliation—VACANT, Dir., 1400 6th St. N., New Ulm, 56073-2099. Tel: 507-359-2966; Fax: 507-354-3667.

Vocations Team—Most Rev. JOHN M. LEVOIR, Team Chm.; Revs. TODD J. PETERSEN, Dir., Diocesan Pastoral Center, 1400 6th St. N., New Ulm, 56073-2099. Tel: 507-359-2966, Ext. 331; 507-342-5155; Fax: 507-354-3667. Email: frtodd@mac.com; CRAIG A. TIMMERMAN, Asst. Dir., Diocesan Pastoral Center, 1400 6th St. N., New Ulm, 56073. Tel: 507-359-2966; Fax: 507-354-3667. Email: fathercraig@gmail.com; Ms. MARGARET MCHUGH, Coord., Vocation Fairs & Other Program Events, Diocesan Pastoral Center, 1400 6th St. N., New Ulm, 56073-2099. Tel: 507-359-2966, Ext. 327; 507-233-5327; Fax: 507-354-3667. Email: mmchugh@dnu.org.

Continuing Education of Clergy—Mrs. KARLA CROSS, Dir., Diocesan Pastoral Center, 1400 6th St. N., New Ulm, 56073-2099. Tel: 507-359-2966, Ext. 323; Fax: 507-354-3667.

Committee for Continuing Education of Clergy—Revs. JOHN A. PEARSON; MARK S. STEFFL; CRAIG A. TIMMERMAN; Sr. DONNA WERMUS, S.S.N.D.

Board of Trustees for Pension Plan for Priests—Most Rev. JOHN M. LEVOIR; Rev. Msgrs. DOUGLAS L. GRAMS, J.C.L.; EUGENE L. LOZINSKI, J.C.L.; Revs. ROBERT P. GOBLIRSCH; STEVEN J. VERHELST; Mr. DONALD GUGGEMOS JR.; Mr. MICHAEL SCHWARTZ; Mr. THOMAS J. HOLZER, Staff Liaison.

Vicar for Retired Priests—Rev. BERNARD J. STEINER (Retired), 1001 N. Garden St., Apt. 105, New Ulm, 56073. Tel: 507-359-3583. Email: bernardsteiner@newulmtel.net.

Organizations in the Diocese of New Ulm

Diocesan Council of Catholic Women—Mrs. AUDREY PROKOSCH, Pres., 24624 U.S. Hwy. 71, Redwood Falls, 56283. Tel: 507-644-3112. Email: amprokosch@gmail.com; Mrs. CHRIS HEIDERSCHEIDT, Pres.-Elect, 26098 190th St., Sleepy Eye, 56085-4366. Tel: 507-794-4201; Rev. Msgr. EUGENE L. LOZINSKI, J.C.L., Diocesan Moderator.

Girl Scouts—Mrs. MARY REITSMA, 4313 N.E. 15th St., Willmar, 56201. Tel: 320-235-3471.

Boy Scouts—Rev. ANDREW J. MICHELS, Chap., St. Mary, 636 1st Ave. N., Sleepy Eye, 56085-1004. Tel: 507-794-4171; Fax: 507-794-5871.

Marriage Encounter—JEFF KODET; RONDI KODET, 34814 280th St., Redwood Falls, 56283. Tel: 507-644-3523.

CLERGY, PARISHES, MISSIONS AND PAROCHIAL SCHOOLS

CITY OF NEW ULM

(BROWN COUNTY)

1—CATHEDRAL OF THE HOLY TRINITY (1856) [CEM] [JC], (Holy Cross area faith community with St. Gregory the Great, Lafayette; St. George, West Newton Township; St. John the Baptist, Searles; St. Mary's, New Ulm.) Rev. Msgr. John A. Richter, Rector; Rev. Matthew J. Wiering, Parochial Vicar.

Res. & Mailing Address: 605 N. State St., 56073-1898. Tel: 507-354-4158; Fax: 507-354-2563. Email: newulmcathedral@hotmail.com. Web: cathedralht.org.

See New Ulm Area Catholic Schools, New Ulm under New Ulm Area Catholic Schools located in the Institution section.

Catechesis/Religious Program—Students 139.

2—ST. MARY (1911) [JC], (Holy Cross area faith community with Cathedral, New Ulm; Searles; Lafayette; West Newton Township.) Rev. Msgr. Douglas L. Grams; Rev. Edward J. Ardolf; Deacon Leonard Fuller.

Church: 417 S. Minnesota St., 56073-2120. Tel: 507-233-9500; Fax: 507-354-8414. Email: stmarys@newulmtel.net. Web: www.stmarys-newulm.com.

See New Ulm Area Catholic Schools, New Ulm under New Ulm Area Catholic Schools located in the Institution section.

Catechesis/Religious Program—Tel: 507-233-9511; Fax: 507-354-8414. Students 193.

OUTSIDE THE CITY OF NEW ULM

APPLETON, SWIFT CO., ST. JOHN (1880) [CEM 2] [JC 2], (Prince of Peace area faith community with Dawson & Madison.) Rev. Brian W. Oestreich.

Mailing Address: 349 E. Reuss Ave., 56208-1516.

Res.: 412 3rd St., W., Madison, 56256. Tel: 507-829-6667. Email: prince-of-peace@hotmail.com.

Church: 350 S. Edquist St., 56208-1516.

Catechesis/Religious Program—Tel: 320-289-1146. Students 72.

ARLINGTON, SIBLEY CO., ST. MARY (1864) [CEM], (Area faith community with Gaylord & Green Isle.) Rev. Keith R. Salisbury.

Mailing Address: P.O. Box 392, 55307-0392.

Res.: 504 7th Ave., N.W., P.O. Box 392, 55307-0392. Tel: 507-964-5413; Fax: 507-964-5425. Email: stmararl@frontiernet.net.

Catechesis/Religious Program—Tel: 507-964-5378. Jane Steinborn, D.R.E. (Elem K-6); Beth Walters, D.R.E. (Jr. & Sr. High 7-12). Students 131.

BARRY, BIG STONE CO., ST. BARNABAS, Closed. For sacramental records contact Holy Rosary, Graceville.

BEARDSLEY, BIG STONE CO., ST. MARY (1884) [CEM], Clustered with Graceville. Sr. Rebecca Littel, O.S.B., Pastoral Assoc.

Res. & Mailing Address: 518 S. Forest St., P.O. Box 299, 56211-0299. Tel: 320-265-6113 (Rectory & Office). Email: saintmary@centurytel.net.

Church: 510 S. Forest St., 56211. Tel: 320-265-6916.

Catechesis/Religious Program—Students 22.

BECHYN, RENVILLE CO., ST. MARY, Closed. For sacramental records contact St. Aloysius, Olivia.

BELGRADE, NICOLLET CO., ST. MICHAEL, Closed. For sacramental records contact St. Paul, Nicollet.

BENSON, SWIFT CO., ST. FRANCIS (1881) [CEM], (St. Isidore the Farmer area faith community with Clontarf; Danvers; De Graff; & Murdock.) Revs. William A. Sprigler; Paul D. Timmerman, Parochial Vicar. In Res., Rev. Samuel Perez Tax. Area Pastoral Leaders:, Deacon Michael Thoennes, Dir. Faith Formation.
Area Office—Tel: 320-842-4271; Fax: 320-843-2264. Email: stfran@embarqmail.com. Web: www.catholicareaparishes.org.
Church: 508 13th St. N., 56215-1228.
Catechesis/Religious Program—Robbie Jennings, Rel. Educ. & Youth Ministry. Students 193.

BIRCH COOLIE, RENVILLE CO., ST. PATRICK, Closed. For sacramental records contact Sacred Heart, Franklin. Earlier records located at St. John, Morton.

BIRD ISLAND, RENVILLE CO., ST. MARY (1879) [CEM], (Heart of Jesus area faith community with Hector; Olivia; & Renville.) Rev. George V. Schmit Jr.
Mailing Address: P.O. Box 500, 55310-0500. Email: stmarybi@yahoo.com. Web: www.afcheaatofjesus.org.
Parish Offices & Rectory: 220 S. 10th St., P.O. Box 500, 55310-0500. Tel: 320-365-3593; Fax: 320-365-4510.
Res.: 240 S. 8th St., P.O. Box 500, 55310-0500. Tel: 320-365-3828.
School—(Grades K-8), 140 S. 10th St., P.O. Box 500, 55310-0500. Tel: 320-365-3693. Email: principal@stmarysschoolbirdisland.com. Web: www.stmarysschoolbirdisland.com. Mrs. Tracy Bertrand, Prin. Lay Teachers 12; Students 123.
Catechesis/Religious Program—Students 75.

CANBY, YELLOW MEDICINE CO., ST. PETER (1897) [CEM], (Good Teacher area faith community with St. Leo; Ghent; & Minneota.) Rev. Craig A. Timmerman.
Res.: 307 W. 4th St., 56220-1211. Tel: 507-223-7304; Fax: 507-223-5776. Email: stpeter@canbylancers.org.
School—(Grades K-6), 410 Ring Ave. N., 56220-1237. Tel: 507-223-7729; Fax: 507-223-7178. Mrs. Jessica Balzarini, Prin. Lay Teachers 5; Students 45.
Catechesis/Religious Program—Students 117.

CLARA CITY, CHIPPEWA CO., ST. CLARA (1890), (Holy Family area faith community with Granite Falls & Montevideo.) Sr. Carole Freking, O.S.F., Pastoral Admin.
Church: 414 N. Main St., P.O. Box 310, 56222-0310. Tel: 320-847-2256; Fax: 320-847-2445. Email: stclara@hcinet.net. Web: saintsjac.org.
Catechesis/Religious Program—Tel: 320-847-2445. Email: bstrommer@hcinet.net. Students 81.

CLARKFIELD, YELLOW MEDICINE CO., ST. ISIDORE, Closed. For sacramental records contact St. Joseph, Montevideo.

CLEMENTS, REDWOOD CO., ST. JOSEPH (ORATORY) (1902) [CEM] Rev. Msgr. Eugene L. Lozinski.
Mailing & Physical Address: P.O. Box 459, Morgan, 56266-0459. Tel: 507-794-4171. Email: stmichaels@redred.com.

CLONTARF, SWIFT CO., ST. MALACHY (1878), (St. Isidore the Farmer area faith community with Benson; Danvers; DeGraff; & Murdock.) Rev. William A. Sprigler.
Mailing Address: 508 13th St. N., Benson, 56215-1228. Tel: 320-842-4271; Fax: 320-843-2264; 320-365-4510. Email: stfran@embarqmail.com.
Church: 300 Armagh St., S.W., 56226.
Catechesis/Religious Program—Robbie Jennings, Dir. Faith Formation & Youth Ministry. Students 19.

COMFREY, BROWN CO., ST. PAUL (1900) [CEM], (Divine Mercy area faith community with Clements; Morgan; Leavenworth; & Sleepy Eye.) Sr. JoAnne Backes, O.S.B., Pastoral Admin.
Res. & Mailing Address: 209 N. Field St., P.O. Box 277, 56019-0277. Tel: 507-877-2361; Fax: 507-877-2361. Email: stpcomfrey@yahoo.com.
Catechesis/Religious Program—Tel: 507-877-9800. Students 44.

COTTONWOOD, LYON CO., ST. MARY (1902) [CEM], (Bread of Life area faith community with Green Valley & Marshall.) Rev. Jack (John) A. Nordick.
Res. & Mailing Address: 255 W. 4th St. S., P.O. Box 228, 56229-0228. Tel: 507-423-5220; Fax: 507-423-5275. Email: stmarys.cottonwood@frontiernet.net. Web: www.holy-redeemer.com.
Catechesis/Religious Program—Students 90.

DANVERS, SWIFT CO., CHURCH OF THE VISITATION (ORATORY) (1885) [CEM], (St. Isidore the Farmer area faith community with Benson; Clontarf; De Graff; & Murdock.) Rev. William A. Sprigler.
Mailing Address: 508 13th St. N., Benson, 56215-1228. Email: stfran@embarqmail.com.

DARWIN, MEEKER CO., ST. JOHN (1861) [CEM], (Seeker of Souls area faith community with Forest City.) Rev. John A. Pearson.
Res. & Mailing: 106 N. 4th St., 55324-6016. Tel: 320-275-2915; 320-693-9496; Fax: 320-275-0198. Email: rectory@stjohnscatholic-darwin.com. Web: www.stjohnscatholic-darwin.com.
Catechesis/Religious Program—Tel: 320-286-2800. Email: johnhansen@embarqmail.com; cnpeterson@xtratyme.com. Students 151.

DAWSON, LAC QUI PARLE CO., ST. JAMES (1898) [CEM], (Prince of Peace area faith community with Appleton & Madison.) Sr. Vivian Petersen, O.S.B., Pastoral Admin.
Res. & Mailing Address: 10th & Locust, P.O. Box 270, 56232-0270. Tel: 320-769-4465. Email: stjames@frontiernet.net; prince-of-peace@hotmail.com.
Catechesis/Religious Program—Students 44.

DE GRAFF, SWIFT CO., ST. BRIDGET (1876) [CEM], (St. Isidore the Farmer area faith community with Benson; Clontarf; Danvers; & Murdock.) Rev. William A. Sprigler.
Mailing Address & Res.: 508 13th St. N., Benson, 56215-1228. Tel: 320-842-4271; Fax: 320-843-2264.
Church: Email: stfran@embarqmail.com. Web: www.catholicareaparishes.org.
Area Office—Tel: 320-842-4271; Fax: 320-843-2264.
Catechesis/Religious Program—Church of St. Francis, 508 13th St. N., Benson, 56215. Michael Thoennes, Dir. Faith Formation. Students 26.

EDEN VALLEY, MEEKER CO., ST. PETER (1903) Closed. For inquiries for parish records contact Assumption Church, Eden Valley, Diocese of St. Cloud.

FAIRFAX, RENVILLE CO., ST. ANDREW (1871) [CEM], (All Saints Area faith community with Franklin; Gibbon; & Winthrop.) Rev. Jeffrey P. Horejsi.
Area Office: Tel: 507-426-7739.
Res. & Mailing Address: 15 S.E. First St., P.O. Box C, 55332-0903. Tel: 507-426-7125. Email: ffgw@centurytel.net.
Catechesis/Religious Program—Tel: 507-426-7742. Connie Serbus, D.R.E. Students 82.

FAXON TOWNSHIP, SIBLEY CO., ST. JOHN-ASSUMPTION (1859) [CEM 2], Clustered with Henderson & Jessenland. Rev. Samuel F. Perez.
Mailing Address: P.O. Box 427, Henderson, 56044.
Church: 26523 200th St., Belle Plaine, 56011-9302. Tel: 507-248-3550. Email: stjos@frontiernet.net.
Catechesis/Religious Program—Students 114.

FOREST CITY, MEEKER CO., ST. GERTRUDE (1857) [CEM], (Seeker of Souls area faith community with Darwin.) Rev. John A. Pearson, Sacramental Min.; Mr. Michael P. McNeil, Pastoral Admin.
Mailing Address: 31626-650th Ave., Litchfield, 55355-4110.
Church: 31608-650th Ave., Litchfield, 55355-4410. Tel: 320-693-7801. Email: stgert@xtratyme.com. Web: www.forministry.com/usmnrcathsgccs.
Res.: 31628-650th Ave., Litchfield, 55355.
Catechesis/Religious Program—Students 36.

FRANKLIN, RENVILLE CO., SACRED HEART (1898) [CEM 2], (All Saints Area faith community with Fairfax; Gibbon; & Winthrop.) Rev. Jeffrey P. Horejsi.
Mailing Address: P.O. Box 175, 55333-0175. Email: ffgw@centurytel.net.
Res.: 15 S.E. First St., P.O. Box C, Fairfax, 55332-0903. Tel: 507-426-7125.
Church: E. Main St., 55333-0175.
Catechesis/Religious Program—Connie Serbus, D.R.E. Students 49.

GAYLORD, SIBLEY CO., ST. MICHAEL (1882), (Ss. Michael, Mary & Brendan area faith community with Arlington & Green Isle. Rev. Keith R. Salisbury.
Res. & Mailing Address: 411 Court Ave., P.O. Box 357, 55334-0357. Tel: 507-237-2851; Fax: 507-237-2383. Email: stmichael@myclearwave.net.
Catechesis/Religious Program—P.O. Box 357, 55334-0357. Angie Weber, D.R.E.; Mr. Timothy Dolan, D.R.E. Students 87.

GHENT, LYON CO., ST. ELOI (1883) [CEM], (Good Teacher Area faith community with Canby; St. Leo; & Minneota.) Rev. Jeremy G. Kucera.
Church: 306 W. McQuestion, 56239-9750. Tel: 507-428-3285. Email: steloi@starpoint.net.
Catechesis/Religious Program—Students 66.

GIBBON, SIBLEY CO., ST. WILLIBRORD (1886) [CEM], (All Saints Area faith community with Fairfax; Franklin; & Winthrop.) Rev. Jeffrey P. Horejsi; Sr. Mary Ann Kuhn, S.S.N.D., Parish Min.
Res. & Mailing Address: 1032 Ash Ave., P.O. Box 436, 55335-0436. Tel: 507-834-6461. Email: ffgw@centurytel.net.
Catechesis/Religious Program—Tel: 507-834-6659. Students 62.

GLENCOE, MCLEOD CO.

1—ST. GEORGE, Closed. For sacramental records, contact St. Pius X, Glencoe.

2—SS. PETER AND PAUL, Closed. For sacramental records, contact St. Pius X, Glencoe.

3—ST. PIUS X (1983) [CEM], (Blessed John Paul II area faith community with Silver Lake & Winsted) Rev. Anthony J. Stubeda.
Res., Church & Mailing Address: 1014 Knight Ave., N., 55336-2300. Tel: 320-864-5162; 320-864-2963 (Rectory); Fax: 320-864-5163. Email: stpiusx@stpiusxglencoe.org.
School—(Grades PreK-6), 1103 E. 10th St., 55336-2399. Tel: 320-864-3214. Email: principal@stpiusxglencoe.org. Ms. Catherine Millerbernd, Prin. Sisters 2; Lay Teachers 6; Students 71.
Catechesis/Religious Program—Tel: 320-864-5162. Students 135.

GRACEVILLE, BIG STONE CO., HOLY ROSARY (1878) [JC], Clustered with Beardsley. Rev. David L. Breu; Deacon Art D. Abel. Tel: 320-748-7573 (Home).
Res. & Mailing Address: 511 Studdart Ave., P.O. Box 7, 56240-0007. Tel: 320-748-7313. Email: choly000@centurytel.net.
Catechesis/Religious Program—517 Studdart Ave., 56240. Tel: 320-748-7501. Students 129.

GRANITE FALLS, YELLOW MEDICINE CO., ST. ANDREW (1885) [CEM], (Holy Family area faith community with Montevideo & Clara City.) Rev. James W. Devorak.
Church: 1094 Granite St., 56241-1355. Fax: 320-564-2335 (Call First).
Res.: 521 Eureka Ave., Montevideo, 56241. Tel: 320-269-2335; Fax: 320-269-7555. Email: standrew@saintsjac.org. Web: www.saintsjac.org.
Catechesis/Religious Program—1056 Fourth St., 56241. Tel: 320-564-2336. Students 106.

GREEN ISLE, SIBLEY CO., ST. BRENDAN (1854) [CEM], (Ss. Michael, Mary & Brendan area faith community with Arlington & Gaylord.) Rev. Keith R. Salisbury.
Res. & Mailing Address: 221 McGrann St., S., P.O. Box 85, 55338-0085. Tel: 507-326-5111; Fax: 507-964-5209. Email: stbrendan@frontiernet.net.
Catechesis/Religious Program—Students 28.

GREEN VALLEY, LYON CO., ST. CLOTILDE (1912) [CEM], (Bread of Life area faith community with Cottonwood & Marshall.) Rev. Jack (John) A. Nordick, Parochial Admin.
Res.: 255 W. 4th, Cottonwood, 56229. Tel: 507-423-5220. Email: linda@stclotilde.com.
Church: 3272-270th Ave., Marshall, 56258-0228. Tel: 507-532-2841.
Catechesis/Religious Program—Students 55.

GREENLEAF, MEEKER CO., ST. COLUMBAN, Closed. For inquiries for sacramental records contact St. Philip, Litchfield.

HECTOR, RENVILLE CO., CHURCH OF ST. JOHN (1878) [CEM], (Heart of Jesus area faith community with Bird Island; Olivia; & Renville.) Mr. Donald A. Clasemann, Pastoral Admin.
Church: 301 Cedar Ave. E., P.O. Box 295, 55342-0295. Tel: 320-848-6437; Fax: 320-848-2407. Email: stjohnshector@frontiernet.net.
Catechesis/Religious Program—Students 60.

HEGBERT, SWIFT CO., ST. AGNES, Closed. For sacramental records, contact St. John, Appleton.

HENDERSON, SIBLEY CO., ST. JOSEPH (1859) [CEM], Clustered with Faxon Township & Jessenland. Rev. Samuel F. Perez.
Res. & Mailing Address: 213 S. 6th St., P.O. Box 427, 56044-7735. Tel: 507-248-3550. Email: stjos@frontiernet.net.
Catechesis/Religious Program—Students 55.

HOLLOWAY, SWIFT CO., ST. JOSEPH, Closed. For sacramental records, contact St. John, Appleton.

HUTCHINSON, MCLEOD CO., CHURCH OF ST. ANASTASIA (1866) [CEM], Clustered with Stewart. Revs. Gerald S. Meidl; Zachary D. Peterson, Parochial Vicar.
Mailing Address: 460 Lake St., S.W., 55350-2349. Email: stanastasia@stanastasia.net. Web: www.stanastasia.net.
Church: 400 Lake St., S.W., 55350-2349. Email: stanastasia@stanastasia.net. Web: www.stanastasia.net.
Res.: 1016 Roe Ave., 55350-2117. Tel: 320-587-6507; Fax: 320-234-6756.
School—(Grades PreK-6) Tel: 320-587-2490. Email: jstoffels@stanastasia.net. Jody Stoffels, Prin.; Sarah Zimmerman, Librarian. Lay Teachers 11; Students 144.
Catechesis/Religious Program—Tel: 320-234-6129. Students 337.

IVANHOE, LINCOLN CO., SS. PETER & PAUL (1900) [CEM], (Christ the King area faith community with Lake Benton; Tyler; & Wilno.) Rev. Ronald V. Huberty.
Res. & Mailing Address: 111 N. Sherwood, P.O. Box 49, 56142-0049. Tel: 507-694-1402; Fax: 507-694-1437.
Catechesis/Religious Program—213 Linwood, P.O. Box 310, Tyler, 56178. Veronica Whelan, D.R.E. & Youth Min. Students 45.

JESSENLAND, SIBLEY CO., ST. THOMAS (ORATORY) (1855) [CEM] Rev. Samuel F. Perez.
Mailing Address: P.O. Box 427, Henderson, 56044-0427. Email: stjos@frontiernet.net.
Church: 31624 Scenic Byway Rd., Henderson, 56044. Tel: 507-248-3550.

KANDIYOHI, KANDIYOHI CO., ST. PATRICK (1868) [CEM], (Jesus Our Living Water area faith community

with Lake Lillian; Willmar; & Spicer.) Revs. Steven J. Verhelst; John C. Ekwoanya, Parochial Vicar.
Res. & Mailing Address: 245 N. 2nd St., P.O. Box 164, 56251-0164. Tel: 320-382-6424. Email: stpatmn@charter.net. Web: ourlivingwater.org/stpatrick.html.
Catechesis/Religious Program—Students 43.

LAFAYETTE, NICOLLET CO., ST. GREGORY THE GREAT (1942) [CEM], (Holy Cross area faith community with Cathedral & St. Mary's, New Ulm; St. John's, Searles; & St. George, West Newton Township.) Rev. John G. Berger.
Res. & Mailing Address: 440 6th St., P.O. Box 5, 56054-0005. Tel: 507-228-8298; Fax: 507-228-8298. Email: stsgg@centurytel.net.
Catechesis/Religious Program—Students 42.

LAKE BENTON, LINCOLN CO., ST. GENEVIEVE (1897) [CEM], (Christ the King area faith community with Ivanhoe; Tyler; & Wilno.) Rev. Ronald V. Huberty.
Res. & Mailing Address: 111 N. Sherwood, P.O. Box 49, Ivanhoe, 56142. Tel: 507-247-3464 (Office); Fax: 507-247-3286.
Church: 119 S. Sherman St., 56149. Tel: 507-368-4232.
Catechesis/Religious Program—Fax: 507-247-3286. Veronica Whelan, D.R.E. - Youth Min. Students 54.

LAKE LILLIAN, KANDIYOHI CO., ST. THOMAS MORE (1934) [CEM], (Jesus Our Living Water area faith community with Kandiyohi; Willmar; & Spicer.) Revs. Steven J. Verhelst; John C. Ekwoanya, Parochial Vicar.
Res. & Mailing Address: P.O. Box 164, Kandiyohi, 56251-0164. Tel: 320-382-6424. Email: stpatmn@charter.net. Web: ourlivingwater.org/stthomas.html.
Church: 781 Second St. E., 56253.
Catechesis/Religious Program—Students 16.

LAMBERTON, REDWOOD CO., ST. JOSEPH (1895) [CEM], (Area faith community with Sanborn, Springfield & Clements.) Mr. Michael A. Pekar Jr., Pastoral Admin.
Res. & Mailing Address: 400 W. 2nd Ave., P.O. Box 458, 56152-0458. Tel: 507-752-7269.
Catechesis/Religious Program—Students 27.

LEAVENWORTH, BROWN CO., CHURCH OF THE JAPANESE MARTYRS (1867) [CEM], (Divine Mercy area faith community with Clements; Comfrey; Morgan; & Sleepy Eye.) Sr. JoAnne Backes, O.S.B., Pastoral Admin.
Office & Church: 30881 County Rd. 24, Sleepy Eye, 56085-4361. Tel: 507-794-6974. Email: jmartyrs@sleepyeyetel.net.
Catechesis/Religious Program—Students 38.

LESTER PRAIRIE, MCLEOD CO., ST. CONRAD, Closed. Incorporated but never organized. No sacramental records.

LITCHFIELD, MEEKER CO., ST. PHILIP (1859) [CEM], (Good Shepherd area faith community with Manannah.) Rev. Joseph A. Steinbeisser.
Parish Offices: 306 N. Holcombe Ave., 55355-2223. Tel: 320-693-3313; Fax: 800-404-1952. Email: stphilip@hutchtel.net. Web: www.thechurchofstphilip.org.
Church: 821 E. 5th St., 55355-2223.
School—(Grades K-5), 225 E. 3rd St. Tel: 320-693-6283. Email: mccarney@stphilipsschool.com. Ms. Diana M. McCarney, Prin. Lay Teachers 7; Students 87.
Catechesis/Religious Program—Tel: 320-593-4776. Students 229.

LUCAN, REDWOOD CO., OUR LADY OF VICTORY (1889) [CEM], (Light of the World area faith community with Seaforth; Wabasso; & Wanda.) Rev. Todd J. Petersen.
Res. & Mailing Address: P.O. Box 96, 56255-0096. Tel: 507-747-2231; Fax: 507-747-2233. Email: ourlady@means.net.
Church: 303-Third St., 56255.
Catechesis/Religious Program—Students 14.

MADISON, LAC QUI PARLE CO., ST. MICHAEL (1884) [CEM], (Prince of Peace area faith community with Appleton & Dawson.) Rev. Brian W. Oestreich.
Church: 412 3rd St. W., 56256-1494. Tel: 320-598-3690; Fax: 320-598-3619. Email: stmike2@frontiernet.net; prince-of-peace@hotmail.com. Web: www.princeofpeaceafc.org.
Catechesis/Religious Program—Students 54.

MANANNAH, MEEKER CO., CHURCH OF OUR LADY (1876) [CEM], (Good Shepherd area faith community with Litchfield.) Rev. Msgr. Francis J. Garvey.
Res.: 57482 CSAH 3, Grove City, 56243-9786. Tel: 320-693-8900; 320-453-7526; Fax: 320-693-8900. Email: ourlady@meltel.net. Web: www.coolparish.org.
Catechesis/Religious Program—Students 95.

MARSHALL, LYON CO., HOLY REDEEMER (1883) [CEM], (Bread of Life area faith community with Cottonwood & Green Valley.) Revs. Paul L. Wolf; Paul A. Schumacher, Parochial Vicar.
Mailing Address: 503 W. Lyon St., 56258-1311.
School—(Grades K-8), 501 S. Whitney. Tel: 507-532-6642; Fax: 507-532-2636. Email: cdesmet@holy-redeemer.com. Carol J. DeSmet, Prin. Lay Teachers 25; Students 255.
Catechesis/Religious Program—503 S. Whitney St., 56258-1995. Tel: 507-532-3602. Lori Timmerman, D.R.E. Students 406.

MIDDLE LAKE, NICOLLET CO., ST. NICHOLAS, Closed. Incorporated but never organized. No sacramental records.

MILROY, REDWOOD CO., ST. MICHAEL (1904) [CEM], (Our Lady of the Prairie area faith community with Tracy & Walnut Grove.) Mr. Richard P. Hamsa, Pastoral Admin.
Res. & Mailing Address: 200 Euclid Ave., 56263. Tel: 507-336-2505. Email: stmichael@means.net.
Church: 400 Cedar St., 56263.
Catechesis/Religious Program—Students 141.

MINNEOTA, LYON CO., ST. EDWARD (1880) [CEM], (Good Teacher area faith community with Canby; Ghent; & St. Leo.) Rev. Jeremy G. Kucera.
Church & Res.: 409 N. Adams St., 56264-9801. Tel: 507-872-6346; Fax: 507-872-5263. Web: www.stedschurch.com.
School—210 W. 4th St. Tel: 507-872-6391. Email: stedward@centurytel.net. Web: stedwardcatholic-school.com. Jason Myhre, Prin. Lay Teachers 11; Students 129.
Catechesis/Religious Program—Tel: 507-428-3285. Students 110.

MONTEVIDEO, CHIPPEWA CO., ST. JOSEPH (1882) [CEM], (Holy Family area faith community with Granite Falls & Clara City.) Rev. James W. Devorak.
Res.: 521 Eureka Ave., 56265-1899. Tel: 320-269-8623. Email: stjoseph@saintsjac.org. Web: www.saintsjac.org.
Church: 512 Black Oak Ave., 56265-1874. Tel: 320-269-5954.
Catechesis/Religious Program—Students 136.

MORGAN, REDWOOD CO., ST. MICHAEL (1890) [CEM], (Divine Mercy area faith community with Clements; Comfrey; Leavenworth; & Sleepy Eye.) Rev. Msgr. Eugene L. Lozinski; Rev. Mark S. Steffl, Admin. In Res., Rev. Mark S. Mallak, Sacramental Min.
Res., Church & Mailing Address: 510 W. 3rd St., P.O. Box 459, 56266-0459. Tel: 507-249-3643. Email: stmichaels@redred.com.
School—(Grades PreK-6), 612 W. 3rd St., P.O. Box 459, 56266-0459. Tel: 507-249-3192; Fax: 507-249-2557. Email: stmichaels@redred.com. Mary Gangelhoff, Supervisory Prin.; Jennifer Janni, Prin. Lay Teachers 5; Students 47.
Catechesis/Religious Program—Tel: 507-644-3523. Email: jrek@redred.com. Students 77.

MORTON, RENVILLE CO., ST. JOHN (1873) [CEM], Clustered with Redwood Falls. Sr. Jodelle Zimmerman, O.S.B., Pastoral Admin.
331 W. 3rd St., P.O. Box 88, 56270-0088.
Res. & Mailing Address: 341 W. 3rd St., P.O. Box 88, 56270-0088. Tel: 507-697-6120. Email: stjohnsmorton@mchsi.com.
Catechesis/Religious Program—Students 50.

MURDOCK, SWIFT CO., CHURCH OF THE SACRED HEART (1879) [CEM], (St. Isidore the Farmer area faith community with Benson; Clontarf; Danvers; & De Graff.) Revs. William A. Sprigler; Paul D. Timmerman, Parochial Vicar.
Res., Church & Mailing Address: 201 Orleans, P.O. Box 9, 56271. Tel: 320-314-2566; 320-842-4271 (Area Office); Fax: 320-843-2264. Email: stfran@embarqmail.com. Web: www.catholicareaparishes.org.
Catechesis/Religious Program—Deacon Michael Thoennes, Dir. Faith Formation. Students 68.

NASSAU, LAC QUI PARLE CO., ST. JAMES (1902) [CEM], Clustered with Ortonville & Rosen. Rev. Robert P. Goblirsch.
Mailing Address: 421 Madison Ave., Ortonville, 56278-2713. Tel: 320-839-2772; Fax: 320-839-2873. Email: secbkpr.stjohns@midconetwork.com.
Catechesis/Religious Program—Students 5.

NICOLLET, NICOLLET CO., ST. PAUL (1907) [CEM 4], (Apostles Peter & Paul area faith community with St. Peter.) Rev. Edward J. Ardolf.
Church & Mailing Address: 410 5th St., P.O. Box 248, 56074-0248. Tel: 507-232-3857.
Catechesis/Religious Program—Students 82.

NORTH MANKATO, NICOLLET CO., HOLY ROSARY (1924) Rev. Peter C. Nosbush.
Res. & Mailing Address: 525 Grant Ave., 56003-2939. Tel: 507-387-6501; Fax: 507-387-7365. Email: hros2@hickorytech.net. Web: www.holyrosarynorthmankato.com.
School—546 Grant Ave., 56003-2937. Tel: 507-345-6765. Web: www.loyolacatholicschools.org. Mrs. Shelley Schultz, Interim High School Prin. School is part of Mankato Area Catholic Schools, Diocese of Winona. Numbers are reported by the Winona Diocese. Students 634.
Catechesis/Religious Program—Students 285.

OLIVIA, RENVILLE CO., ST. ALOYSIUS (1888) [CEM 2] [JC], (Heart of Jesus area faith community with Renville; Hector; & Bird Island.) Rev. Paul H. van de Crommert.
Church: 302 S. 10th St., 56277-1288. Tel: 320-523-2030 (Office); 320-523-1271 (Rectory); Fax: 320-214-2419. Email: saintaloysiuschurch@msn.com.
Catechesis/Religious Program—Tel: 320-523-2030. Students 49.

ORTONVILLE, BIG STONE CO., ST. JOHN (1879), Clustered with Nassau & Rosen. Rev. Robert P. Goblirsch.
Res.: 421 Madison Ave., 56278-2713. Tel: 320-839-2772; Fax: 320-839-2873. Email: secbkpr.stjohns@midconetwork.com. Web: www.bordermissionchain.com.
Catechesis/Religious Program—Tel: 320-839-2873. Email: dre.stjohns@midconetwork.com. Students 105.

RAYMOND, KANDIYOHI CO., SACRED HEART, Closed. For sacramental records, contact St. Clara, Clara City.

REDWOOD FALLS, REDWOOD CO., ST. CATHERINE (1870) [CEM], Clustered with Morton. Rev. Michael M. Doyle.
Church & Mailing Address: 900 E. Flynn St., P.O. Box 383, 56283-0383. Tel: 507-644-2278; Fax: 507-644-2643. Email: stcath@mystcatherine.org.
Res.: 904 E. Flynn St., P.O. Box 383, 56283-0383. Tel: 507-644-8114.
Catechesis/Religious Program—Students 234.

REGAL, KANDIYOHI CO., ST. ANTHONY (MISSION) (1933) [CEM] Closed. Records at Our Lady of the Lakes, Spicer.

RENVILLE, RENVILLE CO., HOLY REDEEMER (1891) [CEM], (Heart of Jesus area faith community with Olivia; Bird Island; & Hector.) Sr. Donna Wermus, S.S.N.D., Pastoral Admin.
Church & Mailing Address: 106 S.E. 3rd St., P.O. Box 401, 56284-0401. Tel: 320-329-3884; Fax: 320-329-3884. Email: hrchurch@centurytel.net. Web: www.afcheartofjesus.org.
Catechesis/Religious Program—Tel: 320-329-8219. Students 61.

ROSEN, LAC QUI PARLE CO., ST. JOSEPH (1885) [CEM], Clustered with Nassau & Ortonville. Rev. Robert P. Goblirsch.
Mailing Address: 421 Madison Ave., Ortonville, 56278-2713. Tel: 320-839-2772; Fax: 320-839-2873. Email: secbkpr.stjohns@midconetwork.com. Web: www.bordermissionchain.com.
Catechesis/Religious Program—Tel: 320-568-2428. Students 48.

ST. LEO, YELLOW MEDICINE CO., ST. LEO (1881) [CEM], (Good Teacher area faith community with Canby; Ghent; & Minneota.) Rev. Craig A. Timmerman.
Church & Mailing Address: 202 W. Church St., 56264. Tel: 507-224-2289. Email: st.peter@canbylancers.org.
Catechesis/Religious Program—Tel: 507-223-7729. Students 23.

SAINT PETER, NICOLLET CO.

1—CHURCH OF ST. PETER (1856) [CEM], (Apostles Peter & Paul area faith community with Nicollet.) Rev. Philip M. Schotzko; Sr. Therese Collison, S.S.N.D., Pastoral Assoc.; Mrs. Kay Osborne, Pastoral Assoc.
Church & Mailing Address: 1801 W. Broadway, P.O. Box 522, 56082-0522. Tel: 507-931-1628; Fax: 507-931-2977. Email: office@churchofstpeter.org. Web: www.churchofstpeter.org.
School—John Ireland School, (Grades K-6) Tel: 507-931-2810. Email: therese.collison@churchofstpeter.org. Web: www-.churchofstpeter.org. Sr. Therese Collison, S.S.N.D., Prin. Sisters 1; Lay Teachers 9; Students 88.

2—IMMACULATE CONCEPTION, Closed. For sacramental records, contact St. Peter's, St. Peter.
Catechesis/Religious Program—Tel: 507-931-3662. Connie Bollum, D.R.E. Students 262.

SANBORN, REDWOOD CO., ST. THOMAS (ORATORY) (1902), (Area faith community with Lamberton & Springfield.) Mr. Michael A. Pekar Jr., Pastoral Admin., (Lamberton).
301 E. Winona St., P.O. Box 176, 56083-0176. Tel: 507-752-7269.

SEAFORTH, REDWOOD CO., ST. MARY (1880) [CEM 2] [JC 2], (Light of the World area faith community with Wabasso; Lucan; & Wanda.) Rev. Todd J. Petersen.
Mailing Address: P.O. Box 239, Wabasso, 56293-0239. Tel: 507-342-5190 (Office); Fax: 507-342-5156. Email: stannesschool@wabassostannesschool.com.
Catechesis/Religious Program—Students 33.

SEARLES, BROWN CO., ST. JOHN THE BAPTIST (1905) [CEM], (Holy Cross area faith community with Cathedral & St. Mary's, New Ulm; Lafayette; & West Newton Township.) Rev. Msgr. John A. Richter, Parochial Admin.

Church & Mailing Address: 18241 First Ave. S., 56073-5171. Tel: 507-359-4244. Email: sjs@newulmtel.net. Web: www.stjohnssearles-.catholicweb.com.
See New Ulm Area Catholic Schools, New Ulm under New Ulm Area Catholic Schools located in the Institution section.
Catechesis/Religious Program—Students 9.

SILVER LAKE, MCLEOD CO.
1—ST. ADALBERT, Closed. For sacramental records, contact Holy Family, Silver Lake.
2—CHURCH OF THE HOLY FAMILY (1993) [CEM 4] Revs. Anthony J. Stubeda; Patrick E. Okonkwo, Parochial Vicar.
Res. & Mailing Address: 720 W. Main St., 55381-0326. Tel: 320-327-2261 (Rectory); Fax: 320-327-6533. Email: office@holyfamilysilverlake.org. Web: www.holyfamilysilverlake.org.
Catechesis/Religious Program—Tel: 320-327-2931. Email: re@holyfamilysilverlake.org. Students 143.
3—ST. JOSEPH, Closed. For sacramental records, contact Holy Family, Silver Lake.

SLEEPY EYE, BROWN CO., ST. MARY (1876) [CEM], (Divine Mercy area faith community with Clements; Comfrey; Leavenworth; & Morgan.) Rev. Msgr. Eugene L. Lozinski; Revs. Mark S. Steffl; Andrew J. Michels, Senior Assoc.; Deacon Mark D. Kober. Tel: 507-794-4682.
Res.: 636 First Ave. N., 56085-1004. Tel: 507-794-4171; Fax: 507-794-5871. Email: saintmaryse@sleepyeyetel.net. Web: www.sesmchurch.com.
School—(Grades PreK-6), 104 St. Mary St. N.W. Tel: 507-794-6141; Fax: 507-794-4841. Email: thelget@sesmschool.com. Web: www.sesmschool-.com. Mary Gangelhoff, Prin.; Miss Jenny Blick, Librarian. Lay Teachers 16; Students 178.
High School—(Grades 7-12) Tel: 507-794-4121; Fax: 507-794-4841. Email: jneubauer@sesmschool.com. Mr. Jerry Neubauer, Prin.; Mary Kate Losleben, Media Center/Lab. Lay Teachers 22; Students 196.
Catechesis/Religious Program—Tel: 507-794-7600; Fax: 507-794-5871. Shauna Molden, D.R.E. Students 126.

SPICER, KANDIYOHI CO., OUR LADY OF THE LAKES (1962) [CEM], (Jesus Our Living Water area faith community with Willmar; Kandiyohi; & Lake Lillian.) Revs. Steven J. Verhelst; Jerome E. Paulson, Parochial Vicar.
Res.: 15525 69th St., N.E., 56288-9659. Tel: 320-796-5664; Fax: 320-796-6310. Email: ourlady@tds.net. Web: www.olol.ourlivingwater.org.
Church & Mailing Address: 6680 153rd Ave. N.E., 56288-9659.
Catechesis/Religious Program—Tel: 320-796-5968. Students 220.

SPRINGFIELD, BROWN CO., ST. RAPHAEL (1874) [CEM], (Vine & Branches area faith community with Lamberton & Sanborn.) Rev. Dennis C. Labat.
Res.: 112 W. Van Dusen St., 56087-1396. Tel: 507-723-4137 (Office); 507-723-4141 (Rectory). Email: straphael@newulmtel.net. Web: www.straphaelmn.org.
School—(Grades PreK-6), 20 W. VanDusen St. Tel: 507-723-4135; Fax: 507-723-5409. Percy Lingen, Prin. Lay Teachers 7; Students 47.
Catechesis/Religious Program—Tel: 507-723-4138. Monica Simmons, Youth Min. & Faith Formation. Students 124.

STEWART, MCLEOD CO., CHURCH OF ST. BONIFACE (1877) [CEM], Clustered with Hutchinson. Rev. Gerald S. Meidl.
Mailing Address: 551 Main St., P.O. Box 202, 55385-0202. Tel: 320-562-2344. Email: stbcc@hutchtel.net.
Catechesis/Religious Program—Students 35.

SWAN LAKE, NICOLLET CO.
1—THE CHURCH OF THE VISITATION, Closed. For sacramental records, contact St. Paul, Nicollet.
2—VISITATION, Closed. For sacramental records, contact St. Paul, Nicollet.

TAUNTON, LYON CO., SS. CYRIL AND METHODIUS (1895) [CEM 2] Closed. For inquiries for parish records contact the chancery.

TRACY, LYON CO., ST. MARY (1885) [CEM], (Our Lady of the Prairie area faith community with Walnut Grove & Milroy.) Rev. Robert J. Mraz.
Mailing Address: 249 6th St., 56175-1114.
Res.: 600 3rd St., P.O. Box 602, Walnut Grove, 56180. Tel: 507-629-4075 (Office); 507-859-2164 (Home); Fax: 507-629-3667 (Office). Email: stmary@iw.net. Web: www.stmarytracy.org.
Church: 285 6th St., 56175.
School—(Grades K-6), 225 6th. St., 56175-1114. Tel: 507-629-3270; Fax: 507-629-3518. Email: stmarys@iw.net. Web: www.stmaryschooltracy.org. Kathleen Vondrocek, Prin. Lay Teachers 5; Students 33.
Catechesis/Religious Program—Tel: 507-629-3667. Email: saintmaryre@iw.net. Students 83.

TYLER, LINCOLN CO., ST. DIONYSIUS (1880) [CEM], (Christ the King area faith community with Ivanhoe; Lake Benton; & Wilno.) Rev. Ronald V. Huberty.
Mailing Address: P.O. Box 310, 56178-0310.
Res.: 111 N. Sherwood, P.O. Box 49, Ivanhoe, 56142-0049. Tel: 507-247-3464 (Office). Email: bjthooft@frontiernet.net.
Church: 203 Linwood St., 56178. Tel: 507-247-5807 (Church & Office); Fax: 507-247-3286.
Catechesis/Religious Program—Veronica Whelan, D.R.E. & Youth Min. Students 153.

VESTA, REDWOOD CO., HOLY NAME, Closed. For sacramental records, contact St. Catherine's, Redwood Falls.

WABASSO, REDWOOD CO., ST. ANNE (1900) [CEM] [JC], (Light of the World area faith community with Lucan; Wanda; & Seaforth.) Rev. Todd J. Petersen.
Mailing Address: 1052 Cedar St., P.O. Box 239, 56293-0239.
Church Address: 950 North St., 56293-0239. Tel: 507-342-5190 (Office); 507-342-5155 (Rectory); Fax: 507-342-5156.
School—(Grades K-6), 1054 Cedar St., P.O. Box 239, 56293-0239. Tel: 507-342-5389; Fax: 507-342-5156. Email: mail@wabassostanneschool.com. Web: inetteacher.com/school/201229. Mary Franta, Prin. Lay Teachers 8; Students 90.
Catechesis/Religious Program—Tel: 507-342-5190. Students 84.

WALNUT GROVE, REDWOOD CO., ST. PAUL (1902) [CEM], (Our Lady of the Prairie area faith community with Tracy & Milroy.) Rev. Robert J. Mraz.
Mailing Address: 600 3rd St., P.O. Box 236, 56180-0236. Tel: 507-859-2164; Fax: 507-859-2375. Email: fatherbob@iw.net. Web: www.smstracy.org.
Catechesis/Religious Program—Tel: 507-629-4075; Fax: 507-629-3667. Students 5.

WANDA, REDWOOD CO., ST. MATHIAS (1871) [CEM], (Light of the World area faith community with Seaforth; Lucan; & Wabasso.) Rev. Todd J. Petersen.
Mailing Address: P.O. Box 239, Wabasso, 56293-0239.
Church: 308 St. Mathias Blvd., 56293. Tel: 507-342-5190 (Office); 507-342-5155 (Rectory); Fax: 507-342-5156. Email: stannesschool@wabassostanneschool.com.
Catechesis/Religious Program—Students 50.

WATKINS, MEEKER CO., CHURCH OF ST. ANTHONY (1889) [CEM] Rev. John H. Brunner.
Res. & Mailing Address: 170 Meeker Ave. S., P.O. Box 409, 55389-0409. Tel: 320-764-2755; Fax: 320-764-2755. Email: stanthony@meltel.net. Web: www.stanthonywatkins.com.
Church: 201 Central Ave. S., 55389-0409.
Catechesis/Religious Program—Tel: 320-764-5722. Students 207.

WEST NEWTON TOWNSHIP, NICOLLET CO., ST. GEORGE (1858) [CEM], (Holy Cross area faith community with Cathedral & St. Mary's, New Ulm; Lafayette; & Searles.) Rev. John G. Berger.
Mailing Address: 440 6th St., P.O. Box 5, Lafayette, 56054-0005. Tel: 507-228-8298.
Church: 63105 Fort Rd., 56073. Tel: 507-228-8298; Fax: 507-228-8298. Email: stsgg@centurytel.net. Web: www.churchofstgeorge.com.
Catechesis/Religious Program—Students 25.

WILLMAR, KANDIYOHI CO., ST. MARY (1871) [CEM], (Jesus Our Living Water area faith community with Spicer; Kandiyohi; & Lake Lillian.) Revs. Steven J. Verhelst; Brian L. Mandel, Parochial Vicar.
Church & Mailing Address: 713 12th St., S.W., 56201-3099. Tel: 320-235-0118; Fax: 320-235-0153. Email: parishoffice@stmaryswillmar.org. Web: www.stmaryswillmar.org.
Catechesis/Religious Program—Tel: 320-235-3982. Students 433.

WILNO, LINCOLN CO., ST. JOHN CANTIUS (1883) [CEM], (Christ the King area faith community with Ivanhoe; Lake Benton; & Tyler.) Rev. Ronald V. Huberty.
Mailing Address: P.O. Box 49, Ivanhoe, 56142-0049.
Church: 111 N. Sherwood, P.O. Box 49, Ivanhoe, 56142-0049. Tel: 507-694-1402; Fax: 507-694-1437.
Catechesis/Religious Program—213 Linwood, P.O. Box 310, Tyler, 56178. Fax: 507-694-1548. Veronica Whelan, D.R.E. & Youth Min. Students 80.

WINSTED, MCLEOD CO., HOLY TRINITY (1869) [CEM 2] Revs. Anthony J. Stubeda; Anthony R. Hesse; Patrick E. Okonkwo; Deacon Michael Thoennes.
Res. & Mailing Address: 111 Winsted Ave. W., P.O. Box 9, 55395-0009. Tel: 320-485-4421; Fax: 320-485-4283. Email: pastor@stpiusx.org. Web: www.winstedholytrinity.org.
School—Holy Trinity Elementary School, (Grades PreK-6), 211 2nd St. N., 55395-0038. Tel: 320-485-2182, Ext. 2160. Email: cmillerbernd@tds.net. Mailing Address: P.O. Box 38, 55395-0038. Cathy Millerbernd, Prin. Lay Teachers 8; Students 129.
High School—Holy Trinity High School, (Grades 7-12), 110 Winsted Ave., P.O. Box 38, 55395-0038. Tel: 320-485-2182; Fax: 320-485-4283. Bill Tschida, Prin. Lay Teachers 12; Students 112.
Catechesis/Religious Program—Tel: 320-485-2182, Ext. 2155; Fax: 320-485-4283. Email: maryjeanhagar@yahoo.com. Students 188.

WINTHROP, SIBLEY CO., ST. FRANCIS DE SALES (1906), (All Saints area faith community with Fairfax; Gibbon; & Franklin.) Rev. Jeffrey P. Horejsi.
Church & Mailing Address: 510 N. Brown St., P.O. Box 447, 55396-0447. Tel: 320-647-5334. Email: ffgw@centurytel.net.
Catechesis/Religious Program—Box C, Fairfax, 55332. Fax: 507-426-7742. Connie Serbus, D.R.E. Students 37.

Chaplains of Public Institutions

APPLETON. *Prairie Correctional Facility*. Rev. Brian W. Oestreich, Volunteer Service Provider.
IVANHOE. *Divine Providence Hospital & Home*.
ST. PETER. *St. Peter Regional Treatment Center*. Rev. John G. Berger, Chap.
WINSTED. *St. Mary's Care Center*. Rev. Eugene M. Brown, Chap. (Retired).

On Special or Other Diocesan Assignment:
Rev. Msgrs.—
Grams, Douglas L., J.C.L.
Lozinski, Eugene L., J.C.L.
Revs.—
Berger, John G.
Labat, Dennis C.
Petersen, Todd J.
Schotzko, Philip M.
Schumacher, Paul A.
Timmerman, Craig A.
Timmerman, Paul D.

On Duty Outside the Diocese:
Rev. Msgr.—
Schaffer, Gregory T., Parroquia San Lucas Toliman, Depto. Solola 07013, Guatemala. Tel: 011-502-7722-0112; Fax: 011-502-7722-0112
Rev.—
Goggin, John T., Parroquia San Lucas Toliman, Depto. Solola 07013 Guatemala. Tel: 011-502-7722-0112; Fax: 011-502-7722-0112

Military Chaplains:
Rev.—
Wagener, John M., Lt. Col. (Retired), 117 E. Summit Ave., San Antonio, TX 78212-2953. Tel: 210-738-3481

Retired:
Rev. Msgr.—
Wyffels, Robert J., 702 3rd Ave., N.W., Apt. 15, Sleepy Eye, 56085.
Revs.—
Adrian, Stephen J., 10410 E. Twilight Dr., Sun Lakes, AZ 85248-6851. Tel: 480-895-0465
Barry, James D., 9300 Collegeville Rd., Apt. 305, Bloomington, 55437. Tel: 952-846-0551. Email: jdbarry35@yahoo.com
Becker, Dennis E., 11208 Co. Rd. 12 N.W., Garfield, 56332. Tel: 320-834-2100. Email: denny-b1@hotmail.com
Behan, Harry P., P.O. Box 35, Saint Peter, 56082-0035.
Bowles, William H., 4595 Bayview Dr., Fort Lauderdale, FL 33308-5330.
Brown, Eugene M., 551 4th St. N., 55395-4523.
Casey, Patrick L., 1322 Alton St., #315, Saint Paul, 55116.
Fink, Frederick T., 1219 Trisco Cove Dr. S.E., Osakis, 56360-4943.
Gross, Richard C., P.O. Box 6, Watkins, 55389. Tel: 320-764-2856
Hackert, Eugene C., 702 3rd Ave. N.W., Sleepy Eye, 56085. Tel: 507-794-2566
Hadusek, Paul J., Minnesota Manor Health Care Center, 700 N. Monroe, Minneota, 56264.
Hansen, Lawrence H., 151 S. Bishop Ave., Unit B13, Secane, PA 19018. Tel: 484-469-4250
Irrgang, Kenneth E., 740 14th St. S. Apt. 13, St. Cloud, 56301-5518. Tel: 320-654-1008. Email: irrgang@charter.net
Jenniges, Leonard J. (STP), Divine Providence Community Home, 700-3rd Ave. N.W., Sleepy Eye, 56085-1099.
Krystosek, Robert H. (GI), P.O. Box 425, Clara City, 56222-0425. Tel: 320-847-2615
Mead, Leland C., 22295 Lakewood Dr., Madison Lake, 56063-9706. Tel: 507-243-3868
Moran, James E., 1021 N. Garden St., Apt. 107, 56073-1559.
Plathe, Anthony H., 1381 Mission Hills Blvd., Clearwater, FL 33759-2767. Tel: 727-773-7225
Rademacher, Germain P., 60297 402nd Ln., 56073. Tel: 507-359-5157; Fax: 507-359-5157

Schaefer, Roman J., Kasper Life Center, P.O. Box 1, Donaldson, IN 46513-0001. Tel: 574-935-1741

Siebenand, Ambrose F., St. Benedict Senior Community, 1810 Minnesota Blvd. S.E., Rm. 126, St. Cloud, 56304-2423. Tel: 320-252-0010

Steiner, Bernard J., 1001 N. Garden St., Apt. 105, 56073-1566.

INSTITUTIONS LOCATED IN THE DIOCESE

[A] NEW ULM AREA CATHOLIC SCHOOLS

NEW ULM. *New Ulm Area Catholic Schools*, 514 N. Washington St., 56073-1897. Tel: 507-354-2719; Fax: 507-354-7071. Web: www.nuacs.com. Rev. Msgr. John A. Richter, Pastoral Coord. & Board Delegate. Consolidated: The two schools consolidated under the above title are as follows:

St. Anthony Elementary School (Grades PreK-12), 514 N. Washington St., 56073. Tel: 507-354-2928; Fax: 507-359-7029. Email: shelly.bauer@nuacs.com. Shelly Bauer, Prin., (Grades Pre K-6). Lay Teachers 19; Students 292.

Cathedral High School, 600 N. Washington St., 56073-1897. Tel: 507-354-4511; Fax: 507-354-5711. Email: peter.roufs@nuacs.com. Peter Roufs, Prin., (Grades 7-12). Priests 1; Lay Teachers 19; Students 214.

[B] GENERAL HOSPITALS

GRACEVILLE. *Graceville Health Center* DBA: Essentia Health Graceville, Holy Trinity Hospital, Graceville Health Center Clinic, Essentia Health Holy Trinity Hospital, Graceville Health Center Home Health, Grace Home, Essentia Health Grace Home, Grace Village., 115 W. 2nd St., P.O. Box 157, 56240-0157. Tel: 320-748-7223; Fax: 320-748-7225. Email: kevin.gish@essentiahealth.org. John Costello, Board Chair; Kevin Gish, CEO. Inpatient Bed Capacity 15; Inpatients 281; Outpatients 8,431; Total Staff 170; Clinic Visits 6,043; Home Health Visits 2,007; Nursing Home 50; Assisted Living 16.

Graceville Health Center DBA: Graceville Health Center, Chokio Medical, Essentia Health Chokio Clinic., 101 S. Main St., Chokio, 56221. Tel: 320-324-7500; Fax: 320-324-7563. Email: kevin.gish@essentiahealth.org. John Costello, Board Chair; Kevin Gish, CEO. Clinic Visits 673; Total Staff 5.

MARSHALL. **Avera Marshall*, 300 S. Bruce St., 56258-1934.

[C] HOMES FOR AGED

GRACEVILLE. *Graceville Health Center dba Essentia Health-Grace Home (SNF) and Grace Village (ALF)* 116 W. 2nd St., P.O. Box 638, 56240. Tel: 320-748-7261; Fax: 320-748-8238. Email: thowell@ghealth.net. John Costello, Board Chair; Todd Howell, CEO. GH Bed Capacity 50; Grace Village Number of Rooms 16; Total Staff 80.

IVANHOE. *Divine Providence Apartments*, 312 E. George St., P.O. Box 136, 56142-0136. Tel: 507-694-1414; Fax: 507-694-1191. Margaret Schmidt, Admin. Total Apartments 7.

NEW LONDON. *Benedictine Living Community of New London*, 100 Glen Oaks Dr., 56273. Tel: 320-354-2231. Certified Beds 62; Residents 53.

SAINT PETER. *Benedictine Living Community of St. Peter*, 1907 Klein St., 56082. Tel: 507-934-2203; Fax: 507-934-8392. Email: linda.nelsen@bhshealth.org. Web: www.bhshealth.org. Long Term Care Beds 79; Total Staff 135.

Benedictine Senior Living Community of St. Peter, 1906 N. Sunrise Dr., 56082. Tel: 507-934-8810; Fax: 507-934-0214. Bed Capacity 46; Total Staff 10.

SLEEPY EYE. *Divine Providence Community Home & Lake Villa Maria Senior Apts.*, 700 3rd Ave. N.W., 56085-1099. Tel: 507-794-3011; 507-794-5333 (Lake Villa); Fax: 507-794-3020. Email: divine@sleepyeyetel.net. Sr. Bernadine Ugolini, D.S.M.P., Supr.; Jayna Groebner, Admin. Daughters of St. Mary of Providence. Sisters 3; Lay Workers 105; Aged Residents 58; Tenants 20; Bed Capacity 58; Total Assisted Annually 110; Total Staff 105.

WINSTED. *Benedictine Living Community of Winsted*, 551 Fourth St. N., 55395.

St. Mary's Care Center (1959) 551 4th St. N., Ste. 101, 55395-0750. Tel: 320-485-2151; Fax: 320-485-4241. Email: christinagamaldi.@bhshealth.org. Web: www.stmaryscarecenter.org. Rev. Eugene M. Brown, Chap. (Retired); Christina A. Gamaldi, Admin. & CEO. Subsidiary of the Benedictine Health System. Bed Capacity 70; Total Staff 164.

[D] RETREAT HOUSES

NEW ULM. *St. Alphonsus Retreat House*, 1400 6th St. N., 56073-2099. Tel: 507-359-2966; Fax: 507-354-3667. Email: dnu@dnu.org.

SLEEPY EYE. *Schoenstatt Sisters of Mary (Secular Institute)* (1926) 27762 County Rd. 27, 56085-9801. Tel: 507-794-7727; Fax: 507-794-7727. Email: schoensttonthelake@schsrsmary.org. Sisters Rita Marie Otto, Supr.; M. Jessica Swedzinski, Youth & Family Min.; M. Alice Kunz, Librarian; M. Deanne Niehaus, Youth Min.; M. Ellen Hoemberg, I.S.S.M., Parish Min.; M. Candace Fier, M.T.S., B.S.N., R.N., Dir. Office of Family Life Educ. & Safe Environment & Coord. Dio NU. Total Staff 6.

[E] YOUTH CENTERS

RENVILLE. *Center for Youth Ministry*, Diocesan Pastoral Center, 1400 6th St. N., 56073-2099. Tel: 507-359-2966; Fax: 507-354-3667. Ms. Margaret Mc Hugh, Dir. Youth Ministry.

[F] MISCELLANEOUS

NEW ULM. *Christ Our Life Capital Campaign*, 1400 Sixth St., N., 56073.

Handmaids of the Heart of Jesus (ACS), 515 N. State St., 56073. Tel: 507-276-9128. Email: handmaids1@gmail.com.

SAINT PETER. *St. Peter Regional Treatment Center*, 100 Freeman Dr., 56082-1599. Tel: 507-931-7100; Fax: 507-931-7711. Rev. John G. Berger, Chap. Mental Health and Chemical Dependency: Patients Assisted Annually 825; Bed Capacity 530; Total Staff 1,256.

RELIGIOUS INSTITUTES OF WOMEN REPRESENTED IN THE DIOCESE

For further details refer to the corresponding bracketed number in the Religious Institutes of Men or Women section.

[]—*Benedictine Sisters of Pontifical Jurisdiction* (Crookston, MN)—O.S.B

[]—*Benedictine Sisters of Pontifical Jurisdiction* (Watertown, SD)—O.S.B.

[]—*Benedictine Sisters of Pontifical Jurisdiction* (Yankton, SD)—O.S.B.

[]—*Benedictine Sisters of Pontifical Jurisdiction* (St. Joseph, MN)—O.S.B.

[0940]—*Daughters of St. Mary of Providence* (Immaculate Conception Province, Chicago, IL)—D.S.M.P.

[]—*Franciscan Clarist Congregation* (Nirmal Pani Province, Kerala State, India)—F.C.C.

[]—*Franciscan Sisters of Little Falls, MN*—O.S.F.

[1870]—*Handmaids of the Heart of Jesus Sisters* (New Ulm, MN)—A.C.J.

[0210]—*Missionary Benedictine Sisters of Pontifical Jurisdiction* (Norfolk, NE)—O.S.B.

[]—*Presentation of the Blessed Virign Mary* (Fargo, ND)—P.B.V.M.

[]—*Schoenstatt Sisters of Mary* (Waukesha, WI)

[2970]—*School Sisters of Notre Dame* (Central Pacific Province/Our Lady of Good Counsel Campus, Province, Mankato, MN) —S.S.N.D.

[]—*Sisters of St. Francis of the Congregation of Our Lady of Lourdes* (Sylvania, OH)—O.S.F.

[1570]—*Sisters of St. Francis of the Holy Family* (Dubuque, IA)—O.S.F.

[3840]—*Sisters of St. Joseph of Carondelet* (St. Paul, MN)—C.S.J.

[3830-03]—*Sisters of St. Joseph of Orange* (Orange, CA)—C.S.J.

[1720]—*Sisters of the Third Order Regular of St. Francis of the Congregation of Our Lady of Lourdes* (Rochester, MN)—O.S.F.

NECROLOGY

† Martinka, Stanley V., (Retired)—Died March 12, 2011

An asterisk (*) denotes an organization that has established tax-exempt status directly with the IRS and is not covered by the USCCB Group Ruling.

Archdiocese of New York

(Archidioecesis Neo-Eboracensis)

His Eminence

EDWARD CARDINAL EGAN, J.C.D., D.D.

Archbishop Emeritus of New York; ordained December 15, 1957; appointed Titular Bishop of Allegheny and Auxiliary Bishop of New York April 1, 1985; consecrated May 22, 1985; appointed Bishop of Bridgeport November 8, 1988; installed December 14, 1988; appointed Archbishop of New York May 11, 2000; installed June 19, 2000; elevated to Cardinal February 21, 2001; retired February 23, 2009. *Res.: 452 Madison Ave., New York, NY 10022.*

Most Reverend

ROBERT A. BRUCATO, D.D.

Retired Auxiliary Bishop of New York; ordained June 1, 1957; appointed Titular Bishop of Temuniana and Auxiliary Bishop of New York July 1, 1997; consecrated August 25, 1997; retired October 31, 2006. *Res.: John Cardinal O'Connor Clergy Residence, 5655 Arlington Ave., Bronx, NY 10471.*

Most Reverend

JOSU IRIONDO, D.D.

Auxiliary Bishop of New York; ordained December 23, 1962; appointed Titular Bishop of Alton and Auxiliary Bishop of New York October 30, 2001; consecrated December 12, 2001. *Res.: St. Anthony of Padua, 832 E. 166 St., Bronx, NY 10459.*

Most Reverend

DOMINICK J. LAGONEGRO, D.D.

Auxiliary Bishop of New York; ordained May 31, 1969; appointed Titular Bishop of Modrus and Auxiliary Bishop of New York October 30, 2001; consecrated December 12, 2001. *Res.: Sacred Heart, 301 Ann St., Newburgh, NY 12550.*

His Eminence

TIMOTHY CARDINAL DOLAN, PH.D.

Archbishop of New York; ordained June 19, 1976; appointed Auxiliary Bishop of St. Louis June 19, 2001; installed August 15, 2001; appointed Archbishop of Milwaukee June 25, 2002; installed as Tenth Archbishop August 28, 2002; appointed Archbishop of New York February 23, 2009; installed April 15, 2009; elevated to Cardinal February 18, 2012. *Office: 1011 First Ave., New York, NY 10022.*

Chancery: 1011 First Ave., New York, NY 10022. Tel: 212-371-1000; Fax: 212-813-9538.

Web: www.ny-archdiocese.org

Most Reverend

JAMES F. McCARTHY, D.D.

Retired Auxiliary Bishop of New York; ordained June 1, 1969; appointed Titular Bishop of Verrona and Auxiliary Bishop of New York May 11, 1999; consecrated June 29, 1999; retired June 15, 2002.

Most Reverend

WILLIAM J. McCORMACK, D.D.

Retired Auxiliary Bishop of New York; ordained February 21, 1959; appointed Titular Bishop of Nicives and Auxiliary Bishop of New York December 23, 1986; consecrated January 6, 1987; retired October 30, 2001. *Res.: 142 E. 29th St., New York, NY 10016.*

Most Reverend

DENNIS J. SULLIVAN, D.D., V.G.

Auxiliary Bishop of New York; ordained May 29, 1971; appointed Titular Bishop of Enera and Auxiliary Bishop of New York June 28, 2004; consecrated September 21, 2004. *Res.: 452 Madison Ave., New York, NY 10022.*

Most Reverend

GERALD T. WALSH, D.D.

Auxiliary Bishop of New York; ordained May 27, 1967; appointed Auxiliary Bishop and Titular Bishop of Altiburus June 28, 2004; consecrated September 21, 2004. *Res.: St. Joseph's Seminary, 201 Seminary Ave., Yonkers, NY 10704.*

SEE ERECTED APRIL 8, 1808.

Square Miles 4,683.

Created an Archdiocese July 19, 1850.

Comprises the Boroughs of Manhattan, Bronx, and Richmond of the City of New York, and the Counties of Dutchess, Orange, Putnam, Rockland, Sullivan, Ulster and Westchester in the State of New York.

Legal Title: Archdiocese of New York.

STATISTICAL OVERVIEW

Personnel	
Cardinals	1
Retired Cardinals	1
Auxiliary Bishops	4
Retired Bishops	3
Priests: Diocesan Active in Diocese	424
Priests: Diocesan Active Outside Diocese	19
Priests: Diocesan in Foreign Missions	1
Priests: Retired, Sick or Absent	186
Number of Diocesan Priests	630
Religious Priests in Diocese	713
Total Priests in Diocese	1,343
Extern Priests in Diocese	215
Ordinations:	
Diocesan Priests	4
Religious Priests	5
Transitional Deacons	1
Permanent Deacons	12
Permanent Deacons in Diocese	379
Total Brothers	312
Total Sisters	2,666
Parishes	
Parishes	369
With Resident Pastor:	
Resident Diocesan Priests	291
Resident Religious Priests	68
Without Resident Pastor:	
Administered by Priests	10
Professional Ministry Personnel:	
Brothers	32
Sisters	100
Lay Ministers	349
Welfare	
Catholic Hospitals	8
Total Assisted	450,000
Health Care Centers	2
Total Assisted	4,700
Homes for the Aged	15
Total Assisted	40,000
Residential Care of Children	31
Total Assisted	1,822
Day Care Centers	473
Total Assisted	8,131
Specialized Homes	83
Total Assisted	5,419
Special Centers for Social Services	1,238
Total Assisted	284,561
Residential Care of Disabled	98
Total Assisted	2,578
Educational	
Seminaries, Diocesan	1
Students from This Diocese	24
Students from Other Diocese	19
Diocesan Students in Other Seminaries	51
Seminaries, Religious	7
Students Religious	89
Total Seminarians	164
Colleges and Universities	10
Total Students	44,412
High Schools, Diocesan and Parish	10
Total Students	4,074
High Schools, Private	40
Total Students	21,736
Elementary Schools, Diocesan and Parish	171
Total Students	47,292
Elementary Schools, Private	25
Total Students	3,822
Catechesis/Religious Education:	
High School Students	6,973
Elementary Students	92,074
Total Students under Catholic Instruction	220,547
Teachers in the Diocese:	
Priests	18
Brothers	27
Sisters	89
Lay Teachers	4,035
Vital Statistics	
Receptions into the Church:	
Infant Baptism Totals	22,926
Minor Baptism Totals	1,655
Adult Baptism Totals	1,022
Received into Full Communion	1,390
First Communions	21,469
Confirmations	18,791
Marriages:	
Catholic	3,514
Interfaith	1,056
Total Marriages	4,570
Deaths	12,338
Total Catholic Population	2,618,755
Total Population	5,819,455

Succession of Prelates—Most Rev. R. LUKE CONCANEN, O.P., D.D., first Bishop; cons. April 24, 1808; died June 19, 1810; Rt. Revs. JOHN CONNOLLY, O.P., D.D., second Bishop; cons. Nov. 6, 1814; died Feb. 6, 1825; JOHN DUBOIS, S.S., D.D., third Bishop; cons. Oct. 29, 1826; died Dec. 20, 1842; Most Rev. JOHN HUGHES, D.D., cons. Titular Bishop of Basileopolis and coadjutor to the Bishop of New York, Jan. 7, 1838; succeeded to the See of New York, Dec. 20, 1842; created first Archbishop, July 19, 1850; died Jan. 3, 1864; His Eminence JOHN CARDINAL McCLOSKEY, D.D., second Archbishop; cons. Titular Bishop of Axiere, and coadjutor to the Bishop of New York, March 10, 1844; translated to the See of Albany, May 21, 1847; promoted to the See of New York, May 6, 1864; created first U.S. Cardinal, Cardinal Priest of the Holy Roman Church, March 15, 1875 under the title of Sancta Maria Supra Minervam; died Oct. 10, 1885; Most Rev. MICHAEL AUGUSTINE CORRIGAN, D.D., third Archbishop; cons. Bishop of Newark, NJ May 4, 1873; promoted to the Archiepiscopal See of Petra and made coadjutor to His Eminence Cardinal McCloskey, Archbishop of

New York, with the right of succession, Oct. 1, 1880; succeeded to the See of New York, Oct. 10, 1885; made Assistant at the Pontifical Throne, April 19, 1887; died May 5, 1902; His Eminence JOHN CARDINAL FARLEY, fourth Archbishop of New York; ord. June 11, 1870; cons. Titular Bishop of Zeugma and Auxiliary to the Archbishop of New York, Dec. 21, 1895; promoted to this See, Sept. 15, 1902; preconized June 22, 1903; made Assistant at the Pontifical Throne, Dec. 4, 1904; created Cardinal Priest of the Holy Roman Church under the Title of Sancta Maria Supra Minervam, Nov. 27, 1911; died Sept. 17, 1918; PATRICK CARDINAL HAYES, fifth Archbishop of New York; ord. Sept. 8, 1892; appt. Auxiliary to the Archbishop of New York, July 3, 1914; cons. Titular Bishop of Tagaste, Oct. 28, 1914; appt. Bishop Ordinary of U.S. Army and Navy Chaplains by the Holy See, Nov. 24, 1917; promoted to the See of New York, March 10, 1919; created Cardinal Priest of the Holy Roman Church under the title of Sancta Maria in Via, March 24, 1924; died Sept. 4, 1938; FRANCIS CARDINAL SPELLMAN, sixth Archbishop of New York; ord. May 14, 1916; appt. Auxiliary Bishop of Boston, July 30, 1932; cons. Sept. 8, 1932; appt. to the See of New York, April 15, 1939; appt. Military Vicar for the Armed Forces of the United States, Dec. 11, 1939; created and proclaimed Cardinal Priest under the title of SS. John and Paul in the Consistory, Feb. 18, 1946; died Dec. 2, 1967; TERENCE CARDINAL COOKE, seventh Archbishop of New York; ord. Dec. 1, 1945; appt. Auxiliary Bishop of New York, Sept. 15, 1965; cons. Dec. 13, 1965; appt. to the See of New York, March 8, 1968; installed and appt. Military Vicar of the United States Armed Forces, April 4, 1968; created and proclaimed Cardinal Priest under the title of SS. John and Paul in the Consistory, April 28, 1969; died Oct. 6, 1983; JOHN CARDINAL O'CONNOR, eighth Archbishop of New York; ord. Dec. 15, 1945; appt. Titular Bishop of Curzola and Auxiliary Bishop to the Military Vicar, April 24, 1979; cons. May 27, 1979; appt. Bishop of Scranton, May 10, 1983; installed June 29, 1983; appt. Archbishop of New York, Jan. 31, 1984; installed March 19, 1984; created Cardinal Priest, May 25, 1985; died May 3, 2000; EDWARD CARDINAL EGAN, J.C.D., D.D., ord. Dec. 15, 1957; appt. Titular Bishop of Allegheny and Auxiliary Bishop of New York April 1, 1985; cons. May 22, 1985; appt. Bishop of Bridgeport Nov. 8, 1988; installed Dec. 14, 1988; appt. Archbishop of New York May 11, 2000; installed June 19, 2000; elevated to Cardinal Feb. 21, 2001; retired Feb. 23, 2009.

Vicar General—Most Rev. DENNIS J. SULLIVAN, D.D., V.G. Fax: 212-826-6020.

Retired Bishops—Most Revs. ROBERT A. BRUCATO, D.D., V.G. (Retired); JAMES F. MCCARTHY, D.D.; WILLIAM J. MCCORMACK, D.D. (Retired).

Episcopal Vicars of the Archdiocese—

South Bronx—Most Rev. JOSU IRIONDO, S.T.L., D.D., Church of St. Anthony of Padua, 832 E. 166 St., Bronx, 10459. Tel: 718-542-7293.

Orange, Sullivan, Ulster, Northern Westchester/ Putnam, Dutchess—Most Rev. DOMINICK J. LAGONEGRO, D.D., Church of the Sacred Heart, 301 Ann St., Newburgh, 12550. Tel: 845-561-2264.

Regional Vicars of the Archdiocese—

Manhattan (West)—Rev. Msgr. THOMAS P. LEONARD, Holy Trinity Church, 213 W. 82nd St., New York, 10024. Tel: 212-787-0634.

Manhattan (North)—Rev. Msgr. GABRIEL LA PAZ, J.C.L., Incarnation Church, 1290 St. Nicholas Ave., New York, 10033. Tel: 212-927-7474.

Manhattan (South)—Rev. Msgr. KEVIN J. NELAN, Our Lady of Guadalupe/St. Bernard Church, 328 W. 14th St., New York, 10014. Tel: 212-243-0265.

Manhattan (East)—Rev. Msgr. THOMAS A. MODUGNO, St. Monica Church, 413 E. 79th St., New York, 10021. Tel: 212-288-6250.

Manhattan (Central Harlem)—Rev. GREGORY CHISHOLM, S.J., Interim, Church of St. Charles Borromeo, 211 W. 141st St., New York, 10030. Tel: 212-281-2100.

Bronx (Northwest)—Rev. Msgr. JOHN J. JENIK, Our Lady of Refuge, 290 E. 196th St., Bronx, 10458. Tel: 718-367-4690.

Bronx (Northeast)—Rev. Msgr. EDWARD M. BARRY, St. Barnabas Church, 409 E. 241st St., Bronx, 10470. Tel: 718-324-1478.

Bronx (East)—VACANT, Our Lady of the Assumption Church, 1634 Mahan Ave., Bronx, 10461. Tel: 718-824-5454.

Staten Island—Rev. Msgrs. JAMES J. DORNEY, Co Vicar, St. Peter's Church, 53 St. Mark's Pl., New Brighton, Staten Island, 10301. Tel: 718-727-2672; PETER G. FINN, M.Div., M.S., M.Ed., Co Vicar, Blessed Sacrament Church, 30 Manor Rd., Staten Island, 10310. Tel: 718-442-1581.

Central Westchester—Rev. Msgr. JOHN T. FERRY, Church of Immaculate Heart of Mary, 8 Carman Rd., Scarsdale, 10583. Tel: 914-723-0276; 914-723-0281.

Northern Westchester and Putnam—Rev. Msgr. GEORGE P. THOMPSON, St. Patrick Church, 7 Pound Ridge Rd., Bedford, 10506. Tel: 914-234-3668.

Westchester (Yonkers)—Rev. LEONARD F. VILLA, St. Eugene, 707 Tuckahoe Rd., Yonkers, 10710. Tel: 914-779-5460.

Westchester (South Shore)—Rev. MARTIN J. BIGLIN, Holy Name of Jesus, 75 Lispenard Ave., New Rochelle, 10801. Tel: 914-636-4856.

Orange—Most Rev. DOMINICK J. LAGONEGRO, D.D., Vicar, 301 Ann St., Newburgh, 12550. Tel: 845-561-2264; Fax: 845-562-7144.

Rockland—Rev. Msgr. EDWARD J. WEBER, St. Francis of Assisi Church, 128 Parrott Rd., West Nyack, 10994. Tel: 845-634-4957.

Dutchess—Rev. Msgr. FRANCIS P. BELLEW, St. Mary's Church, 11 Clinton St., Wappingers Falls, 12590.

Ulster—Rev. GEORGE W. HOMMEL, St. John, 12 Holly Hills Dr., Woodstock, 12498. Tel: 845-679-7696.

Sullivan—Rev. Msgr. EDWARD F. STRAUB, St. Peter's Church, 264 N. Main St., Liberty, 12754. Tel: 845-292-4525.

Vicar for Development—Most Rev. GERALD T. WALSH, D.D., 1011 First Ave., New York, 10022. Tel: 212-371-1000, Ext. 3320.

Vicars for Religious—Sisters CATHERINE CLEARY, P.B.V.M., 1011 First Ave., New York, 10022. Tel: 212-371-1000, Ext. 2576; ROSAMOND BLANCHETT, R.S.H.M. Tel: 212-371-1000, Ext. 2575.

Vicar for Hispanic Affairs— (Vicario, Asuntos Hispanos), Most Rev. JOSU IRIONDO, S.T.L., D.D., St. Anthony of Padua, 832 E. 166 St., Bronx, 10459.

Archbishopric of New York—1011 First Ave., New York, 10022. Tel: 212-371-1000. (Cable Address: Curia New York).

Chancery—1011 First Ave., New York, 10022. Tel: 212-371-1000; Fax: 212-813-9380.

Chancellor and Moderator of the Curia—Rev. Msgr. GREGORY MUSTACIUOLO.

Vice-Chancellors—Rev. Msgr. DOUGLAS J. MATHERS, J.D., J.C.D.; Sr. EILEEN CLIFFORD, O.P.

Secretary to the Archbishop—Rev. JAMES A. CRUZ.

Archbishop's Delegate for Healthcare—KARL P. ADLER, M.D.

Chief Financial Officer—Mr. WILLIAM E. WHISTON.

General Counsel—JAMES P. MCCABE, J.D.

Canon 1742 Panel of Pastors—Rev. WILLIAM B. COSGROVE; Rev. Msgrs. JOSEPH R. GIANDURCO, J.C.D.; JOHN K. GRAHAM; Revs. ROBERT F. GRIPPO; GEORGE W. HOMMEL; MICHAEL F. KEANE; Rev. Msgr. ROBERT W. LARKIN; Rev. THOMAS F. MADDEN; Rev. Msgr. FRANCIS J. MCAREE, S.T.D.; Rev. ROBERT F. MCKEON; Rev. Msgr. KEVIN P. O'BRIEN, Ph.D.; Rev. EDWARD K. RUSSELL.

Archdiocesan Consultors—Most Revs. DENNIS J. SULLIVAN, D.D., V.G.; DOMINICK LAGONEGRO, D.D.; JOSU IRIONDO, D.D.; GERALD T. WALSH, D.D.; Rev. Msgrs. WILLIAM J. BELFORD; JOHN J. JENIK; GREGORY MUSTACIUOLO; EDWARD J. WEBER; Revs. LOUIS R. JEROME; JOHN M. LAGIOVANE; FABIAN LOPEZ; ROBERT M. PANEK.

Metropolitan Tribunal—

Judicial Vicar—Very Rev. WILLIAM S. ELDER, J.C.D.

Associate Judicial Vicar—Rev. RICHARD L. WELCH, C.Ss.R., J.C.D., M.R.E., M.Div.

Judges—Very Rev. WILLIAM S. ELDER, J.C.D.; Rev. Msgr. OSCAR A. AQUINO, J.C.D.; Rev. GEORGE OONNOONNY, J.C.D.; Rev. Msgr. KENNETH J. SMITH, M.A., S.T.B.; Rev. RICHARD L. WELCH, C.Ss.R., J.C.D., M.R.E., M.Div.; Ms. SILVANA BARKAUS, J.C.L., L.L.M.; Revs. RAYMOND DALY, J.C.D.; ANTHONY OMENIHU, J.C.L.; Rev. Msgr. DESMOND J. VELLA, J.C.D., S.T.L., M.S.

Defenders of the Bond—Very Rev. ROBERT HOSPODAR, J.C.L.; Rev. JOSE MARABE, J.C.D.

Promoter of Justice—Very Rev. ROBERT HOSPODAR, J.C.L.

Office Manager—Sr. MARY DANIEL BAUER, F.S.P., B.A.

Tribunal Coordinator—Ms. SILVANA BARKAUS, J.C.L., L.L.M.

Advocates—Ms. CATHERINE A. BARRETT; Ms. LYDIA MARTINEZ; Ms. INGRID PENA; Ms. MARIA BELARDO.

Interdiocesan Tribunal of New York State—201 Seminary Ave., Yonkers, 10704. Tel: 914-968-4301.

Judicial Vicar—Very Rev. MICHAEL T. MARTINE, J.C.L.; Sr. JOAN DUMBROWSKI, Sec. & Notary.

Censors Librorum—Rev. Msgr. FRANCIS J. MCAREE, S.T.D.; Rev. DONALD F. HAGGERTY, S.T.D.; Rev. Msgr. MICHAEL F. HULL, S.T.D.

Archdiocesan Offices and Directors

Apostleship of Prayer—VACANT.

Apostleship of the Sea—Rev. Msgr. KEVIN J. NELAN, Dir., Stella Maris Maritime Center for Seamen, Pier 52, New York, 10019. Tel: 212-265-5020.

Archives—Rev. MICHAEL MORRIS, M.A., M.Div., Archivist; PATRICK MCNAMARA, Ph.D., Archival Mgr., St. Joseph's Seminary, 201 Seminary Ave., Yonkers, 10704. Tel: 914-476-6333.

Black Ministry, Office of—Bro. TYRONE DAVIS, C.F.C., Dir., Cardinal Hayes H.S., 650 Grand Concourse, Bronx, 10451. Mailing Address: P.O. Box 553, New York, 10027.

Building Commission—St. Joseph's Seminary, 201 Seminary Ave., Yonkers, 10704. Tel: 914-476-1058.

Directors—Mr. DAVID MADDOX, Dir.; Mr. KEVIN O'BRIEN, Dir. & Financial Coord.

Assistant Director—KEVIN SHAUGHNESSY.

Consultant—JASON GAYNOR.

Catechetical Office—Sr. JOAN CURTIN, C.N.D. Tel: 212-371-1000, Ext. 2849.

Catholic Charismatic Center— (Centro Carismatico Catolico) Most Rev. JOSU IRIONDO, S.T.L., D.D., Center Dir., 826 E. 166th St., Bronx, 10460. Tel: 212-378-1734.

Catholic Charities—Rev. Msgr. KEVIN L. SULLIVAN, Exec. Dir., 1011 First Ave., New York, 10022. Tel: 212-371-1000 (Consult separate listing).

Catholic Health Care System—KARL P. ADLER, M.D., Chm. Bd. Trustees, 1011 First Ave., New York, 10022. Tel: 212-371-1000; Fax: 212-751-4655.

Catholic Health Care Foundation of the Archdiocese of New York, Inc.—KARL P. ADLER, M.D., Chm., 1011 First Ave., New York, 10022.

Catholic High School Association—1011 First Ave., New York, 10022.

Catholic New York— (See Ecclesiastical Communications Corp.), JOHN WOODS, Editor; Mr. JOSEPH ZWILLING, Assoc. Publisher.

Catholic World Wide Web Corporation—1011 First Ave., New York, 10022.

Cemeteries— (The Trustees of St. Patrick's Cathedral in the City of New York, Inc.) Mr. GEORGE BORRERO, Exec. Dir., 1011 First Ave., New York, 10022. Tel: 212-753-4883.

Central Services— Archdiocese of New York *1011 First Ave., New York, 10022*. Tel: 212-371-1000.

Charismatic Renewal Office—Rev. WILLIAM B. COSGROVE; Sr. PAULINE CINQUINI, S.C., 194 Gaylor Rd., Scarsdale, 10583. Tel: 914-725-1773; Fax: 914-725-5227. Email: charismny@juno.com.

Communications Office (Bureau of Information for the Media)—Mr. JOSEPH ZWILLING, Dir.; Ms. WANDA VASQUEZ, Asst. Dir., Spanish Communications; Rev. LORENZO ATO, 1011 First Ave., New York, 10022. Tel: 212-371-1000, Ext. 2990.

Conciliation and Arbitration, Office of—Rev. Msgr. DOUGLAS J. MATHERS, J.D., J.C.D., Dir., 1011 First Ave., New York, 10022. Tel: 212-371-1000, Ext. 2929.

Coordinator for Special & Pastoral Ministries—Rev. EMILE FRISCHE, M.H.M., 1011 First Ave., New York, 10022. Tel: 212-371-1000, Ext. 2925.

Coordinator of Priest Retiree Affairs—Mrs. MARY B. LYNCH, R.N., Our Lady of Consolation, 3103 Arlington Ave., Bronx, 10463. Tel: 718-548-0888.

Data Systems Center and Telecommunication Office—Mr. ANDREW J. DONNELLY, Dir., 1011 First Ave., New York, 10022. Tel: 212-371-1000.

Deaf, Catholic Center for—Rev. Msgr. PATRICK P. MCCAHILL, Dir., 1011 First Ave., New York, 10022. Tel: 212-988-8563.

Development, Archdiocesan Office of—Most Rev. GERALD T. WALSH, D.D., Vicar for Devel.; HELEN T. LOWE, Exec. Dir., 1011 First Ave., New York, 10022. Tel: 212-371-1000.

Ecclesiastical Assistance Corporation—1011 First Ave., New York, 10022. Tel: 212-371-1000.

Ecclesiastical Communications Corp.—1011 First Ave., New York, 10022. Tel: 212-371-1000.

Ecclesiastical Maintenance Services, Inc.—JOSEPH ROCH, Area Supvr. Tel: 917-560-3916.

Ecclesiastical Properties Corporation—1011 First Ave., New York, 10022.

Office of Ecumenical and Interreligious Affairs—Rev. ROBERT J. ROBBINS, Dir., 1011 First Ave., New York, 10022. Tel: 212-371-1000, Ext. 3076.

Educational Services of the Archdiocese of New York, Inc.—1011 First Ave., New York, 10022.

Education, Department of, Archdiocese of New York—1011 First Ave., New York, 10022. Tel: 212-371-1000. (Consult separate listing)

Family Life/Respect Life Office—Sr. VERONICA MARY, S.V., Dir., 1011 First Ave., New York, 10022. Tel: 212-371-1000, Ext. 3185.

Hispanic Affairs, Office of— (Vicario, Asuntos Hispanos), VACANT.

Holy Childhood Association—Sr. PAULINE CHIRCHIRILLO, P.B.V.M., Mission Educ. Dir., 1011 First Ave., New York, 10022. Tel: 212-371-1000, Ext. 2700.

Holy Name Society Archdiocesan Union of New York—Rev. JAMES P. CONNOLLY, Assoc. Dir.; ANDREW E. LISANTI JR., Pres.; Mr. ANTHONY J. MEROLLA, Exec. Sec., 1905 Tenbroeck Ave., Bronx, 10461-1833. Tel: 718-931-9239.

Hospital Apostolate, Office of the—Rev. Msgr. MARC J. FILACCHIONE, Coord., 1011 First Ave., New York, 10022. Tel: 212-371-1000, Ext. 3065.

Human Resources—VACANT, Dir., 1011 First Ave., New York, 10022. Tel: 212-371-1000, Ext. 2906; Fax: 212-838-0637.

Information, Bureau of and Radio-T.V. Communications— See Communications

Inner City Scholarship Fund, Inc.—1011 First Ave., New York, 10022. Tel: 212-371-1000.

Institutional Commodity Services Corporation—ROBERT SCHIAVI, Dept. Mgr., 1011 First Ave., New York, 10022. Tel: 212-371-1000.

Intercultural Institute—Most Rev. JOSU IRIONDO, S.T.L., D.D., Dir. Tel: 212-371-1000, Ext. 2982.

Instructional T.V. Communications Center—VACANT.

Insurance Division—EDWARD REIGADAS, Dir. Tel: 212-371-1000, Ext. 2626; DANNY HOLTSCLAW, Oper. Mgr., 1011 First Ave., New York, 10022. Tel: 212-371-1000, Ext. 3024.

Inter-Parish Financing, Commission for—Rev. BRIAN P. MCCARTHY, Chm., 1011 First Ave., New York, 10022. Tel: 212-371-1000.

Italian Apostolate, Office of the—Rev. ROBERT J. AUFIERI, Dir., 1011 First Ave., New York, 10022. Tel: 212-371-1000, Ext. 3055.

Justice and Peace, Archdiocesan Office of—Mr. GEORGE HORTON, Dir., 1011 First Ave., New York, 10022. Tel: 212-371-1000.

Legal Affairs, Office of—JAMES P. MCCABE, J.D., Gen. Counsel; RODERICK J. CASSIDY, J.D., Assoc. Gen. Counsel, 1011 First Ave., New York, 10022. Tel: 212-371-1000, Ext. 2440; Fax: 212-826-8795.

Language Institute—1011 First Ave., New York, 10022. Tel: 212-371-1000, Ext. 2982.

Legion of Mary—Rev. GERALD E. MURRAY, Dir., 1011 First Ave., New York, 10022.

Light and Life Evangelization Program— (Luz y Vida) *St. Joseph's Cursillo Center, 523 W. 142nd St., New York, 10031*. Tel: 212-926-7433.

Liturgical Commission, Archdiocesan—Sr. JANET BAXENDALE, S.C., M.A., St. Joseph's Seminary, 201 Seminary Ave., Yonkers, 10704.

Pastoral Life Conference—Revs. THOMAS P. DEVERY. Tel: 212-371-1000, Ext. 2930; THOMAS P. D'ANGELO, Asst., 1011 First Ave., New York, 10022. Tel: 212-371-1000.

Pastoral Services, Archdiocese of New York—1011 First Ave., New York, 10022. Tel: 212-371-1000.

Pension Office, Archdiocesan—Mr. MICHAEL CORRIGAN, Exec. Sec., 1011 First Ave., New York, 10022. Tel: 212-371-1000.

Permanent Diaconate Formation Program—(Programa de Formacion para Diaconos) VACANT.

Priest Personnel, Office of—Rev. THOMAS P. DEVERY, Dir., 1011 First Ave., New York, 10022. Tel: 212-371-1000, Ext. 2930; Fax: 212-826-8173.

Adjunct and International Clergy Office—Deacon JOSEPH SOLANTO, Coord., St. Joseph's Seminary, 201 Seminary Ave., Yonkers, 10704. Tel: 914-968-6200, Ext. 8122.

Priest Personnel Board—Rev. THOMAS P. DEVERY, Chm.

Priest Wellness Office— St. Joseph's Seminary.

Priest Retiree Affairs—VACANT.

Priests Council of the Archdiocese of New York—His Eminence TIMOTHY M. DOLAN, Ph.D., Pres.; Rev. JOSEPH P. LAMORTE, Chm.; Rev. Msgr. JOHN J. JENIK, Vice Chm.; Rev. WILLIAM J. LUCIANO, Recording Sec., 1011 First Ave., New York, 10022. Tel: 212-371-1000, Ext. 2932.

Prison Apostolate—Catholic State Prison Ministerial Association, 1011 First Ave., New York, 10022. Tel: 212-371-1000, Ext. 3204. Email: fr.Richard.Gorman@archny.org. Revs. GEORGE J. DASH, O.F.M.Cap., Pres.; GAMINI E. FERNANDO, Vice Pres.; AUGUSTINE GRAAP, O.Carm., Sec.; Deacon FRANK GOHL, Treas.; Rev. RICHARD F. GORMAN, Esq., Dir. & Contact Person.

Propagation of the Faith, Society for the—Archdiocesan Office, Sr. PAULINE CHIRCHIRILLO, P.B.V.M., Archdiocesan Dir., 1011 First Ave., New York, 10022. Tel: 212-371-1000, Ext. 2700.

Propagation of the Faith, National Office—Rev. Msgr. JOHN E. KOZAR, Natl. Dir., National Office: 366 Fifth Ave., New York, 10001. Tel: 212-563-8700.

Retirement Plan for Priests—VACANT, 1011 First Ave., New York, 10022. Tel: 212-371-1000, Ext. 2934.

Safe Environment Program—Mr. EDWARD MECHMANN, Dir.

St. Joseph's Cursillo Center—Rev. FRANK PELUSO, O.A.R., Dir., 275 West 230th St., Bronx, 10463. Tel: 718-796-4340.

Schools, Superintendent of—Dr. TIMOTHY J. MCNIFF, 1011 First Ave., New York, 10022. Tel: 212-371-1000, Ext. 2802.

**Sovereign Military Hospitaller Order of Saint John of Jerusalem of Rhodes and of Malta* American Association, U.S.A. *1011 First Ave., Rm. 1350, New York, 10022*. Tel: 212-371-1522. Web: www.maltausa.org. Deacon JEFFREY TREXLER, Exec. Dir. & Contact Person.

Spiritual Development, Office of—Rev. EUGENE J. FULTON, Dir., One Pryer Manor Rd., Larchmont, 10538. Tel: 914-235-6839.

Stewardship—CHANNON LUCAS, 1011 First Ave., New York, 10022. Tel: 212-371-1000, Ext. 3305.

Trustees of St. Patrick's Cathedral in the City of New York, Inc.—Rev. Msgr. JAMES K. VAUGHEY, Exec. Dir., Cemeteries; Mr. GEORGE BORRERO, Asst. Exec. Dir., Cemeteries.

Victim Assistance Coordinators—Sr. EILEEN CLIFFORD, O.P. Tel: 212-371-1000, Ext. 2949. Email: victimsassistance@archny.org; Deacon GEORGE COPPOLA. Tel: 917-861-1762. Email: victimassistance@archny.org.

CLERGY, PARISHES, MISSIONS AND PAROCHIAL SCHOOLS

NEW YORK CITY

BOROUGH OF MANHATTAN

1—CATHEDRAL OF ST. PATRICK (Old, 1809; New, 1879) Rev. Msgr. Robert Ritchie, Rector; Revs. Joseph J. Tyrrell, Master of Ceremonies & Parochial Vicar; Jose Marabe (Philippines), Parochial Vicar; Robert Bubel, Parochial Vicar; Deacons Edmundo Ramos; Anthony Gostkowski.
Rectory—460 Madison Ave., 10022. Tel: 212-753-2261; Fax: 212-755-4128.
(Archbishop's Residence), Res.: 452 Madison Ave., 10022. His Eminence Timothy M. Dolan; Most Rev. Dennis J. Sullivan, Vicar Gen.; Rev. Msgrs. William J. Belford, Vicar for Clergy; Gregory Mustaciuolo, Chancellor; Rev. James A. Cruz, Sec. to Archbishop.
Chapel—New York, Sts. Faith, Hope and Charity, Records at St. Patrick Cathedral.

2—ST. AGNES (1873) Revs. Myles P. Murphy; Johny Dominic; David Shiahornu; Deacon Richard Cheu. In Res., Rev. Felix Jones.
Res.: 143 E. 43rd St., 10017. Tel: 212-682-5722; Fax: 212-370-5791. Email: churchofstagnes@aol.com.

3—ST. ALBERT (1916) Closed. Parochial records at Sacred Heart.

4—ALL SAINTS (1879) Rev. Steven Pavignano, O.F.M. In Res., Revs. Francis K. Kim, O.F.M., Exec. Vice Pres., Franciscan Missionary Charities, Inc.; Joseph Kim, O.F.M.; Bro. Glenn W. Humphrey, O.F.M., School Psychologist, Rice High School.
Res.: 47 E. 129th St., 10035. Tel: 212-534-3535; Fax: 212-987-1930.
School—(1900) 52 E. 130th St., 10037. Tel: 212-534-0558; Fax: 212-831-6343. Geneine Morris, Prin. Lay Teachers 8; Students 191.
Catechesis/Religious Program—Students 7.

5—ST. ALOYSIUS (1899), (Jesuit) Revs. Frederick J. Pellegrini, S.J.; Thomas P. Green, S.J.
Res.: 219 W. 132nd St., 10027. Tel: 212-234-2848; Fax: 212-234-6495.
School—(1940) 223 W. 132nd St., 10027. Tel: 212-283-0921; Fax: 212-234-4198. Carol McCarthy, Prin. (Lower School); Courtney Nunns, Prin. (Upper School); John Lavagnino, Pres. Religious 2; Lay Teachers 20; Students 230.
Catechesis/Religious Program—Students 20.

6—ST. ALPHONSUS (1847) Closed. Records at St. Anthony of Padua.

7—ST. AMBROSE (CHAPEL CENTRO MARIA) (1897) Closed. Records at Sacred Heart Church.

8—ST. ANDREW (1842) Revs. James Hayes, S.S.S.; Gode Iwele, O.M.I., Parochial Vicar. Blessed Sacrament Fathers and Brothers.
Res.: 20 Cardinal Hayes Pl., 10007. Tel: 212-962-3972; 212-962-3973; Fax: 212-962-1012. Email: churchofsaintandrewnyc@verizon.net.
Catechesis/Religious Program—
Station—New York Infirmary Beekman Downtown Hospital 170 William St., 10007. Tel: 212-312-5000.
Station—St. Margaret's House 49 Fulton St., 10007. Tel: 212-766-8122.

9—ST. ANN (1911), (Don Orione Fathers) Revs. Mario Guarino, F.D.P.; Pasquale Ruggieri, F.D.P. (Italy).
Res.: 312 E. 110th St., 10029.
School—(1926) 314-318 E. 110th St., 10029. Tel: 212-722-1295; Fax: 212-722-8267. Web: www-.stannsnyc.org. Sr. Josephine Cioffi, Prin. Priests 2; Sisters, Servants of the Immaculate Heart of Mary 1; Lay Teachers 12; Students 340.
Catechesis/Religious Program—Students 210.
Chapel—St. Ann's Convent 319 E. 109 St., 10029. Tel: 212-534-8321.

10—ST. ANN'S ROMAN CATHOLIC CHURCH (1852), Administered from and records located at Immaculate Conception, 414 E. 14th St., New York, NY 10009. Tel: 212-254-0200., 110 E. 12th St., 10003.

11—ANNUNCIATION (1853), (Hispanic), (Piarist Fathers) Revs. Jose A. Gimeno, Sch.P. (Spain), Pastor/Supr.; Jose M. Clavero, Sch.P. (Spain); Luis A. Cruz, Sch.P. (Puerto Rico); Very Rev. Fernando Negro, Sch.P. (Spain); Rev. Javier Vanegas, Sch.P. (Nicaragua).
Res.: 88 Convent Ave., 10027. Tel: 212-234-1919; Fax: 212-281-7205. Email: annunciationchurchnyc@yahoo.com.
School—(1858) 461 W. 131st St., 10027. Tel: 212-281-7174; Fax: 212-281-1732. Omar O. Ortiz, Prin. Lay Teachers 12; Students 204.
Catechesis/Religious Program—Students 262.

12—ST. ANTHONY OF PADUA (Org. 1859; Re-org. 1866), (Italian), (Franciscan) Revs. Joseph F. Lorenzo, O.F.M.; Francis A. Hanudel, O.F.M.; Bro. Courtland Campbell, O.F.M., Pastoral Min.
Res. & Chapel: 154 Sullivan St., 10012. Tel: 212-777-2755; Fax: 212-673-6684. Email: stanthonychurch@aol.com. Web: www.stanthonynyc.org.
Catechesis/Religious Program—Sr. Annette Seiter, O.S.F., D.R.E. Students 60.

13—ASCENSION (1895) Revs. John P. Duffell; Sixto Quezada (Dominican Republic). In Res., Rev. Joseph W. Baker.
Res.: 221 W. 107th St., 10025. Tel: 212-222-0666; Fax: 212-961-1086.
School—(1912) 220 W. 108th St., 10025. Tel: 212-222-5161; Fax: 212-280-4690. Lay Teachers 13; Students 320.
Catechesis/Religious Program—Tel: 212-749-5938; Fax: 212-749-8658. Students 250.
Chapel—Riverside Study Center 330 Riverside Dr., 10025. Tel: 212-222-3285; Fax: 212-316-3629. (Opus Dei)

14—ASSUMPTION (1858) Closed. Records at Sacred Heart Church.

15—BASILICA OF ST. PATRICK'S OLD CATHEDRAL (1809) Rev. Msgr. Donald Sakano; Revs. Andrew Thi; Jonathan Morris, Parochial Vicar; Deacons Hector R. Rodriguez; Paul Vitale. In Res., Rev. Msgr. John B. Ahern (Retired).
Res.: 263 Mulberry St., 10012. Tel: 212-226-8075; Fax: 212-226-1219. Email: info@oldcathedral.org. Web: www.oldcathedral.com.
Catechesis/Religious Program—Students 50.
Chapel—St. Michael [JC] 266 Mulberry St., 10012. Tel: 212-226-2644; Fax: 212-226-1219.

16—ST. BENEDICT THE MOOR (1883) Attended by Sacred Heart of Jesus, New York Rev. Jose Gabriel Piedrahita, Admin.
Res.: 457 W. 51st St., 10019. Tel: 212-265-5020; Fax: 212-977-4116.

17—ST. BERNARD (1868) Closed. Records at Our Lady of Guadalupe-St. Bernard.
Res.: 328 W. 14th St., 10014. Tel: 212-243-0265; Fax: 212-255-8466.
Catechesis/Religious Program—Tel: 212-243-5317; Fax: 212-255-8466. Students 100.

18—BLESSED SACRAMENT (1887) Rev. Msgr. Robert B. O'Connor; Revs. Alfredo Balinong, S.J. (Philippines); Alexis Bastidas (Venezuela).
Res.: 152 W. 71st St., 10023. Tel: 212-877-3111; Fax: 212-799-6233. Web: www.blessedsacramentnyc.com.
School—(1902) 147-151 W. 70th St., 10023. Tel: 212-724-7561; Fax: 212-724-7561. Imella Engel, Prin. Lay Teachers 12; Students 242.
Catechesis/Religious Program—Students 161.
Chapel—Convent of Blessed Sacrament 133 W. 70th St., 10023.
Chapel—St. Agnes' Home 237 W. 74th St., 10023. Tel: 212-874-9203.
Chapel—Archdiocese Teachers Residence 22 W. 70th St., 10023.

19—ST. BONIFACE (1858) Closed. Records at Holy Family Church.

20—ST. BRIGID (1848; 1955), Records at St. Emeric, 185 Ave. D, New York, NY 10009. Tel: 212-228-4494. Rev. Lorenzo Ato, Admin.
Res.: 119 Avenue B, 10009. Tel: 212-228-5400; Fax: 212-254-0334.
School—185 E. Seventh St., 10009. Tel: 212-677-5210; Fax: 212-260-2262. Donna Vincent, Prin. Students 132.
Catechesis/Religious Program—Students 125.

21—ST. CATHERINE OF GENOA (1887) Rev. Msgr. Kenneth J. Smith; Rev. Thelamaque Florvil (Haiti).
Res.: 506 W. 153rd St., 10031. Tel: 212-862-6130; Fax: 212-491-6272. Email: scg@yahoo.com.
Catechesis/Religious Program—Students 125.

22—ST. CATHERINE OF SIENA (1897), (Dominican), Revs. Jordan James Kelly, O.P.; Juan-Diego Brunetta, O.P.; Louis C. Mason, O.P., Hospital Chap.; Bro. Thomas Aquinas Dolan, O.P.; Sr.

Margaret Oettinger, O.P., Hospital Chap. In Res., Rev. John Aquinas Farren, O.P.
Res.: 411 E. 68th St., 10021. Tel: 212-988-8300; Fax: 212-988-6918.
Catechesis/Religious Program—Paul A. Zalonski, D.R.E. Students 35.

23—ST. CECILIA (1873), (Apostles of Jesus) Rev. Peter Mushi, A.J.; Deacon Jose M. Hernandez.
125 E. 105th St., 10029. In Res., Revs. Francis Iroot, A.J.; Chrisanth Mugasha, A.J.
Res.: Tel: 212-534-1350; Fax: 212-410-6177.
Catechesis/Religious Program—Students 159.

24—CHAPEL OF THE SACRED HEARTS OF JESUS AND MARY (1914) [CEM] [JC], Mission of Saint Stephen and Our Lady of Scapular Parish. Records at Saint Stephen and Our Lady of Scapular Parish., 142 E. 29th St., 10016. Tel: 212-683-1675. In Res., His Eminence Edward Cardinal Egan; Rev. Brendan Fitzgerald.
Res.: 325 East 33rd Street, 10016. Tel: 212-213-6027; Fax: 212-213-9136.
Station—N.Y.U. Medical Center, Tel: 212-889-3886.

25—ST. CHARLES BORROMEO (1888) Revs. Gregory Chisholm, S.J.; Thomas Mestriparampil; Deacons Rodney Beckford; Kenneth L. Radcliffe.
Res.: 211 W. 141st St., 10030. Tel: 212-281-2100; Fax: 212-862-1881.
School—(1904) 214 W. 142 St., 10030. Tel: 212-368-6666; Fax: 212-281-1323. Ms. Aleeya Francis, Prin. Sisters of the Blessed Sacrament 2; Lay Teachers 13; Students 190.
Catechesis/Religious Program—Students 60.
Mission—Resurrection 276 W. 151st St., New York Co. 10039. Tel: 212-690-7555; Fax: 212-690-6590.

26—CHURCH OF THE RESURRECTION (1907), Mission of St. Charles Borromeo. Records at St. Charles Borromeo, 211 W. 141st St., New York, NY 10030 (212-281-2100)., 211 W. 141st St., 10030.
Catechesis/Religious Program—Mrs. Marisa Rivera, C.R.E. Students 42.
Mission—Chapel of the Resurrection 276 W. 151st St., 10039. Tel: 212-862-1881; Fax: 212-690-6590. Email: scbharlem211@gmail.com. Web: www.churchofstcharlesborromeoharlem.com.

27—ST. CLARE (1903) Closed. Records at St. Raphael's Church.

28—ST. CLEMENS MARY (1909) Closed. Records at Holy Cross Church, Manhattan.

29—ST. COLUMBA (1845) Rev. Keith G. Fennessy. In Res., Rev. Tomas DelValle.
Res.: 343 W. 25th St., 10001. Tel: 212-807-8876; Fax: 212-989-6548. Email: saintcolumba@verizon.net.
Chapel—Sisters of Congregation of Notre Dame 329 W. 25th St., 10001. Tel: 212-243-1760.
Catechesis/Religious Program—Email: saintcolumbaccd@verizon.net. Students 15.

30—CORPUS CHRISTI (1906) Rev. Raymond M. Rafferty. In Res., Rev. Msgr. Kevin L. Sullivan; Rev. Maurice Mamba (Democratic Republic of Congo).
Res.: 529 W. 121st St., 10027. Tel: 212-666-9350; Fax: 212-531-2487. Email: corpus-christi-nyc@nyc.rr.com. Web: www.corpus-christi-nyc.org.
School—(1907) 535 W. 121st St., 10027. Tel: 212-662-9344; Fax: 212-662-2725. Web: www.ccschoolnyc.org. Dorothy Valla, Prin. Lay Teachers 11; Students 190.
Catechesis/Religious Program—Students 25.

31—ST. CYRIL (1916), (Slovenian), (Franciscan) Rev. Krizolog Cimerman, O.F.M.
Res.: 62 St. Mark's Pl., 10003. Tel: 212-674-3442; Fax: 212-674-3442.

32—SS. CYRIL AND METHODIUS - ST. RAPHAEL (1913; 1886), (Croatian), (Franciscan) Revs. Nikola Pasalic, O.F.M.; Stipe Renic, O.F.M.
Res.: 502 W. 41st St., 10036. Tel: 212-563-3395; Fax: 212-868-1203. Email: crkva.nyc@verizon.net.
Catechesis/Religious Program—Students 85.

33—ST. ELIZABETH (1869) Revs. Daniel S. Kearney; Enrique Salvo, Parochial Vicar; Alberto del Olmo, S.J. (Spain), Parochial Vicar.
Res.: 268 Wadsworth Ave., 10033. Tel: 212-568-8803; Fax: 212-781-2754.
School—(1936) 612 W. 187th St., 10033. Tel: 212-568-7291; Fax: 212-928-2515. Web: www.steliznyc.org. Sisters 3; Lay Teachers 18; Students 360.
Catechesis/Religious Program—Tel: 212-923-4900; Fax: 212-781-2754. Students 382.
Chapel—Sisters Residence 612 W. 187th St., 10033.
Chapel—Cabrini Chapel 701 Ft. Washington Ave., 10040. Tel: 212-923-3536; Fax: 212-923-1871. Email: st.francescabrinishrine@verizon.net.
Isabella Geriatric Center—515 Audubon Ave., 10040. Tel: 212-342-9245.

34—ST. ELIZABETH OF HUNGARY (1891), (Slovak), Rev. Msgr. Patrick P. McCahill.
Res.: 211 E. 83rd St., 10028-2854. Tel: 212-734-5747; 212-988-1903 (TTY); 866-810-3394 (VP); Fax: 212-988-1903. Email: MO65@archny.org. Web: www.stelizabethofhungarynyc.org.
Catechesis/Religious Program—Students 58.

35—ST. EMERIC (1949) Rev. Lorenzo Ato, Admin.
Res.: 185 Avenue D, 10009. Tel: 212-228-4494; Fax: 212-375-1163.
Catechesis/Religious Program—Students 139.

36—EPIPHANY (1868) Rev. Msgrs. Leslie J. Ivers; Walter J. Niebrzydowski, Pastor Emeritus (Retired); Harry J. Byrne, Pastor Emeritus (Retired); Rev. Loyola Amalraj (India), Parochial Vicar. In Res., Rev. Francis Okoli.
Res.: 239 E. 21st St., 10010. Tel: 212-475-1966; Fax: 212-477-0537. Email: epiphanychurch239@gmail.com. Web: www.theepiphanychurch.org.
School—(1869) 234 E. 22nd St., 10010. Tel: 212-473-4128; Fax: 212-473-4392. Web: www.theepiphanyschool.org. Sisters 1; Lay Teachers 35; Students 553.
Catechesis/Religious Program—Students 694.

37—ST. FRANCES CABRINI (1973) Rev. Peter A. Miqueli.
Res.: 564 Main St., Roosevelt Island, 10044. Tel: 212-832-6778 (office).
Catechesis/Religious Program—Students 75.

38—ST. FRANCIS DE SALES (1894), (Don Orione Fathers) Rev. Victor Muzzin, F.D.P. (Italy). In Res., Revs. John A. Kamas, S.S.S.; Matthew Abba (Africa).
Res.: 135 E. 96th St., 10128. Tel: 212-289-0425; Fax: 212-996-2028. Email: sfds.church@yahoo.com.

39—ST. FRANCIS OF ASSISI (1844), (Franciscan. For priests and brothers not listed here, see St. Francis Monastery under Monasteries and Residences of Priests and Brothers.) Revs. Andrew J. Reitz, O.F.M., Guardian; Michael Carnevale, O.F.M.; Anthony M. Carrozzo, O.F.M.; Joseph F. Cavoto, S.A.; John M. Felice, O.F.M.; R. Patrick Fitzgerald, O.F.M.; Robert A. Gavin, O.F.M.; Hugh Hines, O.F.M.; Andrew Hwang, O.F.M. (Korea, South); Vincent A. Laviano, O.F.M.; Felix P. McGrath, O.F.M.; John J. McVean, O.F.M.; Stephen D. Mimnaugh, O.F.M.; James R. O'Connell, O.F.M.; Timothy J. Shreenan, O.F.M.; Bro. Alan J. Thomas; Revs. Kevin Tortorelli, O.F.M.; Thomas Walters, O.F.M.; Bro. Christopher Coccia, O.F.M., Vicar. In Res., Very Rev. John F. O'Connor, O.F.M., Min. Provincial; Revs. Dominic Monti, O.F.M., Vicar Provincial; Brian E. Smail, O.F.M., Vocation Dir.; Bro. Michael Harlan, O.F.M., Sec. of the Province.
Res.: *St. Francis of Assisi Friary*, 135 W. 31st St., 10001. Tel: 212-736-8500; Fax: 212-736-8545. Web: www.stfrancisnyc.org.
Catechesis/Religious Program—Students 29.

40—ST. FRANCIS XAVIER (1847), (Jesuit) Revs. Joseph S. Costantino, S.J.; Peter E. Fink, S.J.; Cassandra Agredo, Dir. Outreach Mission; Patrick Brewis, Dir. Stewardship; Jacqueline Falco, Business Mgr.; John Uehlein, Dir. Music Min.
Office: 55 W. 15th St., 10011. Tel: 212-627-2100; Fax: 212-675-6997. Email: stfrancisxavier@sfxavier.org. Web: http:www.sfxavier.org.
Catechesis/Religious Program—Ms. Luz Marina Diaz, Dir. Faith Formation. Students 72.

41—ST. GABRIEL (1867) Closed. Records at Church of Sacred Hearts of Jesus and Mary.

42—GOOD SHEPHERD (1912), (Capuchin Franciscans) Revs. Robert Abbatiello, O.F.M.Cap., Guardian; Philip Bohan, O.F.M.Cap., Parochial Vicar; Arlen Harris, O.F.M.Cap., Parochial Vicar; Deacons Rafael Then; Antonio Guzman. In Res., Rev. James R. Gavin, O.F.M.Cap.
Res.: 608 Isham St., 10034. Tel: 212-567-1300; Fax: 212-567-1476. Web: www.goodshepherdnyc.org.
School—(1925) 620 Isham St., 10034. Tel: 212-567-5800; Fax: 212-567-5839. Lay Teachers 12; Students 156.
Catechesis/Religious Program—Students 187.
Chapel— 630 Isham St., 10034. Tel: 212-567-1600. (Private)

43—ST. GREGORY (1907) Rev. Msgr. Michael Crimmins; Rev. Luis Pulido.
Res.: 144 W. 90th St., 10024. Tel: 212-724-9766; 212-724-9767; Fax: 212-579-3380.
School—(1913) 138 W. 90th St., 10024. Tel: 212-362-5410; Fax: 212-362-5062. Ms. Donna Gabella, Prin. Lay Teachers 10; Students 192.
Catechesis/Religious Program—Email: stgregnyc@aol.com. Students 60.

44—GUARDIAN ANGEL (1888) Rev. Msgr. Michael F. Hull. In Res., Rev. Philip S. Phan.
Res.: 193 Tenth Ave., 10011-4709. Tel: 212-929-5966; Fax: 212-929-5966.
School—(1911)Tel: 212-989-8280; Fax: 212-352-1467. Maureen McElduff, Prin. Lay Teachers 10; Students 212.

45—ST. HEDWIG (1934) Closed. Parochial records at St. Stanislaus Church.

46—HOLY AGONY (1930), (Spanish), (Vincentian) Revs. Victor Elia, C.M.; Candido Arrizurieta, C.M.; Jesus Arellano, C.M.
Res.: 1834 Third Ave., 10029. Tel: 212-289-5589; Fax: 212-289-8321. Email: milagha2@verizon.net.
Catechesis/Religious Program—Students 115.

47—HOLY CROSS (1852) Rev. Peter M. Colapietro; Mr. Edward Greene, LAMP Missionary.
Res.: 329 W. 42nd St., 10036. Tel: 212-246-4732; Fax: 212-307-5033.
School—(1864) 332 W. 43rd St., 10036. Tel: 212-246-0923; Fax: 212-246-0923. Sr. Mary Theresa Dixon, O.P., Prin. Sisters of St. Dominic of Blauvelt 1; Lay Teachers 10; Students 200.
Convent—Dominican Convent, 460 W. 44th St., 10036. Tel: 212-246-9768.
Chapel—St. Joseph's Home 425 W. 44th St., 10036. Tel: 212-246-5363.

48—HOLY FAMILY (1924) Revs. Robert J. Robbins; Joseph T. Chacko, Parochial Vicar; Bro. Robert V. Fontaine, C.S.C., Pastoral Assoc.
Res.: 315 E. 47th St., 10017-2318. Tel: 212-753-3401; Fax: 212-753-3428. Email: pastor@churchholyfamily.org. Web: www.churchholyfamily.org.
Catechesis/Religious Program—Students 21.

49—HOLY INNOCENTS (1866) Revs. Thomas Kallumady; Owen J. Lafferty. In Res., Revs. William J. Delaney; Oliver Chanama.
Res.: 128 W. 37th St., 10018. Tel: 212-279-5861; Fax: 212-714-9313. Email: pastor@innocents.com. Web: www.innocents.com.

50—HOLY NAME OF JESUS (1868), (Franciscan) Revs. Daniel T. Kenna, O.F.M.; Michael McDonnell, O.F.M.; Michael Tyson, O.F.M.; Lawrence D. Ford, O.F.M.; Evariste Ouedraogo. In Res., Rev. Matthew A. Pravetz, O.F.M.; Deacon Andre Alexandre.
Res.: 207 W. 96th St., 10025. Tel: 212-749-0276; Fax: 212-749-2045. Email: holyname.nyc@aol.com.
School—(1905) 202 W. 97th St., 10025. Tel: 212-749-1240; Fax: 212-749-4363. Mr. John Joven, Prin. Sisters 1; Lay Teachers 17; Students 272.
Catechesis/Religious Program—Tel: 212-749-0276, Ext. 16. Students 162.

51—HOLY ROSARY (1884), (Augustinian) Revs. Gilbert Luis R. Centina III, O.S.A.; Abel Alvarez, O.S.A., Parochial Vicar; Basilio S. Alava, O.S.A., Parochial Vicar.
Res.: 444 E. 119th St., 10035. Tel: 212-534-0740; Fax: 212-534-7572.
School—(1949) 371 Pleasant Ave., 10035. Tel: 212-876-7555; Fax: 212-876-0152. Lay Teachers 10; Students 252.
Catechesis/Religious Program—Students 16.

52—HOLY TRINITY (1898) Rev. Msgr. Thomas P. Leonard; Rev. Gary M. Mead, Parochial Vicar.
Res.: 213 W. 82nd St., 10024. Tel: 212-787-0634; Fax: 212-787-4917. Email: holy213@earthlink.net. Web: www.htcny.org.
Catechesis/Religious Program—Students 140.
Chapel—Chinese Catholic Information Center 86 Riverside Dr., 10024. Tel: 212-787-6969; Fax: 212-787-0351. Web: www.htcny.org.

53—ST. IGNATIUS LOYOLA (1851), (Jesuit) Revs. George M. Witt, S.J.; William J. Bergen, S.J.; James L. Dugan, S.J.; Ugo R. Nacciarone, S.J.; Sr. Kathryn King, Pastoral Assoc.; Ms. Joanne F. Cunneen, Pastoral Assoc.
Res.: 980 Park Ave., 10028. Tel: 212-288-3588; Fax: 212-734-3671.
School—(1854) 48 E. 84th St., 10028. Tel: 212-861-3820; Fax: 212-879-8248. Lay Teachers 33; Students 538.
Day Nursery—240 E. 84th St., 10028. Tel: 212-734-6427; Fax: 212-734-6972. Lay Assistants 28; Capacity 126.
School—Loyola School, Tel: 212-288-3522; Fax: 212-861-1021.
School—Marymount School, 1026 Fifth Ave., 10028. Tel: 212-744-4486; Fax: 212-744-0163.
High School—Regis High School, 55 E. 84th St., 10028. Tel: 212-288-1100; Fax: 212-794-1221.
Catechesis/Religious Program—Tel: 212-861-4764. Ms. Joanne Cunneen, D.R.E. Students 575.

54—IMMACULATE CONCEPTION (1855) Rev. Msgr. Kevin Nelan; Revs. Francis X. Buu; Antony Roche Alfred. In Res., Rev. Msgr. Desmond J. Vella.
Res.: 414 E. 14th St., 10009. Tel: 212-254-0200; Fax: 212-505-7610. Web: www.immaculateconception-nyc.org.
School—(1864) 419 E. 13th St., 10009. Tel: 212-475-2590; Fax: 212-777-2818. Sisters 1; Lay Teachers 9; Students 244.
Catechesis/Religious Program—Students 78.

55—INCARNATION (1908), (Hispanic), Rev. Msgr. Gabriel La Paz; Revs. Felino Reyes Nin; Aroldo Guerra.
Res.: 1290 St. Nicholas Ave., 10033. Tel: 212-927-7474; Fax: 212-928-0315. Web: www.incarnation-nyc.org.
School—(1910) 568-570 W. 175th St., 10033. Tel: 212-795-1030; Fax: 212-795-1564. Lay Teachers 21; Students 552.
Catechesis/Religious Program—Maria Minaya, D.R.E. Students 574.

56—ST. JAMES (1827) Rev. Walter Tonelotto, C.S.,

Admin.
Rectory—23 Oliver St., 10038. Tel: 212-233-0161; Fax: 212-964-0132.
School—(1854) 37 St. James Place, 10038. Tel: 212-267-9289; Fax: 212-227-0065. Mrs. Anne Marie McGoldrick, Vice Prin. Lay Teachers 10; Students 210.
Catechesis/Religious Program—Tel: 212-233-0161. Elba Feliciano, D.R.E. Students 20.

57—ST. JEAN BAPTISTE (1882), (Blessed Sacrament Fathers) Revs. Anthony Schueller, S.S.S.; Ernest R. Falardeau, S.S.S.; Bernard J. Camire, S.S.S.; Christian Christopher, S.S.S.; Deacons Richard Russo; Joseph Pino.
Res.: 184 E. 76th St., 10021. Tel: 212-288-5082; Fax: 212-717-8397. Email: sjbrcc@aol.com. Web: www.stjeanbaptisteny.org.
High School—173 E. 75th St., 10021. Tel: 212-288-1645; Fax: 212-288-6540. Email: information@stjean.org. Web: www.stjean.org. (Girls High School) Sisters of the Congregation of Notre Dame 6; Lay Teachers 30; Students 330.
Catechesis/Religious Program—Tel: 212-472-2853, Ext. 6. Email: robinscott@yahoo.com. Students 65.
Chapel—Sisters' Convent, Tel: 212-472-1230 (Apt. A); 212-472-8821 (Apt. B); Fax: 212-396-2025. Web: www.cnd-m.com.

58—ST. JOACHIM (1888), (Italian), Closed. Parochial records are at Church of St. Joseph.

59—ST. JOHN NEPOMUCENE (1895), (Slovak), Revs. Martin Svitan; Stefan Chanas, Parochial Vicar.
Res.: 411 E. 66th St., 10065. Tel: 212-734-4613; Fax: 212-734-2483. Email: slovakchurch@gmail.com. Web: www.stjohnnepomucene.org.
Chapel—Sisters' Convent 320 E. 66th St., 10065. Tel: 212-737-0221.

60—ST. JOHN THE BAPTIST (1840), (Capuchin) Revs. Thomas Franks, O.F.M.Cap.; John B. Riordan, O.F.M.Cap., Parochial Vicar; Gerard Mulvey, O.F.M.Cap., Parochial Vicar; Bro. Luke Benbrook, O.F.M.Cap., Pastoral Assoc. In Res., Revs. John Clermont, O.F.M.Cap., Missionary Apostolate; Edward Conway, O.F.M.Cap.; Philip Fabiano, O.F.M-.Cap.; Francis Gasparik, O.F.M.Cap., Provincial Min.; Leonard Glavin, O.F.M.Cap. (Retired); Matthias Wesnofske, O.F.M.Cap., Spiritual Asst. of Secular Order of St. Francis; Ramon Frias, O.F.M-.Cap.; Bro. George McCloskey, O.F.M.Cap., Mission & Devel. & Communications Office.
Res.: 210 W. 31st St., 10001-2876. Tel: 212-564-9070; Fax: 212-564-3964.

61—ST. JOHN THE EVANGELIST (1840) [CEM] Rev. Msgr. Douglas J. Mathers; Revs. James P. Connolly, Senior Priest; Joseph Arlagadda.
Res.: 348 E. 55th St., 10022. Tel: 212-753-8418; Fax: 212-826-1848. Email: churchofstjohn@cs.com.
Catechesis/Religious Program—Students 3.

62—ST. JOHN THE MARTYR (1903) Rev. Sean R. Harlow, O.Carm. In Res., Revs. Paul Feeley, O.Carm. (Retired); Sunny Mathew, O.Carm. (India).
Res.: 259 E. 71st St., 10021-4596. Tel: 212-744-4880; 212-744-4881; Fax: 212-628-6662. Email: sjtm@nyc.rr.com.
Catechesis/Religious Program— Regional. See St. Ignatius Loyola, New York.

63—ST. JOSEPH (1829), (Dominican) Revs. John Patrick McGuire, O.P.; Kevin Gillen, O.P.; Very Rev. David Dominic Izzo, O.P.
Res.: 371 Sixth Ave., 10014. Tel: 212-741-1274; Fax: 212-741-2147. Web: www.washingtonsquarecatholic.org.
Catechesis/Religious Program—Thomas Sabatelli, D.R.E. Students 86.

64—ST. JOSEPH (1924), (Scalabrinian) Rev. Walter Tonelotto, C.S.
Res.: 5 Monroe St., 10002. Tel: 212-267-8376; Fax: 212-964-0132. Email: sjch5@aol.com. Web: www.stjosephnyc.org.
School—(1926) One Monroe St., 10002. Tel: 212-233-5152; Fax: 212-267-4357. Frances Acosta, Prin. Lay Teachers 11; Students 235.
Catechesis/Religious Program—Students 10.
Convent—83 Madison St., 10002. Tel: 212-233-5670.

65—ST. JOSEPH (1873) Rev. James Boniface Ramsey. In Res., Rev. Hayden J. Vaverek.
Res.: 404 E. 87th St., 10128. Tel: 212-289-6030; Fax: 212-348-8075. Email: sjosephyorkville@aol.com. Web: www.stjosephsyorkville.org.
School—(1880) 420 E. 87th St., 10128. Tel: 212-289-3057; Fax: 212-289-7239. Lay Teachers 13; Students 329.
Catechesis/Religious Program—Tel: 212-861-4764; Fax: 212-734-3671. Regional. See St. Ignatius Loyola, New York. Students 14.

66—ST. JOSEPH OF THE HOLY FAMILY (1860) Revs. David E. Nolan; Neil J. O'Connell, O.F.M.; Ransford Clarke.
Res.: 405 W. 125th St., 10027. Tel: 212-662-9125.
Catechesis/Religious Program—Students 90.
Convent—400 W. 126th St., 10027.

67—ST. JUDE (1949) Rev. Elias Isla; Deacon Porfirio Rodriguez.
Res.: 431 W. 204th St., 10034. Tel: 212-569-3000; Fax: 212-304-4545.
School—(1953) 433 W. 204th St., 10034. Tel: 212-569-3400; Fax: 212-304-4479. Lay Teachers 16; Students 400.
Catechesis/Religious Program—Tel: 212-569-3002. Students 510.
Chapel—New York, St. Jude Convent

68—ST. LEO (1880) Closed. Parochial records at St. Stephen's Church.

69—ST. LUCY (1900) Rev. Msgr. Oscar A. Aquino, Admin. In Res., Rev. Esviardo Palomino, Pastor Emeritus (Retired).
Res.: 344 E. 104th St., 10029. Tel: 212-534-1470.
School—(1942) 340 E. 104th St., 10029. Tel: 212-534-4021; Fax: 212-354-4130. Consolidated with St. Francis de Sales School to form St. Francis de Sales-St. Lucy Academy (1993).
Catechesis/Religious Program—Diana Naranjo, D.R.E. Students 46.

70—ST. MALACHY'S (1902), (The Actors' Chapel) Revs. Richard D. Baker; Emile Frische, M.H.M.
Res.: 239 W. 49th St., 10019. Tel: 212-489-1340; Fax: 212-262-6224. Email: parishoffice@actorschapel.org. Web: www.actorschapel.org.
Encore Community Services—Tel: 212-581-2910; 212-664-8628; Fax: 212-757-0244. Web: www.encorecommunityservices.org. Sisters Elizabeth Hasselt, O.P., Exec. Dir.; Lillian McNamara, O.P., Dir.; Peggy Gearity, Controller.
Encore Community Center & Programs—Tel: 212-581-2910.
Catechesis/Religious Program—Students 55.

71—ST. MARK THE EVANGELIST (1907), (Holy Spirit Fathers) Rev. Phillip R. Howard, C.S.Sp.
Res.: 65 W. 138th St., 10037. Tel: 212-281-4931; Fax: 212-491-6803.
School—(1912) 55 W. 138th St., 10037. Tel: 212-283-4848; Fax: 212-926-0419. Web: www.saintmarkschool.org. Antwan Allen, Prin. Daughters of Charity of St. Vincent de Paul 1; Lay Teachers 12; Students 249.
Catechesis/Religious Program—Students 18.
Chapel—St. Mark's Convent, Tel: 212-283-5306.

72—ST. MARY (1826) Rev. Msgr. Neil A. Connolly; Rev. Robert J. O'Neil, M.H.M. In Res., Rev. Peter Ma (Retired), (Chinese Apostolate), (Retired).
Res.: 28 Attorney St., 10002. Tel: 212-674-3266; Fax: 212-539-0216. Email: stmaryparish@aol.com.
Catechesis/Religious Program—Students 126.

73—MARY HELP OF CHRISTIANS (1908) Unassigned. (Salesian); Records at: Immaculate Conception, 414 E. 14th St., New York, NY 10009 (212-254-0200)
Res.: 440 E. 12th St., 10009.

74—ST. MARY MAGDALEN (1873), (German), Closed. Parochial records at Immaculate Conception Church.

75—ST. MATTHEW (1902) Closed. Parochial records at Blessed Sacrament Church.

76—ST. MICHAEL (1857) Rev. Myles P. Murphy.
Res.: 424 W. 34th St., 10001. Tel: 212-563-2575.
Catechesis/Religious Program—Students 4.
Chapel—Sacred Heart 419 W. 33rd St., 10001. Tel: 212-947-7668.

77—ST. MICHAEL CHAPEL (1936), (Russian), Rt. Rev. Economos Roman V. Russo, (Newton); Very Protodeacon Christopher LiGreci.
Church: 266 Mulberry St., 10012. Tel: 212-226-2644 (Church); 718-836-7311 (Residence); Fax: 718-921-5290.
Catechesis/Religious Program—Students 13.

78—ST. MONICA (1879) Rev. Msgr. Thomas A. Modugno; Rev. Joseph A. Francis.
Res.: 413 E. 79th St., 10075. Tel: 212-288-6250; Fax: 212-570-1562. Email: info@churchofstmonica.org. Web: www.churchofstmonica.org.
Chapel—St. Monica Convent 404 E. 80th St., 10075. Tel: 212-288-1986.

79—MOST HOLY CRUCIFIX (1925), (Italian), Unassigned. Records at Basilica of St. Patrick's Old Cathedral, 263 Mulberry St., New York, NY 10012. Tel: 212-226-8075.
Res.: 378 Broome St., 10013. Tel: 212-226-2556.

80—MOST HOLY REDEEMER (1844), (Redemptorist) Revs. Sean J. McGillicuddy, C.Ss.R.; James R. Cascione, C.Ss.R. In Res., Revs. Lenin Delgado, C.Ss.R.; Tom McCluskey, C.Ss.R.; Arthur G. Wendel, C.Ss.R., Vicar.
Res.: 173 E. Third St., 10009. Tel: 212-673-4224.
Catechesis/Religious Program—Students 52.

81—MOST PRECIOUS BLOOD (1891), (Italian), [CEM], (Franciscan) Rev. Fabian Grifone, O.F.M., Supr.; Friar Dominic Poirier, O.F.M.
Res.: 109 Mulberry St., 10013. Tel: 212-226-6427; Fax: 212-226-1837. Email: fgrifone@aol.com. Web: www.mostpreciousbloodchurch.net.

82—NATIVITY (1842), (Mission of St. Teresa). Records at St. Teresa, 141 Henry St., New York, NY 10002. Tel: 212-233-0233. Rev. Donald C. Baker; Deacon Arnaldo Rodriguez.
Res.: 141 Henry St., 10002. Tel: 212-674-8590; Fax: 212-674-8789.
Catechesis/Religious Program—Students 50.
Nativity Mission Center—204 Forsyth St., 10002. Tel: 212-477-2472; Fax: 212-473-0538.

83—ST. NICHOLAS (1833), (German), Closed. Parochial records at Most Holy Redeemer Church.

84—NOTRE DAME (1910) Rev. Msgr. John N. Paddack; Revs. Michael K. Holleran; Daniel O'Reilly.
Res.: 405 W. 114th St., 10025. Tel: 212-866-1500; Fax: 212-222-5704. Email: parish@ndparish.org. Web: www.ndparish.org.
Catechesis/Religious Program—Students 25.
St. Luke's Hospital—Tel: 212-523-4000.
Amsterdam Nursing Home—Tel: 212-316-7700.

85—OUR LADY OF ESPERANZA (1912), (Spanish), Rev. Edward K. Russell, Admin.
Res.: 624 W. 156th St., 10032. Tel: 212-283-4340; Fax: 212-283-4388. Email: vze4s75z@verizon.net.
Catechesis/Religious Program—Students 270.

86—OUR LADY OF GOOD COUNSEL (1886) Revs. Kazimierz A. Kowalski; Richard Terga, C.I.C.M. In Res., Very Rev. William S. Elder.
Res.: 230 E. 90th St., 10128. Tel: 212-289-1742; Fax: 212-427-5643.
Catechesis/Religious Program—Students 115.

87—OUR LADY OF GRACE (Stanton St.) (1907) Closed. Parochial records at Church of the Nativity.

88—OUR LADY OF GUADALUPE AT ST. BERNARD'S (1869) Revs. Santiago Rubio (Mexico); Enel Almeus. In Res., Revs. Joseph O'Meara; Patrick Martin.
Res.: 328 W. 14th St., 10014. Tel: 212-243-0265, Ext. 66; Fax: 212-255-8466.
Catechesis/Religious Program—Students 150.
Mission—St. Veronica 149 Christopher St., New York Co. 10014.

89—OUR LADY OF LORETO (1891), (Sicilian), Rev. Msgr. Michael F. Hull.
Res.: 309 Elizabeth St., 10012. Tel: 212-431-9840; Fax: 212-625-9096.
Holy Name Centre for Homeless Men—Tel: 212-226-5848.

90—OUR LADY OF LOURDES (1901) Revs. Fabian Lopez; Fidel Cruz (Mexico); Deacon Pedro O'Brien. In Res., Rev. Lawrence E. Lucas.
Res.: 472 W. 142nd St., 10031. Tel: 212-862-4380, Ext. 10; Fax: 212-862-4126.
School—(1903) 462-468 W. 143rd St., 10031. Tel: 212-926-5820, Ext. 11; Fax: 212-491-6034. Cathy M. Hufnagel, Prin. Lay Teachers 11; Students 282.
Catechesis/Religious Program—Tel: 212-862-4380, Ext. 10; Fax: 212-862-4126. Students 291.
Chapel—Convent of Our Lady of Lourdes 463 W. 142nd St., 10031. Tel: 212-862-4380; Fax: 212-862-4126.

91—OUR LADY OF MT. CARMEL (1884), (Italian), (Pallotine) Rev. Anthony Kelly, S.A.C.
Res.: 448 E. 116th St., 10029-0614. Tel: 212-534-0681; Fax: 212-534-0629.
School—Mt. Carmel-Holy Rosary, 371 Pleasant Ave., 10035. Tel: 212-876-7555; Fax: 212-876-0152. Sisters 1; Lay Teachers 10; Students 180.
Catechesis/Religious Program—Students 300.
Convent—456 E. 116th St., 10029-0614. Tel: 212-427-2381. Sisters of Charity 5.

92—OUR LADY OF PEACE (1918), (Italian), Rev. Bartholomew Daly, M.H.M., Admin. In Res., Rev. Andrew Bielak (Poland).
Res.: 237 E. 62nd St., 10065. Tel: 212-838-3189; Fax: 212-308-4819. Email: olpnyc@aol.com.
Catechesis/Religious Program—Students 20.

93—OUR LADY OF PERPETUAL HELP (1887) Closed. For inquiries for parish records please see Our Lady of Peace.

94—OUR LADY OF POMPEII (1892), (Italian), (Scalabrinian) Revs. John Charles Massari, C.S.; Romulo Montero (Philippines), Pastoral Assoc.; Bro. Michael La Mantia, C.S.
Res.: 25 Carmine St., 10014. Tel: 212-989-6805; Fax: 212-727-3139. Email: pompeiny@aol.com.
School—(1930) 240 Bleecker St., 10014. Tel: 212-242-4147; Fax: 212-691-2361. Email: no34@adnyeducation.org. Web: www.ladyofpompeii.org. Sisters (Apostles of the Sacred Heart of Jesus) 3; Lay Teachers 20; Students 222.
Catechesis/Religious Program—Students 15.

95—OUR LADY OF SORROWS (1867), (Capuchin) Revs. Thomas Faiola, O.F.M.Cap.; Thomas McNamara, O.F.M.Cap.; Bro. Robert Gerdin, O.F.M.Cap., Pastoral Assoc.; Deacon Wallace Zambrana. In Res., Rev. Michael Marigliano, O.F.M.Cap.; Bros. Terence Taffe, O.F.M.Cap.; John Conway, O.F.M.Cap.
Res.: 213 Stanton St., 10002-1898. Tel: 212-475-2321; Fax: 212-475-2452. Email: oloschurch@yahoo.com. Web: www.ourladyofsorrowsny.4lpi.com.
Church: 103 Pitt St., 10002. Tel: 212-673-0900; Fax: 212-982-0166.
Catechesis/Religious Program—Tel: 212-673-0900,

Ext. 306. Students 170.

96—OUR LADY OF THE MIRACULOUS MEDAL (1926) Closed. For inquiries for parish records, see Holy Agony, New York.

97—OUR LADY OF THE ROSARY (1883), Shrine of St. Elizabeth Ann Seton. Rev. Peter Meehan; Rev. Msgr. Timothy Collins, Pastor Emeritus (Retired). In Res., Rev. Robert A. Jeffers (Retired).
Res.: 7 State St., 10004. Tel: 212-269-6865; Fax: 212-809-6850. Email: setonshrine05@netscape.com. Web: www.setonshrine.com.

98—OUR LADY OF VICTORY (1944) Rev. Msgr. Marc J. Filacchione; Revs. Socorro Braganca, O.C.D.; Reynaldo Domagas (Philippines), (Hospital Chap.); Romeo Hontiveros (Philippines).
Res.: 60 William St., 10005. Tel: 212-422-5535; Fax: 212-785-4457. Web: www.ourladyofvictorychurch.org.

99—OUR LADY OF VILNIUS (1905), (Lithuanian), Closed. For inquiries for Sacramental records contact St. Anthony of Padua, 154 Sullivan St., New York, NY 10012.

100—OUR LADY QUEEN OF ANGELS (1886), Closed. Records at: Our Lady of Mt. Carmel, 448 E. 116th St., New York, NY 10029 (212-534-0681)
Res.: 226 E. 113th St., 10029.
School—(1886 and 1955) 229-231 E. 112th St., 10029. Tel: 212-722-9277; Fax: 212-987-8837. Lay Teachers 12; Students 235.
Catechesis/Religious Program—Tel: 212-860-7618; Fax: 212-828-0506. Students 65.
Convent—(Franciscan Sisters of the Renewal), 232 E. 113th St., 10029. Tel: 212-831-3334; Fax: 212-831-3339. Web: www.franciscansisterscfr.com. Sr. Francis O'Donnell, C.F.R., Local Servant.

101—OUR LADY QUEEN OF MARTYRS (1927) Revs. Antonio Almonte; Marco Antonio Ortega, Parochial Vicar; Deacons Narciso Hernandez; Luis Feliz; Delio Fernandez; Bienvenido Valdez.
Res.: 91 Arden St., 10040. Tel: 212-567-2637; Fax: 212-567-1305.
School—(1932) 71 Arden St., 10040. Tel: 212-567-3190; Fax: 212-304-8587. Andrew Woods, Prin. Lay Teachers 14; Students 318.
Catechesis/Religious Program—Tel: 212-942-8604 (CCD Office). Students 300.

102—OUR SAVIOUR (1955) Rev. George W. Rutler.
Res.: 59 Park Ave., 10016. Tel: 212-679-8166; Fax: 212-213-0352. Email: info@oursaviournyc.org. Web: www.oursaviournyc.org.
Catechesis/Religious Program—Students 81.

103—ST. PAUL (1834), (Institute of The Incarnate Word) Revs. Claudio Stewart; Delfin Condori Puma.
Res.: 113 E. 117th St., 10035. Tel: 212-534-4422; Fax: 212-996-5588. Email: par.newyork@ive.org. Web: www.stpaulchurchive.org.
School—(1870) 114-122 E. 118th St., 10035. Tel: 212-534-0619; Fax: 212-534-3990. Email: stpaul@email.com. Lay Teachers 14; Students 280.
Catechesis/Religious Program—Tel: 212-534-4481. Email: ccdstpaul@servidoras.org. Students 467.
Convent—(Sisters of The Servants of the Lord and The Virgin of Matara), St. Paul Convent, 149 E. 117th St., 10035. Tel: 917-492-3668. Email: c.roseduchesne@servidoras.org. Web: www.ssvmusa.org.

104—ST. PAUL THE APOSTLE (1858), (Paulist. See also Paulist Fathers' Motherhouse under Monasteries located in the Institution section.) Revs. Gilbert S. Martinez, C.S.P.; Ronald A. Franco, C.S.P.; Deacon Waldemar Sandoval.
Mailing Address & Office: 405 W. 59th, 10019. Tel: 212-265-3495; Fax: 212-262-9239. Email: webmaster@stpaultheapostle.org. Web: www.stpaultheapostle.org.
Catechesis/Religious Program—Students 150.
Chapel—Oblates of Jesus the Priest, Tel: 212-265-3209; Fax: 212-265-4154.

105—ST. PETER (1785) Revs. Kevin Madigan; Donald T. Fussner (Retired); Alex Joseph (India); Arthur Leone (Retired).
Mailing Address: 22 Barclay St., 10007.
Res.: 18 Vesey St., 10007. Tel: 212-233-8355 (Church); 212-608-4709 (Res.); Fax: 212-285-0497. Email: st.peterschurch1785@verizon.net.
Catechesis/Religious Program—James O'Connor, D.R.E. Students 96.
Chapel—St. Joseph's Chapel 385 South End Ave., 10280. Tel: 212-466-0131. Web: www.sjchapel.org.

106—ST. RAPHAEL (1886) Closed. See Sts. Cyril and Methodius.

107—ST. ROSE (1868) Closed. Parochial records at St. Mary Church.

108—ST. ROSE OF LIMA (1902) Revs. Edward K. Russell; Ramon Lopez. In Res., Rev. Melchor Ferrer, S.D.B.
Res.: 510 W. 165th St., 10032. Tel: 212-568-0091.
School—(1924) 517 W. 164th St., 10032. Lay Teachers 10; Students 260.
Catechesis/Religious Program—Sr. Ramona Liriano, D.R.E. Students 297.
Chapel—St. Rose of Lima Convent 509 W. 164th St., 10032.
Medical Centre—

109—SACRED HEART OF JESUS (1876) Rev. Jose Gabriel Piedrahita.
Res.: 457 W. 51st, 10019. Tel: 212-265-5020; Fax: 212-977-4116. Email: sacredheart51@nyc.rr.com. Web: www.shjsnyc.org.
School—(1892) 456 52nd St., 10019. Tel: 212-246-4784; Fax: 212-707-8382. Lay Teachers 19; Students 227.
Chapel—Centro Maria 539 W. 54th St., 10019. Tel: 212-757-6989; Fax: 212-307-5687.
Chapel—Convent of Sacred Heart 450 W. 51st St., 10019. Tel: 212-397-1396; Fax: 212-397-1397.
Catechesis/Religious Program—Tel: 212-265-5020, Ext. 16; Fax: 212-977-4116. Students 71.

110—ST. SEBASTIAN (1915) Closed. Parochial records at Epiphany Church.

111—ST. STEPHEN AND OUR LADY OF THE SCAPULAR (1848; 1869) Rev. Msgr. Lawrence M. Connaughton. In Res., Most Rev. William J. McCormack (Retired); Rev. Msgr. Walter J. Niebrzydowski (Retired); Revs. Stephen Okeke (Nigeria); Damian Umeokeke; Joseph Nahas.
Res.: 142 E. 29th St., 10016. Tel: 212-683-1675; Fax: 212-683-7921. Email: olsss142@aol.com. Web: www.churchofststephen.com.
Catechesis/Religious Program—Epiphany Church, 239 E. 21st St., 10010. Tel: 212-475-1966; Fax: 212-477-0537. Web: www.epiphanyrcchurch.us. Students 8.
Mission—Chapel of the Sacred Hearts of Jesus and Mary 325 E. 33rd St., New York Co. 10016. Tel: 212-213-6027; Fax: 212-213-9136. Rev. Msgr. Lawrence M. Connaughton, Admin. In Res., His Eminence Edward Cardinal Egan; Rev. Brendan Fitzgerald.
Chapel—Bellevue Hospital, Chapel of Our Lady Helper of the Sick, Tel: 212-561-4440. Rev. Francis Okoli.

112—ST. STANISLAUS BISHOP AND MARTYR (1872), (Polish), (Pauline Fathers) Revs. Bogdan Mikolaj Socha, O.S.P.P.E.; Dominik Pawel Libiszewski, O.S.P.P.E.
Res.: 101 E. Seventh St., 10009. Tel: 212-475-4576; Fax: 212-674-4894. Email: rectory@stanislauschurch.com. Web: www.stanislauschurch.com.
Catechesis/Religious Program—Students 140.

113—ST. STEPHEN (1848) Consolidated in 1990. See Our Lady of Scapular/St. Stephen for details.

114—ST. STEPHEN OF HUNGARY (1902), (Franciscan) Revs. Angelus Gambatese, O.F.M.; William K. Bried, O.F.M. In Res., Rev. Kyle Haden, O.F.M.; Bro. Thomas J. Cole, O.F.M., Guardian; Revs. Allan G. Von Kobs, O.F.M.; Dennis M. Wilson, O.F.M.; Bro. Timothy Miskowski, O.F.M.
Res.: 414 E. 82nd St., 10028. Tel: 212-861-8500; Fax: 212-535-9221. Web: www.saintstephenofhungary.com.
School—(1918) 408 E. 82nd St., 10028. Tel: 212-288-1989; Fax: 212-517-5877. Ms. Katherine Peck, Prin. Lay Teachers 15; Students 235.
Catechesis/Religious Program—Religious Education Program Ms. Jayne Porcelli, D.R.E. Students 65.
Dewitt Nursing Home—211 E. 79th St., 10021. Tel: 212-879-1600.

115—ST. TERESA (1863) Revs. Donald C. Baker; Joseph Guo Zhang Ruan; Mauricio Zapata, Pastoral Assoc. In Res., Rev. Sunny Mathew, O.Carm. (India); Deacons Arnaldo Rodriguez; Patrick So.
Res.: 141 Henry St., 10002. Tel: 212-233-0233; Fax: 212-619-4538.
Church: 141 Henry St., 10002. Tel: 212-233-0233; Fax: 212-619-4538. Email: teresa141henry@hotmail.com. Web: www.teresa141henry.org.
Catechesis/Religious Program—Students 96.
Mission—Church of the Nativity 44 - 2nd Ave., 10003. Tel: 212-674-8590; Fax: 212-619-4530.

116—ST. THOMAS MORE (1950) Rev. Msgr. John A. Boehning; Revs. Jose Tentativa; Edwin Diaz. In Res., Rev. Msgr. Thomas J. Shelley.
Res.: 65 E. 89th St., 10128. Tel: 212-876-7718; Fax: 212-831-5756. Email: m106@archny.org. Web: www.thomasmorechurch.org.
Catechesis/Religious Program—Narnia Clubs, 163 E. 81st St., 10150. Tel: 212-535-9329; Fax: 212-628-8409. Email: info@narniaclubs.com. Web: www.narniaclubs.com. Students 328.

117—ST. THOMAS THE APOSTLE (1889), (African American), [CEM], Records at St. Joseph of the Holy Family, 405 W. 125th St., NY, NY 10027.
Res.: 262 W. 118th St., 10026. Tel: 212-662-2693; Fax: 212-662-4560.
Catechesis/Religious Program—Students 127.

118—TRANSFIGURATION (1827), (Chinese-English), Rev. Raymond J. Nobiletti, M.M.
Res.: 29 Mott St., 10013-5006. Tel: 212-962-5157; Fax: 212-962-5217. Email: transparish@aol.com. Web: www.transfigurationnyc.org.
School—Lower School (1832), (Grades K-4) Tel: 212-962-5265; Fax: 212-964-8964. Email: m110@adnyeducation.org. Web: www.transfigurationschoolnyc.org. Lay Teachers 9; Students 221.
School—Upper School, (Grades 5-8), 37 St. James Pl., 10038. Tel: 212-267-9289; Fax: 212-227-0065. Dr. Patrick Taharally, Prin. (Lower & Upper Schools). Lay Teachers 6; Students 128.
School—Kindergarten School (1954), (Early Childhood Site), 10 Confucius Pl., 10002. Tel: 212-431-8769; Fax: 212-431-8917. Email: e.engtran@adnyeducation.org. Ms. Emily Eng-Tran, Prin. Lay Teachers 23; Students 150.
Catechesis/Religious Program—Students 110.

119—ST. VERONICA (1887), Mission of Our Lady of Guadalupe at St. Bernard. Old records at St. Veronica, 149 Christopher St., New York, NY 10014; Tel: 212-924-5628. New records at Our Lady of Guadalupe at St. Bernard, 328 W. 14th St., New York, NY 10014; Tel: 212-243-0265., 328 W. 14th St., 10014.

120—ST. VINCENT DE PAUL (1841), (French), Rev. Gerald E. Murray. In Res., Revs. Robert J. Poveromo; Gerard Messier, A.A.
Res.: 116 W. 24th St., 10011. Tel: 212-243-4727; Fax: 212-675-0528.
Church: 123 W. 23rd St., 10011.
Catechesis/Religious Program—Students 280.

121—ST. VINCENT FERRER (1867), (Dominican) Revs. Walter Cornelius Wagner, O.P.; Vinod Bruno Mary Shah, O.P.; Bro. John Damian McCarthy, O.P.
Res.: 869 Lexington Ave., 10065-6648. Tel: 212-744-2080; Fax: 212-327-3011. Web: www.csvf.org.
High School—151 E. 65th St., 10065-6607. Tel: 212-535-4680; Fax: 212-988-3455. Web: www.saintvincentferrer.com. Sr. Gail Morgan, O.P., Prin. Dominican Sisters of Our Lady of the Springs 8; Lay Teachers 30; Girls 496.
Catechesis/Religious Program—
Chapel—Dominican Sisters of Our Lady of the Springs 152 E. 66th St., 10065. Tel: 212-744-2375; Fax: 212-249-5355.
Chapel—Dominican Academy 44 E. 68th St., 10065. Tel: 212-744-0195; Fax: 212-744-0375.

BOROUGH OF BRONX

1—ST. ADALBERT (1898), (Polish), Closed. For inquiries for parish records contact the chancery.

2—ST. ANGELA MERICI (1899), (Apostles of Jesus) Revs. Nestorio Agirembabazi, A.J.; John Kalungi, A.J.; Deacon Felipe Sin-Garciga.
Res.: 917 Morris Ave., Bronx, 10451. Tel: 718-293-0984; Fax: 718-293-7325. Email: nagirembabazi@yahoo.com. Web: www.saintangelamerici.net.
Church: E. 163rd St., Bronx, 10451.
School—(1917) 266 E. 163rd St., Bronx, 10451. Tel: 718-293-3365; Fax: 718-293-6617. Lay Teachers 14; Students 323.
Catechesis/Religious Program—Fax: 718-293-0984. Students 163.

3—ST. ANN (1927) Rev. Francis P. Scanlon. In Res., Revs. Misael Bacleon (Philippines); Andrew Ovienloba (Nigeria).
Res.: 3519 Bainbridge Ave., Bronx, 10467. Tel: 718-547-9350; Fax: 718-547-1718. Email: saintannchurch@aol.com.
School—(1928) Bainbridge Ave. & Gun Hill Rd., Bronx, 10467. Tel: 718-655-3449; Fax: 718-547-4020. Mrs. Cecile Rodriguez, Prin. Students 280.
Catechesis/Religious Program—Tel: 718-655-3449; Fax: 718-547-2020. Students 100.

4—ST. ANSELM (1892), (Augustinian Recollects) Revs. Antonio Palacios, O.A.R.; Jose Antonio Rodrigalvarez, O.A.R.; Deacon Apolonio Mejia.
Res.: 685 Tinton Ave., Bronx, 10455. Tel: 718-585-8666; Fax: 718-401-6686.
School—(1908)Tel: 718-993-9464; Fax: 718-292-3496. Ms. Teresa M. Lopes, Prin. Lay Teachers 13; Students 380.
Catechesis/Religious Program—Tel: 718-585-8542. Students 240.

5—ST. ANTHONY (1908) Rev. Joseph J. Kelly; Deacon Frankie Vazquez. In Res., Rev. John J. Piderit, S.J.
Res.: 1496 Commonwealth Ave., Bronx, 10460. Tel: 718-931-4040; 718-931-4041; Fax: 718-863-0202. Email: st.commonwealth@yahoo.com.
School—(1931) 1776 Mansion St., Bronx, 10460. Tel: 718-892-1244; Fax: 718-892-4656. Email: B224@adnyschools.org. Lay Teachers 12; Students 178.
Catechesis/Religious Program—Students 75.

6—ST. ANTHONY (1919) Mission of St. Frances of Rome. Records at Saint Frances of Rome, 4307 Barnes Ave., Bronx, NY 10466. Phone: 718-324-5340; Fax: 718-324-5373.
Res.: 4307 Barnes Ave., Bronx, 10466.
Catechesis/Religious Program—Attendance at Saint Frances of Rome.

7—ST. ANTHONY OF PADUA (1903), (African

American—Hispanic), [CEM] Most Rev. Josu Iriondo; Rev. Benjamin Palacios, D.V.M., Parochial Vicar; Deacon Nelson Duran.
Res.: 832 E. 166th St., Bronx, 10459. Tel: 718-542-7293; Fax: 718-378-1819. Email: stanthony832@aol.com.
Catechesis/Religious Program—Students 198.

8—ST. ATHANASIUS (1907) Rev. Jose Rivas; Deacons Alejandro Rosado; Fernando Vazquez.
Res.: 878 Tiffany St., Bronx, 10459. Tel: 718-328-2558; Fax: 718-328-3121. Email: sachurch878verizon@verizon.net.
School—(1913) 830 Southern Blvd., Bronx, 10459. Tel: 718-542-5161; Fax: 718-542-7584. Email: b227@adnyschool.org. Web: www.athschool.org. Marianne Kraft, Prin. Sisters 1; Lay Teachers 11; Students 315.
Catechesis/Religious Program—Juan A. Sotomayor Jr., C.R.E. Students 125.

9—ST. AUGUSTINE (1849) Rev. Thomas Fenlon; Sr. Dorothy Hall, O.P., Pastoral Assoc.; Rita Velez, Sec. In Res., Rev. Joseph Bernardine Onyia (Nigeria), Chap., Bronx Lebanon Hospital.
Res.: 1183 Franklin Ave., Bronx, 10456. Tel: 718-893-0072; Fax: 718-861-3080. Email: staugbx@optonline.net.
Church: E. 167th St., Bronx, 10456.
Catechesis/Religious Program—Students 85.

10—ST. BARNABAS (1910), (Irish—Italian), Rev. Msgr. Edward M. Barry; Revs. Brendan Gormley; Benjamin Mariasoosai; Deacon Cornelius Manning, (Retired). In Res., Rev. Philip Amankwa-Danguah.
Res.: 409 E. 241st St., Bronx, 10470. Tel: 718-324-1478; Fax: 718-324-1479. Email: stbarnabasbronx@aol.com. Web: www.stbarnabasbronx.org.
School—(1912) 413 E. 241st St., Bronx, 10470. Tel: 718-324-1088; Fax: 718-324-2397. Email: B229@adnyschools.org. Web: www.stbarnabasschool.org. Lay Teachers 16; Students 400.
High School—High School for Girls (1924)*St. Barnabas High School*, 425 E. 240th St., Bronx, 10470. Tel: 718-325-8800; Fax: 718-325-8820. Web: www-.stbarnabashighschool. Sisters 2; Lay Teachers 16; Students 224.
Catechesis/Religious Program—Tel: 718-324-0865. Students 362.
Convent—(Sisters of Life), 445 E. 240th St., Bronx, 10470. Tel: 718-708-6742; Fax: 718-708-6744. Sisters 6; Postulants 8.
Chapel—St. Barnabas High School Chapel Yonkers.

11—ST. BENEDICT (1923) Revs. Stephen P. Norton; Clement Kanu (Africa), Parochial Vicar; Brian P. Taylor, Parochial Vicar; Deacon John Scott.
Res.: 2969 Otis Ave., Bronx, 10465-2198. Tel: 718-828-3403; Fax: 718-829-1304. Email: stbenedict@optonline.net.
School—(1923) 1016 Edison Ave., Bronx, 10465. Tel: 718-829-9557; Fax: 718-319-1898. Sisters 1; Lay Teachers 17; Students 295.
Catechesis/Religious Program—Tel: 718-829-1200. Students 392.
Chapel—St. John 1082 Edison Ave., Bronx, 10465.

12—BLESSED SACRAMENT (1927) Revs. Evaristus C. Ohuche; Raul G. Miguez (Cuba); Deacon Epi Portalatin.
Res.: 1170 Beach Ave., Bronx, 10472. Tel: 718-892-3214; Fax: 718-892-3907. Email: blsacramentchurch@yahoo.com.
School—(1929) 1160 Beach Ave. & 1141 Taylor Ave., Bronx, 10472. Tel: 718-892-0433; Fax: 718-892-3337. Email: b200@adnyschools.org. Miss Herminia Roman, Prin. Lay Teachers 10; Students 275.
Catechesis/Religious Program—Tel: 718-863-4620. Students 92.

13—ST. BRENDAN (1908) Revs. George R. Stewart; Santiago Rubio Clemente; Sancho G. Garrote; Sr. Catherine Naughton, O.P., Senior Outreach Coord.; Deacons Paul Hveem; Orlando Pascal.
Res.: 333 E. 206th St., Bronx, 10467. Tel: 718-547-6655; Fax: 718-547-6579.
School—(1912) 268 E. 207th St., Bronx, 10467. Tel: 718-653-2293; Fax: 718-653-3234. Miss Michele Pasquale, Prin. Lay Teachers 15; Students 345.
Catechesis/Religious Program—Tel: 718-654-6424. Judith Cordero, D.R.E. Students 235.

14—CHRIST THE KING (1926) Revs. Sixto Quezada (Dominican Republic); Abraham Berko-Attah.
Res.: 141 Marcy Pl., Bronx, 10452. Tel: 718-538-5546; Fax: 718-538-3081.
School—Tel: 718-538-5959; Fax: 718-538-6369. Lay Teachers 10; Students 436.
Catechesis/Religious Program—Tel: 718-538-5546; Fax: 718-538-3081. Students 364.
Mission—Ghanaian Mass & Pilgrims

15—ST. CLARE OF ASSISI (1929), (Italian), Revs. Richard Guarnieri; Dennis Cagantas (Philippines); Deacon Thomas Tortorella.
Res.: 1918 Paulding Ave., Bronx, 10462. Tel: 718-863-8974; Fax: 718-931-6909. Email: stclareofassisi@aol.com. Web: www.rc.net/newyork/stclare.
Church: 1027 Rhinelander Ave., Bronx, 10461.
School—(1951) 1911 Hone Ave., Bronx, 10461. Tel: 718-892-4080; Fax: 718-239-1007. Email: b232@adnyschools.org. Janice Desmond, Prin. Lay Teachers 22; Students 434.
Catechesis/Religious Program—Tel: 718-829-9624. Students 150.
Chapel—Bronx, Morningside House Chapel 1000 Pelham Pkwy., Bronx, 10461. Tel: 718-409-8200.

16—ST. DOMINIC (1924), (Italian), Rev. Robert P. Badillo, M.Id.; Deacon Reynaldo Rosado.
Res.: 1739 Unionport Rd., Bronx, 10462. Tel: 718-863-3282; Fax: 718-792-4950.
Catechesis/Religious Program—Our Lady of Solace, 731 Morris Park Ave., Bronx, 10462. Tel: 718-823-9044. Students 160.
Convent—1710 Unionport Rd., Bronx, 10462. Tel: 718-824-2580. Sisters 9.

17—ST. FRANCES DE CHANTAL (1927) Revs. Michael Sullivan; Susai Antony Devasagayam; Deacons John Murphy; George Coppola.
Res.: 190 Hollywood Ave., Bronx, 10465. Tel: 718-792-5500; Fax: 718-792-1824. Email: sfdchantal@gmail.com. Web: www.sfdchantal.org.
School—(1929) 2962 Harding Ave., Bronx, 10465. Tel: 718-892-5359; Fax: 718-892-6937. Ms. Lisa Macchia, Prin. Lay Teachers 10; Students 263.
High School—Preston High School, Established by the Sisters of Divine Compassion., 2780 Schurz Ave., Bronx, 10465. Tel: 718-863-9134.
Catechesis/Religious Program—Ms. Christi Chiapetti. Students 190.
Convent—Convent of Sisters of Life, 198 Hollywood Ave., Bronx, 10465. Tel: 718-863-2264.

18—ST. FRANCES OF ROME (1898) Revs. Francis J. Corry; John P. Sheehan; James P. Clark (Retired); Sr. Ellen Hublitz, O.P., Pastoral Assoc.
Res.: 4307 Barnes Ave., Bronx, 10466. Tel: 718-324-5340; Fax: 718-324-5373.
Church: 761 E. 236th St., Bronx, 10466.
Catechesis/Religious Program—Sr. Kathleen Harrington, P.V.B.M., D.R.E. Students 90.
Mission—St. Anthony 4505 Richardson Ave., Bronx, 10470.
Mission—St. Francis of Assisi 4330 Baychester Ave., Bronx, 10466.

19—ST. FRANCIS OF ASSISI (1928), Mission of Sacred Heart. Records at Sacred Heart, 1253 Shakespeare Ave., Bronx, NY 10452. Tel: 718-293-2766., 1544 Shakespeare Ave., Bronx, 10452. Tel: 718-731-6840; 718-731-6841. Mailing Address: P.O. Box 520013, Bronx, 10452. Fax: 718-731-6841.

20—ST. FRANCIS OF ASSISI (1949) Mission of St. Frances of Rome. Records at Saint Frances of Rome, 4307 Barnes Ave., Bronx, NY 10466. Phone: 718-324-5340; Fax: 718-324-5373.
Res.: 4307 Barnes Ave., Bronx, 10466.
School—4300 Baychester Ave., Bronx, 10466. Tel: 718-994-4650. Mary Jane Helmrich, Prin. Lay Teachers 14; Students 327.
Catechesis/Religious Program—Attendance at Saint Frances of Rome.

21—ST. FRANCIS XAVIER (1928) Revs. Matthew J. Furey; Catalino S. Villaviza; Shanthi Reddy Singareddy. In Res., Rev. Hippolytus Duru (Nigeria).
Res.: 1703 Lurting Ave., Bronx, 10461. Tel: 718-892-3330; Fax: 718-931-6890.
School—(1930) 1711 Haight Ave., Bronx, 10461. Tel: 718-863-0531; Fax: 718-319-1152. Mrs. Angela Deegan, Prin. Lay Teachers 11; Students 286.
Catechesis/Religious Program—Students 124.
Chapel—St. Francis Xavier Convent 1661 Haight Ave., Bronx, 10461. Tel: 718-892-9466; Fax: 718-829-1488.

22—ST. GABRIEL (1939) Revs. John M. Knapp; Lawrence David Ahyuwa; Deacon Eugene Burke. In Res., Revs. George H. Hill; Antony Siviramatu.
Res.: 3250 Arlington Ave., Bronx, 10463. Tel: 718-548-4470; 718-548-4471; Fax: 718-548-6451.
Church: 235th & Netherland Ave., Bronx, 10463. Fax: 718-548-0444.
School—590 W. 235th St., Bronx, 10463. Tel: 718-548-0444; Fax: 718-796-2638. Deborah D. Pitula, Prin. Lay Teachers 11; Students 238.
Catechesis/Religious Program—Tel: 718-548-6585. Mr. Glenn A. McCarthy, D.R.E. Students 90.

23—ST. HELENA (1940) Rev. Msgr. Thomas B. Derivan; Revs. Edmundo Gomez; Jerome Ofoegbu (Nigeria); Joseph Ligory (Sri Lanka).
Res.: 1315 Olmstead Ave., Bronx, 10462. Tel: 718-892-3232; Fax: 718-892-3078. Email: sthelenarc@yahoo.com. Web: www.sthelenabronxny.org.
School—(1941) 2050 Benedict Ave., Bronx, 10462. Tel: 718-892-3234; Fax: 718-892-3924. Richard Meller, Prin. Lay Teachers 13; Students 415.
High School—Msgr. Scanlan High School (1949), (Coed), 915 Hutchinson River Pkwy., Bronx, 10465. Tel: 718-430-0100; Fax: 718-892-8845. Mrs. Emily Padilla-Bradley, Prin. Sisters of St. Dominic (Sparkill, NY) 5; Lay Teachers 26; Students 455.
Catechesis/Religious Program—Tel: 718-892-3234. Students 105.

24—HOLY CROSS (1921) Revs. Peter A. Pomposello; Robert J. Ginel; Deacons Valentin Acabeo; Jaime A. Bello.
Res.: 620 Thieriot Ave., Bronx, 10473. Tel: 718-893-5550; Fax: 718-378-3655. Email: holycross@holycrossbronx.org. Web: www.holycrossbronx.org.
School—(1923 & 1955) 1846 Randall Ave., Bronx, 10473. Tel: 718-842-4492; Fax: 718-842-4052. Lay Teachers 18; Students 393.
Catechesis/Religious Program—Students 256.
Chapel—Chapel of St. Anthony at Holy Cross

25—HOLY FAMILY (1896) Revs. James D. Flanagan; Andrew M. O'Connor, Parochial Vicar; Deacon Dhoel Canals.
Res.: 2158 Watson Ave., Bronx, 10472. Tel: 718-863-9156; Fax: 718-597-5560.
School—(1913) 2169 Blackrock Ave., Bronx, 10472. Tel: 718-863-7280; Fax: 718-931-8690. Lay Teachers 16; Students 325.
Catechesis/Religious Program—2169 Black Rock Ave., Bronx, 10472. Tel: 718-822-8030. Students 195.
Chapel—Holy Family 2155 Blackrock Ave., Bronx, 10472.

26—HOLY ROSARY (1925) Revs. Robert A. Quarato; Osayamen Samson Imhangbe (Nigeria); Sebastian Pandarathikudiyil, V.C. (India); Deacon Joseph Solanto.
Res.: 1510 Adee Ave., Bronx, 10469. Tel: 718-379-4432; 718-379-4654; Fax: 718-379-9028. Email: holyrosarybx@verizon.net.
School—(1927; 1955) 1500 Arnow Ave., Bronx, 10469. Tel: 718-652-1838; Fax: 718-515-9872. Mrs. Maryann Fusco, Prin. Lay Teachers 18; Students 430.
Catechesis/Religious Program—Tel: 718-654-9381. Students 95.
Chapel—Holy Rosary Convent 2755 Woodhull Ave., Bronx, 10469. Tel: 718-798-6435.

27—HOLY SPIRIT (1901) Revs. Ricardo Fajardo (Dominican Republic); Damian Ekete (Nigeria).
Res.: 1940 University Ave., Bronx, 10453. Tel: 718-583-0120; Fax: 718-583-1444. Email: holyspiritbx@yahoo.com.
School—(1913) 1960 University Ave., Bronx, 10453. Tel: 718-583-1570; Fax: 718-583-3378. Lay Teachers 11; Students 256.
Catechesis/Religious Program—Students 275.

28—IMMACULATE CONCEPTION (1853), (German), (Redemptorist) Rev. Francis G. Skelly, C.Ss.R.; Deacon Cristobal Rodriguez. In Res., Revs. Tat-Thang Hoang, C.Ss.R.; Patrick Keyes, C.Ss.R.; Richard Bennett, C.Ss.R.; Frank Mulvaney; Paul Loc; Bros. Laurence J. Lujun; Leo Patin, C.Ss.R.
Res.: 389 E. 150th St., Bronx, 10455. Tel: 718-292-6970; Fax: 718-292-4603.
School—(1854) 378 E. 151st St., Bronx, 10455. Tel: 718-585-4843; Fax: 718-585-6846. Sisters of Christian Charity 3; Lay Teachers 22; Students 510.
Catechesis/Religious Program—Tel: 718-292-6970, Ext. 15. Students 75.
Chapel—Sisters of Christian Charity 365 E. 150th St., Bronx, 10455. Tel: 718-585-8981.

29—IMMACULATE CONCEPTION (1903), (Capuchin) Revs. John Lo Sasso, O.F.M.Cap.; Peter Napoli, O.F.M-.Cap.; Robert Williams, O.F.M.Cap.; Bro. Jesu Perez, O.F.M.Cap., Pastoral Assoc.; Deacons Carlos Mercado; Victor Tosi.
Capuchin Friary: 754 E. Gun Hill Rd., Bronx, 10467. Tel: 718-653-2200; Fax: 718-882-0054.
School—Tel: 718-547-3346; Fax: 718-547-5505. Sr. Latecia Aviles, O.B.T., Prin. Priests 4; Brothers 2; Oblates to the Blessed Trinity 4; Franciscan Missionary Sisters 2; Missionary Sisters of the Catechism 4; Lay Teachers 13; Students 895.

30—ST. JEROME'S (1869) Rev. Gustavo Javier Nieto, I.V.E.
Res.: 230 Alexander Ave., Bronx, 10454. Tel: 718-665-5533; Fax: 718-665-5875. Email: stjeromech@aol.com.
School—(1871) 222 Alexander Ave., Bronx, 10454. Tel: 718-292-4920; Fax: 718-292-3111. Lay Teachers 10; Students 300.
Catechesis/Religious Program—Mrs. Carmen Acevedo, D.R.E. Students 300.

31—ST. JOAN OF ARC (1949) Revs. Paul J. LeBlanc; Jose Mena; Deacons Ismael Camacho; Angel Alvarez.
Res.: 1372 Stratford Ave., Bronx, 10472. Tel: 718-842-2233; Fax: 718-842-4720.
Catechesis/Religious Program—Students 293.

32—ST. JOHN CHRYSOSTOM (1899) Rev. Carlos Rodriguez.
Res.: 985 E. 167th St., Bronx, 10459. Tel: 718-542-6164; Fax: 718-542-0448.
School—(1914) 1144 Hoe Ave., Bronx, 10459. Tel:

718-328-7226; Fax: 718-378-5368. Sr. Mary Elizabeth Mooney, O.P., Prin. Sisters of St. Dominic (Sparkill, NY) 9; Lay Teachers 13; Students 372.
Catechesis/Religious Program—Tel: 718-328-7723. Students 190.

33—St John Nam (1989), (Korean), Revs. Simon Nam; Andrew H. Lee (Korea, South).
Res.: 3663 White Plains Rd., Bronx, 10467. Tel: 718-231-2414; Fax: 718-405-0053. Email: church_of_st_john_nam@hotmail.com.
Catechesis/Religious Program—Students 69.

34—St. John Vianney, Cure of Ars (1960) Rev. Jose A. Serrano; Deacons Al Leasiolagi; Edwin Cruz.
Res.: 715 Castle Hill Ave., Bronx, 10473. Tel: 718-863-4411; Fax: 718-863-1673.
Catechesis/Religious Program—Students 70.

35—St. John's (1886) Revs. Antonio Zabala, O.A.R.; Eliseo Gonzalez, O.A.R., Parochial Vicar; Francis A. Cregan, O.A.R., Parochial Vicar; Deacon Andrew Rivera.
Res.: 3021 Kingsbridge Ave., Bronx, 10463. Tel: 718-548-1221; Fax: 718-548-7774. Email: oarbx@aol.com.
School—(1903) 3143 Kingsbridge Ave., Bronx, 10463. Tel: 718-548-0255; Fax: 718-548-0864. Jayson Bock, Prin. Sisters 2; Lay Teachers 12; Students 226.
Catechesis/Religious Program—Tel: 718-884-2627. Students 168.
Convent—Religious of Jesus and Mary, 3029 Godwin Ter., Bronx, 10463. Tel: 718-548-4902; 718-543-2454.

36—St. Joseph (1873) Revs. Salvatore Sportino; Clement Umoenoh.
Res.: 1949 Bathgate Ave., Bronx, 10457. Tel: 718-731-2504; Fax: 718-731-0478.
School—(1922) 1946 Bathgate Ave., Bronx, 10457. Tel: 718-583-9432; Fax: 718-299-0780. Janine A. Hughes, Prin. Lay Teachers 20; Students 465.
Catechesis/Religious Program—Students 22.

37—St. Lucy (1927) Revs. Nikolin Pergjini; Louis Anderson. In Res., Rev. Msgr. Frederick J. Becker.
Church: 833 Mace Ave., Bronx, 10467. Tel: 718-882-0710; Fax: 718-882-8876.
School—(1955) 830 Mace Ave., Bronx, 10467. Tel: 718-882-2203; Fax: 718-547-8351. Mrs. Jane Stefanini, Prin. Lay Teachers 15; Students 410.
Catechesis/Religious Program—Students 250.

38—St. Luke (1897) Rev. Msgr. Gerald J. Ryan; Rev. Cesar Rafael Bejarano, O.F.M. (Venezuela); Mary Kay Louchart, Pastoral Assoc.; Sharon Joslyn, Pastoral Assoc.
Res.: 623 E. 138th St., Bronx, 10454. Tel: 718-665-6677; Fax: 718-665-0898. Email: stlukes138@aol.com.
School—(1910) 608 E. 139th St., Bronx, 10454. Tel: 718-585-0380; Fax: 718-665-3407. Email: b247@adnyeducation.org. Sisters of St. Dominic (Blauvelt) 1; Lay Teachers 16; Students 330.
Catechesis/Religious Program—Tel: 718-801-5512; Fax: 718-665-6677. Students 590.
Chapel—St. Luke Convent 621 E. 138th St., Bronx, 10454. Tel: 718-292-3016.

39—St. Margaret Mary (1923) Revs. Robert P. Arce; Jose Ambooken (India), Parochial Vicar; Oscar Munoz, Parochial Vicar. In Res.,
Res.: 1914 Morris Ave., Bronx, 10453-5904. Tel: 718-299-4233; Fax: 718-583-3726.
School—(1923) 121 E. 177th St., Bronx, 10453. Tel: 718-731-5905; Fax: 718-731-8924. Sisters of Mercy of the Americas 1; Lay Teachers 13; Students 370.
Catechesis/Religious Program—Students 350.

40—St. Margaret of Cortona (1887) Revs. Brian P. McCarthy; Andrew J. Walsh; David Manvelpillai (Sri Lanka); Nicholas E. Callaghan.
Res.: 6000 Riverdale Ave., Bronx, 10471. Tel: 718-549-8053; Fax: 718-543-3432. Email: smcchurch@optonline.net.
School—(1926) 452 W. 260th St., Bronx, 10471. Tel: 718-549-8580; Fax: 718-884-3298. Email: b248@adnyschools.org. Web: www.stmargaretschool-riverdale.com. Mr. Hugh Keenan, Prin. Lay Teachers 18; Students 280.
Catechesis/Religious Program—Tel: 718-884-9777. Kerry Bader, D.R.E. Students 127.

41—St. Martin of Tours (1897) Rev. Cosme S. Fernandes; Deacon Frankie Lopez.
Res.: 664 Grote St., Bronx, 10457. Tel: 718-295-0913; Fax: 718-295-2344. Email: stmartinoftoursparish@yahoo.com.
Catechesis/Religious Program—Dolores Rodriguez, C.R.E. Students 150.

42—St. Mary (1866) Unassigned. Records at: Our Lady of Grace, 3985 Bronxwood Ave., Bronx, NY 10466 (718-652-4817).
Church: White Plains Rd., Bronx, 10466-3932.
School—(1950) 3956 Carpenter Ave., Bronx, 10466-3932. Tel: 718-547-0500; Fax: 718-547-0532. Lay Teachers 14; Students 300.
Catechesis/Religious Program—Tel: 718-231-2569. Students 100.
Chapel—Convent 3961 Carpenter Ave., Bronx, 10466. Tel: 718-652-2873.
School Chapel—E. 224th St., Bronx, 10466.

43—St. Mary Star of the Sea (1887) Rev. Michael F. Challinor. In Res., Rev. Augustus Onwubiko (Nigeria).
Res.: 595 Minneford Ave., Bronx, 10464-1118. Tel: 718-885-1440; Fax: 718-885-9498. Email: smssci@verizon.net.
Church: 600 City Island Ave., Bronx, 10464.
School—(1931) 580 Minneford Ave., Bronx, 10464. Tel: 718-885-1527; Fax: 718-885-1552. Email: b252@adnycschools.org. Dominican Sisters of Blauvelt 1; Lay Teachers 14; Students 215.
Catechesis/Religious Program—Sr. Bernadette Hannaway, O.S.U., D.R.E. Students 140.
Chapel—Daughters of Mary 176 Kilroe St., Bronx, 10464. Tel: 718-885-1842.
Ursuline Community—596 Minnieford Ave., Bronx, 10464. Tel: 718-885-2139.
Convent—Daughters of Mary Convent

44—St. Michael (1969) Revs. Pat F. Rossi; Benedict Paul, Parochial Vicar.
Res.: 765 Co-Op City Blvd., Bronx, 10475-1601. Tel: 718-671-8050; Fax: 718-320-3776.
Catechesis/Religious Program—Students 31.

45—Nativity of Our Blessed Lady (1924) Rev. Jaime H. Duenas (Retired).
Rectory—1531 E. 233rd St., Bronx, 10466. Tel: 718-324-3531; Fax: 718-798-0628. Email: natychurch@aol.com.
School—(1953) 3893 Dyre Ave., Bronx, 10466. Tel: 718-324-2188; Fax: 718-324-1128. Lay Teachers 15; Students 230.
Catechesis/Religious Program—Students 25.
Convent—1534 E. 233rd St., Bronx, 10466. Tel: 718-325-5355.

46—St. Nicholas of Tolentine (1906), (Augustinian) Revs. Joseph F. Girone, O.S.A.; Joseph Tran. In Res., Revs. William J. Wallace, O.S.A.; Richard Nahman, O.S.A.
Res.: 2345 University Ave., Bronx, 10468. Tel: 718-295-6800; Fax: 718-367-7411.
School—(1907) 2336 Andrews Ave., Bronx, 10468. Tel: 718-364-5110; Fax: 718-561-3964. Lay Teachers 7; Students 255.
Catechesis/Religious Program—Tel: 718-295-6800, Ext. 19. Mr. Jesus de La Rosa, Coord. Faith Formation. Students 304.
Convent—Convent of St. Nicholas of Tolentine, 2341 University Ave., Bronx, 10468. Tel: 718-367-3102.

47—Our Lady of Angels (1924) Revs. Thomas A. Lynch; Urbano Rodrigues, Parochial Vicar; Deacon Carlos Sanchez.
Res.: 2860 Webb Ave., Bronx, 10468. Tel: 718-548-3005; Fax: 718-884-2450. Email: ourladyofangels@hotmail.com.
Church: 2860 Sedgwick Ave., Bronx, 10468.
School—(1928) 2865 Claflin Ave., Bronx, 10468. Tel: 718-549-3503. Web: www.ourladyofangelsschool.org. Sr. Mary Ann Cleary, S.C., Prin. Sisters of Charity of St. Vincent de Paul 3; Lay Teachers 10; Students 250.
Catechesis/Religious Program—Tel: 646-508-3699. Email: ourladyofangels/religioused@hotmail.com. Sr. Maria Corona, P.C., D.R.E.; Sylvia Santiago, C.R.E. Students 262.

48—Our Lady of Grace (1924) Revs. Levelt Germain; Manuel Victor Herrera, Parochial Vicar; Cyprien Emille, Parochial Vicar; Charles Udokang; Deacons W. Joseph Mulryan; Salvatore Mazzella.
Res.: 3985 Bronxwood Ave., Bronx, 10466. Tel: 718-652-4817; Fax: 718-652-2996.
School—Tel: 718-547-9918; Fax: 718-547-7602. Daphne Lewis, Prin. Lay Teachers 18; Students 136.
Catechesis/Religious Program—Students 379.

49—Our Lady of Mercy (Fordham) (1852-1892) Revs. Ambiorix Rodriguez; Conrado Lomibao (Philippines).
Res.: 2496 Marion Ave., Bronx, 10458. Tel: 718-933-4400; Fax: 718-933-5904. Email: office@ourladyofmercyny.org. Web: www.ourladyofmercyny.org.
School—(1907) 2512 Marion Ave., Bronx, 10458. Tel: 718-367-0237; Fax: 718-367-0529. Lay Teachers 12; Students 250.
Catechesis/Religious Program—Sr. Veronica Alcazar, H.M.S.P., D.R.E. Students 195.

50—Our Lady of Mt. Carmel (1906), (Italian), Rev. Eric Rapaglia.
Res.: 627 E. 187th St., Bronx, 10458. Tel: 718-295-3770; Fax: 718-367-2240. Email: FrRapaglia@yahoo.com. Web: www.ourladymtcarmelbx.org.
School—(1925) 189th St. & Bathgate Ave., Bronx, 10458. Tel: 718-295-6080; Fax: 718-561-5205. John T. Riley, Prin. Lay Teachers 14; Students 218.
Catechesis/Religious Program—2380 Belmont Ave., Bronx, 10458. Tel: 718-295-7397; Fax: 718-295-7656. Students 191.
Convent—Suore Missionarie del Catechismo, 2410 Hughes Ave., Bronx, 10458. Tel: 718-329-0390; Fax: 718-329-0390. Sisters 3.

51—Our Lady of Pity (1908), (Hispanic), Records at Sts. Peter & Paul, 833 St. Ann's Ave., Bronx, NY 10456. Rev. Matthew Morreale, O.F.M., Guardian & Pastor; Friar Dominic Poirier, O.F.M.
Res.: 276 E. 151st St., Bronx, 10451. Tel: 718-665-3880.

52—Our Lady of Refuge (1923) [JC] Rev. Msgr. John J. Jenik; Deacon Ronald Sequeria.
Res.: 290 E. 196th St., Bronx, 10458. Tel: 718-367-4690; Fax: 718-365-7644. Web: www.ourladyofrefuge.com.
School—(1923) 2708 Briggs Ave., Bronx, 10458. Tel: 718-367-3081; Fax: 718-367-0741. Lay Teachers 10; Students 300.
Catechesis/Religious Program—Tel: 718-367-3384. Students 240.

53—Our Lady of Solace (1903) Revs. Robert P. Badillo, M.Id.; Gnanapragasm Anthonypillai.
Res.: 731 Morris Park Ave., Bronx, 10462. Tel: 718-863-3282; Fax: 718-792-4950. Email: ols1@verizon.net.
Catechesis/Religious Program—Tel: 718-823-9044. Students 160.

54—Our Lady of the Assumption (1923) Rev. Msgr. Anthony Marchitell; Revs. Anthony Mizzi-Gili; Gnana Prakash (India).
Res.: 1634 Mahan Ave., Bronx, 10461. Tel: 718-824-5454; Fax: 718-824-5456. Email: olaprsh@optonline.net.
School—(1928) 1617 Parkview Ave., Bronx, 10461. Tel: 718-829-1706; Fax: 718-931-2693. Anthony Puleo, Prin. Lay Teachers 9; Students 319.
Catechesis/Religious Program—Tel: 718-904-8464. Students 308.
Chapel—Convent 1639 Parkview Ave., Bronx, 10461. Tel: 718-829-7980.

55—Our Lady of Victory (1909) Rev. Thomas Fenlon; Maria Peguero, Pastoral Assoc. In Res., Rev. Ishamel O. Iwuala, Chap., Bronx Lebanon Hospital.
Res.: 1512 Webster Ave., Bronx, 10457. Tel: 718-583-4044; Fax: 718-583-4764. Email: b217@archny.org.
Catechesis/Religious Program—Ms. Lourdes Reyes, C.R.E. Students 125.

56—Our Saviour (1912), (Yarumal Missionaries) Revs. David Guzman Perez, M.X.Y. (Colombia); Tulio E. Ramirez, M.X.Y. (Colombia).
Res.: 2317 Washington Ave., Bronx, 10458. Tel: 718-295-9600; Fax: 718-295-9607.
Catechesis/Religious Program—Students 135.

57—St. Peter and St. Paul (1897) Rev. Richard Mederich Marcelino Cisneros.
Res.: 833 St. Ann's Ave., Bronx, 10456. Tel: 718-665-3924; Fax: 718-292-5159. Email: ssppchurch@verizon.net.
School—(1911) 838 Brook Ave., Bronx, 10456. Tel: 718-665-2056. Sisters 2; Lay Teachers 15; Students 342.
Catechesis/Religious Program—Students 155.

58—SS. Philip and James (1949) Rev. Steven Masinde.
Res.: 1160 E. 213th St., Bronx, 10469. Tel: 718-547-2203; Fax: 718-231-8160. Email: church@stsphilipandjames.com. Web: www.stsphilipandjames.com.
School—(1953) 1160 E. 213th St., Bronx, 10469. Tel: 718-882-4576; Fax: 718-653-6167. Email: school@stsphilipandjames.com. Web: www.stsphilipandjamesschool.com. Sisters of St. Dominic (Blauvelt) 1; Lay Teachers 11; Students 300.
Catechesis/Religious Program—Students 37.
Chapel—Dominican Sisters Convent 1180 E. 214th St., Bronx, 10469.

59—St. Philip Neri (1898) Rev. Msgr. Kevin P. O'Brien; Rev. Steven Markantonis.
Res.: 3025 Grand Concourse, Bronx, 10468. Tel: 718-733-3200; Fax: 718-733-4390.
School—(1913) 3031 Grand Concourse, Bronx, 10468. Tel: 718-365-8806. Mrs. Janet E. Heed, Prin. Lay Teachers 11; Students 250.
Catechesis/Religious Program—Students 190.
Chapel—Convent of Mount St. Ursula Marion Ave. & 200th St., Bronx, 10468. Tel: 718-365-7410.
Chapel—Kolping Residence Kolping Society, 2916 Grand Concourse, Bronx, 10468. Tel: 718-733-6119.
Chapel—Ursuline Residence 2850 Marion Ave., Bronx, 10468. Tel: 718-295-6094.
St. Mary's Hall—323 E. 198th St., Bronx, 10468. Tel: 718-933-9894. (Ursuline).

60—St. Pius V (1907) Rev. Adolfo Romero-Rios (Argentina); Deacons Raul Padron; Luis A. Torres.
Res.: 420 E. 145th St., Bronx, 10454. Tel: 718-665-6642; Fax: 718-665-4007. Email: st_piusv@hotmail.com. Web: www.freewebs.com/saintpiuschurch.
Catechesis/Religious Program—Students 69.

61—St. Raymond (1842) [CEM 2] Rev. Msgr. John K. Graham. In Res., Revs. Stephen Adu-Kwaning (Ghana); William Brogan; Joseph Darbouze; Fred

Agyman.
Res.: 1759 Castle Hill Ave., Bronx, 10462. Tel: 718-792-4044; Fax: 718-863-8509. Email: strayoffice@yahoo.com.
School—(1860) 2380 E. Tremont Ave., Bronx, 10462. Tel: 718-597-3232; Fax: 718-892-4449. Email: b258@adnyeducation.org. Web: www.strayelem.org. Sr. Patricia Brito, R.J.M., Prin. Lay Teachers 47; Students 859.
High School—(Boys), 2151 St. Raymond Ave., Bronx, 10462. Tel: 718-824-5050; Fax: 718-863-8808. Bro. Daniel Gardner, F.S.C., Prin. Brothers of the Christian Schools 6; Lay Teachers 56; Students 754.
High School—(Girls), 1725 Castle Hill Ave., Bronx, 10462. Tel: 718-824-4220; Fax: 718-829-3571. Email: rayacad@adnyschools.org. Web: www.saintraymondacademy.org. Sr. Mary Ann D'Antonio, S.C., Prin. Sisters 4; Lay Teachers 32; Students 366.
Catechesis/Religious Program—Tel: 718-792-4044, Ext. 238. Sr. Teresa Marie Diaz, P.C.I., D.R.E. Students 210.
St. Raymond's Community Outreach, Inc.—71 Metropolitan Ave., 2nd Fl., Bronx, 10462. Tel: 718-824-0353.
Chapel—Brothers Residence 1754 Castle Hill Ave., Bronx, 10462. Tel: 718-829-1417; Fax: 718-863-8392. Brothers of the Christian Schools 7.

62—ST. RITA OF CASCIA SHRINE CHURCH (1900), (Spanish), Rev. Ramon S. Manrique.
Res.: 448 College Ave., Bronx, 10451. Tel: 718-585-5900; Fax: 718-585-5901. Email: saintritaschurch@aol.com.
Catechesis/Religious Program—452 College Ave., Bronx, 10451. Students 189.

63—ST. ROCH (1899), (Augustinian Recollects) Rev. Jose Martinez, Admin.
Res.: 525 Wales Ave., Bronx, 10455. Tel: 718-292-3833; Fax: 718-292-3834.
Catechesis/Religious Program—Jeanette Guzman, D.R.E. Students 79.

64—SACRED HEART (1875) Rev. Msgr. Robert M. Trainor, Senior Priest; Revs. Joseph E. Franco, Parochial Admin.; Rufino Lecumberri, Senior Priest; Santiago Rubio (Mexico), Parochial Vicar; Deacons Alfonso Ramos; Juan Chaparro.
Res.: 1253 Shakespeare Ave., Bronx, 10452. Tel: 718-293-2766; Fax: 718-293-1581.
School—Sacred Heart School (1950) 95 W. 168th St., Bronx, 10452. Tel: 718-293-4288; Fax: 718-293-4886. Rachel Suarez, Prin.; Abigal Akano, Asst. Prin. (Middle); Patricia Maldonado, Asst. Prin. (Primary). Lay Teachers 26; Students 655.
School—Middle School (1926) 1248 Nelson Ave., Bronx, 10452. Tel: 718-293-6040. Lay Teachers 15; Students 350.
Catechesis/Religious Program— Ms. Migdalia Colon, D.R.E. Students 230.
Mission—St. Francis of Assisi 1544 Shakespeare Ave., Bronx, 10452. Tel: 718-731-6840.

65—SANTA MARIA (1926), (Idente Missionaries) Revs. Martin Esguerra, M.Id.; Cristobal Martin, M.Id., Parochial Vicar.
Res.: 2352 St. Raymond Ave., Bronx, 10462. Tel: 718-828-2380; Fax: 718-828-4296. Email: b265@archny.org. Web: www.santamariaparish.us.
School—(1951) 1510 Zerega Ave., Bronx, 10462. Tel: 718-823-3636; Fax: 718-823-7008. Sr. Diane Mastroianni, A.S.C.J., Prin. Sisters Apostles of the Sacred Heart of Jesus 5; Lay Teachers 18; Students 393.
Catechesis/Religious Program—Bro. Marek Wasilewski, M.Id., D.R.E. Students 77.
Chapel—Santa Maria Convent 1460 Zerega Ave., Bronx, 10462.

66—ST. SIMON STOCK (1919), (Carmelite) Revs. Nelson Belizario, O.Carm.; Christopher J. Iannizzotto, O.Carm., Parochial Vicar.
Res.: 2191 Valentine Ave., Bronx, 10457. Tel: 718-367-1251; Fax: 718-933-8822.
Church: E. 182nd St. & Ryer Ave., Bronx, 10457.
School—2195 Valentine Ave., Bronx, 10457. Tel: 718-367-0453; Fax: 718-733-1441. Web: www.stsimonstockschool.org. Lay Teachers 9; Students 210.
Catechesis/Religious Program—Web: www.saintsimonstockchurch.org. Students 146.

67—ST. THERESA OF THE INFANT JESUS (1927), (Italian), Revs. Robert F. Grippo; Niranjan Rodrigo, Parochial Vicar; Deacon Anthony P. Cassaneto. In Res., Rev. Thomas D'Angelo.
Res.: 2855 St. Theresa Ave., Bronx, 10461. Tel: 718-892-1900; Fax: 718-892-1146.
School—(1954) 2872 St. Theresa Ave., Bronx, 10461. Tel: 718-792-3688; Fax: 718-892-9441. Mrs. Josephine Fanelli, Prin. Lay Teachers 25; Students 365.
Catechesis/Religious Program—Tel: 718-792-8434. Mrs. Marie McCarrick, D.R.E. Students 170.

68—ST. THOMAS AQUINAS (1890) Revs. Librado Godinez; Alex Perez, Parochial Vicar.
Res.: 1900 Crotona Pkwy., Bronx, 10460. Tel: 718-589-5235; Fax: 718-861-3638. Email: secretary@saintthomasaquinasbronx.org. Web: www.stthomasaquinasbronx.org.
School—(1907) 1909 Daly Ave., Bronx, 10460. Tel: 718-893-7600; Fax: 718-378-5531. Lay Teachers 10; Students 232.
Catechesis/Religious Program—1900 Crotona Pkwy., Bronx, 10460. Students 221.
Convent—1899 Daly Ave., Bronx, 10460.

69—ST. VALENTINE (1891), (Polish), Closed. For information for sacramental records, please contact Our Lady of Grace, Bronx.

70—VISITATION (1928) Rev. Msgr. Robert W. Larkin.
Res.: 160 Van Cortlandt Park S., Bronx, 10463. Tel: 718-548-1455; Fax: 718-548-0289.
School—(1932) 171 W. 239th St., Bronx, 10463. Tel: 718-543-2250; Fax: 718-543-3665. Priests 1; Sisters 2; Lay Teachers 8; Students 199.
Catechesis/Religious Program—Students 88.

BOROUGH OF RICHMOND

STATEN ISLAND

1—ST. ADALBERT (Elm Park) (1901), (Polish), Rev. Eugene J. Carrella; Deacon Joseph J. Rentkowski.
Res.: 337 Morningstar Rd., 10303. Tel: 718-442-8476; Fax: 718-727-1241. Email: stadalbert311@aol.com.
School—(1905) 355 Morningstar Rd., 10303. Tel: 718-442-2020; Fax: 718-447-2012. Priests 1; Lay Teachers 10; Students 310.
Catechesis/Religious Program—Students 65.

2—ST. ANN (1914) Revs. Joy Mampilly; John McCarthy.
Res.: 101 Cromwell Ave., 10304. Tel: 718-351-0270; Fax: 718-980-4731.
School—(1955) 125 Cromwell Ave., 10304. Tel: 718-351-4343. Mrs. Bernadette Ficchi, Prin. Presentation Nuns 1; Lay Teachers 12; Students 246.
Catechesis/Religious Program—Mrs. Kathleen Daly, C.R.E. Students 255.

3—ST. ANTHONY (1908) Rev. John J. Wroblewski.
24 Shelly Ave., 10314.
Res.: 24 Shelly Ave., 10314. Tel: 718-761-6660; Fax: 718-761-1029.
Church: 4055 Victory Blvd., 10314.
Catechesis/Religious Program—Students 112.

4—ASSUMPTION/ST. PAUL (1922) Rev. Michael W. Cichon.
Res.: 145 Clinton Ave., 10301. Tel: 718-447-6362; Fax: 718-720-0106.
Catechesis/Religious Program—Students 47.

5—ST. BENEDICTA (1925) Closed. For inquiries for parish records contact Our Lady of Mount Carmel.

6—BLESSED SACRAMENT (1910) Rev. Msgrs. Peter G. Finn; Francis V. Boyle, Pastor Emeritus (Retired); Revs. Michael Moon; Francisco Lanzaderas.
Res.: 30 Manor Rd., 10310. Tel: 718-442-1581; Fax: 718-442-1398.
Church: Manor Rd. & Forest Ave., 10310.
School—(1917) 830 Delafield Ave., 10310. Tel: 718-442-3090; Fax: 718-442-9654. Mrs. Linda Magnusson, Prin. Lay Teachers 24; Students 527.
Catechesis/Religious Program—Tel: 718-448-0378. Students 518.

7—ST. CHARLES (1960) Rev. Msgr. Thomas J. Bergin; Revs. Ronald P. Perez; Albin Roby Antony (India); Antony Das S. Devadhasan (India); Deacons Michael Calafiore; Lawrence Droge; Stephen Tobon.
Res.: 644 Clawson St., 10306. Tel: 718-987-2670; Fax: 718-987-7950. Email: stcharles@verizon.net. Web: www.saintcharles.weebly.com.
School—200 Penn Ave., 10306. Tel: 718-987-0200; Fax: 718-987-8158. Email: si314@adnyschools.org. Lay Teachers 30; Students 678.
Catechesis/Religious Program—Tel: 718-979-6800. Email: mpetrides@stcharlessch.org. Students 446.

8—ST. CHRISTOPHER (1926) Rev. Joseph M. McLafferty.
Res.: 130 Midland Ave., 10306. Tel: 718-351-2452; Fax: 718-351-1174.
School—(1930) 15 Lisbon Pl., 10306. Tel: 718-351-0902; Fax: 718-351-0975. Catherine Falabella, Prin. Lay Teachers 15; Students 285.
Catechesis/Religious Program—130 Midland Ave., 10306. Tel: 718-351-2480; Fax: 718-351-1174. Gloria DePietro, D.R.E. Students 85.

9—ST. CLARE (1921) Rev. Msgr. Richard J. Guastella; Revs. James Essuon (Ghana), Parochial Vicar; Thomas Roslak, Parochial Vicar; Joseph Karikunnel (India), Parochial Vicar; Deacon Richard Mitchell.
Res.: 110 Nelson Ave., 10308. Tel: 718-984-7873; Fax: 718-966-8420.
School—151 Lindenwood Rd., 10308. Tel: 718-984-7091; Fax: 718-227-5052. Jo Rossicone, Prin. Lay Teachers 23; Students 626.
Catechesis/Religious Program—Tel: 718-948-4829. Seton Harney, C.R.E. Students 1,137.

10—ST. CLEMENT (1910) Rev. Msgr. Nicholas J. Soares.
Res.: 207 Harbor Rd., 10303. Tel: 718-442-1688; Fax: 718-442-4689.
Church: 126 Van Pelt Ave., 10303.
Catechesis/Religious Program—Tel: 718-727-6442. Students 358.

11—HOLY CHILD (1966) Revs. Alan Travers; Wilfred Y. Dodo (Nigeria); Edwin H. Cipot; Anne Lukasiewicz, Music Min.
Res.: 4747 Amboy Rd., 10312. Tel: 718-356-5890; Fax: 718-356-5995.
Preschool Office—4747 Amboy Rd., 10312. Tel: 718-356-5159; Fax: 718-356-1933.
School—School of Religion, Tel: 718-356-5277; Fax: 718-227-0898. Marie Ferro, D.R.E. Lay Teachers 75; Students 1,100.
Catechesis/Religious Program—Students 1,100.

12—HOLY FAMILY (1966) [JC] Revs. Austin E. Titus; John M. Mensah (Ghana).
Mailing Address: 366 Watchogue Rd., 10314. Tel: 718-761-6671.
Catechesis/Religious Program—Students 350.

13—HOLY ROSARY (1927) Revs. Robert J. Aufieri; Bernal Stainwall; Stephen G. Challman; Deacon Rosario Tirella. In Res., Rev. Eduardo Amora (Philippines).
Res.: 80 Jerome Ave., 10305. Tel: 718-727-3360; Fax: 718-876-6183. Web: www.hrosarychurch.com.
School—(1955), (Grades PreK-8), 100 Jerome Ave., 10305. Tel: 718-447-1195; Fax: 718-815-5862. Richard Kuberski, Prin. Lay Teachers 13; Students 281.
Catechesis/Religious Program—Tel: 718-273-6695. Laurel Fulcher, C.R.E. Students 260.
Mission—Holy Rosary 207 Sand Ln., 10305.

14—IMMACULATE CONCEPTION (1887) Rev. Peter J. Byrne; Deacon Hector Espinal.
Res.: 128 Targee St., 10304. Tel: 718-447-2165; Fax: 718-447-4835. Email: i303@archny.org.
School—(1908) 104 Gordon St., 10304. Tel: 718-447-7018; Fax: 718-447-4365. Email: si303@adnyschools.org. Mr. Joseph P. Bollini, Prin. Lay Staff 18; Students 217.
Catechesis/Religious Program—Students 157.

15—ST. JOHN NEUMANN (1982) Revs. Robert W. Dillon; John S. Kostek; Lucito T. Purawan.
Res.: 1380 Arthur Kill Rd., 10312. Tel: 718-984-8535; Fax: 718-984-6948. Email: rectory@sjneumann.org.
Catechesis/Religious Program—Tel: 718-966-7327. Students 293.

16—ST. JOHN THE BAPTIST DE LA SALLE (1900), Records at: Immaculate Conception, 128 Targee St., Staten Island, NY 10304. Tel: 718-447-2165.
Res.: 128 Targee St., 10304. Tel: 718-447-2165; Fax: 718-447-4835.
Church: 76 Jackson St., 10304.

17—ST. JOSEPH (1902), (Italian), Very Rev. Michael T. Martine; Rev. Antonio Ferrer.
Parish Office—463 Tompkins Ave., 10305. Tel: 718-816-0047; Fax: 718-816-4529.
Res.: 171 St. Mary's Ave., 10305.
Church: 466 Tompkins Ave., 10305.
School—139 St. Mary's Ave., 10305. Tel: 718-447-7686; Fax: 718-447-7687. Linda Bilotti, Prin. Lay Teachers 13; Students 175.
Catechesis/Religious Program—Students 54.

18—ST. JOSEPH, ST. THOMAS (1848) [CEM] Revs. Robert W. Dillon; Rizalimo P. Garcia, C.M.; Evangelio R. Suaybaguio; Arnel Ranada (Philippines).
Res.: 6097 Amboy Rd., 10309. Tel: 718-356-0294; Fax: 718-948-3885. Web: www.stjstparish.org.
School—50 Maguire Ave., 10309. Tel: 718-356-3344; Fax: 718-227-9531. Joanne DelGeorge, Prin. Lay Teachers 10; Students 335.
Catechesis/Religious Program—Tel: 718-984-1156. Elizabeth Brim, D.R.E. Students 1,600.

19—ST. MARGARET MARY (1926) Rev. Erno Diaz; Deacon Patrick Graham.
Res.: 560 Lincoln Ave., 10306. Tel: 718-351-2612; Fax: 718-987-0446. Email: mmaryrectory@si.rr.com.
School—(1925) 556 Lincoln Ave., 10306. Tel: 718-351-4778; Fax: 718-351-3786. Mrs. Rita Vallebuono, Prin. Lay Teachers 5; Students 75.
Catechesis/Religious Program—Students 124.

20—ST. MARY (1852) [CEM] Rev. Victor J. Buebendorf. In Res., Rev. Michael Arputham.
Res.: 1101 Bay St., 10305. Tel: 718-727-0671; Fax: 718-815-7393. Email: stmaryrosebank@verizon.net.
Catechesis/Religious Program—Students 98.

21—ST. MARY OF THE ASSUMPTION (1853) [CEM], (Jesuit) Rev. Mark C. Hallinan, S.J.; Deacon James Stahlnecker. In Res., Revs. John R. Hyatt, S.J.; Patrick J. Sullivan, S.J.
Res.: 2230 Richmond Ter., 10302. Tel: 718-442-6372; Fax: 718-448-2159. Email: stmaryassumption@hotmail.com.
Catechesis/Religious Program—Students 226.
Mission—Christ the King 182 Park Ave., Richmond Co. 10302.

22—ST. MICHAEL (1922) Rev. Msgr. Nicholas J. Soares.
Res.: 207 Harbor Rd., 10303. Tel: 718-442-1688; Fax: 718-442-4689.
Church: 211-213 Harbor Rd., 10303.
Catechesis/Religious Program—Tel: 718-727-6442. Students 358.

23—OUR LADY HELP OF CHRISTIANS (1898) Revs. D. Francis Dias; Saharaj Arokiasamy (India); Deacons John Singler; Richard Salhany.
Res.: 7396 Amboy Rd., 10307. Tel: 718-317-9772; Fax: 718-317-0038. Web: www.olhcparish.org.
School—(1910 and 1955) 23 Summit St., 10307. Tel: 718-984-1360; Fax: 718-966-9356. Mr. Michael Saldarelli, Prin. Lay Teachers 10; Students 300.
Catechesis/Religious Program—Students 725.

24—OUR LADY OF GOOD COUNSEL (1898), (Augustinian) Revs. Liam Tomas O'Doherty, O.S.A.; James W. Cassidy, Parochial Vicar; Robert Terranova, O.S.A.
Res.: 10 Austin Pl., 10304. Tel: 718-447-1503; Fax: 718-447-7361. Email: ologc@verizon.net. Web: www.ologc.catholicweb.com.
School—(1923) 42 Austin Pl., 10304. Tel: 718-447-7260; Fax: 718-815-7262. Email: si304@adnyschools.org. Web: www.goodcounselsch.org. Mrs. Frances Santangelo, Prin. Lay Teachers 16; Students 317.
Catechesis/Religious Program—Tel: 718-816-0542. Linda Affatato, D.R.E. Students 306.

25—OUR LADY OF MT. CARMEL-ST. BENEDICTA (1913) Revs. Mark C. Hallinan, S.J.; John R. Hyatt, S.J.; Deacon Anthony A. Lagotta, (Retired). In Res., Rev. Matthew F. Roche, S.J.
Res.: 1265 Castleton Ave., 10310. Tel: 718-442-3411; Fax: 718-442-3997. Email: mountcarmelsi@verizon.net.
School—285 Clove Rd., 10310. Tel: 718-981-5131; Fax: 718-981-0027. Email: si306@adnyedu.org.
Catechesis/Religious Program—Students 151.

26—OUR LADY OF PITY (1923) Rev. Msgr. Philip J. Franceschini; Rev. Edwin C. Lanuevo (Philippines); Deacon Michael Venditto.
Res.: 1616 Richmond Ave., 10314. Tel: 718-761-5421; Fax: 718-983-6225. Web: www.churchofourladyofpity.com.
Catechesis/Religious Program—Sr. Marcia Vinje, D.R.E. Students 260.

27—OUR LADY STAR OF THE SEA (1916) Rev. Msgr. Jeffrey Conway; Revs. Robert J. Poveromo, Parochial Vicar; George Perera (Sri Lanka); Joseph Antony Panimayakumar Gaspar (India), Parochial Vicar; Sr. Linda Isola, P.B.V.M., Pastoral Assoc.; Mrs. Debra Emigholz, Business Mgr.
Res.: 5371 Amboy Rd., Huguenot Park, 10312. Tel: 718-984-0593; Fax: 718-984-5203. Web: www.olssparish.org.
School—(1959) 5411 Amboy Rd., 10312. Tel: 718-984-5750. Irma Cummings, Prin.; Josephine Tortorella, Asst. Prin. Lay Teachers 24; Students 733.
Catechesis/Religious Program—5411 Amboy Rd., 10312. Tel: 718-984-1885. Camille Quaglia, D.R.E. Students 1,015.

28—OUR LADY, QUEEN OF PEACE (1922) Revs. Pancrose Kalist; Patrick J. McCarthy.
Res.: 90 Third St., 10306. Tel: 718-351-1093; Fax: 718-351-1784. Email: olqpchurch@verizon.net.
School—(1924) 22 Steele Ave., 10306. Tel: 718-351-0370; Fax: 718-351-0950. Theresa Signorile, Prin. Lay Teachers 22; Students 516.
Catechesis/Religious Program—Tel: 718-979-0989. Students 335.
Mission—Our Lady of Lourdes 130 Cedar Grove Ave., New Dorp Beach, Richmond Co. 10306.

29—ST. PATRICK (1862) Rev. Msgr. John M. McCarthy; Revs. Joseph Victor Maynigo-Arenas (Philippines); Ranulfo Docabo (Philippines). In Res., Rev. Ronelo Anung (Philippines).
Parish Office:—3560 Richmond Rd., 10306. Tel: 718-979-4227; Fax: 718-979-7637. Email: parishadmin@stpatrickssi.org.
Res.: 53 St. Patrick's Pl., 10306. Tel: 718-351-0044; Fax: 718-351-0824.
School—(1919) 3560 Richmond Rd., 10306. Tel: 718-979-8815; Fax: 718-979-4984. Web: www.stpatrickssi.org. Deborah Brochin, Prin. Lay Teachers 22; Students 485.
Catechesis/Religious Program—Tel: 718-979-1272. Students 248.

30—ST. PAUL (1924), Records for Assumption/St. Paul, 145 Clinton Ave., Staten Island, NY 10301 (Tel: 718-447-6362; Fax: 718-720-0106) Rev. Michael W. Cichon.
Res. & Mailing Address: 145 Clinton Ave., 10301. Tel: 718-447-6362; Fax: 718-720-0106.
Catechesis/Religious Program—
Christian Brothers Residence—148 Cassidy Pl., 10301.

31—ST. PETER (1839) [CEM] Rev. Msgr. James J. Dorney; Rev. Glendino Ragsag (Philippines).
Res.: 53 St. Mark's Pl., 10301. Tel: 718-727-2672; Fax: 718-720-9269.
School—300 Richmond Ter., 10301. Tel: 718-447-1796; Fax: 718-447-4240. Miss Margaret Annunziata, Prin. Lay Teachers 11; Students 222.
High School—St. Peter's Boys High School, 200 Clinton Ave., 10301. Tel: 718-447-1676; Fax: 718-447-4027. Mr. John Fodera, Prin.; Bro. James Kelly, F.S.C., Pres. Brothers of the Christian Schools 6; Lay Teachers 29; Students 563.
Catechesis/Religious Program—
St. Joseph, Brothers' House—Tel: 718-447-2815.

32—ST. RITA (1921) Revs. Richard Veras; John F. Reardon, Pastor Emeritus (Retired); Anthony Gonzalez (Philippines), Parochial Vicar.
Res.: 281 Bradley Ave., 10314. Tel: 718-698-3746; Fax: 718-698-4670. Email: mliss@saintritas.net. Web: www.saintritas.net.
School—(1922) 30 Wellbrook Ave., 10314. Tel: 718-761-2504; Fax: 718-761-0014. Adele Kosinski, Prin. Sisters 1; Lay Teachers 20; Students 301.
Catechesis/Religious Program—Email: mgillespie@saintritas.netTel: 718-982-6948. Mary Gillespie, C.R.E. Students 289.
Convent—Dominican Sisters, 61 Wellbrook Ave., 10314. Tel: 718-761-1171. (Roman Congregation of St. Dominic)

33—ST. ROCH (1922) Rev. Leo R. Prince.
Res.: 602 Port Richmond Ave., 10302. Tel: 718-442-4755; Fax: 718-981-4455. Email: strochs@si.rr.com.
School—465 Villa Ave., 10302. Tel: 718-448-2424. Sr. Mary Patricia, Prin. Sisters of St. John the Baptist 4; Lay Teachers 10; Students 95.
Catechesis/Religious Program—Students 107.

34—SACRED HEART (1875) Revs. Louis R. Jerome; Deogracias Lingao, Parochial Vicar. In Res., Rev. Robert J. Navins (Retired).
Res.: 981 Castleton Ave., 10310. Tel: 718-442-0058; Fax: 718-816-8006. Email: sacredheart310@yahoo.com. Web: www.sacredheartsi.com.
School—(1875) 301 N. Burgher Ave., 10310. Tel: 718-442-0347; Fax: 718-440-6978. Web: www.shschool.info. Mrs. Evelyn M. Lacagnino, Prin. Lay Teachers 13; Students 233.
Catechesis/Religious Program—Tel: 718-448-1536; Fax: 718-448-1526. Students 220.

35—ST. STANISLAUS KOSTKA (1923), (Polish), Rev. Jacek Wozny.
Res.: 109 York Ave., 10301. Tel: 718-447-3937; Fax: 718-815-5733.
Catechesis/Religious Program—Students 98.

36—ST. SYLVESTER (1921) Rev. Jacob Thumma (India).
Res.: 854 Targee St., 10304-4517. Tel: 718-727-4639; Fax: 718-273-2950. Email: stsylvesterschurch@yahoo.com.
Catechesis/Religious Program—Tel: 718-420-1374. Students 80.

37—ST. TERESA (1926) Revs. John J. O'Hara; James Ferreira; Vincent Soosai, O.F.M. (India); Deacon Phillip J. Maroon.
Res.: 1634 Victory Blvd., 10314. Tel: 718-442-5412; Fax: 718-442-9041. Email: rectory@saintteresasi.org. Web: www.saintteresasi.org.
School—(1955) 1632 Victory Blvd., 10314. Tel: 718-448-9650; 718-447-6426; Fax: 718-447-6462. Email: si332@education.org. Lay Teachers 15; Students 294.
Catechesis/Religious Program—Tel: 718-981-2632; Fax: 718-981-0026. Students 306.
Mission—St. Nicholas Northern Blvd., Staten Island Co. 10301.
Chapel—St. Nicholas La Bau Ave. & Northern Blvd., 10314.

OUTSIDE THE CITY OF NEW YORK

AMENIA, DUTCHESS CO., IMMACULATE CONCEPTION (1868) [CEM] Rev. Robert K. Wilson. In Res., Deacon David Weinstein.
Res.: 4 Lavelle Rd., Box 109, 12501. Tel: 845-373-8193; Fax: 845-373-8194.
Catechesis/Religious Program—Students 66.
Mission—St. Patrick [CEM] Church St., Millerton, Dutchess Co. 12546.

ARDSLEY, WESTCHESTER CO., OUR LADY OF PERPETUAL HELP (1929) Revs. Philip J. Gagliano; Robert J. Duane, Pastor Emeritus (Retired).
Res.: One Cross Rd., 10502. Tel: 914-693-0030. Email: olphardsley@aol.com.
Catechesis/Religious Program—Tel: 914-693-0037. Email: olphccd@aol.com. Students 353.

ARMONK, WESTCHESTER CO., ST. PATRICK (1966) Rev. John F. Quinn.
Res.: 29 Cox Ave., P.O. Box 6, 10504. Tel: 914-273-9724. Email: armagh@bestweb.net. Web: www.stpatrickinarmonk.org.
Catechesis/Religious Program—Tel: 914-273-8226; Fax: 914-273-4901. Email: patrreled@optonline.net. Allanna Hasselgren, D.R.E. Students 578.

BANGALL, DUTCHESS CO., IMMACULATE CONCEPTION (1919) [CEM] Rev. William A. White, Admin. In Res., Rev. John A. Bida.
Res.: 64 Hunns Lake Rd., P.O. Box 623, 12506-0623. Tel: 845-868-1923; Fax: 845-868-1593. Email: iccrectory@optonline.net.
Catechesis/Religious Program—Students 24.

BARRYTOWN, DUTCHESS CO., SACRED HEART, Closed. Parochial records at St. Christopher, Red Hook.

BEACON, DUTCHESS CO.
1—ST. JOACHIM (Records at St. John the Evangelist).
2—ST. JOHN THE EVANGELIST Revs. David E. Nolan; Fabian Eghiabumhe; Irenaeus Ikhane.
Res.: 2 Oak St., 12508. Tel: 845-838-0915; Fax: 834-838-0919. Email: stsjoachimjohn@optonline.net.
Catechesis/Religious Program—Tel: 845-831-6550. Students 360.

BEDFORD, WESTCHESTER CO., ST. PATRICK (1929) Rev. Msgr. George P. Thompson; Rev. Joseph Domfeh-Boateng (Ghana); Deacon Louis Santore.
Parish Office: 485 State Rd., 10506. Tel: 914-234-3344. Email: patrick485@optonline.net. Web: www.stpatricksbedford.org.
Res.: 7 Pound Ridge Rd., Box 303, 10506. Tel: 914-234-3668; Fax: 914-234-9126. Email: stpatsgt@optonline.net.
School—(1956) State Rd., 10506. Tel: 914-234-7914. Email: w406@adnyschools.org. Web: www.stpatricksbedford.com. Ms. Jennifer Ciavirella, Prin. Lay Teachers 11; Students 180.
Catechesis/Religious Program—Tel: 914-234-3775; Fax: 914-234-0579. Mrs. Pat Perlstein, D.R.E.; Mrs. Karen Schmidt, D.R.E. Students 620.

BLAUVELT, ROCKLAND CO., ST. CATHARINE (1868) [CEM] Rev. Msgr. Emmet R. Nevin; Revs. Michael P. Kerrigan, C.S.P.; Abraham Vallayil, C.M.I.; Deacons John C. Kelleher; John Jurasek.
Res.: 523 Western Hwy., 10913. Tel: 845-359-0542; Fax: 845-365-2387.
Catechesis/Religious Program—Tel: 845-359-4014. Mrs. Audrey Angelini, C.R.E. Students 652.
Chapel—Our Lady Queen of Peace 140 Old Orangeburg Rd., Orangeburg, 10962. Tel: 845-359-1000, Ext. 3588.

BREWSTER, PUTNAM CO., ST. LAWRENCE O'TOOLE (1878) [CEM] Revs. Robert F. McKeon; Eric Twene (Ghana); Richard Gill, L.C.; Deacons Mark Shkreli; John Baffa; Dale Konas.
Res.: 31 Prospect St., 10509. Tel: 845-279-2021; Fax: 845-279-7441.
Catechesis/Religious Program—Tel: 845-279-6098; Fax: 845-279-8165. Theresa Scorca, D.R.E. Students 551.

BRIARCLIFF MANOR, WESTCHESTER CO., ST. THERESA (1926) Rev. Msgr. James K. Vaughey; Rev. L. Praxid DeSilva (Sri Lanka).
Res.: 1394 Pleasantville Rd., 10510. Tel: 914-941-1646; Fax: 914-944-9503. Email: stchurch@optonline.net. Web: www.sainttheresa.org.
School—Tel: 914-762-1050; Fax: 914-941-9483. Lay Teachers 10; Students 200.
Catechesis/Religious Program—Tel: 914-923-3286; Fax: 914-944-9503. Students 468.
Mission—Our Lady of the Wayside Rte. 100, Millwood, Westchester Co. 10546.

BRONXVILLE, WESTCHESTER CO., ST. JOSEPH (1922) Rev. Msgrs. James F. Doyle; Guy Vinci; Rev. Herbert P. DeGaris. In Res., Revs. Dawson Ambosta (India); Joachim Adione.
Res.: 15 Cedar St., 10708. Tel: 914-337-1660; Fax: 914-337-1342.
School—(1951) 30 Meadow Ave., 10708. Tel: 914-337-0261; Fax: 914-395-1192. Mrs. Anne Marie McGoldrick, Prin. Lay Teachers 25; Students 260.
Catechesis/Religious Program—28 Meadow Ave., 10708. Tel: 914-337-6383; Fax: 914-779-8103. Mrs. Antoinette Gilligan, D.R.E. Students 950.

BUCHANAN, WESTCHESTER CO., ST. CHRISTOPHER (1929) Revs. Andrew E. Kurzyna; Clement Kagoma (Africa); Deacon Ronald J. Schlitt.
Res.: 3094 Albany Post Rd., 10511. Tel: 914-737-1046; Fax: 914-737-9320. Email: stchristopher@optonline.net.
Catechesis/Religious Program—Tel: 914-737-1437. Email: olivell@optonline.net. Catherine M. Garnsey, D.R.E. Students 318.

CALLICOON, SULLIVAN CO., HOLY CROSS (1870) [CEM] [JC 2] Rev. Ignatius E. Smith, O.F.M.
Res.: 9719 Rte. 97, P.O. Box 246, 12723. Tel: 845-887-5450; Fax: 845-887-5873. Web: holycrosscallicoon.org.
Catechesis/Religious Program—Students 77.
Mission—St. Patrick, Long Eddy, 12760.
Chapel—Callicoon, Holy Cross Rectory

CARMEL, PUTNAM CO., ST. JAMES THE APOSTLE (1913) Revs. Anthony D. Sorgie; Vincent DePaul Howley; John A. DeBellis; Deacons Charles T. Borsavage; Gerard Cartwright; Anthony Gruerio.
Res.: 14 Gleneida Ave., 10512. Tel: 845-225-2079; Fax: 845-225-5566. Email: stjoll@aol.com.
School—(1954)Tel: 845-225-9365; Fax: 845-228-2859. Lay Teachers 10; Students 264.
Catechesis/Religious Program—Tel: 845-225-6504. Students 1,850.
Mission—Our Lady of the Lake/Mt. Carmel [JC] 1 Doherty Dr., Lake Carmel, Putnam Co. 10512. Tel: 845-228-1235.
Mission—Chapel of Life, Carmel

CHAPPAQUA, WESTCHESTER CO., ST. JOHN AND ST. MARY (1922) Rev. Msgrs. Thomas E. Gilleece;

Patrick Barry; Deacons Charles Devlin; Walter Brady; Mrs. Joan Corso Ferroni, Pastoral Assoc.
Res.: 15 St. John's Pl., 10514. Tel: 914-238-3274; Fax: 914-238-3354. Web: www.sjsmrcc.com.
Catechesis/Religious Program—30 Poillon Rd., 10514. Tel: 914-238-3696. Email: kidsrelig@optimum.net. Students 517.

CHESTER, ORANGE CO., ST. COLUMBA (1875) [CEM] Rev. John S. Bonnici.
Res.: 27 High St., 10918. Tel: 845-469-2108; Fax: 845-469-6165.
Catechesis/Religious Program—Tel: 845-469-9503. Students 196.

COLD SPRING-ON-HUDSON, PUTNAM CO., OUR LADY OF LORETTO (1833) Revs. Brian T. McSweeney; Gabriel Awuafor (Ghana).
Res.: 24 Fair St., 10516. Tel: 845-265-3718; Fax: 845-265-4309.
Catechesis/Religious Program—Tel: 845-265-2594. Email: ollreled@verizon.net. Catherine Garnsey, D.R.E. Students 262.
Mission—St. Joseph's Chapel Garrison, Putnam Co. 10524.

CONGERS, ROCKLAND CO., ST. PAUL (1896) [CEM] Revs. Arthur Mastrolia; John F. Palatucci, Parochial Vicar; Rev. Msgr. John Boachie, Parochial Vicar; Sr. Gloria Jean Henchy, C.D.P., Pastoral Assoc.; Deacons Dominic Buonocore, Parish Mgr.; John W. McSherry; Mark Czerwinski.
Res.: 82 Lake Rd. W., 10920. Tel: 845-268-4464; Fax: 845-268-6790. Web: www.stpaulcongers.net.
School—365 Kings Hwy., Valley Cottage, 10989. Tel: 914-268-6506; Fax: 914-268-1809. Sr. Stephen Gerard, O.P., Prin. Sisters 4; Lay Teachers 10; Students 220.
Catechesis/Religious Program—Tel: 845-268-5442. Rowena Hoblin, C.R.E. Students 800.
Chapel—Sisters' Convent and School, Valley Cottage

CORNWALL-ON-HUDSON, ORANGE CO., ST. THOMAS OF CANTERBURY (1870) [CEM] Rev. Bernard P. Heter; Rev. Msgr. Francis X. Duffy, Pastor Emeritus (Retired); Rev. Dennis M. Dinan; Deacons John V. Pelella; William Stafford.
Res.: 10 Second St., 12520. Tel: 914-534-2547; Fax: 914-534-1357. Email: sthomascanterbury@hvc.rr.com.
Catechesis/Religious Program—Tel: 914-534-9393. Email: stthomasdre@aol.com. Mrs. Judy Valentine, D.R.E. Students 465.

CORTLANDT MANOR, WESTCHESTER CO.
1—ST. COLUMBANUS (Van Cortlandtville) (1950) Rev. Francis J. Samoylo; Rev. Msgr. Patrick J. Keenan, Pastor Emeritus; Rev. Rayappa Thumma, Parochial Vicar; Deacon John J. Coppola.
Res.: 122 Oregon Rd., 10567. Tel: 914-737-4705; Fax: 914-736-7476.
School—122 Oregon Rd., 10567. Tel: 914-739-1200; Fax: 914-739-1109. Lay Teachers 10; Students 220.
Catechesis/Religious Program—Tel: 914-739-2441. Students 310.
Mission—North American Martyrs 55 Oscawana Lake Rd., Putnam Valley, Putnam Co. 10579. Tel: 845-528-6433.
2—HOLY SPIRIT (1966) Rev. Thomas P. Kiely; Deacon Ray Parchen.
Res.: 1969 Crompond Rd., 10567-4113. Tel: 914-737-2316; Fax: 914-737-6882. Email: holyspiritchurch1969@verizon.net.
Catechesis/Religious Program—Tel: 914-734-9243. Email: re_holyspiritchurch1969@verizon.net. Students 635.
Chapel—Cortlandt Manor

CRESTWOOD, WESTCHESTER CO., CHURCH OF THE ANNUNCIATION (1931) Rev. Msgr. Dennis P. Keane; Revs. Salvatore Riccardi, C.P.; Tomislav Mlakic (Croatia); Ivan Lovric (Croatia).
Res.: 470 Westchester Ave., 10707. Tel: 914-779-7345; Fax: 914-961-5688.
School—(1943) 465 Westchester Ave., 10707. Tel: 914-337-8760; Fax: 914-337-8878. Barbara S. Kavanagh, Prin. Sisters 2; Lay Teachers 23; Students 517.
Catechesis/Religious Program—Tel: 914-779-2374. Students 165.

CROTON FALLS, WESTCHESTER CO., ST. JOSEPH (1845) Rev. Msgr. James R. Moore; Revs. Jude Aguwa (Nigeria); Michael Cedro.
Res.: 10 Croton Falls Rd., P.O. Box 719, 10519. Tel: 914-277-3765; 914-277-3877; Fax: 914-277-1823.
School—(1949), (Grades K-8) Tel: 914-277-3783; Fax: 914-277-3238. Lay Teachers 8; Students 108.
Catechesis/Religious Program—14 Croton Falls Rd., 10519. Tel: 914-276-1067. Students 985.
Mission—St. Michael Park Ave., Goldens Bridge, Westchester Co. 10526.
Mission—St. John [CEM] Rte. 116, North Salem, Westchester Co. 10560.

CROTON-ON-HUDSON, WESTCHESTER CO., HOLY NAME OF MARY (1874) Revs. Brian C. Brennan; Nelson Couto (India); Deacon Albert Mazza.
Res.: 110 Grand St., 10520. Tel: 914-271-4797; Fax: 914-271-6841.
School—Holy Name of Mary Montessori School, Tel: 914-271-5182.
Catechesis/Religious Program—114 Grand St., 10520. Tel: 914-271-4254. Students 444.
Mission—Church of the Good Shepherd Benedict Blvd. and Young Ave., Harmon, Westchester Co. 10520.

DOBBS FERRY, WESTCHESTER CO.
1—OUR LADY OF POMPEII (1922), (Italian), Rev. Timothy J. Scannell, Admin.
Rectory—95 Palisade St., 10522. Tel: 914-693-0119; Fax: 914-693-3408.
Catechesis/Religious Program—
2—SACRED HEART (1862) Revs. Timothy J. Scannell; Emmanuel Poovathinal, C.M.I. (India); Deacon Patrick D. Troy.
Res.: 18 Bellewood Ave., 10522. Tel: 914-693-0119; Fax: 914-693-3408. Email: shrectory@aol.com.
Church: Broadway and Ashford Ave., 10522. Tel: 914-693-5541.
Catechesis/Religious Program—Tel: 914-479-1045. Mrs. Mary Perillo, D.R.E.; Ann Kinnally, Business Mgr. Students 288.

DOVER PLAINS, DUTCHESS CO., ST. CHARLES BORROMEO (1859) [CEM] Rev. Anthony J. Giuliano; Deacon James Lawlor.
Res.: 83 Mill St., P.O. Box 9, 12522. Tel: 845-877-9934; Fax: 845-877-9936. Email: stcharlesdover@aol.com.
Catechesis/Religious Program—Tel: 845-832-6989; Fax: 845-832-6989. Students 126.
Mission—Our Lady of Solace Mission Wingdale, Dutchess Co.

EAST KINGSTON, ULSTER CO., ST. COLMAN (1904) Revs. James E. Borstelmann, Admin.; Luke W. McCann, Pastor Emeritus (Retired).
Res.: 18 Brigham St., 12401. Tel: 845-336-8237; Fax: 845-382-1488.
Catechesis/Religious Program—Email: stcolemanff@yahoo.com. Students 71.

ELLENVILLE, ULSTER CO., ST. MARY AND ST. ANDREW (1850) Revs. John W. Lynch; Chinnappa Reddy Aduri.
Res.: 137 S. Main St., 12428. Tel: 845-647-6080; Fax: 845-647-2486.
Catechesis/Religious Program—Bruce Santiago, C.R.E. Students 160.
Mission—Our Lady of Lourdes Kerhonkson, Ulster Co. 12446.

ELMSFORD, WESTCHESTER CO., OUR LADY OF MT. CARMEL (1904) Revs. Robert J. Norris; Andrew Oni (Nigeria).
Res.: 59 E. Main St., 10523. Tel: 914-592-6789; Fax: 914-592-3898.
School—(1929)Tel: 914-592-7575; Fax: 914-345-1591. Web: www.olmc.ws. Sisters of Divine Compassion 4; Lay Teachers 7; Students 219.
Catechesis/Religious Program—Tel: 914-592-4280. Students 150.

FISHKILL, DUTCHESS CO., CHURCH OF ST. MARY, MOTHER OF THE CHURCH (1953) Rev. Msgr. Joseph A. Martin; Revs. Patrick K. Curley; Adolfo Occeno (Philippines); Deacons Joseph R. Hafeman; Michael Decker; John O'Reilly.
Res.: 103 Jackson St., P.O. Box 780, 12524-0499. Tel: 845-896-6400; Fax: 845-896-4575. Email: stmaryfishkill@aol.com.
School—(1955)Tel: 845-896-9561; Fax: 845-896-8477. Mrs. Ellen Anderson, Prin. Lay Teachers 9; Students 299.
Catechesis/Religious Program—100 Jackson St., P.O. Box 780, 12524. Tel: 845-896-6430; Fax: 845-896-6764. Mrs. Eileen Budnik, D.R.E. Students 759.

FLORIDA, ORANGE CO., ST. JOSEPH (1895), (Polish), [CEM] Rev. Joseph M. Tokarczyk.
Res.: 14 Glenmere Ave., 10921. Tel: 845-651-7792; Fax: 845-651-7793. Email: saintjoseph@optonline.net.
Catechesis/Religious Program—19 Glenmere Ave., 10921. Tel: 845-651-4240. Students 284.
Mission—St. Stanislaus 17 Pulaski Hwy., Pine Island, Orange Co. 10969. Tel: 845-258-4426; Fax: 845-651-7793.

FORESTBURGH, SULLIVAN CO., ST. THOMAS AQUINAS (1900) [CEM] Rev. Ivan L. Csete; Deacon Paul A. Rausch.
Res. & Rectory: One Forestburgh Rd., 12777. Tel: 845-791-7400.
Catechesis/Religious Program—1965 Rte. 17K, Montgomery, 12549. Email: ebrasington@hvc.rr.com. Mrs. Brett (Autumn) Cancredi, D.R.E. Students 50.

GARDINER, ULSTER CO., ST. CHARLES BORROMEO (1883) [CEM] Rev. Robert M. Panek.
Res.: 2212 Rte. 44/55, 12525. Tel: 845-255-1374; Fax: 845-256-9050.
Catechesis/Religious Program—Tel: 845-895-2532. Students 136.

GARNERVILLE, ROCKLAND CO., ST. GREGORY BARBARIGO (1961) Revs. Joseph P. LaMorte; Peter Cimbert Ekanem; Deacons Augustine A. Pappalardo; George Albin; Roland Dowen; John Kelly.
Res.: 21 Cinder Rd., 10923. Tel: 845-947-1873; Fax: 845-947-8256.
School—29 Cinder Rd., 10923. Tel: 845-947-1330; Fax: 845-947-4392. Mrs. Cathleen Cassel, Prin. Sisters of St. Dominic (Sparkill) 4; Lay Teachers 14; Students 293.
Catechesis/Religious Program—Tel: 845-429-2775. Mr. Donald Ruzzi, C.R.E. Students 621.

GLASCO, ULSTER CO., ST. JOSEPH (1919) Rev. Msgr. Charles F. Zanotti.
Res.: 61 Glasco Tpke., P.O. Box 208, 12432. Tel: 845-246-5453; Fax: 845-247-9343.
A-Villa St. Dominic—Tel: 914-246-5610, Ext. 51. Rest House for Ladies. Dominican Sisters (Sparkill). Also Known as Corazon Center.
Catechesis/Religious Program—Tel: 845-246-4598. Students 130.

GOSHEN, ORANGE CO., ST. JOHN THE EVANGELIST (1837) [CEM] Rev. Thomas Dicks; Rev. Msgr. Bayani Valenzuela; Revs. Brendan Buckley, O.F.M-.Cap.; Adaly Rosado; Deacons Luis Baerga; Vincent Cookingham.
Res.: 71 Murray Ave., 10924. Tel: 845-294-5328; Fax: 845-294-2577.
School—77 Murray Ave., 10924. Tel: 845-294-6434; Fax: 845-294-7303. Sr. Patricia Langton, O.P., Prin. Sisters 1; Lay Teachers 8; Students 190.
Catechesis/Religious Program—Tel: 914-294-6847. Students 685.
Chapel—Immaculate Conception Convent 73 Murray Ave., 10924.
Station—Orange County Home and Infirmary, Tel: 845-294-7971.
Station—Orange County Jail, Tel: 845-294-6166.
Station—Campbell Hall Nursing Facility Orange. Tel: 845-294-8154.
Arden Hill Hospital—Tel: 845-294-5441.

GREENWOOD LAKE, ORANGE CO., HOLY ROSARY (1954) Rev. Robert J. Sweeney.
Res.: 41 Windermere Ave., 10925-2105. Tel: 845-477-8378; Fax: 845-477-7238. Email: holy_rosary_gwl@yahoo.com.
Catechesis/Religious Program—Tel: 845-477-0906; Fax: 845-477-0906. Students 172.

HARRIMAN, ORANGE CO., ST. ANASTASIA (1899) [CEM] Revs. Michael F. Keane; Eder Tamara (Colombia); Deacons Eugene E. Bormann; James Faulkner; Brian O'Neill.
Res.: 21 N. Main St., P.O. Box 942, 10926. Tel: 845-238-3844; Fax: 845-238-3846. Email: parish.office@saintanastasiachurch.org. Web: www.saintanastasiachurch.org.
Catechesis/Religious Program—Tel: 845-782-5099. Students 550.

HARRISON, WESTCHESTER CO., ST. GREGORY THE GREAT (1911) Rev. Msgr. Francis J. McAree; Revs. James B. Teague; Michael Soosairaj (India); John Edison (India).
Res.: 215 Halstead Ave., 10528. Tel: 914-835-0677; Fax: 914-835-5152. Email: stgreggreat@aol.com. Web: www.stgregorythegreat.com.
Catechesis/Religious Program—94 Broadway, 10528. Tel: 914-835-1278; Fax: 914-835-2070. Students 489.

HARTSDALE, WESTCHESTER CO.
1—CHURCH OF OUR LADY OF SHKODRA (1989), (Albanian), [CEM] Rev. Peter Popovich.
Res.: 361 W. Hartsdale Ave., 10530. Tel: 914-761-3523; Fax: 914-949-2690.
2—SACRED HEART (1926) Rev. Msgr. Patrick J. Carney; Revs. Wenceslaus Rodrigues (India); Philip P. Tah (Nigeria).
Res.: 10 Lawton Ave., 10530. Tel: 914-949-0028; Fax: 914-289-0398.
School—(1953) 59 Wilson St., 10530. Tel: 914-946-7242; Fax: 914-946-7323. Mrs. Virginia Salamone, Prin. Sisters 1; Lay Teachers 10; Students 217.
Catechesis/Religious Program—Tel: 914-428-5043; Fax: 914-428-5043. Email: sacredheart.re@aol.com. Ms. Anne Marie Iozzo, D.R.E. Students 145.
Convent—11 Lawton Ave., 10530. Tel: 914-946-2581.

HASTINGS-ON-HUDSON, WESTCHESTER CO.
1—ST. MATTHEW (1892) Rev. Matthew F. Fernan. In Res., Rev. James Smyth (Retired).
Res.: 616 Warburton Ave., 10706. Tel: 914-478-2822; Fax: 914-478-3681.
Catechesis/Religious Program—Students 185.
2—ST. STANISLAUS KOSTKA (1912), (Polish), Records at: St. Matthew, 616 Warburton Ave., Hastings-on-Hudson, NY 10706 (914-478-2822).
Res.: 616 Warburton Ave., 10706.

HAVERSTRAW, ROCKLAND CO.
1—ST. MARY OF THE ASSUMPTION (1899), (Slovak), Rev. Msgr. Robert J. McCabe, Admin.
Res.: 46 Conklin Ave., 10927. Tel: 845-429-2245; Fax: 845-429-1350. Email: havermar46@optimum.net.

Catechesis/Religious Program—Students 65.

2—ST. PETER (1848) [CEM] [JC] Revs. Thomas F. Madden; Miguel Castillo (Mexico); Fredy Patino Montoya.

Res.: 115 Broadway, 10927. Tel: 914-429-2196; Fax: 914-947-4564. Email: pastor@saintpeterschurch.us. Web: www.saintpeterschurch.us.

School—(1863) 21 Ridge St., 10927. Tel: 914-429-5311; Fax: 845-429-5140. Mrs. Margaret Hamilton, Prin. Lay Teachers 12; Students 271.

Catechesis/Religious Program—21 Ridge St., 10927. Tel: 914-429-8824; Fax: 845-429-2721. Students 643.

Station—Green Hills Home, Tel: 914-429-8411.

Station—Northern Riverview Health Care Center, Tel: 914-429-5381.

HAWTHORNE, WESTCHESTER CO., HOLY ROSARY (1901) Rev. John Fraser. In Res., Rev. Martin Njenga.

Res.: 170 Bradhurst, 10532. Tel: 914-769-0030; Fax: 914-769-3326.

School—(1955) 180 Bradhurst Ave., 10532. Tel: 914-769-0030, Ext. 25.

Catechesis/Religious Program—Tel: 914-769-0030, Ext. 23. Deacon Richard McLaughlin, D.R.E. Students 486.

HIGHLAND FALLS, ORANGE CO., SACRED HEART OF JESUS (1870) [CEM] Rev. Jack Arlotta.

Res.: 353 Main St., 10928. Tel: 845-446-4609; Fax: 845-446-4610. Email: frjack-a@hvc.rr.com. Web: www.sacredheart-highlandfalls.org.

Catechesis/Religious Program—Tel: 845-446-2071. Maryann Brigham, D.R.E. Students 135.

Mission—Blessed Sacrament 794 Rte 9W, Fort Montgomery, Orange Co. 10922.

HIGHLAND MILLS, ORANGE CO., ST. PATRICK (1957) Revs. Gerard P. Travers; Jacob Mattappillil (India); Deacon Paul Weireter.

Res.: 26 Hunter St., 10930. Tel: 845-928-6027; Fax: 845-928-2982. Web: www.stpatrickshm.org.

Catechesis/Religious Program—Tel: 845-928-6688; Fax: 845-928-3189. Louise Pisano, D.R.E. & Youth Min. Students 925.

HIGHLAND, ULSTER CO., ST. AUGUSTINE (1899) Revs. Lawrence Paolicelli; George Kyeremeh (Ghana); Deacons John Bellacicco; Frank S. Ottaviano.

Res.: 55 Main St., 12528. Tel: 845-691-7673; Fax: 845-691-6680.

School—(1958) 35 Phillips Ave. and Elting Pl., 12528. Tel: 845-691-9488; Fax: 845-691-2338. Miss Kathryn Feeney, Prin. Lay Teachers 9; Students 133.

Catechesis/Religious Program—Students 295.

HOPEWELL JUNCTION, DUTCHESS CO.

1—ST. COLUMBA (1992) Rev. Msgr. Gerardo J. Colacicco; Rev. Emmanuel Udoh (Nigeria); Deacons William Alvarado; John Reilly; Warren Testa.

Res.: 835 Rte. 82, P.O. Box 428, 12533. Tel: 845-227-8380; Fax: 845-227-8390. Email: stcolumba@frontiernet.net. Web: www.stcolumba.net.

School—St. Denis-St. Columba, Tel: 845-227-7777; Fax: 845-226-8470. Email: stcol1@aol.com. Web: stcolumba-hopewelljunction.e-paluch.com/school.asp. Sr. Kathleen Marie Gerritse, C.R., Prin. Sisters 3; Lay Teachers 14; Students 363.

Catechesis/Religious Program—P.O. Box 368, Hopewell Jct., 12533. Tel: 845-221-4900. Web: www.stcolumbaonline.org. Sr. Marie Pappas, C.R., D.R.E. Students 1,131.

2—ST. DENIS (1899) [CEM] Revs. Vincent de Paul Howley; Patrick J. Dunne, Parochial Vicar; Deacons Walter Dauerer; Stanley Aviles; Enrico Messina; Robert Pelech; Frank Munoz.

Res. & Office: 598 Beekman Rd., P.O. Box 10, 12533. Tel: 845-227-8382; Fax: 845-227-3951. Email: stdenischurch@optonline.net. Web: www.stdenischurch.org.

The Ark and The Dove Preschool:—604 Beekman Rd., P.O. Box 1139, 12533. Tel: 845-227-5232; Fax: 845-227-0435. Email: noah1@stdenischurch.org.

School—St. Denis-St. Columba, See St. Columba for details., Tel: 845-227-7777; Fax: 845-226-8470. Email: stcol1@aol.com. Web: www.stcolumba.net. Students 363.

Catechesis/Religious Program—604 Beekman Rd., P.O. Box 1139, 12533. Tel: 845-227-3949; Fax: 845-227-0435. Email: stdenisre@stdenischurch.org. Students 606.

HYDE PARK, DUTCHESS CO., REGINA COELI (1863) Revs. Michael L. Palazzo; Raphael Amoako Tawiah; Deacons Frank J. Gohl; Gerard Lindley; Mark O'Sullivan; Peter Dalmer. In Res., Rev. John M. Lagiovane.

Res.: 2 Harvey St., 12538. Tel: 845-229-2134; Fax: 845-229-1668. Email: frontdesk@reginacoelihp.org. Web: www.reginacoeli-hydepark-ny.org.

School—(1955) Albany Post Rd., 12538. Tel: 845-229-8589; Fax: 845-229-1388. Email: coeli@verizon.net. Lay Teachers 17; Students 150.

Catechesis/Religious Program—Tel: 845-229-9139; Fax: 845-229-1668. Students 135.

Mission—St. Paul (1851) Mulford Ave., Staatsburg, Dutchess Co. 12580.

IRVINGTON-ON-THE-HUDSON, WESTCHESTER CO., IMMACULATE CONCEPTION (1873) Rev. Msgr. Raymond J. Byrne; Rev. Ted Onumaegbu.

Res.: 16 N. Broadway, 10533. Tel: 914-591-7480; Fax: 914-591-7806. Email: immacon@optonline.net. Web: www.iccirvington.catholicweb.com.

Catechesis/Religious Program—Tel: 914-591-7740. Email: ccdicc@optonline.net. Students 218.

JEFFERSONVILLE, SULLIVAN CO.

1—ST. GEORGE (1963) [CEM] Merged with St. Francis of Assisi to form St. George-St. Francis, Jeffersonville.

Res.: 12748. Tel: 845-482-4640; Fax: 845-482-3276.

Catechesis/Religious Program—Students 110.

2—ST. GEORGE-ST. FRANCIS (1843; 1909) [CEM] Rev. Ignatius Vu.

Res.: 97 Schoolhouse Hill Rd., P.O. Box 672, 12748. Tel: 845-482-4640; Fax: 845-482-3276. Email: saintgeorgesaintfran@hvc.rr.com.

Catechesis/Religious Program—Students 75.

Mission—St. Francis of Assisi 4020 State Rte. 52, Youngsville, Sullivan Co. 12791.

KATONAH, WESTCHESTER CO., ST. MARY OF THE ASSUMPTION (1908) Revs. Edmund P. Connors; Paul M. Waddell; Deacon George Chiu.

Res.: 117 Valley Rd., 10536. Tel: 914-232-3356; Fax: 914-232-5736. Email: stmarysparish@yahoo.com.

Catechesis/Religious Program—99 Valley Rd., 10536. Tel: 914-232-4648. Mrs. Susan Gmuer, C.R.E. Students 725.

Mission—St. Matthias (1909) 107 Babbitt Rd., Bedford Hills, Westchester Co. 10507.

KINGSTON, ULSTER CO.

1—HOLY NAME OF JESUS (1884) Closed.

2—IMMACULATE CONCEPTION (1896), (Polish), [CEM] Rev. John W. Borzuchowski.

Res.: 467 Delaware Ave., 12401. Tel: 845-331-0846; Fax: 845-331-7647. Email: kbh62@prodigy.net.

Catechesis/Religious Program—Tel: 845-331-7352. Students 35.

3—ST. JOSEPH (1868) Revs. Frank J. Damis; Uldarico De la Pena (Philippines) (MO); George Devanapalle (India); Deacons Richard Frohmiller; Robert Winrow; John Peters; Joseph Doherty.

Res.: 242 Wall St., 12401. Tel: 845-338-1554; Fax: 845-340-1961. Email: sjcr242@earthlink.net.

School—(1869) Wall & Pearl Sts., 12401. Tel: 845-339-4390; Fax: 845-339-7994. Lay Teachers 14; Students 160.

Catechesis/Religious Program—Tel: 845-339-4391; Fax: 845-339-4391. Students 228.

Mission—Msgr. O'Reilly Chapel Zandhoeck Rd., Hurley, 12443.

4—ST. MARY (1842) [CEM] Rev. Edmund M. Burke. In Res., Rev. John Audu (Nigeria), Chap., Kingston Hospital & Parochial Vicar.

Res.: 160 Broadway, 12401. Tel: 845-331-0301; Fax: 845-339-6165.

School—Kingston Catholic School (1867) 159 Broadway, 12401. Tel: 845-331-9318; Fax: 845-331-2674. Jill Albert, Prin. Lay Teachers 12; Students 243.

Catechesis/Religious Program—Students 140.

5—ST. PETER (1858), (German), [CEM] Rev. Edmund M. Burke. In Res., Rev. Marc K. Oliver, Admin.

Res.: 93 Wurts St., 12401-6328. Tel: 914-331-0436; Fax: 914-331-7149.

Catechesis/Religious Program—(Spanish) Students 73.

LAGRANGEVILLE, DUTCHESS CO., BLESSED KATERI TEKAKWITHA (2002) Rev. Msgr. Desmond O'Connor; Rev. Brian Graebe; Deacons John Barone; Andrew Daubman; Robert Horton; Theodore Van De Ven.

Res.: 1925 Rte. 82, 12540. Tel: 845-227-1710; Fax: 845-227-1734. Email: blessedkateri@optonline.net. Web: www.blessedkateriparish.com.

Catechesis/Religious Program—Tel: 845-227-1710, Ext. 3; Fax: 845-226-6150. Email: bktfaithform@optonline.net. Web: www.blessedkateriparish.com. Students 973.

LAKE KATRINE, ULSTER CO., ST. CATHERINE LABOURE (1957) Rev. John T. Kearney; Rev. Msgr. Eugene A. Fowler, Pastor Emeritus (Retired); Deacon John M. Sullivan, (Retired).

Res.: 200 Tuytenbridge Rd., P.O. Box 271, 12449. Tel: 914-382-1133; Fax: 914-382-1051.

Catechesis/Religious Program—Students 106.

LARCHMONT, WESTCHESTER CO.

1—ST. AUGUSTINE (1892) Rev. Msgrs. Thomas R. Kelly; Walter F. Kenny, Pastor Emeritus (Retired); Rev. Joseph Karimatton (India).

Res.: 18 Cherry Ave., 10538. Tel: 914-834-1220; Fax: 914-833-2130. Email: staugustineny@verizon.net. Web: www.staugustineny.org.

Catechesis/Religious Program—Tel: 914-834-9523. Sr. Suzanne Duzen, SS.C.M., D.R.E. Students 575.

2—SS. JOHN AND PAUL (1949) Rev. Msgr. Thomas F. Petrillo; Rev. Salvatore DeStefano; Deacons James Brown; John Shea.

Res.: 280 Weaver St., 10538. Tel: 914-834-5458; Fax: 914-833-5081.

School—(1952)Tel: 914-834-6332; Fax: 914-834-6332. Colleen R. Pettus, Prin. Lay Teachers 14; Students 303.

Catechesis/Religious Program—Tel: 914-834-4597; Fax: 914-834-7493.

LIBERTY, SULLIVAN CO., ST. PETER (1894) [CEM] Rev. Msgr. Edward F. Straub; Deacon John Riley.

Res.: 264 N. Main St., 12754. Tel: 845-292-4525; Fax: 845-292-1627.

Catechesis/Religious Program—Students 155.

LIVINGSTON MANOR, SULLIVAN CO., ST. ALOYSIUS (1899) [CEM] Rev. Msgr. William J. Collins; Rev. Alfred M. Croke, Pastor Emeritus (Retired).

Res.: Church St., Box 206, 12758. Tel: 914-439-5625; Fax: 914-439-5188.

Mission—Sacred Heart (1906) P.O. Box 206, De Bruce, Sullivan Co. 12758.

Mission—Gate of Heaven (1901) Highland Ave., Roscoe, Sullivan Co. 12776.

Catechesis/Religious Program—Students 43.

MAHOPAC, PUTNAM CO., ST. JOHN THE EVANGELIST (1889) Revs. Brian C. Brennan; Miroslaw Pawlaczyk (Poland); Dennis T. Williams; Deacons John Armo; Bernard Moran; John Scarfi.

Res.: 221 E. Lake Blvd., 10541. Tel: 845-628-2006; Fax: 845-628-5970. Email: info@sjemahopac.org.

School—(1955) 239 E. Lake Blvd., 10541. Tel: 845-628-6464; Fax: 845-628-6469. Religious of the Divine Compassion 1; Lay Teachers 15; Students 104.

Catechesis/Religious Program—Students 1,506.

Chapel—Convent of Religious of the Divine Compassion, Tel: 914-628-6497.

MAMARONECK, WESTCHESTER CO.

1—MOST HOLY TRINITY (1874) Revs. Joseph F. Irwin; Joseph Kahumburu (Kenya); Mathew Pazhoor (India); Deacon Augustine DiFiore.

Res.: 320 E. Boston Post Rd., 10543. Tel: 914-698-5944; Fax: 914-698-5274. Email: courtneymht@yahoo.com.

Catechesis/Religious Program—Tel: 914-698-1868. Email: mhtdb@aol.com. Students 196.

2—ST. VITO (1911), (Italian), Rev. Msgr. James E. White; Rev. Edward O'Neil.

Res.: 816 Underhill Ave., 10543. Tel: 914-698-2648; Fax: 914-698-6081. Email: stvitochurch@optonline.net.

Catechesis/Religious Program—826 Underhill Ave., Mamaronek, 10543. Tel: 914-698-2949. Students 301.

MARLBORO, ULSTER CO., ST. MARY (1900) [CEM] Rev. Edward Bader; Deacons Thomas Cornell; Vincent Porcelli; John T. Repke.

Res.: 71 Grand St., P.O. Box 730, 12542. Tel: 845-236-4340; Fax: 845-236-3183.

Catechesis/Religious Program—Tel: 845-236-7791. Mrs. Paula Marton, C.R.E. Students 389.

Mission—Our Lady of Mercy 977 River Rd., Newburgh/Roseton, Orange Co. 12550.

MAYBROOK, ORANGE CO., CHURCH OF THE ASSUMPTION (1907) Revs. Daniel M. O'Hare, Admin.; Benjamin Zirra; Deacon Edward M. Grosso.

Res.: 211 Homestead Ave., P.O. Box 320, 12543. Tel: 845-427-2046.

Catechesis/Religious Program—Tel: 845-427-5318. Students 96.

MIDDLETOWN, ORANGE CO.

1—HOLY CROSS (1999) Rev. Robert D. Porpora; Deacon Robert Buckner.

Res.: 626 County Rte. 22, 10940. Tel: 845-355-4439; Fax: 845-355-4709.

Catechesis/Religious Program—Tel: 845-355-6255. Students 573.

Mission—Our Lady of the Scapular 125 Main St., Unionville, Orange Co. 10988. Tel: 845-726-3222.

2—ST. JOSEPH (1865) [CEM] Rev. Dennis A. Nikolic; Rev. Msgr. John J. Budwick, Parochial Vicar; Rev. Franciso Tejada, Parochial Vicar; Deacons Richard Trapani; Albert Loeffler. In Res., Rev. Msgr. George J. Valastro (Retired).

Res.: 149 Cottage St., 10940. Tel: 845-343-6013; Fax: 845-344-4735.

School—(1889) 113 Cottage St., 10940. Jennifer Langford, Prin. Lay Teachers 11; Students 170.

Catechesis/Religious Program—Tel: 845-343-4415. Angelica Frausto, C.R.E. Students 536.

3—OUR LADY OF MT. CARMEL (1912) Revs. James Sidoti, O.Carm.; Raymond Bagdonis, O.Carm., Parochial Vicar; Patrick McGuigan, O.Carm.; Stephen Huy Tran, O.Carm.; Deacons Edward Woods, Pastoral Assoc.; John Frohbose, Pastoral Assoc. In Res., Revs. Alfred Isacsson, O.Carm.; Robert Greco, O.Carm.; John Logan, O.Carm.

Res.: 90 Euclid Ave., 10940. Tel: 845-343-4121; Fax: 845-343-4433.

School—205 Wawayanda Ave., 10940. Tel: 845-343-8836; Fax: 845-342-1404. Lay Teachers 14; Students 151.

Catechesis/Religious Program—Tel: 845-342-1510. Students 768.
Mission—Our Lady of the Assumption P.O. Box 527, Bloomingburg, Sullivan Co. 12721-0527. Tel: 845-733-1477; Fax: 845-733-6691.
Mission—St. Paul Rte. 17K, Bullville, Orange Co. 10915. Tel: 845-361-3107; Fax: 845-361-4201.

MILLBROOK, DUTCHESS CO., ST. JOSEPH (1890) [CEM] Rev. Msgr. James T. O'Connor; Revs. Samuel Kofi (Ghana); Andrew Nketiah (Ghana).
Res.: 15 North Ave., P.O. Box 439, 12545. Tel: 845-677-3422; Fax: 845-677-3423. Email: stjosephmil@aol.com.
School—(1957)Tel: 845-677-3670; Fax: 845-677-8365. Lay Teachers 10; Students 143.
Catechesis/Religious Program—Tel: 845-677-3273. Students 214.
Mission—(1883) Clinton Corners, Dutchess Co. 12514.
Chapel—Millbrook, Cardinal Hayes Home for Children
Station—Green Briar Home, Tel: 845-677-9997.

MILTON, ULSTER CO., ST. JAMES (1874) Rev. Fred Kempfirl.
Res.: 12 Main St., 12547. Tel: 914-795-6164; Fax: 914-795-6164.
Catechesis/Religious Program—Teresa Green, C.R.E. Students 45.

MONROE, ORANGE CO., SACRED HEART CHURCH (1957) Revs. Thomas J. Byrnes; George Pulparayil (India); Christopher Argano; Deacons Peter Brockmann; Richard McCarthy, (Retired); Angelo Corsaro; Robert Duncan.
Res.: 26 Still Rd., 10950. Tel: 845-782-8510; Fax: 845-782-3593. Email: info@sacredheartchurch.org. Web: www.sacredheartchurch.org.
School—(1964)Tel: 845-783-0365; Fax: 845-782-0354. Catherine Muenkel, Prin. Lay Teachers 15; Students 264.
Catechesis/Religious Program—Tel: 845-782-7420; Fax: 845-782-5192. Sr. Rose O'Rourke, D.R.E. Students 1,047.
Convent—Still Rd., 10950.
Mission—Sacred Heart Chapel 151 Stage Rd., 10950.

MONTGOMERY, ORANGE CO., HOLY NAME OF MARY (1868) [CEM] Revs. Daniel M. O'Hare; Robert Geissler, Pastor Emeritus (Retired); Joseph D. Sullivan, Pastor Emeritus (Retired); Deacon Thomas Jordan.
Res.: 89 Union St., 12549. Tel: 845-457-5276.
Catechesis/Religious Program—Tel: 845-457-1738. Email: hnm469@frontiernet.net. Linda Hummel, D.R.E. Students 165.

MONTICELLO, SULLIVAN CO., ST. PETER (1874) [CEM] Revs. John Tran; Gonzalo Arias (Colombia). In Res., Rev. Stanislaus Ogbonna, C.S.Sp. (Nigeria).
Res.: 10 Liberty St., 12701. Tel: 845-794-5577; Fax: 845-791-1210.
Catechesis/Religious Program—Tel: 845-791-7172. Students 263.
Mission—St. Joseph Mongaup Valley, Sullivan Co.
Mission—St. Anne White Lake, Sullivan Co.

MT. KISCO, WESTCHESTER CO., ST. FRANCIS OF ASSISI (1868) [CEM] Rev. Steven E. Clark. In Res., Rev. Francis Anane.
Res.: 2 Green St., 10549. Tel: 914-666-5986; Fax: 914-666-3859. Email: sanfrankisco@earthlink.net. Web: www.sfamountkisco.org.
Catechesis/Religious Program—12 Green St., Mount Kisco, 10549. Tel: 914-666-3161; Fax: 914-666-5474. Students 228.

MOUNT VERNON, WESTCHESTER CO.

1—ST. MARY (1894) Rev. Alfredo Monteiro (India).
Res.: 23 S. High St., 10550. Tel: 914-664-5855; Fax: 914-663-6097. Email: stmarymv@aol.com. Web: www.stmarys-church.com.
Catechesis/Religious Program—Students 198.

2—OUR LADY OF MOUNT CARMEL (1897), (Italian), Rev. Lawrence J. Quinn.
Res.: 10550. Tel: 914-668-3540; Fax: 914-668-4393.
Catechesis/Religious Program—Victoria Liconia, D.R.E. Students 235.

3—OUR LADY OF VICTORY (1871), Comunidade Catolica de Brasileiros (Missionaries of St. Charles-Scalabrinians) Rev. Heitor Castoldi, C.S.
Res.: 28 W. Sidney Ave., 10550. Tel: 914-668-5861; Fax: 914-668-0161. Email: w475@archny.org. Web: www.churcholv.org.
School—(1898) 38 N. Fifth Ave., 10550. Tel: 914-667-4063; Fax: 914-665-3135. Helena Castilla, Prin. Lay Teachers 14; Students 300.
Catechesis/Religious Program—Students 70.

4—SS. PETER AND PAUL (1929) Rev. John F. Lauri. In Res., Rev. Msgr. Thomas F. Scanlon (Retired); Rev. Brian E. McWeeney.
Res.: 129 Birch St., 10552. Tel: 914-668-9815; Fax: 914-668-6052. Email: sppcmvny@gmail.com.
Catechesis/Religious Program—Tel: 914-668-9880. Students 80.

5—SACRED HEART (1872) Rev. Msgr. Howard W. Calkins; Rev. Benjamin Uzbuegbuman (Nigeria).
Res.: 115 S. Fifth Ave., 10550. Tel: 914-668-7440; Fax: 914-668-1177. Email: sacredheart115@verizon.net.
School—(1895) Second St. & S. Fifth Ave., 10550. Tel: 914-667-1734; Fax: 914-667-1497. Lay Teachers 9; Students 264.
Catechesis/Religious Program—Mrs. Alison Nicholas, D.R.E. Students 264.
Chapel—Sacred Heart Convent 67 S. Fifth Ave., 10550.

6—ST. URSULA (1908) Revs. John T. McLoughlin; Valentine U. Ibeh (Nigeria); Deacons Thomas J. Abbamont; Carl Degenhardt.
Res.: 214 E. Lincoln Ave., 10552. Tel: 914-668-0085; Fax: 914-668-4228.
Catechesis/Religious Program—Tel: 914-699-7964. Ms. Mona Parkinson, C.R.E. Students 63.

NANUET, ROCKLAND CO., ST. ANTHONY (1897) [CEM] Revs. Joseph J. Deponai; Frank W. Bassett Jr.; Ferdinando Caindec; Deacon John R. Maloney. In Res., Rev. Joseph A. DeSanto (Retired).
Res.: 36 W. Nyack Rd., 10954. Tel: 845-623-2138; Fax: 845-623-5556. Email: stanthonys.church@verizon.net.
School—(1953) 32-34 West Nyack Rd., 10954. Tel: 845-623-2311; Fax: 845-623-2406. Email: stanthonysoffice@verizon.net. Sr. Pat Howell, O.P., Prin. Sisters 3; Lay Teachers 8; Students 217.
Catechesis/Religious Program—Tel: 845-624-2230. Email: st.anthony.prep@gmail.com. Ms. Anne Malloy, D.R.E. Students 626.
Mission—St. Anthony Shrine Church 38 W. Nyack Rd., Rockland Co. 10954.

NARROWSBURG, SULLIVAN CO., ST. FRANCIS XAVIER (1862) [CEM 2], (Franciscan) Rev. William Scully, O.F.M.
Res.: 151 Bridge St., 12764. Tel: 845-252-6681; Fax: 845-252-6519. Web: www.stfrancisxavier.net.
Catechesis/Religious Program—Students 24.
Mission—Our Lady of the Lake Rte. 52, Lake Huntington, Sullivan Co. 12752. Tel: 845-252-6681.

NEW CITY, ROCKLAND CO., ST. AUGUSTINE (1957) Revs. William B. Cosgrove; Michael Cedro; Varghese I. Chethipuzha; Deacons Michael G. McCabe; Lawrence O'Toole.
Res.: 140 Maple Ave., 10956. Tel: 845-634-3641; Fax: 845-639-6118. Email: staug@optonline.net. Web: www.staugnewcity.org.
School—Tel: 845-634-7060; Fax: 845-634-8725. Web: www.saintaugustineparishschool.com. Katharine Murphy, Prin. Lay Teachers 10; Students 204.
Catechesis/Religious Program—Tel: 845-634-8462. Email: staugustinereo@yahoo.com. Students 750.

NEW PALTZ, ULSTER CO., ST. JOSEPH (1894), (Capuchin Franciscans) Revs. Bernard M. Maloney, O.F.M.Cap.; Barnabas Keck, O.F.M.Cap., Parochial Vicar; Raphael Iannone, O.F.M.Cap.; Deacon Salvatore P. Patricola, O.F.M.Cap.
Res.: 34 S. Chestnut St., 12561. Tel: 845-255-5635; Fax: 845-255-5679. Email: stjoenp@csdsl.net. Web: www.stjosephnewpaltz.org.
Catechesis/Religious Program—Tel: 845-255-0237; Fax: 845-256-0687. Sr. Philomena Fleck, O.S.B., D.R.E. Students 400.

NEW ROCHELLE, WESTCHESTER CO.

1—BLESSED SACRAMENT (1848) [CEM] Rev. Msgr. William J. Bradley; Rev. Charles Imokhai (Nigeria); Deacons Charles Rizzo; Frank Orlando.
Res.: 15 Shea Pl., 10801. Tel: 914-632-3700; Fax: 914-632-0732.
High School—24 Shea Pl., 10801. Tel: 914-632-2595; Fax: 914-632-3321. Edward Sullivan, Prin. (Coed) Lay Teachers 25; Students 352.
Catechesis/Religious Program—Tel: 914-235-7311. Ms. Gina Rocas-Gardon, D.R.E. Students 312.

2—ST. GABRIEL (1893) Rev. Msgr. Patrick V. McNamara. Email: churchofstgabriels@verizon.net.
Res.: 120 Division St., 10801. Tel: 914-632-0211; Fax: 914-637-8991.
Catechesis/Religious Program—Mrs. Maria Elena Marquez, D.R.E. Students 245.

3—HOLY FAMILY (1913) Rev. Msgrs. Ferdinando D. Berardi; John Mescall, Pastor Emeritus (Retired); Revs. Joseph Okech Adhunga, A.J. (Kenya); George K. Nedumaruthumchalil (India); Deacons Donald Gray; Raymond Hall; Sr. Connie Koch, O.P., Pastoral Asst. for Faith Formation.
Res.: 83 Clove Rd., 10801. Tel: 914-632-0673; Fax: 914-576-8556.
Church: Mayflower Ave. & Mt. Joy Pl., 10801.
Catechesis/Religious Program—Tel: 914-636-6758. Students 380.
Chapel—Ursuline Sisters 1352 N. Ave., 10804. Tel: 914-636-3456; Fax: 914-576-2620.
Chapel—Iona Grammar and Preparatory Schools 173 Stratton Rd., 10804. Tel: 914-633-7744; 914-632-2727; Fax: 914-235-6338.
Chapel—Iona College 715 N. Ave., 10801. Tel: 914-633-2000; Fax: 800-633-2329.
Chapel—St. Joseph's Residence, St. Patrick Prov. 30 Montgomery Circle, 10801. Tel: 914-633-6851; Fax: 914-633-5579.
Chapel—New Rochelle, St. Joseph Chapel, Tel: 914-632-6592; Fax: 914-533-4264.
Chapel—Edmond Rice Hall 33 Pryer Ter., 10804. Tel: 914-636-6194; Fax: 914-636-0021.
Chapel—Opus Dei 99 Overlook Cir., 10804. Tel: 914-235-1201; Fax: 914-235-7805.
Chapel—Holy Cross Brothers Provincialate 85 Overlook Cir., 10804. Tel: 914-632-4468; Fax: 914-632-2490.

4—HOLY NAME OF JESUS (1929) Revs. Martin J. Biglin; Francis Maurice; Deacons Carmine DeMarco; Robert Gontcharuk.
Res.: 75 Lispenard Ave., 10801. Tel: 914-636-4856; Fax: 914-636-8474.
Church: Petersville Rd. and Halligan St., 10801.
School—(1954) 70 Petersville Rd., 10801. Tel: 914-576-6672; Fax: 914-576-6676. Mr. Albert D'Angelo, Prin. Lay Teachers 10; Students 184.
Catechesis/Religious Program—Tel: 914-576-6038. Students 180.
Chapel—Sisters of Charity Convent 78 Petersville Rd., 10801. Tel: 914-636-4354.

5—ST. JOSEPH (1901), (Italian), Revs. Philip J. Caruso; Cosimo R. Fazio, Pastor Emeritus (Retired); Rev. Msgr. John A. Ruvo, Senior Priest.
Res.: 280 Washington Ave., 10801. Tel: 914-632-0675; Fax: 914-633-4264.
Catechesis/Religious Program—St. Joseph School of Religion, 53 Sixth St., 10801. Tel: 914-632-3458. Email: stjoenr@aol.com. Antoinette Rossetti, D.R.E. Students 202.

NEW WINDSOR, ORANGE CO., ST. JOSEPH (1962) Rev. Robert G. Hilfiker; Deacons Joseph Lieby; Anthony Ferraiuolo; Leonard Farmer.
Res.: 4 St. Joseph Pl., 12553. Tel: 845-561-8467; Fax: 845-562-3269. Email: stjoseph@choiceonemail.com.
Catechesis/Religious Program—Tel: 845-561-8475. Students 155.

NEWBURGH, ORANGE CO.

1—ST. FRANCIS OF ASSISI (1909), (Polish), [CEM] Rev. John J. Vondras.
Res.: 145 Benkard Ave., 12550. Tel: 845-561-1317; Fax: 845-561-1337.
School—Now Sacred Heart School, Merged in Sept. 1992., 24 S. Robinson Ave., 12550. Tel: 845-561-1433.
Catechesis/Religious Program—Tel: 845-561-6697. Students 380.

2—ST. MARY (1875) Rev. William A. Scafidi, M.Ss.A.; Deacons John L. Seymour; William Castellane.
Res.: 180 South St., 12550. Tel: 845-562-0862; Fax: 845-562-0876. Web: www.stmary.org.
Catechesis/Religious Program—Maria Castellane, D.R.E. Students 126.

3—ST. PATRICK (1836) [CEM 2] Revs. Fernando A. Hernandez; Bladi J. Socualaya; Sr. Helen Raynor, Spanish Apostolate; Deacons Fred Steup; Donald Halter; William Glover; Dennis White.
Res.: 55 Grand St., 12550. Tel: 914-561-0885; Fax: 914-561-8629.
Catechesis/Religious Program—Tel: 914-561-6470. Ms. Mary Jane Newman, D.R.E. Students 660.
Mission—Our Lady of the Lake Lakeside & Rte. 52, Orange Lake, Orange Co. 12550. Tel: 914-561-9537.

4—SACRED HEART (1912), (Italian), Rev. William A. Scafidi, M.Ss.A.; Deacons Dominick Casadone; Peter Haight; Lawrence Kawula; Thomas Neppl.
Res.: 301 Ann St., 12550. Tel: 845-561-1433; Fax: 845-561-4383. Email: sacredheart.newburgh@verizon.net. Web: www.sacredheart-newburgh.e-paluch.com.
School—(1951) 24 S. Robinson Ave., 12550. Religious 1; Lay Teachers 9; Students 170.
Catechesis/Religious Program—24 S. Robinson Ave., 12550. Tel: 845-561-2589. Students 437.

NYACK, ROCKLAND CO., ST. ANN (1869) Revs. Rees W. Doughty; Simon Gyan-Obeng (Ghana); Fidelis Enzeani (Nigeria); Deacons Thomas Luke Conroy; Charles DeGroat.
Res.: 16 Jefferson St., 10960. Tel: 845-358-4707; Fax: 845-358-3246. Email: st_ann@msn.com. Web: www.stann-nyack.org.
Catechesis/Religious Program—Tel: 845-358-3758. Email: julielepore@verizon.net. Ms. Julie LePore, C.R.E. Students 190.
Convent—150 Third Ave., 10960.

OBERNBURG, SULLIVAN CO., ST. MARY (1854) [CEM], (Franciscan) Rev. Joseph Juracek, O.F.M.; Deacon Lawrence Knack.
Res.: 388 Obernburg Rd., 12767. Tel: 845-482-5541.
Catechesis/Religious Program—Students 25.

OSSINING, WESTCHESTER CO.

1—ST. ANN (1927) Revs. Edward G. Byrne; Alberto Espinal; Deacon Jose DeJesus.
Res.: 25 Eastern Ave., 10562. Tel: 914-941-2556; Fax: 914-923-9239. Email: sarcc25ea@aol.com.
St. Ann's Peas & Karrots Program—(Grades PreK-K), 16 Elizabeth St., 10562. Tel: 914-941-0312. Ms. Cookie Colucci, Dir. Early Childhood Education

Catechesis/Religious Program—Tel: 914-941-2420. Students 605.
Convent—
2—ST. AUGUSTINE (1853) [CEM] Rev. Msgr. Hilary Franco; Rev. Slawomir Ciszkowski (Poland); Deacons Timothy Slominski; Steven DeMartino; Clifford Calanni. In Res., Rev. John A. Vigilanti.
Res.: Eagle Park Rte. 9, 10562. Tel: 914-941-0067; Fax: 914-944-0828.
School—(1893)Tel: 914-941-3849; Fax: 914-941-4342. Sr. Mary Elizabeth Donoghue, Prin. Priests 2; Dominican Sisters of Our Lady of the Springs, Bridgeport, CT 2; Lay Teachers 25; Students 474.
Catechesis/Religious Program—Students 305.
OTISVILLE, ORANGE CO., HOLY NAME (1969) [CEM] Rev. Msgr. Peter Tran Van Phat.
Res.: 45 Highland Ave., P.O. Box 597, 10963. Tel: 845-386-1320; Fax: 845-386-6105. Email: hnojotisville@frontiernet.net.
School—Goshen Central Elementary
High School—Goshen High School
Catechesis/Religious Program—Tel: 845-386-2327. Mrs. Gina Barbona, Coord. Students 12.
PATTERSON, PUTNAM CO., SACRED HEART (1957) Revs. Thomas Lutz; Ponnachan Georgekutty.
Res.: 414 Haviland Dr., 12563. Tel: 845-279-4832; Fax: 845-278-0432.
Catechesis/Religious Program—Mrs. Margaret Cairney, C.R.E. Students 360.
PAWLING, DUTCHESS CO., ST. JOHN THE EVANGELIST (1848) [CEM] Revs. John J. Duff; Vincent Paul Dassanayake (Sri Lanka).
Res.: 39 E. Main St., 12564. Tel: 845-855-5488; Fax: 845-855-1273.
Catechesis/Religious Program—Tel: 845-855-9408. Students 443.
PEARL RIVER, ROCKLAND CO.
1—ST. AEDAN (1966) Rev. Msgr. Joseph P. Penna; Rev. Hrudayaraju Sunkara; Deacon James F. Maher.
Res.: 23 Reld Dr., 10965. Tel: 845-735-7405; Fax: 845-735-4125. Email: staedan@optonline.net.
Catechesis/Religious Program—Tel: 845-735-2036. Email: staedan3@optonline.net. Students 642.
2—ST. MARGARET OF ANTIOCH (1895) Rev. Msgr. John J. O'Keefe. In Res., Revs. Joseph Kuzhichalil (India); Paul Osei-Fosu (Ghana).
Res.: 33 N. Magnolia St., 10965. Tel: 845-735-4746; Fax: 845-735-4744.
School—(1953) 34 N. Magnolia St., 10965. Tel: 845-735-2855; Fax: 845-735-0131. Email: rk499@adnyschools.org. Mrs. Carolyn Slattery, Prin. Lay Teachers 11; Students 245.
Catechesis/Religious Program—Tel: 845-735-5489. Email: smprep@hotmail.com. Mrs. Brenda Lattuca, D.R.E. Students 875.
PEEKSKILL, WESTCHESTER CO., ASSUMPTION (1859) [CEM] Rev. John J. Higgins; Rev. Msgr. Francis J. Ansbro, Pastor Emeritus (Retired); Revs. Vernon P. Wickrematunge (Sri Lanka), Parochial Vicar; Louis Anderson, Parochial Vicar; Deacon James F. Roberts.
Res.: 131 Union Ave., 10566. Tel: 914-737-2071; Fax: 914-737-1633. Email: info@assumptionpeekskill.org. Web: www.assumptionpeekskill.org.
School—(1907) 920 Msgr. Ansbro Way, 10566. Tel: 914-737-0680; Fax: 914-737-1322. Email: school@assumptionpeekskill.org. Lay Teachers 16; Students 201.
Catechesis/Religious Program—Tel: 914-737-2231; Fax: 914-737-2353. Email: ccd@assumptionpeekskill.org. Students 352.
Chapel—Mount St. Francis, Tel: 914-737-3373; Fax: 914-736-9614.
PELHAM, WESTCHESTER CO., ST. CATHARINE (1896) Rev. Peter F. Bannan.
Res.: 25 Second Ave., 10803. Tel: 914-738-1491; Fax: 914-738-0398.
Catechesis/Religious Program—Tel: 914-738-1332. Students 300.
PELHAM MANOR, WESTCHESTER CO., OUR LADY OF PERPETUAL HELP (1954) Revs. Robert J. DeJulio; Oliver Offor; Abraham Vettiyolil; Deacons Joseph McQuade; Daniel Murphy.
Res.: 559 Pelham Manor Rd., 10803. Tel: 914-738-1449; Fax: 914-738-9454. Email: olph@msn.com.
School—(1957) 575 Fowler Ave., 10803. Tel: 914-738-5158. Mrs. Susan Cotronei, Prin. Lay Teachers 10; Students 200.
Catechesis/Religious Program—Tel: 914-738-0670. Students 605.
PHOENICIA, ULSTER CO., ST. FRANCIS DE SALES (1902) [CEM] Revs. George W. Hommel, Admin.; Matthew Azhakath, O.C.D., Parochial Vicar.
Res.: 109 Main St., P.O. Box 25, 12464. Tel: 845-688-5617; Fax: 845-688-5630.
Catechesis/Religious Program—Students 5.
PIERMONT, ROCKLAND CO., ST. JOHN THE BAPTIST (1852) Rev. Msgr. John T. Mulligan.
Res.: 895 Piermont Ave., 10968. Tel: 845-359-0078; Fax: 845-359-2976. Email: stjohnrectory2@optonline.net. Web: www.stjohnspiermont.org.
Catechesis/Religious Program—Students 194.
PINE BUSH, ORANGE CO., THE INFANT SAVIOUR (1951) Rev. Kevin M. Gallagher.
Res.: 22 Holland Ave., 12566. Tel: 845-744-2391; Fax: 845-744-5938.
Catechesis/Religious Program—Tel: 845-744-9944. Students 325.
Mission—Our Lady of the Valley Walker Valley, Ulster Co. 12588.
PINE ISLAND, ORANGE CO., ST. STANISLAUS (1912), (Polish), [CEM], Mission of St. Joseph. Records at St. Joseph, 14 Glenmare Ave., Florida, NY 10921. Rev. Joseph M. Tokarczyk, Admin.
Res.: 17 Pulaski Hwy., 10969. Tel: 845-651-7792.
PINE PLAINS, DUTCHESS CO., ST. ANTHONY (1958) Revs. William A. White; John A. Bida, Parochial Vicar.
Church: 68 Poplar Ave., 12567-5531. Tel: 518-398-7115; Fax: 518-398-9146. Email: stanthonys58@fairpoint.net.
Catechesis/Religious Program—Students 14.
PLATTEKILL, ULSTER CO., OUR LADY OF FATIMA (1960), (Theatine) Rev. John Jaume, C.R.
Res.: 1250 State Rt. 32, P.O. Box 700, 12568. Tel: 845-564-4972; Fax: 845-566-1954. Email: parishoffatima@aol.com.
Catechesis/Religious Program—Students 157.
PLEASANT VALLEY, DUTCHESS CO., ST. STANISLAUS KOSTKA (1903) Revs. John J. Backes; Francis Perry Yawo Azah (Ghana); Deacon John Dunn.
Res.: 1590 Main St., P.O. Box 558, 12569. Tel: 845-635-1700; Fax: 845-635-8675. Email: emmettre@optonline.net. Web: www.saintstanislaus.net.
Catechesis/Religious Program—Students 315.
PLEASANTVILLE, WESTCHESTER CO., HOLY INNOCENTS (1894) [CEM], (Dominican) Very Rev. William Alexander Holt, O.P.; Revs. Daniel Davies, O.P.; Hugh Burns, O.P.; Sean J. McConway, O.P.
Res.: 431 Bedford Rd., 10570. Tel: 914-769-0025; Fax: 914-747-2476.
Catechesis/Religious Program—Tel: 914-769-3297. Students 727.
Mission—Our Lady of Pompeii Saragota and Garrigan, Pleasantville Park, Westchester Co. 10570.
POCANTICO HILLS, WESTCHESTER CO., THE MAGDALENE (1894) Rev. Joseph Dietz. In Res., Rev. Kenneth Chigbo (Nigeria).
Res.: 525 Bedford Rd., Pocantico Hills, Sleepy Hollow, 10591-1216. Tel: 914-631-0529; Fax: 914-332-7958. Email: thmagdalene@archny.org.
Catechesis/Religious Program—Students 200.
PORT CHESTER, WESTCHESTER CO.
1—CORPUS CHRISTI (1925), (Salesians) Revs. Thomas E. Ruekert, S.D.B.; Peter Granzotto, S.D.B.; Javier Aracil, S.D.B.; Vincent Paczkowski, S.D.B., Coord. Youth Min.; Deacon Michael Gizzo, Pastoral Assoc.
Res.: 136 S. Regent St., 10573. Tel: 914-939-3169; Fax: 914-939-7249.
School—Corpus Christi - Holy Rosary School (1959) 135 S. Regent St., 10573. Tel: 914-937-4407; Fax: 914-937-6904. Sr. Lou Ann Fantauzza, F.M.A., Prin. Sisters, Daughters of Mary Help of Christians 4; Lay Teachers 14; Students 277.
Catechesis/Religious Program—Sr. Margaret Rose Buonaiuto, F.M.A., D.R.E. Students 130.
2—OUR LADY OF MERCY (1854) [CEM] Revs. Robert J. Staar; Christopher Johnson, O.C.D. (India), Parochial Vicar; Lawrence Naskar (India), Parochial Vicar.
Res.: 260 Westchester Ave., 10573. Tel: 914-939-0612; Fax: 914-939-2807. Email: olmoffice@verizon.net.
Catechesis/Religious Program—Tel: 914-937-5288. Miss Antoinette Rossetti, D.R.E. Students 226.
3—OUR LADY OF THE ROSARY (1904), (Salesian) Revs. Stephen Schenck, S.D.B.; Richard Alejunas, S.D.B., Coord. Youth Ministry; Tarcisio Dos Santos, S.D.B. (Brazil), Parochial Vicar; Deacon William Vaccaro, Admin.
Church & Mailing Address: 22 Don Bosco Pl., 10573. Tel: 914-939-0547; Fax: 914-937-0692.
Res.: 23 Nicola Pl., 10573. Tel: 914-937-5532.
Catechesis/Religious Program—Students 313.
Chapel—Adoration Chapel
4—SACRED HEART OF JESUS (1917) Rev. Msgr. Peter Gelsomino.
Res.: 229 Willett Ave., 10573. Tel: 914-939-1497; Fax: 914-937-6232.
Catechesis/Religious Program—Frank W. Noriega, D.R.E. Students 75.
PORT EWEN, ULSTER CO., PRESENTATION OF THE BLESSED VIRGIN MARY (1874) Rev. Carl D. Johnson; Deacons John J. Larkin; Marc Fanelli.
Res.: Fr Kelly Dr., P.O. Box 904, 12466. Tel: 845-331-0053; Fax: 845-331-3836. Email: presentationbvm@aol.com.
Catechesis/Religious Program—Students 34.
Mission—Sacred Heart [JC] 1055 Broadway, P.O. Box 200, Esopus, Ulster Co. 12429. Tel: 845-384-6828; Fax: 845-384-6234. Rev. Eugene J. Grohe, C.Ss.R.
PORT JERVIS, ORANGE CO.
1—IMMACULATE CONCEPTION (1851) Revs. George Hafemann; George La Grutta.
Res.: 50 Ball St., Box 712, 12771. Tel: 845-856-8212; Fax: 845-858-8375. Email: st-marys-rectory@hvc.rr.com.
Catechesis/Religious Program—Tel: 845-858-4208. Students 186.
2—MOST SACRED HEART (1899) [CEM], Records at: Immaculate Conception, P.O. Box 712, 50 Ball St., Port Jervis, NY 12771 (845-856-8212/5924), Mailing Address: 12 McAllister St., P.O. Box 712, 12771-0712. Tel: 845-856-8212; Fax: 845-858-8375.
POUGHKEEPSIE, DUTCHESS CO.
1—HOLY TRINITY (1921) Rev. Joseph P. LaMorte. In Res., Rev. Gamini E. Fernando (Sri Lanka).
Res.: 775 Main St., 12603. Tel: 845-452-1863; Fax: 845-485-7569. Email: htpok@hvc.rr.com. Web: www.holytrinitypoughkeepsie.org.
School—(1952) 20 Springside Ave., 12603. Tel: 845-471-0520; Fax: 845-471-0309. Email: d520@adnyschools.org. Mrs. Mary Ann McGivney, Prin. Sister Servants of the Immaculate Heart of Mary 2; Lay Teachers 9; Students 165.
Catechesis/Religious Program—Tel: 845-471-5838; Fax: 845-471-0309. Email: htre@hvc.com. Mrs. Lisa P. Timm, D.R.E. Students 305.
Chapel—Holy Trinity Convent 769 Main St., 12603. Tel: 845-452-3484.
2—ST. JOHN THE BAPTIST (1923), Records at: Our Lady of Mt. Carmel, 11 Mt. Carmel Pl., Poughkeepsie, NY 12601 (845-454-0340).
Res.: 1 Grand St., 12601. Tel: 845-454-0340; Fax: 845-486-8154.
3—ST. JOSEPH (1901), (Polish), (Society of Christ) Rev. Edward W. Traczyk, S.Ch.
Res.: 9 Lafayette Pl., 12601. Tel: 845-452-2333; Fax: 845-452-6686.
Catechesis/Religious Program—Students 8.
Chapel—Poughkeepsie, Rectory
Chapel—Cemetery Chapel 42 Evergreen Ave., 12601.
4—ST. MARTIN DE PORRES (1962) [CEM] Rev. Msgr. James P. Sullivan; Revs. Douglas Y. Crawford; Abraham K. George, M.C.B.S.; Deacons Robert Jarmick, Pastoral Assoc., (Retired); Franklin Hung, Pastoral Assoc.; Victor Salamone, Pastoral Assoc.; Patrick Hogan, Pastoral Assoc.; David Nash, Pastoral Assoc.
Res.: 118 Cedar Valley Rd., 12603. Tel: 845-473-4222; Fax: 845-473-4223. Email: smdppok@optonline.net. Web: www.stmartindeporres.org.
School—122 Cedar Valley Rd., 12603. Tel: 845-452-4428; Fax: 845-452-9013. Web: stmartindeporresschool.org. Mrs. Kathleen Leahy, Prin. Lay Teachers 14; Students 441.
Catechesis/Religious Program—Tel: 845-471-8728. Janet McGuirk, D.R.E.; Ellen Farina, Asst. D.R.E. Students 659.
5—ST. MARY (1873) Revs. George A. Sears; Charles Heston Joseph. In Res., Rev. Msgr. John J. Brinn.
Res.: 231 Church St., 12601-4200. Tel: 845-452-8250; Fax: 845-452-8266.
Catechesis/Religious Program—Tel: 845-471-4747; Fax: 845-471-4747. Students 229.
6—OUR LADY OF MT. CARMEL (1910), (Italian), Revs. Peter J. Kihm; Francis Mfodwo (Ghana); Deacon George F. Cacchione; Mr. Kevin Martin, Parish Mgr.
Res.: 11 Mt. Carmel Pl., 12601. Tel: 845-454-0340; Fax: 845-486-8154.
Catechesis/Religious Program—Email: mtcfaithform@hvc.rr.com. Mrs. Katherine Hamilton, D.R.E. Students 311.
7—ST. PETER (1837) [CEM] Rev. James A. Garisto.
Res.: 6 Father Cody Plaza, Hyde Park, 12601. Tel: 845-452-8580; Fax: 845-471-4800. Web: www.stpetersparishny.com.
Church: *Administration Bldg.*, 171 Salt Point Rd., 12603. Fax: 845-471-4800.
School—(1844) 12 Fr. Cody Plaza, 12601. Tel: 845-471-6600; Fax: 845-454-1674. Email: school@stpetersparishny.org. Web: www.stpetersparishny.org. Lay Teachers 16; Students 220.
Catechesis/Religious Program—Tel: 845-452-8580, Ext. 205. Students 126.
Mission—Our Lady of the Rosary Chapel 299 Hudson View Dr., 12601.
Chapel—Poughkeepsie, Convent of St. Peter
Chapel—Hyde Park, P.J. Kenedy Memorial Chapel of Our Lady of the Way Culinary Institute of America, Albany Post Rd., Hyde Park, 12538. Rev. Marc K. Oliver, Chap.
Chapel—Our Lady Health of the Sick Hudson River Psychiatric Center, Ross Bldg., State Hospital, 12601. Rev. Augustine Graap, O.Carm., Chap.
RED HOOK, DUTCHESS CO., ST. CHRISTOPHER (1875) [CEM] Rev. Thomas J. Curley; Rev. Msgrs. Charles P. Coen, Pastor Emeritus; Joaquim J. Olendzki;

Rev. Xavier S. Santiago (India).
Res.: 7411 S. Broadway, 12571. Tel: 845-758-3732; Fax: 845-758-1214. Email: saintchristopher@earthlink.net.
Catechesis/Religious Program—30 Benner Rd., 12571. Tel: 845-758-5506; Fax: 845-758-5682. Students 308.

RHINEBECK, DUTCHESS CO., THE GOOD SHEPHERD (1901) [CEM] Revs. Jeffrey R. Galens; Arul Sebastian (India).
Res.: 3 Mulberry St., 12572. Tel: 845-876-4583; Fax: 845-876-7884. Email: goodshep1@frontiernet.net. Web: www.goodshepherd12572.com.
Catechesis/Religious Program—Tel: 845-876-7298. Email: gscp@frontier.com. Students 189.
Mission—St. Joseph Church St., Rhinecliff, Dutchess Co. 12574.
Rhinebeck, Ferncliff Nursing Home—Tel: 845-876-2011; Fax: 845-876-4810.
Rhinebeck, Sisters of St. Ursula, Linwood Retreat House—Tel: 845-876-4178; Fax: 845-876-6544.

ROSENDALE, ULSTER CO., ST. PETER (1855) [CEM] Rev. Andrew Florez; Deacon Robert Repke.
Res.: 1017 Keator Ave., P.O. Box 471, 12472. Tel: 845-658-3117; Fax: 845-658-3540.
Catechesis/Religious Program—Tel: 845-658-8911. Students 105.
Mission—Our Lady Help of Christians J.F.K. Ln., High Falls, Ulster Co. 12440.

RYE, WESTCHESTER CO., RESURRECTION (1880) Rev. Msgr. Donald M. Dwyer; Revs. Zacharias Nadackal, C.M.I. (India); Joseph Lim, Parochial Vicar; Epifanio Marcaida (Philippines), Parochial Vicar. In Res., Rev. Msgr. Edward D. O'Donnell (Retired).
Res.: 910 Boston Post Rd., 10580. Tel: 914-967-0142; 914-967-0254; Fax: 914-925-2751. Web: www.resurrectionrye.com.
School—(1906) 116 Milton Rd., 10580. Tel: 914-967-1218; Fax: 914-925-3511. Lay Teachers 30; Students 565.
Catechesis/Religious Program—Tel: 914-925-2754; Fax: 914-925-2758. Email: resprep@optonline.net. Students 1,181.

SAUGERTIES, ULSTER CO.
1—ST. JOHN THE EVANGELIST (1886) Rev. William F. Woodruff, Admin.; Rev. Msgr. William E. Williams, Pastor Emeritus (Retired).
Res.: 915 Rte. 212, 12477. Tel: 845-246-9581; Fax: 845-246-9582.
Catechesis/Religious Program—Students 82.
2—ST. MARY OF THE SNOW (1833) [CEM] Rev. Christopher H. Berean; Deacons Perry Bunyar; Donald Trees; Karl Pietkiewicz; Arnie Hyland; Hank Smith.
Res.: 36 Cedar St., 12477. Tel: 845-246-4913; Fax: 845-246-4996.
School—(1881) 25 Cedar St., 12477. Tel: 845-246-6381. Miss Christine M. Molinelli, Prin. Lay Teachers 10; Students 94; Preschool 9.
Catechesis/Religious Program—Tel: 845-246-7534. Mrs. Kelly Myers, Coord. Students 149.
Chapel—Saugerties, Parish Center

SCARSDALE, WESTCHESTER CO.
1—IMMACULATE HEART OF MARY (1912) Rev. Msgr. John T. Ferry; Revs. Robert P. Henry, Parochial Vicar; Thomas Valavanickal, C.M.I. (India), Parochial Vicar; Matthew S. Ernest; Deacons Ernest F. Salomone; Robert di Targiani; Thomas Cusick.
Res.: 8 Carman Rd., 10583. Tel: 914-723-0276; Fax: 914-722-0628. Email: w534@archny.org. Web: www.ihm-parish.org.
School—(1928) 201 Boulevard, 10583. Tel: 914-723-5608; Fax: 914-723-8004. Email: w534@adnyeducation.org. Web: www.ihmscarsdale-.org. Mrs. Patricia Gatti, Prin. Lay Teachers 17; Students 289.
Catechesis/Religious Program—Tel: 914-723-7593; Fax: 914-723-7209. Email: ihmsor@aol.com. Web: www.ihmreled.org. Mrs. Diane Meade, D.R.E. Students 872.
2—OUR LADY OF FATIMA (1948) Rev. Msgr. Hugh F. McManus; Deacons Michael J. Fox; John J. Kollar; Irene Ingham Kollar, Pastoral Assoc.
Res.: 5 Strathmore Rd., 10583. Tel: 914-723-7421; Fax: 914-723-7229. Web: www.olfchurchscarsdale.org.
School—(1950) 963 Scarsdale Rd., 10583. Tel: 914-723-0460; Fax: 914-722-4571. Email: w525@adnyschools.org. Web: www.olfschoolscarsdale.org. Mrs. Sharyn O'Leary, Prin. Lay Teachers 12; Students 167.
Catechesis/Religious Program—Tel: 914-472-6604; Fax: 914-472-6679. Email: olfreled@aol.com. Students 180.
3—ST. PIUS X (1954) Revs. Francisco Sebastian Bacatan, A.M. (Philippines); Mark Aaron Riomalos, A.M.; Michael de Leon, A.M.; Deacon Theodore A. Gaskin. In Res., Rev. Msgr. William B. O'Brien (Retired).
Res.: 91 Secor Rd., 10583. Tel: 914-725-2755; Fax: 914-725-2782. Email: saintpiusx@optoline.net. Web: www.saintpiusxchurch.com.
Catechesis/Religious Program—Tel: 914-472-5594; Fax: 914-725-2782. Email: stpiusxreled@yahoo.com. Students 250.

SHRUB OAK, WESTCHESTER CO., SAINT ELIZABETH ANN SETON (1963) Rev. Msgr. Thomas P. Sandi; Revs. George C. Lodi; S. Kulandairajan (India); Deacons Michael Wilson; Richard Juliano.
Res.: 1377 E. Main St., 10588. Tel: 914-528-3547; Fax: 914-528-4216. Email: seton@bestweb.net. Web: www.seton-parish.org.
School—1375 E. Main St., 10588. Tel: 914-528-3563; Fax: 914-528-0341. Sr. Gabriel Miriam, S.C., Prin. Sisters 1; Lay Teachers 25; Students 330.
Catechesis/Religious Program—Tel: 914-528-8553. Email: setonre@bestweb.net. Sara Koshofer, C.R.E. Students 1,358.

SLEEPY HOLLOW, WESTCHESTER CO.
1—HOLY CROSS (1921), (Slovak—Polish), Unassigned. Records at: St. Teresa of Avila, 130 Beekman Ave., Sleepy Hollow, NY 10591 (914-631-0720).
Res.: 118 Beekman Ave., 10591.
2—IMMACULATE CONCEPTION (1917) Rev. Msgr. Louis J. Mazza.
Res.: 199 N. Broadway, 10591. Tel: 914-631-0446; Fax: 914-631-4157. Email: iccshny@aol.com.
3—ST. TERESA OF AVILA (1853) Rev. Msgr. Francis P. Gorman; Revs. Jude Egbeji (Nigeria); Asuramonil F. Peri (Sri Lanka).
Res.: 130 Beekman Ave., 10591. Tel: 914-631-0720; Fax: 914-366-6459.
Catechesis/Religious Program—Tel: 914-631-1831. Students 300.

SLOATSBURG, ROCKLAND CO., ST. JOAN OF ARC (1966), (Italian—Irish), Revs. Niranjan Rodrigo, Admin.; John J. McKenna (Retired).
Res.: 32 Eagle Valley Rd., 10974. Tel: 845-753-5239; Fax: 845-753-5341. Email: joanofarcsloats@optonline.net. Web: www.stjoansparish.org.
Catechesis/Religious Program—Tel: 845-753-5193. Students 200.

SPRING VALLEY, ROCKLAND CO., ST. JOSEPH (1894) Revs. Rudolph F. Gonzalez; Patrick Adekola (Nigeria); Jose Soto (Colombia); Dessier Predelus (Haiti); Peter Bakwaph (Nigeria).
Res.: 333 Sneden Pl. W., 10977. Tel: 845-356-0311; Fax: 845-352-8126.
Catechesis/Religious Program—Tel: 845-356-0054. Maureen Foley, D.R.E. Students 800.

STONY POINT, ROCKLAND CO., IMMACULATE CONCEPTION (1889) Rev. Msgr. William J. Foley; Rev. Reji Joseph, C.M.I.; Deacons Philip Marino; John Crapanzano; John Sadowski.
Res.: 26 John St., 10980. Tel: 845-786-2742; Fax: 845-942-2614. Email: r547@archny.org. Web: www.immaculatestonypoint.org.
Catechesis/Religious Program—24 E. Main St., 10980. Tel: 845-786-5298. Email: immaculatereled@verizon.net. Students 461.
Mission—Immaculate Conception 5 Buckberg Rd., Tomkins Cove, Rockland Co. 10986.

SUFFERN, ROCKLAND CO., SACRED HEART (1868) Rev. Msgr. Joseph R. Giandurco; Revs. Angelo J. Micciulla; Cresus Fernando; Deacon Joseph A. Witt. In Res., Rev. Brian Coffey, M.H.M.
Res. & Office: 129 Lafayette Ave., 10901. Tel: 845-357-0035; Fax: 845-368-0393.
School—(1909) 60 Washington Ave., 10901. Tel: 845-357-1684; Fax: 845-357-0318. Mrs. Kathleen Grande, Prin. Lay Teachers 11; Students 205.
Catechesis/Religious Program—Tel: 845-357-6044. Janis Batewell, C.R.E. Students 637.
Chapel—Good Samaritan Hospital 255 Lafayette Ave., 10901. Tel: 845-368-5000.
Chapel—Tagaste Monastery 220 Lafayette Ave., 10901. Tel: 845-357-0067; Fax: 845-369-0625.

TAPPAN, ROCKLAND CO., OUR LADY OF THE SACRED HEART (1952) Revs. George J. Torok, C.O.; John F. Dwyer, Weekend Assoc. (Retired); Francis Conka, C.O. In Res., Revs. Vladimir Chripko, C.O.; Thomas Kunnel, S.D.B.; Martin Kertys, C.O.; Roman Dominic Palecko, C.O.
Res.: 120 King's Hwy., 10983. Tel: 845-359-1230; Fax: 845-359-1410. Email: marywarner@optonline.net.
Catechesis/Religious Program—Tel: 845-365-2141. Email: olshre@optonline.net. Students 519.

TARRYTOWN, WESTCHESTER CO., TRANSFIGURATION (1896), (Carmelite) Revs. Lucian W. Beltzner, O.Carm.; Philip Marani, O.Carm. In Res., Rev. Francis F. Dixon, O.Carm.
Res.: 268 S. Broadway, 10591. Tel: 914-631-1672; Fax: 914-524-9352. Web: www.transfiguration-church.org.
School—(1949) 40 Prospect Ave., 10591. Tel: 914-631-3737; Fax: 914-631-6640. Web: www.transfigurationschool.org. Audrey J. Woods, Prin. Lay Teachers 14; Students 224.
Catechesis/Religious Program—Tel: 914-631-2380; Fax: 914-524-9352. Students 175.

TIVOLI, DUTCHESS CO., ST. SYLVIA (1890) [CEM] Revs. Thomas J. Curley, Admin.; H. Theriault, Pastor Emeritus; Rev. Msgr. Joaquim J. Olendzki, Parochial Vicar.
Res.: 104 Broadway, P.O. Box 95, 12583-0095. Tel: 845-757-2442; Fax: 845-757-3553.
Catechesis/Religious Program— At St. Christopher, Red Hook. Students 80.

TUCKAHOE, WESTCHESTER CO.
1—ASSUMPTION (1911), (Italian), Rev. Eric P. Raaser.
Res.: 53 Winterhill Rd., 10707. Tel: 914-961-3643; Fax: 914-961-0283. Web: www.assumption-immaculate.org.
Catechesis/Religious Program— Clustered with Immaculate Conception, Tuckahoe.
2—IMMACULATE CONCEPTION (1853) [CEM] Revs. Eric P. Raaser; John Francis Antony; Kevin M. Malick; Deacon Anthony Viola.
Res.: 53 Winterhill Rd., 10707. Tel: 914-961-3643; Fax: 914-961-0283. Web: www.assumption-immaculate.org.
School—(1913)Tel: 914-961-3785; Fax: 914-961-6054. Web: www.icschoolonline.org. Ms. Maureen J. Harten, Prin. Lay Teachers 21; Students 359.
Catechesis/Religious Program—Tel: 914-961-1076; Fax: 914-961-4765. Lynn Callahan, D.R.E. Students 720.
Chapel—Sisters Convent, Tel: 914-961-3970.

TUXEDO, ORANGE CO., OUR LADY OF MT. CARMEL (1895) Rev. Joseph A. Emmanuel.
Res.: 5 Tobin Way, Rte. 17, P.O. Box 697, 10987. Tel: 845-351-5284; Fax: 845-251-2002. Email: mtcarmeltuxedo@aol.com; olmc@aol.com.
Catechesis/Religious Program—Students 66.

VALHALLA, WESTCHESTER CO., HOLY NAME OF JESUS (1896) Revs. Joseph A. Blenkle; Philip T. Persico.
Res.: Two Broadway, 10595. Tel: 914-949-2323; Fax: 914-686-6325.
School—Tel: 914-948-1744; Fax: 914-948-1749. Web: www.hnjschool.net. Toni Corso, Prin. Lay Teachers 12; Students 120.
Catechesis/Religious Program—Tel: 914-949-1422. Email: hnjre@aol.com. Students 653.

VERPLANCK, WESTCHESTER CO., ST. PATRICK (1843) [CEM] Rev. Andrew E. Kurzyna.
Res.: 240 11th St., P.O. Box 609, 10596. Tel: 914-737-0635; Fax: 914-788-0584.
Catechesis/Religious Program—Church of St. Christopher, 3094 Albany Post Rd., Buchanan, 10511. Tel: 914-737-1437; Fax: 914-737-9320. Students 17.

WALDEN, ORANGE CO., MOST PRECIOUS BLOOD (1894) Rev. Joseph Fallon.
Res.: 42 Walnut St., 12586. Tel: 845-778-5719; Fax: 845-778-5659. Email: mpbparish@frontiernet.net.
School—180 Ulster Ave., 12586. Tel: 845-778-3028; Fax: 845-778-3785. Email: or554@adnyschools.org. Lay Teachers 10.
Catechesis/Religious Program—Tel: 845-778-7081. Email: mpbreled@aol.com. Students 340.
Mission—St. Benedict Wallkill, Ulster Co. 12589.

WAPPINGERS FALLS, DUTCHESS CO., ST. MARY (1850) [CEM] Rev. Msgr. Francis P. Bellew; Rev. Gnanadhas George Michael (India).
Res.: 11 Clinton St., 12590. Tel: 845-297-6261; 845-297-6262; Fax: 845-297-3227. Email: churchstmary@aol.com. Web: www.catholic-church.org/saintmarys.
School—(1890 and 1955) Convent Ave., 12590. Tel: 845-297-7500; Fax: 845-297-0886. Email: officestmary@yahoo.com. Web: www.stmarywf.org. Mrs. Mary Ellen LaRose, Prin. Lay Teachers 17; Students 185.
Catechesis/Religious Program—Tel: 845-297-7586. Email: sm_ore@yahoo.com. Patricia Manuli, D.R.E. Students 268.
Chapel—Mt. Carmel

WARWICK, ORANGE CO., ST. STEPHEN (1865) [CEM] Revs. Michael P. McLoughlin; Casmir Mung'amo; Deacons Thomas MacDougall; Emmet Noonan.
Res.: 75 Sanfordville Rd., 10990. Tel: 845-986-4028; Fax: 845-986-4109. Web: www.warwickinfo.net/ststephen.
School—Tel: 845-986-3533; Fax: 845-986-7023. Web: ststephen-stedward.org. Lay Teachers 13; Students 206.
Catechesis/Religious Program—Tel: 845-986-2231; Fax: 845-986-5939. Students 981.

WASHINGTONVILLE, ORANGE CO., ST. MARY (1902) [CEM] Revs. Jeffrey E. Maurer; Paul Dmoch; Anthony Omenihu; Deacon Timothy Curran.
Res.: 2 Fr. Tierney Cir., 10992. Tel: 845-496-3730; Fax: 845-496-3159.
Catechesis/Religious Program—Tel: 845-496-4101. Students 1,255.

WEST HARRISON, WESTCHESTER CO., ST. ANTHONY OF PADUA (1952) Revs. Christopher W. Monturo; Peter C. Scaramuzzo.
Res.: 85 Harrison St., 10604. Tel: 914-948-1480;

Fax: 914-948-0488. Email: stanthony@optonline.net. Web: www.stanthonyonline.org.
School—(1957) Gainsborg Ave., 10604. Tel: 914-949-6986; Fax: 914-328-1981. Web: www.rc.net/newyork/stanthonyschool/. Students 48.
Catechesis/Religious Program—Tel: 914-949-0212; Fax: 914-949-6669. Email: stanthonyreled@optonline.net. Students 330.

WESLEY HILLS, ROCKLAND CO., ST. BONIFACE (1966) Rev. Hugh R. Grace; Deacon Peter Venezia.
Res.: 5 Willow Tree Rd., 10952. Tel: 845-354-7307; Fax: 914-354-9046.
Catechesis/Religious Program—Tel: 845-354-7039. Students 61.

WEST HURLEY-WOODSTOCK, ULSTER CO., ST. JOHN (1860) Rev. George W. Hommel.
Res.: 12 Holly Hills Dr., Woodstock, 12498. Tel: 914-679-7696; Fax: 914-679-8393.
Catechesis/Religious Program—Tel: 914-679-2869. Students 100.
Mission—St. Augustine Watson Hollow Rd., West Shokan, Ulster Co. 12494. Tel: 914-657-2190.

WEST NYACK, ROCKLAND CO., ST. FRANCIS OF ASSISI (1964) Rev. Msgr. Edward J. Weber; Deacon Farrell J. Hopkins; Sr. Patricia Hogan, O.P., Pastoral Assoc. In Res., Rev. Gerard F. Rafferty, S.S.L.
Res.: 128 Parrott Rd., 10994. Tel: 845-634-4957; Fax: 845-639-6629. Email: stfrancisassisi@optonline.net. Web: www.stfrancis-assisi.org.
Catechesis/Religious Program—Tel: 845-638-4215. Email: stfrancisprep@optonline.net. Mrs. Nancy Doran, D.R.E. Students 1,332.

WEST POINT, ORANGE CO., CATHOLIC CHAPEL OF THE MOST HOLY TRINITY (1899), Most Holy Trinity is being served under the Archdiocese for Military Services. For inquiries for sacramental records before Jan. 1, 1999, please contact Sacred Heart, Highland Falls. Rev. Msgr. Brian Donahue; Revs. Edson J. Wood, O.S.A., Brigade Chap. U.S. Corps of Cadets; Felix K. Kumai (Nigeria).
United States Military Academy, 699 Washington Rd., 10996. Tel: 845-938-8760; Fax: 845-938-8763.
Catechesis/Religious Program—Tel: 845-938-8761. Cindy Ragsdale, D.R.E. Students 248.

WHITE PLAINS, WESTCHESTER CO.

1—ST. BERNARD (1926) Rev. Robert J. Morris; Deacon Daniel Pellegrin. In Res., Rev. Louis Maram Reddy (India).
Res.: 51 Prospect St., 10606. Tel: 914-949-2111; Fax: 914-949-6044. Email: rectory@stbernardswp.com. Web: www.stbernardswp.com.
Catechesis/Religious Program—Tel: 914-686-8145. Students 441.

2—ST. JOHN THE EVANGELIST (1868) [CEM] Rev. Msgr. Neil Graham; Revs. Timothy S. Wiggins; Paul Chemplamparampil Joseph, C.M.I.; Jaccius Jean Pierre.
Res.: 148 Hamilton Ave., 10601. Tel: 914-949-0439; Fax: 914-421-1202.
Catechesis/Religious Program—Tel: 914-437-5144. Students 233.

3—OUR LADY OF MT. CARMEL (1902), (Italian), (Stigmatine) Revs. Albert Azrak, C.S.S.; Thomas Augustine Badgley; Joseph Henchey, C.S.S.
Res.: 92 S. Lexington Ave., 10606. Tel: 914-948-5909; Fax: 914-328-1946. Web: www.olmcwp.org.
Catechesis/Religious Program—Students 237.

4—OUR LADY OF SORROWS (1929) Revs. Philip J. Quealy; Thomas DeSimone.
Res.: 920 Mamaroneck Ave., 10605. Tel: 914-949-9819; Fax: 914-949-4148. Email: office@olscc.com.
School—(1957) 888 Mamaroneck Ave., 10605. Tel: 914-761-0124; Fax: 914-761-0176. Email: w561@adnyschools.org. Web: www.olscc.com. Sr. Marie Cecile, R.D.C., Prin. Lay Teachers 15; Students 194.
Catechesis/Religious Program—Tel: 914-949-3896. Maryrita Opperman, C.R.E. Students 332.

WOODBOURNE, SULLIVAN CO., IMMACULATE CONCEPTION (1957) [CEM] Rev. John J. Lynch.
Res.: 6317 Rte. 42, P.O. Box 66, 12788. Tel: 845-434-7643; Fax: 845-436-7370. Email: s564@hvc.rr.com.
Catechesis/Religious Program—Tel: 845-436-7370. Students 98.

WURTSBORO, SULLIVAN CO., ST. JOSEPH (1880) [CEM] Rev. Peter J. Madori; Deacon Edward Czerwinski. In Res., Rev. Matthias Ndulaka.
Res.: 180 Sullivan St., P.O. Box 277, 12790. Tel: 845-888-4522; Fax: 845-888-5072.
Catechesis/Religious Program—Students 110.

YONKERS, WESTCHESTER CO.

1—ST. ANN (1947) Revs. Andrew P. Carrozza; John P. McDonagh; James K. Annor-Omen (Ghana).
Res.: 854 Midland Ave., 10704. Tel: 914-965-1555; 914-965-5584; Fax: 914-965-0678.
School—40 Brewster Ave., 10701. Tel: 914-965-4333; Fax: 914-965-1778. Mr. Michael Vicario, Prin. Lay Teachers 10; Students 165.
Catechesis/Religious Program—Students 102.

2—ST. ANTHONY (Nepera Park) (1923) Revs. Karl A. Bauer; Robert Ashman.
Res. & Church: 10 Squire Ave., 10703. Tel: 914-965-2733; Fax: 914-963-2285. Web: www.stanthonys-catholic.org.
School—1395 Nepperhan Ave., 10703. Tel: 914-476-8489; Fax: 914-965-7939. Mrs. Elizabeth Carney, Prin. Lay Teachers 11; Students 241.
Catechesis/Religious Program—Tel: 914-965-5535. Students 91.

3—ST. ANTHONY (Willow St.) Closed. For inquiries for parish records contact Our Lady of Mt. Carmel, Yonkers.

4—ST. BARTHOLOMEW (1910), (Missionaries of St. Paul of Nigeria) Revs. Anthony Bassey, M.S.P.; Donald Eruaga, M.S.P., Parochial Vicar; Deacon Robert A. Clemens.
Res.: 15 Palmer Rd., 10701. Tel: 914-965-0566; Fax: 914-965-9046.
Catechesis/Religious Program—Tel: 914-476-6676. Students 158.

5—ST. CASIMIR (1899), (Polish), (Pauline) Revs. Anzelm Chalupka, O.S.P.P.E.; Michal Czyzewski, O.S.P.P.E.
Res.: 239 Nepperhan Ave., 10701. Tel: 914-963-1254; Fax: 914-969-5204. Email: rectory@saintcasimir.org. Web: www.saintcasimir.org.
School—(1906) 259 Nepperhan Ave., 10701-3461. Tel: 914-965-2730; Fax: 914-965-3347. Helen DiNoia, Prin. Lay Teachers 10; Students 240.
Catechesis/Religious Program—Students 9.

6—CHRIST THE KING (1927) Rev. William J. Luciano.
Res.: 740 N. Broadway, 10701. Tel: 914-963-7474; 914-963-7564; Fax: 914-963-7548. Email: ctkrectory@optonline.net.
Catechesis/Religious Program—Email: rel.ed.ctk@verizon.net. Students 70.

7—ST. DENIS (1910) Revs. Edward P. O'Halloran; Thomas V. Berg.
Res.: 470 Van Cortlandt Park Ave., 10705. Tel: 914-963-8468; Fax: 914-963-7354.
Catechesis/Religious Program—73 Lawrence St., 10705. Rev. Edward P. O'Halloran, D.R.E. Students 100.

8—ST. EUGENE (1949) Revs. Leonard F. Villa; Michael D. Morrow; Leo Perrera.
Rectory—32 Massitoa Rd., 10710. Tel: 914-779-5460; Fax: 914-793-8913. Email: rectory32@optonline.net. Web: www.steugene.info. Parish Office: 31 Massitoa Rd., 10710. Tel: 914-961-2590; Fax: 914-961-2881.
School—(1951) 707 Tuckahoe Rd., 10710. Tel: 914-779-2956; Fax: 914-779-7668. Email: w577@adnyeducation.org. Lay Teachers 17; Students 320.
Catechesis/Religious Program—Tel: 914-793-2158; Fax: 914-337-9868. Marisela DeVictoria, D.R.E. Tel: 914-337-9868. Students 103.

9—IMMACULATE CONCEPTION (1848), (Spanish—Arabic), [CEM] Rev. Msgr. Hugh J. Corrigan; Revs. Sami Totah (Jordan); Virgilio Compentente (Philippines). In Res., Rev. Osvaldo Franklin (Angola).
Res.: 103 S. Broadway, 10701. Tel: 914-963-0156; Fax: 914-963-1803. Email: marys103@optonline.net.
Catechesis/Religious Program—Tel: 914-963-1053. Students 150.
Good Shepherd Arabic Community of St. Mary—Rev. Sami Totah (Jordan), Admin.

10—ST. JOHN THE BAPTIST (1903) Rev. Msgr. J. Christopher Maloney; Revs. Thomas Valenti; Daniel Ulloa, O.P. (Mexico); Deacon Martin J. Olivieri.
Res.: 670 Yonkers Ave., 10704. Tel: 914-963-1486; Fax: 914-375-1115.
School—(1954)Tel: 914-965-2356. Sisters 2; Lay Teachers 14; Students 328.
Catechesis/Religious Program—Tel: 914-965-2338. Sr. Mary Beth Read, O.S.U., D.R.E. Students 155.
Chapel—Convent 176 Sweetfield Circle, 10704. Tel: 914-965-1837.

11—ST. JOSEPH PARISH (1871), (Hispanic), [CEM] Revs. George J. Kuhn; Arthur F. Rojas; Deacon Abraham Santiago.
Res.: 141 Ashburton Ave., 10701. Tel: 914-963-0730; Fax: 914-964-5833.
Catechesis/Religious Program—Students 195.
Convent—Sisters of Charity, Tel: 914-423-1351. Sisters 6.

12—ST. MARGARET OF HUNGARY (1928) Unassigned. Records at: St. Joseph, 141 Ashburton Ave., Yonkers, NY 10701 (914-963-0730)
Res.: 76 Locust Hill Ave., 10701.

13—MOST HOLY TRINITY (1894), (Slovak), Rev. George Oonnoonny.
Res.: 18 Trinity Pl., 10701. Tel: 914-963-0720; Fax: 914-709-0224.
Chapel—Franciscan Friars of the Renewal 15 Trinity Pl., 10701. Tel: 914-476-7279; Fax: 914-476-5033. Rev. James Mary Atkins, C.F.R.

14—OUR LADY OF FATIMA (1977), (Portuguese Center) Rev. Osvaldo Franklin (Angola), Admin.
Portuguese R.C. Center—355 S. Broadway, 10705. Tel: 914-423-9688; Fax: 914-423-8271. Email: fatima1305@verizon.net. Web: www.fatima-port-church.com.
Catechesis/Religious Program—Neide Pires, D.R.E. Students 98.

15—OUR LADY OF MT. CARMEL (1913), (Italian), (Pallottine) Revs. Terzo Vinci, S.A.C.; Chris Salvatori, S.A.C.; Deacons Alfred R. Impallomeni; Nick A. Mazzei Jr.
Res.: 70 Park Hill Ave., 10701. Tel: 914-963-4766; Fax: 914-963-4766. Email: tervinci@optonline.net.
Catechesis/Religious Program—Tel: 914-476-8888; Fax: 914-476-8888. Email: olmcreled@juno.com. Students 325.

16—OUR LADY OF THE ROSARY (1907), Records At: Immaculate Conception/St. Mary, 103 S. Broadway, Yonkers, NY 10701 (914-963-0156). Rev. Msgr. Hugh J. Corrigan, Temporary Admin.
Res.: 226 Warburton Ave., 10701.

17—ST. PAUL THE APOSTLE (1923) Rev. James F. Healy; Sr. Eileen Treanor, P.B.V.M., Parish Ministry; Deacons James J. Hamilton; Rudolfo Teng. In Res., Rev. Philip Thomas Kizhakumpurath, M.S.F.S. (India).
Res.: 602 McLean Ave., 10705. Tel: 914-963-7330; Fax: 914-963-1952. Email: w581@adny.org.
Church: Lincoln Park, 10705.
School—(1949) 77 Lee Ave., 10705. Tel: 914-965-2165; Fax: 914-965-5792. Grace Mallardi, Prin. Lay Teachers 15; Students 201.
Catechesis/Religious Program—Sr. Eileen Treanor, P.B.V.M., D.R.E. Students 126.

18—ST. PETER (1894) Revs. Joseph Espaillat; Julio Vasquez (El Salvador), Parochial Vicar; Deacon Pedro Irizarry.
Res.: 91 Ludlow St., 10705. Tel: 914-963-0822; Fax: 914-968-9305.
School—(1894 and 1955) 204 Hawthorne Ave., 10705. Tel: 914-963-2314; Fax: 914-966-8822. Email: principal@stpetersny.com. Web: www.stpetersny-.com. Sisters 1; Lay Teachers 9; Students 235.
Catechesis/Religious Program—Tel: 914-969-3813. Students 374.

19—SACRED HEART (1891), (Capuchin) Rev. Maurice Moreau, O.F.M.Cap.; Bro. Roger Deguire, O.F.M-.Cap.; Revs. Christopher Dietrich, O.F.M.Cap.; Theodosius Corley, O.F.M.Cap. In Res., Rev. Thomas Murphy, O.F.M.Cap.; Bro. John Shento, O.F.M.Cap.
Res.: 110 Shonnard Pl., 10703. Tel: 914-963-4205; Fax: 914-476-4960.
School—(1893)Tel: 914-963-5318; Fax: 914-709-0250. Web: www.shgsyonkers.org. Lay Teachers 15; Students 253.
High School—34 Convent Ave., 10703. Tel: 914-965-3114; Fax: 914-965-4510. Religious 1; Lay Teachers 24; Students 406.
Sacred Heart Parish High School Foundation, Inc.—34 Convent Ave., 10703. Tel: 914-963-4205; Fax: 914-476-4960.
Catechesis/Religious Program—Students 140.
Convent—27 Convent Ave., 10703. Tel: 914-476-4602.

YORKTOWN HEIGHTS, WESTCHESTER CO., ST. PATRICK (1898) Rev. Joseph Bisignano; Rev. Msgr. Dermot R. Brennan, Pastor Emeritus (Retired); Revs. Daniel Tuite; Thomas L. Kreiser; Augustine Addai (Ghana); Deacon Kevin T. Byrnes.
Res.: 137 Moseman Rd., 10598. Tel: 914-962-5050; 914-962-5051; Fax: 914-962-0595. Email: w583@archny.org. Web: www.stpatricks-yorktown.org.
School—(1953) 117 Moseman Rd., 10598. Tel: 914-962-2211; Fax: 914-243-4814. Lay Teachers 12; Students 261.
Catechesis/Religious Program—Tel: 914-962-5586; Fax: 914-962-3207. Students 1,557.

YOUNGSVILLE, SULLIVAN CO., ST. FRANCIS OF ASSISI (1963) Merged with St. George, Jeffersonville to form St. George-St. Francis, Jeffersonville.

YULAN, SULLIVAN CO., ST. ANTHONY OF PADUA (1907) [CEM], (Franciscan) Rev. Anthony F. Moore, O.F.M.
Res.: 12792. Tel: 845-557-8512; Fax: 845-557-3527. Email: afmofm@hvc.rr.com.
Catechesis/Religious Program—Students 73.
Mission—Sacred Heart Berme Church Rd., Pond Eddy, Sullivan Co. 12770.

Chaplains of Public Institutions
Military Installations

NEW YORK. *National Catholic Community Service*, 487 Park Ave., 10022. Rev. Msgr. Richard Cahill, Dir. (Cardinal Spellman Servicemen's Club)
New York City Veterans Administration Hospital, 406 First Ave., 10022. Revs. Pasquale V. Laghezza, SS.CC., Jose A. Salazar.

BRONX. *Veterans Administration Hospital*, 130 W. Kingsbridge Rd., 10460. Rev. Paul F. O'Connor, O.S.B.

MONTROSE. *Franklin D. Roosevelt Hospital*. Vacant.
WEST POINT. *Stewart Field*. Rev. Nash P. Geany.
West Point.
U.S. Military Academy 10966. Vacant.

Societies

NEW YORK. *Marine and Aviation Department*. Vacant.
New York Fire Department. Rev. Msgr. Marc J. Filacchione.
New York Police Department. Rev. Msgr. Joseph J. Zammit.
New York Postal Service.
New York Sanitation Department. Rev. Peter M. Colapietro.
YONKERS. *Yonkers Fire Department*. Rev. Thomas F. McDonald (Retired).
Yonkers Police Department. Vacant.

Prisons

CITY. *Anna M. Kross Center*, 18-18 Hazen St., East Elmhurst, 11370. Tel: 718-546-3654. Rev. George J. Dash, O.F.M.Cap.
Eric M. Taylor Center, 10-10 Hazen St., East Elmhurst, 11370. Tel: 718-546-5796. Rev. Michael Koncik, C.Ss.R.
George M. Motchan Detention Center, 15-15 Hazen St., East Elmhurst, 11370. Tel: 718-546-4543. Rev. Thomas Mestriparampil.
George Vierno Center, 09-09 Hazen St., East Elmhurst, 11370. Tel: 718-204-5079, Ext. 2254. Rev. Oliver Chanama.
Manhattan Detention Center, 125 White St., 10013. Tel: 212-225-1367. Deacon Miguel Granda.
North Infirmary Command, 15-00 Hazen St., East Elmhurst, 11370. Tel: 718-546-1256. Sr. Amy Henry.
Otis Bantum Correctional Center, 16-00 Hazen St., East Elmhurst, 11370. Tel: 718-546-6617. Revs. Michael Koncik, C.Ss.R., Thomas Mestriparampil.
Robert N. Davoren Center, 11 Hazen St., East Elmhurst, 11370. Tel: 718-546-7223. Sr. Margaret McCabe, C.S.J.
Rose M. Singer Center, 19-19 Hazen St., East Elmhurst, 11370. Sr. Eileen Schelenberg, C.S.J.
Vernon C. Bain Center, 1 Halleck, Bronx, 10474. Tel: 718-579-4371. Rev. Thomas Fenlon, Deacon Miguel Granda.
COUNTY. *Dutchess County Jail*, Poughkeepsie, 12601. Tel: 845-297-5706. Attended by St. Mary, Poughkeepsie, Tel: 845-452-8250.
Orange County Jail. Attended from St. John, Goshen. Tel: 845-294-5328.
Putnam County Jail. Attended by St. James, Carmel. Tel: 845-225-2079.
Rockland County Jail. Attended by St. Augustine, New City. Tel: 845-634-3641.
Sullivan County Jail. Attended by St. Peter, Monticello. Tel: 845-794-5577.
Ulster County Jail, Kingston, 12401. Tel: 845-338-1554. Deacon John Bellacicco.
Westchester County Jail, Box 389, Valhalla, 10595. Tel: 914-347-6132. Rev. Paul Tolve, I.V.Dei, Deacon John Sadowski.
FEDERAL. *Federal Correctional Institution*, Otisville, 10963. Tel: 845-386-5855, Ext. 291. Revs. James McDevitt, Robert D. Porpora.
Metropolitan Correctional Center, 150 Park Row, 10007-1779. Tel: 212-240-9656, Ext. 6454. Rev. Michael O'Hara, O.M.I.
STATE. *Arthur Kill Correctional Facility*, 2911 Arthur Kill Rd., Staten Island, 10309-1197. Tel: 718-356-7333. Rev. Frank Naccarato.
Bayview Correctional Facility, 550 W. 20th St., 10011-2878. Tel: 212-255-7590. Deacon Emmett Noonan.
Beacon Correctional Facility, Box 780, Beacon, 12508-0780. Tel: 845-831-4200. Deacon Frank Gohl.
Bedford Hills Correctional Facility, 247 Harris Rd., Bedford Hills, 10507-2499. Tel: 914-241-3100. Sr. Mary Anne Collins.
Downstate Correctional Facility, Box 445, Fishkill, 12524-0445. Tel: 845-831-6600. Rev. Arecio P. Dormido.
Eastern Correctional Facility, Napanoch, 12458-0338. Tel: 845-647-7400. Deacon Joseph Doherty.
Edgecombe Correctional Facility, 611 Edgecombe Ave., 10032-4398. Tel: 212-923-2575. Deacon Emmett Noonan.
Fishkill Correctional Facility, Box 307, Beacon, 12508. Tel: 845-831-4800. Rev. George J. Dash, O.F.M-.Cap., Deacon Frank Gohl.
Fulton Correctional Facility, 1511 Fulton Ave., Bronx, 10457-8398. Tel: 718-583-8000. Rev. Matthew Ugwoji.
Green Haven Correctional Facility, Stormville, 12582. Tel: 845-221-2711. Rev. Gamini E. Fernando (Sri Lanka), Deacon Robert Buckner.
Lincoln Correctional Facility, 31-33 W. 110 St., 10026-4398. Tel: 212-860-9400. Vacant.
Otisville Correctional Facility, Box 8, Otisville, 10963-0008. Tel: 845-386-1490, Ext. 4830. Rev. Augustine Graap, O.Carm., Deacon Eugene Bormann.
Shawangunk Correctional Facility, Box 750, Wallkill, 12589-0750. Tel: 845-895-2081. Vacant.
Sing Sing Correctional Facility, 354 Hunter St., Ossining, 10562-5442. Tel: 914-941-0108, Ext. 4810. Rev. Matthew Ugwoji.
Sullivan Correctional Facility, P.O. Box AG, Fallsburg, 12733-0116. Tel: 845-434-2080. Rev. Stanislaus Ogbonna, C.S.Sp. (Nigeria).
Taconic Correctional Facility, 250 Harris Rd., Bedford Hills, 10507-2498. Tel: 914-241-3010. Sr. Antonia Maguire, O.S.F.
Ulster Correctional Facility, Berne Rd., P.O. Box 800, Napanoch, 12458. Tel: 914-647-1670, Ext. 4800. Deacon James Faulkner.
Wallkill Correctional Facility, Box G, Wallkill, 12589-0286. Tel: 845-895-2021. Vacant.
Woodbourne Correctional Facility, Pouch 1, Woodbourne, 12788. Tel: 845-434-7730. Rev. Matthias Ndulaka.

Hospitals

BRONX. *St. Barnabas Hospital*, Tel: 718-960-9000. Rev. Matthew Abba, Sr. Miriam Hanratty, O.P., Deacon Victor Pino.
Bronx Psychiatric Center, Tel: 718-931-0600. Vacant.
Bronx-Lebanon Hospital Center, Tel: 718-590-1800; 718-518-5059. Revs. Ishamel O. Iwuala, Joseph Bernardine Onyia (Nigeria).
Calvary Hospital, Tel: 718-518-2114. Revs. Raymond G. Pierini, M.M., P/T Spiritual Counselor, Chux Okochi, Dir. Pastoral Svcs., Anthony Nzegwu.
Jacobi Medical Center. Revs. Sancho G. Garrote, Hippolytus Duru (Nigeria), Chap., Sr. Rosemary Sullivan, F.M.M., Chap.
James F. Peters Medical Center. Rev. Paul F. O'Connor, O.S.B.
Lincoln Medical and Mental Health Center, Tel: 718-579-5000; 718-579-5059. Vacant.
Montefiore Medical Center, Tel: 718-920-4997. Revs. Paul F. Nwobi, Ephrem Pottamplackal, M.C.B.S.
Montefiore Medical Center - North Division. Rev. Msgr. Frederick J. Becker, Vice Pres. Pastoral Svcs., Sr. Catherine McVicar, S.M.
New York Westchester Square Medical Center, Tel: 718-828-2380. Serviced by Santa Maria Parish.
North Central Bronx Hospital, Tel: 718-519-5000. Revs. Hippolytus Duru (Nigeria), Sancho E. Garrote (Philippines). Serviced by Jacobi Medical Chaplain.
Union Hospital, Tel: 718-200-2020. Serviced by St. Barnabas Hospital.
BRONXVILLE. *Lawrence Hospital*. Rev. Joachim Adione, Sr. Florence Mallon, S.C.
CALLICOON. *Community General Hospital*, Tel: 845-887-5530. Serviced by Holy Cross, Callicoon.
CARMEL. *Putnam Hospital Center*, Tel: 845-279-5711. Serviced by St. James the Apostle, Carmel.
CASTLE POINT. *V.A. Hudson Valley Healthcare*, Tel: 845-831-2000, Ext. 5453. Revs. Raymond A. Pavlick, Richard DeLaPena, Joseph W. Hickey (Retired).
COLD SPRING. *Julia L. Butterfield Memorial Hospital*, Tel: 914-265-3642. Serviced by Our Lady of Loretto, Cold Spring.
CORNWALL. *St. Luke's-Cornwall Hospital*, Tel: 845-534-2547. Rev. Peter Claver Ugoagwu, Chap. Serviced by St. Thomas of Canterbury, Cornwall-on-Hudson.
DOBBS FERRY. *St. Cabrini Nursing Home*, Tel: 914-693-6800. Sr. Maryann Calabrese, Rev. Edwin F.D. Robinson, O.F.M., Dir. Pastoral Care.
Dobbs Ferry Pavilion/St. John's Riverside Hospital, Tel: 914-693-0700. Serviced by Sacred Heart, Dobbs Ferry.
ELLENVILLE. *Ellenville Regional Hospital*, Tel: 845-647-6080. Serviced by the Church of St. Mary & St. Andrew, Ellenville.
GOSHEN. *Orange Regional Medical Center*, Tel: 914-294-5441. Serviced by St. John, Goshen.
HARRIS. *Community General Hospital of Sullivan County*, Tel: 845-292-4525. Serviced by St. Peter, Monticello.
HARRISON. *Saint Vincent's Westchester*, Tel: 914-967-6500. Rev. Msgr. John Gallagher.
HAWTHORNE. *Rosary Hill Home*, Tel: 914-769-0114. Rev. Jacob Restrick, O.P., S.T.L.
KINGSTON. *Benedictine Hospital*, Tel: 845-338-2500. Sisters M. Dorothy Huggard, O.S.B., Dir. Pastoral Care, Mary Feehan, O.S.B., Revs. Louis Yaya, Benjamin Zirra.
Kingston City Hospital, Tel: 845-331-3131. Serviced by St. Mary, Kingston.
MANHATTAN. *Bellevue Hospital*. Rev. Frederick O. Nyanguf, A.J.
Beth Israel Medical Center, Tel: 212-420-2759, Ext. 3. Revs. Francis Okoli, Damian Umeokeke.
Bird S. Coler Memorial Hospital and Home, Tel: 212-838-8155. Vacant.
Goldwater Memorial Hospital, Tel: 212-318-8000; 212-318-4738. Rev. Andrew Bielak (Poland).
Gouverneur Hospital, Tel: 212-374-4000. Serviced by St. Teresa, NYC.
Gracie Square, Tel: 212-988-4400. Rev. Michael Koncik, C.Ss.R. Serviced by St. Jean Baptiste, NYC.
Harlem Hospital, Tel: 212-281-4931. Rev. Emmanuel Okpalauwaekwe. Serviced by St. Mark.
Hospital for Special Surgery, Tel: 212-606-1757. Sr. Margaret Oettinger, O.P., Revs. Carl Mason, Michael P. Trainor, O.P.
Lenox Hill Hospital, Tel: 212-439-2547. Rev. Christian Christopher, S.S.S.
St. Luke's-Roosevelt Hospital Center, Tel: 212-523-4000.
Roosevelt Site. Revs. Lionel A. DeSilva, C.S.P. Tel: 212-523-6920, James F. McQuade, C.S.P.
St. Luke's Site. Serviced by Notre Dame, NYC
Manhattan Eye, Ear & Throat Hospital, Tel: 212-838-9200. Serviced by St. Vincent Ferrer.
Manhattan Psychiatric Center, Tel: 212-369-0500, Ext. 2530.
Medical Arts Center Hospital, Tel: 212-755-0200. Serviced by St. Patrick Cathedral.
Memorial Sloan Kettering Cancer Center, Tel: 212-639-5982. Revs. Louis C. Mason, O.P., Michael P. Trainor, O.P.
Metropolitan Hospital. Rev. Michael J. Sala, S.J.
Mount Sinai Medical Center. Vacant.
New York Downtown Hospital - New York Infirmary, Tel: 212-312-5000; 212-233-5300. Rev. Reynaldo Domagas (Philippines). Serviced by St. Andrew, NYC.
New York Eye & Ear Infirmary, Tel: 212-673-3480. Serviced by Immaculate Conception, 414 E. 14th St., NY, NY 1009.
New York Presbyterian-Columbia Medical Center, Tel: 212-305-3101. Rev. Michael M. Ferrer, S.D.B.
Allen Pavilion-Columbia Presbyterian. Rev. Arlen Harris, O.F.M.Cap.
New York Presbyterian Hospital, Tel: 212-746-4690. Revs. Melchor Ferrer, S.D.B., Omumuawuike Madu, C.M.F., Louis C. Mason, O.P., Michael P. Trainor, O.P.
New York University Medical Center, Tel: 212-263-7300. Revs. Chrisanth Mugasha, A.J., Stephen Okeke (Nigeria).
Hospital for Joint Disease. Vacant. Serviced by Immaculate Conception Church, 414 E. 14th St., NY, NY 10009, Tel: 212-254-0200.
Rockefeller University, Tel: 212-570-8000. Serviced by St. Catherine of Siena.
Terence Cardinal Cooke Health Care Center, Tel: 212-360-3993. Revs. Patrick Bonner, Dir. Pastoral Care, Ayub Mwampela.
U.S.V.A. Medical Center, Tel: 212-686-7500. Revs. Ramon Saavedra (Philippines), Jose A. Salazar, Andrew Sioleti, O.F.M.
MIDDLETOWN. *Orange Regional Medical Center*, Tel: 845-343-2424. Serviced by St. Joseph, Middletown.
MONTROSE. *FDR DVA Hospital*. Rev. Robert D. Tracy, O.Carm.
MOUNT KISCO. *Northern Westchester Hospital*, Tel: 914-666-1200. Vacant. Serviced by St. Francis of Assisi, Mt. Kisco.
MOUNT VERNON. *Mount Vernon Hospital*, Tel: 914-664-8000. Rev. Isaac Aganbi.
NEW HAMPTON. *MID Hudson Psychiatric Center*. Rev. George Palparayil. Serviced by visiting priests.
NEW ROCHELLE. *Sound Shore Medical Center*, Tel: 914-632-5000. Vacant. Chaplain, contact hospital operator.
NEWBURGH. *St. Luke-Cornell Hospital*, Tel: 845-561-4400. Rev. Peter Claver Ugoagwu. Serviced by St. Patrick, Newburgh.
NORTH TARRYTOWN. *Phelps Memorial Hospital*, Tel: 914-631-0720. Serviced by St. Theresa's, Sleepy Hollow.
NYACK. *Nyack Hospital*, Tel: 845-358-6200. Deacon James Gorman, Dir., P.C. Serviced By St. Ann, Nyack.
ORANGEBURG. *Rockland Psychiatric Center*. Serviced by area parishes.
OSSINING. *Stony Lodge Hospital*, Tel: 914-941-7400. Serviced by St. Augustine, Ossining.
PEEKSKILL. *Hudson Valley Hospital Center*, Tel: 914-737-9000. Vacant. Serviced by Holy Spirit, Cortlandt Manor.
POMONA. *Dr. Robert L. Yeager Health Center*. Serviced by St. Boniface, Monsey, NY
PORT JERVIS. *Bon Secours Community Hospital*, Tel: 845-856-5351. Rev. Vincent Odikanoro, Deacons Albert W. Perroult, Dir. Pastoral Care, John Nash.
POUGHKEEPSIE. *St. Francis Hospital*, Tel: 845-471-2000. Sr. Marie Bernadette Wyman, Dir. Pastoral Care, Rev. Zeverin Emagalit, Pastoral Care Assoc., Sisters Alice Howley, Pastoral Care Assoc., Marie Colette, O.S.F., Pastoral Care Assoc., Patricia Nugent, Pastoral Care Assoc., Cathy O'Shea, Pastoral Care Assoc., Deacons Frank S. Ottaviano, Pastoral Care Assoc., (Beacon), Dennis White, Pastoral Care Assoc., (Beacon), Rev. Joseph Mali.

Hudson River Psychiatric Center, Tel: 845-452-7378. Rev. Augustine Graap, O.Carm.

Vassar Brothers Hospital 12601. Tel: 845-454-8500. Revs. David A. DeSimone, Charles Heston Joseph. Serviced by St. Mary's Church, 231 Church St., Poughkeepsie, NY 12601, Telephone: 845-452-8250.

RHINEBECK. *Northern Dutchess Hospital*, Tel: 845-876-4583. Serviced by Good Shepherd, Rhinebeck.

RYE. *Rye Psychiatric Hospital Center*, Tel: 914-967-4567. Serviced by Church of the Resurrection, Rye.

STATEN ISLAND. *Richmond University Medical Center*, Tel: 718-818-1234. Revs. Ralph Dawis, Chap., Clement Kalu.

Richmond University Medical Center/Bayley Seton Campus, Tel: 718-354-6000. Revs. Ralph Dawis, Clement Kalu.

Seaview Hospital Rehabilitation Center and Home, Tel: 718-371-3000, Ext. 3284. Rev. George Sabol, O.F.M. Conv.

Staten Island University Hospital North. Revs. John DeLora, Eduardo Amora (Philippines), Percy Joseph Raj.

Staten Island University Hospital South, Tel: 718-260-2000. Revs. John DeLora, Deogracias Linago, Pastoral Care, Percy Joseph Raj.

SUFFERN. *Good Samaritan Hospital*, Tel: 914-357-3300. Rev. James P. Bono, I.V.Dei, Sr. Margaret Strauch, S.S.N.D., Mgr. of Pastoral Care, Rev. Brian Coffey, M.H.M., Chap., Sr. Sheila Mullins, O.P., Chap.

TUXEDO PARK. *Tuxedo Memorial Health Care Center*, Tel: 914-351-4751. Vacant.

VALHALLA. *Blythdale Children's Hospital*, Tel: 914-592-7555. Serviced by Holy Name of Jesus.

Westchester Medical Center, Tel: 914-347-7000. Rev. Kenneth Chigbo (Nigeria). Night coverage by The Magdalene Pocantico Hills.

WARWICK. *St. Anthony Community Hospital*, Tel: 845-986-2276. Rev. Henry Tanto, S.M.M.M.

WASSAIC. *Taconic, D.D.S.O.* Serviced by Immaculate Conception Armenia.

WEST HAVERSTRAW. *Helen Hayes Hospital*, Tel: 845-947-2200. Serviced by Marion Shrine, Salesians.

WHITE PLAINS. *Burke Rehabilitation Center*, Tel: 914-948-0050. Rev. Thomas Collins, Sr. Laura Morgan, F.M.S.C.

New York Hospital - Cornell Medical Center Westchester Division, Tel: 914-949-9819. Served by Our Lady of Sorrows, Mamaroneck, NY.

White Plains Hospital, Tel: 914-681-0600. Serviced by St. Bernard, White Plains.

YONKERS. *St. John's Riverside Hospital*, Tel: 914-964-4444. Rev. Nicholas Nwagwu. Park Care Pavillion (formerly Yonkers General); Night Call-Christ the King, Yonkers, (914-963-7474). Serviced by St. Joseph's, Yonkers.

St. Joseph's Medical Center, Tel: 914-378-7000. Sr. Dolores Doyle, P.B.V.M., Dir. Pastoral Care, Rev. Thomas Murphy, O.F.M.Cap., Sr. Margaret Kelly, S.C.

On Duty Outside the Archdiocese:
Rev. Msgrs.—
Brown, Charles, Congregation Pro, Doctrina Fidei
Irwin, Kevin W., Catholic University of America, Washington, DC.
Meier, John P., Notre Dame Univ., South Bend, IN.
Shelley, Thomas J., Fordham
Stern, Robert L., Catholic Near East Welfare Association, 1011 First Ave., 10022-4195.
Revs.—
Adams, Richard, N. American College, Rome
Altrui, Ronald P., Pennsylvania
Dillon, Richard J., University of Milan.
Euk, Vincent, Trenton, Diocese
Haggerty, Donald, Ethiopia
Imbelli, Robert P., Boston College, Boston, MA.
Martin, William F., Christian Foundation for Children & Adults, P.O. Box 65, Warren, VT 05674.
Quinn, John L., Cross International Catholic Outreach, Pompano Beach, FL.
Sandstrom, Philip, American College, Louvain, Belgium.
Serra, Dominic, Catholic University of America, Washington, DC 20261.
Smarsh, Charles F., University of Maryland.
Tran, Joseph, Hartford Diocese

Graduate Studies:
Revs.—
Cleary, William
Cruz, Eric, Notre Dame, IN.
D'Alliessi, Daniel
Ernest, Matthew S.

Military Chaplains:
Rev. Msgr.—
Hill, Philip W., Office of the Chief of Chaplains, 2700 Army Pentagon, Washington, DC.
Revs.—
Lindblad, Karl-Albert, 2031 Nicklaus Dr., Suffolk, VA 23435. U.S.N.
Mandato, Kieran, 7437 Heatherfield Ln., Box 1799, Alexandria, VA 22315.
Muhm, William M., 4499 Brisbane Way #4, Oceanside, CA 92054.
O'Reilly, Edward M. (Retired)
Pugliese, Francis A., PSC 557, Box 1921, Fpo, AP 96379-1921.

Unassigned:
Revs.—
Baker, Joseph
Nahas, Joseph
Rev. Canon—
Pintabone, John A.

Absent on Sick Leave:
Revs.—
Adams, Walter C. (Retired)
D'Incecco, Alfred
Leo, Arthur R.
Tran, Philip

On Leave of Absence:
Revs.—
Altrui, Ronald P.
Baker, George
Betances-Torres, Martin
Borkowski, Francis
Fanning, John
Kang, Paul
McLucas, James
Selvaraj, Peter

Retired:
Most Revs.—
Brucato, Robert A., D.D., V.G., John Cardinal O'Connor Clergy Residence, 5655 Arlington Ave., Bronx, 10471.
McCormack, William J., D.D., Our Lady of the Scapular and St. Stephen, 142 E. 29, 10016.
Rev. Msgrs.—
Ahern, John B., Our Lady of Loreto, 309 Elizabeth St., 10012.
Ansbro, Francis J., Assumption, 131 Union Ave., Peekskill, 10566.
Bardes, George F., John Cardinal O'Connor Clergy Residence, 5655 Arlington Ave., Bronx, 10471.
Birkle, Walter A., St. John the Baptist, 670 Yonkers Ave., 10704.
Boyle, Francis V., John Cardinal O'Connor Clergy Residence, 5655 Arlington Ave., Bronx, 10471.
Brennan, Dermot R., John Cardinal O'Connor Clergy Residence, 5655 Arlington Ave., Bronx, 10471.
Byrne, Harry J., John Cardinal O'Connor Clergy Residence, 5655 Arlington Ave., Bronx, 10471.
Clyne, Vincent F., 376 Baden Pl., Staten Island, 10306.
Collins, Timothy, John Cardinal O'Connor Clergy Residence, 5655 Arlington Ave., Bronx, 10471.
Cox, James, 999 Shapley Rd., Bainbridge, 13733.
Curran, Hugh D., St. Catherine's Parish, 25 Second Ave., Pelham, 10803.
Duffy, Francis X., John Cardinal O'Connor Clergy Residence, 5655 Arlington Ave., Bronx, 10471.
Dunne, Joseph A., Our Lady of Consolation Residence, 3103 Arlington Ave., Bronx, 10463.
Ford, Robert A., John Cardinal O'Connor Clergy Residence, 5655 Arlington Ave., Bronx, 10471.
Fowler, Eugene A., Ferncliff Nursing Home, 21 Ferncliff Rhinebeck, Rock Tavern, 12575.
Gerathy, Kenneth A., Our Lady of Consolation Residence, 3103 Arlington Ave., Bronx, 10463.
Gillen, John J., St. Benedict, 2969 Otis Ave., Bronx, 10465.
Kenny, Walter F., S.T.D., St. Augustine, 18 Cherry Ave., Larchmont, 10538.
Loughman, Kenneth M., Most Precious Blood, 42 Walnut St., Walden, 12586.
Marinacci, Nicolas, St. Patrick's Old Cathedral, 263 Mulberry St., 10012.
McCormack, Robert, Convent of St. Brigitta, 4 Runkenhage Rd., Danien, CT 06830.
McCorry, Edward J., 5 Daisy Ct., Suffern, 10901.
O'Brien, William B., 142 Garth Rd., Apt. 4T, Scarsdale, 10583.
O'Donnell, Peter C., John Cardinal O'Connor Clergy Residence, 5655 Arlington Ave., Bronx, 10471.
Oliverio, Francis E., 214 Grove St., Cedarhurst, 11516.
Pavis, Victor S., John Cardinal O'Connor Clergy Residence, 5655 Arlington Ave., Bronx, 10471.
Plo, John, c/o Luis Bolinches, 23-9 Pta 27, Valencia 46023 Spain.
Scanlon, Thomas F., Sts. Peter & Paul, 129 Birch St., Mt. Vernon, 10552.
Revs.—
Arold, Richard J., 422 Ocean Blvd., Unit 4B, Long Branch, NJ 07740.
Carroll, Patrick, 49 E. 73rd. St., 10021.
Chiang, John B., 264 Chung Cheng Rd. Shihlin, Taipai 111 Taiwan.
Ciaravolo, Ronald, 213 Fairview Ave., Box 898, Montauk, 11954.
Coleman, John J., Regeis Residence, 3200 Baychester Ave., Bronx, 10475.
Conte, James W., 2156 Catalina Blvd., San Diego, CA 92107.
Conti, John P., 537 Third St., Brooklyn, 11215.
Croke, Alfred M., John Cardinal O'Connor Clergy Residence, 5655 Arlington Ave., Bronx, 10471.
Crotty, John M., John Cardinal O'Connor Clergy Residence, 5655 Arlington Ave., Bronx, 10471.
Daly, Christopher H., John Cardinal O'Connor Clergy Residence, 5655 Arlington Ave., Bronx, 10471.
Delaney, John J., J.D., Mary Manning Walsh Nursing Home, 1339 York Ave., 10021.
DeSanto, Joseph A., 6 Lennox Ct., Bon Aire, Apt. 709, Suffern, 10901.
Dibble, Michael, 5 Corte de la Canada, Martinez, CA 94553.
DiNola, Leonard J., 16 Green St., Somersworth, NH 03878.
DiSenso, Gerard, John Cardinal O'Connor Clergy Residence, 5655 Arlington Ave., Bronx, 10471.
Doyle, Philip R., Box 1088, Carmel, 10512.
Driscoll, Donald, 160 Locust Ave., Scarsdale, 10583.
Duane, Robert J., John Cardinal O'Connor Clergy Residence, 5655 Arlington Ave., Bronx, 10471.
Dumpson, Roland J., Franciscans Handmaids of Mary Convent, 15 W. 124th St., 10027.
Dwyer, John F., Our Lady of the Sacred Heart, 120 Kings Hwy., Tappan, 10983.
Fazio, Cosimo R., Box 1895, New Smyrna Beach, FL 32170.
Fiorillo, Antimo M., Santa Maria Parish, 2352 St. Raymond's Ave., Bronx, 10462.
Fussner, Donald T., St. Peter, 18 Barclay St., 10007.
Geissler, Robert, 196 Azalea Cir., Jackson, NJ 08527.
Gigante, Louis R., P.O. Box 820, Philmont, 12565.
Gussoni, Lino, Via Rodini Tedeschi 19, Piacenza 29100 Italy.
Halborg, John T., 90 LaSalle St., Apt. 9C, 10027.
Hammer, Jefferson J., P.O. Box 589, Pine Bush, 12566.
Hickey, Joseph W., 297 S. Broadway, Apt. 5C, Tarrytown, 10591.
Holihan, John W., Our Lady of Consolation Residence, 3103 Arlington Ave., Bronx, 10463.
Jeffers, Robert A., Our Lady of the Rosary, 7 State St., 10004.
Kennedy, Robert T., J.U.D., J.D., 400 Symphony Cir., Hunt Valley, MD 21030.
Kuolt, Benedict J., John Cardinal O'Connor Clergy Residence, 5655 Arlington Ave., Bronx, 10471.
Lancellotti, Vincent A., John Cardinal O'Connor Clergy Residence, 5655 Arlington Ave., Bronx, 10471.
Leone, Arthur, Our Lady of Good Counsel, 230 E. 90th St., 10128.
Ma, Peter, St. Mary's Parish, 28 Attorney St., 10002.
McAndrew, Joseph P., 5 Crescent Dr., Apt. 45, Warwick, 10990.
McCann, Luke W., Ph.D., 65 Viola Ave., Leonardo, NJ 07737.
McDonald, Bernard J., 160 E. Main St., Port Jervis, 12771.
McDonald, Thomas F., John Cardinal O'Connor Clergy Residence, 5655 Arlington Ave., Bronx, 10471.
McKenna, John J., 196 Azalea Cir., Jackson, NJ 08527.
Navins, Robert J., Sacred Heart, 981 Castleton Ave., Staten Island, 10310.
Neilson, Richard J., P.O. Box 999, South Orleans, MA 02662.
Nielson, Thomas A., 19B Monmouth Ln., Whiting, NJ 08759.
O'Meara, Joseph P., St. Patrick's Old Cathedral, 263 Mulberry St., 10012.
O'Reilly, Edward M., P.O. Box 5592, Hudson, FL 34674.
O'Shea, Gerard, Rt. A1A, Apt. 920, Atlantic Beach, FL 32233.
Palomino, Esviardo, St. Lucy, 344 E. 104 St., 10029.
Pane, Andrew M., 9 Pasadena Rd., Bronxville, 10708.
Pizzuto, Alfred, John Cardinal O'Connor Clergy Residence, 5655 Arlington Ave., Bronx, 10471.
Pucci, Alfred, Holy Family, 366 Watchogue Rd., Staten Island, 10314.
Reardon, John F., John Cardinal O'Connor Clergy Residence, 5655 Arlington Ave., Bronx, 10471.
Smolinski, Joseph J., 11 Dale Ave., Apt. 21,

Highland Falls, 10928.
Smyth, James, St. Matthew, 616 Warburton Ave., Hastings-on-Hudson, 10706.
Sullivan, Joseph D., 603 Mill Pl., Montgomery, 12549.
Tos, Aldo J., 1 Columbus Cir., Apt. 529A, 10019.
Tou, John B., St. Bernadette, 12 Zion Rd., Singapore.
Tubridy, James J., John Cardinal O'Connor Clergy Residence, 5655 Arlington Ave., Bronx, 10471.
Walsh, Ronald J., 87 Star Crest, Sand Lake, 12153.
Whitson, Robley E., 73 W. Shore Rd., New Preston, CT 06777.

Permanent Deacons:
Abbamont, Thomas J., St. Ursula, Mount Vernon
Abels, Gregory, (Leave of Absence)
Acabeo, Valentin, Holy Cross, Bronx
Ackerman, Henry, (Leave of Absence)
Aglietti, Richard, St. Joseph, Millbrook
Albin, George, St. Gregory Barbarigo, Garnersville
Alexandre, Andre, Holy Name, Manhattan
Almanzar, Andres A., Puerto Rico
Alvarado, William, St. Columba, Hopewell Junction
Alvarez, Angel, St. Joan of Arc, Bronx
Alvarez, Robert, (On Leave)
Armo, John, St. John Evangelist, Mahopac
Attridge, James C., St. Peter & Paul the Apostle Parish, Brandenton, FL
Aviles, Stanley, St. Denis, Hopewell Junction
Baffa, John, St. Lawrence O'Toole, Brewster
Barone, John, Blessed Kateri Tekakwitha, La Grangeville
Battersby, William L., St. Mary, Mount Vernon
Beckford, Rodney, St. Charles Borromeo, Manhattan
Bellacicco, John A., St. Augustine, Highland
Bello, James, Holy Cross, Bronx
Bello, Rafael J., (Medical Leave)
Bernal, Enrique, Fort Mill, SC
Biasotti, John C., (Leave of Absence)
Blake, George W., St. Martha, Sarasota, FL
Bormann, Eugene, St. Anastasia, Harriman
Borsavage, Charles T., St. James the Apostle, Carmel
Bouwmans, Philip R., Lords Valley, PA
Brady, Walter, St. John & St. Mary, Chappaqua
Brockmann, Peter, Sacred Heart, Monroe
Brown, James A., SS. John & Paul, Larchmont
Buckley, John J., Sacred Heart Parish, Pinellas Park, FL
Buckner, Robert, Holy Cross, (Middletown) South Centerville
Bunyar, Perry A., Canada
Buonocore, Dominic, St. Paul, Congers
Burke, Eugene F., St. Gabriel, Bronx
Burnett, Robert V., Antigua, WI
Burns, James T., St. Francis Assisi, Englewood, FL
Byrne, Kevin, St. Patrick, Yorktown Heights
Cacchione, George F., Our Lady of Mt. Carmel, Poughkeepsie
Calafiore, Michael R., St. Charles, Staten Island
Calanni, Clifford, St. Augustine, Ossining
Camacho, Ismael, St. Joan of Arc, Bronx
Campoverde, Carlos, Assumption, Peekskill
Canals, Dhoel M., Holy Family, Bronx
Cartwright, Gerard, St. James the Apostle, Carmel
Carvajal, Rafael, Christ the King, Bronx
Casadone, Dominick G., Sacred Heart, Newburgh
Cassaneto, Anthony P., St. Theresa of the Infant Jesus, Bronx
Castellane, William, St. Mary's, Newburgh
Chaparro, Juan, Sacred Heart, Bronx
Charbonneau, Andre, St. Elizabeth, Manhattan
Charlesworth, Myles J., Our Lady of Lourdes Parish, Raleigh, NC
Chiu, George, St. Mary of the Assumption, Katonah
Clemens, Robert A., St. Bartholomew, Yonkers
Colton, Thomas, Albany, NY
Conroy, Luke, St. Ann, Nyack, NY
Cookingham, Vincent, St. John the Evangelist, Goshen, NY
Coppola, George, St. Frances de Chantal, Bronx
Coppola, John J., St. Columbanus, Cortlandt Manor
Corsaro, Angelo, Sacred Heart, Monroe
Cosme, Felix, Gainsville, GA
Cotto, Angel L., Caguas, Puerto Rico
Crapanzano, John, Immaculate Conception, Stony Point, NY
Cruz, Edwin J., St. John Vianney, Bronx
Cunningham, John, St. John the Baptist, Piermont
Curran, Timothy, St. Mary, Washingtonville
Cusick, Thomas, Immaculate Heart of Mary, Scarsdale
Czerwinski, Edward, St. Joseph, Wurtsboro
Czerwinski, Mark, St. Paul, Congers
D'Aiello, Joseph, St. Vincent de Paul, Milford, PA
Da Costa, Orlindo, Our Lady of Fatima, Yonkers
Dalmer, Peter, Regina Coeli, Hyde Park
Damiano, Rocco, St. Mary's, Newburgh
Darlestin, Leones J., (Leave of Absence)
Daubman, Andrew, Blessed Kateri Tekakwitha, La Grangeville
Dauerer, Walter P., St. Denis, Hopewell Junction
De Jesus, Jose L., St. Ann, Ossining
De Maio, Donald J., St. Peter the Apostle, Naples, FL
De Marco, Carmine J., Holy Name of Jesus, New Rochelle
De Meis, John, Our Lady of Grace, Staten Island
De Vivo, Michael, St. Patrick's, York, PA
Dean, Timothy, Sacred Heart, Esopus
Decker, Michael, St. Mary, Mother of the Church, Fishkill
Degenhardt, Carl, St. Ursula, Mount Vernon
DeGroat, Charles, St. Ann's, Nyack
DeMartino, Steven, St. Augustine, Ossining
Deschler, Bernard M., St. Thomas More-St. Edmund, Rockaway Pt., NY
Devlin, Charles, SS. John and Mary, Chappaqua
Di Fiore, Augustine, Most Holy Trinity, Mamaroneck
di Targiani, Robert, (Medical Leave)
Dickson, Donald, (Leave of Absence)
Doherty, Joseph, St. Joseph, Kingston
Donovan, William, (Medical Leave)
Dowen, Roland, St. Gregory Barbarigo Parish, Garnerville
Dringus, William L., Holy Spirit, Albany, NY
Droge, Lawrence, St. Charles Borromeo, Staten Island
Droulette, Donald L., Beltsville, MD
Duncan, Robert, Sacred Heart, Monroe
Dunn, John, St. Stanislaus, Pleasant Valley, NY
Duran, Nelson, St. Anthony of Padua, Bronx
Edgerton, John M., Tarpon Springs, FL
Espinal, Hector, Immaculate Conception, Staten Island
Esposito, Robert A., The Villages, FL
Estela, Jorge, St. Peter's, Haverstraw
Fama, Arthur, St. Anthony of Padua, Redbank, NJ
Fanelli, Marc, Presentation of Blessed Virgin Mary, Port Ewen
Farmer, Leonard, St. Joseph, New Windsor
Faulkner, James, St. Anastasia, Harriman
Feliz, Luis J., Our Lady Queen of Martyrs, Manhattan
Fernandez, Delio, Our Lady Queen of Martyrs, Manhattan
Fernandez, Roberto, (Medical Leave)
Ferraiuolo, Anthony P., St. Joseph, New Windsor
Fontánez, Luis, Orlando, FL
Forte, Joseph, (Leave of Absence)
Fox, Michael J., Our Lady of Fatima, Scarsdale
Francis, James, Sts. Peter and Paul, Bronx
Frohbose, John M., St. Paul, Bullville
Frohmiller, Richard J., St. Joseph, Kingston
Garcia, Rene, Our Lady of Guadalupe, Manhattan
Gaskin, Theodore A., St. Pius X, Scarsdale
Gizzo, Michael, Corpus Christi, Port Chester
Glover, William, St. Patrick, Newburgh
Gohl, Frank, Regina Coeli, Hyde Park
Gomas, Kelly, (Leave of Absence)
Gontcharuk, Robert, Holy Name of Jesus, New Rochelle
González, Faustino, La Coruna, Spain
González, Ismael, Nuestra Senora de la Asuncion, Caguas, Puerto Rico
Gorman, James, Charlotte, NC
Gorzka, Stephen S., (Leave of Absence)
Grady, Paul, (Leave of Absence)
Graham, Patrick, St. Margaret Mary, SI
Granda, Miguel E., St. Gabriel, Bronx
Gray, Donald, Holy Family, New Rochelle
Grosso, Edward, Assumption, Maybrook
Gruerio, Anthony G., St. James, Carmel
Guglielmo, Joseph N., Infant Savior, Pine Bush
Guzman, Antonio, Good Shepherd, Manhattan
Hafeman, Joseph R., St. Mary Mother of the Church, Fishkill
Haight, Peter R., Sacred Heart, Newburgh
Hall, Raymond, Holy Family, New Rochelle
Halter, Donald, St. Patrick, Newburgh
Hamilton, Eugene R., St. Peter, Haverstraw
Hamilton, James J., Our Lady of the Springs, Ocala, FL
Hayes, James R., Regina Coeli, Hyde Park, NY
Hernandez, Jose M., St. Cecilia, Manhattan
Hernandez, Narcisco, Our Lady Queen of Martyrs, Manhattan
Hogan, Patrick J., St. Martin de Porres, Poughkeepsie
Hopkins, Farrell J., (Medical Leave)
Horton, Robert, Blessed Kateri Tekakwitha, La Grangeville
Horvath, Robert J., Sarasota, FL
Hung, Franklin, St. Martin de Porres, Poughkeepsie
Hveem, Paul, St. Brendan's, Bronx
Hyland, Arnold, St. Mary of the Snow, Saugerties
Idehen, Francis, Most Precious Blood, Walden
Impallomeni, Alfred R., Our Lady of Mount Carmel, Yonkers
Irizarry, Pedro, St. Peter, Yonkers
Jarmick, Robert E., St. Martin de Porres, Poughkeepsie
Jean-Gilles, Gabriel, Miami, FL
Jesselli, Stephen, (On Leave)
Johnson, Robert Joseph, (Leave of Absence)
Jordan, Thomas, Holy Name of Mary, Montgomery
Juhasz, Lajos, (Unassigned)
Juliano, Richard, St. Elizabeth Ann Seton; Shrub Oak
Jurasek, John, St. Catharine, Blauvelt
Kawula, Lawrence, Sacred Heart, Newburgh
Kazimir, Martin, Albany, NY
Kelleher, John C., St. Catharine, Blauvelt
Kelly, John, St. Gregory Barbarigo, Garnerville
Kenefick, Cecil, St. Theresa, Briarcliff Manor
Knack, Lawrence F., St. Mary, Obernberg
Knight, Charles C., Our Lady of the Lourdes Parish, Marysville, OH
Koch, George J., Our Lady of the Lourdes, Sun City West, AZ
Kollar, John J., Our Lady of Fatima, Scarsdale
Konas, Dale, St. Lawrence O'Toole, Brewster
Kozinski, Paul, St. Mary, Rosebank, S.I.
Lagotta, Anthony A., (Medical Leave)
Larkin, John J., Presentation of the Blessed Virgin Mary, Port Ewen
Laurato, Vincent I., St. Barnabas, Bronx
Lawlor, James, St. Charles Borromeo, Dover Plains, NY
Le Blanc, Vincent F., Westchester Medical Center, West Harrison
Leasiolagi, Taulafoga, St. John Vianney, Bronx
Li Greci, Christopher, St. Michael Chapel, Manhattan
Lieby, Joseph, St. Joseph, New Windsor
Liegey, Gabriel, St. Patrick, Fairfield, VT
Lindley, Gerard, Regina Coeli, Hyde Park
Loeffler, Albert, St. Joseph, Middletown
Longo, Ralph D., Annunciation, Crestwood
Lopez, Francisco Javier, St. Martin of Tours, Bronx
Lousa, Pedro, (Leave of Absence)
Lugo, Alejandro, St. Cecilia, Manhattan
Mac Dougall, Thomas, St. Stephen the Martyr, Warwick, NY
Maher, James, St. Aedans, Pearl River
Maldonado, Eusebio, Holy Cross, Manhattan
Maloney, John R., St. Anthony, Nanuet
Man, Chi Sum, Transfiguration, Manhattan
Mangino, Charles, (Leave of Absence)
Manning, Cornelius J., St. Barnabas, Bronx
Marino, Philip A., Immaculate Conception, Stony Point
Maroon, Phillip J., St. Teresa of the Infant Jesus, Staten Island
Marquez, Jose, St. Francis of Assisi, Mt. Kisco
Martinez, Luis A., Holy Rosary, Manhattan
Mayeski, Martin, St. Joachim & St. John the Evangelist, Beacon
Mazza, Albert, Holy Name of Mary, Croton-on-Hudson
Mazzei, Nicholas A., Our Lady of Mt. Carmel, Yonkers
Mazzella, Salvatore, Our Lady of Grace, Bronx
McCarthy, Richard, Sacred Heart, Monroe
McGarry, James, St. Catherine of Siena, Sebring, FL
McLaughlin, Richard, Holy Rosary, Hawthorne
McQuade, Joseph, Our Lady of Perpetual Help, Pelham Manor
McSherry, John W., St. Paul, Congers
Meier, Anthony C., Raleigh, NC
Mejia, Apolonio, St. Anselm's, Bronx
Mercado, Carlos V., Immaculate Conception, Bronx
Messina, Enrico, St. Denis, Hopewell Junction
Mitchell, Richard F., St. Clare, Staten Island
Mojica, Jose, San Juan, Puerto Rico
Monegro, Juan, Incarnation, Manhattan
Moran, Bernard, St. John the Evangelist, Mahopac
Morillo, Felix M., Good Shepherd, Orlando, FL
Mueller, William J., (Leave of Absence)
Mulryan, W. Joseph, Our Lady of Grace, Bronx
Munoz, Frank, St. Denis, Hopewell Junction
Munoz, Jose, Mt. Pocono, PA
Murphy, Daniel, Our Lady of Perpetual Help, Pelham Manor
Murphy, John G., St. Frances de Chantal, Bronx
Nash, David, St. Martin de Porres, Poughkeepsie
Nash, John J., Bon Secours Community Hospital, Port Jervis
Neppl, Thomas, Sacred Heart, Newburgh
Nolasco, Rolando, Our Lady of Mercy, Bronx
Noonan, Emmet, St. Stephen the Martyr, Warwick, NY
Nunez, Acadio, (Leave of Absence)
O'Brien, Donald F., Scranton, PA
O'Brien-Lambert, Pedro, Our Lady of Lourdes, Manhattan
O'Connor, Gerard R., (Medical Leave)

O'Neill, Brian, St. Anastasia, Harriman
O'Reilly, John F., St. Mary, Mother of the Church, Fishkill
O'Sullivan, Mark, Regina Coeli, Hyde Park
O'Toole, Lawrence, Charlotte, NC
Olivieri, Martin J., St. John the Baptist, Yonkers
Orlando, Francis B., Blessed Sacrament, New Rochelle
Ortíz, Louis, Ponce, Puerto Rico
Ortíz, Pablo, Puerto Rico
Osgood, Kevin, Colorado Springs, CO
Ottaviano, Frank S., St. Augustine, Highland
Pacheco, Angel, St. Isaac Jogues Parish, Orlando, FL
Padron, Jose R., St. Pius V, Bronx
Pang, Robert, St. John the Baptist, Piermont
Pappalardo, Augustine A., St. Gregory Barbarigo, Garnerville
Parchen, Raymond, Holy Spirit, Cortlandt Manor
Patrona, Joseph, St. Mary, Mt. Vernon
Pelech, Robert, St. Denis, Hopewell Junction
Pelella, John V., St. Thomas of Canterbury, Cornwall-on-Hudson
Pellegrin, Daniel, St. Bernard, White Plains
Pellegrini, Guy A., Annunciation, Crestwood
Pena, Jose, St. Joseph, Spring Valley
Pereira, Joaquim, St. Margaret of Cortona, Riverdale
Perez, Primitivo, Ocala, FL (Unassigned)
Peters, John, St. Joseph, Kingston
Pietkiewicz, Karl J., St. Mary of the Snow, Saugerties
Pino, Joseph, St. Jean Baptiste, Manhattan
Pino, Victor M., (Leave of Absence)
Pipher, Jesse E., Our Lady Queen of Martyrs, Sarasota, FL
Porcel, Carlos M., (Medical Leave)
Porcelli, Vincent, St. Mary, Marlboro, NY
Portalatin, Epimegnio, Blessed Sacrament, Bronx
Powers, John, St. John the Evangelist, Manhattan
Powers, William, (Leave of Absence)
Quigley, Donald M., St. Margaret of Cortona, Bronx
Radcliffe, Kenneth L., Resurrection, Central Harlem
Radzilowicz, John, St. Casimir, Yonkers
Ramos, Alfonso, Sacred Heart, Bronx
Ramos, Edmundo A., St. Patrick's Cathedral, Manhattan
Ramos, Epifanio, Puerto Rico
Ramos, Rafael, Puerto Rico
Rausch, Paul A., St. Thomas Aquinas, Forestburg
Reilly, John P., St. Columba, Hopewell Junction
Rentkowski, Joseph, St. Adalbert, Staten Island
Repke, John W., St. Mary, Marlboro
Repke, Robert, St. Peter's, Rosendale
Rescildo, Ralph J., Southbury, CT
Rettino, P. Robert, Lord's Valley, PA (Medical Leave)
Reynolds, Peter E., St. Columba, Chester
Riley, John M., St. Peter, Liberty
Rivera, Andrew A., St. John, Bronx
Rivera, José A., Aquas Buenas, Puerto Rico
Rizzo, Charles A., Blessed Sacrament, New Rochelle
Rodgers, James, Richmond, VA
Rodriguez, Arnaldo, Nativity, Manhattan
Rodriguez, Cristobal, Immaculate Conception, Bronx
Rodriguez, Hector R., St. Patrick's Old Cathedral
Rodriguez, Porfirio, St. Jude, Manhattan
Rodríguez, Jacinto, San Antonio, Guayama, PR
Romagosa, Guillermo P., (Medical Leave)
Rosado, Alejandro, St. Athanasius, Bronx
Rosado, Odalis R., (Leave of Absence)
Rosado, Reynaldo, St. Dominic, Bronx
Rosado, Ricardo, Broward, FL
Rush, James J., Harrisburg, PA
Russell, Franklyn R., St. Patrick, Newburgh
Russo, Richard J., St. Jean Baptist, Manhattan
Sadowski, John, Immaculate Conception, Stony Point
Sakowicz, Albert, Albany, NY
Salamone, Victor A., St. Martin de Porres, Poughkeepsie
Salhany, Richard, Our Lady Help of Christians, Staten Island
Salomone, Ernest F., Immaculate Heart of Mary, Scarsdale
Sanchez, Carlos, Our Lady of Angels, Bronx
Sanchez, Oscar, Puerto Rico
Sandoval, Waldemar, St. Paul the Apostle, Manhattan
Santiago, Abraham, St. Joseph, Yonkers
Santore, Louis, St. Patrick, Bedford
Scarfi, John, St. John the Evangelist, Mahopac
Schimpf, Robert, St. Joseph, Bronxville
Schlitt, Ronald, St. Christopher, Buchanan
Scott, John, St. Benedict, Bronx, NY
Sepulveda, Miguel A., Puerto Rico
Sequeira, Ronald, O.L. of Refuge, Bronx
Serrano, Jose I., St. Jude, Marion Oaks, FL
Seymour, John L., St. Mary, Newburgh
Shea, John, SS. John and Paul, Larchmont
Shiel, Thomas P., Palm Harbor, FL
Shkreli, Mark, St. Lawrence O'Toole, Brewster
Sica, Generoso, St. Joseph, Croton Falls
Sin-Garciga, Felipe, St. Angela Merici, Bronx
Singler, John A., Our Lady Help of Christians, Staten Island
Slominski, Timothy, St. Augustine, Ossining
Smith, Henry, St. Mary of the Snow, Saugerties
So, Patrick, St. Teresa, Manhattan
Solanto, Joseph P., (Leave of Absence)
Stafford, William, St. Thomas of Canterbury, Cornwall on Hudson, NY
Stahlnecker, James J., St. Mary of the Assumption, Staten Island
Steup, Fredrick C., St. Patrick, Newburgh
Stewart, George, Jay, NY
Suarez, Israel, Guaynabo, Puerto Rico
Sullivan, John D., Lady Lake, FL
Sullivan, John M., (Medical Leave)
Sweeney, Walter F., Sacred Heart of Jesus, Boulder, CO
Tayco, Renato, (Medical Leave)
Taylor, Victor, Atlanta, Georgia
Teng, Rudolph, St. Paul the Apostle, Yonkers
Testa, Warren, St. Columba, Hopewell Junction
Then, Rafael, Good Shepherd, Manhattan
Thompson, Alfred, Holy Child, Staten Island
Tirella, Rosario J., Holy Rosary, Staten Island
Tobin, William D., (Medical Leave)
Tobon, Stephen, St. Charles Borromeo, Staten Island
Topple, Edwin R., St. John the Evangelist, Saugerties
Torres, Luis A., Mayaguez, Puerto Rico
Torres, Luis J., St. Pius V., Bronx
Tortorella, Thomas, St. Clare of Assisi, Bronx
Tosi, Victor, Immaculate Conception, Bronx
Trapani, Richard, St. Joseph, Middletown, NY
Trees, Donald F., St. Mary of the Snow, Saugerties
Treiling, John F., St. Lawrence O'Toole, Brewster
Troy, Patrick D., Sacred Heart, Dobbs Ferry
Vaccaro, William N., Our Lady of the Rosary, Port Chester
Valdez, Bienvenido, Our Lady Queen of Martyrs, Manhattan
Vargas, Thomas A., (Leave of Absence)
Vasquez, Domingo, Davie, FL
Vazquez, Fernando, St. Athanasius, Bronx
Vazquez, Juan F., St. Anthony, Bronx
Velez, Randy, Cooperstown, NY
Venditto, Michael, Our Lady of Pity, Staten Island
Venezia, Ignatius, St. Boniface, Wesley Hills
Verboys, Joseph, St. John of the Cross, Vero Beach, FL
Villanueva, Engracio G., St. Joseph-St. Thomas, Staten Island
Viola, Anthony, Immaculate Conception & Assumption, Tuckahoe
Weinstein, David, Immaculate Conception, Amenia
Weir, John E., (Medical Leave)
Weireter, Paul J., St. Patrick, Highland Mills
Weiss, Robert W., Coatesville, PA
Wengeroth, Edward, (Medical Leave)
White, Dennis, St. Patrick, Newburgh
Whiteman, Robert, J.D., Ed.D., (Leave of Absence)
Wilson, Michael, St. Elizabeth Ann Seton, Shrub Oak, NY
Winrow, Robert P., St. Joseph, Kingston
Witt, Joseph A., Sacred Heart, Suffern
Woods, Edward J., Our Lady of Mt. Carmel, Middletown
Zambrana, Wallace, Our Lady of Sorrows, Manhattan
Zatarga, Michael, St. Joan of Arc, Boca Raton, FL

INSTITUTIONS LOCATED IN THE ARCHDIOCESE

[A] SEMINARIES, ARCHDIOCESAN

YONKERS. *Cathedral Prep Program* (1963) 201 Seminary Ave., 10704. Tel: 914-968-1340; Fax: 914-968-6671. Email: cprep@dunwoodie.edu. Web: www.cathedralprep.com. Revs. Luke M. Sweeney, S.T.L., Dir. of Vocations; Luis F. Saldana, S.T.D (Cand.), Asst. Vocation Dir. Hispanic Vocations; Andrew King, S.T.D. (Cand.).

St. Joseph's Seminary (1896) Archdiocesan Major Seminary, 201 Seminary Ave., 10704-1896. Tel: 914-968-6200; Fax: 914-376-2019. Email: sjs@archny.org. Web: www.ny-archdiocese.org/pastoral/seminary.cfm. Most Rev. Gerald T. Walsh, M.S.W., D.D., Rector; Revs. Joseph Henchey, C.S.S., Spiritual Dir.; Andrew King, S.T.D. (Cand.), Dean of Students & Admissions; Kevin O'Reilly, S.T.D., Academic Dean; Luke M. Sweeney, S.T.L., Vocation Dir.; Charles S. Szivos, M.Div., Spiritual Dir.; Thomas V. Berg, Ph.D., Faculty Sec. Non-Resident Faculty: Priests 15; Sisters 4; Lay Teachers 7; Students 51.

Non-Resident Faculty: Rev. Msgrs. Joseph R. Giandurco, J.C.D.; Michael F. Hull, S.T.D.; John A. Radano, Ph.D.; Revs. Andrew D. Apostoli, C.F.R., M.S.; Solanus Benfatti, C.F.R., S.T.L.; John S. Bonnici, S.T.D.; Peter Dugandzic; Benedict Joseph Groeschel, C.F.R., Ed.D.; Joseph W. Koterski, S.J.; Joseph T. Lienhard, S.J., Dr. Theol. Habil.; Very Rev. Michael T. Martine, J.C.L.; Revs. John O'Neill, Ph.D.; Gerard F. Rafferty, S.S.L., Dir., Assessment; Luis F. Saldana, S.T.D (Cand.); Timothy J. Scannell, Ph.D.; Dr. John Tricamo, Ph.D.; Dr. Stephen Buglione, Ph.D., Psychologist; Dr. Richard Gallagher, M.D., Psychiatrist; Dr. Enrique Aquilar, S.S.D.; Patrick McNamara, Ph.D.; Sisters Janet Baxendale, S.C., M.A.; Marie Pappas, C.R., Ph.D. (Cand); Monica Wood, S.C., M.A., M.L.S., Dir. Library Svcs.; Mary Frances Mills, O.S.F., M.S., Registrar; Ms. Marie Dundon, M.A.; Ms. Jennifer Pascual, D.M.A., Dir. Music.

[B] SEMINARIES, RELIGIOUS OR SCHOLASTICATES

BEACON. *St. Lawrence of Brindisi Friary, Province of the Stigmata of St. Francis*, 180 Sargent Ave., 12508-3993. Tel: 845-831-0394; 845-838-0759 (Infirmary); Fax: 845-831-0918; 845-838-1352 (Infirmary). Rev. Jude Duffy, O.F.M.Cap., Vicar; Bro. Julius Tkaczyk, O.F.M.Cap.; Revs. Achilles Cassieri, O.F.M.Cap., Guardian; Sylvester Catallo, O.F.M.Cap.; Luke Guastella, O.F.M.Cap. (Friary and Infirmary) Priests 6; Brothers 2.

BRONX. *Ciszek Hall* Residence for Jesuit Scholastics and Brothers engaged in Philosophy and Theology Studies at Fordham University., 2502 Belmont Ave., 10458-6282. Tel: 347-329-5857; Fax: 718-365-3166. Revs. Joseph C. Sands, S.J., Rector; Richard Zanoni, S.J., Asst. Rector. Priests 3; Brothers 1. In Res. Rev. Daniel J. Fitzpatrick, S.J.

STATEN ISLAND. *Society of St. Paul*, 2187 Victory Blvd., 10314. Tel: 718-761-0047; Fax: 718-761-0057. Email: provincialoffice@stpauls.us. Web: www.stpauls.us. Bros. Kevin J. Cahill, S.S.P., Book Store Coord.; Lawrence H. Schubert, S.S.P., Bursar's Office; Revs. Edmund C. Lane, S.S.P., Editor-in-Chief; Ernesto Tigreros, S.S.P.; Bros. Edward Donaher, S.S.P., Art Dir.; Robert Konrad, S.S.P., Mktg.; Peter Lyne, S.S.P., Mktg.; Joseph Dubois, S.S.P., Mailing; Vincent Minj, S.S.P., Parish Exhibits; Benedict Santoro, S.S.P.; Rev. Matthew Roehrig, S.S.P., Dir. Mktg.; Bros. Richard Brunner, S.S.P., Personnel Delegate, Supr. Gen.; Emmanuel Cana, S.S.P., Bookstore Dir.; Rev. Arthur Palisada, S.S.P., Translator; Bros. Frank Sadowski, S.S.P., Editorial Office; Joshua Seidl, S.S.P., Parish Exhibits; Revs. Arcangel Cardenas, S.S.P., Spanish Apostolate; Juan Huerta, S.S.P., Spanish Apostolate; Sebastian Lee, S.S.P., Korean Apostolate; Bro. Gerard Roche, S.S.P. Priests 7; Brothers 14.

SUFFERN. *Tagaste Monastery* Major Seminary of the Province of St. Augustine of the Augustinian Recollect Fathers & Brothers. , 220 Lafayette Ave., 10901. Tel: 845-357-0067; Fax: 845-369-0625. Email: tagaste@optonline.net. Web: www.tagastemonastery.org. Revs. Ramon Gaitan, O.A.R., Prior; Frank T. Wilder, O.A.R., Prior; John Oldfield, O.A.R., Vice Prior; Frederic Abiera, O.A.R., Prefect of Students; Marlon Beof, O.A.R., Prefect of Students; John Gruben, O.A.R., Novice Master; Bros. Eric Crelencia, O.A.R.; Joseph Joly, O.A.R.; Jorge Valdevia, O.A.R.; Deacon Ramiro Munoz, O.A.R. Priests 4; Brothers 3; Simple Professed 2.

[C] COLLEGES AND UNIVERSITIES

NEW YORK. *College of Mount Saint Vincent* (Coed); Founded by the Sisters of Charity of Saint Vincent de Paul. Chartered by the University of the State of New York., 6301 Riverdale Ave., 10471-1093. Tel: 718-405-3200; Fax: 718-549-2603. Email: carol.finegan@mountsaintvincent.edu. Web: www.mountsaintvincent.edu. Charles L. Flynn Jr., Ph.D., Pres.; Paul Dovillard, Ph.D., Dean, Undergraduate College; Madeline Melkonian, Vice Pres. Institutional Advancement and College Relations; Dr. Guy Lometti, Provost; Sebastian Derry, Dir. Library. Sisters 3; Lay Faculty 72; Total Enrollment 2,100.

Marymount Manhattan College Chartered by the Univ. of the State of NY., 221 E. 71st St., 10021. Tel: 212-517-0400. Email: vdorgan@mmm.edu. Web: www.mmm.edu. Dr. Judson Shaver, Pres.; Dawn Webber, Vice Pres. Academic Affairs; Christy Gaiti, Vice Pres. Student Affairs (Acting); Paul Ciraulo, Vice Pres. Business & Financial Affairs; Mary Kay Demetry-Jeynes, Dean Courses for Adults; Jeanne Evans, Dir. College Rels. & Institutional Advancement; Sr. Virginia Dorgan,

R.S.H.M., Campus Min. Sisters 3; Students 2,330.

BRONX. **Fordham University* (1841) Second campus and Branch campus at Lincoln Center, New York, NY 10023 and 400 Westchester Ave., West Harrison, NY 10528. Chartered by the Legislature of the State of New York., 441 E. Fordham Rd., 10458. Tel: 718-817-3040; Fax: 718-817-3050. Web: www.fordham.edu. Rev. Joseph M. McShane, S.J., Pres.; Mr. John J. Lordan, Senior Vice Pres., CFO & Treas.; Dr. Stephen Freedman, Provost; Roger Milici, Vice Pres. Devel. & Univ. Rels.; Rev. Msgr. Joseph Quinn, Vice Pres. Mission & Min.; Mr. Frank Simio, Vice Pres. Finance; Dr. Frank J. Sirianni, Vice Pres. Information Technology; Mr. Jeffrey L. Gray, Vice Pres. Students Affairs; Dr. Brian Byrne, Vice Pres. Lincoln Center; Dr. Peter Stace, Vice Pres. for Enrollment; Mr. Marco Valera, Vice Pres. Facilities Mgmt.; John P. Harrington, Dean, Arts & Sciences Faculty; Dr. Nancy Busch, Dean, Graduate School of Arts & Sciences; Dr. Michael Latham, Dean, Fordham College at Rose Hill; Dr. Donna Rapaccioli, Dean, Gabelli Sch., Business; Dr. David Gautschi, Dean, Graduate School Business Admin.; Dr. James Hennessy, Dean, Graduate School Educ.; Michael M. Martin, J.D., Dean, School of Law; Dr. Peter B. Vaughan, Dean, Graduate School of Social Svc.; Rev. Robert R. Grimes, S.J., Dean, Fordham College at Lincoln Center; Dr. Isabelle Frank, Dean, Fordham Sch. Continuing & Professional Studies; John P. Harrington, Interim Dean, Graduate School of Religion & Religious Educ.; Mr. Thomas A. Dunne, Vice Pres. Admin. Priests 44; Sisters 8; Total Staff 3,034; Total Enrollment 15,158.

Manhattan College (1853) 4513 Manhattan College Pkwy., Riverdale, 10471. Tel: 718-862-7200; 800-622-9235; Fax: 718-862-8019. Email: admit@manhattan.edu. Web: www.manhattan.edu. Dr. Brennan O'Donnell, Pres. Priests 1; Brothers 6; Sisters 3; Lay Staff 202; Administrators 190; Lay 186; Total Enrollment 3,657.

NEW ROCHELLE. **The College of New Rochelle* (1904) Founded in 1904 by the Religious of the Order of St. Ursula. Chartered by the Regents of the University of the State of New York. The College is composed of four schools: School of Arts and Sciences (Women); Graduate School; School of New Resources; School of Nursing (Coed)., 29 Castle Pl., 10805. Tel: 914-654-5000; Fax: 914-654-5980. Email: info@cnr.edu. Web: www.cnr.edu. Judith A. Huntington, Pres.; Dr. Joan Bailey, Vice Pres., Mission & Identity; Dr. Ellen Curry Damato, Exec. Vice Pres.; Dr. Dorothy Escribano, Senior Vice Pres. Academic Affairs; Dr. Richard Thompson, Ph.D., Dean School of Arts & Sciences; Dr. Marie Ribarich, Dean, Graduate School; Dr. Mary Alice Donius, Dean School of Nursing; Ms. Elza Dinwiddie-Boyd, Dean of School of New Resources; Keith Borge, Vice Pres. Financial Affairs; Dr. Colette Geary, Vice Pres. Student Svcs.; Rev. J. Joseph Flynn, O.F.M.Cap., Chap.; Ana Fontura, Dean, Gill Library; Helen Wolf, Dir. Campus Ministry. Priests 1; Sisters 5; Total Faculty & Staff 438; Students 4,702.

Iona College (Coed); Education in the tradition of the Christian Brothers. Independent College, 715 North Ave., 10801. Tel: 914-633-2000; Fax: 914-633-2018. Email: webmaster@iona.edu. Web: www.iona.edu. Priests 1; Brothers 10; Sisters 4; Lay Teachers 529; Students 4,065.

Iona College Rockland Graduate Center, 2 Blue Hill Plaza-Concourse Level, P.O. Box 1522, Pearl River, 10965-8522. Tel: 845-620-1350; Fax: 845-620-1260. Joseph E. Nyre, Ph.D., Pres.; Dr. Brian Nickerson, Vice Pres. for Academic Affairs & Interim Provost; Mr. Jonathan C. Ivec, Vice Pres. Finance & Admin.; Mr. Charles Carlson, Vice Provost for Student Devel.; Marilyn Wilkie, Acting Vice Pres. Advancement & External Affairs; Dr. Jeanne Zaino, Interim Dean of School of Arts & Sciences; Dr. Vincent Calluzzo, Dean, Hagan School of Business; Mr. Richard Palladino, Dir. Libraries.

NEWBURGH. *Mt. St. Mary College* (1954) (Coed), 330 Powell Ave., 12550. Tel: 845-561-0800; Fax: 845-569-3416. Email: williams@msmc.edu. Web: www.msmc.edu. Rev. Kevin Mackin, O.F.M., Pres.; Dr. Iris Turkenkopf, Ph.D., Vice Pres. of Academic Affairs; Darlene Benzenberg, Registrar; Rev. Francis Amodio, O.Carm., Chap. & Dir. Campus Min.; Barbara Pertuzzelli, Library Dir. Divisions: Arts & Letters; Education; Business; Nursing; Natural Sciences; Mathematics & Information Technology; Philosophy & Religious Studies; Social Sciences. Sisters 3; Lay Teachers 82; Students 3,152.

ORANGEBURG. *Dominican College* (1952) Chartered by University of the State of New York., 470 Western Hwy., 10962. Tel: 845-848-7800; Fax: 845-359-2313. Email: admissions@dc.edu. Web: www.dc.edu. Sisters Mary Eileen O'Brien, O.P., Ph.D., Pres.; Kathleen Sullivan, O.P., Chancellor; Dr. Thomas Nowak, Vice Pres. Academic Affairs & Academic Dean; John Burke, Vice Pres. Student Devel. & Dean of Students; Anthony Cipolla, Vice Pres. Financial Affairs & Chief Fiscal Officer; Dorothy Filoramo, Vice Pres. Institutional Advancement; Brian Fernandes, Vice Pres. Enrollment Mgmt.; Mary McFadden, Registrar; Dr. William Stagmeyer, Institutional Research; Mr. Joseph Clinton, Athletics; Sr. Barbara McEneany, O.P., Campus Min.; Mr. John Barrie, M.A., M.L.S., Librarian. Sisters 11; Lay Teachers 73; Students 2,058.

Divisions: Dr. Sandra Countee, Allied Health; Dr. Mark Meachem, C.D.R., Arts & Sciences; Dr. Clare Pennino, Business Admin.; Dr. Nancy Di Dona, Nursing; Dr. Barbara Socor, Social Sciences; Dr. Roger Tesi, Educ. Teacher; Rev. Ronald Stanley, O.P., Chap.

SPARKILL. *St. Thomas Aquinas College* 10976. Tel: 845-398-4000; Fax: 845-359-8136. Web: www.stac.edu. Sr. Margaret M. Fitzpatrick, S.C., Ed.D., Pres.; Dr. L. John Duvney, Vice Pres. Academic Affairs. Founded by Dominican Sisters of Sparkill in 1952. Senior coed college, chartered by Univ. of the State of New York. Sisters 2; Lay Professors 65; Students 2,700.

STATEN ISLAND. *St. John's University Staten Island Campus*, 300 Howard Ave., 10301. Tel: 718-390-4545; Fax: 718-390-4520. Web: www.stjohns.edu. Very Rev. Donald J. Harrington, C.M., Pres.; Rev. Patrick J. Griffin, C.M., Exec. Vice Pres. Mission; Dr. Jerrold Ross, Academic Vice Pres. & Dean; Donna Narducci, Assoc. Dean & Dir. Peter J. Tobin College of Business; James O'Keefe, Assoc. Dean College of Professional Studies; Stephen Kuntz, Assoc. Dean, School of Education, Graduate Div.; Kimberly Palmieri, Asst. Dean, Office of Student Affairs; Kelly Rocca, Assoc. Dean, St. John's College; Mark Meng, Librarian. Vincentian Community. Students 2,215.

VALHALLA. **New York Medical College, Administration Bldg.*, 40 Sunshine Cottage Rd., 10595. Tel: 914-594-4600. Web: www.nymc.edu.

[D] DEPARTMENT OF EDUCATION

NEW YORK. *Department of Education, Superintendent of Schools Office*, 1011 First Ave., 10022. Tel: 212-371-1000, Ext. 2800; Fax: 212-758-3018. Email: dr.timothy.mcniff@archny.org. Web: www.nycatholicschools.org. Dr. Timothy J. McNiff, Supt. Schools; Mrs. Doreen DePaolis, Office Mgr.; Ms. Mary Kate Blaine, Chief, Staff.

Office of Finance Tel: 212-371-1011, Ext. 2819; Fax: 212-758-3018. Mr. John Coyne, Exec. Dir.

Vocations Office, 1011 First Ave., 10022. Tel: 212-371-1011, Ext. 2803; Fax: 212-758-3018. Sr. Deanna Sabetta, C.N.D., Vocations Dir. for Rel. Life.

University Apostolate -Campus Ministry, St. Joseph Seminary, 201 Seminary Ave., Yonkers, 10704. Tel: 914-968-6200, Ext. 8252. Rev. Daniel O'Reilly, M.A., Dir.

Associate Superintendents: Sr. Anne Massell, P.B.V.M., Assoc. Supt. Personnel; Mr. Philip Gorrasi, Assoc. Supt. Mission Effectiveness; Ms. Kathleen Curatolo, Assoc. Supt. Professional Recruitment; Mrs. Fran Davies, Assoc. Supt. Communications & Mktg.; Mr. Michael Deegan, Assoc. Supt. Urban Education; Ms. Joanne DeMizio, Assoc. Supt. Curriculum & Staff Devel.; Mr. Ray Vitiello, Assoc. Supt. Public Policy & Student Svcs.; Dr. Joseph Gerics, Assoc. Supt. Secondary Educ.

Assistant Superintendents: Mrs. Madeline Mitrevski, Asst. Supt. Student Information Svcs.

Directors: Sr. Alice Kirk, O.P., Dir., Technology Staff Devel.; Mr. David DiCerto, Asst. Dir. Student Recruitment; Ms. Lucia DiJusto, C.F.P., Admin. Asst.; Mrs. Oneeka Jordan, SIS Helpdesk; Mrs. Connie McCroy, Early Childhood Educ.; Mrs. Eileen Murtha, Special Educ.; Mrs. Lisette Robustelli, Religious Educ.; Ms. Lillian Valentin, Data Collections; Dr. Raymond Cummings Jr., Curriculum Devel. & Assessment.

District Superintendents: Mrs. Roseann Carotenuto, District Supt., Bronx; Mrs. Zoilita Herrera, District Supt., Staten Island; Mrs. Mary Jane Daley, District Supt., Rockland, Orange, Sullivan, Dutchess, & Ulster; Sr. June Clare Tracy, O.P., Ph.D., District Supt., Manhattan; Mr. Philip Gorrasi, District Supt., Westchester/Putnam.

Archdiocesan Drug Abuse Prevention Program, 2789 Schurz Ave., 10465. Tel: 718-904-1333; Fax: 718-823-2177. Mrs. Frances Maturo, Dir.

Mother Francisska Elementary School, 850 Hylan Blvd., Staten Island, 10304. Tel: 718-447-1750; Fax: 718-447-8022. Patricia Cirbos, Education Supvr.

John Cardinal O'Connor School, 16 N. Broadway, Irvington, 10533. Tel: 914-591-9330; Fax: 914-231-7688. Mrs. Donna Taylor, Education Dir.

Joan Ann Kennedy Memorial Preschool, 26 Sharpe Ave., Staten Island, 10302. Tel: 718-876-0939; Fax: 718-816-6507. Dr. Kathryn Meyer, Education Dir.

The Therese Program for Children on the Autistic Spectrum

Bishop Patrick V. Ahern High School, 315 Arlene St., Staten Island, 10314. Tel: 718-982-5084; Fax: 718-982-5114. Ms. Diane Cunningham, Exec. Dir.

Family Life/Respect Life Office, 1011 First Ave., 10022. Tel: 212-371-1000, Ext. 3185; Fax: 212-371-3382. Sr. Mary Elizabeth, S.J., Dir.

Archdiocesan Catechetical Office, 1011 First Ave., 10022. Tel: 212-371-1000, Ext. 2849; Fax: 212-980-1035. Sr. Joan Curtin, C.N.D., Archdiocesan Dir.; Ms. Ivelisse Sanchez, Asst. to Dir. Tel: 212-371-1000, Ext. 2859; Mrs. Nancy Doran, Dir. Catechist Formation. Tel: 212-371-1000, Ext. 2867; Sr. Teresita Morse, R.J.M., Dir. Formation of Catechetical Leaders. Tel: 212-371-1000, Ext. 2858; Mr. Oscar Cruz, Dir. Catechumenate/Family Catechesis/Formation, Adult Catechesis Leaders. Tel: 212-371-1000, Ext. 2851; Mrs. Kathleen Alonzo, Consultant. Tel: 212-371-1000, Ext. 2864; Mr. John Edward, Consultant. Tel: 212-371-1000, Ext. 2986; Mrs. Linda Sgammato, Dir. Special & Early Childhood Rel. Educ. Tel: 212-371-1000, Ext. 2852; Ms. Maureen McKew, Dir. Communications. Tel: 212-371-1000, Ext. 2855; Miss Ann Kearney, Financial Advisor. Tel: 212-371-1000, Ext. 2857; Ms. Anne Malloy, Dir. New York Catholic Bible School. Tel: 212-371-1000, Ext. 2831; Mrs. Linda De Markey, Registrar: New York Catholic Bible School. Tel: 212-371-1000, Ext. 2860; Ms. Cynthia Martinez, Dir. Formation Catholic Youth Ministers/Adolescent Catechesis. Tel: 212-371-1000, Ext. 2831; Mr. James Connell, Webmaster. Tel: 212-371-1000, Ext. 2808.

Child Nutrition and School Management Service, 1011 First Ave., 10128. Tel: 212-371-1000, Ext. 2760; Fax: 212-421-3760. Mr. Edward Albano, Child Nutrition Dir.

Catechetical Regional Offices

Bronx, 4505 Richardson Ave., Bronx, 10470. Tel: 718-547-4212; Fax: 718-547-4231. Ms. Jeannette Chishibanji, Regional Director, Bronx.

Manhattan, c/o Mother Cabrini High School, 701 Fort Washington Ave., 10040. Tel: 212-923-0950; Fax: 212-543-3190. Sr. Catherine Ryan, F.S.P., Regional Dir., Manhattan.

Staten Island, 203 Sand Ln., Staten Island, 10305. Tel: 718-273-3833; Fax: 718-273-9602. Sr. Mary Crucifix Pandullo, C.S.J.B., Regional Director, Staten Island.

Dutchess/Ulster Counties, 26 S. Hamilton Ave., Poughkeepsie, 12601-2599. Tel: 845-471-5427; Fax: 845-471-5427. Mrs. Linda Fitzsimmons, Regional Dir., Dutchess/Ulster.

Central & Southern Westchester/Yonkers, 56 Dunston Ave., Yonkers, 10701. Tel: 914-965-0490; Fax: 914-965-0896. Sr. Zelide M. Ceccagno, M.S.C.S., Regional Dir, Yonkers, SCW & Adult Media Library.

Orange/Sullivan Counties, 19 Glenmere Rd., Florida, 10921. Tel: 845-728-0495; Fax: 845-728-0495.

Blessed Kateri Tekakwitha Center, P.O. Box 1011, Liberty, 12754. Tel: 845-292-9100; Fax: 845-292-9100. Sr. Kevin John Shields, O.P., Regional Dir., Orange/Sullivan Counties.

Rockland/Northern Westchester/Putnam Counties, 24 E. Main St., Stony Point, 10980. Tel: 845-429-4297; Fax: 845-429-4163. Mrs. Peg Hoblin, Regl. Dir., No. Westchester/Putnam/Rockland Counties. Tel: 845-624-3190 (Westchester/Putnam); Fax: 845-624-3190; Sr. Anne Ryan, P.B.V.M., Consultant. Tel: 845-534-3755.

Center for Spiritual Development, 96 Milton Rd., Rye, 10580. Tel: 914-967-7328; Fax: 914-967-7387. Anne Marie Wallace, Ph.D., Dir.

Instructional Television Tel: 914-968-7800; Fax: 914-968-2075. Mr. Michael Lavery, Admin. Dir.

215 Seminary Ave., Yonkers, 10704. Elementary School: Full-Time Sisters 142; Part-Time Sisters 51; Full-Time Brothers 10; Part-Time Brothers 1; Full-Time Order Priests 2; Part-Time Order Priests 3; Full-Time Lay Teachers 3,870; Part-Time Lay Teachers 988; Total Parish Enrollment 76,387; Total Inter-Parish Enrollment 1,709; Total Private Enrollment 4,250; High School: Full-Time Sisters 86; Part-Time Sisters 39; Full-Time Brothers 37; Part-Time Brothers 5; Full-Time Order Priests 27; Part-Time Order Priests 4; Full-Time Diocesan Priests 26; Full-Time Lay Teachers 2,304; Part-Time Lay Teachers 191; Total Diocesan Enrollment 10,588; Parish Enrollment 4,664; Private Enrollment 12,359.

[E] HIGH SCHOOLS

NEW YORK. *St. Agnes Boys High School*, 555 West End Ave., 10024-2795. Tel: 212-873-9100; Fax: 212-873-9292. Email: agneshs@adnyeducation.org. Web: www.staghs.org. Robert J. Conte, Prin. Lay Teachers 18; Total Enrollment 251.

All Hallows Institute aka All Hallows High School

(1909) (Boys), 111 E. 164th St., Bronx, 10452. Tel: 718-293-4545; Fax: 718-410-8298. Email: hallows@adnyeducation.org. Web: www.allhallows.org. Mr. Sean J. Sullivan, Prin.; Mr. Paul Krebbs, Pres. Congregation of Christian Sisters & Brothers 6; Lay Teachers 34; Students 663.

Aquinas High School (Girls), 685 E. 182nd St., Bronx, 10457. Tel: 718-367-2113; Fax: 718-295-5864. Email: aquinashs@adnyeducation.org. Web: www.aquinashs.org. Sisters Margaret Ryan, O.P., Pres.; Catherine Rose Quigley, O.P., Prin.; Celine Geiger, Librarian. Sisters 10; Lay Teachers 40; Students 613.

Cathedral High School (Girls), 350 E. 56th St., 10022. Tel: 212-688-1545; Fax: 212-754-2024. Email: mspagnolo@cathedralhs.org. Web: www.cathedralhs.org. Ms. Maria Spagnuolo, Prin.; Rev. Robert J. Poveromo, Chm. Religion Dept.; Mrs. Rosemary Eivers, Asst. Prin. Priests 1; Sisters 5; Lay Teachers 38; Students 565.

Convent of the Sacred Heart (Girls), One E. 91st St., 10128-0689. Tel: 212-722-4745; Fax: 212-996-1784. Email: coshhs@adnyeducation.org. Web: www.cshnyc.org. Dr. Joseph J. Ciancaglini, Head of School. Religious of the Sacred Heart. Sisters 2; Faculty 57; High School Students 200.

Cristo Rey New York High School, Inc. (2004) 112 E. 106th St., 10029. Tel: 212-996-7000; Fax: 212-427-7444. Web: www.cristoreyny.org. Rev. Joseph P. Parkes, S.J., Pres.; William P. Ford III, Prin.; Brian Heese, Dir. Corp. Work Study Prog. Sisters 2; Jesuit 1; Lay Teachers 18; Students 363.

**Cristo Rey New York High School, Inc.*, 112 E. 106th St., 10029. Tel: 212-996-7000; Fax: 212-427-7444. Email: cristorey@adnyeducation.org. Web: www.cristoreyny.org. Rev. Joseph P. Parkes, S.J., Pres.; William P. Ford III, Prin. Sisters 2; Jesuits 1; Lay Teachers 18; Students 363.

Dominican Academy (Girls), 44 E. 68th St., 10065. Tel: 212-744-0195; Fax: 212-744-0375. Email: dominica@adnyeducation.org. Web: www.dominicanacademy.org. Sisters Barbara Kane, O.P., Prin.; Geraldine Milbert, O.P., Librarian. Dominican Sisters 4; Lay Teachers 22; Students 223.

La Salle Academy (Boys), 44 E. Second St., 10003. Tel: 212-475-8940; Fax: 212-529-3598. Email: lasalle@adnyeducation.org. Web: www.lasalleacademy.org. Dr. William B. Hambleton, Pres.; Bros. James Furlong, F.S.C.; Timothy Jones, F.S.C.; Dr. William Macatee, Prin.; Ms. Patricia Toney, Librarian. Brothers of The Christian Schools. Brothers 5; Lay Teachers 35; Students 336.

In Res. Bros. John Bassett, F.S.C.; Raymond Buck, F.S.C., (Retired); Stephen Caplice, F.S.C., (Retired); Leonard Wojtanowski, C.F.X.

Loyola School (Coed), 980 Park Ave., 10028. Tel: 212-288-3522; Fax: 212-861-1021. Email: loyola@adnyeducation.org. Web: www.loyola-nyc.org. Mr. James F. X. Lyness, Headmaster; Mr. Robert Sheehy, Bd. Chm.; Tony Oroszlany, Pres.; Revs. James J. Curry, S.J.; Michael E. Sehler, S.J. Society of Jesus. Priests 2; Lay Teachers 26; Students 204.

Mother Cabrini High School (1899) (Girls), 701 Ft. Washington Ave., 10040. Tel: 212-923-3540; Fax: 212-781-2051. Email: info@cabrinihs.org. Web: www.cabrinihs.com. Mr. Bruce Segall, Pres.; Ms. Kerry Schmid, Prin.; Mr. Matthew Bizzaro, Campus Min.; Mike Radice, Dir. Advancement; Mr. Daniel Gabriele, Librarian; Angelica Bernier, Dir., Enrollment. Brothers 1; Sisters 2; Lay Teachers 19; Students 307.

Notre Dame School of Manhattan (1912) (Girls), 327 W. 13th St., 10014. Tel: 212-620-5575; Fax: 212-620-0432. Email: ntdamehs@adnyeducation.org. Web: www.cheznous.org. Ms. Jaclyn Brilliant, Prin.; Dr. Virginia O'Brien, Pres.; Ms. Andrea Catenaccio, Librarian. Sisters 5; Lay Teachers 18; Students 310.

Regis High School (1914) (Boys), 55 E. 84th St., 10028. Tel: 212-288-1100; Fax: 212-794-1221. Email: pjudge@regis-nyc.org. Web: www.regis-nyc.org. Rev. Philip G. Judge, S.J., Pres.; Dr. Gary J. Tocchet, Prin.; Ms. Kristin Ross, Asst. Prin.; Mr. Nicholas de Spoelberch, Dean of Students; Revs. Anthony Andreassi, C.O.; Arthur C. Bender, S.J.; James P. Croghan, S.J. Society of Jesus. Priests 4; Lay Teachers 60; Students 530.

Res.: 53 E. 83rd St., 10028.

Rice High School (Boys), 74 W. 124th St., 10027. Tel: 914-636-6194; Fax: 914-636-0021. Email: ricehs@adnyeducation.org. Web: www.ricehs.org. Sr. Patricia J. Ells, C.N.D., Head of School. Congregation of Christian Brothers. Brothers 5; Lay Teachers 25; Students 259.

Xavier High School (Boys), 30 W. 16th St., 10011. Tel: 212-924-7900; Fax: 212-924-0303. Web: www.xavierhs.org. Mr. John R. Raslowsky, Pres.; Mr. Michael Livigni, Headmaster; Mr. Luciano Lovallo, Dean Academics & Asst. Prin.; Miss Janet Bonica, Registrar; Revs. James R. Van Dyke, S.J., Faculty Chap.; Ralph Rivera, S.J., Campus Min.; Dennis Baker, S.J., Teacher History Dept.; Louis Garaventa, S.J., History Dept.; Tracy Tong, Librarian; Brian McCabe, Dean of Students. Society of Jesus., (See listing for Xavier Jesuit Community for additional names of priests and brothers.) Priests 5; Jesuit Scholastics 1; Lay Teachers 74; Students 1,021.

BARDONIA. *Albertus Magnus*, 798 Rte. 304, 10954. Tel: 845-623-8842; Fax: 845-623-0009. Email: albertus@adnyeducation.org. Web: www.albertusmagnus.net. Joseph Troy, Pres. & Prin. Sisters of St. Dominic (Sparkill) 5; Lay Teachers 39; Students 476.

BRONX. *Academy of Mount St. Ursula* (1855) (Girls), 330 Bedford Park Blvd., 10458. Tel: 718-364-5353; Fax: 718-364-2354. Email: mtstursu@adnyeducation.org. Web: www.amsu.org. Rev. John A. Vigilanti, J.C.L., Ph.D., Pres.; Lisa Harrison, Prin.; Haydee Comacho, Librarian. Ursuline Nuns. Sisters 1; Lay Teachers 27; Students 365.

Cardinal Hayes High School (Boys)., 650 Grand Concourse, 10451. Tel: 718-292-6100; Fax: 718-292-9178. Email: hayes@adnyeducation.org. Web: www.cardinalhayes.org. Mr. William D. Lessa, Prin.; Revs. Joseph P. Tierney, M.Div., Pres.; Harry Burke; Robert Harrison. Priests 3; Brothers 2; Sisters 1; Lay Teachers 63; Students 926. In Res. Revs. Matthew Ugwoji; Emmanuel Okpalauwaekwe.

Cardinal Spellman High School, One Cardinal Spellman Pl., 10466. Tel: 718-881-8000; Fax: 718-515-6615. Email: dokeefe@cardinalspellman.org. Web: www.cardinalspellman.org. Mr. Daniel O'Keefe, Prin.; Sr. Veronica Wood, O.S.F., Asst. Prin.; Neil McCarthy, Ph.D., Asst. to Pres.; Revs. Trevor Nicholls, Pres.; John R. Kraljic; John T. Monaghan; James J. O'Shaughnessy; Peter R. Pilsner; Francis J. Principe; Kathy Steves, Librarian. Priests 6; Sisters 2; Lay Teachers 80; Students 1,413. In Res. Rev. Richard F. Gorman, Esq.

St. Catharine Academy (1889) (Girls), 2250 Williamsbridge Rd., 10469-4891. Tel: 718-882-2882; Fax: 718-231-9099. Email: catherin@adnyeducation.org. Web: www.scahs.org. Sisters Ann M. Welch, R.S.M., Prin.; Patricia Wolf, R.S.M., Pres.; Barbara Flynn, Librarian. Sisters 8; Lay Teachers 38; Students 695.

Fordham Preparatory School (1841) (Boys), 441 E. Fordham Rd., 10458. Tel: 718-367-7500; Fax: 718-367-7598. Web: www.fordhamprep.org. John F. Neary, Bd. Chm.; Rev. Kenneth J. Boller, S.J., Pres.; Mr. Robert J. Gomprecht, Prin.; Mr. Dennis M. Ahern, Asst. Prin.; Mrs. Theresa Napoli, Asst. Prin.; Mr. Steven Pettus, Dean of Students; Mr. Michael Lacinak, Dir. Guidance; Revs. John M. Costello, S.J.; Donald G. Devine, S.J.; Mallick J. Fitzpatrick, S.J.; Joseph J. Kamiensky, S.J.; Stanley J. O'Konsky, S.J.; William J. O'Malley, S.J.; Charles D. Sullivan, S.J.; Raymond M. Sweitzer, S.J.; James R. Van Dyke, S.J.; Susan Andrews, M.A., Librarian. Priests 10; Lay Teachers 78; Students 989.

Mount St. Michael Academy, (Grades 6-12), (Boys), 4300 Murdock Ave., 10466. Tel: 718-515-6400; Fax: 718-994-7729. Email: mount@adnyschools.org. Web: www.mountstmichael.org. Dr. Anthony Miserandino, Pres.; Bro. Steve Schlitte, F.M.S., Prin. Brothers 6; Lay Teachers 47; Students 791.

Preston High School (1947) (Girls), 2780 Schurz Ave., 10465. Tel: 718-863-9134; Fax: 718-863-6125. Email: preston@adnyeducation.org. Web: www.prestonhs.org. Mrs. Jane Grendell, Prin.; Linda Youngren, Asst. Prin.; Sr. Loretta Marie Schollhamer, R.D.C., Librarian. Sisters of the Divine Compassion 3; Lay Teachers 40; Students 573.

GOSHEN. *John S. Burke Catholic High School*, 80 Fletcher St., 10924. Tel: 845-294-5481; Fax: 845-294-7957. Email: jbyrnes@burkecatholic.org; burke@adnyeducation.org. Web: www.burkecatholic.org. Rev. Msgr. James T. Byrnes, Ph.D., Prin.; Ms. Sandra Jean, Asst. Prin. for Academics; Mr. Kevin Canty, Asst. Prin. for Student Affairs; Mr. John Dolan, Asst. Prin. P.P.S. & Dir. Admissions; Mrs. Joanne Fitzpatrick, Procurator; Mrs. Joe L. Ruiz, Librarian. Priests 1; Lay Teachers 40; Students 442.

HARTSDALE. *Maria Regina High School*, 500 W. Hartsdale Ave., 10530. Tel: 914-761-3300; Fax: 914-761-0860. Email: mariareg@adnyeducation.org. Web: www.mariaregina.org. Sisters Danielle M. Baran, C.R., Pres., Prin. & Supr.; Mary Krystyna Kobielus, C.R., Librarian. Sisters of the Resurrection, Franciscan Sisters, Dominican Sisters. Sisters 6; Lay Teachers 34; Students 560.

HURLEY. *John A. Coleman Catholic High School* (1967) 430 Hurley Ave., 12443. Tel: 845-338-2750; Fax: 845-388-0250. Email: office@colemancatholic.net. Web: www.colemancatholic.org. Mr. Louis L. Tullo, Prin.; Doreen Kondratowicz, Librarian. Priests 1; Sisters 1; Lay Teachers 28; Students 190.

KATONAH. **The Montfort Academy*, 99 Valley Rd., 10536. Tel: 914-767-0325; Fax: 914-767-0735. Email: sterenzio@themontfortacademy.org; montfort@adnyeducation.org. Web: www.themontfortacademy.org. Steven Terenzio, Headmaster.

NEW ROCHELLE. *Iona Preparatory School* (1916) (Boys), 255 Wilmot Rd., 10804. Tel: 914-632-0714; Fax: 914-632-9760. Email: ionaprep@adnyeducation.org. Web: www.ionaprep.org. Bro. Thomas R. Leto, C.F.C., Pres.; Mrs. Maureen Kiers, Prin.; Mr. Kieran Daly, Dean; Ms. Susan Natale, Dean; Mrs. Barbara Robertson, Chief Advancement Officer; Mrs. Barbara O'Meara, CFO; Kevin Kavanah, Librarian; Bros. James J. Adams, C.F.C.; William R. Harris, C.F.C.; Carmine P. Pellegrino, C.F.C.; Gerard Menezes, C.F.C.; John A. Reynolds, C.F.C. Edmund Rice Christian Brothers North America. Brothers 6; Sisters 1; Lay Teachers 55; Students 787.

Salesian High School, 148 Main St., 10801. Tel: 914-632-0248; Fax: 914-632-5426. Email: salesian@adnyeducation.org. Web: www.salesianhigh.org. Revs. Patrick Angelucci, S.D.B., Dir. & Pres.; James Mulloy, S.D.B.; Thomas Provanzano, S.D.B., Coord. of Youth Ministry; Bros. Donald Caldwell, S.D.B., Guidance; Michael Equino, S.D.B.; Miguel Suarez, S.D.B.; James Zettel, S.D.B.; Sr. Barbara Wright, O.P., Asst. Prin.; John Flaherty, M.A., Prin.; Mr. Christopher Beal, Business Mgr.; Mr. Robert Molinaro, Dean of Students; Mr. Steven Sallustio, Vice Pres. Institutional Advancement; Paul Zaccagnino, Librarian. Priests 3; Brothers 3; Sisters 1; Lay Teachers 36; Students 505.

Ursuline School (1897) (Grades 6-12), (Girls), 1354 North Ave., 10804. Tel: 914-636-3950; Fax: 914-636-3949. Email: ursuline@adnyeducation.org. Web: www.ursuline.pvt.ny.us. Sr. Joan Woodcomb, O.S.U., Treas.; Mrs. Eileen Davidson, Prin.; Kathy Freeman, Librarian. Priests 1; Sisters 7; Lay Teachers 86; Students 770.

POUGHKEEPSIE. *Our Lady of Lourdes High School* (1954) 131 Boardman Rd., 12603. Tel: 845-463-0400; Fax: 845-463-0174. Email: ourladyoflourdes@ollchs.org. Web: www.ollchs.org. Rev. John M. Lagiovane, Prin.; Mr. Michael Krieger, Asst. Prin., Academics; Miss Christine Messina, Campus Min.; Bro. Henry Sawicki, F.M.S., Chm. Science Dept.; Mrs. Catherine Merryman, Asst. Prin. Faculty; Mr. Charles Junjulas Jr., Dean of Men; Mrs. Judith Maher, Dir., Guidance; Rev. John M. Lagiovane, Admissions; Mrs. Maureen Myers, Dean of Women; Ms. Judith Mletzko, Librarian. Brothers 1; Sisters 1; Lay Teachers 45; Students 692.

RYE. *School of the Holy Child*, (Grades 5-12), (Girls), 2225 Westchester Ave., 10580. Tel: 914-967-5622; Fax: 914-967-6476. Email: holychild@adnyeducation.org. Web: www.holychildrye.org. Ann F. Sullivan, Head of School; Joli Moniz, Admissions Dir.; Helen Kostelas, Librarian. Society of the Holy Child Jesus 1; Lay Teachers 59; Students (Upper School) 254; (Middle School) 95.

SOMERS. *John F. Kennedy Catholic High School*, 54 Rte. 138, 10589. Tel: 914-232-5061; Fax: 914-232-3416. Email: jfkhs@adnyeducation.org. Web: www.kennedycatholic.org. Rev. Mark G. Vaillancourt, Ph.D., Pres. & Prin.; Mr. Stephen T. Schmidt, Vice Prin. Academics; Deacon Alfred R. Impallomeni, Vice Prin. Faculty & Student Affairs; Sr. Barbara Heil, R.D.C., Dir. Admissions. Diocesan Priests, Sisters of the Divine Compassion. Priests 3; Sisters 7; Lay Teachers 29; Students 564.

STATEN ISLAND. *St. John Villa Academy High School* (1932) 25 Landis Ave., 10305-3729. Tel: 718-442-6240; Fax: 718-447-6729. Email: sjva@adnyeducation.org. Web: www.sjva.org. Barbara Ann Logan, Prin.; Sr. Eliza McLoughlin, Librarian. Sisters 7; Lay Teachers 31; Girls 508.

St. Joseph by the Sea, High School (Coed), 5150 Hylan Blvd., 10312. Tel: 718-984-6500; Fax: 718-984-6503. Email: josbysea@adnyeducation.org. Rev. Michael P. Reilly, Prin. Priests 3; Sisters 6; Lay Teachers 69; Students 1,271.

St. Joseph Hill Academy (Girls), 850 Hylan Blvd., 10305-2095. Tel: 718-447-1374; Fax: 718-447-3041. Email: joshill@adnyeducation.org. Web: stjhill.org. Angela T. Ferrando, Prin. Daughters of Divine Charity. Sisters 1; Lay Teachers 30; Students 474.

Monsignor Farrell High School, 2900 Amboy Rd., 10306. Tel: 718-987-2900; Fax: 718-987-4241. Email: farrell@adnyeducation.org. Web: www.msgrfarrellhs.org. Rev. Msgr. Edmund J. Whalen, S.T.D., Prin.; Rev. John P. Comiskey; Kathleen Sparnroft, Librarian. Priests 2; Brothers 2; Sisters 2; Lay Teachers 58; Students 872.

Moore Catholic High School, 100 Merrill Ave., 10314. Tel: 718-761-9200; Fax: 718-982-7779. Email: moorecats@adnyeducation.org. Web: www.moorechs.org. Douglas McManus, Prin. Daughters of Our Lady of the Garden 2; Sisters of John the Baptist 1; Lay Teachers 39; Students 574.

Notre Dame Academy High School, 134 Howard Ave., 10301. Tel: 718-447-8878; Fax: 718-447-2926. Email: ntdameac@adnyeducation.org. Web: www.notredameacademy.org. Sr. Patricia Corley, C.N.D., Pres.; Dr. Kathryn Jaenicke, Prin.; Christine Gullo, Librarian. Congregation of Notre Dame. Sisters 2; Lay Teachers 35; Girls 407.

WHITE PLAINS. *Academy of Our Lady of Good Counsel (High School)* (1922) (Girls), 52 N. Broadway, 10603. Tel: 914-949-0178; Fax: 914-682-3531. Email: ldonovan@gcahs.org. Web: www.gcahs.org. Sisters Laura Donovan, R.D.C., Prin.; Mary Alice O'Brien, R.D.C., Librarian. Sisters of the Divine Compassion 5; Dominican Sisters of Hope 1; Lay Teachers 26; Students 364.

Archbishop Stepinac High School, 950 Mamaroneck Ave., 10605. Tel: 914-946-4800; Fax: 914-684-2591. Email: stepinac@adnyeducation.org. Web: www.stepinac.org. Rev. Thomas E. Collins, Pres.; Mr. Paul Carty, Prin.; Sal Poidomani, Librarian. Priests 3; Lay Teachers 38; Students 625.

Staff of School: Rev. Justin S. Cinnante.

[F] SPECIAL SCHOOLS

NEW YORK. *Grace Institute*, 1233 Second Ave., 10065. Tel: 212-832-7605; Fax: 212-486-2869. Email: info@graceinstitute.org. Web: www.graceinstitute.org. Dr. Mary Mulvihill, Exec. Dir. Sisters of Charity, Mt. St. Vincent. Teachers 8; Students 300.

John A. Coleman School, 590 Avenue of the Americas, 10011. Tel: 646-459-3401; Fax: 646-459-3689. Email: sharon.herl@setonpediatric.org. Web: www.setonpediatric.org. Ms. Sharon Herl, Prin.

Lavelle School for the Blind, E. 221st St. and Paulding Ave., 10469. Tel: 718-882-1212; Fax: 718-882-0005. Web: www.lavelleschool.org. William F. Simpson, Supt. Sisters of St. Dominic of Blauvelt. Capacity 183; Lay Teachers 24; Total Staff 132; Total Enrollment 160.

Mount St. Ursula Speech Center, 2885 Marion Ave., Bronx, 10458. Tel: 718-584-7679; Fax: 718-584-7954. Email: msuspeech@aol.com. Sr. Bernadette Hannaway, O.S.U., Admin. Bd. Dirs. Ursuline Nuns. Sisters 1; Lay Clinicians 6; Support Staff 4; Total Staff 10; Total Enrollment 140; Total Assisted Annually 234.

Seton Foundation for Learning, Inc. (1985) 315 Arlene St., Staten Island, 10314. Tel: 718-982-5084; Fax: 718-982-5114. Email: seton@adnyschools.org. Rev. Msgrs. James J. Dorney, Chm.; Peter G. Finn, M.Div., M.S., M.Ed., Co-Chm.; Ms. Diane Cunningham, Exec. Dir.; Thomas J. Vazzana, M.D., Pres. Lay Teachers 14; Assistants 31; Total Enrollment 128.

IRVINGTON. *John Cardinal O'Connor School*, 16 N. Broadway, 10533. Tel: 914-591-9330. Email: jcoconnor@adnyeducation.org. Mrs. Donna Taylor, Prin.

MILLBROOK. *Cardinal Hayes School for Special Children* (1984) 3374 Franklin Ave., P.O. Box CH, 12545. Tel: 845-677-6363; Fax: 845-677-6691. Email: fapers@cardinalhayeshome.org. Web: www.cardinalhayeshome.org. Fred Apers, Exec. Dir. Educational programs for multi-handicapped children. Lay Teachers 7; Capacity 60; Total Enrollment 55.

[G] ELEMENTARY SCHOOLS, PRIVATE

NEW YORK. *Academy of St. Joseph*, (Grades PreK-4), 111 Washington Pl., 10014. Tel: 212-243-5420; Fax: 212-414-4526. Ms. Angela Coombs, Head of School; Norma Courier, Librarian. Lay Teachers 6.

Convent of the Sacred Heart (Girls), 1 E. 91st St., 10128. Tel: 212-722-4745; Fax: 212-996-1784. Web: cshnyc.org. Dr. Joseph J. Ciancaglini, Head of School. Sisters 2; Faculty 94; Elementary School Students 441.

St. John Villa Academy Elementary School, Mailing Address: 57 Cleveland Pl., Staten Island, 10305. Sr. Lucita Bacat, C.S.J.B., Prin. Sisters 9; Lay Teachers 10; Students 418.

Marymount School, (Grades N-12), 1026 Fifth Ave., 10028. Tel: 212-744-4486; Fax: 212-794-5205. Email: calvar@marymountnyc.org. Web: www.marymountnyc.org. Concepcion Alvar, B.S., M.A., Head of School; Lillian Issa, Deputy Head, Dir. Admissions; Alexis Bradford, Dir., Finance; Nora Gibson, Dir., School Affairs; Elizabeth Clarke, Librarian; Cynthia Montes, Librarian. Religious of the Sacred Heart of Mary. Sisters 2; Lay Teachers 108; Students 643.

Nativity Mission Center, Inc. (1971) 204 Forsyth St., 10002. Tel: 212-477-2472; Fax: 212-473-0538. Email: keenan@nynativity.org. Web: www.nativitymission.org. Rev. James F. Keenan, S.J., Pres. & Contact Person. Brothers 2; Priests 1; Sisters 1; Total Staff 11; Students 60.

BRONX. *Saint Ignatius School*, 740 Manida St., 10474-5420. Tel: 718-861-9084; Fax: 718-861-9096. Email: info@nynativity.org. Web: www.nynativity.org. Mr. John Omernick, Prin.

Villa Maria Academy (1887) 3335 Country Club Rd., 10465. Tel: 718-824-3260; Fax: 718-824-7315. Email: villa@adnyschools.org. Web: www.vmany.org. Sr. Teresa Barton, C.N.D., Prin.; Claudia Canzone, Librarian. Congregation of Notre Dame. Sisters 3; Lay Teachers 25; Students 410.

NEW ROCHELLE. *Iona Grammar School*, (Grades K-8), (Boys), 173 Stratton Rd., 10804. Tel: 914-633-7744; Fax: 914-235-6338. Email: pmborchetta@ionagrammer.com. Web: www.ionagrammar.com. Peter M. Borchetta, Pres. & Headmaster; Diana Gooljar, Librarian. Lay Teachers 20; Students 195.

NEWBURGH. *Bishop Dunn Memorial School*, 50 Gidney Ave., 12550. Tel: 845-569-3494; Fax: 845-569-3303. Email: bishdunn@adnyeducation.org. Web: www.bdms.org. Mr. James Delviscio, Prin.; Sr. Frances Irene Fair, Dir. Devel.; Donna Del Conte, Librarian. Dominican Sisters of Hope. Sisters 2; Lay Teachers 15; Students 290.

Nora Cronin Presentation Academy, (Grades 5-8), 120 South St., 12550. Tel: 845-567-0708; Fax: 845-567-0709. Email: presentationacad@aol.com. Web: www.noracroninpresentationacademy.com. Sr. Yliana Hernandez, P.B.V.M., Contact Person, Pres., Prin.

STATEN ISLAND. *Academy of St. Dorothy* (1932) 1305 Hylan Blvd., 10305. Tel: 718-351-0939; Fax: 718-351-0661. Email: dorothy@adnyeducation.org. Sr. Sharon A. McCarthy, S.S.D., Prin. Sisters of St. Dorothy 1; Lay Teachers 15; Students 277.

St. Joseph Hill Academy Elementary (1919) 850 Hylan Blvd., 10305. Tel: 718-981-1187; Fax: 718-448-7016. Email: joshiles@adnyschools.org. Web: www.stjosephhill.org. Mrs. Dorothy Zissler, Prin. Lay Teachers 30; Students 523.

Notre Dame Academy-Elementary School (1903) 78 Howard Ave., 10301. Tel: 718-273-9096; Fax: 718-273-1093. Email: ntdames@adnyeducation.org. Web: www.notredameacademy.org. Sr. Rose Mary Galligan, C.N.D., Prin. Congregation of Notre Dame. Lay Teachers 14; Students 240.

WHITE PLAINS. *Academy of Our Lady of Good Counsel* (Elementary Dept.), 52 N. Broadway, 10603. Tel: 914-761-4423; Fax: 914-997-4195. Email: gdcounes@adnysch.org. Dr. Judith Johnson, Prin. Sisters 1; Lay Teachers 16; Students 163.

[H] THE CATHOLIC CHARITIES OF THE ARCHDIOCESE OF NEW YORK

NEW YORK. *Catholic Charities Alliance*, 1011 First Ave., 10022. Tel: 212-371-1011, Ext. 2400. Rev. Msgr. Kevin L. Sullivan, Pres.

The Catholic Charities of the Archdiocese of New York, 1011 First Ave., 10022. Tel: 212-371-1000; Fax: 212-755-1526. Web: wwwcatholiccharitiesny.org. Rev. Msgr. Kevin L. Sullivan, Exec. Dir.; Joseph Buttigieg, Assoc. Exec. Dir.; Mr. Kenneth Dempsey, CFO; Mr. George B. Horton; Ms. Luz Taverez-Salazar, Special Asst.; Ms. Margaret King, Dir. Inst. Advancement; Mr. Joseph Becker, Agency Relations Liaison; Ms. Mary Ellen Ros, Catholic Charities Dir. Hudson Valley; Mr. Joseph Panepinto, Catholic Charities Dir. Staten Island; Mr. Philip Dorian, Dir. Agency Svcs.

The Ladies of Charity of the Catholic Charities of the Archdiocese of New York, 1011 First Ave., 10022. Tel: 212-371-1000, Ext. 2540; Fax: 212-319-8265. Ms. Dorothea A. McElduff, Exec. Dir.; Rev. Msgr. Peter G. Finn, M.Div., M.S., M.Ed., Spiritual Dir.

Catholic Charities Community Services, Archdiocese of New York, 1011 First Ave., 10022. Tel: 212-371-1000; Fax: 212-826-8795. Ms. Beatriz Diaz, Exec. Dir.; Ms. Anne Tommaso, Dir. Beacon of Hope Svcs. Div.; Ms. Raluca Oncioiu, Dir. Migration & Refugee Svcs.; Mr. Alfred Peck, Dir. Community Outreach Svcs. Div.; Mr. Alec McAuley, Dir. CYO Div.; Ms. Mary Marshall, Dir. Hudson Valley Reg. Svcs.; Ms. Joy Jasper, Dir. Human Resources.

Roman Catholic Fund for Children and Other Purposes, 1011 First Ave., 10022. Tel: 212-371-1000; Fax: 212-826-8795. Rev. Msgr. Kevin L. Sullivan.

Holy Name Centre for Homeless Men, Inc., 18 Bleeker St., 10012. Tel: 212-226-5848. Rev. Msgr. John B. Ahern, Dir. (Retired).

Providence Health Services, 1249 Fifth Ave., 10029. Karl Adler, Pres.

St. Michael's Home, c/o The Catholic Charities of the Archdiocese of New York, 1011 First Ave., 10022. Tel: 212-371-1000. Web: cathwww.org. Bernard E. Reidey, Vice Pres.

GOSHEN. *Catholic Charities Community Services of Orange County*, Administrative Offices: 224 Main St., 10924. Tel: 845-294-5124. Dr. Dean Scher, COO, Exec. Dir.

Early Learning Center, 59 St. John St., 10924. Tel: 845-294-7502. Montessori-based day care for 60 2.9-5 year olds.

Chemical Dependency Clinics: Medically supervised, outpatient clinics for chemically dependent adults and their families.

224 Main St., 10924. Tel: 845-294-5888; Fax: 845-294-1402.

21 Centre St., Middletown, 10940. Tel: 845-343-7675; Fax: 845-343-2501.

101 Carpenter Pl., Monroe, 10950. Tel: 845-782-0295; Fax: 845-782-5164.

280 Broadway, Newburgh, 12550. Tel: 845-562-8255; Fax: 845-562-4140.

Gateway Clinic, 46 Roe St., Newburgh, 12550. Tel: 845-569-0034; Fax: 845-569-0047.

17-19 Sussex St., Port Jervis, 12771. Tel: 845-856-6344; Fax: 845-856-4091.

8 Scofield St., Walden, 12586. Tel: 845-778-5628; Fax: 845-778-5168.

Housing Resource Center, 280 Broadway, Newburgh, 12550. Tel: 845-561-1665; Fax: 845-561-2825. Provides eviction prevention services as part of a collaborative effort among Catholic Charities Community Services of Orange County and the Orange County Department of Social Services.

Student Assistance Services, 10 Orchard St., Middletown, 10940. Tel: 845-344-5565; Fax: 845-344-6982. Chemical dependency awareness, prevention, life skills education; Counseling, assessment, and referral services for students in Pine Bush School District.

Employee Assistance Program: Employee Assistance Programs for 45 corporations, businesses, governments, groups, etc. Provides confidential counseling assessment, and referral services for employees on a self-initiated or supervisor-recommended basis. Training programs and related consultative services provided.

10 Orchard St., Middletown, 10940. Tel: 845-344-5565; Fax: 845-344-6982.

Community Outreach Services--Immigration Services: Provides services to immigrants in need of assistance.

149 Cottage St., Middletown, 10940. Tel: 845-341-1978.

319 Broadway, Newburgh, 12550. Tel: 845-561-3452.

Community Outreach Services-Social Services: Provides information and referral, case management/service coordination, emergency assistance for rent, utilities, transportation, food and clothing (limited by available resources), entitlement assistance and advocacy. Also available to help parishes with CYO programs and to assess needs, evaluate existing service programs, recruit and train volunteers to meet parish needs and facilitate service to the parish.

21 Centre St., Middletown, 10940. Tel: 845-344-4242; Fax: 845-343-2501.

319 Broadway, Newburgh, 12550. Tel: 845-561-3451; Fax: 845-561-2825.

Maternity and Adoption Services: Offers maternity and adoption services to married and unmarried parents including those experiencing an unplanned pregnancy.

224 Main St., 10924. Tel: 845-294-5124, Ext. 302; Fax: 845-294-1369.

Health Insurance: Tel: 845-534-4894; Fax: 845-226-1369. Offers free or low cost health insurance through Family Health Plus and Child Health Plus programs. Coverage includes: check-ups, prenatal care, screenings and preventive care, well-child visits, immunizations, lab tests, x-rays, hospitalization and emergency treatment. (Appointments are set up at various sites in Orange County)

[I] HOUSING

NEW YORK. *Catholic Charities Department of Housing, Housing Development Institute, Inc.*, 1011 First Ave., 10022. Tel: 212-371-1000. Rev. Msgr. Kevin L. Sullivan, Pres.

[J] MENTAL HEALTH SERVICES

NEW YORK. *Catholic Charities Community Services, Beacon of Hope*, 1011 First Ave., 6th Fl., 10022. Tel: 212-371-1000, Ext. 3608; Fax: 212-421-0021. Email: denise.bauer@archny.org. Web: www.catholiccharitiesny.org. Denise Bauer, M.S.W., Dir., Beacon of Hope.

SVCMC Health Services Inc., 130 W. 12th St., Ste. 6-E, 10011. Tel: 212-604-7536. Email: estclair@svcmcny.org. Elizabeth St. Clair Esq., Contact Person.

[K] IMMIGRATION SERVICES

NEW YORK. *Catholic Charities Department of Immigrant Services*, 1011 First Ave. 12th Fl., 10022. Tel: 212-419-3700; Fax: 212-751-3197. Web: www.archny.org. Ms. Raluca Oncioiu, Dept. Dir.

Refugee Resettlement, 1011 First Ave., 12th Fl., 10022. Tel: 212-419-3726; Fax: 212-688-4178.

Project Irish Outreach, 1011 First Ave., 11th Fl., 10022. Tel: 212-371-1000, Ext. 3640; Fax: 212-755-1526.

New York Immigration Hotline, 1011 First Ave., 12th Fl., 10022. Tel: 212-419-3737; 800-566-7636. Lindita Berdynaj, Coord.

Asylum Information and Referral Hotline, 1011 First Ave., 12th Fl., 10022. Tel: 212-419-3737; Fax: 800-354-0365.

[L] COMMUNITY OUTREACH SERVICES DIVISION

NEW YORK. *Catholic Charities Community Services, Community Outreach Services Division*, 1011 First Ave., 10022. Tel: 212-371-1000, Ext. 2039; Fax: 212-317-8719.

Case Management/Social Services:

Central Office, 1011 First Ave., 10022. Tel: 212-371-1000, Ext. 2035; 888-744-7900 (Catholic Charities Helpline).

Central Harlem, 34 W. 134th St., 10030. Tel: 212-862-6401; Fax: 212-862-6421.

Lower Manhattan, 213 Stanton St., 10002. Tel: 212-673-0900.

East Manhattan, St. Cecilia's Church, 125 E. 105th St., 10029. Tel: 212-348-0488; Fax: 212-876-1827.

Washington Hts., 4111 Broadway, 10033. Tel: 212-795-6860; Fax: 212-781-2935.

South Bronx, 402 E. 152nd St., Bronx, 10455. Tel: 718-292-1485; Fax: 718-742-9754.

Staten Island, 120 Anderson Ave., Staten Island, 10302. Tel: 718-448-5757; Fax: 718-448-6749.

Westchester County/Peekskill, Our Lady of the Rosary, 22 Don Bosco Pl., Port Chester, 10573. Tel: 914-939-0547; Fax: 914-965-4241.

Westchester County/Yonkers, 204 Hawthorne Ave., Yonkers, 10701. Tel: 914-476-2700; Fax: 914-965-4241.

Dutchess County, 218 Church St., Poughkeepsie, 12601. Tel: 845-452-1400; Fax: 845-452-3336.

66 Bennett St., Middletown, 10943. Tel: 845-344-4244.

Rockland County, 78 Hudson Ave., Haverstraw, 10927. Tel: 845-942-5791; Fax: 845-429-2938.

Sullivan County, P.O. Box 395, Monticello, 12701. Tel: 845-791-6023; Fax: 845-791-6104.

Ulster County, 59 Pearl St., Kingston, 12401. Tel: 845-340-9170; Fax: 845-340-9596.

Emergency Food Services, 1011 First Ave., 10022. Tel: 212-371-1000, Ext. 2481; Fax: 212-317-8719. Ms. Jeanne McGettigan.

Homelessness Prevention Services:

1011 First Ave., 6th Fl., 10022. Tel: 212-371-1011, Ext. 2030; Fax: 212-753-7827. 2155 Blackrock Ave., Bronx, 10472. Tel: 718-414-1050; Fax: 718-414-1058. Antonio Garcia, Dir.

St. Nicholas Job Center, 132 W. 125th St., Rm. 301, 10027. Tel: 212-666-3124; Fax: 212-666-8406.

Waverly Job Center, 12 W. 14th St., 4th Fl., 10011. Tel: 212-337-0213; Fax: 212-337-0211.

Employment Services, 1011 First Ave., 12th Fl., 10022. Tel: 212-371-1011, Ext. 3719; Fax: 212-319-8719.

Manhattan: Lt. Joseph P. Kennedy, Jr. Memorial Center, 34 W. 134th St., 10037. Tel: 212-862-6401; Fax: 212-862-6421.

Hudson Valley Regional Services:

Catholic Charities Community Services Hudson Valley Regional Services, Poughkeepsie Catholic Center, 218 Church St., Poughkeepsie, 12601. Tel: 845-452-1400; Fax: 845-452-3336. Ms. Mary Marshall, Dir.

Regional Offices:

Dutchess, Poughkeepsie Catholic Center, 218 Church St., Poughkeepsie, 12601. Tel: 845-452-1400; Fax: 845-452-3336. Ms. Mary Marshall.

Rockland, 78 Hudson Ave., Haverstraw, 10927. Tel: 845-942-5791; Fax: 845-429-2938.

Westchester, 22 Don Bosco Pl., Port Chester, 10573. Tel: 914-939-0547; Fax: 914-965-4241.

Sullivan, P.O. Box 395, Monticello, 12701. Tel: 845-791-6023; Fax: 845-791-6104. Rhetta Eason, Regl. Admin.

Ulster, 59 Pearl St., Kingston, 12401. Tel: 845-340-9170; Fax: 845-340-9596. Rhetta Eason, Regl. Admin.

Putnam, 235 Monsignor O'Brien Blvd., Mahopac, 10541. Tel: 845-628-2006, Ext. 115; Fax: 845-628-5970. John Scarfi, Parish Social Min.

[M] SOCIAL AND COMMUNITY DEVELOPMENT

NEW YORK. *Catholic Charities Department of Social and Community Development*, 1011 First Ave., Room 1287, 10022. Tel: 212-371-1000, Ext. 2480; Fax: 212-319-0405. Mr. George B. Horton, Dir. Tel: 212-371-1000, Ext. 2475.

Offices and Staff:

Criminal Justice Ministry Email: kenneth.hoffarth@archny.org.

Justice and Peace Ministry Thomas Dobbins Jr., Outreach Coord. Tel: 212-371-1000, Ext. 2473.

Education Outreach Program Alison Hughes-Kelsick, Dir. Tel: 212-371-1000, Ext. 2450.

Institute for Human Development Melissa Pavone, Dir.

Community Development and The Guild for Dorothy Day Ms. Lourdes Ferrer. Tel: 212-371-1000, Ext. 2474.

Deaf Apostolate Rev. Msgr. Patrick P. McCahill, Dir.

[N] SPECIAL SERVICES FOR THE ELDERLY/HANDICAPPED

BEACON. *Metropolitan Association of Contemplative Communities, Inc.*, 89 Hiddenbrooke Dr., 12508. Tel: 845-831-5572; Fax: 845-831-5579. Web: macc.catholic.org. Sr. Rita Donahue, O.C.D., Contact Person.

[O] SERVICES TO THE DISABLED

NEW YORK. *Catholic Charities Community Services Beacon of Hope House Division, Catholic Charities*, 1011 First Ave., 10022. Tel: 212-371-1000; Fax: 212-421-0021. Email: denise.bauer@archny.org. Web: www.archny.org. Ms. Joy Jasper, Dir. Human Resources; Ms. Anne Tommaso, M.B.A., M.P.A., Dir. of Behavioral Health.

Beacon of Hope House Bronx Congregate Services, 1400 Waters Pl., Bronx, 10461. Tel: 718-892-3494; Fax: 718-892-5507. Ms. Jacqueline Rosario-Perez, M.S.W., Dir. Bronx Congregate Progs.

Terence Cardinal Cooke Residence, 2467 Bathgate Ave., Bronx, 10458. Tel: 718-367-6990; 718-367-5405 (TTY); Fax: 718-365-2544. Kathy Momperrouse, Prog. Supvr.

Beacon of Hope House Staten Island Supervised Programs, 777 Seaview Ave., Bldg. D, 2nd Fl., Staten Island, 10305. Tel: 718-980-1072; Fax: 718-980-1077. Mr. Dennis Scimone, M.S.W., M.P.A., Dir. of Residential Svcs.; Eva Merlo, Admin. Sec.; Ms. Sandy Mormile, Dir. Staten Island & Brooklyn Svcs.

Staten Island Apartment Programs Tel: 718-979-6241; Fax: 718-979-6941. Jillian Maye, Prog. Supvr.

90-92 Hancock St., Staten Island, 10305. Tel: 718-979-6241; Fax: 718-979-6941.

Highbridge Neighborhood Supported Housing Program, 1484 Nelson Ave., Suite A, Bronx, 10452. Tel: 718-503-8106; Fax: 718-293-0939. Deborah Neal, Prog. Mgr.

Kingsborough Intensive Supported Apartment Program, 647 Vanderbilt Ave., Brooklyn, 11238. Tel: 718-398-4556; Fax: 718-398-4807. Ms. Michelle Foster, Prog. Supvr.

East Bronx Supported Housing, 2510 Westchester Ave., Ste. 210, Bronx, 10461. Tel: 718-239-5206; Fax: 718-239-5287. Paul Gregory, Dir. Bronx Supported Housing.

The Clubhouse, 512 Southern Blvd., Bronx, 10455. Tel: 718-993-1078; Fax: 718-993-0216. Ms. Sharon George, Prog. Dir.

New York Catholic Deaf Center, St. Elizabeth of Hungry Church, 211 E. 83rd St., 10028. Tel: 212-988-8563 (Voice); 212-988-1903 (TTY); 866-810-3394 (Video Phone); Fax: 212-988-1903. Web: www.deafcathnyc.org. Rev. Msgr. Patrick P. McCahill, Dir. Total Staff 2; Total Assisted Annually 8,056.

BARRYVILLE. *New Hope Manor*, 35 Hillside Rd., 12719. Tel: 845-557-8353; Fax: 845-557-6603. Email: newhopemnr@aol.com. Web: www.newhopemanor.org. Nicholas A. Roes, Ph.D., Dir.; Bro. Charles Kinney, S.A., Bd. of Directors; Sr. Jeanne Micelli, O.P., Bd. of Directors. See listing in the Miscellaneous section for further details. Bed Capacity 60; Total Assisted Annually 100; Total Staff 50.

Staff: An all-female substance abuse treatment center Sisters Maureen Conway, O.P., Dir. of Education, Housemother, Counselor & Teacher; Patricia Conway, O.P., Housemother, Counselor & Teacher.

[P] YOUTH SERVICES

NEW YORK. *Catholic Youth Organization of the Archdiocese of New York Inc.*, Executive Office, 1011 First Ave., 10022-4187. Tel: 212-371-1000; Fax: 212-826-3347. Chris Gallagher, Pres.; Mr. Alec McAuley, Exec. Dir.

Archdiocesan Committee on Scouting Tel: 914-499-4840; Fax: 212-826-3347. Mr. Seth Peloso, Dir. Opers., NYC; Mr. Monge Codio, Dir. Opers., Hudson Valley Region.

CYO Bronx County Tel: 212-371-1000; Fax: 212-826-3347. Mr. Anthony D'Angelo, County Dir.

Grace Youth Ministry Tel: 212-371-1000, Ext. 3619. Mrs. Carmen Castro, Coord.

Lt. Joseph P. Kennedy, Jr., Memorial Center Tel: 212-862-6401; Fax: 212-862-6421. Deacon Rodney Beckford.

34 W. 134th St., 10037. Tel: 212-862-6401; Fax: 212-862-6421.

CYO Staten Island County Tel: 718-448-4949; Fax: 718-448-0576.

120 Anderson Ave., Staten Island, 10302. Tel: 718-448-4950; Fax: 718-448-0576. Frank Minotti, County Coord.

Staten Island Center Tel: 718-448-4949; Fax: 718-273-8361. Gayle Murphy, After School & Camp Dir.

120 Anderson Ave., Staten Island, 10302. Tel: 718-448-4949; Fax: 718-448-0576.

CYO Westchester/Putnam Offices Tel: 845-623-2785; Fax: 845-624-0889. Frank Magaletta, County Dir.

9 Brookview Blvd., Chestnut Ridge, 10977. Tel: 845-623-2785; Fax: 845-624-0889.

Blair Lodge Youth Ministry Center, Peekskill Rd., Putnam Valley, 10579. Tel: 845-528-5005; Fax: 845-528-6137.

1011 First Ave., 10022. Tel: 845-783-1254; Fax: 212-826-3347.

CYO Orange Office Mr. John Smith, Sports Coord.

P.O. Box 234, Highland Mills, 10930. Tel: 845-534-7700; Fax: 212-826-3347.

CYO Rockland Office Tel: 845-620-1662. Thomas F. Collins.

34 Graney Ct., Pearl River, 10965. Tel: 845-620-1662; Fax: 845-452-3336.

CYO Dutchess Office Tel: 845-452-1400; Fax: 845-452-3336.

Catholic Center, 240 Church St., Poughkeepsie, 12601. Tel: 845-452-1400; Fax: 845-452-3336.

CYO Ulster/Sullivan County Tel: 845-340-9170; Fax: 845-340-9596.

59 Pearl St., Kingston, 12401. Tel: 845-340-9170; Fax: 845-340-9596. Tom Kelly, County Dir.

BRONX. *St. Francis Youth Center, Inc.*, 420 E. 156th St., 10455. Tel: 718-993-3405; 718-402-6235; Fax: 718-993-9997. Bro. Joachim Joseph, C.F.R., Dir.; Yvette Torres, Admin. Brothers 3; Priests 1; Lay Missionaries 1.

GARRISON. *Capuchin Youth and Family Ministries*, 781 Rte. 9D, 10524. Tel: 845-424-3609; Fax: 845-424-4403. Email: cyfm@cyfm.org. Web: www.cyfm.org. P.O. Box 192, 10524. Thomas Brinkmann, Exec. Dir.; Rev. Fred Nickle, O.F.M.Cap., Chap.; Bro. Lake Herman, O.F.M.Cap., Chap. A ministry of the Capuchin Franciscan Province of St. Mary.

[Q] SOCIETY OF ST. VINCENT DE PAUL

NEW YORK. *Society of St. Vincent De Paul, Archdiocesan Central Council of New York* Territory: Archdiocese of New York., 1011 First Ave., 10022. Tel: 212-755-8615; Fax: 212-755-0151. Email: james17022@msn.com. James Young, Pres.; Rev. Msgr. Robert Ritchie, Spiritual Advisor.

The Society of St. Vincent de Paul of the Archdiocese of New York, Inc.

District Council of Manhattan (1846) 1011 First Ave., Ste. 607, 10022. Tel: 212-755-8615; Fax: 212-755-0151. Email: phughes@archny.org. Ms. Pattie Hughes, Pres.

The Society of St. Vincent de Paul in the City of New York, Territory: Manhattan.

District Council of the Bronx, 611 Minneford Ave., City Island, 10464. Tel: 718-885-1197. Tom McMahon, Pres.

District Council of Staten Island, 11 Windham Loop, Apt. 3NN, Staten Island, 10314. Tel: 718-370-2804. Raymond Martin, Pres.

BRONX. *District Council of the Bronx* Territory: Borough of The Bronx & Lower Westchester., 402 E. 152nd St., 10455. Tel: 718-292-9090; Fax: 718-993-6130. Rev. Tom Dicks; Dominick Galdieri, Pres.

The Society of St. Vincent de Paul, District Council of the Bronx, Inc.

[R] INSTITUTIONS FOR DEPENDENT CHILDREN

NEW YORK. *Covenant House Under 21* (Runaway and Homeless Youth.), 460 W. 41st St., 10036. Tel: 212-727-4000; Fax: 212-727-4992. Mr. Kevin M. Ryan, Pres.; Mr. Jerome Kilbane, Exec. Dir. Total Assisted 6,476; Total Staff 245.

Rights of Passage Transition Housing. Bed Capacity 160.

Crisis Center Emergency Shelter. Bed Capacity 170.

Vincent J. Fontana Center for Child Protection, 27

Christopher St., 10014. Tel: 212-660-1323; Fax: 212-660-1319. Email: chuck.caputo@nyfoundling.org. Children & Families 250; Total Staff 12.

BLAUVELT. *Saint Dominic's Home* (1878) 500 Western Hwy., 10913. Tel: 845-359-3400; Fax: 845-359-4253. Email: judyk@stdominicshome.org. Web: www.stdominicshome.org. Judith D. Kydon, Exec. Dir. In Foster Homes 400.

New York Offices, 853 Longwood Ave., Ste. 202, Bronx, 10459. Tel: 917-645-9100; Fax: 917-645-9095. Web: www.stdominicshome.org.

St. Dominic's School Tel: 845-359-3400, Ext. 243; Fax: 845-359-5286. Web: www.stdominicshome-.org. (Serves children and adolescents with emotional disabilities, K-8th grade.) Capacity 80.

Community residences for developmentally disabled Tel: 845-359-3400; Fax: 845-359-3673. Capacity 152.

Community residences for mentally ill Tel: 845-359-3400; Fax: 845-359-7361. Capacity 36.

TORCH (To Reach Children), 2340 Andrews Ave., Bronx, 10468. Tel: 718-365-7238; Fax: 718-584-3057. Web: www.stdominicshome.org.

Friends of St. Dominic's Inc., 500 Western Hwy., 10913. Tel: 845-359-3400; Fax: 845-398-0466. Email: sjm@stdominicshome.org. Web: www.stdominicshome.org/friends. Sr. Joseph Mary Mahoney, O.P., Pres.

BRONX. *Saint Dominic's Home - Prevention Program (ASTAAN)* Parent Aide Counseling Advocacy Information and Referral., 2345 University Ave., 10468. Tel: 718-584-4407; Fax: 718-584-4540. Email: annettet@stdominicshome.org. Web: www.stdominicshome.org. Families 100; Families Served 200.

NANUET. *St. Agatha Home of the New York Foundling Hospital* (Residential.), 135 Convent Rd., 10954. Tel: 845-623-3461. Sisters of Charity of St. Vincent de Paul of New York., Residence for adults with developmental disabilities.; Respite for caregivers of adults and children with developmental disabilities.; Group Home.

OSSINING. *Cardinal McCloskey Emergency Residential School* (1980) 155 N. Highland Ave., 10562. Tel: 914-762-5302; Fax: 914-762-7844. Total Staff 7; Capacity 12; Total Assisted 45.

SPRING VALLEY. *Good Counsel, Inc.*, 22 Linden Ave., 10977. Tel: 845-356-0517; 800-723-8331 (Info & Referrals); Fax: 845-356-0406. Web: www.goodcounselhomes.org; www.postabortionhelp.org. Rev. Benedict Joseph Groeschel, C.F.R., Ed.D., Chm.; Christopher Bell, Exec. Dir.; Nannette Morris, House Mgr. Bed Capacity 47; Total Assisted Annually 221; Total Staff 72.

Good Counsel, Inc., 38 Wiman Pl., Staten Island, 10305. Tel: 718-727-8266; 800-723-8331 (Info. & Referrals); Fax: 718-447-6625. Web: www.goodcounselhomes.org; www.postabortionhelp.org. Christopher Bell, Exec. Dir.; Claudia Marroquin, House Mgr.

Good Counsel, Inc., 1157 Fulton Ave., Bronx, 10456. Tel: 718-312-3980, Ext. 10; 800-723-8331 (For Info & Referrals); Fax: 718-312-3991. Email: delores_morgan@goodcounselhomes.org. Web: www.goodcounselhomes.org. Christopher Bell, Exec. Dir.; Delores Morgan, House Mgr.

Good Counsel/Daystar Program, 275 North St., Harrison, 10528. Tel: 914-925-9834; 800-723-8331 (Info. & Referrals); Fax: 914-925-9101. Web: www-.goodcounselhomes.org; www.postabortion-help.org. Christopher Bell, Exec. Dir.; Luise Mejia, House Dir. Bed Capacity 41; Total Assisted 315; Total Staff 60.

Good Counsel, Inc., 116 Heulings Ave., Riverside, NJ 08075. Tel: 856-393-8169; Fax: 856-393-8420. JoAnn DiNoia, Dir.

WEST PARK. *St. Cabrini Home* (1890) 12493. Tel: 845-384-6500; Fax: 845-384-6001. Email: info@cabrinihome.com. Web: cabrinihome.com. Ilze Earner, Ph.D., Exec. Dir. Served by Missionary Sisters of the Sacred Heart Children 80; Agency Operated Boarding Home 1; Group Homes 6; Missionary Sisters of Sacred Heart 5.

St. Cabrini Home, Inc. Tel: 845-384-6500; Fax: 845-384-6001. Email: infor@cabrinihome.com. Web: www.cabrinihome.com. Residents 210.

VALHALLA. *Cardinal McCloskey Services* (1946) 115 Stevens Ave., 10595. Tel: 914-997-8000; Fax: 914-997-2166. Email: bfinnerty@cardinalmccloskey.org. Web: www.cardinalmccloskeyservices.org. Mrs. Beth Finnerty, Pres. & CEO. Statistical Information: Sisters 2; Hayden House Capacity: 20, 35 Children Served; Foster Boarding Home Total Assisted: 398; Tappan Group Home Capacity: 8, Total Assisted: 9; Therapeutic Foster Boarding Home: 66 Children Served; General Preventative Services Total Assisted: 875 children/365 families; OMH — Family-based Treatment Children Assisted: 9; In Day Care: Site I Capacity: 922 Children Served, Site II: 144 Children Assisted; Site III University Heights: 134 Children Assisted; OPWDD Residence Capacity: 79, 31 Families Assisted; OPWDD Day Habilitation: 18 Consumers Assisted; OPWDD Case Management 99 Consumers Assisted; OPWDD Family Support: 31 Families Assisted; Enhanced Supportive Employment: 4 Consumers Assisted; Medical and Clinical Services: Total Assisted: 728 children.75 families/78 adults; Drop-in-Center: 175 Individuals Served; B2H: 249 Children Served; Rockland Diagnostic: 5 Children Served.

Little Angels Head Start Program Staff 219; Capacity 1,356; Assisted 1,356.

[S] SPECIALIZED CHILD CARING HOMES

NEW YORK. *Good Shepherd Services*, 305 7th Ave., 9th Fl., 10001. Tel: 212-243-7070; Fax: 212-929-3412. Email: plomonaco@goodshepherds.org. Web: www.goodshepherds.org. Sr. Paulette LoMonaco, R.G.S., Exec. Dir. Provides foster care and adoption services and five residential programs for at risk adolescents, a training program for social service workers and a comprehensive range of neighborhood family services to individuals and youth in the Bronx and in Brooklyn. These services include a range of educational support, counseling, after school program, crisis intervention, and advocacy services. Sisters 3; Total Assisted 18,000; Total Staff 850.

Kennedy Child Study Center (1958) 151 E. 67th St., 10065. Tel: 212-988-9500; Fax: 212-570-6690. Email: ppg@kenchild.org. Web: www.kenchild.org. Peter P. Gorham, B.A., M.S.W., M.B.A., Exec. Dir. Preschool Special Education 120; Infant/Parent Services 23.

Case Management Services Tel: 212-988-9500; Fax: 212-327-2601. Family Support Services 20.

Bronx Site, 1028 E. 179th St., Bronx, 10460. Tel: 718-842-0200; Fax: 718-842-1328. Preschool Special Education 160; Infant/Parent Services 100.

Case Management Services Tel: 718-842-0200; Fax: 718-842-1328. Family Support Services 40.

Mission of the Immaculate Virgin (1871) 6581 Hylan Blvd., Staten Island, 10309. Tel: 718-317-2803; 718-317-2600; Fax: 718-317-2830. Email: srynn@mountloretto.org. Web: www.mountloretto.org. Stephen Rynn, Exec. Dir.

Mission of the Immaculate Virgin for the Protection of Homeless and Destitute Children In Res. Rev. Michael P. Reilly.

Intermediate Care Facility Tel: 718-966-6185. Capacity 12.

Day Care Center & Universal Pre-K Tel: 718-317-2849. Capacity 85.

Individual Residential Alternatives

Individual Residential Alternatives (I.R.A.) Tel: 718-317-2803; Fax: 718-317-2830. Capacity 36.

Day Habilitation Program Tel: 718-317-2676. Capacity 8.

Residential & Day Care Tel: 718-317-2600; 718-317-2803; Fax: 718-317-2830. Total Assisted 297; Total Staff 162.

New York Foundling Charitable Corp., 590 Avenue of the Americas, 10011. Tel: 212-633-9300. Web: www.nyfoundling.org. Mr. William Baccaglini, Exec. Dir.

**New York Foundling Hospital Center for Pediatric, Medical and Rehabilitative Care, Inc. dba Elizabeth Seton Pediatric Center* (1987) 590 Avenue of the Americas, 10011. Tel: 646-459-3600; Fax: 646-459-3636. Email: patricia.tursi@setonpediatric.org. Web: www.setonpediatric.org. Patricia A. Tursi, CEO. Sponsored by Sisters of Charity of St. Vincent de Paul of New York. Bed Capacity 136; Total Assisted Annually 206; Total Staff 396.

New York Foundling Hospital, The (Children from Infancy to 21), 590 Avenue of the Americas, 10011. Tel: 212-633-9300; Fax: 212-886-4086. Email: info@nyfoundling.org. Web: www.nyfoundling.org. Mr. William Baccaglini, Exec. Dir. Children & Families 13,000; Total Staff 1,200.

Sr. Una McCormack Maternity Services, Inc. (1997) 1011 First Ave., 10022. Tel: 212-371-1000, Ext. 2100; Fax: 212-755-4110.

MILLBROOK. *Cardinal Hayes Home for Children* (1941) Residential care for developmentally disabled children and young adults., St. Joseph Dr., P.O. Box CH, 12545. Tel: 845-677-6363; Fax: 845-677-6691. Email: fapers@cardinalhayeshome.org. Web: www.cardinalhayeshome.org. Fred Apers, Exec. Dir. Franciscan Missionaries of Mary 5; Capacity of Residential Facilities: Millbrook Intermediate Care Facility 60; Community Intermediate Care Facilities 50.

RHINEBECK. *Astor Learning Center, The* The Astor Learning Center provides individualized special education for children with emotional disturbances in conjunction with the mental health services of the Residential Treatment programs. The ALC serves children between the ages of 5-11 at time of admission., 6339 Mill St., P.O. Box 5005, 12572-5005. Tel: 845-871-1032; Fax: 845-876-2020. Email: skeegan@astorservices.org. Web: www.astorservices.org. Sue Keegan, Prin. Capacity 75; Total Assisted 107; Total Staff 50.

Astor Services for Children & Families Residential Treatment Facility for severe emotionally disturbed-mentally ill boys and girls, ages 5-12., 6339 Mill St., P.O. Box 5005, 12572-5005. Tel: 845-871-1000; Fax: 845-876-2020. Email: jmcguirk@astorservices.org. Web: www.astorservices.org. James McGuirk, Ph.D., Exec. Dir. & CEO. Bed Capacity 20.

Residential Treatment Center (Rhinebeck) Bed Capacity 27; Therapeutic Foster Boarding Homes 30; Family-Based Treatment 10.

Counseling Centers: Red Hook, Poughkeepsie, Beacon and Bronx (Ages birth-18)

Day Treatment Programs (Ages 3-12) Capacity Dutchess Co. 56; Bronx 181; Therapeutic Nursery, Bronx 40; Adolescent Day Treatment 120.

Astor Family Services Program, Bronx (Ages birth-18) Capacity 90.

Head Start-Day Care Centers: Poughkeepsie, Beacon, Millerton, Wingdale, Wappingers Falls, Pine Plains Capacity 418.

Day Care Centers: Beacon, Wingdale Capacity 50.

Special Class Integrated Services (Ages 3-5) Capacity 32.

Early Head Start Capacity 135; Total Assisted 5,515; Total Staff 718.

[T] CHILDREN'S AGENCIES & PROTECTIVE INSTITUTIONS

NEW YORK. *Catholic Guardian Society and Home Bureau* (1908) 1011 First Ave., 10022. Tel: 212-371-1000; Fax: 212-935-7820. Email: jfrein@cgshb.org. Mr. John Frein, Exec. Dir. Intermediate care facilities, individual residential alternatives and family respite support programs for developmentally disabled adults and adolescents. Group home program for boys and girls, ages 13-21 years; foster and kinship family care and adoption services for boys and girls, ages 0-21; provides regular and therapeutic foster homes for boys and girls ages 0-21; and specialized foster homes for children with AIDS and special medical conditions; Child abuse and neglect prevention programs; Specialized group care programs for mother-child population, children with special needs, and assessment services for PINS youth and their families; pregnancy support services; international adoption services; post-adoption services; homeless shelter and aftercare services for women with children; and family day care services. Total Assisted 3,863; Total Staff 1,077.

LINCOLNDALE. *Lincoln Hall*, P.O. Box 600, 10540. Tel: 914-248-7474; Fax: 914-248-8391. Email: pt.lincolnhall@worldnet.att.net. Jack Flavin, Exec. Dir.

City Office, 220 E. 23rd St., 10010. Capacity (Boys) 207; Total Staff 351; Total Assisted 421.

[U] CATHOLIC CHARITIES - CHILD CARING AGENCIES

OSSINING. *The Cardinal McCloskey Emergency Residential School*, 155 N. Highland Ave., 10562. Tel: 914-762-5302; Fax: 914-762-7844. Email: jfedele@cardinalmccloskey.org. Teachers 4; Assistants 2.

STATEN ISLAND. *Sisters of Charity Healthcare System Nursing Home, Inc. dba Saint Elizabeth Anns Health Care & Rehabilitation Center* 91 Tompkins Ave., 10304. Tel: 718-876-1099; Fax: 718-876-1393. Email: pmcgrann@svcmcny.org. Robert Reyes, L.N.H.A., Contact Person.

THORNWOOD. *Catholic World Mission, Inc.* (1998) 590 Columbus Ave., 10594. Tel: 914-773-1368; Fax: 914-773-1438. Web: www.catholicworldmission.org. Rev. Jose Felix Ortega, L.C., Contact Person.

[V] DAY NURSERIES

NEW YORK. *St. Benedict's Day Nursery, Day Care Center*, 21 W. 124th St., 10027. Tel: 212-423-5715; Fax: 212-423-5917. Email: stben124@aol.com. Mrs. Sharon Barbacer, Dir. Handmaids of the Most Pure Heart of Mary 2; Lay Teachers 8; Children 56.

Nazareth Nursery (1901) Montessori Day Care., 214-216 W. 15th St., 10011-6501. Tel: 212-243-1881; Fax: 212-243-1881 (Call First). Web: www.nazarethnursery.org. Sisters Lucy Sabatini, O.S.F., Admin., Educ. Dir. & Prin.; Eleanore Therese Vargas, O.S.F., Asst. Admin. Sisters 2; Capacity 55; Total Staff 14; Lay Teachers 7; Ancillary Staff 6.

Providence Rest Child Day Care Center, Inc. (1991)

3310 Campbell Dr., 10465. Tel: 718-823-3588; Fax: 718-823-3588. Sisters 1; Total Assisted 25; Total Staff 7.

San Jose Day Nursery, 432 W. 20th St., 10011. Tel: 212-929-0839; Fax: 212-924-0891. Sisters Haydee Luisa Fernandez, Supr.; Trinidad Fernandez, Dir. Mothers of the Helpless 6; Children 57.

YONKERS. *Queen's Daughters Day Care Center, Inc.* (1903) 73 Buena Vista Ave., 10701. Tel: 914-969-4491; Fax: 914-969-4491. Email: qddcc@excite.com. Barbara Berrios, Dir. Children 125; Total Staff 20.

[W] GENERAL HOSPITALS

NEW YORK. *Cabrini Medical Center (Cabrini Development Council, Inc.)*, 227 E. 19th St., 10003. Tel: 212-995-6000; Fax: 212-995-6568. Mr. Robert S. Chaloner, Pres. & CEO; Sr. Arlene Primus, M.S.C., Exec. Dir. for Mission & Ministry. Bed Capacity Acute Hospital 467; Available for Use 329; Skilled Nursing Facility at Dobbs Ferry 306; New York City, Beds 240; Missionary Sisters of the Sacred Heart 10; Patients Assisted Annually (includes Homecare Visits) 66,832; Cabrini Hospice Program (Home Care) 900; Total Staff 2,376.

Stuyvesant Polyclinic, Inc. Tel: 212-674-0220; Fax: 212-533-2251. Patients Assisted Annually 62,891.

Sisters of Charity Health Care System Corp., 75 Vanderbilt Ave., Staten Island, 10304. Tel: 718-354-5080. Web: www.schcs.com. Bed Capacity 866; Total Assisted Annually 29,794; Total Staff 4,000.

Bayley Seton Campus Tel: 718-354-6000; Fax: 718-876-1234.

St. Vincent's Medical Center of Richmond

Saint Vincent Catholic Medical Centers of New York, 130 W. 12 St., 10011. Tel: 212-604-2300; Fax: 212-604-7533. Email: mfagan@svcmcny.org. Web: svcmc.org. Henry Amoroso, Pres. & CEO; Lowell Johnson, CFO; Ms. Catherine Callagy, Senior Vice Pres. Fund Devel.; Arthur Webb, COO; Paul Goebel, Chief Administrative Officer. Bed Capacity 662; Total Assisted Annually 300,000; Total Staff 4,545.

St. Vincent's Manhattan, 170 W. 12th St., 10011. Tel: 212-604-7000.

St. Vincent's Westchester, 275 North St., Harrison, 10528. Tel: 914-967-6500; Fax: 914-925-5157.

KINGSTON. *Benedictine Hospital* (1901) 105 Mary's Ave., 12401. Tel: 845-338-2500; Fax: 845-334-3149. Web: www.hahv.org. Sisters Mary Feehan, O.S.B., Senior Vice Pres., Mission Effectiveness; Mary Dorothy Huggard, O.S.B., Dir., Pastoral Care. Sisters of St. Benedict (Federation of St. Scholastica) 4; Capacity 150; Patients Assisted Annually 72,996; Total Staff 738.

PORT JERVIS. *Bon Secours Community Hospital* (1915) 160 E. Main St., 12771. Tel: 845-858-7000; Fax: 845-858-7415. Email: jeff_reilly@bshsi.org. Web: www.bonsecourscommunityhosp.org. Jeff Reilly, Sr. Vice Pres. Opers.; Sr. Rosemary Corr, Chap.; Rev. Vincent Odikanoro. Capacity 141; SNF Beds 46; Patients Assisted Annually 81,802; Total Staff 474.

POUGHKEEPSIE. *St. Francis Hospital*, 241 North Rd., 12601. Tel: 845-483-5000; Fax: 845-485-3762. Web: www.sfhhc.org. Robert L. Savage, Pres. & CEO; Revs. Joseph Mali, Dir. Pastoral Care & Mission Effectiveness; Zeverin Emagalit, Pastoral Care Assoc. Sisters of St. Francis of the Neumann Communities Capacity 333; Outpatient Visits 179,324; Admissions 8,924; Total Staff 1,650.

St. Francis Health Care Foundation, 241 North Rd., 12601. Tel: 845-431-8707; Fax: 845-483-5097.

SUFFERN. *Good Samaritan Hospital of Suffern*, 255 Lafayette Ave., 10901. Tel: 845-368-5000; Fax: 845-368-5430. Web: www.GoodSamHosp.org. Philip A. Patterson, CEO, Bon Secours Charity Health System; Clare Brady, Sr. Vice Pres. Mission; Rev. Jamie Bono, Dir. Pastoral Care. Sisters of Charity of St. Elizabeth 1; Capacity 370; Patients Assisted Annually 165,000; Total Staff 1,575.

WARWICK. *St. Anthony Community Hospital, Inc.* Franciscan System of Warwick, Inc., 15-19 Maple Ave., 10990. Tel: 845-986-2276; Fax: 845-986-2687. Jeff Reilly, SVP; Leah Cerkvenik, EVP; Suzanne Evanoff, Dir. Pastoral Care; Rev. Henry Tanto, Chap. (Retired). Capacity 73; Patients Assisted Annually 34,262.

YONKERS. *St. Joseph's Medical Center* (1888) 127 S. Broadway, 10701. Tel: 914-378-7000; Fax: 914-965-4838. Email: public.relations@saintjosephs.org. Web: saintjosephs.org. Mr. Michael J. Spicer, Pres.; Rev. Thomas Murphy, O.F.M.Cap.; Sr. Dolores Doyle, P.B.V.M., Dir. of Pastoral Care. Bed Capacity 394; Nursing Home Beds 200; Sisters of Charity of St. Vincent de Paul 7; Patients Assisted Annually 340,407; Total Staff 1,411.

[X] SPECIAL HOSPITALS AND SANATORIA FOR INVALIDS

NEW YORK. *Calvary Hospital* (1889) For advanced cancer patients., 1740 Eastchester Rd., Bronx, 10461. Tel: 718-863-6900; Fax: 718-518-2674. Email: sgarry@calvaryhospital.org. Web: www.calvaryhospital.org. Frank A. Calamari, Pres. & CEO; Rev. Chux Okochi, Dir. Pastoral Svcs. Pastoral Staff 20; Accommodations for 225; Patients Assisted Annually 5,519.

Terence Cardinal Cooke Health Care Center, 1249 Fifth Ave., 10029. Tel: 212-360-1000; Fax: 212-289-2739. Email: lgaffney@chcsnet.org. Web: www.tcchcc.org. Laura P. Gaffney, Exec. Dir. Hospital for developmentally disabled. Bed Capacity 50.

Developmental Disabilities Clinic, 1249 Fifth Ave., 10029. Tel: 212-360-3703; Fax: 212-360-3842. Comprehensive Outpatient medical, therapeutic and educational services. On site and off site OMRDD Article 16 services. Patients Assisted Annually 44,000.

Hemodialysis, 1249 Fifth Ave., 10029. Tel: 212-360-3860; Fax: 212-860-3862. 22 End Stage Renal Dialysis Stations; (For information concerning nursing home see Homes for Aged category.) Patients Assisted Annually 22,000.

BRONX. *St. Eleanora's Home for Convalescents* (1901) Sisters of Charity Center, 6301 Riverdale Ave., 10471. Tel: 718-549-9200, Ext. 261; Fax: 718-884-3013. Email: ghanley@scny.org. Web: scny.org. Total Assisted Annually 30; Total Staff 10.

HARRISON. *St. Vincent's Hospital Westchester* (1879) 275 North St., 10528. Tel: 914-967-6500; Fax: 914-925-5157. Web: www.svcmc.org. Bernadette Kingham-Bez. Psychiatric Hospital.; Clergy Consultation Program; Inpatient and outpatient mental health and substance abuse services for adults, adolescents, children and their families. Sites in Harrison, Tuckahoe & White Plains. Services available in Spanish. Capacity 133; Inpatients Assisted Annually 2,891; Sisters of Charity of St. Vincent de Paul 3; All outpatient program admissions 165,000; Partial Hospital 50; Opiod Maintenance Treatment Program 43.

HAWTHORNE. *Rosary Hill Home* (1901) Free home for incurable cancer patients., 10532. Tel: 914-769-0114; Fax: 914-769-3916. Web: www.hawthorne.dominicans.org. Sisters Mary Joseph, O.P., Admin.; Maureen, O.P., Supr. *The Servants of Relief for Incurable Cancer* Professed Sisters of St. Dominic 26; Capacity 72; Patients Assisted Annually 106; Total Staff 47.

[Y] ORDERS OF NURSING SISTERS

NEW YORK. *Little Sisters of the Assumption Family Health Service, Inc.* (1958) 333 E. 115th St., 10029. Tel: 646-672-5200; Fax: 212-348-8284. Email: gcarter@lsafhs.org. Gary Carter, Exec. Dir.

BRONX. *Convent of the Sisters Servants of Mary* Mission: Private nursing in the homes., 3305 Country Club Rd., 10465-1296. Tel: 718-829-0428; Fax: 718-829-2346. Email: servantsmaryny@optonline.com. Web: sistersservantsofmary.org. Sr. Elvia Navarro, S.deM., Mother Supr. Sisters 21.

OSSINING. *Dominican Sisters Family Health Service, Inc. (Central Services/Administration)* (1974) Community-based, certified, voluntary Home Health Agency and Long Term Home Health Care and AIDS Programs serving all of Westchester, Suffolk and the South Bronx. Unique community outreach programs., 299 N. Highland Ave., 10562. Tel: 914-941-1710; Fax: 914-941-0518. Email: VHanrahan@dsfhs.org. Web: www.dsfhs.org. Sisters Virginia Hanrahan, O.P., B.S.N., M.S.N., Ph.D., Pres./CEO; Margaret Flood, O.P., B.S.N., M.A., M.P.A., COO. Total Staff 423; Total Patients 14,000; Total Visits 197,000.

Bronx Office, 279 Alexander Ave., Bronx, 10454. Tel: 718-665-6557; Fax: 718-292-9113. Ana Collado, Admin.

Westchester Office, 299 N. Highland Ave., 10562. Tel: 914-941-1654; Fax: 914-941-1556. Email: EBobb@dsfhs.org. Evelyn Bobb, B.S.N., M.P.A., Admin.

Suffolk County Offices (4 Offices in Suffolk), 103-6 W. Montauk Hwy., Box 209, Hampton Bays, 11946. Tel: 631-728-0181; Fax: 631-728-2943. Email: pash@dsfhs.org. Web: www.dsfhs.org.

Box 678, Wainscott, 11975. Tel: 631-537-6759; Fax: 631-537-7187. Email: pash@dsfhs.org. Web: www.dsfhs.org. Pamella Ash, B.S.N., M.A., Admin., Suffolk Offices.

3237 Rte. 112, Ste. 1, Medford, 11763. Tel: 631-207-1170; Fax: 631-207-0149.

**Family Home Health Care, Inc.* (Licensed Home Health Care Affiliate), 65 S. Broadway, Tarrytown, 10591. Tel: 914-631-7200; Fax: 914-631-2382. Email: dozure@dsfhs.org. Diane Ozure, Admin.

Family Home Health Care, Inc. (Licensed Home Health Care Affiliate), 3237 Rte. 112, Ste. 1, Medford, 11763. Tel: 631-207-1170; Fax: 631-207-0149. Email: pash@dsfhs.org. Pamella Ash, B.S.N., M.A., Admin., Suffolk Offices.

STATEN ISLAND. *Pax Christi Hospice* Hospice Care Services for the terminally ill., 1200 South Ave., Ste. 306, 10314. Tel: 718-876-1022; Fax: 718-876-1803.

[Z] NURSING HOMES

NEW YORK. *Cabrini Center for Nursing & Rehabilitation*, 542 E. 5th St., 10009. Tel: 212-358-3000; Fax: 212-358-6269. Email: mdevlin@cabrini-eldercare.org. Web: www.cabrini-eldercare.org. Sr. Mary Fedlis Ezemaduka, S.J.S., Chap.; Mary Devlin, COO. Total SNF Beds 240; Total Assisted Annually 4,789; Total Staff 305.

Kateri Residence (1981) Skilled Nursing Care/Residential Health Care Facility for the Elderly., 150 Riverside Dr., 10024-2201. Tel: 646-505-3500; Fax: 212-873-0658. Email: hkole@archcare.org. Web: www.archcare.org. Henriette M. Kole, Exec. Dir.; Michael Monahan, Admin.; Tim Moses, Dir. Res. Svcs.; Carmen Vega-Stevens, Dir. Quality Mgmt. & Corp. Compliance Officer; Elliot Schwartz, Medical Dir.; Maureen Boothby, Dir. Nursing Svcs.; Eileen Donovan, Dir. Res. Assessment; Wanda Taylor, Dir. Admissions; Lisa Orriola, Dir. Recreation; Rev. John Anderson, Dir. Pastoral Care; Sisters Miriam Poveda, R.S.H.M., Pastoral Care Assoc.; Padraic Mary McGuinness, O.P., Pastoral Care Assoc.; Mary Pat Gorman-Barry, Dir. Social Svcs.; Sara DeTore, Dir. Rehabilitation Svcs.; Rev. Anthony J. Pleho, Chap. Bed Capacity 520; Total Staff 648.

Mary Manning Walsh Home, 1339 York Ave., 10021. Tel: 212-628-2800; Fax: 212-585-3896. Email: mmwhome@msn.com. Sr. Sean William O'Brien, O.Carm., Admin. Carmelite Sisters for the Aged and Infirm. Total Staff 480; Bed Capacity 362; Total Assisted 724.

Terence Cardinal Cooke Health Care Center Skilled Nursing Facility; Skilled Nursing Facility AIDS Program, 1249 Fifth Ave., 10029. Tel: 212-360-1000; Fax: 212-289-2739. Email: lgaffney@chcsnet.org. Web: www.tcchcc.org. (See Special Hospitals Category for additional services offered from this Health Care Center.) Bed Capacity 523; Bed Capacity 156.

BRONX. *Bon Secours New York Health System, Inc.*, 2975 Independence Ave., 10463-4699. Tel: 718-548-1700; Fax: 718-554-8826. Email: stephen_kazanjian@bshsi.org. Web: www.scherviercares.org. Eileen Malo, CEO; Charles Ignatius, Chap. & Dir. Pastoral Care.

Frances Schervier Home and Hospital

Frances Schervier Housing Development Fund Corporation

Jeanne Jugan Residence (1903) 2999 Schurz Ave., 10465. Tel: 347-329-1800; Fax: 347-329-1815. Email: bxmothersuperior@littlesistersofthepoor.org. Web: www.jjrbronx.org. Sr. Genevieve Nugent, Pres.; Rev. Robert M. Dunn, Chap. Low Income Apartments 20; Skilled 30; Dayshare 20; Bed Capacity 47; Total Staff 60; Total Assisted Annually 90.

Medical Missionaries of Mary, 563 Minneford Ave., 10464-1118. Tel: 718-885-0945; Fax: 718-885-0010. Email: minniefordmmm@verizon.net. Web: www.mmmusa.org. Sisters Siobhan Corkery, M.M.M., Congregational Leader; Therese McDonough, M.M.M., USA Area Leader.

St. Patrick's Home for the Aged and Infirm (1931) 66 Van Cortlandt Park S., 10463. Tel: 718-519-2800; Fax: 718-304-1817. Email: www.admissions@stpatrickshome.org. Web: www.stpatrickshome.org/. Sr. M. Patrick Michael, O.Carm., Admin. Carmelite Sisters for the Aged and Infirm. Sisters 16; Bed Capacity 264; Total Assisted Annually 429; Total Staff 350.

Providence Rest (1922) 3304 Waterbury Ave., 10465. Tel: 718-931-3000; Fax: 718-514-8447. Email: prnh@providencerest.org. Web: www.providencerest.org. Sisters Seline Mary Flores, C.S.J.B., Admin.; Michele Sinnona, Supr. Sisters of St. John the Baptist 19; Bed Capacity 200; Total Assisted 174; Total Staff 310.

St. Vincent de Paul Residence (1992) 900 Intervale Ave., 10459. Tel: 917-645-9200; Fax: 718-589-7010. Email: fcianciotto@chcsnet.org. Web: www.svdpres.org. Mr. Frank Cianciotto, CEO.

DOBBS FERRY. *Cabrini of Westchester*, 115 Broadway, 10522. Tel: 914-693-6800; Fax: 914-693-1731. Web: www.cabrini-eldercare.org. Patricia Krasnausky, Pres. & CEO; Rev. Edwin F.D. Robinson, O.F.M., Dir. Pastoral Care. Missionary Sisters of the Sacred Heart 5; Bed Capacity 304; Home Health Care 250; Total Staff 450; Adult Day Health Care 50.

Cabrini Care at Home, 115 Broadway, 10522. Tel: 914-693-6800, Ext. 500. Email: pkrasnausky@cabrini-eldercare.org. Web:

www.cabrini-eldercare.org. Patricia Krasnausky, Contact Person.

MIDDLETOWN. *St. Teresa's Nursing Home*, 120 Highland Ave., 10940. Tel: 845-342-1033; Fax: 845-344-5631. Email: mchaiken@chcsnet.org. Bed Capacity 98; Total Assisted 98; Total Staff 122.

RHINEBECK. *Ferncliff Nursing Home* (1973) 21 Ferncliff Dr., 12572. Tel: 845-876-2011; Fax: 845-876-4810. Sr. Sean Damien Flynn, O.Carm., B.S., M.B.A., Admin. Member: Catholic Health Care System. Bed Capacity 328; Total Assisted 410; Total Staff 450.

STATEN ISLAND. *Carmel Richmond Healthcare and Rehabilitation Center* (1969) 88 Old Town Rd., 10304-4299. Tel: 718-979-5000; Fax: 718-979-8027. Sr. Maureen T. Murray, O.Carm., Pres. & CEO. Carmelite Sisters for the Aged and Infirm. Bed Capacity 300; Total Assisted Annually 330; Total Staff 350.

Friends of Carmel Richmond, Inc. (1981) Tel: 718-979-5000; Fax: 718-979-8027. Adult Daycare Program. Total Assisted 330; Total Staff 350; Adult Day Healthcare Program Rehabilitation Unit 30.

WARWICK. *Villa Frances at the Knolls* Franciscan Health Partner, Inc., 22 Van Duzer Pl., 10990. Tel: 914-987-5717; Fax: 914-986-1231. Tom Clark, SVP, Long Term Care; Michael Deyo, Admin., Schervier Pavillion; Rev. Henry Tanto (Retired). Capacity 120.

[AA] ADULT RESIDENCES

NEW YORK. *St. Agnes' Residence* For students and working women., 237 W. 74th St., 10023. Tel: 212-874-1361. Nancy Clifford, Admin. Franciscan Fathers of St. Francis Monastery. Daughters of Mary of the Immaculate Conception 2; Accommodations for 99; Total Assisted 104; Total Staff 6.

Centro Maria, Inc. For young students and working women., 539 W. 54th St., 10019. Tel: 212-757-6989; Fax: 212-307-5687. Email: cenmariany@mindspring.com. Web: www.religiosasdemariainmaculada.org. Sr. Hilda Ramirez, R.M.I., Local Supr. Religious of Mary Immaculate 8; Total Assisted Annually 667; Bed Capacity 86.

Cor Mariae, c/o 1011 First Ave., Rm. 1130, 10022. Tel: 212-371-1000, Ext. 2435. Residence for formerly homeless senior women.

The Dwelling Place (1977) For homeless women., 409 W. 40th St., 10018. Tel: 212-564-7887; Fax: 212-695-3642. Sr. Margaret Boyle, P.B.V.M., Admin. Bed Capacity 15; Dinner Program 50; Total Assisted 12,000; Total Staff 6.

El Carmelo Residence, 249 W. 14th St., 10011. Tel: 212-242-8224; Fax: 212-242-7233. Sr. Modesta Perez, Supr.

The Jeanne d'Arc Residence (1896) 253 W. 24th St., 10011. Tel: 212-989-5952; Fax: 212-691-0257. Email: jdresidence@gmail.com. Ms. Eileen C. Piazza, Admin. Women. Accommodations for 140; Sisters of Divine Providence 7; Lay Staff 11; Total Assisted Annually 200.

St. Joseph's Immigrant Home For students and working women., 425 W. 44th St., 10036-4402. Tel: 212-246-5363. Sr. Mary Celine, D.M., Admin. Daughters of Mary of the Immaculate Conception 2; Accommodations for 90.

Kolping Society of New York Men's Residence (Catholic Kolping Society New York, Inc.) (1888) For young Catholic men., 165 E. 88th St., 10128. Tel: 212-369-6647; Fax: 212-987-5652. Email: residence@kolpingny.org. Ernest Endrich, Mgr. Bed Capacity 88; Total Assisted Annually 350; Total Staff 10.

The Leo House (1889) Clergy, Sisters & Other Travelers., 332 W. 23rd St., 10011. Tel: 212-929-1010; Fax: 212-366-6801. Mr. Frank Castro, Exec. Dir. Bed Capacity 70; Total Staff 35.

St. Mary's Residence (1913) For students and young working women., 225 E. 72nd St., 10021. Tel: 212-249-6850; Fax: 212-249-4336. Email: St.MarysRes72@aol.com. Sr. Almaisa Brito, F.D.C., Admin.; Mrs. Lisa Rodriguez, Dir. of Admissions. Daughters of Divine Charity 6; Bed Capacity 150; Total Staff 6.

Sacred Heart Residence Working or studying young ladies ages 19-29., 432 W. 20th St., 10011. Tel: 212-929-5790; Fax: 212-924-0891. Email: sacredheartresidence@hotmail.com. Web: www.sacredheartresidence.com. Sr. Haydee Luisa Fernandez, Admin. Congregation of Mothers of the Helpless. Capacity 30; Total Staff 3.

Thorpe Family Residence, Inc. (1988) 2252 Crotona Ave., 10457. Tel: 718-933-7312; Fax: 718-933-7311. Email: mdeodati@aol.com. Web: thorpeonline.org. Sr. Mary Jane Deodati, R.D.C., Exec. Dir. Residents 65; Total Assisted 130; Total Staff 10.

The Crotona-Thorpe Housing Development Fund Corporation Tel: 845-359-6400; Fax: 845-359-6503. Sr. Irene Ellis, O.P., Pres. (Sub of Thorpe Family Residence, Inc.)

BRONX. *Kolping-on-Concourse*, 2916 Grand Concourse, 10458. Tel: 718-733-6119. Web: www.kolpingresidence.com. Ernest Endrich, Mgr. (Catholic Kolping Society New York, Inc.) Total in Residence 96; Total Assisted Annually 124; Total Staff 11.

DOBBS FERRY. *Cabrini Housing Development Fund Corporation*, c/o of St. Cabrini Nursing Home, Inc., 115 Broadway, 10522. Tel: 914-693-6800, Ext. 500; Fax: 914-693-1731. Email: pkrasnausky@cabrini-eldercare.org. Web: www.cabrini-eldercare.org.

GARRISON. *St. Christopher's Inn* (1908) Temporary shelter for homeless men. Outpatient chemical dependency services & primary healthcare., 21 Franciscan Way, P.O. Box 150, 10524-0150. Tel: 845-335-1000; Fax: 845-335-1017. Email: bdrobach@atonementfriars.org. Web: www.stchristophersinn-graymoor.org. Rev. William Drobach, S.A., Pres. & CEO. Atonement Friars. Total Assisted 1,200; Total Staff 75; Bed Capacity 177; Volunteers 15.

MONTROSE. *Kolping-on-Hudson* (Catholic Kolping Society New York, Inc.), 95 Montrose Point Rd., 10548. Tel: 914-736-0117. Total Assisted 2,000; Total Staff 10.

MOUNT VERNON. *St. Theresa's Residence*, 30 S. 10th Ave., 10550. Tel: 914-664-5900; Fax: 914-664-6733. John Schroeder, Exec. Dir. Bed Capacity 12.

[BB] CATHOLIC CAMPS

NEW YORK. *The Catholic Camp Association Inc.*, 1011 First Ave., 10022. Tel: 212-371-1000.

John V. Mara CYO Camps, Putnam Valley, 10579.

Hill Camp Capacity 120.

Valley Camp Capacity 120; Total Assisted 147; Total in Residence 271; Total Staff 48.

THORNWOOD. *Mission Network Activities USA, Inc.* (1997) 590 Columbus Ave., 10594. Tel: 914-773-1368; Fax: 914-773-1438. Rev. Jose Felix Ortega, L.C., Contact Person.

[CC] COMMUNITY CENTERS

NEW YORK. *Cardinal Spellman Center, Inc.*, 137 E. Second St., 10009. Tel: 212-677-6600; Fax: 212-995-8537. Community Centers foster and promote the positive development of children, youth, their families and other adults by providing or hosting various wholesome activities.

Casita Maria Inc. (1934) 928 Simpson St., 6th Fl., Bronx, 10459. Tel: 718-589-2230; Fax: 718-842-4622. Email: info@casita.us. Web: www.casitamaria.org. Sarah Calderon, Exec. Dir.; Mrs. Jacqueline Weld, Chm. Serves the Bronx, East Harlem, and greater New York City; Casita Maria serves over 5,000 individuals each year through arts, education, and community programs.

Casita Maria-Carver Community Center, 55 E. 102nd St., 10029. Tel: 212-289-2708; 718-589-2230; Fax: 212-360-1947; 718-589-5714. Email: info@casita.us. Lue Ann Eldar, Exec. Dir.; Diana Ayala, Dir. Serves Carver Houses and adjacent areas of East Harlem.

Casita Maria Inc., 928 Simpson St., Bronx, 10459. Tel: 718-589-2230; Fax: 718-589-5714.

Drew-Hamilton CYO Center, 220 W. 143rd St., 10030. Serves Central Harlem.

Lieut. Joseph P. Kennedy, Jr. Memorial Community Center, 34 W. 134th St., 10037. Tel: 212-862-6401, Ext. 410; Fax: 212-862-6421. Deacon Rodney Beckford. Community Centers foster and promote the positive development of children, youth, their families and other adults by providing or hosting various wholesome activities.

Life Experience and Faith Sharing Association, 45 E. 126th St., 10035. Tel: 212-987-0959; Fax: 212-987-0958. Email: lefslitera@aol.com. James Addison, LEFS Team - Mission Co-Coord. & Fin. Coord.; Deborah Byrd, LEFS Team; Deborah Canty, LEFS Team; Timothy Dunnington, LEFS Team; Sr. Dorothy Gallant, S.C., LEFS Team - Mission Co-Coord.; Georgia James, LEFS Team; Vaughn McLamb, LEFS Team; Sr. Cecilia Palange, I.C.M., LEFS Team; Ann Quintano, LEFS Team; Eve Thomas Barber, Assoc. Team Mem.; Frank Brandon, Assoc. Team Mem. LEFSA - Ministry among people who are homeless and formerly homeless. Total Assisted 1,500.

Staten Island CYO Center Serves residents of Port Richmond and surrounding areas.

120 Anderson Ave., Port Richmond, Staten Island, 10302. Fax: 718-273-8361.

HAVERSTRAW. *Catholic Community Services of Rockland, Inc.*, 78 Hudson Ave., 10927. Tel: 845-942-5791; Fax: 845-429-2938. Email: martha.robles@archny.org. Martha Robles, Exec. Dir. Provides emergency services to those in need.

PORT CHESTER. *Don Bosco Community Center of Port Chester, Inc.*, Office of the Pres., 22 Don Bosco Pl., 10573. Tel: 914-939-0323, Ext. 11; Fax: 914-939-3490. Email: boscoalive@yahoo.com. Web: www.donboscocenter.com. Rev. Richard Alejunas, S.D.B., Exec. Dir.

YONKERS. *Casa Juan Diego, Inc.*, 97 Yonkers Ave., 10701. Tel: 914-963-0250; Fax: 914-476-5033. Bro. Philip Allen, C.F.R., Dir. Services to the needy; especially Spanish Speaking immigrants, day laborers.

[DD] MONASTERIES AND RESIDENCES OF PRIESTS AND BROTHERS

NEW YORK. *All Saints Friary* (2002) (Order of Friars Minor-The Franciscans-Province of the Most Holy Name of Jesus), 47 E. 129th St., 10035. Tel: 212-534-3535; Fax: 212-534-7832. Bros. Charles F. Gilmartin, O.F.M.; Glenn W. Humphrey, O.F.M., B.A., M.A., Ph.D.; Revs. Francis K. Kim, O.F.M., B.A., M.Div.; Steven Pavignano, O.F.M. Priests 2; Brothers 2.

"America;" Residence and publication office of the America Press, 106 W. 56th St., 10019. Tel: 212-581-4640; Fax: 212-399-3596. Email: jesuits@americamagazine.org. Web: www.americamagazine.org. Revs. Andrew J. Christiansen, S.J., Editor-in-Chief; Robert C. Collins, S.J.; Vincent P. DeCola, S.J.; Charles A. Frederico, S.J.; Daniel J. Gatti, S.J.; Roger D. Haight, S.J.; Walter J. Modrys, S.J.; James J. Martin, S.J.; Damian O'Connell, S.J.; Leo J. O'Donovan, S.J.; Joseph A. O'Hare, S.J.; Robert F. O'Toole, S.J., Interim Supr.; Joseph P. Parkes, S.J.; J. Peter Schineller, S.J.; John P. Schlegel, S.J., Publisher; Edward W. Schmidt, S.J.; Raymond A. Schroth, S.J.; Michael E. Sehler, S.J.; Thomas R. Slon, S.J.; Michael V. Teuth, S.J.; Bro. Francis W. Turnbull, S.J. Priests 20; Brothers 1.

Atonement Friars, 138 Waverly Pl., 10014-3845. Tel: 212-243-4692; Fax: 212-675-6160. Web: www.atonementfriars.org. Revs. James Loughran, S.A.; Timothy I. MacDonald, S.A., Admin. & Guardian; Elias D. Mallon, S.A.; Charles Sharon, S.A., Admin.; Wilfred Tyrrell, S.A.

Brothers of the Christian Schools of Manhattan College, Inc., 4415 Post Rd., Bronx, 10471. Tel: 718-884-0613; Fax: 718-884-3500. Bros. Timothy Murphy, Pres./Dir.; John Muller, F.S.C., Sec. Total Staff 3; Total in Residence 25.

Calasanzian Fathers (Piarists), 88 Convent Ave., 10027. Tel: 212-234-1919; Fax: 212-281-7205. Email: annunciationchurchnyc@yahoo.com. Revs. Jose A. Gimeno, Sch.P. (Spain), Supr.; Jose M. Clavero, Sch.P. (Spain); Javier Vanegas, Sch.P. (Nicaragua); Luis A. Cruz, Sch.P. (Puerto Rico); Very Rev. Fernando Negro, Sch.P. (Spain).

St. Catherine of Siena Priory, 411 E. 68th St., 10021. Tel: 212-988-8300; Fax: 212-988-6918. Email: stcatsiena@aol.com. Revs. Christopher Johnson, O.P., Prior; Jordan James Kelly, O.P., Subprior; Michael P. Trainor, O.P.; John Aquinas Farren, O.P., S.T.D.; Louis C. Mason, O.P.; Kenneth A. France-Kelly, O.P.; Bro. Thomas Aquinas Dolan, O.P.

St. Clare Friary, 440 W. 36th St., 10018-6326. Tel: 212-594-4108. Email: sground440@aol.com. Web: www.solidgroundministry.com. Rev. James Goode, O.F.M., Ph.D., Local Minister, Pastoral Dir., Solid Ground Ministry; Harold Williams Jr., Affiliate, Solid Ground Prog. Coord.; James P. Newson Jr., Black Catholic Apostolate for Life Asst. *Shrine of Saint Josephine Bakhita* In the Holy Mother of God Chapel, Tel: 212-868-1847. Web: www.solidgroundministry.com. *Solid Ground Ministry: A Franciscan Ministry with African American Families* (1996) Tel: 212-868-1847. Email: sground440@aol.com. Web: www.solidgroundministry.com. *National Black Catholic Apostolate for Life* (1997) Tel: 212-594-4108. Email: tnbcalife@aol.com. Web: www.blackcatholicsforlife.org.

St. Crispin Friary (1987) 420 E. 156th St., Bronx, 10455. Tel: 718-665-2441; Fax: 718-993-4754. Web: www.franciscanfriars.com. *Franciscan Friars of the Renewal* (1987) 420 E. 156th St., Bronx, 10455. Tel: 718-402-8255; Fax: 718-402-5556. Revs. Louis Leonelli, C.F.R., Local Servant; Benedict Joseph Groeschel, C.F.R., Ed.D., Community Council; Bros. Guy LaFranz Bourgeois, C.F.R.; Simon Dankowski, C.F.R.; Mariano Joseph Demma, C.F.R.; Joseph Michael Fino, C.F.R.; Roch Mary Greiner, C.F.R.; Angelo LeFever, C.F.R.; Oisin Martin, C.F.R.; Anthony Ocello, C.F.R.; Crispin Mary Rinaldi, C.F.R. Priests 2; Brothers 6.

Saint Francis Monastery, Inc., 135W. 31 St., 10001. Tel: 212-736-8500. Rev. Andrew J. Reitz, O.F.M., Contact Person.

Franciscan Friars, Holy Name Province, Holy Name Province Provincialate, 129 W. 31st St., 2nd Fl., 10001-3403. Tel: 646-473-0265; Fax: 800-420-1078;

800-605-8542. Email: hnp@hnp.org. Web: www.hnp.org. Very Rev. John F. O'Connor, O.F.M., Pres. & Min. Prov.; Rev. Dominic Monti, O.F.M., Vicar Prov.; Bro. Michael Harlan, O.F.M., Prov. Sec.; Rev. Dennis M. Wilson, O.F.M., Prov. Treas.

The Order of Friars Minor of the Province of the Most Holy Name

Priests of the Province in Residences not listed elsewhere: Revs. David M. Bossman, O.F.M., Seton Hall University, 400 S. Orange Ave., South Orange, NJ 07079-2696. Tel: 973-761-9770; Fax: 973-275-2333; Roch A. Coogan, O.F.M. (Retired); John Coughlin, O.F.M.; James W. Czerwinski, O.F.M.; Francis J. DiSpigno, O.F.M.; Kyle E. Haden, O.F.M.; Michael P. Jones, O.F.M.; Cidouane C. Joseph, O.F.M.; J. Patrick Kelly, O.F.M.; Leonard Lencewicz, O.F.M., St. Anthony Hermitage, 8817 Brys Dr., Tampa, FL 33635. Tel: 813-888-5616; Fax: 813-886-3624; Erick Lopez, O.F.M.; Joseph J. Nangle, O.F.M., Clare House, 708 Rock Creek Church Rd., N.W., Washington, DC 20010; David Phan, O.F.M.; Rene F. Phillips, O.F.M., 850 Thomas Ln., Angola, 14006-9572. Tel: 716-549-7930; C. Raymond Selker, O.F.M.; Benedict M. Taylor, O.F.M., Create Inc., 73 Lenox Ave., 10026. Tel: 212-663-1975; Fax: 212-663-1293; Dac T. Tran, O.F.M.

Priests Abroad: For Information Regarding Vocations to the Brotherhood & Priesthood, write Franciscan Vocation Office, 129 W. 31st St., 2nd Fl., New York, NY 10001-3403. Revs. Howard O'Shea, O.F.M.; Joseph G. Rozansky, O.F.M., JPIC Office of the Order, Curia Generalizia dei Frati Minori, Via S. Maria Mediatrice 25, Rome 00165 Italy; Emerson Rodriguez-Delgado, O.F.M.

Franciscan Province of the Immaculate Conception, 125 Thompson St., 10012. Tel: 212-674-4388; Fax: 212-533-8034. Revs. Primo P. Piscitello, O.F.M., Min. Prov.; Robert M. Campagna, O.F.M., Vicar Prov.; James Goode, O.F.M., Ph.D., Promoter Missions; Bro. Ronald Bolfeta, O.F.M., Prov. Treas. & Prov. Sec.

Friars Minor of the Order of St. Francis, Incorporated, New York, 1871 Franciscan Province of the Immaculate Conception of New York City. Priests 116; Brothers 20; Permanent Deacons 2; Bishops 4. *Franciscan Mission Associates*, 274-280 W. Lincoln Ave., Mount Vernon, 10550. Tel: 914-664-5604; Fax: 914-664-3017. Ms. Madeline Bonnici, Exec. Dir.; Rev. Vit Fiala, O.F.M., Dir. of Secular Franciscans. *Pious League of Saint Anthony*, 151 Thompson St., P.O. Box 700, 10012-0700. Tel: 212-674-4388; Fax: 212-533-8034.

Priests of the Province Abroad: Revs. Francis Walter, O.F.M., General Definitor, Convento S. Francesco, Via Nicolo V, 35, Rome 00165 Italy; Edwin Paniagua, O.F.M., Translator; Antonio Riccio, O.F.M., Guardian.

Military Chaplains: Rev. Michael Travaglione, O.F.M., 23 Bassett St., Fort Bragg, NC 28307.

Retired Military Chaplains: Revs. Edwin Bobrek, O.F.M., 1427 Ave. de las Adelsas, Encinitas, CA 92024. Tel: 619-436-5355; Sigmund Brambilla, O.F.M., 97 Franklin St., Northampton, MA 01060. Tel: 413-584-4482; Jack Hoak, O.F.M., St. Rose of Lima Friary, 35 Center St., Meriden, CT 06450-5685. Tel: 518-273-8622; Fax: 518-273-2731; Charles Soto, O.F.M. (Retired), P.O. Box 4051, Steubenville, OH 43952. Tel: 740-424-9434.

Priests of the Province Residing Elsewhere: Revs. Romano S. Almagno, O.F.M., Sts. Peter & Paul Cathedral Res., 30 Fenner St., Providence, RI 02903; Lucius Annese, O.F.M., 201 E. 19th St., Apt. 8F, 10003. Tel: 212-995-6056; Marion Cascino, O.F.M.; Roderick Crispo, O.F.M.; Simeon C. Distefano, O.F.M., Chap., 1339 York Ave., 10021. Tel: 212-628-2800; Stephen Galambos, O.F.M., 21077 Quarry Hill Rd., Winona, MN 55987. Tel: 507-454-8000; Ronald Gliatta, O.F.M., 3301 N.E. 32nd Ave., Apt. 203, Fort Lauderdale, FL 33308; Ciro Iodice, O.F.M., 1111 Langley St., Fall River, MA 02720. Tel: 508-679-2105; Januarius Izzo, O.F.M., Marian Manor, 130 Dorchester St., South Boston, MA 02127; Richard Martignetti, O.F.M.; Edwin Paniagua, O.F.M., General Curia of Friars Minor, Via S. Maria Mediatrice, 25, Rome 00165 Italy; Emery Parillo, O.F.M.; Clement Procopio, O.F.M., 306 S. 18th St., Cottonwood, AZ 86326. Tel: 928-639-4583; Roberto Siguere, O.F.M., Iglesia de S. Francisco, Barrio Latina, Jutiapa, Jutiapa Guatemala.

Residing in Canada: Revs. Jose Alvin Te, O.F.M.; Gregory Botte, O.F.M., St. Francis Friary, 72 Mansfield Ave., Toronto ON M6J 2B2 Canada. Tel: 416-536-8195; Fax: 416-531-6883; Celestino Canzio, O.F.M., St. Charles Borromeo Friary, 811 Lawrence Ave., Toronto ON M6A 1C3 Canada. Tel: 416-787-0369; Fax: 416-256-4466; Michael D'Cruz, O.F.M., St. Charles Borromeo Friary, 811 Lawrence Ave., Toronto ON M6A 1C3 Canada. Tel: 416-787-0369; Fax: 416-256-4466; Gregory E. Imbroll, O.F.M., St. Charles Borromeo Friary, 811 Lawrence Ave., Toronto ON M6A 1C3 Canada. Tel: 416-787-0369; Fax: 416-256-4466; Giacomo LaSelva, O.F.M.; Frederick Mazzarella, O.F.M., St. Francis Friary, 72 Mansfield Ave., Toronto ON M6J 2B2 Canada. Tel: 416-536-8195; Fax: 416-531-6883; Amedeo Nardone, O.F.M., St. Jane Frances de Chantal Friary, 2747 Jane St., Downsview ON M3L 2E8 Canada. Tel: 416-741-1463; Fax: 416-741-1469; Peter Nguyen Van Quy, O.F.M.; Rohwin Pais, O.F.M., St. Jane Frances de Chantal Friary, 2747 Jane St., Downsview ON M3L 2E8 Canada. Tel: 416-741-1463; Fax: 416-741-1469; Ralph Paonessa, O.F.M., St. Lawrence Friary, 2210 Lawrence Ave. E., Scarborough ON M1P 2P9 Canada. Tel: 416-759-9359; Fax: 416-759-6725; Jimmy Zammit, O.F.M., Immaculate Conception Friary, 2 Richardson Ave., Toronto ON M6M 3R4 Canada. Tel: 416-651-1787; Fax: 416-651-7881. *St. Francis Center for Religious*, 208501 Hwy. #9, Caledon ON L7K OA8 Canada. Tel: 519-941-1747; Fax: 519-941-6961. Bro. Philip Adamo, O.F.M. *St. Peter Friary*, 100 Bainbridge Ave., Woodbridge ON L4L-3Y1 Canada. Tel: 905-851-3600; Fax: 905-856-0171. Revs. Claudio Moser, O.F.M.; James Wells, O.F.M.; Michael Corcione, O.F.M.

The Franciscan Vocation Ministry of Holy Name Province (1901) 129 W. 31st St., 2nd Fl., 10001-3403. Tel: 212-924-1451; 646-473-0265; 800-677-7788; Fax: 800-793-7649. Email: vocation@hnp.org. Web: www.beafranciscan.org. Rev. Brian E. Smail, O.F.M., HNP Vocation Dir.

St. Ignatius Loyola Residence (1866) 53 E. 83rd St., 10028. Tel: 212-288-6200; Fax: 212-606-3460. Revs. Frederick J. Pellegrini, S.J., Interim Rector; Arthur C. Bender, S.J.; William J. Bergen, S.J.; Vincent L. Biagi, S.J.; Vincent M. Cooke, S.J.; James J. Curry, S.J.; Thomas F. Denny, S.J.; James L. Dugan, S.J.; John F. Garvey, S.J.; Philip G. Judge, S.J.; Ugo R. Nacciarone, S.J.; Daniel G. O'Hare, S.J.; Hernan Paredes, S.J.; Michael J. Sala, S.J.; Ramon A. Salomone, S.J., Min.; John R. Sheehan, S.J.; George M. Witt, S.J.; Bros. Edward L. McCarthy, S.J.; Jerome P. Menkhaus, S.J.

Immaculate Conception Friary, 754 E. Gun Hill Rd., 10467. Tel: 212-653-2200. Revs. John LoSasso, O.F.M.Cap.; Peter Napoli, O.F.M.Cap.; Robert Williams, O.F.M.Cap. Capuchin Friars of the Province of the Stigmata of St. Francis. Total Assisted 190; Total Staff 20; Priests 3; Brothers 2.

Institute of the Incarnate Word, Inc., 113 E. 117th St., 10035. Tel: 212-534-5257; Fax: 212-534-5258. Web: www.iveamerica.org. Rev. Gustavo Javier Nieto, I.V.E., Pres.

Jesuit Community at Fordham University (1846) 441 E. Fordham Rd., Spellman Hall, 10458. Tel: 718-817-5322; Fax: 718-733-4456. Rev. John J. Cecero, S.J., Rector/Supr., Jesuit Community at Cardinal Spellman Hall. *Loyola Hall, Jesuit Community* (1929) Tel: 718-817-5322; Fax: 718-733-4456. Revs. Thomas E. Smith, S.J., Supr.; Thomas R. Marciniak, S.J., Minister; Pierce A. Brennan, S.J.; Robert H. Cousineau, S.J.; Joseph V. Dolan, S.J., Sub Min.; Edward T. Dowling, S.J.; Rev. Msgr. Charles J. Fahey (SY); Revs. James J. Fedigan, S.J.; Alfred L. Fiorino, S.J.; Mallick J. Fitzpatrick, S.J.; Matthew C. Flood, S.J.; John R. Keating, S.J.; Donald J. Keefe, S.J.; Gerald J. McIntyre, S.J.; Donald J. Moore, S.J.; Vincent M. Novak, S.J.; Thomas V. O'Connor, S.J.; Louis B. Pascoe, S.J.; Angelo Sujeewa Pathirana, S.J.; Richard J. Regan, S.J.; James A. Sadowsky, S.J.; Victor Salanga, S.J.; Daniel J. Sullivan, S.J.; Jose Vilaplana, S.J. (Spain); Bros. Sebastian A. Boccabella, S.J.; John Glasenapp, O.S.B. *Jesuit Community, Kohlmann Hall* Tel: 718-584-1638; Fax: 718-584-0760. Revs. Raymond M. Sweitzer, S.J., Supr.; Kenneth J. Boller, S.J., Pres., Fordham Prep.; Donald G. Devine, S.J.; James J. Hederman, S.J.; Joseph J. Kamiensky, S.J.; Stanley J. O'Konsky, S.J.; William J. O'Malley, S.J.; Charles D. Sullivan, S.J.; James R. VanDyke, S.J. *Cardinal Spellman Hall, Jesuit Community* (1995) Tel: 718-817-5330; Fax: 718-817-5717. Revs. John J. Cecero, S.J., Rector/Supr.; R. Bentley Anderson, S.J.; Henry J. Bertels, S.J.; Claudio M. Burgaleta, S.J.; Martin Chase, S.J.; Christopher M. Cullen, S.J.; Terrence E. Dempsey, S.J.; John T. Dzieglewicz, S.J.; Philip A. Florio, S.J.; Robert R. Grimes, S.J.; Anton T. Harris, S.J., Min. & Asst. to Rector; Aloysius P. Kelley, S.J.; Joseph W. Koterski, S.J.; Joseph T. Lienhard, S.J.; Nicholas D. Lombardi, S.J.; David P. Marcotte, S.J.; Thomas M. McCoog, S.J.; Paul D. McNelis, S.J.; Joseph M. McShane, S.J., Pres., Fordham Univ.; Mark S. Mossa, S.J.; G. Ronald Murphy, S.J.; Daniel J. O'Brien, S.J.; George W. Quickley, S.J.; Gerard Reedy, S.J.; Patrick J. Ryan, S.J.; Thomas J. Scirghi, S.J.; Gregory S. Waldrop, S.J. Priests 60; Brothers 2; Total in Residence 62.

St. Joseph's Friary (Franciscan Friars of the Renewal); (Postulancy), 523 W. 142nd St., 10031. Tel: 212-234-9089; Fax: 212-234-8871; Tel: 212-281-4355 (Vocations Office). Web: www.franciscanfriars.com. Revs. Luke Mary Fletcher, C.F.R., Local Servant & Postulant Dir.; Isaac Mary Spinharney, C.F.R., Vicar; Gabriel Mary Bakkar, C.F.R., Vocation Dir.; Robert Lombardo, C.F.R.; Bros. John-Mary Johannssen, C.F.R.; Jude Thaddeus Mary Boyden, C.F.R.; Angelus Immaculata Montgomery, C.F.R. Postulants 5. *St. Mary Church*, 17 Pompton Ave., Pompton Lakes, NJ 07442. Tel: 973-835-0374; Fax: 973-835-8173.

Maryknoll House Catholic Foreign Mission Society., 121 E. 39th St., 10016. Tel: 212-697-4470; Fax: 212-697-4472. Email: mklnyc@aol.com. Web: www.maryknoll.org. Rev. Francis T. McGourn, M.M., Dir.

Murray-Weigel Hall, 515 E. Fordham Rd., 10458-5004. Tel: 718-430-4900; Fax: 718-365-8650. Email: jfjoyce@jesuits.net. Revs. Erwin G. Beck, S.J.; Thomas C. Blessin, S.J.; John B. Breslin, S.J., M.A., M.Div., Ph.D.; John M. Buckley, S.J.; Vincent E. Butler, S.J.; Richard L. Caplice, S.J.; James R. Carney, S.J.; Neil J. Carr, S.J.; William B. Cogan, S.J.; John M. Costello, S.J.; John F. Curran, S.J.; Robert W. Dahlke, S.J.; James J. DiGiacamo, S.J.; Joseph F. Fitzpatrick, S.J.; John J. Gallen, S.J.; John J. Gerhard, S.J.; Richard P. Grogan, S.J.; Edward L. Guth, S.J.; Martin S. Hegyi, S.J., B.A., Ph.D. (Hungary); James F. Joyce, S.J., Supr.; Joseph P. Kane, S.J.; Robert G. Kelly, S.J., M.A.T., B.A., S.T.B.; John J. Leonard, S.J.; Charles H. Lohr, S.J.; Edward C. Lynch, S.J.; T. Patrick Lynch, S.J.; John M. McConnell, S.J.; John J. McDonald, S.J.; James A. McDonough, S.J.; Vincent M. McNally, S.J.; Louis A. Mounteer, S.J.; Edward J. Murphy, S.J.; Thomas P. Murphy, S.J.; Harold F.X. O'Donnell, S.J.; Vincent T. O'Keefe, S.J.; Richard J. Pendergast, S.J.; Thomas S. Prout, S.J.; Alfredo S. Quevedo, S.J.; Francis V. Rooney, S.J.; Peter J. Roslovich, S.J.; William J. Scanlon, S.J., Chap. Health Care Facility; Brendan T. Scott, S.J.; Louis E. Soloman, S.J.; Joseph R. Spellerberg, S.J.; John P. St. George, S.J.; Francis J. Staebell, S.J.; Patrick T. Sullivan, S.J.; William M. Sullivan, S.J.; Richard F. Timone, S.J.; Francis P. Valentino, S.J.; Joachim Von Kerssenbrock, S.J.; Thomas F. Walsh, S.J.; James J. Wheeler, S.J.; James J. Yannarell, S.J.; Donald M. Zewe, S.J. Priests 58; Brothers 2.

Brothers: Bros. Francis Christopher Jensen, S.J.; Raymond V. Whalen, S.J.

Our Lady of Consolation Residence Tel: 718-548-0888; Fax: 718-548-7824. 3103 Arlington Ave., Bronx, 10463-3305. Tel: 718-548-0889; 718-548-0889; Fax: 718-548-7824. Email: mblolc@aol.com. Mrs. Mary B. Lynch, R.N., Residence Dir.; Rev. Msgrs. Joseph A. Dunne (Retired); Kenneth A. Gerathy (Retired); Victor S. Pavis (Retired); Revs. William J. Delaney; Leonard J. DiNola (Retired); Antimo M. Fiorillo (Retired); John C. Flynn; John W. Holihan (Retired); Andrew M. Pane (Retired).

Padua Friary (1866) 151 Thompson St., 10012-3110. Tel: 212-254-9553. Revs. Daniel B. Morey, O.F.M., Guardian; Bruno Ciardiello, O.F.M. (Retired); Benedict J. D'Alessandro, O.F.M. (Retired); Louis D. De Tommaso, O.F.M. (Retired); Alban V. Montella, O.F.M. (Retired); Paul Rotondi, O.F.M. (Retired); Louis Troiano, O.F.M. (Retired); Bros. Paschal De Mattia, O.F.M., (Retired); Joseph La Gressa, O.F.M., Dir. Food Svc.

Pallottine Fathers, Society of the Catholic Apostolate, 448 E. 116th St., 10029. Tel: 212-534-0681; Fax: 212-534-0629. Revs. Tony Kelly, S.A.C., Spanish Apostolate; Carlos Cardoso, S.A.C., Assoc. Admin. Total Assisted 300; Total Staff 15.

Paulist Fathers' Motherhouse, 415 W. 59th St., 10019. Tel: 212-265-3209; Fax: 212-265-4154. Email: Paulist59@cs.com. Web: www.paulist.org. Revs. John Behnke, C.S.P., Supr.; Gerald J. Aylward, C.S.P. (Retired); Donald Campbell, C.S.P.; John E. Collins, C.S.P., Preaching Apostolate; Kevin A. Devine, C.S.P.; James M. DiLuzio, C.S.P., Preaching Apostolate; David P. Dwyer, C.S.P., Dir. Young Adult Ministries; Lionel A. DeSilva, C.S.P., Hosp. Chap.; David E. Farnum, C.S.P., Vocation Dir.; James A. Haley, C.S.P., Supr. & General Treas.; Dennis W. Hickey, C.S.P. (Retired); Mark-David Janus, C.S.P., Pres. Paulist Press; James B. Lloyd, C.S.P. (Retired); Kevin A. Lynch, C.S.P., Emeritus Publisher Paulist Press; Joseph F. Mahon, C.S.P. (Retired); Gilbert S. Martinez, C.S.P., Pastor St. Paul the Apostle; Lawrence V. McDonnell, C.S.P. (Retired); James F. McQuade, C.S.P., Hospital Chap.; Robert A. O'Donnell, C.S.P. (Retired); Robert Pinkston, C.S.P. (Retired); Frank Sabatté, C.S.P., Arts Ministry; Jeremiah D. Sullivan, C.S.P. (Retired); Francis M. Sweeney, C.S.P. (Retired); Timothy P.

Tighe, C.S.P., Preaching Apostolate. See also St. Paul the Apostle Parish

Redemptorist Priests and Brothers, C.Ss.R. (1887) (Prov. of Baltimore), Redemptorist Residence, 323 E. 61st St., 10065-8204. Tel: 212-838-1324; Fax: 212-838-4154. Revs. Francis J. O'Rourke, C.Ss.R., B.A., Local Supr.; Russell J. Abata, C.Ss.R., B.A., S.T.D.; Carlyle R. Blake, C.Ss.R.; Robert Cheesman, C.Ss.R., B.A., Retired U.S. Air Force Chap.; Joseph Freund, C.Ss.R., B.A., M.R.E., M.Div., Redemptorist Mission Preaching; Michael Hopkins, C.Ss.R., Consultor & Treas.; Michael Koncik, C.Ss.R., Chap.-Rikers Island, Otis Bateman No. 49 Infirmary Command; James P. Lundy, C.Ss.R.; Raymond P. McCarthy, C.Ss.R., M.Div.; Alex Ortiz, C.Ss.R., B.A., M.Div.; Richard L. Welch, C.Ss.R., J.C.D., M.R.E., M.Div., Tribunal Judge & Assoc. Judicial Vicar; Bro. Christopher A. Colarossi, C.Ss.R.

Society of Jesus, New York Province aka New York Province of the Society of Jesus 39 E. 83rd St., 10028-0810. Tel: 212-774-5500; Fax: 212-794-1036. Email: nykprov@nysj.org. Web: www.nysj.org. Very Rev. David S. Ciancimino, S.J., Prov.; Revs. Vincent L. Biagi, S.J., Asst. for Secondary & Presecondary Educ. & Lay Formation; Thomas H. Feely, S.J., Asst. for Formation for the Maryland & New York Provinces; Charles A. Frederico, S.J., Vocation Dir. for Maryland & New York Provinces; Mr. Nick Napolitano, Asst. Social Min.; Revs. James J. Hederman, S.J., Vocation Promoter for NEN, MAR & NYK Provinces; James F. Keenan, S.J., Dir. Devel.; Walter J. Modrys, S.J., Province Treas.; Ramon A. Salomone, S.J., Asst. to Provincial for Intl.; J. Peter Schineller, S.J., Archivist; Thomas R. Slon, S.J., Exec. Asst. to Prov.; Dr. Jacqueline C. Perez, Province Asst. for Healthcare. a.k.a. Jesuit Seminary and Mission Bureau, Inc.

Jesuit Provincial's Office (1540) 39 E. 83rd St., 10028. Tel: 212-774-5500; Fax: 212-794-1036. Email: nykprov@nysj.org. Web: www.nysj.org.

Priests of the Province Abroad: Revs. Michael P. Hilbert, S.J., Pontificia Universita Gregoriana, Piazza della Pilotta 4,00187, Rome, Italy. Tel: 39-06-6701-5452; Fax: 39-06-6701-5412; Keith F. Pecklers, S.J., Coll Bellarmino, Via del Seminario 120, 00186, Rome, Italy. Tel: 39-06-69527-6638; Fax: 39-06-6701-5413.

Priests of the Province in Residences Not Listed Elsewhere: Revs. George H. Belgarde, S.J., P.O. Box 429, Hogansburg, 13655. Tel: 613-575-2066; Gerard P. Bell, S.J., 15107 Interlachen Dr., Apt. 722, Silver Spring, MD 20906. Tel: 301-438-3753; Gerard H. Ettlinger, S.J., 10-01 162nd St., Apt. 5-D, Whitestone, 11357. Tel: 718-767-5895; Edward J. Mally, S.J., 1S 150 Spring Rd., Apt. 2E, Oakbrook Terrace, IL 60181. Tel: 630-833-0645; Fax: 708-756-6863; Walter J. Smith, S.J., 370 First Ave., Apt. 12C, 10010. Tel: 646-215-5347.

Jesuit Community of the Immaculate Conception (1974) 147 Thompson St., 10012. Tel: 212-663-4615; Fax: 212-866-3241. Email: robjkeck@aol.com. Revs. W. Alan Briceland, S.J., Supr.; Robert J. Keck, S.J., Pastoral Ministry; George M. Anderson, S.J.; Daniel J. Berrigan, S.J.; Gerald T. Huyett, S.J.; John G. McSherry, S.J.; Enrico Raulli, S.J.; Joseph C. Towle, S.J.

St. Vincent de Paul Residence, 900 Intervale Ave., 10459. Tel: 718-589-6965; Fax: 718-589-7010. Email: svdpres@chcn.org. Web: www.svdpres.org. Total Assisted 3,120; Total Staff 8.

St. Vincent Ferrer Priory (1867) Dominican Friars Provincial House (Province of St. Joseph)., 869 Lexington Ave., 10065-6648. Tel: 212-744-2080; Fax: 212-327-3011. Revs. Brian Martin Mulcahy, O.P., B.A., M.Div., Prior Prov.; E. Raymond Daley, O.P., S.T.L., J.C.D., S.T.D., Metropolitan Tribunal; William Robert Gannon, O.P., S.T.L., M.S.W.; Raymond Ferrer Halligan, O.P., S.T.L., A.B., MA.S.S., Subprior, Dominican Foundation; Bernard Lawrence Keitz, O.P., S.T.L., Parochial Ministry; Antoninus Niemiec, O.P., B.A., M.Div., B.F.A., Graduate Studies; Bros. Martin Michael Downey, O.P., M.A., Asst. Prov. Treas.; John Damian McCarthy, O.P., Sexton & Sacristan; Revs. Stanley Robert Azaro, O.P., S.T.L., Th.D.; William Paul Marquis, O.P., B.S., S.T.L., Ph.D., Prov. Syndic; Very Rev. William Alexander Holt, O.P., B.A., M.Div., Prior & Prov. Sec., Missions; Revs. John Albert Langlois, O.P., S.T.D., Socius & Vicar, Prov.; Walter Cornelius Wagner, O.P., J.D., Pastor; Darren Michael Pierre, O.P., S.T.L., M.S., Vicar, Admin.; Vinod Bruno Mary Shah, O.P., B.A., M.A., Parochial Vicar & Promoter, Holy Name Society.

Priests assigned but serving elsewhere: Revs. Ronald Eugene Henery, O.P., S.T.B., Preaching Min.; Frederick Damien Hoesli, O.P., B.A.; John Aedan McKeon, O.P., S.T.B., Preaching Min.; J. Albert Paretsky, O.P., M.A., S.S.L., S.T.D., Assoc. Prof., Biblical Studies; Jacob Restrick, O.P., S.T.L., Chap.; Robert William Vaughn, O.P., S.T.B., M.Ed., Preaching Min.; Jeremy Aquinas Guilbeau, O.P., M.A., S.T.L., Graduate Studies.

Vincentian Fathers, 1834 Third Ave., 10029. Tel: 212-289-5589; Fax: 212-289-8321. Email: milagha2@verizon.net. Revs. Victor Elia, C.M., Supr.; Candido Arrizurieta, C.M.; Jesus Arellano, C.M., Vicar.

Padres Paules Community (Vincentians) Inc.

Xavier Jesuit Community, 30 W. 16th St., 10011. Tel: 212-924-7900; Fax: 212-337-7545. Email: hzen@juno.com. Rev. Gerald J. Chojnacki, S.J., Rector; Mr. Dennis Baker, S.J.; Rev. James J. Bowes, S.J., Treas.; Very Rev. David S. Ciancimino, S.J., Admin.; Revs. Joseph S. Costantino, S.J., Pastor; James P. Croghan, S.J.; Thomas H. Feely, S.J., Admin.; Peter E. Fink, S.J., Asst. Pastor; Daniel Hendrickson, S.J.; James F. Keenan, S.J., Admin.; Edward J. McMahon, S.J.; James L. Pierce, S.J.; John F. Replogle, S.J.; Ralph Rivera, S.J.; Henry J. Zenorini, S.J. (For list of faculty see the high school listing for Xavier High School)

BEACON. *St. Joachim Friary*, 61 Leonard St., 12508. Tel: 845-838-0000. Email: frfred@cyfm.org. Web: www.cyfm.org. Rev. Fred Nickle, O.F.M.Cap., Chap.; Bros. Lake Herman, O.F.M.Cap., Guardian; Carlos Hernandez, O.F.M.Cap. Serving Capuchin Youth and Family Ministries, Garrison, NY

BRONX. *Idente Missionaries - Santa Maria Residence*, 2352 St. Raymond Ave., 10462. Tel: 718-828-2380; Fax: 718-828-4296. Revs. Fernando Real, M.Id., Ph.D., Prov. Supr.; Robert P. Badillo, M.Id., Ph.D.; Martin I. Esquerra, D.Min.; Cristobal Martin, M.Id., Ph.D., Prov. Sec.; Bro. Marek Wasilewski, M.Id., B.A.

John Cardinal O'Connor Residence, 5655 Arlington Ave., 10471. Tel: 718-581-0070. Most Rev. Robert A. Brucato, D.D., V.G. (Retired); Rev. Msgrs. George F. Bardes (Retired); Francis V. Boyle (Retired); Dermot R. Brennan (Retired); Harry J. Byrne (Retired); Timothy Collins (Retired); Francis X. Duffy (Retired); Robert A. Ford (Retired); Peter C. O'Donnell (Retired); Revs. Alfred M. Croke (Retired); John M. Crotty (Retired); Christopher H. Daly (Retired); Gerard DiSenso (Retired); Robert J. Duane (Retired); Benedict J. Kuolt (Retired); Vincent A. Lancellotti (Retired); Thomas F. McDonald (Retired); Alfred Pizzuto (Retired); John F. Reardon (Retired); James J. Tubridy (Retired), Cardinal O'Connor Residence, 5655 Arlington Ave., 10471.

Saint Lawrence Friary, 1027 Grand Concourse, 10452. Tel: 718-293-9180; Fax: 718-293-3384. Revs. Anthony Marie Baetzold, C.F.R., Local Vicar; Bernard Marie Murphy, C.F.R., Local Servant; Bros. Matthew Youssef Hawkins, C.F.R.; Innocent Mariae Montgomery; Ignatius Mary Shin, C.F.R.

Our Lady of the Angels Friary (Franciscan Friars of the Renewal), 427 E. 155th St., 10455. Tel: 718-993-3405; Fax: 718-993-9997. Web: www.franciscanfriars.com. Revs. Stanley Fortuna, C.F.R.; Fidelis Moscinski, C.F.R.; Terrence Messer, C.F.R.; Bros. Joachim Joseph Bellavance, C.F.R., Dir. St. Francis Ctr.; John Joseph Brice, C.F.R., Local Servant, Community Steward; Peter Westall, C.F.R., Local Vicar, Dir. St. Padre Pio Shleter; Piere Toussaint Guiteau, C.F.R., Asst. Dir. Youth for Christ; Isaiah Marie Hofmann, C.F.R., Asst. Dir. Youth for Christ; Mark-Mary Maximilian Ames, C.F.R., Asst. Dir., St. Padre Pio Shelter.

Passionist Residence, 5801 Palisade Ave., 10471. Tel: 718-548-1182; Fax: 718-548-2945. Rev. Columkille Regan; Bro. Michael Moran, C.P., Local Supr. Priests 3; Brothers 1; Total in Residence 4.

Yarumal Mission Society, Inc. (1997) Office of the Pres., 2317 Washington Ave., 10458. Tel: 718-561-8248; Fax: 718-295-9607. Email: imeyusa@aol.com. Web: www.yarumal.org. Revs. David Guzman Perez, M.X.Y., Pres.; Tulio E. Ramirez, M.X.Y. (Colombia).

CORNWALL. *Jogues Retreat Center*, P.O. Box 522, 12518-0522. Tel: 845-534-7570; Fax: 845-534-3276. Email: conroyp48@hotmail.com. Revs. Edward J. Coughlin, S.J., Supr.; J. Peter Conroy, S.J., Asst. to Supr. Sabbatical.

ESOPUS. *Marist Brothers F.M.S. (Province of U.S.A.)* (1942) P.O. Box 197, 12429. Tel: 845-384-6625; Fax: 845-384-6277. Email: brohen@aol.com. Bros. Todd Patenaude, F.M.S., Supr.; Henry J. Sawicki, F.M.S.; Gregory De LaNoy, F.M.S. Brothers 3.

Redemptorist Priests and Brothers C.Ss.R. (Province of Baltimore), Mount Saint Alphonsus, Rte. 9W, P.O. Box 219, 12429. Tel: 845-384-8000; Fax: 845-384-8088. Email: gkeav@aol.com. Web: www.msaretreat.com. Rev. Thomas J. Travers, C.Ss.R.; Bros. Gerard St. Hilaire, C.Ss.R.; Robert Skinner, C.Ss.R. Priests 6; Brothers 3. In Res. Revs. Dennis Billy, C.Ss.R.; Eugene J. Grohe, C.Ss.R.; John Kiwus, C.Ss.R.; Raymond Weithman, C.Ss.R.

GARRISON. *St. Christopher's Friary*, Box 150, 10524-0150. Tel: 845-335-1000; Fax: 845-424-3786. Web: www.stchristophersinn-graymoor.org. Revs. John F. Kiesling, S.A., Guardian; Charles Angell, S.A.; John W. Coppinger, S.A.; William Drobach, S.A.; Robert Warren, S.A.; Bros. Benedict Terasawa, S.A.; Charles Kenny, S.A.; Joseph O'Gara, S.A.; John O'Hara, S.A. Total Staff 60; Total Assisted 1,200.

Franciscan Friars of the Atonement (1898) Graymoor, P.O. Box 300, 10524-0300. Tel: 845-424-3671; 845-424-3672; 845-424-3673; Fax: 845-424-2166. Email: glucrezia@atonementfriars.org. Web: www.atonementfriars.org. Revs. Fred Alvarez, S.A.; Norman Boyd, S.A.; Charles Brozat, S.A.; Alban Carroll, S.A.; Martin Carter, S.A.; Joseph F. Cavoto, S.A.; Kenneth Cienik, S.A., Guardian, St. Paul's Friary; John W. Coppinger, S.A.; Bro. Kieran Cullen, S.A., (Retired); Revs. Joseph Di Mauro, S.A.; David L. Doerner, S.A. (Retired); Walter Gagne, S.A., Dir. Archives & Record Ctr., Guardian St. Paul's Friary; James Gardiner, S.A., Dir. Spiritual Life Center; Carmen Giuliano, S.A.; Bros. Francis Gutman, S.A.; Stephen Hanley, S.A., (Retired); John Baptist Hildreth, S.A.; Daniel Houde, S.A.; Alan LeMay, S.A.; Pius MacIsaac, S.A.; Rev. Martin Madison, S.A.; Bro. Dominic McDonnell, S.A.; Rev. Owen Murphy, S.A. (Retired); Bro. Theodore Novak, S.A.; Rev. Mark O'Connor, S.A.; Bro. Joseph O'Gara, S.A.; Rev. Thomas Orians, S.A., Assoc. Dir. of Campus Min., Felician College, NJ; Bro. DePorres Poncia, S.A.; Revs. George Ribeiro, S.A.; Emil Tomaskovic, S.A.; Peter Taran; Bro. Edmund Sheridan, S.A., (Retired); Rev. Emmanuel Sullivan, S.A.; Bro. Robert Taylor, S.A., (Retired); Rev. Wilfred Tyrell, S.A.; Bro. Liam Young, S.A., Mass Dept. *St. Francis of Assisi Novitiate*, Graymoor, P.O. Box 300, 10524-0300. Tel: 845-424-4055; Fax: 845-424-4673. Rev. Conan Hall, S.A.; Bro. Leo Hall, S.A. *St. Christopher's Inn*, Graymoor, P.O. Box 150, 10524-0150. Tel: 845-424-3616; Fax: 845-424-3786. Revs. Bernard Palka, S.A., Pres. & CEO; Charles Angell, S.A.; William Drobach, S.A., Vice Pres.; Bro. Charles Kenney, S.A.; Rev. John F. Kiesling, S.A., St. Joan of Arc Parish, Toronto ON M6P 1B1 Canada. Tel: 416-762-1026; Fax: 416-762-4194; Bro. Benedict Terasawa, S.A.; Rev. Robert Warren, S.A., Guardian, St. Christopher's Inn. *Graymoor Ecumenical and Interreligious Institute*, 475 Riverside Dr., Rm. 1960, 10115-1999. Tel: 212-870-2330; Fax: 212-870-2001. Rev. James Loughran, S.A., Dir. Tel: 212-807-9694; Fax: 212-870-2001. *Atonement Friars*, 138 Waverly Pl., 10014. Rev. Wilfred Tyrrell, S.A.

Priests of the Province Serving Elsewhere: Revs. David Fitzgerald, S.A., Pastor, St. Andrew the Apostle, Apex, NC; Thomas Gumprecht, S.A., St. Andrew the Apostle, Apex, NC; Francis Eldridge, S.A., St. Odilia's Parish, 522 Hooper Ave., Los Angeles, CA 90011; Bro. Gerard Hand, S.A.; Revs. V. Paul Ojibway, S.A., Santa Maria Parish, 20 Santa Maria Way, Orinda, CA 94563; Boniface Riedmann, S.A. (Retired), Chapel of Our Savior, 475 Westgate Dr., Brockton, MA 02301. *Chapel of Our Savior*, 475 Westgave Dr., Brockton, MA 02301-1819. Tel: 508-583-8357; Fax: 508-586-5510. Bro. Thomas Banacki, S.A.; Revs. Gerald DiGiralamo, S.A., 4 Buttercup Dr., Bohemia, 11716; Robert Langone, S.A., Retreat Dir.; Bro. Louis Marek, S.A.; Rev. Malcolm Martin, S.A., Chapel of Our Savior, 475 Westgate Dr., Brockton, MA 02301; Bro. Savio McNiece, S.A., Chapel of Our Savior, 475 Westgate Dr., Brockton, MA 02301; Revs. Daniel O'Shea, S.A.; Daniel Sylvain, S.A.

Franciscan Friars of the Atonement, Minister General Office (1898) Graymoor, P.O. Box 300, 10524-0300. Tel: 845-424-2113; Fax: 845-424-2166. Email: ministergen@atonementfriars.org. Web: www.atonementfriars.org. Very Rev. James F. Puglisi, S.A., Min. Gen.; Rev. Timothy I. MacDonald, S.A., Vicar Gen. & 1st Gen. Counselor; Bro. Kevin Goss, S.A., Sec. Gen. & 3rd Gen. Counselor; Revs. Elias D. Mallon, S.A., 2nd Gen. Counselor; V. Paul Ojibway, S.A., 4th Gen. Councilor; Charles Sharon, S.A., Personnel Dir. & Assoc. Treas.

Friar-Priests serving in Japan, Diocese of Yokohama: Tel.: 011-81-45-581-6374; Fax: 011-81-45-581-9068. Revs. Pacificus Von Essen, S.A.; Joseph Hiramatsu, S.A. (Japan), Regional Minister; Raymond Rodriquez Luis, S.A.; Bro. Ignatius Kobayashi, S.A. (Japan).

Friars on Assignment: Tel.: 845-424-3671; Fax: 845-424-2166. Revs. Joseph Scerbo, S.A.; Edward Gallagher, S.A. (Retired), Chapel of Our Savior, 475

Westgate Dr., Brockton, MA 02301; James Gardiner, S.A.; Bernard Palka, S.A.
Friars stationed in England: Tel.: 011-44-171-828-4163; Fax: 011-44-171-798-9090. Bro. Denis Burgelin, S.A., (England); Revs. Robert Mercer, S.A. (England); Michael Seed, S.A. (England).
Friars stationed in Canada, Archdiocese of Vancouver: Tel.: 604-277-8353; Fax: 604-275-4034. Revs. Arthur Gouthro, S.A., St. Joseph the Worker Parish, 4451 Williams Rd., Richmond BC V7E 1J7 Canada. (Canada); William Linakis, S.A., 1127 Barclay St., Apt. 1202, Vancouver BC V6E 4C6. (Canada); David Poirier, S.A., St. Joseph the Worker Parish, 4451 Williams Rd., Richmond BC V7E 1J7 Canada. (Canada); Bros. Timothy MacDonald, S.A., St. Joseph the Worker Parish, 4451 Williams Rd., Richmond BC V7E 1J7 Canada. (Canada); Hugh MacIsaac, S.A., (Canada).
Archdiocese of Toronto, Canada: Revs. Damian MacPherson, S.A. (Canada), Dir. Ecumenical & Interfaith Affairs & Guardian Paul Wattson Friary, St. Michael's Rectory, 200 Church St., Toronto ON M5B 1Z2 Canada. Tel: 416-694-0382; Fax: 416-934-3445; Daniel Callahan, S.A.
Friars residing in Italy: Tel.: 011-39-06-687-9552; Fax: 011-39-06-683-3631. Bro. Simon Peter Ango, S.A.; Rev. Edward Boes, S.A., Rector, Church of Sant'Onofrio; Bro. Gregory Lucrezia, S.A., Proc. Gen.; Very Rev. James F. Puglisi, S.A., Minister General; Rev. Brian Terry, S.A. *Graymoor Ecumenical & Interreligious Institute*, 475 Riverside Dr., Rm. 1960, 10115-1999. Tel: 212-870-2330; Fax: 212-870-2001. Email: lmnygeii@aol.com. Web: www.geii.org.
Friars of the Atonement, Inc.
St. Christopher's Inn, Inc.
Union That Nothing Be Lost, Inc.
Paul Wattson Human Resources Fund, Inc., (G.E.I.I.)

HARTSDALE. *Mill Hill Fathers Residence*, 222 W. Hartsdale Ave., 10530-1667. Tel: 914-682-0645; Fax: 914-682-0862. Email: mhmnyoffice@aol.com. Web: www.millhillmissionaries.com. Revs. Terence J. Lee, M.H.M., Admin.; James Brian Coffey, M.H.M.; Bartholomew Daly, M.H.M., Regl. Representative; Emile Frische, M.H.M.; Lester Lonergan, M.H.M. (Retired), 1415 Abbey Pl., Apt. 14, Charlotte, NC 28209; Peter Major, M.H.M.; Robert J. O'Neil, M.H.M.; Gregory P. Rice, M.H.M.

MARYKNOLL. *M.M.A.F. Charitable Trust, Treasury Office*, P.O. Box 306, 10545-0306. Tel: 914-941-7590; Fax: 914-941-3619. Email: rcallahan@maryknoll.org. Rev. Richard B. Callahan, M.M., Contact Person.

Maryknoll Fathers and Brothers 10545-0305. Tel: 914-941-7590; Fax: 914-944-3605. Email: generalcouncil@maryknoll.org. Web: www.maryknoll.org.
General Council: Most Rev. William J. McNaughton, M.M. (Retired); Revs. Edward M. Dougherty, M.M., Supr. Gen. & Pres.; Jose A. Aramburu, M.M., Vicar Gen. & Vice Pres.; Edward J. McGovern, M.M., Asst. Gen.; Paul R. Masson, M.M., Asst. Gen.; Thomas A. Ahearn, M.M. (Retired); Joseph B. Arsenault, M.M. (Retired); Richard Aylward, M.M. (Retired); Paul D. Belliveau, M.M. (Retired); Francis J. Breen, M.M.; J. Ernest Brunelle, M.M. (Retired); Richard B. Callahan, M.M., Treas. Gen.; Charles H. Cappel, M.M. (Retired); John J. Casey, M.M.; Herman W. Cisek, M.M.; George C. Cotter, M.M.; William J. Coy, M.M. (Retired); Wayman P. Deasy, M.M.; Robert L. Depinet, M.M. (Retired); Gilbert J. De Ritis, M.M. (Retired); Robert W. Donnelly, M.M. (Retired); Daniel D. Dolan, M.M. (Retired); Michael A. Duggan, M.M.; Miguel F. d'Escoto, M.M. (Retired); Philip N. Erbland, M.M.; Lawrence W. Flynn, M.M. (Retired); William B. Frazier, M.M.; Herbert T. Gappa, M.M. (Retired); James M. Gilligan, M.M. (Retired); Donald F. Glover, M.M. (Retired); Ronald L. Green, M.M.; Kevin J. Hanlon, M.M.; Joseph A. Heim, M.M. (Retired); James L. Hilgeman, M.M. (Retired); Robert A. Jalbert, M.M.; David J. Jones, M.M. (Retired); John M. Kaserow, M.M.; John E. Keegan, M.M. (Retired); Martin P. Keegan, M.M. (Retired); David C. Kelly, M.M. (Retired); Leo R. Kennedy, M.M (Retired); John R. King, M.M. (Retired); Joseph A. Klecha, M.M. (Retired); David E. LaBuda, M.M.; Joseph P. LaMar, M.M., Asst. Treas. (Retired); Peter M. Le Jacq, M.M.; Robert R. Lefebvre, M.M. (Retired); James W. Lehr, M.M. (Retired); Lawrence J. Lewis, M.M.; Robert J. Lloyd, M.M. (Retired); Martin J. Lowery, M.M.; Ernest C. Lukaschek, M.M.; James J. Madden, M.M.; William T. Madden, M.M. (Retired); Joseph V. McCabe, M.M.; Gerard T. McCrane, M.M. (Retired); Lawrence F. McCulloch, M.M. (Retired); Thomas P. McDonnell, M.M. (Retired); Joseph J. McGahren, M.M. (Retired); Francis T. McGourn, M.M. (Retired); Charles J. McPadden, M.M. (Retired); Carl P. Meulemans, M.M. (Retired); Edward F. Moore, M.M. (Retired); John J. Moran, M.M.; Laurence T. Murphy, M.M. (Retired); Gerald J. Nagle, M.M. (Retired); Paul A. O'Brien, M.M. (Retired); Fernand Paquet, M.M. (Retired); Thomas E. Pesaresi, M.M.; David L. Pfeiffer, M.M.; Robert J. Reiley, M.M. (Retired); Peter L. Ruggere, M.M. (Retired); Leo B. Shea, M.M. (Retired); Michael A. Simone, M.M. (Retired); John C. Sivalon, M.M.; David A. Smith, M.M.; Richard P. Smith, M.M. (Retired); John F. Soltis, M.M. (Retired); Romane St. Vil, M.M.; Kenneth J. Sullivan, M.M.; Raymond F. Sullivan, M.M. (Retired); J. Edward Szendrey, M.M.; Joseph W. Towle, M.M. (Retired); James M. Travis, M.M. (Retired); John C. Tynan, M.M. (Retired); Joseph R. Veneroso, M.M.; Robert W. Vujs, M.M. (Retired); Michael P. Walsh, M.M.; Edward M. Wroblewski, M.M. (Retired); Maurice J. Zerr, M.M. (Retired); Michael O. Zunno (Retired); Bros. John E. Argauer, M.M., (Retired); John J. Blazo, M.M.; Gordon M. Burns, M.M., (Retired); Eugene E. Casper, M.M., (Retired); Brendan J. Corkery, M.M.; Kevin F. Dargan, M.M.; Wayne J. Fitzpatrick, M.M.; Vianney R. Flick, M.M., (Retired); John H. Frangenberg, M.M., (Retired); Thomas A. Hickey, M.M.; Anthony Lopez, M.M.; Victor E. Marshall, M.M., (Retired); Andrew E. Marsolek, M.M.; Adrian R. Mazuchowsla, M.M., (Retired); David E. McKenna, M.M., (Retired); Donald R. Miriani, M.M., (Retired); Frank J. Norris, M.M., (Retired); Albert F. Patrick, M.M., (Retired); William T. Raible, M.M.; DePorres Stilp, M.M., (Retired); Raymond C. Tetrault, M.M. *Maryknoll St. Teresa's Residence*, 10545-0321. Tel: 914-941-4240; 914-941-4247; Fax: 914-923-3407.
Staff: Revs. Richard A. Bell, M.M. (Retired); John P. Hudert, M.M. (Retired) In Res. Revs. Frederick J. Allen, M.M. (Retired); Anthony B. Brodniak, M.M.; Richard L. Brooker, M.M. (Retired); Robert F. Crohan, M.M. (Retired); Clyde F. Davis, M.M.; Emile E. Dumas, M.M.; Alfred J. Fleming, M.M. (Retired); Thomas F. Gibbons, M.M. (Retired); Charles F. Girnius, M.M. (Retired); Fernand L. Gosselin, M.M. (Retired); Robert Golish, M.M. (Retired); John P. Grady, M.M. (Retired); John P. Hudert, M.M. (Retired); Charles T. Huegelmeyer, M.M. (Retired); Daniel P. Jensen, M.M. (Retired); Walter W. Johnson, M.M. (Retired); Richard S. Kardian, M.M. (Retired); John B. Keaney, M.M. (Retired); Thomas H. Keefe, M.M. (Retired); Walter T. Kelleher, M.M. (Retired); John F. Kennedy, M.M.; Joseph R. Lang, M.M. (Retired); Joseph V. Maynard, M.M. (Retired); William E. McCarthy, M.M. (Retired); Francis S. Meccia, M.M.; James P. Nieckarz, M.M. (Retired); James K. Nishimuta, M.M. (Retired); Howard E. O'Brien, M.M. (Retired); John J. O'Brien, M.M. (Retired); Frank T. O'Donnell, M.M. (Retired); Fernand Paquet, M.M. (Retired); Peter J. Petrucci, M.M. (Retired); Arthur J. Prall, M.M. (Retired); John J. Ruessmann, M.M.; Alan J. Ryan, M.M. (Retired); Thomas C. Saunders, M.M. (Retired); James M. Scanlon, M.M. (Retired); Steven S. Scherrer, M.M. (Retired); Charles J. Schmidt, M.M. (Retired); J. David Sullivan, M.M. (Retired); Norbert M. Verhagen, M.M. (Retired); Donald J. Vittengl, M.M. (Retired); Edward F. Walck, M.M. (Retired); John Daly Walsh, M.M.; John J. Walsh, M.M. (Retired); James R. Whitmore, M.M. (Retired); Louis J. Wolken, M.M. (Retired); Peter A. Wu, M.M. (Retired); Robert R. Zahn, M.M. (Retired); Richard E. Zeimet, M.M. (Retired); Bros. Peter Agnone, M.M., (Retired); George Carlonas, M.M, (Retired); Conrad J. Fleisch, M.M., (Retired); John J. Wohead, M.M., (Retired); Goretti A. Zilli, M.M.
Special Assignments: Revs. Patrick A. Bergin, M.M. (Retired); Stephen R. Booth, M.M.; Roy L. Bourgeois, M.M.; Curtis R. Cadorette, M.M.; John P. Casey, M.M. (Retired); Donald J. Doherty, M.M. (Retired); Michael Gould, M.M. (Retired); Scott T. Harris, M.M.; Ralph S. Kroes, M.M. (Retired); Daniel A. Lanza, M.M. (Retired); Francis J. Leong, M.M. (Retired); Robert A. Lilly, M.M. (Retired); Thomas J. Marti, M.M.; Manuel J. Mejia, M.M. (Retired); James P. Noonan, M.M. (Retired); Richard T. Ouellette, M.M. (Retired); Richard E. Paulissen, M.M. (Retired); Gerald J. Persha, M.M. (Retired); Raymond G. Pierini, M.M.; Joseph S. Pulaski, M.M. (Retired); John A. Rich, M.M. (Retired); James R. Roy, M.M. (Retired); Daniel J. Sherman, M.M. (Retired); David J. Schwinghamer, M.M.; John J. Sullivan, M.M. (Retired); Joseph Chuc Tran, M.M.; Wayne T. Weinlader, M.M. (Retired); Gerald M. Wickenhauser, M.M. (Retired); Arthur H. Willie, M.M. (Retired); John F. Wymes, M.M. (Retired).

Maryknoll Fathers and Brothers Charitable Trust, P.O. Box 306, 10545-0306. Tel: 914-941-7590, Ext. 2422; Fax: 914-944-3628. Web: www.maryknoll.org. Revs. Thomas A. Ahearn, M.M., Trustee (Retired); Richard B. Callahan, M.M., Trustee; Wayman P. Deasy, M.M., Trustee; Thomas P. McDonnell, M.M. (Retired); J. Edward Szendrey, M.M., Trustee; Susan J. Dahl, Trustee.

MIDDLETOWN. *St. Albert's Priory*, 72 Carmelite Dr., P.O. Box 908, 10940-0908. Tel: 845-344-2220; Fax: 845-342-4412. Revs. Francis Amodio, O.Carm.; Christopher Byrnes, O.Carm.; Garth Eversley, O.Carm.; John Logan, O.Carm.; Vincent McDonald, O.Carm.; Stephen Huy Tran, O.Carm.; Thomas Zalewski, O.Carm., Prior; Bros. Michael Garraghan, O.Carm.; Dominic Dang Nguyen, O.Carm. *The National Shrine of Our Lady of Mount Carmel*, 70 Carmelite Dr., P.O. Box 2163, 10940-2163. Tel: 845-343-1879; Fax: 845-343-1912. Rev. Thomas Zalewski, O.Carm., Dir.

Brandsma Priory, Carmelite Novitiate, 1 Carmelite Dr., P.O. Box 2127, 10940-0439. Tel: 845-343-2959; Fax: 845-344-1808. Rev. Robert Traudt, O.Carm., Co-Dir. Novices; Very Rev. Michael Kissane, O.Carm., Co-Dir. Novices. Carmelite Friars (North American Prov. of St. Elias and Most Pure Heart of Mary Province).

Carmelite Friars (North American Province of St. Elias) (1931) 68 Carmelite Dr., P.O. Box 3079, 10940-0890. Tel: 845-344-2223; 845-344-2225 (Vocation phone); Fax: 845-344-2210. Email: proelias@frontiernet.net. Web: www.carmelites.com. Very Rev. Mario Esposito, O.Carm., Prior Prov.; Rev. Patrick McGuigan, O.Carm., Prov. Procurator. Tel: 914-344-2224; Bro. Robert Bathe, O.Carm., Vocation Dir. *Office of Lay Carmelites*, 70 Carmelite Dr., P.O. Box 3079, 10940-0890. Tel: 845-344-2476; Fax: 845-956-2474. Email: jsoreth@frontiernet.net. Rev. Garth Eversley, O.Carm., Provincial Delegate Lay Carmelites.

MOUNT VERNON. *St. Bernardine of Siena Friary*, 25 Laurel Ave., 10552-1018. Tel: 914-699-1221; Fax: 914-668-6143. Rev. James Villa, O.F.M., Admin. & Guardian. Franciscan Friars, Province of Immaculate Conception. Priests 3. In Res. Revs. Andre Cirino, O.F.M.; Roderick Crispo, O.F.M.

Kolbe Friary, 274-280 W. Lincoln Ave., 10550. Tel: 914-664-7169. Bro. Angelo Monti, O.F.M., Guardian. Franciscan Friars, Province of the Immaculate Conception.

NEW PALTZ. *St. Joseph Friary*, 34 S. Chestnut St., 12561. Tel: 914-255-5635; Fax: 914-255-5679. Revs. Bernard M. Maloney, O.F.M.Cap.; Raphael Iannone, O.F.M.Cap., Province Property Mgr.; Barnabas Keck, O.F.M.Cap., Parochial Vicar; Deacon Salvatore P. Patricola, O.F.M.Cap. Capuchin Franciscans, Province of St. Mary.

NEW ROCHELLE. *Brothers of Holy Cross of the Eastern Province of the United States of America, Inc.* (1958) 85 Overlook Cir., 10804-4501. Tel: 914-632-4468; 914-632-4469; Fax: 914-632-2490. Email: tdzie@aol.com. Web: www.holycrossbrothers.org. Bros. Jonathan Beebe, C.S.C., B.A., M.A., M.S.W., Councillor; Edward Boyer, C.S.C., B.A., M.A., Councillor; James J. Branigan, C.S.C., B.A., M.S., Councilor; Roger Croteau, C.S.C., B.A., Councilor; Jerome Donnelly, C.S.C., B.A., M.A., Councilor; Mark Knightly, C.S.C., B.A., M.S.W., Asst. Prov.; Stephen J. LaMendola, C.S.C., B.A., M.A., B.S., P.D., Councilor; George Schmitz, C.S.C., B.A., M.A., Steward; William Zaydak, C.S.C., B.A., M.A., Provincial. Professed Brothers (Total in Province) 110. In Res. Bros. Roger Croteau, C.S.C., B.A.; James Rio, C.S.C.

Congregation of Christian Brothers New Rochelle (1906) 21 Pryer Ter., 10804. Tel: 914-636-6194; Fax: 914-636-0021. Email: alb@cbinstitute.org. Brothers Living in Community 5. *Saint Joseph Residence* (1986) 30 Montgomery Cir., 10804. Tel: 914-633-6851; Fax: 914-633-5579. Email: jbm@atgnet.com. Bro. Michael L. Colasuonno, Pastoral Care Coord. Limited care facility for male religious. Total in Residence 20; Total Staff 8.

Saint Joseph's Residence, Inc., 30 Montgomery Cir., 10804-4413. Tel: 914-633-6851; Fax: 914-633-5579. Email: jbm@atgnet.com. Bros. Charles Haynes, Vice Pres. Finance; Kevin M. Griffith, C.F.C.; Thomas C. Higgins, Sec.; James B. Moffett, C.F.C., Vice Pres. Admin. Congregation of Christian Brothers., A facility of limited care for male religious. Total in Residence 20; Total Staff 5.

Salesian Cooperators of St. John Bosco, 148 Main St., 10802-0639. Tel: 914-636-4225; Fax: 914-636-0159. Email: tdunnesdb@aol.com. Mr. James Dolan, Prov. Coord.; Very Rev. Thomas Dunne, S.D.B., Prov. Delegate.

Salesian Provincial House (1959) 148 Main St., P.O. Box 639, 10802-0639. Tel: 914-636-4225; Fax: 914-636-0159. Email: sdbsue@aol.com. Web: www.salesians.org. Very Rev. Thomas Dunne, S.D.B., Prov.; Revs. Robert Bauer, S.D.B.; John Blanco, S.D.B.; Edward Cappelletti, S.D.B.; Steven Dumais, S.D.B.; Michael Mendl, S.D.B.; Terrence O'Donnell, S.D.B.; Sean Rooney, S.D.B.; Robert Savage, S.D.B., Archives; Frank Wolfram, S.D.B., Supr.; Bros. Bruno Busatto, S.D.B.; Thomas Dion, S.D.B.; Emile Dube, S.D.B.;

Thomas Higgs, S.D.B.; Andrew Lacombe, S.D.B.; John Zito, S.D.B. Priests 10; Brothers 4.

PELHAM. *Marist Brothers* (1994) 2 Eden Ter., Poughkeepsie, 12601-4803. Tel: 845-471-8354. Bros. John Malich, F.M.S., Dir.; Kenneth Hogan, F.M.S.; John Nash, F.M.S.

Marist Brothers Champagnat Hall Community (1926) 4300 Murdock Ave., Bronx, 10466. Tel: 718-994-4227, Ext. 32; 718-994-4676; Fax: 718-994-0145. Bros. James Adams, F.M.S., Dir.; David Cooney, F.M.S., Pastoral Care, Dept. Head; Joseph McAlister, F.M.S., Staff, Health Care; Joseph Sacino, F.M.S., Asst. Treas.; Alphonse Matuga, F.M.S.; Robert Ryan, F.M.S.; Anthony Iazzetti, F.M.S.; Nicholas Caffrey, F.M.S.; Emil Denworth, F.M.S.; Valerian Doiron, F.M.S.; Richard Rancourt, F.M.S.; James Gaffney, F.M.S.; Robert Leclerc, F.M.S.; Joseph Scanlon, F.M.S.; Augustine Landry, F.M.S.; James Ryan, F.M.S.; Godfrey Robertson, F.M.S.; Victor Serna, F.M.S.; Edward Vollmer, F.M.S.; Vincent Xavier, F.M.S.

Marist Brothers Community (1993) 26 First Ave., 10803. Tel: 914-738-1218. Bros. John Bantz, F.M.S., Dir.; Larry Gordon, F.M.S.; James McKnight, F.M.S.; Donnell Neary, F.M.S.; Sean Sammon, F.M.S.; Michael Sheerin, F.M.S.

Marist Brothers-St. Benedict Community, 1082 Edison Ave., Bronx, 10465. Tel: 718-931-3744. Bros. Gerald Doherty, Dir.; Frederick Sambor, Dir.; Eugene Birmingham; Armand Lamagna, F.M.S.; Thomas Schady, F.M.S.

Marist Residence, 272 W. 91st St., 10024. Tel: 212-769-4951; Fax: 212-769-4951. Email: FMS91@aol.com. Bros. James Adams, F.M.S., Dir.; Richard Van Houten, F.M.S., Prin.; Emil Denworth, F.M.S.; James Kearney, F.M.S.; George Kopper, F.M.S.

PELHAM MANOR. *St. Vincent's Residence*, 190 Mt. Tom Rd., 10803-3309. Tel: 914-738-6138; Fax: 914-738-6136. Email: pfagan@cpprov.org. Rev. Edward L. Beck, C.P., Supr. & Dir.; Very Revs. Robert H. Joerger, C.P., Provincial Supr.; Robin Ryan, C.P., Vicar Provincial; James O'Shea, C.P., Provincial Consultor; Rev. Paul R. Fagan, C.P., Studies & Itinerant Preacher. The Passionists.

STATEN ISLAND. *St. Francis Friary*, 500 Todt Hill Rd., 10304. Tel: 718-981-3131; Fax: 718-981-2742. Email: bjfarleo@aol.com. Revs. Brennan-Joseph Farleo, O.F.M.Conv., Guardian, Supr. & Preaching Min.; Philip Blaine, O.F.M.Conv., Spiritual Center Dir.; Edward Costello, O.F.M.Conv.; George Sabol, O.F.M. Conv. In Res. Bro. Joseph Freitag. *Friars Minor Conventual Immaculate Conception Province Charitable Trust* Tel: 718-981-3131; Fax: 718-981-2742. Priests 4; Brothers 1.

Scalabrinian Missionaries Scalabrinian Mission Office, The Center for Migration Studies; St. Charles Residence., 209 Flagg Pl., 10304. Tel: 718-351-0232; Fax: 718-979-1241. Email: cms@cmsny.org. Web: www.scalabrini.org. Revs. Rene Manenti, C.S., Dir., Center for Migration Studies & St. Charles Devel. Office; Ezio Marchetto, Asst. Dir., Center for Migration Studies.

THORNWOOD. *Legionaries of Christ*, 582 Columbus Ave., 10594. Tel: 914-749-3900; Fax: 914-749-3939. Email: twlc@legionaries.org. Web: www.legionofchrist.org.

WEST PARK. *Congregation of Christian Brothers*, Santa Maria-on-Hudson, 12493. Tel: 845-384-3006; Fax: 845-750-6290. Bros. Richard E. Pigott, Contact Person; D. D. Crimmins; J. Laurence Heathwood; R.J. Lasik. Total in Residence 4.

WHITE PLAINS. *Capuchin Friars of North America*, 30 Gedney Park Dr., 10605-3599. Tel: 914-761-3008; Fax: 914-948-6429. Email: jmchugh@juno.com. Revs. John Celichowski, O.F.M.Cap., Pres.; Matthew Elshoff, O.F.M.Cap., Vice Pres.; Jerome McHugh, O.F.M.Cap., Sec. & Treas.

St. Conrad Friary (1882) Provincial Headquarters of the Province of St. Mary of the Capuchin Order., 30 Gedney Park Dr., 10605-3599. Tel: 914-761-3008; Fax: 914-948-6429. Email: fgasparik@capuchin.org. Web: www.capuchin.org. Revs. Francis Gasparik, O.F.M.Cap., Min. Prov.; Michael Marigliano, O.F.M.Cap., Vicar Prov.; Jerome McHugh, O.F.M.Cap., Sec. & Treas.; Mr. David LeGare, Dir. Finance; Bros. Richard Therrien, O.F.M.Cap., Prof. Theology at Stepinac H.S.; John Shento, O.F.M.Cap., Dir. Communications; Pius Blandino, O.F.M.Cap., Plant Mgr.; Revs. Paul Engel, O.F.M.Cap., Dir. Downey Side; Joseph Flynn, O.F.M.Cap., Chap., College of New Rochelle; Bro. John Koelle, O.F.M.Cap., Asst. Sec. & Treas.

The Province of St. Mary of the Capuchin Order, (Nature of Apostolate: Provincial Administration, Parishes, Capuchin Food Pantries, Hospital & Prison Chaplains, Preaching, Recruitment). Total in Residence 6; Total Staff 12. *Capuchin Friars International, Inc.* (1984) St. Conrad Friary, 30 Gedney Park Dr., 10605-3599. Tel: 914-761-3008, Ext. 21; Fax: 914-948-6429. Web: www.ofmcap.org. Revs. Luis Eduardo Rubiano, O.F.M.Cap., Treas.; Giampiero Gambaro, O.F.M.Cap., Sec.; Jerome McHugh, O.F.M.Cap., Asst. Sec. Treas.

Capuchin Friars International, Inc. St. Francis of Assisi Foundation, St. Conrad Friary, 30 Gedney Park Dr., 10605-3599. Tel: 914-761-3008, Ext. 21; Fax: 914-948-6429. Dr. Livio Camozzi, Pres.; Bro. Mark Schenk, O.F.M.Cap., Vice Pres.; Revs. Giampiero Gambaro, O.F.M.Cap., Treas.; Jerome McHugh, O.F.M.Cap., Asst. Sec. Treas.

St. Francis of Assisi Foundation

YONKERS. *St. Clare Friary* Residence for Senior Friars., 110 Shonnard Pl., 10703. Tel: 914-423-2392. Revs. Michael Connolly; Senan Taylor, O.F.M.Cap., Guardian; Joel Daniels, O.F.M.Cap.; Darius Devito, O.F.M.Cap.; Andrew Drew, O.F.M.Cap. (Retired); Zachary Grant; Raymond Hand, O.F.M.Cap.; Knute Kenlon, O.F.M.Cap.; James McIntyre, O.F.M.Cap.; Eymard McKinnon; John Proppe, O.F.M.Cap.; Walter O'Brien; Philip Romano, O.F.M.Cap. Capuchin Franciscan Friars, Province of St. Mary. Total in Residence 11; Total Staff 3.

St. Felix Friary (Franciscan Friars of the Renewal), 15 Trinity Plaza, 10701. Tel: 914-476-7279; Fax: 914-476-5033. Web: FranciscanFriars.com. Revs. James Mary Atkins, C.F.R., Local Servant; Jeremiah Shryock, C.F.R., Vicar; Bros. Simon Dankowski, C.F.R.; Justin Alarcon, C.F.R.; Giles Barrie, C.F.R.; Tobias Redfield, C.F.R.; Philip Allen, C.F.R.; David Valenzuela, C.F.R.; Antonio diez deMedina, C.F.R.; Seraphim Roycourt.

St. Leopold's Friary (Franciscan Friars of the Renewal); (House of Studies), 259 Nepperhan Ave., 10701-3461. Tel: 914-965-8143; Fax: 914-709-8986. Web: www.franciscanfriars.com. Rev. Solanus M. Benfatti, C.F.R., S.T.L., Dir., Seminarians; Deacon John Paul Ouellette, C.F.R., Local Vicar; Rev. Andrew D. Apostoli, C.F.R., M.S.; Bro. Francis Edkins, C.F.R.; Rev. Christopher P. Metzger, C.F.R.; Bro. Felix Mary Desilets, C.F.R.; Rev. Lawrence Schroedel, C.F.R.; Bros. Nathanael Mary Lysinger, C.F.R.; Youssef M. Hanna, C.F.R.; Bonaventure Mary Rummell, C.F.R.; Paschal Marie Coby, C.F.R.; Paul Raniero Donnelly, C.F.R.; Christopher McBride, C.F.R.; Luke Joseph Leighton; Ignatius Shin, C.F.R.; Gabriel Joseph Kyte, C.F.R.; Pius Gagne, C.F.R.

[EE] CONVENTS AND RESIDENCES OF SISTERS

NEW YORK. *Academy of St. Dorothy* (1932) 1305 Hylan Blvd., Staten Island, 10305. Tel: 718-987-0677; 718-351-0939; Fax: 718-351-0661. Email: dorothy@adnyeducation.org. Sr. Caridad Portu, S.S.D., Coord. Sisters of St. Dorothy. Sisters 7.

Blessed Trinity Missionary Cenacle, 414 E. 14th St., 10009. Tel: 212-475-1450; Fax: 212-254-8565. Web: MSBTNYC.com. Sr. Sara Butler, M.S.B.T., Ph.D. Missionary Social Work and Parish & Community Services, and Catholic Charities of New York; Nazareth Housing-Work with homeless; seminary education. Missionary Servants of the Most Blessed Trinity 4. *Catholic Charities*, 213 Stanton St., 10002. Tel: 212-777-3111; Fax: 212-677-9057. Email: msbtnyc1@aol.com.

Carmelite Sisters Teresas of St. Joseph, Inc., 249 W. 14th St., 10011. Tel: 212-242-8224; Fax: 212-242-7233. Email: hnascarmelitaj@aol.com. Sr. Angela Perez, Supr.

Convent of Our Lady of the Presentation (1775) 419 Woodrow Rd., 10312. Tel: 718-356-2121; Fax: 718-948-4115. Email: rosemarypssi@aol.com. Motherhouse and Novitiate of the Sisters of the Presentation. Sisters 11.

Corpus Christi Monastery, 1230 Lafayette Ave., 10474-5399. Tel: 718-328-6996; Fax: 718-328-1974. Email: dominicannunsny@verizon.net. Sr. Maria Pia of the Eucharist, O.P., Prioress. Solemnly Professed 10.

The Dwelling Place of New York, Inc., 409 W. 40th St., 10018. Tel: 212-564-7887; Fax: 212-695-3642. Email: nancydpny@aol.com. Sr. Margaret Boyle, P.B.V.M., Admin. For Homeless Women Sisters 2.

Franciscan Handmaids of Mary Convent Generalate of the Franciscan Handmaids of Mary., 15 W. 124th St., 10027. Tel: 212-289-5655; Fax: 212-987-5447. Email: handmaidsofmary@aol.com. Web: www.fhm.members.aol.com/fhm.nyc. Sisters Gertrude Lilly Ihenacho, F.H.M., Congregation Min.; Loretta Theresa Richards, F.H.M., Asst. Cong. Minister Formation, Dir.; Leonie Therese Obinna, F.H.M., Dir. Vocations. Sisters 17; Total Assisted 100.

Other Convents:

Most Pure Heart of Mary Convent, 63 Bayside Ln., Staten Island, 10309. Tel: 718-227-5575. Email: pfsocialjustice@yahoo.com. *St. Edward Food Pantry*, 6581 Hylan Blvd., Staten Island, 10309. Tel: 718-984-1625; Fax: 718-996-0814. Sr. Chala Marie Hill, F.H.M., Dir.

Handmaids of Mary Altar Bread Distribution Service, 6581 Hylan Blvd., Staten Island, 10309. Tel: 718-984-1625; Fax: 718-966-0814. Associates 35.

St. Benedict's Day Nursery (Day Care Center), 21 W. 124 St., 10027. Tel: 212-423-5715; Fax: 212-423-5917. Email: stben124@aol.com. Geneine Morris, Dir.

Franciscan Missionaries of Mary, 3305 Wallace Ave., Bronx, 10467-6519. Tel: 718-547-4693; Fax: 718-325-5102. Email: palfmm@aol.com. Web: www.fmmusa.org.

FMM Provincialate, 3305 Wallace Ave., Bronx, 10467-6519. Tel: 718-547-4693; Fax: 718-325-5102. Email: palfmm@aol.com. Web: www.fmm.org or www.fmmusa.org.

Holy Name of Jesus Convent, 204 W. 97th St., 10025-5620. Tel: 212-678-6901. Email: fmmny97@aol.com. Web: www.fmmusa.org. *Our Lady of Millbrook Convent*, Box K, Millbrook, 12545. Tel: 845-677-6739; Fax: 845-677-6530. Email: fmmch@aol.com. Web: www.fmmusa.org.

Franciscan Sisters of the Poor Foundation, Inc., 708 Third Ave., Ste. 1858, 10017. Tel: 212-818-1987; Fax: 212-808-0096. Email: lchristian@franciscanfoundation.org. Web: www.franciscanfoundation.org.

International Presentation Association of the Sisters of the Presentation of the Blessed Virgin Mary, 211 E. 43rd St., Ste. 1207, 10017-4707. Tel: 212-370-0075; Fax: 212-370-0075. Email: pbvmipa@msn.com. Web: internationalpresentationassociation.org. Sr. Fatima Rodrigo, Contact Person.

St. Joseph Provincialate (1921) 850 Hylan Blvd., Staten Island, 10305. Tel: 718-981-4402; Fax: 718-556-3550. Email: sisterwilliam@gmail.com. Provincialate of the Daughters of Divine Charity (St. Joseph Province). In Province 29.

Missionary Sisters of Our Lady of Perpetual Help, Inc. (1934) *Office of the President*, 371 E. 150th St., Bronx, 10455. Tel: 718-742-2509; Fax: 718-742-2503. Sr. Isaura Flores, M.P.S., Acting Mother Supr.; Melissa Garza, Agent Residence.

Missionary Sisters of the Immaculate Heart of Mary (1897) District House, 238 E. 15th St., Apt. 5, 10003-3901. Tel: 212-677-2959; Fax: 212-475-7455. Email: icmusdist@juno.com. Sr. Kathryn Vercelline, I.C.M., Dist. Leader. *St. Joseph Convent* (1948) 238 E. 15th St., 10003-3901. Tel: 212-254-0658; Fax: 212-475-7455. Sisters 15.

Parish Visitors of Mary Immaculate (1920) 2151 Watson Ave., Bronx, 10472-5401. Tel: 718-823-0350; Fax: 718-823-0350. Sr. Linda Giovanelly, P.V.M.I., Supr. Sisters 5.

**Servants of the Lord and Virgin of Matara, Inc.*, 226 E. 113th St., 10029. Tel: 212-534-4063; Fax: 212-828-8379. Web: ssvmusa.org. Sr. Mary of the Sacred Heart Gaes, Pres.

Shalom Convent, 714 W. 231st St., 10463. Tel: 718-884-1663. Email: kerr714sweeney@verizon.net. Franciscan Sisters of the Poor 3.

Sisters of Charity Center, 6301 Riverdale Ave., 10471-1093. Tel: 718-549-9200, Ext. 230; Fax: 718-884-3013. Web: www.scny.org. Sr. Jane Iannucelli, Pres.

The Sisters of Charity of Saint Vincent de Paul of New York

Sisters of Charity Center

Mount Saint Vincent on Hudson

The Sisters of Charity of Saint Vincent de Paul of New York Pension Trust Total in Congregation 333; In Archdiocese 326.

The Elizabeth Seton Federation, Inc. (1995) Sisters of Charity Center, 6301 Riverdale Ave., Bronx, 10471. Tel: 718-549-9200, Ext. 268; Fax: 718-884-3013. Web: www.sisters-of-charity-federation.org.

Sisters of the Good Shepherd, 337 E. 17th St., 10003-3804. Tel: 212-475-4245; Fax: 212-777-9260.

Sisters of the Good Shepherd-New York City Sisters 2.

Society of Helpers, 385 W. 263rd St., Bronx, 10471. Tel: 718-884-3100. Email: nyhelper@rcn.com. Web: www.helpers.org. Sr. Geraldine Finan, Supr. Sisters 4.

Society of the Sacred Heart, R.S.C.J., 515 E. 118th St., 10035. Tel: 212-876-2276; Fax: 212-996-5277. Email: fgimber@rscj.org. Web: www.RSCJ.org.

Other Residences: *Society of the Sacred Heart, R.S.C.J.*, 501 W. 52nd St., #4E, 10019. Tel: 212-581-3894. *Society of the Sacred Heart, R.S.C.J.*, 515 E. 118th St., 10035. Tel: 212-876-2895. *Society of the Sacred Heart, R.S.C.J.*, 406 E. 80th St., 10075. Tel: 212-288-1986; 212-288-5116 (East River Community); Fax: 212-861-8851.

Visitation Convent (Sisters of Life), 320 E. 66th St., 10021. Tel: 212-737-0221. Sisters 5.

BEACON. *Carmelite Monastery* (2000) 89 Hiddenbrooke Dr., 12508-2230. Tel: 845-831-5572; Fax: 845-831-5579. Email: beaconcarmel@optonline.net. Web: www.carmelitesbeacon.org. Sr. Michaelene Devine,

O.C.D., Prioress. Professed Nuns 18.

BLAUVELT. *Congregation of Sisters of St. Dominic of Blauvelt*, 496 Western Hwy., 10913. Tel: 845-359-5600; Fax: 845-359-5773. Email: choward@opblauvelt.org. Web: www.opblauvelt.org. Sr. Catherine Howard, O.P., Pres.
The Sisters of St. Dominic of Blauvelt, New York Sisters 146; Candidate 1.

BRONX. *The Congregation of The Daughters of Mary, Inc.*, 176 Kilroe St., 10464. Tel: 718-885-1842; Fax: 718-885-1842. Email: dmcityisland@optimum.net. Sr. Agnes Jose, D.M., Sec. & Treas.

Franciscan Sisters of the Renewal (Franciscan Sisters of the Renewal), *Convent of San Damiano*, 1661 Haight Ave., 10461. Tel: 718-829-9466; Fax: 718-239-6321. Web: www.franciscansisterscfr.com. Sr. Agnes Mary Holtz, C.F.R., Local Servant. (Novitiate House, Convent of San Damiano) Sisters 10.

Missionaries of Charity, Inc., 335 E. 145th St., 10451. Tel: 718-292-0019; Fax: 718-292-2929. Sisters M. Leticia, M.C., Regl. Supr.; M. Rose Clara, M.C., Supr. 406 W. 127th St., 10027. Tel: 212-222-7229. Sr. M. Manorama, M.C., Supr. 657 Washington St., 10014. Tel: 212-645-0587. Sr. M. Tonia, M.C., Supr.

Our Lady of Guadalupe Convent, 3537 Bainbridge Ave., 10467. Tel: 718-547-9840; Fax: 718-547-0995. Sisters Lucille Cutrone, C.F.R., Community Servant; Clare Marie Matthiass, C.F.R., Local Servant. (Franciscans Sisters of the Renewal) Sisters 8.

Sisters of Charity Novitiate, Mount Saint Vincent Convent, 6301 Riverdale Ave., 10471. Tel: 718-601-5370, Ext. 272 (Novitiate); 718-601-5370, Ext. 274 (House). Sr. Anne Denise Brennan, Formation/Novice Dir.

Sisters of St. John the Baptist, Provincial Residence, 3308 Campbell Dr., 10465-1358. Tel: 718-518-7820; Fax: 718-518-8930. Email: srmcecile@hotmail.com. Web: baptistines.org. Sr. Mary Cecile Swanton, C.S.J.B., Prov. Supr. In Province 91; In Archdiocese 76.

Mt. St. John Convent, 150 Anderson Hill Rd., Purchase, 10577. Tel: 914-761-7965; Fax: 914-761-2315. Sr. Mary Faith Chanda, C.S.J.B., Supr. (Retired Sisters' Residence) Sisters in Residence 24.

ESOPUS. *Mother of Perpetual Help Monastery*, P.O. Box 220, 12429. Tel: 845-384-6533; Fax: 845-384-6654. Email: rednuns.esopus@gmail.com. Web: www.redemptoristinenunsofnewyork.org/. Sr. Paula Schmidt, O.SS.R., Prioress. Redemptoristine Nuns. Professed Sisters 9.

GARRISON. *Motherhouse and Novitiate of the Franciscan Sisters of the Atonement* (1898) St. Francis Convent - Graymoor, 41 Old Highland Tpke., 10524. Tel: 845-424-3623; Fax: 845-424-3298. Email: nconboy@graymoor.org. Web: www.graymoor.org. Sisters Nancy Conboy, S.A., Min. Gen.; Mary Patricia Galvin, S.A., Coord.
Franciscan Sisters of the Atonement, Inc. Sisters 151.

Our Lady of the Atonement Retreat House, St Francis Convent, 41 Old Highland Tpke., 10524. Tel: 845-424-3300; Fax: 845-230-8400. Email: retreathouse@graymoor.org. Web: www.graymoor.org. Sr. Eleanor White, S.A., Directress. Franciscan Sisters of the Atonement, Graymoor. Sisters 2.

GRAYMOOR. *Mother Lurana House* Adult Social Day Center., 166 Old W. Point Rd., E., Garrison, 10524. Tel: 845-424-3184; Fax: 845-424-4137. Web: www.graymoor.org. Sr. Eileen Waldron, S.A., Admin. Franciscan Sisters of the Atonement.

HARTSDALE. *Institute of the Sisters of Mercy of the Americas, Mid-Atlantic Community*, 150 Ridge Rd., 10530-2205. Tel: 914-328-3200; Fax: 914-328-3761. Web: www.mercymidatlantic.org. Sr. Patricia Vetrano, R.S.M., Pres.
The Sisters of Mercy, Inc. Sisters of Mercy. Sisters of Mercy of the Americas 1,007.

HAVERSTRAW. *Sisters of St. Francis of Peace* (1986) *Congregation Center*, 20 Ridge St., 10927-1198. Tel: 845-942-2527; Fax: 845-429-8141. Email: jgilligan@fspnet.org. Web: www.fspnet.org. Sr. Jeanne Gilligan, F.S.P., Congregation Min.

HAWTHORNE. *Motherhouse & Novitiate of the Sisters of St. Dominic, Congregation of St. Rose of Lima* (1900) 10532. Tel: 914-769-0114; Fax: 914-769-0827. Web: www.hawthorne-dominicans.org. Sr. Mary Francis, O.P., Supr. Gen.; Rev. Martin Connors, O.P., B.A., S.T.B., Chap.
Motherhouse and Dominican Sisters of St. Dominic, Congregation of St. Rose of Lima. Professed Sisters 53; Sisters in Community 55; In Archdiocese 27.

HIGHLAND MILLS. *Religious of Jesus and Mary* (1911) 15 Bethany Dr., 10930-1003. Tel: 845-928-2213; Fax: 845-928-9437. Email: RJMClaireD@aol.com. Web: www.bethanyspiritualitycenter.org. Sr. Claire Dandeneau, R.J.M., Supr. Sisters 12.

HOPEWELL JUNCTION. *St. Aloysius Novitiate*, 306 Beekman Rd., P.O. Box 98, 12533. Tel: 845-226-5671; Fax: 845-226-5671. Email: jstab35097@aol.com. Web: www.oblatestotheblessedtrinity.org. Sr. Gloria Castro, Supr. Gen. Perpetually Professed Sisters 30; Temporary Professed Sisters 5; Novices 4; Postulants 3.

LIBERTY. *Blessed Kateri Tekakwitha Religious Education Center*, Box 1011, 12754. Tel: 845-292-9100; Fax: 845-292-9100. Email: BKT4@verizon.net. Dominican Sisters.

LIVINGSTON MANOR. *Monastic Sisters of Bethlehem and of the Assumption of the Virgin* (1951) 393 Our Lady of Lourdes Camp Rd., 12758. Tel: 845-439-4300; Fax: 845-439-3069. Sr. Amena Figeat, M.S.B.A.V., Supr. Total in Residence 15.

MARYKNOLL. *Maryknoll Communities, Inc.*, 77 Ryder Rd., P.O. Box 133, 10545-0133. Tel: 914-941-7590; Fax: 914-944-3628. Email: rcallahan@maryknoll.org. Web: www.maryknoll.org.

Maryknoll Residential Care Skilled Nursing home for the Maryknoll sisters only., Maryknoll Sisters Center, 10545-0311. Tel: 914-941-9230; Fax: 914-941-0213. Email: pedmiston@mksisters.org. Web: www.maryknoll.org. Sr. Patricia Edmiston, Admin. Bed Capacity 42; Sisters 33.

Maryknoll Sisters Charitable Trust, Treasury Office, P.O. Box 306, 10545-0306. Tel: 914-941-7590; Fax: 914-944-3628. Email: rcallahan@maryknoll.org. Web: www.maryknoll.org. Rev. Richard B. Callahan, M.M., Trustee.

Maryknoll Sisters Contemplative Community Contemplative Community of the Maryknoll Sisters of St. Dominic., P.O. Box 311, 10545-0311. Tel: 914-941-7575; Fax: 914-923-0733. Email: mkcontemplative@optimum.net. Sr. Grace Myerjack, M.M., Coord. Sisters 8.

Maryknoll Sisters of St. Dominic Inc. (1912) P.O. Box 311, 10545-0311. Tel: 914-941-7575; Fax: 914-923-0733. Email: secretariat@mksisters.org. Web: www.maryknoll.org. Sr. Marcelline Yurkovic, M.M., Center-Rogers Coord. Professed Sisters 212; Total in Residence 212.

MILLBROOK. *Franciscan Missionaries of Mary* (1941) P.O. Box K, 12545. Tel: 845-677-6739; Fax: 845-677-9530. Email: fmmch@aol.com. Web: fmmusa.org. Sisters Anne Turbini, F.M.M.; Jacqueline LaVie, F.M.M.; Martha Vu, F.M.M. Sisters 4.

MONROE. *Parish Visitors of Mary Immaculate* (1920) *Marycrest Convent*, 164 Quaker Hill Rd., P.O. Box 658, 10949-0658. Tel: 845-783-2251; Fax: 845-783-2085. Sisters Carole Marie Troskowski, Gen. Supr.; Mary Remias, Juniorate Dir.; Maria Catherine, Novice Dir. A contemplative-missionary community serving the Church by person-to-person evangelization through visiting parish families on behalf of their priests; religious education for children and adults not connected with the Catholic schools, giving spiritual counsel and serving as a liaison for social service needs of family members. Total in Community 57.

Queen of Apostles Convent Provincial Retirement Home and Provincialate of the Sisters of the Catholic Apostolate (Pallottine)., 98 Harriman Heights Rd., 10950. Tel: 845-492-5000; Fax: 845-492-5070. Email: qoaconvent@hotmail.com. Web: www.pallottinesisters.org. Sisters Ann Joachim Firneno, C.S.A.C., Supr.; Olivia Reginella, C.S.A.C., Prov.; Rev. Michael F. Keane, Chap. Sisters 36.

MONSEY. *St. Zita's Villa* Motherhouse and Novitiate of Sisters of Reparation of the Congregation of Mary., 50 Saddle River Rd., N., 10952. Tel: 845-356-2011; Fax: 845-364-6520. Sr. Maureen Francis, S.R.C.M., Supr. Sisters 3.

NEW ROCHELLE. *Ursuline Bedford Park Convent* (1855) 1338 North Ave., 10804. Tel: 914-636-3456; Fax: 914-576-2620. Email: bedfordpark@aol.com. Sr. Kathleen Mary Donohue, O.S.U. Sisters 6.

Ursuline Communities, Inc. (1997) 1338 North Ave., 10804. Tel: 914-712-0060; Fax: 914-712-3134. Email: ursruepr@aol.com.

Ursuline Convent of St. Teresa's, 39 Willow Dr., 10805. Tel: 914-632-1199; Fax: 914-633-5281. Sr. Jeanne Giebelhouse, O.S.U., Supr.
Ursuline Convent of St. Teresa's, New York Sisters 36.

Ursuline Provincialate, 1338 North Ave., 10804-2121. Tel: 914-712-0060; Fax: 914-712-3134. Email: ursruepr@aol.com. Provincialate of the Ursulines of the Roman Union, Eastern Province. Sisters in Province 115.

Ursuline Sisters of Andrews Avenue, Inc. (1995) 1338 North Ave., 10804. Tel: 914-712-0060; Fax: 914-712-3134.

Ursuline Residence, Inc., 1338 North Ave., 10804. Tel: 914-712-0060; Fax: 914-712-3134.

NEW WINDSOR. *Mt. St. Joseph* (1775) Administration Center of the Sisters of the Presentation of the Blessed Virgin Mary of New Windsor., 84 Presentation Way, 12553. Tel: 914-564-0513; Fax: 914-567-0219. Email: pbvmadministration@hvc.rr.com. Web: sistersofthepresentation.org. Sisters Patricia Anastasio, P.B.V.M., Pres.; Margaret Muller, P.B.V.M., Community Archivist. Ministry in the field of academic education in parochial elementary and high schools; pastoral services; health care; social services. Sisters 126.

NEWBURGH. *Daughters of Mary Immaculate* (1898) Italian Apostolate in Sacred Heart Church., 15 Stori Rd., 12550. Tel: 845-565-5034. Sr. Alba Danese, F.M.I., Supr. Total Assisted 180; Total Staff 2.

NYACK. *Sisters of Our Lady of Christian Doctrine aka Institute of Christian Doctrine* Visitation House, 629 N. Midland Ave., 10960-1032. Tel: 845-512-8669; Fax: 845-358-7663. Email: vermettered@aol.com. Web: www.sistersrcd.org. Sr. Rose T. Vermette, R.C.D., Pres. Sisters 21.

Marydell Faith & Life Center, 640 N. Midland Ave., 10960. Tel: 845-358-5399; Fax: 845-358-1671. Email: marydell@netzero.net.

OSSINING. *Dominican Sisters of Hope* (1995) 299 N. Highland Ave., 10562-2327. Tel: 914-941-4420; Fax: 914-941-1125. Email: lelcock@ophope.org. Web: www.ophope.org. Sr. Lorelle Elcock, O.P., Prioress. Total in Community 211.

Dominicare, Inc. (2001) Office of the President, 299 N. Highland Ave., 10562-2327. Tel: 914-941-4420; Fax: 914-941-1125. Email: lelcock@ophope.org. Web: www.ophope.org.

Sisters of St. Dominic Charitable Trust, 299 N. Highland Ave., Bldg. 5, 10562. Tel: 914-941-4455; Fax: 914-502-0574. Email: hdowney@ophope.org. Hugh R. Downey, Trustee.

PEEKSKILL. *Mt. St. Francis, Motherhouse & Infirm of Franciscan Missionary Sisters of Sacred Heart* Canonical Name: Franciscan Missionary Sisters of the Sacred Heart., 250 South St., 10566. Tel: 914-737-5409; Fax: 914-736-9614. Email: sramcfmsc@mail.com. Sr. Anne Matthew Carlone, F.M.S.C., Prov. Supr.
Missionary Sisters of the Third Order of St. Francis

PELHAM. *Sisters of St. Francis of the Neumann Communities* (1893) P.O. Box 8592, 10803. Tel: 914-840-9694; Fax: 914-840-9710. Email: msalerno@sosf.org. Web: www.sosf.org. Sr. Maria Salerno, O.S.F., Leadership; Rev. Knute Kenlon, O.F.M.Cap., Chap. Sisters of St. Francis, Hastings-on-Hudson. Sisters 76; Associates in Region 26.

RHINEBECK. *Linwood Spiritual Center*, 50 Linwood Rd., 12572-2507. Tel: 845-876-4178; Fax: 845-876-1920. Email: rboyle@st-ursula.org; msteeley@st-ursula.org. Web: www.linwoodspiritualctr.org. Sr. Maureen Steeley, S.U., Dir. Spiritual Center. Society of St. Ursula.

RYE. *Convent of the Holy Child*, 25 Convent Ln., 10580-1904. Tel: 914-967-5544; Fax: 914-925-2575. Email: holychildd@aol.com. Sisters of the Holy Child Jesus 22.

SCARSDALE. *Blessed Sacrament Monastery*, 86 Dromore Rd., 10583-1706. Tel: 914-722-1657; Fax: 914-722-1665. Email: obsny@optonline.net. Web: www.catholic.org/macc. Sr. Mary Francis Blackmore, O.S.S., Prioress. Sacramentine Nuns. Sisters 7.

SLOATSBURG. *St. Mary's Villa, Spiritual & Educational Center*, 150 Sisters Servants Ln., P.O. Box 9, 10974-0009. Tel: 845-753-5100; Fax: 845-753-1956. Email: ssminy@aol.com. Sisters Servants of Mary Immaculate.

SPARKILL. *Dominican Convent of Our Lady of the Rosary* (1876) Motherhouse and General Novitiate of Dominican Sisters of Congregation of Our Lady of the Rosary., 175 Rte. 340, 10976-1047. Tel: 845-359-4088; Fax: 845-359-4083. Email: lorraine.larocca@sparkill.org. Web: www.sparkill.org. Sr. Mary Murray, O.P., Pres.; Rev. George Torak, Chap. Sisters 331.

STATEN ISLAND. *Daughters of St. Paul, Pious Society* (1915) 840 Delafield Ave., 10310. Tel: 718-447-5071; Fax: 718-816-1332. Email: statenisland@pauline.org. Web: www.pauline.org. Sr. Mary Thecla Paolini, Supr. Missionary Sisters of the Communications Media. Sisters 7.

Pious Disciples of the Divine Master, Regional and Formation House, 60 Sunset Ave., 10314. Tel: 718-761-2323; 718-494-8597; Fax: 718-494-2123. Email: srnieves@aol.com. Web: www.pddm.us. Sr. M. Nieves Salinas, P.D.D.M., Regl. Supr. Sisters 10.

TARRYTOWN. *Provincial Center, Religious Sacred Heart of Mary*, 50 Wilson Park Dr., 10591-3023. Tel: 914-631-8872; Fax: 914-631-7803. Email: mflannelly@rshmeap.org. Web: www.rshm.org. Sisters Kathleen Fagan, R.S.H.M., Prov. Supr.;

Joanne Safian, R.S.H.M., Prov. Counselor; Margaret Ellen Flannelly, R.S.H.M., Prov. Counselor; Virginia Dorgan, R.S.H.M., Treas.; Mary Alice Young, R.S.H.M., Dir. of Advancement; Lucia Kenny, R.S.H.M., Archivist; Loretta Ruvo, R.S.H.M., Dir. Vocation Promotion; Ms. MaryAnn DeRosa, Provincial Team Sec. Total Staff 16.

WALDEN. *Little Sisters of the Assumption*, Provincial House, 100 Gladstone Ave., 12586. Tel: 845-778-0667; Fax: 845-778-0676. Email: provsec@littlesisters.org. Web: www.littlesisters.org. Sr. Annette Allain, L.S.A., Prov. Sisters in Province 23.

Other residences in New York: *Little Sisters of the Assumption*, 475 E. 115th St., 10029. Tel: 212-369-2097. *Little Sisters of the Assumption*, 310 E. 120th St., 10035. Tel: 917-668-4738; Fax: 212-427-6096.

Little Sisters of the Assumption, 98 Gladstone Ave., 12586-0677. Tel: 845-778-0678. Sr. Annette Allain, L.S.A., Prov. Sisters 1.

WAPPINGERS FALLS. *Monastery of St. Clare - Franciscan Poor Clare Nuns* (1915) 70 Nelson Ave., 12590-1121. Tel: 845-297-1685; Fax: 845-297-7657. Email: claresny@gmail.com. Web: www.poorclaresny.com. Sr. Mary Michael Boisseau, O.S.C., Abbess.

Franciscan Poor Clare Nuns Sisters 12; Postulants 1.

WARWICK. *Mt. Alverno Center, Bon Secours Charity Health System*, 20 Grand St., 10990. Tel: 845-986-2267; Fax: 845-986-9269. Web: www.stanthonycommunityhosp.org. Toni Clark, Senior Vice Pres. Long Term Care; Michael Deyo, Admin., Mt. Alverno Center, Adult Home/Assisted Living Program; Suzanne Evanoff, Pastoral Care; Rev. Henry Tanto, Chap. (Retired). St. Francis Center at the Knolls, Villa Francis at the Knolls.

WHITE PLAINS. *Convent of Our Lady of Good Counsel* Motherhouse of the Sisters of the Divine Compassion., 52 N. Broadway, 10603. Tel: 914-798-1300; Fax: 914-949-5169. Email: smerritt@divinecompassion.org. Web: divinecompassion.org. Sr. Susan Merritt, R.D.C., Pres. Sisters 27.

RDC Center for Counseling and Human Development, Inc. (1991) 52 N. Broadway, 10603. Tel: 914-949-0504; Fax: 914-997-1979. To provide counseling services for laity, religious and clergy. Individual and group counseling are offered as well as marital and family therapy.

YONKERS. *St. Paul the Apostle*, 586 McLean Ave., 10705. Tel: 914-968-8094; Fax: 914-968-0462. Sisters Agnes Mary, S.V., Supr. Gen.; Mary Elizabeth, S.V., Vicar Gen.; Brigid Ancilla Marie, S.V.; Catherine Peter, S.V.; Dorothy Guadalupe, S.V.; Elizabeth Ann, S.V.; Maeve Nativitas, S.V.; Maria Anne Michela, S.V.; Mariea Dolorosa, S.V.

Our Lady of New York, 1955 Needham Ave., Bronx, 10466. Tel: 718-881-8008; Fax: 718-654-2911.

Sacred Heart of Jesus (1991) 450 W. 51st St., 10019. Tel: 212-397-1396; Fax: 212-397-1397. Sisters Rita Marie, S.V, Local Supr.; Ann Catherine, S.V.; Giovanna Mariae, S.V.; Rose Clairvaux, S.V.; Mary Kolbe, S.V.; Fiat Marie, S.V.; Amata Filia, S.V.

Villa Maria Guadalupe, 159 Skymeadow Dr., Stamford, CT 06903. Tel: 203-329-1492; Fax: 203-329-1495. Sisters Mary Karen, S.V., Local Supr.; Rosario John, S.V.; Josamarie Perpetua, S.V.; Marija Joseph, S.V.; Maria Emmanuel, S.V.; Marie-Noel Maximilliene, S.V.; Mary Loretta, S.V.; Mary Teresa, S.V.; John Joseph, S.V.; Talitha Guadalupe, S.V.; Bernadette Therese, S.V.; Mary Louise Concepta, S.V.

St. Francis de Chantal, 198 Hollywood Ave., Bronx, 10465. Tel: 718-863-2264; Fax: 718-792-9645. Sisters Mary Gabriel, S.V., Dir. Novices; Bethany Madonna, S.V.; Antoniana Maria, S.V., Dir. Vocations; Loretto Michael, S.V.; Mariae Agnus Dei, S.V.; Rose Clairvaux, S.V.

St. Barnabas Convent, 445 E. 240th St., Bronx, 10470. Tel: 718-708-6742; Fax: 718-708-6744. Sr. Charlotte Ann Marie, S.V., Local Supr. & Dir., Postulants. Sisters 8.

Visitation Convent, 320 E. 66th St., 10021. Tel: 212-737-0221; 877-777-1277. Sr. Magdalene Theresa, S.V., Local Supr. Sisters 8.

St. Augustine Convent, 2661 Kingston Rd., Scarborough ON M1M 1M3 Canada. Tel: 416-261-7207, Ext. 266; Fax: 416-261-0923. Sr. Mary Rose, S.V., Supr. Sisters 6.

Sisters of Life, 586 McLean Ave., 10705. Tel: 914-968-8094; Fax: 914-968-0462. Sr. Agnes Mary Donovan, S.V., Supr. Gen. Professed Sisters 54; Novices 13; Postulants 8.

[FF] RETREAT HOUSES

BRONX. *St. Joseph's Center*, 275 W. 230th St., 10463. Tel: 718-796-4340. Rev. Jose Luis Martinez, O.A.R., Dir.; Bro. Mario Alvarez, O.A.R., Admin. (Spanish Cursillo Center) Total in Residence 1; Total Staff 2.

ESOPUS. *Marist Brothers of Ulster County* (1994) Mid Hudson Valley Camp - Summer camp for disadvantaged children/Retreat house for youth. Winter youth retreat facility., P.O. Box 197, 12429. Tel: 845-384-6106 (residence); 845-384-6620 (office); Fax: 845-384-6479. Email: esopusdon1@aol.com. Web: www.maristretreathouse.com. Bro. Donald Nugent, F.M.S., Dir. Total Staff 2.

Mount St. Alphonsus Redemptorist Retreat Center, 1001 Broadway, P.O. Box 219, 12429. Tel: 845-384-8000; Fax: 845-384-8088. Web: www.mountsaintalphonsus.org. Revs. Thomas J. Travers, C.Ss.R.; Thomas (Martin) Deely, C.Ss.R.; Charles Brinkmann, C.Ss.R.; Joseph Freund, C.Ss.R., B.A., M.R.E., M.Div. Redemptorist Fathers and Brothers., Groups and individual retreats, conferences, workshops, and days of prayer. Available for Religious Chapters. Capacity 300; Bed Capacity 106.

HIGHLAND MILLS. *Bethany Spirituality Center, Inc.*, 15 Bethany Dr., 10930. Tel: 845-460-3061; Fax: 845-928-2320. Email: info@bethanyspiritualitycenter.org. Web: www.bethanyspiritualitycenter.org. Sr. Eileen Reid, R.J.M., Pres.; Richard C. Green, Dir. Religious of Jesus and Mary. Total in Residence 11.

LARCHMONT. *St. Francis Retreat, Inc.*, 1 Pryer Manor Rd., 10538. Tel: 914-235-6839; Fax: 914-576-6540. Rev. Benedict Joseph Groeschel, C.F.R., Ed.D. Tel: 914-632-3743.

Trinity Retreat, 1 Pryer Manor Rd., 10538. Tel: 914-235-6839; Fax: 914-576-6540. Email: trinityret@aol.com. Revs. Eugene J. Fulton (PSC), Dir.; Benedict Joseph Groeschel, C.F.R., Ed.D., Assoc. Dir.

MIDDLETOWN. *National Shrine of Our Lady of Mount Carmel*, 70 Carmelite Dr., P.O. Box 2163, 10940-2163. Tel: 845-343-1879; Fax: 845-343-1912. Email: nsolmc@warwick.net. Web: www.ourladyofmtcarmelshrine.com. Rev. Thomas Zalewski, O.Carm., Dir. Total Staff 4.

SLOATSBURG. *St. Mary's Villa*, 150 Sisters Servants Ln., P.O. Box 9, 10974-0009. Tel: 845-753-5100; Fax: 845-753-1956. Email: ssminy@aol.com. Sisters Servants of Mary Immaculate., Spiritual and Educational Center. (Retreats) Total in Residence 5; Total Staff 7.

STATEN ISLAND. **Mount Manresa Jesuit Retreat House* (1911) 239 Fingerboard Rd., 10305. Tel: 718-727-3844; Fax: 718-727-4881. Email: info@mountmanresa.org. Web: www.mountmanresa.org. Mr. Fred Herron, Interim Dir.; Ms. Arlene Volsario, Admin.; Revs. Thomas M. Gavin, S.J., Retreat Min.; Matthew F. Roche, S.J., Retreat Min.; Sr. Maureen Skelly, S.C., Retreat Min. Society of Jesus. Total in Residence 4; Total Staff 6.

STONY POINT. *Don Bosco Retreat Center and Marian Shrine* Founded 1947., 174 Filors Ln., 10980-2620. Tel: 914-947-2200; Fax: 914-947-2203. Email: marianshrine@marianshrine.org. Web: www.marianshrine.org. Revs. Augustine Baek, S.D.B., RYC Korean Min.; James Berning, S.D.B., Retreats Coord. & Vice Dir.; William Bucciferro, S.D.B., Shrine Coord. & Delegate for Cooperator Salesians; Richard Crager, S.D.B.; Dominic DeBlase, S.D.B.; Joseph Doran, S.D.B., Chap. Marycrest Convent, Monroe; James McKenna, S.D.B.; Peter Sang Yun Kim, S.D.B.; Franco Pinto, S.D.B.; Waclaw Swierzbiolek, S.D.B., Polish Min.; Chester Szemborski, S.D.B.; Vincent Zuliani, S.D.B.; Bros. Charles Mayer, S.D.B.; Richard Pasiak, S.D.B.; Henry van der Velden, S.D.B.; Polynice Wilgintz, S.D.B.; Bernard Zdanowicz, S.D.B. Total in Residence 17; Total Staff 23.

Marian Shrine (1947) 174 Filors Ln., 10980-2620. Tel: 845-947-2200; Fax: 845-947-2203. Email: marianshrine@marianshrine.org. Web: www.marianshrine.org. Revs. George Atok, S.D.B.; Augustine Baek, S.D.B., RYC Korean Min.; James Berning, S.D.B., Retreats Coord. CYM; William Bucciferro, S.D.B., Shrine Coord. & Delegate for Cooperator Salesians; Joseph Doran, S.D.B., Chap. Marycrest Convent, Monroe; Peter Sang Yun Kim, S.D.B.; John Puntino, S.D.B., Dir.; Waclaw Swierzbiolek, S.D.B., Polish Min.; Chester Szemborski, S.D.B.; Vincent Zuliani, S.D.B.; Bros. Jerome Cincotta, S.D.B.; Michael Eguino, S.D.B.; Charles Mayer, S.D.B.; Richard Pasaik, S.D.B.; Henry van der Velden, S.D.B.; Bernard Zdanowicz, S.D.B. Total in Residence 17; Total Staff 23.

WAPPINGERS FALLS. *Mt. Alvernia Retreat House* 12590. Tel: 845-297-5706; Fax: 845-298-0309. Email: mtalverniarh@optonline.net. Revs. Michael Nappo, O.F.M., Guardian, Retreat Staff; Roch Ciandella, O.F.M., Dir. Retreats; Thomas Garone, O.F.M., Assoc. Dir., Retreats; Armand Padula, O.F.M., Librarian, Parochial Ministry; Bro. Thomas Hollowood, O.F.M., Dir. Maintenance.

WARWICK. *Franciscan Sisters of the Poor Convent*, 24 Grand St., 10990. Tel: 845-986-6799. Email: warwick.convent@optonline.net. Sr. Margaret A. Ferri, S.F.F., Local Community Min.; Rev. Edward Sullivan, O.F.M., Chap. Franciscan Sisters of the Poor.

YONKERS. *Sisters of Mary Reparatrix*, 287 Hayward St., 10704. Tel: 914-376-3245; Fax: 914-423-5721. Sisters Judy Frasietti, S.M.R.; Geraldine McCullagh, S.M.R. Sisters 2.

[GG] UNIVERSITY APOSTOLATES

YONKERS. *University Apostolate* 201 Seminary Ave., 10704. Tel: 914-968-6200, Ext. 8252; Fax: 914-968-6671. Rev. Daniel O'Reilly, M.A., Dir.

Bronx Community College Loew Hall-Room 422, University Ave. & W. 181st St., Bronx, 10453. Tel: 718-289-5954. Web: www.bcc.cuny.edu. Rev. James Sheehan, Campus Min.

City College of New York Baskerville, 204, 137th St. & Convent Ave., 10031. Tel: 212-650-5866. Web: www.ccny.cuny.edu. Mr. Gregory Pope, Campus Min.

Columbia University 110 Earl Hall, 10027. Tel: 212-854-5110. Web: www.columbia.edu. Rev. Daniel O'Reilly, M.A., Campus Min.; Rev. Msgr. John Paddock, Campus Min.; Rev. Marek Pienkowski, O.P., Campus Min.

Culinary Institute of America 93 Wurts St., Kingston, 12401. Tel: 845-331-0436; Fax: 845-340-9596. Email: chaplains@bestweb.net. Web: www.ciachef.edu. Rev. Marc K. Oliver, Campus Min.

Dutchess Community College 93 Wurts St., Kingston, 12401-4509. Tel: 845-331-0436. Web: www.cuny-dutchess.edu. Rev. Marc K. Oliver, Campus Min.

Vassar College St. Raymond Ave., Poughkeepsie, 12604. Tel: 845-437-7000. Web: www.vassar.edu. Ms. Linda Tuttle, Campus Min.

Dominican College 470 Western Hwy., Orangeburg, 10962. Tel: 845-359-7800. Sr. Barbara McEneany, O.P., Dir. Campus Min.; Rev. Ronald Stanley, O.P., Chap., Campus Min.

Fordham University at Rosehill 441 E. Fordham Rd., Bronx, 10458. Tel: 718-817-4500; Fax: 718-817-4505. Email: currie@fordham.edu. Web: www.fordham.edu/cm. Rev. Philip A. Florio, S.J.; Sr. Regina DeVitto, C.N.D., Faith Formation; Randy Jerome, Retreats & CLC; Mr. Denis Kelly; Mr. Robert Minotti, Dir. Music; Lisandro Pena, Liturgy Coord.; Gil Severiano, Sec.; Rev. Erika Crawford, Interfaith Coord.

Fordham Lincoln Center 113 W. 60th St., Lowenstein 217, 10023. Tel: 212-636-6267; 212-636-6268. Rev. John McDonagh; Ms. Joan Cavanagh, Assoc. Dir.; Mr. Patrick Callaghan, Sec.

Herbert H. Lehman College Student Life Bldg., 250 Bedford Park Blvd. W. (222E), Bronx, 10468. Tel: 718-960-4979. Web: www.lehman.cuny.edu. Rev. Neil J. O'Connell, O.F.M., B.A., S.T.B., M.A., Ph.D., Campus Min.

Borough of Manhattan 199 Chambers St., 10009. Tel: 212-220-8000. Web: www.bmcc.cuny.edu. Rev. Neil J. O'Connell, O.F.M., B.A., S.T.B., M.A., Ph.D., Campus Min.

Hostos Community College 475 Grand Concourse (Rm. C371), Bronx, 10451. Tel: 718-518-6873 (Mon-Tues). Web: www.hostos.cuny.edu. Rev. James Sheehan, Campus Min.

Hunter/Baruch College Newman Catholic Center, 695 Park Ave., Rm. 1317 E. Bldg., 10021. Tel: 212-772-4752 (Hunter); 646-312-4762 (Baruch). Web: www.hunter.cuny.edu; www.baruch.cuny.edu. Sr. Barbara Ann Mueller, O.P., Campus Min.

Iona College 715 North Ave., New Rochelle, 10801. Tel: 914-633-2632; Fax: 914-633-2363. Web: www.iona.edu. Mr. Carl Procario-Foley, Dir. Campus Min.; Rev. Francis F. Dixon, O.Carm., Campus Min.; Tiffany Di Nomi, Campus Min.; Jeanne McDermott, Campus Min.

Manhattan College 4513 Manhattan College Pkwy., Bronx, 10471. Tel: 718-862-7972; Fax: 718-862-8073. Email: lois.harr@manhattan.edu. Web: www.manhattan.edu.

Campus Ministry and Social Action Lois Harr, M.A., Dir. Campus Min.; Rev. George H. Hill, M.Div., M.A., Chap. Tel: 718-862-7972; Mr. Kevin McCloskey, Campus Min.; Jennifer Edwards, M.A., Campus Min.

Manhattanville College 2900 Purchase St., Purchase, 10577. Tel: 914-323-5150, Ext. 447; Fax: 914-694-2496. Rev. William Tyrrell, S.A., Campus Min.

Marist College 3399 North Rd., Poughkeepsie, 12601. Tel: 845-575-3130; 845-575-3000, Ext. 2275; Fax: 845-575-3299. Email: francis.kelly@marist.edu. Rev. Richard LaMorte, Chap.; Bro. Frank Kelly, F.M.S., Campus Min.

Mt. St. Mary College 330 Powell Ave., Newburg, 12550. Tel: 845-569-3517. Web: www.msmc.edu. Rev. Francis Amodio, O.Carm., Campus Min.; Carol Gibney, Campus Min.

College of Mt. St. Vincent 6301 Riverdale Ave., Riverdale, 10471. Tel: 718-405-3200; 718-405-3215; 718-405-3216. Web: www.cmsv.edu. Sisters

Cecilia Harriendorff, S.C., Campus Min.; Theresa Capria, S.C.

College of New Rochelle 29 Castle Pl., New Rochelle, 10805. Tel: 914-654-5052; 914-654-5867; Fax: 914-654-5958. Email: hwolf@cnr.edu. Web: www.cnr.edu. Helen Wolf, Dir.; Rev. John Joseph Flynn, O.F.M.Cap., Chap.

New York Maritime College 6 Pennyfield Ave., Fort Schuyler, Bronx, 10465-4198. Tel: 718-409-7200. Web: www.sunymaritime.edu. Dr. Mary Ellen Keefe, Campus Min.

New York University Catholic Center at NYU, 58 Washington Sq. S., 10012. Tel: 212-741-1274. Email: john.mcquire-op@nyu.edu. Web: www.nyu.edu. Rev. John McGuire, O.P., Campus Min.

Office: *St. Joseph's Rectory*, 371 - 6th Ave., 10014. Tel: 212-741-1274; Fax: 212-473-2971.

Pace University One Pace Plaza, 20 Cardinal Hayes Pl., 10038. Tel: 212-962-3972. Web: www.pace.edu. Rev. John McGuire, O.P., Campus Min.

Rockland Community College 145 College Rd., Suffern, 10901. Tel: 845-574-4531; Fax: 845-574-4552. Web: www.sunyrockland.edu. Mr. Michael Ver'Schneider, Campus Min.

St. John's University 300 Howard Ave., Rm. B9, Staten Island, 10301. Tel: 718-390-4473. Web: www.stjohns.edu. Sr. Joan Mahoney, C.N.D., Dir. Campus Min. Tel: 718-390-4473; James Behan Jr., Campus Min.; Melissa Gibilaro, Campus Min.

St. Thomas Aquinas 125 Rte. 340, Sparkill, 10976. Tel: 845-398-4062; Fax: 845-398-4061. Web: www.stac.edu. Sr. Madeleine Murphy, O.P., Campus Min.

SUNY/New Paltz 75 S. Manheim Blvd., New Paltz, 12561. Tel: 845-691-7151. Web: www.newpaltz.edu. Mr. Henry Grimsland, Campus Min.

Wagner College & The College of Staten Island One Campus Rd., Staten Island, 10301. Tel: 718-390-3461 (Wagner); 718-982-2652 (College of Staten Island). Email: elaine.schenk@verizon.net. Web: www.wagner.edu; www.csi.cuny.edu. Sr. Elaine R. Schenk, M.Id., Campus Min.

[HH] MISCELLANEOUS

NEW YORK. *1011 First Avenue, Inc.*, 1011 First Ave., 10022. Tel: 212-371-1000. James P. McCabe, J.D., Gen. Counsel & Contact Person.

Alfred E. Smith Memorial Foundation, Inc., The (1946) 1011 First Ave., 10022-4134. Tel: 212-371-1000, Ext. 3315; Fax: 212-421-1640.

America Press, Inc. (1909) The Business & Editorial Offices, 106 W. 56th St., 10019. Tel: 212-581-4640; Fax: 212-399-3596. Email: america@americamagazine.org. Web: www.americamagazine.org. Revs. Andrew J. Christiansen, S.J., Pres. & Editor-in-Chief; John P. Schlegel, S.J., Publisher; Mr. Albert C. Pierce, Chm. Bd. of Trustees.

American Committee on Italian Migration, Inc., 25 Carmine St., 10014. Tel: 212-247-7373; Fax: 212-265-5793. Email: acimny@aol.com. Web: www.aciminnigra.org. Rev. Joseph Fugolo, C.S., Natl. Exec. Sec. To insure fair immigration policy favoring reunion of families and cultural integration of Italian Americans. Total Staff 3.

American Compassion Services, Inc., 1356 Madison Ave., 3S, 10128. Tel: 646-264-2680. Email: info@fidesco-usa.org. Herve Duteil, Pres.

St. Ansgar Scandinavian Catholic League (1910) 430 E. 20th St., Apt. MB, 10009. Tel: 212-675-0400; Fax: 201-433-3355. Email: viggor@rambusch.com. Web: www.saintansgars.org. Edwin Rambusch, Pres.; Martin Rambusch, Vice Pres. & Sec.; Rev. John T. Halborg, Chap. (Retired); Mr. Viggo B. Rambusch, Treas.

Apostolate for Family Consecration, Inc., St. Joseph East Coast Center, 350 5th Ave., Suite 5900, PMB #26N, 10118-0069. Tel: 212-971-1370. Email: robert@familyland.org. Web: www.familycatechism.com; www.familyland.org. Robert Coniker, Pres.

Association of New York Catholic Homes, Inc., 1011 First Ave., 10022. Tel: 212-371-1000, Ext. 2939. Email: william.whiston@archny.org. Mr. William E. Whiston, Treas. & Contact Person.

Benefice Advantage, 155 E. 56th St., 2nd Fl., 10022. Tel: 718-518-2168; Fax: 718-518-2690. Email: vsampugnaro@chcsnet.org. Vincent Sampugnaro, Human Resources.

Brooklyn Prep Alumni Association (1964) Loyola Hall, Fordham Univ., 10458. Tel: 718-817-5669; Fax: 718-817-5504. Web: www.brooklynprep.org. Rev. Daniel J. Fitzpatrick, S.J., Moderator. Membership 4,780.

Calvary Fund, Inc., 1740 Eastchester Rd., Bronx, 10461. Tel: 718-518-2077; Fax: 718-518-2477. Email: webmaster@calvaryhospital.org. Web: calvaryhospital.org. Frank A. Calamari, Pres.; Richard E. Meyer, Chm.

The Cardinal Cooke Guild, 1011 First Ave., 10022. Tel: 212-371-1000, Ext. 2740; Fax: 212-371-1011 Ext. 2478. Email: abbeykkmoy@aol.com. Web: www.terencecardinalcooke.org. Official organization for the promotion of the Cause of Canonization of the Servant of God Terence Cardinal Cooke. Cause: Dr. Avv. Andrea Ambrosi, Roman Postulator; Rev. Msgr. Joseph R. Giandurco, J.C.D., Vice Postulator; Rev. Benedict Joseph Groeschel, C.F.R., Ed.D., Consultant Guild: Patricia Handal, Coord.

Cardinal Cooke Memorial Foundation, 1011 First Ave., Rm. 1940, 10022. Tel: 212-371-1000; Fax: 212-813-9538.

Cardinal's Fund for Children, 1011 First Ave., Rm. 1130, 10022.

Carmel Housing Development Fund Co., Inc., 1011 First Ave., 10022. Tel: 212-371-1000; Fax: 212-826-8795. Rev. Msgr. Kevin L. Sullivan, Pres.

Catholic Alumni Club of the Archdiocese of New York, 83 Christopher St., 10014. Tel: 212-243-6513. Email: marydplaza@yahoo.com. Web: www.caci.org/cac/newyorkcac.html. Marguerite Cronin, Pres.

Catholic Big Sisters and Big Brothers, 137 E. 2nd St., 2nd Fl., 10009. Tel: 212-475-3291; Fax: 212-475-0280. Email: director@cbsbb.org. Web: www.cbsbb.org. Total Assisted 1,029.

Catholic Daughters of the Americas and Its Courts, 10 W. 71st St., 10023. Tel: 212-877-3041; Fax: 212-724-5923. Email: cdofanatl@aol.com. Web: www.catholicdaughters.org. Joanne Tomassi, Natl. Regent; Mrs. Margaret O'Brien, Contact Person.

Catholic Family and Human Rights Institute, 211 E. 43rd St., Ste. 1306, 10017. Tel: 212-754-5948; Fax: 212-754-9291. Email: c-fam@c-fam.org. Web: www.c-fam.org. Austin Ruse, Pres.; Susan Yoshihara, Ph.D., Exec. Vice Pres.

Catholic Health Care Foundation of the Archdiocese of New York, Inc., 205 Lexington Ave., 3rd Fl., 10016. Tel: 212-752-4735. Email: poconnor@archcare.org. Web: www.archcare.org. Mrs. Patricia O'Connor, Contact Person.

Catholic Health Care System, 205 Lexington Ave., 3rd Fl., 10016. Tel: 212-752-4735. Email: slarue@chcsnet.org. Web: www.chcsnet.org. Karl P. Adler, M.D., Archbishop's Delegate for Health Care.

Catholic High School Association of New York (1928) 1011 First Ave., Rm. 1856, 10022. Tel: 212-371-1000; Fax: 212-758-3018. Email: supt@adnyschools.org. Web: www.ny-archdiocese.org.

Catholic High Schools' Athletic Association of the Archdiocese of New York, 650 Grand Concourse, 10451. Tel: 917-681-4097.

4300 Murdock Ave., Bronx, 10466. Tel: 718-325-6423. Mr. Richard Tricario, Pres.

Catholic Indemnity Insurance Company, c/o 1011 First Ave., 10022. Tel: 212-371-1000; Fax: 212-838-0841. Email: edward.reigadas@archny.org. Edward Reigadas, Sec.

Catholic Interracial Council of N.Y., The, 899 10th Ave., 10019. Tel: 212-237-8600. Gerard W. Lynch, Pres.

**Catholic League for Religious and Civil Rights*, 450 Seventh Ave., 34th Fl., 10123. Tel: 212-371-3191; Fax: 212-371-3394. Email: cl@catholicleague.org. Web: www.catholicleague.org. Dr. William A. Donohue, Pres.; Bernadette Brady, Vice Pres. Total Staff 12.

Catholic Medical Mission Board, Inc., 10 W. 17th St., 10011-5765. Tel: 212-242-7757; Fax: 212-807-9161; 212-242-0930. Email: info@cmmb.org. Web: www.cmmb.org. With nearly 100 years of service since 1912, CMMB (Catholic Medical Mission Board) is the leading U.S.-based Catholic charity focused exclusively on global healthcare. CMMB's medical volunteer, donated medicines, HIV/AIDS, child survival and neglected tropical diseases programs and initiatives focus on making healthcare available to all. In 2010, with revenues of more than $190 million, CMMB worked in nearly 50 countries, serving the poorest of the poor. Specifically, Healing Help, CMMB's medical donation program, delivered supplies valued at more than $163.3 million to 173 hospitals, clinics and other health facilities in 38 countries. MVP, CMMB's medical volunteer program, deployed 68 long-term volunteers and facilitated the placement of an additional 1,595 short-term volunteers in 24 countries. CMMB is headquartered in New York City and maintains a Washington, D.C. office. Globally, it has offices in Haiti, Honduras, Kenya, Peru, South Africa, Southern Sudan, and Zambia and has a regional representative in India.

Officers: Michael Doring Connelly, Chm.; F. William Smullen III, Vice Chm.; Chris Allen, Treas.; Mary Colleen Scanlon, R.N., J.D., Sec.

Members: John E. Celentano; Nicholas D'Agostino III; Ambassador Mark R. Dybul, M.D.; Sr. Patricia Eck, C.B.S.; Stephanie L. Ferguson, Ph.D., R.N., F.A.A.N.; John F. Galbraith; JeanMarie C. Grisi; John D. Herrick; Clarion E. Johnson, M.D.; Henry W. Mann III, Esq.; Maria Rosa Robinson, M.D., M.B.A.; Robert E. Robotti; Rev. Peter Schineller, S.J.; Michael J. Seergy; Most Rev. Joseph M. Sullivan, D.D.; Bill White.

Catholic Near East Welfare Association (CNEWA) (1926) 1011 First Ave., 10022. Tel: 212-826-1480; Fax: 212-826-8979. Email: cnewa@cnewa.org. Web: www.cnewa.org. His Eminence Timothy M. Dolan, Ph.D., Chair & Treas.; Rev. Msgr. John E. Kozar, Pres.; Rev. Guido Gockel, M.H.M., Vice Pres., Middle East & Europe; Mr. Gabriele Delmonaco, Vice Pres., Devel.; Mr. Michael La Civita, Vice Pres., Communications; Mr. Domingo Sotero, Vice Pres., Mgmt.; Mr. Thomas Varghese, Vice Pres., India & Northeast Africa.

Catholic Resources, Inc., 1339 York Ave., 10021. Tel: 646-475-4835. Email: kmcguire@chcsnet.org. Kathryn McGuire, Sr. Vice Pres.

Catholic Spiritual Family, The Work, Inc., 123 E. 38th St., 10016. Tel: 212-677-5680. Email: theworkinc@catholic.org. Web: www.thework-fso.org. Sr. Maria Hugens, F.S.O., Treas.

The Catholic World Wide Web Corporation, 1011 First Ave., 10022. Tel: 212-371-1000. Email: bernard.reidy@archny.org. Web: www.archny.org. Bernard E. Reidy, Archbishop's Delegate for Admin. & Fin.

Centro Altagracia de Fe y Justicia, Inc. (Altagracia Center of Faith and Justice, Inc.), 39 E. 83rd St., 10028. Tel: 212-568-2115; Fax: 212-568-2118. Email: info@centroaltagracia.org. Web: www.centroaltagracia.org. Rev. Gerald J. Chojnacki, S.J., Bd. Chair; Richard Espinal, Exec. Dir.

Centro Carismatico Catolico Hispano De La Arquidiocesis De Nueva York, 826 E. 166th St., Bronx, 10459. Tel: 718-378-1734; Fax: 718-378-1819. Email: centro826@aol.com. Web: www.centrocatolicocarismatico.com. Most Rev. Josu Iriondo, S.T.L., D.D., Dir.

Chapel San Lorenzo Ruiz (Philippine Pastoral Center), 378 Broome St., 10013. Tel: 212-966-1019; Fax: 212-966-1034. Email: chapelofsanlorenzoruiz@gmail.com. Web: www.chapelofsanlorenzo.com. Rev. Erno Diaz, Dir.

Chinese Catholic Information Center, 86 Riverside Dr., 10024. Tel: 212-787-6969. Rev. Paul Chan (Taiwan), Dir. Total in Residence 7; Total Staff 4.

Christ House, Inc. Shared Residence for Religious and Young Men Lacking Family Support., 432 E. 142nd St., Bronx, 10454. Tel: 718-665-8740; Fax: 718-665-1665. Email: christhouse@christhousebronx.com. Mr. Raul Morales, Dir.

The Christophers (1945) 5 Hanover Sq., 10004. Tel: 212-759-4050; Fax: 212-838-5073. Email: mail@christophers.org. Web: www.christophers.org. Mary Ellen Robinson, COO. A multi-media organization reaching millions with the Gospel message. Total Staff 10.

CNEWA UNITED STATES (2003) 1011 First Ave., 10022. Tel: 212-826-1480; Fax: 212-826-8979. Email: cnewa@cnewa.org. His Eminence William Cardinal Keeler, D.D., J.C.D., Pres.; Mr. Gabriele Delmonaco, National Dir.

Committee for Mission Responsibility Society, Inc. The Propagation of the Faith, 1011 First Ave., 10022. Tel: 212-371-1000, Ext. 2700; Fax: 212-371-7220. Email: pchirchirillo@aol.com. Sr. Pauline Chirchirillo, P.B.V.M.

Community of St. Egidio, U.S.A., Inc., 236 E. 15th St., 10003. Tel: 212-663-1483; Fax: 212-663-1483. Email: santegidiousa@gmail.com. Web: www.santegidio.org. Paola Piscitelli, Pres.

Cor Mariae Development Fund Corporation, 1011 First Ave., 10022. Rev. Msgr. Kevin L. Sullivan, Pres. & Contact Person.

Cor Mariae Housing Development Fund, Inc., 1011 First Ave., 10022. Tel: 212-371-1000, Ext. 2400. Rev. Msgr. Kevin L. Sullivan, Pres.

Cornelia Connelly Center for Education, Holy Child Middle School, 220 E. 4th St., 10009. Tel: 212-982-2287; Fax: 212-982-0547. Email: mscerbo@connellycenter.org. Web: www.holychild.com. Mary Claire Scerbo, Dir.; Sr. Marcia Sichol, S.H.C.J., Contact Person.

Courage International, Incorporated, Church of St. John the Baptist, 210 W. 31st St., 10001. Tel: 212-268-1010; Fax: 212-268-7150. Email: NYcourage@aol.com. Web: couragerc.net. Rev. John F. Harvey, O.S.F.S., Dir. Total Staff 4.

Descubriendo El Siglo XXI, Inc. (Discovering XXI Century Inc.) (2001) *Holy Cross Church*, 329 W. 42nd St., 10036. Tel: 212-244-4778; Fax: 212-868-6997. Email: radiosigloxxi@aol.com. Web: www.descubriendoelsiglo21.org. Rev. Tomas Del Valle-Reyes, Pres.

The Dominican Foundation of Dominican Friars, Province of St. Joseph, Inc., 141 E. 65th St., 10065. Tel: 212-535-3664; Fax: 775-542-5511. Web: www.dominicanfriars.org. Very Rev. David Dominic Izzo, O.P., S.T.L., Dir.

Dominican Mission Secretariat Very Rev. David Dominic Izzo, O.P., S.T.L., Dir.

Dominican Friars' Guilds, 141 E. 65th St., 10065. Tel: 212-744-2410; Fax: 212-737-3875.

St. Jude Dominican Missions, 141 E. 65th St., 10065. Tel: 212-744-2410; Fax: 212-737-3875. Email: advancement@opfriars.org. Very Rev. David Dominic Izzo, O.P., S.T.L., Dir.

Dominican Rosary Apostolate, 141 E. 65th St., 10065. Tel: 212-744-2410; Fax: 212-737-3875.

Deserving Poor Boys Priesthood Association, 141 E. 65th St., 10065. Tel: 212-744-2410; Fax: 212-737-3875.

St. Martin de Porres Guild, 141 E. 65th St., 10065. Tel: 212-744-2410; Fax: 212-737-3875.

Dominican Shrine of St. Jude, Inc., St. Catherine of Siena Priory, 411 E. 68th St., 10065-6305. Tel: 212-249-6067; Fax: 212-988-8920. Email: kfrancekelly@dominicanshrineofsaintjude.org. Web: www.dominicanshrineofsaintjude.org. Rev. George Lawrence Concordia, O.P., Ph.D., Admin. Dir.

**The Elizabeth Seton Housing Development Fund Corporation*, 1991 Lexington Ave., 10035. Tel: 212-348-1655; Fax: 212-348-1822. Email: epfeldmann@att.net. Sr. Elizabeth Vermaelon, Pres. Total Assisted 87; Total Staff 3.

Felix Varela Foundation, Inc., The, 1011 First Ave., 10022. Tel: 718-229-8001, Ext. 677; 718-281-9677; Fax: 917-522-9707. Most Rev. Octavio Cisneros, Pres.

Focolare Movement-Manhattan, 429 E. 12th St., 10009. Tel: 212-388-9498. Email: focmny@yahoo.com. Web: www.focolare.org. Flavio Pedroni, Local Dir.

Foundation of the Order of Friars Minor of the Province of the Most Holy Name, 129 W. 31st St., 2nd Fl., 10001-3403. Tel: 646-473-0265; Fax: 800-420-1078. Email: hnp@hnp.org. Web: www.hnp.org. Very Rev. John F. O'Connor, O.F.M., Dir.

St. Frances Cabrini Shrine, Inc., 701 Fort Washington Ave., 10040. Tel: 212-923-3536; Fax: 212-923-1871. Web: www.mothercabrini.com.

St. Francis Counseling Center, Inc., 135 W. 31st St., 10001. Tel: 212-736-8500; Fax: 212-736-8545. Web: www.stfrancisnyc.org. Julie Berwick, L.C.S.W., Dir.

St. Francis Monastery Breadline for the Poor, Inc., 135 W. 31st St., 10001-3439. Tel: 212-736-8500; Fax: 212-736-8545. Email: stfra135@aol.com. Rev. Andrew J. Reitz, O.F.M., Contact Person.

Franciscan Missionary Charities, Inc. (1997) 38 W. 32nd St., Ste. 910-C, 10001. Tel: 917-797-8890; 646-685-7788. Email: cowofm@gmail.com. Revs. Ronald P. Stark, O.F.M., Pres.; Francis K. Kim, O.F.M., B.A., M.Div., Exec. Vice Pres.

Franciscan Missionary Union, Province of the Most Holy Name Headquarters, St. Francis Friary, 135 W. 31st St., 10001-3439. Tel: 888-372-6478. Email: fmu@fmunion.org. Rev. Russell C. Becker, O.F.M., Sec.; Bro. Thomas J. Cole, O.F.M., Dir. The Franciscan Missionary Union maintains 3 Medical Clinics in Lima, Peru. Various social services in Bolivia; local assistance in Taiwan, Japan, Brazil, North Korea, East Africa and Southern US Missions. Friar Missionaries 46.

Franciscans International, Inc., 246 E. 46th St., #1F, 10017-2937. Tel: 212-490-4624; Fax: 212-490-4626. Email: newyork@fiop.org. Web: www.franciscansinternational.org. Sisters Liliane Alam, F.M.M., CFO; Denise Boyle, F.M.D.M., Exec. Dir.; Rev. Michael Lasky, O.F.M.Conv., Acting Dir. of the Americas.

Franciscans of Holy Name Province Benevolence Trust, Inc., 129 W. 31st St., 2nd Fl., 10001-3403. Tel: 646-473-0265; Fax: 800-420-1078. Email: hnp@hnp.org. Web: hnp.org. Very Rev. John F. O'Connor, O.F.M., Dir.

Franciscans of Holy Name Province Sick, Aged and Retired Trust, 129 W. 31st St., 2nd Fl., 10001-3403. Tel: 646-473-0265; Fax: 800-420-1078. Email: hnp@hnp.org. Web: www.hnp.org. Very Rev. John F. O'Connor, O.F.M., Dir.

Franciscans of Holy Name Province Education and Formation Trust, 129 W. 31st St., 2nd Fl., 10001-3403. Tel: 646-473-0265; Fax: 800-420-1078. Email: hnp@hnp.org. Web: www.hnp.org. Very Rev. John F. O'Connor, O.F.M., Dir.

The Fratecelli Corporation, 129 W. 31st St., 2nd Fl., 10001-3403. Tel: 646-473-0265; Fax: 800-420-1078. Email: hnp@hnp.org. Web: www.hnp.org. Very Rev. John F. O'Connor, O.F.M., Pres.

Friends of American Art in Religion, Inc., 143 E. 43rd St., 10017. Tel: 212-682-5722; Fax: 212-370-5791. His Eminence Edward Cardinal Egan, Pres.; Rev. Msgr. Eugene V. Clark, P.A., Sec. & Treas.

The Good Shepherd Volunteers, Inc., 337 E. 17th St., 10003. Tel: 212-475-4245, Ext. 718; Fax: 212-979-8604. Email: gsv@goodshepherds.org. Web: www.gsvolunteers.org. Michele G. Gilfillan, M.A., Dir.

Gregorian University Foundation, The, 106 W. 56th St., 10019. Tel: 212-582-5433; Fax: 212-956-2921. Email: otooler@mindspring.com. Web: www.the-gregorian.com. Rev. Robert F. O'Toole, S.J., Pres.

Guild of Catholic Lawyers, The (1928) 101 Park Ave., 30th Fl., 10178. Tel: 212-808-7847; Fax: 212-808-7897. Rev. George W. Rutler, Spiritual Dir.

Hispanic Catholic Charismatic Center of the Archdiocese of New York, 826 E. 166th St., Bronx, 10459. Tel: 718-378-1734; Fax: 718-378-1819. Email: centro826@aol.com. Web: wwwcentrocatolicocarismatico.com. Most Rev. Josu Iriondo, S.T.L., D.D.

The Housing Fund of the Archdiocese of New York, 1011 First Ave., 10022. Tel: 212-371-1000. Rev. Msgrs. Kevin L. Sullivan, Vice. Pres.; Donald Sakano, Sec. & Treas.

The Human Adventure Corp. Doing Business for Communion and Liberation and Fraternity of Communion and Liberation, USA., 125 Maiden Ln., 15th Fl., 10038. Tel: 212-337-3580; Fax: 212-337-3585. Email: cladministration@clhac.com. Web: www.clonline.org/us. Maurizio Capuzzo, Pres.

Hungarian Catholic League of America, Inc., 414 E. 82 St., 10028. Tel: 212-327-2959; Fax: 212-535-9221. Rev. Msgr. William I. Varsanyi, P.A., Bd. Chm.; A. Petrak, Sec.

Incarnation Children's Center Fund, Inc. (1988) 142 Audubon Ave., 10032. Tel: 212-928-2590, Ext. 32; Fax: 212-928-1500. Email: ccastro@incarnationchildrenscenter.org. Web: www.incarnationchildrenscenter.org. Carolyn Castro, Exec. Dir. Capacity 21.

Institute of the Helpers, 385 W. 263rd St., Bronx, 10471. Tel: 718-884-3100. Sr. Maryellen Moore.

International Catholic Organizations Information Center, Inc., 323 E. 47 St., 10017. Tel: 212-355-5557; Fax: 212-355-5557. Email: ico_center@yahoo.com. Rev. Daniel LeBlanc, O.M.I., Pres. of Board; Bill Barbanes, Admin.

**The Jesuit Collaborative*, c/o New York Province of the Society of Jesus, 38 E. 83rd St., 10028-0810.

Jesuit Seminary and Mission Bureau, Inc., 39 E. 83rd St., 10028. Tel: 212-774-5500; Fax: 212-794-1036. See Jesuit Provincial's office.

St. Joseph's Union of Staten Island, New York Inc., 108 Bedell St., Staten Island, 10309. Tel: 718-984-9296. Sr. Una McCormack, O.P., Treas.

LAMP Ministries, Inc. (1982) 2704 Schurz Ave., Bronx, 10465. Tel: 718-409-5062; Fax: 718-904-0048. Email: tscheuring@lampministries.org. Web: www.lampministries.org. Tom Scheuring, Ph.D., Co-Dir.; Lyn Scheuring, Ph.D., Co-Dir.; Marybeth Greene, Assoc. Dir.; Ed Greene, Assoc. Dir.

LaSalle New York City, Inc., 44 E. 2nd St., 10003. Tel: 212-475-8940; Fax: 212-529-3598. Web: www.lasalleacademy.org. Bros. Franc Byrnes, F.S.C., Chm.; Michael Farrell, F.S.C., Pres. Total Assisted 370; Total Staff 45.

The Lay Fraternity of St. Dominic, Inc., 141 E. 65th St., 10021-6618. Tel: 212-744-2080. Email: fsd@opfriars.org. Ms. Marianne Jablonski, Pres.; Rev. Darren Michael Pierre, O.P., S.T.L., M.S. Tel: 212-288-5872.

Legion of Mary, Office, 1011 First Ave., 10022. Tel: 212-752-7966. Email: ny.senatus@verizon.net. Web: legion-of-mary-ny.org.

**Life Athletes, Inc.*, 1011 First Ave., 10022. Tel: 574-237-9000. Email: chris@lifeathletes.org. Web: www.lifeathletes.org. Christopher J. Godfrey, Pres.

Lumen Dei, 340 W. 53rd St., 10019. Tel: 212-586-4447; Fax: 212-586-1640. Email: newyorkfem2@gmail.com. Web: www.lumendei.org. Rev. Wilberto Reyes-Garced, L.D., Regl. Supr. Priests of Lumen Dei 1; Sisters of Lumen Dei 5.

**The Malta Human Services Foundation*, 1011 First Ave., Rm. 1350, 10022. Tel: 212-371-1522. Web: www.maltausa.org. Deacon Jeffrey Trexler, Exec. Dir. & Contact Person.

Manhattan North Community Services, Inc., 91 Arden St., 10040. Niki Montaluo, Pres.

Maria Droste Services (1982) 171 Madison Ave., Ste. 400, 10016-5110. Tel: 212-889-4042; Fax: 212-889-3936. Email: srros@mariadrosteservices.com. Web: www.mariadrosteservices.com. Betsy Selman-Babinecz, D.C.S.W., L.C.S.W. Dir.

St. Germaine's Services

**Monsignor Robert Fox Memorial Shelter Housing Development, Inc.*, Fox House, 111 E. 117th St., 10035. Tel: 212-534-6634; Fax: 212-427-8507. Email: foxshelter@aol.com. Sr. Florence Speth, S.C., Exec. Dir. Total Assisted 565; Total Staff 17.

National Federation for Life, 1011 First Ave., Rm. 1417, 10022.

National Office of the Devotees of Padre Pio, Inc., 1154 1st Ave., 10065. Tel: 212-838-6549. Mr. Mario Bruscki, Dir.

**Nazareth Housing, Inc.* (1983) 519 E. 11th St., 10009. Tel: 212-777-1010; Fax: 212-777-1867. Web: www.nazarethhousingnyc.org.

New York Catholic Continuum Care, Inc. (NYCCC), 1011 First Ave., 11th Fl., 10022. Tel: 212-371-1011, Ext. 2462. Doug Sansted, Contact Person.

New York Catholic Foundation, Inc., 1011 First Ave., 10022. Tel: 212-371-1000. Email: helen.lowe@archny.org. Web: archny.org. Helen Lowe, Exec. Dir. Devel.

New York Society of the John Paul II Foundation, Inc. (1997) 101 E. 7th St., 10009. Tel: 718-383-8030; Fax: 718-349-2773. Email: polstar.shop@verizon.net. Mr. Michael Pajak, Pres. Tel: 718-383-9587.

Nocturnal Adoration Society of the United States (1900) 184 E. 76th St., 10021. Tel: 212-288-5082; Fax: 212-717-8397. Email: sjbrcc@aol.com. Web: www.stjeanbaptisteny.org. Congregation of the Blessed Sacrament.

North American College of Rome, Alumni Assoc. of, Msgr. Farrell High School, 2900 Amboy Rd., Staten Island, 10306. Tel: 718-987-2900; Fax: 718-987-4241. Rev. Msgr. Edmund J. Whalen, S.T.D.

Northeast Hispanic Catholic Center, 1011 First Ave., 10022. Tel: 212-751-7045; Fax: 212-753-5321. Email: nhcc1011@aol.com. Doris N. Valentin, Interim Exec. Dir.

Parish Assistance Corporation, c/o 1011 First Ave., 10022. Tel: 646-794-3394. Email: charles.sheerin@archny.org. Charles Sheerin, Dir.

**Partnership for Global Justice*, 211 E. 43rd St., Ste. 708, 10017. Tel: 212-682-6481. Email: partnershipforglobaljustice@gmail.com. Web: www.partnershipforglobaljustice.com. Sr. Lucianne Siers, O.P., Dir.

St. Patrick's Cathedral Landmark Foundation, Inc., 1011 1st Ave., 17th Fl., 10022. Tel: 646-794-2789; Fax: 212-758-6925. Web: www.archny.org.

St. Patrick's International Inc., c/o Cullen & Dykman, 44 Wall St., 10005-2407. Tel: 212-732-2000; Fax: 212-742-8260. Email: spsbur@iol.ie. Web: www.spms.org. Rev. Seamus O'Neill, Pres.

Patrons of the Arts in Vatican Museums, 404 E. 87th St., 10128. Tel: 212-289-6030; Fax: 212-348-8075. Rev. James Boniface Ramsey, Pres. Staff 2.

St. Paul's Guild, Inc., 1011 First Ave., Rm. 1940, 10022. Tel: 212-371-1000; Fax: 212-813-9538.

Pauline Books & Media, 64 W. 38th St., 10022. Tel: 212-754-1110; Fax: 212-754-2268. Web: www.pauline.org.

Pauline Books & Media Total Staff 5.

Pax Christi Metro New York (1983) 371 Sixth Ave., 10014. Tel: 212-420-0250; Fax: 212-420-1628. Email: nypaxchristi@igc.org. Web: www.nypaxchristi.org. Rosemarie Pace, B.A., Ed.D., M.S., Dir. We are a regional chapter of Pax Christi USA, the national Catholic movement for peace.

Perpetual Help Center, 294 E. 150th St., Bronx, 10451. Tel: 718-585-3678. Web: www.redemptorists.net. Rev. Daniel Francis, C.Ss.R. Redemptorist Fathers of New York.

Regina Coeli Society First Friday Club for the Catholic Women of New York City Police Dept., P.O. Box 939, 10272-0604. Tel: 646-610-6169. Det. Gloria Felix, Pres.

St. Rose's Settlement, 1011 First Ave., Rm. 1940, 10022. Tel: 212-371-1000; Fax: 212-813-9538.

Scalabrini International Migration Network, 27 Carmine St., 10014-4423. Tel: 212-675-3993; Fax: 212-255-1771. Email: advocacy@simn-cs.net. Web: www.simn-cs.net. Rev. Leonir Mario Chiarello, Dir.

Shrine of St. Jude, Inc., St. Stephen of Hungary Parish, 414 E. 82nd St., 10028. Tel: 800-688-JUDE; Fax: 212-535-9221. Web: www.saintstephenofhungary.org. Very Rev. John F. O'Connor, O.F.M., Pres.; Rev. Angelus Gambatese, O.F.M., Spiritual Dir.; Sr. Natalie M. Runfola, R.S.C.J., Exec. Sec.

Sisters of Charity of New York Charitable Trust (1988) 6301 Riverdale Ave., Bronx, 10471-1093. Tel: 718-549-9200; Fax: 718-884-3013. Web: www.scny.org.

Sisters of Charity Center (1971) 6301 Riverdale Ave., Bronx, 10471-1093. Tel: 718-549-9200, Ext. 261; Fax: 718-884-3013. Web: www.scny.org.

**The Elizabeth Seton Women's Center, Inc.* (1996) 133 W. 70th St., 10023. Tel: 212-579-3657; Fax: 212-579-3659. Email: eswc@aol.com. Sisters Dorothy Metz, Pres.; Arleen Ketchum, S.C., Dir.

The Partnership for Inner-City Education, 1011 First Ave., 18th Fl., 10022. Tel: 646-794-3338; Fax: 212-688-2956. Email: jill.kafka@partnershipnyc.org. Jill Kafka, Exec. Dir.

St. Thomas Aquinas Foundation National Headquarters (Order of Preachers, St. Joseph Prov.), 141 E. 65th St., 10065. Tel: 212-737-5757; Fax: 212-861-4216. Email: provincial@opfriars.org. Web: www.op-stjoseph.org. Very Revs. Brian

Mulcahy, O.P., Pres.; Mark Padrez, O.P., Bd. Member; Charles E. Bouchard, O.P., Bd. Member; Christopher T. Eggleton, O.P., Bd. Member; Rev. William Paul Marquis, O.P., B.S., S.T.L., Ph.D., Treas.

St. Thomas Aquinas Foundation of the Dominican Fathers of the United States (STAF)

Thorpe Family Residence, Inc. (1988) 2252 Crotona Ave., Bronx, 10457. Tel: 718-933-7312; Fax: 718-933-7311. Total Assisted Families 16; Total Staff 10.

Trust for the Center for Migration Studies in New York, 27 Carmine St., 10014-4423. Tel: 212-255-1111; Fax: 212-255-1771. Web: www.cmsny.org. Rev. Matthew Didone.

Saint Vincent's Catholic Medical Centers Foundation, Inc., 170 W. 12th St., Smith 5, 10011. Tel: 212-604-2276; Fax: 212-604-7533. Email: ccallagy@svcmcny.org. Ms. Catherine Callagy, Sr. Vice Pres. Fund Devel.

Voluntas Dei USA, 244 Fifth Ave., Ste. P250, 10001. Tel: 212-726-2286. Email: anthonyciorra@gmail.com. Rev. Anthony J. Ciorra, District Dir.

Xavier Society for the Blind (1900) 154 E. 23rd St., 10010. Tel: 212-473-7800; Fax: 212-473-7801. Rev. John R. Sheehan, S.J., Chm. Bd.

BARRYVILLE. *New Hope Manor*, 35 Hillside Rd., 12719. Tel: 845-557-8353; Fax: 845-557-6603. Email: newhopemnr@aol.com. Web: www.newhopemanor.org. Nicholas A. Roes, Ph.D., Exec. Dir.; Sisters Patricia Conway, O.P., Counselor, House Mother & Teacher; Maureen Conway, O.P., Dir. Education, Counselor & Teacher; Jeanne Micelli, O.P., Bd. Member; Marianne Morelli, O.P., Bd. Member; Margaret Murphy, O.P., Bd. Member; Bro. Charles Kinney, S.A., Bd. Member. Sparkill Dominican Sisters, Sisters of Christian Charity, Franciscan Friars of the Atonement, A live-in therapeutic community for the substance abuse rehabilitation of women, pregnant women, and infants.

BEACON. *Carmelite Communion, Inc.* (2000) 89 Hiddenbrooke Dr., 12508-2230. Tel: 845-831-5572; Fax: 845-831-5579. Email: beaconcarmel@optonline.net. Web: www.carmelitesbeacon.org. Sr. Michaelene Devine, O.C.D., Prioress & Contact Person. Professed Sisters 18.

Metropolitan Association of Contemplative Communities, Inc. (1967) 89 Hiddenbrooke Dr., 12508. Tel: 845-831-5572; Fax: 845-831-5579. Web: macc.catholic.org. Sr. Rita Donahue, O.C.D., Contact Person.

BRONX. *Abraham House, Inc.*, 340 Willis Ave., P.O. Box 305, 10454. Tel: 718-292-9321; Fax: 718-292-5925. Email: apabon@abrahamhouse.org. Robert Murphy, Pres. Total Assisted 6,000; Total Staff 35.

American St. Boniface Society, Incorporated, P.O. Box 1352, 10466-1352. Tel: 718-994-0989; Fax: 718-994-6119. Rev. Joachim Von Kerssenbrock, S.J., Exec. Dir.

St. Anthony Shelter for Renewal, 420 E. 156th St., 10455. Tel: 718-665-2441. Rev. Richard Roemer, C.F.R., Pres.

Calvary Holding Company, Inc., 1740 Eastchester Rd., 10461. Tel: 718-518-2251; Fax: 718-518-2674. Frank A. Calamari, Pres.; Thomas J. Fahey Jr., M.D., Chm.

Focolare Movement, 179 Robinson Ave., 10465. Tel: 718-828-1969; Fax: 718-828-6929. Email: focfny@optonline.net. Maria Teresa Fonza, Local Dir.

Focolare Movement Formation Fund, 179 Robinson Ave., 10465. Tel: 212-636-7328; Fax: 212-636-6899. Web: www.focolare.us. Amelia J. Uelmen Esq., Contact Person.

Foundation of Christ the Redeemer Institute Id of Christ the Redeemer, Men & Women Idente Missionaries., 2352 St. Raymond Ave., 10462. Tel: 718-828-2380; Fax: 718-828-4296.

**Francesco Productions Inc.* (2003) 420 E. 156th St., 10455. Tel: 718-401-1589; Fax: 718-401-8984. Web: www.francescoproductions.com. Kim Yu, Volunteer Mng. Dir.; Rev. Stanley Fortuna, C.F.R., Founder.

Franciscan Mission Outreach, Inc., 420 E. 156th St., 10455. Tel: 718-402-8255; Fax: 718-402-5556. Rev. Mariusz Casimir Koch, C.F.R., Contact Person. Priests 2; Total Staff 2.

Franciscan Renewal Ministries, Inc., 420 E. 156th St., 10455. Tel: 718-665-2441. Rev. Benedict Joseph Groeschel, C.F.R., Ed.D., Sec. & Contact Person.

St. Joseph's Center (1994) For the development of Lay Leaders, Cursillo Center, Marriage Encounter. (Spanish), 275 W. 230th St., 10463. Tel: 718-796-4340; Fax: 718-796-4340. Rev. Jose Luis Martinez, O.A.R., Dir. Total in Residence 2; Total Staff 4; Capacity 45.

St. Joseph's School for the Deaf Childrens Fund, Inc., 1000 Hutchinson River Pkwy., 10465. Tel: 718-828-9000; Fax: 718-792-6631. Email: darles@sjsdny.org. The Children's Fund assists St. Joseph's School for the Deaf in meeting the needs of the children and their educational experiences.

Saint Jutta Foundation, Inc. (1956) c/o Rev. Martin A. Hegyi, S.J., Murray-Weigal Hall, 515 E. Fordham Rd., 10458-5029. Tel: 718-817-3671; Fax: 718-365-8650. Email: hegyi@fordham.edu. Rev. Martin S. Hegyi, S.J., B.A., Ph.D. (Hungary), Contact Person.

**Mercy Center, Inc.* (1990) 377 E. 145th St., 10454-1006. Tel: 718-993-2789; Fax: 718-402-1594. Email: administration@mercycenterbronx.org. Web: www.mercycenterbronx.org. Joseph S. Dirr, Co-Dir.; Sr. Mary Galeone, R.S.M., Co-Dir. Parenting skills courses, business training, support groups, spirituality groups, & ESL. Sisters 4; Total Assisted 2,500; Total Staff 21.

Metro New York Christian Life Communities, Inc., Loyola Faber Hall, Fordham University, 10458. Tel: 718-817-5454; Fax: 718-733-4456. Email: metronyclc@yahoo.com. Web: www.fordham.edu/clc. Rev. Daniel J. Fitzpatrick, S.J., Moderator & Contact Person.

The Saint Padre Pio Shelter Corporation, 427 E. 155th St., 10455. Tel: 718-292-3713; Fax: 718-993-9997. Web: www.franciscanfriars.com. Bros. Peter Marie Westall, C.F.R.; Mark-Mary Ames, C.F.R., Asst. Dir. Total Assisted 18.

Preston Center of Compassion, Inc. (2003) *Office of the President*, 2780 Schurz Ave., 10465. Tel: 718-892-8977. Donna Santarpia, Pres.; Sr. Patricia Warner, R.D.C., Dir.

Rosalie Hall, Inc., 4150 Bronx Blvd., 10466. Tel: 718-920-9800; Fax: 718-920-9896. (Home for Unwed Mothers)

**Tolentine-Zeiser Community Life Center, Inc.*, 2345 University Ave., 10468. Tel: 718-933-6935; Fax: 718-733-1653. Total Assisted 172; Total Staff 12.

Youth Ministries for Peace & Justice, Inc. (1994) 1384 Stratford Ave., 10472. Tel: 718-328-5622; Fax: 718-328-5630. Email: atorres.fleming@ympj.org. Web: www.ympj.org. Alexie Torres-Fleming, Exec. Dir.

BRONXVILLE. *Polish Knights of Malta, Inc.* (1986) 3 Stoneleigh Plaza, #4-E, 10708. Tel: 914-793-4596; Fax: 914-771-4034. Email: witoldsulimirski@cs.com. Mr. Witold S. Sulimirski, Pres.

CORNWALL. *Contemplative Outreach, Ltd.*, 10 Landmark Dr., Ste. 117, P.O. Box 208, 12518. Tel: 845-534-5180. Email: office@coutreach.org. Web: www.contemplativeoutreach.org. Rt. Rev. Thomas Keating, O.C.S.O., Chairperson; Gail Fitzpatrick-Hopler, Pres. Total Staff 12.

DOVER PLAINS. *RDC Loaves and Fishes, Inc.*, 7 Market St., 12522. Tel: 845-877-9076; Fax: 888-316-4540. Web: rdcloavesandfishes.org. Lauren McLeod, Pres.

ELMSFORD. *Leviticus 25:23 Alternative Fund, Inc.* (1983) 33 W. Main St., Rm. 205, 10523. Tel: 914-606-9003; Fax: 914-606-9006. Email: info@leviticusfund.org. Web: www.leviticusfund.org. David C. Raynor, Exec. Dir.; Sr. Margaret Murphy, O.P., Finance Officer; Maryann Sorese, Bus. Devel. Office; Kenneth A. Gold, Loan Officer.

HARTSDALE. *Marian Woods, Inc.* (2001) 152 Ridge Rd., 10530. Tel: 914-750-6000; Fax: 914-750-6100. Frances A. Brooks, Exec. Dir.

Mercy Education Support Fund, Inc., 150 Ridge Rd., 10530. Tel: 914-328-3200, Ext. 410; Fax: 914-328-3761. Email: srpwolf@optonline.net. Sr. Patricia Wolf, R.S.M., Pres. & Contact Person.

HAVERSTRAW. *Franciscan Sisters of Peace*, 20 Ridge St., 10927-1198. Tel: 845-942-2527; Fax: 845-429-8141. Email: jgilligan@fspnet.org. Web: www.fspnet.org. Sr. Jeanne Gilligan, F.S.P., Congregation Minister.

Ladycliff College Alumnae Association, Inc., c/o Franciscan Sisters of Peace, 20 Ridge St., 10927-1198. Tel: 914-446-2973; 914-446-5921.

HAWTHORNE. *Blessed Margaret's Cancer Relief Fund, Inc.*, Rosary Hill Home, 600 Linda Ave., 10532. Tel: 914-769-0114; Fax: 914-769-0827. Sr. Mary Francis, O.P., Pres.

The Rose Hawthorne Guild, 600 Linda Ave., 10532. Tel: 914-769-0114; Fax: 914-769-0827. Sr. Mary Francis, O.P., Pres. & Contact Person.

HIGHLAND MILLS. *Thevenet Montessori School*, (Grades PreK-1), 21 Bethany Dr., 10930. Tel: 845-928-6981; Fax: 845-928-3179. Email: thevenet@frontiernet.net. Sr. Norene Costa, R.J.M., Prin. Religious of Jesus and Mary. Sisters 1; Lay Teachers 9; Students 110.

HYDE PARK. *Focolare Movement National Center (Women's Branch)* (1943) Women's Branch, *Mariapolis Luminosa with offices of Focolare magazine "Living City"*, 200 Cardinal Rd., 12538. Tel: 845-229-0230, Ext. 178. Email: ff.luminosa.ny@focolare.us. Web: livingcitymagazine.com. Marlise Becker, Contact Person. Founded in Trent, Italy in 1943. International Headquarters are in Rome, Italy. Movement was approved in March 1962 with the aim of working toward the fulfillment of Christ's prayer for unity, that all may be one. More than four million people, in all walks of life, married and single, are committed in or connected with the Movement. Centers in over fifty countries. Call for additional information.

Focolare Movement National Center (Men's Branch) (Men), *Mariapolis Luminosa with publishing house New City Press*, 7 Intellect Way, 12538. Tel: 845-229-0307; Fax: 810-222-0307. Email: czmlumi@optonline.net. Web: rc.net/focolare. Antonio Vallejo.

Focolare Movement, Mariapolis Luminosa (Work of Mary), 200 Cardinal Rd., 12538. Tel: 845-229-0307; Fax: 810-222-0307. Web: www.focolare.us. Antonio Vallejo, Contact Person.

Focolare Movement, Women's Branch (East Coast) (Work of Mary), 257 Peace Ave., 12538. Tel: 845-229-9712; Fax: 845-229-1770. Web: www.focolare.us. Marigen Lohla, Co-Dir.

Living City of the Focolare Movement, Inc., 202 Comforter Blvd., 12538. Tel: 845-229-0496; Fax: 845-220-1770. Web: www.livingcitymagazine.com. Amelia J. Uelmen Esq., Contact Person.

New City Press of the Focolare Movement, Inc., 202 Comforter Blvd., 12538. Tel: 845-229-0335; Fax: 845-229-0351. Web: www.newcitypress.com. Amelia J. Uelmen Esq., Contact Person.

JAMAICA. *The Fellowship of the Beloved Disciple* (1980) *Immaculate Conception Monastery*, 86-45 Edgerton Blvd., 11432. Tel: 718-739-6502; Fax: 718-739-7770. Email: lallycp@aol.com. Web: www.unityincommunity.org. Rev. Owen Lally, C.P., Chap.; Yvonne Zeller, Dir.

LARCHMONT. *The Oratory of Divine Love, Inc.*, 1 Pryer Manor Rd., 10538. Tel: 914-643-3743. Email: ycleffi@aol.com. Web: www.oratoryofdivinelove.com. Rev. Benedict Joseph Groeschel, C.F.R., Ed.D., Pres.

LIVINGSTON MANOR. *The Monastic Family of Bethlehem* (1987) 393 Our Lady of Lourdes Camp Rd., 12758. Tel: 845-439-4300; Fax: 845-439-3069.

MARYKNOLL. *The Asian Catholic News Fund*, P.O. Box 306, 10545-0306. Tel: 914-941-7590; Fax: 914-944-3628. Email: rcallahan@maryknoll.org. Web: www.maryknoll.org. Rev. Richard B. Callahan, M.M., Contact Person.

Friends of St. Maria Goretti, U.S.A., Inc., P.O. Box 0043, 10545-0043. Tel: 914-941-7636, Ext. 2273; Fax: 914-945-0715. Email: gzilli@maryknoll.org. Web: www.mariagoretti.org. Mrs. Marie Finn, Pres.; Bro. Goretti A. Zilli, M.M., Sec. Tel: 914-941-6372; 914-941-7590; Rev. William T. Madden, M.M., Treas. (Retired); Mr. Ronald Finn, Vice Pres.

Maryknoll Fathers and Brothers Apostolic Trust, P.O. Box 306, 10545-0306. Tel: 914-941-7590; Fax: 914-944-3628. Web: www.maryknoll.org. Rev. David A. Smith, M.M., Contact Person.

Maryknoll Lay Missioners Foundation, P.O. Box 307, 10545-0307. Tel: 914-762-6364; Fax: 914-762-7362. Email: sstanton@mklm.org. Sam Stanton, Contact Person.

Maryknoll Mission Association of the Faithful (1994) P.O. Box 307, 10545-0307. Tel: 914-762-6364; Fax: 914-944-3576. Email: info@mklm.org. Web: www.mklm.org. Sam Stanton, Exec. Dir.; Margo Cambier, Dir. Mission. Purpose: Maryknoll Lay Missioners (MKLM) is a Catholic organization, comprising single men and women, couples and families, inspired by the mission of Jesus to live and work with poor communities in Africa, Asia and the Americas, responding to basic needs and helping to create a more just and compassionate world. MKLM applies skills and knowledge, raising the quality of life, and restoring hope, by making lasting improvements in the areas of justice and peace, education, health, pastoral care and sustainable development. MKLM recruits, trains and financially supports its missioners solely by public donation.

Maryknoll Missionary Education Trust, P.O. Box 306 Ryder Rd., 10545. Tel: 914-941-7590; Fax: 914-944-3628.

MOUNT VERNON. *St. Dymphna Devotion* (1961) 274-280 W. Lincoln Ave., P.O. Box 598, 10551-0598. Tel: 914-664-5604; Fax: 914-664-3017. Rev. Primo P. Piscitello, O.F.M., Prov.; Ms. Madeline Bonnici, Exec. Dir. Province of the Immaculate Conception.

Franciscan Mission Associates (1961) 274-280 W. Lincoln Ave., P.O. Box 598, 10550. Tel: 914-664-5604; Fax: 914-664-3017. Web: www.franciscanmissionassoc.org. Rev. Primo P. Piscitello, O.F.M., Prov.; Ms. Madeline Bonnici, Exec. Dir. Province of the Immaculate Conception.

MT. KISCO. *Regina Apostolorum, Inc.*, 773 Armonk Rd., 10549. Tel: 914-773-1368; Fax: 914-773-1438. Rev. Jose Felix Ortega, L.C., Contact Person.

NEW ROCHELLE. *Christian Brothers Foundation, Inc.*,

33 Pryer Ter., 10804. Tel: 914-636-6194; Fax: 914-636-0021. Bro. Hugh B. O'Neill, C.F.C., Contact Person.

Marian Residence Fund (1997) 1338 North Ave., 10804. Tel: 914-712-0060; Fax: 914-712-3134. Email: ursruepr@aol.com.

O.S.U. Charitable Trust (1997) 1338 North Ave., 10804. Tel: 914-712-0060; Fax: 914-712-3134. Email: ursruepr@aol.com.

St. Paul's Benevolent, Educational and Missionary Institute, Inc., Province Center, 20 Cedar St., 10801. Tel: 914-633-3130; Fax: 914-738-7652. Web: www.thepassionists.org. Very Rev. Robert H. Joerger, C.P., Contact Person.

Salesian Missions, Inc., 2 Lefevre Ln., 10801. Tel: 914-633-8344; Fax: 914-633-7404. Web: www.salesianmissions.org. Rev. Mark Hyde, S.D.B., Dir.

Songcatchers, Inc., 44 Liberty Ave., 10801. Tel: 914-654-1178 (Day); 914-576-6774 (Eve.); Fax: 914-740-7945. Email: songcatchers@gmail.com. 50 Washington Ave., 10801. Web: www.songcatchers.org. Sr. Beth Dowd, O.S.U., Dir. Program activities for elementary and middle school children, including Choir Camp, Concert Choir, and an After-School Music Program, Early Childhood Music Program. Young adults: volunteer staff of after-school program and camp.

Ursuline Social Outreach, Inc. (1996) 138 Centre Ave., 10805. Tel: 914-633-7298; Fax: 914-633-7393. Email: usoalc@aol.com. David J. Smith, Exec. Dir. Ursuline Outreach sponsors The Adult Learning Center, 138 Centre Ave., New Rochelle, NY 10805. Sisters 3; Volunteers 60; Total Assisted Annually 1,000.

NEWBURGH. **Newburgh Ministry* (1983) 9 Johnston St., P.O. Box 1449, 12551. Tel: 845-561-0070; Fax: 845-561-5087. Sr. Margaret Anderson, O.P., Chairperson, Bd. of Dir.; James McElhinney, Exec. Dir.

Newburgh San Miguel Program dba Newburgh San Miguel Program P.O. Box 284, Chappaqua, 10514. Tel: 914-861-9222. Email: gk@sonocap.com. Rev. Mark J. Connell, D.Min., Pres.& Project Coord.; Greg Kiernan, Dir. Devel.; Sr. Lois Dee, O.P., Prin.

Our Lady of Comfort Women's Center, 91 Ann St., 12550. Tel: 845-561-6267; Fax: 914-565-0572. Nina Faulkner, Treas. Shelter for Women & Children.

Presentation Educational Foundation, Inc., 157 Liberty St., 12550. Tel: 845-567-0708; Fax: 845-567-0709. Web: noracroninpresentationacademy.com. Sr. Yliana Hernandez, P.B.V.M., Pres.

OSSINING. *Dominican Sisters of Hope Ministry Trust*, 299 N. Highland Ave., 10562. Tel: 914-941-4420; Fax: 914-941-1125. Email: ministrytrust@ophope.org. Web: www.ophope.org. Sr. Pat Sullivan, O.P., Interim Chairperson.

PELHAM. *Passionist Communications, Inc.*, P.O. Box 8600, 10803-0440. Tel: 914-738-3344; Fax: 914-738-7652. Email: contact@TheSundayMass.org. Web: www.thesundaymass.org. Rev. Edward L. Beck, C.P.

Passionist Communications Center, P.O. Box 8600, 10803-1417. Tel: 914-738-3344; Fax: 914-738-7652. Email: contact@TheSundayMass.org. Web: www.thesundaymass.org. Rev. Edward L. Beck, C.P., Exec. Producer.

RHINEBECK. **The Astor Home for Children Foundation, Inc.*, 6339 Mill St., P.O. Box 5005, 12572-5005. Tel: 845-871-1117; Fax: 845-876-2020. Email: smoorhead@astorservices.org. Web: www.astorservices.org. Sonia Barnes-Moorhead, Exec. Vice Pres.

RIVERDALE. *Holy Innocents Foundation*, 5272 Post Rd., 10471. Fax: 718-593-0248. Kevin T. O'Reilly, Pres.

RYE. *Legacy Growth, Inc.*, 815 Boston Post Rd., 10580. Tel: 203-795-2800; Fax: 203-281-6051. Rev. Anthony Bannon, L.C.

Legion of Christ North America, Inc., 815 Boston Post Rd., 10580. Tel: 914-773-1368. Rev. Jose Felix Ortega, L.C., Contact Person.

Pastoral Support Services, Inc., 815 Boston Post Rd., 10580. Tel: 914-773-1368. Rev. Jose Felix Ortega, L.C., Sec.

The Resurrection School Foundation, Inc., 910 Bost Post Rd., 10580. Tel: 914-925-2732; Fax: 914-925-3527. Email: info@resurrectionschoolfoundation.com. Web: www.resurrectionschoolfoundation.com. Michael Iuliano, Dir.

SALT POINT. *Camp Veritas*, 1653 Salt Point Tpke., 12578. Tel: 845-266-5784. Email: ryan1@campveritas.com. Web: www.campveritas.com. Ryan Young, Bd. Chairperson.

SCARSDALE. *Catholic Charismatic Renewal Office*, 194 Gaylor Rd., 10583. Tel: 914-725-1773; Fax: 914-725-5227. Email: charismny@optonline.net. Web: www.catholiccharismaticny.org. Sr. Pauline Cinquini, S.C., Co-Liaison; Rev. William B. Cosgrove, Co-Liaison.

Tel: 845-634-3641; Fax: 845-639-6118. Email: frbill@optonline.net.

SLEEPY HOLLOW. *RSHM Life Center, Inc.* (1995) 32-34 Beekman Ave., 10591. Tel: 914-366-9710; Fax: 914-366-9713. Email: susan@rshmlifecenter.org. Web: www.rshmlifecenter.org. Sacred Heart of Mary. Total Assisted 600; Adults 240; Children 360; Total Staff 10.

SLOATSBURG. *St. Mary's Villa, Inc.*, 150 Sisters Servants Ln., P.O. Box 9, 10974-0009. Tel: 845-753-5100; Fax: 845-753-1956. Email: ssminy@aol.com. Sisters Kathleen Hutsko, S.S.M.I., Pres.; Consolata Trudick, S.S.M.I., Sec.

The Blessed Josaphata Fund (2001) 9 Emmanuel Dr., P.O. Box 9, 10974-0009. Tel: 845-753-2840; Fax: 845-753-1956. Email: rmulcahey@sbcq.com; ssminy@aol.com. Richard T. Mulcahey Jr., Esq., Contact Person; Sr. Kathleen Hutsko, S.S.M.I., Provincial Supr.

SPARKILL. *Hallel Institute* (1974) 175 Rte. 340, 10976-1047. Tel: 845-365-2277; Fax: 845-365-2279. Email: hallel@hallel.net. Web: hallel.net. Rev. George J. Torok, C.O., Pres. Total in Residence 40; Total Staff 7.

New York Oratory of St. Philip Neri, Inc., 175 Rte. 340, 10976. Tel: 845-365-2277; Fax: 845-365-2279. Revs. George J. Torok, C.O., Provost; Vladimir Chripko, C.O., Vice Provost & Treas.; Martin Kertys, C.O., Deputy; Frantisek Conka, C.O., Sec.

One to One Learning, Inc. (1997) Office of the President, 175 Rte. 340, 10976. Tel: 845-512-8176; Fax: 845-512-8178. Email: clpangel@aol.com. Sr. Cecilia LaPietra, O.P., Executive Dir.

STATEN ISLAND. *Emmaus Ministries, Ltd.*, c/o Church of St. Clare, 110 Nelson Ave., 10308. Tel: 718-984-7873; Fax: 718-966-8420. Web: www.stclares.com. Monica Brown, Pres.; Rev. Msgr. Joseph P. Murphy, Vice Pres. & Contact Person.

Fort Place Housing Corporation, 78 Fort Place, 10301. Tel: 718-818-5055. Email: mditommaso@svcmcny.org. Marianne DiTommaso, Asst. Sec. Bd. Dirs.

Indian Knanaya Catholic Community of Greater NY, Inc., 94 Wilcox St., 10303. Tel: 914-494-7571; Fax: 914-494-9183. Email: ikcc@hotmail.com. Jose Chummar, Pres.

Korean Catholic Apostolate of Staten Island, Inc., 726 Woolley Ave., 10314. Tel: 718-351-2612; Fax: 718-273-2950. Web: kcasi.org. Rev. Hyunsang Sung, Contact Person.

Pax Christi Hospice, 1200 South Ave., Ste. 306, 10314. Tel: 718-876-1022. Email: mackermann@svcmcny.orgFax: 718-876-1803.

Pax Christi Hospice, 227 E. 19th St., 10003. Tel: 212-995-6480 (Inpatient); 212-995-7474 (Home Care).

Schoenstatt Sisters of Mary, Secular Institute, 337 Cary Ave., 10310-2041. Tel: 718-727-8005. Email: shrineny@schsrsmary.org. Sisters 7; Total Staff 3.

**Sisters of Charity Housing Development, Corp.*, 150 Brielle Ave., 10314-6400. Tel: 718-477-6803; Fax: 718-477-1356. Email: epfeldmann@worldnet.att.net. Eric Feldmann, Exec. Dir.

SUFFERN. *Good Samaritan Foundation for Better Health, Inc.*, 255 Lafayette Ave., 10901-4869. Tel: 845-368-5151; Fax: 845-368-5596. Email: stacey_kirschenbaum@bshsi.org. Web: goodsamhosp.org. Sr. Mary Louise Moran, S.C., Pres.; Stacey Kirschenbaum, Dir. Fundraising arm of Good Samaritan Hospital, Suffern, NY.

TARRYTOWN. *Religious of the Sacred Heart of Mary Charitable Trust*, 50 Wilson Park Dr., 10591. Tel: 914-631-2979; Fax: 914-332-4735. Sr. Bernadette Kenny, Contact Person.

THORNWOOD. *Alpha Omega Family Center, Inc.* (1993) 582 Columbus Ave., 10594. Tel: 914-749-3900; Fax: 914-749-3939. Rev. Jacobo Munoz, L.C., Contact Person.

Arke, Inc., 590 Columbus Ave., 10594. Tel: 914-773-1368. Rev. Jose Felix Ortega, L.C., Contact Person.

Catholic Net, Inc. (1997) 590 Columbus Ave., 10594. Tel: 914-773-1368; Fax: 914-773-1438. Rev. Jose Felix Ortega, L.C., Contact Person.

Consolidated Catholic Administrative Services, Inc. (1999) 590 Columbus Ave., 10594. Tel: 914-773-1368; Fax: 914-773-1438. Rev. Jose Felix Ortega, L.C., Contact Person.

Familia USA, Inc. (1997) 590 Columbus Ave., 10594. Tel: 914-773-1368; Fax: 914-773-1438. Rev. Jose Felix Ortega, L.C., Contact Person.

Helping Hands Medical Missions, Inc. (1997) 590 Columbus Ave., 10594. Tel: 914-749-3900; Fax: 914-749-3939. Rev. Jose Felix Ortega, L.C.

Legion of Christ and Consecrated Regnum Christi Members Assistance Foundation (2002) 590 Columbus Ave., 10594. Tel: 914-773-1368; Fax: 914-773-1438. Rev. Jose Felix Ortega, L.C., Contact Person.

Legion of Christ, Incorporated (1978) 590 Columbus Ave., 10594. Tel: 914-773-1368; Fax: 914-773-1438. Rev. Jose Felix Ortega, L.C., Contact Person.

Mission Network Programs USA, Inc. (1997) 590 Columbus Ave., 10594. Tel: 914-773-1368; Fax: 914-773-1438. Email: cknet@flash.net. Web: catholickidsnet.org. Rev. Jose Felix Ortega, L.C., Contact Person.

Nueva Primavera Inc., 590 Columbus Ave., 10594. Tel: 914-773-1368. Rev. Jose Felix Ortega, L.C., Contact Person.

Youth and Family Encounter, Inc. (1998) 590 Columbus Ave., 10594. Tel: 914-773-1368; Fax: 914-773-1438. Rev. Jose Felix Ortega, L.C., Contact Person.

TUCKAHOE. **Peace Through Divine Mercy, Inc.* (1988) 50 Columbus Ave., #410, 10707. Tel: 914-771-7717. Email: mjkm67@gmail.com. Web: www.peacethroughmercy.com. Kathleen Keefe, Contact Person. Apostolate for priestly and family renewal.

WALDEN. *Little Sisters of the Assumption Family In Mission, Inc.*, 100 Gladstone Ave., 12586. Tel: 212-722-7404; Fax: 212-722-7405. Email: coordinator@lsafim.org. Web: www.lsafim.org. Sr. Annette Allain, L.S.A., Prog. Coord.

WHITE PLAINS. *Children's Rehabilitation Center, Inc.*, 317 North St., 10605. Tel: 646-459-3905; Fax: 646-459-3688. Web: www.setonpediatric.org. William Van Lew, CFO.

Company of St. Paul, 52 Davis Ave., 10605. Tel: 914-946-1019; Fax: 914-946-1019. Rev. Stuart Sandberg, Pres.

Concerts at the Chapel, Inc., White Plains Center of Compassion, 52 N. Broadway, 10603. Tel: 914-798-1201. Web: www.divinecompassion.org. Paula Caracappa, Coord.

Deutschsprachige Katholische Gemeinde New York-German Speaking Catholic Congregation New York, 106 Greenacres Ave., 10606. Tel: 914-831-3165. Rev. Peter Bleeser, Contact Person.

Religious of Divine Compassion Charitable Trust, 52 N. Broadway, 10603. Tel: 914-798-1300; Fax: 914-949-5169. Email: smerritt@divinecompassion.org; smerritt@pace.edu. Web: divinecompassion.org.

The Little Disciple Learning Center, Inc., 348 S. Lexington Ave., 10606. Tel: 914-949-2111. Rev. Robert J. Morris, Contact Person.

WOODBOURNE. *Heart's Home USA* (2003) 2299 Ulster Heights Rd., 12788. Tel: 845-434-5076; Fax: 718-522-2922. Email: info@heartshomeusa.org. Web: www.heartshomeusa.org. Laetitia Pallua de Besset, Pres.

YONKERS. *Finian Sullivan Corporation*, One Father Finian Sullivan Dr., 10703. Tel: 914-969-6159; Fax: 914-969-1503. Email: scorbett@hhmgnt.com. Peter Bassano, Esq., Contact Person.

Jesus Caritas Fraternity, Inc., 4 Curran Ct., 1R, 10710. Tel: 914-961-0050. Email: margebaker@secularinstitutes.org. Mary D. Christensen, Corresponding Sec.

NACAR, Inc., 35 Vark St., 10701. Tel: 914-476-7474; Fax: 914-476-7484. Email: eocsc@aol.com. Web: www.catholic-church.org/nacar. Sr. Ellen Rose O'Connell, S.C., Pres., Emeritus/Archivist.

[II] PERSONAL PRELATURES

NEW YORK. *Prelature of the Holy Cross and Opus Dei* (1928) 139 E. 34th St., 10016. Tel: 646-742-2700; Fax: 646-742-2747. Email: newyork@opusdei.org. Web: www.opusdei.org. Rev. Msgrs. Thomas G. Bohlin, Ph.D., S.T.D., Regl. Vicar for the U.S.; Javier Garcia de Cardenas; Revs. Deogracias Rosales; Robert A. Brisson; James W. Albrecht; John C. Agnew.

Overlook Study Center Tel: 914-235-0199; Fax: 914-637-9597. Revs. Bradley K. Arturi, J.C.D.; Paul Grant.

99 Overlook Cir., New Rochelle, 10804. Tel: 914-235-6128. Rev. Malcolm M. Kennedy.

330 Riverside Dr., 10025. Tel: 212-222-3285; Fax: 212-316-3629.

RELIGIOUS INSTITUTES OF MEN REPRESENTED IN THE ARCHDIOCESE

For further details refer to the corresponding bracketed number in the Religious Institutes of Men or Women section.

[0130]—*Assumptionists*—A.A.

[0140]—*The Augustinians* (Prov. of St. Joseph)—O.S.A.

[0330]—*Brothers of the Christian Schools* (New York Prov.)—F.S.C.

[0600]—*Brothers of the Congregation of Holy Cross*—C.S.C.

[0400]—*Canons Regular of the Order of the Holy Cross* (Prov. of St. Odilia, Minneapolis, MN)—O.S.C.

[0470]—*The Capuchin Friars* (St. Mary Prov.)—O.F.M.Cap.

[0270]—*Carmelite Fathers & Brothers* (St. Elias Prov.)—O.Carm.
[0310]—*Congregation of Christian Brothers* (Eastern U.S.)—C.F.C.
[0220]—*Congregation of the Blessed Sacrament*—S.S.S.
[1330]—*Congregation of the Mission*—C.M.
[1210]—*Congregation of the Missionaries of St. Charles*—C.S.
[1000]—*Congregation of the Passion* (St. Paul Prov.)—C.P.
[0480]—*Conventual Franciscans* (Immaculate Conception Prov.)—O.F.M.Conv.
[0520]—*Franciscan Friars* (Provs. of Most Holy Name of Jesus, Immaculate Conception; Commissariats of Holy Cross, Holy Family)—O.F.M.
[0530]—*Franciscan Friars of the Atonement*—S.A.
[0690]—*Jesuit Fathers and Brothers* (New York Prov.)—S.J.
[0730]—*Legionaries of Christ*—L.C.
[]—*Little Brothers of the Gospel*
[0770]—*The Marist Brothers*—F.M.S.
[0780]—*Marist Fathers* (Northeastern Prov.)—S.M.
[0800]—*Maryknoll*—M.M.
[0830]—*Mill Hill Missionaries*—M.H.M.
[0720]—*The Missionaries of Our Lady of La Salette*—M.S.
[0910]—*Oblates of Mary Immaculate* (Eastern Prov.)—O.M.I.
[0430]—*Order of Preachers-Dominicans* (St. Joseph Prov.)—O.P.
[0150]—*Order of the Augustinian Recollects*—O.A.R.
[1030]—*Paulist Fathers*—C.S.P.
[1040]—*Piarist Fathers*—Sch.P.
[1070]—*Redemptorist Fathers* (Baltimore Prov.)—C.SS.R.
[1190]—*Salesians of Don Bosco* (St. Philip Prov.)—S.D.B.
[1020]—*Society of St. Paul*—S.S.P.
[0990]—*Society of the Catholic Apostolate*—S.A.C.
[1280]—*Stigmatine Fathers and Brothers*—C.S.S.
[1300]—*Theatine Fathers*—C.R.
[0560]—*Third Order Regular of Saint Francis*—T.O.R.

RELIGIOUS INSTITUTES OF WOMEN REPRESENTED IN THE ARCHDIOCESE

[0130]—*Apostles of the Sacred Heart of Jesus*—A.S.C.J.
[0230]—*Benedictine Sisters of Pontifical Jurisdiction*—O.S.B.
[0330]—*Carmelite Sisters for the Aged and Infirm*—O.Carm.
[3110]—*Congregation of Our Lady of the Retreat in the Cenacle*—R.C.
[2410]—*Congregation of the Marianites of Holy Cross*—M.S.C.
[3710]—*Congregation of the Sisters of Saint Agnes*—C.S.A.
[1920]—*Congregation of the Sisters of the Holy Cross*—C.S.C.
[1710]—*Congregation of the Third Order of St. Francis of Mary Immaculate*—O.S.F.
[0760]—*Daughters of Charity of St. Vincent de Paul*—D.C.
[0790]—*Daughters of Divine Charity* (St. Joseph Prov.)—F.D.C.
[0850]—*Daughters of Mary Help of Christians*—F.M.A.
[0860]—*Daughters of Mary of the Immaculate Conception*—D.M.
[0950]—*Daughters of St. Paul*—F.S.P.
[0810]—*Daughters of the Heart of Mary*—D.H.M.
[0420]—*Discalced Carmelite Nuns*—O.C.D.
[1050]—*Dominican Contemplative Nuns*—O.P.
[1070-03]—*Dominican Sisters*—O.P.
[1070-11]—*Dominican Sisters*—O.P.
[1070-05]—*Dominican Sisters*—O.P.
[1070-06]—*Dominican Sisters*—O.P.
[1070-13]—*Dominican Sisters*—O.P.
[1070-16]—*Dominican Sisters*—O.P.
[1070-23]—*Dominican Sisters*—O.P.
[1070-15]—*Dominican Sisters*—O.P.
[1115]—*Dominican Sisters of Peace*—O.P.
[1120]—*Dominican Sisters of the Roman Congregation*—O.P.
[1170]—*Felician Sisters*—C.S.S.F.
[1260]—*Franciscan Handmaids of the Most Pure Heart of Mary*—F.H.M.
[1370]—*Franciscan Missionaries of Mary*—F.M.M.
[1400]—*Franciscan Missionary Sisters of the Sacred Heart* (Peekskill, NY)—F.M.S.C.
[1180]—*Franciscan Sisters of Allegany, New York*—O.S.F.
[1310]—*Franciscan Sisters of Little Falls, Minnesota*—O.S.F.
[1425]—*Franciscan Sisters of Peace*—F.S.P.
[1190]—*Franciscan Sisters of the Atonement*—S.A.
[1440]—*Franciscan Sisters of the Poor*—S.F.P.
[2070]—*Holy Union Sisters*—S.U.S.C.
[]—*Idente Missionaries*—M.Id.
[3790]—*Institute of the Sisters of St. Dorothy*—S.S.D.
[2310]—*Little Sisters of the Assumption*—L.S.A.
[2340]—*Little Sisters of the Poor*—L.S.P.
[2470]—*Maryknoll Sisters of St. Dominic*—M.M.
[2480]—*Medical Missionaries of Mary*—M.M.M.
[2680]—*Misericordia Sisters*—S.M.
[2720]—*Mission Helpers of the Sacred Heart*—M.H.S.H.
[2710]—*Missionaries of Charity*—M.C.
[1360]—*Missionary Franciscan Sisters of the Immaculate Conception*—O.S.F.
[2790]—*Missionary Servants of the Most Blessed Trinity*—M.S.B.T.
[2900]—*Missionary Sisters of St. Charles Borromeo*—M.S.S.C.B.
[2750]—*Missionary Sisters of the Immaculate Heart of Mary*—I.C.M.
[2860]—*Missionary Sisters of the Sacred Heart*—M.S.C.
[2920]—*Mothers of the Helpless*—M.D.
[3030]—*Oblates of the Most Holy Redeemer*—O.SS.R.
[3035]—*Oblates of the Mother of Orphans*—O.M.O.
[3760]—*Order of St. Clare*—O.S.C.
[2010]—*Order of the Most Holy Redeemer*—O.SS.R.
[3160]—*Parish Visitors of Mary Immaculate*—P.V.M.I.
[3450]—*Religious of Jesus-Mary*—R.J.M.
[3460]—*Religious of Mary Immaculate*—R.M.I.
[3465]—*Religious of the Sacred Heart of Mary* (Eastern North American Prov.)—R.S.H.M.
[2519]—*Religious Sisters of Mercy, Alma, MI*—R.S.M.
[3490]—*Sacramentine Nuns*—O.S.S.
[2970]—*School Sisters of Notre Dame*—S.S.N.D.
[1680]—*School Sisters of St. Francis*—O.S.F.
[0980]—*Sister Disciples of the Divine Master*—P.D.D.M.
[1830]—*Sister of the Good Shepherd*—R.G.S.
[3020]—*Sisters Oblates of the Blessed Trinity*—O.B.T.
[0590]—*Sisters of Charity of Saint Elizabeth, Convent Station*—S.C.
[0650]—*Sisters of Charity of St. Vincent de Paul, New York*—S.C.
[0660]—*Sisters of Christian Charity*—S.C.C.
[2360]—*Sisters of Loretto*—S.L.
[2575]—*Sisters of Mercy of the Americas*—R.S.M.
[3000]—*Sisters of Notre Dame de Namur*—S.N.D.deN.
[3080]—*Sisters of Our Lady of Christian Doctrine*—R.C.D.
[3740]—*Sisters of St. Casimir*—S.S.C.
[1510]—*Sisters of St. Francis of the Mission of the Immaculate Virgin*—O.S.F.
[3820]—*Sisters of St. John the Baptist*—C.S.J.B.
[3830-05]—*Sisters of St. Joseph*—C.S.J.
[3890]—*Sisters of St. Joseph of Peace*—C.S.J.P.
[0260]—*Sisters of the Blessed Sacrament for Indians and Colored People*—S.B.S.
[3140]—*Sisters of the Catholic Apostolate (Pallottine)*—C.S.A.C.
[2980]—*Sisters of the Congregation de Notre Dame*—C.N.D.
[0970]—*Sisters of the Divine Compassion*—R.D.C.
[1000]—*Sisters of the Divine Providence of Kentucky*—C.D.P.
[1990]—*Sisters of the Holy Names of Jesus & Mary*—S.N.J.M.
[3320]—*Sisters of the Presentation of the B.V.M.* (Newburgh; Staten Island)—P.B.V.M.
[3320]—*Sisters of the Presentation of the B.V.M.* (Aberdeen, SD)—P.B.V.M.
[3470]—*Sisters of the Reparation of the Congregation of Mary*—S.R.C.M.
[3480]—*Sisters of the Resurrection*—C.R.
[1490]—*Sisters of the Third Franciscan Order (Syracuse)*—O.S.F.
[3600]—*Sisters, Servants of Mary*—S.M.
[2160]—*Sisters, Servants of the Immaculate Heart Of Mary*—I.H.M.
[1890]—*Society of Helpers*—H.H.S.
[2460]—*Society of Mary Repartrix*—S.M.R.
[4040]—*Society of St. Ursula*—S.U.
[4060]—*Society of the Holy Child Jesus*—S.H.C.J.
[4070]—*Society of the Sacred Heart*—R.S.C.J.
[4110]—*Ursuline Nuns*—O.S.U.
[4130]—*Ursuline Sisters (Tildonk)*—O.S.U.
[4230]—*Xaverian Missionary Sisters*—X.M.M.

ARCHDIOCESAN CEMETERIES

AIRMONT. *Cemetery of the Ascension*
HAWTHORNE. *Cemetery of the Gate of Heaven*
LONG ISLAND CITY. *Calvary*
STATEN ISLAND. *Cemetery of the Resurrection*

NECROLOGY

✠ Mestice, Most Rev. Anthony F., Retired Auxiliary Bishop of New York.—Died April 29, 2011
✠ Sheridan, Most Rev. Patrick J., Retired Auxiliary Bishop of New York.—Died Dec. 2, 2011
† Boyle, Rev. Msgr. Patrick J., Rye, NY Resurrection—Died Feb. 16, 2011
† Corrigan, Rev. Msgr. Bernard P., (Retired)—Died Jan. 30, 2011
† Toohy, Rev. Msgr. William J., (Retired)—Died June 12, 2011
† Carson, John F., Yonkers, NY St. Ann.—Died Aug. 3, 2011
† Darby, Thomas J., (Retired)—Died Feb. 9, 2011
† McGarry, Thomas M., (Retired)—Died March 23, 2011
† McGuire, John C., (Retired)—Died March 23, 2011
† McMahon, Bernard, (Retired)—Died Oct. 9, 2011
† Mulloy, Matthew, (Retired)—Died April 22, 2011
† Peluso, Michael J., Staten Island, NY Our Lady of Pity—Died Sept. 27, 2011
† Sullivan, Frederick J., (Retired)—Died Jan. 31, 2011
† Tiercelin, Harry, (Retired)—Died April 6, 2011

An asterisk (*) denotes an organization that has established tax-exempt status directly with the IRS and is not covered by the USCCB Group Ruling.

Diocese of Norwich

(Dioecesis Norvicensis)

Most Reverend

MICHAEL R. COTE, D.D.

Bishop of Norwich; ordained June 29, 1975; appointed Titular Bishop of Cebarades and Auxiliary Bishop of Portland May 9, 1995; ordained July 27, 1995; appointed Bishop of Norwich March 11, 2003; installed May 14, 2003. *Res.: 274 Broadway, Norwich, CT 06360.*

Chancery: 201 Broadway, Norwich, CT 06360. Tel: 860-887-9294; Fax: 860-886-1670.

Web: www.norwichdiocese.org

ESTABLISHED AUGUST 6, 1953.

Square Miles 1,978.

Corporate Title: The Norwich Roman Catholic Diocesan Corporation.

Comprises the Counties of Middlesex, New London, Tolland and Windham in the State of Connecticut and Fishers Island, a portion of Suffolk County in the State of New York.

For legal titles of parishes and diocesan institutions, consult the Chancery Office.

STATISTICAL OVERVIEW

Personnel	
Bishop	1
Priests: Diocesan Active in Diocese	71
Priests: Diocesan Active Outside Diocese	7
Priests: Diocesan in Foreign Missions	1
Priests: Retired, Sick or Absent	32
Number of Diocesan Priests	111
Religious Priests in Diocese	59
Total Priests in Diocese	170
Extern Priests in Diocese	12
Ordinations:	
Diocesan Priests	1
Permanent Deacons in Diocese	69
Total Brothers	25
Total Sisters	177
Parishes	
Parishes	76
With Resident Pastor:	
Resident Diocesan Priests	65
Resident Religious Priests	11
Without Resident Pastor:	
Administered by Priests	13
Missions	6
Pastoral Centers	8
Professional Ministry Personnel:	
Sisters	7
Lay Ministers	41
Welfare	
Homes for the Aged	2
Total Assisted	239
Residential Care of Children	1
Total Assisted	20
Special Centers for Social Services	4
Total Assisted	8,500
Educational	
Diocesan Students in Other Seminaries	5
Seminaries, Religious	1
Students Religious	26
Total Seminarians	31
Colleges and Universities	1
Total Students	237
High Schools, Diocesan and Parish	4
Total Students	2,241
High Schools, Private	2
Total Students	424
Elementary Schools, Diocesan and Parish	15
Total Students	2,519
Catechesis/Religious Education:	
High School Students	2,040
Elementary Students	12,243
Total Students under Catholic Instruction	19,735
Teachers in the Diocese:	
Priests	1
Brothers	4
Sisters	16
Lay Teachers	345
Vital Statistics	
Receptions into the Church:	
Infant Baptism Totals	1,587
Minor Baptism Totals	85
Adult Baptism Totals	55
Received into Full Communion	262
First Communions	1,921
Confirmations	2,030
Marriages:	
Catholic	343
Interfaith	120
Total Marriages	463
Deaths	1,976
Total Catholic Population	238,565
Total Population	692,328

Former Bishops—Most Revs. BERNARD J. FLANAGAN, D.D., J.C.D., ord. Dec. 8, 1931; cons. Nov. 30, 1953; installed Dec. 9, 1953; transferred to See of Worcester, Aug. 12, 1959; retired March 31, 1983; died Jan. 28, 1998; VINCENT J. HINES, D.D., J.C.D., ord. May 2, 1937; appt. Nov. 27, 1959; cons. March 17, 1960; retired June 17, 1975; died April 23, 1990; DANIEL P. REILLY, D.D., ord. May 30, 1953; appt. June 17, 1975; cons. Aug. 6, 1975; transferred to See of Worcester, Oct. 27, 1994; installed Dec. 8, 1994; retired March 9, 2004; DANIEL A. HART, D.D., ord. Feb. 2, 1953; cons. Auxiliary Bishop of Boston Oct. 18, 1976; appt. Sept. 12, 1995; installed Bishop of Norwich Nov. 1, 1995; retired March 11, 2003; died Jan. 14, 2008.

Office of the Bishop—Most Rev. MICHAEL RICHARD COTE, D.D. Tel: 860-887-9294. Email: bpcote@norwichdiocese.net; Mrs. ALICE PUDVAH, Administrative Asst. Tel: 860-887-9294, Ext. 234. Email: alice@norwichdiocese.net.

The Chancery

Chancery—201 Broadway, Norwich, 06360. Tel: 860-887-9294; Fax: 860-886-1670.

Vicar General—Very Rev. LESZEK T. JANIK, J.C.L., V.G. Tel: 860-887-9294, Ext. 231. Email: vicargeneral@norwichdiocese.net; Mrs. CHRISTINE SIART, Sec. Tel: 860-887-9294, Ext. 246. Email: sec.voc@norwichdiocese.net.

Chancellor—Rev. Msgr. ROBERT L. BROWN. Tel: 860-887-9294, Ext. 232; Cell: 860-303-6080. Email: chancellor@norwichdiocese.net; Mrs. BECKY CADY, Sec. Tel: 860-887-9294, Ext. 235. Email: becky@norwichdiocese.net; Mrs. REBECCA MCDOUGAL, Receptionist. Tel: 860-887-9294, Ext. 100.

Vicar for Clergy—Very Rev. DENNIS M. PERKINS. Tel: 860-887-9294, Ext. 258. Email: vicarclergy@norwichdiocese.net; Deacon MICHAEL C. BERSTENE, Dir. Deacon Personnel; Mrs. REBECCA MCDOUGAL, Sec. Tel: 860-887-9294, Ext. 100. Email: rebecca@norwichdiocese.net.

Diaconate: Office of Deacon Personnel—The Chancery, 201 Broadway, Norwich, 06360-4458. Web: www.norwichdeacons.org. Deacon MICHAEL C. BERSTENE, Diocesan Dir., Deacon Personnel. Tel: 860-887-9294; Fax: 860-886-1670. Email: director@norwichdeacons.org; Mrs. REBECCA MCDOUGAL, Sec. Tel: 860-887-9294, Ext. 100; Fax: 860-886-1670. Email: rebecca@norwichdiocese.net.

Diocesan Attorney—MICHAEL E. DRISCOLL ESQ., 22 Courthouse Sq., Norwich, 06360. Tel: 860-889-3321.

Diocesan Attorney Emeritus—JAMES J. DUTTON JR., Esq., K.S.G., 22 Courthouse Sq., Norwich, 06360. Tel: 860-889-3321.

Diocesan Finance Office—Tel: 860-887-9294; Fax: 860-885-1512. WILLIAM J. RUSSELL, CPA, Diocesan Finance Officer. Tel: 860-887-9294, Ext. 241; SUSAN GARDINER, Administrative Asst. Tel: 860-887-9294, Ext. 261; JANET WEST, Finance Analyst. Tel: 860-887-9294, Ext. 243; ANN MARIE OSOWSKI, Benefits Admin. Tel: 860-887-9294, Ext. 245; KAREN HUFFER, Internal Auditor. Tel: 860-887-9294, Ext. 244; JENNIFER BEAUDOIN, Accounting Clerk. Tel: 860-887-9294, Ext. 242; Ms. ROBIN HOLTSCLAW, Risk Mgr. (CMRS). Tel: 800-331-2561; Fax: 860-726-9412.

College of Consultors—Rev. Msgrs. HENRY N. ARCHAMBAULT, P.A., J.C.D.; THOMAS R. BRIDE, P.A., K.C.H.S.; ROBERT L. BROWN; RICHARD P. LAROCQUE; ANTHONY S. ROSAFORTE; Very Revs. MICHAEL T. DONOHUE; LESZEK T. JANIK, J.C.L., V.G.; LAURENCE A.M. LAPOINTE; DENNIS M. PERKINS; Rev. ROBERT WASHABAUGH.

Presbyteral Council—Most Rev. MICHAEL RICHARD COTE, D.D., Pres.; Rev. RICHARD J. RICARD, Chm.; Very Rev. LESZEK T. JANIK, J.C.L., V.G. Members: Rev. Msgrs. HENRY N. ARCHAMBAULT, P.A., J.C.D.; THOMAS R. BRIDE, P.A., K.C.H.S.; ROBERT L. BROWN, Sec.; RICHARD P. LAROCQUE; ANTHONY S. ROSAFORTE; Very Revs. MICHAEL T. DONOHUE; GREGOIRE J. FLUET, Ph.D., V.F., K.H.S.; JAMES P. CARINI; LAURENCE A.M. LAPOINTE; CHARLES R. LEBLANC, V.F.; DENNIS M. PERKINS; MICHAEL L. PHILLIPPINO; TED F. TUMICKI, S.T.L., J.C.L., J.V.; Revs. JOHN N. ANTONELLE, Vice Chm.; GRZEGORZ P. BROZONOWICZ; ROLAND C. CLOUTIER, L.C.S.W.; EDWARD M. DEMPSEY, D.B.A.; GREGORY P. GALVIN; SALVADOR GONZALEZ, O.M.I.; DAVID KASHEN, O.F.M.Conv.; KEVIN M. REILLY; BRIAN J. ROMANOWSKI; MICHAEL S. SMITH; ROBERT WASHABAUGH.

Deans—Very Revs. LAURENCE A.M. LAPOINTE, Willimantic; JAMES P. CARINI, Vernon; Rev. Msgr. HENRY N. ARCHAMBAULT, P.A., J.C.D., Norwich; Very Revs. CHARLES R. LEBLANC, V.F., Putnam; GREGOIRE J. FLUET, Ph.D., V.F., K.H.S., Old Saybrook; MICHAEL T. DONOHUE, New London; MICHAEL L. PHILLIPPINO, Middletown.

Diocesan Pastoral Council—Most Rev. MICHAEL RICHARD COTE, D.D., Chm.; Very Rev. LESZEK T. JANIK, J.C.L., V.G.; Rev. Msgr. ROBERT L. BROWN; Very Rev. TED F. TUMICKI, S.T.L., J.C.L., J.V.; Rev. WALTER M. NAGLE; Mr. TODD POSTLER;

Ms. HELENE LABELLE; Mr. JAMES LANDHERR; Sr. ELISSA RINERE, C.P., J.C.D.; Mrs. ESPERANZA NUGENT; Mr. STEPHEN ST. JOHN; Mrs. ELAINE TRUDO; Mr. ELBERT BURR; Ms. LOIS DUPOINTE; Mr. GEORGE GORTON; Ms. SANDRA GRILLO; Ms. RITA LAJOIE; Mr. KEENAN MARR; Ms. PATRICIA WESTER.

The Tribunal

Diocesan Tribunal—

*Judicial Vicar—*Very Rev. TED F. TUMICKI, S.T.L., J.C.L., J.V.

*Associate Judicial Vicar—*Rev. GEORGE J. RICHARDS JR., J.C.L.

*Defenders of the Bond—*Revs. ROGER J. LAMOUREUX, O.M.I.; JOSEPH CASTALDI, J.C.L.

*Coordinator of the Tribunal—*SALLY J. TOLLES, D.H.S., J.D., J.C.L. Cons. Sec. D.H.S., J.D., J.C.L.

*Judges—*Rev. Msgr. HENRY N. ARCHAMBAULT, P.A., J.C.D.; Very Rev. LESZEK T. JANIK, J.C.L., V.G.; Rev. GEORGE J. RICHARDS JR., J.C.L.; Very Rev. TED F. TUMICKI, S.T.L., J.C.L., J.V.; SALLY J. TOLLES, D.H.S., J.D., J.C.L. Cons. Sec. D.H.S., J.D., J.C.L.; Sr. ELISSA RINERE, C.P., J.C.D.

*Archivist—*Very Rev. GREGOIRE J. FLUET, Ph.D., V.F., K.H.S.

*Auditor/Assessors—*BEATRICE L. THEROUX Consecrated Secular, D.H.S.; Sr. ELISSA RINERE, C.P., J.C.D.; Rev. Msgr. RICHARD P. LAROCQUE; Revs. PAUL J. MURDOCK; BRIAN J. ROMANOWSKI; Ms. JACQUELINE M. KELLER, M.A.

*Administrative Assistant of the Tribunal—*Ms. JACQUELINE M. KELLER, M.A.

*Notaries—*Rev. Msgrs. THOMAS R. BRIDE, P.A., K.C.H.S.; ROBERT L. BROWN; Rev. GEORGE J. RICHARDS JR., J.C.L.; SALLY J. TOLLES, D.H.S., J.D., J.C.L., Cons. Sec.; Ms. JACQUELINE M. KELLER, M.A.; Mrs. ALICE PUDVAH.

Diocesan Offices, Ministries and Societies

*Advisory Ministry Evaluation Committee—*Rev. Msgrs. THOMAS R. BRIDE, P.A., K.C.H.S.; ROBERT L. BROWN, Chm.; Mr. WILLIAM J. RUSSELL, CPA, D.F.O.; Very Rev. DENNIS M. PERKINS; Rev. JOSEPH B. WHITTEL; Sr. MARY A. MCCARTHY, R.S.M.; SALLY J. TOLLES, D.H.S., J.D., J.C.L. Cons. Sec. D.H.S., J.D., J.C.L.; Mrs. NANCY MIGNAULT; Mrs. RELLA BERNABUCCI; Mr. WILLIAM JUZWIC; Dr. JEREMIAH LOWNEY; Dr. ROBERT MILLER, Ph.D.

Annual Catholic Appeal (ACA)— See Development, Diocesan Office.

*Bishop's Liaison with Retired Clergy—*Very Rev. DENNIS M. PERKINS, The Chancery, 201 Broadway, Norwich, 06360-4458. Tel: 860-887-9294, Ext. 258.

*Bishop's Delegate for Safe Environments—*Rev. RICHARD J. RICARD.

*Delegate for Consecrated Life—*SALLY J. TOLLES Cons. Sec. D.H.S., J.D., J.C.L. The Tribunal, Diocese of Norwich, 201 Broadway, Norwich, 06360-4419. Tel: 860-887-9294, Ext. 255.

*Delegate for Internal Investigations—*Mr. VICTOR E. LENDA JR.

*Delegate for Evangelization in Hispanic Ministry—*Rev. MARTIN J. JONES.

*Diocesan Finance Council—*Most Rev. MICHAEL RICHARD COTE, D.D., Chm.; Very Rev. LESZEK T. JANIK, J.C.L., V.G.; Mr. JAMES CRONIN; Mr. PETER LAMALFA; Mr. FRED PERKINS, CPA; Mr. BERNARD PHANEUF; Mr. WILLIAM MCGURK; Mr. TERRENCE CAHILL; Mr. PETER SIPPLES, Attorney.

*Diocesan Panel of Pastors, Canon 1742—*Rev. Msgr. ANTHONY S. ROSAFORTE; Very Rev. DENNIS M. PERKINS; Rev. RICHARD J. RICARD.

Diocesan Pastoral Council— See Chancery listing.

Board of Education— See School Office.

*Board of Conciliation and Arbitration—*SALLY J. TOLLES, D.H.S., J.D., J.C.L. Cons. Sec. D.H.S., J.D., J.C.L.

*Building Commission—*Very Rev. MICHAEL F. DONOHUE, Chm.; Mr. GEORGE SCHILLER; Mr. PAUL LUSSIER; Mr. ELBERT BURR.

Campaigns—

*Campaign for Human Development—*Very Rev. MICHAEL T. DONOHUE, Diocesan Dir., St. Matthias Church, 317 Chesterfield Rd., P.O. Box 25, East Lyme, 06333-0025. Tel: 860-739-5208; Fax: 860-739-0524.

*Catholic Relief Services—*Rev. Msgr. ROBERT L. BROWN, Dir.; Mrs. BECKY CADY, 201 Broadway, Norwich, 06360-4328. Tel: 860-887-9294, Ext. 235.

*Campus Ministry—*Very Rev. LAURENCE A.M. LAPOINTE, Diocesan Dir., Newman Hall, 290 Prospect St., Willimantic, 06226. Tel: 860-423-0856; Fax: 860-456-8083 (See separate category under Institutions for details).

*Middletown—*Rev. HALBERT WEIDNER, C.O., Wesleyan University - The University Chaplains, 171 Church St., Middletown, 06459-3625. Tel: 860-685-2285, Ext. 2706; Fax: 860-685-2821.

*New London—*Very Rev. LAURENCE A.M. LAPOINTE, Catholic Chap., Connecticut College, P.O. Box 5203, New London, 06320-5203. Tel: 860-439-2452; Fax: 860-439-2463.

*Storrs—*Chaplains: Revs. GREGORY C. MULLANEY; JOHN N. ANTONELLE.

*Willimantic—*Very Rev. LAURENCE A.M. LAPOINTE, Campus Min., Eastern Connecticut State University, Newman Hall, 290 Prospect St., Willimantic, 06226-2304. Tel: 860-423-0856; Fax: 860-456-8083.

Catechetical Ministry— See Faith Events, Office of.

Catholic Charities, Diocese of Norwich, Inc.—

*Executive Director—*Mr. MAREK KUKULKA, L.M.F.T., 331 Main St., Norwich, 06360. Tel: 860-889-8346; Fax: 860-889-2658.

*Adolescent Substance Abuse Treatment Program—*ERIN GARDNER, L.C.S.W., Social Worker & Coord. Norwich and New London Office.

*Adoption Program—*SUSAN SEDENSKY, J.D., L.C.S.W., Prog. Coord. Norwich Office.

*Behavioral Health Clinic—*CIRO MASSA, L.C.S.W., L.A.D.C., Dir. Clinic, 331 Main St., Norwich, 06360. Tel: 860-889-8346. 28 Huntington St., New London, 06320. Tel: 860-443-5328; BEN LOCASTRO, L.C.S.W., C.E.A.P., Site Supvr., 553 Portland Cobalt Rd., Portland, 06480. Tel: 860-342-0760.

*Emergency Financial Service—*ROSALINDA BAZINET, B.A., Supvr. New London Office, 28 Huntington St., New London, 06320. Tel: 860-443-5328; Fax: 860-443-6013; SYLVIA LAUDETTE, L.C.S.W., Mgr., Norwich Office, 331 Main St., Norwich, 06360. Tel: 860-889-8346; Fax: 860-889-2658.

*Emergency Financial Assistance—*SEAN FEENEY, Social Worker, 88 Jackson St., P.O. Box 54, Willimantic, 06226. Tel: 860-423-7065.

*Empowering People for Success Program—*COLETTA WILSON, M.S.W., Social Worker, New London Office: 28 Huntington St., New London, 06320. Tel: 860-443-5328; Fax: 860-443-6013. Willimantic Office: 88 Jackson St., Willimantic, 06226. Tel: 860-423-7065; Fax: 860-456-1096; ROSA ALMONTE, Willimantic Office: 88 Jackson St., Willimantic, 06226. Tel: 860-423-7065; Fax: 860-456-1096.

*Family Life Educator/Parish Social Ministry Coordinator—*Ms. SUSAN WILLIAMS, B.A., M.S., Norwich Office: 331 Main St., Norwich, 06360. Tel: 860-889-8346; Fax: 860-889-2658.

*Courage Chaplain—*Rev. VICTOR CHAKER, St. Mary Church, 1600 Main St., P.O. Box 250, Coventry, 06238-0250. Tel: 860-742-0681.

*Housing Program—*JAY GELFOND; VICTORIA GOWLIS, Norwich Office: 331 Main St., Norwich, 06360. Tel: 860-889-8346; Fax: 860-889-2658.

*Immigration—*ROSALINDA BAZINET, B.A.; ALVIANIA HILARIO, New London Office: 28 Huntington St., New London, 06320. Tel: 860-443-5328; Fax: 860-443-6013.

*Office of Family Life—*Ms. SUSAN WILLIAMS, B.A., M.S. Tel: 860-889-8346, Ext. 283; Fax: 860-889-2658. Email: swilliams@ccfsn.org. Web: www.ccfsn.org. Marriage preparation, marriage support and enrichment, natural family planning, parenting education, True Love Waits (chastity/abstinence), Project Rachel (post abortion), separation and divorce, bereavement, singles and singles-again.

*Courage Chaplain—*Rev. VICTOR CHAKER, St. Mary Church, 1600 Main St., P.O. Box 250, Coventry, 06238-0250. Tel: 860-742-0681.

*Pregnancy Program—*SHARON GOODE, Social Worker, Norwich Office: 331 Main St., Norwich, 06360. Tel: 860-889-8346; Fax: 860-889-2658; ROSALINDA BAZINET, B.A., Social Worker, New London Office: 28 Huntington St., New London, 06320. Tel: 860-443-5326; Fax: 860-443-6013.

Catholic Mutual Relief Society— Diocesan Property and Liability Insurance, Ms. ROBIN HOLTSCLAW, Claims/Risk Mgr. Email: rholtsclaw@catholicmutual.org; Office for all claims: Catholic Mutual Group, 467 Bloomfield Ave., Bloomfield, 06002. Tel: 800-331-2561; Fax: 860-726-9412. National Office: Catholic Mutual Relief Society, 10843 Old Mill Rd., Omaha, NE 68154. Tel: 800-228-6108; Fax: 402-551-2943.

Catholic Youth Organization (CYO)— See Faith Events, Office of.

*Cemetery Corporation and Subsidiaries, Diocesan Cemeteries—*Mr. JOSEPH M. MUSCARELLA, Dir. Diocesan Properties; SHIRLEY MCGRATH, Cemetery Mgr., Office, 815 Boswell Ave., Norwich, 06360-2536. Tel: 860-887-1019; Fax: 860-889-4804 (For details on individual cemeteries see separate listing); The following cemeteries are subsidiaries of the Norwich Diocesan Cemetery Corp.

Moosup—All Hallows Cemetery, Green Hallow Rd., Moosup, 06354. Cemetery Office: 815 Boswell Ave., Norwich, 06360-2536. Tel: 860-887-1019.

New London—St. Mary Cemetery of New London Corp., 600 Jefferson Ave., New London, 06320-2412. Tel: 860-443-3465 (Office).

Norwich—St. Mary & St. Joseph Cemetery Corp., 815 Boswell Ave., Norwich, 06360-2536. Tel: 860-887-1019.

Taftville—Sacred Heart Cemetery Corp., Harland Rd., Taftville, 06380. Cemetery Office, 815 Boswell Ave., Norwich, 06360-2536. Tel: 860-887-1019.

Uncasville—St. Patrick Cemetery, Depot Rd., Uncasville, 06382. Cemetery Office, 815 Boswell Ave., Norwich, 06360-2536. Tel: 860-887-1019.

Wauregan—Sacred Heart Cemetery, Wauregan Rd., Wauregan, 06387. Cemetery Office: 815 Boswell Ave., Norwich, 06360-2536. Tel: 860-887-1019.

Westbrook—Resurrection Cemetery Corp., Rte. 145, Westbrook, 06498. Tel: 860-399-6503 (Cemetery Office).

*Censor of Books—*Rev. ROBERT W. CRONIN (Retired), 275 Steele Rd., Apt. B118, West Hartford, 06117. Tel: 860-232-1886; Very Rev. LAURENCE A.M. LAPOINTE, St. Joseph Church, 99 Jackson St., Willimantic, 06226. Tel: 860-423-8439.

Communications, Office of—31 Perkins Ave., Norwich, 06360-3613. Tel: 860-887-3933; Fax: 860-859-1253. Web: www.norwichdiocese.org. Mr. MICHAEL R. STRAMMIELLO, Dir. Email: com@norwichdiocese.net; Ms. MEREDITH MORRISON, Administrative Asst./Webmaster.

Four County Catholic— Official monthly newspaper of the Diocese of Norwich: (No July issue).

*Publisher—*Most Rev. MICHAEL RICHARD COTE, D.D., Bishop of Norwich.

*Executive Editor—*Mr. MICHAEL R. STRAMMIELLO.

*News Editor—*Mrs. TRINA FULTON, 31 Perkins Ave., Norwich, 06360-3613. Tel: 860-886-1281; Fax: 860-859-1253. Email: comtrina@norwichdiocese.net.

*Theological Advisor—*Very Rev. TED F. TUMICKI, S.T.L., J.C.L., J.V.

Community Ministries—

*Middletown—*Mr. RONALD KROM, Exec. Dir.; TERRY CARBONE, Svc. Coord., St. Vincent dePaul Place, 617 Main St., P.O. Box 398, Middletown, 06457-0398. Tel: 860-344-0097; Fax: 860-343-0023. Web: www.svdmiddletown.org.

*Norwich—*JILLIAN CORBIN, Exec. Dir. Email: jcsvdpp@gmail.com; Ms. BETTY ROARTY, Administrative Asst., St. Vincent dePaul Place, 10 Railroad Pl., Norwich, 06360. Tel: 860-889-7374. Email: brsvdpp@yahoo.com. Web: www.svdpp.org.

*Connecticut Catholic Conference—*MICHAEL CARROLL CULHANE, Exec. Dir.; Deacon DAVID REYNOLDS, Legislative Liaison, Connecticut Catholic Conference, 134 Farmington Ave., Hartford, 06105-3784. Tel: 860-524-7882; Fax: 860-525-0750. Email: ccc@ctcatholic.org. Web: www.ctcatholic.org.

*Continuing Education and Formation Commission for the Clergy—*Revs. MICHAEL S. SMITH, Chm.; GRZEGORZ P. BROZONOWICZ; DAVID P. CHOQUETTE; PETER B. LISZEWSKI; WALTER M. NAGLE; MARK D. O'DONNELL; Very Rev. DENNIS M. PERKINS.

*Council of Catholic Women—*Mrs. JUDY PAPPAGALLO, Pres.; Very Rev. CHARLES R. LEBLANC, V.F., Diocesan Spiritual Advisor, Mailing Address: St. Joseph Rectory, P.O. Box 897, North Grosvenordale, 06255-0897. Tel: 860-923-2361. District Spiritual Advisors: Revs. VICTOR CHAKER, Willimantic Deanery; STEPHEN S. GULINO, Norwich Deanery; JOSEPH B. WHITTEL, New London Deanery; DAVID P. CHOQUETTE, Putnam Deanery, Diocesan Mod.; Very Rev. JAMES P. CARINI, Rockville Deanery; Revs. PAUL J. GAUMOND, Shoreline Deanery; JAMES J. SUCHOLET, Middletown Deanery.

*Courage Chaplain—*Rev. VICTOR CHAKER, St. Mary Church, 1600 Main St., P.O. Box 250, Coventry, 06238-0250. Tel: 860-742-0681.

Ecclesia Dei Ministry (Tridentine Rite)—

*Director and Chaplain—*Very Rev. GREGOIRE J. FLUET, Ph.D., V.F., K.H.S., St. Bridget of Kildare, P.O. Box 422, Moodus, 06469-0422. Tel: 860-873-8623.

*Development, Diocesan Office of (DOD)—*Mrs. ANGELA ARNOLD, Exec. Dir. Tel: 860-886-1928, Ext. 13; Fax: 860-886-2651. Email: dod@norwichdiocese.net. Administrative Assistants: SUSAN UNDERHILL. Tel: 860-886-1928, Ext. 10; MARLENE PEER, 197 Broadway, Norwich, 06360-4407. Tel: 860-886-1928, Ext. 11.

Annual Catholic Appeal (ACA)— (See Development, Diocesan Office).

Planned Giving Office—Mrs. MARY LOU GANNOTTI, 197 Broadway, Norwich, 06360. Tel: 860-886-1928, Ext. 15. Email: marylou.gannotti@norwichdiocese.net.

Stewardship Office—Mrs. ANGELA ARNOLD, 197 Broadway, Norwich, 06360. Tel: 860-886-1928, Ext. 13. Email: dod@norwichdiocese.net.

The Catholic Foundation—Mrs. ANGELA ARNOLD, Dir. Tel: 860-886-1928, Ext. 14. Email: dod@norwichdiocese.net.

Diocesan Properties, Office of—Mr. JOSEPH M. MUSCARELLA, Dir., 815 Boswell Ave., Norwich, 06360. Tel: 860-887-1019.

Disabilities-People with— See His Able People, Ministry of

Ecumenism—

Diocesan Commission for Ecumenical and Interreligious Affairs—Deacon LEO N. BERNARD; Ms. KATHLEEN BURTON; SANDRA CALABRO; Mr. CHARLES HENRY SR.; Sr. BARBARA HOBBS, P.B.V.M.; Mr. MARK KRISTOFF; Very Rev. CHARLES R. LEBLANC, V.F.; Rev. MARK D. O'DONNELL; MICHAEL OLOCK; RAFAEL ORTIZ; Rev. FRANCIS C. ROULEAU.

Ecumenical and Interreligious Affairs, Office of—VACANT, Bishop Flanagan Ministry Center, 199 Broadway, Norwich, 06360. Tel: 860-848-2237; Fax: 860-848-2816. Email: ecuminter@norwichdiocese.net.

Evangelization & Catechumenate (RCIA), Office of—See Office of Faith Events

Faith Events, Office of—199 Broadway, Norwich, 06360. Tel: 860-848-2237, Ext. 312; Fax: 860-848-2816. Email: faithevents@norwichdiocese.net. MARGE VANNER, Coord.; PAM PLASSE, Asst. Coord. Advisory Board: MOTHER MARY JUDE LAZARUS, S.C.M.C., Co Chair; Deacon GERALD L. SHAW, Co Chair; Rev. GREGORY BROZONOWICZ; Deacons THOMAS J. CASEY; CHRISTOPHER DESKUS; PETER L. GILL; Mr. BRIAN HENRY; Very Rev. LESZEK T. JANIK, J.C.L., V.G.; Mrs. JILL PATTEN; Mrs. ANNE STAUFFER; Mrs. NANCY MIGNAULT.

Diocesan Catholic Scouting—Tel: 860-848-2237, Ext. 311.

Co Chairs—PAM PLASSE; ISABEL GREENHALGH. Email: faithevents@norwichdiocese.org.

Faith Formation, Office for— See Office of Faith Events

"Four County Catholic"— See Newspaper

Haiti, Diocese of Norwich Outreach to, Inc.— a successor corporation of the two merged corporations, Haitian Ministries for the Diocese of Norwich and Hospice St. Joseph for the Diocese of Norwich. Mrs. KYN TOLSON, Programs Admin., 199 Broadway, Norwich, 06360. Tel: 860-848-2237, Ext. 206. Email: info@outreachtohaiti.org; Ms. ANNA DEBIASI, Dir. Educ. & Devel., 199 Broadway, Norwich, 06360. Tel: 860-848-2237, Ext. 206.

Chaplain and Director of Twinning in Haiti—Rev. FRANCIS ROLEAU.

His Able People, Ministry of— A ministry for persons with disabilities. *Inquiries should be made to: 201 Broadway, Norwich, 06360*. Tel: 860-887-9294, Ext. 100.

Hispanic Ministry—MOTHER MARY JUDE LAZARUS, S.C.M.C., Diocesan Dir., Hispanic Apostolate Office, 61 Club Rd., Windham, 06280-1007. Tel: 860-456-3349; Fax: 860-423-4157. Email: aposthispano@juno.com.

Evangelization—

Delegate for Evangelization in Hispanic Ministry—Rev. MARTIN J. JONES, St. Mary Church, 70 Central Ave., Norwich, 06360. Tel: 860-887-2565.

Hispanic Ministry Board—Clinton: Mr. ALEZANDRO CASTANEDA; Mrs. NORMA GARZON. Middletown: Sr. XINIA RODRIGUEZ, R.O.D.A. New London: Rev. ROBERT WASHABAUGH; Mrs. MARIA TORRES; Mr. VERTILIO RAMOS; Deacon MARIO RAMOS. Norwich: Mr. GEBERTH GAMBOA; Mrs. ZULMA GAMBOA; Rev. GERALD S. KIRBY; Sr. FRANCISCA CANDELARIA, R.O.D.A.; Mr. DAVID FERNANDEZ; Mrs. IRIS FERNANDEZ. Windham: Rev. PAUL J. MURDOCK; Deacon FELIPE SILVA; Mrs. VIRGINIA RODRIGUEZ.

Clinton—

St. Mary of the Visitation Church - Spanish Apostolate—Rev. MICHAEL SEQUEIRA, Pastor, 54 Grove St., Clinton, 06413-1999. Tel: 860-669-8512; Fax: 860-669-9052.

Middletown—

St. Francis of Assisi Church - Spanish Apostolate—Rev. HALBERT WEIDNER, C.O., Admin., 10 Elm St., Middletown, 06457-4426. Tel: 860-347-4684; Fax: 860-347-7669; Sr. XINIA RODRIGUEZ, R.O.D.A., Res.: 28 River Ave., Norwich, 06360. Tel: 860-886-6092.

New London—

St. Mary, Star of the Sea Church - Spanish Apostolate—Rev. ROBERT WASHABAUGH, Pastor; Deacons JESUS DIEZ-CANSECO, 10 Huntington St., New London, 06320-6198. Tel: 860-447-1431; Fax: 860-437-1889. Email: stmarysnl@aol.com; MARIO RAMOS, Res.: 4 Aspen Ln., Ledyard, 06339. Tel: 860-389-4485.

Norwich—

St. Mary Church - Spanish Apostolate—Rev. GERALD S. KIRBY. In Res.: Rev. MARTIN J. JONES; Sr. FRANCISCA CANDELARIA, R.O.D.A., Pastoral Assoc., 70 Central Ave., Norwich, 06360-4794. Tel: 860-887-2565.

Windham—

Iglesia del Sagrado Corazon de Jesus—Rev. PAUL J. MURDOCK, Pastor, Res.: 310 Elizabeth Ln., Stonegate Manor, North Windham, 06256. Pastoral Associates: Sr. FRANCISCA CANDELARIA, R.O.D.A.; Mrs. VIRGINIA RODRIGUEZ; Deacon FELIPE SILVA, 61 Club Rd., Windham, 06280-1007. Tel: 860-423-8617; Fax: 860-423-4157.

Holy Childhood— See Pontifical Association of the Holy Childhood.

Holy Name Societies— Address all mail to: *Holy Name Societies, 201 Broadway, Norwich, 06360-4328*. Tel: 860-887-9294.

Insurance— See Catholic Mutual Relief Society (C.M.R.S.)

Office of Internal Affairs—201 Broadway, Norwich, 06360-4480. Tel: 800-624-7407; 860-889-4455. Mr. VIC LENDA JR., Bishop's Delegate for Internal Investigations; Mrs. MARY SWEENEY, Assistance Coord. Tel: 800-624-7407.

Justice & Peace, Catholic Action for—Rev. JOSEPH B. WHITTEL, Our Lady of Perpetual Help Church, 63 Old Norwich Rd., P.O. Box 329, Quaker Hill, 06375-0329. Tel: 860-443-1875; Fax: 860-437-9869. Email: jbwhittel@hotmail.com.

Lawyers, Guild of Catholic—Mailing Address: 201 Broadway, Norwich, 06360-4328. Tel: 860-887-9294, Ext. 246. MICHAEL E. DRISCOLL ESQ., Pres.; Rev. Msgr. HENRY N. ARCHAMBAULT, P.A., J.C.D., Chap.; Mrs. CHRISTINE SIART, Sec. Tel: 860-887-9294, Ext. 246.

Legion of Mary—VACANT.

Marriage Encounter/Catholic Charities/Family Life Office— (See Catholic Charities & Family Services).

Mercy Xavier Fund—Bro. BRIAN DAVIS, C.F.X., Pres., 181 Randolph Rd., Middletown, 06457. Tel: 860-347-2343; 860-346-7735.

Newspaper— Official monthly newspaper of Diocese of Norwich--"Four County Catholic" Most Rev. MICHAEL RICHARD COTE, D.D., Publisher; Mrs. TRINA FULTON, News Editor, 31 Perkins Ave., Norwich, 06360. Tel: 860-886-1281. Email: comtrina@norwichdiocese.net; Very Rev. TED F. TUMICKI, S.T.L., J.C.L., J.V., Theological Advisor.

Pastoral Planning, Office of—Sr. ELISSA RINERE, C.P., J.C.D., 199 Broadway, Norwich, 06360. Tel: 860-848-2237, Ext. 203; Fax: 860-848-2816. Email: rinere@norwichdiocese.org. Advisory Board: Very Rev. JAMES P. CARINI; MOTHER MARY JUDE LAZARUS, S.C.M.C.; Revs. MARK D. O'DONNELL; MICHAEL S. SMITH; JOSEPH B. WHITTEL; ROLAND C. CLOUTIER, L.C.S.W.

People with Disabilities— (See His Able People, Ministry of).

Planned Giving Office— See Development, Diocesan Office of

Pontifical Association of the Holy Childhood—Rev. WILLIAM J. OLESIK, Mailing Address: St. Matthews Church, P.O. Box 100, Tolland, 06084-0100. Tel: 860-872-0200.

Pontifical Society for the Propagation of the Faith—Rev. WILLIAM J. OLESIK, Dir., Mailing Address: St. Matthews Church, P.O. Box 100, Tolland, 06084-0100. Tel: 860-872-0200.

Prison Ministry for Diocese of Norwich—Ms. SHEREE L. ANTOCH, Dir., 199 Broadway, Norwich, 06360. Tel: 860-848-2237, Ext. 211; Fax: 860-848-2816. Email: prison@norwichdiocese.net.

Brooklyn—

Brooklyn Correctional Institution—59 Hartford Rd., Brooklyn, 06234. Tel: 860-779-4568. Deacon CHRISTOPHER DESKUS, Chap.

Niantic—

York Correctional Institution—201 W. Main St., Niantic, 06357. Tel: 860-691-6529; 860-691-6673. Deacons DENNIS F. DOLAN, Chap.; THOMAS J. CASEY.

Somers—

Northern Correctional Institution—287 Bilton Rd., Somers, 06071. Tel: 860-763-8686. Deacon ROBERT BERND.

Osborn Correctional Institution—100 Bilton Rd., Somers, 06071. Tel: 860-749-8391, Ext. 5476. Deacon MICHAEL TORRES, Chap.; Rev. ZACARIAS PUSHPANATHAN (Immaculate Conception, Hartford).

Willard-Cybulski Correctional Institution—391 Shaker Rd., Enfield, 06082. Tel: 860-763-6106. Deacon LEO B. CONRAD, Chap.

Uncasville—

Corrigan-Radgowski Correctional Institution—986 Norwich-New London Tpke., Uncasville, 06382. Tel: 860-848-5034. Deacons THOMAS J. CASEY, Chap.; CHRISTOPHER DESKUS, Chap.; Rev. MARK D. O'DONNELL (St. Agnes Church, Niantic).

Commission for Human Life and Justice—Rev. JOSEPH B. WHITTEL, Our Lady of Perpetual Help Church, 63 Old Norwich Rd., P.O. Box 329, Quaker Hill, 06375-0329. Tel: 860-443-1875; Fax: 860-437-9869. Email: jbwhittel@hotmail.com.

Project Northeast— A program of Evangelization for the unchurched poor. Rev. RICHARD L. ARCHAMBAULT, Dir., 81 Church St., Putnam, 06260-1809. Tel: 860-928-4078; 860-928-0105; Sr. ELEANOR BALDONI, D.H.S., Assoc. Dir., 22 Pearl Ave., Putnam, 06260-1625. Tel: 860-928-5965.

RCIA— See Evangelization & Catechumenate, Office of

Religious— See Delegate for Consecrated Life

Retirement—

Priests' Retirement Plan Board—Most Rev. MICHAEL RICHARD COTE, D.D.; Very Rev. DENNIS M. PERKINS; Rev. JOSEPH CASTALDI, J.C.L.; Mr. JAMES CRONIN; Rev. DENNIS G. CAREY; Mr. CHARLES HAYES.

Safe Environments, Office of—199 Broadway, Norwich, 06360. Tel: 860-848-2237. Email: ose@norwichdiocese.net. Rev. RICHARD J. RICARD, Bishop's Delegate; Ms. KAREN CAISE, Dir. Tel: 860-848-2237, Ext. 212.

School Office, Diocesan—43 Perkins Ave., Norwich, 06360-4480. Tel: 860-887-4086; Fax: 860-887-9371. Web: www.norwichdso.org. Dr. JOHN F. SHINE, Ph.D., K.M., Supt. Email: superintendentdso@norwichdiocese.net; Sr. BARBARA GOULD, R.S.M., Asst. Supt. Email: asstsuperdso@norwichdiocese.net; Mrs. LOIS PEGG, Sec. Email: adminasstdso@norwichdiocese.net.

Diocesan School Technology Consultant—Ms. SHEILA CERJANEC, Technology Coord. Email: technologydso@norwichdiocese.net; Mrs. ANN G. CROOKS, Elementary School Devel. Coord. Email: developmentdso@norwichdiocese.net.

Board of Education—Most Rev. MICHAEL RICHARD COTE, D.D., Ex Officio; Dr. JOHN F. SHINE, Ph.D., K.M., Supt.; Sr. BARBARA GOULD, R.S.M.; Mr. ALTON BUTTON; Mrs. ROSANNE COFFEY; Very Rev. GREGOIRE J. FLUET, Ph.D., V.F., K.H.S.; Rev. Msgr. ROBERT BROWN; Mrs. KATHRYN CONNELLY; Mr. JOSEPH GRILLO; Mrs. ANNA GLAVAN; Mrs. JAN LEDWIDGE; Dr. ROBERT MILLER, Ph.D., Bd. Chm.; Mr. WILLIAM J. RUSSELL, CPA, D.F.O.

Scouting— (See Faith Events, Office of).

Sick, Ministry to the—Sr. RITA JOHNSON, S.S.N.D., Dir., W.W. Backus Hospital, 326 Washington St., Norwich, 06360-2742. Tel: 860-889-8331. Res.: 7 Otis St., Norwich, 06360. Tel: 860-886-6948.

Soup Kitchen— (See Community Ministries, Saint Vincent de Paul Place). Email: svdpp@sbcglobal.net.

Spanish Speaking Apostolate— (See Hispanic Ministry).

Spiritual Renewal Services—Co-Directors: Rev. RAYMOND D. INTOVIGNE, Rectory: 1600 Main St., P.O. Box 250, Coventry, 06238-0250. Tel: 860-742-0681; Mrs. JUDITH HUGHES, Office, 11 Bath St., P.O. Box 6, Norwich, 06360-5836. Tel: 860-887-0702; 860-887-7667 Prayer Line; Fax: 860-859-1366. Email: renewal@catholicweb.com.

Victim Assistance Coordinator—Mrs. MARY SWEENEY. Tel: 800-624-7407.

Vocation—Rev. GREGORY P. GALVIN, Dir., Res.: St. Thomas Aquinas, 46 N. Eagleville Rd., Storrs, 06268; Mrs. CHRISTINE SIART, Sec. to Dir., 201 Broadway, Norwich, 06360-4328. Tel: 860-887-9294, Ext. 246. Res.: St. Thomas Aquinas, 46 N. Eagleville Rd., Storrs, 06268. Email: vocations@norwichdiocese.net; sec.voc@norwichdiocese.net.

Seminarian Advisory Board—Rev. GREGORY P. GALVIN; Very Revs. MICHAEL L. PHILLIPPINO; LESZEK T. JANIK, J.C.L., V.G.; Revs. KEVIN M. REILLY; MICHAEL C. GIANNITELLI; RICHARD J. RICARD; JOSEPH TITO.

Worship, Office of—Sr. ELISSA RINERE, C.P., J.C.D., Dir., 199 Broadway, Norwich, 06360. Tel: 860-848-2237, Ext. 209; Fax: 860-848-2816. Email: rinere@norwichdiocese.net. Liturgical Commission: Very Rev. JAMES P. CARINI; Rev. STANLEY J. SZCZAPA; Deacon PETER L. GILL; Rev. PAUL J. MURDOCK; Mrs. NANCY MIGNAULT; Dr. SUSAN BERRY; Mr. ANGEL CORREA.

CLERGY, PARISHES, MISSIONS AND PAROCHIAL SCHOOLS

CITY OF NORWICH

(NEW LONDON COUNTY)

1—ST. PATRICK CATHEDRAL (1879) Rev. Msgr. Anthony S. Rosaforte, Rector; Rev. P. Gregorz Jednaki. In Res., Rev. Joseph E. Nichols (Retired).
School—211 Broadway, 06360. Tel: 860-889-4174; Fax: 860-889-0040. Email: stpatrick.cath.sch@snet.net. Catherine Reed, Prin. Lay Teachers 14; Students 234.
Catechesis/Religious Program—Students 139.

2—ST. JOSEPH (1904), (Polish), Rev. Tomasz Sztuber, Admin. In Res., Deacon Thomas A. Lewis.
Res.: 120 Cliff St., 06360-5134. Tel: 860-887-1565; Fax: 860-889-3560.
Catechesis/Religious Program—Tel: 860-887-4565. Students 32.

3—ST. MARY (1845) Rev. Gerald S. Kirby; Sr. Francisca Candelaria, R.O.D.A., Pastoral Assoc. Hispanic Min. In Res., Rev. Martin J. Jones.
Res.: 70 Central Ave., 06360-4794. Tel: 860-887-2565; Fax: 860-892-1692. Email: secretary@stmarys1845.org.
Catechesis/Religious Program—Ss. Peter & Paul, 181 Elizabeth St., 06360. Students 16.

4—SS. PETER AND PAUL (1938) Very Rev. Leszek T. Janik; Rev. Christopher J. Zmuda, Parochial Vicar.
Res.: 181 Elizabeth St., 06360-6199. Tel: 860-887-9857; Fax: 860-886-4728. Email: ssppnorwich@netscape.net.
Catechesis/Religious Program—Students 46.

5—SACRED HEART (Norwichtown) (1902) Rev. Michael J. Gill; Deacon Wayne Sinclair.
Res.: 52 W. Town St., Norwichtown, 06360-2296. Tel: 860-887-1030; Fax: 860-887-6550. Email: sacredheart06360@gmail.com.
Catechesis/Religious Program—Tel: 860-887-1715. Paula Wiencek, C.R.E. Students 45.
Mission—St. John 190 Fitchville Rd., Bozrah, New London Co. 06334.

OUTSIDE THE CITY OF NORWICH

ASHFORD, WINDHAM CO., ST. PHILIP THE APOSTLE (1921) [CEM 2], Yoked with St. Jude, Willington. Rev. Russell F. Kennedy, Admin.
Mailing Address: 64 Pompey Hollow Rd., 06278-1540.
Res.: 25 Old Farms Rd., P.O. Box 240, Willington, 06279-0240. Tel: 860-429-2860 (Office at St. Philip); 860-429-9655 (Res.); Fax: 860-487-5703. Email: church7227@sbcglobal.net. Web: www.saintphilipsaintjude.org.
Catechesis/Religious Program—Raymond Potter, D.R.E. Students 57.

BALLOUVILLE, WINDHAM CO., ST. ANNE (1882) Closed. For inquiries for parish records contact St. Joseph, Dayville.

BALTIC, NEW LONDON CO., ST. MARY OF THE IMMACULATE CONCEPTION (1866) [CEM] Rev. Joseph Tito.
Res.: 70 W. Main St., 06330-1348. Tel: 860-822-6378; Fax: 860-822-6378.
School—St. Joseph, 10 School Hill Rd. Tel: 860-822-6141; Fax: 860-822-1479. Sr. Mary Patrick Mulready, S.C.M.C., Prin. Sisters of Charity of Our Lady, Mother of the Church 2; Lay Teachers 8; Students 115.
Catechesis/Religious Program—Students 85.

BOLTON, TOLLAND CO., ST. MAURICE (1954) Rev. Wojciech Pelczarski, S.D.S., Admin.
Res.: 32 Hebron Rd., 06043-7606. Tel: 860-643-4466; Fax: 860-643-4466. Email: stmauricechurch@sbcglobal.net. Web: www.saintmauricebolton.org.
Catechesis/Religious Program—Students 65.

BROOKLYN, WINDHAM CO., OUR LADY OF LA SALETTE (1968) Rev. John J. O'Neill, M.S., Temp. Admin.
Res.: 21 Providence Rd., P.O. Box 211, 06234-0211. Tel: 860-774-6275; Fax: 860-774-0679.
Catechesis/Religious Program—Students 140.
Mission—Our Lady of Lourdes 41 Cedar Swamp Rd., Hampton, Windham Co. 06247.

CANTERBURY, WINDHAM CO., ST. AUGUSTINE (1978), Yoked with St. John the Apostle, Plainfield. Rev. Arul Rajan Peter, Admin.; Deacon Timothy M. Marshall.
Res.: 144 Westminster Rd., 06331-1417. Tel: 860-546-6074; Fax: 860-546-6074. Email: staugus@charter.net. Web: www.staugustine-canterbury.org.
Catechesis/Religious Program—Tel: 860-546-6225. Students 65.

CHESTER, MIDDLESEX CO., ST. JOSEPH (1885) [CEM] Rev. Patrick Biegler, M.S.A., Admin.; Deacon Lawrence Moneypenny. In Res., Rev. Charles Bak, M.S.A.
Res.: 48 Middlesex Ave., 06412-1309. Tel: 860-526-5495; Fax: 860-526-7880. Web: www.stjosephchester.parishesonline.com.
Catechesis/Religious Program—Tel: 860-526-2152. Students 412.

CLINTON, MIDDLESEX CO., ST. MARY OF THE VISITATION (1934) [CEM] Rev. Michael Sequeira; Deacon Paul Weber.
Res.: 54 Grove St., 06413-1999. Tel: 860-669-8512; Fax: 860-669-9052. Email: godsquad@snet.net. Web: www.stmarysclinton.com.
Catechesis/Religious Program—Tel: 860-669-7375. Email: reledof@snet.net. Gina Offner, D.R.E.; Margo Blake, Youth Min. Students 334.

COLCHESTER, NEW LONDON CO., ST. ANDREW (1860) [CEM 2] [JC 2], Yoked with St. Francis of Assisi, Lebanon. Revs. Marek Masnicki; Benjamin V. Soosaimanickam; Deacon Michael L. Puscas.
Res.: 128 Norwich Ave., 06415-1269. Tel: 860-537-2355; Fax: 860-537-2356. Email: bjpalmer@standrewofcolchester.org. Web: www.sacredheartgroton.org.
Catechesis/Religious Program—Tel: 860-537-5415. Email: cre@standrewofcolchester.org. Students 650.

COLUMBIA, TOLLAND CO., ST. COLUMBA (1960) Rev. Daniel C. Cronin.
Res.: 328 Junction Rtes. 66 & 87, P.O. Box 146, 06237-0146. Tel: 860-228-3735; Fax: 860-228-8777. Email: sec.stcolumba@sbcglobal.net.
Catechesis/Religious Program—Tel: 860-228-3727. Students 92.

COVENTRY, TOLLAND CO., ST. MARY (1877) [CEM] Revs. Victor Chaker; Raymond D. Intovigne, Parochial Vicar.
Res.: 1600 Main St., P.O. Box 250, 06238-0250. Tel: 860-742-0681; Fax: 860-742-1318.
Catechesis/Religious Program—Tel: 860-742-1092. Students 241.
Mission—St. Joseph Eagleville, Tolland Co.

CROMWELL, MIDDLESEX CO., ST. JOHN (1882) Revs. Mark Curesky, O.F.M.Conv.; Bart Karwacki, O.F.M.Conv., Parochial Vicar.
Res.: 5 St. John Ct., 06416-2118. Tel: 860-635-5590; Fax: 860-635-5591. Web: www.saintjohn-cromwell.org.
Catechesis/Religious Program—Tel: 860-635-5156. Email: faithformationsjc@sbcglobal.net. Students 428.

DANIELSON, WINDHAM CO., ST. JAMES (1869) [CEM] Revs. John J. O'Neill, M.S.; Thomas Sickler, M.S.; Elson Kattookkaran, M.S, Parochial Vicar; Deacon Rene N. Barbeau Jr. In Res., Revs. John E. Welch, M.S. (Retired); Joseph Whalen, M.S. (Retired).
Res.: 12 Franklin St., 06239. Tel: 860-774-3900; Fax: 860-774-4205.
School—Tel: 860-774-3281; Fax: 860-779-2137. Ms. Monique Almquist, Prin. Lay Teachers 13; Students 215.
Catechesis/Religious Program—Tel: 860-774-8459. Students 240.
Mission—Our Lady of Peace

DAYVILLE, WINDHAM CO., ST. JOSEPH (1874) [CEM] Rev. Leon J. Susaimanickam, Admin.
Res.: 350 Hartford Pk., Box 487, 06241-2109. Tel: 860-774-8656; Fax: 860-774-8656.
Catechesis/Religious Program—Students 43.

DURHAM, MIDDLESEX CO., NOTRE DAME (1955), Yoked with St. Colman, Middlefield. Revs. Michael C. Giannitelli; James J. Sucholet; Deacons Peter L. Gill; Ronald Blank.
Res.: 272 Main St., 06422-1611. Tel: 860-349-3058; Fax: 860-349-8949. Email: officendc@comcast.net. Web: www.churchofnotredame.org.
Catechesis/Religious Program—Email: drendc@comcast.net. Kum Cha Soja, D.R.E. Students 366.

EAST HAMPTON, MIDDLESEX CO., ST. PATRICK (1879), (Irish), [CEM] Rev. Walter M. Nagle; Sr. Dominic Joseph Valla, A.S.C.J., Pastoral Assoc.
Res.: 47 W. High St., P.O. Box 177, 06424-0177. Tel: 860-267-6646; Fax: 860-267-7807. Email: stpatrick47@sbcglobal.net. Web: www.saintpatrickeh.org.
Catechesis/Religious Program—Students 384.

EAST LYME, NEW LONDON CO., ST. MATTHIAS (Flanders) (1939) Very Rev. Michael T. Donohue; Deacons Steven Reed; Gerald L. Shaw.
Church: 317 Chesterfield Rd., P.O. Box 25, 06333-0025. Tel: 860-739-5208; Fax: 860-739-0524.
Catechesis/Religious Program—Tel: 860-739-5208; Fax: 860-739-0524. Students 201.

ELLINGTON, TOLLAND CO., ST. LUKE (1961) Revs. Thomas Plathottam, C.S.T.; George Villamthanam, C.S.T.; Deacons Harry Grospitch; Frank Hann.
Rectory—141 Maple St., P.O. Box 246, 06029-0246. Tel: 860-875-8552; Fax: 860-872-6548. Email: stluke_ellington@comcast.net. Web: www.stlukeellington.com.
Church: 139 Maple St., 06029.
Catechesis/Religious Program—Tel: 860-875-4951. Email: stluke_dre@comcast.net. Mrs. Nancy Rudek, D.R.E.; Anthony Littizzio, Youth Min. Students 379.
Convent—St. Luke Convent, 8 Berr Ave., 06029-0246.

ESSEX, MIDDLESEX CO., OUR LADY OF SORROWS (1926) Rev. Paul J. Gaumond; Deacon William Kaiser Jr.
Res.: 14 Prospect St., 06426-1049. Tel: 860-767-1284; Fax: 860-767-7874. Web: www.oloschurch.com.
Catechesis/Religious Program—Tel: 860-767-1074. Students 360.

FISHERS ISLAND, SUFFOLK CO., OUR LADY OF GRACE (1902), (Irish), Rev. Joseph Castaldi, Canonical Pastor.
Res.: Alpine Ave., Box 425, NY 06390-0425. Tel: 631-788-7353; Fax: 631-788-7312. Email: olog@fishersisland.net.
Catechesis/Religious Program—Students 3.

GALES FERRY, NEW LONDON CO., OUR LADY OF LOURDES (1960) Rev. Brian J. Converse; Deacon R. Philip Hayes.
Res.: 1650 Rte. 12, 06335-1534. Tel: 860-464-7251; Fax: 860-464-7252. Email: pastor@ololgf.org. Web: www.ololgf.org.
Catechesis/Religious Program—Tel: 860-464-6676. Email: ffo@ololgf.org. Monika Verebelyi, D.R.E. Students 227.

GROTON, NEW LONDON CO.

1—ST. MARY MOTHER OF THE REDEEMER (1964) Rev. Joseph C. Ashe; Deacons Peter H. Danesi III; Paul Wallen; Douglas A. Hoffman.
Res.: 69 Groton Long Point Rd., 06340. Tel: 860-445-1446; Fax: 860-448-7269. Email: st.marys.top@comcast.net. Web: stmarymr.catholicweb.com.
Catechesis/Religious Program—Tel: 860-448-0529. Mrs. Barbara Simoncini, D.R.E.; Mrs. Theresa Seals, D.R.E. Students 293.

2—SACRED HEART (1905) Rev. Dariusz Dudzik.
Res.: 56 Sacred Heart Dr., 06340-4431. Tel: 860-445-2905; 860-445-6648; Fax: 860-445-6648. Web: www.sacredheartgroton.org.
School—Sacred Heart School, (Grades PreK-8), 50 Sacred Heart Dr., 06340-4431. Tel: 460-445-0611; Fax: 860-448-4999. Mr. Larry Fitzgerald, Prin. Lay Teachers 17; Aides 6; Students 202.
Catechesis/Religious Program—Tel: 860-445-2905, Ext. 12. Students 102.

HEBRON, TOLLAND CO., THE CHURCH OF THE HOLY FAMILY (1987) Rev. Michael S. Smith; Deacon Thomas J. Casey.
Mailing Address: P.O. Box 146, 06248-0146. Tel: 860-228-0096; Fax: 860-228-1629.
Catechesis/Religious Program—Tel: 860-228-0096, Ext. 3. Mrs. Rachel Casey, D.R.E. Students 693.

HIGGANUM, MIDDLESEX CO., ST. PETER (1958) Rev. Jan Swiderski.
Res.: 30 St. Peter Ln., P.O. Box 707, 06441-0707. Tel: 860-345-8018; Fax: 860-345-4067.
Catechesis/Religious Program—Tel: 860-345-4726. Students 202.

JEWETT CITY, NEW LONDON CO., ST. MARY (1870), (Polish), [CEM 2], Yoked with St. Catherine of Siena, Preston & St. Thomas the Apostle, Voluntown. Very Rev. Ted F. Tumicki; Rev. Stephen S. Gulino; Deacons Paul R. Baillargeon; Anthony Dombkowski.
Res.: 34 N. Main St., 06351-2012. Tel: 860-376-2044; Fax: 860-376-5771. Email: stmary.church@snet.net. Web: www.stmaryjc.4lpi.com.
Catechesis/Religious Program—Fax: 860-376-5771. Email: psrstmary@hotmail.com. Students 111.

KILLINGWORTH, MIDDLESEX CO., ST. LAWRENCE (1978) Rev. Joseph F. DeCosta; Deacons John A. Balchus; Robert Ferraro.
Res.: 7 Hemlock Dr., 06419-2227. Tel: 860-663-2576; Fax: 860-663-4238. Email: stlawrencec@yahoo.com. Web: www.stlawrencechurch.com.
Catechesis/Religious Program—Tel: 860-663-2943. Students 188.

LEBANON, NEW LONDON CO., ST. FRANCIS OF ASSISI (1945), Yoked with St. Andrew, Colchester. Revs. Marek Masnicki; Benjamin V. Soosaimanickam; Deacon Michael L. Puscas.
Res.: 67 W. Town St., 06249. Tel: 860-642-6711; Fax: 860-642-4032. Email: stfrancisassisi@catholic.org.
Catechesis/Religious Program—M. James Hay, D.R.E.; Mrs. Joann Hay, Asst. D.R.E. Students 164.

MIDDLEFIELD, MIDDLESEX CO., ST. COLMAN (1890), Yoked with Notre Dame, Durham. Revs. Michael C. Giannitelli; James J. Sucholet; Deacons Ronald Blank; Peter L. Gill.
Res.: 145 Hubbard St., P.O. Box 457, 06455-0457. Tel: 860-349-3868; Fax: 860-349-3150.
Catechesis/Religious Program—Ms. Barbara-Jean DiMauro, D.R.E. Students 184.

MIDDLETOWN, MIDDLESEX CO.

1—ST. FRANCIS OF ASSISI (1903) Rev. Halbert Weidner, C.O. In Res., Rev. George Busto, C.O.
Res.: 10 Elm St., 06457-4427. Tel: 860-347-4684;

Fax: 860-347-7669. Web: saintfrancisofassisi.com.
Catechesis/Religious Program—Tel: 860-347-4684, Ext. 18. Students 40.

2—ST. JOHN (1843) [CEM] Very Rev. Michael L. Phillippino; Deacon John Hancock.
Res.: 19 John's Sq., 06457-2201. Tel: 860-347-5626; Fax: 860-638-3633. Email: stjohnsecretary@comcast.net. Web: www.saintjohnchurchmiddletown.com.
School—Tel: 860-347-3202; Fax: 860-347-3537. Email: bobfritzsjs@yahoo.com. Mr. Robert Fritz, Prin. Lay Teachers 19; Students 165.
Catechesis/Religious Program—Mrs. Kathryn Connelly, D.R.E. Students 58.

3—ST. MARY OF CZESTOCHOWA (1903), (Polish), [CEM] Rev. Richard Sliwinski.
Res.: 79 S. Main St., 06457-3606. Tel: 860-347-2365; Fax: 860-347-2110. Email: stmarymdtln@yahoo.com.
School—87 S. Main St., 06457. Tel: 860-347-2978; Fax: 860-347-7267. Web: www.stmarymiddletown-.com. Mrs. Kathleen Dutil, Prin. Lay Teachers 10; Students 202.
Catechesis/Religious Program—Email: stmarysgift@yahoo.com. Susan Ferriaolo, D.R.E. Students 140.

4—ST. PIUS X (1957) Revs. John Gallagher, O.F.M-.Cap.; Samuel Fuller, O.F.M.Cap.; John Rathschmidt, O.F.M.Cap.; Raynold Thibodeau, O.F.M.Cap.; Bro. Eugene Sheehan, O.F.M.Cap. In Res., Revs. James Hammer, O.F.M.Cap.; Bruce Quinn, O.F.M.Cap. (Retired); Ephrem Karwowski, O.F.M.Cap.; Don Bosco Duquette, O.F.M.Cap. (Retired).
Res.: 310 Westfield St., 06457-2047. Tel: 860-347-4441; 860-347-4442; Fax: 860-347-3001. Email: stpiusfriars@snet.net. Web: www.stpius-x.org.
Catechesis/Religious Program—Tel: 860-346-9100. Carol Butler, C.R.E. (6th-Confirmation); Kimberly Molski, C.R.E. (PreK-5th). Students 497.

5—ST. SEBASTIAN (1930), (Italian), [CEM] Rev. James Thaikoottathil, Admin.
Res.: 155 Washington St., 06457-2800. Tel: 860-347-2638; Fax: 860-347-6736 (Office). Email: church6892@att.net. Web: stsebastianct.org.
Catechesis/Religious Program—Students 164.

MONTVILLE, NEW LONDON CO., ST. JOHN THE EVANGELIST (1881) [CEM], Yoked with Our Lady of Perpetual Help, Quaker Hill & Our Lady of the Lakes, Oakdale. Revs. Joseph B. Whittel; Robert F. Buongirno, Temp. Admin.; Richard D. Breton Jr.; Tadeusz Zadorozny (Poland); Deacons William T. Herrmann; Ronald S. Kitlinski. In Res., Rev. Msgr. Robert L. Brown, Chancellor. Tel: 860-887-9294 (Chancery); 860-848-3771 (Private); Cell: 860-303-6080.
Res.: 22 Maple Ave., Uncasville, 06382-2327. Tel: 860-848-1257; Fax: 860-848-1258. Email: stjhh@sbcglobal.net. Web: www.stjohnsuncasville.com.
Catechesis/Religious Program—Tel: 860-848-1409; Fax: 860-848-1258. Sara Waters, D.R.E. Students 19.

MOODUS, MIDDLESEX CO., ST. BRIDGET OF KILDARE (1914) [CEM] Very Rev. Gregoire J. Fluet.
Res.: 75 Moodus-Leesville Rd., P.O. Box 422, 06469-0422. Tel: 860-873-8623; Fax: 860-873-9407.
Catechesis/Religious Program—Students 281.

MOOSUP, WINDHAM CO., ALL-HALLOWS (1859) [CEM], Yoked with Sacred Heart, Wauregan. Rev. Damian Tomiczek, S.D.S.
Res.: 130 Prospect St., 06354-1499. Tel: 860-564-2668; Fax: 860-564-3941. Email: ahcmoosup@yahoo.com. Web: www.allhallowschurch.weebly.com.
Catechesis/Religious Program—Tel: 860-230-0141. Lisa Krauss, D.R.E. (Grades K-Confirmation). Students 86.

MYSTIC, NEW LONDON CO., ST. PATRICK (1870) [CEM] Rev. Kevin M. Reilly.
Res.: 32 E. Main St., 06355. Tel: 860-536-1800; Fax: 860-572-1513. Email: stpatrickchurch@snet.net.
Catechesis/Religious Program—Tel: 860-536-6808; Fax: 860-572-1513. Susan Waters, D.R.E. & Youth Min. Students 139.

NEW LONDON, NEW LONDON CO.

1—ST. JOSEPH (1907) Revs. Joseph Castaldi; Prodeep Chandra Nayak (India); George Mattathilanickal; Deacon Gerard Gaynor Jr.
Res.: 17 Squire St., 06320-4891. Tel: 860-443-5393; Fax: 860-443-0113.
School—Tel: 860-442-1720; Fax: 860-443-5247. Lay Teachers 10; Students 208.
Catechesis/Religious Program—Students 181.

2—ST. MARY, STAR OF THE SEA (1870) Rev. Robert Washabaugh; Deacons Jesus A. Diez Canseco; Mariano Ramos; Sr. Irma Garcia, R.O.D.A., Pastoral Assoc.; Deborah McCann-Connors, Pastoral Assoc. The Oblate Sisters to Divine Love.
Res.: 10 Huntington St., 06320-6198. Tel: 860-447-1431; Fax: 860-437-1889. Email: information@stmarynewlondon.net. Web: www.stmarynl.org.
School—(1879) 16 Huntington St., 06320. Tel: 860-443-7758; Fax: 860-444-2465. Web: www.stmary-schoolnewlondon.com. Anne Tortora, Prin. Lay Teachers 9; Students 108.
Catechesis/Religious Program—Tel: 860-447-1431; Fax: 860-437-1889. Ms. Alvania Tejera, Youth Min. Students 109.

NIANTIC, NEW LONDON CO., ST. AGNES (1922) [JC] Revs. Mark D. O'Donnell; Tomasz Albrecht, Parochial Vicar; Deacon James Delaney.
Res.: 22 Haigh Ave., 06357-3129. Tel: 860-739-9722; Fax: 860-691-2187. Email: saintagnesparish@sbcglobal.net. Web: www.saintagnescatholicchurch.com.
Catechesis/Religious Program—Tel: 860-739-9992. Email: dre.st.agnes@sbcglobal.net. Rhonda Lundgren, Dir., Faith Formation; Kelsey Doherty, Confirmation Coord. Students 225.
Chapel—Crescent Beach, St. Francis Chapel (Summer) [JC]

NORTH GROSVENORDALE, WINDHAM CO., ST. JOSEPH (1872) [CEM], Yoked with St. Stephen, Quinebaug. Very Rev. Charles R. LeBlanc; Rev. Nicholas Mukama Mbogo, Parochial Vicar.
Res.: 12 Main St., P.O. Box 897, 06255-0897. Tel: 860-923-2361; Fax: 860-923-3396. Email: stjoseph18@sbcglobal.net. Web: stjosephng.4lp1.com.
School—26 Main St., P.O. Box 137, 06255-0897. Tel: 860-923-2090; Fax: 860-923-3609. Mrs. Sharon Briere, Prin. Lay Teachers 18; Students 135.
Catechesis/Religious Program—Students 100.
Mission—Sacred Heart, (Closed)

NORTH STONINGTON, NEW LONDON CO., ST. THOMAS MORE (1967) Rev. V. Antony Alaharasan.
Res.: 87 Mystic Rd., 06359. Tel: 860-535-1601; Fax: 860-535-2828. Email: smchurch01@snet.net.
Catechesis/Religious Program—Fax: 860-535-2828. Michael Lloyd, Dir. Faith Formation. Students 108.

OAKDALE, NEW LONDON CO., OUR LADY OF THE LAKES (1966), Yoked with Our Lady of Perpetual Help, Quaker Hill & St. John the Evangelist Church, Montville. Revs. Joseph B. Whittel; Robert F. Buongirno, Temp. Admin.; Richard D. Breton Jr.; Tadeusz Zadorozny (Poland); Deacons William T. Herrmann; Ronald S. Kitlinski. In Res., Rev. Brian J. Romanowski.
Res.: 752 Norwich-Salem Tpke., 06370. Tel: 860-859-1575; Fax: 860-859-3273. Email: parish.office@snet.net. Web: ourladyofthelakes-oakdale.myownparish.com.
Catechesis/Religious Program—Tel: 860-859-8733. Email: faith.formation@att.net. Students 215.

OCCUM, NEW LONDON CO., ST. JOSEPH (1878) Rev. Augustine Naduvilekoot.
P.O. Box 256, Versailles, 06383.
Res.: 11 Baltic Rd., 06360. Tel: 860-822-8020; Fax: 860-822-8007.
Catechesis/Religious Program—Tel: 860-822-6963. Mrs. Monica Bernier, D.R.E. Students 64.
Saint Society Church— (Corporate Title: St. Joseph Church Society of Occum, CT, Inc.)

OLD LYME, NEW LONDON CO., CHRIST THE KING (1934) Rev. Msgr. Thomas R. Bride; Deacon Julius Periera. In Res., Rev. Thomas W. Ahern (Retired).
Office: 1 McCurdy Rd., 06371-1629. Tel: 860-434-1660 (Rectory); 860-434-1669 (Office); Fax: 860-434-7140. Web: christthekingchurch.net.
Catechesis/Religious Program—Tel: 860-434-9873. Louise Young, D.R.E. Students 275.

OLD SAYBROOK, MIDDLESEX CO., ST. JOHN (1884) [CEM] Revs. Grzegorz P. Brozonowicz; Christopher P. Feeney, Parochial Vicar; Deacon Joseph Giuliano.
Res.: 161 Main St., 06475-2367. Tel: 860-388-3787; Fax: 860-388-6008. Web: www.saintjohnchurchos.com.
School—42 Maynard Rd., 06475. Tel: 860-388-0849; Fax: 860-388-6265. Web: www.saintjohnschoolos.org. Sr. Elaine Moorcroft, S.C.M.C., Prin. Sisters 2; Lay Teachers 15; Students 243.
Catechesis/Religious Program—Sr. Gabriel Fassl, S.C.M.C., D.R.E. Students 225.

PAWCATUCK, NEW LONDON CO., ST. MICHAEL (1861) [CEM 2] Very Rev. Dennis M. Perkins.
Res.: 60 Liberty St., 06379. Tel: 860-599-5580; Fax: 860-599-8079. Email: saint.michael@sbcglobal.net.
School—63 Liberty St., 06379. Tel: 860-599-1084. Doris S. Messina, Prin. Lay Teachers 9; Students 161.
Catechesis/Religious Program—Mrs. Crystal F. Wilcox, D.R.E. Students 281.

PLAINFIELD, WINDHAM CO., ST. JOHN THE APOSTLE (1907) [CEM], Yoked with St. Augustine, Canterbury. Rev. Arul Rajan Peter, Admin.; Deacon Leo N. Bernard.
Res.: 10 Railroad Ave., 06374-1215. Tel: 860-564-3313; Fax: 860-564-3314. Email: stjohnplainfield@ct.metrocast.net.
Catechesis/Religious Program—12 Railroad Ave., 06374. Tel: 860-564-8380. Students 100.

POMFRET, WINDHAM CO., MOST HOLY TRINITY (1886), Yoked with St. Mary Church, Putnam. Revs. David P. Choquette; Anthony J. DiMarco; Deacons Pierre M. Desilets; Jorge Escalona.
Res.: 568 Pomfret St., P.O. Box 235, 06258-0235. Tel: 860-928-5830; Fax: 860-928-4035. Email: mhtoffice@sbcglobal.net. Web: www.mostholytrinitypomfret.parishesonline.com.
Catechesis/Religious Program—Email: lyoungwdstk@hotmail.com. Students 138.

PORTLAND, MIDDLESEX CO., ST. MARY (1872) [CEM] Rev. John F. Ashe; Sisters Mary Ida Dolan, R.S.M., Pastoral Assoc.; Laura Marie Meskill, R.S.M., Pastoral Assoc.; Deacon Dana Garry.
Res.: 51 Freestone Ave., 06480. Tel: 860-342-2328; Fax: 860-342-1433. Email: st.mary.rectory@sbcglobal.net.
Catechesis/Religious Program—Tel: 860-342-2308. Students 443.

PRESTON, NEW LONDON CO., ST. CATHERINE OF SIENA (1975), Yoked with St. Mary, Jewett City & St. Thomas the Apostle, Voluntown. Very Rev. Ted F. Tumicki; Rev. Stephen S. Gulino; Deacons Paul R. Baillargeon; Anthony Dombkowski; Mrs. Nancy Mignault, Pastoral Assoc.
Res.: 243 Rte. 164, 06365-8726. Tel: 860-887-9966; Fax: 860-889-7640.
Catechesis/Religious Program—Students 90.

PUTNAM, WINDHAM CO., ST. MARY CHURCH OF THE VISITATION (1866) [CEM], Yoked with Most Holy Trinity Church, Pomfret. Revs. David Choquette; Anthony DiMarco; Deacons Pierre M. Desilets; Jorge Escalona.
Res.: 218 Providence St., 06260-1514. Tel: 860-928-6535; Fax: 860-928-7246. Email: stmarychurchputnam@snet.net. Web: www.stmaryputnam.org.
Catechesis/Religious Program—15 Marshall St., 06260. Tel: 860-928-2032. Mrs. Carol Paul, Dir. Faith Formation. Students 137.

QUAKER HILL, NEW LONDON CO., OUR LADY OF PERPETUAL HELP (1904), (Polish), Yoked with St. John the Evangelist, Montville & Our Lady of the Lakes, Oakdale. Revs. Joseph B. Whittel; Richard D. Breton Jr.; Tadeusz Zadorozny (Poland); Deacons William T. Herrmann; Ronald S. Kitlinski.
Res.: 63 Old Norwich Rd., P.O. Box 329, 06375-0329. Tel: 860-443-1875; Fax: 860-437-9869. Web: ourladyph.org.
Catechesis/Religious Program—59 Old Norwich Rd., 06375. Tel: 860-447-3550. Sr. Michelle Sokol, S.S.J.-T.O.S.F., D.R.E. Students 60.
Convent—Sisters of St. Joseph of Third Order of St. Francis, 59 Old Norwich Rd., P.O. Box 329, 06375. Tel: 860-447-3550.

QUINEBAUG, WINDHAM CO., ST. STEPHEN (1955), Yoked with St. Joseph, North Grosvenordale. Very Rev. Charles R. LeBlanc; Rev. Richard D. Breton Jr., Parochial Vicar.
Mailing Address: 12 Main St., P.O. Box 897, North Grosvenordale, 06255.
Res.: 130 Old Turnpike Rd., 06262. Tel: 860-923-2361; Fax: 860-923-3396. Email: stjoseph18@sbcglobal.net.
Catechesis/Religious Program—Students 18.

ROCKVILLE, TOLLAND CO.

1—ST. BERNARD (1854) [CEM] Revs. Richard J. Ricard; Dennis J. Mercieri; Deacon Michael Berstene.
Res.: 25 St. Bernard Ter., 06066-3217. Tel: 860-875-0753; Fax: 860-871-7460. Email: rectory@saintbernardchurch.org. Web: www.saintbernardchurch.org.
School—(Grades PreSchool), 20 School St., P.O. Box 177, 06066. Tel: 860-875-0753, Ext. 114; Fax: 860-872-2444. Sherry Yarusewicz, Dir. Preschool. Lay Teachers 2; Students 15.
Catechesis/Religious Program—22 School St., 06066. Email: kimberly@saintbernardchurch.orgTel: 860-875-0753, Ext. 119; Fax: 860-871-9570. Kimberly Manganella, D.R.E. Students 304.
Cemetery Office—

2—ST. JOSEPH (1905), (Polish), Revs. Krysztof Drybka, O.S.P.P.E.; Marcin Mikulski, O.S.P.P.E., Parochial Vicar.
Res.: 33 West St., 06066-6154. Tel: 860-871-1970; Fax: 860-872-0333. Email: info@stjosephct.org. Web: www.rc.net/norwich/st_joseph/.
School—41 West St., 06066. Tel: 860-875-4943; Fax: 860-870-4532. Email: sjs@sjro.org. Mrs. Kathy Peck, Prin. Lay Teachers 11; Students 72.
Catechesis/Religious Program—Students 95.

ROGERS, WINDHAM CO., ST. IGNATIUS (1939) Closed. For inquiries for parish records contact St. Joseph, Dayville.

SOMERSVILLE, TOLLAND CO., ALL SAINTS (1915) Rev. Roland C. Cloutier; Deacons James J. Burgess; Walter B. Williams; John J. Abdalla.
Res.: 25 School St., P.O. Box M, 06072-0913. Tel: 860-749-8625; Fax: 860-763-1890. Email:

alstchurch@yahoo.com. Web: www.somersallsaints.org.
Catechesis/Religious Program—Tel: 860-763-0348. Susan L. King, D.R.E. Students 350.

STAFFORD SPRINGS, TOLLAND CO., ST. EDWARD (1869) [CEM] Revs. Thomas Lavin, O.F.M.Conv.; Jude Surowiec, O.F.M.Conv.; David Kashen, O.F.M.Conv. Mailing Address: 6 Benton St., 06076-0433. Tel: 860-684-2705; Fax: 860-684-0757. Email: stedwardparish@stedward-stafford.org. Web: www.stedward-stafford.org.
Res.: 55 High St., 06076.
School—(Grades PreK-8), 25 Church St., 06076. Tel: 860-684-2600; Fax: 860-684-4030. Maryanne Pelletier, Prin. Lay Teachers 10; Students 106.
Catechesis/Religious Program—Students 231.
Mission—St. Joseph, (Summer Chapel), 6 Benton St., Tolland Co. 06076.

STONINGTON, NEW LONDON CO., ST. MARY (1850) [CEM] Rev. Msgr. Richard P. LaRocque.
Res.: 95 Main St., 06378-1219. Tel: 860-535-1700; Fax: 860-535-3433.
Catechesis/Religious Program—Tel: 860-535-4252. Matthew West, D.R.E. Students 107.

STORRS, TOLLAND CO., ST. THOMAS AQUINAS (1947) Revs. Gregory C. Mullaney; John N. Antonelle, Parochial Vicar; Jane Froglay, Music Dir.; Joanne Cichocki, Business Mgr. In Res., Rev. Gregory P. Galvin, Vocation Dir.
Res.: 46 N. Eagleville Rd., Storrs Mansfield, 06268. Tel: 860-429-6436.
Catechesis/Religious Program—Tel: 860-429-6436; Fax: 860-429-2809. Email: thallesta@yahoo.com. Tammy Halle, D.R.E. Students 100.

TAFTVILLE, NEW LONDON CO., SACRED HEART (1883) Rev. Msgr. Henry N. Archambault. In Res., Rev. William J. Flynn (Retired).
Res.: 156 Providence St., P.O. Box 208, 06380. Tel: 860-887-3072; Fax: 860-204-9338. Email: sacred.heart@sbcglobal.net.
School—15 Hunters Ave., 06380-0208. Tel: 860-887-1757; Fax: 860-889-7276. Email: principal.shta@sacredhearttaftville.org. Web: www.sacredhearttaftville.org. Sr. David Riquier, S.C.M.C., Prin. Sisters of Charity of Our Lady, Mother of the Church 3; Lay Teachers 11; Students 209.
Catechesis/Religious Program—Tel: 860-887-3072. Students 49.

TOLLAND, TOLLAND CO., ST. MATTHEW (1964) Very Rev. James P. Carini; Deacon Ronald Freedman. Mailing Address: P.O. Box 100, 06084-0100. Tel: 860-872-0200; Fax: 860-875-4413. Email: parishoffice@stmatthewct.org. Web: www.stmatthewct.org. In Res., Rev. William J. Olesik.
Catechesis/Religious Program—Email: faithformation@stmatthewct.org. Mrs. Cynthia Yaconiello, D.R.E. (Grades K-6); Mrs. Bridget Thurston, Youth Min. (Grades 7-12); Mrs. Ann Marie Galdau, Dir. (Preschool). Students 674.

VERNON, TOLLAND CO., SACRED HEART (1958) [JC] Rev. Stanley J. Szczapa; Mrs. Rella Bernabucci, Pastoral Asst.; Ernest Golnik, Liturgy and Music Dir.; Deacon Lawrence W. Deraleau.
Church: 550 Hartford Tpke., 06066-5000. Tel: 860-875-4563; Fax: 860-872-2535. Email: info@sacredheartchurch.net. Web: www.sacredheartchurch.net.
Catechesis/Religious Program—Students 86.

VOLUNTOWN, NEW LONDON CO., ST. THOMAS THE APOSTLE (1892) [CEM], Yoked with St. Mary, Jewett City & St. Catherine of Siena, Preston. Very Rev. Ted F. Tumicki; Rev. Stephen S. Gulino; Deacons Paul R. Baillargeon; Anthony Dombkowski.
Res.: 61 Preston City Rd., P.O. Box 99, 06384-0099. Tel: 860-376-2293; Fax: 860-376-0287. Web: www.stthomasvoluntown.org.
Catechesis/Religious Program—49 Preston City Rd., 06384. Tel: 860-376-8352. Cathy Becotte, D.R.E. Tel: 860-376-8665. Students 42.
Mission—St. Anne (1891) Rte. 201, Glasgo, New London Co.

WATERFORD, NEW LONDON CO., ST. PAUL (1960) Rev. Dennis G. Carey; Deacon Richard K. Walker.
Res.: 170 Rope Ferry Rd., 06385-2609. Tel: 860-443-5587; Fax: 860-442-9308. Email: stpaulwtfd@sbcglobal.net.
Catechesis/Religious Program—Tel: 860-443-3375. Mrs. Roseann Ward, C.R.E. Students 207.

WAUREGAN, WINDHAM CO., SACRED HEART (1889), (French), [CEM], Yoked with All Hallows, Moosup. Rev. Damian Tomiczek, S.D.S.
Res.: 620 Wauregan Rd., P.O. Box 468, 06387-0468. Tel: 860-564-2668; Fax: 860-564-3941. Email: shcbulletinnews@hotmail.com.
Catechesis/Religious Program—120 Prospect St., Moosup, 06354.

WEST WILLINGTON, TOLLAND CO., ST. JUDE (1981), Yoked with St. Philip, Ashford. Rev. Russell F. Kennedy, Admin.; Deacon Christopher Deskus.
Res.: 25 Old Farms Rd., P.O. Box 240, Willington, 06279-0240. Tel: 860-429-9655; Fax: 860-429-9655. Email: church7227@scbglobal.net. Web: www.saintphilipsaintjude.org.
Catechesis/Religious Program—Tel: 860-429-8604. Muriel J. Goble, D.R.E. Students 64.

WESTBROOK, MIDDLESEX CO., ST. MARK (1962) Rev. Peter B. Liszewski; Deacon Thomas E. Rymut.
Res.: 222 McVeagh Rd., 06498-1512. Tel: 860-399-9207; Fax: 860-399-7751.
Catechesis/Religious Program—Tel: 860-399-6208. Students 253.

WILLIMANTIC, WINDHAM CO.

1—ST. JOSEPH (1859) [CEM] Very Rev. Laurence A.M. LaPointe; Revs. George J. Richards Jr.; Luis Henry Agudelo; Deacon Lawrence Goodwin.
Res.: 99 Jackson St., 06226-3077. Tel: 860-423-8439; Fax: 860-423-6825. Email: stjosephwillimantic@gmail.com.
School—St. Mary-St. Joseph, 35 Valley St., 06226. Tel: 860-423-8479; Fax: 860-423-8365. Sr. Mary Mark Orsulak, S.C.M.C., Prin.
Catechesis/Religious Program—Students 206.
Convent—88 Jackson St., 06226. Tel: 860-423-5122.
Mission—St. Margaret Rte. 14, Scotland, Windham Co. 06264. Tel: 203-423-1791.

2—ST. MARY (1903), (French), Rev. Roger J. Lamoureux, O.M.I.
Res. & Parish Center: 80 Maple Ave., 06226-2733. Tel: 860-423-5835; Fax: 860-423-9933. Email: stmary06226@charter.net. Web: stmarywillimantic.4lpi.com.
Church: 46 Valley St., 06226-2733.
School—St. Mary-St. Joseph, 35 Valley St., 06226. Tel: 860-423-8479; Fax: 860-423-8365. Email: smsj@charterinternet.com. Web: www.sm-sjschool.org. Sr. Mary Mark Orsulak, S.C.M.C., Prin. Sisters 2; Lay Teachers 14; Students 173.
Catechesis/Religious Program—Tel: 860-423-9700. Students 25.
Convent—Sisters of Charity of Our Lady, 88 Jackson St., 06226. Tel: 860-423-5122.
Faith Formulation—Tel: 860-423-9700.

WINDHAM, WINDHAM CO., SAGRADO CORAZON DE JESUS (1991), (Hispanic), Rev. Paul J. Murdock; Sr. Francisca Candelaria, R.O.D.A., Pastoral Assoc.; Deacon Felipe Silva; Mrs. Virginia Rodriguez, Pastoral Assoc.
Mailing Address: 61 Club Rd., 06280-1007. Tel: 860-423-8617; Fax: 860-423-4157. Email: sagradocor@sbcglobal.net.
Catechesis/Religious Program—Students 129.

Chaplains of Public Institutions

NORWICH. *William W. Backus Hospital* 06360. Tel: 860-889-8331. Sr. Rita Johnson, S.S.N.D., Dir., Ministry to Sick.

GROTON. *U.S. Submarine Base-New London* 06349-5013. Tel: 860-694-3232. Rev. Thomas F.X. Hoar, S.S.E., Chap.

MIDDLETOWN. *Connecticut Valley Hospital*, Eastern Dr., P.O. Box 351, 06457. Tel: 860-262-5900; Fax: 860-262-5900. Deacon Peter L. Gill, Chap.
Middlesex Memorial Hospital, 28 Crescent St., 06457-0822. Tel: 860-347-9471, Ext. 6725. Rev. George Busto, C.O., Chap.

NEW LONDON. *Lawrence and Memorial Hospitals*, 365 Montauk Ave., 06320. Tel: 860-442-0711, Ext. 2609. Deacon William H. McGann.
U.S. Coast Guard Memorial Chapel, U.S. Coast Guard Academy, 15 Mohegan Ave., 06320-4195. Tel: 860-444-8482; Fax: 960-701-6729. Rev. Daniel Mode, Lieutenant, L.C.D.R., C.H.C., U.S.N.

On Duty Outside the Diocese:
Rev. Msgr.—
Randall, Kevin S., 3339 Massachusetts Ave., N.W., Washington, DC 20008-3687.
Revs.—
Angelo, Thomas M.
Boudreau, C. Paul
Caiazzo, Nicholas
Gwudz, John S.
Maltese, James L., Parish of Saints Philip and James, 1 Carow Pl, St. James, NY 11780.
Martin, Patrick A., P.O. Box 16, Stafford Springs, 06076.
Romanowski, Brian J.
Rouleau, Francis C.
Smith, Thomas J.

Military Chaplains:
Rev.—
Angelo, Thomas M., Ch. Capt., 23 Wg/MC, Pope AFB, NC 28308.

Absent on Leave:
Revs.—
Bolieau, Henry G.
Dempsey, Edward M., D.B.A., 75 Bushnell St., Hartford, 06114.
Rweyemamu, Justinian B.
Schuh, Karl Christopher
Sennik, Thomas W.
Valliere, Timothy C.

Retired:
Rev. Msgrs.—
Malanowski, Thaddeus F., Queen of the Clergy Residence, 274 Strawberry Hill Ave #205, Stamford, 06902.
West, Willis W.
Revs.—
Ahern, Thomas W.
Almendra, Leoncio T.
Archer, Arthur
Cronin, Robert W., 275 Steel Rd., Apt. B118, West Hartford, 06107.
Drummond, Elsyn J.
Finnerty, Joseph G.
Flynn, William J.
Giaquinto, Albert C., St. Charles Villa, 603 Maiden Choice Ln., Baltimore, MD 21228.
Gruber, Anthony P.
Konopka, Edward M.
LeCours, Sylva P., 40 Hartford Pike, Dayville, 06241.
Liszewski, Francis A.
Marciniak, John, 70 W. 18th Rd., Broad Channel, NY 11693.
McCorry, Patrick G.
McGrail, Charles A., 468 Main St., Apt. 218, Niantic, 06357.
McKenna, Frank W.
McNulty, Robert E., 65 Beach St., P.O. Box 356, Green Harbor, MA 02041.
McNulty, William J., 66 Brown St., Hamden, 06518.
Nichols, Joseph E., Cathedral of St. Patrick, 213 Broadway, 06360.
Pupsys, Adam, 89 Mill Rock Rd., E., Old Saybrook, 06475.
Ramen, Paul F., 350 Pond Hill Rd., Moosup, 06354. Tel: 860-887-2565
Wisneski, Edward, S.T.D., Ph.D., 78 E. Ridge Rd., Middletown, 06457.

Permanent Deacons:
Abdalla, John, (Retired)
Bachand, Francis J., (Retired)
Baillargeon, Paul R., St. Mary, Jewett City; St. Catherine of Siena, Preston & St. Thomas the Apostle, Voluntown
Balchus, John A., St. Lawrence, Killingworth
Barbeau, Rene N., Jr., St. James, Danielson
Barlow, Robert C., St. Andrew, Colchester
Bernard, Leo N., (Retired)
Berstene, Michael C., Diocesan Dir. of Deacon Personnel, St. Bernard, Rockville
Blank, Ronald E., Notre Dame, Durham; St. Coleman, Middlefield
Burgess, James J., All Saints, Somersville
Burke, John J., Jr., Flat Rock, NC
Cannata, Nicholas J., (Retired)
Cartier, L. Roger, Pinellas Park, FL
Casey, Thomas J., Church of the Holy Family, Hebron
Cortese, Benjamin, St. Joseph, Rockville
Cote, Albert J., (Retired)
Cyr, Warren, Prison Ministry, Niantic
Danesi, Peter H., III, St. Mary, Groton
Delaney, James, St. Agnes, Niantic
Deraleau, Lawrence W., Sacred Heart, Vernon
Desilets, Pierre M., St. Mary, Putnam; Most Holy Trinity, Pomfret
Deskus, Christopher, St. Juse, Willington
Diez Conseco, Jesus A., St. Mary, Hispanic Apostolate, New London
Dolan, Dennis F., Prison Ministry, Niantic
Dombkowski, Anthony, St. Mary, Jewett City; St. Catherine of Siena, Preston & St. Thomas the Apostle, Voluntown
Doyle, Dennis A., III, SS. Peter & Paul, Norwich
Escalona, Jorge, Most Holy Trinity, Pomfret
Fecteau, Al R., (Retired)
Ferraro, Robert, St. Lawrence, Killingworth
Freedman, Ronald, St. Matthew, Tolland
Garry, Dana, St. Mary, Portland
Gaynor, Gerard J., Saint Joseph, New London
Gill, Peter L., St. Colman, Middlefield; Notre Dame, Durham
Giuliano, Joseph, St. John, Old Saybrook
Goodwin, Lawrence M., St. Joseph, Williamantic; St. Margaret Mission, Scotland
Grospitch, Harry J., St. Luke, Ellington
Hancock, John, St. John, Middletown
Hann, Frank, St. Luke, Ellington
Hayes, Robert P., Our Lady of Lourdes, Gales Ferry
Herrmann, William, Our Lady of Lakes, Oakdale; St. John the Evangelist, Montville & Our Lady of Perpetual Help, Quaker Hill
Hoffman, Douglas A., St. Mary, Groton

Jolin, Joseph, North Fort Meyers, FL
Kaiser, William, Jr., Our Lady of Sorrows, Essex
King, Mark J., Waxhaw, NC
Kitlinski, Ronald S., Our Lady Perpetual Help, Quaker Hill; St. John the Evangelist, Montville & Our Lady of the Lakes, Oakdale
LaCasse, Roland J., (Retired)
LaPlante, Joseph A., Southwest Harbor, ME
Lewis, Thomas A., St. Joseph, Norwich
Marshall, Timothy M., St. Augustine, Canterbury
McGann, William H., Our Lady of Lourdes, Gales Ferry
McMahon, James R., Sr., Spring Hill, FL
Melendez, Carlos, Port St. Lucie, FL
Moneypenny, Lawrence, St. Joseph, Chester
Nygaard, Melvin G., St. John, Uncasville
O'Reilly, Henry E., (Retired)
Osuba, Jose, Columbia
Pereira, Julias A., Christ the King, Old Lyme
Phaneuf, Bernard A., St. Mary, Putnam
Puscas, Michael L., St. Francis of Assisi, Lebanon; St. Andrew, Colchester
Ramos, Mariano, St. Mary, New London
Reed, Steven W., St. Matthias, East Lyme
Rymut, Thomas E., St. Mark, Westbrook
Shaw, Gerald L., St. Matthias, East Lyme
Silva, Felipe, Sagrado Corazon de Jesus, Windham
Sinclair, Wayne, Sacred Heart, Norwichtown
Tynan, Thomas M., Alexandria, VA
Walker, Richard K.
Wallen, Paul A., (Retired)
Weber, F. Paul, St. Mary of the Visitation, Clinton
Williams, Walter B., All Saints, Somersville
Young, David G., Monica, CA

INSTITUTIONS LOCATED IN THE DIOCESE

[A] SEMINARIES, RELIGIOUS OR SCHOLASTICATES

CROMWELL. *Holy Apostles College and Seminary* (1956) 33 Prospect Hill Rd., 06416-2005. Tel: 860-632-3010; 860-632-3012 (Admissions); Fax: 860-632-3030. Email: rector@holyapostles.edu. Web: www.holyapostles.edu. Rev. Msgrs. David Q. Liptak (HRT); James Turro; Very Revs. Douglas L. Mosey, C.S.B., Ph.D., Pres. & Rector; Gregoire J. Fluet, Ph.D., V.F., K.H.S., Vice Pres.; Addison Hallock, M.S.A., Spiritual Dir.; Revs. Michel Legault, M.S.A.; Bradley Pierce, M.S.A.; Ronan P. Callahan, C.P.; Luis Luna, M.S.A.; David Zercie, M.S.A.; Jude Surowiec, O.F.M.Conv.; John Hillier, Vice Rector; Dominic Anaeto, Ph.D.; Sr. Mary Anne Linder, F.S.E., Dir. Field Educ.; Dr. Cynthia Toolin, Registrar; Mr. William J. Russell, CPA, D.F.O., Finance Officer; Clare Adamo, M.S.L.S., Library Dir. Priests 19; Brothers 2; Sisters 3; Lay Teachers 11; Seminarians 83; College Division Lay Students 288.

[B] HIGH SCHOOLS, DIOCESAN

MIDDLETOWN. *Mercy High School* (1963) 1740 Randolph Rd., 06457-5155. Tel: 860-346-6659; Fax: 860-344-9887. Email: info@mercyhigh.com. Web: www.mercyhigh.com. Sr. Mary A. McCarthy, R.S.M., Prin.; Mrs. Virginia Sullivan, Vice Prin. Student Life; Mrs. Diane Santostefano, Dir. Admissions; Mrs. Marie Leary, Dir., Communications; Mr. Steven Brickey, Vice Prin. Academics; Sr. Peggy O'Neill, R.S.M., Registrar; Miss Ann Derbacher, Campus Min.; Mrs. Patricia Boothroyd, Librarian. Sisters 7; Lay Teachers 63; Students 670; Total Staff 87.

Xavier High School (1963) 181 Randolph Rd., 06457-5635. Tel: 860-346-7735; Fax: 860-346-6859. Email: djaskot@xavierhighschool.org. Web: www.xavierhighschool.org. Bro. Brian Davis, C.F.X., Headmaster; Mr. Nicholas Cerreta, Dean, Students; Mr. Brendan Donohue, Prin.; Mr. Andrew T. Gargano, Academic Dean; Mr. Peter Langevin, Dean Faculty Formation; Mr. David Sizemore, Academic Dean. Brothers of St. Francis Xavier. Brothers 6; Lay Teachers 65; Students 875.

UNCASVILLE. *Saint Bernard School*, 1593 Norwich-New London Tpke., 06382-1399. Tel: 860-848-1271; Fax: 860-848-1274. Email: info@saint-bernard.com. Web: www.saint-bernard.com. Mr. Thomas J. Doherty III, Headmaster. Tel: 860-848-1271, Ext. 146; Rev. Kevin M. Reilly, Chap.

Grades 6-12 Tel: 860-848-1271, Ext. 146 (Prin.); Fax: 860-848-1274. Mrs. Mary C. Dillman, Asst. Headmaster.

[C] HIGH SCHOOLS, PRIVATE

BALTIC. *Academy of the Holy Family* (1874) 54 W. Main St., P.O. Box 691, 06330-0691. Tel: 860-822-9272; Fax: 860-822-1318. Email: principal@ahfbaltic.org. Web: www.ahfbaltic.org. Sr. Mary Loreto Beckstein, S.C.M.C., Prin.; Barbara Gozzo, Librarian. Sisters of Charity of Our Lady Mother of the Church. Sisters 6; Lay Teachers 7; Students 61.

THOMPSON. *Marianapolis Preparatory School*, P.O. Box 304, 06277-0304. Tel: 860-923-9565; Fax: 860-923-3730. Email: mebbitt@marianapolis.org. Web: www.marianapolis.org. Mr. Joseph C. Hanrahan, Headmaster; Rev. Timothy Roth, M.I.C., Chap.; Douglas Daniels, Chief Fin. Operating Officer; Ms. Cheryl Wakely, Librarian. Priests 1; Lay Teachers 41; Students 340.

Congregation of Marians of the Immaculate Conception, P.O. Box 368, 06277-0368. Tel: 860-923-2220; Fax: 860-923-1884. Rev. John Petrauskas, M.I.C.

[D] CHILDREN, RESIDENTIAL CARE FOR

DEEP RIVER. *Mount St. John*, 135 Kirtland St., 06417-1816. Tel: 860-343-1340; Fax: 860-343-1394. Email: decerbod@mtstjohn.org; mckenneyv@mtstjohn.org. Web: www.mtstjohn.org. Mr. Douglas DeCerbo, Exec. Dir.; Mrs. Kathy White, Prin. Boys 32; Bed Capacity 32; Total Assisted Annually 85; Lay Staff 116; Total Staff 116.

[E] HOMES FOR AGED

WINDHAM. *St. Joseph Living Center* (1988) 14 Club Rd., 06280-1000. Tel: 860-456-1107; Fax: 860-450-7114. Email: liverson@wcmh.org. Geralyn Hines-Iversen, Admin.; Dr. Stephen J. Leach, Medical Dir.; Patricia Duffy, R.N., Dir. Nursing Svcs.; Valerie Oliver, R.N., Admissions Coord. & Case Mgr.; Paula Haney, R.P.T., Dir. Rehabilitation Svcs. Sisters 8; Capacity 120; Total Assisted 120; Lay Staff 200; Total Staff 210.

[F] SPECIAL CARE FACILITIES

WILLIMANTIC. *Holy Family Home and Shelter, Inc.*, 88 Jackson St., P.O. Box 884, 06226-0884. Tel: 860-423-7719; Fax: 860-423-3770. Email: sisterpeter@holyfamilywillimantic.org. Web: www.holyfamilywillimantic.org. Bonnie Reilein, Exec. Dir. Email: bonnie@holyfamilywillimantic.org; Sr. M. Peter Bernard, S.C.M.C., Dir. Public Rels. Total Staff 15; Bed Capacity 32; Residents 32; Total Assisted 175.

[G] MONASTERIES AND RESIDENCES OF PRIESTS AND BROTHERS

CROMWELL. *Society of the Missionaries of the Holy Apostles* (1956) 22 Prospect Hill Rd., 06416-2005. Tel: 860-632-3039; Fax: 866-344-8134 (Internal Fax). Rev. Edward C. Doherty, M.S.A.; Very Rev. Addison Hallock, M.S.A., Prov. Supr.; Revs. Daniel Karempelis, M.S.A.; Michael LeGault, M.S.A., Prof.; Barrera Luna, M.S.A., Prof.; William McCarthy, M.S.A.; Bradley Pierce, M.S.A.; George Realmuto, M.S.A.; Robert Sickler, M.S.A.; Thomas Simon, M.S.A.; Richard Skarbek, M.S.A.; Pasquale Taliercio, M.S.A. Society of the Missionaries of the Holy Apostles.

Working Outside the Diocese: Revs. James Anderson, M.S.A.; Robert Anello, M.S.A.; Charles Bak, M.S.A.; Patrick Biegler, M.S.A.; J. Patrick Boyhan, M.S.A.; William Broome, M.S.A.; Robert Burk, M.S.A.; James Downs, M.S.A.; Harold Dunn, M.S.A.; Francis Fajella, M.S.A.; Stanley Grove, M.S.A.; Richard Hite, M.S.A.; Vincent Kilidjian, M.S.A.; Benedict Klucinec, M.S.A.; Peter Kucer, M.S.A.; John R. Lyons, M.S.A.; Michael Nofi, M.S.A.; Gerard Petta, M.S.A.; Laurence Preston, M.S.A.; Edward Przygocki, M.S.A.; Martin Rooney, M.S.A.; Vincent Salamoni, M.S.A.; Jose Salazar, M.S.A.; David Zercie, M.S.A.

GRISWOLD. *Marian Friary of Our Lady of Guadalupe*, 199 Colonel Brown Rd., 06351. Tel: 860-376-6840; Fax: 860-376-6848. Email: friars@figuadalupe.com. Web: www.figuadalupe.com. Revs. Angelo Mary Geiger, F.I., American Supr.; Dominic Savio Mary Murphy, F.I., Guardian, Novice Master; Bonaventure M. McGuire, F.I., Vicar; Friars Augustine M. Arts, F.I.; Roderic Mary Burke, F.I.; Peter Mary Cloonan; Didacus Mary Cortes, F.I.; Joseph Mary Jakopac, F.I.; Jude Mary McFeely, F.I.; Camillo Mary Flannery; John Mary Nguyen; Alphonsus Mary Timossi, F.I. Brothers 4; Priests 3; Novices 4.

MIDDLETOWN. *Congregation of the Brothers of St. Francis Xavier*, 181 Randolph Rd., 06457-5635. Tel: 860-346-8585; Fax: 860-346-6859. Bros. Brian Davis, C.F.X., Headmaster & Dir.; Eugene Behenna, C.F.X.; Labre Dillon, C.F.X.; Thomas Fahey, C.F.X.; J. Robert Houlihan, C.F.X.; Thomas Ryan, C.F.X.; John Sullivan, C.F.X. Total in Residence 7.

THOMPSON. *Marian Fathers* (1673) Marianapolis Prep School, 06277-0368. Tel: 860-923-2220; Fax: 860-923-1194. Email: aragon1948@yahoo.com; troth@marianapolis.org. P.O. Box 368, 06277-0368. Email: bromicl@aol.com; aragon1984@yahoo.com. Rev. Timothy Roth, M.I.C., Supr. & Prov. Council & Prov. Sec.; Bros. Donald Schaefer, M.I.C., Second Councilor; Brian Manian, M.I.C., First Councilor & Fourth Prov. Councilor; Revs. John Petrauskas, M.I.C.; Bernard Backiel, M.I.C., Second Councilor. Total in Residence 5. Bros. & Priests Elsewhere Revs. John Duoba, M.I.C.; Victor Rimselis, M.I.C. In Res. Rev. Jerome Zalonis, M.I.C.

WILLIMANTIC. *Missionary Oblates of Mary Immaculate*, 289 Windham Rd., P.O. Box 55, 06226-0055. Tel: 860-423-8484; Fax: 860-456-5583. Revs. John W. Hanley, O.M.I., Dir., Retreat House; Roger Couture, O.M.I.; Salvador Gonzalez, O.M.I., Dir. & Supr. of the Community; Ronald Meyer, O.M.I.; Bro. Richard Cote, O.M.I. Total in Residence 6; Total Staff 12.

[H] CONVENTS AND RESIDENCES FOR SISTERS

NORWICH. *School Sisters Notre Dame*, 7 Otis St., 06360. Tel: 860-886-6948.

BALTIC. *Holy Family Motherhouse*, 54 W. Main St., 06330-0691. Tel: 860-822-8241; Fax: 860-822-9842. Email: academythe@sbcglobal.net. Web: www.sistersofcharity.com. Sr. M. Anthony, Supr. Gen. Sisters of Charity of Our Lady, Mother of the Church. Professed 59; Junior Professed 2; Novices 1.

Sacred Heart Educational Center-Tutoring Tel: 860-822-6508. Sr. M. Mercedes, Admin.

GROTON. *Society of the Sisters for the Church*, 45 Nicholas Ave., 06340-5024. Tel: 860-445-7258 (Home).

HIGGANUM. *Apostles of the Sacred Heart of Jesus* (1894) Sacred Heart on the Lake, 529 Brainard Hill Rd., 06441-4010. Tel: 860-345-4653; Fax: 860-345-4469. Total in Residence 3.

MIDDLETOWN. *Daughters of Our Lady of the Garden* (1829) Convent and Nursery School., 67 Round Hill Rd., 06457-6119. Tel: 806-346-5765; Fax: 806-346-6361. Sr. Donna Beauregard, F.M.H., Supr.Web: www.sistersolg.org. Total Assisted 82; Total Staff 9.

Sisters of Mercy of the Americas, Northeast Community, 421 High St., 06457. Tel: 860-346-6619. Email: RTGarneau@aol.com. Other residences located in Middletown, Norwich, Portland & Preston Sisters 2.

PUTNAM. *Holy Spirit Provincial House*, 72 Church St., 06260-1810. Tel: 860-928-0891; Fax: 860-928-6496. Sr. Norma Bourdon, D.H.S., Prov.; Rev. Richard L. Archambault, Chap. Daughters of the Holy Spirit. Sisters 56.

Other Locations: *Notre Dame Convent*, 4 Ravine St., 06260. Tel: 860-928-6163. *Provincialate Community*, 31 Ravine St., 06260. Tel: 860-928-7072; 860-928-3882. *All Hallows Convent*, 152 Prospect St., Moosup, 06354. Tel: 860-564-5409.

499 Church St., 06260. Tel: 860-963-0311.

218 Woodstock Ave., Apt. 8, 06260. Tel: 860-928-5894.

70 Proulx St., Apt. C13, Brooklyn, 06234. Tel: 860-779-1291.

Immaculate Conception Convent, Spiritual Renewal Center, 600 Liberty Hwy., 06260-2503. Tel: 860-928-7955; Fax: 860-928-1930. Sr. Igne Marijosius, M.V.S., Prov. Supr. Sisters of the Immaculate Conception of the Blessed Virgin Mary 5; Total in Residence 6; Total Staff 10.

Matulaitis Nursing Home Inc., 10 Thurber Rd., 06260-2522. Tel: 860-928-7976; Fax: 860-963-2378. Email: mnhadm@yahoo.com. Web: matulaitisnh.org. Jane Logan, Admin.; Rev. Izydor Sadowski, S.D.B., Chap. Sisters of the Immaculate Conception of the Blessed Virgin Mary. Sisters 3; Residents 119.

Provincialate Community of the Daughters of the Holy Spirit, 31 Ravine St., 06260-1817. Tel: 860-928-7072. Web: www.fillesstesprit.org. Sisters Norma Bourdon, D.H.S., Prov. Tel: 860-928-7072; Bonnie Morrow, D.H.S., Prov. Councillor & Treas. Tel: 860-928-3882.

WILLIMANTIC. *Sisters of Charity of Our Lady, Mother of the Church*, St. Joseph Convent, 88 Jackson St., 06226. Tel: 860-423-5122. Total in Residence 3; Total Staff 3.

[I] RETREAT HOUSES

NORWICH. *Ministry of His Able People*, 201 Broadway, 06360-4328. Tel: 860-887-9294, Ext. 100.

MYSTIC. *St. Edmund's Retreat, Enders Island*, P.O. Box 399, 06355-0399. Tel: 860-536-0565; Fax: 860-572-7655. Email: admin@endersisland.com. Web: www.endersisland.com. Rev. Thomas F.X. Hoar, S.S.E., Pres.; Mr. Jeffrey J. Anderson, Exec. Dir.; Mrs. Claire St. Clair, Finance Dept.; John J.

Foley II, Chair of Board of Trustees; Robert Wilson, Chair Finance Committee. Total in Residence 1; Total Staff 20.

WILLIMANTIC. *Immaculata Retreat House*, 289 Windham Rd., P.O. Box 55, 06226-0055. Tel: 860-423-8484; Fax: 860-423-5285. Email: immaculata@omict.org. Web: www.immaculataretreat.org. Revs. Roger Couture, O.M.I.; Salvador Gonzalez, O.M.I., Supr.; John W. Hanley, O.M.I., Dir.; Ronald Meyer, O.M.I.; Bro. Richard Cote, O.M.I. Missionary Oblates of Mary Immaculate: U.S. Province. Total in Residence 5; Total Staff 12.

[J] SECULAR INSTITUTES

WINDHAM. *Secular Branch of the Daughters of the Holy Spirit* (2003) 80 Tuckie Rd., 06280. Tel: 860-456-2778. Email: conssecdhs@aol.com. Jane F. Houtman, Consecrated Secular, D.H.S., Regl. Mod.

[K] CAMPUS MINISTRY

WILLIMANTIC. *Campus Ministry* , Eastern Connecticut State University, Newman Hall., 290 Prospect St., 06226. Tel: 860-423-0856; Fax: 860-456-8083. Email: lapointel@easternct.edu. Web: www.norwichdiocese.org. Very Rev. Laurence A.M. LaPointe, Diocesan Dir. Campus Ministry.

Wesleyan University-The University Ministry Office of the University Chaplains, 171 Church St., Middletown, 06459-3625. Tel: 860-685-2277; Fax: 860-685-2821. Rev. Halbert Weidner, C.O., College Chap.

Connecticut College Harkness Chapel, 270 Mohegan Ave., New London, 06320-4196. Tel: 860-439-2452; Fax: 860-439-2463. Email: lalap@conncoll.edu; lapointel@easternet.edu. Very Rev. Laurence A.M. LaPointe, College Chap.

University of Connecticut St. Thomas Aquinas Chapel, 46 N. Eagleville Rd., Storrs, 06268-1710. Tel: 860-429-6436; Fax: 860-429-2809. Email: stthoffice@worldnet.att.net. Revs. Gregory C. Mullaney; John N. Antonelle, Chap. In Res. Rev. Gregory P. Galvin.

[L] MISCELLANEOUS

NORWICH. *The Annual Catholic Appeal of the Diocese of Norwich, Inc.*, 197 Broadway, 06360. Tel: 860-886-1928; Fax: 860-886-2651. Email: dod@norwichdiocese.net. Web: www.norwichdiocesedevelopment.org. Mrs. Angela Arnold, Exec. Dir.

The Catholic Foundation of the Diocese of Norwich, Inc., 197 Broadway, 06360. Tel: 860-886-1928, Ext. 14; Fax: 860-886-2651. Email: dod@norwichdiocese.net. Web: www.norwichdiocesedevelopment.org. Mrs. Angela Arnold, Exec. Dir.

Diocese of Norwich Assisted Living Services, Inc., 201 Broadway, 06360-4480. Tel: 860-887-9294; Fax: 860-886-1670.

The Donor Advised Funds of the Diocese of Norwich, Inc., 201 Broadway, 06360. Tel: 860-887-9294; Fax: 860-886-1670.

CROMWELL. *Basilian Fathers of Connecticut, Inc.* (1987) 33 Prospect Hill Rd., 06416. Tel: 860-632-3010; Fax: 860-632-3030. Email: fr_mosey@juno.com. Very Rev. Douglas L. Mosey, C.S.B., Ph.D., Pres. & Rector.

Marian Housing Corporation, 201 Broadway, 06360-4328. Tel: 860-632-1688; 860-859-0527; Fax: 860-889-2978.

DEEP RIVER. *Edmund Rice Charitable Foundation, Inc.*, 135 Kirtland St., 06417. Tel: 860-343-1340; Fax: 860-343-1394. Email: decerbod@mtstjohn.org.

Mount Saint John Foundation for Charitable Works, Inc., 135 Kirtland St., 06417. Tel: 860-343-1300; Fax: 860-343-1394. Email: decerbod@mtstjohn.org.

MIDDLETOWN. *Mercy Alumnae and Development Office*, 1740 Randolph Rd., 06457. Tel: 860-347-8957; Fax: 860-344-9887. Email: bmiller@mercyhigh.com. Web: www.mercyhigh.com. Barbara P. Miller, Dir. Alumnae & Devel.

Mercy-Xavier Fund Corporation, 181 Randolph Rd., 06457. Tel: 860-346-7735; Fax: 860-346-6859.

Xavier Advancement Office, 181 Randolph Rd., 06457. Tel: 860-347-6079; Fax: 860-346-6859. Email: advancement@xavierhighschool.org. Web: www.xavierhighschool.org. Mr. Michael Tommasi, Dir.; Mr. Joseph E. Lane, Asst. Devel. Office; Mr. John Guerin, Communications Dir. Total Staff 4.

MYSTIC. *St. Edmund's of Connecticut, Inc.*, P.O. Box 399, 06355-0399. Tel: 860-536-0565; Fax: 860-572-7655. Email: admin@endersisland.com. Web: www.endersisland.com. Most Revs. Michael Richard Cote, D.D., Pres.; Thomas Tobin; Very Rev. Michael Cronogue, S.S.E., Supr. General; Rev. Thomas F.X. Hoar, S.S.E., Sec.

PUTNAM. *The Daughters of the Holy Spirit Charitable Trust* (1985) 72 Church St., 06260-1810. Tel: 860-928-0891; Fax: 860-928-6496. Email: bmorrow@snet.net. Sr. Bonnie Morrow, Trustee & Contact Person.

The Holy Spirit Health Care Center, Inc., 72 Church St., 06260. Tel: 860-928-0891; Fax: 860-928-1312. Sr. Norma Bourdon, D.H.S., Prov. & Contact Person; Mr. Gary Spieker, Admin.

WILLIMANTIC. *Saint Joseph's Home for the Aged, Inc.* (1991) 88 Jackson St., 06226. Tel: 860-887-9294; Fax: 860-885-1512. Email: dfo@norwichdiocese.net.

WINDHAM. *Sagrado Corazon de Jesus, Inc. of Windham*, 61 Club Rd., 06280. Tel: 860-423-8617; Fax: 860-423-4157. Email: sagradocor@sbcglobal.net.

RELIGIOUS INSTITUTES OF MEN REPRESENTED IN THE DIOCESE

For further details refer to the corresponding bracketed number in the Religious Institutes of Men or Women section.

[]—*Benedictine Monks*—O.S.B.

[1350]—*Brothers of St. Francis Xavier* (St. Joseph Prov.)—C.F.X.

[0470]—*The Capuchin Friars* (Prov. of St. Mary)—O.F.M. Cap

[0740]—*Congregation of Marians of the Immaculate Conception*—M.I.C.

[]—*Congregation of Priests of St. Basil*—C.S.B.

[]—*Congregation of the Oratory of St. PhilipNeri*—C.O.

[]—*Congregation of St. Therese*—C.S.T.

[0480]—*Conventual Franciscans*—O.F.M.Conv

[0533]—*Franciscan Friars of the Immaculate*—F. I.

[0690]—*Jesuit Fathers and Brothers*—S.J.

[0720]—*The Missionaries of Our Lady of La Salette* (Prov. of Our Lady of the Americas)—M.S.

[]—*Missionary Congregation of the Blessed Sacrament*—M.C.S.B.

[0910]—*Oblates of Mary Immaculate* (Missionary Oblates of Mary Immaculate, U.S. Prov.)—O.M.I.

[]—*Order of St. Paul the First Hermit, Pauline Fathers*—O.S.P.P.E.

[1190]—*Salesians of Don Bosco*—S.D.B.

[]—*Salvatorian Fathers*—S.D.S.

[1260]—*Society of Mary, Marianist*—S.M.

[0440]—*Society of St. Edmund*—S.S.E.

[0590]—*Society of the Missionaries of the Holy Apostles*—M.S.A.

RELIGIOUS INSTITUTES OF WOMEN REPRESENTED IN THE DIOCESE

[0130]—*Apostoles of the Sacred Heart of Jesus*—A.S.C.J.

[]—*Congregation of Notre Dame*—C.N.D.

[]—*Daughters of Our Lady of the Garden*—F.M.H.

[0820]—*Daughters of the Holy Spirit*—D.H.S.

[1190]—*Franciscan Sisters of Atonement*—S.A.

[1410]—*Mill Hill Sisters (Franciscan Missionaries of St. Joseph)*—F.M.S.J.

[2970]—*School Sisters of Notre Dame*—S.S.N.D.

[]—*Sisters Oblates to Divine Love*—R.O.D.A.

[0530]—*Sisters of Charity of Our Lady, Mother of the Church*—S.C.M.C.

[3860]—*Sisters of St. Joseph of Cluny*—S.J.C.

[2575]—*Sisters of Mercy of the Americas*—R.S.M.

[3000]—*Sisters of Notre Dame de Namur* (Connecticut Prov.)—S.N.D.deN.

[3830]—*Sisters of St. Joseph*—S.S.J.

[3930]—*Sisters of St. Joseph of the Third Order of St. Francis*—S.S.J.-T.O.S.F.

[]—*Sisters of St. Martha*—C.S.M.

[]—*Sisters of the Adoration of the Blessed Sacrament*—S.A.B.S.

[]—*Sisters of the Cross and Passion*—C.P.

[2140]—*Sisters of the Poor of the Immaculate Conception of the Blessed Virgin Mary (Lithuanian)*—M.V.S.

[3320]—*Sisters of the Presentation of the B.V.M.*—P.B.V.M.

NECROLOGY

† Flint, Kenneth, (Retired)—Died Sept. 10, 2011
† Lynch, Robert B., (Retired)—Died Aug. 6, 2011
† Pilatowski, Eugene L., (Retired)—Died June 27, 2011

An asterisk (*) denotes an organization that has established tax-exempt status directly with the IRS and is not covered by the USCCB Group Ruling.

Diocese of Oakland

(Dioecesis Quercopolitana)

Most Reverend

SALVATORE J. CORDILEONE

Bishop of Oakland; ordained July 9, 1982; appointed Auxiliary Bishop of San Diego and Titular Bishop of Natchesium July 5, 2002; ordained August 21, 2002; appointed Bishop of Oakland March 23, 2009; installed May 5, 2009. *Office: 2121 Harrison St., Ste. 100, Oakland, CA 94612-3788.*

Most Reverend

JOHN S. CUMMINS, D.D.

Retired Bishop of Oakland; ordained January 24, 1953; appointed Titular Bishop of Lambesi and Auxiliary Bishop of Sacramento February 26, 1974; consecrated May 16, 1974; appointed Bishop of Oakland May 3, 1977; installed June 30, 1977; retired September 30, 2003. *Office: 617 Prospect Ave., Oakland, CA 94610.* Tel: 510-832-5037.

Chancery Office: 2121 Harrison St., Ste. 100, Oakland, CA 94612-3788. Tel: 510-893-4711; Fax: 510-893-0945.

Email: chancellor@oakdiocese.org

Web: www.oakdiocese.org

ESTABLISHED JANUARY 13, 1962.

Square Miles 1,467.

Comprises two Counties in the State of California--viz., Alameda and Contra Costa.

Legal Title: The Roman Catholic Bishop of Oakland, a Corporation Sole.

For legal titles of parishes and diocesan institutions, consult the Chancery Office.

STATISTICAL OVERVIEW

Personnel	
Bishop	1
Retired Bishops	1
Priests: Diocesan Active in Diocese	98
Priests: Diocesan Active Outside Diocese	9
Priests: Retired, Sick or Absent	52
Number of Diocesan Priests	159
Religious Priests in Diocese	164
Total Priests in Diocese	323
Extern Priests in Diocese	45
Ordinations:	
Diocesan Priests	4
Religious Priests	2
Transitional Deacons	1
Permanent Deacons in Diocese	115
Total Brothers	96
Total Sisters	370
Parishes	
Parishes	83
With Resident Pastor:	
Resident Diocesan Priests	48
Resident Religious Priests	17
Without Resident Pastor:	
Administered by Priests	17
Administered by Lay People	1
Missions	1
Pastoral Centers	8
Closed Parishes	1
Professional Ministry Personnel:	
Sisters	20
Lay Ministers	127
Welfare	
Health Care Centers	1
Total Assisted	3,381
Homes for the Aged	2
Total Assisted	264
Day Care Centers	1
Total Assisted	514
Specialized Homes	6
Total Assisted	18,674
Special Centers for Social Services	3
Total Assisted	247,000
Residential Care of Disabled	1
Total Assisted	915
Educational	
Diocesan Students in Other Seminaries	28
Seminaries, Religious	3
Students Religious	335
Total Seminarians	363
Colleges and Universities	2
Total Students	5,394
High Schools, Diocesan and Parish	3
Total Students	1,698
High Schools, Private	6
Total Students	4,059
Elementary Schools, Diocesan and Parish	44
Total Students	11,751
Elementary Schools, Private	2
Total Students	150
Catechesis/Religious Education:	
High School Students	6,418
Elementary Students	20,348
Total Students under Catholic Instruction	50,181
Teachers in the Diocese:	
Priests	41
Brothers	33
Sisters	43
Lay Teachers	2,149
Vital Statistics	
Receptions into the Church:	
Infant Baptism Totals	8,751
Minor Baptism Totals	497
Adult Baptism Totals	343
Received into Full Communion	475
First Communions	7,902
Confirmations	4,187
Marriages:	
Catholic	850
Interfaith	159
Total Marriages	1,009
Deaths	2,393
Total Catholic Population	399,546
Total Population	2,586,396

Former Bishops—Most Revs. FLOYD L. BEGIN, S.T.D., cons. May 1, 1947; appt. Bishop of Oakland on Feb. 21, 1962; died April 26, 1977; JOHN S. CUMMINS, D.D. (Retired), ord. January 24, 1953; appt. Titular Bishop of Lambesi and Auxiliary Bishop of Sacramento February 26, 1974; cons. May 16, 1974; appt. Bishop of Oakland May 3, 1977; installed June 30, 1977; retired Sept. 30, 2003; ALLEN HENRY VIGNERON, D.D., ord. July 27, 1975; appt. Auxiliary Bishop of Detroit and Titular Bishop of Sault Ste. Marie June 12, 1996; cons. July 9, 1996; appt. Coadjutor Bishop of Oakland Jan. 10, 2003; installed Feb. 26, 2003; succeeded to See Oct. 1, 2003; appt. Archbishop of Detroit Jan. 5, 2009; installed Jan. 28, 2009.

Chancery Office—2121 Harrison St., Ste. 100, Oakland, 94612-3788. Tel: 510-893-4711; Fax: 510-893-0945. Office Hours: 8:30 am-4:45 pm, except legal holidays.

Office of the Bishop—Most Rev. SALVATORE J. CORDILEONE, Bishop; Rev. DAVID E. STAAL, Priest Sec. to the Bishop.

Moderator of the Curia and Vicar General—Rev. GEORGE E. MOCKEL.

Chancellor—Sr. GLENN ANNE MCPHEE, O.P.

Chief Financial Officer—Mr. MICHAEL P. CANIZZARO.

Judicial Vicar—Rev. RAYMOND G. BRETON, J.C.L.

Director of Communications and Community Relations—MICHAEL C. BROWN.

Bishop's Representative for Eastern Rite Catholics—Rev. DAVID LINK.

Bishop's Representative for Permanent Deacons—Deacon DAVID REZENDES.

Bishop's Representative for Catholic Charismatics (English)—Ms. ROSEMARIE MULLINS.

Bishop's Representative for Catholic Charismatics (Spanish)—Rev. FRANCISCO J. FIGUEROA-ESQUER.

Catholic Cathedral Corporation of the East Bay (CCCEB)—Mr. MICHAEL P. CANIZZARO, Contact, 2121 Harrison St., Ste. 100, Oakland, 94612-3788. Tel: 510-267-8323; Fax: 510-446-7401. Email: mcanizzaro@oakdiocese.org. Officers: Rev. DAVID E. STAAL, Vice Pres.; Mr. MICHAEL P. CANIZZARO, CFO/Treas.; Mr. WILLIAM UTIC, Sec.

Christ the Light Cathedral Corporation—Mr. MICHAEL P. CANIZZARO, Contact, 2121 Harrison St., Ste. 100, Oakland, 94612-3788. Tel: 510-267-8323; Fax: 510-446-7401. Email: mcanizzaro@oakdiocese.org. Officers: Rev. DAVID E. STAAL, Vice Pres.; Mr. MICHAEL P. CANIZZARO, Treas.; Mr. WILLIAM UTIC, Sec.

John Paul II High School, a California nonprofit religious corporation—Rev. GEORGE E. MOCKEL, Incorporator, 2121 Harrison St., Ste. 100, Oakland, 94612-3788. Tel: 510-893-4711; Fax: 510-893-0945. Email: gmockel@oakdiocese.org. Officers: Mr. JOSEPH L. CONNELL, Ph.D., Pres.; Rev. GEORGE E. MOCKEL, Vice Pres.; Mr. MICHAEL P. CANIZZARO, Treas.; Sr. BARBARA BRAY, S.N.J.M., Sec.

The Roman Catholic Welfare Corporation of Oakland—2121 Harrison St., Ste. 100, Oakland, 94612-3788. Tel: 510-893-4711. Officers: Sr. BARBARA BRAY, S.N.J.M., Pres.; Mrs. LINDA BASMAN, Vice Pres.; Mr. MICHAEL P. CANIZZARO, Sec. & Treas. Members of the Board - Appointed:

Sr. GLENN ANNE MCPHEE, O.P.; Mr. JOSEPH L. CONNELL, Ph.D.

Consultors—Revs. SEAMUS J. FARRELL; ROBERT M. HERBST, O.F.M.Conv., J.C.D.; GEORGE E. MOCKEL; PAULSON MUNDANMANI; PAUL J. SCHMIDT; LARRY E. YOUNG.

Presbyteral Council—Revs. GEORGE ALENGADAN, S.D.B., Sec.; JOHN R. BLAKER; RAYMOND G. BRETON, J.C.L., Vice Chair; DANIEL E. DANIELSON (Retired); SEAMUS J. FARRELL; BRIAN T. JOYCE; JOSE M. LEON; JAMES V. MATTHEWS; RUBEN MORALES; BICH N. NGUYEN, J.C.L.; WILLIAM D. ROSARIO; RONALD G. SCHMIT; LARRY E. YOUNG, Chair. Ex Officio: Rev. GEORGE E. MOCKEL.

Diocesan Pastoral Council—Region 1 - Central: VACANT. Region 2 - Northwest: Ms. ANA GONZALES. Region 3 - Northeast: VACANT. Region 4 - Southwest: Ms. MARY FAIR; CHUCK WOODS. Region 5 - Southwest: YVONNE ALGER-ROUNDS. Deacon Representative: VACANT. Women Religious Representative: Sr. KIM NGUYEN, S.S.N.D. Priest Representatives - Alameda County: Revs. JAY MATTHEWS; KENNETH SALES; JOHNSON C. ABRAHAM. Priest Representatives - Contra Costa County: VACANT. Ex Officio: Rev. GEORGE E. MOCKEL; Sr. GLENN ANNE MCPHEE, O.P.; MICHAEL C. BROWN; DEBRA K. GUNN.

Diocesan Planning Board—Mr. MARK BALES; Mr. J. J. WEST; Ms. MARY FAIR; Mr. MIKE HENDERSHOT; Ms. JOANN MASS; Rev. JOSE ARONG, O.M.I.; Ms. RITA MITCHELL. Ex Officio: Rev. GEORGE E. MOCKEL; DEBRA K. GUNN.

Design Review Board—Revs. PAUL D. MINNIHAN, S.T.D., Liturgy; FRED A. RICCIO; LARRY E. YOUNG; Sr. BARBARA BRAY, S.N.J.M., Educ.; Mr. PAUL BONGIOVANNI, Finance; Mr. MICHAEL P. CANIZZARO, Finance; Mr. DAVID MESSINGER, S.E.; Mr. TED MILHAUS, A.I.A.; Mrs. LISA OBEREMPT, Finance; Mr. DICK RUDOLFF; Mr. MARK ZALESKI; Mr. ALEX HERNANDEZ; Mr. JAMES H. MCCANN.

Diocesan Review Board—Sr. GLENN ANNE MCPHEE, O.P., Victims Assistance Coord.; Revs. ROBERT J. MCCANN, J.C.L.; JAMES J. MCGEE; MARIO HENRY BARSOTTI, (Ret. Judge); Mrs. ROSEMARY BOWER, Ph.D.; Mrs. COLLEEN DAVIES, Esq.; Mr. GEORGE FREUHAN; Mr. FRANK HEFFERNAN; Mr. MICHAEL E. DELEHUNT, Esq.

Deacon Council—Deacons REY ENCARNACION, Pres.; RONALD HORAN, Past Pres.; WILLIAM GALL, Pres.-elect; JOHN ARCHER; RICHARD FOLGER; JOHN KORTUEM; TIMOTHY MOORE, Ex Officio; DAVE REZENDES; Revs. GEORGE ALENGADAN, S.D.B.; NEAL CLEMENS; Mrs. ROSE ENCARNACION.

Lay Ecclesial Ministers Council (LEMC)—Region 1: Ms. ANNE MARIE FOURRE; Ms. SUZY SILVA. Region 2: Mr. WALT SEARS. Region 3: Mr. KEITH MACHI. Region 4: Ms. ELIZABETH ROGERS; Ms. LISA PROMANI. Region 5: Ms. ROBYN LANG; Ms. LUCY SOLTAU. Special Works: Mrs. MARILYN MARCHI; Ms. GLORIA ESPINOZA. Priest Representative: Rev. JOHN PROCHASKA. Ex Officio: Mr. KEITH BORCHERS; Sr. GLENN ANNE MCPHEE, O.P.

Diocesan Finance Council—Mr. DAVID L. ASH; Mr. WILLIAM ATKINSON; Mr. PAUL BONGIOVANNI; Mr. JOHN CALLAGY; Mr. RICHARD CAMPBELL; Mr. MICHAEL P. CANIZZARO; Rev. RICHARD J. CULVER; Mr. PATRICK DEVINE; Mr. GLEN HENTGES; Mr. DAVID MCGRAW; Rev. GEORGE E. MOCKEL; Mr. WILLIAM UTIC; Mr. KIP WIXSON.

Pastoral Leadership Placement Board (PLPB)—Revs. FRED A. RICCIO, Chair; ISMAEL GUTIERREZ, Vice Chair; LEO J. EDGERLY JR.; Mrs. KATHLEEN MURPHY; Sr. ROSALINE NGUYEN, L.H.C.; Revs. JOHN PROCHASKA; ROBERT K. RIEN; Rev. Msgr. ANTONIO VALDIVIA (Retired). Ex Officio: Revs. GEORGE E. MOCKEL; RAYMOND G. BRETON, J.C.L.

Deans—Deanery #1: Rev. RAYMOND SACCA. Deanery #2: Rev. TIMOTHY K. JOHNSON. Deanery #3: Rev. JESUS NIETO-RUIZ. Deanery #4: Rev. JAMES V. MATTHEWS. Deanery #5: Rev. FRED RICCIO. Deanery #6: Rev. DAVID J. FARRUGIA, O.P. Deanery #7: Rev. GARY KLAUER, O.F.M.Conv. Deanery #8: Rev. JAMES J. THOTTAPALLY. Deanery #9: Rev. JOHN KASPER, O.S.F.S. Deanery #10: Rev. LEO ALBAN ASUNCION. Deanery #11: Rev. RICHARD MANGINI. Deanery #12: Rev. RICHARD J. CULVER. Deanery #13: Rev. OLMAN SOLIS. Deanery #14: Rev. ROBERT MENDONCA. Deanery #15: Rev. JOHN PROCHASKA. Deanery #16: Rev. GEOFFREY BARAAN. Deanery #17: Rev. RAMON GOMEZ. Deanery #18: VACANT.

Diocesan Departments

Apostleship of the Sea—Rev. JOSEPH DUONG PHAN, Port Chap., 4001 Seventh St., Oakland, 94607. Tel: 510-444-7885.

Archivist/Records Management—Ms. CARRIE MCCLISH, 2121 Harrison St., Ste. 100, Oakland, 94612-3788. Tel: 510-267-8318; Fax: 510-893-4734.

Campaign for Human Development—Mr. SOLOMON BELETTE, Dir., 433 Jefferson St., Oakland, 94607-3539. Tel: 510-768-3105.

Canon Law Department—

Judicial Vicar & Director—Rev. RAYMOND G. BRETON, J.C.L., 2121 Harrison St., Ste. 100, Oakland, 94612-3788. Tel: 510-267-8330; Fax: 510-836-0611.

Adjutant Judicial Vicars—Revs. ROBERT M. HERBST, O.F.M.Conv., J.C.D.; ROBERT J. MCCANN, J.C.L.

Promoter of Justice—Rev. FRANCISCO V. VICENTE, O.P., J.C.D.

Defenders of the Bond—Rev. DAVID K. O'ROURKE, O.P.; Mr. ROBERT FLUMMERFELT, J.D., J.C.L.

Judges—Revs. RAYMOND G. BRETON, J.C.L.; ROBERT M. HERBST, O.F.M.Conv., J.C.D.; ROBERT J. MCCANN, J.C.L.; HERMAN LEONG, J.C.L.; SERGIO LOPEZ, J.C.D.; BICH N. NGUYEN, J.C.L.

Notaries of the Tribunal—JACQUELINE COMPTON; MARY O'SULLIVAN.

Auditors—Mrs. CAROL IZO; THERESA KOBAK; KAREN LAIBLE; VIOLETA POZO; MARY MCMANUS.

Court of Second Instance—Rev. ROBERT M. HERBST, O.F.M.Conv., J.C.D., Presiding Judge; Mrs. CAROL IZO, Notary.

Catholic Funeral and Cemetery Services—Mr. ROBERT W. SEELIG, Exec. Dir., 4457 Willow Rd., Ste. 100, Pleasanton, 94588. Tel: 925-946-1440 ANTIOCH, Contra Costa County, Holy Angels/Holy Cross Cemetery; HAYWARD, Alameda County, Holy Angels Funeral and Cremation Center/Holy Sepulchre Cemetery and Mausoleum, Holy Angels/Sorensen's Chapel; LAFAYETTE, Contra Costa County, Holy Angels/Queen of Heaven Cemetery; LIVERMORE, Alameda County, Holy Angels/St. Michael's Cemetery; OAKLAND, Alameda County, Cathedral of Christ the Light Mausoleum/Holy Angels/St. Mary's Cemetery; Holy Angels/Cooper's Chapel; SAN PABLO, Contra Costa County, Holy Angels/St. Joseph's Cemetery and Mausoleum.

Legal Title: The Roman Catholic Cemeteries of the Diocese of Oakland, a California nonprofit religious corporation, dba Catholic Funeral and Cemetery Services Officers: Mr. ROBERT W. SEELIG, Pres.; Rev. GEORGE E. MOCKEL, Vice Pres.; Mr. MICHAEL P. CANIZZARO, Sec. & Treas.

Catholic Relief Services—Mr. SOLOMON BELETTE, Dir., 433 Jefferson St., Oakland, 94607-3539. Tel: 510-768-3105.

Catholic Youth Organization and Catholic Scouting—Mr. BILL FORD, Dir., 2121 Harrison St., Ste. 100, Oakland, 94612-3788. Tel: 510-893-5154; Fax: 510-834-5498.

Censor—Rev. ROBERT J. MCCANN, J.C.L., 2121 Harrison St., Ste. 100, Oakland, 94612-3788. Tel: 510-267-8330.

Clergy Services—Rev. NEAL CLEMENS, Dir., 2121 Harrison St., Ste. 100, Oakland, 94612-3788. Tel: 510-267-8307.

Department of Catholic Schools—Sr. BARBARA BRAY, S.N.J.M., Supt., 2121 Harrison St., Oakland, 94612-3787. Tel: 510-628-2152; Mrs. LINDA BASMAN, Asst. Supt. Tel: 510-628-2157; Ms. ELIZABETH GUNERATNE, Interim Asst. Supt. Tel: 510-628-2157; VACANT, Urban Catholic Schools Collaborative Dir.; Mrs. MARGO TANMEN, Controller. Tel: 510-628-2157.

Department for Evangelization and Catechetics—Mr. KEITH BORCHERS, Dir., 2121 Harrison St., Ste. 100, Oakland, 94612-3788. Tel: 510-893-4711; Fax: 510-272-0738; Ms. MARY ANN WIESINGER, Assoc. Dir.

Latino Ministry—Mr. HECTOR D. MEDINA.

Marriage and Family Life Ministry—Mr. EDWARD HOPFNER.

Life and Justice Ministry—Mr. JOHN WATKINS, Coord.

Youth and Young Adult Ministry—Ms. PATTI COLLYER, Coord.

Coordinator of Catechesis and Adult Faith Formation—Mr. SAMUEL VASQUEZ.

St. Joseph Center for the Deaf Catechetical and Faith Formation—VACANT, D.R.E., 25580 Campus Dr., Hayward, 94542-1137. Tel: 510-881-2245 (Voice); 510-881-2248 (Video Phone); 510-881-2247 (TTY); Fax: 510-881-2248. Email: sjcd@sjcd.org. Web: www.sjcd.org.

Special Religious Education Department (SPRED)—Sr. AURORA PEREZ, Dir. Web: www.oakdiocese.org/education/spred.

Development—VACANT, Dir., 2121 Harrison St., Ste. 100, Oakland, 94612-3788. Tel: 510-267-8314.

FACE (Family Aid Catholic Education, Tuition Assistance)—Mr. CHRIS GOOD, Dir., 2121 Harrison St., Ste. 100, Oakland, 94612-3788. Tel: 510-628-2169.

Diocesan Worship—Rev. PAUL D. MINNIHAN, S.T.D., Dir., 2121 Harrison St., Ste. 100, Oakland, 94612-3788. Tel: 510-271-1945. Email: pminnihan@oakdiocese.org.

Episcopal Liturgist—Rev. PAUL D. MINNIHAN, S.T.D., 2121 Harrison St., Ste. 100, Oakland, 94612-3788. Tel: 510-271-1945. Email: pminnihan@oakdiocese.org.

Ethnic Pastoral Centers—

Director of Ethnic & Cultural Services Division—Sr. FELICIA SARATI, C.S.J., 2121 Harrison St., Ste. 100, Oakland, 94612-3788. Tel: 510-273-4998.

Asian/Indian Community—Mrs. BELLA COMELO, 2048 Juneau St., San Leandro, 94577. Tel: 510-357-0940.

Brazilian Community—Mr. JOSE FREITAS, 1500 Elm St., El Cerrito, 94530. Tel: 510-232-4328.

Chinese Pastoral Center—Rev. PAUL FENG CHEN, Dir., 707 C St., Union City, 94587. Tel: 510-471-2609.

Eritrean Community—Rev. GEBRIEL WOLDAI, Bay Area Regl. Dir., 1640 Addison St., Berkeley, 94703. Tel: 510-549-3620.

Ethiopian Community in Formation—Ms. ELIZABETH KRISTOS. Tel: 510-620-0594.

Fijian Community—Mr. SAM DEO, 15207 Hardin St., San Leandro, 94579. Tel: 510-329-8621.

Filipino Community—Ms. FE QUINTO, 1650 Gardner Blvd., San Leandro, 94577. Tel: 510-569-5039.

Indonesian Community—Mr. BEN LIEM, 4013 Yolo Dr., San Jose, 95136-1986. Tel: 408-221-9262.

Kenyan Community—Rev. JAMES K. KARIU, 5641 Esmond Ave., Richmond, 94805. Tel: 510-860-2299.

Kmhmu/Laotian Pastoral Center—Rev. DONALD MACKINNON, C.Ss.R., Chap., 2215 Rose St., Berkeley, 94709. Tel: 510-582-8888.

Korean Pastoral Center—Rev. DOMINIC KIM, Dir., St. Andrew Kim Korean Catholic Pastoral Center, 6226 Camden St., Oakland, 94605. Tel: 510-562-3843.

Nigerian Community—Mr. AMBROSE ANYANWU, 3025 Maple St., Oakland, 94602. Tel: 510-436-6051.

Polish Pastoral Center—Deacon WITOLD CICHON, Dir., 4593 Ridgeline Dr., Antioch, 94531-9393. Tel: 925-779-1027.

Portuguese Community—Mr. MANUEL ALVES, 6752 Montcalm Ave., Newark, 94560-2344. Tel: 510-793-6572.

Tongan Community—Mrs. MELE MAUSIA, 1135 83rd Ave., Oakland, 94621. Tel: 510-927-7131.

Vietnamese Pastoral Center—Sr. ROSALINE NGUYEN, L.H.C., 2121 Harrison St., Ste. 100, Oakland, 94612-3788. Tel: 510-628-2153.

Exorcist—Rev. KENNETH NOBREGA, 2121 Harrison St., Ste. 100, Oakland, 94612-3788. Tel: 510-267-8345.

Facilities, Planning and Services—Mr. ALEX HERNANDEZ, Dir. Tel: 510-267-8355; Mr. JAMES H. MCCANN, Assoc. Dir., 2121 Harrison St., Ste. 100, Oakland, 94612-3788. Tel: 510-267-8308.

Financial Services—Mr. PAUL BONGIOVANNI, Controller, 2121 Harrison St., Ste. 100, Oakland, 94612-3788. Tel: 510-267-8321.

Human Resources—Dr. PENNY PENDOLA, Dir., 2121 Harrison St., Ste. 100, Oakland, 94612-3788. Tel: 510-267-8359.

Safe Environment for Children—Mrs. MARILYN MARCHI, Prog. Coord., 2121 Harrison St., Ste. 100, Oakland, 94612-3788. Tel: 510-267-8315.

Newspaper: "The Catholic Voice"—Mr. ALBERT C. PACCIORINI, Editor, 2121 Harrison St., Ste. 100, Oakland, 94612-3788. Tel: 510-419-1073.

"El Heraldo Catolico"—Mr. ALBERT C. PACCIORINI, Co Editor, 2121 Harrison St., Ste. 100, Oakland, 94612-3788. Tel: 510-419-1073.

Office of Clergy Formation—Rev. GEORGE ALENGADAN, S.D.B., Dir., 2121 Harrison St., Ste. 100, Oakland, 94612-3788. Tel: 510-267-8364.

Pastoral Planning and Stewardship—DEBRA K. GUNN, Dir., 2121 Harrison St., Ste. 100, Oakland, 94612-3788. Tel: 510-628-2186.

Pontifical Association of the Holy Childhood—Rev. GEORGE E. MOCKEL, Interim Dir., 2121 Harrison St., Ste. 100, Oakland, 94612-3788. Tel: 510-267-8317.

Propagation of the Faith—Rev. GEORGE E. MOCKEL, Interim Dir., 2121 Harrisonn St., Ste. 100, Oakland, 94612-3788. Tel: 510-267-8317 Legal Title: Oakland Society for the Propagation of the Faith.

Rector of the Cathedral of Christ the Light—Rev. RAYMOND SACCA, 2121 Harrison St., Ste. 130, Oakland, 94612-3788. Tel: 510-496-7202.

St. Peter the Apostle Society—Rev. GEORGE E. MOCKEL, Interim Dir., 2121 Harrison St., Ste. 100, Oakland, 94612-3788. Tel: 510-267-8317.

Vicars for Religious—Revs. RAYMOND G. BRETON, J.C.L.; ROBERT M. HERBST, O.F.M.Conv., J.C.D., 2121 Harrison St., Ste. 100, Oakland, 94612-3788. Tel: 510-267-8330.

Vocations—Revs. KENNETH NOBREGA, Priestly and Rel. & Dir. for Seminarians. Tel: 510-267-8345; SERGIO LOPEZ, J.C.D., Co-Dir. for Spanish-Speaking Outreach, 2121 Harrison St., Ste. 100, Oakland, 94612-3788. Tel: 510-267-8342.

Organizations—
Confraternity of Eucharistic Devotion (CEDDO)—Mrs. PAMELA HAMILTON, Mod.; Mr. JON HAMILTON SR., Asst. Mod.; Mrs. GLENDA DUBSKY, Sec.; Mrs. VALERIE BURKART, Treas.; Rev. LAWRENCE C. D'ANJOU, Chap. Email: ceddo@oakdiocese.org. Web: www.ceddo.org.
Courage - Oakland Chapter—Chaplains: Revs. JOHN DIREEN. Tel: 510-843-2244; FRANCISCO FIGUEROA-ESQUER. Tel: 510-532-2068.
Cursillo Movement—Rev. LEO J. EDGERLY JR., Spiritual Dir. Tel: 510-530-4343.
Diocesan Council of Catholic Women—STEFFIE SILVIA, 5521 Columbia Ave., Richmond, 94804-5627. Tel: 510-525-7829.
St. Vincent de Paul Society—
Alameda County, Executive Director—Mr. PHILIP ARCA, 9235 San Leandro St., Oakland, 94603. Tel: 510-636-4246; 510-638-7600.
Contra Costa, Executive Director—Mr. RON WESTON, 2210 Gladstone Dr., Pittsburg, 94565. Tel: 925-439-5060, Ext. 19.

CLERGY, PARISHES, MISSIONS AND PAROCHIAL SCHOOLS

CITY OF OAKLAND

(ALAMEDA COUNTY)

1—CATHEDRAL PARISH OF CHRIST THE LIGHT (2008) Revs. Raymond Sacca; Joseph Nguyen, Parochial Vicar; Deacons Eugene Stelly; Rey Encarnacion; Peter Ta; Jorge Angel.
Res.: 2121 Harrison St., 94612. Tel: 510-832-5057; Fax: 510-832-0212. Email: cpctl@oakdiocese.org. Web: www.ctlcathedral.org.
Catechesis/Religious Program—Sr. Kim Trong Nguyen, S.S.N.D., D.R.E. Students 112.

2—ST. ANDREW-ST. JOSEPH (1965), (African American), Merged into Cathedral Parish of Christ the Light, Oakland.

3—ST. ANTHONY (1871) Revs. Jesus Nieto-Ruiz; Peter Son Vo, Parochial Vicar.
Res.: 1535 16th Ave., 94606-4425. Tel: 510-534-2117; Fax: 510-534-2119. Email: sanantonio-oakland@comcast.net. Web: www.stanthonyoakland.parishesonline.com.
School—(Grades K-8), 1500 E. 15th St., 94606. Tel: 510-534-3334; Fax: 510-534-3378. Web: www.stanthonyschool.spruz.com. Sr. Barbara Flannery, C.S.J., Prin. Sisters 1; Lay Teachers 9; Students 198.
Catechesis/Religious Program—Carmen Hernandez, C.R.E. Students 438.

4—ST. AUGUSTINE (1907) Rev. Mark Wiesner; Ms. Karen Miller, Pastoral Assoc.; Robbie Valentine, Office & Facility Admin.; James Gilman, Music Dir.; Mr. Walt Sears, Adult Formation. In Res., Rev. Gabriel Wankar (Nigeria).
Res.: 400 Alcatraz Ave., 94609-1106. Tel: 510-653-8631; Fax: 510-653-4256. Email: saintaugustinechurch@comcast.net.
Catechesis/Religious Program—Tel: 510-653-8631, Ext. 103; Fax: 510-653-4256. Email: saintaugustinechurch@comcast.net. Rebecca Pelle, D.R.E. Students 52.

5—ST. BENEDICT (1930), (African American), Rev. James V. Matthews; Deacon Ronald Tutson. In Res., Rev. Cuthbert Aronyu (Uganda).
Res.: 2245 82nd Ave., 94605-3407. Tel: 510-632-1847; Fax: 510-633-2092. Email: saintbenedictcrh@aol.com.
Catechesis/Religious Program—Students 15.

6—ST. BERNARD (1912), (Hispanic—African American), Revs. Roberto Flores, S.V.D.; Dominic Asare, S.V.D., Parochial Vicar; Deacon Javier Fuentes.
Res.: 1620-62nd Ave., 94621-4221. Tel: 510-632-3013; Fax: 510-632-5286. Email: st.bernard.church@sbcglobal.net.
Catechesis/Religious Program—Students 270.

7—CATHEDRAL OF ST. FRANCIS DE SALES (1886) Merged with St. Mary, Immaculate Conception to form Cathedral Parish of Christ the Light.

8—ST. COLUMBA (1898), (African American), Rev. Aidan McAleenan, Parochial Admin.; Rawn Harbor, Pastoral Assoc.
Res.: 6401 San Pablo Ave., 94608-1233. Tel: 510-654-7600; Fax: 510-654-7615. Email: stcolumba1898@gmail.com. Web: www.stcolumba-oak.com.
Catechesis/Religious Program—Ms. Margaret Roncalli, Dir., Faith Formation. Students 56.

9—ST. CYRIL (1926), (Korean), Merged with St. Lawrence O'Toole, Oakland to form St. Lawrence O'Toole-St. Cyril of Jerusalem, Oakland. For parish records contact St. Lawrence O'Toole-St. Cyril of Jerusalem, Oakland.

10—ST. ELIZABETH (1892), (Hispanic), Revs. Oscar A. Mendez, O.F.M.; Martin Ibarra, O.F.M., Parochial Vicar; Alberto Villafan, O.F.M., Parochial Vicar.
Res.: 1500 34th Ave., 94601-3024. Tel: 510-536-1266; Fax: 510-536-8560. Email: stelizabethchurch@yahoo.com. Web: www.stelizabethoak.org.
School—(Grades PreK-8), 1516 33rd Ave., 94601-3016. Tel: 510-532-7392; Fax: 510-532-0321. Web: www.stelizabeth.us. Sr. Rose Marie Hennessy, O.P., Prin. Sisters 4; Lay Teachers 36; Students 345.
Catechesis/Religious Program—Students 303.

11—ST. JARLATH (1910) Rev. Francisco J. Figueroa-Esquer, Admin. In Res., Rev. Thomas Martin (Australia).
Res.: 2620 Pleasant St., 94602-2125. Tel: 510-532-2068; Fax: 510-532-3745. Email: sjarlath@sbcglobal.net.
School—(Grades K-8), 2634 Pleasant St., 94602-2125. Tel: 510-532-4387; Fax: 510-532-1001. Web: www.stjarlath.org. Rodney Pierre-Antoine, Prin. Brothers 1; Sisters 1; Lay Teachers 10; Students 83.
Catechesis/Religious Program—Students 211.

12—ST. LAWRENCE O'TOOLE, Merged with St. Cyril, Oakland to form St. Lawrence O'Toole-St. Cyril of Jerusalem, Oakland. For parish records contact St. Lawrence O'Toole-St. Cyril of Jerusalem, Oakland.

13—ST. LAWRENCE O'TOOLE-ST. CYRIL OF JERUSALEM (1916) Rev. Nicholas Glisson; Deacon Jeffrey Burns. In Res., Revs. Bich N. Nguyen; Benedict Ehinack (Cameroon).
Res.: 3725 High St., 94619-2107. Tel: 510-530-0761; Fax: 510-530-0974. Email: slotsjc@sbcglobal.net. Web: www.stlawrenceotoole.net.
School—(Grades K-8), 3695 High St., 94619. Tel: 510-530-0266; Fax: 510-530-7568. Web: www.stlawrenceotoole.com. Sally Douthit, Prin. Lay Teachers 18; Students 156.
Catechesis/Religious Program—Tel: 510-530-0775; Fax: 510-530-0775. Email: sharonf@holyfamilysisters.org. Web: www.stlawrenceotoole.net. Students 160.

14—ST. LEO THE GREAT (1911) Rev. Timothy K. Johnson. In Res., Revs. Thomas Ng (Retired); Anatole A. Tiendrebeogo (Burkina Faso); Ignas L. Kilolelo (Tanzania).
Res.: 176 Ridgeway Ave., 94611-5122. Tel: 510-654-6177; Fax: 510-654-4203. Email: stleo@pacbell.net. Web: www.stleothegreat.org.
School—(Grades PreK-8), 4238 Howe St., 94611-4705. Tel: 510-654-7828; Fax: 510-654-4057. Email: sleo@csdo.org. Web: www.stleothegreat.org. Sonya Simril, Prin. Lay Teachers 28; Students 232.
Catechesis/Religious Program—Email: stleo@pacbell.net. Web: www.stleothegreat.org. Students 30.

15—ST. LOUIS BERTRAND (1908), (Hispanic—African American), Rev. Jesus Hernandez Vidal, Admin.; Deacon Earl Johnson.
Res.: 1410-100th Ave., 94603-2506. Tel: 510-568-1080; Fax: 510-635-8618. Email: parish@slboakland.com.
Catechesis/Religious Program—Tel: 510-632-2865. Students 588.

16—ST. MARGARET MARY (1922) Rev. Stanislaw Zak. In Res., Rev. Canon Henry Fragelli, I.C.
Res.: 1219 Excelsior Ave., 94610-2830. Tel: 510-482-0596; Fax: 510-482-2093. Email: stmargaretm@yahoo.com. Web: www.stmargmaryoak.org.
Catechesis/Religious Program—Students 103.

17—MARY HELP OF CHRISTIANS CHURCH (1915), (Spanish), Rev. Jesus Nieto-Ruiz, Parochial Admin.; Deacon Gabriel Hernandez.
Res.: 2611 E. Ninth St., 94601-1404. Tel: 510-534-3501. Email: maryhelpofchrist@aol.com.
Catechesis/Religious Program— Reyna Pina Lupian, D.R.E. Students 96.

18—ST. MARY, IMMACULATE CONCEPTION, Merged into the Cathedral Parish of Christ the Light, Oakland.

19—ST. MARY, IMMACULATE CONCEPTION-ST. FRANCIS DE SALES (1993) Merged into the Cathedral Parish of Christ the Light, Oakland.

20—OUR LADY OF LOURDES (1921) Rev. Seamus D. Genovese.
Res.: 2808 Lakeshore Ave., 94610-3613. Tel: 510-451-1790; Fax: 510-893-6443. Email: lourdesoakland@aol.com. Web: www.lourdesoakland.com.
Catechesis/Religious Program—

21—ST. PASCHAL BAYLON (1955) Rev. Paul D. Minnihan.
Res.: 3700 Dorisa Ave., 94605-4941. Tel: 510-636-0335; Fax: 510-636-0287. Email: office@stpaschaloakland.org. Web: www.stpaschaloakland.org.

22—ST. PATRICK (1879), (African American—Hispanic), Rev. David H. Gill, S.J., Parochial Admin.
Res.: 1023 Peralta St., 94607-1927. Tel: 510-444-1081; Fax: 510-444-1113. Email: howard1023@sbcglobal.net.
School—St. Martin de Porres, St. Patrick Campus, (Grades 6-8), 1630 10th St., 94607-1426. Tel: 510-832-1757; Fax: 510-832-6481. Web: www.stmdp.org. Ms. Ann Magovern, Pres.; Maurice Harper, Prin. Lay Teachers 5; Students 68.
Catechesis/Religious Program—Students 76.

23—SACRED HEART (1876) Revs. Karl Davis, O.M.I.; Jose Arong, O.M.I., Parochial Vicar. In Res., Revs. Nicanor Sarmiento, O.M.I.; Philip Singarayar, O.M.I.; Scott Hill, O.M.I.; Bro. Patrick Chiso, O.M.I.
Res.: 4025 Martin Luther King Jr. Way, 94609-2317. Tel: 510-655-9209; Fax: 510-652-1958.
School—St. Martin de Porres, Sacred Heart Campus, (Grades K-5), 675 41st St., 94609-2380. Tel: 510-652-2220; Fax: 510-652-2294. Web: www.stmdp.org. Ms. Ann Magovern, Pres.; Maurice Harper, Prin. Lay Teachers 8; Students 138.
Catechesis/Religious Program—

24—ST. THERESA OF THE INFANT JESUS (THE LITTLE FLOWER) (1925) Rev. Robert J. McCann. In Res., Rev. Peter L. Chong (Fiji).
Res.: 30 Mandalay Rd., 94618. Tel: 510-547-2777; Fax: 510-653-3575. Email: debbie@sttheresaoakland.org. Web: www.sttheresaoakland.org.
School—(Grades K-8), 4850 Clarewood Dr., 94618. Tel: 510-547-3146; Fax: 510-547-3253. Web: www-.sttheresaschool.org. Judith KoneffKlatt, Prin. Lay Teachers 33; Students 282.
Catechesis/Religious Program—Tel: 510-547-2777, Ext. 39. Email: sharon@sttheresaoakland.org. Students 134.

OUTSIDE THE CITY OF OAKLAND

ALAMEDA, ALAMEDA CO.

1—ST. ALBERT (1976) Merged with St. Philip Neri, Alameda to form St. Philip Neri St. Albert the Great, Alameda.

2—ST. BARNABAS (1925) Rev. Dana P. Michaels, Parochial Admin. In Res., Rev. Robert M. Herbst, O.F.M.Conv.
Res.: 1427 Sixth St., 94501-3760. Tel: 510-522-8933; Fax: 510-522-8380. Email: sbparishoffice@comcast.net. Web: www.rc.net/oakland/st-barnabas.
Catechesis/Religious Program—Tel: 510-337-8962. Students 50.

3—ST. JOSEPH BASILICA (1885) Rev. Fred A. Riccio; Deacon David Young.
Res.: 1109 Chestnut St., 94501-4212. Tel: 510-522-0181; Fax: 510-522-2864. Email: parish@sjbalameda.org. Web: www.sjbalameda.org.
School—St. Joseph Elementary School, (Grades K-8), 1910 San Antonio Ave., 94501-4216. Tel: 510-522-4456; Fax: 510-522-2890. Web: www.stjosephalameda.org. Monica O'Callaghan, Prin. Lay Teachers 30; Students 269.
Please see Saint Joseph Notre Dame High School under High Schools Parochial located in the Institution section.
Catechesis/Religious Program—Tel: 510-522-0181, Ext. 9409. Ms. Anne Marie Fourre, Dir. Faith Formation. Students 239.

4—ST. PHILIP NERI (1925) Merged with St. Albert, Alameda to form St. Philip Neri St. Albert the Great, Alameda.

5—ST. PHILIP NERI-ST. ALBERT THE GREAT (2011) Revs. Joy Kumarthusseril, M.F. (India); JoJo Puthussery, M.F. (India), Parochial Vicar. In Res., Revs. Jerrold F. Kennedy (Retired); George E. Mockel.
School—(Grades K-8), 1335 High St., 94501-3165. Tel: 510-521-0787; Fax: 510-521-2418. Web: www.spnalameda.org. Janis Palana-Allocco, Prin. Lay Teachers 34; Students 271.
Catechesis/Religious Program—Consolidated with St. Philip Neri, Alameda, 3101 Van Buren St., 94501. Tel: 510-373-5200, Ext. 208. Email: cff@saspn.org. Students 128.

ANTIOCH, CONTRA COSTA CO.

1—ST. IGNATIUS OF ANTIOCH (1979) [CEM] Rev. Robert K. Rien, Parochial Admin.; Deacon Gary Hack.
Office: 3351 Contra Loma Blvd., 94509-5468. Tel: 925-778-0768; Fax: 925-778-0845. Email: st.ignatius@sbcglobal.net. Web: www.stignatiusofantioch.com.
Res.: 209 Tanganyika Ct., 94509.
Catechesis/Religious Program—3351 Contra Loma Blvd., 94509-5468. Tel: 925-778-1631. Students 149.

2—MOST HOLY ROSARY (1874), (Hispanic), [CEM] [JC] Revs. Roberto Corral, O.P.; Francisco V. Vicente, O.P., Parochial Vicar; David Bello, O.P., Parochial Vicar; Sisters Alma Mariel Chavira, O.P., Hispanic Ministry; Monica Terrazas, O.P., Hispanic

Ministry; Deacons Charles Silvernale; Jerry Grigg; Mrs. Jackie Hooke, Pastoral Assoc. & Business Admin. In Res., Rev. Edward Krasevac, O.P.
Res.: 1313 A St., 94509-2328. Tel: 925-757-4020; Fax: 925-757-6828. Email: office@holyrosaryca.org. Web: holyrosaryantioch.org.
School—(Grades PreK-8), 25 E. 15th St., 94509. Tel: 925-757-1270; Fax: 925-757-9309. Web: www.holyrosarycatholicschool.org. Susana Lapeyrade-Drummond, Prin. Lay Teachers 62; Students 566.
Catechesis/Religious Program—1313 A St., 94059-2328. Tel: 915-757-9515; Fax: 925-757-9638. Web: holyrosaryantioch.org. Students 680.

BAY POINT, CONTRA COSTA CO., OUR LADY, QUEEN OF THE WORLD (1962) Revs. Richard J. Culver; Peter Ngo Duc Dung, Parochial Vicar.
Res.: 3155 Winterbrook Dr., 94565-3264. Tel: 925-458-4718; Fax: 925-458-3161. Email: wanda@olqw.org. Web: www.olqw.org.
Catechesis/Religious Program—Tel: 925-458-4574; Fax: 925-458-3161. Email: email@olqwre.com. Web: www.olqwre.com. Students 172.

BERKELEY, ALAMEDA CO.

1—ST. AMBROSE (1909) Revs. John Gibson, S.D.B.; Jesse Montes, S.D.B., Parochial Vicar.
Res.: 1145 Gilman St., 94706-2252. Tel: 510-525-2620; Fax: 510-525-5399.
Catechesis/Religious Program—Students 145.

2—HOLY SPIRIT PARISH/NEWMAN HALL (1967) Revs. Bernard Campbell, C.S.P.; Albert Moser, C.S.P., Parochial Vicar; William L. Edens, C.S.P., Parochial Vicar. (Newman Center 1899).
Res.: 2700 Dwight Way, 94704-3113. Tel: 510-848-7812; Fax: 510-848-0179. Email: email@calnewman.org. Web: www.calnewman.org.
Catechesis/Religious Program—Ms. Frances Rojek, D.R.E. Students 135.

3—ST. JOSEPH THE WORKER (1879) Rev. John Direen; Deacon Noe Gonzalez. In Res., Revs. Joseph Thieu Nguyen; Gebriel Woldai.
Res.: 1640 Addison St., 94703-1404. Tel: 510-843-2244; Fax: 510-843-2730. Email: sjwchurch@sbcglobal.net. Web: www.stjosephtheworkerchurch.org.
Catechesis/Religious Program—Tel: 510-843-2244. Students 210.

4—ST. MARY MAGDALEN (1923) Revs. David J. Farrugia, O.P.; Bruno Gibson, O.P., Parochial Vicar. In Res., Revs. Christopher J. Renz, O.P.; Albert Paretsky, O.P.; Michael J. Dodds, O.P.; Michael Sweeney, O.P.
Res.: 2005 Berryman St., 94709-1920. Tel: 510-526-4811; Fax: 510-525-3638.
School—School of the Madeleine, (Grades K-8), 1225 Milvia St., 94709-1932. Tel: 510-526-4744; Fax: 510-526-5152. Web: www.themadeleine.com. Ken Willers, Prin. Lay Teachers 37; Students 313.
Catechesis/Religious Program—Students 55.

BRENTWOOD, CONTRA COSTA CO., IMMACULATE HEART OF MARY (1949), (English—Spanish), Revs. Jerry W. Brown; Carl Tacuyan Arcosa, Parochial Vicar; Fabio Correa Correa, Parochial Vicar; Deacons John Kortuem; Ed Spano; Ron Horan.
Office: 500 Fairview Ave., 94513-1742. Tel: 925-634-4154; Fax: 925-516-9340.
Rectory—1361 Downey Point Dr., 94513-1870. Tel: 925-516-3189.
Catechesis/Religious Program—Students 764.

BYRON, CONTRA COSTA CO., ST. ANNE (1916) Rev. Ronald G. Schmit.
Mailing Address: P.O. Box 476, 94514-0476. Tel: 925-634-6625; Fax: 925-634-4194.
Catechesis/Religious Program—Tel: 925-634-6625, Ext. 224. Email: srbarbara@stannechurchbyron.com. Web: www.stannechurchbyron.com. Students 299.

CASTRO VALLEY, ALAMEDA CO.

1—OUR LADY OF GRACE (1947) Revs. Thomas Verber, O.S.A.; Paul E. Quante, O.S.A., Parochial Vicar; Deacons Matthew Dulka; Nelson Gonsalves.
Res.: 3433 Somerset Ave., 94546-54. Tel: 510-537-0806; Fax: 510-537-6281. Email: olgcv@sbcglobal.net. Web: www.olgcv.org.
School—(Grades K-8), 3427 Somerset Ave., 94546. Tel: 510-581-3155; Fax: 510-581-1059. Web: www.olgschool.org. Ryan Brusco, Prin. Lay Teachers 25; Students 209.
Catechesis/Religious Program—Tel: 510-582-9266; Fax: 510-537-6281. Email: olgrec@sbcglobal.net. Ms. Robyn Lang, D.R.E. Students 180.

2—TRANSFIGURATION (1961) Revs. Mario L. Borges; Terence O'Malley, S.C.J., Parochial Admin.; Deacons Timothy Moore; Burton Rigley; Martin Leach.
Res.: 4000 E. Castro Valley Blvd., 94552-4908. Tel: 510-538-7941; Fax: 510-538-7983. Email: transfig_office@sbcglobal.net. Web: www.transfigchurch.com.
Catechesis/Religious Program—Tel: 510-537-1502. Email: transfigccd@aol.com. Students 296.

CONCORD, CONTRA COSTA CO.

1—ST. AGNES (1964) Rev. Vincent Cotter; Deacon Gerald Waters.
Mailing Address: 3966 Chestnut Ave., 94519-1955. Web: www.stagnesparish.net.
Res.: 3900 Chestnut Ave., 94519-1955. Tel: 925-689-0838; Fax: 925-689-7899. Email: stagnesoffice@comcast.net. Web: www.stagnesparish.net.
School—(Grades K-8), 3886 Chestnut Ave., 94519-1907. Tel: 925-689-3990; Fax: 925-689-3455. Web: www.stagnesconcord.com. Jill Lucia, Prin. Lay Teachers 32; Students 354.
Catechesis/Religious Program—Students 170.

2—ST. BONAVENTURE (1957) Revs. Richard A. Mangini; David Lawrence, S.J., Parochial Vicar; Ronan Rances (Philippines); Deacons William Gall; Mariano Preza, Latino Ministry; Richard Gierak; Christa L. Fairfield, Parish Life Dir.
Res.: 5562 Clayton Rd., 94521-4158. Tel: 925-672-5800; Fax: 925-672-4606. Web: www.stbonaventure.net.
Catechesis/Religious Program— Rosann Halick, D.R.E. Students 632.

3—ST. FRANCIS OF ASSISI (1984), (Formerly Most Precious Blood, 1955) Revs. Ismael Gutierrez, Parochial Admin.; Glenn A. Naguit, Parochial Vicar; Deacons Charles Palomares; John Mazibrook; Fred Schaub, Business Mgr.
Res.: 860 Oak Grove Rd., 94518-3461. Tel: 925-682-5447; Fax: 925-682-5491. Web: www.sfaconcord.com.
School—(Grades K-8), 866 Oak Grove Rd., 94518-3461. Tel: 925-682-5414; Fax: 925-682-5480. Web: www.sfaconcord.org. Sr. James M. Dyer, C.S.J., Prin. Sisters 3; Lay Teachers 15; Students 322.
Catechesis/Religious Program—Ms. Kathleen M. De Lemos, Youth Min. & Teen Sacraments; Mrs. Scarlett Salaverria, D.R.E.-Spanish; Mr. Nathan Cho, D.R.E.-English. Students 486.

4—QUEEN OF ALL SAINTS (1923) [CEM] Revs. Michael Cunningham; Enrique Ballesteros, Parochial Vicar.
Res.: 2390 Grant St., 94520-2245. Tel: 925-825-0350; Fax: 925-825-6975. Email: gaschurch@yahoo.com. Web: www.qaschurch.org.
School—(Grades K-8), 2391 Grant St., 94520-2244. Tel: 925-685-8700; Fax: 925-685-2034. Web: www.qasconcord.org. Lucia Prince, Prin. Lay Teachers 20; Students 206.
Catechesis/Religious Program—Tel: 925-685-8707. Email: nancytomsic@yahoo.com. Nancy Tomsic, D.R.E. Students 989.

CROCKETT, CONTRA COSTA CO., ST. ROSE OF LIMA (1912) Rev. Ciarian Dillon, O.M.I.
Res.: 555 Third Ave., 94525-1114. Tel: 510-787-2052; Fax: 510-787-1199.
Catechesis/Religious Program—Tel: 510-787-1203. Students 17.
Mission—St. Patrick Prospect & Lake Canyon Rd., Port Costa, Contra Costa Co. 94569.

DANVILLE, CONTRA COSTA CO., ST. ISIDORE (1910) Revs. Gerard K. Moran; Paul Coleman (Ireland), Parochial Vicar; Deacons Adam J. Pietras; John Jee. In Res., Rev. Msgr. John T. McCracken, Pastor Emeritus (Retired).
Parish Office:—440 LaGonda Way, 94526-2562. Tel: 925-837-2122; Fax: 925-362-1919. Email: office@st-isidore-danville.org. Web: www.st-isidore-danville.org.
Res.: 445 LaGonda Way, 94526-2522. Tel: 925-837-2122.
School—(Grades K-8), 435 La Gonda Way, 94526. Tel: 925-837-2977; Fax: 925-837-2407. Web: www.stisidore.org. Jean Schroeder, Prin. Lay Teachers 71; Students 640.
Catechesis/Religious Program—Tel: 925-362-1900. Students 855.
Kids Connection—432 La Gonda Way, 94526-2562. Tel: 925-820-7753. Before and after school child care.
Youth Ministry—440 La Gonda Way, 94526-2562. Tel: 925-362-1904; Fax: 925-362-1929. Students 160.

DUBLIN, ALAMEDA CO., ST. RAYMOND (1961) Revs. Lawrence C. D'Anjou, Parochial Admin.; William Rosario, Parochial Vicar; Deacons Joe Sicat, (Retired); John Archer Jr.; David Cloyne; Ms. Diana Bitz, Pastoral Assoc.
Res.: 11555 Shannon Ave., 94568. Tel: 925-828-2460; Fax: 925-828-8610. Email: office@st-raymond-dublin.org. Web: www.st-raymond-dublin.org.
School—(Grades K-8), 11557 Shannon Ave., 94568-1376. Tel: 925-828-4064; Fax: 925-828-2454. Web: www.strayschool.org. Catherine Deehan, Prin. Lay Teachers 33; Students 307.
Catechesis/Religious Program—Tel: 925-574-7414. Email: julie@st-raymond-dublin.org. Students 456.

EL CERRITO, CONTRA COSTA CO.

1—ST. JEROME (1941) Rev. Dante Tamayo, Parochial Admin.; Deacon Benjamin Agustin. In Res., Rev. Antonius G. Aryanto (Indonesia).
Res.: 308 Carmel Ave., 94530-3735. Tel: 510-525-0876; Fax: 510-526-2721. Email: saintjeromechurch@comcast.net. Web: www.stjeromeec.org.
School—(Grades K-8), 320 San Carlos Ave., 94530. Tel: 510-525-9484; Fax: 510-525-5227. Alison Wilkie, Prin. Lay Teachers 20; Students 161.
Catechesis/Religious Program—Students 62.

2—ST. JOHN THE BAPTIST (1925) Revs. Thuong Hoai Nguyen; Rolando Bartolay, Parochial Vicar; Deacon Thomas McGowan.
Res.: 11150 San Pablo Ave., 94530-2131. Tel: 510-232-5659; Fax: 510-236-0960.
School—(Grades K-8), 11156 San Pablo Ave., 94530-2131. Tel: 510-234-2244; Fax: 510-234-3726. Web: www.stjohnec.org. Dina Trombettas, Prin. Lay Teachers 28; Students 229.
Catechesis/Religious Program—Students 18.

EL SOBRANTE, CONTRA COSTA CO., ST. CALLISTUS (1952) Rev. James J. Thottapally, Admin.
Res.: 3580 San Pablo Dam Rd., 94803-2822. Tel: 510-223-1153; Fax: 510-223-1137. Email: st.callistus@sbcglobal.net.
Catechesis/Religious Program—Tel: 510-222-2538. Students 92.

FREMONT, ALAMEDA CO.

1—CORPUS CHRISTI (1914) Rev. Salvador Macias.
Mailing Address: 37968 Third St., 94536. In Res., Deacon Alfonso Perez.
Res.: 37891 Second St., 94536-2926. Tel: 510-790-3207; Fax: 510-790-3227.
Catechesis/Religious Program—Tel: 510-790-3226. Email: ccreled@sbcglobal.net. Students 222.

2—HOLY SPIRIT (1886) [CEM] [JC] Revs. Mathew Vellankal (India); Thomas Khue, Parochial Vicar; Deacons Rudolph Brazil; William Drobick; Richard Yee; Charles Glover. In Res., Rev. John Offor (Nigeria).
Res.: 37588 Fremont Blvd., 94536-3707. Tel: 510-797-1660; Fax: 510-797-7080. Email: hsparish@gmail.com. Web: www.holyspiritfremont.org.
School—(Grades PreK-8), 3930 Parish Ave., 94536. Tel: 510-793-3553; Fax: 510-793-2694. Web: www.holyspiritfmt.com. Susan Buchanan, Prin. Lay Teachers 34; Students 306.
Catechesis/Religious Program—37648 Fremont Blvd., 94536. Tel: 510-456-4974; Fax: 510-456-4991. Email: deenabenton@yahoo.com. Web: www.hscfaithformation.com. Students 534.

3—ST. JAMES THE APOSTLE (1972) Rev. Antony Vazhappilly, S.D.B. (India), Admin.; Deacon Ernesto Dandan.
Res.: 34700 Fremont Blvd., 94555. Tel: 510-792-1962. Email: stjamesapostle@att.net.
Catechesis/Religious Program—Students 76.

4—ST. JOSEPH (OLD MISSION SAN JOSE) (1797) [CEM] Rev. Msgr. Manuel C. Simas; Rev. Rosendo R. Manalo, Parochial Vicar; Deacon Lance Vivet.
Mailing Address: P.O. Box 3276, 94539-0327.
Church: 43148 Mission Blvd., 94539. Tel: 510-656-2364; Fax: 510-656-2438. Email: stjomissj@aol.com. Web: www.stjosephmsj.org.
School—(Grades K-8), 43222 Mission Blvd., 94539-5827. Tel: 510-656-6525; Fax: 510-656-3608. Web: www.sjsmsj.org. P.O. Box 3246, 94539. Jan Cooper, Prin. Sisters 1; Lay Teachers 30; Students 266.
Catechesis/Religious Program—Tel: 510-657-0905; Fax: 510-657-4165. Sr. Mary Teresa Parker, Dir. Faith Formation. Students 268.

5—ST. LEONARD (1959) Merged with Santa Paula, Fremont to form Our Lady of Guadalupe, Fremont.

6—OUR LADY OF GUADALUPE (2000) Revs. John Prochaska; Alexander Q. Castillo, Parochial Vicar; James Sullivan, Parochial Vicar; Deacons Ovide Guesnon; Steven Budnik Sr.; Jorge Lara; Michael Cantlon.
Office: 41933 Blacow Rd., 94538. Tel: 510-657-4043; Fax: 510-657-4055. Email: office@guadalupe-parish.org. Web: www.guadalupe-parish.org.
Res. & Church: 40382 Fremont Blvd., 94538-3409. Tel: 510-656-4921; Fax: 510-226-0714.
School—(Grades K-8), 40374 Fremont Blvd., 94538-3409. Tel: 510-657-1674; Fax: 510-657-3659. Web: www.olgweb.org. Linda Parini, Prin. Sisters 1; Lay Teachers 31; Students 223.
Catechesis/Religious Program—Tel: 510-651-4966. Students 612.

7—SANTA PAULA (1965) Merged with St. Leonard, Fremont to form Our Lady of Guadalupe, Fremont.

HAYWARD, ALAMEDA CO.

1—ALL SAINTS (1898) [CEM] Revs. Anthony W. Herrera, Parochial Vicar; Fernando Cortez, Parochial Vicar; Deacon Lawrence Quinn; Mr. Stephen P. Mullin, Parish Life Dir. In Res., Rev. George Byarugaba (South Africa).
Church: 22824 Second St., 94541-5217. Tel: 510-581-2570; Fax: 510-581-9538.
School—(Grades K-8), 22870 Second St., 94541. Tel: 510-582-1910; Fax: 510-582-0866. Web: www.allsaintshayward.org. Jennifer Diaz, Prin. Lay Teachers 12; Students 218.

Catechesis/Religious Program—Students 298.

2—St. Bede (1955) Revs. Seamus J. Farrell; Jesus Manuel Galvez, O.F.M. Conv., Parochial Vicar; Deacon Denis Ryken, (Retired).
Res.: 26950 Patrick Ave., 94544-3851. Tel: 510-782-2171; Fax: 510-782-9712. Email: st.bedechurch@yahoo.com.
School—(Grades K-8), 26910 Patrick Ave., 94544-3851. Tel: 510-782-3444; Fax: 510-782-2243. Web: www.stbedehay.com. Toni Cosentino, Prin. Lay Teachers 18; Students 226.
Catechesis/Religious Program—Tel: 510-782-4292. Students 727.

3—St. Clement (1951) Revs. Ramon Gomez; Giopre Prado, Parochial Vicar.
Office & Res.: 750 Calhoun St., 94544-4202. Tel: 510-582-7282; Fax: 510-582-1875. Email: saintclement@comcast.net. Web: www.stclement.org.
School—(Grades K-8), 790 Calhoun St., 94544-4202. Tel: 510-538-5885; Fax: 510-538-1643. Web: www.s-clement.org. Mrs. Lana Jang Rocheford, Prin. Lay Teachers 31; Students 262.
Catechesis/Religious Program—Students 469.

4—St. Joachim (1950) Revs. Joseph Sebastian, S.V.D; Mario Roberto Olea, S.V.D., Parochial Vicar.
Res.: 21250 Hesperian Blvd., 94541-5809. Tel: 510-783-2766; Fax: 510-783-2760. Web: stjoachimcatholicchurch.org.
School—(Grades PreK-8) Tel: 510-783-3177; Fax: 510-783-2161. Web: www.stjoachimschool.org. Armond Seishas, Prin. Lay Teachers 36; Students 351.
Catechesis/Religious Program—Tel: 510-785-1818. Students 765.

Lafayette, Contra Costa Co., St. Perpetua (1952) Rev. John Kasper, O.S.F.S., Parochial Admin.; Deacon Luis Rivilla.
Res.: 3454 Hamlin Rd., 94549-5019. Tel: 925-283-0272; Fax: 925-283-6534. Email: office@stperpetua.org. Web: www.stperpetua.org.
School—(Grades K-8), 3445 Hamlin Rd., 94549-5018. Tel: 925-284-1640; Fax: 925-284-5676. Web: www.stperpetua.org. Karen Goodshaw, Prin. Lay Teachers 38; Students 279.
Catechesis/Religious Program—Tel: 925-283-0272, Ext. 204. Students 359.

Livermore, Alameda Co.

1—St. Charles Borromeo (1964) [JC] Rev. Augusto Acob, Parochial Admin.; Deacon Gilbert Pesqueira. In Res., Rev. Richard McCafferty, S.J. (Retired).
Res.: 1315 Lomitas Ave., 94550-6441. Tel: 925-447-4549; Fax: 925-373-7088. Email: office@stcharlesborromeo.org. Web: www.stcharlesborromeo.org.
Catechesis/Religious Program—Students 257.

2—St. Michael (1878), (Spanish), [CEM] Revs. Robert Mendonca; Javier Aguilar, Parochial Vicar; David E. Staal; Deacons David Rezendes; William Archer, Bus. Admin. & Pastoral Assoc.; Manuel Moya. In Res., Revs. Augustine Koilparampil; Walter W. Mayer (Retired).
Res.: 458 Maple St., 94550-3238. Tel: 925-447-1585; Fax: 925-447-0520.
School—(Grades K-8), 345 Church St., 94550-3205. Tel: 925-447-1888; Fax: 925-447-6720. Web: www.smsliv.org. Tim Hooke, Prin. Lay Teachers 27; Students 243.
Catechesis/Religious Program—Tel: 925-447-8814; Fax: 925-447-6720. Patty Malhiot, D.R.E. Students 595.

Martinez, Contra Costa Co., St. Catherine of Siena (1873) [CEM] Rev. Leonardo Asuncion (Philippines), Parochial Admin.; Deacons Alberto Dizon; David Holland.
Parish Office & Mailing Address: 1125 Ferry St., 94553-1720. Email: stcathmtz@yahoo.com. Web: www.stcmtz.org.
Res.: 1100 Estudillo St., 94553-1707. Tel: 925-228-2230; Fax: 925-228-1318. Email: frleostcath@yahoo.com.
School—(Grades PreSchool-PreSchool) Tel: 925-229-2255; Fax: 925-229-2474. Email: scpreschool@comcast.net.
School—(Grades PreK-8), 604 Mellus St., 94553-1639. Tel: 925-228-4140; Fax: 925-228-0697. Web: www.stcath.net. Ms. Sandy Wright, Prin. Lay Teachers 33; Students 179.
Catechesis/Religious Program—Tel: 925-228-2230, Ext. 30. Students 208.

Moraga, Contra Costa Co., St. Monica (1965) Rev. Wayne Campbell.
Res.: 1001 Camino Pablo, 94556-1831. Tel: 925-376-6900; Fax: 925-376-9796. Email: office@stmonicamoraga.com. Web: www.stmonicamoraga.com.
Catechesis/Religious Program—Students 352.

Newark, Alameda Co., St. Edward (1920) Revs. Jeffrey R. Keyes, C.PP.S.; James Franck, C.PP.S., Parochial Vicar; Jaya Babu Nuthulapati, C.PP.S. (India), Parochial Vicar; Sr. Mary Mark Schoenstein, O.P., Pastoral Assoc.; Deacons Ernest Perez, (Retired); Rolito C. Roque; Roger Wedl.
Res.: 5788 Thornton Ave., 94560-3826. Tel: 510-797-0241; Fax: 510-797-4557. Email: parishoffice@stedwardcatholic.org.
School—(Grades K-8) Tel: 510-793-7242; Fax: 510-793-3189. Web: stedwardnewark.org. Mr. Gregory Fonzeno, Prin. Lay Teachers 33; Students 289.
Catechesis/Religious Program—Tel: 510-797-5588. Email: faithformation@stedwardcatholic.org. Students 374.

Oakley, Contra Costa Co., St. Anthony (1925) [JC] Revs. Olman Solis; Kenneth Sales, Parochial Vicar; Ms. Joann Mass, Business Mgr.; Deacons Joseph Tovar; Alan Layden; Frank Bustos, (Retired).
Res.: 971 O'Hara Ave., 94561-5785. Tel: 925-625-2048; Fax: 925-625-4433. Email: jmassstanthony@aol.com. Web: www.stanthonyoakley.org.
Catechesis/Religious Program—Tel: 925-625-2077. Students 424.

Orinda, Contra Costa Co., Santa Maria (1892) Rev. Msgr. Theodore W. Kraus; Deacon Maurice Custodio, (Retired). In Res., Rev. George Alengadan, S.D.B.
Res.: 40 Santa Maria Way, 94563-2605. Tel: 925-254-2426; Fax: 925-254-2468. Email: smoffice@smparish.org. Web: www.santamariaorinda.com.
Catechesis/Religious Program—Students 176.
Convent—50 Santa Maria Way, 94563-2605. Tel: 925-253-0831.

Piedmont, Alameda Co., Corpus Christi (1929) Rev. Leo J. Edgerly Jr. In Res., Revs. Basil DePinto (Retired); Daniel E. Danielson (Retired).
Res.: 322 St. James Dr., 94611-3627. Tel: 510-530-4343; Fax: 510-530-6824. Email: rectory@corpuschristipiedmont.org. Web: www.corpuschristipiedmont.org.
School—(Grades K-8), One Estates Dr., 94611-3341. Tel: 510-530-4056; Fax: 510-530-5926. Web: www-.corpuschristischool.com. Mrs. Kathleen Murphy, Prin. Lay Teachers 32; Students 277.
Catechesis/Religious Program—Students 219.

Pinole, Contra Costa Co., St. Joseph (1947) Revs. Paul J. Schmidt; Mark Amaral, Parochial Vicar; Edilberto S. Castanas, Parochial Vicar; Deacons Leslie Miyashiro; Donaciano Perez.
Parish Center, Office & Mailing Address: 2100 Pear St., 94564-1711. Tel: 510-741-4900; Fax: 510-724-9185. Email: info@sjcpinole.org. Web: www.sjcpinole.org.
Church: 837 Tennent Ave., 94564-1723.
School—(Grades K-8), 1961 Plum St., 94564. Tel: 510-724-0242; Fax: 510-724-9886. Web: www.stjosephpinole.com. Arlene Marseille, Prin. Lay Teachers 33; Students 299.
Catechesis/Religious Program—Students 469.

Pittsburg, Contra Costa Co.

1—Good Shepherd (1965) Rev. Helmut W. Richter; Deacon Ken Wedge.
Res.: 3200 Harbor St., 94565-5444. Tel: 925-432-6404; Fax: 925-432-6748. Web: www.goodshepherdpittsburg.org.
Catechesis/Religious Program—Tel: 925-439-1091. Students 262.

2—St. Peter, Martyr of Verona (1914) Revs. Sergio Mora; Jesus Salvador Quiroz, Parochial Vicar.
Res.: 740 Black Diamond St., 94565-2148. Tel: 925-432-4771; Fax: 925-432-3389.
School—(Grades PreK-8), 425 W. 4th St., 94565-1968. Tel: 925-439-1014; Fax: 925-439-1506. Web: www.stpetermartyrschool.org. Joseph Siino, Prin. Lay Teachers 26; Students 258.
Catechesis/Religious Program—Tel: 925-432-7200. Students 668.

Pleasant Hill, Contra Costa Co., Christ the King (1951) Revs. Brian T. Joyce; Daniel O'Connor, M.H.M. (Ireland), Parochial Vicar; Deacon John Ashmore. In Res., Revs. Brian Timony (Retired); Michael Dibble.
Res.: 199 Brandon Rd., 94523-3220. Tel: 925-682-2486; Fax: 925-682-5021. Email: webmaster@ctkph.org. Web: www.ctkph.org.
School—(Grades K-8), 195 Brandon Rd., 94523. Tel: 925-685-1109; Fax: 925-685-1289. Email: info@ctkschool.org. Web: www.ctkschool.org. Mrs. Kathy Gannon-Briggs, Prin. Lay Teachers 34; Students 324.
Catechesis/Religious Program—Tel: 925-686-1017; Fax: 925-686-6325. Web: www.ctkph.org. Students 1,000.

Pleasanton, Alameda Co.

1—St. Augustine (1901) Merged with St. Elizabeth Seton, Pleasanton to form The Catholic Community of Pleasanton.

2—The Catholic Community of Pleasanton (1901) [CEM] Revs. Padraig Greene, Admin.; Johnson Abraham, Parochial Vicar; Weerasak (Lee) Chompoochan, Parochial Vicar; Deacons Richard Martin; Ernest Freeman, (Retired); Gary Wortham.
Res.: 3999 Bernal, P.O. Box 817, 94566-7264. Tel: 925-846-4489; Fax: 925-426-5061. Web: www.catholicsofpleasanton.org.
Catechesis/Religious Program—Tel: 925-846-3531; Fax: 925-846-3543. Students 1,334.

3—St. Elizabeth Seton (1991) Merged with St. Augustine, Pleasanton to form The Catholic Community of Pleasanton.

Point Richmond, Contra Costa Co., Our Lady of Mercy (1902) Rev. David K. O'Rourke, O.P., Parochial Admin.
Res.: 301 W. Richmond Ave., 94801-3862. Tel: 510-232-1843. Email: dkorop@sbcglobal.net. Web: www.pointrichmondcatholic.org.
Catechesis/Religious Program—Margaret Morkowski, D.R.E. Students 10.

Richmond, Contra Costa Co.

1—St. Cornelius (1952) [CEM] Rev. Filiberto Barrera, Admin. In Res., Revs. George E. Crespin (Retired); Edmund Coppinger (WIL) (Retired); Raymond Ogbemure (Nigeria).
Res.: 205-28th St., 94804-3001. Tel: 510-233-5215; Fax: 510-233-7342.
School—(Grades K-8), 201-28th St., 94804-3001. Tel: 510-232-3326; Fax: 510-232-4071. Web: home.catholicweb.com/stcornelius. Ms. Sherri Moradi, Prin. Lay Teachers 20; Students 165.
Catechesis/Religious Program—Students 350.

2—St. David of Wales (1952) Revs. John R. Blaker; James Kimani Kairu (Kenya), Parochial Vicar.
Res.: 5641 Esmond Ave., 94805-1112. Tel: 510-237-1531; Fax: 510-237-3801. Email: davidofwales@gmail.com. Web: www.davidofwales.googlepages.com.
School—(Grades PreK-8), 871 Sonoma St., 94805-1122. Tel: 510-232-2283; Fax: 510-231-0484. Web: www.stdavidschool.org. Ann Pires, Prin. Lay Teachers 20; Students 165.
Catechesis/Religious Program—Students 8.

3—St. Mark (1912) Rev. Ramiro Flores, Admin.
Res.: 159 Harbour Way, 94801-3553. Tel: 510-234-5886; Fax: 510-236-5711.
Catechesis/Religious Program—Tel: 510-234-5886, Ext. 222. Students 465.

Rodeo, Contra Costa Co., St. Patrick (1923) Revs. Larry E. Young; Rafal P. Duda, Parochial Vicar.
Res.: 902 Spruce Ct., 94572-1549. Tel: 510-313-0829; Fax: 510-799-5681.
Office: 825 Seventh St., 94572-1549. Tel: 510-799-4406. Web: www.stpatrickrodeo.org.
School—(Grades PreK-8), 907 Seventh St., 94572-1549. Tel: 510-799-2506; Fax: 510-799-6781. Web: www.stpatrickschoolrodeo.org. Kelly Stevens, Prin. Lay Teachers 32; Students 348.
Catechesis/Religious Program—Tel: 510-799-4434. Students 311.

San Leandro, Alameda Co.

1—St. Alphonsus Liguori (1955) [CEM] Merged with Our Lady of Grace, Castro Valley. For parish records contact Our Lady of Grace, Castro Valley.

2—Assumption of the Blessed Virgin Mary (1951) Revs. Vincent J. Scott; Christopher Berbena, Parochial Vicar; Deacons Dac Cao; Harry Clyde; George Peters; John Durden Jr. In Res., Rev. Joseph Duong Phan.
Res.: 1100 Fulton Ave., 94577-6210. Tel: 510-352-1537; Fax: 510-352-9155. Email: slassumption@sbcglobal.net. Web: www.churchoftheassumption.net.
School—(Grades K-8), 1851 136th Ave., 94578-1661. Tel: 510-357-8772; Fax: 510-357-7018. Web: www.assumptionschool-sl.org. Pamela Lyons, Prin. Lay Teachers 14; Students 289.
Catechesis/Religious Program—Students 52.

3—St. Felicitas (1952) Revs. Augustine Joseph, Parochial Admin.; Jayson J. Landeza, Parochial Vicar; Deacon Jose Prado, (Retired). In Res., Rev. Tran Thuc Dinh (Vietnam) (Retired).
Res.: 1662 Manor Blvd., 94579-1509. Tel: 510-351-5244; Fax: 510-351-5730. Email: stfelicitaschurch@comcast.net.
School—(Grades K-8), 1650 Manor Blvd., 94579-1509. Tel: 510-357-2530; Fax: 510-357-5358. Web: www.stfelicitas-school.org. Meghan Anne Jorgensen, Prin. Sisters 1; Lay Teachers 25; Students 284.
Catechesis/Religious Program—Tel: 510-483-4880. Sandi Walton, D.R.E. Students 566.

4—St. Leander (1864) Revs. Paul R. Vassar; Gerald Pedrera, Parochial Vicar; Juan Franco, Parochial Vicar; Deacons Dennis Davis; Victor Silveira. In Res., Rev. Thomas Lester (Retired).
Office: 474 W. Estudillo Ave., 94577-3610. Tel: 510-895-5631; Fax: 510-352-3578. Email: stleander@sbcglobal.net.
School—(Grades PreK-8), 451 Davis St., 94577. Tel: 510-351-4144; Fax: 510-483-6060. Web: www-.stleanderschool.org. Lynne Mullen, Prin. Lay Teachers 30; Students 233.
Catechesis/Religious Program—Students 532.

5—Our Lady of Good Counsel (1966) [JC] Rev. Jan Rudzewicz, Parochial Admin.

Rectory—14112 Azores Pl., 94577-6402. Tel: 510-614-2765; Fax: 510-355-1584. Web: www.olgcsanleandro.com.
Church: 2500 Bermuda Ave., 94577-5436.
Catechesis/Religious Program—Nadine Ramos, D.R.E. Students 42.

SAN LORENZO, ALAMEDA CO., ST. JOHN THE BAPTIST (1925) Revs. Michael Lacey; Hugo Franca (Brazil), Parochial Vicar; Deacons Leonard J. Bettencourt, (Retired); Arturo Jimenez; Noe Tuason.
Res.: 264 E. Lewelling Blvd., 94580-1736. Tel: 510-351-5050; Fax: 510-276-0397. Email: stjohnsrectory@gmail.com. Web: www.stjohnsparishslz.org.
School—(Grades PreK-8), 270 E. Lewelling Blvd., 94580-1736. Tel: 510-276-6632; Fax: 510-276-5645. Web: www.stjohnslz.org. Mrs. Alyssia Schwartz, Prin. Lay Teachers 22; Students 273.
Catechesis/Religious Program—Tel: 510-351-5050, Ext. 16; Fax: 510-276-0397. Kathleen Kennedy, D.R.E. Students 348.

SAN PABLO, CONTRA COSTA CO., ST. PAUL (1864) Revs. Gary Klauer, O.F.M.Conv.; Jacob Carazo, O.F.M.Conv., Parochial Vicar; Tammylee Ngo, O.F.M.Conv., Parochial Vicar.
Res.: 1845 Church Ln., 94806-3705. Tel: 510-232-5931; Fax: 510-232-1846. Web: www.saintpaulschurch.org.
School—(Grades K-8), 1825 Church Ln., 94806. Tel: 510-233-3080; Fax: 510-231-8776. Web: www-.stpaulofsanpablo.org. Natalie Lenz-Acuna, Prin. Lay Teachers 18; Students 169.
Catechesis/Religious Program—Students 403.

SAN RAMON, CONTRA COSTA CO., ST. JOAN OF ARC (1979) Revs. Raymond Zielezienski; Paul Christian Mendoza, Parochial Vicar; Deacons Ruben Gomez; Hock Chuan Oey.
Office: 2601 San Ramon Valley Blvd., 94583-1630. Tel: 925-830-0600. Email: parishoffice@sjasr.org. Web: www.sjasr.org.
Res.: 2421 Cuenca Dr., 94583.
Catechesis/Religious Program—Tel: 925-830-4710. Students 1,253.

UNION CITY, ALAMEDA CO.

1—ST. ANNE (1973) Rev. Geoffrey Baraan; Deacons Benigno Calub; Carlos Rabuy. In Res., Rev. Mel Serraon.
Res.: 32223 Cabello St., 94587-0292. Tel: 510-471-7766; Fax: 510-487-6540. Email: stanne@sbcglobal.net. Web: www.sainteannecatholic.org.
Catechesis/Religious Program—Students 835.

2—HOLY FAMILY CATHOLIC ETHNIC MISSION (1933), For parish records contact St. Anne, Union City.

3—OUR LADY OF THE ROSARY (1951) Rev. Jose M. Leon; Deacons Federico Ceja, (Retired); Richard Folger, (Retired); Gustaaf Roemers, (Retired); Luis Trucios. In Res., Rev. Paul Feng Chen.
Res.: 703 C St., 94587-2195. Tel: 510-471-2609; Fax: 510-471-4601. Email: admin@olrchurch.org. Web: www.olrchurch.org.
School—(Grades K-8), 678 B St., 94587-2141. Tel: 510-471-3765. Web: www.olrschool.org. Gloria Galarsa, Prin. Lay Teachers 15; Students 146.
Catechesis/Religious Program—Tel: 510-471-7419. Email: reled@olrchurch.org. Web: www.olrchurch.org. Students 347.

WALNUT CREEK, CONTRA COSTA CO.

1—ST. ANNE (1965) Rev. Joseph Parekkatt, Parochial Admin.
Res.: 1600 Rossmoor Pkwy., 94595-2507. Tel: 925-932-2324; Fax: 925-932-4628.

2—ST. JOHN VIANNEY (1965) Revs. James J. McGee; Luke Ssemakula (Uganda), Parochial Vicar; Deacon Herb Casey.
Res.: 1650 Ygnacio Valley Rd., 94598-3123. Tel: 925-939-7911; Fax: 925-939-0450. Email: staff@sjvianney.org. Web: www.sjvianney.org.
Catechesis/Religious Program—Tel: 925-939-9544. Students 427.

3—ST. MARY (1941) [JC] Revs. Paulson Mundanmani, Admin.; Ruben Morales-Morfin, Parochial Vicar; Deacon Antonio Reyes.
Res.: 1201 Alpine Rd., 94596-4403. Tel: 925-891-8937; Fax: 925-934-1358. Web: www.stmary-wc.org.
School—(Grades PreK-8), 1158 Bont Ln., 94596. Tel: 925-935-5054; Fax: 925-935-5063. Web: www.st-mary.net. Suzanne Edwards, Prin. Sisters 1; Lay Teachers 38; Students 306.
Catechesis/Religious Program—2039 Mt. Diablo Blvd., 94596. Tel: 925-891-8930. Web: www.stmary-wc.org. Students 197.

4—ST. STEPHEN (1966) Rev. Denis A. Des Rosiers.
Res.: 525 Madonna Ln., 94597-2917. Tel: 925-939-3826; Fax: 925-988-0417. Email: keavenyct@sbcglobal.net. Web: saintstephenparish.org.
Church: 1101 Keaveney Ct., 94597-2465.
Catechesis/Religious Program—Students 31.

Chaplains of Public Institutions
Hospitals

OAKLAND. *Children's Hospital*. Sr. Bernice Gotelli, P.B.V.M., Chap. Tel: 510-428-3885, Ext. 2676. Attended by Sacred Heart Parish, Tel: 510-655-9209.
Highland Hospital. Attended by St. Margaret Mary Parish, Tel: 510-482-0596.
Kaiser-Permanente Medical Center. Spiritual Care Services, Tel: 510-752-6281. Attended by St. Leo the Great Parish, Tel: 510-654-6177.
Summit Campus of the Alta Bates Summit Medical Center. Chaplain Office, Tel: 510-869-6784 Attended by Sacred Heart Parish, Tel: 510-655-9209.

ALAMEDA. *Alameda Hospital*. Attended by St. Joseph Basilica, Tel: 510-522-0181.

ANTIOCH. *Delta Memorial Hospital*. Attended by Most Holy Rosary Parish, Tel: 925-757-4020
Kaiser Permanente Deer Valley. Attended by St. Ignatius of Antioch Parish, Tel: 925-778-0768.
Sutter Delta Medical Center. Attended by St. Ignatius of Antioch Parish, Tel: 925-778-0768.

BERKELEY. *Alta Bates Campus of the Alta Bates Summit Medical Center*. Rev. Michael M. Guimon, O.S.M., Chap. Tel: 510-204-6733; Pager: 510-801-0426. Chaplaincy Services, Tel: 510-204-6730.
Herrick Campus of the Alpha Bates Summit Medical Center. Rev. Michael M. Guimon, O.S.M., Chap. Tel: 510-204-6733; Pager: 510-801-0426. Attended by St. Joseph the Worker Parish, Berkeley, Tel: 510-843-2244.

CASTRO VALLEY. *Eden Hospital*. Attended by Our Lady of Grace Parish, Tel: 510-537-0806.

CONCORD. *Mt. Diablo Hospital Medical Center*. Dept. of Spiritual Care, Tel: 925-674-2133

FREMONT. *Kaiser Permanente Medical Center*. Attended by Our Lady of Guadalupe Parish, Tel: 510-657-4043; St. Edward Parish, Tel: 510-797-0241; St. Joseph Parish, Tel: 510-656-2364.
Washington Hospital. Attended by Our Lady of Guadalupe Parish, Tel: 510-657-4043; St. Edward Parish, 510-797-0241; St. Joseph Parish, 510-656-2364

HAYWARD. *Kaiser Permanente Medical Center*. Attended by St. Bede Parish, Tel: 510-781-2171.
St. Rose Hospital. Pastoral Care Office, Tel: 510-264-4050 Attended by St. Bede Parish, Tel: 510-781-2171.

LIVERMORE. *VA Palo Alto Health Care System Home Livermore Division*. Rev. Augustine Koilparampil. Tel: 925-373-4700, Ext. 35369. Attended by St. Michael Parish, Tel: 925-447-1585.
Valley Memorial Hospital. Attended by St. Charles Borromeo Parish, Tel: 925-447-4549.

MARTINEZ. *Contra Costa Regional Medical Center and VA Administrative Skilled Nursing Center*, Tel: 925-370-4178 (Office). Rev. William B. Johnson, Chap. Pager: 925-346-4293, Sr. Moira McPherson, O.P. Tel: 925-370-4178 (Office); 925-228-2230, Ext. 8. Attended by St. Catherine of Siena Parish, Tel: 925-228-2230.

PITTSBURG. *Delta Memorial Hospital*. Attended by Good Shepherd Parish, Tel: 925-432-6404.

PLEASANTON. *Valley Care Medical Center*. Attended by The Catholic Community of Pleasanton, Tel: 925-846-4489; St. Charles Borromeo Parish, Tel: 925-447-4549.

RICHMOND. *Kaiser-Permanente Medical Center*. Attended by St. Cornelius Parish, Tel: 510-233-5215; St. Mark Parish, Tel: 510-234-5886 & St. Paul Parish, Tel: 510-232-5931

SAN LEANDRO. *All Saints Hospital*. Attended by Assumption Parish, Tel: 510-352-1537.
Fairmont Hospital. Attended by Assumption Parish, Tel: 510-352-1537.
George Mark Children's House. (Hospice) Attended by Assumption Parish, Tel: 510-352-1537.
John George Psychiatric Pavillion. Attended by Assumption Parish, Tel: 510-352-1537.
Kindred Hospital. Attended by Assumption Parish, Tel: 510-352-1537.
San Leandro Hospital. Attended by St. Leander Parish, Tel: 510-895-5631.

SAN PABLO. *Doctors Medical Center*. Attended by St. Paul Parish, Tel: 510-232-5931 & St. Callistus Parish, Tel: 510-223-1153.

SAN RAMON. *San Ramon Regional Medical Center*. Attended by St. Joan of Arc Parish, Tel: 925-830-0600.

WALNUT CREEK. *Kaiser-Permanente Medical Center*. Attended by St. Mary Parish, Tel: 925-891-8900.
Walnut Creek Campus of John Muir Memorial Hospital. Pastoral Care Svcs., Tel: 925-947-5281 Rev. William B. Johnson, Chap. Pager: 925-920-8573. Attended by St. John Vianney Parish, Tel: 925-939-7911.

Prisons and Jails

OAKLAND. *Glenn E. Dyer Detention Facility*. Maria Elena Gonzalez. Tel: 510-259-1728. Detention Ministry sponsored by, Cathedral Parish of Christ the Light, Sacred Heart Parish, St. Columba Parish & St. Patrick Parish, Oakland.

BYRON. *Orin Allen Youth Rehabilitation Facility*. Ken Landoline. Tel: 925-513-3632; 510-813-8125. Detention Ministry sponsored by, St. Anthony Parish, Oakley; Immaculate Heart of Mary Parish, Brentwood; Most Holy Rosary Parish, St. Ignatius Parish, Antioch & St. Anne Parish, Byron.

CLAYTON. *Marsh Creek Detention Facility*. Kathleen Barrere. Tel: 925-674-9140. Detention Ministry sponsored by, St. Bonaventure Parish, Queen of All Saints Parish, St. Agnes Parish & St. Francis of Assisi Parish, Concord.

DUBLIN. *Alameda County Santa Rita Jail*. Richard Denoix. Tel: 925-367-5833. Detention Ministry sponsored by, St. Joan of Arc Parish, San Ramon; St. Raymond Parish, Dublin; St. Isidore Parish, Danville.
Federal Prison Corrections Institution. Deacon Ruben Gomez. Tel: 925-901-0543. Detention Ministry sponsored by, St. Joan of Arc Parish, San Ramon; St. Raymond Parish, Dublin & St. Isidore Parish, Danville

MARTINEZ. *John A. Davis Juvenile Hall*. Mr. Ed Chichon. Tel: 510-758-1469. Detention Ministry sponsored by, St. Callistus Parish, El Sobrante; St. Joseph Parish, Pinole; St. Patrick Parish, Rodeo & St. Rose of Lima Parish, Crockett.
Martinez Detention Facility. Deacon Charles Silvernale. Tel: 925-754-1959. Detention Ministry sponsored by, St. Catherine of Siena Parish, Martinez; Christ the King Parish, Pleasant Hill & St. Stephen Parish, Walnut Creek.

RICHMOND. *West County Detention Facility*. Patricia Connelly. Tel: 510-242-2343. (formerly Richmond Jail); Detention Ministry sponsored by, St. Paul Parish, San Pablo; Our Lady of Mercy Parish, Point Richmond; St. Cornelius Parish & St. Mark Parish, Richmond.

SAN LEANDRO. *Juvenile Hall Facility*. Dennis Flannery. Tel: 510-276-7021. Detention Ministry sponsored by, Our Lady of Good Counsel Parish, Church of the Assumption; St. Felicitas Parish & St. Leander Parish, San Leandro.

On Duty Outside the Diocese:
Revs.—
Dong, Quang Minh
Nguyen, Hy, S.S.
Thurston, Anthony
Tompkins, Terry
Wydeven, John L.
Zamora, Clarence

Study Leave:
Rev.—
Kappler, Stephan

Military Chaplains:
Revs.—
Dinh, Van, Chap., Barksdale AFB, 111 Woodvale Cir., Bossier City, LA 71111.
Tran, Joseph, Chap., 90 MW/HC, 7000 Randall Ave., Fe Warren Afb, WY 82005-2974. Tel: 307-773-3434; Fax: 307-773-2821

On Medical Leave:
Rev.—
Goodwin, Patrick

On Duty to Byzantine Ministry in the Diocese:
Rev.—
Hernandez, Anthony

Retired:
Rev. Msgrs.—
Cardelli, Daniel E.
Ferraro, Joseph
McCracken, John T.
Valdivia, Antonio
Revs.—
Andrade, Bernardino
Atwood, Ronald E.
Brylka, Vincent R.
Charm, Robert
Chavez, Ricardo A.
Cleu, Paul
Crespin, George E.
Danielson, Daniel E.
DePinto, Basil
Devine, Paul
Dinh, Tran Thuc (Vietnam)
Fernandes, John
Gagliardi, Richard
Jaques, Domingos
Joyce, Michael
Kennedy, Jerrold F.
Kozina, Vladimir
Lester, Thomas

Lima, John H.
Marshall, William
Mayer, Walter W.
Mifsud, Carmelo
Ng, Thomas
Norkett, Michael P.
Osuna, E. Donald
Palis, Theo
Peiris, Richard
Phan, Anthony Lam
Pickett, James B.
Poon, Stanislaus
Ruffing, Norman
Russell, Kenneth
Schexnayder, James
Snyder, Alexander
Starbuck, James
Timony, Brian

Permanent Deacons:
Agustin, Benjamin, St. Jerome, El Cerrito
Angel, Jorge, Cathedral Parish of Christ the Light
Archer, John, St. Raymond Penafort, Dublin
Archer, William, St. Michael, Livermore
Arteaga, Gustavo, (On duty outside diocese)
Ashmore, John, Christ the King, Pleasant Hill
Baptista, Antonio, (On duty outside diocese)
Barnes, James, (Retired)
Beltran, Juan, (Unassigned).
Bettencourt, Leonard, (Retired), St. John the Baptist, San Lorenzo.
Bothe, William, (Retired)
Brazil, Rudolph, Holy Spirit, Fremont
Budnik, Steven, Sr., Our Lady of Guadalupe, Fremont
Burns, Jeffrey, St. Lawrence O'Toole, Oakland
Bustos, Frank, (Retired), St. Anthony, Oakley
Cabezas, Rigoberto, (Unassigned)
Calub, Benigno, St. Anne, Union City.
Cantlon, Michael, Our Lady of Guadalupe, Fremont
Cao, Dac, Church of the Assumption, San Leandro
Casey, Herb, St. John Vianney, Walnut Creek
Ceja, Federico, (Retired), Our Lady of the Rosary, Union City.
Chen, Clement, (On Duty Outside Diocese).
Cichon, Witold, Polish Pastoral Center, Union City
Cloyne, David, St. Raymond, Dublin
Clyde, Harry, Church of the Assumption, San Leandro
Custodio, Maurice, Santa Maria, Orinda
Dandan, Ernesto, St. James, Fremont
Davis, Dennis, St. Leander, San Leandro
DeLeon, Joseph L., (Out of Diocese)
Dizon, Alberto, St. Catherine of Siena, Martinez
Drobick, William, Holy Spirit, Fremont
Duhe, Gaston J., (Retired)
Dulka, Matthew, Our Lady of Grace, Castro Valley
Durden, John, Jr., Church of the Assumption, San Leandro
Ehling, Rex, (Retired)
Encarnacion, Rey, Cathedral Parish of Christ the Light, Oakland
Evans, Garry, (On Duty Outside the Diocese)
Folger, Richard, (Retired), Our Lady of the Rosary, Union City
Freeman, Ernest, (Retired), Catholic Community of Pleasanton
Fuentes, Javier, St. Bernard, Oakland
Gall, William, St. Bonaventure, Concord
Garcia, James, (On Duty Outside the Diocese)
Gierak, Rich, St. Bonaventure, Concord.
Glover, Chuck, Holy Spirit, Freemont
Gomes, Joseph, (On Duty Outside the Diocese)
Gomez, Ruben, St. Joan of Arc, San Ramon
Gonsalves, Nelson, Our Lady of Grace, Castro Valley
Gonzalez, Noe, St. Joseph the Worker, Berkeley
Grigg, Jerry, Most Holy Rosary, Antioch
Guesnon, Ovide, Our Lady of Guadalupe, Fremont
Hack, Gary, St. Ignatius, Antioch
Hernandez, Gabriel, Mary Help of Christians, Oakland.
Hoblitzell, Ross, (Retired)
Holland, David, St. Catherine of Siena, Martinez
Horan, Ronald, Immaculate Heart of Mary, Brentwood
Jee, John, St. Isidore, Danville
Jimenez, Arturo, St. John the Baptist, San Lorenzo
Johnson, Earl, St. Louis Bertrand, Oakland
Kortuem, John, Immaculate Heart of Mary, Brentwood
Lara, Jorge, Our Lady of Guadalupe, Fremont
Layden, Alan, St. Anthony, Oakley
Leach, Marty, Transfiguration, Castro Valley
Lee, Stanley, (On Duty Outside the Diocese) Philippines
Lewandowski, Daniel, (On Duty Outside the Diocese)
Macachor, Oscar, St. Joachim, Hayward (On Leave)
Madrigal, Ysidro, (Retired)
Martin, Richard, Catholic Community of Pleasanton
Mazibrook, John, St. Francis of Assisi, Concord
McGowan, Thomas, St. John, El Cerrito
Miyashiro, Leslie, St. Joseph, Pinole
Molloy, Ernest, (On Duty Outside the Diocese)
Moore, Timothy, Transfiguration, Castro Valley
Moya, Manuel, St. Michael, Livermore
Nguyen, John, (Retired)
Oey, Hock Chuan, St. Joan of Arc, San Ramon
Palomares, Charles, St. Francis of Assisi, Concord
Pearce, James, (On Duty Outside the Diocese)
Perez, Alfonso, Corpus Christi, Fremont
Perez, Donaciano, St. Joseph, Pinole
Perez, Ernest, (Retired), St. Edward, Newark
Perez, Jose, (Retired)
Pesqueira, Gil, St. Charles Borromeo, Livermore
Peters, George, Church of the Assumption, San Leandro
Pietras, Adam J., St. Isidore, Danville
Prado, Jose, (Retired), St. Felicitas, San Leandro
Preza, Mariano, St. Bonaventure, Concord
Quigley, Edward, (On Duty Outside the Diocese)
Quinn, Lawrence, All Saints, Hayward
Rabuy, Carlos, St. Anne, Union City
Reyes, Antonio, St. Mary, Walnut Creek
Rezendes, David, St. Michael, Livermore
Rigley, Burton, Transfiguration, Castro Valley
Rivilla, Luis, St. Perpetua, Lafayette
Roemers, Gustaaf, (Retired), Our Lady of the Rosary, Union City
Roque, Rolito C., St. Edward, Newark
Ryken, Denis, (Retired), St. Bede, Hayward.
Sicat, Joe, (Retired), St. Raymond, Dublin
Silveira, Victor, St. Leander, San Leandro
Silvernale, Charles, Most Holy Rosary, Antioch.
Spano, Edward, Immaculate Heart of Mary, Brentwood
Stelly, Eugene, Cathedral Parish of Christ the Light, Oakland
Ta, Peter, Cathedral Parish of Christ the Light, Oakland
Taylor, Stephen, (On Duty Outside the Diocese)
Tovar, Joseph, St. Anthony, Oakley
Trucios, Luis, Our Lady of the Rosary, Union City
Tuason, Noe, St. John the Baptist, San Lorenzo.
Tutson, Ron, St. Benedict, Oakland
Vivet, Lance, St. Joseph, Fremont.
Waters, Gerald, St. Agnes, Concord.
Wedge, Ken, Church of the Good Shepherd, Pittsburg.
Wedl, Roger, St. Edward, Newark
Wong, Danny, Chinese Ministry Center, Oakland
Wortham, Gary, Catholic Community of Pleasanton
Yee, Richard, Holy Spirit, Fremont
Young, David, St. Joseph Basilica, Alameda

INSTITUTIONS LOCATED IN THE DIOCESE

[A] SEMINARIES, RELIGIOUS OR SCHOLASTICATES

OAKLAND. *School of Applied Theology Graduate Theological Union-Berkeley* An Affiliate of the Graduate Theological Union, Berkeley; SAT Sabbatical, 5890 Birch Ct., 94618-1627. Tel: 510-652-1651; Fax: 510-420-0542. Email: info@satgtu.org. Web: www.satgtu.org. James I. Briggs, Exec. Dir.; Sr. Maureen Therese McGroddy, R.S.H.M., Dean Students & Admissions. Priests 13; Brothers 7; Sisters 6; Lay Teachers 8; Students 44; Total Staff 4.

Trustees: J. Randall Andrada; Mary V. Clemency; Ron Courtney; Sr. Barbara Dawson, R.S.C.J.; James A. Donahue, Ph.D.; Sr. Mary T. Grove, I.H.M.; Alan Holloway; James I. Briggs; Edward Tywoniak, Ed.D.; Mr. Robert Mallon; Mr. John McMahon.

BERKELEY. *Dominican School of Philosophy and Theology* (St. Albert's College), 2301 Vine St., 94708-1816. Tel: 510-849-2030; Fax: 510-849-1372. Email: info@dspt.edu. Web: www.dspt.edu. Rev. Michael Sweeney, O.P., Pres.; Peter MacLeod, Vice Pres., Administration, CFO; Mr. Michael Chinnavaso, Dir., Devel. & Donor Rels.; Rev. Christopher J. Renz, O.P., Academic Dean; John Knutsen, Dir. Admissions; Rev. Michael Fones, O.P., Co-Dir., Catherine of Siena Inst.; Sherry Anne Weddell, Co-Dir., Catherine of Siena Inst.; Teresa Olson, Registrar; Colleen Powers, Office Admin. & Dir. Student Svcs. Priests 16; Sisters 2; Lay Teachers 2; Students 103.

Faculty (Regular): Revs. Joseph Boenzi, S.D.B.; Michael J. Dodds, O.P.; Edward Krasevac, O.P.; Bryan Kromholtz, O.P.; Eugene Ludwig, O.F.M-.Cap.; Michael T. Morris, O.P.; Albert Paretsky, O.P.; Anselm Ramelow, O.P.; Augustine Thompson, O.P.; Sisters Marianne Farina, C.S.C.; Barbara Green, O.P.; Margarita Vega, Ph.D.

Faculty (Adjunct): Revs. Michael Fones, O.P.; Arthur Lenti, S.D.B.; Hilary Martin, O.P.; Brendan McAnerney, O.P.; Henry Ormond, O.Carm.; Sergius Propst, O.P.; John J. Roche, S.D.B.

Franciscan School of Theology (1968) 1712 Euclid Ave., 94709-1208. Tel: 510-848-5232; Fax: 510-549-9466. Email: info@fst.edu. Web: www.fst.edu. Rev. Joseph P. Chinnici, O.F.M., Pres. & Rector; Bro. William J. Short, O.F.M., Academic Dean; Carolyn Rodkin, Chief Fin. Officer; Vince Nims, Dir., Recruitment; Ms. Clare Ronzani, Dir., Spiritual Formation; Rev. Franklin Fong, O.F.M., Assoc. Devel. Dir.; Bro. John Summers, O.F.M., Assoc. Devel. Dir.; Randi Quaid, Assoc. Devel. Dir.; Mary Morrison, Dir., Student Svcs.; Joyce McConeghey, Admin. Asst., Pres. & Acad. Dean; Jenna Neilson, Registar & Receptionist. Priests 6; Brothers 3; Sisters 2; Deacons 1; Lay Teachers 3; Total Enrollment 80.

Faculty: Revs. Joseph P. Chinnici, O.F.M.; Garrett Galvin, O.F.M.; Michael D. Guinan, O.F.M.; Thomas West, O.F.M.; Bros. John Kiesler, O.F.M.; William J. Short, O.F.M.; Sisters Mary Beth Ingham, C.S.J.; Eva Lumas, S.S.S.; Mary McGann, R.S.C.J.; Deacon Jeffrey Burns, Ph.D.; Ronald Harbor; Darleen Pryds.

Faculty (Adjunct): Rev. Robert J. McCann, J.C.L.; Frances Flynn.

Jesuit School of Theology of Santa Clara University (Berkeley, California Campus) An Ecclesiastical Faculty of Theology under statutes approved by the Holy See. One of two theological centers of the U.S. Jesuit Conference, Society of Jesus. A graduate school of Santa Clara University located at Berkeley. A Member of the Graduate Theological Union (GTU), Berkeley., 1735 LeRoy Ave., 94709-1115. Tel: 510-549-5000; Fax: 510-841-8536. Email: ltran@jstb.edu. Web: www.scu.edu/jst. Rev. Kevin F. Burke, S.J., Dean; Maureen Beckman, Asst. Dean, Enrollment Mgmt. & Marketing; Paul Kircher, Asst. Dean, Students; Revs. Robert W. McChesney, S.J., Dir. New Directions Sabbatical Prog.; Dir. Intercultural Initiatives; George R. Murphy, S.J., Dir. Formation Prog.; Dr. Bruce Lescher, Assoc. Academic Dean; Sr. Grace A. Hogan, O.P., Assoc. Dir. Enrollment Mgmt.; Ms. Lorna Wallace McKeown, Asst. Academic Dean & In-House Registrar; Lan Tran, Dir. Finance & Business Svc.; Maria Vickroy-Peralta, Asst. Dean, Devel. Priests 11; Sisters 5; Lay Teachers 9; Faculty 17; Students 152.

Faculty: (See listing for The Jesuit Community at The Jesuit School of Theology of Santa Clara Univ., California campus, Berkeley) Revs. Thomas E. Buckley, S.J.; Kevin F. Burke, S.J.; John C. Endres, S.J.; Eduardo C. Fernandez, S.J.; David H. Gill, S.J.; George E. Griener, S.J.; Paul A. Janowiak, S.J.; Francis X. McAloon, S.J.; William R. O'Neill, S.J.; Dr. Jerome P. Baggett; Dr. Thomas Cattoi; Dr. Lisa Fullam; Dr. Gina Hens-Piazza; Rev. Paul Janowiak, S.J.; Dr. Bruce Lescher; Dr. Mia M. Mochizuki; Dr. Jean-Francois Racine; Dr. Catherine P. Zeph.

Part-time Emeritus Faculty: Rev. T. Howland Sanks, S.J.; Sisters Mary Ann Donovan, S.C.; Sandra M. Schneiders, I.H.M.

Part-time Adjunct Faculty: Rev. George R. Murphy, S.J.; Sisters Mary Ann Donovan, S.C.; Jane Ferdon, O.P.; Gloria Inez Loya, P.B.V.M.; Julia Prinz, V.D.M.F.; Ms. Clare Ronzani.

[B] COLLEGES AND UNIVERSITIES

OAKLAND. *Holy Names University* (1868) Chartered 1868. Residence and Non-Residence Students., 3500 Mountain Blvd., 94619-1627. Tel: 510-436-1000; Fax: 510-436-1199. Web: www.hnu.edu.

Sisters of the Holy Names of Jesus and Mary, A Corporation

Holy Names University, A Corporation Sisters of the Holy Names of Jesus and Mary. Priests 1; Sisters 4; Lay Professors 48; Students 1,319.

Administration: William J. Hynes, Ph.D., Pres.; Lizbeth Martin, Vice Pres. Academic Affairs; Michael Miller, Vice Pres. Student Affairs & Enrollment Svcs.; Stuart Koop, Vice Pres. Finance & Admin.; Sr. Carol Sellman, S.N.J.M., Vice Pres., Mission Effectiveness; Richard Ortega, Vice Pres. Univ. Advancement; Jeanette Calixto, Registrar; Carrie Rehak, Ph.D., Dir. Campus Ministry; Karen Schneider, Dir. Library Svcs.

Religious Faculty: Sisters Marcia Frideger, S.N.J.M.; Maureen Hester, S.N.J.M.; Christine Patrinos, S.N.J.M.; JoAnne Quinlivan, S.N.J.M.

Religious Staff: Rev. James Conlon.

MORAGA. *St. Mary's College* (1963) Coed. Resident and Non-Resident Students., 1928 St. Mary's Rd., 94556-2715. Tel: 925-631-4000; Fax: 925-376-1847. Web: www.stmarys-ca.edu. Bro. Ronald Gallagher,

F.S.C., Pres.
Saint Mary's College of California Brothers of the Christian Schools, District of San Francisco. Priests 4; Brothers 25; Professors 445; Total Enrollment 4,075.
Alemany Community: Bro. Michael Meister, F.S.C., Prof. Rel. Studies & Theology.
Campus Ministers: Revs. Thomas J. McElligott (SFR), Campus Min.; Salvatore Ragusa, S.D.S., Campus Min.
Faculty: Revs. John Morris, O.P.; Michael A. Russo; Bros. Mel Anderson, F.S.C., Pres. Emeritus; Martin Ash, Alumni Dept.; Michael S. Avila, F.S.C., Prof. Rel. Studies & Theology; William Beatie, F.S.C., Prof. Philosophy; Dominic Berardelli, F.S.C., Spec. Asst. to Pres.; Glenn Bolton, F.S.C., Career Counseling; Kenneth W. Cardwell, F.S.C., Prof. Integral Prog.; Camillus Chavez, F.S.C., Campus Min.; Myron Collins, F.S.C., Prof. Chemistry; Charles Hilken, F.S.C., Prof. History; Richard Lemberg, F.S.C., Librarian, Instructional Svcs.; Bernard LoCoco, F.S.C.; Brenden Madden, F.S.C., Career Counseling; Mark McVann, F.S.C., Prof. Rel. Studies & Theology; Bertrand Nguyen, F.S.C., (Retired); Raphael Patton, F.S.C., Prof. Mathematics; Casimir Reichlin, F.S.C., Spec. Asst. to Pres.; Augustus Rossi, F.S.C., Prof. Chemistry; Dominic John Ruegg, F.S.C., Librarian (Retired); Clarence Schenk, F.S.C., Media Svcs.; Stan Sobczyk, (Retired); Martin Yribarren, F.S.C.

[C] HIGH SCHOOLS, DIOCESAN

OAKLAND. *Bishop O'Dowd High School* (1951) 9500 Stearns Ave., 94605-4720. Tel: 510-577-9100; Fax: 510-638-3259. Email: sphelps@bishopodowd.org. Web: www.bishopodowd.org. Stephen Phelps, Ed.D., Pres.; Pamela Shay, Prin.; Annette Counts, Librarian. Lay Teachers 72; Students 1,125.

St. Elizabeth High School, 1530-34th Ave., 94601. Tel: 510-532-8947; Fax: 510-532-9754. Email: lbrock@stliz-hs.org. Web: www.stliz-hs.org. Sisters Mary Liam Brock, O.P., Prin.; Christopher Miller, O.P., Librarian. Sisters 3; Lay Teachers 16; Students 165.

[D] HIGH SCHOOLS, PAROCHIAL

ALAMEDA. *Saint Joseph Notre Dame High School*, 1011 Chestnut St., 94501-4315. Tel: 510-523-1526; Fax: 510-523-2181. Email: toconnor@sjnd.org. Web: www.sjnd.org. Mr. Simon Chiu, Prin.; Kristopher White, Ed.D., Asst. Prin. Academics; Jennifer Dlugosh, Librarian. Lay Teachers 28; Total Staff 54; Students 408.

[E] HIGH SCHOOLS, PRIVATE

OAKLAND. *Holy Names High School* (1868) 4660 Harbord Dr., 94618-2211. Tel: 510-450-1110; Fax: 510-547-3111. Email: sslyngstad@hnhsoakland.org. Web: www.hnhsoakland.org. Sally Slyngstad, S.N.J.M., Prin.; Kris Waller, Librarian. Sisters of the Holy Names of Jesus and Mary. Sisters 4; Lay Teachers 36; Students 200.

BERKELEY. *Saint Mary's College High School* (1863) 1294 Albina Ave., 94706-2599. Tel: 510-526-9242; Fax: 510-559-6277. Web: www.saintmaryschs.org. Bro. Edmond Larouche, F.S.C., Pres.; Mr. Peter Imperial, Prin.; Mr. Brian Thomas, Librarian. Brothers of the Christian Schools. Brothers 1; Lay Teachers 48; Students 600.

CONCORD. *Carondelet High School* (1965) 1133 Winton Dr., 94518-3527. Tel: 925-686-5353; Fax: 925-671-9429. Email: chs@carondeleths.org. Web: www.carondelet.pvt.k12.ca.us. Sr. Kathleen Lang, C.S.J., Pres.; Mrs. Nancy Libby, Prin.; Mrs. Joan Tracy, M.L.S., Librarian. Sisters of St Joseph of Carondelet. Sisters 4; Lay Teachers 63; Students 802.
Convent: Tel: 925-686-9697.

De La Salle High School of Concord, Inc. dba De La Salle High School (1965) (Boys), 1130 Winton Dr., 94518-3528. Tel: 925-288-8100; Fax: 925-686-3474. Email: higakic@dlshs.org. Web: www.dlshs.org. Mr. Mark DeMarco, Pres.; Bro. Robert J. Wichman, F.S.C., Prin.; Ms. Elaine Seed, Librarian. Brothers of the Christian Schools Brothers 1; Lay Teachers 73; Students 1,027.
Co-Assistant Principals: Mr. Jack Dyer, Student Life; Mr. Roger Hassett, Dir. Campus Ministry; Mrs. Mary Ann Lemire Mattos, Academic Life.

HAYWARD. *Moreau Catholic High School* (1965) 27170 Mission Blvd., 94544. Tel: 510-881-4300; Fax: 510-581-5669. Email: tlee@moreaucatholic.org. Web: www.moreaucatholic.org. Terrence Lee, Pres.; Lauren Lek, Prin.; Catherine Wickboldt, Corp. Treas.; Susan Geiger, Librarian; Rev. Tito Bonoan, Chap. Congregation of Holy Cross. Priests 2; Lay Teachers 54; Students 900.

RICHMOND. *Salesian High School*, 2851 Salesian Ave., 94804. Tel: 510-234-4433; Fax: 510-236-4636. Email: nreina@salesian.com. Web: www.salesian.com. Rev. Nicholas J. Reina, S.D.B., Dir. & Pres.; Mr. Timothy Chambers, Prin.; Rev. John Malloy, S.D.B.; Bros. Anthony Matse, S.D.B., (Retired); Ricardo Ramos, S.D.B.; Sr. Mary Greenan, F.M.A., Coord. Youth Min.; Stephanie Tristan, Dir. Devel. Salesians of St. John Bosco. Priests 1; Brothers 1; Sisters 1; Lay Teachers 27; Students 530. In Res. Rev. Chris Woerz, S.D.B.; Bros. Jerry Weirich, S.D.B.; Gustavo Ramirez, S.D.B.

[F] ELEMENTARY SCHOOLS, PRIVATE

CONCORD. *Wood Rose Academy*, (Grades PreSchool-8), 4347 Cowell Rd., 94518-1807. Tel: 925-825-4644; Fax: 925-825-4645. Email: woodroseacad@sbcglobal.net. Web: www.woodroseacademy.org. Ellen Crnkovich, Prin.; Rosemarie Ramirez, Librarian. Lay Teachers 15; Students 120.

[G] EARLY CHILDHOOD EDUCATION CENTERS

FREMONT. *Dominican Kindergarten*, 43326 Mission Blvd., 94539-5829. Tel: 510-651-7978; Fax: 510-651-7978. Email: sj@dkmsj.com. Web: www.dkmsj.org. Sr. Jane Marie Estoesta, O.P., Dir. & Teacher. Sisters 1; Students 30.

[H] CATHOLIC CHARITIES OF THE DIOCESE OF OAKLAND

OAKLAND. *Catholic Charities of the Diocese of Oakland*, 433 Jefferson St., 94607-3539. Tel: 510-768-3100; Fax: 510-451-6998. Email: info@cceb.org. Web: www.cceb.org. Most Rev. Salvatore J. Cordileone, Pres.; Mr. Solomon Belette, CEO, Sec.; A.R. Neubauer, Chm.; Stephen Wilcox, Vice Chm.; Ben F. Polando, Treas.; Michael C. Brown, Diocesan Representative; Frank Malifrando, Chief Devel. Officer; Cynthia Rothschild, Chief Prog. Officer; Doug Haffer, Legal Immigration Svcs. Div. Dir. Tel: 510-768-3167; 888-277-8608 Legal Immigration Svcs. Toll Free; Cristina Hernandez, Educ. & Employment Div. Dir. Tel: 510-439-4261; Millie Burns, Deputy Dir., Progs., Violence Prevention & Mental Health Svcs. Div. Dir. Tel: 510-768-3188; Carol Leahy, Poverty Div. Dir. Tel: 510-768-3165.
Catholic Charities of the Diocese of Oakland. Total Assisted Annually 21,000.

Oakland Family Service Center, 433 Jefferson St., 94607. Tel: 510-768-3100.

Concord Family Service Center, 3540 Chestnut Ave., Concord, 94519. Tel: 925-825-3099.

Richmond Main Office, 2369 Barrett Ave., Richmond, 94804. Tel: 510-234-5110.

[I] DAY NURSERIES

OAKLAND. *Saint Vincent's Day Home, Inc.* (1911) 1086 Eighth St., 94607-2616. Tel: 510-832-8324; Fax: 510-832-5021. Email: info@svdh.org. Web: www.svdh.org. Corinne M. Mohrmann, Exec. Dir.
Saint Vincent's Day Home, A Corporation, Purpose: Since 1911, Saint Vincent's Day Home's (SVDH) mission has been to serve and act on behalf of the needs, rights and well-being of all young children by offering educational and developmental services and resources to families struggling toward self-sufficiency. SVDH strives to achieve high-quality services while promoting excellence in the field of Child Development and Family Services. Religious 1; Lay Staff 48; Capacity 230; Total Assisted 514; Total Staff 49.

[J] ORGANIZATIONS FOR DEAF AND HARD OF HEARING

HAYWARD. *St. Joseph's Center for Deaf and Hard of Hearing*, 25580 Campus Dr., 94542-1137. Tel: 510-267-8338 (Voice); 866-977-9920 (Video Phone); Fax: 510-893-0945. Email: rherbst@oakdiocese.org. Web: www.sjcd.org. 2121 Harrison St., Ste. 100, 94612-3788.
St. Joseph's Center for the Deaf and Hard of Hearing, A Corporation.

[K] RETIREMENT AND CARE FACILITIES

OAKLAND. *Bishop Begin Villa* (Retired Priests), 3418 E. 18th St., 94601-3004. Tel: 510-536-0719; Fax: 510-261-4516. Revs. Vincent R. Brylka (Retired); Tom J. Edwards; Joseph A. Ferreira (Retired); David Link. Residents 4; Total Assisted 4.

Mercy Retirement and Care Center (1822) (Affiliated with Elder Care Alliance), 3431 Foothill Blvd., 94601-3129. Tel: 510-534-8540; Fax: 510-261-7551. Email: pcreedon@eldercarealliance.org. Web: www.mercyretirementcenter.org. Sr. Patricia Creedon, Admin. Sponsored by the Sisters of Mercy of the Americas - West Midwest Community., Residental Care, Assisted Living and Skilled Nursing. Sisters of Mercy 5; Employees 160; Residents 93; Bed Capacity 107.

Bishop Begin Villa, Retirement Facility for Priests in the Oakland Diocese Extensive community services.

Convalescent Hospital - Skilled Nursing Facility Tel: 510-534-8540; Fax: 510-261-4516. Web: www.mercyretirementcenter.org. Bed Capacity 59; Residents 55.

[L] MONASTERIES AND RESIDENCES OF PRIESTS AND BROTHERS

OAKLAND. *Franciscan Friars (Province of St. Barbara), Arch Street Friary*, 1508 Arch St., Berkeley, 94708-1829. Tel: 510-898-1879. Revs. Garrett Galvin, O.F.M., Guardian; Joseph P. Chinnici, O.F.M.; Franklin Fong, O.F.M.; Michael D. Guinan, O.F.M.; Kenneth Lavarone, O.F.M.; Finian McGinn, O.F.M.; Bros. Rami Fodda, O.F.M.; Louis Khoury, O.F.M.; Nghia Phan, O.F.M.; Joseph Sury, O.F.M.; Ryan Thornton, O.F.M.

Franciscan Friars (Province of St. Barbara), Msg. Oscar A. Romero Friary, 1465 - 35th Ave., 94601. Tel: 510-479-7435. Revs. Oscar A. Mendez, O.F.M.; Alberto Villafan, O.F.M.; Bro. David Cobian, O.F.M., M.Div.

Franciscan Friars of California (Province of St. Barbara), Provincial Office, 1500-34th Ave., 94601-3092. Tel: 510-536-3722; Fax: 510-536-3970. Email: main@sbofm.org. Web: www.sbfranciscans.org. Very Rev. John Hardin, O.F.M., Prov. Min.; Revs. Kenneth Lavarone, O.F.M., Prov. Vicar; Daniel Lackie, O.F.M., Vocations/JPIC Animator; Bros. Peter Boegel, O.F.M., Prov. Sec.; James Swan, O.F.M., Assoc. Treas.; Sr. Elizabeth Konkol, S.S.J.-T.O.S.F., Prov. Min. Assist.; Ms. Guadalupe Aceves, Treas.; Ms. Gerry Carbone, Treas. Asst.; Ms. Reyna Lupian, Accounting; Ms. Gwen Patterson, Treas. Asst. Insurance.
Franciscan Friars of California
St. Anthony Retreat Center, Inc.
St. Anthonys Seminary Priests 3; Total Staff 10.

Franciscan Friars of California (Province of St. Barbara), Office of Franciscan Outreach, 1500 - 34th Ave., 94601-3092. Tel: 916-443-5717. Email: ofmcadev@att.net. Web: www.sbfranciscans.org. Ms. Ali Packard, Devel. Assoc.; Bro. Jeff Shackleton, O.F.M., Publications Editor; Ms. Jonte McQueen, Devel. Asst.

Franciscan Friars of California, (Province of St. Barbara), St. Elizabeth Friary, 1500 34th Ave., 94601-3091. Tel: 510-536-1287; Fax: 510-536-3578. Email: stefriary@mail.com. Web: www.sbfranciscans.org. Bros. Balbino Rodriguez, O.F.M., Guardian; Jeffrey Macnab, O.F.M., Vicar; Revs. William Brand, O.F.M.; Mel Bucher, O.F.M.; Eugene Burnett, O.F.M.; Rigoberto Caloca-Rivas, O.F.M., Ph.D.; Larry Dunphy, O.F.M.; Martin Ibarra, O.F.M.; John Tran Nguyen, O.F.M.; Pedro Vasquez, O.F.M.; Louis Vitale, O.F.M.; Bros. Robert Brady, O.F.M.; Raul Diaz, O.F.M.; Mario Espitia, O.F.M.; Thomas More Ganmy, O.F.M.; Juan Jose Jauregui, O.F.M.; Michael Minton, O.F.M.; Samuel Nasada, O.F.M.; Vincent Nguyen, O.F.M.; Maurice Peltier, O.F.M.; Phillip Polk, O.F.M.; Scott Slattum, O.F.M.; James Swan, O.F.M.; Victor Vega, O.F.M.; Rufino Zaragoza, O.F.M.
Friars of the Province in Residences Not Listed Elsewhere Revs. Barry Brunsman, O.F.M., Los Banos, CA; Garrett Edmunds, O.F.M., Jerusalem, Israel; Elias Galvez, O.F.M., Guaymas, Mexico; John Gibbons, O.F.M., Ussuriysk, Russia; Emerito Gomez, O.F.M., Yabukoa, Puerto Rico; Xavier J. Harris, O.F.M., Belmont, CA; William Minkel, O.F.M., Guaymas, Mexico; Miguel Obregon, O.F.M., Houston, TX; Rodrigo Ortiz, O.F.M., Medellin, Colombia; Sergio Santo, O.F.M., Manila, Philippines; Gary Swirczynski, O.F.M., Fort Worth, TX; Robert Young, O.F.M., Tallahassee, FL; Bros. Leo Gonzales, O.F.M., Jerusalem, Israel; Gerard Saunders, O.F.M., Tierra Blanca, Peru; Ivo Toneck, O.F.M., Guaymas, Mexico.

Jesuit Fathers and Brothers (1972) *Murray Residence Community*, 171 Santa Rosa Ave., 94610-1316. Tel: 510-655-8334; Fax: 510-655-4816. Revs. Thomas C. Weston, S.J., Supr.; John A. Baumann, S.J.; Stephen M. Kelly, S.J.; Lester E. Love, S.J.; Michel Marcil, S.J.

Missionary Oblates of Mary Immaculate United States Province (1953) 290 Lenox Ave., 94610-4625. Tel: 510-452-1550; Fax: 510-893-1272. Email: omi290@comcast.net. Web: www.omiusa.org.
Missionary Oblates of Mary Immaculate United States Province Total in Residence 2; Total Staff 1. In Res. Revs. Don Arel, O.M.I., Dir.; William Hallahan, O.M.I.

Order of Preachers (Province of the Most Holy Name of Jesus - Western Dominican Province) (1914) 5877 Birch Ct., 94618-1626. Tel: 510-658-8722; Fax: 510-658-1061. Email: wdp@opwest.org. Web: www.opwest.org. Very Rev. Mark C. Padrez, O.P., Prior Prov.; Revs. Dominic DeDomenico, O.P., Treas.; Jude Eli, O.P., Dir. Western Dominican

Preaching; Vincent Benoit, O.P., Dir. Province Web Site; John Marie Bingham, O.P., Promoter Holy Name Society, (Knight Commander of the Holy Sepulcher); Michael Fones, O.P., Student Master; Xavier Lavagetto, O.P., Promoter Parish Min.; Steven Maekawa, O.P., Dir. Vocations; Stephen Maria Lopez, O.P., Dir. Promoter Rosary Confraternity; John Morris, O.P., Promoter Social Justice; Joseph Sergoff, O.P., Socius & Vicar to Prov.; Bartholomew J. Hutcherson, O.P., Promoter Campus Min.; Anthony Rosevear, O.P., Novice Master; Patrick LaBelle, O.P., Promoter Ongoing Formation; Bryan Kromholtz, O.P., Regent, Studies; Vincent Serpa, O.P., Promoter & Dominican Laity; Michael Morris, O.P., Promotor Mass Media & Arts; Martin Walsh, O.P., Dir. Dominican Mission Foundation; Allen Duston, O.P., Dir. St. Jude Shrine. Province of the Most Holy Name of Jesus. Total in the Province 152.

Serving in Latin America: Revs. Timothy Conlan, O.P. (Guatemala); Bartholomew dela Torre, O.P. (Mexico); Martin Walsh, O.P.

Serving in Germany: Rev. Richard Schenk, O.P.

Serving in Rome: Revs. Luke D. Buckles, O.P., Prof. Pontificia Universita San Tommaso; Robert Christian, O.P., Prof. Pontificia Universita San Tommaso; Alejandro Crosthwaite, O.P., Prof. Pontificia Universita San Tommaso.

Serving in Israel: Rev. Gregory T. Tatum, O.P., Assoc. Prof. Ecole Biblique et Archeologique Francaise.

Serving in Australia: Rev. Hilary Martin, O.P., Visiting Prof.

Serving in Africa: (Kenya) Bros. Daniel Thomas, O.P.; Emmanuel Taylor, O.P., Residing Student.

Serving in Switzerland: Revs. Michael S. Sherwin, O.P., Assoc. Prof. Univ. Fribourg; Bernard Blankenhorn, O.P., Doctoral Studies.

Order of Preachers (Province of the Most Holy Name of Jesus - Western Dominican Province) (1932) *St. Albert Priory*, Dominican House of Formation, 5890 Birch Ct., 94618-1627. Tel: 510-596-1800; Fax: 510-596-1860. Web: www.op.org/opwest/sap. Very Rev. Reginald Martin, O.P., Prior; Revs. Vincent Benoit, O.P.; Dominic Briese, O.P.; Dominic DeDomenico, O.P., Province Trustee; Finbarr Hayes, O.P.; Michael Fones, O.P., Student Master; Bryan Kromholtz, O.P.; Steven Maekawa, O.P., Dir. Vocations; Hilary Martin, O.P.; Brendan McAnerney, O.P., DominICON Ministry Sacramento, CA; Mark O'Leary, O.P.; Sergius Propst, O.P.; Richard Schenk, O.P.; Edmund K. Ryan, O.P.; John Flannery, O.P., Subprior, Regent of Studies; Augustine Thompson, O.P.; Antoninus Wall, O.P.; Janko Zagar, O.P.; Bros. Kevin Andrew, O.P.; Raymond Bertheaux, O.P.; Christopher Brannan, O.P.; Joseph Mary Do, O.P.; Bradley Elliott, O.P.; Justin Gable, O.P.; Lupe Gonzalez, O.P.; Mark Gorski, O.P.; Peter Junipero Hannah, O.P.; Simon Kim, O.P.; Dennis Klein, O.P.; Corwin Saxon Low, O.P.; Richard Maher, O.P.; Dominic Maichrowicz, O.P.; Pasquale Manalio-Passarelli, O.P.; Gabriel Mosher, O.P.; Dominic Tuan Ngo, O.P.; Michael James Rivera, O.P.; Ambrose Sigman, O.P.; Emmanuel Taylor, O.P.; Christopher Wetzel, O.P.; Peter Yost, O.P. *Order of Preachers (Province of Holy Name of Jesus - Western Dominican Province), Siena House*, 5730 Presley Way, 94618-1633. Tel: 510-654-8735. Revs. Michael T. Morris, O.P., Dominican School of Philosophy and Theology; David K. O'Rourke, O.P., Parish Admin., (Our Lady of Mercy, Richmond, CA); Very Rev. Mark C. Padrez, O.P., Socius & Vicar to Prov. & Supr.; Revs. Terence Reilly, O.P.; Joseph Sergott, O.P.; Leo Tubbs, O.P. Priests 7.

Redemptorist Fathers (Denver Province), 8945 Golf Links Rd., 94605-4124. Tel: 510-562-9740; Fax: 510-562-1406. Email: POBCSS@aol.com. P.O. Box 5007, 94605-4124. Rev. Patrick O'Brien, C.Ss.R., Pres.

Redemptorist Society of California; Redemptorists of Oakland.

BERKELEY. *Capuchin Franciscan Friars, House of Studies*, 1534 Arch St., 94708-1829. Tel: 510-841-2229; Fax: 510-849-0809. Email: piusofmcap@hotmail.com. *Saint Conrad Friary* Tel: 510-841-2229; Fax: 510-849-0809. Revs. James Johnson, O.F.M.Cap.; Peter Vong Mai (Vietnam); Bros. Peter Ciolino, O.F.M.Cap.; Hai Ho, O.F.M.Cap.; Christopher Iwancio, O.F.M.Cap.; Mark Mance, O.F.M.Cap.; Nathaniel Santos, O.F.M.Cap. Friars in Residence 9; Friars in Formation 6; Total Staff 3.

Incarnation Monastery, Camaldolese Benedictines (1979) 1369 La Loma Ave., 94708-2031. Tel: 510-845-0601; Fax: 510-845-0601. Email: facolnaghi@aol.com. Web: www.contemplation.com. Rev. Andrew Colnaghi, Prior. Tel: 510-548-0965; Fax: 510-548-6439. Total in Residence 3. In Res. Revs. Thomas Matus, O.S.B.Cam.; Arthur Poulin, O.S.B.Cam.; Matthew Rios, O.S.B.Cam.

Jesuit Fathers and Brothers, Jesuit Community at Jesuit School of Theology, 1756 LeRoy Ave., 94709-1157. Tel: 510-225-6200; Fax: 510-549-1114. Email: rector@jstb.edu. Web: www.jstbjesuits.org. Revs. Thomas E. Buckley, S.J.; Kevin F. Burke, S.J., Dean; Guillaume (Billy) Birhashwirwa Chabwine, S.J. (Democratic Republic of Congo); Fady Chidiac, S.J. (Lebanon); Dominik Ciolek, S.J. (Poland); Bert Daelemans, S.J. (Belgium); John C. Endres, S.J.; Eduardo C. Fernandez, S.J.; David H. Gill, S.J.; George E. Griener, S.J.; Richard D. Hunt, S.J.; Paul A. Janowiak, S.J.; David W. Johnson, S.J.; Jerome Kerketta, S.J. (India); Joseph Lobo, S.J. (India); Frank A. Majka, S.J.; Robert W. McChesney, S.J.; John T. Mitchell, S.J., Min.; George R. Murphy, S.J.; Sess Julien N'Guessan, S.J. (Cote d'Ivoire); Joseph H. Nguyen, S.J.; Jorge Arturo Ochoa, S.J. (Mexico); Robert J. Ochs, S.J.; William R. O'Neill, S.J.; Stephen Patterson, S.J. (England); Binoy Jacob Pichalakkattu, S.J. (India); T. Howland Sanks, S.J.; Ignatius Sasmita, S.J.; Martin Sebo, S.J. (Slovakia); Anthony E. Sholander, S.J., Rector; Antonius Firmansyah Sihombing, S.J. (Indonesia); Tomislav Spiranec, S.J. (Croatia); Rafal Struginski, S.J. (Poland); Irudayaraj Dominic Sundara Raj, S.J. (India); James Argen Tete, S.J. (India); Anthony S. Valan, S.J. (India); Miran Zvanut, S.J. (Slovenia). (See also listing for The Jesuit School of Theology at Berkeley). Priests 40; Brothers 2; Deacons 5; Total in Residence 81; Scholastics 34.

Marist Fathers and Brothers, 2335 Warring St., 94704-1839. Tel: 510-486-1232; 510-486-1276; Fax: 510-848-7204. Web: www.societyofmaryusa.org. Rev. Thomas E. Ellerman, S.M., Dir. Postulants; Mr. Jack Ridout, Vocations Dir. & Business Mgr.

Marist Society Inc., Seminary Name: St. Peter Chanel Seminary - Marist Pre-novitate Program.

Priests of the Congregation of Holy Cross, Holy Cross Center, 2597 Virginia St., 94709-1108. Tel: 510-548-8515. Revs. Bruce Cecil, C.S.C; Harry Cronin, C.S.C., Dir.; Brent A. Kruger, C.S.C.

Redemptorist Fathers (Denver Province), St. Clement Maria House, Redemptorist West Coast Mission Team, 2215 Rose St., 94709-1430. Tel: 510-981-9005; Fax: 510-981-9004. Email: anphdng@gmail.com. Revs. Anthony Nguyen, C.Ss.R., Rector; Donald MacKinnon, C.Ss.R.; Richard Schiblin, C.Ss.R.; David Tobin, C.Ss.R.; Deacon Dennis Lee, C.Ss.R.

The Redemptorists of Berkeley

Salesians of Don Bosco, Don Bosco Hall, 1831 Arch St., 94709-1309. Tel: 510-204-0800; Fax: 510-704-1925. Email: donboscohallca@gmail.com. Web: www.donboscowest.org. Total in Residence 16; Total Staff 4.

Core Team: Revs. Joseph Boenzi, S.D.B., Councilor; Arthur Lenti, S.D.B., Councilor; John Roche, S.D.B., Prof.; Steven Whelan, S.D.B., Economer.

Students in Residence: Revs. Redentor Coloma, S.D.B. (Papua New Guinea); Chan Rhan Hur (Korea, South); George Kainikunnel, S.D.B. (Sudan); Andrew Ng, S.D.B. (Hong Kong); Samuel Oppong Nkansah, C.S.Sp. (Ghana); Alejandro Rodriguez, S.D.B. (Mexico).

Servites (United States of America Province), 2406 Virginia St., 94709-1206. Tel: 510-849-2726. Revs. Bruce J. Klikunas, O.S.M. (Retired); Michael M. Guimon, O.S.M., Alta-Bates Summit Hospital Chap.; Stephen Ryan, O.S.M. (Retired). Total in Residence 2.

Society of the Precious Blood (Kansas City Province) (1985) 2800 Milvia St., 94703-2209. Tel: 510-841-2777. Revs. David Matz, C.PP.S.; James D. Sloan, C.PP.S.; James Urbanic, C.PP.S. Priests 4.

CASTRO VALLEY. *Conventual Franciscans (Province of St. Joseph of Cupertino), Holy Family Friary*, 19697 Redwood Rd., 94546-3456. Tel: 510-582-7314; Fax: 510-582-7455. Revs. Thomas Czeck, O.F.M.Conv.; Paul Fazio, O.F.M.Conv.; Thomas Hamilton, O.F.M.Conv.; Bruce Lamb, O.F.M.Conv.; Bros. Francisco Cabral, O.F.M.Conv.; Patrick Lytell, O.F.M.Conv.; James Reiter, O.F.M.Conv.; Christopher Saindon, O.F.M.Conv.

[M] CONVENTS AND RESIDENCES FOR SISTERS

OAKLAND. *Adrian Dominican Sisters (Congregation of the Most Holy Rosary)*, 3693 High St., 94619-2105. Tel: 510-530-2621. Adrian Dominican Sisters 3; San Rafael Dominican Sisters 1; Sisters of The Holy Family 1.

Congregation of the Queen of the Holy Rosary (Dominican Sisters of Mission San Jose), St. Elizabeth Convent, 1555-34th Ave., 94601-3062. Tel: 510-532-8344; Fax: 510-533-2365. Web: www.msjdominicans.org. Sisters 13.

Dominican Sisters of Oakford, Bethany House, 919 Aileen St., 94608-2805. Tel: 510-652-0986. Email: bethanyop@gmail.com. Web: www.oakford.op.org. Sisters 2.

Sisters of Mercy of the Americas (West Midwest Community), Mercy Retirement and Care Center, 3431 Foothill Blvd., 94601-3129. Tel: 510-534-8540; Fax: 510-261-7551. Web: www.mercyretirementcenter.org. Sisters 5.

Sisters of Notre Dame de Namur (California Province), 3431 Foothill Blvd., 94601-3129. Tel: 510-533-3162. 3431 Foothill Blvd., 94601-3129. Tel: 510-533-3162. Sisters 13.

Sisters of Sacred Hearts of Jesus and Mary, 7626 Curry Ave., El Cerrito, 94530. Sisters 2.

Sisters of St. Joseph of Carondelet, 1133 Winton Dr., Concord, 94518. Tel: 925-686-9697; Fax: 925-671-9429.

Carondelet Community, 1133 Winton Dr., Concord, 94518-3527. Tel: 925-686-9697; Fax: 925-671-9429. Sisters 5. *Kwanza House Community*, 529 Jean St., 94610-1906. Tel: 510-655-2382; Fax: 510-655-0249. Sisters 2. *Christ the King Community*, 3095 Diablo View Rd., Pleasant Hill, 94523-4535. Tel: 925-280-1562; Fax: 925-685-1289. Sisters 3. *St. Anthony Community*, 428 Coral Reef Rd., Alameda, 94501. Tel: 510-995-8604. Sisters 2.

Bethany Community, 2203 Colonial Ct., Walnut Creek, 94598-1125. Tel: 925-932-2004. Sisters 3.

Via del Sol Community, 720 N. Gate Rd., Walnut Creek, 94598. Tel: 925-287-9611. Sisters 2.

Sisters of the Holy Names of Jesus and Mary (U.S. - Ontario Province), 3500 Mountain Blvd., 94619. Tel: 510-436-1265; Fax: 503-675-7138. Web: www.snjmusontario.org. Sisters 37.

Sisters of the Presentation of the Blessed Virgin Mary (1854) 11 Warren Ave., No. 7, 94611-5457. Tel: 510-420-4556. Sisters 4.

Union of Sisters of the Presentation of the Blessed Virgin Mary (Kildare, Ireland), 1114 - 32nd St., 94608. Tel: 510-547-8284. Sisters 4.

BERKELEY. *Congregation of the Queen of the Holy Rosary (Dominican Sisters of Mission San Jose)*, St. Mary Magdalen Community, 2004 Eunice St., 94709-1932. Tel: 510-527-4817. Email: smls@msjdominicans.org. Web: www.msjdominicans.org. Sisters 5.

Sisters of Charity of the Blessed Virgin Mary, 1746 Addison St., 94703-1567. Tel: 510-841-8791. Email: helen.thompson@comcast.net. Web: www.bvmcong.org.

BRENTWOOD. *Religious Missionary Sisters of the Blessed Sacrament and Mary Immaculate*, 636 - 3rd St., 94513-1357. Tel: 925-513-8154; Fax: 925-516-4847. Email: jverano1960@att.net. Sisters 3.

CONCORD. *Quinhon Missionary Sisters of the Holy Cross*, Provincial House, 1685 Humphrey Dr., 94519-2810. Tel: 925-674-9639; Fax: 925-676-9320. Sr. Rosaline Lieu Nguyen, L.H.C., Novice Directress. *Aspirant House*, 50 Santa Maria Way, Orinda, 94563-2605. Tel: 925-253-0831. Sr. Mary Anh Cong, L.H.C., Aspirants Directress.

St. Felicitas Convent, 1604 Manor Dr., San Leandro, 94579. Tel: 510-351-5577. Sr. Ancilla Tien Le, L.H.C., Supr.

Sisters of St. Joseph of the Third Order of St. Francis, 2301 Mt. Diablo St., 94520-2213. Tel: 925-825-2091; Fax: 925-825-2439. Sisters 6.

EL CERRITO. *Sisters of Mercy of Ireland (U.S. Province)*, St. John the Baptist Convent, 11154 San Pablo Ave., 94530-2131. Tel: 510-233-6769; Fax: 510-233-6058. Sisters 2.

EMERYVILLE. *Sisters of St. Francis of Penance and Christian Charity* (1835) *Casa Guadalupe*, 1231 40th St., Apt. 334, 94608. Tel: 510-655-5944. Web: www.franciscanway.org. *Sophia House*, 3877 Howe St., #210, 94611. Tel: 510-601-8132. *Canticle Community*, 474 Dolores Ave., Apt. 306, San Leandro, 94577. Sisters 4.

FREMONT. *Congregation of the Queen of the Holy Rosary (Dominican Sisters of Mission San Jose)* (1876) 43326 Mission Blvd., 94539-5829. Tel: 510-657-2468; Fax: 510-657-1734. Web: www.msjdominicans.org. Sr. Gloria Marie Jones, O.P., Congregational Prioress. Generalate Motherhouse and Novitiate of the Dominican Sisters of Mission San Jose, Congregation of The Queen of the Holy Rosary. Sisters 101.

Queen of Peace Community Tel: 510-657-2468; Fax: 510-657-1734. Sr. Carmel Marie Silva, O.P., Community Prioress.

St. Joseph Priory Tel: 510-657-2468; Fax: 510-657-1734. Sr. Donna Maria Moses, O.P., Community Prioress.

St. Martin Residence Tel: 510-657-2468; Fax: 510-657-1734. Sr. Jennifer Daniels, O.P., Community Prioress.

Siena Community (1977) Tel: 510-657-2468; Fax: 510-657-1734. Sr. Katherine Jean Cowan, O.P., Community Prioress.

St. Edward Convent (1969) 37088 Arden St.,

Newark, 94560-3702. Tel: 510-793-9447; Fax: 510-793-3189. Sr. Barbara Hagel, O.P., Community Prioress.

St. Elizabeth Convent, 1555-34th Ave., 94601-3062. Tel: 510-532-8344; Fax: 510-533-2365. Sr. Mary Liam Brock, O.P., Community Prioress.

St. Mary Magdalen Convent (1937) 2004 Eunice St., Berkeley, 94709-1926. Tel: 510-527-4817; Fax: 510-527-4818. Sr. Mary LaSalette Fuslier, O.P., Community Prioress.

San Domenico Community Tel: 510-657-2468; Fax: 510-657-1734. Sr. Jarlath McGrath, O.P., Community Prioress.

Sisters of the Holy Family, Motherhouse, 159 Washington Blvd., P.O. Box 3248, 94539-0324. Tel: 510-624-4500; Fax: 510-624-4550. Email: info@holyfamilysisters.org. Web: www.holyfamilysisters.org. Sr. Gladys Guenther, S.H.F., Congregational Pres. Sisters 70.

HERCULES. *Congregation of the Mother of Carmel* (1866) 142 Weiss Ct., 94547-3750. Tel: 510-724-4178. Email: weisscarmel@yahoo.com. Sisters 3.

KENSINGTON. *Discalced Carmelite Nuns of Berkeley, Inc.* (1950) 68 Rincon Rd., 94707-1047. Tel: 510-526-5050. Solemn Professed 2.

LIVERMORE. *Congregation of the Most Holy Name (Dominican Sisters of San Rafael)* (1912) *House of Martha & Mary*, 638 - 36th St., Richmond, 94805-1756. Tel: 510-620-1933. Sisters 4.

NEWARK. *Congregation of the Queen of the Holy Rosary (Dominican Sisters of Mission San Jose)*, St. Edward Convent, 37088 Arden St., 94560-3702. Tel: 510-793-9447; Fax: 510-793-3189 (School). Email: bhagel@msjdominicans.org. Sisters 4.

RICHMOND. *Franciscan Sisters of Little Falls, MN*, 2341 Prince St., Berkeley, 94705-1938. Tel: 510-848-5721. Sisters 1.

Sisters of Social Service, 1712 Euclid Ave., Berkeley, 94709. Tel: 510-387-5913. Email: elumas@att.net. Web: www.sistersofsocialservice.com.

SAN LEANDRO. *Dominican Sisters of Oakford*, Our Lady of Guadalupe House of Formation, 327 Woodland Park, 94577-3732. Tel: 510-569-9189. Email: oakforddominicans@gmail.com. Total in Residence 3; Sisters 3.

Our Lady of Oakford Regional Center, 980 Woodland Ave., 94577. Tel: 510-638-2822; Fax: 510-633-9734.

Marist Missionary Sisters, 1515 Boxwood Ave., 94579-1303. Tel: 510-357-7816. Email: missionarymary55@comcast.net. Web: www.maristmissionarysmsm.org. Sr. Susan Scherkenbach, S.M.S.M. Sisters 4.

WALNUT CREEK. *Sisters of the Holy Family* (1962) 1823 Sunnyvale Ave., 94597-1811. Tel: 925-935-6151; Fax: 925-935-6151. Email: mfaheyshf@aol.com. Web: www.holyfamilysisters.org.

[N] PASTORAL CENTERS

OAKLAND. *Holy Redeemer Center* Spiritual hospitality center., 8945 Golf Links Rd., 94605-4124. Tel: 510-635-6341; Fax: 510-562-1406. Email: pobcssr@aol.com. P.O. Box 5007, 94605. Rev. Patrick O'Brien, C.Ss.R., Dir.

DANVILLE. *San Damiano Retreat* (1961) Retreat House for men, women and married couples., *Franciscan Retreat House*, 710 Highland Dr., P.O. Box 767, 94526-3704. Tel: 925-837-9141; Fax: 925-837-0522. Email: info@sandamiano.org. Web: www.sandamiano.org. Rev. Raymond J. Bucher, O.F.M., Dir. Tel: 925-837-9141; Fax: 925-837-0522. Total in Residence 7; Total Staff 23. In Res. Revs. Stephen Cain, O.F.M.; Rusty Shaughnessey, O.F.M., Retreat Master; Evan Arthur Howard, O.F.M. (Retired); Josef Prochnow, O.F.M.; Bros. Marion Alfonso, O.F.M.; Dennis Duffy, O.F.M.

LAFAYETTE. *Diocesan Youth Retreat Center*, 1977 Reliez Valley Rd., 94549-1505. Tel: 925-934-5802; Fax: 925-934-0642. Email: timohara24@yahoo.com. Web: www.oakdiocese.org/youthretreat. P.O. Box 1505, 94549. Total in Residence 1; Total Staff 1.

WALNUT CREEK. *Holy Family Center* (1982) 1823 Sunnyvale Ave., 94597-1811. Tel: 945-935-6151. Email: mfaheyshf@aol.com. Sr. Marietta Fahey, S.H.F., Dir. Ministries: Personal Growth Programs, Counseling, Spiritual Direction.

[O] NEWMAN CENTERS

OAKLAND. *Holy Names University Campus Ministry* (1868) 3500 Mountain Blvd., 94619-1627. Tel: 510-436-1081; Fax: 510-436-1199. Email: rehak@hnu.edu. Web: www.hnu.edu. Carrie Rehak, Ph.D., Dir. Campus Min.

MORAGA. *St. Mary's College Mission and Ministry Center* P.O. Box 4777, 94575-4777. Tel: 925-631-4366. Web: www.stmarys-ca.edu. Revs. Thomas J. McElligott (SFR), Chap.; Salvatore Ragusa, S.D.S., Asst. Dir., Liturgy & Prayer; Bro. Camillus Chavez, F.S.C., Meditation Coord.; Joanne Angerame, Administrative Asst.; Ms. Marie Lawler, Dir.; Ms. Pamela Thomas, Asst. Dir., Residential Min.; Mr. Anthony Artega, Asst. Dir. Music Ministry; Mr. Denis Block, Asst. Dir., Lasallian Formation; Sr. Jodi Min, O.P., Asst. Dir., Lasallian Mission.

[P] PERSONAL PRELATURES

BERKELEY. *Opus Dei* Prelature of the Holy Cross and Opus Dei, *Garber House*, 1827 Oxford St., 94709-1800. Tel: 510-548-2819; Fax: 510-644-3898. Rev. Jerome L. Jung.

[Q] MISCELLANEOUS LISTINGS

OAKLAND. *Adventus, a California nonprofit public benefit corporation*, 2121 Harrison St., Ste. 100, 94612-3787. Tel: 510-893-4711; Fax: 510-893-0945. Email: mcanizzaro@oakdiocese.org. Mr. Michael P. Canizzaro, Pres.; Mr. James H. McCann, Vice Pres.; John J. Ryan, Sec.; Robert Pohl, Treas. Purpose: To support the mission of the Roman Catholic Diocese of Oakland.

The Benilde Religious & Charitable Trust, c/o Plageman, Lund and Cannon LLP, 155 Grand Ave., Ste. 950, 94612-3500. Tel: 510-899-6100; Fax: 510-899-6101. Email: wplageman@plagemanlund.com. Web: www.plagemanlund.com. Mr. William H. Plageman Jr., Contact Person. Charitable trust fund to benefit the educational activities of the Brothers of the Christian Schools of San Francisco. Lasallian Education Opportunities.

Casa Vincentia Home for single pregnant women, 18-25 yrs., 3210 62nd Ave., 94605-1614. Tel: 510-729-0316; Fax: 510-729-0319. Web: www.casavincentia.org. Barbara Jackson, Exec. Dir. Total in Residence 6; Total Staff 1; Total Assisted Annually 125.

Dominican Community Support Charitable Trust, 5877 Birch Ct., 94618-1626. Tel: 510-658-8722; Fax: 510-658-1061. Very Rev. Mark C. Padrez, O.P., Trustee; Rev. Dominic DeDomenico, O.P., Trustee.

Dominican Missionaries for the Deaf Apostolate, 2121 Harrison St., 94612-3787. Tel: 210-627-6303. Email: tomcoughlin@juno.com. Web: www.dominicanmissionaries.org.

Dominican Sisters Vision of Hope (2000) 1555 34th Ave., 94601-3062. Tel: 510-533-5768; Fax: 510-533-2365. Email: osd@msjdominicans.org. Web: www.visionofhope.org. Sr. John Martin Fixa, O.P., Exec. Dir.

Franciscan Charities, Inc., 1500 34th Ave., 94601-3024. Tel: 510-536-3772; Fax: 510-536-3970.

A Friendly Manor/A Friendly Place, 2298 San Pablo Ave., 94612-1321. Tel: 510-451-8923; Fax: 510-451-8920. Email: afriendlymanor@bcglobal.net. Sr. Maureen Lyons, C.S.J. Purpose: Daytime hospitality center for homeless women. Total Staff 7; Number Served Annually 15,660.

**The Gamelin-California Association* (1991) Rent-subsidized housing for persons with physical disabilities including persons with AIDS., Providence House, 540-23rd St., 94612-1718. Tel: 510-444-0839; Fax: 510-465-5420. Email: barbara.cook@providence.org. Web: www.providencesupportivehousing.org. Barbara Cook, Dir. Units 40; Number Served Annually 48.

Italian Catholic Federation (1924) 8393 Capwell Dr., Ste. 110, 94621-2117. Tel: 510-633-9058; 888-423-1924; Fax: 510-633-9758. Email: info@icf.org. Web: www.icf.org. Rev. Msgr. Daniel E. Cardelli, Diocesan Chap. & Spiritual Dir. (Retired).

Lasallian Educational Opportunities, Inc. (1994) 710 40th St., 94609-2372. Tel: 510-450-0747; Fax: 510-548-1343. Email: ngonza1230@gmail.com. Web: www.theleocenter.org. Deacon Noe Gonzalez, Dir. Total Assisted 180; Total Staff 8.

**Next Step Learning Center, Inc.*, 2222 Curtis St., 94607. Tel: 510-251-1731; Fax: 510-251-8028. Web: www.nextsteplc.org. Gregory Schopf, Pres.; Sisters Rosemary Delaney, S.N.J.M., Vice Pres.; Cynthia Canning, S.N.J.M., Sec.

**Oakland Elizabeth House* (1991) 6423 Colby St., 94618-1309. Tel: 510-658-1380; Fax: 510-658-3160. Email: oakehouse@oakehouse.org. Web: www.oakehouse.org. Tina Humphrey, Exec. Dir. Purpose: Transitional house and program for women and their children. Total Assisted Annually 150.

**PICO National Network* (1972) 171 Santa Rosa Ave., 94610-1316. Tel: 510-655-2801; Fax: 510-655-4816. Email: jbaumann@piconetwork.org. Web: www.piconetwork.org. Revs. John A. Baumann, S.J., Founder & Dir. Special Projects; Michael Mandala, S.J.; Mr. Hank Goldstein, Chm.

Province of Saint Barbara Fraternal Care Trust, 1500 34th Ave., 94601. Tel: 510-536-3722. Trustees Very Revs. Melvin A. Jurisich, O.F.M., Chm.; John Hardin, O.F.M.; Bro. Peter Boegel, O.F.M., Sec.; Mr. Edward J. Dantzig; Mr. Stephen Ethridge.

Redemptorist Vice Province Initiative, 8945 Golf Links Rd., 94605. Tel: 312-739-0900; Fax: 312-782-3773. Email: mjsamis4@aol.com. P.O. Box 5007, 94605. Rev. Patrick O'Brien, C.Ss.R., Dir.; Michael J. Samis, Asst. Sec.

Religious Communities Investment Fund, Inc., 462 Elwood Ave., Ste. 2, 94610. Tel: 510-836-7556; Fax: 510-836-7556. Web: www.rcif.org. Sr. Corinne Florek, O.P., Dir. & Contact Person.

BERKELEY. *Academy of American Franciscan History*, 1712 Euclid Ave., 94709-1208. Tel: 510-548-1755; Fax: 510-549-9466. Email: acadafh@fst.edu. Web: www.aafh.org. Total Staff 1.

Inter-Friendship House Association, Friendship Center, 1646 Addison St., 94703-1404. Tel: 510-843-7675; Fax: 510-843-7675. Web: www.fuyou-berkeley.org. Ken Wong, Chm. Total Staff 1.

Multicultural Institute (1991) 1920 Seventh St., 94710-2011. Tel: 510-848-4075; Fax: 510-848-4095. Email: rcaloca@mionline.org. Web: www.mionline.org. Board of Directors: Revs. William M. Cieslak, O.F.M.Cap., Ph.D.; James Lockman, O.F.M., Ph.D.; Rigoberto Caloca Rivas, O.F.M., Ph.D.; Jon M. Balousek, Treas. Tel: 925-254-8373; John Matzger, Sec.; Philip J. Murphy, M.B.A., Pres.

Administrative Staff: Rev. Rigoberto Caloca-Rivas, O.F.M., Ph.D., Exec. Dir.; Dr. Paula Worby, Ph.D., Assoc. Dir.; Bro. David Cobian, O.F.M., M.Div., Life Skills Prog. Dir.; Rey Gonzalez, Life Skills Prog. Asst.; Rodolfo Lara, Life Skills Prog. Dir.; Cesar Meza-Esviele, Life Skills Prog. Dir.; Enrique Moreno, Life Skills Prog. Asst.

CONCORD. *East Bay Services to the Developmentally Disabled* (1984) 1870 Adobe St., 94520. Tel: 925-825-2091; Fax: 925-825-2439. Nonresidence Serves 850; Residence 65; Total Staff 70.

DANVILLE. *Catholic Professional & Business Breakfast Club of the Diocese of Oakland*, 440 LaGonda Way, 94526. Tel: 415-235-3513. Email: attilab@sbcglobal.net. Web: www.catholicsatwork.org. David R. Manion, Pres.; John Dunican, Treas.

EL CERRITO. *Divine Mercy Eucharistic Society*, 11152 San Pablo Ave., 94530-2131. Tel: 510-412-4715; Fax: 510-412-3537. Email: divinemercyjesus@comcast.net. Web: divinemercywestcoast.org. Thelma Orias, Pres.

Mary's House aka Mary's House of Mercy 1850 Church Ln., San Pablo, 94806-3706. Tel: 510-236-0383; Fax: 510-236-0395. Email: divinemercyjesus@comcast.net. Web: marys-house.org. (ministry of Divine Mercy Eucharistic Society) Total Assisted Annually 16.

FREMONT. *Dominican Sisters of Mission San Jose Foundation (A Nonprofit Corp.)*, 43326 Mission Blvd., 94539-5829. Tel: 510-657-2468; Fax: 510-657-1733. Email: clare.e.fischer@gmail.com. Web: www.msjdominicans.org. Michael Botello, Pres.; Janice Caldwell, Sec. & Treas.; Sr. Francis Clare Fischer, O.P., Foundation Admin.

Pia Backes Support Trust, Dominican Sisters of Mission San Jose, 43326 Mission Blvd., 94539-5829. Tel: 510-657-2468; Fax: 510-683-0712. Email: tan.dmsj@gmail.com. Sr. Mary Liam Brock, O.P., Pres.

LAFAYETTE. *Magnificat S.O.T.I. - Walnut Creek Chapter*, 909 Carol Ln., 94549. Tel: 925-954-7205; Fax: 925-954-7205. Web: www.magnificatsoti.org. Mary L. Johnstone, Coord.

RELIGIOUS INSTITUTES OF MEN REPRESENTED IN THE DIOCESE

For further details refer to the corresponding bracketed number in the Religious Institutes of Men or Women section.

[0140]—*The Augustinians*—O.S.A.

[0330]—*Brothers of the Christian Schools* (Prov. of San Francisco)—F.S.C.

[0200]—*Camaldolese Benedictines*—O.S.B.Cam.

[0470]—*The Capuchin Friars*—O.F.M.Cap.

[0270]—*Carmelite Fathers and Brothers*—O.Carm.

[1130]—*Congregation of the Priests of the Sacred Heart*—S.C.J.

[0480]—*Conventual Franciscans*—O.F.M.Conv.

[0520]—*Franciscan Friars* (Prov. of Santa Barbara)—O.F.M.

[0305]—*Institute of Christ the King Sovereign Priest*—I.C.

[0690]—*Jesuit Fathers and Brothers*—S.J.

[0780]—*Marist Fathers and Brothers*—S.M.

[800]—*Maryknoll Fathers and Brothers*—M.M.

[0830]—*Mill Hill Missionaries*—M.H.M.

[]—*Missionaries of Faith*—M.F.

[0910]—*Oblates of Mary Immaculate* (US Prov.)—O.M.I.

[920]—*Oblates of St. Francis de Sales*—O.S.F.S.

[0430]—*Order of Preachers-Dominicans* (Prov. of the Most Holy Name of Jesus, Western Dominican Prov.)—O.P.

[1030]—*Paulist Fathers*—C.S.P.
[0610]—*Priests of the Congregation of Holy Cross*—C.S.C.
[1070]—*Redemptorist Fathers* (Denver Prov.)—C.SS.R.
[1190]—*Salesians of Don Bosco* (San Francisco Prov.)—S.D.B.
[1240]—*Servites*—O.S.M.
[1290]—*Society of Priests of St. Sulpice*—S.S.
[1200]—*Society of the Divine Savior*—S.D.S.
[0420]—*Society of the Divine Word*—S.V.D.
[1060]—*Society of the Precious Blood* (Prov. of the Pacific)—C.PP.S.

RELIGIOUS INSTITUTES OF WOMEN REPRESENTED IN THE DIOCESE

[1070-13]—*Adrian Dominican Sisters* (Congregation of the Most Holy Rosary)—O.P.
[]—*Congregation of Mother of Carmel*—C.M.C.
[1070-04]—*Congregation of the Most Holy Name* (Dominican Sisters of San Rafael)—O.P.
[1070-12]—*Congregation of the Queen of the Holy Rosary* (Dominican Sisters of Mission San Jose)—O.P.
[0850]—*Daughters of Mary Help of Christians*—F.M.A.
[0420]—*Discalced Carmelite Nuns*—O.C.D.
[1070-30]—*Dominican Sisters of Oakford*—O.P.
[]—*Dominican Sisters of the Christian Doctrine*—O.P.
[1070-03]—*Dominican Sisters (Sinsinawa-Congregation of the Most Holy Rosary)*—O.P.
[1310]—*Franciscan Sisters of Little Falls, Minnesota*—O.S.F.
[2470]—*Maryknoll Sisters of St. Dominic*—M.M.
[2710]—*Missionaries of Charity*—M.C.
[2420]—*Missionary Sisters of the Society of Mary, Marist Missionary Sisters*—S.M.S.M.
[]—*Oblates of Notre Dame*—O.N.D.
[]—*Quinhon Missionary Sisters of the Holy Cross*—L.H.C.
[]—*Religious Missionary Sisters of the Blessed Sacrament and Mary Immaculate*—M.S.S.
[3465]—*Religious of the Sacred Heart of Mary*—R.S.H.M.
[2970]—*School Sisters of Notre Dame*—S.S.N.D.
[0440]—*Sisters of Charity of Cincinnati, Ohio*—S.C.
[0430]—*Sisters of Charity of the Blessed Virgin Mary* (Mt. Carmel, Dubuque, IA)—B.V.M.
[1920]—*Sisters of Holy Cross*—C.S.C.
[2360]—*Sisters of Loretto at the Foot of the Cross*—S.L.
[]—*Sisters of Mercy of Ireland* (U.S. Prov.)—R.S.M.
[2575]—*Sisters of Mercy of the Americas West Midwest Community* (Regional Community of Burlingame, CA)—S.M.
[3000]—*Sisters of Notre Dame de Namur* (California Prov.)—S.N.D.deN.
[1650]—*Sisters of St. Francis of Philadelphia*—O.S.F.
[4080]—*Sisters of Social Service of Los Angeles, Inc.*—S.S.S.
[1630]—*Sisters of St. Francis of Penance and Christian Charity*—O.S.F.
[3840]—*Sisters of St. Joseph of Carondelet* (Los Angeles Prov.)—C.S.J.
[3830-03]—*Sisters of St. Joseph of Orange*—C.S.J.
[3930]—*Sisters of St. Joseph of the Third Order of St. Francis*—S.S.J.-T.O.S.F.
[1960]—*Sisters of the Holy Family*—S.H.F.
[1990]—*Sisters of the Holy Names of Jesus and Mary* (U.S. - Ontario Prov.)—S.N.J.M.
[3320]—*Sisters of the Presentation of the B.V.M.* (San Francisco, CA)—P.B.V.M.
[3680]—*Sisters of the Sacred Hearts of Jesus and Mary*—S.H.J.M.
[1720]—*Sisters of the Third Order of St. Francis of the Congregation of Our Lady of Lourdes*—O.S.F.
[2150]—*Sisters, Servants of the Immaculate Heart of Mary*—I.H.M.
[4070]—*Society of the Sacred Heart*—R.S.C.J.
[3330]—*Union of the Sisters of the Presentation of the Blessed Virgin Mary*—P.B.V.M.

NECROLOGY

† Brainard, Ernest B., (Retired)—Died Dec. 14, 2010
† Deane, Declan, Pleasant Hill, CA Christ the King.—Died Dec. 12, 2010
† Driscoll, James E., (Retired)—Died Oct. 29, 2011

An asterisk (*) denotes an organization that has established tax-exempt status directly with the IRS and is not covered by the USCCB Group Ruling.

Diocese of Ogdensburg

(Dioecesis Ogdensburgensis)

Most Reverend

TERRY R. LAVALLEY

Bishop of Ogdensburg; ordained September 24, 1988; appointed Bishop of Ogdensburg February 23, 2010; installed April 30, 2010. *Mailing Address: P.O. Box 369, Ogdensburg, NY 13669.*

Chancery Office: P.O. Box 369, Ogdensburg, NY 13669. Tel: 315-393-2920; Fax: 866-314-7296.

Web: www.dioogdensburg.org

Square Miles 12,036.

Erected by His Holiness Pius IX, February 16, 1872.

Incorporated by a special act of the Legislature of the State of New York, April 10, 1945, with the title: The Roman Catholic Diocese of Ogdensburg, New York.

Comprises that part of Herkimer and Hamilton Counties north of the northern line of the townships of Ohio and Russia as existing in 1872 with the entire Counties of Lewis, Jefferson, St. Lawrence, Franklin, Clinton and Essex in the State of New York.

For legal titles of parishes and diocesan institutions, consult the Chancery Office.

STATISTICAL OVERVIEW

Personnel	
Bishop	1
Priests: Diocesan Active in Diocese	68
Priests: Diocesan Active Outside Diocese	3
Priests: Retired, Sick or Absent	50
Number of Diocesan Priests	121
Religious Priests in Diocese	5
Total Priests in Diocese	126
Extern Priests in Diocese	6
Ordinations:	
Transitional Deacons	1
Permanent Deacons in Diocese	70
Total Brothers	6
Total Sisters	104
Parishes	
Parishes	99
With Resident Pastor:	
Resident Diocesan Priests	60
Resident Religious Priests	2
Without Resident Pastor:	
Administered by Priests	37
Missions	7
New Parishes Created	1
Closed Parishes	3
Professional Ministry Personnel:	
Sisters	2
Lay Ministers	833
Welfare	
Homes for the Aged	1
Total Assisted	130
Special Centers for Social Services	4
Total Assisted	20,000
Educational	
Diocesan Students in Other Seminaries	7
Total Seminarians	7
High Schools, Diocesan and Parish	2
Total Students	332
Elementary Schools, Diocesan and Parish	13
Total Students	1,989
Catechesis/Religious Education:	
High School Students	1,121
Elementary Students	3,939
Total Students under Catholic Instruction	7,388
Teachers in the Diocese:	
Sisters	13
Lay Teachers	181
Vital Statistics	
Receptions into the Church:	
Infant Baptism Totals	970
Minor Baptism Totals	53
Adult Baptism Totals	42
Received into Full Communion	58
First Communions	918
Confirmations	875
Marriages:	
Catholic	232
Interfaith	68
Total Marriages	300
Deaths	1,609
Total Catholic Population	96,882
Total Population	497,712

Former Bishops—Rt. Revs. EDGAR P. WADHAMS, D.D., ord. Jan. 15, 1850; cons. May 5, 1872; died Dec. 5, 1891; HENRY GABRIELS, D.D., ord. Sept. 21, 1861; cons. May 5, 1892; died April 23, 1921; Most Revs. JOSEPH H. CONROY, D.D., LL.D., ord. June 11, 1881; cons. May 1, 1912; succeeded to the See, Nov. 21, 1921; died March 20, 1939; FRANCIS J. MONAGHAN, S.T.D., LL.D., ord. May 29, 1915; cons. June 29, 1936; succeeded to the See, March 20, 1939; died Nov. 13, 1942; BRYAN J. MCENTEGART, D.D., LL.D., ord. Sept. 8, 1917; cons. Aug. 3, 1943; transferred to Titular See of Aradi, Aug. 19, 1953; appt. June 26, 1953; to Rectorship of Catholic University of America, Washington, D.C.; appt. Bishop of Brooklyn, April 16, 1957; installed June 13, 1957; appt. Archbishop, April 15, 1966; retired and appt. Titular Archbishop of Gabii, July 17, 1968; died Sept. 30, 1968; WALTER P. KELLENBERG, D.D., ord. June 2, 1928; cons. Oct. 5, 1953; appt. to Ogdensburg, Jan. 19, 1954; transferred to See of Rockville Centre, April 16, 1957; installed May 27, 1957; died Jan. 11, 1986; JAMES J. NAVAGH, D.D., ord. Dec. 21, 1929; cons. Sept. 24, 1952; appt. to Ogdensburg, May 8, 1957; transferred to Paterson, Feb. 12, 1963; died in Rome, Oct. 2, 1965; LEO R. SMITH, D.D., ord. Dec. 21, 1929; appt. Auxiliary Bishop of Buffalo, July 9, 1952; cons. Sept. 24, 1952; appt. Bishop of Ogdensburg, Feb. 12, 1963; died in Rome Oct. 9, 1963; THOMAS A. DONNELLAN, D.D., ord. June 3, 1939; appt. March 4, 1964; cons. April 9, 1964; appt. to Atlanta, May 29, 1968; transferred to Archdiocese of Atlanta, July 16, 1968; died in Atlanta, Oct. 15, 1987; STANISLAUS J. BRZANA, S.T.D., LL.D, ord. June 7, 1941; appt. Titular Bishop of Cufruta and Auxiliary of Buffalo, May 24, 1964; cons. June 29, 1964; transferred to Ogdensburg, Oct. 22, 1968; retired Nov. 11, 1993; died March 1, 1997; PAUL S. LOVERDE, D.D., S.T.L., J.C.L., ord. Dec. 18, 1965; appt. Titular Bishop of Ottabia and Auxiliary Bishop of Hartford, Feb. 3, 1988; cons. April 12, 1988; transferred to Ogdensburg, Nov. 11, 1993; installed Jan. 17, 1994; appt. Bishop of Arlington, Jan. 25, 1999; installed March 25, 1999; GERALD M. BARBARITO, D.D., J.C.L., ord. Jan. 31, 1976; appt. Titular Bishop of Gisipa and Auxiliary Bishop of Brooklyn June 28, 1994; cons. Aug. 22, 1994; transferred to Ogdensburg Oct. 26, 1999; installed Jan. 7, 2000; appt. Bishop of Palm Beach July 1, 2003; installed Aug. 28, 2003; ROBERT J. CUNNINGHAM, D.D., J.C.L., ord. May 24, 1969; appt. Bishop of Ogdensburg March 9, 2004; ord. and installed May 18, 2004; appt. Bishop of Syracuse April 21, 2009; installed May 26, 2009.

Diocesan Offices

Unless otherwise noted, all mail for the following offices to go to: *Spratt Memorial Bldg., 604 Washington St., P.O. Box 369, Ogdensburg, 13669.* Office Hours: Mon.-Fri. 8:15-4 (Sept.-June); Summer Hours: 8:45-4.

Office of the Bishop—Most Rev. TERRY R. LAVALLEY, 604 Washington St., P.O. Box 369, Ogdensburg, 13669.

Secretary to the Bishop—VACANT.

Bishop's Office Secretary—LINDA ROSS. Fax: 866-393-7642.

Episcopal Vicar for Worship and Priestly Formation—Rev. DOUGLAS J. LUCIA, J.C.L., Mailing Address: P.O. Box 369, Ogdensburg, 13669. Tel: 315-393-2920; Fax: 866-314-7296. Vocations Director: Rev. BRYAN D. STITT, S.T.L.

Department of Worship—Rev. DOUGLAS J. LUCIA, J.C.L., Dir.

Fiscal Officer—Mr. MICHAEL J. TOOLEY. Fax: 866-314-7296.

Parish Administrative Services Coordinator—Mr. VINCE THOUIN.

Human Resources Director—Ms. KIMBERLY SNOVER.

Insurance Claims and Risk Management Department—Mr. JACK CARTER, Mgr. Tel: 315-393-0441; Fax: 866-519-6423; RITA TULIP, Claims Svc. Representative.

Unless otherwise noted, all mail for the following offices to go to: *Bishop Stanislaus J. Brzana Diocesan Pastoral Center, 622 Washington St., P.O. Box 369, Ogdensburg, 13669.* Office Hours: Mon.-Fri. 8:15-4 (Sept.-June); Summer Hours: 8:45-4.

Episcopal Vicar for Pastoral Services and Moderator of the Curia—Rev. Msgr. JOHN R. MURPHY, S.T.L., M.A.

Chancellor—Sr. JENNIFER VOTRAW, S.S.J.

Episcopal Vicar for Clergy and Director Priest Personnel and Deacons—Rev. JAMES W. SEYMOUR.

Matrimonial Tribunal and Office of Canonical Affairs—

Judicial Vicar and Vicar for Canonical Affairs—Rev. Msgr. HARRY K. SNOW, M.A.Th. , J.C.L., V.F.

Moderator of the Tribunal—Mrs. ELAINE SEYMOUR.

Adjutant Judicial Vicars—Revs. PHILIP T. ALLEN; DOUGLAS J. LUCIA, J.C.L.

Promoter of Justice—Rev. Msgr. PETER R. RIANI, V.F., S.T.D., M.Ed.

Defenders of the Bond—Revs. LAWRENCE E. COTTER, S.T.L., B.S., M.S. (Retired); RAYMOND J. MOREAU; JOSEPH A. MORGAN; ALAN D. SHNOB; JOHN R. YONKOVIG.

Judges—Rev. Msgr. BERNARD E. CHRISTMAN (Retired); Revs. ROBERT L. COTTER (Retired); GILBERT B. MENARD (Retired).

Notary—Mrs. DIANNA L. SHAVER.

Advocates—Mrs. ELAINE SEYMOUR; Rev. Msgrs. DENNIS J. DUPREY, V.F.; JOHN R. MURPHY, S.T.L., M.A.; Revs. DOUGLAS A. DECKER; GARVIN J. DEMARAIS; GARRY B. GIROUX, J.C.L.; ALBERT J. HAUSER; ALAN J. LAMICA; WILLIAM G. REAMER.

Bishop's Delegate for Religious—Sr. ELLEN DONAHUE, S.A.

Development Office— Planned Giving; Stewardship Office Mrs. JANICE SHOEN, Exec. Dir.; Mrs.

VALERIE MATHEWS, Asst. Dir.
Bishops' Fund Appeal—Mrs. VALERIE MATHEWS, Dir.
The Foundation of the Roman Catholic Diocese of Ogdensburg, New York—Mrs. JANICE SHOEN, Exec. Dir.
Evangelization—Sr. MARY EAMON LYNG, S.S.J., Dir.
Formation for Ministry—Mrs. HEIDI MACKO, Dir.
Mission Aid Societies—Sr. MARY ELLEN BRETT, S.S.J., Dir. Fax: 866-314-7296 Society for The Propagation of the Faith; Holy Childhood Association; Society of St. Peter the Apostle; Missionary Union of Clergy and Religious; Ogdensburg Peruvian Apostolate.
Office of Planning—Sr. JENNIFER VOTRAW, S.S.J., Dir.
Department of Communications—Sr. JENNIFER VOTRAW, S.S.J., Dir., Mailing Address: P.O. Box 369, Ogdensburg, 13669. Tel: 315-393-2920; Fax: 866-314-7296.
Bureau of Information—Sr. JENNIFER VOTRAW, S.S.J., Mailing Address: P.O. Box 369, Ogdensburg, 13669. Tel: 315-393-2920; Fax: 866-314-7296.
Newspaper- "The North Country Catholic" Mrs. MARY LOU KILIAN, Editor; CHRISTINE WARD, Editorial Asst., Mailing Address: P.O. Box 326, Ogdensburg, 13669. Tel: 866-314-7296.
Bureau of Media—Mrs. LINDA J. KELLEY, 1900 State Hwy. 11B, Potsdam, 13617. Tel: 315-265-0261; Fax: 315-268-7104.
Cemeteries—Sr. JENNIFER VOTRAW, S.S.J., Mailing Address: P.O. Box 369, Ogdensburg, 13669. Tel: 315-393-2920; Fax: 866-314-7296.

Unless otherwise noted, all mail for the following offices to go to: *Bishop Paul S. Loverde Center for Education and Formation, 100 Elizabeth St., P.O. Box 369, Ogdensburg, 13669*. Fax: 866-314-7296. Office Hours: Mon.-Fri. 8:15-4 (Sept.-June); Summer Hours: 8:45-4.

Episcopal Vicar for Catholic Education—Rev. Msgr. ROBERT H. AUCOIN, S.T.L., M.Ed., Roman Catholic Church of St. Mary's, 17 Lawrence Ave., Potsdam, 13676. Email: raucoin@dioogdensburg.org.
Diocesan Director of Christian Formation—Sr. ELLEN ROSE COUGHLIN, S.S.J. Tel: 315-393-4231; Fax: 866-314-7296.
Department of Christian Formation—
Ogdensburg Regional Center—Mrs. HEIDI MACKO, Dir.
Plattsburgh Regional Center—PAM BALLENTINE, Dir., 23 St. Charles St., Ste. 1, Plattsburgh, 12901. Fax: 518-563-2138.
Watertown Regional Center—Mr. MICHAEL WAGNER, Dir., 866 Arsenal St., Watertown, 13601. Tel: 315-782-3620; Fax: 315-782-2009.
Department of Youth Ministry—Deacon BRIAN T. DWYER.
Catholic Scouting—Rev. BRYAN D. STITT, S.T.L., Diocesan Liaison.
Department of Education—Sisters ELLEN ROSE COUGHLIN, S.S.J., Supt. & Dir. Educ.; SHIRLEY ANNE BROWN, S.S.J., Catholic School Supvr.; PAM BALLENTINE, Dir. Faith Formation.
Family Life Department and Pre-Cana—Directors: Deacon GARY FRANK; Mrs. GAYLE FRANK.

Consultative Bodies

Deans—Rev. JOHN R. YONKOVIG; Rev. Msgrs. LEEWARD J. POISSANT, V.F., Clinton; PETER R. RIANI, V.F., S.T.D., M.Ed., Essex; Revs. JOHN J. LOOBY, Franklin; SONY G. PULICKAL, V.F., Hamilton-Herkimer; ARTHUR J. LABAFF, V.F., Jefferson; CHRISTOPHER C. CARRARA, Lewis; Rev. Msgr. HARRY K. SNOW, M.A.Th. , J.C.L., V.F., St. Lawrence.
Diocesan Consultors—Rev. Msgrs. ROBERT L. LAWLER, P.A.; ROBERT H. AUCOIN, S.T.L., M.Ed.; Revs. DOUGLAS G. COMSTOCK; PIERRE AUBIN, M.S.C.; ARTHUR J. LABAFF, V.F.; DONALD J. MANFRED; JOSEPH A. MORGAN; JOHN J. LOOBY; SCOTT D. FOBARE; KEVIN J. O'BRIEN; DOUGLAS J. LUCIA, J.C.L.
Council of Religious—Sisters RITA MARY MORRISSETTE, O.S.U., Pres.; MARY FRANCES BARNES, D.C., Vice Pres.; ANNUNCIATA COLLINS, S.S.J., Sec.; BERNADETTE DUCHARME, S.C.L., Treas.
Committee on Assignments—Rev. Msgrs. ROBERT L. LAWLER, P.A.; JOHN R. MURPHY, S.T.L., M.A.; Revs. DOUGLAS J. LUCIA, J.C.L.; JAMES W. SEYMOUR; RAYMOND J. MOREAU; CHRISTOPHER C. CARRARA; CLYDE A. LEWIS; ARTHUR J. LABAFF, V.F.; MICHAEL GAFFNEY.

Other Diocesan Offices and Directors

Diocesan Archivist— (see Chancellor's Office) Ms. SALLY RUSAW, Assoc. Archivist.
Apostleship of Prayer—Rev. ALBERT J. HAUSER, Dir., Mailing Address: P.O. Box 369, Ogdensburg, 13669.
Building Commission—Sr. JENNIFER VOTRAW, S.S.J., Mailing Address: P.O. Box 369, Ogdensburg, 13669.
Campus Ministry—*John XXIII College Community, 90 Broad St., Plattsburgh, 12901*. Rev. TIMOTHY G. CANAAN, Dir.; JACKIE ROBERTSEN; Rev. MARK R. REILLY; Sr. CAROL KRAEGER, S.S.J.; Rev. ROBERT L. DECKER; Rev. Msgr. ROBERT H. AUCOIN, S.T.L., M.Ed.; STEVEN YOUNG; Mr. ALAN KNACK; Deacon PHILIP GIARDINO; RITA MAWN; Rev. DOUGLAS J. LUCIA, J.C.L.; Sr. JULIANA RAYMOND, S.S.J.; THOMAS J. PHALON.
Catholic Charities—Sr. DONNA FRANKLIN, D.C., Diocesan Dir., Wadhams Hall, 6866 State Hwy. 37, Ogdensburg, 13669. Tel: 315-393-2255; Fax: 315-393-2402. Ogdensburg Office: Sr. DONNA FRANKLIN, D.C.; JOELLA LAMICA, 716 Caroline St., Ogdensburg, 13669. Tel: 315-393-2660; Fax: 315-393-9362. Watertown Office 812 State St., Watertown, NY 13601. Tel: 315-788-4330; Fax: 315-786-0539.: PENNY MCKENNA, Administrative Asst. Plattsburgh Office: PORTIA TURCO, Dir., 4914 S. Catherine St., Plattsburgh, 12901. Tel: 315-561-0470; Fax: 315-561-0472. Malone Office: JOELLA LAMICA, Dir., Rennie St., Malone, 12953. Tel: 518-483-1460; Fax: 518-483-1478. Tupper Lake Office - Foster Grandparent Program: VIVIAN SMITH, 80 Park St., Ste. 2, P.O. Box 701, Tupper Lake, 12986. Tel: 518-359-7688; Fax: 518-359-3927.
RSVP of Clinton County—MARY CATHERINE GARDNER, 46 Flynn Ave., Plattsburgh, 12901. Tel: 518-566-0944; Fax: 518-566-0945.
RSVP of Essex County—BARBARA BRASSARD, 38 Park Pl., Ste. 3, Port Henry, 12974. Tel: 518-546-3565.
Seaway House—CAROL WHITCOMBE, Dir., 212 Caroline St., Ogdensburg, 13669. Tel: 315-393-3133.
Catholic Relief Services—Sr. DONNA FRANKLIN, D.C., Mailing Address: P.O. Box 296, Ogdensburg, 13669. Tel: 315-393-2255; Fax: 315-393-2402.
Censor Librorum—Rev. LAWRENCE E. COTTER, S.T.L., B.S., M.S. (Retired), Mailing Address: P.O. Box 369, Ogdensburg, 13669.
Charismatic Renewal—Rev. FRANCIS J. CORYER, Liaison, Mailing Address: 1413 Military Tpke., P.O. Box 2223, Plattsburgh, 12901.
Committee for the Continuing Education of Clergy—Rev. SCOTT D. FOBARE, Chm., Mailing Address: St. Patrick's Church, 12 St. Patrick Pl., Port Henry, 12974. Tel: 518-846-7254; Fax: 518-375-3624.
Ecumenical Commission—Rev. DANIEL L. CHAPIN, Chm., Mailing Address: St. Stephen's Church, P.O. Box 38, Croghan, 13327-0038. Tel: 315-346-6958; Fax: 315-346-1200.
Legion of Mary—VACANT.
Natural Family Planning Services—Mr. ANGELO PIETROPAOLI; Mrs. SUZANNE PIETROPAOLI, 36 First St., Malone, 12953.
Permanent Diaconate Program—
Director of Deacon Formation—Rev. Msgr. ROBERT H. AUCOIN, S.T.L., M.Ed., Roman Catholic Church of St. Mary's, 17 Lawrence Ave., Potsdam, 13676.
Priests' Eucharistic League—Rev. ALBERT J. HAUSER, Dir., Mailing Address: P.O. Box 369, Ogdensburg, 13669. Tel: 315-393-2920; Fax: 315-394-7401.
Respect Life Office—Mr. JOHN MINER; COLLEEN MINER.
St. Vincent de Paul Society—VACANT.
Young Adult Ministry—LORRAINE TURGEON.

CLERGY, PARISHES, MISSIONS AND PAROCHIAL SCHOOLS

CITY OF OGDENSBURG

(ST. LAWRENCE COUNTY)

1—ST. MARY'S CATHEDRAL (1748) [CEM] Rev. Joseph A. Morgan, Rector; Sr. Mary Teresa La Brake, G.N.S.H., Pastoral Assoc.; Deacons Francis F. Bateman; David J. Sandburg; John L. White. In Res., Revs. Vicente F. Jazmines; Edward E. Papp (Retired).
Res.: 415 Hamilton St., 13669. Tel: 315-393-3930; Fax: 315-393-6680. Email: sboyer@saintmaryscathedral.net. Web: www.saintmaryscathedral.net.
Catechesis/Religious Program—214 Morris St., 13669. Tel: 315-393-1820; Fax: 315-393-1670. Email: bishopconroydre@verizon.net. Web: www.bishopconroyschool.org. Mrs. Celina Burns, D.R.E. Students 142.

2—NOTRE DAME (1859), (French), [CEM] Rev. F. James Shurtleff; Deacons Thomas Kilian; Mark A. LaLonde; Elizabeth J. Bernhard, Pastoral Assoc.
Res.: 125 Ford Ave., 13669. Tel: 315-393-5050; Fax: 315-393-5962. Email: secretary@ndogd.org. Web: www.notredame-ogdensburg.com.
School—*St. Marguerite D'Youville Academy*, (Grades PreK-6), 315 Gates St., 13699. Tel: 315-393-0165; Fax: 315-394-0499. Mrs. Celina Burns, Prin. Lay Teachers 11; Students 86.
Catechesis/Religious Program—*Bishop Conroy Christian Formation Program*, 214 Morris St., 13669. Tel: 315-393-1820; Fax: 315-393-1670. Mrs. Celina Burns, D.R.E. Students 65.

OUTSIDE CITY OF OGDENSBURG

ADAMS, JEFFERSON CO., ST. CECILIA (1870) [CEM] Rev. Patrick A. Ratigan.
Mailing Address: 17 Grove St., 13605. Email: adamscatholic@yahoo.com. Web: www.stceciliasadams.org.
Catechesis/Religious Program—Students 187.
Mission—*Queen of Heaven* 8900 NYS Rte. 3, Henderson, Jefferson Co. 13650. Tel: 315-232-2392; Fax: 315-232-2817.

ALEXANDRIA BAY, JEFFERSON CO., ST. CYRIL OF ALEXANDRIA (CATHOLIC COMMUNITY OF ALEXANDRIA) (1000 Islands) (1885) [CEM] Rev. Douglas G. Comstock; Deacon Bernard E. Slate.
Catholic Community of Alexandria
Res.: 17 Rock St., 13607. Tel: 315-482-2670; Fax: 815-301-1901. Email: pastor@stcyrils.org. Web: www.stcyrils.org.
Catechesis/Religious Program—Students 89.

ALTONA, CLINTON CO., HOLY ANGELS (1865), (Irish—French Canadian), [CEM] Rev. Gilbert O. Boisvert.
Res.: P.O. Box 113, 12910. Tel: 518-236-5848; Fax: 518-236-4249. Email: holyangels@primelink1.net.
Oratory—*Jericho, St. Alexis*
Catechesis/Religious Program—Students 171.

AU SABLE FORKS, CLINTON CO.

1—CATHOLIC COMMUNITY OF HOLY NAME AND ST. MATTHEW Rev. Kris C. Lauzon; Deacon John J. Ryan.
Res.: 10 Church Ln., P.O. Box 719, 12912. Tel: 518-647-8225; Fax: 518-647-5394.
St. Matthew—Worship Site:
School—(Grades PreK-6), 14207 NYS Rte. 9 N., 12912. Tel: 518-647-8444. Mrs. Christine Reynolds, Prin. Sisters 1; Lay Teachers 7; Students 68.
Catechesis/Religious Program—Students 47.
Mission—*St. Margaret*

2—HOLY NAME (1848) [CEM] Merged with St. Matthew, Black Brook to form Catholic Community of Holy Name and St. Matthew, Au Sable Forks.

BLACK BROOK, CLINTON CO., ST. MATTHEW (1848) [CEM] Merged Now a worship site of Catholic Community of Holy Name and St. Matthew.

BLACK RIVER, JEFFERSON CO., ST. PAUL (1901) Rev. Garvin J. Demarais; Deacon William S. Raven.
Res.: 208 LeRay St., 13612. Tel: 315-773-5672.
Church: 210 LeRay St., 13612.
Catechesis/Religious Program—Students 35.

BLOOMINGDALE, ESSEX CO., ST. PAUL (1897) [CEM 2] Revs. Mark R. Reilly; Paul J. Kelly, Parochial Vicar.
Res.: 27 Bernard St., Saranac Lake, 12983. Tel: 518-891-4616; Fax: 518-891-4619.
Mission—*Assumption of the B.V.M.* 826 NYS Rte. 86, Gabriels, Franklin Co. 12939.
Catechesis/Religious Program—Mary Kay Benham, D.R.E.; Michele Crowley, C.R.E.; Cherie Racette, Asst. Students 35.

BOMBAY, FRANKLIN CO., ST. JOSEPH (1912) [CEM] Rev. Martin E. Cline.
Res.: 20 County Rte. 4, 12914. Tel: 518-358-4518.
Office & Mailing Address: P.O. Box 499, Fort Covington, 12937. Tel: 518-358-2500.
Catechesis/Religious Program—Students 37.

BRASHER FALLS, ST. LAWRENCE CO., ST. PATRICK (1830), (Irish—French), [CEM] Rev. Garry B. Giroux.
Res.: P.O. Box 208, 13613. Tel: 315-389-5401; Fax: 315-389-4066. Email: parish@twcny.rr.com.
Parish Center—Email: parish@twcny.rr.com.
Catechesis/Religious Program— Donna Steenberg, D.R.E.; Bernadette Frohm, D.R.E. Students 57.

BROWNVILLE, JEFFERSON CO., ROMAN CATHOLIC COMMUNITY OF BROWNVILLE AND DEXTER formerly Immaculate Conception of the B.V.M. (1874), (Irish—Italian), Rev. Kevin J. O'Brien.
Res.: 119 W. Main St., P.O. Box 99, 13615. Tel: 315-782-1143; Fax: 315-782-0231. Email: icses@twcny.rr.com.
Immaculate Conception—Worship Site: 13615.
Catechesis/Religious Program—Tel: 315-788-7240. Mrs. Christina M. Corey, D.R.E. Students 154.

BRUSHTON, FRANKLIN CO., ST. MARY'S CHURCH (1870) [CEM] Rev. Christopher J. Looby.
Res.: 1347 Washington St., 12916-0249. Tel: 518-529-7433. Email: office@stmarysbrushton.org.
Catechesis/Religious Program—Tel: 518-529-6580; Fax: 518-529-7433. Ernest Russell Jr., D.R.E. Students 77.

BURKE, FRANKLIN CO., ST. GEORGE (1874) [CEM] Merged with St. Patrick, Chateaugay to form Catholic Community of Burke and Chateaugay.

CADYVILLE, CLINTON CO., ST. JAMES CHURCH (1854) [CEM] Rev. Msgr. Lawrence M. Deno.
Res.: 26 Church Rd., P.O. Box 117, 12918-0117. Tel: 518-293-7026; Fax: 518-293-8246. Web: www.stjamescadyville.org.
Catechesis/Religious Program—Students 85.

CANTON, ST. LAWRENCE CO.
1—ST. MARY (1868) [CEM] Rev. Douglas J. Lucia; Brian P. Walsh, Pastoral Assoc.; Thomas J. Phalon. Tel: 315-386-8425; Deacon James M. Snell.
Res.: 68 Court St., 13617. Tel: 315-386-2543; Fax: 315-386-8870.
School—(Grades PreK-6), 2 Powers St., 13617. Tel: 315-386-3572. Mrs. Marianne Jadlos, Prin. Lay Teachers 10; Students 112.
Catechesis/Religious Program—Ms. Jamie Burns, C.R.E. Students 108.
Oratory—St. Henry-DeKalb Junction
Oratory—St. Paul-Pyrites 24 Pestle St., Russell, St. Lawrence Co. 13684.
2—NEWMAN MINISTRY OF ST. MARY'S PARISH: NEWMAN CENTER (1959), (Campus Parish) Rev. Douglas J. Lucia; Thomas J. Phalon.
Tel: 315-386-8425.
Catechesis/Religious Program—Students 108.

CAPE VINCENT, JEFFERSON CO.
1—THE CATHOLIC COMMUNITY OF CAPE VINCENT, ROSIERE AND CHAUMONT Rev. Pierre Aubin, M.S.C.; Sr. Anne Hogan, S.S.J., Pastoral Assoc.
Box 288, 13618.
Res.: 139 N. Kanady St., Box 288, 13618. Tel: 315-654-2662; Fax: 315-654-4721.
Catechesis/Religious Program—Students 62.
2—ST. VINCENT OF PAUL (1832) [CEM 2] Merged with St. Vincent de Paul, Rosiere & All Saints, Chaumont to form The Catholic Community of Cape Vincent, Rosiere and Chaumont, Cape Vincent.

CARTHAGE, JEFFERSON CO., ST. JAMES MINOR (1818) [CEM 2] [JC] Revs. George F. Maroun; John J. Cosmic (Retired); Sisters Mary Rita Kempney, S.S.J., Pastoral Assoc.; Marie Angele Ellis, S.S.J., Pastoral Assoc.; Deacon Richard J. Staab.
Res.: 327 West St., 13619. Tel: 315-493-3224; Fax: 315-493-3280. Email: stjames@twcny.rr.com.
School—Augustinian Academy, (Grades PreK-8), 317 West St., 13619. Tel: 315-493-1301; Fax: 315-493-0632. Sr. Annunciata Collins, S.S.J., Prin. Sisters of St. Joseph 1; Lay Teachers 12; Students 171.
Catechesis/Religious Program—Students 48.
Convent—Tel: 315-493-1672.

CHAMPLAIN, CLINTON CO., ST. MARY (1861) [CEM 2] Rev. James A. Delbel; Deacon Leonard Patrie.
Res.: 86 Church St., P.O. Box 368, 12919. Tel: 518-298-8244; Fax: 518-298-2879. Email: churchofstmary@yahoo.com.
School—(Grades PreK-6) Tel: 518-298-3372; Fax: 518-298-3886. Email: smaoffice@primelink1.net. Web: www.worldwordweb.com. Sr. Marie Cordata Kelly, S.S.J., Prin.; Mrs. Jean Jesburger, Librarian. Sisters of St. Joseph 2; Lay Teachers 8; Students 49.
Catechesis/Religious Program—Students 41.

CHASM FALLS, FRANKLIN CO., ST. HELEN (1881) [CEM], Malone Catholic Parishes - see detailed information under Notre Dame, Malone., 306 W. Main St., P.O. Box 547, Malone, 12953. Email: mcp@twcny.rr.com. Web: malonecatholic.com.
Oratory—St. Mary, Malone Catholic Parishes -see detailed information under Notre Dame, Malone., Lake Titus, Franklin Co. 12953.
Oratory—St. Joseph, Malone Catholic Parishes - see detailed information under Notre Dame, Malone., Owl's Head, Franklin Co. 12953.
Catechesis/Religious Program—Ms. Tamra Murphy, D.R.E.

CHATEAUGAY, FRANKLIN CO., CATHOLIC COMMUNITY OF BURKE AND CHATEAUGAY formerly St. Patrick's Church (1848) [CEM] Rev. John J. Looby; Deacon Brian T. Dwyer.
Res.: 132 W. Main St., P.O. Box 908, 12920. Tel: 518-497-6673; Fax: 518-497-6165. Email: ccbc@twcny.rr.com.
Catechesis/Religious Program—Students 105.

CHAUMONT, JEFFERSON CO., ALL SAINTS (1922) Merged with St. Vincent de Paul, Cape Vincent & St. Vincent de Paul, Rosiere to form The Catholic Community of Cape Vincent, Rosiere and Chaumont, Cape Vincent.

CHAZY, CLINTON CO., SACRED HEART (1898) [CEM 2] Rev. Raymond J. Moreau.
Res.: 27 Church St., P.O. Box 459, 12921. Tel: 518-846-7650; Fax: 518-846-7655. Email: csacredheart@twcny.rr.com. Web: www.chazysacredheart.org.
Catechesis/Religious Program—Email: religion@twcny.rr.com. Students 146.

CLAYTON, JEFFERSON CO., ST. MARY'S OF CLAYTON (1838) [CEM 2] Rev. Arthur J. LaBaff; Deacons Gary A. Frank; Bruce Wayne Daugherty.
Res.: 521 James St., 13624. Tel: 315-686-3398 (Rectory); 315-686-2638 (Rel. Educ. Office); Fax: 315-686-2700.
Catechesis/Religious Program—Tel: 315-686-2638. Students 113.

COLTON, ST. LAWRENCE CO., ST. PATRICK (1864) [CEM] [JC] Rev. Msgr. Robert H. Aucoin.
Res.: P.O. Box 315, 13625. Tel: 315-262-2871.
Church: 4897A SH56, 13625.
Catechesis/Religious Program—Students 43.
Mission—St. Paul, Closed. Now an oratory., South Colton, St. Lawrence Co. 13687.
Mission—St. Michael, Closed. Now an oratory., Parishville, St. Lawrence Co. 13625.

CONSTABLE, FRANKLIN CO., THE CATHOLIC COMMUNITY OF CONSTABLE, WESTVILLE AND TROUT RIVER (1872) [CEM] Rev. Francis J. Flynn; Deacon Garry N. Burnell.
Res.: 1197 State Rte. 122, P.O. Box 78, 12926. Tel: 518-483-2775 (Rectory); 518-483-0486 (Parish Office); Fax: 518-483-0486.
Catechesis/Religious Program—Students 76.
Mission— 4326 State Rte. 37, Westville, Franklin Co. 12926.

CONSTABLEVILLE, LEWIS CO., ST. MARY (1820) [CEM] [JC 2] Rev. Lawrence E. Marullo.
Rectory—3200 N. Main St., P.O. Box 382, 13325. Tel: 315-397-2556. Email: srectory1@twcny.rr.com.
Catechesis/Religious Program—Students 33.

COOPERSVILLE, CLINTON CO., ST. JOSEPH (1790) [CEM] Revs. Clyde A. Lewis; Normand C. Cote, Pastor Emeritus (Retired).
Mailing Address: P.O. Box 217, Rouses Point, 12979. 82 Mason Rd., Champlain, 12919. Tel: 518-297-7361; Fax: 518-297-3181. Email: stpats@twcny.rr.com.
Catechesis/Religious Program—Tel: 518-846-7180; Fax: 518-846-7655. Email: csacredheart@twcny.rr.com. Students 3.

COPENHAGEN, LEWIS CO., ST. MARY (1901), (Irish—French), [CEM 2] Rev. George F. Maroun; Sr. Mary Rita Kempney, S.S.J., Pastoral Assoc.; Deacon Richard J. Staab.
Res.: 9790 NYS Rte. 12, P.O. Box 12, 13626-0012. Tel: 315-688-2683. Email: stmarycope@westelcom.com.
Catechesis/Religious Program—Students 25.

CROGHAN, LEWIS CO., ST. STEPHEN (1869) [CEM] [JC 3] Rev. Daniel L. Chapin.
Res.: 9748 State Rte. 812, P.O. Box 38, 13327-0038. Tel: 315-346-6958; Fax: 315-346-1200.
Catechesis/Religious Program—Tel: 315-346-6963. Mr. Thomas Schneeberger, D.R.E. Students 129.
Oratory—Belfort, St. Vincent de Paul
Oratory—New Bremen, St. Peter [CEM 3]

CROWN POINT, ESSEX CO., SACRED HEART CHURCH (1874) [CEM] Rev. Kevin D. McEwan; Sr. Carol Daul, S.A., Pastoral Assoc.; Deacon Elliott A. Shaw.
Mailing Address: c/o 22 Father Jogues Pl., Ticonderoga, 12883.
Church: 12928. Tel: 518-597-3924. Email: tipastor@verizon.net. Web: www.smsh.org.
Catechesis/Religious Program—Students 30.

DANNEMORA, CLINTON CO., ST. JOSEPH (1853) [CEM 2] Rev. Donald F. Kramberg; Deacon Edward Mazuchowski. In Res., Rev. Guy F. Edwards. Tel: 518-492-2511, Ext. 4800.
Res.: 179 Smith St., Box 418, 12929-0418. Tel: 518-492-7118; Fax: 518-492-7742. Email: office@stjosephsdannemora.com.
Catechesis/Religious Program—Tel: 518-492-2524. Email: llelynch@aol.com. Lynn Lynch, C.R.E. Students 79.

DEFERIET, JEFFERSON CO., ST. RITA (1900) Rev. Garvin J. Demarais.
Res.: 208 Leray St., Black River, 13612. Tel: 315-773-5672.
Church: 31 Riverside Dr., 13628.

ELIZABETHTOWN, ESSEX CO., ST. ELIZABETH (1881) [CEM] Rev. Msgr. Peter R. Riani.
Res.: 8434 NYS Rte. 9N, P.O. Box 368, 12932. Tel: 518-873-6760.
Catechesis/Religious Program—Students 20.

ELLENBURG, CLINTON CO., ST. EDMUND (1869) [JC 2] Rev. Theodore A. Crosby; Deacon John A. Levison.
Res. & Church: 5526 Rte. 11, P.O. Box 119, 12933-0119. Tel: 518-594-3907 (Office); Fax: 518-594-3222. Email: stedmund@twcny.rr.com. Web: stedmunds.grainofwheat.net.
Catechesis/Religious Program—Fax: 518-594-3222. Mona LaBombard, D.R.E. Students 70.
Oratory—Immaculate Heart of Mary 560 State Rte. 189, Churubusco, 12923.

ESSEX, ESSEX CO., ST. JOSEPH, [CEM] [JC] Merged with St. Philip of Jesus, Willsboro to form Catholic Community of St. Philip of Jesus and St. Joseph of Willsboro.

EVANS MILLS, JEFFERSON CO., ST. MARY (1847) [CEM] Rev. Thomas E. Kornmeyer.
Res.: 8408 S. Main St., 13637. Tel: 315-629-4425 (Rectory); 315-782-4678 (Office); Fax: 315-629-4868. Email: cstmarys@verizon.net.
Catechesis/Religious Program—Students 40.
Mission—St. Joseph Philadelphia, Jefferson Co.
Mission—St. Theresa of Avila Theresa, Jefferson Co.
Oratory—St. Michael (1849) [CEM] Antwerp, Jefferson Co. Tel: 315-659-8372. Antwerp, NY

FORT COVINGTON, FRANKLIN CO., ST. MARY (1837) [CEM 2] Rev. Martin E. Cline.
Res.: 20 County Rte. 4, Bombay, 12914. Tel: 518-358-2500; Fax: 518-358-4471.
Office & Mailing Address: P.O. Box 499, 12937.
Catechesis/Religious Program—Tel: 518-358-2500. Jocelyn Kelly, D.R.E. Students 47.

GLENFIELD, LEWIS CO., ST. MARY (1919) [CEM] Rev. Christopher C. Carrara.
Res.: 5457 Shady Ave., Lowville, 13367. Tel: 315-376-6662; Fax: 315-376-6663.
Catechesis/Religious Program—Tel: 315-376-6662. Students 14.
Mission—St. Thomas (1876) [CEM] Greig, Lewis Co.

GOUVERNEUR, ST. LAWRENCE CO.
1—ST. HENRY (1893) [CEM] Closed. Now an Oratory under St. Mary's, Canton.
2—ST. JAMES (1875) [CEM 2] Rev. Stephen Rocker.
Res.: 164 E. Main St., 13642. Tel: 315-287-0114; Fax: 315-287-0606. Web: stjamesgouv.com.
School—(Grades PreSchool-6), 20 S. Gordon St., 13642. Tel: 315-287-0130; Fax: 315-287-0054. Mrs. Bridgette LaPierre, Prin. Lay Teachers 13; Students 133.
Catechesis/Religious Program—Debra Ward, D.R.E. Students 32.
3—SACRED HEART (1894) Rev. Stephen Rocker; Deacon Peter J. Lawless.
Res. & Mailing Address: 164 E. Main St., 13642. Tel: 315-287-0114; Fax: 315-287-0606. Email: catholic@twcny.rr.com.
Parish Hall: 6 Trout Lake Rd., Edwards, 13635.
Catechesis/Religious Program—Mary Anne Lawless, D.R.E. Students 8.

HAMMOND, ST. LAWRENCE CO., ST. PETER (1905), (French—Irish), [CEM] Merged with The Roman Catholic Community of Morristown, Hammond & Rossie. Now a worship site.

HARRISVILLE, LEWIS CO., ST. FRANCIS SOLANUS (1879), (French—Irish), [CEM] Rev. Robert L. Decker; Deacon Ken Seymour.
Res.: 14355 Maple St., P.O. Box 208, 13648. Tel: 315-543-2421; Fax: 315-543-2421.
Catechesis/Religious Program—Students 26.
Oratory—St. Henry Natural Bridge, Jefferson Co. 13665. Tel: 315-543-2431.

HEUVELTON, ST. LAWRENCE CO., ST. RAPHAEL'S (1880) Rev. James W. Seymour; Deacon Richard L. Van Kirk.
Res.: 5 Clinton St., P.O. Box 377, 13654. Tel: 315-344-2383. Email: saintraphael@twcny.rr.com.
Catechesis/Religious Program—Students 100.

HOGANSBURG, FRANKLIN CO., ST. PATRICK (1834), (Irish), [CEM] [JC] Rev. Martin E. Cline; Mrs. Carol Pulsifer, Pastoral Assoc.
Office & Mailing Address: P.O. Box 499, Fort Covington, 12937.
Res.: 20 County Rte. 4, P.O. Box 156, Bombay, 12914. Tel: 518-358-2500; Fax: 518-358-4471.
Catechesis/Religious Program—Jocelyn Kelly, D.R.E.

HOPKINTON, ST. LAWRENCE CO., CHURCH OF THE HOLY CROSS (1877) [CEM] Rev. Alfred H. Fish.
Res.: P.O. Box 288, St. Regis Falls, 12980. Tel: 518-856-9456.
Catechesis/Religious Program—Students 6.

HOUSEVILLE, LEWIS CO., ST. HEDWIG (1922), (Polish), Rev. Christopher C. Carrara; Michele Rosteck, Pastoral Assoc.
St. Peter's Church: 5457 Shady Ave., Lowville, 13367-1615. Tel: 315-376-6662; Fax: 315-376-6663.
Catechesis/Religious Program—Students 11.

INDIAN LAKE, HAMILTON CO., ST. MARY'S (1958) [CEM] Rev. Philip T. Allen.
Res.: 6333 NYS Rte. 28, 12842. Tel: 518-648-5422; Fax: 518-648-0323.
Catechesis/Religious Program—Students 30.
Mission—St. Paul P.O. Box 332, Blue Mountain Lake, Hamilton Co. 12842.

INLET, HAMILTON CO., ST. ANTHONY OF PADUA (1929) Rev. Shane M. Lynch; Deacon Ronald Ste.-Marie.
Mailing Address: P.O. Box 236, Old Forge, 13420. Tel: 315-357-2811; Fax: 315-369-2049.
Catechesis/Religious Program—Students 16.
St. William—, Seasonal Chapel, Raquette Lake, 13436.

KEENE, ESSEX CO., ST. BRENDAN (1868) Rev. John R. Yonkovig; Deacon Bruce Carley Wadsworth.
Res.: P.O. Box 130, 12942-0130. Tel: 518-523-2200.
Catechesis/Religious Program—Students 3.

KEESEVILLE, CLINTON AND ESSEX COS.
1—CHURCH OF THE IMMACULATE CONCEPTION (THE ROMAN CATHOLIC COMMUNITY OF KEESEVILLE) (1835),

(Irish—French), [CEM] Consolidated with St. John the Baptist, Keeseville to form The Roman Catholic Community of Keeseville.

2—ST. JOHN THE BAPTIST (THE ROMAN CATHOLIC COMMUNITY OF KEESEVILLE) (1853), (French—Irish), [CEM 2] Rev. Msgr. Leeward J. Poissant.
Res.: 1804 Main St., 12944-3745. Tel: 518-834-7100; Fax: 518-834-4612. Email: rcckparish@charter.net.
Immaculate Conception— (1835) Worship Site: Tel: 518-834-2070.
St. John the Baptist— (1853) Worship Site: Tel: 518-834-7600.
Catechesis/Religious Program—1806 Main St., 12944-3745. Tel: 518-578-5632. Students 93.

LAFARGEVILLE, JEFFERSON CO., ST. JOHN THE EVANGELIST (1848) [CEM] Rev. Arthur J. LaBaff.
Res. & Mailing Address: 521 James St., Clayton, 13624. Tel: 315-686-3398; Fax: 315-686-2700.
Church: 35923 Rte.180, 13656. Email: stmarysclayton@westel.com.com.
Catechesis/Religious Program—Students 16.

LAKE CLEAR, FRANKLIN CO., ST. JOHN IN THE WILDERNESS (1887) [CEM] [JC] Revs. Mark R. Reilly; Paul J. Kelly, Parochial Vicar; Sr. Carol Kraeger, S.S.J., Pastoral Assoc.
Mailing Address: 6148 State Rte. 30, P.O. Box 260, 12945. Tel: 518-891-2286. Email: srcarolk@yahoo.com.
Res.: 27 St. Bernard's St., Saranac Lake, 12983. Tel: 518-891-4616; Fax: 518-891-4619. Email: stbernard@roadrunner.com. Web: stbernards-saranaclake.catholicexchange.com.
*Catechesis/Religious Program—Pius X Inter-Parish Religious Education Center*Email: piusxcenter@roadrunner.com. Students 5.
Summer Station—Fish Creek, State Campsite. Tel: 518-891-3239.
Oratory—St. Gabriel Pickett Hall, #105, Paul Smiths, Franklin Co. 12970. Tel: 518-327-6225.

LAKE PLACID, ESSEX CO., ST. AGNES (1896) [CEM] Rev. John R. Yonkovig; Deacon Bruce Carley Wadsworth.
Res.: 169 Hillcrest Ave., 12946. Tel: 518-523-2200; Fax: 518-523-2203. Email: stagnesch@roadrunner.com.
School—(Grades PreK-3), 2322 Saranac Ave., 12946. Tel: 518-523-3771. Catherine Bemis, Prin.; Karen Armstrong, Librarian. Lay Teachers 5; Students 71.
Catechesis/Religious Program—Tel: 518-523-3202. Mrs. Marcia Pilawa, D.R.E. Students 70.

LAKE PLEASANT, HAMILTON CO., ST. JAMES MAJOR (1924) Rev. Sony G. Pulickal.
Res.: 2781 NYS Rte. 8, P.O. Box 214, Speculator, 12164. Tel: 518-548-6275. Email: sjcsac@frontiernet.net.
Catechesis/Religious Program—Students 2.

LISBON, ST. LAWRENCE CO., SS. PHILIP AND JAMES (1872) Rev. James W. Seymour; Sr. Mary Frances Barnes, D.C., Pastoral Assoc.; Elaine Craig, Lay Min.; Marlene Watson, Lay Min.
Mailing Address: 6892 County Rt. 10, P.O. Box 175, 13658. Tel: 315-393-3796. Email: ssp&j@centralny.twcbc.com.
Catechesis/Religious Program—Tel: 315-393-3796. Students 38.

LONG LAKE, HAMILTON CO., ST. HENRY (1899) [JC] Rev. Peter M. Berg.
Res.: 18 Adams Ln., Newcomb, 12852-1701. Tel: 518-582-3671. Email: stetherese@frontiernet.net.
Catechesis/Religious Program—

LOUISVILLE, ST. LAWRENCE CO., ST. LAWRENCE (1930) [CEM] Merged with Sacred Heart, Massena to form Church of Sacred Heart and St. Lawrence, Massena.

LOWVILLE, LEWIS CO., ST. PETER (1870) Rev. Christopher C. Carrara; Michele Rosteck, Pastoral Assoc.; Deacon Ronald J. Pominville.
Res.: 5441 Shady Ave., 13367. Tel: 315-376-6662; Fax: 315-376-6663. Email: stpeters@centralny.twcbc.org. Web: www.stpeters-lowville.org.
Catechesis/Religious Program—Web: stpeters-lowville.org. Margaret Martin, D.R.E. Students 153.

LYON MOUNTAIN, CLINTON CO., ST. BERNARD (1875) [CEM] [JC] Rev. Theodore A. Crosby; Deacon Francis Siskavich.
Res.: 10 Church Pond Rd., P.O. Box 23, 12952. Tel: 518-735-4357; Fax: 518-735-4357. Email: stbernardchurch@adkwireless.net.
Catechesis/Religious Program—Students 17.
Mission—St. Michael [CEM 2] Standish, Clinton Co.

MADRID, ST. LAWRENCE CO., ST. JOHN THE BAPTIST (1869) [CEM] Rev. Msgr. Robert L. Lawler.
Mailing Address: P.O. Box 68, 13660.
Pastor's Residence: 34 Oak St., P.O. Box 187, Waddington, 13694. Tel: 315-388-4466; Fax: 315-388-4722. Email: stmarywadd@aol.com.
Church: North St., 13660-0068. Fax: 315-322-5661.
Catechesis/Religious Program—Students 36.

MALONE, FRANKLIN CO.

1—ST. JOHN BOSCO (1935) [CEM], Malone Catholic Parishes - see detailed information under Notre Dame., 306 W. Main St., P.O. Box 547, 12953.

2—ST. JOSEPH'S (1849), (Irish), [CEM 2], Malone Catholic Parishes - see detailed information under Notre Dame., 306 W. Main St., P.O. Box 547, 12953.

3—NOTRE DAME (1868), (French-Canadian), [CEM] Revs. Joseph W. Giroux; Bryan D. Stitt; Sisters Mary Elizabeth Looby, G.N.S.H., Pastoral Assoc.; Barbara Schiavoni, G.N.S.H., Pastoral Assoc.
Priest's Res.: 11 Church Pl., P.O. Box 547, 12953. Tel: 518-483-4074; Fax: 518-483-4185. Email: mcp@twcny.rr.com. Web: malonecatholic.com.
Office: 306 W. Main St., P.O. Box 547, 12953. Tel: 518-483-1300; Fax: 518-483-1307.
School—Holy Family, (Grades PreK-8), Joint venture Malone Catholic Parishes and 5 other rural parishes., 12 Homestead Pk., 12953. Tel: 518-483-4443; Fax: 518-481-6762. Anne Marie Wiseman, Prin. Sisters 1; Lay Teachers 14; Students 184.
Catechesis/Religious Program—Ms. Tamra Murphy, D.R.E. Combined with St. Joseph, Malone; St. John Bosco, Malone; St. Helen, Chasm Falls, Malone. Students 332.

MASSENA, ST. LAWRENCE CO.

1—THE CATHOLIC COMMUNITY OF ST. MARY'S & ST. JOSEPH'S Rev. J. Michael Gaffney; Sr. Maureen Sweeney, S.S.J., Pastoral Assoc.
105 Cornell Ave, P.O. Box 609, 13662. Tel: 315-764-0239; Fax: 315-796-5526. Email: stsmaryandjoseph@twcny.rr.com. Web: www.stmarymassena.catholicweb.com.
School—Trinity Catholic School, (Grades PreK-6), 188 Main St., 13662. Tel: 315-769-5911; Fax: 315-769-6973. Email: principal@twcny.rr.com. Web: www.trinitycatholicschool.net. Joan Rufa, Prin.; Candace O'Neill, Librarian. Sisters of Saint Joseph and Servants of Mary 2; Lay Teachers 10; Students 215.
Catechesis/Religious Program—Anne Borsellino, D.R.E. (Grades K-12). Students 119.

2—CHURCH OF SACRED HEART AND ST. LAWRENCE (1874) [CEM] Rev. Donald J. Manfred; Sr. Juliana Fitzpatrick, O.S.M., Pastoral Assoc.; Deacons James J. Hotte; Thomas E. Proulx.
212 Main St., 13662.
Res.: 212 Main St., P.O. Box 329, 13662. Tel: 315-769-2469; Fax: 315-769-6973. Email: sacredh@nnymail.com. Web: www.sacredheartmassena.net.
Catechesis/Religious Program—Sr. Edward Marie Tesiero, S.A., Dir. Christian Formation. Students 186.
Convent—188 Main St., P.O. Box 91, 13662. Tel: 315-769-6238.

3—ST. JOSEPH (1947) [JC] Merged with St. Mary's to form The Catholic Community of St. Mary's & St. Joseph's.

4—ST. MARY (1913) [JC] Merged with St. Joseph's to form The Catholic Community of St. Mary's & St. Joseph's.
See Trinity Catholic School under The Catholic Community of St. Mary's & St. Joseph's, Massena.

5—SACRED HEART, Merged with St. Lawrence, Louisville to form Church of Sacred Heart and St. Lawrence, Massena.

MINEVILLE, ESSEX CO., THE CHURCH OF ALL SAINTS (1872) [CEM] Merged with St. Patrick's, Port Henry to form Catholic Community of Moriah, Port Henry.

MOOERS FORKS, CLINTON CO., ST. ANN (1860), (French-Canadian), [CEM] Rev. Gerald A. Cerank; Deacons Tyrone A. Rabideau; Dennis Monty.
Res.: 3062 Rte. 11, P.O. Box 89, 12959. Tel: 518-236-5632; Fax: 518-236-4446.
Catechesis/Religious Program—Tel: 518-236-4436. Students 98.

MOOERS, CLINTON CO., ST. JOSEPH (1910), (French-Canadian), [CEM] Rev. Gerald A. Cerank.
Mailing Address: P.O. Box 89, Mooers Forks, 12959-0089. Tel: 518-236-5632; Fax: 518-236-4446.
83 Maple St., 12958.
Catechesis/Religious Program—73 Maple St., 12958. Tel: 518-236-4436. Students 64.

MORRISONVILLE, CLINTON CO., THE ROMAN CATHOLIC COMMUNITY OF ST. ALEXANDER AND ST. JOSEPH formerly St. Alexander (1897) [CEM] Rev. Scott R. Seymour; Deacon Marvin M. Connor.
Rectory—1349 Military Tpke., Plattsburgh, 12901. Tel: 518-563-6301.
Church: 1 Church St., P.O. Box 159, 12962. Tel: 518-561-5039; Fax: 518-561-5040.
Catechesis/Religious Program— Mrs. Amy Dylong, D.R.E. & Youth Min. Students 85.

MORRISTOWN, ST. LAWRENCE CO., THE ROMAN CATHOLIC COMMUNITY OF MORRISTOWN, HAMMOND AND ROSSIE formerly St. John the Evangelist (1941) Rev. Albert J. Hauser; Deacon Patrick Lyons.
Res.: P.O. Box 216, 13664. Tel: 315-375-6571; Fax: 315-375-4832. Email: stjohns@centralny.twcbc.com.
Worship Sites—
St. Patrick—, Rossie, NY
St. Peter—, Hammond, NY
Catechesis/Religious Program—Students 26.

NEWCOMB, ESSEX CO., ST. THERESE (1950) [CEM] Rev. Peter M. Berg.
Res.: 18 Adams Ln., 12852-1701. Tel: 518-582-3671. Email: stetherese@frontiernet.net.
Catechesis/Religious Program—

NORFOLK, ST. LAWRENCE CO., VISITATION OF THE B.V.M. (1880) [CEM] Rev. Msgr. John R. Murphy, Admin.; Deacon Lawrence A. Connelly. In Res., Rev. Andrew J. Amyot, 11 Hepburn St., 13667. Tel: 315-384-2064.
Church & Rectory: 3 Morris St., P.O. Box 637, 13667. Fax: 315-384-3575. Email: visitationchurch@twcny.rr.com.
Catechesis/Religious Program—Tel: 315-384-4242. Students 35.

NORTH BANGOR, FRANKLIN CO., ST. AUGUSTINE (1887) [CEM] Rev. Christopher J. Looby.
Res.: 1347 Washington St., Brushton, 12916. Tel: 518-483-6674; Fax: 518-483-6674.
Catechesis/Religious Program—Students 161.

NORTH LAWRENCE, ST. LAWRENCE CO., ST. LAWRENCE (1875), (Irish—French), [CEM] Rev. Garry B. Giroux.
Res.: P.O. Box 208, Brasher Falls, 13613. Tel: 315-389-5401; Fax: 315-389-4066. Email: parish@twcny.rr.com.
Catechesis/Religious Program— Clustered with St. Patrick, Brasher Falls. Students 10.

NORWOOD, ST. LAWRENCE CO., ST. ANDREW (1876) [CEM] Rev. Msgr. Harry K. Snow.
Res.: 2 Park Ave., 13668. Tel: 315-353-7303; Fax: 315-353-4650.
Catechesis/Religious Program—Students 48.

OLD FORGE, HERKIMER CO., ST. BARTHOLOMEW (1897) Rev. Shane M. Lynch.
Res.: P.O. Box 236, 13420. Tel: 315-369-3554; Fax: 315-369-2049. Email: stbarts@roadrunner.com.
Catechesis/Religious Program—Students 41.

OLMSTEDVILLE, ESSEX CO., ST. JOSEPH (1871) [CEM 2] Rev. Richard S. Sturtz.
Mailing Address: P.O. Box 368, Schroon Lake, 12870. Tel: 518-251-2565; 518-532-7100; Fax: 518-532-7100.
Rectory—639 Church Rd., P.O. Box 1, 12857.
Catechesis/Religious Program—Tel: 518-251-2565. Students 3.

PERU, CLINTON CO., ST. AUGUSTINE (1883) [CEM] Rev. Alan D. Shnob; Deacon George Grady Benson.
Res.: 3035 Main St., 12972. Tel: 518-643-2439 (Office); 518-643-6759 (Rectory); Fax: 518-643-0960. Email: staugrec@verizon.net. Web: www.peruparish.org.
Catechesis/Religious Program—Tel: 518-643-9498. Students 96.
Oratory—St. Patrick [CEM 2] West Peru, Clinton Co. 12972.

PLATTSBURGH, CLINTON CO.

1—ST. JOHN THE BAPTIST (1873) Merged with Newman Parish, John XXIII College Community to form The Roman Catholic Church of St. John the Baptist, Plattsburgh.

2—ST. JOSEPH (Treadwells Mill) (1935) Merged with St. Alexander, Morrisonville to form The Roman Catholic Community of St. Alexander and St. Joseph.

3—NEWMAN PARISH, JOHN XXIII COLLEGE COMMUNITY (1970) Merged with St. John the Baptist, Plattsburgh to form The Roman Catholic Church of St. John the Baptist, Plattsburgh.

4—OUR LADY OF VICTORY (1907), (French), Rev. William G. Reamer.
Res.: 4919 S. Catherine St., 12901. Tel: 518-561-1842; Fax: 518-561-2269.
Catechesis/Religious Program—Students 61.

5—ST. PETER (1853) [CEM] Rev. Msgr. Dennis J. Duprey; Deacons Mark Bennett, Spiritual Life Dir.; Frank A. Bushey Jr. In Res., Rev. Msgr. Joseph G. Aubin (Retired).
Res.: 114 Cornelia St., 12901. Tel: 518-563-1692; Fax: 518-566-9420. Email: spchurch1692@primelink1.net. Web: www.saintpeterschurch.org.
See Seton Academy Elementary School, Plattsburgh under Elementary Schools, Private in the Institution Section.
Convent—St. Peter's Convent, 5 Caitlin Way, 12903. Tel: 518-566-7315. Email: dshope2@charter.net. Sr. Mary Stephanie Frenette, O.P., Contact Person. Dominican Sisters of Hope Total in Residence 2.
Catechesis/Religious Program—Tel: 518-563-3278. Therese Moen, D.R.E.; Jennifer Campbell, Assoc. D.R.E. Students 130.

6—THE ROMAN CATHOLIC CHURCH OF ST. JOHN THE BAPTIST (1837), (Irish), [CEM 3] Revs. Timothy G. Canaan; Normand C. Cote (Retired).
Res.: 7 Margaret St., 12901. Tel: 518-563-0730;

Fax: 518-563-0754. Email: office@broadstreetcatholics.org.
See Seton Academy Elementary School, Plattsburgh under Elementary Schools, Private in the Institution Section.
Catechesis/Religious Program—Students 70.
Oratory—St. Mary of the Lake (Cumberland Head) (1965) 1202 Cumberland Head Rd., 12901. Rev. Garvin J. Demarais.

PORT HENRY, ESSEX CO., CATHOLIC COMMUNITY OF MORIAH (1854), (Irish), [CEM] Rev. Scott D. Fobare.
Res.: 12 St. Patrick's Pl., 12974. Tel: 518-546-7254; Fax: 518-375-3624. Web: ccofm.grainofwheat.net.
Catechesis/Religious Program—Tel: 518-546-3374. Students 98.
Worship Site: St. Patrick—

PORT LEYDEN, LEWIS CO., ST. MARTIN (1879) [CEM] Rev. Lawrence E. Marullo; Deacon James W. Chaufty.
Res.: 7108 North St., P.O. Box 431, 13433. Tel: 315-348-6104; Fax: 315-348-6353. Email: smartins@frontiernet.net.
Catechesis/Religious Program—Students 29.
Mission—St. John Lyons Falls, Lewis Co. Tel: 315-348-6599.

POTSDAM, ST. LAWRENCE CO., ST. MARY (1841) [CEM] Rev. Msgr. Robert H. Aucoin.
Res.: 17 Lawrence Ave., 13676. Tel: 315-265-9680; Fax: 315-883-1354. Email: info@stmarystpatrick.net. Web: www.stmarystpatrick.net.
Catechesis/Religious Program—Tel: 315-265-9520. Email: ajkane@potsdamcatholic.org. Students 77. Email: syoung@stmarystpatrick.net. Serving SUNY Potsdam and Clarkson Univerities.

RAQUETTE LAKE, HAMILTON CO., ST. WILLIAM (1890), Seasonal chapel of St. Anthony of Padua in Inlet, N.Y. Rev. Shane M. Lynch.
Mailing Address: P.O. Box 236, Old Forge, 13420. Tel: 315-369-3554; Fax: 315-369-2049.

RAYMONDVILLE, ST. LAWRENCE CO., ST. RAYMOND (1920) [CEM] Rev. Msgr. John R. Murphy, Admin. 8828 Rte. 56, 13678.
Res. & Mailing Address: 3 Morris St., Norfolk, 13667. Tel: 315-384-4242; Fax: 315-384-3575.
Catechesis/Religious Program—

REDFORD, CLINTON CO., CHURCH OF THE ASSUMPTION (1853) [CEM] Rev. Donald F. Kramberg; Deacon Edward Mazuchowski.
Res.: 78 Clinton St., 12978. Tel: 518-293-6259; Fax: 518-293-6435. Email: carousel1850@hotmail.com.
Catechesis/Religious Program—Kris Bowman, C.R.E. Students 41.

REDWOOD, JEFFERSON CO., ST. FRANCIS XAVIER (1848) [CEM] Consolidated Worship site of Catholic Community of Alexandria.

ROSIERE, JEFFERSON CO., ST. VINCENT DE PAUL (1871) [CEM] Merged with St. Vincent de Paul, Cape Vincent & All Saints, Chaumont to form The Catholic Community of Cape Vincent, Rosiere and Chaumont, Cape Vincent.

ROUSES POINT, CLINTON CO., ST. PATRICK (1857), (Irish), [CEM] [JC] Rev. Clyde A. Lewis; Deacon Noel A. Hinerth; Jo Anne Ryan, Business Mgr.
Res.: 138 Lake St., P.O. Box 217, 12979. Tel: 518-297-7361; Fax: 518-297-3181. Email: stpats@twcny.rr.com. Web: www.saintpatricks.ws.
Catechesis/Religious Program—9 Liberty St., P.O. Box 217, 12979. Tel: 518-297-2767. Kathy Guay, D.R.E. Students 69.

SACKETS HARBOR, JEFFERSON CO., ST. ANDREW (1886) Rev. Kevin J. O'Brien; Deacon Norman Hunneyman.
Res.: 119 W. Main St., P.O. Box 99, Brownville, 13615. Tel: 315-646-3341.
Catechesis/Religious Program—Students 30.

SAINT REGIS FALLS, FRANKLIN CO., ST. ANN (1883) [CEM] Rev. Alfred H. Fish.
Res.: P.O. Box 288, St. Regis Falls, 12980. Tel: 518-856-9456.
Catechesis/Religious Program—Students 17.
Oratory—St. Peter Santa Clara.

SARANAC LAKE, FRANKLIN CO., ST. BERNARD (1888) [CEM] [JC] Revs. Mark R. Reilly; Paul J. Kelly, Parochial Vicar; Sr. Carol Kraeger, S.S.J., Pastoral Assoc.; Deacons Frederick R. Oberst; Joseph Szwed; Jerome A. Cheney.
Res.: 27 St. Bernard St., 12983. Tel: 518-891-4616; Fax: 518-891-4619. Email: stbernard@roadrunner.com.
School—(Grades K-5) Tel: 518-891-2830. Raymond Dora, Prin. Lay Teachers 7; Students 49.
Catechesis/Religious Program—*Pius X Center* Cherie Racette, Asst.; Michelle Crowley, C.R.E. (Confirmation Prog). Students 100.

SCHROON LAKE, ESSEX CO., OUR LADY OF LOURDES (1883) [CEM] Rev. Richard S. Sturtz.
Res.: 1114 Main St., P.O. Box 368, 12870. Tel: 518-532-7100; Fax: 518-532-7100. Email: ollsjcoffice@verizon.net. Web: www.schroonlakecatholicchurch.com.
Rectory—1114 U.S. Rte. 9, 12870.
Catechesis/Religious Program—Students 38.

SCIOTA, CLINTON CO., ST. LOUIS (1899), (French-Canadian), [CEM] Rev. Gilbert O. Boisvert.
Res.: P.O. Box 113, Altona, 12910. Tel: 518-236-5848; Fax: 518-236-4249.
Catechesis/Religious Program—Tel: 518-236-4436. Students 18.

STAR LAKE, ST. LAWRENCE CO., ST. HUBERT (1893), (French—Irish), [JC] Rev. Robert L. Decker; Deacon Philip F. Giardino.
Res.: 1046 Oswegatchie Trail Rd., P.O. Box 9, 13690. Tel: 315-848-3612; Fax: 315-848-3612. Email: sthubertschurch@gmail.com.
Catechesis/Religious Program—Students 43.
Oratory—St. Anthony of Padua P.O. Box 9, Newton Falls, St. Lawrence Co. 13690.
Oratory—St. Michael P.O. Box 9, Fine, St. Lawrence Co. 13690.

TICONDEROGA, ESSEX CO., ST. MARY (1852) [CEM] Rev. Kevin D. McEwan; Sr. Carol Daul, S.A., Pastoral Assoc.; Deacon Elliott A. Shaw.
Res.: 22 Father Jogues Pl., 12883. Tel: 518-585-7144; Fax: 518-585-3632. Email: stmarysticonderoga@nycap.rr.com. Web: www.smsh.org.
School—(Grades PreK-8), 64 Amherst Ave., 12883. Tel: 518-585-7433; Fax: 518-585-3632. Email: sschoo3@nycap.rr.com. Web: home.nycap.rr.com/tistmarys. Sr. Sharon Anne Dalton, S.S.J., Prin. Sisters 2; Lay Teachers 8; Students 112.
Catechesis/Religious Program—Tel: 518-597-3924. Students 50.

TROUT RIVER, FRANKLIN CO., ST. BRIDGET'S ORATORY (1865) [CEM] Rev. Francis J. Flynn; Deacon Garry Burnell.
Res.: 1197 State Rte. 122, P.O. Box 78, Constable, 12926. Tel: 518-483-2775 (Rectory); 518-483-0486 (Office); Fax: 518-483-1618.

TUPPER LAKE, FRANKLIN CO.
1—ST. ALPHONSUS - HOLY NAME OF JESUS (1890) [CEM] Rev. Douglas A. Decker; Deacons James T. Ellis; Gerald H. Savage; James R. Keough.
Parish Office: *Holy Ghost Parish Center*, 40 Marion St., 12986.
Church: 48 Wawbeck Ave., 12986.
Holy Name Church, 115 Main St., 12986.
Res.: 114 Main St., 12986. Tel: 518-359-9360. Email: stalphon@verizon.net.
Catechesis/Religious Program—Combined with Holy Name of Jesus, Tupper Lake., Tel: 518-359-3405. Students 129.
2—HOLY NAME OF JESUS (Faust) (1904) [CEM] Merged with St. Alphonsus, Tupper Lake to form St. Alphonsus-Holy Name of Jesus, Tupper Lake.

WADDINGTON, ST. LAWRENCE CO., ST. MARY (1826) [CEM 3] Rev. Msgr. Robert L. Lawler.
Res.: 34 Oak St., P.O. Box 187, 13694. Tel: 315-388-4466; Fax: 315-388-4722. Email: rlawler9@twcny.rr.com.
Catechesis/Religious Program—Msgr. Arquett Parish Center, Tel: 315-388-4423. Students 43.

WATERTOWN, JEFFERSON CO.
1—ST. ANTHONY (1913), (Italian), [JC] Rev. Donald A. Robinson; Deacons Richard C. Warner Sr.; John R. Murray.
Res.: 850 Arsenal St., 13601. Tel: 315-782-1190; Fax: 315-786-3489.
Catechesis/Religious Program—Students 95.
2—HOLY FAMILY (1895) Rev. Steven M. Murray; Deacons Edward R. Miller; Michael J. Allan; Patrick J. Bates, Pastoral Assoc.; Sr. Angelica Rebello, S.C.C., Pastoral Assoc. In Res., Rev. Msgr. Paul E. Whitmore (Retired); Rev. Leo A. Wiley (Retired).
Res.: 129 Winthrop St., 13601. Tel: 315-782-2468; Fax: 315-782-4684. Email: hfchurch@twcny.rr.com. Web: www.holyfamilywatertown.org.
Catechesis/Religious Program—Holy Family Religious Education Office, Sterling Pl., 13601. Tel: 315-782-6750. Email: holyfamilyre@yahoo.com. Students 162.
3—OUR LADY OF THE SACRED HEART (1876) [CEM] Rev. Richard Kennedy, M.S.C.; Sr. Diane Marie Ulsamer, S.S.J., Pastoral Assoc.; Deacons William Michael Johnston; John J. Trombly.
Parish Office—320 W. Lynde St., 13601. Tel: 315-782-1474; Fax: 315-782-4939. Email: rwkpng03@mscparish.com. Web: www.olshparish.org.
Catechesis/Religious Program—Sr. Diane Ulsamer, S.S.J., D.R.E. Students 45.
4—ST. PATRICK (1854) [CEM], (Linked with St. Anthony) Rev. Donald A. Robinson; Deacon Kevin Mastellon, Pastoral Assoc.; Sr. Mary William Argy, S.S.J., Pastoral Assoc.; Deacon William G. Schmidt.
Res. & Mailing Address: 123 S. Massey St., 13601-3201. Tel: 315-782-6086 (Pastoral Center); Fax: 315-788-4059. Email: pastoralcenter@stpatswtn.org. Web: stpatrickwatertownny.org.
Catechesis/Religious Program—Mrs. Elizabeth Bamann, D.R.E. Students 141.

WELLS, HAMILTON CO., ST. ANN'S (1890) [CEM] Rev. Sony G. Pulickal.
Mailing Address: P.O. Box 214, Speculator, 12164. Tel: 518-548-6275. Email: sjcsac@frontiernet.net.
Catechesis/Religious Program—Students 8.

WEST CHAZY, CLINTON CO., ST. JOSEPH (1884) [CEM] Rev. J. Roger McGuinness.
Res.: 60 W. Church St., P.O. Box 224, 12992. Tel: 518-493-4521; Fax: 518-493-5880. Email: stjosephs@westelcom.com.
Catechesis/Religious Program—Students 69.

WEST LEYDEN, LEWIS CO., ST. MARY'S NATIVITY (1900) [CEM] Rev. Lawrence E. Marullo.
Mailing Address: 1183 State Rte. 26, P.O.382, Constableville, 13325.
Res.: 1175 State Rte. 26, P.O. Box 382, Constableville, 13325. Tel: 315-397-2556.
Catechesis/Religious Program—Students 16.
Oratory—SS. Peter & Paul

WESTPORT, ESSEX CO., ST. PHILIP NERI (1879) [CEM] Rev. Msgr. Peter R. Riani.
Res.: 8434 NYS Rte. 9N, P.O. Box 368, Elizabethtown, 12932. Tel: 518-873-6760; Fax: 518-873-6530.
Catechesis/Religious Program—Students 3.

WILLSBORO, ESSEX CO.
1—CATHOLIC COMMUNITY OF ST. PHILIP OF JESUS OF WILLSBORO (1909) & ST. JOSEPH OF ESSEX (1872), [CEM] Rev. John M. Demo, Admin.
Mailing Address: P.O. Box 607, 12996.
Res.: 3746 Main St., 12996. Tel: 518-963-4524; Fax: 518-963-7719. Email: stphilip@willex.com.
Catechesis/Religious Program—Students 12.
2—ST. PHILIP OF JESUS (1909) [CEM] Merged with St. Joseph, Essex to form Catholic Community of St. Philip of Jesus and St. Joseph of Willsboro.

WITHERBEE, ESSEX CO., ST. MICHAEL (1911) Closed. For inquiries for parish records contact the chancery.

Chaplains of Public Institutions

FORT DRUM. *U.S. Army Headquarters*. Revs. Ned Blick, Simon Obeng, Mathias Rendon, O.F.M., Curtis Kondik, Jean Claude Kilumbu.

Military and Medical

OGDENSBURG. *St. Lawrence Psychiatric Center*, St. Vincent's Chapel, 13669. Tel: 315-541-2001, Ext. 2414; Fax: 315-541-2049. Rev. Vicente F. Jazmines, Chap.

FORT DRUM. *U.S. Army Headquarters Fort Drum*, Tel: 315-772-5591; Fax: 315-772-6725.

PLATTSBURGH. *Champlain Valley Physicians Hospital Medical Center*, 75 Beekman St., 12901. Tel: 518-561-2000. Rev. William G. Reamer, Chap.

TUPPER LAKE, (SUNMOUNT). *Sunmount Developmental Center*, 403 Park St., 12986. Tel: 518-359-3311; Fax: 518-359-4133. Rev. Paul J. Kelly, Chap.

WATERTOWN. *Samaritan Medical Center*, 830 Washington St., 13601. Tel: 315-785-4000; Fax: 315-785-4195. Sr. Maria Flavia D'Costa, SCC, Chap.

Prisons

OGDENSBURG. *Ogdensburg Correctional Facility*, One Correction Way, 13669. Tel: 315-393-0281. Deacon Thomas F. Kilian, Rev. James W. Seymour.
Riverview Correctional Facility, Box 158, 13669. Tel: 315-393-8400. Rev. James W. Seymour, Deacon Mark A. LaLonde.

ALTONA. *Altona Correctional Facility*, P.O. Box 125, 12910. Tel: 518-236-7841; Fax: 518-236-6235. Deacon John A. Levison.

CAPE VINCENT. *Cape Vincent Correctional Facility* 13618. Tel: 315-654-4100, Ext. 548. Deacon Robert V. Ruddy, Rev. Richard Huber, M.S.C.

DANNEMORA. *Clinton Correctional Facility*, P.O. Box 798, 12929-0798. Tel: 518-492-2511, Ext. 4800. Deacon Larry R. Debiec, Rev. Victor E. Lamore.

GOUVERNEUR. *Gouverneur Correctional Facility*, Scotch Settlement Rd., P.O. Box 370, 13642. Tel: 315-287-7351; Fax: 315-287-2533. Deacons Bruce Dougherty, Thomas F. Kilian.

MALONE. *Barehill Correctional Facility*, Cady Rd., 12953. Tel: 518-483-8411, Ext. 409. Rev. Alan J. Lamica.
Franklin Correctional Facility, P.O. Box 10, 12953-9720. Tel: 518-483-6040, Ext. 2402. Deacon Joseph R. Szwed, Rev. Alan J. Lamica.
Upstate Correctional Facility, P.O. Box 2000, 12953. Tel: 518-483-6997. Deacon Bryan J. Bashaw, Rev. Alan J. Lamica.

MORIAH. *Moriah Shock Incarceration Correctional Facility*, Fisher Hill Rd., P.O. Box 999, Mineville, 12956-0999. Tel: 518-942-7531. Deacon Elliott Shaw.

RAY BROOK. *Adirondack Correctional Facility*, Box 110, 12977-0110. Tel: 518-891-1343. Rev. Victor E. Lamore.
Res.: Star Rte., Box 152, Saranac Lake, 12983. Tel: 518-891-6540.
Federal Correctional Institution, P.O. Box 300, 12977.

Tel: 518-891-5400. Rev. Richard P. Zuk (BRK).

WATERTOWN. *Watertown Correctional Facility* 13601. Tel: 315-782-7490, Ext. 445. Deacon Bruce Dougherty.

On Duty Outside the Diocese:

Revs.—

Hubbard, Jeffrey A., 401 Michigan Ave., N.E., Washington, DC 20017.

Kennehan, John P., St. John's Mercy Hospital, Springfield, MO.

Sestito, Joseph N., 100 Van Tassal Ln., Rome, 13440.

Wertman, Raymond, 2292 Costa Rican Dr., Brahmin #56, Clearwater, FL 34623.

Absent on Sick Leave, Disabled:

Revs.—

Demers, Richard D., St. Augustine's Rectory, 3035 State Rte. 22, Peru, 12972.

Giroux, Harry E. (Retired), St. Joseph's Home, 950 Linden St., 13669.

Helfrich, Peter G., 10 Knoll Brook Rd., Apt. 3, Rochester, 14610.

Retired:

Rev. Msgrs.—

Aubin, Joseph G., St. Peter's Rectory, 114A Cornelia St, Plattsburgh, 12901.

Christman, Bernard E., Indian Harbor Beach, FL 32937.

McAvoy, C. John, 51 Willow Way, Apt. 19, Saranac Lake, 12983.

McCarthy, Robert J., St. Joseph's, 13601.

Whitmore, Paul E., Holy Family Rectory, 129 Winthrop St., 13601.

Revs.—

Beyette, Paul V., HC, Box 218, Loon Lake, 12989.

Cosmic, John J., 39 Anderson Ave., P.O. Box 117, Deferiet, 13628.

Cote, Norman J., St. John the Baptist Rectory, 7 Margaret St., Plattsburgh, 12901.

Cotter, Lawrence E., S.T.L., B.S., M.S., P.O. Box 606, 13669. United Helpers, 8103 State Hwy. 68, 13669.

Cotter, Robert L., 1425 Washington St., 13601.

Crable, John M., Samuel F. Vilas Home, 61 Beckman St., Plattsburgh, 12901.

DeRoche, Wilfred L., 26-5 S. Meadow Village, Carver, MA 02330.

Downs, John L., 8828 State Hwy. 56, Raymondville, 13678.

Hart, Rolland A., 224 Stone Hill Rd., Williston, VT 05495.

Jarecki, Michael S., P.O. Box 627, Winchester, NH 03470.

Keefe, Daniel T., 30 Glen Dr., Apt 1, Plattsburgh, 12901.

Lamitie, Robert O., Star Rte., Box 35 C, Saranac Lake, 12983.

Ledermann, Paul F., 53-885 Avenida Mandoza, La Quinta, CA 92253.

Menard, Gilbert B., 2 Garrett Way, Schuyler Falls, 12985.

O'Reilly, Patrick J., St. Bernard's Rectory, 27 St. Bernard St., Saranac Lake, 12983.

Papp, Edward E., St. Mary's Cathedral, 415 Hamilton St., 13669.

Patterson, Terrence R., Box 288, Potsdam, 13676. Tel: 315-265-2986

Poupore, Norman E., P.O. Box 824, Pierrepont Manor, 13674.

Silver, John E., 2705 Sagittarius Dr., Myrtle Beach, SC 29575.

Wiley, Leo A., Holy Family Church, 129 Winthrop St., 13601.

Permanent Deacons:

Allen, Michael J., Holy Family, Watertown

Bashaw, Bryan J., Malone

Bateman, Francis F., Ogdensburg

Bennett, Mark E., Spritual Life Director, 95 Brinkerhoff St., Plattsburgh, 12901. Church of St. Peter, Plattsburg

Benson, George Grady, Peru

Brousseau, Frederick A., 34 Olympian Dr., Slingerlands, 12159.

Burnell, Garry N., St. Francis of Assisi, Constable

Bushey, Frank A., Jr., 7 Addoms St., Plattsburgh, 12901. Church of St. Peter, Plattsburg

Chaufty, James W., P.O. Box 43, Port Leyden, 13433. St. Martin's Church, Port Leyden; St. John's Church, Lyons Falls

Cheney, Jerome A., Saranac Lake

Cogan, John A., 108 Sunrise Dr., Plattsburgh, 12901. St. John the Baptist, Plattsburg; St. Mary's of the Lake in Cumberland Head

Connelly, Lawrence A., Norfolk

Connor, Marvin M., 459 Irish Settlement Rd., P.O. Box 325, Schuyler Falls, 12985. Roman Catholic Community of St. Alexander and St. Joseph, Morrisonville & Treadwells Mill

Crosby, Patrick, Clayton (Summers Only) (Syracuse Diocese)

Dashnaw, Donald, (Retired Outside Diocese)

Daugherty, Bruce Wayne, Clayton & LaFargeville

Debiec, Larry, Clinton Correctional Facility, Dannemora

Defayette, Gerald R., (Retired), St. Joseph, West Chazy

Diehl, Robert, (Retired), 8 B Wyoming Ave, Whiting, NJ 08759.

Dwyer, Brian T., 543 County Rte. 52, Chateaugay, 12920. Catholic Community, Burke & Chateaugay

Ellis, James T., St. Alphonsus, Tupper Lake

Frank, Gary A., St. Mary, Clayton

Giardino, Philip F., St. Hubert, Star Lake

Gillen, James, Jonesboro, ME

Gilner, Gerard, (Retired), St. Mary, Indian Lake

Hinerth, Noel A., St. Patrick, Rouses Point

Hotte, James J., Sacred Heart, Massena

Hunneyman, Norman L., St. Andrew's, Sackets Harbor; Mercy Center, Watertown

Johnston, William Michael, Our Lady of the Sacred Heart, Watertown

Keough, James R., P.O. Box 585, Inlet, 13360.

Kilian, Thomas F., Gouverneur Correctional Facility, Gouverneur; Notre Dame, Ogdensburg; Ogdensburg Correctional Facility

King, Robert A., (Retired), St. Peter, Plattsburgh

LaLonde, Mark A., Notre Dame, Ogdensburg; Riverview Correctional Facility, Ogdensburg

Lawless, Peter J., Sacred Heart, Edwards

Levison, John A., Altona Correctional Facility, Altona

Looby, Phillip M., St. Francis, Solanus, Harrisville

Lukasiewicz, Jack M., 357 Cemetery Rd., Plattsburgh, 12901. Our Lady of Victory, Plattsburg

Mader, Frederick J., (Retired), St. Paul, Bloomingdale

Mastellon, Kevin, Watertown

Mazuchowski, Edward, St. Joseph, Dannemora

Miller, Edward R., Holy Family, Watertown

Monty, Dennis, St. Ann's, Mooers Forks

Murray, John R., St. Anthony's, Watertown (Syracuse Diocese)

Oberst, Frederick R., St. Bernard, Saranac Lake

Patrie, Leonard L., St. Mary, Champlain

Pominville, Ronald J., St. Peter, Lowville

Proulx, Thomas E., 21 Douglas Rd., Massena, 13662. Church of Sacred Heart, Massena; St. Lawrence Church, Louisville

Rabideau, Tyrone, St. Ann, Mooers Forks

Raven, William S., St. Paul, Black River

Ruddy, Robert V., St. Vincent of Paul & Cape Vincent Correctional Facility, Cape Vincent

Ryan, John J., Holy Name, Ausable Forks

Sandburg, David J., 9535 State Hwy. 37, 13669. St. Mary's Cathedral, Ogdensburg

Savage, Gerald H., St. Alphonsus, Tupper Lake

Schmidt, William G., St. Patrick, Watertown

Seymour, Kenneth A., Harrisville; Star Lake

Sharrow, Thomas D., Schenectady

Shaw, Elliott A., St. Mary's, Ticonderoga; Moriah Shock Incarceration Facility, Mineville

Siskavich, Francis, St. Bernard, Lyon Mountain

Slate, Bernard E., Alexandria Bay

Snell, James M., 10 Morningside Dr., Potsdam, 13676. St. Mary's Church, Canton

Staab, Richard J., St. James, Carthage

Ste.-Marie, Ronald, St. Anthony, Inlet

Stewart, George, St. Margaret, Wilmington; Au Sable Forks (New York Diocese)

Szwed, Joseph, St. Bernard, Saranac Lake; Franklin Correctional Facility, Malone

Trombly, John J., 678 Grant St., 13601.

Van Kirk, Richard L., Heuvelton

Wadsworth, Bruce Carley, Lake Placid

Warner, Richard C., Sr., St. Anthony, Watertown

White, John L., 928 Caroline St., 13669. St. Mary's Cathedral, Ogdensburg

Yarchuk, Andrew, (Retired), 30 Wellington Rd., Webster, 14580.

INSTITUTIONS LOCATED IN THE DIOCESE

[A] HIGH SCHOOLS, INTERPAROCHIAL

PLATTSBURGH. *Seton Catholic Central*, 206 New York Rd., 12903. Tel: 518-561-4031; Fax: 518-563-1193. Email: crussell@setoncatholic.net. Web: www.setoncatholic.net. Catherine Russell, Prin.; Andrew Lauria, Librarian. Lay Teachers 22; Students 125.

WATERTOWN. *Immaculate Heart Central High School*, (Grades 7-12), 1316 Ives St., 13601. Tel: 315-788-4670; Fax: 315-788-4672. Email: ihcadmin@ihchs.org. Web: www.ihcschools.org. Mrs. Lisa Parsons, Prin.; Mr. Pat A. Fontana, Spiritual Dir.; Mr. John Montanoo, Librarian. Priests 1; Sisters 3; Lay Teachers 26; Students 320.

[B] ELEMENTARY SCHOOLS, PRIVATE

PLATTSBURGH. *Seton Academy Elementary School*, (Grades PreK-6), St. Charles St., 12901. Tel: 518-825-7386. Sr. Helen Hermann, S.S.J., Prin.; Kathleen Toner, Asst. Prin.; Kyle Page, Librarian. Religious 1; Lay Teachers 16; Students 217.

WATERTOWN. *Immaculate Heart Central School*, 122 Winthrop St., 13601. Tel: 315-788-7011; Fax: 315-788-7011. Email: kimmurrock@ihcschools.org. Gary F. West, Prin.; Annette Connolly, Vice-Prin.

Immaculate Heart (Central Elementary) (Grades PreK-6) Gary F. West, Prin.; Annette Connolly, Vice-Prin. Sisters 1; Lay Teachers 18.

[C] RELIGIOUS EDUCATION

OGDENSBURG. *Bishop Conroy School of Religion*, 214 Morris St., 13669-1714. Tel: 315-393-1820; Fax: 315-393-1670. Email: bishopconroydre@verizon.net. Mrs. Celina Burns, D.R.E. Lay Teachers 26; Total Staff 1; Students 290.

SARANAC LAKE. *Pius X Center*, (Grades K-10), 27 St. Bernard St., 12983. Tel: 518-891-4616, Ext. 27; Fax: 518-891-4619. Email: piusxcenter@roadrunner.com. Michelle Crowley, Dir. Total Staff 2; Students 100.

WATERTOWN. *Watertown Catechetical Office*, Sterling Pl., 13601. Tel: 315-782-0030. Sisters Diane Marie Ulsamer, S.S.J., Coord.; Noel Chabanel, S.S.J., Outreach Coord. Sisters 2; Students 120.

Special Religious Education Tel: 315-782-0030. Email: specialreligioused@yahoo.com. Sr. Diane Marie Ulsamer, S.S.J., Coord.

[D] CONFERENCE AND RETREAT CENTER

OGDENSBURG. *Wadhams Hall*, 6866 State Hwy. 37, 13669-4420. Tel: 315-393-4231; Fax: 315-393-4249. Email: inquiry@wadhams.edu. Web: www.wadhams.edu. Mr. Jeffrey Ward, A.A.S., Bus. Mgr. Total Staff 6.

[E] SPECIAL HOSPITALS AND HOMES FOR INVALIDS AND AGED

OGDENSBURG. *St. Joseph's Home* (1960) 950 Linden St., 13669. Tel: 315-393-3780; Fax: 315-393-3847. Email: administrator@stjh.org. Web: www.stjh.org. Coleen Steele, Admin. Total Staff 120; Bed Capacity 82; Total Assisted 124.

[F] MONASTERIES AND RESIDENCES OF PRIESTS AND BROTHERS

SARANAC LAKE. *St. Joseph's Friary*, P.O. Box 470, 12983. Tel: 518-891-3494. Bros. Alan Lemay, S.A.; Paschal Steen, T.S.A. Total in Residence 2.

WATERTOWN. *Missionaries of the Sacred Heart*, 668 Thompson St., 13601. Tel: 315-782-3480; Fax: 315-782-0473. Email: rwkpng03@mscparish.com. Revs. Pierre Aubin, M.S.C.; David DeLuca, M.S.C.; Vincent T. Freeh, M.S.C.; Richard Huber, M.S.C.; Richard Kennedy, M.S.C.; Bros. Peter Marceau, M.S.C.; Jean-Paul Paradis, M.S.C.

[G] CONVENTS AND RESIDENCES FOR SISTERS

OGDENSBURG. *Sisters of St. Joseph*, 251 Proctor Ave., 13669. Tel: 315-393-6511. Total in Residence 3.

CARTHAGE. *St. James Convent, Sisters of St. Joseph*, 317 West St., 13619. Tel: 315-493-1672. Email: smacollinsssj@yahoo.com. Total Staff 2; Total in Residence 2.

ELLENBURG CENTER. *Our Lady of the Adirondack's Inc. House of Prayer* (1972) 7270 Star Rd., Rte. 190, 12934-2501. Tel: 518-594-3253. Email: olaprayerhouse@gmail.com. Web: www.ourladyoftheadirondackshouseofprayer.catholicweb.com. Our Lady of the Adirondacks Community. Total Staff 3.

Our Lady of the Adirondacks Community (1990) Email: oadirond@twcny.rr.com. Web: www.ourladyoftheadirondackshouseofprayer.catholicweb.com. Rev. Alan J. Lamica, Spiritual Dir. Tel: 518-529-7433.

Our Lady of the Adirondacks Prayer Association (1972) Tel: 518-594-3253; Fax: 518-594-7143. Email: oadirond@twcny.rr.com. Web: www.ourladyoftheadirondackhouseofprayer.catholicweb.com. Members 170.

LAKE PLACID. *St. Margaret Convent*, 185 Old Military Rd., 12946. Tel: 518-523-2929; Fax: 518-523-5449. Email: mokeefe@mercymidatlantic.org. Sr. M. Camillus O'Keefe, R.S.M., B.A., B.S., Supr. Sisters of Mercy.

MALONE. *St. Joseph's Ursuline Nuns*, 49 Morton St., 12953. Tel: 518-483-2880; Fax: 518-483-5356.

Email: ursulmal@verizon.net. Sisters 2.

MASSENA. *St. Joseph's Convent, Sisters of St. Joseph,* 72 Malby Ave., 13662. Tel: 315-764-0379. Total in Residence 2; Sisters of St. Joseph 2.

Sacred Heart Convent, 188 Main St., P.O. Box 91, 13662. Tel: 315-769-6238. Email: mas-osm@verizon.net. Total in Residence 3.

PLATTSBURGH. *Sisters of Charity of St. Louis* (1910) 60 Club Rd. Unit 204, 12903. Tel: 518-563-7410. Email: srber.du@charter.net.

Sisters of Mercy, 62-64 Court St., 12901. Tel: 518-561-9689; Fax: 518-563-4553. Email: srbnanmarie@gmail.com. Sisters of Mercy Sisters of Mercy 3.

SARANAC LAKE. *Sisters of Mercy of the Americas* (1831) 35 Trudeau Rd., 12983-5635. Tel: 518-891-3234. Email: srmcarolyn@roadrunner.com.

TICONDEROGA. *St. Mary's Convent, Sisters of St. Joseph* (1959) 145 Lake George Ave., 12883. Tel: 518-585-6547; Fax: 518-585-7505. Email: sschoo3@nycap.rr.com. Sr. Sharon Anne Dalton, S.S.J. Total in Residence 2.

TUPPER LAKE. *Dominican Sisters of Hope, Ossining* (1995) 37 Lake St., Apt. 2, 12986. Tel: 518-359-9632.

WATERTOWN. *Precious Blood Monastery, Sister Adorers of the Precious Blood,* 400 Pratt St., 13601. Tel: 315-788-1669; Fax: 315-779-9046. Email: smarilyn@twcny.rr.com. Web: sisterspreciousblood.org. Sr. Marilyn McGillan, A.P.B., Asst. Supr. Total Staff 6; Total in Residence 4.

Sisters of St. Joseph Motherhouse (1880) 1425 Washington St., 13601-4533. Tel: 315-782-3460; Fax: 315-788-2794. Email: bcollinsssj@yahoo.com. Web: www.ssjwatertown.org. Sisters Mary Ellen Brett, S.S.J., Motherhouse Supr.; Bernadette Marie Collins, S.S.J., Major Supr.; Mr. Randy Belina, Motherhouse Admin. Total Staff 25; Total in Residence 31.

[H] INCORPORATED CEMETERIES

BRASHER FALLS. *St. Patrick's Cemetery Association of Brasher Falls, N.Y.,* Box 208, 13613. Tel: 315-389-5401; Fax: 315-389-4066. Email: parish@twcny.rr.com. Web: www.stpatrick-stlawrence.org. Rev. Garry B. Giroux, J.C.L.

CARTHAGE. *St. James Cemetery Corporation,* 327 West St., 13619. Tel: 315-493-3224; Fax: 518-493-3280. Email: stjames@twcny.rr.com.

CROGHAN. *St. Stephen's Cemetery Association, Inc.,* 9748 State Rte. 812, Box 38, 13327. Tel: 315-346-6958; Fax: 315-346-1200. Email: cschnee@twcny.rr.com.

MALONE. *St. Joseph's Cemetery of Malone, N.Y., Inc.,* 306 W. Main St., 12953. Tel: 518-483-1300; Fax: 518-483-1307. Email: mcp@twcny.rr.com. Web: malonecatholic.com.

Notre Dame Cemetery of Malone, N.Y., Inc., Office: 306 W. Main St., 12953. Tel: 518-483-1300; Fax: 518-483-1307. Email: mcp@twcny.RR.com. Web: malonecatholic.com.

PLATTSBURGH. *Mount Carmel Cemetery,* St. John the Baptist Church, 7 Margaret St., 12901. Tel: 518-563-0730; Fax: 518-563-0754. Email: office@stjohnsplattsburgh.org.

WATERTOWN. *Calvary Cemetery Association of Watertown, N.Y.,* 320 W. Lynde St., 13601. Tel: 315-782-1474; Fax: 315-782-4939. Email: rwkpng03@mscparish.com. Priests 1; Total Staff 1.

[I] MISCELLANEOUS LISTINGS

OGDENSBURG. *St. Joseph's Foundation, Inc.,* 950 Linden St., 13669. Tel: 315-394-0463; Fax: 315-393-3847. Email: foundation@stjh.org. Web: www.stjh.org.

CAPE VINCENT. *Mission Project Service,* 139 N. Kanady St., P.O. Box 288, 13618. Tel: 315-654-2662; Fax: 315-654-4721. Email: misprojser@aol.com. Web: www.missionprojectservice.org. Beverly Hennigan, Exec. Dir.; Rev. Pierre Aubin, M.S.C., Dir.

HOGANSBURG. *St. Regis Mission* , (Akwesasne); Reservation and parish on both sides of U.S.-Canadian border, Box 429, 13655. Tel: 613-575-2066. Rev. Jerome Pastores, Pastor. Priests 1; Brothers 1.

Roman Catholic Community Center, Inc. (Kateri Tekakwitha Center) Mrs. Lucille Peters, Rel. Educ. Coord. Tel: 518-358-2931.

LAKE PLACID. *Mercy Care for the Adirondacks, Inc.,* 185 Old Military Rd., 12946. Tel: 518-523-5580; Fax: 518-523-5449. Email: dbeal@adkmercy.org. Web: www.adkmercy.org. Donna Beal, Exec. Dir.

SARANAC LAKE. *Guggenheim Center for Religious Programs,* P.O. Box 664, 12983. Tel: 518-891-0809 (Lodge); 518-891-3323 (Dorm). Mr. Ralph Bennett, Dir. Tel: 518-327-3545.

Res.: P.O. Box 5, Rainbow Lake, 12976. Tel: 518-327-3545.

WATERTOWN. *Sacred Heart Foundation* (1967) 668 Thompson St., 13601. Tel: 315-782-3344; Fax: 315-782-0473. Email: mail@sacredheartfoundation.com. Web: www.sacredheartfoundation.com. Nicholas J. Buduson, Foundation Mgr.

The Federation of Sisters of the Precious Blood, Inc. (1969) 400 Pratt St., 13601. Tel: 315-788-1669; Fax: 315-779-9046. Email: srm1@twcny.rr.com. Web: www.sisterspreciousblood.org. Sr. Mary Jo Divney, A.P.B., Pres. Sisters 55.

RELIGIOUS INSTITUTES OF MEN REPRESENTED IN THE DIOCESE

For further details refer to the corresponding bracketed number in the Religious Institutes of Men or Women section.

[0320]—*Brothers of Christian Instruction* (Alfred, ME)—F.I.C.

[0530]—*Franciscan Friars of the Atonement*—S.A.

[0690]—*Jesuit Fathers and Brothers* (French Canadian Prov. of Montreal)—S.J.

[1110]—*Missionaries of the Sacred Heart*—M.S.C.

RELIGIOUS INSTITUTES OF WOMEN REPRESENTED IN THE DIOCESE

[]—*Congregation of the Sisters of the Cross of Chavanod* (India)

[0760]—*Daughters of Charity of St. Vincent de Paul*—D.C.

[0750]—*Daughters of the Charity of the Sacred Heart of Jesus*—F.C.S.C.J.

[0810]—*Daughters of the Heart of Mary*—D.H.M.

[1070-03]—*Dominican Sisters*—O.P.

[1105]—*Dominican Sisters of Hope*—O.P.

[1190]—*Franciscan Sisters of the Atonement*—S.A.

[1840]—*Grey Nuns of the Sacred Heart*—G.N.S.H.

[2575]—*Institute of the Sisters of Mercy of the Americas* (New York, NY)—R.S.M.

[3580]—*Servants of Mary* (Servite Sisters)—O.S.M.

[0110]—*Sisters Adorers of the Precious Blood*—A.P.B.

[0620]—*Sisters of Charity of St. Louis*—S.C.S.L.

[3840]—*Sisters of St. Joseph of Carondelet*—C.S.J.

[3830-12]—*Sisters of St. Joseph of Watertown*—S.S.J.

[4110]—*Ursuline Nuns*—O.S.U.

Incorporated Cemeteries

CARTHAGE. *St. James Cemetery*

Croghan

St. Stephen's Cemetery Association, Inc.

Malone

St. Joseph's Cemetery of Malone, NY, Inc.

Notre Dame Cemetery of Malone, NY, Inc.

Plattsburgh

Mount Carmel Cemetery

Watertown

Calvary Cemetery Association of Watertown, NY

NECROLOGY

† Phillips, Rev. Msgr. George M., (Retired)—Died Oct. 28, 2011

† Chase, Charles E., (Retired)—Died Jan. 4, 2011

† Gonyo, Roland G., (Absent on Sick Leave)—Died Nov. 16, 2011

† Lamitie, James F., (Retired)—Died Nov. 22, 2010

† McCasland, Howard, Churubusco, NY Immaculate Heart of Mary.—Died Dec. 28, 2010

An asterisk (*) denotes an organization that has established tax-exempt status directly with the IRS and is not covered by the USCCB Group Ruling.

Archdiocese of Oklahoma City

(Archidioecesis Oklahomapolitana)

Most Reverend

PAUL S. COAKLEY

Archbishop of Oklahoma City; ordained May 21, 1983; appointed Bishop of Salina October 21, 2004; installed December 28, 2004; appointed Archbishop of Oklahoma City December 16, 2010; installed February 11, 2011. *Catholic Pastoral Center: 7501 Northwest Expwy., P.O. Box 32180, Oklahoma City, OK 73123.*

Most Reverend

EUSEBIUS J. BELTRAN, D.D.

Archbishop Emeritus of Oklahoma City; ordained May 14, 1960; appointed Bishop of Tulsa February 28, 1978; installed April 20, 1978; appointed Archbishop of Oklahoma City November 24, 1992; installed January 22, 1993; retired December 16, 2010. *Res.: P.O. Box 32180, Oklahoma City, OK 73123.*

Catholic Pastoral Center: 7501 Northwest Expwy., P.O. Box 32180, Oklahoma City, OK 73123. Tel: 405-721-5651; Fax: 405-721-5210.

ESTABLISHED FEBRUARY 6, 1973.

Square Miles 42,470.

Erected into a Vicariate Apostolic by Brief of May 29, 1891. Erected into the Diocese of Oklahoma with the See in Oklahoma City by a Brief of Pope Pius X, August 17, 1905. Name changed to Diocese of Oklahoma City and Tulsa by Bull of Pope Pius XI, November 14, 1930. Erected into Archdiocese of Oklahoma City by a Bull of Pope Paul VI, December 13, 1972. The Province includes the Dioceses of Tulsa and Little Rock.

Comprises the following 46 Counties: Alfalfa, Beaver, Beckham, Blaine, Caddo, Canadian, Carter, Cimarron, Cleveland, Comanche, Cotton, Custer, Dewey, Ellis, Garfield, Garvin, Grady, Grant, Greer, Harmon, Harper, Jackson, Jefferson, Johnston, Kay, Kingfisher, Kiowa, Lincoln, Logan, Love, McClain, Major, Marshall, Murray, Noble, Oklahoma, Pontotoc, Pottawatomie, Roger Mills, Seminole, Stephens, Texas, Tillman, Washita, Woods and Woodward.

For legal titles of parishes and archdiocesan institutions, consult the Pastoral Office.

STATISTICAL OVERVIEW

Personnel	
Archbishops	1
Retired Archbishops	1
Abbots	1
Retired Abbots	3
Priests: Diocesan Active in Diocese	56
Priests: Diocesan Active Outside Diocese	1
Priests: Retired, Sick or Absent	21
Number of Diocesan Priests	78
Religious Priests in Diocese	28
Total Priests in Diocese	106
Extern Priests in Diocese	27
Ordinations:	
Diocesan Priests	1
Permanent Deacons in Diocese	95
Total Brothers	7
Total Sisters	90
Parishes	
Parishes	66
With Resident Pastor:	
Resident Diocesan Priests	57
Resident Religious Priests	9
Missions	45
Closed Parishes	1
Professional Ministry Personnel:	
Brothers	4
Sisters	11
Lay Ministers	68
Welfare	
Catholic Hospitals	7
Total Assisted	331,535
Health Care Centers	2
Total Assisted	280
Homes for the Aged	2
Total Assisted	170
Day Care Centers	2
Total Assisted	197
Other Institutions	4
Total Assisted	179
Educational	
Diocesan Students in Other Seminaries	22
Total Seminarians	22
Colleges and Universities	1
Total Students	734
High Schools, Diocesan and Parish	2
Total Students	1,099
Elementary Schools, Diocesan and Parish	19
Total Students	3,931
Elementary Schools, Private	1
Total Students	239
Non-residential Schools for the Disabled	1
Total Students	5
Catechesis/Religious Education:	
High School Students	3,454
Elementary Students	9,437
Total Students under Catholic Instruction	18,921
Teachers in the Diocese:	
Priests	4
Brothers	7
Sisters	18
Lay Teachers	443
Vital Statistics	
Receptions into the Church:	
Infant Baptism Totals	2,577
Minor Baptism Totals	269
Adult Baptism Totals	198
Received into Full Communion	604
First Communions	2,661
Confirmations	1,533
Marriages:	
Catholic	475
Interfaith	229
Total Marriages	704
Deaths	800
Total Catholic Population	115,954
Total Population	2,069,649

Former Bishops—Rt. Rev. THEOPHILE MEERSCHAERT, D.D., ord. Dec. 23, 1871; appt. first Vicar-Apostolic of Indian Territory and Titular Bishop of Sidyma by Bulls of June 2, 1891; cons. in Natchez, Sept. 8, 1891; appt. first Bishop of Oklahoma, Aug. 23, 1905; made assistant at the pontifical throne, Nov. 30, 1916; died Feb. 21, 1924; Most Revs. FRANCIS C. KELLEY, D.D., LL.D., Ph.D., Litt.D., Bishop of Oklahoma City & Tulsa; ord. Aug. 24, 1893; appt. Bishop of Oklahoma, June 25, 1924; cons. Holy Name Cathedral, Chicago, IL, Oct. 2, 1924; died Feb. 1, 1948; EUGENE J. MCGUINNESS, D.D., Bishop of Oklahoma City & Tulsa; ord. May 22, 1915; cons. Bishop of Raleigh, Dec. 21, 1937; appt. Coadjutor, Oklahoma City and Tulsa "cum jure successionis," Nov. 11, 1944; installed Jan. 10, 1945; succeeded to the See, Feb. 1, 1948; died Dec. 27, 1957; VICTOR J. REED, D.D., Bishop of Oklahoma City & Tulsa; ord. Dec. 21, 1929; cons. March 5, 1958; died Sept. 8, 1971; JOHN R. QUINN, D.D., ord. July 19, 1953; appt. Auxiliary Bishop of San Diego and Titular Bishop of Thisiduo, Oct. 21, 1967; Episcopal ordination, Dec. 12, 1967; transferred to Oklahoma City and Tulsa, Nov. 18, 1971; appt. as Archbishop of the Archdiocese of Oklahoma City, Dec. 13, 1972; installed as Archbishop of Oklahoma City, Feb. 6, 1973; transferred to Archbishop of San Francisco, April 26, 1977; CHARLES A. SALATKA, D.D., ord. Feb. 24, 1945; appt. Titular Bishop of Cariana and Auxiliary of Grand Rapids Dec. 9, 1961; cons. March 6, 1962; appt. Bishop of Marquette Jan. 10, 1968; installed March 25, 1968; appt. Archbishop of Oklahoma City Sept. 27, 1977; installed Dec. 15, 1977; retired Nov. 24, 1992; died March 17, 2003; EUSEBIUS J. BELTRAN, ord. May 14, 1960; appt. Bishop of Tulsa Feb. 28, 1978; installed April 20, 1978; appt. Archbishop of Oklahoma City Nov. 24, 1992; installed Jan. 22, 1993; retired Dec. 16, 2010.

Vicar General—Rev. Msgr. EDWARD J. WEISENBURGER, V.G., M.A., J.C.L.

Regional Vicars—Region I-A: Rev. MICHAEL L. CHAPMAN, B.A., 317 N. Blackwelder, Oklahoma City, 73106. Region I-B: Rev. EDWARD T. MENASCO, Mailing Address: P.O. Box 1227, Norman, 73070. Region II-A: Rev. WILLIAM L. NOVAK, Mailing Address: P.O. Box 850249, Yukon, 73085. Region II-B: Rev. DONALD J. WOLF, 632 N. Kickapoo Ave., Shawnee, 74801-6070. Region III: Rev. RUSSELL L. HEWES, 1300 E. Beverly St., Ada, 74821. Region IV: Rev. PHILIP M. SEETON, 1010 N.W. 82nd St., Lawton, 73505-4103. Region V: Rev. REX A. ARNOLD, 1218 Knox Ave., Clinton, 73601. Region VI: Rev. MICHAEL WHEELAHAN, Mailing Address: P.O. Box 731, Guymon, 73942-0731. Region VII: Rev. JOSEPH M. IRWIN, 110 N. Madison, Enid, 73701. Region VIII: Rev. KEVIN J. RATTERMAN, Mailing Address: P.O. Box 1330, Ponca City, 74602. Region IX: Rev. STEPHEN V. HAMILTON, S.T.L., 406 S. 6th St., Kingfisher, 73750.

Catholic Pastoral Center—7501 Northwest Expwy., P.O. Box 32180, Oklahoma City, 73123. Tel: 405-721-5651; Fax: 405-721-5210. Office Hours: Mon.-Fri. 8:30-4:30.

Chancellor—Mrs. LOUTITIA D. EASON.

Vicar General—Rev. Msgr. EDWARD J. WEISENBURGER, V.G., M.A., J.C.L.

Vicar for Ministries—VACANT.

Archdiocesan Tribunal—7501 Northwest Expwy., P.O. Box 32180, Oklahoma City, 73123. Tel: 405-721-5651.

Judicial Vicar—Rev. RICHARD D. STANSBERRY JR., M.A., M.Div., J.C.L.

Judge—Sr. KATHRYN OLSEN, I.H.M., J.C.L., Assoc. Judge.

Defenders of the Bond—Revs. LOWELL STIEFERMAN; GERARD MACAULAY (Retired).

Advocates—Mrs. JUDY REILLY; Rev. EDWARD T. MENASCO.

Notary—Ms. MARILYN NEWMAN; Ms. CAROL DAVITO, (2nd Instance).

Interdiocesan Tribunal of Second Instance for the Province of Oklahoma City—Mailing Address: P.O.

Box 32180, Oklahoma City, 73123. Tel: 405-721-5651.

Judicial Vicar—Rev. ROBERTO A. QUANT, J.C.L., (2nd Instance).

Adjutant Judicial Vicars—Revs. JOHN K. ANTONY, J.C.L., (2nd Instance); TAM NGUYEN, J.C.L., (2nd Instance).

Judges—Mr. GEORGE RIGAZZI, J.C.L.; Rev. Msgr. EDWARD J. WEISENBURGER, V.G., M.A., J.C.L.; Revs. ROBERT T. DIENERT; PIUS OKOROCHUKWU; MICHAEL A. DODD, J.C.L.

Defenders of the Bond—Revs. BILL H. PRUETT, J.C.L.; ELMER C. SCHWARZ, J.C.L. (Retired) (2nd instance); PETER QUANG LE, J.C.L.; STEPHEN V. HAMILTON, S.T.L.

Notaries—Mrs. TONI NICHOLLS; Mrs. LIZ PARKER; Ms. SUZI BLANCO.

Consultors Archdiocesan—Revs. BRUCE K. NATSUHARA, B.A., S.T.B., S.T.L.; RAYMOND K. ACKERMAN; TIMOTHY D. LUSCHEN; JOHN R. METZINGER; Rev. Msgr. EDWARD J. WEISENBURGER, V.G., M.A., J.C.L.; Rev. JOACHIM SPEXARTH, O.S.B.

Council of Priests Archdiocesan—Revs. JOHN R. METZINGER; BRUCE K. NATSUHARA, B.A., S.T.B., S.T.L., Vice Chm.; TIMOTHY D. LUSCHEN; DONALD J. WOLF; REX A. ARNOLD, Sec. & Treas.; JOSEPH M. IRWIN; JOACHIM SPEXARTH, O.S.B.; RAYMOND K. ACKERMAN; Rev. Msgr. EDWARD J. WEISENBURGER, V.G., M.A., J.C.L.; Revs. JOSEPH A. JACOBI; STEPHEN V. HAMILTON, S.T.L., Chm.

Health Panel, Archdiocesan—Rev. WILLIAM B. ROSS, Chm. (Retired), 1506 W. Walnut, El Reno, 73036. Tel: 405-527-3077.

Personnel Committee—Revs. THOMAS J. BOYER; RAYMOND K. ACKERMAN; CHARLES R. MURPHY, B.S., M.Ed., M.Div.; JOSEPH R. ROSS; Rev. Msgr. EDWARD J. WEISENBURGER, V.G., M.A., J.C.L.

Archdiocesan Offices and Directors

Office of Stewardship and Development—Mr. BARNEY SEMTNER, Dir., Mailing Address: P.O. Box 32180, Oklahoma City, 73123. Tel: 405-721-5651.

Archdiocesan Development Fund— formerly Diocesan Development Fund; also formerly known as Diocesan Fund, Bishop's Fund for Diocesan Development, Mr. THOMAS MAXWELL, Dir., 7501 N.W. Expwy., P.O. Box 32180, Oklahoma City, 73123. Tel: 405-721-5651.

Archdiocese of Oklahoma City Educational Trust Fund—Sr. CATHERINE POWERS, C.N.D., Dir., 7501 N.W. Expwy., P.O. Box 32180, Oklahoma City, 73123.

Catholic Charities of the Archdiocese of Oklahoma City, Inc.—Mr. TIMOTHY O'CONNOR, Dir., 1501 N. Classen Blvd., Oklahoma City, 73106. Tel: 405-523-3000; Fax: 405-523-3030.

Archdiocesan Finance Council—Most Rev. PAUL S. COAKLEY; Revs. RICHARD D. STANSBERRY JR., M.A., M.Div., J.C.L.; TIMOTHY M. FULLER; Mr. JOHN TORBETT; Mr. FLOYD ANDERSON; Mrs. ELLEN FLEMING; Mr. LARRY KUNZ; Mr. MICHAEL MILLIGAN; Mr. MICHAEL R. STERKEL; Mr. DAVID JOHNSON, Business Mgr., Mailing Address: Business Office, P.O. Box 32180, Oklahoma City, 73123. Tel: 405-721-5651.

Building Committee—Mr. DAVID JOHNSON, Mailing Address: P.O. Box 32180, Oklahoma City, 73123. Tel: 405-721-5651.

Catholic Foundation of Oklahoma, Inc.—Mr. BARNEY SEMTNER, Exec. Dir., 7501 Northwest Expwy., P.O. Box 32180, Oklahoma City, 73123. Tel: 405-721-5651.

Catholic Lawyers Guild—Mailing Address: P.O. Box 32180, Oklahoma City, 73123. Tel: 405-721-5651. VACANT, Mailing Address: P.O. Box 1585, Ada, 74821. Tel: 580-332-4811.

Catholic Physicians Guild—Rev. DANIEL MCCAFFREY, Chap., Mailing Address: P.O. Box 32180, Oklahoma City, 73123. Tel: 405-942-4084.

Catholic Social Services—Mr. TIM O'CONNOR, 1501 N. Classen Blvd., Oklahoma City, 73106. Tel: 405-523-3000; Fax: 405-523-3030.

Charismatic Renewal—Rev. MARVIN F. LEVEN, Episcopal Moderator (Retired), Mailing Address: P.O. Box 404, Okarche, 73762. Tel: 405-263-7798.

Communications, Archdiocesan Department of—Mailing Address: P.O. Box 32180, Oklahoma City, 73123. Tel: 405-721-1810; 405-721-5651.

Correction Related Ministry—VACANT.

Council of Catholic Women, Archdiocesan—Rev. ROBERT T. WOOD.

Ecumenical and Interreligious Affairs, Office for Archdiocesan Dir.—VACANT.

Education—Sr. CATHERINE POWERS, C.N.D., Archdiocesan Dir., Mailing Address: P.O. Box 32180, Oklahoma City, 73123. Tel: 405-721-4202; 405-721-5651.

Catholic Schools, Office of—Sr. CATHERINE POWERS, C.N.D., Supt.; Dr. CRIS CARTER, Assoc. Supt., Mailing Address: P.O. Box 32180, Oklahoma City, 73123. Tel: 405-721-4202; 405-721-5651.

Religious Education, Office of—Ms. PATRICIA KOENIG, Dir.; Ms. ANGELA SCHMIDT, Assoc. Dir., Mailing Address: P.O. Box 32180, Oklahoma City, 73123. Tel: 405-721-1415; 405-721-5651.

Pastoral Ministry Office—Sr. M. DIANE KOORIE, R.S.M., Dir., Mailing Address: P.O. Box 32180, Oklahoma City, 73123. Tel: 405-721-1415; 405-721-5651 Affiliated with Kansas Newman College, Wichita, KS and Aquinas Institute, St. Louis, MO.

Campus Ministry, Department of—Rev. JAMES A. GOINS, Mailing Address: 100 E. Stinson, Norman, 73072. Tel: 405-321-0990.

Clergy Education, Department of—Mailing Address: P.O. Box 32180, Oklahoma City, 73123. Tel: 405-721-5651.

Victim Assistance Coordinator—Mrs. JENNIFER GOODRICH, Mailing Address: P.O. Box 32180, Oklahoma City, 73123. Tel: 405-721-5651, Ext. 150. Email: jgoodrich@catharchdioceseokc.org.

Safe Environment Program—Mrs. JANET ENGSTRAND, Coord., Mailing Address: P.O. Box 32180, Oklahoma City, 73123. Tel: 405-721-5651, Ext. 150.

Family Life Department—Mr. GEORGE RIGAZZI, J.C.L., Mailing Address: P.O. Box 32180, Oklahoma City, 73123. Tel: 405-721-8943; 405-721-5651.

Justice and Human Development, Commission for—VACANT.

Legal Counsel—Mr. DOUG EASON, 9211 Lake Hefner Pkwy., Ste. 200, Oklahoma City, 73120. Tel: 405-841-6000.

Master of Ceremonies—Revs. ROBERT T. WOOD; TIMOTHY M. FULLER, Asst.

Ministry to Priests Program—Rev. JOSEPH R. ROSS, Mailing Address: P.O. Box 2546, Lawton, 73502. Tel: 580-355-2054.

Mission "Micatokla"--Archdiocesan Mission of Santiago Atitlan, Guatemala—Mr. DAVID JOHNSON, Mailing Address: P.O. Box 32180, Oklahoma City, 73123. Tel: 405-721-5651; Fax: 405-721-5210.

Newspaper— "The Sooner Catholic" Ms. RAY DYER, Editor, Mailing Address: P.O. Box 32180, Oklahoma City, 73123. Tel: 405-721-1810; 405-721-5651.

Permanent Diaconate—Deacon MAX SCHWARZ, Dir., Mailing Address: P.O. Box 32180, Oklahoma City, 73123. Tel: 405-721-5651.

Priests' Medical Fund— formerly known as Infirm Priest Fund. Rev. Msgr. EDWARD J. WEISENBURGER, V.G., M.A., J.C.L., Mailing Address: P.O. Box 32180, Oklahoma City, 73123. Tel: 405-721-5651.

Priests' Retirement Trust Fund—Most Rev. PAUL S. COAKLEY; Revs. EDWARD T. MENASCO, Mailing Address: P.O. Box 1227, Norman, 73070; MICHAEL L. CHAPMAN, B.A., 317 N. Blackwelder, Oklahoma City, 73106.

Propagation of the Faith, Holy Childhood Assoc., Missionary Cooperation Plan—VACANT, Mailing Address: P.O. Box 32180, Oklahoma City, 73123. Tel: 405-721-5651.

Rural Life—VACANT.

Scouting—Rev. CHARLES R. MURPHY, Mailing Address: P.O. Box 60569, Oklahoma City, 73146. Tel: 580-395-2148.

St. Ann's Home, Inc.—Mrs. DOROTHY JOYCE, Admin., 9400 St. Ann Dr., Oklahoma City, 73162. Tel: 405-728-7888.

St. Francis de Sales Seminary (Legal Title)—Most Rev. PAUL S. COAKLEY; Mr. DAVID JOHNSON, Treas., Mailing Address: P.O. Box 32180, Oklahoma City, 73123.

Vocations and Seminarians—Rev. WILLIAM L. NOVAK, Dir.

Worship and Spiritual Life, Office of—Rev. STEPHEN J. BIRD, Dir.

Youth and Young Adult Ministry, Office of—Mrs. NANCY HOUSH, Dir. Tel: 405-721-5651; Mrs. BECKY JAIME, Assoc. Dir., Mailing Address: P.O. Box 32180, Oklahoma City, 73123. Tel: 405-721-9220; 405-721-5651.

CLERGY, PARISHES, MISSIONS AND PAROCHIAL SCHOOLS

OKLAHOMA CITY

(OKLAHOMA COUNTY)

1—CATHEDRAL OF OUR LADY OF PERPETUAL HELP (1919) [JC] Rev. Msgr. Edward J. Weisenburger; Rev. Thanh Van Nguyen; Deacons William Enos; Paul Lewis; Anthony Le; Sang Ninh.
Res.: 3214 Lake Ave., 73118. Tel: 405-525-2349; Fax: 405-525-3628. Email: olph@cathedralokc.org. Web: www.cathedralokc.org.
School—Bishop John Carroll, 1100 N.W. 32, 73118. Tel: 405-525-0956 (Office); Fax: 405-523-3053. Lay Teachers 15; Students 195.
Catechesis/Religious Program—Tel: 405-525-2349, Ext. 140. Students 183.

2—ST. ANDREW DUNG-LAC (1994), (Vietnamese), [JC] Rev. Dominic Hung Hoang; Deacons Ty V. Nguyen; Kha Nguyen; Sr. Mary Quy Truong.
Mailing Address: 3000 S.W. 55th St., P.O. Box 891584, 73119.
Church: 3000 S.W. 55th St., 73119. Tel: 405-681-2665; 405-681-6918; Fax: 405-681-7951.
Catechesis/Religious Program—Students 345.

3—ST. CHARLES BORROMEO (1954) [JC] Revs. Timothy D. Luschen; Long N. Phan; Deacons Marc LeWand; Bill Gorden; Thomas Phan; Bill King; Alfonso Lopez.
Res.: 5024 N. Grove St., 73122. Tel: 405-789-2595; Fax: 405-789-4394.
School—5000 N. Grove St., 73122. Tel: 405-789-0224; Fax: 405-789-3583. Lay Teachers 20; Students 192.
Catechesis/Religious Program—Students 330.

4—CHRIST THE KING (1949) [JC] Rev. Richard D. Stansberry Jr.; Deacons James Smith; Richard L. Boothe III.
Mailing Address: 8005 Dorset Dr., P.O. Box 20508, 73156-0508. Tel: 405-842-1481; Fax: 405-843-0539. Web: www.ckokc.org.
Rectory—1900 Elmhurst Ave., 73120. Tel: 405-841-6680.
Church: 8005 Dorset Dr., 73120. Tel: 405-842-1481; Fax: 405-843-0539.
School—1905 Elmhurst, 73120. Tel: 405-843-3909; Fax: 405-843-6519. Web: www.ckschool.com. Mrs. Karen Carter, Prin. Lay Teachers 38; Students 508.
Catechesis/Religious Program—Tel: 405-843-4766. Students 213.

5—CHURCH OF THE EPIPHANY OF THE LORD (1976) Revs. Stephen J. Bird; Mariyanandam Pulugujju (India). Tel: 405-722-1993; Alveria Kopp, Pastoral Assoc.; Mrs. Judy Reilly, Pastoral Assoc.; Deacons Robert Heskamp; Richard Fahy.
Res.: 7336 W. Britton Rd., 73132. Tel: 405-722-2110; Fax: 405-722-6719. Email: epiphany@epiphanyokc.com. Web: www.epiphanyokc.com.
Catechesis/Religious Program—Tel: 405-722-0051. Email: redirector@epiphanyokc.com. Mr. Daniel Douglas, D.R.E.; Tracy Osterman, Youth Min.; Bob Waldrop, Music Dir. Students 353.

6—CORPUS CHRISTI (1924), (African American), [JC] Rev. John Zupez, S.J.; Deacons Dunn Cumby; Bernard Hollier.
Res.: 1005 N.E. 15th St., 73117. Tel: 405-239-2854; Fax: 405-235-2122. Email: jzupez@jesuits.net.
Catechesis/Religious Program—Students 24.
Mission—St. Robert Bellarmine 121 N.W. 1st St., P.O. Box 280, Jones, 73049.

7—ST. EUGENE'S (1958) [JC] Revs. Joseph A. Jacobi; William B. Ross (Retired); Deacons Bill Bawden, Dir. Admin.; Chuck Hankins; Alejandro Randolph; Thomas O. Goldsworthy.
Mailing Address: 2400 W. Hefner Rd., P.O. Box 20930, 73156.
Res.: 10804 Greystone Ave., 73120. Tel: 405-752-5098; Fax: 405-751-8722. Web: www.steugenes.org.
School—Tel: 405-751-0067; Fax: 405-302-4254. Mrs. Suzette Williams, Prin. Lay Teachers 27; Students 356.
Catechesis/Religious Program—Students 388.

8—ST. FRANCIS OF ASSISI (1925) [JC] Rev. Charles R. Murphy; Deacon Joe Forgue.
Res.: 1901 N.W. 18th St., P.O. Box 60569, 73106. Tel: 405-528-0485; Fax: 405-524-1260. Web: www.stfrancisokc.com.
School—Rosary, 1919 N.W. 18th St., 73106. Tel: 405-525-9272; Fax: 405-525-5643. Web: www.rosaryschool.com. Mrs. Karen Lynn, Prin. Lay Teachers 25; Students 249.
Catechesis/Religious Program—Students 105.

9—HOLY ANGELS (1924), (Hispanic), [JC] Rev. Michael L. Chapman; Deacon Santos Hernandez.
Res.: 317 N. Blackwelder St., 73106. Tel: 405-232-6572; Fax: 405-235-8334.
Convent—Carmelite Missionaries of St. Teresa, 1522 N.W. Third St., 73106. Tel: 405-231-1935.
Catechesis/Religious Program—Students 505.

10—IMMACULATE CONCEPTION (1892) [CEM] Rev. George Pupius; Deacon James Keene.
Res.: 3901 S.W. 29th St., 73119. Tel: 405-685-4224; Fax: 405-685-4483.
Catechesis/Religious Program—Tel: 405-685-4806. Students 80.

11—ST. JAMES THE GREATER (1954) Rev. Bill H. Pruett; Deacon Marti Gulikers.

Church: 4201 S. McKinley, 73109. Tel: 405-636-6805; Fax: 405-636-6848.
Res.: 4308 S. Blackwelder, 73119. Tel: 405-636-6802; Fax: 405-636-6807. Web: www.stjamesokc.com.
School—1224 S.W. 41st St., 73109. Tel: 405-636-6810; Fax: 405-636-6818. Anne Codding, Prin. Lay Teachers 16; Students 173.
Catechesis/Religious Program—Tel: 405-636-6840. Students 172.

12—ST. JOSEPH (1889) [JC], (Old Cathedral) Rev. Bruce K. Natsuhara. In Res., Rev. George Parackal.
Res.: 307 N.W. 4th St., 73102. Tel: 405-815-6650; Fax: 405-815-6644. Email: stjosephs1@coxinet.net.
Church: 307 N.W. 4th St., 73102.
Catechesis/Religious Program—Students 101.

13—KOREAN MARTYRS (1996), (Korean), Rev. Jinsu Lawrence Kim.
Res.: 7517 S. Linn Ave., 73159. Tel: 405-688-5585; Fax: 405-688-5586.
Church: 2600 S.W. 74th St., 73159. Tel: 405-681-6464; Fax: 405-688-5586.
Catechesis/Religious Program—Students 31.

14—OUR LADY OF MOUNT CARMEL AND ST. THERESE LITTLE FLOWER (1921) [JC] Revs. Raul Reyes, O.C.D.; Luis Castaneda, O.C.D., Supr.; Jesus Sancho, O.C.D.; Henry Bordeaux, O.C.D.
Mailing Address: 1125 S. Walker Ave., 73101-1196. Tel: 405-235-2037; Fax: 405-235-7023.
Catechesis/Religious Program—Students 633.

15—ST. PATRICK (1950) Rev. Thomas McSherry; Deacons Duane Fischer; Forrest Simpson.
Res.: 2121 N. Portland, 73107. Tel: 405-946-4441; Fax: 405-946-4894. Email: info@stpatrickokc.com. Web: www.stpatrickokc.com.
Catechesis/Religious Program—Students 170.

16—ST. PAUL, APOSTLE (1956) [JC] Rev. Maurus P. Jaeb, O.S.B.; Deacon Raymond LaChance.
Res.: 3901 S. Sunnylane Rd., Del City, 73115. Tel: 405-677-4873; Fax: 405-619-0596.
Catechesis/Religious Program—Students 131.

17—ST. PHILIP NERI (Midwest City) (1946) [CEM] Rev. Timothy M. Fuller.
Church & Mailing Address: 1107 Felix Pl., Midwest City, 73110-5331. Tel: 405-737-4476; Fax: 405-741-0531. Email: parish@spnok.org.
Rectory—301 Wilson Dr., Midwest City, 73110-5346.
School—1121 Felix Pl., Midwest City, 73110-5331. Tel: 405-737-4496; Fax: 405-732-7823. Mrs. Mary Dresel, Prin. Lay Teachers 17; Students 193.
Catechesis/Religious Program—Tel: 405-737-4476, Ext. 108. Email: dre@spnok.org. Students 206.

18—SACRED HEART (1911) [JC] Revs. Roberto A. Quant; William M. Lewis.
Res.: 2706 S. Shartel Ave., 73109. Tel: 405-634-2458; Fax: 405-634-2459. Email: sacredheartokc@yahoo.com. Web: www.sacredheartcatholicchurchokc.org.
School—2700 S. Shartel Ave., 73109. Tel: 405-634-5673; Fax: 405-634-7011. Web: www.sacredheartok-c.org. Joana Camacho, Prin. Lay Teachers 12; Students 154.
Catechesis/Religious Program—Tel: 405-634-6448. Email: sacredheartrosamz@cox.net. Students 843.

OUTSIDE OKLAHOMA CITY

ADA, PONTOTOC CO., ST. JOSEPH (1902) Rev. Russell L. Hewes; Deacons Michael Radosevich, (Retired); Dennis D. Fine.
Res.: 1300 E. Beverly St., P.O. Box 1585, 74821. Tel: 580-332-4811; Fax: 580-436-1226.
Catechesis/Religious Program—Students 208.
Mission—St. Francis Xavier 1313 E. 7th St., Sulphur, Murray Co. 73086. Tel: 580-622-3070.

ALTUS, JACKSON CO., PRINCE OF PEACE (1964) Rev. Joseph Sundar Raju Pudota.
Res.: 1500 Falcon Rd., 73521. Tel: 580-482-3363; Fax: 580-482-6657. Email: princeofpeace1766@cableone.net.
Mission—St. Helen Church 507 E. Highview, Frederick, 73542. Tel: 580-335-3298; Fax: 580-335-3953. Email: sthelenchurch@pldio.net.
Catechesis/Religious Program—Students 166.

ALVA, WOODS CO., SACRED HEART (1897) [CEM] Rev. James A. Wickersham.
Res.: 627 12th St., 73717. Tel: 580-327-3006 (office); Fax: 580-327-0710. Email: sacredheartalva@gmail.com.
Mission—Our Mother of Mercy 210 S. Main St., Waynoka, Woods Co. 73860.
Mission—St. Cornelius (1895) 404 S. Massachusetts, Cherokee, Alfalfa Co. 73728. Tel: 580-596-3328.
Catechesis/Religious Program—Tel: 580-327-3006. Students 40.

ANADARKO, CADDO CO., ST. PATRICK'S (1892), (Native American), [JC 5] Rev. Joseph Patrick Schwarz.
Res.: 1115 W. Petree Rd., Box 628, 73005. Tel: 405-247-5255; Fax: 405-247-5249. Email: stpats@sbcglobal.net.
Mission—Our Lady of the Most Holy Rosary Binger. Hwy. 152, Binger, Caddo Co. 73009.
Mission—St. Richard Hwy. 9, Carnegie, Caddo Co. 73015.
Catechesis/Religious Program—Students 58.

ARDMORE, CARTER CO., ST. MARY (1898) [CEM] Rev. Thomas Dowdell.
Mailing Address: 101 E St., S.W., 73401. Email: stmaryardmore@hotmail.com. Web: stmaryardmoreok.org.
Res.: 112 F St. S.W., 73401. Tel: 580-223-0231; Fax: 580-226-2129.
Catechesis/Religious Program—Students 228.

BETHANY, OKLAHOMA CO., LATIN MASS COMMUNITY, See separate listing. See St. Damien of Molokai Chapel, Edmond.

BLACKWELL, KAY CO., ST. JOSEPH'S (1901) Rev. Martin Larok Obwona, F.C. (Uganda); Deacon Bart Brashears.
Res.: 315 W. Blackwell Ave., P.O. Box 578, 74631. Tel: 580-363-2096; Fax: 580-363-2096.
Catechesis/Religious Program—Tel: 580-363-0441; Fax: 580-363-0441. Students 31.

CHANDLER, LINCOLN CO., OUR LADY OF SORROWS (1894) [CEM] Rev. James J. Mickus; Deacon Rusty Wooden.
Res.: 409 Price Ave., P.O. Box 543, 74834. Tel: 405-258-1239; Fax: 405-258-0010.
Mission—St. Louis Hwy. 99 & Eighth Ave., Stroud, Lincoln Co. 74079.
Catechesis/Religious Program—Students 44.

CHICKASHA, GRADY CO., HOLY NAME (1895) [CEM] Rev. Shane L. Tharp.
Res.: 210 S. Seventh St., Box 748, 73023-0748. Fax: 405-224-4434.
Catechesis/Religious Program—Tel: 405-224-6068. Students 129.

CLINTON, CUSTER CO., ST. MARY'S (1944) Rev. Rex A. Arnold; Deacons Pedro Maldonado; William A. Hough.
Res.: 714 S. 12th St., P.O. Box 1295, 73601. Tel: 580-323-0309; 580-323-0345 (Office); Fax: 580-323-1351. Email: frrex@sbcglobal.net. Web: stmarysclintonok.org.
Mission—St. Anne 522 E. 3rd, Cordell, Washita Co. 73632.
Catechesis/Religious Program—1218 Knox Ave., P.O. Box 1295, 73601. Tel: 580-323-0345; Fax: 580-323-0345. Email: k.hubbard@stmarysclintonok.org. Students 181.

DUNCAN, STEPHENS CO., ASSUMPTION (1902) [CEM] Revs. Peter Jandaczek; Joseph Nettem; Deacon James Conway.
Res.: 711 Hickory Ave., 73533. Tel: 580-255-0590; Fax: 580-701-2468. Web: www.assumptionparishonline.org.
Mission—Immaculate Conception Fourth & Comanche, Marlow, Stephens Co. 73055. Tel: 580-658-2365.
Mission—St. Patrick Church 3rd & Ohio, Walters, Cotton Co. 73572.
Mission—San Jose 1117 Lincoln Ave., Ryan, Jefferson Co. 73565. Tel: 580-757-2830.
Mission—St. Thomas Aquinas Chapel 400 E. 'D' St., Waurika, Jefferson Co. 73573.
Catechesis/Religious Program—Maria Martinez, D.R.E. Students 255.

EDMOND, OKLAHOMA CO.

1—ST. DAMIEN OF MOLOKAI CHAPEL (2010) Revs. Joseph Portzer, F.S.S.P., Chap.; Christopher Pelster, F.S.S.P., Asst. Chap.
8455 N.W. 234th Sorghum Mill, 73025. Tel: 405-330-9968.
Catechesis/Religious Program—Students 34.

2—ST. JOHN THE BAPTIST (1889) Rev. John R. Metzinger; Very Rev. Louis Vanderley, O.S.B.; Rev. Balaswamy Konka; Deacons Bill Coyle, Business Mgr.; Gary Peterson, Outreach/Evangelization; Roy Forsythe, Prison Ministry.
Res.: 900 S. Littler Ave., P.O. Box 510, 73083-0510. Tel: 405-340-0691; Fax: 405-340-5715.
School—St. Elizabeth Ann Seton School, 925 South Blvd., 73034-4710. Tel: 405-348-5364; Fax: 405-340-9627. Email: seas@stjohn-catholic.org. Web: www.stjohn-catholic.org/s_e_a_s_.htm. Mrs. Angie Howard, Prin. Lay Teachers 26; Students 460.
Catechesis/Religious Program—Tel: 405-340-9871; Fax: 405-340-3260. Web: www.stjohn-catholic.org/re.htm. Students 685.

3—ST. MONICA (1993) [CEM] Rev. Raymond K. Ackerman.
Mailing Address: 2001 N. Western, 73012. Tel: 405-359-2700; Fax: 405-341-0023.
Res.: 1121 N.W. 199th St., 73012. Tel: 405-330-2699; Fax: 405-330-2699.
Catechesis/Religious Program—Students 441.

EL RENO, CANADIAN CO., SACRED HEART (1890) [CEM] Rev. Mark E. Mason.
Res.: 208 S. Evans Ave., 73036-3636. Tel: 405-262-1405; Fax: 405-262-2251; 405-262-2818. Email: elreno@sacredheart.com.
School—Sacred Heart School, 210 S. Evans, 73036. Tel: 405-262-2284; Fax: 405-262-3818. Shannon Statton, Prin. Teachers 7; Students 104.
Catechesis/Religious Program—Tel: 405-262-2273. Students 175.

ELGIN, COMANCHE CO., ST. ANN (1914), (German), [CEM] Rev. Madineni Prakash; Deacon Thomas E. Biles.
Res.: 8492 St. Hwy. 17, P.O. Box 10, 73538. Tel: 580-492-5914; Fax: 580-492-5908. Email: stann@tds.net.
Mission—Our Lady of Perpetual Help 220 N. A St., Sterling, Comanche Co. 73567.
Mission—Mother of Sorrows 521 E. Wallace, Apache, Caddo Co. 73006.
Catechesis/Religious Program—Students 102.

ELK CITY, BECKHAM CO., ST. MATTHEW'S (1970), (German), [CEM] [JC 3] Rev. Carl William Janocha; Deacons Paul Albert; Jim E. Warnke; Kathy Noble, Music Min.
Mailing Address: 3001 E. Hwy. 66, 73644-9607. Tel: 580-225-0066; Fax: 580-225-3522. Email: stmatthew@cableone.net.
Res.: 2900 E. Highway 66, 73644. Tel: 580-225-3980; Fax: 580-225-3522. Email: stmatthew@cableone.net.
Mission—Queen of All Saints 914 N. 5th St., Sayre, Beckham Co. 73662. Tel: 580-928-5124. Deacon Sherman McKaskle.
Catechesis/Religious Program—Celia Spitz, D.R.E. Students 158.

ENID, GARFIELD CO.

1—ST. FRANCIS XAVIER (1893) [CEM] [JC] Revs. Joseph M. Irwin; Rajesh K. Mankena; Deacon Anthony Crispo.
Res.: 110 N. Madison, P.O. Box 3527, 73702. Tel: 580-237-0812; Fax: 580-237-0909.
School—St. Joseph Catholic School, (Grades PreK-5) Tel: 580-242-4449; Fax: 580-242-3541. Wade Laffey, Prin. Lay Teachers 9; Students 92.
Catechesis/Religious Program—Students 587.
Mission—St. Gregory the Great 1924 W. Willow Rd., Garfield Co. 73703. Tel: 580-233-4589; Fax: 580-233-4590. Email: stgregorys@sbcglobal.net.
Mission—St. Michael [CEM] Main St., Goltry, Alfalfa Co. 73739.

2—ST. GREGORY THE GREAT (1971) See separate listing. Now a mission of St. Francis Xavier, Enid.

GUTHRIE, LOGAN CO., ST. MARY'S (1889) [CEM] Rev. Robert T. Wood; Deacons Roy Ellison; Richard Washko, (Retired).
Mailing Address: 411 N. Elm St., P.O. Box 1556, 73044.
Res.: 411 N. Elm St., P.O. Box 1556, 73044. Tel: 405-282-4239; Fax: 405-282-5610. Email: stmarys@coxinet.net.
School—502 E. Warner Ave., 73044. Tel: 405-282-2071; Fax: 405-282-2924. Email: stmaryscatholic@sbcglobal.net. Mrs. Sheila Whalen-Guthrie, Prin. Lay Teachers 9; Students 154.
Mission—St. Margaret Mary P.O. Box 632, Crescent, Logan Co. 73028. Tel: 405-969-2351.
Catechesis/Religious Program—Students 54.

GUYMON, TEXAS CO., ST. PETER'S (1906), (Hispanic), [CEM] Revs. Michael Wheelahan; Raul Sanchez; Benjamin Bandanadam; Deacons Joe Cruz; Simon Guerra.
Res.: 1220 N. Quinn St., P.O. Box 731, 73942. Tel: 580-338-7212; Fax: 580-338-8746. Email: stpeter@ptsi.net.
Mission—St. Frances Cabrini 101 Ave. C, Beaver, Beaver Co. 73932. Tel: 580-256-5305.
Mission—Sacred Heart 106 N. Albright, P.O. Box 468, Hooker, Texas Co. 73945. Tel: 580-652-2320.
Mission—Good Shepherd S. Ellis at Second, P.O. Box 966, Boise City, Cimarron Co. 73933. Tel: 580-544-3443.
Catechesis/Religious Program—Tel: 405-454-9940. Students 320.

HARRAH, OKLAHOMA CO., ST. TERESA OF AVILA (1907), (Polish), [CEM] Rev. Lucas Raj Pinapati (India).
Res.: 1576 Tim Holt Dr., P.O. Box 418, 73045. Tel: 405-454-2819; Fax: 405-454-0981. Email: info@stteresaharrah.org. Web: www.stteresaharrah.org.
Catechesis/Religious Program—Tel: 405-454-9440. Students 143.
Mission—Saint Vincent de Paul Church 123 S. 9th St., Mcloud, 74851-0585. Tel: 405-964-5606; Fax: 405-964-5606. Email: stvincentmcloud@gmail.com.

HENNESSEY, KINGFISHER CO., ST. JOSEPH'S (1890), (Hispanic), [CEM] Rev. Joseph H. Arledge.
Res.: 211 N. Cherokee St., 73742. Tel: 405-853-4425; Fax: 405-853-2166.
Mission—St. Joseph 101 First St., P.O. Box 117, Bison, Garfield Co. 73720.
Catechesis/Religious Program—Tel: 405-853-2158. Students 119.

HITCHCOCK, BLAINE CO., SACRED HEART MISSION, Closed. For inquiries for parish records contact St. Anthony of Padua Church, Okeene.

KINGFISHER, KINGFISHER CO., SS. PETER AND PAUL (1896) [CEM] Rev. Stephen V. Hamilton; Deacon Terrence R. Rice.

Mailing Address: 309 S. Main, 73750.
Res.: 410 S. 6th St., 73750. Tel: 405-375-4581; Fax: 405-375-3858. Web: www.stspeterandpaul.org.
School—Tel: 405-375-4616; Fax: 405-375-5296. Lay Teachers 8; Students 64.
Catechesis/Religious Program—Students 125.
Mission—St. Rose of Lima 900 N. Clarence Nash Blvd., Watonga, Blaine Co. 73772.

KONAWA, POTTAWATOMIE CO., SACRED HEART (1876) [CEM] Rev. Adrian Vorderlandwehr, O.S.B.
Res.: 47943 Abbey Rd., 74849. Tel: 580-925-2145; Fax: 580-925-2145.
Mission—St. Mary Wanette, Pottawatomie Co.
Catechesis/Religious Program—Students 18.

LAWTON, COMANCHE CO.
1—BLESSED SACRAMENT (1902) Rev. Joseph R. Ross; Deacon Bill Adamson. In Res., Rev. James D.M. Stafford.
Res.: 12 S.W. Seventh St., Box 2546, 73502. Tel: 580-355-2054; Fax: 580-355-2055. Email: blessedsaclawton@sbcglobal.net.
School—St. Mary's, 611 A Ave., 73501. Tel: 580-355-5288; Fax: 580-355-4336. Email: saintmarysknights@juno.com. Lay Teachers 17; Students 130.
Catechesis/Religious Program—Tel: 580-353-8182. Students 120.
2—HOLY FAMILY (1959), (Formerly St. Barbara) Rev. Philip Seeton; Deacons Michael J. Romaka; Jim Coe; David Bunch.
Res.: 1010 N.W. 82nd St., 73505. Tel: 580-536-6351; Fax: 580-536-6352. Email: holyfamilyoffice@sbcglobal.net. Web: www.holyfamilylawton.org.
Catechesis/Religious Program—Tel: 580-536-6355; Fax: 580-536-6352. Email: vickigable@hotmail.com. Students 263.

LEXINGTON, CLEVELAND CO., ST. JOHN THE BAPTIST, Closed. For parish records contact Our Lady of Victory, Purcell.

LOYAL, KINGFISHER CO., ST. JOSEPH MISSION, Closed. For inquiries for parish records contact Sts. Peter & Paul Church, Kingfisher.

MADILL, MARSHALL CO., HOLY CROSS CHURCH (1948) Rev. Oby J. Zunmas.
14 W. Francis St., 73446-3234. Tel: 580-795-3721; Fax: 888-696-2593.
Mission—Good Shepherd 200 N.W. 8th, P.O. Box 127, Marietta, 73448. Tel: 580-276-9604.
Catechesis/Religious Program—Margarita Moreno, D.R.E. (Holy Cross); Carol Steinbock, D.R.E. (Good Shepherd). Students 348.

MANGUM, GREER CO., SACRED HEART (1902) Rev. Jude Shayo, A.J.
Mailing Address: P.O. Box 310, 73554. Tel: 580-782-2657; Fax: 580-782-3397.
Res.: 409 N. Byers, 73554. Tel: 580-726-3925.
Mission—Sts. Peter and Paul 328 S. Randlett St., Hobart, Kiewa Co. 73651. Fax: 580-726-3486. Web: www.stspeter-paul.com.
Mission—Our Lady of Guadalupe 524 E. Chestnut, Hollis, Harmon Co. 73550. Tel: 580-688-2233.
Catechesis/Religious Program—Students 11.

MCLOUD, POTTOWATOMIE CO., ST. VINCENT DE PAUL (1904) See separate listing. Now a mission of St. Teresa of Avila, Harrah.

MEDFORD, GRANT CO., ST. MARY'S (1940) [CEM 3] Rev. Lourdu Reddy Ponnapati (India).
Res.: 214 W. Cherokee, Box 360, 73759. Tel: 580-395-2148; Fax: 580-395-2148.
Mission—St. Mary's Assumption Main & Birch, Wakita, Grant Co. 73771.
Mission—St. Joseph's S. Hwy. 81, Pond Creek, Grant Co. 73766.
Catechesis/Religious Program—Tel: 580-395-2290. Students 33.

MOORE, CLEVELAND CO., ST. ANDREW THE APOSTLE CATHOLIC CHURCH (1962) [CEM] Rev. John W. Feehily; Deacons Jerome Caplinger; Angus Watford.
Res.: 800 N.W. Fifth St., 73160. Tel: 405-799-3334; Fax: 405-799-4880. Web: www.standrewmoore.com.
Catechesis/Religious Program—Tel: 405-799-3334, Ext. 305. Email: mhochla@standrewmoore.com. Linda Hartley, D.R.E.; Margaret Hochla, D.R.E. Students 381.

MUSTANG, CANADIAN CO., CHURCH OF THE HOLY SPIRIT (1983) Rev. James A. Greiner.
Church: 1100 N. Sara Rd., P.O. Box 246, 73064. Tel: 405-376-9435 (Parish Office); 405-376-5218 (Rectory); Fax: 405-376-4929. Email: lonelk67@sbcglobal.net. Web: www.mustangcatholic.com.
Catechesis/Religious Program—Tel: 405-376-5633. Martin Weaver, D.R.E. (High School); Martha Quezada, D.R.E. (PreK-8th). Students 219.

NEWKIRK, KAY CO., ST. FRANCIS OF ASSISI (1894) See separate listing. Now a mission of Church of St. Mary, Ponca City.

NICOMA PARK, OKLAHOMA CO., OUR LADY OF FATIMA (1949) Closed. For inquiries for parish record contact St. Philip Neri, Midwest City.

NORMAN, CLEVELAND CO.
1—CHURCH OF ST. MARK THE EVANGELIST (1991) Revs. Thomas J. Boyer; Sami Chaaya, M.L.M.; Deacon Byron Jacobson.
Mailing Address: 3939 W. Tecumseh Rd., 73072-1708. Tel: 405-366-7676; Fax: 405-366-7842. In Res., Rev. Jim F. Chamberlin.
Res.: 3701 Castlerock Rd., 73072. Tel: 405-447-3085.
Catechesis/Religious Program—Students 352.
2—ST. JOSEPH'S (1896) [CEM] Rev. Edward T. Menasco; Deacons Larry Sousa; Patrick Gabrish; Jeff Willard, Pastoral Assoc.; Steve Lewis; Richard Montedoro.
Mailing Address: 421 E. Acres, P.O. Box 1227, 73070.
Res.: 422 E. Tonhawa, P.O. Box 1227, 73070. Tel: 405-321-8080; Fax: 405-321-4360. Web: www.stjosephsok.org.
Church: 211 N. Porter, 73071.
Catechesis/Religious Program—Tel: 405-321-8084. Students 297.
3—ST. THOMAS MORE UNIVERSITY PARISH (1979) [JC] Rev. James A. Goin; Deacon John D. Pigott; Nolan Reilly, Music Intern; Erin Snow, Dir., Campus Min.; Samuel E. Snow, Business Mgr.
Res.: 1501 Lincoln Ave., 73072. Web: www.stm-ou.org.
Church: 100 E. Stinson St., 73072. Tel: 405-321-0990; Fax: 405-321-0964. Web: www.stm-ou.org.
Catechesis/Religious Program—Lisa Tippitt, C.R.E. Students 155.

OKARCHE, KINGFISHER CO., HOLY TRINITY (1893) [CEM] Rev. Sam Licanda; Deacon Max Schwarz.
Res.: 211 W. Missouri, Box 185, 73762-0185. Tel: 405-263-7930; Fax: 405-263-4518.
School—Box 485, 73762. Tel: 405-263-4422; Fax: 405-263-9753. Tammy Jacobs, Prin. Lay Teachers 14; Students 100.
Catechesis/Religious Program—Tel: 405-263-4640. Students 102.
Mission—Immaculate Heart of Mary 107 Freehome, Calumet, Canadian Co. 73014.

OKEENE, BLAINE CO., ST. ANTHONY'S (1901) [CEM] Rev. Jaroslaw P. Topolewski.
Res.: P.O. Box 767, 73763. Tel: 580-822-3511 (Rectory); 580-822-3544 (Office); Fax: 580-822-3542. Email: stanthony@pldi.net.
Rectory—220 E. Grant, 73763.
Mission—St. Thomas P.O. Box 624, Seiling, Dewey Co. 73663. Tel: 580-922-4376.
Mission—St. Ann 424 S. 6th, P.O. Box 55, Fairview, Major Co. 73737. Tel: 580-227-2270.
Catechesis/Religious Program—Tel: 580-822-3507. Students 34.

PAULS VALLEY, GARVIN CO.
1—ST. CATHERINE OF SIENA (1949) [JC] See separate listing. Now a mission of Our Lady of Victory, Purcell.

PERRY, NOBLE CO., ST. ROSE OF LIMA (1893) [CEM] Rev. Daniel J. Letourneau; Sandy Soulek, Pastoral Assoc.
Mailing Address: P.O. Box 603, 73077-0603.
Res.: 421 Ninth St., 73077. Tel: 580-336-9300; Fax: 580-336-4000. Email: stroseperry@sbcglobal.net. Web: www.saintroseperry.com.
Mission—Sacred Heart Broadway & Lowe, Billings, Noble Co. 74630.
Catechesis/Religious Program—Students 46.

PONCA CITY, KAY CO., CHURCH OF ST. MARY (1893) [CEM] [JC] Revs. Kevin J. Ratterman; John Aram; Deacon Richard Robinson.
Res.: 707 E. Ponca St., Box 1330, 74602. Tel: 580-765-6031; Fax: 580-765-1327. Email: stmarysponcacity@sbcglobal.net. Web: www.stmarypc.com.
School—St. Mary, 415 S. 7th, 74601. Tel: 580-765-1352. Web: www.stmarypc.com/school/school/htm. Teachers 18; Students 145.
Catechesis/Religious Program—Tel: 580-765-7794. Email: stmarydre@sbcglobal.net. Students 132.
Mission—St. Francis of Assisi P.O. Box 101, Newkirk, 74647.

PRAGUE, LINCOLN CO., ST. WENCESLAUS, NATIONAL SHRINE OF THE INFANT JESUS OF PRAGUE (1899), (Czech), [CEM] Rev. M. Price Oswalt.
Res.: 304 Jim Thorpe Blvd., Box 488, 74864. Tel: 405-567-3404; Fax: 405-567-0365.
Mission—St. Michael 217 S. Koonce, P.O. Box 684, Meeker, Lincoln Co. 74855.
Catechesis/Religious Program—Students 19.

PURCELL, MCCLAIN CO., OUR LADY OF VICTORY (1886), (Hispanic), [CEM] Rev. Michael Vaught.
Office: 307 W. Jefferson St., Box 1280, 73080. Tel: 405-527-3077; Fax: 405-527-7842 (Pastor); 405-527-6817 (Office). Email: ourladyofvictory@cebridge.net.
Catechesis/Religious Program—Students 218.
Mission—St. Catherine of Siena 205 W. Bert St., Pauls Valley, 73075. Tel: 405-238-3741; Fax: 405-238-3858.
Mission—St. Peter Church P.O. Box 1280, 73080. E. Second & Quapah, Lindsay, Garvin Co. 73052.

SEMINOLE, SEMINOLE CO., IMMACULATE CONCEPTION (1928) Rev. Basil Keenan, O.S.B.
Mailing Address: P.O. Box 164, 74818-0164.
Res.: 811 W. Wrangler Blvd., 74868. Tel: 405-382-3602; Fax: 405-382-3602. Email: basilosb@hotmail.com.
Chapel—St. Joseph Chapel 702 S. Seminole, Wewoka, 74884.
Catechesis/Religious Program—Students 47.

SHAWNEE, POTTAWATOMIE CO., ST. BENEDICT (1895) [CEM] Rev. Donald J. Wolf; Deacons David Schrupp; William T. Thurman.
Res.: 632 N. Kickapoo, 74801. Tel: 405-275-0001; Fax: 405-214-9181. Email: st.benedict.office@sbcglobal.net. Web: www.stbenedictchurch.net.
Catechesis/Religious Program—Tel: 405-275-5399. Students 174.

SULPHUR, MURRAY CO., ST. FRANCIS XAVIER (1974) See separate listing. Became a mission of St. Joseph, Ada.

TONKAWA, KAY CO., ST. JOSEPH'S (1909) [JC] Rev. Martin Larok Obwona, F.C. (Uganda).
Res.: 320 W. North St., P.O. Box 525, 74653. Tel: 580-628-2416; Fax: 580-363-2096.
Catechesis/Religious Program—Students 46.

UNION CITY, CANADIAN CO., ST. JOSEPH'S (1893) [CEM] Rev. Mark E. Mason; Deacon Lloyd Menz, Pastoral Assoc.
Res.: 403 N. Kate Boevers Ave., Box 100, 73090. Tel: 405-483-5329; Fax: 405-483-5183.
Catechesis/Religious Program—Tel: 405-381-2569. Students 67.

WEATHERFORD, CUSTER CO., ST. EUGENE'S (1960) [CEM 3] Rev. Christopher H. Tran; Deacon Joseph Dubey.
Res.: 704 N. Bryan, 73096. Tel: 580-772-3209; Fax: 580-772-3541 (Fr. Tran); 580-772-2162 (Office). Web: steugenecatholicchurch.org. Email: st-secretary@itlnet.net.
Mission—Blessed Sacrament 520 N. Oklahoma, Thomas, Custer Co. 73669.
Mission—Sacred Heart 204 N. Clark Ave., Hinton, Caddo Co. 73047.
Catechesis/Religious Program—Students 161.

WOODWARD, WOODWARD CO., ST. PETER'S (1905), (German), Rev. Scott A. Boeckman.
Res.: 2020 Oklahoma Ave., 73801. Tel: 580-256-8505; Fax: 580-256-5840. Web: stpeternwok.com.
Mission—Sacred Heart 301 N. Main, Mooreland, Woodward Co. 73852.
Mission—Holy Name 600 S. Main, Shattuck, Ellis Co. 73858.
Mission—St. Joseph 325 S.W. 2nd, Buffalo, Harper Co. 73834.
Catechesis/Religious Program—Tel: 580-256-2966. Email: stpeterdre@sbcglobal.net. Students 245.

YUKON, CANADIAN CO., ST. JOHN NEPOMUK (1889) Rev. William L. Novak; Deacons Jeffrey Kelly; John Teague; Daniel Lombardi.
Mailing Address: 600 Garth Brooks Blvd., P.O. Box 850249, 73085.
Church: 600 S. Garth Brooks Blvd., 73099. Tel: 405-354-2743; Fax: 405-354-2770. Email: parishsecretary@sjnok.org.
School—(Grades PreK-8) Tel: 405-354-2509; Fax: 405-354-8192. Web: www.sjnok.org. Diane Floyd, Prin.; Sue Parizek, Librarian. Lay Teachers 17; Students 207.
Catechesis/Religious Program—Students 344.

Special Assignment:
Revs.—
Bird, Stephen J., Dir., Office of Worship & Spiritual Life, P.O. Box 32180, 73123. Tel: 405-721-5651
Creider, Philip B., St. Gregory's Abbey, Shawnee, OK
Leven, Marvin F., Chap. (Retired), Mercy Health Center, 4300 W. Memorial, 73120.
McCaffrey, Daniel, Natural Family Planning Outreach, 3366 N.W. Expressway, Bldg. D, #630, 73112.
Menasco, Edward T., Diaconate Program, P.O. Box 32180, 73123.
Parackal, George, Chap. St. Anthony Hospital, 1000 N. Lee St., P.O. Box 205, 73101. Tel: 405-272-6263
Ross, Joseph R., P.O. Box 2546, Lawton, 73502. Tel: 580-355-2054

Awaiting Assignment:

Absent on Sick Leave:
Rev.—
Grimes, Price D., Jr., P.O. Box 32180, 73123. Tel: 405-720-9871

Retired:
Revs.—
Bao, Anthony, Belleview Health Center, 6500 N. Portland #674, 73116.
Beckman, Richard J., 1601 Academy Rd., Ponca City, 74604.
Burger, Joseph, Saint Ann Nursing Home, 9400 Saint Ann's Dr. #C13, 73162.
Devlin, Kevin, 1044 W. 80th Ave., Conway Spring, KS 67031.
Gallatin, Paul H., 5700 N.W. 50th St., 73122.
Hanrahan, Denis G., P.O. Box 32180, 73123.
Kolb, Joseph C., P.O. Box 32180, 73123.
Kowalski, Lawrence T., 2084 Lantern Ln., Enid, 73703.
Lamb, Louis J., Saint Ann Retirement Center, 7501 W. Britton Rd., #338, 73132.
Leven, Marvin F., P.O. Box 464, Okarche, 73762.
MacAulay, Gerard, Saint Ann Retirement Center, 7501 W. Britton Rd., #238, 73132.
Michalcka, John J., P.O. Box 32180, 73123.
Moore, Wilbur E., P.O. Box 32180, 73123.
Roberson, Henry, 1141 Pinehurst Dr., Norman, 73072.
Ross, William B., 1506 W. Walnut, El Reno, 73036.
Schwarz, Elmer C., J.C.L., P.O. Box 32180, 73123.
Stieferman, Lowell L., P.O. Box 32180, 73123.
Vas, Joseph S.
Vrana, John P.

Permanent Deacons:
Adamson, Bill, Blessed Sacrament, Lawton
Albert, Paul, St. Matthew, Elk City
Bartlett, Chester A., St. Charles Borromeo, Oklahoma City
Bawden, William, St. Eugene, Oklahoma City
Best, David, (Retired)
Biles, Thomas E., St. Ann, Elgin
Boothe, Richard L., III, Christ the King, Oklahoma City
Brashers, Bart, St. Joseph, Blackwell
Caplinger, Jerome, St. Andrew, Moore
Coe, James, Holy Family, Lawton
Collier, E. Charles
Conway, James, Immaculate Conception, Marlow
Coyle, William St. John the Baptist, Edmond
Crispo, Anthony, St. Francis Xavier, Enid
Cruz, Joseph M., St. Peter, Guymon
Cumby, Dunn, Corpus Christi, Oklahoma City
Dubey, Joseph, St. Eugene, Weatherford
Duclos, Edward, St. Joseph Old Cathedral, Oklahoma City
Ellison, Roy, St. Mary's, Guthrie
Enos, William, Our Lady's Cathedral, Oklahoma City
Estrada, Francisco, St. Mary, Ponca City
Fahy, Richard, Epiphany of the Lord, Oklahoma City
Fine, Dennis D., St. Joseph, Ada
Fischer, Duane, St. Patrick, Oklahoma City
Forgue, Joseph, St. Francis of Assisi, Oklahoma City
Forsythe, Roy, St. John the Baptist, Edmond
Frazier, Dennis, St. Patrick, Oklahoma City
Gabrish, Patrick, St. Joseph, Norman
Goldsworthy, Thomas O.
Gorden, William, St. Charles, Oklahoma City
Guerra, Simon, St. Peter, Guymon
Gulikers, Marti, St. James, Oklahoma City
Hankins, Chuck, St. Eugene, Oklahoma City
Hernandez, Santos, Holy Angels, Oklahoma City
Heskamp, Robert, Epiphany of the Lord, Oklahoma City
Hollier, Bernie, Corpus Christi, Oklahoma City
Hough, William A., St. Mary, Clinton
Hunt, Lee, St. Monica, Edmond
Jacobson, Byron, St. Mark, Norman
Keene, James, Immaculate Conception Church, Oklahoma City
Kelly, Jeffrey, St. John Nepomuk Church, Yukon
Kenny, Philip, St. Peter, Woodward
King, William, St. Charles, Oklahoma City
LaChance, Raymond, St. Paul, Del City
Le, Anthony, Our Lady's Cathedral, Oklahoma City
Leal, George, Sacred Heart Church, Oklahoma City
LeWand, Mark, (Retired)
Lewis, Paul, Our Lady's Cathedral, Oklahoma City
Lewis, Steve, St. Joseph, Norman
Lombardi, Daniel, St. John Nepomuk, Yukon
Lopez, Alfonso, Saint Charles Borromeo, Oklahoma City
Maldonado, Pedro, St. Mary, Clinton
McKaskle, Sherman, Queen of All Saints, Sayre
Means, Gary, St. Cornelius, Cherokee
Mejstrik, Norman, St. Philip Neri, Midwest City
Menz, Lloyd, St. Joseph, Union City
Mobley, Eulis, Prince of Peace, Altus
Montedoro, Richard, St. Joseph, Norman
Nguyen, Kha, St. Andrew Dung Lac, Oklahoma City
Nguyen, Manh San, Chap., Oklahoma County Jail
Nguyen, Ty V., St. Andrew Dung Lac, Oklahoma City
Nieto, Lucio, (Retired)
Ninh, Sang, Our Lady's Cathedral, Oklahoma City
O'Loughlin, Bernard, (Retired)
Ontiveros, Santiago, St. Peter, Woodward
Ortiz, Jose, Our Lady of Victory, Purcell
Painter, Richard, St. Philip, Midwest City
Peterson, Gary, St. John the Baptist, Edmond
Phan, Thomas, St. Charles, Oklahoma City
Pigott, John, St. Thomas More, Norman
Radosevich, Michael, St. Joseph, Ada
Rakosky, Gerald St. Monica, Edmond
Randolph, Alejandro, St. Eugene, Oklahoma City
Rice, Terrence R.
Robinson, Richard, St. Mary, Ponca City
Romaka, Michael J.
Schrupp, David, St. Benedict, Shawnee
Schwarz, Max, Holy Trinity, Okarche
Simpson, Forrest, St. Patrick, Oklahoma City
Smith, James, Christ the King, Oklahoma City
Smits, Robert, St. Patrick, Anadarko
Sousa, Lawrence, St. Joseph, Norman
Teague, John, St. John Nepomuk, Yukon
Thurman, William T.
Vance, Herbert Reeves, Chap., Oklahoma Medical Complex, Oklahoma City
Walker, Rod, Holy Cross, Madill
Wallace, Wenum Ray, Prince of Peace, Altus
Warnke, Jim E., St. Matthew, Elk City
Warren, John, Our Lady of Victory Church, Purcell
Washko, Richard, (Retired)
Watford, Angus, St. Andrew, Moore
Willard, Jeff, St. Joseph, Norman
Wooden, Rusty, Our Lady of Sorrows, Chandler
Young, James G., St. Philip Neri, Midwest City

INSTITUTIONS LOCATED IN THE ARCHDIOCESE

[A] COLLEGES AND UNIVERSITIES

SHAWNEE. *St. Gregory's University* (Coed); Liberal Arts and Sciences, 1900 W. MacArthur Dr., 74804. Tel: 405-878-5100; Fax: 405-878-5198. Email: president@stgregorys.edu. Web: www.stgregorys.edu. Rt. Rev. Lawrence R. Stasyszen, O.S.B., S.T.D., Chancellor; Ron Faulk, Ph.D., Interim Provost; Greg Main, Pres. Priests 3; Brothers 3; Sisters 1; Lay Teachers 25; Total Staff 93; Students 734.

[B] HIGH SCHOOLS, ARCHDIOCESAN

OKLAHOMA CITY. *Bishop McGuinness Catholic High School* (1950) (Coed), 801 N.W. 50th St., 73118. Tel: 405-842-6638; Fax: 405-858-9550; 405-858-9550 (Prin. Office). Email: development@bmchs.org. Web: bmchs.org. Mr. David Morton, Pres. & Prin.; Rev. Daniel Letourneau; Ms. Katherine Marquis, Librarian. Priest/Chaplain 1; Sisters 1; Lay Teachers 66; Students 722; Total Staff 92.

[C] HIGH SCHOOLS, PRIVATE

OKLAHOMA CITY. *Mount St. Mary High School* (1903) (Coed), 2801 S. Shartel Ave., 73109. Tel: 405-631-8865; Fax: 405-631-9209. Email: themount@mountstmary.org. Web: mountstmary.org. Rev. Billy Lewis, Chap.; Mrs. Talita DeNegri, Prin.; Mr. Brian Boeckman, Chm., Rel. Studies Dept.; Mrs. Geraldine Adams, Librarian. Sisters of Mercy of the Americas, Archdiocese of Oklahoma City. Priests 1; Lay Teachers 36; Students 377.

[D] ELEMENTARY SCHOOLS, PRIVATE

OKLAHOMA CITY. *Good Shepherd Catholic School aka Good Shepherd Catholic School at Mercy* 13404 N. Meridian, 73120. Tel: 405-721-4202; Fax: 405-709-2811. Sr. Catherine Powers, C.N.D., Supt., Schools; Dr. Donna Kearns, Ed.D., Prin. Lay Teachers 3; Students 5; PreK Students 3; Elem Students 2; Total Staff 10.

Villa Teresa (1933) (Grades PreK-4), 1216 Classen Dr., 73103. Tel: 405-232-4286; Fax: 405-552-2658. Email: principal@villateresaschool.com. Web: villateresaschool.com. Sisters Veronica Higgins, Prin.; Joseph Marie Gibbons, Librarian. Carmelite Sisters of St. Therese of the Infant Jesus. Sisters 5; Lay Teachers 19; Total Staff 30; Students 239.

NORMAN. *All Saints Catholic School, Inc.* (1996) 4001 36th Ave., N.W., 73072. Tel: 405-447-4600; Fax: 405-447-7227. Email: lschmitt@ascsn.org. Web: www.ascsn.org. Leslie Schmitt, Prin.; Felicia Kizer, Librarian. Lay Teachers 29; Students 455; PreK Students 43; Total Staff 40.

[E] GENERAL HOSPITALS

OKLAHOMA CITY. *St. Anthony Hospital*, 1000 N. Lee St., P.O. Box 205, 73101. Tel: 405-272-7000; Fax: 405-272-7075. Web: www.saintsok.com. Joe Hodges, Pres.; Rev. George Parackal, Chap. A member of SSM Health Care. Bed Capacity 601; Total Staff 2,730; Patients Assisted Annually 141,223.

Bone and Joint Hospital at St. Anthony, 1111 N. Dewey, P.O. Box 205, 73101. Tel: 405-979-8000; Fax: 405-979-8001. Chad Aduddell, Pres. A member of SSM Health Care. Bed Capacity 85; Total Staff 205; Patients Assisted Annually 7,167.

Saint Anthony South Hospital, P.O. Box 205, 73101. Tel: 405-713-5751; Fax: 405-680-4149. Joe Hodges, Pres. A member of SSM Health Care. Bed Capacity 124.

Mercy Health Center Owned and operated by Sisters of Mercy Health System, St. Louis., 4300 W. Memorial Rd., 73120. Tel: 405-755-1515; Fax: 405-752-3811. Email: thomas.edelstein@mercy.net. Web: www.mhso.okla.smhs.com. Di Smalley, Pres. & CEO; Paul Lewis, Dir. Pastoral Svcs. Sisters 2; Bed Capacity 381; Total Staff 3,088; Patients Assisted Annually 19,500.

ARDMORE. *Mercy Memorial Health Center, Inc. (MMHC)*, 1011 14th Ave., N.W., 73401. Tel: 580-220-6611; Fax: 580-220-6580. Email: mindy.burdick@mercy.net. Web: www.mercyok.net. Ms. Mindy Burdick, Pres. Total Staff 873; Bed Capacity 190; Patients Assisted Annually 145,656.

EL RENO. *Mercy El Reno Hospital Corporation*, 2115 Parkview Dr., 73036. Tel: 405-262-2640; Fax: 405-422-2521. Jon Vitiello, CFO; Cindy Carmichael, Contact Person. Total Beds 48; Total Staff 140; Total Assisted 10,000.

GUTHRIE. *Mercy Hospital Logan County, Inc.*, 200 S. Academy, 73044.

HEALDTON. *Healdton Mercy Hospital Corporation*, 3462 Hospital Rd., 73438. Tel: 580-229-0701; Fax: 580-229-0691. Cindy Carmichael, Vice Pres. Rural Devel. Tel: 405-752-3724; Jon Vitiello, CFO. Total Beds 22; Total Staff 41; Total Assisted 7,500.

TISHOMINGO. *Mercy Tishomingo Hospital Corporation*, 1000 S. Byrd St., 73460.

[F] SPECIAL CARE FACILITIES

OKLAHOMA CITY. *St. Ann's Home, Inc.* (1950) 9400 St. Ann's Dr., 73162. Tel: 405-728-7888; Fax: 405-728-1302. Mrs. Dorothy Joyce, Exec. Dir. Sisters 3; Total Staff 115; Bed Capacity 120; Total Assisted 110; Priests 2.

[G] ECUMENICAL CENTERS

OKLAHOMA CITY. *Catholic Pastoral Center*, 7501 Northwest Expwy., 73132. Tel: 405-721-5651; Fax: 405-721-5210. Email: tmaxwell@catharchdioceseokc.org. Web: www.catharchdioceseokc.org. Mr. Thomas Maxwell, Dir.; Sheila Morgan, Events Coord. Used for Archdiocesan Chancery; ecumenical activities; retreat-meeting center for ecumenical and nonprofit organizations; and retired priests' residence.

[H] HOMES FOR THE AGED

OKLAHOMA CITY. *Saint Ann Retirement Center, Inc.*, 7501 W. Britton Rd., 73132. Tel: 405-721-0747; Fax: 405-721-0492. Email: djohnson@catharchdioceseokc.org. Mr. David J. Johnson, Business Mgr. Total Assisted 50; Total Staff 60; Total Independent 120.

Trinity Gardens Apartments, 1501 N. Classen Blvd., 73106. Tel: 405-523-3000; Fax: 405-523-3030. Email: toconnor@catholiccharitiesok.org. Mr. Timothy O'Connor, Contact Person. 58 low income apartments for senior citizens. Affordable Housing Units 58; Total Assisted Annually 64; Total Staff 1.

Catholic Charities, 3825 N.W. 19th St., 73107. Tel: 405-523-3000; Fax: 405-523-3030. Residents 67.

Villa Isenbart, Inc. (1970) c/o Catholic Charities, 1501 Classen Blvd., 73106. Tel: 405-523-3000; Fax: 405-523-3030. Email: toconnor@catholiccharitiesok.org. 40 Apartment Residences for Low-Income Elderly. Apartments (Low-Income) 40; Total Assisted Annually 46; Total Staff 1.

3801 N.W. 19th St., 73107. Tel: 405-947-4143; Fax: 405-947-4199. Mr. Timothy O'Connor, Dir. Residents 41.

EL RENO. *Saint Katharine Drexel Retirement Center, Inc.*, 301 W. Wade, 73036. Tel: 405-262-2920 (Legal Counsel); Fax: 405-295-1950. Email: skdblm@gmail.com. Brenda Miller, Exec. Dir. Bed Capacity 54; Total Assisted Annually 50; Total Staff 25; Apartments 49.

PONCA CITY. *St. Mary's Housing Foundation*, P.O. Box 1330, 74602. Tel: 580-765-7794; Fax: 580-765-1327. Email: stmarysponcacity@sbcglobal.net. 408 S. 8th St., 74601. Rev. Kevin J. Ratterman, Pres. Senior Citizens Residences 6.

Via Christi Village Ponca City, Inc. (1985) (Formerly The Retirement Community Devel. Corp.); Sisters of St. Joseph/Sisters of the Sorrowful Mother of Broken Arrow, OK and Congregation of St. Joseph., 1601 Academy Rd., 74604. Tel: 580-762-0927; Fax: 580-762-0933. Web: www.viachristi.org/villages. Karen McConnell, CEO. Continuum of care for the aged. Total Staff 201; Residents 150; Total Assisted 170.

[I] MONASTERIES AND RESIDENCES OF PRIESTS AND BROTHERS

OKLAHOMA CITY. *Monastery of Our Lady of Mount Carmel and Little Flower*, 1125 S. Walker Ave., 73109. Tel: 405-235-2037; Fax: 405-235-7035. Order of Discalced Carmelites (Oklahoma Province)., Little Flower Clinic: Free medical service for the poor. Total Assisted Annually 1,800.

SHAWNEE. *St. Gregory's Abbey* (1875) Order of St. Benedict, including University, Novitiate, and Mabee-Gerrer Museum of Art., 1900 W. MacArthur Dr., 74804. Tel: 405-878-5491; Fax: 405-878-5189. Email: abbotlawrence@stgregorys.edu. Web: www.monksok.org. Rt. Revs. Lawrence R. Stasyszen, O.S.B., S.T.D., Abbot & University Chancellor; Martin Lugo, O.S.B., Novice Master & Prior; Adrian R. Vorderlandwehr, O.S.B., CPA, Business Mgr; Very Rev. Louis Vanderley, O.S.B.; Revs. Nicholas K. Ast, O.S.B., Univ.Vice Pres. & Chap.; Matthew J. Brown, O.S.B.; Charles J. Buckley, O.S.B., Ph.D., Vocation Dir.; Boniface T. Copelin, O.S.B., Formation Dir.; Brendan Helbing, O.S.B.; Maurus P. Jaeb, O.S.B.; Basil Keenan, O.S.B.; Manuel Magallanes, O.S.B.; Eugene C. Marshall, O.S.B.; Rt. Rev. Charles Massoth, O.S.B., Guest Master (Retired); Rev. Patrick McCool, O.S.B.; Bro. Andrew C. Raple, O.S.B.; Revs. Joachim Spexarth, O.S.B., Subprior; Paul J. Zahler, O.S.B., Ph.D.; Bros. Benet S. Exton, O.S.B.; Isidore D. Harden, O.S.B.; George A. Hubl, O.S.B.; Kevin E. McGuire, O.S.B.; Dominic J. Ramirez, O.S.B.; Simeon Z. Spitz, O.S.B.; Damian S. Whalen, O.S.B., Ph.D.

Benedictine Fathers of Sacred Heart Mission, Inc. Priests 17; Brothers 7. *Saint Gregory's Abbey Benefit Trust*, 1900 W. MacArthur St., 74804-2404. Tel: 405-878-5463; Fax: 405-878-5400. Rt. Rev. Lawrence R. Stasyszen, O.S.B., S.T.D., Trustee & Contact Person.

[J] CONVENTS AND RESIDENCES FOR SISTERS

OKLAHOMA CITY. *Carmelite Sisters of St. Therese of the Infant Jesus Motherhouse* (1917) 1300 Classen Dr., 73103. Tel: 405-232-7926; Fax: 405-236-3170. Email: pmillerok@hotmail.com. Web: www.oksister.com. Sr. Patricia Ann Miller, Gen. Supr. Sisters in Community 18; Resident Sisters 13.

Villa Teresa School

Medical Sisters of St. Joseph, Little Flower Province, c/o 7217 N.W. 121st. St., 73162. Tel: 405-721-4390; Fax: 405-721-4390. Email: oklittleflower@att.net. Sr. Rosemilla Michael, Supr. Sisters 3.

Sisters of Mercy of the Americas (1831) Retirement Center for Sisters of Mercy of Oklahoma., Mercy Health Center Convent, 4300 W. Memorial Rd., 73120. Tel: 405-755-1515; Fax: 405-936-5498. Email: rpower@mercysc.org. Web: www.mercyok.com. Sr. M. Rose Elizabeth Power, R.S.M., Coord. Sisters 14; Staff 20.

PIEDMONT. *Carmel of St. Joseph* (1939) 20,000 N. County Line Rd., 73078-9123. Tel: 405-348-3947; Fax: 405-348-4916. Email: dcn@okcarmel.org. Web: www.okcarmel.org. Sr. Donna Ross, O.C.D., Prioress. Discalced Carmelite Nuns (Cloistered). Professed Sisters 9; Novices 1.

Sisters of Benedict, 728 Richland Rd., S.W., 73078-9324. Tel: 405-373-4565; Fax: 405-373-3392. Email: redplains@mountosb.org. Web: www.mountosb.org/redplains. Sr. Anne Shepard, O.S.B., Prioress. Professed Sisters 7.

[K] CAMPUS MINISTRY & NEWMAN CENTERS

NORMAN. *Campus Ministry for the Archdiocese of Oklahoma City* 100 E. Stinson, 73072. Tel: 405-321-0990; Fax: 405-321-0964. Web: www.stm-ou.org/students. Rev. James A. Goins, Pastor & Dir.; Mrs. K. Erin Snow, J.D., Campus Min. Tel: 405-321-0990, Ext. 205.

University of Oklahoma 100 E. Stinson, 73072. Tel: 405-321-0990; Fax: 405-321-0964. Web: www.stm-ou.org/students. Mrs. K. Erin Snow, J.D., Campus Min.

East Central State University P.O. Box 1585, Ada, 74820. Tel: 580-332-4811; Fax: 580-436-1226. Rev. Russell L. Hewes.

Northwestern Oklahoma State College 627 12th St., Alva, 73717. Tel: 580-327-0339; Fax: 580-327-0710. Rev. Andrew Wickersham.

University of Science & Arts of Oklahoma P.O. Box 748, Chickasha, 73023. Tel: 405-224-7513; Fax: 405-224-4434. Rev. Shane L. Tharp.

University of Central Oklahoma 321 E. Clegern, Edmond, 73034. Tel: 405-340-6300; Fax: 405-340-5715. Rev. John Metzinger.

Oklahoma Panhandle State University P.O. Box 277, Goodwell, 73942. Tel: 580-338-7212; Fax: 580-338-5584. Rev. Michael Wheelahan.

Cameron University P.O. Box 7948, Lawton, 73506. Tel: 580-536-6351. Rev. Philip M. Seeton.

Northern Oklahoma College P.O. Box 525, Tonkawa, 74653. Tel: 580-628-2416; Fax: 580-531-2607. Rev. Larok Martin.

Southwestern Oklahoma State University P.O. Box 407, Weatherford, 73096. Tel: 580-772-3209; Fax: 580-772-3541. Rev. Christopher Tran; Deacon Joe Dubey.

[L] MISCELLANEOUS

OKLAHOMA CITY. *St. Anthony Hospital Foundation, Inc., Oklahoma City, Oklahoma* Member of SSM Health Care, P.O. Box 205, 73101. 826 N.W. 11, 73106. Tel: 405-272-7070; Fax: 405-270-7607. Email: saintsfoundation@ssmhc.com. Web: www.givetosaints.com. Sherry Rhodes, Pres.

Bishop McGuinness Catholic High School Building Trust (2003) 9211 Lake Hefner Pkwy. Ste. 200, 73120. Tel: 405-936-0990; Fax: 405-248-4111. Email: dgeason@telepath.com. Douglas G. Eason, Contact Person.

Catholic Schools Opportunity Scholarship Fund, Inc., 7501 N.W. Expwy., P.O. Box 32180, 73123.

Sister BJ's Pantry, Inc., 1300 Classen Dr., 73103. Tel: 405-837-7068. Sr. Barbara Joseph Foley, C.S.T., Pres. & Contact Person. An apostolate of the Oklahoma Carmelite Sisters of St. Theresa of the Infant Jesus, Oklahoma City, OK.

SSM Health Care of Oklahoma, Inc. (For staff listings please see St. Anthony Hospital located under General Hospitals), 1000 N. Lee, P.O. Box 205, 73101. Tel: 405-272-7000; Fax: 405-272-6477. Joe Hodges, Interim Pres. & CEO.

ARDMORE. *Mercy Memorial Health Center Foundation*, 1011 Fourteenth Ave., N.W., 73401. Tel: 580-220-6712; Fax: 580-220-6170. Email: mindy.burdick@mercy.net. Ms. Mindy Burdick, Pres. & Contact Person; Andre Moore, Exec. Dir.

LAWTON. *Columbia Square, Inc. dba Villanova Apartments* 1501 N. Classen, 73106. Tel: 405-523-3000; 580-248-2550; Fax: 580-248-2550. Email: toconnor@catholiccharities.org. Low Income Apartments for Families 64; Total Assisted 230. 304 W. 4th, 73505. Tel: 405-523-3000; Fax: 405-523-3030. Mr. Tim O'Connor, Pres. Bd. of Dirs.

OKARCHE. *New Leaven Ministries Foundation*, 511 Hunter Dr., P.O. Box 464, 73762. Tel: 405-263-7798. Email: frsamxi@pldi.net. Rev. Marvin F. Leven (Retired).

PIEDMONT. *Red Plains Spirituality Center* Location at Red Plains Monastery, 728 Richland Rd., S.W., 73078-9324. Tel: 405-373-4565; Fax: 405-373-3392. Email: redplains@mountosb.org. Web: www.mountosb.org/redplains. Operated by Benedictine Sisters.

PRAGUE. *National Shrine of the Infant Jesus of Prague, St. Wenceslaus Church*, P.O. Box 488, 74864. Tel: 405-567-3080; Fax: 405-567-0364. 304 Jim Thorpe Blvd., 74864. Tel: 405-567-3404; 405-567-3080; Fax: 405-567-0364; 405-567-3404. Email: shrine_iop@hotmail.com. Novena to the Infant Jesus of Prague takes place the 17th through 25th of each month. Pilgrimages take place on Sunday prior to the 25th of the month.

SHAWNEE. *St. Gregory's University Endowment Foundation*, 1900 W. MacArthur, 74804. Tel: 405-878-5420; Fax: 405-878-5198. Email: fdelehanty@stgregorys.edu. Web: www.stgregorys.edu. Faith Delehanty, Dir. Inst. Advancement.

National Institute on Development Delays, Inc., 1900 W. MacArthur, 74804. Tel: 405-878-5288; Fax: 405-878-5302. Email: frpaul@stgregorys.edu. Web: www.nidd.org. Rev. Paul J. Zahler, O.S.B., Ph.D., Founder/Dir.

Early Developmental Integration Center Tel: 405-878-5289; Fax: 405-878-5302.

C. Harold and Connie Brand Early Child Development Center Tel: 405-878-5289; Fax: 405-878-5302.

Native American Home Start Program formerly Kickapoo Home Start Program Tel: 405-878-5289; Fax: 405-878-5302. Overnight Camp (adults) 30; Child Development Center 45.

Lyle H. Boren Child Development Center Tel: 405-878-5289; Fax: 405-878-5302.

Home Integration, Inc. Tel: 405-878-5289; Fax: 405-878-5302.

St. Michael Foundation, Inc. Tel: 405-878-5289; Fax: 405-878-5302.

RELIGIOUS INSTITUTES OF MEN REPRESENTED IN THE ARCHDIOCESE

For further details refer to the corresponding bracketed number in the Religious Institutes of Men or Women section.

[0200]—*Benedictine Monks*—O.S.B.

[0260]—*Discalced Carmelite Friars* (Oklahoma Prov.)—O.C.D.

[0690]—*Jesuit Fathers* (Missouri Prov.)—S.J.

RELIGIOUS INSTITUTES OF WOMEN REPRESENTED IN THE ARCHDIOCESE

[0100]—*Adorers of the Blood of Christ*—A.S.C.

[0230]—*Benedictine Sisters of Pontifical Jurisdiction*—O.S.B.

[0380]—*Carmelite Sisters of St. Therese of the Infant Jesus*—C.S.T.

[0390]—*Congregation of Missionary Carmelites of St. Therese* (Houston, TX)—C.M.S.T.

[0895]—*Daughters of Our Lady of the Holy Rosary* (New Orleans, LA)—F.M.S.R.

[0420]—*Discalced Carmelite Nuns*—O.C.D.

[]—*Dominican Congregation of Our Lady of the Rosary Lang Son* (Lang Son, Vietnam)—O.P.

[1070-13]—*Dominican Sisters* (Adrian, MI)—O.P.

[1070-06]—*Dominican Sisters* (Newburgh, NY)—O.P.

[1070-03]—*Dominican Sisters* (Sinsinawa, WI)—O.P.

[1070]—*Dominican Sisters of Hope* (Ossining, NY)—O.P.

[1115]—*Dominican Sisters of Peace*—O.P.

[1900]—*Eucharistic Missionaries of St. Theresa* (Mexico)—M.E.S.T.

[1415]—*Franciscan Sisters of Mary*—F.S.M.

[]—*Hermanas Catequistas Guadalupanas*—H.C.G.

[2500]—*Medical Sisters of St. Joseph*—M.S.J.

[1680]—*School Sisters of St. Francis*—S.S.S.F.

[2980]—*Sisters of Congregation de Notre Dame*—C.N.D.

[2575]—*Sisters of Mercy of the Americas*—R.S.M.

[3360]—*Sisters of Providence of St. Mary-of-the-Woods*—S.P.

[3840]—*Sisters of St. Joseph of Carondelet*—C.S.J.

[2150]—*Sisters, Servants of the Immaculate Heart of Mary*—I.H.M.

CEMETERIES

OKLAHOMA CITY. *Resurrection Memorial Cemetery, Inc.*, 7500 W. Britton Rd., 73132. Tel: 405-721-4191; Fax: 405-721-3238. Email: cristford@aol.com. Christina T. Ford, Dir.

NECROLOGY

† Lafferty, David M., Okarche, OK Holy Trinity.—Died Feb. 2, 2011

† Larkin, Kirk S., Lawton, OK Holy Family.—Died April 29, 2011

† O'Toole, Thomas, Ardmore, OK St. Mary.—Died Jan. 12, 2011

Archdiocese of Omaha

(Archidioecesis Omahensis)

Most Reverend

GEORGE J. LUCAS

Archbishop of Omaha; ordained on May 24, 1975; appointed Bishop of the Diocese of Springfield in Illinois on October 19, 1999; ordained a Bishop and installed December 14, 1999; appointed Archbishop of Omaha June 3, 2009; installed July 22, 2009. *Chancery Office: 100 N. 62nd St., Omaha, NE 68132-2795.*

Most Reverend

ELDEN FRANCIS CURTISS

Retired Archbishop of Omaha; ordained May 24, 1958; appointed Bishop of Helena March 4, 1976; consecrated April 28, 1976; appointed Archbishop of Omaha May 4, 1993; installed June 25, 1993; retired June 3, 2009. *Chancery Office: 100 N. 62nd St., Omaha, NE 68132-2795.*

Chancery Office: 100 N. 62nd St., Omaha, NE 68132-2795. Tel: 402-558-3100; Fax: 402-558-3026.

Web: www.archomaha.org

Email: archbishop@archomaha.org

ESTABLISHED AS A VICARIATE-APOSTOLIC JANUARY 6, 1857.

Square Miles 14,051.

Erected a Diocese October 2, 1885; Archdiocese August 7, 1945.

Comprises the Counties of Boyd, Holt, Merrick, Nance, Boone, Antelope, Knox, Pierce, Madison, Platte, Colfax, Stanton, Wayne, Cedar, Dixon, Dakota, Thurston, Cuming, Dodge, Burt, Washington, Douglas and Sarpy in the State of Nebraska.

For legal titles of parishes and archdiocesan institutions, consult the Chancery Office.

STATISTICAL OVERVIEW

Personnel	
Archbishops	1
Retired Archbishops	1
Retired Bishops	1
Abbots	1
Retired Abbots	2
Priests: Diocesan Active in Diocese	132
Priests: Diocesan Active Outside Diocese	8
Priests: Retired, Sick or Absent	45
Number of Diocesan Priests	185
Religious Priests in Diocese	78
Total Priests in Diocese	263
Extern Priests in Diocese	9
Ordinations:	
Diocesan Priests	4
Religious Priests	1
Transitional Deacons	2
Permanent Deacons	14
Permanent Deacons in Diocese	237
Total Brothers	20
Total Sisters	266
Parishes	
Parishes	132
With Resident Pastor:	
Resident Diocesan Priests	93
Resident Religious Priests	2
Without Resident Pastor:	
Administered by Priests	35
Administered by Deacons	1
Administered by Lay People	1
Missions	15
Professional Ministry Personnel:	
Sisters	12
Lay Ministers	101
Welfare	
Catholic Hospitals	3
Total Assisted	190,489
Homes for the Aged	3
Total Assisted	291
Day Care Centers	16
Total Assisted	1,286
Specialized Homes	9
Total Assisted	1,839
Special Centers for Social Services	8
Total Assisted	83,319
Educational	
Diocesan Students in Other Seminaries	28
Total Seminarians	28
Colleges and Universities	2
Total Students	8,793
High Schools, Diocesan and Parish	12
Total Students	2,978
High Schools, Private	5
Total Students	2,608
Elementary Schools, Diocesan and Parish	54
Total Students	13,899
Elementary Schools, Private	1
Total Students	62
Non-residential Schools for the Disabled	1
Total Students	58
Catechesis/Religious Education:	
High School Students	2,448
Elementary Students	14,786
Total Students under Catholic Instruction	45,660
Teachers in the Diocese:	
Priests	28
Scholastics	3
Brothers	2
Sisters	11
Lay Teachers	1,400
Vital Statistics	
Receptions into the Church:	
Infant Baptism Totals	4,100
Minor Baptism Totals	250
Adult Baptism Totals	202
Received into Full Communion	484
First Communions	4,366
Confirmations	3,645
Marriages:	
Catholic	813
Interfaith	445
Total Marriages	1,258
Deaths	1,844
Total Catholic Population	231,695
Total Population	937,293

Former Bishops—Rt. Revs. JAMES O'GORMAN, O.C.S.O., D.D., ord. Dec. 21, 1843; Vicar-Apostolic and Titular Bishop of Raphanea; cons. May 8, 1859; died July 4, 1874; JAMES O'CONNOR, D.D., ord. March 25, 1848; Vicar-Apostolic and Titular Bishop of Dibona; cons. Aug. 20, 1876; appt. first Bishop of Omaha, Oct. 2, 1885; died May 27, 1890; RICHARD SCANNELL, D.D., ord. Feb. 26, 1871; cons. Bishop of Concordia, Nov. 30, 1887; transferred to Omaha, Jan. 30, 1891; died Jan. 8, 1916; Most Revs. JEREMIAH J. HARTY, D.D., ord. April 28, 1878; cons. Archbishop of Manila, P.I., Aug. 15, 1903; transferred to Omaha, May 16, 1916; died Oct. 29, 1927; FRANCIS J. L. BECKMAN, S.T.D., D.D. Bishop of Lincoln and Apostolic Administrator of Omaha from June 1, 1926 to July 4, 1928; JOSEPH FRANCIS RUMMEL, D.D., Bishop of Omaha; appt. March 30, 1928; cons. May 29, 1928; installed July 4, 1928; transferred to the Archdiocese of New Orleans, March 9, 1935; died Nov. 8, 1964; JAMES H. RYAN, D.D., appt. Titular Bishop of Modra, Aug. 15, 1933; cons. Oct. 25, 1933; transferred to See of Omaha, Aug. 3, 1935; installed Nov. 21, 1935; elevated to Archepiscopal dignity, Aug. 7, 1945; died Nov. 23, 1947; GERALD T. BERGAN, D.D., ord. Oct. 28, 1915; appt. Bishop of Des Moines, March 24, 1934; cons. June 13, 1934; promoted to Omaha, Feb. 7, 1948; retired June 18, 1969; made Titular Archbishop of Tacarata; died July 12, 1972; DANIEL E. SHEEHAN, D.D., J.C.D., ord. May 23, 1942; appt. Titular Bishop of Capsu and Auxiliary, Jan. 4, 1964; cons. March 19, 1964; succeeded to See, June 11, 1969; retired May 14, 1992; died Oct. 24, 2000; ELDEN FRANCIS CURTISS, ord. May 24, 1958; appt. Bishop of Helena March 4, 1976; cons. April 28, 1976; appt. Archbishop of Omaha May 4, 1993; installed June 25, 1993; retired June 3, 2009.

Vicar General—Very Rev. MICHAEL W. GREWE, V.G.

Chancery Office—100 N. 62nd St., Omaha, 68132-2795. Tel: 402-558-3100; Fax: 402-558-3026. Email: archbishop@archomaha.org. Office Hours: Mon.-Fri. 8:30-5.

Chancellor—Deacon TIMOTHY F. MCNEIL, J.C.L.

Moderator of the Curia and Vicar for Clergy—Rev. JOSEPH C. TAPHORN, J.C.L.

Finance Director (canonical)—Mr. HERBERT L. KARRER.

Metropolitan Tribunal—100 N. 62nd St., Omaha, 68132.

Judicial Vicar—Rev. JOSEPH C. TAPHORN, J.C.L.

Judges—Rev. RYAN P. LEWIS, J.C.L., S.T.L.; Deacons ROBERT J. OVERKAMP, J.C.L.; TIMOTHY F. MCNEIL, J.C.L.

Promoter of Justice—Rev. R. MICHAEL FITZPATRICK, J.C.L., S.T.L.

Defenders of the Bond—Revs. R. MICHAEL FITZPATRICK, J.C.L., S.T.L.; MICHAEL F. GUTGSELL, J.C.L.; Deacon TIMOTHY F. MCNEIL, J.C.L.

Appeal Court— The Tribunal of the Archdiocese of St. Louis, MO is the Appeal Court for Omaha.

Consultors—Very Rev. MICHAEL W. GREWE, V.G.; Revs. THOMAS E. BAUWENS; R. MICHAEL FITZPATRICK, J.C.L., S.T.L.; NORMAN F. HUNKE; DANIEL L. WITTROCK; MICHAEL F. GUTGSELL, J.C.L.

Deans—Revs. DAMIEN COOK, U.S.E.; ALFRED J. SALANITRO, U.S.C.; GERALD P. MELCHIOR, J.C.L., U.N.E.; HAROLD J. BUSE, U.W.C.; DAMIAN J. ZUERLEIN, Sub. S.; FRANKLIN A. DVORAK, Sub. N.; THOMAS W. WEISBECKER, R.S.W.; ERIC S. OLSEN, R.N.C.; LEO A. RIGATUSO, R.S.E.; ROSS C. BURKHALTER, R.C.; WALTER L. NOLTE, R.N.W.; DAVID M. KORTH, R.N.E.

Finance Council—Most Rev. GEORGE J. LUCAS; Rev. R. MICHAEL FITZPATRICK, J.C.L., S.T.L.; Very Rev. MICHAEL W. GREWE, V.G.; Mr. HERBERT L. KARRER; PAT LACY; Rev. JOSEPH C. TAPHORN, J.C.L.; Mr. RICK WITT; Rev. DAMIAN J. ZUERLEIN; Mr. HERMAN D. WEIST.

Archdiocesan Offices and Directors

Cemeteries—Very Rev. MICHAEL W. GREWE, V.G., Dir.

Censor Librorum—Rev. MATTHEW J. GUTOWSKI.

Omaha Priests Retirement Plan and Trust, The—Most Rev. GEORGE J. LUCAS; Rev. Msgrs. JAMES R. CAIN, J.C.D. (Retired); FRANCIS E. KUBART (Retired); Mr. JAMES KINEEN; Mr. JOSEPH BEVERIDGE; Mr. HERBERT L. KARRER.

Ecumenical Officer—Rev. RYAN P. LEWIS, J.C.L., S.T.L.

Worship Office—Bro. WILLIAM WOEGER, F.S.C., Dir.

Council of Catholic Women, Archdiocesan—Rev. JAMES V. KRAMPER, Archdiocesan Moderator, Mailing Address: P.O. Box 37, Ewing, 68735. Tel: 402-626-7605.

Diaconate Program—Deacon JAMES KEATING, Ph.D., Dir., 100 N. 62nd St., Omaha, 68132. Tel: 402-558-3100.

Catholic Schools Office—Rev. Msgr. JAMES E. GILG, Supt. Schools, Mercy Hall, 3300 N. 60th St., Omaha, 68104. Tel: 402-557-5600.

Office of Evangelization & Catechesis—Mercy Hall, 3300 N. 60th St., Omaha, 68104. WILLIAM BECKMAN, Dir. Tel: 402-557-5610.

Administrative Services Office—Mr. HERBERT L. KARRER, Dir., 100 N. 62nd St., Omaha, 68132. Tel: 402-558-3100; Fax: 402-561-1210.

Information Technology Office—Mr. SHAWN M. BAAS, Dir., Nazareth Hall, 3300 N. 60th St., Omaha, 68104. Tel: 402-557-5500; Fax: 402-827-3793.

Stewardship & Development Office—SHANNAN BROMMER, Dir., Mercy Hall, 3300 N. 60th St., Omaha, 68104. Tel: 402-557-5650; Fax: 402-551-3426.

Family Life Office—Mrs. VALERIE CONZETT, D.Min., L.P.C., Dir., Nazareth Hall, 3300 N. 60th St., Omaha, 68104. Tel: 402-551-9003; 888-800-8352; Fax: 402-551-3050. Email: vhconzett@archomaha.org. Areas of Ministry: Aging, Black Catholics, Disabilities, Hispanic Marriage and Family Life, Marriage and Family Life, Media Center, Natural Family Planning, Respect Life Apostolate, & Rural Life.

Newspaper— "The Catholic Voice" Deacon RANDY GROSSE, Gen. Mgr., 6060 N.W. Radial Hwy., P.O. Box 4010, Omaha, 68104. Tel: 402-558-6611; Fax: 402-558-6614.

Office of Missions & Justice—OMAR GUTIERREZ, Mgr., 100 N. 62nd St., Omaha, 68132. Tel: 402-558-3100; Fax: 402-551-4212.

Propagation of the Faith—OMAR GUTIERREZ, Mgr., 100 N. 62nd St., Omaha, 68132. Tel: 402-558-3100; Fax: 402-551-4212.

Priests' Council—

Officers—Revs. MICHAEL F. GUTGSELL, J.C.L., Pres.; GARY L. OSTRANDER, Vice Pres.; WALTER L. NOLTE, Sec.; DAMIAN J. ZUERLEIN, Treas.

Age Groups—Rev. Msgr. JAMES E. GILG; Revs. GARY L. OSTRANDER; DAMIAN J. ZUERLEIN; FRANK J. BAUMERT; DANIEL L. WITTROCK; JOHN L. PIETRAMALE; MARK T. BERAN; JEFFREY J. MOLLNER.

Religious Orders—Revs. MICHAEL DODD, S.S.C.; DANIEL LENZ, O.S.B.; ROBERT F. O'CONNOR, S.J.

Deans—Revs. ALFRED J. SALANITRO, (USC); DAMIEN COOK, (USE); GERALD P. MELCHIOR, J.C.L., (UNE); THOMAS W. WEISBECKER, (RSW); ERIC S. OLSEN, (RNC); WALTER L. NOLTE, (RNW); LEO A. RIGATUSO, (RSE); DAVID M. KORTH, (RNE); ROSS C. BURKHALTER, (RC); DAMIAN J. ZUERLEIN, (Sub. S.); FRANKLIN A. DVORAK, (Sub.N.); HAROLD J. BUSE, (UWC).

Archbishop's Appointee—Rev. JOSEPH C. TAPHORN, J.C.L.

Ex Officio (Consultors)—Very Rev. MICHAEL W. GREWE, V.G., Vicar Gen.; Revs. THOMAS E. BAUWENS, Consultor; NORMAN F. HUNKE; DANIEL L. WITTROCK; MICHAEL F. GUTGSELL, J.C.L.; R. MICHAEL FITZPATRICK, J.C.L., S.T.L.

St. Cecilia Institute for Sacred Liturgy, Music and the Arts—Bro. WILLIAM J. WOEGER, F.S.C., Dir., 3900 Webster St., Omaha, 68131. Tel: 402-553-5524; Fax: 402-551-2306.

Omaha. Archdiocesan Deposit and Loan Fund, Inc.—A pool of funds from archdiocesan parishes providing low interest loans for capital improvements and new construction by archdiocesan parishes. This nonprofit religious, charitable and educational corporation, whose president is the Archdiocese of Omaha, is duly constituted under the laws of the State of Nebraska. Mr. LEE KARRER, Finance Dir., 100 N. 62nd St., Omaha, 68132. Tel: 402-558-3100; Fax: 402-561-1210.

Omaha. Archdiocesan Retreat and Conference Centers— Located in renovated Sheehan Center; overnight, day and weekend accommodations for teens, young adults and adult groups, large and small meeting space, chapel and food service area. *St. Joseph's Hall, 3330 N. 60th St., Omaha, 68104.* Tel: 402-558-1442; Fax: 402-551-1482. GARY BOSANEK, Dir.

Servant Minister—Rev. THOMAS A. GREISEN.

Victim Outreach and Prevention—MARY BETH HANUS, Mgr., Mercy Hall, 3300 N. 60th St., Omaha, 68104. Tel: 402-827-3798; 888-808-9055. Email: mbhanus@archomaha.org.

Vocations Office—Rev. PAUL C. HOESING, 100 N. 62nd St., Omaha, 68132. Tel: 402-558-3100; Fax: 402-554-0783. Email: pchoesing@archomaha.org. Web: www.archomaha.org/vocations.

CLERGY, PARISHES, MISSIONS AND PAROCHIAL SCHOOLS

CITY OF OMAHA

(DOUGLAS COUNTY)

1—ST. CECILIA CATHEDRAL (1888) Revs. Michael F. Gutgsell; Mark J. McKercher; Paul L. Vasquez.
Res.: 701 N. 40 St., 68131. Tel: 402-551-2313; Fax: 402-551-2306. Email: stceciliacathedral@stceciliacathedral.org. Web: www.stceciliacathedral.org.
School—Tel: 402-556-6655; Fax: 402-502-3048. Paulette Rourke, Prin. Lay Teachers 22; Students 280.
Catechesis/Religious Program—Students 333.

2—ST. ADALBERT (1919) Rev. John L. Pietramale. In Res., Rev. Carl F. Sodoro.
Res.: 2617 S. 31st St., 68105. Tel: 402-345-1621.
Catechesis/Religious Program—2124 S. 32nd Ave., 68105. Tel: 402-341-5604.

3—ST. AGNES (1889), (Irish—Spanish), Merged with Our Lady of Guadalupe, Omaha to form Our Lady of Guadalupe - St. Agnes Parish, Omaha.

4—ST. ANDREW KIM TAEGON CATHOLIC COMMUNITY Rev. Paul Saewan Oh.
2617 S. 31st St., 68105. Tel: 402-345-1621.
Catechesis/Religious Program—Rosa Hwang Po, D.R.E. Students 12.

5—ST. ANN (1917), (Italian—Hispanic), Closed. For inquiries for parish records contact St. Peter, Omaha.

6—ST. ANTHONY (1907), (Lithuanian), Rev. Frank E. Jindra.
Res.: 5219 S. 36th St., 68107. Tel: 402-731-4578.
Catechesis/Religious Program—

7—ASSUMPTION, B.V.M. (1894), (Czech), Rev. Bernard Starman.
Res.: 5434 S. 22nd St., 68107. Tel: 402-734-4500; Fax: 402-734-4501. Email: assumptionbvmparish@cox.net.
Catechesis/Religious Program—Participate in Our Lady of Guadalupe/St. Agnes program., 4930 S. 23rd St., 68107. Tel: 402-738-8240; Fax: 402-827-6764. Students 3.

8—ST. BENEDICT THE MOOR (1919) Rev. Vitalis E. Anyanike; Deacons Frank Barbour; Ernie Spicer.
Res.: 2423 Grant St., 68111. Tel: 402-348-0631; Fax: 402-342-4451. Email: stbenedictomaha@gmail.com.
Catechesis/Religious Program—Students 62.

9—ST. BERNARD (1905) Rev. Gerald P. Melchior; Deacons Donald Kemp, (Retired); Charles Baughman, (Retired); Edwin Osterhaus; Paul Dreismeier; Timothy F. McNeil.
Res.: 3601 N. 65 St., 68104. Tel: 402-551-0269; Fax: 402-551-2311. Web: stbernardomaha.org.
School—Tel: 402-553-4993; Fax: 402-551-4939. James Daro Jr., Prin. Lay Teachers 13; Students 190.
Catechesis/Religious Program—Tel: 402-556-1679. Jerry Brocky, D.R.E. & Youth Dir. Students 17.

10—BLESSED SACRAMENT (1919) Rev. Craig J. Loecker, Admin.
Res.: 3020 Curtis Ave., 68111. Tel: 402-455-5200; Fax: 402-455-8398. Email: admin@blessedsacrament.ohmcoxmail.com. Web: www.blessedsacramentomaha.org.
Catechesis/Religious Program—Students 7.

11—ST. BRIDGET (1887), (Irish), Rev. Frank A. Partusch.
Res.: 4112 S. 26th St., 68107. Tel: 402-733-8811; Fax: 402-731-9937.
Catechesis/Religious Program—Tel: 402-734-5227. Students 41.

12—CHRIST THE KING (1953) Revs. Steven J. Stillmunks; Douglas C. Hall; Deacon Jon Fulcher. In Res., Rev. Christopher N. Onuoha.
Res.: 654 S. 86th St., 68114. Tel: 402-391-3606; Fax: 402-391-1498. Email: troiac@ctkomaha.org. Web: www.ctkomaha.org.
School—831 S. 88th St., 68114. Tel: 402-391-0977; Fax: 402-391-2418. Email: ctkschool@ctkomaha.org. Lay Teachers 24; Students 344.
Catechesis/Religious Program—Tel: 402-391-3624. Email: warnera@ctkomaha.org. Ann Warner, D.R.E.; Diane Sullivan, Dir., Adult Faith Formation. Students 126.

13—ST. ELIZABETH ANN (1981) Revs. Franklin A. Dvorak; Gerald "Chi" Igboanusi, Asst.; Deacons Jack Finney; Ernie Gencarelli; Martin Crowley; Dennis Connor; John Dagerman; Duane Karmazin; David Klein.
Res.: 5419 N. 114th St., 68164. Tel: 402-493-2186; Fax: 402-493-0630.
See St. James-Seton School, Omaha under Elementary Schools, Interparochial located in the Institution section.
Catechesis/Religious Program—Tel: 402-572-0369; Fax: 402-572-0347. Ms. Jo Kusek, D.R.E. Students 175.

14—ST. FRANCES CABRINI (1856) Rev. James F. Clifton, S.J.
Res.: 1334 S. 9th St., 68108. Tel: 402-342-2464; Fax: 402-342-2470. Email: stfrancescabrini.oma@archomaha.org.
Catechesis/Religious Program—Students 150.
See All Saints Catholic School, Omaha under Elementary Schools, Interparochial located in the Institution section.

15—ST. FRANCIS ASSISI, (Polish—Spanish), Rev. William E. Sanderson.
Res.: 3529 Q St., 68107. Tel: 402-731-0204.
Catechesis/Religious Program—Students 246.

16—HOLY CROSS (1922) Rev. Carl A. Salanitro; Deacons George Elster; Timothy A. Mulcahy.
Res.: 4803 William St., 68106. Tel: 402-553-7500; Fax: 402-553-7735.
School—1502 S. 48th St., 68106. Tel: 402-551-3773; Fax: 402-556-1896. Lay Teachers 20; Students 296.
Catechesis/Religious Program—Students 132.

17—HOLY FAMILY (1876) Deacon Ralph L. Hueser, Admin.
Res.: 1715 Izard St., 68102. Tel: 402-345-1062; Fax: 402-344-8136. Email: holyfamilyomaha@cox.net.
Catechesis/Religious Program—

18—HOLY GHOST (1918) Rev. Gregory Benkowski; Deacons Tom Schulte; Paul Eubanks; Andy Sommer; Al Aulner; Tim Leininger.
Res.: 5219 S. 53rd St., 68117. Tel: 402-731-3176; Fax: 402-738-1409. Email: parishsecretary@holyghostomaha.org. Web: www.holyghostomaha.com.
School—(Grades PreK-8), 5203 Q St., 68117. Tel: 402-731-5161; Fax: 402-731-5174. Mrs. Dana Martin, Prin. Lay Teachers 13; Students 106.
Catechesis/Religious Program— Eleanor Morley, D.R.E. Students 93.

19—HOLY NAME (1917) Rev. Frank J. Baumert.
Res.: 3014 N. 45th St., 68104. Tel: 402-451-6622; Fax: 402-457-6901. Email: holynameparish@holynameomaha.org. Web: www.holynameomaha.org.
School—(Grades PreSchool-8) Tel: 402-451-5403; Fax: 402-453-7950. Sofia Kock, Prin. Lay Teachers 16; Students 163.
Catechesis/Religious Program—Students 28.

20—IMMACULATE CONCEPTION, B.V.M. (1897), (Polish), Revs. John A. Brancich, F.S.S.P.; Terrence Gordon, F.S.S.P., Parochial Vicar.
Res.: 2708 S. 24th St., 68108. Tel: 402-342-1074; Fax: 402-505-7616.
See All Saints Catholic School, Omaha under Elementary Schools, Interparochial located in the Institution section.
Catechesis/Religious Program—Students 72.

21—ST. JAMES (1963) Revs. Richard J. Reiser; Roger Kalscheuer; Deacons Jerry Gau; Stan Kurtz; Pat Lenz; Wayne Young; Richard Hopkins; Randy Grosse.
Res.: 9025 Larimore Ave., 68134. Tel: 402-572-0499; Fax: 402-573-9345. Email: rectory@stjamescatholicchurch.org. Web: www.stjamescatholicchurch.org.
See St. James-Seton School, Omaha under Elementary Schools, Interparochial located in the Institution section.
Catechesis/Religious Program—Tel: 402-572-0369; Fax: 402-572-0347. Ms. Jo Kusek, D.R.E. Students 236.

22—ST. JOAN OF ARC (1955) Rev. Daniel F. Soltys; Deacon Ronald R. Ryan. In Res., Rev. Patrick C. Harrison.
Res.: 3122 S. 74th St., 68124. Tel: 402-393-2005; Fax: 402-398-9438.
School—7430 Hascall St., 68124. Tel: 402-393-2314; Fax: 402-393-4405. Lay Teachers 15; Students 162.
Catechesis/Religious Program—Tel: 402-391-1906; 402-393-2315. Email: religioused@sjaomaha.org. Marilyn Opitz, D.R.E. Students 82.

23—ST. JOHN (1897) Revs. Patrick J. Malone, S.J.; Philip R. Amidon, S.J.
Office: 2500 California Pl., 68178. Tel: 402-280-3031; Fax: 402-280-2465.
Catechesis/Religious Program—Students 10.

24—ST. JOHN VIANNEY (1974) Rev. R. Patrick McCaslin; Deacons Frank Telich; John Kronschnabel; Harold Sawtelle; Joseph Choi; Chuck Luczynski.
Res.: 5801 Oak Hills Dr., 68137. Tel: 402-895-0808. Web: www.sjvomaha.org.
Catechesis/Religious Program—Tel: 402-895-0896; Fax: 402-932-1336. Margaret Iossi. Students 352.

25—ST. JOSEPH (1887), (German—Hispanic), Rev. William D. Bond.
Church: 1723 S. 17th St., 68108. Tel: 402-342-1618; Fax: 402-342-2640.
See All Saints Catholic School, Omaha under Elementary Schools, Interparochial located in the Institution section.
Catechesis/Religious Program—Tel: 402-502-1392. Students 441.

26—ST. LEO (1978) Revs. Harold J. Buse; An Duy Phan; Deacons George Knockenhauer; Jerry Steenson; Ira Miller; Reinold ter Kuille; James Shipman.
1920 N. 102nd St., 68114. Tel: 402-397-0407; Fax: 402-397-2887. Email: dina_turco@stleo.net. Web: www.stleo.net.
See St. Pius X-St. Leo School, Omaha under Elementary Schools, Interparochial located in the Institution section.
Catechesis/Religious Program—Tel: 402-397-0407, Ext. 206. Students 326.

27—ST. MARGARET MARY (1919) Revs. Gregory P. Baxter; James M. Weeder. In Res., Revs. Paul C. Hoesing; Joseph C. Taphorn.
Res.: 6116 Dodge St., 68132-2114. Tel: 402-558-2255; Fax: 402-551-6644. Web: www.smmomaha.org.
School—123 N. 61st St., 68132. Tel: 402-551-6663; Fax: 402-551-5631. Lay Teachers 24; Students 551.
Catechesis/Religious Program—Tel: 402-558-9119; Fax: 402-551-5631. Students 138.

28—ST. MARY (1901) Rev. William E. Sanderson.
Res.: 3529 Q St., 68107. Tel: 402-731-0204; Fax: 402-731-0793.
Catechesis/Religious Program—

29—ST. MARY MAGDALENE (1868) Rev. Msgr. James E. Gilg. In Res., Rev. James F. Schwertley (Retired).
Res.: 109 S. 19th St., 68102. Tel: 402-342-4807; Fax: 402-344-0941.
See All Saints Catholic School, Omaha under Elementary Schools, Interparochial located in the Institution section.

30—MARY OUR QUEEN (1963) Revs. Robert K. English; Marc Lim; Deacons Paul Rooney; Steve Floersch; Robert Hamilton; Thomas H. Frankenfield.
Res.: 3535 S. 119th St., 68144. Tel: 402-333-8662; Fax: 402-333-4504. Email: pastor.maryourqueen.oma@archomaha.org. Web: www.maryourqueenchurch.com.
Church: 3504 S. 118th St., 68144.
School—3405 S. 119th St., 68144. Tel: 402-333-8663; Fax: 402-334-3948. Web: www.mogschool.org. Lay Teachers 32; Students 540.
Catechesis/Religious Program—Tel: 402-333-8231, Ext. 225. Barb Eastridge, D.R.E. Students 233.

31—MOTHER OF PERPETUAL HELP (1975), (Church of the Deaf) Marlene Rowe, Lay Coord. Tel: 402-493-7220.
Res.: 5215 Seward St., 68104. Tel: 402-558-4214.

32—OUR LADY OF FATIMA CATHOLIC COMMUNITY Rev. Nguyen Loi.
Rectory—709 S. 28th St., 68105-1511. Tel: 402-341-4560; Fax: 402-341-6483.

33—OUR LADY OF GUADALUPE (1927), (Spanish), Merged with St. Agnes, Omaha to form Our Lady of Guadalupe - St. Agnes Parish, Omaha.

34—OUR LADY OF GUADALUPE - ST. AGNES PARISH Revs. Jose Mendoza (Venezuela); Neal Wilkinson, S.J.; Deacons Joe Ramirez; Duane Bronk; Luis Valadez; Jesus Herrera; Martin Franco.
4930 S. 23rd St., 68107. In Res., Revs. Bill Bernardo Schmitt; Charles Lintz, S.S.C.
Res.: 2221 "Q" St., 68107. Tel: 402-731-0100.
Res.: 2310 O St., 68107. Tel: 402-731-2196; Fax: 402-827-6764.
Catechesis/Religious Program—Tel: 402-738-8240. Marcella Cervantes, D.R.E. Students 569.
Convent—St. Agnes, 5225 S. 23rd St., 68107. Tel: 402-731-1005.

35—OUR LADY OF LOURDES (1917) Rev. John L. Pietramale; Deacons Frank Hilt; Ken Kalkowski. In Res., Rev. David G. Reeson.
Res.: 2110 S. 32nd Ave., 68105. Tel: 402-346-0900; Fax: 402-344-3315. Email: ourladyoflourdesoma@archomaha.org.
School—2124 S. 32nd Ave., 68105. Tel: 402-341-5604. Web: www.omahaourladyoflourdes.com. William Kelly, Prin. Lay Teachers 19; Students 257.
Catechesis/Religious Program—Students 45.

36—ST. PATRICK (1883) Rev. James M. Buckley.
Res.: 1404 Castelar St., 68108. Tel: 402-341-1305; Fax: 402-342-5510. Email: stpatricko@cox.net. Web: www.stpatrickomaha.com.
See All Saints Catholic School, Omaha under Elementary Schools, Interparochial located in the Institution section.
Catechesis/Religious Program—Students 75.

37—ST. PATRICK (ELKHORN) formerly St. Patrick (1868) [CEM] Revs. Gary L. Ostrander; Rodney T. Adams.
Res.: 20500 W. Maple Rd., P.O. Box 10, 68022. Tel: 402-289-4289; Fax: 402-763-9530. Web: www.stpatselkhorn.org.
School—(Grades PreK-8) Tel: 402-289-5407. Donald Ridder, Prin. Lay Teachers 38; Students 771.

38—ST. PETER (1887) Revs. Damien Cook; S. Anthony Weidner; Deacon John Zak.
Catechesis/Religious Program—Tel: 402-289-4947. Mary F. McMahon, D.R.E. Students 723.
Res.: 709 S. 28th St., 68105-1511. Tel: 402-341-4560; Fax: 402-341-6483. Email: secretary@stpeterchurch.net. Web: www.stpeterchurch.net.
Catechesis/Religious Program—Email: secretary@stpeterchurch.net. Sr. Clara Acosta, D.R.E. Students 370.

39—SS. PETER AND PAUL (1917), (Croatian), Rev. Frank E. Jindra.
Res.: 5912 S. 36th St., 68107. Tel: 402-731-4578; Fax: 402-738-8808.
School—Tel: 402-731-4713; Fax: 402-731-2633. Richard Leimbach, Prin. Lay Teachers 14; Students 146.
Catechesis/Religious Program—Tel: 402-733-3344; Fax: 402-731-2633. Bernice Pfeifer, D.R.E. Students 145.

40—ST. PHILIP NERI (1904) Rev. Craig J. Loecker; Deacon Fred Hendricks.
Res.: 8200 N. 30th St., 68112. Tel: 402-455-1289; Fax: 402-455-8398. Web: www.spnomaha.org.
School—8202 N. 31st St., 68112. Tel: 402-455-8666; Fax: 402-453-3620. Rob Laird, Prin. Lay Teachers 13; Students 174.
Catechesis/Religious Program—Tel: 402-455-2190. Email: reducation@hotmail.com. Veronica LeClair, D.R.E. Students 40.

41—ST. PIUS X (1954) Revs. Michael P. Eckley; Kevin Joyce.
Res.: 6905 Blondo St., 68104. Tel: 402-558-8446; Fax: 402-558-4986. Web: www.stpiusxomaha.org.
See St. Pius X-St. Leo School, Omaha under Elementary Schools, Interparochial located in the Institution section.
Catechesis/Religious Program—Tel: 402-558-1898. Patty Griffith, D.R.E. Students 91.

42—ST. RICHARD (1963) Closed. for inquiries for parish records, please contact Holy Name Parish, Omaha.

43—ST. ROBERT BELLARMINE (1966) Revs. Donald W. Shane; Michael B. Voithofer; Deacons Larry Sampier; Thomas Murphy; Michael Fletcher; Robert Jergovie; Jack Miller; Joseph Laird.
Res.: 11802 Pacific St., 68154. Tel: 402-333-8989; Fax: 402-333-5489. Web: www.stroberts.com.
School—(Grades PreK-8), 11900 Pacific St., 68154. Tel: 402-334-1929; Fax: 402-333-7188. Sandra Suiter, Prin. Lay Teachers 41; Students 596.
Catechesis/Religious Program—Tel: 402-333-1959. Deb Poledna, D.R.E. Students 906.

44—ST. ROSE (1919) Rev. Frank A. Partusch. In Res., Rev. Thomas A. Greisen.
Res.: 4102 S. 13th St., 68107. Tel: 402-733-9327; Fax: 402-731-9937. Email: st.roseomaha@cox.net.
Catechesis/Religious Program—

45—SACRED HEART (1890) Rev. Thomas M. Fangman; Deacons Charles Weskirchen; James Chambers; Richard Crotty.
Res.: 2218 Binney St., 68110. Tel: 402-451-5755; 402-451-7897; Fax: 402-451-1731.
School—Tel: 402-451-5858; Fax: 402-451-7480. Lay Teachers 11; Students 132.
Catechesis/Religious Program—2207 Wirt St., 68110. Students 146.

46—ST. STANISLAUS (1919), (Polish), Rev. R. Michael Fitzpatrick; Deacons Daniel Saniuk; James Staroski.
Res.: 4002 J St., 68107. Tel: 402-731-4152; Fax: 402-731-4389. Email: rfitzk@aol.com.
School—(Grades K-8) Tel: 402-731-0484; Fax: 402-733-4898. Lay Teachers 8; Students 92.
Catechesis/Religious Program—At and with SS. Peter & Paul, Omaha. Students 17.

47—ST. STEPHEN THE MARTYR (1989) Revs. James R. Tiegs; Joseph G. Broudou; Jeffrey J. Mollner; Deacons Ernest Abbott Jr.; Dennis Dethlefs; Paul Tomaso; C. Martin Warwick; Jerry Kozney; Wes Kreun.
Res.: 17456 Orchard Ave., 68135. Tel: 402-895-1811. Email: stephen.martyr@stephen.org. Web: www.stephen.org.
Church: 16701 S St., 68135. Tel: 402-896-9675; Fax: 402-896-1990.
School—Tel: 402-896-0754; Fax: 402-861-4640. Dr. Roseanne Williby, Prin. Lay Teachers 40; Students 857.
Catechesis/Religious Program—Tel: 402-896-5683; Fax: 402-861-4590. Mary Maguire, D.R.E. Students 1,030.

48—ST. THERESE OF THE CHILD JESUS (1918) Revs. Vitalis E. Anyanike; Neal Wilkinson, S.J.
Res.: 2423 Grant St., 68111. Tel: 402-348-0631; Fax: 402-342-4451. Email: stbenedictthemoor.oma@archomaha.org.
Church: 1423 Ogden St., 68110.
Catechesis/Religious Program—Felix Cortes, D.R.E. Students 40.

49—ST. THOMAS MORE (1958) Revs. Ryan P. Lewis; Thomas W. Neitzke, S.J.
Res.: 4804 Grover St., 68106. Tel: 402-556-1456; Fax: 402-556-1395. Web: www.stmomaha.org.
School—3515 S. 48th Ave., 68106. Tel: 402-551-9504; Fax: 402-551-9507. Web: www.stmbengals.org. Lay Teachers 19; Students 200.
Catechesis/Religious Program—Tel: 402-551-9507; Fax: 402-551-9507. Students 42.

50—ST. VINCENT DE PAUL (1991) Revs. Daniel J. Kampschneider; Walter Jong-A-Kiem; Deacons William J. Barnes; Gary J. Hennessey; Richard Jizba; Jay Reilly; Mike Poulin, Pastoral Min.; Wendy Everson, Pastoral Min.; Steve Nespor, Dir. Youth Min.; Kathy Mayer, Dir. Worship; Bob Verkuilen, Dir. Devel.
Mailing Address: 14330 Eagle Run Dr., 68164.
Res.: 14217 Eagle Run Dr., 68164. Tel: 402-496-7988 (Parish Office); 402-498-8425 (Rectory); Fax: 402-496-9933 (Parish Office). Web: www.svdpomaha.org.
School—Tel: 402-492-2111. Web: www.svdp-omaha.org. Dr. Barbara Marchese, Prin. Lay Teachers 38; Students 793.
Catechesis/Religious Program—Tel: 402-493-1642; Fax: 402-496-9933. Vicki Smith, D.R.E. Students 586.

51—ST. WENCESLAUS (1877), (Czech), Revs. Thomas E. Bauwens; Kizito Okhuoya; Deacons Donald Cowles; Joe Kulus; Michael J. DeSelm.
Res.: 1516 S. 152nd Ave. Cir., 68144. Tel: 402-330-0304; Fax: 402-330-1476. Web: www.stwenceslaus.org.
School—(Grades PreSchool-8), 15353 Pacific St., 68154. Tel: 402-330-4356; Fax: 402-884-4417. William Huben, Prin. Sisters 1; Lay Teachers 44; Students 896.
Catechesis/Religious Program—Tel: 402-330-1889. Nicholas Emanuel, Dir. Faith Formation. Students 545.

OUTSIDE THE CITY OF OMAHA

ALBION, BOONE CO., ST. MICHAEL (1877) [CEM] Rev. Stanley T. Schmit.
Res.: 524 W. Church St., 68620. Tel: 402-395-2393.
School—Tel: 402-395-2926; Fax: 402-395-2926. Lay Teachers 9; Students 97.
Catechesis/Religious Program—Students 127.

ALOYS, CUMING CO., ST. ALOYSIUS (1891), (German), [CEM] Revs. Gerald E. Gonderinger; Francis W. Lordemann.
Mailing Address: 343 N. Monitor St., West Point, 68788.
Res. & Church: 700 Hwy. 32, West Point, 68788. Tel: 402-372-2188; Fax: 402-372-3563. Email: stmary@yahoo.com. Web: myweb.cableone.net/stmary.
Catechesis/Religious Program—Students 3.

ATKINSON, HOLT CO., ST. JOSEPH (1886) [CEM] Rev. LuVerne W. Steffes.
Res.: 317 W. State St., P.O. Box 220, 68713. Tel: 402-925-2122.
School—Tel: 402-925-2104; Fax: 402-925-2104. Email: stjoeschool@esu8.org. Lay Teachers 5; Students 31.
Catechesis/Religious Program—Students 62.

BANCROFT, CUMING CO., HOLY CROSS (1884), (German), [CEM] Rev. Paul R. Ortmeier.
Res.: P.O. Box 524, Lyons, 68038. Tel: 402-687-2102. Web: www.stjoseph-holycross.com.
Catechesis/Religious Program—Students 48.

BATTLE CREEK, MADISON CO., ST. PATRICK'S (1875) [CEM] Rev. Michael B. Malloy; Deacons Tom Hughes; Melvin Schaecher.
Res.: 107 N. Third St., P.O. Box 40, 68715. Tel: 402-675-2485. Email: stpatrick@frontier.com.
Catechesis/Religious Program—Tel: 402-675-6345. Teresa Wilkinson, D.R.E. Students 98.

Mission—St. Francis de Sales Schoolcraft, Madison Co.

BEEMER, CUMING CO., HOLY CROSS (1913) [CEM] Rev. William J. Safranek.
Res.: 517 Fraisier St. N., P.O. Box 212, 68716. Tel: 402-528-3475; Fax: 402-528-3475. Email: hcbeemer@gpcom.net.
Catechesis/Religious Program—Students 32.

BELLEVUE, SARPY CO.

1—ST. BERNADETTE (1963) Rev. Alfred J. Salanitro; Deacons Ron Casart; Gary Chladek; Pete Digilio, (Retired); Sebastian Enzolera. In Res., Most Rev. Anthony Milone (Retired).
Res.: 7600 S. 42nd St., 68147. Tel: 402-731-4694; Fax: 402-733-4890. Email: terriamac@gmail.com. Web: www.stbernadetteparish.org.
School—Tel: 402-731-3033; Fax: 402-731-8735. Mrs. Lynn Schultz, Prin. Lay Teachers 18; Students 230.
Catechesis/Religious Program—Tel: 402-731-4694, Ext. 305; Fax: 402-733-4890. Jacquelyn Diane Van Ornam, D.R.E. Students 95.

2—ST. MARY (1921) Revs. Dennis A. Hanneman; Mark M. Bridgman; Deacons Ralph Hueser; Duane Iwanski; Chuck L'Archevesque; Andy Foray; John Huck; John Wacha; Lee Mayhan; Gary Bash.
Res.: 811 W. 23rd Ave., 68005. Tel: 402-291-1350; Fax: 402-291-1375. Email: rectory@stmarysbellevue.com. Web: www.stmarysbellevue.com.
School—(Grades PreK-8), 903 W. Mission Ave., 68005. Tel: 402-291-1694; Fax: 402-291-9667. Web: www.stmarysschoolbellevue.com. Cheryl Castle, Prin.; Mary Ellen Reckmeyer, Librarian. Lay Teachers 16; Students 183.
Catechesis/Religious Program—Tel: 402-291-7222; Fax: 402-291-3964. Elizabeth Tomaso, D.R.E. Students 246.

3—ST. MATTHEW THE EVANGELIST CHURCH OF BELLEVUE (1996) Rev. Ronald S. Wasikowski. In Res., Rev. Msgr. Thomas D. Furlong (Retired).
Office: 12210 S. 36th St. Ste. A, 68123. Tel: 402-292-7418; Fax: 402-292-7421. Email: saintmatthew@stmatthewsomaha.org. Web: www.stmatthewsomaha.org.
Res.: 3605 Looking Glass Dr., 68123. Tel: 402-292-7430.
School—(Grades PreSchool-8), 12210 S. 36th St. Ste. B, 68123. Tel: 402-291-2030. Web: www.stmatthewsschool.net. Janet Wilson, Prin. Lay Teachers 14; Students 145.
Catechesis/Religious Program—Students 147.

BLAIR, WASHINGTON CO., ST. FRANCIS BORGIA (1865) [CEM] Rev. Mario D. Rapose; Rebecca Crotty, Bookkeeper.
Res.: 2005 Davis Dr., 68008. Tel: 402-426-3823; Fax: 402-426-5131. Email: office@stfrancisborgia.org.
Catechesis/Religious Program—Deborah Lager, D.R.E. Students 289.

BLOOMFIELD, KNOX CO., ST. ANDREW (1892) [JC] Rev. Michael D. Schmitz.
Res.: 1316 W. 5th St., Crofton, 68730. Tel: 402-388-4814; Fax: 402-388-2680. Email: strosecrofton@gpcom.net.
Catechesis/Religious Program—Tel: 402-373-2696; Fax: 402-373-2233. Barb Jackson, D.R.E. Students 76.

BOW VALLEY, CEDAR CO., SS. PETER AND PAUL, Merged with Sacred Heart, Wynot; Ss. Philip and James, St. James and Immaculate Conception, St. Helena to form Holy Family Church of Cedar County, Hartington.

BOYS TOWN, DOUGLAS CO., IMMACULATE CONCEPTION B.V.M. (1936) Revs. Steven Boes; Valentine J. Peter.
Mailing Address: 13703 Dowd Dr., 68010. In Res., Rev. Msgr. Peter F. Dunne (Retired); Revs. Eugene McReynolds, O.S.B.; Clifford J. Stevens (Retired).
Parish Center: 13900 Dowd Dr., 68010. Tel: 402-498-1464; Fax: 402-493-9575.
Catechesis/Religious Program—The Catholic Center, 13702 Dowd Dr., 68010. Tel: 402-498-1030. Students 199.

BUTTE, BOYD CO, SACRED HEART PARISH OF BOYD COUNTY (1906) [JC 4] Rev. Timothy Podraza.
Res. & Office: 921 Gale St., P.O. Box 8, 68722. Tel: 402-775-2452; 402-775-0067 (Office).
Catechesis/Religious Program—Tel: 402-775-2622. Students 92.

CEDAR RAPIDS, BOONE CO., ST. ANTHONY (1884) [CEM] Rev. Ralph J. Steffensmeier.
Res.: P.O. Box 56, 68627. Tel: 308-358-0773; Fax: 308-358-0773.
Catechesis/Religious Program—Students 50.

CENTRAL CITY, MERRICK CO., ST. MICHAEL (1910) Rev. Msgr. Nelson A. Newman; Deacons Robert Flesch; Richard Larson; Donald Placke.
Res.: 2402 20th Ave., 68826. Tel: 308-946-2855; Fax: 308-946-2214.
Catechesis/Religious Program—Kendra Jefferson, D.R.E. Students 71.

CLARKS, MERRICK CO., ST. PETER (1918) [CEM] Rev. Richard J. Whiteing.
Res.: 315 N. Esther, Box 368, Fullerton, 68638. Tel: 308-536-2574; Fax: 308-536-2574.
Church: 302 N. Dixon St., 68628.
Catechesis/Religious Program—Tel: 308-548-2870. Students 29.

CLARKSON, COLFAX CO.

1—SS. CYRIL AND METHODIUS (1901), (Czech), [CEM] Rev. Timothy W. Forget.
Res.: 120 Cherry St., P.O. Box 457, 68629. Tel: 402-892-3464 (Church Office); 402-892-3064 (Father's Office); Fax: 402-892-9879.
School—St. John Neumann, Tel: 402-892-3474; Fax: 402-892-3474. Lay Teachers 4; Students 31.
Catechesis/Religious Program—Students 85.

2—HOLY TRINITY (1878), (Czech), [CEM] Rev. Leo A. Rigatuso.
Res.: 614 Center St., Howells, 68641. Tel: 402-986-1627; Fax: 402-986-1627.
School— See Elementary Schools, Interparochial under Institutions located in the Archdiocese.
Catechesis/Religious Program—

COLERIDGE, CEDAR CO., ST. MICHAEL (1886), (German—Irish), [CEM] Rev. Jeffery S. Loseke.
Mailing Address: P.O. Box 278, Hartington, 68739.
Res.: 315 S. Madison, 68727. Tel: 402-254-6559; Fax: 402-254-6553. Email: trinitymichael@hartel.net.
Catechesis/Religious Program—Students attend religious education at St. Mary's in Laurel Holy Trinity in Hartington.

COLUMBUS, PLATTE CO.

1—ST. ANTHONY (1913) Rev. Lydell T. Lape; Deacons Michael Placzek; Michael McGuire; Kelly McGowan.
Res.: 562 17th Ave., 68601. Tel: 402-564-3313; Fax: 402-563-1005.
School—1719 6th St., 68601. Tel: 402-564-4767; Fax: 402-564-5530. Web: teachers.esu7.org/stanthony. Norma Cremers, Prin. Lay Teachers 7; Students 145.
Catechesis/Religious Program—Lori Olson, D.R.E. Students 143.

2—ST. BONAVENTURE (1877) [CEM] Revs. Thomas W. Weisbecker; Michael P. Keating. In Res., Rev. Andrew J. Roza; Deacons Daniel Keiter; Arthur Spenner; Lawrence Mielak.
Res.: 1565 18th Ave., 68601. Tel: 402-564-7151; Fax: 402-562-6025. Email: stbons@esu7.org. Web: www.stbons.com.
School—Tel: 402-564-7153; Fax: 402-564-2587. Cheryl Zoucha, Prin. Lay Teachers 15; Students 202.
Catechesis/Religious Program—Gail Benesch, D.R.E.; Belinda Keiter, Youth Min. Students 289.

3—ST. ISIDORE (1963) [JC] Rev. Joseph A. Miksch.
Res.: 3921 20th St., 68601. Tel: 402-564-8993; Fax: 402-564-8955. Email: isidore@megavision.com. Web: www.saintisidores.com.
School—3821 20th St., 68601. Tel: 402-564-2604. Lay Teachers 13; Students 198.
Catechesis/Religious Program—Tel: 402-246-5455. Students 196.

CONSTANCE, CEDAR CO., ST. JOSEPH (1896) [CEM], (Mission of Fordyce) Rev. David L. Fulton.
Mailing Address: P.O. Box 170, Fordyce, 68736. Tel: 402-357-3506. Email: frfulton@hotmail.com. Web: www.stbonifaceparish.org.
See West Catholic Elementary, Fordyce under Elementary Schools, Interparochial located in the Institution section.
Catechesis/Religious Program—Students 5.

CREIGHTON, KNOX CO., ST. LUDGER (1885), (German—Czech), [JC] Rev. Walter L. Nolte.
Res.: 410 Bryant Ave., 68729-2917. Tel: 402-358-3596; Fax: 402-358-3559.
School—Lay Teachers 4; Students 31.
Catechesis/Religious Program—Tel: 402-358-3501. Karen Boyle, D.R.E.; Ellen Huigens, D.R.E.; Darla Frisch, D.R.E. Students 67.
Mission—St. Ignatius Brunswick, Antelope Co.

CROFTON, KNOX CO., ST. ROSE OF LIMA (1906) [CEM] Rev. Michael D. Schmitz; Deacon Frank Fillaus.
Res.: 1316 W. Fifth St., 68730. Tel: 402-388-4814; Fax: 402-388-2680. Email: strosecrofton@gpcom.net.
School—St. Rose School, 1302 W. 5th St., 68730. Tel: 402-388-4393; Fax: 402-388-4393. Email: strose@esu1.org. Web: www.stroseschool.us. Lay Teachers 10; Students 99.
Catechesis/Religious Program—Terry Mueller, D.R.E., (Grades 1-8). Students 86.

DELOIT TOWNSHIP, HOLT CO., ST. JOHN THE BAPTIST (1910) [CEM 2] Rev. James V. Kramper.
Res.: P.O Box 37, Ewing, 68735. Tel: 402-626-7605; Fax: 402-626-7605.
Catechesis/Religious Program—Students 32.

DODGE, DODGE CO., ST. WENCESLAUS (1883), (Czech), [CEM 2] [JC] Rev. Patrick A. McLaughlin.
Res.: 743 Second St., 68633. Tel: 402-693-2235; Fax: 402-693-2236. Web: www.stwenc.org.
School—212 N. Linden St., 68633. Tel: 402-693-2819; Fax: 402-693-2347. Stacy Uttecht, Headmistress. Lay Teachers 4; Students 49.
Catechesis/Religious Program—Tel: 402-693-2347. Students 78.
Mission—Sacred Heart (1874) [CEM] Olean, Colfax Co. Tel: 402-693-2356.
Catechesis/Religious Program—Students 55.

DUNCAN, PLATTE CO., ST. STANISLAUS, [CEM] Rev. Rodney V. Kneifl.
Mailing Address: P.O. Box 155, Platte Center, 68653-0155.
Church: 1120 8th St., 68634. Tel: 402-897-2625; Fax: 402-246-2045. Email: stsjoemike@aol.com.
Catechesis/Religious Program—Students 28.

ELGIN, ANTELOPE CO., ST. BONIFACE (1902), (German), [CEM] Rev. Ross C. Burkhalter; Deacons Dennis Wiehn; Bill Camp.
Res.: 301 S. 2nd St., P.O. Box B, 68636-0433. Tel: 402-843-2345; Fax: 402-843-2253. Email: stboniface.elg@archomaha.org.
School—Tel: 402-843-5460; Fax: 402-843-5842. Email: saintbon@esu8.org. Lay Teachers 6; Students 74.
Catechesis/Religious Program—Students 51.

EMERSON, DAKOTA CO., SACRED HEART (1886) [CEM] Rev. Gerald Leise Jr.
Res.: 601 N. Main St., P.O. Box 250, 68733. Tel: 402-695-2342; Fax: 402-695-2505. Email: catholic@inebraska.com.
Catechesis/Religious Program—Students 55.

EWING, HOLT CO., ST. PETER DE ALCANTARA (1885) [CEM] Rev. James V. Kramper.
Res.: P.O. Box 37, 68735. Tel: 402-626-7605; Fax: 402-626-7605.
Catechesis/Religious Program—Students 116.
Mission—Mission of St. Theresa of Avila, Clearwater, NE (1886) 509 Nebraska St., Clearwater, 68726.

FORDYCE, CEDAR CO., ST. JOHN THE BAPTIST (1909), (German), [CEM] Rev. David L. Fulton; Deacons Marcus Potts; Brian Heine.
Res.: P.O. Box 170, 68736. Tel: 402-357-3506; Fax: 402-357-3795. Email: frfulton@hotmail.com. Web: www.stbonifaceparish.org.
See West Catholic Elementary, Fordyce under Elementary Schools, Interparochial located in the Institution section.
Catechesis/Religious Program—Mary Jean Zavadil, D.R.E. Students 11.
Mission—St. Joseph, Cedar Co. Tel: 402-388-4814.

FORT CALHOUN, WASHINGTON CO., ST. JOHN THE BAPTIST (1883) Revs. Mario D. Rapose; Stephen J. Gutgsell.
Res.: 215 N. 13th St., P.O. Box 148, 68023. Tel: 402-468-5348; Fax: 402-468-4619. Email: sjcc@huntel.net.
Catechesis/Religious Program—Tel: 402-468-5659. Email: religioused@huntel.net. Students 75.

FREMONT, DODGE CO., ST. PATRICK (1858) [CEM] Revs. David Belt; James E. Keiter; Deacons Robert Chapman; Edward Gentrup; LeRoy Spieker; Vic Henry; Dan Mueller; Joe Uhlik; David A. Probst; Andy Kresha; Craig Steel; Thomas Silva.
Rectory—422 E. Fourth St., 68025. Tel: 402-721-6611; Fax: 402-727-8167. Email: stpatsfremont@yahoo.com. Web: www.stpatsfremont.org.
Church: 3400 E. 16th St., 68025. Tel: 402-727-6500.
High School—Archbishop Bergan, Tel: 402-721-9683; Fax: 402-721-5366. Web: www.berganknights.org. Ron Beacom, Prin. Lay Teachers 14; Students 120.
School—Bergan Middle School, (Grades 7-8) Fax: 402-721-5366. Mary Riggert, Librarian. Lay Teachers 8; Students 57.
School—Archbishop Bergan Elementary formerly ABC Elementary (Grades K-6), 1515 N. Johnson Rd., 68025. Tel: 402-721-9766; Fax: 402-721-1180. Kate Hurst, Librarian. Teachers 20; Students 206.
Catechesis/Religious Program—Tel: 402-721-6611, Ext. 15. Email: stpatsfremontrf@yahoo.com. Janae Smith, D.R.E. Students 316.

FULLERTON, NANCE CO., ST. PETER (1917), (Polish), [CEM] Rev. Richard J. Whiteing.
Res.: 315 N. Esther, P.O. Box 368, 68638-0368. Tel: 308-536-2574; Fax: 308-536-2574.
Church: 315 N. Esther St., 68638.
Catechesis/Religious Program—Students 80.

GENOA, NANCE CO., ST. ROSE OF LIMA (1900) [JC] Rev. William D. L'Heureux.
116 N. Elm St., P.O. Box 490, 68640-0490.
Res.: 407 Vine St., P.O. Box 332, Silver Creek, 68663. Tel: 308-773-2282.
Catechesis/Religious Program—Students 89.

GRETNA, SARPY CO.

1—ST. CHARLES BORROMEO (2005) Rev. Norman F. Hunke.
P.O. Box 625, 68028. Tel: 402-916-9730; Fax: 402-916-9740. Email: parish@scbccomaha.org. Web: www.stcharlesomaha.org.
Catechesis/Religious Program—Amanda Hoeke, D.R.E.; Shelly Stonacek, D.R.E. Students 340.

2—St. Patrick (1858), (Irish), [CEM] Very Rev. Michael W. Grewe; Deacons Larry Heck; Steve Grandinetti.
Res.: 214 No. Cherokee Dr., 68028. Tel: 402-332-4428. Church: 508 Angus St., 68028. Tel: 402-332-4444; Fax: 402-332-5107. Email: stpatrick.gre@archomaha.org. Web: www.stpatsgretna.org.
Catechesis/Religious Program—Tel: 402-332-3454. Email: smfagan@archomaha.org. Students 710.

Hartington, Cedar Co., Holy Trinity (1886), (German—Irish), [CEM] [JC] Rev. Jeffery S. Loseke.
Mailing Address: P.O. Box 278, 68739.
Res. & Office: 404 S. Broadway, 68739. Tel: 402-254-6559; Fax: 402-254-6553. Email: trinitymichael@hartel.net.
School—(Grades K-6) Tel: 402-254-6496. Adaline Dreesen, Librarian. Lay Teachers 10; Students 157.
Catechesis/Religious Program—Students 106.

Hooper, Dodge Co., St. Rose of Lima (1885) [CEM 2] Rev. Damien Wee.
Res.: 405 Elk St., P.O. Box 443, 68031. Tel: 402-654-3449; Fax: 402-654-3449. Email: parishroselaw@gmail.com.
Catechesis/Religious Program—Students 35.
Mission—St. Lawrence [CEM] 910 Grant St., Box 443, Dodge Co. 68031.
Catechesis/Religious Program—Students 34.

Howells, Colfax Co.
1—St. John Nepomucene (1893) [CEM] Rev. Leo A. Rigatuso.
Res.: 614 Center St., 68641. Tel: 402-986-1653; Fax: 402-986-0882.
See Howells Community Catholic School, Howells under Elementary Schools, Interparochial located in the Institution section.
Catechesis/Religious Program—Students 30.

2—SS. Peter and Paul (1890), (German), [CEM] Rev. Leo A. Rigatuso.
Res.: 614 Center St., 68641. Tel: 402-986-1653.
See Howells Community Catholic School, Howells under Elementary Schools, Interparochial located in the Institution section.
Catechesis/Religious Program—Students 34.
Mission—Holy Trinity - Heun 1733 Rd. 12, Clarkson, 68629. Tel: 402-986-1627.

Humphrey, Platte Co., St. Francis (1883) [CEM] [JC 2] Revs. John S. Andrews; Wayne Pavela.
Res.: 203 S. 5th, P.O. Box 116, 68642. Tel: 402-923-0913; Fax: 402-923-1931.
School—(Grades K-12) Tel: 402-923-0611; Fax: 402-923-1590. Julie Huettner, Librarian. Priests 1; Lay Teachers 23; Students 213.
Catechesis/Religious Program—Students 213.

Jackson, Dakota Co., St. Patrick (1856) [CEM] Rev. Paul M. Albenesius.
Res.: 203 E. Elk St., P.O. Box 87, 68743. Tel: 402-632-4292.
Catechesis/Religious Program—Tel: 402-632-4258; Fax: 402-632-4312. Claudette Albenesius, D.R.E. Students 78.
Mission—St. Mary [CEM 2] 200 Iowa St., P.O. Box 126, Hubbard, Dakota Co. 68741. Tel: 402-632-4283.

Krakow, Nance Co., SS. Peter and Paul (1893), (Polish), [CEM] Rev. William D. L'Heureux.
P.O. Box 490, Genoa, 68640.
Res.: 407 Vine St., P.O. Box 332, Silver Creek, 68663. Tel: 308-773-2282.
Catechesis/Religious Program—Students 24.

Laurel, Cedar Co., St. Mary (1894) Rev. James F. McCluskey.
Res.: 406 Elm St., P.O. Box 828, 68745. Tel: 402-256-3303; Fax: 402-256-3019. Email: maryann68745@yahoo.com.
Catechesis/Religious Program—Shirley Haahr, D.R.E. Students 53.
Mission—St. Anne [CEM] Dixon, Dixon Co.

Leigh, Colfax Co., St. Mary (1900) [CEM] Rev. Timothy W. Forget.
Res.: 220 W. Third St., P.O. Box 385, 68643. Tel: 402-487-2666; Fax: 402-487-2666. Email: smarlei@frontiernet.net.
Catechesis/Religious Program—Laurie Urban, D.R.E. Students 61.

Lindsay, Platte Co., Holy Family (1895) [CEM] Rev. James F. Novotny.
Res.: 103 E. 3rd St., P.O. Box 68, 68644. Tel: 402-428-2455; Fax: 402-428-5205. Email: lhfp@megavision.com. Web: www.megavision.net/lhf.
School—(Grades 1-6) Tel: 402-428-3455; Fax: 402-428-3231. Email: nmoser@esu7.org. Web: www.lhf.esu7.org. Patty Hemmer, Librarian. Lay Teachers 4; Students 47.
High School—(Grades 7-12) Tel: 402-428-3215; Fax: 402-428-3231. Lay Teachers 9; Students 73.
Catechesis/Religious Program—Students 6.

Lynch, Boyd Co., Assumption B.V.M. (1892) [CEM] Merged with Ss. Peter and Paul, Butte and St. Mary, Spencer to form Sacred Heart Parish of Boyd Co.

Lyons, Burt Co., St. Joseph (1884) [JC] Rev. Paul R. Ortmeier.
Res.: 430 Lincoln St., P.O. Box 524, 68038. Tel: 402-687-2102. Web: www.stjoseph-holycross.com.
Catechesis/Religious Program—Students 67.

Madison, Madison Co., St. Leonard of Port Maurice (1885) [CEM] Rev. Scott A. Hastings; Deacons Lawrence F. Throener; Benjamin Villalobos Jr.
Res.: 504 S. Nebraska St., P.O. Box 368, 68748. Tel: 402-454-3529; Fax: 402-454-6533.
School—Tel: 402-454-3525. Lay Teachers 4; Students 54.
Catechesis/Religious Program—Students 120.

Menominee, Cedar Co., St. Boniface (1882), (German), [CEM] Rev. David L. Fulton; Deacon Clarence Jansen.
Res.: P.O. Box 170, Fordyce, 68736. Tel: 402-357-3506; Fax: 402-357-3795. Email: frfulton@hotmail.com. Web: www.stbonifaceparish.org.
See West Catholic Elementary, Fordyce under Elementary Schools, Interparochial located in the Institution section.
Catechesis/Religious Program—Tel: 402-357-3308. Email: stjohnbon1@gpm.com. Mary Jean Zavadil, C.R.E. Students 42.

Monterey, Cuming Co., St. Boniface (1905), (German), [CEM] Revs. Gerald E. Gonderinger, Admin.; Francis W. Lordemann.
343 N. Monitor St., West Point, 68788.
Res.: 450 12th Rd., West Point, 68788. Tel: 402-372-2188; Fax: 402-372-3563. Email: wpstmary@yahoo.com. Web: myweb.cableone.net/stmary.
Catechesis/Religious Program—Students 7.

Neligh, Antelope Co., St. Francis Rev. John P. Broheimer.
Res.: 702 W. 11th St., P.O. Box 259, 68756. Tel: 402-887-4521; Fax: 402-887-4521 (Call first). Email: stfranciscc@frontiernet.net.
Catechesis/Religious Program—Students 134.

Newcastle, Dixon Co., St. Peter (1873) [CEM] Rev. David F. Liewer; Deacon Dennis Knudsen.
Mailing Address: P.O. Box 898, Ponca, 68770-0898. Church: 403 Annie St., 68757. Tel: 402-755-2773; Fax: 402-755-2773.
Res.: 405 Annie St., P.O. Box 127, 68757. Tel: 402-355-2620 (Rectory).
Catechesis/Religious Program—Susie Day, D.R.E. Students 38.

Norfolk, Madison Co., Sacred Heart (1881), (German), Revs. Daniel R. Andrews; Joseph M. Wray; Scott A. Hastings, Hispanic Ministry; Deacons Jim Doolittle; Theodore Coler; Robert Viergutz.
Office: 204 S. Fifth St., 68701.
Res.: 202 S. Fifth St., 68701. Tel: 402-371-2621; Fax: 402-371-0403. Web: www.sacredheartnorfolk.com.
Sacred Heart Church—Church: 200 S. 5th St., 68701.
St. Mary's Catholic Church—2300 Madison Ave., 68701.
School—Sacred Heart Elementary School, (Grades PreSchool-6), 2301 Madison Ave., 68701. Tel: 402-371-4584 (Pre-School-6); Fax: 402-379-8129 (Pre-School-6). Web: www.sacredheartnorfolk.com. Troy Berryman, Prin. (Pre-School-6); Sherry Stuifbergen, Librarian. Priests 2; Lay Teachers 23; Students 392.
High School—Norfolk Catholic High School (1925), (Grades 7-12), 2300 Madison Ave., 68701. Tel: 402-371-2784 (7-12); Fax: 402-379-2929 (7-12). Email: jeffbellar@ncknights.org. Mr. Jeff Bellar, Prin. & Contact (7-12); Sherry Stuifbergen, Librarian. Priests 2; Lay Teachers 26; Students 296.
Catechesis/Religious Program—Tel: 402-371-8658. Marilyn Kathol, D.R.E. (Pre-School-12); Philip Zimmerman, Adult Formation. Students 450.

North Bend, Dodge Co., St. Charles Borromeo (1892) [JC] Rev. Donald M. Cleary.
Res.: 831 Locust St., P.O. Box 457, 68649. Tel: 402-652-8484; Fax: 402-652-3418. Email: stcharles.nbe@archomaha.org.
Catechesis/Religious Program—Tel: 402-652-8437. Jody Mullally, D.R.E. (Grades K-6). Students 119.

O'Neill, Holt Co., St. Patrick (1877) Revs. Francis A. Nigli; Jeffrey Lorig.
Res.: 301 E. Adams, 68763. Tel: 402-336-1602; Fax: 402-336-1533.
School—(Grades PreSchool-6) Tel: 402-336-2664; Fax: 402-336-2055. Jennie Schneider, Librarian. Lay Teachers 9; Students 130.
High School—(Grades 7-12) Tel: 402-336-4455; Fax: 402-336-1533. Jennie Schneider, Librarian. Lay Teachers 12; Students 116.
Catechesis/Religious Program—Tel: 402-336-1602; Fax: 402-336-1533. Georgia Blumenstock, D.R.E. Students 113.
Mission—St. Joseph Amelia, Holt Co. Tel: 402-482-5283.

Osmond, Pierce Co., St. Mary of the Seven Dolors (1904) [CEM] Rev. Michael J. Swanton.
Res.: 208 E. 5th St., P.O. Box 397, 68765. Tel: 402-748-3340; Fax: 402-748-3433.
School—302 E. 5th St., P.O. Box 427, 68765. Tel: 402-748-3433. Email: cconley_stmarys@huntel.net. Lay Teachers 4; Students 29.
Catechesis/Religious Program—Students 53.

Papillion, Sarpy Co., St. Columbkille (1897) Revs. Damian J. Zuerlein; Kevin W. Vogel; Deacons Eldon Lauber, Pastoral Assoc.; Frank Mascarello; Jerry Overkamp; William Hill; Russ Perry; Duane Thome; Steve Jordan; Bob Stier; John J. Zurek; Eric VandeBerg; Brian Thomas; David Krueger, Stewardship Dir.
Office: 200 E. Sixth St., 68046. Tel: 402-339-3285; Fax: 402-592-4753. Web: www.saintcolumbkille.org.
School—224 E. 5th St., 68046. Tel: 402-339-8706; Fax: 402-592-4147. Lay Teachers 23; Students 517.
Catechesis/Religious Program—Tel: 402-339-0990; Fax: 402-339-3977. Students 673.

Pender, Thurston Co., St. John (1889) [JC] Rev. Gerald Leise Jr.
Res.: 108 N. 5th, P.O. Box 96, 68047. Tel: 402-385-3258; Fax: 402-385-3400. Email: catholic@inebraska.com.
Catechesis/Religious Program—Students 59.

Petersburg, Boone Co., St. John the Baptist (1896) [CEM] Rev. Stanley T. Schmit.
Mailing Address: 4th & Norman Sts., P.O. Box 608, 68652.
Res.: 524 W. Church St., Albion, 68620. Tel: 402-395-2393.
Catechesis/Religious Program—Students 35.

Pierce, Pierce Co., St. Joseph (1905), (German), [CEM] Rev. Keith D. Rezac.
Res.: 118 W. Willow St., 68767. Tel: 402-329-4200; Fax: 402-329-4579.
Catechesis/Religious Program—Students 132.
Mission—St. Paul the Apostle 203 E. Park Ave., Plainview, 68769.

Plainview, Pierce Co., St. Paul (1912) [CEM] Rev. Keith D. Rezac.
Res.: *St. Joseph*, 118 W. Willow, Pierce, 68767. Tel: 402-329-4200; Fax: 402-329-4579.
Catechesis/Religious Program—Students 36.

Platte Center, Platte Co., St. Joseph (1884), (German—Irish), [CEM] [JC] Rev. Rodney V. Kneifl.
Res.: 155 A St., P.O. Box 155, 68653-0155. Tel: 402-246-2255; Fax: 402-246-2045. Email: stsjoemike@aol.com.
Catechesis/Religious Program—Tel: 402-246-5700. Email: stjopre@megavision.com. Angela Dolezal, D.R.E.; Lisa Hoadley, D.R.E. Students 42.

Ponca, Dixon Co., St. Joseph (1890) [CEM] Rev. David F. Liewer.
Mailing Address: P.O. Box 898, 68770.
Church: 420 W. 2nd St., 68770. Tel: 402-755-2773; Fax: 402-755-2773.
Res.: 421 Annie St., P.O. Box 127, Newcastle, 68757. Tel: 402-355-2620.
Catechesis/Religious Program—Wendy Masin, D.R.E.; Jamie Hamar, D.R.E. Students 90.

Raeville, Boone Co., St. Bonaventure (1882), (German), [CEM] Rev. Ross C. Burkhalter.
Res.: 301 S. 2nd St., Box B, Elgin, 68636. Tel: 402-843-2345; Fax: 402-843-2253. Email: stbonaventure.rae@archomaha.org.
Catechesis/Religious Program—Students 3.

Ralston, Douglas Co., St. Gerald (1957) Revs. Owen W. Korte; Anthony L. Espinosa.
Res.: 7859 Lakeview St., 68127. Tel: 402-331-1955; Fax: 402-339-8733. Email: office@stgerald.org. Web: www.stgerald.org.
Church: 9602 Q St., 68127.
School—Tel: 402-331-4223; Fax: 402-331-4523. David Garland, Prin. Lay Teachers 25; Students 418.
Catechesis/Religious Program—Tel: 402-331-4223. Students 284.

Randolph, Cedar Co., St. Frances de Chantal (1892), (German), [CEM] Rev. Michael J. Swanton; Deacon Doug Tunink.
Res.: *St. Jane Frances de Chantal*, 402 N. Bridge St., 68771. Tel: 402-337-0644. Email: stjane@cableone.net.
Catechesis/Religious Program—Tel: 402-337-0341. Sandy Thies, D.R.E. Students 102.

St. Charles, Cuming Co., St. Anthony (1862), (German), [CEM] Revs. Gerald E. Gonderinger; Francis W. Lordemann.
343 N. Monitor St., West Point, 68788.
Res.: 449 15th Rd., West Point, 68788. Tel: 402-372-2188; Fax: 402-372-3563. Email: wpstmary@yahoo.com. Web: myweb.cableone.net/stmary.
Catechesis/Religious Program—Students 11.

St. Edward, Boone Co., St. Edward (1888) [CEM] Rev. Ralph J. Steffensmeier.
Res.: 805 Washington St., P.O. Box A, 68660-0136. Tel: 402-678-2642; Fax: 402-678-2341. Email: stedward@gpcom.net.

Catechesis/Religious Program—Elizabeth Czarnick, D.R.E. (Elementary); Erica Werts, D.R.E. (Jr.-Sr. High). Students 49.

ST. HELENA, CEDAR CO., IMMACULATE CONCEPTION, Merged with Ss. Philip & James, St. James; Ss. Peter & Paul, Bow Valley & Sacred Heart, Wynot to form Holy Family Church of Cedar County.

ST. JAMES, CEDAR CO., SS. PHILIP AND JAMES, Merged with Immaculate Conception, St. Helena; Ss. Peter and Paul, Bow Valley and Sacred Heart, Wynot to form Holy Family Church of Cedar County.

SCHUYLER, COLFAX CO.

1—ST. MARY (1914) Merged with St. Augustine, Schuyler to form Divine Mercy, Schuyler.

2—ST. AUGUSTINE (1878), (Irish—German), Merged with St. Mary, Schuyler to form Divine Mercy, Schuyler.

3—DIVINE MERCY Revs. Carl J. Zoucha; Andrew J. Syring; Deacons Carl Perrin; Marvin Capoun; Danny Hastings.
Parish Office: 308 W. 10 St., 68661. Tel: 402-352-3540; Fax: 402-352-5971.
Res.: 619 Banner, 68661.
Catechesis/Religious Program—320 W. 10th St., 68661. Tel: 402-352-2149. Sara Rojo, D.R.E. Students 711.

SILVER CREEK, MERRICK CO., ST. LAWRENCE (1902), (Polish), [CEM] Rev. William D. L'Heureux.
Res.: 407 Vine St., P.O. Box 332, 68663. Tel: 308-773-2282.
Catechesis/Religious Program—Kris Zelasney, D.R.E. Students 42.

SNYDER, DODGE CO., ST. LEO, [CEM] Rev. Donald M. Cleary.
P.O. Box 188, 68664.
Res.: 831 Locust St., P.O. Box 457, North Bend, 68649. Tel: 402-652-8484; Fax: 402-652-3418. Email: stleo.sny@archomaha.org.
Catechesis/Religious Program—Tel: 402-568-2586. Betty Marxsen, D.R.E. Students 28.

SOUTH SIOUX CITY, DAKOTA CO., ST. MICHAEL (1898) [CEM] Revs. Oscar A. Perez (Venezuela); James R. de Anda.
Office:—P.O. Box 128, 68776.
Res.: 1405 First Ave., 68776. Tel: 402-494-5424; Fax: 402-494-6342.
School—Tel: 402-494-1526; Fax: 402-494-4283. Lay Teachers 14; Students 164.
Catechesis/Religious Program—1414 Third Ave., 68776. Tel: 402-494-2827. Students 650.

SPENCER, BOYD CO., ST. MARY (1892) [CEM 2] Merged with Ss. Peter and Paul, Butte and Assumption B.V.M., Lynch to form Sacred Heart Parish of Boyd Co.

SPRINGFIELD, SARPY CO., ST. JOSEPH (1980) [JC] Rev. Matthew J. Gutowski.
Res.: 102 S. Ninth St., 68059. Tel: 402-253-2889; Fax: 402-253-2949.
Catechesis/Religious Program—Tel: 402-253-2949. Sherry Huntwork, D.R.E. Students 154.

STANTON, STANTON CO., ST. PETER (1893) [JC] Rev. Gerald A. Connealy.
Res.: 1504 Ivy St., P.O. Box 557, 68779. Tel: 402-439-2147; Fax: 402-439-2149. Email: stpeters@stanton.net.
Catechesis/Religious Program—Tel: 402-379-1234; 402-439-2331. Valerie Morfeld, D.R.E.; Karen Petersen, D.R.E. Students 92.

STUART, HOLT CO., ST. BONIFACE (1899) [CEM] Rev. LuVerne W. Steffes.
Res.: 106 E. Fourth, P.O. Box 190, 68780. Tel: 402-924-3262; Fax: 402-924-3262. Email: stboniface@elkhorn.net.
Catechesis/Religious Program—Students 87.

TARNOV, PLATTE CO., ST. MICHAEL (1884), (Polish), [CEM] Rev. Rodney V. Kneifl.
Res.: P.O. Box 155, Platte Center, 68653. Tel: 402-246-2255; Fax: 402-246-2045. Email: stsjoemike@aol.com.
Catechesis/Religious Program—Tel: 402-923-1308. Email: rbrand1@megavision.com. Students 18.

TEKAMAH, BURT CO., ST. PATRICK (1889) [JC] Rev. Mark A. Tomasiewicz.
3480 Hwy. 32, 68061-1542.
Res.: 1323 R St., 68061-1542. Tel: 402-374-1692; Fax: 402-808-2004.
Catechesis/Religious Program—Tel: 402-870-2158. Ashley Olson, D.R.E. Students 83.
Mission—Holy Family [CEM] 2801 Co. Rd. U, Decatur, Burt Co. 68020.

TILDEN, MADISON CO., OUR LADY OF MT. CARMEL (1887) [CEM] Rev. John P. Broheimer.
Res.: P.O. Box 458, 68781. Tel: 402-368-7710; Fax: 402-368-7710.
Catechesis/Religious Program—Tel: 402-368-5919. Corinne Frey, D.R.E. Students 57.

VALLEY, DOUGLAS CO., ST. JOHN (1917) Rev. Lloyd A. Gnirk.
Res.: 209 E. Sunset, P.O. Box 587, 68064. Tel: 402-359-5783; Fax: 402-359-5217.
Catechesis/Religious Program—Tel: 402-625-2717. Connie Schnoes, D.R.E. Students 88.

VERDIGRE, KNOX CO., ST. WENCESLAUS (1884), (Czech—Bohemian), [CEM] Rev. Douglas P. Scheinost.
Res.: 409 S. Third St., P.O. Box 9, 68783-0009. Tel: 402-668-2331; Fax: 402-668-2375.
Catechesis/Religious Program—Students 59.
Mission—St. William 262 Buckeye Rd., P.O. Box 9, Knox Co. 68783-0009. Tel: 402-857-3438. Rev. Douglas P. Scheinost.

WALTHILL, THURSTON CO., ST. JOSEPH (1912), (Native American), Revs. Daniel L. Wittrock; David M. Korth.
Res.: P.O. Box GG, Winnebago, 68071. Tel: 402-846-5550; Fax: 402-878-2760.
Catechesis/Religious Program—Students 8.
Mission—Our Lady of Fatima Revs. Daniel L. Wittrock; David M. Korth.

WAYNE, WAYNE CO., ST. MARY (1881) Rev. Mark T. Beran.
Res.: 412 E. 8th St., 68787. Tel: 402-375-2000; Fax: 402-375-5782.
School—St. Mary's Catholic School, 420 E. 7th St., 68787. Tel: 402-375-2337. Lay Teachers 6; Students 37.
Catechesis/Religious Program—Students 164.

WEST POINT, CUMING CO., ASSUMPTION B.V.M. (1875) [CEM] Revs. Gerald E. Gonderinger; Francis W. Lordemann; Deacons Vincent Maly; Kenneth Batenhorst; David Baumert; Francis Meiergerd.
Res.: 343 N. Monitor St., 68788. Tel: 402-372-2188; Fax: 402-372-3563. Email: wpstmary@yahoo.com. Web: myweb.cableone.net/stmary.
School—Guardian Angel, Tel: 402-372-5328. Web: gacatholicschool.org. Mr. Matthew R. Richardson, Prin. Priests 2; Sisters 1; Lay Teachers 16; Students 175.
Catechesis/Religious Program—Email: ccdstmaryswp@yahoo.com. Sr. Michael Ann O'Donnell, D.R.E. Students 129.

WINNEBAGO, THURSTON CO.

1—ST. AUGUSTINE'S (1909), (Native American), [CEM], (Indian Mission) Revs. Daniel L. Wittrock; David M. Korth.
Res.: 1 Mission Road S., P.O. Box GG, 68071-0766. Tel: 402-878-2402; Fax: 402-878-2760. Web: staugustinemission.org.
School—St. Augustine Indian Mission School, (Grades K-8)Email: dmkorth@archomaha.org. Web: www.staugustinemission.org. Donald Blackbird Jr., Prin.; Sr. Frances Betz, Librarian. Missionary Benedictine Sisters 4; Lay Teachers 10; Students 116.
Mission—St. Cornelius Homer, Dakota Co. 68030. Revs. Daniel L. Wittrock; David M. Korth.
Catechesis/Religious Program—Students 26.

2—OUR LADY OF FATIMA OF MACY, Closed. This is a mission of St. Joseph, Walthill.

WISNER, CUMING CO., ST. JOSEPH (1879), (Irish—German), [CEM] [JC] Rev. William J. Safranek.
Res.: 1318 G Ave. W., P.O. Box 623, 68791. Tel: 402-529-3531. Email: stjoes@gpcom.net.
Catechesis/Religious Program—Tel: 402-529-3891. Anne McManigal, D.R.E. Students 117.

WYNOT, CEDAR CO.

1—HOLY FAMILY PARISH OF CEDAR COUNTY (2000), (German), [JC 4] Rev. Eric S. Olsen.
Parish Office—P.O. Box 65, 68792-0065. Tel: 402-254-3311; 402-357-2465; Fax: 402-357-2766. Email: holyfamily@gpcom.net.
Catechesis/Religious Program—Tel: 402-254-6980. Students 112.

2—SACRED HEART, Merged see Holy Family of Cedar County.

On Duty Outside the Archdiocese:
Revs.—
Dunne, Dermot J., Diocese of St. Petersburg, FL
Hanefeldt, Joseph G., Faculty, North American College, Rome
LaPlante, David W., Archdiocese of Milwaukee
Parrinello, Frank P., Fraternity of St. Peter (F.S.S.P.)

Graduate Studies:
Rev.—
Ofalsa, Rheo C.

Military Chaplains:
Revs.—
DeGuzman, Dennis U., U.S.A.F.
Dillon, Jerome V., Chap., U.S.N.R.
Sohm, Andrew L., U.S.A.F.

On Leave of Absence:
Rev.—
Welsh, Garry A.

Retired:
Rev. Msgrs.—
Brodersen, Charles F., 7323 Shirley St. #303, 68124.
Cain, James R., J.C.D., 7323 Shirley St. #206, 68124.
Dunne, Peter F., Boys Town Center, Boys Town, 68010.
Furlong, Thomas D., 3605 Looking Glass Dr., Bellevue, 68123.
Kubart, Francis E., 7323 Shirley St. #105, 68124.
Nienaber, Robert H., 7323 Shirley St. #312, 68124.
Werner, Cyril J., P.O. Box 562, Hartington, 68739.
Whelan, Bill S., 7323 Shirley St. #101, 68124.
Wiese, Melvern A., 320 E. Decatur St., West Point, 68788.
Wolbach, Richard A., 4001 S. 36th St., 68107.
Revs.—
Adams, Thomas J., 3330 S. 104th Ave., 68124.
Astuto, Lucian S., 15676 Webster St., 68118.
Bartek, William C., 7323 Shirley St. #204, 68124.
Beacom, John F., 841 E. Decatur, West Point, 68788.
Benliro, Fernando C., 9620 W. Russell Rd. #1105, Las Vegas, NV 89148.
Conley, Martin P., 7323 Shirley St. #315, 68124.
Finch, Joseph E., St. Theresa Mortherhouse, 600 Woods Rd., Germantown, NY 12526.
Fitzgerald, William J., 4800 N. 68th St., Unit 133, Scottsdale, AZ 85251.
Kros, Donald M., 50241 Edgewater Rd., Box 51, Lynch, 68748.
Lammers, Ralph A., 7323 Shirley St. #201, 68124.
Lange, Timothy J., 200 Benedictine Ln., Yankton, SD 57078.
Librea, Raphael B., 4803 William St., 68106.
McCaslin, John O., 7323 Shirley St., #305, 68124.
McKamy, Eldon J., 22426 N. Homestead Ln., Sun City West, AZ 85375.
Merwald, Melvin J., 770 N. 93rd St., #4A1, 68114.
Meyer, Emmett F., 508 W. Angus St., Gretna, 68028.
Peschel, Roland A., 7323 Shirley St. #210, 68124.
Petrasic, Martin J., Via Christe, 3636 California St., 68131.
Preisinger, Robert F., 1729 N. 177th Plz., 68118.
Printy, Michael G., 7323 Shirley St. #304, 68124.
Richling, Theodore L., 7323 Shirley St. #102, 68124.
Ryberg, James C., New Cassell, 900 N. 90th St., 68114.
Schlautman, Wayne W., 7323 Shirley St. #301, 68124.
Schmitz, Robert A., 7323 Shirley St. #213, 68124.
Schwartz, Hugh F., 7323 Shirley St. #205, 68124.
Schwertley, James F., 109 S. 19th St., 68102.
Smith, Robert J., 7323 Shirley St. #302, 68124.
Spenner, Jerome I., 7323 Shirley St., #203, 68124.
Stevens, Clifford J., 14100 Crawford St., HQ Bldg., Boys Town, 68010.
Stolinski, Dennis R., 4311 S. 150th St., 68137.
Stortz, Donald L., 626 N. 44th St., 68131.
Swanson, Charles F., 801 S. 52nd St., Apt. 1412, 68106.
Vavrina, Kenneth P., 7323 Shirley St., #314, 68124.
Wilwerding, Anthony P., 7323 Shirley St., #308, 68124.

Permanent Deacons:
Abbott, Ernest, Jr.
Adams, Chuck
Anderson, Andy
Anderson, Dennis
Archbold, Steve
Archibald, Joseph
Aulner, Al
Barbour, Frank
Barnes, William J.
Bartman, Frank
Bash, Gary
Batenhorst, Kenneth F.
Baughman, Charles
Baumert, David
Belcher, Roger A.
Berger, Bill, (On Duty Outside the Diocese)
Bevan, Edward J.
Blanton, Dan, (On Duty Outside the Diocese)
Boettger, Kent, (On Duty Outside the Diocese)
Bollman, James G., (On Duty Outside the Diocese)
Brich, James
Bronk, Duane, (On Duty Outside the Diocese)
Burbach, Bernie, (Retired)
Burton, Thomas
Camp, William J.
Cantrell, Charles D., (On Duty Outside the Diocese)
Capoun, Marvin
Carl, Robert J.
Casart, Ronald
Casner, James

Cerio, Paul M.
Chambers, James
Chapman, Robert
Chladek, Gary F.
Choi, Joseph
Christensen, Dave
Clausen, Donald
Coler, Thomas
Connor, Dennis
Conrad, James J., Jr.
Conzett, Michael
Cowles, Donald
Crotty, Richard
Crowley, Martin
Dagerman, John
Dahlseid, John
Davis, Dennis, (On Duty Outside the Diocese)
DeBlauw, James L., (On Duty Outside the Diocese)
DeSelm, Michael J.
Dethlefs, Dennis
DiGiacomo, Yano
Digilio, John J.
Digilio, Peter
Dineen, Lonnie
Dohmen, Louis
Doolittle, James
Dreismeier, Paul
Drvol, Gregg
Dunn, Donald
Elster, George
Emerson, William
Enzolera, Sebastian
Eubanks, Paul
Ficenic, Terry
Filipcic, Anthony
Fillaus, Frank
Finney, Jack
Fischman, David
Fisher, Ed
Fitzgerald, Thomas
Flesch, Robert
Fletcher, Michael
Floersch, Steve
Foray, Andrew
Franco, Martin
Frankenfield, Thomas H.
French, Gary
Friend, Joseph
Fulcher, Jon
Gau, Jerome
Gencarelli, Ernest
Gentrup, Edward
Goldsmith, Edwin G.
Graff, Francis, (On Duty Outside the Diocese)
Grandinetti, Steve
Gross, Patrick
Grosse, Randy
Gurney, David
Guzman, Luis
Hamilton, Robert
Hanson, Chris
Hastings, Danny
Heck, Lawrence
Heffeman, John, (On Duty Outside the Diocese)
Heine, Brian
Hendricks, Fred
Hennessey, Gary
Henry, Victor R.
Herrara, Jesus
Hesson, Ronald W., (On Duty Outside the Diocese)
Hill, William H., Jr.
Hills, Lyle
Hilt, Frank
Hopkins, Richard
Huck, John
Hueser, Ralph
Hughes, Thomas J.
Hunke, Melvin, (On Duty Outside the Diocese)
Iwanski, Duane
Janda, Dave
Janik, Norman
Jansen, Clarence
Jizba, Richard
Johnson, Donald
Jordan, Steve
Joyce, Kevin
Kaiser, Roland, (On Duty Outside the Diocese)
Kalkowski, Kenneth
Karmazin, Duane
Keating, James, Ph.D.
Keiter, Daniel
Kemp, Donald
Klein, David
Kleinschmitt, Shane
Knockenhauer, George F.
Knudsen, Dennis
Kober, Mark, (On Duty Outside the Diocese)
Koziel, Timothy J.
Kozney, Jerry
Krajicek, Joseph
Kramper, Jim, (On Duty Outside the Diocese)
Kresha, Andrew
Kreun, Wesley
Krieski, Timothy, (On Duty Outside the Diocese)
Kronschnabel, John
Krueger, David
Kube, Norman
Kulus, Joe
Kurtz, Stanley
L'Archevesque, Charles
Laird, Joseph
Larson, Rick
Lauber, Eldon
Leick, Mike
Leininger, Tim
Lenz, Patrick
Livingston, Tom
Long, Harlan
Luczynski, Chuck
Lukowski, Ray
Luna, Stephen
Maly, Vince
Marsh, Douglas
Mascarello, Frank
Matukewicz, Paul
Mayhan, Leo, II
McGowan, Kelly
McGuire, Michael
McNeil, Richard
McNeil, Tim, J.C.L.
Medina, Steven, (On Duty Outside the Diocese)
Meiergerd, Francis
Metzinger, Roger
Mielak, Lawrence
Miller, Carl, (On Duty Outside the Diocese)
Miller, Ira
Miller, Jack
Mines, John
Morello, Carl
Mouton, Gregory, (On Duty Outside the Diocese)
Mruz, Lawrence F.
Mueller, Daniel D.
Mueting, Richard, (On Duty Outside the Diocese)
Mulcahy, Timothy A.
Murphy, James
Murphy, Thomas
Narducci, Warren, (On Duty Outside the Diocese)
Nelson, Richard
Nelson, Sreven
Newell, Mike
Niedergeses, Richard
Nienaber, Harold
O'Donnell, William L., (On Duty Outside the Diocese)
Olsenholler, Jeffery
Osterhaus, Edwin
Overkamp, Jerry, J.C.L.
Palmer, Quentin, (On Duty Outside the Diocese)
Pavlik, Keith
Perchal, Daniel E.
Perrin, Carl A.
Perry, Russ
Pickett, Robert
Placke, Donald
Placzek, Michael
Potts, Marcus
Powers, Paul, (On Duty Outside the Diocese)
Preister, Tim
Pribnow, Otto
Pribnow, Roger D.
Probst, David A.
Ramirez, Joseph
Reese, Mike, (On Duty Outside the Diocese)
Reilly, James L.
Rettenmaier, Gerald J.
Reynolds, Mike
Ricketts, James
Rooney, Paul
Ryan, Ronald R.
Sampier, Larry D.
Sanders, Thomas, (On Duty Outside the Diocese)
Saniuk, Daniel
Sawtelle, Harold
Schaecher, Melvin
Schimonitz, Eugene, (Retired)
Schindel, James
Schlautman, William
Schmit, Vincent
Schulte, Thomas
Schultz, Charles J.
Schumacher, Allan
Seamann, Donald M., (On Duty Outside the Diocese)
Shipman, James
Silva, Thomas
Simmonds, Bud
Small, John
Smith, Marty
Sommer, Andrew
Sommer, Fred
Spenner, Arthur
Spicer, Ernest
Spieker, LeRoy
St. Arnold, Skip
Staroski, Jim
Steel, Craig
Steenson, Gerald
Steffen, Paul
Stier, Robert A.
Sukup, Charles
Tardy, Jim
Telich, Frank
ter Kuille, Reinold
Tharp, Bud
Thoene, Sylvan
Thomas, Brian
Thome, Duane
Throener, Lawrence F.
Tomaso, Paul
Tunink, Douglas G.
Tylutki, Glenn, (On Duty Outside the Diocese)
Uhlik, Joseph R.
Valadez, Luis
Valasek, Thomas W.
VandeBerg, Eric
Viergutz, Robert
Villalobos, Benjamin, Jr.
Villemure, Arthur
Wacha, John
Warwick, Marty
Watson, James
Weeder, Paul
Weskirchen, Charles
Wiehn, Dennis
Young, William
Zak, John J., Jr.
Zurek, John J.

INSTITUTIONS LOCATED IN THE ARCHDIOCESE

[A] COLLEGES AND UNIVERSITIES

OMAHA. *College of Saint Mary* (1923) 7000 Mercy Rd., 68106. Tel: 402-399-2400; Fax: 402-399-2342. Email: enroll@csm.edu. Web: www.csm.edu. Dr. Maryanne Stevens, Pres.; Dr. Christine Pharr, Vice Pres. Academic Affairs; Glen Sisk, Public Rels.; Melissa Tiemann, Librarian. Sisters 4; Lay Teachers 61; Students 1,063.

**Creighton University* (1878) 2500 California Plaza, 68178. Tel: 402-280-2700; Fax: 402-280-2727. Email: president@creighton.edu. Web: www.creighton.edu. Rev. Timothy R. Lannon, S.J., Pres. & Contact; Michael J. LaCroix, M.L.S., M.B.A., Dir., Reinert Alumni Memorial Library. Priests 29; Brothers 1; Sisters 3; Lay Teachers 776; Total Enrollment 7,730; Total Staff 2,754.

The University is comprised of the following schools:

College of Arts and Sciences Tel: 402-280-2431; Fax: 402-280-4729. Dr. Robert Lueger, Dean, College Arts and Sciences.

College of Business Administration Tel: 402-280-2852; Fax: 402-280-2172. Dr. Anthony Hendrickson, Dean, College of Business Admin.

Graduate School and University College/Summer Sessions Tel: 402-280-2424; 402-280-2870; Fax: 402-280-2423; 402-280-5762. Dr. Gail Jensen, Ph.D., Dean, Graduate School.

School of Law Tel: 402-280-2874; Fax: 402-280-3161. Marianne Culhane, J.D., Dean School of Law.

School of Dentistry Tel: 402-280-5061; Fax: 402-280-5094. Dr. Mark A. Latta, D.M.D., M.S., Dean, School of Dentistry.

School of Medicine Tel: 402-280-2600; Fax: 402-280-4027. Dr. Rowen Zetterman, Interim Dean, School of Medicine.

School of Nursing Tel: 402-280-2004; Fax: 402-280-2045. Dr. Eleanor Howell, Dean, School of Nursing.

School of Pharmacy and Health Professions Tel: 402-280-1828; Fax: 402-280-5738. Dr. J. Christopher Bradberry, Ph.D., Dean, School of Pharmacy & Health Professions.

[B] HIGH SCHOOLS, ARCHDIOCESAN

OMAHA. *Roncalli Catholic High School of Omaha* (1964) 6401 Sorensen Pkwy., 68152. Tel: 402-571-7670; Fax: 402-571-3216. Email: jdempsey@roncallicatholic.org; choltz@roncallicatholic.org. Web: www.roncallicatholic.org. Mr. Chad Holtz, Prin.; Rev. Gerald "Chi" Igboanusi, Chap., Pastoral Min.; Mr. James Meister, Activities Dir.; Margie Hladik, Media Specialist; Rev. Lloyd A. Gnirk, Pres. Emeritus; Jeff Dempsey, Pres. Priests 2; Lay Teachers 23; Students 350; Total Staff 38.

V.J. & Angela Skutt Catholic High School (1993) 3131 S. 156th St., 68130. Tel: 402-333-0818; Fax: 402-333-1790. Email: skuttcatholic@gmail.com. Web: www.skuttcatholic.com. Patrick Slattery,

Pres. & Prin.; Jon Burt, Asst. Prin.; Rob Meyers, Asst. Prin.; Michael McMahon, Activities Dir.; Isela Padilla, Librarian. Priests 1; Lay Teachers 50; Students 697; Total Staff 75.

BELLEVUE. *Daniel J. Gross Catholic High School of Omaha*, 7700 S. 43rd St., 68147. Tel: 402-734-2000; Fax: 402-734-4270. Email: cleve@grosscatholic.org. Web: www.grosscatholic.org. Rev. Steve Emanuel, Chap., Campus Min.; Rebecca Cleveland, Pres. & Contact; Dorothy Ostrowski, Prin. Priests 1; Lay Teachers 43; Students 425; Total Staff 60.

COLUMBUS. *Scotus Central Catholic High School*, (Grades 7-12), 1554 18th Ave., 68601. Tel: 402-564-7165; Fax: 402-564-6004. Email: wmorfel@esu7.org. Web: www.scotuscc.org. Mr. Wayne Morfeld, Pres.; Rev. Andrew J. Roza, Chap. & Teacher; Mrs. Cathy Podliska, Librarian. Priests 1; Lay Teachers 27; Students 401.

ELGIN. *Pope John XXIII Central Catholic High School at Elgin*, 303 Remington St., P.O. Box 179, 68636. Tel: 402-843-5325; Fax: 402-843-2297. Email: bgetzfre@esu8.org. Betty Getzfred, Prin.; Revs. Ross C. Burkhalter, Pres.; John P. Broheimer, Theology Teacher; Lauren Vaisvilas, Librarian. Priests 2; School Sisters of St. Francis 1; Lay Teachers 9; Students 90.

HARTINGTON. *Cedar Catholic High School* (1964) 401 S. Broadway, P.O. Box 15, 68739-0015. Tel: 402-254-3906; Fax: 402-254-3976. Email: tkathol@esu1.org. Web: www.cedarcatholic.org. Terry Kathol, Prin.; Rev. Jeffery S. Loseke, Pres.; Marilyn Rastede, Librarian. Priests 3; Sisters 1; Lay Teachers 19; Students 202; Total Staff 22.

WEST POINT. *Central Catholic High School*, 419 E. Decateur, 68788. Tel: 402-372-5326; Fax: 402-372-5327. Web: www.westpointcentralcatholic.org. Mr. Matthew R. Richardson, Prin.; Mary Jo Kampschnieder, Librarian. Priests 2; Franciscan Sisters of Christian Charity 1; Lay Teachers 16; Students 150.

[C] HIGH SCHOOLS, PRIVATE

OMAHA. *Creighton Preparatory School*, 7400 Western Ave., 68114. Tel: 402-393-1190; Fax: 402-393-0260. Email: tmerk@prep.creighton.edu. Web: www.creightonprep.creighton.edu. Revs. Thomas Merkel, S.J., Pres.; James H. Ryan, S.J., Supr.; Mr. John Naatz, Prin.; Revs. Kevin C. Schneider, S.J.; James A. Sinnerud, S.J.; George Sullivan, S.J.; Robert J. Tillman, S.J.; Bro. Edward Gill, S.J.; Mrs. Diane Sands, Librarian; Michael Lex. Priests 6; Scholastics 3; Lay Teachers 74; Students 1,022.

Duchesne Academy of the Sacred Heart (1881) 3601 Burt St., 68131. Tel: 402-558-3800; Fax: 402-558-0051. Email: shaggas@duchesneacademy.org. Web: www.duchesneacademy.org. Mrs. Sheila K. Haggas, Head of School & Contact; Laura Hickman, Prin.; Suzanne Rose, Librarian. Society of the Sacred Heart 3; Lay Teachers 32; Girls 293.

Marian High School, 7400 Military Ave., 68134. Tel: 402-571-2618, Ext. 114; Fax: 402-571-1952. Email: stoohey@omahamarian.org. Web: marianhighschool.net. Susan Toohey, Head of School, Prin. & Contact; Donna Broekemeir, Librarian. Servants of Mary. Lay Teachers 50; Girls 685.

Marian High School Endowment Trust

Marian High School Scholarship Endowment Trust

Mercy High School (1955) 1501 S. 48th St., 68106. Tel: 402-553-9424; Fax: 402-553-0394. Email: hannond@mercyhigh.org. Web: www.mercyhigh.org. Sr. Delores Hannon, R.S.M., Pres. & Contact; Carolyn Jaworski, Prin.; Kathy Redding, Librarian. Sisters of Mercy of the Americas 1; Lay Teachers 36; Girls 388.

ELKHORN. *Mount Michael Benedictine School*, 22520 Mt. Michael Rd., 68022-3400. Tel: 402-289-2541; Fax: 442-289-4539. Email: dpeters@mountmichael.org. Web: www.mountmichael.com. Rt. Rev. Michael Liebl, O.S.B., Abbot; Dr. David Peters, Ed.D., Prin.; Revs. Gregory Congote, O.S.B., Campus Min., Theology Instructor; Richard Thell, O.S.B.; Daniel Lenz, O.S.B.; Louis L. Sojka, O.S.B.; Stephen J. Plank, O.S.B.; Bro. Luke Clinton, Librarian. Priests 6; Sisters 1; Professed Brothers 2; Lay Teachers 23; Students 220.

[D] ELEMENTARY SCHOOLS, INTER-PAROCHIAL

OMAHA. *All Saints Catholic School*, 1335 S. 10th St., 68108. Tel: 402-346-5757; Fax: 402-346-8794. Email: mmburki@archomaha.org. Marlan Burki, Prin. & Contact; Colleen Botsios, Librarian. Serving parishes of St. Frances Cabrini, St. Joseph, St. Mary Magdalene Immaculate Conception, St. Patrick and also St. Peter, St. Rose, St. Bridget Lay Teachers 15; Students 147.

Assumption-Guadalupe Grade School, 5602 S. 22nd St., 68107. Tel: 402-734-4504; Fax: 402-734-4505. Rev. Bernard Starman, Pres.; Nicole Lanum, Prin.; Susan Hobbs, Librarian. Priests 1; Lay Teachers 11; Students 145.

St. James-Seton School, 4720 N. 90th St., 68134. Tel: 402-572-0339; Fax: 402-572-0347. Email: sjsprin@sjsomaha.org. Web: sjsomaha.org. Mrs. Chris Arnold, Prin. & Contact; Nan Forman, Librarian. Lay Teachers 33; Students 648; Total Staff 71.

St. Pius X / St. Leo School (1956) 6905 Blondo St., 68104. Tel: 402-551-6667; Fax: 402-551-8123. Email: joyce.gubbels@spsl.net. Web: www.spsl.net. Mrs. Joyce Gubbels, Prin. & Contact; Mrs. Christy Vogel, Librarian. (Two-parish school) Sisters 1; Lay Teachers 52; Students 805.

FORDYCE. *West Catholic Elementary*, (Grades 1-6), 303 Omaha St., P.O. Box 167, 68736-0167. Tel: 402-357-3507; Fax: 402-357-3551. Email: csbrewer@schools.archomaha.com. Dianne Becker, Librarian; Mary Pinkelman, Office Mgr.; Renae Mainquist, 1-2 Grade Teacher; Teresa Aarens, 3-4 Grade Teacher; Connie Brewer, 5-6 Grade Teacher & Head Teacher; Dianne Becker, Librarian. Serving parishes in Constance, Fordyce & Menominee Lay Teachers 3; Students 24.

HARTINGTON. *East Catholic Elementary* Serving parishes in Bow Valley, St. Helena & Wynot, St. James., 108 W. 889th Rd., 68739-6079. Tel: 402-357-2146; Fax: 402-357-3758. Email: mjklug@schools.archomaha.org. Mary Jean Klug, Head Teacher. Lay Teachers 6; Students 51.

HOWELLS. *Howells Community Catholic School*, 114 N. 6th St., 68641. Tel: 402-986-1689; Fax: 402-986-1689. Carrie Gall, Head Teacher; Rev. Leo A. Rigatuso; Pat Recker, Librarian. Serving parishes in Howells, Olean, Heun, Aloys & Tabor Lay Teachers 4; Students 59.

[E] ELEMENTARY SCHOOLS, PRIVATE

OMAHA. *Jesuit Academy* (1996) 2311 N. 22nd St., 68110. Tel: 402-346-4464; Fax: 402-341-1817. Email: frtom@jesuitmso.org. Web: www.jesuitacademy.org. Rev. Thomas W. Neitzke, S.J., Pres. & Contact; Mr. Patrick Rusca, Prin. Lay Teachers 5; Students 62; Total Staff 11.

[F] SPECIAL EDUCATION

OMAHA. *Madonna School*, 6402 N. 71st Plaza, 68104. Tel: 402-556-1883; Fax: 402-556-7332. Email: jdunlap@madonnaschool.org. Web: www.madonnaschool.org. Jay Dunlap, Pres. Serving Special Needs Students. Lay Teachers 9; Para Teachers 7; Administrators 5; Students 58.

Madonna Shop, 9205 Bedford, 68134. Tel: 402-551-5441; Fax: 402-551-6910. Email: rmoses@mshop.omhcoxmail.com. Robin Moses, Dir. Workshop for physical and mental disabilities Total Staff 9; Total Enrollment 44.

[G] GENERAL HOSPITALS

OMAHA. **Archbishop Bergan Mercy Medical Center* (1910) 7500 Mercy Rd., 68124. Tel: 402-398-6060; Fax: 402-398-6920. Web: alegent.com. Marie Knedler, Admin.; Revs. Sally Carlson, Dir. Alegent Health Pastoral Care; Carl F. Sodoro, Chap.; Ron Elliott, Chap. & Team Lead; Mary Mason, Chap.; Sr. Dorothy Rolf, Chap.; Rev. Kit Billings, Chap.; Julia Knezetic, Chap.; Marian Standeven, Operations Leader Mission Svcs./Community Affairs. Affiliate of Catholic Health Initiatives. Priests 1; Sisters 1; Bed Capacity 400; Patients Assisted Annually 100,292; Total Staff 1,875.

**Bergan Mercy Foundation, Inc.* Tel: 402-343-4438; Fax: 402-343-4316. Paul Strawhecker, Chief Devel. Officer; Beth Llewellyn, Vice Pres. Mission Integration.

O'NEILL. *Avera St. Anthony's Hospital* (1952) 300 N. 2nd St., 68763. Tel: 402-336-2611; Fax: 402-336-5135. Email: Ron.Cork@avera.org. Web: www.avera-sta.org. Ronald J. Cork, Pres. & CEO. Sponsored by Sisters of the Presentation of the B.V.M. of Aberdeen, SD & Benedictine Sisters of Sacred Heart Monastery, Yankton, SD., Attended by St. Patrick Church. Bed Capacity 25; Bassinets 6; Patients Assisted Annually 23,552; Total Staff 272.

WEST POINT. *Franciscan Care Services, Inc. dba St. Francis Memorial Hospital* 430 N. Monitor St., 68788-1595. Tel: 402-372-2404; Fax: 402-372-2360. Email: rbriggs@fcswp.org. Web: www.fcswp.org. Ronald O. Briggs, CEO & Contact; Deacon Vince Maly, Chap. Franciscan Sisters of Christian Charity. Sisters 4; Bed Capacity 25; Patients Assisted Annually 66,645; Total Staff 230.

[H] NURSING AND CONVALESCENT HOMES

OMAHA. *Mercy Villa*, 1845 S. 72nd St., 68124. Tel: 402-391-6224; Fax: 402-390-8691. Email: vsilvestri@mercywmw.org. Sr. Virginia Silvestri, O.S.M., Community Care Coord. Retirement Home for the Sisters of Mercy of the Americas for the West Midwest Community. Resident Sisters 37; Total Assisted 37; Total Staff 59; Bed Capacity 46.

New Cassel Retirement Center, 900 N. 90th St., 68114. Tel: 402-393-2277; Fax: 402-393-3784. Web: www.newcassel.org. Mr. Joseph H. Schulte, Admin.; Rev. Robert F. Preisinger (Retired); Mary Kerres, Dir. Pastoral Care. School Sisters of St. Francis. Sisters 4; Aged Residents 179; Total Staff 75.

WEST POINT. *Franciscan Care Services, Inc. dba St. Joseph Retirement Community* (1905) 320 E. Decatur, 68788. Tel: 402-372-3477; Fax: 402-372-6600. Web: www.fcswp.org. Jerry Wordekemper, Admin. Franciscan Sisters of Christian Charity (Manitowoc, WI) 3; Residents 75; Total Assisted Annually 65; Total Staff 37.

[I] FAMILY SERVICE CENTERS

OMAHA. *Catholic Charities*, Daniel E. Sheehan Center, 3300 N. 60th St., 68104. Tel: 402-554-0520; Fax: 402-554-0365. Email: catholiccharities@ccomaha.org. Web: www.ccomaha.org.

Catholic Charities, Inc. Satellite Offices and Services:

Christ Child Center, 1248 S. 10th St., 68108. Tel: 402-342-4566; Fax: 402-342-4541. Email: ChristChildMain@ccomaha.org. Marilyn Sims, Prog. Dir. Services: youth programs; aquatics; senior svcs.

Columbus Center, 3020 18th St., Columbus, 68601. Tel: 402-563-3833; Fax: 402-562-8714. Email: ColumbusClinic@ccomaha. org. Shelli Cornwell, Dir. Behavioral Health. Services: Assessments, Mental health/substance abuse assessments: adult and youth; Outpatient treatment; Medication management; Residential treatment, co-occurring: adult.

Christ Child Learning Center, 2201 S. 11th St., 68108. Tel: 402-341-1880; Fax: 402-933-2941. Email: ChristChildLearning@ccomaha.org. Kim Berg, Prog. Dir. Services: Day care; Pre-School.

Domestic Violence Services - The Shelter Tel: 402-558-5700. Email: FrancesH@ccomaha.org. France Hauptman, L.M.H.P., L.C.S.W., Prog. Dir. Services: 24-hour crisis line; counseling & advocacy; emergency shelter & temporary housing.

Msgr. Kelligar House, 4439 S. 33rd St., 68107. Tel: 402-827-3495; Fax: 402-827-3595. Email: KHouse@ccomaha.org. Michelle Wadum-Lechner, Clinical Mgr. Services: Intermediate residential treatment.

Journeys Tel: 402-898-4135; Fax: 402-898-4139. Email: JourneysBldg@ccomaha.org. Teri Speck, Dir. Behavioral Health. Services: Substance abuse/mental health assessments: adolescent; Residential treatment: Adolescent.

Journeys Outpatient, 740 N. 129th St., 68154. Tel: 402-504-4099; Fax: 402-898-4139. Email: JourneysBldg@ccomaha.org. Teri Speck, Dir. Behavioral Health. Services: Substance abuse/ mental health Assessments: adolescent; Outpatient treatment: adolescent.

Juan Diego Center, 5211 S. 31st St., 68107. Tel: 402-731-5413; Fax: 402-731-5865. Email: JuanDiegoCenter@ccomaha.org. John Synowiecki, Dir. Govt. Rels.; Elisha Novak, Dir. Immigration Legal Assistance; Ana Barrios, Dir. Juan Diego Prog.; Adriana Zambrano, Dir. Microbusiness Training. Services: Government Relations and Public Policy; Immigration Legal Assistance; Juan Diego Program; Latina Resource Center; Mircrobusiness Training & Development; Food Assistance; Family Enrichment Program.

Christ Child North Center, 2111 Emmet St., 68110. Tel: 402-453-6363; Fax: 402-934-5313. Email: ChristChildNorth@ccomaha.org. Marilyn Sims, Prog. Dir. Services: Community forums; Family enrichment program; Senior services. Food Assistance.

Omaha Campus for Hope, 1490 N. 16th St., 68102. Tel: 402-827-0570; Fax: 402-827-0580. Email: OCHBLdg@ccomaha.org. Michael Phillips, Dir. Behavioral Health. Services: Emergency detoxification services - adults; Residential treatment - adults: short term; intermediate; co-occurring substance abuse & mental health disorders.

Sheehan Center, 3300 N. 60th St., 68104. Tel: 402-554-0520; Fax: 402-554-0365. Email: catholiccharities@ccomaha.org. John Griffith, Exec. Dir.; Emily Cunningham Kozlik, Dir. Devel.; Theresa Ross, Dir. Fin.; Sharon Robson, Senior Dir. Human Resources; Sue Malloy, Prog. Mgr. Pregancy Counseling & Adoption. Services: Adoption services and support; Mental health/substance abuse assessments: adult; Outpatient treatment; Pregnancy counseling and support.

St. James Manor, 3102 N. 60th St., 68104. Tel: 402-551-4243; Fax: 402-558-8013. Email: StJamesManor@ccomaha.org. Deb Lang, Dir. Services: affordable housing.

[J] MONASTERIES AND RESIDENCES OF PRIESTS AND BROTHERS

OMAHA. *Jesuit Community at Creighton University*, 2500 California Plaza, 68178. Tel: 402-280-2744; Fax: 402-280-5590. Email: jesuits@creighton.edu. Web: magis.creighton.edu/cujesuits/. Revs. Robert F. O'Connor, S.J., Rector; Sunny Augustine, S.J.; Philip R. Amidon, S.J.; Andrew Alexander, S.J.; Thomas E. Bannantine, S.J.; Charles R. Baumann, S.J.; Burnell B. Bisbee, S.J.; Hubert G. Boschert, S.J.; Raymond A. Bucko, S.J.; Robert O. Burns, S.J.; Gregory I. Carlson, S.J.; James F. Clifton, S.J.; Paul Coelho, S.J.; Christopher S. Collins, S.J.; John D. Cuddigan, S.J., Pastoral Ministry; Donald A. Doll, S.J.; Robert J. Dufford, S.J.; Michael J. Flecky, S.J.; William F. Gerut, S.J.; Lawrence D. Gillick, S.J.; M. Dennis Hamm, S.J.; William J. Harmless, S.J.; Richard J. Hauser, S.J.; Bro. James F. Heidrick, S.J.; Revs. William T. Johnson, S.J.; Howard E. Kalb, S.J.; Kevin F. Kersten, S.J.; Charles T. Kestermeier, S.J.; Timothy R. Lannon, S.J.; Patrick J. Malone, S.J.; Dennis P. McNeilly, S.J.; Thomas S. McShane, S.J., Prof.; James L. Michalski, S.J.; Thomas W. Neitzke, S.J.; Richard W. Ott, S.J.; Anand Pereira, S.J.; Francis A. Prokes, S.J.; Perry L. Robinson, S.J.; M. Ross Romero, S.J.; John P. Schlegel, S.J., Pres., Creighton Univ.; Thomas J. Shanahan, S.J.; Thomas A. Simonds, S.J.; David L. Smith, S.J.; Albert R. Thelen, S.J.; Robert J. Tillman, S.J.; Neal Wilkinson, S.J.; M. John Wymelenberg, S.J.; Eric A. Zimmer, S.J.; Bros. Robert E. Smith, S.J.; Michael R. Wilmot, S.J.
Jesuit Community at Creighton University Priests 44; Brothers 4.

ELKHORN. *Mount Michael Benedictine Abbey* (1954) 22520 Mount Michael Rd., 68022-3400. Tel: 402-289-2541; Fax: 402-289-4539. Email: abbot@mountmichael.org. Web: www.mountmichael.org. Rt. Revs. Theodore Wolff, O.S.B.; Michael Liebl, O.S.B., Abbot; Raphael Walsh, O.S.B.; Revs. Gregory Congote, O.S.B.; Adrian Liable, O.S.B.; Nathanael Foshage, O.S.B.; Eugene McReynolds, O.S.B.; Richard Thell, O.S.B., Prior; John Hagemann, O.S.B.; Daniel Lenz, O.S.B.; Louis L. Sojka, O.S.B., Subprior & Contact; Stephen J. Plank, O.S.B.; Bro. Jerome Kmiecik, O.S.B. Mount Michael Benedictine Abbey Priests 11; Professed Brothers 13; Total Assisted 220; Total Staff 60.

ST. COLUMBANS. *Missionary Society of St. Columban* (Corporate Title: Missionary Society of St. Columban), 68056. Tel: 402-291-1920; Fax: 402-291-8693. Email: directorusa@columban.org. Web: www.columban.org. Revs. Arturo Aguilar, S.S.C., Regl. Dir.; Salvatore Caputo, S.S.C., Ph.D. (Retired), (Providence, RI); Michael Dodd, S.S.C.; Edward Dolan, S.S.C. (Retired), (Providence, RI); Charles Lintz, S.S.C.; Anthony Mortell, S.S.C.; Charles O'Rourke, S.S.C.; Edward Quinn, S.S.C.; William Schmitt, S.S.C.; Thomas Shaughnessy, S.S.C.; Colm Stanley, S.S.C., (Omaha, NE); Richard Steinhiber, S.S.C., (Omaha, NE); Paul White, S.S.C. (Retired), (Omaha, NE). Regional Headquarters and Administration Offices of the Columban Fathers in the United States Priests 14.
Other Assignments: Revs. Donald Kelley, S.S.C. (Retired), Brownsville; Peter Cronin, S.S.C., Buffalo; Vincent McCarthy, S.S.C. (Retired), Buffalo; Thomas Walsh, S.S.C. (Retired), Buffalo; Charles Flaherty, S.S.C. (Retired), Boston; Leo Distor, S.S.C., Chicago; Charles Duster, S.S.C., Omaha; Thomas Glennon, S.S.C., Omaha; Francis Grady, S.S.C. (Retired), Providence; Timothy Mulroy, S.S.C., Chicago; Francis Royer, S.S.C. (Retired), Chicago; John Smith, S.S.C., Chicago; John Wanaurny, S.S.C., San Bernardino; Clarence Beckley, S.S.C. (Retired), Dubuque; Michael Donnelly, S.S.C., El Paso; William Morton, S.S.C., El Paso; Kevin Mullins, S.S.C., El Paso; Dennis O'Mara, S.S.C., El Paso; Albert Utzig, S.S.C., San Bernardino; John Brannigan, S.S.C., Los Angeles; Yong Hoon Choi, S.S.C., Los Angeles; Thomas Cusack, S.S.C., Los Angeles; George DaRoza, S.S.C., Los Angeles; Gerard Dunne, S.S.C., Los Angeles; Peter Kenny, S.S.C., Los Angeles; Thomas Reynolds, S.S.C., Los Angeles; Edward Roberts, S.S.C., Palm Beach; Denis Bartley, S.S.C., Providence; John Buckley, S.S.C., Providence; Francis Carroll, S.S.C., Providence; Charles Degnan, S.S.C., Providence; James Dwyer, S.S.C., Providence; Norbert Feld, S.S.C., Providence; Victor Gaboury, S.S.C. (Retired), Providence; Brian Gallagher, S.S.C., Providence; John Hogan, S.S.C., Providence; Francis Keaney, S.S.C., Boston; Oliver Kennedy, S.S.C., Providence; John Marley, S.S.C., Providence; Daniel McGinn, S.S.C., Providence; Joseph McSweeney, S.S.C., Providence; Joseph McSweeny, S.S.C., Omaha; John Moran, S.S.C., Providence; Paul O'Malley, S.S.C. (Retired), Providence; Robert O'Rourke, S.S.C. (Retired), Providence; Paul Richardson, S.S.C., Providence; John Roche, S.S.C., Providence; Alban Sueper, S.S.C. (Retired), Providence; William Sullivan, S.S.C., Providence; William Sweeney, S.S.C., Providence; John Lagomarsino, S.S.C., Sacramento; Gerard O'Shaughnessy, S.S.C., San Bernardino; Brendan O'Sullivan, S.S.C., San Bernardino; Bernard Toal, S.S.C., Providence; Robert Clark, S.S.C., San Diego; Finbar Maxwell, S.S.C., San Jose; William Brunner, S.S.C., Sioux City; Cathal Gallagher, S.S.C., Sioux Falls; Mark Mengel, S.S.C., Springfield, MA; Robert Mosher, S.S.C., El Paso, TX; Thomas Vaughan, S.S.C. (Retired), St. Paul; Gerald Wilmsen, S.S.C. (Retired), Superior.

SCHUYLER. *Benedictine Mission House*, 1123 Rd. I, P.O. Box 528, 68661-0528. Tel: 402-352-2177; Fax: 402-352-2176. Email: monastery@benedictinemissionhouse.com. Web: www.benedictinemissionhouse.com. Revs. Mauritius Wilde, O.S.B., Prior & Contact; Volker Futter, O.S.B., Subprior; Thomas Aquinas Leitner, O.S.B.; Paul L. Kasun, O.S.B. Brothers 3.

[K] CONVENTS AND RESIDENCES FOR SISTERS

OMAHA. *Monastery of St. Clare* (1878) 3626 N. 65th Ave., 68104. Tel: 402-558-4916; Fax: 402-558-5046. Web: www.omahapoorclare.org. Sr. Mary Clare Brown, Contact. Poor Clares (Second Order of St. Francis)., Attended by Jesuit Fathers. Sisters 8.

Motherhouse of the Servants of Mary, Convent of Our Lady of Sorrows, 7400 Military Ave., 68134. Tel: 402-571-2547; Fax: 402-573-6055. Web: www.osms.org. Sisters Mary Gehringer, O.S.M., Prov. & Contact; Carol Kowalski, O.S.M., Asst. Prov. Professed 82; Sisters in Motherhouse 33.

Provincial Motherhouse and Novitiate of the Notre Dame Sisters (1853) 3501 State St., 68112. Tel: 402-455-2994; Fax: 402-455-3974. Email: notredamesisters@notredamesisters.org. Web: www.notredamesisters.org. Sr. Celeste Wobeter, N.D., Prov. Pres. Professed 45; Sisters in Motherhouse 15.

Sisters of Mercy of the Americas West Midwest Community, Inc. (2008) 7262 Mercy Rd., 68124-2389. Tel: 402-393-8225; Fax: 402-393-8145. Email: info@mercywmw.org. Web: www.mercywestmidwest.org. Sisters Judith Frikker, R.S.M., Pres.; Judith Frikker, R.S.M., Substitute Pres.; Sheila Megley, R.S.M., Treas.; Judith Cannon, R.S.M., Sec.; Kathy Thornton, R.S.M., Leadership Team; Michelle Gorman, R.S.M., Leadership Team; Kim Kinsel, Community Operating Officer; Carol Kelley, Community Fin. Officer; Sandy Goetzinger-Comer, Dir. Communications. Sisters 740; Associates 536.

Knowles Mercy Spirituality Center, 2304 Campanile Rd., Waterloo, 68069. Tel: 402-359-4288; Fax: 402-359-4843. Email: kmscenter@mercywmw.org. Web: www.kmscenter.org. Marisa Gilbert, Dir. Overnight Capacity 15; Daytime Capacity 60; Staff 6.

Sisters of the Good Shepherd (R.G.S.), 1106 N. 36th St., 68131. Tel: 402-551-2966; Fax: 402-292-2046. Email: ellen.dolan@stmarysbellevueebm. Web: www.goodshepherdsisters.org.

NORFOLK. *Immaculata Monastery* (1923) 300 N. 18th St., 68701-3687. Tel: 402-371-3438; Fax: 402-371-0127. Email: rtoffosb@gmail.com. Web: www.norfolk-osb.org. Sr. Pia Portmann, O.S.B., Prioress.
Immaculata Monastery, Priory Motherhouse and Novitiate of the Missionary Benedictine Sisters Sisters 37; Personnel 14.

[L] SECULAR INSTITUTES

OMAHA. *Cor Unum Family Inc.*, 7323 Shirley St., #101, 68124. Tel: 402-933-9812. Email: bwhelanl@cox.net. Rev. Msgr. Bill S. Whelan, Contact Person (Retired).

Institute of the Apostolic Oblates (1950) 6762 Western Ave., 68132. Tel: 402-553-4418; Fax: 402-553-1388. Email: aoomaha@prosanctity.org. Web: www.prosanctity.org. Teresa J. Monaghen, Natl. Moderator; Franca Salvo, Local Moderator, & Contact Person; Joan Christine Patten, Vocation Dir. A secular institute for women with the aim of promoting the apostolate of interior life, the universal call to holiness, and the Pro Sanctity Movement.

Apostolic Sodales formerly Apostolic Sodales - Secular Institute (1962) 11002 N. 204 St., Elkhorn, 68022. Tel: 402-731-2196; Fax: 402-731-2196. Web: http://apostolic-sodales.org. Revs. Thomas W. Weisbecker, First Natl. Bro.; Frank E. Jindra, Spiritual Dir.; Carl J. Zoucha, Contact Person. A Secular Institute for priests with the aim of promoting the spirituality of the Cenacle, brotherhood among priests, and forming the Church as a family.

ELKHORN. *Pro Sanctity Movement* (1947) 11002 N. 204th St., 68022. Tel: 402-289-2670; Fax: 402-289-1938. Email: psm@prosanctity.org. Web: www.prosanctity.org. Teresa Monaghen, Local Pro Sanctity Dir. & Contact. Tel: 402-289-2670; Jessica L. Kary, Natl. Pro Sanctity Dir. Dir. Ecclesial organization: Promotes apostolates of holiness; teaches, supports and guides people seeking to deepen their spiritual life.

[M] FOUNDATIONS AND TRUST FUNDS

OMAHA. *The Institute for Priestly Formation Foundation*, 2500 California Plaza, 68178-0207. Tel: 402-546-6384. Mr. P. Thomas Pogge, Exec. Dir.

The Omaha Archdiocesan Educational Foundation, Inc.

The Office of Stewardship and Development formerly The Office of Stewardship, Planning and Development 3212 North 60th St., P.O. Box 4130, 68104-0130. Tel: 402-554-8493; Fax: 402-554-8402. Email: mejewell@archomaha.org.

Archbishop Sheehan Adult Education Endowment Trust

All Saints Catholic School Educational Endowment Trust

Black Students Catholic Educational Endowment Trust

Black Student Catholic Scholarship Trust Fund, 68104. A trust for the purpose of providing eligible black Catholic students scholarships and assistance for Catholic high school education. The board of 10 trustees for a nonprofit religious and educational corporation, whose president is the Archbishop of Omaha oversees the affairs of this trust.

Music in Catholic Schools Endowment Trust

Roncalli Catholic High School Educational Endowment Trust

Roncalli Catholic High School Scholarship Endowment Trust

Religious Education Evangelization Commission Endowment Trust

The Catholic Voice Educational Endowment Trust

The Omaha Archdiocesan Parish Foundation, Inc.

St. Michael Church Endowment Trust, Albion.

St. Michael Church Educational Endowment Trust, Albion.

St. Aloysius Parish Endowment Trust, Aloys.

St. Aloysius Parish Educational Endowment Trust Aloys, NE

St. Joseph Parish Endowment Trust, Amelia.

St. Joseph Parish Educational Endowment Trust, Amelia.

St. Joseph Parish Endowment Trust, Atkinson.

St. Joseph Church Educational Endowment Trust, Atkinson.

Holy Cross Parish Endowment Trust, Bancroft.

Holy Cross Parish Educational Endowment Trust, Bancroft.

St. Patrick Parish Endowment Trust, Battle Creek.

St. Patrick Parish Educational Endowment Trust, Battle Creek.

Holy Cross Parish Endowment Trust, Beemer, 68716.

Holy Cross Parish Educational Endowment Trust, Beemer.

St. Mary Church Endowment Trust, Bellevue.

St. Mary Church Educational Endowment Trust, Bellevue.

St. Matthew the Evangelist Parish Endowment Trust, Bellevue, 68123.

St. Francis Borgia Parish Endowment Trust, Blair.

St. Francis Borgia Parish Educational Endowment Trust, Blair.

St. Andrew Parish Endowment Trust, Bloomfield.

St. Andrew Parish Educational Endowment Trust, Bloomfield.

SS. Peter and Paul Parish Endowment Trust, Bow Valley.

SS. Peter and Paul Parish Educational Endowment Trust, Bow Valley.

East Catholic Elementary School Educational Endowment Trust, Bow Valley.

St. Ignatius Parish Endowment Trust, Brunswick.

St. Ignatius Parish Educational Endowment Trust, Brunswick.

SS. Peter and Paul Parish Endowment Trust, Butte.

SS. Peter and Paul Parish Educational Endowment Trust, Butte.

St. Anthony Parish Endowment Trust, Cedar Rapids.

St. Anthony Parish Educational Endowment Trust, Cedar Rapids.

St. Michael Catholic Church Parish Endowment Trust, Central City.

St. Michael Parish Educational Endowment Trust, Central City.

St. Peter Parish Endowment Trust, Clarks.

St. Peter Parish Educational Endowment Trust, Clarks.

SS. Cyril and Methodius Parish Endowment Trust, Clarkson.

SS. Cyril and Methodius Parish Educational Endowment Trust, Clarkson.

Holy Trinity Church of Colfax, County Parish and

Cemetery Endowment Trust Fund, Clarkson, 68629.
St. Theresa of Avila Parish Endowment Trust, Clearwater.
St. Theresa of Avila Parish Educational Endowment Trust, Clearwater.
St. Theresa Church of Clearwater Cemetery Endowment Trust Fund, Clearwater, 68726.
St. Michael Parish Endowment Trust, Coleridge.
St. Michael Parish Educational Endowment Trust, Coleridge.
St. Anthony Parish Endowment Trust, Columbus.
St. Anthony Parish Educational Endowment Trust, Columbus.
St. Anthony Elementary School Endowment Trust, Columbus.
St. Bonaventure Church Endowment Trust, Columbus.
St. Isidore Church Endowment Trust, Columbus.
St. Isidore Parish Educational Endowment Trust, Columbus.
St. Isidore Elementary School Endowment Trust, Columbus.
Scotus Central Catholic High School Endowment Trust, Columbus.
St. Joseph Parish Endowment Trust, Constance.
St. Joseph Parish Educational Endowment Trust, Constance.
St. Ludger Parish Endowment Trust, Creighton.
St. Ludger Parish Educational Endowment Trust, Creighton.
St. Joseph Church of Constance Endowment Trust Fund, Crofton, 68730. Rev. Joseph G. Broudou, Contact Person.
St. Rose Church Cemetery Endowment Trust Fund, Crofton, 68730. Rev. Joseph G. Broudou, Contact Person.
St. Rose of Lima Parish Endowment Trust, Crofton.
St. Rose of Lima Parish Educational Endowment Trust, Crofton.
Holy Family Parish Endowment Trust, Decatur.
Holy Family Parish Educational Endowment Trust, Decatur.
St. Anne Parish Endowment Trust, Dixon.
St. Anne Parish Educational Endowment Trust, Dixon.
St. Anne Church of Dixon Cemetery Endowment Trust Fund, Dixon, 68732.
St. Wenceslaus Parish Endowment Trust, Dodge.
St. Wenceslaus Church Educational Endowment Trust, Dodge.
St. Stanislaus Parish Endowment Trust, Duncan.
St. Stanislaus Parish Educational Endowment Trust, Duncan.
St. Boniface Parish Endowment Trust, Elgin.
St. Boniface Parish Educational Endowment Trust, Elgin.
St. Boniface School Endowment Trust, Elgin.
Pope John XXIII Central Catholic High School Endowment Trust, Elgin.
St. Patrick Parish Endowment Trust, Elkhorn.
St. Patrick School Endowment Trust, Elkhorn.
St. Patrick School Tuition Assistance Endowment Trust, Elkhorn.
Mt. Michael Foundation, Inc., Elkhorn.
Sacred Heart Parish Endowment Trust, Emerson.
Sacred Heart Parish Educational Endowment Trust, Emerson.
St. Peter de Alcantara Parish Endowment Trust, Ewing.
St. Peter de Alcantara Parish Educational Endowment Trust, Ewing.
St. Theresa Church of Clearwater Cemetery Endowment Trust Fund, Ewing, 68735. Rev. William J. Safranek, Contact.
St. John the Baptist Parish Endowment Trust, Fordyce.
St. John the Baptist Parish Educational Endowment Trust, Fordyce.
West Catholic Educational Endowment Trust, Fordyce.
St. John the Baptist Parish Endowment Trust, Fort Calhoun.
St. John the Baptist Church Educational Endowment Trust, Fort Calhoun.
St. Patrick Catholic Church Endowment Trust, Fremont.
St. Patrick Parish Educational Endowment Trust, Fremont.
Archbishop Bergan Jr./Sr. Catholic High School Educational Endowment Trust, Fremont.
St. Peter Catholic Church Endowment Trust, Fullerton.
St. Peter Parish Educational Endowment Trust, Fullerton.
St. Rose of Lima Parish Endowment Trust, Genoa.
St. Rose of Lima Parish Educational Endowment Trust, Genoa.
St. Patrick Parish Endowment Trust, Gretna.
St. Patrick Parish Educational Endowment Trust, Gretna.
Holy Trinity Parish Endowment Trust, Hartington.
Holy Trinity Parish Educational Endowment Trust, Hartington.
Holy Trinity Grade School Endowment Trust, Hartington.
Cedar Catholic High School Educational Endowment Trust, Hartington.
Holy Trinity Parish Endowment Trust, Heun.
Holy Trinity Parish Educational Endowment Trust, Heun.
Holy Trinity Parish of Colfax County Parish and Cemetery Endowment Trust Fund Heun, NE
St. Cornelius Parish Endowment Trust, Homer.
St. Cornelius Parish Educational Endowment Trust, Homer.
St. Rose of Lima Parish Endowment Trust, Hooper.
St. Rose of Lima Parish Educational Endowment Trust, Hooper.
St. John Nepomucene Parish Endowment Trust, Howells.
St. John Nepomucene Parish Educational Endowment Trust, Howells.
SS. Peter and Paul Parish Endowment Trust, Howells.
SS. Peter and Paul Parish Educational Endowment Trust, Howells.
SS. Peter and Paul Catholic Church Endowment for Howells Community Catholic School, Howells.
St. Mary Parish Endowment Trust, Hubbard.
St. Mary Parish Educational Endowment Trust, Hubbard.
St. Francis Parish Endowment Trust, Humphrey.
St. Francis Parish Educational Endowment Trust, Humphrey.
St. Francis Church of Humphrey Cemetery Endowment Trust Fund, Humphrey, 68642.
St. Patrick Parish Endowment Trust, Jackson.
St. Patrick Parish Educational Endowment Trust, Jackson.
SS. Peter and Paul Parish Endowment Trust, Krakow.
SS. Peter and Paul Parish Educational Endowment Trust, Krakow.
St. Anne Church of Dixon Cemetery Endowment Trust Fund, Laurel, 68745. Rev. James F. McCluskey.
St. Mary Parish Endowment Trust, Laurel.
St. Mary Parish Educational Endowment Trust, Laurel.
St. Mary Parish Endowment Trust, Leigh.
St. Mary Parish Cemetery Endowment Trust, Leigh.
Holy Family Parish Endowment Trust, Lindsay.
Holy Family Parish Educational Endowment Trust, Lindsay.
Assumption Parish Endowment Trust, Lynch.
Assumption Parish Educational Endowment Trust, Lynch.
Assumption Parish Cemetery Endowment Trust, Lynch.
St. Joseph Parish Endowment Trust, Lyons.
St. Joseph Parish Educational Endowment Trust, Lyons.
Our Lady of Fatima Parish Endowment Trust, Macy.
Our Lady of Fatima Parish Educational Endowment Trust, Macy.
St. Leonard Parish Endowment Trust, Madison.
St. Leonard Parish Educational Endowment Trust, Madison.
St. Boniface Parish Endowment Trust, Menominee.
St. Boniface Parish Educational Endowment Trust, Menominee.
St. Boniface's Church Cemetery Endowment Fund Menominee, NE
St. Boniface Parish Endowment Trust, Monterey.
St. Boniface Parish Educational Endowment Trust, Monterey.
Sacred Heart Parish Endowment Trust, Naper.
Sacred Heart Parish Educational Endowment Trust, Naper.
St. Francis of Assisi Parish Endowment Trust, Neligh.
St. Francis of Assisi Parish Educational Endowment Trust, Neligh.
St. Peter Parish Endowment Trust, Newcastle.
St. Peter Parish Educational Endowment Trust, Newcastle.
St. William Parish Endowment Trust, Niobrara.
St. William Parish Educational Endowment Trust, Niobrara.
Sacred Heart Parish Endowment Trust, Norfolk.
Sacred Heart Parish Religious Education Endowment Trust, Norfolk.
Sacred Heart Elementary School Educational Endowment Trust, Norfolk.
Norfolk Catholic High School Educational Endowment Trust, Norfolk.
St. Charles Borromeo Parish Endowment Trust, North Bend.
St. Charles Borromeo Parish Educational Endowment Trust, North Bend.
Sacred Heart Parish Endowment Trust, Olean.
Sacred Parish Educational Endowment Trust, Olean.
Church of the Assumption Endowment Trust
Church of the Assumption Educational Endowment Trust
Church of the Assumption Scholarship Educational Endowment Trust
Blessed Sacrament Parish Endowment Trust
Blessed Sacrament Parish Educational Endowment Trust
Blessed Sacrament School Educational Endowment Trust
Christ the King Parish Endowment Trust
Christ the King Educational Endowment Trust
Holy Cross Parish Endowment Trust
Holy Family Parish Endowment Trust
Holy Family Parish Educational Trust
Holy Ghost Parish Endowment Trust
Holy Ghost Parish Educational Endowment Trust
Holy Name Parish Endowment Trust
Holy Name Parish Educational Endowment Trust
Holy Name Elementary School Endowment Trust Omaha, NE
Immaculate Conception Parish Endowment Trust
Immaculate Conception Parish Educational Endowment Trust
Mary Our Queen Educational Endowment Trust
Mary Our Queen Parish Endowment Trust, 68198.
Mother of Perpetual Help Parish Endowment Trust
Mother of Perpetual Help Parish Educational Endowment Trust
Our Lady of Fatima Parish Endowment Trust
Our Lady of Fatima Parish Educational Endowment Trust
Our Lady of Guadalupe Parish Endowment Trust
Our Lady of Guadalupe Educational Endowment Trust, 68131.
Our Lady of Lourdes Parish Endowment Trust Tel: 402-346-0900.
Our Lady of Lourdes Parish Educational Endowment Trust Tel: 402-346-0900.
Our Lady of Lourdes School Educational Endowment Trust
Sacred Heart Parish Endowment Trust
Sacred Heart Parish Educational Endowment Trust
St. Adalbert Parish Endowment Trust
St. Adalbert Parish Educational Endowment Trust
St. Agnes Parish Endowment Trust
St. Agnes Parish Educational Endowment Trust
St. Anthony Parish Endowment Trust
St. Anthony Parish Educational Endowment Trust
St. Benedict Parish Endowment Trust
St. Benedict Parish Educational Endowment Trust
St. Bernadette Parish Endowment Trust
St. Bernadette Parish Educational Endowment Trust
St. Bernard Parish Memorial Endowment Trust
St. Bernard Parish Religious Education Endowment Trust
St. Bridget Parish Endowment Trust
St. Bridget Parish Educational Endowment Trust
St. Cecilia Cathedral Endowment Trust
St. Elizabeth Ann Parish Endowment Trust
St. Elizabeth Ann Parish Educational Endowment Trust
St. Francis of Assisi Church of South Omaha Endowment Trust
St. Francis of Assisi Church of South Omaha Educational Endowment Trust
St. Frances Cabrini Parish Endowment Trust
St. Frances Cabrini Parish Educational Endowment Trust
St. James Parish Endowment Trust
St. James Parish Educational Endowment Trust
St. James/Seton School Educational Endowment Fund
St. Joan of Arc Parish Endowment Trust
St. Joan of Arc Parish Educational Endowment Trust
St. Joan of Arc Grade School Educational Endowment Trust
St. John Parish Endowment Trust
St. John Parish Educational Endowmwnt Trust
St. John Vianney Church of Millard Parish Endowment Trust
St. John Vianney Parish Educational Endowment Trust
St. Joseph Parish Endowment Trust
St. Joseph Parish Educational Endowment Trust
St. Leo Parish Endowment Trust
St. Leo Parish Educational Endowment Trust
St. Margaret Mary Parish Endowment Trust
St. Margaret Mary Parish Educational Endowment Trust
St. Margaret Mary School Educational Endowment Trust
St. Mary's Church of Tabor Parish and Cemetery Endowment Trust Fund, 100 North 62nd St., 68132. Tel: 402-986-1627; Fax: 402-986-1627.
St. Mary Parish Endowment Trust
St. Mary Parish Educational Endowment Trust
St. Mary Elementary School Endowment Trust

St. Patrick Parish Endowment Trust
St. Patrick Church Educational Endowment Trust
St. Peter Parish Endowment Trust
St. Peter Parish Educational Endowment Trust
SS. Peter and Paul Church Endowment Trust
SS. Peter and Paul Parish Educational Endowment Trust
SS. Peter and Paul Elementary School Educational Endowment Trust
St. Philip Neri Church Endowment Trust
St. Philip Neri Parish Educational Endowment Trust
St. Pius X Parish Endowment Trust
St. Pius X Parish Educational Endowment Trust
St. Pius X/St. Leo School Educational Endowment Trust
St. Richard Parish Endowment Trust
St. Robert Bellarmine Parish Endowment Trust
St. Rose Parish Endowment Trust
St. Rose Parish Educational Endowment Trust
St. Stanislaus Parish Endowment Trust
St. Stanislaus Parish Educational Endowment Trust

St. Stephen the Martyr Parish Endowment Trust
St. Stephen the Martyr Parish Educational Endowment Trust
St. Stephen the Martyr Elementary School Educational Endowment Trust
Teachers' Salary Endowment Trust Fund of St. Stephen Church of Omaha, 68198.
St. Therese of the Child Jesus Parish Endowment Trust
St. Therese of the Child Jesus Parish Educational Endowment Trust
St. Thomas More Parish Endowment Trust
St. Thomas More Parish Educational Endowment Trust
St. Thomas More School Educational Endowment Trust
St. Vincent de Paul Parish Endowment Trust
St. Vincent de Paul Parish Educational Endowment Trust
St. Wenceslaus Parish Endowment Trust
St. Wenceslaus Parish Educational Endowment Trust

St. Patrick Foundation, Inc., O'Neill.
St. Mary School Foundation, Inc., O'Neill.
St. Patrick Parish Educational Endowment Trust, O'Neill, 68763.
St. Mary of the Seven Dolors Parish Endowment Trust, Osmond.
St. Columbkille Parish Endowment Trust, Papillion.
St. Columbkille Educational Endowment Trust, Papillion.
St. John the Baptist Parish Endowment Trust, Pender.
St. John the Baptist Parish Educational Endowment Trust, Pender.
St. John the Baptist Parish Endowment Trust, Petersburg.
St. John the Baptist Parish Educational Endowment Trust
St. John the Baptist Center Maintenance Endowment Trust, Petersburg.
St. John the Baptist Church of Petersburg Cemetery Endowment Trust, Petersburg, 68652.
St. Joseph Parish Endowment Trust, Pierce.
St. Joseph Parish Educational Endowment Trust, Pierce.
St. Paul Parish Endowment Trust, Plainview.
St. Paul Parish Educational Endowment Trust, Plainview.
St. Joseph Parish Endowment Trust, Platte Center.
St. Joseph Parish Educational Endowment Trust, Platte Center.
St. Joseph Parish Endowment Trust, Ponca.
St. Joseph Parish Educational Endowment Trust, Ponca.
St. Mary Parish Endowment Trust, Primrose.
St. Mary Parish Educational Endowment Trust, Primrose.
St. Bonaventure Parish Endowment Trust, Raeville.
St. Bonaventure Parish/Pope John XXIII High School Educational Endowment Trust, Raeville.
St. Gerald Parish Endowment Trust, Ralston.
St. Gerald Parish Educational Endowment Trust, Ralston.
St. Gerald School Educational Endowment Trust, Ralston.
St. Frances de Chantal Parish Endowment Trust, Randolph.
St. Frances de Chantal Parish Educational Endowment Trust, Randolph.
St. Frances de Chantal of Randolph Cemetery Endowment Trust Fund, Randolph, 68771.
St. Anthony Parish Endowment Trust, St. Charles.
St. Anthony Parish Educational Endowment Trust, St. Charles.
St. Edward Parish Endowment Trust, St. Edward.
St. Edward Parish Educational Endowment Trust, St. Edward.
St. Edward's Church of St. Edward Cemetery Endowment Trust Fund, St. Edward, 68660.
Immaculate Conception Parish Endowment Trust, St. Helena.
Immaculate Conception Parish Educational Endowment Trust, St. Helena.
SS. Philip and James Parish Endowment Trust, St. James.
SS. Philip and James Parish Educational Endowment Trust, St. James.
St. John Parish Endowment Trust, St. John.
St. Francis de Sales Parish Endowment Trust, Schoolcraft.
St. Augustine Parish Endowment Trust, Schuyler.
St. Augustine Parish Educational Endowment Trust, Schuyler.
St. Mary Parish Endowment Trust, Schuyler.
St. Mary Parish Educational Endowment Trust, Schuyler.
St. Lawrence Parish Endowment Trust, Scribner.
St. Lawrence Parish Educational Endowment Trust, Scribner.
St. Lawrence Parish Endowment Trust, Silver Creek.
St. Lawrence Parish Educational Endowment Trust, Silver Creek.
St. Lawrence Church of Silver Creek Cemetery Endowment Trust Fund, Silver Creek, 68663.
St. Leo Parish Endowment Trust, Snyder.
St. Leo Parish Educational Endowment Trust, Snyder.
St. Michael Parish Endowment Trust, South Sioux City.
St. Michael Educational Endowment Trust, South Sioux City.
St. Mary Catholic Church Endowment Trust, Spencer.
St. Mary Parish Educational Endowment Trust, Spencer.
St. Mary Cemetery Endowment Trust, Spencer.
St. Joseph Parish Endowment Trust, Springfield.
St. Joseph Parish Educational Endowment Trust, Springfield.
St. Peter Parish Endowment Trust, Stanton.
St. Peter Parish Educational Endowment Trust, Stanton.
St. Boniface Parish Endowment Trust, Stuart.
St. Boniface Parish Educational Endowment Trust, Stuart.
St. Boniface Elementary School Endowment Trust, Stuart.
St. Mary Parish Endowment Trust, Tabor.
St. Mary Parish Educational Endowment Trust, Tabor.
St. Mary's Church of Tabor Parish and Cemetery Endowment Trust Fund
St. Michael Parish Endowment Trust, Tarnov.
St. Michael Parish Educational Endowment Trust, Tarnov.
St. Patrick Parish Endowment Trust, Tekamah.
St. Patrick Parish Educational Endowment Trust, Tekamah.
Our Lady of Mt. Carmel Parish Endowment Trust, Tilden.
Our Lady of Mt. Carmel Parish Educational Endowment Trust, Tilden.
St. John the Evangelist Parish Endowment Trust, Valley.
St. John the Evangelist Parish Educational Endowment Trust, Valley.
St. Wenceslaus Church Parish Endowment Trust, Verdigre.
St. Wenceslaus Parish Educational Endowment Trust, Verdigre.
St. Joseph Parish Endowment Trust, Walthill.
St. Joseph Parish Educational Endowment Trust, Walthill.
St. Mary Parish Endowment Trust, Wayne.
St. Mary Parish Educational Endowment Trust, Wayne.
Church of the Assumption of the B.V.M. Parish Endowment Trust, West Point.
Church of the Assumption of the B.V.M. Parish Educational Endowment Trust, West Point.
Guardian Angels Grade School Educational Endowment Trust, West Point.
West Point Central Catholic High School Educational Endowment Trust, West Point.
West Point Central Catholic High School Activity Center Endowment Trust
St. Augustine Indian Mission Endowment Trust, Winnebago.
St. Augustine Indian Mission Educational Endowment Trust, Winnebago.
St. Augustine Indian Mission Tuition Relief Educational Endowment Trust, Winnebago.
FEATHERS, Winnebago, 68071. Rev. David M. Korth, Contact & Dir. An endowment, duly constituted under the laws of the State of Nebraska as a nonprofit religious, charitable and educational corporation, to provide scholarships to Native American children of the Winnebago nation to attend high school, grade school, college.
St. Joseph Parish Endowment Trust, Wisner.
St. Joseph Parish Educational Endowment Trust, Wisner.
Sacred Heart Parish Endowment Trust, Wynot.
Sacred Heart Parish Educational Endowment Trust, Wynot.

ELKHORN. *Mount Michael Foundation*, 22520 Mount Michael Rd., 68022-3400. Tel: 402-289-2541; Fax: 402-289-4539. Rt. Rev. Michael Liebl, O.S.B., Abbot.

FORDYCE. *Cemetery Endowment for St. Boniface Church*, Box 170, 68736. Tel: 402-357-3506; Fax: 402-357-3795. Rev. David L. Fulton, Contact Person, Pastor.

ST. COLUMBANS. *Columban Fathers Regional Administration*, P.O. Box 10, 68056-0010. Tel: 402-291-1920; Fax: 402-291-8693. Email: stcolneus@aol.com. Web: www.columban.org. Dan Eminger, Treas.
St. Columban's Central Administration Web: columban.org.
St. Columban's Medical and Retirement Tel: 402-291-1920; Fax: 402-291-4984.
St. Columban's Gift Annuity Trust Tel: 402-291-1920; Fax: 402-291-4984.
St. Columban's Education Trust Tel: 402-291-1920; Fax: 402-291-4984.
St. Columban's Priests Health Program Trust Tel: 402-291-1920; Fax: 402-291-4984.
St. Columban's Retirement Fund Trust Tel: 402-291-1920; Fax: 402-291-4984.
St. Columban's Masses in Trust Tel: 402-291-1920; Fax: 402-291-4984.
St. Columban's Donors/Personal Trust Tel: 402-291-1920; Fax: 402-291-4984.
St. Columban's Regional Trust Tel: 402-291-1920; Fax: 402-291-4984.
St. Columban's Burse Estate Trust Tel: 402-291-1920; Fax: 402-291-4984.
St. Columban's Gift Annuity Trust California Tel: 402-291-1920; Fax: 402-291-4984.

NORFOLK. *Missionary Benedictine Sisters Foundation, Immaculata Monastery*, 300 N. 18th St., 68701. Tel: 402-379-3438; Fax: 402-371-0127. Email: rtoffosbe@gmail.com. Web: www.norfolk-osb.org. Sr. Rita Marie Tofflemire, Contact Person.

SCHUYLER. *St. Benedict Center Endowment Fund* (2000) 1126 Rd. "I", P.O. Box 528, 68661-0528. Tel: 402-352-8819; Fax: 402-352-8884. Email: Retreats@StBenedictCenter.com. Web: www.StBenedictCenter.com. Rev. Germar Neubert, O.S.B., Contact at Benedictine Mission House/Christ the King Priory. An endowment for the purpose of providing for the support and benefit of development, maintenance and supplemental funding of programs and services of St. Benedict Center and the receipt and management of gifts and bequests to the same center. The nonprofit, charitable and educational corporation is duly constituted under the laws of the State of Nebraska.
St. Benedict Center A nonprofit, ecumenical retreat and conference center, founded by the Missionary Benedictines of Christ the King Priory, Schuyler, NE. As Benedictines we share our hospitality and spirituality with those who search for personal and spiritual growth. We welcome individuals and groups of all Christian denominations, as they seek God in a peaceful and quiet setting. We provide an atmosphere that is conducive to prayer, rest and renewal for laity, clergy and religious., 1126 Rd. I, P.O. Box 528, 68661-0528. Tel: 402-352-8819; Fax: 402-352-8884. Email: Retreats@StBenedictCenter.com. Web: www.StBenedictCenter.com.
Benedictine Mission House Endowment Trust, 1123 Rd. "I", P.O. Box 528, 68661-0528. Tel: 402-352-2177. Email: monastery@benedictinemissionhouse.com. Web: www.benedictinemissionhouse.com. Rev. Volker Futter, O.S.B., Contact Person & Treas.

[N] MISCELLANEOUS

OMAHA. *Archdiocese of Omaha Youth Camp*, 100 N. 62nd St., 68132. Tel: 402-332-3384; Fax: 402-332-3384.
Beginning Experience of Omaha, Inc., 3214 N. 60th St., 68104-3495. Tel: 402-551-9003, Ext. 1304; 888-800-8352. Email: paseier@archomaha.org. Pat Seier, Coord.
Bethlehem House (2002) 2301 S. 15th St., 68108. Tel: 402-502-9224. Email: gfreimuth@cox.net. Web: www.bethlehemhouseomaha.com. Gina Freimuth, Exec. Dir., 1404 Castelar St., 68108. Tel: 402-341-1305; Fax: 402-342-5511. Provides housing, spiritual and pastoral support to women facing crisis pregnancy for up to 10 weeks after delivery. Staff 4.
C.M.G. Agency, Inc., 10843 Old Mill Rd., 68154-2600. Tel: 800-228-6108, Ext. 2413; Fax:

402-551-2943. Email: ppeterson@catholicmutual.org. Paul Peterson, Contact & Sec. An insurance agency supporting the religious and business activities of the Catholic Mutual Relief Society of America and The Catholic Relief Insurance Company of America.

Cathedral Arts Project, Inc., 100 N. 62nd St., 68132. Tel: 402-558-3100, Ext. 3007; Fax: 402-558-3026. Email: WJWOEGER@archomaha.org. Web: www.cathedralartsproject.org. Bro. William J. Woeger, F.S.C., Exec. Dir. & Contact.

**Catholic Charities Foundation*, 3300 N. 60th, 68104-3402. Tel: 402-554-0520; Fax: 402-829-9268. Email: catholiccharities@ccomaha.org. Web: www.ccomaha.org. John Griffith, Pres. & Contact.

Catholic Jail and Prison Ministry (1998) 701 S. 28th St., 68105-1511. Tel: 402-342-7142; Fax: 402-330-5842. Email: RPVON@prodigy.net. Richard P. Vondenkamp, Dir.

Catholic Mutual of Canada, 10843 Old Mill Rd., 68154-2600. Tel: 800-228-6108, Ext. 2413; Fax: 402-551-2943. Email: ppeterson@catholicmutual.org. Paul Peterson, Contact Person & Vice Pres. To support the religious and business activities of the Catholic Mutual Relief Society of America and its subsidiary Catholic Relief Insurance Company of America.

Catholic Relief Insurance Company II, c/o 100 N. 62nd St., 68132. Tel: 800-228-6108. Email: ppeterson@catholicmutual.org. Web: www.catholicmutual.org. Paul Peterson, Vice Pres., C.M.G.

Catholic Umbrella Pool (1987) 10843 Old Mill Rd., 68154-2600. Tel: 402-551-8765; Fax: 402-551-2943. Email: mintrieri@catholicmutual.org. Mr. Michael A. Intrieri, Admin.

Christ Child Society of Omaha (1906) 1248 S. 10th St., 68108. Tel: 402-342-4566; Fax: 402-342-4541. For programming, see Catholic Charities.

Christian Family Movement (CFM), 3514 N. 63rd St., 68104. Tel: 402-558-1710. Deacon Edwin Osterhaus, Contact; Sheila Osterhaus, Contact.

Christian Urban Education Service (1974) 2207 Wirt St., 68110. Tel: 402-451-5755; Fax: 402-451-1731. Email: sacredheart@sacredheart-cues.org. Web: www.sacredheart-cues.org. Rev. Thomas M. Fangman, Exec. Dir. of CUES.

Christians Encounter Christ, 1938 S. 149th Cir., 68144. Tel: 402-334-2597. Rick Ekstrom, Contact. Purpose: To promote the transferring of environments through Christian leaders who are willing to live and share their principles of being Christian. Through the ongoing development of their Christian Personality, strengthened by their 4th Day, these leaders strive to instill the spirit and sense of gospel to all environments in which they are actively involved.

CUP Re, Inc., c/o 100 N. 62nd St., 68132. Tel: 802-651-0168. Web: www.catholicumbrellapool.org. William Russell, Pres.

Equestrian Order of the Holy Sepulchre of Jerusalem, Northern Lieutenancy, 11808 W. Center Rd., Ste. 100, 68114-4434. Tel: 402-504-1600; 402-676-6410; Fax: 402-504-1601. Thomas R. Burke, Vice Pres.

FOCCUS, Inc. USA formerly FOCCUS, Inc. (1986) 3330 N. 60th St., 68104. Tel: 402-827-3735; 877-883-5422 (Toll free); Fax: 402-551-3050. Email: foccus@foccusincusa.com. Web: www.foccusincusa.com. Mrs. Valerie Conzett, D.Min., L.P.C., Dir., Family Life Office. A marriage education ministry offering research-based marriage preparation and marriage enrichment materials and services supporting family life around the world.

Francis House-Men's Shelter (1975) 1702 Nicholas St., 68102. Tel: 402-341-1821; Fax: 402-341-5270. Email: information@sienafrancis.org. Web: www.sienafrancis.org. Mike Saklar, Exec. Dir. (Men's Sheltering) Total Assisted Monthly 700; Total Staff 33.

Heart of Mary Publishing Company, Incorporated (1991) 2216 Poppleton Ave., 68108-3436. Tel: 402-342-9265; Fax: 402-342-9094. Email: srmarylucy@aol.com. Web: www.heartofmaryministry.com. Sr. Mary Lucy Astuto, D.E.F., M.S., Pres.

Holy Name Housing Corp., 3014 N. 45th St., 68104. Tel: 402-453-6100; Fax: 402-451-7187. Sr. Marilyn Ross, R.S.M., Exec. Dir. & Contact.

IXIM, Spirit of Solidarity, 200 E. 6th St., Papillion, 68046. Tel: 402-339-3285; Fax: 402-592-4753. Web: ixim.org. Rev. Damian J. Zuerlein, Contact Person.

St. James Manor, Inc., 3102 No. 60th St., 68104. Tel: 402-551-4243; Fax: 402-558-8023. Email: debl@ccomaha.org. John Griffith, Pres. & Contact.

Latino Catholic Scholarship Fund, 5434 S. 22nd St., 68107. Tel: 402-734-4500; Fax: 402-734-4501. Email: bgstarman@archomaha.org. Web: www.archomaha.com. Rev. Bernard Starman, Contact Person. Receives and distributes funds as financial aid to Latino students attending Catholic schools.

Legion of Mary, 702 W. 11th St., Neligh, 68756. Tel: 402-887-4521. Rev. John P. Broheimer, Spiritual Dir.

**Maria Regina Cleri*, P.O. Box 540657, 68154. Vicki Herout, Contact Person.

Marriage Encounter, 704 I St., Central City, 68826. Tel: 308-946-3568. Web: www.archomaha.com/lunks/wwme. Pat Benson, Local Contact; Janelle Benson, Local Contact.

McAuley Ministry Fund (1995) 7262 Mercy Rd., 68124-2389. Tel: 402-393-8225; Fax: 402-393-8145. Email: info@mercywmw.org. Web: www.mercywestmidwest.org. Sr. Judith Frikker, R.S.M., Pres. (Provides support to the mission of the Sisters of Mercy of the Americas West Midwest Community Inc.).

Mercy Holdings (1979) 7262 Mercy Rd., 68124-2389. Tel: 402-393-8225; Fax: 402-393-8145. Email: info@mercywmw.org. Web: www.mercywestmidwest.org. Sr. Judith Frikker, R.S.M., Contact.

Mercy Housing Midwest, 7300 Edna Ct., La Vista, 68128. Tel: 303-830-3371; Fax: 303-830-3301. Email: poroark@mercyhousing.org.

Mercy House, 2904 N. 45th St., 68104. Tel: 303-830-3371; Fax: 303-830-3301.

Mercy Northglen, 3303 Portia St., Ste. 2B, Lincoln, 68521. Tel: 303-830-3371; Fax: 303-830-3301.

Mercy Western Manor, 2200 W. Q St., Unit 8, Lincoln, 68528. Tel: 303-830-3371; Fax: 303-830-3301.

Mercy Crestview Village, 7300 Edna Ct., La Vista, 68128. Tel: 303-830-3371; Fax: 303-830-3301.

Mercy Oakwood Gardens, 7262 Mercy Rd., 68124. Tel: 303-830-3371; Fax: 303-830-3301. To provide affordable housing to the economically poor.

The Most AMYable Roman Catholic Lending Library, Inc. (2001) 5404 William St., 68106-2355. Tel: 402-553-1837. Email: rogjud@yahoo.com. Roger Elliott, Pres.; Judy Elliott, Vice Pres. Purpose: a nonprofit religious, charitable and educational corporation is duly constituted under the laws of the State of Nebraska and operated by a Board of Directors for the purpose of collecting and lending orthodox Catholic books and magazines, videos and audiotapes, compact and video discs, prayer petitions and Rosary Decade Group.

New Cassel Foundation, 900 N. 90th St., 68114-2704. Tel: 402-393-2277; Fax: 402-393-3784. Web: www.newcassel.org. Ric Miller, Pres. & Contact. A nonprofit religious, charitable and educational corporation, duly constituted under the laws of the State of Nebraska, to provide support and benefit for the New Cassel Retirement Center and the Franciscan Centre.

New Covenant Center: Education for Justice and Peace (1982) 2830 Caldwell St., 68131. Tel: 402-345-1368. Email: mcosssf@juno.com. Sr. Maureen Connolly, S.S.S.F., M.Div., M.A., B.A., Prog. Coord.

Notre Dame Housing, Inc. (1996) 3501 State St., 68112-1709. Tel: 402-455-2994; Fax: 402-455-3974. Email: jconnealy@notredamesisters.org. Web: www.notredamesisters.org. Sr. Joy Connealy, N.D., Contact. Purpose: To provide housing for elderly and persons of low-income or otherwise unable to afford market rate housing.

Notre Dame Living Center, Inc. (1996) 3501 State St., 68112-1709. Tel: 402-455-2994; Fax: 402-455-3974. Email: jconnealy@notredamesisters.org. Web: www.notredamesisters.org. Sr. Joy Connealy, N.D., Contact. Purpose: Provides affordable housing to the elderly, particularly those of low-income status.

Pope Paul VI Institute for the Study of Human Reproduction (1982) 6901 Mercy Rd., 68106. Tel: 402-390-6600; Fax: 402-390-9851. Email: popepaul@popepaulvi.com. Web: www.popepaulvi.com. Thomas W. Hilgers, M.D., Dir.

Siena House-Women's Shelter (1975) 1702 Nicholas St., 68102. Tel: 402-341-1821; Fax: 402-341-5270. Email: information@sienafrancis.org. Web: www.sienafrancis.org. Mike Saklar, Exec. Dir. (Women's Sheltering) Total Staff 33; Total Assisted Monthly 150.

Siena/Francis House Recovery Program (1975) P.O. Box 217-DTS, 68101. Tel: 402-341-1821; Fax: 402-341-5270. Email: information@sienafrancis.org. Web: www.sienafrancis.org. 1702 Nicholas St., 68102. Mike Saklar, Dir. & Contact. Total Staff 33; Total Assisted Monthly 85.

Society of St. Vincent de Paul, 3802 Leavenworth St., #300, 68105. Tel: 402-346-5445; Fax: 402-885-8255. Email: svdpomaha@hotmail.com. Web: svdpomaha.com/home. Deacon Joseph Haird, Spiritual Dir.; Roy Gertig, District Council Pres.

Teachers' Salary Endowment Trust Fund of St. Stephen Church of Omaha, St. Stephen Church of Omaha, 16701 "S" St., 68135. Tel: 402-896-9675; Fax: 402-896-1990. Email: t.jorgensen@stephen.org. Web: www.stephen.org. Purpose: providing endowment support for teachers employed by St. Stephen Church of Omaha. Priests 2.

TEC, Box 4130, 68104. Tel: 402-554-8493; Fax: 402-554-8402. Email: rmramos@archomaha.org. Web: www.archomaha.org. Ms. Rita Ramos, Coord. Youth Ministry.

St. Vincent de Paul Store, Inc., 2101 Leavenworth St., 68102. Tel: 402-341-1688; 402-341-4942; Fax: 402-341-9079. Web: www.svdpomaha.org.

GRETNA. *Holy Family Shrine* Mailing Address: P.O. Box 507, 68028. Tel: 402-332-4565. Email: holyfamilyshrine@hotmail.com. Web: www.holyfamilyshrine.com. 23132 Pflug Rd., 68028. Matthew Sakowski, Caretaker. A place of pilgrimage, prayer and resource for the public and private prayer. This nonprofit religious, charitable and educational corporation is duly constituted under the laws of the State of Nebraska and operated by a Board of Trustees.

LYNCH. *Niobrara Valley House of Renewal*, P.O. Box 163, 68746. Tel: 402-569-3433. Rev. Douglas P. Scheinost, Pastor.

OAKDALE. *Tintern Retreat and Resource Center*, 52619 843 Rd., 68761. Tel: 402-776-2188. Email: tintern@gpcom.net. Web: www.tintern.homestead.com. Becky Kerkman, Mgr. & Contact.

PLATTE CENTER. *Servants of the Heart of the Father*, P.O. Box 218, 68653. Tel: 402-246-9214; Fax: 402-246-9232. Email: sothotf@aol.com. Web: www.sothotf.org. Rev. Rodney V. Kneifl, Contact Person.

RAEVILLE. *St. Bonaventure's Church of Raeville Cemetery Endowment Trust Fund*, 2305 SR Rd., 68652.

[O] PUBLIC ASSOCIATIONS OF THE CHRISTIAN FAITHFUL

OMAHA. *Christian Life Community-North Central Region (CLC)* (1998) 2500 California Plaza, 68178. Tel: 402-280-2692; Fax: 402-280-5590. Email: jzsj@creighton.edu. Rev. John D. Zuercher, S.J., Contact & Regional Ecclesial Asst. A public association of the Christian faithful of Pontifical Right providing spiritual support and guidance in the Jesuit tradition of the Spiritual Exercises.

Franciscan Sisters of Joy, Franciscan Sisters of Joy, 8141 Farnam Dr., #403, 68114. Tel: 402-551-0347. Email: jmueller@creighton.edu. Sr. Joan Mueller, O.S.C., Ph.D., Clare Sister.

Institute for Priestly Formation formerly INSTITUTE FOR PRIESTLY FORMATION, CREIGHTON UNIVERSITY 2500 California Plaza, 68178. Tel: 402-546-6384; Fax: 402-280-3529. Email: ipf@creighton.edu. Web: www.creighton.edu/ipf. Rev. Richard J. Gabuzda, Exec. Dir. Purpose: To offer programs and support for the integration of theological study, spiritual growth and direction, and retreat experiences for diocesan seminarians and priests.

[P] PRIVATE ASSOCIATIONS OF THE FAITHFUL

OMAHA. *Brides of the Victorious Lamb, Inc.*, 5215 S. 36th St., 68107. Tel: 402-490-8458. Email: intercessorrelief@gmail.com. Web: www.intercessorrelief.com. Rev. Gregory P. Baxter, S.T.L., Contact Person.

Daughters of the Eternal Father (2002) 2216 Poppleton Ave., 68108-3436. Tel: 402-342-1032; Fax: 402-342-9094. Email: srmarylucy@aol.com. Web: www.omahadef.org. Sr. Mary Lucy Astuto, D.E.F., M.S., Foundress.

Seraphic Sisters of the Eucharist, 705 S. 28th St., 68105. Tel: 402-346-6845; Fax: 402-341-6483. Email: seraphicsisters@yahoo.com. Web: seraphicsisters-ne.org. Sisters Clara Maria Acosta-Millan, S.S.E., Supr.; Lourdes Candida-Cano, Asst.

RELIGIOUS INSTITUTES OF MEN REPRESENTED IN THE ARCHDIOCESE

For further details refer to the corresponding bracketed number in the Religious Institutes of Men or Women section.

[0200]—*Benedictine Monks*—O.S.B.

[0330]—*Brothers of the Christian Schools* (St. Louis, MO)—F.S.C.

[0690]—*Jesuit Fathers and Brothers* (Wisconsin Prov.)—S.J.

[1065]—*Priestly Fraternity of St. Peter*

[0370]—*Society of St. Columban*—S.S.C.

RELIGIOUS INSTITUTES OF WOMEN REPRESENTED IN THE ARCHDIOCESE

[0230]—*Benedictine Sisters of Pontifical Jurisdiction*—O.S.B.

[1070-03]—*Dominican Sisters*—O.P.
[1115]—*Dominican Sisters of Peace*—O.P.
[1230]—*Franciscan Sisters of Christian Charity*—O.S.F.
[1430]—*Franciscan Sisters of Our Lady of Perpetual Help*—O.S.F.
[2575]—*Institute of the Sisters of Mercy of the Americas*—R.S.M.
[0210]—*Missionary Benedictine Sisters*—O.S.B.
[2690]—*Missionary Catechists of Divine Providence*
[2960]—*Notre Dame Sisters*—N.D.
[3760]—*Order of St. Clare*—O.S.C.
[2970]—*School Sisters of Notre Dame*
[1680]—*School Sisters of St. Francis* (Our Lady of Angels Prov.)—O.S.F.
[3580]—*Servants of Mary*—O.S.M.
[0430]—*Sisters of Charity of the Blessed Virgin Mary*—C.S.J.
[1630]—*Sisters of St. Francis of Peace and Christian Charity* (Denver Prov.)—O.S.F.
[1640]—*Sisters of St. Francis of Perpetual Adoration* (Colorado Springs, CO)—O.S.F.
[1830]—*Sisters of the Good Shepherd*—R.G.S.
[3270]—*Sisters of the Most Precious Blood* (O'Fallon, MO)—C.PP.S.
[3320]—*Sisters of the Presentation of the B.V.M.*—P.B.V.M.
[4070]—*Society of the Sacred Heart*—R.S.C.J.

ARCHDIOCESAN CEMETERIES

OMAHA. *Calvary*
Holy Sepulchre
St. Mary
St. Mary Magdalene
Resurrection

NECROLOGY

† Krejci, Rev. Msgr. Albert L., (Retired)—Died Feb. 17, 2011
† Meister, Rev. Msgr. Andrew H., (Retired)—Died April 25, 2011
† O'Donnell, Rev. Msgr. Edward C., (Retired)—Died Jan. 30, 2011
† Ciurej, Richard S., (Retired)—Died Jan. 2, 2011
† Hunkeler, Edward J., (Retired)—Died Aug. 12, 2011
† Kenny, James E., (Retired)—Died May 21, 2011
† McMahon, Aloysius J., (Retired)—Died May 17, 2011

An asterisk (*) denotes an organization that has established tax-exempt status directly with the IRS and is not covered by the USCCB Group Ruling.

Diocese of Orange in California

(Arausicanae in California)

Most Reverend

TOD DAVID BROWN, D.D.

Bishop of Orange; ordained May 1, 1963; appointed Bishop of Boise December 27, 1988; Episcopal Ordination April 3, 1989; appointed Bishop of Orange June 29, 1998; installed September 3, 1998. *Office: Marywood Center, 2811 E. Villa Real Dr., Orange, CA 92867.*

Most Reverend

DOMINIC MAI LUONG

Auxiliary Bishop of Orange; ordained May 21, 1966; appointed Auxiliary Bishop of Orange and Titular Bishop of Cebarades April 25, 2003; installed June 11, 2003. *Office: Marywood Center, 2811 E. Villa Real Dr., Orange, CA 92867.*

Chancellor's Office: 2811 E. Villa Real Dr., P.O. Box 14195, Orange, CA 92863-1595. Tel: 714-282-3000; Fax: 714-282-4202.

Web: www.rcbo.org

Email: sgiacomi@rcbo.org

ESTABLISHED JUNE 18, 1976.

Square Miles 782.

Comprises the County of Orange in the State of California.

Diocesan Patron: Our Lady of Guadalupe.

Legal Titles: (Prot. No. CD 528-76)
The Roman Catholic Bishop of Orange, a Corporation Sole.
Diocese of Orange Education and Welfare Corporation.
Catholic Charities of Orange.
For legal titles of parishes and diocesan institutions, consult the Diocesan Pastoral Service Office

STATISTICAL OVERVIEW

Personnel	
Bishop	1
Auxiliary Bishops	1
Abbots	1
Priests: Diocesan Active in Diocese	119
Priests: Diocesan Active Outside Diocese	7
Priests: Retired, Sick or Absent	41
Number of Diocesan Priests	167
Religious Priests in Diocese	87
Total Priests in Diocese	254
Extern Priests in Diocese	32
Ordinations:	
Diocesan Priests	6
Religious Priests	3
Transitional Deacons	5
Permanent Deacons	13
Permanent Deacons in Diocese	105
Total Brothers	8
Total Sisters	326
Parishes	
Parishes	57
With Resident Pastor:	
Resident Diocesan Priests	47
Resident Religious Priests	6
Without Resident Pastor:	
Administered by Priests	4
Missions	5
Pastoral Centers	5
Professional Ministry Personnel:	
Sisters	23
Lay Ministers	280
Welfare	
Catholic Hospitals	3
Total Assisted	1,563,232
Health Care Centers	5
Total Assisted	28,376
Homes for the Aged	1
Total Assisted	60
Day Care Centers	2
Total Assisted	530
Specialized Homes	5
Total Assisted	563
Special Centers for Social Services	9
Total Assisted	3,840,014
Other Institutions	2
Total Assisted	172
Educational	
Diocesan Students in Other Seminaries	33
Total Seminarians	33
High Schools, Diocesan and Parish	3
Total Students	4,216
High Schools, Private	4
Total Students	2,280
Elementary Schools, Diocesan and Parish	32
Total Students	11,245
Elementary Schools, Private	3
Total Students	1,432
Catechesis/Religious Education:	
High School Students	11,794
Elementary Students	31,002
Total Students under Catholic Instruction	62,002
Teachers in the Diocese:	
Priests	7
Brothers	2
Sisters	19
Lay Teachers	1,366
Vital Statistics	
Receptions into the Church:	
Infant Baptism Totals	13,893
Minor Baptism Totals	744
Adult Baptism Totals	510
Received into Full Communion	933
First Communions	13,221
Confirmations	6,993
Marriages:	
Catholic	1,722
Interfaith	399
Total Marriages	2,121
Deaths	2,784
Total Catholic Population	1,291,505
Total Population	3,166,461

Former Bishops—Most Revs. WILLIAM R. JOHNSON, appt. Titular Bishop of Biera and Auxiliary Bishop of Los Angeles, Feb. 9, 1971; cons. March 25, 1971; installed as first Bishop of Orange, June 18, 1976; died July 28, 1986; NORMAN F. MCFARLAND, D.D., J.C.D., ord. June 15, 1946; appt. Titular Bishop of Bida and Auxiliary of San Francisco, June 5, 1970; cons. Sept. 8, 1970; appt. Apostolic Administrator, Dec. 6, 1974; appt. Bishop of Reno-Las Vegas, Feb. 10, 1976; installed March 31, 1976; appt. Bishop of Orange, Dec. 29, 1986; installed Feb. 24, 1987; retired June 30, 1998; died April 16, 2010.

Vicar General—Rev. Msgr. MICHAEL HEHER, V.G., Office: Marywood Center.

Chancellor—Mrs. SHIRL GIACOMI, Office: Marywood Center.

Moderator of the Curia—Rev. Msgr. MICHAEL HEHER, V.G., Office: Marywood Center.

Director of Clergy Personnel—Rev. BINH T. NGUYEN, Office: Marywood Center.

Secretary to the Bishop—Rev. BINH T. NGUYEN, Office: Marywood Center.

Vicar for Religious Communities—Sr. EYMARD FLOOD, O.S.C., Office: Marywood Center.

Vicar for Priests—Rev. CHRISTOPHER SMITH, Office: Marywood Center.

Vicar for Faith Formation—Rev. GERALD M. HORAN, O.S.M., Office: Marywood Center.

Diocesan Pastoral Service Office—2811 E. Villa Real Dr., P.O. Box 14195, Orange, 92863-1595. Tel: 714-282-3000; Fax: 714-282-3029. Office Hours: Mon.-Fri. 9-5.

Office of Canonical Services—2811 E. Villa Real Dr., P.O. Box 14195, Orange, 92863-1595. Tel: 714-282-3080; Fax: 714-282-3087. Rev. Msgr. DOUGLAS COOK, J.C.L., Dir. Canonical Svcs.

Judicial Vicar—Rev. Msgr. DOUGLAS COOK, J.C.L.

Adjutant Judicial Vicars—Rev. Msgr. TUAN JOSEPH PHAM, J.C.L.; Rev. VIET PETER HO, J.C.L.

Promoter of Justice—Rev. SY NGUYEN, J.C.L.

Judges—Rev. Msgrs. JOHN G. CAMPBELL, J.C.L. (Retired); ARTHUR A. HOLQUIN, S.T.L.; Rev. JAMES HARTNETT; Rev. Msgr. DOUGLAS COOK, J.C.L.; Revs. JOSEPH M. NETTEKOVEN; THEODORE OLSON; JACK SEWELL, J.C.L.; MINH CONG BUI, J.C.L.; FERNANDO ENGEL, J.C.L.; Sisters MARGARET ANNE RAMSDEN, S.F.C.C., J.C.L.; ANNE GIBLIN, R.S.C., J.C.L.; Ms. PEGGY JEAN PAOLI, J.C.L.

Defender of the Bond—Rev. JOHN CARONAN, O.Praem., J.C.L.

Ecclesiastical Notaries—LINDA BRAUN; PAULA LYNN; LILLIAN ESQUIVEL; SUSAN STANKIS; KIM BUI; KASSANDRA FLORES.

Newman Apostolate—Rev. JOHN FRANCIS VU, S.J., Mailing Address: P.O. Box 523, Garden Grove, 92842. Tel: 949-856-0211.

Diocesan Pastoral Council—Mrs. SHIRL GIACOMI, Chancellor. Tel: 714-282-3115.

Parish Councils and Parish Development—Mrs. SHIRL GIACOMI, Chancellor, Office: Marywood Center.

Diaconate—Deacon FRANK CHAVEZ, Office: Marywood Center.

Clergy Personnel Board—Revs. TIMOTHY FREYER; ENRIQUE J. SERA; BINH T. NGUYEN; MICHAEL ST. PAUL; JOHN W. MONEYPENNY; Rev. Msgr. MICHAEL

HEHER, V.G.; Rev. EFRAIN FLORES; Rev. Msgr. DONALD ROMITO.

Sexual Misconduct and Oversight Review Board (SMORB)—RON LOWENBERG, Chm.; Rev. BRUCE PATTERSON; JAMES BURNS; JOSEPH M. CERVANTES, Ph.D., ABPP; PAUL COBLE ESQ.; WILLIAM J. COLLINS, M.D.; GENE HOWARD; Sr. KATHLEEN MARIE PUGHE, C.S.J.; DARLYNE PETTINICHIO; Honorable MICHAEL BRENNER, (Retired); DIANE GOMEZ-VALENZUELA, M.S.W. Staff: MARIA RULLO SCHINDERLE ESQ.; LISA EMPTING.

Media Relations—STEPHEN BOHANNON, Office: Marywood Center.

Orange Diocesan Council of Catholic Women—Sr. EYMARD FLOOD, O.S.C., Moderator; JACKIE BRANDON, Pres., Office: Marywood Center.

General Counsel—Ms. MARIA RULLO SCHINDERLE.

Priests' Relief—Rev. CHRISTOPHER SMITH, Office: Marywood Center.

Council of Priests—Most Revs. TOD DAVID BROWN, D.D.; DOMINIC M. LUONG, D.D., V.G.; Rev. Msgrs. J. MICHAEL MCKIERNAN; DOUGLAS COOK, J.C.L.; MICHAEL HEHER, V.G.; J. MICHAEL MCKIERNAN; Revs. JOHN E. JANZE; STEVEN SALLOT; KERRY BEAULIEU; EDWARD POETTGEN, Chm.; THEODORE OLSON; BINH T. NGUYEN, Auditor; JUAN CABOBOY; SY NGUYEN, J.C.L.; JOSEPH ROBILLARD; JOSEPH KNERR; ROBERT CAPONE; JOSEPH THUONG TRAN; JAMES C. RIES; BENEDICT YANG; MICHAEL-DWIGHT COLIN GALINADA; CHRISTOPHER HEATH; BRUCE PATTERSON; JOHN FRANCIS VU, S.J.; JOHN W. MONEYPENNY; Rev. Msgr. ARTHUR A. HOLQUIN, S.T.L.; Revs. MICHAEL L. HARVEY, O.F.M.; CHARBEL R. GRBAVAC, O.Praem.

Observers—Mrs. SHIRL GIACOMI, Chancellor; Deacon FRANK CHAVEZ.

Consultors—Most Rev. TOD DAVID BROWN, D.D.; Rev. Msgrs. DOUGLAS COOK, J.C.L.; J. MICHAEL MCKIERNAN; MICHAEL HEHER, V.G.; Most Rev. DOMINIC M. LUONG, D.D., V.G.; Rev. STEVEN SALLOT; Rev. Msgr. ARTHUR A. HOLQUIN, S.T.L.; Revs. THEODORE OLSON; JOHN E. JANZE; SY NGUYEN, J.C.L.; MICHAEL L. HARVEY, O.F.M.; EDWARD POETTGEN.

Pastoral Care— (of families in all stages) MICHAEL DONALDSON, Dir.

Propagation of the Faith—LINCOLN NGUYEN, Coord., Office: Marywood Center.

Council for Religious—Sisters EYMARD FLOOD, O.S.C., Dir.; BRID O'SHEA, R.S.C.; JANE RUDOLPH, O.P.; BREDA CHRISTOPHER, P.B.V.M.; REGINA HERRERA, M.E.S.S.T.; BERNICE JORDAN, C.S.J.; ELIA CARO, O.S.F.

Office for Faith Formation—Rev. GERALD M. HORAN, O.S.M.

Children's Faith Formation Advisory Council—Mrs. PAM BENDER; Ms. RENATE GOUTIER; Mrs. KATHY HERNANDEZ; Mrs. ROSE ANTOGNOLI; Sr. CECILIA TRANG PHAM, L.H.C.; Mr. JOSE SALAS; Ms. STELLA HEUMANN. Staff: Rev. GERALD M. HORAN, O.S.M.; Dr. KATHLEEN SCHINHOFEN, Assoc. Dir., Office of Faith Formation; Mrs. NANCY HARDY.

Catholic Schools and Parish Faith Formation—Rev. GERALD M. HORAN, O.S.M., Vicar for Faith Formation; Mrs. SALLY TODD, Assoc. Supt., Office: Marywood Center; Mr. GREGORY DHUYVETTER, Supt.; Mrs. NANCY HARDY, Dir. Parish Faith Formation; Dr. KATHLEEN SCHINHOFEN, Assoc. Dir. Faith Formation; Ms. DEB MCGRATH, Controller Dept. of Catholic Schools.

Safe Environment Coordinator—NORMA AGUERRO.

Young & Young Adult Ministries—Mr. ARMANDO CERVANTES, Coord. Office: Marywood Center.

Diocesan Consultative Schools Board— Office: Marywood Center Membership: Rev. GERALD M. HORAN, O.S.M., Ex Officio; Mrs. SALLY TODD, Ex Officio; Rev. STEVEN SALLOT; Mr. GREGORY DHUYVETTER, Ex Officio; Mrs. CINDY BOBRUK, Ex Officio; Ms. DEB MCGRATH, Ex Officio; Mrs. KARI BRETSCHGER; Mr. CHUCK PACKARD; Mr. PAUL CARREY; Mrs. SUE GARCIA; Ms. ADRIANNA LOPEZ, Recording Sec.; Mrs. SUSAN KAVANAUGH; Mrs. CRYSTAL SMITH; Mr. THOMAS DELANEY.

Vocations Office—Rev. JOHN NENEMAN, Dir., Office: Marywood Center.

Catholic Campaign for Human Development—Local Board: Deacon JAMES MERLE, Dir.; JOYCE COTTAGE; Deacons GARY MUCHO; ROBERT SOIKKELI; Ms. JUDY DONCKELS; Ms. JEANNIE MOLLENAUER; Mr. RUBEN BARRON; Ms. GRACE PINE.

Diocesan Offices and Directors

Apostleship of Prayer—Rev. JOSEPH M. NETTEKOVEN, 2050 W. Ball Rd., Anaheim, 92804. Tel: 714-774-2595.

Archivist—Rev. WILLIAM KREKELBERG, Office: Mission Basilica San Juan Capistrano, 31522 Camino Capistrano, San Juan Capistrano, 92675-0691.

Boy Scouts/Girl Scouts—Rev. MICHAEL P. HANIFIN, Office: Santa Clara de Asis Church, 22005 Avenida de la Paz, Yorba Linda, 92887-2745.

Liturgical Commission—Rev. Msgr. ARTHUR A. HOLQUIN, S.T.L., Ex Officio; Mr. JAIME ROMERO; Mrs. REGINA KIM; Rev. Msgr. J. MICHAEL MCKIERNAN; Deacon FRANK CHAVEZ; Ms. LESA TRUXAW, Ex Officio; Dr. JOAN H. TIMMERMAN; Revs. BINH T. NGUYEN; CRAIG M. BUTTERS; Mr. MARK PURCELL; Rev. EUGENE LEE; Mr. JOSEPH BAZYOUROS, Chm.; Deacon TOM MCGUIRE.

Building and Renovation Committee of the Liturgical Commission—Rev. Msgrs. J. MICHAEL MCKIERNAN; ARTHUR A. HOLQUIN, S.T.L.; TUAN JOSEPH PHAM, J.C.L.; Ms. LESA TRUXAW, Chm., Office: Marywood Center; Mr. MICHAEL SHAFFER; JOSEPH BAZYOURUS.

Land Advisory Board—Most Rev. TOD DAVID BROWN, D.D.; Rev. EDWARD POETTGEN; Mr. ARTHUR BIRTCHER; Mr. LOU ODDO; Mr. TERENCE K. BARRY, Chm.; Ms. SHARON HENNESSEY; Mr. R. RAND SPERRY; Rev. Msgr. MICHAEL HEHER, V.G.; Mr. J. BARNEY PAGE. Staff: Mr. PHIL RIES; LILY FUNK; JOE NOVOA; Mrs. SHIRL GIACOMI; Ms. MARIA RULLO SCHINDERLE.

Diocesan Construction Board—Most Rev. TOD DAVID BROWN, D.D.; JACK W. FLEMING; Rev. KENNETH A. SCHMIT; Mr. ARTHUR BIRTCHER, Chm.; Mr. EDWARD REYNOLDS; Mr. RICHARD HEIM; Ms. MARY WESTBROOK; Ms. TRUDY MAZZARELLA. Staff: Rev. Msgr. MICHAEL HEHER, V.G.; Mr. PHIL RIES; JOE NOVOA, Dir. Construction; Mrs. SHIRL GIACOMI; LOY GIBSON, Comm. Sec.

Diocesan Finance Council—Most Rev. TOD DAVID BROWN, D.D.; Rev. Msgrs. LAWRENCE J. BAIRD, P.A.; MICHAEL HEHER, V.G.; Mr. TIMOTHY BUSCH; Ms. MAUREEN FLANAGAN, C.F.A., Chm.; Sr. MARY BERNADETTE MCNULTY, C.S.J.; Mr. JEFFREY D. LITTELL, Vice Chm.; Mr. PAUL SCHLOEMER; Mrs. SHIRL GIACOMI, Chancellor; Mr. THOMAS GREELEY; Rev. TUYEN VAN NGUYEN; Mr. FRANK SURYAN JR.; Mr. PAUL SCHLOEMER; Ms. ANNETTE WALKER; Ms. JAN NGUYEN. Staff: Mr. PHIL RIES, Dir. Finance; JOANNE MCALPINE; Rev. BINH T. NGUYEN; Mr. KEVIN LARSON; Ms. MARIA RULLO SCHINDERLE.

Director of Finance—Mr. PHIL RIES, Dir.; Mr. KEVIN LARSON, Controller, Office: Marywood Center.

Catholic Charities of Orange—TERESA SMITH, M.S.W., L.C.S.W., Exec. Dir., 1820 E. 16th St., Santa Ana, 92701. Tel: 714-347-9605; Fax: 714-542-3020.

Cemeteries—Mr. MICHAEL WESNER, Dir., Office: Marywood Center.

Ministry to Priests—Rev. CHRISTOPHER SMITH, Vicar for Priests.

Cursillo Movement—Deacon DOUG COOK, Exec. Spiritual Dir.; Revs. DAVID VUELVAS-ARIAS, Spiritual Dir., Hispanic Cursillo; SY NGUYEN, J.C.L., Spiritual Dir., Vietnamese Cursillo, Office: Marywood Center.

Catholic Deaf Center—NANCY LOPEZ, Dir., 1800 E. 17th St., Ste. 100, Santa Ana, 92705. Tel: 714-547-0824 (Voice); Teletype: 714-547-7103; Fax: 714-547-7195. Email: nlopez@rcbo.org. Web: www.rcbo.org.

Detention Ministry/Restorative Justice—Deacon PHILLIP GOODMAN, 1820 W. Orangewood Ave., Ste. 101, Orange, 92868. Tel: 714-634-9909; Fax: 714-634-9910.

Library/Media Center—APRIL CIPO, Coord.

Institute of Pastoral Ministry—Mrs. OLIVIA CORNEJO, Dir. Office: Marywood Center.

Ecumenical and Interreligious Affairs—Rev. AL BACA; Ms. MARY SUSA; Very Rev. HUGH C. BARBOUR, O.Praem.; Mr. FEDERICO SAYRE; Dr. BRAD HAWKINS; Mr. DONALD ROSS; Mr. EUGENE O'TOOLE; Mr. JAMES NIELSON; Mr. HOWARD YOUNG; Rev. JOHN MONESTERO; Mr. ANTHONY VULTAGGIO, Chm.; Mr. DARREL KING; Mrs. ORALIE ENOS; Dr. H. MICHAEL HERSH; Sr. JEANNE FALLON, C.S.J.; Ms. IRMA ESPINOSA; Mr. GREG KELLEY; Judge DAVID MCEACHEN; Rev. CHRISTIAN MONDOR, O.F.M.; Sr. ERNESTINE VELARDE, O.D.N.; Mrs. ADRIANNE WITTHOEFT.

Natural Family Planning—Mrs. PATRICIA POINTDEXTER, B.S., R.N., C.F.C.P., C.F.C.E., Coord., Office: Catholic Charities of Orange County, Inc., 1820 E. 16th St., Santa Ana, 92701. Tel: 714-347-9600.

Engaged Encounter—KEENAN STANLEY; LORI STANLEY.

Marriage Encounter - English—WALLY CLAUDIO; MARIA CLAUDIO.

Marriage Encounter - Spanish—SANTOS VASQUEZ; MARIA LUISA VASQUEZ.

Vietnamese Community Couples Retreat—Mr. KY VU; Mrs. CAY DINH VU, 24862 Branch Ave., Lake Forest, 92630. Tel: 949-472-5083.

Retrouvaille - English—GARY LOPEZ; MARY LOPEZ.

Retrouvaille - Spanish—MARTIN RAMOS; ANGELICA RAMOS.

Office of Hispanic Ministry—Deacon GUILLERMO TORRES, Dir., Office: Marywood Center.

Holy Childhood—LINCOLN NGUYEN, Coord., Office: Marywood Center.

Catholic Relief Services—Mrs. SHIRL GIACOMI, Chancellor.

Risk Management and Insurance Services—Mr. MICHAEL SHAFFER, Dir., Office: Marywood Center.

Legion of Mary—

English—TERI FODOR, Pres. Tel: 714-533-1550.

Vietnamese—THACH LUU, Pres.

Worship—Ms. LESA TRUXAW, Dir., Office: Marywood Center.

Respect Life, Justice and Peace—GEORGEANN LOVETT, Dir. Office: Marywood Center.

Catecumenate—Ms. LESA TRUXAW, Dir., Office: Marywood Center.

Advancement (Orange Catholic Foundation)—Mrs. CINDY BOBRUK, Exec. Dir., Office: Marywood Center.

Victim Assistance Coordinator—RITA COLLINS-FAULKNER, Ph.D. Tel: 800-364-3064. Email: rita50@speakeasy.net.

CLERGY, PARISHES, MISSIONS AND PAROCHIAL SCHOOLS

CITY OF ORANGE

1—CATHEDRAL OF THE HOLY FAMILY (1921) Rev. Msgr. Douglas Cook, Rector; Revs. Bao Q. Thai, Parochial Vicar; Timothy Nguyen, Parochial Vicar; Deacons Richard Lovett; Tom McGuine; Carlos Euyoque. In Res., Rev. Rafael Luevano.

Res.: 566 S. Glassell St., 92866. Tel: 714-639-2900; Fax: 714-639-8022. Email: parish@hfcathedral.org. Web: www.hfcathedral.org.

School—530 S. Glassell St., 92866. Tel: 714-538-6012; Fax: 714-633-5892. Lay Teachers 31; Students 495.

Catechesis/Religious Program—Tel: 714-639-2900, Ext. 235; Fax: 714-516-9949. Students 441.

2—LA PURISIMA (1964) Revs. Vincent Hung Pham, Admin.; Avelino Orozco; Deacons Anthony Bube; Tin Nguyen; Paul Amorino.

Res.: 11712 N. Hewes, 92869. Tel: 714-633-5800; Fax: 714-633-8364. Email: info@lapurisima.net. Web: www.lapurisima.net.

School—Tel: 714-633-5411; Fax: 714-633-1588. Email: lps@lpcs.net. Web: www.lpcs.net. Mrs. Debbie Vallas, Prin. Lay Teachers 17; Students 219.

Catechesis/Religious Program—Tel: 714-633-5344. Students 970.

3—ST. NORBERT (1963) Revs. Patrick Rudolph; Agustin Escobar; Kiet A. Ta; Deacons Joseph Esparza; Juan Espinoza; Janine Kilgore, Liturgy Director. In Res., Rev. Antonio Zapata (Retired).

Res.: 300 E. Taft Ave., 92865. Tel: 714-637-4360; Fax: 714-637-4311. Email: info@stnorbertchurch.org. Web: www.stnorbertchurch.org.

School—Tel: 714-637-6822; Fax: 714-637-1604. Email: sshaia@stnorbertchurch.org. Lay Teachers 15; Students 304.

Catechesis/Religious Program—Tel: 714-998-1070. Mrs. Carmen Estrada, Hispanic Min. Dir.; Edith Marik, D.R.E.; Ms. Charlene Dumitru, Adult Faith Formation Dir.; Kirsten King, Youth Min. Dir. Students 854.

ORANGE COUNTY OUTSIDE THE CITY

ALISO VIEJO, CORPUS CHRISTI (1999) [CEM] Rev. Fred K. Bailey.

27231 Aliso Viejo Pkwy., 92656. Tel: 949-389-9008; Fax: 949-831-6540. Email: corpuschristi@corpuschristialisoviejo.org. Web: www.avcatholics.org.

Catechesis/Religious Program—Students 413.

ANAHEIM

1—ST. ANTHONY CLARET (1955) Revs. Rudolph J. Preciado; Bill T. Cao; Miguel A. Hernandez; Deacons August Mones; Jose Luis Reynoso.

Res.: 1450 E. La Palma Ave., 92805. Tel: 714-776-0270; Fax: 714-776-6022. Email: stanthonyclaret@yahoo.com.

Catechesis/Religious Program—Tel: 714-778-1399; Fax: 714-956-2701. Margarita Navarro, D.R.E. Students 1,358.

2—ST. BONIFACE (1860) Revs. Timothy Freyer; Gregory Marquez; Nicolas T. Nguyen.

Res.: 120 N. Janss St., 92805. Tel: 714-956-3110; Fax: 714-399-0566. Email: stboniface120@aol.com. Web: stbonifaceonline.org.

Catechesis/Religious Program—Tel: 714-772-3060; Fax: 714-399-0568. Students 1,450.

3—ST. JUSTIN MARTYR (1958) Revs. Joseph Robillard; Thomas Paul K. Naval, A.M., Parochial Vicar; Francis Ng, Parochial Vicar; Deacons Raymond

Duthoy; Jose Ferreras; Kalini Folau; Ramon Leon; Louis Liu. In Res., Rev. John Monestero.
Res.: 2050 W. Ball Rd., 92804. Tel: 714-774-2595; Fax: 714-774-9849. Web: www.saintjustin.org.
Church: Ball Rd. and Empire, 92804.
School—2030 W. Ball Rd., 92804. Tel: 714-772-4902; Fax: 714-772-2092. Lay Teachers 12; Students 206.
Catechesis/Religious Program—Tel: 714-535-6111 (English); Fax: 714-774-9849 (English). Students 736.
Mission—Sacred Heart 10852 Harcourt, Orange Co. 92804. Tel: 714-821-3133; Fax: 714-821-1498.

4—San Antonio de Padua Del Cañon Church (1977) Revs. Joseph M. Nettekoven; Seamus A. Glynn, Pastor Emeritus (Retired); John R. LeVecke, S.J.; Deacon Doug Cook.
Res.: 5800 E. Santa Ana Canyon Rd., 92807. Tel: 714-974-1416; Fax: 714-974-9630. Web: sanantonio-parish.org.
See St. Francis of Assisi School, Yorba Linda under Multi-Parish Schools located in the Institution section.
Catechesis/Religious Program—Tel: 714-974-2053. Carolyn Buehler, D.R.E. Students 929.

Brea, St. Angela Merici (1962) Revs. Michael-Dwight Colin Galinada; Martin Nguyen; Deacons Jim Merle; Benjamin Flores; Jose Luis Rodriguez.
Res.: 585 Walnut St., 92821. Tel: 714-529-1821; Fax: 714-529-0569. Email: office@stangelabreachurch.org. Web: stangelabreachurch.org.
Church: Walnut and Fir, 92821.
School—575 S. Walnut Ave., 92821. Tel: 714-529-6372; Fax: 714-529-7755. Religious 1; Lay Teachers 16; Students 288.
Catechesis/Religious Program—Tel: 714-529-2311. Students 865.

Buena Park, St. Pius V (1948) Revs. Theodore Olson; Khoi Phan, Parochial Vicar; Salvador Landa; Deacons Rey Marin; William Yang.
Res.: 7691 Orangethorpe Ave., 90621. Tel: 714-522-2193; Fax: 714-522-1730. Web: stpius5.org.
School—7681 Orangethorpe Ave., 90621. Tel: 714-522-5313; Fax: 714-522-1767. Web: stpius5school.net. Lay Teachers 19; Students 482.
Catechesis/Religious Program—Tel: 714-522-3971. Email: sre@stpius5.org. Students 971.

Capistrano Beach, San Felipe de Jesus (1950), (Hispanic), Rev. Steven Sallot; Deacon Victor Samano.
Mailing Address: *c/o St. Edward the Confessor*, 33926 Calle La Primavera, Dana Point, 92629.
Church: Domingo St. & Sepulveda, 92624.
Catechesis/Religious Program—Tel: 949-493-8918. Students 178.

Costa Mesa

1—St. Joachim (1947) Revs. Enrique J. Sera; Martin Phuoc Bui; Gilberto Escobedo.
Mailing Address: 1964 Orange Ave., 92627.
Res.: 1943 Orange Ave., 92627. Tel: 949-574-7400; Fax: 949-574-7407. Email: tstuddert@stjoachimcostamesa.com. Web: www.stjoachimparish.com.
School—Tel: 949-574-7411; Fax: 949-646-8948. Lay Teachers 16; Students 308; Teacher Aides 7; Day Care Personnel 1.
Catechesis/Religious Program—Tel: 949-574-7400; Fax: 949-575-7407. Students 718.

2—St. John the Baptist (1960) Revs. Augustine R. Puchner, O.Praem.; Philip T. Smith, O.Praem.; Andrew Tran, O.Praem.; Godfrey E. Bushmaker, O.Praem.; Deacon Paul Cho. In Res., Revs. Robert Hodges, O.Praem.; Norbert J. Wood, O.Praem.
Res.: 1015 Baker St., 92626. Tel: 714-540-2214; Fax: 714-540-5902. Email: info@sjboc.org. Web: www.sjbcostamesa.org.
School—1021 Baker St., 92626. Tel: 714-557-5060; Fax: 714-557-9263. Web: www.sjbschool.net. Sr. M. Vianney Ennis, S.M., Prin. Sisters of Mercy 2; Lay Teachers 22; Students 600.
Catechesis/Religious Program—Tel: 714-546-4102. Christina Ford, D.R.E. (English); Sisters Thu-Huong Nguyen, L.H.C., D.R.E. (Vietnamese); Bertha Rafael, M.C., D.R.E. (Spanish). Students 680.

Cypress, St. Irenaeus (1961) Revs. Patrick Moses; Daniel B. Reader; Venancio Amidar; Deacons Jose Campos; Jerry Pyne.
Res.: 5201 Evergreen Ave., 90630. Tel: 714-826-0760; Fax: 714-826-1608. Email: parish@sticypress.org. Web: www.sticypress.org.
School—9201 Grindlay St., 90630. Tel: 714-827-4500; Fax: 714-827-2930. Email: office@stischoolcypress.org. Lay Teachers 20; Students 335.
Catechesis/Religious Program—9211 Grindlay St., 90630. Tel: 714-826-1140; Fax: 714-826-1608. Email: rbradley@sticypress.org. Students 850.

Dana Point, St. Edward the Confessor (1969) Revs. Steven Sallot; Loc Tran; Mario Juarez, Parochial Vicar; Christopher Heath; Deacon Ron Tiberi.
Mailing Address: 33926 Calle La Primavera, 92629.
Res.: 24451 Alta Vista Dr., 92629. Tel: 949-496-1307; Fax: 949-496-1557. Web: www.stedward.com.
School—33866 Calle La Primavera, 92629. Tel: 949-496-1241; Fax: 949-496-1819. Lay Teachers 25; Students 657.
Catechesis/Religious Program—Tel: 949-496-6011. Students 714.

Fountain Valley, Holy Spirit (1972) Rev. Msgr. Tuan Joseph Pham; Revs. Benjamin Tran; Jeffrey A. Droessler; Deacon Phillip Goodman.
Mailing Address: 17270 Ward St., 92708.
Res.: 16806 Mt. Olsen Cir., 92708. Tel: 714-963-1811; Fax: 714-968-1775. Email: office@hsccfv.org. Web: www.hsccfv.org.
Catechesis/Religious Program—Tel: 714-963-7871; 714-964-8767; Fax: 714-968-1775. Email: faithformation@hsccfv.org. Roz Esh, C.R.E. (English); Sisters Cecilia Trang Pham, L.H.C., Dir. Faith Formation; Ann Marie Han Dang, L.H.C., C.R.E. (Vietnamese). Students 920.

Fullerton

1—St. Juliana Falconieri (1965) Revs. Frank Falco, O.S.M.; Paul M. Gins, O.S.M., Parochial Vicar; Deacons Gerhard P. Stadel; William Schlater, (Retired). In Res., Rev. Patrick Donovan, O.S.M.
Res.: 1316 N. Acacia Ave., 92831. Tel: 714-879-1965; Fax: 714-526-6673. Email: info@stjulianachurch.org. Web: www.stjulianachurch.org.
School—1320 N. Acacia Ave., 92831. Tel: 714-871-2829; Fax: 714-871-8465. Web: www.stjulianaschool.org. Lay Teachers 16; Part-Time Teachers 4; Students 279.
Catechesis/Religious Program—Michael McHenry, Dir. Faith Formation. Students 221.

2—St. Mary's (1912) Revs. James C. Ries; Armando Virrey, Parochial Vicar; Deacons Carlos Gonzalez; Manuel Chavira.
Res.: 400 W. Commonwealth Ave., 92832. Tel: 714-525-2500; Fax: 714-525-3837. Web: saintmarys-fullerton.catholicweb.com.
See school listing under St. Philip Benizi, Fullerton for details.
Catechesis/Religious Program—Students 540.

3—St. Philip Benizi (1958) Revs. David Gallegos, O.S.M.; Justin M. Pisciotta, O.S.M., Parochial Vicar; Deacons Richard Glaudini; Chuck Doidge; Richard Doubletree; Antonio Luna; Philip Hardjadinata. In Res., Rev. Gerald M. Horan, O.S.M.
Parish Office: 235 S. Pine Dr., 92833. Tel: 714-871-3610; Fax: 714-871-5827. Email: philipbenizi@aol.com. Web: benizi.us.
Res.: 5210 Somerset, Buena Park, 90621.
School—Annunciation Catholic School, 215 S. Pine Dr., 92833-3293. Tel: 714-871-6121; Fax: 714-992-4167. Web: annunciationcs.org. Ms. Barbara Barreda, Prin. Lay Teachers 12; Students 127.
Catechesis/Religious Program—Tel: 714-870-0561. Mrs. Maria Barrientos, Dir. Faith Formation; Jorge Ledezma, Youth Min. & Confirmation Coord. Students 356.

Garden Grove

1—St. Callistus (1961) Revs. Tuyen Nguyen; Joseph Long Kim Nguyen; Juan B. Navarro, Parochial Vicar; Joseph Thuong Tran, Parochial Vicar; Deacons Joseph Khiet Nguyen; Jose Serrano; Guillermo Torres.
Res.: 12921 Lewis St., 92840. Tel: 714-971-2141; Fax: 714-971-9112.
Church: Garden Grove Blvd. and Lewis St., 92840.
St. Callistus Preschool—12132 Haster St., 92840. Tel: 714-750-6777.
School—(Grades PreSchool-8), 12901 Lewis St., 92840. Tel: 714-971-2023; Fax: 714-971-2031. Sisters 1; Lay Teachers 15; Students 217.
Catechesis/Religious Program—Tel: 714-971-2091. Maureen Ross, D.R.E. Students 1,729.

2—St. Columban (1953) Revs. Juan Caboboy; Brendan Manson; Tuan Nguyen; Kiem Van Tran; Deacon Anthony Carrasco.
Res.: 10801 Stanford Ave., 92840. Tel: 714-534-1174; Fax: 714-534-1937. Web: www.saintcolumbanchurch.org.
School—10855 Stanford Ave., 92840. Tel: 714-534-3947; Fax: 714-590-9153. Religious Sisters of Charity 2; Lay Teachers 12; Students 234.
Catechesis/Religious Program—Tel: 714-537-2015. Students 1,314.

Huntington Beach

1—St. Bonaventure (1965) Revs. Joseph Knerr; Angelos Sebastian, Parochial Vicar; Khoa Vo, Parochial Vicar; Deacons Jim Andersen; Scott Ford; Vincent Tran; Son Hoang. In Res., Rev. John R. Keller (Retired).
Res.: 16400 Springdale St., 92649. Tel: 714-846-3350; 714-846-3359; Fax: 714-840-0480. Email: email@stbonaventure.org. Web: www.saintbonaventureparish.org.
School—16377 Bradbury Ln., 92647. Tel: 714-846-2472; Fax: 714-840-0498. Judy Luttrell, Prin. Union of the Sisters of the Presentation of the Blessed Virgin Mary 6; Lay Teachers 27; Students 616.
Catechesis/Religious Program—Tel: 714-846-2472. Laraine Soule, D.R.E. Students 1,190.

2—St. Mary's by the Sea (1977) Rev. Quang Vinh Chu, Admin.
Res.: 321 10th St., 92648. Tel: 714-536-6913; Fax: 714-536-2464. Email: officesmbs@gmail.com. Web: stmarysbythesea.net.
Catechesis/Religious Program—Students 69.

3—SS. Simon and Jude (1912) Revs. Michael L. Harvey, O.F.M.; Richard Juzix, O.F.M.; Deacon Bill Cobbett; Sr. Maureen Sheehan, B.V.M., Pastoral Assoc.; Christina Sumpter, Pastoral Admin. In Res., Rev. Christian Mondor, O.F.M.
Res.: 20444 Magnolia St., 92646. Tel: 714-962-3333; Fax: 714-965-6456. Email: ssj@ssj.org. Web: www.ssj.org.
School—20400 Magnolia St., 92646. Tel: 714-962-4451; Fax: 714-968-1329. Web: www.ssj.org/school/. Lay Teachers 35; Students 579.
Catechesis/Religious Program—Tel: 714-963-0014. Web: www.ssj.org/faith/index.html. Nancy Cunningham, Dir. Faith Formation. Students 660.

4—St. Vincent de Paul (1977) Revs. Jerome T. Karcher; Robert Capone; Deacon Gerard Wallace.
Res.: 8345 Talbert Ave., 92646. Tel: 714-842-3000; Fax: 714-842-6780. Email: svdp@svdphb.org. Web: www.svdphb.org.
Catechesis/Religious Program—Tel: 714-842-3000; Fax: 714-842-6780. Email: reled@svdphb.org. Students 586.

Irvine

1—St. Elizabeth Ann Seton (1976) Rev. Thomas Pado; Deacon Steve Greco.
Res.: 9 Hillgate, 92612-3265. Tel: 949-854-1000; Fax: 949-854-0079. Web: www.seasirvine.org.
Catechesis/Religious Program—Students 187.
Mission—Queen of Life Chapel 2532 Dupont Dr., 92612. Tel: 949-474-7368; Fax: 781-207-0713. Email: tbush@bushfirm.com.

2—St. John Neumann (1978) Rev. Msgr. Donald Romito; Rev. Anthony Hien T. Vu, Parochial Vicar. In Res., Revs. John M. Joyce (Retired); Michael Tung Nguyen.
Res.: 5101 Alton Pkwy., 92604-8605. Tel: 949-559-4006; Fax: 949-857-4788. Email: parishoffice@sjnirvine.org. Web: www.sjnirvine.org.
Catechesis/Religious Program—Tel: 949-786-6105; Fax: 949-786-6102. Email: religioused@sjnirvine.org. Kellie De Leo, D.R.E.; Juliana Gerace, Dir. Youth Min. Students 555.

3—St. Thomas More (1996) [CEM] Revs. John E. Janze; George Blais; William Krekelberg, Parochial Vicar; Deacon Tony Patronite; Theresa Nault, Office & Business Mgr.; Cari Maas, Music Dir. In Res., Rev. Alex H. Ha.
Res.: 51 Marketplace, 92602. Tel: 949-551-8601; Fax: 949-551-5879.
Catechesis/Religious Program—Barbara Catiller, D.R.E.; David Calavitta, Youth Min. Students 857.

La Habra, Our Lady of Guadalupe (1947) Revs. Justin H. MacCarthy; William Hubbard, Parochial Vicar; Edward Becker, Parochial Vicar.
Res.: 900 W. La Habra Blvd., 90631. Tel: 562-691-0533; Fax: 562-694-8328. Web: www.olglahabra.org.
School—Tel: 562-697-9726; Fax: 562-905-0095. Web: www.olgvikings.com. Lay Teachers 22; Students 387.
Catechesis/Religious Program—Tel: 562-691-2104; Fax: 562-697-6391. Students 717.

Ladera Ranch, Holy Trinity (2005) Rev. Reynold Furrell; Deacon Randall McMahon; Andy Albritton, Music & Media Dir.
1600 Corporate Dr., 92694. Tel: 949-218-3131; Fax: 949-388-1311. Email: frreynold@holytrinityladera.org. Web: www.holytrinityladera.org.
Catechesis/Religious Program—Patti Wieckert, Youth Min., Confirmation & Jr. High; Joe Schleicher, D.R.E.; Lauren McCaul, Faith Formation Coord. Students 735.

Laguna Beach, St. Catherine of Siena (1923) Revs. Eamon T. O'Gorman; Marito F. Rebamontan, Senior Priest.
Res.: 1042 Temple Ter., 92651. Tel: 949-494-9701; Fax: 949-497-2610. Email: info@stcathlagunabeach.org. Web: www.stcathlagunabeach.org.
School—30516 S. Coast Hwy., 92651. Tel: 949-494-7339; Fax: 949-376-5752. Web: www.saintcatherinelaguna.com. Lay Teachers 14; Students 185.
Catechesis/Religious Program—Tel: 949-494-9701, Ext. 119. Students 193.

Laguna Niguel, St. Timothy (1980) Rev. Msgr. John Urell; Rev. Paw Lwin, Parochial Vicar.
Rectory—29182 Via San Sebastian, 92677.
Church: 29102 Crown Valley Pkwy., 92677. Tel: 949-249-4091; Fax: 949-249-4094. Web: www.st-timsrc.org.

Catechesis/Religious Program—Tel: 949-495-4126. Students 512.

LAGUNA WOODS, ST. NICHOLAS (1965) Revs. Richard A. Delahunty; Thai Paul Minh Trinh. In Res., Rev. Timothy MacCarthy (Retired).
Res.: 24252 El Toro Rd., 92637. Tel: 949-837-1090; Fax: 949-837-9510.
Catechesis/Religious Program—Tel: 949-837-7676. Students 464.

LAKE FOREST, SANTIAGO DE COMPOSTELA (1979) Revs. David Gruver; William Barman; Deacons Carlos Euyoque; Don Jensen. In Res., Rev. Rosendo Silva, L.C.
Res.: 21682 Lake Forest Dr., 92630. Tel: 949-951-8599; Fax: 949-951-2687. Email: admin@santiagodecomp.com. Web: www.santiago-catholicchurch.org.
See Serra Catholic School, Rancho Santa Margarita under Multi-Parish Schools located in the Institution section.
Catechesis/Religious Program—Tel: 949-951-0792; Fax: 949-951-2687. Email: re@santiagodecomp.com. Students 768.

LOS ALAMITOS, ST. HEDWIG (1960) Revs. Kenneth A. Schmit; Christopher Tuan Pham; Deacons Larry Hurst; Gary Mucho.
Res.: 11482 Los Alamitos Blvd., 90720. Tel: 562-296-9000; Fax: 562-296-9099. Web: sainthedwigparish.org.
School—3591 Orangewood Ave., 90720. Tel: 562-296-9060; Fax: 562-296-9089. Email: parishschool@sainthedwigparish.org. Lay Teachers 25; Students 497.
Catechesis/Religious Program—Tel: 562-296-9040. Students 402.

MISSION VIEJO, ST. KILIAN (1970) Revs. Bruce Patterson; Wayne Adajar, Parochial Vicar; Deacons Bob Kelleher; Mark Martin.
26872 Estanciero Dr., 92691. Email: gmoonll@cox.net.
Res.: 25672 Morales, 92691. Tel: 949-586-4440; Fax: 949-454-1043. Email: stkilians@cox.net. Web: stkilianchurch.org.
See Serra Catholic School, Rancho Santa Margarita under Multi-Parish Schools located in the Institution section.
Catechesis/Religious Program—Tel: 949-586-4550; Fax: 949-454-1043. Email: skre@cox.net. Marcia Burns, D.R.E. Students 717.

NEWPORT BEACH

1—OUR LADY OF MOUNT CARMEL (1923) Rev. Msgr. Lawrence J. Baird; Rev. John B. Weling, Parochial Vicar; Deacon Stephen Mutz. In Res., Rev. Sean Condon (Ireland), Senior Priest (Retired).
Res.: 1441 W. Balboa Blvd., 92661-1163. Tel: 949-673-3775; Fax: 949-673-3137. Email: olmc@olmc.net. Web: www.olmc.net.
Catechesis/Religious Program—Tel: 949-673-2719; Fax: 949-673-3137. Students 244.
Chapel—St. John Vianney 314 Marine Ave., Balboa Island, 92662-1206. Tel: 949-673-3775, Ext. 3; Fax: 949-673-3801.

2—OUR LADY QUEEN OF ANGELS (1961) Revs. Kerry Beaulieu; Joseph D. Nguyen; David Klunk, Parochial Vicar; Deacon Jim Arnold. In Res., Rev. Msgr. Wilbur Davis (Retired).
Res.: 2046 Mar Vista Dr., 92660. Tel: 949-644-0200; Fax: 949-644-1349. Web: www.olqa.org.
School—Tel: 949-644-1166; Fax: 949-644-6213. Email: eryan@olqa.org. Web: www.olqaschool.org. Lay Teachers 29; Students 460.
Catechesis/Religious Program—Tel: 949-219-1497; Fax: 949-644-1349. Students 641.

PLACENTIA, ST. JOSEPH (1953) Revs. Timothy Ramaekers; Benedict Yang; Deacon Jorge Ramirez.
Res.: 717 N. Bradford Ave., 92870-4514. Tel: 714-528-1487; Fax: 714-579-3791.
School—801 N. Bradford Ave., 92870-4515. Tel: 714-528-1794; Fax: 714-528-0668. Web: www.sjsplacentia.org. Lay Teachers 15; Students 287.
Catechesis/Religious Program—Tel: 714-528-1487; Fax: 714-579-3791. Sarah Rooney, Faith Formation Coord.; Eloisa Ramirez, Spanish Faith Formation Coord. Students 534.
Mission—Santa Teresita 636 Van Buren Ave., Atwood, Orange Co. 92811.

RANCHO SANTA MARGARITA, SAN FRANCISCO SOLANO CHURCH (1989) [CEM] Revs. Craig M. Butters; Martin Tran; Deacon Carl Swanson.
Res.: 22082 Antonio Pkwy., 92688-1993. Tel: 949-589-7767; Fax: 949-589-7768. Email: information@sfsolano.org. Web: www.sfsolano.org.
See Serra Catholic School, Rancho Santa Margarita under Multi-Parish Schools located in the Institution section.
Catechesis/Religious Program—Tel: 949-589-1709; Fax: 949-589-2840. Mrs. Mary Ann Taeger, D.R.E. Students 931.

SAN CLEMENTE, OUR LADY OF FATIMA (1947) Revs. Jack Sewell; Paul Flynn, O.S.A. (Ireland).
Res.: 105 La Esperanza, 92672. Tel: 949-492-4101; Fax: 949-492-4856. Email: lrojas@olfchurch.net. Web: www.olfchurch.net.
School—Tel: 949-492-7320; Fax: 949-492-3793. Web: http://olfschool.net. Lay Teachers 13; Students 201.
Catechesis/Religious Program—Tel: 949-492-4101; Fax: 949-492-4856. Students 455.

SAN JUAN CAPISTRANO, MISSION BASILICA - SAN JUAN CAPISTRANO (1776) [CEM] Rev. Msgr. Arthur A. Holquin, Pastoral Rector; Rev. Timothy J. Peters, Parochial Vicar; Deacon David Sire. In Res., Rev. Michael M. Pontarelli, O.S.M.
Res.: 31522 Camino Capistrano, 92675. Tel: 949-234-1360; Fax: 949-248-2008 (Parish Office). Web: www.misssionparish.org.
School—31641 El Camino Real, 92675. Tel: 949-234-1385; Fax: 949-248-2178. Lay Teachers 15; Students 290.
Catechesis/Religious Program—Tel: 949-234-1370; Fax: 949-248-2056. Margot Santos, D.R.E. & Dir. Hispanic Ministries. Students 550.

SANTA ANA

1—CHRIST OUR SAVIOR CATHEDRAL (2005) Rev. Msgr. J. Michael McKiernan, Rector.
2000 W. Alton Ave, 92704. Tel: 714-444-1500. Email: parishoffice@christoursaviorcathedral.com. Web: coscp.org. In Res., Rev. Viet Peter Ho; Deacon Frank Chavez.
Catechesis/Religious Program—Mr. Luis Ramirez, D.R.E. Students 360.

2—ST. ANNE'S (1923), (Hispanic), Revs. Antonio Lopez-Flores, O.Praem; Ramon Cisneros; Randy Guillen (NEW); Deacon Francisco Martinez.
Res.: 109 W. Borchard Ave., P.O. Box 2425, 92707. Tel: 714-835-7434; 714-835-7435; Fax: 714-835-4506.
School—1324 S. Main St., 92707. Tel: 714-542-9328; Fax: 714-542-3431. Sisters 2; Lay Teachers 17; Students 213.
Catechesis/Religious Program—Tel: 714-542-1213; Fax: 714-542-6608. Students 752.

3—ST. BARBARA CATHOLIC CHURCH (1962) Revs. Richard C. Kennedy; Raphael Xuan Nguyen; Michael Mai Khai Hoan, Senior Priest; Sergio Ramos; Deacon Joseph Anh Nguyen. In Res., Rev. Jose Luis Jimenez, O.A.R. (Retired).
Res.: 730 S. Euclid St., 92704. Tel: 714-775-7733; Fax: 714-775-9467. Email: st_barbara_church@hotmail.com.
School—5306 W. McFadden Ave., 92704. Tel: 714-775-9477; Fax: 714-775-9468. Email: sbs@stbarbara.com. Web: www.stbarbara.com. Lay Teachers 19; Students 367.
Catechesis/Religious Program—Tel: 714-775-9475. Students 855.

4—ST. GEORGE (CHALDEAN CATHOLIC) Rev. Zuhair G. Toma (LA).
Mailing Address: 4807 W. McFadden, 92704. Tel: 714-531-7760; Fax: 714-775-1442.

5—IMMACULATE HEART OF MARY (1960) Revs. Edward Poettgen; Hector Bedoya; Carlos Leon; Deacons Gerardo de Santos; Adolfo Ramirez. In Res., Rev. Ignatius Lau (Retired).
Res.: 1100 S. Center St., 92704. Tel: 714-751-5335; Fax: 714-662-0130. Email: m40manuela@msn.com.
School—Tel: 714-545-8185; Fax: 714-545-2362. Lay Teachers 10; Students 187.
Catechesis/Religious Program—Tel: 714-546-5186. Students 1,625.

6—ST. JOSEPH (1887) Revs. John W. Moneypenny; Leonel M. Vargas.
Res.: 727 Minter St., 92701. Tel: 714-542-4411; Fax: 714-542-9770. Email: sjpostmaster@stjosephsa.org. Web: www.stjosephsa.org.
School—608 Civic Center Dr. E., 92701. Tel: 714-542-2704; Fax: 714-542-2132. Email: bsnyder@stjoesa.org. Web: www.stjoesa.org. Lay Teachers 9; Students 234.
Catechesis/Religious Program—717 N. Minter St., 92701. Tel: 714-550-8096; Fax: 714-245-2319. Students 587.

7—OUR LADY OF GUADALUPE (1927), (Hispanic), Rev. David Vuelvas-Arias.
Res.: 541 E. Central Ave., 92707. Tel: 714-540-0902; Fax: 714-540-3053.
Catechesis/Religious Program—Tel: 714-540-9231. Rosa Castro, D.R.E. Students 642.

8—OUR LADY OF GUADALUPE (1938), (Hispanic), Revs. Alfredo de Dios, O.A.R.; Juan Jose Guzman, O.A.R.; Deacons Ulises Feliciano, O.A.R.; Miguel Gonzalez.
Res.: 1322 E. Third St., 92701. Tel: 714-836-4142; Fax: 714-836-7417. Email: olguadalupesa@hotmail.com.
Catechesis/Religious Program—Tel: 714-973-0279. Deacon Domingo Garza, D.R.E. Students 1,665.

9—OUR LADY OF LA VANG (2006) Revs. Joseph Luan Nguyen, Admin.; Long Vu; Deacon Rigoberto Maldonado.
Res.: 288 S. Harbor Blvd., 92704. Tel: 714-775-6200; Fax: 714-775-6226. Email: parish@ourladyoflavang.org. Web: www.ourladyoflavang.org.
Catechesis/Religious Program—Students 424.

10—OUR LADY OF THE PILLAR (1965), (Hispanic), Revs. Anthony Palos, O.A.R.; Euben Capacillo; Jose Luis Martinez, O.A.R.; Gabino Perez, O.A.R.; Deacon Luis Gallardo.
Res.: 1622 W. 6th St., 92703. Tel: 714-543-1700; Fax: 714-543-9640.
Catechesis/Religious Program—Tel: 714-542-4684. Students 1,300.

SEAL BEACH

1—ST. ANNE'S (1921) Rev. Msgr. Michael Heher; Revs. Robert S. Vidal, Pastor Emeritus; Duy T. Le; Deacon Gary Mucho.
Res.: 340 Tenth St., 90740. Tel: 562-431-0721; Fax: 562-431-3050. Email: stannesealbeach@yahoo.com. Web: www.stannesealbeach.org.
Catechesis/Religious Program—Tel: 562-431-8524; Fax: 562-431-3050. Sr. Samuel Marie Settar, O.S.F., D.R.E. Students 129.

2—HOLY FAMILY (1969) Rev. James Hartnett. In Res., Rev. Msgr. Brian Coghlan (Retired).
Res.: 13900 Church Pl., 90740. Tel: 562-430-8170; Fax: 562-493-4643.

STANTON, ST. POLYCARP (1961) Revs. Michael St. Paul, Admin.; Joseph Duc Hoang; Deacons Binh Chu; Larry Leone; Ramiro Lopez. In Res., Rev. Joseph C. Nguyen.
Res.: 8100 Chapman Ave., 90680. Tel: 714-893-2766; Fax: 714-898-6675. Web: www.stpolycarp.org.
School—8182 Chapman Ave., 90680. Tel: 714-893-8882; Fax: 714-897-3357. Web: www.saintpolycarp-school.com. Lay Teachers 10; Students 174.
Catechesis/Religious Program—Tel: 714-892-3158. Students 346.

TUSTIN, ST. CECILIA (1957), (Spanish—Vietnamese), Revs. Al Baca; Thomas De Nguyen-Dang; Vincent O. Gilmore, O.Praem.; Deacons Don Ngo; Martin Ruiz.
Res.: 1301 Sycamore, 92780. Tel: 714-544-3250; Fax: 714-838-1996. Web: www.stcecilia.org.
School—1311 Sycamore, 92780. Tel: 714-544-1533; Fax: 714-544-0643. Email: school@stceciliak8.org. Lay Teachers 18; Students 317.
Catechesis/Religious Program—Tel: 714-838-4466. Students 746.

WESTMINSTER, BLESSED SACRAMENT (1947) Revs. Tuan Ngoc Pham; Joseph Droessler; Efrain Flores; Danh Ngoc Trinh; Deacons Matt Calabrese; Arturo Gimenez; Hao Nguyen; Joseph Stripling.
Res.: 14072 S. Olive St., 92683. Tel: 714-892-4489; Fax: 714-892-5560. Email: bscparishoffice@socal.rr.com. Web: www.blessedsacramentparish.com.
School—14146 S. Olive St., 92683. Tel: 714-893-7701; Fax: 714-891-7186. Email: blsdsacramentsch@covet.net. Roisin McAree, Prin. Lay Teachers 16; Students 305.
Catechesis/Religious Program—14144 S. Olive St., 92683. Tel: 714-897-2142; Fax: 714-892-5560. Ana Marie Gimenez, D.R.E. Students 1,550.

YORBA LINDA

1—ST. MARTIN DE PORRES (1970) Revs. Sy Nguyen; Ian Bustonera; Deacon Denis F. Zaun.
Mailing Address: 19767 Yorba Linda Blvd., 92886. Tel: 714-970-2771; Fax: 714-970-5654. Web: www.smdpyl.org.
School—St. Francis of Assisi, 5330 Eastside Cir., 92887. Tel: 714-695-3700; Fax: 714-695-3704. Web: www.stfrancis-yorbalinda.com. Thomas Waszak, Prin. Lay Teachers 27; Students 439.
Catechesis/Religious Program—Tel: 714-970-2171; Fax: 714-970-5654. Mrs. Pam Bender, D.R.E. (Children); Cindy Piszyk, D.R.E. (Adult); Katie Balanos, D.R.E. (Youth). Students 600.

2—SANTA CLARA DE ASIS (2001) Rev. Michael P. Hanifin; Deacon Robert Soikkeli.
Mailing Address & Office: 22005 Avenida de la Paz, 92887. Tel: 714-970-7885; Fax: 714-970-2618. Email: webmaster@scdayl.org. Web: www.scdayl.org.
Catechesis/Religious Program—Students 283.

Chaplains Of Public Institutions

ORANGE. *UCI Medical Center*, 101 The City Dr. S., 92868. Tel: 714-634-5678. Rev. Joseph Son Nguyen. (Served by St. Callistus Parish.)
12921 Lewis St., Garden Grove, 92840. Tel: 714-971-2141.

COSTA MESA. *Fairview Developmental Center*, 2501 Harbor, 92626. Tel: 714-545-9331. Mary Brosseau.

SANTA ANA. *All Adult and Juvenile Jail Facilities*, 1820 W. Orangewood Ave., Ste. 101, 92868. Tel: 714-634-9909; Fax: 714-634-9910. Deacon Phillip Goodman, Dir. Email: pgoodman@rcbo.org, Elita Ferreras, Juvenile Facilities, Fred Lapuza, Adult Facilities, Deacon Martin Ruiz, Hispanic Ministry.

Special Assignment:
Most Rev.—
Luong, Dominic M., D.D., V.G.
Rev. Msgrs.—
Cook, Douglas, J.C.L.

Heher, Michael, V.G.
Revs.—
Doktorczyk, Steve
Grace, John, O.S.A.
Ho, Viet Peter, J.C.L.
Horan, Gerald M., O.S.M.
Krekelberg, William
Luevano, Rafael
Moreland, J. Gordon, S.J., Dir., House of Prayer for Priests, 7734 Santiago Canyon Rd., 92869.
Neneman, John
Nguyen, Binh T.
Smith, Christopher

On Duty Outside the Diocese:
Revs.—
Shimotsu, John M., Military
Sweeney, Kevin, Military

Military Chaplains:
Revs.—
Shimotsu, John M.
Sweeney, Kevin

Awaiting Assignment:
Revs.—
Schneider, Troy D.
Tran, Quan Dinh

Absent on Sick Leave:
Revs.—
DiStefano, Joseph
Justice, Joseph Charles
Monestero, John

Inactive Leave:
Rev.—
McAndrew, John P. (Retired)

Education Leave:
Rev.—
Sun Kim, Simon Chung, Washington, D.C.

Administrative Leave:
Rev.—
Nguyen, Anh Tuan

Retired:
Rev. Msgrs.—
Caceres, Alonso
Campbell, John G., J.C.L.
Coghlan, Brian
Davis, Wilbur
Keenan, John C.
McGowan, Anthony
McLaughlin, William
Revs.—
Bebek, Dominic
Benedicto, Benjamin
Block, John
Bradley, John A.
Buckman, Frank
Condon, Sean (Ireland)
Conlon, Colmbanus
Dunning, James Patrick
Fry, James Q.
Ha, Thomas Do Thanh
Huynh, Andrew
Joyce, John M.
Keller, J. Rod
Kolberg, Lawrence R.
Lau, Ignatius
Luongo, John
MacCarthy, Timothy
McAndrew, John P.
Nguyen, Tien Duc
Sheahan, John A.
Shetter, John
Skonezny, Raymond
Vu, Joachim

Permanent Deacons:
Amorino, Paul, La Purisima, Orange
Anderson, James, St. Bonaventure, Huntington Beach
Arnold, James, Our Lady Queen of Angels, Newport Beach
Barth, John, (On Duty Outside the Diocese)
Bourne, Scotty, (On Duty Outside the Diocese)
Boyer, Charles, St. John Neuman, Irvine
Brenes-Rios, Anthony, (On Duty Outside the Diocese)
Bube, Anthony, La Purisima, Orange
Calabrese, Matt, Blessed Sacrament, Westminster
Campos, Jose, St. Ireaneus, Cypress
Canlas, Fred, St. Joachim, Costa Mesa
Carrasco, Anthony, St. Columban, Garden Grove
Carver, Timothy, (On Leave)
Chavez, Frank, Christ Our Savior Cathedral, Santa Ana
Chavez, Jose Manuel, Our Lady of Guadalupe, La Habra
Chavira, Manuel, St. Mary, Fullerton
Cho, Paul, St. John the Baptist, Costa Mesa
Chu, Binh, St. Polycarp, Stanton
Chung, Peter, St. Thomas Korean Center, Anaheim
Cobbett, William, SS. Simon and Jude, Huntington Beach
Cook, Douglas, San Antonio de Padua, Anaheim Hills
Dao, Jerry, Immaculate Heart of Mary, Santa Ana
Davis, Clyde, (On Duty Outside the Diocese)
Dennis, Irving, (On Duty Outside the Diocese)
DeSantos, Gerardo, Immaculate Heart of Mary, Santa Ana
Doidge, Chuck, St. Philip Benizi, Fullerton
Doubletree, Richard, St. Philip Benizi, Fullerton
Duthoy, Raymond, St. Justin Martyr, Anaheim
Erwin, Glenn, Our Lady of Mt. Carmel, Newport Beach
Esparza, Joseph, St. Norbert, Orange
Espinoza, Juan, St. Norbert, Orange
Euyoque, Carlos, Santiago de Compostela, Lake Forest
Faulk, Edward, (On Duty Outside the Diocese)
Ferreras, Jose, St. Justin Martyr, Anaheim
Fletcher, Michael, (On Duty Outside the Diocese)
Flores, Benjamin, St. Angela Merici, Brea
Folau, Kalini, Tongan Community
Ford, Scott, St. Bonaventure, Huntington Beach
Gallardo, Luis, Our Lady of the Pillar, Santa Ana
Garza, Domingo, Our Lady of Guadalupe, Santa Ana
Gimenez, Arturo, Blessed Sacrament, Westminster
Glaudini, Richard, St. Philip Benizi, Fullerton
Gonzales, Carlos, St. Mary, Fullerton
Gonzalez, Miguel, Our Lady of Guadalupe, Santa Ana
Goodman, Phillip, Holy Spirit, Fountain Valley
Greco, Steve, Elizabeth Ann Seton, Irvine
Griffin, Gary, Mission Basilica, San Juan Capistrano
Hardjadinata, Philip, Indonesian Community
Hernandes, Alfredo, St. Boniface, Anaheim
Hoang, Son, St. Bonaventure, Huntington Beach
Hurst, Larry, St. Hedwig, Los Alamitos
Jensen, Don, Santiago de Compostela, Lake Forest
Kelleher, Robert, St. Kilian, Mission Viejo
Kim, Peter, Korean Martyrs Catholic Center, Westminster
Lechner, Joel, (On Duty Outside Diocese)
Lee, Moon Chul, Korean Martyrs
Leon, Ramon, St. Justin Martyr, Anaheim
Leone, Larry, St. Polycarp, Stanton
Leuta, Filipo, Samoan Community
Liu, Louis, Chinese Catholic Community, Santa Ana
Lopez, Ramiro, St. Polycarp, Stanton
Lovett, Richard, Holy Family Cathedral, Orange
Luna, Antonio, St. Philip Benizi, Fullerton
Luna, Frank, (Retired)
Maldonado, Rigoberto, Our Lady of La Vang, Santa Ana
Marin, Reynaldo, St. Pius V, Buena Park
Martin, Mark, St. Kilian, Mission Viejo
Martinez, Francisco, St. Anne, Santa Ana
McGuine, Thomas, (On Duty Outside the Diocese)
McMahon, Randall, Holy Trinity, Ladera Ranch
Melton, Harold, (On Duty Outside the Diocese)
Merle, James, St. Angela Merici, Brea
Mezquita, Fernando, (On Duty Outside the Diocese)
Milam, Jay, St. Boniface, Anaheim
Miller, Gerald, (On Duty Outside the Diocese)
Mones, August, St. Anthony Claret, Anaheim
Mucho, Richard "Gary", St. Hedwig, Los Alamitos
Mutz, Stephen, Our Lady of Mt. Carmel, Newport Beach
Navarro, Carlos, (Leave of Absence)
Ngo, Dong Dinh, St. Cecilia, Tustin
Nguyen, Anh Phuong, St. Barbara, Santa Ana
Nguyen, Hao, Blessed Sacrament, Westminster
Nguyen, Joseph Khiet, St. Callistus, Garden Grove
Nguyen, Tin, La Purisima, Orange
Oh, Nicholas, Korean Martyrs Catholic Center
Patronite, Tony, St. Thomas More, Irvine
Pleitez, Cruz, St. Boniface, Anaheim
Pyne, Gerald, St. Iranaeus, Cypress
Ramirez, Adolfo, Immaculate Heart of Mary, Santa Ana
Ramirez, Jorge, St. Joseph, Placentia
Reynoso, Jose Luis, St. Anthony Claret, Anaheim
Rodriguez, Fidel, St. Pius V, Buena Park
Rodriguez, Jose Luis, St. Angela Merici, Brea
Romero, Rafael, St. Joseph, Santa Ana
Ruiz, Martin, St. Cecilia, Tustin
Salgado, Eddie, St. Catherine of Siena, Laguna Beach
Samano, Victor, San Felipe de Jesus, Capistrano Beach
Schlater, William, St. Juliana Falconieri, Fullerton
Serrano, Jose, St. Callistus, Santa Ana
Sire, David, Mission Basilica San Juan Capistrano, San Juan Capistrano
Sokkeli, Bob, Santa Clara de Asis, Yorba Linda
Song, Thomas, St. Thomas Korean Center, Anaheim
Stadel, Gerhard P., St. Juliana Falconieri, Fullerton
Stripling, Joseph, Blessed Sacrament, Westminster
Sullivan, Neill, (Retired)
Swanson, Carl, San Francisco Solano, Rancho Santa Margarita
Swift, Bernard, (Retired)
Thompson, Wayne, St. Nicholas, Laguna Woods
Tiberi, Ron, St. Edward the Confessor, Dana Point
Torres, Guillermo, St. Callistus, Garden Grove
Tran, Vincent, St. Bonaventure, Huntington Beach
Wallace, Gerard, St. Vincent de Paul, Huntington Beach
Yang, William, Hmong Community, Buena Park
Zaun, Denis, St. Martin de Porres, Yorba Linda

INSTITUTIONS LOCATED IN THE DIOCESE

[A] SEMINARIES AND SCHOLASTICATES FOR RELIGIOUS

MIDWAY CITY. *St. Patrick's Novitiate*, 7820 Bolsa Ave., 92655. Tel: 714-897-8181; Fax: 714-898-9020. Email: BrosStPatrick@aol.com. Web: www.patricianbrothers.com. Bro. Aquinas Cassin, F.S.P., Supr. Conducted by the Brothers of St. Patrick. Brothers 5.

SILVERADO. *St. Michael's Norbertine Postulancy, Novitiate and Juniorate* (1959) 19292 El Toro Rd., 92676. Tel: 949-858-0222; Fax: 949-858-4583. Rt. Rev. Eugene J. Hayes, O.Praem., Abbot; Revs. Thomas W. Nelson, O.Praem., Dir. Formation; Ambrose Criste, O.Praem., Novice Master; Very Rev. Hugh C. Barbour, O.Praem., Prof. Philosophy; Revs. Gregory M. Dick, O.Praem., Prof. Scripture; Sebastian A. Walshe, O.Praem., Prof. Philosophy; John Henry Hanson, O.Praem.; Chrysostom Anthony Baer, O.Praem. Conducted by the Norbertine Fathers., For listing of other Norbertine priests working in the Diocese, refer to St. Michael College Prep High School. Priests 6; Total Enrollment 24.

[B] COLLEGES AND UNIVERSITIES

ORANGE. *St. Joseph College, Orange* Branch Campus of University of San Francisco; St. Joseph Library., 480 S. Batavia St., 92868. Tel: 714-633-8121; Fax: 714-744-3166. Sisters Eileen McNerney, C.S.J., Gen. Sec.; Christine Hilliard, C.S.J., Librarian.

[C] HIGH SCHOOLS, DIOCESAN

FULLERTON. *Rosary High School* (Girls), 1340 N. Acacia Ave., 92831. Tel: 714-879-6302; Fax: 714-879-0853. Email: rosary@rosaryhs.org. Web: www.rosaryhs.org. Annette Zaleski, Prin. & Interim Pres.; Winnie Stokes, Librarian. Lay Teachers 45; Students 587; Total Staff 33.

RANCHO SANTA MARGARITA. *Santa Margarita Catholic High School*, 22062 Antonio Pkwy., 92688. Tel: 949-766-6000; Fax: 949-766-6005. Email: information@smhs.org. Web: www.smhs.org. Mr. Paul Carrey, Pres.; Mr. Raymond R. Dunne, Prin. & Contact Person; Jolene Finn, Librarian. Sisters 3; Lay Teachers 97; Students 1,592.

SANTA ANA. *Mater Dei High School* (1950) (Coed), 1202 W. Edinger Ave., 92707-2191. Tel: 714-754-7711; Fax: 714-754-1880. Email: admissions@materdei.org. Web: www.materdei.org. Ms. Frances Clare, Prin. & Contact; Mr. Patrick Murphy, Pres.; Nancy Ryan, Librarian. Lay Teachers 141; Students 2,049; Total Staff 178.

[D] HIGH SCHOOLS, PRIVATE

ANAHEIM. *Cornelia Connelly School of the Holy Child* (1961) (Girls), 2323 W. Broadway, 92804. Tel: 714-776-1717; Fax: 714-776-2534. Email: cornelia@connellyhs.org. Web: www.connellyhs.org. Sr. Francine Gunther, S.H.C.J., Head of School; Martha Izabal Serrano, Asst. Head; Heather Daugherty, Librarian. Society of the Holy Child Jesus. Lay Teachers 20; Students 200; Total Staff 35.

Servite High School, A California Corporation, 1952 W. La Palma, 92801. Tel: 714-774-7575; Fax: 714-774-1404. Email: mail@servitehs.org. Web: www.servitehs.org. Mr. Peter S. Bowen, Pres.; Mr. Michael P. Brennan, Prin.; Mrs. Olga Hofreiter, Asst. Prin. Academic Affairs; Mr. Andrew A. Katnic, Asst. Prin. Student Affairs; Jacqui Engelman, Librarian. Servite Friars. Priests 3;

Brothers 1; Lay Teachers 75; Students 960; Total Staff 134.

SAN JUAN CAPISTRANO. *JSerra Catholic High School*, 26351 Junipero Serra Rd., 92675. Tel: 949-493-9307; Fax: 949-493-9308. Web: www.jserra.org. Mr. Frank Talarico, Pres.; Thomas R. Waszak, Prin.; Mr. Eric Stroupe, Vice Pres. Academics; Dr. Sharon Anderson, Vice Pres. Student Svcs.; Jeanne Swedo, Librarian. Priests 3; Lay Teachers 57.

SILVERADO. *St. Michael's Preparatory School* (Boarding school for boys), 19292 El Toro Rd., 92676-9710. Tel: 949-858-0222; Fax: 949-858-7365. Email: stmichaelsprep@juno.com. Web: www.stmichaelsprep.org. Revs. Gabriel D. Stack, O.Praem., Headmaster; Claude Williams, O.Praem., Asst. Dean Students; John Henry Hanson, O.Praem.; Alphonsus B. Hermes, O.Praem.; Jerome M. Molokie, O.Praem.; Justin S. Ramos, O.Praem.; James G. Smith, O.Praem., Treas.; Victor S. Szczurek, O.Praem.; Sebastian Walsh, O.Praem.; Charles W. Willingham, O.Praem.; Brendan Hanking, O.Praem. Priests 10; Seminarians 6; Lay Teachers 6; Students 64; Total Staff 23.

[E] ELEMENTARY SCHOOLS AND DAY NURSERIES, PRIVATE

ANAHEIM. *St. Catherine's Military Academy* (1889) 215 N. Harbor Blvd., 92805. Tel: 714-772-1363; Fax: 714-772-3004. Email: admissions@stcatherinesacademy.org. Web: stcatherinesacademy.org. Sr. Johnellen Turner, O.P., Admin. & Prin.
St. Catherine's Military Academy, a Corp. Dominican Sisters of Mission San Jose 10; Lay Teachers 16; Students 154; Total Staff 62.

SANTA ANA. *Santa Clara Day Nursery and Kindergarten*, 1021 N. Newhope, 92703. Tel: 714-554-8850; Fax: 714-554-5886. Email: clarisas@netzero.net. Sisters Susana Guzman, M.C., Contact; Maria Socorro Miranda, Prin. Poor Clare Missionary Sisters (M.C.). Sisters 13; Children 95; Total Staff 13.

TUSTIN. *Saint Jeanne de Lestonnac School* (1961) 16791 E. Main, 92780. Tel: 714-542-4271; Fax: 714-542-0644. Email: srsharon@sjdlschool.com. Web: www.sjdlschool.com. Sisters Doris Louise Valdez, O.D.N., Pres.; Sharon Maria Lamprecht, O.D.N., Prin.; Catherine Zimmerman, Librarian. Sisters of the Company of Mary 7; Adrian Dominican 1; Lay Teachers 31; Students 435; Total Staff 8.

[F] MULTI-PARISH SCHOOLS

RANCHO SANTA MARGARITA. *Serra Catholic School* (1995) 23652 Antonio Pkwy., 92688-1993. Tel: 949-888-1990; Fax: 949-635-1921. Email: serra@serraschool.org. Web: www.serraschool.org. Angeline Trudell, Pres.; Mrs. Cathy Muzzy, Prin. (Gr. 5-8); Mrs. Carol Reiss, Prin. (Gr. K-4). Lay Teachers 62; Students 1,008; Total Staff 148.

YORBA LINDA. *St. Francis of Assisi Catholic School* (1998) 5330 East Side Cir., 92887. Tel: 714-695-3700; Fax: 714-695-3704. Email: office@sfayl.org. Web: www.sfayl.org. Thomas Waszak, Prin.; Avelina Oliver, Librarian. Lay Teachers 28; Students 414; Total Staff 52.

[G] GENERAL HOSPITALS

ORANGE. *St. Joseph Hospital of Orange* (1929) 1100 W. Stewart Dr., 92868. Tel: 714-771-8000, Ext. 8020; Fax: 714-744-8600. Steve Moreau, Pres. & CEO; Alan Garrett, Exec. Vice Pres. & COO; Linda Simon, Vice Pres. Mission Integration; Rev. Elly S. Tavarro. Inpatients 21,218; Outpatients 272,085; Beds 525; Other Employees 3,800; Nurses 1,000.

FULLERTON. *St. Jude Medical Center* (1957) 101 E. Valencia Mesa Dr., 92835-3875. Tel: 714-992-3000; Fax: 714-992-3029. Email: sisterclaudette.desforges@stjoe.org. Web: www.stjudemedicalcenter.org. Revs. William Caffrey, S.V.D., Chap.; Ignacio Estrada, S.V.D., Chap.; Timothy Freyer, Chap.; Gregory Marquez, Chap.; Sal Landa, Chap.; Timothy F. Bushy, Dir., Mission Svcs. & Spiritual Care; Sr. Claudette Des Forges, C.S.J., Vice Pres. Mission Integration; Judy Eugenio, Chap.; Sr. Josepha Ha, C.H.C., Chap.; Bill Boylan, Chap.; Luis Dicares, Chap. Bed Capacity 384; Nurses 656; Total Staff 2,900; Total Assisted Inpatient & Outpatient 1,000,000.

LAGUNA BEACH. *Mission Hospital Laguna Beach (MHLB)*, 31872 Coast Hwy., 92651. Tel: 949-499-7133; Fax: 949-499-8682. St. Joseph Health System. Bed Capacity/Operational 103; Patients Assisted: Inpatients 19,842; Outpatients 41,937; Staff 331.

MISSION VIEJO. *Mission Hospital Regional Medical Center (MHMV)*, 27700 Medical Center Rd., 92691. Tel: 949-364-1400; Fax: 949-364-2056. Email: kenneth.mcfarland@stjoe.org. Web: www.mission4health.com. Kenn McFarland, Interim Pres. & CEO; Cynthia H. Mueller, Vice Pres., Mission Integration. St. Joseph Health System. Total Staff 2,286; Patients Assisted: Inpatient Days 74,778; Outpatients 133,372; Bed Capacity 304.

[H] SPECIAL SERVICES

ORANGE. *Loyola Institute for Spirituality*, 480 S. Batavia St., 92868. Tel: 714-997-9587; Fax: 714-997-9588. Email: office@loyolainstitute.org. Web: www.loyolainstitute.org. Revs. Stephen Corder, S.J., Exec. Dir.; Felix N.W. Just, S.J., Dir. Biblical Educ.; David C. Robinson, S.J., Assoc. Dir.; Bro. Charles Jackson, S.J., Assoc. Dir.; Sr. M. Barbra Ostheimer, S.N.D., Assoc. Dir.; Wini Chuidian, Fin. Officer; Cynthia Guzman, Office Mgr.

ANAHEIM. *St. Thomas Korean Catholic Center*, 412 N. Crescent Way, 92801. Tel: 714-772-3995; Fax: 714-772-3636. Email: stthomas@stkcc.org. Web: www.stkcc.org. Revs. Alex K. Kim, Dir.; Eugene Lee, Assoc. Dir.; Deacons Peter Chung; Thomas Song.

SANTA ANA. *St. Francis Home for the Aged* (1944) 1718 W. 6th St., 92703. Tel: 714-542-0381; Fax: 714-542-4654. Email: stfrancishome@sbcglobal.net. Web: www.st-francis-home.org. Sr. Elia Caro, O.S.F., Admin. & Contact Person. Franciscan Sisters of the Immaculate Conception, Inc. Sisters 16; Bed Capacity 70; Total Assisted 60; Total Staff 23.
Vietnamese Catholic Center, 1538 N. Century Blvd., 92703. Tel: 714-554-4211; 714-554-5565; Fax: 714-265-1161. Email: srtuoi@yahoo.com. Web: www.vncatholic.org. Rev. Joseph Nguyen Thai, Coord. & Contact Person. Total in Residence 2; Total Staff 5.

SILVERADO. *St. Michael's Summer Camp* Boys aged 7-12 years., St. Michael's Abbey, 19292 El Toro Rd., 92676-9701. Tel: 949-858-0222, Ext. 226; Fax: 949-858-4583. Rev. Patrick D. Foutts, O.Praem., Contact. Capacity 120; Total in Residence 95; Total Staff 25.

WESTMINSTER. *Korean Catholic Ministry*, 7655 Trask Ave., 92683. Tel: 714-897-6510; Fax: 714-897-0832. Email: church@kmccoc.org. Web: www.kmccoc.org. Rev. John Hogan, S.S.C., Dir. Korean Martyrs Center & Contact Person.

YORBA LINDA. *Pope John Paul II Polish Center*, 3999 Rose Dr., 92886. Tel: 714-996-8161; Fax: 714-996-8161. Web: www.polishcenter.org. Revs. Henry Noga, S.V.D., Dir.; David C. Robinson, S.J., Assoc. Dir.; John Francis Vu, S.J., Chap., U.C. Irvine.

[I] MONASTERIES AND RESIDENCES OF PRIESTS AND BROTHERS

ANAHEIM. *Manresa Jesuit Residence*, 401 W. Leonora St., 92805-2634. Tel: 714-991-7765; Fax: 714-991-7798. Email: office@loyolainstitute.org. Web: loyolainstitute.org. Rev. Stephen Corder, S.J., Exec. Dir., Loyola Institute for Spirituality; Bro. Charles Jackson, S.J., Assoc. Dir.; Revs. Felix N.W. Just, S.J., Dir. Biblical Educ.; David C. Robinson, S.J., Assoc. Dir.; John Francis Vu, S.J.
Servite Fathers and Brothers Servite Friars, Servite Priory, 1922 W. La Palma Ave., 92801-3544. Tel: 714-774-8869; Fax: 714-774-6792. Web: www.servite.org. Revs. Perry McCoy, O.S.M.; Edward M. Penonzek, O.S.M.; Bro. Christopher M. Moran, O.S.M. *Servite High School*, 1952 W. La Palma Ave., 92801-3595. Tel: 714-774-7575; Fax: 714-774-1401. Web: www.servitehs.org.

FULLERTON. *Servite Fathers and Brothers*, St. Juliana Falconieri, 1316 N. Acacia, 92831. Tel: 714-879-1971; Fax: 714-526-6673. Email: info@stjulianachurch.org. Web: www.stjulianachurch.org. Rev. Frank Falco, O.S.M., Contact Person. Total in Residence 3; Total Staff 3. *St. Philip Benizi*, 235 S. Pine Dr., 92833-3294. Tel: 714-871-3613.

HUNTINGTON BEACH. *Franciscan Friars*, Sts. Simon & Jude, 20444 Magnolia St., 92646. Tel: 714-962-3333; Fax: 714-965-6456. Email: ssj@ssj.org. Web: www.ssj.org. Rev. Dan Lackie, O.F.M., Contact Person.

MIDWAY CITY. *Brothers of St. Patrick, St. Patrick's Novitiate*, 7820 Bolsa Ave., 92655. Tel: 714-897-8181; Fax: 714-898-9020. Bros. Aquinas Cassin, F.S.P., Supr. (Retired); Joseph Anoop, F.S.P.; Benedict Mavelil, F.S.P.; Kevin Minihan, F.S.P.; Matthew Regan, F.S.P., (Retired).

SANTA ANA. *Augustinian Recollects*, Our Lady of Guadalupe, 1322 E. 3rd St., 92701-5104. Tel: 714-836-4142; Fax: 714-836-7417. Rev. Alfredo de Dios, O.A.R., Contact Person. *Our Lady of the Pillar*, 1622 6th St., 92703. Tel: 714-543-1700; Fax: 714-543-9640. Rev. Anthony Palos, O.A.R.

SILVERADO. *Norbertine Fathers of Orange Inc.* (1959) For detailed information regarding the high school and seminary, please refer to High Schools, Private and Seminaries and Scholastics for Religious in the Institution section., St. Michael's Abbey (O.Praem.), 19292 El Toro Rd., 92676-9710. Tel: 949-858-0222; Fax: 949-858-4583. Rt. Rev. Eugene J. Hayes, O.Praem., Abbot; Very Rev. Hugh C. Barbour, O.Praem., Prior; Revs. James G. Smith, O.Praem., Subprior; Jordan S. Anderson, O.Praem.; Chrysostom Anthony Baer, O.Praem; Godfrey E. Bushmaker, O.Praem.; John Caronan, O.Praem., J.C.L.; Leo J. Celano, O.Praem.; Ambrose Criste, O.Praem.; Gregory M. Dick, O.Praem.; Vincent O. Gilmore, O.Praem.; Francis M. Gloudeman, O.Praem.; Charbel R. Grbavac, O.Praem.; Brendan R. Hankins, O.Praem.; John Henry Hanson, O.Praem.; Alphonsus B. Hermes, O.Praem.; Joseph K. Horn, O.Praem.; Gerlac A. Horvath, O.Praem. (Retired); Bernard M. Johnson, O.Praem.; Jerome M. Molokie, O.Praem.; Thomas W. Nelson, O.Praem.; Augustine R. Puchner, O.Praem.; Justin S. Ramos, O.Praem.; Adrian Sanchez, O.Praem.; Benedict M. Solomon, O.Praem.; Gabriel D. Stack, O.Praem.; Victor S. Szczurek, O.Praem.; Sebastian A. Walshe, O.Praem.; Claude A. Williams, O.Praem.; Charles W. Willingham, O.Praem. For detailed information concerning St. Michael's Abbey and St. Michael's College Preparatory High School please refer to the Seminary and High School categories in this diocese. Priests 46; Clerics 17; Postulants 5; Deacons 2.

WESTMINSTER. *Columban Fathers, Korean Martyrs Catholic Center*, 7655 Trask Ave., 92683. Tel: 714-897-6510; Fax: 714-897-0832. Email: church@kmccoc.org. Web: www.kmccoc.org. Rev. John Hogan, S.S.C. Tel: 714-897-2825.

[J] CONVENTS AND RESIDENCES FOR SISTERS

ORANGE. *Congregation of the Sisters of the Holy Cross, Inc.*, 540 S. LaVeta Park Cir., Apt. 49, 92868.
Sisters of the Holy Cross, Inc.
Sisters of St. Joseph of Orange Motherhouse Community, 480 S. Batavia, 92868. Tel: 714-633-8121; Fax: 714-744-3165. Sr. Eileen McNerney, C.S.J., Gen. Sec. & Contact Person. Sisters 21. *Regina Residence Community*, 430 S. Batavia St., 92868. Tel: 714-744-3109; Fax: 714-744-3163. Sisters 51. *Nazareth Community*, 940 W. Palmyra, 92868. Tel: 714-771-4706. Email: nazarethcommunity@yahoo.com. Sisters 3. *Casa Esperanza Community*, 954 W. Palmyra, 92868. Tel: 714-639-1030. Sisters 2. *St. Joseph Hospital Community*, P.O. Box 5600, 92863-5600. Tel: 714-771-8000; 714-771-8040. Sisters 9. *Greengrove Community*, 2075 Greengrove St., 92865. Tel: 714-974-9079. Email: csjgr@earthlink.net. Sisters 2. *Valencia Community*, 5742 E. Valencia Dr., 92869. Tel: 714-639-2665. Email: csjval@yahoo.com. Sisters 3. *Palmyra Community*, 1000 W. Palmyra St., 92868-3812. Tel: 714-997-0590. Email: sisters@sbcglobal.net. Sisters 2.
Westwood Community, 2014 N. Westwood Ave., Santa Ana, 92706-3542. Tel: 714-689-8667. Sisters 3.
Union of Sisters of the Presentation of the Blessed Virgin Mary, 343 E. Chestnut, 92867. Tel: 714-283-2496; Fax: 714-283-4159. Email: orangePBVM@aol.com. Web: pbvmunion.org. Sr. Breda Christopher, P.B.V.M., Contact Person. Sisters 3.

ANAHEIM. *Dominicans, Mission San Jose dba St. Catherine Academy St. Catherine's Academy*, 215 N. Harbor Blvd., 92805-2596. Tel: 714-772-1363; Fax: 714-772-3004. Email: scms@msjdominicans.org. Web: www.stcatherinesmilitary.com. Sr. Johnellen Turner, O.P., Admin., Prin. & Contact Person. Sisters 17.

BREA. *Sisters of St. Clare*, 446 S. Poplar Ave., 92821-6649. Tel: 714-256-1278. Sr. Anne Otter, Contact Person. Sisters 2. St. Clare's Garden, 449 S. Pine Ave., 92821-6649. Tel: 714-257-1113; Fax: 714-257-1068. Sr. Briegeen Moore, O.S.C., Contact Person.

BUENA PARK. *Sisters of Our Lady of Perpetual Help* (1932) 6751 Western Ave., 90621. Tel: 714-521-1345; Fax: 714-521-7611. Email: solphca@hanmail.net. Sr. Maura Cho, S.O.L.P.H., Pres. & Contact. Sisters 8.

COSTA MESA. *Sisters of Mercy of Ireland* (1959) St. John the Baptist Convent, 2960 Mendoza Dr., 92626. Tel: 714-545-2116; Fax: 714-557-9263. Email: mvianney@sjbschool.net. Sr. Mary Vianney, S.M., Prin. & Contact Person.
Sisters of St. Joseph of Orange (1946) *St. Joachim School*, 1964 Orange Ave., 92627. Tel: 949-547-7411, Ext. 409; Fax: 949-646-8948. Email: skm@

stjoachimparish.com. Sr. Kathleen Marie, C.S.J., Prin.

CYPRESS. *Union of the Sisters of the Presentation of the Blessed Virgin Mary*, 5151 Evergreen Ave., 90630. Tel: 714-527-4844; Fax: 714-527-5189. Sr. Mary Dunlea, P.B.V.M., Contact Person. Sisters 5.

DANA POINT. *Sisters of St. Joseph of Orange* (1912) Dana Point Community, 33392 Via Lenita, 92629. Tel: 949-488-0433. Email: csjdana@earthlink.net. Sr. Martha Ann Fitzpatrick, Contact Person.

FULLERTON. *Sisters of St. Joseph of Orange*, East Alto Community, 1601 E. Alto Ln., 92831. Tel: 714-526-3141. Email: csjoalto@adelphia.net. Sr. Judith Fergus, Contact Person. Sisters 3. *St. Jude Hospital Community*, 3642 Coronado Dr., 92835. Tel: 714-879-7159. Sisters 2.

GARDEN GROVE. *Eucharistic Missionaries of the Most Holy Trinity*, 11892 E. Lampson Ave., 92840. Tel: 714-530-5727; Fax: 714-636-5192. Email: virginiamesst@hotmail.com. Sisters Virginia Herrera, M.E.S.S.T., Local Supr.; Carmen Juarez, Contact Person. Sisters 4.

Religious Sisters of Charity, St. Columban Convent, 12555 Westlake St., 92840. Tel: 714-534-1003. Email: rscgg@aol.com. Sr. Bernadette Moran, Contact Person. Sisters 3.

Sisters of St. Joseph of Orange, Garden Grove Community, 9731 Acacia Ave., 1- C, 92841. Tel: 714-530-4695. Sr. Rebecca Rodriguez, Contact Person.

HUNTINGTON BEACH. *Sisters of Charity of the Blessed Virgin Mary*, SS. Simon & Jude Convent, 20512 Tobermory Cir., 92646-5837. Tel: 714-968-2237; Fax: 714-965-6456. Web: www.bvmcong.org. Sr. Maureen Sheehan, B.V.M., Pastoral Assoc.

Sisters of the Presentation of the Blessed Virgin Mary, St. Bonaventure Convent, 16441 Bradbury Ln., 92647. Tel: 714-846-6212; Fax: 714-840-0480. Email: presentation@linkline.com. Web: www.gnofn.org/~presis/. Sr. Annunciata Murtagh, P.B.V.M., Contact Person. Sisters 4.

LAKE FOREST. *School Sisters of St. Francis* (1874) 23333 Ridge Rte. Dr. #31, 92630-2846. Tel: 949-951-8681. Email: generalate@sssf.org. Web: www.sssf.org. Sisters Agnes Steiner, S.S.S.F., Contact Person; Paula Jane Tupa, S.S.S.F., Admin. & Dir. Education, Escalade Academy. Sisters 2.

SANTA ANA. *Franciscan Missionary Sisters of the Immaculate Conception* (1944) 1718 W. 6th St., 92703. Tel: 714-542-0381; 714-542-8352; Fax: 714-542-4654. Email: stfrancishome@sbcglobal.net. Web: www.st-francis-home.org. Sisters 16; Total Staff 23; Total Assisted 60.

Poor Clare Missionary Sisters of the Blessed Sacrament, 1019 N. Newhope St., 92703-1534. Tel: 714-554-8850; Fax: 714-554-5886. Email: clarisas@netzero.net. Sr. Susana Guzman, M.C., Contact Person. Sisters 14.

Sisters of St. Joseph of Carondelet, Hogar de San Jose, 507 N. Linwood Ave., 92701. Tel: 714-541-6480; Cell: 714-454-6221. Email: adcsj@sbcglobal.net. Sr. Barbara Anne Stowasser, C.S.J., Prov. *St. Joseph*

Sisters of St. Joseph of Orange, Casa Guadalupe Community, 414 S. Broadway, 92701. Tel: 714-834-9381. Email: csj414@yahoo.com. Mailing Address: 480 S. Batavia St., 92868. Sisters 4.

Bethany, 480 S. Batavia, 92868. Tel: 714-289-6761; Fax: 714-289-6760. Email: csjbeth@csjorange.org. Sr. Louise Ann Micek, Dir. Sisters 4. *Olive Street Community*, 2109 N. Olive St., 92706. Tel: 714-542-3380. Email: 2109csj@sbcglobal.net. Sisters 4.

Taller San Jose, 801 N. Broadway, 92707. Tel: 714-543-5105; Fax: 714-543-5032. Email: ssmith@tallersanjose.org. Shawna Smith, Exec. Dir. Sisters 2.

Sisters of the Company of Mary, St. Anne Convent, 1339 S. Broadway, 92707. Tel: 714-558-1340; Fax: 714-542-3431. Email: saintanneschool@sbcglobal.net. Sisters 5.

Sisters of the Lovers of the Holy Cross, 1401 S. Sycamore St., 92707. Tel: 714-973-1951; Fax: 714-667-0711. Web: www.lhcla.org. Sisters 10. 920 N. Bewley St., 92703. Tel: 714-554-9385; Fax: 714-554-5925. Email: grace_duc@yahoo.com. Web: www.lhcla.org. Sr. Grace Duc Le, L.H.C., Contact Person. Sisters 15.

Society Devoted to the Sacred Heart, 2927 S. Greenville St., 92704. Tel: 714-557-4538; Fax: 714-668-9780. Web: www.sdsh.org. Sisters 6. *Sacred Heart Convent*, 2911 S. Greenville St., 92704. Tel: 714-751-6335; Fax: 714-546-0873. Sisters 6.

SEAL BEACH. *Franciscans, Syracuse*, 328 1/2 10th St., 90740. Tel: 562-493-4630. Email: sealbeachsam@yahoo.com.

SILVERADO. *Rosarian Dominicans* (1972) St. Michael's Convent, 19292 El Toro Rd., 92676. Tel: 949-858-0487. Sisters 8.

TUSTIN. *Adrian Dominicans*, St. Jeanne de Lestonnac Convent, 16791 E. Main St., 92780. Tel: 714-720-3693; Fax: 714-835-0648. Email: srterry@sjdlschool.com. Web: www.sjdlschool.com.

Sisters of the Company of Mary (1607) 16791 E. Main St., 92780-4034. Tel: 714-541-3125; Fax: 714-835-0648. Email: elviraodn@yahoo.com. Web: www.lestonnac.org. Sr. Elvira Rios, O.D.N., Prov. Sec. & Contact Person. Sisters 19.

Lestonnac Retreat Center: (1961) Tel: 714-541-3125; Fax: 714-835-0648.

Lestonnac Residence: (1980) Tel: 714-541-3125; Fax: 714-835-0648.

WESTMINSTER. *Korean Sisters of Our Lady of Perpetual Help*, 7655 Trask Ave., 92683. Tel: 714-373-2556; Fax: 714-897-0832.

[K] CATHOLIC CHARITIES

SANTA ANA. *Catholic Charities of Orange County, Inc.* (1976) 1820 E. 16th St., 92701. Tel: 714-347-9600; Fax: 714-542-3020. Email: tsmith@ccoc.org. Web: www.ccoc.org. Teresa Smith, M.S.W., L.C.S.W., Exec. Dir. & CEO. Total Staff 43; Total Assisted 153,008.

Columbian Disability Camps Orange, CA.; Weekend getaway and ACE camp., 5140 Box Canyon Ct., Yorba Linda, 92887. Tel: 714-347-9627; Fax: 714-542-8482. Web: recreationcampoc.com. Mailing Address: 2811 E. Villa Real Dr., 92867. Meghan Schinderle, Co-Dir.; Katie Webb, Co-Dir.

Casa Santa Maria, 7551 Orangethorpe Ave., Buena Park, 90621. Tel: 714-523-1734; Fax: 714-542-3020. Ofelia Aranda, Advocate. Independent senior housing living project.

Counseling Services, 1820 E. 16th St., 92701. Tel: 714-347-9643; Fax: 714-542-3020.

Doris Cantlay Drop In Center Tel: 714-668-1130; Fax: 714-957-2523. Xang Yang, Dir.

Employment Services, Anaheim. Tel: 714-347-9664; Fax: 714-635-9896. Thu Tran, Contact Person.

Independent Senior Housing Living Project Casa Santa Maria, 7551 Orangethorpe Ave., Buena Park, 90621-1015. Tel: 714-994-1404; Fax: 714-994-0853. Patricia Warg, Res. Mgr.

Resettlement, Immigration & Citizenship Services Tel: 714-347-9664; Fax: 714-542-3541. Thu Tran, Prog. Dir.

[L] RETREAT HOUSES

ORANGE. *Center for Spiritual Development*, 434 S. Batavia St., 92868-3907. Tel: 714-744-3175, Ext. 4406; Fax: 714-744-3176. Email: csdinfo@csjorange.org. Web: www.thecsd.com. Julie Mussche, Dir. & Contact. Total Staff 9.

House of Prayer for Priests (1983) 7734 E. Santiago Canyon Rd., 92869. Tel: 714-639-9740. Email: jgmhop@yahoo.com. Rev. J. Gordon Moreland, S.J., Dir. & Contact Person. Total in Residence 2; Total Staff 1; Total Assisted 1,500. In Res. Rev. Patrick B. Philbin, S.M. (Retired).

Marywood Retreat Center Marywood provides the atmosphere on your journey to serve others. The beautiful grounds of Marywood offer centrally located facilities in Orange County for retreats, conferences, trainings, workshops, staff development days, camps and school events during the week or weekends. Overnight accomodations are available., 2811 E. Villa Real Dr., 92867. Tel: 714-282-3098 (Days Mon-Fri); Fax: 714-282-4228. Email: esandoval@rcbo.org. Web: www.rcbo.org. Elizabeth Sandoval, Facilities Coord.; Doug Fisher, Facilities Mgr. Tel: 714-282-3121. Email: dfisher@rcbo.org. Overnight Guest Accommodations 200; Day Guest 600; Total Staff 8.

FULLERTON. *Pro Sanctity Spirituality Center, Retreat House* (1979) 205 S. Pine Dr., 92833. Tel: 714-956-1020. Email: apostolico@aol.com. Web: caprosanctity.org. Capacity: 26 overnight, 32 day use

Pro Sanctity Movement (1947) Tel: 714-956-1020. Renee Jarecki, Dir.; Palmira Tafani, Counselor.

LA HABRA. *Villa Maria House of Prayer* (1978) 1252 N. Citrus Dr., 90631-2652. Tel: 562-691-5838. Sr. Grace Ann Loperena, C.S.J., Contact Person. Sisters of St. Joseph of Carondelet. Sisters 3.

SANTA ANA. *Heart of Jesus Retreat Center*, 2927 S. Greenville St., 92704. Tel: 714-557-4538; Fax: 714-668-9780. Email: heartofjesusrc@sbcglobal.net. Society Devoted to the Sacred Heart. Total Staff 5.

[M] NEWMAN CENTERS

FULLERTON. *California State University Fullerton, Newman Center* (1966) St. Juliana Falconieri, 1316 N. Acacia Ave., 92831-1202. Tel: 714-871-1086; Fax: 714-526-6673. Email: donovanpj7@roadrunner.com. Web: www.newman-csuf.com. Rev. Patrick Donovan, O.S.M., Chap., Dir., Treas., Newman Catholic Club. Tel: 714-871-1086.

IRVINE. *U.C.I. Interfaith Center* P.O. Box 6030, 92616-6030. Tel: 949-856-0211; 949-753-3373; Fax: 714-639-9313. Web: spirit.dos.uci.edu/ucc. Rev. John Francis Vu, S.J., Dir. Campus Ministry & Chap.

[N] SECULAR INSTITUTES

FULLERTON. *Institute of the Apostolic Oblates, Inc. (House of Professed Apostolic Oblates)* (1950) 2125 W. Walnut Ave., 92833. Tel: 714-956-1020. Email: ApostolicO@aol.com. Renee A. Jarecki, Mod. House of Formation for Professed Apostolic Oblates. Secular Institute of the Apostolic Oblates, Inc.

[O] MISCELLANEOUS LISTINGS

ORANGE. *American Federation Pueri Cantores*, 615 E. Chapman Ave., #200, 92866. Tel: 714-633-7554; Fax: 714-516-1531. Email: info@pcchoirs.org. Web: www.pcchoirs.org. Jan Schmidt, Exec. Dir.

Christ Our Savior Cathedral Fund, Inc., c/o Diocese of Orange, 2811 E. Villa Real Dr., 92867. Tel: 714-282-3011.

St. Joseph Health Ministry, 500 S. Main St., Ste. 1000, 92868. Tel: 714-347-7778; 714-347-7586; Fax: 714-347-7501.

St. Joseph Health System, 500 S. Main St., Ste. 1000, 92868. Tel: 714-347-7500; Fax: 714-347-7663. Web: www.stjhs.org. William Noce, Bd. Chm.; Ms. Deborah Proctor, Pres. & CEO.

St. Joseph Health System Foundation, 500 S. Main St., Ste. 1000, 92868. Tel: 714-347-7500; Fax: 714-347-7663. Gabriela Robles, Dir., Community Outreach.

St. Jude Hospital Yorba Linda aka St. Joseph Heritage Healthcare St. Joseph Health System, 500 S. Main St., 92868-4515. Tel: 714-347-7579; Fax: 714-347-7590. C. R. Burke.

Orange Catholic Foundation (2000) 2811 E. Villa Real Dr., 92867-1999. Tel: 714-282-3021; Fax: 714-282-3029. Web: www.oc-foundation.org.

Orange County Catholic Alumni Club, P.O. Box 6054, 92863-6054. Tel: 714-502-8086. Email: orangecountyCAC@juno.com. Web: www.occaci.com.

Sisters of St. Joseph Healthcare Foundation, 480 S. Batavia St., 92868. Tel: 714-633-8121; Fax: 714-744-3135. Email: rfox@csjorange.org. Sr. Theresa LaMetterey, C.S.J., Exec. Dir.

**Society of St. Vincent de Paul*, 180 S. Cypress St., 92866.

FULLERTON. *St. Jude Memorial Foundation*, P.O. Box 4138, 92834. Tel: 714-992-3033; Fax: 714-446-5430. Lynne Bolen, Contact Person.

Western Catholic Educational Association, 2651 E. Chapman Ave., Ste. 216, 92831. Tel: 714-447-9834; Fax: 714-447-9846. Email: wcea214@sbcglobal.net. Web: westwcea.org. Bro. William Carriere, F.S.C., Exec. Dir.

IRVINE. **Council of Orange County - Society of St. Vincent de Paul*, 8014 Marine Way, 92618. Tel: 949-653-2900; Fax: 949-653-9155.

Our Lady of Peace Korean Catholic Center, 6789 Quail Hill Pkwy., #206, 92603.

LAGUNA WOODS. **St. Michael's Abbey Foundation*, 24361 El Toro Rd., Ste. 220, 92637-2757.

SANTA ANA. *Project SUCCESS*, 5306 W. McFadden Ave., 92704. Tel: 714-775-9485; Fax: 714-531-5868. Email: info@project-success.org. Web: www.project-success.org.

RELIGIOUS INSTITUTES OF MEN REPRESENTED IN THE DIOCESE

For further details refer to the corresponding bracketed number in the Religious Institutes of Men or Women section.

[]—*Alagard Ni Maria*—A.M.
[0150]—*Augustinian Recollects*—O.A.R.
[]—*Brothers of St. Patrick*—F.S.P.
[0520]—*Franciscan Fathers*—O.F.M.
[0690]—*Jesuit Fathers and Brothers*—S.J.
[]—*Legionnaires of Christ*—L.C.
[0780]—*Marist Fathers*—S.M.
[0900]—*Norbertine Fathers*—O.Praem.
[1240]—*Servite Fathers and Brothers*—O.S.M.

RELIGIOUS INSTITUTES OF WOMEN REPRESENTED IN THE DIOCESE

[]—*Congregation of Servants of Jesus, The High Priest*—S.J.P.
[3832]—*Congregation of the Sisters of St. Joseph*—C.S.J.
[1070-13]—*Dominican Sisters* (Adrian, MI)—O.P.
[]—*Dominican Sisters* (Mission San Jose)—O.P.
[]—*Dominican Sisters* (Western Australia)—O.P.
[]—*Eucharistic Missionaries of the Most Holy Trinity*—M.E.S.S.T.
[]—*Family of Mary of the Visitation*—F.M.V.
[1350]—*Franciscan Missionary Sisters of the Immaculate Conception*—O.S.F.
[1540]—*Franciscan Sisters* (Syracuse, IA)—O.S.F.

[]—*Korean Order of Discaled Carmelites*—O.C.D.
[2390]—*Lovers of the Holy Cross Sisters*—L.H.C.
[2490]—*Medical Missionary Sisters*—M.M.S.
[]—*Missionaries of the Holy Spirit*—M.S.P.S.
[2840]—*Poor Clare Missionaries of Blessed Sacrament*—M.C.
[3280]—*Presentation Sisters of Blessed Virgin Mary*—P.B.V.M.
[3400]—*Religious Sisters of Charity*—R.S.C.
[2575]—*Religious Sisters of Mercy of the Americas*—R.S.M.
[]—*Religious Sisters of the Sacred Heart of Mary*—R.S.H.M.
[]—*Rosarian Dominican Sisters*—O.P.
[]—*School Sisters of Notre Dame*—S.S.N.D.
[1680]—*School Sisters of St. Francis*—S.S.S.F.
[]—*Sisters for Christian Community*—S.F.C.C.
[0430]—*Sisters of Charity of the Blessed Virgin Mary*—B.V.M.
[]—*Sisters of Notre Dame*—S.N.D.
[]—*Sisters of Our Lady of Perpetual Help*—S.O.L.P.H.
[3770]—*Sisters of St. Clare*—O.S.C.
[3830-03]—*Sisters of St. Joseph* (Orange)—C.S.J.
[3840]—*Sisters of St. Joseph of Carondelet*—C.S.J.
[]—*Sisters of St. Joseph of Concordia*—C.S.J.
[0700]—*Sisters of the Company of Mary*—O.D.N.
[1990]—*Sisters of the Holy Names of Jesus and Mary*—S.N.J.M.
[4050]—*Sisters of the Society Devoted to the Sacred Heart*—S.D.S.H.
[]—*Sisters, Servants of the Immaculate Heart of Mary*—I.H.M.
[]—*Society of Jesus*—S.J.
[4060]—*Society of the Holy Child Jesus*—S.H.C.J.

DIOCESAN CEMETERIES

ORANGE. *Holy Sepulcher*, 7845 Santiago Canyon Rd., 92869. Tel: 714-532-6551; Fax: 714-288-8441. Email: holysepulcher@rcbo.org. Dow Gras, Cemetery Mgr.

ANAHEIM. *Holy Cross Cemetery*, Mailing Address: c/o *Holy Sepulcher*, 7845 Santiago Cyn, 92869. 619 S. Euclid, 92802. Tel: 714-532-6551.

HUNTINGTON BEACH. *Good Shepherd Cemetery and Mausoleum*, 8301 Talbert Ave., 92646. Tel: 714-847-8546; Fax: 714-842-9979. Email: goodshepherd@rcbo.org. Guadalupe Ramirez, Mgr.

LAKE FOREST. *Ascension*, 24754 Trabuco Rd., 92630. Tel: 949-837-1331; Fax: 949-837-9013; 949-837-9013. Email: ascension@rcbo.org. Kevin M. Haynes, Supt. Mgr.

NECROLOGY

† Pierse, Rev. Msgr. James J., Seal Beach, CA Holy Family.—Died Feb. 22, 2011
† Chen, Rafael, (Retired)—Died May 4, 2011
† Croal, Thomas, (Retired)—Died May 29, 2011
† Fee, George Patterson, (Retired)—Died May 30, 2011
† Ho, Matthias, (Retired)—Died Jan. 25, 2011
† Kinzer, Gary—Died Oct. 5, 2011

An asterisk (*) denotes an organization that has established tax-exempt status directly with the IRS and is not covered by the USCCB Group Ruling.

Diocese of Orlando

(Dioecesis Orlandensis)

Most Reverend

JOHN G. NOONAN

Bishop of Orlando; ordained September 23, 1983; appointed Auxiliary Bishop of Miami June 21, 2005; ordained Titular Bishop of Bonusta and Auxiliary Bishop of the Archdiocese of Miami August 24, 2005; appointed Bishop of Orlando October 23, 2010; installed as Fifth Bishop of the Diocese of Orlando December 16, 2010. *Chancery: 50 E. Robinson St., Orlando, FL 32801.* Tel: 407-246-4800. *Mailing Address: P.O. Box 1800, Orlando, FL 32802.*

Most Reverend

NORBERT L. DORSEY, C.P., D.D., S.T.D.

Bishop Emeritus of Orlando; ordained April 28, 1956; appointed Auxiliary Bishop of Miami January 10, 1986; ordained Titular Bishop of Mactaris and Auxiliary Bishop of the Archdiocese of Miami March 19, 1986; appointed Bishop of Orlando March 20, 1990; installed as Third Bishop of Orlando May 25, 1990; retired November 13, 2004. *Office: 50 E. Robinson St., Orlando, FL 32801. Mailing Address: P.O. Box 1800, Orlando, FL 32802.*

Chancery: 50 E. Robinson St., Orlando, FL 32801. Mailing Address: P.O. Box 1800, Orlando, FL 32802. Tel: 407-246-4800; Fax: 407-246-4942.

Web: www.orlandodiocese.org

Email: cbrinati@orlandodiocese.org

ESTABLISHED JUNE 18, 1968.

Square Miles 9,611.

Comprises the Counties of Brevard, Lake, Marion, Orange, Osceola, Polk, Seminole, Sumter and Volusia in the State of Florida.

For legal titles of parishes and diocesan institutions, consult the Chancery.

STATISTICAL OVERVIEW

Personnel	
Bishop	1
Retired Bishops	1
Priests: Diocesan Active in Diocese	81
Priests: Diocesan Active Outside Diocese	3
Priests: Diocesan in Foreign Missions	1
Priests: Retired, Sick or Absent	47
Number of Diocesan Priests	132
Religious Priests in Diocese	71
Total Priests in Diocese	203
Extern Priests in Diocese	58
Ordinations:	
Diocesan Priests	1
Transitional Deacons	3
Permanent Deacons	5
Permanent Deacons in Diocese	188
Total Brothers	15
Total Sisters	108
Parishes	
Parishes	80
With Resident Pastor:	
Resident Diocesan Priests	68
Resident Religious Priests	12
Missions	12
Professional Ministry Personnel:	
Brothers	2
Sisters	26
Lay Ministers	208
Welfare	
Health Care Centers	3
Total Assisted	1,224
Day Care Centers	5
Total Assisted	146
Specialized Homes	2
Total Assisted	26
Special Centers for Social Services	9
Total Assisted	120,000
Residential Care of Disabled	1
Total Assisted	116
Other Institutions	2
Total Assisted	291
Educational	
Diocesan Students in Other Seminaries	23
Students Religious	13
Total Seminarians	36
High Schools, Diocesan and Parish	5
Total Students	2,619
Elementary Schools, Diocesan and Parish	30
Total Students	10,274
Non-residential Schools for the Disabled	1
Total Students	60
Catechesis/Religious Education:	
High School Students	3,749
Elementary Students	18,579
Total Students under Catholic Instruction	35,317
Teachers in the Diocese:	
Brothers	4
Sisters	9
Lay Teachers	1,121
Vital Statistics	
Receptions into the Church:	
Infant Baptism Totals	5,651
Minor Baptism Totals	535
Adult Baptism Totals	295
Received into Full Communion	495
First Communions	5,911
Confirmations	4,748
Marriages:	
Catholic	815
Interfaith	328
Total Marriages	1,143
Deaths	3,677
Total Catholic Population	393,230
Total Population	4,199,193

Former Bishops—Most Revs. WILLIAM D. BORDERS, D.D., ord. May 18, 1940; appt. Bishop of Orlando, May 2, 1968; cons. June 14, 1968; transferred to Baltimore, March 25, 1974 as Archbishop; died April 19, 2010.; THOMAS J. GRADY, D.D., ord. April 23, 1938; appt. Second Bishop of Orlando, Nov. 9, 1974; installed Dec. 16, 1974; retired May 25, 1990; died April 21, 2002; NORBERT L. DORSEY, C.P., D.D., S.T.D. (Retired), ord. April 28, 1956; appt. Titular Bishop of Mactaris and Auxiliary Bishop of Miami Jan. 10, 1986; cons. March 19, 1986; appt. Bishop of Orlando March 20, 1990; installed as Third Bishop of Orlando May 25, 1990; retired Nov. 13, 2004; THOMAS G. WENSKI, ord. May 15, 1976; appt. Titular Bishop of Kearney and Auxiliary Bishop of Miami June 24, 1997; cons. Sept. 3, 1997; appt. Coadjutor Bishop of Orlando July 1, 2003; installed Aug. 22, 2003; appt. Fourth Bishop of Orlando Nov. 13, 2004; appt. Archbishop of Miami April 20, 2010.

Chancery—50 E. Robinson St., Orlando, 32801. Tel: 407-246-4800; Fax: 407-246-4942. Email: eworley@orlandodiocese.org. Web: www.orlandodiocese.org. *Mailing Address: P.O. Box 1800, Orlando, 32802.*

Vicar General and Chancellor for Canonical Affairs—Very Rev. GREGORY PARKES, J.C.L., Mailing Address: P.O. Box 1800, Orlando, 32802. Tel: 407-246-4846. Email: gparkes@orlandodiocese.org.

Chancellor for Administration—CAROL BRINATI, Mailing Address: P.O. Box 1800, Orlando, 32802-1800. Tel: 407-246-4800. Email: cbrinati@orlandodiocese.org.

Presbyteral Council—

President—Most Rev. JOHN NOONAN Diocese of Orlando.

Ex Officio Members—Very Revs. ESAU GARCIA, V.F., (South Central Dean); JOHN GIEL, V.F., J.C.L., (Northern Dean); SEAN HESLIN, V.F., (Southern Dean); STAN MURRAY, V.F., (Eastern Dean); GREGORY PARKES, J.C.L., V.G., Chancellor for Canonical Affairs; STEPHEN D. PARKES, V.F., (North Central Dean); PETER PUNTAL, V.F., (Western Dean); RICHARD WALSH, Vicar Gen.; Rev. MIGUEL A. GONZALEZ, Vicar for Priests; Very Rev. PAUL HENRY, Vicar for Priests.

Representative by Age—Revs. KARL BERGIN, (25-45); RICHARD W. TROUT, (46-64); NICHOLAS KING, (65 & over).

Representative - Secular Priests Not Incardinated—Rev. ROY V. ECO.

Representative - Religious Priests—Rev. BENJAMIN A. BERINTI, C.PP.S., V.F.

Representative - Retired Priests—Rev. Msgr. DAVID PAGE (Retired).

Appointed Members—Revs. YBAIN F. RAMIREZ; JEAN GAETAN BOURSIQUOT.

Chief Financial Officer—BRYAN JOSEPH, Mailing Address: P.O. Box 1800, Orlando, 32802. Tel: 407-246-4831. Email: bjoseph@orlandodiocese.org.

Marriage Tribunal—50 E. Robinson St., Orlando, 32801. Tel: 407-246-4850.

Judicial Vicar—Very Rev. FERNANDO GIL, J.D., J.C.D., 50 E. Robinson St., Orlando, 32801. Tel: 407-246-4854.

Director of Tribunal—Very Rev. FERNANDO GIL, J.D., J.C.D.

Promoter of Justice—Sr. LUCY VAZQUEZ, O.P., J.C.D.

Defenders of the Bond—Very Rev. GREGORY PARKES, J.C.L.; Rev. JOSE BAUTISTA, J.C.L.; Sr. LUCY VAZQUEZ, O.P., J.C.D.

Judges—Revs. PAIGE BLAKELY, J.C.L. (Retired); JOSE BAUTISTA, J.C.L.; JOSEPH V. BELLERIVE, J.C.D.; CROMWELL CABRISOS, J.C.L.; Very Revs. JOHN GIEL, V.F., J.C.L.; FERNANDO GIL, J.D., J.C.D.

Regional Advocates—Sisters PATRICIA O'MALLEY, S.N.D.deN. Tel: 386-668-1426; JOYCE ROHLIK, B.V.M., Resurrection, Lakeland, 33813. Tel: 863-646-3556.

Deans—Very Revs. JOHN GIEL, V.F., J.C.L., Northern Deanery; ESAU GARCIA, V.F., Central Deanery South; STEPHEN D. PARKES, V.F., Central Deanery North; STAN MURRAY, V.F., Eastern Deanery; PETER PUNTAL, V.F., Western Deanery; SEAN HESLIN, V.F., Southern Deanery.

Vicars for Clergy—Revs. PAUL J. HENRY; MIGUEL A. GONZALEZ.

Vicar for Religious—Rev. ROBERT D'AVERSA, T.O.R., Mailing Address: P.O. Box 1800, Orlando, 32802.

Moderator for Women Religious—Sr. ELIZABETH MURPHY, O.S.F., Mailing Address: P.O. Box 1800, Orlando, 32802.

Sister's Council—Sr. VIRGINIA WEST, S.N.D.deN., Pres., Mailing Address: P.O. Box 1800, Orlando, 32802.

Diocesan Offices and Organizations

Archivist and Librarian—HYUN PETERSON, Dir., Mailing Address: P.O. Box 1800, Orlando, 32802. Tel: 407-246-4920.

Catholic Charities of Central Florida, Inc.—CHRISTOPHER GARDNER, Chm., Bd. Directors; VACANT, Pres. & CEO.

Cemetery, San Pedro—Very Rev. A. GILES SCHINELLI, T.O.R., Dir., Mailing Address: San Pedro Center, 2400 Dike Rd., Winter Park, 32792. Tel: 407-671-6322.

Censor of Books—Rev. STEVEN OLDS, S.T.D., St. Vincent de Paul Seminary, 10701 S. Military Trail, Boynton Beach, 33436; Very Rev. ESAU GARCIA, V.F., Mailing Address: P.O. Box 1800, Orlando, 32802. Tel: 407-246-4814.

Liturgy—Very Rev. ROBERT E. WEBSTER, Dir., Mailing Address: P.O. Box 1800, Orlando, 32802. Tel: 407-246-4861.

Liturgical Music—CHARLES THATCHER, Dir., Mailing Address: P.O. Box 1800, Orlando, 32802. Tel: 407-246-4862.

Propagation of the Faith—Rev. JOHN M. MCCORMICK, Dir., St. James Cathedral, 215 N. Orange Ave., Orlando, 32801. Tel: 407-422-2005.

Victim Assistance Coordinator—HEIDI PECKHAM, Mailing Address: P.O. Box 1800, Orlando, 32802. Tel: 407-246-4866; 407-246-7179 (HOTLINE). Email: hpeckham@orlandodiocese.org.

Secretariat for Administration—BRYAN JOSEPH, Sec. & CFO, Mailing Address: P.O. Box 1800, Orlando, 32802. Tel: 407-246-4831. Email: bjoseph@orlandodiocese.org.

Diocesan Finance Committee—JOSEPH F. BERT, Chm., Mailing Address: P.O. Box 1800, Orlando, 32802.

Fiscal Management—BRYAN JOSEPH, CFO.

Comptroller—ROGER BARNES, Mailing Address: P.O. Box 1800, Orlando, 32802. Tel: 407-246-4832.

Design and Construction Services—VACANT, Mailing Address: P.O. Box 1800, Orlando, 32802. Tel: 407-246-4870.

Human Resources—THERESA SIMON, Sr. Dir., Mailing Address: P.O. Box 1800, Orlando, 32802. Tel: 407-246-4830. Email: tsimon@orlandodiocese.org.

Information Technology—JACK PAIGE, Sr. Dir., Mailing Address: P.O. Box 1800, Orlando, 32802. Tel: 407-246-4839. Email: jpaige@orlandodiocese.org.

Insurance Committee—Dr. MARGARET CURRAN, Chm., Mailing Address: P.O. Box 1800, Orlando, 32802. Tel: 407-246-4835.

Secretariat for Evangelization—DANIEL HARDESTER, Sec., Mailing Address: P.O. Box 1800, Orlando, 32802. Tel: 407-246-4895. Email: dhardester@orlandodiocese.org.

Advocacy and Justice - Respect Life—DEBORAH STAFFORD SHEARER, Dir., Mailing Address: P.O. Box 1800, Orlando, 32802. Tel: 407-246-4819; Fax: 407-246-4942.

Communications—TERESA PETERSON, Dir., Mailing Address: P.O. Box 1800, Orlando, 32802. Tel: 407-246-4811. Email: tpeterson@orlandodiocese.org.

Hispanic Communications— (Buena Nueva FM; El Clarin) TOMAS EVANS, Dir., Mailing Address: P.O. Box 1800, Orlando, 32802. Tel: 407-246-4926.

Media Center—DANIEL HARDESTER, Dir., 50 E. Robinson St., Orlando, 32801. Tel: 407-246-4895; Fax: 407-246-4935.

Mission Office, Sister Diocese—Sr. BERNADETTE MACKAY, O.S.U., Dir., Mailing Address: P.O. Box 1800, Orlando, 32802. Tel: 407-246-4890; Fax: 407-246-4892.

Newspaper— "The Florida Catholic" TERESA PETERSON, Mailing Address: P.O. Box 1800, Orlando, 32802. Tel: 407-246-4811. Email: tpeterson@orlandodiocese.org.

Secretariat for Faith Formation—HENRY FORTIER, Sec. & Supt. Schools, Mailing Address: P.O. Box 1800, Orlando, 32802. Tel: 407-246-4904; Fax: 407-246-4940. Email: hfortier@orlandodiocese.org.

Diocesan School Board—JOSEPH STANTON, Chm. Bd., Mailing Address: P.O. Box 1800, Orlando, 32802. Tel: 407-246-4904; Fax: 407-246-4940.

Faith Formation—DENNIS JOHNSON JR., Sr. Dir., Mailing Address: P.O. Box 1800, Orlando, 32802. Tel: 407-246-4910; Fax: 407-246-4935.

Schools—HENRY FORTIER, Sec. & Supt. Schools, Mailing Address: P.O. Box 1800, Orlando, 32802. Tel: 407-246-4904; Fax: 407-246-4940. Email: hfortier@orlandodiocese.org.

Secretariat for Pastoral Ministries—HEIDI PECKHAM, Sec., Mailing Address: P.O. Box 1800, Orlando, 32802. Tel: 407-246-4866. Email: hpeckham@orlandodiocese.org.

Campus Ministry—DENNIS JOHNSON JR., Dir., Mailing Address: P.O. Box 1800, Orlando, 32802. Tel: 407-246-4867.

Catholic Campus Ministry at University of Central Florida—Mailing Address: P.O. Box 677145, Orlando, 32867. Tel: 407-382-7063. Rev. SCOTT M. CIRCE, Campus Min.

Ethnic Ministries—Rev. JOHN M. MCCORMICK, Dir. Tel: 407-422-2005.

African Ministry—Rev. EMMANUEL AKALUE.

Portuguese/Brazilian Ministry—Rev. MOACIR BALEN, C.S.

Filipino Ministry—Rev. ROY V. ECO.

Haitian Ministry—Rev. JEAN GAETAN BOURSIQUOT.

Hispanic Ministry—TOMAS EVANS, Dir., Mailing Address: P.O. Box 1800, Orlando, 32802. Tel: 407-246-4931.

Korean Ministry—Rev. ANDREW KYUNG-CHUL LEE.

Polish Ministry—Rev. ANDRZEJ JURKIEWICZ.

Vietnamese Ministry—Rev. CHAU J. NGUYEN.

Family Life and Pastoral Care—DIGNA MONTANEZ, Co Mgr.; GIGI SANTIAGO, Co Mgr., Mailing Address: P.O. Box 1800, Orlando, 32802. Tel: 407-246-4881.

Farmworker Ministry and Hope CommUnity Center—Sisters GAIL GRIMES, S.N.D.deN., Admin.; ANN KENDRICK, S.N.D.deN., Community Rels. Coord., 1016 N. Park Ave., Apopka, 32712. Tel: 407-880-4673; Fax: 407-464-0854. Web: www.hcc-offm.org.

Permanent Diaconate—Deacons DAVID L. GRAY, Dir.; JOHN RUMPLASH, Assoc. Dir. Formation, Mailing Address: P.O. Box 1800, Orlando, 32802. Tel: 407-246-4875; Fax: 407-246-4942.

Priestly Life and Ministry—Rev. RICHARD W. TROUT, Dir., P.O. Box 1800, Orlando, 32802. Tel: 407-246-4875.

Priest Personnel—Very Rev. RICHARD WALSH, Dir., Mailing Address: P.O. Box 1800, Orlando, 32802. Tel: 407-246-4875.

San Pedro Spiritual Development Center—Very Rev. A. GILES SCHINELLI, T.O.R., San Pedro Center, 2400 Dike Rd., Winter Park, 32792. Tel: 407-671-6322.

Cursillos de Cristiandad—VACANT, Mailing Address: P.O. Box 1800, Orlando, 32802. Tel: 407-246-4876.

Foundations for Lay Ministry Program—Directors: CAROL STANTON, Ph.D.; Rev. BENJAMIN A. BERINTI, C.PP.S., V.F., Mailing Address: San Pedro Center, 2400 Dike Rd., Winter Park, 32792. Tel: 407-671-6322.

Tourism Ministry—Basilica of the National Shrine of Mary, Queen of the Universe, 8300 Vineland Ave., Orlando, 32821. Tel: 407-239-6600. Very Rev. PAUL HENRY, Rector.

Apostleship of the Sea Chaplain— Port Canaveral: Deacon WILLIAM WANCA SR., 720 Mullet Rd., Ste. N, Cape Canaveral, 32920. Tel: 321-431-2700.

Airport Ministry, Orlando International Airport—Rev. ROBERT F. SUSANN, M.S., Airport Chap. Tel: 407-947-5453.

Vocations—Rev. JORGE TORRES, Dir., Mailing Address: P.O. Box 1800, Orlando, 32802. Tel: 407-246-4875; Fax: 407-246-4937. Email: jtorres@orlandodiocese.org.

Youth and Young Adult Ministry—MICHELLE FISCHER, Dir., Mailing Address: P.O. Box 1800, Orlando, 32802. Tel: 407-246-4911; Fax: 407-246-4935. Email: mfischer@orlandodiocese.org.

Girl Scouting—MICHELLE FISCHER, Mailing Address: P.O. Box 1800, Orlando, 32802. Tel: 407-246-4867.

Other Diocesan Organizations

Catholic Charities of Central Florida, Inc.—CHRISTOPHER GARDNER, Chm., Bd. Directors; VACANT, Pres. & CEO, Mailing Address: Central Office, 1819 N. Semoran Blvd., Orlando, 32807-3598. Tel: 407-658-1818; Fax: 407-282-2891. Web: www.cflcc.org; Central Regional Office: 1771 N. Semoran Blvd., Orlando, 32807-3598. Tel: 407-658-1818. Southern Regional Office: 3800 E. Eau Gallie Blvd., Ste. 101, Melbourne, 32934. Tel: 321-636-6144. Eastern Regional Office: 207 White St., Daytona Beach, 32114-3427. Tel: 386-255-6521. Western Regional Office: 1801 E. Memorial Blvd., Lakeland, 33801-5528. Tel: 863-686-7153.

Immigration Services—

Refugee Resettlement—RICHARD LOGUE, Dir., 1771 N. Semoran Blvd., Ste. C, Orlando, 32807-3598. Tel: 407-658-0110; Fax: 407-249-5699.

Prison Ministry—Deacon DAVID L. GRAY, Dir., Mailing Address: P.O. Box 1800, Orlando, 32802. Tel: 407-246-4868.

**Pathways to Care, Inc.*DAWN ZINGER, Dir., Mailing Address: 430 Plumosa Ave., Casselberry, 32707. Tel: 407-388-0245. Web: pathwaystocare.org/.

**Catholic Foundation of Central Florida, Inc.*ALLAN KEEN, Chm., Bd. Directors; JAMES EDWARDS, Mailing Address: P.O. Box 4905, Orlando, 32801-4905. 50 E. Robinson St., Orlando, 32801. Tel: 407-246-4841; Fax: 407-246-4939.

**Hope Community Center, Inc.*Sisters GAIL GRIMES, S.N.D.deN., Admin.; ANN KENDRICK, S.N.D.deN., Community Rels. Coord., Mailing Address: 1016 N. Park Ave., Apopka, 32712. Tel: 407-880-4673; Fax: 407-464-0854. Web: www.hcc-offm.org.

CLERGY, PARISHES, MISSIONS AND PAROCHIAL SCHOOLS

CITY OF ORLANDO

(ORANGE COUNTY)

1—ST. JAMES CATHEDRAL (1881) Revs. John M. McCormick, Rector; Nicholas A. Tocco; Deacon David L. Gray.
Church: 215 N. Orange Ave., 32801. Tel: 407-422-2005; Fax: 407-422-2009. Email: info@stjcc.net. Web: www.stjamesorlando.com.
School—505 E. Ridgewood St., 32803. Tel: 407-841-4432; Fax: 407-648-4603. Email: stjcs@stjcs.com. Web: www.stjcs.com. Mrs. Gerri Gendall, Prin. Lay Teachers 29; Students 455.
Catechesis/Religious Program—Students 310.
Mission—St. Ignatius Kim Korean Mission 1518 E. Muriel St., Orange Co. 32806. Tel: 407-895-8858; Fax: 407-895-8858. Rev. Andrew Kyung C. Lee.

2—ST. ANDREW (1957) Rev. Vigny Joseph Bellerive; Deacons Jose Cruz; Rafael Hernandez.
Res.: 430 Cinnamon Bark Ln., 32835. Tel: 407-293-0730; Fax: 407-293-0739. Email: lstandrewcatho@cfl.rr.com. Web: www.standrew-orlando.org.
School—877 Hastings St., 32808. Tel: 407-295-4230; Fax: 407-290-0959. Email: sand@doschool.org. Web: www.standrewcatholicschool.org. Lay Teachers 19; Students 342.
Catechesis/Religious Program—Students 105.

3—BLESSED TRINITY (1965) Revs. Roland Nadeau, M.S.; William Slight, M.S. In Res., Revs. Robert F. Susann, M.S., Airport Chap.; Joseph Gosselin, M.S.
Res.: 4545 Anderson Rd., 32812. Tel: 407-277-1702; Fax: 407-277-1973. Email: info@blessedtrinityorlando.org. Web: blessedtrinityorlando.org.
Catechesis/Religious Program—Tel: 407-277-1702; Fax: 407-277-1973. Students 283.

4—ST. CHARLES BORROMEO (1954) Revs. Augustine Clark; Alvaro Jimenez, Parochial Vicar; Deacons Paul Volkerson; Jose D. Naveo.
Res.: 4001 Edgewater Dr., 32804. Tel: 407-293-9556; Fax: 407-293-9213. Web: www.stcharlesorlando.org.
School—4005 Edgewater Dr., 32804. Tel: 407-293-7691; Fax: 407-295-9839. Web: www.stcharles-orlando.org. Lay Teachers 27; Students 388.
Preschool—Students 23.
Catechesis/Religious Program—Tel: 407-293-9556, Ext. 121. Students 88.

5—GOOD SHEPHERD (1956) Revs. Joseph O'Neil, M.S.; Stephen J. Krisanda, M.S.; Baiju Augustine Avittappally, M.S.; Terry Niziolek, M.S.; Deacons John T. Crotty; Confesor De Jesus; Vicente Rivera; Felix Morillo.
Mailing Address: 5900 Oleander Dr., 32807. Tel: 407-277-3939; Fax: 407-273-5148.
Res.: 567 Hewett Dr., 32807. Tel: 407-275-6381.
School—Tel: 407-277-3973; Fax: 407-277-2605.

Email: jhartmann@goodshepherd.org. Web: www-.goodshepherd.org. Lay Teachers 45; Students 546.
Good Shepherd Early Childhood Educational Ctr.—Tel: 407-277-3939, Ext. 220. Email: mjimenez@goodshepherd.org. Lay Teachers 12; Students 56.
Catechesis/Religious Program—Tel: 407-277-3939, Ext. 211. Email: lmediavilla@goodshepherd.org. Laura Mediavilla, C.R.E. Students 358.

6—HOLY CROSS (1992) Very Rev. Esau Garcia; Rev. John Walsh; Deacons Celso Diaz; Ramon Morales; Kenneth N. Money; Mary Shelton, Liturgy Dir.; Dennis Cote, Business Mgr.; Jose F. Velez, Music Dir.
Res.: 12600 Marsfield Ave., 32837. Tel: 407-438-0990; Fax: 407-438-4090.
Catechesis/Religious Program—Elsie V. Torres, D.R.E. (K-5); Tina Shannon, Middle School & Senior High Youth Coord. Students 739.

7—HOLY FAMILY (1975) [JC] Revs. William Ennis; Justin Vakko, O.C.D.; Peter Cordeno; Deacons Charles Mallon; Patrick Kenneth McAvoy; Robert J. Pleus; John R. Martin; Carl Orbon; Carl Lawrence Brockman.
Res.: 5125 S. Apopka-Vineland Rd., 32819. Tel: 407-876-2211; Fax: 407-876-1167. Email: hfoffice@hfcchurch.com. Web: www.holyfamilyorlando.org.
School—5129 S. Apopka-Vineland Rd., 32819. Tel: 407-876-9344; Fax: 407-876-8775. Web: www.hfc-school.com. Sr. Dorothy Sayers, M.P.F., Prin. Sisters 1; Lay Teachers 30; Students 640.
Catechesis/Religious Program—Tel: 407-876-6331; Fax: 407-876-8775. Students 1,100.

8—ST. ISAAC JOGUES (1987) Rev. Jose Munoz; Deacons Pedro Laboy; Orlando Lendoiro; Alan Espinoza; Rafael Mejia.
Mailing Address: 4301 S. Chickasaw Tr., 32829. Tel: 407-249-0906; Fax: 407-273-3236. Email: stisaac@st-isaac.org. Web: st-isaac.org.
Catechesis/Religious Program—Students 725.

9—ST. JOHN VIANNEY (1959) Revs. Miguel A. Gonzalez; Juan Daniel Petrino; Rex Familar; Deacons Ovidio A. Ossa; Thomas P. Breaud.
Res.: 6200 S. Orange Blossom Tr., 32809. Tel: 407-855-5391; Fax: 407-859-3631. Web: www.sjvorlando.org.
School—Tel: 407-855-4660; Fax: 407-857-7932. Web: www.sjvs.org. Sr. Elizabeth Murphy, O.S.F., Prin. Sisters of St. Francis of Philadelphia 2; Lay Teachers 35; Students 588.
Catechesis/Religious Program—Tel: 407-855-5391, Ext. 235. Sr. Linda L. Gaupin, C.D.P., D.R.E. Students 304.

10—ST. JOSEPH (1962), (Polish—Filipino), Revs. Robert W. Brown; Larry Lossing (Retired); Andrzej Jurkiewicz.
Res.: 1501 N. Alafaya Tr., 32828. Tel: 407-275-0841; Fax: 407-275-0841.
Catechesis/Religious Program—Students 455.

11—ST. MAXIMILIAN KOLBE (2006) Rev. David Scotchie. 4013 Alcott Cir., 32828-4886. Email: office@avaloncatholic.org. Web: www.avaloncatholic.org.
Catechesis/Religious Program—Denise Kriscunas, D.R.E. Students 626.

12—ST. PHILIP PHAN VAN MINH CATHOLIC CHURCH (2004) Revs. Chau J. Nguyen; Chien Nguyen.
Mailing Address: 15 W. Par St., 32804. Email: vanphong@philipminhparish.org. Web: philipminhparish.org.
Catechesis/Religious Program—Students 349.

OUTSIDE THE CITY OF ORLANDO

ALTAMONTE SPRINGS, SEMINOLE CO.

1—ANNUNCIATION (1982) Very Rev. Stephen D. Parkes; Revs. Mark R. Wajda; Stephen A. Baumann.
Mailing Address: P.O. Box 915887, Longwood, 32791-5887. Tel: 407-869-9472; Fax: 407-869-4661. Web: www.churchofannunciation.org.
Res.: 1020 Montgomery Rd., 32714.
School—Annunciation Catholic Academy, (Grades K-8) Tel: 407-774-2801; Fax: 407-774-2826. Lay Teachers 29; Students 512.
Catechesis/Religious Program—Tel: 407-869-0934; Fax: 407-869-4661. Students 815.

2—ST. MARY MAGDALEN (1959) Revs. Charles I. Mitchell; Edward J. Thompson; Rick Voor; Deacons Henry Libersat, (Retired); Jerry Kelly; Marshall Ashby Gibbs; Juan Cruz; Lois Locey, Pastoral Assoc.
Res.: 861 Maitland Ave., 32701. Tel: 407-831-1212; Fax: 407-831-1560. Email: office@stmarymagdalen.org. Web: www.stmarymagdalen.org.
Adult Day Care—Employees 9; Total Assisted 11.
School—869 Maitland Ave., 32701. Tel: 407-339-7301; Fax: 407-339-9556. Email: stmarymagdalen@smmschool.org. Web: www.smmschool.org. Sisters 1; Lay Teachers 36; Students 504.
Catechesis/Religious Program—Tel: 407-831-1212, Ext. 233. Email: larannw@stmarymagdalen.org. Students 391.

APOPKA, ORANGE CO., ST. FRANCIS OF ASSISI (1966) Revs. Charles J. Deeney, O.M.I.; Tomas Hurtado, Parochial Vicar; Deacons Frank Diaz; Laurence Herbert; James G. Shelley; Jesus Davila.
Res.: 834 S. Orange Blossom Trail, 32703-6560. Tel: 407-886-4602; Fax: 407-886-9758. Email: stfrancisofassisi@catholicweb.com. Web: home.catholicweb.com/stfrancisofassisi/.
Catechesis/Religious Program—Students 525.

BAREFOOT BAY, BREVARD CO., ST. LUKE (1986) [JC] Rev. Yvon Hache; Deacon John Dunlop.
Res.: 5055 Micco Rd., 32976. Tel: 772-664-9310; Fax: 772-664-3374.
Catechesis/Religious Program—Students 19.

BARTOW, POLK CO., ST. THOMAS AQUINAS (1956) Rev. Eugene Grytner, S.D.S.; Deacon Mark M. King.
Res.: 1305 E. Mann Rd., 33830. Tel: 863-533-8578; Fax: 863-533-5090.
Catechesis/Religious Program—Students 102.
Mission—St. Elizabeth Ann Seton
Mission—Our Lady of Guadalupe 2150 Bomber Rd., Wahneta, Polk Co. 33880. Tel: 863-299-3854; Fax: 863-299-8247. Rev. Norman Farland.

BELLEVIEW, MARION CO., ST. THERESA (1951) Rev. David P. Vivero Jr.
Res. & Church: 11528 S.E. U.S. Hwy. 301, 34420-4430. Tel: 352-245-4506; Fax: 352-245-1521. Web: www.sttheresacatholicchurch.org.
Catechesis/Religious Program—Tel: 352-245-5300; Fax: 352-245-1521. Email: sttheresare@cfl.rr.com. Students 90.

BUSHNELL, SUMTER CO., ST. LAWRENCE (1959) Rev. Pedro Zapata; Deacons Bruno Wiencek; Miguel A. Beltran.
Office & Mailing Address: 320 E. Dade Ave., 33513. Tel: 352-793-7788; Fax: 352-793-4787. Email: stlawbush@gmail.com.
Res.: 223 E. Vermont Ave., 33513. Tel: 352-426-1953 (Emergency Phone).
Catechesis/Religious Program—Students 89.

CANDLER, MARION CO., IMMACULATE HEART OF MARY (1983) Rev. Felicito S. Baybay.
Mailing Address: P.O. Box 310, 32111. Tel: 352-687-4031; Fax: 352-687-1811.
Catechesis/Religious Program—Tel: 352-687-8818. Students 56.

CASSELBERRY, SEMINOLE CO., ST. AUGUSTINE (1969) Revs. Ybain F. Ramirez; William J. Neumann, Vicar; Deacon Isreal Colon.
Office & Church: 375 N. Sunset Dr., 32707. Tel: 407-695-3262; Fax: 407-699-8998. Email: samainoffice@embarqmail.com. Web: www.staugustinecc.org.
Rectory—
Catechesis/Religious Program—Students 197.

CELEBRATION , OSCEOLA CO., CORPUS CHRISTI (2005) Very Rev. Gregory Parkes.
Mailing Address: 1050 Celebration Ave., 34747. Tel: 321-939-1491; Fax: 321-939-1494. Web: www.celebrationcatholic.org.
Catechesis/Religious Program—Students 223.

CLERMONT, LAKE CO.

1—BLESSED SACRAMENT (1961) Very Rev. Robert E. Webster; Revs. Jose Augusto Cadavid; Cromwell Cabrisos; Deacons Rafael Gonzales; Fernando Molina; Fred Grant; Luis Roman; Jim Maubach; Ismael Pineiro.
720 12th St., 34711. Email: frbob@blessedsacramentcc.com. Web: www.blessedsacramentcc.com.
Res.: 1675 Grandiflora Ave., 34711. Tel: 352-394-3562; 352-242-9047; Fax: 352-241-0062. Email: frbob@blessedsacramentcc.com. Web: www.blessedsacramentcc.com.
Catechesis/Religious Program—Tel: 352-394-3562, Ext. 103. Students 700.
Mission—Mission Outreach - Santo Toribio Romo Mascotte, 34753. Fax: 352-241-0064.

2—ST. FAUSTINA CATHOLIC CHURCH (2006) Rev. Jean Hugues Desir.
Mailing Address: P.O. Box 135576, 34713-5576. Web: stfaustina.org.
Catechesis/Religious Program—Students 71.

COCOA BEACH, BREVARD CO., CHURCH OF OUR SAVIOUR (1956) Very Rev. Sean Heslin; Rev. Kiskama Lemor, C.S.Sp.
Res.: 5301 N. Atlantic Ave., 32931. Tel: 321-783-4554; Fax: 321-868-6743. Email: oursaviourchurch@cfl.rr.com. Web: www.oursaviourparish.org.
School—Tel: 321-783-2330; Fax: 321-784-6330. Web: www.oursaviour-school.org. Lay Teachers 15; Students 148.
Catechesis/Religious Program—Students 175.

COCOA, BREVARD CO., BLESSED SACRAMENT (1967) Rev. Anthony F. Quinlivan, C.Ss.R.; Deacons Richard J. Basso; Eugene O'Hern.
5135 N. U.S. Hwy. 1, 32927.
Office: 5135 N. Cocoa Blvd., 32927. Tel: 321-632-6333; Fax: 321-631-2560. Email: debbielbailey@bellsouth.net. Web: www.blessedsacramentcocoa.org.
Catechesis/Religious Program—Students 86.

DAYTONA BEACH, VOLUSIA CO.

1—BASILICA OF SAINT PAUL (1881) Rev. Timothy P. Daly; Deacons Vernon W. Hart; Rick Ferranti.
Res.: 317 Mullally St., 32114. Tel: 386-252-5422; Fax: 386-252-1936. Web: www.basilicaofsaintpaul.com.
School—Tel: 386-252-7915; Fax: 386-238-7903. Web: www.stpaulpanthers.org. Lay Teachers 15; Students 163.
Catechesis/Religious Program—Students 75.

2—OUR LADY OF LOURDES (1953) Rev. Philip J. Egitto.
Res.: 201 University Blvd., 32118. Tel: 386-255-0433; Fax: 386-238-1175. Web: www.ourladyoflourdesdaytona.com.
School—1014 N. Halifax, 32118. Tel: 386-252-0391; Fax: 386-238-1175. Email: sodell@lourdesacademy.net. Web: lourdesacademy-.net. Lay Teachers 18; Students 261.
Catechesis/Religious Program—Students 42.

DELAND, VOLUSIA CO., ST. PETER'S CHURCH (1883) Revs. Thomas Connery; Raul Adrain Valdez; Deacons Chester DeMarsh; Robert LaPlante; Gerard Smith; Robert Joseph Kinsey.
Mailing Address: 359 New York Ave., P.O. Box 3700, 32721.
Res.: 359 W. New York Ave., 32720. Tel: 386-822-6000; Fax: 386-822-6034.
School—Tel: 386-822-6010; Fax: 386-822-6013. Mr. Peter Randlov, Prin. Lay Teachers 23; Students 262.
Catechesis/Religious Program—Rick Grinstead, D.R.E. & Youth Min. Students 438.
Mission—San Jose Mission 165 Emporia Rd., Barberville, Volusia Co. 32005. Tel: 386-749-9372.

DEBARY, VOLUSIA CO., ST. ANN'S (1961) Revs. Peter J. Henry; David C. Gillis, Parochial Vicar; Deacon James Kiney Lathan.
Mailing Address: P.O. Box 530218, 32753-0218.
Office: 26 Dogwood Tr., 32713. Tel: 386-668-8270; Fax: 386-668-8471. Email: stannsdebary@comcast.net. Web: www.stannsdebary.com.
Res.: 10 Larkspur Ln., 32713. Tel: 386-668-8619.
Catechesis/Religious Program—Email: religiousedkid@comcast.net. Students 207.

DELTONA, VOLUSIA CO.

1—ST. CLARE (1989), (Anglo—Hispanic), Rev. Carlos Bedoya.
2961 Day Rd., 32738. Tel: 386-789-9990; Fax: 386-789-2430.
Catechesis/Religious Program—Students 157.

2—OUR LADY OF THE LAKES (1970) Revs. Francisco Aquino (Philippines); Frank Cerio.
Res.: 1310 Maximilian St., 32725. Tel: 386-574-2131; Fax: 386-860-0074. Email: olladmin@cfl.rr.com.
Catechesis/Religious Program—Students 171.

DUNNELLON, MARION CO., ST. JOHN THE BAPTIST (1976) Rev. Emmanuel Akalue; Deacons Fred Crawford Jr.; Joseph Interlandi; Santos N. Santiago.
Res.: 7545 S. Hwy. 41, 34432. Tel: 352-489-3166; Fax: 352-489-3156. Email: mail@stjohncc.com. Web: www.stjohncc.com.
Catechesis/Religious Program—Students 66.

EUSTIS, LAKE CO., ST. MARY OF THE LAKES (1912) Rev. Gilbert Medina.
Res.: 218 Ocklawaha Ave., 32726-4840. Tel: 352-483-3500; Fax: 352-483-1370. Email: stmaryl@mpinet.net.
Catechesis/Religious Program—Tel: 352-483-3500, Ext. 13. Students 213.

HAINES CITY, POLK CO., ST. ANN (1969), (Anglo—Hispanic), [JC], (Formerly Transfiguration) Revs. Robert W. Mitchell; Jesus Arroyave (Colombia); Deacons Jose Ramos; Hector Colon.
Mailing Address: 1311 E. Robinson Dr., P.O. Box 1285, 33845. Tel: 863-422-4370; Fax: 863-421-2522. Email: office@stannhc.org. Web: www.stannhc.org.
Catechesis/Religious Program—Students 352.

INDIALANTIC, BREVARD CO., HOLY NAME OF JESUS (1959) Revs. Anthony R. Welle, Parochial Admin.; Joseph Bui; Rev. Msgrs. David Page (Retired); David Page (Retired); Bernard Christman (Retired); Rev. Frank Brett (Retired); Deacons Charles Foy; Joseph Richiuso; Vincent Trunzo; Joseph Gassman; John Farrell.
Res.: 3050 Hwy. A1A, 32903. Tel: 321-773-2783; Fax: 321-777-0929. Email: hnjparish@hnj.org. Web: www.hnj.org.
School—3060 Hwy. A1A, 32903. Tel: 321-773-1630; Fax: 321-773-7148. Email: hnj@hnj.org. Ms. Mary Ellen Massey, Prin. Pre-School: 3-4 years. Lay Teachers 27; Students 286.
Catechesis/Religious Program—Tel: 321-773-2783, Ext. 120. Students 599.

KISSIMMEE, OSCEOLA CO.

1—St. Catherine of Siena (1994) Revs. Jose Bautista (Colombia); Nazaire Massillon (Haiti), Parochial Vicar; Deacons Juan R. Vargas; Angel R. Morales; Esteban Cruz; Ernesto Nunez.
Office: 2750 E. Osceola Pkwy., 34743. Tel: 407-344-9607; Fax: 407-344-9160. Email: stcatherineofsiena@cfl.rr.com. Web: homecatholicweb.com/stcatherineofsiena.
Res. & Mailing Address: P.O. Box 450698, 34745-0698.
Catechesis/Religious Program—Students 332.

2—Holy Redeemer (1917) Revs. Timothy P. Labo; Percival P. Devera; Rodolfo Ramon (Cuba); Deacons Manuel Lacsamana; Tommy Tate; Eliezer Maldonado.
Res.: 1603 N. Thacker Ave., 34741. Tel: 407-847-2500; 407-846-3700; Fax: 407-847-9687. Web: hredeemer.org.
School—(1993), (Grades PreK-8), 1800 W. Columbia Ave., 34741. Tel: 407-870-9055; Fax: 407-870-2214. Larry Thompson, Prin.; Sr. Eileen Fichtner, Librarian. Sisters of St. Joseph 1; Lay Teachers 18; Students 259.
Catechesis/Religious Program—Tel: 407-870-8196; Fax: 407-870-2214. Email: re@hredeemer.org. Mrs. Rose Dzejak, D.R.E. Students 407.

Lady Lake, Lake Co., St. Timothy (1985) Revs. Edward Waters; Gerald Shovelton (Retired); Eugene R. Weis (ROC) (Retired); Deacons Russell Anderberg, (Retired); John Sullivan; Frederick Giel; Nicholas Deutsch, (Retired); Ronald L'Huillier, (Retired); George Mattison; Richard R. Kaseta.
1351 Paige Pl., 32159. Tel: 352-753-0989; Fax: 352-753-9602. Web: www.sttimothycc.com. In Res., Rev. Gerard M. Cunningham (WDC).
Catechesis/Religious Program—Students 100.

Lake Wales, Polk Co., Holy Spirit (1927) Rev. Anthony Bluett; Rev. Msgr. Leo Dobosiewicz (Retired); Deacons John C. Avery; Samuel Ralph Knight.
Res.: 644 S. 9th St., P.O. Box 232, 33853. Tel: 863-676-1556; Fax: 863-676-2962.
Catechesis/Religious Program—Tel: 863-678-1083. Students 249.
Mission—St. Leo the Great 10721 E. Leisure, 33898. Nalcrest, Polk Co. 33856. Tel: 863-679-1919.

Lakeland, Polk Co.

1—St. Anthony Catholic Church (1982) Rev. Nicholas J. O'Brien; Deacon Francisco Hernandez.
Church: 820 Marcum Rd., 33809-4306. Tel: 863-858-8047; Fax: 863-859-1036. Web: www.stanthonyparish.com.
School—(Grades PreK-8), 924 Marcum Rd., 33809. Tel: 863-858-0671; Fax: 863-858-0876. Web: www.saintanthonycatholicschool.com. Mrs. Janet Peddecord, Prin. Lay Teachers 13; Students 199.
**St. Anthony's Catholic School Endowment Fund, Inc.*
Catechesis/Religious Program—Students 120.

2—Church of the Resurrection (1963) Revs. Matthew Mello; Ngugi Bernard Kiratu, Parochial Vicar; Domingo N. Gonzalez (Retired); Deacons Joseph B. Wortman; Antonio Martinez; Donald Andrew.
Res.: 3855 S. Florida Ave., 33813-1109. Tel: 863-646-3556; Fax: 863-644-8697. Email: info@churchoftheres.net. Web: www.churchoftheres.net.
School—(1990), (Grades PreK-8), 3720 Old Hwy. 37, 33813. Tel: 863-644-3931; Fax: 863-648-0625. Email: office@rcslakeland.org. Web: www.rcslakeland.org. Dr. Christopher Benedetti, Prin. Lay Teachers 31; Students 414.
Catechesis/Religious Program—Tel: 863-644-0585. Students 452.

3—St. John Neumann (1988) Rev. Frank Buck, Admin.; Deacon George Ferrioli; John Knox, Liturgy Dir.; Patricia DeSilvestro, Pastoral Min. Coord.; Mike Bucklen, Business Mgr.
Res. & Church: 501 E. Carter Rd., 33813. Tel: 863-607-9892.
Ministry Center: 603 E. Carter Rd., 33813.
Catechesis/Religious Program—Donna Cooper, Faith Formation Coord. Students 402.

4—St. Joseph's (1898) [JC] Revs. John Caulfield; Ramon Bolatete; Franklin Salazar. In Res., Rev. Felix Banos (Retired).
Res.: 210 W. Lemon St., P.O. Box 30, 33802. Tel: 863-682-0555; Fax: 863-686-9546.
School—310 McDonald St., 33803. Tel: 863-686-6415; Fax: 863-687-8074. Web: www.stjosephlakeland.org. Lay Teachers 20; Students 214.
Catechesis/Religious Program—Students 190.

Leesburg, Lake Co., St. Paul's (1954) Very Rev. John Giel; Revs. Gianni Agostinelli, C.S.; Waldemar Maciag (Poland); Deacons Michael Francis McGinnity; Sam Damiano; George Lenhardt.
Res.: 1330 Sunshine Ave., 34748. Tel: 352-787-6354; Fax: 352-787-5971.
School—1304 Sunshine Ave., 34748. Tel: 352-787-4657; Fax: 352-787-0324. Lay Teachers 16; Students 157.
Catechesis/Religious Program—Tel: 352-787-6354; Fax: 352-787-5971. Students 69.
Catholic Community Television Network (CCTN)—Tel: 352-326-2286. Web: www.cctn.org.
St. Paul's Thrift Shop—1321 Sunshine Ave., 34748. Tel: 352-787-3388.
St. Paul's Gift Shop—Tel: 352-365-6804.

Longwood, Seminole Co., Church of the Nativity (1960) Revs. Ralph DuWell, Parochial Admin.; John Kudiyiruppilulaltannan, Parochial Vicar; Deacons John Mire Gravois; Walter A. Skinner Jr.
Res.: 3255 N. Ronald Reagan Blvd., 32750. Tel: 407-322-3961; Fax: 407-322-3981. Email: info@nativity.org. Web: nativity.org.
Catechesis/Religious Program—Students 509.

Melbourne Beach, Brevard Co., Immaculate Conception (1978) Rev. Joseph A. Nolan; Deacons Howard Pettengill Jr.; Michael J. Biennas.
Res.: 3780 S. Hwy. A1A, 32951. Tel: 321-725-0552; Fax: 321-727-8218.
Catechesis/Religious Program—Tel: 321-726-8111. Students 61.

Melbourne, Brevard Co.

1—Ascension (1959) Rev. Edmund J. Tobin; Deacons Michael J. McElwee; Sergio Colon; Tom Stauffacher.
Mailing Address: 2950 N. Harbor City Blvd., 32935-6259. Tel: 321-254-1595; Fax: 321-255-3490. Web: www.ascensioncatholic.net.
School—Tel: 321-254-5495; Fax: 321-259-0993. Web: www.ascensioncatholicsch.org. Lay Teachers 31; Students 496.
Catechesis/Religious Program—Tel: 321-254-1595, Ext. 3080. Students 299.

2—Our Lady of Lourdes (1931), (Hispanic), Rev. Karl Bergin, Parochial Admin.; Deacons Richard Beauton; Arcelio Perez; Edward C. Stives; Vincent Accardi. In Res., Revs. Carl Feil, O.S.M. (Retired); Joseph J. Rimshaw, S.S.J. (Retired).
Res.: 1626 Oak St., 32901-4517. Tel: 321-723-3636; Fax: 321-951-8029. Email: admin@oll-church.com. Web: oll-church.com.
School—420 E. Fee Ave., 32901. Tel: 321-723-3631; Fax: 321-723-7408. Email: school@ollmelbourne.org. Web: www.ollmelbourne.org. Lay Teachers 15; Students 184.
Catechesis/Religious Program—Email: carolynziarno@oll-church.com. Students 215.

Merritt Island, Brevard Co., Divine Mercy Catholic Community (1964) Rev. Michael A. Farrell.
Res.: 1940 N. Courtenay Pkwy., 32953. Tel: 321-452-5955; Fax: 321-455-2268.
School—Tel: 321-452-0263; Fax: 321-453-7573. Lay Teachers 21; Students 196.
Catechesis/Religious Program—Students 230.
Convent—1930 N. Courtenay Pkwy., 32953. Tel: 321-452-1279.

Mims, Brevard Co., Holy Spirit (1967) Rev. Andrzej Wojtan.
Office & Res.: 2399 Holder Rd., 32754-2103. Tel: 321-269-2282; Fax: 321-269-2252.
Catechesis/Religious Program—Tel: 321-269-7785. Students 164.

Mount Dora, Orange Co., St. Patrick's (1973), (Hispanic), [CEM] Revs. Robert D'Aversa, T.O.R.; Blase Romano, T.O.R.; Gianni Agostinelli, C.S.; Deacons William Fisher Jr.; Paul Gaucher.
Res.: 1323 Olympia Ave., 32757. Tel: 352-383-8556; Fax: 352-383-8443.
Catechesis/Religious Program—Tel: 352-383-8556, Ext. 34. Students 239.

New Smyrna Beach, Volusia Co.

1—Our Lady Star of the Sea (1973) Rev. John S. Murray.
Res.: 4000 S. Atlantic Ave., 32169. Tel: 386-427-4530; Fax: 386-427-1331.
Catechesis/Religious Program—Tel: 386-427-4530, Ext. 11. Students 34.

2—Sacred Heart (1926) Revs. John F. Murray, C.Ss.R.; Edward J. Gray, C.Ss.R.; Francis Nelson, C.Ss.R.; Alistair McKay; Deacons Thomas Murray; Darrel Cevasco, C.Ss.R.
Mailing Address: P.O. Box 729, 32170.
Res.: 998 Father Donlan Dr., 32168. Tel: 386-428-6426; Fax: 386-423-4088. Email: r_sacred@bellsouth.net. Web: sacredheartnsb.org.
School—1003 Turnbull St., 32168. Tel: 386-428-4732; Fax: 386-428-4087. Email: lsvajko@sacredheartcatholic.com. Web: sacredheartcatholic.com. Sisters of Notre Dame (Toledo) 2; Lay Teachers 10; Students 238.
Catechesis/Religious Program—Tel: 386-428-6956. Email: abaker@sacredheartcatholic.com. Andy Baker, D.R.E. & Youth Min. Students 140.
Mission—St. Gerard 3171 S. Ridgewood Ave., Edgewater, Volusia Co. 32141. Tel: 386-428-6930.

Ocala, Marion Co.

1—Blessed Trinity (1922) Revs. Patrick J. Sheedy; Roy V. Eco; Alfonso Cely; Deacons James G. Schwartz; James Boerstler; Heriberto Berrios. In Res., Rev. Michael O'Keeffe.
Res.: 5 S.E. 17th St., 34471. Tel: 352-629-8092; Fax: 352-351-8872. Email: mail@blessedtrinity.org. Web: blessedtrinity.org.
School—Tel: 352-622-5808; Fax: 352-622-1660. Email: btschool@btschool.org. Web: btschool.org. Lay Teachers 39; Students 687.
Catechesis/Religious Program—Students 272.
Mission—Christ the King 14045 N. U.S. Hwy. 301, P.O. Box 129, Citra, 32113. Tel: 352-595-5605.
Mission—Guadalupe Catholic Mission 11153 W. Hwy. 40, 34482. Tel: 352-291-2695.

2—St. Jude's Catholic Community (1983) Rev. Barthelemy Garcon, S.M.M.; Deacons Santos N. Santiago; Jose I. Serrano; Edward C. Wilson.
Church: 443 Marion Oaks Dr., 34473-3203. Tel: 352-347-0154; Fax: 352-347-5211. Email: office@stjude-marioaks.org.
Catechesis/Religious Program—Elba Santiago, C.R.E.; Cathy O'Donnell, Music Min. Students 63.

3—Our Lady of the Springs (1982) Revs. Andrew Mallick; George Maniangattu, Parochial Vicar; Deacons James Hamilton, (Retired); John Warren Howell.
Office: 4047 N.E. 21st St., 34470. Tel: 352-236-2230; Fax: 352-236-1475. Web: www.ourladyofthesprings.org.
Catechesis/Religious Program—Students 30.
Mission—St. Joseph of the Forest Silver Springs. 17301 E. Hwy. 40, Ocala National Forest, Marion Co. 34488. Tel: 352-625-4222; Fax: 352-625-4922. Email: stjosephforest@embarqmail.com.
Mission—St. Hubert of the Forest 55600 Veterans Dr., Astor, Lake Co. 32102. Tel: 352-759-3983; Fax: 352-759-3982. Web: www.sthubertsmission.com. Mailing Address: P.O. Box 715, Astor, 32102.

4—Queen of Peace (1987) Revs. Patrick J. O'Doherty; Alex Panakal, O.C.D., Curate.
Res.: 6455 S.W. State Rd. 200, 34476. Tel: 352-854-2181; Fax: 352-854-7840. Email: queen_of_peace@embarqmail.com.
Catechesis/Religious Program—Students 30.

Ormond Beach, Volusia Co.

1—St. Brendan (1960) Rev. Thomas G. Barrett. In Res., Rev. James T. Queen (Retired).
Res.: 136 Banyan Dr., 32176. Tel: 386-441-1505; Fax: 386-441-0774. Web: www.stbrendanchurchormond.org.
School—Tel: 386-441-1331. Email: stb@stbrendanormond.org. Web: stbrendanormond.org. Lay Teachers 25; Students 180.
Catechesis/Religious Program—Tel: 386-441-1505, Ext. 307. David Sikorra, D.R.E.; Janice Leach, Music Dir. Students 70.

2—Prince of Peace (1966) Revs. Bill Zamborsky; Stephen Ogonwa (Nigeria), Parochial Vicar; Deacon Bruce Gesinski.
Res.: 600 S. Nova Rd., 32174. Tel: 386-672-5272; Fax: 386-677-3224. Web: www.princeofpeaceormond.org.
Catechesis/Religious Program—Tel: 386-672-5272, Ext. 26. Email: dre@princeofpeaceormond.org. Students 270.

Oviedo, Seminole Co., Most Precious Blood Catholic Church (2005) Revs. Scott M. Circe; Hector Vazquez Saad, Parochial Vicar.
Mailing Address: P.O. Box 622288, 32762-2288. Tel: 407-365-3231; Fax: 407-365-3313. Email: scirce@oviedocatholic.org. Web: www.oviedocatholic.org.
Catechesis/Religious Program—Students 860.

Palm Bay, Brevard Co.

1—St. Joseph (1914) [CEM] Rev. Robert J. Hoeffner; Deacons Alfred P. Somma; Michael Patrick Mintern.
Res.: 5330 Babcock St., N.E., 32905. Tel: 321-727-1565; Fax: 321-676-2579. Email: hoeffnerr@st-joe.org. Web: www.st-joe.org.
School—5320 Babcock St. N.E., 32905. Tel: 321-723-8866; Fax: 321-727-1181. Email: stokesc@st-joe.org. Lay Teachers 15; Students 206.
Catechesis/Religious Program—Email: wyattl@st-joe.org. Students 300.

2—Our Lady of Grace (1989) Rev. Leo Hodges; Deacons William T. Wanca Sr., Pastoral Assoc.; Jack H. Rhine; Albert Gutierrez; Kevin Crawford.
Church & Mailing Address: 300 Malabar Rd. S.E., 32907-3005. Tel: 321-725-3066; Fax: 321-725-9534. Email: ourladyofgrace@cfl.rr.com. Web: www.ourladyofgracechurch.com.
Res.: 949 Haas St., 32907. Tel: 321-726-8742.
Catechesis/Religious Program—Teachers 176.

Poinciana, Kissimmee Co., St. Rose of Lima (1994) Unassigned.
Rectory—3860 Pleasant Hill Rd., Kissimmee, 34746. Tel: 407-932-5004; Fax: 407-932-0407. Email: office@fl-saintroseoflima.com. Web: www.fl-saintroseoflima.com.
Catechesis/Religious Program—Students 394.

Port Orange, Volusia Co.

1—Epiphany (1962) Very Rev. John Bosco Maison; Deacons Michael Nugent; Richard G. Meyer.

Res.: 201 Lafayette St., 32127. Tel: 386-767-6111; Fax: 386-767-0017. Email: epiphanychurch@cfl.rr.com. Web: catholicchurchofepiphany.com.
Catechesis / Religious Program—Students 125.

2—OUR LADY OF HOPE (1981) [CEM] Revs. Christopher Hoffmann; Joseph Pinchock (Retired); Deacons Thomas A. Tagye, Pastoral Assoc.; Michael Samuel Pettit.
Mailing Address: P.O. Box 290216, 32129.
Res.: 4675 S. Clyde Morris Blvd., P.O. Box 290216, 32129. Tel: 386-788-6144; Fax: 386-761-8840.
Catechesis / Religious Program—Tel: 386-788-6747. Email: hopedre@cfl.rr.com. Maureen Kealhoffer, C.R.E. Students 265.

ROCKLEDGE, BREVARD CO., ST. MARY'S (1917) [JC] Revs. Nicholas King; Terence J. Farrelly, Pastor Emeritus (Retired); Luis Osorio.
Mailing Address: 75 Barton Ave., 32955. Tel: 321-636-6834; Fax: 321-632-4301. Email: secretary@stmarysrockledge.org. Web: www.stmarysrockledge.org.
School—Tel: 321-636-4208; Fax: 321-636-0591. Email: info@stmarys-school.org. Web: www.stmarys-school.org. Lay Teachers 21; Students 310.
Catechesis / Religious Program—Tel: 321-633-9985. Email: faithformation@stmarysrockledge.org. Students 111.

SAINT CLOUD, OSCEOLA CO., ST. THOMAS AQUINAS (1968) Revs. Kent A. Walker; Lionel Pacheco, Parochial Vicar.
Mailing Address: P.O. Box 700368, 34770-0368.
Res.: 721 Brown Chapel Rd., 34769. Tel: 407-891-3639. Email: info@stacatholic.org. Web: www.stacatholic.org.
Church: 700 Brown Chapel Rd., 34769. Tel: 407-957-4495; Fax: 407-957-1771.
School—800 Brown Chapel Rd., 34769. Tel: 407-957-1772; Fax: 407-957-8700. Web: www.staschool.info. Lay Teachers 20; Students 259.
Catechesis / Religious Program—Tel: 407-957-4057. Students 473.

SANFORD, SEMINOLE CO., ALL SOULS (1911) [CEM] Revs. Richard W. Trout; Mark Christopher (Retired); Ken Metz; Edward McCarthy (Retired); Mrs. Vicki Fordham, Dir. Opers.
Res.: 301 W. 8th St., 32771. Tel: 407-322-3795; Fax: 407-322-1131. Web: www.allsoulssanford.org.
School—810 S. Oak Ave., 32771. Tel: 407-322-7090; Fax: 407-321-7255. Email: office@allsoulscatholicschool.org. Web: allsoulscatholicschool.org. Lay Teachers 15; Students 281.
Catechesis / Religious Program—Email: mlfess@allsoulssanford.org. Students 401.

SUMMERFIELD, MARION CO., ST. MARK THE EVANGELIST (2005) Revs. Jerzy Maj, O.S.P.P.E.; Tadeuz Olzacki, Parochial Vicar; Deacons Robert A. Esposito, Pastoral Assoc.; John Rumplasch; Don Curtis, Business Mgr.; Melanie O'Donnell, Music Min.
7081 S.E. Hwy. 42, 34491. Tel: 352-347-9317; Fax: 352-347-9749. Email: stmarkoffice@aol.com. Web: www.stmarkrcc.com.
Catechesis / Religious Program—Twinned with St. Timothy's. Students 11.

TITUSVILLE, BREVARD CO., ST. TERESA (1958) Revs. Krzysztof Bugno, S.D.S.; Aland Jean, C.I.C.M.; Deacon Donald Boland.
Res.: 203 Ojibway Ave., 32780. Tel: 321-268-3441; Fax: 321-268-3270. Web: home.catholicweb.com/saintteresa/index.cfm.
School—Tel: 321-267-1643; Fax: 321-268-5124. Email: jzackel@steresa-titusville.org. Web: www.stteresa-titusville.org. Sisters of Mercy (Gort, Ireland) 1; Lay Teachers 17; Students 184.
Catechesis / Religious Program—Tel: 321-268-0440. Students 163.
Convent—Sisters of Mercy, 3380 Muirfield Dr., 32780. Tel: 321-267-1610; Fax: 321-267-1610. Sisters 2.
Convent—Sisters of Notre Dame, Chardon, Ohio, 1735 Harrison #130, 32780. Tel: 321-264-4274.

VIERA, BREVARD CO., ST. JOHN THE EVANGELIST (2001) Revs. R. Bradley Beaupre, C.S.C.; Peter J. Walsh, C.S.C.; Donald G. Mainardi (Retired); Manfred Dreilich, Dir. Liturgy & Music; Deacons Hugh W. Muller; James B. Seidel; James D. Stokes.
Mailing Address: 5655 Stadium Pkwy., 32940. Tel: 321-637-9650; Fax: 321-637-9651. Email: office@stjohnviera.org. Web: www.stjohnviera.org.
Catechesis / Religious Program—Vincent Castellano, Dir. Faith Formation. Students 392.

WILDWOOD, SUMTER CO.

1—SAN PEDRO DE JESUS MALDONADO MISSION (2006) Unassigned.210 Wonders St., 34785. Tel: 352-787-9208.
Catechesis / Religious Program—Cecilia Montavlo, D.R.E. Students 64.

2—ST. VINCENT DE PAUL (2005) Rev. Peter A. Sagorski; Deacons John Claude Curtin; Joseph Pius Piyasiri Gabriel; Joseph F. Mador; Dana McCarthy; Byron Anthony Otradovec; Frank J. Campione; Daniel James Pallo; Richard F. Radford; Daniel G. Miller Sr.; Gregory Bruce Senholzi.
5323 E. CR 462, 34785. Tel: 352-330-0220; Fax: 352-748-6106. Web: www.sumtercatholic.org.
Catechesis / Religious Program—Frank Webber, Dir. Faith Formation. Students 25.

WINTER GARDEN, ORANGE CO., RESURRECTION (1967) Revs. Moacir Balen, C.S.; German Vargas, C.S., Parochial Vicar; Bob Pautienus, Business Mgr.
Res.: 358 Floral Ave., 34787-4338.
Church & Mailing Address: 1211 Winter Garden Vineland Rd., 34787. Tel: 407-656-3113; Fax: 407-654-4935. Email: resurrectionwg@earthlink.net. Web: www.resurrectionwg.org.
Catechesis / Religious Program—Sr. Patricia Sipan, S.N.D., Faith Formation Dir. & RCIA; Nancy Parker, D.R.E.; Jon Sarta, Music Min., Liturgy & Youth Min. Students 855.

WINTER HAVEN, POLK CO.

1—ST. JOSEPH'S (1923) Very Rev. Peter Puntal; Rev. Fracilus Petit-Homme, S.M.M.; Deacons Nuoc Van Dang; John E. Landry.
Res.: 532 Ave. M N.W., 33881. Tel: 863-294-3144; Fax: 863-299-9709. Web: www.stjosephwh.org.
School—535 Avenue M, N.W., 33881. Tel: 863-293-3311; Fax: 863-299-7894. Web: www.stjosephwh-school.org. Lay Teachers 35; Students 373.
Catechesis / Religious Program—Students 423.

2—ST. MATTHEW (1973) [CEM 2] Rev. Charles Viviano.
Res.: 558 Cody Caleb Dr., 33884.
Church: 1991 Overlook Dr., 33884. Tel: 863-324-3040; Fax: 863-324-9181. Email: stmatthew@stmatthewwh.com. Web: stmatthewwh.com.
Catechesis / Religious Program—Students 252.

WINTER PARK, ORANGE CO., ST. MARGARET MARY (1947) Very Rev. Richard Walsh; Revs. Vilaire Philius; Glenn Charest; Deacons Robert Kreps; Nemesio Gubatan.
Res.: 526 N. Park Ave., 32789. Tel: 407-647-3392; Fax: 407-647-4492. Web: www.stmargaretmary.org.
School—142 E. Swoope Ave., 32789. Tel: 407-644-7537; Fax: 407-644-7357. Web: www.smmknight-.org. Lay Teachers 37; Students 594.
Catechesis / Religious Program—Tel: 407-647-5171; Fax: 407-647-4492. Students 582.

WINTER PARK, SEMINOLE CO., SAINTS PETER AND PAUL (1967) Revs. Derk Schudde; Fidel Rodriguez; Deacons Al Castellana; Norman Levesque; Donald M. Warner; Scott Lindeman.
Res.: 5300 Old Howell Branch Rd., 32792. Tel: 407-657-6114; Fax: 407-657-9375. Email: mail@stspp.net. Web: www.stspp.net.
Catechesis / Religious Program—Fax: 407-657-9530. Students 550.

WINTER SPRINGS, SEMINOLE CO., ST. STEPHEN (1985) Revs. John J. Bluett; George W. Dunne, S.S.S. (Ireland).
Res.: 575 Tuskawilla Rd., 32708. Tel: 407-699-5683; Fax: 407-699-8408. Email: ststephen@st-stephen.com. Web: st-stephen.com.
Catechesis / Religious Program—Students 909.

Shrines

Basilica of the National Shrine of Mary Queen of the Universe (1986) Revs. Paul J. Henry; Martin Gerber; Barry Dowd; Sharon Mayer, Interim Dir. Opers.; Sharon Mayer, Dir. Devel.; William Picher, Dir. Music.
Mailing Address: 8300 Vineland Ave., 32821.
Res.: 7468 Lake Willis Dr., 32821. Tel: 407-239-8631. Email: shrine@maryqueenoftheuniverse.org. Web: maryqueenoftheuniverse.org.

Special Assignment:
Rev.—
Gohring, William, Fire Dept. & Hospital Chap.

On Duty Outside the Diocese:
Revs.—
Krisman, Ronald, J.C.L.
Mueller, Michael, U.S. Military
Olds, Steven, S.T.D., St. Vincent de Paul Seminary, Boynton Beach, FL
Payne, Jeremiah L., Graduate Studies Rome
Ruse, Fred R.
Stahl, Allen M. (Retired), U.S. Military

Retired:
Most Rev.—
Dorsey, Norbert L., C.P., D.D., S.T.D., 5566 Jessamine Ln., 32809.
Rev. Msgrs.—
Caverly, Patrick J., P.A., V.G., Annunciation Catholic Church, P.O. Box 915887, Longwood, 32791.
Fernandez, Manuel, P.O. Box 703, Mount Dora, 32756.
Gimeno, Fabian G., 2708 Emerald Lake Ct., Kissimmee, 34744.
Harte, F. Joseph, P.O. Box 691805, 32869.
Page, David, P.O. Box 33252, Indialantic, 32903.
Very Revs.—
Chavarria, Jerome L., C.Ss.R., St. Alphonsus Villa, P.O. Box 548, New Smyrna Beach, 32170.
Conley, Seraphin J., T.O.R., Villa Madonna, 4385 Saxon Ave., New Smyrna Beach, 32169.
Revs.—
Arboleda, Vidal, 10237 Chorlton Cir., 32832.
Aschmann, Karl, C.Ss.R., St. Alphonsus Villa, P.O. Box 548, New Smyrna Beach, 32170-0548.
Banos, Felix, P.O. Box 30, Lakeland, 33802-0030.
Benitez, Edward, P.O. Box 1524, Davenport, 33837.
Blakely, Paige, J.C.L., P.O. Box 1336, New Smyrna Beach, 32170.
Bonar, Clyde A., 2235 Coldstream Dr., Winter Park, 32792. Tel: 407-622-6237
Brown, Stephan, S.V.D., St. Anthony Catholic Church, 820 Marcum Rd., Lakeland, 33809.
Carboy, Daniel, C.Ss.R., St. Alphonsus Villa, P.O. Box 548, New Smyrna Beach, 32170.
Cooney, Sean K., 9610 Abbot Ct., 32817. Tel: 407-657-1961
Daigle, Eugene, C.Ss.R., St. Alphonsus Villa, P.O. Box 548, New Smyrna Beach, 32170-0548.
Douglass, Vincent, C.Ss.R., St. Alphonsus Villa, P.O. Box 548, New Smyrna Beach, 32170-0548.
Farrelly, Terence J., 56 Barton Ave., Rockledge, 32955. Tel: 321-636-9099
Feil, Carl, O.S.M., Our Lady of Lourdes Catholic Church, 1626 Oak St., Melbourne, 32901.
Finley, William, 2501 Q. St., N.W., Apt. 426, Washington, DC 20007.
Fryar, James, F.S.S.P., Queen of Peace Catholic Church, 6455 S.W. State Rd. 200, Ocala, 34476.
Fucheck, Robert, 1444 Highland Pl., Lady Lake, 32162.
Garcia, Emilio, P.O. Box 1757, Dunnellon, 34430.
Giglio, Michael E., V.F., Church of the Epiphany, 201 Lafayette St., Daytona Beach, 32127.
Gonzalez, Carlos, S.D.W., Sons & Daughters of Divine Will, 5580 Jack Brack Rd., Saint Cloud, 34771.
Gonzalez, Domingo N., P.O. Box 5756, Lakeland, 33807. Tel: 863-644-2461
Gorney, Joseph, C.Ss.R., St. Alphonsus Villa, P.O. Box 548, New Smyrna Beach, 32170-0548.
Graves, Robert, S.D.W, Sons & Daughters of Divine Will, 5580 Jack Brack Rd., Saint Cloud, 34771.
Hamilton, Edward A., 400 Alderbrook Dr., Wayne, PA 19087. Tel: 610-949-0443
Hanley, William, 1340 Natal St., N.W., Palm Bay, 32907.
Hannon, Michael, 210 Gretchen Ct., Oldsmar, 34677. Tel: 727-781-7619
Hayden, Joseph M., 2354 Mulligan Dr., Lakeland, 33810.
Holland, Cajetan, C.S.C., Holy Cross Fathers, 325 Arthur Ave., Cocoa Beach, 32931.
Hunt, Robert, 4213 Summit Creek Blvd., Apt. 7310, 32837.
Jordan, Patrick, 133 Oak Ln., Lake Helen, 32744.
Joseph, William, Flat 42 The Lumiere Bldg., 544 Romford Rd, London E7 8AY, United Kingdom.
Kelly, George F., C.Ss.R., St. Alphonsus Villa, P.O. Box 548, New Smyrna Beach, 32170-0548.
Kurber, Robert, 12204 Manado St., 32837. Tel: 407-240-1642
Lambour, Stephen, C.S.C., Holy Cross Fathers, 325 Arthur Ave., Cocoa Beach, 32931.
Londono, Hugo, P.O. Box 1496, Ormond Beach, 32175. Tel: 386-441-6548
Long, Joseph J., C.S.C., Blessed Sacrament Catholic Church, 5135 N. U.S. 1, Cocoa, 32927.
Lossing, Larry, 1702 Elaine St., Altamonte Springs, 32701.
Mainardi, Donald G., 1025 Rockledge Dr., #505, Rockledge, 32955. Assisting Divine Mercy
McCarthy, Edward, S.T.L., D.Min., 31036 Nocatee Tr., Sorrento, 32776.
McMackin, Thomas P., Prince of Peace, 1103 Monticello Ln., #2, Port Orange, 32129. Tel: 386-846-5578
Mitchell, Peter, St. Thomas Aquinas Catholic Church, 1305 E. Mann Rd., Bartow, 33830.
Mitzi, John, 410 Marsh Point Cir., Saint Augustine, 32084.
Morelos, Gustavo, S.D.W., Sons & Daughters of Divine Will, 5580 Jack Brack Rd., Saint Cloud, 34771.
Murphy, James, C.S.C., Holy Cross Brothers, 325 Arthur Ave, Cocoa Beach, 32931.
Mutsko, Frank J., 473 Valverda Dr., Lady Lake, 32162.
O'Carroll, Patrick J., 5055 Micco Rd., Barefoot Bay, 32976.
O'Leary, Raymond J., Sherwin Condo, 2555 S. Atlantic Ave., Unit 1601, Daytona Beach, 32118. Tel: 386-788-6144
Oser, Ronald E., Prince of Peace Catholic Church, 600 S. Nova Rd., Ormond Beach, 32174.

Palmese, Anthony, 443 Marion Oaks Dr., Ocala, 34473-3203.
Pinchock, Joseph, Our Lady of Hope Catholic Church, 4675 S. Clyde Morris Blvd., Port Orange, 32119.
Quinn, Peter, 2967 S. Atlantic Ave., #907, Daytona Beach, 32116.
Remski, Howard, R.S.S.P., Queen of Peace Catholic Church, 6455 S.W. State Rd., Ocala, 34476.
Roberts, Joseph, Our Lady of the Lakes Catholic Church, 1310 Maximilian St., Deltona, 32725.
Rojas, Tito Nels, J.C.L., 5550 E. Michigan St., Unit 3320, 32822.
Ross, Kenneth, 604 White Plains Rd., Eastchester, NY 10709.
Schneider, Edward, 1665 Glen Ethel Ln., Longwood, 32779.
Seelman, Patrick, T.O.R., San Pedro Center, 2400 Dike Rd., Winter Park, 32792.
Serraino, Fred, C.S.C., Holy Cross Fathers, 325 Arthur Ave., Cocoa Beach, 32931.
Sheedy, Valentine, Oceans 3, 3043 S. Atlantic Ave., Apt. 202, Daytona Beach, 32118.
Silvia, Kenneth J., C.S.C., Holy Cross Fathers, 325 Arthur Ave., Cocoa Beach, 32931.
Traupman, Robert, 2999 N.W. 48th Ave., #251, Lauderdale Lakes, 33313. Tel: 954-533-4478
Wawrzycki, Andrew, 15015 Broadway Ave., Snohomish, WA 98296.
Winter, Donald J., C.Ss.R., St. Alphonsus Villa, P.O. Box 548, New Smyrna Beach, 32170-0548.
Zammit, Francis X., P.O. Box 291242, Port Orange, 32129. Tel: 386-761-1388

Permanent Deacons:
Abreu, Rosendo, St. Augustine, Casselberry
Accardi, Vincent Joseph, Our Lady of Lourdes, Melbourne
Almodovar, Ismeal, Resurrection, Winter Garden
Anderberg, Russell, St. Timothy, Lady Lake
Andrew, Donald, Church of the Resurrection, Lakeland
Avery, John C., Holy Spirit, Lake Wales
Barbieri, Robert, St. Peter, Deland
Basso, Richard, Blessed Sacrament, Cocoa
Beauton, Richard William, Our Lady of Lourdes, Melbourne
Beltran, Miguel A., St. Vincent de Paul, Wildwood
Berrios, Heriberto, Blessed Trinity, Ocala
Biennas, Michael, Immaculate Conception, Melbourne Beach
Boerstler, James, Blessed Trinity, Ocala
Boland, Donald, St. Teresa, Titusville
Bonneau, Louis, Immaculate Heart of Mary, Candler
Breaud, Thomas P., St. John Vianney, Orlando
Brockman, Carl Lawrence, Holy Family, Orlando
Campione, Frank J., St. Vincent de Paul, Wildwood
Castellana, Al, Sts. Peter & Paul, Winter Park
Cater, Thomas, Our Lady of the Springs, Ocala
Collier, John
Colon, Hector, St. Ann, Haines City
Colon, Isreal, St. Augustine, Casselberry
Colon, Sergio, Ascension, Melbourne
Contreras, Juan, St. Rose of Lima, Poinciana
Crawford, Fred J., Jr., St. John the Baptist, Dunnellon
Crawford, Kevin, Our Lady of Grace, Palm Bay
Crotty, John, Good Shepherd, Orlando
Cruz, Estaban, St. Catherine of Siena, Kissimmee
Cruz, Jose F., St. Andrew, Orlando
Cruz, Juan, St. Mary Magdalen, Orlando
Curtin, Claude J., St. Vincent de Paul, Wildwood
Daidone, Salvatore, Most Precious Blood, Oviedo
Damiano, Samuel J., St. Paul, Leesburg
Dang, Nuoc Van, St. Joseph, Winter Haven
Davila, Jesus, St. Francis of Assisi, Apopka
DeJesus, Confesor, Good Shepherd, Orlando
DelGiudice, John, St. Thomas Aquinas, St. Cloud
DeMarsh, Chester, Prince of Peace, Ormond Beach
Deutsch, Nicholas, St. Timothy, Lady Lake
Diaz, Celso, Holy Cross, Orlando
Diaz, Frank, St. Francis of Assisi, Apopka
Dunlop, John, St. Luke, Barefoot Bay
Durden, Donathan L., Divine Mercy, Merritt Island
Espinoza, Alan, St. Isaac Jogues, Orlando
Esposito, Robert A., St. Mark the Evangelist, Summerfield
Falotico, Francis E., Our Lady of Grace, Palm Bay
Farrell, John, Holy Name of Jesus, Indialantic
Ferranti, Richard L., Basilica of St. Paul, Daytona Beach
Ferriola, Constantino, Nativity, Longwood
Ferrioli, George, St. John Neumann
Fisher, William, Jr., St. Patrick, Mount Dora
Gabriel, Joseph Pius Piyasiri, St. Vincent de Paul, Wildwood
Garcia, Jose M., Good Shepherd, Orlando
Gassman, Joseph, Holy Name of Jesus, Indialantic
Gaucher, Paul, St. Patrick, Mt. Dora
Gaudioso, Robert D., St. Rose of Lima, Poinciana
Gesinski, Bruce, Prince of Peace, Ormond Beach
Gibbs, Marshall Ashby, St. Mary Magdalen, Altamonte Springs
Giel, Frederick, St. Timothy, Lady Lake
Gonzales, Rafael, Blessed Sacrament, Clermont
Gonzalez, Jose M., St. Isaac Jogues, Orlando
Grant, Frederick M., Blessed Sacrament, Clermont
Gravois, John Mire, Nativity, Longwood
Gray, David L., Cathedral of St. James, Orlando
Gubatan, Nemesio, St. Margaret Mary, Winter Park
Gutierrez, Albert, Our Lady of Grace, Palm Bay
Hamilton, James J., Our Lady of the Springs, Ocala
Hart, Vernon W., Basilica of St. Paul, Daytona
Herbert, Laurence Matthew, St. Francis of Assisi, Apopka
Hernandez, Francisco, St. Joseph, Lakeland
Hernandez, Rafael, St. Andrew, Orlando
Howell, John Warren, Our Lady of the Springs, Ocala
Humphrey, Frank, Our Lady Star of the Sea, New Symrna Beach
Interlandi, Joseph, St. John the Baptist, Dunnellon
Kaseta, Richard, St. Timothy, Lady Lake
Kelly, Gerard H., St. Mary Magdalen, Altamonte Springs
King, Mark M.
Kinsey, Robert Joseph, St. Peter, DeLand
Knight, Samuel Ralph, Holy Spirit, Lake Wales
Kreps, Robert P., St. Margaret Mary, Winter Park
L'Huillier, Ron, St. Timothy, Lady Lake
Laboy, Pedro, St. Isaac Jogues, Orlando
Lacsamana, Manuel, Holy Redeemer, Kissimmee
Lafleur, Normand R., St. Theresa, Belleview
Lammers, John, St. Joseph of the Forest Mission, Silver Springs
Landry, John E., St. Joseph, Winter Haven
LaPlante, Robert, St. Peter, DeLand
Lathan, James Kiney, St. Ann, DeBary
Lendoiro, Orlando, St. Isaac Jogues, Orlando
Leonhardt, George, Jr., St. Paul, Leesburg
Levesque, Norman, Saints Peter and Paul, Winter Park
Libersat, Henry, St. Mary Magdalen, Altamonte Springs
Lindeman, Scott, Sts. Peter and Paul, Winter Park
Mador, Joseph F., St. Vincent de Paul, Wildwood
Maldonado, Eliezer, St. Catherine of Siena, Kissimmee
Mallon, Charles A., Holy Family, Orlando
Martin, James T., Holy Spirit, Lake Wales
Martin, John R., Holy Family, Orlando
Martinez, Antonio, Church of the Resurrection, Lakeland
Mastrangelo, Eugene Kearns, St. Brendan, Ormond Beach
Mattison, George, St. Timothy, Lady Lake
McAvoy, Patrick Kenneth, Holy Family, Orlando
McCarthy, Dana G., St. Vincent de Paul Mission, Wildwood
McElwee, Michael J., Ascension, Melbourne
McGinnity, Michael Francis, St. Paul, Leesburg
Mejia, Rafael, St. Isaac Jogues, Orlando
Meyer, Richard G., Epiphany, Port Orange
Miller, Daniel G., Sr., St. Vincent de Paul Mission, Wildwood
Mintern, Michael Patrick, St. Joseph, Palm Bay
Molina, Fernando, Blessed Sacrament, Clermont
Money, Kenneth N., Holy Cross, Orlando
Mongan, Patrick, Church of Our Savior, Cocoa Beach
Montanez, Felix, St. Isaac Jogues, Orlando
Morales, Angel R., St. John Vianney, Orlando
Morales, Ramon, Holy Cross, Orlando
Morillo, Felix M., Good Shepherd Parish, Orlando
Mukri, Kevin, St. Timothy, Lady Lake
Muller, Hugh W., St. John the Evangelist, Viera
Multeri, James R., St. Maximilian Kolbe, Avalon Park
Murello, Andrew Frank, St. Mary's, Rockledge
Murphy, Michael J., St. Mary's, Rockledge
Murray, Thomas A., Sacred Heart, New Smyrna Beach
Naveo, Jose D., St. Charles Borromeo, Orlando
Neris, Susano, Holy Redeemer, Kissimmee
Nugent, Michael J., Church of the Epiphany, Port Orange
Nunez, Ernesto, St. Catherine of Siena, Kissimmee
O'Hern, Eugene J., Blessed Sacrament, Cocoa
Orbon, Carl, Holy Family, Orlando
Ortiz, Jacinto, St. Rose of Lima, Poinciana
Ossa, Ovidio A., St. John Vianney, Orlando
Otradovec, Byron Anthony, St. Vincent de Paul, Wildwood
Oullette, Lucain, St. Matthew, Winter Haven
Pacheco, Angel, St. Isaac Jogues, Orlando
Pagan, Miguel A., St. Maximilian Kolbe, Avalon Park
Pallo, Daniel James, St. Vincent de Paul, Wildwood
Pellosie, John
Perez, Arcelio, Our Lady of Lourdes, Melbourne
Pettengill, Howard, Jr., Immaculate Conception, Melbourne Beach
Pettit, Michael Samuel, Our Lady of Hope, Port Orange
Pineiro, Ismael, Blessed Sacrament, Clermont
Pleus, Robert J., Holy Family, Orlando
Radford, Richard F., St. Vincent de Paul, Wildwood
Ramos, Jose Vidal, St. Rose of Lima, Poinciana
Ramos, Jose A., St. Ann, Haines City
Reilly, Eugene, Hospital Ministry
Rhine, Jack H., Our Lady of Grace, Palm Bay
Richiuso, Joseph, Holy Name of Jesus, Indialantic
Rinderle, Edward, St. Peter, Deland
Rivera, Vicente, Good Shepherd, Orlando
Rodriguez, Diego N., Church of the Resurrection, Lakeland
Roe, Robert Steven, St. Joseph, Lakeland
Roman, Luis A., Blessed Sacrament, Clermont
Rumplasch, John A., St. Mark the Evangelist, Summerfield
Santiago, Santos N., St. Jude, Ocala
Schwartz, James G., Blessed Trinity, Ocala
Seidel, James B., St. John the Evangelist, Viera
Senholzi, Gregory Bruce, St. Vincent de Paul
Serrano, Jose I., St. Jude, Ocala
Shaefer, Edward, Queen of Peace, Ocala
Shelley, James G., St. Francis of Assisi. Apopka
Shortell, Mike, Blessed Sacrament, Clermont
Skinner, Walter A., Jr., Nativity Catholic Church, Longwood
Smith, Gerard F., St. Peter, DeLand
Somma, Alfred P., St. Joseph, Palm Bay
Stauffacher, Thomas, Ascension, Melbourne
Stilwell, Lee
Stives, Edward C., Our Lady of Lourdes, Melbourne
Stokes, James D., St. John the Evangelist, Viera
Sullivan, John D., St. Timothy, Lady Lake
Tagye, Thomas A., Our Lady of Hope, Port Orange
Tate, Tommy L., Holy Redeemer, Kissimmee
Thomas, Walter D., St. Timothy, Lady Lake
Timmes, William, St. Margaret Mary, Winter Park
Torres, Gilberto, Our Lady of the Lakes, Deltona
Trunzo, Vincent, Holy Name of Jesus, Indialantic
Vargas, Juan R., St. Catherine of Siena, Kissimmee
Volkerson, Paul, St. Charles Borromeo, Orlando
Wade, James L., St. Anthony, Lakeland
Wanca, William T., Sr., Our Lady of Grace, Palm Bay
Warner, Donald M., Sts. Peter & Paul, Winter Park
Webb, Charles, St. Theresa, Belleview
Whale, William E., Church of the Epiphany, Port Orange
Wiencek, Bruno, St. Lawrence, Bushnell
Wilson, Edward C., St. Jude, Ocala
Wortman, Joseph B., Church of the Resurrection, Lakeland

INSTITUTIONS LOCATED IN THE DIOCESE

[A] HIGH SCHOOLS, DIOCESAN AND PAROCHIAL

ORLANDO. *Bishop Moore Catholic High School Inc.* (1954) 3901 Edgewater Dr., 32804. Tel: 407-293-7561; Fax: 407-296-8135. Email: kanem@bishopmoore.org. Web: www.bishopmoore.org. Maureen Kane, Pres.; Thomas Doyle, Prin.; Scott Brogan, Asst. Prin.; Jean Hoffman, Asst. Prin.; Matt Gorden, Dean of Men; Tanya Jarvis, Dean of Women; Rev. Rick Voor, Chap.; Deacon Bill Timmes, Chap. Sisters 1; Lay Teachers 70; Students 1,133; Total Staff 18.

DAYTONA BEACH. *Father Lopez Catholic High School, Inc.*, 3918 LPGA Blvd., 32124. Tel: 386-253-5213; Fax: 386-252-6101. Email: lsayago@fatherlopez.org. Web: www.fatherlopez.org. Lee Sayago, Prin. Lay Teachers 24; Total Staff 50; Students 346.

LAKELAND. *Santa Fe Catholic High School, Inc.* (1960) 3110 Highway 92 E., 33801. Tel: 863-665-4188; Fax: 863-665-4151. Email: gcote@santafecatholic.org. Web: www.santafecatholic.org. Gwen Cote, Pres.; Matthew Franzino, Prin.; Trish Deal, Librarian. Sisters 1; Lay Teachers 21; Students 247; Brothers 1.

MELBOURNE. *Central Catholic High School, Inc.*, 100 E. Florida Ave., 32901. Tel: 321-727-0793; Fax: 321-727-1134. Email: burkem@melbournecc.org. Web: melbournecc.org. Michael Burke, Pres.; Rev. Karl Bergin; Tom Armstrong, Prin.; Janet Keany, Librarian. Priests 1; Lay Teachers 38; Students 373.

OCALA. *Trinity Catholic High School, Inc.* (2000) 2600

S.W. 42nd St., 34471. Tel: 352-622-9025; Fax: 352-861-8164. Email: daubin@tchs.us. Web: www.trinitycatholichs.org. Bro. Daniel Aubin, F.S.C., Pres.; Rev. Patrick J. Sheedy, School Pastor; Mrs. Jacquelyn Gehrsitz, Prin.; Mrs. Lila Vivi, Librarian. Brothers 3; Lay Teachers 42; Students 520.

[B] SPECIAL SCHOOLS

ORLANDO. *Morning Star School* (1960) 954 Leigh Ave., 32804-2299. Tel: 407-295-3077; Fax: 407-522-1700. Email: mss954@aol.com. Kathryn Harding, Ph.D., Prin. School for Exceptional Children. Lay Teachers 8; Students 60.

[C] HOUSING ACCOMMODATIONS FOR THE ELDERLY

ORLANDO. *St. Joseph's Garden Courts, Inc.*, 1515 N. Alafaya Trail, 32828. Tel: 407-382-0808; 407-470-1357 (Catholic Charities); Fax: 407-382-0812; 407-657-5648 (Catholic Charities).

Monsignor Bishop Manor, Inc., 815 Borders Cir., Ste. 144, 32808. Tel: 407-293-3339; Fax: 407-293-0085. Total Staff 6; Total in Residence 300.

DAYTONA BEACH. *Casa San Pablo*, 401 N. Ridgewood Ave., 32114. Tel: 386-253-2828; Fax: 386-253-0842. Barbara D. Mitchell, Admin. Total in Residence 64; Total Staff 7.

MELBOURNE. *Ascension Manor* (1995) 2960 Pineapple Ave., 32935. Tel: 321-757-9828; Fax: 321-752-9437; Teletype: 800-955-8771. Email: ascensionmanor@carteretmgmt.com. Josephine Stratford, Mgr. Total in Residence 79; Total Staff 9.

OCALA. *Trinity Villas I, Inc.*, 3728 N.E. 8th Pl., 34470-1093. Tel: 352-694-5507; Fax: 352-694-1434. Email: dcrawford@trinityvilla.cfcoxmail.com. Debra Crawford, Mgr. Total in Residence 98; Total Staff 5.

Trinity Villas II, Inc., 3728 N.E. 8th Pl., 34470-1093. Tel: 352-694-5507; Fax: 352-694-1434. Email: dcrawford@trinityvilla.cfcoxmail.com. Debra Crawford, Mgr. Total in Residence 64; Total Staff 3.

ORMOND BEACH. *Prince of Peace Housing, Inc. dba Prince of Peace Villas* (1996) 664 S. Nova Rd., 32174. Tel: 386-673-5080; Fax: 386-673-2008. Email: cmartin@carteretmgmt.com. Carol Martin-Ryan, Mgr. Total in Residence 72; Total Staff 5.

PORT ORANGE. *Epiphany Manor* (1989) 4792 S. Ridgewood Ave., 32127. Tel: 386-767-2556; Teletype: 800-955-8771; Fax: 386-761-0490. Email: cstefano@carteretmgmt.com. Cheryl Stefano, Mgr. Total Residence 76; Total Staff 5; Apartment Units 72.

SAINT CLOUD. *St. Anthony Garden Courts*, 444 Hamilton Park Cir., 34769.

WINTER HAVEN. *Episcopal Catholic Apartments* (1974) 500 Ave. L, N.W., 33881. Tel: 863-299-4481; Fax: 863-299-5719; Teletype: 800-955-8771. Haley Alam, Admin. Apartments 199; Total Staff 15.

[D] FAMILY CARE FACILITIES

SAINT CLOUD. *Bishop Grady Villas* (2004) 401 Bishop Grady Ct., 34769. Tel: 407-892-6078; Fax: 407-892-3081. Web: www.bishopgradyvillas.org. Kevin Johnson, Exec. Dir. Bed Capacity 48; Total Assisted Annually 116; Full Time Equivalents 40.

[E] RETREAT CENTERS

WINTER PARK. *San Pedro Spiritual Development Center*, 2400 Dike Rd., 32792. Tel: 407-671-6322; Fax: 407-671-3992. Email: info@sanpedrocenter.org. Web: www.sanpedrocenter.org. Total in Residence 5; Total Staff 16.

Friars on Staff: Very Rev. A. Giles Schinelli, T.O.R., Admin.; Revs. David Kaczmarek, T.O.R.; John Vianney Cunningham, T.O.R.; Bro. Truong Tello Vu, T.O.R.; Rev. Benjamin A. Berinti, C.PP.S., V.F. Friars in Residence: Rev. Patrick Seelman, T.O.R. (Retired).

[F] MONASTERIES AND RESIDENCES OF PRIESTS AND BROTHERS

COCOA BEACH. *Congregation of Holy Cross, United States Province*, 325 Arthur Ave., 32931-4005. Tel: 321-799-8383; Fax: 321-783-6312. Email: christopherlodge68@gmail.com. Revs. Joseph J. Long, C.S.C. (Retired); James Murphy, C.S.C., Asst. Supr. (Retired); Laurence Olszewski, C.S.C.; Bros. William Farrell, C.S.C.; Dennis Fleming, C.S.C., Supr.; Herman Zaccarelli, C.S.C.; Revs. George B. Mulligan, C.S.C.; Kenneth J. Silvia, C.S.C. (Retired); Fred Serraino, C.S.C. (Retired); Louis A. Mango, C.S.C.; Thomas J. Shea, C.S.C. Priests 8; Brothers 3; Total Staff 4.

DELAND. *Augustinian Monks of the Primitive Observance*, 2075 Mercers Fernery Rd., 32720. Tel: 386-736-4321. Email: monks@augustinianmonks.com. Web: www.augustinianmonks.com. Rev. Seamus, O.S.A.Prim., Abbot/Pres.

KISSIMMEE. *Presentation Brothers*, 1602 Pettis Blvd., 34741-3117. Tel: 407-846-2033. Email: fpm1802@Juno.com. Web: www.presentationbrothers.com. Bros. Francis Sebo, F.P.M.; Francis Schafer, F.P.M., Prov. Supr.; James Needham, F.P.M., Community Leader.

NEW SMYRNA BEACH. *St. Alphonsus Villa-Redemptorist Fathers and Brothers*, 318 N. Riverside Dr., P.O. Box 548, 32170-0548. Tel: 386-428-6481. Revs. Glenn D. Parker, C.Ss.R., Rector; Karl Aschmann, C.Ss.R. (Retired); John Barry, C.Ss.R. (Retired); Daniel Carboy, C.Ss.R. (Retired); Eugene Daigle, C.Ss.R. (Retired); Vincent Douglass, C.Ss.R. (Retired); Joseph Gorney, C.Ss.R. (Retired); George F. Kelly, C.Ss.R. (Retired); Bro. David Skarda, C.Ss.R., (Retired); Rev. Donald J. Winter, C.Ss.R. (Retired); Bros. Frank Roberts, C.Ss.R.; Christopher Walsh, C.Ss.R., Admin. Total in Residence 12; Total Staff 8.

Redemptorist Fathers of the Vice Province of Richmond, 313 Hillman St., P.O. Box 1529, 32170. Tel: 386-427-3094; Fax: 386-423-1270. Email: vpofrichmond@aol.com. Very Rev. Jerome L. Chavarria, C.Ss.R., Vice Prov. & Supr. (Retired); Revs. Glenn D. Parker, C.Ss.R., Consultor; Peter Sousa, C.Ss.R., Vice Prov. Vicar.

Redemptorists Fathers of Florida, Inc.; Redemptorists Fathers of South Carolina; Redemptorists Fathers of North Carolina, Inc.; Redemptorists Fathers of Virginia, Incorporated; Redemptorists Fathers of Georgia, Incorporated. Total in Residence 1; Total Staff 1.

Villa Madonna, 4385 Saxon Dr., 32169. Tel: 386-427-4660. Email: seraphintor@aol.com. Very Rev. Seraphin J. Conley, T.O.R. (Retired). Email: seraphintor@aol.com.

OCALA. *Congregation of Christian Brothers* (1802) (Congregation) (Edmund Rice Christian Brothers North America), 1384 S.E. 54th Pl., 34480-5760. Tel: 352-622-1374; Fax: 352-861-8164. Email: daubin@tchs.org. Web: www.trinitycatholichs.org. Bros. Daniel Aubin, F.S.C., Pres.; F. Damian Ryan, C.F.C.; Francis Gammaro, C.F.C. Edmund Rice Brothers 2; De La Salle Christian Brothers 1.

WINTER PARK. *Franciscan Friars, T.O.R., San Pedro Friary*, 2400 Dike Rd., 32792. Tel: 407-671-6322; Fax: 407-671-3992. Email: info@sanpedrocenter.org. Web: www.sanpedrocenter.org. Very Rev. A. Giles Schinelli, T.O.R.; Revs. David Kaczmarek, T.O.R.; Vianney Cunningham, T.O.R.; Bro. Truong Tello Vu, T.O.R.; Rev. Benjamin A. Berinti, C.PP.S., V.F. For detailed information of staff and residences in this diocese, please see Retreat Centers in the Institution section. Priests 4; Brothers 1; Total in Residence 5; Total Staff 16. In Res. Rev. Patrick Seelman, T.O.R. (Retired).

[G] CAMPUS MINISTRY

ORLANDO. *Catholic Campus Ministry at the University of Central Florida* 12094 Collegiate Way, 32817. Tel: 407-382-7063; Fax: 407-382-7073. Email: info@ccmknights.com. Web: www.ccmknights.com. Mailing Address: P.O. Box 677145, 32867. Revs. Scott M. Circe, Campus Min.; Hector Vazquez, Campus Min.; Tony Marco, Assoc. Campus Min.

Embry-Riddle Aeronautical University (1926) *Office of Campus Ministry-Interfaith Chapel*, Interfaith Chapel, 600 S. Clyde Morris Blvd., Daytona Beach, 32114-3900. Tel: 386-226-6580; Fax: 386-226-7370. Email: dbcsu@erau.edu. Web: www.dbcsu.org.

600 S. Clyde Morris Blvd., Daytona Beach, 32114-3900. Tel: 386-226-6581; Fax: 386-226-7370. Email: dalyt@erau.edu. Rev. Timothy P. Daly, Catholic Chaplain, Catholic Ministry.

DELAND. *Stetson University Catholic Campus Ministry* 359 W. New York Ave., 32720. Tel: 386-822-6000; Fax: 386-822-6034. Web: www.stpeterdeland.net. Rev. Thomas Connery; Rick Grinstead, Campus Min. Total Staff 2.

LAKELAND. *Florida Southern College Newman Center* c/o St. Joseph, 210 W. Lemon St., 33815. Tel: 863-682-0555; Fax: 863-686-9546. Email: rayboletti@msn.com. Web: www.stjosephlakeland.org. Rev. Ramon Bolatete, Chap. Total in Residence 1; Total Staff 1.

MELBOURNE. *Florida Institute of Technology Campus Ministry* (1958) 150 W. University Blvd., 32901-6988. Tel: 321-674-8045; Fax: 321-674-8938. Email: dbailey@fit.edu. Web: www.fit.edu. Rev. Douglas S. Bailey, S.D.S. Total Staff 1.

WINTER PARK. *Rollins College Campus Ministry* c/o St. Margaret Mary, 526 Park Ave. N., 32789. Tel: 407-647-3392; Fax: 407-647-4492. Web: stmargaretmary.org.

[H] MISCELLANEOUS

ORLANDO. **Catholic Volunteers in Florida, Inc.*, P.O. Box 536476, 32853-6476. Tel: 407-382-7071; Fax: 407-382-7073. Email: volunteer@cvif.org. Web: www.cvif.org. Sr. Florence Bryan, S.S.J., Dir. Site Placements/Formation; Mrs. Valarie Amica, Prog. Dir.; Ms. Elaine Fowler, Exec. Dir. National recruitment for statewide (FL) placement of full-time volunteers in one-year service assignments. Co-sponsored by Florida's bishops, Sisters of St. Joseph of St. Augustine, FL, and New Hope Charities. The Episcopal Advisor is Bishop John G. Noonan of the Diocese of Orlando. Lay Volunteers 19; Total Staff 3.

The Florida Catholic Serving the Dioceses of Orlando, Palm Beach & Venice., Mailing Address: P.O. Box 4993, 32802. Tel: 407-373-0075; Fax: 407-373-0087. Carol Brinati, Associate Publisher.

RELIGIOUS INSTITUTES OF MEN REPRESENTED IN THE DIOCESE

For further details refer to the corresponding bracketed number in the Religious Institutes of Men or Women section.

[]—*Augustinian Monks of the Primitive Observance*—OS.S.A.
[0140]—*Augustinian Priests*—O.S.A.
[]—*Congregation of Christian Brothers* (Eastern U.S. American Province)—C.F.C.
[0600]—*Congregation of Holy Cross*—C.S.C.
[0220]—*Congregation of the Blessed Sacrament*—S.S.S.
[0610]—*Congregation of the Holy Cross (Southern Province)*—C.S.C.
[]—*Congregation of the Holy Spirit*
[1000]—*Congregation of the Passion*—C.P.
[0720]—*Missionaries of Our Lady of LaSalette*—M.S.
[]—*Missionaries of St. Charles*—C.S.
[]—*Missionhurst Congregation of the Immaculate Heart of Mary*—C.I.C.M.
[]—*Montfort Missionaries*
[1310]—*Most Holy Trinity Fathers*—O.SS.T.
[0910]—*Oblates of Mary Immaculate*—O.M.I.
[0200]—*Order of St. Benedict*—O.S.B.
[1010]—*Pauline Fathers*—O.S.P.P.E.
[]—*Presentation Brothers*—F.P.M.
[1070]—*Redemptorist Fathers* (Baltimore Province)—C.Ss.R.
[]—*Redemptorists*—C.SS.R.
[0420]—*Society of the Divine Word*—S.V.D.
[0690]—*Society of Jesus*—S.J.
[1200]—*Society of the Divine Savior*—S.D.S.
[]—*Society of the Divine Savior (Polish Province)*
[1060]—*Society of the Precious Blood (Cincinnati Province)*—C.PP.S.
[]—*Sons of the Divine Will*
[]—*St. Joseph Society of the Sacred Heart*—S.S.J.
[0560]—*Third Order Regular of Saint Francis (Province of the Immaculate Conception)*—T.O.R.

RELIGIOUS INSTITUTES OF WOMEN REPRESENTED IN THE DIOCESE

[]—*Adrian Dominican Sisters*—O.P.
[]—*Benedictine Sisters of Tanzania*—O.S.B.
[]—*Congregation of Divine Providence*
[1230]—*Franciscan Sisters of Christian Charity*—O.S.F.
[]—*Immaculate Heart of Mary Reparatrix*
[]—*Incarnatio Consecratio Mission*
[]—*Irish Sisters of Mercy*
[]—*Mission Catechist Sisters*—M.C.S.
[]—*Mission Helpers of Sacred Heart*
[]—*Missionary Sisters of the Incarnation Consecration Mission*—I.C.M.
[3760]—*Order of St. Clare*—O.S.C.
[]—*Religious Sisters Filippini*
[]—*Servants of Mary*
[]—*Sinsinawa Dominican Sisters*—O.P.
[]—*Sisters for Christian Community*—S.F.C.C.
[0440]—*Sisters of Charity of Cincinnati, Ohio*—S.C.
[]—*Sisters of Charity of the Blessed Virgin Mary*
[0660]—*Sisters of Christian Charity*—S.C.C.
[0990]—*Sisters of Divine Providence*—C.D.P.
[1650]—*Sisters of St. Francis of Philadelphia*—O.S.F.
[]—*Sisters of the Good Shepherd*
[3900]—*Sisters of St. Joseph of St. Augustine, Florida* (St. Augustine, FL)—S.S.J.
[3840]—*Sisters of St. Joseph of Carondolet*—C.S.J.
[2360]—*Sisters of Loretto at the Foot of the Cross*—S.L.
[]—*Sisters of Mercy of the Americas*
[2990]—*Sisters of Notre Dame*—S.N.D.
[]—*Sisters of Notre Dame-Chardon*
[]—*Sisters of Notre Dame de Namur*
[3320]—*Sisters of the Presentation of the Blessed Virgin Mary*—P.B.V.M.
[]—*Sisters of St. Dominic (Adrian)*
[]—*Sisters of St. Dominic (St. Catherine de Ricci)*
[]—*Sisters of St. Francis of Christian Charity*

[]—*Sisters of St. Francis of the Holy Family*
[]—*Sisters of St. Joseph*
[]—*Sisters of the Holy Names of Jesus and Mary*
[]—*Sisters of the Immaculate Heart of Mary*
[]—*Sisters of the Living Word*
[]—*Ursuline Nuns*—O.S.U.

NECROLOGY

† Granahan, Gerry—Died Dec. 22, 2010
† McNicholas, Stephen—Died June 5, 2011

An asterisk (*) denotes an organization that has established tax-exempt status directly with the IRS and is not covered by the USCCB Group Ruling.

Diocese of Owensboro

(Dioecesis Owensburgensis)

Most Reverend

WILLIAM F. MEDLEY

Bishop of Owensboro; ordained May 22, 1982; appointed Bishop of Owensboro December 15, 2009; ordained February 10, 2010. *Mailing Address: 600 Locust St., Owensboro, KY 42301.*

Most Reverend

JOHN J. MCRAITH, D.D.

Bishop Emeritus of Owensboro; ordained February 21, 1960; appointed October 23, 1982; consecrated December 15, 1982; retired January 5, 2009. *Res. & Mailing: 529 Cedar St., Owensboro, KY 42301.*

CREATED DECEMBER 9, 1937.

Square Miles 12,502.

Erected February 23, 1938.

Comprises the following thirty-two Counties in the western part of the State of Kentucky: Allen, Ballard, Breckinridge, Butler, Caldwell, Calloway, Carlisle, Christian, Crittenden, Daviess, Edmonson, Fulton, Graves, Grayson, Hancock, Henderson, Hickman, Hopkins, Livingston, Logan, Lyon, McCracken, McLean, Marshall, Muhlenberg, Ohio, Simpson, Todd, Trigg, Union, Warren and Webster.

For legal titles of parishes and diocesan institutions, consult the Catholic Pastoral Center.

Catholic Pastoral Center: 600 Locust St., Owensboro, KY 42301. Tel: 270-683-1545; Fax: 270-683-6883.

Web: www.rcdok.org

Email: kevin.kauffeld@pastoral.org

STATISTICAL OVERVIEW

Personnel	
Bishop	1
Retired Bishops	1
Priests: Diocesan Active in Diocese	53
Priests: Diocesan Active Outside Diocese	3
Priests: Retired, Sick or Absent	20
Number of Diocesan Priests	76
Religious Priests in Diocese	18
Total Priests in Diocese	94
Extern Priests in Diocese	11
Ordinations:	
Diocesan Priests	1
Religious Priests	2
Permanent Deacons in Diocese	5
Total Sisters	186
Parishes	
Parishes	79
With Resident Pastor:	
Resident Diocesan Priests	39
Resident Religious Priests	11
Without Resident Pastor:	
Administered by Priests	28
Administered by Deacons	1
Professional Ministry Personnel:	
Sisters	12
Lay Ministers	67
Welfare	
Catholic Hospitals	1
Total Assisted	282,290
Homes for the Aged	2
Total Assisted	195
Day Care Centers	3
Total Assisted	223
Specialized Homes	1
Total Assisted	18
Special Centers for Social Services	2
Total Assisted	9,030
Educational	
Diocesan Students in Other Seminaries	17
Total Seminarians	17
Colleges and Universities	1
Total Students	681
High Schools, Diocesan and Parish	3
Total Students	732
Elementary Schools, Diocesan and Parish	15
Total Students	3,016
Catechesis/Religious Education:	
High School Students	846
Elementary Students	3,011
Total Students under Catholic Instruction	8,303
Teachers in the Diocese:	
Priests	4
Sisters	15
Lay Teachers	317
Vital Statistics	
Receptions into the Church:	
Infant Baptism Totals	939
Minor Baptism Totals	86
Adult Baptism Totals	122
Received into Full Communion	259
First Communions	925
Confirmations	987
Marriages:	
Catholic	203
Interfaith	147
Total Marriages	350
Deaths	506
Total Catholic Population	49,721
Total Population	879,747

Former Bishops—Most Revs. FRANCIS R. COTTON, D.D., First Bishop of Owensboro; ord. June 17, 1920; appt. Dec. 16, 1937; cons. Feb. 24, 1938; died Sept. 25, 1960; HENRY J. SOENNEKER, D.D., Second Bishop of Owensboro; ord. May 26, 1934; appt. March 10, 1961; cons. April 26, 1961; installed May 9, 1961; retired June 17, 1982; died Sept. 24, 1987; JOHN J. MCRAITH, ord. Feb. 21, 1960; appt. Oct. 23, 1982; cons. Dec. 15, 1982; retired Jan. 5, 2009.

Catholic Pastoral Center—600 Locust St., Owensboro, 42301. Tel: 270-683-1545; Fax: 270-683-6883. Refer all official business to this address.

Vicar General—Rev. J. PATRICK REYNOLDS, J.C.L., Res.: St. Thomas More, 5645 Blandville Rd., Paducah, 42001-8722. Tel: 270-534-9000.

Vicar of Clergy—Rev. DARRELL VENTERS, St. Jerome, 20 State Rte. 339 N., Fancy Farm, 42039. Mailing Address: P.O. Box 38, Fancy Farm, 42039-0038.

Chancellor—Mr. KEVIN KAUFFELD.

Archivist—Ms. SARAH PATTERSON.

Diocesan Tribunal—

Judicial Vicar—Very Rev. J. MICHAEL CLARK, J.C.L.

Adjutant Judicial Vicar—VACANT.

Defender of the Bond—Rev. JOSEPH M. MILLS, J.C.L. (Retired).

Judges—Revs. LEONARD J. ALVEY; JOHN R. VAUGHAN, J.C.D.; RICHARD MEREDITH; TITUS AHABYONA, J.C.L.

Advocates— Priests and pastoral ministers of the diocese.

Director/Auditor and Case Promoter—Ms. LOUANNE PAYNE.

Notaries—Mrs. MARY ANN KURZ; Ms. SANDY MORRIS.

Clinical Psychologists (Peritus)—WILLIAM G. BACH, M.D.

Diocesan Boards and Councils

Diocesan Pastoral Council—

Consultors—Revs. ANTHONY BICKETT; D. ANDREW GARNER; BRUCE MCCARTY; JERRY RINEY; GERALD CALHOUN (Retired); DARRELL VENTERS; MICHAEL WILLIAMS.

Deans—Revs. FRANK RUFF, G.H.M., Bowling Green; RANDY HOWARD, Eastern; BENJAMIN F. LUTHER, Hopkinsville; ANTHONY J. SHONIS, Central; MARK A. BUCKNER, Owensboro West; PATRICK M. BITTEL, Owensboro East; TOM BUCKMAN, Paducah; JASON WAYNE MCCLURE, The Lakes; ERIC D. RILEY, Fancy Farm.

Age Group Six Representative—Rev. JOSEPH M. MILLS, J.C.L. (Retired).

Priests' Council—Revs. FRANK RUFF, G.H.M.; ANTHONY J. SHONIS; RANDY HOWARD; ERIC D. RILEY; BENJAMIN F. LUTHER; JASON WAYNE MCCLURE; PATRICK M. BITTEL; MARK A. BUCKNER; TOM BUCKMAN; D. ANDREW GARNER; MICHAEL WILLIAMS; BRUCE MCCARTY; ANTHONY BICKETT; JERRY RINEY; J. PATRICK REYNOLDS, J.C.L.; DARRELL VENTERS; JOSEPH M. MILLS, J.C.L. (Retired).

Council of Religious—Sisters PAM MUELLER, O.S.U., Pres.; EULA JOHNSON, S.C.N., Treas.; DEBRA A. BAILEY, A.D.; ELAINE BURKE, O.S.U., Sec.; MARGARET ALOKAN, O.S.F., J.C.L.; SHARON MILLER, G.H.M.S.

Pastoral Office for Administration—Mr. ERNIE TALIAFERRO, CFO; KAY HARDIN, Assoc. Dir.

Pastoral Office for Stewardship—Mr. KEVIN KAUFFELD, Dir.

Diocesan Finance Council—Mr. HOMER BARTON; Ms. JANET BERRY; Sr. BARBARA JEAN HEAD, O.S.U.; CHRIS D. MELTON; Mr. CHARLES KAMUF; Mr. JOSEPH HANCOCK; Mr. BOB OGLE; Revs. BRAD WHISTLE; J. PATRICK REYNOLDS, J.C.L.; Mr. BRYAN BORDERS; Mr. MIKE THOMPSON.

Pastoral Office for Education—

Superintendent of Schools—Mr JAMES P. MATTINGLY.

Director of Office for Faith Formation—Sr. ETHEL MARIE BIRI, S.S.N.D., Dir. Lay Ministry & Formation; Ms. ELAINE ROBERTSON, Dir. Faith Formation.

Committee for Education—Revs. JOHN M. THOMAS; LARRY HOSTETTER, S.T.D.; Sr. KARLA KAELIN, O.S.U.; Mr. THOMAS MALEWITZ; Mr. BILL GRANT;

Mr. GARY ERVIN; Ms. PAULA PAYNE; Mr. GEORGE BARBER; Ms. DUSTI BENSON; Ms. KIM HARDESTY; Ms. VICKIE STUMPH; Ms. JEANNE NASH.

Director of Ecumenism—Rev. ANTHONY BICKETT.

Youth Ministry—Ms. MELINDA PRUNTY, Dir.

Gasper River Catholic Youth Camp and Retreat Center—Mr. BEN WARRELL, Dir.

Director of Communications and Editor of the Diocesan Newspaper— "Western Kentucky Catholic" MEL HOWARD.

Television and Radio Broadcast Communications—Rev. JOHN R. MEREDITH, Dir.; Mr. CLIFF RUSSELL, Broadcast Consultant.

Pastoral Office for Worship—Rev. LARRY MCBRIDE, Dir.; Ms. MARTHA HAGAN, Assoc. Dir.; Mr. MIKE BOGDAN, Dir. Office for Music.

Diocesan Liturgical Committee—Revs. CARL MCCARTHY; LARRY MCBRIDE; ANTHONY BICKETT; JOHN M. THOMAS; Sisters GEORGIA ACKER, O.P.; GERI HOYE, O.P.; Ms. MARTHA HAGAN; Ms. PATTY BROWN; Mr. MICHAEL BOGDAN; Ms. CLEO HIGDON; Sr. ALICIA COOMES, O.S.U.

Pastoral Office for Spiritual Life—Sr. ANN MCGREW, O.S.U., Dir., Mount St. Joseph, 8001 Cummings Rd., Maple Mount, 42356. Tel: 270-229-0200; Fax: 270-229-0279.

Cursillo—Sr. ELAINE BURKE, O.S.U., Mount St. Joseph, 8001 Cummings Rd., Maple Mount, 42356. Tel: 270-229-4103, Ext. 720; Fax: 270-229-0279; CECILIA HAMILTON, Lay Dir., 4324 Landsdowne N., Owensboro, 42303. Tel: 270-926-4176.

Catholic Charities—RITA HEINZ, Dir. Programs, 600 Locust St., Owensboro, 42301. Tel: 270-683-1545. Board Members: MARK PFIEFER, Ex Officio; Revs. ED BRADLEY, Ex Officio; C. PHILLIP RINEY, Ex Officio; TIM HAMMOND, Ex Officio; Sr. JOSEPH ANGELA BOONE, O.S.U.; DAVID MUDD; ROSE LOWERY; DAN FORTIER; CLAIRE HAMMOND; MARLA BERTSCHINGER; KATHLEEN BAUMGARTEN; MARGARET FENWICK; VANCE WEBB; IGNATIUS C. PAYNE JR.; NICK NICHOLS.

Catholic Campaign for Human Development—RICHARD MURPHY, Dir.

Catholic Relief Service—RICHARD MURPHY, Dir.

Pastoral Office for Social Concerns—RICHARD MURPHY, Dir.

Social Concerns Committee—RICHARD MURPHY; LIZ FRANCIS; Ms. BONNY PRUDHOMME; MARTHA CRABTREE; BERNADETTE HOWARD; SUZANNE ROSE; VERONICA WILHITE; Ms. DONNA FAVORS; STEPHANIE ELDER; Sr. SUZANNE SIMS, O.S.U.

Office for Safe Environment for the Protection of Children and Young People—Ms. MOLLY THOMPSON, Coord.

Respect Life Office—RICHARD MURPHY.

African-American Office—VERONICA WILHITE, Dir.

Hispanic Office—LUIS AJU, Dir.

Justice for Immigrants—VACANT.

Pastoral Office of Family Life—TAMI SCHNEIDER, Dir.

Family Life Committee—TAMI SCHNEIDER; KEN RASP; KATHY RASP; AMANDA REFFITT; NATHAN REFFIT; DREW HARDESTY; RACHE HARDESTY; LORI LEWIS; FRANK STRASSER; MARIE STRASSER; MARTHA WINN; RUSS CARRICO; ELLEN CARRICO; SARAH RICE; AUSTIN RICE; AARON CARRICO; STEPHANIE CARRICO; SUZANNE PADGETT; TONYA BARR; Rev. MICHAEL WILLIAMS.

Natural Family Planning—Billings Ovulation Method: MICHELLE ROBERTS, Owensboro; MARTHA WINN, Bowling Green. Creighton Model Method: SUZANNE PADGETT, Owensboro; PATTI GUTIERREZ, Owensboro; AMANDA REFFITT, Owensboro.

Society for the Propagation of the Faith—Rev. RAY CLARK.

Vicar of Clergy—Rev. DARRELL VENTERS.

Priest Personnel Committee—Revs. J. PATRICK REYNOLDS, J.C.L., Vicar Gen.; D. ANDREW GARNER, Dir. Vocations; ERIC D. RILEY; BRUCE MCCARTY; LARRY MCBRIDE; LEONARD ALVEY, Ed.S.; JASON WAYNE MCCLURE; DARRELL VENTERS, Vicar of Clergy.

Vocations Office—Rev. D. ANDREW GARNER, Dir. Tel: 270-314-8152; Fax: 270-683-6883; Dr. FRED LITKE, Assoc. Dir., Catholic Pastoral Center, 600 Locust St., Owensboro, 42301-2130. Tel: 270-683-1545.

Ongoing Formation of Priests—Rev. RICHARD MEREDITH, St. Pius Tenth Parish, 3814 U.S. 60 E., Owensboro, 42303. Tel: 270-684-4745; Fax: 270-684-2709.

**Roman Catholic Diocese of Owensboro Charitable Trust Fund, Inc.*Mr. ERNIE TALIAFERRO; Most Rev. WILLIAM F. MEDLEY; Mr. KEVIN KAUFFELD.

Organizations

St. Vincent de Paul Society—IGNATIUS C. PAYNE JR., Diocesan Council Pres., 3880 Bordeaux Loop, S., Owensboro, 42303. Tel: 270-683-6525.

Scouting Activities—Rev. KENNETH MIKULCIK, Chap., Catholic Pastoral Center, 600 Locust St., Owensboro, 42301. Tel: 270-683-1545.

Holy Childhood Association—Rev. RAY CLARK.

Teens Encounter Christ—Rev. ERIC D. RILEY, Mailing Address: St. Joseph Parish, 702 W. Broadway St., Mayfield, 42066. Tel: 270-247-2843.

Legion of Mary—Rev. BENJAMIN F. LUTHER, Dir. Marian Chapters.

Serra Club—Rev. RAY CLARK, Chap.

Owensboro Chapter—GARY JACKSON, Pres. Tel: 270-926-4221.

Holy Name, Henderson Chapter—LARRY DENTON, Pres. Tel: 270-827-1368.

Mercy Health Partners - Lourdes, Inc.—1530 Lone Oak Rd., P.O. Box 7100, Paducah, 42002-7100. Tel: 270-444-2444; Fax: 270-444-2980. STEVEN GRINNELL, Pres. & CEO.

Victim Assistance Coordinator—RITA HEINZ. Tel: 270-683-1545. Email: heinzr@pastoral.org.

Birthright—TERRI LAHUGH, Dir., 512 W. 7th St., Owensboro, 42301. Tel: 270-683-1103. Email: birthright839@bellsouth.net. Hours: Mon.-Fri. 9am-noon.

Daughters of Isabella—Very Rev. Msgr. BERNARD POWERS, State Chap. (Retired); ANN NEWBY, State Regent. Tel: 270-685-4001; SHEILA THOMSON, Owensboro Circle #241 Regent. Tel: 270-683-2397; MARTHA FLOYD, Paducah Circle #258 St. Francis de Sales. Tel: 270-443-1640.

CLERGY, PARISHES, MISSIONS AND PAROCHIAL SCHOOLS

CITY OF OWENSBORO

(DAVIESS COUNTY)

1—ST. STEPHEN CATHEDRAL (1839) Revs. John R. Vaughan; Brandon Williams, Parochial Vicar; Sr. Therese Francis Walker, M.S.B.T., Pastoral Assoc. & Dir. Faith Formation; Deacon Dirck Curry; Mr. Michael Conley, Dir. Music Ministry; Chris Warren, Business Mgr.
Res.: 610 Locust St., 42301. Tel: 270-683-6525; Fax: 270-683-3621. Web: www.ststephencathedral.org.
Catechesis/Religious Program—Students 32.
Chapel—Blessed Sacrament [CEM] 602 Sycamore St., 42301. Tel: 270-926-4741. Veronica Wilhite, Admin.

2—BLESSED MOTHER (1948) Rev. John R. Meredith; Brett Ballard, Dir. Music; Russ Hayden, Business Mgr. & Admin.; Darlene Quinn, Office Asst.
Office: 601 E. 23rd St., 42303. Tel: 270-683-8444; Fax: 270-683-6423.
Res.: 515 E. 22nd St., 42303. Tel: 270-663-1398.
Catechesis/Religious Program—Nicholas Hardesty, D.R.E.; Christina Best, Youth Min. Students 90.

3—THE IMMACULATE (1954) Rev. Anthony Jones; Susan Belcher, Sec.
Parish Office—2516 Christie Pl., 42301. Tel: 270-683-0689; Fax: 270-926-9016.
Res.: 2601 Christie Pl., 42301.
Catechesis/Religious Program—Diane Willis, D.R.E. Students 114.

4—SS. JOSEPH AND PAUL (1887) Revs. Carl McCarthy; Jose Carmelo Jimenez (Mexico).
Mailing Address: 609 E. 4th St., 42303. Tel: 270-683-5641; Fax: 270-685-4766. Web: www.stjpc.org.
Catechesis/Religious Program—423 Clay St., 42303. Tel: 270-683-5641. Students 76.
Mission—Good Samaritan Refugee Home 1601 Pearl St., Daviess Co. 42303.

5—OUR LADY OF LOURDES (1959) Rev. Brad Whistle.
Res.: 4029 Frederica St., 42301. Tel: 270-684-5369; Fax: 270-683-8008. Web: www.lourdescatholicchurch.com.
Catechesis/Religious Program—Drew Hardesty, D.R.E. Students 87.
Our Lady of Lourdes Day Care—4005 Frederica St., 42301. Tel: 270-926-6516. Children 69.

6—ST. PIUS TENTH (1957) Rev. Julian Ibemere (Nigeria); Marisa Cooper, Business Mgr.
Mailing Address: 3418 US 60 E., 42303. In Res., Rev. Titus Ahabyona (Uganda).
Res.: 3512 E. Sixth St., 42303. Tel: 270-684-5517; 270-684-4745 (Office); Fax: 270-684-2709. Web: stpiustenthparish.org.
Catechesis/Religious Program—Nancy Greenwell, D.R.E.; Matt Hunt, Youth Min. Students 160.
St. Pius Tenth Day Care—Tel: 270-684-7456. Children 76.

7—PRECIOUS BLOOD (1960) Rev. Bruce McCarty.
3306 Fenmore St., 42301. Tel: 270-684-6888; Fax: 270-684-1304.
Catechesis/Religious Program—Sr. Rosanne Spalding, O.S.U., D.R.E. Students 58.
Precious Blood Day Care—3400 Fenmore St., 42301. Tel: 270-683-3012. Children 78.

8—ST. RAPHAEL (1842) [CEM] Closed. Records at Diocesan Archives, 600 Locust St., Owenboro, Tel: 270-683-1545. St. Raphael Cemetery, est. 1847, became interparochial when church burned in 1983.

OUTSIDE THE CITY OF OWENSBORO

AURORA, MARSHALL CO., ST. HENRY (1967) [CEM] Rev. Babu Kulathumkal, H.G.N. (India).
Church: 16097 U.S. Hwy. 68 E., Hardin, 42048. Tel: 270-474-8058; Fax: 270-474-9867. Web: sainthenryparish.com.
Catechesis/Religious Program—Students 13.

AXTEL, BRECKINRIDGE CO., ST. ANTHONY (1812) [CEM] Rev. Roy Anthony Stevenson.
Res.: 1654 S. Hwy. 79, Hardinsburg, 40143. Tel: 270-257-2132; Fax: 270-257-2137. Email: padrefalls@att.net.
Catechesis/Religious Program—Students 59.

BARDWELL, CARLISLE CO., ST. CHARLES (1891) [CEM] Rev. Richard Cash.
Res.: 6922 State Rte. 408, 42023. Tel: 270-642-2586; Fax: 270-642-2222. Email: ssdcpastor@wk.net. Web: www.stcharles-bardwell.org.
Catechesis/Religious Program—Students 37.

BEAVER DAM, OHIO CO., HOLY REDEEMER (1962) Rev. Eric D. Riley.
13th & Madison Sts., P.O. Box 106, 42320. Tel: 270-274-3414.
Office: P.O. Box 106, 42320. Tel: 270-274-3414; Fax: 270-274-4245.
Catechesis/Religious Program—Students 55.

BIG CLIFTY, GRAYSON CO., ST. MARY, Closed. Records kept at St. Paul's Church, 1821 St. Paul Rd., Leitchfield, KY 42754. Tel: 270-242-7436.

BOWLING GREEN, WARREN CO.

1—HOLY SPIRIT (1970) Revs. Jerry Riney; Steve Hohman, Parochial Vicar.
Office: 4754 Smallhouse Rd., 42104. Tel: 270-842-7777. Web: www.holyspiritcatholic.org.
Catechesis/Religious Program—Lori Lewis, D.R.E. Students 145.

2—ST. JOSEPH (1859) Revs. D. Andrew Garner; Joshua A. McCarty, Parochial Vicar; John McAllister, Dir. Faith Formation; Deacon Robert Imel.
Office: 434 Church Ave., 42101. Tel: 270-842-2525; Fax: 270-843-9624. Web: www.stjosephbg.com.
Res.: 401 Church Ave., 42101. Tel: 270-843-7568.
Catechesis/Religious Program—Students 127.

BROWN'S VALLEY, DAVIESS CO., ST. ANTHONY (1902) [CEM] Very Rev. J. Michael Clark.
Church: 261 St. Anthony Rd., Utica, 42376. Tel: 270-733-4341. Email: stabv@bellsouth.net. Web: www.stanthony.church-builder.com.
Catechesis/Religious Program—Students 45.

CADIZ, TRIGG CO., ST. STEPHEN (1966) Rev. Babu Kulathumkal, H.G.N. (India).
Res.: 1698 Canton Rd., 42211. Tel: 270-522-3801; Fax: 270-522-3901. Email: ststephencath387@bellsouth.net.
Catechesis/Religious Program—Ms. April Washer, C.R.E. Students 19.

CALHOUN, MCLEAN CO., ST. SEBASTIAN (1871) [CEM] Rev. John Okoro (Nigeria).
180 State Rte. 136 W., 42327-9521.
Res.: 445 Main St., 42327-9521. Tel: 270-273-9268; Fax: 270-273-3185.
Catechesis/Religious Program—Students 32.

CALVERT CITY, MARSHALL CO., ST. PIUS TENTH (1954) Rev. Anthoni Ottagon, H.G.N.
Office: 777 Fifth Ave., P.O. Box 495, 42029. Tel: 270-395-4727; Fax: 270-395-5747. Email: stpiusx@newwavecomm.net. Web: www.stpiusx.us.
Res.: 723 Fifth Ave., 42029.
Church: 777 Fifth Ave., 42029.
Catechesis/Religious Program—Betty Lou Derry, C.R.E. Students 44.

CENTRAL CITY, MUHLENBERG CO., ST. JOSEPH (1886) Rev. Benjamin F. Luther; Sisters Rose Karen Johnson, O.S.U., Pastoral Assoc.; Rose Theresa Johnson, O.S.U., Pastoral Assoc.
Res.: 113 S. Third St., 42330. Tel: 270-754-1164; Fax: 270-754-1164.
Catechesis/Religious Program—Students 35.

CLARKSON, GRAYSON CO., ST. ELIZABETH OF HUNGARY (1906) [CEM] Rev. Martin E. Hayes.
Res.: 1821 St. Paul Rd., Leitchfield, 42754. Tel: 270-242-7436.
Church: 306 Clifty Ave., 42726. Tel: 270-242-4414. Email: stpaulgrayson@msn.com.
Catechesis/Religious Program—Students 4.

CLINTON, HICKMAN CO., ST. JUDE Rev. Shijo Vadakumkara, H.G.N. (India).
Mailing Address: 304 Mayfield Rd., 42031. Email: stjudeclinton@hotmail.com.
Church: 306 Mayfield Rd., 42031. Tel: 270-653-6869.
Catechesis/Religious Program—Students 11.

CLOVERPORT, BRECKINRIDGE CO., ST. ROSE (1857)

[CEM] Rev. Dan Kreutzer.
Res.: 118 Chestnut St., 40111. Tel: 270-788-6422; Fax: 270-788-6930.
Catechesis/Religious Program—Students 30.

CURDSVILLE, DAVIESS CO., ST. ELIZABETH Rev. Bruce McCarty; Judy Schadler, Contact Person.
Mailing Address: 6143 First St., P.O. Box 9-A, 42334. Tel: 270-229-4134. Email: selizabethville@gmail.com.

DAWSON SPRINGS, HOPKINS CO., RESURRECTION Rev. Bruce Fogle.
Church: 530 Industrial Park Rd., 42408. Tel: 270-383-4743; 270-797-8665.
Catechesis/Religious Program—Students 11.

EARLINGTON, HOPKINS CO., IMMACULATE CONCEPTION (1847) Rev. Bruce Fogle.
Res.: 112 S. Day St., 42410. Tel: 270-383-4743. Email: immaculatecc@bellsouth.net.
Catechesis/Religious Program—Students 11.

EDDYVILLE, LYON CO., ST. MARK CHURCH (1990) Rev. Thomas Shaiju, H.G.N. (India).
Res.: 302 Peachtree Ln., 42038. Tel: 270-365-6786.
Catechesis/Religious Program—Students 14.

ELKTON, TODD CO., ST. SUSAN (1965) Revs. Frank Ruff, G.H.M., Sacramental Min.; Daniel C. Dillard, Parochial Vicar; Heriberto Rodriguez, Parish Life Coord.
221 Allensville St., P.O. Box 788, 42220. Tel: 270-265-5263 (Office); Fax: 270-265-5288 (Office).
Catechesis/Religious Program—Students 35.

FANCY FARM, GRAVES CO., ST. JEROME (1836) [CEM] Rev. Darrell Venters.
Res.: P.O. Box 38, 42039. Tel: 270-623-8181; Fax: 270-623-6341. Email: stjerome@wk.net. Web: stjeromefancyfarm.org.
Catechesis/Religious Program—Students 188.

FANCY FARM, HICKMAN CO., ST. DENIS (1914) [CEM] Rev. Richard Cash.
Mailing Address: 6922 State Rte. 408, Bardwell, 42023. Tel: 270-642-2586; Fax: 270-642-2222.
Catechesis/Religious Program—Students 19.

FORDSVILLE, OHIO CO., ST. JOHN THE BAPTIST (1893) Rev. Jean Rene Kalombo (Democratic Republic of Congo); Sr. Marie Michael Hayden, O.S.U., Pastoral Assoc.
66 Smith St., 42343. P.O. Box 127, 42343. Tel: 270-276-3619. Email: sjbccfordsville@bellsouth.net.
Catechesis/Religious Program—Students 11.

FRANKLIN, SIMPSON CO., ST. MARY (1880) [CEM] Rev. Robert Drury.
Res.: 403 N. Main St., P.O. Box 388, 42135-0388. Tel: 270-586-4515; Fax: 270-586-4549. Email: ccfk@bellsouth.net.
Catechesis/Religious Program—Students 38.

FULTON, FULTON CO., ST. EDWARD Rev. Shijo Vadakumkara, H.G.N. (India).
Res.: 504 Eddings St., 42041. Tel: 270-472-2742. Email: stedwardky@bellsouth.net.
Catechesis/Religious Program—Students 26.

GRAND RIVERS, LIVINGSTON CO., ST. ANTHONY OF PADUA (1986) Rev. Anthoni Ottagon, H.G.N.
Res.: 1518 J.H. O'Bryan Ave., P.O. Box 447, 42045. Church: Tel: 270-362-7121. Email: stpiusx@newwavecomm.net.
Catechesis/Religious Program—Students 2.

GRAYSON SPRINGS, GRAYSON CO., ST. AUGUSTINE (1815) [CEM] Rev. Brian A. Johnson.
Res. & Mailing Address: c/o St. Anthony Church, 1256 St. Anthony Church Rd., Clarkson, 42726. Tel: 270-242-4791; Fax: 270-242-2601.
Catechesis/Religious Program—Students 13.

GUTHRIE, TODD CO., STS. MARY & JAMES (1950) Revs. Frank Ruff, G.H.M., Sacramental Min.; Daniel C. Dillard, Parochial Vicar; Heriberto Rodriguez, Parish Life Coord.
313 3rd St., 42234. P.O. Box 325, 42234. Tel: 270-483-2571. Email: saintsusan@bellsouth.net.
Catechesis/Religious Program—Students 28.

HARDINSBURG, BRECKINRIDGE CO., ST. ROMUALD (1811) [CEM] Rev. Anthony Bickett.
Res.: 394 N. Hwy. 259, 40143. Tel: 270-756-2356; Fax: 270-756-2099. Email: stromuald@bbtel.com. Web: www.stromuald.org.
Catechesis/Religious Program—Students 100.

HAWESVILLE, HANCOCK CO., IMMACULATE CONCEPTION (1871) [CEM] Rev. Chrispin Q. B. Oneko.
430 Main Cross, P.O. Box 219, 42348.
Res.: 190 Judith Lynn, P.O. Box 219, 42348. Tel: 270-927-8419; Fax: 270-927-6783.
Catechesis/Religious Program—Students 58.

HENDERSON, HENDERSON CO., HOLY NAME OF JESUS (1886) [CEM] Revs. Larry McBride; Anthony J. Shonis, Parochial Vicar.
Res.: 511 Second St., 42420. Tel: 270-826-2096; Fax: 270-827-1494. Web: www.holynameparish.net.
School—(Grades PreK-8), 628 Second St., 42420. Tel: 270-827-3425; Fax: 270-827-4027. Web: www.holynameschool.org. Sandy Fleming, Prin. Ursuline Sisters 1; Lay Teachers 29; Students 481.
Catechesis/Religious Program—Students 145.

HENSHAW, UNION CO., ST. AMBROSE (1832) [CEM] Rev. Gregory G. Trawick; Sr. Alicia Coomes, O.S.U., Pastoral Assoc.
Res.: *c/o St. Francis Borgia*, P.O. Box 256, Sturgis, 42459. Tel: 270-333-5915; Fax: 270-333-4342.
Church: 5914 S.R. 270 W., Morganfield, 42437. Tel: 270-333-1832; Fax: 270-333-1833. Email: stambrosercc@gmail.com. Web: www.saintambrosekentucky.org.
Catechesis/Religious Program—Tel: 270-333-2806. Students 11.

HICKMAN, FULTON CO., SACRED HEART (1853) Rev. Shijo Vadakumkara, H.G.N. (India); Butch Busby, Contact Person.
Res.: 411 Moulton St., 42050-1327. Tel: 270-236-2071.
Catechesis/Religious Program—1203 Lattus Rd., 42050. Tel: 270-236-4604. Students 7.

HOPKINSVILLE, CHRISTIAN CO., SS. PETER AND PAUL (1872) Revs. Richard Meredith; Daniel C. Dillard.
Res.: 902 E. Ninth St., 42240. Tel: 270-885-8522; Fax: 270-885-5296. Web: www.stsppchurch.org.
Catechesis/Religious Program—Students 85.
School—(Grades PreK-8) Tel: 270-886-0172; Fax: 270-887-9924. Web: www.stsppschool.org. Sarah Kranz, Prin. Lay Teachers 10; Students 160.

IRVINGTON, BRECKINRIDGE CO., HOLY GUARDIAN ANGELS (1898) [CEM] Rev. Dan Kreutzer.
301 W. High St., 40146. Tel: 270-547-2137. Email: hguardianangel@yahoo.com.
Catechesis/Religious Program—Students 26.

KNOTTSVILLE, DAVIESS CO., ST. WILLIAM (1887) [CEM] Rev. Patrick M. Bittel.
Res.: 6007 St. Lawrence Rd., Philpot, 42366. Tel: 270-281-4802; Fax: 270-281-9556.
School—Mary Carrico Memorial School, (Grades PreK-8) Tel: 270-281-5526; Fax: 270-281-9556. Email: mcarrico144@yahoo.com. Raymond Montgomery, Prin. Lay Teachers 5; Students 91.
Catechesis/Religious Program—Students 62.

LACENTER, BALLARD CO., ST. MARY (1907) [CEM] Rev. J. Patrick Reynolds.
Church: 624 Broadway, P.O. Box 570, 42056. Tel: 270-665-5551 (Office); Fax: 270-665-5551. Email: stmcc@brtc.net.
Catechesis/Religious Program—Rene Doublin, D.R.E. Students 26.

LEITCHFIELD, GRAYSON CO., ST. JOSEPH'S, [CEM] Rev. Randy Howard.
Res.: 109 W. Walnut St., 42754. Tel: 270-259-3028; Fax: 270-259-9860.
Catechesis/Religious Program—Students 46.

LEWISPORT, HANCOCK CO., ST. COLUMBA (1850) [CEM] Rev. Chrispin Q. B. Oneko.
815 Pell St., 42351. Mailing Address: P.O. Box 358, 42351.
Res.: 190 Judith Lynn, P.O. Box 219, Hawesville, 42348. Tel: 270-927-8419; Fax: 270-927-6783.
Catechesis/Religious Program—Students 34.

LIVERMORE, MCLEAN CO., ST. CHARLES BORROMEO (1917) Rev. John Okoro (Nigeria).
Mailing Address: 180 Hwy. 136 W., Calhoun, 42327.
Church: 506 Hill Ave., 42352. Tel: 270-273-3185; 270-273-9268 (Res.); Fax: 270-273-3185. Email: stsebch@bellsouth.net.
Res./Rectory: 445 Main St., Calhoun, 42327.
Catechesis/Religious Program—Students 10.

MADISONVILLE, HOPKINS CO., CHRIST THE KING (1969) Rev. John M. Thomas; Patricia L. Brown, Pastoral Assoc.
Res.: 1600 Kingsway Dr., 42431. Tel: 270-821-5494; Fax: 270-825-8612. Email: christthekingchu@bellsouth.net. Web: www.ctkmadisonville.org.
School—(Grades PreK-8) Tel: 270-821-8271. Email: christschool@bellsouth.net. Beth Herrmann, Prin.; SuzAnne Wilson, Librarian. Lay Teachers 8; Students 102.
Catechesis/Religious Program—Students 35.
Preschool—Tel: 270-821-3954. Students 62.

MARION, CRITTENDEN CO., ST. WILLIAM (1962) [CEM] Rev. Gregory G. Trawick.
1308 N. Adams, Sturgis, 42459. Mailing Address: P.O. Box 343, 42064.
Res.: 1317 N. Main, Sturgis, 42459.
Church: 860 S. Main St., 42064. Tel: 270-965-2477. Email: saintwilliam@att.net.

MAYFIELD, GRAVES CO., ST. JOSEPH (1887) [CEM] Rev. Eric D. Riley; Sr. Eloisa Aquino, Hispanic Ministry.
Res.: 702 W. Broadway St., 42066. Tel: 270-247-2843; Fax: 270-247-6835. Web: www.stjosephmayfield.com.
School—St. Joseph Catholic School, (Grades PreK-6), 112 S. 14th St., 42066. Tel: 270-247-4420; Fax: 270-247-2612. Susan Brinkley, Prin. Lay Teachers 4; Students 41.
Catechesis/Religious Program—Students 92.

MCQUADY, BRECKINRIDGE CO., ST. MARY-OF-THE-WOODS (1870) [CEM 2] Rev. Roy Anthony Stevenson.
1654 Hwy. 79 S., Hardinsburg, 40143.
Church: 4711 Hwy. 105 S., Hardinsburg, 40143. Tel: 270-756-2093; Fax: 270-257-2137. Email: tmalewitz@mac.com.
Catechesis/Religious Program—Mrs. Gale Hinton, C.R.E. Students 24.

MORGANFIELD, UNION CO., ST. ANN (1877) [CEM] Rev. Gerald H. Baker.
Res.: 304 Church St., 42437. Tel: 270-389-2287; Fax: 270-389-0219.
Catechesis/Religious Program—Students 53.

MORGANTOWN, BUTLER CO., HOLY TRINITY (1958) Rev. Jean Rene Kalombo (Democratic Republic of Congo).
766 Logansport Rd., P.O. Box 222, 42261.
Res.: 117 13th Rd., P.O. Box 106, Beaver Dam, 42320. Tel: 270-274-3414.
Catechesis/Religious Program—Students 3.

MURRAY, CALLOWAY CO., ST. LEO (1933) Rev. Jason Wayne McClure; Deacon Joseph R. Ohnemus.
Res.: 401 N. 12th St., 42071. Tel: 270-753-3876; Fax: 270-759-2074.
Catechesis/Religious Program—Allison Loomis, D.R.E. & Campus Min. Students 130.

OAK GROVE, CHRISTIAN CO., ST. MICHAEL THE ARCHANGEL (1995) Rev. David W. Kennedy; Deacon Jack Cheasty.
Church: 448 State Line Rd., P.O. Box 505, 42262. Tel: 270-640-9850; Fax: 270-640-9850.
Catechesis/Religious Program—Students 150.

PADUCAH, MCCRACKEN CO.

1—ST. FRANCIS DE SALES (1848) [CEM] Revs. Brian Roby; Uwem Enoh, Parochial Vicar.
Church: 116 S. Sixth St., 42001. Tel: 270-442-1923; Fax: 270-443-4616. Email: sfds@vci.net. Web: www.stfrancisdesalespaducah.org.
Catechesis/Religious Program—Gina Smith, D.R.E. Students 88.

2—ST. JOHN THE EVANGELIST (1839) Rev. Tom Buckman.
Parish Office: 6705 Old U.S. Hwy. 45, 42003. Tel: 270-554-3810; Fax: 270-534-9163. Web: www.stjohnspaducah.com.
Catechesis/Religious Program—Paducah Faith Formation, 1241 Elmdale Rd., 42003. Tel: 270-443-0295; Fax: 270-443-0295. Students 22.

3—ROSARY CHAPEL Revs. Brian Roby; Uwem Enoh, Parochial Vicar.
Catechesis/Religious Program—Students 9.
Chapel— 711 Ohio St., P.O. Box 1481, 42001. Tel: 270-444-6383; Fax: 270-444-0553. Email: rosary@bellsouth.net.

4—ST. THOMAS MORE (1944) [CEM] Revs. J. Patrick Reynolds; Ryan Harpole, Parochial Vicar; James Hess, Liturgy & Music Dir.; Sr. Esther Ardonez, Hispanic Ministry; Nicole Strasser, Youth Min.; Donna Tarantino, Dir. Ministries & Volunteers; Missy Eckenberg, Dir. Devel.; Steve DuPerrieu, Office Mgr.
Church: 5645 Blandville Rd., 42001-8722. Tel: 270-534-9000; Fax: 270-534-4339. Email: bulletin@stmore.org. Web: www.stmore.org.
Catechesis/Religious Program—Faith Formation, 1241 Elmdale Rd., 42003. Tel: 270-443-0295. Students 125.

PEONIA, GRAYSON CO., ST. ANTHONY (1822) [CEM] Rev. Brian A. Johnson.
Res.: 1256 St. Anthony Church Rd., Clarkson, 42726. Tel: 270-242-4791. Email: stanthony@usdol.net.
Catechesis/Religious Program—Students 24.

PHILPOT, DAVIESS CO., ST. LAWRENCE (1821) [CEM] Rev. Patrick M. Bittel.
Res.: 6007 St. Lawrence Rd., 42366. Tel: 270-281-4802; Fax: 270-281-9556. Web: www.swsl.org.
Catechesis/Religious Program—Mary Helen Rhodes, D.R.E. Students 22.

PRINCETON, CALDWELL CO., ST. PAUL (1874) [CEM] Rev. Thomas Shaiju, H.G.N. (India).
Res.: 813 S. Jefferson, 42445. Tel: 270-365-6786 (Rectory); 270-365-3645 (Office). Email: pesolomon@bellsouth.net.
Catechesis/Religious Program—Students 14.

PROVIDENCE, WEBSTER CO., HOLY CROSS Rev. Bruce Fogle.
112 S. Day St., Earlington, 42410.
Church: 730 North Highway 41A, 42450. Tel: 270-383-4743.
Catechesis/Religious Program—Students 3.

REED, HENDERSON CO., ST. AUGUSTINE (1896) [CEM] Rev. Suresh Bakka (India).
Res.: 81 Church St., 42301. Tel: 270-764-1691; Fax: 270-764-0444.
Church: 16777 Hwy. 60 E., 42451. Tel: 270-764-5599. Web: www.gus-n-pete.org.
Catechesis/Religious Program—Students 36.

ROME, DAVIESS CO., ST. MARTIN (1885) Rev. Maury D. Riney, Parochial Admin.
Church: 5856 Kentucky 81, 42301. Tel: 270-685-0339; Fax: 270-684-5444. Email: stmartinrome@gmail.com.

RUSSELLVILLE, LOGAN CO., SACRED HEART (1873) Rev. Masilamani Suvakkin, H.G.N. (India).
Res.: 296 W. 6th St., 42276. Tel: 270-726-6963; Fax: 270-726-2232. Email: email@sacredheartrussellville.org. Web:

www.sacredheartrussellville.org.
Catechesis / Religious Program—Students 79.

ST. JOSEPH, DAVIESS CO., ST. ALPHONSUS (1854) [CEM] Rev. J. Raymond Goetz.
Mailing Address: 7925 KY 500, 42301. Tel: 270-229-4164.
Res.: 7950 Cummings Rd., 42301. Tel: 270-229-4530. Email: st.alphonsus@att.net.
Catechesis / Religious Program—Students 72.

ST. PAUL, GRAYSON CO., ST. PAUL (1810) [CEM] Rev. Martin E. Hayes.
Res.: 1821 St. Paul Rd., Leitchfield, 42754. Tel: 270-242-7436.
School—(Grades PreK-8), 1812 St. Paul Rd., Leitchfield, 42754. Tel: 270-242-7483. Email: saintpaulschool@windstream.net. Sr. Anne Michelle Mudd, O.S.U., Prin. Lay Teachers 3; Students 18.
Catechesis / Religious Program—Students 43.

SCOTTSVILLE, ALLEN CO., CHRIST THE KING (1964) Rev. Dennis Holly, G.H.M.; Catherine Grapes, Office Admin.
Res.: 298 Bluegrass Dr., P.O. Box 463, 42164. Tel: 270-237-4404. Email: christtheking@nctc.com. Web: www.scottsvilleky.catholicweb.com.
Catechesis / Religious Program—Students 26.

SEBREE, WEBSTER CO., ST. MICHAEL (1977) Rev. Al Bremer; Patti Gutierrez, Parish Life Coord.
Office: P.O. Box 705, 42455. Tel: 270-835-2584; Fax: 270-835-2584. Email: stmichaelsebree@gmail.com. 57 Watkins Sebree Rd., 42455.
Catechesis / Religious Program—Students 55.

SORGHO, DAVIESS CO., ST. MARY MAGDALENE (1907) [JC] Rev. Mark A. Buckner.
Office: 7232 Kentucky 56, 42301. Tel: 270-771-4436; Fax: 270-771-4478. Email: pattibartley@yahoo.com.
Res.: Tel: 270-302-2464.
Catechesis / Religious Program—Tel: 270-771-4438. Debi Hopkins, D.R.E. Students 72.

STANLEY, DAVIESS CO., ST. PETER OF ALCANTARA (1873) [CEM 2] Rev. Suresh Bakka (India).
Res.: 81 Church St., 42301. Tel: 270-764-1983; Fax: 270-764-0444. Email: lschreeker@stpeterandstaugustine.com. Web: www.stpeterandstaugustine.com.
Catechesis / Religious Program—Students 25.

STURGIS, UNION CO., ST. FRANCIS BORGIA (1952) Rev. Gregory G. Trawick.
Mailing Address: P.O. Box 256, 42459.
Church: 1317 N. Main St., 42459. Tel: 270-333-5915; Fax: 270-333-4342. Email: saintfrancisborgia@yahoo.com.
Catechesis / Religious Program—1317 N. Main St., 42459. Tel: 270-333-2806; Fax: 270-333-4342. Students 15.

SUNFISH, EDMONSON CO., ST. JOHN THE EVANGELIST (1830) [CEM] Rev. Randy Howard.
Mailing Address: 109 W. Walnut, Leitchfield, 42754.
Church: 430 St. John Church Rd., 42284. Tel: 270-259-3028; Fax: 270-259-9860.

UNIONTOWN, UNION CO., ST. AGNES (1859) [CEM] Rev. Terry Devine.
Mailing Address: P.O. Box 607, 42461.
Office: 504 Mulberry St., 42461. Tel: 270-822-4416; Fax: 270-822-5316.
Res.: 407 Fifth St., 42461. Tel: 270-822-4780 (Rectory). Email: stagnes@owens.twcbc.com.
Church: 413 Fifth St., 42461.
Catechesis / Religious Program—Students 118.

WAVERLY, UNION CO.
1—ST. PETER (1909) [CEM] Rev. Freddie Byrd.
Res.: 201 E. Market St., 42462. Tel: 270-389-4224. Email: stpeter.sacredheart@gmail.com.
Catechesis / Religious Program—Students 36.
2—SACRED HEART (1812) [CEM] Rev. Freddie Byrd. 201 E. Market St., 42462. Tel: 270-389-4224.
Church: 674 St. Rt. 141 N., Morganfield, 42437. Tel: 270-389-4224. Email: stpeter.sacredheart@gmail.com.
Catechesis / Religious Program—Students 5.

WAX, GRAYSON CO., ST. BENEDICT (1830) [CEM] Rev. Brian A. Johnson.
Mailing Address: 1256 St. Anthony Church Rd., Clarkson, 42726.
Catechesis / Religious Program—James Clemons, Dir. Students 10.
St. Anthony Church—Wax Rd., 42726. Tel: 270-242-4791.

WHITESVILLE, DAVIESS CO., ST. MARY OF THE WOODS (1845) [CEM] Rev. David P. Johnson.
Res.: 10503 Franklin St., 42378. Tel: 270-233-4529.
Church: 10534 Main Cross, P.O. Box 1, 42378. Tel: 270-233-4196; Fax: 270-233-5557.
School—St. Mary's Grade School, (Grades PreSchool-8) Tel: 270-233-5253; Fax: 270-233-9360. Sr. Suzanne Sims, O.S.U., Prin.; Peggy Clark, Librarian. Lay Teachers 12; Students 140.
Catechesis / Religious Program—Students 174.

Non-Parochial Assignments:
Revs.—
Alvey, Leonard J., Brescia University, 717 Frederica St., 42301.
Clark, Ray, Chap., Passionist Monastery, 8564 Crisp Rd., 42378. Prison Ministry
Hostetter, Larry, S.T.D., Pres., Brescia University, 717 Frederica St., 42301.
Mikulcik, Kenneth, Study Canon Law, St. Paul University, Ottawa, Cananda
Riney, Maury D., Chap., Owensboro Medical Health System, 42301. Carmel Home, 2501 Old Hartford Rd., 42303.

On Duty Outside the Diocese:
Revs.—
Puryear, Stan, Missionary, Diocese of Bani, Dominican Republic
Roof, Frank, Dept. of Veterans Affairs Medical Center, 1201 Northwest 16th St., Miami, FL 33125.

Absent on Leave:
Revs.—
Arflack, Gregory A.
Ausenbaugh, J. Andrew
Hayes, Gary
Karl, Kevin
Patterson, Ralph
Payne, Gary
Ulrich, Steve
Weider, Henry
Wheatley, Carroll (Retired)

Retired:
Very Rev. Msgrs.—
Hancock, George, Bishop Cotton Apts, 2501 1/2 Old Hartford Rd., Apt. 6, 42303.
Powers, Bernard, P.O. Box 9A, Curdsville, 42334.
Revs.—
Calhoun, Gerald, 1110 Rose Creek Dr., Madisonville, 42431.
Clemons, Delma
Glahn, Carl, Carmel Home, 2501 Old Hartford Rd., 42303.
Miller, Joseph C., 20333 Fairwood Dr., Neves, MN 56467.
Mills, Joseph M., J.C.L., Bishop Cotton Apts, 2501 1/2 Old Hartford Rd., 42303.
Powell, Paul, J.C.L., St. Martin Parish, 5856 KY 81, 42301.
Powers, Aloysius, Bishop Cotton Apts, 2501 1/2 Old Hartford Rd., Apt. 6, 42303.
Powers, Richard, 10500 McIntyre Rd., 42301.
Riney, Philip C., Bishop Cotton Apts, 2501 1/2 Old Hartfort Rd., 42303.
Willett, William David

INSTITUTIONS LOCATED IN THE DIOCESE

[A] COLLEGES AND UNIVERSITIES

OWENSBORO. *Brescia University*, 717 Frederica St., 42301. Tel: 270-685-3131; Fax: 270-686-6422. Web: www.brescia.edu. Rev. Larry Hostetter, S.T.D., Pres.; Sisters Cheryl Clemons, O.S.U., Ph.D., Vice Pres. Academic Affairs & Academic Dean; Helena Fischer, O.S.U., Registrar; Rev. Leonard J. Alvey, Prof. & Counselor; Dr. Marc Pugliese, Dir. Ministry Formation; Sr. Judith Riney, O.S.U., Dir. Library Svcs. Priests 4; Sisters 12; Administrators 6; Lay Teachers 40; Students 681.

[B] HIGH SCHOOLS, INTER-PAROCHIAL

OWENSBORO. *Owensboro Catholic High School*, 1524 W. Parrish Ave., 42301. Tel: 270-684-3215; Fax: 270-684-7050. Email: gates.settle@owensborocatholic.org. Web: www.owensborocatholic.org/schools/ochs. Mr. Gates Settle, Prin.; Ms. Sherry Orth, Rel. Dept. Chair; Ms. Amy Lambert, Dean of Students; Mr. Keith Osborne, Devel. Dir.; Ms. Marilyn Pace, Librarian. Lay Teachers 39; Students 456.

PADUCAH. *St. Mary High School*, 1243 Elmdale Rd., 42003. Tel: 270-442-1681, Ext. 232; Fax: 270-442-7920. Email: laly@smss.org. Web: www.smss.org. Lisa Aly, Prin.; Rhonda Webb, Librarian. Lay Teachers 13; Students 175.

WHITESVILLE. *Trinity High School* 42378. Tel: 270-233-5533; Fax: 270-233-9293. Web: www.trinityhs.com. Ms. Connie Morgan, Prin. Lay Teachers 14; Students 104.

[C] ELEMENTARY SCHOOLS, INTER-PAROCHIAL

OWENSBORO. *Owensboro Catholic Elementary 4-6 Campus*, (Grades 4-6), 525 E. 23rd St., 42303. Tel: 270-683-6989; Fax: 270-684-5956. Email: tracy.conkright@owensborocatholic.org. Ms. Tracy Conkright, Prin.; Theresa Sauer, Librarian. Lay Teachers 17; Students 275.

Owensboro Catholic Elementary K-3 Campus, (Grades K-3), 4017 Frederica St., 42301. Tel: 270-684-7583; Fax: 270-684-4938. Email: lori.whitehouse@owensborocatholic.org. Web: www.owensborocatholic.org. Ms. Lori Whitehouse, Prin.; Sherry Durham, Librarian. Religious 1; Lay Teachers 24; Students 412.

Owensboro Catholic Middle School, (Grades 7-8), (Owensboro Catholic Middle School), 2540 Christie Pl., 42301. Tel: 270-683-0480; Fax: 270-683-0495. Email: ann.flaherty@owensborocatholic.org. Web: www.owensborocatholic.org. Ms. Ann Flaherty, Prin.; Ms. Margie Ebelhar, Librarian. Lay Teachers 18; Students 201.

BOWLING GREEN. *St. Joseph Interparochial School*, (Grades PreSchool-8), 416 Church Ave., 42101-1887. Tel: 270-842-1235; Fax: 270-842-9072. Email: janlange@stjosephschoolbg.org. Web: stjosephschoolbg.org. Janice Lange, Prin.; Sally Jackson, Librarian. Lay Teachers 26; Students 338.

HARDINSBURG. *St. Romuald School*, (Grades PreK-8), 408 N. Hwy. 259, 40143. Tel: 270-756-5504; Fax: 270-756-2099. Email: srissecretary@hotmail.com. Mr. Rob Cox, Prin. Lay Teachers 13; Students 235.

MORGANFIELD. *St. Ann Interparochial School*, (Grades PreK-8), 320 S. Church St., 42437-1600. Tel: 270-389-1898; Fax: 270-389-1834. Email: beth.hendrickson@st-ann.com. Web: www.st-ann.com. Beth Hendrickson, Prin.; Ms. Charlotte Hollis, Librarian. Lay Teachers 16; Students 219.

PADUCAH. *St. Mary Elementary*, (Grades PreK-5), 377 Highland Blvd., 42003. Tel: 270-442-1681, Ext. 251; Fax: 270-442-7920. Email: nmornar@smss.org. Web: www.smss.org. Nancy Mornar, Prin.; Lisa Jett, Media Specialist. Lay Teachers 24; Students 253.

St. Mary Middle School, (Grades 6-8), 1243 Elmdale Rd., 42003. Tel: 270-442-1681, Ext. 232; Fax: 270-442-7920. Web: www.smss.org. Lisa Aly, Prin.; Rhonda Webb, Librarian. Lay Teachers 12; Students 128.

[D] GENERAL HOSPITALS

PADUCAH. *Mercy Health Partners-Lourdes, Inc.*, 1530 Lone Oak Rd., P.O. Box 7100, 42002-7100. Tel: 270-444-2444; Fax: 270-444-2980. Web: www.elourdes.com. Steven Grinnell, Pres. & CEO; Ms. Marianne Potina, Vice. Pres. of Mission Integration. Catholic Health Partners. Bed Capacity 240; Patients Assisted Annually 282,289; Total Staff 1,425.

McAuley Manor, Inc. Tel: 270-575-0050; Fax: 270-415-9165. Email: lmidyett@mercyhousing.org. Housing for Elderly.

Mercy Manor, Inc. Tel: 270-415-9166; Fax: 270-415-9165. Email: lmidyett@mercyhousing.org. Apartments for Elderly.

Dublin Manor, Inc. Apartments for the Elderly, Tel: 270-441-0026; Fax: 270-444-2980. Email: lmidyett@mercyhousing.org.

Lourdes Foundation, Inc., 1530 Lone Oak Rd., 42002-7100. Tel: 270-444-2205; Fax: 270-444-2732. Web: www.elourdes.com.

Mercy Regional Emergency Medical System Tel: 270-443-6529; Fax: 270-444-9128.
Mercy Regional Emergency Medical System

[E] HOMES FOR AGED

OWENSBORO. *Carmel Home*, 2501 Old Hartford Rd., 42303. Tel: 270-683-0227; Fax: 270-688-0630. Sr. M. Francis Teresa Scully, Carmel., D.C.J., Admin. & Supr.; Rev. Maury D. Riney, Chap. Carmelite Sisters of the Divine Heart of Jesus. Sisters 5; Residents 113; Bed Capacity 115; Total Staff 104; Total Assisted Annually 142.

KNOTTSVILLE. *Bishop Soenneker Home* Residential Care of the Handicapped/Disabled Elderly., 42366. Tel: 270-281-4881; Fax: 270-281-5804. Residents 52; Total Staff 29; Total Assisted Annually 68.

[F] MONASTERIES AND RESIDENCES OF PRIESTS AND BROTHERS

AUBURN. *Fathers of Mercy*, 806 Shaker Museum Rd., 42206. Tel: 270-542-4146; Fax: 270-542-4147. Email: missions@fathersofmercy.com. Web: www.fathersofmercy.com. In Res. Very Rev. David

M. Wilton, C.P.M., Supr. Gen.; Revs. John Agapito, C.P.M.; Joseph Aytona, C.P.M., Treas. Gen.; Ben Cameron, C.P.M., 1st Councillor, Asst. Gen. Mission Dir.; Louis Caporiccio, C.P.M., House Superior, Novice Master; William Casey, C.P.M., 2nd Councillor; James P. Costigan, C.P.M.; Christopher Crotty, C.P.M.; Louis Guardiola, C.P.M.; Wade Menezes, C.P.M.; George L. McInnis, C.P.M.; Anthony M. Stephens, C.P.M., Vocations Dir., Student Master, 3rd Councillor; Thomas Sullivan, C.P.M., 4th Councillor.

[G] CONVENTS AND RESIDENCES FOR SISTERS

OWENSBORO. *The Glenmary Center*, P.O. Box 22264, 42304-2264. Tel: 270-686-8401; Fax: 270-686-8759. Web: www.glenmarysisters.org. Sr. Sharon Miller, G.H.M.S., Pres. Home Mission Sisters of America, Inc. aka Glenmary Sisters. Professed Sisters in Community 10.

Service to the Home Missions Total Assisted Annually 10,000; Total Staff 9.

MAPLE MOUNT. *Mount St. Joseph*, 8001 Cummings Rd., 42356. Tel: 270-229-4103; Fax: 270-229-4127. Web: www.ursulinesmsj.org. Sr. Sharon Sullivan, O.S.U., Ph.D., Congregational Leader; Ms. Sarah Patterson, Archivist Contact. Motherhouse and Convent of the Ursuline Nuns of the Congregation of Paris. Professed Sisters in Community 159.

WHITESVILLE. *Passionist Nuns/St. Joseph's Monastery*, 8564 Crisp Rd., 42378-9782. Tel: 270-233-4571; Fax: 270-233-4356. Email: nunsp@bellsouth.net. Web: www.passionistnuns.org. Sr. Catherine Marie Schuhmann, C.P., Supr. Religious of the Passion of Jesus Christ, (Passionist Nuns, Cloistered Contemplative). Postulants 1; Junior Professed 1; Final Vows 12; Affiliate 1; Novices 1.

[H] RETREAT CENTERS

BOWLING GREEN. *Gasper River Catholic Youth Camp & Retreat Center*, 2695 Jackson Bridge Rd., 42101. Tel: 270-781-2466. Web: www.gasperriverretreatcenter.org. Email: ben.warrell@pastoral.org. Mr. Ben Warrell, Dir. (A diocesan-owned entity)

MAPLE MOUNT. *Mount Saint Joseph Conference and Retreat Center*, 8001 Cummings Rd., 42356. Tel: 270-229-0200; Fax: 270-229-0279. Email: msj.center@maplemount.org. Web: www.msjcenter.org. Sr. Ann McGrew, O.S.U., Dir.

[I] NEWMAN CENTERS

BOWLING GREEN. *Western Kentucky University Catholic Campus Center St. Thomas Aquinas Chapel*, 1403 College St., P.O. Box 10170, 42102-4770. Tel: 270-843-3638; Fax: 270-843-3326. Email: mew_62@hotmail.com. Web: www.wkucatholiccenter.com. Rev. Michael E. Williams, Dir.; Mary E. Reding, Campus Min. Students 1,651.

MURRAY. *Murray State University Newman House* 401 N. 12th St., 42071. Tel: 270-753-3876; Fax: 270-759-2074. Email: allie@stleoky.org. Web: www.msunewmanhouse.com. Allison Loomis, Campus Min.; Rev. Jason Wayne McClure, Chap. Students 800.

[J] MISCELLANEOUS LISTINGS

OWENSBORO. *Cathedral Preschool*, 600 Locust St., 42301. Tel: 270-926-1652; Fax: 270-683-3621. Email: pam.weafer@pastoral.org. Pam Weafer, Dir. Teachers 4; Students 132.

The Catholic Foundation of Western Kentucky, 600 Locust St., 42301. Tel: 270-683-1545; Fax: 270-683-6883. Email: ja@pastoral.org. Web: www.rcdok.org. Mr. Kevin Kauffeld, Contact Person.

Centro Latino, 524 Locust St., 42301. Tel: 270-683-2541; Fax: 270-684-5819. Email: ocentrolatino@aol.com. Total Staff 4; Total Assisted Annually 8,565.

**Daniel Pitino Shelter, Inc.*, 501 Walnut St., 42301. Tel: 270-688-9000; Fax: 270-688-0093. Email: dpsjim@hotmail.com. Web: www.pitinoshelter.org. Provides soup kitchen seven days a week, shelter for 65 homeless, education facilities and medical services for those unable to pay. Total Assisted Annually 469; Employees 11; Volunteers 210.

St. Gerard Life Home, 600 Locust St., 42301. Tel: 270-852-8328; Fax: 270-683-6883. Email: adoptions@pastoral.org. Rita Heinz, Catholic Charities Dir. Birthmother housing and pregnancy outreach.

Gideon Productions, Inc., 515 E. 22nd St., 42303. Tel: 270-688-9040; Fax: 270-688-9040. Email: frjohn@gideonproductions.com. Web: www.gideonproductions.com. Rev. John R. Meredith, Dir.; Mr. Cliff Russell, Broadcast Consultant.

**Glenmary Sisters Charitable Trust*, P.O. Box 22264, 42301. Tel: 270-686-8401; Fax: 270-686-8759.

Interparish Deposit Loan Fund Corp., 600 Locust St., 42301-2130. Tel: 270-683-1545; Fax: 270-683-6883. Email: ernie.taliaferro@pastoral.org. Web: www.owensborodio.org. Mr. Ernie Taliaferro, Contact Person.

Owensboro Catholic Consolidated School System, 1524 W. Parrish Ave., 42301. Tel: 270-686-8896; Fax: 270-686-8997. Email: ken.rasp@owensborocatholic.org. Web: www.owensborocatholic.org. Ken Rasp, Dir.

**The Roman Catholic Diocese of Owensboro Kentucky Charitable Trust Fund, Inc.*, 600 Locust St., 42301. Tel: 270-683-1545; Fax: 270-683-6883. Email: ernie.taliaferro@pastoral.org. Web: www.owensborodio.org. Mr. Ernie Taliaferro.

BOWLING GREEN. *Diocesan Shrine of Mary Mother of the Church and Model of all Christians*, St. Joseph, 434 Church St., 42101. Tel: 270-842-2525; Fax: 270-754-1164.

HORSE BRANCH. *St. Francis Community Center*, 768 Horsebranch Loop, 42349. Tel: 270-274-4385. Sr. Luisa Bickett, O.S.U., Pastoral Outreach Min.

PADUCAH. *St. Mary School System*, 1243 Elmdale Rd., 42003. Tel: 270-442-1681, Ext. 273; Fax: 270-442-7920. Email: afarmer@smss.org. Web: www.smss.org.

St. Mary School System Benefit Fund, 1243 Elmdale Rd., 42003. Tel: 270-442-1681, Ext. 273; Fax: 270-442-7920. Email: afarmer@smss.org. Web: www.smss.org. Dr. Angela Farmer, Contact Person.

PRINCETON. *Heralds of Good News of St. Paul, Inc.*, 813 S. Jefferson St., 42445. Tel: 270-365-6786. Rev. Thomas Shaiju, H.G.N. (India), Dir. & Contact Person.

RELIGIOUS INSTITUTES OF MEN REPRESENTED IN THE DIOCESE

For further details refer to the corresponding bracketed number in the Religious Institutes of Men or Women section.

[0820]—*Congregation of the Fathers of Mercy*—C.P.M.

[0570]—*Glenmary Home Missioners* (Glendale OH)—G.H.M.

[]—*Heralds of Good News* (India)—H.G.N.

RELIGIOUS INSTITUTES OF WOMEN REPRESENTED IN THE DIOCESE

[]—*Africa Province of the Franciscan Sisters of the Immaculate Conception* (Glasgow, Scotland, Nigeria Province)—O.S.F.

[0360]—*Carmelite Sisters of the Divine Heart of Jesus*—Carmel D.C.J.

[]—*Holy Cross Sisters USA Provinces*—S.C.S.C.

[2080]—*Home Mission Sisters of America*—G.H.M.S.

[2575]—*Institute of the Sisters of Mercy of the Americas* (Cincinnati, OH; Detroit, MI)—R.S.M.

[2790]—*Missionary Servants of the Most Blessed Trinity*—M.S.B.T.

[]—*Missioneras del Sagrado Corazon de Jesus Ad Gentes*—M.A.G.

[3170]—*Religious of the Passion of Jesus Christ*—C.P.

[1070-03]—*Sinsinawa Domincan Sisters*—O.P.

[0500]—*Sisters of Charity of Nazareth*—S.C.N.

[]—*Sisters of St. Benedict*—O.S.B.

[2260]—*Sisters of the Lamb of God*—A.D.

[1760]—*Sisters of the Third Order of St. Francis of Penance and Charity* (Tiffin, OH)—O.S.F.

[1720]—*Sisters of the Third Order Regular of St. Francis of the Congregation of Our Lady of Lourdes* (Rochester, MN)—O.S.F.

[4120]—*Ursuline Nuns, of the Congregation of Paris*—O.S.U.

INTERPAROCHIAL CEMETERIES

OWENSBORO. *Mater Dolorosa*, 1860 W. 9th St., 42301. 5404 Leitchfield Rd., 42303. Tel: 270-926-8097; Fax: 270-926-8038. Email: dolorosa3@juno.com. Mr. Art Hodde, Dir. Staff 5.

St. Raphael Cemetery Est. 1847, 6025 Hayden Bridge Rd., 42301. 600 Locust St., 42301-2130. Tel: 270-683-1545; Fax: 270-683-6883.

Resurrection, 5404 Leitchfield Rd., 42303. Tel: 270-926-8097; Fax: 270-926-8038. Email: dolorosa3@juno.com. Mr. Art Hodde, Dir.

BOWLING GREEN. *St. Joseph Cemetery Foundation, Inc., St. Joseph Cemetery Foundation*, P.O. Box 10334, 42102. Tel: 270-842-2525 (St. Joseph Parish); 270-842-7777 (Holy Spirit Parish). Mr. Ray Grudzielanek, Chief Oper. Mgr.

PADUCAH. *Mt. Carmel Interparochial Cemetery* (1893) 116 S. 6th St., 42001. Tel: 270-442-1923. Rev. Brian Roby, Dir.

NECROLOGY

† Reisz, Leonard, (Retired)—Died Feb. 17, 2011

† Rhodes, Joseph, (Retired)—Died Dec. 6, 2010

† Tiell, Maurice J., (Retired)—Died Oct. 11, 2011

An asterisk (*) denotes an organization that has established tax-exempt status directly with the IRS and is not covered by the USCCB Group Ruling.

Diocese of Palm Beach

(Dioecesis Litoris Palmensis)

Most Reverend

GERALD M. BARBARITO

Bishop of Palm Beach; ordained January 31, 1976; appointed Auxiliary Bishop of Brooklyn June 28, 1994; installed August 22, 1994; appointed Bishop of Ogdensburg October 26, 1999; appointed Bishop of Palm Beach July 1, 2003; installed August 28, 2003. *Office: 9995 N. Military Tr., Palm Beach Gardens, FL 33410.*

The Pastoral Center Office: 9995 N. Military Tr., Palm Beach Gardens, FL 33410. Tel: 561-775-9500; Fax: 561-775-9556. *Mailing Address: P.O. Box 109650, Palm Beach Gardens, FL 33410-9650*

Web: diocesepb.org

Email: info@diocesepb.org

ESTABLISHED OCTOBER 24, 1984.

Square Miles 5,115.

Comprises the Counties of Palm Beach, Martin, Indian River, Okeechobee and St. Lucie in the State of Florida.

Legal Corporate Title: The Diocese of Palm Beach.

For legal titles of parishes and diocesan institutions, consult the Chancery.

STATISTICAL OVERVIEW

Personnel	
Bishop	1
Retired Bishops	1
Priests: Diocesan Active in Diocese	82
Priests: Diocesan Active Outside Diocese	3
Priests: Retired, Sick or Absent	22
Number of Diocesan Priests	107
Religious Priests in Diocese	30
Total Priests in Diocese	137
Extern Priests in Diocese	3
Ordinations:	
Diocesan Priests	2
Transitional Deacons	1
Permanent Deacons	7
Permanent Deacons in Diocese	105
Total Brothers	1
Total Sisters	105
Parishes	
Parishes	50
With Resident Pastor:	
Resident Diocesan Priests	44
Resident Religious Priests	6
Missions	3
Pastoral Centers	1
Professional Ministry Personnel:	
Brothers	1
Sisters	47
Lay Ministers	66
Welfare	
Homes for the Aged	5
Total Assisted	436
Special Centers for Social Services	26
Total Assisted	10,000
Educational	
Seminaries, Diocesan	1
Students from This Diocese	9
Students from Other Diocese	68
Diocesan Students in Other Seminaries	6
Total Seminarians	15
High Schools, Diocesan and Parish	3
Total Students	1,457
Elementary Schools, Diocesan and Parish	14
Total Students	4,206
Elementary Schools, Private	2
Total Students	498
Total Students under Catholic Instruction	6,176
Teachers in the Diocese:	
Priests	4
Sisters	13
Lay Teachers	533
Vital Statistics	
Receptions into the Church:	
Infant Baptism Totals	3,284
Minor Baptism Totals	276
Adult Baptism Totals	176
Received into Full Communion	335
First Communions	3,744
Confirmations	2,476
Marriages:	
Catholic	480
Interfaith	126
Total Marriages	606
Deaths	2,062
Total Catholic Population	243,363
Total Population	1,922,300

Former Bishops—Most Revs. THOMAS V. DAILY, D.D., ord. Jan. 10, 1952; appt. Titular Bishop of Bladia and Auxiliary Bishop of Boston, Dec. 31, 1974; cons. Feb. 11, 1975; appt. first Bishop of Palm Beach, July 17, 1984; installed Oct. 24, 1984; transferred to Bishop of Brooklyn, Feb. 20, 1990; J. KEITH SYMONS, D.D., ord. May 18, 1958; appt. Auxiliary Bishop of St. Petersburg, Jan. 16, 1981; cons. March 19, 1981; appt. second Bishop of Pensacola-Tallahassee, Sept. 29, 1983; installed Nov. 8, 1983; appt. second Bishop of Palm Beach, June 2, 1990; installed July 31, 1990; resigned June 2, 1998; ANTHONY J. O'CONNELL, D.D., ord. March 30, 1963; appt. Bishop of Knoxville, May 27, 1988; ord. and installed Sept. 8, 1988; appt. Bishop of Palm Beach Nov. 6, 1998; resigned March 8, 2002; SEAN P. O'MALLEY, O.F.M.Cap., Ph.D., ord. Aug. 29, 1970; appt. Coadjutor May 30, 1984; appt. Bishop of St. Thomas, Virgin Islands; ord. Aug. 2, 1984; installed Oct. 16, 1985; appt. Bishop of Fall River June 16, 1992; installed Aug. 11, 1992; appt. Bishop of Palm Beach Sept. 3, 2002; installed Oct. 19, 2002; appt. Archbishop of Boston July 1, 2003; installed July 30, 2003.

The Pastoral Center—Mailing Address: P.O. Box 109650, Palm Beach Gardens, 33410-9650. Tel: 561-775-9500; Fax: 561-775-9556. *9995 N. Military Tr., Palm Beach Gardens, 33410.*

Vicar General—Very Rev. CHARLES E. NOTABARTOLO, V.G.

Moderator of Curia—Very Rev. CHARLES E. NOTABARTOLO, V.G.

Episcopal Secretary—Rev. BRIAN KING.

Executive Secretary to Bishop—Mrs. ANNETTE RUSSELL.

Chancellor—Mrs. LORRAINE SABATELLA, B.A.

Coordinator of Archives and Records—Mrs. MERKE BARONI.

Matrimonial Tribunal—

Judicial Vicar—Rev. Msgr. THOMAS J. KLINZING, J.C.L.

Adjutant Judicial Vicar—Rev. GLEN J. POTHIER, J.C.L., D.Th.

Judges—Rev. Msgr. THOMAS J. KLINZING, J.C.L.; Rev. GLEN J. POTHIER, J.C.L., D.Th.; Rev. Msgr. KEITH BRENNAN, J.C.D.

Defender of the Bond—Rev. FRANCISCO OSORIO, J.C.L.

Assessors—Rev. Msgr. JAMES M. BURKE (Retired); Very Rev. MICHAEL W. EDWARDS, V.F.; Rev. KEVIN NELSON, M.A., M.Div.

Promoter of Justice—Rev. DAMIAN TOWEY, C.P., J.C.D.

Notaries—Mrs. LORRAINE SABATELLA, B.A.; Mr. SANDI MARTINEZ, M.A.; Mrs. HELEN COUGHTER, B.A.; Mrs. DEBORAH DUXBURY, B.A.; Ms. ALICE RIVERA.

Director of the Tribunal—Mr. SANDI MARTINEZ, M.A.

Case Directors & Secretaries—Mr. SANDI MARTINEZ, M.A.; Mrs. HELEN COUGHTER, B.A.; Mrs. DEBORAH DUXBURY, B.A.; Ms. ALICE RIVERA.

Advocates—Rev. Msgr. JAMES M. BURKE (Retired); Deacon SAM BARBARO; Rev. GERALD GRACE, S.T.D.; Deacons MARTIN SERRAES; DENNIS T. DEMES, Ph.D.; Rev. KEVIN NELSON, M.A., M.Div.; Deacon JAMES BROOKS, A.S.; Mrs. LYNN POWELL; Mrs. KAREN TURNBULL, A.A.

Vicars Forane—Very Revs. MICHAEL W. EDWARDS, V.F., Northern Deanery; ALFREDO HERNANDEZ, V.F., Central Deanery; Very Rev. Canon THOMAS J. SKINDELESKI, V.F., Southern Deanery; Very Rev. AIDAN HYNES, V.F., Cathedral Deanery.

Vocations—Rev. THOMAS LAFRENIERE, Dir. Tel: 561-775-9555.

Religious—Rev. JOSEPH SANTA-BIBIANA, S.D.B., Episcopal Delegate.

Diaconate—Deacons MARTIN SERRAES, Episcopal Delegate; DENNIS T. DEMES, Ph.D., Dir. Formation. Tel: 561-775-9540.

Chief Financial Officer—Mr. DENIS HAMEL. Tel: 561-775-9518.

Consultative Bodies

Consultors—Rev. Msgr. THOMAS J. KLINZING, J.C.L.; Very Revs. MICHAEL W. EDWARDS, V.F.; CHARLES E. NOTABARTOLO, V.G.; Revs. GERALD GRACE, S.T.D.; RICHARD MURPHY.

Presbyteral Council—Ex Officio: Very Rev. CHARLES E. NOTABARTOLO, V.G., Vicar Gen.; Rev. Msgr. THOMAS J. KLINZING, J.C.L., Judicial Vicar; Very Revs. MICHAEL W. EDWARDS, V.F., Vicar Forane - Northern Deanery; AIDAN HYNES, V.F., Vicar Forane - Cathedral Deanery; ALFREDO HERNANDEZ, V.F., Vicar Forane - Central Deanery; Very Rev. Canon THOMAS J. SKINDELESKI, V.F., Vicar Forane - Southern Deanery; Rev. RICHARD MURPHY. Elected Members: Very Rev. THOMAS E. BARRETT; Revs. MICHAEL DRISCOLL, O.Carm.; RICHARD E. GEORGE II; GERALD GRACE, S.T.D.; Rev. Msgr. JOHN MCMAHON (Retired); Revs. JOSEPH M. PAPES; GLEN J. POTHIER, J.C.L., D.Th.; NESTOR RODRIGUEZ; ELIFETE ST. FORTE; Very Rev. PAUL WIERICHS, C.P.

Diocesan Offices

Background Screening—KELLIE JOHNSON. Tel: 561-775-9530.

Building, Construction, Real Estate Office—Rev.

RICHARD MURPHY, Episcopal Delegate. Tel: 561-775-9514; MICHAEL LOCKWOOD, Dir. Tel: 561-775-9523.

Catholic Charities Administrataive Offices—Mrs. SHEILA GOMEZ, Exec. Dir. Tel: 561-775-9573; DIANN JASINSKI, Assoc. Dir. Tel: 561-775-9567; JUDY EVANS, Mgr. Human Resources. Tel: 561-775-9564.

Cemetery: Our Lady Queen of Peace—10941 Southern Blvd., West Palm Beach, 33411. Rev. ZBIGNIEW A. RUDNICKI, Dir.; Mr. THOMAS JORDAN, Admin. Tel: 561-793-0711.

Communications—DIANNE LAUBERT, Dir. Tel: 561-775-9529. Email: dlaubert@diocesepb.org; LINDA REEVES, Florida Catholic Editor. Tel: 561-775-9528. Email: flcath@diocesepb.org.

Development—Deacon MICHAEL MINTERN, Dir. Tel: 561-775-9519. Email: mmintern@diocesepb.org; LYNDSAY VONBOKERN, Devel. Coord. Tel: 561-775-9590; Fax: 561-799-9527.

Ecumenism—Deacon DENNIS T. DEMES, Ph.D., Episcopal Delegate. Tel: 561-775-9540.

Education—

Schools Office—Mr. GARY GELO, Supt. Tel: 561-775-9546. Email: ggelo@diocesepb.org; Mrs. MARIE PRIVUZNAK, Asst. Supt. Tel: 561-775-9532.

Office of Catechetical Leadership, Youth Ministry Formation and Young Adult—Mr. ANTHONY MARCHICA, Dir. Tel: 561-775-9548; MARIE DRIVER, Sec. & Media Coord. Tel: 561-775-9549.

School of Christian Formation (English & Spanish)—Deacon JAIME ZAPATA, Dir. Tel: 561-775-9506.

Employee Services— (see also Insurance Services) Mrs. ANA JAROSZ, Dir. Tel: 561-775-9525; GRETCHEN CARD, Human Resources Asst. Tel: 561-775-9503.

Family Life/Marriage—Mrs. JANICE PETERSEN MINSHEW, Coord. Tel: 561-775-9557.

Finance—Mr. DENIS HAMEL, CFO. Tel: 561-775-9518; CHRIS GRANT, Controller. Tel: 561-775-9515.

Haitian Ministry—Rev. YVES GEFFRARD, Episcopal Delegate. Tel: 561-466-9617.

Hispanic Ministry—Deacon JAIME ZAPATA, Dir. Tel: 561-775-9506.

Information Technology—MIKE IRISH, Dir. Tel: 561-775-9504; CARLOS MESA, Network Admin. Tel: 561-775-9542; SCOTT LOMBARDI, Web Devel. Tel: 561-775-9505.

Insurance Services— (see also Employee Services) Mrs. ANA JAROSZ, Dir. Tel: 561-775-9525; SANDY MAULDEN, Benefits Asst. Tel: 561-775-9574.

Internal Services—Ms. MARIAN LOYND, Dir. Tel: 561-630-2694.

Liturgy—Rev. BRIAN KING, Dir.; Mrs. JEANNE CLARK, Coord. Tel: 561-775-9539.

Permanent Diaconate/Diaconate Formation Program—Deacons MARTIN SERRAES, Episcopal Delegate. Tel: 561-775-9540; DENNIS T. DEMES, Ph.D., Dir. Formation. Tel: 561-775-9541; Mrs. LYNN POWELL, Permanent Diaconate & Diaconate Formation Asst. Tel: 561-775-9540.

Propagation of the Faith & Missionary Cooperative Plan—Very Rev. MICHAEL W. EDWARDS, V.F., Dir. Tel: 772-567-5129; Mrs. BETTY MCKINLEY, Sec. Tel: 561-775-9598.

Real Estate—Rev. RICHARD MURPHY, Episcopal Delegate. Tel: 561-775-9514.

Religious Men and Women—Episcopal Delegate: Rev. JOSEPH SANTA-BIBIANA, S.D.B.

Safe Environments—Mrs. KATHRYN JOHANSEN, Coord. Tel: 561-775-9593.

Seminarians—Rev. THOMAS LAFRENIERE, Dir. Tel: 561-775-9555.

Vocations—Rev. THOMAS LAFRENIERE, Dir. Tel: 561-775-9555.

Young Adult Ministry—Mr. ANTHONY MARCHICA, Dir. Tel: 561-775-9548.

Catholic Charities Services and Offices

Executive Director—Mrs. SHEILA GOMEZ.

Associate Director—DIANN JASINSKI.

Catholic Charities Administrative Offices—9995 N. Military Trail, Palm Beach Gardens, 33410-9650. Tel: 561-775-9560; Fax: 561-625-5906. *Mailing Address: P.O. Box 109650, Palm Beach Gardens, 33410-9650.*

After-School Program—

Pahokee Pals—1200 E. Main St., Pahokee, 33476. Tel: 561-924-5677; Fax: 561-924-3595. *Mailing Address: P.O. Box 664, Pahokee, 33476.*

Counseling Services—

Counseling—

West Palm Beach—900 54th St., West Palm Beach, 33407. Tel: 561-254-6558; 561-215-0208; Fax: 561-863-5379. *Mailing Address: P.O. Box 8246, West Palm Beach, 33407.*

Stuart—1111 S. Federal Hwy., Ste. 110, Stuart, 34994. Tel: 772-283-0541; Fax: 772-220-9894.

Palm Beach—St. Edward Catholic Church, 144 N. County Rd., Palm Beach, 33480-3916. Tel: 561-891-0379; Fax: 561-514-3528.

Vero Beach—St. Helen Catholic Church, 2005 Tallahassee Ave., Vero Beach, 32960. Tel: 772-778-5411; Fax: 772-562-2209. *Mailing Address: P.O. Box 2927, Vero Beach, 32960.*

Delray Beach—840 George Bush Blvd., Bldg. D, Delray Beach, 33483. Mailing Address: 1040 S. Federal Hwy., Ste. 101, Delray Beach, 33483. Tel: 561-504-5097; 561-215-0208; Fax: 561-266-0693.

Boca Raton—298 S.W. 3rd St., Boca Raton, 33432. Mailing Address: 370 S.W. 3rd St., Boca Raton, 33432. Tel: 561-847-5131; Fax: 561-368-6420.

Port St. Lucie—7410 S. Federal Hwy., Ste. 105, Port Saint Lucie, 34952. Tel: 772-283-0541; Fax: 772-204-9566.

Elder Services—

Elder Affairs—900 54th St., West Palm Beach, 33407. Tel: 561-842-2406; Fax: 561-863-5379. *Mailing Address: P.O. Box 8246, West Palm Beach, 33407.* AMY FARIELLO.

Health Related Services—

Interfaith Health & Wellness/Wellness Ministry—900 54th St., West Palm Beach, 33407. Tel: 561-842-2406; Fax: 561-863-5379. *Mailing Address: P.O. Box 8246, West Palm Beach, 33407.* BERNADETTE MACY.

Immigration Services—

Immigration Legal Services—TIMOTHY KEOHANE, 900 54th St., West Palm Beach, 33407. Tel: 561-494-0928; Fax: 561-202-2310. Mailing Address: P.O. Box 8246, West Palm Beach, 33407; RENEE ARNAO, 1111 S. Federal Hwy., Ste. 216, Stuart, 34994. Tel: 772-463-0445; Fax: 772-872-0311; MARIA CHRISTINA MARQUEZ, 15305 S.W. Adams Ave., Indiantown, 34956. Tel: 772-597-2812; Fax: 772-597-2813. Mailing Address: P.O. Box 67, Indiantown, 34956.

Outreach—900 54th St., West Palm Beach, 33407. Mailing Address: P.O. Box 8246, West Palm Beach, 33407. Tel: 561-844-6124.

Pregnancy Services—

Birthline—1040 S. Federal Hwy., Ste. 101, Delray Beach, 33483. Tel: 561-278-0894; Fax: 561-274-7056. *3452 W. Boynton Beach Blvd., Boynton Beach, 33436.* Tel: 561-738-2060; Fax: 561-732-0750. MARY RODRIGUEZ.

Lifeline—900 54th St., West Palm Beach, 33407. Tel: 561-842-5301; Fax: 561-842-5302. *Mailing Address: P.O. Box 8246, West Palm Beach, 33407.* MARY RODRIGUEZ.

Refugee Services—

Refugee and Resettlement—900 54th St., West Palm Beach, 33407. Tel: 561-863-9255; Fax: 561-863-1680. *Mailing Address: P.O. Box 8246, West Palm Beach, 33407.* EMMA SOLER.

Substance Addiction Ministry—9995 N. Military Trail, Palm Beach Gardens, 33410-9650. Mailing Address: P.O. Box 109650, Palm Beach Gardens, 33410-9650. Tel: 561-775-9527; Fax: 561-625-5906. Mr. ERIK A. VAGENIUS.

Office of Black Catholic Ministry—Mailing Address: P.O. Box 8246, West Palm Beach, 33407. Tel: 561-758-3061; Fax: 561-863-5379. LORRAINE LYLES.

Prison Ministry—Mailing Address: P.O. Box 109650, Palm Beach Gardens, 33410-9650. Tel: 561-775-9553; Fax: 561-625-5906. Mr. THOMAS LAWLOR.

Transitional Housing—

Samaritan Center—3650 41st St., Vero Beach, 32967. Tel: 772-770-3039; Fax: 772-567-0812. TRACEY SEGAL.

Respect Life Ministry—Mailing Address: P.O. Box 109650, Palm Beach Gardens, 33410-9650. Tel: 561-775-9565; Fax: 561-625-5906. Mr. DONALD KAZIMIR; DONNA GARDNER, Post Abortion Healing & Project Rachel.

Organizations and Movements

Charismatic Movement—

English—Mr. JOHN DEAN, Dir. Tel: 772-562-5954. Email: jdeaneph320@earthlink.net.

Spanish—Tel: 561-793-8544. Rev. FRANCISCO J. OSORIO, J.C.L.

Christ Child Society—

Boca Raton—AGNES GREGORY. Tel: 561-482-3067.

North Palm Beach—MARY BISHOP. Tel: 561-795-0134.

Stuart—CHERYL MACKIE. Tel: 772-299-7852.

Con El, Healthcare Ministry to the Third World—DOROTHY MARTIN. Tel: 561-659-2822.

Council of Catholic Women—Rev. CLEMENS HAMMERSCHMITT, Spiritual Moderator. Tel: 561-966-8878; MYRNA WONG, Pres. Tel: 772-335-5160.

Cursillo Movement—

English—Tel: 561-747-9330. Deacon JOSEPH POLLOCK, Spiritual Advisor; Mr. JERRY SULLIVAN, Lay Dir.

Spanish—Tel: 561-964-4168. Sr. MARGARITA GOMEZ, R.M.I., S.T.L., D.Min., Spiritual Advisor; ALICIA M. FERNANDEZ, Lay Dir.

Damas Catolicas en Acion—Rev. NESTOR RODRIGUEZ, Spiritual Moderator; LILIA MARIA GIBBONS, Founder & Dir.

Knights of Columbus—Very Rev. Canon THOMAS J. SKINDELESKI, V.F. Tel: 561-276-6892; PETER J. BISHOP, Membership Admin. Tel: 561-795-0134.

Legion of Mary, Palm Beach Curia—Rev. DANIS RIDORE, Spiritual Moderator. Tel: 561-276-6892; GLORIA PAT STEWART, Pres. Tel: 561-659-4160.

CLERGY, PARISHES, MISSIONS AND PAROCHIAL SCHOOLS

CITY OF PALM BEACH GARDENS

(PALM BEACH GARDENS), CATHEDRAL OF ST. IGNATIUS LOYOLA (1984) Very Rev. Thomas E. Barrett, Rector; Revs. Edgar Mazariegos; Paul Chung Nguyen.

Res.: 9999 N. Military Tr., 33410. Tel: 561-622-2565; Fax: 561-624-9489. Web: www.stignatiuspb.com. Email: office@stignatiuspb.com.

See All Saints Catholic School, Jupiter under Interparochial Schools located in the Institution section.

Catechesis/Religious Program—Students 242.

OUTSIDE THE CITY OF PALM BEACH GARDENS

BELLE GLADE, PALM BEACH CO., ST. PHILIP BENIZI (1961) Revs. Joseph Santa-Bibiana, S.D.B.; Omar Oswaldo Guillen, S.D.B.; Bro. Robert Malusa, S.D.B., Youth Ministry.

Res.: 710 S. Main St., 33430-4202. Tel: 561-996-3870; Fax: 561-996-1281. Email: philip710@comcast.net.

Catechesis/Religious Program—Tel: 561-996-5928; Fax: 561-996-1281. Students 393.

BOCA RATON, PALM BEACH CO.

1—ASCENSION (1968) Revs. Charles Hawkins; Peter Van Nguyen; Deacon Lon Phillips.

Res.: 7250 N. Federal Hwy., 33487-1606. Tel: 561-997-5486; Fax: 561-997-5862. Email: ascensioncatholicchurch@ascensioncatholicchurch.net. Web: ascensioncatholicchurch.net.

Catechesis/Religious Program—Students 160.

2—ST. JOAN OF ARC (1956) Rev. Msgr. Michael D. McGraw, M.Ss.A.; Revs. Jimmy Hababag (Philippines); Tomasz Bochnak; Deacon William Watzek.

Res.: 370 S.W. 3rd St., 33432. Tel: 561-392-0007; Fax: 561-392-0074. Web: www.stjoan.org.

School—501 S.W. 3rd Ave., 33432. Tel: 561-392-7974; Fax: 561-368-6671. Sr. Ellen Murphy, R.S.M., Prin. Sisters 3; Lay Teachers 30; Students 563.

Catechesis/Religious Program—Tel: 561-391-4345; Fax: 561-962-6002. Students 641.

Convent—500 S.W. 4th Ave., 33432. Tel: 561-368-6655 (Sisters of Mercy).

3—ST. JOHN THE EVANGELIST (1992) Rev. Michael O'Flaherty.

Res.: 10300 Yamato Rd., 33498. Tel: 561-488-1373; Fax: 561-488-5562. Email: stjohnbocaraton@bellsouth.net.

Catechesis/Religious Program—Students 405.

4—ST. JUDE (1979) Very Rev. Michael Kissane, O.Carm; Revs. Richard Champigny, O.Carm.; Guy Fiano, O.Carm. In Res., Rev. Michael Driscoll, O.Carm.

Church: 21689 Toledo Rd., 33433. Tel: 561-392-8172. Web: www.stjudeboca.org.

Rectory & Priory: 2235 S.W. 16th Pl., 33486-8560. Tel: 561-750-1937.

Early Learning Center—Tel: 561-392-9579; Fax: 561-362-0845. Total Staff 7; Students 50.

School—Tel: 561-392-9160; Fax: 561-392-5815. Miss Debbie Armstrong, Prin. & Preschool Dir. Lay Teachers 36; Students 305.

Catechesis/Religious Program—Tel: 561-362-8597; Fax: 561-362-0845. Email: linda@stjudeboca.org. Students 65.

5—OUR LADY OF LOURDES (1977) Rev. Francis Reardon.

Res.: 22094 Lyons Rd., 33428. Tel: 561-483-2440.

Catechesis/Religious Program—Tel: 561-483-2440, Ext. 1429; Fax: 561-558-1434. Email: rdannunzio@lourdesboca.org. Students 675.

BOYNTON BEACH, PALM BEACH CO.

1—ST. MARK (1952) Revs. Richard T. Florek, O.F.M.Conv.; Samuel Zebron, O.F.M.Conv.; Germain Kopaczynski, O.F.M.Conv.; Sr. Mary Joan Millecan, Contact Person, St. Mark Pastoral Care.

Res. & St. Mark Pastoral Care: 643 St. Mark Pl., 33435. Tel: 561-734-9330; 561-735-3530 (Pastoral

Care); Fax: 561-735-3463.
School—730 N.E. 6th Ave., 33435. Tel: 561-732-9934; Fax: 561-732-0501. Dr. Joseph Finley, Prin. Lay Teachers 28; Students 196.
Catechesis/Religious Program—Students 200.

2—ST. THOMAS MORE (1972) Revs. Julian P. Harris; Alex J. Vargas; Peter Truong; Deacons William Cresswell; Silvio Menendez; Mark Lizardi; Gerard Palermo.
Res.: 10935 S. Military Tr., 33436. Tel: 561-737-3095; Fax: 561-737-8697. Web: stmbb.org.
School—Thomas More Preschool, Tel: 561-737-3770. Adriana Palazzi, Dir.
Catechesis/Religious Program—Tel: 561-737-3521; Fax: 561-737-3596. Email: formationdirector@stmbb.org. Students 522.

DELRAY BEACH, PALM BEACH CO.

1—EMMANUEL (1983) Revs. Timothy Sockol; Raymond P. Hubert, Pastor Emeritus (Retired).
Res.: 15700 S. Military Tr., 33484. Tel: 561-496-2480; Fax: 561-496-5755.
Catechesis/Religious Program—Students 88.

2—OUR LADY OF PERPETUAL HELP MISSION (1987) Rev. Roland Desormeaux, C.S.
Church & Res.: 510 S.W. Eighth Ave., 33444-2448. Tel: 561-276-4880; Fax: 561-276-7036. Email: perpetualchurch@aol.com.
Catechesis/Religious Program—Students 149.

3—OUR LADY QUEEN OF PEACE (1963) Revs. Carlos Anklan, C.S.; Vincenzo Ronchi, C.S. In Res., Rev. Hector Sartori, C.S.
Res.: 9600 W. Atlantic Ave., 33446. Tel: 561-499-6234; Fax: 561-499-5513. Email: hanklan@aol.com. Web: www.queenofpeacemission.org.
Catechesis/Religious Program—Students 327.

4—ST. VINCENT FERRER (1941) Very Rev. Canon Thomas J. Skindeleski; Rev. Danis Ridore (Canada); Deacons Lee Levenson; Joseph Nick Nowak; Bruce Turnbull; Keith Skinner.
Res.: 840 George Bush Blvd., 33483. Tel: 561-276-6892; Fax: 561-276-8068. Email: svfoffice@bellsouth.net. Web: www.stvincentferrer.com.
School—810 George Bush Blvd., 33483. Tel: 561-278-3868; Fax: 561-279-9508. Mrs. M. Vikki Delgado, Prin. Little Servant Sisters of the Immaculate Conception 3; Lay Teachers 25; Students 240.
Catechesis/Religious Program—Tel: 561-279-8041; Fax: 561-276-6274. Students 133.

FELLSMERE, INDIAN RIVER CO., OUR LADY OF GUADALUPE MISSION (1991) Revs. John Morrissey; Ducasse Francois (Haiti).
Catechesis/Religious Program—Students 168.
Mission— Rte. 512, P.O. Box 9, Indian River Co. 32948. Tel: 772-571-9875; Fax: 772-571-8321. Email: olg@bellsouth.net.

FORT PIERCE, ST. LUCIE CO.

1—ST. ANASTASIA (1911) Revs. Richard E. George II; Mark Mlay, A.L.C.P. (Tanzania).
Res.: 407 S. 33rd St., 34947. Tel: 772-461-2233; Fax: 772-461-2242. Web: www.stanastasiachurch.org.
School—401 S. 33 St., 34947. Tel: 772-461-2232; Fax: 772-468-2037. Email: info@stanna.org. Web: www.stanna.org. Dr. Kevin Hoeffner, Prin. Lay Teachers 41; Students 506.
Catechesis/Religious Program—Email: stanastasiayouth@gmail.com (Youth); susanoconnor2010@gmail.com (Religious Ed.). Students 60.

2—ST. MARK THE EVANGELIST (1972) Revs. Michael J. McNally; Camillus Temba, A.L.C.P.; Deacon Paul Lauer.
Res.: 1924 Zephyr Ave., 34982. Tel: 772-461-8150; Fax: 772-464-2367. Email: stmarkssecretary@bellsouth.com.
Catechesis/Religious Program—Tel: 772-464-8955. Email: drestmark@bellsouth.net. Students 84.

3—NOTRE DAME MISSION (1995) Revs. Richard E. George II; Yves Geffrard (Haiti).
Res.: 217 N. U.S. Hwy. #1, 34950. Tel: 561-466-9617; Fax: 561-466-4075.
Catechesis/Religious Program—Tel: 772-335-9540. Students 24.

HIGHLAND BEACH, PALM BEACH CO., ST. LUCY (1968) Rev. Gerald Grace.
Res.: 3510 S. Ocean Blvd., 33487. Tel: 561-278-1280; Fax: 561-278-8509. Email: stlucys@bellsouth.net.
Catechesis/Religious Program—Students 6.

HOBE SOUND, MARTIN CO., ST. CHRISTOPHER (1960) Very Rev. Aidan Hynes.
Res.: 12001 S.E. Federal Hwy., 33455. Tel: 772-546-5150; Fax: 772-546-8820. Email: office@stchrishobesound.com. Web: stchrishobesound.com.
See All Saints Catholic School, Jupiter under Interparochial Schools located in the Institution section.
Catechesis/Religious Program—Students 230.

INDIANTOWN, MARTIN CO., HOLY CROSS (1960) Revs. Francisco Osorio; Juan de la Calle, Pastor Emeritus.
Mailing Address: 15927 S.W. 150th St., P.O. Box 999, 34956. Tel: 772-597-2798; Fax: 772-597-2741. Email: holcros1@itspeed.net.
Res.: 15670 Famel Blvd., 34956. Tel: 772-597-3935.
Catechesis/Religious Program—Students 192.

JENSEN BEACH, MARTIN CO., ST. MARTIN DE PORRES (1973) Revs. James Molgano; Thomas J. Rynne, Pastor Emeritus (Retired); Marco Tulio DeLeon.
Res.: 2555 N.E. Savanna Rd., 34957. Tel: 772-334-4214; Fax: 772-334-8627. Email: info@stmartindp.com. Web: www.stmartindp.com.
Catechesis/Religious Program—Tel: 772-334-4492. Email: info@stmartindp.com. Students 143.

JUPITER, PALM BEACH CO., ST. PETER (1987) Revs. Donald T. Finney; Sabas Mallya; Raciel Trevino; Deacons Stephen McMahon; Donald Battison; Joseph Pollock; Byron Champagne; Stephen Scienzo.
Res.: 1701 Indian Creek Pkwy., 33458. Tel: 561-575-0837; Fax: 561-575-6784. Email: parish@stpetercatholicchurch.com. Web: stpetercatholicchurch.com.
See All Saints Catholic School, Jupiter under Interparochial Schools located in the Institution section.
Catechesis/Religious Program—Students 570.

LAKE WORTH, PALM BEACH CO.

1—ST. MATTHEW (1992) Rev. Clemens Hammerschmitt.
Res. & Mailing: 6090 Hypoluxo Rd., 33463-7312. Tel: 561-966-8878; Fax: 561-968-1238.
Catechesis/Religious Program—Tel: 561-966-1538. Students 287.

2—SACRED HEART (1917) Revs. Joseph M. Papes; Peter Van Nguyen, Pastor Emeritus; Quesnel Delvard, S.D.B.
Res.: 425 N. M St., 33460. Tel: 561-582-4736; Fax: 561-588-5238.
School—410 N. M St., 33460. Tel: 561-582-2242; Fax: 561-547-9699. Candace Tamposi, Prin. Sisters 1; Lay Teachers 19; Students 185.
Catechesis/Religious Program—Tel: 561-582-4736, Ext. 200. Students 111.

LANTANA, PALM BEACH CO., HOLY SPIRIT (1964) Revs. Kevin Nelson; Ronald Schulz, Pastor Emeritus (Retired).
Res. and Mailing: 1000 Lantana Rd., P.O. Box 3978, 33465. Tel: 561-585-5970; Fax: 561-575-8482. Email: hspiritlantana@gmail.com. Web: holyspiritlantana.com.
Catechesis/Religious Program—Tel: 561-585-5970, Ext. 301. Students 126.

NORTH PALM BEACH, PALM BEACH CO.

1—ST. CLARE (1960) Revs. William D. O'Shea; Giuseppe Savaia.
Res.: 821 Prosperity Farms Rd., 33408. Tel: 561-622-7477; Fax: 561-624-0022. Email: stclare821@aol.com.
School—Tel: 561-622-7171; Fax: 561-627-4426. Web: stclareschool.com. Mr. Andrew J. Houvouras, Prin. Lay Teachers 31; Students 413.
Catechesis/Religious Program—Students 102.

2—ST. PAUL OF THE CROSS (1970) Rev. Arthur Venezia.
Res.: 10970 Jack Nicklaus Dr., 33408. Tel: 561-626-1873; Fax: 561-626-4383. Email: paulcross@bellsouth.net. Web: paulcross.org.
See All Saints Catholic School, Jupiter under Interparochial Schools located in the Institution section.
Catechesis/Religious Program—Email: joanné reled@bellsouth.net. Students 134.

OKEECHOBEE, OKEECHOBEE CO., SACRED HEART (1964) Rev. Hugh Duffy.
Mailing Address: P.O. Box 716, 34973.
Res.: 901 S.W. 6th St., 34974. Tel: 863-763-3727; Fax: 863-763-9334. Email: heartokeechobee@earthlink.net.
Catechesis/Religious Program—Tel: 863-763-2745. Students 535.

PAHOKEE, PALM BEACH CO., ST. MARY (1933) Rev. John J. Mericantante.
Res.: 1200 E. Main St., 33476. Tel: 561-924-7305; Fax: 561-924-9394. Web: www.stmaryofpahokee.com.
Catechesis/Religious Program—Tel: 561-924-5888. Students 161.

PALM BEACH, PALM BEACH CO., ST. EDWARD (1926) Rev. Msgr. Thomas J. Klinzing.
Res.: 144 N. County Rd., 33480. Tel: 561-832-0400; Fax: 561-833-3359.
Catechesis/Religious Program—Students 67.

PALM BEACH GARDENS, PALM BEACH CO., ST. PATRICK (1987) Revs. Brian Flanagan; Brian Campbell.
Res.: 13591 Prosperity Farms Rd., 33410. Tel: 561-626-8626; Fax: 561-622-6471. Email: stpatpbg@yahoo.com. Web: www.stpatrickchurch.org.
Rectory—2549 Hope Ln. W., 33410.
See All Saints Catholic School, Jupiter under Interparochial Schools located in the Institution section.
Catechesis/Religious Program—Students 170.

PALM CITY, MARTIN CO., HOLY REDEEMER (1983) Revs. Martin B. Mulqueen; John A. Kasparek.
Mailing Address: P.O. Box 916, 34991. Web: www.holyredeemercc.org.
Catechesis/Religious Program—Tel: 772-463-1579; Fax: 772-286-8792. Email: religed@holyredeemercc.org. Students 560.

PALM SPRINGS, PALM BEACH CO., ST. LUKE (1961) Rev. Adrian Torres. In Res., Revs. Thomas LaFreniere; Elifete St. Forte.
Res.: 2892 S. Congress Ave., 33461. Tel: 561-965-8980; Fax: 561-965-1384. Email: parish@st.lukeparish.com. Web: www.stlukeparish.com.
School—Tel: 561-965-8190; Fax: 561-965-2404. Suzanne Sandelier, Prin. Lay Teachers 12; Students 178.
Catechesis/Religious Program—Tel: 561-965-8190, Ext. 212. Students 604.

PORT ST. LUCIE, ST. LUCIE CO.

1—ST. BERNADETTE (2001) Revs. Victor A. Ulto; Son Linh Hoang; Deacons Edward Breitfelder; Steven Dove.
Church: 350 N.W. California Blvd., 34986. Tel: 772-336-9956; Fax: 772-336-5266. Email: stbernadetteslw@aol.com. Web: stbernadettescatholicchurch.org.
Catechesis/Religious Program—Students 308.

2—ST. ELIZABETH ANN SETON (1993) Revs. Edmund L. Szpieg; Carl Hellwig.
Church: 930 S.W. Tunis Ave., 34953-3351. Tel: 772-336-0282; Fax: 772-336-1494.
Catechesis/Religious Program—Tel: 772-336-0363; Fax: 772-336-1494. Students 435.

3—HOLY FAMILY (1987) Revs. Thomas F. Cauley; Eduardo Medina.
Mailing Address: 2330 Mariposa Ave., 34952. Tel: 772-335-2385; Fax: 772-335-2517.
Catechesis/Religious Program—Tel: 772-337-4313. Students 367.

4—ST. LUCIE (1961) Rev. Mark Szanyi, O.F.M.Conv.; Rev. Msgr. James M. Burke, Pastor Emeritus (Retired); Revs. Peter C. Dolan, Pastor Emeritus (Retired); Michael Englert, O.F.M.Conv.; Vincent Rubino, O.F.M.Conv.; Deacons Richard Moser; Carlos Melendez.
Res.: 425 S.W. Irving St., 34983. Tel: 772-878-1215; Fax: 772-878-1299. Web: www.stlucie.cc.
Catechesis/Religious Program—290 S.W. Prima Vista, Port Saint Lucie, 34983. Students 388.

RIVIERA BEACH, PALM BEACH CO., ST. FRANCIS OF ASSISI (1948) Revs. Arthur Obin, O.M.I.; Gilmond Boucher, O.M.I.; Deacon Richard Lyles.
Res.: 200 W. 20th St., 33404-6160. Tel: 561-842-2482; Fax: 561-863-2985.
Catechesis/Religious Program—Students 10.

ROYAL PALM BEACH, PALM BEACH CO., OUR LADY QUEEN OF THE APOSTLES (1988) Revs. Zbigniew A. Rudnicki; Laurent Assenga, A.L.C.P.; Deacons Stephen Hayes; Luis J. Castellanos.
Res.: 100 Crestwood Blvd. S., 33411. Tel: 561-798-5661; Fax: 561-798-5663. Web: www.olqa.cc.
Catechesis/Religious Program—Students 470.

SEBASTIAN, INDIAN RIVER CO., ST. SEBASTIAN (1981) Revs. John Morrissey; Ducasse Francois (Haiti); Deacon Steven Guess.
Mailing Address: 13075 U.S. Hwy. 1, 32978. Tel: 772-589-5790; Fax: 772-388-0084. Email: office@stsebastian.com. Web: www.stsebastian.com.
Catechesis/Religious Program—Tel: 772-589-4147. Students 170.

STUART, MARTIN CO.

1—ST. ANDREW (1999) Rev. John A. Barrow.
Church & Mailing: 2100 S.E. Cove Rd., 34997. Tel: 772-781-4415; Fax: 772-781-2906.
Catechesis/Religious Program—Students 80.

2—ST. JOSEPH (1916) Revs. Noel McGrath (Ireland); Juan Raul Cardenas; Albert Dello Russo.
Res.: 1200 E. 10th St., 34996. Tel: 772-287-2727; Fax: 772-287-4998. Email: noelm@sjcflorida.org. Web: sjcflorida.org.
School—Tel: 772-287-6975; Fax: 772-287-4733. Mrs. Mary Preston, Prin. Lay Teachers 30; Students 295.
Catechesis/Religious Program—Tel: 772-287-2727, Ext. 109. Jeanne Caron, D.R.E. Students 281.

TEQUESTA, PALM BEACH CO., ST. JUDE (1962) Very Rev. Charles E. Notabartolo; Revs. Thomas Vengayil, Pastor Emeritus; Benedict Ndeyekiyo Mosha, A.L.C.P. (Tanzania).
Mailing Address: P.O. Box 3726, 33469.
Res.: 204 U.S. Hwy. One, 33469. Tel: 561-746-7974; Fax: 561-743-6127. Email: infostjude@bellsouth.net. Web: www.stjudecatholicchurch.com.
See All Saints Catholic School, Jupiter under Interparochial Schools located in the Institution section.
Catechesis/Religious Program—Tel: 561-746-1890; Fax: 561-743-6127. Students 206.

VERO BEACH, INDIAN RIVER CO.

1—ST. HELEN (1919) Very Rev. Michael W. Edwards;

Rev. Msgr. Irvine Nugent, Pastor Emeritus (Retired); Revs. Tri Pham; Jean Wesner Boulin.
Res.: 2085 Tallahassee Ave., P.O. Box 2927, 32961. Tel: 772-567-5129; Fax: 772-567-1061. Email: sthelenchurch@hotmail.com. Web: sthelenvero.org.
School—2050 Vero Beach Ave., 32960. Tel: 772-567-5457; Fax: 772-567-4823. Howard Avril, Prin. Lay Teachers 16; Students 233.
Catechesis/Religious Program—2025 20th Ave., 32960. Tel: 772-562-5954; Fax: 772-562-2209. Email: sthelenre@bellsouth.net. Students 218.

2—HOLY CROSS (1981) Revs. Richard Murphy; Michael Massaro, C.S.C.; John B. O'Hare, Pastor Emeritus (Retired).
Res.: 500 Iris Ln., 32963. Tel: 772-231-0671; Fax: 772-234-5653.
Catechesis/Religious Program—Students 178.

3—ST. JOHN OF THE CROSS (1989) Revs. John J. Pasquini; John A. Crowley, Pastor Emeritus (Retired); David C. Downey; Deacons Charles Mallory; Eugene Hoch; Joseph Verboys.
Res.: 7550 26th St., 32966. Tel: 772-563-0057; Fax: 772-563-9176.
Catechesis/Religious Program—Email: stjohnofthecross@bellsouth.net. Students 54.

WELLINGTON, PALM BEACH CO.

1—ST. RITA (1980) Revs. Donald Munro; Yves Francois; Michael Parrotta (FAR) (Retired). In Res.,
Res.: 13645 Paddock Dr., 33414. Tel: 561-793-8544; Fax: 561-793-4082. Email: saintrita@bellsouth.net. Web: www.saintrita.com.
Catechesis/Religious Program—Whole Community Catechesis Faith Formation, Tel: 561-795-4321; Fax: 561-795-5478. Email: stritadonna@bellsouth.net. Students 950.

2—ST. THERESE DE LISIEUX (2000) Rev. Brian Lehnert; Deacons Alfred C. Payne; Robert Rodriguez.
Mailing Address: 11800 Lake Worth Rd., 33449.
Rectory—3760 Cypress Edge Dr., Lake Worth, 33467. Tel: 561-784-0689; Fax: 561-784-8346.
Catechesis/Religious Program—Students 426.

WEST PALM BEACH, PALM BEACH CO.

1—ST. ANN (1895) Revs. Nestor Rodriguez; James Murtagh, Pastor Emeritus (Retired); John D'Mello; Andre Dumarsais Pierre-Louis.
Our Lady Faith Haitian Center—Tel: 561-805-7712.
Res.: 310 N. Olive Ave., 33401. Tel: 561-832-3757; Fax: 561-659-1465.
School—Tel: 561-832-3676; Fax: 561-832-1791. Dr. Patrice A. Scheffler, Prin. Lay Teachers 19; Students 244.
Catechesis/Religious Program—Tel: 561-832-3676, Ext. 315; Fax: 561-659-7024. Students 65.
St. Ann Place Outreach to the Homeless—2107 N. Dixie Hwy., 33407. Tel: 561-805-7708. Sr. Carleen Cekal, S.S.N.D., Dir.

2—HOLY NAME OF JESUS (1954) Revs. Gavin Badway; Andrew Brierley; Norbert Jean-Pierre (Haiti).
Res.: 345 S. Military Tr., 33415. Tel: 561-683-3555; Fax: 561-683-1051. Email: hnjchurch@aol.com. Web: www.holynameofjesuschurch.net.
School—Tel: 561-683-2990; Fax: 561-683-0803. Web: holynameofjesusschool.org. Michael Smith, Prin. Lay Teachers 10; Students 168.
Catechesis/Religious Program—Tel: 561-683-3555, Ext. 111. Email: sranne@holynameofjesuschurch.net. Students 454.

3—ST. JOHN FISHER (1963) Rev. Mario Castaneda.
Res.: 4001 N. Shore Dr., 33407. Tel: 561-842-1224; Fax: 561-842-8750. Email: stjohnfisher4001@aol.com.
Catechesis/Religious Program—Students 44.

4—ST. JULIANA (1949) Very Rev. Alfredo Hernandez; Revs. Jose Crucet; Dominic Toan Tran.
Res.: 4500 S. Dixie Hwy., 33405. Tel: 561-833-9745; Fax: 561-833-4992. Web: www.stjulianacatholicchurch.com.
School—4355 S. Olive Ave, 33405. Tel: 561-655-1922; Fax: 561-655-8552. Email: info@saintjuliana.org. Web: www.saintjuliana.org. Dr. Serena Brasco, Prin. Lay Teachers 20; Students 229.
Catechesis/Religious Program—4514 S. Dixie Hwy., 33405. Tel: 561-833-1278; Fax: 561-833-4992. Students 374.

5—MARY IMMACULATE (1974) Rev. Tomasz Makowski.
Res.: 390 Sequoia Dr., 33409. Tel: 561-686-8128; Fax: 561-686-6893.
Catechesis/Religious Program—Students 67.

Released from Diocesan Assignment:
Revs.—
Gallagher, John, Evangelization study and writing
Guerin, Louis T., M.Div., St. Vincent de Paul Regional Seminary, Boynton Beach, 33436-4899.
Lacy, Aidan, St. Mary's Medical Center, P.O. Box 24620, 33416-4620.
O'Flanagan, Thomas P., US Navy Chap.
O'Toole, Timothy, Cross International Catholic Outreach

Retired:
Rev. Msgrs.—
Burke, James M.
McMahon, John
Nugent, Irvine
Revs.—
Block, John G.
Calle, Juan de la
Christopher, Mark
Crowley, John A.
Devereaux, Martin C.
Dockerill, Walter
Dolan, Peter C.
Guinan, Frank
Hubert, Raymond P.
Kuczborski, Joseph
MacGabhann, Kevin
Murphy, Richard
Murtagh, James
O'Hare, John B.
O'Loughlin, Frank
Profeta, Salvatore
Rynne, Thomas J.
Schulz, Ronald
Skehan, John A.

Permanent Deacons:
Ambroise, Emile
Baker, Philip
Barbaro, Sam
Bartlett, Matthew
Battison, Donald
Beaudoin, John
Beres, Ronald
Blake, Richard
Bloom, David
Bott, Gerald
Breitfelder, Edward
Brooks, James
Caceres, Edgard
Castellanes, Luis
Champagne, Byron
Crary, Lawrence
Creelman, Wayne
Cresswell, William
Culhane, Neil
Cunningham, John
Cuseo, Anthony
deGroat, Charles
Delgado, Alberto
Demes, Dennis T., Ph.D.
DiMauro, Joseph
Dingee, Richard
Dove, Steven
Draughon, Woodworth R., Jr.
Ervin, Martin
Fathauer, Ronald
Ferguson, William
Fischer, Edward
Garamella, Robert
Gaucher, Paul
Gluhosky, Frank
Golden, Robert
Guess, Steven
Hamilton, Jack
Hankle, David
Hayes, Stephen
Hoch, Eugene
Jacobs, William
Klimazewski, Norbert
Lacey, James
Lauer, Paul
Levenson, Lee
Lizardi, Mark
Loafman, Frank
Loh, Lester
Lopez, Jesus
Lucente, Salvatore
Lyles, Richard
Mallory, Charles
Mancuso, Terry
Mares, Jose Antonio
Mazzella, Peter
McBride, Peter
McMahon, Stephen
Melendez, Carlos
Menendez, Silvio
Meyer, James
Mintern, Michael
Moser, Richard
Mostler, John
Munoz, Miguel
Murray, Paul
Nowak, Nick
O'Connell, Joseph
Ortiz, Jose
Pagliara, Daniel
Palermo, Gerard
Parlee, Charles W.
Parrilli, James
Payne, Alfred C.
Phillips, Lon
Pierce, Jack
Plucinski, Andrew
Pollock, Joseph
Pope, Robert
Powell, David R.
Raisch, Jack
Rich, William
Rivera, Angel
Rodriguez, Robert
Santana, Richard
Sawney, Ira (Grenada)
Schopfer, Richard
Scienzo, Stephen
Seppanen, Henry
Serraes, Martin
Sherman, Gregory
Skinner, Keith
Sullivan, John
Turnbull, Bruce
Venezia, Richard
Verboys, Joseph
Voegele, Richard
Watzek, William
Weir, Charles
Wesley, Albert
Whalen, Charles
White, George
Zapata, Jaime
Zatarga, Michael

INSTITUTIONS LOCATED IN THE DIOCESE

[A] SEMINARIES, RELIGIOUS OR SCHOLASTICATES

BOYNTON BEACH. *St. Vincent de Paul Regional Seminary*, 10701 S. Military Tr., 33436. Tel: 561-732-4424; Fax: 561-737-2205. Web: svdp.edu. Rev. Msgr. Keith R. Brennan, J.C.D. (STA), Rector & Pres.; Rev. Steven Olds, S.T.D. (ORL), Dean Spiritual Formation; Rev. Msgr. Andrew Anderson, J.C.D. (MIA); Dr. Sixto Garcia, Ph.D.; Dr. Antonio Lopez, Ph.D.; Mr. Art Quinn, B.A., M.A., M.S., Ed.S., Library Dir.; Most Rev. Raymond Lessard, D.D., S.T.L., J.C.L.; Rev. Msgr. Michael Muhr, S.P., M.Div., M.A.; Revs. Jose Juan Quijano, S.T.L., S.T.D. (MIA); Louis T. Guerin, M.Div., Dean Pastoral Formation; Jose N. Alfaro (MIA), Vice Rector, Dean of Students, Human Formation; Michael J. Flynn, M.Div., S.T.L. (PT), Liturgy Dir.; Sr. Margarita Gomez, R.M.I., S.T.L., D.Min.; Dr. Emilio Chavez, S.T.D., Ph.D.; Dr. Carol Razza, Ed.D.; Mr. Stanton Cadow, Dir., Inst. Devel.; Mr. Keith Parker, Campus Admin.; Dr. Joyce Martinez, B.A., M.Ed., Ed.D., Dir. Language; Revs. William L. Burton, O.F.M.; Jeremiah L. Payne (ORL); Deacon Dennis T. Demes, Ph.D., Academic Dean.

[B] HIGH SCHOOLS, DIOCESAN AND PAROCHIAL

BOCA RATON. *Pope John Paul II High School, Inc.*, 4001 N. Military Tr., 33431. Tel: 561-314-2100; Fax: 561-989-8582. Email: pjphs@pjpii.org. Web: www.pjpii.org. Dr. Michael J. Coury, Pres.; Sr. Eileen Sullivan, O.P., Prin.; Ms. Diane DeMarco, Campus Min.; Mr. Christopher Kilian, Asst. Prin.; Mrs. Susan Hanley, Media Specialist. Sisters 2; Lay Teachers 41; Students 475.

FORT PIERCE. *John Carroll High School, Inc.* (1962) 3402 Delaware Ave., 34947-6116. Tel: 772-464-5200; Fax: 772-464-5233. Email: jcchs@johncarrollhigh.com. Web: www.johncarrollhigh.com. Very Rev. Thomas E. Barrett, Pres.; Mr. Ben C. Hopper, Prin.; Elaine Welker, Media Specialist. Priests 1; Lay Teachers 30; Students 420.

WEST PALM BEACH. *Cardinal Newman High School, Inc.*, 512 Spencer Dr., 33409-3616. Tel: 561-683-6266; Fax: 561-683-7307. Email: jclarke@cardinalnewman.com. Web: www.cardinalnewman.com. Rev. David W. Carr, Pres.; John F. Clarke, Prin.; Ms. Susan Stephenson, Asst. Prin. Student Life; Ms. Theresa Fretterd, Asst. Prin. Academics; Rev. Andre Dumarsais Pierre-Louis, Chap.; Nelle Martin, Media Specialist. Priests 3; Lay Teachers 48; Students 575.

[C] INTERPAROCHIAL SCHOOLS

JUPITER. *All Saints Catholic School*, 1759 Indian Creek Pkwy., 33458. Tel: 561-748-8994; Fax: 561-748-8979. Email: ascs@allsaintsjupiter.org. Web: www.allsaintsjupiter.org. Mrs. Mary Beth Quick, Prin.; Mrs. Kim Maihack, Librarian. Lay Teachers 33; Total Enrollment 438.

[D] SCHOOLS, PRIVATE

INDIANTOWN. *Hope Rural School*, (Grades PreK-5), 15929 S.W. 150th St., 34956. Tel: 772-597-2203; Fax: 772-597-2259. Email: hopesch@onearrow.net. Sisters Mary Dooley, S.S.N.D., Dir.; Katherine Kinnally, S.S.N.D., Prin. Sisters 2; Lay Teachers 11; Students 126.

WEST PALM BEACH. *Holy Cross Catholic Preschool & Center*, 930 Southern Blvd., 33405. Tel: 561-366-8026; Fax: 561-366-8577. Email: holycrosscpc@aol.com. Ana M. Fundora, Exec. Dir. Sisters 2; Lay Teachers 19; Students 90.

**Rosarian Academy*, (Grades PreK-8), 807 N. Flagler Dr., 33401. Tel: 561-832-5131; Fax: 561-820-8750. Email: info@rosarian.org. Web: www.rosarian.org. Virginia Devine, Prin.; Betty Sayer, Librarian. Sisters of St. Dominic (Adrian, MI). Sisters 3; Lay Teachers 45; Students 355.

[E] GENERAL HOSPITALS

WEST PALM BEACH. *St. Mary's Hospital, Inc.*, 901 45th St., 33407-2495. Affiliated Support Organizations: *Women's Health Services, Inc.*

[F] HOMES FOR AGED

WEST PALM BEACH. *Lourdes-Noreen McKeen Residence for Geriatric Care*, 315 Flagler Dr. S., 33401. Tel: 561-655-8544; Fax: 561-650-8952. Web: www.lnmr.org. Sr. Mary Anne Dennehy, O.Carm., Admin.; Rev. Chinnappan M. Devaraj, O.F.M., Chap.

[G] PERSONAL PRELATURES

DELRAY BEACH. *Prelature of the Holy Cross and Opus Dei*, 4409 Frances Dr., 33445. Tel: 561-498-1249; Fax: 561-498-0054. Rev. Victor Cortes.

[H] MONASTERIES AND RESIDENCES OF PRIESTS AND BROTHERS

NORTH PALM BEACH. *Our Lady of Florida Spiritual Center*, 1300 U.S. Hwy. No. 1, 33408. Tel: 561-626-1300; Fax: 561-627-3956. Email: malbee@cpprov.org. Web: www.ourladyofflorida.org. Very Rev. Paul Wierichs, C.P., Dir.; Revs. Damian Towey, C.P., J.C.D.; Emmanuel Gardon, C.P.; Fidelis Connelly, C.P.; Patrick Daugherty, C.P.; John Connor, C.P. Priests 6.

VERO BEACH. *Paulist Fathers Residence*, 1225 20th Ave., 32960. Tel: 772-562-0500; Fax: 772-794-9810. Revs. William J. Cantwell, C.S.P.; James M. Brucz, C.S.P.; Michael J. Martin, C.S.P.

[I] CONVENTS AND RESIDENCES FOR SISTERS

DELRAY BEACH. *Christ the King Monastery of St. Clare* (Solemn Vows, Papal Enclosure), 3900 Sherwood Blvd., 33445-5655. Tel: 561-498-3294; Fax: 561-498-2281. Email: ctkmdelray@comcast.net. Sr. Leanna Chrostowski, O.S.C., Abbess. Cloistered Sisters 9.

STUART. *Congregation of the Sisters of the Most Holy Soul of Christ*, 1042 E. 9th St., 34996. Tel: 772-286-5720. Email: sschusa@yahoo.com. Web: sistersofthemostholysoulofchrist.com. Sr. Martina Bednarz, C.A.C.H., Supr.

WEST PALM BEACH. *Adrian Dominican Sisters, Florida Mission Chapter*, 810 N. Olive Ave., 33401-3710. Tel: 561-832-6521; Fax: 561-832-0365. Email: alees@adriandominicans.org. Web: www.adriandominicans.org. Sr. Anne Liam Lees, O.P., Chapter Prioress.

Congregation of the Sisters of the Holy Cross, 2335 Edgewater Dr., 33406. Tel: 561-434-7593.

[J] RETREAT HOUSES

LANTANA. *The Cenacle Spiritual Life Center*, 1400 S. Dixie Hwy., 33462-5492. Tel: 561-249-1621; Fax: 561-249-1623. Email: cenaclefl@aol.com. Web: www.cenaclesisters.org. Spiritual Life Center for laity and religious. Sisters 3.

NORTH PALM BEACH. *Our Lady of Florida Spiritual Center*, 1300 U.S. Hwy. No. 1, 33408. Tel: 561-626-1300; Fax: 561-627-3956. Email: malbee@cpprov.org. Web: www.ourladyofflorida.org.

[K] MISCELLANEOUS LISTINGS

PALM BEACH GARDENS. *Catholic Charities Foundation of the Diocese of Palm Beach, Inc.*, 9995 N. Military Tr., 33410.

Catholic Charities of the Diocese of Palm Beach, Inc., P.O. Box 109650, 34410-9650. 9995 N. Military Tr., 34410. Tel: 561-775-9560; Fax: 561-625-5906.

Con El, Inc., P.O. Box 109650, 33410-9650.

Diocesan Council of Catholic Women, c/o P.O. Box 109650, 33410. Rev. Clemens Hammerschmitt, Diocesan Moderator; Myrna Wong, Pres. Tel: 772-335-5160.

Diocese of Palm Beach, Inc., P.O. Box 109650, 33410-9650.

Diocese of Palm Beach Burse Fund Trust

Diocese of Palm Beach Endowment Trust

Diocese of Palm Beach Health Plan Trust Very Rev. Charles E. Notabartolo, V.G., Chm.; Rev. Louis T. Guerin, M.Div., Chm.

Diocesan Pension Plan Trust Very Rev. Charles E. Notabartolo, V.G., Chm.

Diocese of Palm Beach Savings Fund Trust, Diocese of Palm Beach, P.O. Box 109650, 33410-9650. Mr. Denis Hamel, Chm.

Diocesan Property & Liability Insurance Committee Rev. Richard Murphy, Chm.

The Florida Catholic of Palm Beach, Inc., P.O. Box 109650, 33410-9650. Linda Reeves, Editor.

Helping Hands Scholarship Fund, Diocese of Palm Beach, Tel: 561-775-9547. P.O. Box 109650, 33410-9650.

BOCA RATON. *Christ Child Society of Boca Raton*, P.O. Box 811025, 33481-1025. Tel: 561-482-3067; Fax: 561-482-3087. Email: agnesgreg@aol.com.

Cross International Catholic Outreach, Inc., 2700 N. Military Tr., 33432. Tel: 561-392-9212, Ext. 104; Fax: 561-367-0564. Email: info@crossinternational.org. Web: www.crosscatholic.org. Mailing Address: P.O. Box 273908, 33427-3908. Mr. James J. Cavnar, Pres.

Friends of Newman, Inc., 370 S.W. 3rd St., 33432.

BOYNTON BEACH. *St. Vincent de Paul Regional Seminary Endowment Trust*, 10701 S. Military Tr., 33436.

GREENACRES. *Villa Madonna*, 4809 Lake Worth Rd., 33463-3455. Tel: 561-963-1900; Fax: 561-963-1476. Email: villamadonnamgr@spm.net. Sharon VanGorder, Resident Mgr.

JENSEN BEACH. *Villa Assumpta, Inc.*, 2539 N.E. Mission Dr., 9-8, 34957. Tel: 561-334-0009; Fax: 561-334-2168. Email: villaassumptamgr@spm.net. Janice Foci, Resident Mgr.

NORTH PALM BEACH. *Christ Child Society of Palm Beach*, P.O. Box 14441, 33408. Tel: 561-795-0134. Email: mbishop110@aol.com.

PORT ST. LUCIE. *Villa Seton, Inc.*, 3300 S.W. Chartwell St., 34953. Tel: 772-344-6969; Fax: 772-344-7822. Email: villasetonmgr@spm.net. Peggy McShane, Resident Mgr.

RIVIERA BEACH. **St. Vincent de Paul Salvage Store of West Palm Beach, Inc.*, 2647 Old Dixie Hwy., West Palm Beach, 33404-4119. Tel: 561-967-9699. Email: svdppalmbeach@att.net. Richard Persek, Pres.

Villa Franciscan, Inc., 2101 Avenue F, 33404. Tel: 561-840-0444; Fax: 561-840-9444. Email: villafranciscanmgr@spm.net. Web: villafranciscan.catholicweb.com. John Bralich Jr., Resident Mgr.

STUART. *Christ Child Society of Stuart*, P.O. Box 2007, 34995. Tel: 772-299-7852. Cheryle Mackie, Pres.

VERO BEACH. **St. Sebastian Conference of St. Vincent de Paul Society, Inc.*, 5480 85th St., 32967-5544.

**St. Vincent de Paul Society of Indian River County, Incorporated*, 1745 14th Ave., 32960.

WELLINGTON. *Magnificat Palm Beach Center, Inc.*, 1420 Sailboat Cir., 33414. Tel: 561-793-0343; Fax: 561-793-0343. Diane Bailey, Treas.; Dr. Carol Razza, Ed.D., Coord.

WEST PALM BEACH. *Villa Regina*, 2660 Haverhill Rd. N., 33417. Tel: 561-478-3900; Fax: 561-478-9787. Email: villareginamgr@spm.net. Faye Crommell, Resident Mgr.

RELIGIOUS INSTITUTES OF MEN REPRESENTED IN THE DIOCESE

For further details refer to the corresponding bracketed number in the Religious Institutes of Men or Women section.

[]—*Apostolic Life Community of Priests in the Opus Spiritus Sancti* (Tanzania)—A.L.C.P.

[0030]—*Congregation of St. Paul*—C.S.P.

[0610]—*Congregation of the Holy Cross*—C.S.C.

[0650]—*Congregation of the Holy Ghost of Ireland*—C.S.Sp.

[1000]—*Congregation of the Passion*—C.P.

[0260]—*Discalced Carmelite Friars*—O.C.D.

[0520]—*Franciscan Friars* (Holy Name Prov.)—O.F.M.

[0470]—*Franciscan Friars, Capuchin (Province of St. Augustine)*—O.F.M.Cap.

[0480]—*Franciscans Friars, Conventual*—O.F.M.Conv.

[1210]—*Missionaries of St. Charles Borromeo*—C.S.

[0910]—*Oblates of Mary Immaculate*—O.M.I.

[0920]—*Oblates of St. Francis de Sales*—O.S.F.S.

[0270]—*Order of Carmelites*—O.Carm.

[1040]—*Piarist Fathers*—Sch.P.

[1190]—*Salesians of Don Bosco*—S.D.B.

[0690]—*Society of Jesus*—S.J.

[0370]—*Society of St. Columban*

[1060]—*Society of the Precious Blood*—C.PP.S.

RELIGIOUS INSTITUTES OF WOMEN REPRESENTED IN THE DIOCESE

[0330]—*Carmelite Sisters for the Aged and Infirm*—O.Carm.

[0685]—*Claretian Missionary Sisters*—R.M.I.

[3710]—*Congregation of St. Agnes*—C.S.A.

[1930]—*Congregation of the Sisters of the Holy Cross*—C.S.C.

[1710]—*Congregation of the Third Order of St. Francis of Mary Immaculate*—O.S.F.

[]—*Consecrated Virgin*—C.V.

[1070-03]—*Dominican Sisters* (Sinsinawa, WI)—O.P.

[1070-13]—*Dominican Sisters* (Adrian, MI)—O.P.

[]—*Dominican Sisters of Blawville* (New York)

[1070-16]—*Dominican Sisters of Hope*—O.P.

[]—*Dominican Sisters of Peace*

[1070-17]—*Dominican Sisters of St. Catherine de Ricci*—O.P.

[1180]—*Franciscan Sisters of Allegany, NY*—O.S.F.

[1845]—*Guadalupan Missionaries of the Holy Spirit*—M.G.Sp.S

[]—*Hermitage of the Diocese of Palm Beach*

[2300]—*Little Servant Sisters of the Immaculate Conception*

[2470]—*Maryknoll Sisters of St. Dominic*—M.M.

[2490]—*Medical Mission Sisters*—M.M.S.

[3760]—*Order of St. Clare*—O.S.C.

[3110]—*Religious of Our Lady of the Cenacle*—R.C.

[3465]—*Religious of the Sacred Heart of Mary*—R.S.H.M.

[2970]—*School Sisters of Notre Dame*—S.S.N.D.

[]—*Sisters for Christian Community*—S.F.C.C.

[0590]—*Sisters of Charity of St. Elizabeth* (Convent Station, NJ)—S.C.

[2110]—*Sisters of Humility of Mary*—H.M.

[2560]—*Sisters of Mary Reparatrix*—S.M.R.

[2520]—*Sisters of Mercy* (Dublin, Ireland)—R.S.M.

[2575]—*Sisters of Mercy of the Americas*—R.S.M.

[1630]—*Sisters of St. Francis of Penance and Christian Charity*—O.S.F.

[3840]—*Sisters of St. Joseph of Carondelet*—C.S.J.

[3900]—*Sisters of St. Joseph of St. Augustine*—S.S.J.

[0260]—*Sisters of the Blessed Sacrament*—S.B.S.

[1990]—*Sisters of the Holy Names of Jesus and Mary*—S.N.J.M.

[]—*Sisters of the Most Holy Soul of Jesus*—C.A.C.H.

[2150]—*Sisters, Servants of the Immaculate Heart of Mary*—I.H.M.

DIOCESAN CEMETERIES

ROYAL PALM BEACH. *Our Lady Queen of Peace Catholic Cemetery, Inc.*, 10941 Southern Blvd., 33406. Tel: 561-793-0711; Fax: 561-793-0182. Email: info@ourqueen.org. Web: www.ourqueen.org. Rev. Zbigniew A. Rudnicki, Dir.; Mr. Thomas Jordan, Admin.

NECROLOGY

† Saporito, Rev. Msgr. Cosmo—Died 2011

† Fenech, Francis X., Lake Worth, FL Sacred Heart.—Died Jan. 27, 2011

† Lechiara, Francis J., Palm Beach, FL Saint Edward.—Died May 12, 2011

† Redden, Gerald Donald, Fort Pierce, FL San Juan Diego Pastoral Center.—Died May 20, 2011

An asterisk (*) denotes an organization that has established tax-exempt status directly with the IRS and is not covered by the USCCB Group Ruling.

Diocese of Paterson

(Dioecesis Patersonensis)

Most Reverend

ARTHUR J. SERRATELLI

Bishop of Paterson; ordained December 20, 1968; appointed Titular Bishop of Enera and Auxiliary Bishop of Newark July 3, 2000; Episcopal ordination September 8, 2000; appointed Bishop of Paterson June 1, 2004.

Most Reverend

FRANK J. RODIMER, D.D., J.C.D.

Retired Bishop of Paterson; ordained May 19, 1951; appointed Bishop of Paterson December 13, 1977; ordained and installed February 28, 1978; retired June 1, 2004. *Res.: 1082 Greenpond Rd., Green Pond, NJ 07435.*

Diocesan Center: 777 Valley Rd., Clifton, NJ 07013. Tel: 973-777-8818; Fax: 973-777-8976.

Web: www.patersondiocese.org

ESTABLISHED DECEMBER 9, 1937.

Square Miles 1,214.

Comprises the Counties of Passaic, Morris and Sussex in the State of New Jersey.

For legal titles of parishes and diocesan institutions, consult the Chancery Office.

STATISTICAL OVERVIEW

Personnel	
Bishop	1
Retired Bishops	1
Abbots	2
Retired Abbots	4
Priests: Diocesan Active in Diocese	147
Priests: Diocesan Active Outside Diocese	17
Priests: Retired, Sick or Absent	93
Number of Diocesan Priests	257
Religious Priests in Diocese	136
Total Priests in Diocese	393
Extern Priests in Diocese	20
Ordinations:	
Diocesan Priests	9
Transitional Deacons	6
Permanent Deacons in Diocese	207
Total Brothers	46
Total Sisters	710
Parishes	
Parishes	111
With Resident Pastor:	
Resident Diocesan Priests	92
Resident Religious Priests	7
Without Resident Pastor:	
Administered by Priests	12
Pastoral Centers	5
Professional Ministry Personnel:	
Brothers	1
Sisters	24
Lay Ministers	109
Welfare	
Catholic Hospitals	3
Total Assisted	1,001,000
Homes for the Aged	8
Total Assisted	440
Residential Care of Children	1
Total Assisted	70
Day Care Centers	5
Total Assisted	1,400
Specialized Homes	2
Total Assisted	1,500
Special Centers for Social Services	12
Total Assisted	70,000
Residential Care of Disabled	12
Total Assisted	90
Educational	
Seminaries, Diocesan	1
Students from This Diocese	11
Diocesan Students in Other Seminaries	46
Seminaries, Religious	2
Students Religious	6
Total Seminarians	63
Colleges and Universities	2
Total Students	2,043
High Schools, Diocesan and Parish	3
Total Students	2,274
High Schools, Private	4
Total Students	1,380
Elementary Schools, Diocesan and Parish	36
Total Students	8,355
Elementary Schools, Private	3
Total Students	565
Catechesis/Religious Education:	
High School Students	9,050
Elementary Students	32,586
Total Students under Catholic Instruction	56,316
Teachers in the Diocese:	
Priests	10
Brothers	6
Sisters	97
Lay Teachers	908
Vital Statistics	
Receptions into the Church:	
Infant Baptism Totals	6,585
Minor Baptism Totals	195
Adult Baptism Totals	148
Received into Full Communion	248
First Communions	6,727
Confirmations	5,140
Marriages:	
Catholic	897
Interfaith	170
Total Marriages	1,067
Deaths	3,164
Total Catholic Population	425,273
Total Population	1,142,767

Former Bishops—Most Revs. THOMAS H. MCLAUGHLIN, S.T.D., LL.D., cons. July 25, 1935; transferred to Paterson, Dec. 16, 1937; died March 17, 1947; THOMAS A. BOLAND, S.T.D., LL.D., cons. July 25, 1940; transferred to Paterson, June 21, 1947; transferred to Newark as Archbishop, Nov. 15, 1952; died March 16, 1979; JAMES A. MCNULTY, D.D., appt. Auxiliary Bishop of Newark, Aug. 2, 1947; cons. Oct. 7, 1947; appt. Bishop of Paterson, April 9, 1953; transferred to Diocese of Buffalo, Feb. 12, 1963; died Sept. 4, 1972; JAMES J. NAVAGH, D.D., cons. Sept. 24, 1952; appt. Bishop of Ogdensburg, May 8, 1957; transferred to Bishop of Paterson, Feb. 12, 1963; died Oct. 2, 1965; LAWRENCE B. CASEY, D.D., appt. Auxiliary Bishop of Rochester, Feb. 10, 1953; cons. May 5, 1953; appt. Bishop of Paterson, March 9, 1966; died June 15, 1977; FRANK J. RODIMER, D.D., J.C.D. (Retired), appt. Bishop of Paterson Dec. 13, 1977; ord. Feb. 28, 1978; resigned June 1, 2004.

Vicar General and Moderator of the Curia—Rev. Msgr. JAMES T. MAHONEY, Ph.D., V.G.

Chief Operating Officer—Mr. THOMAS A. BARRETT.

Chief Financial Officer—VACANT.

Episcopal Vicars—

Education—Rev. PAUL S. MANNING.

Evangelization—Rev. GENO SYLVA, S.T.D.

Pastoral Administration—Rev. HERNAN ARIAS.

Deans—Revs. ANTONIO RODRIGUEZ, Passaic; JOHN T. CONNOLLY, M.Div., Clifton; PHILIP A. LEBEAU, Northeast Morris; DARIUSZ K. KAMINSKI, Paterson; JOHN P. PILIPIE, Sussex; Rev. Msgrs. T. MARK CONDON, J.C.L., S.T.L., Mid-Passaic; JOSEPH J. GOODE, M.Ch.A., Southwest Morris; Revs. ROBERT J. MITCHELL, Southeast Morris; P. CHRISTOPHER MULDOON, Western Morris; JUDE S. SALUS, O.S.B., Eastern Morris; JOHN DEMATTIA, Northern Morris; Rev. Msgr. PATRICK G. PANOS, Northern Passaic.

Chancellor/Delegate for Religious—Sr. MARY EDWARD SPOHRER, S.C.C.

Vice Chancellors—Revs. MARC A. MANCINI, J.C.L.; KEVIN CORCORAN; Sr. CATHERINE MCDONNELL, O.P., (Urban Ministry).

Archivist—Rev. Msgr. RAYMOND J. KUPKE, Ph.D.

Priest Secretary to the Bishop—Rev. KEVIN CORCORAN.

Secretary to the Bishop—Mrs. BARBARA FIERRO.

Secretary to the Vicar General and Chancellor—Mrs. ARLINE PERRO.

Secretary to the Vice Chancellors—Mrs. KERRY TIMONEY.

Diocesan Counsel—KENNETH F. MULLANEY JR.

Diocesan Tribunal—

Judicial Vicar—Rev. Msgr. EDWARD J. KURTYKA, P.A., J.C.D.

Adjutant Judicial Vicar—Rev. Msgr. JOSEPH T. ANGINOLI, J.C.L.

Advocates—Revs. JOHN T. CONNOLLY, M.Div.; VINCENT B. GROGAN, O.F.M., J.C.D.

Auditors—Revs. JOHN P. HANLEY (Retired); MANUEL GUEVARA.

Defenders of the Bond—Rev. Msgrs. T. MARK CONDON, J.C.L., S.T.L.; GEORGE F. HUNDT, J.C.L.

Canonical Advisor—Rev. Msgr. JOSEPH J. GOODE, M.Ch.A.

Associate Judges—Revs. MARC A. MANCINI, J.C.L.; MICHAEL J. BURKE, S.T.M., J.D.; Rev. Msgr. JOHN J. CARROLL, Ed.D.; Rev. JOHN T. CATOIR, J.C.D. (Retired); Rev. Msgrs. JOHN E. HART; JOHN J. DEMKOVICH (Retired); HERBERT K. TILLYER, P.A., M.Ch.A.

Administrative Assistants and Notaries—Mrs. SHAWN VACCA; Mrs. MARY BETH LEONHARD.

Consulting Psychologists and Experts—Revs. RICHARD MUCOWSKI, O.F.M.; GREGORY A.

BATTAFARANO, O.Carm., M.S., L.P.C.; Mr. JOSEPH DE CHRISTOFANO, L.C.S.W.; Mrs. MARY DE CHRISTOFANO, M.S.W., L.C.S.W.

Minister to Priests—Rev. Msgr. PETER J. DOODY.

Vocations Office—737 Valley Rd., Clifton, 07013. Tel: 973-777-2955; Fax: 973-777-4597. Revs. HUBERT JURJEWICZ, Dir.; BENJAMIN WILLIAMS, Asst. Dir.

Vocations Board—Revs. HERNAN ARIAS; SIGMUND PEPLOWSKI; T. KEVIN CORCORAN; MARC A. MANCINI, J.C.L.

Consultative Bodies—

Presbyteral Council—Rev. Msgr. JOHN E. HART, Chm.; Revs. PATRICK RICE, Vice Chm.; DAVID MCDONNELL; EIDER REYES; Rev. Msgrs. LOUIS J. BIHR; JOHN J. CARROLL, Ed.D.; Revs. FRANK P. AGRESTI; BRIAN SULLIVAN; Rev. Msgrs. JAMES H. O'RORKE (Retired); GEORGE F. HUNDT, J.C.L.; JAMES T. MAHONEY, Ph.D., V.G.; Revs. MICHAEL RODAK; ANTONIO RODRIGUEZ; JUDE S. SALUS, O.S.B.

College of Consultors—Rev. Msgr. JOHN E. HART, Chm.; Revs. PATRICK RICE, Vice Chm.; DAVID MCDONNELL; Rev. Msgr. JAMES H. O'RORKE (Retired); Revs. EIDER REYES; MICHAEL RODAK; Rev. Msgr. LOUIS J. BIHR; Rev. BRIAN SULLIVAN; Rev. Msgrs. GEORGE F. HUNDT, J.C.L.; JAMES T. MAHONEY, Ph.D., V.G.; Revs. MARC A. MANCINI, J.C.L.; ANTONIO RODRIGUEZ.

College of Deans—Rev. ROBERT J. MITCHELL, Chm.

Finance Council—LORRAINE HRICIK-DEL GUERCIO, Chm.; Sr. MARY EDWARD SPOHRER, S.C.C.; Mr. STANTON J. FEELEY; Mr. THOMAS A. BARRETT; Mr. JOHN BERGER; Mr. JAMES GARIBALDI; Mr. CHARLES PASCARELLA; Mr. MICHAEL RESCOE; Rev. Msgr. JAMES T. MAHONEY, Ph.D., V.G.; Mr. WILLIAM MCLAUGHLIN; Mr. EUGENE R. SYLVA; Mr. BRAD WATSON.

Theological Commission—Rev. Msgrs. JOHN E. HART; T. MARK CONDON, J.C.L., S.T.L.; Sr. KATHLEEN FLANAGAN, S.C., Ph.D.; Dr. JAMES INCARDONA, Ph.D.; Rev. ALEKSY KOWALSKI, Ph.D.; Rev. Msgr. RAYMOND J. KUPKE, Ph.D.; Revs. ANTHONY J. MASTROENI, S.T.D., J.D.; CHARLES J. PARR, Ph.D. (Retired); Rev. Msgr. HERBERT K. TILLYER, P.A., M.Ch.A.; Dr. DIANNE TRAFLET, J.D., S.T.D.

Pastoral Council—Mrs. JANET HOVEN, Chm.

Justice and Peace Commission—Rev. PATRICK RICE, Chm.

Liturgical Commission—VACANT, Chm.

Hispanic Commission—Mr. ALVARO CAMARGO, Pres.

Black Catholic Ministries Commission—Mrs. RUTH LAWSON, Chm.

Education Council—Mr. EDWIN PETERSON, Chm.

Diocesan Secretariats

Communications Secretariat—Mailing Address: 775 Valley Rd., P.O. Box 1887, Clifton, 07015. Tel: 973-278-3202; Fax: 973-279-2265. Mr. RICHARD A. SOKERKA, Exec. Sec. & Dir. Communications; Mr. JOSEPH CECE, Webmaster. Email: cecej@infonetdev.com.

Diocesan Newspaper, "The Beacon"—Tel: 973-279-8845. Mr. RICHARD A. SOKERKA, Editor & Gen. Mgr.; Mr. MICHAEL WOJCIK, News Editor.

Media Resource Center—777 Valley Rd., Clifton, 07013. Tel: 973-777-8818. Ms. MARYANNE NILAN, Consultant.

Secretariat for Evangelization—777 Valley Rd., Clifton, 07013. Tel: 973-777-8818. Rev. GENO SYLVA, S.T.D., Vicar for Evangelization; Mr. PHILIP A. RUSSO, Exec. Sec.

Office of Family Life—Mrs. MARIE RYAN, Consultant.

Natural Family Planning—Rev. JOHN P. HANLEY, Spiritual Dir. (Retired); Mrs. MARIE RYAN, Consultant.

Respect Life—Dr. MARY MAZZARELLA, Consultant.

Director of Catechesis as Evangelization—Rev. DEREK ANDERSON, S.O.L.T.

Catechetical Leaders Association—SUE REILLY.

Diocesan Commission on Evangelization and Catechesis—Mr. ALLAN WRIGHT.

Office of Multicultural Ministries—Rev. ENRIQUE CORONA, Consultant.

Commission for Hispanic Catholic Ministry—Mr. ALVARO CAMARGO.

Office of Worship and Spirituality—Rev. Msgr. T. MARK CONDON, J.C.L., S.T.L., Dir.

Liturgical Commission—Rev. Msgr. T. MARK CONDON, J.C.L., S.T.L.

Diocesan Chapter, National Pastoral Musicians—Mr. PAUL CUSTLER.

Diocesan Choir—Mr. PAUL CUSTLER.

Office of Youth Ministry—Mr. PHILIP A. RUSSO, Consultant.

Outreach to Generation "Y"— (18-22) Mr. BRIAN HONSBERGER, Consultant.

Catholic Scouting—

Boy Scouting—Rev. BRIAN P. QUINN, Chap.

Girl Scouting—Rev. FRANK P. AGRESTI, Chap.

Ecumenical Officer—Rev. CHARLES J. PARR, Ph.D. (Retired), 82 Sunrise Rd., Pompton Plains, 07444.

Related Organizations—

Catholic Deaf Society—Rev. Msgrs. JOSEPH J. GOODE, M.Ch.A., Mod., 24 Ann Rd., Long Valley, 07853. Tel: 908-850-0263; THOMAS J. TRAPASSO, S.T.L., Asst. Mod. (Retired).

Charismatic Renewal—Rev. NICHOLAS BOZZA, Liaison. Tel: 973-347-0032.

English Cursillos—Mr. MIKE WILSON, Lay Dir.; Rev. RAYMOND ORAMA, Spiritual Advisor.

Spanish Cursillos—LUIS SALERNA, Lay Dir.; WILLIAM TORRES; Rev. BRANDO IBARRA, Spiritual Advisor.

Retrouvaille—Contact Couple: PAT GALLO; TOM GALLO. Tel: 732-238-0234.

World Wide Marriage Encounter—Executive Couple: MICHAEL MORGAN; EILEEN MORGAN. Tel: 973-827-9606. Registration Couple: EILEEN PEREZ; RALPH PEREZ. Tel: 800-499-6552.

Secretariat for Pastoral Administration—775 Valley Rd., Clifton, 07013. Tel: 973-777-2955.

Vicar for Pastoral Administration—Rev. HERNAN ARIAS.

Clergy Personnel Office—Rev. Msgrs. RAYMOND M. LOPATESKY, Dir.; THOMAS J. COLETTA, Asst. Dir.; Mrs. ROSEMARY J. DONNELLY, Administrative Asst.; Rev. JUDE S. SALUS, O.S.B., Dir. Newly Ordained Priests.

Deacon Internship Program—Rev. DARIUSZ K. KAMINSKI.

Priestly Life Committee—Revs. HERNAN ARIAS; PAWEL F. SZUREK; MARK OLENOWSKI; STANLEY C. BARRON; DAVID MCDONNELL.

Mission Office—24 DeGrasse St., Paterson, 07505. Tel: 973-278-3491. Rev. Msgr. JOHN J. DEMKOVICH, Dir. (Retired); Rev. STANLEY C. BARRON, Assoc. Dir.

Office of Health Care Ministry—Rev. MARTIN ROONEY, Coord.

Office of the Permanent Diaconate—205 Madison Ave., Madison, 07940. Tel: 973-443-9300; Fax: 973-443-4140; 973-777-8976. Deacon KEVIN CLEARY, Dir.

Permanent Diaconate Program—Rev. FRANK P. AGRESTI, Spiritual Dir.

Director of the Diaconate Program—Deacon KEVIN CLEARY.

Victim Assistance Coordinator—Ms. PEGGY ZANELLO. Tel: 973-879-1489.

Division of Finance and Budget—777 Valley Rd., Clifton, 07013. Tel: 973-777-8818. Mr. THOMAS A. BARRETT, COO.

Division of Finance and Budget—Mr. BRAD WATSON, CFO; Ms. JOLANTA LONDENE, Controller; Mr. TIMOTHY POTTER, Dir. Devel.; Ms. XANDRA LAW, Asst.; VACANT, Assoc. Dir.

Diocesan Cemeteries Office—58 McLean Blvd., Paterson, 07513. Tel: 973-279-2900. Rev. PETER VB. WELLS, Dir.; Mr. JOHN M. CAVANAUGH, Asst. Dir.

Office of Business Administration—Deacon ROBERT AYERS, Business Mgr.; Mr. JAMES FIERRO, Diocesan Facilities Mgr.; REBECA RUIZ, Diocesan Architect.

Office of Human Resources—Mr. DENNIS BUTLER, Chief Human Resources & Compliance Officer; Mrs. VIRGINIA EMAUS, Employee Benefits; Mr. RICHARD ZICCARDI, Risk Mgr.

Youth and Protection—Mrs. JOAN VALK, Coord.

School Division—777 Valley Rd., Clifton, 07013. Tel: 973-777-8818. Rev. PAUL S. MANNING, Vicar for Educ.; Mr. JOHN R. ERIKSEN, Supt.; MARY DEBRA BAIER, Deputy Supt.; Mr. JOHN FANELLI, Asst. Supt. Technology; Mr. CHRISTOPHER STEFANSKI, Technology Assoc.; Mrs. FRANCES TUITE, Educ. Council Pres.; Sr. JUNE MORRISSEY, S.C., Pres. Elementary Principals' Assoc.

Secretariat for Catholic Charities—777 Valley Rd., Clifton, 07013. Tel: 973-777-8818; Fax: 973-523-6183. Mr. JOSEPH F. DUFFY, Exec. Sec. Tel: 973-777-8818, Ext. 278; Rev. EDWARD LAMBRO, Dir. Devel. & Public Rels. Tel: 973-777-8818, Ext. 294.

Hispanic Information Center—186 Gregory Ave., Passaic, 07055. Tel: 973-779-7022. Mr. LORENZO HERNANDEZ, Dir.

Catholic Family and Community Services—Mrs. DIANE SILBERNAGEL, Exec. Dir.; Mr. ROBERT JACOB, Assoc. Dir. & CFO; Ms. CATHERINE SPINA, Admin. Asst.; Revs. MICHAEL J. BURKE, S.T.M., J.D., Staff Attorney; RICHARD BAY, Special Project Coord.

Aging Services—Tel: 973-279-4300. Ms. LINDA WARD, Sussex County. Tel: 973-209-0123; Ms. RITA KELLY, Passaic County. Tel: 973-279-7100, Ext. 33.

Adoption and Counseling Services—476 17th Ave., Paterson, 07504. Tel: 973-523-9595. Rev. THOMAS MCGRATH, Dir.

Friendship Corner—279 Carroll St., Paterson, 07509. Tel: 973-569-0001. Ms. OLGA GONZALEZ, Dir.

Mount Saint Joseph Children's Center—124 Shepherds Ln., Totowa, 07512. Tel: 973-595-5720. Ms. PATRICIA S. VERDUIN, Dir.

Multi-Lingual Center—24 DeGrasse St., Paterson, 07501. Tel: 973-279-7100. Ms. ROSE KARADASHIAN, Dir.

Partnership for Social Services—48 Wyker Rd., Franklin, 07416. Tel: 973-827-4702. Sr. THOMASINA GEBHARD, S.S.M., Dir.

Marian Aids Ministry—Sr. MARIA ELIZABETH WHILIFER, Dir.

Father English Multi-Purpose Community Center—435 Main St., Paterson, 07501. Tel: 973-881-0280. Mr. JOSEPH MELOSH, Dir.

Preschool Day Care Center Programs— A Child's World-El Mundo del Nino; Mr. JOSEPH MURRAY, Dir.

El Mundo de Colores—44 Ward St., Paterson, 07505. Tel: 973-523-0919. Ms. LAURA ZARIFE, Dir.

After School Programs—Ms. AIDA ZARATE, Dir.

Teenage After School Program—Mr. JUAN GONZALEZ, Dir.

Work Assistance Program—Mr. JUAN GONZALEZ, Dir.

Senior and Disabled Transportation—MICHAEL DRAKEFORD, Dir.

Emergency Food and Clothing Programs—Mr. CARLOS ROLDAN, Dir.

Passaic Teen Center—228 Hope Ave., Passaic, 07055. Tel: 973-473-5755. CAROLYN ARTALE, Dir.

Youth Haven— (Shelter-Crisis Intervention) *212 Slater St., Paterson, 07501.* Tel: 973-881-1661. CAROLYN ARTALE, Dir.

Hope House— (Catholic Social Services of Morris County, Inc.) *19-21 Belmont Ave., Dover, 07801.* Tel: 973-361-5555. Mrs. DIANE SILBERNAGEL, Exec. Dir.; JULIE M. WILLIS, Assoc. Dir.; Ms. KELLY STAGER, Dir. Devel. & Publicity; Ms. KRIS ERNST, Dir. Behavioral Health Svcs.; JIJU KOTTARTHIL, Chief Accountant.

Department for Persons with Disabilities—1 Catholic Charities Way, P.O. Box 2539, Oak Ridge, 07438. Tel: 973-406-1100. Mr. SCOTT MILLIKEN, Exec. Dir.; Ms. JOANNA MILLER, Asst. Exec. Dir.; Sr. JOAN KATHLEEN GERCKE, S.S.J., Staffing & Pastoral Care Coord.; Mr. ROCCO ZAPPILE, CFO; Mr. CHRISTOPHER BRANCATO, Dir. Devel.

Group Homes—Murray House, 86 Allwood Place, Clifton, 07015. Tel: 973-470-5694. Ms. PAMELA VANECK, Dir. *Barnet House, 52 Lenox Ave., Pompton Lakes, 07442.* Tel: 973-409-2764. LAUREN MARCINIAK, Dir. *Finnegan House, 1049 Weldon Rd., Oak Ridge, 07438.* Tel: 973-697-1246. Ms. LYNNE ROCKSTROH, Dir. *Alexander House, 1049 Weldon Rd., Oak Ridge, 07438.* Tel: 973-697-1812. Ms. CLARA BECK, Dir. *Columbus House, 1048 Weldon Rd., Oak Ridge, 07438.* Tel: 973-697-1644. Ms. CHERYL SLATE, Dir. *Fitzpatrick House, 215 Mountain Ave., Pompton Lakes, 07442.* Tel: 973-248-1569. PAM BARRETT, Dir. *Wehrlen House, 18 Bisset Dr., West Milford, 07480.* Tel: 973-208-1883. MARCIA CARBERRY, Dir. *Gruenert Employment Center, 725 Rte. 15 S., Lake Hopatcong, 07849.* Tel: 973-663-9102. Mrs. KATHY DE YOUNG, Dir. *Basile Apartment, Brittany Chase, Wayne, 07470.* Tel: 973-409-2767. Mr. JEFFREY ONDIMU. *Calabrese House, 829 Littleton Rd., Parsippany, 07054.* Tel: 973-299-8360. LORI EVANS, Dir. *Wallace House, 447 Glen Rd., Sparta, 07871.* Tel: 973-276-3470. Ms. KIM WALTER, Dir. *Keleher Apartments, 124 Barrister Dr., Butler, 07405.* Tel: 973-409-2761. Ms. ISABEL MARTE, Dir.

Straight and Narrow, Inc.—508 Straight St., Paterson, 07503. Tel: 973-345-6000. Mr. DAVID J. MACTAS, Exec. Dir.; Dr. JUSTYNA DMOWSKI, Psy.D., Dir. Clinical Svcs.; Ms. SARA PASQUINO, Dir. Alpha-II Prog.; Dr. HAYMAN RAMBARAN, Dir. Straight and Narrow Detox/Medical Unit; Ms. JUDY KURTZER, Dir., Alpha I & III Programs; Mr. VITO ANDRISANI, Out-Patient Svcs., 508 Straight St., Paterson, 07503; Rev. Msgr. LOUIS J. BIHR, Dir. Pastoral Care Unit. *Admissions Department, 508 Straight St., Paterson, 07503.* CAROLINE MODRZEJEWSKI, Dir. *Mens Residential Services, 396 Staight St., Paterson, 07503.* Ms. JUDY KURTZER, Dir. *Womens Residential Services, 396 Straight St., Paterson, 07503.* Ms. KAREN ROCCISANO. *Msgr. Wall Center, 230 E. Ridgewood Ave., Bldg. 10, Paramus, 07652.* Ms. NANCY DIMITROVSKI, Dir. *Family Success Center, 101 Cedar St., Paterson, 07501.* ADELA CACERES, Dir. *Adolescent Residential Services, 396 Straight St., Paterson, 07503.* Ms. REINA RIVAS, Dir. *Intoxicated Drivers Resource Center, 182 First St., Passaic, 07055. 230 E. Ridgewood Ave., Paramus, 07652.* Mr. KENNETH HARDING, Dir.

La Vida Child Care Center, 396 Straight St., Paterson, 07503. Dr. Anna De Molli, Dir. *La Vida Child Care Center II, 116 Jackson St., Paterson, 07501.* Dr. Anna De Molli, Dir. *Straight and Narrow Apartments, 390 Straight St., Paterson, 07503.* Mr. Angelo Zecca. *Straight and Narrow Apartments II, 380 Straight St., Paterson, 07503.* Mr. Dwayne Brookins.

Migrant Ministry—Community of Our Lady of Guadalupe, 12 Columba St., Morristown, 07960. Tel: 908-647-0280. Rev. Raphael Pisso, S.T., Dir.; Luis Arias, Asst. Dir.

Affiliated Organizations—

Apostleship of Prayer—Rev. Msgr. Christopher C. DiLella, Dir., 26 Green Village Rd., Madison, 07040. Tel: 973-377-4000.

Diocesan Council of Catholic Women—Rev. Msgr. Joseph A. Ciampaglio, Dir.; Mrs. Maureen Joyce, Pres., 8 Glenwood Mountain Rd., Sussex, 07461.

Diocesan Holy Name Federation—Mr. Frank Steiner, Pres.

Legion of Mary—Rev. Msgr. John J. Demkovich, Spiritual Dir. (Retired); Mrs. Lucy Leone, Pres., 63 Monroe St., Passaic, 07055. Tel: 973-779-0427.

Priests Eucharistic League—Rev. Msgr. Christopher C. DiLella, Dir.

CLERGY, PARISHES, MISSIONS AND PAROCHIAL SCHOOLS

CITY OF PATERSON

(Passaic County)

1—Cathedral of St. John the Baptist (1820) [CEM] Rev. Msgr. Mark J. Giordani; Revs. Ruben Dario Castillo (Colombia); Manuel Guevara, Parochial Vicar; Deacons Jose Pomales; Guido Pedraza; Hector Castellanos. In Res., Rev. Msgr. Patrick E. Brown.
Res.: 381 Grand St., 07505. Tel: 973-345-4070; Fax: 973-345-7831.
Catechesis/Religious Program—Students 342.

2—St. Agnes (1883) Rev. Luis A. Rendon, Admin.; Deacons Gilberto Vazquez; Pedro Cruz.
Res.: 681 Main St., 07503. Tel: 973-279-0250; Fax: 973-357-1218.
Catechesis/Religious Program—Students 130.

3—St. Anthony's (1909), (Italian), Revs. Eider Reyes; Amadito Flores, Parochial Vicar; Deacon Pedro Cruz.
Res.: 138 Beech St., 07501. Tel: 973-742-9695; Fax: 973-881-0522.
Catechesis/Religious Program—Students 49.

4—Blessed Sacrament (1911), (Italian), Revs. Ramon Orama, Admin.; Misael Jaramillo, Parochial Vicar.
Res.: 224 E. 18th St., 07524. Tel: 973-523-5002; Fax: 973-523-3766.
School—(1953) 289-Sixth Ave., 07524. Tel: 973-278-8787; Fax: 973-278-6436. Sr. Noreen Holly, S.C., Prin. Maestre Pie Filippini (Religious Teachers Filippini) 4; Lay Teachers 8; Students 136.
Catechesis/Religious Program—Students 100.

5—St. Bonaventure (1877) Revs. Daniel P. Grigassy, O.F.M.; Christopher VanHaight, O.F.M., Parochial Vicar; Deacons Joseph Balough; Anthony Fierro.
Res.: 174 Ramsey St., 07501. Tel: 973-279-1016; Fax: 973-279-2507.
Catechesis/Religious Program—Students 194.

6—St. Casimir's (1911), (Lithuanian), Rev. John P. Hanley, Admin. (Retired). In Res., Rev. Patrick Magee, F.L.H.F.
Res.: 501 W. Broadway, 07522. Tel: 973-595-8446; Fax: 973-790-0778.

7—St. George (1897) Rev. Robert W. Wisniefski, Admin.; Deacon Eugenio Morales.
Res.: 408 Getty Ave., 07503. Tel: 973-742-0350; Fax: 973-754-0657.

8—St. Gerard Majella (1962) Revs. Rijo Johnson, S.D.V.; Lorenzo Gomez, S.D.V., Parochial Vicar; Robert Vass, S.D.V., Parochial Vicar. In Res., Rev. Charles J. Waller.
Res.: 501 W. Broadway, 07522. Tel: 973-595-8446; Fax: 973-790-0778.
School—(1965)Tel: 973-595-5640; Fax: 973-595-5475. Sisters 1; Lay Teachers 9; Students 235.
Catechesis/Religious Program—Students 67.

9—St. Joseph's (1867) Rev. Robert W. Wisniefski; Deacons Ronald Romano; Hector Casillas.
Res.: 399 Market St., 07501. Tel: 973-278-0030.
See Pope John Paul II School, Clifton under Elementary Schools, Diocesan located in the Institution section.
Catechesis/Religious Program—Students 162.

10—St. Mary's (1873), (Auxilium Christianorum) Rev. Jorge I. Rodriguez; Deacons Antonio Salierno; Juan Carlos Carnero; Jose Trinidad.
Res.: 410 Union Ave., 07502. Tel: 973-790-8651; Fax: 973-790-8534.
Catechesis/Religious Program—Students 115.

11—St. Michael the Archangel (1903), (Italian), Revs. Rijo Johnson, S.D.V.; Lorenzo Gomez, S.D.V., Parochial Vicar; Robert Vass, S.D.V., Parochial Vicar; Jimson Varchese, S.D.V.
Res.: 70 Cianci St., 07501-1831. Tel: 973-523-8413. Email: st-michaelschurch@yahoo.com.
Catechesis/Religious Program—Combined with St. Gerard, Majella Students 8.

12—Our Lady of Lourdes (1882) Revs. Ramon Orama, Admin.; Misael Jaramillo, Parochial Vicar; Deacons Mario Munoz; Raul Pamplona.
Res.: 440 River St., 07524-1902. Tel: 973-742-2142; Fax: 973-345-9136. Email: blessedpastor@aol.com. Web: www.miracleoflourdes.org.

13—Our Lady of Pompei (1916), (Italian), Revs. Frank P. Agresti; Sal J. Panagia, Pastor Emeritus (Retired); Deacon Henry Gallo.
Res.: 70 Murray Ave., 07501. Tel: 973-742-1969; Fax: 973-742-1335.
Catechesis/Religious Program—Students 54.

14—Our Lady of Victories (1882) Rev. Msgr. Thomas J. Coletta; Deacon Maximo Paulino.
Res.: 100 Fair St., 07501. Tel: 973-279-0487; 973-279-0527; Fax: 973-977-8506. Email: olvjude@verizon.net. Web: www.olvjude.org.
Catechesis/Religious Program—Students 151.

15—St. Stephen's (1903), (Polish), Rev. Dariusz K. Kaminski; Deacon Candelario Espinal.
Res.: 86 Martin St., 07501. Tel: 973-742-2822; Fax: 973-742-1679.
Catechesis/Religious Program—Students 40.

16—St. Therese (1926) Rev. Luciano Cruz; Deacons Nicholas Varsalona; Raul Pamplona; Luis Ramirez.
Res.: 80 13th Ave., 07504. Tel: 973-881-0400; Fax: 973-881-7638.
Catechesis/Religious Program—Students 50.

OUTSIDE THE CITY OF PATERSON

Andover, Sussex Co., Good Shepherd (1979) [CEM] Rev. Msgrs. Martin McDonnell; Richard A. Steiger, Pastor Emeritus (Retired); Deacons Thomas Sullivan; Edmund Galinski; Keith Harris; Mrs. Sharon Matuza, Pastoral Assoc.
Office: Rte. 517 (48 Tranquility Rd.), P.O. Box 464, 07821. Tel: 973-786-6631; 973-786-5520 (Res.); 973-786-5811 (CEM); Fax: 973-786-5233.
Catechesis/Religious Program—Tel: 973-786-6632. Students 550.

Boonton, Morris Co.

1—SS. Cyril and Methodius (1907), (Slovak), [CEM] Rev. Zbigniew Tyburski.
Res.: 215 Hill St., 07005. Tel: 973-334-0139; Fax: 973-402-9512. Web: stcyrilboonton.org.
Catechesis/Religious Program—Students 20.

2—Our Lady of Mount Carmel (1847) [CEM] Rev. Thomas H. Fallone.
Res.: 910 Birch St., 07005. Tel: 973-334-1017; Fax: 973-335-1833.
School—(1868) 205 Oak St., 07005. Tel: 973-334-2777; Fax: 973-334-0975. Lay Teachers 12; Students 131.
Catechesis/Religious Program—Students 285.

Branchville, Sussex Co., Our Lady Queen of Peace (1951) Rev. Msgr. William P. Stober.
Res.: 209 Rte. 206, 07826. Tel: 973-948-3185; Fax: 973-948-4799.
Catechesis/Religious Program—Tel: 973-948-2741. Students 182.

Budd Lake, Morris Co., St. Jude (1946) Revs. Joseph J. Orlandi; James Moss, Parochial Vicar (part-time); Deacons Anthony C. Siino; Paul M. Wisniewski; John M. Sanker; Joanne Lawlar, Pastoral Assoc.
Res.: 17 Mt. Olive Rd., 07828. Tel: 973-691-1561; Fax: 973-691-9060. Web: www.stjudeparish.org.
Catechesis/Religious Program—Students 534.

Butler, Morris Co., St. Anthony (1878) [CEM] Revs. Michael Jones, O.F.M.; James W. Czerwinski, O.F.M.
Res.: 65 Bartholdi Ave., 07405. Tel: 973-838-0031; Fax: 973-838-0649.
School—(1882)Tel: 973-838-0854; Fax: 973-838-1460. Lay Teachers 11; Students 207.
Catechesis/Religious Program—Students 325.
Parish House—71 Bartholdi Ave., 07405. Tel: 973-838-8585.

Cedar Knolls, Morris Co., Notre Dame of Mt. Carmel (1917) Rev. Jude S. Salus, O.S.B.; Deacons Joseph Harris; Victor Lupi; Ronald Forino; Matthew McMahon; Alfredo Fanelli; David Collins; Henry de Mena; James Butkus.
Office: 75 Ridgedale Ave., 07927. Tel: 973-538-1358; Fax: 973-538-7403.
Catechesis/Religious Program—Students 925.

Chatham Township, Morris Co., Corpus Christi (1966) Rev. Msgr. James T. Mahoney.
Res.: 234 Southern Blvd., 07928. Tel: 973-635-0070; Fax: 973-635-5518. Email: jmahoney@corpuschristi.org. Web: www.corpuschristi.org.
Catechesis/Religious Program—Students 1,450.

Chatham, Morris Co., St. Patrick's (1874) Rev. Robert J. Mitchell; Deacons Joseph A. Wisneski; Mark Nixon.
Parish Office: 41 Oliver St., 07928.
Res.: 85 Washington Ave., 07928. Email: info@st-pats.org. Web: www.st-pats.org.
School—(1872) 45 Chatham St., 07928. Tel: 973-635-4623; Fax: 973-635-2311. Lay Teachers 28; Students 338.
Catechesis/Religious Program—Students 811.

Chester, Morris Co., St. Lawrence the Martyr (1950) Rev. Msgr. Paul F. Knauer; Rev. Enrique Corona, Parochial Vicar; Deacon Frank Owens.
Res.: Main St., P.O. Box 730, 07930. Tel: 908-879-5371; Fax: 908-879-7701.
Catechesis/Religious Program—Main St., P.O. Box 31, 07930. Tel: 908-879-6714; Fax: 908-879-7701. Students 833.

Clifton, Passaic Co.

1—St. Andrew the Apostle (Allwood) (1938) Rev. Msgr. Richard A. Rusconi; Deacons Robert G. Ayers; Richard J. Goglia.
Res.: 400 Mt. Prospect Ave., 07012. Tel: 973-779-6873; Fax: 973-779-0573.
School—(1953) 418 Mt. Prospect Ave., 07012. Tel: 973-473-3711; Fax: 973-473-6611. Sisters of the Presentation 1; Lay Teachers 10; Students 215.
Catechesis/Religious Program—Tel: 973-779-6873; Fax: 973-779-0573. Students 183.

2—St. Brendan (1945) Revs. Frank W. Weber; Robert W. Wisniefski, Admin. In Res., Rev. Msgr. Francis Matarazzo (Retired); Rev. Peter Clark.
Res.: 154 E. First St., 07011. Tel: 973-772-1115; Fax: 973-772-0497. Email: weber01@aol.com. Web: www.st-brendan.org.
School—(1946) 154 E. First St., 07011. Tel: 973-772-1149; Fax: 973-772-5547. Lay Teachers 15; Students 370.
Catechesis/Religious Program—Tel: 973-772-6775; Fax: 973-772-6213. Students 170.

3—St. Clare (1913) Revs. Peter VB. Wells; Thomas J. Fitzgerald. In Res., Rev. Joseph J. Garbarino.
Res.: 69 Allwood Rd., 07014. Tel: 973-777-7588; Fax: 973-249-6825.
School—(1959)Tel: 973-777-7582; Fax: 973-473-0127. Religious 1; Lay Teachers 14; Students 175.
Catechesis/Religious Program—Students 94.

4—SS. Cyril and Methodius (1913), (Slovak), Revs. John T. Connolly, Admin.; Hector Melendez. In Res., Rev. Msgr. John J. Demkovich (Retired); Rev. Richard Bay.
Res.: 218 Ackerman Ave., 07011. Tel: 973-546-4390; Fax: 973-546-3269. Email: cyrilmethodius1@verizon.net.
Catechesis/Religious Program—Students 81.

5—St. John Kanty (1930), (Polish), Revs. Raphael Zwolenkiewicz, O.F.M.Conv.; Miroslaw Podymniak, O.F.M.Conv.; Roger Haas, O.F.M.Conv.; Deacon Robert Altilio.
Res.: 49 Speer Ave., 07013. Tel: 973-779-0564; 973-779-4102 (Office); Fax: 973-773-0857. Email: sjkrcch@optonline.net. Web: www.saintjohnkanty.org.
Catechesis/Religious Program—Tel: 973-779-6214. Students 227.

6—St. Paul (1914) Rev. Leonardo Jaramillo; Deacons Joseph Puskas; Peter Casamento.
Res.: 124 Union Ave., 07011. Tel: 973-546-2746; 973-772-0117; Fax: 973-340-2083.
Catechesis/Religious Program—Students 105.

7—St. Philip the Apostle (1943) Revs. Paul S. Manning; Brian P. Quinn, Parochial Vicar; Deacon Nicholas Veliky. In Res., Rev. Msgr. P. Kevin Flanagan (Retired).
Res.: 797 Valley Rd., 07013. Tel: 973-779-6200; Fax: 973-779-2959. Web: www.stphilip.org.
School—(1954)Tel: 973-779-4700; Fax: 973-779-0932. Email: bzito@stphilip.org. Web: www.saintphilipschool.org. Lay Teachers 28; Students 419.
Catechesis/Religious Program—Tel: 973-779-1439. Students 392.

8—Sacred Heart (1897), (Italian), Rev. John T. Connolly; Rev. Msgr. Julian B. Varettoni, Pastor Emeritus (Retired); Rev. Andrew T. Perretta. In Res., Rev. Richard Bay, 21 Varettoni Pl., 07011.
Res.: 145 Randolph Ave., 07011. Tel: 973-546-6012; Fax: 973-546-1814. Email: church@sacredheartclifton.com.
Catechesis/Religious Program—Students 68.

Convent Station, Morris Co., St. Thomas More (1966) Rev. Joseph G. Farias, Admin.
Res.: Madison Ave., Box 286, 07961. Tel: 973-267-5330.
Catechesis/Religious Program—Tel: 973-267-5585. Students 18.

DENVILLE, MORRIS CO., ST. MARY'S (1926) Revs. Martin G. Glynn; Richard V. Tartaglia; Deacons Michael Allgaier; John Flynn.
Res.: 15 Myers Ave., 07834. Tel: 973-627-0269; Fax: 973-627-6355.
School—(1954)Tel: 973-627-2606; Fax: 973-627-9316. Sisters 1; Lay Teachers 15; Students 256.
Catechesis/Religious Program—Tel: 973-627-8276. Students 604.

DOVER, MORRIS CO.
1—ST. MARY'S (1845) [CEM] Rev. John DeMattia; Deacons Thomas P. Beirne; Stuart A. Hartnett.
Res.: 425 W. Blackwell St., 07801. Tel: 973-366-0184; Fax: 973-366-5377.
Catechesis/Religious Program—Students 230.
2—OUR LADY QUEEN OF THE MOST HOLY ROSARY (1959), (Hispanic), Revs. Brendan J. Murray, Admin.; Benjamin Williams, Parochial Vicar; Nelson Betancur, Parochial Vicar.
Res.: 77 Richards Ave., 07801. Tel: 973-361-2725; Fax: 973-361-4058. Email: holyrosary@verizon.net.
Catechesis/Religious Program—Students 316.
3—SACRED HEART (1904) Revs. Brendan J. Murray; Benjamin Williams, Parochial Vicar; Nelson Betancur, Parochial Vicar. In Res., Rev. Carmen Buono.
Res.: 4 Richards Ave., 07801. Tel: 973-366-0060; Fax: 973-366-8636. Web: sacredheart-dover.com.
Catechesis/Religious Program—Students 157.

EAST HANOVER, MORRIS CO., ST. ROSE OF LIMA (1957) Rev. Owen B. Moran; Deacons Frank Para, Pastoral Assoc.; Vincent Leo Jr.
Res.: 312 Ridgedale Ave., 07936. Tel: 973-887-5572; Fax: 973-884-0476. Web: saintroseoflimachurch.org.
School—(1961)Tel: 973-887-6990; Fax: 973-887-8655. Lay Teachers 10; Students 151.
Catechesis/Religious Program—Tel: 973-887-0357. Students 503.

FLANDERS, MORRIS CO., ST. ELIZABETH ANN SETON (1985) Rev. Stanley C. Barron; Deacons Dennis King; Frank Puglia.
Res.: 61 Main St., 07836. Tel: 973-927-1629; Fax: 973-927-0327. Email: steliz@hughes.net. Web: stelizabethschurch.org.
Catechesis/Religious Program—Tel: 973-927-7077; Fax: 973-927-0093. Students 830.

FLORHAM PARK, MORRIS CO., HOLY FAMILY (1951) Revs. Frederick Walters; William J. Mooney; Deacons William F. Ward; Peter Flore; Mrs. Barbara Froetscher, Pastoral Assoc.; Mrs. Patricia Danishek, Pastoral Assoc.; Mrs. Virginia Akhoury, Pastoral Assoc.
Res.: 1 Lloyd Ave., 07932. Tel: 973-377-1817; Fax: 973-377-6350.
School—(1954)Tel: 973-377-4181; Fax: 973-377-0273. Sisters of Christian Charity 1; Lay Teachers 16; Students 162.
Catechesis/Religious Program—Tel: 973-377-3101. Students 608.

FRANKLIN, SUSSEX CO., IMMACULATE CONCEPTION (1867) [CEM] Rev. Boguslaw Kobus.
Res.: 75 Church St., 07416. Tel: 973-827-9575; Fax: 973-827-7375. Web: immaculateconceptionfranklin.org. Email: icchurch@ptd.net.
Catechesis/Religious Program—Tel: 973-827-9501. Email: church@icrschool.com. Students 341.

GREEN POND, MORRIS CO., ST. SIMON THE APOSTLE (Rockaway Twp.) (1942) Rev. Daniel Staniskis, Admin.
Res.: 1010 Green Pond Rd., 07435. Tel: 973-697-4699; Fax: 973-697-1784.
Catechesis/Religious Program—Students 96.

HAMBURG, SUSSEX CO., ST. JUDE THE APOSTLE (1966) Rev. William B. Collins.
Res.: 4-24 Beaver Run Rd., P.O. Box 1, 07419. Tel: 973-827-8030; Fax: 973-827-8382. Email: stjudehamburg@embarqmail.com. Web: www.stjudehamburg.org.
Catechesis/Religious Program—Tel: 973-827-2280. Students 300.

HASKELL, PASSAIC CO., ST. FRANCIS OF ASSISI (1905) Rev. Lancelot Reis; Deacon Jose Rivera.
Res.: 868 Ringwood Ave., 07420. Tel: 973-835-0480; Fax: 973-835-3277. Email: stfrancis@optonline.net. Web: stfrancishaskell.org.
School—(1912)Tel: 973-835-3268; Fax: 973-616-7644. Lay Teachers 11; Students 162.
Catechesis/Religious Program—Tel: 973-835-1946. Students 261.

HAWTHORNE, PASSAIC CO., ST. ANTHONY'S (1908) Rev. Msgr. Raymond J. Kupke; Revs. Luis Carlos Moreno, Parochial Vicar; Roberto Amador, Parochial Vicar; Deacons Richard J. Brudzynski; George Forshay; Anthony E. Bernardine; Gerald Fadlalla.
Res.: 276 Diamond Bridge Ave., 07506. Tel: 973-427-1478; Fax: 973-427-4826. Email: info@stanthony-hawthorne.org. Web: www.stanthony-hawthorne.org.
School—(1912) 270 Diamond Bridge Ave., 07506. Tel: 973-423-1818; Fax: 973-423-6065. Sisters 3; Lay Teachers 12; Students 242.
Catechesis/Religious Program—Tel: 973-427-7873. Students 683.

HEWITT, PASSAIC CO., OUR LADY QUEEN OF PEACE (1921) Revs. Michael Rodak, Admin.; Adam Muda; Deacons Charles Roche; Joseph Verboys; Philip Thiuri.
Res.: 1911 Union Valley Rd., 07421. Tel: 973-728-8162; Fax: 973-728-4650. Web: www.olopnj.com.
Catechesis/Religious Program—Students 383.

HIGHLAND LAKES, SUSSEX CO., OUR LADY OF FATIMA (1954) Rev. Msgr. Robert B. Carroll.
Mailing Address: 184 Breakneck Rd, P.O. Box 242, 07422. Tel: 973-764-4457; Fax: 973-764-4504. Email: olfatima@warwick.net. Web: olfatima-highlandlksnj.catholicweb.com.
Catechesis/Religious Program—Students 339.

HOPATCONG, SUSSEX CO., ST. JUDE'S (1931) Rev. George J. Gothie; Deacon Thomas Friel.
Res.: 40 Maxim Dr., 07843. Tel: 973-398-6377; Fax: 973-398-0121. Email: reled@stjudehopatcong.org. Web: www.stjudehopatcong.org.
Catechesis/Religious Program—Students 170.

KINNELON, MORRIS CO., OUR LADY OF THE MAGNIFICAT (1961) [CEM] Rev. Msgr. John J. Carroll.
Res.: 2 Miller Rd., 07405. Tel: 973-838-6838; Fax: 973-838-0710. Web: olmchurch.org.
Catechesis/Religious Program—Tel: 973-838-0567; Fax: 973-838-0409. Sr. Ellen Denise O'Connor, F.S.P. Students 667.

LAKE HOPATCONG, MORRIS CO., OUR LADY STAR OF THE SEA (Jefferson Twp.) (1910) Rev. P. Christopher Muldoon; Deacon Alberto R. Totino.
Res.: 237 Espanong Rd., P.O. Box 337, 07849. Tel: 973-663-0211; Fax: 973-663-4302. Email: olsos@optonline.net. Web: www.olsoslh.org.
Catechesis/Religious Program—Tel: 973-663-0124; Fax: 973-663-2118. Students 382.

LINCOLN PARK, MORRIS CO., ST. JOSEPH'S (1922) Revs. Philip A. LeBeau; Robert J. Norton, O.F.M., Parochial Vicar; Deacons Stephen J. Marabeti; Joseph Parlapiano.
Res.: 216 Comly Rd., 07035. Tel: 973-696-4411; Fax: 973-305-8466. Email: stjoelp@optonline.net. Web: www.stjosephsonline.org.
Catechesis/Religious Program—Students 405.

LITTLE FALLS, PASSAIC CO., OUR LADY OF THE HOLY ANGELS (1883) Rev. Msgr. T. Mark Condon; Revs. David Pickens; Ricardo Ortega, Parochial Vicar; Deacon Joseph Sisco.
Res.: 473 Main St., 07424. Tel: 973-256-5200; Fax: 973-256-0185.
Catechesis/Religious Program—Tel: 973-256-5200. Students 471.

LONG VALLEY, MORRIS CO.
1—ST. LUKE (1982) Rev. Michael J. Drury.
Res.: P.O. Box 416, 07853. Tel: 908-876-3515; Fax: 908-876-5277.
Church: 265 W. Mill Rd., 07853.
Catechesis/Religious Program—Students 1,100.
2—ST. MARK THE EVANGELIST (1986) Rev. Msgr. Joseph J. Goode; Rev. Abuchi Nwosu, Parochial Vicar.
Office: 59 Spring Ln., 07853.
Res.: 24 Ann Rd., 07853. Tel: 908-850-0652; Fax: 908-850-0648. Email: frjoe.stm@comcast.net.
Catechesis/Religious Program—Students 379.

MADISON, MORRIS CO., ST. VINCENT MARTYR (1805) [CEM] Rev. Msgr. George F. Hundt; Rev. Jesus A. Gaviria.
Res.: 26 Green Village Rd., 07940. Tel: 973-377-4000; Fax: 973-377-8242.
School—(1848)Tel: 973-377-1104; Fax: 973-377-2632. Lay Teachers 29; Students 417.
Catechesis/Religious Program—Tel: 973-966-1771. Students 715.

MCAFEE, SUSSEX CO., ST. FRANCIS DE SALES (1963) Rev. Msgr. John V. Boland.
Mailing Address: P.O. Box 785, 07428. Tel: 973-827-3248; Fax: 973-827-7534.
Catechesis/Religious Program—Tel: 973-827-7534; Fax: 973-827-3248. Email: jane@stfrancisvernon.org; melory@st.francisvernon.org. Web: www.stfrancis-vernon.org. Students 800.

MENDHAM, MORRIS CO., ST. JOSEPH'S (1853) [CEM] Rev. Msgr. Joseph T. Anginoli; Rev. Pawel Bala, Parochial Vicar; Deacon Robert F. Santos.
6 New St., 07945. Tel: 973-543-5950; Fax: 973-543-6025.
School—(1963)Tel: 973-543-7474; Fax: 973-543-7817. Lay Teachers 19; Students 236.
Catechesis/Religious Program—Students 687.

MONTAGUE, SUSSEX CO., ST. JAMES THE GREATER (1943) Rev. Wayne F. Varga; Deacon Wayne Von Doehren.
Res.: 75 River Rd., 07827. Tel: 973-948-2296; Fax: 973-948-4634. Email: stjamesthomas@aol.com.
Catechesis/Religious Program—122 C.R. 645, Sandyston, 07826. Fax: 973-948-7007. Students 43.

MONTVILLE, MORRIS CO., ST. PIUS X (1959) Rev. Mark Olenowski; Deacons Jack Callahan; Patrick Mann.
Parish Ministry Office—Tel: 973-335-2894; Fax: 973-394-0069.
Res.: 24 Changebridge Rd., 07045. Tel: 973-331-1706.
School—(1963)Tel: 973-335-1253; Fax: 973-335-2392. Sr. June Morrissey, S.C., Prin. Religious 2; Lay Teachers 12; Students 244.
Catechesis/Religious Program—24 Changebridge Rd., 07045. Tel: 973-335-2894, Ext. 108. Students 1,014.

MORRIS PLAINS, MORRIS CO., ST. VIRGILIUS (1881) Rev. Msgr. Francis J. Duffy; Rev. Richard Kilcomons; Deacons Sylvester Mazzoccoli; Thomas Harenchar; Merle Sisler; Rich Pinto; Frank Para; Ken Rado.
Res.: 250 Speedwell Ave., 07950. Tel: 973-538-1418; Fax: 973-538-2992. Email: parishoffice@stvirgil.org. Web: www.stvirgil.org.
School—(1910) 238 Speedwell Ave., 07950. Tel: 973-539-7267; Fax: 973-292-5157. Mr. Jerry Fazio, Prin. Lay Teachers 14; Students 137.
Catechesis/Religious Program—Tel: 973-267-1366. Students 598.

MORRISTOWN, MORRIS CO.
1—ASSUMPTION OF THE BLESSED VIRGIN MARY (1848) [CEM] Rev. Msgr. John E. Hart; Rev. Philip-Michael Tangora, Parochial Vicar; Deacons P. Michael Hanly; William Harty; Brian D. Beyerl. In Res., Rev. Dennis J. Crowley.
Res.: 91 Maple Ave., 07960. Tel: 973-539-2141; Fax: 973-984-0632. Email: assumption@assumptionparish.org. Web: assumptionparish.org.
School—(1850) 63 MacCulloch Ave., 07960. Tel: 973-538-0590; Fax: 973-984-3632. Sisters of Charity 1; Lay Teachers 45; Students 520.
Catechesis/Religious Program—Tel: 973-267-5638; Fax: 973-984-0632. Students 750.
2—ST. MARGARET OF SCOTLAND (1885) Revs. Hernan Arias; Jared J. Brogan, Parochial Vicar; Michael Lee, Parochial Vicar; Deacon Tim Holden.
Res.: 6 Sussex Ave., 07960. Tel: 973-538-0874; Fax: 973-538-4581. Email: stmargaret07960@yahoo.com.
Catechesis/Religious Program—Tel: 973-267-8354. Students 262.

MOUNT ARLINGTON, MORRIS CO., OUR LADY OF THE LAKE (1888) Revs. Hugh P. Murphy; Desmond O'Connor, S.P.S.
Res.: One Park Ave., 07856. Tel: 973-398-0240; Fax: 973-398-3667.
Catechesis/Religious Program—Tel: 973-601-1475. Students 298.

MOUNT HOPE, MORRIS CO., ST. BERNARD'S (1855) Rev. Alfred J. Lampron, Admin.
Res.: 446 Mt. Hope Rd., Wharton, 07885-2814. Tel: 973-627-0066; Fax: 973-627-3631. Email: stbernardsmth@verizon.net.
Catechesis/Religious Program—Students 4.

MOUNTAIN LAKES, MORRIS CO., ST. CATHERINE OF SIENA (1956) Revs. Peter Filipkowski; Thomas Mangieri.
Res.: 10 N. Pocono Rd., 07046. Tel: 973-334-7131; Fax: 973-334-3202.
Catechesis/Religious Program—Tel: 973-334-5257. Students 685.

NETCONG, MORRIS CO., ST. MICHAEL'S (1873) [CEM] Rev. Nicholas Bozza; Deacons Joseph Keenan; Stuart Murphy; Richard F. Bias.
Res.: 4 Church St., 07857. Tel: 973-347-0032; Fax: 973-347-1560.
School—(1922), (Grades PreK-8), (School operated by The Catholic Academy of Sussex County Inc.), 10 Church St., 07857. Tel: 973-347-0039; Fax: 973-347-0054. Lay Teachers 14; Students 212.
Catechesis/Religious Program—Tel: 973-347-1465. Students 321.

NEW VERNON, MORRIS CO., CHRIST THE KING (1956) Rev. Patrick G. O'Donovan.
Res.: Blue Mill Rd., P.O. Box 368, 07976. Tel: 973-539-4955; Fax: 973-267-7070. Web: www.churchofchristtheking.org.
Catechesis/Religious Program—Students 388.

NEWTON, SUSSEX CO., ST. JOSEPH (1854) [CEM] Rev. Brian Sullivan; Deacons Gerald Hanifan; Alfred Kucinski; Larry D'Amico; Thomas Zayac.
Res.: 17 Elm St., 07860. Tel: 973-383-1985; Fax: 973-383-8164. Email: stjoseph727@yahoo.com.
Catechesis/Religious Program—Tel: 973-383-8413. Students 405.

OAK RIDGE, MORRIS CO., ST. THOMAS, THE APOSTLE (1949) [CEM] Rev. Msgr. John E. Fitzpatrick.
Res.: 5635 Berkshire Valley Rd., 07438. Tel: 973-208-0090; Fax: 973-208-0092.
Catechesis/Religious Program—Tel: 973-208-0096. Students 168.

OGDENSBURG, SUSSEX CO., ST. THOMAS OF AQUIN (1881) [CEM] Rev. John P. Pilipie; Deacons Edward Reading; Dominic Zampella.
Res.: 53 Kennedy Ave., 07439. Tel: 973-827-3190; Fax: 973-827-2885. Email: stthomasofaquin@embarqmail.com. Web: www.stthomasofaquin.org.
Catechesis/Religious Program—Students 120.

PARSIPPANY, MORRIS CO.

1—ST. ANN (1982) Rev. Timothy Dowling; Sr. Frances Sanzo, S.S.C., Pastoral Assoc.; Mrs. Ginny Bissig, Pastoral Assoc.; Deacons Alfred Frank; Leonard Deo.
Res.: 781 Smith Rd., 07054. Tel: 973-884-1986; Fax: 973-884-0940.
Catechesis/Religious Program—Students 312.

2—ST. CHRISTOPHER (1944) Revs. Joseph G. Buffardi; Marcin Walka; Deacons John J. Kelly; Edward Lally; Henry Rohrman; Richard A. Gaydo; Alan Lucibello. In Res., Rev. Msgr. Frank B. Ferraioli (Retired).
Res.: 1050 Littleton Rd., 07054. Tel: 973-539-7050; Fax: 973-539-3601.
See separate listing under Elementary Schools, Diocesan in the Institution section.
Catechesis/Religious Program—Tel: 973-539-6208. Students 400.

3—ST. PETER THE APOSTLE (1938) Rev. Msgr. Herbert K. Tillyer; Rev. L. Richard Hardy; Sr. Sylvia Berzinski, S.S.C., Pastoral Assoc.; Rev. Raimundo Rivera, Parochial Vicar; Deacons Louis Chiocco; Robert A. Lang; Joseph Marsicovete; Peter Cistaro.
Res.: 179 Baldwin Rd., 07054. Tel: 973-334-2090; Fax: 973-334-5397. Email: stpeterpar@optonline.net. Web: saintpetertheapostle.org.
See separate listing under Elementary Schools, Diocesan in the Institution section.
Catechesis/Religious Program—189 Baldwin Rd., 07054. Tel: 973-335-9713; Fax: 973-334-5397. John Cammarata, D.R.E. Students 538.

PASSAIC, PASSAIC CO.

1—ST. ANTHONY OF PADUA (1917), (Italian), Rev. Brando Ibarra.
Res.: 95 Myrtle Ave., 07055. Tel: 973-777-4793; Fax: 973-779-6864. Email: info@stanthonypassaic.com. Web: stanthonypassaic.com.
Catechesis/Religious Program—Students 293.

2—ASSUMPTION OF THE BLESSED VIRGIN MARY (1891), (Slovak), Revs. Edgar Ruiz, Admin.; Jose Lopez, Parochial Vicar.
Res.: 63 Monroe St., 07055. Tel: 973-779-0427; Fax: 973-472-5033.
Catechesis/Religious Program—Students 245.

3—HOLY ROSARY (1918), (Polish), Revs. Stefan Las; Marek Miarecki.
Res.: 6 Wall St., 07055. Tel: 973-473-1578; Fax: 973-473-1773. Email: holyrosarypass@optonline.net.
Catechesis/Religious Program—Students 442.

4—HOLY TRINITY (1900), (German), Revs. Antonio Rodriguez; Bernardo Velasquez, Parochial Vicar.
Res.: 226 Harrison St., 07055. Tel: 973-778-9763; Fax: 973-778-7582.
Catechesis/Religious Program—Students 500.

5—ST. JOSEPH'S (1892), (Polish), Revs. Stanley Lesniowski; Andrzej Puchalski.
Res.: 7 Parker Ave., 07055. Tel: 973-473-2822; Fax: 973-473-2855.
Catechesis/Religious Program—Students 212.

6—ST. NICHOLAS (1868) [CEM] Rev. Edgar Ruiz, Admin.; Rev. Msgr. Felipe N. Carvajal, Pastor Emeritus (Retired); Rev. Jose Lopez, Parochial Vicar.
Res.: 153 Washington Pl., 07055. Tel: 973-779-7867; Fax: 973-815-1893. Email: stnicholasrc@prodigy.net.
Catechesis/Religious Program—Tel: 973-779-7867; Fax: 973-815-1893. Students 64.

7—OUR LADY OF FATIMA (1954), (Hispanic), Revs. Gilberto Gutierrez; Bernardo Velasquez, Parochial Vicar.
Res.: 32 Exchange Pl., 07055. Tel: 973-472-0815; Fax: 973-472-0250.
Catechesis/Religious Program—Students 215.

8—OUR LADY OF MT. CARMEL (1902), (Italian), Rev. Ignatius Zampino, O.F.M.Cap. In Res., Rev. Vincent Liuzzo, O.F.M.Cap.
Res.: 10 St. Francis Way, 07055. Tel: 973-473-0246; Fax: 973-473-3404. Email: ladyofmtcarmel@verizon.net. Web: ladyofmtcarmel.org.
Catechesis/Religious Program—Students 38.

9—ST. STEPHEN'S (1902), (Magyar), Rev. Laszlo Vas.
Res.: 223 Third St., 07055. Tel: 973-779-0332; Fax: 973-778-4263.
Catechesis/Religious Program—Students 3.

PEQUANNOCK, MORRIS CO.

1—HOLY SPIRIT (1949) Rev. John F. Tarantino; Deacons Michael Scruggs; Gary Zack.
Res.: 318 Newark-Pompton Tpke., 07440. Tel: 973-696-1234; Fax: 973-305-9390. Email: info@holyspiritchurchnj.org.
School—(1956) 330 Newark-Pompton Tpke., 07440. Tel: 973-835-5680; Fax: 973-835-1757. Maestre Pie Filippini (Religious Teachers Filippini) 2; Lay Teachers 20; Students 255.
Catechesis/Religious Program—330 Newark-Pompton Tpke., 07440. Tel: 973-835-5696. Students 135.
Convent—Tel: 973-694-2111.

2—OUR LADY OF FATIMA CHAPEL (TRIDENTINE) (1994) Rev. Benoit Guichard, F.S.S.P.; Damian Sypher, F.S.SP.; Rev. Robert Boyd, F.S.S.P.
Res.: 32 West Franklin Ave., 07440. Tel: 973-694-6727. Web: www.olfchapel.org.
School—Kolbe Immaculata School, 18 First St., 07440. Tel: 973-694-1034; Fax: 973-694-1304. Mary Pat Baxter, Prin. Lay Teachers 11; Students 65.
Catechesis/Religious Program—Students 70.

POMPTON LAKES, PASSAIC CO., OUR LADY OF THE ASSUMPTION (1906) Revs. Frank Sevola, O.F.M.; Lawrence Anderson (O.F.M); Richard Husted, O.F.M.; Gonzalo Torres, O.F.M.; Deacons Thomas Kimak; Hal Clark.
Parish Office—17 Pompton Ave., 07442. Tel: 973-835-0374; Fax: 973-835-8173.
St. Mary's Friary: 37 Pompton Ave., 07442. Tel: 973-839-1975. Email: smc@stmarys-pompton.org. Web: www.stmarys-pompton.org.
School—(1951) 25 Pompton Ave., 07442. Tel: 973-835-2010; Fax: 973-835-7529. Carol LaSalle, Prin. Lay Teachers 10; Students 244.
Catechesis/Religious Program—Tel: 973-835-7750; Fax: 973-616-6307. Students 1,827.

POMPTON PLAINS, MORRIS CO., OUR LADY OF GOOD COUNSEL (1962) Rev. Paul O'Donnell Duggan; Deacons Edward Jaroszewski; Herb D. Coyne; Carmen Restaino. In Res., Rev. Charles J. Parr (Retired).
Res.: 155 W. Pkwy., P.O. Box 218, 07444. Tel: 973-839-2447; Fax: 973-839-9492.
Catechesis/Religious Program—Tel: 973-839-3311. Students 775.

PROSPECT PARK, PASSAIC CO., ST. PAUL'S (1924) Rev. Msgr. Edward J. Kurtyka. In Res., Rev. Michael A. Burke.
Res.: 286 Haledon Ave., 07508. Tel: 973-790-8169.
Catechesis/Religious Program—Tel: 973-790-8135. Students 82.

RANDOLPH, MORRIS CO.

1—ST. MATTHEW THE APOSTLE (1988) Rev. Daniel W. Murphy; Deacons Edward Keegan; Richard A. Brady; John Dugger; Jim Hackett.
Res.: 335 Dover-Chester Rd., 07869. Tel: 973-584-1101; Fax: 973-584-0499. Email: st.matthews@st.matthewsrandolph.org. Web: www.stmatthewsrandolph.org.
Catechesis/Religious Program—Students 655.

2—RESURRECTION (1978) Rev. John Andrew Connell; Deacons Roger Lacouture; Kenneth Weaver; Raymond Latour; Richard Reck; Richard Van Glahn.
Res.: 651 Millbrook Ave., 07869. Tel: 973-895-4224; Fax: 973-895-3224. Web: www.resurrectionparishnj.org.
Catechesis/Religious Program—Tel: 973-895-4226. Students 1,042.

RINGWOOD, PASSAIC CO., ST. CATHERINE OF BOLOGNA (1917) Rev. Msgr. Patrick G. Panos; Rev. Paul Barboutz; Deacons James Elliott; Richard Michalski.
Res.: 112 Erskine Rd., 07456. Tel: 973-962-7032; Fax: 973-962-1776. Email: scobsecretary@optonline.net. Web: www.scobp.org.
School—(1948)Tel: 973-962-7131; Fax: 973-962-0585. Franciscan Sisters of Philadelphia 1; Lay Teachers 14; Students 265.
Catechesis/Religious Program—Tel: 973-962-6081. Students 445.

ROCKAWAY, MORRIS CO.

1—ST. CECILIA'S (1869) [CEM] Revs. Sigmund A. Peplowski; Daniel O'Mullane, Parochial Vicar; Marcin Michalowski, Parochial Vicar; Deacons John F. Taylor; Paul D. Willson.
Office: 90 Church St., 07866.
Res.: 70 Church St., 07866. Tel: 973-627-0313; 973-627-0316; Fax: 973-627-4811. Email: stcec@optonline.net. Web: www.st-cecilia.org.
School—(1958) Halsey Ave., 07866. Tel: 973-627-6003; Fax: 973-627-5217. Sisters of Christian Charity 2; Lay Teachers 12; Students 200.
Catechesis/Religious Program—Tel: 973-252-0760. Students 1,060.
Convent—100 Church St., 07866. Tel: 973-627-6533.

2—SACRED HEART (1923), (Slovak), Revs. Sigmund A. Peplowski; Daniel O'Mullane, Parochial Vicar; Marcin Michalowski, Parochial Vicar. In Res., Rev. Stephen Sniscak.
Res.: 63 E. Main St., 07866. Tel: 973-627-0422; Fax: 973-627-6249.
School—(1965) 40 E. Main St., 07866. Tel: 973-627-7689. Sisters of the Sorrowful Mother 1; Lay Teachers 10; Students 259.
Catechesis/Religious Program—Students 51.

ROCKAWAY TOWNSHIP, MORRIS CO., ST. CLEMENT, POPE AND MARTYR (1964) Rev. James J. Termyna; Deacon Harry Dachisen.
Res.: 154 Mt. Pleasant Ave., Dover, 07801. Tel: 973-366-7095; Fax: 973-366-6083. Email: parishoffice@stclement-rtwp.org. Web: www.stclement-rtwp.org.
Catechesis/Religious Program—Tel: 973-366-7547. Students 338.

SANDYSTON, SUSSEX CO., ST. THOMAS THE APOSTLE (1941) Rev. Wayne F. Varga; Deacon Wayne Von Doehren.
Mailing Address: 210 Rte. 206 N., 07826. Tel: 973-948-2296. Email: stjamesthomas@aol.com.
Catechesis/Religious Program—122 C.R. 645, 07826. Fax: 973-948-7007. Students 106.

SCHOOLEY'S MOUNTAIN, MORRIS CO., OUR LADY OF THE MOUNTAIN (1954) [CEM] Rev. Msgr. Joseph J. Goode; Rev. Abuchi Nwosu, Parochial Vicar.
Res.: 2 E. Springtown Rd., Long Valley, 07853. Tel: 908-876-4395; Fax: 908-876-3744.
Catechesis/Religious Program—Tel: 908-876-4003. Students 686.

SPARTA, SUSSEX CO.

1—BLESSED KATERI TEKAKWITHA (1988) Rev. Patrick Rice; Deacons Andrew Calandriello; Gerard Leary; Charles Mathias; Tony Chiocco; Barry O'Brien; Joseph Cote; Glen P. Murphy.
Office: 427 Stanhope Rd., 07871. Tel: 973-729-1682; Fax: 973-729-0702. Email: office@blessedkateri.org. Web: www.blessedkateri.org.
Res.: 11 Cherry Tree Ln., 07871. Tel: 973-729-2892.
Catechesis/Religious Program—Tel: 973-729-0489. Students 702.

2—OUR LADY OF THE LAKE (1935) Revs. David McDonnell; Gregorz Golba, Parochial Vicar; Deacon Edward Maron.
Res.: 294 Sparta Ave., 07871. Tel: 973-729-6107; Fax: 973-729-7203. Email: info@ourladyofthelake.org. Web: www.ourladyofthelake.org.
School—(1954), (School operated by The Catholic Academy of Sussex County Inc.), Tel: 973-729-9174; Fax: 973-729-0318. Dr. Catherine Duncan, Librarian. Lay Teachers 38; Students 540.
Catechesis/Religious Program—Students 895.

STIRLING, MORRIS CO., ST. VINCENT DE PAUL (1886) [CEM] Revs. A. Richard Carton; Leonardo Lopez, Parochial Vicar; Deacons Peter J. O'Neill; Brian F. Mather.
Res.: Bebout Ave., 07980. Tel: 908-647-0118; Fax: 908-647-5992.
School—(1955)Tel: 908-647-0421; Fax: 908-647-3878. Sisters 2; Lay Teachers 19; Students 200.
Catechesis/Religious Program—Tel: 908-647-6772. Students 475.

STOCKHOLM, SUSSEX CO., ST. JOHN VIANNEY (1958) Rev. Matthew J. Twiggs; Deacons James Camarrano; Kevin L. Combs.
Res.: 2823 Rte. 23, P.O. Box 505, 07460. Tel: 973-697-6550; Fax: 973-697-6882. Web: www.sjvianneyparish.org.
Catechesis/Religious Program—Tel: 973-764-7071. Students 238.

SUCCASUNNA, MORRIS CO., ST. THERESE (1957) Revs. Marc A. Mancini; Vidal Gonzales, Parochial Vicar; William Santeliz, Parochial Vicar; Deacons Anthony Signorelli; Bruce Olsen.
Res.: 7 Hunter St., 07876. Tel: 973-584-8271; Fax: 973-584-0684. Email: stthereseoffice@optonline.net.
School—(1963) 135 Main St., 07876. Tel: 973-584-0812; Fax: 973-584-2029. Sisters 1; Lay Teachers 10; Students 270.
Catechesis/Religious Program—Tel: 973-584-9444; Fax: 973-584-9492. Students 801.

SUSSEX, SUSSEX CO., ST. MONICA (1881) Rev. Charles A. Perricone; Carol Bezak, Pastoral Assoc.
Res.: 33 Unionville Ave., 07461. Tel: 973-875-4521; Fax: 973-875-7538.
Catechesis/Religious Program—Students 124.

SWARTSWOOD, SUSSEX CO., OUR LADY OF MT. CARMEL (1951) Rev. Brian Ditullio, Admin.; Deacons Anthony P. Barile Jr.; Robert T. Davis; Edward J. Muller.
Mailing Address: P.O. Box 124, 07877. Tel: 973-383-3566; Fax: 973-383-3831.
Catechesis/Religious Program—Tel: 973-579-2355. Students 155.

TOTOWA BOROUGH, PASSAIC CO., ST. JAMES OF THE MARCHES (1926) Revs. J. Patrick Ryan; Marek Kysiak (Poland), Parochial Vicar.
Res.: 32 St. James Pl., 07512. Tel: 973-790-0288; Fax: 973-790-7064. Email: stjameschurch@optonline.net.
Catechesis/Religious Program—31 St. James Pl. Tel: 973-790-4860; Fax: 973-790-4644. Students 450.

WAYNE, PASSAIC CO.

1—ANNUNCIATION (1963) Rev. Msgr. Peter J. Doody; Deacon Joseph C. Crowley Jr.
Res.: 45 Urban Club Rd., 07470. Tel: 973-694-5700; Fax: 973-694-5706. Web: www.abumwayne.org.
Catechesis/Religious Program—Tel: 973-694-0787. Students 148.

2—HOLY CROSS (1925) Rev. Msgr. Christopher C. DiLella, Admin.; Rev. Charles J. Parr, Pastor Emeritus (Retired).
Res.: 17 Van Duyne Ave., 07470. Tel: 973-696-1065; Fax: 973-696-3641. Email: holycrosswayne@verizon.net.

Catechesis/Religious Program—Tel: 973-696-3500. Students 45.

3—IMMACULATE HEART OF MARY (1956) Rev. Daniel A. Kelly; Deacon Daniel Galvin.
Res.: 580 Ratzer Rd., 07470. Tel: 973-694-3400; Fax: 973-694-3459. Email: ihmchurch@aol.com. Web: www.ihmwaynenj.org.
School—(1958)Tel: 973-694-1225; Fax: 973-872-9043. Lay Teachers 16; Students 205.
Catechesis/Religious Program—Tel: 973-694-4891. Students 605.

4—OUR LADY OF CONSOLATION (1963) Rev. Michael D. Lombardo; Deacon John Schuler.
Res.: 1799 Hamburg Tpke., 07470. Tel: 973-839-3444; Fax: 973-839-9695.
School—(1967)Tel: 973-839-2323; Fax: 973-616-5379. Lay Teachers 15; Students 168.
Catechesis/Religious Program—Students 366.

5—OUR LADY OF THE VALLEY (1960) Rev. Msgr. Christopher C. DiLella; Rev. ST Sutton, Parochial Vicar; Deacons Vincent Cocilovo; Michael J. Malecki.
Office: 630 Valley Rd., 07470. Tel: 973-694-4585; Fax: 973-696-4430.
Res.: 614 Valley Rd., 07470. Web: www.olvwayne.org.
Catechesis/Religious Program—630 Valley Rd. Tel: 973-696-8307. Students 625.

WEST MILFORD TOWNSHIP, PASSAIC CO., ST. JOSEPH (1765) Rev. Steven Shadwell, Admin.; Deacons Milton Smilek; Anthony Curcio; Benjamin LoParo; Harry White. In Res., Rev. Francis Kelly.
Res.: 454 Germantown Rd., 07480. Tel: 973-697-6100; Fax: 973-697-3716. Web: www.stjoseph-nj.org.
Catechesis/Religious Program—Tel: 973-208-0636. Students 360.

WHIPPANY, MORRIS CO., OUR LADY OF MERCY (1854) [CEM] Revs. Sean McDonnell; Janusz Rzadca, Parochial Vicar.
Res.: 9 Parsippany Rd., 07981. Tel: 973-887-0050; Fax: 973-887-0991. Email: olmchwhip@aol.com. Web: www.ourladyofmercyparish.com.
School—90 Whippany Rd., 07981. Tel: 973-887-2611; Fax: 973-887-6629. Ms. Elizabeth Ventola, Prin. Lay Teachers 17; Students 200.
Catechesis/Religious Program—94-96 Whippany Rd. Tel: 973-887-0767. Students 283.

Chaplains of Public Institutions

Hospitals

PATERSON. *St. Joseph Hospital*, 703 Main St., 07503. Tel: 973-754-2000; 973-754-2060 (Office). Mr. William McDonald, Pres. & CEO, Revs. Martin Rooney, Francis Enrico Conde, Chap., Edward A. Collins, Thomas G. Rainforth, Christopher Anyanwu, Volodymyr Baran, Chap.
Preakness Hospital, P.O. Box V, 07509. Tel: 973-278-6800. Rev. James Moss.

DENVILLE. *St. Clare Hospital*, Pocono Rd., 07834. Tel: 973-627-3000. Revs. Ifeanyi Iwu, Chap., Paul Nwambu, Chap., Stephen Sniscak, Chap.

DOVER. *Dover General Hospital*, Jardine St., 07801. Tel: 973-939-3000. Rev. Henry Tanto.

MORRIS PLAINS. *Greystone Park Psychiatric Hospital* 07950. Tel: 973-538-1800. Rev. Simon P. Gallagher, O.S.B.

MORRISTOWN. *Morristown Memorial Hospital*, 100 Madison Ave., 07960. Tel: 973-540-5307. Revs. Zbigniew Kluba, Dennis J. Crowley, Sisters Teresa Chiappa, S.S.C., Jo Mascera, S.S.C.

NEWTON. *Newton Memorial Hospital*, 175 High St., 07860. Tel: 973-383-2121. Vacant.

PASSAIC. *St. Mary Hospital*, 211 Pennington Ave., 07055. Tel: 973-473-1000. Revs. Sam Frapaul, O.F.M.Cap., Stanley Robel, O.F.M.Cap.

POMPTON PLAINS. *Chilton Memorial Hospital* 07444. Tel: 973-831-5000. Rev. Robert J. Norton, O.F.M., Chap., Deacons Edward Jaroszewski, Gil Leifer, Larry White.

TOTOWA. *North Jersey Developmental Center*. Rev. Louis J. Scurti.

WAYNE. *St. Joseph's Wayne Hospital*, Hamburg Tpke., 07470. Tel: 973-942-6900. Rev. Thomas G. Rainforth.

Correctional Facilities

PATERSON. *Passaic County Jail*. Rev. Msgr. Mark J. Giordani, Rev. Luis A. Rendon.

MORRISTOWN. *Morris County Jail*. Rev. Hernan Arias, Coord. Prison Ministry.

NEWTON. *Sussex County Jail*. Rev. A. Richard Carton.

Colleges

NEWTON. *Sussex County Community College*. Carol Bezak, Campus Min.

RANDOLPH. *County College of Morris*. Deacon Richard Galdo, Campus Min.

Special Assignment:
Rev. Msgr.—
Bihr, Louis J., 296 Straight St., 07501.
Revs.—
Corcoran, T. Kevin, 178 Derrom Ave., 07504.
Lambro, Edward, 476 17th Ave., 07504. Tel: 973-523-4456
McGrath, Thomas, 476 17th Ave., 07504. Tel: 201-523-9595

On Duty Outside the Diocese:
Revs.—
Bono, James P., Warwick, NY
Briganti, Philip J., El Paso, TX
Glabik, Peter S., Orchard Lake, MI
Grasso, Richard, Ormond Beach, FL
Holterhoff, Edward G., Morro Bay, CA
Joly, Michael D., Yorktown, VA
Kanzic, Gerald, Pittsburgh, PA
McLoughlin, Brendan, Denville, NJ
Pavlick, Raymond A., Walden, NY
Reading, Edward, Ortley Beach, NJ
Savitt, Alan F., Clifton, NJ
Stephenson, Alphonse J., Point Pleasant, NJ
Vitillo, Robert J., Geneva, Switzerland
Weis, John H., Sebewaing, MI

Graduate Studies:
Revs.—
Garbarino, Joseph J., Fordham University
Waller, Charles J.

Military Chaplains:
Rev. Msgr.—
Cusack, John J., USAF
Revs.—
O'Grady, Frank, USA
Parisi, Michael, USN

Unassigned:
Rev. Msgrs.—
Brown, Patrick E.
Naughton, William M.
Revs.—
Biegun, Marek
Davis, Joseph P.
Mastroeni, Anthony J., S.T.D., J.D.
Scurti, Louis J.

Absent on Leave:
Rev. Msgr.—
Tamayo, Elias
Revs.—
Cramer, William N.
Erwin, Patrick O.
Long, David P., S.T.L., J.C.L.
Mabango, Ashiono Anthony
Scott, James C.
Treglio, Vincent

Medical Leave:
Rev.—
Drogon, Greg

Retired:
Most Rev.—
Rodimer, Frank J., D.D., J.C.D., 1082 Green Pond Rd., Green Pond, 07435.
Rev. Msgrs.—
Amandolare, Ronald J., 34 Timberline Dr., Little Egg Harbor Twp, 08087.
Boland, Eugene, 2 Tulip Crescent, Unit 1A, Little Falls, 07424.
Carey, Leo P., Nazareth Village, Main St., Box 635, Chester, 07930.
Carvajal, Felipe N., 30 Park Ave., Garfield, 07026.
Cassidy, Charles C., 15 Sea Girt Ln., Waretown, 08758.
Ciampaglio, Joseph M., 32 Greenways Ln., Lakewood, 08701.
Conway, Michael, 2510 S.W. 81st Ave., Apt. 308, Davie, FL 33328.
Corr, John F., 83 Primose Tr., Morristown, 07960.
Demkovich, John J., 218 Ackerman Ave., Clifton, 07011.
Diachak, Robert, Nazareth Village, 11 Meadow Ln., P.O. Box 745, Chester, 07930.
Dudak, George A., Nazareth Village, Main St., Chester, 07930.
Ferraioli, Frank B., 1050 Littleton Rd., Parsippany, 07054.
Ferrito, Joseph L., 15 Sea Girt Ln., Waretown, 08758.
Flanagan, P. Kevin, 797 Valley Rd., Clifton, 07013.
Introini, Elso C., 34 San Carlos St., Toms River, 08757.
Lasch, Kenneth E., J.C.D., 41 Elm St., Apt. 2-E, Morristown, 07960.
Lee, Thaddeus, P.O. Box 21, Passaic, 07055.
Longua, Paul A., The Atrium at Wayne, 1120 Alps Rd., Wayne, 07470.
Madden, Brendan P., Nazareth Village, Main St., Chester, 07930.
Matarazzo, Francis, 154 E. 1st St., Clifton, 07011.
McBride, Peter A., Nazareth Village, Main St., Chester, 07930.
McCarthy, William, 3 Winding Wood Dr., Sayreville, 08872.
McHugh, Peter J., Nazareth Village, P.O. Box 745, Chester, 07930.
Murray, James H., 19 Pocono Rd., Apt. 83, Denville, 07834.
O'Rorke, James H., 41 Spruce Hill Ct., Hamburg, 07419.
Puma, Vincent E., St. Vincent's Nursing Home, 315 E. Lindsley Rd., Cedar Grove, 07009.
Rauscher, Martin F., 41 Elm St., Apt. 4E, Morristown, 07960.
Rocco, Remigio G., P.O. Box 93, Layton, 07851.
Russo, Charles J., 27 Livingston Rd., Morristown, 07960.
Ryan, Leo P., Main St., Box 635, Chester, 07930.
Schinski, Stanley E., Main St., Box 635, Chester, 07930.
Scott, Patrick J., 400 Mt. Prospect Ave., Clifton, 07012.
Steiger, Richard A., 28 Carriage Ln., Newton, 07860.
Trapasso, Thomas J., S.T.L., Main St., Box 635, Chester, 07930.
Tully, Ronald J.
Varettoni, Julian B., 486 Rt. 46, Hackettstown, 07840.
Wehrlen, John B., 22 Morning Glory Ct., Toms River, 08755.
Revs.—
Bradley, Charles, 4017 Whitehall Way, Alpharetta, GA 30004.
Catoir, John T., J.C.D., Nazareth Village, Main St., Chester, 07930.
Costigan, George, 85 Richard Mine Rd., Dover, 07801.
Coutinho, Absalom, Bradenton, FL 34282.
Davey, Edward M., Nazareth Village, Main St., Chester, 07930.
Dillon, Edward J., 1754 River Rd., Upper Black Eddy, PA 18972.
Hanley, John P., 501 W. Broadway, 07524.
Heekin, John M., 3912 S. Ocean Blvd., Apt. 505, Highland Beach, FL 33487.
Hertel, James R., J.C.D., 2 Ann St., Unit F112, Clifton, 07013.
Hewitt, Kenneth R., 490 Windemere Ave., Mount Arlington, 07856.
Hooper, Robert K., Nazareth Village, 11 Meadow Ln., Box 635, Chester, 07930.
Iovino, Paul, 23 Mission Way, Barnegat, 08005.
Jacobs, Richard A., 91 Maple Ave., Catskill, NY 12414.
Klein, John J., Nazareth Village, 11 Meadow Ln., Box 635, Chester, 07930.
Klim, Vincent, Nazareth Village, Main St., Chester, 07930.
Krajewski, Paul A., 10 Prime Rose Ln., Mount Arlington, 07856.
Kuzhippallil, George, P.O. Box 164, Broadway, 08808.
LoGatto, Joseph J., Via Fontanella, Cosenza, Italy.
Lugo, Joseph W., 78 Chestnut St., Bridgewater, 08807.
Mazza, Victor J., 1 Scenic Dr., Unit 903, Highlands, 07732.
McHugh, Dennis, Our Lady's Shrine, Knock, County Mayo, Ireland.
Mullan, Patrick, Nazareth Village, Main St., Box 635, Chester, 07930.
Murphy, Joseph E., Nazareth Village, Main St., Box 635, Chester, 07930.
Mushinsky, John E., 22 Boston Rd., Neptune, 07753.
Nix, Albert P., P.O. Box 564, Sparta, 07871.
O'Connor, John H., 6 Condict St., Morris Plains, 07950.
O'Kielty, James P. (ARL), 134 Christendom Dr., Front Royal, VA 22630.
O'Riordan, Jeremiah, Nazareth Village, Main St., Chester, 07930.
Oliveri, Richard H., 433 18th Ave., Brick, 08724.
Panagia, Sal J., Great George Village, Le Touquet, Unit 4, Vernon, 07462.
Parr, Charles J., Ph.D., 155 W. Pkwy., Pompton Plains, 07444.
Pisarcik, John G., 302 Regent St., Dover, DE 19904-3392.
Rento, Richard G., 33 Murray Ln., Lavalette, 08735.
Scolamiero, Dominic A., 1968 Sailor's Quay, 34 N. Pier, Brick, 08723.
Sella, Donald J., P.O. Box 1108, Fajardo, PR 00738.
Shema, George T., Nazareth Village, Main St., Box 635, Chester, 07930.
Smith, James A.D., Nazareth Village, Main St., Box 635, Chester, 07930.
Sordillo, Ronald, 306 Mountain Ave., New Providence, 07974.
Stepien, Allen F., 5 New Briar Ln., Clifton, 07012.

Permanent Deacons:
Acevedo, Pedro, (Retired)
Allgaier, Michael, St. Mary, Denville
Altilio, Robert M., St. John Kanty, Clifton
Ayers, Robert, St. Andrew, Clifton
Balough, Joseph, St. Bonaventure, Paterson
Bandel, Arthur, (Unassigned)
Barile, Anthony P., Jr., Our Lady of Mount Carmel, Swartswood
Beirne, Thomas P., St. Mary, Dover
Bernardine, Anthony E., St. Anthony, Hawthorne
Beyerl, Brian D., Assumption, Morristown
Bianchi, Roland, Archdiocese of Newark
Bias, Richard F., St. Michael, Netcong
Biersbach, Raymond, St. Mark, Long Valley
Boscia, Edward F., St. Thomas, Ogdensburg
Brady, Richard A., St. Matthew, Randolph
Brudzynski, Richard, St. Anthony, Hawthorne
Butkus, James A., Notre Dame, Cedar Knolls
Calandriello, Andrew, Blessed Kateri Tekakwitha, Sparta
Callahan, Jack, St. Pius X, Montville
Cammarano, James, St. John Vianney, Stockholm
Carnero, Juan Carlos, St. Mary, Paterson
Casamento, Peter, Diocese of Charleston, SC
Casillas, Hector, St. Joseph, Paterson
Cassidy, Joseph, (Retired)
Castellanos, Hector, St. John Cathedral, Paterson
Cedrone, David, Our Lady Queen of Peace, West Milford
Chimileski, Raymond J., St. Luke, Long Valley
Chiocco, Anthony F., Blessed Kateri Tekakwitha, Sparta
Chiocco, Louis, St. Peter the Apostle, Parsippany
Cistaro, Peter, St. Peter the Apostle, Parsippany
Clark, Hal G., St. Mary, Pompton Lakes
Cleary, Kevin, St. Luke, Long Valley
Cocilovo, Vincent, Our Lady of the Valley, Wayne
Collins, David, Notre Dame, Cedar Knolls
Combs, Kevin L., St. Francis De Sales, McAfee
Cortes, Jesus, (Unassigned)
Coyne, Herb D., Our Lady of Good Counsel, Pompton Plains
Crowley, Joseph C., Jr., Annunciation, Wayne
Cruz, Pedro, St. Agnes, Paterson
Curcio, Anthony, Jr., St. Joseph, West Milford
D'Amico, Larry, St. Joseph, Newton
Dachisen, Harry, St. Clement Pope and Martyr, Rockaway Township
DaSilva, Joao, Morristown Memorial Hospital
Davila, Jesus, (Unassigned)
Davis, Robert T., Our Lady of Mount Carmel, Swartswood
de Mena, Henry, Notre Dame, Cedar Knolls
Delgado, Alberto, (Unassigned)
Deo, Leonard, St. Ann, Parsippany
DiLorenzo, Anthony, Diocese of Venice, FL
Dolan, Eugene P., (Leave of Absence)
Drury, Brian, (Unassigned)
Duarte, Hildebrando A., Diocese of Trenton, NJ
Dugger, John, St. Matthew, Randolph
Elliott, James, St. Catherine of Bologna, Ringwood
Espinal, Candelario, St. Stephen, Paterson
Fadalla, Gerald J., St. Anthony, Hawthorne
Fanelli, Alfredo, Notre Dame of Mt. Carmel, Cedar Knolls
Ferry, Daniel F., Diocese of Richmond, VA
Fierro, Anthony O., St. Bonaventure, Paterson
Fiore, Peter M., Holy Family, Florham Park
Flynn, Jack, St. Mary, Denville
Forino, Ronald, Notre Dame of Mount Carmel, Cedar Knolls
Forshay, George W., St. Anthony, Hawthorne
Frank, Alfred E., St. Ann, Parsippany
Friel, Thomas, St. Jude, Hopatcong
Galinski, Edmund V., Good Shepherd, Andover
Gallo, Henry, (Retired)
Galvin, Daniel, Immaculate Heart of Mary, Wayne
Gaydo, Richard A., St. Christopher, Parsippany
Gibbons, Thomas P., Our Lady of the Mountain, Schooley's Mountain
Gil, Luis, St. John the Baptist, Paterson
Goglia, Richard J., St. Andrew, Clifton
Gordon, Gary, Morristown Memorial Hospital
Gunther, Stephen A., (Unassigned)
Hackett, Jim, St. Matthew the Apostle, Randolph
Hanifen, Gerald B., St. Joseph, Newton
Hanly, P. Michael, Assumption, Morristown
Harenchar, Thomas G., St. Virgil, Morris Plains
Harris, Joseph, Notre Dame, Cedar Knolls
Harris, Keith, Good Shepherd, Andover
Hartnett, Stuart A., St. Mary, Dover
Harty, William, (Retired)
Head, Robert C., Our Lady of the Mountain, Schooley's Mountain
Healy, Philip, (Retired)
Healy, Thomas F., Jr., St. Luke, Long Valley
Higgins, Edward J., (Retired)
Holden, Timothy M., St. Margaret, Morristown
Hussey, William E., (Retired)
Hyle, Henry, (Leave of Absence)
Jaroszewski, Edward, Our Lady of Good Counsel Church, Pompton Plains
Keegan, Edward, St. Matthew, Randolph
Keenan, Joseph, St. Michael, Netcong
Kelly, John, St. Christopher, Parsippany
Kimak, Thomas J., St. Mary, Pompton Lakes
King, Dennis, St. Elizabeth Ann Seton, Flanders
Klose, Albert P., (Retired)
Kronyak, Thomas, (Unassigned)
Kucinski, Al, St. Joseph, Newton.
Lacouture, Roger, (Retired)
Lally, Edward J., St. Christopher, Parsippany
Lang, Robert A., St. Peter the Apostle, Parsippany
Latour, Raymond, Resurrection, Randolph
Leary, Gerard, Blessed Kateri Tekakwitha, Sparta
Lebron, Florencio G., (Leave of Absence)
Leo, Vincent, Jr., St. Rose of Lima, East Hanover
Llibre, John, (Retired)
Lo Paro, Ben, St. Joseph, West Milford
Long, William P., (Retired)
Lucibello, Allan J., St. Christopher, Parsippany
Lupi, Victor, Notre Dame, Cedar Knolls
Malecki, Michael J., Our Lady of the Valley, Wayne
Mallory, Charles, (Unassigned)
Mann, Patrick, St. Pius X, Montville
Marabeti, Stephen J., St. Joseph Church, Lincoln Park
Maron, Edward, Our Lady of the Lake, Sparta
Marsicovete, Joseph, St. Peter the Apostle, Parsippany
Mather, Brian F., St. Vincent de Paul, Stirling
Mathias, Charles T., Bl. Kateri Tekakwitha, Sparta
Mazzaccoli, Sylvester A., St. Virgil Church, Morris Plains
McCabe, Mark, (Retired)
McMahon, Matthew, Notre Dame of Mount Carmel, Cedar Knolls
Meyer, John, St. Mark, Long Valley
Michalski, Richard, St. Catherine of Bologna, Ringwood
Morales, Eugenio, SS. Cyril and Methodius, Clifton
Morton, Robert, St. Clement, Rockaway Twp.
Muller, Edward J., Our Lady of Mount Carmel, Swartswood
Munoz, Mario, Our Lady of Lourdes, Paterson
Murphy, Glen P., Blessed Kateri Tekakwitha, Sparta
Murphy, Stuart, St. Michael, Netcong
Natafalusy, Stephen P., (Retired)
Nixon, Mark G., St. Patrick, Chatham
Nolan, Richard, (Leave of Absence)
O'Brien, Barry, Blessed Kateri Tekakwitha, Sparta
O'Leary, Donald, (Leave of Absence)
O'Neill, Peter J., St. Vincent de Paul, Stirling
Ochner, Ronald, Our Lady of Good Counsel, Pompton Plains
Olsen, Bruce, St. Therese, Succasunna
Owens, Frank, St. Lawrence the Martyr, Chester
Pamplona, Raul, Our Lady of Lourdes, Paterson
Para, Frank, St. Virgil, Morris Plains
Parlapiano, Joseph J., St. Joseph, Lincoln Park
Paulino, Maximo, Our Lady of Victories, Paterson
Pedraza, Guido, St. John the Baptist, Paterson
Pilek, John F., (Leave of Absence)
Pinto, Richard, St. Virgil, Morris Plains
Pisano, Vincent F., (Unassigned)
Pomales, Jose, St. John Cathedral, Paterson
Pringle, Robert H., Consolation, Wayne
Puglia, Frank, St. Elizabeth Ann Seton, Flanders
Puleo, Paul A., (Retired)
Puskas, Joseph, St. Paul, Clifton
Quinn, Joseph, Notre Dame of Mt. Carmel, Cedar Knolls
Rado, Kenneth, St. Virgil, Morris Plains
Ramirez, Edward, St. Nicholas, Passaic
Ramirez, Luis, St. Therese, Paterson
Reading, Edward J., St. Thomas of Aquin, Ogdensburg
Reck, Richard, Resurrection, Randolph
Restaino, Carmen, Our Lady of Good Counsel, Pompton Plains
Richardson, Joseph, Our Lady of Magnificat, Kinnelon
Rivera, Jose M., St. Francis of Assisi, Haskell
Roche, Charles, Our Lady Queen of Peace, Hewitt
Rohrman, Harry, St. Christopher, Parsippany
Romano, Ron, St. Joseph, Paterson
Salierno, Anthony, St. Mary, Paterson
Sanchez, Armando, Archdiocese of Lima, Peru
Sanker, John M., St. Jude, Budd Lake
Santiago, Manuel, Diocese of St. Petersburg, FL
Santos, Robert F., St. Joseph, Mendham
Schenker, Jerome, (Leave of Absence)
Schuler, John, Our Lady of Consolation, Wayne
Scrone, Daniel, Diocese of St. Augustine, FL
Scruggs, Michael K., Holy Spirit, Pequannock
Sheehan, Patrick, Diocese of Charleston, SC
Signorelli, Anthony, St. Therese, Succasunna
Siino, Anthony C., St. Jude, Budd Lake
Silva, Percy, (Leave of Absence)
Simeone, Enio, (Retired)
Sisco, Joseph, Our Lady of Holy Angels, Little Falls
Sisler, Merle F., St. Virgil, Morris Plains
Sisson, Stanley, (Retired)
Smilek, Milton, St. Joseph, West Milford
Sullivan, Thomas, Good Shepherd, Andover
Taylor, John F., St. Cecilia, Rockaway
Tenga, Charles, (Retired)
Thiuri, Phillipe, (Leave of Absence)
Totino, Alberto R., Our Lady Star of the Sea, Lake Hopatcong
Trinidad, Jose M., (Leave of Absence)
Turner, John, (Retired)
Van Glahn, Richard, Resurrection, Randolph
Van Orman, Patrick, (Retired)
Varsalona, Nicholas, St. Therese Church, Paterson
Vazquez, Gilberto, St. Agnes, Paterson
Veliky, Nicholas, St. Philip the Apostle, Clifton
Verboys, Joseph R., Our Lady Queen of Peace, Hewitt
Vesota, Robert, (Retired)
Von Doehren, Wayne, St. James, Montague; St. Thomas, Hainesville
Walker, John, (Leave of Absence)
Wallace, Michael J., Passaic County Youth Detention Center
Ward, William, Holy Family, Florham Park
Weaver, Kenneth, Resurrection, Randolph
Whelan, Edward, St. Elizabeth Ann Seton, Flanders
White, Harry, St. Joseph, West Milford
Willson, Paul D., St. Cecelia, Rockaway
Wisneski, Joseph A., St. Patrick, Chatham
Wisniewski, Paul M., (Leave of Absence)
Zack, Gary, Holy Spirit, Pequannock
Zampella, Dominic, St. Thomas of Aquin, Ogdensburg
Zayac, Thomas, St. Joseph, Newton

INSTITUTIONS LOCATED IN THE DIOCESE

[A] SEMINARIES, RELIGIOUS OR SCHOLASTICATES

BOONTON. *Domus Bartimaeus* (Diocesan House of Discernment), 913 Birch St., 07005. Tel: 973-588-7814. Rev. Hubert Jurjewicz, Dir. Seminarians 11.

[B] COLLEGES AND UNIVERSITIES

MENDHAM. *Assumption College for Sisters*, 350 Bernardsville Rd., 07945-2923. Tel: 973-543-6528; Fax: 973-543-1738. Email: acs@acs350.org. Web: www.acs350.org. Sisters Joseph Spring, S.C.C., Pres.; Gerardine Tantsits, S.C.C., Academic Dean & Registrar; Theresa Bower, S.C.C., Librarian; Patricia McGrady, Treas. Conducted by Sisters of Christian Charity. Religious 12; Lay Staff 11; Students 43.

MORRISTOWN. *College of Saint Elizabeth*, 2 Convent Rd., 07960-6989. Tel: 973-290-4000; 973-290-4475; Fax: 973-290-4485. Web: www.cse.edu. Rev. Msgr. Thomas J. McDade (NEW), Scholar in Res.; Sr. Francis Raftery, S.C., Pres.; Katherine Buck, Vice Pres. Student Life; Maria Cammarata, Vice Pres. Finance & Admin. and Treas.; Anthony Colabraro, Comptroller; James Dlugos, Vice Pres. & Dean Academic Affairs; Dr. Carol Strobeck, Dean, Women's College & Undergraduate Studies; Mrs. Donna Tatarka, Dean Admissions; Amira Unver, Librarian. Sisters of Charity of St. Elizabeth., Full-time Admin. and Faculty: Priests 1; Religious 13; Lay Teachers 205; Students 2,000.

[C] HIGH SCHOOLS, DIOCESAN

DENVILLE. *Morris Catholic High School* 07834. Tel: 973-627-6674; Fax: 973-627-4351. Email: mchs@morriscatholic.org. Web: www.morriscatholic.org. Michael St. Pierre, Pres.; Dr. Jeanne Gradone, Prin.; Rev. Carmen Buono, Chap. Priests 1; Sisters 3; Lay Teachers 38; Students 458.

SPARTA. *Pope John XXIII High School* School operated by The Catholic Academy of Sussex County, Inc., 07871. Tel: 973-729-6125; Fax: 973-729-4313. Email: pjhs@popejohn.org. Rev. Msgr. Kieran A. McHugh, Pres.; Mrs. Gloria Shope, Prin. Lay Teachers 79; Students 970.

WAYNE. *De Paul Catholic High School*, 1512 Alps Rd., 07470. Tel: 973-694-3702; Fax: 973-633-5381. Email: asciaino@dpchs.org. Web: depaulcatholic.org. Rev. Michael Donovan, Pres.; Anthony J. Sciaino, Prin. Sisters 1; Brothers 1; Lay Teachers 72; Students 842.

[D] HIGH SCHOOLS, PRIVATE

CONVENT STATION. *Academy of St. Elizabeth* 07961. Tel: 973-290-5200; Fax: 973-290-5232. Sr. Patricia Costello, O.P, Prin. Sisters of Charity. Sisters 3; Lay Teachers 25; Students 225.

MORRISTOWN. *Delbarton School*, 230 Mendham Rd., 07960. Tel: 973-538-3231; Fax: 973-538-8836. Email: homepage@delbarton.org. Web: www.delbarton.org. Bro. Paul J. Diveny, O.S.B.,

Headmaster; Mr. Charles Ruebling, Asst. Headmaster; Mrs. Anne Leckie, Dean of Faculty; Dr. David Donovan, Dir. Admissions; Mr. David Hajduk, Dir. Campus Min. Day School for Boys. (Grades 7-12) Monks 10; Laymen 68; Students 542.

Villa Walsh Academy 07960. Tel: 973-538-3680; Fax: 973-538-6733. Email: villawalsh@aol.com. Web: www.villawalsh.org. Sr. Patricia Pompa, M.P.F., Prin. College Preparatory for girls (Grades 7-12). Conducted by Religious Teachers Filippini Sisters 5; Lay Teachers 32; Students 255.

NORTH HALEDON. *Mary Help of Christians Academy*, 659-723 Belmont Ave., 07508. Tel: 973-790-6200; Fax: 973-790-6125. Email: principal@maryhelp.org. Web: www.maryhelp.org. Sr. Kim Keraitis, F.M.A., Prin.; Lillian Brunetti, Librarian. Daughters of Mary Help of Christians (Salesian Sisters). Sisters 11; Lay Teachers 26; Students 320.

[E] ELEMENTARY SCHOOLS, DIOCESAN

PARSIPPANY. *All Saints Academy*, 189 Baldwin Rd., 07054. Tel: 973-334-4704; Fax: 973-334-0622. Ms. Judy Berg, Pres. Sisters 1; Lay Teachers 15; Students 245.

TOTOWA. *Academy of Saint Francis of Assisi*, 400 Totowa Rd., 07512. Tel: 973-956-8824; Fax: 976-956-9430. Email: office@academyofstfrancis.org. Web: www.academyofstfrancis.org. Mrs. Linda Kostenko, Prin. Serves Our Lady of the Holy Angels, Little Falls & St. James, Totowa Lay Teachers 11; Students 247.

[F] REGIONAL ELEMENTARY SCHOOLS

FRANKLIN. *Immaculate Conception Regional School*, (Grades PreK-8), School operated by The Catholic Academy of Sussex County, Inc., 65 Church St., 07416. Tel: 973-827-3777; Fax: 973-827-8728. Email: dispagna@icrschool.com. Web: www.icrschool.com. Ms. Diane Di Spagna, Prin. Serves Immaculate Conception, Franklin; Our Lady of Fatima, Highland Lakes; St. John Vianney, Stockholm; St. Monica, Sussex; St. Thomas of Aquin, Ogdensburg; St. Francis De Sales, McAfee; St. Jude, Hamburg Lay Teachers 16; Students 216.

NEWTON. *St. Joseph Regional School* School operated by The Catholic Academy of Sussex County, Inc., Jefferson St., 07860. Tel: 973-383-2909; Fax: 973-383-6353. Email: sjrs@nac.net. Web: www.sjccsorg. Ms. Linda Nick, Prin. Serves St. Joseph, Newton; Our Lady Queen of Peace, Branchville; Our Lady of Mount Carmel, Swartswood Lay Teachers 12; Students 194.

[G] PRIVATE PRESCHOOL

FLORHAM PARK. *Magic Kingdom Day Nursery*, 88 Brooklake Rd., 07932. Tel: 973-966-9762; Fax: 973-377-3994. Email: magickingdom2008@yahoo.com. Sr. M. Antonietta Raucci, S.D.V., Prin. Vocationist Sisters. Sisters 14; Lay Teachers 4; Students 84.

NEWTON. *Camp Auxilium Learning Center* School operated by The Catholic Academy of Sussex County, Inc., 14 Old Swartswood Rd., 07860. Tel: 973-383-2621; Fax: 973-383-3214. Email: campauxilium@nac.net. Web: www.campauxilium.org. Sr. Theresa Samson, F.M.A., Prin. Salesian Sisters. Sisters 5; Lay Teachers 9; Students 241.

PARSIPPANY. *St. Elizabeth Nursery and Montessori School, Inc.*, 499 Park Rd., 07054. Tel: 973-540-0721; Fax: 973-540-9186. Email: saintelizabeths@yahoo.con. Web: www.stelizabethschool.com. Sisters Gina Maria Amico, F.S.S.E., Delegate General; Cathy Lynn Cummings, F.S.S.E., Prin. Students 333.

[H] EVANGELIZATION CENTERS

MADISON. *St. Paul Inside The Walls: The Catholic Center for Evangelization at Bayley-Ellard*, 205 Madison Ave., 07940. Tel: 973-377-1004; Fax: 973-377-1952. Rev. Geno Sylva, S.T.D., Dir.; Sr. Mary Joseph Schultz, S.C.C., Resource Dir.; Mr. Daniel Ferrari, Music Dir.; Ms. Virginia Kamenitzer, Prog. Dir.; Mr. Dennis Rodano, Business Mgr.; Ms. Patricia Terranella, Admin. Asst.; Ms. Ivannia Vega-McTighe, Lay Min. Formation Leadership; Mr. Allan Wright, Academic Dean Evangelization In Res. Rev. Derek Anderson, S.O.L.T.

[I] CHILDREN'S CENTERS

TOTOWA. *Mt. St. Joseph Children's Center*, 124 Shepherds Ln., 07512. Tel: 973-595-5720; Fax: 973-595-1930. Ms. Patricia S. Verduin, Dir. Residential school for classified emotionally disturbed boys, 6-14, referred from public school districts. Under the direction of Catholic Family and Community Services. Residents 37.

[J] RETREAT HOUSES & HOUSES OF PRAYER

BRANCHVILLE. *Sanctuary of Mary-Our Lady of the Holy Spirit*, 252 Wantage Ave., 07826. Tel: 973-875-7625. Rev. James Mulligan, S.O.L.T.

CHESTER. *Hermits of Bethlehem in the Heart of Jesus*, 82 Pleasant Hill Rd., 07930. Tel: 908-879-7059; Fax: 908-879-7059. Rev. Eugene C. Romano, Desert Father; Bros. Giuseppe Crispino; Raphael Joseph Peres; Bernard Streidel. Priests 1; Sisters 6; Brothers 3.

FLORHAM PARK. *Vocationist Fathers Retreat Center*, 90 Brooklake Rd., 07932. Tel: 973-966-6262; Fax: 973-593-8381. Email: info@vocationist.org. Web: www.vocationist.org.

MENDHAM. *Quellen Spiritual Center*, 350 Bernardsville Rd., 07945. Tel: 973-543-6528, Ext. 217; Fax: 973-543-9459. Email: quellen@scceast.org. Web: www.quellenspiritualcenter.org. Sr. Teresa Skierkowski, S.C.C., Dir.

Villa Pauline 07945. Tel: 973-543-9058. Retreat House for Men & Women Sisters of Christian Charity 5.

MORRISTOWN. *Loyola House of Retreats*, 161 James St., 07960. Tel: 973-539-0740; Fax: 973-898-9839. Email: retreathouse@loyola.org. Web: www.loyola.org. Revs. Gerald J. McIntyre, S.J., Supr.; Charles Moutenot, S.J., Pres. & Dir. Spiritual Progs.; Edmund W. Nagle, S.J.; William P. Poorten, S.J.; William J. Rakowicz, S.J.; Kirk R. Reynolds, S.J.; Thomas F. Walsh, S.J. Society of Jesus. Priests 7.

St. Mary's Abbey Retreat Center, 230 Mendham Rd., 07960. Tel: 973-538-5231, Ext. 2100; Fax: 973-538-7109. Email: abbeyretreat@juno.com. Web: delbarton.org. Rev. Patrick M. Hurley, O.S.B., Dir. & Guestmaster.

MOUNT ARLINGTON. *Claremount Retreat Center*, 35 Windemere Ave., 07856. Tel: 973-601-1475; Fax: 973-234-5292. Email: claremount@optonline.net. Sr. Maryann Kasica, C.S.S.F., Dir.

NEWTON. *Sacred Heart Retreat Center*, 20 Old Swartswood Rd., 07860. Tel: 973-383-2620; Fax: 973-383-3083. Email: shcenter@nac.net. Sr. Theresa Kelly, F.M.A., Dir. Daughters of Mary Help of Christians (Salesian Sisters of St. John Bosco). Sisters 4.

[K] GENERAL HOSPITALS

PATERSON. *St. Joseph's Hospital and Medical Center*, 703 Main St., 07503. Tel: 973-754-2000; Fax: 973-754-3273. Mr. William McDonald, Pres. & CEO; Sr. Maryanne Campeotto, S.C., Vice Pres., Mission; Revs. Martin Rooney, Dir. Mission Svcs.; Christopher Anyanwu; Edward A. Collins, Chap.; Thomas G. Rainforth, Chap. Sisters of Charity of St. Elizabeth 35; Bed Capacity 1,000; Patients Assisted Annually 315,607.

DENVILLE. *Saint Clare's Health Services, Inc. dba Saint Clare's Health System* 25 Pocono Rd., 07834. Tel: 973-983-5588; Fax: 973-983-5655. Email: torr@saintclares.org. Web: www.saintclares.org. Edward J. McManus, Chm.; Mr. Leslie D. Hirsch, M.P.H., Pres. & CEO.

Affiliates:

Saint Clare's Hospital, Inc. Tel: 973-625-6194; Fax: 973-625-6184.

Saint Clare's Foundation, Inc. Tel: 973-983-5303; Fax: 973-983-5312.

St. Francis Life Care Corporation Tel: 973-586-6003; Fax: 973-586-6030.

Visiting Nurse Association of Saint Clare's, Inc., Sparta, 07871. Tel: 973-729-7078; Fax: 973-729-7057.

Saint Clare's Community Care, Inc., 07834. Tel: 973-983-1540; Fax: 973-983-1530.

Saint Clare's Hospital, Inc., 25 Pocono Rd., 07834. Tel: 973-625-6194; Fax: 973-625-6184. Email: ccoronel@saintclares.org. Web: www.saintclares.org. Edward J. McManus, Chm.; Mr. Leslie D. Hirsch, M.P.H., Pres. & CEO. (Parent Corp.: Saint Clare's Health Services) Patients Assisted Annually 369,371; Bed Capacity 584.

Campuses:

Saint Clare's Hospital-Denville Tel: 973-625-6194; Fax: 973-625-6184.

Saint Clare's Hospital-Boonton Township Tel: 973-316-1808; Fax: 973-316-1839.

Saint Clare's Hospital-Sussex Tel: 973-702-2980; Fax: 973-702-2893.

Saint Clare's Hospital-Dover Tel: 973-989-3525; Fax: 973-989-3560.

Pastoral Care Department: Revs. Paul Nwambu; Henry Tanto; Victor Razumov; Stephen Sniscak; Sisters Susan Evelyn, R.S.M.; Mary Ellen Joyce, S.S.M.; Saundra McKeta, S.M.I.C.; Frances Renn, S.S.M.; Kurt Danna-Storm.

PASSAIC. *St. Mary's Hospital*, 350 Blvd., 07055. Tel: 973-365-4300; Fax: 973-471-5531. Email: sniffenm@smh-passaic.org. Web: www.smh-passaic.org. Michael J. Daniel, Pres. & CEO; Revs. Stephen Hoyt, O.F.M.Cap.; Sam Frapaul, O.F.M.Cap.; Sr. Dolores Cervi, S.S.D. Sisters of Charity of St. Elizabeth 3; Bed Capacity 292; Patients Assisted Annually 257,139.

St. Mary's Health Corporation

St. Mary's Hospital Foundation Tel: 973-365-9605. Bruce Byrne, Exec. Dir.

[L] HOMES FOR AGED

PATERSON. *St. Joseph Rest Home for Aged Women* Conducted by Daughters of Charity of the Most Precious Blood, 46 Preakness Ave., 07522. Tel: 973-956-1921; Fax: 973-956-1582. Sr. Maria Goretti Chaloux, D.C.P.B., Supr. Residents 18.

DENVILLE. *St. Francis Health Resort*, 122-126 Diamond Spring Rd., 07834. Tel: 973-627-5000; Fax: 973-627-6389. Email: jthone@saintclares.org. Web: www.saintfrancisres.com. Sr. M. Johnice Thone, S.S.M., Exec. Dir. Senior Living Community Sisters of the Sorrowful Mother 6; Bed Capacity 100; Apartments 62; Guests 150.

Franciscan Oaks Independent Living Units & Health Center, 21 Pocono Rd., 07834. Tel: 973-586-5000; Fax: 973-586-5039. Sponsored by Sisters of the Sorrowful Mother.

TOTOWA. *St. Joseph's Home for the Elderly*, 140 Shepherd Ln., 07512. Tel: 973-942-0300; Fax: 973-942-7201. Email: info@littlesistersofthepoor.org. Sr. Margaret Hogarty, L.S.P., Admin./Supr.; Rev. Evan Greco, O.F.M., Chap. Conducted by Little Sisters of the Poor Sisters 14; Residents 110.

[M] RESIDENCES FOR WOMEN

WAYNE. *Bethany Residence*, 738 Rte. 23, 07470. Tel: 973-628-8109. Cora Ladung, Admin. Residents 12.

[N] MONASTERIES AND RESIDENCES OF PRIESTS AND BROTHERS

PATERSON. *Saint Michael's Friary*, 190 Butler St., 07524. Tel: 973-345-7082; Fax: 973-345-7083. Revs. Agustino Miguel Torres, C.F.R.; Bernard Marie Murphy, C.F.R.; Leo Fisher, C.F.R.; Bros. Damiano Marie Vaissade, C.F.R.; Diego Jose Rivera, C.F.R.; Xavier Meiergard, C.F.R. Franciscan Friars of the Renewal.

BUTLER. *St. Anthony Friary*, 63 Bartholdi Ave., 07405. Tel: 973-838-4080; Fax: 973-492-5483. Revs. Christian F. Camadella, O.F.M.; Bernard R. Creighton, O.F.M., Vicar; Kevin M. Cronin, O.F.M.; James W. Czerwinski, O.F.M.; Edward J. Donohue, O.F.M.; Hugh Eller, O.F.M.; Vincent B. Grogan, O.F.M., J.C.D.; Thomas R. Hartle, O.F.M.; Thomas E. Kelly, O.F.M.; John J. Kull, O.F.M.; Daniel J. Lanahan, O.F.M.; Claude T. Lenehan, O.F.M.; Stephen Lynch, O.F.M.; Jeremiah V. McGinley, O.F.M.; Cassian A. Miles, O.F.M.; Guy Morgan, O.F.M.; John J. Pierce, O.F.M.; Leon C. Ristuccia, O.F.M.; Edwin F.D. Robinson, O.F.M.; Paul G. Sinnema, O.F.M.; Rayner F. Williams, O.F.M.; Bros. Peter X. Ahlheim, O.F.M.; Octavio A. Duran, O.F.M.; Robert M. Frazetta, O.F.M.; William P. Mann, O.F.M.; Richard McFeeley, O.F.M., Guardian; John E. Quinn, O.F.M.; Frank B. Waywood, O.F.M. Order of Friars Minor. Priests 21; Brothers 6. *Franciscan Ministry of the Word* Tel: 973-838-4093. Web: www.franmow.org. Rev. Kevin M. Cronin, O.F.M.

CLIFTON. *Holy Face of Jesus Monastery*, 1697 State Hwy. 3, P.O. Box 691, 07012. Tel: 973-778-1177; Fax: 973-778-3809. Email: holyface@worldnet.att.net. Revs. Bernard Schinn, O.S.B., Supr.; Louis-Marie Navaratne, O.S.B. Sylvestrine Benedictine Monks. Priests 2.

FLORHAM PARK. *Father Justin Vocationary*, 90 Brooklake Rd., 07932. Tel: 973-966-6262; Fax: 973-593-8381. Email: info@vocationist.org. Web: www.vocationist.org. Revs. Ignatius Okoroji, S.D.V., Supr.; Vernon Kohlmann, S.D.V.

MORRISTOWN. *St. Mary's Abbey*, Delbarton, 230 Mendham Rd., 07960. Tel: 973-538-3231; Fax: 973-538-7109. Email: osbmonks@delbarton.org. Web: www.osbmonks.org. Rt. Revs. Giles P. Hayes, O.S.B., Abbot; Brian H. Clark, O.S.B., Abbot Emeritus; Gerard P. Lair, O.S.B., Abbot Emeritus; Very Rev. Bruno A. Ugliano, O.S.B., Prior; Revs. Jerome Borski, O.S.B., Subprior; Benet W. Caffrey, O.S.B.; Justin Capato, O.S.B.; Gabriel M. Coless, O.S.B.; Richard F. Cronin, O.S.B.; Anthony G. Sargent, O.S.B.; Edward Seton Fittin, O.S.B.; Donal R. Fox, O.S.B.; Simon P. Gallagher, O.S.B.; John E. Hesketh, O.S.B.; Patrick M. Hurley, O.S.B.; Beatus T. Lucey, O.S.B.; James O'Donnell, O.S.B., Treas.; Hilary O'Leary, O.S.B., Novice Master; Rembert F. Reilly, O.S.B.; Wilfred G. Schulz, O.S.B.; Joachim B. Schweitzer, O.S.B.; Andrew T. Smith, O.S.B.; Luke L. Travers, O.S.B.; Basil J. Wallace, O.S.B.; Bros. John Babicz, O.S.B.; Michael De Saye, O.S.B.; Paul J. Diveny, O.S.B.; Jeremiah R. Grosse, O.S.B.; Tarcisius Hoang-Hoa, O.S.B.; Jonathan M. Hunt, O.S.B.;

James Konchalski, O.S.B.; Dennis Monaghan, O.S.B.; Liam S. Mullin, O.S.B.; Kieran M. Shiek, O.S.B.; Demetrius M. Thomas, O.S.B.; Kevin M. Tidd, O.S.B.; Joseph Voltaggio, O.S.B. Priests 29; Serving Outside the Diocese 6; Brothers 14.

In Res. Revs. Alberto O. Khanh, O.Cist.; Vincent Liem Tran Van Hoa, O.Cist.

Resident Outside the Abbey: Revs. Timothy J. Brennan, O.S.B.; Elias R. Lorenzo, O.S.B.; Karl J. Roesch, O.S.B.; Jude S. Salus, O.S.B.; Benedict M. Worry, O.S.B.; Bro. Brendan A. Tumulty, O.S.B.

NEWTON. *St. Paul's Abbey*, 289 U.S. Hwy. 206 S., P.O. Box 7, 07860-0007. Tel: 973-383-2470; Fax: 973-383-5782. Email: osbnewton@catholic.or.kr. Rt. Revs. Joel P. Macul, O.S.B., Abbot; Augustine J. Hinches, O.S.B., (Resigned); Very Rev. Samuel Kim, O.S.B., Prior; Revs. Augustine So, O.S.B.; Bosco Kim, O.S.B.; Peter Ahn, O.S.B.; Odilo Yi, O.S.B. Order of St. Benedict, Congregation of St. Ottilien., (Formerly the Little Flower Monastery) Priests 11; Lay Monks 8.

Priests Residing Outside the Monastery: Rt. Rev. Justin E. Dzikowicz, O.S.B., Namibia; Revs. Peter W. Blue, O.S.B., Inkamana Abbey, P/Bag X9333, Vryheid, 3100, South Africa. Tel: 27-34-982-2577; Patrick J. Bonner, O.S.B., Florida; Damian J. Milliken, O.S.B., P.O. Box 213, Lushoto. Tel: 255-2726-40210; Fax: 255-2726-40212.

OAK RIDGE-MILTON. *St. Stanislaus B. M. Friary*, 2 Manor Dr., 07438. Tel: 973-697-7757. Deacon Jerzy P. Krzyskow. Capuchin Fathers. Brothers 1.

RINGWOOD. *Holy Name Friary, Inc.*, 2 Morris Rd., 07456. Tel: 973-962-7200; Fax: 973-962-9766. Email: hnfringwood@netscape.net. Revs. A. Francis Soucy, O.F.M., Supr. & Contact Person; Giles Bello, O.F.M.; Charles Brozat, S.A.; Lawrence A. Burke, O.F.M.; Leo Clifford, O.F.M.; Matthew Conlin, O.F.M.; Brennan Connolly, O.F.M.; Brian Flynn, O.F.M.; Robert Grix, O.F.M.Cap.; Martin Hanhauser, O.F.M.; Bonaventure Hayes, O.F.M.; Joseph Kiernan, O.F.M.; Eric F. Kyle, O.F.M.; Robert Lynch, O.F.M.; Francis Majewski, O.F.M.Cap.; Theodore A. McNally, O.F.M.; Kenan Morris, O.F.M.; Joel Munzing, O.F.M.; Owen Murphy, S.A.; Philip W. Nielsen, O.F.M.; Reginald Redlon, O.F.M.; Boniface Riedman, S.A.; Finian A. Riley, O.F.M.; Cyril Seaman, O.F.M.; Aloysius Siracus, O.F.M.; Lambert F. Valentine, O.F.M.; Bros. Kieran Cullen, S.A.; Fintan Duffy, O.F.M.; Steven Hanley, S.A.; John Hildreth, O.F.M.; Ennis Thomas, O.F.M. Priests 25; Brothers 3.

STIRLING. *Shrine of St. Joseph*, 1050 Long Hill Rd., 07980. Tel: 908-647-0208; Fax: 908-647-5770. Email: religious@stshrine.org. Web: stshrine.org. Revs. Peter Krebs, S.T., Custodian; Gary Banks, S.T.; Ralph Frisch, S.T.; Joseph Keenan, S.T.; Conrad Schmitt, S.T.; Rafael Piso, S.T.; Bros. John Skrodinsky, S.T., Esq.; Martin Pacholek, S.T. Priests 6; Brothers 2; Sisters 5. *Trinity House at the Shrine of St. Joseph*, 1292 Long Hill Rd., 07980.

WAYNE. *P.I.M.E. Missionaries Residence*, 34 Grandview Dr., 07470. Tel: 973-694-1790; Fax: 973-694-0444. Email: pimenj@optonline.net. Web: www.pimeusa.org. Rev. Giancarlo Ghezzi, P.I.M.E.

Xaverian Missionary Fathers, Provincial House, 12 Helene Court, 07470. Tel: 973-942-2975; Fax: 973-942-5012. Email: xavwayne@optonline.net. Web: www.xaviermissionaries.org. Revs. Carl S. Chudy, S.X., Prov.; Frank B. Grappoli, S.X., Rector & Treas.

Mission Assignments: Makeni, Sierra Leone: Most Rev. George Biguzzi, S.X., Bishop of Makeni; Revs. Luigi Brioni, S.X.; Eugene Montesi, S.X.

Belem, Brazil: Rev. Danilo Lago, S.X.

Burundi: Rev. Pierino Zoni, S.X.

Cameroon: Revs. Rene Lovat, S.X.; Fernandes de Araujo Herondi, S.X.

Sao Paulo, Brazil: Rev. Gino Nasini, S.X.

Jakarta, Indonesia: Rev. Franco Qualizza, S.X.

Bogota, Colombia: Rev. Mauro Loda, S.X.

Torreon, Mexico: Revs. Dan Boschetto, S.X.; Ramon Cerratos, S.X.; Pablo Nieves, S.X.

Taiwan: Revs. Edi Foschiatto, S.X.; Martino Roia, S.X.; Joe Vignato, S.X.

Japan: Revs. Renato Filippini, S.X.; Frank Sottocornula, S.X.

Mozambique: Revs. Horacio Perez, S.X.; Dario Maso, S.X.

[O] CONVENTS AND RESIDENCES FOR SISTERS

PATERSON. *Daughters of Charity of the Most Precious Blood*, 46 Preakness Ave., 07522. Tel: 973-956-1921; Fax: 973-956-1582. Sr. Maria Goretti Chaloux, D.C.P.B., Supr. Sisters 10.

Missionary Sisters of the Immaculate Conception of the Mother of God, 779 Broadway, 07514-1329. Tel: 973-279-3790; Fax: 973-742-8231. Email: egsmic@optonline.net. Sr. Eleanor Goekler, S.M.I.C., Prov. Coord.

Missionary Sisters of the Immaculate Conception of the Mother of God, 396 E. 38th St., 07504-1414. Tel: 973-279-2885; Fax: 973-742-8281. Email: smcketa@optonline.net. Sisters 5.

Missionary Sisters of the Immaculate Conception of the Mother of God, St. Bonaventure Convent, 146 Danforth Ave., 07501. Tel: 973-357-1915. International House for Studies

Missionary Sisters of the Immaculate Conception of the Mother of God, 374-18th Ave., 07504-1333. Tel: 973-653-3323. Sisters 3.

Missionary Sisters of the Immaculate Conception, Inc., 779 Broadway, 07514. Tel: 973-279-3790; Fax: 973-742-8231.

BOONTON. *Society of the Sisters of the Church*, 24 Deer Hill Ct., 07005. Tel: 973-299-8365; Fax: 973-884-0940. Email: SRBW@ssoc.org. Web: www.ssoc.org. Sr. Frances Sanzo, S.S.C., Coord. Sisters 12.

CHESTER. *Carmel of the Immaculate Heart of Mary*, 80 Pleasant Hill Rd., 07930-2135. Tel: 908-879-4990; Fax: 908-879-0884. Email: hermcarm@gti.net. Sr. Mary of Jesus and St. Joseph, O.Carm., Desert Mother. Hermits of Our Lady of Mt. Carmel Sisters 4.

CONVENT STATION. *Motherhouse of the Sisters of Charity*, P.O. Box 476, 07961-0476. Tel: 973-290-5000; Fax: 973-290-5335. Email: escharity@aol.com. Web: www.scnj.org. Sr. Maureen Shaughnessy, S.C., Gen. Supr. Professed Sisters 60.

DENVILLE. *Our Lady of Sorrows Convent, Sisters of Sorrowful Mother*, 9 Pocono Rd., 07834. Tel: 973-627-9008. Web: www.ssmfranciscans.org.

Residences: *Our Lady of Sorrows Convent, Sisters of Sorrowful Mother*, 9 Pocono Rd., 07834. Tel: 973-983-8456; Fax: 973-270-0187. Sisters 12. *Lake House Community, Sisters of Sorrowful Mother*, 22 Wyker Rd., Franklin, 07416. Tel: 973-827-0191. Sisters 2.

FLORHAM PARK. *St. Anne Villa*, P.O. Box 476, Convent Station, 07961. Tel: 973-292-6555; Fax: 973-867-1560. Email: mfarrell@saintannevilla.org. Sr. Marian Farrell, S.C., Admin.; Rev. Jerome Borski, O.S.B., Chap. Sisters of Charity of St. Elizabeth., Home for retired and infirm Sisters Bed Capacity 101.

Sister Joanna House of Formation, 88 Brooklake Rd., 07932. Tel: 973-966-9762; Fax: 973-377-3994. Email: vocationist@yahoo.com. Sisters Gelsomina Mosca, Supr. & Prin.; Louisa Garcione, S.D.V., Delegate. Sisters 15.

GLADSTONE. *Mt. St. John Convent*, 22 St. John's Dr., 07934. Tel: 908-234-0640; Fax: 908-781-7814. Email: baptistines@worldnet.att.net. Web: www.baptistines.home.att.net. Sr. Angelita Vazzano, C.S.J.B., Admin. Sisters of St. John the Baptist. Sisters 3.

HALEDON. *Institute of the Daughters of Mary Help of Christians*, 655 Belmont Ave., 07508. Tel: 973-790-7963; Fax: 973-790-6482. Email: secretarysua@aol.com. Web: www.salesiansisters.org. Sisters Karen Dunn, F.M.A., Prov.; Carmen Pena, F.M.A., Supr.; Rev. Armindo Simao Laranjinha, S.D.B., Chap. Provincialate of Daughters of Mary Help of Christians Daughters of Mary Help of Christians (Salesian Sisters) 102.

MENDHAM. *Mallinckrodt Convent-Motherhouse and Novitiate of the Sisters of Christian Charity*, 350 Bernardsville Rd., 07945. Tel: 973-543-6528; Fax: 973-543-9459. Web: scceast.org. Sr. Joan Daniel Healy, S.C.C., Prov. Supr. Daughters of the Blessed Virgin Mary of the Immaculate Conception. Sisters 46; Novices 3; Postulants 2.

MORRISTOWN. *St. Lucy Provincialate of the Religious Teachers Filippini, Novitiate, Villa Walsh Academy*, 455 Western Ave., 07960-4928. Tel: 973-538-2886; Fax: 973-538-6107. Email: bjtakacs@filippiniusa.org. Web: www.filippiniusa.org. Sisters Betty Jean Takacs, M.P.F., Prov.; Dolores Bianchi, M.P.F., Supr.; Elaine Bebyn, M.P.F., Dir. Formation.

Pontifical Institute of the Religious Teachers Filippini Sisters 97; Novices 1; Junior Professed 1.

Monastery Discalced Carmelite Nuns of the Most Blessed Virgin Mary of Mt. Carmel, 189 Madison Ave., 07960. Tel: 973-539-0773. Sr. Therese Katulski, O.C.D., Prioress. Professed Nuns 11; Novices 1.

MOUNT ARLINGTON. *Felician Sisters of St. Francis of Assisi Convent*, 37 Windemere Ave., 07856. Tel: 973-601-3383. Sr. Mary Lorene Pivinski, C.S.S.F., Local Supr. Professed Sisters 4.

PARSIPPANY. *St. Francis of Assisi Novitiate-Franciscan Sisters of St. Elizabeth*, 499 Park Rd., 07054. Tel: 973-539-3857; Fax: 973-539-3347. Email: srcathylynn@yahoo.com. Web: www.franciscansisters.com. Sr. Gina Maria Amico, F.S.S.E., Delegate Gen. Perpetually Professed Sisters 42; Temporarily Professed Sisters 11.

STIRLING. *Holy Trinity Convent*, 1026 Long Hill Rd., 07980. Tel: 908-647-6584. Sr. Sophia Kozikowska, Supr. Servants of Jesus 7.

WOODLAND PARK. *Missionary Sisters of the Immaculate Conception of the Mother of God*, Generalate, 47 Garden Ave., 07424. Tel: 973-279-1484; Fax: 973-279-2991. Email: smicgen@optonline.net. Sr. Maria Do Livramento Oliveira, S.M.I.C., Coord. Gen. Sisters 4.

The Society of Sisters for the Church, 396 Rifle Camp Rd., West Paterson, 07424. Tel: 718-894-8564. Web: www.ssc-usa.org. Sr. Loretta Rybacki, S.S.C., Pres. Sisters 19.

[P] NEWMAN CENTERS

HALEDON. *William Paterson University of New Jersey* 219 Pompton Rd., 07508. Tel: 973-720-3524; 973-595-6184; Fax: 973-595-5312. Email: frhubert@jesuscampus.net. Web: www.jesuscampus.net. Rev. Hubert Jurejewicz, Campus Min., Prince of Peace Chapel, Wayne. Jesus Christ, Prince of Peace Chapel Catholic Campus Ministry Center.

MADISON. *Drew University Catholic Campus Ministry* 07940. Tel: 973-408-3027. Email: jfarias@drew.edu. Sr. Mary Joseph Schultz, S.C.C., Campus Min.

Fairleigh Dickinson University Catholic Campus Ministry Fairleigh Dickinson University, 285 Madison Ave., 07940. Tel: 973-443-8651; Fax: 973-287-5330. Email: madisonccm@aol.com. Sr. Mary Joseph Schultz, S.C.C., Campus Min.

[Q] MISCELLANEOUS LISTINGS

PATERSON. *St. Anthony's Guild* 07509. Tel: 973-777-1915; Fax: 973-777-5687. Email: anthonian@aol.com. Web: www.anthonian.org. Rev. David I. Convertino, O.F.M., Dir. Membership organization supports the work of The Franciscan Friars of Holy Name Province.

The Association of the Marian Apostolate of Mercy, Inc., 31 St. James Pl., Totowa, 07512. Tel: 973-956-5969; Fax: 973-956-0979. Email: marianassociates@gmail.com. Sr. Maria Elizabeth Whilifer, Pres.; Judith A. Bonnesen, Treas.; Rev. Msgr. Paul L. Bochicchio, V.F. (NEW).

Cor Jesu Mission Fund Inc, 1048 E. 26th St., 07513. Tel: 973-278-2540. Revs. Anthony J. Mastroeni, S.T.D., J.D., Pres.; Eugene C. Romano, Vice Pres.; Sr. Mary Taylor, R.S.C.J., Treas.

Martin de Porres Village Corporation, Green St., 07501. Tel: 973-881-8022; Fax: 973-881-0149. Rev. Msgr. Herbert K. Tillyer, P.A., M.Ch.A., Pres. Sponsoring Martin De Porres, Vill.

Sr. Merita Learning Center, Martin De Porres Village, 1 Green St., 07501. Tel: 973-881-7115; Fax: 973-881-0748. Sr. Christina Schoen, F.S.P., Dir.

Province of the Immaculate Conception of the Missionary Sisters of the Immaculate Conception 1996 Trust Fund, 779 Broadway, 07514. Tel: 973-279-3790; Fax: 973-742-8231. Email: smicmissionarysisters@yahoo.com. Sr. Joanne Riggs, S.M.I.C., Trustee.

Riese Corporation, c/o R.P. Marzulli Co., 264 Belleville Ave., Bloomfield, 07003. Tel: 973-743-2300; Fax: 973-743-8021. Rev. Msgr. Herbert K. Tillyer, P.A., M.Ch.A., Pres. Sponsoring Governor Paterson Towers, Maurice Brick Residence, Brestel Residence, William F. Hinchcliffe Pavilion, Ralph J. Diverio Residence, Murray M. Bisgaier Residence, William Levine Residence.

CHESTER. *Nazareth Village* Retirement residence for diocesan priests., 11 Meadow Ln., Box 635, 07930. Tel: 908-879-6991; Fax: 908-879-7461. Email: nazarethvillage@hotmail.com. Web: www.nazarethvillage.com. Rev. Msgr. Raymond M. Lopatesky, Dir. In Res. Rev. Msgrs. Leo P. Carey (Retired); Robert M. Diachek; George A. Dudak (Retired); Brendan P. Madden (Retired); Peter A. McBride (Retired); Peter J. McHugh (Retired); Leo P. Ryan (Retired); Stanley E. Schinski (Retired); Thomas J. Trapasso, S.T.L. (Retired); Revs. John T. Catoir, J.C.D. (Retired); Edward M. Davey (Retired); Robert K. Hooper (Retired); John J. Klein (Retired); Vincent Klim (Retired); Patrick Mullan (Retired); Joseph E. Murphy (Retired); James P. O'Kielty; Jeremiah O'Riordan (Retired); George T. Shema (Retired); James A.D. Smith (Retired); Ronald Sordillo (Retired).

CLIFTON. *Casa Guadalupe*, House of Discernment for women contemplating religious life.737 Valley Rd., 07013. Tel: 973-737-1456. Email: holly@casaguadalupe.net. Web: www.casaguadalupe.net. Ms. Holly Lawmaster, Dir.; Rev. Agustino Miguel Torres, C.F.R., Spiritual Dir.

Casa Guadalupe, Inc. Women 8.

CONVENT STATION. *Seton Health Care, Inc., Convent of Saint Elizabeth*, P.O. Box 476, 07961. Tel: 973-290-5450; Fax: 973-290-5335. Email: rmoynihan@

scnj.org. Web: www.scnj.org. Sr. Rosemary Moynihan, S.C., Pres.

MORRISTOWN. *College of St. Elizabeth, Center for Theological and Spiritual Development* 2 Convent Rd., 07960. Tel: 973-290-4354, Ext. 4491; Fax: 973-290-4312. Email: ibaratte@cse.edu. Web: www.cse.edu/center.

PASSAIC. *St. Jude Media Ministries*, 63 Monroe St., 07055. Tel: 908-879-1460; Fax: 908-879-7461. Email: jcatoir@aol.com. Web: www.messengerofjoy.com. Rev. John T. Catoir, J.C.D., Dir. (Retired).

POMPTON LAKES. *Pathways Counseling Center, Inc.*, 16 Pompton Ave., 07442. Tel: 973-835-6337; Fax: 973-616-4688. Email: pegb@pathwayscounseling.org. Web: www.pathwayscounseling.org. Ms. Mathilda Catarina, Ph.D., Clinic Dir.; Ms. Peg Buczek, Admin. Mgr.

RINGWOOD. *NCPC, Inc.*, 112 Erskine Rd., 07456. Tel: 973-962-7032. Most Rev. Arthur J. Serratelli, S.T.D., S.S.L., D.D., Pres.; Rev. Msgr. Patrick G. Panos, Sec.

SPARTA. *The Catholic Academy of Sussex County, Inc.*, 28 Andover Rd., 07871. Tel: 973-729-6125. Most Rev. Arthur J. Serratelli, S.T.D., S.S.L., D.D., Pres.; Rev. Msgr. James T. Mahoney, Ph.D., V.G., Vice Pres.; Sr. Mary Edward Spohrer, S.C.C., Sec. & Treas.; Rev. Msgr. Kieran A. McHugh, Dir. The Academy operates Pope John XXIII H.S.; Rev. George Brown School; Immaculate Conception School; St. Joseph's School; St. Michael's School; Camp Auxilium Center.

Pope John XXIII High School Special Project Foundation, Inc, 28 Andover Rd., 07871. Most Rev. Arthur J. Serratelli, S.T.D., S.S.L., D.D., Pres.; Rev. Msgr. Kieran A. McHugh, Agent.

WAYNE. *Consortium of Catholic Schools of the Roman Catholic Diocese of Paterson, Inc.*, 1502 Alps Rd., 07470. Tel: 973-694-3702, Ext. 213; Fax: 973-696-1327. Most Rev. Arthur J. Serratelli, S.T.D., S.S.L., D.D., Pres.; Rev. Msgr. James T. Mahoney, Ph.D., V.G., Vice Pres.; Mary Debra Baier, Dir.; Sr. Mary Edward Spohrer, S.C.C., Sec. & Treas.

Siena Village, 1000 Siena Village, 07470. Tel: 973-696-2811; Fax: 973-696-2721. Email: aldors@aol.com. Sr. Alice Matthew, O.P., Dir.

RELIGIOUS INSTITUTES OF MEN REPRESENTED IN THE DIOCESE

For further details refer to the corresponding bracketed number in the Religious Institutes of Men or Women section.

[0200]—*Benedictine Monks* (St. Mary, St. Paul Abbeys; Holy Face of Jesus Monastery)—O.S.B.
[0470]—*The Capuchin Friars*—O.F.M.Cap
[0480]—*Conventual Franciscans*—O.F.M.Conv
[0520]—*Franciscan Friars* (Holy Name Prov.)—O.F.M.
[0690]—*Jesuit Fathers and Brothers* (New York Prov.)—S.J.
[0840]—*Missionary Servants of the Most Holy Trinity* (Silver Spring, MD)—S.T.
[1050]—*Pontifical Institute for Foreign Missions*—P.I.M.E.
[1190]—*Salesians of Don Bosco* (Turin, Italy)—S.D.B.
[1340]—*Vocationist Fathers*—S.D.V.
[1360]—*Xaverian Missionary Fathers* (Wayne)—S.X.

RELIGIOUS INSTITUTES OF WOMEN REPRESENTED IN THE DIOCESE

[0230]—*Benedictine Sisters of Pontifical Jurisdiction*—O.S.B.
[0740]—*Daughters of Charity of the Most Precious Blood*—D.C.P.B.
[0850]—*Daughters of Mary Help of Christians*—F.M.A.
[]—*Daughters of the Most Pure Heart of the Most Holy Virgin Mary* (Passaic)
[0420]—*Discalced Carmelite Nuns*—O.C.D.
[1070-06]—*Dominican Sisters*—O.P.
[1070-18]—*Dominican Sisters*—O.P.
[1115]—*Dominican Sisters of Peace*—O.P.
[1170]—*Felician Sisters*—C.S.S.F.
[1400]—*Franciscan Missionary Sisters of the Sacred Heart* (Peekskill)—F.M.S.C.
[]—*Hermits of Our Lady of Mt. Carmel*—H.O.Carm.
[2340]—*Little Sisters of the Poor*—L.S.P.
[2760]—*Missionary Sisters of the Immaculate Conception of the Mother of God*—S.M.I.C.
[3430]—*Religious Teachers Filippini*—M.P.F.
[1700]—*School Sisters of the Third Order of St. Francis*—O.S.F.
[3560]—*Servants of Jesus* (Starling)—S.J.
[3580]—*Servants of Mary*—O.S.M.
[0590]—*Sisters of Charity of Saint Elizabeth, Convent Station*—S.C.
[0660]—*Sisters of Christian Charity*—S.C.C.
[3820]—*Sisters of St. John the Baptist*—C.S.J.B.
[3830]—*Sisters of St. Joseph* (Chestnut Hill, PA)—C.S.J.
[3890]—*Sisters of St. Joseph of Peace*—C.S.J.P.
[1830]—*Sisters of the Good Shepherd*—R.G.S.
[3320]—*Sisters of the Presentation of the B.V.M.*—P.B.V.M.
[4100]—*Sisters of the Sorrowful Mother (Third Order of St. Francis)*—S.S.M.
[]—*The Society of the Sisters of the Church* (Passaic)
[4210]—*Vocationist Sisters*—S.D.V.

NECROLOGY

† Casey, Joseph M., (Retired)—Died July 25, 2011
† McLaughlin, Anthony J., (Unassigned)—Died Oct. 16, 2011
† McLeod, David, (Retired)—Died April 11, 2011
† Quinlan, John J., Swartswood, NJ Our Lady of Mt. Carmel—Died Jan. 22, 2011
† St. Martin, Jean-Claude, Rockaway, NJ St. Cecilia's & Sacred Heart—Died Feb. 11, 2011

An asterisk (*) denotes an organization that has established tax-exempt status directly with the IRS and is not covered by the USCCB Group Ruling.

Diocese of Pensacola-Tallahassee

(Dioecesis Pensacolensis-Tallaseiensis)

Most Reverend

GREGORY L. PARKES

Bishop of Pensacola-Tallahassee; ordained June 26, 1999; appointed Bishop of Pensacola-Tallahassee March 20, 2012. *Office: 11 North B St., Pensacola, FL 32502.* Tel: 850-435-3500.

Most Reverend

JOHN H. RICARD, S.S.J.

Bishop Emeritus of Pensacola-Tallahassee; ordained May 25, 1968; ordained Auxiliary Bishop of Baltimore July 2, 1984; appointed Bishop of Pensacola-Tallahassee January 21, 1997.

Monsignor James Amos Pastoral Center: 11 North B St., Pensacola, FL 32502. Tel: 850-435-3500; Fax: 850-436-6424. *Mailing Address: P.O. Drawer 13284, Pensacola, FL 32591*

Web: www.ptdiocese.org

Email: chancellor@ptdiocese.org

ESTABLISHED NOVEMBER 6, 1975.

Square Miles 14,044.

Comprises the following Counties: Bay, Calhoun, Escambia, Franklin, Gadsden, Gulf, Holmes, Jackson, Jefferson, Leon, Liberty, Madison, Okaloosa, Santa Rosa, Taylor, Wakulla, Walton and Washington Counties.

For legal titles of parishes and diocesan institutions, consult the Pastoral Center.

STATISTICAL OVERVIEW

Personnel	
Bishop	1
Retired Bishops	1
Priests: Diocesan Active in Diocese	51
Priests: Diocesan Active Outside Diocese	8
Priests: Diocesan in Foreign Missions	1
Priests: Retired, Sick or Absent	15
Number of Diocesan Priests	75
Religious Priests in Diocese	14
Total Priests in Diocese	89
Extern Priests in Diocese	15
Ordinations:	
Diocesan Priests	3
Transitional Deacons	1
Permanent Deacons in Diocese	62
Total Brothers	5
Total Sisters	23
Parishes	
Parishes	49
With Resident Pastor:	
Resident Diocesan Priests	39
Resident Religious Priests	4
Without Resident Pastor:	
Administered by Priests	6
Missions	8
Professional Ministry Personnel:	
Brothers	3
Sisters	11
Lay Ministers	57
Welfare	
Catholic Hospitals	49
Total Assisted	98,527
Homes for the Aged	2
Total Assisted	890
Special Centers for Social Services	4
Total Assisted	49,525
Other Institutions	2
Total Assisted	43
Educational	
Diocesan Students in Other Seminaries	11
Total Seminarians	11
High Schools, Diocesan and Parish	2
Total Students	690
Elementary Schools, Diocesan and Parish	7
Total Students	1,801
Catechesis/Religious Education:	
High School Students	808
Elementary Students	3,776
Total Students under Catholic Instruction	7,086
Teachers in the Diocese:	
Sisters	6
Lay Teachers	185
Vital Statistics	
Receptions into the Church:	
Infant Baptism Totals	994
Minor Baptism Totals	116
Adult Baptism Totals	159
Received into Full Communion	357
First Communions	1,062
Confirmations	998
Marriages:	
Catholic	203
Interfaith	120
Total Marriages	323
Deaths	595
Total Catholic Population	63,091
Total Population	1,399,521

Former Bishops—Most Revs. RENE H. GRACIDA, D.D., ord. May 23, 1959; appt. Titular Bishop of Masuccaba and Auxiliary of Miami, Dec. 6, 1971; cons. Jan. 25, 1972; appt. first Bishop of Pensacola-Tallahassee, Oct. 1, 1975; installed Nov. 6, 1975; transferred to Bishop of Corpus Christi, May 19, 1983; J. KEITH SYMONS, D.D., Bishop of Pensacola-Tallahassee; ord. May 18, 1958; Titular Bishop of Siguritanus and Auxiliary of St. Petersburg; appt. Jan. 16, 1981; cons. March 19, 1981; Bishop of Pensacola-Tallahassee; appt. Sept. 29, 1983; installed Nov. 8, 1983; transferred to Bishop of Palm Beach, June 2, 1990; JOHN M. SMITH, J.C.D., D.D., Bishop of Pensacola-Tallahassee; ord. May 27, 1961; Titular Bishop of Tre Taverne and Auxiliary of Newark; appt. Dec. 1, 1987; cons. Jan. 25, 1988; Bishop of Pensacola-Tallahassee; appt. June 25, 1991; installed July 31, 1991; transferred to Coadjutor Bishop of Trenton, Nov. 21, 1995; appt. Bishop of Trenton July 1, 1997; JOHN H. RICARD, S.S.J. (Retired), ord. May 25, 1968; ord. Auxiliary Bishop of Baltimore July 2, 1984; appt. Bishop of Pensacola-Tallahassee Jan. 21, 1997; retired March 11, 2011.

Monsignor James Amos Pastoral Center—11 North B St., Pensacola, 32502. Tel: 850-435-3500; Fax: 850-436-6424. *Mailing Address: P.O. Drawer 13284, Pensacola, 32591.*

Office of the Bishop—VACANT, Exec. Sec.

Chancellor—Rev. Msgr. MICHAEL V. REED, J.C.L.

Child and Youth Protection—

Moderator of the Curia—Rev. Msgr. MICHAEL V. REED, J.C.L.

Vicar for Priests—VACANT.

Vicar for Permanent Deacons and Chairman—Very Rev. JOSEPH P. CALLIPARE.

Delegate for Religious—Sr. MARGARET KUNTZ, A.S.C.J.

Vicars Forane—VACANT, Northwest Vicariate Forane; Very Rev. EUGENE D. CASSERLY, M.Ch.A., Southwest Vicariate Forane; Rev. Msgr. MICHAEL A. CHERUP, West Central Vicariate Forane; Very Revs. PETER LAWRENCE ZALEWSKI, East Central Vicariate Forane; KEVIN JOHNSON, Eastern Vicariate Forane.

Vicar General—Rev. Msgr. LUKE HUNT, V.G.

Diocesan Tribunal—Mailing Address: P.O. Drawer 13284, Pensacola, 32591. Tel: 850-436-6454; Fax: 850-436-6457. Direct all matters regarding Marriage Dispensations and questions to Tribunal Office.

Judicial Vicar—Rev. Msgr. JAMES J. FLAHERTY, J.C.L., J.V.

Associate Judicial Vicar—VACANT.

Advocate—VACANT.

Judges—Rev. Msgr. JAMES J. FLAHERTY, J.C.L., J.V.; Deacon DANIEL M. MCAULIFFE, J.C.L.

Promoter of Justice—Rev. Msgr. MICHAEL V. REED, J.C.L.

Auditor—RUBY B. RIVAIS.

Defender of the Bond—Very Rev. EUGENE D. CASSERLY, M.Ch.A.

Notary—RUBY B. RIVAIS.

College of Consultors—Rev. Msgr. JAMES J. FLAHERTY, J.C.L., J.V.; Rev. MICHAEL FOLEY; Rev. Msgr. MICHAEL W. TUGWELL; Very Rev. PETER LAWRENCE ZALEWSKI; Rev. Msgrs. MICHAEL V. REED, J.C.L.; LUKE HUNT, V.G.

Administrative Council—Rev. Msgrs. JAMES J. FLAHERTY, J.C.L., J.V.; MICHAEL V. REED, J.C.L., Chancellor; JOHN GODLEWSKI; Mr. KEVIN VICKERY; MARK DUFVA; JOHN KENNEDY; Rev. Msgr. LUKE HUNT, V.G.

Council of Priests—VACANT.

Executive Committee of Permanent Deacons—Very Rev. JOSEPH P. CALLIPARE, Vicar for Permanent Deacons & Chm.; Deacons PAUL GRAAFF; STEPHEN WULF; DANIEL M. MCAULIFFE, J.C.L.; ROGER GALLAGHER; LOU FETE; SANTIAGO MOLINA; RICHARD LURTON.

Council of Sisters—Sisters MAUREEN JOSEPH KIRWAN,

S.C., Pres.; MARGUERITE GIBBS, I.H.M., Vice Pres.

Priests' Pension Plan, Board for—Rev. Msgrs. LUKE HUNT, V.G.; MICHAEL V. REED, J.C.L.; MICHAEL P. MOONEY; MICHAEL A. CHERUP; Very Rev. JOSEPH P. CALLIPARE; Rev. Msgrs. JOHN T. CASSIDY; JOHN V. O'SULLIVAN. Consultants: JOHN GODLEWSKI; ROBERT EMMANUEL ESQ.

Priest Personnel Board—VACANT.

Diocesan Commissions, Departments, and Offices

Apostleship of the Sea, Office of the—Rev. PETER MCLAUGHLIN, Chap., Mailing Address: P.O. Box 12423, Pensacola, 32591-2423. Tel: 850-435-3500.

Archivist—CARLISLE SEMMES, Ed.D., Mailing Address: P.O. Box 13284, Pensacola, 32591. Tel: 850-435-3500.

Commission for African American Catholics—GABRIEL M. BROWN, Chm., Mailing Address: P.O. Drawer 13284, Pensacola, 32591. Tel: 850-435-3500.

Building & Renovation, Diocesan Commission for—Rev. Msgrs. LUKE HUNT, V.G.; MICHAEL V. REED, J.C.L.; JOHN GODLEWSKI; JOHN KENNEDY; Rev. PAUL T. WHITE; J. PATRICK REMICH; ROBERT BENNETT, Chm.; AMY BINEGAR, Mailing Address: P.O. Drawer 13284, Pensacola, 32591. Tel: 850-435-3500.

Campus Ministry—Mailing Address: P.O. Drawer 13284, Pensacola, 32591. Tel: 850-435-3500. Rev. JAMES PAUL VALENZUELA, Pensacola-University of West Florida: Nativity of Our Lord Parish, 9945 Hillview Dr., Pensacola, 32514. Tel: 850-477-3221. Tallahassee-Florida Agricultural & Mechanical University, St. Eugene Chapel: Rev. EJIOFOR UGWU, M.S.P., Dir. & Chap., 701 Gamble St., Tallahassee, 32310. Tel: 850-222-6482. Florida State University: Rev. CHRISTOPHER LEBLANC, Dir., Mailing Address: P.O. Box 2395, Tallahassee, 32316. Tel: 850-222-9630.

Catholic Daughters of the Americas—Rev. ROBERT F. MORRIS, Court Chap.; Mrs. JOYCE PFEIFFER, Regent, 304 N. Sunset Blvd., Gulf Breeze, 32507.

Catholic Women, Diocesan Council of—CAROL GIGUERE, Pres., 19 Newcastle Ct., Niceville, 32578. Tel: 850-897-4998.

Catholic Charities of Northwest Florida—MARK DUFVA, Exec. Dir., Mailing Address: 1000 W. Garden St., Pensacola, 32502. Tel: 850-435-3516.

Pensacola Office—LINDSEY CANNON, Regl. Dir., 1815 N. 6th Ave., Pensacola, 32503. Tel: 850-436-6410; Fax: 850-436-6439. Email: cathchar@cc.ptdiocese.org. Fort Walton Beach Office: CAROLYN KETCHEL, Regl. Dir., 11 First St., S.E., Fort Walton Beach, 32548. Tel: 850-244-2825; Fax: 850-664-9146. Email: ketchelc@cc.ptdiocese.org. Panama City Office: DIANE WILLIAMS, Regl. Dir., 3128 E. 11th St., Panama City, 32401. Tel: 850-763-0475; Fax: 850-763-2969. Email: williamsd@cc.ptdiocese.org. Tallahassee Office: ANSEL STEADMAN, Regl. Dir., Mailing Address: P.O. Box 20165, Tallahassee, 32316. Tel: 850-222-2180; Fax: 850-681-6963. Email: cathchartal@cc.ptdiocese.org.

Campaign for Human Development, Office of—LINDSAY MYERS, Dir., 1000 W. Garden St., Pensacola, 32502. Tel: 850-435-3516.

Justice and Peace, Office of—Catholic Charities, 1000 W. Garden St., Pensacola, 32502. Tel: 850-435-3516.

Liaison for Diocesan Disaster Relief—

Charismatic Renewal, Diocesan Commission for—Rev. EUGENE PATHE, Moderator; KIM JONES, Chair, 909 Maplewood Ave., Tallahassee, 32303. Email: alwaysps1@gmail.com.

Cursillo Movement—VACANT, Spiritual Dir.; CATHY CURRIER, Diocesan Lay Dir., 102 Jamie Ct., Crestview, 32539. Tel: 850-689-0190.

Ecumenical & Interreligious Affairs, Office of—VACANT, Dir.

Finance, Department of—JOHN GODLEWSKI, Dir., Mailing Address: P.O. Drawer 13284, Pensacola, 32591. Tel: 850-435-3500.

Human Resources—ROBIN JONES.

Internal Review—MIKE NOWLAN.

Communications— "The Catholic Compass" PEGGY DEKEYSER.

Real Estate/Construction—ROBERT BENNETT.

Information Technology—CELESTE DURAND.

Accounting—PAULA BEAUCHAMP.

Cemetery, Office of—Deacon STEPHEN WULF, Dir., Holy Cross Cemetery, 1300 E. Hayes St., Pensacola, 32503. Tel: 850-432-0878; Fax: 850-434-9032; FRED MCEVOY, Dir., Calvary Cemetery, 4298 Country Club Blvd., Sunny Hills, 32428. Tel: 850-773-2165.

Finance, Diocesan Commission for—ROBERT EMMANUEL ESQ., Chm.; Rev. Msgrs. LUKE HUNT, V.G., Sec.; MICHAEL V. REED, J.C.L.; BLAISE ADAMS; DENNIS MCKINNON; ROBERT HAMEL; ERIC NICKELSEN; J. PATRICK REMICH; JOHN GODLEWSKI, Mailing Address: P.O. Drawer 13284, Pensacola, 32591. Tel: 850-435-3500.

Holy Name Society—Rev. Msgr. MICHAEL V. REED, J.C.L., Mailing Address: P.O. Drawer 13284, Pensacola, 32591. Tel: 850-435-3500.

Independent Review Board—Mailing Address: P.O. Drawer 13284, Pensacola, 32591. Tel: 850-435-3500; Fax: 850-436-6424. Rev. DOUGLAS G. HALSEMA; Mrs. STEPHANIE ALFT; Mrs. ANGELA GUILLAUME; Dr. ANITA NUSBAUM; ROBERT EMMANUEL ESQ.; SHELLY REYNOLDS CLAUBAUGH; KELLY MEEK; PAUL JANSEN.

Knights of Columbus—Rev. Msgr. LUKE HUNT, V.G., Diocesan Chap., Mailing Address: P.O. Box 1057, Gulf Breeze, 32562. Tel: 850-934-0222; Fax: 850-934-2804.

Legion of Mary—Rev. HECTOR R.G. PEREZ, S.T.D., Diocesan Spiritual Dir., 900 W. Garden St., Pensacola, 32502. Tel: 850-432-9362.

Liturgy, Office of—Rev. PAUL T. WHITE, Dir., 100 Francis St., Mary Esther, 32569. Tel: 850-581-2556.

Department of Pastoral Ministry—Rev. Msgr. JAMES J. FLAHERTY, J.C.L., J.V., Dir., Mailing Address: P.O. Drawer 13284, Pensacola, 32591. Tel: 850-435-3500; Fax: 850-436-6424.

Catechetics—Sr. MARGARET KUNTZ, A.S.C.J. Email: kuntzm@ptdiocese.org.

Adult Faith Formation—STEPHANIE MCNEILL. Email: mcneills@ptdiocese.org.

Youth—LISA KURNIK ScoutingEmail: kurnikl@ptdiocese.org.

Marriage—VACANT.

Ethnic Concerns—

Hispanic Ministry, Office of—Co Directors: Rev. NICHOLAS FRANK SCHUMM; Sr. MARGARET KUNTZ, A.S.C.J.

Orders & Ministries, Commission for—Mailing Address: P.O. Drawer 13284, Pensacola, 32591. Tel: 850-435-3500; Fax: 850-436-6424. Rev. Msgr. MICHAEL W. TUGWELL; Rev. THOMAS J. GUIDO; Rev. Msgrs. JOHN V. O'SULLIVAN; MICHAEL V. REED, J.C.L.

Office of the Permanent Diaconate and Permanent Deacon Formation—Very Rev. JOSEPH P. CALLIPARE, Vicar for Permanent Deacons, 11 N. "B" St., Pensacola, 32502. Tel: 850-435-3552; Fax: 850-435-3565. Email: calliparej@ptdiocese.org.

Permanent Deacon Formation Team—Very Rev. JOSEPH P. CALLIPARE, Dir.; Rev. DOUGLAS G. HALSEMA, Spiritual Formation; Deacon TIMOTHY M. WARNER, Esq., Pastoral Formation; Rev. PAUL T. WHITE, Liturgical Formation.

Permanent Deacon Formation Board— Committee for Admissions and Scrutinies Ms. CAROLINE BUSH; Ms. JANE BRIM; Very Rev. JOSEPH P. CALLIPARE, Chm.; Deacon JOHN DURKIN; Rev. DOUGLAS G. HALSEMA; Mrs. BETTY ANN LURTON; Deacons GARY MCBRIDE; JOHN PARNHAM; TIMOTHY M. WARNER, Esq.; Rev. PAUL WHITE.

Permanent Deacon Deanery Representatives—Deacons DANIEL M. MCAULIFFE, J.C.L., West Central; LOU FETE, Eastern; ROGER GALLAGHER, East Central; PAUL GRAAFF, Northwest; RICHARD LURTON, At-Large; SANTIAGO MOLINA, At-Large; STEPHEN WULF, Southwest.

Continuing Education & Formation—Rev. Msgr. JAMES J. FLAHERTY, J.C.L., J.V., Dir., 11 N. B St., Pensacola, 32502.

Propagation of the Faith, Office of—Rev. Msgr. FRANCIS S. SZCZYKUTOWICZ, Dir., 2056 Sunny Hills, Sunny Hills, 32428-2929. Tel: 850-773-3406.

Respect Life Committee—Co Chairmen: Deacons ROGER GALLAGHER. Email: rogercrna@aol.com; MARK SCHNEIDER. Email: maslas1@embarqmail.com.

Schools, Department of—Mr. KEVIN VICKERY, Supt. Schools; DONNA BASS, Asst. to Supt. Schools & Teacher Certification, Mailing Address: P.O. Drawer 13284, Pensacola, 32591. Tel: 850-435-3500; Fax: 850-436-6424. Email: ptschools@ptdiocese.org.

Holy Childhood Association—Mr. KEVIN VICKERY, Dir.

Catholic Youth Sports League—LEONARDO CRUZ, Dir.

Seminarian Candidate Review Board—Rev. ROY C. MARIEN; Rev. Msgr. STEPHEN C. BOSSO; WILLIAM NADICKSBERND; Sr. SUSAN MARIE KRUPP, A.S.C.J.; Mrs. LINDA BARRETT; ROSEMARY MASON, Mailing Address: P.O. Drawer 13284, Pensacola, 32591. Tel: 850-435-3500.

Seminarians, Office of—Rev. Msgr. STEPHEN C. BOSSO, Dir.; MICHELE JOHNSTON, Staff Asst., Mailing Address: P.O. Drawer 13284, Pensacola, 32591. Tel: 850-435-3552. Email: johnstonm@ptdiocese.org.

Vocations, Office of—Rev. WILLIAM PHILIP GANCI; MICHELE JOHNSTON, Staff Asst., Mailing Address: P.O. Drawer 13284, Pensacola, 32591. Tel: 850-435-3552. Email: johnstonm@ptdiocese.org.

Serra Club—Pensacola: Rev. MICHAEL J. NIXON; J. PATRICK REMICH, Pres. Tallahassee: CHRIS KROLL, Pres.

Stewardship & Development, Office of—JOHN KENNEDY, Dir.

Victim Assistance Coordinators—DANIELLE MALONE, L.M.H.L. Tel: 850-438-3131, Ext. 17. Email: maloned@ptdiocese.org; Dr. JAMES GAGNON, M.S.W., L.C.S.W. Tel: 850-877-0205.

CLERGY, PARISHES, MISSIONS AND PAROCHIAL SCHOOLS

GREATER PENSACOLA

(ESCAMBIA COUNTY)

1—CATHEDRAL OF THE SACRED HEART (1905) Rev. Msgr. Michael V. Reed, Rector; Rev. Matthew Cameron Worthen, Parochial Vicar; Deacons Jean White, (Retired); John Durkin; John Parnham; Paul Graaff.

Mailing Address: 1212 E. Moreno St., 32503. Apostles of the Sacred Heart. In Res., Rev. Msgr. George Sindik (Retired).

Res.: 1101 E. Mallory St., 32503. Tel: 850-438-3131; Fax: 850-436-6428. Email: reedm@sch.ptdiocese.org. Web: www.shc.ptdiocese.org.

School—Sacred Heart Cathedral School, (Grades K-8), 1603 N. 12th Ave., 32503. Tel: 850-436-6440; Fax: 850-436-6444. Raymond Thompson, Prin.; Mary Fritz, Librarian.

Catechesis/Religious Program—Tel: 850-438-3131; Fax: 850-436-6428. Students 114.

Convent—3531 Monteigne Dr., 32503. Tel: 850-438-0560.

2—ST. ANNE (Brownsville) (1953) Closed. For inquiries for sacramental records, please see the Cathedral of the Sacred Heart, Pensacola.

3—ST. ANNE'S (Bellview) (1964) Rev. John J. Licari; Deacons Thomas Gordon; Donald Krehely.

Res.: 5200 Saufley Field Rd., 32526-1626. Tel: 850-456-5966; Fax: 850-453-3138. Web: www.stannebv.org.

Catechesis/Religious Program—Students 114.

4—ST. ANTHONY OF PADUA (1941), (African American), Rev. Msgr. Michael V. Reed; Deacons Jean White, (Retired); John Durkin; John Parnham; Paul Graaff.

Mailing Address: c/o 1212 E. Moreno St., 32503. Tel: 850-324-5655; Fax: 850-944-5299. Email: reedm@ptdiocese.org. Web: www.ptdiocese.org.

Res. & Church: 1804 N. Davis Hwy., 32503. Tel: 850-436-6422.

Catechesis/Religious Program—Twinned with The Cathedral of the Sacred Heart., *Community Center*, 1805 N. 6th Ave., 32503.

5—HOLY SPIRIT (1976) Rev. Msgr. James J. Flaherty; Rev. J. Thomas Dillon, Parochial Vicar; Deacons Lloyd Krueger; Robert Gregerson, (Atlanta).

Res.: 1145 Freeboard Blvd., 32507. Tel: 850-492-5300. Church: 10650 Gulf Beach Hwy., 32507. Tel: 850-492-0837; Fax: 850-492-4968.

Catechesis/Religious Program—Tel: 852-492-0837, Ext. 211. Students 90.

6—ST. JOHN THE EVANGELIST (1851) [CEM] Rev. Msgr. James J. Flaherty; Rev. J. Thomas Dillon. Email: dillonj@clergy.ptdiocese.org; Deacon Gerard Williamson.

Office: 303 S. Navy Blvd., 32507. Tel: 850-455-0356; Fax: 850-453-5109. Email: office@stjohn.ptdiocese.org. Web: www.stjohn.ptdiocese.org.

School—(Grades K-8), 325 S. Navy Blvd., 32507. Tel: 850-456-5218; Fax: 850-456-5956. Web: www.sjsw.ptdiocese.org. Mrs. Ann Williams, Prin. Lay Teachers 16; Students 183.

Catechesis/Religious Program—Email: reled@stjohn.ptdiocese.org. Students 64.

Convent—

7—ST. JOSEPH (1891) [CEM] Rev. Patrick Foley; Sr. Maureen Joseph Kirwan, S.C., Pastoral Assoc.; Deacon Eugene Pallone.

Mailing Address: P.O. Box 13566, 32591. Tel: 850-436-6461; Fax: 850-436-6462. Email: admin@stjoseph.ptdiocese.org. Web: www.stjosephchurchpensacola.parishonline.com.

Res.: 141 W. Intendencia St., 32502. Tel: 850-436-6461; Fax: 850-436-6462. Email: admin@stjoseph.ptdiocese.org. Web: www.stjosephchurchpensacola.parishesonline.com.

Catechesis/Religious Program—Tel: 850-436-6461; Fax: 850-436-6462. Gail Rothschild, D.R.E. Students 46.

8—LITTLE FLOWER (1945) Rev. James Thoyalil, V.C. (India); Deacons Reymond Castellano; Stephen

Wulf.
Res.: 6495 Lillian Hwy., P.O. Box 3009, 32516. Tel: 850-455-5641; Fax: 850-455-4508. Email: office@ptlittleflower.org.
School—(Grades K-8) Tel: 850-455-4851; Fax: 850-457-8982. Sr. Barbara Zipoli, A.S.C.J., Prin. Lay Teachers 18; Students 170.
Catechesis/Religious Program—Tel: 850-455-8434. Students 107.

9—ST. MARY (1941) Rev. Dominic Phan Sa; Deacon Herman Lux.
Res. & Mailing Address: 401 Van Pelt Ln., 32505. Tel: 850-478-2797; Fax: 850-478-2739. Email: stmaryca@bellsouth.net.
Catechesis/Religious Program—Tel: 850-478-2797; Fax: 850-478-2739. Students 30.

10—ST. MICHAEL (1781) Rev. Peter A. McLaughlin (CAM).
Mailing Address: P.O. Box 12423, 32591-2423.
Res.: 19 N. Palafox St., 32501. Tel: 850-438-4985; Fax: 850-433-9758. Email: fosterl@stmichael.ptdiocese.org. Web: www.stmichael.ptdiocese.org.
Catechesis/Religious Program—Students 15.

11—NATIVITY OF OUR LORD (1969) Rev. Msgr. Michael P. Mooney; Rev. James Paul Valenzuela, Parochial Vicar; Deacons Randall Comeau, (Retired); Dennis Dobransky; John Bartoszewicz, (Retired). In Res., Rev. Msgr. Raymond Mullins (Retired).
Res.: 9945 Hillview Dr., 32514-5702. Tel: 850-477-3221; Fax: 850-478-5584.
Catechesis/Religious Program—Tel: 850-477-3221, Ext. 5. Email: mzeni@nativityofourlordcc.org. Web: nativityofourlordcc.org. Students 284.

12—OUR LADY QUEEN OF MARTYRS (1977), (Vietnamese), Rev. Paul Cao.
Res.: 3295 S. Barrancas Ave., 32507. Tel: 850-455-2712. Email: ourladyqueenofmartyrs@gmail.com.
Catechesis/Religious Program—Tel: 850-455-2712; Fax: 850-455-0264. Students 46.

13—ST. PAUL (1963) Revs. Douglas G. Halsema; Michael J. Nixon, Parochial Vicar; Deacons John P. Morgan, (Retired); Robert Leblanc; Richard Lurton.
Res.: 1700 Conway Dr., 32503. Tel: 850-434-2551; Fax: 850-436-6449. Email: parishoffice@stpaulcatholic.net. Web: www.stpaulcatholic.net.
School—3121 Hyde Park Rd., 32503. Tel: 850-436-6435; Fax: 850-436-6437. Ms. Lorelei Darga, Prin. Lay Teachers 25; Students 211.
Catechesis/Religious Program—Fax: 850-436-6449. Email: clarkeb@stpaulcatholic.net. Students 202.

14—ST. STEPHEN (1922) Rev. Hector R.G. Perez.
Res.: 900 W. Garden St., 32502. Tel: 850-432-9362; Fax: 850-435-9946.
Catechesis/Religious Program—Tel: 850-432-9362; Fax: 850-435-9946. Email: fhrgp3@cox.net. Students 43.

15—ST. THOMAS MORE (1954) Rev. Msgr. John T. Cassidy.
Mailing Address: 510 Bayshore Dr., 32507. Tel: 850-456-2543; Fax: 850-455-5203. Email: bayshore@stm.gccoxmail.com.
Catechesis/Religious Program—Fax: 850-455-5203. Students 15.

CITY OF TALLAHASSEE

(LEON COUNTY)

1—CO-CATHEDRAL OF ST. THOMAS MORE (1968) Rev. Msgr. Michael W. Tugwell, Rector; Rev. Christopher LeBlanc, Parochial Vicar; Deacon Santiago Molina.
Res.: 832 W. Tennessee St., P.O. Box 2395, 32304. Tel: 850-222-7371; 850-222-9630 (Office); Fax: 850-222-6430.
For a complete listing, see John Paul II Catholic High School located under High Schools, Diocesan in the Institution section.
Catechesis/Religious Program—Students 120.
Chapel—St. Eugene, Florida A&M University [JC] 701 W. Gamble St., 32310. Tel: 850-222-6482; Fax: 850-222-6482. Rev. Ejiofor Ugwu, M.S.P.

2—BLESSED SACRAMENT (1845) Rev. Msgr. John V. O'Sullivan; Revs. Juan Pedro Hernandez, Parochial Vicar; Timothy Michael Holeda II, Parochial Vicar; Deacons Charles L. Fete; Rudolph Raymaker; Patrick Dallet; Michael Nixon.
Res.: 624 Miccosukee Rd., 32308. Tel: 850-222-1321; Fax: 850-222-9772. Web: www.bsc.ptdiocese.org.
School—Trinity Catholic, (Grades K-8), 706 E. Brevard St., 32308. Tel: 850-222-0444; Fax: 850-224-5067. Mrs. Janet Gendusa, Prin. Lay Teachers 31; Students 484.
For a complete listing, see John Paul II Catholic High School located under High Schools, Diocesan in the Institution section.
St. John Neumann Retreat Center—685 Miccosukee Rd., 32308. Tel: 850-224-2971. Sr. Christine Kelly, S.S.J., Dir.
Catechesis/Religious Program—Students 156.

3—GOOD SHEPHERD (1973) Revs. Michael Foley; James Christian Winkeljohn, Parochial Vicar; William Philip Ganci, Parochial Vicar; Deacons Edward Melvin III; Gerald Haynes; Thomas McBrearty; Mark Schneider.
4665 Thomasville Rd., 32309-2512. Tel: 850-893-1837; 850-893-2381; Fax: 850-894-6912. Email: goodshepherd@gs.ptdiocese.org. Web: www.goodshepherdparish.org.
For a complete listing, see John Paul II Catholic High School located under High Schools, Diocesan in the Institution section.
Catechesis/Religious Program—Bette Scaringe, D.R.E. Students 744.

4—ST. LOUIS (1979) Very Rev. Kevin Johnson; Deacons Nelson Madera; Robert Macko.
3640 Fred George Rd., 32303.
Res.: 4151 Miraflores Ln., 32303. Tel: 850-562-5140. Email: stlouischurch@embarqmail.com.
Catechesis/Religious Program—Tel: 850-562-5140; Fax: 850-562-3117. Students 47.

OUTSIDE THE CITIES OF PENSACOLA AND TALLAHASSEE

APALACHICOLA, FRANKLIN CO., ST. PATRICK (1851) [JC] Rev. Roger Latosynski.
Res.: 27 Sixth St., P.O. Box 550, 32329. Tel: 904-653-9453; Fax: 850-653-4528. Email: stpatcath@gtcom.net. Web: www.stpatrickmass.com.
Catechesis/Religious Program—Thomasine Brock, Dir., Faith Formation; Monica Moron, Dir., Faith Formation. Students 13.

BAYOU GEORGE, BAY CO., OUR LADY OF THE ROSARY Rev. W. P. Brown.
Res.: 5622 Julie Dr., Panama City, 32404. Tel: 850-769-5067; Fax: 850-769-1229.
Catechesis/Religious Program—Tel: 850-769-5067; Fax: 850-769-1227. Students 25.
Mission—Our Lady Queen of Peace P.O. Box 213, Fountain, Bay Co. 32438. Tel: 850-722-0466; Fax: 850-722-0466.

BLOUNTSTOWN, CALHOUN CO., ST. FRANCIS OF ASSISI (1972) [CEM] Rev. Chuck Collins.
Res.: 16498 S.W. Gaskin St., 32424. Tel: 850-674-4482; Fax: 850-674-4482. Email: stfrancisassisi@gtcom.net.
Catechesis/Religious Program—Students 20.

BONIFAY, HOLMES CO., BLESSED TRINITY (1979) Rev. Richard Dawson.
Res.: 2331 Hwy. 177A, 32425. Tel: 850-547-3735; Fax: 850-547-7477. Email: btbonifay@embarqmail.com.
Catechesis/Religious Program—Students 11.

CANTONMENT, ESCAMBIA CO., ST. JUDE THADDEUS (1945) [CEM] [JC] Revs. George Thekku; Thomas Koyickal, Parochial Vicar; Deacons Thomas Simard; Bradley M. Seabrook.
Res.: 303 Rocky Ave., 32533. Tel: 850-968-6189; Fax: 850-968-1578. Email: ustjudethadde@panhandle.rr.com. Web: stjudecantonment.com.
Mission—St. Elizabeth of Hungary 303 Rocky Ave., Escambia Co. 32533. Tel: 850-587-2550.
Catechesis/Religious Program—Students 18.

CHATTAHOOCHEE, GADSDEN CO., HOLY CROSS PARISH (1979) Rev. Chuck Collins.
Res.: 4034 Memorial Blue Star Hwy., 32324. Tel: 850-663-4610.

CHIPLEY, WASHINGTON CO., ST. JOSEPH THE WORKER (1968) Rev. George Sammut.
Res.: P.O. Box 266, 32428. Tel: 850-638-7654.
Catechesis/Religious Program—Students 7.

CRAWFORDVILLE, WAKULLA CO., ST. ELIZABETH ANN SETON (1975) [CEM] Rev. Edward T. Jones.
Mailing Address: 3609 Coastal Hwy., 32327. Tel: 850-926-1797; Fax: 850-926-1737.
Catechesis/Religious Program—Students 63.

CRESTVIEW, OKALOOSA CO., OUR LADY OF VICTORY (1954) Revs. John B. Cayer; Kurian Manikuttiyil, Parochial Vicar; Deacon Kenneth Mayfield.
Office: 550 Adams Dr., 32536. Tel: 850-682-4622; Fax: 850-689-0335. Email: olvadmin@olv.ptdiocese.org. Web: www.olv.ptdiocese.org.
Catechesis/Religious Program—Tel: 850-682-4622, Ext. 15; Fax: 850-689-0335. Students 250.

DE FUNIAK SPRINGS, WALTON CO., ST. MARGARET (1931) Rev. Richard Dawson; Deacon Walter D. Harris.
Mailing Address: P.O. Box 590, 32435-0590. Tel: 850-892-9247; Fax: 850-892-2065.
Res.: 247 U.S. Hwy. 331 N., Box 590, 32435. Tel: 850-892-9247; Fax: 850-892-2065. Email: stmargaret@embarqmail.com.
Catechesis/Religious Program—Tel: 850-892-9247; Fax: 850-892-2065. Students 67.

DESTIN, OKALOOSA CO., CORPUS CHRISTI (1977) Rev. Robert F. Morris.
Res.: 307 Beach Dr., 32541. Tel: 850-654-5422; Fax: 850-837-3807. Email: corpuschristic@aol.com.
Catechesis/Religious Program—Tel: 850-654-5423; Fax: 850-837-3807. Students 70.

FORT WALTON BEACH, OKALOOSA CO., ST. MARY CHURCH (1914) Rev. Msgr. Michael A. Cherup; Rev. Craig Smith, Parochial Vicar; Deacons Robert J. Saxer; Walter Richardson; Daniel M. McAuliffe.
Res.: 110 St. Mary Ave., S.W., 32548. Tel: 850-243-3742; Fax: 850-243-1271. Email: smcfwb@saintmarychurchfwb.org. Web: www.saintmarychurchfwb.org.
School—(Grades K-8), 110 Robinwood Dr., 32548. Tel: 850-243-8913; Fax: 850-243-7895. Mrs. Regina Nadicksbernd, Prin.; Kathleen Piccione, Librarian. Priests 1; Religious 1; Lay Teachers 27; Students 418.
Catechesis/Religious Program—Tel: 850-244-1833; Fax: 850-243-1271. Students 20.

FOUNTAIN, BAY CO., OUR LADY QUEEN OF PEACE MISSION Rev. William P. Brown.
Mailing Address: 5622 Julie Dr., Panama City, 32404. Tel: 850-722-0466; Fax: 850-722-0466.
Church: 18005 Lazy Ln., 32438. Tel: 850-769-5067; Fax: 850-769-1227.
Catechesis/Religious Program—Students 24.

FREEPORT, WALTON CO., CHRIST THE KING MISSION (1984) Rev. Thomas S. Collins; Deacon Dave Casey.
Mailing Address: *c/o St. Rita*, 137 Moll Dr., Santa Rosa Beach, 32459.
Church: 15542 U.S. Hwy. 3315, 32439. Tel: 850-267-2558; Fax: 850-267-3711.

GULF BREEZE, SANTA ROSA CO.

1—ST. ANN (1948) Rev. Msgr. Luke Hunt; Rev. Paul Francis Lambert, Parochial Vicar; Deacon Kenneth McClure.
Res.: 100 Daniel Dr., P.O. Drawer 1057, 32561. Tel: 850-932-2859; Fax: 850-934-2804. Email: info@stanngulfbreeze.org. Web: www.stanngulfbreeze.org.
School—St. Ann Discovery School, Tel: 850-932-9330; Fax: 850-934-2804. Jean Jones, Dir. (Learning Center) (Age 8 wks.-Pre-K) Teachers 36; Students 111.
Catechesis/Religious Program—Tel: 850-932-2859, Ext. 234; Fax: 850-934-2804. Students 348.
Mission—Our Lady of the Assumption Pensacola Beach. 920 Via de Luna, P.O. Box 1057, Santa Rosa Co. 32561. Tel: 850-934-0222; Fax: 850-934-6020.

2—SAINT SYLVESTER (1979) Revs. John F. Kelly; Alvaro Pio Gonzalez (Colombia), Parochial Vicar.
Church & Office: 6464 Gulf Breeze Pkwy, 32563. Tel: 850-939-3020; Fax: 850-936-5366. Email: saintsylv@stsylv.org. Web: www.stsylv.org.
Rectory—7083 Brighton Oaks Blvd., Navarre, 32566. Tel: 850-936-1215.
Catechesis/Religious Program—Sandra Nicholas, D.R.E. Students 311.

LANARK VILLAGE, FRANKLIN CO., SACRED HEART OF JESUS (1960) Rev. Edward T. Jones, Admin.
Res.: 109 Elm St., P.O. Box 729, 32323. Tel: 850-697-3445.

MADISON, MADISON CO., ST. VINCENT DE PAUL (1907) Rev. Viet Tan Huynh. In Res., Rev. Joseph C. Schwab, O.M.I.
Res.: 186 N.W. Sumter St., 32340-2048. Tel: 850-973-2428.
Catechesis/Religious Program—Students 12.

MARIANNA, JACKSON CO., ST. ANNE (1947) [JC] Rev. George Sammut.
Res.: 3009 Fifth St., P.O. Box 1547, 32447. Tel: 850-482-3734; Fax: 850-482-7241.
Catechesis/Religious Program—Tel: 850-482-3734; Fax: 850-482-7241. Students 38.

MARY ESTHER, OKALOOSA CO., ST. PETER (1975) Rev. Paul T. White; Deacon David P. Robinson.
Res.: 100 Francis St., 32569. Tel: 850-581-2556; Fax: 850-581-2640. Email: office@stpeter.ptdiocese.org. Web: www.stpeter.ptdiocese.org.
Catechesis/Religious Program—Tel: 850-581-7263. Students 89.

MEXICO BEACH, BAY CO., OUR LADY OF GUADALUPE MISSION (1980) Closed. For inquiries for parish records contact the chancery.

MILTON, SANTA ROSA CO., ST. ROSE OF LIMA (1957) [JC] Rev. Msgr. Stephen C. Bosso; Rev. Richard Lee Schamber, Parochial Vicar; Deacons Thomas Kennell; Chris Christopher; Jeffrey Massey.
Church: 6451 Park Ave., 32570. Tel: 850-623-3600; Fax: 850-983-3043. Email: srlparish@srl.ptdiocese.org. Web: www.stroselima.parishesonline.com.
Res.: 5965 Sleepy Hollow, 32570. Tel: 850-983-1449.
Catechesis/Religious Program—Students 195.

MIRAMAR BEACH, WALTON CO., CHURCH OF THE RESURRECTION (1981) Rev. Thomas J. Guido; Deacon Matthew Rezmer.
Rectory—
Church: 259 Miramar Beach Dr., 32550. Tel: 850-837-0357; Fax: 850-837-2062.
Catechesis/Religious Program—Tel: 850-837-0357; Fax: 850-837-2062. Email: marilyn@rcc-destin.org. Marilyn Austin, D.R.E. & Youth Ministry; Steve McCown, Music Min. Students 100.

MONTICELLO, JEFFERSON CO., ST. MARGARET (1917) Rev. Viet Tan Huynh.
Res.: c/o 186 Sumter St., Madison, 32340. Tel: 850-973-2428.
Church: U.S. Hwy. 90 E., 32344. Tel: 850-997-3622; Fax: 850-973-2825.
Catechesis/Religious Program—Students 40.

NICEVILLE, OKALOOSA CO.
1—CHRIST OUR REDEEMER (1989) Rev. Robert Johnson; Deacons Joaquin Trevino; James Murray; William E. Schaal; Miguel Nolla; Carmen Marshall-Claude, Youth Min.; Adam Ubowski, Music Min.
Res.: 1028 White Point Rd., 32578. Tel: 850-897-7797; Fax: 850-897-2422. Email: coroffice@gmail.com.
Catechesis/Religious Program—Tel: 850-897-2974; Fax: 850-897-2422. Email: coreducate@gmail.com; coryouth@gmail.com. Web: www.corcatholic.org. Lisa Hall, D.R.E. Students 247.
2—HOLY NAME OF JESUS (1960) Rev. Dominic Dat Tran; Deacons Louis Marini; Willie O'Neal; James Cox; Gary McBride; Thomas Fraites; John Shin.
Res.: 1200 Valparaiso Blvd., 32578-2946. Tel: 850-678-7813; Fax: 850-678-5775. Email: holyname@holynamechurch.org. Web: www.holynamechurch.org.
Catechesis/Religious Program—Tel: 850-678-6790; Fax: 850-678-5775. Email: b.younger@holynamechurch.org. Students 201.

PANAMA CITY BEACH, BAY CO., ST. BERNADETTE (1956) Revs. Ted Sosnowski, C.R. (Poland); Paul Smith, Parochial Vicar; Deacon Dale Johnson; Juli Roock, Business Mgr.; Yvette Valenti, Youth Min.
Res.: 1214 Moylan Rd., 32407. Tel: 850-249-4100; Fax: 850-233-1177. Web: www.stbernadette.com.
Child Development Center—Tel: 850-230-0009; Fax: 850-230-6989. Juli Roock, Dir. Lay Teachers 27; Students 122.
Catechesis/Religious Program—Tel: 850-249-1200. Shirley Merglewski, D.R.E. Students 104.
St. Bernadette John Lee Outreach Center— (2003) 1329 Moylan Rd., 32407. Tel: 850-236-5252. Email: stbernadette@knology.net.

PANAMA CITY, BAY CO.
1—ST. DOMINIC (1890) Very Rev. Peter Lawrence Zalewski; Revs. Benedict Klucinec, M.S.A.; Kevin McQuone; Dominic Dieu Tran, S.D.D.; Deacon Roger Gallagher. In Res., Rev. John Selleck.
Res.: 3308 E. 15th St., 32405-7414. Tel: 850-785-4574; Fax: 850-872-0800. Web: www.stdominic.ptdiocese.org.
Catechesis/Religious Program—Tel: 850-763-7393; Fax: 850-872-0800. Students 320.
2—ST. JOHN THE EVANGELIST (1945) Rev. Roy C. Marien; Deacons Timothy M. Warner; Earl C. Mirus; George Walters.
Res.: 1008 Fortune Ave., 32401. Tel: 850-763-1821; Fax: 850-784-1739. Email: stj.office@knology.net. Web: www.stjohnpc.ptdiocese.org.
School—1005 Fortune Ave., 32401. Tel: 850-763-1775; Fax: 850-784-4461. Email: stjohns@knology.net. Web: www.stjohncatholicschool-.com. Kendall F. McKee, Prin. Lay Teachers 14; Students 108.
Catechesis/Religious Program—Email: stj.dre@knology.net. Mary Fry, D.R.E. Students 49.
3—SS. PETER & PAUL MISSION (1981), (Vietnamese), [JC] Rev. Dominic Dieu Tran, S.D.D.
Mailing Address: 1003 East Ave., 32401.
Res.: 3308 E. 15th St., 32405. Tel: 850-785-4574.
Catechesis/Religious Program—Students 53.

PENSACOLA BEACH, ESCAMBIA CO., OUR LADY OF THE ASSUMPTION MISSION (1979) Unassigned.Mailing Address: P.O. Box 1057, Gulf Breeze, 32562. Tel: 850-934-0222; Fax: 850-934-6020. Web: www.stangulfbreeze.org. See St. Ann, Gulf Breeze.
920 Via de Luna, 32561. Tel: 850-934-0222.
Catechesis/Religious Program—Tel: 850-934-0222; Fax: 850-934-6020. Students 7.

PERRY, TAYLOR CO., IMMACULATE CONCEPTION (1914) Rev. Bernard Jakubco, M.S.C.
Res.: 2750 S. Byron Butler Pkwy., 32348. Tel: 850-584-3169; Fax: 850-584-3169. Email: immac@fairpoint.net.
Catechesis/Religious Program—Students 37.
Center—Tel: 850-584-8853.

PORT ST. JOE, GULF CO., ST. JOSEPH (1925) Rev. Philip Fortin.
Res.: 2006 Monument Ave., P.O. Box 820, 32457-0820. Tel: 850-229-1922; Fax: 850-229-1585. Email: stjoseph@fairpoint.net.
Church: 20th & Monument Sts., 32457-0820.
Catechesis/Religious Program—Tel: 850-227-1417. Students 42.
Mission—San Blas Catholic Mission 7524 Capesan Blas Rd., Gulf Co. 32456.
Mission—St. Lawrence Mission 788 N. Hwy. 71, Wewahitchka, Gulf Co. Tel: 850-639-5787.

QUINCY, GADSDEN CO., ST. THOMAS THE APOSTLE (1957) Rev. Nicholas Frank Schumm.
Res. & Mailing Address: Hwy. 90 & 27 N. Shadow St., P.O. Box 549, 32351. Tel: 850-627-2350; Fax: 850-627-6755. Email: st_thomas@tds.net. Web: www.stthomas-quincy.parishesonline.com.
Catechesis/Religious Program—Tel: 850-627-2350; Fax: 850-627-6755. Students 142.
Hispanic Ministry Office of St. Thomas—Religious Education Office. Fax: 850-627-6755.

SANTA ROSA BEACH, WALTON CO., ST. RITA (1982) Rev. Thomas S. Collins; Deacon David Casey.
Mailing Address: 137 Moll St., 32459. Tel: 850-267-2558; 850-622-2751 (Rectory); Fax: 850-267-3711. Email: saintritacatholic.church@mchsi.com. Web: saintritaparish.org.
Res.: Tel: 850-267-2558; Fax: 850-267-3711.
Catechesis/Religious Program—Students 240.
Mission—Christ the King Catholic Mission Freeport, Walton Co.

SUNNY HILLS, WASHINGTON CO., ST. THERESA (1972) Rev. Msgr. Francis S. Szczykutowicz.
Res.: 2056 Sunny Hills Blvd., 32428. Tel: 850-773-3406; Fax: 850-773-7008. Email: fr_frank@bellsouth.net.
Catechesis/Religious Program—Tel: 850-773-3406; Fax: 850-773-7008.

WEWAHITCHKA, GULF CO., ST. LAWRENCE MISSION, Mailing Address: P.O. Box 820, Port St. Joe, 32457. Email: stjoseph@gtcom.net. 788 N. Hwy. 71, 32465. Tel: 850-227-1417.

WOODVILLE, LEON CO., ST. STEPHEN THE PROTOMARTYR (1979) Rev. Msgr. John V. O'Sullivan, Admin.
Mailing Address: P.O. Box 208, 32362. Tel: 850-421-9094.
Res.: 1997 Natural Bridge Rd., 32362. Tel: 850-926-1797; Fax: 850-926-1737. Email: seascp@aol.com.
Catechesis/Religious Program—Students 4.

Chaplains of Public Institutions

PENSACOLA. *Escambia County Jail*. Deacon Dennis Dobransky.
Saufley Field Federal Prison Camp. Vacant.
TALLAHASSEE. *Federal Correctional Institution*. Deacon Ted Horbowy.
CHATTAHOOCHEE. *Florida State Hospital*. Rev. Chuck Collins.
CHIPLEY. *Washington Correctional Institution*. Rev. John Selleck.
CRAWFORDVILLE. *Wakulla Correctional Institution*. Deacons Lou Fete, Marcus Hepburn, Santiago Molino, Madera Nelson.
CRESTVIEW. *Okloosa Correctional Facility*. Deacons James Cox, Daniel M. McAuliffe, J.C.L.
EGLIN. *Eglin Federal Prison Camp Eglin Air Force Base*. Deacon Gary McBride.
MARIANNA. *Florida Correctional Institutions*.
SNEADS. *Apalachee Correctional Institution*.
WEWAHITCHKA. *Gulf Coast Institution*. Rev. John Selleck.

On Duty Outside the Diocese:
Revs.—
Flynn, Michael J., M.Div., S.T.L., St. Vincent de Paul Regional Seminary, Boynton Beach, FL
O'Brien, Dennis J. South America.
Ssemakula, Yozefu B., Studying outside Diocese (Notre Dame, IN)
Stewart, Paul

Military Chaplains:
Revs.—
Knox, Sean Vincent, Randolph AFB.
Krzywicki, Lance P., Chap., ILVA, 1, 07029, Tempio Paosania, Italy.
McClanahan, Robert P., Jr., Chap., Cmdr.
Voyt, Stephen A., Lt. Col., Hickam AFB, HI 96853.

On Leave of Absence:
Revs.—
Bluett, James K.
Castillo, Richard

Retired:
Rev. Msgrs.—
Bowles, Richard J.
Crawford, C. Slade
Mullins, Raymond
Sindik, George
Revs.—
Altenbaugh, Richard L.
Dolan, Hugh
Gray, John
Hevia, Todd O.
Hogarty, Paul
Jorden, James A.
Joseph, William
Kiem, Anthony
Kirby, Edward A.
Lambert, James J.
O'Shea, David T.

Permanent Deacons:
Barrows, Stanley, (Retired), (On Duty Outside Diocese)
Bartoszewicz, John M., (Retired), Nativity of Our Lord Parish, Pensacola
Brinkworth, Gary, (On Duty Outside Diocese)
Casey, David R., St. Rita, Santa Rosa Beach
Castellano, Reymond, Little Flower, Pensacola
Christopher, Chris, St. Rose of Lima, Milton
Cirabisi, Sal
Comeau, Randall O., (Retired), Nativity of Our Lord, Pensacola
Cox, James, Holy Name of Jesus, Niceville
Dallet, Patrick, Blessed Sacrament, Tallahassee
Dobransky, Dennis, Nativity of Our Lord, Pensacola
Durkin, John, Cathedral of the Sacred Heart, Pensacola
Fete, Charles L., Blessed Sacrament, Tallahassee
Fraites, Thomas J., Holy Name of Jesus, Niceville
Gallagher, Roger, St. Dominic, Panama City
Gardner, James L., (Retired), (On Duty Outside Diocese)
Gordon, Thomas, St. Anne, Pensacola
Graaff, Paul, Cathedral of the Sacred Heart, Pensacola
Gregerson, Robert, Holy Spirit, Pensacola (Archdiocese of Atlanta) (Extern)
Harris, Walter D., St. Margaret, Defuniak Springs
Haynes, Gerald, Good Shepherd, Tallahassee
Horbowy, Thaddeus, Tallahassee, Archdiocese of Galveston-Houston (Extern)
Howell, John, (On Duty Outside Diocese)
Johnson, Dale R., (Retired), St. Bernadette, Panama City Beach
Kennell, Thomas H., St. Rose of Lima, Milton
Krehely, Donald, (Retired), St. Anne, Pensacola
Kreppein, John, (Retired), (On Duty Outside Diocese)
Krueger, Lloyd, Holy Spirit, Pensacola
L'Huillier, Ron, (On Duty Outside Diocese)
Landry, Alduce, (Retired), (On Duty Outside Diocese)
Leblanc, Robert, St. Paul, Pensacola
Lee, Charles, (On Duty Outside Diocese)
Lurton, Richard, St. Paul, Pensacola
Lux, Herman, St. Mary, Pensacola (Diocese of Altoona-Johnstown) (Extern)
Macko, Robert, St. Louis, Tallahassee
Madera, Nelson I., (Retired), St. Louis, Tallahassee
Marini, Louis, (Retired), Holy Name of Jesus, Niceville
Massey, Jeffrey, St. Rose of Lima, Milton
Mayfield, Kenneth, Our Lady of Victory, Crestview (Archdiocese of Los Angeles) (Extern)
McAuliffe, Daniel, St. Mary, Ft. Walton Beach
McBrearty, Thomas, Good Shepherd, Tallahassee
McBride, Gary, Holy Name of Jesus, Niceville
McClure, Kenneth, St. Ann, Gulf Breeze
Melvin, Edward, III, Good Shepherd, Tallahassee
Mirus, Earl C., St. John the Evangelist, Panama City
Molina, Santiago, St. Thomas More, Tallahassee
Morgan, John P., (Retired), St. Paul, Pensacola
Murphy, Michael, (On Duty Outside Diocese)
Murray, James, Christ Our Redeemer, Blue Water Bay
Nixon, Michael, Blessed Sacrament, Tallahassee
Nolla, Miguel, Christ Our Redeemer, Niceville
O'Neal, Willie, (Retired), Holy Name of Jesus, Niceville
Pallone, Eugene, St. Joseph, Pensacola
Parnham, John, Cathedral of the Sacred Heart, Pensacola
Provencher, Conrad, (Retired), St. Bernadette, Panama City Beach (Diocese of Trenton) (Extern)
Raymaker, Rudolph, (Retired), Blessed Sacrament, Tallahassee
Renick, John, M.D., (Retired), (On Duty Outside Diocese)
Rezmer, Matthew, Resurrection, Miramar Beach
Richardson, Walter H., (Retired), St. Mary, Fort Walton Beach
Robinson, David P., (Retired), St. Peter, Mary Esther
Rose, Joseph, (Retired), (On Duty Outside Diocese)
Saxer, Robert J., (Retired), St. Mary, Fort Walton Beach
Schaal, William E., (Retired), Christ Our Redeemer, Blue Water Bay
Schneider, Mark, Good Shepherd, Tallahassee
Scott, John, (On Duty Outside Diocese)
Seabrook, Bradley M., (Retired), St. Jude, Cantonment
Shin, John, Holy Name of Jesus, Niceville
Simard, Thomas, St. Jude; St. Elizabeth, Cantonment
Trevino, Joaquin D., (Retired), Christ Our Redeemer, Blue Water Bay
Walters, George, St. John the Evangelist, Panama City

Warner, Timothy M., Esq., St. John the Evangelist, Panama City
White, Jean, (Retired), Cathedral of the Sacred Heart
Williamson, Gerard, (Retired), St. John the Evangelist, Pensacola
Wulf, Stephen, Little Flower, Pensacola
Zmuda, Henry, (On Duty Outside the Diocese)

INSTITUTIONS LOCATED IN THE DIOCESE

[A] HIGH SCHOOLS, DIOCESAN

PENSACOLA. *Pensacola Catholic High School*, 3043 W. Scott St., 32505. Tel: 850-436-6400; Fax: 850-436-6405. Email: kmartin@pensacolachs.org. Web: pensacolachs.org. Sr. Kierstin Martin, A.S.C.J., Prin.; Rebecca Frandsen, Librarian. Sisters 1; Lay Teachers 50; Students 570; Total Staff 59.

TALLAHASSEE. *John Paul II Catholic High School* (2001) 5100 Terrebone Dr., 32311-7848. Tel: 850-201-5744; Fax: 850-205-3299. Email: srecronan@jpiichs.org. Web: www.jpiichs.org. Sr. Ellen Cronan, A.S.C.J., Prin.; MaryAnn Hensarling, Librarian. Sisters 3; Lay Teachers 16; Students 119; Total Staff 4.

[B] GENERAL HOSPITALS

PENSACOLA. *The Mother Seton Guild of Sacred Heart Hospital, Inc.*, 5151 N. 9th Ave., 32504. Tel: 850-416-7883. Ms. Janet Shelby, Pres.

Sacred Heart Foundation, Inc. (1984) 5151 N. 9th Ave., 32504. Tel: 850-416-4660; Fax: 850-416-4664. Email: hroberts@shhpens.org. Web: sacred-heart.org. P.O. Box 2700, 32513-2700. Tel: 850-416-4660; Fax: 850-416-4664. Roger Webb, Chm. Bed Capacity 466; Total Assisted Annually 2,637; Total Staff 10.

Sacred Heart Health System, Inc. DBA: Sacred Heart Hospital of Pensacola; Sacred Heart Hospital on the Emerald Coast; Sacred Heart Hospital on the Gulf., 5151 N. Ninth Ave., 32504. Tel: 850-416-7000; Fax: 850-416-6119. Email: lskaiser@shhpens.org. Web: sacred-heart.org. Laura S. Kaiser, Pres. & CEO. Annual Admissions 32,326; Total Staff (includes SHHP, SHHEC & SHHG) 5,000; Total Number of Admissions & Outpatient Encounters 98,527; Bed Capacity (SHHP) 466; Bed Capacity (SHHEC) 58; Bed Capacity (SHHG) 25.

Sacred Heart Health Ventures, Inc., 5151 N. Ninth Ave., 32504. Tel: 850-416-6500; Fax: 850-416-6119. Email: kemmanue@shhpens.org. Karen Emmanuel, Gen. Counsel.

Sacred Heart Hospital Administration, 5151 N. 9th Ave., 32504. Tel: 850-416-7000; Fax: 850-416-6119. Web: www.sacred-heart.org.

[C] HOMES FOR AGED

PENSACOLA. *Haven of Our Lady of Peace, Inc.* (2000) 1900 Summit Blvd., 32503. Tel: 850-436-5900; Fax: 850-436-5959. Email: miperez@shhpens.org. Martha Perez, Vice Pres./Admin. Bed Capacity 120; Total Staff 198; Total Assisted Annually 782.

[D] APARTMENTS FOR THE ELDERLY AND HANDICAPPED

TALLAHASSEE. *Casa Calderon, Inc.*, 800 W. Virginia St., 32304. Tel: 850-222-4026; Fax: 850-561-6868. Email: karkoel@aol.com. Rev. Msgr. Michael W. Tugwell, Pres.; Ms. Barbara Bolden, Mgr. Total Assisted 111; Total Staff 5.

[E] MONASTERIES AND RESIDENCES FOR PRIESTS AND BROTHERS

TALLAHASSEE. *Brotherhood of Hope*, 2302 Mission Rd., 32304-2629. Tel: 850-580-3553; Fax: 850-576-2384. Web: www.brotherhoodofhope.org. Bros. Adam Neri; Stephen Quense; Clinton Reed; Jason Zink.

Missionary Servants of the Most Holy Trinity, 7997 Mahan Dr., P.O. Box 10429, 32302-2429. Tel: 850-224-4955. Email: fvrst@mail.instal.com. Revs. Dennis M. Berry, S.T., Custodian; Raul Ventura, S.T.; Raymond Calixte, S.T.; Bro. Eliezer Lopez, S.T.

[F] CONVENT AND RESIDENCES FOR SISTERS

APALACHICOLA. *Martin House* (1982) 24 Apaco Ave, 32320. Tel: 850-653-8774. Email: jdreaop@hotmail.com. Sisters Jeanne Drea, O.P.; Mary Alice Neylon, O.P. Sisters (Sinsinawa Dominican Congregation of the Most Holy Rosary) 3.

SUNNY HILLS. *Vestiarki Sisters of Jesus (Poland)* (1882) 3919 Vistula Dr., 32428. Tel: 850-773-3302. Sisters 4; Total Assisted 3.

[G] HOMELESS SHELTERS

PANAMA CITY. *St. Barnabas House*, 2943 E. 11th St., 32401. Tel: 850-763-0475; Fax: 850-763-2969. Email: cathcharpc@cc.ptdiocese.org. c/o Catholic Charities, 3128 E. 11th St., 32401. Deborah Walton, Coord. Bed Capacity 22; Total in Residence 20; Total Staff 3; Total Assisted Annually 34.

Naomi House, 2941 E. 11th St., 32401. Tel: 850-763-0475; Fax: 850-763-2969. Email: cathcharpc@cc.ptdiocese.org. c/o Catholic Charities, 3128 E. 11th St., 32401. Bed Capacity 4; Total Staff 3; Total Assisted Annually 9.

[H] MISCELLANEOUS

PENSACOLA. *The Catholic Foundation of Northwest Florida, Inc.*, 11 N. B St., 32502. Tel: 850-435-3500; Fax: 850-435-3568. Web: www.ptdiocese.org. John Godlewski, Dir. Fin.

Diocese of Pensacola-Tallahassee Education Foundation, Inc., 11 N. B St., 32501. Tel: 850-435-3500; Fax: 850-436-6424. Email: ptschools@ptdiocese.org. Web: www.ptdiocese.org.

St. Michael Cemetery Foundation, Inc., P.O. Box 13602, 32591. Tel: 850-436-4643. Web: www.stmichaelscemetery.org.

TALLAHASSEE. *Florida Catholic Conference* (1969)Office: 201 W. Park Ave., 32301-7760. Tel: 850-222-3803; Fax: 850-681-9548. Email: flacathconf@flacathconf.org. Web: www.flacathconf.org. D. Michael McCarron, Ph.D., Exec. Dir.

Martyrs of La Florida Missions, Incorporated, P.O. Box 12062, 32317. Tel: 850-663-8161. Heather Jordan, Sec.

RELIGIOUS INSTITUTES OF MEN REPRESENTED IN THE DIOCESE

For further details refer to the corresponding bracketed number in the Religious Institutes of Men or Women section.

[]—*Brothers of Hope* (Benedictine - St. Meinrad, IN)
[1080]—*Congregation of the Resurrection* (Chicago Prov.)—C.R.
[]—*Missionaries of the Sacred Heart*—M.S.C.
[0840]—*Missionary Servants of the Most Holy Trinity*—S.T.
[]—*Missionary Society of St. Paul of Nigeria* (Gwagwalda-Abuja)—M.S.P.
[0910]—*Oblates of Mary Immaculate* (Eastern American Prov.)—O.M.I.
[0520]—*Order of Friars Minor, Franciscans*—O.F.M.
[0975]—*Society of our Lady of the Most Holy Trinity*—S.O.L.T.
[1335]—*Vincentian Congregation*—V.C.

RELIGIOUS INSTITUTES OF WOMEN REPRESENTED IN THE DIOCESE

[0130]—*Apostles of the Sacred Heart of Jesus*—A.S.C.J.
[1070-03]—*Dominican Sisters*—O.P.
[1070-13]—*Dominican Sisters*—O.P.
[0590]—*Sisters of Charity of Saint Elizabeth, Convent Station*—S.C.
[2575]—*Sisters of Mercy of the Americas* (Baltimore, MD)—R.S.M.
[3830-06]—*Sisters of St. Joseph of Buffalo*—S.S.J.
[3900]—*Sisters of St. Joseph of St. Augustine, Florida*—S.S.J.
[]—*Vestiarki Sisters of Jesus* (Poland)—V.S.J.

NECROLOGY

(No Deaths)

An asterisk (*) denotes an organization that has established tax-exempt status directly with the IRS and is not covered by the USCCB Group Ruling.

Diocese of Peoria

(Dioecesis Peoriensis)

Most Reverend

DANIEL R. JENKY, C.S.C.

Bishop of Peoria; ordained April 6, 1974; appointed Auxiliary Bishop of Fort Wayne-South Bend and Titular Bishop of Amantia October 21, 1997; consecrated December 16, 1997; appointed Bishop of Peoria February 12, 2002; installed April 10, 2002. *Office: 419 N.E. Madison Ave., Peoria, IL 61603.*

Chancery: 419 N.E. Madison Ave., Peoria, IL 61603. Tel: 309-671-1550; Fax: 309-671-1576.

ESTABLISHED 1877.

Square Miles 16,933.

A cross-section of Illinois, bounded on the north by the Counties of Whiteside, Lee, De Kalb, Grundy and Iroquois, and on the east by Kendall, Grundy, Kankakee and Ford, and on the south by Adams, Brown, Cass, Menard, Sangamon, Macon, Moultrie, Douglas and Edgar; comprising the Counties of Bureau, Champaign, Dewitt, Fulton, Hancock, Henderson, Henry, Knox, La Salle, Livingston, Logan, Marshall, Mason, McDonough, McLean, Mercer,Peoria, Piatt, Putnam, Rock Island, Schuyler, Stark, Tazewell, Vermilion, Warren and Woodford.

For legal titles of parishes and diocesan institutions, consult the Chancery.

STATISTICAL OVERVIEW

Personnel	
Bishop	1
Abbots	1
Retired Abbots	2
Priests: Diocesan Active in Diocese	119
Priests: Diocesan Active Outside Diocese	14
Priests: Retired, Sick or Absent	56
Number of Diocesan Priests	189
Religious Priests in Diocese	36
Total Priests in Diocese	225
Extern Priests in Diocese	14
Ordinations:	
Transitional Deacons	4
Permanent Deacons in Diocese	120
Total Brothers	8
Total Sisters	202
Parishes	
Parishes	157
With Resident Pastor:	
Resident Diocesan Priests	124
Resident Religious Priests	19
Without Resident Pastor:	
Administered by Priests	14
Missions	25
Pastoral Centers	5
Professional Ministry Personnel:	
Sisters	18
Lay Ministers	19
Welfare	
Catholic Hospitals	9
Total Assisted	2,255,991
Homes for the Aged	3
Total Assisted	332
Day Care Centers	2
Total Assisted	241
Specialized Homes	1
Total Assisted	33
Special Centers for Social Services	1
Total Assisted	28,305
Educational	
Diocesan Students in Other Seminaries	36
Total Seminarians	36
Colleges and Universities	1
Total Students	403
High Schools, Diocesan and Parish	5
Total Students	2,640
Elementary Schools, Diocesan and Parish	37
Total Students	9,452
Catechesis/Religious Education:	
High School Students	1,300
Elementary Students	10,897
Total Students under Catholic Instruction	24,728
Teachers in the Diocese:	
Priests	13
Brothers	2
Sisters	10
Lay Teachers	978
Vital Statistics	
Receptions into the Church:	
Infant Baptism Totals	2,334
Minor Baptism Totals	142
Adult Baptism Totals	229
Received into Full Communion	427
First Communions	2,406
Confirmations	3,170
Marriages:	
Catholic	461
Interfaith	291
Total Marriages	752
Deaths	2,066
Total Catholic Population	149,176
Total Population	1,492,335

Former Bishops—Most Revs. JOHN LANCASTER SPALDING, D.D., cons. May 1, 1877; resigned Sept. 11, 1908; Titular Archbishop of Scitopolis; appt. Oct. 14, 1908; died Aug. 25, 1916; EDMUND M. DUNNE, D.D., ord. June 24, 1887; cons. Sept. 1, 1909; died Oct. 17, 1929; JOSEPH H. SCHLARMAN, Ph.D., J.C.D., ord. June 29, 1904; cons. June 17, 1930; named Assistant at Papal Throne, Nov. 16, 1950; Archbishop ad personam; appt. June 27, 1951; died Nov. 10, 1951; WILLIAM E. COUSINS, D.D., ord. April 23, 1927; Titular Bishop of Forma and Auxiliary Bishop of Chicago; appt. Dec. 17, 1948; cons. March 7, 1949; Bishop of Peoria; appt. May 21, 1952; Archbishop of Milwaukee; appt. Dec. 17, 1958; died Sept. 14, 1988; JOHN B. FRANZ, D.D., ord. June 13, 1920; Bishop of Dodge City; appt. May 29, 1951; cons. Aug. 29, 1951; transferred to Peoria, Aug. 8, 1959; installed Nov. 4, 1959; retired June 1, 1971; died July 3, 1992; EDWARD W. O'ROURKE, D.D., ord. May 28, 1944; Bishop of Peoria; appt. May 24, 1971; cons. July 15, 1971; retired Jan. 23, 1990; died Sept. 29, 1999; JOHN J. MYERS, J.C.D., ord. Dec. 17, 1966; appt. Coadjutor Bishop of Peoria July 7, 1987; ord. Sept. 3, 1987; succeeded to Bishop of Peoria, Jan. 23, 1990; appt. Archbishop of Newark July 24, 2001; installed Oct. 9, 2001.

Bishop's Office—419 N.E. Madison Ave., Peoria, 61603. Tel: 309-671-1550; Fax: 309-671-1576. Please direct all calls for the Bishop's Office to this number; Office Hours: Mon.-Fri. 8:30-4:30.

Vicars General—Rev. Msgrs. PAUL E. SHOWALTER, P.A., V.G.; JAMES E. KRUSE, J.C.L., Mailing Address: Spalding Pastoral Center, 419 N.E. Madison Ave., Peoria, 61603. Tel: 309-671-1550; Fax: 309-671-1576.

Chancellor—Ms. PATRICIA GIBSON, J.C.L., Spalding Pastoral Center, 419 N.E. Madison Ave., Peoria, 61603. Tel: 309-671-1550; Fax: 309-671-1576.

Director of the Curia—Ms. PATRICIA GIBSON, J.C.L., Spalding Pastoral Center, 419 N.E. Madison Ave., Peoria, 61603. Tel: 309-671-1550; Fax: 309-671-1576.

Vice Chancellors—Deacons ROBERT POMAZAL; ROBERT SONDAG; Rev. Msgr. STANLEY L. DEPTULA, 419 N.E. Madison Ave., Peoria, 61603-3720. Tel: 309-671-1550; Fax: 309-671-1595.

Director of Development—JOHN J. GIBSON, Spalding Pastoral Center, 419 N.E. Madison Ave., Peoria, 61603. Tel: 309-671-1550; Fax: 309-671-1595.

Director of Finance—Mr. JOHN BANNON, Spalding Pastoral Center, 419 N.E. Madison Ave., Peoria, 61603. Tel: 309-671-1550; Fax: 309-671-1597.

Legal Department—Ms. PATRICIA GIBSON, J.C.L., Spalding Pastoral Center, 419 N.E. Madison Ave., Peoria, 61603-3720. Tel: 309-671-1550; Fax: 309-671-1576.

Diocesan Tribunal—Sr. MARIANNE BURKHARD, O.S.B., J.C.L., Spalding Pastoral Center, 419 N.E. Madison Ave., Peoria, 61603. Tel: 309-671-1550; Fax: 309-677-6798.

Judicial Vicar—Rev. Msgr. JASON A. GRAY, J.C.L.

Defender of the Bond—Rev. Msgr. RICK J. OBERCH.

Promoter of Justice—Rev. Msgr. RICK J. OBERCH.

Adjutant Judicial Vicar—Rev. Msgr. JAMES E. KRUSE, J.C.L.

Director of the Tribunal—Sr. MARIANNE BURKHARD, O.S.B., J.C.L.

Judges—Sr. MARIANNE BURKHARD, O.S.B., J.C.L.; Ms. ADELA MARIA KIM, J.C.L.; Rev. Msgrs. J. BRIAN REJSEK, J.C.L.; JASON A. GRAY, J.C.L.

Advocates—Mrs. CHERYL CRISS; Mrs. COLLEEN McCULLA; Mrs. LINDA THOMAS.

Notaries—Mrs. DEBRA WILLIAMS; Mrs. DIANE HAHN; DEBRA ANNE HILL.

Diocesan College of Consultors—Rev. Msgrs. PAUL E. SHOWALTER, P.A., V.G., Vicar Gen.; JOHN J. PRENDERGAST; JEROME HAM (Retired); DALE L. WELLMAN; Rev. THADDEUS PRACZ; Rev. Msgr. GERALD T. WARD; Rev. WILLIAM T. MILLER, I.C., Spalding Pastoral Center, 419 N.E. Madison Ave., Peoria, 61603. Tel: 309-671-1550; Fax: 309-671-1576.

Vicariates and Vicars—Rev. Msgrs. GERALD T. WARD, Bloomington-Lincoln; ALBERT W. HALLIN, P.A., Champaign; Revs. THADDEUS PRACZ, Danville; JAMES G. PALLARDY, Henry-Kewanee; ROBERT D. SPILMAN, La Salle; JEFFREY D. STIRNIMAN, Assoc. Vicar; Rev. Msgrs. DALE L. WELLMAN, Rock Island; RICHARD A. PRICCO, Macomb; ERNEST E. PIZZAMIGLIO, Galesburg; PHILIP HALFACRE, Ottawa; TIMOTHY NOLAN, Pekin; MICHAEL C. BLISS, Peoria; THOMAS E. MACK, Pontiac.

Diocesan Offices and Directors

Finance Council (Canon 492)—Most Rev. DANIEL ROBERT JENKY, C.S.C.; Rev. Msgrs. PAUL E. SHOWALTER, P.A., V.G.; JAMES E. KRUSE, J.C.L.; Sr. DIANE MARIE McGREW, O.S.F.; Revs. JAMES G. PALLARDY; ROBERT D. SPILMAN; Bro. WILLIAM DYGERT, C.S.C.; Mr. DAN DALY; Mr. LEON HINTON; Mr. VERNON WEGERER; Mr. DANIEL REYNOLDS; Mr. JOHN BANNON; JOHN J. GIBSON; Ms. PATRICIA GIBSON, J.C.L.; Mr. DON WESTERN; Ms. RITA KRESS; Mr. ROBERT BRADY, Spalding Pastoral Center, 419 N.E. Madison Ave., Peoria, 61603. Tel: 309-671-1550; Fax: 309-671-1595.

Liturgy, Churches and Chapels—Rev. Msgr. STANLEY L. DEPTULA, 419 N.E. Madison Ave., Peoria, 61603. Tel: 309-671-1550; Fax: 309-671-1573.

Catholic Cemeteries—Deacon ROBERT W. MYERS SR., Spalding Pastoral Center, 419 N.E. Madison Ave., Peoria, 61603. Tel: 309-671-1550; Fax: 309-671-1595.

Catholic Education Office—Bro. WILLIAM DYGERT,

C.S.C., Supt., Catholic Schools, Spalding Pastoral Center, 419 N.E. Madison Ave., Peoria, 61603. Tel: 309-671-1550; Fax: 309-671-1595. Associate Superintendents: PATRICIA KELLOGG; Mr. KENNETH J. SANDERSON; Mr. VINCENT MCCLEAN, Ph.D., Dir., Office of Catechetics.

Respect Life & Human Dignity—Mr. TIM RODER, Dir., Spalding Pastoral Center, 419 N.E. Madison Ave., Peoria, 61603. Tel: 309-671-1550; Fax: 309-671-1581.

Catholic Relief Services—Rev. Msgr. PAUL E. SHOWALTER, P.A., V.G., 419 N.E. Madison Ave., Peoria, 61603. Tel: 309-671-1550; Fax: 309-671-1576.

Catholic Women, Council of—Rev. Msgr. DALE L. WELLMAN, Moderator, 1608 13th St., Moline, 61265. Tel: 309-762-2362.

Censor Librorum—Rev. Msgr. PHILIP HALFACRE, St. Michael the Archangel Church, 801 Lundy St., Streator, 61364.

Clergymen's Aid, Inc.—Most Rev. DANIEL ROBERT JENKY, C.S.C., Trustee & Ex Officio; Rev. Msgrs. PAUL E. SHOWALTER, P.A., V.G., Trustee & Ex Officio; DOUGLAS HENNESSY, Pres.; Revs. GREG NELSON; ROBERT D. SPILMAN, Vice Pres.; MARK A. DESUTTER; DONALD HENDERSON; JEFFREY D. STIRNIMAN, Sec.; Rev. Msgr. DALE L. WELLMAN; Rev. PATRICK M. RIORDAN, 419 N.E. Madison Ave., Peoria, 61603. Tel: 309-671-1550; Fax: 309-671-1595.

Commission for Ecumenism—Rev. Msgr. ALBERT W. HALLIN, P.A., 416 County Rd. 1100 N., Seymour, 61875. Tel: 217-863-2190.

Communications, Diocesan Office of—VACANT, Spalding Pastoral Center, 419 N.E. Madison, Peoria, 61603. Tel: 309-671-1550; Fax: 309-671-1595.

Conciliation and Arbitration Process—Rev. Msgr. PAUL E. SHOWALTER, P.A., V.G., Spalding Pastoral Center, 419 N.E. Madison Ave., Peoria, 61603-2720. Tel: 309-671-1550; Fax: 309-671-1576.

Cursillo Program—Rev. TERRY A. CASSIDY, Spiritual Advisor; Deacon JOHN SKENDER, Diocesan Dir., Spalding Renewal Center, 401 N.E. Madison Ave., Peoria, 61603. Tel: 309-676-5587.

Diocesan Office of Development and Stewardship—JOHN J. GIBSON, Dir., Spalding Pastoral Center, 419 N.E. Madison Ave., Peoria, 61603. Tel: 309-671-1550; Fax: 309-671-1595.

Diocesan Evangelization Office—CRAIG DYKE, Dir., Spalding Pastoral Center, 419 N.E. Madison Ave., Peoria, 61603. Tel: 309-671-1550.

Diocesan Office of Finance—Mr. JOHN BANNON, Dir., Finance Office: Spalding Pastoral Center, 419 N.E. Madison Ave., Peoria, 61603. Tel: 309-671-1550; Fax: 309-671-1597.

Diocesan Hispanic Ministry Office—Rev. FREDI GOMEZ TORRES, Dir., St. Bernard's School, 512 E. Kansas, Peoria, 61603. Tel: 309-682-5823; Fax: 309-682-6030.

Diocesan Office of Human Resources—KAREN SMALL, Dir., Spalding Pastoral Center, 419 N.E. Madison Ave., Peoria, 61603. Tel: 309-671-1550; Fax: 309-671-1583.

Diocesan Pastoral Council—Rev. Msgr. PAUL E. SHOWALTER, P.A., V.G., Spalding Pastoral Center, 419 N.E Madison Ave., Peoria, 61603. Tel: 309-671-1550; Fax: 309-671-1576.

Diocesan Personnel Board—Rev. Msgr. PAUL E. SHOWALTER, P.A., V.G., Spalding Pastoral Center, 419 N.E. Madison Ave., Peoria, 61603. Tel: 309-671-1550; Fax: 309-671-1576.

Diocesan Director of Music—SHERRY SECKLER, Ph.D. Tel: 309-672-6447.

Divine Worship, Office of—Rev. Msgr. STANLEY L. DEPTULA, 419 N.E. Madison Ave., Peoria, 61603. Tel: 309-671-1550; Fax: 309-671-1573.

Office of Marriage and Family—Mr. TIM RODER, Dir., Spalding Pastoral Center, 419 N.E. Madison Ave., Peoria, 61603. Tel: 309-671-1550; Fax: 309-671-1581.

Office of Pastoral Services—Mr. TIM RODER, Dir., Spalding Pastoral Center, 419 N.E. Madison Ave., Peoria, 61603. Tel: 309-671-1550; Fax: 309-671-1581.

Holy Childhood Association—Rev. Msgr. PAUL E. SHOWALTER, P.A., V.G., 419 N.E. Madison Ave., Peoria, 61603. Tel: 309-671-1550.

Office of Victims Assistance—Deacon ROBERT SONDAG, 419 N.E. Madison Ave., Peoria, 61603. Tel: 309-671-1550; Fax: 309-671-1576.

Newspaper--"The Catholic Post"—Mr. THOMAS DERMODY, Editor-in-Chief, 419 N.E. Madison Ave., Peoria, 61603. Tel: 309-671-1550; Fax: 309-671-1579.

Nurses, Council of—VACANT.

Permanent Diaconate, Office of—Rev. Msgr. TIMOTHY NOLAN, Spalding Pastoral Center, 419 N.E. Madison Ave., Peoria, 61603. Tel: 309-671-1550; Fax: 309-671-1581.

Priests' Eucharistic League—Rev. Msgr. PAUL E. SHOWALTER, P.A., V.G., Spalding Pastoral Center, 419 N.E. Madison Ave., Peoria, 61603. Tel: 309-671-1550; Fax: 309-671-1576.

Propagation of the Faith—Rev. Msgr. PAUL E. SHOWALTER, P.A., V.G., 419 N.E. Madison Ave., Peoria, 61603. Tel: 309-671-1550; Fax: 309-671-1576.

Priests' Purgatorial Society—Rev. Msgr. PAUL E. SHOWALTER, P.A., V.G., Spalding Pastoral Center, 419 N.E. Madison Ave., Peoria, 61603. Tel: 309-671-1550; Fax: 309-671-1576.

Rural Life Conference—Rev. LUKE A. SPANNAGEL, Dir., 1001 N. Towanda Barnes Rd., Bloomington, 61705. Email: fr_spannagel@cdop.org.

Presbyteral Council—Rev. Msgr. GERALD T. WARD, Pres., Spalding Pastoral Center, 419 N.E. Madison, Peoria, 61603. Tel: 309-671-1550; Fax: 309-671-1576.

Catholic Charities—Sr. ANA PIA CORDUA, S.C.T.J.M., Pres.; SCOTT HASSETT, Interim Exec. Dir., 2900 W. Heading Ave., Peoria, 61604. Tel: 309-636-8000; Fax: 309-671-0253. Bloomington Offices, 603 N. Center St., Bloomington, 61701. Tel: 309-829-6307; Fax: 309-829-3254. 502 S. Morris Ave., Bloomington, 61704. Tel: 309-820-7616; Fax: 309-820-7657. Champaign Office, 1315 A Curt Dr., Champaign, 61820. Tel: 217-352-5179; Fax: 217-352-0318. Danville Office, 102 N. Robinson, Danville, 61832. Tel: 217-443-1772; Fax: 217-443-1701. Galesburg Office, 292 N. Chambers, Galesburg, 61401. Tel: 309-342-1136; Fax: 309-342-1891. LaSalle Office, 542 Crosat, LaSalle, 61301. Tel: 815-223-4007; Fax: 815-223-4550. LaSalle Office, 548 Crosat, La Salle, 61301. Tel: 815-223-0318. Lincoln Office. Tel: 217-732-3771; Fax: 217-735-1738. Macomb Office, 310 E. Washington St., Macomb, 61455. Tel: 309-833-1791; Fax: 309-836-1462. Rock Island Office, 4703 44th St., Rock Island, 61201. Tel: 309-788-9581; Fax: 309-788-9608.

TEC—Deacon ROBERT HEIPLE, Diocesan Spiritual Dir., Spalding Renewal Center, 401 N.E. Madison Ave., Peoria, 61603. Tel: 309-676-4001; Fax: 309-676-4022. Email: tecinfo@peoriacursillotec.com.

Vocations Office—Rev. Msgr. BRIAN K. BROWNSEY, Dir., Spalding Pastoral Center, 419 N.E. Madison Ave., Peoria, 61603. Tel: 309-671-1550; Fax: 309-671-1581. Assistant Directors: Rev. Msgrs. STANLEY L. DEPTULA; JAMES E. KRUSE, J.C.L.; Rev. DAVID P. RICHARDSON, St. Philomena, 3300 N. Twelve Oaks Dr., Peoria, 61604.

Christ Child Society of Central Illinois—Mailing Address: P.O. Box 1563, Peoria, 61655. Tel: 309-677-7697. Email: christchildsociety@gmail.com. JOAN WEBER, Pres.

*Christ Child Society of the Quad Cities—Mailing Address: P.O. Box 6184, Rock Island, 61201*Email: ccsqc@yahoo.com. SHELLY HUISKAMP.

CLERGY, PARISHES, MISSIONS AND PAROCHIAL SCHOOLS

CITY OF PEORIA

(PEORIA COUNTY)

1—ST. MARY'S CATHEDRAL (1846) Rev. Msgr. Stanley L. Deptula, Rector; Most Rev. Daniel Robert Jenky, C.S.C.; Deacon Toby Tyler.
Office & Mailing: 509 E. Kansas, 61603. Tel: 309-682-1221; Fax: 309-682-3462.
Res.: 607 N.E. Madison Ave., 61603. Tel: 309-682-5823; Fax: 309-682-6030.
Catechesis/Religious Program—Students 260.

2—ST. ANN (1994) Rev. Terry A. Cassidy; Deacons Joseph Koeppel; William Sloman; Stephen Cenek; Bruce Steiner; Sr. Judith Croegaert, O.S.B., Pastoral Assoc.
Mailing Address: 1010 S. Louisa St., 61605. Tel: 309-674-5072; Fax: 309-655-1566. Email: stann_parish@comcast.net.
Catechesis/Religious Program—Students 86.

3—ST. BERNARD'S (1903) Rev. Msgr. Stanley L. Deptula; Rev. Christopher A. Layden.
525 E. Kansas Ave., 61603. Mailing Address: 509 E. Kansas Ave., 61603. Tel: 309-682-5823; Fax: 309-682-3462. Email: b.stbernards@comcast.net.
Catechesis/Religious Program— In conjunction with St. Peter's Parish and St. Mary's Cathedral.

4—ST. BONIFACE'S (1881), (German), Closed. For inquiries for parish records contact St. Ann, Peoria.

5—ST. CECILIA'S, Closed. For Sacramental records write St. Philomena, 3300 N. Twelve Oaks Dr., Peoria, IL 61604.

6—HOLY FAMILY (1956) Revs. John P. Grigus, O.F.M.Conv.; Robert Cook, O.F.M.Conv.; Deacon Joseph Lahood.
Res.: 3720 N. Sterling Ave., 61615. Tel: 309-688-3427; Fax: 309-688-2174. Web: www.peoriaholyfamily.com.
School—2329 W. Reservoir, 61615. Tel: 309-688-2931; Fax: 309-681-5687. Trina Schmidt, Prin. Lay Teachers 17; Students 209.
Catechesis/Religious Program—Email: holyfamilydre@hotmail.com. Mary Donahue, D.R.E. Students 40.

7—ST. JOHN'S (1890), (Irish), Closed. For inquiries for parish records contact St. Ann, Peoria.

8—ST. JOSEPH (1976) Revs. Lawrence W. Zurek, O.F.M.; Luis Aponte-Merced, O.F.M.; Robert Weakley, O.F.M.
Mailing Address: 504 Fulton St., 61602. Tel: 309-676-0726; Fax: 309-673-6330.
Church: 103 Richard Pryor Pl., 61605.
Southside Catholic Child Care Center—1010 W. Johnson, 61605. Tel: 309-674-7340.

9—ST. JUDE (1975) [CEM] Revs. Patrick Henehan; Paul Carlson, Parochial Vicar; Deacons Thomas Rapach; Roger Hunter.
Res.: 10811 N. Knoxville Ave., 61615. Tel: 309-243-7811; Fax: 309-243-7810. Email: stjude@stjudechurchpeoria.org. Web: www.stjudechurchpeoria.org.
Catechesis/Religious Program—Tel: 309-243-7811, Ext. 212; 309-243-7811, Ext. 213; Fax: 309-243-7810. Students 325.

10—ST. MARK'S (1891) Rev. Msgr. Brian Brownsey; Rev. Kevin Lucas, Parochial Vicar; Deacon John Skender. In Res., Rev. Joseph Charles Kitheka (Kenya).
Res.: 1113 W. Bradley Ave., 61606-1722. Tel: 309-673-1263; Fax: 309-637-1484. Email: stmark@mtco.com.
School—711 N. Underhill, 61606. Tel: 309-676-7131; Fax: 309-677-8060. Web: www.saint-mark.net. Mr. Jimmie Moore, Prin. Lay Teachers 15; Students 179.
Catechesis/Religious Program—Tel: 309-497-2838. Students 50.

11—ST. PETER'S (1897) Rev. Msgr. Stanley L. Deptula; Rev. Christopher A. Layden; Deacon Richard Zimmerman.
Catechesis/Religious Program—Anita Keck, D.R.E. Students 10.

12—ST. PHILOMENA (1945) [JC] Rev. David P. Richardson. In Res., Rev. Patrick O'Neal.
Res.: 3300 N. Twelve Oaks Dr., 61604-1464. Tel: 309-682-8642; Fax: 309-682-8955. Email: rectory@stphils.com. Web: www.stphils.com.
School—3216 N. Emery Ave., 61604. Tel: 309-685-1208; Fax: 309-681-5676. Email: school@stphils.com. Sisters of St. Francis of the Immaculate Conception 1; Lay Teachers 24; Students 421.
Catechesis/Religious Program—Tel: 309-685-1677, Ext. 202. Mrs. Judith Martin, D.R.E. Students 37.
St. Philomena Endowment Trust—

13—SACRED HEART (1879), (German), Revs. Lawrence W. Zurek, O.F.M.; Luis Aponte-Merced, O.F.M. In Res., Rev. Robert Weakley, O.F.M.
Res.: 504 Fulton St., 61602. Tel: 309-494-9602 (Rectory); 309-673-6317 (Parish Offices); Fax: 309-673-6330. Email: sacredheartpeoria@comcast.net. Web: www.sacredheartpeoria.com.

14—ST. THOMAS (1937) Rev. Msgr. William A. Watson; Rev. Thomas Taylor; Sr. Rachel Bergschneider, O.S.B., Pastoral Assoc. & D.R.E.; Deacon Francis L. Eaton.
Res.: 904 E. Lake Ave., Peoria Heights, 61616. Tel: 309-688-3446; Fax: 309-688-3467.
School—4229 N. Monroe, Peoria Heights, 61616. Tel: 309-685-2533; Fax: 309-681-7262. Mrs. Maureen Bentley, Prin. Lay Teachers 26; Students 465.
Catechesis/Religious Program—Students 121.

15—ST. VINCENT DE PAUL (1962) Rev. Msgr. Jason A. Gray; Rev. Donald Henderson; Deacons Robert W. Myers Sr.; Thomas DeBernardis.
Res.: 6001 N. University St., 61614. Tel: 309-691-3602; Fax: 309-691-3687. Email: svdppeoria@hotmail.com. Web: svdppeoria.com.
School—Tel: 309-691-5012; Fax: 309-683-1036. Dr. James Minick, Prin. Lay Teachers 25; Students 450.
Catechesis/Religious Program—Tel: 309-691-5012, Ext. 162. Students 631.

OUTSIDE THE CITY OF PEORIA

ABINGDON, KNOX CO., SACRED HEART (1924) Revs. William T. Miller, I.C.; Joseph Presley, I.C.
Res. & Mailing: 506 N. Main St., 61410. Tel: 309-462-3421. Email: scrdhrt@abingdon.net.
Catechesis/Religious Program—Students 3.

ALEDO, MERCER CO., ST. CATHERINE'S CHURCH (1914) [CEM] Rev. John Thieryoung.
Res.: 106 N.E. Fourth, 61231. Tel: 309-582-7500.
Catechesis/Religious Program—Students 122.

Mission—St. Anthony, Matherville
Mission—St. John, Viola
Mission—St. Mary's

ALEXIS, WARREN CO., ST. THERESA'S (1877), (Swedish), [CEM] Rev. Dennis E. Spohrer.
Res.: 131 N. Main St., P.O. Box 26, 61412. Tel: 309-843-0000.
Catechesis/Religious Program—Students 15.

ANDALUSIA, ROCK ISLAND CO., ST. PATRICK CHURCH (1974) Rev. S. Stephen Engelbrecht.
Res.: Box 249, 61232. Tel: 309-798-2098; Fax: 309-798-2840. Email: stpt@mchsi.com. Web: stpatrickandalusia.org.
Catechesis/Religious Program—Students 50.

ANNAWAN, HENRY CO., SACRED HEART (1893) [CEM] Rev. Sebastian Tumusiime, Admin.
Res.: 305 W. South Ave., 61234. Tel: 309-935-6911.
Catechesis/Religious Program—Students 22.
Mission—St. Mary's St. Mary's Rd., Hooppole, Henry Co. 61258.

ARLINGTON, BUREAU CO., ST. PATRICK'S (1864) [CEM] Rev. Patrick Fixsen.
Mailing Address: Box 159, Cherry, 61317.
Res.: 212 S. Main St., Cherry, 61317. Tel: 815-894-2006.
Catechesis/Religious Program—Students 33.

ATKINSON, HENRY CO., ST. ANTHONY'S (1870), (Belgian), [CEM] Rev. Robert Anthony Lee; Deacon Nicholas Simon.
Res.: 204 W. Main St., P.O. Box 210, 61235-0210. Tel: 309-936-7900; Fax: 309-936-7900. Web: www.saintanthonysatkinson.org.
Catechesis/Religious Program—Students 19.

BARTONVILLE, PEORIA CO., ST. ANTHONY (1969) Rev. David C. Heinz; Deacon Louis Tomlianovich.
Res.: 2525 Skyway Rd., 61607. Tel: 309-697-0645; Fax: 309-697-2188. Email: saintanthony1@comcast.net.
Catechesis/Religious Program—Students 120.

BEMENT, PIATT CO., ST. MICHAEL Rev. Bruce Lopez; Deacon Gene Triplett.
Res.: 1301 N. Market St., Monticello, 61856. Tel: 217-762-2566; Fax: 217-762-8666. Web: www.stphilomenaonline.org.
Catechesis/Religious Program— (With St. Philomena)

BENSON, WOODFORD CO., ST. JOHN (1873) [CEM] Rev. Msgr. Charles J. Beebe.
Res.: 508 W. Randolph, Roanoke, 61561. Tel: 309-923-3031; Fax: 309-923-3031. Email: msgrbeebe@cdop.org.
Catechesis/Religious Program—Michelle Boland, Coord. Students 6.

BLACKSTONE, LIVINGSTON CO., ST. BERNARD, Closed. For inquiries for sacramental records contact St. Michael the Archangel, Streator.

BLOOMINGTON, MCLEAN CO.

1—HOLY TRINITY (1853) [CEM] Rev. Msgr. Douglas Hennessy; Rev. Julius Turyatoranwa; Deacons Brendan Carolan; Robert Hermes; James Gore.
Mailing Address: 711 N. Main St., 61701. Tel: 309-829-2197; Fax: 309-829-2243. Web: www.holytrinitybloomington.org.
School—Holy Trinity Elementary School, (Grades PreSchool-5), 1909 E. Lincoln, 61701. Tel: 309-662-3712; Fax: 309-663-9115. Students 493.
School—Holy Trinity Junior High, (Grades 6-8), 705 N. Roosevelt, 61701. Tel: 309-828-7151; Fax: 309-827-8131. Web: www.holytrinitycatholicschool.org. Mrs. Kay O'Brien, Prin. Lay Teachers 34; Students 181.
Catechesis/Religious Program—Tel: 309-828-8242. Students 150.

2—ST. MARY'S (1867), (German), [CEM] Revs. Ric Schneider, O.F.M.; Gregg Petri, O.F.M.; Bro. Kevin Duckson, O.F.M.; Deacons Darrel Petri; Jose Montenegro.
Res.: 527 W. Jackson St., 61701. Tel: 309-827-8526; Fax: 309-829-3061. Web: stmarysparish.catholicweb.com.
School—603 W. Jackson St., 61701. Tel: 309-828-5954. Web: www.stmarysschool.net. Lay Teachers 15; Students 172.
Catechesis/Religious Program—Students 282.

3—ST. PATRICK CHURCH OF MERNA (1890) [CEM] Rev. Msgr. Gerald T. Ward; Rev. Luke A. Spannagel, Parochial Vicar; Sr. Rita Ann Bregenhorn, O.S.U., Pastoral Assoc.
Church: 1001 N. Towanda Barnes Rd., IL 61705. Tel: 309-662-7361; Fax: 309-664-6167. Email: office@stpatrickmerna.org. Web: www.stpatrickmerna.org.
Catechesis/Religious Program—Students 676.

4—ST. PATRICK'S (1892) [JC] Rev. Peter Zorjan, Admin.
Res.: 1209 W. Locust St., 61701. Tel: 309-829-1355; Fax: 309-828-0577. Email: s.patricks@comcast.net. Web: www.historicsaintpatricks.org.
Catechesis/Religious Program—Students 30.

BRADFORD, STARK CO., ST. JOHN THE BAPTIST (1876) [CEM] Rev. Vien Van Do.
Mailing Address: 303 N. Galena, Wyoming, 61491.
Res.: 218 First St., Box 310, 61421. Tel: 309-897-4081; Fax: 309-897-8007.
Catechesis/Religious Program—Students 27.

BRIMFIELD, PEORIA CO., ST. JOSEPH'S (1852), (Irish), [CEM] Rev. John M. Verrier.
Mailing Address: P.O. Box 199, 61517.
Res.: 314 W. Clay St., 61517. Tel: 309-446-3275; Fax: 309-446-9409.
Catechesis/Religious Program—Students 74.
Mission—St. James Williamsfield, Knox Co. 61489. Tel: 309-446-3275.

BUDD, LIVINGSTON CO., ST. BERNARD'S, Closed. For parish records contact Church of the St. Michael the Archangel, Streator.

BUSHNELL, MCDONOUGH CO., ST. BERNARD (1877) Rev. Thomas B. Holloway.
Res.: 376 W. Hail St., 61422. Tel: 309-772-2333; Fax: 309-772-2112.
Catechesis/Religious Program—Students 27.

CAMP GROVE, MARSHALL CO., ST. PATRICK (1866), (Irish), [CEM] Rev. Vien Van Do.
Mailing Address: 303 N. Galena, Wyoming, 61491.
Res.: 115 W. Camp St., 61424. Tel: 309-493-5261.
Catechesis/Religious Program— Attend St. Dominic, Wyoming.

CAMPUS, LIVINGSTON CO., SACRED HEART (1882), (Irish), [CEM] Rev. Ronald Dodd.
205 N. Elm St., 60920.
Res.: 313 W. Hamilton, Odell, 60460. Tel: 815-998-2197.
Catechesis/Religious Program—Ms. Myrna Masching, D.R.E.

CANTON, FULTON CO., ST. MARY'S (1862) [CEM 2] Rev. Daniel Ebker.
Mailing Address: 139 E. Chestnut St., 61520-2728. Email: stmaryscn@sbcglobal.net.
Res.: 140 N. 2nd Ave., 61520. Tel: 309-647-1473.
Catechesis/Religious Program—Tel: 309-647-1476. Students 83.

CARTHAGE, HANCOCK CO., IMMACULATE CONCEPTION (1860) [CEM] Revs. Anthony J. Trosley; Thomas R. Szydlik.
Mailing Address: 190 N. Wells St., P.O. Box 147, Nauvoo, 62354.
Res.: 125 N. Fayette, 62321. Tel: 217-357-3087.
Catechesis/Religious Program—Carrie Carroll, D.R.E. Students 40.

CHAMPAIGN, CHAMPAIGN CO.

1—HOLY CROSS (1912) Rev. Stephen A. Willard; Deacons Henry Hart; Edward Mohrbacher; Robert J. Ulbrich.
Res.: 405 W. Clark St., 61820. Tel: 217-352-8748; Fax: 217-366-2929. Email: office@holycrosschampaign.org.
School—410 W. White St., 61820. Tel: 217-356-9521; Fax: 217-356-1745. Email: meyersm@holycrosselem.org. Web: www.holycrosselem.org. Mrs. Rose Costello, Prin. Lay Teachers 27; Students 313.
Catechesis/Religious Program—Tel: 217-352-8748; Fax: 217-366-2929. Marc Cardaronella, D.R.E. Students 56.

2—ST. JOHN'S CATHOLIC CHAPEL (1918), (For Catholic Students at the University of Illinois) Rev. Msgrs. Gregory K. Ketcham; Edward J. Duncan, Pastor Emeritus (Retired); Revs. Charles Klamut; Anthony Co.
Newman Hall—604 E. Armory Ave., 61820. Tel: 217-344-1184; Fax: 217-344-4957. Email: info@sjcnc.org. Web: www.sjcnc.org.
Catechesis/Religious Program—Shawn Reeves, D.R.E.

3—ST. MARY'S (1854) [CEM] Rev. Joseph T. Hogan.
Res.: 612 E. Park St., 61820. Tel: 217-352-8364; Fax: 217-352-6859. Email: stmary@stmary-cu.org. Web: stmary-cu.org.
Catechesis/Religious Program—Students 22.

4—ST. MATTHEW (1965) Rev. Msgr. Mark J. Merdian; Revs. Robert Lampitt; Johndamaseni Zilimu (Tanzania).
Res.: 1303 Lincolnshire Dr., 61821. Tel: 217-359-4224; Fax: 217-359-9846. Web: www.stmatt.net.
School—1307 Linconshire Dr., 61821. Tel: 217-359-4114; Fax: 217-359-8319. Petrece Klein, Prin. Lay Teachers 23; Students 417.
Catechesis/Religious Program—Students 172.
Convent—Sisters of St. Francis of the Martyr St. George, 1719 Robert Dr., 61821. Tel: 217-351-5139.

CHATSWORTH, LIVINGSTON CO., SS. PETER AND PAUL (1877), (German—Irish), [CEM] Rev. Binh K. Tran.
Res.: 406 N. Fifth St., P.O. Box 546, 60921. Tel: 815-635-3127; Fax: 815-635-3756.
Mission—St. James Box 583, Forrest, Livingston Co. 61741.
Catechesis/Religious Program—Students 14.

CHENOA, MCLEAN CO., ST. JOSEPH'S (1859) [CEM] Rev. Carl LoPresti.
Res.: 225 W. Owsley, 61726. Tel: 815-945-2561; Fax: 815-945-7634.
Catechesis/Religious Program—Students 25.
Mission—St. Mary Lexington, McLean Co.

CHERRY, BUREAU CO., HOLY TRINITY (1904) [CEM] Rev. Patrick Fixsen.
Res.: 212 S. Main, P.O. Box 159, 61317. Tel: 815-894-2006; Fax: 815-894-2158.
Catechesis/Religious Program—Students 78.

CHILLICOTHE, PEORIA CO., ST. EDWARD (1900) [CEM] Rev. Keith A. Walder; Deacons Gregory Serangeli; Bob Pomazal.
Res.: 1216 N. 6th St., 61523. Tel: 309-274-3809; Fax: 309-274-3834.
School—1221 N. Fifth St., 61523. Tel: 309-274-2994; Fax: 309-274-4141. Mr. John Meisinger, Prin. Lay Teachers 13; Students 97.
Catechesis/Religious Program—Students 78.

CLINTON, DE WITT CO., ST. JOHN THE BAPTIST CATHOLIC CHURCH (1879) Rev. James P. Henning, O.F.M.Conv.
Res.: 612 N. Plum, Farmer City, 61842. Tel: 309-928-3855; Fax: 309-928-9147.
Church: 502 N. Monroe St., 61727. Tel: 217-935-3727; Fax: 217-935-4101.
Catechesis/Religious Program—Fax: 217-935-4101. Students 66.

COAL VALLEY, ROCK ISLAND CO., ST. MARIA GORETTI (1972) Rev. James P. DeBisschop; Sr. Sandra Brunenn, O.S.B., Pastoral Assoc.; Deacon Charles Breeden.
Res.: 220 E. 22nd Ave., P.O. Box 159, 61240. Tel: 309-799-3414; Fax: 309-799-3436. Email: smg@smgcv.org. Web: www.smgcv.org.
Catechesis/Religious Program—Tel: 309-799-7283. Students 84.

COLFAX, MCLEAN CO., ST. JOSEPH'S (1850) Rev. Carl LoPresti.
Res.: 107 W. North, P.O. Box 169, 61728. Tel: 309-723-6229; Fax: 309-723-6229.
Catechesis/Religious Program—Students 23.

COLONA, HENRY CO., ST. PATRICK'S (1941) Rev. Duane C. Jack; Deacon Al Angelo.
Res.: 201 First St., 61241. Tel: 309-792-3854; Fax: 309-792-8630. Email: stpatcolona@qconline.com.
Catechesis/Religious Program—Tel: 309-949-3700. Rose Roe, C.R.E. Students 140.

CREVE COEUR, TAZEWELL CO., SACRE COEUR (1954) Rev. Attilio Morelli.
Res.: 301 Roosevelt St., 61610. Tel: 309-698-7270; Fax: 309-699-0350.
Church: 601 Rusche Ln., 61610. Tel: 309-699-8511.
Catechesis/Religious Program—Kimberly Nieves, Volunteer C.R.E. Students 15.

CULLOM, LIVINGSTON CO., ST. JOHN'S (1881) [CEM], St. John's is served by clergy of St. Mary's, Pontiac Rev. Msgr. Thomas E. Mack; Rev. David Sabel; Deacons George Wagner; R.J. Wallace.
Res.: 119 E. Howard, Pontiac, 61764. Tel: 815-844-7683.
Church: 113 W. Van Alstyne St., P.O. Box 376, 60929. Tel: 815-689-2367.
Catechesis/Religious Program—Students 35.

DALZELL, BUREAU CO., ST. THOMAS MORE (1934), (Italian), Rev. Robert Rayson. In Res., Rev. Msgr. Thomas Badovsky.
Res.: 302 Chestnut, 61320. Tel: 815-663-6201.
Catechesis/Religious Program—Jyll Pozzi, D.R.E. Students 12.

DANVILLE, VERMILION CO.

1—HOLY FAMILY (1978) [CEM] Rev. Thaddeus Pracz; Deacon Richard Smith.
Church: 444 E. Main St., 61832. Tel: 217-431-5100; Fax: 217-431-5103.
Catechesis/Religious Program—Students 102.

2—ST. PAUL'S (1915) Rev. Greg Nelson.
Res.: 1303 N. Walnut St., 61832. Tel: 217-442-5313; Fax: 217-442-5356. Web: www.stpauldanville.org.
School—1307 N. Walnut St., 61832. Tel: 217-442-3880; Fax: 217-442-5852. Mr. Robert Rice, Prin. Lay Teachers 22; Students 377.
Catechesis/Religious Program—Students 41.

DELAVAN, TAZEWELL CO., ST. MARY'S (1867) [CEM] Rev. Gerald J. Verdun.
Res.: 505 E. 4th St., P.O. Box 769, 61734. Tel: 309-244-8516.
Mission—St. Joseph's Hopedale, Tazewell Co.
Catechesis/Religious Program—Students 48.

DEPUE, BUREAU CO., ST. MARY'S (1908) [CEM] Rev. Kevin G. Creegan.
Res.: 312 Park St., Box 19, 61322. Tel: 815-447-2552; Fax: 815-447-2552.
Catechesis/Religious Program—Students 100.
Mission—St. Mary Main St., P.O. Box 271, Tiskilwa, Bureau Co. 61368. Tel: 815-646-4451.

DOWNS, MCLEAN CO., ST. MARY'S (1910) Rev. Msgr. Gerald T. Ward; Rev. Luke A. Spannagel, Parochial Vicar.
Church: 108 E. Washington St., P.O. Box 66, 61736. Tel: 309-378-4679; Fax: 309-378-4679. Email: churchofstmary@verizon.net.
Catechesis/Religious Program—Students 81.

DUNLAP, PEORIA CO., ST. CLEMENT'S, Closed. For inquiries for parish records contact St. Jude, 10811

N. Knoxville, Peoria, IL 61615.
DWIGHT, LIVINGSTON CO., ST. PATRICK'S (1862), (Irish), [CEM] Rev. James E. Rickey.
Res.: 126 W. Mazon Ave., P.O. Box 70, 60420. Tel: 815-584-3522; Fax: 815-584-3518.
Catechesis/Religious Program—Tel: 815-584-3110; Fax: 815-584-3518. Heather Boucher, D.R.E. Students 92.
EAGLE TOWNSHIP, LA SALLE CO., ANNUNCIATION OF BLESSED VIRGIN MARY (1869), (Irish), [CEM] Rev. Charles A. McCarthy, C.S.Sp.
Res.: Rte 1, 957 N. 17th Rd., Tonica, 61370. Tel: 815-856-2502; Fax: 815-856-2503.
Church: 1205 State Rte 18 E., Streator, 61364. Tel: 815-672-6500.
Catechesis/Religious Program— Attend Grand Ridge and St. Anthony's, Streator
EARLVILLE, LA SALLE CO., ST. TERESA OF AVILA (1904) [CEM 2] Rev. Chris G. Haake.
Res.: 221 W. Union St., 60518-8181. Tel: 815-246-4321; Fax: 815-246-4341. Email: st.teresa.earlville@mchsi.com. Web: st.teresa.earlville.home.mchsi.com.
Catechesis/Religious Program—Students 39.
EAST MOLINE, ROCK ISLAND CO.
1—ST. ANNE (1919) Rev. Greg Jozefiak.
Res.: 555 18th Ave., 61244. Tel: 309-755-5071; Fax: 309-755-5343. Email: mbanaszek@olgca.us. Web: www.stanne-em.us.
School—Our Lady of Grace Catholic Academy, 602 17th Ave., 61244. Tel: 309-755-9771; Fax: 309-755-7407. Email: office@olgca.org. Web: www.olgca.org. Linda Vandervennet, Prin. Lay Teachers 11; Students 150.
Catechesis/Religious Program—Students 270.
2—ST. MARY'S (1907), (English—Spanish), Parish Suspended. Rev. Paco Trujillo.
Mailing Address: 412 10th St., Moline, 61265. Tel: 309-764-1562; Fax: 309-764-0317.
School—Our Lady of Grace Catholic Academy, 602 17th Ave., 61244. Tel: 309-755-9771.
Catechesis/Religious Program—Twinned with St. Anne, East Moline and Our Lady of Guadalupe, Silvis., 800 17th St., Silvis, 61282. Tel: 309-792-3867; Fax: 309-792-2241.
EAST PEORIA, TAZEWELL CO., ST. MONICA CHURCH (1898) Rev. Msgr. James E. Kruse; Deacons Charles Robbins; Stephen Racki III.
Res.: 303 Campanile Dr., 61611. Tel: 309-694-2061. Email: st_monicas@hotmail.com.
Catechesis/Religious Program—Tel: 309-699-8458. Students 25.
EL PASO, WOODFORD CO., ST. MARY'S (1863) [CEM 2] Rt. Rev. Roger F. Corpus, O.S.B.
Res.: 79 W. Third, P.O. Box 197, 61738. Tel: 309-527-4555; Fax: 309-527-7750.
Catechesis/Religious Program—Tel: 309-527-3958. Beth Miller, D.R.E. Students 89.
ELKHART, LOGAN CO., ST. PATRICK (1856) Rev. Jeffrey G. Laible.
Mailing Address: 316 S. Logan St., Lincoln, 62656. Tel: 217-732-4019.
Catechesis/Religious Program—Students 30.
Mission—St. Thomas Aquinas Mount Pulaski, Logan Co.
Catechesis/Religious Program—Students 30.
ELMWOOD, PEORIA CO., ST. PATRICK'S (1870), (Irish), [CEM] Rev. Paul Stiene, I.C.
Mailing Address: 802 W. Main St., P.O. Box 440, 61529. Tel: 309-742-4921; Fax: 309-742-4921.
Catechesis/Religious Program—Students 42.
EUREKA, WOODFORD CO., ST. LUKE (1982) [JC] Rev. Eugene A. Radosevich.
Church & Mailing Address: 904 E. Regan Dr., P.O. Box 226, 61530. Tel: 309-467-4855. Email: stluke@mtco.com.
Catechesis/Religious Program—Marcia Brogly, C.R.E. Students 6.
FAIRBURY, LIVINGSTON CO., ST. JOHN THE BAPTIST (1857) [CEM] Rev. Scott Archer.
Res.: 110 E. Ash, 61739. Tel: 815-692-2555.
Catechesis/Religious Program—Students 59.
Mission—St. Rose Strawn, Livingston Co.
FARMER CITY, DE WITT CO., SACRED HEART (1899) [CEM] Rev. James P. Henning, O.F.M.Conv.; Deacons John Leonard; Scott Whitehouse.
Res.: 612 N. Plum St., 61842. Tel: 309-928-3855; Fax: 309-928-9147. Email: shchurch612@frontier.com.
Catechesis/Religious Program—Students 37.
Mission—St. John Bellflower, McLean Co.
FARMINGTON, FULTON CO., ST. MATTHEW'S (1904) Rev. Bruce King, I.C.; Deacon Gary Schultz.
Res.: 156 E. Vernon St., 61531. Tel: 309-245-4001; Fax: 309-245-4351.
Catechesis/Religious Program—Students 37.
GALESBURG, KNOX CO.
1—CORPUS CHRISTI (1885) [CEM] Revs. William T. Miller, I.C.; Joseph Presley, I.C.
Res.: 273 S. Prairie St., 61401. Tel: 309-343-8256; Fax: 309-343-4793. Email: gare2@galesburg.net.
School—Costa Catholic Academy, 2726 Costa Dr., 61401. Tel: 309-344-3151; Fax: 309-344-1594. James Kovac, Prin. Operates with Immaculate Heart and St. Patrick. Lay Teachers 18; Students 260.
Catechesis/Religious Program—Students 117.
2—IMMACULATE HEART OF MARY (1956) Rev. Msgr. Ernest E. Pizzamiglio; Deacons Michael Mannino; Rod Gray.
Res.: 2401 N. Broad St., 61401-1203. Tel: 309-344-3108; Fax: 309-344-1205. Email: ihm@grics.net. Web: www.parishesonline.com/ihomc.
See Costa Catholic Academy, Galesburg under Corpus Christi, Galesburg for details.
Catechesis/Religious Program—Students 54.
3—ST. PATRICK'S (1863) [JC] Revs. William T. Miller, I.C.; Joseph Presley, I.C.; Deacon James D. Haneghan.
Res.: 858 S. Academy St., 61401. Tel: 309-343-9874; Fax: 309-343-9944. Email: stpatrickschurch@galesburg.net.
See Costa Catholic School, Galesburg under Corpus Christi, Galesburg for details.
Catechesis/Religious Program—Students 24.
GALVA, HENRY CO., ST. JOHN'S (1882), (Swedish), [CEM] Rev. John R. Burns; Deacon John V. Holevoet.
Church: 212 N.E. 1st St., 61434. Tel: 309-932-2409; 309-334-2180 (Office); Fax: 309-334-2137. Email: stjohnchurch@winco.net.
Catechesis/Religious Program—Students 57.
GENESEO, HENRY CO., ST. MALACHY'S (1866) Rev. Michael G. Pakula; Deacons Harley Chaffee; Thomas Wachtel; Larry Honzel; Robert O'Rourke; Arthur Ries.
Res.: 551 E. Ogden Ave., 61254. Tel: 309-944-2250; Fax: 309-944-5319. Email: church@saintmalachy.org. Web: www.saintmalachy.org.
School—595 E. Ogden Ave., 61254. Tel: 309-944-3230. Mr. Stan Griffin, Prin. Lay Teachers 7; Students 121.
Catechesis/Religious Program—Tel: 309-944-3518. M. Elizabeth Fristensky, D.R.E. Students 177.
GEORGETOWN, VERMILION CO., ST. ISAAC JOGUES (1942) Rev. John Paninski, M.S.
Res.: 109 W. Seventh St., 61846-1404. Tel: 217-662-6708.
Catechesis/Religious Program—Students 6.
GRANVILLE, PUTNAM CO., SACRED HEART OF JESUS (1908), (Italian), [CEM] Rev. Patrick DeMeulemeester.
Res.: 311 Hennepin St., P.O. Box 217, 61326. Tel: 815-339-2138; Fax: 815-339-2880. Email: shgsph@mchsi.com.
Catechesis/Religious Program—Students 70.
HAVANA, MASON CO., ST. PATRICK'S (1865) [CEM] Rev. David Whiteside; Deacons Stanley Buczko; Jon Dosher.
Res.: 545 S. Orange, 62644. Tel: 309-543-6373; Fax: 309-543-3241.
Catechesis/Religious Program—Students 62.
Mission—Immaculate Conception 505 S. Adams, Manito, Mason Co. 61546. Tel: 309-968-6826. Deacons William Meyer; Robert Sondag.
HENNEPIN, PUTNAM CO., ST. PATRICK'S (1865) [CEM] Rev. Patrick DeMeulemeester.
Res.: 10 St. & Dore, P.O. Box 217, Granville, 61326. Tel: 815-925-7500; 815-339-2138 (Office); Fax: 815-339-2880. Email: shgsph@mchsi.com.
Catechesis/Religious Program—Students 41.
HENRY, MARSHALL CO.
1—ST. JOSEPH'S (1878) [CEM 2] Rev. Thomas R. Mizeur.
1002 School St., P.O. Box 75, 61537. Email: iccc@grics.net. In Res., Sisters Anita Pauwels, O.S.F.; Alice Rogers, O.S.F.
Tri-Parish Offices: 415 N. High St., Lacon, 61540. Tel: 309-246-5145; Fax: 309-246-5417.
Church: 1002 N. School St., 61537. Tel: 309-364-2063 (Convent).
Catechesis/Religious Program—Students 8.
2—ST. MARY'S (1851) [CEM 2] Rev. Thomas R. Mizeur.
Tri-Parish Offices: 415 N. High St., Lacon, 61540. Tel: 309-246-5145.
Res.: 401 South St., 61537. Tel: 309-364-2525; Fax: 309-246-5417. Email: iccc@grics.net.
Church: 401 South St., P.O. Box 75, 61537. Tel: 309-364-2525; Fax: 309-246-5417.
Catechesis/Religious Program—Mary Ann Magnuson, D.R.E. Twinned with St. Joseph's, Henry Students 55.
HOOPESTON, VERMILION CO., ST. ANTHONY CHURCH (1877) Rev. Geoffrey Horton.
Church: 423 S. Third St., P.O. Box 414, 60942. Tel: 217-283-6211; Fax: 217-283-6252. Email: stanthony@avenuebroadband.com.
Catechesis/Religious Program—Tel: 219-283-6249. Email: drestanthony@gmail.com. Students 60.
HOOPPOLE, HENRY CO., ST. MARY'S, Attended by Annawan. Temporarily closed.
IVESDALE, CHAMPAIGN CO., ST. JOSEPH'S (1863), (Irish), [CEM] Rev. Msgr. Albert W. Hallin.
Church: P.O. Box 175, 61851. Tel: 217-863-2190; Fax: 217-863-2616.
Catechesis/Religious Program—James Brewer, D.R.E. Students 45.
KEWANEE, HENRY CO.
1—ST. FRANCIS OF ASSISI (1906) Rev. James G. Pallardy.
410 W. Central Blvd., 61443. Tel: 309-852-2761; Fax: 309-852-0222.
1009 N. Burr St., 61443.
Catechesis/Religious Program—Students 66.
2—ST. MARY'S CATHOLIC CHURCH (1855) [CEM 2] Rev. James G. Pallardy; Deacons Martin Van Meltebeck; John T. Mock.
Res.: 406 W. Central Blvd., 61443-2010. Tel: 309-852-4549; Fax: 309-853-4106. Email: stmarykewanee@hotmail.com.
School—Visitation, 107 S. Lexington, 61443. Tel: 309-856-7451; Fax: 309-852-4259. Mr. David Hobin, Prin. Lay Teachers 12; Students 117.
Catechesis/Religious Program—Tel: 309-856-5451. Deacon Martin Van Meltebeck, D.R.E. Students 70.
KICKAPOO, (EDWARDS) PEORIA CO., ST. MARY OF KICKAPOO (1837) Rev. Joseph Dondanville.
Res.: 9910 W. Knox St., Kickapoo (Edwards), 61528. Tel: 309-691-2030 (Church); Fax: 309-691-2898.
School—Tel: 309-691-3015. Gail Hulse, Prin. Lay Teachers 9; Students 110.
Catechesis/Religious Program—Students 68.
LA SALLE, LA SALLE CO.
1—ST. HYACINTH'S (1875) [CEM] Very Rev. Robert Rayson; Rev. Adam Stimpson, Parochial Vicar.
Res. & Church: 913 Fifth St., 61301. Tel: 815-223-1459; Fax: 815-223-0520.
School—Trinity Catholic Academy, 650 Fourth St., 61301. Tel: 815-223-8523; Fax: 815-223-5366. Mr. Roy Pesch, Prin. Lay Teachers 9; Students 134.
Catechesis/Religious Program—Students 200.
2—ST. PATRICK'S (1838), (Irish), [CEM] Very Rev. Robert Rayson; Rev. Adam Stimpson, Parochial Vicar.
Res.: *c/o Resurrection Church*, 913 Fifth St., 61301. Tel: 815-223-1459.
Church: 725 Fourth St., 61301. Tel: 815-223-0641; Fax: 815-223-0523.
School—Trinity Catholic Academy, (Grades PreSchool-8) Tel: 815-223-1166; Fax: 815-223-7650. Mr. Daniel Schmitt, Prin. Lay Teachers 21; Students 210.
Catechesis/Religious Program— Attend at St. Hyancinth, La Salle.
3—RESURRECTION (1979), (Suspended) Very Rev. Robert Rayson; Rev. Adam Stimpson.
Res.: 913 Fifth St., 61301. Tel: 815-223-1459; Fax: 815-223-1580.
4—SHRINE OF QUEEN OF THE HOLY ROSARY (1925), (Italian), [JC], (Suspended) Very Rev. Robert Rayson, Rector; Rev. Adam Stimpson, Parochial Vicar.
Res.: *c/o Priest Res.*, 913 5th St., 61301. Tel: 815-223-1459.
Church: 725 4th St., 61301. Tel: 815-233-7129.
Catechesis/Religious Program— Attend at Resurrection, La Salle.
LACON, MARSHALL CO., IMMACULATE CONCEPTION (1853) [CEM] Rev. Thomas R. Mizeur; Deacon J. Robert Murphy. In Res., Revs. Arthur D. Meyer (Retired); Harold F. Schmitt; Ronald Enderlin.
Office & Rectory: 415 N. High St., 61540. Tel: 309-246-5145; Fax: 309-246-5417. Email: iccc@grics.net.
Church: 418 N. Center St., 61540.
Catechesis/Religious Program—Katie Bogner, D.R.E. Students 40.
LADD, BUREAU CO., ST. BENEDICT'S (1893), Parish Suspended.
Res.: 314 Bureau St., 61329. Tel: 815-894-2319; Fax: 815-894-2265.
LEONORE, LA SALLE CO., SS. PETER AND PAUL'S (1860), (German), [CEM] Rev. Charles A. McCarthy, C.S.Sp.
Res.: 957 N. 17th Rd., Tonica, 61370. Tel: 815-856-2502; Fax: 815-856-2503.
Catechesis/Religious Program—Students 10.
LEWISTOWN, FULTON CO., ST. MARY'S (1865) [CEM] Revs. Daniel Ebker; Gabriel Msoka, A.J., Parochial Vicar.
Res.: 705 N. Broadway St., 61542. Tel: 309-547-3226; Fax: 309-547-3226. Email: stmaryscn@sbcglobal.net.
Catechesis/Religious Program—Students 2.
Mission—St. Michael St. David, Fulton Co.
LINCOLN, LOGAN CO., HOLY FAMILY (1857) [CEM 2] Revs. Jeffrey G. Laible; Glenn J. Fontana; Simon L. Taabu (Tanzania).
Res.: 316 S. Logan St., 62656. Tel: 217-732-4019; Fax: 217-735-2650. Web: www.holyfamilylincoln.com.
School—Carroll Catholic School, (Grades PreSchool-8), 111 Fourth St., 62656. Tel: 217-732-7518; Fax:

217-732-7518. Web: www.carrollcatholic.com. Vanessa Tibbs, Volunteer Librarian. Lay Teachers 9; Students 113.
Catechesis/Religious Program—Holy Family Religious Education Center, Tel: 217-735-3520. Students 99.
Mission—St. Mary's Atlanta, Logan Co. 61723.

LORETTO, LIVINGSTON CO., ST. MARY'S (1873), (German), Closed. For inquiries contact St. Patrick, Dwight.

LOSTANT, LA SALLE CO., ST. JOHN THE BAPTIST'S (1862) [CEM] Rev. Luke Poczworowski, O.F.M.Conv.
Res.: P.O. Box 486, Wenona, 61377. Tel: 815-853-4558; Fax: 815-853-0111. Email: smary1867@mchsi.com.
Church: 301 S. Sheridan, 61334. Tel: 815-368-3339.
Catechesis/Religious Program—Joan Morse, D.R.E. Combined with St. Mary's, Wenona Students 140.

MACOMB, MCDONOUGH CO., ST. PAUL'S (1854) [CEM] Rev. Msgr. Richard A. Pricco; Deacon Lawrence Adams.
Res.: 309 W. Jackson, 61455. Tel: 309-833-2496. Web: www.stpaul.macomb.com.
School—(Grades PreK-6), 322 W. Washington St., 61455. Tel: 309-833-2470; Fax: 309-833-2470. Email: stpaul@macomb.com. Mrs. Barbara Shrode, Prin. Lay Teachers 8; Students (K-6) 135; Preschool 46.
Catechesis/Religious Program—325 W. Jackson St., 61455. Tel: 309-837-1024. Students 50.
Mission—Sacred Heart Tennessee, McDonough Co.

MAHOMET, CHAMPAIGN CO., OUR LADY OF THE LAKE (1981) Rev. Msgr. James K. Ramer; Deacon Edward Mueller.
501 W. State St., P.O. Box 109, 61853.
Res.: Tel: 217-586-5153; Fax: 217-586-5924.
Catechesis/Religious Program—Tel: 217-840-6283. Mr. Roger L. Phelps, D.R.E. Students 390.

MARSEILLES, LA SALLE CO., ST. JOSEPH'S (1881) Rev. Msgr. J. Brian Rejsek.
Res.: 200 Broadway St., 61341. Tel: 815-795-2240.
Catechesis/Religious Program—Tel: 815-795-2251. Students 60.

MATHERVILLE, MERCER CO., ST. ANTHONY'S CHURCH (1916) [CEM 2] Rev. John Thieryoung.
Office: c/o 106 N.E. 4th St., Aledo, 61231. Tel: 309-582-7500.
Catechesis/Religious Program—Students 77.
Mission—St. John Viola, Mercer Co. 61486. Tel: 309-596-2950.

MENDOTA, LA SALLE CO., HOLY CROSS (1863) [CEM] Revs. Fredi Gomez Torres; Gary W. Blake, Parochial Vicar; Deacons Vincent Slomian; Raymond Fischer.
Res.: 1010 Jefferson St., 61342. Tel: 815-538-6151; Fax: 815-539-5014. Web: holycrossmendota.com.
School—1008 Jefferson St., 61342. Tel: 815-539-7003; Fax: 815-539-9082. Mrs. Anita Kobilsek, Prin. Lay Teachers 13; Students 127.
Catechesis/Religious Program— Karen Zolper, D.R.E. Students 280.

METAMORA, WOODFORD CO.
1—ST. MARY OF LOURDES (1831) [CEM] Rev. Neri Greskoviak, O.F.M.; Bro. Xavier Gedeon, O.F.M., Pastoral Assoc.; Deacons Jack Gaetz; Robert Heiple; William Read; Larry DeCapp.
Res.: 424 Lourdes Church Rd., 61548. Tel: 309-383-4460; Fax: 309-383-4467. Email: stmarylo@ontco.com. Web: www.germantownhills.com/lourdes.
Catechesis/Religious Program—Students 175.
2—ST. MARY'S (1864), (German), [CEM] Rev. Donald F. Roszkowski; Deacon Joseph Lowry; Sharon Elbert, Business Mgr.
Res.: 415 W. Chatham St., P.O. Box 319, 61548. Tel: 309-367-4407; Fax: 309-367-9456. Email: lselbert@mtco.com. Web: stmarysmetamora.com.
School—Tel: 309-367-2528; Fax: 309-367-2169. Ryan Bustle, Prin. Lay Teachers 15; Students 139.
Catechesis/Religious Program—Alan Anderson, D.R.E. Students 105.
Mission—St. Elizabeth Washburn, Woodford Co.

MILAN, ROCK ISLAND CO., ST. AMBROSE (1924) Rev. Anthony M. Ego.
Res.: 312 W. First St., 61264. Tel: 309-787-4593; Fax: 309-787-6403. Email: stambrosemilan@att.net. Web: www.ambroseparish.org.
Catechesis/Religious Program—Tel: 309-787-6403. Diane Hansen, D.R.E. Students 60.

MINONK, WOODFORD CO., ST. PATRICK'S (1878) [CEM] Rev. Luke Poczworowski, O.F.M.Conv.
Res.: 207 W. Third St., Wenona, 61377.
Church & Office: 420 E. Sixth St., Box 107, 61760-0107. Tel: 309-432-2700; Fax: 815-432-3399.
Catechesis/Religious Program—Students 71.

MOLINE, ROCK ISLAND CO.
1—CHRIST THE KING (1967) Rev. Donald L. Levitt.
Parish Center—3205 60th St., 61265. Tel: 309-762-4634; Fax: 309-762-7848. Email: ctkenter@netexpress.net. Web: christtheking.org.
Catechesis/Religious Program—Tel: 309-762-4634, Ext. 206. Sharon Dodd, D.R.E. (PreK-6 & Junior High); Sr. Charlotte Seubert, F.S.P.A., Adult Faith Dir.; Paul Fritch, Youth Min.; Kim Van DeRostyne, Youth Min. Students 229.
2—ST. MARY'S (1875) [CEM] Rev. Francisco Trujillo; Deacon Russ W. Swim.
Res.: 412 10th St., 61265. Tel: 309-764-1562; Fax: 309-764-0317. Email: stmarysmolineil@hotmail.com. Web: www.parishesonline.com.
Catechesis/Religious Program—Tel: 309-762-6575. Meaghan Terry, D.R.E. Students 289.
3—SACRED HEART (1906), (Belgian), Rev. Msgr. Dale L. Wellman; Rev. Thomas Gibson; Sr. Kathleen Mullin, Pastoral Assoc.; Deacons Dennis De Vooght; Patrick Murphy.
Lee Parish Center—1608 13th St., 61265. Tel: 309-762-2362; Fax: 309-757-5502. Email: shchurch@sacredheartmoline.org.
School—Seton Catholic School, (Grades PreK-8), 1320 16th Ave., 61265. Tel: 309-757-5502; Fax: 309-762-0545. Sisters 1; Lay Teachers 36; Students 508.
Catechesis/Religious Program— Sara Tucker, D.R.E. Students 102.

MONMOUTH, WARREN CO., IMMACULATE CONCEPTION (1864) [CEM] Rev. Anthony Bernas; Deacon William Clark.
Church: 210 W. Broadway, 61462. Tel: 309-734-7533; Fax: 309-734-7120.
School—115 North B St., 61462. Tel: 309-734-6037; Fax: 309-734-6082. Kathryn Bennett, Prin. Lay Teachers 13; Students 184.
Catechesis/Religious Program—Rita Selby, D.R.E. Students 63.

MONTICELLO, PIATT CO., ST. PHILOMENA (1888) Rev. Bruce Lopez; Deacon Gene Triplett.
Res.: 1301 N. Market St., 61856. Tel: 217-762-2566; Fax: 217-762-8666. Web: www.stphilomenaonline.org.
Catechesis/Religious Program—Students 144.

MORTON, TAZEWELL CO., BLESSED SACRAMENT (1957) Rev. Mark A. DeSutter; Deacons Rick Miller; David Steeples; Kevin Zeeb.
Res.: 225 E. Greenwood St., 61550. Tel: 309-266-9721. Web: www.mortonblessedsacrament.org.
School—233 E. Greenwood St., 61550. Tel: 309-263-8442; Fax: 309-263-8443. Mr. Michael Birdoes, Prin. Lay Teachers 18; Students 293.
Catechesis/Religious Program—Tel: 309-266-6791. Students 225.

NAUVOO, HANCOCK CO., SS. PETER AND PAUL (1848), (German), [CEM 2] Revs. Anthony J. Trosley; Thomas R. Szydlik; Mark O. Miller.
Res.: 190 N. Wells St., P.O. Box 147, 62354. Tel: 217-453-2428; Fax: 217-453-2427. Email: ssppnauvoo@gmail.com.
School—Tel: 217-453-2511. Email: sppskids@mchsi.com. Lisa Gray, Prin. Lay Teachers 7; Students 70.
Catechesis/Religious Program—Students 25.
Mission—Sacred Heart Dallas City, Hancock Co. 62330.

NORMAL, MCLEAN CO., EPIPHANY (1966) [JC] Rev. Msgr. Eric S. Powell.
Parish Office: 1000 E. College Ave., 61761. Tel: 309-452-2585; Fax: 309-452-4851. Email: office@epiphanyparish.com. Web: www.epiphanyparish.com.
Res.: 1006 E. College Ave., 61761.
School—1002 E. College Ave., 61761. Tel: 309-452-3268; Fax: 309-454-8087. Web: epiphanyschools.org. Michael Lootens, Prin. Lay Teachers 24; Students 375.
Catechesis/Religious Program—Mary Ellen Kiley, C.R.E. Students 272.

ODELL, LIVINGSTON CO., ST. PAUL'S (1873), (Irish), [CEM 2] Rev. Ronald Dodd.
Res.: 313 W. Hamilton, P.O. Box 307, 60460. Tel: 815-998-2197; Fax: 815-998-2197. Email: stpaul.odell@mchsi.com.
School—Tel: 815-998-2194; Fax: 815-998-1514. Email: stpaulodell@catholic.org. Mr. Ed Condon, Prin. Lay Teachers 6; Students 54; Religious 1.
Catechesis/Religious Program—
Mission—Sacred Heart 205 N. Elm St., P.O. Box 68, Campus, 60920.

OGLESBY, LA SALLE CO., HOLY FAMILY (1953) Rev. Michael J. Andrejek.
Res.: 311 N. Woodland Ave., 61348. Tel: 815-883-8233; Fax: 815-883-8771.
School—336 Alice Ave., 61348. Tel: 815-883-8916; Fax: 815-883-8943. Mrs. Jyll Jasick, Prin. Lay Teachers 14; Students 145.
Catechesis/Religious Program—Students 110.

OHIO, BUREAU CO., IMMACULATE CONCEPTION CHURCH (1875), (Irish), [CEM] Rev. Thomas Shaw.
Res.: *c/o St. John's*, 204 N. Main St., Walnut, 61376-0370. Tel: 815-379-2602; Fax: 815-379-2302.
Church: 101 N. Main St., P.O. Box 358, 61349.
Catechesis/Religious Program—Gayle Thomas, D.R.E. Students 17.

ORION, HENRY CO., MARY, OUR LADY OF PEACE (1960) Rev. James P. DeBisschop.
Res.: 1402 10th St., P.O. Box 175, 61273-0175. Tel: 309-526-8422; Fax: 309-526-8469.
Catechesis/Religious Program—Students 124.

OTTAWA, LA SALLE CO.
1—ST. COLUMBA (1844), (Irish), [CEM] Revs. David M. Kipfer; Raymond P. Guthrie.
Res.: 122 W. Washington St., 61350. Tel: 815-433-0700; Fax: 815-433-0305. Email: stcolumbaottawa@hotmail.com. Web: www.geocities.com/scsottawa/.
School—Marquette Academy, (Grades PreK-12), 1110 LaSalle St., 61350. Tel: 815-433-1199; Fax: 815-433-1219.
Catechesis/Religious Program—Students 118.
Mission—St. Mary's 2098 E. 22nd Rd., Grand Ridge, La Salle Co. 61235. Tel: 815-433-0700.
2—ST. FRANCIS OF ASSISI (1858) [CEM] Rev. Jules Adator, S.M.A., Admin.
Res.: 820 Sanger St., 61350. Tel: 815-434-0969; Fax: 815-434-1073.
Catechesis/Religious Program—Mrs. Mary Mann, D.R.E. Students 107.
3—ST. MARY'S (1927) Rev. Jules Adator, S.M.A., Admin.
Mailing Address: 2005 Center St., P.O. Box 2552, Ottawa (Naplate), 61350. Tel: 815-433-2404; Fax: 815-433-9458.
Catechesis/Religious Program—
Convent—2005 Center St., 61350. Tel: 815-433-2637. Dominican Sisters 2.
4—ST. PATRICK'S (1893), (Irish), Rev. Joseph P. Donton.
Res.: 726 W. Jefferson St., 61350. Tel: 815-434-0768; Fax: 815-434-0793.
Catechesis/Religious Program—Mrs. Mary Mann, D.R.E. Students 129.
Convent—2005 Center St., 61350. Tel: 815-433-2637.

PEKIN, TAZEWELL CO., ST. JOSEPH'S (1863) [CEM 2] Rev. Msgr. Timothy Nolan; Rev. James Pankiewicz, Parochial Vicar; Deacons Charles Murray; Martin Pogioli; Mark Wilder; Ernie Whited; Tim Blanchard.
Res.: 303 S. Seventh St., 61554. Tel: 309-347-6108; Fax: 309-347-6959.
School—300 S. Sixth St., 61554. Tel: 309-347-7194; Fax: 309-347-7196. Shannon Rogers, Prin. Lay Teachers 13; Students 200.
Catechesis/Religious Program—Tina Sondag, D.R.E. Students 149.

PENFIELD, CHAMPAIGN CO., ST. LAWRENCE'S (1898) [CEM] Rev. Michael L. Menner.
Res.: P.O. Box 49, 61862. Tel: 217-595-5560; 217-595-5620 (Office).
Catechesis/Religious Program—Students 31.
Mission—St. Charles Borromeo Homer, Champaign Co. 61849.

PERU, LA SALLE CO.
1—ST. JOSEPH'S (1854) [CEM] Rev. Harold L. Datzman, O.S.B.
Res.: 1925 5th St., P.O. Box 608, 61354. Tel: 815-223-0718; Fax: 815-223-5690.
Catechesis/Religious Program—Kristi Bejster, D.R.E. Students 29.
2—ST. MARY (1867), (Irish), Rev. William M. Gardner.
Res.: 1109 Pulaski St., 61354. Tel: 815-223-0315.
Church: 1325 Sixth St., 61354.
See Peru Catholic School System, Peru under St. Joseph's, Peru for details.
Catechesis/Religious Program—Students 3.
3—ST. VALENTINE (1891), (Polish), [CEM] Rev. William M. Gardner.
Res.: 1109 Pulaski St., 61354. Tel: 815-223-0315.
See Peru Catholic School System, Peru under St. Joseph's, Peru for details.
Catechesis/Religious Program—Students 48.

PESOTUM, CHAMPAIGN CO.
1—ST. JOSEPH (1904), (German), [CEM] Closed. Sacramental records are located at St. Mary Philo, Pesotum.
2—ST. MARY (1875), (German), [CEM] Rev. Bowan Schmitt.
Res.: P.O. Box 266, Philo, 61864. Tel: 217-684-5107 (Parish Office); 217-684-2571 (Rectory); Fax: 217-684-2217. Email: churchstthomasphilo@comcast.net.
Catechesis/Religious Program— See St. Thomas, Philo

PETERSTOWN, LA SALLE CO., SS. PETER AND PAUL (1872) [CEM] Revs. Gary W. Blake; Fredi Gomez Torres.
Res.: 1010 Jefferson St., Mendota, 61342. Tel: 815-538-6151; Fax: 815-539-5014.

PHILO, CHAMPAIGN CO., ST. THOMAS (1869) [CEM] Rev. Bowan Schmitt.
Res.: 310 E. Madison, P.O. Box 266, 61864. Tel: 217-684-2571; 217-684-5107 (Parish Office).
School—Tel: 217-684-2309; Fax: 217-684-2217. Web: www.stthomasphilo.org. Mrs. Gwendolyn Roche, Prin. Lay Teachers 10; Students 106.
Catechesis/Religious Program—Tel: 217-684-5701. Combined with Immaculate Conception Mission

and St. Mary, Pesotum. Students 73.
Mission—Immaculate Conception [CEM] Bongard, Champaign Co. 61864.

PONTIAC, LIVINGSTON CO., ST. MARY'S (1877) [CEM] Rev. Msgr. Thomas E. Mack; Rev. David Sabel, Parochial Vicar.
Res.: 119 E. Howard St., P.O. Box 374, 61764. Tel: 815-844-7683; Fax: 815-842-4345.
School—414 N. Main St., 61764. Tel: 815-844-6585; Fax: 815-844-6987. Mr. Richard Morehouse, Prin. Lay Teachers 12; Students 179.
Catechesis/Religious Program—Students 75.
Mission—St. Joseph Flanagan, Livingston Co. 61740. Tel: 815-844-7683.

PRINCETON, BUREAU CO., ST. LOUIS (1865) Rev. Jeffrey D. Stirniman.
Res.: 616 S. Gosse Blvd., 61356. Tel: 815-879-0181; Fax: 815-879-0181. Email: rectory@stlchurch.comcastbiz.net.
School—(Grades PreSchool-8), 631 Park Ave. W., 61356. Tel: 815-872-8521; Fax: 815-879-8010. Email: stlouiscs@comcast.net. Web: www.stlschool.net. Mrs. Mary Paula Schmitt, Prin. Sisters 1; Lay Teachers 10; Students 95.
Catechesis/Religious Program—Tel: 815-872-7016. Students 100.

PRINCEVILLE, PEORIA CO., ST. MARY OF THE WOODS (1867) [CEM] Rev. Patrick M. Riordan; Deacon Frederick J. Kruse.
Res.: 119 Saint Mary St., 61559-9244. Tel: 309-385-4370; 309-385-2578 (Office); Fax: 309-385-1754. Email: smowmo@verizon.net.
Catechesis/Religious Program—Students 45.

RANSOM, LA SALLE CO., ST. PATRICK'S (1883) [CEM] Rev. Msgr. J. Brian Rejsek.
Mailing Address: 200 Broadway, Marseilles, 61341. Tel: 815-795-2240.
Church: 110 Wallace, 60470.
Catechesis/Religious Program—

RANTOUL, CHAMPAIGN CO., ST. MALACHY (1888) [CEM] Revs. Steven Bird; Stanley J. Malinowski, Pastor Emeritus (Retired).
Res.: 340 E. Belle Ave., Ste. 1, 61866. Email: stmalachychurch@catholicweb.com. Web: stmalachychurch.catholicweb.com.
School—340 E. Belle Ave., 61866. Tel: 217-892-2011; Fax: 217-892-5780. Email: stmalachyschool@catholicweb.com. Web: stmalachy-school.catholicweb.com. Mr. James Flaherty, Prin. Sisters 1; Lay Teachers 13; Students 160.
Catechesis/Religious Program—Sr. Sara Koch, O.P., C.R.E. Students 40.
Convent—Dominican Sisters (Springfield), 304 E. Belle Ave., 61866. Tel: 217-892-2870.

RAPIDS CITY, ROCK ISLAND CO., ST. JOHN THE BAPTIST (1857) [CEM] Rev. Glenn Harris.
Res.: 1416 Third Ave., P.O. Box 250, 61278. Tel: 309-496-2414. Email: stjohnrc@mchsi.com.
Catechesis/Religious Program—Fax: 309-496-3414. Students 66.
Mission—St. Mary 708 State Ave., Rte. 84, Hampton, Rock Island Co. 61256. Tel: 309-496-3414.

RARITAN, HENDERSON CO., CHURCH OF ST. PATRICK (1876), (Irish), Rev. Kenneth J. Hummel.
Res.: P.O. Box 24, 61471. Tel: 309-837-3989.
Catechesis/Religious Program—Students 33.

ROANOKE, WOODFORD CO., ST. JOSEPH (1874) Rev. Msgr. Charles J. Beebe.
Res.: 508 W. Randolph, 61561. Tel: 309-923-3031; Fax: 309-926-3031.
Catechesis/Religious Program—Michelle Boland, Coord. CCD; Cathy Bilow, Dir. Youth Prog. Students 62.

ROCK ISLAND, ROCK ISLAND CO.
1—ST. JOSEPH'S (1876), (Suspended) Rev. Steven P. Loftus.
2208-4th Ave., 61201.
2—ST. MARY (1851), (German), (Formerly Immaculate Conception) Revs. Steven P. Loftus; George J. Schroeder, Pastor Emeritus (Retired).
Rectory—2208 4th Ave., 61201-8904. Tel: 309-788-3422; Fax: 309-788-9367.
Catechesis/Religious Program—Julie Nonnenman, D.R.E. Students 49.
3—ST. PIUS X (1955) Revs. R. Michael Schaab; Jerry Logan; Deacons Timothy Granet; Paul Martin; Philip Sailer; Joseph Dockery-Jackson.
Res.: 2502 29th Ave., 61201. Tel: 309-793-7373; Fax: 309-793-7376.
See Jordan Catholic School of Rock Island, Inc., Rock Island under Elementary Schools, Inter-Parochial located in the Institution section.
Catechesis/Religious Program—Students 120.
4—SACRED HEART (1900) Rev. Steven P. Loftus.
Res.: *St. Mary's Church*, 2208 4th Ave., 61201. Tel: 309-788-3322. Email: shrec@qconline.com.
School—Jordan Catholic School of Rock Island, Tel: 309-793-7350; Fax: 309-793-7361. Web: www-.jordanschool.com. Lay Teachers 30; Students 537. See Jordan Catholic School of Rock Island, Inc., Rock Island under Elementary Schools, Inter-Parochial located in the Institution section.
Catechesis/Religious Program—Students 35.

RUSHVILLE, SCHUYLER CO., ST. ROSE (1870) [JC] Rev. William Keebler, Admin.
Res.: 319 N. Franklin St., P.O. Box 194, 62681-0292. Tel: 217-322-3424; Fax: 309-833-1560.
Catechesis/Religious Program—Students 44.

RUTLAND, LA SALLE CO., SACRED HEART (1895), (Irish), [CEM] Closed. Now a mission of St. Ann, Toluca.

ST. AUGUSTINE, KNOX CO., ST. AUGUSTINE (1863) [CEM] Rev. Thomas B. Holloway.
Mailing Address: c/o 376 W. Hail, Bushnell, 61422. Tel: 301-462-3421; 309-772-2333.
Catechesis/Religious Program—Students 10.

SENECA, LA SALLE CO., ST. PATRICK'S (1856) [CEM] Unassigned.
Parish Center—176 W. Union, 61360. Tel: 815-357-6239. Email: stpatrickseneca@hotmail.com.
Catechesis/Religious Program—Tel: 815-357-8509. Students 134.

SEYMOUR, CHAMPAIGN CO., ST. BONIFACE (1878) [CEM] Rev. Msgr. Albert W. Hallin.
Church & Res.: 416 County Rd., 1100 N., 61875. Tel: 217-863-2190; Fax: 217-863-2190.
Catechesis/Religious Program—

SHEFFIELD, BUREAU CO., ST. PATRICK'S (1854) [CEM] Rev. Sebastian Tumusiime.
Res.: 305 W. South Ave., Annawan, 61234. Tel: 309-935-6911.
Church: 231 W. Atkinson St., P.O. Box 514, 61361-0038.
Catechesis/Religious Program—Mary Jo Nelson, D.R.E. Students 14.

SILVIS, ROCK ISLAND CO., OUR LADY OF GUADALUPE (1927) Rev. Greg Jozefiak.
Res.: 800 17th St., 61282. Tel: 309-792-3867; Fax: 309-792-2241. Web: www.olgsilvis.net.
Catechesis/Religious Program—Cheri Smith, D.R.E.

SPRING VALLEY, BUREAU CO.
1—ST. ANNE'S, Closed. For sacramental records contact St. Anthony Church, Spring Valley.
2—ST. ANTHONY (1904), (Italian), Rev. Robert D. Spilman.
Res.: 510 Richard A. Mautino Dr., P.O. Box 150, 61362-0150. Tel: 815-663-3731; Fax: 815-663-0012.
Catechesis/Religious Program—Tel: 815-663-3731. Students 84.
3—IMMACULATE CONCEPTION (1884) [CEM] Rev. Robert D. Spilman.
Mailing Address: P.O. Box 150, 61362.
Res.: 510 Richard A. Mautino Dr., 61362. Tel: 815-663-3731; Fax: 815-663-0012.
Catechesis/Religious Program—Tel: 815-664-2022. Students 59.
4—SS. PETER AND PAUL'S (1891), (Polish), [CEM], Parish Suspended. Rev. Robert D. Spilman.
Mailing Address: P.O. Box 150, 61362.
Mission—St. Gertrude

STREATOR, LA SALLE CO.
1—ST. ANTHONY OF PADUA (1881) [CEM] Closed. Sacramental records are located at St. Michael the Archangel Church, Streator, IL.
2—ST. CASIMIR (1916), (Polish), [CEM], (Suspended) Sacramental records are located at St. Michael the Archangel Church, Streator. IL.
3—IMMACULATE CONCEPTION (1868) [CEM] Closed. Sacramental records are located at St. Michael the Archangel Church, Streator, IL.
4—ST. MICHAEL THE ARCHANGEL CHURCH (2010) Rev. Msgr. Philip Halfacre; Rev. Dustin P. Schultz, Parochial Vicar.
Mailing Address: 513 S. Shabbona St., 61364.
Church: 801 Lundy St., 61364. Tel: 815-672-2474; Fax: 815-672-2040.
School—St. Michael the Archangel School, (Grades K-8), 410 S. Park St., 61364.
Catechesis/Religious Program—Sr. Alice Ann Harcharik, O.S.F., D.R.E. Students 257.
5—ST. STEPHEN'S (1884), (Slovak), [CEM 2] Closed. Sacramental records are located at St. Michael the Archangel Church, Streator, IL.

THOMASBORO, CHAMPAIGN CO., ST. ELIZABETH OF HUNGARY (1893) [CEM] Rev. Msgr. Albert W. Hallin. In Res., Rev. Stanley J. Malinowski (Retired).
Res.: 100 Church St., Box 307, 61878. Tel: 217-643-3395; Fax: 217-643-2217. Email: stelizabethparish@mchsi.com.
Catechesis/Religious Program—Students 8.

TISKILWA, BUREAU CO., ST. MARY'S (1881) [CEM] Closed. Now a mission of St. Mary, Depue.

TOLONO, CHAMPAIGN CO., ST. PATRICK'S (1859) [CEM] Rev. John Cyr.
Res.: 212 E. Washington St., P.O. Box K, 61880. Tel: 217-485-5194.
Catechesis/Religious Program—

TOLUCA, MARSHALL CO., ST. ANN'S (1895), (Italian), [CEM] Rev. Edward S. Kopec.
Res.: 311 W. Santa Fe Ave., Box 165, 61369. Tel: 815-452-2043.
Catechesis/Religious Program—Students 15.
Mission—Sacred Heart Rutland, La Salle Co. 61358.

URBANA, CHAMPAIGN CO., ST. PATRICK'S (1901) Rev. Joseph T. Hogan; Deacon Clifford Maduzia.
Res.: 612 E. Park St., Champaign, 61820.
Church: 708 W. Main St., 61801. Tel: 217-367-2665; Fax: 217-383-1002. Web: www.stpaturbana.org.
Catechesis/Religious Program—Carolyn McElrath, D.R.E. Students 290.

UTICA, LA SALLE CO., ST. MARY (1858) [CEM] Rev. Msgr. James J. Swaner.
Res.: 303 Division St., 61373. Tel: 815-667-4677. Email: stmaryutica@att.net.
Catechesis/Religious Program—Students 69.

WALNUT, BUREAU CO., ST. JOHN THE EVANGELIST (1912) Rev. Thomas Shaw.
Res.: 204 N. Main St., P.O. Box 370, 61376-0370. Tel: 815-379-2602; Fax: 815-379-2302. Email: stjohns1912@mchsi.com.
Catechesis/Religious Program—Students 33.

WAPELLA, DE WITT CO., ST. PATRICK CHURCH (1858) [CEM] Rev. Peter A. Pilon.
Res.: 308 S. Locust St., 61777. Tel: 217-935-9242 (Res.); 217-935-8510 (Office).
Catechesis/Religious Program—Students 49.

WARSAW, HANCOCK CO., SACRED HEART (1874), (German), [CEM] Revs. Anthony J. Trosley; Thomas R. Szydlik, Parochial Vicar; Mark O. Miller, Parochial Vicar.
Res.: 245 S. 9th St., 62379. Tel: 217-256-3657. Email: shc@mchsi.com.
Catechesis/Religious Program—Students 20.
Mission—St. Mary 560 Lakeview Ave., Hamilton, Hancock Co. 62341. Deacon Greggory Golemo.

WASHBURN, WOODFORD CO., ST. ELIZABETH, [CEM] Closed. Now a mission of St. Mary, Metamora.

WASHINGTON, TAZEWELL CO., ST. PATRICK'S (1941) Rev. Msgr. John J. Prendergast; Rev. Ryan Bredemeyer, Parochial Vicar; Deacons Paul Neakrase; Joseph Venzon.
Res.: 705 E. Jefferson, 61571. Tel: 309-444-3524; Fax: 309-444-7070. Email: churchoffice@stpatswashington.com. Web: www.stpatswashington.com.
School—100 N. Harvey, 61571. Tel: 309-444-4345; Fax: 309-444-7100. Email: schooloffice@stpatswashington.com. Dr. Sharon Weiss, Prin. Lay Teachers 20; Students 228.
Catechesis/Religious Program—Keo Thompson, C.R.E. Students 242.

WEDRON, LA SALLE CO., ST. JOSEPH'S (1947) Rev. John G. Waugh.
Mailing Address: Box 60, 60557.
Res.: 3609 E. 2351 Rd., Serena, 60549. Tel: 815-792-2622.
Catechesis/Religious Program—Students 35.

WENONA, MARSHALL CO., ST. MARY'S (1867) [CEM] Rev. Luke Poczworowski, O.F.M.Conv.
Res.: 207 W. Third St., P.O. Box 486, 61377. Tel: 815-853-4558; Fax: 815-853-0111. Email: smary1867@mchsi.com.
Catechesis/Religious Program—Students 140.
Mission—Immaculate Conception Mt. Palatine, La Salle Co. Closed temporarily.

WESTVILLE, VERMILION CO.
1—ST. MARY'S (1903) [CEM] Rev. Timothy J. Sauppe.
Res.: 231 N. State St., 61883. Tel: 217-267-3334; Fax: 217-267-3334. Email: stmary1903@yahoo.com.
Catechesis/Religious Program—Students 47.
2—SS. PETER AND PAUL, Closed. For inquiries for parish records contact St. Mary's, Westville.

WOODHULL, HENRY CO., ST. JOHN'S (1889), (Swedish), [CEM 2] Rev. John R. Burns; Deacon Joseph O'Tool.
Res.: 390 E. Highway Ave., P.O. Box 249, 61490. Tel: 309-334-2180; Fax: 309-334-2137. Email: stjohnchurch@winco.net.
Catechesis/Religious Program—Students 26.
Mission—St. John Vianney 313 S. West St., Cambridge, Henry Co. 61238. Email: stjohn@geneseo.net.

WYOMING, STARK CO., ST. DOMINIC'S (1881) [CEM] Rev. Vien Van Do.
Res.: 303 N. Galena Ave., 61491. Tel: 309-695-4031; Fax: 309-695-4412.
Catechesis/Religious Program—Students 29.

Chaplains of Public Institutions

DANVILLE. *Veterans' Administration Hospital*, Tel: 217-442-8000.

DWIGHT. *Dwight Correctional Center*, Tel: 815-584-3522. Rev. James E. Rickey. Attended from St. Patrick's, Dwight.

LINCOLN. *Logan Correctional Center*, Tel: 217-947-2714; 309-244-8516. Rev. Jeffrey G. Laible, Holy Family Parish, Lincoln.

PONTIAC. *Illinois State Penitentiary*. Attended from St. Paul, Odell
Res.: 811 Hill St., 61704. Tel: 815-842-1150.

SHERIDAN. *Illinois Industrial School for Boys*. Rev. John G. Waugh, Chap.

On Duty Outside the Diocese:
Rev. Msgrs.—
Rohlfs, Steven P., S.T.D., V.G., Rector, Mt. St. Mary's Seminary, Emmitsburg, MD
Soseman, Richard, M.A., J.C.L., Rome, Italy
Swetland, Stuart W., S.T.D., Professor, Mt. St. Mary's Seminary, Emmitsburg, Md
Revs.—
Campbell, Dwight
Caster, Gary C.
Grandon, Douglas, Archdiocese of Denver
Henseler, J. Thomas, Diocese of Springfield, IL
Hochstatter, Theodore, East Africa
Hummel, Kenneth J., Archdiocese of Cincinnati
Myers, James E., 32 Middlefield Rd., Menlo Park, CA 94025.
Ohm, Edward U., (Military)
Reese, Benjamin
Vitaliano, Dominic J., (Military)
Wilder, Daniel J.

On Leave of Absence:
Revs.—
Gallagher, Francis
Morlan, Lawrence A.
Small, Jeffrey
Windy, Jeff

Retired:
Rev. Msgrs.—
Duncan, Edward J., Denver, CO
Fitzpatrick, Donnelly J.
Fitzsimmons, Richard, 830 Garfield Ave., Batavia, 60510.
Ham, Jerome
Higgins, E. Edward
O'Connor, Robert W.
Very Rev.—
Flattery, John J., 20967 Walnut Hill Rd., Danville, 61834.
Revs.—
Anderson, Joseph W., 545 W. Paseo del Canto, Green Valley, AZ 85614.
Barclift, Richard L.
Brajkovich, Thomas R., 114 S. 2nd St. #3, Chillicothe, 61523.
Bresnahan, Richard F., 2435 - 29th St., Moline, 61265.
Carney, Edward, 1295 Millpoint Rd., East Peoria, 61611.
Collins, Patrick, 609 Campbell Rd., P.O. Box 221, Douglas, MI 49406.
Crawford, Richard E., 1414 S. Monroe, Streator, 61364.
Enderlin, R. E.
Fritz, Henry H., O.S.B.
Harkrader, Edward O., 545 S. Fifth St., Princeton, 61356.
Heyd, Joseph J., O.S.B.
Hoffman, Robert, 343 Hickory Ct., Oakwood, 61858.
Horzen, Bernard A., O.S.B.
Kelly, Thomas F., W6881 W. Lake Shore Dr., Elkhorn, WI 53121.
King, John, Little Ireland Rd., R.R. 1 P.O. Box 1936, Starrucca, PA 18462.
Kolczaski, Richard, 1001 Monks Ave., Peru, 61354.
Kretz, James C.
Lukoskie, Raymond M., 2102 LeClaire St., Warsaw, 62379.
Mai-Chi-Than, Joseph M., 904 Switchgrass Ln., Champaign, 61822.
Malinowski, Stanley J., P.O. Box 307, Thomasboro, 61878.
Maloy, Dale, 1709 Char-Lu Dr., Mendota, 61342.
Mann, Robert G., 19614 Star Ridge Dr., Sun City West, AZ 85375.
Meismer, Paul J.
Meyer, Arthur D.
Meyer, Gerald J.
Mullen, Richard, 2414 Heritage Dr., Champaign, 61822.
O'Connor, Robert D., Kahl Home, 1101 W. 9th St., Davenport, IA 52804.
O'Riley, Dennis H., 225 E. Autumn, Oakwood, 61858.
Onderko, John M., 2200 36th St., Rock Island, 61201.
Prendergast, Robert E., P.O. Box 548, Kewanee, 61443.
Raney, Richard E., 21460 Bay Village Dr., #236, Fort Myers Beach, FL 33931-4337.
Remm, George F., P.O. Box 6136, Champaign, 61826.
Roche, David, 413 E Second St., Minonk, 61760.
Royer, Thomas J.
Ryan, William A., 610 E. First St., #2-6, Spring Valley, 61362.
Schladen, Robert, P.O. Box 6105, 61601.
Schroeder, George J., 16 Waverly Dr., Rock Island, 61201.
Thompson, George M., 3026 55th St., Moline, 61265.
Verhoye, Gerard A., 202 N. State, Box 603, Atkinson, 61235.

Permanent Deacons:
Adams, John L., St. Paul's, Macomb
An, Yi-Ning Michael, Epiphany, Normal
Angelo, Alfredo W., Jr., St. Patrick, Colona
Beltramini, Robert, St. Joseph's, Peru
Blanchard, Timothy, St. Joseph, Pekin
Bradford, Bruce, Sacred Heart, Peoria
Breeden, Charles, St. Maria Goretti, Coal Valley
Briggs, James W., St. Anne's, E. Moline
Buczko, Stanley, St. Patrick, Havana
Burton, John, St. Joseph's, Brimfield and St. James, Williamsfield
Buyck, Jerry, Christ the King, Moline
Carolan, Brendan, Holy Trinity, Bloomington
Cenek, Stephen, St. Ann, Peoria
Chaffee, Harley, St. Malachy, Genesco
Clark, William H., Immaculate Conception, Monmouth and St. Theresa's Alexis.
Cleary, Mark, Epiphany, Normal
Crutcher, Steven, St. Patrick of Merna, Bloomington
Curry, Dirck, D.O., Epiphany, Normal
DeBernardis, Thomas, St. Vincent de Paul, Peoria
DeCapp, Larry, St. Mary of Lourdes, Metamora
DeVooght, Dennis, Sacred Heart, Moline
Dockery-Jackson, Joseph, St. Pius X, Rock Island
Dosher, Jon, St. Patrick, Havana
Eaton, Francis, St. Thomas, Peoria Heights
Efinger, Donald, (Working Outside the Diocese)
England, Robert, (Retired)
Ensenberger, Tony, St. Paul, Macomb
Filzen, Bernard R., (Retired)
Fischer, Raymond, Holy Cross, Mendota
Gaetz, Dale, St. Mary, Lourdes
Golemo, Greggory, Sacred Heart, Warsaw; St. Mary, Hamilton
Gore, James, Holy Trinity, Bloomington
Granet, Timothy, St. Pius X, Rock Island
Gray, Rodney, Immaculate Heart of Mary, Galesburg
Gray, William, Dir. of Rural Life, Sts. Peter and Paul, Nauvoo
Grimler, Richard, (Working Outside the Diocese)
Hammond, Richard G., St. Anthony, Bartonville
Haneghan, James, St. Patrick, Galesburg
Hart, Henry, Holy Cross, Champaign; Spiritual Director Champaign Cursillo
Heckman, M. Andrew, St. Elizabeth, Thomasboro; Director of Worship, St. John's Chapel, Champaign
Heipel, Robert, St. Mary of Lourdes, Metamora
Hermes, Robert, Holy Trinity, Bloomington
Holevoet, John V., St. John, Woodhull; St. John, Galva
Honzel, Larry, St. Malachy, Geneseo
Hunter, Roger, St. Jude, Peoria
Kettering, Jack M., St. Pius X, Rock Island
Kim, Byung-Joon (Paul), St. Mary, Champaign
Koeppel, Joseph, St. Ann's, Peoria
Kovachevich, Victor, St. Patrick of Merna, Bloomington
Kruse, Frederick J., Dir. King's House, Henry, IL
La Hood, Joseph, Holy Family, Peoria; Prison Ministry
Lalande, John, (Working Outside the Diocese)
Landry, John, (Retired)
Leonard, John, St. John's, Bellflower; Sacred Heart, Farmer City
Levy, Matthew, Our Lady of Guadalupe, Silvis
Lowry, Joseph, St. Mary of Lourdes, Metamora
Maduzia, Clifford, St. Patrick, Urbana
Mannino, Michael, Immaculate Heart of Mary, Galesburg
Martin, Paul, St. Pius X, Rock Island
Maubach, James, St. Patrick, Washington
Meyer, William, Immaculate Conception, Manito; St. Patrick, Havana
Miller, Rick, Blessed Sacrament, Morton
Mock, John, (Retired)
Mohrbacher, Edward, Holy Cross, Champaign
Montenegro, Jose, St. Mary, Bloomington
Moran, Thomas, Blessed Sacrament, Morton
Mueller, Edward, Our Lady of the Lake, Mahomet
Murphy, John P., St. Louis, Princeton; St. Mary's, Tiskilwa
Murphy, John R., Immaculate Conception, Lacon
Murphy, Patrick, Sacred Heart, Moline
Murray, Charles, St. Joseph, Pekin
Myers, Robert, St. Vincent de Paul, Peoria; Executive Dir. Catholic Cemetery Assn. of Peoria
Neakrase, Paul, St. Patrick, Washington
O'Rourke, Robert, St. Malachy, Geneseo
O'Tool, Joseph, St. John, Woodhull
Petri, Darrel, St. Mary, Bloomington
Pinheiro, Edwin, (On Leave of Absence)
Pogioli, Martin, St. Joseph, Pekin
Pomazal, Robert, Vice Chancellor, St. Edward, Chillicothe
Pool, Michael, St. Patrick of Merna, Bloomington
Racki, Stephen, III, St. Patrick of Merna, Bloomington
Randazzo, Frank G.
Rapach, Thomas, St. Jude's, Peoria
Read, William, Diocese Dir., Cursillo-Tec; St. Mary's of Lourdes, Metamora
Reising, David, St. Philomena, Peoria
Ries, Arthur, St. Malachy, Geneseo
Robbins, Charles, St. Monica, E. Peoria
Sailer, Philip, St. Pius X, Rock Island
Sandoval, Henry, (On Leave of Absence)
Schultz, Gary, St. Matthew, Farmington
Serangeli, Gregory, St. Edward's, Chillicothe; Director of Evangelization, Diocese of Peoria
Simon, Nicholas, St. Anthony, Atkinson
Sims, Fred, (Working Outside the Diocese)
Skender, John, St. Mark, Peoria
Sloman, William, St. Francis Medical Center & St. Ann, Peoria
Slomian, Vincent, Holy Cross, Mendota
Smith, Richard, Holy Family, Danville
Sondag, Robert, Immaculate Conception, Manito
Steeples, David, Blessed Sacrament, Morton
Steiner, Bruce, St. Ann, Peoria
Swim, Russ, St. Mary, Moline
Tomlianovich, Louis A., St. Anthony's, Bartonville
Triplett, Gene, St. Philomena, Monticello; St. Michael, Bement
Tyler, Raymond Toby, Cathedral of St. Mary of the Immaculate Conception, Peoria
Ulbrich, Robert J., Holy Cross, Champaign
Van Meltebeck, Martin, St. Mary, Kewanee
Van Wassenhove, Raymond, (Retired)
Vargas, Ausencio, Hispanic Ministry, St. Mary's Cathedral
Venzon, Joseph, St. Patrick, Washington
Vogelbaugh, Bob, Sacred Heart, Moline
Wachtel, Thomas, St. Malachy, Geneseo
Wagner, George, St. Mary's, Pontiac; St. John, Cullom; St. Joseph, Flanagan
Waldschmidt, Robert, (Retired)
Wallace, Ray, St. Mary's, Pontiac; St. John, Cullom; St. Joseph, Flanagan
Whited, Ernie, St. Joseph, Pekin
Whitehouse, Scott, Sacred Heart, Farmer City
Wilder, Mark, St. Joseph, Pekin
Zeeb, Kevin, Blessed Sacrament, Morton
Zimmerman, Richard, St. Peter, Peoria
Zulz, Charles, St. Mary's, Wenona; St. Patrick's Minonk; St. John's, Lostant

INSTITUTIONS LOCATED IN THE DIOCESE

[A] SEMINARIES, RELIGIOUS OR SCHOLASTICATES

PEORIA. *Rosminian House*, 2327 W. Heading Ave., 61604. Tel: 309-676-6341; Fax: 309-676-1087. Email: frwtmic@gmail.com. Rev. William T. Miller, I.C., Supr. Priests 2; Total Staff 2.

PERU. *St. Bede Abbey* (1891) 24 W. US Hwy 6, 61354. Tel: 815-223-3140; Fax: 815-223-8580. Email: frphilip@st-bede.com. Web: stbedeabbey.org. Benedictine Fathers and Brothers. Priests 19; Brothers 8.

Staff: Rt. Revs. Claude J. Peifer, O.S.B., (Retired Abbot); Marion E. Balsavich, O.S.B., (Retired Abbot); Roger F. Corpus, O.S.B., (Retired Abbot); Philip D. Davey, O.S.B., Abbot; Rev. Michael Calhoun, Prior; Very Rev. Dominic M. Garramone, O.S.B., Subprior & CFO; Revs. Gabriel G. Bullock, O.S.B.; Harold L. Datzman, O.S.B.; Patrick A. Fennell, O.S.B.; Henry H. Fritz, O.S.B. (Retired); Kevin D. Gorman, O.S.B. (Retired); Ambrose B. Hessling, O.S.B. (Retired); Joseph J. Heyd, O.S.B (Retired); Bernard A. Horzen, O.S.B. (Retired); Ronald L. Margherio, O.S.B.; Matthew C. Mazzuchelli, O.S.B.; James M. Murray, O.S.B.; Samuel D. Pusateri, O.S.B.; Arthur G. Schmit, O.S.B.; Bros. David Freeman, O.S.B.; Elias Luis Candelaria Garcia, O.S.B.; Nathaniel Grossman, O.S.B.; Gregory Jarzombek, O.S.B.; George J. Matsuoka, O.S.B., (Retired); Luke E. McLachlan, O.S.B.; Robert Pondant, O.S.B.; Anthony P. Shaughnessy, O.S.B.

[B] HIGH SCHOOLS, DIOCESAN AND INTER-PAROCHIAL

PEORIA. *Peoria Notre Dame High School*, 5105 N. Sheridan, 61614. Tel: 309-691-8741; Fax: 309-691-0875. Web: peorianotredame.com. Mr. Charlie Roy, Prin.; Sr. Margaret Schulz, C.S.J., Asst. Prin.; Mr. Tim Speck, Asst. Prin.; Rev. Paul

Carlson; Mrs. Maureen Vadis, Librarian. Tel: 309-691-8741; Fax: 309-691-0875. Priests 2; Sisters 1; Lay Teachers 55; Students 797.

Peoria Notre Dame Scholarship Trust, 5105 N. Sheridan Rd., 61614. Rev. Msgr. William A. Watson, Pres.

Peoria Notre Dame High School Foundation, St. Thomas Parish, 904 E. Lake Ave., Peoria Heights, 61616. Tel: 309-688-3446. Email: s.cicciarelli@pndhs.org. Most Rev. Daniel Robert Jenky, C.S.C., Contact Person.

BLOOMINGTON. *Central Catholic High School*, 1201 Airport Rd., 61704-2534. Tel: 309-661-7000; Fax: 309-661-7010. Email: jallen@blmcchs.org. Web: www.blmcchs.org. Mrs. Joy Allen, Prin.; Rev. Peter A. Pilon; Ann Cox, Librarian. Priests 1; Lay Teachers 29; Students 377.

CHAMPAIGN. *High School of St. Thomas More*, 3901 N. Mattis Ave., 61822. Tel: 217-352-7210; Fax: 217-352-7213. Email: admin@hs-stm.org. Web: www.hs-stm.org. Tim Millage, Prin.; Rev. Robert Lampitt, Chap.; Joy Mortensen, Librarian. Priests 1; Lay Teachers 30; Students 300.

DANVILLE. *Schlarman Academy* 61832. Tel: 217-442-2725; Fax: 217-442-0293. Email: pstitt@schlarman.com. Web: www.schlarman.com. Mr. Robert Rice, Prin.; Rev. Geoffrey Horton, Chap. Lay Teachers 40; Students 195.

OTTAWA. *Marquette Academy of Ottawa, Inc.*, 1000 Paul St., 61350. Tel: 815-433-0125; Fax: 815-433-2632. Email: brick@marquetteacademy.net. Web: marquetteacademy.net. Brooke Rick, Prin.; Rev. Dustin P. Schultz, Chap. Priests 5; Lay Teachers 51; Students 477.

ROCK ISLAND. *Alleman High School* (1949) 1103 40th St., 61201. Tel: 309-786-7793; Fax: 309-786-7834. Email: allemanhs@mchsi.com. Web: www.allemanhighschool.org. Colin Letendre, Prin.; Revs. Daniel J. Mirabelli, C.S.V., Dir. of Devel.; Steven P. Loftus, Chap.; Nancy Morris, Librarian. Sisters 3; Lay Teachers 23; Students 450.

[C] HIGH SCHOOLS, PRIVATE

PERU. *St. Bede Academy* (1890) 24 W. U.S. Hwy. 6, 61354-2903. Tel: 815-223-3140; Fax: 815-223-8580. Web: www.st-bede.com. Mrs. Michelle Mershon, Prin. Benedictine Fathers and Brothers. Benedictine Priests 3; Brothers 2; Lay Teachers 20; Students 298.
Administration: Dr. Ted Struck, Supt.; Bro. Robert Pondant, O.S.B., Registrar; Rev. Ronald L. Margherio, O.S.B., Chap.; Very Rev. Dominic M. Garramone, O.S.B., CFO; Mr. Bernie Moore, Asst. Prin.; Mr. Robert Leclercq, Dir. Guidance; Mrs. Eve Postula, Treas. & Business Mgr.

[D] ELEMENTARY SCHOOLS INTER-PAROCHIAL

EAST MOLINE. *Our Lady of Grace Catholic Academy*, 603 18th Ave., 61244. Tel: 309-755-9771; Fax: 309-755-7407. Email: office@olgca.org. Web: www.olgca.org. Most Rev. Daniel Robert Jenky, C.S.C., Contact Person; Linda Vandervennet, Prin.; Sylvia Standaert, Librarian. Lay Teachers 11.

LA SALLE. *Trinity Catholic Academy*, 650 Fourth St., 61301. Tel: 815-223-8523; Fax: 815-223-7450. Email: trinitycatholic@insightbb.com. Web: www.asd.com. Mr. Dan Schmitt, Prin.; Mrs. Sue Calderon, Librarian. Lay Teachers 14; Students 177.

MOLINE. *Seton Catholic School*, (Grades PreK-8), 1320-16th Ave., 61265. Tel: 309-757-5500; Fax: 309-762-0545. Email: jbarrett@setonschool.com. Web: www.setonschool.com. Mrs. Jane Barrett, Prin. Sisters 1; Lay Teachers 35; Students 567.

ROCK ISLAND. *Jordan Catholic School of Rock Island, Inc.* Directs the Elementary School System for the Rock Island-Milan area, operating facilities at St. Ambrose and St. Pius X. Parishes in Rock Island., 2901-24th St., P.O. Box 3490, 61204-3490. Tel: 309-793-7350; Fax: 309-793-7361. Web: www.jordanschool.com. Michael Daly, Prin.; Gail Bain, Librarian. Lay Teachers 24; Students 406.

Commission on Education for Jordan Catholic School, P.O. Box 3490, 61204-3490. Tel: 309-793-7350; Fax: 309-793-7361.

WEST PEORIA. *Immaculate Conception Pre-Kindergarten*, 2408 W. Heading Ave., 61604-5096. Tel: 309-674-6168; Fax: 309-674-2006. Email: imfosf@yahoo.com. Web: westpeoriasisters.org. Sr. M. Elaine Haertjens, O.S.F., Dir. Sponsored by the Sisters of St. Francis of the Immaculate Conception. Students 9.

[E] CATHOLIC CHARITIES OF THE DIOCESE PEORIA

PEORIA. *Catholic Charities of the Diocese of Peoria*, 419 N.E. Madison Ave., 61603. Tel: 309-636-8000; Fax: 309-674-1664. Email: communications@ccdop.org. Web: www.ccdop.org. Sr. Ana Pia Cordua, S.C.T.J.M., Pres.; Scott Hassett, Interim Exec. Dir. Total Institutional Staff 30; Other Staff 367; Total Assisted 28,305.

Catholic Charities Administration, 419 N.E. Madison Ave., 61603. Tel: 309-636-8000; Fax: 309-674-1664. Web: www.ccdop.org. Adoption, child care, food pantry, foster care, Latino and immigrant outreach, residential care for youth and senior services; abstinence & character building, educational program; counseling; pregnancy planning & family support services; youth, family & community outreach; Intact family services.

Catholic Charities Branch Offices
Catholic Charities Branch Offices:
603 N. Center St., Bloomington, 61701. Tel: 309-829-6307; Fax: 309-829-3254. Web: www.c-cdop.org.
502 S. Morris Ave., Bloomington, 61701. Tel: 309-820-7617; Fax: 309-820-7657. Web: www.c-cdop.org.
1315A Curt Dr., Champaign, 61821. Tel: 217-352-5179; Fax: 217-352-7817. Web: www.ccdop.org.
102 N. Robinson, Danville, 61832. Tel: 217-443-1772; Fax: 217-443-1701. Web: www.ccdop.org.
292 N. Chambers, Galesburg, 61401. Tel: 309-342-1136; Fax: 309-342-1891. Web: www.ccdop.org.
815 2nd St., La Salle, 61301. Tel: 815-223-4007; Fax: 815-224-4550. Web: www.ccdop.org.
2100 W. 5th St., Lincoln, 62656. Tel: 217-732-3771; Fax: 217-735-1738. Web: www.ccdop.org.
123 S. McArthur St., Macomb, 61455-0355. Tel: 309-833-1791; Fax: 309-836-1462. Web: www.c-cdop.org.

Fort Armstrong, 4703 44th St., Ste. 4, Rock Island, 61201. Tel: 309-788-9581. Web: www.ccdop.orgFax: 309-788-9608.
Catholic Charities Outreach Offices:
Streator Outreach Office, 125 S. Vermillion St., Ste. 12, Streator, 61364.
2900 W. Heading Ave., West Peoria, 61604. Tel: 309-636-8000.

[F] CHILDREN'S HOMES

PEORIA. *Catholic Charities Foster Care Program*, 419 N.E. Madison Ave., 61603. Tel: 309-636-8000; Fax: 309-671-1046. Web: www.ccdop.org. Sr. Ana Pia Cordua, S.C.T.J.M., Pres.; Scott Hassett, Interim Exec. Dir.; Greg Westbrook, Program Admin. Clients placed in Foster Care during year 1,180; Total Staff 189.

Guardian Angel Home, 419 N.E. Madison Ave., 61603. Tel: 309-636-7500; Fax: 309-673-3405. Web: www.ccdop.org. Sr. Ana Pia Cordua, S.C.T.J.M., Pres.; Scott Hassett, Interim Exec. Dir. Treatment for Abused and Neglected Youth. Total Staff 30; Capacity 16; Served 27.

[G] DAY CARE CENTERS

PEORIA. *Jesu Children's Enrichment Centers*, 419 N.E. Madison Ave., 61603. Tel: 309-636-7550; Fax: 309-671-8905. Email: jesu@rogys.com. Total Staff 25; Capacity 104; Served 104.

South Side Catholic Child Care Center, 1010 W. Johnson St., 61605. Tel: 309-674-7340; Fax: 309-497-3740. Joyce Jackson, Dir. Children 128; Total Staff 20.

[H] GENERAL HOSPITALS

PEORIA. *Saint Francis Medical Center*, Mailing Address: 1175 St. Francis Ln., East Peoria, 61611. 530 N.E. Glen Oak Ave., 61637-0002. Mr. Keith Steffen, Pres. & CEO; Rev. Msgr. Michael C. Bliss, Dir., Pastoral Care. Sponsored and owned by the Sisters of the Third Order of St. Francis. Sisters of the Third Order of St. Francis 9; Bed Capacity 616; Patients Assisted Annually 970,358; Total Staff 6,206.

OSF Healthcare System (1880) 800 N.E. Glen Oak Ave., 61603-3200. Tel: 309-655-2850; Fax: 309-655-6869. Web: www.osfhealthcare.org. Sponsored and owned by the Sisters of the Third Order of St. Francis. Total Assisted Annually 2,450,400; Total Staff 13,029; Bed Capacity 1,424.

BLOOMINGTON. *OSF St. Joseph Medical Center*, 2200 E. Washington, 61701. Tel: 309-662-3311; Fax: 309-662-7143. Web: osfhealthcare.org. Mr. Kenneth J. Natzke, Pres.& CEO; Rev. Deogratias Kiwanuka, Dir., Pastoral Care. Sponsored and owned by the Sisters of the Third Order of St. Francis. Bed Capacity 155; Total Assisted Annually 369,715; Total Staff 1,123.

DANVILLE. *Provena United Samaritans Medical Center*, 812 N. Logan, 61832. Tel: 217-443-5000; Fax: 217-443-1965. Web: www.provena.org/usmc. Michael L. Brown, Pres. & CEO.
Provena Hospitals. Sisters 2; Capacity 174; Patients Assisted Annually 87,122; Total Staff 701.

GALESBURG. *St. Mary Medical Center*, 3333 N. Seminary St., 61401-1299. Tel: 309-344-3161; Fax: 309-344-9498. Web: osfhealthcare.org. Mailing Address: 1175 St. Francis Ln., East Peoria, 61611. Mr. Richard S. Kowalski, Chief Exec. Officer; Rev. Deus-Dedit B. Byabato, Chap.; Deacon David Steeples, Dir., Pastoral Care. Sisters of the Third Order of St. Francis 2; Patients Assisted Annually 187,482; Capacity 138; Total Staff 659.

The Galesburg St. Mary Medical Center Foundation, 3333 N. Seminary St., 61401.

MONMOUTH. *OSF Holy Family Medical Center*, 1000 W. Harlem Ave., 61462-1099. Tel: 309-734-3141; Fax: 309-734-3029. Mailing Address: 1175 St. Francis Ln., East Peoria, 61611. Patricia Luker, Pres. & CEO; Rev. Dennis E. Spohrer, Chap. Bed Capacity 23; Total Assisted Annually 74,435; Total Staff 218.

PONTIAC. *OSF Saint James-John W. Albrecht Medical Center*, 2500 W. Reynolds, 61764. Tel: 815-842-2828; Fax: 815-842-4912. Web: osfhealthcare.org. David T. Ochs, Pres. & CEO; Deacon George Wagner, Dir., Pastoral Care. Sponsored and owned by the Sisters of the Third Order of St. Francis. Capacity 42; Patients Assisted Annually 172,542; Total Staff 397.

SPRING VALLEY. *St. Margaret's Hospital*, 600 E. First St., 61362. Tel: 815-664-5311; Fax: 815-664-1335. Email: admin@aboutsmh.org. Web: www.aboutsmh.org. Timothy Muntz, Pres. & CEO; Deacon John Murphy, Pastoral Care Dir. Sisters of Mary of the Presentation 1; Bed Capacity 69; Patients Assisted Annually 234,995; Total Staff 685.

STREATOR. *St. Mary's Hospital*, 111 Spring St., 61364. Tel: 815-673-2311; Fax: 815-673-4541. Web: www.stmaryshospital.org. Sr. Laura Northcraft, Pastoral Care Dir. Hospital Sisters Third Order of St. Francis. Sisters 1; Patients Assisted Annually 62,475; Bed Capacity 127; Bassinets 6; Total Staff 545.

URBANA. *Provena Covenant Medical Center*, 1400 W. Park St., 61801. Tel: 217-337-2000; Fax: 217-337-4541. Web: www.provena.org/covenant. Sr. Mary Robert Morton, S.S.C.M., Supr.; Michael L. Brown, Pres. & CEO; Sr. Mary Robert Morton, S.S.C.M., Dir. & Pastoral Min.
Provena Covenant Medical Center. Sisters 6; Capacity 210; Patients Assisted Annually 96,867; Total Staff 889.

[I] SPECIAL HOSPITALS AND SANATORIA

LACON. *St. Joseph Nursing Home*, 401 Ninth St., 61540. Tel: 309-246-2175; Fax: 309-246-3609. Email: lisa.helms@provena.org. Web: www.stjosephnursinghome-lacon.com. Lisa A. Helms, Admin.; Rev. Harold F. Schmitt, Chap. Daughters of St. Francis of Assisi. Bed Capacity 93; Total Assisted 110; Total Staff 137.

PEORIA HEIGHTS. *Saint Clare Home*, 5533 N. Galena Rd., 61614. Tel: 309-682-5428; Fax: 309-682-8478. Web: osfhealthcare.org. Rev. Msgr. Michael C. Bliss, Chap.; Don Dabbs, Interim Admin. Sponsored and owned by the Sisters of the Third Order of St. Francis., Skilled nursing facility. Bed Capacity 98; Total Assisted Annually 202; Total Staff 84.

[J] HOMES FOR AGED

PEORIA. *St. Augustine Manor*, 1301 N.E. Glendale Ave., 61603. Tel: 309-674-7069; Fax: 309-494-6547. Jeri Myers, Residential Mgr. Residents 33; Total Assisted Annually 33; Total Staff 4.

St. Joseph's Home of Peoria dba St. Joseph's Homecare 2408 W. Heading Ave., West Peoria, 61604. Tel: 309-673-7425; Fax: 309-674-2006. Email: sjhcoffice@yahoo.com. Web: osfsisterswpeoria.org. Sr. Mary Barbara Buckley, O.S.F., Admin. Tel: 309-673-7425; Fax: 309-673-7431. Sisters of St. Francis of the Immaculate Conception. Total Assisted Annually 20; Staff 9.

[K] MONASTERIES AND RESIDENCES FOR PRIESTS AND BROTHERS

GEORGETOWN. *La Salette Missionaries, c/o St. Isaac Jogues Parish*, 109 W. Seventh St., 61846-1404. Tel: 217-662-6708. Rev. John Paninski, M.S., c/o St. Isaac Jogues Parish, Georgetown.
La Salette Fathers, Inc. Priests 1; Total Staff 1.

PRINCEVILLE. *Congregation of St. John*, 11223 W. Legion Hall Rd., 61559. Tel: 309-385-1193; Fax: 309-385-1830. Web: www.stjean.com; www.communityofstjohn.com. Revs. Joseph Mary Brown, C.S.J., Prior; Nathan Cromley, C.S.J. Priests 4; Professed Brothers 5; Novices 2; Postulants 2.

[L] CONVENTS AND RESIDENCES FOR SISTERS

PEORIA. *St. Francis Medical Center Convent*, 740 N.E. Glen Oak Ave., 61603. Tel: 309-655-2083; 309-655-4840. Email: sistermaryjohn.harvey@osfhealthcare.org. Web: franciscansisterspeoria.org. Mailing Address: *St. Francis Medical Center*, 1175 St. Francis Ln., East Peoria, 61611. Sr. Mary John Harvey, O.S.F., Supr. The Sisters of the Third Order of St. Francis 8.

Immaculate Conception Convent (1891) 2408 W. Heading Ave., 61604-5096. Tel: 309-674-6168; Fax: 309-674-2006. Email: imfosf@yahoo.com. Web: westpeoriasisters.org. Sr. Paula Vasquez, O.S.F., Pres. Motherhouse of the Sisters of St. Francis of the Immaculate Conception. Sisters 37; Professed Sisters 37.

Missionaries of Charity Convent (1991) 506 Hancock St., 61603. Tel: 309-495-9490. Sr. M. Alokesh, M.C., Supr. Sisters 5; Total Assisted 9,807; Total Volunteer Staff 2.

The Poor Clares Tel: 309-682-3182; Fax: 309-682-3182. Web: www.poorclaresjoliet.org. Sisters 4.

Our Lady of the Angels Convent, 3432 W. Baskin Ridge, 61604. Tel: 309-682-3182; Fax: 309-682-3182.

EAST PEORIA. *Motherhouse, The Sisters of the Third Order of St. Francis*, 1175 Saint Francis Ln., 61611-1299. Tel: 309-699-7215. Web: www.franciscansisterspeoria.org. Sr. Judith Ann Duvall, O.S.F., Major Supr. Sisters in Residence 17; Total Sisters in Community 30.

Mt. Alverno Novitiate, 1175 Saint Francis Ln., 61611-1299. Tel: 309-699-9313. Web: www.franciscansisterspeoria.org. Rev. Msgr. Rick J. Oberch, Chap. Novitiate of The Sisters of the Third Order of St. Francis., Members of the Novitiate are currently residing at St. Francis Medical Center Convent.

HENRY. *Servants of the Pierced Hearts of Jesus and Mary*, P.O. Box 165, 61537. Tel: 309-364-3084; Fax: 309-364-2783. Web: www.piercedhearts.org. Sr. Delia Maria Morales, Supr.

LACON. *St. Joseph Motherhouse and Novitiate* 61540. Tel: 309-246-2175; Fax: 309-246-2708. Email: sradriana@centurytel.net. Web: www.laconfranciscans.org. Sr. Loretta Matas, Provincial Supr. Congregation of the Daughters of St. Francis of Assisi - American Province. Sisters 9; Sisters in Community (Professed) 13.

PEORIA HEIGHTS. *Franciscan Sisters of John the Baptist*, 1209 E. Lake Ave., 61616. Tel: 309-688-3500. Email: fsjbpeoria@yahoo.com. Web: www.sistersofjohnthebaptist.org. Sr. M. Vaclava Ballon, F.S.J.B., Supr. Professed Sisters 8.

PRINCEVILLE. *Sisters of St. John* (1999) 11227 W. Legion Hall Rd., 61559. Tel: 309-385-2550; Fax: 309-385-2550. Sr. Marie Segolene, S.J., Supr. Sisters 18.

ROCK ISLAND. *St. Mary Monastery* (1874) 2200-88th Ave. W., 61201-7649. Tel: 309-283-2100; Fax: 309-283-2200. Email: benedictines@smmsisters.org. Web: www.smmsisters.org. Sr. Phyllis McMurray, O.S.B., Prioress. Benedictine Sisters. Sisters in Community 51.

Benet House Retreat Center Tel: 309-283-2108; Fax: 309-283-2200. Email: retreats@smmsisters.org. Web: www.smmsisters.org. Sr. Charlotte Sonneville, O.S.B., Dir.

WEST PEORIA. *Mother of Peace Home* (1970) 2408 W. Heading Ave., 61604. Tel: 309-673-4657; Fax: 309-674-2006. Email: iccmoph@yahoo.com. Web: osfsisterswpeoria.org. Sr. Mary Ann Mehuys, O.S.F., Admin. Total in Residence 7; Total Staff 16.

[M] NEWMAN CENTERS

PEORIA. *Newman Foundation at Bradley University & Illinois Central College* 1116 W. College Ave., 61606-1728. Tel: 309-674-0208 (Office); Fax: 309-497-3759. Email: info@bradleynewman.org. Web: bradleynewman.org. Rev. Kevin Lucas, Asst. Chap. Total in Residence 1; Total Staff 7; Total Assisted 3,471.

CHAMPAIGN. *St. John's Catholic Newman Center at the University of Illinois, Urbana-Champaign* 604 E. Armory Ave., 61820. Tel: 217-344-1266; Fax: 217-344-4957. Email: info@sjcnc.org. Web: www.sjcnc.org. Rev. Msgrs. Edward J. Duncan, Emeritus (Retired); Gregory K. Ketcham, Dir. & Chap.; Revs. Charles Klamut; Anthony Co. Total in Residence 8; Newman Center Residence 582; Newman Center Staff 120; Total Staff 8.

MACOMB. *St. Francis of Assisi Newman Center* (1945) 1401 W. University Dr., 61455. Tel: 309-837-3988; Fax: 309-837-4179. Web: www.wiucatholic.org. Sr. Janice Keenan, O.S.F., Dir.; Rev. Thomas B. Holloway, Chap.; Sr. Marion Lemon, O.S.F., Campus Min.; Megan Willis, Campus Min.

NORMAL. *John Paul II Catholic Newman Center, St. Robert Bellarmine Chapel* 501 S. Main St., 61761. Tel: 309-452-5046; Fax: 309-452-3845. Email: srsilvia@isucatholic.org. Web: www.isucatholic.org. Sr. Silvia Tarafa, S.C.T.J.M., Dir. Total Staff 3.

ROCK ISLAND. *Augustana College Catholic Campus Ministry* 639-38th St., 61201. Tel: 309-794-7272; Fax: 309-794-7422. Email: marilynring@augustana.edu. Sr. Marilyn Ring, O.S.B. Total Staff 1.

[N] PERSONAL PRELATURES

URBANA. *Opus Dei* Prelature of the Holy Cross and Opus Dei, Lincoln Green Foundation, 715 W. Michigan Ave., 61801. Tel: 217-367-6650; Fax: 217-344-2987. Email: pdowbor@juno.com. Web: www.opusdei.org.

[O] MISCELLANEOUS

PEORIA. *Archbishop Fulton J. Sheen Foundation* (1996) 419 N.E. Madison, 61603. Tel: 309-671-1550; Fax: 309-671-1573. Email: info@sheencause.org. Web: www.archbishopsheencause.org. Rev. Msgr. Stanley L. Deptula, Exec. Dir.; Most Rev. Daniel R. Jenky, C.S.C., Pres.

Family Resource Center, 321 Main St., 61602. Tel: 309-673-1713. Jan Smith, Dir.

Franciscan Spirituality and Resource Center 2408 W. Heading Ave., 61604. Tel: 309-674-6168; Fax: 309-674-2006. Web: westpeoriasisters.org. Sisters Betty Jean Haverback, O.S.F., Contact Person; Diane VandeVoorde, O.S.F., Contact Person.

Jordan Catholic School of Rock Island, Inc., 419 N.E. Madison Ave., 61603. Tel: 309-671-1550. Most Rev. Daniel R. Jenky, C.S.C., Contact Person.

Nazareth House, NFP, 419 N.E. Madison Ave., 61603. Tel: 309-671-1550. Most Rev. Daniel R. Jenky, C.S.C., Contact Person.

Notre Dame High School of Peoria, Inc 61614. Tel: 309-691-8741; Fax: 309-691-0875. Email: c.roy@pndhs.org. Web: peorianotredame.com.

Seton Catholic School of Moline, Inc., 419 N.E. Madison Ave., 61603. Tel: 309-671-1550. Most Rev. Daniel R. Jenky, C.S.C., Contact Person.

SHARE Food Program of Central Illinois, Inc., 419 N.E. Madison Ave., 61603. Tel: 309-671-1550.

STM Boosters, Inc., Mailing Address: 3901 N. Mattis Ave., Champaign, 61822. Tel: 309-671-1550.

St. Vincent De Paul Society, 419 N.E. Madison Ave., 61603. Tel: 309-671-1550; Fax: 309-671-1576. Diocesan Council and Particular Council of Peoria.

ALEDO. *Family of Mary*, 1331 230th St., 61231. Tel: 309-372-4654. Email: triumph@winco.net.

BLOOMINGTON. *Central Catholic High School of Bloomington, Inc.* (1898)Mailing Address: 1201 Airport Rd., 61704. Tel: 309-661-7000; Fax: 309-661-7010. Mrs. Joy Allen, Contact Person, 1201 Airport Rd., 61704. Email: jallen@blmcchs.org. Web: www.blmcchs.org.

CHAMPAIGN. *Provena Home Care*, 1501 Interstate Dr., 61822. Tel: 217-355-4120; Fax: 217-355-4121. Email: Dianna.Moody@provena.org. Web: www.provenahealth.org. Thomas F. Nehring, System Vice Pres., Mission & Leadership Devel.

The High School of St. Thomas More of Champaign, Inc., 3901 N. Mattis, 61822. Tel: 217-352-7210; Fax: 217-352-7213. Email: tmillage@hs-stm.org. Web: www.hs-stm.org.

DANVILLE. *Schlarman Academyof Danville, Inc.* (1946) 61832. Tel: 217-442-2725; Fax: 217-442-0293. Email: brice@schlarman.com. Web: www.schlarman.com.

LA SALLE. *Starved Rock-LaSalle Manor, Inc.*, 1135 S. 10th St., 61301. Tel: 815-223-0557; Fax: 815-223-0559. Mailing Address: 26 W. 171 Roosevelt Rd., Wheaton, 60187-0667. Ms. Susan Dillberg, Contact Person. Housing Units 48; Residents 118; Staff 2.

LACON. *St. Francis of Assisi Fund, NFP*, 507 N. Prairie St., 61540-1152. Tel: 309-246-2175; Fax: 309-246-2708. Web: www.laconfranciscans.org. Sr. Loretta Matas, Pres.

Religious Sisters Aid, NFP, 507 N. Prairie St., 61540-1152. Tel: 309-246-2175; Fax: 309-246-2708. Web: laconfranciscans.org. Sr. Adriana Zdila, Pres.

MOLINE. *The Order of the Legion of Little Souls of the Merciful Heart of Jesus*, 428 39th St., 61265-1641. Tel: 309-797-8491; Fax: 309-643-6270. Email: littlesoul@ureach.com. Web: www.littlesouls.org. Teresa I. Huyten, Dir.; Revs. Michael L. Menner, Diocesan Chap.; John R. Burns, Natl. Chap.

NORMAL. *Homes of Hope, Inc.*, 401 Pine St., Ste. 1, 61761. Tel: 309-862-0607; Fax: 309-452-7131. Email: homesofhope1@frontier.com. Maureen McIntosh, Dir. Total Staff 30; Bed Capacity 17; Total Assisted Annually 17.

ROCK ISLAND. *Alleman High School of Rock Island, Inc.* 61201. Tel: 309-786-7793; Fax: 309-786-7834. Email: allemanhs@mchsi.com. Web: www.allemanhighschool.org.

RELIGIOUS INSTITUTES OF MEN REPRESENTED IN THE DIOCESE

For further details refer to the corresponding bracketed number in the Religious Institutes of Men or Women section.

[]—*Apostles of Jesus - Peoria Community*
[0200]—*Benedictine Monks* (St. Bede Abbey)—O.S.B.
[]—*Congregation of St. John*—C.S.J.
[1320]—*Clerics of St. Viator*—C.S.V.
[0480]—*Conventual Franciscans*—O.F.M.Conv
[0520]—*Franciscan Friars* (Prov. of St. John the Baptist)—O.F.M.
[0300]—*Institute of Charity* (Rome, Italy)—I.C.
[0720]—*The Missionaries of Our Lady of La Salette*—M.S.

RELIGIOUS INSTITUTES OF WOMEN REPRESENTED IN THE DIOCESE

[0230]—*Benedictine Sisters of Pontifical Jurisdiction*—O.S.B.
[0920]—*Congregation of the Daughters of St. Francis of Assisi, (American Prov.)*—D.S.F.
[2100]—*Congregation of the Humility of Mary*—C.H.M.
[1920]—*Congregation of the Sisters of the Holy Cross*—C.S.C.
[1730]—*Congregation of the Sisters of the Third Order of St. Francis, Oldenburg, IN*—O.S.F.
[1710]—*Congregation of the Third Order of St. Francis of Mary Immaculate, Joliet, IL*—O.S.F.
[0760]—*Daughters of Charity of St. Vincent de Paul*—D.C.
[1070-03]—*Dominican Sisters*—O.P.
[1070-10]—*Dominican Sisters*—O.P.
[]—*Franciscan Sisters of John the Baptist*
[1450]—*Franciscan Sisters of the Sacred Heart*—O.S.F.
[1770]—*Hospital Sisters of the Third Order of St. Francis*—O.S.F.
[2575]—*Institute of the Sisters of Mercy of the Americas*—R.S.M.
[2710]—*Missionaries of Charity*—M.C.
[3230]—*Poor Handmaids of Jesus Christ*—P.H.J.C.
[2970]—*School Sisters of Notre Dame*—S.S.N.D.
[1680]—*School Sisters of St. Francis*—O.S.F.
[3520]—*Servants of the Holy Heart of Mary*—S.S.C.M.
[]—*Servants of the Pierced Hearts of Jesus and Mary* (Miami, FL)
[0430]—*Sisters of Charity of the Blessed Virgin Mary*—B.V.M.
[0660]—*Sisters of Christian Charity*—S.C.C.
[2450]—*Sisters of Mary of the Presentation*—S.M.P.
[3360]—*Sisters of Providence of Saint Mary-of-the-Woods, Indiana*—S.P.
[1540]—*Sisters of Saint Francis, Clinton, Iowa*—O.S.F.
[1705]—*The Sisters of St. Francis of Assisi*—O.S.F.
[1580]—*Sisters of St. Francis of the Immaculate Conception*—O.S.F.
[3840]—*Sisters of St. Joseph of Carondelet*—C.S.J.
[]—*Sisters of the Community of St. John*
[]—*Sisters of the Holy Cross*—C.S.C.
[]—*Sisters of the Sacred Heart and of the Poor* (Mexico)
[1820]—*Sisters of the Third Order of St. Francis (East Peoria, Illinois)*—O.S.F.
[]—*Sisters of the Visitation*

CEMETERIES/CEMETERY ASSOCIATIONS

PEORIA. *Catholic Cemetery Association of Peoria, IL*, 7519 N. Allen, 61614. Tel: 309-691-5889; Fax: 309-690-4737. Email: ccapeo@ameritech.net. Web: www.cdop.org/cemetery. Rev. Msgr. Paul E. Showalter, P.A., V.G. Operates St. Mary's Cemetery, St. Joseph's Cemetery and Resurrection Cemetery in Peoria.

BLOOMINGTON. *Bloomington-Normal Catholic Cemetery Association*, 1800 E. Eastland Dr., 61704. Tel: 309-663-1968.

DANVILLE. *Resurrection Catholic Cemetery Association of Danville, IL*, 818 Wendt, 61832. Tel: 217-431-5114; Fax: 217-431-0918.

FARMER CITY. *St. Joseph Cemetery Association of Farmer City, IL*, 612 N. Plum St., 61842. Tel: 309-928-3855; Fax: 309-928-9147. Email: shchurch612@frontier.com.

GALESBURG. *St. Joseph's Cemetery Association of Galesburg, IL*, P.O. Box 539, 61402-0539. Tel: 309-342-6512.

PEKIN. *Catholic Cemetery Association of Pekin, IL*, Mailing Address: 303 S. 7th St., 61554. Tel: 309-347-6109; Fax: 309-347-6959.

ROCK ISLAND. *Calvary Cemetery Association of Rock Island, IL* 61201. Tel: 309-788-6197; Fax: 309-788-6734. Email: info@calvarycemetaryri.com. Web: www.calvarycemetaryri.com.

NECROLOGY

† Boyle, Rev. Msgr. Raymond J., Seneca, IL St. Patrick's—Died Dec. 28, 2011

† Zube, Rev. Msgr. Joseph A., (Retired)—Died April 5, 2011

† Bies, Michael, Odell, IL St. Paul's—Died Dec. 16, 2010

† Dietzen, John J., (Retired)—Died March 27, 2011

† Shea, Thomas, Bloomington, IL St. Patrick Church of Merna—Died 2011

An asterisk (*) denotes an organization that has established tax-exempt status directly with the IRS and is not covered by the USCCB Group Ruling.

The Personal Ordinariate of the Chair of Saint Peter

Reverend Monsignor

JEFFREY N. STEENSON

Ordinary of the Personal Ordinariate of the Chair of St. Peter; ordained priest 2009; appointed the first Ordinary of the Personal Ordinariate of the Chair of Saint Peter on January 1, 2012.

ESTABLISHED JANUARY 1, 2012.

7809 Shadyvilla Ln., Houston, TX 77055. Tel: 713-609-9292.

Web: www.usordinariate.org

Email: office@usordinariate.org

Curial Officials

Chancellor—MARGARET POLL CHALMERS, J.D., J.C.D. *Vicar General*—Very Rev. R. SCOTT HURD.

An asterisk (*) denotes an organization that has established tax-exempt status directly with the IRS and is not covered by the USCCB Group Ruling.

Archdiocese of Philadelphia

(Archidioecesis Philadelphiensis)

His Eminence

CARDINAL JUSTIN RIGALI

Archbishop Emeritus of Philadelphia; ordained a priest April 25, 1961; appointed Archbishop and President of the Pontifical Ecclesiastical Academy June 8, 1985; Episcopal ordination September 14, 1985; appointed Archbishop of St. Louis January 25, 1994; installed March 15, 1994; appointed Archbishop of Philadelphia July 15, 2003; installed October 7, 2003; created Cardinal Priest October 21, 2003; retired July 19, 2011. *Office: P.O. Box 11886, Knoxville, TN 37939.*

Most Reverend

MARTIN N. LOHMULLER, J.C.D., D.D.

Auxiliary Bishop Emeritus of Philadelphia; ordained June 3, 1944; appointed Auxiliary Bishop of Philadelphia and Titular Bishop of Ramsbury February 11, 1970; consecrated April 2, 1970; retired October 11, 1994. *Res.: 1410 Almshouse Rd., Jamison, PA 18929.*

Most Reverend

LOUIS A. DESIMONE, D.D.

Auxiliary Bishop Emeritus of Philadelphia; ordained May 10, 1952; appointed Auxiliary Bishop of Philadelphia and Titular Bishop of Cillio June 27, 1981; consecrated August 12, 1981; retired April 2, 1997. *Res.: St. Justin Martyr Rectory, 1222 Hagysford Rd., Narberth, PA 19072.*

Most Reverend

ROBERT P. MAGINNIS, D.D.

Auxiliary Bishop Emeritus of Philadelphia; ordained May 13, 1961; appointed Auxiliary Bishop of Philadelphia and Titular Bishop of Siminia January 24, 1996; consecrated March 11, 1996; retired June 8, 2010. *Res.: St. Edmond Home for Children, 320 S. Roberts Rd., Rosemont, PA 19010.*

Most Reverend

CHARLES J. CHAPUT, O.F.M. CAP.

Archbishop of Philadelphia; ordained August 29, 1970; appointed Bishop of Rapid City April 11, 1988; Episcopal ordination July 26, 1988; appointed Archbishop of Denver February 18, 1997; installed April 7, 1997; appointed Archbishop of Philadelphia July 19, 2011; installed September 8, 2011. *Office: 222 N. 17th St., Philadelphia, PA 19103-1299.*

AS CHRIST LOVED THE CHURCH

The Chancery: 222 N. 17th St., Philadelphia, PA 19103-1299. Tel: 215-587-4538; Fax: 215-587-3907.

Web: www.archphila.org

Email: chancery@adphila.org

Most Reverend

MICHAEL J. FITZGERALD

Auxiliary Bishop of Philadelphia; ordained May 17, 1980; appointed Auxiliary Bishop of Philadelphia and Titular Bishop of Tamallula June 22, 2010; consecrated August 6, 2010. *Office: 222 N. 17th St., Rm. 530, Philadelphia, PA 19103-1299.* Tel: 215-965-8280; Fax: 215-965-8283.

Most Reverend

JOHN J. MCINTYRE

Auxiliary Bishop of Philadelphia; ordained May 16, 1992; appointed Auxiliary Bishop of Philadelphia and Titular Bishop of Bononia June 8, 2010; consecrated August 6, 2010. *Office: 222 N. 17th St., Rm. 830, Philadelphia, PA 19103-1299.* Tel: 215-965-8190; Fax: 215-965-8193.

Most Reverend

TIMOTHY C. SENIOR

Auxiliary Bishop of Philadelphia; ordained May 18, 1985; appointed Auxiliary Bishop of Philadelphia and Titular Bishop of Floriana June 8, 2009; ordained July 31, 2009. *Office: 222 N. 17th St., Rm. 1200, Philadelphia, PA 19103-1299.* Tel: 215-587-4507; Fax: 215-587-4545.

Most Reverend

DANIEL E. THOMAS

Auxiliary Bishop of Philadelphia; ordained May 18, 1985; appointed Auxiliary Bishop of Philadelphia and Titular Bishop of Bardstown June 8, 2006; ordained July 26, 2006. *Office: 222 N. 17th St., Rm. 930, Philadelphia, PA 19103-1299.* Tel: 215-965-8275; Fax: 215-965-8278.

DIOCESE ESTABLISHED APRIL 8, 1808.

Square Miles 2,202.

Erected an Archdiocese February 12, 1875.

Comprises all the City and County of Philadelphia, and the Counties of Bucks, Chester, Delaware and Montgomery in the State of Pennsylvania.

Patrons of the Diocese: I. Immaculate Conception B.V.M., December 8; II. Saints Peter and Paul, Apostles, June 29. This Archdiocese was solemnly consecrated to the Sacred Heart of Jesus on the Feast of Saint Teresa of Avila, October 15, 1873. On May 23, 1952, the Archdiocese of Philadelphia was solemnly consecrated to the Immaculate Heart of Mary at the Shrine of Our Lady of Fatima, Portugal.

For legal titles of parishes and archdiocesan institutions, consult The Chancery.

STATISTICAL OVERVIEW

Personnel	
Retired Cardinals	1
Archbishops	1
Auxiliary Bishops	4
Retired Bishops	3
Abbots	1
Retired Abbots	1
Priests: Diocesan Active in Diocese	387
Priests: Diocesan Active Outside Diocese	18
Priests: Retired, Sick or Absent	135
Number of Diocesan Priests	540
Religious Priests in Diocese	356
Total Priests in Diocese	896
Extern Priests in Diocese	34
Ordinations:	
Diocesan Priests	3
Religious Priests	2
Transitional Deacons	5
Permanent Deacons	19
Permanent Deacons in Diocese	266
Total Brothers	101
Total Sisters	2,700
Parishes	
Parishes	266
With Resident Pastor:	
Resident Diocesan Priests	227
Resident Religious Priests	26
Without Resident Pastor:	
Administered by Priests	15
Missions	6
Pastoral Centers	17
Closed Parishes	2
Professional Ministry Personnel:	
Brothers	1
Sisters	60
Lay Ministers	164
Welfare	
Catholic Hospitals	6
Total Assisted	778,591
Health Care Centers	1
Total Assisted	150
Homes for the Aged	32
Total Assisted	6,252
Residential Care of Children	2
Total Assisted	419
Day Care Centers	1
Total Assisted	43
Specialized Homes	3
Total Assisted	1,749
Special Centers for Social Services	15
Total Assisted	103,334
Residential Care of Disabled	7
Total Assisted	892
Other Institutions	20
Total Assisted	21,004
Educational	
Seminaries, Diocesan	1
Students from This Diocese	49
Students from Other Diocese	87
Diocesan Students in Other Seminaries	1
Seminaries, Religious	11
Students Religious	30
Total Seminarians	80
Colleges and Universities	11
Total Students	45,922
High Schools, Diocesan and Parish	17
Total Students	16,502
High Schools, Private	16
Total Students	7,537
Elementary Schools, Diocesan and Parish	163
Total Students	51,688
Elementary Schools, Private	18
Total Students	4,611
Non-residential Schools for the Disabled	4
Total Students	206
Catechesis/Religious Education:	
High School Students	1,229
Elementary Students	50,259
Total Students under Catholic Instruction	178,034
Teachers in the Diocese:	
Priests	85
Brothers	31
Sisters	406
Lay Teachers	8,827
Vital Statistics	
Receptions into the Church:	
Infant Baptism Totals	12,725
Minor Baptism Totals	621
Adult Baptism Totals	453

Received into Full Communion....... 373
First Communions................. 11,908
Confirmations.................... 11,083
Marriages:
Catholic........................ 2,847
Interfaith...................... 1,174
Total Marriages................. 4,021
Deaths.......................... 10,629
Total Catholic Population....... 1,464,263
Total Population................ 4,008,994

Former Bishops—Most Revs. MICHAEL FRANCIS EGAN, O.F.M., D.D., cons. Oct. 28, 1810; died July 22, 1814; HENRY CONWELL, D.D., cons. Sept. 24, 1820; died April 22, 1842; FRANCIS PATRICK KENRICK, D.D., cons. June 6, 1830; transferred to Baltimore in 1851; died July 8, 1863; JOHN NEPOMUCENE NEUMANN, C.Ss.R., D.D., cons. March 28, 1852; died Jan. 5, 1860; Canonized June 19, 1977.

Former Archbishops—Most Revs. JAMES FREDERIC WOOD, D.D., cons. coadjutor, cum iure successionis, April 26, 1857; Bishop of Philadelphia, Jan. 5, 1860; appt. Archbishop Feb. 12, 1875; Sacred Pallium, June 17, 1875; died June 20, 1883; PATRICK JOHN RYAN, D.D., cons. April 14, 1872; Bishop of Tricomia and Coadjutor with right of succession to the Archbishop of St. Louis; appt. Titular Archbishop of Salamis, Jan. 6, 1884; Archbishop of Philadelphia, June 8, 1884; died Feb. 11, 1911; EDMOND FRANCIS PRENDERGAST, D.D., cons. Feb. 24, 1897, Titular Bishop of Scillio; Auxiliary Bishop of Philadelphia; Archbishop of Philadelphia, May 27, 1911; died Feb. 26, 1918; His Eminence DENNIS CARDINAL DOUGHERTY, D.D., appt. Bishop of Nueva Segovia, P.I., April 7, 1903; cons. June 14, 1903; transferred to Jaro, P.I., April 19, 1908; transferred to Buffalo Nov. 30, 1915; transferred to Philadelphia April 30, 1918; installed as Archbishop of Philadelphia July 10, 1918; Pallium conferred May 6, 1919; created Cardinal Priest, March 7, 1921; died May 31, 1951; JOHN CARDINAL O'HARA, C.S.C., appt. Military Delegate of Armed Forces and Titular Bishop of Mylasa Dec. 11, 1939; cons. Jan. 15, 1940; transferred to Buffalo March 10, 1945; transferred to Philadelphia Nov. 28, 1951; installed as Archbishop of Philadelphia Jan. 9, 1952; Pallium conferred Jan. 12, 1953; created Cardinal Priest Dec. 15, 1958; died Aug. 28, 1960; JOHN CARDINAL KROL, D.D., J.C.D., ord. Feb. 20, 1937; appt. Titular Bishop of Cadi and Auxiliary Bishop of Cleveland July 11, 1953; cons. Sept. 2, 1953; appt. Archbishop of Philadelphia Feb. 11, 1961; created Cardinal Priest June 26, 1967; retired Feb. 11, 1988; died March 3, 1996; ANTHONY CARDINAL BEVILACQUA, D.D., M.A., J.C.D., J.D., ord. June 11, 1949; appt. Auxiliary Bishop of Brooklyn Oct. 7, 1980; cons. Nov. 24, 1980; appt. Bishop of Pittsburgh Oct. 7, 1983; installed Dec. 12, 1983; installed Archbishop of Philadelphia Feb. 11, 1988; Created Cardinal Priest June 28, 1991; retired July 15, 2003; died Jan. 31, 2012.; CARDINAL JUSTIN RIGALI (Retired), ord. a priest April 25, 1961; appt. Archbishop and President of the Pontifical Ecclesiastical Academy June 8, 1985; episcopal ord. Sept. 14, 1985; appt. Archbishop of St. Louis Jan. 25, 1994; installed March 15, 1994; appt. Archbishop of Philadelphia July 15, 2003; installed Oct. 7, 2003; Created Cardinal Priest Oct. 21, 2003; retired July 19, 2011.

Vicars General—Most Revs. DANIEL E. THOMAS; TIMOTHY C. SENIOR; JOHN J. MCINTYRE; MICHAEL J. FITZGERALD.

Office of the Archbishop—Most Rev. CHARLES J. CHAPUT, O.F.M.Cap., Archbishop of Philadelphia; FRANCIS X. MAIER, Sr. Advisor; Rev. BRIAN P. HENNESSY, J.C.L., M.A., M.Div., Sec. to the Archbishop, 222 N. 17th St., Philadelphia, 19103-1299. Tel: 215-587-3800.

Office of the Moderator of the Curia—Most Rev. TIMOTHY C. SENIOR. Tel: 215-587-4507; Fax: 215-587-4545; Rev. Msgr. ARTHUR E. RODGERS, Ph.D., Coord. Archdiocesan Planning Initiatives. Tel: 215-587-5663.

Deans—Revs. ROLAND D. SLOBOGIN, M.Div., Deanery 1 - Eastern Delaware County, Saint Charles Borromeo Rectory, 3422 Dennison Ave., Drexel Hill, 19026. Tel: 610-623-3800; 610-623-3801; ROBERT C. VOGAN, M.Div., Deanery 2 - Western Delaware County, Saint Joseph Rectory, 3255 Concord Rd., Aston, 19014-1905. Tel: 610-497-3340; Rev. Msgr. DANIEL J. KUTYS, M.Div., Deanery 3 - Western Chester County, Ss. Peter and Paul Rectory, 1325 Boot Rd., West Chester, 19380. Tel: 610-692-2216; 610-692-2911; Rev. JOSEPH C. DIECKHAUS, J.C.L., M.Div., Deanery 4 - Northern Chester County, Ss. Philip and James Rectory, 107 N. Ship Rd., Exton, 19341. Tel: 610-363-6536; Rev. Msgrs. JOSEPH J. NICOLO, M.Div., Deanery 5 - Western Montgomery County, Saint Helena Rectory, 1489 DeKalb Pike, Blue Bell, 19422. Tel: 610-275-7711; MICHAEL T. MCCULKEN, M.Div., Deanery 6 - Main Line, Bridgeport and Roxborough, Saint Mathias Rectory, 128 Bryn Mawr Ave., Bala Cynwyd, 19004-3099. Tel: 610-664-0207; STEPHEN P. MCHENRY, Ph.D., M.A., M.Div., Deanery 7 - Eastern Montgomery County, Northwest Philadelphia, Saint Anthony of Padua Rectory, 259 Forrest Ave., Ambler, 19002-5999. Tel: 215-646-4742; 215-646-4743; Revs. WILLIAM C. KAUFMAN, M.Div., Deanery 8 - South Philadelphia, Northern Liberties, Saint Richard Rectory, 3010 S. 18th St., Philadelphia, 19145. Tel: 215-468-4777; 215-468-4778; JOHN F. BABOWITCH, M.Div., Deanery 9 - West Philadelphia, Center City, Saint Barnabas Rectory, 6300 Buist Ave., Philadelphia, 19142-3098. Tel: 215-726-1119; 215-726-1120; Rev. Msgr. JAMES D. BEISEL, M.A., M.Div., Deanery 10 - Central/Upper Bucks County, Saint Robert Ballarmine Rectory, 856 Euclid Ave., Warrington, 18976. Tel: 215-343-0315; 215-343-0592; Revs. THOMAS J. DUNLEAVY, M.Div., Deanery 11 - Upper Northeast Philadelphia/Lower Bucks County, Saint Anselm Rectory, 12670 Dunks Ferry Rd., Philadelphia, 19154. Tel: 215-637-3525; THOMAS M. HIGGINS, M.Div., Deanery 12 - Lower Northeast Philadelphia, Holy Innocents Rectory, 1337 E. Hunting Park Ave., Philadelphia, 19124-4938. Tel: 215-743-2600.

Office for Consecrated Life—

Vicar for Consecrated Life—Rev. Msgr. JOSEPH J. ANDERLONIS, S.T.D., Office: 222 N. 17th St., Philadelphia, 19103-1299. Tel: 215-587-3795; Fax: 215-587-3790.

The Chancery—Rev. Msgr. GERARD C. MESURE, J.D., J.C.D., M.A., Chancellor; Revs. SEAN P. BRANSFIELD, M.Div., M.A., J.C.L.; JAMES M. OLIVER, J.C.D., M.A., M.Div., Vice Chancellor, 222 N. 17th St., Philadelphia, 19103-1299. Tel: 215-587-4538; Fax: 215-587-3907.

Archivist—JOSEPH J. CASINO, M.A., M.S.L.S., Office, 100 E. Wynnewood Rd., Wynnewood, 19096-3001. Tel: 610-667-2125; Fax: 610-667-2730.

Metropolitan Tribunal—222 N. 17th St., Philadelphia, 19103-1299. Tel: 215-587-3750; Fax: 215-587-0508. Communications should be sent to the above address.

Judicial Vicar—Rev. Msgr. PAUL A. DIGIROLAMO, J.C.D., M.A., M.Div.

Assistant Judicial Vicars—Revs. SEAN P. BRANSFIELD, M.Div., M.A., J.C.L.; EDUARDO G. MONTERO, J.C.L.

Archdiocesan Judges—Revs. JOSEPH C. DIECKHAUS, J.C.L., M.Div.; STEVEN J. HARRIS, J.C.D.; Rev. Msgr. SAMUEL E. SHOEMAKER, J.C.D.; Sr. CARLOTTA BARTONE, S.H.C.J., J.C.L.

Promoters of Justice—Rev. Msgr. GERARD C. MESURE, J.D., J.C.D., M.A.; Rev. JAMES M. OLIVER, J.C.D., M.A., M.Div.

Defenders of the Bond—Rev. Msgrs. JOHN P. BOLAND, M.A. (Retired); JAMES J. GRAHAM, J.C.D., M.Div.; GERARD C. MESURE, J.D., J.C.D., M.A.; Rev. JAMES M. OLIVER, J.C.D., M.A., M.Div.; Rev. Msgr. ROBERT J. POWELL, D.M.A, M.A., M.Div.; Revs. JOHN D. REARDON, M.Div.; VINCENT F. WELSH, J.C.L., M.A.

Approved Advocates—Revs. JOSEPH W. BONGARD, M.A., M.Div.; JOSEPH E. HOWARTH, M.A.L.S.; Rev. Msgrs. KENNETH P. MCATEER, M.Div.; JOSEPH J. NICOLO, M.Div.; Sr. CAROL MOCKUS, C.S.F.N.; Deacons JOHN M. BETZAL; EDWARD A. KONARSKI.

Notary—ADAM A. DICKERSON, M.A.

Office for General Counsel—TIMOTHY R. COYNE ESQ., Gen. Counsel. Tel: 215-587-0511; Fax: 215-587-0512.

Office for Information Technology—FRANZ FRUEHWALD, M.B.A., Chief Information Officer. Tel: 215-854-7067; Fax: 215-854-7079.

Office for Audit Services—Mr. MARC A. FISHER, CPA, Dir. Tel: 215-587-3995; Fax: 215-587-2430.

Department for Media Affairs—

Office for Communications—DONNA FARRELL, Dir. Tel: 215-587-3747; Fax: 215-587-3875.

Newspaper - "The Catholic Standard and Times", "PHAITH" Magazine—MATTHEW GAMBINO, Dir. & Gen. Mgr. Tel: 215-587-3698; Fax: 215-587-3979.

Office for Financial Services—

All addresses are 222 N. 17th St., Philadelphia, PA 19103.

Acting Chief Financial Officer Pro Tem—JOSEPH J. SWEENEY JR., M.B.A., N.H.A. Tel: 215-587-3943.

Assistant Controller—JOSEPH MCCORMICK. Tel: 215-587-3898.

Educational Financial Services—DAVID J. MAGEE, M.B.A., Ed.D., Dir. Tel: 215-587-3755; Fax: 215-587-3525.

Investment Services—Mr. ROBERT J. GUNN, Dir. Tel: 215-587-3969; Fax: 215-965-1711.

Office for Insurance Services—CHARLES J. DEBEVEC, C.P.C.U., Dir. Tel: 215-587-3644; Fax: 215-587-2498.

Office for Research and Planning—ROBERT J. MILLER, Ed.D., Dir. Tel: 215-587-3545; Fax: 215-587-3817.

Office for Stewardship and Development—Rev. Msgr. FRANCIS W. BEACH, M.Div., Archbishop's Delegate & Exec. Dir.; SHANNON JORDAN, Assoc. Dir. Tel: 215-587-5650; Fax: 215-587-2442. Email: develop@adphila.org.

Secretariat for Catholic Education

All addresses are: 222 N. 17th St., Philadelphia, PA 19103-1299 unless otherwise indicated.

Secretary for Catholic Education—Dr. RICHARD MCCARRON. Tel: 215-587-3700; Fax: 215-587-5644.

Office of Catholic Education—Dr. RICHARD MCCARRON, Sec. for Catholic Educ.; Mr. JASON BUDD, Deputy Sec. Catholic Educ.; Ms. MARY E. ROCHFORD, Supt. Schools; Ms. DEBORAH BACHOR, Asst. Supt. Elementary Educational Svcs.; Dr. THOMAS F. ROONEY JR., Ed.D., Asst. Supt., Secondary Schools. Directors: Mrs. EILEEN WILSON, Dir. Elementary Educational Svcs.; Sr. EDWARD WILLIAM QUINN, I.H.M., Dir. Elementary Curriculum & Instruction; Dr. CAROL CARY, Dir. Secondary Curriculum & Instruction; PETER BALZANO, Dir. Secondary School Svcs.; Sr. MARIE ESTHER HART, I.H.M., Coord. Science Initiatives; Mrs. REGINA DIGUILIO, Exec. Dir. for Institutional Advancement; Mrs. JACQUELINE COCCIA, Dir. Elementary Educational Svcs.; Mrs. THERESA RYAN-SZOTT, Dir. Secondary Personnel; JOSEPH KONECKI, Dir. Technology K-12.

Office for Catechetical Formation—Rev. JOHN J. AMES, S.T.D., M.A., M.Div., Deputy Sec. Catechetical Formation; Mrs. ANN MENNA, Dir. Parish Elementary Rel. Educ.; Ms. ELIZABETH A. RIORDAN, Dir. Secondary Rel. Educ. & Staff Devel.

Office for Youth and Young Adults—Mr. JOHN J. TAGUE, M.A., M.B.A., Dir.; Ms. MARIA C. RICHARDSON, Asst. to Dir., 222 N. 17th St., Philadelphia, 19103-1299. Tel: 215-965-4637; Fax: 215-965-4629.

Parish Youth and Young Adult Ministry—Program and Region Coordinators: Mr. DANIEL R. FINOCCHIO, Region III; Ms. SUSAN C. MATOUR, Region I; Ms. AMANDA G. COWLEY, Regions II, IV.

Catholic Scouting—Ms. PATRICIA ANTONACCI, Co-ord.

Archdiocesan Boy Scouts—Rev. Msgr. JOHN B. WENDRYCHOWICZ, Chap.

Community Service Corps—KATHLEEN PFEFFER, Coord.

Athletic Ministry—Ms. CAROL BEAUSOLEIL, Coord.

Secretariat for Catholic Human Services

All addresses are: 222 N. 17th St., Philadelphia, PA 19103. Tel: 215-587-3900, unless otherwise indicated.

Secretary for Catholic Human Services—JOSEPH J. SWEENEY JR., M.B.A., N.H.A. Tel: 215-587-3908; GARY MILLER, CFO. Tel: 215-587-3892; CARL F. SHEPPARD, Chief Human Resources Officer. Tel: 609-661-3080; FRANZ FRUEHWALD, M.B.A., Chief Information Officer. Tel: 215-965-1737; EDWARD J. LIS, M.A., M.Div., Dir. Catholic Mission Integration. Tel: 215-965-1710; ANNE H. AYELLA, Dir. Catholic Relief Svcs., 111 S. 38th St., Philadelphia, 19104. Tel: 267-262-8901; SUZANNE O'GRADY-LAURITO, Coord. Catholic Campaign for Human Devel. Tel: 215-790-9536.

Catholic Charities of the Archdiocese of Philadelphia—JOSEPH J. SWEENEY JR., M.B.A., N.H.A., Sec. Catholic Human Svcs. Tel: 215-587-3908; JAMES AMATO, L.S.W., Deputy Sec. Catholic Social Svcs. Tel: 215-587-3754; GARY MILLER, CFO. Tel: 215-587-3892; AMY STONER, L.S.W., A.C.S.W., Dir. Community-Based Prevention Svcs. Tel: 215-587-3590; KATHLEEN EMERY, M.S.W., M.Ed., Dir. Community-Based & Specialized Svcs. Tel: 215-587-3906; DEBORAH WAGNER, L.S.W., Dir. Housing & Homeless Svcs. Tel: 215-854-7080; JOSEPH LAVORITANO, Dir., St. Gabriel's System, 227 N. 18th St., Philadelphia, 19103. Tel: 215-665-8777; MARK E. FITZGERALD, M.S.W., N.H.A., Dir. Developmental Progs. Div., Administrative Office, 1797 S. Sproul Rd., Springfield, 19064. Tel: 484-475-2469.

Catholic Health Care Services—JOSEPH J. SWEENEY JR., M.B.A., N.H.A., Sec. Catholic Human Svcs. & Diocesan Coord. for Health Care Affairs. Tel: 215-587-3908; STUART K. SKINNER, R.N., M.B.A., N.H.A., Deputy Sec. & CEO Catholic Health Care Svcs. and Dir. Facility-Based Svcs. Tel: 215-587-2436; 215-587-3663; MICHAEL CZEKNER, M.B.A., C.M.A., CFO. Tel: 215-242-2062; MARGARET M. FULLMER, M.H.A., N.H.A., Dir. Mktg. Svcs. Tel: 215-587-3663; KELLY WRIGHT, M.S.W., N.H.A., Dir. Prog. Devel. & Administrative Support. Tel: 215-587-2487; JUDITH P. HORVATH, R.N., M.B.A., N.H.A., Dir. Clinical Oper. Tel: 215-587-3663; JOHN M. WAGNER, Dir. Project Devel. Tel: 215-587-3589; JOSEPH J. SWEENEY JR., M.B.A., N.H.A., Diocesan Coord. for Health Care Affairs. Tel: 215-587-3908.

Information Technology Services (ITS) Division—FRANZ FRUEHWALD, M.B.A., CIO. Tel: 215-965-1737.

Information Systems—MICHAEL LEIDEN, Dir. Tel: 215-854-7061.

Information Technology—M. LEE MYERS, Dir. Tel: 267-663-0031.

Nutritional Development Services—111 S. 38th St., Philadelphia, 19104. Tel: 267-262-8905. LORRAINE M. KNIGHT, M.Ed., Dir.

Office of Community Development—JOHN M. WAGNER, Dir. Tel: 215-587-3589.

For detailed information please see Catholic Social Services of the Archdiocese of Philadelphia in the Institution Section (J).

Secretariat For Evangelization

All addresses are: 222 N. 17th St., Philadelphia, PA 19103-1299. Fax: 215-587-3561, unless otherwise indicated.

Secretariat for Evangelization—Most Rev. JOHN J. MCINTYRE, Auxiliary Bishop of Philadelphia. Tel: 215-965-8190; Fax: 215-965-8193.

Office of the Vicar for Cultural Ministries—

Vicar for Cultural Ministries—Rev. BRUCE LEWANDOWSKI, C.Ss.R. Tel: 215-667-2822.

Office for Black Catholics—BILL BRADLEY, Dir. Tel: 215-587-3535.

Office for Hispanic Catholics—VACANT, Dir. Tel: 215-667-2820; BLANCA HERRERA, Asst. Dir. Tel: 215-667-2824; Fax: 215-667-2825.

Catholic Institute for Evangelization—Sr. RUTH BOLARTE, I.H.M., Dir. Tel: 215-324-8291; Fax: 215-324-8730.

Office for Pastoral Care for Migrants and Refugees—JAMES KING, B.A., M.A., Dir. Tel: 215-587-3540.

African Apostolate—Rev. KIERAN O. UDEZE, Chap./Coord., Cathedral Basilica of SS. Peter & Paul, 18th St. & the Benjamin Franklin Pkwy., Philadelphia, 19103. Tel: 215-561-1313.

Apostleship of the Sea—Rev. DOMINIC ISAAC, Chap./Coord., Apostleship of the Sea, 475 N. Fifth St., Philadelphia, 19123. Tel: 215-922-2562.

Chinese Apostolate—Rev. THOMAS BETZ, O.F.M.Cap., Chap./Coord. Tel: 215-922-0999.

Filipino Apostolate—Rev. EFREN V. ESMILLA, M.Div., Chap., Our Lady of Hope Rectory, 5200 N. Broad St., Philadelphia, 19141. Tel: 215-329-8100.

French Apostolate— Contact: Office for Pastoral Care for Migrants and Refugees. Tel: 215-587-3540.

Haitian Apostolate—Rev. ALBERT GARDY VILLARSON, O.M.I., Chap./Coord., Incarnation of Our Lord Rectory, 5105 N. 5th St., Philadelphia, 19120. Tel: 215-329-2320.

Indian Apostolate, Syro Malankara Rite—Rev. CHANLIS CHACKO, Chap./Coord., St. Jude Syro-Malankara Catholic Church, 244-258 W. Cheltenham Ave., Philadelphia, 19126. Tel: 215-673-8127.

Indian Apostolate-Knanayan Comm. Syro-Malabar Rite—Revs. MATHEW MANAKKATT, Chap./Coord. Tel: 215-947-3500; JOHN P. MELEPURAM, Pastor, St. Thomas Syro-Malabar Catholic Church, 608 Welsh Rd., Philadelphia, 19115. Tel: 215-808-4052.

Indian Apostolate, Latin Rite—Rev. RAJU B. SELVARAJ PILLA, Chap./Coord., Our Lady of Grace Rectory, 225 Bellevue Ave., Penndel, 19047. Tel: 215-757-7700.

Indonesian Apostolate— Contact Office for Pastoral Care for Migrants and Refugees. Tel: 215-587-3540.

Japanese Apostolate— Contact Office for Pastoral Care for Migrants and Refugees. Tel: 215-587-3540.

Korean Apostolate—Revs. JOHN SUNG WOO PARK, Holy Angels, 7000 Old York Rd., Philadelphia, 19126. Tel: 215-548-5535; SIMON HYUNG-MIN HA, Chap./Coord., Holy Cross, Bishop & Springfield Rds., Springfield, 19064. Tel: 610-626-3321.

Pakistani Apostolate—Rev. DOMINIC ISAAC, Chap./Coord., St. William, Rising Sun Ave. & Devereaux St., Philadelphia, 19111. Tel: 215-745-1389.

Portuguese and Brazilian Apostolates—Rev. GELSO DADATT, St. Martin of Tours, 5450 Roosevelt Blvd., Philadelphia, 19124. Tel: 215-533-0593.

Vietnamese Apostolate—Rev. Msgr. JOSEPH T. TRINH, Chap./Coord., St. Helena Rectory, 6161 N. 5th St., Philadelphia, 19120. Tel: 215-424-1300.

Office for Ecumenical and Interreligious Affairs—Rev. Msgr. MICHAEL J. CARROLL, M.A., Dir. (Retired); Sr. JUDITH KREIPE, I.H.M., Asst. Dir. Tel: 215-587-3624.

Office for Formation of the Laity—MARYANNE HARRINGTON, Dir. Tel: 215-587-0500; VACANT, Asst. Dir.

Family Life Office—DOMINIC LOMBARDI, M.A., S.T.L., Dir. Tel: 215-587-5639; ANN HANINCIK, M.T.S., Asst. Dir. Marriage Preparation. Tel: 215-587-3639.

Prison Ministry Program—VACANT, Chap.; LAURA FORD, Admin. Tel: 215-331-3640.

Respect Life Office—STEVEN BOZZA, M.A., Dir. Tel: 215-587-5661. Web: www.archdiocese-phl.org/evangelization/resplife/resplife.htm.

AIDS Ministry Program—STEVEN BOZZA, M.A., Dir. Tel: 215-587-5661.

Department for Pastoral Care for Persons with Disabilities—Sr. KATHLEEN SCHIPANI, I.H.M., M.Ed., M.A., Admin. Tel: 215-587-3913; 866-892-6063 (VP); 215-587-0510 (TDD).

Deaf Apostolate—Sr. KATHLEEN SCHIPANI, I.H.M., M.Ed., M.A., Admin. Tel: 215-587-3913 (TDD); 866-892-6063 (VP); Rev. ANTHONY T. RUSSO, C.Ss.R., Coord., Visitation B.V.M. Tel: 215-423-9547 (TDD); 866-970-0840 (VP); 215-634-1133 (Voice); Fax: 215-634-6662. Web: www.archphila.org/evangelization/resplife/resplife.htm. For information on Mass schedule call office or visit our web site.

Department for Pro-Life Activities—STEVEN BOZZA, M.A., Dir. Tel: 215-587-5661.

Pontifical Mission Society for the Propagation of the Faith—Rev. Msgr. JAMES T. MCDONOUGH, M.S.W., L.L.D., Dir. (Retired); MICHELE MEIERS, Asst. Dir. Tel: 215-587-3944.

Pontifical Mission Society of St. Peter Apostle—Rev. Msgr. JAMES T. MCDONOUGH, M.S.W., L.L.D., Dir. (Retired). Tel: 215-587-3944.

Pontifical Mission Society - Holy Childhood Association—MAUREEN RILLING, Mission Coord. Tel: 215-587-3945.

Pontifical Missionary Union—Rev. Msgr. JAMES T. MCDONOUGH, M.S.W., L.L.D., Dir. (Retired). Tel: 215-587-3944.

Office for Divine Worship—Rev. G. DENNIS GILL, M.Div., S.L.L., Dir. Tel: 215-587-3537; VACANT, Asst. Dir.

Office for Liturgical Music—Dr. JOHN ROMERI, M.M., ChM, AAGO, Ph.D., Dir. Tel: 215-587-3696.

Secretariat For Clergy

All addresses are: 222 N. 17th St., Philadelphia, PA 19103-1299 unless otherwise indicated.

Office for Clergy—Rev. Msgr. DANIEL J. SULLIVAN, M.Div.; Rev. JAMES M. OLIVER, J.C.D., M.A., M.Div., Asst. Vicar for Clergy.

Department Retired Clergy—Rev. Msgr. WILLIAM A. DOMBROW, M.Div.

Permanent Diaconate Department—Rev. Msgr. GREGORY J. PARLANTE, M.A., M.Div., Assoc. to Vicar for Clergy; Deacon JAMES T. OWENS, Dir. Associates to the Administrator: Deacons ERNEST W. ANGIOLILLO; MARK H. DILLON; CHARLES G. LEWIS; PAUL J. MCBLAIN.

St. Charles Borromeo Seminary—Rev. SHAUN L. MAHONEY, S.T.D., M.Div., Rector, 100 E. Wynnewood Rd., Wynnewood, 19096. Tel: 610-667-3394.

Vocation Office for Diocesan Priesthood—Rev. KEVIN J. GALLAGHER, M.Div., St. Charles Borromeo Seminary, 100 E. Wynnewood Rd., Wynnewood, 19096. Tel: 610-667-5778.

Secretariat For Temporal Services

All addresses are: 222 N. 17th St., Philadelphia, PA 19103-1299 unless otherwise indicated.

Temporal Services—Mr. JAMES J. BOCK JR., Sec. Tel: 215-587-3959; Fax: 215-965-1711; Mrs. MARLENE M. LOGLISCI, M.B.A., S.P.H.R., C.E.L.S., Deputy Sec. & Dir. Tel: 215-587-3910; Fax: 215-587-3572.

Catholic Cemeteries Office—Mr. ROBERT WHOMSLEY, Dir. Tel: 215-895-3450; Fax: 215-895-3458.

Human Resources Office—Mrs. MARLENE M. LOGLISCI, M.B.A., S.P.H.R., C.E.L.S., Deputy Sec. & Dir. Tel: 215-587-3910; Fax: 215-587-3572.

Office for General Services—Mr. GEORGE G. SHARRETTS, Dir. Tel: 215-587-3633; Fax: 215-965-7553.

Office for Special Projects/Closures—Tel: 215-587-3519 (Special Projects); 215-587-3996 (closures); Fax: 215-587-2481.

Office of Property Services—Tel: 215-587-3560; Fax: 215-587-0599.

Archdiocesan Offices, Boards, Commissions and Committees

All addresses are: 222 N. 17th St., Philadelphia, PA 19103-1299 unless otherwise indicated.

Board of Trustees of Lay Employees Retirement Plan—Most Rev. CHARLES J. CHAPUT, O.F.M.Cap., Chm.; Mr. JAMES J. BOCK JR., Vice Chm.

Diocesan Priests' Compensation and Benefits Committee—Rev. Msgr. DANIEL J. SULLIVAN, M.Div., Chm.; Rev. EDWARD H. BELL, M.Div.; Rev. Msgr. PAUL A. DIGIROLAMO, J.C.D., M.A., M.Div.; Revs. WILLIAM G. DONOVAN, M.Div., Ph.L., Ph.D.; WILLIAM B. DOONER, M.Div.; TIMOTHY M. JUDGE, M.Div.; WILLIAM C. KAUFMAN, M.Div.; Rev. Msgr. DANIEL J. KUTYS, M.Div.; Mr. ROBERT J. SIMS.

Building Committee—Rev. ROBERT C. VOGAN, M.Div., Chm., (Drawings of building plans are reviewed by this committee).

Censores Librorum—Revs. J. BRIAN BRANSFIELD, M.Div., M.A., S.T.L.; ROBERT A. PESARCHICK, M.A., S.T.L., S.T.D.; Rev. Msgr. JOSEPH G. PRIOR, M.Div., M.A., S.S.L., S.T.D.; Rev. JOSEPH T. SHENOSKY, S.T.D., M.A., M.Div.

College of Consultors—Most Revs. DANIEL E. THOMAS; TIMOTHY C. SENIOR; JOHN J. MCINTYRE; MICHAEL J. FITZGERALD; Rev. Msgrs. GERARD C. MESURE, J.D., J.C.D., M.A., Consultant; DANIEL J. SULLIVAN, M.Div.; Rev. JOHN F. BABOWITCH, M.Div.; Rev. Msgr. JAMES D. BEISEL, M.A., M.Div.; Rev. THOMAS J. DUNLEAVY, M.Div.; Rev. Msgr. DANIEL J. KUTYS, M.Div.; Rev. SHAUN L. MAHONEY, S.T.D., M.Div.; Rev. Msgr. MICHAEL T. MCCULKEN, M.Div.

Council of Priests—Most Rev. CHARLES J. CHAPUT, O.F.M.Cap. Ex Officio: Most Revs. DANIEL E. THOMAS; TIMOTHY C. SENIOR; JOHN J. MCINTYRE; MICHAEL J. FITZGERALD; Rev. Msgr. DANIEL J. SULLIVAN, M.Div. Deans: Revs. ROLAND D. SLOBOGIN, M.Div., Deanery 1; ROBERT C. VOGAN, M.Div., Deanery 2; Rev. Msgr. DANIEL J. KUTYS, M.Div., Deanery 3; Rev. JOSEPH C. DIECKHAUS, J.C.L., M.Div., Deanery 4; Rev. Msgrs. JOSEPH J. NICOLO, M.Div., Deanery 5; MICHAEL T. MCCULKEN, M.Div., Deanery 6; STEPHEN P. MCHENRY, Ph.D., M.A., M.Div., Deanery 7; Revs. WILLIAM C. KAUFMAN, M.Div., Deanery 8; JOHN F. BABOWITCH, M.Div., Deanery 9; Rev. Msgr. JAMES D. BEISEL, M.A., M.Div., Deanery 10; Revs. THOMAS J. DUNLEAVY, M.Div., Deanery 11; THOMAS M. HIGGINS, M.Div., Deanery 12. By Appointment: Rev. SHAUN L. MAHONEY, S.T.D., M.Div. By Election: Revs. CHRISTOPHER R. COOKE, M.A., M.Div.; THOMAS R. BETZ, O.F.M.Cap.; Rev. Msgr. JOSEPH W. MURRAY, M.A. (Retired); Rev. BRUCE LEWANDOWSKI, C.Ss.R. Consultant: Rev. Msgr. GERARD C. MESURE, J.D., J.C.D., M.A.

Educational Fund— Office of the Chief Financial Officer. Tel: 215-587-3943.

Information Line, Archdiocesan—Tel: 215-587-3600.

Interparochial Cooperation, Commission for—Rev. THOMAS M. HIGGINS, M.Div., Chm., Holy Innocents Rectory, 1337 E. Hunting Park Ave., Philadelphia, 19124-4938. Tel: 215-743-2600.

Legion of Mary—Rev. FRANCIS G. LENDACKY, St. Agnes-St. John Nepomucane Rectory, 319 Brown St., Philadelphia, 19123-2228. Tel: 215-627-0340.

Parish Sites and Boundaries, Commission for—Rev. Msgr. JAMES D. BEISEL, M.A., M.Div., Chm.

Pastors Review Board—Rev. JOHN F. BABOWITCH, M.Div.; Rev. Msgr. JAMES D. BEISEL, M.A., M.Div.; Rev. THOMAS J. DUNLEAVY, M.Div.; Rev. Msgrs. DANIEL J. KUTYS, M.Div.; MICHAEL T. MCCULKEN, M.Div.

Pennsylvania Catholic Conference— (Harrisburg) Board of Governors: Most Rev. CHARLES J. CHAPUT, O.F.M.Cap. Administrative Board: Most Rev. TIMOTHY C. SENIOR. Department on Communications: DONNA FARRELL; MATTHEW GAMBINO. Education Department: Dr. RICHARD MCCARRON; Ms. MARY E. ROCHFORD. Social Concerns: JOSEPH J. SWEENEY JR., M.B.A., N.H.A.

Office for Child and Youth Protection—LESLIE J. DAVILA, M.S., Dir. Tel: 215-587-3880; Fax: 215-587-2466.

CLERGY, PARISHES, MISSIONS AND PAROCHIAL SCHOOLS

CITY OF PHILADELPHIA

(PHILADELPHIA COUNTY)

1—CATHEDRAL BASILICA OF SS. PETER AND PAUL (1846) Rev. Msgr. Arthur E. Rodgers; Revs. Edward P. Burke; Charles J. Kennedy; Deacons Epifanio DeJesus; Joseph A. Micucci. In Res., Revs. G. Dennis Gill; Kieran O. Udeze (Nigeria).
Res.: 1723 Race St., 19103. Tel: 215-561-1313; 215-561-1314; Fax: 215-561-1580. Web: www.cathedralphila.org.
Chapel—Our Lady of the Miraculous Medal 1903 Spring Garden St., 19130.

2—ST. ADALBERT (1904), (Polish), Rev. Thaddeus Gorka.
Res.: 2645 E. Allegheny Ave., 19134. Tel: 215-739-3500; Fax: 215-739-5706.
See Our Lady of Port Richmond Regional School, Philadelphia under Regional Parish Schools located in the Institution Section.

3—ST. AGATHA-ST. JAMES (1976), Consolidated. Revs. James T. McGuinn; Benjamin Nwanonenyi; George Strausser.
Res.: 3728 Chestnut St., 19104. Tel: 215-386-9732; Fax: 215-386-9734. Web: saintsaj.org.

4—ST. AGNES-ST. JOHN NEPOMUCENE (1907), (Slovak), Consolidated January 1, 1980. Rev. Francis G. Lendacky.
Res.: 319 Brown St., 19123. Tel: 215-627-0340.

5—ALL SAINTS (Bridesburg) (1860) [CEM] Rev. William E. Grogan.
Res.: 2651 Buckius St., 19137. Tel: 215-535-4411; Fax: 215-744-6533. Email: allsaintsphl@aol.com.
See Pope John Paul II Regional Catholic School, Philadelphia under Regional Parish Schools located in the Institution section.
Catechesis/Religious Program—Students 56.

6—ALL SAINTS CHAPEL, Closed. (1877-1977) Formerly located at Philadelphia General Hospital, 700 Civic Center Blvd. Spiritual records are kept at St. Agatha-St. James Church. Tel: 215-386-9732; 386-9733.

7—ST. ALOYSIUS (1894-2003), (German), Closed. Formerly located at 26th & Tasker Sts. Spiritual records are kept at worship site of St. Gabriel Church, Tel: 215-463-4060.

8—ST. ALPHONSUS, Closed. (1852-1972) Formerly located at 1400 S. Fourth St. Spiritual records are kept at Sacred Heart of Jesus Church. Tel: 215-465-4050; 465-4051.

9—ST. AMBROSE (1923) Revs. James N. Catagnus; John M. Harkins.
Res.: 405 E. Roosevelt Blvd., 19120. Tel: 215-329-7900; 215-329-7901; Fax: 215-329-9206.
Church: C St. & Roosevelt Blvd., 19120.
Catechesis/Religious Program—Tel: 215-455-8160. Students 80.

10—ST. ANDREW (1924), (Lithuanian), Rev. Peter M. Burkauskas.
Res.: 1913 Wallace St., 19130. Tel: 215-765-2322; Fax: 215-765-0124.

11—ST. ANNE (1845) [CEM] Revs. Edward E. Brady; Joseph M. Arnholt.
Res.: 2328 E. Lehigh Ave., 19125. Tel: 215-739-4590; Fax: 215-739-0983. Email: stannephil@comcast.net. Web: www.saintanne.net.
School—2343 E. Tucker St., 19125. Tel: 215-634-4231; Fax: 215-427-0608. Timothy Archer, Prin. Lay Teachers 10; Students 195.
Catechesis/Religious Program—Cedar & Tucker Sts., 19125. Students 52.

12—ANNUNCIATION B.V.M. (1860) Rev. John E. Calabro.
Res.: 1511 S. 10th St., 19147. Tel: 215-334-0159; Fax: 215-462-5065.
School—12th & Wharton Sts., 19147. Tel: 215-465-1416; Fax: 215-465-0308. Lay Teachers 11; Students 226.
Catechesis/Religious Program—Mary Ellen Carroll, D.R.E. Students 50.

13—ST. ANSELM (1962) Revs. Thomas J. Dunleavy; Daid M. Friel. In Res., Rev. John E. Fitzgerald (Retired); Deacons Dennis P. Warner; Gerald J. Whartenby.
Res.: 12670 Dunks Ferry Rd., 19154. Tel: 215-637-3525; Fax: 215-637-4915. Email: stanselm.church@verizon.net. Web: www.stanselmparish.com.
School—12650 Dunks Ferry Rd., 19154. Tel: 215-632-1133; Fax: 215-632-3264. Mrs. Geraldine Murphy, Prin. Lay Teachers 23; Students 408.
Catechesis/Religious Program—Students 175.

14—ST. ANTHONY OF PADUA (1886-1999) Closed. Formerly located at 2321 Fitzwater St. Spiritual records are kept at St. Charles Borromeo Church. Tel: 215-735-0600.

15—ASCENSION OF OUR LORD (1899) Rev. Andris Alexis Moronta, I.V.E.; Deacon Leo Gladnick.
Res.: 725 E. Westmoreland St., 19134. Tel: 215-739-1670; Fax: 215-739-1455.
Catechesis/Religious Program— Deacon Leo Gladnick, D.R.E. Students 40.

16—ASSUMPTION B.V.M., Closed. (1848-1995) Formerly located at 1131 Spring Garden St. Spiritual records are kept at St. John the Evangelist Church. Tel: 215-563-4145.

17—ST. ATHANASIUS (1928) Rev. Joseph F. Okonski; Deacon Fred Poellnitz. In Res., Rev. Anayo Naa, C.Ss.R. (Nigeria).
Res.: 2050 Walnut Ln., 19138. Tel: 215-548-2700; Fax: 215-548-7453.
See St. Athanasius-Immaculate Conception School, Philadelphia under Regional Parish Schools located in the Institution section.
Catechesis/Religious Program—Students 36.

18—ST. AUGUSTINE (1796), First foundation of Augustinian Order in U.S.A. Rev. James D. McBurney, O.S.A. In Res., Revs. Paul F. Morrisey, O.S.A.; James D. Paradis, O.S.A.
Res.: 243 N. Lawrence St., 19106-1195. Tel: 215-627-1838; Fax: 215-627-3911. Email: staug243@verizon.net. Web: www.staugustinechurch.com.
See St. Mary Interparochial School, Philadelphia under Regional Parish Schools located in the Institution section.
Catechesis/Religious Program—Students 7.

19—ST. BARBARA (1921) Rev. Msgr. Wilfred J. Pashley.
Res.: 5359 Lebanon Ave., 19131. Tel: 215-473-1044; Fax: 215-473-5252. Email: saintbarbara5359@aol.com.
Catechesis/Religious Program—Students 2.
Convent—5336 Diamond St., 19131. Tel: 215-477-3839.

20—ST. BARNABAS (1919) Rev. John F. Babowitch; Deacons John J. Ellis; John J. Kreczkevich.
Res.: 6300 Buist Ave., 19142-3098. Tel: 215-726-1119; 215-726-1120; Fax: 215-726-1180.
Mary, Mother of Peace Area Catholic School. For further information see Regional Parish Schools in the Institution section.
Catechesis/Religious Program—Tel: 215-724-8728; Fax: 215-729-2315. Sr. Susan Bruno, I.H.M., D.R.E. Students 12.
Convent—6328 Buist Ave., 19142-3097. Tel: 215-729-1572.

21—ST. BARTHOLOMEW (1919) Rev. John J. LaRosa.
Res.: 5600 Jackson St., 19124. Tel: 215-831-1224; 215-831-1225; Fax: 215-831-0467. Email: stbartrectory@yahoo.com. Web: stbartsparish.org.
Catechesis/Religious Program—Students 65.

22—ST. BENEDICT (1922) Rev. George B. Moore; Deacon James L. Mahoney.
1942 E. Chelten Ave., 19138.
Res.: 1940 E. Chelten Ave., 19138. Tel: 215-924-4401; Fax: 215-924-4390. Email: george.moore289@gmail.com.
Catechesis/Religious Program—Students 14.

23—ST. BERNARD (1927) Revs. Joseph N. Accardi; David B. Machain (Retired); Deacon Richard F. Hunter.
Res.: 7341 Cottage St., 19136. Tel: 215-333-0446; Fax: 215-333-3215.
Catechesis/Religious Program—Students 67.

24—ST. BONAVENTURE (1889-1993) Closed. Formerly located at 9th & Cambria Sts. Spiritual records are kept at St. Veronica Church. Tel: 215-228-4878.

25—ST. BONIFACE (1865-2006) Closed. Formerly located at 174 W. Diamond St. Spiritual records are kept at Visitation B.V.M. Church. Tel: 215-634-1133.

26—ST. BRENDAN (1925-1934) Closed. Formerly located at 507 Manheim St. Spiritual records are kept at St. Francis of Assisi Church. Tel: 215-842-1287.

27—ST. BRIDGET (1853) Rev. Joseph P. Devlin. In Res., Rev. John B. Flanagan.
Res.: 3667 Midvale Ave., 19129. Tel: 215-844-4126; Fax: 215-842-2536. Email: stb@stbridgeteastfalls.org. Web: stbridgeteastfalls.org.
School—3636 Stanton St., 19129. Fax: 215-844-4089. Lay Teachers 17; Students 200.
Catechesis/Religious Program—Students 20.
Convent—3665 Midvale Ave., 19129.

28—ST. CALLISTUS (1921) Rev. Francis Yacobi, O.F.M.Cap.
Res.: 700 N. 67th St., 19151-3614. Tel: 215-473-4417; Fax: 215-473-6728. Email: st.callistusparish@yahoo.com.

29—ST. CARTHAGE (1915-2000) Closed. Formerly located at 525 Cobbs Creek Pkwy. Spiritual records are kept at St. Cyprian Church. Tel: 215-747-3250.

30—ST. CASIMIR (1893) Closed. Formerly located at 324-328 Wharton St. Spiritual records are kept at St. Andrew Church. Tel: 215-765-2322.

31—ST. CATHERINE OF SIENA (1910-1972) Closed. Formerly located at 436 W. Penn St. Spiritual records are kept at St. Vincent de Paul Church. Tel: 215-438-2925.

32—ST. CECILIA (1911) Revs. Charles E. Bonner; James T. McCabe; Mardean E. Miller; Deacon Patrick J. Diamond.
Res.: 535 Rhawn St., 19111. Tel: 215-725-1240; Fax: 215-725-2130. Email: stcecilia.swagner@verizon.net.
School—525 Rhawn St., 19111. Tel: 215-725-8588; Fax: 215-725-0247. Sisters of the Immaculate Heart of Mary 6; Lay Teachers 28; Students 661.
Catechesis/Religious Program—Tel: 215-725-2821. Students 156.

33—CHAPEL OF OUR LADY OF THE MIRACULOUS MEDAL (LA MILAGROSA) (1912), (Spanish), Attended by Cathedral Basilica of SS. Peter and Paul, 1723 Race St., Philadelphia, PA 19103. Tel: 215-561-1313; 1314.
Church: 1903 Spring Garden St., 19130.
Catechesis/Religious Program—Students 16.

34—ST. CHARLES BORROMEO (1868) Rev. Edward P. Kuczynski; Deacon William C. Mayes.
Res.: 902 S. 20th St., 19146. Tel: 215-735-0600; Fax: 215-735-6630.
Church: 20th & Christian Sts., 19146.
Catechesis/Religious Program—Tel: 215-735-6898; Fax: 215-732-6253. Students 25.

35—CHRIST THE KING (1963) Rev. James A. Callahan. In Res., Rev. Michael G. Speziale.
Res.: 3252 Chesterfield Rd., 19114. Tel: 215-632-1144; Fax: 215-632-4933. Email: ctk@christthekingparish.net. Web: www.christthekingparish.net.
School—3205 Chesterfield Rd., 19114. Tel: 215-632-1375; 215-637-3838. Web: www.christthekingschool-.net. Sisters of St. Joseph 2; Lay Teachers 19; Students 355.
Catechesis/Religious Program—Tel: 215-632-2144. Students 93.

36—ST. CHRISTOPHER (1950) Rev. Msgr. Joseph P. Garvin; Revs. Thomas J. Gardner; Engelbert G. Michel. In Res., Rev. Msgr. John P. Boland (Retired); Rev. Dennis J.W. O'Donnell; Deacon Richard S. Malamut.
Res.: 13301 Proctor Rd., 19116. Tel: 215-673-5177; Fax: 215-698-0585. Web: www.stchrisparish.org.
School—13305 Proctor Rd., 19116. Tel: 215-673-5787; Fax: 215-673-8511. Web: www.saintchris.angelcities.com. Lay Teachers 30; Students 562.
Catechesis/Religious Program— James Malinowski, D.R.E. Students 215.

37—ST. CLEMENT (1865-2004) Closed. Spiritual records are kept at Divine Mercy Parish. Tel: 215-727-8300.

38—ST. COLUMBA (1895-1993) Closed. Formerly located at 2340 W. Lehigh Ave. Spiritual records are kept at St. Martin de Porres Church. Tel: 215-228-8330; 228-8331.

39—CORPUS CHRISTI, Closed. (1912-1987) Formerly located at 29th & Allegheny Ave. Spiritual records are kept at St. Martin de Porres Church. Tel: 215-228-8330; 228-8331.

40—SAINT CYPRIAN (2000) Rev. Msgr. Federico A. Britto. In Res., Rev. Dominic Hoang Minh Tien.
Res.: 525 Cobbs Creek Pkwy., 19143. Tel: 215-747-3250; Fax: 215-747-2372. Email: sntcyprian@verizon.net. Web: www.saintcyprian.net.
Catechesis/Religious Program—Students 30.

41—DIVINE MERCY PARISH (2004) Rev. Michael S. Olivere.
Res.: 6667 Chester Ave., 19142-1397. Tel: 215-727-8300; Fax: 215-727-5932. Email: divinemercyparish@comcast.net. Web: divinemercyrc.com.
School—Mary, Mother of Peace Regional Parish School, 64th and Buist Ave., 19142. Tel: 215-729-3603. Sr. Janet Walters, I.H.M., Prin. For further information see Regional Parish Schools in the Institution section.
Catechesis/Religious Program—Mary Finnegan, C.R.E. Students 30.

42—ST. DOMINIC (1849) [CEM] Revs. Edward T. Kearns; Charles C. Garst, O.S.F.S.; Michael J. Heim; Deacon Mark A. Salvatore. In Res., Rev. Jacob John.
Res.: 8504 Frankford Ave., 19136. Tel: 215-624-5502; 215-624-5503; Fax: 215-333-1750. Email: stdominicphilapa@hotmail.com. Web: stdominicphilapa.e-paluch.com.
School—8512 Frankford Ave., 19136. Tel: 215-333-6703; Fax: 215-333-9930. Sr. Shaun Thomas, I.H.M., Prin. Sisters, Servants of the Immaculate Heart of Mary 5; Lay Teachers 23; Students 415.
Catechesis/Religious Program—Tel: 215-624-5301. Students 70.
Convent—8510 Frankford Ave., 19136. Tel: 215-333-0144.

43—ST. DONATO (1910), (Italian), Rev. Ferdinand Buccafurni.
Res.: 403 N. 65th St., 19151. Tel: 215-747-4131; Fax: 215-747-7884.
School—405 N. 65th St., 19151. Tel: 215-748-2994; Fax: 215-748-0288. Amelia Luci, Prin. Lay Teachers 12; Students 220.
Catechesis/Religious Program—Students 9.

44—ST. EDMOND (1912) Rev. Maurice C. Avicolli, O.Praem.; Deacon James J. Stewart.
Res.: 2130 S. 21st St., 19145. Tel: 215-334-3755; Fax: 215-334-2081.

Catechesis / Religious Program—Students 9.

45—ST. EDWARD THE CONFESSOR (1865-1993) Closed. Spiritual records are kept at Visitation B.V.M. Church. Tel: 215-634-1133; 228-8331.

46—ST. ELIZABETH (1872-1993) Closed. Spiritual records are kept at St. Martin De Porres Church. Tel: 215-228-8330; 228-8331.

47—EPIPHANY OF OUR LORD (1889) Rev. John Pidgeon; Rev. Msgr. Richard T. Powers (Retired). In Res., Rev. Dennis J. Witalec; Deacon Frederick C. Druding.
Res.: 110 Tree St., 19148. Tel: 215-334-1035; Fax: 215-334-7885.
School—1248 Jackson St., 19148. Tel: 215-467-5385; Fax: 215-336-5103. Patricia Cody, Prin. Lay Teachers 15; Students 295.
Catechesis / Religious Program—Tel: 215-467-5621. Marge Jarman, C.R.E. Students 74.

48—ST. FRANCIS DE SALES (1890) Rev. John D. Hand; Barbara McGee, Business Mgr.
Res.: 4625 Springfield Ave., 19143. Tel: 215-222-5819; Fax: 215-222-5821. Web: www.saintfrancisdesales.net.
School—917 S. 47th St., 19143. Tel: 215-387-1749; Fax: 215-387-6605. Sr. Mary McNulty, I.H.M., Prin. Sisters, Servants of the Immaculate Heart of Mary 6; Lay Teachers 22; Students 517.
Catechesis / Religious Program—Tel: 215-222-3382. Sr. Alice Marie Daly, I.H.M., D.R.E. Students 42.
Convent—912 S. 47th St., 19143. Tel: 215-727-3929. Email: ihm912@comcast.net.

49—ST. FRANCIS OF ASSISI (1899) Rev. Eugene F. Sheridan, C.M. In Res., Revs. Joseph V. Cummins, C.M.; Timothy V. Lyons, C.M.; Marvin A. Navas, C.M.
Res.: 4821 Greene St., 19144. Tel: 215-842-1287; Fax: 215-842-3338.
Catechesis / Religious Program—Students 20.

50—ST. FRANCIS XAVIER (1839) Revs. Paul C. Convery, C.O.; Brian R. Gaffney, C.O.; Deacon Vincent J. Thompson. In Res., Very Rev. Georges G. Thiers, C.O., Provost; Rev. Philip G. Bochanski, C.O.
Res.: 2319 Green St., 19130. Tel: 215-765-4568; Fax: 215-765-4049.
School—641 N. 24th St., 19130. Tel: 215-763-6564; Fax: 215-236-2818. Lay Teachers 12; Students 210.
Catechesis / Religious Program—Students 32.
Oratory— 2321 Green St., 19130.

51—ST. GABRIEL (1895) Rev. John C. Zagarella, O.Praem.; Sisters Marian Gregory, I.H.M., Pastoral Min.; Felice Marie, I.H.M., Pastoral Min.
Res.: 2917 Dickinson St., 19146. Tel: 215-463-4060; Fax: 215-755-2680. Web: stgabesphila.com.
School—St. Gabriel School, 2917 Dickinson St., 19146. Tel: 215-468-7230; Fax: 215-468-2554. Sr. Noreen James Friel, I.H.M., Prin. Consolidated school for St. Gabriel Parish, St. Aloysius Parish & King of Peace Parish, Philadelphia, PA. Sisters 7; Lay Teachers 10; Students 206.
Catechesis / Religious Program—Tel: 215-334-0374. Mr. Chris Marano, Youth Min. Students 30.
Convent—2916 Dickinson St. Tel: 215-334-2620.

52—ST. GEORGE (1902), (Lithuanian), Rev. Msgr. Joseph J. Anderlonis.
Res.: 3580 Salmon St., 19134. Tel: 215-739-3102; Fax: 215-739-7217.
School—2700 E. Venango St., 19134. Tel: 215-634-8803. Lay Teachers 10; Students 202.
Convent—3570 Salmon St., 19134. Tel: 215-739-0472.

53—GESU (1868-1993) Closed. Formerly located at 18th & Thompson Sts. Spiritual records are kept at St. Malachy Church. Tel: 215-763-1305.

54—GOOD SHEPHERD (1925-2004) Closed. Spiritual records are kept at Divine Mercy Parish. Tel: 215-727-8300.

55—ST. GREGORY, Closed. (1895-1981) Formerly located at 52nd & Warren Sts. Spiritual records are kept at St. Rose of Lima Church. Tel: 215-877-2991, 2992.

56—ST. HEDWIG (1907-2000), (Polish), Closed. Formerly located at 24th & Brown Sts. Spiritual records are kept at St. Francis Xavier Church, Tel: 215-765-4568.

57—ST. HELENA (1924) Rev. Msgr. Joseph T. Trinh; Deacons Victor Seda; Huan C. Tran. In Res., Rev. Edward A. Pelczar; Deacon Brouycie P. Isley.
Res.: 6161 N. Fifth St., 19120-1422. Tel: 215-424-1300; Fax: 215-424-9152.
School—6101 N. Fifth St., 19120. Tel: 215-549-2947; Fax: 215-549-5947. Sisters of St. Joseph 1; Lay Teachers 20; Students 375.
Catechesis / Religious Program—Students 39.

58—ST. HENRY (1916-1993), (German), Closed. Formerly located at 4400 N. 5th St. Spiritual records are kept at Incarnation of Our Lord Church. Tel: 215-329-2320; 329-2321.

59—HOLY ANGELS (1906), (Korean), Rev. John Sung Woo Park.
Res.: 7000 Old York Rd., 19126. Tel: 215-548-5535; 215-548-5536; Fax: 215-224-6615.
Catechesis / Religious Program—Bernard Suh, C.R.E. Students 200.

60—HOLY CHILD (1909-1993) Closed. Formerly located at 5200 N. Broad St. Spiritual records are kept at Our Lady of Hope Church. Tel: 215-329-8100; 329-8164.

61—HOLY CROSS (1890) Rev. James M. Cox; Deacon Francis B. Urmson.
Res.: 6440 Greene St., 19119. Tel: 215-438-2921; Fax: 215-848-7953.
School—144 E. Mt. Airy Ave., 19119. Tel: 215-242-0414; Fax: 215-242-0414. Lay Teachers 12; Students 160.
Catechesis / Religious Program—Students 18.
Convent—148 E. Mt. Airy Ave., 19119. Tel: 215-247-0262.

62—HOLY FAMILY (1885) Rev. Francis X. McKee. In Res., Rev. Msgr. John E. Breslin (Retired).
Res.: 234 Hermitage St., 19127. Tel: 215-482-0450; Fax: 215-482-7531. Email: rectory234@aol.com. Web: www.holyfamilyphilly.org.
School—Holy Child Catholic School, 242 Hermitage St., 19127. Tel: 215-487-2796; 215-483-0903; Fax: 215-242-0214. Web: holychildmyk.org. Michael J. Patterson, Prin. Regional school for Holy Family, St. John the Baptist, St. Josaphat, St. Lucy and St. Mary of the Assumption parishes. Lay Teachers 26; Students 214.
Catechesis / Religious Program—Manayunk Area CCD, 240 Hermitage St., 19127. Fax: 215-483-4471. Students 48.

63—HOLY INNOCENTS (1927) Revs. Thomas M. Higgins; Vincent Tung The Pham; Deacon Jorge L. Vera.
Res.: 1337 E. Hunting Park Ave., 19124. Tel: 215-743-2600; Fax: 215-743-8041. Email: holyinnocents@comcast.net.
See Holy Innocents Area Catholic School, Philadelphia under Regional Parish Schools located in the Institution section.
Catechesis / Religious Program—Tel: 215-743-5909. Students 250.

64—HOLY NAME OF JESUS (Fishtown) (1904) Rev. Kevin B. McGoldrick; Deacon John G. Boyle.
Res.: 701 E. Gaul St., 19125-2896. Tel: 215-739-3960; Fax: 215-739-7597. Web: www.holyname-fishtown.org.
Catechesis / Religious Program—Students 15.

65—HOLY REDEEMER (1941), (Chinese), Unassigned. Mission Chapel of the Church of St. John the Evangelist.
School—915 Vine St., 19107. Tel: 215-922-0999; Fax: 215-922-6674. Web: www.holyredeemer.cc. Lay Teachers 12; Students 279.
Catechesis / Religious Program—Students 57.
Parish House—916 Wood St., 19107. Tel: 215-592-7552.

66—HOLY SPIRIT (1964) Rev. Mark S. Kunigonis; Deacon Albert George.
Res.: 1900 Geary St., 19145. Tel: 215-334-4242; Fax: 215-334-8787. Web: www.holyspirit-phl.org.
School—1845 Hartranft St., 19145. Tel: 215-389-0715; Fax: 215-336-7719. Web: www.holyspiritschool-phl.org. Lay Teachers 11; Students 239.
Catechesis / Religious Program—Students 26.

67—HOLY TRINITY, (German), [CEM] Closed. (1788-2009) Formerly located at 6th & Spruce Sts. Spiritual records are kept at Old St. Mary's, Philadelphia. Tel: 215-923-7930.

68—ST. HUBERT (1924-1940) Closed. Formerly located at Torresdale and Cottman Aves. from 1924-1940. Spiritual records transferred to St. Bernard Church. Tel: 215-333-0446.

69—ST. HUGH OF CLUNY (1922) Revs. Andris Alexis Moronta, I.V.E.; Marcelo R. Lopresti, I.V.E.; Deacon Jose L. Lozada-Figueroa.
Res.: 145 W. Tioga St., 19140. Tel: 215-634-1800; Fax: 215-427-0303.
School—3501 N. Mascher St., 19140. Tel: 215-863-8048; Fax: 215-634-2690. Sisters of St. Joseph 3; Lay Teachers 6; Students 141.
Catechesis / Religious Program—Fax: 215-427-0303. Students 172.

70—ST. IGNATIUS OF LOYOLA (1893) Rev. Jeffrey M. Stecz.
Rectory—636 N. 43rd St., 19104. Tel: 215-386-5065; Fax: 215-386-2832. Email: oms-si@yahoo.com. Web: www.oms-stignatius.com.
School—Our Mother of Sorrows-St. Ignatius School, 1008 N. 48th St., 19131. Tel: 215-473-5828. Sr. Owen Patricia Bonner, S.S.J., Prin.
Catechesis / Religious Program—Sr. Stephanie Henry, S.B.S., D.R.E. Students 20.
Convent—644 N. 43rd St., 19104. Tel: 215-386-0302.
Chaplaincy—St. Ignatius Nursing Home. Tel: 215-349-8800; Fax: 215-222-3078.

71—IMMACULATE CONCEPTION (1869) Closed. Formerly located at 1020 N. Front St., Philadelphia, PA, 19123. Spiritual Records are kept at St. Michael Church. Tel: 215-739-2358.

72—IMMACULATE CONCEPTION (1902) Rev. Charles P. Strollo, C.M. In Res., Revs. Michael J. Carroll, C.M.; Gregory P. Cozzubbo, C.M.; Carl L. Pieber, C.M.
Res.: 1020 E. Price St., 19138. Tel: 215-843-9468; Fax: 215-843-6570. Web: immaculateconception-phila.net.
See St. Athanasius-Immaculate Conception School, Philadelphia under Regional Parish Schools located in the Institution section.
Catechesis / Religious Program—Tel: 215-843-9468; Fax: 215-843-6570. Students 14.
Shrine—*Our Lady of the Miraculous Medal* 500 E. Chelten Ave., 19144. Tel: 215-848-1985. Web: www-.cammonline.org.

73—IMMACULATE HEART OF MARY (1952) Rev. Msgr. Joseph P. McGeown; Revs. Armand D. Garcia; Paul Obrimski; Deacon George W. Kletzel.
Res.: 819 Cathedral Rd., 19128. Tel: 215-483-1000; Fax: 215-483-1732. Email: ihmparish@comcast.net. Web: www.ihmphila.org.
School—815 Cathedral Rd., 19128. Tel: 215-482-2029; Fax: 215-482-1075. Lay Teachers 31; Students 431.
Catechesis / Religious Program—Tel: 215-483-4266. Students 65.

74—INCARNATION OF OUR LORD (1900) Rev. Sean F. O'Neill; Deacons Felipe Cruz; Jose Hernandez. In Res., Revs. Paul T. Maina; Albert Gardy Villarson, O.M.I., (Haitian Apostolate).
Res.: 5105 N. Fifth St., 19120. Tel: 215-329-2320; Fax: 215-329-6149. Web: www.incarnationofourlord.org.
School—Tel: 215-457-2779; Fax: 215-457-1328. Sr. Mary Anne Sweeney, I.H.M., Prin. Sisters, Servants of the Immaculate Heart of Mary 6; Lay Teachers 14; Students 372.
Catechesis / Religious Program—Students 165.
Convent—401 W. Lindley Ave., 19120. Tel: 215-329-0672.

75—SAINT IRENAEUS (1966-2004) Closed. Formerly located at 2728 S. 73rd St. Spiritual records are kept at Divine Mercy Parish. Tel: 215-727-8300. Worship Site of Divine Mercy Parish.

76—ST. JAMES (1850-1976) Consolidated with St. Agatha to form St. Agatha-St. James. See separate listing for details.

77—ST. JEROME (1955) Revs. Dennis P. Boyle; Carl Graczyk, O.F.M.; Anthony T. Rossi. In Res., Rev. Ignatius Marneni; Deacon Charles Pavonarius.
Res.: 8100 Colfax St., 19136. Tel: 215-333-4461; Fax: 215-333-6791. Email: stjeromeparish@catholicexchange.com. Web: www.stjeromeparish.com.
School—3031 Stamford St., 19136. Tel: 215-624-0637; Fax: 215-624-5711. Sharon Nendza, Prin. Lay Teachers 29; Students 555.
Catechesis / Religious Program—Students 48.

78—ST. JOACHIM (1845) [CEM] Rev. Steven P. Wetzel, O.S.F.S.
Res.: 1527 Church St., 19124. Tel: 215-535-0580; Fax: 215-831-1788. Web: www.stjoachims.org.
See Holy Innocents Area Catholic School, Philadelphia under Regional Parish Schools located in the Institution section.
Catechesis / Religious Program—Students 31.

79—ST. JOAN OF ARC (1919) Rev. John J. Large. 1676 Ruan St., 19124. Tel: 215-535-4036; Fax: 215-535-1267.
Rectory—2025 E. Atlantic St., 19134. Tel: 215-535-4641; Fax: 215-535-5138.
See Holy Innocents Area Catholic School, Philadelphia under Regional Parish Schools located in the Institution section.
Catechesis / Religious Program—Maggie Purr, D.R.E. Students 8.

80—ST. JOHN CANTIUS (1892), (Polish), Revs. Joseph J. Zingaro; Konstanty J. Pruszynski.
Res.: 4415 Almond St., 19137. Tel: 215-535-6667; Fax: 215-535-7107. Email: sjc4415@comcast.net.
School—Pope John Paul II Regional Catholic, 4435 Almond St., 19137. Tel: 215-535-3446; Fax: 215-535-3858. Web: pjp2rcs.com. Linda Milewski, Prin. Regional school for St. John Cantius and All Saints parishes. Lay Teachers 16; Students 173.
Catechesis / Religious Program—Students 40.

81—ST. JOHN NEPOMUCENE, (Slovak), Consolidated with St. Agnes January 1, 1980. Spiritual records transferred to St. Agnes-St. John Nepomucene, 319 Brown St., Philadelphia, PA 19123. Tel: 215-627-0340.

82—ST. JOHN THE BAPTIST (1831) [CEM] Revs. James A. Lyons; Michael V. Marrone; Deacon Gaspero P. Baratta.
Res.: 146 Rector St., 19127. Tel: 215-482-4600; Fax: 215-482-2976. Email: sjbphila@aol.com. Web: stjohnmanayunk.org.
Catechesis / Religious Program—Students 40.

83—ST. JOHN THE EVANGELIST (1830) [CEM] Revs. John Daya, O.F.M.Cap.; Senan Glass, O.F.M.Cap.; Anselm Martin, O.F.M.Cap.; Roger White, O.F.M-.Cap.; Bro. James Gavin, O.F.M.Cap. In Res., Revs.

Thomas Betz, O.F.M.Cap.; Piotr Kwiatek, O.F.M-.Cap; Benjamin R. Regotti, O.F.M.Cap.
Res.: 21 S. 13th St., 19107. Tel: 215-563-4145; Fax: 215-563-1770. Web: www.stjohnsphilly.com.
See St. Mary Interparochial School, Philadelphia under Regional Parish Schools located in the Institution section.
Mission—Holy Redeemer Chinese Church 915 Vine St., 19107. Tel: 215-922-0999; Fax: 215-922-6674.

84—ST. JOSAPHAT (1898), (Polish), Rev. Leonard A. Lewandowski. In Res., Rev. Tijo Joy Mullakara.
Res.: 124 Cotton St., 19127. Tel: 215-483-4470; Fax: 215-483-4037.
See Holy Child Catholic School, Philadelphia under Regional Parish Schools located in the Institution section.
Catechesis/Religious Program—Students 53.

85—ST. KATHERINE OF SIENA (1922) Revs. Paul M. Kennedy; Ronald J. Ferrier; William J. Monahan; Deacon James J. Duffy; Carol Buchsbaum, Business Mgr. In Res., Rev. Msgr. Francis A. Carbine (Retired).
Res.: 9700 Frankford Ave., 19114-2896. Tel: 215-637-7548; Fax: 215-637-0146. Email: skschurch@skschurch.com. Web: www.skschurch-.com; home.catholicweb.com/saintkatherineofsienaphiladelphia.
School—9720 Frankford Ave., 19114. Tel: 215-637-2181; Fax: 215-637-4867. Web: www.sksgradeschool-.com. Mr. Thomas Armbruster, Prin. Sisters of the Holy Family of Nazareth 3; Sisters, Servants of the Immaculate Heart of Mary 1; Lay Teachers 26; Students 561.
Catechesis/Religious Program—Tel: 215-637-1464. Email: prep@skschurch.com. Students 86.

86—KING OF PEACE (1926-2004), (Italian), Closed. Spiritual records are kept at St. Gabriel Church, Tel: 215-463-4060.

87—ST. LADISLAUS (1906-2003), (Polish), Closed. Formerly located at 1650 W. Hunting Park Ave. Spiritual records are kept at St. Josaphat Church, Tel: 215-483-4470.

88—ST. LAURENTIUS (1882), (Polish), Rev. Francis A. Gwiazda.
Res.: 1608 E. Berks St., 19125. Tel: 215-739-1776; 215-739-9387; Fax: 215-739-9663. Email: stlaurentius@netzero.net.
School—1612 E. Berks St., 19125. Tel: 215-423-8834; Fax: 215-426-4675. Email: aplauren06@nni.com. Web: userweb.nni.com/ aplauren06. Felician Sisters of St. Francis 1; Lay Teachers 14; Students 209.
Catechesis/Religious Program—Students 236.
Convent—1648 E. Berks St., 19125. Tel: 215-739-4447.

89—ST. LEO (1884) Rev. Joseph L. Farrell. In Res., Rev. Joseph E. O'Brien (Retired).
Res.: 6658 Keystone St., 19135. Tel: 215-333-0340; Fax: 215-333-7590. Email: stleotacony@hotmail.com. Web: www.saintleos.com.
Catechesis/Religious Program—Tel: 215-331-3399. Students 82.

90—ST. LUCY (1905), (Italian), Rev. Charles Zlock.
Res.: 4503 Smick St., 19127. Tel: 215-483-0554; Fax: 215-483-2450.
See Holy Child Catholic School, Philadelphia under Regional Parish Schools located in the Institution section.

91—ST. LUDWIG (1891-1975), (German), Closed. Formerly located at 28th & Master Sts. Spiritual records are kept at St. Francis Xavier Church. Tel: 215-765-4568.

92—ST. MADELEINE SOPHIE (1925) Rev. James M. Cox; Deacon Francis Urmson.
Res.: 6440 Greene St., 19119. Tel: 215-438-2921; Fax: 215-848-7953. Email: smg0398@comcast.net. See Holy Cross Parish School, Philadelphia.
Catechesis/Religious Program—Students 4.

93—ST. MALACHY (1850) Rev. Msgr. Kevin C. Lawrence. In Res., Rev. J. Jerome Wild.
Res.: 1429 N. 11th St., 19122. Tel: 215-763-1305; Fax: 215-763-2023. Email: ccsm@stmalachy.us. Web: www.saintmalachyparish.com.
School—1419 N. 11th St., 19122. Tel: 215-232-0696; Fax: 215-236-1434. Lay Teachers 12; Students 215.
Catechesis/Religious Program—Students 33.

94—SAINT MARTHA (1966) Rev. Alexander Masluk; Rev. Msgr. John J. Miller; Deacon Raymond F. Gwynn Sr. In Res., Rev. James J. Collins.
Res.: 11301 Academy Rd., 19154-3304. Tel: 215-632-3720; Fax: 215-632-7737. Web: stmarthachurch.com.
School—11321 Academy Rd., 19154-3304. Tel: 215-632-0320; Fax: 215-632-5546. Lay Teachers 21; Students 374.
Catechesis/Religious Program—Students 115.

95—ST. MARTIN DE PORRES (1993) Rev. Stephen D. Thorne.
Res.: 2340 W. Lehigh Ave., 19132. Tel: 215-228-8330; Fax: 215-221-6516.
School—23rd St. & Lehigh Ave., 19132. Tel: 215-223-6872; Fax: 215-223-4126. Sisters of St. Joseph 5; Lay Teachers 17; Students 398.
Catechesis/Religious Program—Students 15.

96—ST. MARTIN OF TOURS (1923) Revs. John F. Meyers; Christopher R. Cooke; Deacon Stanley M. Zaleski; Sr. Eileen Maguire, S.S.J., Pastoral & Social Min. In Res., Rev. Gelso Dadatt.
Res.: 5450 Roosevelt Blvd., 19124. Tel: 215-535-2962; Fax: 215-535-3091. Email: stmartinsphila@aol.com. Web: www.smtparish.org.
School—Loretto Ave. & Sanger St., 19124. Fax: 215-533-1579. Sisters of the Immaculate Heart of Mary 6; Lay Teachers 20; Students 443.
Catechesis/Religious Program—Fax: 215-535-3091. Email: ccd@smtparish.org. Brenda Pineda, C.R.E. Students 120.

97—ST. MARY MAGDALEN DE PAZZI, (Italian), Closed. (1852-2000). Formerly located at 712 Montrose St. Spiritual records are kept at Saint Paul Church. Tel: 215-923-0355.

98—ST. MARY OF CZESTOCHOWA, (Polish), Closed. (1927-2000) Formerly located at 59th St. and Elmwood Ave. Spiritual records are kept at St. Barnabas Church. Tel: 215-726-1119; 1120.

99—ST. MARY OF THE ASSUMPTION (1849), (German), [CEM] Rev. Charles Zlock.
Res.: 176 Conarroe St., 19127. Tel: 215-482-4264; Fax: 215-508-1731. Web: www.stmarymanayunk-.com.
See Holy Child Catholic School, Philadelphia under Regional Parish Schools located in the Institution section.
Catechesis/Religious Program—Students 78.

100—ST. MARY OF THE ETERNAL, (Italian), Closed. (1911-1976) Formerly located at 2222 W. Clearfield St. Spiritual records are kept at St. Martin de Porres. Tel: 215-228-8330.

101—MATER DOLOROSA (1911), (Italian), Rev. John J. Large. In Res., Rev. Cornelius F. Kilty, O.S.F.S.
Res.: 1676 Ruan St., 19124. Tel: 215-535-4036; 215-743-4718; Fax: 215-535-1267. Email: materdolorosachurch@verizon.net. Web: materdolorosachurch.net.
See Holy Innocents Area Catholic School, Philadelphia under Regional Parish Schools located in the Institution section.
Catechesis/Religious Program—Students 25.

102—MATERNITY B.V.M. (1870) Revs. Paul S. Quinter; James C. Otto; Deacons Phillip Heaney; Charles R. Lindsay. In Res., Rev. Msgr. Bernard E. Witkowski (Retired).
Res.: 9220 Old Bustleton Ave., 19115-4686. Tel: 215-673-8127; 215-676-5144; Fax: 215-673-6597. Web: maternitybvm.catholicweb.com.
School—9322 Bustleton Ave., 19115. Tel: 215-673-0235; Fax: 215-671-1347. Lay Teachers 20; Students 532.
Catechesis/Religious Program—Tel: 215-673-4010. Sr. Mary Beth Geraghty, R.S.M., D.R.E. Students 156.
Convent—Tel: 215-673-8118.

103—ST. MATTHEW (1927) Rev. Msgr. Charles E. McGroarty; Revs. Thomas J. Cavanaugh; Steven J. Marinucci; Deacon Robert Burns. In Res., Rev. Msgr. Thomas J. Kelley (Retired).
Res.: 3000 Cottman Ave., 19149. Tel: 215-333-0585; Fax: 215-333-0757. Web: www.stmattsparish.com.
School—3040 Cottman Ave., 19149. Tel: 215-333-3142. Sisters, Servants of the Immaculate Heart of Mary 8; Lay Teachers 40; Students 825.
Catechesis/Religious Program—Students 100.
Convent—3040 Cottman Ave., 19149. Tel: 215-333-8214.

104—ST. MICHAEL (1831) [CEM] Rev. Msgr. John J. Miller; Bonnie Hackett, Coord. Parish Svcs.
Res.: 1445 N. Second St., 19122. Tel: 215-739-2358; Fax: 215-739-5766. Web: www.saintmichael.catholicweb.com.
Catechesis/Religious Program—Students 30.

105—ST. MICHAEL MISSION, Closed. Spiritual records are kept at Our Lady of Calvary Church. Tel: 215-637-7515.

106—ST. MICHAEL OF THE SAINTS, Closed. (1924-1982) Formerly located at 4811 Germantown Ave. Spiritual records kept at St. Francis of Assisi Church. Tel: 215-842-1287.

107—ST. MONICA (1895) Revs. Joseph J. Kelley; James C. Rodia, O.Praem.; Deacon Leonard D. DeMasi. In Res., Rev. Msgr. James E. Connelly (Retired).
Res.: 2422 S. 17th St., 19145. Tel: 215-334-4170; 215-334-4171; Fax: 215-389-6045. Web: www.saintmonicaparish.net.
School—Junior School, 1720 Ritner Ave., 19145. Tel: 215-334-3777; Fax: 215-389-0355.
School—Senior School, 2500 S. 16th St., 19145. Tel: 215-467-5338; Fax: 215-467-4599. Servants of the Immaculate Heart of Mary 6; Lay Teachers 23; Students 445.
Catechesis/Religious Program—Tel: 215-334-1659; Fax: 215-389-0355. Students 161.

108—MOST BLESSED SACRAMENT, Closed. (1901-2008) Formerly located at 56th St. & Chester Ave. Spiritual records are kept at St. Francis de Sales Church, Philadelphia. Tel: 215-222-5819.

109—MOST PRECIOUS BLOOD OF OUR LORD, Closed. (1907-1993) Formerly located at 28th & Diamond Sts. Spiritual records are kept at St. Martin De Porres Church. Tel: 215-228-8330.

110—MOTHER OF DIVINE GRACE (1926), (Italian), Rev. Walter J. Benn. In Res., Rev. Stephen H. Paolino.
Res.: 2918 E. Thompson St., 19134. Tel: 215-739-0353; Fax: 215-739-9910.
School—2612 E. Monmouth St., 19134. Tel: 215-426-7325; Fax: 215-426-0753. Lay Teachers 10; Students 234.
Catechesis/Religious Program—

111—NATIVITY OF THE BLESSED VIRGIN MARY (1882) Revs. Dennis Z. Fedak; Richard P. Connors; James P. Gorman. In Res., Rev. Daniel J. Moriarity (Retired).
Res.: 2535 E. Allegheny Ave., 19134. Tel: 215-739-2735; Fax: 215-739-2748. Email: nativitybvm@aol.com. Web: www.nativityphiladelphia.4lpi.com.
Catechesis/Religious Program—Students 50.

112—ST. NICHOLAS OF TOLENTINE (1912), (Italian), Revs. Nicholas Martorano, O.S.A.; John Brynes, O.S.A.; James R. Keating, O.S.A. In Res., Revs. W. Howard McGraw, O.S.A.; Denis G. Wilde, O.S.A.
Res.: 910 Watkins St., 19148. Tel: 215-463-1326; Fax: 215-463-0888. Web: www.stnicksphila.com.
Church: Ninth St. below Morris St., 19148.
School—913 Pierce St., 19148. Tel: 215-468-0353; Fax: 215-334-9661. Religious Sisters Filippini 3; Religious 2; Lay Teachers 13; Students 280.
Catechesis/Religious Program—Students 73.

113—OLD ST. JOSEPH'S (1733) Revs. Daniel M. Ruff, S.J.; Edward T. O'Donnell, S.J. In Res., Revs. Dennis M. Linehan, S.J. (Retired); James F. McAndrews, S.J. (Retired); Gerald J. McGlone, S.J.; Terrence Toland, S.J. (Retired).
Res.: 321 Willings Aly., 19106. Tel: 215-923-1733; 215-923-1734; Fax: 215-574-8529. Web: www.oldst-joseph.org.
See St. Mary Interparochial School, Philadelphia under Regional Parish Schools located in the Institution section.
Catechesis/Religious Program—Christine Szczepanowski, C.R.E. Students 50.

114—OLD ST. MARY'S (1763) [CEM] Rev. Msgr. Paul A. DiGirolamo.
Res.: 252 S. Fourth St., 19106. Tel: 215-923-7930. Web: www.oldstmary.com.
See St. Mary Interparochial School, Philadelphia under Regional Parish Schools located in the Institution section.

115—OUR LADY HELP OF CHRISTIANS (1885), (German), Rev. Dennis Z. Fedak.
Res.: 2535 E. Allegheny Ave., 19134.
Church: 3160 Gaul St., 19134. Tel: 215-739-2211; Fax: 215-739-9272.
Catechesis/Religious Program—Students 110.
See Our Lady of Port Richmond Regional School, Philadelphia under Regional Parish Schools located in the Institution Section.
Convent—Tel: 215-739-7890.

116—OUR LADY OF ANGELS (1907-2006), (Italian), Closed. Formerly located at 4970 Master St. Spiritual records are kept at St. Donato Church. Tel: 215-747-4131.

117—OUR LADY OF CALVARY (1958) Revs. John P. Paul; William S. Kirk; Lawrence F. Kozak.
Res.: 11024 Knights Rd., 19154. Tel: 215-637-7515; Fax: 215-637-7517. Web: www.ourladyofcalvary.org.
School—11023 Kipling Ln., 19154. Tel: 215-637-1648; Fax: 215-637-3810. Sisters of the Holy Family of Nazareth 6; Lay Teachers 38; Students 860.
Catechesis/Religious Program—Students 240.

118—OUR LADY OF CONSOLATION (1917), (Italian), Rev. Dennis J. Carbonaro; Deacon Joseph M. Cella.
Res.: 7056 Tulip St., 19135. Tel: 215-333-0442; 215-333-5774; Fax: 215-333-2884. Web: www.olctacony.org.
School—Princeton & Edmund Sts., 19135. Tel: 215-624-0505. Web: www.olcph.org. Mr. Stephen DiCicco, Prin. Religious 1; Lay Teachers 10; Students 199.
Catechesis/Religious Program—Students 50.

119—OUR LADY OF GOOD COUNSEL (1898-1932) Closed. Formerly located at 816 Christian St. Spiritual records are kept at St. Paul Church. Tel: 215-923-0355.

120—OUR LADY OF HOPE (1993) Revs. Efren V. Esmilla; Rayford E. Emmons; Deacons William Champagne; Israel Rosario; Felipe Hernandez; Homer A. Panganiban.
Res.: 5200 N. Broad St., 19141-1628. Tel: 215-329-8100; 215-329-8164; Fax: 215-324-4660. Email: olhphiladelphia@aol.com.
Catechesis/Religious Program—Students 20.

121—OUR LADY OF LORETO (1932-2000), (Italian), Closed. Formerly located at 6214 Grays Ave. Spiritual records are kept at St. Barnabas Church. Tel: 215-726-1119; 1120.

122—OUR LADY OF LOURDES (1894) Rev. James W. Mayer, O.de.M.
Res.: 6315 Lancaster Ave., 19151. Tel: 215-473-2874; Fax: 215-473-2878. Email: dbaker@ourladylourdes.org. Web: www.ourladylourdes.org.
Parish Center: 1920 N. 63rd St., 19151. Tel: 215-473-1669; Fax: 215-473-1670.
School—1940 N. 63rd St., 19151. Tel: 215-877-2727; Fax: 215-877-6042. Sisters of Our Lady of Mercy 4; Lay Teachers 14; Students 220.
Catechesis/Religious Program—Students 44.

123—OUR LADY OF MERCY (1889-1984) Closed. Formerly located at Broad St. & Susquehanna Ave. Spiritual records are kept at St. Malachy Church. Tel: 215-763-1305.

124—OUR LADY OF MT. CARMEL (1896) Revs. Francis J. Cauterucci; Chanlis Chacko.
Res.: 2319 S. Third St., 19148. Tel: 215-334-7766; Fax: 215-334-3269. Web: www.ourladymountcarmel.net.
School—2329 S. Third St., 19148. Tel: 215-334-0584; Fax: 215-336-4519. Sisters of Mercy 2; Lay Teachers 7; Students 145.
Catechesis/Religious Program—Students 24.
Convent—251 Ritner St., 19148. Tel: 215-334-6800.

125—OUR LADY OF POMPEII (1914-1993), (Italian), Closed. Formerly located at 6th St. & Erie Ave. Spiritual records are kept at St. Veronica Church. Tel: 215-228-4878.

126—OUR LADY OF RANSOM (1955) Rev. Thomas M. Sodano; Deacon Ralph J. Shirley. In Res., Rev. Edward L. Rauch, O.S.F.S. (Retired).
Res.: 6701 Calvert St., 19149. Tel: 215-332-6166; Fax: 215-332-6811. Email: olorbulletin@yahoo.com. Web: www.oloransom.org.
School—6740 Roosevelt Blvd., 19149. Tel: 215-332-4352. Lay Teachers 10; Students 225.
Catechesis/Religious Program—Tel: 215-708-2495. Students 60.
Convent—Tel: 215-624-1954.

127—OUR LADY OF THE BLESSED SACRAMENT (1910-1972) Closed. Formerly located at 712 N. Broad St. Spiritual records are kept at the Cathedral Basilica of SS. Peter and Paul. Tel: 215-561-1313; 561-1314.

128—OUR LADY OF THE BLESSED SACRAMENT (2005) Rev. Paul Kuppe, O.F.M.Cap.; Deacon Richard G. Nightingale.
Mailing Address: 345 N. 63rd St., 19139. Tel: 215-476-6511; Fax: 215-476-3230. Web: www.olobs.org.
School—344 N. Felton St., 19139. Tel: 215-474-4011; Fax: 215-474-7807.
Catechesis/Religious Program—Mark Gonzalez, Dir. Faith Formation. Students 40.

129—OUR LADY OF THE HOLY ROSARY (Germantown) (1928-1977), (Italian), Closed. Formerly located at 528 E. Haines St. Spiritual records are kept at Immaculate Conception Church. Tel: 215-843-9468.

130—OUR LADY OF THE HOLY SOULS (1909-1993) Closed. Formerly located at 19th & Tioga Sts. Spiritual records are kept at Our Lady of Hope Church. Tel: 215-329-8100.

131—OUR LADY OF THE ROSARY (1886-2005) Closed. Formerly located at 345 N. 63rd St. Spiritual records are kept at Our Lady of the Blessed Sacrament Church. Tel: 215-476-6511.

132—OUR LADY OF VICTORY (1899-2005) Closed. Formerly located at 5412 Vine St. Spiritual records are kept at Our Lady of the Blessed Sacrament Church. Tel: 215-476-6511.

133—OUR MOTHER OF CONSOLATION (1855) Very Rev. Robert L. Bazzoli, O.S.F.S.; Rev. James R. Yeakel, O.S.F.S.
Res.: 9 E. Chestnut Hill Ave., 19118. Tel: 215-247-0430; Fax: 215-247-2506. Email: bbazzoli@omcparish.com. Web: omcparish.com.
School—17 E. Chestnut Hill Ave., 19118. Tel: 215-247-1060; Fax: 215-247-0590. Email: bhagy@omcparish.com. N. Bruce Hagy, Prin. Lay Teachers 12; Students 176.
Catechesis/Religious Program—Email: jrussell@omcparish.com. Students 115.
Convent—23 E. Chestnut Hill Ave., 19118. Tel: 215-247-0552.

134—OUR MOTHER OF SORROWS (1852) Rev. Jeffrey M. Stecz.
St. Ignatius of Loyola, 636 N. 43rd St., 19104. Tel: 215-386-5065.
Rectory—1030 N. 48th St., 19131. Tel: 215-878-0875; Fax: 215-878-7420. Email: oms_si@yahoo.com. Web: www.oms-stignatius.com.
School—Our Mother of Sorrows-St. Ignatius School, 1020 N. 48th St., 19131. Tel: 215-473-5828; Fax: 215-477-3096. Web: www.omssi.org. Sr. Owen Patricia Bonner, S.S.J., Prin. Sisters of St. Joseph 3; Lay Teachers 10; Students 310.
Catechesis/Religious Program— Mrs. Jennifer Simmons, D.R.E. Students 205.

135—ST. PATRICK (1839) Rev. Daniel E. Mackle. In Res., Rev. Msgr. Louis A. D'Addezio (Retired).
Res.: 242 S. 20th St., 19103. Tel: 215-735-9900; Fax: 215-732-0998. Email: stpatricksparish@aol.com.
School—St. Mary Interparochial School, Tel: 215-923-7522.
See St. Mary Interparochial School, Philadelphia under Regional Parish Schools located in the Institution section.
Catechesis/Religious Program—Students 25.

136—ST. PAUL (1843) Rev. Gerald P. Carey.
Res.: 808 S. Hutchinson St., 19147. Tel: 215-923-0355; Fax: 215-923-1803. Web: stpaulparishsouthphilly.com.
Worship Site: St. Mary Magdalen de Pazzi Church—712 Montrose St., 19147.
Catechesis/Religious Program—Students 140.

137—ST. PETER CLAVER (1889-1985) Closed. Formerly located at 12th & Lombard Sts. Spiritual records are kept at St. John the Evangelist Church. Tel: 215-563-4145.

138—ST. PETER THE APOSTLE (1842) [CEM] Revs. Alfred E. Bradley, C.Ss.R.; Matthew T. Allman, C.Ss.R.; Varghese Kocherry, C.Ss.R.; Gordon L. Cannoles, C.Ss.R.; Mark Wise, C.Ss.R.; Deacons Jose Miguel Betancourt; Juan Ramos. In Res., Revs. Richard Boever, C.Ss.R.; Gerard Brinkman, C.Ss.R.; John M. Hamrogue, C.Ss.R.; Donald Miniscalco, C.Ss.R.; Rev. Msgr. George Tomichek, D.C.
Church, Rectory & Mailing Address: 1019 N. Fifth St., 19123. Tel: 215-627-2386; Fax: 215-627-2366. Email: stpetersoffice@comcast.net.
School—1009 N. Fifth St., 19123. Tel: 215-922-5958. Sr. Rose Federici, S.S.N.D. School Sisters of Notre Dame 1; Lay Teachers 11; Students 238.
Catechesis/Religious Program— Sr. Clare Marsico, I.H.M., D.R.E. Students 45.
Convent—1005 N. 5th St., 19123. Tel: 215-627-3954.
Shrine—St. John Neumann, Tel: 215-627-3080; Fax: 215-627-3296. Mary Argenbright, Office Mgr.

139—ST. PHILIP NERI (1840) Revs. James M. Oliver; Francis Piro (Retired).
Res.: 218 Queen St., 19147. Tel: 215-468-1922; Fax: 215-465-3147. Email: stphilipneri@comcast.net. Web: churchofstphilipneri.org.

140—ST. RAPHAEL (1904-1989) Closed. Formerly located at 86th St. & Tinicum Ave. Spiritual records are kept at Divine Mercy Parish. Tel: 215-727-8300.

141—ST. RAYMOND OF PENAFORT (1941) Rev. Christopher M. Walsh.
Res.: 1350 Vernon Rd., 19150. Tel: 215-549-3760; Fax: 215-549-1271. Email: pastor@saintraymond.net. Web: www.saintraymond.net.
School—7940 Williams Ave., 19150. Tel: 215-548-1919; Fax: 215-548-1925. Lay Teachers 10; Students 300.
Catechesis/Religious Program—Students 40.

142—RESURRECTION OF OUR LORD (1928) Rev. Joseph E. Howarth; Deacons Joao A. Ferreira; Dennis J. Friel. In Res., Rev. Joseph E. Tustin, O.S.F.S.
Res.: 2000 Shelmire Ave., 19152. Tel: 215-745-3211; Fax: 215-745-0587. Web: www.resurrectphila.org.
School—2020 Shelmire Ave., 19152. Tel: 215-742-1127; Fax: 215-742-0947. Email: resurrectionschool@yahoo.com. Web: www.resurrection.org/school. Mrs. Joan Stulz, Prin. Lay Teachers 24; Students 478.
Catechesis/Religious Program—Tel: 215-742-0947. Students 82.

143—ST. RICHARD (1924) Rev. William C. Kaufman.
Res.: 3010 S. 18th St., 19145. Tel: 215-468-4777; Fax: 215-468-3161. Web: www.strichardchurch.org.
School—19th & Pollock Sts., 19145. Tel: 215-467-5430. Lay Teachers 11; Students 262.
Catechesis/Religious Program—Dennis Mueller, D.R.E. Students 60.

144—ST. RITA OF CASCIA (1907) Revs. Joseph A. Genito, O.S.A., Pastor & Shrine Dir.; William A. Recchuti, O.S.A; Daniel McLaughlin, O.S.A. In Res., Revs. Michael Scuderi, O.S.A.; Eugene DelConte, O.S.A.
Res. & Friary: 1166 S. Broad St., 19146. Tel: 215-546-8333; Fax: 215-732-3510. Email: ritashrine@aol.com. Web: www.saintritashrine.org.
Shrine—The National Shrine of St. Rita of Cascia 1166 S. Broad St., 19146. Tel: 215-546-8333; Fax: 215-732-3510.

145—ST. ROSE OF LIMA (1921) Rev. Msgr. Wilfred J. Pashley.
Res.: 1535 N. 59th St., 19151. Tel: 215-877-2991; Fax: 215-877-8255. Email: saintroseoflima@aol.com.
School—1516 N. Wanamaker St., 19131. Tel: 215-473-6030; Fax: 215-473-2338. Sisters, Servants of the Immaculate Heart of Mary 3; Lay Teachers 11; Students 220.

146—SACRED HEART (1913-1977), (Hungarian), Closed. Formerly located at Mascher & Master Sts. Spiritual records are kept at St. Michael Church. Tel: 215-739-2358.

147—SACRED HEART OF JESUS (1871) Revs. Robert T. Feeney; William E. Dean. In Res., Rev. John J. Bradley (Retired).
Res.: 1404 S. Third St., 19147-6099. Tel: 215-465-4050; 215-465-4051; Fax: 215-465-0400. Web: www.sacredheartsp.com.
School—1329 Moyamensing Ave., 19147. Tel: 215-462-4129; Fax: 215-462-9429. Web: www.sacredheartsp.com. Sr. Patricia Mount, I.H.M., Prin. Sisters of the Immaculate Heart of Mary 5; Lay Teachers 10; Students 196.
Convent—1420 S. Third St., 19147. Tel: 215-463-8719. Sr. Kathleen Schipani, I.H.M., Supr.

148—ST. STANISLAUS (1891-2006), (Polish), Closed. Formerly located at 242 Fitzwater St. Spiritual records are kept at St. Philip Neri Church. Tel: 215-468-1922.

149—STELLA MARIS (1954) Rev. John R. DiOrio.
Res.: 2901 S. 10th St., 19148. Tel: 215-465-2336; 215-465-2337; Fax: 215-465-1061.
Catechesis/Religious Program—Students 100.
Convent—2929 S. 10th St., 19148. Tel: 215-462-1111.

150—ST. STEPHEN (1843-1993) Closed. Formerly located at Broad & Butler Sts. Spiritual records are kept at Our Lady of Hope Church. Tel: 215-329-8100.

151—ST. TERESA OF AVILA (1853-1972) Closed. Formerly located at Broad & Catherine Sts. Spiritual records are kept at St. Rita Church. Tel: 215-546-8333.

152—ST. THERESE OF THE CHILD JESUS (1925) Rev. Msgr. David H. Benz; Deacon Edward M. Purnell.
Res.: 6611 Ardleigh St., 19119. Tel: 215-438-5279; Fax: 215-438-8031.
Catechesis/Religious Program—Tel: 215-438-5279. Students 25.

153—ST. THOMAS AQUINAS (1885) Rev. Msgr. Hugh Joseph Shields; Rev. Joseph Dinh C. Huynh (Vietnam).
Res.: 1719 Morris St., 19145. Tel: 215-334-2312; Fax: 215-755-9369. Email: staparish@yahoo.com. Web: www.staquinas.com.
School—18th & Morris Sts., 19145. Tel: 215-334-0878; Fax: 215-334-2357. Email: sta.school@yahoo.com. Lay Teachers 9; Students 208.
Day Care—1616 S. 18th St. Tel: 215-334-9442; Fax: 215-334-8221. Staff 15; Children 100.
Catechesis/Religious Program—Students 1.

154—ST. TIMOTHY (1928) Revs. Stephen F. Leva; Patrick G. McCormick; Deacon Edward F. Hanley.
Res.: 3001 Levick St., 19149. Tel: 215-624-6188; Fax: 215-624-1316. Web: www.st-tims.org.
School—3033 Levick St., 19149. Tel: 215-338-9797; Fax: 215-331-6457. Lucille Hillerman, Prin. Lay Teachers 22; Students 481.
Catechesis/Religious Program—Tel: 215-338-9797, Ext. 123. Students 113.
Convent—3033 Levick St., 19149. Tel: 215-624-8333.

155—TRANSFIGURATION OF OUR LORD (1905-2000) Closed. Formerly located at 5533 Cedar Ave. Spiritual records are kept at St. Cyprian Church. Tel: 215-747-3250.

156—ST. VERONICA (1872) Rev. Eduardo Coll, I.V.E.; Deacon Rafael Maldonado.
Res.: 533 W. Tioga St., 19140. Tel: 215-228-4878; 215-225-5677; Fax: 215-228-0381. Email: par.philadelphi@ive.org.
School—Sixth & Tioga St., 19140. Tel: 215-225-1575; Fax: 215-225-2595. Sr. Mary Ann Bolger, I.H.M., Prin. Sisters, Servants of the Immaculate Heart of Mary 3; Lay Teachers 8; Students 172.
Catechesis/Religious Program—Tel: 215-228-4878. Sr. Maria de Foy, S.S.V.M., D.R.E. Students 170.
Convent—Sisters, Servants of the Immaculate Heart of Mary, 3521 N. Sixth St., 19140. Tel: 215-223-9107. Sr. Victoria Ferraro, I.H.M., Supr.
Convent—Katharine Drexel Sisters, Servants of the Lord and the Virgin of Matara, 632 W. Erie Ave., 19140. Tel: 215-225-9888.

157—ST. VINCENT DE PAUL (1851) Rev. Richard J. Rock, C.M. In Res., Revs. Orlando Cardona, C.M.; Ignatius Suparno, C.M. (Indonesia).
Res.: 109 E. Price St., 19144. Tel: 215-438-2925; Fax: 215-438-4856. Web: www.saint-vincent-church.org.
See the Depaul Catholic School, Philadelphia under Regional Parish Schools located in the Institution section.
Catechesis/Religious Program—Students 55.

158—VISITATION B.V.M. (1874) Revs. John Olenick, C.Ss.R.; James A. Brennan, C.Ss.R.; Thomas McCluskey, C.Ss.R.; Luong Uong, C.Ss.R.; Deacon Edwin Manzano. In Res., Revs. Bruce Lewandowski, C.Ss.R.; Anthony T. Russo, C.Ss.R.
Res.: 2625 B St., 19125. Tel: 215-634-1133; Fax: 215-634-6662. Email:

visitationchurch@visitationbvm.com. Web: www.visitationbvm.net.
School—300 E. Lehigh Ave., 19125. Tel: 215-634-7280; Fax: 215-634-4062. Sisters of St. Joseph 5; Lay Teachers 24; Students 500.
Catechesis/Religious Program—Ms. Norma Rivera, D.R.E. Students 353.
Cardinal Bevilacqua Community Center—2646 Kensington Ave., 19125. Tel: 215-426-9422; Fax: 215-426-9426. Sr. Karen Owens, S.S.J., Dir.

159—ST. WILLIAM (1920) Revs. Joseph G. Watson; Stephen McCarthy; Deacon Louis Malfara. In Res., Rev. Dominic Isaac.
Res.: 6200 Rising Sun Ave., 19111. Tel: 215-745-1389; Fax: 215-745-2650. Web: www.churchofstwilliam.org.
School—Main School, Rising Sun and Robbins St., 19111. Tel: 215-342-4488. Sr. Catherine Clark, I.H.M., Prin.
School—Middle School, Rising Sun and Devereaux Aves., 19111. Tel: 215-725-2574. Sisters, Servants of the Immaculate Heart of Mary 4; Lay Teachers 14; Students 300.
Catechesis/Religious Program—Tel: 215-745-0921. Sr. Maryan Chappetto, I.H.M., D.R.E. Students 101.
Convent—6226 Rising Sun Ave., 19111. Tel: 215-745-3513.

OUTSIDE THE CITY OF PHILADELPHIA

ABINGTON, MONTGOMERY CO., OUR LADY HELP OF CHRISTIANS (1953) Rev. Anthony W. Janton; Deacon Joseph T. Rooney. In Res., Rev. John P. Melepuram.
Res.: 1500 Marian Rd., 19001. Tel: 215-886-3456; Fax: 215-886-7312. Web: www.olhc-parish.org.
Preschool—Tel: 215-887-8503. Lay Teachers 8; Students 49.
School—Elkins & Crater Rds., 19001. Tel: 215-887-3067; Fax: 215-887-3250. Lay Teachers 16; Students 210.
Catechesis/Religious Program—Tel: 215-672-7074. Dianne Donohue. Students 163.

AMBLER, MONTGOMERY CO.

1—ST. ANTHONY OF PADUA (1886) [CEM] Rev. Msgr. Stephen P. McHenry; Rev. John T. Lyons; Deacons David E. Jones; Kevin Gentilcore.
Res.: 259 Forest Ave., 19002-5903. Tel: 215-646-4742; Fax: 215-646-4864. Web: www.saintanthony-parish.org.
See St. Anthony - St. Joseph Elementary School, Ambler under Regional Parish Schools located in the Institution section.
Catechesis/Religious Program—260 Forest Ave., 19002. Tel: 215-646-6150. Students 292.

2—ST. JOSEPH (1920) Rev. Eugene M. Tully; Deacon Francis Clark.
Res.: 16 S. Spring Garden St., 19002-4797. Tel: 215-646-0494; Fax: 215-643-6389. Email: maccard@verizon.net.
Catechesis/Religious Program—Students 116.

ARDMORE, MONTGOMERY CO., ST. COLMAN (1907) Rev. James C. Sherlock; Deacon David B. Schaffer. In Res., Rev. John A. Freeman (Retired).
Res.: 11 Simpson Rd., 19003. Tel: 610-642-0545; 610-649-4775; Fax: 610-642-6853. Email: stcolmanchurch@gmail.com. Web: www.stcolmanardmore.com.
See SS. Colman-John Neumann School, Bryn Mawr under Regional Parish Schools located in the Institution section.
Catechesis/Religious Program—Students 80.

ARDSLEY, MONTGOMERY CO., QUEEN OF PEACE (1954) Rev. Lawrence F. Crehan; Joseph Costello, Business Mgr.
Res.: 820 North Hills Ave., 19038. Tel: 215-887-1838; Fax: 215-887-8328. Email: queenofpeaceparish@comcast.net. Web: www.queenofpeaceparish.net.
See Good Shepherd Catholic Regional School, Ardsley, under Regional Parish Schools located in the Institution Section.
Catechesis/Religious Program—Tel: 215-886-3014. Aileen M. O'Brien, C.R.E. Students 175.
Convent—825 North Hills Ave., 19038. Tel: 215-887-4785.

ASTON, DELAWARE CO., ST. JOSEPH (1947) Revs. Robert C. Vogan; William S. Lange; Rev. Msgr. Richard J. Skelly (Retired); Deacon John M. Betzal.
Res.: 3255 Concord Rd., 19014. Tel: 610-497-3340; Fax: 610-497-3383. Email: stjoseph256@comcast.net. Web: www.stjosephaston.org.
School—Tel: 610-494-0147. Email: stjosephschooloffice@comcast.net. Ms. Anne Cook, Prin. Lay Teachers 14; Students 186.
Catechesis/Religious Program—Tel: 610-494-4358. Email: cmaugeri@stjoseph.org. Ms. Catherine Maugeri, D.R.E. Students 310.

AVONDALE, CHESTER CO., ST. ROCCO (2010) Rev. Msgr. Francis J. Depman; Rev. Andres Garcia.
Parish Center: 9016 Gap Newport Pike, P.O. Box 1019, 19311. Tel: 610-268-3365; Fax: 610-268-5064. Email: mail@stroccochurch.org.
Church: 333 Sunny Dell Rd., 19311.
Convent—Sisters, Servants of the Lord and the Virgin of Matara, 420 Auburn Rd., 19311. Tel: 610-268-0675.
Mission—Santa Maria, Madre de Dios 29 Gap Newport Pike, P.O. Box 1019, 19311. Tel: 610-268-1515. Email: mail@missionsantamaria.org. Web: www.missionsantamaria.org.

BALA CYNWYD, MONTGOMERY CO., ST. MATTHIAS (1906) Rev. Msgr. Michael T. McCulken; Rev. James A. Grant; Mr. John Yura, Business Mgr.; Brandon Artman, Dir. Parish Svcs. & Music. In Res., Rev. Charles E. Gormley (Retired).
Res.: 128 Bryn Mawr Ave., 19004-3013. Tel: 610-664-0207; Fax: 610-664-3559. Email: matthias@saintmatthias.org. Web: saintmatthias.org.
Catechesis/Religious Program—120 Bryn Mawr Ave., 19004-3013. Tel: 610-664-1942. Students 93.
Convent—108 Highland Ave., 19004. Tel: 610-667-1399.

BENSALEM, BUCKS CO.

1—ST. CHARLES BORROMEO (1903) Rev. Msgr. Joseph P. Duncan; Rev. Richard K. McFadden, Parochial Vicar.
Res.: 1731 Hulmeville Rd., 19020. Tel: 215-638-3625; Fax: 215-245-8578. Web: stcharles-bensalem.myownparish.com.
School—(Grades PreK-8), 1704 Bristol Pike, 19020. Tel: 215-639-3456; Fax: 215-639-0496. Web: stcharlesbensalem.org. Sisters, Servants of the Immaculate Heart of Mary 2; Lay Teachers 20; Students 367.
Catechesis/Religious Program—Tel: 215-638-3650. Students 115.
Convent—1080 Kings Ave., 19020. Tel: 215-639-0113. Sisters Servants of the Immaculate Heart of Mary 8.

2—ST. ELIZABETH ANN SETON (1976) Rev. Michael J. Lonergan; Deacons William A. Cella; Stephen A. Guckin.
1200 Park Ave., 19020-4652. Tel: 215-245-6122; Fax: 215-245-4211. Web: www.seasparish.info.
Catechesis/Religious Program—Tel: 215-638-1498. Students 105.

3—SAINT EPHREM (1966) [CEM] Rev. Msgr. Kenneth P. McAteer; Revs. Stephen F. Katziner; Richard E. Rudy; Deacons Edward J. Dymek Jr.; James P. DeBow.
Res.: 5400 Hulmeville Rd., 19020. Tel: 215-245-1698; Fax: 215-245-4787.
School—5340 Hulmeville Rd., 19020. Tel: 215-639-9488; Fax: 215-639-0206. Sisters, Servants of the Immaculate Heart of Mary 4; Lay Teachers 25; Students 470.
Catechesis/Religious Program—Tel: 215-639-4895. Students 227.
Convent—5300 Hulmeville Rd., 19020. Tel: 215-638-1024.

4—OUR LADY OF FATIMA (1954) Rev. Msgr. Edward M. Deliman; Rev. Victor P. Warkulwiz, M.S.S.; Deacon Adolfo Crespo.
Res.: 2933 Street Rd., 19020. Tel: 215-639-4254; Fax: 215-639-4589. Email: olf.pastor@verizon.net.
Parish Center—Tel: 215-639-1916.
Catechesis/Religious Program—2915 Street Rd., 19020. Tel: 215-638-3256. Sr. Sonia Avi, D.R.E. Students 175.

BERWYN, CHESTER CO., ST. MONICA (1897) [CEM] Rev. William A. Trader.
Res.: 635 First Ave., 19312. Tel: 610-644-0110; Fax: 610-695-0850. Web: www.saintmonicachurch.org.
School—601 First Ave., 19312. Tel: 610-644-8848; Fax: 610-695-8515. Mrs. Lisa Hoban, Prin. Lay Teachers 15; Students 156.
Catechesis/Religious Program—Tel: 610-647-4757. Mary Pizzano, D.R.E. Students 292.

BOOTHWYN, DELAWARE CO., ST. JOHN FISHER (1971) Rev. Gregory J. Hickey.
Res.: 4225 Chichester Ave., 19061. Tel: 610-485-0441; Fax: 610-859-2109. Web: www.stjohnfisherchurch.com.
See Holy Saviour-St. John Fisher School, Linwood under Regional Parish Schools located in the Institution section.
Catechesis/Religious Program—Tel: 610-485-0581. Students 246.

BRIDGEPORT, MONTGOMERY CO.

1—ST. AUGUSTINE (1892) [CEM] Rev. Scott D. Brockson.
Res.: 464 Ford St., 19405. Tel: 610-272-4088; Fax: 610-272-6396. Email: staugustine@comcast.net. Web: www.saintaugustinechurch.net.
Catechesis/Religious Program—Students 52.
Worship Site: Our Lady of Sorrows—421 Coates St., 19405.

2—OUR LADY OF MT. CARMEL (1924), (Italian), Rev. Salvatore J. Pronesti.
Res.: 502 Ford St., 19405. Tel: 610-272-3479; Fax: 610-272-5449. Email: olmcoffice@comcast.net. Web: www.olmcchurch.net.
Catechesis/Religious Program—Tel: 610-272-3479; Fax: 610-272-5449. Students 59.

3—OUR MOTHER OF SORROWS (1926-2001), (Slovak), Closed. Spiritual records are kept at St. Augustine, Bridgeport. Tel: 610-272-4088.

BRISTOL, BUCKS CO.

1—ST. ANN (1906), (Italian), Revs. Gerard F. Lynch, O.SS.T.; Thomas A. Morris, O.SS.T.
Res.: 357 Dorrance St., P.O. Box 1175, 19007. Tel: 215-788-2128; Fax: 215-781-9782. Email: office@stannbristol.com. Web: www.stannbristol.com.
Catechesis/Religious Program—418 Jefferson Ave., 19007. Tel: 215-788-2030; Fax: 215-788-2979. Students 95.
Convent—430 Jefferson Ave., 19907. Tel: 215-788-2531.
Mission—Sacred Heart of Jesus Main St., Tullytown, Bucks Co. 19007.

2—ST. MARK (1845) [CEM] Revs. Dennis M. Mooney; Augusto M. Concha.
Res.: 1025 Radcliffe St., 19007. Tel: 215-788-2493; Fax: 215-785-4121. Email: office@saintmarkchurch.net. Web: www.saintmarkchurch.net.
School—1024 Radcliffe St., 19007. Tel: 215-785-0973; Fax: 215-781-0268. Mrs. Angelina Clair, Prin. Lay Teachers 12; Students 186.
Catechesis/Religious Program—Tel: 215-788-2319. Mary Leonhauser, C.R.E. Students 133.

BROOKHAVEN, DELAWARE CO., OUR LADY OF CHARITY (1952) Revs. Brian A. Izzo; Richard C. Williams (Retired).
Res.: 231 Upland Rd., 19015. Tel: 610-872-6192; Fax: 610-872-1120.
School—(Grades PreK-8), 249 Upland Rd., 19015. Tel: 610-874-0410; Fax: 610-874-5879. Lay Teachers 13; Students 174.
Catechesis/Religious Program—Tel: 484-480-5469. Students 184.

BROOKLINE, DELAWARE CO., ANNUNCIATION B.V.M. (1927) Rev. Mark J. Haynes. In Res., Rev. Tadeusz Pacholczyk.
Res.: 410 Sagamore Rd., Havertown, 19083. Tel: 610-449-1613; Fax: 610-449-7041. Web: www.annunciationparish.com.
School—411 Brookline Blvd., Havertown, 19083. Tel: 610-446-8430; Fax: 610-446-0627. Sisters of Mercy 1; Lay Teachers 14; Students 201.
Catechesis/Religious Program—Tel: 610-449-9858. Students 340.
Convent—421 Brookline Blvd., Havertown, 19083. Tel: 610-449-4065.

BROOMALL, DELAWARE CO., ST. PIUS X (1955) Revs. James Hutchins; Albert J. Santorsola; Rev. Msgr. John J. Jagodzinski; Deacons Joseph E. Iannucci; Stephen C. Kazanjian. In Res., Rev. Edward J. Casey.
Res.: 220 Lawrence Rd., 19008. Tel: 610-353-4880; Fax: 610-356-1084. Email: stpiusxbusinessoffice@comcast.net. Web: www.saintpius.net.
School—204 Lawrence Rd., 19008. Tel: 610-356-7222; Fax: 610-356-5380. Sisters, Servants of the Immaculate Heart of Mary 6; Lay Teachers 22; Students 415.
Catechesis/Religious Program—Tel: 610-353-6950; Fax: 610-356-1084. Students 409.

BRYN MAWR, DELAWARE CO., ST. JOHN NEUMANN (1964) Rev. James J. McKeaney; Sr. Carol Kelly, S.S.J., Dir. Parish Ministries.
Res.: 380 Highland Ln., 19010. Tel: 610-525-3100; Fax: 610-525-6363. Email: sjnparish@verizon.net.
See SS. Colman-John Neumann School, Byrn Mawr under Regional Parish Schools located in the Institution section.
Catechesis/Religious Program—Students 125.

BRYN MAWR, MONTGOMERY CO., OUR MOTHER OF GOOD COUNSEL (1885) Revs. John T. Denny, O.S.A.; Dennis M. McGowan, O.S.A.; Deacon William C. Harkin, O.S.A. In Res., Rev. Francis A. Sirolli, O.S.A.
Res.: 31 Pennswood Rd., 19010. Tel: 610-525-0147; Fax: 610-525-0157. Email: omgc@omgcparish.org. Web: www.omgcparish.org.
Catechesis/Religious Program—Students 110.

BUCKINGHAM, BUCKS CO., OUR LADY OF GUADALUPE (2000) Rev. Msgr. Joseph P. Gentili; Deacon Robert P. Gohde.
Parish Office—5175 Cold Spring Creamery Rd., Ste. #5, Doylestown, 18902. Tel: 267-247-5374; Fax: 267-247-5402.
Res.: 3243 Ash Mill Rd., Doylestown, 18902.
Catechesis/Religious Program—Students 563.

CENTER SQUARE, MONTGOMERY CO., ST. HELENA (1919) Rev. Msgr. Joseph J. Nicolo; Rev. George J. Szparagowski; Deacon A. Kenneth Belanger.
Res.: 1489 DeKalb Pike, Blue Bell, 19422. Tel: 610-275-7711; Fax: 610-275-7610. Web: www.sainthelena-centersquare.net.
School—1499 DeKalb Pike, Blue Bell, 19422. Tel: 610-279-3345. Web: www.sainthelenaschool.org.

Sisters of Mercy 1; Lay Teachers 29; Students 504.
Catechesis/Religious Program—Tel: 610-279-3870. Students 282.
Convent—Tel: 610-272-1383.

CHADDS FORD, DELAWARE CO., ST. CORNELIUS (1963) Rev. Msgr. Gregory J. Parlante; Rev. Dominic M. Chiaravalle; Deacons Ronald L. Lewis; Harry J. Morris; John J. Todor. In Res., Rev. Philip J. Lowe.
Res.: 160 Ridge Rd., 19317. Tel: 610-459-2502; Fax: 610-459-3942. Email: stcorn1@comcast.net. Web: saintcornelius.org.
School—St. Cornelius School, Tel: 610-459-8663; Fax: 610-459-7728. Students 207.
Catechesis/Religious Program—Tel: 484-840-9250; Fax: 610-459-3942. Students 650.

CHALFONT, BUCKS CO., ST. JUDE (1962) Rev. Msgr. James P. McCoy; Rev. Robert G. Suskey; Mr. Robert T. O'Sullivan, Business Mgr.; Deacons John T. Riordan; Claude B. Granese; Timothy P. Lynch.
Res.: 321 W. Butler Ave., 18914-2329. Tel: 215-822-0179; Fax: 215-822-0638. Email: office@stjudechalfont.org. Web: www.stjudechalfont.org.
School—323 W. Butler Ave., 18914-2329. Tel: 215-822-9225; Fax: 215-822-0722. Email: semrsm@stjudeschool.com. Web: www.stjudeschool.com. Sr. Elizabeth Marley, R.S.M., Prin. Sisters 1; Lay Teachers 24; Students 363.
Catechesis/Religious Program—Tel: 215-822-7553. Email: prep@stjudeschool.com. Alice Patcella, D.R.E. Students 538.

CHELTENHAM, MONTGOMERY CO.

1—ST. JOSEPH (1953) Rev. William S. Harrison.
Parish Center—7631 Waters Rd., 19012-1318. Tel: 215-635-5533; Fax: 215-635-4578.
Catechesis/Religious Program—Students 50.

2—PRESENTATION OF BLESSED VIRGIN MARY (1890) Rev. William S. Harrison; Sr. Joan B. Melley, S.S.J., Parish Svcs. Dir.
Res.: 100 Old Soldiers Rd., 19012. Tel: 215-379-1364; 215-379-1599; Fax: 215-379-2054.
School—105 Old Soldiers Rd., 19012. Tel: 215-379-3798; Fax: 215-379-4430. Web: www.presentationbvm.org/school. Lay Teachers 13; Students 260.
Catechesis/Religious Program—Tel: 215-379-2054. Students 75.
Convent—107 Old Soldiers Rd., 19012. Tel: 215-379-8343.

CHESTER, DELAWARE CO.

1—ST. ANTHONY OF PADUA (1908-1993), (Italian), Closed. Formerly located at 308 W. 3rd St. Spiritual records are kept at Saint Katharine Drexel Church, Chester. Tel: 610-872-3731.

2—ST. HEDWIG (1902-1993), (Polish), Closed. Formerly located at 4th & Hayes Sts. Spiritual records are kept at Sacred Heart Church, Clifton Heights. Tel: 610-623-0409.

3—IMMACULATE HEART OF MARY (1873-1993) Closed. Formerly located at 2nd & Norris Sts. Spiritual records are kept at Saint Katharine Drexel Church, Chester. Tel: 610-872-3731.

4—SAINT KATHARINE DREXEL (1993) Rev. Msgr. Joseph C. McLoone; Rev. Peter J. Welsh; Deacons Michael J. Finn; John J. Pileggi.
1920 Providence Ave., 19013. Tel: 610-872-3731; Fax: 610-872-0545. Web: www.stkatharinedrexelparish.org. In Res., Rev. Angelo J. Hernandez.
Catechesis/Religious Program—Students 39.
Convent—1902 Providence Ave., 19013. Tel: 610-876-4916.
Saint Katharine Drexel Center—2nd & Norris St., 19013. Tel: 610-872-3731; Fax: 610-872-0545.

5—ST. MICHAEL (1842-1993) Closed. Formerly located at 7th St. & Avenue of the States. Spiritual records are kept at Saint Katharine Drexel Church, Chester. Tel: 610-872-3731.

6—OUR LADY OF VILNA (1924-1972), (Lithuanian), Closed. Formerly located at 4th & Madison Sts. Spiritual records are kept at Saint Katharine Drexel, Chester. Tel: 215-872-3731.

7—RESURRECTION OF OUR LORD (1911-1993) Closed. Formerly located at 9th St. & Highland Ave. Spiritual records are kept at Saint Katharine Drexel Church, Chester. Tel: 610-872-3731.

8—ST. ROBERT (1922-1993) Closed. Formerly located at 20th St. & Providence Ave. Spiritual records are kept at Saint Katharine Drexel Church, Chester. Tel: 610-872-3731.

CLIFTON HEIGHTS, DELAWARE CO., SACRED HEART (1910), (Polish), Rev. Jan Palkowski.
Res.: 316 E. Broadway, 19018. Tel: 610-623-0409; Fax: 610-623-2926. Email: shc316@aol.com. Web: www.sacredheart-cliftonheights.net.
Catechesis/Religious Program—Students 15.
Mission—St. Hedwig Chapel 4th & Hayes Sts., Chester, Delaware Co. 19013.

COATESVILLE, CHESTER CO.

1—ST. CECILIA (1869) [CEM] Revs. Francis J. Mulranen; Nicholas J. Dininni, Coord. Hispanic Ministry, N. Chester Co.; Deacon Frederick H. Kerr. In Res., Rev. Semanhyia Boateng-Mensah.
Res.: 99 N. 6th Ave., 19320. Tel: 610-384-0422; Fax: 610-384-4415.
See Pope John Paul II Regional Catholic Elementary School, West Brandywine under Regional Parish Schools located in the Institution section.
Regional Religious Education Program—Tel: 610-384-0900. Felicia Navarro, D.R.E. Students 113.
Convent—603 E. Lincoln Hwy., 19320. Tel: 610-384-0733; Fax: 610-384-5730.

2—ST. JOSEPH (1924), (Slovak), Rev. John V. Oulds.
Res.: 404 Charles St., 19320. Tel: 610-384-0360; Fax: 610-384-8545. Email: sjrectory@comcast.net. Web: www.stjosephcoatesville.org.
See Pope John Paul II Regional Catholic Elementary School, West Brandywine under Regional Parish Schools located in the Institution section.
Catechesis/Religious Program—Students 54.

3—OUR LADY OF THE ROSARY (1917), (Italian), Rev. Thomas J. Brennan; Deacon Richard Stoughton.
Res.: 80 S. 17th Ave., 19320. Tel: 610-384-1415; Fax: 610-383-6592. Email: FatherB@olrcc.org. Web: www.olrcc.org.
See Pope John Paul II Regional Catholic Elementary School, West Brandywine under Regional Parish Schools located in the Institution section.
Catechesis/Religious Program—Tel: 610-384-1415. Students 127.

4—ST. STANISLAUS KOSTKA (1907), (Polish), [CEM] Rev. John V. Oulds.
Res.: 209 W. Lincoln Hwy., 19320. Tel: 610-384-1172; Fax: 610-384-8545. Email: ststanskostkacc@aol.com.
See Pope John Paul II Regional Catholic Elementary School, West Brandywine under Regional Parish Schools located in the Institution section.
Catechesis/Religious Program—Students 2.

COLLEGEVILLE, MONTGOMERY CO., ST. ELEANOR (1911) Rev. Msgr. Patrick E. Sweeney; Rev. Jonathan J. Dalin; Deacon Joseph DeRosa.
Res.: 647 Locust St., 19426. Tel: 610-489-1647; Fax: 610-489-7469. Email: church@steleanor.com. Web: www.steleanor.com.
School—Tel: 610-489-9434, Ext. 2225; Fax: 610-489-6137. Email: mpaulhamus@steleanor.com. Web: www.steleanorschool.com. Lay Teachers 27; Students 504.
Catechesis/Religious Program—Tel: 610-489-4677, Ext. 2233. Email: religiousEd@steleanor.com. Students 1,115.

COLLINGDALE, DELAWARE CO., ST. JOSEPH (1916) Rev. Michael J. Reilly; Deacons Paul McBlain; Thomas L. Taylor. In Res., Rev. James R. Casey.
Res.: 500 Woodlawn Ave., 19023. Tel: 610-583-4530; Fax: 610-583-7730. Email: parishrectory@stjosephcollingdale.org. Web: www.saintjoseph-collingdale.com.
Catechesis/Religious Program—Tel: 610-586-1520. Mary Carney, Dir. Faith Formation. Students 75.

CONSHOHOCKEN, MONTGOMERY CO.

1—SS. COSMAS AND DAMIAN (1912), (Italian), Rev. Gasper A. Genuardi; Deacon Joseph C. Carr. In Res., Rev. John J. McKenzie, O.S.A.
Res.: 209 W. Fifth Ave., 19428. Tel: 610-828-0101; Fax: 610-828-5294. Email: sscdchurch@aol.com. Web: sscosmasanddamian.com.
See SS. Cosmas & Damian Primary Campus, Conshohocken under Regional Parish Schools located in the Institution section.
Catechesis/Religious Program—Students 90.

2—ST. MARY (1905), (Polish), [CEM] Rev. Msgr. Gerard C. Mesure; Deacon Thomas P. Quinn. In Res., Rev. John Arthur McGinnis (FAR) (Retired).
Res.: 140 W. Hector St., 19428. Tel: 610-828-0260; Fax: 610-828-9665. Email: stmaryconshy@verizon.net.
Catechesis/Religious Program—Mrs. Kathleen Pulli, D.R.E.

3—ST. MATTHEW (1851) [CEM] [JC 2] Rev. J. Thomas Heron. In Res., Rev. John J. Ames.
Res.: 219 Fayette St., 19428. Tel: 610-828-0424; Fax: 610-825-5168.
See Conshohocken Catholic School, Conshohocken under Regional Parish Schools located in the Institution section.
Catechesis/Religious Program—Email: stmatthewdre@verizon.net. Web: www.stmatthewchurch.com. Students 141.
Convent—Third Ave. & Harry St., 19428. Tel: 610-828-0174.

CROYDON, BUCKS CO., ST. THOMAS AQUINAS (1922) Rev. Michael J. Davis; Deacon John J. Gallagher.
Res.: 126 Walnut Ave., 19021-5496. Tel: 215-788-2989; 215-788-5813; Fax: 215-788-7626.
Catechesis/Religious Program—Students 85.

DARBY, DELAWARE CO., BLESSED VIRGIN MARY (1913) Rev. Joseph M. Corley. In Res., Rev. Edward J. Kennedy.
Res.: 1101 Main St., 19023. Tel: 610-583-2128; Fax: 610-583-9829. Email: bvmrectory@rcn.com. Web: www.bvm-darby.com.
School—47 MacDade Blvd., 19023. Tel: 610-586-0638; Fax: 610-586-1582. Sisters, Servants of the Immaculate Heart of Mary 3; Lay Teachers 10; Students 215.
Catechesis/Religious Program—Tel: 610-586-2490. Students 15.

DOWNINGTOWN, CHESTER CO., ST. JOSEPH (1851) [CEM] Rev. Msgr. Joseph C. McLoone; Rev. Brian M. Kean; Deacon Edward R. Schiappa. In Res., Revs. Edward J. Jablonski; Matthew W. Guckin.
Res.: 338 Manor Ave., 19335. Tel: 610-269-8294; Fax: 610-269-2487.
School—340 Manor Ave., 19335. Tel: 610-269-8999; Fax: 610-269-2252. Sisters, Servants of the Immaculate Heart of Mary 5; Lay Teachers 31; Students 637.
Catechesis/Religious Program—Tel: 610-873-8798; Fax: 610-873-5466. Mrs. Kathryn Thomas, D.R.E. Students 791.
Convent—336 Manor Ave., 19335. Tel: 610-269-8314.

DOYLESTOWN, BUCKS CO., OUR LADY OF MOUNT CARMEL (1850) [CEM] Rev. Msgr. Charles H. Hagan; Revs. John C. Crowley; James J. Mulligan; Paschal U. Onunwa (Nigeria); Deacons George Corwell; James J. Fowkes.
Res.: 235 E. State St., 18901. Tel: 215-348-4190; Fax: 215-348-3104. Web: www.ourladymtcarmel.org.
School—225 E. Ashland St., 18901. Tel: 215-348-5907; Fax: 215-348-5671. Sisters of St. Francis of Philadelphia 1; Lay Teachers 25; Students 355.
Catechesis/Religious Program—Tel: 215-345-7089; Fax: 215-345-4216. Cindy Balceniuk, D.R.E. Students 1,150.
Convent—209 E. State St., 18901. Tel: 215-348-4663.

DREXEL HILL, DELAWARE CO.

1—ST. ANDREW (1916) Rev. Msgr. Albin J. Grous; Revs. James F. Sullivan; Girard J. Cusatis (Retired).
Res.: 3500 School Ln., 19026. Tel: 610-259-1169. Email: info@standrewdh.com. Web: www.standrewdh.com.
School—529 Mason Ave., 19026. Tel: 610-259-5145; Fax: 610-284-6956. Sisters of St. Joseph 1; Lay Teachers 16; Students 317.
Catechesis/Religious Program—Students 185.
Convent—535 Mason Ave., 19026. Tel: 610-259-6130.

2—ST. BERNADETTE (1947) Revs. John J. Kelly; Robert F. Lucas; Deacons Frank B. Burke; Thomas P. Fitzpatrick.
Res.: 1035 Turner Ave., 19026. Tel: 610-789-7676; Fax: 610-789-9539. Web: www.stbl.org.
School—1001 Turner Ave., 19026. Fax: 610-789-0890. Lay Teachers 17; Students 267.
Catechesis/Religious Program—Tel: 610-853-1740. Kyleen B. Roe, Dir., Faith Formation. Students 233.
Convent—

3—ST. CHARLES BORROMEO (1849) [CEM] Revs. Roland D. Slobogin; Daniel P. Devine; Deacon John H. Farrell.
Res.: 3422 Dennison Ave., 19026. Tel: 610-623-3800; Fax: 610-284-9583. Web: stcharlesdrexelhill.org.
Catechesis/Religious Program—Tel: 610-259-4389. Students 130.

4—ST. DOROTHY (1947) Revs. Michael D. Murphy; John D. Silcox Jr.
Res.: 4910 Township Line Rd., 19026. Tel: 610-789-7788; 610-789-7338; Fax: 610-789-6936.
School—1225 Burmont Rd., 19026. Tel: 610-789-4100. Web: www.stdots.org. Lay Teachers 20; Sisters of Mercy 2; Students 423.
Catechesis/Religious Program—Tel: 610-853-1499. Students 326.
Convent—1201 Burmont Rd., 19026. Tel: 610-789-4112.

EAST GOSHEN, CHESTER CO., SS. PETER AND PAUL (1967) Rev. Msgr. Daniel J. Kutys; Rev. James J. Whelan; Deacons Thomas J. Horan; Robert F. Pierce.
Res.: 1325 Boot Rd., West Chester, 19380. Tel: 610-692-2216; Fax: 610-692-7103. Web: www.sspeterandpaulrc.org.
School—(Grades PreK-8), 1327 Boot Rd., West Chester, 19380-5901. Tel: 610-696-1000; Fax: 484-631-0181. Email: school@sspeterandpaulrc.org. Mrs. Margaret Egan, Prin. Lay Teachers 27; Students 430.
Catechesis/Religious Program—Tel: 610-692-5886; Fax: 484-631-0182. Email: lpjte@verizon.net. Patricia B. Ehrhart, D.R.E. Students 385.

EAST LANSDOWNE, DELAWARE CO., ST. CYRIL OF ALEXANDRIA (1928) Rev. Dominic Tran Minh Duc. In Res., Rev. James P. Olson.
Res.: 153 Penn Blvd., 19050-2698. Tel: 610-623-5160; Fax: 610-622-2479. Web: saintcyril.org.
School—716 Emerson Ave., 19050. Tel: 610-623-1113; Fax: 610-623-2427. Sr. Barbara Montague, I.H.M., Prin. Sisters, Servants of the Immaculate

Heart of Mary 4; Lay Teachers 12; Students 208.
Catechesis/Religious Program—Fax: 610-622-2479. Students 25.
Convent—171 Penn Blvd., 19050. Tel: 610-623-6590.

EDDYSTONE, DELAWARE CO., ST. ROSE OF LIMA (1890) Rev. Gerald D. Canavan; Deacons Anthony J. DiIenno; Lawrence P. Schnepp.
Res.: 1901 Chester Pike, 19022. Tel: 610-876-6170; Fax: 610-876-6128.
See St. Madeline-St. Rose, Ridley Park under Consolidated Parish Schools located in the Institution section.
Catechesis/Religious Program—Students 158.

ELKINS PARK, MONTGOMERY CO., ST. JAMES (1923) Rev. Edward A. Windhaus. In Res., Rev. Quan H. Tran.
Res.: 8320 Brookside Rd., 19027. Tel: 215-635-6210; Fax: 215-635-3346. Email: stjameselkinspark@comcast.net. Web: www.stjamesparish.net.
Catechesis/Religious Program—Students 79.

ESSINGTON, DELAWARE CO., ST. MARGARET MARY ALACOQUE (1921) Rev. Anthony F. Orth.
Res.: 500 Wanamaker Ave., 19029. Tel: 610-521-9177; Fax: 610-595-0230. Email: stmarectory@comcast.net. Web: stmargaretmaryalacoque.net.
Catechesis/Religious Program—Students 54.

EXTON, CHESTER CO., SS. PHILIP AND JAMES (1959) Rev. Joseph C. Dieckhaus; Deacons James E. Bogdan; Charles W. Polley Jr.
Res.: 107 N. Ship Rd., 19341. Tel: 610-363-6536; Fax: 610-524-7359. Web: www.sspj.net.
School—721 E. Lincoln Hwy., 19341. Tel: 610-363-6530; Fax: 610-363-6495. Sr. Helen Thomas McCann, Prin. Sisters, Servants of the Immaculate Heart of Mary 4; Lay Teachers 20; Students 526.
Catechesis/Religious Program—Tel: 610-363-1307. Sr. Eunice Marie, I.H.M., D.R.E. Students 526.
Convent—105 N. Ship Rd., 19341. Tel: 610-363-2263.

FAIRLESS HILLS, BUCKS CO., ST. FRANCES CABRINI (1953) Rev. Msgr. Michael P. McCormac; Deacons Mace M. Mazzoni; Louis F. Hoelzle.
Res.: 325 S. Oxford Valley Rd., 19030. Tel: 215-946-4040; Fax: 215-943-1116.
See Holy Family Regional Catholic School, Levittown, under Regional Parish Schools located in the Institution Section.
Catechesis/Religious Program—Tel: 215-946-1115. Email: saintfrancescabrini@verizon.net. Audrey Wilson, D.R.E. Students 153.

FALLSINGTON, BUCKS CO., ST. JOSEPH THE WORKER (1956) Rev. Donald G. Birch. In Res., Rev. Mark J. Hunt.
Res.: 9172 New Falls Rd., 19054. Tel: 215-945-4486; Fax: 215-945-3292. Web: www.sjtw.org.
See Holy Family Regional Catholic School, Levittown, under Regional Parish Schools located in the Institution Section.
Catechesis/Religious Program—Tel: 215-945-4680. Students 168.

FEASTERVILLE, BUCKS CO., ASSUMPTION B.V.M. (1950) Rev. William F. McGeown; Deacon Robert J. Stewart; Sr. Diane Wolf, S.S.J., Pastoral Assoc. In Res., Rev. John E. Donia.
Res.: 1900 Meadowbrook Rd., 19053. Tel: 215-357-1221; Fax: 215-357-2283. Web: www.abvmfeasterville.org.
School—Tel: 215-357-5499. Sisters, Servants of the Immaculate Heart of Mary 5; Lay Teachers 13; Students 199.
Catechesis/Religious Program—Tel: 215-357-3445. Mrs. Joyce Boag, D.R.E. Students 254.
Convent—55 Bristol Rd., 19053. Tel: 215-355-3898.

FLOURTOWN, MONTGOMERY CO., ST. GENEVIEVE (1953) Rev. Msgr. Michael J. Matz. In Res., Rev. Carl F. Janicki; Deacons Joseph Nines; Michael G. Conroy.
Res.: 1225 Bethlehem Pike, 19031. Tel: 215-836-2828; Fax: 215-836-7218. Email: rectory@stgensparish.com. Web: www.stgensparish.com.
School—1237 Bethlehem Pike, 19031. Tel: 215-836-5644; Fax: 215-836-0159. Web: www.stgens.com. Sisters of St. Joseph 3; Lay Teachers 18; Students 235.
Catechesis/Religious Program—Tel: 215-836-1994. Students 161.
Worship Site: Seven Dolors Church—1200 E. Willow Grove Ave., Wyndmoor, 19038. Tel: 215-836-2828; Fax: 215-836-7218.

GLADWYNE, MONTGOMERY CO., ST. JOHN BAPTIST VIANNEY (1927) Rev. Msgr. Donald E. Leighton. In Res., Rev. Msgr. Francis W. Beach.
Res.: 1110 Vaughans Ln., 19035. Tel: 610-642-0938; Fax: 610-642-1432.
Catechesis/Religious Program—350 Conshohocken State Rd., 19035. Mrs. MaryAnne Monroe, C.R.E. Students 120.

GLEN MILLS, DELAWARE CO., ST. THOMAS THE APOSTLE (1729) [CEM] Revs. Francis P. Groarke; John H. Roebuck.
Res.: 430 Valley Brook Rd., 19342. Tel: 610-459-2224; Fax: 610-459-2677.
School—Tel: 610-459-8134; Fax: 610-459-8120. Lay Teachers 35; Students 364.
Catechesis/Religious Program—Tel: 610-459-3477. Mary Sassani, D.R.E. Students 545.
Chaplaincies— Glen Mills Schools; Delaware County Prison; Brinton Manor; Rosehill; Riddle Hospital; 4 Seasons Assisted Living.

GLENOLDEN, DELAWARE CO., ST. GEORGE (1923) Rev. Christopher J. Papa.
Res.: 22 E. Cooke Ave., 19036-1497. Tel: 610-237-1633; Fax: 610-237-9626. Web: www.stgeorgeparish.org.
Catechesis/Religious Program—Students 81.
Convent—11 E. Lamont Ave., 19036-1497. Tel: 484-318-5092.

GLENSIDE, MONTGOMERY CO., ST. LUKE THE EVANGELIST (1905) Revs. Joseph D. Brandt; John F. McBride; Deacon Thomas M. Croke.
Res.: 2316 Fairhill Ave., 19038. Tel: 215-572-0128; Fax: 215-572-0482. Email: stlukerc@aol.com. Web: www.stlukerc.org.
School—2336 Fairhill Ave., 19038. Tel: 215-884-0843; Fax: 215-884-4607. Sr. William Adele, S.S.J., Prin. Sisters of St. Joseph 3; Lay Teachers 23; Students 321.
Catechesis/Religious Program—2330 Fairhill Ave., 19038. Tel: 215-884-2080. Email: prep@stlukerc.org. Students 300.
Convent—2324 Fairhill Ave., 19038. Tel: 215-884-0225.

HATBORO, MONTGOMERY CO., ST. JOHN BOSCO (1953) Revs. Gary J. Kramer; Gerald C. Ronan; Deacon Daniel J. Rouse.
Parish Office Center—215 E. Cty. Line Rd., 19040-1244.
Res.: 235 E. County Line Rd., 19040. Tel: 215-672-7280; Fax: 215-672-1105. Web: www.saintjohnbosco.org.
Catechesis/Religious Program—Tel: 267-803-0774. Email: cflack@saintjohnbosco.org. Students 354.
Convent—189 E. County Line Rd., 19040.

HATFIELD, MONTGOMERY CO., ST. MARIA GORETTI (1953) Rev. Andrew C. Brownholtz; Joseph Rydzewski, Business Mgr.; Eileen Ericsson, Music Dir.
Res.: 1601 Derstine Rd., 19440. Tel: 215-721-0199; Fax: 215-721-4320. Web: www.stmariagoretti.net.
School—2980 Cowpath Rd., 19440. Tel: 215-721-9098; Fax: 215-721-3394. Lay Teachers 14; Students 192.
Catechesis/Religious Program—Tel: 215-721-6559. Julie Clymer, D.R.E.; Joseph Cruice, Youth Min. Students 596.

HAVERTOWN, DELAWARE CO., ST. DENIS (1825) [CEM] Rev. Msgr. James J. Graham; Deacons Francis J. Connors; John F. Schlegel. In Res., Rev. Msgr. Bernard J. Trinity (Retired); Rev. Daniel M. Kredensor.
Res.: 2401 St. Denis Ln., 19083. Tel: 610-446-0200; Fax: 610-446-4638. Web: www.stdenishavertown.org.
School—300 E. Eagle Rd., 19083. Tel: 610-446-4608; Fax: 610-446-5705. Web: www.saintdenisschool.com. Sr. Gerald Helene, O.S.F., Prin. Lay Teachers 20; Students 350.
Catechesis/Religious Program—Tel: 610-449-7892; Fax: 610-446-5705. Students 362.
Convent—Tel: 610-446-1263.

HIGHLAND PARK, DELAWARE CO., ST. LAURENCE (1917) Rev. James E. Goerner; Rev. Msgr. Richard Malone; Deacon Mark Wallace. In Res., Rev. Joseph C. McCaffrey.
Res.: 30 St. Laurence Rd., Upper Darby, 19082. Tel: 610-449-0600; 610-449-0601; Fax: 610-449-4299.
School—8245 W. Chester Pike, 19082. Tel: 610-789-2670; Fax: 610-789-1128. Web: www.saintlaurence-.org. Sisters, Servants of the Immaculate Heart of Mary 13; Lay Teachers 21; Students 375.
Catechesis/Religious Program—Tel: 610-449-0600, Ext. 15. Students 75.
Convent—Tel: 610-449-7042.
H.O.P.E. Program—Tel: 610-449-0600; Fax: 610-449-4299.

HILLTOWN, BUCKS CO., OUR LADY OF THE SACRED HEART (1919) [CEM] Rev. Michael J. Kelly; Deacons Vincent G. Ceneviva; J. Gerry Murphy. In Res., Rev. John D. Schiele.
Res.: 9 Broad St., 18927. Tel: 215-822-9224; Fax: 215-712-0278. Web: www.olsh-hilltown.web.officelive.com.
See St. Agnes-Sacred Heart School, Hilltown under Regional Parish Schools located in the Institution section.
Catechesis/Religious Program—Tel: 215-822-9020. Students 598.

HOLLAND, BUCKS CO., ST. BEDE THE VENERABLE (1965) Rev. Msgr. John C. Marine; Rev. Harold B. McKale. In Res., Rev. Msgr. Robert J. Grudowski (Retired).
Res.: 1071 Holland Rd., 18966. Tel: 215-357-5720; Fax: 215-396-0704. Web: www.st-bede.org.
School—1053 Holland Rd., 18966. Tel: 215-357-4720; Fax: 215-355-9526. Margi Slomiany, Prin. Lay Teachers 21; Students 291.
Catechesis/Religious Program—Tel: 215-357-2130; Fax: 215-357-0232. Students 700.

HORSHAM, MONTGOMERY CO., ST. CATHERINE OF SIENA (1963) Rev. Joseph F. Rymdeika; Deacon Timothy Urbanski; Joshua Jenkins, Dir. Parish Svcs. In Res., Rev. John C. Nguyen.
Res.: 321 Witmer Rd., 19044. Tel: 215-672-2881; Fax: 215-674-1025. Web: stcatherineschurch.org.
School—317 Witmer Rd., 19044. Tel: 215-674-1904; Fax: 215-674-1466. Lay Teachers 19; Students 222.
Catechesis/Religious Program—Tel: 215-674-8549. Students 372.
Convent—319 Witmer Rd., 19044. Tel: 215-672-7221.

HUNTINGDON VALLEY, MONTGOMERY CO., ST. ALBERT THE GREAT (1962) Rev. Msgr. Paul V. Dougherty; Revs. Mathew Manakatt; Charles D. Smith (Retired); Deacons Michael J. Kolakowski; Edward J. Morris; Sr. Marie Rachfalski, O.S.F., Parish Svcs. Dir.
Res.: 212 Welsh Rd., 19006. Tel: 215-947-3500; Fax: 215-938-9071. Email: rectory@stalbertthegreat.org.
School—Tel: 215-947-2332; Fax: 215-938-9360. Cynthia Koons, Prin. Lay Teachers 26; Students 455.
Catechesis/Religious Program—Tel: 215-947-3641. Sr. Patricia Gannon, S.S.J., D.R.E. Students 270.

JAMISON, BUCKS CO., ST. CYRIL OF JERUSALEM (1965) Rev. Msgr. Robert J. Powell; Rev. Michael A. Filippello; Deacons Joseph F. Windish; Joseph Owen. In Res., Most Rev. Martin N. Lohmuller.
Res.: 1410 Almshouse Rd., 18929. Tel: 215-343-1288; Fax: 215-343-3924.
Catechesis/Religious Program—Tel: 215-343-3139. Students 755.

JENKINTOWN, MONTGOMERY CO., IMMACULATE CONCEPTION (1866) Rev. David E. Diamond; Deacons Paul Hagerty; Alvin Clay.
Res.: 604 West Ave., 19046-2708. Tel: 215-884-4022; 215-887-0181; Fax: 215-887-4163.
School—606 West Ave., 19046-2708. Tel: 215-887-1312; Fax: 215-887-5517. Diane Greco, Prin. Lay Teachers 18; Students 195.
Catechesis/Religious Program—Tel: 215-885-5586. Ms. Marie McGuigan, D.R.E. Students 140.

KENNETT SQUARE, CHESTER CO., ST. PATRICK (1869) [CEM] Rev. Victor F. Sharrett; Deacon James K. Madonna. In Res., Rev. Andres Garcia.
Res.: 218 Meredith St., 19348. Tel: 610-444-2128. Email: stpatkennett@verizon.net. Web: www.rc.net/philadelphia/st_patrick/.
Parish Office—205 Lafayette St., 19348. Tel: 610-444-4364; Fax: 610-444-2129.
School—210 Meredith St., 19348. Tel: 610-444-3104; Fax: 610-444-3166. Web: www.stpatskennettsquare.org. Lay Teachers 22; Students 214.
Catechesis/Religious Program—Tel: 610-444-2214. Marianne Kane, D.R.E. Students 225.

KIMBERTON, CHESTER CO., ST. BASIL THE GREAT (1965) Rev. Gary T. Pacitti.
Res.: 2300 Kimberton Rd., Box 637, 19442-0637. Tel: 610-933-2110; 610-933-4730; Fax: 610-933-0627. Email: church@stbasils.org. Web: www.stbasils.org/church.
School—Tel: 610-933-2453; Fax: 610-933-7590. Email: arufo@stbasils.org. Web: www.stbasils.org. Lay Teachers 15; Students 213.
Catechesis/Religious Program—Tel: 610-935-1261. Email: dre@stbasil.org. Students 242.
Convent—Sisters of St. Francis Residence, Tel: 610-933-2345.

KING OF PRUSSIA, MONTGOMERY CO., MOTHER OF DIVINE PROVIDENCE (1954) Rev. Martin T. Cioppi; Deacon Mark H. Dillon. In Res., Rev. Msgr. Joseph W. Murray (Retired); Rev. William Dickinson.
Res.: 333 Allendale Rd., 19406-1640. Tel: 610-265-4178; Fax: 610-265-1653. Email: mdpinfo@mdpparish.com. Web: mdpparish.com.
School—405 Allendale Rd., 19406. Tel: 610-265-2323; Fax: 610-265-1816. Web: www.mdpschool-.com. Lay Teachers 19; Students 238.
Catechesis/Religious Program—Tel: 610-337-2173. Students 270.

LAFAYETTE HILL, MONTGOMERY CO., ST. PHILIP NERI (1945) Rev. Msgr. Charles P. Vance; Deacon Salvatore R. Bianco. In Res., Rev. Kevin J. Gallagher.
Res.: 437 Ridge Pike, 19444. Tel: 610-828-5717; 610-834-1975; Fax: 610-834-0392.
School—3015 Chestnut St., 19444. Tel: 610-828-3082; Fax: 610-828-2943. Sisters of St. Joseph 2; Lay Teachers 26; Students 462.
Catechesis/Religious Program—Tel: 610-834-9868. Students 257.
Convent—Tel: 610-828-2866.

LANSDALE, MONTGOMERY CO., ST. STANISLAUS (1876) [CEM] Rev. Msgr. Joseph A. Tracy; Revs. Philip M.

Forlano; John R. Weber; Deacons Charles G. Lewis; C. Stephens Vondercrone; Raymond C. Wellbank.
Res.: 51 Lansdale Ave., 19446-2972. Tel: 215-855-3133; Fax: 215-855-5478. Email: ststan@comcast.net. Web: www.ststanislaus.com.
School—493 E. Main St., 19446-2898. Tel: 215-368-0995; Fax: 215-393-4869. Diane E. McCaughan, Prin. Lay Teachers 25; Students 357.
Catechesis/Religious Program—Tel: 215-855-9893. Email: ststansbl@comcast.net. Bridget Letukas, C.R.E. Students 256.

LANSDOWNE, DELAWARE CO., ST. PHILOMENA (1898) Revs. Jason Kulczynski; Ukachukwu Onyeabor.
Res.: 41 E. Baltimore Ave., 19050. Tel: 610-622-2420; Fax: 610-622-1215. Web: saintphilomena-pa.org.

LENNI, DELAWARE CO., ST. FRANCIS DE SALES (1894) [CEM] Rev. Michael A. Colagreco; Deacon Paul A. Quinn.
Res.: 35 New Rd., P.O. Box 97, 19052. Tel: 610-459-2203; Fax: 610-459-5029. Web: www.sfdschurch.org.
School—39 New Rd. Tel: 610-459-0799; Fax: 610-558-3058. Sisters of St. Francis of Philadelphia 2; Lay Teachers 11; Students 169.
Catechesis/Religious Program—Tel: 610-459-0554. Students 224.
Convent—28 New Rd., Aston, 19014. Tel: 610-459-2501.
Station—Fair Acres Geriatric Center Lima. Tel: 610-891-5600.
Station—Granite Farms Est. Media. Tel: 610-358-3440.
Station—Riddle Village Media. Tel: 610-891-3777.
Station—The Residence at Glen Riddle Media. Tel: 610-358-9933.
Station—Riddle Hospital Media. Tel: 610-566-9400.
Station—Penn State Lima Campus Media. Tel: 610-892-1350.
Station—Williamson School Media. Tel: 610-566-1776.

LEVITTOWN, BUCKS CO.

1—IMMACULATE CONCEPTION B.V.M. (1954) Rev. Timothy F. O'Sullivan. In Res., Rev. Christopher D. Lucas.
Res.: 5201 Emilie Rd., 19057-2505. Tel: 215-946-1638; 215-946-1639; Fax: 215-946-2149. Web: www.immaculateconceptionparish.com.
See Holy Family Regional Catholic School, Levittown, under Regional Parish Schools located in the Institution Section.
Catechesis/Religious Program—Tel: 215-595-6096. Students 145.
Convent—Tel: 215-945-4664.

2—ST. MICHAEL THE ARCHANGEL (1953) Revs. Michael C. DiIorio; Charles J. Sullivan; Deacon William F. Shire.
Res.: 66 Levittown Pkwy., 19054. Tel: 215-945-1166; Fax: 215-945-6988. Web: www.stmichaellvt.org/church.
School—130 Levittown Pkwy., 19054. Tel: 215-943-0222; Fax: 215-943-9068. Web: www.stmichaellvt.org. Lay Teachers 15; Students 260.
Catechesis/Religious Program—Tel: 215-547-2518. Janet Fiatoa, C.R.E. Students 254.
Convent—88 Levittown Pkwy., 19054. Tel: 215-486-5840.

3—QUEEN OF THE UNIVERSE (1955) Revs. Michael F. Hennelly; John J. Farry.
Res.: 2443 Trenton Rd., 19056. Tel: 215-945-8750; Fax: 215-945-0413. Web: www.quparish.com.
See Holy Family Regional Catholic School, Levittown, under Regional Parish Schools located in the Institution Section.
Catechesis/Religious Program—Tel: 215-945-2704. Email: quprep341@gmail.com. Students 366.
Convent—2505 Trenton Rd., Bucks Co. 19056. Tel: 215-945-6116.

LIMERICK, MONTGOMERY CO., BLESSED TERESA OF CALCUTTA (2006) Rev. Paul C. Brandt; Deacons David M. Kubczak; Thomas G. Phillips.
Mailing Address: P.O. Box 229, 19468. Web: www.blteresacalcutta.org.
Office: 1228 Main St., Linfield, 19468. Tel: 610-287-2525; Fax: 610-495-9928.
Res.: 284 Swamp Pike, Schwenksville, 19473.
School—(Grades K-8), 256 Swamp Pike, Schwenksville, 19473. Tel: 610-287-2500; Fax: 610-287-2543.
Catechesis/Religious Program—Students 567.

LINFIELD, MONTGOMERY CO., ST. CLARE (1963-2006) Closed. Formerly located at 1228 Main St., Linfield. Spiritual records are kept at Blessed Teresa of Calcutta Church. Tel: 610-287-2525.

LINWOOD, DELAWARE CO., HOLY SAVIOUR (1915) Rev. John J. Sibel; Deacon John J. DuBois.
Res.: 108 E. Ridge Rd., 19061-4327. Tel: 610-485-2520; 610-485-2521; Fax: 610-485-7727. Email: holysaviour@verizon.net.
See Holy Saviour-St. John Fisher, Linwood under Regional Parish Schools located in the Institution section.
Catechesis/Religious Program—Tel: 610-485-2520; Fax: 610-485-7727. Students 254.
Convent—116 E. Ridge Rd., 19061. Tel: 484-485-7942.

LOWER MAKEFIELD, BUCKS CO., ST. JOHN THE EVANGELIST (1964) Rev. Msgr. Joseph G. Prior; Deacon James E. Hartmann.
Res.: 752 Big Oak Rd., Morrisville, 19067. Tel: 215-295-4102; Fax: 215-295-3128. Email: rectoryoffice@stjohnpa.org. Web: www.stjohnpa.org.
School—728 Big Oak Rd., Morrisville, 19067. Tel: 215-295-0629; Fax: 215-295-6258. Lay Teachers 17; Students 207.
Catechesis/Religious Program—Tel: 215-295-9239. Students 352.

MALVERN, CHESTER CO., ST. PATRICK (1915) Revs. Christopher Redcay; Arul Amalraj, O.Praem.; Deacon Lawrence P. Froio. In Res., Rev. Kevin P. McCabe.
Res.: 126 Woodland Ave., 19355. Tel: 610-647-2345; Fax: 610-647-4997. Web: www.stpatrickmalvern.org.
School—115 Channing Ave., 19355. Tel: 610-644-5797; Fax: 610-647-0535.
Catechesis/Religious Program—118 Woodland Ave., 19355. Tel: 610-296-8899; Fax: 610-296-8384. Students 296.

MANOA, DELAWARE CO., SACRED HEART (1927) Rev. Henry J. McKee; Deacons John J. Suplee; Thomas J. Woods. In Res., Rev. Paul J. O'Donnell.
Res.: 105 Wilson Ave., Havertown, 19083. Tel: 610-449-3000; Fax: 610-449-2364. Email: shpmckee@comcast.net.
School—Tel: 610-446-9198; Fax: 610-446-4861. Sisters, Servants of the Immaculate Heart of Mary 2; Lay Teachers 12; Students 239.
Catechesis/Religious Program—Tel: 610-446-7597; Fax: 610-446-3176. Sr. Kathleen McCafferty, S.S.J., D.R.E. Students 295.
Convent—Tel: 610-446-7597.

MAPLE GLEN, MONTGOMERY CO., ST. ALPHONSUS (1963) Rev. Msgr. Thomas J. Owens; Rev. Quan M. Trinh; Deacon Peter H. Burghart.
Res.: 33 Conwell Dr., 19002. Tel: 215-646-4600; Fax: 215-646-0180. Email: rectory@stalphonsus.com. Web: www.stalphonsusparish.com.
School—29 Conwell Dr., 19002. Tel: 215-646-0150; Fax: 215-646-7150. Lay Teachers 30; Students 385.
Catechesis/Religious Program—Tel: 215-643-7938. Web: www.stalphonsus.com. Students 210.
Convent—1563 Temple Dr., 19002. Tel: 215-646-6644.

MARCUS HOOK, DELAWARE CO., IMMACULATE CONCEPTION (1917), (Italian), Rev. Joseph A. Amalfitano.
Res.: 21 W. Eighth St., 19061. Tel: 610-485-1026; Fax: 610-485-7819.
Catechesis/Religious Program—Students 42.

MEDIA, DELAWARE CO.

1—ST. MARY MAGDALEN (1963) Rev. Msgr. Ralph J. Chieffo; Deacons E. Peter Zurbach; James A. DiFerdinand. In Res., Revs. William J. Chiriaco; John E. Mulgrew (Retired).
Res.: 2400 N. Providence Rd., 19063. Tel: 610-566-8821; Fax: 610-566-1005. Email: frralphsmm@verizon.net; info@stmarymagdalen.net. Web: www.stmarymagdalen.net.
School—2430 N. Providence Rd., 19063. Tel: 610-565-1822; Fax: 610-627-9670. Email: smsoffice@comcast.net. Lay Teachers 26; Students 416.
Catechesis/Religious Program—Tel: 610-565-5782. Email: prep@stmarymagdalen.net. Students 156.

2—NATIVITY OF THE BLESSED VIRGIN MARY (1868) [CEM] Rev. Edward H. Bell. In Res., Revs. Daniel J. Cavanaugh, Senior Priest (Retired); James W. Donlon (Retired).
Res.: 30 E. Franklin St., 19063. Tel: 610-566-0185; Fax: 610-566-2873. Email: nativitybvm@comcast.net. Web: www.nativity-bvm.org.
School—Gayley St., 19063. Tel: 610-566-6881; Fax: 610-566-3910. Web: www.nativitybvmschool.org. Mrs. Mary Ann Johnston, Prin. Lay Teachers 18; Students 180.
Catechesis/Religious Program—Students 295.

MILMONT PARK, DELAWARE CO., OUR LADY OF PEACE (1922) Rev. Louis P. Bellopede.
Res.: 501 Belmont Ave., 19033-3308. Tel: 610-532-8081; 610-532-8082; Fax: 610-532-7402.
Catechesis/Religious Program—Students 85.

MORRISVILLE, BUCKS CO., HOLY TRINITY (1900) [CEM] Rev. John C. Eckert; Deacon Warren C. Leonard.
Res.: 201 N. Pennsylvania Ave., 19067. Tel: 215-295-3045; Fax: 215-295-8317. Email: holytrinityrcc@aol.com. Web: www.holytrinitymorrisville.org.
School—Osborne Ave. & Stockham Ave., 19067. Tel: 215-295-6900; Fax: 215-337-9079. Mrs. Elaine McDowell, Prin. Lay Teachers 11; Students 221.
Catechesis/Religious Program—Tel: 215-295-3079. Students 120.

MORTON, DELAWARE CO., OUR LADY OF PERPETUAL HELP (1907) Rev. Msgr. John M. Savinski; Rev. Richard Smith; Deacon David N. Fosbenner.
Res.: O.L.P.H. Ct., 2130 Franklin Ave., 19070. Tel: 610-543-1046; Fax: 610-543-6150. Email: olph0101@comcast.net. Web: www.olphmorton.org.
School—#5 O.L.P.H. Ct., 2130 Franklin Ave., 19070. Tel: 610-543-8350; Fax: 610-544-3203. Sisters of St. Francis of Philadelphia 4; Lay Teachers 20; Students 302.
Catechesis/Religious Program—Tel: 610-543-5448. Students 286.
Convent—#3 O.L.P.H. Ct., 2130 Franklin Ave., 19070. Tel: 610-543-0186.

NARBERTH, MONTGOMERY CO., ST. MARGARET (1900) Rev. Robert J. Chapman; Sr. Anne Marie Stegmaier, I.H.M., Parish Svcs. Dir. In Res., Rev. Stephen J. Dougherty.
Res.: 208 N. Narberth Ave., 19072. Tel: 610-664-3770; Fax: 610-664-5001. Email: stmargrectory@comcast.net. Web: www.saintmarg.org.
School—227 N. Narberth Ave., 19072. Tel: 610-664-2640; Fax: 610-664-4677. Email: secretary@saint-margaret.org. Web: www.saint-margaret.org. Sisters of Mercy 1; Lay Teachers 15; Students 270.
Catechesis/Religious Program—Tel: 610-664-5715. Students 160.

NEW GARDEN TOWNSHIP, CHESTER CO., ST. GABRIEL OF THE SORROWFUL MOTHER (1988) Rev. Richard J. Maisano.
Mailing Address: P.O. Box 709, Avondale, 19311. Tel: 610-268-0296; Fax: 610-268-5022. Email: stgabriel@kennett.net. Web: www.stgabrielavondalepa.org.
Catechesis/Religious Program— Brian G. Jefferes, C.R.E. Students 165.

NEW HOPE, BUCKS CO., ST. MARTIN OF TOURS (1885) [CEM] Rev. W. Frederick Kindon; Deacon Edward S. Jones.
Res.: 1 Riverstone Cir., 18938. Tel: 215-862-5472; Fax: 215-862-1829. Email: frkindon@stmartinoftours.org. Web: www.stmartinoftours.org.

NEWTOWN SQUARE, DELAWARE CO., ST. ANASTASIA (1912) Rev. Msgr. Philip J. Cribben; Revs. Christopher P. Landis; James E. Dalton, O.S.F.S.; Deacon Thaddeus C. Raczkowski. In Res., Rev. Jaehwa John Lee.
Res.: 3301 W. Chester Pike, 19073. Tel: 610-356-1613; Fax: 610-356-8332. Email: pcribben@saintannies.org. Web: www.saintanastasia.net.
School—3309 W. Chester Pike, 19073. Tel: 610-356-6225; Fax: 610-356-5748. Web: www.saintannies.org. Sisters of St. Joseph 2; Lay Teachers 37; Students 640.
Catechesis/Religious Program—Tel: 610-356-5069. Students 450.
Convent—3305 W. Chester Pike, 19073. Tel: 610-356-0273.

NEWTOWN, BUCKS CO., ST. ANDREW (1880) [CEM] Rev. Msgr. Michael C. Picard; Revs. Kenneth C. Brabazon; Eugene C. Wilson; Deacons Edward E. Duese; Richard G. Napoli. In Res., Revs. Richard B. Landry, M.S.; Paul N. Belhumer.
Res.: 81 Swamp Rd., 18940. Tel: 215-968-2262; Fax: 215-579-9344. Web: standrewnewtown.com.
School—51 Wrights Rd., 18940. Tel: 215-968-2685; Fax: 215-968-4795.
Preschool—51 Wrights Rd., 18940. Tel: 215-968-2685; Fax: 215-968-4795. Lay Teachers 42; Students 700.
Catechesis/Religious Program—Tel: 215-968-6929. Students 1,000.

NORRISTOWN, MONTGOMERY CO.

1—ST. FRANCIS OF ASSISI (1923) Rev. Vincent F. Welsh; Deacon James Mahar.
Res.: 600 Hamilton St., 19401. Tel: 610-272-0402; Fax: 610-272-1794. Web: www.saintfrancisnorristown.com.
School—Oak & Buttonwood Sts., 19401. Tel: 610-272-0501; Fax: 610-272-8011. Email: contact@sfacatholic.org. Web: www.sfacatholic.org. Sisters of St. Joseph 2; Lay Teachers 14; Students 176.
Catechesis/Religious Program—Email: pugh.katherine4@gmail.com. Students 99.
Convent—Tel: 610-272-3686.

2—HOLY SAVIOUR (1903), (Italian), Rev. Msgr. Charles L. Sangermano. In Res., Revs. Alan J. Okon Jr.; Francis J. Sabatini (Retired).
Res.: 407 E. Main St., 19401. Tel: 610-275-0958; Fax: 610-275-8464. Web: www.holysaviour.com.
School—Our Lady of Victory Regional School, 351 E. Johnson Hwy., 19401. Tel: 610-275-2990. Lay Teachers 12; Students 190.
Catechesis/Religious Program—Students 110.
Mission—Our Lady of Mount Carmel 460 Fairfield Rd., Plymouth Meeting, Montgomery Co. 19462. Tel: 610-277-7739.

3—ST. PATRICK (1835) [CEM] Rev. Augustus C. Puleo; Jeff Mitchell, Business Mgr.; Laureen Zbyszinski, Operations Mgr.
Res.: 714 DeKalb St., 19401. Tel: 610-272-1408; Fax: 610-275-0238. Web: www.stpatrickchurch.com.
Catechesis/Religious Program—Religious Educ. Bldg., 703 Green St., 19401. Tel: 610-272-4500. Mary Ann Mitchell, D.R.E. Students 200.
Convent—Missionaries of Charity, 630 DeKalb St., 19401. Tel: 610-277-5962.

4—ST. PAUL (1963) Rev. Harry E. McCreedy; Sr. Rosellen Bracken, R.S.M., Parish Svcs. Dir.; Mary Rose Edmonds, Business Mgr. In Res., Rev. Msgr. Henry B. Degnan (Retired).
Res.: 2007 New Hope St., 19401. Tel: 610-279-6725; Fax: 610-275-6771. Web: www.saintpaulcatholicchurcheastnorriton.net.
School—Our Lady of Victory Catholic Regional School, 351 E. Johnson Hwy., 19401. Tel: 610-275-2990; Fax: 610-275-0470. Lay Teachers 12; Students 130.
Catechesis/Religious Program—Tel: 610-279-5330. Mrs. Meg Farrell, D.R.E. Students 91.

5—ST. TERESA OF AVILA (1918) Rev. Msgr. Andrew J. Golias; Deacon Francis C. Lally.
Res. & Mailing Address: 1260 S. Trooper Rd., 19403-3659. Tel: 610-666-5820; Fax: 610-666-7511. Email: starectory@verizon.net. Web: www.stteresaofavilaparish.com.
School—2550 S. Parkview Dr., 19403. Tel: 610-666-6069; Fax: 610-666-0195. Web: www.stteresaofavila-.com. Darlene Adams, Prin. Lay Teachers 14; Students 168.
Catechesis/Religious Program—Tel: 610-666-0644. Ms. Mary Katherine Roach, D.R.E. Students 237.

6—ST. TITUS (1962) Rev. Thomas P. Kletzel.
Res.: 3006 Keenwood Rd., East Norriton, 19403. Tel: 610-279-4990; Fax: 610-279-8640. Web: www.sttitus.org.
School—3000 Keenwood Rd., East Norriton, 19403. Tel: 610-279-6043; Fax: 610-279-8090. Elizabeth Veneziale, Prin. Lay Teachers 15; Students 181.
Catechesis/Religious Program—Tel: 610-279-5662. Mrs. Claire Boyle, C.R.E. Students 85.

NORTH WALES, MONTGOMERY CO.

1—MARY, MOTHER OF THE REDEEMER (1987) Rev. Msgr. John T. Conway; Revs. Keith J. Chylinski; William J. Teverzczuk; Deacons George H. Klinger; Joseph W. Lonergan; Lou Tonelli, Business Mgr.; Maria D. Stumpf, Dir. Parish Svcs. In Res., Rev. Msgr. James J. Shields (Retired).
Res.: 1325 Upper State Rd., 19454. Tel: 215-362-7400; 215-362-8966; Fax: 215-362-4127. Web: mmredeemer.org.
School—1321 Upper State Rd., 19454. Tel: 215-412-7101; Fax: 215-412-7197. Mrs. Denise Judge, Prin.
Catechesis/Religious Program—Tel: 215-412-2251; Fax: 215-412-7197. Nancy Franks, D.R.E. Students 806.

2—ST. ROSE OF LIMA (1919) Rev. Msgr. Daniel A. Murray. In Res., Rev. Kevin J. Kelly; Deacon Edward A. Konarski.
Res.: 428 S. Main St., 19454-3224. Tel: 215-699-4617; Fax: 215-699-4452.
School—425 W. Pennsylvania Ave., 19454-3498. Tel: 215-699-8831; Fax: 215-661-1691. Lay Teachers 17; Students 154.
Catechesis/Religious Program—Tel: 215-699-4434. Joanne M. Tragesser, D.R.E. Students 171.

NORWOOD, DELAWARE CO., ST. GABRIEL (1891) Rev. Samuel A. Verruni; Deacon Gary W. Guy. In Res., Rev. Peter C. Igwilo.
Res.: 233 Mohawk Ave., 19074. Tel: 610-586-1225; Fax: 610-586-6068. Email: office2@stgabrielnorwood.org. Web: www.stgabrielnorwood.org.
School—20 E. Cleveland Ave., 19074. Tel: 610-532-3234; Fax: 610-532-5523. Lay Teachers 14; Students 175.
Catechesis/Religious Program—Tel: 610-532-5057. Email: religiousedu@stgabrielnorwood.org. Students 300.

ORELAND, MONTGOMERY CO., HOLY MARTYRS (1949) Rev. Michael J. Ryan. In Res., Revs. Charles J. Noone (Retired); Raymond F. Tribuiani (Retired).
Res.: 120 Allison Rd., 19075. Tel: 215-884-8575; Fax: 215-884-5924. Web: www.holymartyrschurch.net.
Preschool—207 Ulmer Ave., 19075. Tel: 215-887-2044.
Catechesis/Religious Program—Tel: 215-884-8575. Students 205.

OTTSVILLE, BUCKS CO., ST. JOHN THE BAPTIST (1743) [CEM] Revs. Simione R. Volavola; Anthony Ripp, M.S.C.; Deacon Ernest D'Angelo.
Res.: 4050 Durham Rd., 18942. Tel: 610-847-5521. Web: www.stjohnsottsville.org.
School—Tel: 610-847-5523; Fax: 610-847-8549. Email: principal@stjohnsottsville.org. Lay Teachers 19; Students 147.
Catechesis/Religious Program—Tel: 610-847-5522; Fax: 610-847-5522. Students 235.

OXFORD, CHESTER CO., SACRED HEART (1914) Rev. Gregory J. Hamill; Deacon Francis Murphy.
Res.: 203 Church Rd., 19363. Tel: 610-932-5040; Fax: 610-932-5041. Web: sacredheartchurchoxford.org.
School—Tel: 610-932-3633; Fax: 610-932-6051. Mr. Steven Brunner, Prin.
Catechesis/Religious Program—Tel: 610-932-5863. Mrs. Maryanne Fazio, Dir. Faith Formation. Students 370.

PAOLI, CHESTER CO., ST. NORBERT (1956) Revs. Michael J. Lee, O.Praem.; Carl Braschoss, O.Praem.; Deacons William Masapollo; John P. Lozano.
Res.: 50 Leopard Rd., 19301. Tel: 610-644-1655; Fax: 610-644-1928. Web: www.stnorbert.org.
School—Greenlawn & Leopard Rds., 19301. Tel: 610-644-1670; Fax: 610-644-0201. Lay Teachers 19; Students 199.
Catechesis/Religious Program—Tel: 610-644-1670, Ext. 122. Students 428.

PARKESBURG, CHESTER CO., OUR LADY OF CONSOLATION (1853) [CEM] Rev. Victor J. Eschbach; Deacon Eugene Favinger. In Res., Rev. John Van De Paer, C.I.C.M.
Res.: 603 W. Second Ave., 19365. Tel: 610-857-3510; Fax: 610-857-2353. Email: olc@comcast.net. Web: www.olcchurch.org.
See Coatesville Area Catholic Elementary School, Coatesville under Regional Parish Schools located in the Institution section.
Catechesis/Religious Program—603 W. 2nd Ave., 19365. Tel: 610-857-1003. Delores Cain, D.R.E. Students 307.
Mission—St. Malachy (1838) [CEM] 76 St. Malachi Rd., Cochranville, Chester Co. 19330. Tel: 610-857-3510; Fax: 610-857-2353.

PENN VALLEY, MONTGOMERY CO., ST. JUSTIN MARTYR (1964-2009) Closed. Formerly located at 1222 Hagysford Rd., Narberth. Spiritual records are kept at St. John Baptist Vianney, Gladwyne. In Res., Most Rev. Louis A. DeSimone; Rev. Russell J. DeSimone, O.S.A.
Res.: 1222 Hagysford Rd., Narberth, 19072. Tel: 610-664-0165; Fax: 610-664-5612.

PENNDEL, BUCKS CO., OUR LADY OF GRACE (1908) [CEM] Revs. William B. Dooner; James R. DeGrassa; Deacon Dominic A. Garritano. In Res., Rev. Raju Pilla.
Res.: 225 Bellevue Ave., 19047. Tel: 215-757-7700; 215-757-7786; Fax: 215-757-5377. Web: ourladyofgrace-penndel.org.
School—300 Hulmeville Ave., 19047. Tel: 215-757-5287; Fax: 215-757-6199. Web: www.olgschool-penndel.org. Mrs. Denise Lewis, Prin. Lay Teachers 20; Students 339.
Catechesis/Religious Program—Tel: 215-757-5530. Students 448.
Parish Service Center—338 Hulmeville Ave., 19047. Tel: 215-757-5052; Fax: 215-757-5530.

PENNSBURG, MONTGOMERY CO., ST. PHILIP NERI (1919) [CEM] Rev. Robert A. Roncase; Deacon Michael J. Franks Sr. In Res., Rev. Raymond W. Smart (Retired).
Res.: 1325 Klinerd Rd., 18073. Tel: 215-679-9275; 215-679-9330; Fax: 215-679-0386. Email: spnofc@comcast.net. Web: www.spnparish.org.
School—Sixth & Washington Sts., East Greenville, 18041. Tel: 215-679-7481; Fax: 215-679-8370. Web: www.spnelementary.com. Students 132.
Catechesis/Religious Program—Tel: 215-541-3120; Fax: 215-541-1398. Students 225.

PHOENIXVILLE, CHESTER CO.

1—ST. ANN (1905) [CEM] Rev. John J. Newns; Deacon Daniel T. Giblin. In Res., Rev. Joseph A. Heim, M.M. (Retired).
Res.: 602 S. Main St., 19460. Tel: 610-933-3732; Fax: 610-935-7958. Email: stannphx@comcast.net. Web: www.churchofsaintann.org.
See Holy Family School, Phoenixville under Regional Parish Schools located in the Institution section.
Catechesis/Religious Program—Tel: 610-755-1077; Fax: 610-935-7958. Email: youthstann@comcast.net. Students 402.

2—HOLY TRINITY (1903), (Polish), [CEM] Rev. Michael W. Rzonca.
Res.: *Sacred Heart Rectory*, 148 Church St., 19460. Tel: 610-933-3830; Fax: 610-935-9261. Email: holytrinityphoenixville@verizon.net. Web: www.holytrinity-phoenixville.net.
Church: 217 Dayton St., 19460.
See Holy Family School, Phoenixville under Regional Parish Schools located in the Institution section.
Catechesis/Religious Program—Students 10.
Convent—Bernardine Sisters of the Third Order of St. Francis, 221 Dayton St., 19460. Tel: 610-983-9446.

3—ST. MARY OF THE ASSUMPTION (1840) [CEM 2] Rev. John S. Hutter; Deacon Albert T. Derivan.
Res.: 212 Dayton St., 19460. Tel: 610-933-2526; Fax: 610-935-1706. Web: www.stmaryassumption-.org.
See Holy Family School, Phoenixville under Regional Parish Schools located in the Institution section.
Catechesis/Religious Program—Students 158.

4—SACRED HEART (1900), (Slovak), [CEM] Rev. Michael W. Rzonca.
Res.: 148 Church St., 19460. Tel: 610-933-3830; Fax: 610-935-9261. Email: sacredheartphoenixville@verizon.net. Web: www.sacredheart-phoenixville.net.
See Holy Family School, Phoenixville under Regional Parish Schools located in the Institution section.
Catechesis/Religious Program—Students 35.

PLYMOUTH MEETING, MONTGOMERY CO., EPIPHANY OF OUR LORD (1957) Rev. Joseph J. Quindlen; Deacons Kenneth P. Clancy; Emil J. Wernert. In Res., Rev. James J. Kelly (Retired).
Res.: 3050 Walton Rd., 19462-2361. Tel: 610-828-8634; Fax: 610-828-1802. Email: epiphanych@comcast.net. Web: www.epiphanyofourlord.com.
School—3040 Walton Rd., 19462-2361. Tel: 610-825-0160; Fax: 610-825-0460. Web: www.eols.org. Miss Miriam A. Havey, Prin. Lay Teachers 16; Students 198.
Catechesis/Religious Program—Tel: 610-825-6790; Fax: 610-825-0460. Email: religious.education@eols.org. Web: www.eols.org. Heddy Martorelli, C.R.E. Students 188.

POTTSTOWN, MONTGOMERY CO.

1—ST. ALOYSIUS (1856) [CEM 2] Rev. Joseph L. Maloney; Deacon James Anderson.
Parish Office: 223 Beech St., 19464. Tel: 610-326-5877; Fax: 610-326-0901.
Res.: 1016 E. High St., 19464. Web: saintaloysius.net.
School—(Grades PreK-8), 220 N. Hanover St., 19464. Tel: 610-326-6167; Fax: 610-970-9960. Jack Schulte, Prin. Lay Teachers 17; Students 274.
Catechesis/Religious Program—Tel: 610-326-5877, Ext. 146. Students 235.

2—HOLY TRINITY (1899-2004), (Slovak), Closed. Spiritual records are kept at St. Aloysius Church, Pottstown. Tel: 610-326-5877. Worship site of St. Aloysius Church, Pottstown.

3—ST. PETER (1924-2006), (Polish), Closed. Formerly located at 1128 South St. Spiritual records are kept at Blessed Teresa of Calcutta, Limerick. Tel: 610-287-2525.

PRIMOS, DELAWARE CO., ST. EUGENE (1955) Rev. Joseph M. McDermott; Deacon James V. Walsh. In Res., Rev. Msgr. Michael J. Burke (Retired).
Res.: 200 S. Oak Ave., 19018. Tel: 610-626-2866; Fax: 610-626-1904. Email: steugene55@rcn.com. Web: www.sainteugenechurch.net.
School—110 S. Oak Ave., 19018. Tel: 610-622-2909; Fax: 610-622-6358. Web: sainteugeneschool.org. Lay Teachers 10; Students 234.
Catechesis/Religious Program—Students 112.

QUAKERTOWN, BUCKS CO., ST. ISIDORE (1886) [CEM] Revs. Frederick J. Riegler; Richard J. McAndrews; Deacon Richard S. Haddon Sr.
Parish Office: 603 W. Broad St., 18951. Email: stisidorechurch@comcast.net. Web: www.stisidores.org.
Res.: 2545 W. Pumping Station Rd., 18951. Tel: 215-536-4389; Fax: 215-536-4137.
School—603 W. Broad St., 18951. Tel: 215-536-6052; Fax: 215-536-8647. Lay Teachers 15; Students 264.
Catechesis/Religious Program—Tel: 215-536-6498. Students 456.

RICHBORO, BUCKS CO., ST. VINCENT DE PAUL (1968) Rev. Joseph J. McLaughlin; Deacons John M. Golaszewski; William F. Iacobellis.
Res.: 654 Hatboro Rd., 18954-1039. Tel: 215-357-5905; Fax: 215-953-8190. Web: www.svdp-richboro.org.
Catechesis/Religious Program—Tel: 215-322-1932. Sr. Alice Gallagher, S.S.J., D.R.E. Students 464.
Convent—Sisters of St. Joseph, 624 Hatboro Rd., 18954-1039. Tel: 215-942-9152.

RIDLEY PARK, DELAWARE CO., ST. MADELINE (1908) Rev. Louis P. Bellopede; Deacon Michael J. Alexander.
Res.: 110 Park St., 19078. Tel: 610-532-6880; Fax: 610-532-6653.
Church: Penn St. & Morton Ave., 19078.
See St. Madeline-St. Rose School, Ridley Park under Regional Parish Schools located in the Institution section.
Catechesis/Religious Program—Tel: 610-583-6120. Students 215.

RIEGELSVILLE, BUCKS CO., ST. LAWRENCE (1974) [JC] Rev. Gavin W. Muir.
Res.: 345 Elmwood Ln., 18077. Tel: 610-749-2684; Fax: 610-749-2695. Email: saintlawrence@verizon.net. Web:

parishesonline.com/scripts/hostedsites/org.asp?ID=7320.
Catechesis/Religious Program—Students 96.

ROSLYN, MONTGOMERY CO., ST. JOHN OF THE CROSS (1953) Rev. David A. Fernandes; Deacon Raymond Jacobucci. In Res., Rev. Aloysius Ochasi (Nigeria).
Res.: 2741 Woodland Rd., 19001. Tel: 215-659-4460; Fax: 215-659-2551. Web: www.stjohnofthecrossparish.org.
See Good Shepherd Catholic Regional School, Ardsley under Regional Parish Schools located in the Institution Section.
Catechesis/Religious Program—Tel: 215-659-1451. Students 130.
Convent—Grey Nuns of the Sacred Heart, 2803 Woodland Rd., 19001. Tel: 215-659-4483.

ROYERSFORD, MONTGOMERY CO., SACRED HEART (1973) Rev. Peter J. DiMaria.
Res.: 838 Walnut St., P.O. Box 64, 19468. Tel: 610-948-5915; 610-948-4087; Fax: 610-948-0573. Web: sacredheartroyersford.org.
School—Lewis Rd. & Washington St., 19468. Tel: 610-948-7206; Fax: 610-948-6508. Lay Teachers 14; Students 176.
Catechesis/Religious Program—Tel: 610-792-2997. Laura Hritz, C.R.E. Students 376.

RYDAL, MONTGOMERY CO., ST. HILARY OF POITIERS (1962) Rev. Kevin P. Murray; Deacon John K. Hunter.
Res.: 820 Susquehanna Rd., 19046. Tel: 215-884-3252; Fax: 215-884-5342. Email: sthilaryrydal@comcast.net.
School—920 Susquehanna Rd., 19046. Tel: 215-887-4520; Fax: 215-887-6337. Students 244.
Catechesis/Religious Program—Students 120.

SCHWENKSVILLE, MONTGOMERY CO., ST. MARY (1926) Rev. Charles J. McElroy. In Res., Rev. Stephen P. DeLacy.
Res.: 40 Spring Mount Rd., 19473. Tel: 610-287-8156; Fax: 610-287-4226. Web: www.churchofsaintmary.org.
School—Tel: 610-287-7757. Lay Teachers 24; Students 319.
Catechesis/Religious Program—Tel: 610-287-4517. Students 439.

SECANE, DELAWARE CO., OUR LADY OF FATIMA (1952) Rev. Msgr. George A. Majoros; Revs. Joseph W. Dragon; Thomas P. Gillin. In Res., Rev. Vincent R. Morabito.
Res.: 1 Fatima Dr., 19018. Tel: 610-532-5800; Fax: 610-532-6937. Web: www.olfsecane.org.
School—10 Fatima Dr., 19018. Tel: 610-586-7539; Fax: 610-586-0117. Web: olfschool/secane.com. Sisters, Servants of the Immaculate Heart of Mary 2; Lay Teachers 12; Students 230.
Catechesis/Religious Program—Tel: 610-586-3633. Students 155.
Convent—5 Fatima Dr., 19018. Tel: 610-532-1190.

SELLERSVILLE, BUCKS CO., ST. AGNES (1919) [CEM] Rev. Msgr. John B. Wendrychowicz; Rev. Timothy J. Buckley; Deacons Harry Tucker; Harry D. Antrim.
Res.: 445 N. Main St., 18960. Tel: 215-257-2128; Fax: 215-257-4561. Web: www.stagneschurch.org.
See St. Agnes-Sacred Heart School, Hilltown under Regional Parish Schools located in the Institution section.
Catechesis/Religious Program—Tel: 215-257-1811; Fax: 215-257-0525. Email: stagnesprep@gmail.com. Web: www.stagnesprep.org. Students 355.

SHARON HILL, DELAWARE CO., HOLY SPIRIT (1892) Rev. Martin E. Woodeshick; Deacon Albert Rayner. In Res., Rev. Msgr. Daniel J. Kehoe, Pastor Emeritus (Retired).
Res.: 1028 School St., 19079. Tel: 610-583-2220; Fax: 610-583-5130.
Catechesis/Religious Program—Tel: 610-583-2220. Sr. Maureen Murray, R.S.M., D.R.E. Students 8.

SOUTH COVENTRY, CHESTER CO., ST. THOMAS MORE (1968) Rev. Hugh J. Dougherty.
Res.: 2101 Pottstown Pike, Pottstown, 19465. Tel: 610-469-9304; Fax: 610-469-9315.
Catechesis/Religious Program—Tel: 610-469-9302. Students 557.

SOUTHAMPTON, BUCKS CO., OUR LADY OF GOOD COUNSEL (1923) Rev. Msgr. Anthony J. D'Angelico; Revs. John J. Kilgallon; Michael Pawelko.
Res.: 611 Knowles Ave., 18966-4198. Tel: 215-357-1300, Ext. 100; Fax: 215-357-4452. Web: www.olgc.org.
School—Tel: 215-357-1300, Ext. 101. Mr. Frank Mokriski, Prin. Lay Teachers 29; Students 420.
Catechesis/Religious Program—Tel: 215-357-1300, Ext. 107. Students 395.

SPRING CITY, CHESTER CO., ST. JOSEPH (1919) Rev. Charles R. O'Hara. In Res., Rev. Donato P. Silveri.
Res.: 3640 Schuylkill Rd., 19475. Tel: 610-948-7760; Fax: 610-948-8509. Email: st.joes@comcast.net. Web: www.stjosephspringcity.com.
Catechesis/Religious Program—Tel: 610-792-4535. Email: stjosephprep@comcast.net. Andrea Jackowski, D.R.E. Students 211.

SPRINGFIELD, DELAWARE CO.

1—ST. FRANCIS OF ASSISI (1923) Revs. Louis C. Bier; Thomas J. Furey; Joseph J. Meehan (Retired); Deacons Arthur M. McGuire; William T. Baxter.
Res.: 136 Saxer Ave., 19064. Tel: 610-543-0848; Fax: 610-604-0283. Web: www.sfaparish.org.
School—112 Saxer Ave., 19064. Tel: 610-543-0546; Fax: 610-544-9431. Lay Teachers 17; Students 280.
Catechesis/Religious Program—Students 461.

2—HOLY CROSS (1948) Revs. John D. Gabin; Edward C. Kelly; Sr. Mary Carmela Sandusky, R.S.M., Pastoral Min.; Deacon Joseph N. Gousie Sr. In Res., Rev. Msgr. Paul F. Curran (Retired); Rev. Simon Hyung-Min Ha.
Res.: 651 E. Springfield Rd., 19064. Tel: 610-626-3321; Fax: 610-622-2920.
School—240 N. Bishop Ave., 19064. Tel: 610-626-1709; Fax: 610-626-1859. Lay Teachers 14; Students 261.
Catechesis/Religious Program—Tel: 610-626-1057; Fax: 610-626-8057. Students 220.
Convent—Tel: 610-626-2492.

3—ST. KEVIN (1955) Rev. John C. Moloney; Deacons Thomas Eichman; Leonard Diana. In Res., Rev. Thomas P. Gillin.
Rectory—200 W. Sproul Rd., 19064-2016. Tel: 610-544-8777; 610-544-8778; Fax: 610-544-7832.
School—Tel: 610-544-4455; Fax: 610-544-7092. Lay Teachers 16; Students 210.
Catechesis/Religious Program—Tel: 610-544-3236; Fax: 610-544-7382. Students 212.
Convent—Tel: 610-544-4535.

STOWE, MONTGOMERY CO., ST. GABRIEL OF THE SORROWFUL MOTHER (1929) Rev. Thomas A. Nasta.
Parish Center—127 E. Howard St., 19464-6707. Tel: 610-326-5127; Fax: 610-326-5749.
Res.: 421 Jefferson St., 19464-6736.
Catechesis/Religious Program—Tel: 610-327-5376. Students 33.

STRAFFORD, CHESTER CO., OUR LADY OF THE ASSUMPTION (1908), (Italian), [CEM] Rev. Msgr. Joseph T. Marino; Rev. Salvatore M. Riccio; Deacon John P. Rose. In Res., Rev. Msgr. James T. McDonough (Retired).
Res.: 35 Old Eagle School Rd., 19087-2577. Tel: 610-688-1178; 610-688-6147; Fax: 610-293-9680. Web: www.olastrafford.org.
Preschool—135 Fairfield Ln., 19087. Tel: 610-688-5277; Fax: 610-688-4540. Students 92.
Catechesis/Religious Program—Tel: 610-688-6590. Students 121.

SWARTHMORE, DELAWARE CO., NOTRE DAME DE LOURDES (1959) Rev. Karl A. Zeuner; Deacons James Basilio; Michael McAndrews.
Res.: 950 Michigan Ave., 19081. Tel: 610-544-1270; Fax: 610-544-4310. Email: rectory@notredamedelourdes.net.
School—990 Fairview Rd., 19081. Tel: 610-328-9330; Fax: 610-328-3955. Lay Teachers 14; Students 214.
Catechesis/Religious Program—Students 184.

SWEDESBURG, MONTGOMERY CO., SACRED HEART (1907), (Polish), Rev. Scott D. Brockson.
Res.: 120 Jefferson St., 19405. Tel: 610-275-1750; Fax: 610-275-0480. Web: sacredheart-swedesburg.net.
Catechesis/Religious Program—Students 60.
Convent—635 E. Fourth St., 19405. Tel: 610-239-1785. Sr. Klara Slonina, Supr. Sisters Servants of the Most Sacred Heart

TROOPER, MONTGOMERY CO., VISITATION B.V.M. (1954) Rev. Msgr. Thomas A. Murray; Revs. Edward J. Kelly; Michael J. Saban; Deacons Vincent M. Drewicz; Patrick J. Mandracchia. In Res., Rev. Msgr. Ignatius L. Murray (Retired).
Res.: 196 N. Trooper Rd., Norristown, 19403. Tel: 610-539-5572; Fax: 610-539-3240. Web: www.visitationbvm.org.
School—190 N. Trooper Rd., Norristown, 19403. Tel: 610-539-6080; Fax: 610-630-7946. Sisters of the Holy Family of Nazareth 2; Lay Teachers 36; Students 623.
Catechesis/Religious Program—Tel: 610-539-6211. Roseanne Terranova, D.R.E. Students 450.
Convent—Tel: 610-539-5558.

UPPER DARBY, DELAWARE CO., ST. ALICE (1922) Rev. Peter N. Quinn.
Res.: 150 Hampden Rd., 19082. Tel: 610-352-1431; Fax: 610-352-1432.
Catechesis/Religious Program—Tel: 610-352-0725; Fax: 610-352-7288. Students 45.

UPPER GWYNEDD, MONTGOMERY CO., CORPUS CHRISTI (1964) Rev. Msgr. Thomas P. Flanigan; Rev. John F. Wackerman; Deacons Francis E. Langsdorf; William W. Evans; Sr. Eleanor McNichol, S.S.J., Parish Min.
Res.: 900 Sumneytown Pike, Lansdale, 19446. Tel: 215-855-1311; Fax: 215-855-3631. Web: corpuschristilansdale.org.
School—920 Sumneytown Pike, Lansdale, 19446. Tel: 215-368-0582; Fax: 215-361-5927. Email: ccsprin@fast.net. Sisters of St. Joseph 1; Lay Teachers 32; Students 504.
Catechesis/Religious Program—Tel: 215-362-2292. Trish Keen, D.R.E. Students 755.
Convent—1622 Supplee Rd., Lansdale, 19446. Tel: 215-368-0737.

UPPER UWCHLAN, CHESTER CO., SAINT ELIZABETH (2000) Rev. Msgr. Thomas M. Mullin; Deacon Barry R. Midwood.
Parish Office & Church: 100 St. Elizabeth Dr., P.O. Box 695, Uwchlan, 19480-0695. Tel: 610-321-1200; Fax: 610-646-6513. Email: steuucc@stelizabethparish.org. Web: www.stelizabethparish.org.
Res.: 2 Fox Ridge Rd., Glenmoore, 19343-9546. Tel: 610-321-9616.
School—120 Saint Elizabeth Dr., P.O. Box 780, Uwchlan, 19480-0780. Tel: 610-646-6540; Fax: 610-646-6541. Email: bdougherty@stelizabethparish.org. Bernadette Dougherty, Prin. Students 346.
Catechesis/Religious Program—Tel: 610-646-6545. Email: religioused@stelizabethparish.org. Students 854.

VILLANOVA, DELAWARE CO., ST. THOMAS OF VILLANOVA PARISH (1848) Revs. Joseph L. Narog, O.S.A.; Arthur W. Johnson, O.S.A. In Res., Rev. Allan Fitzgerald, O.S.A.
Office: 1229 E. Lancaster Ave., Rosemont, 19010. Tel: 610-525-4801. Web: www.stthomasofvillanova.org.
Res.: 1242 Montrose Ave., Rosemont, 19010.
St. Thomas of Villanova Preschool—1236 Montrose Ave., Rosemont, 19010. Tel: 610-525-7554; Fax: 610-525-6041.
Catechesis/Religious Program—Students 274.

WALLINGFORD, DELAWARE CO., ST. JOHN CHRYSOSTOM (1952) Rev. Edward J. Hallinan; Deacons Raymond Vadino; Walter Lance.
Res.: 617 S. Providence Rd., 19086. Tel: 610-874-3418; Fax: 610-872-1741. Email: sjcparish@yahoo.com. Web: www.saintjohnchrysostom.net.
School—607 S. Providence Rd., 19086. Tel: 610-876-7110; Fax: 610-876-5923. Email: stjohnprincipal@comcast.net. Web: www.sjcschool-news.org. Lay Teachers 19; Students 159.
Catechesis/Religious Program—605 S. Providence Rd., 19086. Tel: 610-872-4673. Email: stjohnreligiouseducation@comcast.net. Students 339.
Convent—Tel: 610-872-7194.

WARMINSTER, BUCKS CO., NATIVITY OF OUR LORD (1956) Rev. Angelo R. Citino.
Res.: 625 W. Street Rd., 18974. Tel: 215-675-1925; Fax: 215-674-3787. Email: frcitino@nativityofourlord.org.
Parish Office Center: 605 W. Street Rd., 18974. Fax: 267-803-1777. Web: www.nativityofourlord.org.
School—585 W. Street Rd., 18974. Tel: 215-675-2820; Fax: 215-675-9413. Email: rmaddaloni@nativity-school.org. Web: www.nativity-school.org. Lay Teachers 28; Students 498.
Catechesis/Religious Program—Tel: 215-672-5316; Fax: 215-675-9413. Email: astolarik@nativity-school.org. Students 295.
Convent—605 W. Street Rd., 18974. Tel: 215-672-0147.

WARRINGTON, BUCKS CO.

1—ST. JOSEPH (1922) Rev. Joseph C. Bordonaro; Deacon Karl Hartmann.
Res.: 1795 Columbia Ave., 18976. Tel: 215-672-3020; Fax: 215-672-3114. Web: www.saintjosephchurch.us.
See St. Joseph-St. Robert Bellarmine School, Warrington under Regional Parish Schools located in the Institution section.
Catechesis/Religious Program—Tel: 215-672-9990. Mrs. Cathy Cain, D.R.E. Students 252.
Station—Willow Grove Joint Reserve Base Willow Grove. Tel: 215-443-6002.

2—ST. ROBERT BELLARMINE (1968) Rev. Msgr. James D. Beisel; Rev. Matthew J. Tralies; Deacon George E. Morris Jr.
Res.: 856 Euclid Ave., 18976. Tel: 215-343-0315; Fax: 215-343-8592.
School - See St. Joseph-St. Robert Bellarmine School, Warrington under Regional Parish Schools located in the Institution section.
Catechesis/Religious Program—850 Euclid Ave., 18976. Tel: 215-343-9433. Students 577.

WAYNE, CHESTER CO., ST. ISAAC JOGUES (1970) Rev. Stephen A. Moerman.
Res.: 50 W. Walker Rd., 19087. Tel: 610-687-3366; Fax: 610-293-9529. Email: rectory@stisaac.org. Web: www.stisaac.org.
Preschool—Tel: 610-687-2481, Ext. 6; Fax: 610-293-9529. Email: anna@stisaac.org.
Catechesis/Religious Program—Tel: 610-687-2481, Ext. 4. Email: reled@stisaac.org. Louis M. Valenti, D.R.E. Students 255.
Youth Ministry—Tel: 610-687-2481, Ext. 5. Email:

jaquilantr@stisaac.org.

WAYNE, DELAWARE CO., ST. KATHARINE OF SIENA (1893) Rev. Msgr. Hans A.L. Brouwers; Sisters Kathleen Callaghan, S.S.J., Dir. Parish Life & Ministry; Elizabeth O'Hara, S.S.J., Parish Svcs. Dir. In Res., Rev. Msgr. Michael J. Carroll (Retired).
Res.: 104 S. Aberdeen Ave., 19087. Tel: 610-688-4584; Fax: 610-688-7951. Email: rectory@stkatharineofsiena.org. Web: www.stkatharineofsiena.org.
School—229 Windermere Ave., 19087. Tel: 610-688-5451; Fax: 610-688-6796. Email: school@stkatharineofsiena.org. Frank Tosti, Prin. Lay Teachers 25; Students 435.
Catechesis/Religious Program—Tel: 610-688-7890. Email: religioused@stkatharineofsiena.org. Barbara Seaman, D.R.E. Students 345.
Convent—235 Windermere Ave., 19087. Tel: 610-688-0655.

WEST BRANDYWINE, CHESTER CO., ST. PETER (1963) Rev. Michael J. Fitzpatrick. In Res., Rev. Emmanuel K. Iheaka; Deacons Thomas C. Concitis; James T. McAvoy.
Parish Office: 2835 Manor Rd., 19344. Tel: 610-380-9045; Fax: 610-380-9049.
Res.: 284 Vincent Dr., Honey Brook, 19344. Web: www.saintpeterchurch.net.
See Pope John Paul II Regional Catholic Elementary School, West Brandywine under Regional Parish Schools located in the Institution section
Regional Religious Education Program—2875 Manor Rd. Tel: 610-384-3145. Patrice A. Peterson, D.R.E. Students 385.

WEST CHESTER, CHESTER CO.

1—ST. AGNES (1793) [CEM] Rev. Msgr. Nelson J. Perez; Revs. Anthony J. Cossavella; Laurence J. Gleason; Deacons Victor Gonzalez; Patrick M. Stokely.
Res.: 233 W. Gay St., 19380. Tel: 610-692-2990; Fax: 610-692-9623. Email: info@saintagnesparish.org. Web: saintagnesparish.org.
School—211 W. Gay St., 19380. Tel: 610-696-1260; Fax: 610-436-9631. Sisters, Servants of the Immaculate Heart of Mary 4; Lay Teachers 24; Students 344.
Catechesis/Religious Program—207 W. Gay St., 19380. Tel: 610-436-4640; Fax: 610-719-1961. Students 482.
Convent—205 W. Gay St., 19380. Tel: 610-692-9430.

2—SS. SIMON AND JUDE (1961) Revs. Michael J. Gerlach; Jeffrey M. Rott; Mr. Ronald B. Avellino, Business Mgr.; Deacons Joseph A. Ruggiero; C. William Shearer.
Res.: 8 Cavanaugh Ct., 19382. Tel: 610-696-3624; Fax: 610-696-3971. Email: rectory@simonandjude.org. Web: www.simonandjude.org.
School—6 Cavanaugh Ct., 19382. Tel: 610-696-5249; Fax: 610-696-4682. Sisters, Servants of the Immaculate Heart of Mary 4; Lay Teachers 24; Students 414.
Catechesis/Religious Program—Tel: 610-692-3118. Sisters Barbara Jude Gentry, I.H.M., D.R.E.; Mary Beth Coyle, Coord. Evangelization & Adult Faith Formation. Students 545.
Convent—Tel: 610-692-4394.

WEST CONSHOHOCKEN, MONTGOMERY CO., ST. GERTRUDE (1888) Rev. Msgr. Gerard C. Mesure; Deacon Thomas P. Quinn.
Res.: *St. Mary Rectory*, 140 W. Hector St., Conshohocken, 19428.
Church: 209 Merion Ave., Conshohocken, 19428. Tel: 610-828-0268; Fax: 610-828-7024. Email: stgerts1888@aol.com.

WEST GROVE, CHESTER CO., ASSUMPTION B.V.M. (1873) [CEM] Revs. William S. Murphy; Kenneth Putz; Joyce Malchione, Business Mgr.; Deacons Jeffrey S. Hanna; Thomas Hannan; Michael DeGrasse. In Res., Rev. Msgr. Francis J. Depman.
Parish Office: 105 W. Evergreen St., 19390. Tel: 610-869-2722. Email: abvm@comcast.net. Web: www.assumptionbvmwestgrove.org.
Res.: 107 W. Evergreen St., 19390. Tel: 610-869-2722; Fax: 610-869-3252.
School—290 State Rd., 19390. Tel: 610-869-9576; Fax: 610-869-4049. Email: assumptionwestgrove@comcast.net. Danielle White, Prin. Lay Teachers 17; Students 206.
Catechesis/Religious Program—Tel: 610-869-8575. Kristine McNicholas, D.R.E. Students 598.

WEST CHESTER, CHESTER CO., ST. MAXIMILIAN KOLBE (1986) Rev. Msgr. Robert J. Carroll; Rev. Marc F. Capizzi; Deacons William L. Hickey; Alfred Mauriello. In Res., Rev. John J. Nordeman.
Res.: 15 E. Pleasant Grove Rd., 19382. Tel: 610-399-6936; Fax: 610-399-4828. Email: saintmax@comcast.net. Web: www.stmax.org.
School—(Grades PreK-8), 300 Daly Dr., 19382. Tel: 610-399-8400; Fax: 610-399-4684. Students 311.
Catechesis/Religious Program—Tel: 610-399-9642. Students 545.

WILLOW GROVE, MONTGOMERY CO., ST. DAVID (1919) Rev. Msgr. Richard T. Bolger; Revs. Leo P. Oswald; John J. Shelley (Retired).
Res.: 316 N. Easton Rd., 19090. Tel: 215-657-0252; Fax: 215-659-6516. Email: stdavidparish@comcast.net. Web: www.stdavidparish.org.
School—401 N. Easton Rd., 19090. Tel: 215-659-6393; Fax: 215-659-6377. Sisters, Servants of the Immaculate Heart of Mary 6; Lay Teachers 16; Students 240.
Catechesis/Religious Program—Tel: 215-659-4059. Students 304.
Convent—400 N. Easton Rd., 19090. Tel: 215-659-0445.

WYNDMOOR, MONTGOMERY CO., SEVEN DOLORS (1916-2003) Closed. Formerly located at 1200 E. Willow Grove Ave. Spiritual records are kept at St. Genevieve Church, Tel: 215-836-2828.

WYNNEWOOD, MONTGOMERY CO., PRESENTATION B.V.M. (1954) Rev. Eduardo G. Montero; Deacon Ernest W. Angiolillo.
Res.: 204 Haverford Rd., 19096. Tel: 610-642-8341; Fax: 610-896-1970. Web: www.presbvm.com.
Catechesis/Religious Program—Students 75.
Parish Center: 240 Haverford Rd., 19096. Tel: 610-642-8341.

YARDLEY, BUCKS CO., ST. IGNATIUS OF ANTIOCH (1920) [CEM] [JC] Rev. Msgr. Samuel E. Shoemaker; Rev. Bernard J. Taglianetti; Deacons Myron A. Moskowitz; Robert J. Skawinski.
Res.: 999 Reading Ave., 19067. Tel: 215-493-3377; Fax: 215-493-0450. Email: contact@stignatiusyardley.org. Web: www.stignatiusyardley.org.
School—997 Reading Ave., 19067. Tel: 215-493-3867; Fax: 267-573-3550. Web: www.sisschool.org. Lay Staff 24; Students 240.
Catechesis/Religious Program—Tel: 215-493-5204; Fax: 215-493-0956. Students 574.

YEADON, DELAWARE CO., ST. LOUIS (1928) Rev. John P. Collins; Deacon Charles R. Amen.
Res.: 821 W. Cobbs Creek Pkwy., 19050. Tel: 610-623-0553; Fax: 610-623-8191. Web: www.stlix-.org; www.stlouischurchyeadon.org.
Catechesis/Religious Program—

Chaplains of Public Institutions

PHILADELPHIA. *Philadelphia Federal Detention Center*, 700 Arch St., 19106. Tel: 215-521-4000. Rev. Benjamin R. Regotti, O.F.M.Cap.
Philadelphia Prison System, 8001 State Rd., 19136. Tel: 215-276-2288. Vacant.
Veterans Administration Medical Center, University & Woodland Aves., 19104. Tel: 215-823-5800, Ext. 2776. Revs. Michael A. Lipareli, Ukachukwu Onyeabor.

COATESVILLE. *Veterans Administration Medical Center* 19320. Tel: 215-384-7711, Ext. 190. Revs. Semanhyia Boateng-Mensah, Emmanuel K. Iheaka.

GRATERFORD. *Graterford State Correctional Institution* 19426. Tel: 215-489-4151. Vacant.

NORRISTOWN. *Norristown State Hospital* 19401. Tel: 215-270-1104. Vacant.

SPRING CITY. *Southeastern Pennsylvania Veterans Center* 19475. Tel: 215-948-2400. Rev. Donato P. Silveri.

On Special or Other Archdiocesan Assignment:
Most Revs.—
Fitzgerald, Michael J., 222 N. 17th St., 19103.
McIntyre, John J., 222 N. 17th St., 19103.
Senior, Timothy C., 222 N. 17th St., 19103.
Thomas, Daniel E., 222 N. 17th St., 19103.
Rev. Msgrs.—
Anderlonis, Joseph J., S.T.D., Vicar, Office for Consecrated Life, Saint George Rectory, 3580 Salmon St., 19134.
Beach, Francis W., M.Div., St. John Baptist Vianney Rectory, 1110 Vaughans Lane, Gladwyne, 19035. Delegate of the Archbishop, Stewardship and Development for the Archdiocese of Philadelphia
Dombrow, William A., M.Div., Rector, Villa Saint Joseph, 1436 Landowne Ave., Darby, 19023.
Mesure, Gerard C., J.D., J.C.D., M.A., Chancellor, Office of the Chancellor, Saint Mary Rectory, 140 West Hector St., Conshohocken, 19428.
Parlante, Gregory J., M.A., M.Div., Assoc. to the Vicar for Clergy, Office for Permanent Deacons, Saint Cornelius Rectory, 160 Ridge Rd., Chadds Ford, 19317.
Sullivan, Daniel J., M.Div., Vicar for Clergy, Sisters of Mercy Convent, 515 Montgomery Ave., Merion Station, 19066.
Revs.—
Ames, John J., S.T.D., M.A., M.Div., Deputy Sec., Office for Catechetical Formation, Saint Matthew Rectory, 219 Fayette St., Conshohocken, 19428.
Bransfield, Sean P., M.Div., M.A., J.C.L., Archdiocesan Judge, Metropolitan Tribunal, Cardinal's Residence, 5700 City Ave., 19131.
Collins, James J., S.O.E.D., Faculty, Holy Family University, 9701 Frankford Ave., 19114.
Endres, James F., Admin., Regina Coeli Residence for Priests, 685 York Rd., Warminster, 18974.
Farley, Bernard C., Chap., Saint John Neumann Nursing Home, 10400 Roosevelt Blvd., 19116.
Gill, G. Dennis, M.Div., S.L.L., Dir., Office for Worship, Cathedral Basilica SS. Peter and Paul, 1723 Race St., 19103.
Hennessy, Brian P., J.C.L., M.A., M.Div., Admin. Sec., Office of the Archbishop, Cardinal's Residence, 5700 City Ave., 19131.
Hernandez, Angelo J., Coord., Hispanic Ministry (Delaware County), St. Katharine Drexel Rectory, 1920 Providence Ave., Chester, 19013.
Hunt, Mark J., S.T.L., S.T.D., Prof., Holy Family Univ. - Newtown Campus, Saint Joseph the Worker Rectory, 9172 New Falls Rd., Fallsington, 19054.
Jablonski, Edward J., M.Div., Chap., St. Martha Manor, St. Joseph Rectory, 460 Manor Ave., Downingtown, 19335.
Janicki, Carl F., Dir. Campus Ministry, Cabrini College, Saint Genevieve Rectory, 1225 Bethlehem Pike, Flourtown, 19031.
Judge, Timothy M., M.Div., Chap., Holy Redeemer Health Systems, 521 Moredon Rd., Huntingdon Valley, 19006.
Kennedy, Charles J., Chap., LaMilagrosa, Cathedral Basilica SS. Peter & Paul, 1723 Race St., 19103.
Kennedy, Edward J., Chap., St. Francis Country House, Blessed Virgin Mary Rectory, 1101 Main St., Darby, 19023.
Kloda, Marshall J., M.Div., Chap., Nazareth Hospital, 2601 Holme Ave., 19152.
Kuczynski, Edward P., M.Div., Chap., St. Monica Manor, Saint Charles Borromeo Rectory, 902 S. 20th St., 19146.
Lee, Jaehwa John, M.S., Chap., Bryn Mawr, Haverford and Swarthmore Newman Centers, St. Anastasia Rectory, 3301 West Chester Pike, Newtown Square, 19073.
Lowe, Philip J., Ed.D., Faculty - Neumann College, Holy Saviour Rectory, 108 E. Ridge Rd., Marcus Hook, 19061.
Marneni, Ignatius, Chap., Immaculate Mary Home, St. Jerome Rectory, 8100 Colfax St., 19136.
McGuinn, James T., M.A., M.Div., Chap., Univ. of Pennsylvania Newman Center, Saint Agatha/Saint James Rectory, 3728 Chestnut St., 19104.
McKay, Douglas M., Chap., Holy Family Home, 5300 Chester Ave., 19143.
McKelvey, James P., M.Div., Chap., Camilla Hall, P.O. Box 100, Immaculata, 19345.
Nordeman, John J., M.A., M.Div., Chap., West Chester Univ. Newman Ctr., Saint Maximilian Kolbe Rectory, 15 E. Pleasant Grove Rd., West Chester, 19382.
O'Donnell, Dennis J.W., Ph.D., Dir., Holy Redeemer Health System, Saint Christopher Rectory, 13301 Proctor Rd., 19116.
Oliver, James M., J.C.D., M.A., M.Div., Asst. Vicar for Clergy, Saint Phillip Neri Rectory, 218 Queen St., 19147.
Pelczar, Edward A., Chap., Temple Univ. Hospital, Saint Helena Rectory, 6161 N. Fifth St., 19120.
Rogers, Christopher B., M.A., Dir., Campus Ministry, Immaculata Univ., 1145 King Rd., Immaculata, 19345.
Sperger, Herbert J., M.Div., Rector, St. Joseph's-In-The-Hills Retreat House, Daylesford Abbey, 220 S. Valley Rd., Paoli, 19301.
Swope, Mark G., M.B.E., M.Div., Chap., Provincialate, Sisters of Holy Redeemer, 521 Moredon Rd., Huntingdon Valley, 19006.
Wild, J. Jerome, S.T.L., M.A., M.Div., Chap., Temple Univ. Newman Center, Saint Malachy Rectory, 1429 N. 11th St., 19122.

On Duty Outside the Archdiocese:
Rev. Msgr.—
Burns, Vincent P., Glenmary Home Missioners, P.O. Box 465618, Cincinnati, OH 45246.
Revs.—
Bonavitacola, John M., Our Lady of Mount Carmel Parish, 2121 S. Rural Rd., Tempe, AZ 85282.
Bransfield, J. Brian, M.Div., M.A., S.T.L., U.S-.C.C.B. Secretariat of Evangelization and Catechesis, 3211 4th St., N.E., Washington, DC 20017.
Concha, Alfonso J., M.Div., Institute for Continuing Theological Education, Vatican City, Italy 00120.
Fairbanks, Gregory J., H.Ed., Pontifical Council for Promoting Christian Unity 00120 Vatican City State.

Funk, Peter C., Diocese of Beaumont, 9920 N. Major Dr., P.O. Box 3948, Beaumont, TX 77713.
Marczewski, Robert, S.T.L., M.Div., SS. Cyril and Methodius Seminary, 3535 Indian Trail, Orchard Lake, MI 48324.
Menei, Francis T., Saint Richard Parish, 201 Adele Ave., Manheim, 17545.

Military Chaplains:
Rev. Msgr.—
McManus, Gerald D.
Revs.—
Coffey, Joseph L.
Foley, Francis P.
Lea, Joseph P.
McDermott, Stephen C.

Graduate Studies:
Revs.—
Check, Ronald, M.A., M.Div., Casa Santa Maria, Dell 'Umilta 30, Rome, Italy.
DiGuglielmo, Anthony J., M.Div., Franciscan Monastery, 1400 Quincy St., N.E., Washington, DC 20017.
Yetman, Robert C., M.A., M.Div., Franciscan Monastery, 1400 Quincy St., N.E., Washington, DC 20017.

Absent on Sick Leave:
Rev. Msgr.—
Graf, John W.
Revs.—
Bajorek, James R.
Witalec, Dennis J.

Retired:
Rev. Msgrs.—
Barszczewski, Francis A., S.T.L., M.S.L.S., Villa Saint Joseph, 1436 Lansdowne Ave., Darby, 19023-1298.
Boland, John P., M.A., Saint Christopher Rectory, 13301 Proctor Rd., 19116-3716.
Breslin, John E., Holy Family Rectory, 234 Hermitage St., 19127.
Burke, Michael J., M.Div., Saint Eugene Rectory, 200 S. Oak Ln., Primos, 19018.
Campbell, Hugh P., 40 Greenbriar Rd., Perryville, MD 21903.
Carbine, Francis A., M.A., Saint Katherine of Siena Rectory, 9700 Frankford Ave., 19114-2896.
Carroll, Michael J., M.A., Saint Katherine of Siena Rectory, 104 S. Aberdeen Ave., Wayne, 19087.
Conahan, John J., Osprey Point #13, 1731 U.S. Rte. 9 S., Ocean View, NJ 08230.
Connelly, James E., S.T.L., H.E.D., St. Monica Rectory, 2422 S. 17th St., 19145.
Cunningham, Joseph C., Villa Saint Joseph, 1436 Lansdowne Ave., Darby, 19023-1298.
Curran, Paul F., Holy Cross Rectory, 651 E. Springfield Rd., Springfield, 19064.
D'Addezio, Louis A., M.A., Saint Patrick Rectory, 242 S. 20th St., 19103.
Degnan, Henry B., St. Paul Rectory, 2007 New Hope St., Norristown, 19401.
Dreger, Francis X., 2700 W. Brigantine Ave., Brigantine, NJ 08203.
Galyo, John M., Villa Saint Joseph, 1436 Lansdowne Ave., Darby, 19023.
Grudowski, Robert J., Saint Bede the Venerable Rectory, 1071 Holland Rd., Holland, 18966.
Howard, James J., 9224 Grace Ln., 19115.
Jaworowski, Anthony E., Villa St. Joseph, 1436 Lansdowne Ave., Darby, 19023.
Kane, Joseph T., Villa St. Joseph, 1436 Lansdowne Ave., Darby, 19023-1298.
Kehoe, Daniel J., Holy Spirit Rectory, 1028 School St., Sharon Hill, 19079.
Kelley, Thomas J., St. Matthew Rectory, 3000 Cottman Ave., 19149.
McBride, James P., 10 E. Maple St., Tresckow, 18254.
McDonough, James T., M.S.W., L.L.D., Our Lady of the Assumption Rectory, 35 Old Eagle School Rd., Strafford, 19087.
McGuire, Anthony W., 400 E. Allens Ln., 19119-1103.
McManus, Robert T., 72 Parkridge Dr., Bryn Mawr, 19010.
Menna, Francis A., Villa Saint Joseph, 1436 Lansdowne Ave., Darby, 19023-1298.
Monaghan, Charles J., Villa Saint Joseph, 1436 Lansdowne Ave., Darby, 19023-1298.
Mortimer, James E., 406 Solly Ave., 19111.
Murray, Ignatius L., Visitation B.V.M. Rectory, 196 N. Trooper Rd., Norristown, 19403-2665.
Murray, Joseph W., M.A., Mother of Divine Providence Rectory, 333 Allendale Rd., King Of Prussia, 19406-1640.
Nace, Arthur J., Villa St. Joseph, 1436 Lansdowne Ave., Darby, 19023.
O'Brien, Bartholomew J., Saint Mary's Manor, 701 Lansdale Ave., Lansdale, 19446-2900.
O'Brien, John F., Villa Saint Joseph, 1436 Landsdowne Ave., Darby, 19023-1298.
O'Donnell, William J. J., M.A., Regina Coeli Residence for Priests, 685 York Rd., Warminster, 18974.
Powers, Richard T., Epiphany of Our Lord Rectory, 1121 Jackson St., 19148.
Ricci, Philip C., P.O. Box 371, Conshohocken, 19428.
Schmidt, Francis X., 110 Nester Dr., Valley Forge Crossing, Norristown, 19403.
Sharkey, John A., Villa Saint Joseph, 1436 Lansdowne Ave., Darby, 19023-1298.
Shields, James J., Mary, Mother of the Redeemer Rectory, 1325 Upper State Rd., North Wales, 19454.
Skelly, Richard J., Saint Joseph Rectory, 256 Concord Rd., Aston, 19014-1905.
Statkus, Francis J., 208 E. Trenton Ave., Wildwood Crest, NJ 08260.
Trinity, Bernard J., Saint Denis Rectory, 2401 Saint Denis Ln., Havertown, 19083.
Walsh, Vincent M., J.C.D., Villa Saint Joseph, 1436 Lansdowne Ave., Darby, 19023-1298.
Witkowski, Bernard E., Maternity B.V.M. Rectory, 9220 Old Bustleton Ave., 19115.
Revs.—
Ambrogi, James J., 40 Schoolhouse Ln., Broomall, 19008.
Anziano, James J., M.D., Regina Coeli Residence for Priests, 685 York Rd., Warminster, 18974.
Bartos, Francis J., Villa Saint Joseph, 1436 Lansdowne Ave., Darby, 19023-1298.
Benonis, Richard R., St. Margaret of Scotland Rectory, P.O. Box 1359, Maggie Valley, NC 28751.
Bowen, Joseph D., Saint Mary's Manor, 701 Lansdale Ave., Lansdale, 19446-2900.
Boyle, George J., Villa Saint Joseph, 1436 Lansdowne Ave., Darby, 19023-1298.
Bradley, John J., Sacred Heart of Jesus Rectory, 1404 S. Third St., 19147-6099.
Breen, Robert H., Villa Saint Joseph, 1436 Lansdowne Ave., Darby, 19023-1298.
Burgoyne, Sidney C., Ph.D., Villa Saint Joseph, 1436 Lansdowne Ave., Darby, 19023-1298.
Cahill, Edward B., M.A., Villa St. Joseph, 1436 Lansdowne Ave., Darby, 19023-1298.
Callahan, Joseph W., Villa Saint Joseph, 1436 Lansdowne Ave., Darby, 19023-1298.
Cavanaugh, Daniel J., Nativity B.V.M. Rectory, 30 E. Franklin St., Media, 19063.
Chow, Luke L., 422 Black Matt Rd., Douglassville, 19518.
Chwieroth, Edward J., D'Youville Manor, 1750 Quarry Rd., Yardley, 19067.
Coates, John T., Saint Mary's Manor, 701 Lansdale Ave., Lansdale, 19446-2900.
Cornely, Francis J., Regina Coeli Residence for Priests, 685 York Rd., Warminster, 18974.
Crowe, George W., Saint John Vianney Center, 151 Woodbine Rd., Downingtown, 19335.
Cusatis, Girard J., St. Andrew Rectory, 3500 School Ln., Drexel Hill, 19026.
Cusick, Eugene G., Villa Saint Joseph, 1436 Lansdowne Ave., Darby, 19023.
Dieckhaus, Anthony W., 1005 Saint James Pl., Cape May, NJ 08204.
Dinda, John J., Villa Saint Joseph, 1436 Lansdowne Ave., Darby, 19023-1298.
Donlon, James W., Nativity B.V.M. Rectory, 30 E. Franklin St., Media, 19063.
Donnelly, William P., Villa St. Joseph, 1436 Landsdowne Ave., Darby, 19023-1298.
Dougherty, Daniel J., 244 Baltimore Pike, Apt. 135, Glen Mills, 19342.
Doyne, David A., St. Francis Country House, 1412 Lansdowne Ave., Darby, 19023-1218.
Duffy, Thomas J., Regina Coeli Residence for Priests, 685 York Rd., Warminster, 18974.
Durney, Charles W., Saint Francis Country House, 1412 Lansdowne Ave., Darby, 19023-1218.
Feeney, Thomas M., Villa St. Joseph, 1436 Lansdowne Ave., Darby, 19023-1298.
Fitzgerald, John E., St. Anselm Rectory, 12669 Dunks Ferry Rd., 19154.
Fitzgibbons, John A., St. John Vianney Center, 151 Woodbine Rd., Downingtown, 19335-3080.
Foley, Peter J., Mount Nazareth, 2755 Holme Ave., 19152.
Franey, John A., P.O. Box 336, Perryville, MD 21903.
Freeman, John A., St. Colman Rectory, 11 Simpson Rd., Ardmore, 19003-2812.
Gallagher, Daniel J., Villa Saint Joseph, 1436 Lansdowne Ave., Darby, 19023-1298.
Gallagher, Francis M., M.A., P.O. Box 597, Ambler, 19002-0597.
Gallagher, John P., Ph.D., Villa Saint Joseph, 1436 Lansdowne Ave., Darby, 19023-1298.
Gallen, Francis H., St. Martha Manor, 470 Manor Ave., Downingtown, 19335.
Garzarelli, Santo R., St. Francis Country House, 1412 Lansdowne Ave., Darby, 19023-1218.
Gormley, Charles E., Saint Matthias Rectory, 128 Bryn Mawr Ave., Bala Cynwyd, 19004.
Gormley, James W., Villa St. Joseph, 1436 Lansdowne Ave., Darby, 19023-1298.
Graf, Henry C., Regina Coeli Residence for Priests, 685 York Rd., Warminster, 18974.
Herron, Francis X., 9 N. Pelham Ave., Longport, NJ 08403.
Himsworth, Raymond J., 3218 Waterstreet Rd., Collegeville, 19426.
Hughes, James F., 257 N. State Rd., Apt. 19A, Springfield, 19064.
Jung, Joseph B., Villa Saint Joseph, 1436 Lansdowne Ave., Darby, 19023-1298.
Kelly, Francis E., 4972 Skippack Pike, P.O. Box 259, Creamery, 19430-0259.
Kelly, James J., Epiphany of Our Lord Rectory, 3050 Walton Rd., Norristown, 19462.
Krick, Howard K., Regina Coeli Residence for Priests, 685 York Rd., Warminster, 18974.
Locke, James E., 31 Ocean Rd., Ocean City, NJ 08226.
Machain, David B., Saint Bernard Rectory, 7341 Cottage St., 19136.
Maguire, Connell J., 2800 N. Ocean Dr., Apt. B15 A, Riviera Beach, FL 33404.
Maher, Edmund J., Villa St. Joseph, 1436 Landsdowne Ave., Darby, 19023-1298.
Maloney, Wilfred F., 1007 Fownes Ave., Brigantine, NJ 08203.
Martin, James J., Saint Francis Country House, 1412 Lansdowne Ave., Darby, 19023-1218.
McCloskey, Joseph W., Villa St. Joseph, 1436 Lansdowne Ave., Darby, 19023-1298.
McFadden, John R., 100 Markham Way, P.O. Box 1383, Albrightsville, 18210.
McLaughlin, James J., M.A., Villa Saint Joseph, 1436 Lansdowne Ave., Darby, 19023-1298.
McNamara, Donald P., 618 Ashford Rd., Wilmington, DE 19803.
McNamee, John P., c/o Saint Malachy Rectory, 1429 N. 11th St., 19122.
McVeigh, James E., P.O. Box 14, Middlebury Center, 16935.
Meehan, Joseph J., M.S., St. Francis of Assisi Rectory, 136 Saxer Ave., Springfield, 19064-2333.
Melle, James J., 11 Haines Rd., East Norriton, 19403.
Moriarity, Daniel J., Nativity B.V.M. Rectory, 2535 E. Allegheny Ave., 19134.
Mulgrew, John E., M.A., Saint Mary Magdalen Rectory, 2400 N. Providence Rd., Media, 19063-1998.
Murphy, Joseph T., 812 Rowland Ave., Cheltenham, 19012.
Nevins, John J., Motherhouse, Grey Nuns of the Sacred Heart, 1750 Quarry Rd., Morrisville, 19067-3998.
Noone, Charles J., Holy Martyrs Rectory, 120 Allison Rd., Oreland, 19075-1896.
O'Brien, Joseph E., Saint Leo Rectory, 6658 Keystone St., 19135.
Piro, Francis, St. Philip Neri Rectory, 218 Queen St., 19147.
Pohl, Jerome H., 2982 Richmond St., 19134.
Romano, Harry A., Villa St. Joseph, 1436 Landsdowne Ave., Darby, 19023-1298.
Sabatini, Francis J., Holy Saviour Rectory, 407 E. Main St., Norristown, 19401-5119.
Scarcia, John J., M.Div., P.O. Box 884, Eagle Lake, FL 33839.
Schifalacqua, Ildebrando E., 113 Eldredge Ave., West Cape May, NJ 08204.
Sheehan, Michael J., M.Div., M.B.A., 239 Crittenden Dr., Newtown, 18940-1323.
Shelley, John J., St. David Rectory, 316 N. Easton Rd., Willow Grove, 19090-2501.
Small, William T., M.A., 34731 Come About Cir., Millsboro, DE 19966.
Smart, Raymond W., Saint Philip Neri Rectory, 1325 Klinerd Rd., Pennsburg, 18073.
Smith, Charles D., M.A., Saint Albert the Great Rectory, 212 Welsh Rd., Huntingdon Valley, 19006-6598.
Smith, Gerald S., St. Mary's Manor, 701 Lansdale Ave., Lansdale, 19446-2900.
Smith, William J., Saint Francis Country House, 1412 Lansdowne Ave., Darby, 19023-1218.
Speitel, Edmond J., 248A Wesley Ave., Ocean City, NJ 08226.
Stec, Joseph C., M.A., Villa Saint Joseph, 1436 Lansdowne Ave., Darby, 19023-1298.
Tribuiani, Raymond F., M.Div., St. Mary's Manor, 701 Lansdale Ave., Lansdale, 19446-2900.
White, Stephen C., J.D., 122 Marlin St., Folsom, 19033-1288.
Wiedmann, Paul A., Villa St. Joseph, 1436 Lansdowne Ave., Darby, 19023-1298.
Williams, Richard C., Our Lady of Charity Rectory,

231 Upland Rd., Brookhaven, 19015-3124.
Wilz, John C., M.A., Villa St. Joseph, 1436 Lansdowne Ave., Darby, 19023-1218.

Permanent Deacons:
Dalton, James E., O.S.F.S., Saint Anastasia Church, Newton Square
Alexander, Michael J., Saint Madeline Church, Ridley Park
Amen, Charles R., Saint Louis Church, Yeadon
Anderson, James, Jr., St. Aloysius Church, Pottstown
Andrews, Edward J.
Angiolillo, Ernest W., Presentation B.V.M. Church, Wynnewood
Antrim, Harry D., St. Agnes Church, Sellersville
Arno, Michael R., Diocese of St. Petersburg, FL
Baratta, Gaspero P., St. John the Baptist Church
Basilio, James A., Notre Dame De Lourdes Church, Swarthmore
Baxter, William T., Saint Francis of Assisi Church, Springfield
Belanger, A. Kenneth, St. Helena Church, Blue Bell
Betancourt, Jose M., St. Peter the Apostle Church
Betzal, John M., St. Joseph Church, Aston
Bianco, Salvatore R., St. Philip Neri Church, Lafayette Hill
Bingham, Dennis J., Archdiocese of Baltimore, MD
Bizal, Francis M.
Bogdan, James E., SS. Philip and James Church, Exton
Bonilla, Victor M.
Boyle, John G., Holy Name of Jesus Church
Brandon, Lawrence G.
Burghart, Peter H., St. Alphonsus Church, Maple Glen
Burke, Francis B., St. Bernadette, Drexel Hill
Burns, James H.
Burns, Robert C., St. Matthew Church
Butcavage, Thomas E.
Calabrese, Peter J., Archdiocese of Baltimore, MD
Campbell, John J.
Carr, Joseph C., SS. Cosmas and Damian Church, Conshohocken
Catanese, Ralph M.
Cavaliere, Francis M.
Cella, Joseph M., Our Lady of Consolation Church
Cella, William A., Saint Elizabeth Ann Seton Church, Bensalem
Ceneviva, Vincent G., Our Lady of Sacred Heart Church, Hilltown
Champagne, William E., Our Lady of Hope Church
Clancy, Kenneth P., Epiphany of Our Lord Church, Plymouth Meeting
Clark, Francis T., St. Joseph Church, Ambler
Clay, Alvin A., Immaculate Conception Church, Jenkintown
Colgan, Francis M.
Concitis, Thomas C., St. Peter Parish Office, West Brandywine
Connors, Francis J., Saint Dennis Church, Havertown
Conroy, Michael G., St. Genevieve Church, Flourtown
Corwell, George V., Our Lady of Mt. Carmel Church, Doylestown
Coyle, Joseph P.
Coyne, Richard C.
Crespo, Adolfo, Our Lady of Fatima Church, Bensalem
Croke, Thomas M., St. Luke the Evangelist Church, Glenside
Cruz, Felipe, Incarnation of Our Lord Church
D'Amico, John J., Diocese of Phoenix, AZ
D'Angelo, Ernest, St. John the Baptist Church, Ottsville
Davaro, John J.
Dayoc, Michael J.
DeBow, James P., St. Ephrem Church, Bensalem
DeGrasse, Michael J., Assumption B.V.M. Church, West Grove
DeJesus, Epifanio, Cathedral Basilica of SS. Peter & Paul
DeMasi, Leonard D., St. Monica Church
Derivan, Albert T., St. Mary of the Assumption Church, Phoenixville
DeRosa, Joseph R., St. Eleanor Church, Collegeville
Diamond, Patrick J., Saint Cecilia Church, Philadelphia
Diana, Leonard J., St. Kevin Church, Springfield
DiFerdinand, James A., St. Mary Magdalen Church, Media
DiIenno, Anthony J., Saint Rose of Lima Church, Eddystone
Dillon, Mark H., Mother of Providence Church, King of Prussia
Drewicz, Vincent M., Visitation B.V.M. Church, Norristown
Druding, Frederick C., Epiphany of Our Lord Church
DuBois, John J., Holy Saviour Church, Linwood
Duess, Edward E., Saint Andrew Church, Newton
Duffy, James J., St. Katherine of Siena
Dymek, Edward J., Jr., St. Ephrem Church, Bensalem
Eichman, Thomas E., St. Kevin Church, Springfield
Eliason, William F.
Ellis, John J., St. Barnabas Church
Evans, William W., Corpus Christi Church, Lansdale
Farrell, John H., Saint Charles Borromeo Church, Drexel Hill
Favinger, M. Eugene, Our Lady of Consolation Church, Parkesburg
Ferreira, Joao A., Resurrection of Our Lord Church
Finn, Michael J., Saint Katharine Drexel Church, Chester
Fitzpatrick, Thomas P., St. Bernadette Church, Drexel Hill
Fosbenner, David N., Our Lady of Perpetual Help Church, Morton
Fowkes, James J., Our Lady of Mount Carmel Church, Doylestown
Frankenberger, Robert
Franks, Michael J., Sr., St. Philip Neri Church, Pennsburg
Fremont, Richard L., St. Elizabeth Church, Uwchlan
Friel, Dennis J., Resurrection of Our Lord Church, Philadelphia
Froio, Lawrence P., St. Patrick Church, Malvern
Gallagher, John J., St. Thomas Aquinas Church, Croydon
Garritano, Dominic A., Our Lady of Grace Church, Penndel
Gellentien, Robert P.
Gentilcore, Kevin F., St. Anthony of Padua Church, Ambler
George, Albert J., Holy Spirit Church
Giblin, Daniel T., St. Ann Church, Phoenixville
Gladnick, Leo T., Ascension of Our Lord Church
Gohde, Robert P., Our Lady of Guadalupe Church, Buckingham
Golaszewski, John M., St. Vincent De Paul Church, Richboro
Gonzalez, Victor, St. Agnes Church, West Chester
Gousie, Joseph N., Sr., Holy Cross Church, Springfield
Granese, Claude B., St. Jude Church, Chalfont
Guckin, Stephen A., Saint Elizabeth Ann Seton Church, Bensalem
Guy, Gary W., St. Gabriel Church, Norwood
Gwynn, Raymond F., Sr., St. Martha Church
Haddon, Richard S., Sr., St. Isidore Church, Quakertown
Hagerty, Paul B.
Hanley, Edward F., St. Timothy Church
Hanna, Jeffrey S., Assumption B.V.M. Church, West Grove
Hannan, Thomas J., Assumption B.V.M. Church, West Grove
Harrison, A. Gerald
Hartmann, James E., St. John the Evangelist Church, Morrisville
Hartmann, Karl J., St. Joseph Church, Warrington
Heaney, Philip E., Maternity B.V.M. Church
Hernandez, Felipe, Our Lady of Hope Church
Hernandez, Jose, Incarnation of Our Lord Church
Hickey, William L., Saint Maximilian Kolbe Church, West Chester
Hoelzle, Louis F., Saint Francis Cabrini Church, Fairless Hills
Hopkins, Stephen
Horan, Thomas J., SS. Peter & Paul Church, West Chester
Houser, Joseph F.
Hunter, John K., St. Hilary of Poitiers Church, Rydal
Hunter, Richard F., St. Bernard Church
Huynh, Trac Mai
Hynes, John
Iacobellis, William F., St. Vincent De Paul Church, Richboro
Iannucci, Joseph E., St. Pius X Church, Broomall
Isley, Brouycie P., St. Helena Church
Jacobucci, Raymond, Saint John of the Cross Church, Roslyn
Jones, David E., St. Anthony of Padua Church, Ambler
Jones, Edward S., Saint Martin of Tours Church, New Hope
Kane, James D., Sr.
Kazanjian, Stephen C., St. Pius X Church, Broomall
Kern, Paul R.
Kerr, Frederick H., St. Cecilia Church, Coatesville
Kletzel, George W., Immaculate Heart of Mary Church
Klinger, George H., Mary, Mother of the Redeemer Church, North Wales
Kolakowski, Michael J., Saint Albert the Great Church, Huntington Valley
Konarski, Edward A., St. Rose of Lima Church, North Wales
Kreczkevich, John J., St. Barnabas Church
Kretsch, Donald J.
Kruckenberger, William F.
Kubczak, David M., Blessed Teresa of Calcutta Church, Limerick
Lally, Francis C., Saint Teresa of Avila Church, Norristown
Lance, Walter C., St. John Chrysostom Church, Wallingford
Langsdorf, Francis E., Corpus Christi Church, Lansdale
Leahy, Eugene R.
Leonard, Warren C., Holy Trinity, Morrisville
Leonhardt, George W., Jr., Diocese of Orlando, FL
Lewis, Charles G., St. Stanislaus Church, Lansdale
Lewis, Ronald L., St. Cornelius Church, Chadds Ford
Lindsay, Charles R., Maternity B.V.M. Church
Lonergan, Joseph W., Mother of the Redeemer Church, North Wales
Lozada, Jose Luis, St. Hugh of Cluny Church
Lozano, John P., St. Norbert Church, Paoli
Lynch, Timothy P., St. Jude Church, Chalfont
Lyon, James E.
Madonna, James K., St. Patrick Church, Kennett Square
Mahar, James, St. Francis of Assisi Church, Norristown
Mahoney, James L., St. Benedict Church
Makoid, Eric T., Diocese of St. Petersburg, FL
Malamut, Richard S., St. Christopher Church
Maldonado, Rafael, St. Veronica Church
Malfara, Louis S., St. William Church
Mandracchia, Patrick J., Visitation B.V.M. Church, Norristown
Manzano, Edwin R., Visitation B.V.M. Church
Maresca, Armand J.
Masapollo, William M., St. Norbert Church, Paoli
Mauriello, Alfred J., St. Maximilian Kolbe, West Chester
Mayes, William C., St. Charles Borromeo Church
Mazzoni, Mace M., St. Frances Cabrini Church, Fairless Hills
McAndrews, Michael J., Notre Dame DeLourdes Church, Swarthmore
McAvoy, James T., St. Peter Church, Brandywine
McBlain, Paul J., St. Joseph Church, Collingdale
McGovern, Clement J.
McGuire, Arthur M., St. Francis of Assisi Church, Springfield
Mendez, Jose M.
Micucci, Joseph A., Cathedral Basilica SS. Peter & Paul
Midwood, Barry R., St. Elizabeth Church, Glenmoore
Morales, Jose A., Diocese of St. Petersburg, FL
Morris, Edward J., Saint Albert the Great Church, Huntingdon Valley
Morris, George E., Jr., St. Robert Bellarmine Church, Warrington
Morris, Harry J., St. Cornelius Church, Chadds Ford
Moskowitz, Myron A., St. Ignatius Church, Yardley
Murphy, Francis X., Sacred Heart Church, Oxford
Murphy, James G., Our Lady of the Sacred Heart Church, Hilltown
Napoli, Richard G., St. Andrew Church, Newtown
Nightingale, Richard G., Our Lady of the Blessed Sacrament Church
Niland, Joseph W.
Nines, Joseph L., St. Genevieve Church, Flourtown
Oliver, Joseph M.
Orlando, Joseph P., Diocese of Camden, NJ
Owen, Joseph T., St. Cyril of Jerusalem Church, Jamison
Owens, James T., Office for Permanent Deacons, St. Charles Seminary, Wynnewood
Panganiban, Homer A., Our Lady of Hope Church
Pavonarius, Charles A., St. Jerome Church
Phillips, Thomas G., Blessed Teresa of Calcutta Church, Limerick
Pierce, Robert F., SS. Peter & Paul Church, West Chester
Pileggi, John J., Saint Katherine Drexel Church, Chester
Poellnitz, Fredrick E., St. Athanasius Church
Polley, Charles W., Jr., SS. Philip and James Church, Exton
Purnell, Edward M., St. Theresa of the Child Jesus Church
Quinn, Paul A., St. Francis De Sales Church, Lenni
Quinn, Thomas P., St. Mary Church, Conshohocken
Raczkowski, Thaddeus C., Saint Anastasia Church, Newton Square
Radetsky, William R.
Ramos, Juan F., St. Peter the Apostle
Rayner, Albert E., Holy Spirit Church, Sharon Hill
Riordan, John T., St. Jude Church, Chalfont
Rooney, Joseph T., Our Lady Help of Christians

Church, Abington
Rosario, Israel, Our Lady of Hope Church
Rose, John P., Our Lady of the Assumption Church, Strafford
Rouse, Daniel J., St. John Bosco Church, Hatboro
Ruggiero, Joseph A., SS. Simon and Jude Church, West Chester
Ryan, Frederick M.
Salvatore, Mark A., St. Dominic Church
Schaffer, David B., M.A., M.S., Saint Colman Church, Ardmore
Schiappa, Edward R., St. Joseph Church, Downingtown
Schlegel, John F., St. Denis Rectory, Havertown
Schnepp, Lawrence P., St. Rose of Lima Church, Eddystone
Seda, Victor I., St. Helena Church
Sexton, Joseph F.
Shearer, C. William, SS. Simon and Jude Church, West Chester
Shields, Thomas A.
Shire, William F., St. Michael the Archangel Church, Levittown
Shirley, Ralph J., Our Lady of Ransom Church
Simpson, Harry J.
Skawinski, Robert J., St. Ignatius Church, Yardley
Smith, Calvin C.
Stam, Bernardus C., Diocese of Wilmington, DE
Stevens, Allen T., Jr., Archdiocese of New Orleans, LA
Stewart, James J., St. Edmond Church
Stewart, Robert J., Assumption B.V.M. Church, Feasterville
Stokely, Patrick M., St. Agnes Church, West Chester
Stoughton, Richard L., Our Lady of the Rosary Church, Coatesville
Suplee, John J., Sacred Heart Church, Havertown
Taylor, Thomas L., St. Joseph Church, Collingdale
Thompson, James A.
Thompson, Vincent J., St. Francis Xavier- The Oratory Church, Philadelphia
Tielemans, Mathieu M.
Tobin, Charles A., Diocese of Camden, NJ
Todor, John J., St. Cornelius Church, Chadds Ford
Tormey, James M., Diocese of Wilmington, DE
Tracy, Robert J.
Tran, Huan C., Saint Helena Church, Philadelphia
Tucker, Henry E., St. Agnes Church, Sellersville
Upcavage, Joseph R.
Urbanski, Timothy E., St. Catherine of Siena Church, Horsham
Urmson, Francis B., Holy Cross Church
Vadino, Raymond M., St. John Chrysostom Church, Wallingford
Vera, Jorge L.
Vondercrone, C. Stephens, St. Stanislaus Church, Lansdale
Wagner, Anthony E., Temple University Newman Center
Walker, James
Wallace, Mark M., St. Laurence Church, Upper Darby
Walsh, James V., St. Eugene Church, Primos
Warner, Dennis P., St. Anselm Church
Wellbank, Raymond C., St. Stanislaus Church, Lansdale
Wernert, Emil J., Epiphany of Our Lord, Plymouth Meeting
Whartenby, Gerald J., St. Anselm Church
Windish, Joseph F., St. Cyril of Jerusalem Church, Jamison
Wirth, Richard D.
Wojewodka, Boleslaw S.
Woods, Thomas J., Sacred Heart Church, Havertown
Zaleski, Stanley M., St. Martin of Tours Church
Ziff, Joel M.
Zurbach, E. Peter, St. Mary Magdalen Church, Media

INSTITUTIONS LOCATED IN THE ARCHDIOCESE

[A] SEMINARIES, ARCHDIOCESAN

WYNNEWOOD. *Theological Seminary of St. Charles Borromeo, Overbrook*, Administration: 100 E. Wynnewood Rd., 19096. Tel: 610-667-3394; Fax: 610-667-7635. Web: www.scs.edu. Revs. Shaun L. Mahoney, S.T.D., M.Div., Rector; Joseph W. Bongard, M.A., M.Div., Vice Rector, Provost; Elaine K. Rice, M.B.A., Vice Pres., Finance & Opers.; Revs. Robert A. Pesarchick, M.A., S.T.L., S.T.D., Academic Dean, Theology Division; Patrick J. Welsh, M.Div., M.A., S.S.L., Dean of Men, Theology Division & Dir. Liturgy; Dr. Kelly Bowring, B.S., M.A., S.T.L., S.T.D., Academic Dean, Graduate School of Theology and Program of Catholic Studies (GST); Jared Haselbarth, M.A., Asst. Dean Graduate School of Theology and Program of Catholic Studies (GST); Rev. Robert B. McDermott, M.Div., Dean of Men, College Division; David L. Osborne, M.A., M.B.A., Dir. Devel.; Revs. Joseph F. Gleason, M.Div., M.S., M.A., Dir. Spiritual Formation, Theology Division; Anthony J. Costa, M.Div., M.A., S.T.L., S.T.D., Dir. Spiritual Formation, College Division; Deacons James T. Owens, Dean, Permanent Diaconate Division; Paul J. McBlain, Dean, Permanent Diaconate Division; Mary D. D'Urso, M.B.A., Dir. Fin. Svcs.; Cait Kokolus, M.S.L.S., M.A., M.S., Vice Pres. Information Svcs. & Assessment And Director of Ryan Memorial Library; Lawrence A. Heyman, Ed.M., M.S., Registrar; James F. Growdon, M.A., M.A., Academic Dean, College Div.; Nicholas Mancini, Dir. Safety & Security; Steven D. Sankey, Dir. Information Technology; Rev. Joseph T. Shenosky, S.T.D., M.A., M.Div., Dir. Pastoral And Apostolic Formation,. Priests 22; Sisters 3; Lay Staff 24; Permanent Deacons 3; College Division Seminarians 54; Pre-Theology Seminarians 19; Theology Division Seminarians 66; Seminarians From Archdiocese of Philadelphia 49; Seminarians From Other Dioceses 87; Seminarians From Religious Communities 3; Permanent Diaconate Division: Aspirants 19; Candidates 59; Graduate School Of Theology And Program Of Catholic Studies 460.

Full Time Instructional Faculty: Rev. Msgr. Michael K. Magee, M.Div., M.A., S.S.L., S.T.L., S.T.D.; Revs. Patrick J. Brady, M.Div., S.S.L., S.T.D.; Dennis J. Billy, C.Ss.R., M.A., M.M.R.Sc., S.T.D., Th.D., D.Min.; William G. Donovan, M.Div., Ph.L., Ph.D.; Stephen J. Dougherty, M.Div., M.A.; Frank A. Giuffre, M.Div., M.A., S.S.L.; Michael H. Spitzer, M.Div., M.A., S.T.L.; Kelly Anderson, M.A., S.T.L., S.T.B.; Ene Andrilli, M.L.S.; Candida Antonelli, M.Ed., Ed.D.; Peter J. Colosi, M.Phil., M.A., Ph.D.; James M. Despres, M.A.; Janet Haggerty, M.A., Ph.D.; James Humble, M.S.L.S.; Theodore E. Kiefer, M.A., D.M.A.; Atherton C. Lowry, M.A., Ph.D.; Mark J. Mourachian, M.A.

Adjunct Faculty: Rev. Msgr. David I. Fulton, S.T.L., J.C.L., S.T.D., J.C.D.; Revs. J. Michael Beers, B.A., Ph.D., S.T.B., S.S.L.; Sean P. Bransfield, M.Div., M.A., J.C.L.; Mark J. Hunt, S.T.L., S.T.D.; Daniel E. Mackle, M.Div., M.A.; James P. Olson, M.Div., M.A., S.T.L.; Vincent Small, B.A., M.A.; Sisters Mary Elizabeth Kratzinger, S.S.J., M.A.; Kathleen Schipani, I.H.M., M.Ed., M.A.; S. Rita Small, R.S.M., M.A.; Kristi Bushner, M.A., J.D.; Robert Crewalk, B.A.; Helen Heinz, M.A., Ph.D.; Franklin Lane, M.A.; Judith M. Owens, M.A.

[B] SEMINARIES, RELIGIOUS OR SCHOLASTICATES

PHILADELPHIA. *Brothers of the Christian Schools*, Jeremy House, 6633 Ardleigh St., 19119-3824. Tel: 215-843-1884; Fax: 215-843-1617. Email: jeremyhouse@juno.com. Bro. Richard Buccina, F.S.C., Dir. Professed Brothers 4; Postulants 4.

DePaul Novitiate, 5710 Magnolia St., 19144. Tel: 215-843-1581; Fax: 215-844-9634. National Novitiate for the Congregation of the Mission (Vincentians). Priests 4; Brothers 2. In Res. Revs. Elmer Bauer III, C.M., Supr.; William M. Allegretto, C.M., Asst. Supr.; Stephen F. Cantwell, C.M.; Miles J. Heinen, C.M.; Bros. Peter A. Campbell, C.M., Treas.; Carmen V. Ciardullo.

St. Vincent's Seminary, 500 E. Chelten Ave., 19144-1296. Tel: 215-713-2400; Fax: 215-844-2085. Email: cmphila88@aol.com. Web: www.cmeast.org. Very Rev. Msgr. Michael J. Carroll, C.M., Prov., Eastern Province; Revs. Gregory P. Cozzubbo, C.M., Asst. Prov.; Bernard M. Tracey, C.M., B.A., M.Div., Supr.; Elmer Bauer III, C.M., Prov. Treas. & Second Councillor; Carl L. Pieber, C.M., Dir. Miraculous Medal Association; John W. Carven, C.M., Prov. Archivist; Mr. Allen Andrews, Exec. Dir. Finance. Central House of the Eastern Province of the Congregation of the Mission, (Vincentians). Residence for retired priests & brothers.

PAOLI. *Daylesford Abbey*, 220 S. Valley Rd., 19301-1900. Tel: 610-647-2530; Fax: 610-651-0219. Email: nobertines@daylesford.org. Web: www.daylesford.org. Revs. Ronald J. Rossi, O.Praem., Abbot Emeritus; Richard J. Antonucci, O.Praem., Abbot; Andrew D. Ciferni, O.Praem., Prior; Very Rev. Steven J. Albero, O.Praem., Subprior; Revs. John Joseph Novielli, O.Praem., Vocations Dir.; Joseph A. Serano, O.Praem., Treas.

Norbertine Fathers, Inc. Priests 25; Brothers 6.

SPRINGFIELD. *Servants of Charity Sd.C.*, 1795 S. Sproul Rd., 19064. Tel: 610-328-3406; Fax: 610-328-1019. Email: servantsofcharity@comcast.net. Web: www.servantsofcharity.org. Revs. Paul Oggioni, Sd.C; A. Pravin Vinodh-Raj, Sd.C.; Dennis M. Weber, Sd.C. Congregation of the Servants of Charity. Priests 4; Candidates 1. In Res. Rev. Elie Saade.

[C] COLLEGES AND UNIVERSITIES

PHILADELPHIA. *Chestnut Hill College*, 9601 Germantown Ave., 19118-2693. Tel: 215-248-7000; Fax: 215-248-7155. Email: chcapply@chc.edu. Web: www.chc.edu. Sisters Carol Jean Vale, S.S.J., Ph.D., Pres.; Mary Josephine Larkin, S.S.J., Dean Library & Info. Resources. Sisters 17; Lay Teachers 69; Students 2,281.

Holy Family University (1954) 9801 Frankford Ave., 19114. Tel: 215-637-7700; Fax: 215-637-3787. Email: fonley@holyfamily.edu. Web: www.holyfamily.edu. Sr. Francesca Onley, C.S.F.N., Ph.D., Pres.; Revs. James MacNew, Chap. & Campus Ministry; Mark J. Hunt, S.T.L., S.T.D., Dept. of Rel. Studies; James J. Collins, S.O.E.D., Dept. of Religious Studies; Lori Schwabenbauer, Librarian. Congregation of the Sisters of the Holy Family of Nazareth. Sisters 5; Lay Faculty 85; Undergraduate Students 2,137; Graduate Students 1,068.

**St. Joseph's University* Regis Hall, 5600 City Ave., 19131. Tel: 610-660-1000; Fax: 610-660-1201. Web: www.sju.edu. Under the direction of the Jesuit Fathers. Incorporated January 29, 1851. Priests 17; Sisters 1; Lay Teachers 740; Students 8,950.

Jesuit Fathers Tel: 610-660-1400; Fax: 610-664-6640. Revs. Mark C. Aita, S.J., M.D.; Anthony J. Berret, S.J.; Bruce M. Bidinger, S.J.; John M. Braverman, S.J.; Thomas J. Brennan, S.J.; William J. Byron, S.J.; Joseph F. Chorpenning, O.S.F.S., S.T.L., Ph.D.; Peter A. Clark, S.J.; Mario Farrugia, S.J.; Joseph J. Feeney, S.J.; Vincent J. Genovesi, S.J.; Joseph J. Godfrey, S.J.; Daniel R.J. Joyce, S.J.; Brendan G. Lally, S.J.; Joseph L. Lombardi, S.J.; Dennis E. McNally, S.J.; Nicholas J. Rashford, S.J.; James D. Redington, S.J.; Patrick H. Samway, S.J.; Bros. Joseph A. Koczera, S.J.; Gerald E. Peltz, S.J.; Sr. Elizabeth Ann Linehan, R.S.M.; Evelyn Minick, Librarian.

LaSalle University, 1900 W. Olney Ave., 19141. Tel: 215-951-1000; Fax: 215-951-1488. Bro. Michael J. McGinniss, F.S.C., Ph.D., Pres.; Joseph R. Marbach, Ph.D., Provost & Vice Pres. Academic Affairs; Matthew S. McManness, Vice Pres. Fin. & Admin.; R. Brian Elderton, M.Ed., Vice Pres. Univ. Advancement; John F. Dolan, Vice Pres. Enrollment Svcs.; James E. Moore, Ph.D., Vice Pres. Student Affairs, Dean Students; Thomas A. Keagy, Ph.D., Dean, School of Arts and Sciences; Paul R. Brazina, C.P.A., Dean, School of Business Admin.; Zane Robinson Wolf, Ph.D., R.N., F.A.A.N., Dean, School of Nursing; James C. Plunkett, Exec. Dir., Admissions; Joseph Y. Ugras, Ph.D., C.M.A., Dean, College Professional & Continuing Studies; Bro. Robert J. Kinzler, F.S.C., Dir. University Ministry & Svc.; John S. Baky, Dir. Connelly Library. (Incorporated under the auspices of the Brothers of the Christian Schools) Brothers 10; Sisters 1; Lay Teachers 233; Students 7,953.

ASTON. *Neumann University*, One Neumann Dr., 19014-1298. Tel: 610-558-5501; Fax: 610-558-5643. Email: neumann@neumann.edu. Web: www.neumann.edu. Dr. Rosalie M. Mirenda, Ph.D., Pres.; Rev. Jude Michael Krill, O.F.M.Conv., Chap.; John Michael Powell, Librarian. Sponsored by the Sisters of St. Francis of Philadelphia., Opened September 1965. Priests 2; Sisters 30; Administrators 125; Faculty and Staff 216; Adjuncts 204; Lay Teachers 187; Students 3,084.

GWYNEDD VALLEY. *Gwynedd-Mercy College*, 1325 Sumneytown Pike, P.O. Box 901, 19437. Tel: 215-646-7300; Fax: 215-641-5556. Email: dobbs.a@gmc.edu. Web: www.gmc.edu. Rev. John Collins, C.S.S.R., Chap. Sisters of Mercy 5; Sisters 1; Brothers 1; Lay Teachers 79; Students 2,370.

IMMACULATA. *Immaculata University* (1920) 19345. Tel: 610-647-4400; Fax: 610-647-7635. Web: www.immaculata.edu. Sisters R. Patricia Fadden, I.H.M., Pres.; Ann Heath, I.H.M., Ph.D., Vice Pres. for Academic Affairs; Theresa Grentz, Vice Pres. for Institutional Advancement; Janice Bates, M.A., Registrar; Dr. Samuel Wrightson, Dean College of Lifelong Learning; Dr. Janet Kane, Dean College of Graduate Studies; Sr. Elaine Glanz, I.H.M., Dean College of Undergraduate Studies; Robert Cole, Vice Pres. Univ. Communications; Robert Forest, Dir. Financial Aid; Erin Ebersole, Dir. Inst. Research, Planning & Assessment; Jeffrey Rollison, Exec. Dir. Library. Conducted by Sisters, Servants of the Immaculate Heart of Mary. Sisters 21; Total Staff 107; Enrollment 4,244.

RADNOR. *Cabrini College* (1957) 610 King of Prussia Rd., 19087-3698. Tel: 610-902-8100; Fax: 610-902-8436. Email: lplummer@cabrini.edu. Web: www.cabrini.edu. Dr. Marie A. George, Pres.; Stephanie Salinis, Campus Min. Missionary Sisters of the Sacred Heart. Priests 2; Sisters 1; Lay Teachers 299; Students 3,291.

ROSEMONT. *Rosemont College of the Holy Child Jesus* 19010-1699. Tel: 610-527-0200; Fax: 610-527-0341. Email: shirsh@rosemont.edu. Web: www.rosemont.edu. Sharon Latchaw Hirsh, Ph.D., Pres.; Jeanne Marie Hatch, S.H.C.J., Vice Pres., Mission; Michael McDonald, Dir. of Campus Ministry; Catherine M. Fennell, Exec. Dir. Library Svcs.; Joseph T. Rogers, Dir. Institutional Research. Sisters of the Holy Child Jesus 2; Lay Teachers 138; Students 1,232.

VILLANOVA. *Villanova University*, 800 Lancaster Ave., 19085. Tel: 610-519-7499; Fax: 610-519-5333. Email: Stephen.Merritt@Villanova.edu. Web: www.villanova.edu. Revs. Peter M. Donohue, O.S.A., Pres. & Bd. Trustee; Raymond F. Dlugos, O.S.A., Bd. Trustee; Paul W. Galetto, O.S.A., Bd. Trustee; Very Rev. Anthony M. Genovese, O.S.A., Bd. Trustee; Revs. Joseph L. Narog, O.S.A., Bd. Trustee; James D. Paradis, O.S.A., Bd. Trustee; Very Rev. Bernard C. Scianna, O.S.A., Bd. Trustee; Bro. Robert Thornton, O.S.A., Bd. Trustee; Richard P. Brennan, Bd. Trustee; Kimble A. Byrd, Esq., Bd. Trustee; James D. Danella, Bd. Trustee; James C. Davis, Bd. Trustee; Denise L. Devine, Bd. Trustee; Nance K. Dicciani, Ph.D., Bd. Trustee; Peter L. Fong, Bd. Trustee; Daryl J. Ford, Ph.D., Bd. Trustee; William M. Gibson, Bd. Trustee; Justin G. Gmelich, Bd. Trustee; Patricia H. Imbesi, Bd. Trustee; John P. Jones III, Bd. Trustee; Catherine M. Keating, Bd. Trustee; Sheila F. Klehm, Bd. Trustee; Patrick G. Lapore, Bd. Trustee; Leonard J. LoBiondo, Bd. Trustee; Anne Welsh McNulty, Bd. Trustee; Thomas Mulroy, Bd. Trustee; Mary D. Naylor, Ph.D., Bd. Trustee; James V. O'Donnell, Bd. Trustee; Terence M. O'Toole, Bd. Trustee; James F. Orr III, Bd. Trustee; Joseph V. Topper Jr., Bd. Trustee; Paul A. Tufano Esq., Bd. Trustee. Founded 1842 by the Augustinians, Province of St. Thomas of Villanova. Colleges of Liberal Arts and Sciences, Engineering, Nursing; The School of Law, the School of Business. Part-time and Continuing Education, Graduate Studies. Priests 28; Lay Teachers 632; Students 10,467; Clerical Faculty: Total Staff 16; Full-Time Enrollment 6,352; Part-Time Enrollment 515.

Administration: Ann Diebold, Vice Pres. Univ. Communications; Revs. Kail C. Ellis, O.S.A., Vice Pres. Academic Affairs; John P. Stack, O.S.A., Vice Pres. Student Life; Mr. Michael J. O'Neill, Vice Pres. Univ. Advancement; Barbara E. Wall, Vice Pres. Mission & Min.; Ms. Dorothy A. Malloy, Vice Pres. Univ. Counsel; Mr. Kenneth G. Valosky, Vice Pres. Admin. & Finance; Mr. Stephen Fugale, Vice Pres. & CIO Information Tech. Svcs.; Rev. George F. Riley, O.S.A., Special Asst. to Pres. External Affairs; Dr. Helen K. Lafferty, Univ. First College Prof.; John Y. Gotanda, J.D., Dean, Law School; Kevin D. Clark, Interim Dean Villanova School of Business; JeanAnn Linney, Ph.D., Dean of Liberal Arts & Sciences; Dr. Gary Gabriele, Dean of Engineering; Mr. Paul Pugh, Dean of Students; Dr. M. Louise Fitzpatrick, Dean College of Nursing; Mr. Stephen R. Merritt, Dean Office of Enrollment Mgmt.; Sr. Beth Hassel, P.B.V.M., Dir. Ctr. for Faith & Learning; Mr. Vincent Nicastro, Dir. Athletics; Revs. Robert P. Hagan, O.S.A., Asst. Athletic Dir.; Joseph D. Calderone, O.S.A., Chap., Law School; John P. Betoni, O.S.A., Graduate Studies Asst.; Kevin DePrinzio, O.S.A., Campus Min.; Thomas Murnane, O.S.A., Office of Univ. Admission; Francis Chambers, O.S.A., Assoc. Dir. of Univ. Admission; Dennis J. Gallagher, O.S.A., Archivist; Joseph S. Mostardi, O.S.A., Campus Min.; Bro. Michael Duffy, O.S.A., Campus Min.

Clerical Faculty: Revs. Stephen J. Baker, O.S.A., Adjunct; Richard G. Cannuli, O.S.A., Dir. Art Gallery, Curator Univ. & Art Collection, Chair of Theatre Dept.; Francis J. Caponi, O.S.A., Office of Theology & Religious Studies; David A. Cregan, O.S.A., Theatre Production; Edmund J. Dobbin, O.S.A., Theology & Rel. Studies; John J. Farrell, O.S.A. (Retired); Joseph L. Farrell, O.S.A., Assoc. Vice Pres. Mission & Min.; Allan Fitzgerald, O.S.A., Dir. Augustinian Institute; John J. Hagen, O.S.A., Adjunct; Richard Jacobs, O.S.A.; Charles P. Laferty, O.S.A., Adjunct; Martin Laird, O.S.A.; Joseph Loya, O.S.A.; Lee J. Makowski, O.S.A.; James J. McCartney, O.S.A., Faculty; Neil J. McGettigan, O.S.A., Adjunct (Retired); Robert J. Murray, O.S.A.; Joseph Ryan, O.S.A.; Michael J. Scanlon, O.S.A.; Joseph P. Lucia, Dir. Falvey Library.

[D] HIGH SCHOOLS, ARCHDIOCESAN

PHILADELPHIA. *Archbishop Ryan High School* Opened September 7, 1966., 11201 Academy Rd., 19154-3397. Tel: 215-637-1800; Fax: 215-637-8833. Email: information@archbishopryan.com. Web: www.archbishopryan.org. Mr. Michael J. McArdle, Pres.; Revs. Rene Barczak, O.F.M.; John E. Donia; Michael G. Speziale, School Min.; Helen T. Chaykowsky, Prin.; Mary Lorenzo Brelsford, Librarian. Franciscan Friars, Order of Friars Minor. Priests 2; Sisters 3; Lay Teachers 83; Total Staff 94; Students 1,615.

Father Judge High School for Boys Opened September 1954., 3301 Solly Ave., 19136-2396. Tel: 215-338-9494; Fax: 215-338-0250. Email: jcampellone@fatherjudge.net. Web: fatherjudge.com. Revs. Joseph G. Campellone, O.S.F.S., Pres.; Jack Kolodziej, O.S.F.S., Asst. Prin.; Bro. James Williams, O.S.F.S.; Rev. James E. Dalton, O.S.F.S., Prin.; Sandra Kolander, Librarian. Oblates of St. Francis de Sales. Priests 4; Sisters 3; Brothers 1; Lay Teachers 62; Students 1,250.

St. Hubert's Catholic High School for Girls Opened September 1941., 7320 Torresdale Ave., 19136. Tel: 215-624-6840; Fax: 215-624-5940. Email: contactus@huberts.org. Web: www.huberts.org. Sr. Mary E. Smith, I.H.M., Pres.; Rev. Thomas M. Sodano, Dir. School Ministry; Ms. Regina Craig, Prin. Priests 1; Sisters 13; Lay Teachers 42; Students 775.

SS. John Neumann and Maria Goretti Catholic High School (Formerly Southeast Catholic High School, St. John Neuman High School for Boys, St. Maria Goretti High School for Girls); (Boys and Girls 2004), 1736 S. Tenth St., 19148-1694. Tel: 215-465-8437; Fax: 215-462-2410. Web: www.neumanngorettihs.org. John Murawski Jr., Pres.; Rev. Jason Kulczynski, School Min.; Mrs. Patricia C. Sticco, Prin. Priests 1; Sisters 2; Lay Teachers 39; Students 800.

John W. Hallahan Catholic Girls High School Opened September 18, 1901., 311 N. 19th St., 19103-1198. Tel: 215-563-8930; Fax: 215-563-3809. Email: jhpres@adphila.org. Web: www.jwhallahan.com. Mrs. Sandra R. Young, Pres.; Rev. Stephen H. Paolino, School Min.; Ms. Mary Kirby, Prin.; Kathleen Kroos, Librarian. Priests 1; Sisters 3; Lay Teachers 27; Students 571.

Little Flower Catholic High School for Girls Opened September 1, 1939., 1000 W. Lycoming St., 19140. Tel: 215-455-6900; Fax: 215-329-0478. Web: www.LittleFlowerHighSchool.org. Sisters Kathleen Klarich, R.S.M., Prin.; Donna Shallo, I.H.M., Pres.; Rev. Joseph C. McCaffrey, M.B.A., M.Div., School Min.; Brooke Hauer, Librarian. Sisters 3; Lay Teachers 33; Students 747.

Roman Catholic High School for Boys Opened September 8, 1890., 301 N. Broad St., 19107. Tel: 215-627-1270; 215-627-1570; Fax: 215-627-4979. Email: r.oneill@cahillite.com. Web: www.cahillite.com. Revs. John B. Flanagan, Pres.; James R. Casey, School Min.; Mr. Robert O'Neill, Prin.; Eric Rosenberger, Librarian. Priests 2; Sisters 2; Lay Teachers 47; Students 1,096.

West Philadelphia Catholic High School West Catholic High School for Boys opened in 1916. West Catholic High School for Girls opened in 1926. Consolidated September, 1989., 4501 Chestnut St., 19139. Tel: 215-386-2244; Fax: 215-222-1651. Email: westcatholic@hotmail.org. Web: www.westcatholic.org. Bro. Timothy Ahern, F.S.C., Pres.; Sr. Mary E. Bur, I.H.M., Prin.; Mrs. Carol Tulba, Librarian. Priests 1; Sisters 7; Brothers 5; Lay Teachers 28; Students 444.

DOWNINGTOWN. *Bishop Shanahan High School*, 220 Woodbine Rd., 19335. Tel: 610-518-1300; Fax: 610-343-6220. Email: rplunkett@shanahan.org. Web: www.shanahan.org. Sisters Regina Plunkett, I.H.M., Pres.; Maureen L. McDermott, I.H.M., Ph.D., Prin.; Revs. Matthew W. Guckin, M.Div., School Min.; Kevin P. McCabe; Alice Dowling, Librarian. (Coed) Formerly St. Agnes High School opened in 1909; became diocesan high school September 1957, moved from West Chester to Downingtown in 1998. Sisters, Servants of the Immaculate Heart of Mary 8; Priests 2; Lay Teachers 60; Students 1,205.

DREXEL HILL. *Archbishop Prendergast High School* Opened September 1956. Restructured 2006. See Monsignor Bonner and Archbishop Prendergast Catholic High School.

Monsignor Bonner and Archbishop Prendergast Catholic High School, 401-403 N. Lansdowne Ave., 19026-1196. Tel: 610-259-0280; Fax: 610-259-1630. Web: www.bonnerhigh.com; www.prendie.com. Revs. James P. Olson, M.Div., M.A., S.T.L., Pres.; Thomas R. Urian; Matthew Wayock, Dir. School Min.; William Brannick, Prin.; Sr. Elizabeth Flavin, S.S.J., Librarian. (Boys) Opened September 1953 as Archbishop Prendergast High School for Boys. New name adopted September 1956. Restructured 2006. Priests 2; Sisters 8; Lay Teachers 77; Students 1,200.

FAIRLESS HILLS. *Conwell-Egan Catholic High School*, 611 Wistar Rd., 19030. Tel: 215-945-6200; Fax: 215-945-6206. Email: cecinfo@conwell-egan.org. Web: conwell-egan.org. Janet Dollard, Pres.; Dr. Kathleen Herpich, Prin.; Larine Lodise, Guidance Dir.; Rev. Christopher D. Lucas, Campus Min.; Geraldine Brennan, Librarian. Formerly Bishop Egan High School, Fairless Hills, and Bishop Conwell High School, Levittown. Priests 2; Sisters 6; Brothers 1; Lay Teachers 35; Students 700.

LANSDALE. *Lansdale Catholic High School*, 700 Lansdale Ave., 19446-2995. Tel: 215-362-6160; 215-242-6160 (Philadelphia); Fax: 215-362-5746. Email: jcasey@lansdalecatholic.com. Web: www.lansdalecatholic.com. Timothy P. Quinn, Prin.; James W. Casey, Pres.; Rev. John D. Schiele. Opened 1949. 1983 joined the System of Secondary Schools in Philadelphia. Priests 1; Lay Teachers 37; Students 785.

RADNOR. *Archbishop John Carroll High School* Opened September 1967., 211 Matson Ford Rd., 19087. Tel: 610-688-7610; Fax: 610-688-8326 (Prin.); 610-971-0827 (Pres.). Email: carroll@jcarroll.org. Web: www.jcarroll.org. Rev. Edward J. Casey, M.Div., Pres.; Joseph Denelsbeck, M.Ed., Prin.; Deacon Thomas G. Phillips, Dir. Campus Min.; Charmane Gates, Librarian. Priests 3; Sisters 3; Lay Teachers 47; Students 960.

ROYERSFORD. *Pope John Paul II High School* (2010) 181 Rittenhouse Rd., 19468. Tel: 484-975-6500. Web: www.pjphs.org. Revs. Alan J. Okon Jr., Pres.; Stephen P. DeLacy, School Min. Students 909.

SPRINGFIELD. *Cardinal O'Hara High School* (Coed) Opened September, 1963., 1701 S. Sproul Rd., 19064. Tel: 610-544-3800; Fax: 610-544-1189. Web: cohs.com. William J. McCusker, Ed.D., Pres.; Marie Rogai, Prin.; Revs. William J. Chiriaco; Paul J. O'Donnell, M.Div., School Min.; Geraldine Brennan, Librarian. Priests 2; Sisters 1; Lay Teachers 78; Students 1,400.

WARMINSTER. *Archbishop Wood Catholic High School* Opened September 1964., 655 York Rd., 18974. Tel: 215-672-5050; Fax: 215-672-9572 (Academic Office); 212-672-5451 (Business Office). Web: www.archwood.org. Gary V. Zimmaro, Pres.; Mrs. Mary Harkins, M.A., Prin.; Rev. John C. Nguyen, School Min. Priests 2; Sisters 4; Lay Teachers 60; Students 1,050.

WYNCOTE. *Bishop McDevitt High School*, 125 Royal Ave., 19095-1198. Tel: 215-887-5575; Fax: 215-887-1371. Email: bmcdhs1@nni.com. Web: www.mcdevitths.org. Salvatore DiNenna, Ed.D., Pres.; Revs. Kevin J. Kelly; Quan H. Tran; Rosemary Naab, Prin.; Glenda Rieffel, Librarian. Opened September 1958. Priests 2; Sisters 3; Lay Teachers 35; Students 635.

[E] VOCATIONAL HIGH SCHOOLS

PHILADELPHIA. *Mercy Vocational High School*, 2900 W. Hunting Park Ave., 19129-1803. Tel: 215-226-1225; Fax: 215-228-6337. Email: generalinfo@mercyvhs.org. Web: www.mercyvocational.org. Sisters Rosemary Herron, R.S.M., Pres.; Susan Walsh, R.S.M., Prin.; Catherine Glatts, Vice Prin.; Sr. Emily Connor, R.S.M., School Min.; Frances Skiendzielewski, Librarian. Sisters of Mercy 12; Lay Teachers 40; Students 378.

[F] HIGH SCHOOLS, PRIVATE

PHILADELPHIA. *St. Joseph's Preparatory School*, Office of the President, 1733 W. Girard Ave., 19130. Tel: 215-978-1950; Fax: 215-765-1710. Web: www.sjprep.org. Rev. George W. Bur, S.J., Pres.; Mr. Michael Gomez, Prin.; Dennis Hart, Dean of Students; Mr. Timothy O'Shaughnessy, CFO; Mr. Joseph Nawn, Asst. Prin. Instruction & Learning; Mrs. Rose Marie Kettinger, Registrar/Asst. Prin. for Academic Programs & Records; Rev. Bruce A. Maivelett, S.J., Dir. of Ignatian Identity; Albert Zimmerman, Dir. Devel.; Mrs. Sonia Nelson, Librarian. Priests 4; Sisters 1; Lay Teachers 80; Students 990.

Nazareth Academy High School, 4001 Grant Ave., 19114-2999. Tel: 215-637-7676; Fax: 215-637-8523. Email: jacobs@nazarethacademyhs.org. Web: www.nazarethacademyhs.org. Sisters Mary Joan Jacobs, C.S.F.N., Ed.D., Prin.; M. Clarissa Mroz, C.S.F.N., Librarian. Sisters 11; Lay Teachers 43; Girls 414.

BENSALEM. *Holy Ghost Preparatory School*, 2429 Bristol Pike, 19020. Tel: 215-639-2102; Fax: 215-639-4225. Email: jduaime@holyghostprep.org. Web: www.holyghostprep.org. Revs. Jeffrey T.

Duaime, C.S.Sp., Pres. Tel: 215-639-2102; Christopher H. McDermott, C.S.Sp., Chap.; Philip Agber, C.S.Sp.; Mr. Michael O'Toole, Prin.; Mr. Vincent Profy, Ed.D., Librarian. Spiritan Fathers 3; Lay Teachers 47; Males 508.

BRYN MAWR. *Country Day School of the Sacred Heart*, 480 Bryn Mawr Ave., 19010. Tel: 610-527-3915; Fax: 610-527-0942. Email: smacdonald@cdssh.org. Web: www.cdssh.org. Sr. Matthew Anita MacDonald, S.S.J., Head of School; Rev. Thomas P. Gillin, M.S., Chap.; Catherine Scholl, Librarian. Sisters 2; Lay Teachers 45; Students 353.

DEVON. *Devon Preparatory School* 19333. Tel: 610-688-7337; Fax: 610-688-2409. Email: info@devonprep.com. Revs. James J. Shea, Sch.P., Prin.; Richard S. Wyzykiewicz, Sch.P., Chap. & Rector; Jose' A. Basols, Sch.P.; Javier Renteria, Sch.P.; Mr. Paul J. Sanborn, Librarian. Piarist Fathers. Priests 3; Lay Teachers 34; Students 260.

FLOURTOWN. *Mt. St. Joseph Academy*, 120 W. Wissahickon Ave., 19031. Tel: 215-233-3177; Fax: 215-233-4734. Email: kbrabson@msjacad.org. Web: www.msjacad.org. Sr. Kathleen Brabson, S.S.J., Pres.; Dr. Judith Caviston, Prin. Sisters of St. Joseph 9; Lay Teachers 57; Students 560.

GWYNEDD VALLEY. *Gwynedd-Mercy Academy*, 1345 Sumneytown Pike, 19437-0902. Tel: 215-646-8815; Fax: 215-646-4361. Web: www.gmahs.com. Sr. Patricia Flynn, R.S.M., Prin.; Marilyn Duffy, Librarian. Sisters 5; Lay Teachers 40; Girls 380.

HOLLAND. *Villa Joseph Marie High School*, 1180 Holland Rd., 18966. Tel: 215-357-8810; Fax: 215-357-2477. Email: dkoop@vjmhs.org. Web: www.vjmhs.org. Mary T. Michel, Pres.; Diana Koopman, Prin. Lay Teachers 35; Students 360.

MALVERN. *Malvern Preparatory School for Boys*, 418 S. Warren Ave., 19355-2707. Tel: 484-595-1194; Fax: 484-595-1118. Web: www.malvernprep.org. Revs. Stephen J. Baker, O.S.A., Prior Faculty; Francis J. Caponi, O.S.A.; Harry J. Erdlen, O.S.A., Campus Min.; Augustine M. Esposito, O.S.A., M.Div., M.A., Ph.D.; James R. Flynn, O.S.A., Headmaster; Thomas J. Meehan, O.S.A.; Mr. James Stewart, Pres.; Mrs. Elizabeth Driscoll, Librarian. Priests 5; Lay Teachers 75; Students 618.

Villa Maria Academy High School, 370 Old Lincoln Hwy., 19355. Tel: 610-644-2551; Fax: 610-644-2866. Email: info@vmahs.org. Web: www.vmahs.org. Sr. Marita Carmel, I.H.M., Prin.; Mrs. Celeste Dougherty, Librarian. Sisters, Servants of the Immaculate Heart of Mary 11; Lay Teachers 51; Girls 430.

MERION. *Merion Mercy Academy*, 511 Montgomery Ave., Merion Station, 19066. Tel: 610-664-6655; Fax: 610-664-6322. Email: mma@merion-mercy.com. Web: www.merion-mercy.com. Sr. Barbara Buckley, R.S.M., Prin.; Ashley Esposito, Dir. Media Center. Day School for Girls. Sisters of Mercy 14; Lay Teachers 49; Students 487.

VILLANOVA. *Academy of Notre Dame de Namur*, 560 Sproul Rd., 19085. Tel: 610-687-0650; Fax: 610-687-1912. Web: www.ndapa.org. Veronica Collins Harrington, Pres.; Ms. Anne T. Carroll, Jr. School Dir.; Joseph D'Angelo, Prin.; Ms. Mary Buxton, Librarian. Sisters 1; Lay Teachers 63.

WYNDMOOR. *LaSalle College High School*, 8605 Cheltenham Ave., 19038. Tel: 215-233-2911; Fax: 215-233-1418. Email: admissions@lschs.org. Web: www.lschs.org. Bro. Richard Kestler, F.S.C., Pres.; Mr. Joseph Marchese, Prin.; Bro. James F. Rieck, F.S.C., Religious Supr.; Donna Long, Librarian; Mr. Kevin Dougherty, Admin/Fin Aid Director. Priests 1; Brothers of the Christian Schools 10; Lay Teachers 89; Students 1,060.

[G] REGIONAL PARISH SCHOOLS

PHILADELPHIA. *St. Athanasius-Immaculate Conception School*, 7105 Limekiln Pike, 19138. Tel: 215-424-5045; Fax: 215-927-6615. Email: saic@sa-ic.org. Sisters Joan Alminde, S.S.J., Prin.; Arleen McNicholas, S.S.J., Librarian. Regional school for St. Athanasius Parish and Immaculate Conception Parish. Sisters 4; Lay Teachers 12; Students 302.

Holy Child Catholic School, 242 Hermitage St., 19127. Tel: 215-487-2796; Fax: 215-487-9134. Email: hccsprincipal@gmail.com. Web: teacherweb.com/PA/HolyChildCatholicSchool/SchoolHomePage/SDHP1.stm. Michael J. Patterson, Prin. Regional school for Holy Family, St. Lucy and St. Mary of the Assumption parishes.

Holy Innocents Area Catholic School, 1312 E. Bristol St., 19124. Tel: 215-743-5909; Fax: 215-743-0199. Email: holyinnocentsaces@juno.com. Sr. Regina Mullen, I.H.M., Prin.; Mrs. Carol Hockensmith, Librarian. Area School for St. Joan of Arc, St. Joachim, Mater Dolorosa, Holy Innocents; Ascension of Our Lord, St. Hugh of Cluny Sisters, Servants of the Immaculate Heart of Mary 8; Lay Teachers 14; Students 300.

St. Mary Interparochial School, 5th & Locusts Sts., 19106. Tel: 215-923-7522; Fax: 215-923-8502. Email: stmary@cavtel.net. Jeanne M. Meredith, Prin.; Barbara Brown, Librarian. Regional school for Old St. Joseph Parish, Old St. Mary Parish, St. John the Evangelist Parish, St. Augustine Parish, St. Mary Magdalen de Pazzi and St. Patrick. Lay Teachers 10; Students 242.

Mary, Mother of Peace, 6334 Buist Ave., 19142. Tel: 215-729-3603; Fax: 215-729-2315. Sr. Janet Walters, I.H.M., Prin. Regional school for Divine Mercy and St. Barnabas. Sisters 2; Lay Teachers 13; Students 253.

Our Lady of Port Richmond Regional School, 3233 Thompson St., 19134. Tel: 215-739-1920; Fax: 215-739-0519. Sisters Mary Ripp, S.C.C., Prin.; Angela Abbruzzese, S.C.C., Librarian. Regional School for St. Adalbert, Nativity of the Blessed Virgin Mary and Our Lady Help of Christians. Sisters 3; Lay Teachers 24.

Pope John Paul II Regional School, (Grades PreK-8), 4435 Almond St., 19137. Tel: 215-535-3446; Fax: 215-535-3858. Web: pjp2rcs.com. Linda Osik-Milewski, Prin.; Anna Marie Kelly, Librarian. Regional School for St. John Cantius and All Saints Parishes. Lay Teachers 16; Students 230.

The DePaul Catholic School, 44 W. Logan St., 19144. Tel: 215-842-1266; Fax: 215-842-1400. Email: info@thedepaulcatholicschool.org. Web: thedepaulcatholicschool.org. Sr. Cheryl Ann Hillig, D.C., Prin. Regional school for St. Francis of Assisi Parish and Saint Vincent de Paul Parish. Sisters 2; Lay Teachers 33; Priests 2; Students 294.

AMBLER. *St. Anthony - St. Joseph Elementary School*, 260 Forest Ave., 19002. Tel: 215-646-6150; Fax: 215-654-5254. Email: sasjprincipal@gmail.com. Web: www.sa-sj.org. Kathleen Dilts, Prin.; Rosa Costanzo, Librarian. Regional school for St. Anthony of Padua Parish and St. Joseph Parish. Sisters of St. Joseph 1; Lay Teachers 12; Students 164.

ARDSLEY. *Good Shepherd Catholic Regional School*, 835 N. Hills Ave, 19038. Tel: 215-886-4782; Fax: 215-517-6708. Email: spatriciahealey@gscregional.org. Web: www.gscregional.org. Sr. Patricia Healey, I.H.M., Prin. Sisters, Servants of the Immaculate Heart of Mary 1; Lay Teachers 20; Students 236.

BRYN MAWR. *SS. Colman-John Neumann School*, 372 Highland Ln., 19010. Tel: 610-525-3266; Fax: 610-525-6103. Web: www.scjnschool.org. Catherine Blumstein, Prin. Regional school for St. Colman Parish and St. John Neumann Parish. Lay Teachers 19; Students 224.

CONSHOHOCKEN. *Conshohocken Catholic School*, 205 Fayette St., 19428. Tel: 610-828-2007; Fax: 610-825-8796. Email: conshohockencatholic@yahoo.com. Patricia J. Kaeser, Prin.; Sr. Mary Pat Watson, Librarian. Regional school for SS. Cosmas & Damian Parish and St. Matthew Parish.

St. Matthew Elementary Campus, 205 Fayette St., 19428. Tel: 610-828-2007; Fax: 610-825-8796.

SS. Cosmas & Damian Primary Campus (Grades PreK-K), 130 W. 5th Ave., 19428. Tel: 610-828-0755; Fax: 610-828-5191. Sisters 4; Lay Teachers 17; Students 200.

HILLTOWN. *St. Agnes-Sacred Heart School*, 100 Broad St., P.O. Box 31, 18927. Tel: 215-822-9174; Fax: 215-822-7942. Web: www.sashschool.com. Margaret Graham, Prin.; Patti Alber, Librarian. Regional School for St. Agnes, Sellersville and Sacred Heart, Hilltown. Lay Teachers 18.

LEVITTOWN. *Holy Family Regional Catholic School*, 2477 Trenton Rd., 19056. Tel: 215-269-9600; Fax: 215-269-9609. Web: www.hfrcs.org. John Mundy, Prin. Sisters of St. Joseph 1; Sisters, Servants of the Immaculate Heart of Mary 3; Lay Teachers 28; Students 536.

LINWOOD. *Holy Saviour-St. John Fisher School*, 122 E. Ridge Rd., 19061. Tel: 610-485-0363; Fax: 610-485-7809. Email: mrworrilow@holysaviorstjohnfisherschool.com. Monica Malseed. Regional school for Holy Saviour Parish and St. John Fisher Parish. Lay Teachers 15; Students 196.

NORRISTOWN. *Our Lady of Victory Regional Catholic School*, 351 E. Johnson Hwy., 19401. Tel: 610-275-2990; Fax: 610-275-0470. Angela Ciccanti, Prin.; Frances Luthy, Librarian. Regional school for Holy Saviour, St. Patrick and St. Paul parishes. Lay Teachers 14; Students 150.

PHOENIXVILLE. *Holy Family School*, 221 Third Ave., 19460. Tel: 610-933-7562; Fax: 610-933-8823. Email: abraca@myholyfamily.com. Web: www.myholyfamilyschool.org. Mrs. Ann Marie Braca, Prin.; Mrs. Josephine Bachi, Librarian. Regional school for St. Ann Parish, Holy Trinity Parish, St. Mary of the Assumption Parish, Sacred Heart Parish and St. Joseph, Spring City. Lay Teachers 24; Students 430.

RIDLEY PARK. *St. Madeline-St. Rose School*, 500 Tome St., 19078. Tel: 610-583-3662; Fax: 610-583-3683. Email: smsrprincipal@comcast.net. Web: www.smsr-central.net. Dennis Reitano, Prin. Regional school for St. Madeline Parish and St. Rose of Lima Parish. Lay Teachers 14; Students 250.

WARRINGTON. *St. Joseph-St. Robert School*, 850 Euclid Ave., 18976. Tel: 215-343-5100; Fax: 215-343-7434. Web: stjstr.org. Mrs. Deborah R. Jaster, Prin.; Marie Orzechowski, Librarian. Regional school for St. Joseph Parish and St. Robert Bellarmine Parish. Lay Teachers 15; Students 272.

WEST BRANDYWINE. *Pope John Paul II Regional Catholic Elementary School*, 2875 Manor Rd., 19320. Tel: 610-384-5961; Fax: 610-384-5730. Email: abmcguire@hotmail.com. Web: www.popejohnpaul2sch.org. Sr. Anne B. McGuire, Prin.; Elizabeth Powell, Librarian. Area school for St. Cecilia, St. Joseph, St. Stanislaus and Our Lady of the Rosary, Coatesville, and St. Peter Parish, West Brandywine. Servants of the Immaculate Heart of Mary 3; Lay Teachers 28; Students 605.

[H] ELEMENTARY SCHOOLS, PRIVATE

PHILADELPHIA. *The Gesu School*, 1700 W. Thompson Sts., 19121. Tel: 215-763-3660; 215-763-9077 (Development); Fax: 215-763-9844. Email: neil@gesuschool.org. Web: www.gesuschool.org. Bryan Carter, Pres.; Sr. Ellen Convey, I.H.M., Prin.; Rev. Neil L. Ver'Schneider, S.J., Vice Prin.; Sr. Patricia McGrenra, I.H.M.; Vivian Ehret, Librarian. Priests, Society of Jesus 1; Sisters, Servants of the Immaculate Heart of Mary 2; Lay Teachers 29; Students 452.

**La Salle Academy*, (Grades 3-8), 1434 N. 2nd St., 19122. Tel: 215-739-5804; Fax: 215-739-1664. Email: jeannemcgowan2002@yahoo.com. Web: www.lasalleacademy.net. Sr. Jeanne McGowan, S.S.J., Pres.; Teresa Diamond, Prin. Sisters 2; Lay Teachers 13; Students 90.

**St. Martin de Porres School*, 2300 W. Lehigh Ave., 19132. Tel: 215-223-6872; 877-689-6006 (Development); Fax: 215-233-4126. Email: apmartin1993@gmail.com. Web: www.fsmdpschool.org. John (Jack) Donnelly, Board Chm.; Rev. Stephen D. Thorne, M.A., M.Div., Pres.; Sisters Nancy Fitzgerald, S.S.J., Prin.; Meghan V. Patterson, S.S.J., Vice Prin. Sisters 5; Lay Teachers 15; Students 390.

Nazareth Academy Grade School, 4701 Grant Ave., 19114. Tel: 215-637-7777; Fax: 215-637-5696. Email: nazarethacademygradeschool@yahoo.com. Web: www.nazarethacademy.net. Sisters Mary Ann Allton, C.S.F.N., Prin.; M. Anita Pasternak, C.S.F.N., Vice Prin.; M. Yvette Ortiz, C.S.F.N., Finance Dir.; Mrs. Nancy Lydon, Librarian. Sisters of the Holy Family of Nazareth 5; Lay Teachers 16; Students 232.

Norwood-Fontbonne Academy, 8891 Germantown Ave., 19118. Tel: 215-247-3811; Fax: 215-247-8405. Email: mbeirne@norfon.org. Web: www.norwoodfontbonneacademy.org. Sisters Mary Helen Beirne, S.S.J., Ed.D., Head of School; Monica Osaben, S.S.J., Dir. Business Opers.; Mrs. Deborah Wood, Dir. Upper Grades (4-8); Mrs. Nancy Peluso, Dir. Lower Grades (PreK-3); Mr. William Dennis, Dir. Campus Min.; Theresa Hutsell, Asst. Dir. Campus Min.; Mrs. Joanne Baillie, Dir. Admissions; Ms. Stephanie Belzer, Dir. Institutional Advancement; Ms. Shannon Craig, Librarian. Sisters of St. Joseph 5; Lay Teachers 33; Students 399.

BRYN MAWR. *St. Aloysius Academy*, (Grades PreK-8), 401 S. Bryn Mawr Ave., 19010. Tel: 610-525-1670; Fax: 610-525-5140. Email: soar@staloysiusacademy.org. Web: www.staloysiusacademy.org. Sr. Stephen Ann Roderiguez, I.H.M., Ed.D., Prin.; Mary Jane McGough, Librarian. Sisters, Servants of the Immaculate Heart of Mary 9; Lay Teachers 43; Students 215.

CHESTER. *Drexel Neumann Academy*, (Grades PreK-9), 1901 Potter St., 19013-5497. Tel: 610-872-7358; Fax: 610-872-7833. Sisters Margaret Gannon, O.S.F., Pres.; Catherine McGowan, S.S.J., Prin.

DREXEL HILL. *Holy Child Academy*, (Grades N-8), 475 Shadeland Ave., 19026. Tel: 610-259-2712; Fax: 610-259-1862. Email: acoll@holychildacademy.com. Web: holychildacademy.com. Mrs. Anita P. Coll, Head of School. Lay Teachers 23; Students 166.

IMMACULATA. *Villa Maria Academy*, 1140 King Rd., 19345-0600. Tel: 610-644-4864; Fax: 610-647-6403. Email: office@villamaria.org. Web: www.villamaria.org. Sr. Mary Ellen Tennity, I.H.M., Prin.; Sarah Connelly, Librarian. Sisters,

Servants of the Immaculate Heart of Mary 6; Lay Teachers 35; Girls 325.

MERION. *Waldron Mercy Academy*, 513 Montgomery Ave., Merion Station, 19066. Tel: 610-664-9847; Fax: 610-664-6364. Email: wma@waldronmercy.org. Web: www.waldronmercy.org. Mr. Stephen Stritch, Prin.; Sr. Joellen McDonnell, R.S.M., Admissions Dir.; Lucille Morinelli, Librarian. Private, co-educational elementary school with child care, preschool & Montessori programs. Sisters of Mercy 4; Lay Teachers 40; Students 525.

RADNOR. *Armenian Sisters Academy* Montessori for ages 3-6. Elementary for ages 7-14., 440 Upper Gulph Rd., 19087. Tel: 610-687-4100; Fax: 610-687-2430. Email: SISTEREMMA@ASAPHILA.ORG. Web: www.asaphila.org. Sr. Emma Moussayan, Prin. Sisters 4; Lay Teachers 22; Students 134.

ROSEMONT. *Rosemont School of the Holy Child*, 1344 Montgomery Ave., 19010. Tel: 610-992-1000; Fax: 610-922-1030. Email: info@rosemontschool.org. Web: www.rosemontschool.org. Sr. Mary Broderick, S.H.C.J., Head of School; Mr. Thomas Lengel, Prin.; Catherine Stuart, Librarian. Sisters of the Holy Child Jesus 1; Lay Teachers 36; Students 315.

SPRING HOUSE. *Gwynedd-Mercy Academy Elementary School*, (Grades K-8), *Elementary School*, 816 Norristown Rd., P.O. Box 241, 19477. Tel: 215-646-4916; 215-646-2406 (Business Office); Fax: 215-646-7250. Email: mkenney@gmaelem.org. Web: www.gmaelem.org. Sr. Anne Crampsie, R.S.M., Prin.; Ms. Marilynne Dickinson, Curriculum Coord.; Ms. Katherine Palladino, Librarian. Sisters of Mercy 1; Lay Teachers 44; Students 488; Total Staff 56.

WYNCOTE. *Ancillae-Assumpta Academy*, (Grades PreK-8), (Coed), 2025 Church Rd., 19095. Tel: 215-885-1636; Fax: 215-885-2740. Email: kharp@ancillae.org; mgillespie@ancillae.org. Kerry Harp, Dir.; Sr. Maureen Gillespie, A.C.J., Prin.; Rosanne Zajko, Librarian. Handmaids of the Sacred Heart of Jesus 5; Lay Teachers 65; Students 574.

WYNDMOOR. *Regina Coeli Academy*, 1108 E. Willow Grove Ave., 19038-7663. Tel: 215-836-2208; Fax: 215-836-7250. Email: info@reginacoeliacademy.com. Web: www.reginacoeliacademy.com. Mr. Tim Murnane, Chm. Bd.; Mr. Joseph W. Austin, Headmaster. A private independent school PreK-8. Classical curriculum and formation in the Catholic faith. Lay Faculty 15; Students 75.

YARDLEY. *Grey Nun Academy* (Coed Day School), 1750 Quarry Rd., 19067. Tel: 215-968-4151; Fax: 215-860-7418. Email: mfinnegan@gnaedu.org. Web: www.gnaedu.org. Marianne R. Finnegan, Prin.; Sr. Martha Moyle, G.N.S.H., Asst. Prin.; Linda Rowan, Librarian. Grey Nuns of the Sacred Heart 1; Lay Teachers 24; Students 198.

[I] SPECIAL EDUCATION

PHILADELPHIA. *St. Lucy Day School for Children with Visual Impairments and Archbishop Ryan Academy for the Deaf*, 4251 L St., 19124. Tel: 215-289-4220; Fax: 215-289-4229. Email: APLucy01@nni.com. Web: www.slds.org. Sr. M. Margaret Fleming, I.H.M., Prin. Sisters, Servants of the Immaculate Heart of Mary 4; Lay Teachers 6; Students 39.

Our Lady of Confidence Day School, Willow Grove. Tel: 215-657-9311; Fax: 215-657-9312. Email: apConf01@nni.com. Web: www.ourladyofconfidence.org. Mentally Challenged. Sisters Servants of the Immaculate Heart of Mary 3; Lay Teachers 8.

Main School and Office, 314 N. Easton Rd., Willow Grove, 19090-2506. Tel: 215-657-9311; Fax: 215-657-9312. Email: APConf01@nni.com.

Bishop McDevitt High School, 125 Royal Ave., Wyncote, 19095-1198. Tel: 215-587-5575, Ext. 247; Fax: 215-657-9312. Sr. Judith Moeller, I.H.M., Prin.

WYNNEWOOD. *St. Katherine Day School*, 930 Bowman Ave., 19096. Tel: 610-667-3958; Fax: 610-667-3625. Email: APKath01@nni.com. Margaret Devaney, Prin. Children with Developmental Delay and/or Multiple Impairments. Lay Teachers 11; Students 86.

[J] CATHOLIC SOCIAL SERVICES OF THE ARCHDIOCESE OF PHILADELPHIA

PHILADELPHIA. *Catholic Social Services of the Archdiocese of Philadelphia*, 222 N. 17th St., 19103-1202. Tel: 215-587-3900; Fax: 215-587-2479. Email: CHSweb@chs-adphila.org. Web: www.css-phl.org. Joseph J. Sweeney Jr., M.B.A., N.H.A., Sec., Catholic Human Svcs.; Gary Miller, CFO; James Amato, L.S.W., Deputy Sec.; Kathleen Emery, M.S.W., M.Ed., Dir. Community-Based & Specialized Svcs.; Amy Stoner, L.S.W., A.C.S.W., Dir. Community-Based Prevention Svcs.; Deborah Wagner, L.S.W., Dir. Housing & Homeless Svcs. All addresses unless otherwise indicated.

St. Gabriel's System, 227 N. 18th St., 19103. Tel: 215-665-8777; Fax: 215-665-6621. Web: www.saintgabrielsystem.org. Joseph Lavoritano, M.A., M.Ed., N.C.S.P., Dir. - Youth Svcs.

Developmental Programs Division Office, 1797 S. Sproul Rd., Springfield, 19064. Tel: 484-475-2469; Fax: 610-543-5397. Web: www.cssmrserv.org. Mark E. Fitzgerald, M.S.W., N.H.A., Dir. Devel. Programs Div.

Adoption Services Tel: 215-331-2443; Fax: 215-457-5418. Robert Montoro, M.S.W., Prog. Supvr.

Child Care/Foster Home Services Tel: 267-331-2488; Fax: 215-457-5418. Teresa Thompson, L.S.W., Dir. Community - Based Svcs.

Philadelphia County Community-Based Prevention Services Amy Stoner, L.S.W., A.C.S.W., Dir.

Casa del Carmen Family Services, 4440 N. Reese St., 19140. Tel: 267-331-2500; Fax: 215-329-6722. Griselle Newman, M.A., Admin.

Northeast Philadelphia Family Service Center, 7340 Jackson St., 19136. Tel: 215-624-5920; Fax: 215-624-9197. Renee Hudson-Small, L.S.W., Admin.

Southwest Philadelphia Family Service Center, 6214 Grays Ave., 19142. Tel: 215-724-8550. Renee Hudson-Small, L.S.W., Admin.

Suburban Counties Community-Based & Specialized Services Tel: 610-279-7372. Kathleen Emery, M.S.W., M.Ed., Dir.

Bucks County Family Service Centers, 100 Levittown Pkwy., Levittown, 19054. Tel: 215-945-2550; Fax: 215-945-3595.

Middle Bucks County, 607 W. Street Rd., Warminster, 18974.

Upper Bucks County, 427 N. Main St., Sellersville, 18960. Gail McCoach, L.C.S.W., Admin.

Chester County Family Service Centers, 140 N. Darlington St., West Chester, 19380. Tel: 610-344-7028; Fax: 610-344-0762. 105 Prospect Ave., West Grove, 19390. Tel: 610-869-6500; Fax: 610-869-6258. Mary Ann Nagel, M.S.S., L.S.W., Prog. Mgr.

Delaware County Family Service Center, 240 N. Bishop Ave., Springfield, 19064. Tel: 610-626-6550; Fax: 610-626-2069. Gail McCoach, L.C.S.W., Admin.

130 E. 7th St., Chester, 19013. Tel: 610-876-7101; Fax: 610-876-9183. Alana Schafer, L.C.S.W., Admin.

Montgomery County Family Service Center, 353 E. Johnson Hwy., Norristown, 19401. Tel: 610-279-7372; Fax: 610-270-0626. Elizabeth Peteraf, L.C.S.W., Prog. Mgr.

Specialized Services, 227 N. 18th St., 19103. The offices are all located at the Holy Family Center unless otherwise noted.

Immigration and Refugee Services Tel: 215-854-7019; Fax: 215-854-7100. Mark Shea Esq., Admin.

Senior Adult Services Tel: 215-854-7087; Fax: 215-965-5712. Kathleen Newman, Asst. Admin.

Housing/Homeless Services Division, 222 N. 17th St., 19103. Tel: 215-854-7080; Fax: 215-587-2479. Deborah Wagner, L.S.W., Dir.

Corporations of Group Homes

St. Joseph House for Boys, 222 N. 17th St., 19103.

St. Joseph Catholic Home for Children, 222 N. 17th St., 19103.

St. Vincent's Services, 222 N. 17th St., 19103.

[K] RESIDENTIAL SERVICES FOR CHILDREN

PHILADELPHIA. *St. Vincent Homes, Administrative Office Building*, 1509 Church St., 19124. Tel: 215-992-5402; Fax: 215-992-5198. Web: www.stvincenthome.org. Richard Pytlewski, M.S.W., Admin.; Theresa Metz, Dir., Social Work. Operates the following programs for court adjudicated dependent females ages 12-21 who suffer from abuse and neglect. All facilities are staffed 24/7. Capacity 74; Total Staff 87.

St. Joachim's Hall Group Home (16 females ages 12-21), 1509 Church St., 19124. Tel: 215-992-5402; Cell: 267-574-1100; Fax: 215-992-5189.

St. Joseph's Hall Group Home (12 females ages 12-21), 477 E. Locust Ave., 19144. Tel: 215-849-1316; Cell: 215-300-2315; Fax: 215-842-0387.

St. Joan of Arc Hall (16 females ages 12-21), 3556 Frankford Ave., 19134. Tel: 215-992-5070; Cell: 215-275-4560; Fax: 215-624-8355.

Guardian Angel Mother/Baby Prog. (10 teen mothers ages 12-21 and 10 babies), 157 W. Carpenter Ln., 19111. Tel: 215-849-9029; Cell: 215-200-6651; Fax: 215-849-0651.

Maternity Group Home (10 females ages 12-21 who are pregnant), 104 E. Township Line Rd., Havertown, 19083. Tel: 610-446-0105; Cell: 215-200-6605; Fax: 610-446-1532.

AMBLER. *St. Mary's Villa for Children and Families*, 701 S. Bethlehem Pike, P.O. Box 388, 19002-0388. Tel: 215-643-7676; Fax: 215-542-9219. Email: fryer.diana@hfi-pgh.org. Web: www.hfi.org. Diana L. Fryer, Exec. Dir. Family centered organization providing residential care and treatment to youth ages 7-18. St. Mary's is committed to helping children, preserving families and strengthening communities by providing residential treatment and outpatient mental health counseling. It strives to empower children and families to lead responsible lives and develop healthy relationships built on faith, hope and love. Sisters of the Holy Family of Nazareth 1; Capacity 87; Total Staff 118; Total Assisted Annually 169.

BENSALEM. *St. Francis - St. Joseph Homes for Children*, 3400 Bristol Pike, 19020. Tel: 215-638-9310; Fax: 215-638-2498. Email: fswiack@chs-adphila.org. Web: www.sfsj.org. Francis E. Swiacki Jr., L.S.W., Admin. Provides residential treatment at 8 sites for boys, ages 12 to 20; also Supervised Living for boys 17 & older. Total Assisted 196; Capacity 102; Total Staff 100.

[L] RESIDENTIAL SCHOOLS FOR MENTALLY CHALLENGED CHILDREN AND ADULTS

SPRINGFIELD. *Cardinal Krol Center*, 1799 S. Sproul Rd., 19064. Tel: 484-475-2467; Fax: 610-543-5387. Web: developmentalprogramsphilly.org. Rev. Dennis M. Weber, Sd.C., Dir. of Mission Identity. A residential facility for 131 male adults with developmental/intellectual disabilities which provides an environment, both day and residential, that contributes to the individuals own growth and development by fulfilling their potential in the physical, mental, emotional, social, psychological, and spiritual areas of their lives. Priests 3; Residential Capacity 131; Day Program 45; Total Assisted Annually 200; Total Staff 300.

Divine Providence Village, 686 Old Marple Rd., 19064. Tel: 484-908-6501; Fax: 610-544-1710. Rosemary Bellenghi, M.S.W., Admin.; Rev. Paul Oggioni, Sd.C, Chap. Care & specialized training for developmentally disabled females. Capacity 96.

Don Guanella School, 1797 S. Sproul Rd., 19064-1195. Tel: 484-475-2467; Fax: 610-328-2136. Email: fr.dweber@chs-adphila.org. Web: developmentalprogramsphilly.org. Rev. Dennis M. Weber, Sd.C., Dir. of Mission Identity & Integration. Provides specialized care and residential treatment program for boys with developmental/intellectual disabilities ages 6-21. Capacity: Residents 25; Day Students 100.

[M] RESIDENTIAL HOMES FOR PHYSICALLY HANDICAPPED CHILDREN

ROSEMONT. *St. Edmond's Home for Children*, 320 S. Roberts Rd., 19010. Tel: 610-525-8800; Fax: 610-525-2693. Web: cssmrserv.org. Denise Clofine, M.Ed., Admin.; Rev. Dennis M. Weber, Sd.C., Chap. Licensed I.C.F./M.R. Home for children ages birth to 21 with severe/profound intellectual and physical disabilities. Capacity 40; Total Staff 160.

[N] PROTECTIVE INSTITUTIONS

PHILADELPHIA. *St. Gabriel's System*, Administrative Offices, 227 N. 18th St., 19103. Tel: 215-665-8777; Fax: 215-665-8821. Email: jlavoritano@chs-adphila.org. Web: www.saintgabrielssystem.org. Joseph Lavoritano, M.A., M.Ed., N.C.S.P., Exec. Dir. Administrative and Intake services for residential treatment; Day Treatment for Court-committed delinquent boys, ages 12-17. (See St. Gabriel's Hall, De LaSalle in Towne, De LaSalle Vocational and St. Gabriel's System Reintegration Services and Brother Rousseau Academy). Total Staff 426; Total Assisted 3,000.

AUDUBON. *St. Gabriel's Hall*, Box 7280, 19407-7280. Tel: 215-247-2776 (Philadelphia); 610-666-7970 (Audubon); Fax: 610-666-1479. Email: jlavoritano@chs_adphila.org. Joseph Lavoritano, M.A., M.Ed., N.C.S.P., Exec. Dir.; Bro. Brian Henderson, F.S.C., Dir. Offers residential treatment for court-committed delinquent boys, ages 10-18.

[O] DAY TREATMENT CENTERS

PHILADELPHIA. *De La Salle-In-Towne Day Treatment Center*, 25 S. Van Pelt St., 19103. Tel: 215-567-5500; Fax: 215-567-6922. Email: cgaus@chs-adphila.org. Charles E. Gaus, Dir. A community-based day treatment program for court-committed delinquent boys, ages 14-17. Capacity 110; Total Staff 35; Total Assisted 260.

BENSALEM. *De La Salle Vocational Day Treatment Center*, Box 344, 19020. Tel: 215-464-0344; Fax: 215-638-3767. Email: jlogan@chs-adphila.org. Mr. James Logan, M.S.S., Dir. A community based day treatment program for court-committed delinquent boys, ages 15-18. Capacity 125; Total Staff 37.

[P] SENIOR COMMUNITY CENTERS

PHILADELPHIA. *St. Anne's Senior Community Center*, 2607 E. Cumberland St., 19125. Tel: 215-423-2772; Fax: 215-423-2423. Barbara Jo Hartzell, Center Coord. Total Staff 6; Total Assisted 11,288.

St. Charles Senior Community Center, 1941 Christian St., 19146. Tel: 215-790-9530; Fax: 215-790-9765. Kathy Boles, Center Coord.

Norris Square Senior Community Center, 2121 N. Howard St., 19133. Tel: 215-423-7241; Fax: 215-634-7751. Bethzaida Butler Lopez, Center Coord. Total Assisted 120; Total Staff 10.

Star Harbor Senior Community Center, 4700 Springfield Ave., 19143. Tel: 215-724-4414; Fax: 215-726-7496. Ernestine Patterson, Center Coord.

[Q] OUTREACH CENTERS

PHILADELPHIA. *Casa del Carmen*, 4400 N. Reese St., 19140. Tel: 215-329-5660; Fax: 215-329-6722. Griselle Newman, M.A., Admin. Offers emergency crisis social services to the Spanish speaking community in Philadelphia and surrounding areas.

Drueding Center, 413 W. Master St., 19122. Tel: 215-769-1830; Fax: 215-787-0999. Email: acollins@holyredeemer.com. Web: www.druedingcenter.org. Anne Marie Collins, Exec. Dir. Sponsor: Sisters of the Holy Redeemer, C.S.R., Subsidiary of Holy Redeemer Health System; Provides transitional housing and support services for homeless women with children; daycare is provided for the children.

Marketing/Public Affairs Department, c/o 1602 Huntingdon Pike, Meadowbrook, 19046. Tel: 215-938-3226; Fax: 215-938-3232.

St. Francis Inn, 2441 Kensington Ave., 19125. Tel: 215-423-5845; Fax: 215-423-2289. Email: stfrancisinn@aol.com. Web: www.stfrancisinn.org. Rev. Michael A. Duffy, O.F.M., Contact Person. Hot meals for the poor. Priests 1; Brothers 3; Sisters 2; Lay Staff 9.

St. Benedict Thrift Store, 437 W. Girard Ave., 19122. Tel: 215-235-1848. A clothing and furniture thrift store operated by Franciscans.

Thea Bowman's Women's Center, 2858 Kensington Ave., 19134. Tel: 215-739-1137. Sr. Xavier Kozubal, C.S.F.N., Contact Person. Women's day activity center.

St. John's Hospice for Men, 1221 Race St., 19107. Tel: 215-563-7763; Fax: 215-563-0108. Web: www.saintjohnshospice.org. Kevin Barr, M.R.S., M.B.A., Prog. Dir. Staffed by Catholic Social Services Archdiocese of Philadelphia. Total Assisted 50,000; Total Staff 33.

The Good Shepherd Program of St. John's Hospice, 1225 Race St., 19107. Tel: 215-569-1101; Fax: 215-569-1622. Kevin Barr, M.R.S., M.B.A., Prog. Dir.

McAuley House, 1800 Morris St., 19145. Tel: 215-271-5166; Fax: 215-271-1601. Marcia Cedeno, Prog. Supvr.

Mercy Hospice, 334 S. 13th St., 19107. Tel: 215-545-5153; Fax: 215-545-1872. Yvonne Branch, Dir. Provides residential case management and referral services to homeless women, women in recovery who are single or are with their children. Mercy Hospice also provides lunch Monday thru Friday from 12:00 - 12:45 p.m. to homeless women and children. Showers, clothing and the use of a telephone are available on a limited basis. Total Staff 26.

Visitation Homes, 2638 Kensington Ave., 19125. Tel: 215-425-2080; Fax: 215-425-1412. Sara Frisby-Simms, Prog. Dir. Residential service program for families making the transition from homelessness to permanent housing. The program offers 18 furnished one to three bedroom apartments and on site case management and life skill services. Referrals come through the City's Office of Emergency Shelter and Services. For a period of up to 2 years, residents are helped to achieve economic self sufficiency and address the other issues which led to their homelessness.

Women of Hope Lombard, 1210 Lombard St., 19147. Tel: 215-732-1341; Fax: 215-732-0659. Susan Stier, Prog. Dir. Residential Facility for chronically mentally ill homeless women. Capacity 24.

Women of Hope-Vine, 251 N. Lawrence St., 19106. Tel: 215-592-9116; Fax: 215-592-0650. Sr. Maureen Crissy, R.S.M., Prog. Dir. Residential facility for chronically mentally ill homeless women. Capacity 22; Total Staff 23; Total Assisted 23.

CHESTER. *Bernardine Center*, 2625 W. Ninth St., 19013. Tel: 610-497-3225; Fax: 610-497-3659. Email: director@bernardinecenter.org. Web: www.bernardinecenter.org. Sr. Sandra Lyons, O.S.F., Dir. West Side Brunch, Emergency Food Cupboard, Supercupboard Program, Advocacy, Computer Lab, English as a Second Language (ESL), Computer Classes, Parenting Classes, Anger Management Classes. Sisters 3.

[R] DAY CARE CENTERS

PHILADELPHIA. *Casa del Carmen Day Care Center*, 4400 N. 5th St., 19140. Tel: 215-457-4325; Fax: 215-457-4339. Mailing Address: 4400 N. Reese St., 19140. Griselle Newman, M.A., Admin.

St. Monica Day Care Center, 1720 W. Ritner St., 19145. Tel: 215-334-6001; Fax: 215-467-4599. Email: DOCIHM@comcast.net. Web: stmonicaparish.net. Sr. Colleen Dougherty, I.H.M., Admin. Sister, Servants of the Immaculate Heart of Mary. Total Staff 12; Total Assisted 120.

[S] GENERAL HOSPITALS

PHILADELPHIA. *St. Agnes Continuing Care Center*, 1900 S. Broad St., 19145. Tel: 215-339-4220. Web: www.mercyhealth.org. H. Ray Welch, Pres. & CEO Mercy Health System; Sr. Kate O'Donnell, O.S.F., Vice Pres. Mission & Healthy Comm. Opened May 15, 1888.; Affiliate of Catholic Health East/Mercy Health System. Bed Capacity 58; Total Staff 414; Total Assisted Annually 931.

Mercy Philadelphia Hospital, 501 S. 54th St., 19143. Tel: 215-748-9300; Fax: 215-748-9709. Web: www.mercyhealth.org. H. Ray Welch, Pres. & CEO, Mercy Health System; Kathryn C. Conallen, CEO; Sr. Megan Brown, R.S.M., Vice Pres., Mission Svcs. Opened July 2, 1918. Incorporated May 1, 1969. Affiliate of Catholic Health East/Mercy Health System. Sisters of Mercy 11; Bed Capacity 214; Patients Assisted Annually 76,037; Total Staff 1,043.

Nazareth Hospital, 2601 Holme Ave., 19152. Tel: 215-335-6039; Fax: 215-335-6598. Web: www.mercyhealth.org. H. Ray Welch, Pres. & CEO, Mercy Health System; Christina Fitzpatrick, CEO; Mary Ann Carter, Vice Pres. Comm. Outreach Mission. Affiliate of Catholic Health East & Mercy Health System. Bed Capacity 233; Total Staff 1,362; Patients Assisted Annually 153,852.

DARBY. *Mercy Fitzgerald Hospital*, 1500 Lansdowne Ave., 19023-1291. Tel: 610-237-4030; Fax: 610-237-4202. Web: www.mercyhealth.org. H. Ray Welch, Pres. & CEO Mercy Health Systems; Brian Finestein, F.A.C.H.E., CEO; Sr. Angela Fellin, R.S.M., Chap.; Revs. Paul J. DeAntoniis, O.Praem, Chap.; Joseph C. Laenen, O.Praem., Chap.; Christal Rozario, Chap. Opened July 1, 1933. Incorporated May 1, 1969.; Affiliate of Catholic Health East & Mercy Health System.

HUNTINGDON VALLEY. *Holy Redeemer Health Care Corporation and Foundation*, 667 Welsh Rd., 19006. Tel: 215-938-4650; Fax: 215-938-4671. Web: www.holyredeemer.com. Parent Corporation of Holy Redeemer Health System; Sponsor: Sisters of the Holy Redeemer, C.S.R. Total Staff 3,487; Total Assisted 212,000.

Marketing & Public Affairs Department, c/o 1602 Huntingdon Pike, Meadowbrook, 19046. Tel: 215-938-3226; Fax: 215-938-3232.

HRH Management Corporation, 667 Welsh Rd., 19006. Tel: 215-938-4650; Fax: 215-938-4671. Web: www.holyredeemer.com. Affiliate of Holy Redeemer Health System. Sponsor: Sisters of the Holy Redeemer, C.S.R.

LANGHORNE. *St. Mary Medical Center*, Langhorne-Newton Rd., 19047. Tel: 215-710-2000; Fax: 215-710-2298. Email: trivera@stmaryhealthcare.org. Web: www.stmaryhealthcare.org. Gregory T. Wozniak, Pres. & CEO; Richard Brochu, Admin., Spiritual Care. Opened February 21, 1973.; Affiliate of Catholic Health East. Bed Capacity 366; Patients Assisted Annually 210,220; Total Staff 2,734.

Langhorne MRI, Inc., Langhorne-Newton Rd., 19047. Tel: 215-710-2000; Fax: 215-710-2298.

MEADOWBROOK. *Holy Redeemer Hospital and Medical Center*, 1648 Huntingdon Pike, 19046. Tel: 215-947-3000; Fax: 215-938-3945. Email: kreilly@holyredeemer.com. Web: www.holyredeemer.com. Patrice Morris, Vice Pres. Mission Integration. Sponsor: Sisters of the Holy Redeemer, C.S.R., Subsidiary of Holy Redeemer Health System, Inc.; Acute care community hospital, providing a broad spectrum of services, including preventive, rehabilitative, emergency and obstetrical care plus pastoral counseling. Bed Capacity 244; Total Assisted 14,700; Total Staff 1,630.

NORRISTOWN. *Mercy Suburban Hospital* (1944) 2701 DeKalb Pike, 19401. Tel: 610-278-2002; Fax: 610-272-4642. Web: www.mercyhealth.org. H. Ray Welch, Pres. & CEO Mercy Health Systems; Jeffrey Snyder, FACHE, FHFMA, CEO; Sr. Ann O'Connell, R.S.M., Vice Pres. Mission Svcs. Affiliate of Catholic Health East/Mercy Health System Bed Capacity 129; Total Assisted Annually 96; Total Staff 1,000.

[T] SPECIALIZED HOSPITALS

PHILADELPHIA. *Mount Nazareth*, 2755 Holme Ave., 19152. Tel: 215-338-8992; Fax: 215-338-8752. Sr. Regina Wieczezynski, Supr. Sisters of the Holy Family of Nazareth., Home for retired and infirm sisters. Resident Sisters 33; Total Assisted Annually 30; Total Staff 19.

ASTON. *Assisi House*, 600 Red Hill Rd., 19014. Tel: 610-459-8990; Fax: 610-558-5344. Email: JLAMANNA@osfPHILA.org. Web: www.osfphila.org. Sr. Jane La Manna, O.S.F., Admin.; Rev. Francis Sariego, O.F.M.Cap. Home for retired Sisters of St. Francis of Philadelphia. Capacity 120; Total Assisted Annually 142; Total Staff 192.

DARBY. *Villa Saint Joseph*, 1436 Lansdowne Ave., 19023-1298. Tel: 610-586-8535; Fax: 610-586-2810. Rev. Msgr. William A. Dombrow, M.Div., Rector; Helen McConnell, R.N., M.S., Admin. Home for aged, infirm and convalescent priests of the Archdiocese of Philadelphia. Sisters 1; Total Staff 60; Residents 62.

DOWNINGTOWN. *Guest House at Saint John Vianney Center*, 151 Woodbine Rd., 19335. Tel: 610-269-2600; Fax: 610-873-8028. Web: www.sjvcenter.org. Mr. Edward Maguire, Admin. An integrated dual diagnosis program, offering specialized treatment for co-occurring mental health and substance abuse disorders for religious and clergy.

St. John Vianney Center, 151 Woodbine Rd., 19335. Tel: 610-269-2600; Fax: 610-518-2020. Web: www.sjvcenter.org. Mr. Edward Maguire, Admin. Center for Behavioral Healthcare for Priests, Brothers, and Sisters. Bed Capacity 50; Total Assisted Annually 122; Total Staff 100.

IMMACULATA. *Camilla Hall Nursing Home*, King and Frazier Rds., P.O. Box 100, 19345-0100. Tel: 610-644-1152; Fax: 610-695-0691. Email: ch@camillahall.org. Sisters Anne Veronica Burrows, I.H.M., Admin.; Patricia McGuigan, I.H.M., Supr.; Rev. James P. McKelvey, M.Div., Chap. Sisters, Servants of the Immaculate Heart of Mary. Bed Capacity 220; Skilled Care 75; Residents 185; Total Staff 178.

MERION STATION. *McAuley Convent*, 517 Montgomery Ave., 19066. Tel: 610-667-2775; Fax: 610-667-9650. Sisters Mary Anne Basile, Supr. & Admin.; Mary Bonaventure, R.S.M., Dir. of Nursing. Infirmary for Religious Sisters of Mercy. Total Staff 50; Total Assisted 36.

WARMINSTER. *Regina Coeli Residence for Priests*, 685 York Rd., 18974. Tel: 215-441-4642. Rev. James F. Endres, Admin.; Helen McConnell, R.N., M.S., Admin. Home for retired priests of the Archdiocese of Philadelphia. Total Staff 5; Total in Residence 11.

[U] AFFILIATED SERVICES

PHILADELPHIA. **Holy Redeemer Home Care and Hospice* Holy Redeemer Support Services, 12265 Townsend Rd., Ste. 400, 19154. Tel: 215-671-9200; Fax: 215-671-1950. Web: www.holyredeemer.com. Toni Hague, R.N., Senior Vice Pres. Affiliate of Holy Redeemer Health System. Sponsor: Sisters of the Holy Redeemer; Medicare certified home health agency serving patients in their own homes; Medicare certified hospice program serving terminally ill patients and their families.

Marketing/Public Affairs Department, c/o 1602 Huntingdon Pike, Meadowbrook, 19046. Tel: 215-938-3226; Fax: 215-938-3232.

PHOENIXVILLE. *St. Mary's Franciscan Shelter*, 209 Emmett St., 19460. Tel: 610-933-3097; Fax: 610-917-9845. Email: stmarysfs@verizon.net. Web: stmarysfs.org. Total Staff 6; Families Assisted 30. Staff: Sr. Christine Kranichfeld, Exec. Dir.; Kate Garges.

[V] NURSING AND CONVALESCENT HOMES

PHILADELPHIA. *St. Ignatius Nursing Home*, 4401 Haverford Ave., 19104. Tel: 215-349-8800; Fax: 215-222-3078. Email: jmeacham@stignatiusnursinghome.org. Web: www.stignatiusnursinghome.org. John W.

Meacham, Admin. Attended from St. Ignatius Church. Felician Sisters 3; Bed Capacity 176; Total Assisted 423; Total Staff 225; Total in Residence 176.

Immaculate Mary Home Opened March 1976., 2990 Holme Ave., 19136-1829. Tel: 215-335-2100; Fax: 215-331-1016. Email: vgibbonne@chs-adphila.org. Web: www.immaculatemaryhome.org. Veronica Gibbone, N.H.A., Admin.; Sr. Patricia Bove, O.S.F., Pastoral Care Coord. Capacity 296; Total Assisted Annually 290; Total Staff 416.

St. John Neumann Nursing Home, 10400 Roosevelt Blvd., 19116. Tel: 215-698-5600; Fax: 215-698-5755. Web: www.stjohnneumannhome.org. Michelle Bieszczad, C.N.H.A., Admin.; Rev. Bernard C. Farley, Chap. Sisters of the Holy Family of Nazareth. Bed Capacity 226; Total Assisted 221; Total Staff 337.

St. Monica Manor, 2509 S. 4th St., 19148. Tel: 215-271-1080; Fax: 215-271-6290. Web: www.stmonicamanor.org. Jeffrey S. Cox, N.H.A., Admin. Bed Capacity 180; Total Assisted 175; Total Staff 227.

Sacred Heart Free Home for Incurable Cancer, 1315 W. Hunting Park Ave., 19140. Tel: 215-329-3222; Fax: 215-329-4197. Email: sistermarieedward@gmail.com. Web: www.sacredheartphila.org. Sisters Marie Edward, O.P., Supr.; Mary Barbara, O.P., Admin.

The Servants of Relief for Incurable Cancer Dominican Sisters of Hawthorne., Opened April 27, 1930.; Attended by Oblates of St. Francis de Sales. Bed Capacity 37; Total Assisted 94; Total Staff 32.

DARBY. *St. Francis Country House* Opened June 30, 1913., 1412 Lansdowne Ave., 19023-1218. Tel: 610-461-6510; Fax: 610-461-3558. Web: www.sfch-ph1.org. Rev. Edward J. Kennedy, Chap. Capacity 273; Total Assisted Annually 458; Total Staff 400.

DOWNINGTOWN. *St. Martha Manor*, 470 Manor Ave., 19335. Tel: 610-873-8490; Fax: 610-873-5927. Web: www.stmarthamanor.org. Maureen Reisinger, N.H.A., Sr. Admin.; Rev. Edward J. Jablonski, M.Div., Chap. Capacity 120; Total Assisted Annually 117; Total Staff 204.

FLOURTOWN. *Saint Joseph Villa*, 110 W. Wissahickon Ave., 19031-1898. Tel: 215-836-4179; Fax: 215-248-7889. Email: apprichd@stjosephvilla.org. Web: www.stjosephvilla.org. Sr. Dorothy Apprich, S.S.J., Admin. Bed Capacity 324; Licensed Beds 106; Convent Beds 216; Total Staff 400.

LANSDALE. *St. Mary Manor*, 701 Lansdale Ave., 19446. Tel: 215-368-0900; Fax: 215-362-2891. Web: www.stmarymanor.org. Maria GioVinco, Admin.; Rev. Msgr. Joseph L. Logrip, M.A., M.Div., Chap. Immaculate Heart of Mary Sisters. Total Assisted Annually 183; Total Staff 246.

[W] LONG TERM RESIDENCES FOR THE ELDERLY

PHILADELPHIA. *Holy Family Home*, 5300 Chester Ave., 19143-4993. Tel: 215-729-5153; Fax: 215-727-5332. Sr. Marie Edward, L.S.P., Pres.; Rev. Douglas M. McKay, Chap. Little Sisters of the Poor. Total Staff 100; Residents 97.

St. John Neumann Place, 2600 Moore St., 19145. Tel: 215-463-1101. Web: www.stjohnneumannplace.org. Lisa Marie Grillo, Social Svcs. Coord. Tel: 215-463-0410.

St. Joseph Housing Corporation, Mount St. Joseph Convent, 9701 Germantown Ave., 19118-2694. Tel: 215-248-7200; Fax: 215-248-7277. Email: msjc@ssjphila.net. Web: www.ssjphila.org.

Staffed by the Sisters of St. Joseph. Total Staff 4; Total in Residence 105.

DARBY. *Little Flower Manor* All Skilled Nursing Care., 1201 Springfield Rd., 19023. Tel: 610-534-6000; Fax: 610-534-6039. Staffed by Sisters of the Divine Redeemer. Total Staff 185; Patients Assisted Annually 239.

DOWNINGTOWN. *Catholic Health Care Services-Villa Saint Martha*, 490 Manor Ave., 19335. Tel: 610-873-5300; Fax: 610-873-2855. Email: admissions.vsm@chs-adphila.org. Web: www.vsm-phl.org. Earle Kimble, N.H.A., Senior Admin.; Rev. Edward J. Jablonski, M.Div., Chap. Independent Living, Assisted Living, Memory Support Assisted Living. Units 120; Total Staff 75; Total Assisted Annually 140.

ELVERSON. *St. Mary of Providence Center*, 227 Isabella Rd., 19520. Tel: 610-942-4166; Fax: 610-942-4259. Email: stmaryofprov@comcast.net. Web: stmaryofprov-pa.org. Sr. Noreen Franzina, D.S.M.P., Supr.; Rev. Andrew J. Latsko, Chap. Residence for Senior Citizens. Center of Spirituality, Retreats and Days of Recollection. Sisters 3; Capacity 39; Overnight and Day Retreats 110; Total Staff 19; Total in Residence 46.

FLOURTOWN. *Bethlehem Retirement Village*, 100 W. Wissahickon Ave., 19031. Tel: 215-233-0998; Fax: 215-233-9052. Email: joliverssj@yahoo.com. Sr. Judith Oliver, S.S.J., Mgr. Staffed by the Sisters of St. Joseph. Apartments 100; Total Staff 4; Total in Residence 102.

HUNTINGDON VALLEY. *Redeemer Village - Redeemer Village II*, 1551 Huntingdon Pike, 19006. Tel: 215-947-8168. Web: www.holyredeemer.com. *Marketing/Public Affairs Department*, Holy Redeemer Health System, c/o 1602 Huntingdon Pike, Meadowbrook, 19046. Joseph Munizza, Dir., Redeemer Village. Sisters of the Holy Redeemer, C.S.R., Subsidiary of Holy Redeemer Health System. Low income housing for the elderly or handicapped, subsidized by HUD. Apartments 151.

Redeemer Village II, 1551 Huntingdon Pike, 19006. Tel: 215-947-8168. Sisters of the Holy Redeemer, C.S.R., Subsidiary of Holy Redeemer Health System, Inc. Low income housing for the elderly or handicapped, subsidized by HUD. Apartments 49.

VENTNOR. *Villa St. Joseph by the Sea* Summer residence for aged, infirm, and convalescent priests of the Archdiocese of Philadelphia., 114 S. Princeton Ave., 08406. Tel: 609-823-9383. Email: hmcconnell@chs.adphila.org. Rev. Msgr. William A. Dombrow, M.Div., Rector; Helen McConnell, R.N., M.S., Admin.

YARDLEY. *D'Youville Manor*, 1750 Quarry Rd., 19067. Tel: 215-579-1750; Fax: 215-579-3054. Web: www.dyouvillemanor.org. Cecile F. Shocket, M.S.N., R.N., N.H.A., Admin. Operated by Grey Nuns of the Sacred Heart. Personal care residence for the elderly. Capacity 51; Total Staff 42; Total in Residence 41.

[X] RESIDENCES FOR WOMEN

PHILADELPHIA. *St. Mary's Residence*, 247 S. 5th St., 19106. Tel: 215-922-4228; Fax: 215-922-0192. Kathleen Nelson, Prog. Dir. Catholic Social Services. Residents 36; Total Staff 7.

[Y] MONASTERIES AND RESIDENCES OF PRIESTS AND BROTHERS

PHILADELPHIA. *Augustinian Community (O.S.A.)*, 910 Watkins St., 19148. Tel: 215-463-1326; Fax: 215-463-0888. Web: www.stnicksphila.com. Revs. James R. Keating, O.S.A., Prior; John Brynes, O.S.A.; Nicholas Martorano, O.S.A., Treas.; Howard McGraw, O.S.A.; Denis G. Wilde, O.S.A. Priests 5; Total Staff 6; Total Assisted 150.

The Brothers of the Christian Schools, Roncalli Community, 6519 N. 12th St., 19126. Tel: 215-424-4032. Bros. Thomas McPhillips, F.S.C., Dir.; Joseph Burke, F.S.C.; Gerard Molyneaux, F.S.C.

Brothers of the Christian Schools, St. Mary's Community, 7018 Boyer St., 19119-1801. Tel: 215-248-2434; Fax: 215-248-4327. Email: st.maryshall@verizon.net. Bro. Edward Davis, F.S.C., Dir. Total in Residence 3.

Congregation of the Mission, St. Vincent's Seminary, 500 E. Chelten Ave., 19144-1203. Tel: 215-713-2400; Fax: 215-844-2085. Email: cmphila88@aol.com. Web: www.cmeast.org. Central House of the Congregation of the Mission (Vincentian Community), Eastern Province. Novitiate, Central Shrine of the Miraculous Medal in the United States, The Central Association of the Miraculous Medal and St. Catherine's Infirmary, Assisted Living Facility, The Brother Bertrand Ducournau Archives of the Eastern Province of the Congregation of the Mission. Total in Residence 42.

Provincial Administration: Very Rev. Msgr. Michael J. Carroll, C.M., Prov.; Revs. Gregory P. Cozzubbo, C.M., Asst. Prov.; Elmer Bauer III, C.M., Prov. Treas.; Mr. Allen Andrews, Exec. Dir. Finance.

House Administration: Revs. Bernard M. Tracey, C.M., B.A., M.Div., Supr.; Joseph V. Agostino, C.M., Asst. Supr.; William J. O'Brien, C.M., Treas. In Res. Revs. Joseph V. Agostino, C.M.; William J. Bamber, C.M.; Robert J. Brandenberger, C.M.; John J. Buckley, C.M.; John W. Carven, C.M., Prov. Archivist; John J. Cusack, C.M.; Gerald E. Deitzer, C.M.; Daniel E. Donovan, C.M.; William P. Finn, C.M.; Frederick J. Gaulin, C.M.; William P. Goff, C.M.; William J. Gormley, C.M.; Walter F. Graham, C.M.; Aloysius P. Grass, C.M.; John J. Hodnett, C.M.; Stephen J. India, C.M.; Richard J. Kehoe, C.M.; John V. Kennedy, C.M.; Michael J. Kennedy, C.M.; Thomas R. Kennedy, C.M.; Thomas S. Krafinski, C.M.; Daniel J. Kramer, C.M.; Francis A. Lynch, C.M.; Francis X. Maguire, C.M.; Thomas P. Mallaghan, C.M.; Robert P. Maloney, C.M.; Walter J. Menig, C.M.; William J. O'Brien, C.M.; Alfred R. Pehrsson, C.M.; Michael J. Shea, C.M.; William W. Sheldon, C.M.; Harold G. Skidmore, C.M.; James E. Smith, C.M.; Robert J. Stone, C.M.; Robert Swain, C.M.; Bernard M. Tracey, C.M., B.A., M.Div.; Louis P. Trotta, C.M; Michael J. Tumulty, C.M.; Robert R. Vignola, C.M.; Bros. Stephen Kennedy, C.M.; Francis Mallaghan, C.M.; Augustine Towey, C.M.

Vincentian Fathers of the Eastern Province of the Congregation of the Mission serving on special assignments other than the Motherhouse:

Rome, Italy: Very Rev. G. Gregory Gay, C.M.

Bolivia: Rev. Aidan R. Rooney, C.M.

Illinois: Rev. Dennis H. Holtschneider, C.M.

Michigan: Revs. John T. Maher, C.M.; Vincent J. O'Malley, C.M.; Francis W. Sacks, C.M.

Father Louis Brisson Residence, 3301 Solly Ave., 19136-2340. Tel: 215-624-1604; Fax: 215-332-3478. Revs. Leon V. Bonikowski, O.S.F.S., Oblate Mission of Appeals; Joseph G. Campellone, O.S.F.S., Pres.; John V. DiFilippo, O.S.F.S. (Retired); Dominick F. Finn, O.S.F.S.; John Fisher, O.S.F.S.; Jack Kolodziej, O.S.F.S.; Robert G. Mulligan, O.S.F.S.; William Nessel, O.S.F.S. (Retired); Bro. James F. Williams, O.S.F.S., Rel. Supvr. Total Staff 5; Total in Residence 11.

Gesu School Jesuit Community and Outreach Center (S.J.), 1700 W. Thompson St., 19121. Tel: 215-763-3660; Fax: 215-763-9844. Email: neil@gesuschool.org. Rev. Neil L. Ver'Schneider, S.J., Contact Person. Total Assisted 300; Total Staff 1.

Jesuit Community, Arrupe House, 1226 N. 18th St., 19121. Tel: 215-765-1875; Fax: 215-978-1920. Email: bmaivelett@sjprep.org. Revs. George W. Bur, S.J., Pres. St. Joseph Prep.; Bruce A. Maivelett, S.J., Dir. Mission/Ministry St. Joseph's Prep; Neil L. Ver'Schneider, S.J., Admin. Gesu School; Jeffrey P. Putthoff, S.J., Dir. Hope Works; Bro. Robert J. Carson, S.J., Mission & Min., St. Joseph's Prep.; Rev. Richard S. McCouch, S.J., Asst. To The Provincial For Schools. Residence of Jesuit Fathers and Brothers.

Monastery of Our Lady of Mercy, 6398 Drexel Rd., 19151-2596. Tel: 215-879-0594; Fax: 215-877-7625. Email: vocations@orderofmercy.org. Web: www.orderofmercy.org. Rev. Matthew H. Phelan, O.de.M, Local Supvr.; Bro. Martin Jarocinski, O.de.M., Archivist/Vocational Asst. Order of the B.V.M. of Mercy (Mercedarian Friars)., Pre-Novitiate House of Studies for the Order. Total in Residence 4.

Order of Friars Minor of the Province of the Most Holy Name aka Holy Name Province The Franciscans, 1802 E. Hagert St., 19125. Tel: 215-423-2859; Fax: 215-423-3875. Revs. William DeBiase, O.F.M.; Michael A. Duffy, O.F.M.; Patrick Sieber, O.F.M.; Bros. Xavier de la Huerta, O.F.M.; Fred Dilger, O.F.M.; John Gill, O.F.M.

The Philadelphia Congregation of The Oratory of St. Philip Neri, 2321 Green St., 19130-3196. Tel: 215-765-4568; Fax: 215-765-4049. Very Rev. Georges G. Thiers, C.O., Provost; Revs. Paul C. Convery, C.O., Vicar; Philip G. Bochanski, C.O.; Brian R. Gaffney, C.O.

St. Pius X Residence, 10821 Knights Rd., 19154. Tel: 215-632-1300. Revs. Rene Barczak, O.F.M.; Carl Graczyk, O.F.M.; Francis Berna, O.F.M. Order of Friars Minor, Assumption B.V.M. Province.

The Brothers of the Christian Schools Jeremy House, 6633 Ardleigh St., 19119-3824. Tel: 215-843-1884; Fax: 215-843-1617. Bro. Richard Buccina, F.S.C., Dir. Professed Brothers 4; Postulants 4.

ARDMORE. *Bellesini Friary*, 111 Argyle Rd., 19003. Tel: 610-642-1420. Revs. Anthony P. Burrascano, O.S.A.; Joseph L. Farrell, O.S.A.; Kevin DePrinzio, O.S.A.

AUDUBON. *Christian Brothers (F.S.C.), St. Gabriel Hall Community*, 1350 Pawlings Rd., P.O. Box 7280, 19407-7280. Tel: 215-247-2776; 610-666-7970; Fax: 610-666-0743.

BENSALEM. *Congregation of the Holy Spirit*, Spiritan Hall, 2401 Bristol Pike, 19020. Tel: 215-638-0845; Fax: 215-639-5438. Email: jduaime@aol.com. Web: www.spiritans.org. Revs. Jeffrey T. Duaime, C.S.Sp., Supr.; Philip Agber, C.S.Sp.; Christopher H. McDermott, C.S.Sp., Bursar. Faculty Residence for Priests Teaching at Holy Ghost Preparatory School.

BRYN MAWR. *Augustinians Friars (O.S.A.)*, Our Mother of Good Counsel Community, 31 Pennswood Rd., 19010-3475. Tel: 610-525-0147; Fax: 610-525-0157. Email: frjmartinez@omgcparish.org. Revs. John T. Denny, O.S.A., Pastor and Contact Person; Dennis M. McGowan, O.S.A.; Francis A. Sirolli, O.S.A.

DEVON. *Piarist Fathers (Order of the Pious Schools)*, 363 Valley Forge Rd., 19333. Tel: 610-688-7337; Fax: 610-688-2409. Email: coeurdeleon@earthlink.net; richardwyzykiewicz@yahoo.com. Total Staff 2; Total in Residence 4.

Priests who teach at Devon Preparatory School: Revs. James J. Shea, Sch.P., Headmaster; Richard S. Wyzykiewicz, Sch.P., Rector; Jose' A. Basols, Sch.P.; Javier Renteria, Sch.P.

DOYLESTOWN. *Pauline Fathers Monastery, Shrine of Our Lady of Czestochowa*, 654 Ferry Rd., P.O. Box

2049, 18901. Tel: 215-345-0607; Fax: 215-348-2148. Email: info@czestochowa.us. Web: www.czestochowa.us. Office: Tel: 215-345-0600; 215-345-0601; Fax: 215-348-2148. Very Rev. Joseph M. Olczak, O.S.P.P.E., Prov.; Revs. Michael Czyzewski, O.S.P.P.E.; Jan Kolmaga, O.S.P.P.E.; Marek Lacki, O.S.P.P.E., Prov. Sec.; Tadeusz Lizinczyk, Prior; Jan Michalak, O.S.P.P.E., Subprior; Bartlomiej Marciniak, O.S.P.P.E.; Lucius Tyrasinski, O.S.P.P.E.; Rafal Walczyk, O.S.P.P.E., Shrine Dir.; Tomasz Wilk, O.S.P.P.E.; Stephen Z. Wozniczka, O.S.P.P.E.; Bros. Tomasz Fabiszewski, O.S.P.P.E.; Kazimierz Kania, O.S.P.P.E.; Bernard Kluczkowki, O.S.P.P.E.; Piotr Lisiecki, O.S.P.P.E.; Casimir Pasnik.

FAIRLESS HILLS. *St. Anthony Friary*, 607 Wistar Rd., 19030. Tel: 215-943-4810; Fax: 215-943-7410. Revs. Fidelis F. Weber, T.O.R., Guidance Dir. & Local Min.; Neil Saller, T.O.R.; Bro. Lawrence Hilferty, T.O.R. Franciscan Friars T.O.R., Faculty residence for priests and brothers who teach at Conwell-Egan Catholic High School. Total in Residence 3.

LAVEROCK. *Brothers of Charity (F.C.)*, Triest Hall, 7720 Doe Ln., 19038. Tel: 215-887-6361; Fax: 215-877-6372. Email: jfitzfc@aol.com. Web: www.brothersofcharity.org. Bro. John Fitzgerald, F.C., Regl. Supr. Total Staff 4; Total in Residence 10.

MALVERN. *Augustinian Friars (O.S.A.), Malvern Prep School, St. Augustine Friary at Albers Hall*, 418 S. Warren Ave., 19355-2707. Tel: 484-595-1193; Fax: 484-595-5765. Web: www.augustinians.org. Revs. Francis J. Caponi, O.S.A., Assoc. Prof., Villanova Univ.; Christopher J. Drennen, O.S.A.; Harry J. Erdlen, O.S.A., Prior & Campus Min.; James R. Flynn, O.S.A., Headmaster; Thomas J. Meehan, O.S.A. Total in Residence 5; Students 620.

MERION STATION. *Jesuit Community at St. Joseph's University*, 261 City Ave., 19066. Tel: 610-660-1400; Fax: 610-664-6640. Email: vgenoves@stu.edu. Web: www.sju.edu/jesuits. *Loyola Center and Manresa Hall* Revs. Mark C. Aita, S.J., M.D.; Bruce M. Bidinger, S.J.; Patrick P. Brannan, S.J.; John M. Braverman, S.J.; Thomas J. Brennan, S.J.; Francis F. Burch, S.J.; William J. Byron, S.J.; Peter A. Clark, S.J.; Jerome B. Coll, S.J.; James A. Devereux, S.J.; Paul A. Donovan, S.J.; James M. English, S.J.; Henry J. Erhart, S.J.; Joseph J. Feeney, S.J.; Joseph A. Fitzmyer, S.J.; Vincent J. Genovesi, S.J., Rector; Thomas F. Gleeson, S.J.; Edgar Graham, S.J.; Michael A. Hricko, S.J., Asst. for Jesuit Svcs.; Chap., Manresa Hall; Edward A. Jarvis, S.J.; Daniel R.J. Joyce, S.J.; John J. Kelly, S.J.; Brendan G. Lally, S.J.; Joseph L. Lombardi, S.J.; Thomas P. Martin, S.J.; Thomas D. Masterson, S.J.; John J. Mawhinney, S.J.; John W. McDaniel, S.J.; William J. McGrath, S.J.; Dennis E. McNally, S.J.; James W. Moore, S.J.; Vincent M. O'Brien, S.J.; Eugene J. Power, S.J.; Nicholas J. Rashford, S.J.; Anthony P. Roberts, S.J.; Francis E. Skechus, S.J.; Herbert F. Smith, S.J.; Martin R. Tripole, S.J.; John Woodward, S.J.; Bros. Lee S. Colombino, S.J.; Donald Dixon, S.J.; Robert A. Larouere, S.J.; John J. McLane, S.J.; Gerald E. Peltz, S.J.; William J. Sudzina, S.J.; Mr. Joseph A. Koczera, S.J. Priests 47; Brothers 6; Jesuits 1. *St. Alphonsus House*, 5800 Overbrook Ave., 19131. Tel: 215-477-9220; Fax: 215-477-1519. Revs. Anthony J. Berret, S.J.; Mario Farrugia, S.J.; Joseph J. Godfrey, S.J.; James D. Redington, S.J.; Patrick H. Samway, S.J. Priests 5.

Residing Elsewhere: Revs. Robert S. Curry, S.J., Chap., St. John Vianney Ctr., 151 Woodbine Rd., Downingtown, 19335; Thomas F.X. Wheeler, S.J., Infirmary Chap., McAuley Convent, 517 Montgomery Ave., 19066-1296. Tel: 610-660-7841; Fax: 610-667-9680.

PAOLI. *Daylesford Abbey*, 220 S. Valley Rd., 19301-1900. Tel: 610-647-2530; Fax: 610-651-0219. Email: norbertines@daylesford.org. Web: www.daylesford.org. Revs. Ronald J. Rossi, O.Praem., Abbot Emeritus; Richard J. Antonucci, O.Praem., Abbot; John Joseph Novielli, O.Praem., Dir. Devel. & Vocation; Very Rev. Steven J. Albero, O.Praem., Prior; Revs. Joseph A. Serano, O.Praem., Treas.; Carl Braschoss, O.Praem.; Andrew D. Ciferni, O.Praem.; Joseph P. McLaughlin, O.Praem.; Theodore J. Antry, O.Praem.; Maurice C. Avicolli, O.Praem.; Michael T. Collins, O.Praem.; Francis X. Cortese, O.Praem.; William R. Craig, O.Praem.; Bro. Francis Danielski, O.Praem.; Revs. Paul J. DeAntoniis, O.Praem; William J. Kelly, O.Praem.; Blaise R. Krautsack, O.Praem.; Joseph C. Laenen, O.Praem.; David T. Lawlor, O.Praem.; Michael J. Lee, O.Praem.; Thomas O. Meulemans, O.Praem.; James C. Rodia, O.Praem.; Domenic A. Rossi, O.Praem.; Thomas J. Rossi, O.Praem.; Nicholas R. Terico, O.Praem.; Charles T. Urban, O.Praem.; John C. Zagarella, O.Praem.; Bros. Blase G. Corso, O.Praem.; James Garrey, O.Praem.; John B. Ginder, O.Praem.; A. Gerard Jordan, O.Praem.; Joseph P. Mulholland, O.Praem.; Rev. Carl Braschoss, O.Praem.

Norbertine Fathers, Inc. Priests 27; Brothers 4.

ROSEMONT. *Saxony Hall*, 110 Montrose Ave., 19010-1509. Tel: 610-520-4510; Fax: 610-520-4510. Revs. Robert P. Hagan, O.S.A., Prior; Stephen J. Baker, O.S.A., Treas.; Martin S. Laird, O.S.A.; James J. McCartney, O.S.A.; Joseph Loya, O.S.A.; John J. McKenzie, O.S.A. Total in Residence 6.

SPRINGFIELD. *Servants of Charity (Sd.C.)* Don Guanella Village, Cardinal Krol Center, 1799 S. Sproul Rd., 19064. Tel: 484-475-2467; Fax: 610-543-5397. Email: fr.dweber@chs-adphila.org. Rev. Dennis M. Weber, Sd.C., Prov. Counselor/U.S. Rep. Total in Residence 5.

VILLANOVA. *St. Augustine Friary*, 214 Ashwood Rd., 19085. Tel: 610-527-0325. Revs. T. Shawn Tracy, O.S.A., Prior; Francis J. Barr, O.S.A.; Edward Dixey, O.S.A.; James E. Martinez, O.S.A.; James V. Vitali, O.S.A. Priests 5.

Fray de Leon Community, Burns Hall - West Campus, Villanova University, 800 E. Lancaster Ave., 19085. Tel: 610-519-5020. Revs. Joseph S. Mostardi, O.S.A., Prior; David A. Cregan, O.S.A.; Peter M. Donohue, O.S.A.; Bro. Michael Duffy, O.S.A. Augustinians. Total in Residence 4. P.O. Box 340, 19085. Tel: 610-527-3330, Ext. 279; Fax: 610-527-0618.

St. John Stone Friary, 37 Aldwyn Ln., 19085. Tel: 610-527-7925. Revs. John E. Deegan, O.S.A.; Arthur B. Chappell, O.S.A.; Kail C. Ellis, O.S.A., Prior; Michael J. Scanlon, O.S.A.

Provincial Offices of the Order of St. Augustine, Province of St. Thomas of Villanova, P.O. Box 340, 19085-0340. Tel: 610-527-3330; Fax: 610-520-0618. Email: secretary@augustinian.org. Web: www.augustinian.org. Very Rev. Anthony M. Genovese, O.S.A., Prior Prov. Tel: 610-527-3330, Ext. 225; Revs. Martin L. Smith, O.S.A., Prov. Treas. Tel: 610-527-3330, Ext. 226; John J. Sheridan, O.S.A., Prov. Archivist. Tel: 610-527-3330, Ext. 247; Michael H. Bielecki, O.S.A., Prov. Sec. Tel: 610-527-3330, Ext. 223; Anthony P. Burrascano, O.S.A., Mission Office. Tel: 610-527-3330, Ext. 238; Kevin DePrinzio, O.S.A., Dir. Vocations. Tel: 610-527-3330, Ext. 284; Joseph S. Mostardi, O.S.A., Dir. Office of the Augustinian Volunteers. Tel: 610-527-3330, Ext. 279.

St. Thomas Monastery, 800 E. Lancaster Ave., 19085. Tel: 610-519-7500; Fax: 610-519-5040. Revs. John P. Betoni, O.S.A.; Michael H. Bielecki, O.S.A.; John E. Bresnahan, O.S.A.; Robert M. Burke, O.S.A.; Donald X. Burt, O.S.A.; Angus N. Carney, O.S.A.; Thomas J. Casey, O.S.A.; Francis E. Chambers; William M. Cleary, O.S.A.; Edmund J. Dobbin, O.S.A.; Edward C. Doherty, O.S.A.; Edward E. Doran, O.S.A.; Joseph A. Duffey (Retired); Thomas P. Dwyer, O.S.A.; John J. Farrell, O.S.A. (Retired); Francis A. Farsaci, O.S.A.; John J. Ferrence, O.S.A.; John J. Fitzgerald, O.S.A.; Dennis J. Gallagher, O.S.A.; James L. Galligan, O.S.A.; Very Rev. Anthony M. Genovese, O.S.A., Prior Prov.; Revs. Karl A. Gersbach, O.S.A.; Joseph J. Getz, O.S.A.; Adrian Gilligan, O.S.A.; James G. Glennon, O.S.A.; Edward V. Griffin, O.S.A.; John J. Hagen, O.S.A., Subprior; Roger M. Hanouille, O.S.A.; Joseph A. Jordan, O.S.A.; Cherubin F. Kerr, O.S.A.; Charles P. Laferty, O.S.A.; Martin Laird, O.S.A.; John F. Lipp, O.S.A.; George P. Magee, O.S.A.; Lee J. Makowski, O.S.A.; Gordon E. Marcellus, O.S.A.; Gary N. McCloskey, O.S.A., Prior; Neil J. McGettigan, O.S.A. (Retired); William A. McGuire, O.S.A.; Daniel J. Menihane; Ralph J. Monteiro, O.S.A.; Thomas M. Murnane, O.S.A.; Robert J. Murray, O.S.A.; James L. Nolan, O.S.A.; Joseph X. O'Connor, O.S.A.; Bernard J. O'Dowd, O.S.A.; J. Thomas Pohto, O.S.A., Treas.; Walter J. Quinn, O.S.A.; Jorge A. Reyes, O.S.A.; George F. Riley, O.S.A.; Joseph G. Ryan, O.S.A.; Augustus C. Sandmann, O.S.A.; Joseph C. Schnaubelt, O.S.A.; John J. Sheridan, O.S.A.; Martin L. Smith, O.S.A.; Joseph A. Spinelli, O.S.A.; John P. Stack, O.S.A.; Robert E. Steinman, O.S.A.; Michael P. Sullivan, O.S.A. Total Staff 64; Total in Residence 59.

St. Thomas of Villanova Friary, 109 Willowburn Rd., 19085-1313. Tel: 610-527-0856; Fax: 610-527-8812. Revs. Richard G. Cannuli, O.S.A.; Joseph D. Calderone, O.S.A., Prior; Paul W. Galetto, O.S.A.; Bro. Robert Thornton, O.S.A., Treas.

WYNDMOOR. *Christian Brothers (F.S.C.)*, LaSalle High School Community, 8605 Cheltenham Ave., 19038. Tel: 215-233-3030; Fax: 215-233-0297. Email: rieck@lschs.org. Web: www.lschs.org. Bro. James F. Rieck, F.S.C., Contact Person. Total in Residence 14.

Villa de Sales Oblate Residence, 8501 Flourtown Ave., 19038. Tel: 215-836-1472; Fax: 215-836-1472. Revs. Joseph F. Chorpenning, O.S.F.S., S.T.L., Ph.D.; Charles F. Engelhardt, O.S.F.S.; Thomas P. Gallagher, O.S.F.S.; William A. Guerin, O.S.F.S.; Charles J. Norman, O.S.F.S., M.A., Ph.D.; Very Rev. Richard T. Reece, O.S.F.S., M.S., Ph.D.; Revs. Robert G. Reece, O.S.F.S., M.S., Ph.D.; Albert J. Smith, O.S.F.S., M.S. Total in Residence 9.

[Z] CONVENTS AND RESIDENCES OF SISTERS

PHILADELPHIA. *Assumption Hall*, Sisters of St. Joseph, 8900 Norwood Ave., 19118-2711. Tel: 215-247-3665; 215-248-2564. Sr. Marjorie Lawless, S.S.J., Contact. Residence for Norwood-Fontbonne Academy Faculty. Total Staff 15.

Assumption House, 1001 S. 47th St., 19143. Tel: 215-386-5016; Fax: 215-386-1780. Email: rabowman227@juno.com. Sr. Clare Teresa, R.A.

Blessed Trinity Mother Missionary Cenacle, 3501 Solly Ave., 19136. Tel: 215-335-7550; Fax: 215-335-7559. Email: msbtphl@msbt.org. Web: msbt.org. Sisters Joan Marie Keller, M.S.B.T., Gen. Custodian; Ellen Kieran, M.S.B.T., Gen. Sec. Generalate, Novitiate and Candidacy of the Missionary Servants of the Most Blessed Trinity. Mother Boniface Center. Total Staff 22; Total in Residence 63.

Carmelite Monastery, 66th Ave. and Old York Rd., 19126. Tel: 215-424-6143; Fax: 215-424-6143. Sr. Barbara of the Holy Ghost, O.C.D., Prioress.

Congregation of the Sisters of St. Felix, St. Ignatius Convent, 4401 Haverford Ave., 19104. Tel: 215-222-2296; Fax: 215-222-3078. Sr. Mary Agatha Cebula, C.S.S.F., N.H.A., Local Min.

Daughters of Charity, 449 E. Locust Ave., 19144-1323. Tel: 215-438-3536; Fax: 215-438-5232. Email: philadtrs@aol.com. Web: dc-northeast.org. Sr. Patricia Evanick, D.C., Supr. Total in Residence 5.

Daughters of St. Paul Convent, 9610 Evans St., 19115. Tel: 215-969-5068. Email: philadelphia@paulinemedia.com. Web: www.pauline.org. Sr. Patricia Maresca, F.S.P., Supr. Sisters 4.

Emmaus Convent, 5358 Cedar Ave., 19143. Tel: 215-471-7260. Email: rsmemmaus@aol.com. Sisters of Mercy (R.S.M.). Total in Residence 3.

St. Francis Convent, 1727 S. 11th St., 19148. Tel: 215-463-7343. Email: gpfrancia@verizon.net. Residence of Sisters of St. Francis of Philadelphia employed at John W. Hallahan High School, St. Nicholas Elementary School, St. Thomas Aquinas Elementary School, Children's Aid Society, University of Pennsylvania, Assisi House (Retirement), and Neuman University.

Franciscan Sisters of Allegany (O.S.F.), 2622 Potter St., 19125. Tel: 215-739-6441.

Handmaids of the Sacred Heart of Jesus, 1242 S. Broad St., 19146-3119. Tel: 215-468-6368; Fax: 215-271-1488. Email: cbanh1@juno.com. Web: acjusa.org. Sr. Cam Banh, A.C.J., Supr. Total in Residence 4.

Hannah House, Sisters of St. Joseph, 2458 N. 16th St., 19132. Tel: 215-221-0211; Fax: 215-228-7070. Email: ginjenkins@verizon.net. Sr. Virginia Jenkins, S.S.J., Contact Person. Sisters 2.

Immaculate Heart Convent, 7310 Torresdale Ave., 19136. Tel: 215-332-8299; Fax: 215-332-6077. Email: ihc@comcast.net. Sr. Mary Theresa Flynn, I.H.M., Supr. Faculty Residence for Sisters, Servants of the Immaculate Heart of Mary, teaching at St. Hubert High School. Total in Residence 11.

Immaculate Heart Convent, 4904 Chestnut St., 19139. Tel: 215-474-8971. Sr. Mary K. Lydon, I.H.M., Supr. Faculty Residence for Sisters, Servants of the Immaculate Heart of Mary, who teach at West Philadelphia Catholic High School. Total Staff 3; Total in Residence 6.

St. Joseph Convent, 7300 Torresdale Ave., 19136. Tel: 215-338-4884. Email: ssjtorr@netcarrier.com. Faculty Residence for Sisters of St. Joseph, who teach at St. Martin of Tours, St. Hubert High School and St. Vincent's Homes.

Little Sisters of the Poor, Holy Family Home, 5300 Chester Ave., 19143. Tel: 215-729-5153; Fax: 215-729-5158.

Little Workers of the Sacred Hearts, Sacred Hearts Convent, 160 Carpenter Ln., 19119-2563. Tel: 215-843-2266.

Mary Immaculate Convent, 1731 S. 11th St., 19148. Tel: 215-468-9133; Fax: 215-336-7463. Email: maryim1731@yahoo.com. Sr. Dorothy Mayer, I.H.M., Supr. Faculty Residence for Sisters, Servants of the Immaculate Heart of Mary, who teach at SS. John Neuman and Maria Goretti Catholic High School and John W. Hallahan High School. Total in Residence 15; Total Staff 15.

Medical Mission Sisters, North American Sector, 8400 Pine Rd., 19111. Tel: 215-742-6100; Fax: 215-342-3948. Email: mmsorg@

medicalmissionsisters.org. Web: www.medicalmissionsisters.org. Sisters Suzanne Maschek, M.M.S., SNA Coord.; Maria Hornung, M.M.S., SNA Coord.; Rose Kershbaumer, M.M.S., SNA Coord. Sisters in Sector 120; Total in Residence 83.

St. Michael Hall, 9001 Germantown Ave., 19118. Tel: 215-247-3698. Email: SSJsmhall@aol.com. Faculty Residence for Sisters of St. Joseph who staff Chestnut Hill College. Total in Residence 11.

Monastery of the Visitation Nuns, 5820 City Ave., 19131-1295. Tel: 215-473-5888; Fax: 215-473-7512. Email: viznunphil@aol.com. Sr. Antoinette Marie Walker, V.H.M., Supr. Jesuit priests from St. Joseph's University, Chaplains. Total Staff 6; Total in Residence 6.

Mother of Peace House, 2622 Potter St., 19125. Tel: 215-739-6441. Franciscan Sisters of Allegany.

Mt. St. Joseph Convent, 9701 Germantown Ave., 19118-2694. Tel: 215-248-7200; Fax: 215-248-7277. Email: msjc@ssjphila.org. Web: ssjphila.org. Sr. Anne Patricia Myers, S.S.J., Congregational Pres. Motherhouse of the Sisters of St. Joseph of Chestnut Hill, Philadelphia.

Nazareth Convent, Religious Sisters of Mercy, 6369 Woodbine Ave., 19151. Tel: 215-477-3022. Sr. Kathleen Lyons, R.S.M., Contact Person & Treas.

Peace Hermitage, 8400 Pine Rd., 19111. Tel: 215-342-2039; 215-742-6100, Ext. 149; Fax: 215-342-3948. Society of Catholic Medical Missionaries (Medical Mission Sisters). Total in Residence 2.

School Sisters of Notre Dame, Visitation Community, 3978 Constance Rd., 19114. Tel: 215-824-0754. Email: sisterbernie@yahoo.com. Web: www.ssnd.org. Sr. Bernadette Marie Ravenstahl, S.S.N.D., Contact.

Sister Servants of the Holy Spirit of Perpetual Adoration (S.Sp.S.A.P.), Convent of Divine Love, 2212 Green St., 19130. Tel: 215-567-0123; Fax: 215-569-8314. Email: conventofdivinelove@verizon.net. Web: www.adorationsisters.org. Sr. Mary Caritas, S.Sp.S.A.P., Supr.; Rev. Philip G. Bochanski, C.O., Chap.

Sisters of St. Francis of Philadelphia, Santa Chiara, 2238 S. 12th St., 19148. Tel: 215-465-2227. Email: RRBARBAOSF@aol.com. Sisters Residence for those who work at Assisi House, Aston, and Epiphany Church.

Sisters of St. Francis of Philadelphia, Canticle House, 1624 Mifflin St., 19145. Tel: 215-551-2586. Web: www.osfphila.org.

Sisters of St. Joseph, Neumann House, 58 E. Northwestern Ave., 19118. Tel: 215-248-7200; Fax: 215-248-7277. Email: msjc@ssjphila.org. Web: ssjphila.org. Total in Residence 4.

Sisters of St. Joseph of Philadelphia, Immaculate Heart of Mary Convent, 823 Cathedral Rd., 19128. Tel: 215-482-8540. Sisters in Residence 5.

Sisters of St. Joseph of Philadelphia Convent, 6818 Cresheim Rd., 19119. Tel: 215-438-7515. Total in Residence 8.

Sisters of St. Joseph of Philadelphia Elizabeth House, 138 W. Carpenter Ln., 19119-2563. Tel: 215-849-3362. Sr. Mary Elizabeth Hamm, S.S.J., Contact Person.

Sisters of St. Joseph of Philadelphia, Fournier Community, Administration, 9701 Germantown Ave., 19118-2694. Tel: 215-248-7200; Fax: 215-248-7277. Email: msjc@ssjphila.org. Web: ssjphila.org. Sr. Mary Theresa Shevland, Contact Person. Sisters 3.

Sisters of the Good Shepherd, 5356 Chew Ave., 19138. Tel: 215-843-9411; Fax: 215-843-3141. Email: srnora@coraservices.org. Neighborhood ministry, mediation program.

Sisters of the Holy Child, 2362 E. York St., 19125-3029. Tel: 215-423-9514.

Sisters of the Holy Family of Nazareth, 2755 Home Ave., 19152. Tel: 215-543-0016; Fax: 215-338-8752. Email: skiepura@nazarethcsfn.org. Web: nazarethcsfn.org. Sr. Sally Marie Kiepura, C.S.F.N., Prov. Supr.

Sisters of the Holy Family of Nazareth, 9801 Frankford Ave., 19114. Tel: 267-341-3735; Fax: 267-341-3702.

Sisters of the Holy Family of Nazareth, Jesus of Nazareth Convent (aka Mount Nazareth), 2755 Holme Ave., 19152. Tel: 215-338-8992; Fax: 215-338-8752. Sr. Regina Wieczezynski, Supr. Staff 22; Total in Residence 38.

Sisters of the Holy Family of Nazareth, Infant Jesus Convent, 2723 Holme Ave., 19152-2015. Tel: 215-335-6380; Fax: 215-335-3764. Email: nazcon@aol.com. Web: www.csfn.org. Total in Residence 22.

Sisters of the Holy Redeemer, Angelus Community, 705 Medary Ave., 19126. Tel: 215-276-2187; Fax: 215-914-4111. Email: kkaufmann@holyredeemer.com. Web: www.sistersholyredeemer.org. Total in Residence 2.

ARDMORE. *Missionary Sisters of the Holy Rosary (M.S.H.R.)*, 205 Cricket Ave., 19003. Tel: 610-896-1786. Web: holyrosarymissionarysisters.org. Total in Residence 3.

ASTON. *Anna Bachmann House*, 606 S. Convent Rd., 19014. Tel: 610-558-3240. Web: www.osfphila.org. Sr. Eileen Walsh, O.S.F., Contact Person.

Convent of Our Lady of Angels, 609 S. Convent Rd., 19014. Tel: 610-459-4125; Fax: 610-459-0195. Email: smonteleone@osfphila.org. Web: www.osfphila.org. Sr. Esther Anderson, Congregational Min. Motherhouse of the Sisters of St. Francis of Philadelphia.

Mt. Alvernia Convent, 602A S. Convent Rd., 19014. Tel: 610-459-5989. Sr. Kathleen M. Winkelman, O.S.F., Contact Person. Sisters of St. Francis of Philadelphia. Total in Residence 3.

Sisters of St. Francis, 607 S. Convent Rd., 19014. Tel: 610-358-5417. Email: cwright@osfphila.org. Web: www.osfphila.org. Sr. Donna Desien, O.S.F., Congregational Sec.

Sisters of St. Francis of Philadelphia, 6 Red Hill Rd., 19014. Tel: 610-459-1113.

Sisters of St. Francis of Philadelphia, Our Lady of the Valley Convent, 10 Red Hill Rd., 19014-1119. Tel: 610-358-4008. Web: www.osfphila.org. Sr. Ann David Strohminger, O.S.F., Contact. Total in Residence 4.

Sisters of St. Francis of Philadelphia, Visitation Convent 609 S. Convent Rd., 19014. Tel: 610-558-7731. Web: www.osfphila.org. Sr. Donna Desien, O.S.F., Congregational Sec. Total in Residence 4.

Sisters of St. Francis of Philadelphia, Assisi House, 600 Red Hill Rd., 19014. Tel: 610-459-8990; Fax: 610-558-5344. Email: jlamanna@osfphila.org. Web: www.osfphila.org. Total in Residence 95; Total Staff 192.

Sisters of St. Francis of Philadelphia, Portiuncula Convent, 610 Red Hill Rd., 19014. Tel: 610-558-5350; Fax: 610-558-5344. Email: portiuncula@hotmail.com. Sisters 10.

Sisters of St. Francis of Philadelphia (Assumption Convent), Assumption Convent, 609 S. Convent Rd., 19014. Tel: 610-558-7672. Web: www.osfphila.org. Sr. Donna Desien, O.S.F., Congregational Sec. Total in Residence 4.

Sisters of St. Francis of Philadelphia, TAU Convent, 4000 Concord Rd., 19014. Tel: 610-494-7322. Sr. Helen Budzik, O.S.F., Contact. Total in Residence 4.

AVONDALE. *Blessed Marie Catherine Formation Program*, 100 S. Williamson Rd., 19311. Tel: 610-268-1373. Sr. M. Ephesus, Supr.

BENSALEM. *St. Michael Hall*, 1663 Bristol Pike, 19020. Tel: 215-244-9900; 215-638-0865; Fax: 215-244-6222. Email: stmichhall@aol.com.

Sisters of the Blessed Sacrament The Infirmary of the Sisters of the Blessed Sacrament.

Sisters of the Blessed Sacrament, 1663 Bristol Pike, 19020-5702. Tel: 215-244-9900; Fax: 215-244-8174. Web: www.katharinedrexel.org. Sr. Patricia Suchalski, S.B.S., Pres.

Sisters of the Blessed Sacrament for Indians and Colored People, Motherhouse of the Sisters of the Blessed Sacrament for Indians and Colored People. Total in Residence 78; Total Staff 86.

BROOKHAVEN. *Sisters of St. Francis of Philadelphia, Claddagh House*, 160 Meadowbrook Ln., 19015. Tel: 610-490-5367; Fax: 610-490-5367. Email: mirmurray@comcast.net. Web: www.osfphila.org. Total in Residence 3.

BRYN MAWR. *Missionary Sisters of the Holy Rosary*, 741 Polo Rd., 19010. Tel: 610-520-1974; Fax: 610-520-2002. Email: helenamcneill@comcast.net. Web: www.holyrosarymissionarysisters.com. Total in Residence 3.

Society of the Holy Child Jesus, 700 Old Lancaster Rd., 19010. Tel: 610-527-5076; Fax: 610-527-4671. Email: apenrose@juno.com. Retirement Residence for Sisters of the Holy Child Jesus. Total in Residence 5.

CHELTENHAM. *Sisters of the Good Shepherd (Contemplative)*, 7633 Waters Rd., 19012. Tel: 215-782-8627; Fax: 215-782-8741. Sr. Martha Cardenas, Supr. Total in Residence 7.

CHESTER. *Bernardine Sisters of St. Francis*, Sacred Heart Convent, 2601 W. Tenth St., 19013-2004. Tel: 610-497-9788; 610-497-2368; Fax: 610-497-3659. Email: conlab2@verizon.net. Total in Residence 8.

Missionaries of Charity, Gift of Mary, 2714 W. 9th St., 19013. Tel: 610-494-7424. Sr. Maria Burkhita, M.C., Supr. Total Assisted 300; Total Staff 5.

DREXEL HILL. *St. Joseph Convent*, 435 N. Lansdowne Ave., 19026-1190. Tel: 610-622-0440; Fax: 610-259-5606. Email: sosjdrexelhill@yahoo.com. Faculty residence for Sisters of St. Joseph who teach at Msgr. Bonner and Archbishop Prendergast Catholic High School and West Philadelphia Catholic High School.

ERDENHEIM. *Sisters of St. Joseph of Philadelphia*, Divine Shepherd Convent, 927 Bethlehem Pike, 19038. Tel: 215-836-2082. Total in Residence 6.

Sisters of St. Joseph of Philadelphia, Nazareth House, 931 Bethlehem Pike, 19038. Tel: 215-836-2613. Total in Residence 5.

ELVERSON. *Daughters of St. Mary of Providence (D.S.M.P.)*, 227 Isabella Rd., 19520. Tel: 610-942-4166; Fax: 610-942-4259. Email: stmaryofprov@comcast.net. Web: stmaryofprov-pa.org. Sr. Noreen Franzina, D.S.M.P., Supr. Total in Residence 3; Total Staff 19.

ESSINGTON. *Bernardine Sisters of St. Francis*, St. Margaret Mary Convent, 546 Wanamaker Ave., 19029. Tel: 610-521-3286; Fax: 610-521-3280.

FALLSINGTON. *Grey Nuns of the Sacred Heart, St. Joseph the Worker Convent*, 9168 New Falls Rd., 19054-1805. Tel: 215-269-9783. Total in Residence 5.

FLOURTOWN. *St. Rita Convent*, 1410 Bethlehem Pike, 19031. Tel: 215-836-1615. Email: sima1pa@verizon.net. Sisters Marianne Beatty, R.S.M., Admin.; Maureen B. McCann, R.S.M., Coord. Sisters of Mercy of the Americas. Total in Residence 2.

Sisters of St. Joseph of Philadelphia, Mt. St. Joseph Academy, 120 W. Wissahickon Ave., 19031-1899. Tel: 215-233-4368; Fax: 215-233-4734. Email: ssjmountcon@verizon.net. Total in Residence 14.

Sisters of St. Joseph of Philadelphia, St. Joseph Villa Staff Visitation Community, 110 W. Wissahickon Ave., 19031-1898. Tel: 215-836-4179; Fax: 215-248-7802. Email: visitationcommunity@msn.com. Total 11.

FOX CHASE MANOR. *Sisters of St. Basil the Great (O.S.B.M.)* Motherhouse of the Sisters of St. Basil., 710 Fox Chase Rd., 19046-4198. Tel: 215-663-9153; Fax: 215-379-4843. Email: province@stbasils.com. Web: www.stbasils.com. Sr. Dorothy Ann Busowski, O.S.B.M., Prov. Supr.

Basilian Spirituality Center, 710 Fox Chase Rd., Jenkintown, 19046-4198. Tel: 215-780-1227; Fax: 215-379-4843.

GLENSIDE. *Medical Mission Sisters* (Society of Catholic Medical Missionaries, Inc.), 2230 Mt. Carmel Ave., 19038. Tel: 215-886-4036. Email: eunice@medicalmissionsisters.org. Web: medicalmissionsisters.org. Total in Residence 3.

GWYNEDD VALLEY. *Religious Sisters of Mercy - St. Joseph Convent*, 1349 Sumneytown Pike, P.O. Box 902, 19437-0902. Tel: 215-646-5259.

Religious Sisters of Mercy - Transfiguration Convent, 1325 Sumneytown Pike, P.O. Box 901, 19437-0901. Tel: 215-641-5512; Fax: 215-641-5509. Email: mcmahon.c@gmc.edu. Web: www.gmc.edu.

HAVERFORD. *Handmaids of the Sacred Heart of Jesus*, 616 Coopertown Rd., 19041. Tel: 610-642-5715; Fax: 610-642-6788. Sr. Dorothy Beck, A.C.J., Local Coord.

Handmaids of the Sacred Heart of Jesus Provincialate, 616 Coopertown Rd., 19041. Tel: 610-642-5715; Fax: 610-642-6788. Email: dbeck@ancillae.org. Web: www.ancillae.org. Sr. Dorothy Beck, A.C.J., Prov. Supr. and Local Supr. Total in Residence 10.

HUNTINGDON VALLEY. *Sisters of the Holy Redeemer Provincialate*, 521 Moredon Rd., 19006. Tel: 215-914-4100; Fax: 215-914-4111; 215-914-4171. Email: amhaas@holyredeemer.com. Web: www.sistersholyredeemer.org. Sisters Anne Marie Haas, C.S.R., Prov. Supr.; Ellen M. Marvel, C.S.R., Formation Dir.; Revs. Timothy M. Judge, M.Div., Chap.; Aloysius Ochasi (Nigeria), Chap.; Dennis J.W. O'Donnell, Ph.D., Dir. Integrated Health Svcs.; Mark G. Swope, M.B.E., M.Div., Chap. Holy Redeemer Health System. Total in Residence 13.

St. Teresa of Avila Convent, 619 Moredon Rd., 19006. Tel: 215-947-0135; Fax: 215-914-4111. Email: sranita@holyredeemer.com. Web: www.sistersholyredeemer.org. Total in Residence 2.

IMMACULATA. *Sisters, Servants of the Immaculate Heart of Mary (I.H.M.)*, Pacis Hall, P.O. Box 700, 19345-0700. Tel: 610-889-1668; Fax: 610-695-0691 (Camilla Hall). Email: pacishall03@netzero.net. Sr. Joan Carroll, I.H.M., Supr. Total in Residence 35.

Sisters, Servants of the Immaculate Heart of Mary (I.H.M.), 1145 King Rd., P.O. Box 400, 19345-0400. Tel: 610-647-4400, Ext. 3660; Fax: 610-640-5890. Email: gillet@immaculata.edu. Web: www.ihmimmaculata.org. Total in Residence 44.

Sisters, Servants of the Immaculate Heart of Mary, (I.H.M.), King & Frazer Rds., P.O. Box 100, 19345. Tel: 610-644-1152; Fax: 610-695-0691. Email: ch@camillahall.org.

Villa Maria House of Studies, 1140 King Rd., 19345-0200. Tel: 610-647-2160; Fax: 610-889-4874. Email: s.rita.lenihan@ihmimmaculata.org.

Villa Maria House of Studies, Motherhouse of the Sisters, Servants of the Immaculate Heart of Mary, Ministry in the field of Academic Education at all levels, Congregation Retirement and Health Care Center, Pastoral Ministry, Diocesan and Parish Administration, Literary Center, Spirituality Center, Directors of Religious Education, Guidance/Counseling, Ministry to Hispanics. Total in Congregation 864.

JENKINTOWN. *Sisters of the Holy Redeemer*, St. Elizabeth Convent, 615 Fox Chase Rd., 19046. Tel: 215-379-0112; Fax: 215-914-4111. Email: srcmsuya@hotmail.com. Web: www.sistersholyredeemer.org. Total in Residence 3.

LANGHORNE. *Monastery of St. Clare, Poor Clares*, 1271 Langhorne-Newtown Rd., 19047-1297. Tel: 215-968-5775; Fax: 215-968-6254. Email: stclare@poorclarepa.org. Web: www.poorclarepa.org. Cloistered Contemplative Nuns., Prayer and Altar Bread Ministry.

San Damiano Convent, 104 Alberts Way, 19047. Tel: 215-860-7185.

Sisters of St. Francis of Philadelphia Total in Residence 3.

Sisters of St. Francis of Philadelphia, St. Mary Medical Center Convent, 1207 Langhorne-Newton Rd., 19047-1233. Tel: 215-757-9494. Total in Residence 8.

Sisters of St. Francis of Philadelphia, Franciscan Residence, 113 Alberts Way, 19047. Tel: 215-860-1059. Sisters serving at St. Mary Medical Center.

LANSDALE. *Religious of the Assumption, Assumption Convent*, 506 Crestview Rd., 19446. Tel: 215-368-4427 (Main House); 215-362-6296. Email: ra.lansdale@verizon.net; filapost@aol.com.

MALVERN. *Villa Maria Academy Convent*, 370 Old Lincoln Hwy., 19355. Tel: 610-647-4878; Fax: 610-644-2866. Email: info@vmahs.org. Web: www.vmahs.org. Sisters, Servants of the Immaculate Heart of Mary (I.H.M.). Total in Residence 9.

MEADOWBROOK. *Sisters of the Holy Redeemer*, Emmanuel Convent, 1616 Huntingdon Pike, 19046. Tel: 215-938-5650; Fax: 215-914-4111. Email: kkaufmann@holyredeemer.com. Web: www.sistersholyredeemer.org. Total in Residence 4.

MERION. *Sisters of Mercy of the Americas, Mid-Atlantic Community, Sisters of Mercy Convent*, 515 Montgomery Ave., Merion Station, 19066. Tel: 610-664-6650; Fax: 610-664-3429. Email: pcarroll@mercymidatlantic.org. Web: www.sistersofmercymerion.org. Sisters Patricia Vetrano, R.S.M., Pres.; Patricia Carroll, R.S.M., Local Coord. Sisters 86.

Sisters of Mercy of the Americas, Mid-Atlantic Community, Inc., 515 Montgomery Ave., Merion Station, 19066. Tel: 610-664-6650; Fax: 610-664-3429. Web: www.mercymidatlantic.org. Sisters Patricia Vetrano, R.S.M., Pres.; Kathleen Keenan, R.S.M., Leadership Team; Catherine Darcy, R.S.M., Leadership Team; Honora Nicholson, R.S.M., Leadership Team; Patricia Smith, R.S.M., Leadership Team. As of January 1, 2007 the Sisters of Mercy of the Americas, Regional Communities of Brooklyn, Dallas, Hartsdale, Merion and Watchung merged to create the Sisters of Mercy of the Americas, Mid-Atlantic Community, Inc. Sisters 1,007.

MORTON. *Sisters of St. Francis of Philadelphia (O.S.F.)*, 2130 Franklin Ave., Ct. No. 3, 19070-1217. Tel: 610-543-0186. Email: aboos@osfphila.org. Total in Residence 5; Total Staff 5.

NEWTOWN. *Grey Nuns of the Sacred Heart*, 4 Stockton Ct., 18940. Tel: 215-968-0735. Email: pgearygnsh@aol.com. Sisters Jean Liston, G.N.S.H.; Patricia Geary, G.N.S.H. Total in Residence 2.

NORRISTOWN. *Missionaries of Charity*, 630 DeKalb St., 19401-3944. Tel: 610-277-5962. Sr. Maria Jasmin, M.C., Supr. Services include Food Distribution and Emergency Night Shelter. Sisters 5.

ORELAND. *Grey Nuns of the Sacred Heart*, 1315 Bruce Rd., 19075. Tel: 215-885-0235. Total in Residence 1.

RADNOR. *Armenian Sisters of the Immaculate Conception*, 440 Upper Gulph Rd., 19087. Tel: 610-688-9360; Fax: 610-687-2430. Email: sisteremma@asaphila.org. Web: www.asaphila.org. Sr. Emma Moussayan, Supr. Total in Residence 4.

Missionary Sisters of the Sacred Heart of Jesus (Cabrini Sisters), Cabrini College Convent Gatehouse, 610 King of Prussia Rd., 19807-3698. Tel: 610-995-1210; Fax: 610-995-1210. Email: vandusen49@aol.com. Web: www.mothercabrini.org.

ROSEMONT. *American Province Archives, Sisters of the Holy Child Jesus*, 1308 Wendover Rd., 19010. Tel: 610-525-8951; Fax: 610-525-8952. Email: hmayer@shcj.org. Web: www.shcj.org. Sr. Helena Mayer, S.H.C.J., Archivist.

Holy Child Center, 1341 Montgomery Ave., 19010. Tel: 610-525-9900; Fax: 610-525-0662. Email: apenrose@shcj.org. Web: www.shcj.org. Total in Residence 30; Total Staff 58.

Society of the Holy Child Jesus, Provincial Office, 1341 Montgomery Ave., 19010-1628. Tel: 610-626-1400; Fax: 610-525-2919. Email: mbuckley@shcj.org. Web: www.shcj.org. Sr. Mary Ann Buckley, S.H.C.J., Prov. Leader.

Society of the Holy Child Jesus American Province, Inc.

ROSLYN. *Grey Nuns of the Sacred Heart, Grey Nuns Novitiate House, St. Joseph the Worker Convent*, 2801 Woodland Rd., 19001. Tel: 215-659-4483. Total in Residence 4.

SPRINGFIELD. *St. Anthony Convent*, 1715 S. Sproul Rd., 19064. Tel: 610-544-4066. Residence for Sisters of St. Francis of Philadelphia who serve in various ministries of the Archdiocese. Total Staff 4; Total in Residence 4.

Immaculate Heart of Mary Convent, 1725 S. Sproul Rd., 19064. Tel: 610-544-0275. Email: ihspringfield@hotmail.com. Sr. Georgine Marie Williamson, I.H.M., Supr. Faculty Residence for Sisters, Servants of the Immaculate Heart of Mary, who teach in Cardinal O'Hara High School and Msgr. Bonner and Archbishop Prendergast High School.

St. Joseph Convent, 1705 S. Sproul Rd., 19064. Tel: 610-544-4230. Email: ssjoh@nni.com. Sr. Mary Beth Kratzinger, S.S.J. Sisters of St. Joseph Faculty House, Cardinal O'Hara High School. Total in Residence 10.

Our Lady of Mercy Convent, 1735 S. Sproul Rd., 19064. Tel: 610-544-0238. Faculty Residence for Sisters of Mercy who teach in Cardinal O'Hara and Mercy Vocational High Schools and who serve in other various ministries.

STRAFFORD. *Our Lady of the Assumption Convent*, 139 Fairfield Ln., 19087. Tel: 610-688-7889. Email: olaihm@comcast.net. Sr. Cynthia Ann Mumma, I.H.M., Supr. Sisters, Servants of the Immaculate Heart of Mary. Total in Residence 6.

UPPER DARBY. *Dominican Sisters Administrative Offices, Dominican Congregation of St. Catherine de Ricci*, 131 Copley Rd., 19082. Tel: 215-635-6027; Fax: 610-352-1947. Email: cealop1@verizon.net. Web: www.elkinsparkop.org. Sr. Anne Lythgoe, O.P., Pres.

WARMINSTER. *Sisters of St. Joseph of Philadelphia*, Nativity of Our Lord Convent, 605 W. Street Rd., 18974. Tel: 215-672-0147; Fax: 215-675-9413. Residence of Sisters St. Joseph.

WYNNEWOOD. *Sisters of the Holy Child Jesus (S.H.C.J.)*, Connell House, 105 Old Forest Rd., 19096. Tel: 610-649-8462. Web: www.shcj.org. Total in Residence 4.

YARDLEY. *Grey Nuns of the Sacred Heart, Augustine Hall*, 1750 Quarry Rd., 19067-3998. Tel: 215-968-5733. Total in Residence 7.

Grey Nuns of the Sacred Heart, Generalate, 1750 Quarry Rd., 19067-3998. Tel: 215-968-4236; Fax: 215-860-5612. Email: jlanigan@greynun.org. Web: www.greynun.org. Sr. Julia C. Lanigan, G.N.S.H., Pres.

The Grey Nuns of the Sacred Heart, Inc.

Grey Nuns of the Sacred Heart, Motherhouse, 1750 Quarry Rd., 19067-3998. Tel: 215-968-4236; Fax: 215-968-6656. Email: webmaster@greynun.org. Sr. Elaine Fahey, G.N.S.H., Coord. Total in Residence 54.

Motherhouse of the Grey Nuns of the Sacred Heart, 1750 Quarry Rd., 19067-3998. Tel: 215-968-4236; Fax: 215-860-5612. Email: webmaster@greynun.org. Web: greynun.org. Sisters Julia C. Lanigan, Pres.; Elaine Fahey, G.N.S.H., Coord., Motherhouse Community. Location of the Motherhouse, Generalate, and Congregational Offices. Total in Residence 45.

[AA] RETREAT HOUSES

PHILADELPHIA. *Marianist Province of the United States dba NACMS* 1341 N. Delaware Ave., Ste. 301, 19125-4300. Tel: 215-634-4116. Email: mwyman@sm-usa.org. Web: www.nacms.org; www.marianist.com. The Marianist Center is committed to the spirit of Mary. This spirit mission fosters spiritual growth and formation, the building of lay faith/action communities and social justice according to the unique gifts of the Marianist tradition. Programs offered in Spirituality, Mary & Community Building for groups, staff, faculty, and parishes, as well as special day long programs specially designed for families. Total Staff 6; Total Assisted 600.

Mother Boniface Center, 3501 Solly Ave., 19136. Tel: 215-335-7541; Fax: 215-335-7541. Email: mbcretreat@msbt.org. Sponsored by Missionary Servants of the Most Blessed Trinity. Mid-week and weekend programs; retreats, days of recollection, scripture study, meetings, workshops and hosting programs. Capacity 57; Total Staff 6; Total in Residence 4.

ASTON. *Clare House*, 608 B. Legion Rd., 19014. Tel: 610-459-4077; Fax: 610-558-5377. Email: fsc@osfphila.org. Web: www.fscaston.org. Sr. Christa Thompson, O.S.F. Directed and Private Retreats. 5 Hermitages on property also. Staffed by Sisters of St. Francis of Philadelphia. Capacity 6; Total Staff 2; Total Guests 441; Total Guests at Hermitages 283.

Franciscan Spiritual Center, 609 S. Convent Rd., 19014. Tel: 610-558-6152; Fax: 610-558-5377. Email: fsc@osfphila.org. Web: www.fscaston.org. Sr. Christa Marie Thompson, O.S.F., Dir. Private, directed and group retreats. Spiritual, human development and holistic programs. Staffed by the Sisters of St. Francis Philadelphia.

DOYLESTOWN. *Shrine of Our Lady of Czestochowa*, 654 Ferry Rd., P.O. Box 2049, 18901. Tel: 215-345-0600; 215-345-0601; Fax: 215-348-2148. Email: info@czestochowa.us. Web: czestochowa.us.

HAVERFORD. *Saint Raphaela Center*, 616 Coopertown Rd., 19041. Tel: 610-642-5715; Fax: 610-642-6788. Email: acjhaverford1@aol.com. Web: straphaelacenter.org. Sr. Margaret Scott, A.C.J., Local Supr.

MALVERN. *St. Joseph's-in-the-Hills* (The Malvern Retreat House), 315 S. Warren Ave., P.O. Box 315, 19355-0315. Tel: 610-644-0400; Fax: 610-644-4363. Email: mail@malvernretreat.com. Web: malvernretreat.com. Rev. Herbert J. Sperger, M.Div., Rector. Tel: 610-644-0400, Ext. 28; James A. Fitzsimmons, Pres.; Francis J. Marx, Chm. Owned and Operated by Catholic Laity since 1921, we serve the spiritual needs of lay men and women of all ages, clergy and religious of many denominations and provide a place of peaceful hospitality. Annual Retreatants over 21,000; Private Rooms 350.

[BB] NEWMAN APOSTOLATE

PHILADELPHIA. *Newman Apostolate for Archdiocese of Philadelphia* 222 N. 17th St., 19103. Tel: 215-587-4544; Fax: 215-964-1749. Email: frjames@adphila.org. Web: www.archdiocese-phl.org/offices/na.htm. Rev. John J. Ames, S.T.D., M.A., M.Div., Deputy Sec.

Full Time Chaplaincies:

Drexel University Newman Center, 30 S. 33rd St., 19104-2509. Tel: 215-590-8760; Fax: 215-587-8634. Web: www.drexel.edu/newmancenter. Rev. James T. McGuinn, M.A., M.Div., Chap.

Temple University Newman Center, 2129 N. Broad St., 19122-1193. Tel: 215-232-3779; Fax: 215-235-7302. Email: wildjer@temple.edu. Web: www.temple-newmancenter.org. Rev. J. Jerome Wild, S.T.L., M.A., M.Div., Chap.; Sr. Ann Raymond Welte, I.H.M, Asst. to Chap.

Tri-College Newman Cluster-Bryn Mawr, Haverford and Swarthmore Colleges St. Kevin, 200 Sproul Rd., Newtown Square, 19073. Tel: 610-544-4415. Rev. Jaehwa John Lee, M.S., Chap.

University of Pennsylvania Newman Hall, 3720 Chestnut St., 19104-6189. Tel: 215-898-7575; Fax: 215-386-5899. Email: frjim@newman.upenn.edu. Web: www.newman.upenn.edu. Rev. James T. McGuinn, M.A., M.Div., Newman Chap.

West Chester University Newman Center, 409 Trinity Dr., West Chester, 19382-5362. Tel: 610-436-0891; Fax: 610-436-6247. Email: fathernordeman@yahoo.com. Web: www.wcunewman.org. Rev. John J. Nordeman, M.A., M.Div., Chap.; Sarah Bacza, Asst. Dir.

Part-time Chaplaincies:

Tenet Hahnemann (Center City Campus) Tel: 215-561-1313. Chaplaincy Vacant.

Arcadia University St. Luke the Evangelist Church, 2316 Fairhill Ave., Glenside, 19038-4107. Tel: 215-572-0128. Rev. Msgr. J. Michael Flood, Chap.

Bucks County Community College St. Andrew Church, 81 Swamp Rd., Newtown, 18940. Tel: 215-968-2262. Rev. Msgr. Michael C. Picard, M.A.

Cheney University Tel: 610-399-2353. Chaplaincy Vacant.

Community College of Philadelphia 19130. Chaplaincy Vacant.

Delaware County Community College St. Anastasia Church, 3301 W. Chester Pk., Newtown Square, 19073. Tel: 610-356-3303; 610-359-5206. Chaplaincy Vacant.

Delaware County Community College Math Science Dept., Media, 19063. Tel: 610-359-5206.

St. Anastasia, 3301 West Chester Pike, Newtown Square, 19073. Tel: 610-356-1613; 610-356-3303; Fax: 610-356-8332.

Delaware Valley College of Science and Agriculture St. Jude Church, 321 W. Butler Ave., Chalfont, 18914-2329. Tel: 215-822-0179; Fax: 215-822-0638.

Rev. James B. McCoy.

Harcum College Our Mother of Good Counsel, 31 Pennswood Rd., Bryn Mawr, 19010. Tel: 610-526-6050. Sharon Watson, Dean of Student Affairs.

Lincoln University Sacred Heart Church, 101 Church Rd., Oxford, 19363. Tel: 610-932-5040. Rev. Gregory J. Hamill, M.A., M.Div., Chap.

Montgomery County Community College St. Helena Church, P.O. Box 5085, Center Square, 19422. Tel: 610-275-7711. Rev. Msgr. Joseph J. Nicolo, M.Div., Chap.

Pennsylvania State University-Abington Our Lady Help of Christians, 1500 Marian Rd., Abington, 19001. Tel: 215-886-3456.

Pennsylvania State University - Delaware County Campus St. Francis de Sales Church, 33 New Rd., Box 97, Lenni, 19062. Tel: 610-459-2203.

Pennsylvania State University-Great Valley Campus 19104. Chaplaincy Vacant

Philadelphia College of Pharmacy and Science St. Francis de Sales Church, 4625 Springfield Ave., 19143. Tel: 215-222-5819.

Philadelphia University St. Bridget Church, 3667 Midvale Ave., 19129-1712. Tel: 215-844-4126. Rev. Joseph P. Devlin, M.A., M.Div., Chap.

Roxborough Memorial School of Nursing St. John the Baptist, 146 Rector St., 19107. Tel: 215-482-4600. Rev. James A. Lyons, M.Div., Chap.

Temple University, Ambler Campus St. Alphonsus Church, 33 Conwell Dr., Maple Glen, 19002. Tel: 215-646-4600; Fax: 215-646-0180. Web: www.libertynet.org/~tunewman.

Thomas Jefferson University , Chaplaincy Vacant.

University of the Arts Assoc. Dean's Office, Broad and Pine Sts., 19102. Tel: 215-875-2236. Chaplaincy Vacant.

University of the Sciences in Philadelphia 600 S. 43rd St., 19104. Tel: 215-596-8800. Rev. Louis C. Bier, St. Francis de Sales.

Ursinus College St. Eleanor Church, 647 Locust St., Collegeville, 19426-2541. Tel: 610-489-1647; Fax: 610-489-7469. Rev. Msgr. Patrick E. Sweeney, Chap.

Widener University Blessed Katherine Drexel Church, 20th and Providence Ave., Chester, 19013-5695. Tel: 610-872-0545. Rev. Msgr. Joseph C. McLoone, M.A., Chap., St. Katharine Drexel.

[CC] MISCELLANEOUS LISTINGS

PHILADELPHIA. **American Academy of the Sacred Arts*, 1629 Porter St., 19145. Tel: 215-339-5041. Sr. Mary Paula Beierschmitt, I.H.M., Pres. Purpose is to glorify God in the cultural disciplines through the creation of original art, educational outreach and ecumenical dialogue.

Br. Rousseau Academy, 7201 Milnor St., 19135. Tel: 215-624-5600; Fax: 215-624-3108. Larry Patrick, M.P.A., Dir.

Catholic Health Care Services, 222 N. 17th St., 19103. Tel: 215-587-3663; Fax: 215-587-3773. Web: www.catholichealthcareservices.org.

Catholic Heritage Center, c/o Archdiocese of Philadelphia, 222 N. 17th St., 19103-1299. The Catholic Heritage Center, a proposed state-of-the-art, multi-purpose facility is owned by the Archdiocese of Philadelphia. It will include a museum featuring both permanent and temporary exhibits on Catholic history, heritage, art and culture, a research library and archives, and an education resource center. Project is currently on hold.

Catholic Kolping Society, 9130 Academy Rd., 19114. P.O. Box 52651, 19115. Tel: 215-676-8977. Email: phlkolping@aol.com. Web: www.kolpingphilly.com. Rev. Engelbert G. Michel, Praeses; Frank Staub, Pres.; Mr. Earl Asimos, Treas.

Catholic League For Persons With Disabilities, 11621 Banes St., 19116. Tel: 215-725-9746; 215-676-0394. Rev. Edmund J. Maher, Spiritual Dir. (Retired).

Catholics United for the Faith (St. John Neumann Philadelphia Area Chapter), 183 Hillcrest Ave., 19118. Tel: 215-247-2585; Fax: 215-247-2585. Email: annemwilson@yahoo.com. Mrs. Anne M. Wilson, Chm.

The Central Association of the Miraculous Medal, 475 E. Chelten Ave., 19144-5785. Tel: 215-848-1010; 800-523-3674; Fax: 215-848-1014. Email: lizanne@cammonline.org. Web: www.miraculousmedal.org. Rev. Carl L. Pieber, C.M., Exec. Dir.; Rob Silbaugh, Dir., Devel.

Change for Change aka Change for Global Change 9701 Germantown Ave., 19118-2694. Tel: 215-248-7220; Fax: 215-248-7277. Email: changeforglobalchange@earthlink.net. Change for Global Change exists to address the global problem of sustainability through education, donations and grants to not-for-profit organizations for projects to aid those who have little or no means to provide a sustainable life for themselves.

CORA Services, 8540 Verree Rd., 19111. Tel: 215-342-7660; 215-535-2957 (Neumann Center); Fax: 215-745-9857. Email: info@coraservices.org. Web: www.coraservices.org. James F. Harron, CEO.

CORA Services, Inc., Philadelphia, Pennsylvania, Services provided for children, families and teen pregnancy. Programs available: counseling, speech and language, remediation, Early Childhood, Drug & Alcohol, and Occupational Therapy. Total Assisted 19,000; Total Staff 174.

CSFN Mission & Ministry, Inc., Sisters of the Holy Family of Nazareth, Holy Family Prov., 2755 Holme Ave., 19152. Tel: 215-335-4802; Fax: 215-335-4804. Email: ltfelici@aol.com.

Daughters of St. Paul, 9610 Evans St., 19115. Tel: 215-969-5068; Fax: 215-969-6422. Email: philadelphia@paulinemedia.org. Web: www.pauline.org. Sisters Patricia Maresca, F.S.P., Supr.; Mary Peter Martin, F.S.P.; Cynthia Guza.

**Depaul, USA*, 5725 Sprague St., 19138-1721. Tel: 215-438-1955; Fax: 215-438-1944. Email: charles.levesque@depaulusa.org. Web: www.depaulusa.org. Charles W. Levesque, Exec. Dir. Depaul USA offers homeless and disadvantaged people the opportunity to fulfill their potential and move towards an independent and positive future. Depaul USA is part of Depaul International and works in the spirit of St. Vincent de Paul and St. Louise De Marillac, believing that everyone should have a place to call home and a stake in their community.

Fournier Retirement Fund Corporation, Mount St. Joseph Convent, 9701 Germantown Ave., 19118-2694. Tel: 215-248-7205; Fax: 215-248-7277. Email: msjc@ssjphila.org. Web: www.ssjphila.org. Sr. Joanne Fehrenbach, S.S.J., Gen. Sec. & Contact Person.

Franciscan Volunteer Ministry, Inc., P.O. Box 29276, 19125. Tel: 215-427-3070; Fax: 215-427-3059. Email: fvmedir@gmail.com. Web: www.franciscanvolunteerministry.org. Katie Sullivan, Exec. Dir.; Matt Johnson, Assoc. Dir. Purpose: To create and run a Franciscan lay volunteer program in the United States.

**Friends of St. Martin de Porres School*, P.O. Box 660, West Chester, 19381-0660. 2300 W. Lehigh Ave., 19132.

Good Shepherd Mediation Program, 5356 Chew Ave., 19138. Tel: 215-843-5413; Fax: 215-843-2080. Email: gsmediation@phillymediators.org. Web: www.phillymediators.org. Cheryl Cutrona, Exec. Dir.

Good Shepherd Corporation, Philadelphia, Pennsylvania

IHM Center for Literacy, 425 W. Lindley Ave., 19120-3340. Tel: 215-457-2232; Fax: 215-457-1611. Email: ihmesl@verizon.net. Web: mysite.verizon.net/ihmesl/. Sisters Mary Regina Schuyler, I.H.M., Dir.; Janice Owen, I.H.M., Site Coord. Full-time program with courses in; English for Speakers of Other Languages (ESOL)

929 S. Farragut St., 19143-3695. Tel: 215-382-0292; Fax: 215-382-4662. Email: ihmesl2@verizon.net.

**International Institute for Culture, Ivy Hall*, 6331 Lancaster Ave., 19151. Tel: 215-877-9910; Fax: 215-877-9911. Web: www.iiculture.org. John M. Haas, Ph.D., S.T.L., Pres. Purpose: for the evangelization of culture through international conferences, language and cultural programs, etc., which reflect the rich cultural heritage of the Catholic Church which serves to bring people to the Person of Jesus Christ.

Katherine Kiernan Chateau, Inc., c/o Catholic Social Services, 222 N. 17th St., Ste. 300, 19103. Tel: 215-587-3903; Fax: 215-587-2479. Email: CHSweb@chs-adphila.org.

Marianist Lay Network of North America (MLNNA), 1341 N. Delaware Ave., #301, 19125-4300. Tel: 215-634-4116. Email: laymarianist@gmail.com. Web: marianist.com/lay.

Medical Mission Sisters Supplemental Subsidy Fund, Inc., 8400 Pine Rd., 19111. Tel: 215-742-6100; Fax: 215-742-2602. Sr. Frances Vaughan, M.M.S., Pres. Bd.

Missionary Cenacle Apostolate, 3501 Solly Ave, 19136. Tel: 410-772-5799. Pat Regan, Treas.; Alma Robles, Gen. Custodian. The MCA is a branch of the Missionary Cenacle Family. Lay people called to be missionaries in the Church in the providence of everyday life. MCA members live and work in the United States, Mexico, Puerto Rico, Colombia, and Costa Rica.

National Catholic Bioethics Center, 6399 Drexel Rd., 19151. Tel: 215-877-2660; Fax: 215-877-2682. Email: postmaster@ncbcenter.org. Web: www.ncbcenter.org. John M. Haas, M.Div., S.T.L., Ph.D., Pres. Tel: 215-877-2660; Donald J. Powers, Vice Pres. Fin. Tel: 401-289-0680; Mark E. Bradford, Exec. Vice Pres. Tel: 215-871-2009; Rev. Tadeusz Pacholczyk, Dir. Educ.; Edward J. Furton, M.A., Ph.D., Dir. Publications; Marie T. Hilliard, J.C.L., Ph.D., R.N., D.M., Dir. Bioethics & Pub. Policy; Rev. Alfred Cioffi, S.T.D., Ph.D.

National Shrine of Saint Rita of Cascia, 1166 S. Broad St., 19146. Tel: 215-546-8333; Fax: 215-732-3510. Email: ritashrine@aol.com. Web: www.saintritashrine.org. Rev. Joseph A. Genito, O.S.A., Dir. Center of Devotion to Saint Rita in the United States.

Sisters of Saint Joseph Welcome Center, 728 E. Allegheny Ave., 19134-2428. Tel: 215-634-1696; Fax: 215-634-0760. Email: emarnien@earthlink.net. Web: www.ssjwelcomecenter.org. Sisters Eileen Marnien, Dir.; Marian Behrle, Dir. Literacy Prog. Sisters 4.

Society of Catholic Medical Missionaries Generalate, Inc. (Effective 1991), 8400 Pine Rd., 19111. Tel: 215-742-6100; Fax: 215-342-3948. Email: generalate@medicalmissionsisters.org.uk. Web: www.medicalmissionsisters.org. Sisters Sue Sopczynski, M.M.S., General Treas.; Agnes Lanfermann, M.M.S., Pres. Corporation collects funds for charitable and missionary work, for Medical Mission Sisters; Assists in operation of hospitals, clinics and primary health care programs; Assists in care of poor, sick and infirm, in U.S. and overseas; Assists in training and educating men and women in medicine and nursing, and other health professions; Trains candidates for the Community; Provides assisted living care to sick and elder Medical Mission Sisters.

Society of St. Vincent de Paul of Philadelphia, 901 E. Luzerne St., 19124. Tel: 215-288-9540; Fax: 215-288-9540. Email: careygroberts@comcast.net. Dom Visco, Pres.; Carey G. Roberts, Exec. Dir. Catholic Lay Organization serving those in need with spiritual, moral, material and financial support regardless of race, creed, etc.

The Saint Thomas More Society of Philadelphia, 2600 One Commerce Sq., 19103-7098. Tel: 215-564-8000; Fax: 215-564-8120. Email: momara@stradley.com. Web: www.stmsphl.org. Robert T. Miller Esq., Pres. Purpose: The Society is an association of Catholic lawyers organized to strengthen the religious and charitable commitment of its members and to promote high ethical standards in the legal profession, as exemplified by the life of Saint Thomas More.

The Warner Perpetual Trust for the Benefit of Catholic Charities, Provident National Bank, P.O. Box 7648, 19101. Tel: 610-585-5698; Fax: 610-358-4275.

The Warner Perpetual Trust for the Benefit of Catholic Charities of the Archdiocese of Philadelphia, (The "Perpetual" Trust)

ASTON. *Sisters of St. Francis Foundation*, 609 S. Convent Rd., 19014. Tel: 610-558-7713; Fax: 610-558-5357. Email: mvdgeest@osfphila.org. Web: www.osfphila.org. Sr. Mary Vandergeest, O.S.F., Exec. Dir. Purpose: Raises funds to fulfill the needs of the Ministries and Retired Sisters of the Sisters of St. Francis of Philadelphia.

Sisters of St. Francis of Philadelphia, Charitable Trust II, Our Lady of Angels Convent, 609 S. Covent Rd., 19014. Tel: 610-558-7733; Fax: 610-459-0195. Email: eanderson@osfphila.org. Web: www.osfphila.org. Sr. Esther Anderson, O.S.F., Congregational Min.

BALA CYNWYD. *The Papal Foundation*, 150 Monument Rd., 19004. Tel: 610-535-6340; 610-535-6341; Fax: 610-535-6343. Email: jcoffey@thepapalfoundation.com. Web: www.thepapalfoundation.com. Mr. James V. Coffey, M.A., Contact Person.

CONSHOHOCKEN. *Mercy Health System of Southeastern PA*, One West Elm St., 19428. Tel: 610-567-6106; Fax: 610-567-6150. Email: kkeenan@mercyhealth.org. Web: www.mercyhealth.org. H. Ray Welch, Pres. & CEO Mercy Health System; Sisters Mary Christine McCann, R.S.M., Bd. Chm.; Kathleen Keenan, R.S.M., Senior Vice Pres., Mission & Sponsorship. Mercy Health System is a regional health corporation of Catholic Health East, sponsored by the Sisters of Mercy.

The health care services operated by Mercy Health System include:

Mercy Philadelphia Hospital Tel: 215-748-9300; Fax: 215-748-9709.

Mercy Fitzgerald Hospital Tel: 610-237-4030; Fax: 610-237-4202.

Mercy Suburban Hospital Tel: 610-278-2002; Fax: 610-272-4642.

St. Agnes Continuing Care Center Tel: 215-339-4220; Fax: 215-339-5650.

St. Agnes Continuing Care Center Foundation Tel: 215-339-4220; Fax: 215-339-5650.

Nazareth Hospital Tel: 215-335-6039; Fax: 215-335-6598.

Nazareth Health Care Foundation Tel: 215-335-6159; Fax: 215-335-6265.

N.E. Physician Services, Inc. Tel: 215-335-6039; Fax:

215-335-6598.

Keystone Mercy Health Plan Tel: 215-937-8201; Fax: 215-937-8202.

Mercy Management Services Tel: 610-567-6106; Fax: 610-567-6150.

Mercy Health Foundation Tel: 610-567-5205; Fax: 610-567-6150.

Mercy Home Health Tel: 610-690-2526; Fax: 610-690-4644.

Mercy Court Tel: 610-623-3083; Fax: 610-259-1414.

DOWNINGTOWN. *Catholic Clinical Consultants*, 151 Woodbine Rd., 19335. Tel: 610-269-2600; Fax: 610-518-2020. Rev. Msgr. Michael T. McCulken, M.Div., Pres.; Dr. Anthony Mele, Psy.D., Dir. Catholic Consultants. Provides outsourced management, clinical and behavioral health consulting to skilled nursing facilities, assisted living facilities, adult day programs and other community-based elder care programs.

EXTON. **Theology of the Body Institute*, 479 Thomas Jones Way, Ste. 100, 19341. Tel: 215-302-8200; Fax: 215-302-8200. Web: tobinstitute.org. Jen Settle, Dir. of Programs. Purpose: To educate and train men and women to understand, live and promote the Theology of the Body and to ensure that the teachings of John Paul II are promoted faithfully and effectively.

FLOURTOWN. *Saint Joseph Guild*, 110 W. Wissahickon Ave., P.O. Box 36, 19031-0036. Tel: 215-248-7838; Fax: 215-248-7802. Email: sjguild19@aol.com. Web: www.ssjphila.org. Sr. Frances DeLisle, S.S.J., Coord.

FORT WASHINGTON. *John Paul II Foundation for Peace, Justice & Human Rights, The Copernicus House*, 1 Reiff Mill Rd., Ambler, 19001. Tel: 215-646-4420; Fax: 215-628-8944. Email: KEENCORNER@aol.com.

HUNTINGDON VALLEY. **Holy Redeemer Health System*, 667 Welsh Rd., 19006. Tel: 215-938-4650; 215-938-3236. Web: www.holyredeemer.com. Michael B. Laign, Pres. & CEO. Sponsor: Sisters of the Holy Redeemer, C.S.R., Parent organization which maintains, manages, and operates the health care system composed of the various corporations sponsored and established by the Sisters of the Holy Redeemer, C.S.R. as follows: Holy Redeemer Health Care Corporation and Foundation; Holy Redeemer Health System; Holy Redeemer Hospital and Medical Center; St. Joseph's Manor; The Lafayette-Redeemer; Holy Redeemer Active and Retirement Living Communities; Holy Redeemer Home Care and Hospice; Holy Redeemer Transitional Care Unit; Holy Redeemer Physician and Ambulatory Services; Redeemer Village; Redeemer Village II; Drueding Center/ Project Rainbow; HRH Management Corporation; Convents Provincialate; Angelus Convent; Emmanuel Convent; Our Lady of Peace Convent; St. Elizabeth Convent.

Holy Redeemer Hospital and Medical Center Tel: 215-947-3000. Web: www.holyredeemer.com.

St. Joseph's Manor Tel: 215-938-4000. Web: www.holyredeemer.com. Benjamin Pieczynski, Admin.

The Lafayette - Redeemer Tel: 215-214-2877. Benjamin Pieczynski, Group Vice Pres.

Holy Redeemer Health Care Corporation and Foundation Tel: 215-938-4650. Web: www.holyredeemer.com.

Holy Redeemer Home Care and Hospice Tel: 800-678-8678. Web: www.holyredeemer.com.

Holy Redeemer Transitional Care Unit Tel: 215-947-3000.

IMMACULATA. *Enserv Inc.*, 1145 King Rd., 19345. Tel: 610-647-4400, Ext. 3147; Fax: 610-251-1668.

JENKINTOWN. **PNFPN-Philadelphia Natural Family Planning Network*, P.O. Box 220, 19046. Tel: 215-885-8388. Web: pnfpn.org. Lester A. Ruppersberger, D.O., Pres. PNFPN is a network of persons dedicated to the promotion of Natural Family Planning (NFP). Our mission is to explain its practice, effectiveness, benefits and underlying moral principles as understood and taught by the Catholic Church.

KING OF PRUSSIA. *Rachel's Vineyard Ministries (International Headquarters)*, 808 N. Henderson Rd., 19406. Tel: 610-354-0555 Toll Free: 877-HOPE-4-ME (877-4673-3463); 877-467-3463 (877 HOPE-4-ME); Fax: 610-354-0311. Email: t.burke@rachelsvineyard.org; k.burke@rachelsvineyard.org. Web: www.rachelsvineyard.org. Theresa Burke, Ph.D., L.P.C., N.C.P., Founder & Exec. Dir.; Kevin Burke, M.S.S., L.S.W., Assoc. Dir. Purpose: to provide retreats offering emotional and spiritual healing after abortion; and continuing education for professionals, clergy and lay persons.

MEADOWBROOK. **Holy Redeemer Physician and Ambulatory Services*, 1648 Huntington Pike, 19046. Tel: 215-938-3713; Fax: 215-938-4610. Web: www.holyredeemer.com. Michele Urofsky, Exec. Vice Pres. Sponsor: Sisters of the Holy Redeemer C.S.R., Affiliate of Holy Redeemer Health System; Nonprofit corporation formed to establish, operate and maintain family health clinics and practices, laboratories, dispensaries, buildings, and facilities relating to these purposes, and provide the services of physicians and other health care professionals in connection with the provision of health care services at Holy Redeemer Hospital and Medical Center, and other hospitals, clinics and health care facilities.

MERION STATION. *The Mercy Foundation*, 515 Montgomery Ave., 19066-1297. Tel: 610-664-6650; Fax: 610-664-3429. Sr. Christine McCann, R.S.M., Pres. Email: pvetrano@mercymidatlantic.org.

Sisters of Mercy of the Americas Mid-Atlantic Community, Inc., 515 Montgomery Ave., 19066. Tel: 610-664-6650; Fax: 610-664-3429. Web: www.mercymidatlantic.org. Sr. Patricia Vetrano, R.S.M., Pres.

NEWTOWN SQUARE. *Catholic Health East*, 3805 West Chester Pike, Ste. 100, 19073-2304. Tel: 610-355-2004; Fax: 610-271-9600. Email: sshare@che.org. Web: www.che.org. Ms. Judith M. Persichilli, Pres. & CEO. Catholic Health East is a multi-institutional, Catholic health system co-sponsored by 9 religious congregations: Franciscan Sisters of Allegany in St. Bonaventure, NY; Sisters of Providence in Holyoke, MA; Sisters of Mercy of the Americas-Northeast Community; Sisters of Mercy of the Americas-Mid-Atlantic Community; Sisters of Mercy of the Americas-South Central Community; Sisters of Mercy of the Americas-New York, Pennsylvania, Pacific West Community; the Sisters of St. Joseph of St. Augustine, FL; Sisters of Charity of Seton Hill, Greensburg, PA; Sisters, Servants of the Immaculate Heart of Mary, Scranton, Pennsylvania; and Hope Ministries, a Public Juridic Person of Pontifical Right within Catholic Health East, Newtown Square, PA. Founded in 1997, Catholic Health East facilities serve communities through 18 regional systems in 11 eastern states.

Continuing Care Management Services Network, 3805 West Chester Pike, Ste. 100, 19073-2304. Tel: 610-355-2000; Fax: 610-355-2050. Email: jcapassol@che.org. Web: www.che.org. Mr. John Capasso, Pres. & CEO.

Global Health Ministry, 3805 West Chester Pike, Ste. 100, 19073-2304. Tel: 610-355-2003; Fax: 610-271-9600. Email: mmcginley@globalhealthministry.org. Web: www.globalhealthministry.org. Sr. Mary Jo McGinley, R.S.M., Pres. & Exec. Dir.

UPPER DARBY. *Dominican Pastoral Counseling*, 131 Copley Rd., 19082. Tel: 215-635-6027; Fax: 610-352-1947. Email: cealop1@verizon.net. Web: www.elkinsparkop.org. Sr. Ceal Warner, O.P., Gen. Councilor.

Lucy Eaton Smith Fund, 131 Copley Rd., 19082. Tel: 215-635-6027; Fax: 610-352-1947. Email: cealop1@verizon.net. Web: www.elkinsparkop.org. Sr. Ceal Warner, O.P., Gen. Councilor.

VILLANOVA. *Augustinian Volunteers*, Business Office: 214 Ashwood Rd., 19085. Tel: 610-527-3330, Ext. 291; Fax: 610-520-0618. Email: osavol@gmail.com. Web: www.osavol.org. Patrick DiDomenico, Dir.; Hannah Kunberger, Assoc. Dir.; Shannon Keough, Asst. Dir. A faith-based lay volunteer program serving the poor in the Archdioceses of Chicago, Boston and New York and the Diocese of San Diego.

WAYNE. **Catholic Leadership Institute*, 440 E. Swedesford Rd., Ste. 3040, 19087. Tel: 610-363-1315; Fax: 610-363-3731. Email: info@CatholicLeaders.org. Web: www.CatholicLeaders.org. Most Rev. Gregory M. Aymond, D.D., M.Div., Episcopal Mod.; Timothy C. Flanagan, Founder & Chair; Matthew F. Manion, Pres. & CEO; Rev. William Dickinson, National Dir. Leadership Devel. Lay organization providing leadership training and personal development programs to help clergy, religious and lay leaders reach their God given potential as Catholic leaders and Christian witnesses in their family, workplace, community and Church.

YEADON. *Mercy Court*, 550 S. Lansdowne Ave., 19050. Tel: 610-623-3083; Fax: 610-259-1414. Email: mercycourt@comcast.net. Paula S. Wisdo, Prog. Mgr. Sisters of Mercy., Low income apartments for independent living for older adults. Total Apartments 100; Total Staff 5.

RELIGIOUS INSTITUTES OF MEN REPRESENTED IN THE ARCHDIOCESE

For further details refer to the corresponding bracketed number in the Religious Institutes of Men or Women section.

[0140]—*Augustinians* (Prov. of St. Thomas Villanova)—O.S.A.

[0290]—*Brothers of Charity*—F.C.

[0330]—*Brothers of the Christian Schools* (Baltimore Prov.)—F.S.C.

[0900]—*Canons Regular of Premontre*—O.Praem.

[0470]—*Capuchin Friars*—O.F.M.Cap.

[0650]—*Congregation of the Holy Spirit* (Eastern Prov.)—C.S.Sp.

[0860]—*Congregation of the Immaculate Heart of Mary (Missionhurst)*—C.I.C.M.

[1330]—*Congregation of the Mission* (Eastern Prov.)—C.M.

[]—*Institute of the Incarnate Word*—I.V.E.

[]—*Legionaries of Christ*—L.C.

[0850]—*Missionaries of Africa*—M.Afr.

[0825]—*Missionaries of the Blessed Sacrament*—M.S.S.

[1110]—*Missionaries of the Sacred Heart* (American Prov.)—M.S.C.

[0840]—*Missionary Servants of the Most Holy Trinity*—S.T.

[0910]—*Oblate Missionaries of Mary Immaculate*—O.M.I.

[0920]—*Oblates of St. Francis de Sales*—O.S.F.S.

[0520]—*Order of Friars Minor* (Assumption B.V.M. & Most Holy Name Provs.)—O.F.M.

[0970]—*Order of Our Lady of Mercy*—O.deM.

[1310]—*Order of the Holy Trinity*—O.SS.T.

[1010]—*Pauline Fathers*—O.S.P.P.E.

[0950]—*The Philadelphia Congregation of the Oratory of Saint Philip Neri*—C.O.

[1040]—*Piarist Fathers*—Sch.P.

[1070]—*Redemptorist Fathers* (Baltimore Prov.)—C.SS.R.

[1220]—*Servants of Charity*—S.C.

[0690]—*Society of Jesus (Jesuits)* (Maryland Prov.)—S.J. Society of Mary (Marianists) S.M.

[0560]—*Third Order Regular of Saint Francis* (Prov. of the Most Sacred Heart)—T.O.R.

RELIGIOUS INSTITUTES OF WOMEN REPRESENTED IN THE ARCHDIOCESE

[1070-13]—*Adrian Dominican Sisters*—O.P.

[2120]—*Armenian Sisters of the Immaculate Conception*—C.I.C.

[1810]—*Bernardine Sisters of the Third Order of St. Francis*—O.S.F.

[0760]—*Daughters of Charity of St. Vincent de Paul*—D.C.

[0940]—*Daughters of St. Mary of Providence*—D.S.M.P.

[0420]—*Discalced Carmelite Nuns*—O.C.D.

[1070-23]—*Dominican Sisters of Hawthorne*—O.P.

[1105]—*Dominican Sisters of Hope*—O.P.

[]—*Dominican Sisters of Our Lady of the Rosary*—O.P.

[1115]—*Dominican Sisters of Peace*—O.P.

[1070-17]—*Dominican Sisters of St. Catherine de Ricci*—O.P.

[1170]—*Felician Sisters*—C.S.S.F.

[1180]—*Franciscan Sisters of Allegany, New York*—O.S.F.

[1840]—*Grey Nuns of the Sacred Heart*—G.N.S.H.

[1870]—*Handmaids of the Sacred Heart of Jesus*—A.C.J.

[]—*Holy Spirit Sisters of Tanzania*—A.C.L.S.

[2310]—*Little Sisters of the Assumption*—L.S.A.

[2340]—*Little Sisters of the Poor*—L.S.P.

[2345]—*Little Workers of the Sacred Hearts*—P.O.S.C.

[2490]—*Medical Mission Sisters*—M.M.S.

[2710]—*Missionaries of Charity*—M.C.

[2790]—*Missionary Servants of the Most Blessed Trinity*—M.S.B.T.

[2730]—*Missionary Sisters of the Holy Rosary*—M.S.H.R.

[2800]—*Missionary Sisters of the Most Sacred Heart of Jesus of Hiltrup*—M.S.C.

[2860]—*Missionary Sisters of the Sacred Heart* (Eastern Prov.)—M.S.C.

[3060]—*Oblates Sisters of St. Francis de Sales*—O.S.F.S.

[3730]—*Order of St. Basil the Great*—O.S.B.M.

[3760]—*Order of St. Clare*—O.S.C.

[0950]—*Pious Society Daughters of St. Paul*—F.S.P.

[3390]—*Religious of the Assumption*—R.A.

[3430]—*Religious Teachers Filippini*—M.P.F.

[2970]—*School Sisters of Notre Dame*—S.S.N.D.

[]—*Servants of the Lord and of the Virgin of Matara*—S.S.V.M.

[3540]—*Sister Servants of the Holy Spirit of Perpetual Adoration*—S.Sp.S.deA.P.

[3630]—*Sister Servants of the Most Sacred Heart of Jesus*—S.S.C.J.

[0500]—*Sisters of Charity of Nazareth*—S.C.N.

[0660]—*Sisters of Christian Charity*—S.C.C.

[2575]—*Sisters of Mercy of the Americas, Merion, PA*—R.S.M.

[3000]—*Sisters of Notre Dame de Namur*—S.N.D.deN.

[2670]—*Sisters of Our Lady of Mercy*—S.O.L.M.
[3893]—*Sisters of Saint Joseph of Philadelphia*—S.S.J.
[1650]—*Sisters of St. Francis of Philadelphia*—O.S.F.
[0260]—*Sisters of the Blessed Sacrament for Indians and Colored People*—S.B.S.
[0970]—*Sisters of the Divine Compassion*—R.D.C.
[1830]—*Sisters of the Good Shepherd*—R.G.S.
[1970]—*Sisters of the Holy Family of Nazareth*—C.S.F.N.
[2000]—*Sisters of the Holy Redeemer*—C.S.R.
[2060]—*Sisters of the Most Holy Trinity*—O.SS.T.
[2160]—*Sisters Servants of the Immaculate Heart of Mary* (Scranton)—I.H.M.
[2170]—*Sisters, Servants of the Immaculate Heart of Mary (Immaculata)*—I.H.M.
[4060]—*Society of the Holy Child Jesus*—S.H.C.J.
[4120]—*Ursuline Sisters of the Immaculate Conception*—O.S.U.
[4190]—*Visitation Nuns*—V.H.M.

ARCHDIOCESAN CEMETERIES

PHILADELPHIA. *Cathedral*, 1032 N. 48th St., 19131. Tel: 215-477-8918; Fax: 215-477-8313.
Holy Sepulchre, Cheltenham Ave. & Ivy Hill Rd., 19150. Tel: 215-247-0691; Fax: 215-886-0298.
New Cathedral, 2nd & Butler Sts., 19140. Tel: 215-634-3212; Fax: 215-634-1733.

BENSALEM. *Resurrection*, 5201 Hulmeville Rd., 19020. Tel: 215-639-0965; Fax: 215-639-4532.

CHALFONT. *St. John Neumann*, 3797 County Line Rd., 18914. Tel: 215-822-0680; Fax: 215-822-5159.

COATESVILLE. *All Souls*, 3215 Manor Rd., 19320. Tel: 484-288-6140; Fax: 484-288-6147.

NEWTOWN. *All Saints*, 291 W. Durham Rd., 18940.

SPRINGFIELD. *SS. Peter and Paul*, 1600 S. Sproul Rd., 19064. Tel: 610-544-4933; Fax: 610-544-6467.

WEST CONSHOHOCKEN. *Calvary*, Gulph & Matsonford Rd., 19428. Tel: 610-525-2214; Fax: 610-525-6247.

WEST GROVE. *Holy Saviour*

YEADON. *Holy Cross*, 626 Bailey Rd., 19050. Tel: 610-626-2206; 215-476-3656; Fax: 610-623-6247.

NECROLOGY

✠ Bevilacqua, His Eminence Anthony Cardinal, Archbishop emeritus of Philadelphia.—Died Jan. 31, 2012
✠ Foley, His Eminence John Patrick Cardinal, Grand Master emeritus of the Equestrian Order of the Holy Sepulchre of Jerusalem.—Died Dec. 11, 2011
† Busco, Rev. Msgr. John J., (Retired)—Died Nov. 8, 2011
† Flood, Rev. Msgr. James J., (Retired)—Died Jan. 17, 2011
† Foley, Rev. Msgr. James J., (Retired)—Died June 21, 2011
† Hanlon, Rev. Msgr. Andrew J., (Retired)—Died Feb. 16, 2011
† Matteo, Rev. Msgr. James P., (Retired)—Died April 1, 2011
† Meehan, Rev. Msgr. Francis X., (Retired)—Died July 22, 2011
† Nugent, Rev. Msgr. Arthur W., (Retired)—Died Feb. 10, 2011
† Doyle, Thomas F., (Retired)—Died Dec. 9, 2010
† Foster, John J., (Retired)—Died June 6, 2011
† Graham, Joseph B., Philadelphia, PA St. Jerome—Died Dec. 28, 2010
† Hagenbach, George G., (Retired)—Died Aug. 1, 2011
† Hoy, Daniel J., (Retired)—Died July 25, 2011
† Jakows, Ronald M., Philadelphia, PA Annunciation B.V.M.—Died Feb. 2, 2011
† McGee, Leo J., (Retired)—Died Oct. 15, 2111
† McGinnis, James J., (Retired)—Died Oct. 26, 2010
† Murphy, James J., (Retired)—Died March 7, 2011
† Sweeney, Joseph J., (Retired)—Died Oct. 16, 2011
† Walsh, John M., (Retired)—Died March 23, 2011
† Wesolowski, Edmund C., (Retired)—Died Jan. 7, 2011

An asterisk (*) denotes an organization that has established tax-exempt status directly with the IRS and is not covered by the USCCB Group Ruling.

Diocese of Phoenix

(Dioecesis Phoenicensis)

Most Reverend

THOMAS J. OLMSTED, J.C.D.

Bishop of Phoenix; ordained July 2, 1973; appointed Coadjutor Bishop of Wichita February 16, 1999; Episcopal ordination April 20, 1999; appointed Bishop of Wichita October 4, 2001; appointed Bishop of Phoenix November 25, 2003; installed December 20, 2003. *Office: 400 E. Monroe St., Phoenix, AZ 85004-2336.*

Most Reverend

THOMAS J. O'BRIEN

Bishop Emeritus of Phoenix; ordained May 7, 1961; consecrated January 6, 1982; installed January 18, 1982; retired June 18, 2003. *Mailing Address: 400 E. Monroe St., Phoenix, AZ 85004-2336.*

Most Reverend

EDUARDO A. NEVARES

Auxiliary Bishop of Phoenix; ordained July 18, 1981; appointed Titular Bishop of Natchesium and Auxiliary Bishop of Phoenix May 11, 2010; episcopal ordination July 19, 2010. *Office: 400 E. Monroe St., Phoenix, AZ 85004-2336.*

ESTABLISHED DECEMBER 2, 1969.

Square Miles 43,967.

Comprises the Counties of Maricopa; Mohave; Yavapai & Coconino not to include the territorial boundaries of the Navajo Indian Reservation; Pinal--that portion of land known as the Gila River Indian Reservation in the State of Arizona.

Patroness of Diocese: Our Lady of Guadalupe.

For legal titles of parishes and diocesan institutions, consult the Chancery Office.

Diocesan Pastoral Center: 400 E. Monroe St., Phoenix, AZ 85004-2336. Tel: 602-257-0030; 602-354-2000; Fax: 602-354-2427.

Web: www.diocesephoenix.org

Email: contact-us@diocesephoenix.org

STATISTICAL OVERVIEW

Personnel	
Bishop	1
Auxiliary Bishops	1
Retired Bishops	1
Priests: Diocesan Active in Diocese	88
Priests: Diocesan Active Outside Diocese	2
Priests: Retired, Sick or Absent	38
Number of Diocesan Priests	128
Religious Priests in Diocese	94
Total Priests in Diocese	222
Extern Priests in Diocese	63
Ordinations:	
Transitional Deacons	1
Permanent Deacons in Diocese	231
Total Brothers	13
Total Sisters	173
Parishes	
Parishes	92
With Resident Pastor:	
Resident Diocesan Priests	63
Resident Religious Priests	19
Without Resident Pastor:	
Administered by Priests	7
Administered by Deacons	2
Administered by Lay People	1
Missions	23
Pastoral Centers	3
Professional Ministry Personnel:	
Brothers	2
Sisters	33
Lay Ministers	1,780
Welfare	
Catholic Hospitals	1
Total Assisted	115,355
Health Care Centers	1
Total Assisted	14,383
Homes for the Aged	21
Total Assisted	1,031
Day Care Centers	4
Total Assisted	717
Specialized Homes	10
Total Assisted	3,528
Special Centers for Social Services	39
Total Assisted	1,687,416
Residential Care of Disabled	24
Total Assisted	132
Other Institutions	1
Total Assisted	1,215
Educational	
Diocesan Students in Other Seminaries	24
Total Seminarians	24
High Schools, Diocesan and Parish	5
Total Students	3,516
High Schools, Private	1
Total Students	1,322
Elementary Schools, Diocesan and Parish	36
Total Students	9,091
Catechesis/Religious Education:	
High School Students	4,838
Elementary Students	22,066
Total Students under Catholic Instruction	40,857
Teachers in the Diocese:	
Priests	5
Scholastics	1
Brothers	3
Sisters	40
Lay Teachers	897
Vital Statistics	
Receptions into the Church:	
Infant Baptism Totals	9,413
Minor Baptism Totals	778
Adult Baptism Totals	327
Received into Full Communion	1,748
First Communions	8,709
Confirmations	9,805
Marriages:	
Catholic	833
Interfaith	173
Total Marriages	1,006
Deaths	3,050
Total Catholic Population	800,149
Total Population	4,369,735

Former Bishops—Most Revs. EDWARD A. MCCARTHY, D.D., installed Bishop of the Diocese of Phoenix, Dec. 2, 1969; transferred to Coadjutor Archbishop of Miami, July 7, 1976; installed Sept. 17, 1976; died June 7, 2005; JAMES S. RAUSCH, D.D., Ph.D., installed March 22, 1977; died May 18, 1981; THOMAS J. O'BRIEN, D.D. (Retired), ord. May 7, 1961; cons. Jan. 6, 1982; installed Bishop of the Diocese of Phoenix Jan. 18, 1982; retired June 18, 2003.

Vicars General—Most Rev. EDUARDO A. NEVARES, V.G. Tel: 602-354-2477; Rev. FREDRICK J. ADAMSON, V.G. Tel: 602-354-2476.

Moderator of the Curia—Rev. FREDRICK J. ADAMSON, V.G., Diocesan Pastoral Center, 400 E. Monroe, Phoenix, 85004. Tel: 602-354-2180.

Diocesan Office—400 E. Monroe St., Phoenix, 85004-2336. Tel: 602-257-0030; 602-354-2000; Fax: 602-354-2427.

Chancellor—Sr. JEAN STEFFES, C.S.A., 400 E. Monroe St., Phoenix, 85004-2336. Tel: 602-354-2470; Fax: 602-354-2427.

Assistant Chancellor—Rev. MICHAEL L. DISKIN, 400 E. Monroe St., Phoenix, 85004-2336. Tel: 602-354-2471; Fax: 602-354-2427.

College of Consultors—Revs. FREDRICK J. ADAMSON, V.G.; ROBERT ALIUNZI, A.J., V.F.; MICHAEL L. DISKIN; RICHARD R. FELT, V.F., Chm.; CHRISTOPHER J. FRASER, J.C.L.; JOHN LANKEIT; DAVID SANFILIPPO; DANIEL VOLLMER.

Deans—Revs. ROBERT ALIUNZI, A.J., V.F., Northwest Deanery; RICHARD R. FELT, V.F., East Deanery; CHARLES G. KIEFFER, V.F., Central Deanery; KIERAN KLECZEWSKI, V.F., Southwest Deanery; DANIEL MCBRIDE, V.F., South Deanery; PATRICK MOWRER, V.F., North Deanery; DENNIS O'ROURKE, V.F., Northeast Deanery.

Presbyteral Council—Revs. FREDRICK J. ADAMSON, V.G.; ROBERT ALIUNZI, A.J., V.F.; TIMOTHY R. DAVERN, J.C.L.; MICHAEL L. DISKIN; BENOIT DRAPEAU, C.J.M.; JOHN D. EHRICH, S.T.L.; RICHARD R. FELT, V.F.; CHRISTOPHER J. FRASER, J.C.L.; DAVID KELASH; DONALD KLINE; WILLIAM "BILLY" J. KOSCO, Vice Chm.; JOHN LANKEIT, Sec.; GREG MENEGAY; Most Revs. EDUARDO A. NEVARES, V.G.; THOMAS J. OLMSTED, J.C.D.; Revs. GARY R. REGULA; HANS P. RUYGT; DAVID SANFILIPPO; ALONSO SAENZ; GREG SCHLARB; DANIEL VOLLMER, Chm.

Diocesan Tribunal—Office: 400 E. Monroe St., Phoenix, 85004-2336. Tel: 602-354-2275; Fax: 602-354-2424.

Judicial Vicar—Rev. CHRISTOPHER J. FRASER, J.C.L.

Adjutant Judicial Vicar—Rev. ERNESTO REYNOSO, J.C.L.

Director—NICOLE M. DELANEY, J.C.L.

Diocesan Judges—AMY M. ARNOLD, J.C.L.; Rev. CHARLES G. KIEFFER, V.F.; Deacon WILLIAM FINNEGAN, J.C.L.; Rev. TIMOTHY R. DAVERN, J.C.L.

Defenders of the Bond—Revs. ROBERT J. CARUSO; PETER P. DOBROWSKI; JOHN D. EHRICH, S.T.L.; ROBERT FLUMMERFELT, J.D., J.C.L.; DANIELA KNEPPER, J.C.L.; Sr. ELLEN SINCLAIR, S.D.S.

Advocates—Sr. BRIDGET CHAPMAN, M.M.; SANDRA J. CONSIGLIO, M.A.; Rev. PATRICK FARLEY; DEBORAH

MALATIN; WILLIAM AHEARN; CYNTHIA BENZING; Deacon ROBERT CAMPAS; Rev. H. FRED LECLAIRE, C.M.F.; ASENCION MURGA; Deacon JAMES FOGLE; JOZETTE NELMS; Rev. MICAH MUHLEN, O.F.M.; Deacon MILFORD SUIDA; CAMILLE O'MELIA; JAMES O'MELIA; DONNA WICKER; JOAN EDEL; TED EDEL; Deacons CHARLES VOSS; PATRICK TOILOLO; WILLIAM JENKINS; JOHN MACKEN; RYAN QUINN; SUSAN PIETRO; SHERRY BROOKS.

Auditors—NICOLE M. DELANEY, J.C.L.; JUSTINA SANCHEZ; CONSTANCE MANAK.

Promoter of Justice— ad causam AMY M. ARNOLD, J.C.L.

Censor Librorum—Rev. TIMOTHY R. DAVERN, J.C.L.

Notaries—ASENCION MURGA; CONSTANCE MANAK; PATRICIA FISCHER; LINDSAY MARTINEZ; JORGE ERIVES; DEBORAH MALATIN; DAN KERESTES.

Appellate Case Coordinator—CONSTANCE MANAK.

Diocesan Offices

Archives—MARIA BETERAN, Archivist, 400 E. Monroe St., Phoenix, 85004-2336. Tel: 602-354-2475.

Arizona Catholic Conference—Mr. RONALD JOHNSON, Exec. Dir., 400 E. Monroe St., Phoenix, 85004-2336. Tel: 602-354-2390; Fax: 602-354-2466; 602-354-2394.

Black Catholic Ministry—ISAIAH "KIT" MARSHALL, Dir., Diocesan Center, 400 E. Monroe St., Phoenix, 85004. Tel: 602-354-2025.

Buildings & Properties—JOHN MINIERI, Dir. Real Property & Facilities, Diocesan Center, 400 E. Monroe St., Phoenix, 85004-2336. Tel: 602-354-2161; Fax: 602-354-2440.

Catholic Campaign for Human Development/Catholic Relief Services—LISA LALIBERTE, Dir., Diocesan Center, 400 E. Monroe St., Phoenix, 85004-2336. Tel: 602-354-2125.

Catholic Cemeteries— St. Francis, Holy Redeemer, Holy Cross, Queen of Heaven, Calvary, All Souls Rev. MICHAEL L. DISKIN, Spiritual Advisor; GARY L. BROWN, Exec. Dir., Administrative Offices, 2033 N. 48th St., Phoenix, 85008. Tel: 602-267-1329; Fax: 602-685-1516. Calvary Cemetery, 201 W. University, Flagstaff, 86001. Tel: 928-220-2317; Fax: 928-774-1105 (Call First). St. Francis Cemetery, 2033 N. 48th St., Phoenix, 85008. Tel: 602-267-1329; Fax: 602-267-7942. Holy Redeemer Cemetery, 23015 N. Cave Creek Rd., Phoenix, 85040. Tel: 480-513-3243; Fax: 480-513-3293. Holy Cross Cemetery, 10045 W. Thomas Rd., Avondale, 85323. Tel: 623-936-1710; Fax: 623-936-6605. Queen of Heaven Cemetery, 1500 E. Baseline Rd., Mesa, 85204. Tel: 480-892-3729; Fax: 480-813-2826. All Souls Cemetery, 700 N. Bill Gray Rd., Cottonwood, 86326. Tel: 928-649-1998. Mortuary Location: Queen of Heaven Mortuary, 1562 E. Baseline Rd., Mesa, 85204. Tel: 480-892-3729; Fax: 480-813-2826.

"The Catholic Sun"— (Diocesan Newspaper) ROB DEFRANCESCO, Assoc. Publisher; JOHN DAVID LONG-GARCIA, Editor, 400 E. Monroe St., Phoenix, 85004-2336. Tel: 602-354-2139; Fax: 602-354-2429. Email: info@catholicsun.org. Web: www.catholicsun.org.

Child and Youth Protection/Victim Assistance Coordinator—PAUL PFAFFENBERGER, 400 E. Monroe, Phoenix, 85004. Tel: 602-354-2396; Fax: 602-354-2496. Email: ppfaffenberger@diocesephoenix.org.

Communications Office—ROB DEFRANCESCO, 400 E. Monroe, Phoenix, 85004-2336. Tel: 602-354-2130; Fax: 602-354-2429.

Corporate Compliance—MONIKA DALEY, 400 E. Monroe St., Phoenix, 85004-2336. Tel: 602-354-2491.

Diaconate Office—Deacons JAMES TRANT, Dir., 400 E. Monroe St., Phoenix, 85004. Tel: 602-354-2011; Fax: 602-354-2437; DOUGLAS BOGART, Assoc. Dir. Tel: 602-354-2012.

Ecumenical and Interreligious Affairs—Rev. MICHAEL L. DISKIN, Dir., 400 E. Monroe, Phoenix, 85004. Tel: 602-354-2471; Fax: 602-354-2427.

Education and Evangelization, Division of—MARYBETH MUELLER, Exec. Dir., 400 E. Monroe, Phoenix, 85004. Tel: 602-354-2341; Fax: 602-354-2444.

Ethnic Ministries, Division of—Most Rev. EDUARDO A. NEVARES, V.G., Dir. Tel: 602-354-2477; IGNACIO RODRIGUEZ, Assoc. Dir., 400 E. Monroe, Phoenix, 85004. Tel: 602-354-2042; Fax: 602-354-2459.

Family Catechesis/Parish Leadership Support—400 E. Monroe St., Phoenix, 85004. RYAN HANNING, Dir. Tel: 602-354-2321; CARMEN PORTELA, Dir. (Spanish). Tel: 602-354-2031.

Finance Office—JOSEPH ANDERSON, Diocesan Finance Officer, 400 E. Monroe St., Phoenix, 85004-2336. Tel: 602-354-2185; Fax: 602-354-2448.

Hispanic Ministry, Office of—JOSE ROBLES, Dir., 400 E. Monroe St., Phoenix, 85004. Tel: 602-354-2041.

Holy Childhood Association—MARGO GONZALEZ, Dir., 400 E. Monroe, Phoenix, 85004. Tel: 602-354-2005; Fax: 602-354-2442.

Human Resources (Personnel and Benefits)—JOY STEWART, Mgr. Parish Human Resources, 400 E. Monroe, Phoenix, 85004. Tel: 602-354-2201; Fax: 602-354-2428.

John Paul II Resource Center—KATRINA ZENO, Coord., 400 E. Monroe St., Phoenix, 85004-2336. Tel: 602-354-2179.

Kino Institute and Library—

Executive Director—MARYBETH MUELLER. Tel: 602-354-2341.

Librarian—Sr. DARCY PELETICH, O.S.F., M.A., M.L.S. Tel: 602-354-2311.

Director of Parish Leadership Credentialing and Certification—ERIC J. WESTBY, 400 E. Monroe St., Phoenix, 85004-2336. Tel: 602-354-2320.

Lay Employee Retirement Plan—MARK KRYSIAK, 400 E. Monroe St., Phoenix, 85004-2336. Tel: 602-354-2189.

Legal/Office of the General Counsel—JOHN KELLY, Attorney, 400 E. Monroe, Phoenix, 85004. Tel: 602-354-2474; Fax: 602-354-2427.

Marriage and Respect Life, Office of—MIKE PHELAN, Dir., 400 E. Monroe, Phoenix, 85004. Tel: 602-354-2355; Fax: 602-354-2431.

Medical Ethics Board—Rev. JOHN D. EHRICH, S.T.L., Chm., 2312 E. Campbell, Phoenix, 85016-5597.

Native American Ministry, Office of—Rev. DALE JAMISON, O.F.M., Dir., 400 E. Monroe St., Phoenix, 85004. Tel: 602-354-2050.

Natural Family Planning, Office of—CINDY LEONARD, Coord., 400 E. Monroe St., Phoenix, 85004. Tel: 602-354-2122; Fax: 602-354-2124.

Parish Administrative Services Office—MARK KRYSIAK, Dir., 400 E. Monroe St., Phoenix, 85004-2336. Tel: 602-354-2189.

Priests' Assurance Association—Revs. STEVEN KUNKEL, Pres., Christ the King, 1551 E. Dana Ave., Mesa, 85204-1719. Tel: 480-964-1719; TIMOTHY DAVERN, J.C.L., J.V.; MICHAEL DISKIN; CHRISTOPHER J. FRASER, J.C.L.; L. PIERRE HISSEY; CHAD KING; GREG MENEGAY; ANTHONY SIGMAN; ROBERT SKAGEN (Retired); PAUL G. SULLIVAN.

Priests, Vicar for—Rev. DAVID SANFILIPPO.

Priest Personnel—Rev. DAVID SANFILIPPO, Vicar for Priests, 400 E. Monroe, Phoenix, 85004. Tel: 602-354-2480; Fax: 602-354-2427.

Advisory Board for the Continuing Formation of Priests—Rev. DAVID SANFILIPPO, 400 E. Monroe, Phoenix, 85004. Tel: 602-354-2480.

Priestly Life and Ministry Board—Revs. JOSEPH BUI; KIERAN KLECZEWSKI, V.F.; EMILE "BUD" PELLETIER; FAUSTO PENAFIEL; PETER ROSSA; DAVID SANFILIPPO, Chm.; Rev. Msgr. ANTONIO SOTELO (Retired).

Priests' Placement Board—Rev. DAVID SANFILIPPO, 400 E. Monroe, Phoenix, 85004. Tel: 602-354-2480. Members: Revs. CHARLES GORAIEB; DONALD J. KLINE; DOUGLAS E. LORIG; THADDEUS MCGUIRE; ERNESTO REYNOSO, J.C.L.; NIKKI WESTBY; Rev. CHAUNCEY WINKLER.

Prisons, Catholic Ministries To—Deacon PETER MURPHY, Dir., 400 E. Monroe St., Phoenix, 85004. Tel: 602-354-2485. Email: dcnmurphy@diocesephoenix.org.

Youth at Risk—KEVIN STARRS, Coord., 400 E. Monroe, Phoenix, 85004. Tel: 602-518-0377.

Propagation of the Faith—MARGO GONZALEZ, Dir., 400 E. Monroe, Phoenix, 85004. Tel: 602-354-2005; Fax: 602-354-2442.

Religious, Office of—Sr. JEAN STEFFES, C.S.A., Dir., 400 E. Monroe, Phoenix, 85004. Tel: 602-354-2470; Fax: 602-354-2427.

Renewal Ministries, Catholic—Rev. ANDRES ARANGO, eud., Liaison, c/o St. Jerome Parish, 10815 N. 35th Ave., Phoenix, 85029-4299. Tel: 602-942-5555.

Safe Environment Training, Office of—MELANIE TAKINEN, Dir., 400 E. Monroe St., Phoenix, 85004-2336. Tel: 602-354-2208.

Schools, Catholic—MARYBETH MUELLER, Supt. Schools. Tel: 602-354-2341; Sr. MELITA M. PENCHALK, O.S.B.M., Asst. Supt. School. Tel: 602-354-2343; CECILIA FRAKES, Asst. Supt., 400 E. Monroe, Phoenix, 85004. Tel: 602-354-2342; Fax: 602-354-2432.

Scouting, Catholic Committee on—Rev. DENNIS O'ROURKE, V.F., Liaison, St. Gabriel, 32648 N. Cave Creek Rd., Cave Creek, 85331. Tel: 480-595-0883; Fax: 480-595-0886.

Stewardship Office— (Charity & Development Appeal) Rev. GREGORY SCHLARB, Vicar, 400 E. Monroe St., Phoenix, 85004. Tel: 602-354-2215; Fax: 602-354-2432; MISSIE D'ANNOY, Dir. Stewardship. Tel: 602-354-2216; CARYN MERON, Dir. Research & Planning. Tel: 602-354-2484.

Vocations Office—Revs. PAUL G. SULLIVAN, Dir., 400 E. Monroe, Phoenix, 85004. Tel: 602-257-2004; Fax: 602-354-2442. Email: frsullivan@diocesephoenix.org; MATTHEW LOWRY, Assoc. Dir., 520 W. Riordan Rd., Flagstaff, 86001. Tel: 928-779-2903; Fax: 928-779-0698.

Worship and Liturgy, Office of—Revs. KIERAN KLECZEWSKI, V.F., Exec. Dir. Tel: 602-354-2113; JOHN MUIR, Asst. Dir., 400 E. Monroe St., Phoenix, 85004. Tel: 602-354-2110.

CLERGY, PARISHES, MISSIONS AND PAROCHIAL SCHOOLS

CITY OF PHOENIX

(MARICOPA COUNTY)

1—SS. SIMON AND JUDE ROMAN CATHOLIC CATHEDRAL (1953) Revs. John Lankeit, Rector; Raul Lopez Marzetti; Matthew Henry; Deacons Charles Shaw; Tony West; Juan Guzman, (Retired). In Res., Most Rev. Thomas J. Olmsted.

Res.: 6351 N. 27th Ave., 85017. Tel: 602-242-1300; Fax: 602-249-3768.

School—(Grades K-8) Tel: 602-242-1299. Sr. Raphael Quinn, I.B.V.M., Prin.; Ms. Gail Castro, Librarian. Sisters 1; Lay Teachers 20; Students 475.

Santa Rosa Hall—1903 W. Ocotillo Rd., 85017.

Convent—Sisters of Loreto (I.B.V.M.), Tel: 602-242-2544.

2—ST. AGNES ROMAN CATHOLIC PARISH (1940) Revs. Bradley L. Peterson, O.Carm., Admin.; Patrick Gavin, O.Carm.; Deacon Jesse Sanchez.

Church & Res.: 1954 N. 24th St., 85008. Tel: 602-244-0349; Fax: 602-244-0054.

School—(Grades PreSchool-8), 2311 E. Palm Ln., 85006. Tel: 602-244-1451. Denise Campbell, Prin.; Ms. Teri Kucera, Librarian. Lay Teachers 14; Students 208.

3—ST. ANTHONY ROMAN CATHOLIC PARISH (1943) Revs. Alfredo Frutades, I.V.E.; Rolando Santoianni, I.V.E.; Miguel Zavala, I.V.E.; Deacon Lowell O'Grady.

Church & Res.: 909 S. First Ave., 85003. Tel: 602-252-1771; Fax: 602-258-4714.

Convent—Sister Servants of the Lord and the Virgin of Matura, S.S.V.M.

Center-St. Pius X—, Closed 2004. Currently used for Unity Mass for Black Catholic Ministry, the Croatian Community and the Sudanese Community.

4—ST. AUGUSTINE ROMAN CATHOLIC PARISH (1970) Revs. Carlos Gomez; Jose Garibaldi Ballesteros Urias; Deacons James Hamilton, (Retired); Lorenzo McKnight; Ricardo Gonzalez.

Church: 3630 N. 71st Ave., 85033. Tel: 623-849-3131; Fax: 623-849-5689.

5—ST. BENEDICT ROMAN CATHOLIC PARISH (1985) Rev. Gary R. Regula; Deacons John Benware; Douglas Davaz.

Church: 16223 S. 48th St., 85048. Tel: 480-961-1610; Fax: 480-961-1794.

School—St. John Bosco Catholic School, (Grades PreSchool-8), 16035 S. 48th St., 85048. Tel: 480-219-4848; Fax: 480-219-5767. Email: sconner@sjbosco.org. Web: www.sjbosco.org. Shelley Conner, Prin.; Theresa Harvey, Librarian. Lay Teachers 30; Students 518.

6—ST. CATHERINE OF SIENA ROMAN CATHOLIC PARISH (1947) Revs. Alonso Saenz; Thielo Ramirez; Deacon Carlos Terrazas.

Res.: 6401 S. Central Ave., 85042. Tel: 602-276-5581; Fax: 602-276-2119.

School—(Grades K-8), 6413 S. Central Ave., 85040. Tel: 602-276-2241, Ext. 251; Fax: 602-268-7886. Ms. Catherine Lucero, Prin. & Preschool Dir. Lay Teachers 12; Students 210.

School—Preschool Lay Teachers 4; Students 31.

7—CORPUS CHRISTI ROMAN CATHOLIC PARISH (1985) Revs. Albert F.H. Hoorman; Rafael Bercasio; Deacons Alexander Gaudio, (Retired); Patrick Flynn, (Retired); Philip Simeone; Robert England.

Res.: 3550 E. Knox, 85044. Tel: 480-893-8770; Fax: 480-893-3291.

8—ST. EDWARD CONFESSOR ROMAN CATHOLIC PARISH (1976) Revs. Oscar Gutierrez, M.D.M., Parochial Admin.; Martin Munoz, M.D.M.

Mailing Address: P.O. Box 27948, Tempe, 85285.

Church: 4410 E. Southern Ave., 85042. Tel: 602-268-2632; Fax: 602-268-8909.

9—ST. FRANCIS XAVIER ROMAN CATHOLIC PARISH (1928) Revs. Daniel J. Sullivan, S.J.; John Auther, S.J.; John M. Martin, S.J.; David J. Robinson, S.J.; Deacon Thomas Klein.

Church: 4715 N. Central Ave., 85012-1796. Tel: 602-279-9547; Fax: 602-248-8968.

School—(Grades PreK-8) Tel: 602-266-5364. Kim Cavnar, Prin.; Mary Ellen Olivieri, Librarian. Lay Teachers 37; Students 588.

10—ST. GREGORY ROMAN CATHOLIC PARISH (1947)

Rev. Emile Pelletier Jr.; Deacons Lee Kloft, (Retired); Edward Bolton, (Retired); Angel Guzman. In Res., Most Rev. Eduardo A. Nevares; Rev. David Sanfilippo.
Res.: 3424 N. 18th Ave., 85015. Tel: 602-264-4488; Fax: 602-266-5210.
School—(Grades PreSchool-8), 3440 N. 18th Ave., 85015. Tel: 602-266-9527. Maureen DeGrose, Prin. Sisters 2; Lay Teachers 29; Students 296.

11—HOLY FAMILY ROMAN CATHOLIC PARISH (1968) Revs. Oscar Gutierrez, M.D.M.; Martin Munoz, M.D.M.
Mailing Address: P.O. Box 27948, Tempe, 85285.
Church: 6802 S. 24th St., 85040. Tel: 602-268-2632; Fax: 602-268-8909.

12—IMMACULATE HEART OF MARY ROMAN CATHOLIC PARISH (1924) Revs. Alfredo Frutades, I.V.E.; Rolando Santoianni, I.V.E.; Miguel Zavala, I.V.E.; Deacon Lowell O'Grady.
Church: 909 E. Washington St., 85034. Tel: 602-253-6129; Fax: 602-253-4210.

13—ST. JEROME ROMAN CATHOLIC PARISH (1962) Revs. Andres Arango, C.J.M.; Benoit Drapeau, C.J.M.; Deacons Schubert Wenzel; William Bidleman, (Retired); Dick Rein; William DeMarco.
Church: 10815 N. 35th Ave., 85029. Tel: 602-942-5555; Fax: 602-504-9115.
School—(Grades PreSchool-8) Tel: 602-942-5644. Carl Hodus, Prin. Lay Teachers 17; Students 261.

14—ST. JOAN OF ARC ROMAN CATHOLIC PARISH (1979) Revs. Donald J. Kline; Nicholas A. Floridi; Deacon James Springer, (Retired).
Church: 3801 E. Greenway Rd., 85032-4698. Tel: 602-867-9171; Fax: 602-482-7930.
School—Preschool, 2yrs.-PreK, Tel: 602-867-9179. Debbie Hilliard, Dir. Students 35.

15—ST. JOSEPH ROMAN CATHOLIC PARISH (1969) Rev. John Greb; Deacon Shawn French. In Res., Deacon James Trant.
Res.: 11001 N. 40th St., 85028. Tel: 602-996-5120; Fax: 602-996-4011.

16—ST. LUKE ROMAN CATHOLIC PARISH (1985) Rev. Pawel Stawarczyk.
Church: 19644 N. Seventh Ave., 85027. Tel: 623-582-0561; Fax: 623-434-3182.

17—ST. MARK ROMAN CATHOLIC PARISH (1946) Revs. Charles G. Kieffer, Canonical Pastor; Fausto Penafiel; Francisco Alejo, O.F.M.
Res.: 400 N. 30th St., 85008. Tel: 602-267-0503; Fax: 602-275-7261.

18—ST. MARTIN DE PORRES ROMAN CATHOLIC PARISH (1973) Revs. Oscar Gutierrez, M.D.M.; Martin Munoz, M.D.M.
Mailing Address: P.O. Box 27948, Tempe, 85285-7948.
Church: 3851 W. Wier Ave., 85041. Tel: 602-276-2466; Fax: 602-232-2147.

19—ST. MARY'S ROMAN CATHOLIC BASILICA (1881) Revs. Vincent Mesi, O.F.M.; Micah Muhlen, O.F.M. In Res., Rev. Luis Baldonado, O.F.M. (Retired).
Res.: 231 N. Third St., 85004. Tel: 602-354-2100; Fax: 602-354-2060.

20—MATER MISERICORDIAE MISSION Rev. J. Terra, F.S.S.P.
1537 W. Monroe St., 85007. Tel: 602-253-6090. Web: www.phoenixlatinmass.org.

21—ST. MATTHEW ROMAN CATHOLIC PARISH (1939) Rev. Raymond J. Ritari; Deacons Anthony Beltran; Matias Valle.
Church: 320 N. 20th Dr., 85009. Tel: 602-258-1789; Fax: 602-258-6507.
School—(Grades K-8), 2038 W. Van Buren, 85009. Tel: 602-254-0611. Gena McGowan, Prin. Lay Teachers 16; Students 190.

22—MOST HOLY TRINITY ROMAN CATHOLIC PARISH (1951) Revs. Alphonsus Bakyil, S.O.L.T.; Daniel Lemence, S.O.L.T.; Deacons J.R. Dalisay, D.S.; Donald Kuban.
Res.: 8620 N. Seventh St., 85020. Tel: 602-944-3375; Fax: 602-943-2323.
School—(Grades PreK-8), 535 E. Alice Ave., 85020. Tel: 602-943-9058. Michael Brennan, Prin. & Dir. (Preschool). Sisters 2; Lay Teachers 11; Students 124.
Convent—Sisters of the Society of Our Lady of the Most Holy Trinity, Tel: 602-568-0601.

23—OUR LADY OF CZESTOCHOWA ROMAN CATHOLIC PARISH (2008) Rev. Jacek Wesolowski, S.Ch.
Church: 2828 W. Country Gables Dr., 85053. Tel: 602-212-1172; Fax: 602-212-1173.
Convent—Missionary Sisters of Christ the King for Polonia, Tel: 602-680-7646. Sr. Bozena Blad, M.Ch.R., Supr.

24—OUR LADY OF FATIMA MISSION Rev. Paul G. Sullivan, Interim Parochial Admin., 1414 S. 17th Ave., 85007. Tel: 602-258-5504.
1418 S. 17th Ave., 85007. Tel: 602-254-4944.
Convent—Missionaries of Charity, Gift of Mary Convent, 1414 S. 17th Ave., 85007. Tel: 602-258-5504.

25—OUR LADY OF THE VALLEY ROMAN CATHOLIC PARISH (1973) Rev. Edward J. Kaminski, C.S.C., Admin.; Deacons Robert Manthie; Richard Meidl.
Church: 3220 W. Greenway Rd., 85053. Tel: 602-993-1213; Fax: 602-993-1223.

26—ST. PAUL ROMAN CATHOLIC PARISH (1976) Revs. Gregory J. Schlarb; Robert Binta; Deacons Bill Vivio; Guy Goubeaux. In Res., Rev. Michael J. Boyle, C.M.
Church: 330 W. Coral Gables Dr., 85023. Tel: 602-942-2608; Fax: 602-548-0708.

27—ST. PHILIP THE DEACON MISSION, A QUASI-PARISH Revs. Charles G. Kieffer, Canonical Pastor; Fausto Penafiel; Francisco Alejo, O.F.M.
615 N. 20th St., Maricopa Co. 85006. Tel: 602-253-1076.

28—SACRED HEART ROMAN CATHOLIC PARISH (1962) Rev. Msgr. Antonio Sotelo (Retired); Ms. Ann Conway, Parish Life Coord.; Deacon Jose Olivares.
Church: 1421 S. 12th St., 85034. Tel: 602-258-2089.

29—ST. THERESA ROMAN CATHOLIC PARISH (1955) Revs. Charles G. Kieffer; Francisco Colasito; Deacons Colin Campbell; Sione Hola. In Res., Rev. William Schmid.
Church: 5045 E. Thomas Rd., 85018. Tel: 602-840-0850; Fax: 602-840-0871.
School—(Grades PreSchool-8), 5001 E. Thomas Rd., 85018. Tel: 602-840-0010. Ms. Maureen Fyan, Prin.; Catherine Downey, Dir. (Preschool); Amy Enahas, Librarian. Lay Teachers 37; Students 530.

30—ST. THOMAS THE APOSTLE ROMAN CATHOLIC PARISH (1950) Revs. John D. Ehrich; Oliver Vietor; Deacons Thomas Bills; Douglas Bogart; Ken Miller, (Retired).
Church: 2312 E. Campbell Ave., 85016-5597. Tel: 602-954-9089; Fax: 602-956-3454.
School—(Grades K-8), 4510 N. 24th St., 85016. Tel: 602-954-9088. Mary Coffman, Prin.; Meg Bushard, Librarian. Sisters 3; Lay Teachers 28; Students 499.
Convent—4550 N. 24th St., 85016. Tel: 602-368-5238. Dominican Srs. of Mary, Mother of the Eucharist.

31—VIETNAMESE MARTYRS PARISH ROMAN CATHOLIC PARISH (2004) Revs. Joseph Nguyen, O.P.; Tich Van Ngo, O.P.
2915 W. Northern Ave., 85051. Tel: 602-395-0421.

32—ST. VINCENT DE PAUL ROMAN CATHOLIC PARISH (1957) Revs. Kilian McCaffrey; Robert Bolding; Deacons William Jenkins; Lorenzo Salazar, (Retired); Ernesto Ramirez.
Church: 3140 N. 51st Ave., 85031. Tel: 623-247-6871; Fax: 623-247-4457.
School—(Grades PreSchool-8), 3130 N. 51st Ave., 85031. Tel: 623-247-8595; Fax: 623-245-0132. Sr. Julie Kubasak, D.C., Prin. Sisters 3; Lay Teachers 19; Students 436.
Convent—Daughters of Charity, 3130 N. 51st Ave., 85031. Tel: 623-247-8916.

OUTSIDE THE CITY OF PHOENIX

ANTHEM, MARICOPA CO., ST. ROSE PHILIPPINE DUCHESNE ROMAN CATHOLIC PARISH (2004) Rev. Mark Harrington; Deacons William Clower; John D'Amico.
2825 W. Rose Canyon Cir., 85086. Tel: 623-465-9740; Fax: 623-742-7031.

ASHFORK, YAVAPAI CO. , ST. ANNE ROMAN CATHOLIC MISSION, A QUASI-PARISH Rev. Bruno Cuario.
47047 7th St., 86320. Mailing Address: P.O. Box 525, Ash Fork, 86320. Tel: 928-637-2458.

AVONDALE, MARICOPA CO., ST. THOMAS AQUINAS ROMAN CATHOLIC PARISH Revs. Kieran Kleczewski; Jorge Canez, Parochial Vicar; Deacons Al Scheller, (Retired); Milford Suida; Jason Robinson; Edgar Carnecer.
Church: 13720 W. Thomas Rd., 85323. Tel: 623-935-2151; Fax: 623-935-5044.
School—(Grades PreK-8) Mr. Patrick Reardon, Prin. Lay Teachers 20; Students 312.

BAGDAD, YAVAPAI CO., ST. FRANCIS OF ASSISI ROMAN CATHOLIC PARISH (1959) Rev. Leonardo J. Vargas, Admin.
Mailing Address: P.O. Box 768, 86321.
Church & Rectory: 220 Cook St., 86321. Tel: 928-633-2389.

BAPCHULE, PINAL CO., ST. PETER (1950) Rev. Dale Jamison, O.F.M., Canonical Pastor; Deacon Peter Fejes.
Mailing Address: P.O. Box 545, Sacaton, 85147. Tel: 520-560-2690.
1500 N. St. Peter Rd., 85151.
School—(Grades K-8), 1500 N. St. Peter Rd., P.O. Box 10840, 85151. Tel: 520-315-3835; Fax: 520-315-3963. Sr. Martha Mary Carpenter, O.S.F., Prin. Sisters 6; Lay Teachers 7; Students 195.
Convent—Franciscan Sisters of Christian Charity (Manitowoc, WI), P.O. Box 10840, 85151. Tel: 520-315-3645.
Mission—Holy Family Blackwater Rd., Blackwater, Pinal Co. Tel: 520-562-3716. P.O. Box 1058, Coolidge, 85228.
Mission—Our Lady of Victory Sacaton Flats, Pinal Co. Tel: 520-562-3716. P.O. Box 1442, Sacaton, 85147.
Mission—St. Anne Santan, Pinal Co. Tel: 520-562-3716. P.O. Box 1297, Sacaton, 85147.
Mission—St. Anthony S. Church St., Sacaton, Pinal Co. Tel: 520-562-3716. P.O. Box 783, Sacaton, 85147.
Field House at St. Anthony— Sisters 2.
Mission—St. Francis 16657 N. Church St., Maricopa, Pinal Co. 85139.

BLACK CANYON CITY, YAVAPAI CO., ST. PHILIP BENIZI ROMAN CATHOLIC MISSION, A QUASI-PARISH Rev. Mark Harrington, Canonical Pastor; Deacon Leslie Stokes.
34621 Black Canyon Hwy., P.O. Box 138, 85324. Tel: 623-374-5392; Fax: 623-374-9768.

BUCKEYE, MARICOPA CO., SAINT HENRY ROMAN CATHOLIC PARISH (1956) Rev. William "Billy" J. Kosco; Deacons George Cameron; Mark Gribowski; Victor Leon.
Church: 128 S. Third St., 85326. Tel: 623-386-6407; Fax: 623-386-4328.

BULLHEAD CITY, MOHAVE CO., ST. MARGARET MARY ROMAN CATHOLIC PARISH (1947) Revs. Peter P. Dobrowski; Julius Kayiwa; Deacons Richard Eckert; John Del Quadro.
Church: 1691 N. Oatman Rd., 86442. Tel: 928-758-7117; Fax: 928-758-2345.

CAMP VERDE, YAVAPAI CO., ST. FRANCES CABRINI ROMAN CATHOLIC PARISH (1962) Revs. Reynaldo Clutario, S.O.L.T.; Alvin Cayetano, S.O.L.T.
Res.: P.O. Box 1677, 86322-1677. Tel: 928-567-3543.
Church: 781 S. Cliffs Pkwy., 86322. Tel: 928-567-3543; Fax: 928-567-7058.

CAREFREE, MARICOPA CO., OUR LADY OF JOY ROMAN CATHOLIC PARISH (1972) Revs. Patrick Farley; Herbert Hauck.
Mailing Address: P.O. Box 1359, 85377.
Church: 36811 N. Pima Rd., 85377. Tel: 480-488-2229 (Church); Fax: 480-488-1085.
School—(Grades K) Tel: 480-595-6409. Christine Tax, Dir. Lay Teachers 7; Students 43.

CASHION, MARICOPA CO., ST. WILLIAM ROMAN CATHOLIC PARISH (1973) Rev. Mario Garcia-Icedo, Admin.; Deacon James Cascio.
Mailing Address: P.O. Box 329, 85329.
Church: 11003 W. Third St., 85329. Tel: 623-936-6115; Fax: 623-936-8308.
Chapel—Our Lady of Guadalupe Santa Maria. 6807 Lower Buckeye Rd., Maricopa Co. 85043.

CAVE CREEK, MARICOPA CO., ST. GABRIEL ROMAN CATHOLIC PARISH (2002) Revs. Dennis O'Rourke; Benedict Onegiu, Parochial Vicar; Deacons James Fogle; Robert Torigian; James Sejba.
32648 N. Cave Creek Rd., 85331. Tel: 480-595-0883; Fax: 480-595-0886.
School—Annunciation Catholic School, (Grades 1-3) Dr. Sharon Pristash, Prin. Lay Teachers 6; Students 72.

CHANDLER, MARICOPA CO.

1—ST. ANDREW THE APOSTLE ROMAN CATHOLIC PARISH (1985) Revs. John R. Coleman; Richard McGuire, O.S.C.; Deacons Ernest Garcia; Donald Crawford; David Runyan.
Church: 3450 W. Ray Rd., 85226. Tel: 480-899-1990; Fax: 480-917-8475.

2—ST. MARY ROMAN CATHOLIC PARISH (1937) Revs. Daniel McBride; Johnrita Adegboyega; Alfredo Valdez Molina; Deacons Bruce Bennett; Mike Kronschnabel; Manuel Olivas; Garry Jolliffe.
Church: 230 W. Galveston, 85225. Tel: 480-963-3207; Fax: 480-814-9417.
School—St. Mary-Basha Catholic Elementary, (Grades K-8), 200 W. Galveston, 85225. Tel: 480-963-4951. Sr. Mary Norbert Long, S.C., Prin. Sisters of Charity of Seton Hill 2; Lay Teachers 24; Students 483.
Convent—Sisters of Charity, Seton Hill, 496 W. Ivanhoe, 85225. Tel: 480-963-5038.

CHINO VALLEY, YAVAPAI CO., ST. CATHERINE LABOURE ROMAN CATHOLIC MISSION, A QUASI-PARISH Rev. H. Fred LeClaire, C.M.F., Admin.; Deacon Michael Holmes.
2062 N. Hwy. 89, 86323. Mailing Address: P.O. Box 152, 86323-0152. Tel: 928-636-4071; Fax: 928-636-1945. Email: stcathlab@juno.com.

CONGRESS, YAVAPAI CO., GOOD SHEPHERD OF THE DESERT MISSION, **Quasi-Parish.** Rev. Msgr. George Highberger, Canonical Pastor.
P.O. Box 1134, Yavapai Co. 85332. Tel: 928-427-6328.

COTTONWOOD, YAVAPAI CO., IMMACULATE CONCEPTION ROMAN CATHOLIC PARISH (1966) Rev. David Kelash; Deacons James Brown; David Kaminsky; Onofre Duran, (Retired).
Church: 700 N. Bill Gray Rd., 86326. Tel: 928-634-2933; Fax: 928-634-3326.
School—St. Joseph Catholic School, (Grades PreK-8), 2715 E. Hwy. 89A, P.O. Box 370, 86326. Tel: 928-649-0624; Fax: 928-649-1191. Email: info@stjcmvv.com. Web: www.sjcms.net. Greg Kirkham, Prin. Lay Teachers 8; Students 97.

Mission—St. Cecilia Clarkdale, Yavapai Co. Currently site for Tridentine Mass. Closed 2002, for sacramental records contact Immaculate Conception, Cottonwood.
Mission—Holy Family, (Closed 2004), Jerome, Yavapai Co.

DOLAN SPRINGS, MOHAVE CO., OUR LADY OF THE DESERT MISSION, A QUASI-PARISH Rev. Peter P. Dobrowski, Canonical Pastor.
15385 N. Pierce Ferry Rd., 86441. Tel: 928-767-7117; Fax: 928-758-7117.

EL MIRAGE, MARICOPA CO., SANTA TERESITA ROMAN CATHOLIC PARISH (1968) Rev. Stephen Schack; Deacon Jose Orozco.
P.O. Box 67, 85335. Tel: 623-583-8183; Fax: 623-583-2963.
Church: 14016 N. Verbena St., 85335.

FLAGSTAFF, COCONINO CO., SAN FRANCISCO DE ASIS ROMAN CATHOLIC PARISH (1997) Revs. Patrick Mowrer; Victor Yakubu; Michael Accinni Reinhardt; Deacons Lawrence Whelan; James Bret; Ronald Johnson; Robert Olberding; Dennis Revering; James Arnold, (Retired); Douglas Rade, (Retired).
Mailing Address: 2257 E. Cedar Ave., 86004-1918. Tel: 928-779-1341; Fax: 928-779-5124.
Holy Trinity Newman Center—520 W. Riordan Rd., 86002. Tel: 928-779-2903; Fax: 928-779-0698. Rev. Matthew Lowry, Chap. & Asst. Dir. Vocations.
School—San Francisco de Asis, (Grades PreSchool-8), 320 N. Humphrey, 86001. Tel: 928-779-1337; Fax: 928-774-1943. Mary Frances Malinoski, Prin. Lay Teachers 13; Students 219.
Convent—Institute of the Blessed Virgin Mary Loretto Sisters, 202 S. Kendrick, 86001. Tel: 520-744-3680.
Chapel—Nativity of B.V.M. 16 W. Cherry Ave., 86001.
Chapel—Our Lady of Guadalupe 224 S. Kendrick, 86001.
Chapel—St. Pius X 2257 E. Cedar Ave., 86004.

FOUNTAIN HILLS, MARICOPA CO., ASCENSION ROMAN CATHOLIC PARISH (1976) Rev. John T. McDonough; Deacons Richard Smith; Phillip LoCascio.
Church: 12615 Fountain Hills Blvd., 85268. Tel: 480-837-1066; Fax: 480-837-9093.
Mission—St. Dominic 25603 N. Danny Ln., Ste. 2, Rio Verde, Maricopa Co. 85263. Tel: 480-471-2112.

GILA BEND, MARICOPA CO., ST. MICHAEL ROMAN CATHOLIC PARISH (1963) Rev. Kieran Kleczewski, Parochial Admin.
Mailing Address: 13720 W. Thomas Rd., Avondale, 85323. Tel: 623-935-2151 (St. Thomas Aquinas).
Church: 314 Dodson St., 85337-0357.

GILBERT, MARICOPA CO.
1—ST. ANNE ROMAN CATHOLIC PARISH (1943) Revs. David Sanfilippo, Interim Canonical Pastor; Charles Casale, Parochial Vicar; Deacons Joe Spadafino; Keith Boswell; Joseph Cady. In Res., Rev. Stephen Adrian (Retired).
Church: 440 E. Elliot Rd., 85299-0228. Tel: 480-892-0905; Fax: 480-505-6034.
Convent—Carmelite Sisters, M.C.S.T.N.J., 206 E. Palo Verde St., 85296. Tel: 480-633-3729.
2—ST. MARY MAGDALENE ROMAN CATHOLIC PARISH Revs. Greg Menegay; Matthew Jacob, D.S.; Deacons Robert Carey; Craig Hintze; Gerald O'Toole; William Shea, (Retired).
Mailing Address: 2654 E. Williams Field Rd., 85296. Tel: 480-279-6737; Fax: 480-279-6786.
Church: 2654 E. Williams Field Rd., 85296.

GLENDALE, MARICOPA CO.
1—ST. HELEN ROMAN CATHOLIC PARISH (1974) Revs. R. Bruce Downs; James J. Ferguson, C.S.C.; Deacons Joseph Shinske, (Retired); Robert Campas; John Mickel.
Church: 5510 W. Cholla, 85304. Tel: 623-979-4202; Fax: 623-412-1226.
2—ST. JAMES ROMAN CATHOLIC PARISH (1982) Revs. Robert Aliunzi, A.J.; John R. Ssegawa, A.J.; Deacons Alan Bowslaugh; Frank Devine; Jack O'Connor, (Retired).
Church: 19640 N. 35th Ave., 85308. Tel: 623-581-0707; Fax: 623-581-0110.
Res.: 18225 N. 35th Dr., 85308. Tel: 623-843-0421.
3—ST. LOUIS THE KING ROMAN CATHOLIC PARISH (1962) Revs. Michael L. Diskin, Canonical Pastor; Joseph Bui; Deacons Joseph Stickney; Eduardo Zavala.
Church: 4331 W. Maryland Ave., 85301. Tel: 623-930-1127; Fax: 623-930-1129.
School—(Grades PreK-8) Tel: 623-939-4260. Jane Daigle, Prin.; Jennifer Weworski, Preschool Dir. Lay Teachers 11; Students 214.
4—OUR LADY OF PERPETUAL HELP ROMAN CATHOLIC PARISH (1947) Revs. Michael Straley; Jose Jesus Lopez; Deacons Albert Gonzalez; Anthony Lopez; Robert Myers; Dennis Raczkowski.
Church: 5614 W. Orangewood Ave., 85301. Tel: 623-939-9785; Fax: 623-934-8854.
School—(Grades PreSchool-8), 7521 N. 57th Ave., 85301. Tel: 623-931-7288. Sr. Mary Doris Anne Okere, I.H.M., Prin. Sisters 4; Lay Teachers 11; Students 176.
Chapel—Our Lady of Guadalupe 6733 N. 55th Ave., 85301.
5—ST. RAPHAEL ROMAN CATHOLIC PARISH (1974) Rev. Edward J. Kaminski, C.S.C., Canonical Pastor; Deacons Richard Meidl; Robert Manthie.
Church: 5525 W. Acoma, 85306. Tel: 602-938-4227; Fax: 602-978-0305.
6—ST. THOMAS MORE ROMAN CATHOLIC PARISH (1997) Rev. James Turner; Deacons Roy Drapeau; Richard Kijewski.
6180 W. Utopia Rd., 85308-7111. Tel: 623-566-8222; Fax: 623-825-1468.

GOODYEAR, MARICOPA CO., SAINT JOHN VIANNEY ROMAN CATHOLIC PARISH (1956) Revs. Tom Eckert, C.S.C.; John Korcsmar, C.S.C.; Paul Ybarra, C.S.C.; Deacon Greg Galloway.
Church: 539 La Pasada Blvd., 85338. Tel: 602-932-3313; Fax: 602-932-1896.
School—(Grades PreSchool-8) Tel: 623-932-2434. Sr. Cecilia Henry, F.M.A., Prin.; Cindi Zulegu, Dir. Sisters 3; Lay Teachers 17; Students 225.
Convent—F.M.A., Salesian Sisters, 15 W. Loma Linda Blvd., Avondale, 85323. Tel: 623-932-2652; Fax: 623-932-1243.

GRAND CANYON, COCONINO CO., EL CRISTO REY ROMAN CATHOLIC PARISH (1960) Revs. Patrick Mowrer, Canonical Pastor; Boniface Akara, C.M.F. Mailing Address: P.O. Box 505, 86023. Tel: 928-638-2390.
Church: 44 Albright Ave., 86023.

GUADALUPE, MARICOPA CO., OUR LADY OF GUADALUPE ROMAN CATHOLIC PARISH (1970) Rev. Joseph A. Baur, O.F.M., Admin.; Deacon Santo Bernasconi.
Church: 5445 San Angelo St., 85283. Tel: 480-839-2860.
Res.: 9004 Calle Maravilla, 85283. Tel: 480-839-2376.

KINGMAN, MOHAVE CO., ST. MARY ROMAN CATHOLIC PARISH (1906) Rev. Matthew Krempel, O.F.M., Parochial Admin.; Deacons Anthony Picciano, (Retired); Philip Wisely.
Church: 302 E. Spring St., 86401. Tel: 928-753-3359; Fax: 928-753-2581.

LAKE HAVASU CITY, MOHAVE CO., OUR LADY OF THE LAKE ROMAN CATHOLIC PARISH (1969) Revs. Chauncey Winkler; Thomas Kawai; Deacons Thomas C. Coe; Jeffrey Arner; Gilbert Lopez; John Navaretta; Patrick Toilolo; Thomas DeFilippis, (Retired).
Church: 1975 Daytona Dr., 86403. Tel: 928-855-2685; Fax: 928-855-7172.
School—Preschool & Kindergarten, (Grades PreK-K) Tel: 928-855-0154. and Kindergarten Lay Teachers 5; Students 37.

LAVEEN, MARICOPA CO., ST. JOHN THE BAPTIST (1950) Deacon James Trant, Parish Life Coord.; Rev. Dale Jamison, O.F.M., Canonical Pastor; Deacons Clement Anselmo; Ron Poulin.
Mailing Address: P.O. Box 693, 85339-0693. Tel: 520-550-2034; Fax: 520-550-4873. 5407 W. Pecos Rd., 85339.
Mission—St. Catherine 3986 S. Santa Cruz Rd., 85339. Tel: 602-292-4466.
Mission—St. Francis of Assisi, Pima-Maricopa Indian Community, Salt River., 3040 N. Longmore, Scottsdale, 85256. Tel: 602-292-4466.
Mission—San Lucy 1120C St., Gila Bend, Pinal Co. 85337. Tel: 602-354-2050.
Blessed Kateri Tekakwitha Spirituality Center/St. John's Convent—Tel: 520-550-5522. Deacon James Trant.
Chapel—St. Paschal Baylon 400 E. Oak, Mesa, 85204. Tel: 602-292-4466.

MAYER, YAVAPAI CO., ST. JOSEPH ROMAN CATHOLIC MISSION, A QUASI-PARISH Rev. Reynaldo Clutario, S.O.L.T.
10901 S. Hwy. 69, 86333. Mailing Address: P.O. Box 171, 86333-0171. Tel: 928-632-4018.

MESA, MARICOPA CO.
1—ALL SAINTS ROMAN CATHOLIC PARISH (1972) Rev. Robert J. Caruso; Deacons T. Vincent Neely, (Retired); Reed Santa, (Retired); Gordon Aird; Bernard Filzen; Albro Wilson; Michael Carr; Winfred Clapham; John Scott.
Church: 1534 N. Recker Rd., 85205. Tel: 480-985-7655; Fax: 480-396-0837.
2—ST. BRIDGET ROMAN CATHOLIC PARISH (1985) Rev. W. Scott Brubaker; Deacon Paul Hursh.
Res.: 2850 E. Lockwood St., 85213. Tel: 480-924-9138.
Church: 2213 N. Lindsay Rd., 85213. Tel: 480-924-9111; Fax: 480-924-3103.
3—CHRIST THE KING ROMAN CATHOLIC PARISH (1959) Revs. Steven Kunkel; Camilo de Villa, Parochial Vicar; Deacons Willard Capistrant; Ronald Ruiz; Tom Bishop; Neil Tift.
1505 E. Dana Ave., 85204.
Church: 1551 E. Dana Ave., 85204. Tel: 480-964-1719; Fax: 480-844-4498.
School—(Grades PreSchool-8) Tel: 480-844-4480. Don Graff, Prin. Lay Teachers 18; Students 236.
Convent—Parish Visitors of Mary Immaculate (P.V.M.I.), 1534 E. Dana Ave., 85204. Tel: 480-969-2384.
4—ST. COLUMBA KIM ROMAN CATHOLIC MISSION, A QUASI PARISH Rev. Young Chang Lee, Parochial Admin.
1375 N. McClintock Dr., Chandler, 85226. Tel: 480-446-7121.
5—HOLY CROSS ROMAN CATHOLIC PARISH (1978) Revs. Richard R. Felt; John Shetler, Parochial Vicar; Jun Baula; Deacons Thomas Ferreira; James Gersitz; Gene Messer; Joe Scaccia; William Finnegan; Ignacio Ixta.
Church: 1244 S. Power Rd., 85206. Tel: 480-981-2021; Fax: 480-981-6844.
6—QUEEN OF PEACE ROMAN CATHOLIC PARISH (1934) Revs. Charles Goraieb; Thomas Bennett, L.C., Parish Admin.; Jesus G. Ty, Parochial Vicar; Deacons John Riedel; Richard Areyzaga; Santiago Rodriguez; Jamie Whitford; Thomas Phelan; Richard Yanez.
Church: 141 N. Macdonald St., 85201. Tel: 480-969-9166; Fax: 480-969-8102.
School—(Grades PreK-8), 109 N. Macdonald St., 85201. Tel: 602-969-0226. Sr. Dorothy Zeller, S.S.N.D., Prin. Sisters 1; Lay Teachers 12; Students 185.
7—ST. TIMOTHY ROMAN CATHOLIC PARISH (1978) Revs. Charles Goraieb; John Parks; Deacons Thomas Bolduc; Richard Petersen; Kevin Bassett; Abram Calderon; Florian Hurrish, (Retired). In Res., Rev. Oliver Mohan, O.M.I. (Retired).
Church: 1730 W. Guadalupe, 85202. Tel: 480-775-5200; Fax: 480-820-7984.
School—St. Timothy Preschool, (Grades PreK-8) Tel: 480-775-5237. Monica Glick, Dir. Lay Teachers 6; Students 91.
School—St. Timothy Catholic School, (Grades K-8), 2520 S. Alma School Rd., 85210. Tel: 480-775-2650; Fax: 480-775-2651. Maureen Vick, Prin. Lay Teachers 15; Students 202.

NEW RIVER, MARICOPA CO., GOOD SHEPHERD MISSION, A QUASI-PARISH Rev. Mark Harrington, Canonical Pastor.
45033 N. 12th St., 85087. Tel: 623-465-9740; Fax: 623-742-7031.

PEORIA, MARICOPA CO., ST. CHARLES BORROMEO ROMAN CATHOLIC PARISH (1968) Rev. Loren Gonzales; Deacons Gustavo Arteaga; Edward Molina, (Retired).
Mailing & Church: 8615 W. Peoria Ave., 85345-0819.
Res.: 8617 W. Peoria Ave., 85345. Tel: 623-979-3418; Fax: 623-412-2397.

PRESCOTT, YAVAPAI CO., SACRED HEART ROMAN CATHOLIC PARISH (1877) Revs. Arthur Gramaje, C.M.F.; Daryl Olds, C.M.F.; Valentin Ramon; Gerald Caffrey, C.M.F.; Richard Wozniak, C.M.F.; Deacons Thomas Kayser, (Retired); John Lamon, (Retired); Charles Tony Humphrey; Peter Balland; Thomas Gregory, (Retired); Joseph Bueti.
Church: 150 Fleury Ave., 86301. Tel: 928-445-3141; Fax: 928-717-1074.
School—(Grades PreSchool-8), 131 N. Summit Ave., 86301. Tel: 928-445-2621; Fax: 928-445-0966. Pamela Dickerson, Prin. Sisters 1; Lay Teachers 12; Students 171.
Convent—Institute of the Blessed Virgin Mary, 229 N. Summit St., 86301. Tel: 928-445-7861.

PRESCOTT VALLEY, YAVAPAI CO., ST. GERMAINE ROMAN CATHOLIC PARISH (1984) Rev. Daniel Vollmer; Deacons Robert Palmer; Wayland Moncrief.
Church: 7997 E. Dana Dr., 86314. Tel: 928-772-6350; Fax: 928-772-4413.

QUEEN CREEK, MARICOPA CO., OUR LADY OF GUADALUPE ROMAN CATHOLIC PARISH Revs. Craig Friedley; Heriberto Serrano; Deacon David Barraza.
Mailing Address: P.O. Box 856, 85142-0856. Tel: 480-987-0315; Fax: 480-888-1159.
Church: 20615 E. Ocotillo Rd., 85242.
School—Our Lady of Guadalupe School, (Grades PreSchool-K) Anne Marie Romley, Dir. Lay Teachers 8; Students 24.

SCENIC, MOHAVE CO., LA SANTISIMA TRINIDAD MISSION, A QUASI-PARISH Rev. Thomas J. Hallsten, Canonical Pastor; Sr. Maria Guadalupe Magana, H.J., Mission Coord.
3735 Scenic Blvd., Mohave Co. 86432. Mailing Address: P.O. Box 344, Beaver Dam, 86432.

SCOTTSDALE, MARICOPA CO.
1—ST. BERNADETTE ROMAN CATHOLIC PARISH (1995) Revs. Peter Rossa; Jose D. Cornelia, D.S.; Deacons Ronald Little; James Hostutler; James Mickens; Alfred Homiski.
Church: 16245 N. 60th St., 85254. Tel: 480-905-0221; Fax: 480-905-0249.
School—Blessed Pope John XXIII Catholic School Community, (Grades K-8), 16235 N. 60th St., 85254. Tel: 480-905-0939; Fax: 480-905-0955. Email: popejohnXXIII@diocesephoenix.org. Preston Colao,

Prin. Lay Teachers 25; Students 612.

2—ST. BERNARD OF CLAIRVAUX ROMAN CATHOLIC PARISH (1994) Revs. Brian Bell; William W. Faiella, C.S.C.; Deacon Alan Hungate.
Church: 10755 N. 124th St., 85259. Tel: 480-661-9843; Fax: 480-614-8092.

3—BLESSED SACRAMENT ROMAN CATHOLIC PARISH (1974) Rev. Patrick Robinson; Rev. Msgr. George Schroeder; Deacons Clemens Czapinski, (Retired); Robert Evans; Fred Giesner, (Retired); James Nazzal. In Res., Rev. Thomas A. Walsh (Retired).
Church: 11300 N. 64th St., 85254. Tel: 480-948-8370; Fax: 480-951-3844.
School—Preschool, (Grades PreSchool-K) Tel: 480-998-9466. Heather Fraher, Dir. Lay Teachers 7; Students 40.

4—ST. DANIEL THE PROPHET ROMAN CATHOLIC PARISH (1961) Rev. Thaddeus McGuire; Deacons Martin Dippre; John Barelli; Roy Anderson, (Retired); Jesus Morales.
Church: 1030 N. Hayden Rd., 85257. Tel: 480-945-8437; Fax: 480-945-4335.
Convent—Daughters of Mary, 7830 E. Roosevelt, 85257.

5—ST. MARIA GORETTI ROMAN CATHOLIC PARISH (1967) Rev. Douglas E. Lorig; Deacons Charles Voss; John Berger; Carmene Carbone; Louis Cornille.
Res.: 8344 E. Edward Ave., 85250.
Church: 6261 N. Granite Reef Rd., 85250. Tel: 480-948-8380; Fax: 480-948-8815.
School—Preschool, (Grades PreSchool-K) Tel: 480-948-8815; Fax: 480-948-3606. Kathleen Bies, Dir. Lay Teachers 4; Students 94.

6—OUR LADY OF PERPETUAL HELP ROMAN CATHOLIC PARISH (1949) Rev. Msgr. Thomas Hever; Rev. Chad King, Parochial Vicar; Deacons Jack Ehrlich; Irving Fleming, (Retired). In Res., Rev. Patrick Smith (Retired).
Church & Res.: 7655 E. Main St., 85251. Tel: 480-947-4331; Fax: 480-874-3798.
School—(Grades K-8), 3801 N. Miller Rd., 85251. Tel: 480-874-3720; Fax: 480-874-3767. Ms. Donna Lauro, Prin. Brothers 1; Sisters 1; Lay Teachers 28; Students 473.
Convent—Sisters of Charity, 7634 E. Second St., 85251. Tel: 480-945-3867.

7—OUR LADY OF THE ANGELS CONVENTUAL CHURCH, at the Franciscan Renewal Center. Revs. Peter Kirwin, O.F.M., Rector; Joseph Schwab, O.F.M., Parochial Admin.; Bro. Sebastian Sandoval, O.F.M.; Deacon Herve Lemire.
5802 E. Lincoln Dr., 85253. Tel: 480-948-7460; Fax: 480-948-2325. Email: casa@thecasa.org. Web: www.thecasa.org. In Res., Rev. Alonso De Blas, O.F.M.

8—ST. PATRICK ROMAN CATHOLIC PARISH (1980) Revs. Eric Tellez; Andre Dargis; William P. Healy (Retired); Deacons James Hoyt; John Meyer.
Church: 10815 N. 84th St., 85260. Tel: 480-998-3843; Fax: 480-998-5218.

SEDONA, YAVAPAI CO.

1—CHAPEL OF THE HOLY CROSS Dr. Charles E. Reaume, Admin.
780 Chapel Rd., 86336. Tel: 928-282-4069; Fax: 928-282-3701. Mailing Address: P.O. Box 1043, 86339.

2—ST. JOHN VIANNEY ROMAN CATHOLIC PARISH (1965) Rev. J.C. Ortiz; Deacons Ronald Martinez; Donald Henkiel, (Retired).
Mailing Address: P.O. Box 3909, West Sedona, 86340-3909.
Church: 180 Soldiers Pass Rd., West Sedona, 86340. Tel: 928-282-7545; Fax: 928-282-1798.

SELIGMAN, YAVAPAI CO., ST. FRANCIS ROMAN CATHOLIC PARISH (1940) Rev. Bruno Cuario, Canonical Pastor.
P.O. Box 309, 86337. Tel: 928-422-3354.
Church: 104 Schoeny, 86337.

SUN CITY WEST, MARICOPA CO., OUR LADY OF LOURDES ROMAN CATHOLIC PARISH (1979) Revs. David M. Ostler; Michael Ashibuogwu; Deacons George Koch, (Retired); Jerome Reicks, (Retired); Maurice Arnold, (Retired); Ronald TenBarge; Dominick Bonaiuto.
Church Location: 19002 N. 128th Ave., 85375. Tel: 623-214-5180; Fax: 623-214-1246.
Church Location: *Prince of Peace*, 14818 W. Deer Valley Dr., 85375. Fax: 623-584-2073.

SUN CITY, MARICOPA CO.

1—CHURCH OF ST. JOACHIM & ST. ANNE ROMAN CATHOLIC PARISH (1961) Rev. John Ebbesmier; Deacons Stephen Weiss; Charles Heeter, (Retired).
Mailing Address: P.O. Box 748, Youngtown, 85363.
Church: 11625 111th Ave., 85351-3746. Tel: 623-972-1179; Fax: 623-972-1170.

2—ST. CLEMENT OF ROME ROMAN CATHOLIC PARISH (1970) Revs. John Slobig; Augustine Ogumere, C.S.Sp.; Deacons Michael Phelan; Stanley Giza, (Retired); Irving Dennis, (Retired); Lee Beatrice.
Church: 15800 Del Webb Blvd., 85351. Tel: 623-974-5867; Fax: 623-974-0562.

3—ST. ELIZABETH SETON ROMAN CATHOLIC PARISH (1976) Rev. Joseph P. McGaffin; Deacons Paul Csuy, (Retired); Larry Grey; David Opsahl.
Church: 9728 Palmeras Dr., 85373. Tel: 623-972-2129; Fax: 623-974-0654.

SUN LAKES, MARICOPA CO., ST. STEVEN ROMAN CATHOLIC PARISH (1988) Revs. L. Pierre Hissey; Regidor Carreon (Retired); Deacons Richard Corwin; Frank Danna, (Retired); Louis Pardini, (Retired); James Gall.
Church: 24827 S. Dobson Rd., 85248. Tel: 480-895-9266; Fax: 480-895-9304.

SURPRISE, MARICOPA CO., ST. CLARE OF ASSISI ROMAN CATHOLIC PARISH Revs. Hans P. Ruygt; Sylvester Modebei; Deacons Stephen Martin, (Retired); Donnan Lukaszewski; Theodore Micek, (Retired); Vincent Torres, (Retired); Joseph Badame.
Church: 17111 W. Bell Rd., 85374. Tel: 623-546-3444; Fax: 623-975-5615.

TEMPE, MARICOPA CO.

1—ALL SAINTS ROMAN CATHOLIC NEWMAN CENTER Revs. Robert Clements; John Muir.
230 E. University Dr., 85281-3700. Tel: 480-967-7823; Fax: 480-967-1741. Web: www.newmanasu.org. In Res., Rev. Paul G. Sullivan.

2—CHURCH OF THE RESURRECTION ROMAN CATHOLIC PARISH (1970) Revs. Romeo Dionisio, Parochial Admin.; Arthur Nave, Parochial Vicar; Deacons Richard Cuprak; Wayne Morten; William Malatin. In Res., Rev. Joseph G. Krynen (Retired).
Church: 3201 S. Evergreen Rd., 85282. Tel: 480-838-0207; Fax: 480-756-1501.

3—HOLY SPIRIT ROMAN CATHOLIC PARISH (1973) Revs. Thomas J. Hallsten, Parochial Admin.; Timothy Davern; Deacons Stephen Beard; Gary Johnson.
*Rectory—*1871 E. Libra Dr., 85283.
Church: 1800 E. Libra Dr., 85283. Tel: 480-838-7474; Fax: 480-838-6720.

4—ST. MARGARET ROMAN CATHOLIC PARISH (1972) Rev. John P. Keefe, C.S.C.; Deacons Frank G. Galarza, Parish Life Coord.; Joseph Thomas Swisher; Pedro Mesa.
Church: 2435 E. McArthur Dr., 85281. Tel: 480-967-0379; Fax: 480-967-3825.

5—OUR LADY OF MT. CARMEL ROMAN CATHOLIC PARISH (1932) Revs. John Bonavitacola, Parochial Admin.; Bernard Green, S.D.S.; Craig Friedley; Deacons James Brett; Thomas Glenn. In Res., Rev. Ernesto Reynoso.
Church: 2121 S. Rural Rd., 85282. Tel: 480-967-8791; Fax: 480-967-4919.
School—(Grades K-8), 2117 S. Rural Rd., 85282. Tel: 480-967-5567; Fax: 480-967-6030. Dr. Vincent Sheridan, Prin. Lay Teachers 28; Students 415.
School—Little Lambs Preschool, 3-4yrs., Tel: 480-966-1753. Molly Gorman, Dir. Lay Teachers 2; Students 51.

TOLLESON, MARICOPA CO., BLESSED SACRAMENT ROMAN CATHOLIC PARISH (1953) Revs. Pedro Velez Prensa, Parochial Vicar; Paul Passant; Deacons Jose Garza; Peter Murphy; Sergio Estupinan; Anthony Chavez, (Retired).
Church: 512 N. 93rd Ave., 85353.
Res.: 312 N. 93rd Ave., 85353. Tel: 623-936-7107; Fax: 623-936-9536.

WICKENBURG, MARICOPA CO., ST. ANTHONY OF PADUA ROMAN CATHOLIC PARISH (1941) Rev. Msgr. George Highberger.
Church: 232 N. Tegner St., 85390. Tel: 928-684-2096; Fax: 928-684-3539.
Mission—Our Lady of Guadalupe 50627 Eagle Eye Rd., P.O. Box 96, Aguila, Maricopa Co. 85320.

WILLIAMS, COCONINO CO., ST. JOSEPH'S ROMAN CATHOLIC PARISH (1928) Rev. Bruno Cuario.
Church: 900 W. Grant, 86046. Tel: 928-635-2430; Fax: 928-635-0177.

YARNELL, YAVAPAI, ST. MARY MEDIATRIX MISSION, A QUASI PARISH Rev. Leonardo J. Vargas, Canonical Pastor.
17343 Hwy. 89, P.O. Box 706, 85362. Tel: 928-427-0276. Email: st_marys_mission@diocesephoenix.org.

Chaplains of Public Institutions

PHOENIX. *Arizona State Hospital*, 2500 E. Van Buren St., 85008. Tel: 602-244-1331. Deacon James Cascio, Chap.

Banner Good Samaritan Medical Center, 1111 E. McDowell Rd., 85006. Tel: 602-239-2000; 602-839-2000. Revs. Fidelis Igwenwanne, Chap., Vincent Mesi, O.F.M., Interim Chap.

John C. Lincoln Hospital - N. Mountain. Responsibilty of Most Holy Trinity Parish, Phoenix; 602-944-3375., 2500 E. Dunlap, 85020. Tel: 602-943-2381.

St. Joseph's Hospital, P.O. Box 2071, 85001. Tel: 602-406-3275. Rev. Milton N. Adamson, C.S.C., Chap., Bonnie McCulley, Dir. Chap. Svcs.

St. Luke's Medical Center. Responsibility of St. Mark, Phoenix; 602-267-0503., 1800 E. Van Buren St., 85006. Tel: 602-251-8100.

Maricopa County Medical Center, 2601 E. Roosevelt St., 85008. Tel: 602-344-5011; 602-344-5437. Rev. Mathews Munjanath, Chap.

Phoenix Indian Medical Center, 4212 N. 16th St., 85016. Tel: 602-263-1576. Responsibility of St. Francis Xavier, Phoenix; 602-279-9547.

Sky Harbor Interfaith Chaplaincy, Sky Harbor International Airport, Terminal 4, Level 3. Tel: 602-244-1346. Web: phoenix.gov/skyharborairport/customer-service/travelers-in-crisis.html. Deacons John Barelli, Chap., Edward Bolton, Chap., Joseph Cady, Chap., Philip Simeone, Chap.

United States Veterans Affairs Medical Center, 650 E. Indian School Rd., 85012. Tel: 602-222-6422. Revs. Kenneth Kleiber, Chap., Matthias Crehan, O.F.M., Chap.

CHANDLER. *Chandler Regional Hospital*, 475 S. Dobson Rd., 85224. Tel: 480-728-5650. Rev. Tim Bushy, Chap.

GILBERT. *Mercy Gilbert Medical Center*, 3555 S. Val Vista Dr., 85296. Tel: 480-728-8000. Rev. Tim Bushy, Chap.

LUKE AIR FORCE BASE. *Luke Catholic Community*, 58 FW/HC, 13968 Shooting Star St., 85309-1932. Tel: 623-856-6211; Fax: 623-856-6968. Deacon James Pfleger, Chap.

MESA. *Banner Desert Medical Center*, 1400 S. Dobson Rd., 85202. Tel: 480-412-3198. Rev. Romeo Dionisio, Chap.

PRESCOTT. *United States Veterans Hospital (Prescott)*, 500 Hwy. 89 N., 86313. Tel: 928-445-4860. Rev. Gerald Caffrey, C.M.F., Chap.

SCOTTSDALE. *Scottsdale Healthcare Osborn*, 7400 E. Osborn Rd., 85251. Tel: 480-882-4000. Rev. Patrick Smith, Chap. (Retired).

SUN CITY. *Banner Boswell Medical Center*, 10401 W. Thunderbird Blvd., 85351. Tel: 623-977-7211. Rev. Larry W. Weidner, Chap.

Special Assignment:
Rev. Msgr.—
Sotelo, Antonio, Prison Chap. (Retired), 700 W. University Dr., #154, Tempe, 85281. Tel: 480-967-0379
Revs.—
Fenlon, Brian, Hospice Chap. (Retired), Hospice of the Valley, 6710 N. 79th Pl., Scottsdale, 85250-7921. Tel: 480-998-2557
Weidner, Larry W., Chap., Banner Boswell Medical Center, 10401 W. Thunderbird Rd., 85351. Tel: 623-977-7211

On Leave:
Rev.—
Draves-Arpaia, Cornelius

Retired:
Most Rev.—
O'Brien, Thomas J., D.D., 400 E. Monroe, 85004.
Rev. Msgrs.—
Malone, Alan, Eyrecourt, Ballinasloe, Galway, Co. Ireland.
McMahon, John J., Mt. Claret Center, 4633 N. 54th St., 85018.
Moyer, Richard W., 3302 N. 7th St., #133, 85014.
O'Grady, Michael, 6301 N. 34th Ln., 85017.
Sotelo, Antonio, 700 W. University Dr., #154, Tempe, 85281.
Revs.—
Bartel, Franklin L., 10351 W. Burnett Rd., Peoria, 85382.
Baumann, Lawrence L., 4040 E. Comanche Dr., Cottonwood, 86326.
Bormann, Charles P., 4901 E. Smokehouse Tr., Cave Creek, 85331.
Boyle, Thomas, 325 W. Holly St., 85003.
Brogan, Leo, 3990 Centre St., Unit 401, San Diego, CA 92103.
Cunningham, John F., 16709 E. Frye Rd., Gilbert, 85297.
D'Eon, Earl, St. Clement of Rome, 15800 Del Webb Blvd., 85351-1698.
Feit, Matthias, 4633 N. 54th St., 85018.
Fenlon, Brian, 6710 N. 79th Pl., Scottsdale, 85250.
Fernandez, Frank, 4112 E. Paradise Dr., 85028.
Gauthier, John C., 8931 Ferry Rd., New Roads, LA 70760-2078.
Gillespie, Joseph, 715 W. Lynwood St., 85007-1912.
Groves, Edmund, St. Paul's Convent, Bushmount, Clonakilty, Co. Cork Ireland.
Hanley, John, 4633 N. 54th St., 85018.
Harnischfeger, William, 10626 Mimosa Dr., 85351.
Healy, William P., 8514 E. Via De Los Libros, Scottsdale, 85258.
Hennessy, Joseph I., 24418 S. Starcrest, Sun Lakes, 85248.
Kotnis, Gregory M., 15735 W. Arrowhead Dr., Suprise, 85374.
Krynen, Joseph G., Resurrection Parish, 3201 S. Evergreen Rd., Tempe, 85282.
Minogue, Michael J., 13018 W. Rosewood Dr., El Mirage, 85335.

O'Carroll, Eugene, 3609 W. Questa Dr., Glendale, 85310.
O'Dea, Thomas, Ballycanally, Ennis, Co. Clare, Ireland.
Parker, Charles, 725 S. Power Rd., #105, Mesa, 85206.
Ryan, Richard, 18615 N. 125th Ave., 85375.
Sigman, Louis Anthony, 1272 E. La Costa Pl., Chandler, 85226.
Simlik, Frank P., 10713 W. El Dorado Dr., 85351.
Skagen, Robert, 3422 W. Del Monico Ln., 85051.
Smith, Patrick, Our Lady of Perpetual Help Parish, 7655 E. Main St., Scottsdale, 85251.
Voss, Robert J., 10742 N. 140th Pl., Scottsdale, 85259.
Waldron, William, 10417 Saratoga Cir., 85351-2210.
Walsh, Thomas A., Blessed Sacrament, 11300 N. 64th St., Scottsdale, 85254.
Wasielewski, Henry R., P.O. Box 939, Tempe, 85280-0939.
Zappitelli, Francis, P.O. Box 17906, Fountain Hills, 85269.

Permanent Deacons:
Aird, Gordon, All Saints, Mesa
Anderson, Roy, (Retired), St. Daniel the Prophet, Scottsdale
Anselmo, Clement, St. John the Baptist, Laveen
Anselmo, Thomas A., (Retired)
Areyzaga, Richard, Queen of Peace, Mesa
Arner, Jeffrey, Our Lady of the Lake, Lake Havasu City
Arnold, James, (Retired), San Francisco de Asis, Flagstaff
Arnold, Maurice, (Retired), Our Lady of Lourdes/ Prince of Peace, Sun City West
Arteaga, Gustavo, St. Charles Borromeo, Peoria
Babbits, Oliver, (Retired), St. Timothy, Mesa
Badame, Joseph, St. Claire of Assisi, Surprise
Balland, Peter, Sacred Heart, Prescott
Barelli, John, St. Daniel the Prophet, Scottsdale
Barraza, David, Our Lady of Guadalupe, Queen Creek
Bassett, Kevin, St. Timothy, Mesa
Battista, James, (Retired)
Beard, Stephen, Holy Spirit, Tempe
Beatrice, Lee, (Retired), St. Clement of Rome, Sun City
Beltran, Anthony, (Retired), St. Matthew, Phoenix
Bennett, Bruce, Ed.D., St. Mary, Chandler
Benware, John, St. Benedict, Phoenix
Berger, John, St. Maria Goretti, Scottsdale
Bernasconi, Santino, Our Lady of Guadalupe, Guadalupe
Bidleman, William, (Retired), St. Jerome, Phoenix
Bilinski, John, (Retired), St. Henry, Buckeye
Bishop, Thomas, Christ the King, Mesa
Bogart, Douglas, St. Thomas the Apostle, Phoenix
Bolduc, Thomas, St. Timothy, Mesa
Bolton, Edward, (Retired), St. Gregory, Phoenix
Bonaiuto, Dominick, Our Lady of Lourdes, Sun City West
Boswell, Keith, St. Anne, Gilbert
Bowslaugh, Alan, St. James, Glendale
Bret, James, San Francisco De Asis, Flagstaff
Brett, James, Our Lady of Mount Carmel, Tempe
Brown, James, Immaculate Conception, Cottonwood
Bueti, Joseph, Sacred Heart, Prescott
Cady, Joseph, St. Anne, Gilbert
Calderon, Abram, St. Timothy, Mesa
Cameron, George, (Retired), St. Henry, Buckeye
Campas, Robert, St. Helen, Glendale
Campbell, Colin, St. Theresa, Phoenix
Capistrant, Willard, Christ the King, Mesa
Carbone, Carmene, St. Maria Goretti, Scottsdale
Carey, Robert, St. Mary Magdalene, Gilbert
Carnecer, Edgar, St. Thomas Aquinas Parish, Avondale
Carr, Michael, All Saints, Mesa
Cascio, James, St. William, Cashion
Chavez, Anthony, (Retired), Blessed Sacrament, Tolleson
Clapham, Winfred, All Saints, Mesa
Clower, William, St. Rose Phillipine Duchesne, Anthem
Coe, Thomas, Our Lady of the Lake, Lake Havasu City
Cornille, Louis, St. Maria Goretti, Scottsdale
Corwin, Richard, (Retired), St. Steven, Sun Lakes
Crawford, Donald, St. Andrew the Apostle, Chandler
Csuy, Paul, (Retired), St. Elizabeth Seton, Sun City
Cuprak, Richard, (Retired), Resurrection, Tempe
Czapinski, Clemens, (Retired), Blessed Sacrament, Scottsdale
D'Amico, John, St. Rose Phillipine Duchesne, Anthem
Dalisay, J.R., D.S., Most Holy Trinity, Phoenix
Danna, Frank, (Retired), St. Steven, Sun Lakes
Davaz, Douglas, St Benedict, Phoenix
DeFilippis, Thomas, (Retired), Our Lady of the Lake
Del Quadro, John, St. Margaret Mary, Bullhead City
DeMarco, William, St. Jerome, Phoenix
Dennis, Irving, (Retired), St. Clement of Rome, Sun City
Devine, Frank, St. James, Glendale
Dippre, Martin, (Retired), St. Daniel the Prophet, Scottsdale
Drapeau, Roy, St. Thomas More, Glendale
Duran, Onofre, (Retired), Immaculate Conception, Cottonwood
Eckert, Richard, (Retired), St. Margaret Mary, Bullhead City
Ehrlich, Jacob, Our Lady of Perpetual Help, Scottsdale
England, Robert, (Retired), Corpus Christi, Phoenix
Estupinan, Sergio, Blessed Sacrament, Tolleson
Evans, Robert, Blessed Sacrament Parish, Scottsdale
Fejes, Peter, St. Peter, Bapchule
Ferreira, Thomas, Holy Cross, Mesa
Filzen, Bernard, All Saints, Mesa
Finnegan, William, J.C.L., Holy Cross, Mesa
Fleming, Irving, (Retired), Our Lady of Perpetual Help, Scottsdale
Flynn, Patrick, (Retired), Corpus Christi, Phoenix
Fogle, James, St. Gabriel, Cave Creek
French, Shawn, St. Joseph Catholic Church, Phoenix
Galarza, Frank, St. Margaret, Tempe
Gall, James, St. Steven, Sun Lakes
Galloway, Gregory, St. John Vianney, Goodyear
Garcia, Ernest, St. Andrew the Apostle, Chandler
Garza, Jose, Blessed Sacrament, Tolleson
Gaudio, Alexander, (Retired), Corpus Christi, Phoenix
Gersitz, James, Holy Cross, Mesa
Giesner, Fred, (Retired), Blessed Sacrament, Scottsdale
Giza, Stanley, (Retired), St. Clement of Rome, Sun City
Glenn, Thomas, Our Lady of Mount Carmel, Tempe
Gonzalez, Albert, Our Lady of Perpetual Help, Glendale
Gonzalez, Ricardo, St. Augustine, Phoenix
Gonzalez, Ronald, St. Thomas More
Goubeaux, Guy, St. Paul, Phoenix
Gouveia, Americo, (Retired)
Gregory, Thomas, (Retired), Sacred Heart, Prescott
Grey, Larry, St. Elizabeth Seton, Sun City
Gribowski, Mark, St. Henry, Buckeye
Guzman, Angel, St. Gregory, Phoenix
Guzman, Juan, (Retired), Ss. Simon & Jude, Phoenix
Hamilton, James, (Retired), St. Augustine, Phoenix
Hanson, Lee, (Retired), Our Lady of Lourdes Parish, Sun City West
Heeter, Charles, (Retired), St. Joachim & St. Anne, Sun City
Henkiel, Donald, (Retired), St. John Vianney Catholic, Sedona
Hernandez, Jose, (Retired)
Hickcox, Edward, (Retired)
Hintze, Craig, St. Mary Magdalene, Gilbert
Holmes, Michael, St. Catherine Laboure, Chino Valley
Homiski, Alfred, St. Bernadette, Scottsdale
Hostutler, James, St. Bernadette, Scottsdale
Hoyt, James, St. Patrick, Scottsdale
Humphrey, Charles Tony, Sacred Heart, Prescott
Hungate, Alan, St. Bernard of Clairvaux, Scottsdale
Hurrish, Florian, (Retired), St. Timothy, Mesa
Hursh, Paul, St. Bridget, Mesa
Ixta, Ignacio, Holy Cross, Mesa
Jenkins, William, St. Vincent de Paul, Phoenix
Johnson, Gary, Holy Spirit, Tempe
Johnson, Ronald, San Francisco de Asis, Flagstaff
Jolliffe, Garry, (Retired), St. Mary Parish, Chandler
Kaminsky, David, Immaculate Conception, Cottonwood
Kayser, Thomas, (Retired), Sacred Heart, Prescott
Kijewski, Richard, St. Thomas More, Glendale
Klein, Thomas, St. Francis Xavier, Phoenix
Kloft, Lee, (Retired), St. Gregory, Phoenix
Koch, George, (Retired), Our Lady of Lourdes/ Prince of Peace, Sun City West
Kronschnabel, Michael, St. Mary, Chandler
Kuban, Donald, (Retired), Most Holy Trinity, Phoenix
Kulinowski, Kenneth, (Retired), St. Thomas Byzantine, Gilbert
Lamon, John, Sacred Heart Parish, Prescott
Lemire, Herve, Our Lady of the Angels, Scottsdale
Leon, Victor, St. Henry, Buckeye
Lessard, Joseph, (Retired), Mount Claret, Phoenix
Little, Ronald, St. Bernadette, Scottsdale
LoCascio, Phillip, Ascension, Fountain Hills
Lopez, Anthony, Our Lady of Perpetual Help, Glendale
Lopez, Gilbert, Our Lady of the Lake, Lake Havasu City
Lukaszewski, Donnan, St. Clare of Assisi, Surprise
Malatin, William, Resurrection, Tempe
Manthie, Robert, St. Raphael, Glendale
Martinez, Ronald, St. John Vianney, Sedona
McKnight, Lorenzo, St. Augustine, Phoenix
Meidl, Richard, St. Raphael, Glendale
Mesa, Pedro, St. Margaret, Tempe
Messer, Gene, Holy Cross, Mesa
Meyer, John, St. Patrick, Scottsdale
Micek, Theodore, (Retired), St. Henry, Buckeye
Mickel, John, St. Helen, Glendale
Mickens, James, St. Bernadette, Scottsdale
Miller, Kenneth, (Retired), St. Thomas the Apostle, Phoenix
Molina, Edward, (Retired), St. Charles Borromeo, Peoria
Moncrief, Wayland, St. Germaine, Prescott Valley
Morales, Jesus, St. Daniel the Prophet, Scottsdale
Morton, Dwight, (Unassigned)
Morton, Wayne, Resurrection, Tempe
Murphy, Peter, Dir., Prison Ministry; Blessed Sacrament, Tolleson
Myers, Robert P., (Retired), Our Lady of Perpetual Help, Glendale
Navaretta, John, Our Lady of the Lake, Lake Havasu City
Nazzal, James, Blessed Sacrament, Scottsdale
Neely, Theodore, (Retired), All Saints, Mesa
O'Connor, John, (Retired), St. James, Glendale
O'Grady, Lowell, Immaculate Heart of Mary, Phoenix
O'Toole, Gerald, St. Mary Magdalene, Gilbert
Olberding, Robert, San Francisco de Asis, Flagstaff
Olivarez, Jose, Sacred Heart, Phoenix
Olivas, Manuel, St. Mary, Chandler
Opsahl, David, St. Elizabeth Seton, Sun City
Orozco, Jose, Santa Teresita, El Mirage
Palmer, Robert, St. Germaine, Prescott Valley
Pardini, Louis, (Retired), St. Steven, Sun Lakes
Petersen, Richard, St. Timothy, Mesa
Pfleger, James, Luke Air Force Base, Glendale
Phelan, Michael, St. Clement of Rome, Sun City
Phelan, Thomas J., III, (Retired), Queen of Peace, Mesa
Picciano, Anthony, St. Mary Catholic Church, Kingman
Poulin, Ronald, St. John the Baptist, Laveen
Raczkowski, Dennis, Our Lady of Perpetual Help, Glendale
Rade, Douglas, (Retired), San Francisco de Asis, Flagstaff
Ramirez, Ernesto, St. Vincent de Paul, Phoenix
Reicks, Jerome, (Retired), Our Lady of Lourdes/ Prince of Peace, Sun City West
Rein, Richard, St. Jerome, Phoenix
Revering, Dennis, San Francisco de Asis, Flagstaff
Riedel, John, Queen of Peace, Mesa
Robinson, Jason, St. Thomas Aquinas, Avondale
Rodriguez, Santiago, (Retired), Queen of Peace, Mesa
Ruiz, Ronald, Christ the King, Mesa
Runyan, David, St. Andrew the Apostle, Chandler
Salazar, Lorenzo, (Retired), St. Vincent de Paul, Phoenix
Sanchez, Jesse, St. Agnes, Phoenix
Santa, Reed, (Retired), All Saints, Mesa
Scaccia, Joseph, Holy Cross, Mesa
Scheller, Albert, (Retired), St. Thomas Aquinas, Avondale
Scott, John, All Saints Catholic Church, Mesa
Sejba, James, (Retired), St. Gabriel, Cave Creek
Shaw, Charles, Ss. Simon & Jude Cathedral, Phoenix
Shea, William, (Retired), St. Mary Magdalene, Gilbert
Shinske, Joseph, (Retired), St. Helen, Glendale
Simeone, Philip, Corpus Christi, Phoenix
Smith, Barry, (Retired)
Smith, Richard, Ascension, Fountain Hills
Spadafino, Joseph, St. Anne, Gilbert
Springer, James, (Retired), St. Joan of Arc, Phoenix
Stickney, Joseph, St. Louis the King, Glendale
Stokes, Leslie, St. Philip Benizi, Black Canyon City
Suida, Milford, St. Thomas Aquinas, Avondale
Swisher, Joseph Thomas, St. Margaret, Tempe
TenBarge, Ronald, Our Lady of Lourdes/Prince of Peace, Sun City West
Terrazas, Carlos, St. Catherine of Siena, Phoenix
Tift, Neil, Christ the King, Mesa
Toilolo, Patrick, Our Lady of the Lake, Lake Havasu City
Torigian, Robert, St. Gabriel, Cave Creek
Torres, Vincent, (Retired), St. Clare of Assisi, Surprise
Trant, James, Dir. Office of Diaconate, St. Francis of Assisi Mission, Scottsdale

Valle, Matias, St. Matthew, Phoenix
Valverde, George, (Retired)
Vivio, William, St. Paul, Phoenix
Voss, Charles, St. Maria Goretti, Scottsdale
Weiss, Stephen, St. Joachim & St. Anne, Sun City
Wenzel, Schubert, St. Jerome, Phoenix
Wenzler, Joseph, St. Clare of Assisi, Surprise
West, Tony, SS. Simon & Jude Cathedral, Phoenix
Whelan, Laurence, (Retired), San Francisco de Asis, Flagstaff
Whitford, Jaime, Queen of Peace Parish, Mesa
Wilson, Ronald, All Saints, Mesa
Wisely, Philip, St. Mary, Kingman
Yanez, Richard, (Retired), Queen of Peace, Mesa
Zavala, Eduardo, St. Louis the King, Glendale

INSTITUTIONS LOCATED IN THE DIOCESE

[A] HIGH SCHOOLS, DIOCESAN

PHOENIX. *Bourgade Catholic High School*, 4602 N. 31st Ave., 85017. Tel: 602-973-4000; Fax: 602-973-5854. Email: krother@bourgade.org. Web: www.bourgadecatholic.org. Ms. Kathryn Rother, Prin.; Mrs. Vicki Kikgarriff, Asst. Prin., Cirriculum & Instruction. Email: vkilgarriff@bourgade.org; Lori Pieper, Asst. Prin., Student Svcs.; Rev. Matthew Henry, Chap.; Angela Rohde, Librarian. Chaplains 1; Lay Teachers 35; Students 404.

St. Mary's Roman Catholic High School, 2525 N. Third St., 85004. Tel: 602-251-2500; Fax: 602-251-2595. Email: sfessler@smknights.org. Web: www.smknights.org. Mrs. Suzanne Fessler, Prin.; Mr. Robert Rogers, Asst. Prin.; Rev. Robert Bolding, Chap.; Carey Hausbeck, Academic Counselor; Catherine Clarke, Librarian. Priests 1; Sisters 2; Lay Teachers 29; Students 503.

Xavier College Preparatory Roman Catholic High School, 4710 N. Fifth St., 85012. Tel: 602-277-3772; Fax: 602-279-1346. Email: sjfphx@xcp.org. Web: www.xcp.org. Sisters M. Joan Fitzgerald, B.V.M., Prin.; Lynn Winsor, B.V.M., Vice Prin.; Rev. Chad King, Chap.; Mary Harkins, Librarian. Priests 1; Sisters 5; Lay Teachers 77; Students 1,168.

CHANDLER. *Seton Catholic Preparatory High School*, 1150 N. Dobson Rd., 85224. Tel: 480-963-1900; Fax: 480-963-1974. Email: pcollins@setonchs.org. Web: www.setoncatholic.org. Patricia Collins, Prin.; Rev. William Schmid, Chap.; Michelle Nowak, Librarian. Priests 1; Lay Teachers 43; Students 554.

SCOTTSDALE. *Notre Dame Preparatory Roman Catholic High School*, 9701 E. Bell Rd., 85260. Tel: 480-634-8200; Fax: 480-634-8299. David D. Gonsalves, Prin.; Jane Tompkins, Asst. Prin.; David Harris, Asst. Prin. & Dean; Rev. John Parks, Chap.; Lillian Vancel, Librarian. Priests 2; Sisters 1; Deacons 1; Lay Teachers 77; Students 887.

[B] HIGH SCHOOLS, PRIVATE

PHOENIX. *Brophy College Preparatory*, 4701 N. Central Ave., 85012. Tel: 602-264-5291; Fax: 602-234-1669. Web: www.brophyprep.org. Rev. Edward Reese, S.J., Pres.; Patrick Higgins, Dean of Students; Robert E. Ryan III, Prin.; Seamus Walsh, Asst. Prin. Curriculum & Instruction; Jim Bopp, Asst. Prin., Student Activities; Mr. A. Joseph Helm Jr., Dir., Legacy; Carol Ford, Controller; Revs. Harry T. Oliver, S.J., Rel. Studies Dept.; Philip S. Postell, S.J., Dir., Alumni Relations; Mr. Christopher Calderon, S.J., World Language Dept.; Mr. Marc P. Valadao, S.J., Religious Studies Dept.; Rev. E. Louis Bishop, S.J.; Jennie Oleksak, Librarian. Jesuit Fathers., Boys Day School. Priests 4; Jesuit 6; Lay Teachers 85; Students 1,322.

[C] GENERAL HOSPITALS

GILBERT. *Mercy Gilbert Medical Center dba Catholic Healthcare West* 3555 S. Val Vista Dr., 85297. Tel: 480-728-8337; Fax: 480-728-9640. Web: www.mercygilbert.org. Martin G. Breeden, Vice Pres. Mission Integration. Sponsored by Sisters of Mercy of the Americas-West Midwest Community. Bed Capacity 212; Total Assisted Annually 115,355; Total Staff 1,317.

[D] HOMES FOR THE AGED & HANDICAPPED

PHOENIX. *Avondale Senior Village*, 10830 W. Apache St., Bldg. 1, Avondale, 85323. Tel: 623-936-5452; Fax: 623-936-5320. Web: www.mercyhousing.org. Mailing Address: P.O. Box 1180, Cashion, 85329. Shelly Hare, Property Mgr. Units 41; Total Assisted Annually 45; Total Staff 2.

Camelot Casitas, 1907 E. Virginia, 85006. Tel: 602-276-7554; Fax: 602-276-7538. Web: www.mercyhousing.org. *CIO Casa de Shanti*, 5236 S. 5th St., 85040. Sherry Nolen. Units 8; Total Assisted Annually 11; Total Staff 1.

Casa De Merced, 62 N. 92nd Dr., Tolleson, 85353. Tel: 623-936-9668; Fax: 623-936-9658. Web: www.mercyhousing.org. Mary Camarena, Property Mgr. Units 41; Total Assisted Annually 45; Total Staff 2.

Casa de Shanti, 5236 S. 5th St., 85040. Tel: 602-276-7554; Fax: 602-276-7538. Web: www.mercyhousing.org. Sherry Nolen, Property Mgr. Total Staff 2; Total Served Annually 32.

El Mirage Senior Village, 12424 W. Thunderbird Rd., El Mirage, 85335. Tel: 623-875-1688; Fax: 623-875-1685. Web: www.mercyhousing.org. Units 41; Total Assisted Annually 43; Total Staff 2.

Guadalupe Senior Village, 9403 S. Avenida Del Yaqui, Guadalupe, 85283. Tel: 480-897-3273; Fax: 480-897-3274. Web: www.mercyhousing.org. Shelly Hare, Property Mgr. Units 22; Total Assisted Annually 25; Total Staff 2.

Mercy Court (Family), 2945 W. Colter St., 85017. Tel: 602-246-1863; Fax: 602-246-2004. Web: www.mercyhousing.org. Kasey Loll, Property Mgr. Total Staff 5; Total Served Annually 388; Units 124.

Peoria Place Apartments, CIO Mercy Housing PMB 256, 1525 N. 39th Ave., 85009. Tel: 480-820-5234; Fax: 480-755-2298. Web: www.mercyhousing.org. Sherry Nolen, Property Mgr. Units 14; Total Assisted Annually 21; Total Staff 1.

Plazas de Merced, 3002 E. Cactus Rd., 85032. Tel: 602-936-9668; Fax: 602-493-0307. Web: www.mercyhousing.org. Sherry Nolan, Property Mgr. Units 25; Total Assisted Annually 26; Total Staff 2.

Roeser Senior Village Apartments, 454 E. Roeser Rd., 85040. Tel: 602-268-5100; Fax: 602-268-5425.

Sweetwater Gardens Apartments (Handicapped), 2035 E. Sweetwater, 85022. Tel: 602-867-4549; Fax: 602-867-4414. Total Assisted Annually 28; Units 24.

Vista Alegre, 6515 W. Maryland Ave., Glendale, 85301. Tel: 623-937-0418; Fax: 623-937-0425. Web: www.mercyhousing.org. Janet Weidler, Property Mgr. Units 60; Total Assisted Annually 78; Total Staff 2.

AVONDALE. *Vianney Villas Apartments* (Retirement)-HUD Rent Subsidized, 750 S. Fourth St., 85323. Tel: 623-932-2036; Fax: 623-932-1134. Total Assisted Annually 56.

GILBERT. *Page Commons* (Senior), 170 N. Oak St., 85233. Tel: 480-813-4609; Fax: 480-813-4658. Web: www.mercyhousing.org. Jennifer Strassburg, Property Mgr. Total Staff 4; Total Served Annually 176; Units 100.

KINGMAN. *Amy Neal Retirement Center*, 3700 Western Ave., 86401-3080. Tel: 928-757-7016. HUD rent subsidized.

Kingman Heights Apartments, 1020 Detroit Ave., 86401. Tel: 928-753-2425; Fax: 928-753-2590. (Retirement)- HUD rent subsidized. Total Assisted Annually 34; Units 33.

LAKE HAVASU CITY. *Becket House Apartments* (Retirement), 865 Cashmere Dr., 86404. Tel: 928-855-7178. Total Assisted Annually 50; Units 50.

Havasu Hills Tel: 928-855-4743. Total Assisted Annually 50; Units 50.

MESA. *Mesa Senior Meadows*, 333 E. 6th St., 85201. Tel: 480-615-7893; Fax: 480-615-7894. Web: www.mercyhousing.org. Jill Fuller, Property Mgr. Units 41; Total Assisted Annually 46; Total Staff 2.

Villas de Merced (Family), 520 N. Mesa Dr., 85201. Tel: 480-649-0338; Fax: 480-649-0298. Web: www.mercyhousing.org. Total Staff 4; Total Served Annually 254.

PAYSON. *Pineview Manor Apartments*, 304 S. Clark Rd., 85541. Tel: 928-474-1317. Email: pnewman@fsl.org. Total Assisted Annually 29; Total Staff 1.

WICKENBURG. *Padua Hills Apartments* (Retirement)-HUD Rent Subsidized, 460 S. West Rd., 85390. Tel: 928-684-7034. Total Assisted Annually 27; Units 25.

WILLIAMS. *St. Agnes Apartments* (Retirement), 200 S. Ninth, 86046. Tel: 928-635-2913. Total Assisted Annually (Apartments) 25; Total Assisted Annually (Food Bank) 3,500; Housing 30.

[E] CONVENTS AND RESIDENCES OF SISTERS

PHOENIX. *Institute of Blessed Virgin Mary (I.B.V.M.)* (Regional House), 2521 W. Maryland Ave., 85017. Tel: 602-433-0658; Fax: 602-864-8620. Email: maryward@q.com. Web: ibvm.org. Sr. Kay Foley, I.B.V.M., Provincial. Sisters 3.

Institute of the Blessed Virgin Mary - Loreto, 7887 N. 16th St., #101, 85020. Tel: 602-331-9135. Sisters 2.

Institute of the Blessed Virgin Mary - Loreto, 26 W. Northern Ave., 85021. Tel: 602-371-0327. Sisters 2.

Missionaries of Charity, 1414 S. 17th Ave., 85007. Tel: 602-258-5504. Sr. Marine, M.C., Local Supr. Sisters 4.

Our Lady of Guadalupe Monastery Sisters of St. Benedict, 8502 W. Pinchot Ave., 85037. Tel: 623-848-9608. Sr. Linda Campbell, O.S.B., Prioress. Sisters 3; Oblates 24.

Sisters of Charity of the Blessed Virgin Mary (Xavier Convent), 311 E. Highland Ave., 85012. Tel: 602-264-0445. Sr. Joan Nuckols, B.V.M., Community Representative. Sisters 7.

Sisters of Divine Savior, 323 E. Elm St., 85012-1703. Tel: 602-274-0228. Email: srgeorgene@yahoo.com. Web: www.sdssisters.org. Sr. Georgene Faust, S.D.S., Cluster Coord. for Region. Sisters 7.

Sisters of Notre Dame de Namur, 6635 S. 14th Way, 85042-4459. Tel: 602-243-9929. Sisters 2.

Union of Sisters of the Presentation of the Blessed Virgin Mary, 729 W. Wilshire Dr., 85007. Tel: 602-271-9687; Fax: 602-253-9166. Email: teresa6085501@yahoo.com. Sisters 4.

GILBERT. *Missionary Carmelites of St. Therese of the Child Jesus*, 206 E. Palo Verde St., 85296. Tel: 480-633-3729. Sr. Guadalupe H. Rodriguez, M.C.S.T.N.J., Local Supr. Sisters 4.

MESA. *Sisters of Notre Dame de Namur* (Casa Guadalupe), 548 W. Third St., 85201. Tel: 480-964-3685; Fax: 480-655-9975. Email: mesasnd@aol.com. Sisters 8.

TONOPAH. *The Poor Clares of Perpetual Adoration, Our Lady of Solitude Monastery*, 9020 N. 381st Ave., P.O. Box 639, 85354. Tel: 480-245-9614. Email: desertnuns@msn.com. Sisters 5.

[F] MONASTERIES AND RESIDENCES OF PRIESTS AND BROTHERS

PHOENIX. *Carmelite Community*, 1717 W. Flower, 85015. Tel: 602-274-3189. Revs. Tiernan O'Callaghan, O.Carm. (Retired); Silvan Boyle, O.Carm. (Retired). Priests 2.

Crosier Community of Phoenix (Canons Regular of the Order of the Holy Cross), P.O. Box 32705, 85064-2705. Tel: 602-224-0434; Fax: 602-224-0722. Email: ddonnay@crosier.org. Web: www.crosier.org. Revs. David N Donnay, O.S.C., Prior, 454 E. Roeser Rd., 85040; Stephan Bauer, O.S.C.; John Christ, O.S.C.; Richard McGuire, O.S.C.; Louis R. Mraz, O.S.C. (Retired); Robert J. Rossi, O.S.C.; Philip Suehr, O.S.C. (Retired); Gerald Thaar, O.S.C. (Retired); Bros. Neil Emon, O.S.C., (Retired); Dale Ettel, O.S.C.; Gabriel Guerrero, O.S.C., (Retired), P.O. Box 32705, 85064; James Lewandowski, O.S.C., 454 E. Roeser Rd., 85040; Gregory Madigan, O.S.C., (Retired); James Scher, O.S.C., Subprior, 454 E. Roeser Rd., 85040; Gus Schloesser, O.S.C.; Timothy Tomczak, O.S.C., P.O. Box 32705, 85064. Priests 8; Brothers 8.

Crosier Provincial House Province of St. Odilia, 4423 N. 24th St., Ste. 400, 85016-5584. Tel: 602-443-7100; Fax: 602-443-7101. Email: provincial@crosier.org. Web: www.crosier.org. Revs. Thomas A. Enneking, O.S.C., Prior; Michael Cotone, O.S.C.; Timothy Conlon, O.S.C., (on exclaustration); Carrie Powell, Prov. Asst. Priests 3; Total Staff 5. Crosiers Serving Abroad Revs. Steven Henrich, O.S.C.; James Hentges, O.S.C.; Glen Lewandowski, O.S.C.

Disciples of Hope, 9241 N. 36th Dr., 85051. Tel: 602-327-7257. Priests 3.

Holy Cross Congregation/Casa Santa Cruz, 7126 N. Seventh Ave., 85021. Tel: 602-944-6000; Fax: 602-944-1221. Revs. Milton N. Adamson, C.S.C., Supr.; Duane Balcerski, C.S.C.; James R. Blantz, C.S.C.; William W. Faiella, C.S.C.; James J. Ferguson, C.S.C., Asst. Supr.; John P. Keefe, C.S.C.; Joseph F. O'Donnell, C.S.C. (Retired); Stephen J. Sedlock; James W. Thornton, C.S.C. (Retired); Richard P. Zang, C.S.C.; Bro. Ronald G. Whelan, C.S.C. Priests 10; Brothers 1.

Society of Jesus, 120 E. Mariposa St., 85012. Tel: 602-264-5291. Revs. John M. Martin, S.J., Supr.; E. Louis Bishop, S.J.; Harry T. Olivier, S.J.; Philip S. Postell, S.J.; Edward Reese, S.J., Pres., Brophy Prep.; Daniel J. Sullivan, S.J., St. Francis Xavier Parish; John Auther, S.J.; David J. Robinson, S.J.

St. Therese Priory, 75 E. Mariposa St., #3, 85012-1631. Tel: 602-604-2365. Revs. Valentine Boyle, O.Carm.; Charles Kurgan, O.Carm.

[G] RETREAT HOUSES

PHOENIX. *Mount Claret Roman Catholic Retreat Center*, 4633 N. 54th St., 85018. Tel: 602-840-5066; Fax: 602-840-5732. Deacon John Mickel, Dir.; Thomas McGuire, Assoc. Dir. Priests 4. In

Res. Rev. Msgrs. John J. McMahon (Retired); Gilbert J. Rutz (Retired); Revs. Matthias Feit (Retired); John Hanley (Retired).

Our Lady of Guadalupe Retreat/Conference Center, 8502 W. Pinchot, 85037. Tel: 623-848-9608. Email: lramenta@benedictinesistersphoenix.org. Web: benedictinesistersphoenix.com. Conference Center Overnight Capacity 25; Conference Center Daytime Capacity 70; Scholastica House Daytime Capacity 30; Scholastica House Overnight Capacity 2.

BLACK CANYON CITY. *Our Lady of Silence Hermitage: A House of Prayer for Priests*, 19950 St. Joseph Rd., 85324. Tel: 623-374-9204. Rev. Eugene Florea, Dir.

CORNVILLE. *Living Water Retreat Center*, P.O. Box 529, 86325. Tel: 928-634-4421; Fax: 928-634-0005. Web: www.livingwaterretreatcenter.com. (Owned and operated by City of the Lord)

SCOTTSDALE. *Franciscan Renewal Center, Inc. (Casa de Paz Y Bien)*, 5802 E. Lincoln Dr., 85253. Tel: 480-948-7460; Fax: 480-948-2325. Email: casa@thecasa.org. Web: www.thecasa.org. Revs. Joseph Schwab, O.F.M., Exec. Dir.; Alonso De Blas, O.F.M.; Peter Kirwin, O.F.M.; Bro. Mario Vasquez, O.F.M. Priests 3; Brothers 1.

[H] NEWMAN CENTERS

PHOENIX. *Arizona State University All Saints Catholic Newman Center*, 230 E. University Dr., Tempe, 85281. Tel: 480-967-7823. Revs. Robert Clements, Dir.; John Muir, Assoc. Dir. (Tempe) In Res. Rev. Paul G. Sullivan.

Holy Trinity Catholic Newman Center 520 W. Riordan Rd., Flagstaff, 86001. Tel: 928-779-2903; Fax: 928-779-0698. Email: info@naunewman.org. Web: www.naunewman.org. Rev. Matthew Lowry, Chap. & Assoc. Vocations Dir.

Yavapai College, Emery Riddle Aeronautical University Sacred Heart Parish, 150 Fleury Ave., Prescott, 86301. Tel: 928-445-3141; Fax: 928-717-1074. (Prescott)

[I] ACADEMIES OF RELIGIOUS TEACHING

PHOENIX. *Kino Institute*, 400 E. Monroe, 85004. Tel: 602-354-2300; Fax: 602-354-2251. Web: www.kinoinstitute.org. MaryBeth Mueller, Exec. Dir. Education & Evangelization; Eric J. Westby, Dir. Parish Leadership Credentialing & Certification; Sisters Maria Celia Molina, SNDdeN, M.Th., Coord. Caminante & Agua Viva; Darcy Peletich, O.S.F., M.A., M.L.S., Librarian; Gina Milligan, Coord. Admin. Svcs. Tel: 602-906-9798; Luz Lobato, Senior Admin. Asst. Program for Catechetical Studies & Adult Leadership Formation.

[J] MISCELLANEOUS LISTINGS

PHOENIX. *Andre House of Arizona*, 213 S. 11th Ave., 85007-3132. Tel: 602-255-0580; Fax: 602-257-4415. Email: director@andrehouse.org. Web: www.andrehouse.org. P.O. Box 2014, 85001-2014. Tel: 602-255-0580; Fax: 602-257-4415. Rev. Eric Schimmel, C.S.C., Dir.; Bro. Richard Armstrong, C.S.C. Hospitality House, Indiana Province of the Congregation of Holy Cross.

**Catholic Charities Community Services*, 4747 N. 7th Ave., 85013. Tel: 602-285-1999; Fax: 602-285-0311. Web: www.catholiccharitiesaz.org. Stuart Seim, Pres.; Robert Brown, CEO; Kristen Schmidt, M.S.W., Ph.D., Vice Pres.

Catholic Charities Regional Service Centers:

Catholic Charities Community Services, Phoenix, 1825 W. Northern Ave., 85021. Tel: 602-997-6105; Fax: 602-943-0377. Cathy Peterson, Dir., Progs. Opers.

Catholic Charities Community Services, Flagstaff, 460 N. Switzer Canyon Dr., Ste. 400, Flagstaff, 86001. Tel: 928-774-9125; Fax: 928-774-0697. Antoinette Sablan, Site Dir.; Cathy Peterson, Vice Pres., Progs.

Catholic Charities Community Services, Yavapai, 434 W. Gurley St., Prescott, 86301. Tel: 928-778-2531; Fax: 928-771-9531.

Catholic Charities Community Services, West Valley, 7400 W. Olive Ave., Ste. 10, Peoria, 85345. Tel: 623-486-9868; Fax: 623-486-9988. Cathy Tompkins, M.S., C.P.C., Dir., Head Start. 51 Head Start Classrooms

Catholic Charities Parish & Community Engagement, 4747 N. 7th Ave., 85013. Tel: 602-285-1999; Fax: 602-285-0311. Deborah DiCarlo, Dir.

Catholic Charities Residential Facilities:

Dignity House Tel: 602-361-0578. Alanna Reichart, Prog. Supvr. Group living for homeless women leaving prostitution.

Housing for Hope, Inc., 4747 N. 7th Ave, 85013. Tel: 602-650-4848. William Schultz, Principal Officer. Housing for poor & needy individuals & families.

My Sister's Place Tel: 480-821-1024. Domestic Violence Shelter

Catholic Community Foundation, 400 E. Monroe St., 85004-2336. Tel: 602-354-2400; Fax: 602-354-2423. Donna Marino, Exec. Dir.

Catholic Education Arizona, 2025 N. Third St., #165, 85004-1425. Tel: 602-218-6542; Fax: 602-218-6623. Email: pmulligan@catholictuition.org. Web: www.catholictuition.org. Paul S. Mulligan, M.T.S., Exec. Dir.; Rick Toerne, Pres.

The Catholic Retreat for Young Singles, Inc., P.O. Box 16064, 85011. Tel: 602-920-1491. Email: theo@tigno.com. Theo Tigno, Pres.

Christ Child Society, 4633 N. 54th St., 85018-1904. Tel: 602-667-3355. Julianne Berkel, Pres.; Janice Grogan, Treas.

Crosier Missions, 4423 N. 24th St., Ste. 400, 85016-5584. Tel: 602-443-7100; Fax: 602-443-7101. Email: cpowell@crosier.org. Web: www.crosier.org. Bro. Albert Becker, O.S.C., Dir. Devel. Total Staff 1.

Cursillo Movement, 4633 N. 54th St., 85018. Tel: 602-840-5066; Fax: 602-840-5732. Email: phoenixcursillo@me.com. Rev. Donald J. Kline, Spiritual Dir.; Deacon Jesse Sanchez, Assoc. Spiritual Dir.; Rosa Maria Estrada, Office Asst.

**Diocesan Council for the Society of St. Vincent De Paul*, P.O. Box 13600, 85002. Tel: 602-254-3338; 602-266-4673; Fax: 602-261-6829. Web: www.stvincentdepaul.net. Joseph J. Riley, Board Pres.; Stephen J. Zabilski, Exec. Dir.

Foundation for Senior Living, 1201 E. Thomas Rd., 85014. Tel: 602-285-1800. Email: gmikkelsen@fsl.org.

Affordable Services for Seniors, Inc., 1201 E. Thomas Rd., 85014. Tel: 602-285-1800. Email: shastings@fsl.org. Mr. Guy Mikkelsen, Pres.

Foundation for Senior Adult Living, Inc. Tel: 602-285-1800; Fax: 602-285-1838. Email: jgreene@fsl.org. Sweetwater Gardens (Apartments for the Handicapped), Phoenix; Kingman Heights Apartments, Kingman.

FSL Management Tel: 602-285-1800; Fax: 602-285-1838. Email: smikkelsen@fsl.org.

FSL Programs Tel: 602-285-1800; Fax: 602-285-1838. Email: lmartin@fsl.org. Ms. Linda Martin, Dir. Adult Day Health Care Centers; In-Home Care Services; Home Safety & Repair Program; Community Action Programs/Senior Centers; Adult Foster Care; Oasis (Older Adult Service & Information System); Pathways Program (Resources and Referral-Care Management).

FSL Real Estate Services Tel: 602-285-1800; Fax: 602-285-1838. Email: shastings@fsl.org. Mr. Guy Mikkelsen, Contact Person.

FSL Rural Development Tel: 602-285-1800; Fax: 602-285-1838. Email: jgreene@fsl.org. Becket House Apartments, Lake Havasu City; Vianney Villas Apartments, Avondale; Padua Hills Apartments, Wickenburg; St. Agnes Apartments, Williams, Amy Neal Retirement Center, Kingman.

FSL Home Improvements, 1201 E. Thomas Rd., 85014. Tel: 602-285-1800; Fax: 602-285-1838. Email: ksmith@fsl.org.

FSL Pathways, 1201 E. Thomas Rd., 85014. Tel: 602-285-1800; Fax: 602-285-1838. Email: chill@fsl.org. Carolyn Hill, Contact Person. Assisted Group Living Program (11 Houses), Phoenix.

Payson Senior Living, Inc., 1201 E. Thomas Rd., 85014. Tel: 602-285-1800; Fax: 602-285-1838. Email: jgreene@fsl.org. (Pineview Manor Apartments, Payson)

St. Clair Senior Living, 1201 E. Thomas Rd., 85014. Tel: 602-285-1800. Email: shastings@fsl.org. Mr. Guy Mikkelsen, Pres.

FSL Christopher Properties, 1201 E. Thomas Rd., 85014.

St. Joseph the Worker (Job Service), P.O. Box 13503, 85002-3503. 1125 W. Jackson St, 85007. Tel: 602-417-9854; Fax: 602-258-4940. Email: info@sjwjobs.org. Web: www.sjwjobs.org. Pat Moroney, Chm. Bd. & Pres.; Amy Caffarello, Exec. Dir.; Charles A. Gagnard II, Vice Chm. & Sec.; Carl Johnson, Treas. To assist homeless, low-income, and other disadvantaged individuals in their efforts to become self-sufficient through quality employment.

Saint Mary's Scholarship & Benefit Fund, 2525 N. Third St., 85004. Tel: 602-251-2511; Fax: 602-251-2595. Email: abayless@smknights.org. Web: www.smknights.org. Christopher Fahrendorf, Pres.; Angelyn Bayless.

CHANDLER. *The Catholic Singles Ministry, Inc.*, 4589 W. Ivanhoe St., 85226. Tel: 480-961-5311. Email: kmp.email@att.net. Web: www.catholicsinglesministry.org. Karina Penaranda, Contact Person.

GOODYEAR. *St. John Vianney School Development Fund*, 539 La Pasada Blvd., 85338. Tel: 623-932-3313; Fax: 623-932-1896. Email: teckert@sjvaz.net. Web: www.stjohnvianneyparish.com. Rev. Thomas J. Eckert, C.S.C., Pres.

MESA. **Life Teen, Inc.*, 2222 S. Dobson Rd., Ste. 601, 85202. Tel: 480-820-7001; Fax: 480-820-8653. Email: randyr@lifeteen.com. Web: www.lifeteen.com; www.catholicyouthministry.com. Randy Raus, Pres.

SCOTTSDALE. **Franciscan Friars of Arizona at the Franciscan Renewal Center*, 5802 E. Lincoln Dr., 85253. Tel: 480-948-7460; Fax: 480-948-2325.

**Mercy Housing Southwest*, Mailing Address: 4802 E. Ray Rd., Ste. 23, PMB 256, 85044. 401 W. Baseline Rd., Ste. 208, Tempe, 85283-5349. Tel: 602-952-9525; Fax: 480-755-2298. Email: swheelock@mercyhousing.org. Jennifer Erixon, Pres.

TEMPE. **City of the Lord*, 711 W. University Dr., 85281-3411. Tel: 480-968-5895; Fax: 480-921-9175. Email: bobcarmody@cityofthelord.org. Web: www.cityofthelord.org. Robert Carmody, Pres.; James R. Jones, Vice Pres.; James Hyde, Sec. & Treas.

**Friends of the Orphans*, 8925 E. Pima Center Pkwy., Ste. 145, Scottsdale, 85258. Tel: 480-967-9449. Email: infosw@friendsus.org. P.O. Box 25507, 85285-5507. Tel: 480-967-9449; Fax: 480-967-9288. Web: www.friendsoftheorphans.org. Deacon James Hoyt, Regl. Dir. Deacons 1; Total Staff 4; Total Assisted 3,700.

**Youth Arise North America dba Caritas In Veritate International; Partnership for China* 2121 S. Rural Rd., 85282. Tel: 480-344-5213; 202-997-8888; Fax: 480-967-5567. Henry Cappello, Pres.; Brad Hahn, Sec.

RELIGIOUS INSTITUTES OF MEN REPRESENTED IN THE DIOCESE

For further details refer to the corresponding bracketed number in the Religious Institutes of Men or Women section.

[]—*Apostles of Jesus*—A.J.

[0200]—*Benedictine Monks* (San Luis Obispo)—O.S.B.

[0600]—*Brothers of the Congregation of Holy Cross*—C.S.C.

[0400]—*Canons Regular of the Order of the Holy Cross*—O.S.C.

[0270]—*Carmelite Fathers and Brothers* (Prov. of Most Pure Heart of Mary)—O.Carm.

[0350]—*Cistercian Order of the Strict Observance (Trappists)*—O.C.S.O.

[0360]—*Claretian Missionaries* (Western Prov.)—C.M.F.

[]—*Congregation of the Holy Spirit*—C.S.Sp.

[1330]—*Congregation of the Mission Western Province*—C.M.

[]—*Disciples of Hope*—D.S.

[]—*Eudists-Congregation of Jesus & Mary*—EUD

[0520]—*Franciscan Friars* (Prov. of Santa Barbara; Prov. of Our Lady of Guadalupe; Prov. of St. John the Baptist)—O.F.M.

[]—*Institute of the Incarnate Word*—I.V.E.

[0690]—*Jesuit Fathers and Brothers* (California Prov.)—S.J.

[]—*Miles Jesu*—M.J.

[0830]—*Mill Hill Missionaries*—M.H.M.

[0910]—*Oblates of Mary Immaculate*—O.M.I.

[0430]—*Order of Preachers (Dominicans)* (Canada)—O.P.

[1065]—*Priestly Fraternity of St. Peter*—F.S.S.P.

[0610]—*Priests of the Congregation of Holy Cross*—C.S.C.

[1260]—*Society of Christ*—S.Ch.

[0975]—*Society of Our Lady of the Most Holy Trinity*—S.O.L.T.

[1200]—*Society of the Divine Savior* (North American Prov.)—S.D.S.

RELIGIOUS INSTITUTES OF WOMEN REPRESENTED IN THE DIOCESE

[0230]—*Benedictine Sisters of Pontifical Jurisdiction* (Duluth, MN)—O.S.B.

[0990]—*Congregation of Divine Providence* (Pittsburgh, PA)—C.D.P.

[2715]—*The Congregation of Missionary Sisters of Christ the King for Polish Immigrants* (Poznan, Poland; Chicago, IL)—M.Chr.

[3710]—*Congregation of the Sisters of St. Agnes* (Fond du Lac, WI)—C.S.A.

[1780]—*Congregation of the Sisters of Third Order of St. Francis of Perpetual Adoration* (LaCrosse, WI)—F.S.P.A.

[1710]—*Congregation of the Third Order of St. Francis of Mary Immaculate* (Joliet, IL)—O.S.F.

[0760]—*Daughters of Charity* (Los Altos Hills, CA)—D.C.

[0850]—*Daughters of Mary Help of Christians* (San Antonio, TX)—F.M.A.

[]—*Daughters of Mary Immaculate* (Chaldean; Bagdad, Iraq)—D.M.I.

[]—*Daughters of Mary, Mother of the Church* (Naga City, Philippines)—D.M.

[1070-03]—*Dominican Sisters* (Sinsinawa, WI)—O.P.

[1070-13]—*Dominican Sisters* (Adrian, MI)—O.P.

[]—*Dominican Sisters of Mary Mother of the Eucharist* (Ann Arbor, MI)—O.P.

[1115]—*Dominican Sisters of Peace* (Columbus, OH)—O.P.

[1120]—*Dominican Sisters of Roman Congregation* (Lewiston, ME)—O.P.

[1170]—*Felician Sisters* (Chicago, IL)—C.S.S.F.

[1230]—*Franciscan Sisters of Christian Charity* (Manitowoc, WI)—O.S.F.

[1910]—*Hermanas de Congregacion San Josefinas* (Mexico City)—H.J.

[2370]—*Institute of the Blessed Virgin Mary (Loretto Sisters)* (Prov. Wheaton, IL)—I.B.V.M.

[2740]—*Maryknoll Sisters of St. Dominic* (Maryknoll, NY)—M.M.

[]—*Missionarias Carmelitas de Santa Teresa del Nino Jesus* (Pueblo, Mexico)—M.C.S.T.N.J.

[2710]—*Missionaries of Charity* (Calcutta, India; Pacifica, CA)—M.C.

[]—*Missionaries of the Kingship of Christ, a Secular Institute* (Bethesda, MD)—S.I.M.

[3130]—*Our Lady of Victory Missionary Sisters* (Huntington, IN)—O.L.V.M.

[3210]—*Poor Clares of Perpetual Adoration* (Tonopah, AZ)—P.C.P.A.

[2970]—*School Sisters of Notre Dame* (Central Pacific Province)—S.S.N.D.

[1680]—*School Sisters of St. Francis* (Milwaukee, WI)—S.S.S.F.

[3590]—*Servants of Mary Servite Sisters* (Lady Smith, WI)—O.S.M.

[0570]—*Sisters of Charity of Seton Hill, Greensburg, Pennsylvania*—S.C.

[0430]—*Sisters of Charity of the B.V.M.* (Dubuque, IA)—B.V.M.

[2575]—*Sisters of Mercy of the Americas* (Buffalo, NY; Omaha, NE)—R.S.M.

[3000]—*Sisters of Notre Dame de Namur* (Cincinnati, OH)—S.N.D.deN.

[1540]—*Sisters of St. Francis* (Clinton, IA)—O.S.F.

[1705]—*The Sisters of St. Francis of Assisi* (Milwaukee, WI)—O.S.F.

[1570]—*Sisters of St. Francis of the Holy Family* (Dubuque, IA)—O.S.F.

[3830-15]—*Sisters of St. Joseph* (Concordia, KS)—C.S.J.

[3840]—*Sisters of St. Joseph of Carondelet* (Los Angeles, CA)—C.S.J.

[3930]—*Sisters of St. Joseph of the Third Order of St. Francis* (Stevens Point, WI)—S.S.J.-T.O.S.F.

[1030]—*Sisters of the Divine Savior* (Milwaukee, WI)—S.D.S.

[2183]—*Sisters of the Immaculate Heart of Mary Mother of Christ* (Nigeria; Minneapolis, MN)—I.H.M.

[3730]—*Sisters of the Order of St. Basil the Great* (Uniontown, PA)—O.S.B.M.

[3260]—*Sisters of the Precious Blood* (Dayton, OH)—C.PP.S.

[3105]—*Sisters of the Society of Our Lady of the Most Holy Trinity* (Bosque, NM)—S.O.L.T.

[2150]—*Sisters, Servants of the Immaculate Heart of Mary* (Monroe, MI)—I.H.M.

[3160]—*The Parish Visitors of Mary Immaculate* (Monroe, NY)—P.V.M.I.

[3330]—*Union of the Sisters of the Presentation of the B.V.M.* (Phoenix, AZ)—P.B.V.M.

NECROLOGY

† Mitchell, William J.—Died Dec. 23, 2010

† Morales, Raul, (Retired)—Died Dec. 4, 2010

† Peacock, Francis A.—Died July 16, 2010

An asterisk (*) denotes an organization that has established tax-exempt status directly with the IRS and is not covered by the USCCB Group Ruling.

Diocese of Pittsburgh

(Dioecesis Pittsburgensis)

Most Reverend

DAVID A. ZUBIK

Bishop of Pittsburgh; ordained May 3, 1975; appointed Auxiliary Bishop of Pittsburgh and Titular Bishop of Jamestown February 18, 1997; consecrated April 6, 1997; appointed Bishop of Green Bay October 10, 2003; installed December 12, 2003; appointed Bishop of Pittsburgh July 18, 2007; installed September 28, 2007. *Office: 111 Blvd. of the Allies, Pittsburgh, PA 15222-1618.*

NOTHING IS IMPOSSIBLE WITH GOD

Most Reverend

WILLIAM JOHN WALTERSHEID

Auxiliary Bishop of Pittsburgh; ordained July 11, 1992; appointed Auxiliary Bishop of Pittsburgh and Titular Bishop of California February 25, 2011; consecrated April 25, 2011. *Office: 111 Blvd. of the Allies, Pittsburgh, PA 15222-1618.*

Most Reverend

WILLIAM J. WINTER, V.G., S.T.D.

Retired Auxiliary Bishop of Pittsburgh; ordained December 17, 1955; appointed Auxiliary Bishop of Pittsburgh and Titular Bishop of Uthina December 27, 1988; consecrated February 13, 1989; retired May 20, 2005. *Res.: St. John Vianney Manor, 2600 Morange Rd., Pittsburgh, PA 15205.*

ESTABLISHED AUGUST 8, 1843.

Square Miles 3,754.

Comprises the Counties of Allegheny, Beaver, Lawrence, Washington, Greene, and Butler in the State of Pennsylvania.

Legal Title: The Diocese of Pittsburgh and each parish in the diocese are organized as separate Pennsylvania Charitable Trusts.

Pastoral Center: 111 Blvd. of the Allies, Pittsburgh, PA 15222-1618. Tel: 412-456-3000.

Web: www.diopitt.org

Email: communications@diopitt.org

STATISTICAL OVERVIEW

Personnel	
Bishop	1
Auxiliary Bishops	1
Retired Bishops	1
Priests: Diocesan Active in Diocese	253
Priests: Diocesan Active Outside Diocese	11
Priests: Diocesan in Foreign Missions	1
Priests: Retired, Sick or Absent	111
Number of Diocesan Priests	376
Religious Priests in Diocese	97
Total Priests in Diocese	473
Extern Priests in Diocese	16
Ordinations:	
Diocesan Priests	4
Transitional Deacons	3
Permanent Deacons	43
Permanent Deacons in Diocese	84
Total Brothers	34
Total Sisters	1,072
Parishes	
Parishes	208
With Resident Pastor:	
Resident Diocesan Priests	166
Resident Religious Priests	8
Without Resident Pastor:	
Administered by Priests	33
Administered by Religious Women	1
Professional Ministry Personnel:	
Brothers	1
Sisters	46
Lay Ministers	229
Welfare	
Catholic Hospitals	1
Total Assisted	221,990
Health Care Centers	1
Homes for the Aged	9
Total Assisted	1,970
Specialized Homes	4
Total Assisted	30,770
Special Centers for Social Services	7
Total Assisted	115,178
Residential Care of Disabled	1
Total Assisted	73
Educational	
Seminaries, Diocesan	1
Students from This Diocese	21
Diocesan Students in Other Seminaries	16
Total Seminarians	37
Colleges and Universities	3
Total Students	13,630
High Schools, Diocesan and Parish	8
Total Students	3,281
High Schools, Private	4
Total Students	694
Elementary Schools, Diocesan and Parish	85
Total Students	16,539
Elementary Schools, Private	3
Total Students	723
Non-residential Schools for the Disabled	2
Total Students	163
Catechesis/Religious Education:	
High School Students	3,803
Elementary Students	38,533
Total Students under Catholic Instruction	77,403
Teachers in the Diocese:	
Priests	2
Brothers	11
Sisters	55
Lay Teachers	1,635
Vital Statistics	
Receptions into the Church:	
Infant Baptism Totals	5,043
Minor Baptism Totals	160
Adult Baptism Totals	260
Received into Full Communion	478
First Communions	6,438
Confirmations	6,635
Marriages:	
Catholic	1,446
Interfaith	571
Total Marriages	2,017
Deaths	7,795
Total Catholic Population	634,736
Total Population	1,915,363

Former Bishops—Rt. Revs. MICHAEL J. O'CONNOR, S.J., D.D., ord. June 1, 1833; cons. Aug. 15, 1843; transferred to Erie and then to Pittsburgh Dec. 20, 1853; resigned May 23, 1860; entered the Society of Jesus Dec. 22, 1860; died at Woodstock College, MD, Oct. 18, 1872; MICHAEL DOMENEC, C.M., D.D., ord. June 30, 1839; cons. Dec. 9, 1860; transferred to Allegheny, Jan. 11, 1876; resigned July 29, 1877; died at Tarragona, Spain, Jan. 5, 1878; JOHN TUIGG, D.D., ord. May 14, 1850; cons. March 19, 1876; transferred to as Apostolic Administrator of Allegheny 1877; died at Altoona Dec. 7, 1889; RICHARD PHELAN, D.D., ord. May 4, 1854; cons. Aug. 2, 1885; Titular Bishop of Cibyra and Coadjutor to the Rt. Rev. John Tuigg; succeeded to Bishop Tuigg, Dec. 7, 1889; died at Idlewood Dec. 20, 1904; Most Revs. J. F. REGIS CANEVIN, D.D., ord. June 4, 1879; cons. Titular Bishop of Sabrata and Coadjutor, Feb. 24, 1903; succeeded to the See of Pittsburgh, Dec. 20, 1904; resigned Nov. 26, 1920; Titular Archbishop of Pelusium; appt. Jan. 9, 1921; died at Pittsburgh March 22, 1927; HUGH C. BOYLE, D.D., ord. July 2, 1898; succeeded to the See of Pittsburgh, June 16, 1921; cons. June 29, 1921; died at Pittsburgh Dec. 22, 1950; His Eminence JOHN CARDINAL DEARDEN, D.D., S.T.D., ord. Dec. 8, 1932; Titular Bishop of Sarepta and Coadjutor Bishop of Pittsburgh; appt. March 13, 1948; cons. May 18, 1948; succeeded to the See, Dec. 22, 1950; assistant at the Pontifical Throne, Oct. 15, 1957; installed at the Archdiocese of Detroit, Dec. 18, 1958; created Cardinal, April 28, 1969; died at Southfield, MI Aug. 1, 1988; JOHN CARDINAL WRIGHT, D.D., S.T.D., ord. Dec. 8, 1935; appt. May 10, 1947; cons. June 30, 1947; transferred to Bishop of Worcester, Jan. 28, 1950; transferred to Pittsburgh, Jan. 23, 1959; to the Roman Curia as Prefect of the Sacred Congregation for the Clergy; appt. April 23, 1969; created Cardinal, April 28, 1969; died at Cambridge, MA, Aug. 10, 1979; Most Rev. VINCENT M. LEONARD, D.D., ord. June 16, 1935; appt. Titular Bishop of Arsacal and Auxiliary, Feb. 28, 1964; cons. April 21, 1964; succeeded to the See, June 1, 1969; resigned June 30, 1983; died at Pittsburgh Aug. 28, 1994; His Eminence ANTHONY CARDINAL BEVILACQUA, D.D., J.C.D., J.D., ord. June 11, 1949; appt. Oct. 4, 1980; cons. Nov. 24, 1980; Bishop of Pittsburgh; appt. Oct. 10, 1983; installed Dec. 12, 1983; appt. Archbishop of Philadelphia, Feb. 11, 1988; created Cardinal, June 29, 1991; resigned Oct. 7, 2003; DONALD CARDINAL WUERL, ord. Dec. 17, 1966; appt. Titular Bishop of Rosemarkie and Auxiliary Bishop of Seattle Dec. 3, 1985; cons. Jan. 6, 1986; appt. and canonically installed Bishop of Pittsburgh Feb. 12, 1988; liturgically installed March 25, 1988; appt. Archbishop of Washington May 16, 2006; installed June 22, 2006; created Cardinal Nov. 20, 2010.

Pastoral Center—111 Blvd. of the Allies, Pittsburgh, 15222-1618. Tel: 412-456-3000. All official correspondence should be directed to this office.

Vicars General—Most Rev. WILLIAM J. WALTERSHEID; Very Rev. RONALD P. LENGWIN, V.G., M.Div.

Episcopal Vicars—Very Revs. FREDERICK L. CAIN, V.E., M.Div.; PHILIP N. FARRELL, V.E., M.A., M.Div.; ROBERT F. GUAY, V.E., M.Div., V.G.; SAMUEL J. ESPOSITO, V.E.

Vicar for Clergy—Most Rev. WILLIAM J. WALTERSHEID.

Vicar for Clergy Personnel—Very Rev. HARRY R. BIELEWICZ, V.E., M.Div.

Vicar for Canonical Services—Very Rev. LAWRENCE A. DINARDO, V.E., J.C.L.

Regional Vicars—

Vicariate 1—Very Rev. ROBERT F. GUAY, V.E., M.Div., V.G., Sisters of the Holy Spirit Motherhouse, 5246 Clarwin Ave., Pittsburgh, 15229. Tel: 412-456-5644.

Vicariate 2—Very Rev. FREDERICK L. CAIN, V.E., M.Div., Sisters of Saint Francis of the Providence of God, 1401 Hamilton Rd., Pittsburgh, 15234. Tel: 412-456-5645.

Vicariate 3—Very Rev. SAMUEL J. ESPOSITO, V.E.

Vicariate 4—Very Rev. PHILIP N. FARRELL, V.E., M.A., M.Div., 125 Franklin St., Butler, 16001. Tel: 412-456-5649.

Chancellor—ARLENE M. MCGANNON, D.Min. Tel: 412-456-3129.

Vice Chancellor—Very Rev. BRIAN J. WELDING, V.J., J.C.D., S.T.L. Tel: 412-456-3135.

Bishop's Office—Most Rev. DAVID ALLEN ZUBIK, D.D.; Mrs. JUDITH A. STYPERK, Exec. Asst.

General Secretary—Very Rev. RONALD P. LENGWIN, V.G., M.Div. Tel: 412-456-3131; Fax: 412-456-3197.

Associate General Secretary—ARLENE M. MCGANNON, D.Min. Tel: 412-456-3129.

Vicar for Canonical Services—Very Rev. LAWRENCE A. DINARDO, V.E., J.C.L., Address all correspondence to: 111 Blvd. of the Allies, Pittsburgh, 15222-1698. Tel: 412-456-3135; Fax: 412-456-3183.

Director, Department for Canon and Civil Law Services—Very Rev. LAWRENCE A. DINARDO, V.E., J.C.L., Address all correspondence to: 111 Blvd. of the Allies, Pittsburgh, 15222-1698. Tel: 412-456-3135; Fax: 412-456-3183.

Assistant Director, Department for Canon and Civil Law Services—Very Rev. BRIAN J. WELDING, V.J., J.C.D., S.T.L. Tel: 412-456-3135.

Matrimonial Concerns, Office for—Revs. RICHARD M. LELONIS, J.C.L., Dir.; LOUIS L. DENINNO, J.C.L., M.Div., Asst. Dir., Address all correspondence to: 2900 Noblestown Rd., Pittsburgh, 15205-4227. Tel: 412-456-3033; Fax: 412-456-3118.

Tribunal Office—Address all correspondence to: 2900 Noblestown Rd., Pittsburgh, 15205-4227. Tel: 412-456-3033; Fax: 412-456-3118.

Judicial Vicar—Very Rev. BRIAN J. WELDING, V.J., J.C.D., S.T.L.

Moderator of the Tribunal—Mr. JAY CONZEMIUS, J.C.L.

Adjutant Judicial Vicar—Rev. BENEDETTO P. VAGHETTO, J.C.L.

Judges—Revs. ROBERT J. AHLIN, J.C.L.; JAMES R. BEDILLION, J.C.L.; LOUIS L. DENINNO, J.C.L., M.Div.; Mr. JAY CONZEMIUS, J.C.L.; Very Rev. LAWRENCE A. DINARDO, V.E., J.C.L.; Rev. WILLIAM P. FEENEY, M.Div.; Very Rev. ROBERT F. GUAY, V.E., M.Div., V.G.; Mrs. RITA F. JOYCE, J.D., J.C.L.; Revs. JAMES E. KUNKEL, S.T.M.; RICHARD M. LELONIS, J.C.L.; JAMES P. MCDONOUGH, S.T.L., J.C.L.; THOMAS M. O'DONNELL, M.Div. (Retired); JOSEPH C. SCHEIB, J.C.L., M.Div., M.A.; CHARLES W. SPEICHER, Ph.D., S.T.M.

Promoter of Justice—Very Rev. LAWRENCE A. DINARDO, V.E., J.C.L.

Defenders of the Bond—Rev. Msgr. WILLIAM M. OGRODOWSKI, V.E., S.T.L.; Revs. JAMES L. BRUNEY, M.Div.; DENNIS J. COLAMARINO; BENEDETTO P. VAGHETTO, J.C.L.

Notaries—Ms. MARTHA J. BRAUN; Ms. SYLVIA VEHEC; Ms. PHYLLIS GEINZER.

Secretary for Catholic Education—Rev. KRIS D. STUBNA, S.T.D.

Secretary for Clergy—Very Rev. HARRY R. BIELEWICZ, V.E., M.Div., Episcopal Vicar for Clergy Personnel; Mrs. RITA E. FLAHERTY, M.S.W., Diocesan Assistance Coord., 111 Blvd. of the Allies, Pittsburgh, 15222-1618. Tel: 412-456-3060; Fax: 412-456-3188; Tel: 888-808-1235 (Toll Free Victim's Assistance Hotline).

Secretary for Evangelization and Social Concerns—Deacon ALEXANDER WROBLICKY, 111 Blvd. of the Allies, Pittsburgh, 15222-1618. Tel: 412-456-3156; Fax: 412-456-3180.

Department for Consecrated Life—Sr. GERALDINE MARIE WODARCZYK, C.S.F.N., Delegate for Rel., 111 Blvd. of the Allies, Pittsburgh, 15222. Tel: 412-456-3067.

Priest Council—Most Rev. DAVID ALLEN ZUBIK, D.D.; Very Rev. HARRY R. BIELEWICZ, V.E., M.Div.; Revs. CHARLES S. BOBER, S.T.D.; THOMAS J. BURKE, M.Div.; Very Revs. FREDERICK L. CAIN, V.E., M.Div.; LAWRENCE A. DINARDO, V.E., J.C.L.; Rev. MARK A. ECKMAN, M.Div.; Very Rev. SAMUEL J. ESPOSITO, V.E.; Rev. REGIS M. FARMER, D.Min.; Very Rev. PHILIP N. FARRELL, V.E., M.A., M.Div.; Rev. WILLIAM P. FEENEY, M.Div.; Very Rev. JOHN FOGARTY, C.S.Sp.; Revs. JOSEPH M. FREEDY; ANTHONY GARGOTTA; Very Rev. ROBERT F. GUAY, V.E., M.Div., V.G.; Rev. JOHN R. HANEY, M.Div.; Very Rev. GERALD LABA, C.P.; Revs. DANIEL J. LANGA; EUGENE F. LAUER (Retired); Very Rev. RONALD P. LENGWIN, V.G., M.Div.; Rev. MATTHEW R. MCCLAIN; Very Rev. JOSEPH M. MELE, Ph.D.; Revs. JEREMIAH T. O'SHEA; JOHN W. SKIRTICH; THOMAS A. SPARACINO, M.Div.; BENEDETTO P. VAGHETTO, J.C.L.; Most Rev. WILLIAM J. WALTERSHEID; Rev. DANIEL W. WHALEN, S.T.L., J.D.; Most Rev. WILLIAM J. WINTER, V.G., S.T.D. (Retired).

College of Consultors—Most Rev. DAVID ALLEN ZUBIK, D.D.; Very Revs. ROBERT F. GUAY, V.E., M.Div., V.G.; FREDERICK L. CAIN, V.E., M.Div.; SAMUEL J. ESPOSITO, V.E.; PHILIP N. FARRELL, V.E., M.A., M.Div.; RONALD P. LENGWIN, V.G., M.Div.; Revs. CHARLES S. BOBER, S.T.D.; THOMAS J. BURKE, M.Div.; MARK A. ECKMAN, M.Div.; REGIS M. FARMER, D.Min.; JOHN W. SKIRTICH; BENEDETTO P. VAGHETTO, J.C.L.; Most Rev. WILLIAM J. WALTERSHEID.

Diocesan Development Board—PATRICK M. JOYCE, Ph.D., Chm.; Mr. WAYNE C. BOETTCHER; Rev. RICHARD A. INFANTE, M.F.A., M.L.S., M.Div., M.A.; (Ret.) Judge MAUREEN LALLY-GREEN; Mr. AMBROSE MURRAY; Mr. FREDERICK P. O'BRIEN; Ms. SUSAN L. RAUSCHER; Rev. KRIS D. STUBNA, S.T.D.

Diocesan Finance Council—Most Rev. DAVID ALLEN ZUBIK, D.D.; Very Rev. RONALD P. LENGWIN, V.G., M.Div.; Mr. WAYNE C. BOETTCHER; Mrs. KATHLEEN W. BUECHEL; Ms. KATHLEEN GEIS; Mr. HOWARD HANNA III; Mr. MICHAEL J. HANNON; Mr. FREDERICK P. O'BRIEN; Mr. CHRISTOPHER G. PONTICELLO, Esq., J.D.; Mr. CHRISTOPHER SOBEL; Mr. JAMES C. STALDER.

Clergy Personnel Board—Rev. FRANK D. ALMADE, Ph.D.; Very Revs. RONALD P. LENGWIN, V.G., M.Div.; HARRY R. BIELEWICZ, V.E., M.Div., Chm.; Deacon STEPHEN J. BYERS; Very Rev. FREDERICK L. CAIN, V.E., M.Div.; Rev. MARK A. ECKMAN, M.Div.; Very Revs. SAMUEL J. ESPOSITO, V.E.; PHILIP N. FARRELL, V.E., M.A., M.Div.; ROBERT F. GUAY, V.E., M.Div., V.G.; Rev. JOHN R. HANEY, M.Div.; Rev. Msgr. JOSEPH R. LAMONDE; Very Rev. JOSEPH M. MELE, Ph.D.; Revs. ROBERT M. MILLER, S.T.L.; TERRENCE P. O'CONNOR, M.Div., J.D.; JOHN W. SKIRTICH; LOUIS F. VALLONE, M.Div.; Most Rev. WILLIAM J. WALTERSHEID; Rev. DANIEL W. WHALEN, S.T.L., J.D.

Diocesan Administration

Administrative Procedures, Office for—Mrs. RITA F. JOYCE, J.D., J.C.L., Admin. Tel: 412-456-3135.

Adult and Family Faith Formation, Office for—Mrs. MAUREEN H. WOOD, M.R.E., Dir. Tel: 412-456-3160; Deacon STEPHEN J. BYERS, Asst. Tel: 412-456-3124.

Archives and Record Center—Mr. KENNETH A. WHITE, Dir.; Mr. BURRIS E. ESPLEN IV, Archivist, 4721 Fifth Ave., Pittsburgh, 15213-2915. Tel: 412-456-3158.

Diocesan Assistance Coordinator—Mrs. RITA E. FLAHERTY, M.S.W. Tel: 412-456-3060. Email: rflaherty@diopitt.org.

Auditors/Analysts, Office for the—Mr. JAMES E. STIERHEIM, Supvr. Tel: 412-456-3029.

Black Catholics, Ethnic and Cultural Communities, Dept. for—Mrs. MARGRETTA STOKES TUCKER, M.Ed., Dir. Tel: 412-456-3170.

Blind Persons— Refer to Disabilities, Dept. for Persons with

Educational Budget and Planning, Office for—Mr. ROY CARTIER, M.B.A., M.R.P., Dir. Tel: 412-456-3108.

Building Commission—Very Rev. RONALD P. LENGWIN, V.G., M.Div.; Mr. JAMES J. ZIELINSKI, Exec. Sec. Tel: 412-456-3034.

Building Services, Office for—Mrs. DARLENE M. HOLZER, Dir. Tel: 412-456-3016.

Business Services, Dept. for—Mr. FREDERICK P. O'BRIEN, CFO & Dir. Tel: 412-456-3137.

Campus Ministry, Office for—Rev. W. PETER HORTON, M.A., M.Div., Dir., 1010 McNeilly Rd., Pittsburgh, 15226-2513. Tel: 412-456-3140.

Canon and Civil Law Services, Dept. for—Very Revs. LAWRENCE A. DINARDO, V.E., J.C.L., Dir.; BRIAN J. WELDING, V.J., J.C.D., S.T.L., Asst. Dir. Tel: 412-456-3135.

Canonical Services, Office for—Very Revs. LAWRENCE A. DINARDO, V.E., J.C.L., Vicar; BRIAN J. WELDING, V.J., J.C.D., S.T.L., Asst. Dir. Tel: 412-456-3135.

Catechetical Ministries and Catechesis, Office for—Mrs. SHARON T. TYBOROWSKI HACHMAN, Dir. Tel: 412-456-3110.

Catholic Charities—Ms. SUSAN L. RAUSCHER, Exec. Dir., 212 9th St., Pittsburgh, 15222. Tel: 412-456-6999. Allegheny County, 212 9th St., Pittsburgh, 15222. Tel: 412-456-6999. Beaver County, 3582 Brodhead Rd., Ste. 108, Monaca, 15601. Tel: 724-775-0758. Butler County, 407 A W. Jefferson St., Butler, 16001. Tel: 724-287-4011. Greene County, 72 E. High St., Waynesburg, 15370. Tel: 724-627-6410. Lawrence County, 413 Highland Ave., New Castle, 16101. Tel: 724-658-5526. Washington County, 331 S. Main St., Washington, 15301. Tel: 724-228-7722. Roselia Center, 624 Clyde St., Pittsburgh, 15213. Tel: 412-682-4410; 412-682-4411. St. Joseph's House of Hospitality, 1635 Bedford Ave., Pittsburgh, 15219. Tel: 412-471-0666.

Catholic Charities Health Care Center, Inc.—ANNETTE FETCHKO, Admin. & Contact Person, 212 Ninth St., Pittsburgh, 15222. Tel: 412-456-6911.

Challenges: Options in Aging—Shenley Square, 2706 Mercer Rd., New Castle, 16105-1422.

Catholic Cemeteries Assoc., The—Ms. ANNABELLE MCGANNON, Exec. Dir., 718 Hazelwood Ave., Pittsburgh, 15217-2807. Tel: 412-521-9133.

Catholic Schools, Dept. for—ROBERT L. PASERBA, Ed.D., Supt. Catholic Schools; Sr. MARY JO MUTSCHLER, S.C., Asst. Supt. Catholic Elementary Schools; Mr. DONALD A. TETI, M.Ed., Asst. Supt. Catholic Secondary Schools; RONALD T. BOWES, D.A., Asst. Supt. Public Policy & Devel. Tel: 412-456-3090.

Educational Consultants, Elementary, Office for—2900 Noblestown Rd., Pittsburgh, 15205. Tel: 412-456-3070. Mr. MICHAEL C. KILLMEYER, M.Ed., M.S.; Sisters CATHERINE ANN KOLLER, C.D.P., M.A.; LORETTA KRALL, C.S.J., M.A.; CECILIA GRANDILLO, M.A.

Educational Consultants, Secondary, Office for—111 Boulevard of the Allies, Pittsburgh, 15222. Tel: 412-456-3070. EDWARD G. SCHEID, Ph.D.

Elementary School Catechesis and Faith Formation, Office for—111 Blvd. of the Allies, Pittsburgh, 15222. Tel: 412-456-3115. HOLLY JOY PENZENSTALDER.

Secondary School Catechesis and Faith Formation, Office for—1010 McNeilly Rd., Pittsburgh, 15226. Tel: 412-456-3140. Mr. CHRISTOPHER J. CHAPMAN.

Institutional Ministries—111 Blvd. of the Allies, Pittsburgh, 15222. Rev. Msgr. JOSEPH R. LAMONDE. Tel: 412-456-3060.

Charismatic Prayer Groups—Rev. JOHN P. SWEENEY, M.Div., Moderator, St. Bonaventure Parish, 2001 Mount Royal Blvd., Glenshaw, 15116-2099. Tel: 412-486-2606.

Chief Facilities Officer—Mr. MICHAEL J. ARNOLD. Tel: 412-456-3093.

Chief Financial Officer—Mr. FREDERICK P. O'BRIEN. Tel: 412-456-3137.

Church Relations, Office for—MAUREEN LALLY-GREEN, Dir. (Ret.) JudgeTel: 412-456-3164.

Communications Commission—Mr. ROBERT P. LOCKWOOD, Chm. Tel: 412-456-3020.

Communications, Dept. for—Mr. ROBERT P. LOCKWOOD, Dir.

Continuing Education of Clergy, Office for—Rev. TERRENCE P. O'CONNOR, M.Div., J.D., Dir., St. Paul Seminary, 2900 Noblestown Rd., Pittsburgh, 15205-4227. Tel: 412-456-3048.

Cultural Diversity, Commission—Mrs. BESS BIAMONTE, Chm. Tel: 412-456-3170; Mrs. MARGRETTA STOKES TUCKER, M.Ed., Diocesan Liaison.

Deaf Persons— Refer to Disabilities, Dept. for Persons with

Diaconate, Office for the—Deacon STEPHEN J. BYERS, Dir. Tel: 412-456-3124.

Diocesan National Black Catholic Congress Leadership Team—VACANT, Team Leader. Tel: 412-456-3170; Mrs. MARGRETTA STOKES TUCKER, M.Ed., Diocesan Liaison.

Disabilities, Dept. for Persons with—Mrs. LORETTA UHLMANN, Dir.; Rev. WALTER G. RYDZON, M.Div., Chap. to Deaf Persons; Deacon TIM KILLMEYER, Asst. to Chap. Tel: 412-456-3119 (Voice); 412-456-3122 (TTY).

Ecumenical and Interfaith Commission—Very Rev. RONALD P. LENGWIN, V.G., M.Div., Chm. Tel: 412-456-3021.

Media and Technology, Dept. for—Deacon JEFFREY A. HIRST, Dir., St. Paul Seminary, 2900 Noblestown Rd., Pittsburgh, 15205-4227. Tel: 412-456-3120.

Envisioning Ministry, Dept. for—MARY ANN GUBISH, D.Min., Dir. Tel: 412-456-3047.

Ethnic Ministries, Office for—Chaplain to Korean Catholic Community: Rev. JONG-SUP KIM.

Chaplain to Latino Catholic Community: Rev. DANIELE VALLECORSA, S.T.L. Chaplain to Vietnamese Catholic Community: Rev. DAM D. NGUYEN, M.Div. Tel: 412-456-3170.

Financial Services, Office for—Mr. WAYNE C. BOETTCHER, Dir. Tel: 412-456-3025.

Central Accounting Services—Tel: 412-456-3030.

Parish Accounting Services—Tel: 412-456-3025.

Foundation, Catholic Diocese of Pittsburgh—PATRICK M. JOYCE, Ph.D., Dir. Tel: 412-456-3085.

Health Care Liaison, Office of the—Very Rev. LAWRENCE A. DINARDO, V.E., J.C.L. Tel: 412-456-3135.

Human Dignity, Department for—Mrs. HELENE PAHARIK, Dir. Tel: 412-456-3156.

Information Technology— Services provided by Vital Solutions International. Mr. EDWARD HANEY, Dir. Tel: 412-456-3152.

Insurance/Employee Benefits, Office for—Mr. DAVID S. STEWART, A.R.M., Dir. Tel: 412-456-3045.

Justice and Peace Commission—VERONICA C. MORGAN-LEE, Ph.D., Chm.; Mrs. HELENE PAHARIK, Liaison. Tel: 412-456-3156.

Lay Personnel, Office for—Mrs. DARLENE M. HOLZER, Dir. Tel: 412-456-3016.

Learning Media Center—Deacon JEFFREY A. HIRST, Dir., St. Paul Seminary, 2900 Noblestown Rd., Pittsburgh, 15205-4227. Tel: 412-456-3120.

Legal Services, Office for—Mrs. RITA F. JOYCE, J.D., J.C.L., Gen. Counsel; KRISTIN M. BOOSE, J.D., Asst. Gen. Counsel; PAUL IURLANO, Legal Counsel; Mr. CHRISTOPHER G. PONTICELLO, Esq., J.D., Assoc. Gen. Counsel. Tel: 412-456-3126.

Matrimonial Concerns, Office for—Revs. RICHARD M. LELONIS, J.C.L., Dir.; LOUIS L. DENINNO, J.C.L., M.Div., Canonical Consultant, 2900 Noblestown Rd., Pittsburgh, 15205-4227. Tel: 412-456-3076.

Diocesan Review Board—Very Rev. LAWRENCE A. DINARDO, V.E., J.C.L., Exec. Sec. Tel: 412-456-3135.

Media and Technology, Department for—Deacon JEFFREY A. HIRST, Dir., St. Paul Seminary, 2900 Noblestown Rd., Pittsburgh, 15205. Tel: 412-456-3120.

Ministries, Institute for—Sr. MARY ANN CORR, S.C., Dir., 111 Blvd. of the Allies, Pittsburgh, 15222. Tel: 412-456-3068.

Mission Office—Very Rev. RONALD P. LENGWIN, V.G., M.Div., Dir. Tel: 412-456-3065.

Music, Office for—Rev. JAMES J. CHEPPONIS, M.Div., M.A., Dir.; Mr. DONALD FELLOWS, Assoc. Dir., St. Paul Seminary, 2900 Noblestown Rd., Pittsburgh, 15205-4227. Tel: 412-456-3042.

Natural Family Planning Advisory Committee—Deacon STEPHEN J. BYERS, Chm. Tel: 412-456-3124; Mrs. MAUREEN H. WOOD, M.R.E., Diocesan Liaison. Tel: 412-456-3160.

Newspaper— "Pittsburgh Catholic" Mr. ROBERT P. LOCKWOOD, Gen. Mgr.; Mr. WILLIAM CONE, Editor, 135 First Ave., #200, Pittsburgh, 15222-1506. Tel: 412-471-1252.

Parish Life and Lay Leadership, Secretariat for—Mr. JOHN P. FLAHERTY, M.A., Sec. Tel: 412-456-3146.

Pastoral Formation, Office for—Sr. CINDY ANN KIBLER, S.H.S. Tel: 412-456-3053.

Payroll, Office for—Mr. JOHN G. CVETIC, Dir. Tel: 412-456-3006.

Peace, Justice and Human Development, Office for—Mrs. HELENE PAHARIK, Dir. Tel: 412-456-3156.

Pilgrimage Office—Very Rev. RONALD P. LENGWIN, V.G., M.Div., Dir. Tel: 412-456-3065.

Pornography, Commission to Counter—Mrs. NORMA NORRIS, Chm.; Mrs. HELENE PAHARIK, Diocesan Liaison. Tel: 412-456-3156.

Post-Ordination Formation, Department for—Very Rev. JOSEPH M. MELE, Ph.D., Dir., St. Paul Seminary, 2900 Noblestown Rd., Pittsburgh, 15205-4227. Tel: 412-456-3048.

Pre-Ordination Formation, Department for—Very Rev. JOSEPH M. MELE, Ph.D., St. Paul Seminary, 2900 Noblestown Rd., Pittsburgh, 15205-4227. Tel: 412-456-3048.

Priestly Vocations, Office for—Rev. JOSEPH M. FREEDY, Dir. Tel: 412-456-3123.

Parish Property, Planning and Development, Office for—Mr. JAMES J. ZIELINSKI, Dir., 135 First Ave., Pittsburgh, 15222. Tel: 412-456-3034.

Property, Planning and Development, Department for—Mr. MICHAEL J. ARNOLD.

Catholic Institute Property, Planning and Development, Office for—Mr. RAYMOND FRANKS.

Protection of Children and Young People, Office for the—Mr. RONALD W. RAGAN, M.P.A., Dir., St. Paul Seminary, 2900 Noblestown Rd., Pittsburgh, 15205. Tel: 412-456-5633.

Public and Community Affairs, Office for—Very Rev. RONALD P. LENGWIN, V.G., M.Div., Dir. Tel: 412-456-3021.

Religious Education, Dept. for—Mrs. JUDITH A. KIRK, Dir. Tel: 412-456-3112.

Respect Life, Office for—Mrs. HELENE PAHARIK, Dir. Tel: 412-456-3156.

Retired Priests, Delegate—Rev. LEROY A. DIPIETRO, Delegate. Tel: 412-732-2797.

Retired Priests, Residences for—SUSAN COLLINS, Admin., Cardinal Dearden Center, 4721 Fifth Ave., Pittsburgh, 15213-2915. Tel: 412-687-8022. St. John Vianney Manor, 2600 Morange Rd., Pittsburgh, 15205-4268. Tel: 412-928-0825.

St. Paul Cathedral—Very Rev. DONALD P. BREIER, M.Div., Rector & Pastor, 108 N. Dithridge St., Pittsburgh, 15213-2694. Tel: 412-621-4951.

St. Paul Seminary—Very Rev. JOSEPH M. MELE, Ph.D., Rector; Rev. TERRENCE P. O'CONNOR, M.Div., J.D., Vice Rector, Dir. Spiritual Formation.

Society for the Propagation of the Faith—Very Rev. RONALD P. LENGWIN, V.G., M.Div., Dir. Tel: 412-456-3065.

Stewardship and Development, Office for—PATRICK M. JOYCE, Ph.D., Dir.; Mrs. DOLORES C. NYPAVER, Asst. Dir.; Mr. PAUL F. STABILE, Dir. Planned Giving. Tel: 412-456-3085.

Television and Radio Production— Refer to Media and Technology, Department for

Theological Commission—Rev. JOSEPH J. KLEPPNER, S.T.L., Ph.D., Chm. Tel: 412-456-3100.

Vision Impairments, Persons with— Refer to Disabilities, Dept. for Persons with

Worship Commission—Rev. JAMES R. GRETZ, Chm. Tel: 412-456-3041.

Worship, Dept. for—Rev. JAMES R. GRETZ, Dir., St. Paul Seminary, 2900 Noblestown Rd., Pittsburgh, 15205-4227. Tel: 412-456-3041.

Youth and Young Adult Ministry, Dept. for—Mrs. JOYCE A. GILLOOLY, M.Ed., Dir.; Mr. CHRISTOPHER J. CHAPMAN, Assoc. Dir.; Mr. GARY RONEY, Assoc. Dir.; Deacon VICTOR P. SATTER, 1010 McNeilly Rd., Pittsburgh, 15226-2513. Tel: 412-456-3140.

CLERGY, PARISHES, MISSIONS AND PAROCHIAL SCHOOLS

CITY OF PITTSBURGH, PROPER

(ALLEGHENY COUNTY)

1—ST. PAUL CATHEDRAL (1834) Very Rev. Donald P. Breier; Revs. Michael J. Roche, Parochial Vicar; Steven M. Palsa, Parochial Vicar. In Res., Revs. Daniele Vallecorsa; Barry P. O'Leary.
Res.: 108 N. Dithridge St., 15213. Tel: 412-621-4951; Fax: 412-621-1079. Email: info@saintpaulcathedral.org. Web: www.saintpaulcathedral.org.
Catechesis/Religious Program—125 N. Craig St., 15213. Tel: 412-621-9444. Students 43.

2—ST. AGNES, Closed. For sacramental records contact St. Paul Cathedral.

3—ST. ANN, (Hungarian), Closed. See St. Stephen.

4—ST. AUGUSTINE, (German), Closed. See Our Lady of the Angels.

5—ST. BEDE (1922) Rev. Edward M. Bryce; Sr. Mary Elizabeth Schrei, S.C., Pastoral Assoc. In Res., Revs. William Okot, A.J.; John Twinomujuni.
Res.: 509 S. Dallas Ave., 15208. Tel: 412-661-7222; Fax: 412-661-9337. Web: www.catholic-church.org/stbedepgh.
School—6920 Edgerton Ave., 15208. Tel: 412-661-9425; Fax: 412-661-0447. Lay Teachers 28; Students 362.
Catechesis/Religious Program—Students 86.

6—ST. BENEDICT THE MOOR (1889), (African American), Rev. Richard J. Zelik, O.F.M.Cap., Admin.; Deacon Reynold Wilmer.
Mailing Address: *Administrative Center*, 164 Washington Pl., 15219.
Rectory—91 Crawford St., 15219. Tel: 412-471-0257; Fax: 412-471-1345. Email: churchoffice@stbenedictthemoor.org. Web: www.stbenedictthemoor.org.
School—631 Watt St., 15219. Tel: 412-682-3755; Fax: 412-682-4058. Email: stben@stbenedictthemoorschool.org. Web: www.stbenedictthemoorschool.org. Sisters of St. Joseph 5; Lay Teachers 13; Students 265.
Catechesis/Religious Program—Students 30.
Convent—Tel: 412-621-0519.

7—ST. CATHERINE OF SIENA (Beechview) (1902) Rev. James M. Bachner; Deacon Thomas O'Neill.
Res.: 1810 Belasco Ave., 15216. Tel: 412-531-2135; Fax: 412-531-8543. Email: saintcatherine15216@yahoo.com.
Catechesis/Religious Program—Tel: 412-561-0399. Students 75.

8—ST. CHARLES LWANGA PARISH (1992) Rev. David H. Taylor. Consolidated from the following churches: Corpus Christi, Holy Rosary, Mother of Good Counsel, Our Lady Help of Christians, Our Lady of the Most Blessed Sacrament, SS. Peter & Paul, and St. Walburga.
Res.: 7114 Kelly St., 15208. Tel: 412-731-3020; Fax: 412-731-1615. Email: frdht@aol.com.
See Sister Thea Bowman Catholic Academy, Pittsburgh under Consolidated Schools located in the Institution section.
Catechesis/Religious Program—Email: nadinepowell@verizon.net. Students 21.

9—CORPUS CHRISTI, Closed. See St. Charles Lwanga.

10—ST. ELIZABETH OF HUNGARY, (Slovak), Closed. See St. Patrick-St. Stanislaus Kostka.

11—EPIPHANY (1902), (Irish), Rev. John L. McKenna; Most Rev. William J. Waltersheid; Revs. Cornelius W. McCaulley (Retired); John Odeyemi (Nigeria).
Res.: 164 Washington Pl., 15219-3502. Tel: 412-471-0257; Fax: 412-471-1345. Email: churchoffice@epiphanychurch.net. Web: www.epiphanychurch.net.

12—HOLY FAMILY, (Polish), Closed. See Our Lady of the Angels.

13—HOLY ROSARY, Closed. See St. Charles Lwanga.

14—ST. HYACINTH, (Polish), Closed. See St. Regis.

15—IMMACULATE CONCEPTION (1905), (Italian), Merged with St. Joseph, Pittsburgh to form Immaculate Conception-St. Joseph, Pittsburgh.

16—IMMACULATE CONCEPTION-ST. JOSEPH (2001), (German), Revs. John E. Dinello; Vincent F. Kolo; Douglas A. Boyd.
Res.: 4712 Liberty Ave., 15224. Tel: 412-682-2354; Fax: 412-682-6766. Email: macsj2@verizon.net.
School—321 Edmond St., 15224. Tel: 412-621-5199; Fax: 412-621-5601.
Catechesis/Religious Program—Students 27.

17—IMMACULATE HEART OF MARY (1897), (Polish), Rev. Joseph E. Swierczynski.
Res.: 3058 Brereton Ave., 15219. Tel: 412-621-5170; Fax: 412-621-7445.
Catechesis/Religious Program—Tel: 412-682-2886; Fax: 412-682-6889. Twinned with Our Lady of Angels. Students 15.

18—ST. JOACHIM, Closed. See St. Rosalia.

19—ST. JOHN THE BAPTIST, Closed. See Our Lady of the Angels.

20—ST. JOSEPH (1872), (German), Merged with Immaculate Conception, Pittsburgh to form Immaculate Conception-St. Joseph, Pittsburgh.

21—ST. KIERAN, Closed. See St. Matthew.

22—ST. LAWRENCE O'TOOLE (East End) (1897) Rev. James G. Graham.
Res.: 5323 Penn Ave., 15224. Tel: 412-363-1771; Fax: 412-363-7552.
Catechesis/Religious Program—

23—ST. MARTIN (West End) Closed. See Guardian Angels.

24—ST. MARY ASSUMPTION (Lawrenceville) Closed. See St. Matthew.

25—ST. MARY OF MERCY (1870) Rev. John L. McKenna.
Mailing Address: *Administrative Center*, 164 Washington Pl., 15219. In Res., Very Rev. Ronald P. Lengwin; Revs. Thomas M. O'Donnell (Retired); Theo Mbaegbu (Nigeria) (PIt); Francis Oranefo (Nigeria).
Res.: 202 Stanwix St., 15222. Tel: 412-261-0110; Fax: 412-261-0113. Email: services_stmaryofmercy@verizon.net. Web: www.stmaryofmercy.org.

26—ST. MARY'S (Lawrenceville) Closed. See Our Lady of the Angels.

27—ST. MATTHEW (1993), Consolidated from St. Kieran and St. Mary Assumption. Rev. Joseph J. Janiszeski, T.O.R.
Res.: 5322 Carnegie St., 15201. Tel: 412-781-6701; Fax: 412-781-1331.
Catechesis/Religious Program— Combined with Our Lady of Angels.

28—MOTHER OF GOOD COUNSEL, (Italian), Closed. See St. Charles Lwanga.

29—OUR LADY HELP OF CHRISTIANS, (Italian), Closed. See St. Charles Lwanga.

30—OUR LADY OF THE ANGELS (1993) [CEM], Consolidated from St. Augustine, Holy Family, St. John the Baptist and St. Mary. Revs. John D. Harvey, O.F.M.Cap.; Michael P. Greb, O.F.M.Cap. In Res., Rev. Reginald Russo, O.F.M.Cap.; Bro. David Cira, O.F.M.Cap.
Res.: 225 37th St., 15201. Tel: 412-682-0929; Fax: 412-682-6889. Email: parish@oloa.org. Web: www.oloa.org.
Catechesis/Religious Program—Gene Ritter, D.R.E.;

Faye Ritter, D.R.E. Students 45.
31—OUR LADY OF THE MOST BLESSED SACRAMENT, Closed. See St. Charles Lwanga.
32—ST. PATRICK (Strip District) Closed. See St. Patrick-St. Stanislaus Kostka.
33—ST. PATRICK-ST. STANISLAUS KOSTKA (1993), (Polish), Rev. Harry E. Nichols. Consolidated with St. Stanislaus, St. Patrick and St. Elizabeth of Hungary. In Res., Rev. Albert Schempp, M.I.
Res. & Parish Office: 57 21st St., 15222. Tel: 412-471-4767; Fax: 412-471-1209. Email: saintsinthestrip@comcast.net. Web: www.saintsinthestrip.org.
Catechesis/Religious Program—Students 8.
34—SS. PETER AND PAUL (East Liberty) Closed. See St. Charles Lwanga.
35—ST. PHILOMENA (Squirrel Hill) Closed. See St. Bede.
36—ST. RAPHAEL (1911) Rev. Joseph E. Sioli.
Res.: 1118 Chislett St., 15206. Tel: 412-661-3100; Fax: 412-661-4105. Email: straphaelchurch@verizon.net.
School—(Grades PreSchool-8), 1154 Chislett St., 15206. Tel: 412-661-0288; Fax: 412-661-0428. Email: straph@verizon.net. Web: www.straphaelelementaryschool.net. Lay Teachers 10; Students 150.
Catechesis/Religious Program—Tel: 412-661-0290 (Sunday Only). Students 37.
37—ST. REGIS (1993), Merged with St. Hyacinth (Polish). Rev. Daniele Vallecorsa.
Mailing Address: 3235 Parkview Ave., 15213.
Res.: *St. Paul Cathedral Rectory*, 108 N. Dithridge St., 15213. Tel: 412-621-4951; Fax: 412-681-1175. Email: 51101@diopitt.org.
Catechesis/Religious Program—Students 85.
38—ST. ROSALIA (1993), Merged with St. Joachim. Rev. Joseph W. Reschick. In Res., Rev. Joseph C. Beck.
Res.: 411 Greenfield Ave., 15207. Tel: 412-421-5766; Fax: 412-421-4529. Email: strosaliaparish@verizon.net. Web: www.strosaliaparish.org.
School—Tel: 412-521-3005; Fax: 412-521-2763. Lay Teachers 12; Students 147.
Catechesis/Religious Program—Tel: 412-521-7836. Students 51.
39—SACRED HEART (1872) Revs. Robert J. Grecco; Mark J. Skertich, Parochial Vicar. In Res., Rev. Edward S. Litavec (Retired).
Res.: 310 Shady Ave., 15206. Tel: 412-661-0187; Fax: 412-661-7932. Email: sacredheartshadyside@comcast.net.
School—325 Emerson St., 15206. Tel: 412-441-1582; Fax: 412-441-2798. Email: info@shes-pgh.org. Web: www.sacredheartpgh.org. Sisters of Charity 1; Sisters of St. Joseph 1; Lay Teachers 22; Students 440.
Catechesis/Religious Program—Students 490.
40—ST. STANISLAUS (Strip District), (Polish), Closed. See St. Patrick-St. Stanislaus Kostka.
41—ST. STEPHEN (1993), Merged with St. Ann. Rev. Daniel L. Walsh, C.S.Sp.
Mailing Address: 5115 Second Ave., 15207. Tel: 412-421-9210; Fax: 412-421-6421. Email: ststephen@verizon.net.
Res.: 131 E. Elizabeth St., 15207. Tel: 412-421-9210.
Catechesis/Religious Program—134 E. Elizabeth St., 15207. Tel: 412-421-4748; Fax: 412-421-4748. Students 45.

SOUTH SIDE

1—ST. ADALBERT, (Polish), Closed. See Prince of Peace.
2—ST. BASIL (1907) Rev. James R. Torquato. In Res., Rev. Joseph C. Scheib.
Res.: 1735 Brownsville Rd., 15210. Tel: 412-882-9763; Fax: 412-882-2476. Email: 06701@diopitt.org.
Catechesis/Religious Program—Students 140.
3—ST. CANICE (Knoxville) Closed. See St. John Vianney.
4—ST. CASIMIR, (Lithuanian), Closed. See Prince of Peace.
5—ST. GEORGE (Allentown) Closed. See St. John Vianney.
6—GUARDIAN ANGELS (West End) (1994) [CEM], Merged with St. James and St. Martin. Rev. Donald N. Buchleitner, Admin.
Res.: 1030 Logue St., 15220. Tel: 412-921-4077; Fax: 412-922-4945.
7—ST. HENRY, Closed. See St. John Vianney.
8—HOLY ANGELS (1903) Rev. Robert J. Ahlin.
Res.: 408 Baldwin Rd., 15207. Tel: 412-461-6906; Fax: 412-461-0961. Email: cheryl@holyangelshays.org. Web: www.holyangelshays.com.
Catechesis/Religious Program—Tel: 412-461-6909, Ext. 23. Email: elaine@holyangelshays.org. Students 290.
9—HOLY INNOCENTS (1900) Rev. Donald N. Buchleitner.
Res.: 3011 Landis St., 15204. Tel: 412-331-0268; Fax: 412-331-1219. Email: hiparish@verizon.net.
10—ST. JAMES (West End) Closed. See Guardian Angels.
11—ST. JOHN THE EVANGELIST, Closed. See Prince of Peace.
12—ST. JOHN VIANNEY (Hilltop) (1994) [CEM], Consolidation of the following churches: St. Canice, St. George, St. Henry and St. Joseph. Rev. Thomas R. Wilson, Admin.; Chuck Mazur, Business Mgr.; Mark L. Carver, Parish Music Dir.
823 Climax St., 15210. Tel: 412-381-8300; Fax: 412-431-3790. Email: sjv@sjvpgh.org. Web: www.sjvpgh.org.
Catechesis/Religious Program—Tel: 412-381-5581. Students 55.
13—ST. JOSAPHAT, (Polish), Closed. See Prince of Peace.
14—ST. JUSTIN (Mt. Washington) (1917) Rev. Walter G. Rydzon.
Res.: 539 Boggs Ave., 15211. Tel: 412-381-9878; 412-381-9825 (TTY); Fax: 412-381-0371. Email: stjustinchurch@cs.com. Web: www.saintjustins.org. Catholic Deaf Community.
Catechesis/Religious Program—Tel: 412-381-3774; Fax: 412-381-0371. Students 90.
15—ST. MARY OF THE MOUNT (Mt. Washington) (1873) Rev. Michael J. Stumpf.
Res.: 403 Grandview Ave., 15211. Tel: 412-381-0212; Fax: 412-381-9921. Email: smom@smomp.org. Web: www.smomp.org.
School—Bishop Leonard-St. Mary of the Mount Academy, 115 Bigham St., 15211. Tel: 412-431-4645; Fax: 412-381-0770. Web: www.blsmma.org. Sisters of the Immaculate Heart of Mary 2; Lay Teachers 10; Students 140.
Catechesis/Religious Program—Tel: 412-381-3310. Students 45.
16—ST. MATTHEW, (Slovak), Closed. See Prince of Peace.
17—ST. MICHAEL, (German), Closed. See Prince of Peace.
18—OUR LADY OF LORETO (1959) Rev. Robert J. Miller. In Res., Very Rev. Harry R. Bielewicz, Vicar for Clergy.
Res.: 1905 Pioneer Ave., 15226. Tel: 412-341-6161; Fax: 412-341-3399. Email: ollpari@aol.com.
Catechesis/Religious Program—Tel: 412-341-6163. Email: pscherwin@verizon.net. Students 91.
Convent—1901 Pioneer Ave., 15226. Tel: 412-343-1377.
19—ST. PAMPHILUS (1960) Rev. Alexis Anania, O.F.M.; Deacon Leon F. Miles. In Res., Friar John-Michael Pinto, O.F.M.
Res.: 948 Tropical Ave., 15216. Tel: 412-341-1000; 412-531-8449; Fax: 412-341-6956.
Church: 1000 Tropical Ave., 15216.
Catechesis/Religious Program—Tel: 412-561-0330. Students 35.
20—ST. PETER, Closed. See Prince of Peace.
21—ST. PIUS X (1954) Rev. Robert J. Miller.
Res.: 3040 Pioneer Ave., 15226. Tel: 412-563-5423; Fax: 412-561-3868. Email: saint.piusx@verizon.net. Web: www.spxchurch.org.
See Brookline Regional Catholic School, Pittsburgh under Consolidated Schools located in the Institution section.
Catechesis/Religious Program—Tel: 412-563-1588. Students 74.
22—PRINCE OF PEACE (1992) [CEM 6], Consolidated from the following churches: St. Adalbert, St. Casimir, St. John the Evangelist, St. Josaphat, St. Matthew, St. Michael and St. Peter. Rev. Bernard M. Harcarik.
Mailing Address: 81 S. 13th St., 15203-1897. In Res., Rev. Eugene F. Laver.
Res.: 162 S. 15th St., 15203-1897. Tel: 412-481-8380; Fax: 412-431-0209. Email: 49801@diopitt.org.
Catechesis/Religious Program—Tel: 412-381-5458. Students 42.
23—RESURRECTION (Brookline) (1909) Rev. Frank Mitolo. In Res., Revs. Victor J. Rocha (Retired); John E. Suhoza (Retired).
Res.: 1100 Creedmoor Ave., 15226. Tel: 412-563-4400; Fax: 412-563-4403. Email: ressi@earthlink.net. Web: www.eressi.com.
Catechesis/Religious Program—Tel: 412-343-9551. Students 192.
24—ST. VINCENT (Esplen) Closed. See St. John of God, McKees Rocks.
25—ST. WENDELIN (Carrick) (1873) Rev. Edwin J. Wichman.
Res.: 2728 Custer Ave., 15227. Tel: 412-882-1480; Fax: 412-884-2334.
Catechesis/Religious Program—Tel: 412-882-3414. Students 105.

NORTH SIDE

1—ST. AMBROSE, Merged with St. Boniface to form Holy Wisdom.
2—ANNUNCIATION, Closed. See Incarnation of the Lord.
3—ST. BONIFACE, Merged with St. Ambrose to form Holy Wisdom.
4—ST. CYRIL OF ALEXANDRIA (1924) Rev. James L. Bruney.
Res.: 3854 Brighton Rd., 15212. Tel: 412-761-1552; Fax: 412-761-3318. Email: saintcyrilchurch@yahoo.com.
School—Tel: 412-761-5043; Fax: 412-761-0840. Lay Teachers 13; Students 200; Preschool 25.
Catechesis/Religious Program—Tel: 412-734-0505. Email: stcyrilreled@yahoo.com. Jean D. Donato, D.R.E. Students 90.
5—ST. FRANCIS XAVIER, Closed. See Risen Lord.
6—ST. GABRIEL ARCHANGEL, (Slovak), Closed. See Risen Lord.
7—HOLY WISDOM (1994) [CEM 3] Very Rev. Lawrence A. DiNardo. In Res., Rev. Louis L. DeNinno.
Res.: 1025 Haslage Ave., 15212-3429. Tel: 412-231-1071; Fax: 412-231-1072. Email: office@holywisdomparish.org. Web: www.holywisdomparish.org.
Catechesis/Religious Program—Tel: 412-321-3186; Fax: 412-321-7807. Twinned with St. Peter, North Side. Students 61.
8—INCARNATION OF THE LORD (1993), Consolidated from Annunciation and Nativity of Our Lord. Rev. David D. DeWitt.
Mailing Address: 4071 Franklin Rd., 15214. Tel: 412-931-2911; Fax: 412-931-2832. Email: fdavidd@gmail.com.
Catechesis/Religious Program— Site used is: Educ. Center at Risen Lord Parish, 3250 California Ave., Pittsburgh PA 15212. Students 36.
9—ST. JOSEPH, Closed. See St. Peter.
10—ST. LEO, Closed. See Risen Lord.
11—MOST HOLY NAME OF JESUS (Troy Hill) (1868), (German), [CEM] Rev. Lawrence R. Smith; Deacon G. Gregory Jelinek.
Res.: 1700 Harpster St., 15212-4393. Tel: 412-231-2994; Fax: 412-231-7180. Email: mostholyhname@hotmail.com. Web: www.mostholynameofjesusparish15212.org.
See Northside Catholic School, Pittsburgh under Consolidated Schools located in the Institution section.
Catechesis/Religious Program—Tel: 412-231-3002; 412-759-9835. Students 120.
Chapel—St. Anthony's Chapel (1880)Tel: 412-323-9504. Sr. Margaret Liam Glenane, S.A., Asst. Dir.
12—NATIVITY OF OUR LORD, Closed. See Incarnation of the Lord.
13—OUR LADY QUEEN OF PEACE, Closed. See St. Peter.
14—ST. PETER (1993), (Polish), [CEM], Consolidated from St. Cyprian, St. Mary's, Mary Immaculate & Our Lady, Queen of Peace, St. Joseph, St. Peter and St. Wenceslaus. Rev. Vincent E. Zidek, O.S.B.
Res.: 720 Arch St., 15212. Tel: 412-321-0711; Fax: 412-321-7807. Email: stpeter@winbeam.com. Web: www.stpeterparish.org.
See Northside Catholic School, Pittsburgh under Consolidated Schools located in the Institution section.
Catechesis/Religious Program—907 Middle St., 15212. Tel: 412-321-3186. Email: patkammersell@comcast.net. Students 50.
15—REGINA COELI, (Italian), Closed. For sacramental records contact St. Cyril of Alexandria.
16—RISEN LORD (1993), Consolidated from the following churches: St. Francis Xavier, St. Gabriel Archangel, St. Leo and Our Lady of Perpetual Help. Rev. David D. DeWitt.
Rectory & Office: 3250 California Ave., 15212. Tel: 412-761-1507; Fax: 412-761-6454. Email: risenlord@choiceonemail.com.
Catechesis/Religious Program—Alda Walker, D.R.E.; Karen Smay, D.R.E. Students 40.
17—ST. WENCESLAUS, Closed. See St. Peter.

OUTSIDE THE CITY OF PITTSBURGH

ALEPPO TOWNSHIP, ALLEGHENY CO., ST. MARY (1852) [CEM] Rev. David J. Jastrab.
Mailing Address: 444 Glenfield Rd., Sewickley, 15143. Tel: 412-741-6460; Fax: 412-749-9271. Email: bcox@saintmaryaleppo.org. Web: www.saintmaryaleppo.org.
Catechesis/Religious Program—Tel: 412-741-3959. Email: b_venturella@saintmaryaleppo.org. Students 100.

ALIQUIPPA, BEAVER CO., ST. TITUS (1994) [CEM 2] [JC 2], Merged with St. Joseph, West Aliquippa. Rev. Paul C. Householder.
Res.: 952 Franklin Ave., 15001. Tel: 724-378-8561; Fax: 724-378-4851. Email: sttituschurch@comcast.net.
Catechesis/Religious Program—Tel: 724-375-7940. Students 70.

ALLISON PARK, ALLEGHENY CO., ST. URSULA (1908) Revs. Garrett D. Dorsey; Ernest Strelinski.
Res.: 3937 Kirk Ave., 15101. Tel: 412-486-6700; Fax: 412-486-2562. Email: ursula@stursula.com.
School—Tel: 412-486-5511; Fax: 412-492-7295. Sisters 1; Lay Teachers 14; Students 147.
Catechesis/Religious Program—Tel: 412-486-3374;

Fax: 412-486-3374. Students 165.

AMBRIDGE, BEAVER CO.

1—CHURCH OF CHRIST THE KING, Closed. See Good Samaritan.

2—DIVINE REDEEMER, Closed. See Good Samaritan.

3—GOOD SAMARITAN (1994) [CEM], Consolidated from the following churches: St. Veronica, Divine Redeemer, St. Stanislaus, Christ the King and Holy Trinity. Revs. Joseph A. Carr; Michael R. Peck, Parochial Vicar.

Mailing Address: *Administrative Center*, 725 Glenwood Ave., 15003. Web: www.goodsam1.org.

Res.: 923 Melrose Ave., 15003. Tel: 724-385-0356 (Resident); 724-266-6565 (Office); Fax: 724-266-5570.

Catechesis/Religious Program—Combined with St. John the Baptist, Baden., Tel: 724-266-6565, Ext. 12. Email: ccd@goodsam1.org. Students 140.

4—HOLY TRINITY, (Croatian), Closed. See Good Samaritan.

5—ST. STANISLAUS, Closed. See Good Samaritan.

6—ST. VERONICA, Closed. See Good Samaritan.

ASPINWALL, ALLEGHENY CO., ST. SCHOLASTICA (1903) Rev. Kenneth R. White.

Res.: 309 Brilliant Ave., 15215. Tel: 412-781-0186; Fax: 412-781-4316. Email: parish@saintscholastica.com. Web: www.saintscholastica.com.

See Christ the Divine Teacher Catholic Academy, Pittsburgh under Consolidated Schools located in the Institution section.

Catechesis/Religious Program—Tel: 412-781-0608. Students 415.

AVELLA, WASHINGTON CO., ST. MICHAEL (1917) [CEM] Rev. Pierre G. Sodini.

Res.: 95 Highland Ave., 15312. Tel: 724-587-3570; Fax: 724-587-5203. Email: stmike@hky.com.

Catechesis/Religious Program—Students 59.

BADEN, BEAVER CO., ST. JOHN THE BAPTIST (1866) [CEM] Revs. Joseph A. Carr; Michael R. Peck, Parochial Vicar.

Administrative Center, 375 Linmore Ave., P.O. Box 171, 15005. Tel: 724-869-2280; Fax: 724-869-0305.

Res.: 923 Melrose Ave., Ambridge, 15003. Tel: 724-385-0356. Email: stjohnsbadenpa@yahoo.com.

Catechesis/Religious Program—Tel: 724-266-6565, Ext. 12. Email: ccd@goodsam1.org. This information is combined with Good Samaritan, Ambridge. Students 15.

BAIRDFORD, ALLEGHENY CO., ST. VICTOR (1919) Rev. Charles W. Speicher.

Res.: 527 Bairdford Rd., P.O. Box 149, 15006. Tel: 724-265-2070; Fax: 724-265-6316.

Catechesis/Religious Program—535 Bairdford Rd., 15006. Tel: 724-265-4040; Fax: 724-265-6313. Students 338.

BALDWIN BORO, ALLEGHENY CO., ST. ALBERT THE GREAT (1956) Rev. James R. Orr.

Mailing Address: 3198 Schieck St., 15227. Tel: 412-884-7744; Fax: 412-884-2300. Email: saintalbert@comcast.net.

Res.: 114 Green Glen Dr., 15227.

Catechesis/Religious Program—Tel: 412-884-8282. Students 260.

BEAVER FALLS, BEAVER CO.

1—DIVINE MERCY (1994), (Polish), [CEM], Consolidated from St. Mary and Holy Trinity. Rev. James B. Farnan.

Mailing Address: 605 Tenth St., 15010.

Res.: 3908 6th Ave., 15010. Tel: 724-846-4585; Fax: 724-846-6868.

School—609 Tenth St., 15010. Tel: 724-846-5955; Fax: 724-846-1894. Web: www.dmacademy.com. Lay Teachers 10; Students 89.

Catechesis/Religious Program—3908 6th Ave., 15010. Tel: 724-601-8301; Fax: 724-843-7575. Email: saintphilomena@verizon.net. Web: beavercountycatholic.com. Students 90.

2—HOLY TRINITY, (Polish), Closed. See Divine Mercy.

3—ST. PHILOMENA (1948) Rev. James B. Farnan.

Res.: 3908 Sixth Ave., 15010. Tel: 724-843-7375; Fax: 724-843-7575. Email: fatherjimfarnan@yahoo.com. Web: beavercountycatholic.com.

Catechesis/Religious Program—Students 100.

BEAVER, BEAVER CO., SS. PETER AND PAUL (1830) [CEM] Unassigned. In Res., Rev. William J. Schwartz.

Res.: 200 Third St., 15009. Tel: 724-775-4111; Fax: 724-775-1117. Email: office@ssppbeaver.org. Web: www.ssppbeaver.org.

School—370 E. End Ave., 15009. Tel: 724-774-4450; Fax: 724-774-5192. Email: school@ssppbeaver.org. Lay Teachers 14; Students 143.

Catechesis/Religious Program—Students 266.

BELLEVUE, ALLEGHENY CO., ASSUMPTION OF THE BLESSED VIRGIN MARY ON THE BEAUTIFUL RIVER (1903) Revs. Dennis M. Buranosky; Richard J. Tusky, Parochial Vicar.

Res.: 45 N. Sprague Ave., 15202. Tel: 412-766-6660; Fax: 412-766-4836. Email: parish@assumptionchurch.org. Web: www.assumptionchurch.org.

School—35 N. Jackson Ave., 15202. Tel: 412-761-7887; Fax: 412-761-7620. Web: www.assumption-church.org. Lay Teachers 9; Part-time 5; Students 104.

Catechesis/Religious Program—Tel: 412-766-4046. Email: mtaylor@assumptionchurch.org. Students 200.

BENTLEYVILLE, WASHINGTON CO.

1—AVE MARIA (1994) [CEM 2], Consolidated from St. Luke, St. Clement and St. Joseph. Rev. Gary W. Krummert.

Res.: 126 Church St., 15314-1406. Tel: 724-239-3591; Fax: 866-910-7782. Email: 06001@diopitt.org.

Catechesis/Religious Program—Students 119.

Ave Maria Religious Education Center—Oak St., P.O. Box 590, Ellsworth, 15331. Tel: 724-239-2226. Email: avemariacenter@fairpoint.net.

2—ST. LUKE, Closed. See Ave Maria, Ellsworth.

BESSEMER, LAWRENCE CO., ST. ANTHONY (1909) Merged with St. Lawrence, Hillsville to form Christ the King, Hillsville.

BETHEL PARK, ALLEGHENY CO.

1—ST. GERMAINE (1957) Rev. John J. Baver; Mary Beth Green, Pastoral Assoc.

Res.: 7003 Baptist Rd., 15102. Tel: 412-833-0661; Fax: 412-833-4036. Email: church_stgermaine@comcast.net.

School—*St. Katharine Drexel School*, 7001 Baptist Rd., 15102. Tel: 412-833-0223; Fax: 412-347-0361. Email: principal@stkatharinedrexelschool.org. Web: www.stkatharinedrexelschool.org. Lay Teachers 12; Students 77.

Catechesis/Religious Program—Tel: 412-833-6662. Students 196.

2—ST. THOMAS MORE (1953) Revs. Mark A. Eckman; Daniel J. Langa.

Res.: 126 Fort Couch Rd., 15241. Tel: 412-833-0031; Fax: 412-833-5995. Email: parishoffice@stmpgh.org. Web: www.stmpgh.org.

School—134 Fort Couch Rd., 15241. Tel: 412-833-1412; Fax: 412-833-5597. Email: rileys@stmcs.org. Web: www.stmcs.org. Lay Teachers 35; Students 480.

Catechesis/Religious Program—Tel: 412-835-6996; Fax: 412-283-0256. Students 720.

3—ST. VALENTINE (1931) Revs. Albert L. Zapf; Jeremiah T. O'Shea, Parochial Vicar & Senior Priest.

Res.: 2710 Ohio St., 15102. Tel: 412-835-4415; Fax: 412-835-4417. Email: svoffice@comcast.net. Web: www.stvals.org.

Catechesis/Religious Program—2709 Mesta St., 15102. Tel: 412-835-3780. Students 510.

BLAWNOX, ALLEGHENY CO.

1—ST. EDWARD (1938) Merged to form St. Pio of Pietrelcina Parish, Pittsburgh.

2—ST. PIO OF PIETRELCINA PARISH (2011) Rev. Joseph F. Keenan.

Res.: 450 Walnut St., 15238. Tel: 412-828-4066; Fax: 412-828-3084.

Catechesis/Religious Program—Students 100.

BOBTOWN, GREENE CO., ST. IGNATIUS OF ANTIOCH (1924) Rev. Lawrence V. Holpp.

Res.: P.O. Box 63, 15315. Tel: 724-839-7122; Fax: 724-839-7315.

Catechesis/Religious Program—Students 28.

BRADDOCK HILLS, ALLEGHENY CO., SACRED HEART (1897), (Polish), Merged with Good Shepherd, Braddock.

BRADDOCK, ALLEGHENY CO., GOOD SHEPHERD (1985), Merged with Sacred Heart, Braddock Hills. Rev. Thomas J. Burke.

Mailing Address: 1024 Maple Way, 15104. Email: gshepoffice@comcast.net. Web: www.goodshepherdbraddock.org.

Res.: 1600 Brinton Rd., 15221. Tel: 412-271-1515; Fax: 412-271-1222.

School—1025 Braddock Ave., 15104. Tel: 412-271-2492; Fax: 412-271-3248. Email: admin@goodshepherdfamily.org. Jacqueline Fazio, Prin. Sisters 1; Lay Teachers 10; Students 114.

Catechesis/Religious Program—Tel: 412-271-2630. Email: missjoan2@verizon.net. Students 40.

Convent—Tel: 412-271-1736.

BRENTWOOD, ALLEGHENY CO., ST. SYLVESTER (1924) Very Rev. John M. Bachkay.

Res.: 3754 Brownsville Rd., 15227. Tel: 412-882-8593; Fax: 412-882-0153. Email: office@stsylvesterparish.org. Web: www.saintsylvesterparish.org.

School—30 W. Willock Rd., 15227. Tel: 412-882-9900. Lay Teachers 10; Students 230.

Catechesis/Religious Program—Tel: 412-881-4142; 412-882-8593, Ext. 219. Students 265.

BRIDGEVILLE, ALLEGHENY CO.

1—ST. AGATHA (1894) Closed. See Holy Child.

2—ST. ANTHONY (1915), (Lithuanian), Closed. See Holy Child.

3—ST. BARBARA (1894) [CEM] Rev. Richard E. Ward.

Res.: 45 Prestley Rd., 15017-1971. Tel: 412-221-5152; Fax: 412-221-7935. Email: stbarb@comcast.net.

Catechesis/Religious Program—Students 275.

4—HOLY CHILD (1994) [CEM], Consolidated from St. Agatha and St. Anthony. Revs. Richard C. Yagesh; Robert J. Meyer, Senior Priest.

Res.: 212 Station St., 15017. Tel: 412-221-5213; Fax: 412-257-2461. Email: holychildparish@verizon.net. Web: www.holychildparish.org.

School—Tel: 412-221-4720; Fax: 412-257-9742. Email: stholychild@comcast.net. Sisters 1; Lay Teachers 13; Students 132.

Catechesis/Religious Program—Tel: 412-221-6514. Students 560.

BULGER, WASHINGTON CO., ST. ANN (1917) Rev. Robert M. Staszewski.

Res.: 967 Grant St., Box 488, 15019-0488. Tel: 724-796-3791; 724-796-9151 (Social Hall); Fax: 724-796-5173. Email: annchurc@icubed.com.

Catechesis/Religious Program—Students 42.

BURGETTSTOWN, WASHINGTON CO., OUR LADY OF LOURDES (1916) [CEM] Rev. Robert P. Connolly.

Res.: 1109 Main St., 15021. Tel: 724-947-3363; Fax: 724-947-9348. Email: olol@verizon.net.

Catechesis/Religious Program—Tel: 724-947-5076. Email: olotccd@verizon.net. Students 101.

BUTLER, BUTLER CO.

1—ST. FIDELIS OF SIGMARINGEN (1995) Revs. James F. Murphy; George Palick.

Res.: 125 Buttercup Rd., 16001. Tel: 724-482-2690; Fax: 724-482-2315. Email: stfidel@aol.com. Web: www.saintfidelis.org.

Catechesis/Religious Program—Tel: 724-482-2362. Joan Pilat, D.R.E. Students 382.

2—ST. MICHAEL THE ARCHANGEL (1909), (Italian—French), [CEM] Rev. James W. Dolan.

Res.: 432 Center Ave., 16001. Tel: 724-282-4107; Fax: 724-282-3156. Email: stmikearchl@zoominternet.net.

See Butler Catholic School, Butler under Consolidated Schools located in the Institution section.

Catechesis/Religious Program—Tel: 724-282-9365. Students 65.

3—ST. PAUL (1867) [CEM] Revs. Steven V. Neff; Thomas L. Gillespie, Parochial Vicar; Gerald J. Lutz, Senior Priest (Retired); Deacon Mitchell M. Natali.

Res.: 128 N. McKean St., 16001. Tel: 724-287-1759; Fax: 724-287-2081. Email: stpaulchurch@zoominternet.net. Web: www.stpaulbutler.org.

See Butler Catholic School, Butler under Consolidated Schools located in the Institution section.

Catechesis/Religious Program—Students 250.

4—ST. PETER (1821), (German), [CEM] Rev. James W. Dolan.

Res.: 127 Franklin St., 16001. Tel: 724-287-2743; Fax: 412-291-3233. Email: office@specialandloved.com. Web: www.specialandloved.com.

See Butler Catholic School, Butler under Consolidated Schools located in the Institution section.

Catechesis/Religious Program—Students 103.

5—ST. WENDELIN (1863) [CEM] Revs. Steven V. Neff; Thomas L. Gillespie, Parochial Vicar.

Res.: 210 Saint Wendelin Rd., 16002-1065. Tel: 724-287-0820; Fax: 724-287-6253. Email: parish@stwendelinbutler.org; 59201@diopitt.org. Web: www.stwendelinbutler.org.

Preschool—Tel: 724-285-4986. Students 23.

School—(Grades K-8), 211 Saint Wendelin Rd., 16002. Tel: 724-285-4986. Lay Teachers 9; Students 66.

Catechesis/Religious Program—Students 122.

CABOT, BUTLER CO., ST. JOSEPH (1904) Revs. Ward Stakem, O.F.M.Cap.; Mark Carter, O.F.M. Cap., Parochial Vicar.

Res.: 315 Stoney Hollow Rd., 16023. Tel: 724-352-2149; Fax: 724-352-7174. Email: stjosephcabot@zoominternet.net. Web: www.stjosephcabot.4lpi.com.

Catechesis/Religious Program—Tel: 724-352-3030; Fax: 724-352-3443. Email: sjreled@zoominternet.net. Includes Good Shepherd through grade 8. Students 312.

CALIFORNIA, WASHINGTON CO., ST. THOMAS AQUINAS (1888) [CEM] Rev. George J. Moneck.

Res.: 213 Fourth St., 15419. Tel: 724-938-3204; Fax: 724-938-0434.

Catechesis/Religious Program—Tel: 724-938-7775. Students 45.

CANONSBURG, WASHINGTON CO.

1—ST. GENEVIEVE, (Polish), Closed. See St. Patrick.

2—ST. PATRICK (1993) [CEM], Merged with St. Genevieve. Revs. John J. Batykefer; F. Raymond Trance; John D. Nanz, Chap.; Deacon Joseph Cerenzia.

Res.: 317 W. Pike St., 15317. Tel: 724-745-6560; Fax: 724-746-1112. Email: stpatparish@verizon.net. Web: www.stpatrickparish.net.

School—Hutchinson & Murdock Sts., 15317. Tel: 724-745-7977; Fax: 724-746-9778. Email: stpat@pulsenet.com. Web: www.stpatschool.org. Priests 2; Lay Teachers 16; Students 213.
Catechesis/Religious Program—Tel: 724-745-3787. Students 559.

CARMICHAELS, GREENE CO., ST. HUGH (1951), (Polish), Rev. John M. Bauer.
Res.: 408 Rt. 88, 15320. Tel: 724-966-7270; Fax: 724-966-9118. Email: sthugholcpc@windstream.net.
Catechesis/Religious Program—Students 132.

CARNEGIE, ALLEGHENY CO.

1—ST. ELIZABETH ANN SETON (1992), (Italian—German), [CEM] [JC 4], Consolidated from the following churches: Holy Souls, St. Ignatius de Loyola, Immaculate Conception, St. Joseph, St. Luke and St. Vincent de Paul, Walkers Mill. Revs. David G. Poecking; Robin Evanish.
Mailing Address: 206 Mary St., 15106-2489.
Res.: 125 Finley Ave., 15106-2489. Tel: 412-276-1011; Fax: 412-276-0816.
Catechesis/Religious Program—127 Finley Ave., 15106. Tel: 412-279-8118. Students 218.

2—HOLY SOULS, Closed. See St. Elizabeth Ann Seton.

3—ST. IGNATIUS DE LOYOLA, (Polish), Closed. See St. Elizabeth Ann Seton.

4—IMMACULATE CONCEPTION, (Polish), Closed. See St. Elizabeth Ann Seton.

5—ST. JOSEPH, (German), Closed. See St. Elizabeth Ann Seton.

6—ST. LUKE, Closed. See St. Elizabeth Ann Seton.

CASTLE SHANNON, ALLEGHENY CO., ST. ANNE (1889) [CEM] Rev. Robert J. Cedolia. In Res., Rev. Hugh J. Lang (Retired).
Res.: 400 Hoodridge Dr., 15234. Tel: 412-531-5964; Fax: 412-531-6901.
School—4040 Willow Ave., 15234. Tel: 412-561-7720; Fax: 412-561-7927. Lay Teachers 12; Students 149.
Catechesis/Religious Program—Tel: 412-561-0101. Students 424.

CECIL, WASHINGTON CO., ST. MARY (1909) [CEM] Rev. Stan M. Gregorek.
Res.: 10 St. Mary's Ln., 15321. Tel: 412-221-1560; Fax: 412-221-9544. Email: stmarysch@comcast.net. Web: www.stmarycecil.org.
Catechesis/Religious Program—19 Cecil Elementary Dr., 15321. Tel: 412-221-0595. Students 200.

CENTER TOWNSHIP, BEAVER CO., ST. FRANCES CABRINI (1961) Revs. Joseph J. Kleppner; Mariusz Mularczyk, Parochial Vicar; Brenda Kostial, Music Dir.
Res.: 115 Trinity Dr. Center Twp., Aliquippa, 15001. Tel: 724-775-6363; Fax: 724-775-3848. Email: sfcabrini@comcast.net. Web: www.sfcabriniparish.org.
Catechesis/Religious Program—Tel: 724-774-4888. Deanna Stacho, D.R.E.; Bob Summers, Youth Min. Students 446.

CENTER TOWNSHIP, BUTLER CO., ST. ANDREW (1964) Rev. James G. Salberg.
Res.: 1660 N. Main St. Ext., Butler, 16001. Tel: 724-287-7781; Fax: 724-287-7346. Email: standrewbutler@zoominternet.net.
Catechesis/Religious Program—Students 140.

CHARLEROI, WASHINGTON CO.

1—SS. CYRIL AND METHODIUS, (Slovak), Closed. See Mary Mother of the Church.

2—ST. JEROME, Closed. See Mary Mother of the Church.

3—MARY MOTHER OF THE CHURCH (1992) [CEM], Consolidated from SS. Cyril & Methodius, St. Jerome and Mother of Sorrows. Rev. Gerald S. Mikonis.
Res.: 624 Washington Ave., 15022-1932. Tel: 724-483-5533; Fax: 724-483-0122.
Catechesis/Religious Program—Students 175.

4—MOTHER OF SORROWS, (Italian), Closed. See Mary Mother of the Church.

CHICORA, BUTLER CO., MATER DOLOROSA (1875) Rev. Joseph P. Pudichery.
Res.: 409 N. Main St., P.O. Box 243, 16025. Tel: 724-445-2275; Fax: 724-445-7507. Email: materdol@zoominternet.net. Web: www.materdolorosa-stjoe.webs.com.
Catechesis/Religious Program—Email: stj@zoominternet.net. Combined with St. Joseph, North Oakland. Students 50.

CHIPPEWA TOWNSHIP, BEAVER CO., CHRIST THE DIVINE TEACHER (1969) Rev. Kim J. Schreck; Deacon Harry J. DeNome.
Res.: 116 Thorndale Dr., Beaver Falls, 15010. Tel: 724-846-3818; Fax: 724-846-3819. Email: cdt-church@comcast.net.
Catechesis/Religious Program—Tel: 724-847-4750. Email: cdtreled@comcast.net. Students 277.

CHURCHILL BOROUGH, ALLEGHENY CO., ST. JOHN FISHER (1960) Rev. Carl J. Gentile (Retired).
Res.: 33 Lewin Ln., 15235. Tel: 412-241-4722; Fax: 412-241-4653.
Catechesis/Religious Program—Tel: 412-241-4653. Students 192.

CLAIRTON, ALLEGHENY CO.

1—ST. CLARE OF ASSISI (1994) [CEM], Consolidated from the following churches: St. Joseph, St. Paulinus and St. Clare. Rev. Charles J. Baptiste.
Mailing Address: 460 Reed St., 15025. Tel: 412-233-7870; Fax: 412-233-0742. Email: stclareparish2@comcast.net. Web: stclarepa.home-.comcast.net. In Res., Rev. Albert J. Semler (Retired). Tel: 412-233-7828.
Catechesis/Religious Program—Students 20.

2—ST. JOSEPH, Closed. See St. Clare of Assisi.

3—ST. PAULINUS, Closed. See St. Clare of Assisi.

CLARKSVILLE, WASHINGTON CO., ST. THOMAS (1992), (Polish—Italian), Rev. J. Francis Frazer.
Res.: 30 Main St., 15322. Tel: 724-377-2588; Fax: 724-377-0707. Email: stthomas@windstream.net.
Catechesis/Religious Program—Students 45.

CONWAY, BEAVER CO., OUR LADY OF PEACE (1941) Rev. John P. Fitzgerald; Deacon James T. Weiland.
Res.: 1000 3rd Ave., 15027. Tel: 724-869-3024; Fax: 724-869-3025. Email: olop@verizon.net.
Catechesis/Religious Program—Tel: 724-869-4723. Email: olopdre@verizon.net. Students 237.

CORAOPOLIS, ALLEGHENY CO., ST. JOSEPH (1891) [CEM] Rev. Richard S. Jones; Mr. Jim Crable, Pastoral Asst.; Virginia Ambrose, Dir. Music; Anne Mankowski, Bookkeeper & Parish Sec.
Res.: 1304 Fourth Ave., 15108. Tel: 412-264-6162; Fax: 412-264-5370. Email: st.josephparish@verizon.net.
Catechesis/Religious Program—Tel: 412-262-9252. Email: jindovina@gaggle.net. Judene Indovina, D.R.E. Students 100.

COYLESVILLE, BUTLER CO., ST. JOHN THE EVANGELIST (1853) [CEM] Rev. Donald R. Bischof.
Res.: 668 Clearfield Rd., Fenelton, 16034-9743. Tel: 724-287-7590; Fax: 724-287-3550. Email: stjohnchurch@zoominternet.net.
Catechesis/Religious Program—Tel: 724-287-0426. Email: stjohnccd@zoominternet.net. Students 110.

CRAFTON, ALLEGHENY CO., ST. PHILIP (1839), (Irish), [CEM] Rev. Walter W. Dworak.
Res.: 50 W. Crafton Ave., 15205. Tel: 412-922-6300; Fax: 412-920-7310. Email: parishoffice@saintphilipchurch.org. Web: www.saintphilipchurch.org.
School—52 W. Crafton Ave., 15205. Tel: 412-928-2742. Web: www.spsangelway.org. Sisters of Charity 1; Lay Teachers 22; Students 368.
Catechesis/Religious Program—Tel: 412-928-2742, Ext. 8. Students 160.

CRANBERRY TOWNSHIP, BUTLER CO.

1—ST. FERDINAND (1961) Revs. John P. Gallagher; Edward J. Kunco; George R. Dalton; Barbara McCarthy, Pastoral Assoc.
Res.: 2535 Rochester Rd., 16066-6496. Tel: 724-776-2888; Fax: 724-776-2378. Web: www.stferd.org.
Catechesis/Religious Program—Tel: 724-776-9177; Fax: 724-776-6640. Email: sue@stferd.org. Students 1,136.
Saint Ferdinand Parish Charitable Trust - A Pennsylvania Charitable Trust.

2—ST. KILIAN (1917) Rev. Charles S. Bober; Deacons Ralph W. Bachner Jr.; Robert M. Marshall; William Caruer.
Res.: 7076 Franklin Rd., 16066-5302. Tel: 724-625-1665; Fax: 724-625-1922. Email: parish@saintkilian.org. Web: www.saintkilian.org.
School—Rosanne Kwiatkowski, Prin. Faculty 27; Students 557.
Catechesis/Religious Program—Students 928.

CREIGHTON, ALLEGHENY CO., HOLY FAMILY (East Deer Twp.) (1949) Rev. Miroslaw Stelmaszczyk.
Res.: 787 Freeport Rd., 15030. Tel: 724-224-1626; Fax: 724-224-0609.
Catechesis/Religious Program—Students 21.

CRESENT, ALLEGHENY CO., ST. CATHERINE OF SIENA (1959) Revs. Louis F. Vallone; Robert J. Zajdel.
Res.: 199 McGovern Blvd., Crescent, 15046. Tel: 724-457-7026; Fax: 724-457-3292.
Catechesis/Religious Program—Students 92.

DARLINGTON, BEAVER CO., ST. ROSE OF LIMA (1854) [CEM] Rev. Kim J. Schreck.
Res.: 3357 Constitution Blvd., 16115. Tel: 724-843-0152; Fax: 724-843-7810.
Catechesis/Religious Program—Students 125.

DONORA, WASHINGTON CO.

1—ST. CHARLES, Closed. See Our Lady of the Valley.

2—ST. DOMINIC, (Slovak), Closed. See Our Lady of the Valley.

3—HOLY NAME OF THE BLESSED VIRGIN MARY, Closed. See Our Lady of the Valley.

4—OUR LADY OF THE VALLEY (1992) [CEM], Consolidated from the following churches: St. Charles Borromeo, St. Dominic, Holy Name of the Blessed Virgin Mary and St. Philip Neri. Rev. Pierre M. Falkenhan.
Mailing Address: 571 Thompson Ave., 15033.
Res.: 1 Park Manor Rd., 15033. Tel: 724-379-4777; Fax: 724-379-6242.
Catechesis/Religious Program—Students 77.

5—ST. PHILIP NERI, (Italian), Closed. See Our Lady of the Valley.

DUQUESNE, ALLEGHENY CO.

1—CHRIST THE LIGHT OF THE WORLD (1994) [CEM 2], Consolidated from St. Hedwig and Holy Name. Rev. Dennis J. Colamarino.
Res.: 32 S. First St., 15110. Tel: 412-469-0196; Fax: 412-466-6845. Email: office@christthelightoftheworld.org. Web: www.christthelightoftheworld.org.
Catechesis/Religious Program—Students 135.

2—HOLY NAME, Closed. See Christ the Light of the World.

3—ST. JOSEPH (1897), (German), [CEM] Rev. Dennis J. Colamarino.
Res.: 817 W. Grant Ave., 15110. Tel: 412-466-1304; Fax: 412-466-3013. Email: stjosephchurch1@verizon.net.
Catechesis/Religious Program— Twinned with Christ the Light of the World. Students 28.

EAST MCKEESPORT, ALLEGHENY CO., ST. ROBERT BELLARMINE (1951) Rev. John D. Brennan.
Res.: 1313 Fifth Ave., 15035. Tel: 412-824-2644; Fax: 412-824-4786. Email: strobertbellarmine@comcast.net. Web: www.geocities.com/strobbel.
Catechesis/Religious Program—Tel: 412-824-3688; Fax: 412-824-5330. Email: srbcf@comcast.net. Students 173.

EAST PITTSBURGH, ALLEGHENY CO.

1—ST. HELEN, (Slovak), Closed. See Holy Cross.

2—HOLY CROSS (1994), Consolidated from St. William and St. Helen. Rev. Miroslaus A. Wojcicki.
Res.: 905 Main St., 15112. Tel: 412-829-1146; Fax: 412-816-2059.

3—ST. WILLIAM, Closed. See Holy Cross.

ELIZABETH, ALLEGHENY CO., ST. MICHAEL (1851) [CEM] Rev. Thomas A. Wagner.
Res.: 101 McLay Dr., 15037. Tel: 412-751-0663; Fax: 412-751-2161. Email: stmichael1@verizon.net.
Catechesis/Religious Program—Students 239.

ELLWOOD CITY, LAWRENCE CO.

1—ST. AGATHA (1895), (Territorial), Merged with Purification of the Blessed Virgin Mary, Ellwood City to form Holy Redeemer, Ellwood City.

2—HOLY REDEEMER PARISH (2000) [CEM] Revs. Mark L. Thomas; Louis F. Pascazi; Joseph J. Dascenzo (Retired).
300 Crescent Ave., Ste. 1, 16117. Tel: 724-758-4411; Fax: 724-752-1466. Email: holydmrec@zoominternet.net. Web: www.holyredeemerparishpgh.com.
School—311 Lawrence Ave., 16117. Tel: 724-758-5591; Fax: 724-758-0705. Email: info@holyredeemerschool.com. Web: www.holyredeemerschool.com. Religious 3; Lay Teachers 14; Students 83.
Catechesis/Religious Program—603 Bridge St., 16117. Tel: 724-752-1271; 724-758-5562; Fax: 724-752-1271. Email: hrreledu@zoominternet.net. Web: www.holyredeemerpgh.com. Students 465.
Convent—300 Crescent Ave., 16117. Tel: 724-758-3741.

3—PURIFICATION OF THE BLESSED VIRGIN MARY (1914) Merged with St. Agatha, Ellwood City to form Holy Redeemer, Ellwood City.

ELRAMA, ALLEGHENY CO., ST. ISAAC JOGUES (1950) Rev. Robert J. Boyle.
Mailing Address: 3609 Washington Ave., Finleyville, 15332.
Church: 1216 Collins Ave., Jefferson Hills, 15025. Tel: 412-384-4406; Fax: 412-384-5740. Email: stisaac@comcast.net.
Catechesis/Religious Program—Students 51.

EMSWORTH, ALLEGHENY CO., SACRED HEART (1891) Rev. Dam D. Nguyen.
Res.: 154 Orchard Ave., 15202. Tel: 412-761-6651; Fax: 412-766-8298.
Catechesis/Religious Program—Tel: 412-761-3806. Students 125.

ETNA, ALLEGHENY CO., ALL SAINTS (1902) Rev. John L. Gudewicz.
Res.: 19 Wilson St., 15223-1798. Tel: 412-781-0530; Fax: 412-784-8769. Email: allsaintsetna@comcast.net.
Catechesis/Religious Program—Tel: 412-781-5183; Fax: 412-781-5273. Email: allsaintsreled@comcast.net. Students 166.
Social Service—Tel: 412-781-0530.

EVANS CITY, BUTLER CO., ST. MATTHIAS (1939) Rev. William E. Dorner.
Res.: *St. Gregory*, 2 W. Beaver St., Zelienople, 16063. Tel: 724-452-7245; Fax: 724-452-4064.
Church: 417 E. Main St., P.O. Box 545, 16033-0545. Tel: 724-538-5331; Fax: 724-538-8237. Email: st.matthias.ec.pc@gmail.com. Web: www.ritzerthall.org.
Catechesis/Religious Program—Students 72.

FINLEYVILLE, WASHINGTON CO., ST. FRANCIS OF ASSISI (1893) [CEM] Rev. Robert J. Boyle; Deacon Victor P. Satter.
Res.: 3609 Washington Ave., 15332. Tel: 724-348-7145; Fax: 724-348-7522. Email: stfran2@verizon.net.
Catechesis / Religious Program—Tel: 724-348-6190. Students 108.

FOREST HILLS, ALLEGHENY CO., ST. MAURICE (1949) Rev. John W. Skirtich.
Res.: 2001 Ardmore Blvd., 15221. Tel: 412-271-0809; Fax: 412-271-2415. Email: stmauriceparish-office@comcast.net. Web: www.stmauriceparish.org.
School—Tel: 412-351-5403; Fax: 412-273-9114. Email: principal@stmauriceschool.org. Web: www-.stmauriceschool.org. Sisters 1; Lay Teachers 21; Students 235.
Catechesis / Religious Program—Tel: 412-271-6606; Fax: 412-271-2415. Students 96.

FRANKLIN PARK BOROUGH, ALLEGHENY CO.
1—ST. JOHN NEUMANN (1979) Rev. Albin C. McGinnis.
Res.: 2230 Rochester Rd., 15237. Tel: 412-366-2020; Fax: 412-366-2866. Email: 25701@diopitt.org. Web: www.stjohnneumannpgh.org.
Catechesis / Religious Program—2230 Rochester Rd., 15237. Tel: 412-366-5885. Students 630.
2—SAINTS JOHN AND PAUL (1994) Rev. Joseph R. McCaffrey.
Res.: 2586 Wexford-Bayne Rd., Sewickley, 15143. Tel: 724-935-2104; Fax: 724-935-8320. Email: info@stsjohnandpaul.org. Web: www.stsjohnandpaul.org.
Catechesis / Religious Program—Students 1,131.

FREDERICKTOWN, WASHINGTON CO.
1—ST. MICHAEL THE ARCHANGEL, Closed. See St. Oliver Plunkett, Marianna.
2—ST. OLIVER PLUNKETT (1994) [CEM] Unassigned. Consolidated from Saints Mary & Ann, Marianna, and St. Michael Archangel, Fredericktown.
Res.: 73 Welcome St., Box 638, 15333. Tel: 724-377-0128; Fax: 724-377-0129. Email: stoliverplunkett@windstream.net.
Catechesis / Religious Program—Students 62.

FREEDOM, BEAVER CO., ST. FELIX (1906) [CEM] Rev. James Menkhus, O.F.M.Cap.
450 13th St., 15042. Tel: 724-775-1476; Fax: 724-775-5684. Email: secretary@stfelix.comcastbiz.net.
Catechesis / Religious Program—Students 60.

GLADE MILLS, BUTLER CO., HOLY SEPULCHER (1955) Rev. John B. Gizler III.
Res.: 1304 E. Cruikshank Rd., Butler, 16002. Tel: 724-586-7610; Fax: 724-586-7247. Email: hsc.office@zoominternet.net. Web: www.holysepulcher.org.
School—6515 Old Rte. 8, Butler, 16002. Tel: 724-586-5022; Fax: 724-586-5073. Lay Teachers 12; Students 150.
Catechesis / Religious Program—Tel: 724-586-7276. Email: hsfaith/formation@zoominternet.net. Students 526.

GLASSPORT, ALLEGHENY CO.
1—ST. CECILIA, Closed. See Queen of the Rosary.
2—QUEEN OF THE ROSARY (1994), Consolidated from Holy Cross and St. Cecilia. Rev. Casimir Kedzierski.
Res.: 530 Michigan Ave., 15045. Tel: 412-672-7209; Fax: 412-672-6390. Email: gorglasspt@comcast.net. Web: www.queenoftherosaryparish.homestead.com.
School—St. Joseph Regional School See Consolidated Schools under Institutions located in the Diocese.
Catechesis / Religious Program—Students 51.

GLENSHAW, ALLEGHENY CO.
1—ST. BONAVENTURE (1957) Revs. John P. Sweeney; Matthew R. McClain.
Res.: 2001 Mt. Royal Blvd., 15116. Tel: 412-486-2606; Fax: 412-492-9329. Email: st_bonnie@hotmail.com.
School—Tel: 412-486-2606, Ext. 301; Fax: 412-487-8657. Lay Teachers 27; Students 285.
Catechesis / Religious Program—Tel: 412-486-2606, Ext. 200. Students 300.
2—ST. MARY OF THE ASSUMPTION (1834) [CEM] Revs. John A. Marcucci; John Donahue; Deacon Francis J. Dadowski Jr.
Res.: 2510 Middle Rd., 15116. Tel: 412-486-4100; Fax: 412-486-4150. Email: rectory@stmaryglenshaw.org. Web: www.stmaryglenshaw.org.
School—Tel: 412-486-7611; Fax: 412-487-9509. Sisters of Divine Providence 1; Lay Teachers 16; Students 261.
Catechesis / Religious Program—Tel: 412-486-5521; Fax: 412-486-5177. Students 56.

GREEN TREE, ALLEGHENY CO., ST. MARGARET (1938) Rev. Francis J. Murhammer.
310 Mansfield Ave., 15220.
Res.: 912 Alice St., 15220. Tel: 412-921-0745; Fax: 412-921-0707. Email: saintmargaret@verizon.net.
School—915 Alice St., 15220. Tel: 412-922-4765; Fax: 412-922-4647. Email: cmilitzer@stmargschool.com. Web: www.stmargschool.com. Lay Teachers 19; (Pre-school 8) 288.
Catechesis / Religious Program—Tel: 412-921-1613; Fax: 412-921-0707. Email: smosdre@gmail.com. 225.

HARMAR, ALLEGHENY CO., ST. FRANCIS OF ASSISI (1940) Merged to form St. Pio of Pietrelcina Parish, Pittsburgh.

HARWICK, ALLEGHENY CO., OUR LADY OF VICTORY (1944) Rev. Alan E. Morris.
Res.: 1319 Low Grade Rd., 15049. Tel: 724-274-8575; Fax: 724-274-0529. Email: olov1@verizon.net.
Catechesis / Religious Program—Tel: 724-274-6445. Email: olovr.ed@verizon.net. Students 185.

HERMAN, BUTLER CO., ST. MARY OF THE ASSUMPTION (1842) [CEM] Revs. Ward Stakem, O.F.M.Cap.; Mark Carter, O.F.M. Cap.
Res.: 821 Herman Rd., Butler, 16002. Tel: 724-285-3285; Fax: 724-285-4715. Email: saintmaryinhermanfr@zoominternet.net.
Catechesis / Religious Program—Students 127.

HILLSVILLE, LAWRENCE CO.
1—CHRIST THE KING (2000) [CEM 2] Rev. James A. Downs; Deacon John J. Carran.
Mailing Address: P.O. Box 23, 16132. Tel: 724-667-7721; Fax: 724-667-0827.
Catechesis / Religious Program—Students 118.
2—ST. LAWRENCE (1904), (Italian), Merged with St. Anthony, Bessemer to form Christ the King, Hillsville.

HOLIDAY PARK, ALLEGHENY CO., OUR LADY OF JOY (1968) Rev. David A. Driesch; Gregory Callaghan, Pastoral Assoc. In Res., Rev. Ladis Cizik.
Res.: 2000 O'Block Rd., 15239. Tel: 412-795-3388; Fax: 412-793-5308. Web: www.ourladyofjoy.org.
Catechesis / Religious Program—Tel: 412-795-4389. Students 460.

HOMESTEAD, ALLEGHENY CO.
1—ST. ANNE, Closed. See St. Maximilian Kolbe, Homestead.
2—ST. ANTHONY, Closed. See St. Maximilian Kolbe, Homestead.
3—ST. MARY MAGDALENE, Closed. See St. Maximilian Kolbe, Homestead.
4—ST. MAXIMILIAN KOLBE (1992) [CEM 3], Consolidated from the following churches: St. Anne, Homestead; St. Anthony, Homestead; St. Margaret, Homestead; St. Mary Magdalene, Homestead; St. Michael, Homestead; SS. Peter & Paul, Homestead. Rev. E. Daniel Sweeney. In Res., Revs. Mark W. Glasgow. Tel: 412-462-1807; Robert G. Turner (Retired).
Parish Center: 363 W. 11th Ave. Ext., 15120. Tel: 412-461-1054; Fax: 412-462-1744. Email: stmaximiliankolbe@comcast.net. Web: home.catholicweb.com/stmaximiliankolbe.
Catechesis / Religious Program—Students 40.
5—SS. PETER AND PAUL, (Lithuanian), Closed. See St. Maximilian Kolbe, Homestead.

HOPEWELL TOWNSHIP, BEAVER CO., OUR LADY OF FATIMA (1954) Rev. Howard W. Campbell.
Res.: 2270 Brodhead Rd., Aliquippa, 15001. Tel: 724-375-7626; Fax: 724-375-0219.
School—Tel: 724-375-7565. Lay Teachers 12; Students 147; Preschool 28.
Catechesis / Religious Program—Tel: 724-378-8020. Students 357.

IMPERIAL, ALLEGHENY CO., ST. COLUMBKILLE (1908) [CEM] Rev. Domenic Mancini.
Res.: 103 Church Rd., 15126. Tel: 724-695-7325; Fax: 724-695-9202.
Catechesis / Religious Program—101 Church Rd., 15126. Tel: 724-695-2146. Students 493.

INDUSTRY, BEAVER CO., ST. CHRISTINE, Closed. See St. Blaise, Midland.

INGRAM, ALLEGHENY CO., ASCENSION (1967) Very Rev. Brian J. Welding.
Res.: 114 Berry St., 15205. Tel: 412-921-1230; Fax: 412-922-1279. Email: ascension.church1@verizon.net.
Catechesis / Religious Program—Tel: 412-922-6808. Students 90.

JEFFERSON HILLS, ALLEGHENY CO., ST. THOMAS A'BECKET (1957) Rev. Robert L. Seeman; Sr. Mary Judith Seman, S.C.N., Social Ministry.
Res.: 509 Gill Hall Rd., 15025. Tel: 412-655-2885; Fax: 412-655-0615. Email: becketst@comcast.net.
Church: 139 Gill Hall Rd., 15025.
Catechesis / Religious Program—Tel: 412-653-4322; Fax: 412-653-9979. Sr. Dolores Ann Therasse, S.C.N., D.R.E. Students 515.
Convent—Tel: 412-655-4122.

KENNEDY TOWNSHIP, ALLEGHENY CO., ST. MALACHY (1953) Rev. Michael J. Maranowski.
Res.: 343 Forest Grove Rd., Coraopolis, 15108. Tel: 412-771-5483; Fax: 412-331-7312.
School—(Grades PreSchool-8) Tel: 412-771-4545; Fax: 412-771-0922. Email: schooloffice@stmalachyschool.net. Web: stmalachyschool.net. Lay Teachers 12; Students 192; Preschool 14.
Catechesis / Religious Program—Tel: 412-771-7480. Students 342.

KOPPEL, BEAVER CO.
1—QUEEN OF HEAVEN (1992) Closed. For inquiries for parish records contact the chancery. Consolidated from St. Monica, Wampum and St. Teresa, Koppel.
2—ST. TERESA, Closed. See Queen of Heaven.

LAWRENCE, WASHINGTON CO., ST. ELIZABETH, Closed. See St. Mary, Cecil.

LIBERTY BORO, ALLEGHENY CO., ST. EUGENE, Closed. See St. Mark, Port Vue.

LYNDORA, BUTLER CO.
1—ST. JOHN (1904), (Slovak), Closed. See St. Fidelis of Sigmaringen, Butler.
2—ST. STANISLAUS KOSTKA (1919), (Polish), Merged with St. Conrad, Meridian and St. John, Lyndora, to form St. Fidelis, Butler.

MCDONALD, WASHINGTON CO., ST. ALPHONSUS (1892) Rev. Gary W. Oehmler.
Res.: 219 W. Lincoln Ave., 15057. Tel: 724-926-2984; Fax: 724-926-5120.
Catechesis / Religious Program—Students 128.

MCKEES ROCKS, ALLEGHENY CO.
1—SS. CYRIL AND METHODIUS, (Polish), Closed. See St. John of God.
2—ST. FRANCIS DE SALES, Closed. See St. John of God.
3—ST. JOHN OF GOD (1993) [CEM 2], Consolidated from the following churches: St. Francis de Sales, SS. Cyril & Methodius, St. Maria Goretti Chapel, St. Mark, St. Mary Help of Christians, Mother of Sorrows and St. Vincent, Pittsburgh. Revs. Louis F. Vallone; Robert J. Zajdel, Parochial Vicar; Deacon Robert J. Stein. In Res., Rev. Regis J. Ryan (Retired).
Parish Office—1011 Church Ave., 15136. Tel: 412-771-5646; Fax: 412-331-0678. Web: www.sjogparish.com.
Catechesis / Religious Program—Tel: 412-331-8501; Fax: 412-331-8500. Students 225.
4—ST. MARIA GORETTI CHAPEL, Closed. See St. John of God.
5—ST. MARK, (Slovak), Closed. See St. John of God.
6—ST. MARY HELP OF CHRISTIANS, (German), Closed. See St. John of God.
7—MOTHER OF SORROWS, (Italian), Closed. See St. John of God.

MCKEESPORT, ALLEGHENY CO.
1—CORPUS CHRISTI PARISH Rev. Stephen A. Kresak.
2515 Versailles Ave., 15132. Tel: 412-672-0765; Fax: 412-672-2220.
2—HOLY TRINITY, Closed. See St. Martin de Porres.
3—ST. MARTIN DE PORRES (1993) [CEM 3] Closed. For inquiries for parish records contact the chancery.
4—ST. MARY, (German), Closed. See St. Martin de Porres.
5—ST. MARY CZESTOCHOWA (1893), (Polish), [CEM] Closed. For inquiries for parish records contact the chancery.
6—ST. PATRICK (1993) [CEM], Merged with St. Denis, Versailles and St. Perpetua, McKeesport. Rev. Vincent P. Velas.
Res.: 310 32nd St., 15132. Tel: 412-673-4110; Fax: 412-678-7259. Email: stpatmck@comcast.net.
Catechesis / Religious Program—305 32nd St., 15132. Students 18.
7—ST. PERPETUA, Closed. See St. Patrick, Versailles.
8—ST. PETER, Closed. See St. Martin de Porres.
9—ST. PIUS V (1903) [CEM] Closed. For inquiries for parish records contact the chancery.
10—SACRED HEART, (Croatian), Closed. See St. Martin de Porres.
11—ST. STEPHEN (1899), (Hungarian), Closed. See St. Pius V.

MEADOW LANDS, WASHINGTON CO., OUR LADY OF THE MIRACULOUS MEDAL (1949) [JC] Rev. Carmen A. D'Amico.
Res.: 300 Pike St., Box 366, 15347. Tel: 724-222-1911; Fax: 724-222-5688. Email: olmm@comcast.net. Web: www.miraculousmedalchurch.org.
Catechesis / Religious Program—Tel: 724-228-9088; 724-228-8575 (CCD Activities Center); Fax: 724-228-1488. Email: rgeckehs@comcast.net. Students 136.

MERIDIAN, BUTLER CO., ST. CONRAD, Merged with St. John and St. Stanislaus Kostka, Lyndora to form St. Fidelis, Butler.

MIDLAND, BEAVER CO., ST. BLAISE (1994) Rev. Michael L. Yaksick.
Res.: 772 Ohio Ave., 15059. Tel: 724-643-4050; Fax: 724-643-6533. Email: stblaisechurch@verizon.net. Web: www.stblaise.org.
Catechesis / Religious Program—Tel: 724-643-4663. Students 215.

MILLVALE, ALLEGHENY CO.
1—ST. ANN, Closed. See Holy Spirit.
2—ST. ANTHONY, (German), Closed. See Holy Spirit.
3—HOLY SPIRIT (1994), Consolidated from St. Anthony and St. Ann. Rev. Daniel W. Whalen.
Res.: 608 Farragut St., 15209. Tel: 412-821-4424; Fax: 412-253-4732. Email: office@holyspiritmillvale.org.
Catechesis / Religious Program—Tel: 412-821-2099.

Students 105.
4—ST. NICHOLAS, (Croatian), Closed. See the new St. Nicholas.
5—ST. NICHOLAS (1894), (Croatian), [JC 2] Rev. Daniel W. Whalen.
Administrative Center—24 Maryland Ave., 15209-2738. Tel: 412-821-3438; Fax: 412-821-8726.
Catechesis/Religious Program— Clustered with Holy Spirit Parish, Millvale. Students 5.
MONACA, BEAVER CO., ST. JOHN THE BAPTIST (1888) [CEM] Rev. George F. Chortos; Anthony Giordano, Pastoral Assoc.
Res.: 1409 Pennsylvania Ave., 15061. Tel: 724-775-3940; Fax: 724-775-6886. Email: st.johns.church@verizon.net.
School—1501 Virginia Ave., 15061. Tel: 724-775-5774; Fax: 724-775-2997. Email: sjsmon@verizon.net. Web: www.stjohn-monaca.org. Lay Teachers 11; Students 177; Preschool 45.
Catechesis/Religious Program—Tel: 724-650-5866. Students 210.
MONONGAHELA, WASHINGTON CO.
1—ST. ANTHONY (1904), (Italian—Slovak), [CEM] Merged with Transfiguration, Monongahela to become St. Damien of Molokai Parish, Monongahela.
2—ST. DAMIEN OF MOLOKAI PARISH Rev. George F. Chortos.
Res.: 722 W. Main St., 15063. Tel: 724-258-7742; Fax: 724-258-8733.
Catechesis/Religious Program—Students 85.
3—TRANSFIGURATION (1865) [CEM 2] Merged with St. Anthony, Monongahela to become St. Damien of Molokai Parish, Monongahela.
MONROEVILLE, ALLEGHENY CO.
1—ST. BERNADETTE (1955) Rev. Anthony Gargotta; Deacon Michael W. Kelly.
Res.: 245 Azalea Dr., 15146. Tel: 412-373-0050; Fax: 412-374-8113. Email: parishoffice@stbrnadet.org. Web: www.stbrnadet.org.
School—(Grades PreK-8) Tel: 412-372-7255; Fax: 412-372-7649. Email: schooloffice@stbrnadet.org. Sisters 2; Lay Teachers 23; Students 337.
Catechesis/Religious Program—Tel: 412-373-1797. Email: mvkopper@stbrnadet.org. Students 370.
2—NORTH AMERICAN MARTYRS (1960) Rev. Joseph G. Luisi.
Res.: 2526 Haymaker Rd., 15146. Tel: 412-373-0330; Fax: 412-380-1306.
School—(Grades PreSchool-6) Tel: 412-373-0889. Lay Teachers 20; Students 108; Preschool 41.
Catechesis/Religious Program—Tel: 412-349-0942. Students 250.
MOON TOWNSHIP, ALLEGHENY CO., ST. MARGARET MARY (1956) Revs. Andrew C. Fischer; James P. Holland, Parochial Vicar; Deacon Robert Sabatelle.
Res.: One Parish Place, 15108-2697. Tel: 412-264-2573; Fax: 412-264-4327. Email: contactus@stmargaretmary-moon.org. Web: st.margaretmary.org.
Catechesis/Religious Program—Tel: 412-264-9368. Email: reoffice@stmargaretmary-moon.org. Students 558.
MT. LEBANON, ALLEGHENY CO.
1—ST. BERNARD (1919) Revs. David J. Bonnar; Richard J. Wesoloski, Parochial Vicar; Brian W. Noel, Parochial Vicar.
Res.: 311 Washington Rd., 15216. Tel: 412-561-3300; Fax: 412-563-0211. Web: www.stbernardchurch.com.
School—(Grades PreK-8), 401 Washington Rd., 15216. Tel: 412-341-5444; Fax: 412-341-2044. Web: www.stbschool.com. Lay Teachers 19; Students 308.
Catechesis/Religious Program—401 Washington Rd., 15216. Tel: 412-561-0199; Fax: 412-561-1005. Web: stbernardchurch.com/ccd. Students 792.
2—ST. WINIFRED (Pittsburgh) (1960) Rev. Kevin J. Dominik; Deacon Joseph J. Kosko Jr.
Res.: 550 Sleepy Hollow Rd., 15228. Tel: 412-344-5010; Fax: 412-563-7279. Email: winoffice@comcast.net. Web: www.stwinifred.org.
Catechesis/Religious Program—Tel: 412-563-1414. Mary Ann Budd, Dir. Faith Formation K-6; Dianne Falvo, Dir. Music Ministries; Dana Mahr, Dir. Faith Formation 7-12. Students 236.
MUNHALL, ALLEGHENY CO.
1—ST. MARGARET, Closed. See St. Maximilian Kolbe, Homestead.
2—ST. MICHAEL, (Slovak), Closed. See St. Maximilian Kolbe, Homestead.
3—ST. RITA (1936), (Slovak), Revs. W. David Schorr; Nicholas Mastrangelo, Parochial Vicar.
Mailing Address: 219 W. Schwab Ave., 15120. Tel: 412-461-4204; Fax: 412-462-5484. Email: stritaparish@verizon.net. Web: www.stritaparish15120.com.
Res.: 1 Majka Dr., West Mifflin, 15122. Tel: 412-461-8087; Fax: 412-461-0142.
Catechesis/Religious Program—Combined with Resurrection, West Mifflin., Tel: 412-461-5787. Students 141.
4—ST. THERESE OF LISIEUX (1925) Revs. James G. Young; Nicholas Mastrangelo, Parochial Vicar; E. Daniel Sweeney, Parochial Vicar; Ms. Lori Ellis, Pastoral Assoc.
Res.: 1 St. Therese Ct., 15120-3701. Tel: 412-462-8161; Fax: 412-462-4817. Email: st.therese@st-therese.net. Web: www.st-therese.net.
School—3 St. Therese Ct., 15120. Tel: 412-462-8163; Fax: 412-462-5865. Email: sttheresemunhall@yahoo.com. Web: www.sttherese-munhall.org. Sisters of Charity 2; Lay Teachers 17; Students 245.
Catechesis/Religious Program—Students 245.
MUSE , WASHINGTON CO., HOLY ROSARY (1963) Rev. George T. DeVille.
Res.: One Orchard St., P.O. Box 447, 15350-0447. Tel: 724-745-3531; Fax: 724-745-0669.
Catechesis/Religious Program—Clyde House, D.R.E. Students 199.
NATRONA HEIGHTS, ALLEGHENY CO.
1—BLESSED SACRAMENT, Closed. See Our Lady of the Most Blessed Sacrament.
2—OUR LADY OF PERPETUAL HELP, Closed. See Our Lady of the Most Blessed Sacrament.
3—OUR LADY OF THE MOST BLESSED SACRAMENT (1992), (Slovak), Consolidated from Most Blessed Sacrament and Our Lady of Perpetual Help. Revs. James K. Mazurek; William P. Siple, Parochial Vicar; Deacon Patrick Wood.
Res.: 1526 Union Ave., 15065-2008. Tel: 724-226-4900; Fax: 724-224-3559. Email: olmbschurch1@verizon.net. Web: www.olmbs.org.
Catechesis/Religious Program—800 Montana Ave., Natrona Hts., 15065. Tel: 724-224-3339; Fax: 724-226-8655. Email: olmbsccd@verizon.net. Students 180.
NATRONA, ALLEGHENY CO.
1—ST. JOSEPH (1992) [CEM] [JC], Merged with St. Ladislaus and St. Mathias. Revs. James K. Mazurek; William P. Siple, Parochial Vicar; Deacon Patrick G. Wood.
Mailing Address: 1526 Union Ave., Natrona Heights, 15065. Tel: 724-224-1336; Fax: 724-224-3559. Email: stjosephnatrona@verizon.net.
Res.: 1283 10th Ave., Natrona Heights, 15065.
High School—800 Montana Ave., Natrona Heights, 15065. Tel: 724-224-5552; Fax: 724-224-0235. Students 205.
Catechesis/Religious Program—Tel: 724-224-3339. Email: olmbsccd@verizon.net. Clustered with Our Lady of the Most Blessed Sacrament, Natrona Heights. Students 35.
2—ST. LADISLAUS, (Polish), Closed. See St. Joseph.
3—ST. MATHIAS, Closed. See St. Joseph.
NEMACOLIN, GREENE CO., OUR LADY OF CONSOLATION (1923), (Polish), [CEM] Rev. John M. Bauer.
Res.: 408 Rte. 88, Carmichaels, 15320. Tel: 724-966-7270; Fax: 724-966-9118. Email: sthugholcpc@windstream.net.
Mission—Sacred Heart Rices Landing, Greene Co.
Mission—St. Mary Crucible, Greene Co.
NESHANNOCK, LAWRENCE CO., ST. CAMILLUS (1959) Rev. Thomas J. Lewandowski; Sr. Barbara Ann Johnston, C.S.J., Pastoral Assoc.
Res.: 314 W. Englewood Ave., New Castle, 16105-1806. Tel: 724-652-9471; Fax: 724-654-1430. Email: rectory@stcamillusparish.org.
Catechesis/Religious Program—Sr. Mary Slick, H.S.M., D.R.E. Students 356.
NEW BEDFORD, LAWRENCE CO., ST. JAMES (1844) [CEM] Rev. James A. Downs.
Res.: 4019 US 422, Pulaski, 16143. Tel: 724-964-8276; Fax: 724-964-1108. Email: stjamestheapostle@comcast.net. Web: www.stjames-church.com.
Catechesis/Religious Program—Students 118.
NEW BRIGHTON, BEAVER CO.
1—SS. CYRIL AND METHODIUS, (Slovak), Closed. See Holy Family.
2—HOLY FAMILY (1994) [CEM], Consolidated from St. Joseph and SS. Cyril and Methodius. Rev. Thomas E. Kredel; Larry Tavlarides, Music Dir.
Rectory & Office: 1851 3rd Ave., 15066. Tel: 724-847-3538; 724-847-3548; Fax: 724-847-3585. Email: hfpl8001@verizon.net.
Church: 521 7th Ave., 15066.
Catechesis/Religious Program—Tel: 724-846-9622. Joe Kralic, D.R.E. Students 131.
3—ST. JOSEPH, Closed. See Holy Family.
NEW CASTLE, LAWRENCE CO.
1—ST. JOSEPH THE WORKER (1888) [JC] Rev. Victor J. Molka Jr.
Res.: 1111 S. Cascade St., 16101. Email: cascade1111@comcast.net. Web: www.stjoeworker.org.
Catechesis/Religious Program—Tel: 724-654-9739; Fax: 724-654-7076. Email: ladyjoe04@aol.com. Students 177.
2—ST. LUCY, (Italian), Closed. See St. Vincent de Paul.
3—MADONNA OF CZESTOCHOWA, Closed. See Mary, Mother of Hope.
4—ST. MARGARET, Closed. See St. Vincent de Paul.
5—ST. MARY, Closed. See Mary, Mother of Hope.
6—MARY, MOTHER OF HOPE (1993), (Irish—Polish), [CEM] [JC], Consolidated from St. Mary and Madonna of Czestochowa. Rev. Victor J. Molka Jr.
Res.: 124 N. Beaver St., 16101. Tel: 724-658-2564. Email: 2psecmmoh@comcast.net. Web: www.marymotherofhope.com.
Catechesis/Religious Program—Tel: 724-658-2564, Ext. 21. Students 196.
7—ST. MICHAEL, (Slovak), Closed. See St. Vincent de Paul.
8—SS. PHILIP AND JAMES, (Polish), Closed. See St. Vincent de Paul.
9—ST. VINCENT DE PAUL (1993) [CEM 2], Consolidated from the following churches in New Castle: St. Lucy, St. Michael, SS. Philip & James, St. Margaret; and Holy Cross, West Pittsburg. Revs. Frank D. Almade, Admin.; Sean M. Francis, Parochial Vicar; Deacon S. Daniel Kielar.
Res.: One Lucymont Dr., 16102. Tel: 724-652-5829; Fax: 724-656-0413. Email: svdppastor@verizon.net.
Catechesis/Religious Program—Students 85.
10—ST. VITUS (1901), (Italian), [JC] Revs. Frank D. Almade, Admin.; Sean M. Francis, Parochial Vicar.
Res.: 910 S. Mercer St., 16101. Tel: 724-652-3422; Fax: 724-652-2322.
School—915 S. Jefferson St., 16101. Tel: 724-654-9297; Fax: 724-654-9364. Lay Teachers 9; Students 129.
Catechesis/Religious Program—Tel: 724-654-9371. Students 359.
NORTH OAKLAND, BUTLER CO., ST. JOSEPH (1845) [CEM] Rev. Joseph P. Pudichery.
Res.: 864 Chicora Rd., P.O. Box 243, Chicora, 16025. Tel: 724-445-2275; Fax: 724-445-7507. Email: stj@zoominternet.net. Web: materdolorosa-stjoe.webs.com.
Catechesis/Religious Program—Combined with Mater Dolorosa. Students 19.
NORTH ROCHESTER, BEAVER CO., ST. PUDENTIANA, Closed. See St. Cecilia, Rochester.
O'HARA TOWNSHIP, ALLEGHENY COUNTY, ST. JOSEPH (1845) Rev. Thomas R. Miller; Mrs. Suzanne M. Gilch, Pastoral Assoc.
Mailing Address: 342 Dorseyville Rd., 15215. Email: parishoffice@stjosephohara.com.
Res.: 330 Dorseyville Rd., 15215. Tel: 412-963-8885, Ext. 311. Web: www.stjosephohara.com.
Catechesis/Religious Program—342 Dorseyville Rd., 15215. Tel: 412-963-8885, Ext. 301. Email: ccd@stjosephohara.com. Students 337.
OAKDALE, ALLEGHENY CO., ST. PATRICK (1866) [CEM] Rev. Gary W. Oehmler.
Res.: 7322 Noblestown Rd., 15071. Tel: 724-693-9260; Fax: 724-693-9247. Email: stpatrickparish@comcast.net. Web: www.saint-patrick-parish.com.
Catechesis/Religious Program—Tel: 724-693-8447. Email: saintpatyouth@yahoo.com. Students 103.
OAKMONT, ALLEGHENY CO., ST. IRENAEUS (1907) Rev. Frank M. Kurimsky.
Res.: 387 Maryland Ave., 15139. Tel: 412-828-3065; Fax: 412-828-1587.
School—(Grades PreSchool-8), 637 Fourth St., 15139. Tel: 412-828-8444; Fax: 412-828-8749. Sr. Carol Ann Papp, O.S.F., Prin. Lay Teachers 15; Students 109.
Catechesis/Religious Program—Tel: 412-828-9450. Students 237.
OVERBROOK, ALLEGHENY CO., ST. NORBERT (1914), (German), Rev. Mark A. Thomas.
Mailing Address: 2413 Saint Norbert St., 15234.
Res.: 3754 Brownsville Rd., 15227. Tel: 412-882-8593; 412-881-2474; Fax: 412-881-6728. Email: office@saintnorbertparish.org. Web: www.saintnorbertparish.org.
Catechesis/Religious Program—Tel: 412-881-2040. Email: ccd@saintnorbertparish.org. Students 52.
PENN HILLS, ALLEGHENY CO.
1—ST. BARTHOLOMEW (1950) Sr. Dorothy Pawlus, C.S.F.N., Parish Life Collaborator.
Res.: 111 Erhardt Dr., 15235. Tel: 412-242-3374; Fax: 412-242-1488. Email: office@stbartsparish.com. Web: www.stbartsparish.com.
School—Tel: 412-242-2511; Fax: 412-242-8317. Email: school@stbartsparish.com. Lay Teachers 13; Students 180.
Catechesis/Religious Program—Tel: 412-242-7207. Email: denise@stbartsparish.com; colleen@stbartsparish.com. Students 70.
2—ST. GERARD MAJELLA (1964) Rev. Martin F. Barkin.
Rectory—Res.: 121 Dawn Dr., Verona, 15147. Tel: 412-793-3333; Fax: 412-793-4726. Email: saintgerardmajella@comcast.net.
Catechesis/Religious Program—Tel: 412-793-3959. Students 102.

3—St. Susanna (1960) Rev. Martin F. Barkin.
Res.: 200 Stotler Rd., 15235-3554. Tel: 412-798-5596; Fax: 412-798-0479. Email: saintsusanna@verizon.net. Web: www.stsusannapennhills.parishesonline.com.
Catechesis/Religious Program—Tel: 412-798-3591. Email: stsusannare@verizon.net. Students 49.

Perrysville, Allegheny Co., St. Teresa of Avila (1867) [CEM] Revs. Robert J. Vular; Michael A. Zavage; Deacons David R. Witter; Jack Miller.
Res.: 1000 Avila Ct., 15237. Tel: 412-367-9001; Fax: 412-366-8415.
School—800 Avila Ct., 15237. Tel: 412-367-9001, Ext. 530; Fax: 412-364-1172. Religious 1; Lay Teachers 18; K-8 254; Preschool 27.
Catechesis/Religious Program—Tel: 412-367-9001, Ext. 549; Fax: 412-548-0009. Students 603.
Convent—900 Avila Ct., 15237. Tel: 412-367-9001, Ext. 544.

Peters Township, Washington Co., St. Benedict the Abbot (1962) Revs. Robert M. Miller; Paul W. Merkovsky; Deacon John L. Layton; Dennis Gehlrlein, Pastoral Assoc.
Res.: 120 Abington Dr., McMurray, 15317. Tel: 724-941-9406; Fax: 724-941-9517. Email: staff@stbenedicttheabbot.org. Web: www.stbenedicttheabbot.org.
Catechesis/Religious Program—Tel: 724-941-9587. Colette Speca, Dir. Faith Formation; Janet Roberto, Young Adult Min. Students 1,300.

Pitcairn, Allegheny Co., St. Michael (2010) Closed. For inquiries for parish records contact the chancery.

Pleasant Hills, Allegheny Co., Saint Elizabeth of Hungary (1942) Revs. Dale E. DeNinno; Nicholas J. Argentieri; Deacon Joseph Compomizzi.
Res.: One Grove Pl., 15236. Tel: 412-882-8744; Fax: 412-882-8320. Email: stelizabethchurch@steliz.com. Web: www.stelizabethparish.org.
School—Tel: 412-881-2958; Fax: 412-882-0111. Web: www.steliz.com. Lay Teachers 25; Students 335.
Catechesis/Religious Program—Tel: 412-882-5023; Fax: 412-207-1647. Students 350.
Chapel of Convenience—St. David, Baldwin Boro, 15236. Tel: 412-882-8744.

Plum, Allegheny Co., St. Januarius (1946) Rev. Peter R. Pilarski (Retired).
Res.: 1450 Renton Rd., 15239. Tel: 412-793-4439; Fax: 412-793-7135. Email: stjanplum@verizon.net. Web: stjanuarius.org.
Catechesis/Religious Program—Students 100.

Port Vue, Allegheny Co.
1—St. Joseph, Closed. See St. Mark.
2—Saint Mark Parish (1993) Rev. Daniel T. Straughn.
Administration Center—1101 Romine Ave., 15133. Tel: 412-678-6275; Fax: 412-673-1393.
Port Vue Worship Site—1125 Romine Ave., 15133.
Res. & Liberty Worship Site—3210 Liberty Way, Liberty Borough, 15133. Tel: 412-678-6275.
School—St. Joseph Regional School, Tel: 412-678-0659; Fax: 412-678-1301. See Consolidated Schools under Institutions located in the Diocese.
Catechesis/Religious Program—Students 150.

Prospect, Butler Co., St. Christopher at the Lake (1974) Rev. Joseph E. Feltz.
Res.: 229 N. Franklin St., 16052. Tel: 724-865-2430; Fax: 724-865-1120. Email: stchristopher@zoominternet.net. Web: christophermoraine.org.
Catechesis/Religious Program—Tel: 724-865-9840. Students 94.

Rankin, Allegheny Co., Visitation of the Blessed Virgin Mary, (Croatian), Closed. See Word of God, Swissvale.

Reserve Township, Allegheny Co., St. Aloysius (1892) Rev. Lawrence R. Smith.
3616 Mt. Troy Rd., 15212. Tel: 412-821-2351; Fax: 412-821-6480. Web: www.staloysius.us.
Res.: 1700 Harpster St., 15212. Tel: 412-231-2994; Fax: 412-231-7180.
Catechesis/Religious Program—Students 38.

Richeyville, Washington Co., St. Agnes (1994) Rev. John E. Forbidussi.
Res.: Box 406, 15358. Tel: 724-632-5858.
Catechesis/Religious Program—Students 38.

Richland Township, Allegheny Co., Saint Richard (1992) Rev. Thomas A. Sparacino.
3841 Dickey Rd., Gibsonia, 15044.
Res.: 5717 Wesleyann Dr., Gibsonia, 15044. Tel: 724-444-1971; Fax: 724-444-6001. Email: amy@saintrich.org. Web: www.saintrich.org.
Catechesis/Religious Program—Students 911.

Robinson Township, Allegheny Co., Holy Trinity (Moon Run) (1944) Rev. Kenneth R. Keene; Rev. Msgr. Joseph R. Lamonde; Deacon Tim Killmeyer.
Res.: 5718 Steubenville Pike, McKees Rocks, 15136-1311. Tel: 412-787-2140; 412-787-2143; Fax: 412-787-3799. Email: htrobins@comcast.net. Web: holytrinityrobinson.org.
School—(Grades PreK-8), 5720 Steubenville Pike, Mc Kees Rocks, 15136-1311. Tel: 412-787-2656; Fax: 412-787-9487. Email: holy-trinity-school@comcast.net. Web: www.holy-trinity-school.org. Lay Teachers 30; Students 373.
Catechesis/Religious Program—Tel: 412-859-3467. Cathy Wilkinson, D.R.E.; D. Carl Stovek, Youth & Young Adult Min. Students 385.

Rochester, Beaver Co., St. Cecilia (1856), (German—Italian), [CEM] Revs. James Menkhus, O.F.M.Cap.; John Getsy, O.F.M.Cap. In Res., Rev. William Gillum, O.F.M.Cap.
Office/Rectory: 628 Virginia Ave., 15074. Tel: 724-775-0801; Fax: 724-774-3056. Email: secretary@stcecilia.comcastbiz.net. Web: www.stceciliaroch.org.
Res.: *St. Fidelis Friary*, 372 East End Ave., Beaver, 15009.
Church: 632 Virginia Ave., 15074.
Catechesis/Religious Program—633 California Ave., 15074. Tel: 724-775-2761. Students 210.
See St. Fidelis Friary under Monasteries & Residences of Priests & Brothers in the Institution section.

Roscoe, Washington Co., St. Joseph (1904) Rev. George J. Moneck.
Res.: 105 Good St., Box 486, 15477. Tel: 724-938-2324; Fax: 724-938-2983.
Catechesis/Religious Program—Students 30.

Ross Township, Allegheny Co., St. Sebastian (North Hills) (1952) Revs. John R. Rushofsky; John L. O'Shea; Deacon Richard R. Cessar.
Res.: 311 Siebert Rd., 15237. Tel: 412-364-8999; Fax: 412-364-6330. Email: info@saintsebastianparish.org. Web: www.saintsebastianparish.org.
School—307 Siebert Rd., 15237. Fax: 412-364-5891. Email: mail@saintsebastianparish.org. Web: www.saintsebastianparish.org. Lay Teachers 32; Students 456.
Catechesis/Religious Program—Students 576.

Russellton, Allegheny Co., Transfiguration (1916) [CEM] Rev. John C. Vojtek.
Res.: 15 Poma St., 15076. Tel: 724-265-1030; Fax: 724-265-1032. Email: rctransroman@consolidated.net.
Church: 100 McKrell Rd., 15076-1305.
Catechesis/Religious Program—Tel: 724-265-3581. Web: www.trccd.catholicweb.com. Maryetta Filotei, D.R.E. Students 48.

Scott Township, Allegheny Co.
1—Our Lady of Grace (1947) Rev. Richard A. Infante.
Res.: 310 Kane Blvd., 15243. Tel: 412-279-7070; Fax: 412-279-2385. Email: rectory@olgscott.org. Web: www.olgscott.org.
School—1734 Bower Hill Rd., 15243. Tel: 412-279-6611; Fax: 412-279-6755. Lay Teachers 25; Students 320.
Catechesis/Religious Program—1730 Bower Hill Rd., 15243. Tel: 412-276-0277; Fax: 412-276-0277. Students 305.
2—SS. Simon and Jude (1955) Rev. Daniel J. Maurer. In Res., Revs. Kris D. Stubna; James R. Gretz.
Res.: 1607 Greentree Rd., 15220. Tel: 412-563-3189; Fax: 412-563-8524. Email: ssjparish@ssjpitt.org. Web: ssjparish.org.
Catechesis/Religious Program—Tel: 412-563-3189, Ext. 209. Students 140.

Sewickley, Allegheny Co., St. James (1863) [CEM] Very Rev. Daniel A. Valentine; Deacon Robert Sabatelle. In Res., Rev. Matthew Tosello (Retired).
Res.: 200 Walnut St., 15143. Tel: 412-741-6650; Fax: 412-741-4782. Email: saintjamesparish@comcast.net. Web: www.saintjames-church.com.
School—(Grades K-8), 201 Broad St., 15143. Tel: 412-741-5540; Fax: 412-741-9038. Email: srchristysjs@yahoo.com; srdianesjs@yahoo.com. Web: www.stjamesschool.us. Dr. Gayle Salvatore, Librarian. (10 full-time/11 part-time) 21; Students 224; Preschool 18.
Catechesis/Religious Program—Tel: 412-741-6766. Email: stjamesreled@comcast.net. Students 416.

Sharpsburg, Allegheny Co.
1—St. John Cantius (1906), (Polish), Closed. See Saint Juan Diego Parish.
2—Madonna of Jerusalem (1904), (Italian), Closed. See Saint Juan Diego Parish.
3—St. Mary (1994) [CEM] Closed. See Saint Juan Diego Parish.
4—Saint Juan Diego Parish (2009) [CEM] Rev. Michael W. Decewicz.
201 9th St., 15215-2304. Tel: 412-784-8700; Fax: 412-781-1101. Email: saintjuandiegopgh@verizon.net. Web: www.saintjuandiegopgh.org.
Catechesis/Religious Program—Students 80.

Slippery Rock, Butler Co., St. Peter (1938) [CEM] Rev. Kevin G. Poecking.
(Administration & Chapel), Res. & Parish Center: 342 Normal Ave., 16057. Tel: 724-794-2880; Fax: 724-794-1255. Email: parishoffice@rockcatholic.org.
Church: 670 S. Main St., 16057.
Catechesis/Religious Program—Katrina Boosel, D.R.E. Students 211.
Mission—*St. Anthony Church* 232 Boyers Rd., Forestville, Butler Co. 16035.

South Park, Allegheny Co.
1—St. Joan of Arc (1923) Rev. Phillip Pribonic.
Res.: 6414 Montour St., 15129. Tel: 412-833-2400; Fax: 412-835-1764. Web: www.mystjoan.org.
School—6470 Library Rd., 15129. Tel: 412-833-2433. Lay Teachers 12; Students 75.
Catechesis/Religious Program—Tel: 412-835-3724. Students 384.
2—Nativity (1905) Rev. John E. Hissrich.
Res.: 5802 Curry Rd., 15236. Tel: 412-655-3000; Fax: 412-650-4658. Email: nativitychurch@comcast.net.
Attending St. Katharine Drexel School at Nativity parish in Bethel Park.
Catechesis/Religious Program—5807 Curry Rd., 15236. Tel: 412-655-1565. Students 225.

Springdale, Allegheny Co., St. Alphonsus (1901) Rev. Kenneth E. Kezmarsky.
Res.: 750 Pittsburgh St., 15144-1699. Tel: 724-274-5084; Fax: 724-274-7035. Email: stalphonsus@verizon.net. Web: www.stalphonsuschurch.com.
Catechesis/Religious Program—Tel: 724-274-2547. Students 110.

Swissvale, Allegheny Co.
1—St. Anselm, Closed. See Word of God.
2—Saint Barnabas, (Slovak), Closed. See Word of God.
3—Madonna del Castello (1920), (Italian), Revs. John Lynam; Joseph B. Codori, Parochial Vicar.
Res.: 2021 S. Braddock Ave., 15218. Tel: 412-271-5666; Fax: 412-271-2335.
Catechesis/Religious Program—Fax: 412-271-2335. Students 26.
4—Word of God (1994), (Irish—Croatian), Consolidated from the following churches: St. Anselm, St. Barnabas and Visitation of the Blessed Virgin Mary, Rankin. Rev. Michael John Lynam.
Res.: 2021 S. Braddock Ave., 15218. Tel: 412-241-1372; Fax: 412-271-2335. Email: wordogod1994@verizon.net. Web: members.bellatlantic.net/~wordogod.
School—7436 McClure Ave., 15218. Tel: 412-371-8587. Sisters of Charity 3; Lay Teachers 13; Students 145.
Catechesis/Religious Program—Students 45.

Tarentum, Allegheny Co.
1—St. Clement, Closed. See Holy Martyrs.
2—Holy Martyrs (1992), (Slovak), [CEM] [JC 2], Consolidated from St. Clement and Sacred Heart, St. Peter. Rev. Aaron J. Kriss.
Res.: 353 W. Ninth Ave., 15084. Tel: 724-224-0770; Fax: 724-224-7070. Email: holymartyrsparish@verizon.net. Web: holymartyrsparish.org.
Catechesis/Religious Program—344 W. 9th Ave., 15084. Tel: 724-224-1234. Email: holymartyrseducation@verizon.net. Students 82.
3—Sacred Heart - St. Peter, Closed. See Holy Martyrs.

Turtle Creek, Allegheny Co., St. Colman (1882) Rev. James E. Kunkel.
Res.: 100 Tri-Boro Ave., 15145. Tel: 412-823-2564; Fax: 412-823-6350. Email: stcolman@verizon.net.
Catechesis/Religious Program—Tel: 412-823-9114. Students 75.

Unity, Allegheny Co., St. John the Baptist (1915) [CEM] Revs. Thomas J. Galvin; Michael Suslowski.
Res.: 444 St. John St., 15239. Tel: 412-793-4511; 412-793-4580; Fax: 412-793-4311. Email: stjohnthebaptistparish@comcast.net. Web: www.stjohnthebaptistparish.net.
School—418 Unity Center Rd., 15239. Tel: 412-793-0555; Fax: 412-793-4001. Web: www.stjohnthebaptistschool.org. Lay Teachers 16; Students 193.
Catechesis/Religious Program—Tel: 412-795-6536. Email: reled@stjohnthebaptist.org. Web: www.stjohnreled.org. Students 417.

Upper St. Clair, Allegheny Co.
1—St. John Capistran (1968) Rev. James J. Chepponis.
Res.: 1610 McMillan Rd., 15241. Tel: 412-221-6275; Fax: 412-257-3789. Email: sjohncap@comcast.net.
Catechesis/Religious Program—Tel: 412-221-5445. Email: sjcreled@comcast.net. Students 320.
2—St. Louise de Marillac (1961) Revs. Michael A. Caridi; John F. Naugle; Deacon William F. Strathmann Jr.; Sr. M. Faith Balawejder, C.S.S.F., Pastoral Assoc.; Greg Fincham, Music Min.
Res.: 320 McMurray Rd., 15241. Tel: 412-833-1010; Fax: 412-833-6624. Email: jfrench@stlouisedemarillac.org.
School—310 McMurray Rd., 15241. Tel: 412-835-0600; Fax: 412-835-2898. Email: kklase@stlouisedemarillac.org. Web: www.stlouiseschoolpa.org. Ken Klase, Prin. Lay Teachers 21;

(K-8) 475.
Catechesis/Religious Program—Tel: 412-835-1155; Fax: 412-833-3952. Lynn Lachut, C.R.E.; Jason Zych, Youth Min. Students 1,060.

VERONA, ALLEGHENY CO., ST. JOSEPH (1866) [CEM] Rev. Philip J. Przybyla.
Res.: 825 Second Ave., 15147-1498. Tel: 412-795-5114; Fax: 412-828-1236. Email: joevchurch@verizon.net.
School—Tel: 412-828-7213; Fax: 412-828-4008. Email: stjosephelementary@comcast.net. Lay Teachers 15; Students 180.
Catechesis/Religious Program—Tel: 412-828-7715. Email: stjosephreled@comcast.net. Students 75.

VERSAILLES, ALLEGHENY CO., ST. DENIS, Closed. See St. Patrick, McKeesport.

WAMPUM, LAWRENCE CO., ST. MONICA, Closed. See Queen of Heaven, Koppel.

WASHINGTON, WASHINGTON CO.

1—ST. HILARY (1919) Rev. Thomas D. O'Neil.
Res.: 320 Henderson Ave., 15301. Tel: 724-222-4087; Fax: 724-222-2130. Email: sthilary@linequest.net. Web: www.sthilaryparish.org.
Catechesis/Religious Program—340 Henderson Ave., 15301. Tel: 724-222-1381. Students 111.

2—IMMACULATE CONCEPTION (1855) [CEM 2] Revs. William P. Feeney; Michael R. Ruffalo; Nicholas A. Spirko; Sr. Margaretta Nussbaumer, C.D.P., Pastoral Assoc.
Worship Site: Sacred Heart, Claysville, PA—
Res.: 119 W. Chestnut St., 15301. Tel: 724-225-1425; Fax: 724-229-7946. Email: ic.wash@verizon.net. Web: www.icwash.org.
School—111 W. Spruce St., 15301. Tel: 724-225-1680; Fax: 724-225-4651. Lay Teachers 21; Students 243; Preschool 66.
Catechesis/Religious Program—135 W. Chestnut St., 15301. Tel: 724-225-0382. Students 366.

WAYNESBURG, GREENE CO., ST. ANN (1839) [CEM] Rev. Richard J. Thompson.
Res.: 232 E. High St., 15370. Tel: 724-627-7568; Fax: 724-627-3735. Email: stannchurch@windstream.net.
Catechesis/Religious Program—Students 137.

WEST ALIQUIPPA, BEAVER CO., ST. JOSEPH, Closed. See St. Titus, Aliquippa.

WEST MIFFLIN, ALLEGHENY CO.

1—ST. AGNES (1867) [CEM] Rev. Joseph R. Grosko, Admin.
Res.: 622 St. Agnes Ln., 15122. Tel: 412-466-6545. Email: stagnes2@msn.com. Web: www.stagneswm.com.
School—(Grades PreSchool-8), 653 St. Agnes Ln., 15122. Tel: 412-466-6238; Fax: 412-466-2013. Sisters of the Holy Spirit 2; Lay Teachers 9; Students 140.
Catechesis/Religious Program—
Convent—Sisters of the Holy Spirit, 635 St. Agnes Ln., 15122. Tel: 412-466-3554.

2—HOLY SPIRIT (1963) Rev. John B. Lendvai.
Res.: 2603 Old Elizabeth Rd., 15122-2558. Tel: 412-346-0477; Fax: 412-466-4983. Email: hsrectory2603@comcast.net.
Catechesis/Religious Program—Tel: 412-346-0475; 412-346-0476 (Music Office); Fax: 412-466-3444. Email: hsccd@comcast.net. Students 189.

3—HOLY TRINITY (1901), (Slovak), [CEM] Rev. Joseph R. Grosko.
Res.: 529 Grant Ave. Ext., 15122. Tel: 412-466-6545; Fax: 412-466-6968. Email: h.trinity@verizon.net.

4—RESURRECTION (1936) Revs. W. David Schorr; Nicholas Mastrangelo.
Res.: 1 Majka Dr., 15122.
Catechesis/Religious Program—Combined with St. Rita., Tel: 412-461-5787. Sr. Charlotte Trojan, O.S.F., D.R.E. Students 130.

WEST PITTSBURG, LAWRENCE CO., HOLY CROSS, Closed. See St. Vincent de Paul, New Castle.

WEST SUNBURY, BUTLER CO.

1—ST. ALPHONSUS (1841) [CEM] [JC 3], Merged with Epiphany, St. Paschal and St. Louis, West Sunbury. Rev. James R. Bedillion.
Res.: 202 W. State St., P.O. Box 246, 16061. Tel: 724-476-1476; Fax: 724-476-1477. Email: stalphparish@zoominternet.net.
Catechesis/Religious Program—Students 85.

2—ST. LOUIS, Closed. See St. Alphonsus, Boyers.

WEST VIEW, ALLEGHENY CO., ST. ATHANASIUS (1905) Revs. Robert A. Norton; Jeffrey T. Molnar. In Res., Rev. Leroy A. DiPietro.
Res.: 7 Chalfonte Ave., 15229. Tel: 412-931-4624; Fax: 412-939-3516. Web: www.stathanasiuswv.org.
Catechesis/Religious Program—Tel: 412-931-4624, Ext. 213. Students 263.

WEXFORD, ALLEGHENY CO.

1—ST. ALEXIS (1961) Rev. Paul J. Zywan.
Res.: 10090 Old Perry Hwy., 15090. Tel: 724-935-4343; Fax: 724-935-1270. Email: parish@stalexis.org. Web: www.stalexis.org.
School—(Grades PreK-8) Tel: 724-935-3940; Fax: 724-935-6070. Email: school@stalexis.org. Lay Teachers 17; Students 270.
Catechesis/Religious Program—Tel: 724-935-0877. Email: dre@stalexis.org. Kate Bianco, D.R.E.; Paula Green, D.R.E. Asst. Students 290.

2—ST. ALPHONSUS (1840) [CEM] [JC] Revs. Peter P. Murphy; Robert W. Fleckenstein, Parochial Vicar.
Res.: 201 Church Rd., 15090. Tel: 724-935-1151. Email: stalphonsus@zoominternet.net. Web: www.stals.org.
School—Tel: 724-935-1152; Fax: 724-935-1110. Email: stals@zoominternet.net. Sisters 1; Lay Teachers 22; Students 450.
Catechesis/Religious Program—Tel: 724-935-1160; Fax: 724-934-3788. Students 550.

WHITE OAK BORO, ALLEGHENY CO., ST. ANGELA (1958) Very Rev. Stephen M. Chervenak.
Office: 1640 Fawcett Ave., 15131. Tel: 412-672-9641; Fax: 412-672-1576. Email: st.angela.merici@verizon.net.
Res.: 1732 Fawcett Ave., 15131.
School—1640R Fawcett Ave., 15131. Tel: 412-672-2360; Fax: 412-672-0880. Lay Teachers 12; Students 217.
Catechesis/Religious Program—Tel: 412-672-0913; Fax: 412-672-1576. Students 95.

WHITEHALL, ALLEGHENY CO., ST. GABRIEL OF THE SORROWFUL VIRGIN (1944) Revs. John R. Haney; Kenneth A. Sparks, Parochial Vicar.
Res.: 5200 Greenridge Dr., 15236. Tel: 412-881-8115; 412-881-8117; Fax: 412-440-0160. Email: stgabeschurch@yahoo.com.
School—Tel: 412-882-3353; Fax: 412-882-2125. Lay Teachers 22; Students 420; Preschool 75.
Catechesis/Religious Program—5302 Greenridge Dr., 15236. Tel: 412-881-7950. Students 310.

WILDWOOD, ALLEGHENY CO., ST. CATHERINE OF SWEDEN (1953) Revs. Regis M. Farmer; Patrick Barkey; Deacon Clifford M. Homer.
Res.: 4701 Sylvan Dr., Allison Park, 15101.
Church: 2554 Wildwood Rd., P.O. Box 246, 15091. Tel: 412-486-6001; Fax: 412-486-6004. Email: info@stcatherineofsweden.org. Web: www.stcatherineofsweden.org.
Catechesis/Religious Program—Email: ccd@stcatherineofsweden.org; reledsec@stcatherineofsweden.org. Students 652.

WILKINSBURG, ALLEGHENY CO., ST. JAMES (1869) Rev. Warren W. Metzler.
Res.: 718 Franklin Ave., 15221. Tel: 412-241-1392; Fax: 412-241-6625. Email: stjameswilk@aol.com. Web: www.stjameswilkinsburg.org.
Catechesis/Religious Program—Tel: 412-242-2246; Fax: 412-241-6625. Students 22.

WILMERDING, ALLEGHENY CO.

1—ST. JUDE THE APOSTLE (1994) [CEM], Consolidated from St. Aloysius and St. Leocadia. Rev. Norbert J. Campbell.
Res.: 405 Westinghouse Ave., 15148. Tel: 412-823-8390; Fax: 412-823-8399.
Catechesis/Religious Program—Tel: 412-823-1066.

2—ST. LEOCADIA, (Polish), Closed. See St. Jude the Apostle.

ZELIENOPLE, BUTLER CO., ST. GREGORY (1906) [CEM] Rev. William E. Dorner.
Res.: 2 W. Beaver St., 16063. Tel: 724-452-7245; Fax: 724-452-4064. Email: stgreg.parish@zoominternet.net. Web: www.stgregzelie.org.
School—115 Pine St., 16063. Tel: 724-452-9731; Fax: 724-452-4064. Email: stgreg.school@zoominternet.net. Lay Teachers 12; Students 250.
Catechesis/Religious Program—Students 300.

Chaplains of Public Institutions

ALLEGHENY COUNTY. *Depaul Institution*, Tel: 412-924-1012. Rev. Walter G. Rydzon, M.Div. Tel: 412-381-9878.
Pittsburgh International Airport, Tel: 412-472-3526. Rev. Robert E. McCreary, O.F.M.Cap. Tel: 724-774-1242.

BEAVER COUNTY. *McGuire Memorial Home*, Tel: 724-843-3400, Ext. 1127. Rev. William Gillum, O.F.M.Cap., Dir. Pastoral Care. Tel: 724-775-0801 Home; 724-843-3400, Ext. 1127 Work. (Vacant)

Hospitals

ALLEGHENY COUNTY. *Children's Hospital*, Tel: 412-692-5325. Sr. Lisa Balcerek, C.S.J., Rev. Douglas A. Boyd, Support Chap. UPMC Chaplains, Tel: 412-692-7253
St. Clair Memorial Hospital, Tel: 412-561-4900. Attended by Our Lady of Grace, Pittsburgh. Tel:412-279-7070
Heritage Valley Sewickley, Tel: 412-741-6600. Deacon Stephen M. Deskevich. Tel: 412-741-6600, Ext. 1752.
Jefferson Regional Medical Center, Tel: 412-469-5000. Rev. Robert J. Boyle, V.F. Tel: 724-348-7145.
Life Care Hospital of Pittsburgh, Tel: 412-247-2585. Attended by St. James, Wilkinsburg. Tel:412-241-1392
Magee-Women's Hospital, Tel: 412-647-1000. Rev. Douglas A. Boyd, Support Chap., Sr. Nora Egan, C.S.J. Tel: 412-641-4525.
McKeesport UPMC. Corpus Christi Parish 412-672-0765, Tel: 412-664-2000.
Mercy Health System of Pittsburgh-Pittsburgh Mercy Hospital, Tel: 412-232-8111. Revs. Gerald Kanzik, John G. Oesterle. Tel: 412-232-8198, Albert Schempp, M.I.
Ohio Valley General Hospital, Tel: 412-777-6161. Attended by St. Malachy. Tel: 412-771-5483 and St. John of God. Tel: 412-771-5646
UPMC Passavant Hospital, Tel: 412-367-6700. Sr. Caritas Marshall, C.S.J. Tel: 412-367-6700. Sacramental Coordination by St. Catherine of Sweden Parish.
UPMC Shadyside Hospital, Tel: 412-623-2121. Revs. Vincent F. Kolo. Tel: 412-623-1691, Douglas A. Boyd, Support Chap.
UPMC St. Margaret Hospital, Tel: 412-767-4672. St. Scholastica Parish & Madonna of Jerusalem Parish: Tel: 412-784-8700; Pastoral Care, Tel: 412-784-4749 & Juan Diego Parish: Tel: 412-784-8700
UPMC University of Pittsburgh Medical Center, Tel: 412-647-7560. Rev. John Obasi. Tel: 412-647-7560. Patient and Family Support, Tel: 412-647-7615
West Penn Allegheny Health System-Alle-Kiski Medical Center, Tel: 724-224-5100. Attended by Our Lady of the Most Blessed Sacrament, Natrona Heights. Tel: 724-226-4900
West Penn Allegheny Health System-Allegheny General, Tel: 412-359-3131. Revs. David Moczulski, O.F.M. Tel: 412-359-4269, Gilbert Z. Puznakoski. Tel: 412-359-4269.
West Penn Allegheny Health System-Forbes Regional, Tel: 412-858-2960; 412-456-5645. Sacramental coordination by Pastoral Vicariate Region Two.
Western Pennsylvania Hospital, Tel: 412-578-5000. Rev. Douglas A. Boyd, Support Chap. Tel: 412-682-5353.

BEAVER COUNTY. *Heritage Valley Beaver*, Tel: 724-728-7000. Revs. William J. Schwartz. Tel: 724-775-4111, Robert E. McCreary, O.F.M.Cap. Tel: 724-774-1242.

BUTLER COUNTY. *Butler Memorial Hospital*, Tel: 724-283-6666. Attended by St. Paul Parish. Tel: 724-287-1759.
UMPC Passavant Health Center. Butler County, PA 724-452-5400 St. Gregory Parish, 724-452-7245

GREENE COUNTY. *Greene County Memorial*, Tel: 724-627-3101. Attended by St. Ann, Waynesburg. Tel:724-627-7568

LAWRENCE COUNTY. *Ellwood City Hospital*, Tel: 724-752-0081. Attended by Holy Redeemer Parish, Ellwood City. Tel:724-758-4441.
Jameson Hospital North Campus. Lawrence County, PA 724-658-9001 Rev. Sean M. Francis, Coord. Pastoral Care. Tel: 724-652-3422.
Jameson Hospital South Campus. Lawrence County, PA 74-658-9001 Mary Mother of Hope Parish, 724-658-2564

WASHINGTON COUNTY. *Mon Valley Hospital*. St. Damien of Molokai Parish 724-258-7742, Tel: 724-258-2000.
Washington Hospital, Tel: 724-225-7000. Attended by Immaculate Conception, Washington. Tel:724-225-1425
West Penn Allegheny Health System-Canonsburg Hospital, Tel: 724-745-6100. Rev. John D. Nanz, D.Div. Tel: 724-745-6560.

Veterans Administration Hospitals

ALLEGHENY COUNTY. *VA Hospital Pittsburgh*, Tel: 412-688-6000, Ext. 6729. Tel: 412-688-6000; Tel: 1-866-482-7488 (24-Hour)
University Drive. Rev. Robert Craig, O.F.M.Cap. Tel: 412-682-6430 Home; 412-683-3000 Work.
Highland Drive. Rev. Mark W. Glasgow. Tel: 412-462-1807 Residence.
H.J. Heinz III (Aspinwall). Rev. Robert Craig, O.F.M-.Cap. Tel: 412-683-3000 Work.
VA Pittsburgh Health Care System. Univeristy Drive Division / Highland Drive Division 412-688-6000 / 866-482-7488 Revs. Robert Craig, O.F.M.Cap., Charles Soto, O.F.M., Mark W. Glasgow, Pastoral Care. Tel: 412-954-4001. HJ Heinz progressive Care Center 412-822-2222 / 866-482-7488

BUTLER COUNTY. *VA Medical Center Butler*, Tel: 800-362-8262. Rev. William J. Ritzert, Chap. (Retired). Tel: 724-477-5009.

Rehabilitation, Nursing and Geriatric Care Facilities

ALLEGHENY COUNTY. *Arden Courts*. Attended by Rev. Ladis Cizik '87 Tel: 412-795-3388
Arden Courts North Hills. St. Theresa of Avila 412-367-9001, Tel: 412-369-7887.
Asbury Heights, Tel: 412-341-1030. Attended by St. Bernard, Mt. Lebanon. Tel: 412-561-3300.
Baldwin Health Care, Tel: 412-885-8400. Attended

by St. Elizabeth of Hungary, Pittsburgh. Tel: 412-882-8744.
Baptist Home. Allegheny County, PA 412-563-6550 St. Winifred Parish 412-344-5010
Beverly Healthcare Mt. Lebanon, Tel: 412-257-4444. Attended by St. Thomas More. Tel: 412-833-0031.
Beverly Manor Nursing Home, Tel: 412-856-7570. Rev. Ladis Cizik. Tel: 412-795-3388.
Canterbury Place, Tel: 412-622-9000. Attended by Our Lady of the Angels, Pittsburgh. Tel: 412-682-0929.
Cedars of Monroeville, Tel: 412-373-3900. Attended by Rev. Ladis Cizik '87 Tel: 412-795-3388
Children's Institute, St. Bede, Tel: 412-661-7222; Fax: 412-420-2400.
Collins Nursing Center. St. Bede Parish. Tel: 412-661-7222., Tel: 412-661-1740.
Concordia at Rebecca. Allegheny County, PA 724-444-0600 St. Victor Parish 724-265-2070
Concordia of Fox Chapel. Allegheny County, PA 412-767-5808 St. Pio of Pietrelcina 412-828-4066
Concordia of South Hills. Allegheny County, PA 412-278-1300 Our Lady of Grace Parish 412-279-7070
Consulate Health Care. Allegheny County, PA 412-767-4998 St. Victor Parish 724-265-2070
Country Meadows. Allegheny County, PA 412-257-2474 Holy Child Parish 412-221-5213
DT Watson Rehab Hospital, Tel: 412-741-9000. Attended by St. James, Sewickley. Tel: 412-741-6650.
Forbes Hospice. Allegheny County, PA 412-578-7208 Rev. Joseph C. Beck. Tel: 412-421-5766.
Forbes Road Nursing Center, Tel: 412-665-3232. Rev. Joseph C. Beck. Tel: 412-421-5766.
Golden Living Center Monoreville. Allegheny County, PA 412-856-7570 Rev. Ladis Cizik. Tel: 412-795-3388.
Golden Living Center Oakmont. Allegheny County, PA 412-828-7300 St. Ireneaus Parish 412-828-3065
Hamilton Hills Personal Care. Rev. Ladis Cizik. Tel: 412-795-3388.
Health South Hospital of Pittsburgh, Tel: 412-856-2400. Rev. Joseph C. Beck. Tel: 412-421-5766.
Healthsouth Harmarville Hospital, Tel: 412-826-4929. St. Mary of the Assumption, 412-486-4100
Heartland Health Care Center. St. Bede Parish. Tel: 412-661-7222., Tel: 412-665-2400.
Heritage Shadyside, Tel: 412-422-5100. Attended by St. Rosalia, Pittsburgh. Tel: 412-421-5766.
Independence Court of Mt. Lebanon, Tel: 412-341-4400. Attended by St. Ann, Castle Shannon. Tel: 412-531-5964; St. Thomas More, Bethel Park. Tel: 724-883-0031
Independent Court of Monroeville, Tel: 412-373-3030. Rev. Joseph C. Beck. Tel: 412-421-5766.
Kane Regional Center - Glen Hazel, Tel: 412-422-6800. Rev. Joseph C. Beck. Tel: 412-422-6839.
Kane Regional Center - McKeesport, Tel: 412-675-8600. Sr. Thomas Joseph Gaines, S.C. Tel: 412-675-8640.
Kane Regional Center - Ross, Tel: 412-369-2000. Rev. Ambrose Mouthevil. Attended by St. Sebastian. Tel: 412-364-8999.
Kane Regional Center - Scott, Tel: 412-429-3000. Rev. Gilbert Z. Puznakoski. Tel: 412-279-7070.
Kindred Hospital Pittsburgh. Allegheny County, PA 412-494-5500 St. Columbkille Parish 724-695-7325
Kindred Hospital Pittsburgh North Shore. Allelgheny County, PA 412-323-5800 St. Peter Parish 412-321-0711
Ladies of the Grand Army Republic (LGAR), Tel: 412-825-9000. Rev. Ladis Cizik. Tel: 412-795-3388.
Little Sisters of the Poor, Tel: 412-761-5373. Rev. John A. Geinzer, S.T.L. , M.Ed.
Longwood at Oakmont, Tel: 412-826-5917. St. Irenaeus. Tel: 412-828-3065
Manorcare Health Services, Highland Dr., 15212. Tel: 412-831-6050. Attended by St. Thomas More. Tel: 412-833-0031.
Manorcare Health Services Green Tree, Greentree Rd., 15212. Tel: 412-344-7744. Attended by SS. Simon & Jude, Tel: 412-563-3189.
Manorcare Health Services McMurray. Attended by St. Benedict the Abbot. Tel: 724-941-9406., McMurray Rd., 15212. Tel: 412-941-3080.
Manorcare Health Services Monroeville, Tel: 412-856-7071. Rev. Ladis Cizik. Tel: 412-795-3388. Tel: 412-856-7071
Manorcare Health Services North Hills, Tel: 412-369-9955. Rev. Joseph C. Beck. Tel: 412-421-5766.
Marian Manor, Inc., Tel: 412-563-6866. Rev. John F. Walsh. Tel: 412-561-2373.
Oakmont Nursing Center, Tel: 412-828-7300. Attended by St. Irenaeus, Oakmont. Tel: 412-828-3065
Presbyterian Seniorcare Westminister Place, Tel: 412-826-6136. Rev. Ladis Cizik. Tel: 412-795-3388. Attended by St. Irenaeus, Oakmont.
Providence Point Nursing Home. Allegheny County, PA 412-276-4500 Our Lady of Grace Parish 412-279-7070
Ridgepoint, Tel: 412-653-6870. Attended by Nativity, South Park Twp. Tel: 412-655-3000.
Riverview Center for Jewish Seniors, Tel: 412-521-5900. Attended by St. Rosalia, Pittsburgh. Tel: 412-421-5766.
Seneca Manor Assisted Living. Rev. Ladis Cizik. Tel: 412-795-3388. Tel: 412-798-6000
Seneca Place. Rev. Ladis Cizik. Tel: 412-795-3388. Tel: 412-798-8000
Shadyside Nursing and Rehabilitation Center. Attended by St Bede Parish. Tel: 412-661-7222., Tel: 412-362-3500.
Southwestern Nursing and Rehabilitation Center, Tel: 412-466-0600, Ext. 5989. Attended by Holy Spirit, West Mifflin. Tel: 412-466-5048
Sunrise Assisted Living. Rev. Ladis Cizik. Tel: 412-795-3388. Tel: 412-380-2589
UPMC Rehabilitation Hospital, Tel: 412-420-2400. Attended by St. Bede, Pittsburgh. Tel: 412-661-7222.
Vincentian Collaborative System, Tel: 412-630-9980. Sr. Laverne Sihelnik, V.S.C.
Vincentian de Marillac Home. Attended by St. Raphael, Tel: 412-661-3100; 412-361-2833.
Vincentian Home, Tel: 412-366-5600. Sisters Karen Kellerski. Tel: 412-366-5600, Ext. 569, Linda Soltis, SCN. Tel: 412-366-5600, Ext. 567.
Vincentian Regency Home, Tel: 412-366-8540. Sr. Denise Hibel. Tel: 412-366-8540
Woodhaven Convalescent Center, Tel: 412-856-4770. Rev. Joseph C. Beck. Tel: 412-421-5766.

BEAVER COUNTY. *Beaver Elder Care Rehab*. Beaver County, PA 724-375-0345 St. Titus Parish 724-378-8561
Blair Personal Care Home. Beaver County, PA 724-843-2209 Holy Redeemer Parish 724-758-4411
Friendship Ridge Skilled Nursing, Tel: 724-775-7100. Rev. William J. Schwartz. Tel: 724-775-7100.
Hunter's Personal Care. Beaver County, PA 724-378-1205 St. Titus Parish 724-378-8561
Maplewood Personal Care. Beaver County, PA 724-266-4485 Good Samaritan Parish 724-266-6565
Providence Care Center. Beaver County, PA 724-846-8504 Divine Mercy Parish 724-846-4585
Villa St. Joseph, Tel: 724-869-6300. Rev. David E. Scharf. Tel: 724-869-6522.

BUTLER COUNTY. *Autumn Grove Care Center*. Butler County, PA 724-735-4224 St. Peter Parish 724-794-2880
Concordia Luteran Ministries. Butler County, PA 724-352-1571 St. Joseph Parish 724-352-2149
Creek Meadows. Butler County, PA 724-452-7378 St. Gregory Parish 724-452-7245
Evergreen Nursing Center. Butler County, PA 724-452-6970 St. Gregory Parish 724-452-7245
St. John Specialty Care Center. Attended by St. Kilian Parish, Tel: 724-625-1665 or Tel: 724-625-1571.
Sunnyview Home, Tel: 724-282-1800. Attended by St. Paul Parish. Tel: 724-287-1759.
Sunrise of Cranberry. Attended by St. Kilian Parish, Tel: 724-625-1665 or Tel: 724-779-4300.
UPMC/Passavant Cranberry and UPMC Cranberry Place. Attended by St. Killian Parish, Tel: 724-625-1665, 724-775-5350, or Tel: 724-772-5350
Valencia Woods at St. Barnabas. Attended by St. Kilian Parish, Tel: 724-625-1665 or Tel: 724-625-4000.
Worthington of Adams. Attended by St. Kilian Parish, Tel: 724-625-1665 or Tel: 724-779-5020.

GREENE COUNTY. *Beverly Health Care*, Tel: 724-852-2020. Attended by St. Ann, Waynesburg. Tel: 724-627-7568.
Rolling Meadows, Tel: 724-627-3153. Attended by St. Ann, Waynesburg. Tel: 724-627-7568.

LAWRENCE COUNTY. *Almira Home*, Tel: 724-652-4131. Rev. Sean M. Francis, Coord. Pastoral Care. Tel: 724-652-3422.
Belvedere Residence, Inc., Tel: 724-924-2191. Rev. Sean M. Francis, Coord. Pastoral Care. Tel: 724-652-3422.
Castle Manor, Tel: 724-654-4377. Rev. Sean M. Francis, Coord. Pastoral Care. Tel: 724-652-3422.
Cedar Manor, Tel: 724-654-8050. Rev. Sean M. Francis, Coord. Pastoral Care. Tel: 724-652-3422.
Edison Manor Nursing & Rehab. Lawrence County, PA 724-652-6340 Rev. Sean M. Francis, Coord. Pastoral Care. Tel: 724-652-3422.
Golden Hill Nursing, Inc., Tel: 724-654-7791. Rev. Sean M. Francis, Coord. Pastoral Care. Tel: 724-652-3422.
Haven Convalescent Home, Tel: 724-654-8833. Rev. Sean M. Francis, Coord. Pastoral Care. Tel: 724-652-3422.
Highland Hall Care Center, Tel: 724-658-4781. Rev. Sean M. Francis, Coord. Pastoral Care. Tel: 724-652-3422.
Hillview Manor, Tel: 724-658-1521. Rev. Sean M. Francis, Coord. Pastoral Care. Tel: 724-652-3422.
Jameson Care Center. Lawrence County, PA 724-596-3411 St. Camillus Parish 724-652-9471
Majors Manor, Tel: 724-924-9568. Rev. Sean M. Francis, Coord. Pastoral Care. Tel: 724-652-3422.
Overlook Nursing Home. St. Camillus Parish 724-652-9471, Tel: 724-946-3511.
Shenango United Presbyterian Home. St. Camillus Parish 724-652-9471, Tel: 724-946-3516.
Silver Oak Nursing. Mary Mother of Hope Parish 724-658-2564, Tel: 724-652-3863.
Southpoint at Jameson PCH. Lawrence County, PA 724-658-1100 Mary Mother of Hope Parish 724-658-2564

WASHINGTON COUNTY. *Beverly South Hills*, Tel: 724-746-1300. Rev. John D. Nanz, D.Div. Tel: 724-745-6560. Tel: 724-745-6560, Tel: 724-746-1300
Canon House, Tel: 724-745-7771. Rev. John D. Nanz, D.Div. Tel: 724-745-6560. Tel: 724-745-6560, Tel: 724-745-7771
Charles House Home for the Aged, Tel: 724-745-6355. Rev. John D. Nanz, D.Div. Tel: 724-745-6560. Tel: 724-745-0950, Tel: 724-745-6355
Greenery Nursing Home, Tel: 724-745-8000. Rev. John D. Nanz, D.Div. Tel: 724-745-6560. Tel: 724-745-6560, Tel: 724-745-8000
Havencrest. Washington County, PA 724-258-3000 St. Damien of Molokai Parish 724-258-7742
Horizon Senior Care, Tel: 724-746-5040. Rev. John D. Nanz, D.Div. Tel: 724-745-6560. Tel: 724-745-6560, Tel: 724-746-5040
Humbert Lane Health Care. Immaculate Conception Parish 724-225-1425, Tel: 724-228-4740.
Kade's Nursing Home, Tel: 724-222-2148. St. Hilary Parish 724-222-4087
Mon Valley Care Center. Washington County, PA 724-310-1111 St. Damien of Molokai Parish 724-258-7742
Presbyterian Senior Care, Tel: 724-222-4300. Immaculate Conception Parish 724-225-1425
Rest Haven Personal Care Home, Tel: 724-745-3333. Rev. John D. Nanz, D.Div. Tel: 724-745-6560.
Washington County Health Center. Immaculate Conception, Washington 724-225-1425, Tel: 724-228-5010.

Mental Health Facilities

ALLEGHENY COUNTY. *Western Psychiatric Institute & Clinic*, Tel: 412-647-3060. Attended by UPMC Chaplains. Tel: 412-647-7615.

WASHINGTON COUNTY. *Bradley Center South*, Tel: 724-746-1212; 724-746-2400. Tel: 724-746-1212

Correctional Institutions

ALLEGHENY COUNTY. *Allegheny County Jail*, Tel: 412-350-2000. Rev. G. Malcolm McDonald. Tel: 412-350-2057, Deacons Thomas O'Neill, Ross Decal.
SCI Pittsburgh, Tel: 412-761-1955. Revs. Thomas J. Dansak, Barry P. O'Leary. Tel: 412-561-3300.
Shuman Center, Tel: 412-661-6806. Social Services. Tel: 412-665-4135.

BEAVER COUNTY. *Beaver County Jail*. Saints Peter and Paul. Tel: 724-775-4111; St. Titus Parish 724-378-8561

BUTLER COUNTY. *Butler County Jail*. St. Paul Parish (724-287-1759)

GREENE COUNTY. *State Correctional Institute at Greene*, Tel: 724-852-2902. Rev. J. Francis Frazer. Tel: 724-377-2588 Parish, Deacons James A. Kenny, James M. Sheil.
Waynesburg County Jail, Tel: 724-627-7780. St. Ann Parish (724-627-7780)

LAWRENCE COUNTY. *Lawrence County Jail*. Mary Mother of Hope Parish 724-658-2564, Tel: 724-654-5384.
Youth Development Center, Tel: 412-656-7300. Rev. John W. Rebel (Retired). Tel: 724-964-8276, Sr. Yvonne Dursh.

WASHINGTON COUNTY. *Washington County Jail*, Tel: 412-561-7557. Attended by Immaculate Conception, Washington. Tel: 724-225-1425.

Graduate Studies:
Very Rev.—
Yurochko, Dennis P., S.T.L., Casa Santa Maria, Via dell'Umilta 30, Rome 00187 Italy.
Revs.—
Donley, Christopher D., North American College 000120 Vatican City State.
Kunz, Thomas W., Casa Santa Maria, Via dell'Umilta 30, Rome 00187 Italy.
Verona, Adam M., North American College 00120 Vatican City State.

On Duty Outside the Diocese:
Rev. Msgrs.—
Kozar, John E., Catholic Near E. Welfare Assoc., 1011 First Ave., New York, NY 10022-4195.
Roos, H. Jules, Centro de Obras Sociales, Apartado 473, Chimbote, Peru.
Revs.—
Bleichner, Howard P., Sulpicians, 2-1151 E. Cliff Dr., Santa Cruz, CA 95062.

Taylor, Augustus R., Jr., 3726 Olmsted St., Los Angeles, CA 90018-4129.
Wehner, James A., S.T.D., Pontifical College Josephinum, 7625 N. High St., Columbus, OH 43235.
Whalen, Timothy F., M.Div., Orchard Lake Schools, 3535 Indian Tr., Orchard Lake, MI 48324.
Zadroga, Jean-Luc P., O.S.B., St. Vincent Archabbey, Latrobe, 15650.

Military Chaplains:
Revs.—
Brzek, Jon J., 4935 Crommelin St., Honolulu, HI 96818-5022.
Glasgow, Mark W., Chap. VA Medical Center, St. Maximilian Kolbe, 363 11th Ave. Ext., Homestead, 15120.

Absent on Sick Leave:
Revs.—
Jordan, John M.
Menegay, David C.
Patriquin, Garry D.
Shulik, Bernard P.
Smoley, Rudolph F.

Retired:
Rev. Msgrs.—
Findlan, Joseph G., St. John Vianney Manor, 2600 Morange Rd., 15205.
Seli, John J., The Place at Merritt Island, 535 Crockett Blvd. Apt 143, Merritt Island, FL 32953-5008.
Revs.—
Ayoob, John, 2349 Railroad St., #1502, 15222.
Bergman, Charles B., St. John Vianney Manor, 2600 Morange Rd., 15205.
Boccardi, Raymond C., 300 Crescent Ave., Ellwood City, 16117.
Bovard, William R., St. John Vianney Manor, 2600 Morage Rd., 15205.
Chortos, Donald, 2611 Plantation Rd., Charlotte, NC 28270.
Cirilli, Matthew R., 708 Sturbridge Ln., Export, 15632.
Conley, Roy H., St. John Vianney Manor, 2600 Morange Rd., 15205.
Connolly, Brian W., Gateway Towers, Unit 21M, 320 Fort Duquesne Blvd., 15222.
Corbett, John B., Vincentian Home, 111 Perrymont Rd., 15237.
Costello, Bernard B., Cardinal Dearden Center, 4721 Fifth Ave., 15213.
Czapinski, Richard J., c/o 92 Locust Ct., 15237-2626.
Dascenzo, Joseph J., Holy Redeemer Parish, 300 Crescent Ave. Ste 1, Ellwood City, 16117.
DeBlasio, Dominck A., 117 Buffalo St., Freeport, 16229.
DeCarlo, Philip J., 801 Somerville Dr., 15243.
DeLuca, Anthony G., 304 Malcolm Ct., Monroeville, 15146.
Dixon, David C., St. John Vianney Manor, 2600 Morange Rd., 15205.
Dixon, Jerome A., J.C.L., Little Sisters of the Poor, 1020 Benton Ave., 15212.
Dougherty, Eugene J., St. John Vianney Manor, 2600 Morange Rd., 15205.
Duch, Robert G., Ph.D., 411 Hickory Ct., 15238.
Elanjileth, J. Matthew, 1500 Fifth Ave. Kelly Bldg., Mc Keesport, 15132.
Erdeljac, Frank G., M.Div., P.O. Box 479, West Pittsburg, 16160.
Fay, William J., 124 Rana Ln., Gibsonia, 15044.
Ferris, Thomas B., Little Sisters of the Poor, 1028 Benton Ave., 15212.
Fisher, Donald C., M.A., 20 Kosciusko Way, 15203.
Garvey, James W., Most Holy Name of Jesus Parish, 1700 Harpster St., 15212.
Gentile, Carl J., V.F., 337 W. 12th Ave. Ext, Homestead, 15120.
Graff, Francis C., 1863 Mahan School Rd., Blairsville, 15717.
Gualtieri, Raymond A., 4940 Brightwood Rd., Apt. A102, Bethel Park, 15102.
Gutierrez, Alvin P., 3401 Rigel St., 15212.
Harvey, John A., Arrowood #359, 512 N. Lewis Run Rd., West Mifflin, 15122.
Henry, Leo G., Vincentian Home, 111 Perrymont Rd., 15237.
Herrmann, Robert W., Guardian Angels Parish, 1030 Logue St., 15220.
Hoffmann, Edward, Vincentian Home, 111 Perrymont Rd., 15237.
Jackovic, George V., 124 Bennington Dr., Canonsburg, 15317.
Jones, Donald R., 202 Williamsburg Dr., Elizabeth, 15037-2442.
Jurewicz, Francis Z., 339 Valley Ave., Wall, 15148.
Keane, John J., 850 Baldwin St., Apt. 415, 15234.
Kirby, Thomas M., Sisters of the Divine Redeemer, 999 Rock Run Rd., Elizabeth, 15037.
Kohler, William F., Our Lady of Fatima Parish, 2270 Brodhead Rd., Aliquippa, 15001.
Koser, Albert C., St. John Vianney Manor, 2600 Morange Rd., 15205.
Krah, James B., Little Sisters of the Poor, 1020 Benton Ave. Apt 2105, 15212.
Kurutz, Joseph V., 1317 Berryman Ave., Bethel Park, 15102.
Laboon, Joseph D., 6887 Brompton Dr., Lakeland, FL 33809.
Lachowicz, Francis B., 169 Royal Oak Dr., White Oak, 15131.
Lang, Hugh J., St. Anne Parish, 400 Hoodridge Dr., 15234.
Lauer, Eugene F., Prince of Peace Parish, 81 S. 13th St., 15203.
Le, Trieu Ngoc, c/o 517 Ap Binh An 1, Xa An Hoa, Huyen Chau Thanh - Tinh An Giang, Vietnam.
Litavec, Edward S., Sacred Heart Parish, 310 Shady Ave., 15206.
Lutz, Gerald J., St. Paul Parish, 128 N. McKean St., Butler, 16001.
MacVeigh, Michael C., St. John Vianney Manor, 2600 Morange Rd., 15205.
Maida, Thaddeus S., 44045 Five Mile Rd., Plymouth, MI 48170.
Manion, Thomas F., Cardinal Dearden Center, 4721 Fifth Ave., 15213-2915.
Markell, John W., 938 Broadway, East Mc Keesport, 15035.
Maurer, Russell J., St. Malachy Parish, 343 Forest Grove Rd., Coraopolis, 15108-3797.
McCaulley, Cornelius W., S.T.L., Epiphany Parish, 164 Washington Pl., 15219.
McColligan, Raymond, St Anne's Home, 685 Angela Dr., Greensburg, 15601.
McDermott, Michael A., 1237 Chartiers Ave., Mc Kees Rocks, 15136.
McIlvane, Donald W., 265 46th St., Apt. 1207, 15201.
Mueller, Richard J., 889 Charlamagne Blvd., Naples, FL 34112.
Nee, Thomas M., Overlook Green, 5250 Meadowgreen Dr., 15236.
O'Brien, Patrick J., S.T.D., M.S.Ed., 5703 Holden St., 15205.
O'Donnell, Thomas M., M.Div., St. Mary of Mercy, 202 Stanwix St., 15222.
O'Malley, John J., 1103 N. Highland Ave., 15206.
O'Toole, John M., 2731 N.E. 14th St. Apt. 319, Pompano Beach, FL 33062.
Oldenski, Kenneth E., 6698 41st St. Cir. E., Sarasota, FL 34243.
Palko, John A., Little Sisters of the Poor, 1028 Benton Ave., 15212.
Petrarulo, John D., St. John Vianney Manor, 2600 Morange Rd., 15205.
Pilarski, Peter R., 3885 Brookside Ln. Apt. 207, Murrysville, 15668.
Polak, Michael J., St. John Vianney Manor, 2600 Morange Rd., 15205.
Ragni, Richard R., Cardinal Dearden Center, 4721 Fifth Ave., 15213.
Reardon, Robert J., St. John Vianney Manor, 2600 Morange Rd., 15205.
Rebel, John W., St. Cyril of Alexandria Parish, 3854 Brighton Rd., 15212.
Ritzert, William J., 954 Gameland Rd., Chicora, 16025.
Rocha, Victor J., Resurrection Parish, 1100 Creedmoor Ave., 15226-2299.
Rutkowski, Theodore A., S.T.L., 2848 Darlington Rd., Beaver Falls, 15010.
Rutledge, William G., St. Mary of the Assumption Parish, 2510 Middle Rd., Glenshaw, 15116.
Ryan, Regis J., St. John of God Parish, 1011 Church Ave., Mc Kees Rocks, 15136.
Savage, Paul J., S.T.L., Villa Saint Joseph, 1030 State St., Baden, 15005.
Schleicher, Edward R., St. Mary of the Assumption, 2510 Middle Rd., Glenshaw, 15116.
Semler, Albert J., St. Clare of Assisi, 460 Reed St., Clairton, 15025.
Smith, Thomas E., 592 Meadowbrook Rd., Trafford, 15085.
Sobon, Walter A., V.F., M.Ed., 402 Red Deer Ln., Coraopolis, 15108.
Suhoza, John E., Resurrection Parish, 1100 Creedmoor Ave., 15226.
Szarnicki, Henry A., St. John Vianney Manor, 2600 Morange Rd., 15205.
Terdine, Richard G., Cardinal Dearden Center, 4721 Fifth Ave., 15213.
Tosello, Matthew, Ph.D., St. James Parish, 200 Walnut St., Sewickley, 15143.
Trzeciakowski, Edward J., St. John Vianney Manor, 2600 Morange Rd., 15205.
Turner, Robert G., 3904 Main St., Apt. 2, Munhall, 15120.
Utz, Raymond M., Cardinal Dearden Center, 4721 Fifth Ave., 15213.
Vecchio, Michael J., 5775 Fernley Dr. W., Apt. 76, West Palm Beach, FL 33415.
Wichmanowski, Walter F., Vincentian Home, 111 Perrymont Rd., 15237.
Wilt, George A., St. John Vianney Manor, 2600 Morange Rd., 15205.

Permanent Deacons:
Babcock, Michael J., St. Albert the Great, Baldwin
Bachner, Ralph W., Jr., St. Kilian, Adams/Cranberry Townships
Bane, John J., (Retired)
Barth, Robert V., (Retired)
Basko, Joseph N., St. Frances Cabrini, Center Twp.
Batz, William G., St. Thomas More, Bethel Park
Berna, Thomas J., St. Stephen, Hazelwood
Bibro, Mark S., St. Pius X, Brookline; Our Lady of Loreto, Brookline
Byers, Stephen J., St. Bonaventure, Glenshaw
Carran, John J., Christ the King, Bessemer/Hillsville; St. James the Apostle, Pulaski
Carver, William H., St. Kilian, Adams/Cranberry Twps.
Cerenzia, Joseph A., St. Patrick, Canonsburg
Cessar, Richard R., St. Sebastian, Ross Twp.
Christmann, Edwin P., St. Peter, Slippery Rock
Comer, Gary L., St. Athanasius, West View
Como, Gerard A., St. Thomas a Becket, Jefferson Hills
Compomizzi, Joseph, St. Elizabeth of Hungary, Pleasant Hills
Dacal, Rosendo F., All Saints, Etna
Dadowski, Francis J., Jr., St. Mary of the Assumption, Glenshaw
DeNome, Harry J., Christ the Divine Teacher, Chippewa Twp.; St. Rose of Lima, Darlington
Deskevich, Stephen M., Sacred Heart, Emsworth
DiSanto, Dale J., St. Angela Merici, White Oak
Eckhardt, Frederick N., St. Bernard, Mount Lebanon
Fitzpatrick, Richard T., Our Lady of the Angels, Lawrenceville
Gaines, George W., St. Fidelis of Sigmaringen, Lyndora/Meridian
Gleason, Kenneth V., (Retired)
Grab, James R., St. Basil, Carrick
Gruseck, David J., St. Christopher, Prospect
Heiles, Albert E., Jr., St. Alphonsus, Wexford
Hirst, Jeffrey A., Immaculate Conception, Washington
Homer, Clifford M., St. Catherine of Sweden, Hampton Twp./Wildwood
Jelinek, G. Gregory, Most Holy Name of Jesus, Troy Hill; St. Aloysius, Reserve Township
Kelly, Michael W., St. Bernadette, Monroeville
Kenny, James A., St. Germaine, Bethel Park
Kielar, S. Daniel, St. Vincent de Paul, New Castle
Killmeyer, Tim M., Holy Trinity, Robinson Township
Kisak, Stephen J., Holy Spirit, Millvale: St. Nicholas, Millvale/North side
Kleifgen, Richard C., St. Anne, Castle Shannon
Kondrich, Keith G., Word of God, Rankin/Swissvale; Madonna del Costello, Swissvale
Kosko, Joseph J., Jr., St. Winifred, Mt. Lebanon
Koslosky, Robert E., Incarnation of the Lord, Observatory Hill/Perry North; Risen Lord, Marshall/Shadeland
Krulikowski, Thomas E., St. Barbara, Bridgeville
Kuhns, Elbert A., St. Thomas, Clarksville
Lander, Kevin L., St. Margaret, Green Tree
Layton, John L., St. Benedict the Abbot, Peters Twp.
Leonard, James F., (Outside Diocese)
Longo, Richard A., Resurrection, Brookline
Lopus, Thomas A., Ss. John and Paul, Franklin Park/Marshall Twp.
Ludwikowski, Jeffrey J., St. Alexis, Wexford
Mackin, James S., Ss. Simon and Jude, Scott Twp.
Marshall, Robert M., St. Kilian, Adams/Cranberry Twps.
McMullen, Robert G., St. Mary of the Mount, Mount Washington
Meyer, Joseph C., Jr., (Retired)
Miles, Leon F., St. Pamphilus, Beechview
Miller, John C., St. Teresa of Avila, Perrysville
Mills, Thomas B., St. Valentine, Bethel Park
Mobley, Anton V., Our Lady of the Miraculous Medal, Meadow Lands
Molitor, Gary, St. Richard, Richland Twp.
Natali, Mitchell M., St. Paul, Butler
Nizan, Daniel E., St. Stephen, Hazelwood
O'Keefe, Charles L., (Retired)
O'Neill, Thomas J., St. Catherine of Sienna, Beechview
Palamara, William R., St. Athanasius, West View
Pikula, Stephen C., Corpus Christi, McKeesport
Poroda, Alexander J., II, St Damien of Molokai, Monongahela
Ragan, John E., St. Michael, Elizabeth
Raymond, Thomas W., St. Oliver Plunkett, Fredericktown/Mariana

Riley, Herbert E., Jr., St. Colman, Turtle Creek
Rubio, Silverio, (Outside Diocese)
Satter, Victor P., St. Francis of Assisi, Finleyville
Sheil, James M., St. Ann, Waynesburg
Stein, Robert J., St. John of God, McKees Rocks
Strathmann, William F., Jr., St. Louis de Marillac, Upper Saint Clair
Sutton, Lawrence R., Ph.D., Our Lady of Grace, Scott Township
Tucek, Richard M., North American Martyrs, Monroeville/Pitcairn
Vannucci, Joseph R., St. John the Baptist, Unity
Vukotich, Charles J., Jr., St. Thomas More, Bethel Park
Weiland, James T., Our Lady of Peace, Conway
White, Andrew J., Sr., St. Sylvester, Brentwood
Wilmer, Reynold, St. Benedict the Moor, Hill District; Epiphany, Uptown; St. Mary of Mercy, The Point/Gateway Center
Witter, David R., St. Teresa of Avila, Perrysville
Wood, Patrick G., Our Lady of the Most Blessed Sacrament, Natrona Heights; St. Joseph, Natrona
Yanniello, Gary J., Holy Child, Bridgeville

INSTITUTIONS LOCATED IN THE DIOCESE

[A] SEMINARIES, RELIGIOUS OR SCHOLASTICATES

PITTSBURGH. *Saint Paul Seminary* (1965) *College & Pre-Theology*, 2900 Noblestown Rd., 15205. Tel: 412-456-3048; Fax: 412-456-3187. Email: seminaryprog@diopitt.org. Web: www.diopitt.org. Rev. Terrence P. O'Connor, M.Div., J.D., Dir. Spiritual Format/Vice Rector; Very Rev. Joseph M. Mele, Ph.D., Rector; Rev. Benedetto P. Vaghetto, J.C.L., Spiritual Dir.; Sr. Cindy Ann Kibler, S.H.S., Dir. Pastoral Formation. Priests 3; Sisters 1; Students (attending Duquesne University) 16.

[B] COLLEGES AND UNIVERSITIES

PITTSBURGH. *Carlow University* (1929) 3333 Fifth Ave., 15213. Tel: 412-578-6059; Fax: 412-578-6668. Email: admission@carlow.edu. Web: www.carlow.edu. Dr. Mary Hines, Pres.; Dr. Margaret McLaughlin, Ph.D., Vice Pres. for Academic Affairs & Provost; Elaine Misko, Librarian. Sisters of Mercy. Sisters 1; Lay Teachers 80; Total Staff 373; Total Enrollment 2,200.

Duquesne University of the Holy Spirit (1878) 600 Forbes Ave., 15282. Tel: 412-396-6000; Fax: 412-396-4334. Web: www.duq.edu. Dr. Charles J. Dougherty, Pres.; Revs. William F. Crowley, C.S.Sp. (Retired); John Fogarty; Sean M. Hogan, C.S.Sp., Exec. Vice Pres. Student Life; Sean Kealy, C.S.Sp.; Raymond D. French, C.S.Sp.; James P. McCloskey, C.S.Sp., Vice Pres. Mission & Identity; Naos McCool, C.S.Sp., Asst. Dean Student Formation School of Educ.; Peter I. Osuji, Campus Min.; John A. Sawicki, C.S.Sp.; Jocelyn Gregoire, C.S.Sp.; Casimir Lawrence Nyaki, Asst. Professor, Philosophy; Eugene Uzukwu, C.S.Sp., Assoc. Prof. of Theology; George J. Spangenberg, C.S.Sp., Visiting Instructor Intl. Educ. The Spiritans. Priests 13; Faculty 502; Students 10,011; Total Staff 1,622.

The University is coeducational and comprises the following Colleges, Schools and Institutes:

College of Liberal Arts Tel: 412-396-6389; Fax: 412-396-4859. Dr. James Swindal, Acting Dean, College & Graduate School of Liberal Arts.

School of Business Administration Tel: 412-396-6238; Fax: 412-396-4764. Dr. Alan Miciak, Dean.

School of Music Tel: 412-396-6080; Fax: 412-396-5479. Dr. Edward Kocher, Dean.

School of Law Tel: 412-396-6300; Fax: 412-396-5219. Ken Gormley, Dean.

School of Leadership and Professional Advancement Tel: 412-396-5600; Fax: 412-396-5072. Dr. Dorothy Bassett, Dean.

School of Education Tel: 412-396-6093; Fax: 412-396-5585. Dr. Olga Welch, Dean.

School of Nursing Tel: 412-396-6550; Fax: 412-396-6346. Dr. Eileen Zungolo, Dean.

School of Pharmacy Tel: 412-396-6380; Fax: 412-396-1810. Dr. J. Douglas Bricker, Dean, Mylan School of Pharmacy.

School of Health Sciences Tel: 412-396-6652; Fax: 412-396-5554. Dr. Gregory Frazer, Dean; Dr. David W. Seybert, Dean Bayer School of Natural & Environmental Sciences. Tel: 412-396-4900; Dr. Ralph L. Pearson, Provost & Academic Vice Pres.; Mr. Stephen Schillo, Vice Pres., Mgmt. & Business; Rev. Sean M. Hogan, C.S.Sp., Exec. Vice Pres. Student Life; Linda S. Drago, Esq., Gen. Counsel & Univ. Sec.; Dr. Laverna Saunders, Librarian.

La Roche College (1963) 9000 Babcock Blvd., 15237-5898. Tel: 412-536-1201; Fax: 412-536-1199. Email: karen.willoughby@laroche.edu. Web: www.laroche.edu. Sr. Candace Introcaso, C.D.P., Ph.D., Pres.; Michael Andreola, Vice Pres. Inst. Advancement; Colleen Ruefle, Vice Pres. for Student Life; Rev. W. Peter Horton, M.A., M.Div., Campus Min.; Dr. Howard Ishiyama, Vice Pres. for Academic Affairs; Dr. Rosemary McCarthy, Ph.D., Vice Pres. for Academic Affairs & Dean of Graduate Students & Adult Educ.; Robert Vogel, Vice Pres. Finance & CFO; Sr. Michele Bisbey, C.D.P., Div. Chair Humanities; George Zaffuto, Vice Pres. Admin. Svcs.; William Firman Jr., Vice Pres., Enrollment Mgmt. & Mktg.; Mary Beth Fetchko, Special Asst. to Pres. & Gen. Counsel; Laverne Collins, Librarian. Sisters of Divine Providence. Priests 3; Sisters 8; Lay Teachers 178; Total Staff 298; Students 1,419.

[C] HIGH SCHOOLS, DIOCESAN

PITTSBURGH. *Bishop Canevin High School, Inc.* (1957) 2700 Morange Rd., 15205. Tel: 412-922-7400; Fax: 412-922-7403. Email: mainoffice@bishopcanevin.org. Web: www.bishopcanevin.org. Mr. Kenneth M. Sinagra, Prin.; Rev. Michael A. Zavage, Chap.; Susan Rakaczky, Librarian. Priests 1; Sisters 1; Lay Teachers 30; Students 390.

Central Catholic High School, Inc. (1927) 4720 Fifth Ave., 15213. Tel: 412-621-8189; Fax: 412-208-0555. Email: principal@centralcatholichs.com. Web: www.centralcatholichs.com. Bros. Richard Grzeskiewicz, F.S.C., Pres.; Robert Schaefer, F.S.C., Prin.; Mary Sickles, Librarian. The school is a Diocesan institution under the care of the Brothers of the Christian Schools (F.S.C.). Priests 2; Brothers 10; Lay Teachers 53; Students 835; Total Staff 72.

North Catholic High School, Inc. (1939) 1400 Troy Hill Rd., 15212. Tel: 412-321-4823; Fax: 412-321-0599. Email: principal@north-catholic.org. Web: www.north-catholic.org. Dr. Michael J. Pendred II, Prin.; Mr. Frank Orga, Pres. Lay Teachers 17; Total Staff 29; Students 265.

Oakland Catholic High School, Inc. (1989) 144 N. Craig St., 15213. Tel: 412-682-6633; Fax: 412-682-2496. Email: webmaster@oaklandcath.org. Web: www.oaklandcath.org. Dr. Maureen Marsteller, Prin.; Katherine D. Freyvogel, Pres.; Mrs. Milana Galagaza Sopko, Librarian. Priests 1; Lay Teachers 49; Total Staff 14; Students 609.

BADEN. *Quigley Catholic High School, Inc.* (1967) 200 Quigley Dr., 15005. Tel: 724-869-2188; Fax: 724-869-3091. Email: office@qchs.org. Web: www.qchs.org. Mrs. Rita McCormick, Prin.; Mr. Mitchell Yanyanin, Librarian. Sisters 1; Lay Teachers 17; Students 146; Total Staff 21.

MCKEESPORT. *Serra Catholic High School, Inc.* (1961) 200 Hershey Dr., 15132. Tel: 412-751-2020; Fax: 412-751-3488. Email: 73781@diopitt.org. Web: www.serrahs.com. Timothy Chirdon, Prin.; Mrs. Wendy Seibert, Librarian. Lay Teachers 25; Students 355; Total Staff 25.

MT. LEBANON. *Seton-LaSalle Catholic High School, Inc.* (1979) 1000 McNeilly Rd., 15226. Tel: 412-561-3583; Fax: 412-561-9097. Email: schoolinfo@slshs.org. Web: www.slshs.org. Lauren Martin, Prin.; Stephanie Schmidt, Librarian. Consolidated South Hills Catholic & Elizabeth Seton High Schools. Lay Teachers 36; Students 501; Total Staff 12.

Under the care of Sisters of Charity. Rev. James M. Bachner, M.Div., Chap.

NATRONA HEIGHTS. *Saint Joseph High School, Inc.*, 800 Montana Ave., 15065. Tel: 724-224-5552; Fax: 724-224-3205. Beverly K. Kaniecki, Prin.

[D] HIGH SCHOOLS, PRIVATE

PITTSBURGH. *Vincentian Academy* (1932) 8100 McKnight Rd., 15237. Tel: 412-364-1616; Fax: 412-367-5722. Web: www.vincentianacademy.org. Sr. Camille Panich, S.C.N., Prin.; John Fedko, Pres. Sisters of Charity of Nazareth 4; Lay Teachers 23; Students 231; Total Staff 35.

CORAOPOLIS. *Our Lady of the Sacred Heart High School* (1932) 1504 Woodcrest Ave., 15108. Tel: 412-264-5140; Fax: 412-264-4143. Email: info@olsh.org. Web: www.olsh.org. Tim Plocinik, Prin.; Mary Patterson, Librarian. Felician Sisters, C.S.S.F., State approved day high school. Sisters 2; Lay Teachers 28; Students 356; Total Staff 45.

[E] CONSOLIDATED SCHOOLS

PITTSBURGH. *Bishop Leonard-Saint Mary of the Mount Academy*, 115 Bigham St., 15211. Tel: 412-431-4645; Fax: 412-381-0770. Mr. Joe Garrity, Prin.; Sr. Janet Milan, Librarian. (Elementary)

Brookline Regional Catholic School, (Grades PreK-8), (Brookline), 2690 Waddington Ave., 15226. Tel: 412-563-0858; Fax: 412-341-5610. Email: brookregcath@yahoo.com. Web: www.brcschool.com. Janet Salley Rakoczy, Prin. Serving the parishes of Our Lady of Loreto, St. Pius X and Resurrection. Lay Teachers 12; Students 148; Total Staff 12.

Christ the Divine Teacher Catholic Academy, (Grades PreK-8), (Aspinwall), 205 Brilliant Ave., 15215. Tel: 412-781-7927; Fax: 412-781-0891. Email: cdtca@consolidated.net. Sr. Dorothy Dolak, S.C.N., Prin. Serving 24 parishes (Regional). Lay Teachers 13; Students 152; Total Staff 13.

Northside Catholic, 3854 Brighton Rd., 15212.

Sister Thea Bowman Catholic Academy, (Grades PreK-8), Elementary, 721 Rebecca Ave., 15221. Tel: 412-242-3515; Fax: 412-241-3199. Sr. Marie Margaret Wolf, Prin. (Elmentary); Mrs. Rita Canton, Prin. (Middle School); Sr. Mary Helen O'Donnell, Librarian.

BETHEL PARK. *Saint Katharine Drexel School*, 7001 Baptist Rd., 15102. Tel: 412-833-0223; Fax: 412-347-0361. Linda M. Bechtol, Prin. (Elementary-Merger)

BUTLER. *Butler Catholic School* (1969) 515 E. Locust St., 16001. Tel: 724-285-4276; Fax: 724-285-4896. Email: bcsoffice@butlercatholic.org. Web: www.butlercatholic.org. Sr. John Ann Mulhern, C.D.P., Prin. Serving the parishes of St. Paul, St. Michael, St. Fidelis, St. Andrew and St. Peter's, Butler. Lay Teachers 19; Students 235; Preschool 35.

MONONGAHELA. *Madonna Catholic Regional School* (1998) (Grades PreSchool-8), 731 Chess St., 15063. Tel: 724-258-3199; Fax: 724-258-6764. Email: madonnacatholicregional@earthlink.net. Web: www.madonnacatholic.org. Sharon Loughran Brown, Prin. Email: sharon@madonnacatholic.com. Serving the parishes of Mary, Mother of the Church, Our Lady of the Valley, and St. Damien of Molokai. Lay Teachers 10; Students 130; Total Staff 15.

PORT VUE. *St. Joseph Regional School*, (Grades PreK-8), 1125 Romine Ave., 15133. Tel: 412-678-0659; Fax: 412-678-1301. Email: dtima@stjoesregional.com. Web: www.stjoesregional.com. Mrs. Dianne Tima, Prin. Serving the parishes of Queen of Rosary, Corpus Christi, St. Mark, St. Patrick. Lay Teachers 12; Students 152; Total Staff 17.

[F] ELEMENTARY SCHOOLS, PRIVATE

PITTSBURGH. *The Campus School Of Carlow University* (1963) (Grades PreK-8), 3333 5th Ave., 15213. Tel: 412-578-6158; Fax: 412-578-6676. Email: mapeduto@carlow.edu. Web: www.campusschool.carlow.edu. Michelle Peduto, Prin.; Amy Collins, Librarian. Sisters of Mercy. Sisters 1; Lay Teachers 30; Students 250; Total Staff 33.

ALLISON PARK. *Providence Heights Alpha School*, 9000 Babcock Blvd., 15101. Tel: 412-366-4455; Fax: 412-635-6317. Web: www.alphaschool.org. Sr. Paulita Kuzy, C.D.P., Prin.; Courtney Dalessandro, Librarian. Sisters of Divine Providence. Sisters 6; Lay Teachers 26; Students 209.

[G] DEPARTMENT OF SPECIAL EDUCATION

PITTSBURGH. *DePaul School for Hearing and Speech* (1908) 6202 Alder St., 15206. Tel: 412-924-1012; Fax: 412-924-1036. Email: mjmac@depaulinst.com. Web: www.speakmiracles.org. Dr. Ruth Auld, Exec. Dir.; Mary Jo McAtee, Prin. Auditory-Oral day school for children with hearing, speech and language impairments. Sisters 1; Lay Teachers 16; Students 60.

NEW BRIGHTON. *McGuire Memorial* (1963) 2119 Mercer Rd., 15066-3437. Tel: 724-843-3400; Fax: 724-847-2004. Email: mcgm@mcguirememorial.org. Web: www.mcguirememorial.org. Residential Facility-Intermediate Care for Developmentally Challenged; Private School, Licensed Adult Training, Community Homes, Employment Option Center. Priests 1; Sisters 3; Lay Teachers 26; Lay Staff 500; ICP Residents 73; Additional Services: Adult Training 153; Community Living Residents 79; Private Academic School 88; Bed Capacity 143; Total Assisted Annually 350.

WEXFORD. **St. Anthony School Programs*, 2000 Corporate Dr., Ste. 580, 15090. Tel: 724-940-9020; Fax: 724-940-9064. Email: lgeorge@stanthonyschoolprograms.com. Lisa George, Program Dir. Resource rooms for students with special needs in 4 elementary schools, 2 high schools and 1 Post-Secondary Program. Lay Teachers 9; Students 106; Total Staff 42.

[H] CHILD CARE INSTITUTIONS

PITTSBURGH. *Franciscan Child Day Care Center*, 1401 Hamilton Rd., 15234-2399. Tel: 412-882-5085; Fax: 412-885-7210. Email: fcdcc@osfprov.org. Web: www.osfprov.org/fcdcc.htm. Mrs. Sandra Merlo, Dir.; Sr. Barbara Zilch, O.S.F., Pres. Total Assisted 99; Total Staff 28.

Holy Family Institute (1900) 8235 Ohio River Blvd., 15202. Tel: 412-766-4030; Fax: 412-766-5434. Email: schott.sandra@hfi-pgh.org. Web: www.hfi-pgh.org. Sr. Linda Yankoski, C.S.F.N., Ed.D., Pres. & CEO. Sisters of the Holy Family of Nazareth., Holy Family Institute is committed to helping children, preserving families and strengthening communities by providing an integrated network of social services and programs. These programs and services include in-home family counseling services, traditional and community-based residential services, a youth workforce development program, the SNAP (Stop Now and Plan) program, Parent-Child Home Program (early learning and literacy), Strong Families Collaborative (financial stabilization), substance abuse and addiction counseling, foster care program, energy assistance programs and specialized schools for grades K through 12. C.S.F.N. 2; St. Joseph Sisters 2; Total Staff 272.

Mt. Alvernia Day Care & Learning Center, 146 Hawthorne Rd., 15209. Tel: 412-821-4302; Fax: 412-821-3318. Web: www.sosf.org. Sisters of St. Francis of the Neumann Communities., Provides infant, toddler, and preschool care as well as before- and after-school care for school age children, school age care on non-school days and summer. Total Assisted 275; Total Staff 45.

Providence Connections, Inc. (1994) Corporate Office, 3113 Brighton Rd., 15212-2456. Tel: 412-766-3860; Fax: 412-766-6775. Email: cwinschel@providenceconnections.org. Web: www.providenceconnections.org. Sr. Carolyn Winschel, C.D.P., Ph.D., Exec. Dir. Staff 7.

Providence Family Support Center (1994) 3113 Brighton Rd., 15212-2456. Tel: 412-766-6730; Fax: 412-766-6775. Web: www.providenceconnections.org. Total Assisted 670; Total Staff 30.

Vincentian Child Development Center, 8150 McKnight Rd., 15237. Tel: 412-366-8588; Fax: 412-366-7315. Email: jparagi@vcs.org. Jill Paragi, Dir.

[I] GENERAL HOSPITALS

PITTSBURGH. *UPMC Mercy* (An affiliate of the University of Pittsburgh Medical Center), 1400 Locust St., 15219. Tel: 412-232-8111; Fax: 412-232-7380. Web: www.upmcmercy.com. Will Cook, M.H.A., Pres. Bed Capacity 487; Patients Assisted Annually 221,990; Total Staff 2,604.

[J] HOMES FOR THE AGED

PITTSBURGH. *Little Sisters of the Poor Home for the Aged* (1839) 1028 Benton Ave., 15212. Tel: 412-307-1100; Fax: 412-307-1104. Email: mspittsburgh@littlesistersofthepoor.org. Web: www.littlesistersofthepoor-pittsburgh.org. Sr. Judith Meredith, Supr. & Admin.; Rev. John A. Geinzer, S.T.L. , M.Ed. Sisters 9; Total Staff 100; Bed Capacity 88; Total Assisted Annually 100.

Marian Manor Corp. (1956) 2695 Winchester Dr., 15220-4099. Tel: 412-440-4424 (Admin.); 412-440-4343 (Nursing); Fax: 412-440-4426. Web: www.vcs.org. Rev. John F. Walsh. Sisters of the Holy Spirit 7; Total Staff 284; Total Assisted Annually 541; Residents 184; Child Day Care 72.

[K] REHABILITATION, NURSING AND GERIATRIC CARE FACILITIES

PITTSBURGH. *Marian Hall Home, Inc.* (1970) 934 Forest Ave., 15202-1118. Tel: 412-761-1999; Fax: 412-761-2556. Email: marian27@verizon.net. Sr. Marian Sgriccia, O.S.F., Admin. Purpose: to provide programs, facilities, and services, including, but not limited to, residential personal care, and long-term care homes for the elderly, ill, or disabled, including supportive services. Total in Residence 60; Total Assisted Annually 100; Total Staff 45.

The Community at Holy Family Manor, Inc., 301 Bellevue Rd., 15229-2194. Tel: 412-931-6996; Fax: 412-931-7255. Web: chfmanor.org. Sr. Catherine Fedewa, C.S.F.N., Exec. Dir. Programs operating under The Community at Holy Family Manor: Mt. Nazareth Learning Center; Nazareth Housing Services; Holy Family Manor Personal Care Home. Bed Capacity 60; Total Assisted Annually 1,745; Total Staff 82.

Vincentian de Marillac (1943) 5300 Stanton Ave., 15206. Tel: 412-361-2833; Fax: 412-361-1237. Email: mcoyne@vcs.org. Linda Schoyer, Pastoral Care; Maureen M. Coyne, B.S., M.S.W., M.P.M., L.N.H.A., Admin. Catholic, skilled nursing home. Total Staff 79; Bed Capacity 50; Total Assisted Annually 108.

Vincentian Home (1924) 111 Perrymont Rd., 15237. Tel: 412-366-5600; Fax: 412-366-1408. Web: www.vcs.org. Sr. Anne Kull, S.C.N., Admin. Sisters of Charity of Nazareth. Sisters 7; Total Staff 275; Bed Capacity 164; Total Assisted Annually 400; Assisted Living: Total Assisted 70; Total Staff 35.

ALLISON PARK. *Vincentian Regency* (1966) 9399 Babcock Blvd., 15101. Tel: 412-366-8540; Fax: 412-369-9789. Email: magenovich@vcs.org. Web: www.vcs.org. Sr. Mary Ann Genovich, S.C.N., Admin. Sisters of Charity of Nazareth. Bed Capacity 143; Total Assisted Annually 400; Total Staff 220.

Providence Manor, 9000 Babcock Blvd., 15101.

BADEN. **Villa St. Joseph of Baden, Inc.*, 1030 State St., 15005. Tel: 724-869-6310; Fax: 724-869-6399. Email: mmurray@villastjoseph.org. Sr. Judith Maroni, C.S.J., Pres.; Ms. Mary M. Murray, N.H.A., M.P.H., Exec. Dir. Purpose: to provide a home-like environment for 120 nursing home residents in need of skilled nursing, rehabilitation and long term intermediate care. Our mission of "competent and compassionate care" is carried out daily by our staff who focus on building relationships, while providing therapy, clinical nursing, activities, spiritual and other support in a holistic manner. Specialty services include short term rehabilitation, dementia care and home-like long term living. Beds for Patients with Dementia or Alzheimer's 30; Total Assisted Annually 204; Total Staff 200; Bed Capacity 120.

[L] PERSONAL PRELATURES

PITTSBURGH. *Prelature of the Holy Cross and Opus Dei* (1928) Warwick House, 5090 Warwick Ter., 15213. Tel: 412-683-8448; Fax: 412-687-3806. Email: info@warwickhouse.org. Web: www.opusdei.org. Revs. Rene J. Schatteman; Martin J. Miller.

[M] MONASTERIES AND RESIDENCES OF PRIESTS AND BROTHERS

PITTSBURGH. *St. Augustine Friary*, 221 36th St., 15201. Tel: 412-682-6430; Fax: 412-682-6148. Web: www.capuchin.com. Revs. Robert Craig, O.F.M.Cap., Chap., VA PGH Health Care Systems; Gervase Degenhardt, O.F.M.Cap., Chap., Sisters of St. Francis, Millvale; Philip Fink, O.F.M.Cap., Guardian; Francis Fugini, O.F.M.Cap., Dir. for Missions; Vernon Busch, O.F.M.Cap., Pastoral Supply; Bertin Roll, O.F.M.Cap., Dir. Emeritus of Archconfraternity of Christian Mothers (Retired); DeSales Young, O.F.M.Cap.; William Henn, O.F.M.Cap., Prof. Pontifical Gregorian Univ.; Otmar Gallagher, O.F.M.Cap. (Retired); Edward Laurent, O.F.M.Cap., Pastoral Supply; Maurice Sheehan, O.F.M.Cap., Academic Dean, Holy Apostles Seminary; John Pfannenstiel, O.F.M.Cap., Dir. Seraphic Mass Assn.
In Res. Revs. Regis Schlick, O.F.M.Cap.; Victor Kriley, O.F.M.Cap., Pastoral Supply; Charles Knoll, O.F.M.Cap.; Bonaventure Stefun, O.F.M.Cap.; Jerome Dunn, O.F.M.Cap.; Bro. Robert Toomey, O.F.M.Cap., Exec. Sec.

Cardinal Dearden Center, 4721 5th Ave., 15213. Tel: 412-687-8022. Revs. Bernard B. Costello (Retired); John M. Jordan; Thomas F. Manion (Retired); Richard R. Ragni (Retired); Richard G. Terdine (Retired); Raymond M. Utz (Retired).

Congregation of the Oratory of St. Philip Neri, The Pittsburgh Oratory, 4450 Bayard St., 15213. Tel: 412-681-3181; Fax: 412-681-2922. Email: frdavid@pittsburghoratory.org. Web: www.pittsburghoratory.org. Very Rev. Drew P. Morgan, C.O., Dir. Newman Inst., Provost; Revs. David S. Abernethy, C.O., Novice Master & Formation Dir. & Vice Provost; Michael J. Darcy, C.O., Grad Student; Joshua Kibler, C.O., Campus Min. & Dir.; Stephen Lowery, C.O., Campus Min.; Bros. Paul Werley, C.O., Novice & Seminarian; Dennis Di Benedetto, C.O., Novice & Seminarian; Peter Gruber, C.O., Novice; Jonathan Crist, C.O., Novice. Total Staff 5.

St. Conrad Friary (1983) 9448 Babcock Blvd., Allison Park, 15101. Tel: 412-364-8240; Fax: 412-366-8331. Web: www.capuchin.com. Rev. John Gesty, O.F.M.Cap.; Very Rev. W. David Nestler, O.F.M.Cap., Prov. Min.; Rev. Angelus Shaughnessy, O.F.M.Cap., Dir. Archonfraternity of Christian Mothers; Bro. Richard Lubomski, O.F.M.Cap., Guardian. Total in Residence 4.

Franciscan Friars, T.O.R., Queen of Peace Friary, 5324 Carnegie St., 15201. Tel: 412-449-1020; Fax: 412-449-1035. In Res. Bro. Michael Tripka, T.O.R., Librarian; Revs. Carol Napoli, T.O.R., (Retired); Joseph Markalonis, T.O.R., Hospital Chap.; Thomas Bourque, T.O.R., Local Min. & Dir. Planning & Mission Effectiveness.

St. John Vianney Manor, 2600 Morange Rd., 15205. Tel: 412-928-0825; 412-928-0908; Fax: 412-928-1947. Retired priests' residence. Total in Residence 22; Total Staff 8. In Res. Most Rev. William J. Winter, V.G., S.T.D. (Retired); Rev. Msgr. Joseph G. Findlan (Retired); Revs. Charles B. Bergman (Retired); William R. Bovard (Retired); Roy H. Conley (Retired); Edward M. Czemerda; David C. Dixon (Retired), St. John Vianney Manor, 2600 Morange Rd., 15205; Eugene J. Dougherty (Retired); Michael C. MacVeigh (Retired); Malcolm McDonald; Kevin F. McKnight; Robert J. Meyer; John D. Petrarulo (Retired); Michael J. Polak (Retired); Robert J. Reardon (Retired); David E. Scharf; Edward R. Schleicher (Retired); Bernard P. Shulik; Rudolph F. Smoley; Henry A. Szarnicki (Retired); Edward J. Trzeciakowski (Retired); George A. Wilt (Retired); Albert C. Koser (Retired).

St. Paul of the Cross Monastery Monastery & Retreat Center., 148 Monastery Ave., S.S., 15203. Tel: 412-381-1188 (Monastery); 412-381-7676 (Retreat Center); Fax: 412-481-5049 (Monastery); 412-431-3044 (Retreat Center). Web: www.catholic-church.org/stpaulsmonastery/. Very Rev. Gerald Laba, C.P., Rector & Retreat Dir.; Revs. Donald Ware, C.P., Asst. Local Supr.; William Davin, C.P.; Timothy Fitzgerald, C.P., Auxiliary Retreat Staff; John F. McMillan, C.P.; Edwin Moran, C.P.; Bro. Matthew Krawchyk, C.P.; Revs. Joseph Sedley, C.P.; Vincent Segotta, C.P.; Patrick Geinzer, C.P.; Paul Vaeth, C.P., Aux. Retreat Staff; Jerome Vereb, C.P.; Bro. Paul Morgan, C.P.

Society of The Divine Word, 207 Lytton, 15213. Tel: 412-683-4030; Fax: 412-683-5033. Revs. Walter Ostrowski, S.V.D., Mission Dir. Tel: 412-683-0640; Raymond Hober, S.V.D.; Bros. John DeBold, S.V.D.; Gerard Raker, S.V.D., Supr. Total in Residence 4.

AVALON. *Holy Family Friary* (Friars Minor), The Franciscans., 232 S. Home Ave., 15202-2899. Tel: 412-761-2550; Fax: 412-202-2559. Revs. David Moczulski, O.F.M., Guardian Chaplain: Allegheny General Hsp. Sisters of the Holy Family of Nazareth; Richard Portasik, O.F.M. (Retired); Leonard Cornelius, O.F.M., Vicar; Bros. Paschal Dierks, O.F.M., (Retired); Felix Nowakowski, O.F.M. Friars 5.

BEAVER. *St. Fidelis Friary*, 372 East End Ave., 15009. Tel: 724-774-1242 (main). Email: stcecilia@verizon.net. Web: www.stceciliaroch.org. Church: *St. Cecilia*, 632 Virginia Ave., Rochester, 15074. Tel: 725-775-0801; Fax: 724-774-3056. Revs. James Menkhus, O.F.M.Cap.; William Talentino, O.F.M. Cap. Capuchin Friars. In Res. Revs. Robert E. McCreary, O.F.M.Cap.; William Gillum, O.F.M.Cap.

BETHEL PARK. *Congregation of the Holy Spirit Province of the United States*, 6230 Brush Run Rd., 15102. Tel: 412-831-0302. Very Rev. John Fogarty, C.S.Sp., Prov. Supr.

Holy Spirit Fathers and Brothers Provincialate, 6230 Brush Run Rd., 15102. Tel: 412-831-0302; Fax: 412-831-0970. Email: usprovince@spiritans.org. Web: www.spiritans.org. Very Rev. John Fogarty, C.S.Sp., Prov. Supr.; Rev. Girard J. Kohler, C.S.Sp., Mission Procurator; Bro. Michael Suazo, C.S.Sp., Province Sec. Residents 2; Total Staff 5.

BUTLER. *St. Mary's Friary*, 821 Herman Rd., 16002. Tel: 724-282-1485; Fax: 724-285-4715. Revs. Mark Carter, O.F.M. Cap., Parochial Vicar; John Carey, O.F.M.Cap., Replacement Ministry; DePaul Ripko, O.F.M.Cap., Replacement Ministry; Gary Stakem, O.F.M.Cap., Replacement Ministry; Ward Stakem, O.F.M.Cap., Pastor & Guardian; Bro. Joseph Day, O.F.M.Cap. Capuchin Franciscan Friars, Province of St. Augustine Priests 5; Brothers 1.

[N] CONVENTS AND RESIDENCES FOR SISTERS

PITTSBURGH. *St. Benedict Monastery* (1870) Benedictine Sisters of Pontifical Jurisdiction, 4530 Perrysville Ave., 15229-2296. Tel: 412-931-2844; Fax: 412-931-8970. Email: osbpgh@osbpgh.org. Web: www.osbpgh.org. Sr. Benita DeMatters, O.S.B., Prioress. Motherhouse and Novitiate of the Benedictine Sisters in the Diocese. Sisters 52.

Ladies of Bethany (1919) 1004 Oglethorpe Ave., 15201-2151. Tel: 412-781-4022.

Motherhouse, Sisters of the Holy Spirit (S.H.S.) (Ross Township), 5246 Clarwin Ave., 15229-2208. Tel: 412-931-1917; Fax: 412-931-4324. Email: SRSHS@verizon.net. Web: www.sistersoftheholyspirit.com. Sr. Grace Fabich, S.H.S., Gen. Supr.; Very Rev. Robert F. Guay, V.E., M.Div., V.G., Chap. Professed Sisters 39; Total in Community 39.

Mount Assisi Convent, Motherhouse of the School Sisters of the Third Order Regular of St. Francis United States Province, 934 Forest Ave., 15202. Tel: 412-761-6004; Fax: 412-761-0290. Email:

administrationusa@verizon.net. Web: schoolsistersosf.org.
Civil Law Entity: The School Sisters of the Third Order Regular of St. Francis, a Pennsylvania corporation. Sisters 91; Residents 34; Total Staff 6. In Res. Rev. Richard M. Lelonis, J.C.L., Chap.

Our Lady of Sorrows Convent of the Passionist Nuns (1910) 2715 Churchview Ave., 15227. Tel: 412-881-1155; Fax: 412-881-1091. Sr. Joyce Foga, C.P., Supr. Motherhouse and Novitiate of the Religious of the Passion. (Passionist Nuns). Professed Sisters 10.

Sisters of Charity of Nazareth, Sisters of Charity of Nazareth Pittsburgh Campus, 8200 McKnight Rd., 15237. Tel: 412-364-3000; Fax: 412-364-9055. Rev. Reginald Russo, O.F.M.Cap., Chap. (formerly VSCs)

Sisters of Mercy of the Americas - New York, Pennsylvania, Pacific West Community, Convent of Mercy, 3333 Fifth Ave., 15213. Tel: 412-578-6225; Fax: 412-578-6180. Rev. Robert J. George, Chap. Convent of Mercy Total Professed Sisters 476; Associates 394.

Sisters of St. Francis of the Providence of God, St. Francis Convent Motherhouse, 3603 McRoberts Rd., 15234-2314. Tel: 412-882-9911; Fax: 412-885-7210. Email: usa@osfprov.org. Web: www.osfprov.org. Sr. Joanne Brazinski, O.S.F., USA Prov. Min.; Very Rev. Frederick L. Cain, V.E., M.Div., Chap. Sisters 51.

Sisters of St. Francis of the Providence of God-Generalate (1922) 1401 Hamilton Rd., 15234-2364. Tel: 412-885-7211; Fax: 412-885-7215. Email: sjgardner@osfprov.org. Web: www.osfprov.org. Sr. Janet Gardner, O.S.F., General Min. Professed 95; Novices 1; Total in Community 96.

Sisters of the Holy Family of Nazareth, 285 Bellevue Rd., 15229-2195. Tel: 412-931-4778; Fax: 412-931-9746. Web: www.csfn.org.
Sisters of the Holy Family of Nazareth, Holy Family Province USA Inc.

Union of Our Lady of Charity Sisters of Our Lady of Charity (1872) 4100 Vinceton St., 15214. Tel: 412-931-2299; Fax: 412-931-6044. Sr. Sheila Rooney, Local Supr. North American Union of the Sisters of Our Lady of Charity, Inc. Sisters 3.

ALLISON PARK. *Congregation of The Sisters of Divine Providence of Allegheny County* (1881) *Providence Heights Motherhouse*, 9000 Babcock Blvd., 15101-2793. Tel: 412-635-5402; Fax: 412-635-5416. Email: srmfranciscdp@hotmail.com. Web: www.divineprovidenceweb.org. Sr. Mary Francis Fletcher, C.D.P., Prov. Dir. & Pres. Motherhouse of the Sisters of Divine Providence in the Diocese (Pittsburgh); Novitiate of the Sisters of Divine Providence (Granite City, IL). In Motherhouse 75; In Province (including Puerto Rico) 241.

BADEN. *Sisters of St. Joseph* (1869) St. Joseph Convent Motherhouse, 1020 State St., 15005. Tel: 724-869-2151; 412-761-3700; Fax: 724-869-3336. Email: msconnell@stjoseph-baden.org. Web: www.stjoseph-baden.org. Sr. Mary Pellegrino, C.S.J., Congregational Moderator; Rev. David E. Scharf, Chap. Total in Community 204; Residents 30.

BEAVER FALLS. *Felician Sisters of North America, Inc. Congregation of the Sisters of St. Felix of Cantalice, Our Lady of Hope Province*, 871 Mercer Rd., 15010. Tel: 724-384-5300; Fax: 724-384-5301. Sr. Mary Christopher Moore, C.S.S.F., Pres.

CORAOPOLIS. *Our Lady of the Sacred Heart Convent* (1932) 1500 Woodcrest Ave., 15108. Tel: 412-264-2890; Fax: 412-264-7047. Email: sconniet@feliciansisters.org. Web: www.feliciansna.org. Sr. Mary Christopher Moore, C.S.S.F., Prov. Min. Home of the Felician Sisters of Pennsylvania C.S.S.F. Professed 74.

ELIZABETH. *Divine Redeemer Motherhouse* (1912) 999 Rock Run Rd., 15037-2613. Tel: 412-751-8600; Fax: 412-751-0355. Email: sisrosemarysdr@aol.com. Web: www.sistersofthedivineredeemer.org. Sr. Rosemary Horvath, S.D.R., Prov.; Rev. Thomas M. Kirby, Chap. (Retired). Motherhouse and Novitiate of the Sisters of the Divine Redeemer. Total in Community 19.

MILLVALE. *Sisters of St. Francis of the Neumann Communities, Western Pennsylvania Region, St. Francis Convent*, 146 Hawthorne Rd., 15209. Tel: 412-821-2200; Fax: 412-821-3318. Email: jbich@sosf.org. Rev. Gervase Degenhardt, O.F.M.Cap., Chap. Attended by Capuchin Fathers from St. Augustine, Pittsburgh. In the Region 107; In the Regional House 80; Associates 39.

VILLA MARIA. *Sisters of the Humility of Mary, Inc.* (1854) *Villa Maria Community Center*, 288 Villa Dr., P.O. Box 914, 16155. Tel: 724-964-8861; Fax: 724-964-8082. Email: info@humilityofmary.org. Web: www.humilityofmary.org. Sr. Susan Schorsten, H.M., Major Supr. Professed Sisters in Congregation 165; Sisters in Residence 45; Residents 43.

[O] RETREAT HOUSES

PITTSBURGH. *Franciscan Spirit and Life Center*, 3605 McRoberts Rd., 15234-2340. Tel: 412-881-9207; Fax: 412-885-7247. Email: fslc@osfprov.org. Sisters of St. Francis of the Providence of God., Purpose: To provide a facility to individuals for retreats and spiritual programs.; Overnight accommodations for 25. Conference room and dining facility. Three hermitages available on daily, overnight or weekly basis. Total Staff 2.

Martina Spiritual Renewal Center, Inc. (1986) 5244 Clarwin Ave., 15229-2208. Tel: 412-931-9766; Fax: 412-931-1823. Email: martinaspiritual@verizon.net. Web: sistersoftheholyspirit.com. Sisters Grace Fabich, S.H.S., Pres.; Donna Smith, S.H.S., Co- Dir.; Mary Lou Witkowski, S.H.S. To provide a facility to individuals and groups for retreats and spiritual programs. Ministry of the Sisters of the Holy Spirit.

St. Paul of the Cross Retreat Center, 148 Monastery Ave., 15203. Tel: 412-381-7676; 412-381-7677; Fax: 412-431-3044. Email: stpaulrcpa@cpprov.org. Web: catholic-church.org/stpaulsretreatcenter. Rev. Patrick Geinzer, C.P., Aux. Retreat Team; Very Rev. Gerald Laba, C.P., Rector & Retreat Dir.; John Colaizzi, Bus. Admin.; Revs. Michael Salvagna, C.P., Aux. Retreat Team; Paul Vaeth, C.P., Aux. Retreat Team; Timothy Fitzgerald, C.P., Aux. Retreat Team; Donald Ware, C.P., Aux Retreat Team. Total in Residence 3; Total Staff 25.

ALLISON PARK. *Kearns Spirituality Center* (1983) 9000 Babcock Blvd., 15101-2713. Tel: 412-366-1124; Fax: 412-635-6318. Email: kearnsscl@pghcdp.org. Web: www.divineprovidenceweb.org. Sisters Agnes Raible, C.D.P., Dir.; Mary Joan Coultas, C.D.P., Prog. Coord. Sisters of Divine Providence., Conference room for 250; overnight accommodations for 60; dining facilities for 70. Call for more information on programs offered. Total Staff 6.

BETHEL PARK. *The Spiritan Center*, 6230 Bush Run Rd., 15102. Tel: 412-835-3510; Fax: 412-835-3541. Email: spiritancenter@juno.com. Revs. John J. Costello, C.S.Sp.; William F. Crowley, C.S.Sp. (Retired); Joseph L. Kelly, C.S.Sp.; Francis J. Kichak, C.S.Sp.; Girard J. Kohler, C.S.Sp.; Raymond J. Kulwicki, C.S.Sp.; Richard J. LeClair, C.S.Sp.; Ralph J. Poirier, C.S.Sp.; Norbert T. Rosso, C.S.Sp.; Joseph A. Seiter, C.S.Sp.; Thomas P. Sharkey, C.S.Sp.; John P. Skaj, C.S.Sp.; Leonard J. Tuozzolo, C.S.Sp.; John R. Weber, C.S.Sp.; John L. Yates, C.S.Sp.; Bro. Michael Suazo, C.S.Sp. Total in Residence 16; Total Staff 19.

GIBSONIA. *Providence Villa*, 10745 Babcock Blvd., 15044-6094. Tel: 724-444-8055; Fax: 724-444-8058. Email: providencevilla@yahoo.com. Web: www.divineprovidenceweb.org. Sisters Marilyn Seidel, C.D.P., Dir.; Leona Ulewicz, C.D.P., Asst. Dir.

[P] OFFICES FOR CAMPUS MINISTRY

PITTSBURGH. *Office for Campus Ministry La Roche College*, 9000 Babcock Blvd., 15237. Tel: 412-536-1050, Ext. 141; Fax: 412-536-1048. Email: hortonp1@laroche.edu. Rev. W. Peter Horton, M.A., M.Div., Dir.

Art Institute of Pittsburgh St. Mary of Mercy, Stanwix St., 15212-5296. Tel: 412-321-0711. Rev. Nicholas Vaskov.

La Roche College (1963) 9000 Babcock Blvd., 15237. Tel: 412-536-1050; Fax: 412-536-1048. Rev. W. Peter Horton, M.A., M.Div.

Carlow University 3333 5th Ave., 15213. Tel: 412-578-6069. Mrs. Siobhan DeWitt.

Carnegie-Mellon University Ryan Catholic Newman Center, 4450 Bayard St., 15213. Tel: 412-681-3181; Fax: 412-681-2922. Revs. Joshua Kibler, C.O., Dir., Campus Ministry; Stephen Lowery, C.O.

Chatham College Ryan Catholic Newman Center, 4450 Bayard St., 15213. Tel: 412-681-3181; Fax: 412-681-2922. Revs. Joshua Kibler, C.O., Dir Campus Ministry; Stephen Lowery, C.O.

Community College of Allegheny County - Boyce Campus St. Bernadette Church, 5245 Azalea Dr., Monroeville, 15146. Tel: 412-373-0050; Fax: 412-374-8113. Rev. Anthony Gargotta.

Community College of Allegheny County - Northside Campus St. Peter Church, 720 Arch St., 15212-5296. Tel: 412-321-0711; Fax: 412-321-7807. Rev. Vincent Zidek, O.S.B.

Community College of Allegheny County - South Campus Holy Spirit Church, 2603 Old Elizabeth Rd., West Mifflin, 15122. Tel: 412-466-5048; Fax: 412-466-4983. Rev. John B. Lendvai.

Community College of Allegheny County - North Hills Campus St. Teresa of Avila, 1000 Avila Ct., 15237-2176. Tel: 412-367-9001; Fax: 412-366-8415. Rev. Robert J. Vular.

Duquesne University Campus Ministry, 15282. Tel: 412-396-6020. Rev. Raymond D. French, C.S.Sp.; Mr. Matt Walsh, Dir.; Stephen Steinbeiser, Dir. Music & Liturgy; Luci-Jo DiMaggio, Campus Min.; Linda Donovan, Campus Min.; Katherine Lecci, Campus Min.; Debbie Kostosky, Campus Min.

Geneva College Campus Ministry, 289 Ridge Rd., New Brighton, 15066. Tel: 724-846-5978. Rev. James B. Farnan, Dir.

Pennsylvania State University, Beaver Campus 824 Ohio River Bend, Apt. #3, Sewickley, 15143. Tel: 724-773-3839. Mr. Gary M. Slifkey, M.A., M.S., Dir.

Point Park College St. Mary of Mercy Church, 202 Stanwix St., 15222. Tel: 412-261-0110; Fax: 412-261-0113. Rev. Nicholas Vaskov.

Robert Morris College, Moon Township Campus Mr. Gary M. Slifkey, M.A., M.S.

University of Pittsburgh Ryan Catholic Newman Center, 4450 Bayard St., 15213. Tel: 412-681-3181; Fax: 412-681-2922. Revs. Joshua Kibler, C.O., Dir., Campus Ministry; Stephen Lowery, C.O.

California University (California) St. Thomas Aquinas Church, 4th & Union Streets, California, 15419. Tel: 724-938-3204; Fax: 724-938-0434. Rev. George J. Moneck, Dir.

Westminster College St. Camillus Church, 313 W. Englewood Ave., New Castle, 16105. Tel: 724-652-9471; Fax: 724-654-1430. Rev. Thomas J. Lewandowski.

Slippery Rock University, Newman Center (Slippery Rock) 342 Normal Ave., Slippery Rock, 16057. Tel: 724-794-8459; Fax: 724-794-1150. Rev. Kevin G. Poecking, Dir.; Ms. Diane Magliocca, Campus Min.

Washington and Jefferson College (Washington) Immaculate Conception, 119 W. Chestnut St., Washington, 15301. Tel: 724-225-1425. Rev. Michael R. Ruffalo.

Waynesburg College (Waynesburg) St. Ann Church, 232 E. High St., Waynesburg, 15370. Tel: 724-627-7568. Rev. Richard J. Thompson.

Office for Institutional Ministries 111 Blvd. of the Allies, 15222. Tel: 412-456-3057; Fax: 412-456-3188. Email: jlamonde@diopitt.org.

[Q] MISCELLANEOUS LISTINGS

PITTSBURGH. *The Capuchin Franciscan Volunteer Corps, Inc.*, 220 37th St., 15201. Tel: 412-682-6011; Fax: 412-682-0506. Email: capcorpseast@gmail.com. Web: www.capuchin.com. Rev. John Pfannenstiel, O.F.M.Cap., Dir. Province of St. Augustine of the Capuchin Order., Purpose: To promote, train, supervise and support Catholic lay missions and missionaries throughout the world, especially in conjunction with the ministries and fraternities of the Capuchin Order.

Catholic Diocese of Pittsburgh Foundation dba Sharing In Faith Our Catholic Legacy 111 Blvd. of the Allies, 15222. Tel: 412-456-3085; Fax: 412-456-3169. Email: stewardship@diopitt.org. Web: www.diopitt.org.

Catholic Employers Benefits Plan Delaware Trust, 111 Blvd. of the Allies, 15222. Tel: 412-456-3137; Fax: 412-456-3139. Email: benefits@diopitt.org. Mr. Frederick P. O'Brien, Dir.

The Catholic Historical Society of Western Pennsylvania, Mailing Address: P.O. Box 194, 15230. 108 N. Dithridge St., 15213. Tel: 412-343-0860. Email: joycecho@aol.com. Web: www.catholichistorywpa.org. Blanche McGuire, Pres. Purpose: To promote the teaching of the Catholic Church in the United States, especially the Church in Western Pennsylvania; to recognize the growth, development and contribution of the Catholic Church by the preservation of artifacts, records and documents related to that history; to make available the results of research and study.

The Catholic Institute of Pittsburgh, PA, 111 Blvd. of the Allies, 15222. Tel: 412-456-3137; Fax: 412-456-3139. Email: fobrien@diopitt.org. Mr. Frederick P. O'Brien, CFO.

Catholic Long Term Care Network of Western Pennsylvania, Inc., 111 Blvd of the Allies, 15222. Tel: 412-630-9980. Web: www.cltcn.org. A collaborative effort of six religious communities and the Diocese of Pittsburgh. The sponsors operate four skilled nursing facilities and three assisted living-personal care homes. Sponsors: Little Sisters of the Poor, School Sisters of St. Francis, Sisters of St. Joseph, Sisters of the Holy Spirit, Sisters of St. Basil the Great, Vincentian Sisters of Charity.

Chimbote Foundation, 111 Blvd. of the Allies, 15222-1618. Tel: 412-456-3085; Fax: 412-456-3169. Email: rlengwin@diopitt.org. Web: www.diopitt.org.

Christ Child Society of Pittsburgh (1992) P.O. Box 11324, 15238-1324. Tel: 412-682-4102. Joyce Orr, Pres.; Laura A. Merzlak, Vice Pres.; Rev. Kevin G. Poecking, Spiritual Advisor. Purpose: To foster a personal love of Christ expressed in service for needy children and youths. Total Assisted 900;

Volunteers 59.

Cursillo Movement-Diocese of Pittsburgh, 1138 Windmill Ln., 15237. Tel: 412-221-1560. Email: pghcursillo@gmail.com. Web: www.cursillo.org/ pittsburgh. Rev. Stan M. Gregorek, Spiritual Advisor; Gary Smith, Ph.D., Lay Dir.

Elizabeth Seton Center Inc. (1985) 1900 Pioneer Ave., 15226. Tel: 412-561-8400; Fax: 412-561-8488. Email: srbarb@setoncenter.com. Web: www.setoncenter.com. Sr. Barbara Ann Boss, S.C., CEO. Care Programs for Children and Adults; Senior Citizens Center; School of Art. Sisters of Charity 8; Total Assisted 2,500; Total Staff 80.

Epiphany Association, 820 Crane Ave., 15216-3050. Tel: 412-341-7494; Fax: 412-341-7495. Email: samuto@epiphanyassociation.org. Web: www.epiphanyassociation.org. Purpose: Under the auspices of its Epiphany Academy of Formative Spirituality, the Association strives with God's help to meet the needs of parents, pastors, teachers, counselors, chaplains, and directors in pursuit of a deeper understanding of the spiritual life in accordance with the wisdom of their faith and formation traditions. Total Staff 7.

St. Francis Academy Corporation, 1401 Hamilton Rd., 15234. Tel: 412-882-9911; Fax: 412-885-7210. Email: usa@osfprov.org. Sr. Joanne Brazinski, O.S.F., Pres.

Holy Family Community Services (1900) 8235 Ohio River Blvd., 15202. Tel: 412-766-4030; Fax: 412-766-5434. Email: yankoski.linda@hfi-pgh.org. Web: www.hfi-pgh.org. Sr. Linda Yankoski, C.S.F.N., Ed.D., Pres. & CEO. Holy Family Community Services is committed to empowering children and families to lead responsible lives and develop healthy and meaningful relationships built on faith, hope and love through a network of integrated programs and services. These programs and services include in-home family counseling services, traditional and community-based residential services, a youth workforce development program, The SNAP (Stop Now and Plan) program, Parent-Child Home Program (early learning and literacy), Strong Families Collaborative (financial stabilization), substance abuse and addiction counseling, foster care program, energy assistance programs and specialized schools for grades K through 12. Children 2,174; Families 8,100.

Holy Family Foundation (1992) 8235 Ohio River Blvd., Ste. 200, 15202. Tel: 412-766-4030; Fax: 412-766-5434. Web: www.hfi-pgh.org. Sr. Linda Yankoski, C.S.F.N., Ed.D., Pres. & CEO. The Holy Family Foundation was incorporated in 1992 to promote & support the public charitable works & educational purposes of Holy Family Institute and any other exempt activities affiliated with Holy Family Institute.

**Holy Family Learning, Inc. aka d/b/a Holy Family International College Preparatory Program* 8235 Ohio River Blvd., 15202. Tel: 412-766-4030; Fax: 412-766-5434. Web: www.hfi-cpp.org. Sr. Linda Yankoski, C.S.F.N., Ed.D., Pres. & CEO. Family International-College Preparatory Program (HFI-CPP), in collaboration with independent private schools, is committed to providing international students with a comprehensive education and residential program. The focus of the program is to help the students develop proficiency in reading, speaking and writing English; obtain excellent academic credentials and strong moral values, who will be condsidered viable candidates to the top colleges and universities in the United States. HFI-CPP values include the development of discipline, concern for others, patience, grace, dignity and the ability to respond positively to adversity. Children Served 25.

Institutional Common Fund Trust, 111 Blvd. of the Allies, 15222. Tel: 412-456-3137.

Institutional Deposit and Loan Fund Trust, 111 Blvd. of the Allies, 15222. Tel: 412-456-3137.

Knights of Columbus Bishop of Pittsburgh Diocese Project, P.O. Box 9691, 15226-0691. Tel: 724-422-7136 (Treas.). Project for benefit of St. Anthony School Programs and McGuire Memorial.

Mercy Outreach Ministries, Inc., 3333 Fifth Ave., 15213. Tel: 412-578-6202; Fax: 412-578-6180. Email: fmcdonough@carlow.edu. Sr. Fidelis McDonough, R.S.M., Contact Person.

Millvale Franciscans, Inc., 146 Hawthorne Rd., 15209. Tel: 412-821-2200; Fax: 412-821-3318. Email: jbich@sosf.org. Betsy Miksic, Contact Person. Sisters of St. Francis of the Neumann Communities.

Mount Assisi Academy Preschool (1980) 934 Forest Ave., 15202. Tel: 412-761-0381; Fax: 412-761-0290. Sr. Bernadine Marie Stemnock, O.S.F., Prov. Min. Sisters 2; Lay Teachers 4; Students 90.

Mount Nazareth Center, Inc. (1986) 285 Bellevue Rd., 15229-2195. Tel: 412-931-4778, Ext. 2180; Fax: 412-931-9746. Sisters of the Holy Family of Nazareth, Holy Family Province.

National Institute for Newman Studies, 211 N. Dithridge St., 15213. Tel: 412-681-4375; Fax: 412-681-4376. Email: admin@ninsdu.org. Web: www.newmanstudiesinstitute.org. Kevin Mongrain, Ph.D., Exec. Dir.; Catharine Ryan, M.A., Asst. Dir.; Jude Rutkowski, B.A., Exec. Asst.; Damon McGraw, M.A.R., Exec. Research Fellow.

Nazareth Family Foundation (1996) 285 Bellevue Rd., 15229. Tel: 412-931-4778, Ext. 2180; Fax: 412-931-9746. Email: srcindy@juno.com. Sr. Cynthia Meyer, C.S.F.N., Pres. Purpose: To promote family life through financial support of facilities, programs, and services which enhance individual and family well-being. Total Assisted 3,200.

Nazareth Global Missions, Inc., 285 Bellevue Rd., 15229. Tel: 412-931-4778, Ext. 2180; Fax: 412-931-9746. Email: srmichelec@juno.com.

North Catholic Endowment Fund, 111 Blvd. of the Allies, 15222. Tel: 412-456-3100; Fax: 412-456-3101. Email: education@diopitt.org. Web: www.diopitt.org.

Parish Common Fund Trust, 111 Blvd. of the Allies, 15222.

Parish Deposit and Loan Fund Trust, 111 Blvd. of the Allies, 15222.

Pension Plan for the Diocese of Pittsburgh (Lay Pension Plan), 111 Blvd. of the Allies, 15222. Tel: 412-456-3137; Fax: 412-456-3139. Email: benefits@diopitt.org. Mr. Frederick P. O'Brien, Dir.

Pittsburgh Catholic Publishing Associates (1954) Purpose: To promote for Catholics and other readers an understanding of the mission and teachings of the Church and its role in the community., 135 First Ave., Ste. 200, 15222-1513. Tel: 412-471-1252; Fax: 412-471-4228. Email: info@pittsburghcatholic.org. Web: www.pittsburghcatholic.org. Mr. Robert P. Lockwood, Gen. Mgr.; Ms. Carmella A. Weismantle, Opers. Mgr.; Mr. William Cone, Editor. Total Staff 15.

Pittsburgh Mercy Health System, Inc., 3333 Fifth Ave., McAuley Hall, 15213. Tel: 412-578-6675; Fax: 412-697-0266. Web: www.pmhs.org. Sr. Susan Welsh, R.S.M., Pres. & CEO.

Parent company of the following subsidiaries:

Mercy Life Center Corporation dba Mercy Behavioral Health Tel: 412-323-4556; Fax: 412-323-4507.

McAuley Ministries, 3333 Fifth Ave., McAuley Hall, 15213. Tel: 412-578-6223; Fax: 412-697-0266. Michele Rone Cooper, Exec. Dir.

Portiuncula Foundation of the Sisters of St. Francis of the Neumann Communities, 146 Hawthorne Rd., 15209. Tel: 412-821-2200; Fax: 412-821-3318. Sr. Marlene Kline, O.S.F., Exec. Dir. Sisters of St. Francis of the Neumann Communities.

Priests' Benefit Plan of the Diocese of Pittsburgh (1955) 111 Blvd. of the Allies, 15222. Tel: 412-456-3060; Fax: 412-456-3139. Email: centralaccounting@diopitt.org. Rev. Charles S. Bober, S.T.D., Chm. Purpose: To provide certain retirement and health-related benefits to eligible priests.

Procurator Assurance, Inc., c/o 111 Boulevard of the Allies, 15222. Tel: 412-456-3137; Fax: 412-456-3139. Email: insurance@diopitt.org. Mr. Frederick P. O'Brien, Dir.

Scholastic Opportunity Scholarship Program, 111 Blvd. of the Allies, 15222. Tel: 412-456-3100; Fax: 412-456-3101. Email: kstubna@diopitt.org. Web: www.diopitt.org. Rev. Kris D. Stubna, S.T.D., Contact Person.

Sisters of St. Francis of the Providence of God Ministries Corporation, 3603 McRoberts Rd., 15234-2314. Tel: 412-882-9911; Fax: 412-885-7210. Email: usa@osfprov.org. Web: www.osfprov.org. Sr. Joanne Brazinski, O.S.F., Pres. Program: Franciscan Spirit and Life Center.

**Society of Saint Vincent de Paul*, Council of Pittsburgh, 1243 N. Franklin St., 15233. Tel: 412-321-1071; Fax: 412-321-9131. Email: council@svdppitt.org. Web: www.svdppitt.org. Mark Stephen Bibro, Pres.; Keith G. Kondrich, B.A., Exec. Dir. Total Assisted 119,399; Total Staff 135.

Saint Thomas More Society (1960) 428 Blvd. of the Allies, 15219. Tel: 412-225-6973. Email: bill@cwkenny.com. C. William Kenny, Pres.

Tri-Diocesan Sisters Leadership Conference, 144 DePaul Center Rd., Greensburg, 15601. Tel: 724-836-0406; Fax: 724-836-8280. Email: ghartzog@scsh.org. Sisters Jeanne Marie Ulica, O.S.F., Co-Chm. Tel: 412-761-6004; Fax: 412-761-0290; Grace Hartzog, S.C., Co-Chm.

Vincentian Collaborative System, 8250 Babcock Blvd., 15237. Tel: 412-630-9980; Fax: 412-348-0186. Email: vcsinfo@vcs.org. Web: www.vcs.org. Raymond E. Washburn, B.S., Pres. & CEO. Purpose: To provide coordination and supervision of facilities and services operating under the auspices of the Sisters of Charity of Nazareth.

Vincentian Collaborative System Charitable Foundation, 8250 Babcock Blvd., 15237. Tel: 412-548-4055; Fax: 412-348-0186.

Vincentian Collaborative System Rehabilitation Services (2000) 111 Perrymont Rd, 15237. Tel: 412-348-1593; Fax: 412-348-1597. Email: lparkinson@vcs.org. Linda Parkinson, Dir., Vincentian Collaborative System Rehabiitation Svcs.

ALLISON PARK. *Divine Providence Foundation*, 9000 Babcock Blvd., 15101. Tel: 412-635-5402; Fax: 412-635-5416. Email: maryjbeatty@hotmail.com. Sr. Mary Francis Fletcher, C.D.P., Pres. Purpose: To perform public charitable works in the area of health care and education.

Sisters of Divine Providence Charitable Trust (1985) 9000 Babcock Blvd., 15101-2793. Tel: 412-635-5402; Fax: 412-635-5416. Email: srmfranciscdp@hotmail.com. Web: www.divineprovidenceweb.org. Mary Dieter, Chm.

BADEN. *The City of God Foundation*, 1020 State St., 15005. Tel: 724-869-6592; Fax: 724-869-4932. Jane Spellacy, Coord.

**Girls Hope of Pittsburgh, Inc.*, 1020 State St., 15005. Tel: 724-869-2868; Fax: 724-869-6576. Email: girlshope@bhgh.org. Sr. Sharon Costello, C.S.J., Exec. Dir. Purpose: To provide a supportive home environment and a quality education through college for girls who have potential for leadership but who because of poverty, abuse, neglect or abandonment cannot remain in their own homes. Total Assisted 22; Total Staff 10.

BEAVER FALLS. *Felician Sisters of North America Endowment Trust*, 871 Mercer Rd., 15010. Tel: 724-384-5300; Fax: 724-384-5301. Sr. Mary Christopher Moore, C.S.S.F., Trustee.

Felician Sisters of North America Real Estate Holding Corporation, 871 Mercer Rd., 15010. Tel: 724-384-5300; Fax: 724-384-5301. Sr. Mary Christopher Moore, C.S.S.F., Pres.

Felician Sisters of North America Real Estate Trust, 871 Mercer Rd., 15010. Tel: 724-384-5300; Fax: 724-384-5301. Sr. MaryAnne Olekszyk, C.S.S.F., Trustee.

Felician Sisters of North America Retirement and Continuing Care Trust, 871 Mercer Rd., 15010. Tel: 724-384-5300. Sr. Nancy Marie Jamroz, C.S.S.F., Trustee.

Felician Sisters of North American Marian Corporation, 871 Mercer Rd., 15010. Tel: 724-384-5300; Fax: 724-384-5301. Sr. Mary Christopher Moore, C.S.S.F., Pres.

BETHEL PARK. *Spiritan Mission Endowment Trust*, 6230 Brush Run Rd., 15102. Tel: 412-831-0302; Fax: 412-831-0970. Email: usprovince@spiritans.org. Web: www.spiritans.org.

Spiritan Support Trust, 6320 Brush Run Rd., 15102. Tel: 412-831-0302; Fax: 412-831-0970. Email: usprovince@spiritans.org. Web: www.spiritans.org. Very Rev. John Fogarty, C.S.Sp., Prov. Supr.

CLAIRTON. *Sisters Place, Inc.* (1993) 418 Mitchell Ave., 15025. Tel: 412-233-3903; Fax: 412-233-3904. Email: info@sistersplace.org. Web: www.sistersplace.org. Jeff Anderson, Pres.; Sr. Mary Parks, C.S.J., Exec. Dir. Purpose: To provide housing and supportive services to women and children who are homeless. Total Staff 11; Families 32.

CRANBERRY TOWNSHIP. *Magnificat Pittsburgh*, 114 Bayberry Ln., 16066. Tel: 724-452-1150. Kay Burkot, Contact Person.

ELIZABETH. *Divine Redeemer Health Care Ministries Corp.* (1990) 999 Rock Run Rd., 15037-2613. Tel: 412-751-8600; Fax: 412-751-0355. Email: sisrosemarysdr@aol.com. Web: www.sistersofthedivineredeemer.org.

Sisters of Divine Redeemer Charitable Trust (1990) 999 Rock Run Rd., 15037-2613. Tel: 412-751-8600; Fax: 412-751-0355. Email: sisrosemarysdr@aol.com. Web: www.sistersofthedivineredeemer.org.

MCKEESPORT. *Auberle*, 1101 Hartman St., 15132-1500. Tel: 412-673-5856, Ext. 1310; Fax: 412-267-5275. Email: johnly@auberle.org. Web: www.auberle.org. Stephanie Walsh, COO; John Patrick Lydon, CEO. Purpose: To provide services to at risk children and their families. Total in Residence 130; Total Staff 230.

Pauline Auberle Foundation (1952) 1101 Hartman St., 15132-1500. Tel: 412-673-5856, Ext. 1310; Fax: 412-267-5275. Email: johnly@auberle.org. Web: www.auberle.org. John Patrick Lydon, CEO; Bridget Clement, Dir. of Devel. Promote the health, education and welfare of children and families. Total Staff 4.

VILLA MARIA. *The Center for Learning*, Customer Service Office: 2105 Evergreen Rd., P.O. Box 910, 16155. Tel: 800-767-9090; Fax: 888-767-8080.

Email: mwall@centerforlearning.org. Web: www.centerforlearning.org; cflreligion.org. Melanie Wall, Pres. & CEO. Educational Publisher of values-based curriculum and online professional development: Religion for Catholic schools and parishes; English/Language Arts, Social Studies and Novel/Drama Curriculum Units for all schools; Owned and operated by the Sisters of the Humility of Mary. Directed by an Ecumenical Lay Board. Administration-business office in Villa Maria.

Administrative/Editorial Office, 29313 Clemens Rd. Ste 2E, Westlake, OH 44145. Tel: 440-250-9341; Fax: 440-250-9715.

Sisters of the Humility of Mary Charitable Trust, Villa Maria Community Center, 288 Villa Dr., P.O. Box 313, 16155. Tel: 724-964-8861; Fax: 724-964-8082. Email: cmarshall@hmministry.org. Web: www.humilityofmary.org. Sr. Carolyn Marshall, H.M., Contact Person.

Villa Maria Education & Spirituality Center (1989) 16155. Tel: 724-964-8886; Fax: 724-964-8815. Email: jmkudlacz@humilityofmary.org. Web: www.villaprograms.com. Jane Marie Kudlacz, H.M., Pres. & CEO. VMESC provides and promotes educational and spiritual experiences in a unique setting for people of all ages, faiths and economic status. Total Assisted 10,000; Total Staff 13.

Villa Maria Residential Services, 380 Villa Dr., P.O. Box 230, 16155. Tel: 724-964-8920, Ext. 3340; Fax: 724-964-1321. Email: kmcculloh@humilityofmary.org. Web: www.humilityofmary.org. Kathleen McCulloh, Pres. & CEO. (Villa Maria Apartments); Housing for low & moderate income for senior citizens 58 & over. Apartments 40.

WEXFORD. **St. Anthony Charitable Foundation*, 2000 Corporate Dr., Ste. 580, 15090. Tel: 724-940-9020; Fax: 724-940-9064.

**St. Anthony Programs*, 2000 Corporate Dr., Ste. 580, 15090. Tel: 724-940-9020; Fax: 724-940-9064.

RELIGIOUS INSTITUTES OF MEN REPRESENTED IN THE DIOCESE

For further details refer to the corresponding bracketed number in the Religious Institutes of Men or Women section.

[0200]—*Benedictine Monks* (St. Vincent Archabbey)—O.S.B.

[0330]—*Brothers of the Christian Schools* (Prov. of Baltimore)—F.S.C.

[0470]—*The Capuchin Friars* (Prov. of St. Augustine)—O.F.M.Cap.

[0650]—*Congregation of the Holy Spirit* (Eastern Prov.)—C.S.Sp.

[1000]—*Congregation of the Passion* (Eastern Prov.)—C.P.

[0520]—*Franciscan Friars* (Immaculate Conception & St. John the Baptist)—O.F.M.

[0950]—*Oratorians*—C.O.

[]—*Society of the Brother-Servants of the Holy Spirit*—B.H.S.

[0420]—*Society of the Divine Word*—S.V.D.

[0560]—*Third Order Regular of Saint Francis* (Prov. of Sacred Heart of Jesus)—T.O.R.

RELIGIOUS INSTITUTES OF WOMEN REPRESENTED IN THE DIOCESE

[0230]—*Benedictine Sisters of Pontifical Jurisdiction*—O.S.B.

[3730]—*Byzantine Sisters of Saint Basil the Great*—O.S.B.M.

[]—*Daughters of Mary Mother of Mercy*

[1070-02]—*Dominican Sisters of Our Lady of the Springs of Bridgeport*—O.P.

[1115]—*Dominican Sisters of Peace*—O.P.

[1170]—*Felician Sisters*—C.S.S.F.

[1190]—*Franciscan Sisters of Atonement*—S.A.

[2575]—*Institute of the Sisters of Mercy of the Americas* (Pittsburgh, PA)—R.S.M.

[]—*Ladies of Bethany*—L.B.

[2340]—*Little Sisters of the Poor*—L.S.P.

[2720]—*Mission Helpers of the Sacred Heart*—M.H.S.H.

[3071]—*North American Union Sisters of Our Lady of Charity*—O.L.C.

[3170]—*Religious of the Passion of Jesus Christ*—C.P.

[3430]—*Religious Teachers Filippini* (St. Lucy Filippini Prov.)—M.P.F.

[2970]—*School Sisters of Notre Dame*—S.S.N.D.

[1690]—*School Sisters of St. Francis*—O.S.F.

[0500]—*Sisters of Charity of Nazareth*—S.C.N.

[0570]—*Sisters of Charity of Seton Hill, Greensburg, Pennsylvania*—S.C.

[0990]—*Sisters of Divine Providence*—C.D.P.

[1805]—*Sisters of St. Francis of the Neumann Communities*—O.S.F.

[1660]—*Sisters of Saint Francis of the Providence of God*—O.S.F.

[3830-13]—*Sisters of Saint Joseph*—C.S.J.

[1620]—*Sisters of St. Francis of Millvale, Pennsylvania*—O.S.F.

[1020]—*Sisters of the Divine Redeemer*—S.D.R.

[1970]—*Sisters of the Holy Family of Nazareth*—C.S.F.N.

[2040]—*Sisters of the Holy Spirit*—S.H.S.

[2110]—*Sisters of the Humility of Mary*—H.M.

[2160]—*Sisters, Servants of the Immaculate Heart of Mary*—I.H.M.

[4160]—*Vincentian Sisters of Charity*—V.S.C.

DIOCESAN CEMETERIES

PITTSBURGH. *The Catholic Cemeteries Association of the Diocese of Pittsburgh* (1952) *Central Office*, 718 Hazelwood Ave., 15217-2807. Tel: 412-521-9133; Fax: 412-521-7019. Web: www.ccapgh.org.

All Saints Catholic Cemetery & Mausoleum (Braddock Catholic), 1560 Brinton Rd., 15221-4899. Tel: 412-271-5950; Fax: 412-271-8219.

Calvary Catholic Cemetery & Mausoleum, 718 Hazelwood Ave., 15217-2807. Tel: 412-421-9959; Fax: 412-421-3670.

Christ Our Redeemer Catholic Cemetery & Mausoleum (North Side Catholic), 204 Cemetery Ln., 15237-2722. Tel: 412-931-2206; Fax: 412-931-2229.

St. Mary Catholic Cemetery, c/o Calvary Cemetery, 718 Hazelwood Ave., 15217-2807. Tel: 412-421-9959; Fax: 412-621-6439.

St. Stanislaus Catholic Cemetery & Mausoleum & St. Anthony Catholic Cemetery, 700 Soose Rd., 15209-1544. Tel: 412-821-4324; Fax: 412-821-4718.

Queen of Heaven Catholic Cemetery & Mausoleum, 2900 Washington Rd., McMurray, 15317-3278. Tel: 724-941-7601; Fax: 724-942-2550.

Resurrection Catholic Cemetery & Mausoleum, 100 Resurrection Rd., Moon Township, 15108-7759. Tel: 724-695-2999; Fax: 724-695-3032.

Sacred Heart Catholic Cemetery and Mausoleum, 97 Sacred Heart Rd., Monongahela, 15063-9605. Tel: 724-258-2885; Fax: 724-258-2275.

Good Shepherd Catholic Cemetery & Mausoleum, 733 Patton St., Monroeville, 15146-4530. Tel: 412-824-0355; Fax: 412-823-9083.

Saint Joseph Catholic Cemetery & Mausoleum, 1443 Lincoln Hwy., North Versailles, 15137-2448. Tel: 412-823-9111; Fax: 412-823-6655.

Holy Souls Catholic Cemetery, c/o Resurrection Catholic Cemetery , 100 Resurrection Rd., Moon Township, 15108-7759. Tel: 724-695-2999; Fax: 724-695-3032.

Our Lady of Hope Catholic Cemetery & Mausoleum, 1898 Bakerstown Rd., Tarentum, 15084-3213. Tel: 724-224-2785; Fax: 724-224-0211.

Holy Savior Catholic Cemetery, 4629 Bakerstown Rd., Gibsonia, 15044-8993. Tel: 724-625-3822; Fax: 724-625-3880.

Mount Carmel Catholic Cemetery & Mausoleum, 7601 Mt. Carmel Rd., Verona, 15147-1518. Tel: 412-241-1260; Fax: 412-241-5041.

NECROLOGY

† Bradley, Dennis J., Pittsburgh, PA Saint John Vianney Manor—Died Dec. 10, 2010

† Franco, Robert M., Pittsburgh, PA Saint John Vianney Manor—Died Aug. 19, 2010

† Kuenzig, Peter A., (Retired)—Died Dec. 4, 2010

† McCormley, Hugh J., (Retired)—Died Sept. 15, 2010

† Murphy, Thomas R., (Retired)—Died Sept. 19, 2010

† Parsons, Harry E., (Retired)—Died May 9, 2011

† Pesanka, Nicholas A., (Health Leave of Absence)—Died Jan. 21, 2011

† Rager, Patrick F., (Health Leave of Absence)—Died July 20, 2010

† Saladna, George E., Springdale, PA Saint Alphonsus—Died April 17, 2011

† Schweitzer, Robert J., New Castle, PA Saint Joseph the Worker—Died Aug. 25, 2010

An asterisk (*) denotes an organization that has established tax-exempt status directly with the IRS and is not covered by the USCCB Group Ruling.

Diocese of Portland (In Maine)

(Dioecesis Portlandensis)

Most Reverend

RICHARD JOSEPH MALONE

Bishop of Portland; ordained priest May 20, 1972; appointed Auxiliary Bishop of Boston and Titular Bishop of Aptuca January 27, 2000; ordained March 1, 2000; appointed Bishop of Portland February 10, 2004; installed March 31, 2004. *Office: 510 Ocean Ave., Portland, ME 04103-4936. Mailing Address: P.O. Box 11559, Portland, ME 04104-7559.*

Most Reverend

JOSEPH JOHN GERRY, O.S.B.

Retired Bishop of Portland; ordained priest June 12, 1954; ordained Titular Bishop of Praecausa and Auxiliary Bishop of Manchester April 21, 1986; appointed Bishop of Portland December 21, 1988; installed February 21, 1989; retired February 10, 2004. *Mailing Address: St. Anselm Abbey, 100 St. Anselm Dr., Manchester, NH 03102-1310.*

Chancery: 510 Ocean Ave., P.O. Box 11559, Portland, ME 04104-7559. Tel: 207-773-6471; Fax: 207-773-0182.

ESTABLISHED JULY 29, 1853.

Square Miles 33,040.

Comprises the State of Maine.

Corporate Title: Roman Catholic Bishop of Portland, a Corporation Sole.

For the legal titles of other diocesan-related institutions, please consult Chancery.

STATISTICAL OVERVIEW

Personnel	
Bishop	1
Retired Bishops	1
Priests: Diocesan Active in Diocese	60
Priests: Diocesan Active Outside Diocese	1
Priests: Retired, Sick or Absent	82
Number of Diocesan Priests	143
Religious Priests in Diocese	27
Total Priests in Diocese	170
Extern Priests in Diocese	11
Ordinations:	
Diocesan Priests	1
Transitional Deacons	1
Permanent Deacons	9
Permanent Deacons in Diocese	43
Total Brothers	13
Total Sisters	285
Parishes	
Parishes	57
With Resident Pastor:	
Resident Diocesan Priests	34
Resident Religious Priests	3
Without Resident Pastor:	
Administered by Priests	20
Missions	18
New Parishes Created	4
Closed Parishes	11
Professional Ministry Personnel:	
Sisters	4
Lay Ministers	39
Welfare	
Catholic Hospitals	3
Total Assisted	445,575
Homes for the Aged	6
Total Assisted	589
Day Care Centers	1
Total Assisted	215
Special Centers for Social Services	2
Total Assisted	715
Residential Care of Disabled	4
Total Assisted	1,984
Educational	
Diocesan Students in Other Seminaries	9
Total Seminarians	9
Colleges and Universities	1
Total Students	3,103
High Schools, Diocesan and Parish	1
Total Students	241
High Schools, Private	2
Total Students	682
Elementary Schools, Diocesan and Parish	10
Total Students	2,088
Elementary Schools, Private	1
Total Students	167
Catechesis/Religious Education:	
High School Students	859
Elementary Students	5,334
Total Students under Catholic Instruction	12,483
Teachers in the Diocese:	
Priests	1
Scholastics	2
Sisters	4
Lay Teachers	246
Vital Statistics	
Receptions into the Church:	
Infant Baptism Totals	1,288
Minor Baptism Totals	177
Adult Baptism Totals	86
Received into Full Communion	115
First Communions	1,648
Confirmations	1,747
Marriages:	
Catholic	373
Interfaith	211
Total Marriages	584
Deaths	2,645
Total Catholic Population	193,392
Total Population	1,274,932

Former Bishops—Very Rev. J. COSKERY, V.G., of Baltimore, The first Bishop-Elect, declined the nomination; Rt. Revs. DAVID W. BACON, D.D., ord. Dec. 13, 1838 in Baltimore, MD; cons. Bishop of Portland April 22, 1855; died Nov. 5, 1874; JAMES AUGUSTINE HEALY, D.D., ord. June 10, 1854 in Paris, France; cons. Bishop of Portland June 2, 1875; died Aug. 5, 1900; His Eminence WILLIAM CARDINAL O'CONNELL, ord. June 8, 1884; cons. Bishop of Portland, May 19, 1901; named Coadjutor Archbishop of Boston, Feb. 8, 1906; succeeded to the See of Boston, Aug. 30, 1907; created Cardinal, Nov. 27, 1911; died April 22, 1944; Rt. Revs. LOUIS S. WALSH, D.D., ord. Dec. 23, 1882 in Rome, Italy; cons. Bishop of Portland Oct. 18, 1906; died May 12, 1924.; JOHN GREGORY MURRAY, D.D., ord. April 14, 1900 in Louvain, France; cons. Bishop of Portland April 28, 1920; transferred to the Archdiocese of St. Paul, Oct. 29, 1931; died Oct. 11, 1956; Most Revs. JOSEPH EDWARD MCCARTHY, D.D., ord. July 4, 1903; cons. Bishop of Portland Aug. 24, 1932; died Sept. 8, 1955; DANIEL JOSEPH FEENEY, D.D., LL.D., ord. May 21, 1921; appt. Titular Bishop of Sita and Auxiliary of Portland, June 22, 1946; cons. Sept. 12, 1946; Apostolic Administrator of the Diocese; appt. July 27, 1948; Coadjutor "cum jure successionis"; appt. March 4, 1952; succeeded to See, Sept. 8, 1955; died Sept. 15, 1969; PETER LEO GERETY, D.D., ord. June 29, 1939; appt. Titular Bishop of Crepedula and Coadjutor Bishop of Portland March 4, 1966; cons. June 1, 1966; appt. Apostolic Administrator, Feb. 18, 1967; succeeded to See, Sept. 15, 1969; transferred to Archdiocese of Newark, April 2, 1974; EDWARD C. O'LEARY, D.D., ord. June 15, 1946; Titular Bishop of Moglaena and Auxiliary Bishop of Portland; appt. Nov. 17, 1970; cons. Jan. 25, 1971; Apostolic Administrator; appt. June 29, 1974; ninth Bishop of Portland, Dec. 4, 1974; installed Dec. 18, 1974; resigned Sept. 27, 1988; died April 2, 2002; JOSEPH J. GERRY, O.S.B., D.D. (Retired), ord. June 12, 1954; cons. Titular Bishop of Praecausa and Auxiliary Bishop of Manchester April 21, 1986; appt. Bishop of Portland Dec. 21, 1988; installed Feb. 21, 1989; retired Feb. 10, 2004.

Vicars General—Rev. Msgrs. MICHAEL J. HENCHAL, J.C.L., V.G.; ANDREW DUBOIS, V.G.

Chancery—510 Ocean Ave., P.O. Box 11559, Portland, 04104-7559. Tel: 207-773-6471; Fax: 207-773-0182. Office Hours: Mon.-Fri. 9-4:30 Labor Day to Memorial Day; Mon.-Thurs. 8-5, Fri. closed, Memorial Day to Labor Day. Closed Holidays. This is the address for all offices unless otherwise listed.

Moderator of the Curia—Rev. Msgr. ANDREW DUBOIS, V.G.. Email: andrew.dubois@portlanddiocese.org.

Chancellor—Sr. RITA-MAE BISSONNETTE, R.S.R., J.C.L.. Email: ritamae.bissonnette@portlanddiocese.org.

Vicar for Priests—Rev. PAUL A. PLANTE. Tel: 207-864-3795. Email: paul.plante@portlanddiocese.org.

Director of Communications—Ms. SUSAN Y. BERNARD. Email: sue.bernard@portlanddiocese.org.

Vicars Forane—Very Revs. JEAN-PAUL LABRIE, V.F.; RICHARD C. MALO, V.F.; JOSEPH E. DANIELS; PHILIP A. TRACY, V.F.; LAWRENCE J. CONLEY (Retired); JOHN R. SKEHAN.

Diocesan Consultors—Rev. Msgrs. J. JOSEPH FORD; RENE T. MATHIEU; MARC B. CARON, S.T.L.; ANDREW DUBOIS, V.G.; Rev. PAUL A. PLANTE; Rev. Msgrs. PAUL F. STEFANKO, J.C.L.; MICHAEL J. HENCHAL, J.C.L., V.G.

Diocesan Review Board—Mr. KEVIN GILDART, Chm.; Mrs. KATHLEEN ROSSI; Ms. MELISSA CILLEY; Rev. NORMAND E. CARPENTIER; Sr. MAUREEN WALLACE, R.S.M.; Mrs. EDNA CHACE; Dr. ANNE PULSIFIER; Honorable ALEXANDER MAC NICHOL. Staff: Rev. Msgr. ANDREW DUBOIS, V.G.; Ms. RUTH OAKLEY;

Rev. Msgr. MICHAEL J. HENCHAL, J.C.L., V.G.

Diocesan Offices and Directors

Department of Pastoral and Educational Services—

Diocesan Office of Lifelong Faith Formation—Mr. MICHAEL LAVIGNE, Dir. Email: michael.lavigne@portlanddiocese.org.

Youth & Young Adult Ministry Coordinator—Mr. JOSEPH MAILHOT. Email: joe.mailhot@portlanddiocese.org.

Retreat Coordinator—Ms. SARAH HOUDE. Email: sarah.houde@portlanddiocese.org.

Faith Formation Outreach Coordinator—Mrs. JUDY MICHAUD, 46 St. Agatha Ave., Frenchville, 04745. Tel: 207-543-7731. Email: judy.michaud@portlanddiocese.org.

Catholic Schools Superintendent—Sr. ROSEMARY T. DONOHUE, S.N.D., Ph.D. Email: rosemary.donohue@portlanddiocese.org.

Office for Missions—Ms. RUTH OAKLEY. Email: ruth.oakley@portlanddiocese.org.

Director of Chaplaincies—Rev. Msgr. ANDREW DUBOIS, V.G.

Latin Mass—Rev. ROBERT PARENT, Coord., 1313 Riverside Dr., Auburn, 04210-9662. Tel: 207-212-3218.

Hospital Chaplaincy—Rev. Msgr. ANDREW DUBOIS, V.G.

Hispanic Ministry—Sr. PAT PORA, R.S.M., Dir.

Prison Ministry—

Ecumenical & Interreligious Services—Rev. RICHARD E. SENGHAS, Coord. (Retired).

Charismatic Renewal—Rev. RICHARD P. RICE (Retired), 66 Ward Circle, Brunswick, 04011-9342.

Campus Ministry—Rev. WILFRED P. LABBE.

Catholic Scouting—Rev. NATHAN D. MARCH, Chap., Mailing Address: Catholic Committee on Scouting, P.O. Box 1540, Lewiston, 04241-1540. Tel: 207-777-1200. Email: nathan.march@portlanddiocese.org.

Resource Center—Rev. NORMAND P. RICHARD, Coord.

Department of Financial Services—Mr. DAVID P. TWOMEY JR., CPA, Dir. Email: david.twomey@portlanddiocese.org.

Parish Financial Services—Ms. ANDREA LAPLANTE, Dir. Email: andrea.laplante@portlanddiocese.org.

Controller—Mrs. LAURIE J. DOWNEY, CPA. Email: laurie.downey@portlanddiocese.org.

Human Resources—Ms. ELIZABETH ALLEN, Dir. Email: elizabeth.allen@portlanddiocese.org.

Director of Property Management—Mr. JAMES SOMMA. Email: james.somma@portlanddiocese.org.

Risk Management—Mr. JOHN CAVALLARO, Dir. Email: john.cavallaro@portlanddiocese.org.

DICON - Diocesan Construction—Mr. GREG STONE, Supt. Email: greg.stone@portlanddiocese.org.

Safe Environment—Mr. THOMAS MESCHINELLI, Coord. Email: thom.meschinelli@portlanddiocese.org.

Information Technology—Mr. MICHAEL MOORE, Dir. Email: michael.moore@portlanddiocese.org.

Department of Canonical Services—Rev. Msgr. PAUL F. STEFANKO, J.C.L.

Tribunal—

Officialis—Rev. Msgr. PAUL F. STEFANKO, J.C.L. Email: paul.stefanko@portlanddiocese.org.

Promoter of Justice—Rev. Msgr. MICHAEL J. HENCHAL, J.C.L., V.G. Email: michael.henchal@portlanddiocese.org.

Defenders of the Bond—Ms. SHANNON FOSSETT. Email: shannon.fossett@portlanddiocese.org; Mr. STEPHEN GARBITELLI, J.C.L. Email: stephen.garbitelli@portlanddiocese.org; Mr. GEORGE G. PAVLOFF, J.C.D. Email: george.pavloff@portlanddiocese.org; Sr. RITA-MAE BISSONNETTE, R.S.R., J.C.L.

Advocates—Ms. SHANNON FOSSETT; Mr. STEPHEN GARBITELLI, J.C.L.; Sr. RITA-MAE BISSONNETTE, R.S.R., J.C.L.

Notaries—Mrs. NAJLIA KERRIGAN. Email: nash.kerrigan@portlanddiocese.org; Mrs. MARY DELANEY. Email: mary.delaney@portlanddiocese.org.

Associate Judges—Rev. JOSEPH J. KOURY, J.C.D. Email: joseph.koury@portlanddiocese.org; Sr. RITA-MAE BISSONNETTE, R.S.R., J.C.L.; Rev. Msgr. MICHAEL J. HENCHAL, J.C.L., V.G.

Guardian—Rev. Msgr. ANDREW DUBOIS, V.G.

Office Coordinator—Rev. Msgr. PAUL F. STEFANKO, J.C.L.

Office of Due Process— (examination of violation of rights within the church)

Director—Ms. SHANNON FOSSETT.

Department of Administrative & Ministerial Services—Rev. Msgr. ANDREW DUBOIS, V.G.

Diocesan Office of Communications—Ms. SUSAN Y. BERNARD, Dir.

Harvest Magazine—Ms. LOIS CZENIAK, Editor. Email: lois.czeniak@portlanddiocese.org.

Diocesan Office of Public Policy—Mr. MARC R. MUTTY. Email: marc.mutty@portlanddiocese.org.

Office of Professional Responsibility—Deacon JOHN S. BRENNAN, Dir. Tel: 866-829-4437 (Toll Free); 207-321-7836 (Office); Cell: 207-650-0492. Email: john.brennan@portlanddiocese.org.

Diaconate—Rev. Msgr. CHARLES M. MURPHY, S.T.D., V.F., Dir. (Retired).

Ministry to Priests—Rev. PAUL A. PLANTE, Vicar.

Vocations—Rev. ROBERT C. VAILLANCOURT. Email: robert.vaillancourt@portlanddiocese.org.

Seminarians—Rev. FRANK J. MURRAY. Email: frank.murray@portlanddiocese.org.

Delegate for Religious—Sr. RITA-MAE BISSONNETTE, R.S.R., J.C.L.

Office of Support and Assistance Ministry— (Victims Assistance) Ms. RUTH OAKLEY. Email: ruth.oakley@portlanddiocese.org; Ms. CAROLYN BLOOM, Independent Clinician. Tel: 207-782-1051. Email: cbloomlcsw@gmail.com.

Department of Development Services—Ms. PATRICIA M. LONG, Dir. Email: patricia.long@portlanddiocese.org.

Catholic Charities Maine— Development Services: Ms. KRISTEN WELLS, Dir., Mailing Address: P.O. Box 10660, Portland, 04104-6060. Tel: 207-781-8550; Fax: 207-781-8560. Email: kristen.wells@portlanddiocese.org.

Catholic Foundation of Maine—Mr. CHRISTOPHER REILLY, Exec. Dir. Email: christopher.reilly@portlanddiocese.org.

Annual Appeal—Ms. PATRICIA M. LONG, Dir. Email: patricia.long@portlanddiocese.org.

Campaign for Human Development—Ms. BONITA BAGLEY, Mailing Address: P.O. Box 10660, Portland, 04104-6060. Tel: 207-781-8550; Fax: 207-781-8560. Email: bbagley@ccmaine.org.

Catholic Relief Services—Ms. RUTH OAKLEY.

Diocesan Priests' Benefit Plan - Trustees—Most Rev. RICHARD JOSEPH MALONE, D.D., S.T.L., Th.D., Pres.; Rev. PAUL A. PLANTE; Rev. Msgr. J. JOSEPH FORD, Chm.; Revs. CLAUDE J. ALBERT, Treas. (Retired); PHILIP A. TRACEY; ROBERT D. LARIVIERE; TIMOTHY J. NADEAU, Sec.; NORMAND E. CARPENTIER.

Diocesan Archivist—Sr. RITA-MAE BISSONNETTE, R.S.R., J.C.L. Contact Chancellor's Office:

Diocesan Board of Education—Sr. ROSEMARY T. DONOHUE, S.N.D., Ph.D., Exec. Sec.; Ms. KATHLEEN MCLAUGHLIN. Members: Rev. RICHARD C. MCLAUGHLIN; Ms. DENISE GOULET; Mrs. DONNA JACQUES; Mr. ROGER F.R. KARL, P.E.; Mr. MATTHEW RANCOURT, Chm.; Mrs. ANDREE TOSTEVIN; Dr. BARBARA ANN ARNOLDO; Sgt. JONATHAN SHAPIRO; Revs. LOUIS J. PHILLIPS; JAMES F. LAFONTAINE, S.J.; Mr. DONALD FOURNIER; Ms. PAULA MOSES.

Diocesan Bureau of Housing—Most Rev. RICHARD JOSEPH MALONE, D.D., S.T.L., Th.D., Bishop of Portland & Pres.; Mr. DAVID P. TWOMEY JR., CPA, Treas.; THOMAS KELLY ESQ., Clerk.

Diocesan Finance Council—Most Rev. RICHARD JOSEPH MALONE, D.D., S.T.L., Th.D.; Rev. Msgr. ANDREW DUBOIS, V.G.; Mr. JOSEPH MALONE; VINCENT VERONEAU; CYNTHIA NICKLESS; ROBERTSON BREED; GREGG H. GINN, Chm.; GREGORY ST. ANGELO; MARK FERNANDEZ; RICHARD RODERICK. Ex Officio Members: Sr. RITA-MAE BISSONNETTE, R.S.R., J.C.L.; Mr. DAVID P. TWOMEY JR., CPA, Finance Officer. Staff: Mrs. LAURIE J. DOWNEY, CPA; Ms. ANDREA LAPLANTE.

Diocesan Pastoral Council—Most Rev. RICHARD JOSEPH MALONE, D.D., S.T.L., Th.D., Pres. Ex Officio: Rev. Msgr. ANDREW DUBOIS, V.G.; Sr. RITA-MAE BISSONNETTE, R.S.R., J.C.L., Chancellor. Appointed Members: Mr. KEVIN BIRCH; Dr. DOUGLAS JORGENSEN; Mrs. WENDY JORGENSEN; Sr. ELAINE LACHANCE, S.C.I.M.; Ms. TERRI MAHER, Co Chm.; Deacon JOHN MCAULIFFE JR.; Ms. MARTHA MULDOON; Mr. MICHAEL POULIN; Sgt. JONATHAN SHAPIRO, Co Chm.; Ms. ELAINE SIPE; Mr. PAUL TULLY.

Liturgical Commission—Rev. Msgr. MARC B. CARON, S.T.L., Dir.

General Counsel—Mr. THOMAS KELLY, Robinson Kriger & McCallum, 12 Portland Pier, Portland, 04101-4713. Tel: 207-772-6565.

Maine Diocesan Council of Catholic Women—Most Rev. RICHARD JOSEPH MALONE, D.D., S.T.L., Th.D., Episcopal Chm.; Sr. CAROL MARTIN, P.F.M., Diocesan Moderator; RUTH WARREN.

Newman Apostolate—Rev. WILFRED P. LABBE. Pastoral Associates: Rev. THOMAS LEQUIN; Ms. BERNICE MURPHY; Rev. FRANK MURRAY.

Personnel Board—Rev. Msgr. ANDREW DUBOIS, V.G.; Rev. NORMAND E. CARPENTIER; Rev. Msgrs. J. JOSEPH FORD; MARC B. CARON, S.T.L.; Very Rev. JEAN-PAUL LABRIE, V.F. Ex Officio Members: Most Rev. RICHARD JOSEPH MALONE, D.D., S.T.L., Th.D., Pres.; Rev. Msgr. MICHAEL J. HENCHAL, J.C.L., V.G., Vicar Gen.; Revs. FRANK J. MURRAY, Dir., Seminarians; PAUL A. PLANTE, Vicar for Priests.

Pontifical Association of Holy Childhood—Ms. RUTH OAKLEY.

Pontifical Society for the Propagation of the Faith—Ms. RUTH OAKLEY.

CLERGY, PARISHES, MISSIONS AND PAROCHIAL SCHOOLS

CITY OF PORTLAND

(CUMBERLAND COUNTY)

1—CATHEDRAL OF THE IMMACULATE CONCEPTION (1853) Revs. Louis J. Phillips, Rector; Gregory P. Dube, Parochial Vicar; Michael J. Seavey, Parochial Vicar; Michele Bernier, Pastoral Coord.; Denis Lafreniere, Business Mgr. In Res., Very Rev. Lawrence J. Conley (Retired).

Office, Res. & Mailing Address: 307 Congress St., 04101-3695. Tel: 207-773-7746 (Rectory); Fax: 207-879-5547. Email: portlandcathedral@portlanddiocese.org. Web: www.portlandcathedral.org.

Catechesis/Religious Program—Tel: 207-772-6597; Fax: 207-879-5547. Ms. Grace Tucci Libby, P.C.L. Students 102.

2—ST. CHRISTOPHER'S (Peaks Island) (1923) Revs. Louis J. Phillips, Admin.; Michael J. Seavey, Parochial Vicar; Gregory P. Dube, Parochial Vicar.

Mailing Address: 307 Congress St., 04101-3695. Tel: 207-773-7446. Email: portlandcathedral@portlanddiocese.org. Web: www.cluster21portland.org.

Church: 15 Central Ave., Peaks Island, 04108.

Catechesis/Religious Program—

Mission— Long Island, Cumberland Co.

3—ST. DOMINIC'S, Merged See Sacred Heart/St. Dominic's, Portland.

4—ST. JOSEPH'S (1909) Closed. See Our Lady of Hope Parish, Portland.

5—ST. LOUIS (1915), (Polish), Revs. Louis J. Phillips, Admin.; Michael J. Seavey, Parochial Vicar; Gregory P. Dube, Parochial Vicar.

Mailing Address: 307 Congress St., 04101-3695. Tel: 207-773-7746; Fax: 207-879-5547. Email: portlandcathedral@portlanddiocese.org. Web: www.stlouischurch.net. In Res., Rev. Paul R. Marquis, Chap.

Res.: 279 Danforth St., 04102-3798. Web: www.stlouischurch.net.

Catechesis/Religious Program—Students 10.

6—OUR LADY OF HOPE PARISH Revs. James F. Lafontaine, S.J.; John R. d'Anjou, S.J., Parochial Vicar; Richard D. Bertrand, S.J., Parochial Vicar; Robert F. Regan, S.J., Senior Priest; Mary Gordon, Business Mgr. In Res., Revs. Robert V. Paskey, S.J.; Albin A. Andrus (Retired); Harold D. Moreshead (Retired); Normand P. Richard.

Mailing Address & Office: 673 Stevens Ave., 04103-2640. Tel: 207-979-7026; Fax: 207-797-2679.

Res.: 492 Ocean Ave., 04103. Tel: 207-775-3032; Fax: 207-874-7514.

Worship Sites:—

St. Joseph Church—673 Stevens Ave., 04103-2640.

St. Patrick Church—1342 Congress St., 04102.

St. Pius X Church—492 Ocean Ave., 04103.

School—St. Brigid School, 695 Stevens Ave., 04103-2682. Tel: 207-797-7073; Fax: 207-797-7078. Mr. Edward P. Buckley, Prin. Lay Teachers 29; Students 400.

Catechesis/Religious Program—Students 83.

7—ST. PATRICK'S (1922) Closed. See Our Lady of Hope Parish, Portland.

8—ST. PETER'S (1911), (Italian), Revs. Louis J. Phillips, Admin.; Michael J. Seavey, Parochial Vicar; Gregory P. Dube, Parochial Vicar.

Mailing Address: 307 Congress St., 04101-3695. Tel: 207-773-7746; Fax: 207-879-5547. Email: portlandcathedral@portlanddiocese.org. In Res., Rev. Msgr. Andrew Dubois.

Church: 72 Federal St., 04101. Tel: 207-773-0748; Fax: 207-879-0557. Web: www.stpeterschurchportland.org.

Catechesis/Religious Program—Ms. Grace Tucci Libby, P.C.L. Students 50.

9—ST. PIUS X (1962) Closed. See Our Lady of Hope Parish, Portland.

10—SACRED HEART/ST. DOMINIC (1997) Revs. Louis J. Phillips, Admin.; Michael J. Seavey, Parochial Vicar; Gregory P. Dube, Parochial Vicar.

Mailing Address: 307 Congress St., 04101-3695. Tel: 207-773-7746; Fax: 207-879-5547. Email: portlandcathedral@portlanddiocese.org. Web: www.shsdp.com.

Church: 80 Sherman St., 04101-2290. Tel: 207-772-6182; Fax: 207-772-9615. Web: www.shsdp.org.

Catechesis/Religious Program—Students 25.

OUTSIDE THE CITY OF PORTLAND

ASHLAND, AROOSTOOK CO., ST. MARK'S, [CEM 3] Merged See Parish of the Precious Blood, Caribou.

AUBURN, ANDROSCOGGIN CO.

1—IMMACULATE HEART OF MARY PARISH (2008) Revs. Richard C. McLaughlin; Robert L. Lupo, Parochial Vicar; Sr. Elizabeth A. Platt, C.O.C., Pastoral Coord.; Deacon Denis Mailhot; Linda Bracket, Business Mgr.

Mailing Address, Res. & Office: *Parish Center*, 24 Sacred Heart Pl., 04210-4938. Tel: 207-782-8096 (Office); 207-786-8577 (Res.); Fax: 207-782-9032.

Churches:—

Sacred Heart Church—8 Sacred Heart Pl., 04210.

St. Louis Church—80 Third St., 04210.

St. Philip's Church—2365 Turner Rd., 04210.

Catechesis/Religious Program—Tel: 207-786-9045. Sandra Tardiff, D.R.E. Students 109.

2—ST. LOUIS (1902) Merged See Immaculate Heart of Mary Parish, Auburn.

3—ST. PHILIP'S (1968) Merged See Immaculate Heart of Mary Parish, Auburn.

4—SACRED HEART (1923) Merged See Immaculate Heart of Mary Parish, Auburn.

AUGUSTA, KENNEBEC CO.

1—ST. ANDREW'S (1968) Merged See St. Michael Parish, Augusta.

2—ST. AUGUSTINE'S (1888) [CEM 2] Merged See St. Michael Parish, Augusta.

3—ST. MARY OF THE ASSUMPTION (1834) [CEM 2] Merged See St. Michael Parish, Augusta.

4—ST. MICHAEL PARISH (2007) [CEM 4] Revs. Francis P. Morin, Admin.; Kevin J. Martin, Parochial Vicar; Gail Gould, Pastoral Coord.; Noreen Hare, Business Mgr.

Office & Mailing Address: 24 Washington St., 04330-4239. Tel: 207-623-8823; Fax: 207-623-7574.

Res.: 41 Western Ave., 04330-6324. Tel: 207-620-1125.

Churches:—

St. Augustine Church—1 Kendall St., 04330.

St. Mary of the Assumption Church—41 Western Ave., 04330.

St. Joseph Church—1 Lincoln St., Gardiner, 04345.

St. Denis Church—298 Grand Army Rd., Whitefield, 04353.

St. Francis Xavier Church—130 Rte. 133, Winthrop, 04364.

School—(Grades PreK-8), 56 Sewall St., 04330-7327. Tel: 207-623-3491; Fax: 207-623-2971. Jon Caron, Prin. Lay Teachers 12; Students 238.

Catechesis/Religious Program—Tel: 207-623-8823. Students 180.

BAILEYVILLE, WASHINGTON CO., ST. JAMES THE GREATER (1905) Merged See Blessed Kateri Tekakwitha Parish, Calais.

BANGOR, PENOBSCOT CO.

1—ST. JOHN'S (1856) Merged See Saint Paul the Apostle Parish, Bangor.

2—ST. MARY (1872) Merged See Saint Paul the Apostle Parish, Bangor.

3—SAINT PAUL THE APOSTLE PARISH (2009) [CEM] Revs. Timothy J. Nadeau, Admin.; Seamus P. Griesbach, Parochial Vicar; Deacons Timothy R. Dougherty; Michael E. Whalen; Mr. Thomas Pendergast, Dir. Pastoral Admin.; Cheryl Whalen, Business Mgr. In Res., Revs. Roland P. Nadeau, Chap.; Apolinary Kavishe, A.J., Chap.

Office, Rectory & Mailing Address: 207 York St., 04401-5442. Tel: 207-217-6740; Fax: 207-217-6730.

Res. for Chaplains: 521 N. Main St., Brewer, 04412-1219. Tel: 207-989-5388.

Churches:—

St. John Church—207 York St., 04401-5442.

St. Mary Church—768 Ohio St., 04401-3106.

St. Joseph Church—521 N. Main St., Brewer, 04412-1219.

St. Theresa Church—440 S. Main St., Brewer, 04412-2327.

St. Matthew Church—70 Western Ave., Hampden, 04444-1427.

St. Gabriel Church—435 S. Main St., Winterport, 04496.

School—All Saints Catholic School, (Grades K-8), P.O. Box 1749, 04401-1749. Tel: 207-947-7063; Fax: 207-942-2398. Web: allsaintsmaine.org. Joseph Gallant, Prin. St. Mary's and St. John's Campuses. Lay Teachers 21; Students 246.

School—St. Mary's Campus, (Grades PreK-2), 768 Ohio St., 04401-3165. Tel: 207-947-7063; Fax: 207-942-7356.

School—St. John's Campus, (Grades 3-8), 166 State St., 04401-5320. Tel: 207-947-0955; Fax: 207-942-2398.

Catechesis/Religious Program—Anne Marie Coleman, Dir. Faith Formation. Students 337.

BAR HARBOR, HANCOCK CO.

1—HOLY REDEEMER (1907) [CEM] Closed. See Parish of the Transfiguration, Bar Harbor.

2—PARISH OF THE TRANSFIGURATION (2011) Rev. John O'Hara; Deacon Joseph LaPlante.

Res.: 21 Ledgelawn Ave., 04609-1303. Tel: 207-288-3535.

Worship Sites:—

Holy Redeemer Church—21 Ledgelawn Ave., 04609-1303.

St. Ignatius Church—8 Lookout Way, Northeast Harbor, 04679.

Our Lady Star of the Sea Chapel—, Little Cranberry Island Islesford, ME (only summers)

St. Peter's Church—5 Ocean House Hill Rd., Manset, 04656.

Catechesis/Religious Program—Students 20.

BATH, SAGADAHOC CO., ST. MARY (1849) Merged See All Saints Parish, Brunswick.

BELFAST, WALDO CO., ST. FRANCIS OF ASSISI (1891) Merged See Saint Brendan the Navigator Parish, Camden.

BENEDICTA, AROOSTOOK CO., ST. BENEDICT'S (1834) [CEM] Rev. Joel R. Cyr; Deacon Danny Watson.

Mailing Address: P.O. Box 27, 04733-0024. Tel: 207-365-4294; Fax: 207-365-7378.

Catechesis/Religious Program—Tel: 207-365-4269. Anna Robinson, D.R.E. Students 8.

BERWICK, YORK CO.

1—OUR LADY OF PEACE (1927) Closed. See Parish of the Ascension of the Lord, Kittery.

2—OUR LADY OF THE ANGELS, [CEM] Closed. See Parish of the Ascension of the Lord, Kittery.

BIDDEFORD, YORK CO.

1—ST. ANDRE'S (1899) [JC] Closed. See Good Shepherd Parish, Saco.

2—ST. JOSEPH'S (1870) Merged See Good Shepherd Parish, Saco.

3—ST. MARY'S (1855) [CEM] Closed. See Good Shepherd Parish, Saco.

BINGHAM, SOMERSET CO., ST. PETER'S (1920) Merged See Christ the King Parish, Skowhegan.

BOOTHBAY HARBOR, LINCOLN CO., OUR LADY, QUEEN OF PEACE (1928) Merged See All Saints Parish, Brunswick.

BRADLEY, PENOBSCOT CO., ST. ANN (1934) [JC] Merged See Parish of the Resurrection of the Lord, Old Town.

BREWER, PENOBSCOT CO.

1—ST. JOSEPH'S (1926) [JC] Merged See Saint Paul the Apostle Parish, Bangor.

2—ST. TERESA'S (1894) Merged See Saint Paul the Apostle Parish, Bangor.

BRIDGTON, CUMBERLAND CO., ST. JOSEPH (1971) Revs. Joseph J. Koury, Admin.; Paul H. Dumais.

Rectory—174 S. High St., 04009. Tel: 207-647-2334; Fax: 207-647-2334.

Church & Mailing Address: 225 S. High St., 04009-4104.

Catechesis/Religious Program—Students 54.

Mission—St. Elizabeth Ann Seton 857 Main St., P.O. Box 332, Fryeburg, Oxford Co. 04037-0332. Tel: 207-935-4245.

BRUNSWICK, CUMBERLAND CO.

1—ALL SAINTS PARISH, [CEM 2] Revs. Frank J. Murray; Normand E. Carpentier, Parochial Vicar; Frederick Morse, Parochial Vicar; Martha Corkery, Pastoral Coord.; Donald Leaver, Business Mgr.

Office & Mailing Address: 132 McKeen St., 04011-2980. Tel: 207-725-2624; Fax: 207-725-4436.

Churches:—

St. Mary Church—144 Lincoln St., Bath, 04530-2198. Tel: 207-443-3423; Fax: 207-443-5692.

St. Charles Church—132 McKeen St., 04011-2980.

St. John the Baptist Church—39 Pleasant St., 04011-2279.

Our Lady Queen of Peace Church—82 Atlantic Ave., Boothbay Harbor, 04538-2129. Tel: 207-633-2680; Fax: 207-633-2611.

St. Patrick Church—Academy Hill Rd., Newcastle, 04553-3473. Tel: 207-563-6038; Fax: 207-563-3218.

St. Ambrose Church—27 Kimball St., Richmond, 04357-1106. Tel: 207-737-4713; Fax: 207-737-4713.

St. Katharine Drexel Church—Harpswell, 04079.

School—St. John's Catholic School, (Grades PreK-8), 37 Pleasant St., 04011-2279. Tel: 207-725-5507; Fax: 207-782-5507. Mrs. Andree Tostevin, Prin. Lay Teachers 13; Students 167.

Catechesis/Religious Program—Tel: 207-725-2624. Amy Ford, D.R.E. Students 260.

2—ST. CHARLES (1930) Merged See All Saints Parish, Brunswick.

3—ST. JOHN THE BAPTIST (1877) [CEM] Merged See All Saints Parish, Bath.

BUCKSPORT, HANCOCK CO., ST. VINCENT DE PAUL (1892) [CEM] Merged See Stella Maris Parish, Ellsworth.

CALAIS, WASHINGTON CO.

1—BLESSED KATERI TEKAKWITHA PARISH, [CEM] Rev. James S. Plourde, Admin.; Sr. Janice Murphy, R.S.M., Pastoral Assoc. Tel: 207-853-2944.

Mailing Address: P.O. Box 898, 04619-0898.

Res. & Office: 31 Calais Ave., 04619. Tel: 207-454-0680; Fax: 207-454-0081.

Churches:—

Immaculate Conception Church—31 Calais Ave., 04619.

St. Ann Church—Peter Dana Point Rd., Indian Twp, 04668.

St. Ann Sipayik Church—126 Bayview Dr., Perry, 04667.

St. James the Greater Church—56 Summit St., Baileyville, 04694.

St. John the Evangelist Church—39 Hersey Ln., Pembroke, 04666.

St. Joseph Church—51 Washington St., Eastport, 04631.

Catechesis/Religious Program—Students 87.

2—IMMACULATE CONCEPTION (1859) Merged See Blessed Kateri Tekakwitha Parish, Calais.

CAMDEN, KNOX CO.

1—SAINT BRENDAN THE NAVIGATOR PARISH (2009) [CEM 2] Rev. Mark S. Reinhardt; Katie Benedict, Business Mgr.

Res. & Office: 7 Union St., 04843-2015. Tel: 207-236-4785; Fax: 207-236-9422.

Churches:—

St. Francis of Assisi Church—81 Court St., Belfast, 04915-6134.

St. Mary of the Isles—Islesboro, 04848.

Our Lady of Good Hope Church—7 Union St., 04843.

Our Lady of Peace Church—North Haven, 04853.

St. Bernard Church—150 Broadway, Rockland, 04841-2698.

St. James Church—Thomaston-0486.

Catechesis/Religious Program—Students 168.

2—OUR LADY OF GOOD HOPE (1967) Merged See Saint Brendan the Navigator Parish, Camden.

CAPE ELIZABETH, CUMBERLAND CO., ST. BARTHOLOMEW (1968) Rev. Msgrs. Michael J. Henchal; Paul F. Stefanko, Parochial Vicar; Thomas Sheehan, Business Mgr.

Church & Res.: 8 Two Lights Rd., 04107-2624. Tel: 207-799-5528; Fax: 207-799-2161. Web: www.saintbarts.com.

Catechesis/Religious Program—Students 84.

CARIBOU, AROOSTOOK CO.

1—HOLY ROSARY (1896) Merged See Parish of the Precious Blood, Caribou.

2—PARISH OF THE PRECIOUS BLOOD (2009) [CEM 10] Very Rev. Jean-Paul Labrie; Revs. Aaron L. Damboise, Parochial Vicar; Raymond P. Morency, Parochial Vicar; Janet Beckwith, Pastoral Coord.; Michael Lagasse, Business Mgr.

Mailing Address: P.O. Box 625, 04736-0625.

Res. & Office: 31 Thomas Ave., 04736. Tel: 207-498-2536; Fax: 207-498-2537.

Churches:—

St. Mark's Church—Allen Farm Rd., Ashland, 04732.

Our Lady of the Lakes—Portage, 04768.

St. Catherine—Washburn, 04786.

Holy Rosary Church—31 Thomas Ave., 04736-1721.

Sacred Heart Church—1143 Van Buren Rd., 04736-3527.

St. Joseph Church—117 Main St., Mars Hill, 04758-0000.

St. Denis Church—143 Main St., Fort Fairfield, 04742-1223.

St. Louis Church—100 Main St., Limestone, 04750-1116.

St. Therese Church—Stockholm, 04783-0000.

Nativity of the Blessed Virgin Mary Church—6 Roberts St., Presque Isle, 04769-0813.

Catechesis/Religious Program—Students 224.

3—SACRED HEART (1881) Merged See Parish of the Precious Blood, Caribou.

DAIGLE, AROOSTOOK CO., HOLY FAMILY, Closed. For inquiries for parish records please contact St. John Vianney Parish, Fort Kent

DEXTER, PENOBSCOT CO.

1—ST. ANNE'S (1893) Merged See Our Lady of the Snows Parish, Dexter.

2—OUR LADY OF THE SNOWS PARISH (2007) Revs. Kent R. Ouellette, Admin.; Paul G. Murray, Parochial Vicar; Jane Young, Pastoral Coord.

Mailing Address: P.O Box 193, 04930-0193.

Office: 60 Free St., 04930. Tel: 207-924-7104; Fax: 207-924-7993. Email: olofthesnows@portlanddiocese.org. Web: www.ourladyofthesnowsme.org.

Res.: 45 High St., Dover Foxcroft, 04426. Tel: 207-564-2612.

Churches:—

St. Anne Church—59 Free St., 04930.

St. Thomas Aquinas Church—45 High St., Dover Foxcroft, 04426.

Sts. Francis & Paul the Apostle Church—128 Riverside St., Milo, 04463.

Catechesis/Religious Program—Students 52.

DOVER-FOXCROFT, PISCATAGUIS CO., ST. THOMAS AQUINAS (1898) Merged See Our Lady of the Snows Parish, Dexter.

EAGLE LAKE, AROOSTOOK CO., ST. MARY'S (1892) [CEM] Merged See St. John Vianney Parish, Fort Kent.

EAST MILLINOCKET, PENOBSCOT CO.
1—CHRIST THE DIVINE MERCY PARISH (2007) Rev. Joel R. Cyr; Deacon Daniel Watson, Pastoral Coord.; Charleen Rossignol, Business Mgr.
Mailing Address: P.O Box 400, 04430-0400.
Office: 58 Center St., P.O. Box 400, 04430-0400. Tel: 207-723-5902; 207-746-3333; Fax: 207-746-8188; 207-723-6395.
Res.: 58 Cedar St., 04430-1031.
Churches:—
St. Peter's Church—58 Cedar St., 04430.
St. Martin of Tours Church—Colby St., Millinocket, 04462.
Catechesis/Religious Program—
2—ST. PETER'S (1907) Merged See Christ the Divine Mercy Parish, East Millinocket.
EASTPORT, WASHINGTON CO., ST. JOSEPH (1828) [JC] Merged See Blessed Kateri Tekakwitha Parish, Calais., P.O. Box 369, Baileyville, 04694-0369.
ELLSWORTH, HANCOCK CO.
1—ST. JOSEPH (1862) [CEM] Revs. Scott M. Mower, Admin.; Bruce Siket, Parochial Vicar; Laurence Fernaldi, Business Mgr.
Res.: 231 Main St., 04605-1613. Tel: 207-667-2342; Fax: 207-667-2043. Email: stjoseph.church@roadrunner.com.
Catechesis/Religious Program—Students 73.
Mission—Our Lady of the Lake, (summers only), Green Lake, Hancock Co.
Mission—St. Margaret, (summers only), Winter Harbor, Hancock Co.
2—STELLA MARIS PARISH (2008) [CEM 2] Revs. Scott M. Mower, Admin.; Bruce Siket, Parochial Vicar.
Res.: 60 Franklin St., P.O. Box S, Bucksport, 04416-1219. Tel: 207-469-3322; Fax: 207-469-3375.
Office: 231 Main St., 04605-1613. Tel: 207-667-2342; Fax: 207-667-2043. Email: stellamaris@roadrunner.com.
Worship Sites:—
Our Lady of Hope Church—137 Perkins St., Castine, 04421.
St. Mary Star of the Sea—8 Granite St., Stonington, 04681.
St. Vincent de Paul—64 Franklin St., Bucksport, 04416.
Catechesis/Religious Program—Students 41.
FAIRFIELD, SOMERSET CO., IMMACULATE HEART OF MARY (1871) Merged See Corpus Christi Parish, Waterville.
FALMOUTH, CUMBERLAND CO., HOLY MARTYRS (1968) Closed. See Parish of the Holy Eucharist, Yarmouth.
FARMINGTON, FRANKLIN CO., ST. JOSEPH'S (1885) Rev. Thomas Lequin.
Mailing Address: 133 Middle St., 04938-1598. Tel: 207-778-2778; Fax: 207-778-0268. Email: stjoefarm@myfairpoint.net.
Res.: 1 Church St., Jay, 04239-1801. Tel: 207-897-2173.
Catechesis/Religious Program—Claire Andrews, D.R.E. Students 34.
FORT FAIRFIELD, AROOSTOOK CO., ST. DENIS (1894) [CEM 2] Merged See Parish of the Precious Blood, Caribou.
FORT KENT, AROOSTOOK CO.
1—ST. JOHN VIANNEY PARISH (2007) [CEM 10] Rev. James L. Nadeau; Dennis Bouchard, Parish Life Coord.
Office & Res.: 26 E. Main St., 04743-1395. Tel: 207-834-5656; Fax: 207-834-7461. Email: stlouis@myfairpoint.net.
Churches:—
St. Mary Church—3443 Aroostock Rd., Eagle Lake, 04739.
St. Louis Church—26 E. Main St., 04743.
St. Charles Church—912 Main St., St. Francis, 04774.
St. Joseph Church—7 Church St., Wallagrass, 04781.
Catechesis/Religious Program—Lisa Charette, D.R.E. K-6; Betsy Nadeau, D.R.E. Jr. High 7-8; Carolyn Bouchard, Youth Min. 9-12. Students 408.
2—ST. LOUIS (1870) [CEM 3] Merged See St. John Vianney Parish, Fort Kent.
FRENCHVILLE, AROOSTOOK CO., ST. LUCE'S (1843) [CEM] Merged See Our Lady of the Valley, St. Agatha.
GARDINER, KENNEBEC CO., ST. JOSEPH'S (1863) [CEM] Merged See St. Michael Parish, Augusta.
GORHAM, CUMBERLAND CO., ST. ANNE (1967) Rev. Joseph J. Koury, Admin.
Mailing Address: 299 Main St., 04038. Tel: 207-839-4857; Fax: 207-839-3082. Email: stannegorham@portlanddiocese.org. Web: www.stannegorham.com.
Catechesis/Religious Program—Tel: 207-839-3082. Sr. Jackie Moreau, R.S.M., D.R.E. Students 120.
Mission—Our Lady of Sebago Rt. 114, East Sebago, Cumberland Co.
GRAND ISLE, AROOSTOOK CO., ST. GERARD-MT. CARMEL (1930) [CEM] Merged See Notre Dame du Mont Carmel Parish, Madawaska.
GRAY, CUMBERLAND CO., ST. GREGORY (1967) Closed. See Parish of the Holy Eucharist, Yarmouth.
GREENVILLE, PISCATAQUIS CO., HOLY FAMILY (1916) [CEM] Very Rev. Richard C. Malo.
Office, Mailing & Res. Address: 145 Pritham Ave., P.O. Box 457, 04441-0457. Tel: 207-695-2262.
Catechesis/Religious Program—Tel: 207-695-2009. Lucy Fay, D.R.E. Students 2.
Mission—St. Joseph's [CEM] Rockwood, Somerset Co.
HALLOWELL, KENNEBEC CO., SACRED HEART (1878) Rev. George W. Hickey.
Res.: 12 Summer St., 04347-1121. Tel: 207-623-3424; Fax: 207-623-3424.
Catechesis/Religious Program—Parish Hall, 5 Summer St., 04347-1121. Tel: 207-623-3807. Karen Jones, D.R.E.; Terri Trott, Youth Min. Students 40.
HAMLIN, AROOSTOOK CO., ST. JOSEPH (1920) [CEM] Merged See Saint Peter Chanel Parish, Van Buren.
HAMPDEN, PENOBSCOT CO., ST. MATTHEW (1968) Merged See Saint Paul the Apostle Parish, Bangor.
HOULTON, AROOSTOOK CO., ST. MARY OF THE VISITATION (1839) [CEM] Rev. David R. Raymond; Deacons Albert Burleigh; Ronald Ouellette.
Res.: 112 Military St., 04730-2507. Tel: 207-532-2871; Fax: 207-532-4401. Email: maryagnespaul@portlanddiocese.org.
Catechesis/Religious Program—Tel: 207-532-0953. Students 101.
HOWLAND, PENOBSCOT CO., ST. LEO THE GREAT (1945) [CEM] Revs. Roger Cyr, O.M.I.; James MacGee, O.M.I., Parochial Vicar.
Mailing Address: P.O. Box 329, 04448-0329. Tel: 207-732-3495.
Rectory—18 River Rd., 04448.
Catechesis/Religious Program—Tel: 207-732-3495. Students 17.
INDIAN TOWNSHIP, WASHINGTON CO., ST. ANN (1929), (Native American), Merged See Blessed Kateri Tekakwitha Parish, Calais.
ISLAND FALLS, AROOSTOOK CO., ST. AGNES (1920) [CEM] Rev. David R. Raymond; Deacons Albert Burleigh; Ronald Ouellette.
Office & Mailing Address: 112 Military St., Houlton, 04730. Tel: 207-532-2871; Fax: 207-532-4401. Email: maryagnespaul@portlanddiocese.org.
Church: Sewall St., 04747. Tel: 207-463-2210.
Catechesis/Religious Program—Tel: 207-528-2737. Students 6.
Mission—St. Paul 34 Katahdin St., Patten, Penobscot Co. 04765.
JACKMAN, SOMERSET CO., ST. ANTHONY (1892) [CEM] Very Rev. Richard C. Malo.
Mailing Address: P.O. Box 338, 04945-0338.
Res.: 145 Pritham Ave., Greenville, 04441. Tel: 207-695-2262.
Church: 336 Main St., 04945-5213. Tel: 207-668-2881.
Catechesis/Religious Program—Students 5.
JAY, FRANKLIN CO., ST. ROSE OF LIMA (1894) [CEM] Rev. Thomas Lequin.
Office, Mailing Address & Res.: One Church St., 04239-1801. Tel: 207-897-2173; Fax: 207-897-2478. Email: saintrose@myfairpoint.net.
Catechesis/Religious Program—Tel: 207-897-2173. Students 81.
KENNEBUNK, YORK CO., ST. MARTHA'S (1909) Merged See Holy Spirit Parish, Wells.
KITTERY, YORK CO.
1—PARISH OF THE ASCENSION OF THE LORD Very Rev. John R. Skehan; Rev. Joseph W. Cahill, Parochial Vicar; Deacon Roger M. Normand, Pastoral Assoc.
Office & Rectory: 6 Whipple Rd., 03904-1758. Fax: 207-439-0442.
Worship Sites:—
Our Lady of Peace Church—, (Saw Mill Hill, Berwick, ME).
St. Christopher-by-the-Sea Church—1 Lilac Ln., York, 03909-1020.
St. Raphael's Church—6 Whipple Rd., 03904-1758.
Star of the Sea Church—, 13 Church St., Freeport, York Beach, ME (seasonal).
Catechesis/Religious Program—Rose Cronin, D.R.E. Students 403.
2—ST. RAPHAEL'S (1916) Closed. See Parish of the Ascension of the Lord, Kittery.
LEWISTON, ANDROSCOGGIN CO.
1—HOLY CROSS (1923) [JC] Merged See Prince of Peace Parish, Lewiston.
2—HOLY FAMILY (1923) Merged See Prince of Peace Parish, Lewiston.
3—ST. JOSEPH'S (1857) [JC] Closed. See Prince of Peace Parish, Lewiston.
4—ST. MARY'S, Closed. For inquiries for parish records contact Prince of Peace Parish, Lewiston.
5—ST. PATRICK'S (1887) [CEM] Closed. See Prince of Peace Parish, Lewiston.
6—SS. PETER AND PAUL BASILICA (1870) Merged See Prince of Peace Parish, Lewiston.
7—PRINCE OF PEACE PARISH (2009) [CEM] Rev. Msgr. Marc B. Caron; Rev. Nathan D. March, Parochial Vicar; Bro. Irenee Richard, O.P.; Patricia Gavula, Pastoral Coord.; Gil La Pointe, Business Mgr.
Mailing Address: P.O. Box 1540, 04241-1540. In Res., Revs. Paul M. Pare (Retired); Maurice N. Morin (Retired).
Catholic Center—16 Ste. Croix St., P.O. Box 1540, 04241-1540. Tel: 207-777-1200; Fax: 207-786-9223.
Res.: 607 Sabattus St., 04240-4193.
Churches:—
Basilica of Ss. Peter & Paul—27 Bartlett St., 04240.
Holy Cross Church—1080 Lisbon St., 04240.
Holy Family Church—607 Sabattus St., 04240.
See St. Dominic Academy, Auburn under High Schools, Regional located in the Institution section.
Catechesis/Religious Program—Donald Smith, Dir. Faith Formation. Students 175.
LIMERICK, YORK CO., ST. MATTHEW (1921) Rev. Albert B. Colpitts, Admin.; Deacon Paul Lissandrello.
Res.: 19 Dora Ln., 04048-3527. Tel: 207-793-2244; Fax: 207-793-2191. Email: stmatthew19@roadrunner.com. Web: www.stmatthewlimerick.org.
Catechesis/Religious Program—Students 145.
LIMESTONE, AROOSTOOK CO., ST. LOUIS, Merged See Parish of the Precious Blood, Caribou.
LINCOLN, PENOBSCOT CO., ST. MARY (1902) Revs. Roger Cyr, O.M.I.; Myles Cyr, O.M.I., Parochial Vicar.
Res.: 164 Main St., P.O. Box 310, 04457-0310. Tel: 207-794-6333; Fax: 207-794-8044.
Catechesis/Religious Program—Students 46.
Mission—St. James Kingman, Penobscot Co.
Mission—Sacred Heart Winn, Penobscot Co.
Mission—St. Ann Danforth, Washington Co. Tel: 207-448-2959; Fax: 207-448-2959.
Mission—Guardian Angel Vanceboro, Washington Co.
LISBON FALLS, ANDROSCOGGIN CO.
1—SS. CYRIL AND METHODIUS, (Slovak), Closed. See Holy Trinity, Lisbon Falls.
2—HOLY TRINITY (1995) [CEM 3] Rev. Lionel G. Chouinard, Admin.
Res.: 7 Highland Ave., 04252-1105.
Church, Office & Mailing: 67 Frost Hill Ave., 04252-1126. Tel: 207-353-2792 (Office); Fax: 207-353-6192. Email: holytrinity@portlanddiocese.org. Web: www.portlanddiocese.org.
Catechesis/Religious Program—Students 71.
LISBON, ANDROSCOGGIN CO., ST. ANNE'S, Closed. See Holy Trinity, Lisbon Falls.
LUBEC, WASHINGTON CO., SACRED HEART (1913) Merged See Saint Peter the Fisherman Parish, Machias.
LYMAN, YORK CO., ST. PHILIP (1981) [JC] Merged See Good Shepherd Parish, Saco.
MACHIAS, WASHINGTON CO.
1—HOLY NAME OF JESUS (1828) Merged See Saint Peter the Fisherman Parish, Machias.
2—SAINT PETER THE FISHERMAN PARISH (2008) Rev. Eugene F. Gaffey; Deacon James J. Gillen, Business Mgr.
Mailing Address: P.O. Box 248, 04654-0248.
Office: 11 Free St., 04654. Tel: 207-255-3731.
Res.: 14 Hamilton St., Lubec, 04652. Tel: 207-733-2214.
Churches:—
Holy Name of Jesus Church—10 Free St., 04654.
Sacred Heart Church—14 Hamilton St., Lubec, 04652.
St. Michael Church—Elm St., Cherryfield, 04622.
Catechesis/Religious Program—Students 12.
MADAWASKA, AROOSTOOK CO.
1—ST. DAVID'S (1872) [CEM] Merged See Notre Dame du Mont Carmel Parish, Madawaska.
2—NOTRE DAME DU MONT CARMEL PARISH (2007) [CEM 4] Revs. Jacques La Pointe, O.F.M., Admin.; David P. Cote, Parochial Vicar; Deacon Donald R. Clavette; Roger Lagasse, Business Mgr.
Mailing Address: P.O. Box 128, 04756-0128.
Office: 337 Thomas St., 04756. Tel: 207-728-7531; Fax: 207-728-4217.
Res.: 774 Main St., 04756. Tel: 207-728-3366.
Churches:—
St. Gerard-Mt. Carmel Church—361 Main St., Grand Isle, 04746.
St. Thomas Aquinas Church—337 Thomas St., 04756.
St. David Church—774 Main St., 04756. Tel: 207-728-6472.
Catechesis/Religious Program—Tel: 207-728-7135. Ann Marie Clavette, D.R.E. Students 182.
3—ST. THOMAS AQUINAS (1929) [CEM] Merged See Notre Dame du Mont Carmel Parish, Madawaska.
MADISON, SOMERSET CO., ST. SEBASTIAN (1907) [CEM] Merged See Christ the King Parish, Skowhegan.
MARS HILL, AROOSTOOK CO., ST. JOSEPH (1927) Merged See Parish of Precious Blood, Caribou.
MECHANIC FALLS, ANDROSCOGGIN CO., OUR LADY OF RANSOM (1931) Merged See Blessed Teresa of Calcutta Parish, Norway.

MEXICO, OXFORD CO., ST. THERESA (1926) [JC] Merged See Parish of the Holy Savior, Rumford.

MILLINOCKET, PENOBSCOT CO., ST. MARTIN OF TOURS (1899) Merged See Christ the Divine Mercy Parish, East Millinocket.

MILO, PISCATAQUIS CO., ST. FRANCIS XAVIER (1929) Merged See Our Lady of the Snows Parish, Dexter.

NEWCASTLE, LINCOLN CO., ST. PATRICK (1796) [CEM] Merged See All Saints Parish, Brunswick.

NORTH VASSALBORO, KENNEBEC CO., ST. BRIDGET'S (1911) Merged See Corpus Christi Parish, Waterville.

NORTHEAST HARBOR, HANCOCK CO., ST. IGNATIUS (1929) Closed. See Parish of the Transfiguration, Bar Harbor.

NORWAY, OXFORD CO.

1—BLESSED TERESA OF CALCUTTA PARISH (2008) Revs. Richard C. McLaughlin; Robert L. Lupo, Parochial Vicar.
Mailing Address, Office & Res.: 32 Paris St., 04268. Tel: 207-743-2606; Fax: 207-743-6601.
Churches:—
Our Lady of Ransom Church—117 Elm St., Mechanic Falls, 04256.
St. Catherine of Sienna Church—32 Paris St., 04268.
St. Mary Church—276 King St., Oxford, 04270.
Catechesis/Religious Program—Sandra Tardif, D.R.E. Students 61.

2—ST. CATHERINE OF SIENNA (1914) Merged See Blessed Teresa of Calcutta Parish, Norway.

OAKLAND, KENNEBEC CO., ST. THERESA (1963) Merged See Corpus Christi Parish, Waterville.

OLD ORCHARD BEACH, YORK CO., ST. MARGARET'S (1926) Merged See Good Shepherd Parish, Saco.

OLD TOWN, PENOBSCOT CO.

1—ST. ANN CHURCH, INDIAN ISLAND (1688), (Native American), Merged See Parish of the Resurrection of the Lord, Old Town.

2—HOLY FAMILY (1992) [JC] Merged See Parish of the Resurrection of the Lord, Old Town.

3—ST. JOSEPH'S, Closed. All records at Parish of the Resurrection of the Lord, Old Town.

4—ST. MARY'S, Closed. All records at Parish of the Resurrection of the Lord, Old Town.

5—PARISH OF THE RESURRECTION OF THE LORD (2009) Rev. Wilfred P. Labbe; Linda Lawrence, Business Mgr.
Office & Res.: 429 Main St., 04468-1718. Tel: 207-827-4000; Fax: 207-827-2113.
Churches:—
St. Ann Church—84 Main St., Bradley, 04411.
St. Ann Church—6 Down St., Indian Island, 04468.
Holy Family Church—429 Main St., 04468.
Our Lady of Wisdom Newman Center Chapel—83 College Ave., Orono, 04473. Tel: 207-866-2155; Fax: 207-866-4543.
Catechesis/Religious Program—Tel: 207-827-2377. Students 100.

OQUOSSOC, FRANKLIN CO., OUR LADY OF THE LAKES (1927) Rev. Paul A. Plante.
Mailing Address: P.O. Box 333, 04964-0333.
Res.: 43 Rangeley Ave., 04964-0333. Tel: 207-864-3795.
Catechesis/Religious Program—
Mission—St. Luke Rangeley, Franklin Co.
Mission—St. John Stratton, Franklin Co.
Mission—Richard H. Bell Memorial Chapel Sugarloaf U.S.A., Franklin Co.

ORONO, PENOBSCOT CO.

1—ST. MARY'S (1888) [JC] Closed. See Parish of the Resurrection of the Lord, Old Town.

2—OUR LADY OF WISDOM PERSONAL CAMPUS PARISH (1946) Merged See Parish of the Resurrection of the Lord, Old Town.

PERRY, WASHINGTON CO., ST. ANN (Pleasant Point) (1907), (Native American), Merged See Blessed Kateri Tekakwitha Parish, Calais.

PITTSFIELD, SOMERSET CO., ST. AGNES (1909) Revs. Kent R. Ouellette, Admin.; Paul G. Murray, Parochial Vicar; Jane Young, Pastoral Coord.
P.O. Box 193, Dexter, 04930-0193.
Res.: 45 High St., Dover Foxcroft, 04426. Tel: 207-564-2612. Email: stagnespittsfield@portlanddiocese.org. Web: www.ourladyofthesnowsme.org.
Office: 60 Free St., Dexter, 04930. Tel: 207-924-7104; Fax: 207-924-7993.
Church: 238 Detroit St., 04967.
Catechesis/Religious Program—Students 36.

PRESQUE ISLE, AROOSTOOK CO., NATIVITY OF B.V.M. (1895) [CEM 2] Merged See Parish of the Precious Blood, Caribou.

RICHMOND, SAGADAHOC CO., ST. AMBROSE (1866) Merged See All Saints Parish, Bath.

ROCKLAND, KNOX CO., ST. BERNARD'S (1857) [CEM 2] Merged See Saint Brendan the Navigator Parish, Camden.

RUMFORD, OXFORD CO.

1—ST. ATHANASIUS-ST. JOHN (1906) [JC] Merged See Parish of the Holy Savior, Rumford.

2—PARISH OF THE HOLY SAVIOR (2008) [CEM] Very Rev. Philip A. Tracy; Elaine McKenna, Business Mgr.
Office: 126 Maine Ave., 04276-2259. Tel: 207-364-4556; Fax: 207-364-2686.
Res.: 7 Brown St., Mexico, 04257. Tel: 207-364-2753.
Churches:—
St. Athanasius & St. John Church—126 Maine Ave., 04276.
Our Lady of the Snows Church—32 Paris Rd., Bethel, 04217. Tel: 207-824-2933.
School—(Grades PreK-8), 115 Maine Ave., 04276-2208. Tel: 207-364-2528. Barbara Pelletier, Prin. Lay Teachers 6; Students 48.
Catechesis/Religious Program—Laura Koch, P.C.L. Students 50.

ST. AGATHA, AROOSTOOK CO.

1—ST. AGATHA'S (1889) Merged See Our Lady of the Valley, St. Agatha.

2—OUR LADY OF THE VALLEY (2006) [CEM 3], Worships at St. Luce Church, Frenchville, St. Agatha Church, St. Agatha & St. Joseph Church, Sinclair. Rev. L. Philip Cyr; Sharon Ouellette, Business Mgr.
Mailing Address: P.O. Box 10, 04772-6161.
Res.: 379 Main St., 04772-6161. Tel: 207-543-7447. Email: stajl@ainop.com.
Catechesis/Religious Program—Tel: 207-543-7366; Fax: 207-543-6193. Janice Young, D.R.E. Students 128.
Mission—St. Michael's Chapel [CEM 2] Birch Point Rd., Madawaska, Aroostook Co. 04756.

ST. FRANCIS, AROOSTOOK CO., ST. CHARLES (1894) [CEM 4] Merged See St. John Vianney Parish, Fort Kent.

ST. JOHN, AROOSTOOK CO., ST. JOHN, Merged See St. John Vianney Parish, Fort Kent.

SABATTUS, ANDROSCOGGIN CO., OUR LADY OF THE ROSARY (1975) Rev. Lionel G. Chouinard, Admin.
Office: 131 High St., 04280-4250. Tel: 207-375-6951; Fax: 207-375-4135. Email: olrparish@portlanddiocese.org.
Catechesis/Religious Program—Tel: 207-375-6581. Students 9.
Mission—St. Francis Greene, Androscoggin Co.

SACO, YORK CO.

1—GOOD SHEPHERD PARISH (2008) [CEM 2] Rev. Msgr. Rene T. Mathieu; Revs. Pichaimuthu Antonydass, H.G.N., Parochial Vicar; Daniel Baillargeon, Parochial Vicar; Elizabeth Williams, Pastoral Coord.; Deacons Kevin N. Jacques; Robert M. Parenteau; David Gadbois, Business Mgr.
Office: 271 Main St., 04072-1510. Tel: 207-282-3321; Fax: 207-284-2274. Email: goodshepherd@portlanddiocese.org. Web: www.goodshepherdparish.us.
Res.: 43 Center St., Biddeford, 04005.
Churches:—
St. Brendan Church—Lester B. Orcutt Blvd., Biddeford, 04005. (Summers Only)
St. Joseph's Church—178 Elm St., Biddeford, 04005.
Most Holy Trinity Church—271 Main St., 04072.
St. Margaret Church—6 Saco Ave., Old Orchard Beach, 04064.
St. Philip Church—404 Goodwins Mills Rd., Alfred, 04002.
School—St. James School, (Grades PreK-8), 25 Graham St., Biddeford, 04005-3297. Tel: 207-282-4084; Fax: 207-286-3693. Ms. Patricia Berthiaume, Prin.; Alice Souza, Librarian. Lay Teachers 16; Students 230.
Catechesis/Religious Program—Students 265.

2—MOST HOLY TRINITY (1916) Merged See Good Shepherd Parish, Saco.

3—NOTRE DAME DE LOURDES (1929) [JC] Closed. See Good Shepherd Parish, Saco.

SANFORD, YORK CO.

1—HOLY FAMILY (1923) [JC] Merged See Saint Therese of Lisieux Parish, Sanford.

2—ST. IGNATIUS MARTYR (1892) [CEM] Closed. See Saint Therese of Lisieux Parish, Sanford.

3—SAINT THERESE OF LISIEUX PARISH (2007) [CEM 2] Rev. Robert D. Lariviere, Admin.; Gerald Coutu, Pastoral Assoc.
Churches:—
Holy Family Church—66 North Ave., 04073.
Notre Dame Church—10 Payne St., Springvale, 04083.
Office: *Pastoral Center*, 66 North Ave., 04073-2997. Tel: 207-324-2420; 207-324-6040; Fax: 207-324-6630.
Res.: 10 Payne St., Springvale, 04083-1312. Tel: 207-324-6041.
School—St. Thomas Consolidated School, (Grades PreK-6) Tel: 207-324-5832; Fax: 207-324-2549. Web: www.saintthomassanford.org. Mrs. Donna Jacques, Prin. Lay Teachers 13; Students 140.
Catechesis/Religious Program—Shelly Carpenter, D.R.E. Students 111.

SCARBOROUGH, CUMBERLAND CO., ST. MAXIMILIAN KOLBE (1988) Rev. Msgrs. Michael J. Henchal; Paul F. Stefanko, Parochial Vicar.
Mailing Address: P.O. Box 57, 04070-0057.
Church, Res. & Parish Offices: 150 Black Point Rd., 04070-9349. Tel: 207-883-0334; Fax: 207-883-4246. Email: stmax@maine.rr.com. Web: www.saintmax.com.
Catechesis/Religious Program—Tel: 207-883-1742. Email: stmaxre@maine.rr.com. Kathy Sparda, D.R.E. Students 391.

SINCLAIR, AROOSTOOK CO., ST. JOSEPH (1936) [CEM] Merged See Our Lady of the Valley, St. Agatha.

SKOWHEGAN, SOMERSET CO.

1—CHRIST THE KING PARISH (2007) [CEM 2] Rev. John C. Mazzei, Admin.
P.O. Box 369, 04976-0369.
Churches:—
St. Peter Church—Owens St., Bingham, 04920. Tel: 207-672-3912.
St. Sebastian Church—161 Main St., Madison, 04950. Tel: 207-696-3203.
Notre Dame Church—273 Water St., 04976.
Office & Res.: 273 Water St., 04976. Tel: 207-474-2039; Fax: 207-474-2039.
Catechesis/Religious Program—Students 56.

2—NOTRE DAME DE LOURDES (1881) [CEM] Merged See Christ the King Parish, Skowhegan.

SOUTH BERWICK, YORK CO., ST. MICHAEL (1886) [CEM] Merged See Parish of the Ascension of the Lord, Kittery.

SOUTH PORTLAND, CUMBERLAND CO.

1—CHURCH OF THE HOLY CROSS (1913) Rev. Msgrs. Michael J. Henchal; Paul F. Stefanko, Parochial Vicar; Thomas Sheehan, Business Mgr.
124 Cottage Rd., 04116-3716.
Parish Office—29 Aspen Ave., 04106-5328. Tel: 207-772-7489; Fax: 207-772-7480. Web: www.hcsj.org.
Res.: 150A Blackpoint Rd., Scarborough, 04074. Tel: 207-883-0334.
School—(Grades PreK-8), 436 Broadway, 04106-2996. Tel: 207-799-6661; Fax: 207-799-8345. Web: www.holycrossme.com. Sr. Theresa Rand, R.S.M., Prin.; Jenny Hall, Librarian. Sisters of Mercy 1; Lay Teachers 16; Students 163.
Catechesis/Religious Program—Tel: 207-773-8710; Fax: 207-772-7480. Theresa Cloutier, D.R.E. Joint Program with St. John the Evangelist, South Portland. Students 87.

2—ST. JOHN THE EVANGELIST (1940) Rev. Msgrs. Michael J. Henchal; Paul F. Stefanko, Parochial Vicar; Thomas Sheehan, Business Mgr.
Office: 29 Aspen Ave., 04106-5328. Tel: 207-772-7489; Fax: 207-772-7480. Web: www.hcsj.org.
Church: 611 Main St., 04106.
Catechesis/Religious Program—Joint Program with Holy Cross, South Portland., Tel: 207-773-8710; Fax: 207-772-7480.

SPRINGVALE, YORK CO., NOTRE DAME (1887) [CEM] Merged See Saint Therese of Lisieux Parish, Sanford.

STOCKHOLM, AROOSTOOK CO., ST. THERESE (1926) Merged See Parish of the Precious Blood, Caribou.

STONINGTON, HANCOCK CO., ST. MARY STAR OF THE SEA (1931) Merged See Stella Maris Parish, Ellsworth.

VAN BUREN, AROOSTOOK CO.

1—ST. BRUNO - ST. REMI (1991) [CEM] Merged See Saint Peter Chanel Parish, Van Buren.

2—SAINT PETER CHANEL PARISH (2007) [CEM 2] Revs. Jacques La Pointe, O.F.M., Admin.; David P. Cote, Parochial Vicar; Roger Lagasse, Business Mgr.
Office: 174 Main St., 04785-1237. Tel: 207-868-2718.
Churches:—
St. Joseph Church—1779 Hamlin Rd., Hamlin, 04785.
St. Bruno-St. Remi Church—174 Main St., 04785.
Catechesis/Religious Program—Students 165.

3—ST. REMI (1923) Closed. See listing for Saint Peter Chanel Parish, Van Buren.

WALLAGRASS, AROOSTOOK CO., ST. JOSEPH'S (1890) [CEM 3] Merged See St. John Vianney Parish, Fort Kent.

WATERVILLE, KENNEBEC CO.

1—CORPUS CHRISTI PARISH (2007) [CEM] Very Rev. Joseph E. Daniels; Rev. John "Jack" Dickinson, Parochial Vicar; Kim Suttie, Pastoral Coord.; Doris Smith, Business Mgr.
Office: 70 Pleasant St., 04901-5405. Tel: 207-872-2281; Fax: 207-877-0675. Web: www.corpuschristimaine.org.
Res.: 72 Pleasant St., 04901.
Churches:—
Immaculate Heart of Mary—21 High St., Fairfield, 04937.
St. Bridget Church—Main St., North Vassalboro, 04962.
Saint Theresa Church—35 Church St., Oakland, 04963.
Notre Dame Church—112 Silver St., 04901.
Sacred Heart Church—72 Pleasant St., 04901.
St. John Church—26 Monument St., Winslow, 04901.

St. Helena—Belgrade Lakes, 04918. (Summers only)
School—St. John Regional Catholic School, (Grades PreK-6), 15 S. Garand St., Winslow, 04901. Tel: 207-872-7115; Fax: 207-872-2500. Ms. Claudette Massey, Prin.; Doreen White, Librarian. Lay Teachers 12; Students 135.
Catechesis/Religious Program—Tel: 207-872-2373. Students 206.
2—NOTRE DAME, Merged See Corpus Christi Parish, Waterville.
3—PARISH OF THE HOLY SPIRIT (1996) [JC] Merged See Corpus Christi Parish, Waterville.
4—SACRED HEART, Merged See Corpus Christi Parish, Waterville.
WELLS, YORK CO.
1—HOLY SPIRIT PARISH (2008) Rev. Thomas M. Murphy, Admin.; Deacon Darrell Blackwell. In Res., Rev. Brendan G. Harnett.
Office & Res.: 236 Eldridge Rd., 04090-4050. Tel: 207-646-5605; Fax: 207-646-9437.
Churches:—
St. Martha Church—30 Portland Rd., Kennebunk, 04043-6631. Tel: 207-985-6252; Fax: 207-985-7740.
St. Mary Church—236 Eldridge Rd., 04090-4050.
All Saints Church—, (summers only), 45 School St., Ogunquit, 03907.
Catechesis/Religious Program—Mrs. Rosanne Smith, D.R.E. Students 272.
2—ST. MARY (1970) Merged See Holy Spirit Parish, Wells.
WESTBROOK, CUMBERLAND CO.
1—ST. ANTHONY OF PADUA PARISH (2005) [CEM] Revs. Joseph J. Koury, Admin.; Reginald R. Brissette, Senior Priest.
Res., Office & Mailing Address: 63 Dana Ct., 04092-2912. Tel: 207-857-0490; Fax: 207-857-0494. Email: stanthonyparish@fairpoint.net. Web: www.stanthonysparish.org.
Catechesis/Religious Program—Students 101.
2—ST. EDMUND (Prides Corner) (1975) Closed. See St. Anthony of Padua, Westbrook.
3—ST. HYACINTH (1892) [CEM] Merged See St. Anthony of Padua, Westbrook.
4—ST. MARY'S (1920) [JC] Closed. See St. Anthony of Padua, Westbrook.
WHITEFIELD, LINCOLN CO., ST. DENIS (1818) [CEM] Merged See St. Michael Parish, Augusta.
WILTON, FRANKLIN CO., ST. MARY, Closed. All records at St. Joseph, Farmington.
WINDHAM, CUMBERLAND CO., OUR LADY OF PERPETUAL HELP (1974) Revs. Joseph J. Koury, Admin.; Reginald R. Brissette, Senior Priest; Paul H. Dumais, Parochial Vicar; Deacon Frank Chambers.
Res.: 919 Roosevelt Tr., 04062-5641. Tel: 207-892-8288; Fax: 207-893-1072. Web: www.ourlady.com.
Catechesis/Religious Program—Students 123.
Mission—St. Raymond Chapel 584 Webbs Mill Rd., Raymond, Cumberland Co. 04071. Tel: 207-892-8288.
WINSLOW, KENNEBEC CO., ST. JOHN THE BAPTIST (1926) [JC] Merged See Corpus Christi Parish, Waterville.
WINTERPORT, WALDO CO., ST. GABRIEL (1850) Merged See Saint Paul the Apostle Parish, Bangor.
WINTHROP, KENNEBEC CO., ST. FRANCIS XAVIER (1910) [JC] Merged See St. Michael Parish, Augusta.
YARMOUTH, CUMBERLAND CO.
1—PARISH OF THE HOLY EUCHARIST Rev. Msgr. J. Joseph Ford; Rev. Peter Kaseta, O.F.M.Cap., Parochial Vicar; Deacon Dennis J. Popadak.
Mailing Address: 326 Main St., 04096-7933. In Res., Rev. John McHugh, O.F.M.Cap.
Office & Rectory: 266 Foreside Rd., Falmouth, 04105. Tel: 207-847-6890; Fax: 207-846-6003.
Res. of Capuchins: 24 N. Raymond Rd., Gray, 04039-7724.
Worship Sites:—
Holy Martyrs of North America Church—266 Foreside Rd., Falmouth, 04105.
Sacred Heart Church—
St. Gregory Church—
St. Jude Church—134 Main St., Freeport, 04034.
Catechesis/Religious Program—Ann Peacock, D.R.E.; Debra Gagnon, D.R.E. Students 403.
2—SACRED HEART (1876) [CEM] Closed. See Parish of the Holy Eucharist, Yamouth.
YORK HARBOR, YORK CO., ST. CHRISTOPHER-BY-THE-SEA (1947) Closed. See Parish of the Ascension of the Lord, Kittery.

Chaplains of Public Institutions

PORTLAND. *St. Joseph's Manor*, Tel: 207-797-0600. Rev. Joseph R. McKenna (Retired), Mrs. Agnes LaStoria, Pastoral Care.
Maine Medical Center, Tel: 207-871-0111. Revs. Gregory P. Dube, Paul R. Marquis, Chap.
Mercy Hospital, Tel: 207-879-3358. Rev. Robert V. Paskey, S.J., Sr. Patricia Mooney, R.S.M., Pastoral Care.
AUGUSTA. *Augusta Mental Health Institute*, Tel: 207-289-7334. Served by the staff of St. Michael Parish, Augusta.
Maine General Medical Center, Tel: 207-626-1000. Served by the staff of St. Michael Parish, Augusta.
Togus VA Medical Center, Togus. Tel: 207-623-8411, Ext. 5176. Rev. Raymond R. Lagace, O.F.M.
BANGOR. *Eastern Maine Medical Center*, Tel: 207-943-7000. Rev. Apolinary Kavishe, A.J. Taylor Hospital, Bangor Convalescent Center,
St. Joseph's Hospital, Tel: 207-262-1798. Rev. Roland P. Nadeau, Chap., Judith Young, Dir., Pastoral Care.
BIDDEFORD. *Southern Maine Medical Center*, Tel: 207-283-3663. Served by Good Shepherd Parish, Biddleford.
LEWISTON. *Central Maine Medical Center*, Tel: 207-795-0111. Mr. Michael B. Tyne, Pastoral Care, Rev. Donald Gagne, S.M.
St. Mary's Regional Medical Center. Rev. D. Joseph Manship, Sr. Suzanne Beaudoin, S.S.Ch.
Campus Ave., P.O. Box 291, 04243-0291. Tel: 207-777-8520. Sr. Madeline Normand, P.M., Mr. Kenneth Rancort.
SOUTH PORTLAND. *Maine Youth Center*. Vacant.
WARREN. *Maine State Prison*, Thomaston. Tel: 207-828-4921. Deacon Frederick J. Harrigan.
Super Maximum Facility & Minimum Facility, Tel: 207-273-5300. Deacon Frederick J. Harrigan.
WATERVILLE. *Mid-Maine Medical Center*, Tel: 207-872-1000. Margaret Crowell.

Special or Other Diocesan Assignment:
Rev. Msgr.—
Dubois, Andrew, V.G., P.O. Box 11559, 04104-7559. Tel: 207-773-6471. Res.: St. Peter Rectory, 72 Federal St., 04101.
Revs.—
Bouchard, Robert P., P.O. Box 11559, 04104-7559.
Cote, Paul E., P.O. Box 11559, 04104-7559.
Gendreau, Claude R., P.O. Box 11559, 04104-7559.
Gendreau, Michael P., P.O. Box 11559, 04104-7559.
Greenleaf, Daniel P., Theological College, 401 Michigan Ave., N.E., Washington, DC 20017-1518.
LaBree, Paul, P.O. Box 11559, 04104-7559.
Michaud, James L., P.O. Box 5296, Ellsworth, 04605-5296.
Morin, Eddy, P.O. Box 129, Saint David, 04773-0129.
Nolette, Mark P., 205 Windsor Neck Rd., Windsor, 04363-3202. Tel: 207-236-4785
Richard, Normand P., P.O. Box 11559, 04104-7559. Tel: 207-773-6471
Vaillancourt, Robert C., Res.: 16 Ste. Croix St., Lewiston, 04240.

Retired:
Rev. Msgrs.—
Begin, Raymond F., S.T.L., J.C.D., Winter, 4951 Summer Tree Rd., Venice, FL 34293-4254. Tel: 941-493-6869. Summer, 19 Northwood Dr., Windham, 04062-5306. Tel: 207-892-0771
Gleason, Paul D., Mount Carmel Nursing Home, 235 Myrtle St., Manchester, NH 03104-4314. Tel: 307-627-3811
Goudreau, Joseph L., 2516 1st Rd. S., Arlington, VA 22204-1921. Tel: 703-521-0918
Lavoie, Robert G., Mt. St. Joseph Home, 7 Highwood St., #6, 04901-5740. Tel: 207-660-6096
Murphy, Charles M., S.T.D., V.F., P.O. Box 378, Kennebunkport, 04046-0378. Tel: 207-967-3788
Nicknair, Leopold G., Cross Winds Residential Care, 40 Village Rd., Fort Kent, 04743-1031. Tel: 207-834-6105
Tatarczuk, Vincent A., P.O. Box 218, Raymond, 04071-0218. Tel: 207-655-3672
Very Rev.—
Conley, Lawrence J., Cathedral Rectory, 307 Congress St., 04101-3695. Tel: 207-773-7746
Revs.—
Albert, Claude J., 32 Portland Rd., Kennebunk, 04043-6631. Tel: 207-641-3311
Albert, James R., P.O. Box 128, Fort Kent, 04743-0128.
Amato, Antonio, Mallview Terrace, 27A Marston St., Apt. 311, Lewiston, 04240-6171. Tel: 207-795-5095
Andrus, Albin A., St. Patrick Rectory, 1342 Congress St., 04102-2117. Tel: 207-879-0827
Auger, Raymond D., 4675 Appletree Cir., Apt. A, Boynton Beach, FL 33436-1231. Tel: 752-561-0417
Bill, J. Armand, 402A Sandpiper Dr., Fort Pierce, FL 34982-5122. Tel: 561-467-1011
Boisvert, Ralph, P.O. Box 733, Augusta, 04332. Tel: 207-446-1013
Cameron, Hilary J., St. Catherine's Hall, 242 Walton St., Apt. 103, 04103-3381. Tel: 207-899-3329
Caron, Antonin R., 79 Fairlawn Ave., Lewiston, 04240-4132.
Chabot, Roger P., Winter: 2516 Hayes St., #7, Hollywood, FL 33020-3459. Summer: 58 Larry Dr., Monmouth, 04259-6504. Tel: 207-513-6218
Clogan, Paul M., P.O. Box 28428, Austin, TX 78755-8428.
Concannon, Stephen F., Our Lady Miraculous Medal, 289 Lafayette Rd., Hampton, NH 03842-2109. Tel: 603-926-2206
Coughlin, Paul E., P.O. Box 424, Springvale, 04083-0424.
Cyr, L. Chanel, Leisure Gardens, 4 Dewberry Dr., Apt. 5, Presque Isle, 04769-3172. Tel: 207-760-8452
Davis, John P., 68 Webster Ave., Lewiston, 04240-6463. Tel: 207-784-6235
Dumoulin, Marcel L.
Farley, Thomas J., Roncalli Apartments, 144 State St., #203, Augusta, 04330-7467. Tel: 207-446-8114
Feeney, John J., 75 State St., Box 108, 04101-3746. Tel: 207-780-1494
Girouard, Robert J., St. Joseph Manor, 1133 Washington Ave., 04103-3629.
Goudreau, George W., 419 Franklin St., Rumford, 04276-2103. Tel: 207-364-7884
Gower, James M., 73 School St., Bar Harbor, 04609-1618. Tel: 207-288-0906
Irving, Alfred E., 57 C St., Groton, CT 06340. Tel: 207-380-5620
Jacques, Alfred, Summer: 137 W. Front St., Skowhegan, 04976-1165. Tel: 207-858-0362. Winter: 4907 Colonnade Ave., Holiday, FL 34690-5974. Tel: 727-934-5698
Jacques, Donald W., 17 Lorisa Ln., Milford, NH 03055-4108. Tel: 603-672-1981
Knox, James, 31 Clearview Dr., Scarborough, 04074-8319. Tel: 207-883-9652
L'Heureux, Ernest L., 64 Lebonan St., Sanford, 04073-3825. Tel: 207-459-7090
Labarre, Renald D., 31 Beacon Ave., Biddeford, 04005-2917. Tel: 207-615-1378
Lavoie, Rene G., 32 Portland Rd., Kennebunk, 04043-6631. Tel: 207-595-1985
Lebel, Maurice T., 64 Flintlock Village #64, Wells, 04090-5326. Tel: 207-641-8790
Lee, Thomas M.
Leveille, Rudolph J., 65 Juniper St., Bangor, 04401-4163. Tel: 207-942-9715
Levesque, Gerald A., Deering Pavillion, 880 Forest Ave., Apt. 4-17, 04103-4163. Tel: 207-409-5445
Levesque, Sylvio J., 4 Choate Ln., Apt. 215, Hallowell, 04347-1469. Tel: 207-263-9231
MacDonough, Richard, S.S., St. John's Seminary, 5012 Seminary Rd., Camarillo, CA 93012-2500.
Martel, C. James, 163 N. Parish Rd., Turner, 04282-0016. Tel: 207-225-3001
McAllister, Donald, Bishop Gendron Res., Apt. 3, 195 Dover Point Rd., Dover, NH 03820-4693. Tel: 603-742-2612
McKenna, Joseph R., 100 State St., #321, 04101-3729. Tel: 207-775-1084
Moreshead, Harold D., St. Patrick Rectory, 1342 Congress St., 04102-2107. Tel: 207-828-8638
Morin, Maurice N., Holy Family Rectory, 607 Sabattus St., Lewiston, 04240-4193. Tel: 207-782-8928
Morrison, James J., St. Joseph Rehabilitation Center & Residence Unit B, 1133 Washington Ave., 04103-3629. Tel: 207-797-0600
Mulkern, Stephen M., 1258 Washington Ave., 04103-3649. Tel: 207-797-3519
Nadeau, Real J., 3333 N.E. 34th St., Apt. 422, Fort Lauderdale, FL 33308-6932. Tel: 954-309-8269
Nadeau, Richard A., Deering Pavilion, 880 Forest Ave., Apt. 5-08, 04103-4128. Tel: 207-797-4629
Neault, Armand R., 54 Blacksmith Rd., #11, Wells, 04090-5748. Tel: 207-646-6417
Nguyen, Thanh, 115F Birchwood Dr., Apt. F, Bristol, CT 06010-2876. Tel: 860-585-6663
Nicknair, Harold W., (Winter), 5725 80th St. N., Unit #411, St. Petersburg, FL 33709-5836. Tel: 727-545-7876. (Summer), 757 Main St., #22, South Portland, 04106-5425. Tel: 207-828-8835
Ouellette, Richard R., P.O. Box 154, Saint Francis, 04774-0154. Tel: 207-398-4475
Paquet, Hubert J., 46 Wentworth St., Biddeford, 04005-3153. Tel: 207-286-9674
Pare, Paul M., Holy Family Rectory, 607 Sabattus St., Lewiston, 04240-4193. Tel: 207-782-8728
Parent, Royal J.
Pechillo, Arthur C., St. Francis Rectory, 130 Rte. 133, Winthrop, 04364-1356. Tel: 207-623-8823
Picard, Raymond, 8 Lufkin Rd., North Yarmouth, 04097-6045. Tel: 207-809-1049
Piselli, Costanzo J., 67 Village Green Dr., 04901-4444. Tel: 207-873-2961
Poussard, Bertrand R., St. Joseph Rehabilitation Center & Residence, 1133 Washington Ave., Unit D, 04103-3629. Tel: 207-878-5488
Reagan, Robert, P.O. Box 1471, Greenville, 04441-1471. Tel: 207-695-2092
Rice, Richard P., 66 Ward Cir., Brunswick, 04011-9342. Tel: 207-373-1832

Roux, G. Albert, 944 Sabattus St., Lewiston, 04240-3712. Tel: 207-783-3590

Senghas, Richard E., 15 Piper Rd., Apt. J320, Scarborough, 04074-7555. Tel: 207-833-6394

Thibodeau, Clement D., 12 St. Anne Ave., Apt. C-6, Caribou, 04736-6131. Tel: 207-498-2037

Tracy, Philip Michael, 148 Breakwater Dr., #404, South Portland, 04106-1656. Tel: 207-767-6501

Welch, Bernard J., 126 Hildreth Rd, P.O. Box 266, Harpswell, 4079-0266.

INSTITUTIONS LOCATED IN THE DIOCESE

[A] COLLEGES AND UNIVERSITIES

STANDISH. *Saint Joseph's College*, 278 Whites Bridge Rd., 04084-5263. Tel: 207-893-7711; Fax: 207-893-7867. Email: klemanski@sjcme.edu. Web: www.sjcme.edu. Mr. Kenneth Lemanski, Interim Pres.; Dr. Randall Krieg, Vice Pres. for Academic Affairs & Dean of the College; Reis Hagerman, Vice Pres. for Student Life; Deacons John McAuliffe Jr.; Daniel Sheridan; Philip Yauch, Vice Pres. & Chief Fin. Officer; Sr. Kathleen Sullivan, R.S.M., Vice Pres. for Mission Integration. Email: ksullivan@sjcme.edu. Sisters 4; Deacons 2; Lay Professors 138; Graduate Students 1,235; Undergraduate Students 1,015; Undergraduate Students in Distance Education 853; Students 3,103.

Residential College Program Tel: 207-893-6641; Fax: 207-893-7861. Rachelle Davis, Dir. Library Svcs. Full-Time Enrollment 1,244; Part-Time Enrollment 1,859.

[B] HIGH SCHOOLS, REGIONAL

AUBURN. *St. Dominic Academy* (1941) (Grades PreK-12), Grades 7-12: 121 Gracelawn Rd., 04210-0452. Tel: 207-782-6911; Fax: 207-795-6439. Email: Donald.Fournier@PortlandDiocese.org. Web: www.st-dominic.net. Grades Pre-K to 6: 17 Baird St., Lewiston, 04240-5001. Tel: 207-783-9323; Fax: 207-783-9491. Mr. Donald Fournier, Prin.; Joline Giruard, Vice Prin. (Gr. 7-12); Don Bilodeau, Vice Prin. (PreK-6). Sisters 1; Lay Teachers 41; Students 565.

[C] HIGH SCHOOLS, PRIVATE

PORTLAND. *Catherine McAuley High School* (1969) 631 Stevens Ave., 04103-2690. Tel: 207-797-3802; Fax: 207-797-3804. Email: peg.downing@mcauleyhs.org. Margaret Downing, Prin.; Deidre Dupree, Librarian. Sisters of Mercy 1; Lay Teachers 20; Girls 174.

Cheverus High School (1917) 267 Ocean Ave., 04103-5798. Tel: 207-774-6238; Fax: 207-828-0207. Web: www.cheverus.org. Rev. William R. Campbell, S.J., Pres.; John H.R. Mullen, Prin. Faculty resides at St. Ignatius Residence. See separate listing for details. Priests 1; Brothers 1; Lay Teachers 44; Students 510.

[D] ELEMENTARY SCHOOLS, PRIVATE

WATERVILLE. *Mount Merici School* (1911) (Grades N-6), 152 Western Ave., 04901-5215. Tel: 207-873-3773; Fax: 207-873-6377. Email: info@mountmerici.org. Web: www.mountmerici.org. Susan H. Cote, Prin. Lay Teachers 11; Students 166.

[E] CATHOLIC CHARITIES MAINE, INC.

PORTLAND. *Catholic Charities Maine*, P.O. Box 10660, 04104-6060. 307 Congress St., 04101-3695. Tel: 207-781-8550; Fax: 207-781-8560. Web: www.ccmaine.org. Most Rev. Richard Joseph Malone, D.D., S.T.L., Th.D., Pres.; Mr. Stephen P. Letourneau, CEO; Ms. Constance Browning Jones, Human Resources Dir. Tel: 207-781-8550.

St. Elizabeth's Child Development Center, 87 High St., 04101-3811. Tel: 207-871-7444; Fax: 207-871-1178. P.O. Box 10660, 04104-6060.

St. Michael's Center, 1066 Kenduskeag Ave., Bangor, 04401. Tel: 207-941-2855; Fax: 207-941-2835. Email: pvestal@main.org. Web: www.ccmaine.org. P.O. Box 10660, 04104-6060. Paul Vestal Jr., Dir. Functional Family Therapy and Case Management Services. Total Assisted Annually 759.

[F] SPECIAL RESIDENTIAL SERVICES

BIDDEFORD. *St. Andre Home, Inc.*, Admin. Office, 283 Elm St., 04005-3093. Tel: 207-282-3351; Fax: 207-282-8733. Web: www.SaintAndreHome.org. Mr. Peter Fitzpatrick, Exec. Dir. Pregnant and Parenting Young Women, Adoption Services, Infant Foster Care Homes, Emergency Placement; Public Information-Education; Community Outreach Services; Residences in Biddeford, Lewiston, Bangor. Total Assisted Annually 796.

St. Andre Housing, Inc., 39 Sullivan St., 04005. Tel: 207-282-9610. Mr. David Twomey, Contact Person. Tel: 207-773-6471, Ext. 7823; Fax: 207-773-0182. Sponsor: Roman Catholic Diocese of Portland., Purpose: to provide low income housing for the elderly in the Biddeford, Maine area. Total Assisted Annually 35.

P.O. Box 11559, 04104-7559.

LEWISTON. **St. Martin de Porres Residence, Inc.*, Mailing Address: P.O. Box 7227, 04243-7227. 23 Bartlett St., 04243-7227. Tel: 207-786-4690; Fax: 207-786-8866. Email: mdeporres@roadrunner.com. Bro. Irenee Richard, O.P., Exec. Dir. Served 140.

[G] HOMES FOR THE AGED

PORTLAND. *Deering Pavilion*, 880 Forest Ave., 04103. Tel: 207-797-8777; Fax: 207-797-8963. Email: deerpav@maine.rr.com. Web: www.deeringpavilion.com. Helen McGuinness, Exec. Dir. Apartments 200; Residents 220.

St. Joseph's Manor (1975) 1133 Washington Ave., 04103-3629. Tel: 207-797-0600; Fax: 207-797-4168. Web: www.saintjosephsmanor.org. Most Rev. Richard Joseph Malone, D.D., S.T.L., Th.D., Pres. Bed Capacity 165; Served 780; Total Staff 225.

AUGUSTA. *Roncalli Apartments, Inc.*, Mailing Address: P.O. Box 11559, 04104-7559. Tel: 207-773-6471, Ext. 7823; Fax: 207-773-0182. 144 State St., 04330. Tel: 207-512-4248; Fax: 207-512-4250. Mr. David P. Twomey Jr., CPA, Treas. Sponsor: Roman Catholic Diocese of Portland., Purpose: to provide very low and extremely low cost housing for the elderly in the capital city of the state. Units 30; Residents 32.

BANGOR. *St. Xavier's Home*, P.O. Box 11559, 04104-7559. 119 Somerset St., 04401. Tel: 207-942-2108. Mr. David Twomey, Treas. & Contact Person. Tel: 207-773-6471; Fax: 207-773-0182. Sponsor: Roman Catholic Diocese of Portland., Purpose: to provide very low and extremely low cost housing for the elderly in the Bangor, Maine area. Units 19; Residents 18.

BIDDEFORD. *St. Andre Health Care & Facility*, 407 Pool St., 04005-9716. Tel: 207-282-5171; Fax: 207-282-5372. Email: aotis-higgins@standre.org. Web: standre.org. Andrea Otis-Higgins, CEO & Admin. Sponsored by Covenant Health Systems, Inc., Tewksbury, MA. Bed Capacity 96; Total Staff 162; Total Assisted Annually 336.

LEWISTON. **St. Marguerite d'Youville Pavilion*, 102 Campus Ave., 04240-6019. Tel: 207-777-4200; Fax: 207-777-4255. Web: www.stmarysmaine.com. Sr. Suzanne Beaudoin, S.S.Ch., Dir. Chaplaincy; Rev. D. Joseph Manship, Chap.; Elizabeth Lowe, Chap.; Philip Jean, Office Admin. Sponsored by St. Mary's Health System. Bed Capacity 210; Total Staff 388; Total Assisted Annually 744.

St. Mary's Residences (Formerly: Maison Marcotte), 100 Campus Ave., 04240-6040. Tel: 207-786-0062; Fax: 207-777-8570. Web: www.stmarysmaine.com. Sponsored by St. Mary's Health System. Total in Residence 130.

WATERVILLE. *Mt. St. Joseph Holistic Care Community*, 7 Highwood St., 04901-5797. Tel: 207-873-0705; Fax: 207-873-6626. Email: msj@mtsj.org. Web: www.mtsj.org. Sr. Claire Labbee, C.S.J., Pastoral Care; Kerry Sirois, Exec. Dir., 04901. Sisters of St. Joseph of Lyons, C.S.J. Assisted Living 27; Nursing Facility 111; Bed Capacity 138; Total Assisted Annually 140; Total Staff 250. In Res. Rev. Msgr. Robert G. Lavoie (Retired).

Seton Village Inc., P.O. Box 11559, 04104-7559. 1 Carver St., 04901-5739. Tel: 207-873-0178; Fax: 207-873-1233. Most Rev. Richard Joseph Malone, D.D., S.T.L., Th.D., Bishop of Portland, Pres.; Mr. David P. Twomey Jr., CPA, Treas. Tel: 207-773-6471, Ext. 7823; Fax: 207-773-0182; Mr. Harlan Cooper, Admin. Purpose: to provide very low and extremely low cost housing for the elderly in the Waterville, Maine area. Units 140; Guests 148.

[H] GENERAL HOSPITALS

PORTLAND. **Mercy Hospital*, 144 State St., 04101-3776. Tel: 207-879-3000; Fax: 207-879-3429. Web: www.mercyhospital.org. Ms. Eileen Skinner, Pres. & CEO; Rev. John T. Crabb, S.J., Dir. Pastoral Care; Mr. Michael Gendreau, Vice Pres. Mission Effectiveness. Lay Nurses (RN's and LPN's) 357; Bed Capacity 230; Emergency Visits 28,617; Inpatient Admissions 7,983; Outpatient Visits 293,256; Patients Assisted Annually 91,643; Total Staff 1,340.

BANGOR. *St. Joseph Hospital*, 360 Broadway, 04401-3974. Tel: 207-262-1000; Fax: 207-262-1922. Email: mary.prybylo@sjhhealth.com. Web: www.stjoeshealing.com. Sponsored by Covenant Health Systems. Felician Sisters 2; Lay Nurses 294; Bed Capacity 112; Total Staff 982; Patients Assisted Annually 101,510.

Pastoral Care Dept., 360 Broadway, 04401. Tel: 207-262-1798; Fax: 207-262-1922. Rev. Roland P. Nadeau; Judith Young, Dir. Pastoral Care.

BUCKSPORT. *Bridgewell, Inc.*, Box 836, 04416. Tel: 207-469-7616; Fax: 207-469-7616. Sr. Miriam Devlin, S.M.I.C., Contact Person. Health Care Research & Education.

LEWISTON. *St. Mary's Health System* (Formerly: Sisters of Charity Health System, Inc.), P.O. Box 7291, 04243-7291. Tel: 207-777-8802; 207-777-8546 Lori J. Tame; Fax: 207-777-8800. Web: www.stmarysmaine.com. Lee Myles, Pres. & CEO. Sponsored by Covenant Health Systems, Tewksbury, MA.

Services Include:

St. Mary's WorkMed Tel: 207-753-3080; Fax: 207-753-3088. Occupational Health Program.

St. Mary's Health Steps Tel: 207-777-8898; Fax: 207-777-3499.

St. Mary's Development Tel: 207-777-8863; Fax: 207-755-3380.

St. Mary's Maine Covenant Tel: 207-777-8553; Fax: 207-777-8562.

St. Mary's Take Charge Tel: 207-777-8898; Fax: 207-755-3499. Health screening programs.

**St. Mary's Regional Medical Center* (1880) Campus Ave., P.O. Box 291, 04243-0291. Tel: 207-777-8802; Fax: 207-777-8800. Web: www.stmarysmaine.com. Lee Myles, Pres. & CEO; Sisters Madeleine Normand, P.M., Chap.; Suzanne Beaudoin, S.S.Ch., Dir. & Chaplaincy Svcs.; Rev. D. Joseph Manship, Chap.; Kenneth Rancourt, Chap. Sponsored by St. Mary's Health System. Sisters 2; Nurses 281; LPN's 3; CNA's 110; Bed Capacity 171; Patients Assisted Annually 252,422; Total Staff 1,419.

St. Mary's Lifeline Tel: 207-777-8827; Fax: 207-777-8570. Serving 714.

St. Mary's Nutrition Center of Maine Tel: 207-513-3847; Fax: 207-782-7560. Nutrition services.

Neighborhood Housing Initiative, Inc., P.O. Box 7291, 04243-7291. Tel: 207-777-8802; Fax: 207-777-8800. Web: www.stmarysmaine.com. Lee Myles, Pres. & CEO. Sponsored by St. Mary's Health System.

[I] MONASTERIES AND RESIDENCES OF PRIESTS AND BROTHERS

PORTLAND. *St. Ignatius Residence (The Jesuits of Maine)*, 492 Ocean Ave., 04103-4936. Tel: 207-775-3032; Fax: 207-775-1229. Rev. James F. Lafontaine, S.J., Supr. Jesuit Fathers (New England Prov.). Priests 8.

ALFRED. *Notre Dame Institute*, 133 Shaker Hill Rd., P.O. Box 159, 04002-0159. Email: notredamefic@roadrunner.com. Bros. Jerome Lessard, F.I.C., Prov. Supr. Tel: 207-324-0067; Fax: 207-490-2370; James Lacasse, F.I.C., Supr. Tel: 207-324-6612; Fax: 207-324-9772; Rev. Theodore Letendre, F.I.C., Dir. of Spiritual Ctr. Provincial House of Brothers of Christian Instruction. *Notre Dame Spiritual Center* Tel: 207-324-1017; Fax: 207-324-5044. Rev. Theodore Letendre, F.I.C. Tel: 207-324-1017. Brothers 11.

KENNEBUNK. *St. Anthony's Friary*, 28 Beach Ave., 04043-7628. Tel: 207-967-2011; Fax: 207-967-0423. Email: jonasbac@gmail.com. Web: www.framon.net. Most Rev. Paul A. Baltakis, O.F.M., Retired Bishop; Revs. Placid Barius, O.F.M., Delegate of Province; Gabriel Baltrusaitis, O.F.M.; John J. Bacevicius, O.F.M., Vicar & Pastoral Ministry; Andrew R. Bisson, O.F.M., Pastoral Ministry; Francis Giedgaudas, O.F.M.; Raimundas Bukauskas, O.F.M., Pastoral Ministry & Treasurer; Aurelijus Gricius, O.F.M., Guardian & Pastoral Ministry. Priests 8.

[J] CONVENTS AND RESIDENCES OF SISTERS

PORTLAND. *Frances Warde Convent*, 37 Capisic St., 04102-2203. Tel: 207-772-1140; Fax: 207-772-1873. Sr. Maura Murphy, R.S.M., Facilitator. Sisters 16.

Monastery of the Precious Blood (1934) 166 State St., 04101-3703. Tel: 207-774-0861; Fax: 207-774-3253. Sr. Mary Jo Divney, A.P.B., Supr. Adorers of the Precious Blood 4.

Sisters of Charity, 41 Tamarlane, 04103-4257. Tel: 207-773-8607; Fax: 207-874-6086.

Sisters of Mercy of the Americas, 84 Plymouth St., 04103-2005. Tel: 207-797-6957. Sr. Mary M. Morey, R.S.M., Contact Person. Sisters of Mercy of the Americas 2.

Sisters of Mercy of the Americas-Northeast Community, Life & Ministry Office: 966 Riverside St., 04103-1046. Tel: 207-797-7861; Fax: 207-797-0416. Sr. Maureen Wallace, R.S.M., Life & Ministry Admin.

ACTON. *The Sisters of the Presentation of Mary of Maine, Inc. Presentation Villa*, 246 Rte. 109,

04001. Tel: 603-669-1080. Email: tgagne@presmarynh.org. Web: www.presentationofmary.com. 495 Mammoth Rd., Manchester, NH 03104-5463. Sr. Theresa Gagne, P.M., Treas.

AUBURN. *Companions of Christ*, 503 Park Ave., 04210-8526. Tel: 207-784-5960. Email: elizabeth.platt@portlanddiocese.org. Sr. Elizabeth Platt, C.O.C., Contact Person. Sisters 2.

AUGUSTA. *St. Augustine*, 5 Kendall St., 04330. Tel: 207-622-2494; Fax: 207-261-4074. Sr. Rachel Boucher, P.M., Supr. Sisters of the Presentation of Mary. Sisters 2.

BANGOR. *St. Joseph Convent*, 360 Broadway, 04401-3979. Tel: 207-262-1124; Fax: 207-262-1925. Email: srbarbara@sjhhealth.com. Sr. Barbara Theresa Martis, C.S.S.F., Contact Person. Felician Sisters 6.

BIDDEFORD. *St. Joseph's Convent*, 409 Pool St., 04005. Tel: 207-283-9051; Fax: 207-286-9418. Email: scimpro@gwi.net. Sr. Theresa Therrien, S.C.I.M., Supr. Sisters of the Immaculate Heart of Mary (Good Shepherd) 34.

Marie Fitzbach Convent, 290 Elm St., 04005. Tel: 207-282-2714. Email: fitzbach@gwi.net. Sr. Annette Nadeau, S.C.I.M., Supr. Servants of the Immaculate Heart of Mary (Good Shepherd Sisters) 6.

Marie Joseph Spiritual Center, 10 Evans Rd., 04005. Tel: 207-284-5671; Fax: 207-286-1371. Email: mariejosephcenter@yahoo.com. Web: www.mariejosephspiritual.org. Sr. Gertrude Robitaille, P.M., Supr. Sisters of the Presentation of Mary 10.

Provincial Residence, 409 Pool Rd., 04005. Tel: 207-282-4976; Fax: 207-282-7376. Email: scimpro@gwi.net. Sr. Theresa Therrien, S.C.I.M., Prov. Supr. Servants of the Immaculate Heart of Mary.

CASCO. *Community of the Resurrection A Lataste Community, Inc.*, P.O. Box 284, 04015-0284. Tel: 207-627-7184; Fax: 207-627-7184. Email: comres1@juno.com. Sr. Renata Camenzind, Supr. Total in Residence 6.

LEWISTON. *Dominican Sisters of the Roman Congregation*, Provincial Residence, 123 Dumont Ave., Apt. 1, 04240-6107. Tel: 207-782-3535; Fax: 207-782-0435. Email: moniqueb@megalink.net. Web: www.crsdop.org; www.dominicanroman.us. Sr. Monique Belanger, O.P., Prov. Prioress.

Holy Cross, 201 Webster St., 04240-5546. Tel: 207-782-0263. Sr. Cecile Mondor, P.M., Supr. Sisters of the Presentation of Mary 3.

OLD ORCHARD BEACH. *Sisters of Our Lady of the Holy Rosary, Regional Formation House*, 25 Portland Ave., 04064-2211. Tel: 207-934-0592. Sisters Maureen Bellerose, R.S.R., Regl. Coord.; Carole Jean Lappa, R.S.R., Formation Dir. Sisters 2; Novices 1.

PLEASANT POINT. *St. Ann's Convent*, P.O. Box 126, Perry, 04667-0126. Tel: 207-853-2944. Email: janicemurphy@mainline.net. Sr. Janice Murphy, R.S.M., Pastoral Assoc.

ST. AGATHA. *Our Lady of Wisdom Community*, 40 St. Agatha Housing Dr., 04772-6124. Tel: 207-543-7523; Fax: 207-543-7575. Sr. Candide Corriveau, D.W., Coord.

SABATTUS. *Dominican Sisters*, 61 Lisbon Rd., 04280-4209. Tel: 207-375-6583; Fax: 207-375-2694. Email: Lucille49@myfairpoint.net. Sr. Lucille Fournier, O.P., Prioress. Dominican Sisters of the Roman Congregation 9.

SOUTH PORTLAND. *Our Lady of Mercy Convent* (1991) 265 Cottage Rd., 04106. Tel: 207-767-5804. Email: eboyd@maine.rr.com. Sr. Karen Hopkins, R.S.M., Supr. Gen. Diocesan Sisters of Mercy of Portland 7.

WATERVILLE. *Blessed Sacrament Convent*, 101 Silver St., 04901. Tel: 207-872-7072; Fax: 207-873-2317. Email: servantsinfo@blesacrament.org. Web: www.blesacrament.org. Sr. Josephine Roney, S.S.S., Supr. Servants of the Blessed Sacrament. Sisters 11.

Ursuline Sisters, 1 Saint Angela Way, 04901-4640. Tel: 207-873-3515; Fax: 207-873-4926. Email: laurijm@myfairpoint.net. Sr. Laurianne Michaud, O.S.U., Prioress. Ursuline Sisters 7.

WHITEFIELD. *Little Franciscans of Mary*, 298 Grand Army Rd., 04353-3419. Tel: 207-549-3945. Email: carol.martin@portlanddiocese.org. Sr. Carol Martin, P.F.M., Contact Person. Little Franciscans of Mary 2.

WINSLOW. *Provincialate of the Sisters of St. Joseph*, 93 Halifax St., 04901-6930. Tel: 207-873-4512; Fax: 207-873-1976. Email: gmdube@roadrunner.com. Web: www.csjwinslowmaine.org. Sisters Gilla Dube, C.S.J., Prov. Supr.; Claire Labbee, C.S.J., Asst. Sisters in the Province 29.

[K] HERMITAGES

ELLSWORTH. *John of the Cross Monastery*, 19 Trinity Way, 04605-2800. Tel: 207-664-0026. Sr. Margaret Dorgan, D.C.M. Carmelite Sisters 2.

ST. ALBANS. *Divine Mercy Hermitage* (1995) 57 Bryant Rd., 04971-7327. Tel: 207-938-3730; Fax: 207-938-3730. Email: srmm3@yahoo.com. Sr. Margaret Mary Cuddeback.

Sky-Arch Hermitage, 47 Bryant Rd., 04971-7327. Email: sky-arch@hotmail.com. Sr. B. Emmanuel Bryant.

WINDSOR. *Transfiguration Hermitage*, 205 Windsor Neck Rd., 04363-3202. Tel: 207-445-8031. Email: benedicite@fairpoint.net. Web: www.transfigurationhermitage.org. Sr. Elizabeth Wagner, Contact Person. Number of Hermits 2.

[L] RETREAT HOUSES

ALFRED. *Notre Dame Retreat & Spiritual Center*, 133 Shaker Hill Rd., P.O. Box 159, 04002-0159. Tel: 207-324-6160; Fax: 207-324-5044. Email: spiritualcenter2002@yahoo.com. Rev. Theodore Letendre, F.I.C., Dir.

BIDDEFORD. *Marie Joseph Spiritual Center*, 10 Evans Rd., 04005. Tel: 207-284-5671; Fax: 207-286-1371. Email: mariejosephcenter@yahoo.com. Web: www.mariejosephspiritual.org. Sr. Janice Perrault, P.M., Dir. Sisters of the Presentation of Mary. Served 3,784.

FRENCHVILLE. *Christian Life Center*, P.O. Box 128, Madawaska, 04756-0128. Tel: 207-543-6193; Fax: 207-543-6193. Email: clc4me@roadrunner.com. Web: clc4me.org. 444 US Route 1, 04745. Deacon Donald R. Clavette, Dir.

[M] NEWMAN CENTERS

PORTLAND. *University of New England-Westbrook College*
Office: 673 Stevens Ave., 04103. Tel: 207-797-7026; Fax: 207-797-2679. Rev. James F. Lafontaine, S.J.

University of Southern Maine Portland Campus, P.O. Box 11559, 04104-7559. Alexandra Stauble, Campus Min.

Gorham Campus Alexandra Stauble, Campus Min. Tel: 207-839-4857.

BIDDEFORD. *University of New England* P.O. Box 11559, 04104-7559. Alexandra Stauble, Campus Min. Ministry Provided by Good Shepherd, Saco.

BRUNSWICK. *Bowdoin College* P.O. Box 11559, 04104-7559. All Saints Parish, 132 McKeen St., 04011. Rev. Frank Murray, Campus Chap.; Alexandra Stauble, Campus Min.

Newman Center 04011. Tel: 207-576-3135.

CASTINE. *Maine Maritime Academy* 158 Franklin St., P.O. Box S, 04416. Tel: 207-469-3312. Rev. Bruce Siket, Campus Chap.

FARMINGTON. *University of Maine at Farmington* Newman Campus Ministry, 04938. 133 Middle St., 04938-1598. Tel: 207-778-2778; Fax: 207-778-0268. Email: stjoefarm@myfairpoint.net. P.O. Box 11559, 04104-7559. Rev. Thomas Lequin, Campus Chap.; Monique Claverie, Campus Min.

FORT KENT. *University of Maine at Fort Kent* St. John Vianney Parish, 26 E. Main St., 04743-1395. Tel: 207-834-5656; Fax: 207-834-7461. Email: stlouis@fairpoint.net. Served by personnel at St. John Vianney Parish, Fort Kent.

LEWISTON. *Bates College* 163 Wood St., 04240. Tel: 207-782-8096; Fax: 207-782-9032. Web: www.bates.edu/admin/offices/chaplain. P.O. Box 11559, 04104-7559. Rev. Nathan D. March, Campus Chap. Served by the personnel of the Lewiston Parishes.

MACHIAS. *University of Maine at Machias* Mailing Address: P.O. Box 11559, 04104-7559. Rev. Eugene F. Gaffey.

ORONO. *University of Maine Parish of the Resurrection of the Lord*, 83 College Ave., 04473-1596. Tel: 207-866-2155; Fax: 207-866-4543. Web: www.umaine.edu/newman. Rev. Wilfred P. Labbe; Kristine B. Moody, Campus Min.; JoAnn C. Hall, Campus Min.

PRESQUE ISLE. *University of Maine at Presque Isle* P.O. Box 11559, 04104-7559. Rev. Aaron L. Damboise, Campus Chap., Holy Rosary Rectory, P.O. Box 625, Caribou, 04736-0625.

SOUTH PORTLAND. *Southern Maine Community College* c/o Holy Cross Parish 29 Aspen Ave., 04106-5328. Tel: 207-772-7489; Fax: 207-772-7480. Mailing Address: P.O. Box 11559, 04104-7559. Rev. Msgr. Michael J. Henchal, J.C.L., V.G.

STANDISH. *Saint Joseph's College* 278 Whites Bridge Rd., 04084-5263. Tel: 207-893-7792; Fax: 207-893-6605. Mr. Frank Daggett, Dir. Campus Min.; Rev. John McHugh, O.F.M.Cap., Chap. Campus Ministry Office.

WATERVILLE. *Colby College* 70 Pleasant St., 04901-5405. Tel: 207-872-2281. Rev. John (Jack) Dickinson, Campus Chap., c/o Parish of the Holy Spirit, 70 Pleasant St., 04901-5405; Laura McCown, Campus Min. Dean of Students Office, Colby College.

Thomas College Mid Maine Campus Ministry, 04901. Tel: 207-872-3559. Email: Daniel.Baillargeon@PortlandDiocese.org. P.O. Box 11559, 04104-7559. Rev. John (Jack) Dickinson, Campus Chap.; Laura McCown, Campus Min. Dean of Students Office, Colby College.

[N] MISCELLANEOUS LISTINGS

PORTLAND. **Catholic Foundation of Maine*, 510 Ocean Ave., P.O. Box 11559, 04104-7559. Tel: 207-773-6471; 207-321-7835; Fax: 207-773-0182. Email: christopher.reilly@portlanddiocese.org. Mr. Christopher Reilly, Exec. Dir. & Contact Person.

St. Joseph Child Development Center, c/o Catholic Charities Maine, P.O. Box 10660, 04104. Tel: 207-782-2711; Fax: 207-782-8741. Email: stjosephinfo@ccmaine.org. Ms. Donna Bissonette, Teaching Dir. Number Served 115.

Maine Catholic Radio Network Inc., Mailing Address: P.O. Box 11559, 04104-7559. Tel: 207-773-6471, Ext. 7810; Fax: 207-773-0182. Email: sue.bernard@portlanddiocese.org. 510 Ocean Ave., 04104. Sue Bernard, Contact Person.

The Presence Radio Network, Inc, P.O. Box 10660, 04104-6060. Tel: 207-689-9939. Email: cnickless@maine.rr.com. Cynthia Nickless, Exec. Dir.

RELIGIOUS INSTITUTES OF MEN REPRESENTED IN THE DIOCESE

For further details refer to the corresponding bracketed number in the Religious Institutes of Men or Women section.

[0320]—*Brothers of Christian Instruction*—F.I.C.
[0520]—*Franciscan Friars*—O.F.M.
[0585]—*Heralds of Good News*—H.G.N.
[0690]—*Jesuit Fathers and Brothers* (New England Prov.)—S.J.
[0780]—*Marist Fathers* (Boston Prov.)—S.M.
[0800]—*Maryknoll*—M.M.
[]—*Missionary Institute of Apostles of Jesus* (U.S.A. Zone)—A.J.
[0910]—*Oblates of Mary Immaculate* (Prov. of St. John the Baptist)—O.M.I.
[0430]—*Order of Preachers (Dominicans)* (Canadian Prov.)—O.P.
[0610]—*Priests of the Congregation of Holy Cross*—C.S.C.
[0110]—*Society of African Missions*—S.M.A.
[0925]—*Society of Our Lady of the Most Holy Trinity*—S.O.L.T.

RELIGIOUS INSTITUTES OF WOMEN REPRESENTED IN THE DIOCESE

[]—*Community of the Resurrection*
[]—*Companions of Christ*—C.O.C.
[3100]—*Congregation of Our Lady of the Holy Rosary*—R.S.R.
[0960]—*Daughters of Wisdom*—D.W.
[]—*Diocesan Carmelites of Maine*—D.C.M.
[2655]—*Diocesan Sisters of Mercy*—R.S.M.
[1120]—*Dominican Sisters of the Roman Congregation*—O.P.
[1170]—*Felician Sisters*—C.S.S.F.
[1430]—*Franciscan Sisters of Our Lady of Perpetual Help*—O.S.F.
[2575]—*Institute of the Sisters of Mercy of the Americas*—R.S.M.
[2280]—*Little Franciscan of Mary*—P.F.M.
[2760]—*Missionary Sisters of the Immaculate Conception of the Mother of God*—S.M.I.C.
[3500]—*Servants of the Blessed Sacrament*—S.S.S.
[3550]—*Servants of the Immaculate Heart of Mary*—S.C.I.M.
[0610]—*Sisters of Charity of St. Hyacinthe (Grey Nuns)*—S.C.S.H.
[3000]—*Sisters of Notre Dame de Namur*—S.N.D.deN.
[3750]—*Sisters of St. Chretienne*—S.S.Ch.
[3870]—*Sisters of St. Joseph (Lyons, France)*—C.S.J.
[0150]—*Sisters of the Assumptions*—S.A.S.V.
[0110]—*The Sisters of the Precious Blood*—A.P.B.
[3310]—*Sisters of the Presentation of Mary*—P.M.
[4110]—*Ursuline Nuns (Roman Union)* (Northeastern Prov.)—O.S.U.

DIOCESAN CEMETERIES

BANGOR. *Mount Pleasant Catholic Cemetery*, 449 Ohio St., 04401. Tel: 207-947-4322. 207 York St., 04401-5442. Mr. Kenneth Hutchinson, Supt.

BIDDEFORD. *St. Joseph Cemetery*, 120 West St., P.O. Box 391, 04005. Tel: 207-282-0747. Email: stjosephscemetery@portlanddiocese.net.

LEWISTON. *St. Peter Cemetery*, 217 Switzerland Rd., 04240. Tel: 207-782-8721; Fax: 207-784-3432. Gerard J.B. Raymond, Exec. Dir.

SOUTH PORTLAND. *Calvary Cemetery*, 1461 Broadway,

04106. Tel: 207-773-5796; Fax: 207-773-5796. Email: calvarycem@portlanddiocese.org. Web: www.portlanddiocese.net/calvary. Mr. Richard Nee, Supt.

WATERVILLE. *St. Francis Catholic Cemetery*, 78 Grove St., 04901. Tel: 207-872-2770; Fax: 207-872-2770. Email: stfrancem@myfairpoint.net. Web: www.portlanddiocese.net/stfranciscemetery. P.O. Box 575, 04903-0575. Mr. Michael W. Hebert, Mgr.

NECROLOGY

† Arps, Joseph W. Jr., (Retired)—Died March 25, 2011
† Chouinard, Marcel G., (Retired)—Died Aug. 6, 2011
† Laplante, Laurent R., (Retired)—Died May 1, 2011
† Plante, Georges J., (Retired)—Died Aug. 9, 2011
† Rokos, Richard V., (Retired)—Died March 22, 2011

An asterisk (*) denotes an organization that has established tax-exempt status directly with the IRS and is not covered by the USCCB Group Ruling.

Archdiocese of Portland in Oregon

(Archidioecesis Portlandensis in Oregon)

Most Reverend

JOHN G. VLAZNY, D.D.

Archbishop of Portland in Oregon; ordained December 20, 1961; appointed Auxiliary Bishop of Chicago and Titular Bishop of Stagno October 31, 1983; consecrated December 13, 1983; appointed Bishop of Winona May 19, 1987; installed July 29, 1987; appointed Archbishop of Portland in Oregon October 28, 1997; installed December 19, 1997.

Most Reverend

KENNETH D. STEINER, D.D.

Retired Auxiliary Bishop of Portland in Oregon; ordained May 19, 1962; appointed Titular Bishop of Avensa and Auxiliary Bishop of Portland in Oregon December 6, 1977; ordained March 2, 1978l; retired Nov. 25, 2011. *Office: 2838 E. Burnside St., Portland, OR 97214.*

Square Miles 29,717.

Erected as a Vicariate-Apostolic December 1, 1843

Created Archdiocese of Oregon City, July 24, 1846; Name changed by Papal Decree to "Archdiocese of Portland in Oregon," September 26, 1928

Comprises that part of the State of Oregon lying between the summit of the Cascades and the Pacific Ocean.

For legal titles of parishes and archdiocesan institutions, consult the Archdiocesan Pastoral Center

Archdiocesan Pastoral Center: 2838 E. Burnside St., Portland, OR 97214-1895. Tel: 503-234-5334; Fax: 503-234-2545.

Web: www.archdpdx.org

Email: @archdpdx.org

STATISTICAL OVERVIEW

Personnel	
Archbishops	1
Retired Bishops	1
Abbots	2
Retired Abbots	3
Priests: Diocesan Active in Diocese	100
Priests: Diocesan Active Outside Diocese	5
Priests: Retired, Sick or Absent	45
Number of Diocesan Priests	150
Religious Priests in Diocese	144
Total Priests in Diocese	294
Extern Priests in Diocese	15
Ordinations:	
Diocesan Priests	3
Religious Priests	4
Transitional Deacons	11
Permanent Deacons	8
Permanent Deacons in Diocese	79
Total Brothers	78
Total Sisters	388
Parishes	
Parishes	124
With Resident Pastor:	
Resident Diocesan Priests	83
Resident Religious Priests	25
Without Resident Pastor:	
Administered by Priests	11
Administered by Deacons	2
Administered by Religious Women	1
Administered by Lay People	2
Missions	22
Pastoral Centers	1
Professional Ministry Personnel:	
Brothers	2
Sisters	15
Lay Ministers	152
Welfare	
Catholic Hospitals	10
Total Assisted	2,271,321
Health Care Centers	12
Total Assisted	22,597
Homes for the Aged	8
Total Assisted	3,016
Day Care Centers	4
Total Assisted	2,506
Specialized Homes	7
Total Assisted	913
Special Centers for Social Services	16
Total Assisted	1,038,507
Residential Care of Disabled	3
Total Assisted	8
Educational	
Seminaries, Diocesan	1
Students from This Diocese	35
Students from Other Diocese	116
Diocesan Students in Other Seminaries	18
Students Religious	29
Total Seminarians	82
Colleges and Universities	2
Total Students	5,805
High Schools, Diocesan and Parish	3
Total Students	1,494
High Schools, Private	7
Total Students	4,184
Elementary Schools, Diocesan and Parish	38
Total Students	8,312
Elementary Schools, Private	2
Total Students	405
Catechesis/Religious Education:	
High School Students	3,742
Elementary Students	12,838
Total Students under Catholic Instruction	36,862
Teachers in the Diocese:	
Priests	11
Scholastics	3
Brothers	4
Sisters	23
Lay Teachers	1,181
Vital Statistics	
Receptions into the Church:	
Infant Baptism Totals	5,794
Minor Baptism Totals	446
Adult Baptism Totals	424
Received into Full Communion	656
First Communions	5,098
Confirmations	2,476
Marriages:	
Catholic	683
Interfaith	281
Total Marriages	964
Deaths	1,785
Total Catholic Population	415,725
Total Population	3,327,110

Former Bishops—Most Revs. FRANCIS NORBERT BLANCHET, D.D., First Vicar Apostolic of Oregon Territory; cons. July 25, 1845, Titular Bishop of Drasa; appt. Archbishop of Oregon City, July 24, 1846 when the Vicariate was erected into an ecclesiastical province; resigned 1880; died June 18, 1883; CHARLES JOHN SEGHERS, D.D., cons. June 29, 1873; Bishop of Vancouver Island, British Columbia; coadjutor to the Archbishop of Oregon City, Dec. 10, 1880; Archbishop, Dec. 20, 1880; resigned 1884; and transferred to Vancouver Island, British Columbia; died Nov. 28, 1886; WILLIAM H. GROSS, C.Ss.R., D.D., Archbishop of Oregon City; cons. Bishop of Savannah, GA April 27, 1873; promoted by His Holiness Leo XIII Feb. 1, 1885 from Savannah to the Archiepiscopal See of Oregon City; died Nov. 14, 1898; ALEXANDER CHRISTIE, D.D., Archbishop of Oregon City; consecrated June 29, 1898, Bishop of Vancouver Island, B.C.; promoted by His Holiness Leo XIII February 12, 1899 from Vancouver Island to the Archiepiscopal See of Oregon City; died April 6, 1925; EDWARD D. HOWARD, D.D., LL.D., Titular Archbishop of Albule; ord. June 12, 1906; cons. Titular Bishop of Isauria and Auxiliary Bishop of Davenport, April 6, 1924; appt. to the See of Oregon City, April 30, 1926; asst. at the Pontifical Throne, May 2, 1939; transferred to the Titular See of Albule and as Archbishop of Portland in Oregon, Dec. 9, 1966; died Jan. 2, 1983; ROBERT JOSEPH DWYER, D.D., Ph.D., ord. June 11, 1932; cons. Bishop of Reno, Aug. 5, 1952; appt. Archbishop of Portland in Oregon, Dec. 9, 1966; resigned Jan. 22, 1974; died March 24, 1976; CORNELIUS MICHAEL POWER, D.D., J.C.D., ord. June 3, 1939; appt. Bishop of Yakima, Feb. 5, 1969; cons. May 1, 1969; appt. Archbishop of Portland in Oregon, Jan. 22, 1974; retired July 3, 1986; died May 22, 1997; WILLIAM J. LEVADA, S.T.D., ord. Dec. 20, 1961; appt. Titular Bishop of Capri and Auxiliary Bishop of Los Angeles, March 29, 1983; appt. Archbishop of Portland in Oregon, July 1, 1986; installed Sept. 21, 1986; appt. Coadjutor Archbishop of San Francisco, Aug. 17, 1995; transferred to Oct. 24, 1995; FRANCIS E. GEORGE, O.M.I., Ph.D., S.T.D., ord. Dec. 21, 1963; appt. Bishop of Yakima July 10, 1990; installed Sept. 21, 1990; appt. Archbishop of Portland in Oregon, April 29, 1996; installed May 27, 1996; appt. Archbishop of Chicago April 8, 1997; installed May 7, 1997.

Office of the Archbishop

Archdiocesan Pastoral Center—2838 E. Burnside St., Portland, 97214-1895. Tel: 503-234-5334; Fax: 503-234-2545.

Vicars and Directors

Vicar General and Moderator of the Curia—Rev. Msgr. DENNIS O'DONOVAN, Pastoral Center, 2838 E. Burnside St., Portland, 97214. Tel: 503-233-8331; Fax: 503-234-2545.

Vicar for Clergy—Rev. DONALD BUXMAN.

Finance Officer—JO WILLHITE.

Department Directors—
Business Affairs—PAULETTE FURNESS.
Clergy—Rev. DONALD BUXMAN.
Education—ROBERT MIZIA.
Chancellor/Public Services—MARY JO TULLY.
Pastoral Services—Rev. Msgr. DENNIS O'DONOVAN.
Evangelization Services—Deacon THOMAS GORNICK.

Chancellor—MARY JO TULLY.

College of Consultors—Most Revs. JOHN G. VLAZNY, D.D.; KENNETH D. STEINER, D.D.; Revs. PATRICK BRENNAN, J.C.L.; TODD MOLINARI; LIAM CARY; Rev. Msgrs. RICHARD HUNEGER; DENNIS O'DONOVAN; Revs. RICHARD D. SIRIANNI; VINCENT TRUJILLO, O.S.B.; JOHN KERNS; GEORGE WOLF; LUAN Q. TRAN; PETER SMITH.

Area Vicars—Rev. JAMES MAYO, Downtown Portland; Rev. Msgr. CHARLES LIENERT, Northeast Portland; Revs. MICHAEL EVERNDEN, C.S.P., Southeast Portland; CHARLES E. ZACH, East Portland Suburban; MAXY D'COSTA, S.F.X., South Portland Suburban; WILLIAM C. MOISANT, West Portland Suburban; PATRICK MCNAMEE, Beaverton Suburban; DONALD GUTMANN, Yamhill County; PETER ARTEAGA, M.Sp.S., Tualatin Valley; LUAN Q. TRAN, Columbia County; KENNETH SAMPSON, North Coast; ANGEL PEREZ, Marion County; GARY L. ZERR, Metropolitan Salem; ED COLEMAN, Santiam; ANDREW R. THOMAS, Albany-Corvallis; RICHARD ROSSMAN, Metropolitan Eugene; KARL SCHRAY, South Coast; SEAN WEEKS, Southern Oregon.

Personnel Board—Rev. Msgr. CHARLES LIENERT; Revs. STEPHEN STOBIE; DAVID BROWN; RONALD C. MILLICAN; KELLY VANDEHEY, J.C.L. Ex Officio: Rev. DONALD BUXMAN; Rev. Msgr. DENNIS O'DONOVAN; Most Rev. JOHN G. VLAZNY.

Tribunal

Judicial Vicar—Rev. PATRICK BRENNAN, J.C.L.; LINDA WEIGEL, J.C.L., Dir. Tel: 503-233-8380.
Adjutant Judicial Vicars—Revs. KELLY VANDEHEY, J.C.L.; PETER SMITH.
Judges—Revs. PATRICK BRENNAN, J.C.L.; CARL GIMPL; MICHAEL JOHNSTON; JAMES MAYO; MICHAEL PATRICK, J.C.L.; KELLY VANDEHEY, J.C.L.; PETER SMITH, J.C.L.

Defenders of the Bond—Rev. Msgr. GREGORY MOYS; Sr. MAUREEN ABBOTT, S.P.; LINDA WEIGEL, J.C.L.

Auditor— By appointment

Case Instructor—SUSAN OUFFOUE.

Notaries—SUSAN OUFFOUE; CONNIE CANARIOS; MARGARET NOLAN.

Advocates— Priests and pastoral ministers by appointment.

Archdiocesan Offices and Agencies

Archives—DAN HASKINS, Records Mgr. Tel: 503-233-8334. 2838 E. Burnside St., Portland, 97214-1895.

Building Commission—Most Rev. JOHN G. VLAZNY, D.D.; Rev. Msgr. DENNIS O'DONOVAN; Revs. JOSEPH HEUBERGER; LESLIE M. SIEG; JIM KIRKPATRICK; BRIAN SHEA; JIM EVANS; ROBERT BOILEAU; JOSEPH GEHLEN; MICHAEL KINNE; DELIA WILSON; PAULETTE FURNESS, Ex Officio; SAMUEL RODRIQUEZ; Rev. PATRICK MCNAMEE; MARY FRANCES CASCIATO.

Business Affairs—PAULETTE FURNESS, Dir., 2838 E. Burnside St., Portland, 97214-1895. Tel: 503-233-8356.

Campus Ministry—Deacon THOMAS GORNICK, Contact, 2838 E. Burnside St., Portland, 97214-1895. Tel: 503-233-8395.

Catholic Charities, Inc.—PIETRO R. FERRARI, Exec. Dir., 2740 S.E. Powell Blvd., Portland, 97202. Tel: 503-231-4866.

Catholic Deaf Ministry—Sr. LINDA ROBY, B.V.M., Dir., 2838 E. Burnside St., Portland, 97214. Tel: 503-233-8398 (V/TTY).

"Catholic Sentinel"— (Official Newspaper of the Archdiocese), Most Rev. JOHN G. VLAZNY, D.D., Publisher-in-Chief; JOHN J. LIMB, Publisher; ROBERT PFOHMAN, Editor, 5536 N.E. Hassalo St., Portland, 97213-3638. Tel: 503-281-1191. Mailing Address: P.O. Box 18030, Portland, 97218-0030.

Catholic Youth Organization/Camp Howard—Sr. KRISTA VON BORSTELL, S.S.M.O., Exec. Dir., 825 N.E. 20th Ave., Oregon Plaza, Ste. 120, Portland, 97232. Tel: 503-231-9484.

Cemeteries—Rev. Msgr. DENNIS O'DONOVAN, Dir. Tel: 503-234-5334; TIM CORBETT, Supt., Mt. Calvary Cemetery, 333 S.W. Skyline Blvd., Portland, 97221. Tel: 503-292-6621. Gethsemani Cemetery, 11666 S.E. Stevens Rd., Portland, 97266. Tel: 503-659-1350. Mount Calvary Cemetery, Eugene, 300 Mary Lane, Eugene, 97405. Tel: 541-686-8722.

Child Protection/Victim Assistance Office—CATHY SHANNON, Dir., 2838 E. Burnside St., Portland, 97214-1895. Tel: 503-416-8810 Victim Assistance; 503-233-8302 Child Protection. Email: cshannon@archdpdx.org.

Clergy Personnel—Rev. DONALD BUXMAN, Vicar for Clergy, 2838 E. Burnside St., Portland, 97214-1895. Tel: 503-233-8366.

Communications—BUD BUNCE, Dir., 2838 E. Burnside St., Portland, 97214-1895. Tel: 503-233-8373.

Continuing Education for Clergy—Rev. JOHN KERNS. Board Members: Revs. ELWIN SCHWAB; GEORGE WOLF; MICHAEL PATRICK, J.C.L.; SEAN WEEKS; PETER O'BRIEN; DONALD BUXMAN, 2838 E. Burnside St., Portland, 97214-1895. Tel: 503-233-8368.

Diaconate Office—Rev. Msgr. RICHARD HUNEGER, Dir.; Deacon VERN KORCHINSKI, Assoc. Dir., 2838 E. Burnside St., Portland, 97214-1895. Tel: 503-233-8368.

Ecumenical and Interreligious Affairs—Rev. RICHARD D. SIRIANNI; MARY JO TULLY, 2838 E. Burnside St., Portland, 97214. Tel: 503-233-8323.

Evangelization Services—Deacon THOMAS GORNICK, Dir., 2838 E. Burnside St., Portland, 97214-1895. Tel: 503-233-8335; MICHAL HORACE, Dir. Youth/Young Adult Ministry. Tel: 503-233-8310; CLAIRE WOODRUFF, D.R.E. Tel: 503-233-8367.

Finance Council—Most Rev. JOHN G. VLAZNY, D.D.; Revs. KENNETH SAMPSON; STEVE GEER; RICHARD D. SIRIANNI; Rev. Msgr. DENNIS O'DONOVAN; DOUG WHITE; TOM EYER; PAULETTE FURNESS; DOUG TOLLEFSON; ARTHUR SCHULTE JR., Ph.D.; ROBERT BELDING; CAMERON WILLIAMS; CAROLYN WINTER; BRIAN WILLIAMS; MICHAEL FAHEY; JO WILLHITE, Chm.; JAMES SCHALLER; SANDRA SURAN; EDWARD HERINCKX, 2838 E. Burnside St., Portland, 97214-1895. Tel: 503-233-8359.

Financial Services—JO WILLHITE, Dir., 2838 E. Burnside St., Portland, 97214-1895. Tel: 503-233-8359.

Hispanic Ministries—RAUL VELAZQUEZ, Dir., 2838 E. Burnside St., Portland, 97214. Tel: 503-233-8324.

Historical Commission—MARY BETH HERKERT, Pres., 2838 E. Burnside St., Portland, 97214-1895. Tel: 503-234-5334.

Holy Childhood, Pontifical Association of—MARY JO TULLY, Dir., 2838 E. Burnside St., Portland, 97214-1895. Tel: 503-233-8323.

Human Resources—BARBARA BALTZ, Dir., 2838 E. Burnside St., Portland, 97214-1895. Tel: 503-233-8370.

Life, Justice and Peace—MATT CATO, Dir., 2838 E. Burnside St., Portland, 97214-1895. Tel: 503-233-8361; Rev. TIMOTHY MOCKAITIS, Assoc. Dir. Respect for Life Activities.

Liturgical Commission—Sr. JEREMY GALLET, S.P., Ex Officio; Revs. JAMES MAYO; JOSEPH S. MCMAHON; RICHARD RUTHERFORD, C.S.C.; Sr. LORETTA SCHAFF, O.S.F.; MARY JO TULLY; AGNES ZUEGER.

Marriage, Family Life and Aging—Deacon THOMAS GORNICK, Contact, 2838 E. Burnside St., Portland, 97214-1895. Tel: 503-233-8395.

Ministry Formation—JERILYN FELTON, Dir., 2838 E. Burnside St., Portland, 97214-1895. Tel: 503-234-5334; HEATHER WYCOFF, Mgr., Griffin Center, 11957 S.E. Fuller Rd., Milwaukie, 97222. Tel: 503-652-7476.

Mission Office—MARY JO TULLY, Dir., 2838 E. Burnside St., Portland, 97214-1895. Tel: 503-233-8323.

Oregon Catholic Conference—Most Rev. JOHN G. VLAZNY, D.D., Pres.; VACANT, Vice Pres.; Rev. Msgr. DENNIS O'DONOVAN, Sec. & Treas., 2838 E. Burnside St., Portland, 97214-1895. Tel: 503-234-5334.

Oregon Catholic Press—Most Rev. JOHN G. VLAZNY, D.D., Publisher-in-Chief; JOHN J. LIMB, Publisher, 5536 N.E. Hassalo St., Portland, 97213-3638. Tel: 503-281-1191. Mailing Address: P.O. Box 18030, Portland, 97218-0030.

Pastoral Services—Rev. Msgr. DENNIS O'DONOVAN, 2838 E. Burnside St., Portland, 97214-1895. Tel: 503-234-5334.

People with Disabilities—DOROTHY DESMARTEAU-COUGHLIN, Dir., 2838 E. Burnside St., Portland, 97214-1895. Tel: 503-233-8399 (V/TTY).

Pro-Life Activities— (See Life, Justice and Peace)

Project Rachel—2740 S.E. Powell Blvd., #7, Portland, 97202. Tel: 800-249-8074.

Propagation of the Faith, Pontifical Society for the—MARY JO TULLY, Dir., 2838 E. Burnside St., Portland, 97214-1895. Tel: 503-233-8323.

Religious Education— (See Evangelization Services)

Refugee Resettlement—CECILIA BARICEVIC, Prog. Mgr., 2740 S.E. Powell Blvd., Portland, 97202. Tel: 971-222-1883.

Resource Development—DOUG TOLLEFSON, Dir., 2838 E. Burnside St., Portland, 97214-1895. Tel: 503-233-8336.

St. Mary's Home for Boys—FRANCIS MAHER, Exec. Dir., 16535 S.W. Tualatin Valley Hwy., Beaverton, 97006. Tel: 503-649-5651.

School Office—ROBERT MIZIA, Supt. Tel: 503-233-8300; Sr. ELIZABETH LARSON, O.S.B., Asst. Supt., School Personnel & Faith Formation; JULIE VOGEL, Dir. Instructional Svcs. & Accreditation.

Special Assistant to the Archbishop—Mr. TODD COOPER, Dir., 2838 E. Burnside St., Portland, 97214-1895. Tel: 503-233-8386.

Stewardship Office—DOUG TOLLEFSON, Dir., 2838 E. Burnside St., Portland, 97214-1895. Tel: 503-233-8336.

Vocations—Rev. JOHN HENDERSON, Dir., 2838 E. Burnside St., Portland, 97214-1895. Tel: 503-233-8368.

Worship—Sr. JEREMY GALLET, S.P., Dir., 2838 E. Burnside St., Portland, 97214-1895. Tel: 503-233-8342.

Youth and Young Adult Ministry— (See Evangelization Services)

CLERGY, PARISHES, MISSIONS AND PAROCHIAL SCHOOLS

CITY OF PORTLAND

(MULTNOMAH COUNTY)

PORTLAND

1—CATHEDRAL OF THE IMMACULATE CONCEPTION (1851) Rev. Patrick Brennan; Deacons Thomas Gornick; Craig Joseph Casey.
Res.: 1716 N.W. Davis St., 97209. Tel: 503-228-4397; Fax: 503-242-2568. Web: www.maryscathedral.org.
School—(Grades K-8), 110 N.W. 17th Ave., 97209. Tel: 503-275-9370; Fax: 503-243-3819. Order of Servants of Mary 2; Lay Teachers 16; Students 199.
Catechesis/Religious Program—Students 15.

2—ST. AGATHA (1911) Rev. Nathan Zodrow, O.S.B.
Office: 1430 S.E. Nehalem St., 97202. Tel: 503-236-4747; Fax: 503-236-6407. Email: stagathapdx@gmail.com. Web: www.stagatha.us.
School—(Grades PreK-8), 7960 S.E. 15th Ave., 97202. Tel: 503-234-5500; Fax: 503-232-7240. Email: sarah.lutz@stagatha.us. Web: www.stagatha.us/school. Stacie Dunn, Librarian. Lay Teachers 15; Students 175.

3—ALL SAINTS (1917) Rev. Richard Thompson.
Res.: 3847 N.E. Glisan, 97232. Tel: 503-232-4305; Fax: 503-238-8847. Email: parish@allsaintsportland.org. Web: www.allsaintsportland.org.
School—(Grades PreSchool-8), 601 N.E. 39th Ave., 97232. Tel: 503-236-6205; Fax: 503-236-0781. Email: office@allsaintsportland.org. Web: www.school.allsaintsportland.org. Lay Teachers 33; Students 435.
Catechesis/Religious Program—Students 175.

4—ST. ANDRE BESSETTE CHURCH (1919), (Downtown Chapel), Rev. Stephen P. Newton, C.S.C. In Res., Rev. Ronald P. Raab, C.S.C.
Res.: 601 W. Burnside St., 97209. Tel: 503-228-0746; Fax: 503-972-1063. Web: www.saintandrechurch.org.

5—ST. ANDREW (1907) Rev. Msgr. Charles Lienert.
Res.: 806 N.E. Alberta St., 97211. Tel: 503-281-4429; Fax: 503-281-4411. Email: ouroffice@standrewchurch.com. Web: www.standrewchurch.com.
Catechesis/Religious Program—Students 137.

6—ST. ANTHONY (1917) Rev. Patrick Donoghue.
Parish Office: 3720 S.E. 79th Ave., 97206. Tel: 503-771-6039; Fax: 503-772-0107. Email: stanthonyportland@archdpdx.org. Web: www.stanthonypdx.com.

7—ASCENSION (1892) Revs. Ben R. Innes, O.F.M.; Jorge Hernandez, O.F.M., Parochial Vicar; Jose Luis Nerio, O.F.M.
Mailing Address: 743 S.E. 76th Ave., 97215. Tel: 503-256-3897; Fax: 503-257-4681. Email: veronica-ascension@qwestoffice.net. Web: ascensionpdx.org.
Rectory—Ascension Friary, 404 S.E. 68th Ave., 97215.
Catechesis/Religious Program—Tel: 503-256-3897, Ext. 21; Fax: 503-257-4681. Email: sharon-ascension@qwestoffice.net. Sharon Grigar, Pastoral

Assoc.; Maria Solis, Dir. Hispanic Ministry. Students 240.

8—ASSUMPTION (1909) Closed. For inquiries for parish records contact the chancery. (Holy Cross)

9—ST. BIRGITTA (1954) Rev. Luan Q. Tran.
Church: 11820 N.W. St. Helens Rd., 97231-2319. Tel: 503-286-3929; Fax: 971-230-0546. Email: stbirgitta@msn.com. Web: stbirgitta.com.
Chapel—Portland, Chapel of Our Lady of Sinj

10—BLESSED SACRAMENT (1913) Closed. For inquiries for parish records please contact Holy Cross, Portland.

11—ST. CHARLES (1914) Rev. Elwin Schwab, Priest Moderator; Sr. Phyllis Jaszkowiak, Pastoral Admin.; Joan Winchester, Pastoral Assoc.
Parish Center—5310 N.E. 42nd, 97218. Tel: 503-281-6461; Fax: 503-281-6828. Email: stchas@stcharlespdx.org. Web: www.stcharlespdx.org.
Catechesis/Religious Program—Email: anitak@stcharlespdx.org. Students 30.

12—CHURCH OF ST. JOSEPH THE WORKER (1885) Rev. John Amsberry; Deacon Michael Caldwell.
Res.: 2310 S.E. 148th Ave., 97233. Tel: 503-761-8710; Fax: 503-761-8545. Web: www.stjosephtheworkerpdx.org.
Catechesis/Religious Program—Tel: 503-762-2704; Fax: 503-761-8545. Students 155.

13—CHURCH OF ST. MICHAEL THE ARCHANGEL (1894), (Italian), Rev. James Mayo; Deacon Charles Amsberry, Pastoral Assoc.
Res.: 424 S.W. Mill St., 97201. Tel: 503-228-8629; Fax: 503-827-7689. Email: secretary@stmichaelportland.org.

14—ST. CLARE (1913) Rev. Charles A. Wood.
Res.: 8535 S.W. 19th Ave., 97219. Tel: 503-244-1037; Fax: 503-246-2665. Email: office@saintclarechurch.org. Web: www.saintclarechurch.org.
School—(Grades PreK-8) Tel: 503-244-7600; Fax: 503-293-2076. Debbi Monahan, Prin.; Lynn Napoli, Librarian. Lay Teachers 19; Students 224.
Catechesis/Religious Program—Tel: 503-244-1037, Ext. 104. Email: jean@saintclarechurch.org. Students 50.

15—ST. ELIZABETH OF HUNGARY (1953) Rev. Jim Kolb, C.S.P.
Res.: 4112 S.W. Sixth Ave. Dr., 97239. Tel: 503-222-2168; Fax: 503-274-2438.
Catechesis/Religious Program—Students 11.

16—ST. FRANCIS OF ASSISI (1876) Rev. Robert Krueger, Moderator (Retired); Valerie Chapman, Pastoral Admin.
Mailing Address: 1131 S.E. Oak St., 97214. Email: office@stfrancispdx.org. Web: www.stfranpdx.catholicweb.com.
Res.: 1136 S.E. Oak St., 97214. Tel: 503-232-5880; Fax: 503-232-6449.
Catechesis/Religious Program—Students 12.

17—HOLY CROSS CATHOLIC CHURCH (1901) Rev. Mark Bachmeier; Deacon Jose Gutierrez; Ana Carmina Perez, Hispanic Ministry.
Office:—5227 N. Bowdoin St., 97203. Tel: 503-289-2834; Fax: 503-283-7056. Email: office@holycrosspdx.org. Web: www.holycrosspdx.org.
School—(Grades K-8), 5202 N. Bowdoin St., 97203. Tel: 503-289-3010; Fax: 503-286-5006. Nancy Jordan, Librarian. Sisters 1; Lay Teachers 12; Students 198.
Chapel—Christ The Teacher, University of Portland 5000 N. Willamette Blvd., 97203. Tel: 503-283-7311; Fax: 503-283-7399.
Catechesis/Religious Program—Students 146.

18—HOLY FAMILY (1931) Rev. George Wolf.
Business Office: 3732 S.E. Knapp, 97202. Tel: 503-774-1428; Fax: 503-774-1854. Email: churchlady18@comcast.net. Web: www.holyfamilyportland.org.
Res.: 3708 S.E. Flavel. Tel: 971-266-8055.
Church: 7525 Cesar E. Chavez Blvd., 97202.
School—(Grades PreSchool-8), 7425 Cesar E. Chavez Blvd., 97202. Tel: 503-774-8871; Fax: 503-774-8872. Email: christyrobinson@holyfamilyportland.org. Christy Robinson, Prin.; Marylee Williamson, Librarian. Lay Teachers 15; Students 249.
Catechesis/Religious Program—Tel: 503-774-1428, Ext. 123 (D.R.E.); 503-774-1428, Ext. 107 (Youth Min.); Fax: 503-774-1854. Students 160.

19—HOLY REDEEMER (1906) Rev. John J. Dougherty, C.S.C.; Deacons Robert Lukosh; John Rilatt.
Church: 25 N. Rosa Parks Way, 97217. Tel: 503-285-4539; Fax: 503-285-0666. Email: holyredeemerchurch@comcast.net. Web: www.holyredeemerpdx.org.
School—(Grades PreK-8), 127 N. Rosa Parks Way, 97217. Tel: 503-283-5197; Fax: 503-283-9479. Sr. Alice Weaver, S.N.J.M., Librarian; Pam Peterson, Librarian. Sisters 4; Lay Teachers 15; Students 269.
Catechesis/Religious Program—Students 269.

20—HOLY ROSARY PARISH & DOMINICAN PRIORY (1894) Revs. Francis Hung Le, O.P.; Vincent Kelber, O.P., Sub-Prior. In Res., Revs. Paul A. Duffner, O.P. (Retired); Thomas More J. McGreevy, O.P. (Retired); Brian T.B. Mullady, O.P.
Res.: 375 N.E. Clackamas St., 97232. Tel: 503-235-3163; Fax: 503-235-3551. Web: holyrosarypdx.org.
Confraternity of the Most Holy Rosary—P.O. Box 3617, 97208. Tel: 503-236-8393; Fax: 503-236-8394.
Catechesis/Religious Program—Students 199.

21—ST. IGNATIUS (1907) [JC] Revs. Christopher S. Weekly; Thomas Royce, S.J., Parochial Vicar; John Ridgway, S.J., Parochial Vicar.
Res.: 3400 S.E. 43rd Ave., 97206. Tel: 503-777-1491; Fax: 503-777-3142. Email: office@stignatiusparish.org. Web: www.stignatiusparish.org.
School—(Grades K-8), 3330 S.E. 43rd St., 97206. Tel: 503-774-5533; Fax: 503-788-1134. Email: jmatcovich@stignatiusschool.org. Web: www.stignatiusschool.org. Susanne Lohkamp, Librarian. Sisters of the Holy Names of Jesus and Mary 1; Lay Teachers 14; Students 198.
Convent—Sisters of the Holy Names of Jesus and Mary, 4130 S.E. Brooklyn, 97206. Tel: 503-231-6538. Sisters 1.
Catechesis/Religious Program—Students 28.

22—IMMACULATE HEART OF MARY (1885) Rev. Nicolaus Marandu.
Res.: 2926 N. Williams Ave., 97227-1628. Tel: 503-287-3724; Fax: 503-287-5011. Email: immaculateheartportland@archdpdx.org. Web: www.immaculateheartchurch.org.

23—ST. JOHN FISHER (1959) Rev. Msgr. Tim Murphy; Deacon Scott Kolbet, Pastoral Assoc.; Kaycie Hoffman, Librarian.
Res.: 7007 S.W. 46th Ave., 97219. Tel: 503-244-4945; Fax: 503-452-8570.
School—(Grades K-8) Tel: 503-246-3234; Fax: 503-246-4117. Administrators 1; Lay Teachers 17; Aides 2; Students 222.
Catechesis/Religious Program—Tel: 503-244-4945; Fax: 503-452-8570. Janice Benson, D.R.E. Students 36.

24—ST. JUAN DIEGO CATHOLIC CHURCH formerly St. Juan Diego Parish (2002) Rev. John Kerns; Kathy Yee, Pastoral Assoc.
Church: 5995 N.W. 178th Ave., 97229. Tel: 503-644-1617; Fax: 503-644-1617 (call first). Web: www.stjuandiego.org.
Catechesis/Religious Program—Bridget Becker, Dir. Faith Formation; Janette Strand, Parish Music Coord.; Peggy Brice, Office Mgr. & Book Keeper. Students 150.

25—KOREAN MARTYRS CATHOLIC CHURCH (1990), (Korean), [JC] Rev. Gi Hyeon (Simon) Shin.
Office & Church: 10840 S.E. Powell Blvd., 97266. Email: chrkor@yahoo.com.
Catechesis/Religious Program—Tel: 503-661-8468. Students 90.

26—ST. MARY MAGDALENE (1911), (The Madeleine) Rev. Michael Biewend.
Res.: 3123 N.E. 24th Ave., 97212. Tel: 503-281-5777; Fax: 503-281-0673. Web: www.themadeleine.edu.
School—(Grades K-8), 3240 N.E. 23rd Ave., 97212. Tel: 503-288-9197; Fax: 503-280-1196. Susan J. Steele, Prin. Lay Teachers 21; Students 253.
Catechesis/Religious Program—Students 48.

27—OUR LADY OF LAVANG (1999), (Vietnamese), Revs. Bartholomew Dat H. Pham, S.D.D.; Peter Khoi Anh Hoang Doan, S.D.D.; Joseph Phiet Trong Vu, C.Ss.R.; Francis Quyet Bui, S.D.D.
5404 N.E. Alameda Dr., 97213. Tel: 503-249-5892; Fax: 503-249-1776.
Catechesis/Religious Program—Students 1,050.
Mission—St. Andrew Dung-Lac 13715 S.W. Walker Rd., Beaverton, Washington Co. 97005. Tel: 503-643-9528; Fax: 503-644-8486.

28—OUR LADY OF SORROWS (1917) Rev. Ronald C. Millican; Deacon An Vu.
Res.: 5313 S.E. Knight St., 97206. Tel: 503-775-6731; Fax: 503-775-6732.
Church & Mailing Address: 5239 S.E. Woodstock Blvd., 97206-6822.
Catechesis/Religious Program—Students 22.

29—ST. PATRICK (1885) Rev. Lucas Laborde.
Church: 1623 N.W. 19th Ave., 97209. Tel: 503-222-4086; Fax: 503-222-6642. Web: sites.google.com/site/stpatrickpdx.
Catechesis/Religious Program—

30—ST. PETER (1911) Rev. David E. Zegar; Brendan Mallon, Pastoral Assoc.; Amparo Piedrahita, Hispanic Min.
Mailing Address: 8623 S.E. Woodstock Blvd., P.O. Box 97266, 97266. Tel: 503-777-3321; Fax: 503-777-3351. Email: stpeterportland@archdpdx.org.
Res.: 5736 S.E. 86th St., 97266. Tel: 503-777-1026.
Catechesis/Religious Program—Tel: 503-777-3322. Students 127.

31—ST. PHILIP NERI (1912) Revs. Charles J. Brunick, C.S.P.; Michael Evernden, C.S.P.; James R. McCauley, C.S.P.
Res.: 2411 S.E. Tamarack Ave., 97214. Tel: 503-231-4955; Fax: 503-736-1383. Email: info@stphilipneripdx.org. Web: www.stphilipneripdx.org.
Catechesis/Religious Program—Students 45.

32—ST. PIUS X (Cedar Mill) (1953) Rev. Craig Boly, S.J.; Deacon Robert Little.
Office: 1280 N.W. Saltzman Rd., 97229. Tel: 503-644-5264; Fax: 503-626-6540. Web: www.stpius.org/.
School—(Grades K-8), 1260 N.W. Saltzman Rd., 97229. Tel: 503-644-3244; Fax: 503-646-6568. Margaret Burd, Librarian. Lay Teachers 21; Students 339.
Catechesis/Religious Program—Tel: 503-644-5264. Students 193.

33—QUEEN OF PEACE, Closed. For inquiries for parish records contact the chancery. (Holy Cross).

34—ST. RITA (1923) Rev. Donald Buxman, Pastoral Moderator; Lisa Porter, Pastoral Admin.
Mailing Address: 10029 N.E. Prescott St., 97220. Tel: 503-252-3403; Fax: 503-256-9682.
Catechesis/Religious Program—Students 31.

35—ST. ROSE OF LIMA (1911) Rev. Peter Smith; Deacon Donald Ciffone.
Res.: 2727 N.E. 54th Ave., 97213. Tel: 503-281-5318; Fax: 503-284-8350.
School—Archbishop Howard School, (Grades PreSchool-8), 5309 N.E. Alameda St., 97213. Tel: 503-281-1912; Fax: 503-281-0554. Email: principal@archbishophoward.org. Web: www.archbishophoward.org. Donna Vandiver, Librarian. Lay Teachers 13; Students 215.
Catechesis/Religious Program—Students 215.

36—SACRED HEART (1893) Rev. Bruce Brown, Admin. (Retired).
Res.: 3910 S.E. 11th Ave., 97202. Tel: 503-231-9636; Fax: 503-231-1766. Email: sheart@att.net. Web: www.sacredheartportland.org.

37—ST. STANISLAUS (1907), (Polish), Rev. Piotr Dzikowski, S.Ch.
Res.: 3916 N. Interstate Ave., 97227-1063. Tel: 503-281-7532; Fax: 503-281-7532. Web: www.ststanislausparish.com.
Catechesis/Religious Program—Christ Our Life Students 47.

38—ST. STEPHEN (1907) Rev. Petrus B. Hoang.
Res.: 1112 S.E. 41st Ave., 97214. Tel: 503-234-5019; Fax: 503-239-5985.
Catechesis/Religious Program—Students 5.

39—ST. THERESE OF THE CHILD JESUS (1955) Rev. Steve Geer.
Res.: 1224 N.E. 131st Pl., 97230. Tel: 503-256-5850; Fax: 503-253-3560. Email: church@stthereseor.org. Web: www.stthereseor.org.
School—(Grades PreSchool-8) Tel: 503-253-9400; Fax: 503-253-9571. Email: st.therese@comcast.net. Web: www.stthereseschool.org. Sisters of the Holy Child Jesus 1; Lay Teachers 13; Students 261.
Catechesis/Religious Program—Students 65.

40—ST. THOMAS MORE (1936) Rev. Richard D. Sirianni.
Church: 3525 S.W. Patton Rd., 97221. Tel: 503-222-2055; Fax: 503-242-1831. Email: stmparish@stmpdx.org.
School—(Grades K-8), 3521 S.W. Patton Rd., 97221. Tel: 503-222-6105; Fax: 503-227-5661. Email: stmschool@stmpdx.org. Web: www.stmpdx.org. Lay Teachers 20; Students 220.
Catechesis/Religious Program—Tel: 503-222-2055, Ext. 14; Fax: 503-242-1861. Email: stmre@yahoo.com; mschuster@stmpdx.org. Students 104.

OUTSIDE THE CITY OF PORTLAND

ALBANY, LINN CO., OUR LADY OF PERPETUAL HELP (ST. MARY) (1885) Rev. Andrew R. Thomas; Kathleen Reilly, Pastoral Assoc.
Res.: 706 Ellsworth St., S.W., 97321. Tel: 541-926-1449; Fax: 541-926-2191. Email: stmarys_albany@comcast.net. Web: www.stmarysalbany.com.
School—St. Mary, (Grades PreK-8), 815 Broadalbin St., S.W., 97321-2469. Tel: 541-928-7474; Fax: 541-926-9342. Email: stmarysch@proaxis.com. Web: www.proaxis.com/~stmarysch. Christina Meadows, Prin. Lay Teachers 13; Students 94.
Catechesis/Religious Program—Fax: 541-926-2191. Students 222.

ALOHA, WASHINGTON CO., ST. ELIZABETH ANN SETON (1982) Rev. Louis Urbanski; Deacon Jesus Espinoza, Pastoral Assoc., Hispanic Ministry; Ann Billings, Bookkeeper & Admin. Asst.
Res.: 3145 S.W. 192nd Ave., 97006. Tel: 503-649-9044; 503-649-6211; Fax: 503-848-2915. Email: admin@seas-aloha.org. Web: seas-aloha.org.
Catechesis/Religious Program—Tel: 503-649-9044. Email: re@seas-aloha.org. Sandi Campos, Dir. Faith Formation. Students 315.

ASHLAND, JACKSON CO., OUR LADY OF THE MOUNTAIN (1887) Rev. Sean Weeks; Deacon James McVeigh.
Res.: 987 Hillview Dr., 97520. Tel: 541-482-1146;

Fax: 541-488-5174. Email: olmop@mind.net. Web: www.ourladymt.org.
Catechesis/Religious Program—Students 187.

ASTORIA, CLATSOP CO., ST. MARY, STAR OF THE SEA (1874) [JC] Rev. Kenneth Sampson.
Rectory—828 14th St., 97103.
Church: 1465 Grand Ave., 97103. Tel: 503-325-3671; Fax: 503-325-7983 (Office). Email: amyr@stmaryastoria.com. Web: www.stmaryastoria.com.
School—(Grades PreK-8) Lay Teachers 14; Students 117.
Mission—St. Francis de Sales 867 5th Ave., Hammond, Clatsop Co. 97121.
Catechesis/Religious Program—Students 53.

BANDON, COOS CO., HOLY TRINITY (1883) [CEM] Rev. Michael Patrick.
Res.: 355 Oregon Ave., S.E., 97411. Tel: 541-347-2309; Fax: 541-347-9256. Web: www.holytrinitybandon.com.
Mission—St. John the Baptist P.O. Box 884, Port Orford, Curry Co. 97465. Tel: 541-253-6250.
Catechesis/Religious Program—Students 42.

BEAVERTON, WASHINGTON CO.

1—ST. CECILIA (1876) Revs. Patrick McNamee; Ysrael Bien.
Res.: 5105 S.W. Franklin Ave., 97005. Tel: 503-644-2619; Fax: 503-626-7204.
School—(Grades PreSchool-8) Tel: 503-644-2619, Ext. 3; Fax: 503-646-4217. Web: www.stcecilia.pvt.k12.or.us. Lay Teachers 17; Students 270.
Catechesis/Religious Program—Students 265.

2—HOLY TRINITY (1962) [CEM] Rev. David Gutmann.
Church: 13715 S.W. Walker Rd., 97005. Tel: 503-643-9528; Fax: 503-644-8486. Email: parish@h-t.org. Web: www.h-t.org.
School—(Grades K-8), 13755 S.W. Walker Rd., 97005. Tel: 503-644-5748; Fax: 503-643-4475. Email: holytrinity@pvt.k12.or.us. Web: www.holytrinity.pvt.k12.or.us. Lay Teachers 14; Students 258.
Catechesis/Religious Program—Students 155.

BROOKINGS, CURRY CO., STAR OF THE SEA (1923) Rev. Luan D. Nguyen; Deacon Leo H. Appel II.
Mailing Address: Box 1066, 97415. 820 Old County Rd., 97415. Tel: 541-469-2313; Fax: 541-469-9644. Email: starofsea820@nwtec.com. Web: www.starofthesea-catholicchurch.com.
Mission—St. Charles Borromeo 94323 Gauntlet, P.O. Box 529, Gold Beach, Curry Co. 97444. Tel: 541-247-2453.
Catechesis/Religious Program—

CANBY, CLACKAMAS CO., ST. PATRICK (1882) [CEM] Rev. John Waldron.
Res.: 498 N.W. Ninth, P.O. Box 730, 97013. Tel: 503-266-9411; Fax: 503-263-2293. Email: stpatricks@canby.com. Web: www.stpatcanby.org.
Catechesis/Religious Program—488 N.W. 9th, 97013. Tel: 503-266-2401. Email: stpatrickreligiouseducation@yahoo.com. Students 162.

CENTRAL POINT, JACKSON CO., SHEPHERD OF THE VALLEY (1978) Rev. Mike Walker.
Office: 600 Beebe Rd., 97502. Tel: 541-664-1050; Fax: 541-664-9312. Email: churchoffice@shepherdcatholic.com. Web: www.shepherdcatholic.com.
Catechesis/Religious Program—Students 200.

COOS BAY, COOS CO., ST. MONICA (1888) Rev. Jeyamani Paul (India).
Mailing Address: 357 S. 6th St., 97420.
Church: 97420. Tel: 541-267-7421; Fax: 541-267-8491. Email: stmchurch@frontier.com. Web: www-.saintmonicacoosbay.org.

COQUILLE, COOS CO., HOLY NAME (1915) Rev. John F. McGuire.
50 S. Dean St., 97423.
Res.: 22 S. Dean St., 97423. Tel: 541-396-3849.
Catechesis/Religious Program—Students 6.
Mission—Sts. Ann and Michael 209 Second St., Myrtle Point, Coos Co. 97458. Tel: 541-396-3849.

CORNELIUS, WASHINGTON CO., ST. ALEXANDER (1881), (Hispanic), Rev. David E. Schiferl.
Mailing Address: P.O. Box 644, 97113. Tel: 503-359-0304; Fax: 503-992-8634. Email: dschiferl@msn.com.
Res.: 268 N. 17th Ave., 97113. Tel: 503-992-0133.
Catechesis/Religious Program—Students 303.

CORVALLIS, BENTON CO., ST. MARY (1861) [CEM] Revs. Stephen Clovis; Ignacio Llorente; Deacons Francis Potts; Chris Anderson; Lynette Martin, Admin. Asst.
Res.: 501 N.W. 25th St., 97330. Tel: 541-757-1988; Fax: 541-757-2788. Web: www.smcatholic.com.
Catechesis/Religious Program—Students 305.

COTTAGE GROVE, LANE CO., OUR LADY OF PERPETUAL HELP (1897) Rev. Roy L. Antunez, S.J.; Deacon Kenneth E. Boone.
Res.: 1025 N. 19th St., 97424. Tel: 541-942-3420; Fax: 541-942-4712.
Mission—St. Philip Benizi 552 Holbrook, Creswell, Lane Co. 97426. P.O. Box 706, Creswell, 97426.
Catechesis/Religious Program—1025 N. 19th St., 97424. Tel: 541-942-4712. Betty Krumlauf, D.R.E. Students 102.

DALLAS, POLK CO., ST. PHILIP (1920) [JC] Rev. Michael Johnston.
Office: 825 S.W. Mill St., 97338. Tel: 503-623-2440.
Catechesis/Religious Program—Students 95.

ESTACADA, CLACKAMAS CO., ST. ALOYSIUS (1924) [JC] Rev. Patrick F. Walsh.
P.O. Box 1199, 97023.
Catechesis/Religious Program—Tel: 503-630-2416. Students 18.

EUGENE, LANE CO.

1—ST. JUDE (1969) Rev. Thomas D. Yurchak.
Office: 4330 Willamette, 97405. Tel: 541-344-1191; Fax: 541-345-6001. Email: parishstjude@comcast.net.
Catechesis/Religious Program—Students 47.

2—ST. MARK (1961) Rev. Richard Rossman; Deacon Darrell Meter.
Res.: 1760 Echo Hollow Rd., 97402. Tel: 541-689-0725; Fax: 541-689-0569. Email: saintmark1760@hotmail.com. Web: www.saintmarkeugene.org.
Catechesis/Religious Program—Tel: 541-689-1054. Email: christdiva@gmail.com. Students 60.

3—ST. MARY (1887) [CEM] Revs. Mark V. Bachmeier; Mariano Regalado Escano; Bryce McProud; Deacon Thomas Altenhofen.
Church: 1062 Charnelton St., 97401. Tel: 541-342-1139; Fax: 541-334-6996. Email: info@stmaryeugene.com. Web: www.stmaryeugene.com.
Catechesis/Religious Program—Students 196.

4—ST. PAUL CATHOLIC CHURCH (1955) Rev. David Brown.
Res.: 1201 Satre St., 97401. Tel: 541-686-2345; Fax: 541-686-0037.
School—(Grades PreK-8) Tel: 541-344-1401; Fax: 541-344-2572. Lay Teachers 17; Students 292.
Catechesis/Religious Program—Students 50.

5—ST. PETER (1955) [JC] Rev. Richard Rossman; Deacon David Sorensen.
Res.: 1150 Maxwell Rd., 97404. Tel: 541-688-1051; Fax: 541-688-9434. Email: stpetercc@stpetereugene.org. Web: www.stpetereugene.org.
Catechesis/Religious Program—Tel: 541-689-0782. Email: stpeterff@stpetereugene.org. Paula J. Voborsky, D.R.E. Students 45.

6—ST. THOMAS MORE CHURCH formerly St. Thomas More (1915), (Catholic Campus Ministry) Rev. Daniel Rolland, O.P.; Corinne M. Lopez, D.R.E. In Res., Rev. Francis Goode, O.P.
Res.: 1386 E. 18th, 97403. Tel: 541-343-0065.
Church: 1850 Emerald St., 97403. Tel: 541-343-7021; Fax: 541-686-8028. Web: www.uonewman.org.
St. Thomas More Community—, Canonical Religious House of the Western Province.

FLORENCE, LANE CO., ST. MARY, OUR LADY OF THE DUNES (1951) Rev. Roger M. Fernando.
Church: 85060 U.S. Hwy. 101 S., Box 2640, 97439. Tel: 541-997-2312; Fax: 541-902-0417. Email: stmary@oregonfast.net. Web: www.oregonfast.net/stmary.
Catechesis/Religious Program—Students 38.

FOREST GROVE, WASHINGTON CO., ST. ANTHONY (1908) [JC] Rev. Jeffrey Meeuwsen; Lani Vandehey, Pastoral Assoc. Tel: 503-357-8147.
Res.: 1660 Elm St., 97116. Tel: 503-357-2989; Fax: 503-357-2217. Web: www.safg.org.
Catechesis/Religious Program—Students 156.

GERVAIS, MARION CO., SACRED HEART-ST. LOUIS (1847) [CEM] Rev. Ronald Nelson.
Office: 605 7th St., P.O. Box 236, 97026. Tel: 503-792-4231; Fax: 503-792-3749. Email: sachrt@xpressdata.net; secretary@sacredheart-stlouis.org.
School—(Grades K-8), 515 7th St., 97026. Tel: 503-792-4541; Fax: 503-792-3826. Email: lashindler@gervais.com. Lucy Shindler Shawn, Prin.; Marion Zellner, Librarian. Lay Teachers 5; Students 59.
Catechesis/Religious Program—Students 120.

GRAND RONDE, YAMHILL CO., ST. MICHAEL (1860) Rev. Terry O'Connell; Deacon David Briedwell, Pastoral Admin.
Res.: 48520 S.W. Hebo Rd., 97347. Tel: 503-879-5480; Fax: 503-879-5480.

GRANTS PASS, JOSEPHINE CO., ST. ANNE (1896) Rev. William Holtzinger; Deacon Robert Chapin.
Res.: 1131 N.E. 10th St., 97526. Tel: 541-476-2240; Fax: 541-476-2194. Email: office@stannechurch.com. Web: www.stannechurch.com.
Parish Center—Tel: 541-479-4848.
School—(Grades PreK-8) Tel: 541-479-1582; Fax: 541-956-4028. Web: www.saintannecatholic-school.org. Frankie Bytheway, Prin. Lay Teachers 8; Students 85.
Kelly Youth Center—Tel: 541-476-5802. Natalie Scott, Youth Min.
Catechesis/Religious Program—Students 188.
Mission—St. Patrick of the Forest 407 W. River St., Cave Junction, Josephine Co. 97523. Tel: 541-592-3658; Fax: 541-592-3580.
Mission—Our Lady of the River Mission 3625 N. River Rd., Gold Hill, Jackson Co. 97525. Tel: 541-582-1373.

GRESHAM, MULTNOMAH CO.

1—ST. ANNE (1957) Rev. Jose Luis Gonzalez.
Res.: 1015 S.E. 182nd Ave., 97233-5099. Tel: 503-665-4935; Fax: 503-661-2116.
Catechesis/Religious Program—Students 325.

2—ST. HENRY (1913) Rev. Charles E. Zach; Deacon Del DeSart.
Office: 346 N.W. First St., 97030. Tel: 503-665-9129; Fax: 503-665-8238. Email: sthenry_gresham@archdpdx.org. Web: www.sthenrygresham.org.
Catechesis/Religious Program—Students 201.

HILLSBORO, WASHINGTON CO., ST. MATTHEW (1902) [CEM] Revs. Peter Arteaga, M.Sp.S.; Pablo Sanchez, M.Sp.S.; Jose Ortega, M.Sp.S.
Church: 475 S.E. 3rd Ave., 97123-4499. Tel: 503-648-1998; Fax: 503-648-4489. Email: parishoffice@stmatthewhillsboro.org. Web: www.stmatthewhillsboro.org.
School—(Grades K-8), 221 S.E. Walnut St., 97123. Tel: 503-648-2512; Fax: 503-648-4518. Email: pdunn@stmatthewschoolhillsboro.org. Bev Wood, Librarian. Lay Teachers 15; Students 267.
Catechesis/Religious Program—Tel: 503-648-1998, Ext. 230. Email: mteeter@stmatthewhillsboro.org. Students 320.

INDEPENDENCE, POLK CO., ST. PATRICK CHURCH (1908) Rev. Msgr. Carl Gimpl.
Office: 1275 E St., 97351. Tel: 503-838-1242; Fax: 503-838-3856. Email: stpatrick97351@yahoo.com.
Res.: 1258 E St., 97351. Tel: 503-838-6442.
Catechesis/Religious Program—Students 229.

JORDAN, LINN CO., OUR LADY OF LOURDES (1885) [CEM] [JC 2] Rev. Ed Coleman.
Res.: 39043 Jordan Rd., Scio, 97374. Tel: 503-394-2437; Fax: 503-394-7045.
Catechesis/Religious Program—Tel: 503-769-2050. Deanne Sumpter, D.R.E. Students 8.
Mission—St. Patrick 7th St., Lyons, Linn Co. 97358. Tel: 503-394-2603; Fax: 503-394-7045.

JUNCTION CITY, LANE CO., ST. HELEN (1916) [CEM] Rev. Marco Escano.
Res.: 1350 W. 6th Ave., 97448. Tel: 541-998-8053; Fax: 541-998-9474. Email: churchrosehelen@qwestoffice.net.
Catechesis/Religious Program—Students 36.

KEIZER, MARION CO., ST. EDWARD (1967) Rev. Gary L. Zerr.
Office: 5303 River Rd. N., 97303. Tel: 503-393-5323. Email: grace@sainteds.com. Web: www.sainteds.com.
Catechesis/Religious Program—Fax: 503-463-5439. Students 305.

LAKE OSWEGO, CLACKAMAS CO., OUR LADY OF THE LAKE (1890) [CEM] Revs. Joseph S. McMahon; Robert Wolf; Deacon Charles Corey.
Mailing Address: 650 A Ave., 97034-2943. Tel: 503-636-7687; Fax: 503-636-9415. Email: office@ollparish.com. Web: www.ollparish.com.
School—(Grades K-8), 716 A Ave., 97034-2943. Tel: 503-636-2121; Fax: 503-635-7760. Email: jcodd@ollschool-lakeoswego.org. Web: www.ollschool-lakeoswego.org. Joan M. Codd, Prin.; Connie D. Gasperina, Librarian. Lay Teachers 18; Students 222.
Catechesis/Religious Program—Tel: 503-636-7687; Fax: 503-636-9415. Email: srjan@ollparish.com. Laura Patton, D.R.E. Students 270.

LEBANON, LINN CO., ST. EDWARD (1903) Rev. Peter O'Brien; Deacon Richard E. Triska.
Office: 100 Main St., 97355. Tel: 541-258-5333; Fax: 541-258-2511. Email: stedwardslebanon@comcast.net.
Res.: 251 Second St., 97355.
Catechesis/Religious Program—Tel: 541-258-2224. Students 115.

LINCOLN CITY, LINCOLN CO., ST. AUGUSTINE (1925) [CEM] Rev. Amancio J. Rodrigues; Deacon William Ennis.
1139 N.W. Hwy. 101, 97367. Tel: 541-994-2216; Fax: 541-994-6554. Email: staugustinechurch@embarqmail.com.
Rectory—1139 N.W. Inlet St., 97367.
Catechesis/Religious Program—Students 27.

MCMINNVILLE, YAMHILL CO., ST. JAMES (1876) [CEM] Rev. Terry O'Connell.
Res.: 1145 N.E. First St., 97128. Tel: 503-472-5232; Fax: 503-472-4414.
School—(Grades PreK-5), 206 N. Kirby St., 97128. Tel: 503-472-2661; Fax: 503-472-5201. Lay Teachers 9; Students 104.
Catechesis/Religious Program—Students 195.
Mission—St. Martin de Porres 407 Ferry St., Dayton, Yamhill Co. 97114. Tel: 503-864-2378; Fax:

503-864-3211.

MEDFORD, JACKSON CO., SACRED HEART OF JESUS (1928) [JC] Revs. Kelly Vandehey; Jesus Angelo Te; Deacon Ron Filardi.
Church: 517 W. Tenth St., 97501. Tel: 541-779-4661; Fax: 541-774-9474. Web: www.sacredheartmedford.org.
School—Sacred Heart School, (Grades PreSchool-8), 431 S. Ivy, 97501. Tel: 541-772-4105; Fax: 541-732-0633. Email: sgray@shcs.org. Web: www.shcs.org. Shirley Gray, Prin.; Susie Schweitzer, Librarian. Lay Teachers 19; Students 266.
Mission—St. Joseph 280 N. 4th, Jacksonville, Jackson Co. 97530.
Catechesis/Religious Program—Students 427.

MILWAUKIE, CLACKAMAS CO.

1—CHRIST THE KING (1961) Rev. David Shaw; Deacon Jim Pittman.
Res.: 7414 S.E. Michael Dr., 97222. Tel: 503-659-1475, Ext. 301; Fax: 503-659-6138. Email: office@ctk.cc. Web: www.ctk.cc.
School—(Grades K-8) Tel: 503-785-2411; Fax: 503-794-9607. Email: office@ctkweb.org. Web: www.ctk-web.org. Joseph Bridgeman, Prin. Lay Teachers 15; Students 231.
Catechesis/Religious Program—Tel: 503-785-2413. Email: religiouseducation@ctk.cc. Students 68.

2—ST. JOHN THE BAPTIST (1912) Revs. Maxy D'Costa, S.F.X.; Mark Gikenyi, Parochial Vicar.
Res.: 10955 S.E. 25th, 97222. Tel: 503-654-5449; Fax: 503-653-9567. Email: parishoffice@sjbcatholicchurch.org. Web: www.sjbcatholicchurch.org.
School—(Grades PreSchool-8), 10956 S.E. 25th, 97222. Tel: 503-654-0200; Fax: 503-654-8419. Web: www.sjbcatholicschool.org. Sisters 2; Lay Teachers 13; Students 206.
Catechesis/Religious Program—Tel: 503-659-2760; Fax: 503-653-9567. Email: reoffice@sjbcatholicchurch.org. Students 190.

MOLALLA, CLACKAMAS CO., ST. JAMES (1938) Rev. Theodore R. Prentice.
Res.: 301 Frances St., 97038. Tel: 503-829-2080; Fax: 503-829-2806.
Catechesis/Religious Program—Students 115.

MONROE, BENTON CO., ST. ROSE OF LIMA (1883) [CEM] Rev. Marco Escano.
Mailing Address & Office: *c/o St. Helen*, 1350 W. 6th Ave., Junction City, 97448.
Church: 470 S. Fifth, 97456. Tel: 541-998-8053; Fax: 541-998-9474. Email: churchrosehelen@qwestoffice.net.
Catechesis/Religious Program—Students 10.

MOUNT ANGEL, MARION CO., ST. MARY (1881), (German), [CEM 2] Rev. Philip Waibel, O.S.B.
Res.: 575 E. College St., 97362. Tel: 503-845-2296; Fax: 503-845-2297. Web: www.stmarymtangel.org.
Catechesis/Religious Program—Tel: 503-845-4282. Email: kabaldwin@hotmail.com. Students 422.
Mission—Holy Rosary [CEM] Scotts Mills, Marion Co.

MYRTLE CREEK, DOUGLAS CO., ALL SOULS (1952) [JC] Rev. William A. Ryan, O.S.A.
Res.: 1242 N.E. Spruce St., P.O. Box 810, 97457. Tel: 541-863-3271; Fax: 541-863-6759. Email: allsoulsparish@gmail.com.
Catechesis/Religious Program—Students 19.
Mission—Holy Family 243 Marshall Ave., P.O. Box 136, Glendale, Douglas Co. 97442.

NEWBERG, YAMHILL CO., ST. PETER (1907) Rev. Donald Gutmann.
Res.: 2315 N. Main, 97132-6081. Tel: 503-538-4312; Fax: 503-538-5693. Email: stpeter.office@frontier.com.
Catechesis/Religious Program—Email: lkrehbiel@archdpdx.org. Laurie Krehbiel, C.R.E. Students 131.

NEWPORT, LINCOLN CO., SACRED HEART PARISH (1889) [JC] Rev. Brian V. Allbright.
Rectory—140 N.W. 10th St., 97365.
Church: 927 N. Coast Hwy., P.O. Box 843, 97365. Tel: 541-265-5101. Email: sacredheartchurch@charterinternet.com.
Mission—St. Mary 231 E. Logsden Rd., Siletz, Lincoln Co. 97380. Tel: 541-444-1164.
Catechesis/Religious Program—Students 132.

NORTH BEND, COOS CO., HOLY REDEEMER (1906) [JC] Rev. Karl Schray.
Res.: 2250 16th St., 97459. Tel: 541-756-6901; Fax: 541-756-3234.
Catechesis/Religious Program—Tel: 541-756-0161. Students 78.

NORTH PLAINS, WASHINGTON CO., ST. EDWARD (1913) [CEM] Rev. Jeffrey Meeuwsen, Admin.
Mailing Address: P.O. Box 507, 97133.
Church: 10990 N.W. 313th Ave., 97133. Tel: 503-647-2131 (Parish); Fax: 503-647-7527. Email: mail@stedwardnp.net.
Catechesis/Religious Program—Tel: 503-647-2131. Students 95.

OAKRIDGE, LANE CO., ST. MICHAEL CATHOLIC CHURCH (1941) Rev. Kenneth Olsen.
Res.: 1584 Canal St., Springfield, 97477. Tel: 541-782-3262. Email: pmorrison@archdpdx.org.
Church: 76387 Crestview St., 97463.
Mission—St. Henry [JC] 38925 Dexter Rd., P.O. Box 65, Dexter, Lane Co. 97431. Tel: 541-937-3033.
Catechesis/Religious Program—Students 10.

OREGON CITY, CLACKAMAS CO., ST. JOHN THE APOSTLE (1842) [CEM] Rev. Msgr. Richard Huneger.
Res.: 417 Washington St., 97045. Tel: 503-742-8200; Fax: 503-742-8219. Email: sja@sja-catholicchurch.com. Web: www.sja-catholicchurch.com.
School—(Grades PreSchool-8) Tel: 503-742-8230; Fax: 503-742-8239. Email: principal@sja-eagles.com. Web: sja-eagles.com. Machelle Nagel, Prin.; Jean Wease, Librarian. Lay Teachers 16; Students 268.
Catechesis/Religious Program—Students 110.

OREGON CITY-REDLAND, CLACKAMAS CO., ST. PHILIP BENIZI (1969) Rev. Paschal Ezurike, Admin.
Res.: 18211 S. Henrici Rd., 97045. Tel: 503-631-2882; Fax: 503-631-7443. Web: www.philipbenizi.org.
Catechesis/Religious Program—Tel: 503-631-7124. Students 55.

RAINIER, COLUMBIA CO., NATIVITY B.V.M. (1910) Rev. Henry Rufo; Linda Bailey, Business Mgr.
Res.: 204 E. C St., P.O. Box 340, 97048. Tel: 503-556-5641. Email: parish_office@nativityofbvm.org.
Catechesis/Religious Program—Students 13.
Mission—St. John the Baptist (1917) 100 High St., Clatskanie, Columbia Co. 97016.

REEDSPORT, DOUGLAS CO., ST. JOHN THE APOSTLE (1924) Rev. Roger M. Fernando.
Res. & Rectory: 12 Saint Johns Way, 97467. Tel: 541-271-5621. Email: stjohns@presys.com.
Catechesis/Religious Program—Students 6.

ROCKAWAY, TILLAMOOK CO., ST. MARY BY THE SEA (1927) [JC] Rev. Laurence L. Gooley, S.J., Parish Admin.
Mailing Address: P.O. Box 390, 97136.
Church: 275 S. Pacific St., 97136. Tel: 503-355-2661 (Office); Fax: 503-355-9611.

ROSEBURG, DOUGLAS CO., ST. JOSEPH (1867) [CEM] Rev. Panneer Selvam.
Rectory—2425 W. Military Rd., 97471.
Church: 800 W. Stanton St., 97471. Tel: 541-673-5157; Fax: 541-672-5022.
Catechesis/Religious Program—Students 115.

ROY, WASHINGTON CO., ST. FRANCIS OF ASSISI (1908) [CEM] Rev. Michael Vuky.
Res.: 39135 N.W. Harrington Rd., Banks, 97106. Tel: 503-324-2231.
School—(Grades K-8), 39085 N.W. Harrington Rd., Banks, 97106. Tel: 503-324-2182; Fax: 503-324-7032. Tia Wren, Librarian. Sisters 1; Lay Teachers 5; Students 92.
Catechesis/Religious Program—Students 22.

ST. HELENS, COLUMBIA CO., ST. FREDERIC (1910) Rev. Joseph Barita.
Church: 175 S. 13th St., 97051. Tel: 503-397-0148; Fax: 503-366-3870. Email: stfred@comcast.net.
Catechesis/Religious Program—Tel: 503-397-0366. Students 40.

ST. LOUIS, MARION CO., ST. LOUIS, Closed. For sacramental records contact Sacred Heart-St. Louis, Gervias.

ST. PAUL, MARION CO., ST. PAUL (1839) [CEM] Rev. Msgr. Gregory Moys.
Res.: 20217 Christie St., N.E., P.O. Box 454, 97137. Tel: 503-633-4611.
School—(Grades PreK-8), 20327 Christie St., N.E., P.O. Box 188, 97137. Tel: 503-633-4622; Fax: 503-633-4624. Email: sppsoffice@stpaultel.com. Web: www.saintpaulparochial.org. Amanda Merrill, Prin.; Mike York, Librarian. Religious 1; Lay Teachers 5; Students 89.

SALEM, MARION CO.

1—ST. JOSEPH (1864) [JC] Revs. Todd Molinari; Henry Guillen-Vega.
Church: 721 Chemeketa St., N.E., 97301. Tel: 503-581-1623; Fax: 503-581-7271. Email: carolyn@stjosephchurch.com. Web: stjosephchurch.com.
School—(Grades PreK-6), 373 Winter St., N.E., 97301. Tel: 503-581-2147; Fax: 503-399-7045. Email: school@stjosephchurch.com. Web: www.stjoseph.com/school. Sisters of the Holy Names of Jesus and Mary 1; Lay Teachers 9; Students 191.
Catechesis/Religious Program—Tel: 503-585-5095. Email: re@stjosephchurch.com. Students 919.

2—QUEEN OF PEACE (1963) Rev. Timothy Mockaitis; Darlene Joynt, Pastoral Asst.
Office: P.O. Box 3016, 97302. Tel: 503-364-7202; Fax: 503-364-5882. Web: www.qpsalem.org.
School—(Grades K-6), 4227 Lone Oak Rd., S.E., 97302. Tel: 503-362-3443; Fax: 503-589-9411. Email: school@qpsalem.org. Debilyn Janota, Prin. Lay Teachers 13; Students 145.
Catechesis/Religious Program—Tel: 503-364-7202; Fax: 503-364-5882. Tricia Boyle, D.R.E. (PreK-Elementary); Cheri Posedel, D.R.E. (Grades 6-12); Bryce Herrmann, Coord. Faith Formation. Students 265.

3—ST. VINCENT DE PAUL (1925) [JC] Rev. Joseph Heuberger; Deacon Jose Roman Mendez; Patty Douglass, Pastoral Assoc.
Res.: 1025 Columbia St., N.E., 97301-7265. Tel: 503-363-4589; Fax: 503-363-9493. Email: stvdp@qwestoffice.net. Web: www.stvincentsalem.org.
School—(Grades PreK-6) Tel: 503-363-8457; Fax: 503-363-1516. Email: st.vincent@comcast.net. Web: www.stvincentsalem.org. David Spink, Librarian. Lay Teachers 5; Students 81.
Catechesis/Religious Program—1010 Columbia St. N.E., 97301-7207. Tel: 503-363-2166; Fax: 503-363-2339. Sheila Machado, D.R.E.; Lisa Mangers, Youth Min. (Young Adults). Students 435.

SANDY, CLACKAMAS CO., ST. MICHAEL THE ARCHANGEL (1898) Rev. Patrick F. Walsh.
Res.: 18090 S.E. Langensand Rd., 97055-9427. Tel: 503-668-4446; Fax: 503-668-4446.
Mission—St. John the Evangelist
Catechesis/Religious Program—Students 65.

SCAPPOOSE, COLUMBIA CO., ST. WENCESLAUS (1911) [CEM] Rev. James R. Stange.
Parish Office—Tel: 503-543-2110; Fax: 503-543-5159.
Res.: 51555 Old Portland Rd., 97056.
Catechesis/Religious Program—Tel: 503-543-7425; Fax: 503-543-5159. Students 110.

SCIO, LINN CO., ST. BERNARD (1912) Rev. Peter O'Brien.
Mailing Address: P.O. Box 45, 97374. Tel: 503-394-2625.
38810 Cherry St., 97374. Tel: 541-258-5333.
Catechesis/Religious Program—Tel: 503-394-3732. James Brown, D.R.E. at St. Bernard; Betty Beary, D.R.E. at St. Thomas.
Mission—St. Thomas 647 Third St., Jefferson, Marion Co. 97352. Tel: 541-327-2343.

SEASIDE, CLATSOP CO., OUR LADY OF VICTORY (1913) Rev. Nicholas Nilema, A.L.C.P./O.S.S.; Deacon Vern Korchinski.
P.O. Box 29, 97138.
Church: 120 Oceanway, 97138. Tel: 503-738-6161; Fax: 503-738-6182. Email: olvoffice@seasurf.net.
Mission—St. Peter the Fisherman, Tel: 503-436-2876.
Catechesis/Religious Program—Students 38.

SHADY COVE, JACKSON CO., OUR LADY OF FATIMA (1955) Rev. Mike Walker.
Office & Mailing Address: P.O. Box 116, 97539.
Office: 37 Church Ln., 97539.
Church: 56 Williams Ln., 97539. Tel: 541-878-2479.
Catechesis/Religious Program—

SHAW, MARION CO., ST. MARY - SHAW formerly St. Mary (1906) [CEM] Rev. Irudayaraj Amalanathan, Admin.
Mailing Address: P.O. Box 338, Aumsville, 97325-0338. Tel: 503-362-6159; Fax: 503-371-6435.
Res.: 9168 Silver Falls Hwy., S.E., P.O. Box 338, Aumsville, 97325.
Catechesis/Religious Program—Students 24.

SHERIDAN, YAMHILL CO., GOOD SHEPHERD (1908) Rev. Terry O'Connell; Deacon David J. Briedwell, Pastoral Admin.
Church: 127 N.E. Hill St., 97378. Tel: 503-843-2206; Fax: 503-843-2206.

SHERWOOD, WASHINGTON CO., ST. FRANCIS (1921) Rev. Thomas McCarthy, S.J.; Deacon William Bloudek.
Mailing Address & Church: 15651 S.W. Oregon St., 97140. Tel: 503-625-6185. Email: office@stfrancissherwood.org. Web: www.stfrancissherwood.org.
Res.: 22942 S.W. Pine St., 97140. Tel: 503-625-6851; Fax: 503-625-5914.
School—(Grades K-8), 15643 S.W. Oregon St., 97140. Tel: 503-625-0497; Fax: 503-625-0564. Web: www.stfrancissherwood.org. Lay Teachers 13; Students 189.
Catechesis/Religious Program—Tel: 503-625-6187; Fax: 503-625-5914. Students 166.

SILVERTON, MARION CO., ST. PAUL (1914) [CEM] Rev. William Hammelman, O.S.B.
Church: 1410 Pine St., 97381. Tel: 503-873-2044; Fax: 503-873-0304. Email: stpaulsilverton@frontier.com. Web: saintpaulsilverton.org.
Catechesis/Religious Program—Students 230.

SPRINGFIELD, LANE CO., ST. ALICE (1947) Rev. David Leo Jaspers.
Res.: 1520 F St., 97477-4161. Tel: 541-747-7041; Fax: 541-746-5213.
Catechesis/Religious Program—Students 92.

STAYTON, MARION CO., IMMACULATE CONCEPTION (1903) [CEM] Revs. Ed Coleman; Raul Marquez.
Res.: 1077 N. Sixth Ave., 97383. Tel: 503-769-2656; Fax: 503-769-5621. Web: www.immacstayton.org.
School—St. Mary, (Grades PreSchool-8), 1066 N. 6th St., 97383. Tel: 503-769-2718; Fax: 503-769-0560. Email: principal@stmarystayton.org. Web: www.stmarystayton.org. Lay Teachers 14; Students

222.
Catechesis/Religious Program—Email: gschmitt@archdpdx.org. Students 119.
Mission—St. Catherine of Siena First & Ivy, Mill City, 97360.

SUBLIMITY, MARION CO., ST. BONIFACE (1879) [CEM] Rev. Irudayaraj Amalanathan.
Res.: 375 S.E. Church St., 97385. Tel: 503-769-5664; Fax: 503-769-4292. Email: boniface@wvi.com.

SUTHERLIN, DOUGLAS CO., ST. FRANCIS XAVIER (1957) Rev. Panneer Selvam.
Mailing Address: 800 Stanton St., Roseburg, 97470. Tel: 541-673-5157 (Office); Fax: 541-672-5022.

SWEET HOME, LINN CO., ST. HELEN CATHOLIC CHURCH formerly St. Helen (1953) Rev. Fred Jeffrey Anthony; Deacon Robert Malone.
600 Sixth Ave., 97386.
Res.: 815 Fifth Ave., 97386. Tel: 541-367-2530. Email: sthelen@centurylink.net.
Catechesis/Religious Program—Students 53.
Mission—Holy Trinity 104 Blakely Ave., P.O. Box 145, Brownsville, Linn Co. 97327.

TIGARD, WASHINGTON CO., ST. ANTHONY (1878) [CEM] Revs. Leslie M. Sieg; Paul Materu, A.L.C.P.; Deacons Art Schmidt; Marco Espinoza.
Res.: 9905 S.W. McKenzie St., 97223. Tel: 503-639-4179; Fax: 503-624-2364. Email: office@stanthonytigard.org. Web: www.stanthonytigard.org.
School—(Grades PreK-8), 12645 S.W. Pacific Hwy., 97223. Fax: 503-620-5117. Email: school@stanthonytigard.org. Karen Bolliger, Prin. Lay Teachers 23; Students 381.
Catechesis/Religious Program—Students 598.
Mission—Mission of the Atonement 7400 S.W. Scholls Ferry Rd., Beaverton, Washington Co. 97008. Tel: 503-646-1344.

TILLAMOOK, TILLAMOOK CO., SACRED HEART (1890) [CEM] Rev. Joseph Sebasty.
2411 Fifth St., 97141. Tel: 503-842-6647; Fax: 503-842-3897.
Catechesis/Religious Program—Tel: 503-842-8984. Students 78.
Mission—St. Joseph P.O. Box 9, Cloverdale, Tillamook Co. 97112. Tel: 503-392-3685.

TUALATIN, CLACKAMAS CO., RESURRECTION CATHOLIC CHURCH formerly Church of the Resurrection (1981) Rev. William C. Moisant.
Mailing Address: 21060 S.W. Stafford Rd., 97062. Tel: 503-638-1579; Fax: 503-638-8754. Email: resurrec@teleport.com. Web: www.resurrection-catholic-parish.org.
Catechesis/Religious Program—Anna Arnesen Mosey, Dir. Faith Formation. Students 307.

VENETA, LANE CO., ST. CATHERINE OF SIENA (1954) Rev. J. Michael Morrissey.
Res.: 25181 E. Broadway Ave., P.O. Box 277, 97487-0277. Tel: 541-935-3933; Fax: 541-935-4184. Email: st.cofsienaveneta@aol.com.
Catechesis/Religious Program—Students 22.

VERBOORT, WASHINGTON CO., VISITATION B.V.M. (1875), (Dutch), [CEM] Rev. Michael Vuky.
Church: 4285 N.W. Visitation Rd., Forest Grove, 97116. Tel: 503-357-3860; Fax: 503-359-0819.
School—(Grades PreK-8), 4189 N.W. Visitation Rd., Forest Grove, 97116. Tel: 503-357-6990; Fax: 503-359-0819. Email: churchsecretary@vcsknights.org. Lay Teachers 9; Students 131.
Catechesis/Religious Program—Tel: 503-357-4190. Students 26.

VERNONIA, COLUMBIA CO., ST. MARY OF IMMACULATE CONCEPTION (1923) Rev. Luan Q. Tran, Admin.
Church: 960 Missouri Ave., P.O. Box 312, 97064. Tel: 503-429-8841; Fax: 503-429-8841 (call first). Email: stmarys08@agalis.net.
Catechesis/Religious Program—Tel: 503-429-8092. Students 33.

WALDPORT, LINCOLN CO., ST. ANTHONY (1949) Rev. Thomas Michael Layton, Admin.
685 N. Broadway, 97394. Mailing Address: P.O. Box 770, 97394. Tel: 541-563-3246; Fax: 541-563-3734. Email: stanthony@peak.org. Web: www.pioneer.net/~stanthony.
Catechesis/Religious Program—Students 12.

WILSONVILLE, CLACKAMAS CO., ST. CYRIL (1926) Rev. Stephen A. Stobie.
Church: 9205 S.W. Fifth St., 97070. Tel: 503-682-2332; Fax: 503-685-9294. Email: st.cyril@integra.net. Web: www.stcyrilparish.org.
Catechesis/Religious Program—Students 54.

WOODBURN, MARION CO., ST. LUKE (1899) [CEM] Revs. Angel A. Perez; Cary Ordiales Reniva, Parochial Vicar.
Office: 417 Harrison St., 97071. Tel: 503-981-5011; Fax: 503-981-5012. Email: st.luke@wbcable.net. Web: www.stlukewoodburn.com.
School—(Grades K-8), 529 Harrison St., 97071. Tel: 503-981-7441; Fax: 503-982-4697. Lay Teachers 11; Students 161.
Catechesis/Religious Program—Students 354.
Mission—St. Agnes 3052 D St., Hubbard, Marion Co. 97032.

YAMHILL, YAMHILL CO., ST. JOHN (1911) Rev. James Coleman, Admin.
Mailing Address: P.O. Box 580, 97148. Tel: 503-662-4291.
Catechesis/Religious Program—Students 85.

SOUTHEAST ASIAN VICARIATE

PORTLAND, MULTNOMAH CO., SOUTHEAST ASIAN VICARIATE (1982), Please refer to Our Lady of Lavang Church, Portland, OR., 5404 N.E. Alameda Dr., 97213.
Catechesis/Religious Program—Students 180.
Mission—St. Andrew Dung Lac 13715 S.W. Walker Rd., Beaverton, Washington Co. 97005. Tel: 503-643-9528; Fax: 503-644-8486.

Chaplains of Public Institutions

PORTLAND. *Department of Veterans' Affairs Medical Center*, 3710 S.W. U.S. Veterans' Hospital Rd., Box 1034, 97207. Tel: 503-220-8262, Ext. 57027; 503-220-8262, Ext. 57201; Fax: 503-721-1049. Rev. William E. Wickham, C.S.C.
Oregon Health Sciences University, 3181 S.W. Sam Jackson Park Rd., 97239. Tel: 503-222-2168. Rev. Jim Kolb, C.S.P. Tel: 503-222-2168.

EUGENE. *Lane County Adult Corrections*, 101 W. Fifth Ave., 97401. Tel: 541-682-2174; Fax: 541-682-2278. Sisters Margaret Graziano, S.N.J.M., Carol Lee, S.N.J.M.

NORTH BEND. *Shutter Creek Correctional Institution*, 95200 Shutters Landing Ln., 97459-0303. Tel: 541-756-6666; 541-756-6901; Fax: 541-756-6888. Rev. Karl Schray, Catholic Volunteer.

ROSEBURG. *U.S. Veterans' Administration Hospital*, 913 N.W. Garden Valley Blvd., 97470-6513. Tel: 541-673-5157. Rev. Paneer Selvam.

SALEM. *Hillcrest Youth Correctional Facility*, 2450 Strong Rd., 97302. Tel: 503-986-0421; Fax: 503-986-0406.
Mill Creek Correctional Facility, 5465 Turner Rd. S.E., 97317. Tel: 503-378-2601. Rev. Victor Perez, Chap.
Oregon State Correctional Institution, 3405 Deer Park Dr., S.E., 97310. Tel: 503-373-0100. Rev. Victor Perez.
Oregon State Penitentiary, 2605 State St., 97310. Tel: 503-373-1673. Rev. Victor Perez, Chap.
Santiam Correctional Institution, 4005 Aumsville Hwy., S.E., 97301-9112. Tel: 503-378-2144. Rev. Victor Perez, Chap.

SHERIDAN. *Federal Correctional Institution*, 27072 Ballston Rd., 97378-9601. Tel: 503-843-6357. Vacant.

WHITE CITY. *U.S. Veterans Affairs Domiciliary* 97503. Tel: 541-826-2111, Ext. 3321. Felix Vistal, Chap.

WILSONVILLE. *Coffee Creek Correctional Facility*, 24499 S.W. Grahams Ferry Rd., 97070. Tel: 503-570-6604; Fax: 503-570-6617. Vacant.

WOODBURN. *MacLaren Youth Correctional Facility*, 2630 N. Pacific Hwy., 97071. Tel: 503-981-9531, Ext. 315; Fax: 503-982-4414. Vacant.

Special Assignment:
Revs.—
Betschart, Joseph, North American College 00120 Vatican City State.
Carey, Raymond, P.O. Box 3019, Salem, 97302.
Maslowsky, Michael, 8601 S.W. Terwilliger Blvd., 97219.

On Duty Outside the Archdiocese:
Revs.—
Cihak, John, Villa Stritch, Via della Nocetta 63, Roma 00164 Italy.
Clark, David, The Von Hugel Institute, St. Edmund's College, Cambridge CB3 England.
King, Martin, 51 FW/HC, Unit 2067, Apo, AP 96278.

Absent on Leave:
Revs.—
Barricks, Robert, 3511 S.E. Vineyard Rd., Milwaukie, 97267.
Frison, Theodore, 4843 S.E. 30th, #38, 97202.
Hoang, Joseph, P.O. Box 3535, Bay City, 97107.

Retired:
Rev. Msgrs.—
Campbell, Francis, 7575 S.W. Danielle Ave., Beaverton, 97008.
Dernbach, Arthur, St. John Vianney Residence, 4630-A S.W. St. John Vianney Way, Beaverton, 97007.
Pham, James Ninh Van, 1949 S.W. Phyllis Pl., Gresham, 97080.
Revs.—
Altstock, Edward, St. John Vianney Residence, 4630-C S.W. St. John Vianney Way, Beaverton, 97007.
Baccellieri, Joseph, 13055 S.E. Stark St., #41, 97233.
Beno, Joseph, c/o 10375 S.W. Cormorant Dr., Beaverton, 97007.
Betts, John C., P.O. Box 3177, Albany, 97321.
Bliven, Edmond, St. John Vianney Residence, 4595-A S.W. St. John Vianney Way, Beaverton, 97007.
Brennan, Cathal, c/o 1701 Wood Duck St. N.E., Silverton, 97381.
Brouillard, John, 17704 N.W. Shadyfir Loop, Space 39, Beaverton, 97006.
Brown, Bruce, 6005 Skyline Dr., West Linn, 97068.
Chun, Francis, 4525-B S.W. St. John Vianney Way, Beaverton, 97007.
Cullings, David Ronald, 638 Wimbleton Ct., Eugene, 97401.
Cunniff, Vincent, St. John Vianney Residence, 4655-D S.W. St. John Vianney Way, Beaverton, 97007.
DePra, Italo, 78 Bonita Rd., Chula Vista, CA 91911.
Dieringer, James J., P.O. Box 683, Pacific City, 97135.
Domin, John M., 14645 S.W. Farmington, Beaverton, 97007.
Dowd, James, 1875 N.E. Country Club Dr., Canby, 97013.
Durand, Donald, 62 N.W. Ava, Gresham, 97030.
Flach, Carl, J.C.L., Maryville Nursing Home, 14645 S.W. Farmington Rd., Beaverton, 97007.
Fleming, Brendan, c/o P.O. Box 91538, 97291.
Galluzzo, James, 1314 N.W. Irving, #512, 97209.
Hume, Kenneth, 19453 Stillmeadow Dr., Oregon City, 97045.
Jacobson, Gary, St. John Vianney Residence, 4595-B S.W. St. John Vianney Way, Beaverton, 97007.
Janes, David, 90971 Hwy. 101, #74, Warrenton, 97146.
Knusel, Frank, 34799 N. Honeyman Rd., Scappoose, 97056.
Krall, Jack, 1167 N.W. Wallula, #E-331, Gresham, 97030.
Krueger, Robert, 1136 S.E. Oak, 97214.
Lau, Michael, 8065 S.W. Laurelwood Ct., 97225.
McGrann, John, 336 S.E. 50th Ave., #1, 97215.
McHugh, Donald, 4525 S.W. St. John Vianney Way, Apt. C, Beaverton, 97007.
Moore, Neil, 1619 N.W. Bridgeway Ln., Beaverton, 97006.
Mosbrucker, Jacob A., 3828 N.E. 79th St., 97213.
Nguyen, Joseph Hau Duc, S.E. Asian Vicariate, 5404 N.E. Alameda Dr., 97213.
Palladino, Robert J., 43330 E. Marmot Rd., Sandy, 97055.
Quintal, Gerald, 835 Sundown Dr., North Otis, 97368.
Remington, Leo, 8012 N. Interstate Ave., 97217.
Reynolds, Daniel, St. John Vianney Residence, 4655-C S.W. St. John Vianney Way, Beaverton, 97007.
Sassano, Rock, 71403 Fishhawk Rd., Birkenfeld, 97016.
Sprauer, Michael, 2838 E. Burnside St., 97214.
Vandehey, Scott A., 4630-B S.W. St. John Vianney Way, Beaverton, 97007.
Waddill, Dale T., 208 Madison St., Oregon City, 97045-2535.
Weber, Theodore, 14460 S.E. Sieben Creek Dr., Clackamas, 97015.

Permanent Deacons:
Altenhofen, Thomas, St. Mary, Eugene
Amsberry, Charles, St. Michael, Portland
Anderson, Chris, St. Mary, Corvallis
Appel, Leo Henry, II, Star of the Sea, Brookings
Bloudek, William, St. Francis, Sherwood
Bozulich, Martin, Holy Redeemer, North Bend
Briedwell, David, Good Shepherd, Sheridan; St. Michael, Grand Ronde
Brinker, Kenneth, St. Peter, Portland
Burke, Harold, Immaculate Heart, Portland
Caldwell, Michael, St. Joseph the Worker, Portland
Casey, Craig Joseph, Cathedral, Portland, OR
Cervantes, Ricardo, Our Lady of the Mountain, Ashland
Chapin, Robert L., Jr., St. Anne, Grants Pass
Ciffone, Donald, St. Rose, Portland
Corey, Charles, Our Lady of the Lake, Lake Oswego
Cramer, Paul, Nativity of the Blessed Virgin Mary, Rainier
Delgado, Gerald Matthew, St. John the Baptist, Milwaukie
DeSart, Del, St. Henry, Gresham
Desmarais, Dennis, St. Juan Diego, Portland
Diehm, Brian, St. Thomas More, Portland
Dooley, Timothy, Holy Family, Portland
Edmonson, Brett Michael, Holy Trinity, Beaverton
Ennis, William, St. Augustine, Lincoln City

Espinoza, Jesus, St. Alexander, Cornelius
Espinoza, Marco, St. Anthony, Tigard
Fillo, Kevin Michael, St. Matthew, Hillsboro
Garcia, Felix, Shepherd of the Valley, Central Point
Giger, Gerald, St. Patrick, Canby
Gonzalez, Jose, St. Anne, Gresham
Gornick, Thomas, Cathedral, Portland
Gutierrez, Jose, Holy Cross, Portland
Hammes, David, St. Cecilia, Beaverton
Hix, Jim, St. John the Baptist, Milwaukie
Jacob, Ramon, St. Andrew, Portland
Kolbet, Scott Allen, St. John Fisher, Portland
Korchinski, Vernard, Our Lady of Victory, Seaside
Larner, Martin, Jr., St. Mary, Albany
Little, Robert, St. Pius X, Portland
Lukosh, Robert, Holy Redeemer, Portland
Luz, John, (Unassigned)
Malone, Robert, St. Helen, Sweet Home
McVeigh, James G., Our Lady of the Mountain, Ashland
Mendez, Jose, St. Vincent de Paul, Salem
Morin, Edward, (Retired), (Unassigned)
Page, Robert, St. Patrick, Independence
Park, William Thomas, St. Stephen, Portland
Partlow, David, (Retired)
Pham, Michael Chau, Our Lady of Lavang, Portland
Pham, Nghia (Paul), Our Lady of Lavang, Portland
Philip, Donald, (Unassigned)
Pittman, James Allen, Christ the King, Milwaukie
Potts, Francis, St. Mary, Corvallis
Rasca, Leo, St. Joseph, Salem
Richardson, Bill, St. Cecilia, Beaverton
Ries, John D., (Retired)
Rilatt, John, Holy Redeemer, Portland
Rodriguez, Raul, St. James, McMinnville
Romeo, Jimenez, St. Andrew, Portland
Schmidt, Arthur, St. Anthony, Tigard
Seifer, Leo, St. Mary, Mount Angel
Soper, Leonard, St. Benedict Lodge, McKenzie Bridge
Sorensen, David E., St. Peter, Eugene
Stenbeck, John H., St. Joseph, Roseburg
Tabor, Stephen, Immaculate Conception, Stayton
Triska, Richard, St. Edward, Lebanon
Vandecoevering, Allen, St. Joseph, Salem
Vu, An, Our Lady of Sorrows, Portland
Wagner, Daniel, St. Ignatius, Portland
Walker, Lawrence, St. Pius X, Portland
Williams, Richard, St. John the Baptist, Port Orford; Mission of Holy Trinity, Bandon

INSTITUTIONS LOCATED IN THE ARCHDIOCESE

[A] SEMINARIES AND SCHOLASTICATES

PORTLAND. *Franciscan Formation Community*, 5323 S.E. Knight St., 97206. Tel: 503-287-9223. Web: www.sbfranciscans.org. Bro. Robert Rodrigues, O.F.M., Postulant Dir. Brothers 1; Postulants 4.

Jesuit Novitiate of Sheridan Orgeon, 3301 S.E. 45th Ave., 97206. Tel: 503-774-5699; Fax: 503-775-6335. Rev. Thomas J. Lamanna, S.J., Rector & Dir. Novices. Priests 1; Novices 5.

MOUNT ANGEL. *Felix Rougier House of Studies*, 585 E. College St., 97362. Tel: 503-845-1181; Fax: 503-845-1189. P.O. Box 499, St. Benedict, 97373. Revs. Jose Gerardo Alberto, M.Sp.S., Supr.; Joel Quezada, M.Sp.S., Vice Supr. Priests 2; Brothers 10.

ST. BENEDICT. *Mount Angel Seminary* 97373. Tel: 503-845-3951; Fax: 503-845-3128. Email: registrar@mtangel.edu. Very Rev. J. Richard Paperini, Pres. & Rector; Rt. Rev. Peter Eberle, O.S.B., Vice-Rector & Dir. of Human Formation (Retired); Rev. Paschal Cheline, O.S.B., Vice Rector, Dir. Spiritual Life; Dr. Elaine Park, S.S.L., S.T.D., Academic Vice Pres.; Revs. Paul Peri, Dir. Pastoral Formation; Ralph Recker, O.S.B., Dir. of Admission, Student Svcs. & Formation Dir.; Marina Keys, Registrar; Tamara Swanson-Orr, Dir. Immigration Svcs. & Business Mgr.; Dr. Seynow House, Ph.D., Assoc. Dean, Graduate School, Theology; Dr. Creighton Lindsey, Ph.D., Assoc. Dean, Undergraduate School. Priests 17; Deacons 1; Sisters 3; Lay Teachers 19.
Formation Directors: Rt. Rev. Peter Eberle, O.S.B. (Retired); Revs. Ralph Recker, O.S.B.; Liem Nguyen, O.S.B.; Rory Pitstick; Joel Quezada, M.Sp.S.; Terrence P. Tompkins.

[B] COLLEGES AND UNIVERSITIES

PORTLAND. **University of Portland*, 5408 N. Strong St., 97203. Tel: 503-943-7911; Fax: 503-943-7401. Email: webmaster@up.edu. Web: www.up.edu. Drew Harrington, Dir. Library. Endowed by the Congregation of Holy Cross; established 1901. Priests 10; Brothers 1; Sisters 3; Lay Teachers 197; Adjunct Faculty 120; Students 3,974.
Executive Officers of the University: Rev. William Beauchamp, C.S.C., Pres.; Bro. Donald J. Stabrowski, C.S.C., Provost; Rev. Mark Poorman, C.S.C., Exec. Vice Pres.; James Lyons, Vice Pres. Univ. Rels.; Alan P. Timmins, Vice Pres. Financial Affairs; James Ravelli, Vice Pres., Univ. Opers.; Madeline Doll, Admin. Asst., CSC Office.
Faculty Staff: Revs. Jeffrey Allison, C.S.C.; Robert Antonelli, C.S.C.; William Beauchamp, C.S.C.; Michael T. Belinsky, C.S.C.; Gary Chamberland, C.S.C.; Jeffrey Cooper, C.S.C.; John Donato, C.S.C., Assoc. Vice Pres. Student Life; Mark Ghyselinck, C.S.C.; Charles Gordon, C.S.C.; Patrick Hannon, C.S.C.; Thomas Hosinski, C.S.C.; James Lies, C.S.C.; Charles McCoy, C.S.C.; Joseph Moyer, C.S.C.; Francis Murphy, C.S.C., Rel. Supr.; Gerry Olinger, C.S.C.; Claude Pomerleau, C.S.C.; Mark Poorman, C.S.C.; Randall C. Rentner, C.S.C.; Richard Rutherford, C.S.C.; Ronald Wasowski, C.S.C.; Arthur F. Wheeler, C.S.C.; Bro. Thomas Giumenta, C.S.C. In Res. Revs. Richard Berg, C.S.C. (Retired); George C. Bernard, C.S.C. (Retired); William Hund, C.S.C. (Retired); James Rigert, C.S.C. (Retired); Charles D. Sherrer, C.S.C. (Retired); William E. Wickham, C.S.C.; John Wironen, C.S.C.; Bros. Ken Allen, C.S.C., (Retired); Donald J. Stabrowski, C.S.C., Provost.
Following is the Academic Structure of the University: Bro. Donald J. Stabrowski, C.S.C., Provost.
College of Arts and Sciences Tel: 503-943-7760; Fax: 503-943-7804. Rev. Stephen C. Rowan, Dean.
School of Nursing Tel: 503-943-7509; Fax: 503-943-7729. Dr. Joanne R. Warner, Interim Dean.
School of Business Administration Tel: 503-943-7224; Fax: 503-943-8041. Dr. Robin D. Anderson, Dean.
School of Engineering Tel: 503-943-7314; Fax: 503-943-7316. Dr. Sharon A. Jones, Dean; Jason S. McDonald, Dean, Admissions. Tel: 503-943-7751. Email: mcdonaja@up.edu.
School of Education Tel: 503-943-7315; Fax: 503-943-8042. Email: watzke@up.edu.
Graduate School Tel: 503-943-7107. Dr. Thomas G. Greene, Dean; Drew Harrington, Dean, Library. Tel: 503-943-7111; Fax: 503-943-7491.

MARYLHURST. *Marylhurst University*, P.O. Box 261, 97036. Tel: 503-636-8141; Fax: 503-636-9526. Email: studentinfo@marylhurst.edu. Web: www.marylhurst.edu. Judith Johansen, J.D., Pres.; Dr. David Plotkin, Provost & Contact Person; Nancy Hoover, Librarian. Sisters 5; Lay Teachers 260; Students 1,917.

[C] HIGH SCHOOLS, ARCHDIOCESAN

PORTLAND. *Central Catholic High School* (1939) (Coed), 2401 S.E. Stark St., 97214. Tel: 503-235-3138; Fax: 503-233-0073. Email: pcorrado@centralcatholichigh.org. Web: www.centralcatholichigh.org. Rev. Timothy Murphy, Pres. Emeritus; John Garrow, Prin.; Sr. Maureen Kalsch, S.S.M.O., Assoc. Prin. Academics; John Harrington, Pres.; Natalie Patterson, Librarian; Nanette Martin, Contact Person & Registrar. Priests 1; Sisters 2; Lay Teachers 53; Students 830.

EUGENE. *Marist Catholic High School* formerly Marist High School (Coed), 1900 Kingsley Rd., 97401. Tel: 541-686-2234; Fax: 541-342-6451. Email: jconroy@marisths.org. Web: www.marisths.org. Rev. David Ronald Cullings, Chap. (Retired); Jay Conroy, Prin. & Contact; Tony Huck, Librarian. Priests 1; Lay Teachers 39; Students 512.

STAYTON. *Regis Catholic High School* formerly Regis High School (1963) (Coed), 550 W. Regis St., 97383. Tel: 503-769-2159; Fax: 503-769-1706. Email: principal@regishighschool.net. Web: www.regishighschool.net. Joan Gilles, Prin.; Jula Galvin, Librarian. Lay Teachers 17; Students 132.
Regis High School Foundation, 550 W. Regis St., 97383. Tel: 503-769-2159; Fax: 503-769-1706. Email: principal@regishighschool.net. Web: www.regishighschool.net.

[D] HIGH SCHOOLS, PRIVATE

PORTLAND. *De La Salle North Catholic High School (Coed)*, 7528 N. Fenwick Ave., 97217. Tel: 503-285-9385; Fax: 503-285-9546. Email: mpowell@delasallenorth.org. Web: www.delasallenorth.org. Matthew D. Powell, Pres.; Tim Joy, Prin.; Chris Frazier, Vice Prin.; Drake Shelton, Dean, Students; Bro. Joe Kirk, F.S.C.; Lillian Knight, Librarian. Sisters 1; Brothers 2; Lay Teachers 17; Students 269.

Jesuit High School (1956) (Coed), 9000 S.W. Beaverton-Hillsdale Hwy., 97225-2491. Tel: 503-292-2663; Fax: 503-292-0134. Email: jgladstone@jesuitportland.org. Web: www.jesuitportland.org. Mr. John J. Gladstone, Pres. & Contact Person; Mrs. Sandra Satterberg, Prin.; Mr. Paul Hogan, Academic Vice Prin.; Mr. James Naggi, Vice Prin. Admin. Svcs.; Michael J. Schwab, Vice Pres. Devel.; Mr. Chris Smart, Vice Prin. Student Life; Mrs. Erin Deklotz, Admissions Dir.; Mr. Donald Clarke, Campus Min.; Gregory Lum, Librarian. The Society of Jesus. Priests 4; Community: Priests 6; Lay Staff 123; Students 1,237.
Faculty: Rev. Joel K. Adams, S.J., J.K., Supr. In Res. Revs. Craig Boly, S.J.; William E. Hayes, S.J.; Edward P. McTighe, S.J.; Lawrence F. Robinson, S.J.; Paul Grubb, S.J.

St. Mary's Academy (1859) (Girls), 1615 S.W. Fifth Ave., 97201. Tel: 503-228-8306; Fax: 503-223-0995. Email: pat.barr@stmarysdpdx.org. Web: www.stmaryspdx.org. Patricia Barr, Prin.; Cindy Daniels, Librarian. Lay Teachers 50; Students 641.

BEAVERTON. *Valley Catholic Middle & High Schools*, (Grades 7-12), (Coed), 4275 S.W. 148th Ave., 97007. Tel: 503-644-3745; Fax: 503-646-4054. Web: www.valleycatholic.org. Mr. Ross Thomas, Prin. Sisters of St. Mary of Oregon Sisters 1; Lay Teachers 40; Students 452.

MEDFORD. *St. Mary's School*, (Grades 6-12), (Coed), 816 Black Oak Dr., 97504. Tel: 541-773-7877; Fax: 541-772-8973. Email: bspillane@smschool.us. Web: www.smschool.us. Frank Phillips, Head of School; Bernyne Spillane, Business Office; Carol Monders, Librarian; Frank Phillips, Prin. Lay Teachers 48; Lay Staff 23; Students 450.

MILWAUKIE. *LaSalle Catholic College Preparatory* formerly Lasalle High School (1966) La Salle Catholic College Preparatory; (Coed), 11999 S.E. Fuller Rd., 97222. Tel: 503-659-4155; Fax: 503-659-2535. Email: tdudley@lsprep.org. Web: www.lsprep.org. Thomas R. Dudley, Prin., Admin. & Contact Person; Denise L. Jones, Pres.; Colette Cassinelli, Librarian. Lay Teachers 46; Students 634.

SALEM. **Archbishop Francis Norbert Blanchet School dba Blanchet Catholic School* (1995) (Grades 6-12), 4373 Market St., N.E., 97301. Tel: 503-391-2639; Fax: 503-399-1259. Email: info@blanchetcatholicschoolcom. Web: www.blanchetcatholicschool.com. Tony Guevaro, Prin. Lay Teachers 25; Students 375.

[E] ELEMENTARY SCHOOLS, AREA

EUGENE. *O'Hara Area Elementary Catholic School* (1889) (Grades PreSchool-8), 715 W. 18th, 97402. Tel: 541-485-5291; Fax: 541-484-9138. Web: www.oharaschool.org. Mrs. Tammy Conway, Prin.; Lynn Gori, Librarian; Ellen Booth, Librarian. Comprised of students from the following parishes in Eugene: St. Jude, St. Mark, St. Mary, St. Paul, St. Peter, St. Alice, the Newman Center, Our Lady of Perpetual Help, St. Catherine, St. Helen, St. Henry, Nativity Ukrainian Catholic Church Lay Teachers 31; Students 522.

[F] ELEMENTARY SCHOOLS, PRIVATE

PORTLAND. **St. Andrew Nativity School* (2000) (Grades 6-8), 4925 N.E. 9th Ave., 97211. Tel: 503-335-9600; Fax: 503-335-9494. Email: info@nativityportland.com. Web: www.nativityportland.com. Mike Chambers, Prin.; Loretta Wiltgen, Pres.; Carol Ramsey, Librarian. Lay Teachers 8; Students 63.

Franciscan Montessori Earth School/St. Francis Academy, 14750 S.E. Clinton St., 97236. Tel: 503-760-8220; Fax: 503-760-8333. Email: info@fmes.org. Web: www.fmes.org. Sr. Kathleen Ann Cieslak, F.S.E., Prin. Staffed by Franciscan Sisters of the Eucharist. Franciscan Sisters of the Eucharist 5; Lay Teachers 28; Students 277.

BEAVERTON. *Valley Catholic Elementary School*, (Grades K-5), 4420 S.W. St. Mary's Dr., 97007. Tel: 503-626-7781; 503-718-6500; Fax: 503-718-6520. Email: jmanning@valleycatholic.org. Web: www.valleycatholic.org. Joe Manning, Interim Prin. & Contact Person; Bob Weber, Pres.; Shauna Jasperson, Librarian. Sisters of St. Mary of Oregon Sisters 2; Lay Teachers 19; Students 342.

[G] SOCIAL AND MINISTERIAL SERVICES

PORTLAND. *Catholic Charities of the Archdiocese of Portland in Oregon*, 2740 S.E. Powell Blvd., 97202. Tel: 503-231-4866; Fax: 503-231-4327. Email: dkeenan@catholiccharitiesoregon.org. Web: www.catholiccharitiesoregon.org. Pietro R. Ferrari, Exec. Dir.; Richard Deml, C.P.A., CFO. CSS Group Homes 96; Resettlement Services 775; Total persons annually served by CSS 130,238.

Catholic Charities Social Service Division of Portland, 2740 S.E. Powell Blvd., 97202. Tel: 503-231-4866; Fax: 503-231-4327. Douglas Alles, Social Svc. Dir. Programs include: crisis pregnancy counseling, adoption services, mental health, case management, domestic violence intervention, parent/child development services, refugee resettlement, resident services, Hispanic health outreach, ministry to the elderly, Project Rachel, Immigration Legal Services, housing and social services for homeless women, anti-human trafficking, trafficking victims assistance, affordable housing for low income families and individuals, gang outreach and prevention, Hispanic school support, financial counseling and healthcare worker employee assistance.

Catholic Youth Organization/Camp Howard, 825 N.E. 20th, Ste. 120, 97232-2295. Tel: 503-231-9484; Fax: 503-231-9531. Web: www.cyocamphoward.org. Sr. Krista Von Borstel, S.S.M.O., Exec. Dir. Programs include: Youth recreation & camping.

Catholic Community Services of Lane County, 1025 G. St., Springfield, 97477. Tel: 541-345-3628; Fax: 541-744-2272. Web: www.cclc.org. Thomas Mulhern, Exec. Dir. Programs include: Emergency shelter, utilities, and food, single mothers shelter, drug dependent mothers shelter, family shelter, young parents program, family self-sufficiency program.

Catholic Community Services of Mid-Willamette Valley and the Central Coast, 3737 Portland Rd., N.E., Salem, 97301. Tel: 503-390-2600; Fax: 503-390-6648. Web: www.ccswv.org. Jim Seymour, Exec. Dir. Programs include: Center for delinquent youth, developmentally & physically disabled group homes, shelter for displaced youth, counseling center, Hispanic mental health outreach, child abuse, parent/newborn program.

Catholic Charities In Southern Oregon, 724 S. Central Ave., Ste. 210, Medford, 97501. Tel: 541-779-0803; Fax: 541-245-5368. Programs include: Immigration legal services.

[H] CHILD DEVELOPMENT CENTERS

PORTLAND. *Providence Health & Services-Oregon dba *Providence Child Center* 830 N.E. 47th Ave., 97213. Tel: 503-215-2400; Fax: 503-215-0660. Patricia Budo, Operations Admin.

Sisters of Providence in Oregon. Total Staff 242.

Providence Health & Services-Oregon dba Center for Medically Fragile Children Tel: 503-215-2400; Fax: 503-215-2424. The Center for Medically Fragile Children at Providence Child Center is the only nursing facility in the Northwest providing skilled nursing care for children with complex medical needs in a residential setting. Fifty-eight beds are dedicated to children needing long-term chronic care, short-term assessment and/or respite care, and end-of-life care. Total Assisted 90.

Providence Health & Services-Oregon dba Providence Montessori School Tel: 503-215-2400; Fax: 503-215-0660. Email: montessorischool@providence.org. Web: www.providence.org/montessori. Preschool and elementary education for children ages 3 to 7 with a broad array of developmental needs and abilities. Students 275.

Providence Health & Services-Oregon dba Providence Wee Care Tel: 503-215-6832; Fax: 503-215-0333. Child development program for children of Providence Medical Center employees and the community, ages 6 weeks to 6 years. Developmental and age-appropriate activities support child's growth and developement. Students 113.

Providence Health & Services-Oregon dba Providence Neurodevelopmental Center for Children Tel: 503-215-2233; Fax: 503-215-2478. Providence Neurodevelopmental Center for Children (PNCC) provides diagnostic and therapy services for children with complex developmental medical needs as well as children with developmental delays. Total Assisted 1,705.

[I] RESIDENTIAL SCHOOLS FOR YOUTHS WITH EMOTIONAL-SOCIAL PROBLEMS

BEAVERTON. *St. Mary's Home for Boys, Inc.*, 16535 S.W. Tualatin Valley Hwy., 97006. Tel: 503-649-5651; Fax: 503-649-7405. Francis Maher, Exec. Dir. & Contact Person. Residential & day treatment center for behaviorally & emotionally disturbed children. Out patient mental health services. Staff 115; Students 172.

[J] GENERAL HOSPITALS

PORTLAND. *Providence Health & Services-Oregon dba Providence Portland Medical Center* (1941) 4805 N.E. Glisan St., 97213. Tel: 503-215-1111; 503-215-6833; Fax: 503-215-6858. Email: bruce.cwiekowski@providence.org. Web: www.providence.org. Revs. Jon Buffington (EST); Kevin T. Clarke, S.J., Chap.; Bruce Cwiekowski, Dir. Pastoral Care & Contact. Tel: 503-215-6833; Fax: 203-215-5619; Rev. John Hubbard, Presbyterian Chap.; Revs. Augustine Manyama, A.J., Chap.; Vernetta Ollison, Chap.; Barnabas Shayo, A.J., Chap.; Jon Sturm, Chap.; Herbert Wheatley, Chap.; Sr. Mary Coakley, O.S.F., Chap.; Mary Follen, On Call Chap.; Patti Fetterman, Admin. Asst.; Martha Leven, Lay Chap. (Catholic); Mary Ann Henry, Lay Chap. (Catholic); Gordon MacDonald, Chap. (Catholic); Jason Mann, Chap.; Sabine Maresco, Chap.; Jean McQuiggin, Chap. (Catholic); Andrea Partenheimer, Music Thanatologist; Stephanie Orscheln, On Call Chap.; James Stephens, Chap.; Sandra J. Walker, E.L.C.A., Clinical Pastoral Educ. Supvr.

Providence Health Systems, Oregon Region Priests 6; Sisters 1; Bed Capacity 483; Total Staff 3,417; Patients Assisted Annually 761,243.

Providence Portland Medical Foundation, 4805 N.E. Glisan, 97213. Tel: 503-215-6187; Fax: 503-215-0530. Carolyn Winter, Chief Development Officer for Oregon; Kelly Buechler, Exec. Dir.

Providence Health & Services-Oregon dba Providence St. Vincent Medical Center 9205 S.W. Barnes Rd., 97225. Tel: 503-216-1234; Fax: 503-216-2468. Web: www.providence.org. Revs. Francis Njau, A.J., Catholic Chap.; Godfred Ocun, A.J., Catholic Chap. & Dir. Pastoral Svcs.; Constantine Shikuku, Chap.; Peter Siamoo, Catholic Chap.; Sr. Patricia Valentine, S.N.J.M., Catholic Chap.; Rev. Dean Schrock, Chap.; Barbara Blair, Protestant Child Life Specialist; Janice Burger, Admin., Providence St. Vincent Medical Center & Contact Person; Ovidiu Peter Cotuna, Protestant Chap.; Charlene K. Epp, Protestant Chap.; Richard Gilbert, Protestant Chap.; Jean Keith-Altemus, Protestant Chap.; Laura A. Moya, Music Thanatologist; Ms. Judith A. McGowan, Catholic Chap.; Ashton Roberts, Protestant Chap.; Ms. Shiela Schaeffer, Catholic Chap.; Ms. Christine Wallace, Protestant Chap.; Beth Warrick, Protestant Life Specialist; Sr. Lynda Thompson, S.N.J.M., Mission Integration Dir.

Providence Health System., Providence Health System. Priests 4; Sisters 2; Total Staff 3,962; Bed Capacity 523; Patients Assisted Annually 456,215.

**St. Vincent Medical Foundation, Portland* Tel: 503-216-2226; Fax: 503-216-4140.

EUGENE/SPRINGFIELD. **Sacred Heart Medical Center*, P.O. Box 10905, 97440. Tel: 541-222-7300; Fax: 541-222-2270. Web: www.peacehealth.org. 3333 RiverBend Dr., Springfield, 97477. Roger Saydack, Interim COO & Admin.; Tom Reitinger, Interim CEO, PeaceHealth OR; Robert V. Scheri, Dir. Mission Svcs, & Spiritual Care & Chap.; Revs. J. Noel Hickie (BAK), Priest Chap.; Kenneth Olsen, Priest Chap.; David Waggoner, Chap.; Ann-Marie Lemire, Chap.; Gordon Ruddick, Chap.; Micki Shirey, Chap.; Edward Harrod, Chap.; Patricia Hoenshell, Chap.; Margie Sherman, Chap.; Angel Scott, Chap.; Marcella Fox, Chap. Sisters of St. Joseph of Peace., Div. of PeaceHealth. Sisters 2; Bed Capacity 438; Total Staff 2,865; Patients Assisted Annually 154,410.

FLORENCE. *Peace Harbor Hospital*, 400 Ninth St., 97439. Tel: 541-997-8412; Fax: 541-997-2913. Email: pbyers@peachhealth.org. Web: www.peacehealth.org. Rick Yecny, Regl. CEO; Sr. Noreen Terrault, C.S.J.P., Pastoral Care; Peggy Byers, Contact Person. Critical access hospital owned and operated by Peace Health, Bellevue, WA. Bed Capacity 21; Total Staff 525; Patients Assisted Annually 15,320.

MEDFORD. *Providence Health & Services-Oregon dba Providence Medford Medical Center* 1111 Crater Lake Ave., 97504-6225. Tel: 541-732-5000; Fax: 541-732-5872. Rev. James Clifford, O.S.A., Dir., Mission & Spiritual Care; Sr. Patricia Marie Landin, S.S.M.O., Chap.; Josue Delgado, Chap.; John Dungey, Chap.; April Tavares, Chap.

Providence Health System-Oregon dba Providence Medford Medical Center Priests 1; Sisters 1; Bed Capacity 168; Total Staff 1,056; Patients Assisted Annually 152,659.

**Providence Community Health Foundation, Medford*, 940 Royal Ave., Ste. 410, 97504. Tel: 541-732-6766; Fax: 541-772-2861. Email: jodi.barnard@providence.org. Web: www.providence.org/medford/foundation.

MILWAUKIE. *Providence Health & Services-Oregon dba *Providence Milwaukie Hospital* (1968) 10150 S.E. 32nd Ave., 97222. Tel: 503-513-8300; Fax: 503-513-8191. Email: Denise.Anderson@providence.org. Web: www.providence.org/milwaukie. Denise Anderson, Dir. Pastoral Care & Mission Integration; Chuck Altig, Chap.; Linda Smith, Chap.; Judith Kleinstein, Chap.; Alexander Wendeheart, Chap.

Providence Health System & Service, Oregon Region. Bed Capacity 77; Total Staff 521; Patients Assisted Annually 125,746.

**Providence Milwaukie Foundation, Milwaukie* (1988) Tel: 503-513-8625; Fax: 503-513-8319. Keith Hyde, Exec. Dir.

NEWBERG. *Providence Health & Services-Oregon dba Providence Newberg Medical Center* 1001 Providence Dr., 97132-1887. Tel: 503-537-1555; Fax: 503-537-1800. Alan Olive, Chief Exec.; Jack R. Sumner, Dir. Finance & Contact Person; Diana Endicott, Chap.; Harry Litzenberg, Chap.; Gordon Powell, Chap.; Lee Shafer, Chap.; William Larson, Chap.; John Mahaffy, Chap.; Rev. Gregg Selander, Mission & Spiritual Care Dir.; Thomas Struck, Chap.; Ken Vandenhoek, Chap.; Sr. Suzette Bautista, Mission & Spiritual Care Assoc. Sisters 1; Bed Capacity 40; Total Staff 527; Patients Assisted Annually 125,746.

OREGON CITY. *Willamette Falls Hospital dba Providence Willamette Falls Medical Center* 1500 Division St., 97045. Tel: 503-656-1631; Fax: 503-650-6807. Web: www.providence.org. Russ Reinhard, Admin.; Elizabeth Sublette, CFO; Catherine Elia, Dir., Spiritual Leadership; Julie Dir-Munoz, Chap.; Rev. Jon Sturm, Chap.; Alexander Wendeheart, Chap.; Mary Peterson, On Call Chap. Bed Capacity 143; Total Staff 680; Patients Assisted Annually 69,599.

Providence Willamette Falls Medical Foundation, 1500 Division St., 97045. Tel: 503-656-1631; Fax: 503-650-6807.

ROSEBURG. *Mercy Medical Center, Inc.*, 2700 Stewart Pkwy., 97471. Tel: 541-673-0611; Fax: 541-677-2391. Web: www.mercyrose.org. Kelly C. Morgan, Pres. & CEO; John S. Kasberger, Vice Pres. Fin., CFO. Tel: 541-677-2458; Marvin Gwaltney, Vice Pres., Mission Services; Rev. Cletus Osuji, Catholic Chap. Bed Capacity 174; Total Staff 1,183; Patients Assisted Annually 191,113.

Mercy Foundation, Inc., 2700 Stewart Pkwy., 97471. Tel: 541-677-4818; Fax: 541-677-4891.

Linus Oakes, Inc., 2700 Stewart Pkwy., 97471. Tel: 541-677-4800; Fax: 541-677-2106.

SEASIDE. *Providence Health & Services-Oregon dba Providence Seaside Hospital* 725 S. Wahanna Rd., 97138-7735. Tel: 503-717-7000; Fax: 503-717-7505. Email: mary.trudell@providence.org. Web: www.providence.org/northcoast. Krista Farnham, Admin.; Mary Trudell, Contact Person.

Sisters of Providence in Oregon. Bed Capacity 45; Total Staff 368; Patients Assisted Annually 79,522.

**Providence Seaside Hospital Foundation, Inc.* Tel: 503-717-7601; Fax: 503-717-7505.

[K] RETIREMENT AND ASSISTED LIVING

PORTLAND. **St. Anthony Village (activity of St. Anthony Village Enterprise)*, 3560 S.E. 79th Ave., 97206. Tel: 503-775-4414; Fax: 503-771-9189. Email: kmarshall@worldspark.org. Web: www.villagesage.com. Rev. Michael Maslowsky, Pres.; Karen Marshall, Admin. & Contact Person; Emily Dunlap, Leasing Coord. Assisted living facility centered around Catholic Parish. Independent, assisted living and memory care unit. Total Assisted Annually 169; Bed Capacity 126; Staff 64.

**Assumption Village (activity of St. Anthony Village Enterprise)* (2002) 9121 N. Burr Ave., 97203. Tel: 503-283-5644; Fax: 503-283-5692. Web: www.villagesage.org. Rev. Michael Maslowsky, Pres.; Rosemarie Davis, Leasing Coord.; Derrick Landis, Admin. Retirement Village, Senior independent and assisted living, chapel with daily Mass multiple activities, gardens, intergenerational interaction with neighborhood and local social service agencies. Total Staff 35; Bed Capacity 107; Total Assisted Annually 102.

BEAVERTON. *Maryville Nursing Home*, 14645 S.W. Farmington Rd., 97007. Tel: 503-643-8626; Fax: 503-520-1435. Kathleen Parry, Admin. & Contact Person; Delores Focht, Dir. Nurses. Bed Capacity 155; Hospice Care 45; Total Assisted Annually 470; Total Staff 220.

MOUNT ANGEL. *Providence Health & Services-Oregon dba Providence Benedictine Nursing Center* 540 S. Main St., 97362-9532. Tel: 503-845-6841; Fax: 503-845-9229. Web: www.providence.org/benedictine. Emily Dazey, Exec. Dir.; Rev. Aelred Yockey, O.S.B., Chap.; Rev. Dana McBrien, Interfaith Chap. Providence Health & Services. Total Staff 190; Patients Assisted Annually 589.

Providence Benedictine Orchard House Tel: 503-845-2544; Fax: 503-845-2560. Personalized Living Center (ALF). Total Staff 25; Bed Capacity 50; Assisted 81.

Providence Benedictine Home Health Tel: 503-845-9226; Fax: 503-845-9880. Total Staff 55; Patients Assisted Annually 1,454.

[L] MONASTERIES AND RESIDENCES OF PRIESTS

PORTLAND. *Ascension Friary* (Province of St. Barbara, Franciscan Friars of Oregon, Franciscan Friars of California), 404 S.E. 68th Ave., 97215. Tel: 503-954-2180. Revs. Ben R. Innes, O.F.M., Guardian; Jorge Hernandez, O.F.M.; Jose Luis Nerio, O.F.M.

Colombiere Community, 3220 S.E. 43rd Ave., 97206-3104. Tel: 503-595-1930; Fax: 503-595-1929.

Web: www.nwjesuits.org. Revs. Roy L. Antunez, S.J.; Thomas J. Bunnell, S.J.; Peter D. Byrne, S.J., Supr.; Gerald T. Cobb, S.J.; Richard H. Ganz, S.J.; James R. Laudwein, S.J.; Patrick J. Lee, S.J., Prov.; John J. Morris, S.J.; John V. Murphy, S.J.; Brad R. Reynolds, S.J.; John Ridgway, S.J.; Thomas Royce, S.J.; Michael A. Tyrrell, S.J.; William D. Voger, S.J.; Christopher S. Weekly. Priests 19.

The Grotto, The National Sanctuary of Our Sorrowful Mother (1924) 85th and N.E. Sandy Blvd., P.O. Box 20008, 97294-0008. Tel: 503-254-7371; 503-254-7372 (Monastery); Fax: 503-254-7948. Revs. John M. Topper, O.S.M., Prior & Exec. Dir.; Robert S. Anderson, O.S.M. Priests 4; Brothers 2. In Res. Revs. Ignatius M. Kissel, O.S.M., Shrine Staff; Damian M. Kobus, O.S.M. (Retired); Deogracias Alejandria, O.S.M., Shrine Staff.

Holy Cross Fathers & Brothers, C.S.C. - University of Portland, 5000 N. Willamette Blvd., 97203. Tel: 503-943-8024; Fax: 503-943-7313. Email: csc@up.edu. Revs. Jeffrey Allison, C.S.C.; Robert Antonelli, C.S.C.; William Beauchamp, C.S.C.; Michael T. Belinsky, C.S.C.; Richard Berg, C.S.C. (Retired); George C. Bernard, C.S.C. (Retired); Gary Chamberland, C.S.C.; Jeffrey Cooper, C.S.C.; John Donato, C.S.C.; Mark Ghyselinck, C.S.C.; Charles Gordon, C.S.C.; Patrick Hannon, C.S.C.; Thomas Hosinski, C.S.C.; William Hund, C.S.C. (Retired); James Lies, C.S.C.; Charles McCoy, C.S.C.; Joseph Moyer, C.S.C.; Francis Murphy, C.S.C., Supr.; Gerry Olinger, C.S.C.; Claude Pomerleau, C.S.C.; Mark Poorman, C.S.C.; Randall C. Rentner, C.S.C.; James Rigert, C.S.C. (Retired); Richard Rutherford, C.S.C.; Charles D. Sherrer, C.S.C. (Retired); Ronald Wasowski, C.S.C.; Arthur F. Wheeler, C.S.C.; William E. Wickham, C.S.C.; John Wironen, C.S.C.; Bros. Ken Allen, C.S.C., (Retired); Thomas Giumenta, C.S.C.; Donald Stabrowski, C.S.C.

Students on Scholarship from the CSC Community Rev. Silvester Makwali.

Holy Rosary Priory, 375 N.E. Clackamas St., 97232-1103. Tel: 503-235-3163; Fax: 503-235-3551. Very Rev. Gerald A. Buckley, O.P., Prior; Revs. Paul A. Duffner, O.P. (Retired); Francis Hung Le, O.P.; Vincent Kelber, O.P.; Thomas More J. McGreevy, O.P. (Retired); Brian T.B. Mullady, O.P.

Jesuit Provincial Office (Society of Jesus, Oregon Prov.), 3215 S.E. 45th Ave., 97206. Tel: 503-226-6977; Fax: 503-228-6741. Email: oregonprov@nwjesuits.org. Web: www.nwjesuits.org. P.O. Box 86010, 97286-0010. Revs. Peter D. Byrne, S.J., Asst. Parishes & Spiritual Ministries; Patrick J. Lee, S.J., Prov.; Michael A. Tyrrell, S.J., Socius Treas.; Patrick J. Twohy, S.J., Dir. Rocky Mountain Mission / NW, Asst. for Native Ministries; Mr. William Lockyear, CFO; Rev. Gerald T. Cobb, S.J., Asst. for Formation; Ms. Cindy Reopelle, Asst. for Secondary & Middle Schools; Asst. for Jesuit-lay Partnerships; Ms. Kathleen Marks, R.N., Asst. for Health Care; Rev. John C. Bentz, S.J., Vocation Dir. Priests 23; Novices 5.

Oregon Province Priests serving outside the U.S.: Revs. Joseph B. Danel, S.J.; Dan T. Mai, S.J.; John J. McLain, S.J.; Bartholomew J. Murphy, S.J.; Michael J. Schultheis, S.J.; Gary N. Smith, S.J.; Quan M. Tran, S.J.; Alan G. Yost, S.J.; Bro. James P. Selinsky, S.J.

AMITY. *Brigittine Priory of Our Lady of Consolation - The Order of the Most Holy Savior* (1976) 23300 Walker Ln., 97101. Tel: 503-835-8080; Fax: 503-835-9662. Email: monks@brigittine.org. Web: www.brigittine.org. Bro. Bernard Ner Suguitan, O.Ss.S., Prior & Contact. Professed 7; Novices 2.

BANKS. *Missionaries of the Holy Spirit, M.Sp.S., Provincial House (Christ the Priest Province)*, 39085 N.W. Harrington Rd., 97106. P.O. Box 130, 97106. Tel: 503-324-2492; Fax: 503-324-2493. Revs. Domenico DiRaimando, M.Sp.S., Prov. Supr.; Juan Jose Gonzalez, M.Sp.S., Prov. Councilor; Bro. Santos Mendoza, M.Sp.S.

CORVALLIS. **Saint John Society*, 2121 N.W. Monroe, 97330. Tel: 541-753-1392; Fax: 541-753-1392. Email: stjohnsociety@socsj.org. Web: www.socsj.org. Priests 2; Brothers 5.

HILLSBORO. *Missionaries of the Holy Spirit, M.Sp.S.*, 642 S.E. 20th Ct., 97123. Revs. Pedro Arteaga, M.Sp.S.; Jose Ortega, M.Sp.S.; Pablo Sanchez, M.Sp.S.

LAFAYETTE. *The Cistercian (Trappist) Abbey of Our Lady of Guadalupe* (1948) P.O. Box 97, 97127. Tel: 503-852-7174; Fax: 503-852-7748. Email: community@trappistabbey.org. Rt. Rev. Peter McCarthy, O.C.S.O., Abbot; Revs. Dismas Gannon, O.C.S.O., Prior; Casey Bailey, O.C.S.O., Novice Master; Martin Cawley, O.C.S.O.; Timothy Clark, O.C.S.O.; Howard Curtis, O.C.S.O.; Joseph-Benedict Donnelly, O.C.S.O.; Francis King, O.C.S.O.; Richard Layton, O.C.S.O., Business Mgr.; Timothy Michell, O.C.S.O.; Peter Plakut, O.C.S.O.; Mark Weidner, O.C.S.O. Order of Cistercians of the Strict Observance. Solemnly Professed 30; Priests 12; Total in Community 31.

MOUNT ANGEL. *Discalced Carmelite Friars (OCD)*, 300 Humpert Ln., 97362. Tel: 503-845-2240 Carmelite House of Studies. *Carmelite House of Studies*, P.O. Box 260, 97362. Tel: 503-845-2240 Carmelite House of Studies; Fax: 503-845-2243. Rev. Jan Lundberg, O.C.D., Rector. Priests 2; Brothers 6.

Missionaries of the Holy Spirit, M.Sp.S., 585 E. College St., 97362. Tel: 503-845-1182; Fax: 503-845-1189. P.O. Box 499, St. Benedict, 97373. Tel: 503-845-1181; Fax: 503-845-1189. Revs. Jose Gerardo Alberto, M.Sp.S., Rector; Joel Quezada, M.Sp.S., Vice Supr. Serving the Felix Rougier House of Studies.

MYRTLE CREEK. *Augustinian Community*, P.O. Box 810, 97457-0116. Tel: 541-863-3271; Fax: 541-863-6759. Email: frbillosa@gmail.com. Revs. James Clifford, O.S.A.; William A. Ryan, O.S.A., Regl. Supr.

ST. BENEDICT. *Mt. Angel Abbey* 97373. Tel: 503-845-3030; Fax: 503-845-3594. Email: postmaster@mtangel.edu. Web: www.mountangelabbey.org. Rt. Revs. Gregory Duerr, O.S.B., Abbot & Prior; Nathan Zodrow, O.S.B. (Retired); Peter Eberle, O.S.B. (Retired); Joseph Wood, O.S.B. (Retired); Revs. Timothy Sander, O.S.B.; Athanasius Buchholz, O.S.B.; Benedict Suing, O.S.B.; Leo Rimmele, O.S.B.; Augustine DeNoble, O.S.B.; Bede Partridge, O.S.B.; Bruno Becker, O.S.B.; Cosmas White, O.S.B.; Alexander Plasker, O.S.B.; Paschal Cheline, O.S.B.; Edmund Smith, O.S.B.; Vincent Trujillo, O.S.B., Prior; William Hammelman, O.S.B.; Jeremy Driscoll, O.S.B.; Paul Thomas, O.S.B.; Philip Waibel, O.S.B.; Marius Walter, O.S.B.; Jerome Young, O.S.B.; Aelred Yockey, O.S.B.; Pius X Harding, O.S.B.; Thomas Thien Dang, O.S.B.; Vincent Liem Nguyen, O.S.B.; Michael Mee, O.S.B.; Odo Recker, O.S.B., Subprior; Ralph Recker, O.S.B.; Ezekiel Lotz, O.S.B.; Martin Grassel, O.S.B.; Joseph Nguyen, O.S.B. Priests 31; Monks in Perpetual Vows 47; Brothers 16.

[M] CONVENTS AND RESIDENCES FOR SISTERS

PORTLAND. *Convent of Sisters of Reparation of the Sacred Wounds of Jesus, Novitiate*, 2120 S.E. 24th Ave., 97214-5504. Tel: 503-236-4207; Fax: 503-236-3400. Email: repsrs@comcast.net. Web: www.reparationsisters.org. Sr. Mary of the Angels, S.R., Supr. Gen. Sisters 2; Private Vows 1; Donne Members 168.

Convent of the Good Shepherd, 562 N. Rosa Parks Way, 97217. Tel: 503-283-4931; Fax: 503-283-4933. Sr. Cathleen Boerboom, Contact Person. Sisters 3.

Holy Spirit Sisters (1950) 2736 N.E. 54th Ave., 97213. Tel: 503-239-0328; Fax: 503-239-0328. Email: hssportland@gmail.com. Sr. Emiliana E. Moshi, Contact Person. Sisters 6.

"Rose Hall" Reparation and Prayer Center, 2120 S.E. 24th Ave., 97214-5504. Tel: 503-236-4207; Fax: 503-236-3400. Email: mmangels@comcast.net. Web: www.reparationsisters.org. Sr. Mary of the Angels, S.R., Dir.

Sister Adorers of the Holy Cross Convent (1670) 7408 S.E. Alder, 97215. Tel: 503-254-3284; Fax: 503-255-3097. Email: mtgportland@gmail.com. Sr. Mary Trinh Nguyen, M.T.G., Supr. & Contact Person.

Adorers of the Holy Cross Sisters, First foundation in the United States in 1976, founded by Bishop Pierre Lambert de la Motte. Represented in the Archdiocese of Portland in Oregon, the Diocese of Arlington, VA and the Diocese of Sacramento, CA. Sisters 12; Candidates 3.

BEAVERTON. *Convent, Franciscan Missionary Sisters of Our Lady of Sorrows* (1939) 3600 S.W. 170th Ave., 97006-5099. Tel: 503-649-7127; Fax: 503-259-9507. Email: sisters@olpretreat.org. Web: www.olpretreat.org. Sr. Anne Marie Warren, O.S.F., Supr. Gen., Contact Person. Sisters 17.

The Lovers of Thuthiem Holy Cross Sisters, 7361 S.W. 175th Ter., 97007. Tel: 503-259-8767; Fax: 503-259-8767. Email: ngoan55@hotmail.com. Sr. Maria Ngoan Nguyen, Supr. Sisters 6.

Sisters of St. Mary of Oregon (1886) 4440 S.W. 148th Ave., 97007. Tel: 503-644-9181; Fax: 503-646-1102. Email: srcharleneh@ssmo.org. Web: www.ssmo.org. Sisters Charlene Herinckx, S.S.M.O., Supr. Gen.; Rita Watkins, S.S.M.O., Local Supr.; Rev. Godfred Ocun, A.J., Chap. Motherhouse of the Sisters of St. Mary of Oregon. Professed Sisters 65.

BRIDAL VEIL. *Franciscan Sisters of the Eucharist Convent* (1973) *Administrative Center*, 48100 E. Columbia R. Hwy., Box 23, 97010. Tel: 503-695-2375; Fax: 503-695-2368. Email: fsebridalveil@fsecommunity.org. Web: www.fsecommunity.org. Sr. Helen Jean Brinkman, F.S.E., Supr. & Contact Person. Sisters 7.

EUGENE. *Carmel of Maria Regina* (1957) (Contemplative Order), 87609 Green Hill Rd., 97402. Tel: 541-345-8649; Fax: 541-345-4857. Sr. Elizabeth Mary, O.C.D., Prioress. Professed Sisters 10.

MARYLHURST. *Convent of the Holy Names*, P.O. Box 398, 97036. Tel: 503-675-2449; Fax: 503-675-2453. Email: meholohan@snjmuson.org. Web: www.snjmusontario.org. Sr. Kathleen Kirchen, S.N.J.M., Campus Coord. Provincial House of the Sisters of the Holy Names of Jesus & Mary, S.N.J.M. Sisters 151.

MOUNT ANGEL. *Queen of Angels Monastery* (1882) 840 S. Main St., 97362-9527. Tel: 503-845-6141; Fax: 503-845-6585. Email: qamosb@yahoo.com. Web: www.benedictine-srs.org. Sr. Donna Marie Chartraw, O.S.B., Prioress. Monastery of the Benedictine Sisters of Mt. Angel.; See separate listing for Shalom Prayer Center (retreat center) and St. Joseph Shelter (special center for social services and assistance). Sisters 39.

WEST LINN. *Convent of the Society of the Holy Child Jesus*, 19622 Sun Cir., 97068. Tel: 503-577-3619. Sisters 5.

[N] RETREAT HOUSES

BEAVERTON. *Our Lady of Peace Retreat* (1953) 3600 S.W. 170th Ave., 97006-5099. Tel: 503-649-7127; Fax: 503-259-9507. Email: sisters@olpretreat.org. Web: www.olpretreat.org. Sr. Anne Marie Warren, O.S.F., Supr. Gen. & Contact Person. Franciscan Missionary Sisters of Our Lady of Sorrows 17.

GOLD HILL. *St. Rita's Retreat Center*, P.O. Box 310, 97525. Tel: 541-855-1333. Email: strita@rvi.net. Rev. Stephen J. Fister, Dir. & Contact Person.

MCKENZIE BRIDGE. *St. Benedict Lodge Dominican Retreat & Conference Center* (1955) 56630 N. Bank Rd., 97413-9614. Tel: 541-822-3572 (Office & Dominican Res.). Email: tfdeman@msn.com. Web: sblodge.opwest.org. Revs. Thomas DeMan, O.P., Chap. & Contact; Kieran Jeremiah Healy, O.P., Chap. & Dir.; David Willis Geib, O.P., Chap. & Asst. Dir.; Deacon Leonard Soper.

46052 McKenzie Hwy., Vida, 97488. Tel: 541-896-0284. Email: dcnlgjms@earthlink.net.

MILWAUKIE. *Franciscan Spiritual Center* (2002) *Lake Plaza South*, 6902 S.E. Lake Rd. #300, 97267. Tel: 503-794-8542; Fax: 503-794-8556. Email: info@francisspctr.com. Web: francisspctr.com. Mary Erickson, Dir.; Sisters Mary Jo Chaves, O.S.F., Spiritual Dir.; Celeste Clavel, O.S.F., Business Mgr.; Emma Holdener, O.S.F., Office Mgr. & Body-work; Guadalupe Medina, O.S.F., Hispanic Ministry. Sisters of St. Francis of Philadelphia., Spiritual direction; day retreats; workshops and body-work. Sisters 4; Staff 8.

MOUNT ANGEL. *Benedictine Sisters Shalom Prayer Center*, 840 S. Main St., 97362-9527. Tel: 503-845-6773; Fax: 503-845-6585. Email: shalom@mtangel.net. Web: www.benedictine-srs.org/shalom. Sr. Dorothy Jean Beyer, O.S.B., Dir. & Contact Person. Sisters 4.

ST. BENEDICT. *Mount Angel Abbey Retreat House* 97373. Tel: 503-845-3025; Fax: 503-845-3027. Email: retreat@mtangel.edu. Web: www.mountangelabbey.org. Rev. Pius X Harding, O.S.B., Guest Master.

[O] SOCIETY OF ST. VINCENT DE PAUL

PORTLAND. **Society of St. Vincent de Paul Portland Council* (1869) Portland Council, P.O. Box 42157, 97242-0157. Tel: 503-235-7837; Fax: 503-233-5581. Email: annap@svdppdx.org. Web: svdppdx.org. 5120 S.E. Milwaukie Ave., 97202. Fax: 503-233-5581. Anna Plaster, Exec. Dir. & Contact Person. Staff 13; Total Assisted Annually 467,897.

EUGENE. *Society of St. Vincent de Paul* Archdiocesan Council., 705 S. Seneca St., P.O. Box 24608, 97402. Tel: 541-687-5820; Fax: 541-683-9423. Email: svdp@svdp.us. Web: www.svdp.us. Louise (Molly) Westling, Pres.

St. Vincent de Paul Society of Lane County, Inc. Eugene Council., 705 Seneca Rd., P.O. Box 24608, 97402. Tel: 541-687-5820; Fax: 541-683-9423. Email: info@svdp.us. Web: www.svdp.us. Louise (Molly) Westling, Pres.; Terrence R. McDonald, Exec. Dir. & Contact Person.

MEDFORD. *Society of St. Vincent de Paul* (1982) Rogue Valley District Council, P.O. Box 1663, 97501. Tel: 541-772-3828; Fax: 541-772-6886. Email: vincent@mind.net. Web: www.stvincentdepaulmedford.info. Dennis Mihocko, Pres. Total Assisted Annually 94,400; Volunteers 250.

SALEM. **St. Vincent de Paul Society of Mid-Williamette Valley* (1957) 3745 Portland Rd., N.E., 97303. Tel: 503-364-3210; Fax: 503-361-7475. Email: shari@svdpsalem.org. P.O. Box 7864,

97303. Jerry Boschler, District Council Pres.; Shari Crawford, Exec. Dir. Total Assisted Annually 102,145.

SUTHERLIN. *Council of Douglas County of the Society of St. Vincent dePaul* (1997) 112 E. Central, P.O. Box 949, 97479. Tel: 541-459-3394. Email: svdp@qwest.net. Camille Hong, Pres.; Delia M. Lester, Treas.

[P] NEWMAN CENTERS

PORTLAND. *Lewis & Clark College* 0615 S.W. Palatine Hill Rd., P.O. Box 171, 97219. Tel: 503-768-7080; Fax: 503-768-7084. Email: schaff@clark.edu. Web: www.lclark.edu/~newman. Sr. Loretta Schaff, O.S.F., Campus Min. Tel: 503-768-7080.

Portland State University Newman Center St. Michael Church, 424 S.W. Mill St., 97201. Tel: 503-222-1725; Fax: 503-827-7689. Web: www.pdxcatholic.org. Rev. Lucas Laborde, Campus Minister.

University of Portland Campus Ministry, 5000 N. Willamette Blvd., 97203. Tel: 503-943-7131; Fax: 503-943-8567. Email: ministry@up.edu. Web: www.up.edu. Revs. Gary Chamberland, C.S.C., Dir. Campus Ministry; Michael T. Belinsky, C.S.C., Asst. Dir. Faith Formation; Vinci Paterson, Asst. Dir. Faith Formation; Maureen Briare, Assoc. Dir. for Music; Stacey Noem, Asst. Dir. for Faith Formation; Josh Noem, Asst. Dir. for Faith Formation; Theresa McCreary, Program Asst.

ASHLAND. *Southern Oregon University (Ashland)* , Walsh Memorial Newman Center, 1150 Ashland St., 97520. Tel: 541-482-0825; Fax: 541-488-5174. Email: olmyouthaya@gmail.com. Web: www.newmansou.com. Rev. Sean Weeks, Chap.

CORVALLIS. *Newman Center at Oregon State University (Corvallis)* Newman Center, 2127 N.W. Monroe St., 97330. Tel: 541-752-6818. Email: newmancenter@socsj.org. Web: www.osunewman.org. Rev. Ignacio Llorente, Office Dir.

Trinity Court (Student Housing) 2200 N.W. Jackson, 97330. Tel: 503-245-7899. Rev. Steve Clovis, Chap.

EUGENE. *Lane Community College* 1850 Emerald St., 97403. Tel: 541-343-7021; Fax: 541-686-8028.

University of Oregon (Eugene) Newman Center, St. Thomas More Catholic Parish, 1850 Emerald St., 97403. Tel: 541-343-7021; Fax: 541-686-8028. Web: www.uonewman.org. Rev. Daniel Rolland, O.P.; Corinne M. Lopez, Dir. Faith Formation.

FOREST GROVE. *Pacific University (Forest Grove)* (1849) 2043 College Way, 97116. Tel: 503-352-2035; Fax: 503-352-2933. James Butler, Campus Min.; Nicki Butler, Campus Minister; Jessica Crenshaw, Coord. Campus Min.; Rev. Jeffrey Meeuwsen, Chap.

St. Anthony Church 1660 Elm St., 97116. Tel: 503-357-8075; Fax: 503-357-2217. Email: jmeeuwsen@stanthonysforestgrove.org. Web: www-.stanthonysforestgrove.org.

MARYLHURST. *Marylhurst University* 17600 Pacific Hwy., 97036. Tel: 800-634-9982; 503-636-8141; Fax: 503-636-9526. Email: jsaalfeld@marylhurst.edu. Sr. Joan Saalfeld, S.N.J.M., Vice Pres., Mission Integration.

MCMINNVILLE. *Linfield College (McMinnville) St. James Church*, 1145 N.E. First St., 97128. Tel: 503-472-5232. Email: mdouglass@stjamesmac.com. Michael Douglass, Campus Min.

MONMOUTH. *Western Oregon University (Monmouth)* 315 N. Knox, 97361. Tel: 503-838-1242; 503-606-0113 (Campus House). Email: catholic_campus_ministry@hotmail.com. Rev. Carl Gimpl, Chap.; Lisa Silbernagel, Campus Min. Tel: 503-606-0113.

SALEM. *Willamette University (Salem) St. Joseph Church*, 721 Chemeketa St., N.E., 97301. Tel: 503-581-1623; Fax: 503-581-7271. Rev. Todd Molinari; Sarah Kresse, Youth & Young Adult Minister; Rolando Moreno, Pastoral Asst.

[Q] MISCELLANEOUS

PORTLAND. *Blanchet House of Hospitality* (1952) P.O. Box 4145, 97208. Tel: 503-226-3911; Fax: 503-222-4071. Email: blanchetcntr@aol.com. Web: www.BlanchetHouse.org. Brian Ferschweiler, Exec. Dir. Tel: 503-807-4330. Served 290,000.

Brotherhood of the People of Praise, 7709 N. Denver Ave., 97217. Tel: 503-230-9999. Email: frpeter6901@yahoo.com. Rev. Peter Smith, J.C.L., Contact Person.

Catholic Broadcasting Northwest, Inc., KBVM-FM 88.3 (1989) P.O. Box 5888, 97228-5888. Tel: 503-285-5200; Fax: 503-285-3322. Email: info@kbvm.fm. Web: www.kbvm.fm. Tony Galati, Exec. Dir. Total Staff 7.

**The Gamelin-Oregon Association-Emilie House* (1986) 5520 N.E. Glisan, 97213-3170. Tel: 503-236-9779; Fax: 503-239-1867. Email: shannan.stickler@providence.org. Web: www.providence.org. Shannan Stickler, Dir. & Contact. Providence Health and Services., 41 apartments for the elderly and mobility impaired subsidized by the Department of Housing and Urban Development.

**Jesuit Volunteer Corps Northwest* (1956) P.O. Box 3928, 97208-3928. Tel: 503-335-8202; Fax: 503-249-1118. Email: info@jvcnorthwest.org. Web: www.jvcnorthwest.org. Jeanne Haster, Exec. Dir. & Contact Person.

St. Joseph the Worker Corporate Internship Program, Inc., 7528 N. Fenwick, 97217. Tel: 503-285-9385, Ext. 104; Fax: 503-285-9546. Email: mjacobson@delasallenorth.org. Web: www.delasallenorth.org. Michael Jacobson, Dir.

**St. Joseph the Worker Job Fund*, 605 N.W. Couch St., 97209. Tel: 503-222-5720; Fax: 503-241-7375. Email: pj@macdcenter.org. Pat Janik, Exec. Dir. & Contact Person; Marylee King, Dir. Staff 2; Total Assisted 8.

Macdonald Center and Residence, 605 N.W. Couch St., 97209. Tel: 503-222-5720, Ext. 3; Fax: 503-241-7375. Email: mk@macdcenter.org. Web: www.macdcenter.org. Pat Janik, Exec. Dir.; Marylee King, Center Dir. & Contact. Staff 40; Total People Served 1,606.

Oregon Catholic Conference (1979) 2838 E. Burnside St., 97214. Tel: 503-233-8387; Fax: 503-235-2630. Most Revs. John G. Vlazny, D.D., Pres.; Kenneth D. Steiner, D.D., Dir.; Rev. Msgr. Dennis O'Donovan, Sec. & Treas.

Parish Funds Trust, 2838 E. Burnside St., 97214-1895. Tel: 503-234-5334; Fax: 503-234-2545. Leonard Vuylsteke, Admin. Trustee.

Paulist Fathers Catholic Center for Evangelization, 2408 S.E. 16th Ave., 97214. Tel: 503-231-4955, Ext. 103; Fax: 503-736-1383. Email: info@stphilipneripdx.org. Web: www.stphilipneripdx.org. Revs. Charles J. Brunick, C.S.P., Dir. N.W. Center Evangelization & Reconciliation; Michael Evernden, C.S.P.; James R. McCauley, C.S.P.; Jeanne McPherson, Business Mgr. Priests 4.

Sharing Our Faith, Shaping Our Future, Capital Campaign, 2838 E. Burnside St., 97214-1895. Tel: 503-234-5334; Fax: 503-234-2545. Leonard Vuylsteke, Board Ex Officio & Contact Person.

Sisters of the Holy Names of Jesus and Mary, Community Support Charitable Trust, P.O. Box 398, Marylhurst, 97036. Tel: 503-675-7123; Fax: 503-675-7138. Email: snjnkirk@yahoo.com. Mangnerite Kirk, Contact Person.

BEAVERTON. *Our Lady of Peace Institute in Catholic Teaching*, 3600 S.W. 170th Ave., 97006. Tel: 503-649-7127; Fax: 503-259-9507. Email: sisters@olpretreat.org. Web: www.olpretreat.org. Sr. Anne Marie, O.S.F., Coord. & Contact Person. Staff 5; Students 30.

Sisters of St. Mary of Oregon Campus Schools Corporation, 4440 S.W. 148th Ave., 97007-2745. Tel: 503-644-9181; Fax: 503-646-1102. Email: Bweber@valleycatholic.org. 4275 S.W. 148th Ave., 97007-2745. Bob Weber, Pres. Sisters 4; Lay Teachers 63; Students 889.

Valley Catholic Middle & High Schools (Grades 7-12), (Coed)

Valley Catholic Elementary School (Grades K-6)

Sisters of St. Mary of Oregon Little Flower Development Center, 4440 S.W. 148th Ave., 97007. Tel: 503-644-9181; Fax: 503-646-1102. Bob Weber, Pres. Sisters 1; Lay Teachers 35; Students 191.

Sisters of St. Mary of Oregon Ministries Corporation, 4440 S.W. 148th Ave., 97007-2745. Tel: 503-644-9181; Fax: 503-646-1102. Sr. Adele Marie Altenhofen, S.S.M.O., Pres.

LAKE OSWEGO. *Holy Names Heritage Center Inc.*, 17425 Holy Names Dr., 97034. Tel: 503-607-0595; Fax: 503-607-0609. Email: smcevoy@snjmuson.org. Web: www.holynamesheritagecenter.org. Mailing Address: P.O. Box 398, Marylhurst, 97036. Tel: 503-675-7114. Sheila McEvoy, S.N.J.M., Contact Person.

**Mary's Woods at Marylhurst, Inc.*, 17400 Holy Names Dr., 97034. Tel: 503-675-2004; Fax: 503-675-2015. Email: ssharma@marywoods.com. Web: www.maryswoods.com. Sisters Mary Breiling, S.N.J.M., Pres. Bd. Dirs.; Roswitha Frawley, S.N.J.M., Mission Dir.; Marrin A. Kaiser, Ph.D., CFO; Lynn Szender, Dir. Marie Rose Health Center; Diane Hood, COO & CFO. Current Residency 419.

MARYLHURST. *Holy Names Sisters Foundation* (1859) *c/o Development Office*, P.O. Box 411, 97036-0411. Tel: 503-697-6435; Fax: 503-697-6436. Email: acarr@snjmuson.org. Web: www.sistersoftheholynames.org/oregon. Vicki Cummings, CFO; Sisters Kathleen Kircher, S.N.J.M., Pres.; Mary Breiling, S.N.J.M., Sec.; Adrianna Carr, Exec. Dir.

Sisters of the Holy Names of Jesus and Mary U.S.-Ontario Province Corporation, P.O. Box 398, 97036. Tel: 503-675-7125; Fax: 503-675-7138. Email: meholohan@snjmuson.org. Web: www.snjmusontario.org. Sisters Mary Ellen Holohan, S.N.J.M., Provincial Supr.; Marcia Frideger, S.N.J.M., Vice Pres.; Jane Hibbard, S.N.J.M., Leadership Team; Mariellen Blaser, S.N.J.M., Leadership Team; Kathleen Hilton, S.N.J.M., Treas./Sec.

MILWAUKIE. *La Salle High School Educational Foundation*, 11999 S.E. Fuller Rd., 97222. Tel: 503-353-1417; Fax: 503-496-1754. Email: mwinningham@lsprep.org. Web: www.lsprep.org. Mr. Matthew Winningham, Treas. & Contact Person.

MOUNT ANGEL. *Benedictine Foundation of Oregon* (1980) Box 912, 97362. Tel: 503-845-2556; Fax: 503-845-4345. Email: benfoundation@mtangel.net. Web: www.benedictine-srs.org. Steven Ritchie, Exec. Dir. & Contact Person.

Carmelite House of Studies, 300 Humpert Ln., P.O. Box 260, 97362. Tel: 503-845-2240; Fax: 503-845-2243. Revs. Jan Lundberg, O.C.D., Rector, Student Master & Contact Person; John Melka, O.C.D. Priests 2; Seminarians 6.

**Fr. Bernard Youth Center, Inc.*, P.O. Box 790, 97362-0790. Tel: 503-845-4097; Fax: 503-845-2208.

St. Joseph's Shelter (1988) 925 S. Main, 97362-9527. Tel: 503-845-6147; Fax: 503-845-2815. Email: sjshelter@mtangel.net. Web: stjosephshelter.org. Sr. Marcella Parrish, S.S.M.O., Admin. & Contact Person. Special center for social services and assistance. Total Staff 6; Total People Served 122; Total Shelter Nights 20,242; Total Meals Served 18,242.

SALEM. *Salem Catholic Schools Foundation*, 643 Union St. N.E., Ste. 200, 97301. Tel: 503-371-9068; Fax: 503-362-0513. Email: kevin@mannixlawfirm.com.

ST. BENEDICT. *The Abbey Foundation of Oregon* (2002) One Abbey Dr., 97373. Tel: 503-845-3066; Fax: 503-845-3075. Web: www.mountangelabbey.org. Rev. Martin Grassel, O.S.B., Treas. & Contact Person.

RELIGIOUS INSTITUTES OF MEN REPRESENTED IN THE ARCHDIOCESE

For further details refer to the corresponding bracketed number in the Religious Institutes of Men or Women section.

[]—*Apostles of Jesus*—A.J.

[]—*Apostolic Life Community Of Priests (Holy Spirit Fathers)*—A.L.C.P.

[0140]—*The Augustinians*—O.S.A.

[0200]—*Benedictine Monks* (Mt. Angel, OR)—O.S.B.

[0895]—*Brigittine Monastery of Our Lady of Consolidation*—O.Ss.S.

[]—*Brotherhood of the People of Praise*

[0330]—*Brothers of the Christian Schools*—F.S.C.

[0350]—*Cistercians Order of the Strict Observance (Trappists)*—O.C.S.O.

[]—*Discalced Carmelite Friars*—O.C.D.

[]—*Domus Dei Clerical Society of Apostolic Life*—S.D.D.

[0520]—*Franciscan Friars* (Prov. of Santa Barbara)—O.F.M.

[0690]—*Jesuit Fathers and Brothers* (Oregon Prov.)—S.J.

[0660]—*Missionaries Of The Holy Spirit*—M.Sp.S.

[0430]—*Order of Preachers (Dominicans)* (Western Prov.)—O.P.

[1030]—*Paulist Fathers*—C.S.P.

[0610]—*Priests of the Congregation of Holy Cross*—C.S.C.

[]—*St. John Society*—S.S.J.

[1240]—*Servites* (Western Prov.)—O.S.M.

[1260]—*Society of Christ*—S.Ch.

[]—*Society of the Missionaries of St. Francis Xavier*—S.F.X.

RELIGIOUS INSTITUTES OF WOMEN REPRESENTED IN THE ARCHDIOCESE

[]—*Adrian Dominican Sisters*—O.P.

[0230]—*Benedictine Sisters of Pontifical Jurisdiction* (Mount Angel, OR)—O.S.B.

[]—*Benedictine Sisters of St. Benedict Monastery*—O.S.B.

[0420]—*Discalced Carmelite Nuns*—O.C.D.

[]—*Dominican Sisters of Caldwell, NJ*—O.P.

[1390]—*Franciscan Missionary Sisters of Our Lady of Sorrows*—O.S.F.

[]—*Holy Spirit Sisters*—A.L.C.S.

[1250]—*The Institute of the Franciscan Sisters of the Eucharist*—F.S.E.

[2575]—*Institute of the Sisters of Mercy of the Americas* (Omaha, NE)—R.S.M.

[]—*The Lovers of The Holy Cross Sisters*—T.H.C.S.

[]—*Maryknoll Missionary Sisters*—M.M.

[]—*Missionaries of the Rosary of Fatima*—M.R.F.

[]—*Oblates of Saint Martha*—O.S.M.
[]—*Religious Sisters of Mercy of Alma, Mich.*—R.S.M.
[3590]—*Servants of Mary (Servite Sisters)*—O.S.M.
[0430]—*Sisters of Charity of the Blessed Virgin Mary*—B.V.M.
[2990]—*Sisters of Notre Dame* (Denver, CO)—S.N.D.
[3350]—*Sisters of Providence* (Mother Joseph Province)—S.P.
[3360]—*Sisters of Providence of St.-Mary-of-the-Woods, IN*—S.P.
[3475]—*Sisters of Reparation of the Sacred Wounds of Jesus*—S.R.
[]—*Sisters of St. Francis* (Clinton, Iowa)—O.S.F.
[]—*Sisters of St. Dominic* (Blauvelt, NY)—O.P.
[1650]—*The Sisters of St. Francis of Philadelphia*—O.S.F.
[3890]—*Sisters of St. Joseph of Peace* (Western Prov.)—C.S.J.P.
[3960]—*Sisters of St. Mary of Oregon*—S.S.M.O.
[1830]—*The Sisters of the Good Shepherd*—R.G.S.
[1990]—*Sisters of the Holy Names of Jesus and Mary*—S.N.J.M.
[]—*Sisters Servants of the Immaculate Heart of Mary*—I.H.M.
[4060]—*Society of the Holy Child Jesus* (American Prov.)—S.H.C.J.
[4155]—*Vietnamese Adorers of the Holy Cross*—M.T.G.

ARCHDIOCESAN CEMETERIES

PORTLAND. *Gethsemani*
Mount Calvary
EUGENE. *Mount Calvary*
SALEM. *St. Barbara*

NECROLOGY

† Alvares, Augustine, (Retired)—Died Oct. 31, 2011
† Borho, Charles D., (Retired)—Died July 9, 2011
† Cieslinski, Robert, (Retired)—Died Aug. 4, 2011
† Gothe, Marcus, (Retired)—Died Dec. 20, 2010
† Hemming, Philip Michael, (Retired)—Died July 16, 2011
† Linehan, Cornelius, (Retired)—Died Feb. 26, 2011

An asterisk (*) denotes an organization that has established tax-exempt status directly with the IRS and is not covered by the USCCB Group Ruling.

Diocese of Providence

(Dioecesis Providentiensis)

Most Reverend

THOMAS J. TOBIN

Bishop of Providence; ordained July 21, 1973; appointed Titular Bishop of Novica and Auxiliary Bishop of Pittsburgh, November 3, 1992; consecrated December 27, 1992; appointed Fourth Bishop of Youngstown installed February 2, 1996; appointed eighth Bishop of Providence March 31, 2005; installed May 31, 2005. *Office: One Cathedral Sq., Providence, RI 02903-3695.*

Bishop's Office & Chancery Office: One Cathedral Square, Providence, RI 02903-3695. Tel: 401-278-4500; Fax: 401-278-4621.

Web: www.dioceseofprovidence.org

Most Reverend

ROBERT C. EVANS

Auxiliary Bishop of Providence; ordained July 2, 1973; appointed Titular Bishop of Aquae Regiae and Auxiliary Bishop of Providence October 15, 2009; consecrated December 15, 2009. *Office: One Cathedral Square, Providence, RI 02903-3695.*

Most Reverend

ROBERT E. MULVEE

Bishop Emeritus of Providence; ordained June 30, 1957; appointed Auxiliary Bishop of Manchester and Titular Bishop of Summa February 15, 1977; consecrated April 14, 1977; appointed Bishop of Wilmington February 19, 1985; installed April 11, 1985; appointed Coadjutor Bishop of Providence February 9, 1995; succeeded to See June 11, 1997; retired March 31, 2005. *Res.: 30 Fenner St., Providence, RI 02903-3603. Mailing Address: One Cathedral Sq., Providence, RI 02903-3695.* Tel: 401-278-4679; Fax: 401-273-0687.

Most Reverend

LOUIS E. GELINEAU

Bishop Emeritus of Providence; ordained June 5, 1954; appointed Bishop of Providence December 6, 1971; consecrated January 26, 1972; retired June 11, 1997. *Res.: St. Antoine Residence, 10 Rhodes Ave., North Smithfield, RI 02896.* Tel: 401-767-3500.

ESTABLISHED APRIL 16, 1872.

Square Miles 1,085.

Corporate Title: Roman Catholic Bishop of Providence, a corporation sole

Comprises the State of Rhode Island.

STATISTICAL OVERVIEW

Personnel	
Retired Archbishops	1
Bishop	1
Auxiliary Bishops	1
Retired Bishops	4
Abbots	1
Retired Abbots	2
Priests: Diocesan Active in Diocese	169
Priests: Diocesan Active Outside Diocese	5
Priests: Retired, Sick or Absent	97
Number of Diocesan Priests	271
Religious Priests in Diocese	108
Total Priests in Diocese	379
Extern Priests in Diocese	10
Ordinations:	
Diocesan Priests	2
Transitional Deacons	3
Permanent Deacons in Diocese	90
Total Brothers	71
Total Sisters	458
Parishes	
Parishes	142
With Resident Pastor:	
Resident Diocesan Priests	125
Resident Religious Priests	8
Without Resident Pastor:	
Administered by Priests	9
Missions	6
Pastoral Centers	1
New Parishes Created	1
Closed Parishes	3
Professional Ministry Personnel:	
Brothers	2
Sisters	18
Lay Ministers	81
Welfare	
Catholic Hospitals	1
Total Assisted	200,000
Homes for the Aged	7
Total Assisted	44,472
Day Care Centers	2
Total Assisted	115
Specialized Homes	2
Total Assisted	182
Special Centers for Social Services	6
Total Assisted	62,300
Other Institutions	5
Total Assisted	46,500
Educational	
Seminaries, Diocesan	1
Students from This Diocese	10
Students from Other Diocese	17
Diocesan Students in Other Seminaries	10
Total Seminarians	20
Colleges and Universities	3
Total Students	7,841
High Schools, Diocesan and Parish	4
Total Students	2,003
High Schools, Private	8
Total Students	3,535
Elementary Schools, Diocesan and Parish	31
Total Students	7,570
Elementary Schools, Private	4
Total Students	1,418
Catechesis/Religious Education:	
High School Students	7,456
Elementary Students	21,590
Total Students under Catholic Instruction	51,433
Teachers in the Diocese:	
Priests	28
Brothers	13
Sisters	38
Lay Teachers	1,160
Vital Statistics	
Receptions into the Church:	
Infant Baptism Totals	3,508
Minor Baptism Totals	294
Adult Baptism Totals	158
Received into Full Communion	327
First Communions	4,479
Confirmations	4,667
Marriages:	
Catholic	956
Interfaith	182
Total Marriages	1,138
Deaths	4,761
Total Catholic Population	621,015
Total Population	1,052,567

Former Bishops—Rt. Revs. THOMAS F. HENDRICKEN, D.D., cons. first Bishop of Providence, April 28, 1872; died June 11, 1886; MATTHEW HARKINS, D.D., cons. second Bishop of Providence, April 14, 1887; died May 25, 1921; Most Revs. WILLIAM A. HICKEY, D.D., ord. Dec. 22, 1893; appt. Coadjutor Bishop of Providence, Cum jure successionis, March 10, 1919; cons. Titular Bishop of Claudiopolis, April 10, 1919; succeeded to the See of Providence, May 25, 1921; died Oct. 4, 1933; FRANCIS P. KEOUGH, D.D., cons. fourth Bishop of Providence, May 22, 1934; appt. Archbishop of Baltimore, Nov. 29, 1947; died Dec. 8, 1961; RUSSELL J. MCVINNEY, D.D., appt. May 29, 1948; cons. July 14, 1948 fifth Bishop of Providence; died Aug. 10, 1971; LOUIS E. GELINEAU, D.D., S.T.L., J.C.L. (Retired), appt. Dec. 6, 1971; cons. sixth Bishop of Providence, Jan. 26, 1972; retired June 11, 1997; ROBERT E. MULVEE (Retired), ord. June 30, 1957; appt. Auxiliary Bishop of Manchester and Titular Bishop of Summa Feb. 15, 1977; cons. April 14, 1977; appt. Bishop of Wilmington Feb. 19, 1985; installed April 11, 1985; appt. Coadjutor Bishop of Providence Feb. 9, 1995; succeeded to See June 11, 1997; retired March 31, 2005.

Vicars General—Most Rev. ROBERT C. EVANS, D.D., J.C.L.; Rev. Msgr. ALBERT A. KENNEY, S.T.L.

Episcopal Vicars and Secretaries—

Vicar for Judicial Matters—Rev. Msgr. RONALD P. SIMEONE, M.Div., J.C.L.

Secretary for Diocesan Administration—Rev. Msgr. ALBERT A. KENNEY, S.T.L.

Secretary for Catholic Education and Evangelization—Mr. DAVID M. BEAUDOIN, D.Min.

Secretary for Ministerial Services—Most Rev. ROBERT C. EVANS, D.D., J.C.L.

Secretary for Planning & Financial Services—Rev. Msgr. RAYMOND B. BASTIA.

Secretary for Catholic Charities and Social Ministry—Mr. JOHN J. BARRY III.

Deans—Very Revs. WILLIAM J. LEDOUX, Deanery No. I; HENRY P. ZINNO JR., Deanery No. II; RANDOLPH G. CHEW, Deanery No. III; NORMAN W. BOURDON, Deanery No. IV; PAUL R. GRENON, Deanery No. V; Rev. Msgr. BARRY R.L. CONNERTON, Deanery No. VI; Very Rev. JAMES J. VERDELOTTI, Deanery No. VII; Rev. Msgrs. PAUL D. THEROUX, S.T.B., J.C.L., Deanery No. VIII; JOHN W. LOLIO, Deanery No. IX; Very Rev. ROGER A. HOULE, Deanery No. X; Rev. Msgr. ANTHONY MANCINI, V.F., Deanery No. XI; Very Rev. MAURICE L. BRINDAMOUR, V.F., Deanery No. XII.

Bishop's Office & Chancery Office—One Cathedral Sq., Providence, 02903-3695. Tel: 401-278-4500; Fax: 401-278-4654. Rev. MICHAEL A. COLELLO, Administrative Sec. to the Bishop. Office Hours: Mon.-Fri. 8:30-4:30.

Vicars General—Most Rev. ROBERT C. EVANS, D.D., J.C.L. Tel: 401-278-4500; Fax: 401-278-4654; Rev. Msgr. ALBERT A. KENNEY, S.T.L. Tel: 401-278-4535; Fax: 401-278-4621.

Delegate for Canonical Affairs—Rev. Msgr. WILLIAM I.

VARSANYI, P.A., J.C.D. Tel: 401-278-4520.
Moderator of the Curia—Rev. Msgr. ALBERT A. KENNEY, S.T.L. Tel: 401-278-4519; Fax: 401-278-4621.
Chancellor—Rev. TIMOTHY D. REILLY, S.T.B., J.C.L. Tel: 401-278-4663; Fax: 401-278-4515.
Assistant Chancellor—Rev. DEAN PATRICK PERRI, J.C.L., S.T.L. Tel: 401-278-4670; Fax: 401-278-4622.
Diocesan Tribunal—
Judicial Vicar—Rev. Msgr. RONALD P. SIMEONE, M.Div., J.C.L. Tel: 401-278-4666; Fax: 401-278-4622.
Judges—Rev. Msgr. PAUL D. THEROUX, S.T.B., J.C.L.; Revs. DEAN PATRICK PERRI, J.C.L., S.T.L.; BRICE LEAVINS, O.F.M.
Assessor and Auditor—Rev. EDWARD J. MCGOVERN (Retired).
Promoter of Justice—Rev. Msgr. WILLIAM I. VARSANYI, P.A., J.C.D.
Defenders of the Bond—Most Rev. LOUIS E. GELINEAU, D.D., S.T.L., J.C.L. (Retired); Rev. DAVID W. MASELLO, J.C.L. (part-time).
Advocate—Rev. TIMOTHY D. REILLY, S.T.B., J.C.L. (part-time).
Assessor and Counselor—Mrs. NANCY GOULD.
Notaries—Mrs. PATRICIA COSTA; Mrs. LINDA L. NASTARI.
Secretary—Rev. Msgr. RONALD P. SIMEONE, M.Div., J.C.L., Sec.
Council of Priests—One Cathedral Sq., Providence, 02903-3695. Tel: 401-278-4518; Fax: 401-278-4623.
Officers—Most Rev. THOMAS J. TOBIN, Pres.; Rev. FRANCIS P. KAYATTA, Moderator; Rev. Msgr. ALBERT A. KENNEY, S.T.L., Sec.
Council Members—Most Rev. ROBERT C. EVANS, D.D., J.C.L.; Rev. Msgr. RAYMOND B. BASTIA; Revs. VICTOR T. SILVA; DAVID F. GAFFNEY, M.Div.; JAY A. FINELLI; DENNIS J. KIETON; KENNETH J. SUIBIELSKI; RICHARD P. DESAULNIERS; STANLEY T. NAKOWICZ; EDWARD J. MCGOVERN (Retired); EDWARD S. CARDENTE; GERARD J. CARON; JOHN C. CODEGA; JAIME A. GARCIA; FRANCIS A. O'LOUGHLIN; FRANCIS C. SANTILLI; MARCIANO ESCOBAR ALBA, C.S.
College of Consultors—Most Rev. ROBERT C. EVANS, D.D., J.C.L.; Rev. Msgr. RAYMOND B. BASTIA; Revs. DAVID F. GAFFNEY, M.Div.; FRANCIS P. KAYATTA; EDWARD J. MCGOVERN (Retired); GERARD J. CARON; FRANCIS C. SANTILLI; MARCIANO ESCOBAR ALBA, C.S.
Finance Council—Most Revs. THOMAS J. TOBIN, Pres.; ROBERT C. EVANS, D.D., J.C.L.; Rev. Msgrs. ALBERT A. KENNEY, S.T.L.; PAUL D. THEROUX, S.T.B., J.C.L.; RAYMOND B. BASTIA; RICHARD D. SHEAHAN; Rev. ROBERT P. PERRON; Sr. DOROTHY SCHWARZ, S.S.D.; The Hon. LAUREEN D'AMBRA; Mr. ALMON HALL; Mr. WILLIAM WRAY; Mr. GLENN CREAMER; Mrs. VIRGINIA ROBERTS; Mrs. MARGARET RUGGIERI; Mrs. PATRICIA SMOLLEY. Staff: Mr. MICHAEL F. SABATINO, CPA; Mr. ANTHONY T. GWIAZDOWSKI.
Chief Financial Officer—Mr. MICHAEL F. SABATINO, CPA.

Diocesan Offices and Directors

Diocesan Administration—
Secretariat for Diocesan Administration—One Cathedral Sq., Providence, 02903-3695. Tel: 401-278-4519; Fax: 401-278-4621. Rev. Msgr. ALBERT A. KENNEY, S.T.L.
Archives—Mrs. LISA A. VESPIA, Archives Clerk, One Cathedral Sq., Providence, 02903-3695. Tel: 401-278-4522.
Censors of Books—Rev. DAVID L. STOKES; Bro. THOMAS J. WHITE, O.P.
Communications— (Legal Title: Diocesan Catholic Telecommunications Network of Rhode Island); (News Media, TV, Public Relations) Mr. MICHAEL GUILFOYLE, Dir. Communications; Ms. KAREN DAVIS, Public Affairs Mgr., One Cathedral Sq., Providence, 02903-3695. Tel: 401-278-4600; Fax: 401-278-4659.
Telecommunications— (Produces Catholic Programming, Liaison with State Interconnect and CATV Companies, ETWN Liaison) Miss SUSAN MCCARTHY. Tel: 401-278-4609.
Website Coordinator—Mrs. LAURA H. TESTA. Tel: 401-278-4602; Fax: 401-278-4659.
Education and Compliance—Lt. ROBERT N. MCCARTHY, Dir., 80 St. Mary's Dr., Cranston, 02920. Tel: 401-941-0760; Fax: 401-941-1195; 401-943-2763.
Government Liaison—Rev. BERNARD A. HEALEY, Dir., 184 Broad St., Providence, 02903-4029. Tel: 401-421-7833, Ext. 104; 401-333-1568.
Human Resources Office—Mr. WILLIAM G. MEYER III, Dir., One Cathedral Square, Providence, 02903-3695. Tel: 401-278-4584; Fax: 401-751-0049.
Newspaper— "Rhode Island Catholic", Diocesan weekly. RICK SNIZEK, Editor; Rev. BERNARD A. HEALEY, Theological Consultant & Editorial Writer, 184 Broad St., Providence, 02903-4080. Tel: 401-272-1010; Fax: 401-421-8418.
Propagation of the Faith— (Legal Title: Society for the Propagation of the Faith, Diocese of Providence) Rev. Msgr. WILLIAM I. VARSANYI, P.A., J.C.D., Dir. Email: wvarsanyi@dioceseofprovidence.org; Ms. PAULA MOLLO, Sec., One Cathedral Sq., Providence, 02903-3695. Tel: 401-278-4519. Email: pmollo@dioceseofprovidence.org.
Catholic Relief Services—Rev. Msgr. WILLIAM I. VARSANYI, P.A., J.C.D. Tel: 401-278-4520. Email: wvarsanyi@dioceseofprovidence.org.
Holy Childhood Association—Rev. Msgr. WILLIAM I. VARSANYI, P.A., J.C.D. Tel: 401-278-4519. Email: wvarsanyi@dioceseofprovidence.org.
Ministerial Services—
Secretariat for Ministerial Services—Most Rev. ROBERT C. EVANS, D.D., J.C.L., Sec., One Cathedral Sq., Providence, 02903-3695. Tel: 401-278-4518; Fax: 401-278-4623.
Ongoing Formation of Priests—Rev. MARCEL L. TAILLON, Dir., One Cathedral Square, Providence, 02903-3695. Tel: 401-278-4516; Fax: 401-278-4515.
Priests' Personnel—Most Rev. ROBERT C. EVANS, D.D., J.C.L., Dir., One Cathedral Sq., Providence, 02903-3695. Tel: 401-278-4518; Fax: 401-278-4623.
Ecumenical Officer—Rev. JOHN A. KILEY, Ecumenical Officer (Retired).
Clergy Benefit Fund— (Legal Title: Our Lady, Queen of the Clergy) Most Rev. ROBERT C. EVANS, D.D., J.C.L., Dir.
Permanent Diaconate—Deacon PAUL J. SULLIVAN, Dir., One Cathedral Sq., Providence, 02903-3695. Tel: 401-278-4650; Fax: 401-278-4515.
Religious—Sr. JACQUELINE DICKEY, S.S.Ch., One Cathedral Sq., Providence, 02903-3695. Tel: 401-278-4633.
Council of Religious—Sr. JACQUELINE DICKEY, S.S.Ch., Coord.
Seminary of Our Lady of Providence— House of Formation for college students and pre-theologians) Revs. CHRISTOPHER M. MAHAR, S.T.L., Rector; DAVID F. GAFFNEY, M.Div., Spiritual Dir.; TIMOTHY D. REILLY, S.T.B., J.C.L., Asst. Spiritual Dir.; Dr. MICHAEL HANSEN, Dir. Human Formation, 485 Mt. Pleasant Ave., Providence, 02908. Tel: 401-331-1316; Fax: 401-521-4192. Email: mhansen@dioceseofprovidence.org.
Senior Priest Advisor—Very Rev. ROGER A. HOULE, Mailing Address: P.O. Box 236, North Scituate, 02857-0236. Tel: 401-647-2255.
Vocations—Rev. MICHAEL J. NAJIM, M.Div., Dir., 485 Mt. Pleasant Ave., Providence, 02908. Tel: 401-831-8011; Fax: 401-521-4192; Sr. JACQUELINE DICKEY, S.S.Ch., Assoc. Dir. Rel. Vocations, One Cathedral Sq., Providence, 02903-3695. Tel: 401-278-4633; Rev. CARL B. FISETTE, Asst. Dir. of Vocations.
Secretariat for Catholic Education and Evangelization—Mr. DAVID M. BEAUDOIN, D.Min., Sec., One Cathedral Sq., Providence, 02903-3695. Tel: 401-278-4625. Email: dbeaudoin@dioceseofprovidence.org.
Black Catholic Ministry—Mrs. PATTY JANUARY, Coord.; Rev. ANDREW MCNAIR, L.C., Chap., One Cathedral Sq., Providence, 02903-3695. Tel: 401-278-4552. Email: pjanuary@dioceseofprovidence.org.
Catholic Campus Ministry—Deacon MICHAEL D. NAPOLITANO, Dir., c/o RI College Campus Ministry, RIC Donovan Dining Center, Unity Center, 600 Mt. Pleasant Ave., Providence, 02908-1991. Tel: 401-456-8168. Email: campus.ministry@ric.edu.
Catholic Schools—Mr. DANIEL FERRIS, Supt., One Cathedral Square, Providence, 02903-3695. Tel: 401-278-4550.
Handicapped Persons Apostolate—Rev. Msgr. GERARD O. SABOURIN, Dir., One Cathedral Sq., Providence, 02903-3695. Tel: 401-278-4630. Email: gsabourin@dioceseofprovidence.org.
Deaf and Hard of Hearing Apostolate—VACANT.
SPRED (Special Religious Education)—Mrs. COLLEEN TOUCHETTE, One Cathedral Sq., Providence, 02903-3695. Tel: 401-658-1174. Email: spredprov@earthlink.net.
Religious Education—Miss LISA M. GULINO, Dir., 34 Fenner St., Providence, 02903-3603. Tel: 401-278-4646. Email: lgulino@dioceseofprovidence.org.
Worship—Mrs. NANCY SMITH, Coord., One Cathedral Sq., Providence, 02903. Tel: 401-278-4586. Email: worship@dioceseofprovidence.org.
Comprehensive Youth Ministry—Miss LOUISE DUSSAULT, Dir., One Cathedral Sq., Providence, 02903-3695. Tel: 401-278-4626. Email: ldussault@dioceseofprovidence.org. Web: www.ymcyoprov.org.
Catholic Scouting-Boy Scouts, Girl Scouts, Camp Fire—Rev. ANGELO N. CARUSI, Chap. Tel: 401-278-4626; Sr. DIANE RUSSO, R.S.M., Pastoral Assoc.
Catholic Youth Organization—Tel: 401-278-4626.
Youth Summer Camp—Mother of Hope Camp, Box W, Chepachet, 02814. Tel: 401-568-3580.
Marriage Preparation and Enrichment—Deacon STEPHEN R. COTE, Coord., 34 Fenner St., Providence, 02903-3603. Tel: 401-278-4577; 401-278-4576. Email: marriage@dioceseofprovidence.org.
Social Ministry—
Secretariat for Catholic Charities and Social Ministry—Mr. JOHN J. BARRY III, Sec., One Cathedral Sq., Providence, 02903-3695. Tel: 401-421-7833, Ext. 205; Fax: 401-274-5450. Email: jbarry@dioceseofprovidence.org.
Community Services and Catholic Charities— (Legal Title: Diocesan Bureau of Social Services) Ms. KATHLEEN MCKEON, Supvr. & Coord., One Cathedral Sq., Providence, 02903-3695. Tel: 401-421-7833, Ext. 206; Fax: 401-453-6135. Email: kmckeon@dioceseofprovidence.org.
AIDS Ministry—Mr. JAMES JAHNZ, One Cathedral Sq., Providence, 02903-3695. Tel: 401-421-7833, Ext. 226; Fax: 401-453-6135. Email: jjahnz@dioceseofprovidence.org.
Catholic Campaign for Human Development and Catholic Charities Advocacy Fund—Mr. JOHN J. BARRY III. Tel: 401-421-7833, Ext. 204.
Chaplains of Public Institutions— Catholic Chaplaincy Team (All Correctional and Detention Institutions) Mrs. MARTHA PAONE. Tel: 401-462-5238. *Youth Correctional Training School*, VACANT. Tel: 401-462-5238.
Clearinghouse Program—Ms. KATHLEEN MCKEON. Tel: 401-421-7833, Ext. 206.
Community Advocacy—VACANT.
Hispanic Ministry—Ms. AIDA HIDALGO, Dir., One Cathedral Sq., Providence, 02903-3695. Tel: 401-421-7833, Ext. 233; Fax: 401-453-6135. Email: ahidalgo@dioceseofprovidence.org.
Immigration and Refugee Services—STELLA CARRERA, Coord. Tel: 401-421-7833, Ext. 229; Fax: 401-277-9027. Email: scarrera@dioceseofprovidence.org.
Interfaith Community Dire Emergency Fund/ Emergency Assistance Network—Mr. JAMES JAHNZ, Coord. Tel: 401-421-7833, Ext. 207; Fax: 401-453-6135.
Peace and Justice—VACANT. Tel: 401-421-7833, Ext. 206; Fax: 401-453-6135.
Elder Care Services— Respite Care; Friendly Visitor Mr. HECTOR MUNOZ. Tel: 401-421-7833, Ext. 211; Fax: 401-453-6135. Email: hmunoz@dioceseofprovidence.org.
Community Services and Advocacy -South County—114 High St., Wakefield, 02879. Tel: 401-783-3149; Fax: 401-783-3149. Ms. BRENDA FAY.
Community Services and Advocacy - West Warwick Satellite—145 Washington St., West Warwick, 02893. Tel: 401-823-6211; Fax: 401-615-1410. Mrs. CHARLOTTE SANTILLI.
Community Services and Advocacy - Woonsocket Satellite—190 N. Main St., Woonsocket, 02895. Tel: 401-762-2849; Fax: 401-762-2849. Mr. RICHARD ZALEWSKI.
Life and Family Ministry— (Legal Title: Retreat House of the Immaculate Heart of Mary) *One Cathedral Sq., Providence, 02903-3695*. Tel: 401-421-7833, Ext. 218; 401-453-6135; Fax: 401-331-4484.
Adoption Searches—PETER MAGNOTTA, M.S.W., L.I.C.S.W., C.C.D.P.-D. Tel: 401-421-7833, Ext. 217; Fax: 401-453-6135. Email: pmagnotta@dioceseofprovidence.org.
Evaluations for Maturity for Marriage—PETER MAGNOTTA, M.S.W., L.I.C.S.W., C.C.D.P.-D. Tel: 401-421-7833, Ext. 217; Mrs. CAROL OWENS, Elizabeth Ministry. Tel: 401-421-7833, Ext. 218. Email: rl.outreach@dioceseofprovidence.org.
Hispanic Parish Outreach—Mr. SILVIO CUELLAR, Coord. Tel: 401-421-7833, Ext. 220. Email: rl.spanish@dioceseofprovidence.org.
Project Rachel—Mrs. CAROL OWENS. Tel: 401-421-7833, Ext. 218.
Rachel's Vineyard's Retreats—Mrs. CAROL OWENS, Liaison. Tel: 401-421-7833, Ext. 218.
Respect Life Program—Mrs. CAROL OWENS. Tel: 401-421-7833, Ext. 218 (Gabriel Project); Mr. SILVIO CUELLAR. Tel: 401-421-7833, Ext. 220.
Project Hope/Projecto Esperanza— (Legal Title: Project Hope/Projecto Esperanza) Mr. JAMES JAHNZ, Prog. Supvr., 474 Broadway, Pawtucket, 02860. Tel: 401-728-0515; Fax: 401-728-2330. Email: jjahnz@dioceseofprovidence.org.
St. Martin de Porres Multi-Service Center— (Legal Title: St. Martin de Porres Center) Ms. ESTHER

E. PRICE, 160 Cranston St., Providence, 02907-2396. Tel: 401-274-6783; Fax: 401-274-5930.

Health Care Ministries—One Cathedral Sq., Providence, 02903-3695. Tel: 401-421-7833, Ext. 204.

Planning and Financial Services—

Secretariat for Planning and Financial Services— Rev. Msgr. RAYMOND B. BASTIA, Vicar; Mr. MICHAEL F. SABATINO, CPA, CFO, One Cathedral Sq., Providence, 02903-3695. Tel: 401-278-4540; Fax: 401-831-1786.

*Diocesan Facilities Department—*Ms. CAROL ANN NELSON, Dir. Facilities; Mr. MAXIME E. GIROUARD JR., Field Project Mgr. & Environmental Engineer, One Cathedral Sq., Providence, 02903-3695. Tel: 401-278-4636; Fax: 401-278-4658; Mr. MICHAEL D. FALCONE, Field Project Mgr.

*Cemeteries—*Rev. ANTHONY W. VERDELOTTI, Dir.; Mr. ARTHUR F. LURGIO, Assoc. Dir., 80 St. Mary's Drive, Cranston, 02920. Tel: 401-944-8383.

*Evangelization & Pastoral Planning—*Rev. Msgr. JACQUES L. PLANTE, Dir., One Cathedral Sq., Providence, 02903-3695. Tel: 401-278-4610.

*Fiscal Office—*J. TIMOTHY KOCAB, Diocesan Controller, One Cathedral Sq., Providence, 02903-3695. Tel: 401-278-4616; Fax: 401-751-6808.

*Insurance Commission—*Rev. Msgr. RAYMOND B. BASTIA, Chm., One Cathedral Sq., Providence, 02903-3695. Tel: 401-278-4547.

*Catholic Mutual Group—*Mr. GREG CARLSON, Claims & Risk Mgr., 80 St. Mary's Dr., Cranston, 02920-5200. Tel: 401-944-5375; 401-944-5379; Fax: 401-944-5380. Email: Mmurphy@catholicmutual.org.

*Management Information Services—*Ms. MARGARET RYAN, Dir., One Cathedral Sq., Providence, 02903-3695. Tel: 401-278-4611.

*Parish Financial Assistance—*Mrs. CATHERINE MESSIER, Dir.; Mr. BRIAN RICHARDS, Parish Business Analyst. Tel: 401-278-4573; Ms. KATHERINE HARRINGTON; Mrs. COLLEEN PETRECCA, One Cathedral Sq., Providence, 02903-3695. Tel: 401-278-4544.

Stewardship and Development— (Annual Appeal, Stewardship, Planned Giving, Major Gifts, Anchor of Hope Fund) Mr. ANTHONY T. GWIAZDOWSKI, Dir., One Cathedral Sq., Providence, 02903. Tel: 401-277-2121.

Catholic Charity Fund Appeal— (Legal Title: Catholic Charity Fund) Tel: 401-277-2121.

Catholic Foundation of R.I.— (Legal Title: Catholic Foundation of Rhode Island) Tel: 401-277-2121. ANDREA H. KRUPP, Esq., Dir.

*Victim Assistance—*PAULA LOUD, Dir. Office of Outreach & Prevention. Tel: 401-946-0728; Fax: 401-946-1587. Email: ploud@dioceseofprovidence.org.

CLERGY, PARISHES, MISSIONS AND PAROCHIAL SCHOOLS

CITY OF PROVIDENCE

(PROVIDENCE COUNTY)

1—CATHEDRAL OF SS. PETER AND PAUL (1837) Rev. Msgr. Anthony Mancini, Rector.
SS. Peter and Paul's Church, Providence, RI In Res., Most Rev. Robert E. Mulvee (Retired); Revs. Romano Almagno, O.F.M.; Michael A. Colello; Robert W. Hayman (Retired).
Res.: 30 Fenner St., 02903. Tel: 401-331-2434 (Office); Fax: 401-273-0687.
*Catechesis/Religious Program—*Students 3.

2—ST. ADALBERT (1902), (Polish), Rev. Marek S. Kupka.
Saint Adalbert's Church
Res.: 866 Atwells Ave., 02909-2596. Tel: 401-351-9306; Fax: 401-351-9306. Web: www.stadalberts.us.
*Convent—*Tel: 401-831-3336. Sisters Mary Bernice Pikul, Supr.; Janice M. Gaudette, Parish Min. Felician Sisters of St. Francis 2.
*Catechesis/Religious Program—*864 Atwells Ave., 02909-2596. Students 32.

3—ST. AGNES (1904) Rev. Normand J. Godin.
St. Agnes Church
Res.: 351 Branch Ave., 02904. Tel: 401-861-7265; Fax: 401-454-6839. Email: stagnesprov@verizon.net.
*Catechesis/Religious Program—*Tel: 401-331-2547. Students 92.

4—ST. ANN (1895), (Italian), Rev. Michael J. Menna. Mailing Address: P.O. Box 9207, 02940-9207.
Saint Ann's Catholic Church of Providence, Rhode Island
Res.: 2 Russo St., 02904. Tel: 401-861-5111; Fax: 401-751-5453. Email: stann1@cox.net.
*Catechesis/Religious Program—*Tel: 401-862-0029. Students 28.

5—ASSUMPTION OF THE BLESSED VIRGIN MARY (1871) Rev. Gildardo Suarez (Colombia).
The Church of the Assumption, Providence, Rhode Island In Res., Rev. Robert M. Beirne (Retired).
Res.: 791 Potters Ave., 02907. Tel: 401-941-1248; Fax: 401-781-4887. Email: assumptionsouthprovidence@yahoo.com. Web: www.assumbvm.com.
*Catechesis/Religious Program—*Tel: 401-941-3768. Email: rel_edu.assumption@yahoo.com. Students 220.
Mission—St. Anthony (Olneyville) (1900)
Saint Anthony's Church Corporation, Rhode Island

6—ST. AUGUSTINE (1929) Rev. Msgr. Barry R.L. Connerton; Revs. Michael J. McMahon; Adam A. Young. (Legal title: Saint Augustine's Church, Providence, Rhode Island) In Res., Rev. Edward J. Byington (FR) (Retired).
Res.: 20 Old Rd., 02908. Tel: 401-831-3503; Fax: 401-421-9060. Email: staugprov@cox.net. Web: www.staugprov.com.
School—(Grades PreK-8), 635 Mt. Pleasant Ave., 02908. Tel: 401-831-1213; Fax: 401-831-4256. Mrs. Kathleen Morry, Prin. Sisters 1; Lay Teachers 26; Students 290.
*Catechesis/Religious Program—*Students 373.

7—ST. BARTHOLOMEW (1907), (Italian), Rev. Camillo Lando, C.S., Admin.; Deacon Robert L. Gallo, Pastoral Assoc.
Saint Bartholomew's Church Corporation
Res.: 297 Laurel Hill Ave., 02909-3897. Tel: 401-944-4466; Fax: 401-946-5866. Email: stbartholomewparish@hotmail.com.
*Catechesis/Religious Program—*Fax: 401-946-5866. Students 140.

8—BLESSED SACRAMENT (1888) Rev. Angelo N. Carusi; Deacon Jimmie H. Owen.
The Church of the Blessed Sacrament in Providence, Rhode Island In Res., Revs. Jose C. Cardenas Bonilla, C.S.; Albert A. Ranallo Jr.
Res.: 239 Regent Ave., 02908. Tel: 401-751-7575; Fax: 401-621-9605. Email: blessacprov@aol.om. Web: www.blessedsacramentpvd.org.
School—(Grades PreK-8), 240 Regent Ave., 02908. Tel: 401-831-3993. June Spencer, Prin. Lay Teachers 20; Students 285.
*Catechesis/Religious Program—*Students 75.

9—ST. CASIMIR (1919), (Lithuanian), [JC] Rev. Dean Patrick Perri, Admin.
Mailing Address: 350 Smith St., 02908.
Saint Casimir's Church, Providence, Rhode Island
Res.: 239 Regent Ave., 02908. Tel: 401-421-7070; Fax: 401-751-7085.

10—ST. CHARLES BORROMEO (1874), (French), Rev. Jaime A. Garcia; Deacons Jose Rico, Pastoral Assoc.; Joseph Braga.
Saint Charles Borromeo Roman Catholic Church, Providence, Rhode Island In Res., Rev. Francis J. Giudice (Retired).
Res.: 178 Dexter St., 02907. Tel: 401-421-6441; Fax: 401-421-4009.
*Catechesis/Religious Program—*Students 316.

11—ST. EDWARD (1874) Revs. Edward S. Cardente; Nolasco Tamayo Alvarez (Colombia).
The Church of St. Joseph Geneva Rhode Island
Res.: 10 Caxton St., 02904. Tel: 401-353-3120; Fax: 401-353-5126.
Church: 997 Branch Ave., 02904. Tel: 401-331-4035. Email: stanthonynp@cox.net.
*Catechesis/Religious Program—*Tel: 401-353-5215. Students 52.

12—GENESIS COMMUNITY, Closed. For inquiries for parish records contact Cathedral of SS. Peter & Paul, Providence.

13—ST. HEDWIG, Closed. For inquiries for sacramental records contact St. Adalbert Parish, Providence.

14—HOLY CROSS (1949), (Italian), Rev. David C. Procaccini; Deacon John J. Natalizia.
Corporation of the Church of the Holy Cross
Res.: 18 King Philip St., 02909. Tel: 401-274-5225; Fax: 401-274-6635. Email: parishoffice@holycross.necoxmail.com.
*Catechesis/Religious Program—*Tel: 401-751-1144. Mrs. June Carnevale, D.R.E. Students 95.

15—HOLY GHOST (1889), (Italian), Rev. Camillo Lando, C.S.
Corporation of the Church of the Holy Ghost, Rhode Island
Res.: 472 Atwells Ave., 02909. Tel: 401-421-3551; Fax: 401-421-3557. Email: hgcri@cox.net. Web: www.geocities.com/holyghostc.
See Holy Ghost School, Providence located in the Institution section under Bread of Life Schools, Urban Catholic Schools Consortium.
*Catechesis/Religious Program—*Students 14.

16—HOLY NAME OF JESUS (1882), (Cape Verdean), Rev. Joseph D. Santos Jr. (Portugal).
Church of the Holy Name of Jesus at Providence, Rhode Island In Res., Rev. John Wydeven (OAK).
Res.: 99 Camp St., 02906-1799. Tel: 401-272-4515; Fax: 401-272-4616. Email: theholyname@cox.net. Web: http://members.cox.net/holynamechurch.
*Catechesis/Religious Program—*Students 48.

17—IMMACULATE CONCEPTION, Closed. For inquiries for sacramental records contact St. Patrick Parish, Providence.

18—ST. JOHN, Closed. Sacramental records are located at St. Mary Church, Providence.
St. John Church of Providence Rhode Island.

19—ST. JOSEPH (Foxpoint) (1851) Rev. Msgr. Raymond B. Bastia; Sr. Mary Ellen Maytum, R.S.M., Pastoral Min.
St. Joseph's Church Providence Rhode Island In Res., Revs. Henry J. Bodah; Dean Patrick Perri; Daniel M. Trainor (Retired); Louis M. Diogo (Retired); Donal R. Kehew (Retired).
Res.: 92 Hope St., 02906. Tel: 401-421-9137; Fax: 401-621-5349. Email: stjoe1851@cox.net. Web: www.saintjoesprov.org.
*Catechesis/Religious Program—*Students 42.

20—ST. MARON Rev. Timothy D. Reilly.
Church of St. Maron in Providence
Res.: One Cathedral Square, 02903-3695. Tel: 401-278-4663; Fax: 401-278-4621.

21—ST. MARY (Broadway) (1853) Revs. Steven R. Patti, O.F.M.; Scott F. Brookbank, O.F.M.
Mailing Address: 538 Broadway, 02909-3329.
St. Mary's Church Providence Rhode Island In Res., Rev. Charles J. O'Connor, O.F.M.
Res.: 214 Broadway, 02903. Tel: 401-274-3434. Email: fsevola@stfrancischapel.com.
*Catechesis/Religious Program—*Students 75.

22—ST. MICHAEL THE ARCHANGEL (South Providence) (1859) Revs. Daniel J. Sweet; Jacques Eddy Chavannes (Haiti); Deacon Juan Andres Perez.
St. Michael's Providence, Rhode Island
Res.: 239 Oxford St., 02905. Tel: 401-781-7210; Fax: 401-461-6164.
*Catechesis/Religious Program—*Students 335.

23—OUR LADY OF CHARITY Rev. Msgr. William I. Varsanyi.
Church of Our Lady of Charity of Providence
Res.: One Cathedral Sq., 02903-3695.

24—OUR LADY OF LOURDES (1904), (French), Rev. Brice Leavins, O.F.M., Admin.; Deacon Anthony J. Wendoloski Jr.
Church of Our Lady of Lourdes
Res.: 901 Atwells Ave., 02909. Tel: 401-272-8127; Fax: 401-861-0226.
*Catechesis/Religious Program—*Students 9.

25—OUR LADY OF MT. CARMEL (1921), (Italian), Rev. Angelo N. Carusi, Admin.
Church of Our Lady of Mount Carmel, Providence
Res.: 12 Spruce St., 02903. Tel: 401-274-2113; Fax: 401-453-1221.
*Catechesis/Religious Program—*Students 31.

26—OUR LADY OF THE ROSARY (1886), (Portuguese), Revs. Joseph A. Escobar; Antonio M. Paiva, Pastor Emeritus (Retired).
Church of Our Lady of the Rosary
Res.: 463 Benefit St., 02903. Tel: 401-421-5621; Fax: 401-421-0783. Email: rosary463@aol.com.
*Catechesis/Religious Program—*Tel: 401-273-1685. Email: olrccd463@aol.com. Elisa Guerra Thibeault, D.R.E. Students 308.

27—ST. PATRICK (1841) Rev. James T. Ruggieri; Deacon Charles Andrade; Eduardo Birbuet, Pastoral Assoc.
St. Patrick's Church, Providence, Rhode Island
Res.: 152 Holden St., 02908. Tel: 401-421-7070; Fax: 401-751-7085. Email: stpatrickprov@yahoo.com. Web: www.stpatrick-providence.org.
School—St. Patrick Academy, (Grades 7-9), 244 Smith St., 02908. Tel: 401-421-9300; Fax: 401-421-0810. Email: steveray8@netscape.net. Web: www.st-patrickacademyri.com. Mr. Stephen M. Raymond, Prin. Lay Teachers 9; Students 71.
Catechesis/Religious Program—c/o Blessed Sacrament Church, 239 Regent Ave., 02908. Students 197.

28—ST. PIUS V (1918) Revs. Peter A. Judd, O.P.; Hyacinth Marie Cordell, O.P.; Donald P. Thibault, O.P.
Saint Pius Church, Providence, Rhode Island In Res., Revs. John L. Sullivan, O.P.; Frank I. Sutman, O.P.; John P. Burchill, O.P.
Res.: 55 Elmhurst Ave., 02908. Tel: 401-751-4871; Fax: 401-273-1089. Email: receptionist@stpiusvchurch.net. Web: http://stpiusvchurch.net.
School—(Grades PreK-8), 49 Elmhurst Ave., 02908. Tel: 401-421-9750; Fax: 401-455-3928. Sr. Mary Veronica Keller, O.P., Prin. Religious 4; Lay Teachers 16; Students 241.
*Catechesis/Religious Program—*Tel: 401-751-4871; Fax: 401-273-1089. Students 65.
*Convent—*30 Elmhurst Ave., 02908.

29—ST. RAYMOND (1911) Rev. Edward L. Pieroni.
Saint Raymond's Church Corporation

Res.: 2 Matilda St., 02904-1812. Tel: 401-351-4224; Fax: 401-274-3350. Email: catholichurch@straymonds.com. Web: www.straymonds.com.
Church: 1240 N. Main St., 02904. Tel: 401-351-4224; Fax: 401-274-3350.
Catechesis/Religious Program—Students 27.

30—St. Sebastian (1915) Rev. Msgr. John J. Darcy.
Church of Saint Sebastian
Res.: 67 Cole Ave., 02906. Tel: 401-751-0196; Fax: 401-273-2753. Email: office@stsebastianri.org. Web: www.stsebastianri.org. In Res., Rev. Ernest H. Berthelette.
Catechesis/Religious Program—Tel: 401-272-6062. Students 66.

31—St. Teresa of Avila (Olneyville) (1883) Closed. For inquiries for sacramental records contact Blessed Sacrament, Providence.
Saint Teresa's Church Providence, Rhode Island

32—St. Thomas (Fruit Hill) (1886) Rev. John P. Soares; Deacon Albert DePetrillo.
St. Thomas' Church of Manton Rhode Island
Res.: 65 Fruit Hill Ave., 02909-5598. Tel: 401-272-7118; Fax: 401-272-8431. Email: stthomas@cox.net.
See St. Thomas Regional School, Providence under Regional Elementary Schools located in the Institution section.
Catechesis/Religious Program—Tel: 401-272-1443; Fax: 401-272-8431. Students 169.

OUTSIDE THE CITY OF PROVIDENCE

Barrington, Bristol Co.

1—Holy Angels (1913), (Italian), Rev. Raymond J. Ferrick.
Holy Angel's Church Corporation
Res.: 341 Maple Ave., 02806. Tel: 401-245-7743; Fax: 401-245-9698.
Catechesis/Religious Program—341 Maple Ave., 02806. Tel: 401-247-1764. Students 53.

2—St. Luke (West Barrington) (1942) Revs. Robert F. Hawkins; Lukasz J. Willenberg.
Saint Luke's Church Corporation, Barrington In Res., Rev. Msgr. Albert A. Kenney.
Res.: 108 Washington Rd., 02806-1133. Tel: 401-246-1212; Fax: 401-246-1301. Email: pastor@stlukesparish.com. Web: www.stlukesparish.com.
School—(Grades PreK-8), 10 Waldron Ave., 02806. Tel: 401-246-0990; Fax: 401-246-2120. Maureen Jannetta, Prin.; Nancy Brex, Librarian. Lay Teachers 19; Students 249.
Catechesis/Religious Program—110 Washington Rd., 02806. Tel: 401-246-1363. Angela Christianson, D.R.E. (Grades 1-5); Diane Comerford, D.R.E. (Grades 6-10). Students 806.

Bristol, Bristol Co.

1—St. Elizabeth (1913), (Portuguese), Revs. Jared J. Costanza; Scott J. Pontes; Deacon James E. Conley.
Saint Elizabeth's Church of Bristol
Res.: 577 Wood St., 02809-2395. Tel: 401-253-8366; Fax: 401-253-7695. Email: office@saintelizabethchurch.net.
Catechesis/Religious Program—Tel: 401-253-3501. Students 392.

2—St. Mary (1869) [CEM] Rev. Barry J. Gamache; Deacons Paul Bisbano; Bernard G. Theroux.
Saint Mary's Church, Bristol, Rhode Island
Res.: 330 Wood St., 02809. Tel: 401-253-3300; Fax: 401-253-4057. Web: www.stmarybristolri.org.
Catechesis/Religious Program—Tel: 401-253-2270. Students 203.
Mission—Our Lady of Prudence Prudence Island, Newport Co. 02872.

3—Our Lady of Mount Carmel (1917), (Italian), [JC] Very Rev. Henry P. Zinno Jr.; Rev. Stephen J. Dandeneau.
Church of Our Lady of Mount Carmel, Bristol
Res.: 141 State St., 02809. Tel: 401-253-9449; Fax: 401-253-5687. Email: hpz612@yahoo.com. Web: www.olmc-bristol.org.
School—(Grades PreK-8), 127 State St., 02809. Tel: 401-253-8455; Fax: 401-254-8234. Filippini Sisters 4; Lay Teachers 11; Students 165.
Catechesis/Religious Program—131 State St., 02809. Tel: 401-253-5052. Students 205.

Burrillville, Providence Co.

1—St. Joseph (Pascoag) (1884) Rev. Clifford J. Cabral; Deacon Anthony E. Muscatelli.
Saint Joseph's Roman Catholic Church of Pascoag, RI
Res.: 183 Sayles Ave., P.O. Box 188, Pascoag, 02859-0188. Tel: 401-568-2411; Fax: 401-568-2586.
Catechesis/Religious Program—Students 252.

2—Our Lady of Good Help (Mapleville) (1905) Rev. Robert L. Marciano; Deacon Richard J. Lapierre.
Eglise de Notre Dame de Bonsecours
Res.: 1063 Victory Hwy., Mapleville, 02839. Tel: 401-568-5272; Fax: 401-568-5351. Email: pat@olgh.necoxmail.com. Web: www.ourladyofgoodhelp.org.
Catechesis/Religious Program—Ms. Patricia Ducharme, D.R.E. (Grades 1-5). Students 199.

3—St. Patrick (Harrisville) (1854) [CEM] [JC 2] Rev. Bernard M. O'Reilly.
St. Patrick's Church, Burrillville, Rhode Island
Res.: 45 Main St., Harrisville, 02830. Tel: 401-568-5600; Fax: 401-568-7132.
Catechesis/Religious Program—Students 81.
Mission—St. Louis Chapel Old Victory Hwy., Glendale, Providence Co. 02826.

4—St. Theresa of the Child Jesus (Nasonville) (1923) [CEM] Rev. Gerard J. Caron.
Church of Saint Teresa of the Child Jesus, Nasonville
Res.: 35 Dion Dr., Harrisville, 02830. Tel: 401-568-8280; Fax: 401-567-9238. Email: cindy@sttheresas.necoxmail.com.
Catechesis/Religious Program—Tel: 401-568-3057. Students 87.

Central Falls, Providence Co.

1—Holy Spirit Parish (2009) [CEM], Consolidation of the following three parishes: Holy Trinity, (Legal Title: Church of the Holy Trinity, Central Falls); Notre Dame, (Legal Title: Notre Dame Church); and St. Matthew, (Legal Title: Saint Matthew's Church of Central Falls). Rev. Otoniel J. Gomez.
Res.: 1030 Dexter St., 02863-1717. Tel: 401-726-2600; 401-725-1748; 401-723-5326; Fax: 401-722-0224. Email: the.holy.spirit.parish@gmail.com. Web: www.holyspiritcentralfalls.parishesonline.com.
Catechesis/Religious Program—Tel: 401-722-3717. Students 211.

2—Holy Trinity (1989) Merged See Holy Spirit Parish, Central Falls.

3—St. Joseph (1906), (Polish), Rev. Dariusz J. Jonczyk.
St. Joseph's Church of Central Falls
Res.: 391 High St., 02863-3109. Tel: 401-723-5427; Fax: 401-726-5971.
Catechesis/Religious Program—Students 54.

4—St. Matthew's (1906), (French), Merged See Holy Spirit Parish, Central Falls.

5—Notre Dame (1873), (French), Merged See Holy Spirit Parish, Central Falls.

Charlestown, Washington Co., St. Mary (Carolina) (1946) Rev. Paul E. Desmarais; Deacons Paul A. Theroux; John S. Shea.
Saint Mary's Church Corporation, Carolina
Res.: 437 Carolina Back Rd., P.O. Box 475, Carolina, 02812. Tel: 401-364-7214; Fax: 401-213-6327. Email: stmjparish@stmj.org. Web: www.stmj.org.
Catechesis/Religious Program—Email: stmj.dre@aol.com. Students 262.
Mission—St. James 2079 Mat. School House Rd., Washington Co. 02813. Tel: 401-364-7214.

Coventry, Kent Co.

1—SS. John and Paul (1955) Very Rev. Paul R. Grenon; Revs. Derek J. Puleo; Eddy E. Lopez-Bolanos; Deacon Robert Persson.
SS. John and Paul Parish Corporation, Coventry In Res., Rev. John J. Duggan (Ireland) (Retired).
Res.: 341 S. Main St., 02816. Tel: 401-821-5764; Fax: 401-828-5351. Email: ssjp341@stjp.necoxmail.com. Web: www.stsjohnpaulri.com.
Father John V. Doyle School—343 South Main St., 02816. Tel: 401-821-3756; Fax: 401-828-5351. Email: rido3467@ride.ri.net. Web: www.ri.net/rinet/fr_doyle. Mr. J. Robert McDermott, Prin.; Mr. James Manning, Vice Prin. Lay Teachers 25; Students 390.
Catechesis/Religious Program—Tel: 401-821-4780; Fax: 401-828-5351. Email: annssjp@stjp.necoxmail.com. Students 1,010.

2—Our Lady of Czenstochowa (Quidnick) (1905), (Polish), Rev. Stephen P. Amaral.
Church of Our Lady of Czenstochowa
Res.: 445 Washington St., 02816. Tel: 401-821-7991; Fax: 401-821-8714. Email: olczenstochowa@aol.com.
Catechesis/Religious Program—Students 100.

3—St. Vincent de Paul (Anthony) (1937), (French), Rev. Michael A. Kelley. (Legal title: Church of Saint Vincent de Paul, Anthony, Rhode Island).
Res.: 6 St. Vincent de Paul St., 02816. Tel: 401-821-8719; Fax: 401-827-5071.
Catechesis/Religious Program—2 St. Vincent de Paul St., 02816. Tel: 401-828-3090. Students 96.

Cranston, Providence Co.

1—St. Ann (1858) Rev. Farrell E. McLaughlin. (Legal title: St. Anne's Church, Cranston, Rhode Island). In Res., Rev. Peter G. Young, Senior Priest (Retired).
Res.: 1493 Cranston St., 02920. Tel: 401-942-2767; Fax: 401-942-2773. Email: stannrcchurch1@cox.net. Web: www.st-ann-parish.org.
Catechesis/Religious Program—Tel: 401-942-2767, Ext. 19. Students 122.

2—Holy Apostles (1991) Rev. Msgr. Richard D. Sheahan.
Holy Apostles Church, Cranston, Rhode Island
Res.: 800 Pippin Orchard Rd., 02921. Tel: 401-946-5586; Fax: 401-946-5066. Email: parishoffice@holyapostles.com. Web: www.holyapostles.com.
Catechesis/Religious Program—Students 1,197.

3—Immaculate Conception (Oaklawn) (1958) Rev. Ronald E. Brassard; Deacons Thomas R. Raspallo; Carmine Forlingieri; Michelle Colgan-Larney, Pastoral Assoc.
Immaculate Conception Church Corporation, Cranston
Res.: 237 Garden Hills Dr., 02920. Tel: 401-942-1854; Fax: 401-942-2897. Web: www.iccri.com.
See Immaculate Conception Catholic Regional School, Cranston under Regional Elementary Schools in the Institution section.
Catechesis/Religious Program— Barbara Prata, D.R.E.; Christopher J. Bordeleau, Youth Min. Students 550.

4—St. Mark (Garden City) (1950) Rev. Anthony W. Verdelotti.
Saint Mark's Church Corporation of Cranston In Res., Rev. Joseph F. Craddock.
Res.: 9 Garden Ct., 02920. Tel: 401-942-1616. Email: stmarkri@aol.com. Web: www.stmarkri.org.
Catechesis/Religious Program—Tel: 401-942-3231. Email: stmarkccd@aol.com. Students 252.

5—St. Mary (Knightsville) (1925), (Italian), (Santa Maria della Civita) Very Rev. James J. Verdelotti; Rev. David G. Thurber Jr.; Deacon Armand R. Ragosta.
Saint Mary's Church, Cranston
Res.: 1525 Cranston St., 02920-5297. Tel: 401-942-1492; Fax: 401-946-2531.
School—(Grades PreK-8) Tel: 401-944-4107; Fax: 401-944-2395. Miss Lisa Lepore, Prin.; Leah Montagano, Librarian. Lay Teachers 13; Students 231.
Catechesis/Religious Program—Tel: 401-944-1323; Fax: 401-944-2461. Students 247.

6—St. Matthew (Auburn) (1909) Revs. James R. Collins; Victor T. Silva.
St. Matthew's Church Corporation In Res., Rev. Chinnaiah Yerrnini.
Res.: 15 Frances Ave., 02910. Tel: 401-461-7172; Fax: 401-461-7339. Email: stmatthew@stmatthew.necoxmail.com.
Church: Elmwood & Park Ave., 02910.
Catechesis/Religious Program—Tel: 401-781-4568. Sr. Mercian Hassett, R.S.M., D.R.E. Students 245.

7—St. Paul (Edgewood) (1907) Revs. Robert H. Forcier; Albert P. Marcello III; Sr. Mary Ann Rossi, C.N.D., Pastoral Assoc.
Saint Paul's Church of Edgewood
Res.: One St. Paul Pl., 02905. Tel: 401-461-5734; Fax: 401-785-3613. Email: stpauledgewoodri@aol.com. Web: www.saintpaulcranston.com.
School—(Grades PreK-8), 1789 Broad St., 02905. Tel: 401-941-2030; Fax: 401-941-0644. Email: rid06826@ride.ri.net. Web: www.saintpaulschool-cranston.com. Mr. John F. Corry, Prin. Lay Teachers 17; Students 215.
Catechesis/Religious Program—Tel: 401-941-5576. Julie Bradley, D.R.E. Students 198.

Cumberland, Providence Co.

1—St. Aidan (1962) Rev. Donald L. Depatie.
St. Aidan Church Corporation, Cumberland In Res., Rev. William F. Sears (Retired).
Res.: 1460 Diamond Hill Rd., 02864. Tel: 401-333-5897; Fax: 401-333-5078.
Catechesis/Religious Program—Students 175.

2—St. Joan of Arc (Cumberland Hill) (1929) Very Rev. Norman W. Bourdon.
Saint Joan's Church, Cumberland, Rhode Island
Res.: 3357 Mendon Rd., 02864-2195. Tel: 401-658-2084; Fax: 401-658-2086. Email: stjoanschurch@gmail.com.
Catechesis/Religious Program—Tel: 401-658-0734. Students 350.

3—St. John Baptist Mary Vianney (Diamond Hill) (1953) Rev. Raymond C. Theroux; Deacon Paul H. Lambert.
Saint John Baptist Mary Vianney Church Corporation, Diamond Hill
Res.: 3609 Diamond Hill Rd., 02864. Tel: 401-333-6060; Fax: 401-334-4548. Email: rctheroux@verizon.net. Web: www.sjvparish.org.
Catechesis/Religious Program—3655 Diamond Hill Rd., 02864. Tel: 401-333-2347. Students 946.

4—St. Joseph (Ashton) (1872) [CEM] Rev. John W. Hunt.
St. Joseph's Church, Ashton, Rhode Island
Res.: 1303 Mendon Rd., P.O. Box 7005, 02864. Tel: 401-333-4013; Fax: 401-333-4013. Email: stjosephashton@catholicexchange.com. Web: www.stjosephashtonri.org.
Catechesis/Religious Program—Tel: 401-333-4014. Students 205.

5—Our Lady of Fatima (Valley Falls) (1953), (Portuguese), Revs. Dennis J. Kieton; Domingos M. da Cunha.
Church of Our Lady of Fatima, Valley Falls
Res.: Fatima Dr., 02864. Tel: 401-723-6719; Fax:

401-723-1698. Email: olf@olfchurch.com. Web: www.olfchurch.com.
Catechesis/Religious Program—Tel: 401-724-3454; Fax: 401-723-1698. Email: ccd@olfchurch.com. Students 261.

6—ST. PATRICK (Valley Falls) (1861) [CEM 2] Rev. Lawrence E. Toole.
St. Patrick's Church Corporation, Valley Falls, Rhode Island
Res.: 301 Broad St., 02864. Tel: 401-725-0344.
Catechesis/Religious Program—Tel: 401-725-0344. Students 70.

EAST GREENWICH, KENT CO., OUR LADY OF MERCY (1853) [CEM] Rev. Msgr. John W. Lolio; Rev. Charles R. Grondin.
Our Lady of Mercy, Greenwich, Rhode Island
Res.: 65 Third St., 02818. Tel: 401-884-4968; Fax: 401-884-1415.
Catechesis/Religious Program—Tel: 401-884-1061. Students 939.
Convent—Sisters of Mercy, 36 Fourth Ave., 02818. Tel: 401-884-9292.
Convent—Sisters of St. Lucy Filippini, 66 Fifth Ave., 02818. Tel: 401-886-4753.

EAST PROVIDENCE, PROVIDENCE CO.

1—ST. BRENDAN (Riverside) (1909) Revs. John C. Codega; Przemyslaw Lepak.
St. Brendan's Church
Res.: 60 Turner Ave., Riverside, 02915. Tel: 401-433-2600; Fax: 401-433-3336. Email: office@stbren.com. Web: www.stbren.com.
Catechesis/Religious Program—Tel: 401-433-2680. Tamara Primmer, D.R.E. Students 450.

2—ST. FRANCIS XAVIER (1915), (Portuguese), Rev. Msgr. Victor M. Vieira; Rev. Richard A. Narciso.
Saint Francis Xavier's Church
Res.: 81 N. Carpenter St., 02914. Tel: 401-434-1878; Fax: 401-438-1950. Email: msgrvieira@cox.net. Web: saintfrancisxavierchurch.com.
Catechesis/Religious Program—Tel: 401-434-3153; 401-434-9421. Students 475.

3—ST. MARGARET (Rumford) (1888) Rev. Msgr. William J. McCaffrey; Deacon John F. Needham, Pastoral Assoc.
Saint Margaret's Church Corporation, East Providence Rhode Island
Res.: 1098 Pawtucket Ave., Rumford, 02916. Tel: 401-438-3230; Fax: 401-438-4221. Email: office-stmargaretchurch@cox.net. Web: www.stmargaretchurch.org.
School—(Grades PreK-8), 42 Bishop Ave., Rumford, 02916. Tel: 401-434-2338; Fax: 401-431-0266. Email: jrezendes@stmargaretsch.org. Mr. John P. Rezendes, Prin. Lay Teachers 16; Students 220.
Catechesis/Religious Program—Tel: 401-435-4755. Email: sara@zapcreative.net. Ms. Sara D. Hickey, D.R.E. Students 230.

4—ST. MARTHA (1956) Rev. David E. Green.
St. Martha's Church Corporation, East Providence
Res.: 2595 Pawtucket Ave., 02914. Tel: 401-434-4060; Fax: 401-434-4849.
Catechesis/Religious Program—Tel: 401-434-7030. Students 197.

5—OUR LADY OF LORETO (1920), (Italian—Brazilian), Rev. Stanley T. Nakowicz.
Church of Our Lady of Loreto, East Providence
Res.: 346 Waterman Ave., 02914. Tel: 401-434-3535; Fax: 401-434-8204. Email: loreto5@oll.necoxmail.com.
Catechesis/Religious Program—Students 67.

6—SACRED HEART (1876) Rev. Peter S. DiTullio, S.d.C.
Church of the Sacred Heart
Res.: 118 Taunton Ave., 02914. Tel: 401-434-0326. Email: pdtsc@hotmail.com.
School—(Grades K-8), 56 Purchase St., 02914. Tel: 401-434-1080; Fax: 401-434-1080. Email: rid04407@ride.ri.net. Sr. Nancy McLennon, D.S.M.P., Prin. Lay Teachers 13; Students 160.
Nursery-Day Care—101 Taunton Ave., 02914. Tel: 401-434-2462. Total Staff 7; Children 75.
Catechesis/Religious Program—Students 42.

EXETER, WASHINGTON CO., BLESSED KATERI TEKAKWITHA CATHOLIC COMMUNITY (1981) Rev. Msgr. Gerard O. Sabourin, Admin.
84 Exeter Rd., 02822. Tel: 401-212-0855.
Catechesis/Religious Program—Students 39.

FOSTER, PROVIDENCE CO., ST. PAUL THE APOSTLE (1972) Rev. M.J. Bernard Dore.
St. Paul's Church Corporation, Foster
Res.: 116A Danielson Pike, 02825-1468. Tel: 401-647-3664; Fax: 401-647-3680. Email: church@stpaulsfoster.org. Web: www.rc.net/providence/stpaul.
Catechesis/Religious Program—Mr. Fernando Botelho, D.R.E. Students 148.

GLOCESTER, PROVIDENCE CO., ST. EUGENE (Chepachet) (1956) Rev. TJ Varghese.
St. Eugene's Church Corporation, Chepachet
Res.: 1251 Putnam Pike, P.O. Box A, Chepachet, 02814. Tel: 401-568-5102; Fax: 401-567-7847. Web: www.sainteugeneschurch.org.
Catechesis/Religious Program—Students 294.

HOPKINTON, WASHINGTON CO.

1—ST. JOSEPH (Hope Valley) (1939) Rev. Michael J. Leckie.
Saint Joseph's Church, Hope Valley
Res.: 1105 Main St., P.O. Box 388, Hope Valley, 02832. Tel: 401-539-8311. Email: stjosephhv@verizon.net. Web: www.stjosephhv.org.
Catechesis/Religious Program—Tel: 401-539-8312. Students 166.

2—OUR LADY OF VICTORY (Ashaway) (1946) Rev. David A. Piacentini.
Church of Our Lady of Victory, Ashaway
Res.: 169 Main St., Ashaway, 02804. Tel: 401-377-8830; Fax: 401-377-8830. Email: lmolv@yahoo.com.
Catechesis/Religious Program—Tel: 401-377-8435; Fax: 401-377-8830. Email: ggolv@yahoo.com. Students 159.

JAMESTOWN, NEWPORT CO., ST. MARK (Jamestown) (1909) [CEM] Rev. William J. O'Neill.
Saint Mark Church of Jamestown
Res.: 60 Narragansett Ave., 02835. Tel: 401-423-1421; Fax: 401-423-2067. Email: stmarkjtn@cox.net. Web: www.stmarkjtn.org.
Catechesis/Religious Program—Students 194.

JOHNSTON, PROVIDENCE CO.

1—ST. BRIGID (Thornton) (1915) Rev. Robert A. Rochon.
Saint Brigid's Church of Johnston
Res.: 1231 Plainfield, 02919. Tel: 401-944-2232; Fax: 401-944-0306. Email: stbrigidjohnston1@verizon.net. Web: www.parishesonline.com/stbrigidjohnston.
Catechesis/Religious Program—Tel: 401-946-3399. Students 103.

2—OUR LADY OF GRACE (1913), (Italian), Rev. Msgr. Carlo F. Montecalvo.
Church of Our Lady of Grace
Res.: 4 Lafayette St., 02919. Tel: 401-231-2220; Fax: 401-231-3905. In Res., Rev. Alfred P. Almonte, C.S.
Catechesis/Religious Program—Tel: 401-231-8959. Students 130.

3—ST. ROBERT BELLARMINE (1963) Rev. John G. LaPointe; Deacon Joseph Tumminelli.
St. Robert Bellarmine Church Corporation, Johnston
Res.: 1804 Atwood Ave., 02919-3215. Tel: 401-232-5600; Fax: 401-231-5793. Email: srbp1804@aol.com. Web: www.strobertsparish.org.
Catechesis/Religious Program—Tel: 401-232-9321; Fax: 401-231-5793. Students 339.

4—ST. ROCCO (1903), (Italian), Revs. Charles Zanoni, C.S.; Mario Titotto, C.S.; Deacon Robert P. Troia.
Saint Rocco Church of Johnston In Res., Rev. Michael Tarro, C.S. (Retired).
Res.: 927 Atwood Ave., 02919. Tel: 401-942-5203; Fax: 401-464-6422. Email: churchofstrocco@verizon.net.
School—(Grades PreK-8), 931 Atwood Ave., 02919. Tel: 401-944-2993; Fax: 401-944-3019. Lorraine Moschella, Prin. Lay Teachers 25; Students 293.
Catechesis/Religious Program—Tel: 401-944-6040. Sr. Rose Alfieri, C.P., D.R.E. Students 260.

LINCOLN, PROVIDENCE CO.

1—ST. AMBROSE (Albion) (1905) [CEM] Rev. Bernard A. Healey; Deacon Robert McAdam.
St. Ambrose Church, Albion, Rhode Island
Res.: 191 School St., P.O. Box 67, Albion, 02802. Tel: 401-333-1568; Fax: 401-333-8941. Email: stambrosechurch@cox.net. Web: www.stambrosechurch.org.
Catechesis/Religious Program—Tel: 401-334-3735. Students 181.

2—ST. JAMES (Manville) (1874) [CEM] Rev. Richard P. Desaulniers.
Saint James Church of Manville, Rhode Island
Res.: 33 Division St., Box 60, Manville, 02838. Tel: 401-766-1558. Email: claudette@stjames.necoxmail.com.
Catechesis/Religious Program—57 Division St., Manville, 02838. Tel: 401-769-2676. Students 140.

3—ST. JUDE (Lincoln) (1946) Rev. Bernard C. Lavin; Deacon L.J. (Bud) Remillard.
St. Jude's Church, Lincoln
Res.: 301 Front St., 02865. Tel: 401-725-8140; Fax: 401-726-4946. Web: www.saintjude.us.
Catechesis/Religious Program—Tel: 401-725-8120. Sr. Mary Higgins, R.S.M., D.R.E. (Grades 1-6); Keri Carvalho, D.R.E. (Grades 7-10). Students 543.

LITTLE COMPTON, NEWPORT CO., ST. CATHERINE OF SIENA (1930) [CEM] Rev. Gerald W. Hussey.
St. Catherine's Church Corporation, Little Compton
Res.: 74 Simmons Rd., P.O. Box 208, 02837-0208. Tel: 401-635-4420; Fax: 401-635-2214. Email: gwh1178@cox.net.
Catechesis/Religious Program—Students 136.

MIDDLETOWN, NEWPORT CO., ST. LUCY (Middletown) (1952) Rev. John W. O'Brien; Deacon John E. Croy; Sr. Sheila Murphy, S.S.J., Pastoral Min.
Saint Lucy's Church Corp.
Res.: 909 W. Main Rd., 02842-6351. Tel: 401-847-6153; Fax: 401-846-1545. Email: stlucyoffice@gmail.com. Web: www.stlucy.org.
Catechesis/Religious Program—Colette Savaria, Coord. Faith Formation; Jane Parillo, Adult Faith Formation; Colleen Earnshaw, Confirmation & Baptism Coord. Students 301.

NARRAGANSETT, WASHINGTON CO.

1—ST. MARY, STAR OF THE SEA (Point Judith) (1960) Rev. Francis P. Kayatta.
St. Mary, Star of the Sea Church Corporation, Point Judith
Res.: 864 Pt. Judith Rd., 02882. Tel: 401-783-4449; Fax: 401-783-0986. Email: stmary's@dioceseofprovidence.org.
Catechesis/Religious Program—Tel: 401-789-7308; Fax: 401-783-0986. Students 202.

2—ST. THOMAS MORE (1917) Revs. Marcel L. Taillon; Carl B. Fisette; Deacon Paul J. Sullivan.
St. Thomas More Church, Narragansett Pier, Rhode Island
Res.: 53 Rockland St., 02882. Tel: 401-789-7682; Fax: 401-783-8646. Email: sthomasmore@cox.net. Web: www.stthomasmoreri.org.
Catechesis/Religious Program—Tel: 401-783-2113. Students 272.
Chapel—St. Veronica Chapel 1035 Boston Neck Rd., 02882.

NEW SHOREHAM, WASHINGTON CO., ST. ANDREW (Block Island) (1917) [JC] Rev. Joseph Protano Jr.
Saint Andrew's Church Corporation, Block Island
Res.: Spring St., P.O. Box 279, Block Island, 02807. Tel: 401-466-5519; Fax: 401-466-3118. Email: standrewblockisland@verizon.net.
Catechesis/Religious Program—Students 27.

NEWPORT, NEWPORT CO.

1—ST. AUGUSTIN (1911) Rev. John T. McNulty; Sr. Josephine St. Leger, S.J.C., Pastoral Assoc.
Saint Augustin's Church of Newport
Res.: 2 Eastnor Rd., 02840. Tel: 401-847-0518; Fax: 401-848-2411. Email: staugstn@intap.net.
Catechesis/Religious Program—Students 48.

2—JESUS SAVIOUR (1926), (Portuguese), Rev. Francis A. O'Loughlin; Deacons James N. Dunbar; James R. Rudnik.
Church of Jesus-Saviour, Newport
Res.: One Vernon Ave., 02840. Tel: 401-847-1267; Fax: 401-846-3375. Email: jsaviour@verizon.net. Web: www.jsaviournewportri.org.
Catechesis/Religious Program—Tel: 401-846-4095. Students 122.

3—ST. JOSEPH (1885) Rev. Raymond B. Malm.
Saint Joseph's Church of Newport, Rhode Island
Res.: 5 Mann Ave., 02840. Tel: 401-847-0065; Fax: 401-849-2195. Email: bernice@stjosephsnewport.org. Web: www.stjosephnewport.org.
Catechesis/Religious Program—Tel: 401-847-9248; Fax: 401-849-2195. Students 121.

4—ST. MARY (1826) [CEM] Rev. George B. McCarthy.
St. Mary's, Newport, Rhode Island
Res.: 12 William St., P.O. Box 547, 02840. Tel: 401-847-0475; Fax: 401-845-9497. Email: stmaryre@aol.com. Web: www.rc.net/providence/stmary.
Catechesis/Religious Program—Tel: 401-846-6057. Students 150.

NORTH KINGSTOWN, WASHINGTON CO.

1—ST. BERNARD (Wickford) (1874) [CEM] Rev. John E. Unsworth; Deacons Ronald DePietro; Joseph Turcotte.
St. Bernard's Roman Catholic Church of Wickford, Rhode Island
Office: St. Bernard Parish Center: 415 Tower Hill Rd., Wickford, 02852. Tel: 401-295-0387; Fax: 401-295-1713. Email: parishcenter@sbcwickford.org. Web: www.sbcwickford.org.
Church: 275 Tower Hill Rd., Wickford, 02852.
Catechesis/Religious Program—Email: sbc.gof@verizon.net. Kriss Auger, D.R.E. Students 520.

2—ST. FRANCIS DE SALES (Davisville) (1960) Revs. Bertrand L. Theroux; D. Andrew Messina.
St. Francis de Sales Church Corporation, North Kingstown
Res.: 381 School St., 02852. Tel: 401-884-2105; Fax: 401-885-4315. Email: parishoffice@saintfds.org. Web: www.saintfds.org.
Catechesis/Religious Program—Tel: 401-885-3639. Kathleen Kane, D.R.E. Students 478.

NORTH PROVIDENCE, PROVIDENCE CO.

1—ST. ANTHONY (1944), (Italian), Rev. Edward S. Cardente; Deacon Anthony Cipriano.
Saint Anthony's Church Corporation, North Providence
Res.: 5 Gibbs St., 02904. Tel: 401-353-3120; Fax: 401-353-5126. Email: stanthonynp@cox.net.
Catechesis/Religious Program—Tel: 401-353-5125. Maryann Pallotta, D.R.E. Students 363.

2—ST. LAWRENCE (Centredale) (1907)
Saint Lawrence Church of Centredale, Closed. For

inquiries for parish records contact Mary Mother of Mankind Parish, North Providence.

3—MARY, MOTHER OF MANKIND (1967) Rev. Joseph A. Pescatello.
Mary, Mother of Mankind Church Corporation, North Providence In Res., Rev. Robert F. Caul (Retired).
Res.: 25 Fourth St., 02911. Tel: 401-231-3542; Fax: 401-232-0965.
Catechesis/Religious Program—Tel: 401-231-3544. Students 193.

4—PRESENTATION OF THE BLESSED VIRGIN MARY (Marieville) (1912), (French—Italian), Rev. Louis T. Natalizia; Deacon Louis A. Vani.
The Church of the Presentation of the Blessed Virgin Mary
Res.: 1081 Mineral Spring Ave., 02904. Tel: 401-722-7140; Fax: 401-722-6617. Email: pbvm1081@cox.net.
Catechesis/Religious Program—Tel: 401-722-7007 (Rel. Ed. Center). Maryann Dempsey, D.R.E. Students 83.

NORTH SMITHFIELD, PROVIDENCE CO., ST. JOHN THE EVANGELIST (Slatersville) (1872) [CEM] Rev. Raymond A. Tetreault; Deacon N. David Bouley.
St. John's Church Society, Rhode Island
Res.: 63 Church St., Box 266, Slatersville, 02876. Tel: 401-762-0946; Fax: 401-762-0944. Email: stjohn02876@yahoo.com. Web: www.stjohnslatersville.4lpi.com.
Catechesis/Religious Program—Tel: 401-762-0966. Mrs. Celeste Baillargeon, C.R.E. Students 469.

PAWTUCKET, PROVIDENCE CO.

1—ST. ANTHONY (1926), (Portuguese), Rev. Jose F. Rocha.
Saint Anthony's Church Corporation, Pawtucket
Res.: 32 Lawn Ave., 02860. Tel: 401-723-9138; Fax: 401-725-5616. Email: stanthony32@pawtucket.necoxmail.com. Web: members.tripod.com/stanthonysparish.
Catechesis/Religious Program—Students 135.

2—BLESSED POPE JOHN PAUL II PAWTUCKET RHODE ISLAND, 697 Central Ave., 02861-2191.

3—ST. CECILIA (1910), (French), Merged with St. Leo the Great, Pawtucket to form Blessed Pope John Paul II Pawtucket Rhode Island.
Saint Cecilia's Church Corporation

4—ST. EDWARD (1904) Rev. Charles H. Galligan.
St. Edward's Church of Pawtucket
Office: 58 Hancock St., 02860. Tel: 401-725-7036; Fax: 401-722-2386. Email: stedwardschurch@verizon.net.
Church: 396 Weeden St., 02860.
Catechesis/Religious Program—Students 50.

5—HOLY FAMILY PARISH, PAWTUCKET (2009), Merger of the following parishes: St. Joseph, Pawtucket, est. 1873 (Legal title: St. Joseph's Church); Our Lady of Consolation, Pawtucket, est. 1895 (Legal title: Church of Our Lady of Consolation, Rhode Island); Sacred Heart of Jesus, Pawtucket, (Irish), est. 1872 (Legal title: The Church of the Sacred Heart of Jesus of Pawtucket, Rhode Island) Rev. Robert P. Perron.
Res.: 195 Walcott St., 02860. Tel: 401-724-9190; Fax: 401-724-9314. Email: leg0203@aol.com.
Catechesis/Religious Program—Students 94.

6—IMMACULATE HEART OF MARY (1979), (Cape Verdean), (An operation of Church of St. Maron in Providence) Rev. Arlindo A. Amaro, C.S.Sp., Admin.
Res.: 35 Clay St., Central Falls, 02863. Tel: 401-725-1126; Fax: 401-726-4119.
Church: 291 High St., 02860. Tel: 401-725-5456.
Catechesis/Religious Program—Students 52.

7—ST. JOHN THE BAPTIST (1884), (French), Rev. Gerald G. Harbour; Deacon Vicente Caban.
The Church of St. John the Baptist of Pawtucket Rhode Island
Res.: 69 Quincy Ave., 02860. Tel: 401-722-9054; Fax: 401-724-3514. Email: st.johnthebaptist@verizon.net.
Catechesis/Religious Program—Students 191.

8—ST. JOSEPH (1873) Closed. See Holy Family Parish, Pawtucket
St. Joseph's Church

9—ST. LEO THE GREAT (1916), (Irish), Merged with St. Cecilia, Pawtucket to form Blessed Pope John Paul II Pawtucket Rhode Island.
Church of Saint Leo the Great in Pawtucket

10—ST. MARIA GORETTI (1953) Rev. Robert L. Bailey; Deacon Thomas Boutier.
St. Maria Goretti Church Corporation, Pawtucket
Res.: 165 Power Rd., 02860. Tel: 401-725-4355; Fax: 401-729-5711.
Catechesis/Religious Program—Students 102.

11—ST. MARY OF THE IMMACULATE CONCEPTION (1829) [JC] Very Rev. William J. Ledoux; Deacon C. Patrick Sheehy.
The Church of the Immaculate Conception of Pawtucket, Rhode Island
Res.: 103 Pine St., P.O. Box 518, 02862. Tel: 401-722-5425; Fax: 401-729-0341. Email: stmarypawt@cox.net.
Catechesis/Religious Program—Mrs. Madeleine Porter, D.R.E. Students 100.

12—OUR LADY OF CONSOLATION (1895) Closed. See Holy Family Parish, Pawtucket.
Church of Our Lady of Consolation Rhode Island

13—SACRED HEART OF JESUS (1872), (Irish), Closed. See Holy Family Parish, Pawtucket.
The Church of the Sacred Heart of Jesus of Pawtucket, Rhode Island

14—ST. TERESA OF THE CHILD JESUS (1929) Rev. Joseph Paquette.
Church of Saint Teresa of the Child Jesus, Pawtucket, Rhode Island In Res., Revs. John J. McElroy (Retired); Thomas J. Ferland.
Res.: 358 Newport Ave., 02861. Tel: 401-722-4470; Fax: 401-722-2958. Email: mlombardi@stteresa.necoxmail.com. Web: www.rc.net/providence/stteresa.
School—(Grades PreK-8), 140 Woodhaven Rd., 02861. Tel: 401-726-1414; Fax: 401-722-6998. Mary Carney, Prin. Lay Teachers 19; Students 213.
Catechesis/Religious Program—Tel: 401-723-2266; 401-722-8650. Liza Roach, D.R.E. Students 218.

PORTSMOUTH, NEWPORT CO.

1—ST. ANTHONY (1901) Rev. Daniel J. Gray.
Saint Anthony's Church of Portsmouth
Res.: 2836 E. Main Rd., P.O. Box 570, 02871. Tel: 401-683-0089; Fax: 401-683-9680. Email: stanthonych@msn.com.
Catechesis/Religious Program—Tel: 401-683-3636. Students 65.

2—ST. BARNABAS (1963) Very Rev. Randolph G. Chew.
St. Barnabas Church Corporation, Portsmouth
Res.: 1697 E. Main Rd., 02871. Tel: 401-683-1343; Fax: 401-683-5065. Email: sbchurch@stbarnabas.necoxmail.com. Web: www.stbarnabasportsmouth.4lpi.com.
Catechesis/Religious Program—Tel: 401-683-3147. Email: faithformation@stbarnabas.necoxmail.com. Students 594.

SCITUATE, PROVIDENCE CO., ST. JOSEPH (North Scituate) (1940) Very Rev. Roger A. Houle; Deacon Paul A. Ullucci.
144 Danielson Pk., P.O. Box 236, North Scituate, 02857.
Saint Joseph's Church Corporation, North Scituate In Res., Rev. Eugene R. Lessard (Retired).
Res.: 151 Danielson Pk., P.O. Box 236, North Scituate, 02857. Tel: 401-647-2255; Fax: 401-647-2968. Email: dmc948@sj.necoxmail.com.
Catechesis/Religious Program—Tel: 401-647-2650 (D.R.E.); Fax: 401-647-2968. Mrs. Lisa Woodhead, D.R.E.; Richard Audet, Youth Min.; Laurie Audet, Youth Min. Students 413.

SMITHFIELD, PROVIDENCE CO.

1—ST. MICHAEL (Georgiaville) (1875) Rev. Richard A. Valentine.
St. Michael's Church, Georgiaville, Rhode Island
Res.: 80 Farnum Pike, Georgiaville, 02917. Tel: 401-231-5119; Fax: 401-231-0523. Email: info@stmikegeo.necoxmail.com. Web: www.stmichaelsmithfield.org.
Catechesis/Religious Program—Tel: 401-231-1340. Students 424.

2—ST. PHILIP (Greenville) (1852) Revs. Francis C. Santilli; Jeremy J. Rodrigues; Juniper Sistare, C.F.R.; Deacons Harris J. Gederman; Carlo J. Sabetti.
St. Philip's Church Greenville Rhode Island
Res.: 622 Putnam Ave., Greenville, 02828-1403. Tel: 401-949-1500; Fax: 401-949-3504. Email: office@saintphilip.com. Web: www.saintphilip.com.
School—(Grades PreK-8), 618 Putnam Ave., Greenville, 02828. Tel: 401-949-1130; Fax: 401-949-1141. Email: dwalsh@stphilipschool.com. Darlene Walsh, Prin. Sisters of Mercy of the Americas 1; Lay Teachers 21; Students 281.
Catechesis/Religious Program—Tel: 401-949-0330; Fax: 401-949-5630. Email: stphilipred@yahoo.com. Marianne Jasinski, C.R.E. Students 987.

SOUTH KINGSTOWN, WASHINGTON CO.

1—CHRIST THE KING (Kingston) (1950) Rev. Joseph D. Creedon.
Christ the King Church Corporation, Kingston
Res.: 180 Old North Rd., Kingston, 02881. Tel: 401-783-7459; Fax: 401-789-3671. Email: info@ctkri.org. Web: www.ctkri.org.
Catechesis/Religious Program—Tel: 401-789-0417. Students 664.

2—ST. FRANCIS OF ASSISI (Wakefield) (1879) [CEM] Rev. Msgr. Paul D. Theroux; Rev. Joseph R. Upton; Deacon Paul O. Iacono; Mary Ellen Battey, Music Min.; Miss Kelli McNulty, Parish Business Mgr.
Saint Francis's Church
Res.: 114 High St., Wakefield, 02879-3141. Tel: 401-783-4411; Fax: 401-783-9667. Email: saintfrancis00@aol.com. Web: stfranciswakefield.com.
Catechesis/Religious Program—Tel: 401-792-8684. Barbette Cullen, D.R.E.; Mrs. Diane Castro, C.R.E. Students 663.
Chapel—St. Romuald Chapel Wakefield. 61 Atlantic Ave., Matunuck, Washington Co. 02879.

TIVERTON, NEWPORT CO.

1—ST. CHRISTOPHER (1910) Rev. Peter J. Andrews; Deacon Jesse L. Martins.
Saint Christopher's Church of Tiverton
Res.: 1554 Main Rd., 02878. Tel: 401-624-6644; Fax: 401-624-9889. Web: www.sstandctiverton.org.
Church: 1584 Main Rd., 02878.
Catechesis/Religious Program—Students 64.

2—HOLY GHOST (North Tiverton) (1913) Rev. Jay A. Finelli.
Church of the Holy Ghost, North Tiverton
Res.: 311 Hooper St., 02878. Tel: 401-624-8131; Fax: 401-625-5156. Email: secretary@holyghostcc.org; pastor@holychostcc.org. Web: www.holyghostcc.org.
Catechesis/Religious Program—Tel: 401-624-3664. Email: ccd@holyghostcc.org. Students 127.

3—ST. MADELEINE SOPHIE (1948), (Portuguese), Rev. Gerald W. Hussey.
Saint Madeleine's Church Corporation of Tiverton
Res.: 35 Lake Rd., 02878. Tel: 401-624-4226; Fax: 401-624-3848.
Catechesis/Religious Program—Students 79.

4—ST. THERESA (1960) Rev. Peter J. Andrews; Deacon Jesse L. Martins.
St. Theresa's Parish Corporation, Tiverton
Res.: 265 Stafford Rd., 02878. Tel: 401-624-8746; Fax: 401-625-5384. Web: www.sstandctiverton.org.
Catechesis/Religious Program—Students 224.

WARREN, BRISTOL CO.

1—ST. ALEXANDER (1915), (Italian), [CEM] Rev. David W. Masello, Admin.
Saint Alexander's Church Corporation, Warren
Res.: 221 Main St., 02885. Tel: 401-245-6369; Fax: 401-247-5455. Email: stalex02885@aol.com.
Catechesis/Religious Program—Tel: 401-247-1764. Students 20.

2—ST. CASIMIR (1908), (Polish), [JC] Closed. For Inquiries for parish records please see St. Mary of the Bay, Warren.
Saint Casimir's Church of Warren

3—ST. MARY OF THE BAY (1851) [CEM] Rev. Peter J. Gower.
Church of Saint Mary of the Bay
Res. and Parish House: 645 Main St., 02885. Tel: 401-245-7000, Ext. 11; Fax: 401-245-7093. Email: stmaryofthebay@aol.com. Web: www.stmaryofthebay.com.
Catechesis/Religious Program—Tel: 401-245-7000, Ext. 21. Twinned with St. Jean Baptiste, Warren. Students 275.
Mission—St. Jean Baptiste (1877)
The Church of Saint Jean Baptiste of Warren Rhode Island

4—ST. THOMAS THE APOSTLE (1952), (Portuguese), Rev. John E. Abreu; Deacon Benjamin Barboza.
Saint Thomas the Apostle Church Corporation
Res.: 500 Metacom Ave., 02885-2808. Tel: 401-245-4469; Fax: 401-245-4527. Email: stthomasap500@fullchannel.net.
Catechesis/Religious Program—Tel: 401-245-4488. Anne Furtado, C.R.E. Students 69.

WARWICK, KENT CO.

1—ST. BENEDICT (Conimicut) (1914) Rev. Roland L. Simoneau.
St. Benedict's Church, Conimicut
Res.: 135 Beach Ave., 02889. Tel: 401-737-9492; Fax: 401-739-0974. Email: stbenedictswarwick@juno.com.
Catechesis/Religious Program—70 Transit St., 02889. Tel: 401-738-2545. Students 153.

2—ST. CATHERINE (Apponaug) (1916) Rev. Richard M. Friedrichs; Deacon John F. Baker.
Saint Catherine's Roman Catholic Church of Warwick, Rhode Island In Res., Rev. Edward A. Sousa Jr.
Res.: 3252 Post Rd., 02886. Tel: 401-737-4455. Email: pastor@stcat.necoxmail.com. Web: www.stcatherineswarwick.org.
Catechesis/Religious Program—Tel: 401-737-6234; Fax: 401-736-0960. Kathleen Pesta, D.R.E.; Kelly Francoeur, D.R.E. Students 121.

3—ST. CLEMENT'S (1961) Merged with St. Rose of Lima to form St. Rose of Lima/St. Clement, Warwick. (Legal title: St. Clement Church Corporation, Warwick).

4—ST. FRANCIS OF ASSISI (Hillsgrove) (1943) Rev. Pierre J. Plante.
Saint Francis Church Corporation, Hillsgrove
Res.: 596 Jefferson Blvd., 02886. Tel: 401-737-5191; Fax: 401-737-1159. Email: stfrancis737@cox.net. Web: www.stfranciswarwick.com.
Catechesis/Religious Program—Students 76.
Convent—249 Chestnut St., 02888. Tel: 401-781-2464.

5—ST. GREGORY THE GREAT (Cowesett) (1961) Rev. Alfred V. Ricci; Deacon Paul F. Kirk.
St. Gregory the Great Church Corporation, Warwick

In Res., Rev. David F. Ricard.
Res.: 360 Cowesett Rd., 02886. Tel: 401-884-1666; Fax: 401-884-2448. Email: info@stgregorychurchri.com. Web: www.stgregorychurchri.com.
Catechesis / Religious Program—Tel: 401-884-0797. Students 669.

6—ST. KEVIN (1956) Revs. Douglas J. Spina; Roman R. Manchester.
St. Kevin's Church Corporation, Warwick
Res.: 333 Sandy Ln., 02889. Tel: 401-737-2638; Fax: 401-732-2832.
School—(Grades PreK-8), 39 Cathedral Rd., 02889. Tel: 401-737-7172; Fax: 401-738-2832. Web: www-.saintkevinschool.org. Roger R. Parent, Prin. Lay Teachers 26; Students 150.
Catechesis / Religious Program—Tel: 401-739-6309. Donna Forte, D.R.E.; Mary Beth Hoxie, D.R.E. Students 400.

7—ST. PETER (Pawtuxet) (1933) Rev. Roger C. Gagne; Deacon Robert M. Morisseau.
St. Peter's Church, Warwick, Rhode Island In Res., Rev. Msgr. Nicholas J. Iacovacci (Retired).
Res.: 350 Fair St., 02888. Tel: 401-467-4895; Fax: 401-785-9282. Email: charlene0226@aol.com. Web: http://stpeterswarwick.com.
School—(Grades PreK-8), 120 Mayfair Rd., 02888. Tel: 401-781-9242; Fax: 401-467-5673. Mrs. Joan Sickinger, Prin. Lay Teachers 15; Students 208.
Catechesis / Religious Program—Tel: 401-461-5691. Email: dre.st.peters.warwick2@juno.com. Margaret Andreozzi, D.R.E.; Elaine Morisseau, D.R.E. Students 290.

8—ST. RITA (Oakland Beach) (1935) Rev. Peter J. D'Ambrosia.
Saint Rita's Church Corporation, Oakland Beach
Res.: 722 Oakland Beach Ave., 02889. Tel: 401-738-1800; Fax: 401-738-1806. Email: st.rita3@verizon.net.
Catechesis / Religious Program—Students 291.

9—STS. ROSE & CLEMENT (1998), Consolidation of St. Rose of Lima and St. Clement. (Legal Title: St. Clement's Church Corporation, Warwick) (Legal Title: St. Rose's Church Corporation, Warwick). Rev. Edward J. Wilson Jr.; Deacon Noel Edsall.
Res.: 171 Inman Ave., 02886-1700. Tel: 401-739-0212; Fax: 401-732-4144. Email: office@ssrc4.necoxmail.com. Web: www.ssrcparish.com.
School—St. Rose of Lima, (Grades PreK-8), 200 Brentwood Ave., 02886. Tel: 401-739-6937; Fax: 401-737-4632. Email: stroseoflimaschool@cox.net. Web: www.saintroseschool.com. Mrs. Jeannine N. Fuller, Prin.; Mrs. Geraldine Grant, Librarian; Mrs. Mauren DiChristofaro, Librarian. Lay Teachers 16; Students 241.
Catechesis / Religious Program—111 Long St., 02886. Cheryl Berube, D.R.E. Students 313.

10—ST. ROSE OF LIMA (Greenwood) (1950) Merged with St. Clement to form St. Rose of Lima/St. Clement, Warwick. (Legal title: Saint Rose's Church Corporation, Warwick).

11—ST. TIMOTHY (Hoxie) (1950) Rev. Barry M. Meehan; Deacon Charles McCarthy.
Saint Timothy's Church Corporation, Warwick
Res.: 1799 Warwick Ave., 02889. Tel: 401-739-9552; Fax: 401-738-2466. Email: sttim@aol.com.
Catechesis / Religious Program—Tel: 401-738-9079. Students 144.

12—ST. WILLIAM (Norwood) (1933) [CEM] Rev. Frank S. Salmani. (Legal title: Saint William Church Corporation, Norwood).
Res. & Church: 200 Pettaconsett Ave., 02888. Tel: 401-781-7226; Fax: 401-781-4177.
Catechesis / Religious Program—Tel: 401-781-0343. Students 76.

WEST WARWICK, KENT CO.

1—ST. ANTHONY (Riverpoint) (1925), (Portuguese), Rev. Fernando A. Cabral (Portugal).
Saint Anthony's Church Corporation, River Point
Res.: 10 Sunset Ave., 02893. Tel: 401-821-8342. Email: stanthonyswwri@hotmail.com.
Catechesis / Religious Program—Students 146.

2—CHRIST THE KING (Centreville) (1931), (French), Rev. Timothy J. Lemlin; Deacon William J. Schofield.
Church of Christ the King, West Warwick
Parish Office: 130 Legris Ave., 02893. Tel: 401-821-9228.
Res.: 120 Legris Ave., 02893.
Catechesis / Religious Program—130 Legris Ave., 02893. Ms. Christine Duggan, D.R.E.; Mrs. Susan A. Vargas, Youth Min. Students 125.

3—ST. JAMES (1908) Merged with St. John the Baptist, West Warwick to form SS. John and James Parish, West Warwick.

4—SS. JOHN AND JAMES PARISH (2003) [CEM] Rev. Andrew McNair, L.C.; Deacons Paul M. Shea; Jose Farjardo.
Res.: 20 Washington St., 02893-4919. Tel: 401-821-7323; Fax: 401-826-7274. Email: ssjohnandjames@cox.net. Web: www.ssjohnandjames.org/parish.
Catechesis / Religious Program— Mrs. Christine Daneault, D.R.E. Students 142.

5—ST. JOHN THE BAPTIST (Arctic) (1874), (French), [CEM] Merged with St. James, West Warwick to form SS. John and James Parish, West Warwick.

6—ST. JOSEPH (Natick) (1873) Rev. Charles H. Downing.
St. Joseph's Church, Natick RI
Res.: 854 Providence St., 02893-1140. Tel: 401-821-4072; Fax: 401-821-2408. Email: downing@dioceseofprovidence.org.
School—(Grades PreK-8), 850 Wakefield St., 02893. Tel: 401-821-3450. Mr. Richard Keenan, Prin.; Karen McLaughlin, Librarian. Lay Teachers 21; Students 281.
Catechesis / Religious Program—Students 120.

7—ST. MARY (Crompton) (1844) [CEM] Rev. Thomas D. O'Neill.
St. Mary's Church, Crompton Rhode Island
Res.: 70 Church St., 02893. Tel: 401-821-5555. Email: stmaryschurch1@cox.net.
Catechesis / Religious Program—Tel: 401-828-8756. Students 71.

8—OUR LADY OF GOOD COUNSEL (Phenix) (1897), (French), [CEM] Rev. Paul R. Lemoi; Deacon Raymond LaFrance.
Church of Our Lady of Good Counsel, Warwick RI
Res.: 62 Pleasant St., 02893. Tel: 401-821-6428; Fax: 401-821-2472. Email: olgc60@juno.com.
Catechesis / Religious Program—Tel: 401-822-1869. Students 76.

9—SS. PETER AND PAUL (Phenix) (1853) [CEM] Rev. Robert J. Giardina.
SS. Peter and Paul's Church, Phoenixville, Rhode Island
Res.: 48 Highland St., 02893-5699. Tel: 401-821-2198.
Catechesis / Religious Program—Students 79.

10—SACRED HEART CHURCH (Natick) (1929), (Italian), Rev. Richard A. Bucci.
Church of the Sacred Heart, Natick RI
Res.: 820 Providence St., 02893. Tel: 401-821-4184; Fax: 401-828-8883. Email: sacredheartww@cox.net.
Catechesis / Religious Program—Students 69.

WESTERLY, WASHINGTON CO.

1—ST. CLARE (Misquamicut) (1946) Rev. Kenneth J. Suibielski; Deacons Stephen R. Cote; W. Carl LaFleur.
Saint Clare's Church Corporation, Misquamicut
Res.: 4 Saint Clare Way, Misquamicut, 02891. Tel: 401-348-8765; Fax: 401-315-5273. Email: stclareri2@cox.net.
Catechesis / Religious Program—Students 141.

2—IMMACULATE CONCEPTION (1885), (Italian), [CEM] Revs. Giacomo D. Capoverdi Jr.; Jacek Ploch; Deacon John D. McGregor.
Mailing Address: P.O. Box 556, 02891-0556. Tel: 401-596-2130; Fax: 401-348-2153.
Church of the Immaculate Conception of Westerly, Rhode Island
Res.: 111 High St., 02891. Tel: 401-596-2130; Fax: 401-348-2351. Email: icc@immcon.com.
Catechesis / Religious Program—Tel: 401-596-0900; Fax: 401-348-2153. Mrs. Catherine Kimmel, C.R.E. (Grades 1-10). Students 238.

3—ST. PIUS X (1955) Rev. Raymond N. Suriani; Deacon Francis J. Valliere.
St. Pius X Parish Corporation, Westerly In Res., Rev. Francis J. Giudice (Retired).
Res.: 44 Elm St., 02891. Tel: 401-596-2535; Fax: 401-596-9930. Email: stpiusx@cox.net.
School—32 Elm St., 02891. Tel: 401-596-5735; Fax: 401-596-5791. Web: www.westerlystpiusxshcool.org. Henry Fiore Jr., Prin. Lay Teachers 18; Students 206.
Catechesis / Religious Program—Tel: 401-596-8530. Email: chrismagowan@cox.net. Christine Magowan, D.R.E. Students 127.

4—ST. VINCENT DE PAUL (Bradford) (1946) Rev. David A. Piacentini.
Saint Vincent's Church Corporation, Bradford
Res.: 7 Church St., P.O. Box 277, Bradford, 02808. Tel: 401-377-2289; Fax: 401-377-8830. Email: lmolv@yahoo.com.
Catechesis / Religious Program—Tel: 401-377-8435. Email: ggolv@yahoo.com. Students 146.

WOONSOCKET, PROVIDENCE CO.

1—ST. AGATHA (1953) Rev. Msgr. John C. Allard; Rev. Timothy J. Gorton; Deacon Eugene Garceau.
Saint Agatha's Church Corporation, Woonsocket In Res., Rev. John D. Dreher (Retired).
Res.: 34 Joffre Ave., 02895. Tel: 401-767-2950; Fax: 401-767-2951.
Catechesis / Religious Program—Students 126.

2—ALL SAINTS PARISH (2009) [JC], An alliance of the following three parishes: Our Lady of Victories, (French), est. 1909, (Legal title: Church of Notre Dame des Victoires); St. Aloysius, (French) est. 1902, (Legal title: Saint Aloysius Church of Woonsocket); and St. Ann, (French) est. 1890 (Legal title: St. Ann's Church Corporation of Woonsocket RI). Revs. Dennis A. Reardon; Hugo Carmona (Colombia).
Res.: 323 Rathbun St., 02895. Tel: 401-762-1100; 401-766-0370; Fax: 401-765-6321.
Catechesis / Religious Program—Tel: 401-766-5771. Students 231.

3—ST. ALOYSIUS (1902) Merged See All Saints Parish, Woonsocket.

4—ST. ANN (1890) Merged See All Saints Parish, Woonsocket.

5—ST. ANTHONY (1924), (Italian), [JC] Rev. Msgr. Ronald P. Simeone.
Saint Anthony's Church, Woonsocket, RI
Res.: 128 Greene St., 02895. Tel: 401-766-2640; Fax: 401-766-2640. Email: saintanthonywoonsocket@verizon.net.
Catechesis / Religious Program—Students 27.

6—ST. CHARLES (1846) [CEM] Rev. Gerald F. Finnegan, S.J.
St. Charles Borromeo's Church, Woonsocket, RI
Res.: 190 N. Main St., 02895-3140. Tel: 401-766-0176; Fax: 401-766-0185. Email: fr_finnegan@stcharlesborromeo.com. Web: www.stcharlesborromeo.com.
Catechesis / Religious Program—Tel: 401-766-3088. Students 10.

7—HOLY FAMILY (1902), (French), [JC] Rev. Edward G. St-Godard.
Church of the Holy Family
Res.: 414 S. Main St., 02895. Tel: 401-762-0830; Fax: 401-762-3441. Email: holyfamilyri@verizon.net.
Catechesis / Religious Program—Students 18.

8—ST. JOSEPH (East Woonsocket) (1929), (French-Canadian), Revs. Michael J. Woolley; Marcin A. Mioduszewski.
Saint Joseph's Church, Woonsocket
Res.: 1200 Mendon Rd., 02895-3999. Tel: 401-766-0626; Fax: 401-766-1632. Web: www.saintjosephwoonsocket.org.
Catechesis / Religious Program—1210 Mendon Rd., 02895. Tel: 401-766-8233. Michelle T. Barrette, D.R.E. Students 178.
Station—Woonsocket Health Center, Tel: 401-765-2100; Fax: 401-232-7275.
Station—Wyndemere Woods, Tel: 401-762-4226; Fax: 401-766-5548.

9—OUR LADY OF VICTORIES (1909) Merged See All Saints Parish, Woonsocket.

10—OUR LADY, QUEEN OF MARTYRS (1953) Very Rev. Maurice L. Brindamour.
Our Lady, Queen of Martyrs Church Corporation, Woonsocket
Res.: 1409 Park Ave., 02895-6597. Tel: 401-762-5117; Fax: 401-765-8875. Email: parish@olqm.necoxmail.com. Web: www.olqm.info. School: See Monsignor Gadoury Regional School, Woonsocket, under The Greater Woonsocket Catholic Regional School System in the Institution section.
Catechesis / Religious Program—Tel: 401-767-2576. Students 150.

11—PRECIOUS BLOOD (1843), (French), [CEM] Rev. Msgr. John C. Allard; Rev. Timothy J. Gorton.
The Church of the Precious Blood Corporation, Woonsocket, RI In Res., Rev. Roger L. Marot (Retired).
Res.: 94 Carrington Ave., 02895. Tel: 401-762-0326; 508-883-6600 (Cemetery); Fax: 401-767-2951. Email: sapbcym6-12@cox.net.
Catechesis / Religious Program—34 Joffre Ave., 02895. Tel: 401-767-2950. Students 35.

12—SACRED HEART (1895) Rev. Ronald J. Bengford.
Church of the Sacred Heart Woonsocket, RI
Res.: 415 Olo St., 02895. Tel: 401-766-3150; Fax: 401-766-6864. Email: shcwoonsocket@cox.net. Web: www.sacredheartri.catholicweb.com.
Catechesis / Religious Program—Students 37.

13—ST. STANISLAUS (1905), (Polish), [JC] Revs. Dariusz J. Jonczyk, Admin.; Marcin A. Mioduszewski.
Saint Stanislaus Kostka Church of Woonsocket
Res.: 174 Harris Ave., 02895. Tel: 401-762-0021.
Catechesis / Religious Program—Students 45.

Chaplains of Public Institutions

PROVIDENCE. *Miriam Hospital*, 164 Summit Ave., 02906. Tel: 401-274-3700. Rev. Edward L. Pieroni. Res.: 2 Matilda St., 02904-1812.
Rhode Island Hospital, 593 Eddy St., 02902. Tel: 401-277-4000. Revs. Jacques Eddy Chavannes (Haiti), Joseph F. Craddock, Dir. Catholic Chaplaincy, Jose Q. dos Reis, Albert A. Ranallo Jr, Chinnaiah Yerrnini, Elsa Menegozzo, Team Member.
Roger Williams Hospital, 825 Chalkstone Ave., 02908. Tel: 401-456-2000. Pastoral care provided by local parishes.
Veterans Administration Hospital, Davis Park, 02908. Tel: 401-273-7100. Rev. John L. Wydeven (OAK).

BURRILLVILLE. *Rhode Island-Zambarano State Hospital*.

. Pastoral care provided by Office of Health Ministries.

CRANSTON. *Department of Corrections*. Mrs. Martha Paone, Chap. Coord.
1 Cathedral Sq., 02903.
Eleanor Slater Hospital. Rev. Msgr. Gerard O. Sabourin.

NEWPORT. *Newport Hospital*. Rev. Francis A. O'Loughlin.
Res.: 1 Vernon Ave., 02840. Tel: 401-847-0065.

NORTH SMITHFIELD. *St. Antoine Residence*. Most Rev. Louis E. Gelineau, D.D., S.T.L., J.C.L. (Retired).
Landmark Medical Center, Fogarty Unit. Pastoral care provided by local parishes.

PAWTUCKET. *Memorial Hospital of Rhode Island*. Pastoral care provided by local parishes.

SOUTH KINGSTOWN. *South County Hospital*. Rev. Msgr. Paul D. Theroux, S.T.B., J.C.L.
Res.: 114 High St., Wakefield, 02879-3141. Tel: 401-782-8000.

WARWICK. *Kent County Memorial Hospital*. Rev. David F. Ricard.
Res.: 41 Sandro Dr., 02886.

WESTERLY. *The Westerly Hospital*, 25 Wells St., 02891. Tel: 401-596-6000. Pastoral care provided by local parishes.

WOONSOCKET. *Landmark Medical Center, Woonsocket Unit*. Pastoral care provided by local parishes.

On Duty Outside the Diocese:
Revs.—
Grant, W. Douglas, c/o Archdiocese of Nassau, P.O. Box N-8187, Nassau Bahamas.
Kelley, Edward J., Chap., U.S. Army
LaMontagne, Bernard L., St. Mary of Woods, IN 47876.
Prendiville, Edmond P., 2480 Presidental Way-Envoy 1202, West Palm Beach, FL 33401.
Sheehan, Peter J., U.S. Navy Catholic Chap., 300 Preserve Ave. E., Port Royal, SC 29935.

Graduate Studies:
Rev.—
Nixon, George K., Pontifical North American College 00120 Vatican City State.

Absent on Leave:
Revs.—
Abruzzese, Joseph A.
Carpentier, Robert A.
Fisette, Kevin R.
Jimenez-Londono, Fredy A.
Petrocelli, John N.
Scagnelli, Peter J.
Stowe, Gregory P.

Retired:
Most Revs.—
Boland, Ernest B., O.P., Providence College, 02918.
Gelineau, Louis E., D.D., S.T.L., J.C.L., 10 Rhodes Ave., North Smithfield, 02896.
Mulvee, Robert E., 30 Fenner St., 02903.
Pearce, George H., S.M., D.D., 10 Rhodes Ave, N., North Smithfield, 02896.
Roque, Francis X., 255 Landsdowne Rd., Warwick, 02888.
Rev. Msgrs.—
Dziob, Michael W., 493 Mt. Pleasant Ave., 02908.
Frappier, George L., 341 Ballou St., 02895.
Halloran, John C., 36 Coffey Ave., Narragansett, 02882.
Iacovacci, Nicholas J., 350 Fair St., Warwick, 02888.
Murray, William F., c/o Robert Murray, 333 Sunset Ave., #412, Palm Beach, FL 33480.
Revs.—
Allard, George L., 493 Mt. Pleasant Ave., Apt. 14, 02908.
Beaulieu, Raymond A., 350 Bush Rd., Jupiter, FL 33458.
Behan, George P., 95 Third St., Newport, 02840.
Beirne, Gerald E., 75 Circuit Dr., Narragansett, 02882.
Beirne, Robert M., 791 Potters Ave., 02907.
Blain, Lionel A., Villa at St. Antoine, 400 Mendon Rd., North Smithfield, 02896.
Blais, Robert L., 10 Hall St., West Warwick, 02893.
Bolton, Paul J., 2520 N.W. 1st Ave., Pompano Beach, FL 33064.
Bouressa, Donald J., P.O. Box 787, Narragansett, 02882.
Brassil, Kevin J., 252 Williams St., 02906.
Cardoso, Reinaldo M., 964 Main St., Pawtucket, 02860.
Caul, Robert F., 25 Fourth St., North Providence, 02911.
Charland, Paul A., 3 Sherwood Valley Ln., Coventry, 02816.
Collins, Raymond F., P.O. Box 507, Saunderstown, 02874.
Courtemanche, Normand L., 58 Bouvier Ave., Manville, 02838.
Davenport, Christopher M., 110 Booth Ave., Pawtucket, 02861.
Dean, Frederic D., 493 Mt. Pleasant Ave., Apt. 10, 02908-3329.
Demers, Normand J., c/o 1 Cathedral Sq., 02903.
Diogo, Louis M., 92 Hope St., 02906.
Dreher, John D., 34 Joffre Ave., 02895.
Duggan, John J. (Ireland), SS. John & Paul Rectory, 341 S. Main St., Coventry, 02816.
Duhaime, James H., 152 Elmdale Rd., North Scituate, 02857.
Dyer, Raymond E., 15 Sumner Brown Rd., Cumberland, 02864-1297.
Farley, James W., P.O. Box 254, Dayville, CT 06249.
Finerty, D. Bryan, 15323 Lime Dr., Punta Gorda, FL 33955.
Fitzgerald, Edmund H., 125 Bucklin St., Apt. 4, Pawtucket, 02861.
Gibowski, Boguslaw T., 400 Sand Rd., North Haverhill, NH 03774.
Giudice, Francis J., 178 Dexter St., 02907.
Gray, John W., 505 Church Ave., Warwick, 02889.
Greaves, John G., 2730 Sailors Way, Naples, FL 34109-7643.
Gregoire, Wilfrid G., 34 Joffre Ave., 02895.
Hamilton, James J., 73 Spring Grove Ave, Warwick, 02889.
Hayman, Robert W., M.A., Ph.D., 30 Fenner St., 02903.
Hazebrouck, Maurice L., c/o One Cathedral Sq., 02903.
Heaney, John F., 1 Scenic Heights Dr., Westerly, 02891.
Henry, Joseph P., 225 Capstan St., Jamestown, 02835.
Hogan, Ralph R., 493 Mt. Pleasant Ave., Apt. 8, 02908.
Horgan, Joseph E., 25 Leading St., Johnston, 02919.
Hynes, James P., 493 Mt. Pleasant Ave., Apt. 3, 02908.
Iwuc, Anthony D., 493 Mt. Pleasant Ave., Apt. 6, 02908.
Johnson, Edward D., 230 Collins Industrial Way, Apt. 362, Lawrenceville, GA 30043.
Kachel, Czeslaw L., 493 Mt. Pleasant Ave., 02908.
Keefe, Francis J., 493 Mt. Pleasant Ave., Apt. 15, 02908.
Keenan, Thomas L., 268 Parkview Dr., 02906.
Kehew, Donal R., 92 Hope St., Apt. 7, 02906.
Kelly, Raymond M.
Kiley, John A., 247 Highland St., 02895.
Laporte, Paul J., 218 Baxter St., Pawtucket, 02861.
Lavin, John J., 56 Boxwood Ave., Cranston, 02910.
Lessard, Eugene R., P.O. Box 236, North Scituate, 02857-0236.
Lonardo, Alfred C., P.O. Box 228, Jamestown, 02835.
Lynch, Cornelius B., 125 Bucklin St., Apt. 15, Pawtucket, 02861.
Maher, Charles E., 188 Col. John Gardner Rd., Narragansett, 02882.
Marot, Roger L., 94 Carrington Ave., 02895.
Maynard, Richard C., 400 Narragansett Pkwy., Apt. S. B4, Warwick, 02888.
McDermott, Charles B., 860 N. Quidnessett Rd., North Kingstown, 02852.
McElroy, John J., 358 Newport Ave., Pawtucket, 02861.
McGeough, Jude P., St. Elizabeth Manor, 1 Dawn Hill Rd., Bristol, 02809.
McGovern, Edward J., 493 Mt. Pleasant Ave., Apt. 1, 02908.
McKenna, Eugene J., 30 Blackberry Hill Dr., Wakefield, 02879.
Micarelli, Edmond C., c/o 1 Cathedral Sq., 02903.
Mongeon, Peter M. (NO), 26 Fairview Ave., Cranston, 02905.
Murphy, William F., 493 Mount Pleasant Ave., Apt. 12, 02908.
O'Hara, Francis W., 36 Eden Crest Dr., Cranston, 02920.
Oliveira, Joel D. (BO), 155 Fort St., East Providence, 02914.
Paiva, Antonio M., 463 Benefit St., 02903.
Pincince, Gerald P., 2280 S. Flagler Ave., Flagler Beach, FL 32136.
Quinn, Charles P., 32 Lakeview Ter., Pascoag, 02859.
Rafferty, Raymond J., 400 Mendon Rd., North Smithfield, 02896.
Randall, Robert J., P.O. Box 5617, Wakefield, 02880.
Reynolds, Paul F., 964 Main St., Pawtucket, 02860.
Schenick, Joseph D., 493 Mt. Pleasant Ave., Apt. 2, 02908.
Sears, William F., 1460 Diamond Hill Rd., Cumberland, 02864.
Slota, Frederick V., 84 Kulas Rd., West Warwick, 02893.
Smith, Nicholas P., 493 Mt. Pleasant Ave., 02908.
Stark, Philip M., 54 Meadow Brook Ave., Cumberland, 02864. (Extern Priest)
Strumski, Matthew J., 400 Mendon Rd., Rm. 216, North Smithfield, 02896.
Tanguay, William H., c/o One Cathedral Sq., 02903.
Tarro, Michael, C.S., 927 Atwood Ave., Johnston, 02919-6290.
Tetrault, Raymond L., 66 Appleton St., 02909.
Trainor, Daniel M., 92 Hope St., Apt. 4, 02906-2099.
Turillo, B. Samuel, 196 Lansdowne Rd., Warwick, 02888.
Walsh, Clyde J., 964 Main St., Pawtucket, 02860.
Walsh, Richard A., 309 Spring St., Newport, 02840.
Watterson, John E., 700 Shore Dr., #1108, Fall River, MA 02721.
Young, Peter G., 1493 Cranston St., Cranston, 02920.

Permanent Deacons:
Alessio, Robert G., (Leave of Absence)
Andrade, Charles, St. Patrick, Providence
Archambault, Bernard L., (Retired)
Bacon, Normand J., (Retired)
Baker, John F., St. Catherine, Warwick
Barboza, Benjamin, St. Thomas the Apostle, Warren
Batalon, Raymond E., (Retired)
Bisbano, Paul, St. Mary, Bristol
Bouley, N. David, St. John, Slatersville
Boutier, Thomas F., St. Maria Goretti, Pawtucket
Braga, Joseph F., St. Charles, Providence
Caban, Vicente, St. John the Baptist, Pawtucket
Ceprano, Peter A., (Retired)
Cipriano, Anthony, St. Anthony, No. Providence
Conley, James E., St. Elizabeth, Bristol
Corey, John A., Blessed Kateri Tekakwitha Catholic Community, Exeter
Cote, Stephen R., Diocesan Marriage Prep. Coord.
Croy, John E., St. Lucy, Middletown
Dadlez, Mark A., (Retired)
DePetrillo, Albert, Hopkins Manor, North Providence
DePietro, Ronald H., St. Bernard, North Kingstown
DiOrio, Dominic P., St. Martha, E. Providence
Dunbar, James N., Jesus Saviour, Newport
Edsall, Noel, SS. Rose & Clement, Warwick
Fajardo, Jose, SS. John and James, West Warwick
Forlingieri, Carmine, (Retired)
Gagnon, Laurence O., (Leave of Absence)
Gallo, Robert L., St. Bartholomew, Providence
Garceau, Eugene, St. Agatha, Woonsocket
Garcia, Luis, (Leave of Absence)
Gederman, Harris J., St. Philip, Greenville
Geoffroy, Roland R., (Leave of Absence)
Gomez, Oscar, (Leave of Absence)
Hanrahan, Charles L., (Leave of Absence)
Horton, Gregory R., (Leave of Absence)
Iacono, Paul O., St. Francis of Assisi, South Kingstown
Johnson, Loring F., (Retired)
Kirk, Paul, D.D.S., St. Gregory the Great, Warwick
Konold, Paul C., (Leave of Absence)
LaFleur, Norman R., (Leave of Absence)
LaFleur, W. Carl, St. Clare, Westerly
LaFrance, Raymond, (Retired)
Lambert, Paul H., St. John Vianney, Cumberland
Lapierre, Richard J., Our Lady of Good Help, Mapleville
Levesque, Raymond E., (Retired)
Lopez, Pedro, Our Lady of Mt. Carmel, Providence
Lopez, Rony, Assumption of the BVM, Providence
Lucian, Robert C., (Retired)
MacLure, Robert, (Retired)
Martins, Jesse L., St. Theresa, Tiverton
Masse, Kevin P., (Leave of Absence)
Masse, Paul, (Leave of Absence)
McAdam, Robert, St. Ambrose, Lincoln
McCarthy, Charles F., St. Timothy, Warwick
McGregor, John D., Immaculate Conception, Westerly
Morisseau, Robert M., St. Peter, Warwick
Muscatelli, Anthony E., St. Joseph, Burrillville
Napolitano, Michael D., Chap., Rhode Island College, Providence
Natalizia, John J., Holy Cross, Providence
Needham, John F., St. Margaret, East Providence
Nova, Leocadio, (Leave of Absence)
O'Hara, Thomas P., (Retired)
Ouellette, Lucien, (Retired)
Owen, Jimmie H., Blessed Sacrament, Providence
Pelland, Robert W., Holy Spirit, Central Falls
Perez, Juan Andres, St. Michael, Providence
Persson, Robert, SS. John & Paul, Coventry
Ragosta, Armand R., St. Mary, Cranston
Raspallo, Thomas R., Immaculate Conception, Cranston
Remillard, Lionel J., St. Jude, Lincoln

Riccio, Raymond L., Chap., State Hospitals
Rico, Jose, St. Charles Borromeo, Providence
Risi, Stephen M., Mary, Mother of Mankind, North Providence
Rose, Joseph, (Retired)
Rudnik, James R., Jesus Saviour, Newport
Sabetti, Carlo J., St. Philip, Greenville
Schofield, William J., Christ the King, West Warwick
Shea, John S., St. Mary, Charlestown
Shea, Paul M., SS. John & James, West Warwick
Sheehy, C. Patrick, St. Mary, Pawtucket
Stone, Francis J., (Retired)
Sullivan, Paul J., St. Thomas More, Narragansett
Tanguay, Paul A., Chap., ACI, Cranston
Theroux, Bernard G., Chap., R.I. Veteran's Home
Theroux, Paul A., St. Mary, Carolina
Troia, Robert, St. Rocco's, Thornton
Tumminelli, Joseph, St. Robert Bellarmine, Johnston
Turbitt, Robert A., II, (Leave of Absence)
Turcios, Jose, Holy Ghost, Providence
Turcotte, Joseph G., St. Bernard, North Kingstown
Ullucci, Paul A., St. Joseph, Scituate
Urrico, Francis X., (Leave of Absence)
Valliere, Francis J., St. Pius X, Westerly
Vani, Louis A., Presentation of the Blessed Virgin Mary, North Providence
Walsh, James T., St. Aidan, Cumberland
Wendoloski, Anthony, Our Lady of Lourdes, Providence

INSTITUTIONS LOCATED IN THE DIOCESE

[A] SEMINARIES, DIOCESAN

PROVIDENCE. *Seminary of Our Lady of Providence*, 485 Mt. Pleasant Ave., 02908. Tel: 401-331-1316; Fax: 401-521-4192. Web: www.olpseminary.com. Revs. Carl B. Fisette, Asst. Dir. Vocations; Christopher M. Mahar, S.T.L., Rector; Michael J. Najim, M.Div., Vocation Dir.; David F. Gaffney, M.Div., Dir. of Spir. Form.; Timothy D. Reilly, S.T.B., J.C.L., Asst. Dir. Spir. Form.
Seminary of Our Lady of Providence, House of Formation for College Students and Pre-Theologians. Total Staff 7; Students 27.

[B] COLLEGES AND UNIVERSITIES

PROVIDENCE. *Providence College*, One Cunningham Sq., 02918. Tel: 401-865-1000; Fax: 401-865-2057. Email: pcadmiss@providence.edu. Web: www.providence.edu. Revs. Brian J. Shanley, O.P., Pres.; Kenneth Sicard, O.P., Exec. Vice Pres. & Treas.; Dr. Hugh V. Lena, Provost & Senior Vice Pres. Academic Affairs; John Sweeney, Senior Vice Pres. Finance & Business & CFO; Rev. Brendan Murphy, O.P., Vice Pres. Student Affairs Admin.; Mr. Edward J. Caron, Vice Pres. College Rels.; Rev. Mark S. Nowel, O.P., Dean Undergraduate & Graduate Studies; Mr. David Wegrzyn, Senior Vice Pres. Inst. Advancement; Revs. Michael J. Cuddy, O.P., Chap.; Joseph J. Guido, O.P., Vice Pres. Mission & Ministry; Marifrances McGinn, Vice Pres. & General Counsel; Robert Driscoll, Assoc. Vice Pres. & Athletic Dir.; Kathleen M. Alvino, Assoc. Vice Pres. Human Resources.
Providence College, Conducted by the Dominican Friars. Dominican Priests Teaching 23; Diocesan Priests Teaching 3; Sisters Teaching 2; Lay Professors 246; Undergraduate Students 3,791; Graduate Students 684; School of Continuing Educ. 498.

NEWPORT. *Salve Regina University* (1934) 100 Ochre Point Ave., 02840-4192. Tel: 401-847-6650; Fax: 401-847-0372. Email: sruadmis@salve.edu. Web: www.salve.edu. Rev. Kris M. von Maluski, Chap.; Sisters M. Therese Antone, R.S.M., Chancellor; Jane Gerety, R.S.M., Pres.; Dr. Laura O'Toole, Dean Undergraduate Studies; Dr. Dean de la Motte, Vice Pres. Academic Affairs; Dr. Leona Misto, R.S.M., Vice Pres. Mission Integration & Planning; William B. Hall, Vice Pres. Admin. & CFO; Dr. Laura E. McPhie-Oliveira, Vice Pres. Enrollment Svcs.; Frederick C. Promades, Dir. Institute Research; Aida Mirante, Dir. Financial Aid; Michael Semenza, Vice Pres. Univ. Relations Advancement; Kathleen Boyd, Dir. Library Svcs.; John Quinn, Dean of Students; Thomas H. Brennan, Assoc. Vice Pres. Technology & CIO; Rev. Michael T. Malone, C.S.Sp., Assoc. Prof.; Michael N. Grandchamp, Assoc Vice Pres. Fin. & Controller; Diane F. Blanchette, Assoc. Vice Pres. Human Resources & AAO; Kristine Hendrickson, Assoc. Vice Pres. Univ. Relations & CCO.
Salve Regina University Sisters of Mercy of the Americas. Priests 1; Sisters 6; Lay Teachers 111; Students: Men 864; Women 1,740.

[C] HIGH SCHOOLS, DIOCESAN

PAWTUCKET. *St. Raphael Academy*, 123 Walcott St., 02860. Tel: 401-723-8100; Fax: 401-723-8740. Web: www.saintrays.org. Rev. Mark A. Sauriol, Chap.; Maryann Donahue-Lynch, Pres. & Prin.
Saint Raphael Academy, Conducted by the Brothers of the Christian Schools. Priests 1; Brothers 1; Sisters 1; Lay Teachers 30; Boys 202; Girls 158.

SOUTH KINGSTOWN. *The Prout School*, 4640 Tower Hill Rd., Wakefield, 02879. Tel: 401-789-9262; Fax: 401-782-2262. Email: info@theproutschool.org. Web: www.theproutschool.org. Gary R. Delneo, Prin.; Rev. Joseph R. Upton, Chap.
The Prout School Priests 1; Lay Teachers 47; Staff & Admin. Personnel 18; Boys 264; Girls 379.

WARWICK. *Bishop Hendricken High School* (1959) 2615 Warwick Ave., 02889. Tel: 401-739-3450; Fax: 401-732-8261. Email: hawks@hendricken.com. Web: www.hendricken.com. Joseph T. Brennan Jr., Prin.; Revs. David F. Gaffney, M.Div., Chap.; Jose Q. dos Reis, Chap. of the Brothers; Mr. John A. Jackson, Pres.; Priscilla Fox, Librarian.
Bishop Hendricken High School Congregation of Christian Brothers. Priests 1; Brothers 3; Sisters 1; Lay Teachers 85; Boys 913.

[D] HIGH SCHOOLS, REGIONAL

PAWTUCKET. *Bishop Francis P. Keough Regional High School* (1971) 145 Power Rd., 02860. Tel: 401-726-0335; Fax: 401-726-0336. Email: biskeo@netscape.net. Web: www.bishopkeough.org. Jeanne H. Leclerc, Prin.; Dorothy Young, Librarian. Sisters 1; Lay Teachers 12; Girls 90.

[E] HIGH SCHOOLS, PRIVATE

PROVIDENCE. *La Salle Academy*, (Grades 7-12), 612 Academy Ave., 02908. Tel: 401-351-7750; Fax: 401-444-1782. Email: dkavanagh@lasalle-academy.org. Web: www.lasalle-academy.org. Bro. Michael McKenery, F.S.C., Pres.; Mr. Donald Kavanagh, Prin.; Rev. Michael J. Najim, M.Div., Chap.; Roseanne Trissler, Librarian; Andrea Hajian, Librarian.
St. John Baptist de LaSalle Institute, Conducted by the Brothers of the Christian Schools. Priests 1; Brothers 6; Lay Teachers 120; Students 1,481; Total Staff 157.

EAST PROVIDENCE. *St. Mary Academy - Bay View, St. Mary Academy-Bayview*, 3070 Pawtucket Ave., Riverside, 02915. Tel: 401-434-0113, Ext. 156; Fax: 401-434-0335. Email: emcauliffe@bayviewacademy.org. Web: www.smabv.org. Sr. Elizabeth McAuliffe, R.S.M., Ed.D., Pres.; Ms. Colleen Gribbin, Prin.; Ms. Kathleen Gendron, Librarian. Sisters of Mercy Northeast Community. Sisters 5; Lay Teachers 51; Girls 458.

PORTSMOUTH. *Portsmouth Abbey School*, 285 Cory's Ln., 02871. Tel: 401-683-2000; Fax: 401-683-5888. Email: fathercaedmon@portsmouthabbey.org. Web: www.portsmouthabbey.org. Rt. Rev. W. Caedmon Holmes, O.S.B., Abbot; Dr. James DeVecchi, Prin.; Roberta Stevens, Librarian.
Order of St. Benedict in Portsmouth, Rhode Island Priests 10; Brothers 3; Lay Teachers 44; Students 358.

SOUTH KINGSTOWN. *Immaculate Conception Academy, Inc.*, 4780 Tower Hill Rd., Wakefield, 02879. Tel: 401-782-6200; Fax: 401-782-6209. Email: cwilders@inteducators.org. Rev. Nikola Derpich, L.C., Chap.; Siobhan O'Connor, Prin.; Ms. Caroline Wilders, Dir. Teachers 8; Boarding School Students 70.

WARREN. *Our Lady of Fatima High School* (1965) (Grades 7-12), 360 Market St., Rte. 136, 02885. Tel: 401-245-4449; Fax: 401-245-1380. Web: www.fatimahs.org; www.findfatima.org. Sr. Mary Margaret Souza, S.S.D., Prin.; Ellen Bennett, Librarian. Sisters of St. Dorothy. Sisters 3; Lay Teachers 10; Students 80.

WOONSOCKET. *Mount Saint Charles Academy* (1924) (Grades 7-12), 800 Logee St., 02895-5599. Tel: 401-769-0310; Fax: 401-762-2327. Email: richerh@mountsaintcharles.org. Web: mountsaintcharles.org. Herve Richer, Pres.; Edwin F. Burke, Prin.; Mrs. Amy Blanchette, Librarian.
Mount Saint Charles Academy, Inc. Brothers of the Sacred Heart. Priests 1; Brothers 10; Sisters 1; Lay Teachers 60; Students 875.

[F] ELEMENTARY SCHOOLS, PRIVATE

PROVIDENCE. *San Miguel School* (1993) 525 Branch Ave., 02904. Tel: 401-467-9777; Fax: 401-785-4976. Web: www.sanmiguelprov.org. Bro. Lawrence Goyette, F.S.C., Exec. Dir. Brothers 2; Lay Teachers 11; Students 64.

CUMBERLAND. *Mercymount Country Day School* (1948) 35 Wrentham Rd., 02864. Tel: 401-333-5919; Fax: 401-333-5150. Email: ride5179@ride.ri.net. Web: www.mercymount.org. Sisters Martha Mulligan, R.S.M., Prin.; Diane Russo, R.S.M., Librarian. Sisters of Mercy Northeast Community. Sisters 4; Brothers 1; Lay Teachers 29; Students 460.

EAST PROVIDENCE. *St. Mary Academy-Bay View*, (Grades PreK-8), *St. Mary Academy-BayView*, 3070 Pawtucket Ave., Riverside, 02915. Tel: 401-434-0113, Ext. 156; Fax: 401-434-0335. Web: www.bayviewacademy.org. Mrs. Cynthia Lorincz, Prin.; Sr. Elizabeth McAuliffe, R.S.M., Ed.D., Pres.; Therese Quigley, Librarian. Sisters of Mercy Northeast Community., Day Pupils. Sisters 1; Lay Teachers 11; Girls 260.

NEWPORT. *Cluny School*, (Grades PreK-8), (Day School), 75 Brenton Rd., 02840. Tel: 401-847-6043; Fax: 401-848-5678. Email: mcaswell@clunyschool.org. Web: clunyschool.org. Sisters Joan Van der Zydem, S.J.L., Provincial; Luke Parker, S.J.C., Vice Provincial; Mrs. Meredith Caswell, Prin.; Sisters Ann Marie Liston, S.J.C., Sec. & Treas.; Maria Rocha, Dir.; Genevieve Marie Vigil, S.J.C., (Retired).
St. Joseph of Cluny Sisters' School, Inc. Sisters 2; Lay Teachers 6; Students 178.

PORTSMOUTH. *St. Philomena School* (1953) (Grades PreK-8), 324 Cory's Ln., 02871. Tel: 401-683-0268; Fax: 401-683-6554. Email: mainoffice@saintphilomena.org. Web: www.saintphilomena.org. Donna Bettencourt-Glavin, Prin.; Jeffrey Moniz, Vice Prin.; Jeanne Staats, Librarian. Sisters Faithful Companions of Jesus. Lay Teachers 30; Students 490.

[G] REGIONAL ELEMENTARY SCHOOLS

PROVIDENCE. *St. Thomas Regional School*, (Grades K-8), 15 Edendale Ave., 02911. Tel: 401-351-0403; Fax: 401-351-0403 (call first). Email: mcdimuccio@cox.net. Mary DiMuccio, Prin. Lay Teachers 10; Students 177.

BURRILLVILLE. *Father Holland Catholic Regional Elementary School*, (Grades PreK-8), 180 Sayles Ave., Pascoag, 02859. Tel: 401-568-4589; Fax: 401-567-9069. Email: frholland@cox.net. Shawn A. Capron, Prin.; Christine Goulet, Librarian. Lay Teachers 10; Students 146.

CRANSTON. *Immaculate Conception Catholic Regional School*, (Grades PreK-8), 235 Garden Hills Dr., 02920. Tel: 401-942-7245; Fax: 401-943-5738. Email: sjennings@iccrschool.org. Web: www.iccrschool.org. Mrs. Sandra Jennings, Prin.; Kristine Mahone, Librarian. Lay Teachers 26; Students 374.

EAST GREENWICH. *Our Lady of Mercy Regional School* (1950) (Grades PreK-8), 55 Fourth Ave., 02818. Tel: 401-884-1618; Fax: 401-885-3138. Email: sjbarry@olmschool.org. Web: www.olmschool.org. Sr. Jeanne Barry, Prin.; Camille Craybas, Librarian. Priests 1; Sisters 2; Lay Teachers 25; Administrators 2; Students 405.

MIDDLETOWN. *All Saints Academy* (1971) (Grades PreSchool-8), 915 W. Main Rd., 02842. Tel: 401-848-4300; Fax: 401-848-5587. Email: rid40001@ride.ri.net. Web: allsaintsacademy.org. John T. Finnegan, Ph.D., Prin. Lay Teachers 13; Students 151.

PAWTUCKET. *Woodlawn Catholic Regional School* (1972) (Grades PreK-8), 61 Hope St., 02860. Tel: 401-723-3759; Fax: 401-722-4090. Web: www.woodlawncrs.org. Veronica Procopio, Prin. Sisters 1; Lay Teachers 8; Students 184.

WAKEFIELD. *Monsignor Matthew F. Clarke Regional School* (1967) (Grades PreK-8), 5074 Tower Hill Rd., 02880. Tel: 401-789-0860; Fax: 401-789-3164. Email: pmurphy@monsignorclarkeschool.org. Web: www.monsignorclarkeschool.org. Patricia Murphy, Prin. Lay Teachers 27; Students 380.

WARWICK. *Overbrook Academy at Our Lady of Providence Center* (Boarding School), 836 Warwick Neck Ave., 02889. Tel: 401-737-2850; Fax: 401-737-2884. Email: information@overbrookacademy.org. Web: www.overbrookacademy.com. Miss Kristina Pinero, Dir.; Rev. Nikola Derpich, L.C., Chap. Lay Teachers 16; Students 168.

[H] THE GREATER WOONSOCKET CATHOLIC REGIONAL SCHOOL SYSTEM

WOONSOCKET. *Greater Woonsocket Catholic Regional School System*, Office: 77 Federal St., 02895. Mailing: P.O. Box 487, 02895-0487. Tel: 401-762-1095; Fax: 401-767-5901. Web: www.gwcrs.org. Mrs. Paula Hurteau, Admin.
Greater Woonsocket Catholic Regional School System

Member Schools

WOONSOCKET
Good Shepherd Catholic Regional School (Grades 3-8), 1210 Mendon Rd., 02895. Tel: 401-767-5906;

Fax: 401-767-5905. Email: goodshepherdschool@cox.net. Web: www.gwcrs.org. Mr. Larry Poitras, Prin.; Joyce Broulliard, Librarian. Lay Teachers 16; Students 232.

Monsignor Gadoury Regional Primary School (Grades PreK-2), Three year old program, 1371 Park Ave., 02895. Tel: 401-767-5902; Fax: 401-767-5923. Email: mgprincipal@yahoo.com. Mary Chabot, Prin. Sisters 1; Lay Teachers 7; Students 174.

[I] BREAD OF LIFE SCHOOLS, URBAN CATHOLIC SCHOOLS CONSORTIUM

PROVIDENCE. *Bread of Life Schools, Urban Catholic Schools Consortium*, 155 Gordon Ave., 02905. Tel: 401-781-2370. Annmarie Bucci, Dir. Fin.

Member Schools

PROVIDENCE

Bishop McVinney Regional School (Grades PreK-8), 155 Gordon Ave., 02905. Tel: 401-781-2370; Fax: 401-785-2618. Email: bishopmcvinney@yahoo.com. Mr. Louis Hebert, Prin.; Carol Kamnski, Librarian.

Catholic Association for Regional Education Lay Teachers 10; Students 230.

CENTRAL FALLS

St. Elizabeth Ann Seton Academy (1995) (Grades PreK-8), 909 Lonsdale Ave., 02863. Tel: 401-728-6230; Fax: 401-723-9532. Email: principal@setonacademyri.org. Web: www.setonacademyri.org. Mrs. Maria Rocheleau, Prin.; Therese M. Rogers, Admin. Asst. Lay Teachers 18; Students 221.

[J] CHILD CARING FACILITIES

PROVIDENCE. *Group Home for Adolescent Boys* (Whitmarsh House), 1055 N. Main St., 02904. Tel: 401-351-7230; Fax: 401-421-0198. Bro. John McHale, O.L.P., Dir. Lay Teachers 5; Boys 40.

NARRAGANSETT. *Ocean Tides*, 635 Ocean Rd., 02882-1314. Tel: 401-789-1016; Fax: 401-788-0924. Email: brob@oceantides.org. Web: www.oceantides.org. Bros. Brendan Gerrity, F.S.C., Pres.; John McGann, F.S.C., Social Svcs.; John Norton, F.S.C., Court Liaison; Joseph Schafer, F.S.C., Dir. Social Svcs.; Peter Clifford, F.S.C., Admin. Asst.; Jane E. Genereux, Prin.

Ocean Tides, Inc. Brothers 5; Lay Teachers 25; Lay Staff 38; Students 112.

[K] GENERAL HOSPITALS

PROVIDENCE. *St. Joseph Health Services of Rhode Island* (1892) 21 Peace St., 02907. Tel: 401-456-4080; Fax: 401-456-4089. Web: www.saintjosephri.com. Kenneth H. Belcher, Pres. & CEO; Rev. John J. Rainone, Dir. Pastoral Care; Sisters Jolly Joseph, Assoc. Chap.; Madeline Rita, Assoc. Chap.

Includes:

St. Joseph Center for Health & Human Services Tel: 401-456-4321; Fax: 401-456-4089. Dr. Abdel Hammo, M.D., Medical Dir.

NORTH PROVIDENCE. *St. Joseph Health Services of Rhode Island - Our Lady of Fatima Hospital* (1954) 200 High Service Ave., 02904. Tel: 401-456-3000; 401-456-3050; Fax: 401-456-3028; 401-456-3640. Web: www.fatimahospital.com. Revs. John J. Rainone, Dir. Pastoral Care; Edward A. Sousa Jr., Chap.; Sr. Madeleine Guertin, Assoc. Chap.; Deacon Anthony J. Wendoloski Jr., Assoc. Chap.; Carol Ross, Acting Dir. School Nursing. Student Nurses 100; Bed Capacity 386; Patients Assisted Annually 200,000; Total Staff 1,850.

Southern New England Rehabilitation Center Tel: 401-456-4500; Fax: 401-456-4501. Web: www.snerc.com. Jon A. Mukand, M.D., Ph.D., Medical Dir. A joint venture of St. Joseph Hospital and Rhode Island Hospital.

Corporate Care Occupational Health Services Tel: 401-456-4020; Fax: 401-456-4203. Dr. Jay Burstein, M.D., Medical Dir.

St. Joseph Center for Psychiatric Services Tel: 401-456-4437; Fax: 401-456-4078. Ronald Gobeil, D.O., Medical Dir.

St. Joseph Health Services Foundation, 200 High Service Ave., 02904. Tel: 401-456-3070. Email: obrown@saintjosephri.com. Web: www.saintjosephri.com. Otis Brown, Vice Pres. Devel. & Public Affairs.

[L] HOMES FOR AGED

CUMBERLAND. *Mount St. Rita Health Centre* (1971) 15 Sumner Brown Rd., 02864. Tel: 401-333-6352; Fax: 401-333-1012. Email: mail@mountstrita.org. Web: www.mountstrita.org. Deborah Beards, Admin.

Mount St. Rita Health Centre Inc., Licensed Nursing Home. Residents 98; Total Staff 160.

NEWPORT. *St. Clare Home* (1909) 309 Spring St., 02840. Tel: 401-849-3204; Fax: 401-849-5780. Email: mbdaigneault@stclarehome.org. Web: stclarehome.org. Mary Beth Daigneault, Admin.; Rev. Richard A. Walsh, Chap. (Retired).

The Saint Clare Home, Nursing Facility. Daughters of the Holy Spirit 2; Lay Nurses 16; Lay Employees 52; Residents 47; Total Assisted Annually 90; Total Staff 70.

NORTH KINGSTOWN. *Scalabrini Villa* (1957) 860 N. Quidnessett Rd., 02852. Tel: 401-884-1802; Fax: 401-884-4727. Email: admin@scalabrinivilla.com. Web: www.scalabrinivilla.com. Sr. Lolita Rodriguez, F.A.S., Supr. Tel: 401-884-4594.

Scalabrini Villa Inc., Full Skilled Nursing Facility. Franciscan Apostolic Sisters 3; Residents 120; Total Staff 126; Total Assisted 43,800.

NORTH SMITHFIELD. *St. Antoine Residence* (1913) 10 Rhodes Ave., 02896. Tel: 401-767-3500; Fax: 401-769-5249. Email: wfargnoli@stantoine.net. Web: www.stantoine.net. Wendy Fargnoli, Exec. Dir.

Saint Antoine Residence Residents 260; Total Staff 415.

The Villa at Saint Antoine (2000) 400 Mendon Rd., 02896-6999. Tel: 401-767-2574; Fax: 401-767-2581. Email: wfargnoli@stantoine.net. Web: www.stantoine.net. Ms. Jean Larkin, Dir.

The Frassati Residence Total Staff 62; Total Assisted 90.

PAWTUCKET. *Jeanne Jugan Apartments*, 310 Sayles Ave., 02860. Tel: 401-723-4314; Fax: 401-723-4316. 964 Main St., 02860. Apartments for Elderly 27; Residents 30; Total Staff 1.

Jeanne Jugan Residence, 964 Main St., 02860. Tel: 401-723-4314; Fax: 401-723-4316. Email: pwadministrator@littlesistersofthepoor.org. Rev. Msgr. William I. Varsanyi, P.A., J.C.D., Chap.

Jeanne Jugan Residence of the Little Sisters of the Poor Little Sisters of the Poor 12; Residents 100; Total Staff 86; Total Assisted 104. In Res. Revs. Reinaldo M. Cardoso (Retired); Paul F. Reynolds (Retired); Clyde J. Walsh (Retired).

[M] CAMPS AND COMMUNITY CENTERS

PROVIDENCE. *St. Martin de Porres Multi-Purpose Center*, 160 Cranston St., 02907. Tel: 401-274-6783; Fax: 401-274-5930. Email: estherdioceseofprovidence@yahoo.com. Ms. Esther E. Price, Dir.

St. Martin de Porres Center Total under care 2,100; Total Assisted 2,500; Total Staff 13.

The McAuley Corporation dba McAuley Ministries 622 Elmwood Ave., P.O. Box 73195, 02907. Tel: 401-941-9013; Fax: 401-941-6862. Email: dwolfe@mcauleyri.org. Web: www.mcauleyri.org. Donald P. Wolfe, Exec. Dir.

The McAuley Corporation, DBA McAuley Ministries. Sisters of Mercy of the Americas Northeast Community.

McAuley Ministries - McAuley House (1975) 622 Elmwood Ave., P.O. Box 27009, 02907-3352. Tel: 401-941-9013; Fax: 401-941-6862. Web: www.mcauleyri.org. Rev. Mary Margaret Earl, Admin. Meal site assisting 10,000 homeless annually. Total Staff 5.

McAuley Ministries - McAuley Village (1990) 325 Niagara St., 02907. Tel: 401-467-3630; Fax: 401-467-2760. Web: www.mcauleyri.org. Kathryn O'Hare, Admin. Transitional Housing and Child Care assisting 23 families, 40 children in Daycare. Total Staff 20.

McAuley Ministries - The Warde-robe (1997) 1286 Broad St., Central Falls, 02863. Tel: 401-729-0405. Web: www.mcauleyri.org. Donna Benetti, Admin. Clothing and housewares for the working poor. Total Assisted Annually 10,000; Total Staff 4.

BURRILLVILLE. *Mother of Hope Camp*, Mailing Address: 1 Cathedral Sq., 02903. Tel: 401-278-4626. Web: www.ymcyoprov.org. Box W, Chepachet, 02814. Tel: 401-568-3580. Maria Piccirilli, Dir.

Mother of Hope Camp

CRANSTON. *Rejoice in Hope Youth Center*, 804 Dyer Ave., 02920. Tel: 401-942-6571; Fax: 401-943-8686. Email: rejoiceinhope@juno.com. Pat Kane, Dir.

EAST PROVIDENCE. *Emmaus Youth Center*, 25 Metropolitan Park Dr., Riverside, 02915. Tel: 401-433-4327; Fax: 401-433-1320. Web: www.ymcyoprov.org. Pat Kane, Dir.; Phil Ricci, Admin.

WARWICK. *OLP Center, Inc.*, 836 Warwick Neck Ave., 02889. Tel: 401-739-6850; Fax: 401-738-8058. Email: info@aldrichmansion.com. Web: Aldrichmansion.com. Mrs. Paulette M. Turcotte, Dir.

OLP Center, Inc. Staff 10.

WOONSOCKET. *Fr. Marot CYO Center* (1970) 53 Federal St., P.O. Box 518, 02895-0518. Tel: 401-762-3252; Fax: 401-762-3255. Email: frmarotcyocenter@choiceonemail.com. Rev. Msgr. John C. Allard, Chap.; Gina M. Czerwinski, Dir.; Mr. Roland Berard, Admin.

CYO of Northern Rhode Island, Inc.

[N] PERSONAL PRELATURES

PROVIDENCE. *Prelature of the Holy Cross and Opus Dei*, Mathewson House, 224 Bowen St., 02906. Tel: 401-272-7834; Fax: 401-272-7854. Email: info@opusdei.org. Web: www.opusdei.org. Rev. George Crafts.

[O] MONASTERIES AND RESIDENCES OF PRIESTS AND BROTHERS

PROVIDENCE. *Brothers of Our Lady of Providence* (1959) 1055 N. Main St., 02904. Tel: 401-351-7230; Fax: 401-421-0198. Bro. John McHale, O.L.P., Supr. Brothers 1.

St. Francis Friary, 214 Broadway, 02903. Tel: 401-274-3434; Fax: 401-453-0034. Email: spatti@stfrancischapel.com. Web: stfrancischapel.com. 538 Broadway, 02909. Tel: 401-274-3434; Fax: 401-453-0034. Revs. Steven R. Patti, O.F.M., Guardian & Exec. Dir.; Scott F. Brookbank, O.F.M.; Michael S. Joyce, O.F.M.; Charles J. O'Connor, O.F.M., Vicar.

St. Francis Weybosset Street Chapel, Inc. Franciscan Friars. Priests 4.

St. John Vianney Residence (1978) 493 Mt. Pleasant Ave., 02908. Tel: 401-331-9870; Fax: 401-331-5092. Rev. Edward J. McGovern, Admin. (Retired). Residence for Senior Priests. Priests 14.

Residents: Rev. Msgr. Michael W. Dziob (Retired); Revs. George L. Allard (Retired); Frederic D. Dean (Retired); Jose Q. Dos Reis; Ralph R. Hogan (Retired); James P. Hynes (Retired); Anthony D. Iwuc (Retired); Czeslaw L. Kachel (Retired); Francis J. Keefe (Retired); William F. Murphy (Retired); John J. Rainone; Joseph D. Schenick (Retired); Nicholas P. Smith (Retired).

St. Pius House, 55 Elmhurst Ave., 02908. Tel: 401-751-4871; Fax: 401-273-1089. Revs. John P. Burchill, O.P.; Hyacinth Marie Cordell, O.P.; Frank I. Sutman, O.P.; Donald P. Thibault, O.P.

Dominican Fathers Priests 5.

St. Thomas Aquinas Priory at Providence College, 333 Eaton St., 02918-0001. Tel: 401-865-2101 (office); Fax: 401-865-2959.

Priory of St. Thomas Aquinas Dominican Friars. Bishops in Residence 1; Priests in Residence 43; Brothers in Residence 1; Priests residing outside the Priory 6.

Assigned & Residing in the Priory: Most Rev. Ernest B. Boland, O.P., Bishop Emeritus of Multan (Retired); Revs. Edward T. Myers, O.P., Prior; Jon Alexander, O.P.; John E. Allard, O.P.; J. Iriarte Andujar, O.P.; Nicanor P.G. Austriaco, O.P.; Albino F. Barrera, O.P.; Peter Batts, O.P.; Edward L. Cleary, O.P.; Paul M. Conner, O.P.; Michael J. Cuddy, O.P.; G. Adrian Dabash, O.P.; James A. Driscoll, O.P.; Thomas J. Ertle, O.P.; William David Folsey, O.P.; Joseph J. Guido, O.P.; G. Nicholas Ingham, O.P.; Terence Keegan, O.P.; Bernard F. Langton, O.P.; Richard A. McAlister, O.P.; Thomas P. McCreesh, O.P.; J. Stuart McPhail, O.P.; Robert A. Morris, O.P.; David Brendan Murphy, O.P.; Robert D. Myett, O.P.; Mark D. Nowel, O.P.; David T. Orique, O.P.; John S. Peterson, O.P.; Jacob Petri, O.P.; R. Gabriel Pivarnik, O.P.; Matthew D. Powell, O.P.; Kevin D. Robb, O.P.; Paul E. Seaver, O.P.; Brian J. Shanley, O.P.; Kenneth Sicard, O.P.; Joseph Torchia, O.P.; John C. Vidmar, O.P.; Walter Urban Voll, O.P.

Assigned but Living Outside the Priory: Revs. George L. Cochran, O.P., (Columbus, OH); Ralph T. Hall, O.P. (Retired); James Ferrer Quigley, O.P., (North American College, Rome, Italy).

BRISTOL. *St. Columban's Retirement House*, 65 Ferry Rd., Box 65, 02809. Tel: 401-253-6909; Fax: 401-253-7099. Revs. Denis Bartley, S.S.C. (Retired); John Buckley, S.S.C.; Salvatore S. Caputo, S.S.C.; Francis P. Carroll, S.S.C., Supr.; Charles Degnan, S.S.C. (Retired); Edward Dolan, S.S.C.; James Dwyer, S.S.C.; Norbert F. Feld, S.S.C. (Retired); Victor Gaboury, S.S.C. (Retired); Brian Gallagher, S.S.C. (Retired); Francis Grady, S.S.C.; John Hogan, S.S.C.; Francis Keaney, S.S.C. (Retired); John Marley, S.S.C. (Retired); Daniel McGinn, S.S.C. (Retired); Joseph McSweeney, S.S.C.; John Moran, S.S.C. (Retired); Paul O'Malley, S.S.C.; Robert O'Rourke, S.S.C. (Retired); Richard L. Pankratz, S.S.C.; Paul Richardson, S.S.C. (Retired); John F. Roche, S.S.C. (Retired); Alban Sueper, S.S.C. (Retired); William F. Sullivan, S.S.C.; William F. Sweeney, S.S.C.; Bernard Toal, S.S.C.

St. Columban's Foreign Mission Society Priests 23.

BURRILLVILLE. *Brothers of the Sacred Heart Provincial House*, 685 Steere Farm Rd., Pascoag, 02859-4601. Tel: 401-568-8686; 401-568-3361; Fax: 401-568-1450. Email: NEprovincial@bshne.org. Bros. Robert Croteau, S.C., Prov. Supr. of New England Prov.; Robert T. Gagne, S.C., Accounts Mgr.; Paul J. Hebert, S.C., Exec. Asst. for Missions; Leo Labbe, S.C., Local Supr.; Willie

A. Morin, S.C., Prov. Sec.; Daniel St. Jacques, S.C., Vocation Dir.

The Order of the Brothers of the Sacred Heart of New England, Inc. Brothers 23.

NARRAGANSETT. *Christian Brothers' Center*, 635 Ocean Rd., 02882. Tel: 401-789-0244; Fax: 401-783-5303. Email: jdl@cbc.necoxmail.com. Web: www.fscdena.org. Bro. Edmond Precourt, F.S.C., Exec. Dir.; Mrs. Mary Gorman, Health Care Coord.

Brothers of the Christian Schools, Long Island-New England Province Brothers of the Christian Schools. Brothers 27.

PORTSMOUTH. *Abbey of St. Gregory the Great* (1918) 285 Cory's Lane, 02871. Tel: 401-683-2000; Fax: 401-683-5888. Email: fathercaedmon@portsmouthabbey.org. Web: www.portsmouthabbey.org. Rt. Revs. W. Caedmon Holmes, O.S.B., Abbot; F. Mark Serna, O.S.B., Retired Abbot (Retired); Matthew Stark, O.S.B., Retired Abbot (Retired); Very Rev. R. Ambrose Wolverton, O.S.B., Prior; Revs. Julian Stead, O.S.B.; F. Philip Wilson, O.S.B.; A. Damian Kearney, O.S.B.; Michael Stafford, O.S.B.; P. Geoffrey Chase, O.S.B.; Christopher Davis, O.S.B.; T. Edmund Adams, O.S.B.; P. Paschal Scotti, O.S.B.

Order of St. Benedict in Portsmouth, Rhode Island Benedictines of the English Congregation. Abbots 3; Priests 13; Brothers 3.

WOONSOCKET. *Brothers of the Sacred Heart* (1821) 800 Logee St., 02895. Tel: 401-769-0313; Fax: 401-769-0065. Email: mscbrotherwillie@hotmail.com. Bro. Roland Champagne, S.C., Local Supr. Brothers 8.

St. John's Residence, 159 Earle St., 02895. Tel: 401-766-9677. Email: bobbreault@hotmail.com. Web: www.Brothersofthesacredheart.org. Bros. Robert F. Breault, S.C., Supr. & Dir.; Alan Aubin, S.C.; Robert Croteau, S.C.; Robert T. Gagne, S.C.; Tom Greer, S.C.; Marcel Leclerc, S.C. Brothers 6.

[P] CONVENTS AND RESIDENCES FOR SISTERS

BARRINGTON. *Monastery of Discalced Carmelites* (1930) 25 Watson Ave., 02806-4009. Tel: 401-245-3421; Fax: 401-245-6872. Email: sllbarr@juno.com. Web: home.att.net/~barringtoncarmel. Sr. Susan L. Lumb, Prioress.

Monastery of Discalced Carmelites at Nayatt, Barrington, RI Professed Sisters 14; Postulants 1.

BRISTOL. *Mt. St. Joseph Spiritual Life Center and Provincialate* formerly Mt. St. Joseph Spiritual Life Center , 13 Monkeywrench Ln., 02809-2916. Tel: 401-253-5434; Fax: 401-253-5344; 401-253-4630. Sr. Dorothy Schwarz, S.S.D., Provincial & Local Coord. Sisters of St. Dorothy. Sisters 4.

CUMBERLAND. *Sisters of Mercy of the Americas Northeast Community, Inc.* (1851) 15 Highland View Rd., 02864-1124. Tel: 401-333-6333; Fax: 401-333-6450. Email: info@mercyne.org. Sisters Lindora Cabral, R.S.M., Pres.; Jacqueline Marie Kieslich, R.S.M., Vice Pres.; Patricia Sullivan, R.S.M., Leadership Team; Donna Conroy, R.S.M., Leadership Team; Kathleen Turley, R.S.M., Leadership Team; Eleanor Little, R.S.M., Archivist; Susan Jenkinson, M.A., Dir., Ministry; Sisters Kathleen Pritty, R.S.M., Dir. Justice; Patricia Moriarty, R.S.M., Dir. Vocation/Incorporation; Ann McGovern, R.S.M., Dir.Vocation/Incorporation; Dale Jarvis, R.S.M., Vocations Min.; Angela Gaffney, Dir., Communications; Gerald Sullivan, COO.

Sisters of Mercy of the Americas Northeast Community, Inc. Sisters 728; Associates 386.

Sisters of Mercy of the Americas Northeast Community, Inc., Administrative Offices formerly Sisters of Mercy 15 Highland View Rd., 02864-1124. Tel: 401-333-6333; Fax: 401-333-6450.

Mercycrest Convent, 125 Wrentham Rd., 02864. Tel: 401-333-5283. *Mercymount Convent*, 75 Wrentham Rd., 02864. Tel: 401-333-0158. Sisters of Mercy 3.

MIDDLETOWN. *Cluny Provincial House* (1807) 7 Restmere Ter., 02842. Tel: 401-846-4757; 401-846-4826 (Prov.); Fax: 401-846-4826 (Office). Email: clunyusa@hotmail.com. St. Joseph of Cluny Sisters' School. Sisters 2,838; Sisters in Diocese 10; Sisters in Cluny Provincial of U.S.A. & Canada 23.

Provincial House Tel: 401-846-4826; Fax: 401-846-4826. Sisters Joan Van der Zyden, S.J.C., Prov. Supr.; Luke Parker, S.J.C., Vice Provincial. *St. Joseph of Cluny Convent* Tel: 401-847-3637; Fax: 401-846-4826. Sr. Joan Van der Zyden, S.J.C., Local Supr.

NEWPORT. *St. Clare Convent, Cutting Memorial*, 301 Spring St., 02840. Tel: 401-846-1025.

The Saint Clare Home Daughters of the Holy Spirit 2.

Corpus Christi Carmel, 516 Broadway, 02840. Tel: 401-847-6165. Web: www.corpuschrsticarmelite.org. Corpus Christi Carmelite Sisters. Sisters 2.

Javouhey House (2002) 78 Carroll Ave., 02840. Tel: 401-849-5124; Fax: 253-484-7155. Email: clunyjh@cox.net. Sr. Ann Marie Liston, S.J.C., Local Coord. Sisters of St. Joseph of Cluny 5.

NORTH KINGSTOWN. *Holy Family Convent*, 1 Wright Ln., 02852. Tel: 401-294-3554. Email: theresinascully@aol.com. Web: www.passionistsisters.org. Sr. Theresina Scully, C.P., Province Leader.

Sisters of the Holy Cross and Passion, Provincial Office of the Sisters of the Cross and Passion. Sisters 3.

NORTH PROVIDENCE. *Daughters of Mary Mother of Mercy*, 2 Pope St., 02904. Tel: 401-353-8654; Fax: 401-353-5126. Sisters 3.

Franciscan Missionaries of Mary (1903) 399 Fruit Hill Ave., 02911. Tel: 401-353-5800; Fax: 401-353-2674. Email: fmmalc@aol.com. Web: www.fmmusa.org.

Franciscan Missionaries of Mary

Holy Family Community, 399 Fruit Hill Ave., 02911. Tel: 401-353-5800; Fax: 401-353-2674. Sr. Elizabeth A. Conyers, F.M.M., Supr. Sisters 12.

Our Lady, Queen of Peace, Assisted Living Community, 399 Fruit Hill Ave., 02911. Tel: 401-353-5800; Fax: 401-354-8296. Sisters Pauline Baris, F.M.M., Supr.; Pauline Williams, F.M.M., Admin. Sisters 13.

Trinity Community, Assisted Living Community, 399 Fruit Hill Ave., 02911. Tel: 401-353-5800. Sr. Maria C. Zunzarren, F.M.M., Supr. Sisters 16.

Our Lady of the Lourdes Convent, 385 Fruit Hill Ave., 02911. Tel: 401-353-6381. Sisters Rosemarie Higgins, F.M.M., Supr.; Yvette Hubert, F.M.M.; Aline Giroux, F.M.M. Sisters 5.

Bethany, (House of On-Going Formation), 397 Fruit Hill Ave., 02911. Tel: 401-353-5860. Email: bethanyfmm@verizon.net. Sr. Yvette Hubert, F.M.M., Dir.

De Chappotin Community, 399 Fruit Hill Ave., 02911. Tel: 401-353-9412; Fax: 401-353-2674. Sr. Rosalie McNaughton, F.M.M., Supr. Sisters 5.

NORTH SMITHFIELD. *Franciscan Missionaries of Mary*, Ein Karim Community, 318 Mendon Rd., 02896. Tel: 401-766-8242; Fax: 401-766-6492. Email: karimfmm@aol.com. Sr. Joyce C. Gardella, F.M.M., Coord. Sisters 4.

SOUTH KINGSTOWN. *Congregation of the Sisters of Divine Providence Generalate* (1851) Tel: 401-782-1785; Fax: 401-782-6967.

Mother of Providence Convent, 12 Christopher St., Wakefield, 02879. Tel: 401-782-1785; Fax: 401-782-6967. Sr. Janet Folkl, C.D.P., Gen. Supr.

WEST GREENWICH. *Mary of Nazareth Novitiate*, 28 Victory Hwy., 02817. Tel: 401-392-1007; Fax: 401-392-1009. Franciscan Missionaries of Mary 5.

WOONSOCKET. *Emmanuel House*, 67 Highland St., 02895. Tel: 401-766-0525.

Franciscan Apostolic Sisters (1953) 94 Carrington Ave., 02895. Tel: 401-762-0326, Ext. 28. Email: smofas@yahoo.com; srloufas@yahoo.com. Web: www.geocities.com/franapsisters. Sr. Ma. Magdalena B. Obispo, F.A.S., Local Animator. Sisters 2. 860 N. Quidnessett Rd., North Kingstown, 02852. Tel: 401-884-4594. Web: www.geocities.com/franapsisters. Sr. Ma. Magdalena B. Obispo, F.A.S., Local Animator/Regional Animator. Sisters in U.S. 15.

[Q] RETREAT HOUSES

CUMBERLAND. *Mercy Lodge*, 6 Summer Brown Rd., 02864. Tel: 401-333-2801. 15 Highland View Rd., 02864-1124. Tel: 401-333-6333; Fax: 401-333-6450.

Sisters of Mercy of the Americas, Northeast Community, Inc.

NORTH PROVIDENCE. *Bethany Renewal Center*, 397 Fruit Hill Ave., 02911. Tel: 401-353-5860. Email: bethanyfmm@aol.com. Web: www.fmmusa.org. Sr. Yvette Hubert, F.M.M. Conducted by the Franciscan Missionaries of Mary.

[R] NEWMAN CENTERS

PROVIDENCE. *Brown University* Box 1931, 02912. Tel: 401-863-2344; Fax: 401-863-9359. Email: catholic@brown.edu. Web: www.brown.edu/students/Brown_Catholic. Rev. Henry J. Bodah, Chap.; Angela Howard McParland, Catholic Campus Min. Priests 1; Total Staff 2.

Johnson & Wales University Catholic Campus Ministry-CBCSI Bldg., 8 Abbott Park Place, 02903.

Rhode Island College Catholic Campus Ministry, Donovan Lower Level, 600 Mt. Pleasant Ave., 02908. Tel: 401-456-8346; Fax: 401-456-2849 (Call first). Email: campusministry@ric.edu. Web: www.ric.edu/chaplain. Deacon Michael Napolitano.

BRISTOL. *Roger Williams University* Catholic Chaplain's Office, 1 Old Ferry Rd., 02809. Tel: 401-254-3433. Rev. Stephen J. Dandeneau.

SMITHFIELD. *Bryant University* 1150 Douglas Pk., Box 33, 02917-1284. Tel: 401-232-6045; Fax: 401-232-6362. Email: revjp@bryant.edu. Rev. Robert L. Marciano, Chap.

SOUTH KINGSTOWN. *University of Rhode Island Catholic Center* 90 Chapel Way, Kingston, 02881. Tel: 401-874-2324; Fax: 401-874-9099. Web: www.uricatholiccenter.org. Revs. Joseph D. Creedon; S. Matthew Glover, Chap.

[S] SECULAR INSTITUTES

GREENVILLE. *Regnum Christi*, 60 Austin Ave., 02828. Tel: 401-949-2820; Fax: 401-949-2310; 401-949-0291. Email: mtrevinousa@inteducators.org. Web: www.regnumchristi.org. Ms. Monica Trevino, Dir.

MANVILLE. *Oblate Missionaries of Mary Immaculate* (1952) P.O. Box 303, 02838. Tel: 603-362-9960; Fax: 603-362-9960. Email: pjlabbe1@juno.com. Web: www.inst.secular-ommi.com. Miss Ruth A. Valois.

[T] MISCELLANEOUS LISTINGS

PROVIDENCE. **The Haitian Project, Inc.*, 160 Broad St., 02903. P.O. Box 6891, 02940.

**Mandamiento Nuevo Corporation*, 184 Broad St., 02903. Tel: 401-421-7833, Ext. 104; Fax: 401-274-5450.

Miscellaneous Listings for the Diocese of Providence Mailing address for all Providence listings, Chancery Office: 1 Cathedral Sq., 02903. Tel: 401-278-4663; Fax: 401-278-4515. Email: treilly@dioceseofprovidence.org. Web: www.dioceseofprovidence.org. Rev. Timothy D. Reilly, S.T.B., J.C.L., Chancellor. For further information contact:

All Saints Catholic Community, Woonsocket, RI

Catholic Association for Regional Education

Catholic Charity Fund

Catholic Foundation of Rhode Island

Catholic Information Center of Newport

Catholic Inner City Apostolate, Inc.

Catholic Investment Trust, Inc.

Catholic Teachers' College of Providence

Charismatic Renewal, 909 Westmain Rd., Middletown, 02842-6351. Tel: 401-847-6153. Rev. John W. O'Brien.

Christ the Redeemer Academy

Cursillo Movement

200 Pettaconsett Ave., Warwick, 02888. Tel: 401-781-7226. Rev. Frank S. Salmani, Spiritual Dir.

461 Shady Valley Rd., Coventry, 02816. Tel: 401-392-1252. Edward Overton, Lay Coord.

The Church of the Immaculate Conception, North Providence

De LaSalle Academy Corporation

DiMed Corp.

Diocesan Administration Corporation Tel: 401-278-4616; Fax: 401-751-6808. J. Timothy Kocab, Diocesan Controller.

Diocesan Catholic Telecommunications Network of Rhode Island

Diocesan Plant Fund

Diocesan Service Corporation Tel: 401-278-4616; Fax: 401-751-6808.

F.A.C.E. of Rhode Island (Financial Aid for Children's Education of Rhode Island)

Father Barry CYO Center

Holy Name Society

The Holy Spirit Catholic Community, Central Falls, RI

House of the Good Shepherd of Providence

Homes for Hope Foundation

Inter-Parish Loan Fund, Inc.

LaSalle Academy

Little Sisters of the Assumption of Woonsocket

Marian Association of Northern Rhode Island

The Mercy Home and School

Mother of Hope Novitiate

Mont St. Francois of Woonsocket, RI formerly Mount St. Francois of Woonsocket, RI

Nazareth Home

New England Conference of Diocesan Directors of Religious Education

Occult Awareness Ministry

Our Lady of Peace Retreat House

Our Lady of Providence Preparatory Seminary

Our Lady, Queen of the Clergy

Parish Investment Group

Pius X Salvage Bureau

Retreat House of the Immaculate Heart of Mary

The Rhode Island Catholic Orphan Asylum (St. Aloysius Home)

Rhode Island Home for Working Boys

Roman Catholic Bishop of Providence A Corporation Sole.

St. Benedict's Hearth Corporation, East Providence.

Saint Casimir's Church of Warren

St. Dominic Savio Youth Center

Saint Francis House
Saint Hedwig's Church Corporation, Providence
St. John's Church of Providence
Saint Margaret's Home
Saint Maria Society
St. Mary Academy of the Visitation
Saint Raphael's Industrial Home and School
St. Vincent de Paul Home, Woonsocket
Saint Vincent de Paul Infant Asylum
Stella Maris Home for Convalescents
The Holy Ghost School
Vision of Hope, Inc.

BURRILLVILLE. *Father Andre Coindre Charitable Trust*, 685 Steere Farm Rd., Pascoag, 02859-4601. Tel: 401-568-3361, Ext. 3202; Fax: 401-568-1450. Email: rgagne@bshne.org. Bro. Robert Croteau, S.C., Treas. & Provincial.

CUMBERLAND. *Northeast FIDES, Inc.*, 15 Highland View Rd., 02864-1124. Tel: 401-333-6333; Fax: 401-333-6450. Sr. Jacqueline Marie Kieslich, R.S.M., Pres.
Northeast FIDES, Inc.

MAPLEVILLE. *Society of St. Vincent de Paul of Providence*, 525 Maureen Cir., 02839. Tel: 401-568-4709; Fax: 401-568-4709. Email: jmar10@cox.net. Web: www.svdpri.org. James Martufi, Pres., Diocesan Council of Providence.

NARRAGANSETT. *Saint Benilde Community Support Charitable Trust*, 635 Ocean Rd., 02882-1314. Tel: 401-789-0244; Fax: 401-783-5303. Email: ddetjefsc@yahoo.com. Bro. David Detje, F.S.C., Sec. & Treas.

NORTH PROVIDENCE. *Franciscan Missionaries of Mary* (1903) 399 Fruit Hill Ave., 02911. Tel: 401-353-5800; Fax: 401-353-2674. Email: almafmm@yahoo.com. Web: www.fmmusa.org.
Mission Resource Center (1988) Tel: 401-353-4470. Email: mmottefmm@gmail.com. Sr. Mary Motte, F.M.M., Dir.

NORTH SMITHFIELD. *Hombre Nuevo (RI), Inc.* (1993) 275 Mechanic St., 02896-7718. Tel: 914-773-1368; Fax: 914-773-1438.

PASCOAG. *The Charles Lwanga Charitable Trust*, 685 Steere Farm Rd., 02859-4601. Tel: 401-568-3361, Ext. 3202; Fax: 401-568-9810. Email: rgagne@bshne.org. Bro. Robert Croteau, S.C., Treasurer & Provincial.

SMITHFIELD. *Conference of Regional Treasurers*, P.O. Box 17372, 02917. Tel: 401-349-4960; Fax: 401-349-4970. Email: vgladu@bmtconsults.com. Virginia Gladu, Contact Person.
LC Pastoral Services, Inc., 60 Austin Ave., Greenville, 02828. Tel: 401-949-2820; Fax: 401-949-2310. Rev. Jose F. Ortega, L.C., Contact Person.
Mater Ecclesiae, Inc. (1993) 60 Austin Ave., Greenville, 02828. Tel: 401-949-2820; Fax: 401-949-2310; 401-949-0291. Email: matere@ids.net. Web: www.regnumchristi.org. Luly Fernandez, Contact Person.
Vocation Action Circle, Inc., 60 Austin Ave., Greenville, 02828. Tel: 914-773-1368; Fax: 914-773-1438. Rev. Jose F. Ortega, L.C., Contact Person.

SOUTH KINGSTOWN. *Ocean Pastoral Center, Inc.*, 4780 Tower Hill Rd., Wakefield, 02879. Tel: 914-773-1368. Rev. Jose F. Ortega, L.C., Contact Person.
Overbrook, Incorporated, 4780 Tower Hill Rd., Wakefield, 02879. Tel: 914-773-1368. Rev. Jose F. Ortega, L.C., Contact Person.

WEST WARWICK. *Tides Family Services*, 215 Washington St., 02893. Tel: 401-822-1360; Fax: 401-823-4694. Email: mail@tidesfs.org. Web: www.tidesfs.org. Bro. Michael Reis, F.S.C., CEO. Total Staff 125; Total Assisted 2,000.
Branch Offices:
Youth New Futures, 790 Broad St., 02907. Tel: 401-467-8888; Fax: 401-467-8899.
Youth New Futures, 242 Dexter St., Pawtucket, 02860. Tel: 401-724-8100; Fax: 401-724-8899.
Preserving Families Network, 242 Dexter St., Pawtucket, 02860. Tel: 401-724-8201; Fax: 401-724-8899. 215 Washington St., 02893. 790 Broad St., 02905.
Outreach and Tracking Program, 242 Dexter St., Pawtucket, 02860. Tel: 401-724-8380; Fax: 401-724-8899.
Woonsocket Outreach Project, 55 Main St., Ste. 1, Woonsocket, 02895. Tel: 401-766-9320; Fax: 401-766-9324.
Learning Centers:
242 Dexter St., Pawtucket, 02860. Tel: 401-724-8060; Fax: 401-724-8899.
790 Broad St., 02907. Tel: 401-467-8228; Fax: 401-467-8899.
222 Washington St., 02893. Tel: 401-823-0157; Fax: 401-823-4694.
Youth Diversion Projects:
215 Washington St., 02893. Tel: 401-822-1360; Fax: 401-823-4694.
242 Dexter St., Pawtucket, 02860. Tel: 401-724-8380; Fax: 401-724-8899.
Preserving Families Network
242 Dexter St., Pawtucket, 02860. Tel: 401-724-8380; Fax: 401-724-8899.
55 Main St., Ste. 1, Woonsocket, 02895. Tel: 401-766-9320; Fax: 401-766-9324.
790 Broad St., 02907. Tel: 401-467-8888; Fax: 401-467-8899.
215 Washington St., 02893. Tel: 401-822-1360; Fax: 401-823-4694.

RELIGIOUS INSTITUTES OF MEN REPRESENTED IN THE DIOCESE

For further details refer to the corresponding bracketed number in the Religious Institutes of Men or Women section.

[0200]—*Benedictine Monks*—O.S.B.
[]—*Brothers of Our Lady of Providence*—O.L.P.
[0330]—*Brothers of the Christian Schools* (New England-Long Island Prov.)—F.S.C.
[1100]—*Brothers of the Sacred Heart*—S.C.
[0310]—*Congregation of Christian Brothers*—C.F.C.
[0650]—*Congregation of the Holy Spirit* (Portuguese Prov. & Irish Prov.)—C.S.SP.
[0520]—*Franciscan Friars* (Prov. of the Most Holy Name)—O.F.M.
[0730]—*Legionaires of Christ*—L.C.
[0780]—*Marist Fathers*—S.M.
[1210]—*Missionaries of St. Charles (Scalabrinians)*—C.S.
[0430]—*Order of Preachers (Dominicans)* (Prov. of St. Joseph)—O.P.
[1220]—*Servants of Charity*—S.C.
[0690]—*Society of Jesus*—S.J.
[0370]—*Society of St. Columban*—S.S.C.

RELIGIOUS INSTITUTES OF WOMEN REPRESENTED IN THE DIOCESE

[0350]—*Carmelite Sisters (Corpus Christi)*—O.Carm.
[0990]—*Congregation of Divine Providence*—C.D.P.
[]—*Daughters of Mary Mother of Mercy*—D.M.M.M.
[]—*Daughters of St. Mary of Providence*—D.S.M.P.
[0820]—*Daughters of the Holy Spirit*—D.H.S.
[0420]—*Discalced Carmelite Nuns*—O.C.D.
[1105]—*Dominican Sisters of Hope*—O.P.
[1115]—*Dominican Sisters of Peace*—O.P.
[1100]—*Dominican Sisters of the Presentation*—O.P.
[1070-05]—*Dominicans* (Amityville)—O.P.
[1070-13]—*Dominicans* (Adrian)—O.P.
[1070-15]—*Dominicans* (Blauvelt)—O.P.
[1070-07]—*Dominicans* (St. Cecilia of Nashville, TN)—O.P.
[1070-17]—*Dominicans* (de'Ricci)—O.P.
[1170]—*Felician Sisters*—C.S.S.F.
[]—*Franciscan Apostolic Sisters*—F.A.S.
[1370]—*The Franciscan Missionaries of Mary*—F.M.M.
[1180]—*Franciscan Sisters of Allegheny*—O.S.F.
[3790]—*Institute of the Sisters of St. Dorothy*—S.S.D.
[2340]—*Little Sisters of the Poor*—L.S.P.
[2470]—*Maryknoll Missionaries*—M.M.
[1360]—*Missionary Franciscan Sisters of the Immaculate Conception*—M.F.I.C.
[3230]—*Poor Handmaids of Jesus Christ*—P.H.J.C.
[3450]—*Religious of Jesus and Mary*—R.J.M.
[2070]—*Religious of the Holy Union of the Sacred Hearts*—S.U.S.C.
[4070]—*Religious of the Sacred Heart*—R.S.C.J.
[3430]—*Religious Teachers Filippini*—M.P.F.
[2970]—*School Sisters of Notre Dame*—S.S.N.D.
[2575]—*Sisters of Mercy of the Americas*—R.S.M.
[3000]—*Sisters of Notre Dame de Namur*—S.N.D.deN.
[3720]—*Sisters of Saint Anne*—S.S.A.
[3750]—*Sisters of St. Chretienne*—S.S.CH.
[0590]—*Sisters of St. Elizabeth, Convent Station*—S.C.
[3860]—*Sisters of St. Joseph of Cluny*—S.J.C.
[3830]—*Sisters of St. Joseph of Springfield*—S.S.J.
[]—*Sisters of the Adoration of the Blessed Sacrament*—S.A.B.S.
[0150]—*Sisters of the Assumption*—S.A.S.V.
[2980]—*Sisters of the Congregation of Notre Dame*—C.N.D.
[3180]—*Sisters of the Cross and Passion*—C.P.
[3310]—*Sisters of the Presentation of Mary*—P.M.
[3320]—*Sisters of the Presentation of the B.V.M.*—P.B.V.M.
[4040]—*Society of St. Ursula*—S.U.
[4048]—*Society of the Sisters, Faithful Companions of Jesus*—F.C.J.

DIOCESAN CEMETERIES

PROVIDENCE. *St. Patrick's*
BARRINGTON. *Maria Del Campo*
CRANSTON. *St. Ann's*
CUMBERLAND. *Resurrection*
EAST PROVIDENCE. *Gate of Heaven*
MIDDLETOWN. *St. Columba*
PAWTUCKET. *St. Francis*
Mount St. Mary's
WEST GREENWICH. *St. Joseph*

NECROLOGY

† DeLellis, Francis V., (Retired)—Died Feb. 17, 2011
† Freitas, Fernando P., (Retired)—Died Feb. 19, 2011
† Heaney, Joseph P., (Retired)—Died March 17, 2011
† Hynes, Joseph P., (Retired)—Died Oct. 7, 2011
† LeThiez, Alphonse D., (Retired)—Died Nov. 17, 2011
† Randall, John F., (Retired)—Died June 14, 2011

Diocese of Pueblo

(Dioecesis Pueblensis)

CARITAS CHRISTI URGET NOS

Most Reverend

FERNANDO ISERN, D.D.

Bishop of Pueblo; ordained April 16, 1993; appointed Bishop of Pueblo October 15, 2009; ordained and installed December 10, 2009. *Pastoral Center: 101 N. Greenwood, Pueblo, CO 81003.*

Catholic Pastoral Center: 101 N. Greenwood, Pueblo, CO 81003. Tel: 719-544-9861; Fax: 719-544-5202.

Web: www.dioceseofpueblo.org

Email: officeofbishop@dioceseofpueblo.org

Square Miles 48,155.

Diocesan Patron: St. Therese of the Child Jesus. Secondary Patroness: Our Lady of Guadalupe.

Erected a Diocese November 15, 1941.

Comprises the 29 Counties of Alamosa, Archuleta, Baca, Bent, Conejos, Costilla, Crowley, Custer, Delta, Dolores, Fremont, Gunnison, Hinsdale, Huerfano, Kiowa, La Plata, Las Animas, Mesa, Mineral, Montezuma, Montrose, Otero, Ouray, Prowers, Pueblo, Rio Grande, Saguache, San Juan and San Miguel in the southern and western part of the State of Colorado.

For legal titles of parishes and diocesan institutions, consult the Finance Office.

STATISTICAL OVERVIEW

Personnel	
Bishop	1
Retired Bishops	1
Priests: Diocesan Active in Diocese	30
Priests: Diocesan Active Outside Diocese	4
Priests: Diocesan in Foreign Missions	1
Priests: Retired, Sick or Absent	22
Number of Diocesan Priests	57
Religious Priests in Diocese	17
Total Priests in Diocese	74
Extern Priests in Diocese	5
Ordinations:	
Diocesan Priests	1
Permanent Deacons	3
Permanent Deacons in Diocese	51
Total Brothers	2
Total Sisters	53
Parishes	
Parishes	52
With Resident Pastor:	
Resident Diocesan Priests	31
Resident Religious Priests	5
Without Resident Pastor:	
Administered by Priests	12
Administered by Deacons	1
Missions	46
Professional Ministry Personnel:	
Brothers	2
Sisters	11
Lay Ministers	54
Welfare	
Catholic Hospitals	5
Total Assisted	714,068
Health Care Centers	2
Total Assisted	5,000
Homes for the Aged	1
Total Assisted	850
Special Centers for Social Services	6
Total Assisted	316,000
Educational	
Diocesan Students in Other Seminaries	7
Total Seminarians	7
Elementary Schools, Diocesan and Parish	3
Total Students	800
Elementary Schools, Private	1
Total Students	140
Catechesis/Religious Education:	
High School Students	1,917
Elementary Students	3,824
Total Students under Catholic Instruction	6,688
Teachers in the Diocese:	
Sisters	1
Vital Statistics	
Receptions into the Church:	
Infant Baptism Totals	1,173
Minor Baptism Totals	56
Adult Baptism Totals	171
First Communions	891
Confirmations	698
Marriages:	
Catholic	186
Interfaith	47
Total Marriages	233
Deaths	1,392
Total Catholic Population	73,264
Total Population	665,906

Former Bishops—Most Revs. JOSEPH CLEMENT WILLGING, D.D., First Bishop of Pueblo; ord. June 20, 1908; appt. Dec. 6, 1941; cons. Feb. 24, 1942; Assistant at Pontifical Throne, Feb. 20, 1958; died March 3, 1959; CHARLES A. BUSWELL, ord. July 9, 1939; appt. Bishop of Pueblo Aug. 8, 1959; cons. Sept. 30, 1959; installed Oct. 6, 1959; retired Sept. 18, 1979; died June 14, 2008.; ARTHUR N. TAFOYA, D.D., ord. May 12, 1962; appt. Bishop of Pueblo July 1, 1980; cons. and installed Sept. 10, 1980; retired Dec. 10, 2009.

Chancery—101 N. Greenwood Ave., Pueblo, 81003. Tel: 719-544-9861; Fax: 719-544-5202. Office Hours: Mon.-Fri. 7-12 & 1-5.

Vicar General—Rev. JAMES E. KING, V.G. Tel: 719-544-9861, Ext. 141.

Moderator of the Curia—Rev. MICHAEL L. PAPESH. Tel: 719-544-9861, Ext. 182.

Chancellor—Rev. Msgr. MARK A. PLEWKA, J.C.L., J.V. Tel: 719-544-9861, Ext. 162.

Vice Chancellor—Rev. MICHAEL L. PAPESH. Tel: 719-544-9861, Ext. 182.

Diocesan Tribunal—

Judicial Vicar—Rev. Msgr. MARK A. PLEWKA, J.C.L., J.V.

Defensores Vinculi—Rev. GEORGE V. FAGAN, J.C.L.; Ms. DONI R. NEEDHAM. Tel: 719-544-9861, Ext. 161.

Judicial Expert—Rev. Msgr. MARVIN J. KAPUSHION, M.S.W., J.C.L., L.C.S.W. (Retired).

Secretarial to the Tribunal—Ms. DONI NEEDHAM. Tel: 719-544-9861, Ext. 161.

Judge—Rev. Msgr. MARK A. PLEWKA, J.C.L., J.V.

Ecclesiastical Notaries—Mrs. THERESA R. FARLEY; Ms. DONI NEEDHAM; Deacon JAKE ARELLANO; Rev. MARK T. BETTINGER.

College of Consultors— Ex Officio: Rev. JAMES E. KING, V.G. Tel: 719-544-9861, Ext. 123; Rev. Msgrs. MARK A. PLEWKA, J.C.L., J.V. Tel: 719-544-9861, Ext. 162; THOMAS M. ADRIANS. Tel: 719-544-9861, Ext. 193; Revs. MICHAEL L. PAPESH. Tel: 719-544-9861, Ext. 182; CARLOS A. ALVAREZ. Tel: 719-647-1500; DERREK SCOTT. Tel: 719-589-5829; JOHN B. FARLEY. Tel: 970-242-6121; PAT VALDEZ, C.R. Tel: 970-563-7308; CHARLES A. SENA, V.F. Tel: 719-336-7759; Rev. Msgr. EDWARD H. NUÑEZ. Tel: 719-647-1500.

Deans—Revs. PAT VALDEZ, C.R., Durango Deanery; DERREK SCOTT, Alamosa Deanery; CHARLES A. SENA, V.F., La Junta Deanery; CARLOS A. ALVAREZ, Pueblo North Deanery; JOHN B. FARLEY, Grand Junction Deanery; Rev. Msgr. EDWARD H. NUÑEZ, Pueblo South Deanery.

Diocesan Offices

Administrative Services—

Moderator of the Curia—Rev. MICHAEL L. PAPESH. Tel: 719-544-9861, Ext. 182.

Office of Lifelong Catechesis—Sr. BETTY WERNER, O.P., Dir. Tel: 719-544-9861, Ext. 114.

Communications—Mrs. KATHERINE CHRISMAN, Dir. Tel: 719-544-9861, Ext. 110.

Finance—Tel: 719-544-9861, Ext. 141. Rev. JAMES E. KING, V.G., Finance Officer. Tel: 719-544-9861, Ext. 123; Mr. ROBERT HAIN, Dir. Tel: 719-544-9861, Ext. 141.

Finance Advisory Council—Rev. JAMES E. KING, V.G., Contact Person, 101 N. Greenwood, Pueblo, 81003. Tel: 719-544-9861, Ext. 123.

Foundation—Mrs. KATHLEEN TILLMAN. Tel: 719-544-9861, Ext. 131.

Human Resources—Mrs. THERESA R. FARLEY, Dir. Tel: 719-544-9861, Ext. 171.

Institutional Ministries—Deacon DANIEL T. LEETCH JR. Tel: 719-544-9861, Ext. 117.

Superintendent of Catholic Schools—Sr. BETTY WERNER, O.P. Tel: 719-544-9861, Ext. 114.

Stewardship—Mrs. KATHLEEN TILLMAN, Dir. Tel: 719-544-9861, Ext. 131.

Tribunal—Rev. Msgr. MARK A. PLEWKA, J.C.L., J.V., Dir. Tel: 719-544-9861, Ext. 162.

Vocations—Rev. MICHAEL CHRISMAN.

Deacon Commission—Deacons VINCENT ROGALSKI, Chair; LLOYD HAWES, Grand Junction Deanery; MICHAEL LACONTE, Pueblo South Deanery; JERRY LEBLANC, Alamosa Deanery; STEVE LUMBERT, Pueblo North Deanery; DOUGLAS MANLEY, La Junta Deanery; MILTON VAN CLEAVE, Durango Deanery.

Office of Worship—Mr. JOSEPH CHRISMAN, Dir. Tel: 719-544-9861, Ext. 115.

Catholic Charismatic Renewal—Liaison: Rev. DONALD P. MALIN, Coord., Mailing Address: Pope John Paul II, 353 S. Pagosa Blvd., Pagosa Springs, 81147. Tel: 970-731-5744.

Respect Life Office—Deacon DARRELL PAGELS, Coord. Tel: 719-544-3690.

Diocesan Liturgical Commission—Mr. JOSEPH CHRISMAN, Contact Person. Tel: 719-544-9861, Ext. 115.

Diocesan Newspaper— "Today's Catholic" Most Rev. FERNANDO ISERN, D.D., Publisher, 101 N. Greenwood St., Pueblo, 81003. Tel: 719-544-9861; Mrs. KATHERINE CHRISMAN, Asst. to Publisher. Tel: 719-544-9861, Ext. 110.

Catholic Charities of the Diocese of Pueblo, Inc.—Mr. JOE MAHONEY, Dir., 429 W. 10th St., Ste. 101, Pueblo, 81003. Tel: 719-544-4233; Fax: 719-544-4215.

Victim Assistance Coordinator—Mr. JOE MAHONEY. Tel: 719-544-4233.

The Bishop Charles A. Buswell Trust—Most Rev. FERNANDO ISERN, D.D., 101 N. Greenwood Ave., Pueblo, 81003. Tel: 719-544-9861, Ext. 122.

Boy Scouts of America—Deacon MIKE ROVELLA, Chap., Mailing Address: 1660 Sneffles, Montrose, 81401. Tel: 970-249-3319, Ext. 15; RIK BERGETHON, Catholic Committee Chm., 159 McNeil Rd., Pueblo, Co 81001. Tel: 719-544-1255.

Clergy Benefit Society of the Diocese of Pueblo, Inc.—Rev. JAMES E. KING, V.G., Contact Person.

Diocesan Council of Catholic Women—Rev. RICHARD F. BECKER, Mod., 235 N. Convent St., Trinidad, 81082. Tel: 719-846-3369, Ext. 25.

Diocesan Pastoral Council—Rev. MICHAEL L. PAPESH, Contact Person, 101 N. Greenwood Ave., Pueblo, 81003. Tel: 719-544-9861, Ext. 182.

Father John Powers Memorial Basketball League, Inc.—Mr. ROBERT J. DOUGLASS, Contact Person, 144 Harvard Ave., Pueblo, 81004. Tel: 719-544-7192.

Girl Scouts of America—Mrs. VICTORIA KAMPA, 4777 Flicker Dr., Pueblo, 81008. Tel: 719-545-1768.

Catholic Campaign for Human Development—Mr. JOE MAHONEY, 429 W. 10th St., Ste. 101, Pueblo, 81003. Tel: 719-544-4233.

Nocturnal Adoration Society—Sr. GORGONIA PARCERO, S.S.S., 311 E. Mesa Ave., Pueblo, 81006. Tel: 719-545-PRAY.

Presbyteral Council—Most Rev. FERNANDO ISERN, D.D., Pres. Ex Officio: Rev. JAMES E. KING, V.G.; Rev. Msgr. MARK A. PLEWKA, J.C.L., J.V.; Rev. MICHAEL L. PAPESH; Rev. Msgr. THOMAS M. ADRIANS. Elected: Revs. DERREK D. SCOTT; PAT VALDEZ, C.R.; JOHN B. FARLEY; CHARLES A. SENA, V.F.; CARLOS A. ALVAREZ; Rev. Msgr. EDWARD H. NUÑEZ; Revs. KEVIN NOVACK; TOMAS CARVAJAL-BASTO, C.R. Appointed: Rev. UJU PATRICK OKEAHIALAM, C.S.Sp.

Clergy Assembly—Rev. Msgr. THOMAS M. ADRIANS, Chm., 1708 Horseshoe Dr., Pueblo, 81001. Tel: 719-542-9248; Deacon STEVE LUMBERT, Sec.; Rev. Msgr. LEONARD E. RACKI, Treas. (Retired).

Clergy Personnel—Rev. Msgr. THOMAS M. ADRIANS, Chm.

SEARCH—Ms. SANDY HANSEN, 2 Bearclaw Ct., Pueblo, 81001. Tel: 719-542-6513; 719-320-2707. Email: sandyrose@searchretreatcenter.org; sandyrose@netzero.net.

Legion of Mary—LAURA DEISLA, 2808 W. 29th St., Pueblo, 81008. Tel: 719-406-1791.

CLERGY, PARISHES, MISSIONS AND PAROCHIAL SCHOOLS

CITY OF PUEBLO

(PUEBLO COUNTY)

1—SACRED HEART CATHEDRAL (1872) Rev. Msgr. Leonard E. Racki, Rector (Retired).
Parish Office:—414 W. 11th St., 81003. Tel: 719-544-5175; Fax: 719-586-9922. Email: shcathedral@qwestoffice.net. Web: cathedralofthesacredheart-pueblo.com.
Catechesis/Religious Program—Margaret Ursick Leetch, Faith Formation Coord. Students 98.

2—ST. ANNE (1956) Deacon Steve Lumbert, Parish Life Coord.
Res.: 2701 E. 12th St., 81001-4708. Tel: 719-545-2644; Fax: 719-544-0959. Email: splsrus@hotmail.com.
Catechesis/Religious Program—Marianne Ortega, C.R.E. Students 36.

3—ST. ANTHONY OF PADUA, Closed. For inquiries for parish records contact the chancery.

4—CHRIST THE KING (1957) Rev. Msgr. Thomas M. Adrians; Deacon Steve Escalera.
1708 Horseshoe Dr., 81001. Tel: 719-542-9248; Fax: 719-545-9826.
Catechesis/Religious Program—Laura Escalera, D.R.E. Students 216.
Convent—11 MacNaughton Rd., 81001. Tel: 719-543-2466; Fax: 719-545-9826.

5—ST. FRANCIS XAVIER (1903) Rev. Uju Patrick Okeahialam, C.S.Sp., Parish Admin.; Deacons Marco Vegas; Paul Villegas.
611 Logan Ave., 81004. Tel: 719-564-1125; Fax: 719-564-1141.
Catechesis/Religious Program—Elizabeth Mestas, C.R.E. Students 158.
Mission—Our Lady of Lourdes Beulah, Pueblo Co.

6—HOLY FAMILY (1954) Rev. Tomas Carvajal-Basto, C.R.; Deacon Philip Medina.
Mailing Address: 2827 Lakeview Ave., 81005. Tel: 719-564-2696; Fax: 719-564-4396.
Catechesis/Religious Program—Pam Evanoff, C.R.E. Students 149.
Mission—St. Aloysius (1936) Rye, Pueblo Co. Rev. Msgr. Marvin J. Kapushion (Retired).

7—HOLY ROSARY (1954) Rev. James E. King.
Office: 2400 W. 22nd St., 81003. Tel: 719-545-7219.
Catechesis/Religious Program—Christine Armstrong, D.R.E. Students 17.

8—ST. JOSEPH (1960) Revs. William T. Gleason; Jose Mario Murillo, Parochial Vicar; Deacon Peter A. Massaro.
Office: 1145 S. Aspen Rd., 81006. Tel: 719-544-1886; Fax: 719-544-5137.
Catechesis/Religious Program—Maria Lopez, D.R.E. Students 305.

9—ST. LEANDER (1902) Rev. Anthony A. Wojcinski; Deacon Edward Riccillo.
Office: 1402 E. Seventh St., 81001. Tel: 719-544-8411; Fax: 719-544-8202.
Catechesis/Religious Program—Jari Trujillo-Santesteven, D.R.E. Students 135.

10—ST. MARY HELP OF CHRISTIANS (1895) Rev. Ben Bacino; Deacons David A. Cockson; Rick Oreskey; Darrell Pagels.
217 E. Mesa Ave., 81006. Tel: 719-296-8778; Fax: 719-562-1195.
Catechesis/Religious Program—Belinda Castro, C.R.E. Students 100.

11—OUR LADY OF GUADALUPE CHAPEL (1968) Closed. For inquiries for parish records please contact St. Leander, Pueblo.

12—OUR LADY OF MT. CARMEL (1901) Rev. Joseph A. Vigil.
421 Clark St., 81003. Tel: 719-542-5952; Fax: 719-542-2310.
Catechesis/Religious Program—Theresa Almeda, C.R.E. Students 227.

13—OUR LADY OF THE ASSUMPTION (1949) Closed. For inquiries for parish records contact the chancery.

14—OUR LADY OF THE MEADOWS (1979) Rev. James E. King.
23 Starling Dr., 81005. Tel: 719-561-3580; Fax: 719-561-1271.
Catechesis/Religious Program—Christine Armstrong, D.R.E. Students 112.

15—ST. PATRICK (1882) Closed. For inquiries for parish records contact the chancery.

16—ST. PAUL THE APOSTLE (2009) Rev. Carlos Alvarez; Deacon Michael Sanchez.
1132 W. Oro Grande Dr., P.O. Box 7199, 81007.
Catechesis/Religious Program—Students 203.

17—ST. PIUS X (1955) Rev. John Ozella; Deacon Roy Stringfellow.
Parish Center—3130 Morris Ave., 81008. Tel: 719-542-4264; Fax: 719-583-8103.
Catechesis/Religious Program—Students 57.

18—SHRINE OF ST. THERESE (1948) Rev. Msgr. Edward H. Nunez; Deacons John Wertz; Buddy P. Rodriguez.
300 Goodnight Ave., 81004. Tel: 719-542-1788; Fax: 719-542-2130.
Catechesis/Religious Program—Sarah Nelson, C.R.E. Students 125.

OUTSIDE THE CITY OF PUEBLO

AGUILAR, LAS ANIMAS CO., ST. ANTHONY (1875), (Spanish—Italian), [CEM] [JC] Rev. Martin Frias.
Mailing Address: P.O. Box 577, 81020. Tel: 719-941-4124; Fax: 719-941-4124.
Catechesis/Religious Program—Leslie Velarde, C.R.E. Students 17.

ALAMOSA, ALAMOSA CO., SACRED HEART (1887) Revs. Derrek Scott; Andres Ayala; Michael Chrisman; Mrs. Marianne Dunne, Pastoral Assoc.; Sr. Johnette Sawyer, Pastoral Assoc.
Mailing Address: 726 3rd St., P.O. Box 547, 81101. Tel: 719-589-5829 (Parish Center); Fax: 719-589-5820.
Catechesis/Religious Program—Students 234.

AVONDALE, PUEBLO CO., SACRED HEART (1960), (Spanish), Revs. William T. Gleason; Jose Mario Murillo.
Mailing Address: P.O. Box 279, 81022. Tel: 719-947-3092; Fax: 719-947-3005.
Catechesis/Religious Program—Students 50.

CANON CITY, FREMONT CO., ST. MICHAEL (1880) Rev. Kevin Novack; Deacon Merle E. Runck.
1029 College Ave., 81212. Tel: 719-275-7549; Fax: 719-275-7540. Email: stmikes@ris.net.
Catechesis/Religious Program—1016 Mystic, 81212. Tel: 719-275-3368. Students 80.

CAPULIN, CONEJOS CO., ST. JOSEPH (1912), (Hispanic), [CEM] Revs. Baykil Williams, S.O.L.T.; Scott Giuliani, S.O.L.T.
Mailing Address: P.O. Box 40, 81124. Tel: 719-274-5304; Fax: 719-274-4454.
Catechesis/Religious Program—Sr. Mary Ann Richwald, S.O.L.T., C.R.E. Students 198.
Mission—Our Lady of the Valley 19617 S. Hwy. 285, La Jara, Conejos Co. 81140. Tel: 719-274-5647.
Mission—St. Therese of the Child Jesus 115 Main St., Manassa, Conejos Co. 81141.
Mission—St. Anthony 18900 County Rd. 28, Los Sauces, Conejos Co. 81151.
Mission—Our Lady of the Immaculate Conception 211 Blanca St., Romeo, Conejos Co. 81148.

CENTER, SAGUACHE CO., ST. FRANCIS JEROME (1951), (San Juan Catholic Community) Revs. Derrek Scott; Andres Ayala; Michael Chrisman; Deacons Donald Lamb; Jerry LeBlanc; Jesus Ruiz.
781 Warden St., 81125. Mailing Address: P.O. Box 590, Monte Vista, 81144. Tel: 719-852-2673; Fax: 719-852-0623.
Catechesis/Religious Program—Students 90.
Mission—St. Agnes P.O. Box 590, Monte Vista, 81144.

CONEJOS, CONEJOS CO., OUR LADY OF GUADALUPE (1857) [CEM] Rev. Sergio Cardenas-Robles, C.R.
Mailing Address: P.O. Box 305, Antonito, 81120. Tel: 719-376-5985; Fax: 719-376-2530. 6633 Co. Rd. 13, 81129.
Catechesis/Religious Program—Students 66.
Mission—St. Augustine 305 8th Ave., Antonito, 81120.
Mission—Sagrada Familia 17344 Co. Rd. G, Lobatos, Conejos Co. 81120.
Mission—San Juan Nepomuceno y San Cayetano 684 Co. Rd. B, Ortiz, Conejos Co. 81120.
Mission—San Antonio de Padua 13148 Co. Rd. C, San Antonio, Conejos Co. 81120.
Mission—San Pedro y San Rafael 5308 Co. Rd. 10.75, San Rafael, Conejos Co. 81120.
Mission—San Isidro Brador Las Mesitas, Conejos Co.

CORTEZ, MONTEZUMA CO., ST. MARGARET MARY (1945) Rev. Pat Valdez, C.R.
Mailing Address: 28 E. Montezuma, 81321. Tel: 970-565-7308 (Office); Fax: 970-565-0822.
Catechesis/Religious Program—Kevin Ketterell, D.R.E. Students 76.
Mission—St. Jude 313 N. Pine, Dove Creek, Dolores Co. 81324.

CRESTED BUTTE, GUNNISON CO., QUEEN OF ALL SAINTS (1883) Attended by St. Peter Parish, Gunnison. Rev. Steven J. Murray; Deacons Vincent Rogalski; John Stroop; Joseph W. Fitzpatrick.
Mailing Address: 400 W. Georgia Ave., Gunnison, 81230.
Tel: 970-641-0808; Fax: 970-641-4592.
Catechesis/Religious Program—401 Sopris, 81224. Students 28.

DEL NORTE, RIO GRANDE CO., HOLY NAME OF MARY (1879) [CEM], (San Juan Catholic Community) Revs. Derrek Scott; Andres Ayala; Michael Chrisman; Deacons Donald Lamb; Jerry LeBlanc; Jesus Ruiz.
Mailing Address: P.O. Box 590, Monte Vista, 81144. Tel: 719-852-2673; Fax: 719-852-0623. 645 Pine St., 81132.
Catechesis/Religious Program—Amanda Rivera, C.R.E. Students 45.
Mission—St. Francis of Assisi Los Valdeses, Rio Grande Co.
Mission—San Jose Agua Ramon, Rio Grande Co.
Mission—Holy Family South Fork, Rio Grande Co.
Mission—St. John the Baptist La Garita, Saguache Co.
Mission—Immaculate Conception Creede, Mineral Co.

DELTA, DELTA CO., ST. MICHAEL (1911) Rev. Canice Enyiaka.
Parish Office: 628 Meeker St., 81416. Tel: 970-874-3300; Fax: 970-874-4015.
Res.: 628 Meeker St., 81416. Tel: 970-874-5116.
Catechesis/Religious Program—Students 90.
Mission—St. Philip Benizi P.O. Box 713, Cedaredge, Delta Co. 81413. Tel: 970-856-6495.

DURANGO, LA PLATA CO.

1—ST. COLUMBA (1881) Rev. James F. Koenigsfeld; Deacon Milton Van Cleave; Mary Therese Ralph, Pastoral Assoc.
1830 E. Second Ave., 81301. Tel: 970-247-0044; Fax: 970-385-5737.
School—(Grades PreK-8) Tel: 970-247-5527; Fax: 970-382-9355. Kevin C. Chick, Prin. Lay Teachers 27; Students 227.
Catechesis/Religious Program—Beth Parrott, D.R.E. Students 110.

2—SACRED HEART (1906), (Hispanic), Rev. Joseph Gallegos, C.R.; Deacons Jose Benito Martinez; Toby Romero.
254 E. Fifth Ave., 81301. Tel: 970-247-3997; Fax: 970-375-2385. Email: birdsheart@frontier.net.
Catechesis/Religious Program—Students 110.

FLORENCE, FREMONT CO., ST. BENEDICT (1895) Rev. Vincente Paz en la Casa; Deacon Michael Patterson.
622 W. Second St., 81226. Tel: 719-784-4879; Fax: 719-784-2070.
Catechesis/Religious Program—Joyce Archuletta, C.R.E. Students 61.

FRUITA, MESA CO., SACRED HEART (1890) Rev. Michael N. Smith, S.J.
Mailing Address: 513 E. Aspen Ave., 81521. Tel: 970-858-9605; Fax: 970-639-8010. Email: sacredheartfruita@yahoo.net. Web: sacredheartfruita.org. 503 E. Aspen Ave., 81521.
Catechesis/Religious Program—Students 85.
GARDNER, HUERFANO CO., SACRED HEART (1912) Rev. Martin Frias; Deacon John Luginbill.
Mailing Address: P.O. Box 86, Walsenburg, 81089. Tel: 719-738-1204; Fax: 719-738-1206.
GRAND JUNCTION, MESA CO.
1—IMMACULATE HEART OF MARY (1955) Rev. John B. Farley; Deacon Leo Truscott; Beverly Goodrich, Pastoral Assoc.
790 26 1/2 Rd., 81506. Tel: 970-242-6121; Fax: 970-256-0276.
Catechesis/Religious Program—Irene Fritzler, D.R.E. Students 347.
Mission—St. Ann 535 W. 1st St., Palisade, Mesa Co. 81526. Tel: 970-464-5157.
Station— Debeque.
Station— Collbran.
2—ST. JOSEPH (1884) Rev. Edmundo Valera; Chris Klein, Liturgy Dir.; Deacon Douglas Van Houten.
Mailing Address: 230 N. Third, 81501. Tel: 970-243-0209; Fax: 970-243-7493.
School—Holy Family School, (Grades K-8), 786 26 1/2 Rd., 81506. Tel: 970-242-6168; Fax: 970-242-4244. Sr. Ann Ashwood-Piper, C.S.J., Prin.; Anita Keenan, Librarian. Sisters 3; Lay Teachers 54; Students 387.
Catechesis/Religious Program—Sr. Rebecca Wolf, D.R.E. Students 233.
GUNNISON, GUNNISON CO., ST. PETER (1881) Rev. Steven J. Murray; Deacons Vincent Rogalski, Pastoral Assoc.; Lloyd Hawes.
Catechesis/Religious Program—400 W. Georgia Ave. Tel: 970-641-0808; Fax: 970-641-4592. Students 82.
Mission—St. Rose of Lima
HOLLY, PROWERS CO., ST. FRANCES OF ROME (1920) Revs. Charles A. Sena, Admin.; Damasus Okoro, C.S.Sp.
Church: 130 S. Fifth St., P. O. Box 130, 81047. Tel: 719-537-6688. Email: stfrances@live.com.
Catechesis/Religious Program—Debra Crossland, C.R.E.; Stephanie Gonzales, C.R.E. Students 82.
Mission—St. Mary Bristol, Prowers Co.
IGNACIO, LA PLATA CO., ST. IGNATIUS PARISH (1898) Rev. Doug Hunt; Deacons John O'Hare; Larry Tucker.
Mailing Address: 15449 Hwy. 172, P.O. Box 1350, 81137. Tel: 970-563-4241; Fax: 970-563-1032.
Catechesis/Religious Program—Students 32.
Mission—St. Bartholemew
Mission—SS. Peter & Rose R.R. 2, Arboles, Archuleta Co. 81137.
LA JUNTA, OTERO CO., OUR LADY OF GUADALUPE/ST. PATRICK (1889) Revs. Alphonsus Ihuoma; Henry Aguwa.
202 Lincoln Ave., Box 1181, 81050. Tel: 719-384-4342; 719-384-4372; Fax: 719-384-7894.
Catechesis/Religious Program—Students 110.
LAMAR, PROWERS CO., ST. FRANCIS DE SALES-OUR LADY OF GUADALUPE (1907) Revs. Charles A. Sena; Damasus Okoro, C.S.Sp.; Deacons Allan J. Medina; Henry J. Wertin.
600 E. Parmenter St., 81052. Tel: 719-336-7759; Fax: 719-336-0291.
Catechesis/Religious Program—Tel: 719-336-7750. Students 254.
LAS ANIMAS, BENT CO., ST. MARY (1910) Revs. Alphonsus Ihuoma; Henry Aguwa.
714 Elm Ave., 81054. Tel: 719-456-1104; Fax: 719-456-1104.
Catechesis/Religious Program—Students 47.
MANCOS, MONTEZUMA CO., ST. RITA (1914) Rev. Pat Valdez, C.R.
Mailing Address: 28 E. Montezuma Ave., Cortez, 81321. Tel: 970-565-7308; Fax: 970-565-0822.
Catechesis/Religious Program—Students 76.
Mission—Our Lady of Victory Church Dolores, 81323.
Mission—Immaculate Heart of Mary Chapel Rico.
MONTE VISTA, RIO GRANDE CO., ST. JOSEPH (1920), (San Juan Catholic Community) Revs. Derrek Scott; Michael Chrisman; Andres Ayala; Deacons Don Lamb. Tel: 719-852-3773; Jerry LeBlanc; Jesus Ruiz.
425 Batterson, P.O. Box 590, 81144. Tel: 719-852-2673; Fax: 719-852-0623.
Catechesis/Religious Program—Loren Santistevan, C.R.E. Students 123.
Station— Lariate.
Station—Juniper Village Nursing Center, Tel: 719-852-5138.
Station—Colorado State Veterans Center Homelake. Tel: 719-852-5118.
Station—High Valley Manor, Tel: 719-852-5711.
MONTROSE, MONTROSE CO., ST. MARY (1906) Rev. Mark T. Bettinger; Deacons Dennis Putnam, (Retired); Michael Rovella; Scott McIntosh.
Parish Center & Church: 1855 St. Mary's Dr., 81401. Tel: 970-249-3319; Fax: 970-249-9088.
Catechesis/Religious Program—Students 205.
Mission—Our Lady of Fatima, Tel: 970-323-5146.
OURAY, OURAY CO., ST. DANIEL THE PROPHET (1883) Rev. Nathanael Foshage, O.S.B.
Mailing Address: P.O. Box 565, 81427. Tel: 970-325-4373.
Catechesis/Religious Program—Valerie Hill, D.R.E. Students 21.
Mission—St. Patrick 1005 Reece, Silverton, San Juan Co. 81433.
PAGOSA SPRINGS, ARCHULETA CO.
1—IMMACULATE HEART OF MARY (1923), (Hispanic), [CEM] Rev. Donald P. Malin; Deacon Patrick McKenzie.
Mailing Address: 353 S. Pagosa Blvd., 81147. Tel: 970-731-5744; Fax: 970-731-2151.
Catechesis/Religious Program—Students 100.
Mission—St. Francis Frances, Archuleta Co.
Mission—St. John Baptist Pagosa Junction, Archuleta Co.
Mission—St. James Trujillo, Archuleta Co.
Station— Chromo.
2—POPE JOHN PAUL II PARISH Rev. Donald P. Malin; Deacon Patrick McKenzie.
353 S. Pagosa Blvd., 81147. Tel: 970-731-5744; Fax: 970-731-2151.
Catechesis/Religious Program—Students 100.
PAONIA, DELTA CO., SACRED HEART (1923) Rev. Pius Nwauzor.
235 N. Fork Ave., P.O. Box 988, 81428. Tel: 970-527-3214; Fax: 970-527-5468.
Catechesis/Religious Program—Students 34.
Mission—St. Margaret Mary 331 Bridge St., Hotchkiss, Delta Co. 81419. Tel: 973-872-2117.
ROCKY FORD, OTERO CO., ST. PETER (1910) Rev. Paul Ekeh; Deacons Douglas Manley; Terry Marinelli.
1209 Swink Ave., 81067. Tel: 719-254-3565; Fax: 719-254-3921.
Catechesis/Religious Program—Marilyn Marinelli, D.R.E. Students 107.
Mission—St. Joseph the Worker, Closed. Sacramental records can be found at St. Peter, Rocky Ford, 1209 Swink Ave., Rocky Ford, CO 81067-1899.
Mission—St. Peter Chapel 905 Main St., Ordway, Crowley Co. 81063. Tel: 719-267-4645.
Mission—Mary Queen of Heaven 602 7th St., P.O. Box 214, Fowler, Otero Co. 81039. Tel: 719-263-4455.
SAN LUIS, COSTILLA CO., SANGRE DE CRISTO (1881), (Hispanic), [CEM] Rev. Heriberto Torres, C.R.; Deacon Margarito Duarte.
Res.: P.O. Box 326, 81152. Tel: 719-672-3685; 719-672-3020 (Rectory); Fax: 719-672-0300.
Church: 511 Church Pl., P.O. Box 326, 81152.
Catechesis/Religious Program—Students 59.
Mission—St. James Blanca, Costilla Co.
Mission—Holy Family Fort Garland, Costilla Co.
Mission—Immaculate Conception Chama, Costilla Co.
Mission—San Acacio San Acacio, Costilla Co.
Mission—SS. Peter and Paul San Pedro, Costilla Co.
Mission—St. Isidro San Isidro, Costilla Co.
Mission—St. Francis of Assisi San Francisco, Costilla Co.
Mission—Sacred Heart of Jesus Garcia, Costilla Co.
SILVERTON, SAN JUAN CO., ST. PATRICK (1883) Rev. Nathanael Foshage, O.S.B.
Mailing Address: P.O. Box 565, Ouray, 81427. Tel: 970-325-4373.
Catechesis/Religious Program—Students 12.
SPRINGFIELD, BACA CO., OUR LADY OF THE ANNUNCIATION (1932) Revs. Charles A. Sena, Admin.; Damasus Okoro, C.S.Sp.
140 Kansas St., 81073. Mailing Address: P.O. Box 174, 81073. Tel: 719-336-7759.
Catechesis/Religious Program—Students 30.
Station— Walsh.
TELLURIDE, SAN MIGUEL CO., ST. PATRICK (1896) Rev. Nathanael Foshage, O.S.B., Supvr.; Deacon Michael Doehrman, Parish Dir.
Mailing Address: P.O. Box 398, 81435. Tel: 970-728-3387.
Catechesis/Religious Program—Students 22.
Mission—Our Lady of Sorrows P.O. Box 451, Nucla, 81424.
TRINIDAD, LAS ANIMAS CO.
1—ST. JOSEPH, TRINIDAD AREA CATHOLIC COMMUNITY, Closed. For inquiries for parish records contact Most Holy Trinity, 719-846-3369.
2—MOST HOLY TRINITY (1885) [CEM] Revs. Richard F. Becker; Kenny Udumka; Deacon Phil Martin.
235 N. Convent St., 81082. Tel: 719-846-3369; Fax: 719-846-4856.
Catechesis/Religious Program—Bro. Harry Gonzales, D.R.E. Students 417.
Mission—St. Isidore Vigil, Las Animas Co.
Mission—St. Ignatius Segundo, Las Animas Co.
3—OUR LADY OF MT. CARMEL, Closed. For inquiries for parish records contact Most Holy Trinity, 719-846-3369.
VINELAND, PUEBLO CO., ST. THERESE (1928) Revs. William T. Gleason; Jose Mario Murillo.
Mailing Address: 1145 S. Aspen Rd., 81006. Tel: 719-948-2410; 719-544-1886; Fax: 719-544-5137.
Catechesis/Religious Program—Maria Lopez, D.R.E. Students 37.
WALSENBURG, HUERFANO CO., ST. MARY (1896) [CEM] Rev. Martin Frias; Deacon John Luginbill; Sr. Carol Tlach, S.N.D., Pastoral Assoc.
Mailing Address: P.O. Box 86, 81089. Tel: 719-738-1204; Fax: 719-738-1206.
Catechesis/Religious Program—Students 37.
Mission—Christ the King P.O. Box 752, La Veta, Huerfano Co. 81055.
Mission—Sacred Heart P.O. Box 228, Gardner, Huerfano Co. 8104.
WESTCLIFFE, CUSTER CO., OUR LADY OF THE ASSUMPTION (1870) Rev. Vicente Paz en La Casa; Deacon Michael Patterson.
Mailing Address: 109 S. Fifth St., P.O. Box 359, 81252. Tel: 719-783-3507; Fax: 719-783-3510. Email: ola.westcliffe@gmail.com.
Catechesis/Religious Program—Joan Kohler, D.R.E. Students 29.

Chaplains of Public Institutions

PUEBLO. *Colorado Mental Health Institute at Pueblo*, Tel: 719-546-4435. Vacant.
St. Mary Corwin Medical Center, 1008 Minnequa Ave., 81004. Tel: 719-560-4000. Deacon Marco Vegas.
Parkview Hospital, Tel: 719-584-7306. Rev. Michael C. DeSciose, 400 W. 17th, 81003.

On Duty Outside the Diocese:
Revs.—
Haberman, C. Robert, Asst. Professor/Dir. of Campus Min., 50 Acadia, San Rafael, CA 94901. Tel: 415-479-1249
Mondji, Jean-Marie, Diocese of Belleville, IL
Perez, Jesse L. (Retired), Diocese of Colorado Springs, CO
Wertin, Matthew, Ottawa, Ontario, Canada

Absent on Leave:
Rev.—
Bonfadini, Leo

Retired:
Rev. Msgrs.—
Delaney, Howard L., 5-A Bonnymede, 81001. Tel: 719-542-4387
Holland, George T., Life Care, 2118 Chatalet, Rm. 103-A, 81005. Tel: 719-561-8697
Huber, Daniel R., 1648 Weatherby Ln., 81008.
Kapushion, Marvin J., M.S.W., J.C.L., L.C.S.W., 620 E. Routt, 81004. Tel: 719-545-4599
Racki, Leonard E., 31 Terrace Dr., 81001. Tel: 719-583-1988
Revs.—
Cerwonka, Clarence J. (SY), Most Holy Rosary Church, P.O. Box 248, Maine, NY 13802. Tel: 607-862-3216
Corbett, Michael E., Pueblo Regent Retirement Residence, 100 San Carlos Rd., 81005.
Costanzo, John J., 4947 King St., Denver, 80221. Tel: 303-477-4853
Gallagher, Maurice O., 1420 Murillo Ln., Boone, 81025. Tel: 719-947-9812
Grimes, Raymond P., St. Mary Parish, 652 Elm Ave., Las Animas, 81054-1738.
Marcantonio, Clement, LRMC 799 CMR 402, Apo, AE 09180.
O'Flynn, John, 23 Churchill Pl., 81001.
Perez, Jesse L., 321 E. 6th St., Salida, 81201.
Pettit, Edward G. (DEN), Mesa Towers, 260 Lamar Ave., #411, 81004. Tel: 719-595-0217
Plough, James H., 711-B Fountainhead Blvd., Grand Junction, 81506. Tel: 970-255-1228
Powers, William V., 1414 E. 8th St., 81001. Tel: 719-542-1688
Quinn, Thomas J., S.J., P.O. Box 607, South Fork, 81154. Tel: 719-657-3147
Roche, Ron, 1912 Vinewood Ln., 81005. Tel: 719-565-0813
Rykowski, Jerome A., 1175 Nininger Rd., Hastings, MN 55033.
Schoening, Sylvester H., Hermitage, 1250 Mountain View Ln., P.O. Box 553, Norwood, 81423. Tel: 970-327-4346
Smigiel, Walter J., 3517 Atlantic Dr., Colorado Springs, 80910. Tel: 719-596-4294

Permanent Deacons:
Arellano, Jake
Cockson, David A., St. Mary, Pueblo
Doehrman, Michael J., Parish Dir., Telluride/Nucla
Duarte, Margarito, Sangre de Cristo, San Luis
Escalera, Stephen, Christ the King, Pueblo
Fitzpatrick, Joseph W., Queen of All Saints, Crested Butte
Hawes, Lloyd, St. Peter, Gunnison
LaConte, Michael, Sacred Heart, Avondale
Lamb, Donald, St. Joseph, Monte Vista
LeBlanc, Jerry, San Juan Catholic Community
Leetch, Daniel T., Jr., Our Lady of Guadalupe/St. Patrick, La Junta; Dir., Inst. Ministries
Luginbill, John, St. Mary, Walsenburg
Lumbert, Steven, Pastoral Life Admin., St. Anne, Pueblo
Manley, Douglas, St. Peter, Rocky Ford
Marinelli, Terry, St. Peter, Rocky Ford
Martin, Philip, Holy Trinity, Trinidad
Martinez, Jose Benito, Sacred Heart, Durango
Massaro, Peter A., St. Joseph, Pueblo
McIntosh, Scott, St. Mary, Montrose
McKenzie, Patrick, Immaculate Heart of Mary, Pagosa Springs
Medina, Allan J., St. Francis de Sales/Our Lady of Guadalupe, Lamar
Medina, Philip, Holy Family, Pueblo
O'Hare, John, St. Ignatius, Ignacio & St. Bartholomew, Bayfield
Oreskey, Richard, St. Mary Help of Christians, Pueblo
Pagels, Darrell, Christ the King, Pueblo
Patterson, Michael, St. Mary, Pueblo; Our Lady of the Assumption, Westcliffe
Putnam, Dennis, (Retired), St. Mary, Montrose
Riccillo, Edward, St. Leander, Pueblo
Rodriguez, Buddy P., CSU-P/County Jail Ministry
Rogalski, Vincent, Queen of All Saints, Crested Butte
Romero, Octaviano, Sacred Heart, Durango
Rovella, Mike, St. Mary, Montrose
Runck, Merle, St. Michael, Canon City
Sadler, Jerome, St. Mary, Seaview, WA
Sanchez, Michael, St. Paul the Apostle, Pueblo West
Shafer, Jacob, Sacred Heart Cathedral
Stringfellow, Roy, St. Pius X, Pueblo
Stroop, John, Queen of All Saints, Crested Butte
Truscott, Leo, Immaculate Heart of Mary, Grand Junction
Tucker, Lawrence, St. Ignatius, Ignacio
Van Cleave, Milton, St. Columba, Durango
Van Houten, Douglas, St. Joseph, Grand Junction
Vegas, Marco, Holy Family, Pueblo
Villegas, Paul, St. Francis, Pueblo
Wertin, Henry, St. Francis de Sales, Lamar
Wertz, John, Shrine of St. Therese, Pueblo
Yatch, Lawrence, St. Michael, Canon City

INSTITUTIONS LOCATED IN THE DIOCESE

[A] ELEMENTARY SCHOOLS, DIOCESAN

PUEBLO. *St. Therese Catholic School*, (Grades PreK-8), 320 Goodnight Ave., 81004. Tel: 719-561-1121; Fax: 719-561-2252. Web: www.sttherese-school.org. John Brainard, Prin.; Mrs. Sally Stricca, Librarian. Lay Teachers 17; Total Enrollment 163.

DURANGO. *St. Columba*, (Grades PreK-8), 1801 E. 3rd Ave., 81301-5072. Tel: 970-247-5527; Fax: 970-382-9355. Email: office@stcolumbaschooldurango.org. Kevin C. Chick, Prin.; Sabrina Buckley, Librarian. Teachers 26; Students 192.

GRAND JUNCTION. *Holy Family Catholic School*, (Grades PreSchool-8), 786 26 1/2 Rd., 81506. Tel: 970-242-6168; Fax: 970-242-4244. Web: holyfamily-gj.org. Sr. Ann Ashwood-Piper, C.S.J., Prin.; Anita Keenan, Librarian. Sisters 2; Lay Teachers 54; Students 387.

[B] ELEMENTARY SCHOOLS, PRIVATE

PUEBLO. *St. John Neumann Catholic Schools*, (Grades PreK-8), 2415 E. Orman Ave., 81004. Tel: 719-561-9419; Fax: 719-561-4718. Email: joyce.baca.anderson@john-neumann.com. Web: www.john-neumann.com. Joyce Baca-Anderson, Prin. & Admin. Lay Teachers 18; Students 147.

[C] GENERAL HOSPITALS

PUEBLO. *Centura Health-St. Mary-Corwin Medical Center*, 1008 Minnequa Ave., 81004. Tel: 719-557-4000; Fax: 719-557-5823. Web: www.stmarycorwin.org. Mr. Rob Ryder, CEO; Eileen Perez, Contact Person; Deacon Marco Vegas, Chap.; Ms. Michele Des Lauriers, Mission Integration; Sr. Darleen Maloney, O.S.F. An operating unit of Catholic Health Initiatives Colorado (an affiliate of Catholic Health Initiatives). Bed Capacity 408; Total Staff 1,165; Patients Assisted Annually 159,184.

CANON CITY. *Centura Health-St. Thomas More Hospital*, 1338 Phay Ave., 81212. Tel: 719-285-2000; Fax: 719-285-2016. Web: www.stthomas.org. Sheri Trahern, Chief Admin. Officer; Rev. Tema Godwin Nnamezie, Chap. An operating unit of Catholic Health Initiatives Colorado (an affiliate of Catholic Health Initiatives). Bed Capacity 55; Patients Assisted Annually 47,560; Staff 380.

DURANGO. *Mercy Regional Medical Center* 81301. Tel: 970-247-4311. Web: www.mercydurango.org. Kirk Dignum, Ph.D., CEO. An operating unit of Catholic Health Initiatives Colorado (an affiliate of Catholic Health Initiatives). Beds 82; Patients Assisted Annually 127,372; Total Staff 905. Chaplains: John Boyd, Chief Medical & Mission Officer; Diana McKenna, Contact & Dir., Mission & Spiritual Care.

GRAND JUNCTION. *Marillac Clinic, Inc.*, 2333 N. 6th St., 81501. Tel: 970-255-1782; 970-255-1799; Fax: 970-255-1711. Email: steve.hurd@stmarygj.org. Steve Hurd, Ph.D., Exec. Dir.
Sisters of Charity of Leavenworth Health System Total Staff 68; Total Assisted 26,963.
St. Mary Hospital and Medical Center, 2635 N. 7th St., P.O. Box 1628, 81501. Tel: 970-298-2273. Email: pmontgomery@stmarygj.com. Web: www.stmarygj.org. Mr. Michael J. McBride, FACHE; Pat Montgomery, Exec. Asst. Sisters of Charity of Leavenworth, Kansas 10; Bed Capacity 346; Patients Assisted Annually 400,575; Total Staff 2,050.

[D] SPECIAL CARE FACILITIES

PUEBLO. *Centura Health-Villa Pueblo*, 1111 Bonforte Blvd., 81001. Tel: 719-545-5911; Fax: 719-544-1354. Greg Warnick, Exec. Dir.; Karen Burnham, Chap. An operating unit of Catholic Health Initiatives Colorado (an affiliate of Catholic Health Initiatives).

CANON CITY. *Centura Health-Progressive Care Center*, 1338 Phay Ave., 81212. Tel: 719-285-2540; Fax: 719-285-2256. Helen Whitener, Admin. An operating unit of Catholic Health Initiatives Colorado (an affiliate of Catholic Health Initiatives). Bed Capacity 116; Total Staff 90.

[E] MONASTERIES AND RESIDENCES OF PRIESTS AND BROTHERS

TRINIDAD. *Trinidad Area Catholic Community*, Rectory, 235 N. Convent St., 81082. Tel: 719-846-3360; Fax: 719-846-4856. Email: rbecker712@aol.com. Revs. Richard F. Becker, Supr.; Kenny Udumka, Parochial Vicar.

[F] CONVENTS AND RESIDENCES FOR SISTERS

PUEBLO. *Servants of the Blessed Sacrament*, 311 E. Mesa Ave., 81006. Tel: 719-545-7729; Fax: 719-542-3094. Email: ssspueblo@juno.com. Web: www.blesacrament.org. Sisters 4.

[G] NEWMAN CENTERS

PUEBLO. *Campus Ministry - Diocese of Pueblo* 101 N. Greenwood St., 81003. Tel: 719-544-9861, Ext. 116; Fax: 719-544-5202. Deacon Daniel T. Leetch Jr.
Adams State College (Alamosa) United Campus Ministry College Center, Rm. 329, P.O. Box 1164, Alamosa, 81102-9986. Tel: 719-587-7516. Ms. Shirley Atencio, Campus Minister.
Fort Lewis College (Durango) Fort Lewis College Center for Campus Ministry, 1830 E. 2nd Ave., Durango, 81301. Tel: 970-247-0044. Ms. Wivina Vigil, Campus Minister.
Colorado Mesa University (Grand Junction) Newman Center, 875 Bunting, Grand Junction, 81501. Tel: 970-241-3670. Hunter Darrouzet, Campus Min.
Western State College (Gunnison) St. John of the Cross Neumann Center, 600 E. Georgia Ave., Gunnison, 81230. Abram Muenzberg, Campus Min.
Colorado State University - Pueblo 419 Petroleum Ave., Florence, 81226. Tel: 719-549-2089. Joyce Archuletta, Campus Min.

[H] RETREAT WORK

CRESTONE. *Spiritual Life Institute of America, Inc.*, P.O. Box 219, 81131. Tel: 719-256-4778. Email: nada@spirituallifeinstitute.org. Web: www.spirituallifeinstitute.org. Rev. Eric Haarer, Prior; Sr. Connie Bielecki, Contact; Susan Ryan, Contact. Priests 1; Sisters 1.

FLORENCE. *Trinity Ranch Conference & Renewal Center, Inc.*, Mailing Address: 1061 County Rd. 290, 81226. Tel: 719-784-9701. Rev. Maurice C. Haefling, O.S.B., Vicar & Admin.

WHITEWATER. *Whitewater Community, Inc.*, 8250 Kannah Creek Rd., 81527. Tel: 970-241-3847. Sr. Mary M. Glenn, Contact. Benedictine Sisters 3.

[I] MISCELLANEOUS

PUEBLO. **Catholic Diocese of Pueblo Foundation*, 101 N. Greenwood St., 81003. Tel: 719-544-9861, Ext. 131; Fax: 719-544-5202. Email: ktillman@dioceseofpueblo.org. Web: www.dioceseofpueblo.org. Mrs. Kathleen Tillman, Exec. Dir.
St. Charles Community, 18 Dartmouth, 81005. Tel: 719-566-1620. Mr. Ed Sajbel, Contact Person.
Deacon Candidate Formation Council, 101 N. Greenwood St., 81003. Tel: 719-544-9861. Web: dioceseofpueblo.org.
Pueblo Community Soup Kitchen, Inc., 422 W. Seventh, 81003. Tel: 719-545-6540. Carolyn Manley, Dir.; Tim Perry, Coord.
S.E.T. of Pueblo, Inc. A division of Catholic Health Initiatives Colorado., 1925 E. Orman Ave., 81004. Tel: 719-557-3886; Fax: 719-557-3880. Email: cindylau@centura.org. Cindy Lau, Exec. Dir.; Sr. Jacqueline Riggio, S.C., Asst. Dir. Purpose: A ministry to low-income, disadvantaged, and underserved persons, providing wellness clinics, fitness and education for empowerment and transformation. Enroll children into federal and state healthcare programs and provide community resource referrals to clients.
SEARCH of Pueblo, 2 Bear Claw Ct., 81001. Tel: 719-542-6513; 719-320-2707. Email: sandyrose@searchretreatcenter.org. Ms. Sandy Hansen, Coord.
Serra Club of Pueblo, 5426 Stonemoor Dr., 81005. Tel: 719-566-0511. Mrs. Sally Stricca, Pres.; Deacon Jacob Shafer, State Governor, 999 W. Fortino Blvd., #240, 81008. Tel: 719-562-0321.
Sisters for Christian Community, 1081 Lynx Dr., 81007. Tel: 719-547-2416; Fax: 719-547-4401. Email: watkins.13@juno.com. Sr. Sallie Watkins, S.F.C.C., Ph.D., Sec. & Contact.

DURANGO. *Mercy Health Foundation*, 1010 Three Springs Blvd., 81301. Tel: 970-764-2804; Fax: 970-764-2809. Email: karenmidkiff@centura.org. Ms. Karen Midkiff, Exec. Dir. & Contact. Affiliate of Catholic Health Initiatives.

GRAND JUNCTION. *Grand Valley Catholic Outreach*, 245 S. 1st St., 81501. Tel: 970-241-3658; Fax: 970-254-1262. Email: kabland@catholicoutreach.org. Web: www.catholicoutreach.org. Sr. Karen Bland, O.S.B., Exec. Dir.
Grand Valley Peace and Justice, c/o St. Joseph Church, 230 N. 3rd St., 81501. Tel: 970-243-0136; Fax: 970-243-7493. Email: gvpeace@acsol.net. Web: gvpeacejustice.net. Julie Mamo, Exec.; Ms. Sherry Cole, Project Coord.
St. Mary's Hospital Foundation, 2635 N. 7th St., P.O. Box 1628, 81502-1628. Tel: 970-298-1954; Fax: 970-298-7605. Email: smhfoundation@stmarygj.org. Web: www.stmarygj.org.
St. Mary's Physical Medicine & Rehabilitation, P.O. Box 1628, 81502. 2686 Patterson Rd., 81506. Tel: 970-298-6005. Valerie Hedgecock, Supvr.

PAGOSA SPRINGS. *Archuleta Housing Corporation*, 703 San Juan St., P.O. Box 355, 81147-0355. Tel: 970-264-2195; Fax: 970-264-4229. Email: archie@centurytel.net.

RELIGIOUS INSTITUTES OF MEN REPRESENTED IN THE DIOCESE

For further details refer to the corresponding bracketed number in the Religious Institutes of Men or Women section.

[]—*Apostles of Jesus*—A.J.
[0200]—*Benedictine Monks*—O.S.B.
[]—*Congregation of the Holy Spirit*—C.S.Sp.
[0260]—*Discalced Carmelite Monks*—O.C.D.
[0690]—*Jesuit Fathers and Brothers* (Missouri Prov.)—S.J.
[]—*Society of Our Lady of the Most Holy Trinity*—S.O.L.T.
[]—*Sons of Mary Mother of Mercy*—S.M.M.M.
[1300]—*Theatine Fathers* (Rome, Italy)—C.R.

RELIGIOUS INSTITUTES OF WOMEN REPRESENTED IN THE DIOCESE

[0230]—*Benedictine Sisters of Pontifical Jurisdiction* (Chicago, IL; Covington, KY; Colorado Springs, CO; Yankton, SD)—O.S.B.
[3765]—*Capuchin Poor Clares*—O.S.C.Cap.
[0420]—*Discalced Carmelite Nuns*—O.C.D.
[1115]—*Dominican Sisters of Peace*—O.P.
[2575]—*Institute of the Sisters of Mercy of the*

Americas—R.S.M.

[3500]—*Servants of the Blessed Sacrament*—S.S.S.

[]—*Sisters for Christian Community*—S.F.C.C.

[0440]—*Sisters of Charity of Cincinnati, Ohio*—S.C.

[0480]—*Sisters of Charity of Leavenworth, Kansas*—S.C.L.

[1570]—*Sisters of St. Francis of Rochester, MN*—O.S.F.

[3830-15]—*Sisters of St. Joseph*—C.S.J.

[]—*Society of Our Lady of the Most Holy Trinity Sisters*—S.O.L.T.

CEMETERIES, DIOCESAN AND PAROCHIAL

AGUILAR. *St. Anthony* (St. Anthony Parish)

CAPULIN. *St. Joseph* (St. Joseph Parish)

CONEJOS. *Conejos; Las Mesitas; Ortiz* (Our Lady of Guadalupe Parish)

DEL NORTE. *St. Francis of Assisi* (Holy Name of Mary Parish)

FRUITA. *Fruita Catholic* (Sacred Heart Parish)

PAGOSA SPRINGS. *St. John the Baptist; St. Andrew Avelino; St. Francis; and St. James* (Pope John Paul II & Immaculate Heart of Mary Parish)

RYE. *Mount Olivet*
The Rye Mount Olivet Cemetery., (St. Aloysius Mission Parish)

SAN LUIS. *San Luis; San Pedro; San Acacio; San Francisco; and Chama* (Sangre de Cristo Parish)

TRINIDAD. *Trinidad Catholic* Legal Title: Trinidad Catholic Cemetery Assoc. (Cemetery Bd.)

WALSENBURG. *St. Mary* Legal Title: St. Mary South Cemetery (St. Mary Parish)

WESTCLIFFE. *Silver Cliff Assumption Catholic* (Our Lady of the Assumption Parish)

NECROLOGY

† Doll, Rev. Msgr. William P., (Retired)—Died May 8, 2011

† Cavanagh, Michael J., (Retired)—Died July 13, 2011

† Danowski, Alexander J., (Retired)—Died July 5, 2011

† Friel, James E., (Retired)—Died Feb. 12, 2011

An asterisk (*) denotes an organization that has established tax-exempt status directly with the IRS and is not covered by the USCCB Group Ruling.

Diocese of Raleigh

(Dioecesis Raleighiensis)

Most Reverend

MICHAEL F. BURBIDGE, Ed.D., D.D.

Bishop of Raleigh; ordained May 19, 1984; appointed Auxiliary Bishop of Philadelphia and Titular Bishop of Cluain Iraird June 21, 2002; consecrated September 5, 2002; appointed Fifth Bishop of Raleigh June 8, 2006; installed August 4, 2006. *Res.: 219 W. Edenton St., Raleigh, NC 27603. Office: 715 Nazareth St., Raleigh, NC 27606.* Tel: 919-821-9700.

Most Reverend

F. JOSEPH GOSSMAN, D.D., J.C.D.

Retired Bishop of Raleigh; ordained December 17, 1955; appointed Titular Bishop of Aguntum and Auxiliary Bishop of Baltimore July 15, 1968; ordained September 11, 1968; appointed Fourth Bishop of Raleigh April 8, 1975; installed May 19, 1975; retired June 8, 2006. *Res.: 715 Nazareth St., Raleigh, NC 27606. Office: 2401 Crusader Dr., Raleigh, NC 27606.* Tel: 919-851-6218.

Catholic Center: 715 Nazareth St., Raleigh, NC 27606. Tel: 919-821-9700; Fax: 919-821-9705.

Web: www.dioceseofraleigh.org

Square Miles 31,875.

Established as Vicariate-Apostolic of North Carolina by Pope Pius IX, March 3, 1868.

Established as Diocese of Raleigh by Pope Pius XI, December 12, 1924.

Comprises the following Counties in the State of North Carolina: Alamance, Beaufort, Bertie, Bladen, Brunswick, Camden, Carteret, Caswell, Chatham, Chowan, Columbus, Craven, Cumberland, Currituck, Dare, Duplin, Durham, Edgecombe, Franklin, Gates, Granville, Greene, Halifax, Harnett, Hertford, Hoke, Hyde, Johnston, Jones, Lee, Lenoir, Martin, Moore, Nash, New Hanover, Northampton, Onslow, Orange, Pamlico, Pasquotank, Pender, Perquimans, Person, Pitt, Robeson, Sampson, Scotland, Tyrrell, Vance, Wake, Warren, Washington, Wayne and Wilson.

For legal titles of parishes and diocesan institutions, consult the Chancery.

STATISTICAL OVERVIEW

Personnel	
Bishop	1
Retired Bishops	1
Priests: Diocesan Active in Diocese	62
Priests: Diocesan Active Outside Diocese	1
Priests: Retired, Sick or Absent	27
Number of Diocesan Priests	90
Religious Priests in Diocese	50
Total Priests in Diocese	140
Extern Priests in Diocese	32
Ordinations:	
Diocesan Priests	1
Transitional Deacons	1
Permanent Deacons in Diocese	57
Total Brothers	5
Total Sisters	45
Parishes	
Parishes	77
With Resident Pastor:	
Resident Diocesan Priests	49
Resident Religious Priests	19
Without Resident Pastor:	
Administered by Priests	6
Administered by Religious Women	3
Missions	18
Pastoral Centers	5
Professional Ministry Personnel:	
Brothers	5
Sisters	19
Welfare	
Special Centers for Social Services	10
Total Assisted	56,153
Educational	
Diocesan Students in Other Seminaries	23
Total Seminarians	23
High Schools, Diocesan and Parish	2
Total Students	1,247
High Schools, Private	1
Total Students	151
Elementary Schools, Diocesan and Parish	30
Total Students	7,742
Catechesis/Religious Education:	
High School Students	4,362
Elementary Students	16,453
Total Students under Catholic Instruction	29,978
Teachers in the Diocese:	
Priests	1
Sisters	5
Lay Teachers	588
Vital Statistics	
Receptions into the Church:	
Infant Baptism Totals	5,231
Minor Baptism Totals	553
Adult Baptism Totals	190
Received into Full Communion	332
First Communions	5,107
Confirmations	2,758
Marriages:	
Catholic	546
Interfaith	303
Total Marriages	849
Deaths	1,116
Total Catholic Population	218,672
Total Population	4,654,373

Former Bishops of Diocese—Most Revs. WILLIAM J. HAFEY, D.D., cons. June 24, 1925; transferred to the See of Scranton, PA, Oct. 2, 1937; installed Nov. 15, 1937; died May 12, 1954; EUGENE J. MCGUINNESS, D.D., cons. Dec. 21, 1937; transferred to the See of Oklahoma City and Tulsa, OK, Dec. 8, 1944; installed Jan. 10, 1945; died Dec. 27, 1957; VINCENT S. WATERS, D.D., cons. May 15, 1945; installed June 6, 1945; died Dec. 3, 1974; F. JOSEPH GOSSMAN, D.D., J.C.D. (Retired), ord. Dec. 17, 1955; appt. Titular Bishop of Aguntum and Auxiliary Bishop of Baltimore July 15, 1968; ord. Sept. 11, 1968; appt. Fourth Bishop of Raleigh April 8, 1975; installed May 19, 1975; retired June 8, 2006.

Former Bishops of Vicariate-Apostolic—His Eminence JAMES CARDINAL GIBBONS, D.D., consecrated Aug. 16, 1868, Titular Bishop of Adramyttum, first Vicar-Apostolic; transferred to Richmond, VA, July 30, 1872; promoted to the See of Baltimore, Oct. 3, 1877; created Cardinal-Priest of S. Maria in Trastevere, June 7, 1886; died March 24, 1921; Most Rev. JOHN J. KEANE, consecrated Bishop of Richmond and Vicar-Apostolic of North Carolina, Aug. 25, 1878; transferred to the Titular See of Jasso, Aug. 12, 1888; elevated to the Archepiscopal Dignity with the title of Archbishop of Damascus, Jan. 9, 1897; transferred to the See of Dubuque, July 24, 1900; resigned April 3, 1911; appt. Titular Archbishop of Cios, April 28, 1911; died June 23, 1918; Rt. Revs. H. P. NORTHROP, consecrated Titular Bishop of Rosalia and Vicar-Apostolic of North Carolina, Jan. 8, 1882; transferred to Charleston, Jan. 27, 1883; died June 7, 1916; LEO HAID, O.S.B. Vicar Apostolic of North Carolina and Abbot-Ordinary of Belmont Abbey consecrated Titular Bishop of Messene, July 1, 1888; died July 24, 1924.

Office of the Bishop—715 Nazareth St., Raleigh, 27606. Tel: 919-821-9702; Fax: 919-821-9779.

Vicar General—Rev. Msgr. DAVID D. BROCKMAN, V.G., S.T.L., J.C.L., 715 Nazareth St., Raleigh, 27606. Tel: 919-821-9708.

Vicar Judicial & Chancellor—Rev. Msgr. GIRARD M. SHERBA, V.J., J.C.D., Ph.D., 2401 Crusader Dr., Raleigh, 27606-2120. Tel: 919-821-9756.

Chancery—2401 Crusader Dr., Raleigh, 27606-2120. Tel: 919-821-8145; Fax: 919-821-9733.

Chief Financial Officer/Chief Operating Officer—Mr. RUSSELL C. ELMAYAN, M.B.A., M.P.S., CFO, 715 Nazareth St., Raleigh, 27606. Tel: 919-821-9704.

Deans—Very Revs. SAMUEL JAMES BUCHHOLZ, V.F., Albemarle; WILLIAM J. UPAH, V.F., Piedmont; MARCOS LEON-ANGULO, V.F., Cape Fear; Rev. Msgr. JEFFREY A. INGHAM, V.F., Fayetteville; Very Revs. GREGORY D. SPENCER, V.F., New Bern; JAMES F. GARNEAU, V.F., Ph.D., Newton Grove Deanery; MARK G. REAMER, O.F.M., V.F., Raleigh; JUSTIN KERBER, C.P., V.F., Tar River.

Diocesan Attorney—CHARLES F. POWERS III, Mailing Address: P.O. Box 10096, Raleigh, 27605-0096. Tel: 919-783-1008.

Diocesan Consultors—Rev. Msgr. DAVID D. BROCKMAN, V.G., S.T.L., J.C.L.; Very Rev. JAMES F. GARNEAU, V.F., Ph.D.; Rev. Msgr. JEFFREY A. INGHAM, V.F.; Rev. ERNEST J. RUEDE; Rev. Msgrs. MICHAEL P. SHUGRUE; GIRARD M. SHERBA, V.J., J.C.D., Ph.D.; Rev. JOSEPH G. VETTER.

Diocesan Tribunal—2401 Crusader Dr., Raleigh, 27606. Tel: 919-821-9759. All rogatorial commissions should be directed to the Tribunal.

Vicar Judicial—Rev. Msgr. GIRARD M. SHERBA, V.J., J.C.D., Ph.D.

Adjutant Vicar Judicial—VACANT.

Defender of the Bond—Very Rev. STEPHEN SMITH, O.P., J.C.D.

Promoter of Justice—Rev. JOSEPH G. MULRONEY, J.C.L.

Diocesan Judges—Rev. Msgrs. THOMAS P. HADDEN (Retired); DAVID D. BROCKMAN, V.G., S.T.L., J.C.L.

Director of the Tribunal—Mrs. VIKKI NEWELL.

Notaries—Mrs. VIKKI NEWELL; Mrs. ANNE SPEICHER; SUSAN STANTON; Mrs. ANNE WOLFF.

Council of Priests—Very Rev. SAMUEL JAMES BUCHHOLZ, V.F.; Rev. Msgr. MICHAEL G. CLAY, D.Min.; Very Rev. JAMES F. GARNEAU, V.F., Ph.D.;

Rev. Msgr. JEFFREY A. INGHAM, V.F.; Very Revs. JUSTIN KERBER, C.P., V.F.; MARCOS LEON-ANGULO, V.F.; DANIEL D. OSCHWALD; MARK G. REAMER, O.F.M., V.F.; Rev. ERNEST J. RUEDE; Rev. Msgr. MICHAEL P. SHUGRUE; Revs. FERNANDO TORRES; JOSEPH G. VETTER; Very Revs. WILLIAM J. UPAH, V.F.; GREGORY D. SPENCER, V.F.; Revs. ROBERT M. HUSSEY, S.J.; DONALD F. STAIB; Rev. Msgr. JOHN A. WALL (Retired). Ex Officio: Rev. Msgrs. DAVID D. BROCKMAN, V.G., S.T.L., J.C.L.; GIRARD M. SHERBA, V.J., J.C.D., Ph.D.; Very Revs. CARLOS ARCE-FLORES, V.F.; STEPHEN SMITH, O.P., J.C.D.

Council of Women Religious—Sisters BARBARA MARIE CADY, S.U.; JOANNA WALSH, F.C.J.; MARY JEAN KOREJWO, S.N.D.; MARY AGNES RYAN, I.H.M.; Rev. Msgr. GIRARD M. SHERBA, V.J., J.C.D., Ph.D., Ex Officio; Sisters MARY ANN CZAJA, C.S.A.; CHRIS GELLINGS, I.H.M.; THERESINE GILDEA, C.D.P.; CAROL LOUGHNEY, I.H.M.; RITA PERL, S.N.D.; LOIS MACGILVRAY, S.N.J.M.; SHIRLEY SIMPSON, C.S.C.; KIERAN WILLIAMS, I.H.M.

Vicar for Priests—Very Rev. STEPHEN SMITH, O.P., J.C.D., Mailing Address: P.O. Box 12927, Raleigh, 27605. Tel: 919-833-1893; Fax: 919-833-1449.

Bishop's Delegate for Religious—Rev. Msgr. GIRARD M. SHERBA, V.J., J.C.D., Ph.D.

Diocesan Offices and Departments

All addresses are 715 Nazareth St., Raleigh, NC 27606 unless noted otherwise.

Business Services—MICHAEL D'ERCOLE, Dir. Tel: 919-821-9727.

Computer Services—Mr. JOHNALLAN TALLANT. Tel: 919-821-9719.

Stewardship and Advancement—Mr. TIMOTHY BRESLIN. Tel: 919-821-9721.

Property and Construction—Mr. ARTHUR WESCHE. Tel: 919-821-9726.

Catholic Charities of the Diocese of Raleigh, Inc.—Ms. KATHLEEN WALSH, M.S.W., A.C.S.W., Dir. Tel: 919-821-9752.

Catholic Formation and Education—Dr. MICHAEL J. FEDEWA, Ed.D., Supt. Tel: 919-821-9748.

Campus Ministry—Dr. MICHAEL J. FEDEWA, Ed.D., Dir., Office of Catholic Formation and Education, 715 Nazareth St., Raleigh, 27606.

Department of Catholic Formation and Evangelization—Sr. ROSE MARIE ADAMS, I.H.M., Dir. Tel: 919-821-9746.

Office of Catechesis and Faith Formation—MARY DISANO, Coord. Tel: 919-821-9710.

Office of Evangelization—Mr. ROBERT JONES. Tel: 919-821-9740.

Office of Lay Ministry Formation—Ms. BEATRICE CALLERY. Tel: 919-821-9715.

Office of Marriage and Family Life—Mrs. LINDA BEDO. Tel: 919-821-9753.

Youth and Young Adult Ministry—VACANT. Tel: 919-821-9770.

Communications—Mr. FRANK MOROCK, Dir. Tel: 919-821-9732.

NC Catholics Magazine—Mr. RICHARD REECE, Editor. Tel: 919-821-9736.

Web Administrator—Mrs. MICHELLE KING. Tel: 919-821-9737.

Ecumenical Commission—Bro. WILLIAM MARTYN, S.A. Tel: 919-847-8205.

Human Resources—GARY ROSIA, Dir. Tel: 919-821-9711.

Office of African Ancestry Ministry and Evangelization—Very Rev. MARCOS LEON-ANGULO, V.F., Vicar. Tel: 919-821-9762; Mrs. LAUREN M. GREEN, Dir. Tel: 919-821-9762.

Office for Child & Youth Protection—Dr. JOHN A. PENDERGRASS, Dir. Tel: 866-535-7233.

Office of Hispanic Ministry—Very Rev. CARLOS ARCE-FLORES, V.F., Vicar. Tel: 919-821-9738.

Office of Permanent Diaconate—Very Rev. JAMES F. GARNEAU, V.F., Ph.D., Dir., P.O. Box 1145, Mount Olive, 28365. Tel: 919-658-4023.

Office for Vocations and Seminarian Formation—Rev. BERNARD E. SHLESINGER III, Dir., 226 Hillsborough St., Raleigh, 27603. Tel: 919-832-6279.

Office of Divine Worship—Mr. GERARD T. HALL, Dir., 226 Hillsborough St., Raleigh, 27603. Tel: 919-832-6281.

Office of Pro-Life—JACKIE BONK. Tel: 919-645-4438.

Miscellaneous Offices—

Apostleship of the Sea—Rev. Msgr. FRANCIS R. MOESLEIN (Retired), 2106 Joslyn Dr., Morehead City, 28557-9200. Tel: 252-726-3579.

Censor Librorum—VACANT.

Holy Childhood Pontifical Association—Very Rev. ROBERT J. KUS, Dir., St. Mary Catholic Church, 412 Ann St., Wilmington, 28401. Tel: 910-762-5491.

Home Mission Society of the Diocese of Raleigh—Very Rev. JAMES F. GARNEAU, V.F., Ph.D., Dir., P.O. Box 1145, Mount Olive, 28365. Tel: 919-658-4023.

Pontifical Mission Societies in the United States—Very Rev. ROBERT J. KUS, Dir., St. Mary, 412 Ann St., Wilmington, 28401. Tel: 910-762-5491.

Victim Assistance Coordinator—Ms. KATHLEEN WALSH, M.S.W., A.C.S.W. Tel: 919-821-9752.

CLERGY, PARISHES, MISSIONS AND PAROCHIAL SCHOOLS

CITY OF RALEIGH

(WAKE COUNTY)

1—CATHEDRAL OF THE SACRED HEART (1834) Very Revs. Daniel D. Oschwald, Rector; Salvatore A. Busichio; Rev. Francisco Javier Garcia Gonzalez, Parochial Vicar; Deacon Michael Boyd Alig. In Res., Rev. Lourduraj Alapaty.
Office & Res.: 219 W. Edenton St., 27603-1724. Tel: 919-832-6030 (Office); 919-836-1790 (Res.); Fax: 919-833-4667. Web: www.sacredheartcathedral.org.
School—(Grades PreK-8), 204 Hillsborough St., 27603. Tel: 919-832-4711; Fax: 919-832-8329. Web: www.cathedral-school.net. Mrs. Donna Moss, Prin. Lay Teachers 15; Students 274.
Catechesis/Religious Program—Students 258.

2—CATHOLIC STUDENT CENTER, NORTH CAROLINA STATE UNIVERSITY (1974) Mailing Address: 600 Bilyeu St., 27606. Tel: 919-833-9668; Fax: 919-833-1194.
Doggett Center at Aquinas House—600 Bilyeu St., 27606. Tel: 919-833-9668; Fax: 919-833-1194. Rev. Anthony De Candia, Campus Min.

3—ST. FRANCIS OF ASSISI (1982) [CEM] Very Rev. Mark G. Reamer, O.F.M.; Revs. David J. McBriar, O.F.M.; William E. McConville, O.F.M.; Emmet Murphy, O.F.M.
Res.: 11401 Leesville Rd., 27613. Tel: 919-847-8205; Fax: 919-870-1790.
Early Childhood Learning Center—Nancy Bourke, Prin. Lay Teachers 26; Students 199.
School—The Franciscan School, 10000 St. Francis Dr. Fax: 919-847-9558. Web: www.franciscan-school.org. Jennifer Bigelow, Prin. Lay Teachers 46; Students 682.
Catechesis/Religious Program— Maureen Leahy, D.R.E. (Grades PreK-5, Faith Formation); Jennifer Fiduccia, D.R.E. (Middle School & High School Faith Formation). Students 1,027.

4—ST. JOSEPH (1968) Rev. Msgr. John J. Williams.
Office: 2817 Poole Rd., 27610. Tel: 919-231-6364; Fax: 919-231-9884.
Res.: 2809 Poole Rd., 27610.
Catechesis/Religious Program—Deborah Pergerson, D.R.E. Students 239.

5—ST. LUKE THE EVANGELIST (1985) Rev. Msgr. John F. O'Connor; Deacon Michael Sanchez.
Church & Res. Address: 12333 Bayleaf Church Rd., 27614-9165. Tel: 919-848-1533; Fax: 919-848-0662. Web: www.stluketheevangelist.org.
Catechesis/Religious Program—Tel: 919-848-3197. Students 237.

6—OUR LADY OF LOURDES (1954) [CEM] Revs. John J. Forbes III; David M. Chiantella, Parochial Vicar; Sr. Mary Agnes Ryan, I.H.M., Pastoral Assoc.; Deacons Myles J. Charlesworth; D. Thomas Mack; Dorthea Bitler, Dir. Devel. In Res., Very Rev. Carlos Arce-Flores.
Office: 2718 Overbrook Dr., 27608. Tel: 919-861-4600; Fax: 919-861-4620. Web: www.ourladyoflourdescc.org.
3600 Rock Creek Dr., 27608. Tel: 919-301-8322.
School—2710 Overbrook Dr., 27608. Tel: 919-861-4610; Fax: 919-861-4630. Dr. Robert Benjamin Scripko, Prin. Sisters of Notre Dame 2; Lay Teachers 23; Students 524.
Catechesis/Religious Program—Tel: 919-861-4614. Joan Samuels Rose, D.R.E. (Min. Faith Formation); Emily West, D.R.E. (Youth Ministry). Students 227.

7—ST. RAPHAEL THE ARCHANGEL (1966) [CEM] Revs. Robert M. Hussey, S.J.; Bruce Bavinger, S.J.; Michael Proterra, S.J.; Deacons Jorge Rodriguez; Hector Velazco.
Res.: 5801 Falls of Neuse Rd., 27609. Tel: 919-865-5700; Fax: 919-865-5701.
School—St. Raphael, 5815 Fall of Neuse Rd., 27609. Tel: 919-865-5750; Fax: 919-865-5751. Mr. Barry Thomas, Prin. Students 420.
St. Raphael Catholic Early Childhood Center—Carrie Griffith, Dir. Students 184.
Catechesis/Religious Program—Jeanne Lewin, D.R.E.; Andrea Beyrer, Youth Min. Coord. Students 648.

OUTSIDE THE CITY OF RALEIGH

AHOSKIE, HERTFORD CO., ST. CHARLES BORROMEO (1944) Rev. J. William Long.
Res.: P.O. Box 605, 27910. Tel: 252-332-2939.
Catechesis/Religious Program—Students 26.
Mission—St. Anne Scotland Neck, Halifax Co.

APEX, WAKE CO.

1—ST. ANDREW THE APOSTLE (1983) [CEM] Revs. David E. Fitzgerald, S.A.; Thomas Gumprecht, S.A.; Joseph Madden, O.F.M.Conv.
Res.: 304 Gentlewoods Dr., Cary, 27518. Tel: 919-303-7732. Email: standrewapex@aol.com. Web: www.saintandrew.org.
Church: 3008 Old Raleigh Rd., 27502. Tel: 919-362-0414; Fax: 919-362-5778. Email: standrewapex@aol.com. Web: www.saintandrew.org.
Catechesis/Religious Program—Tel: 919-362-0685. Katie Fortunato, D.R.E.; Cathy Rusin, Dir. Adult Formation & RCIA Coord.; Theresa Reed, Youth Min.; Cheryl Koller, Music Min.; Lucille T. Wargo, Admin. Students 983.

2—ST. MARY MAGDALENE (1997) Rev. Donald F. Staib.
625 Magdala Pl., 27502. Tel: 919-657-4800; Fax: 919-657-4805. Web: www.stmm.net.
School—625 Magdala Pl., 27502. Tel: 919-657-4800; Fax: 919-657-4805. Robert Cadran, Prin. Lay Teachers 56; Students 623.
Catechesis/Religious Program—Students 862.

BURGAW, PENDER CO., ST. JOSEPH (1908) [CEM] Rev. John Alex Gonzalez.
Church & Res.: 1303 Hwy. 117 S., 28425. Tel: 910-259-2601.
Catechesis/Religious Program—Evelyn McCreary, D.R.E., (St. Joseph); Jason Clark, D.R.E.; Frances Braks, D.R.E. (Transfiguration). Students 60.
Mission—Transfiguration (1953) 506 E. Main St., P.O. Box 1601, Wallace, Duplin Co. 28466. Tel: 910-285-1876.

BURLINGTON, ALAMANCE CO., BLESSED SACRAMENT (1929) Revs. Paul Gabriel, O.F.M.Conv.; Jacek K. Leszczynski, O.F.M.Conv.
Mailing Address: P.O. Box 619, 27216. Tel: 336-226-8796; Fax: 336-227-2896. Web: www.blessedsacramentnc.org. In Res., Revs. Briant Cullinane, O.F.M.Conv.; Gerald Waterman, O.F.M.Conv., Campus Min.
Res.: 514 Parkview Dr., 27215. Tel: 336-222-1401.
School—515 Hillcrest Ave., 27215. Tel: 336-570-0019; Fax: 336-570-9623. Mr. Salvatore Michael Trento, Prin. Lay Teachers 20; Students 176.
Catechesis/Religious Program—Students 558.

BUTNER, GRANVILLE CO., ST. BERNADETTE (1957) Sr. Carol Loughney, I.H.M., Pastoral Admin.
Parish House & Mailing Address: 311 Eleventh St., 27509. Tel: 919-575-4744; Fax: 919-575-4744. Web: mysite.verizon.net/st_bernadette.
Church: 804 West D. St., 27509. Tel: 919-575-4744; Fax: 919-575-4744. Email: st_bernadette@frontier.com.
Catechesis/Religious Program—Students 130.

BUXTON, DARE CO., OUR LADY OF THE SEAS (1935) Mission; Parish Erected (2002) Rev. Robert Brown, O.S.F.S.
Mailing Address: 48478 Hwy. 12, P.O. Box 399, 27920. Tel: 252-995-6613; Fax: 252-995-6398. Email: olssecretary@aol.com. Web: www.ourladyoftheseas.org.
Catechesis/Religious Program—Students 18.

CARY, WAKE CO., ST. MICHAEL THE ARCHANGEL (1962) Revs. Douglas Reed; Joseph Kalu Oji, C.S.Sp.; Jaime Perez Restrepo, Parochial Vicar; Bro. William Martyn, S.A.; Deacons Patrick Daniel Pelkey; Terry Mancuso.
Res.: 804 High House Rd., 27513. Tel: 919-468-6100; Fax: 919-468-6130. Email: office@stmichaelcary.org. Web: www.stmichaelcary.org.
School—810 High House Rd., 27513. Tel: 919-468-6150; Fax: 919-468-6160. Mr. John Yelenic, Prin.
Catechesis/Religious Program—Tel: 919-468-6174. Students 1,735.

CASTLE HAYNE, NEW HANOVER CO., ST. STANISLAUS (1914), (Polish), [CEM] Rev. Ryszard Kolodziej.
Church & Res.: 4849 Castle Hayne Rd., 28429-4849. Tel: 910-675-2336 (Office); Fax: 910-675-3116. Email: ststans4@ec.rr.com. Web: ststans-nc.org.
Catechesis/Religious Program—Students 42.

CHAPEL HILL, ORANGE CO.

1—NEWMAN CATHOLIC STUDENT CENTER, UNIVERSITY OF NORTH CAROLINA (1968) Rev. Msgr. John A. Wall (Retired).
Res.: 218 Pittsboro St., 27516-2738. Tel: 919-929-3730; Fax: 919-929-3778.
Catechesis/Religious Program—Students 163.

2—ST. THOMAS MORE (1940) Revs. Scott E. McCue; James M. Labosky, Parochial Vicar; Deacon Phil Rzewnicki; Mary Ellen McGuire, Pastoral Assoc.
Parish Offices—940 Carmichael St., 27514-4203. Tel: 919-942-1040; Fax: 919-942-6193. Web: church.st-thomasmore.org.
Res. (Parochial Vicar): 211 McCauley St., 27516. Tel: 919-240-4705.
Rectory—301 Rossburn Way, 27516. Tel:

919-967-8485.
School—(Grades K-8), 920 Carmichael St., 27514. Tel: 919-929-1546; Fax: 919-929-1783. Web: school.stthomasmore.org. Michael Ashton, Prin.; Joanna Williams, Librarian; Elaine Lopez, Librarian. Lay Teachers 36; Students 405.
Catechesis/Religious Program—Tel: 919-933-1041. Jim Hynes, Elementary Faith Formation & Adult Faith Educ.; Georgie Clemens, Total Youth Ministry; Annette Horlbeck, Junior Youth Ministry. Students 894.

CLAYTON, JOHNSTON CO., ST. ANN (1935) Rev. Msgr. Michael G. Clay.
Church: 4057 Hwy. 70 Business W., 27520. Tel: 919-934-2084; Fax: 919-934-4639. Web: www.st-annschurch.org.
Catechesis/Religious Program—Email: faithform.stann@yahoo.com. Students 481.

CLINTON, SAMPSON CO., IMMACULATE CONCEPTION (1910) Rev. Mark J. Betti.
104 E. John St., 28328. Tel: 910-592-1384; Fax: 910-299-0429.
Catechesis/Religious Program—Sr. Maxine Tancraitor, C.D.P., D.R.E. Students 123.
Mission—San Juan 1710 Old U.S. Hwy. 701, Ingold, Sampson Co.

DUNN, HARNETT CO., SACRED HEART (1916) Rev. Paul M. Parkerson.
Mailing Address: P.O. Box 535, 28335. Tel: 910-891-1972; Fax: 910-891-5767. Web: www.sacredheartdunnnc.org.
Res.: 311 S. Orange Ave., 28334. Tel: 910-892-3414; Fax: 910-891-5767.
Catechesis/Religious Program—Dr. Mary Ann Chiodo, D.R.E. Students 89.

DURHAM, DURHAM CO.
1—HOLY CROSS (1939), (African American), Rev. Raymond J. Donaldson, S.J.
Church: 2438 S. Alston Ave., 27713. Tel: 919-957-2900; Fax: 919-957-2901. Web: www.holycrossdurham.org.
Res.: 510 Massey Ave., 27701.
Catechesis/Religious Program—Tel: 919-957-2900, Ext. 22. Ava Thompson, D.R.E. Students 69.

2—HOLY INFANT (1970) [CEM] Rev. David J. Devlin, O.S.F.S.
Res.: 5000 Southpark Dr., 27713-9470. Tel: 919-544-7135; Fax: 919-544-1799. Email: lyndad@holyinfantchurch.org. Web: holyinfantchurch.org.
Catechesis/Religious Program—Tel: 919-544-7135, Ext. 18. Students 142.

3—IMMACULATE CONCEPTION (1906) Revs. Daniel McLellan, O.F.M.; Lawrence Hayes, O.F.M., Parochial Vicar; William McIntyre, O.F.M., Parochial Vicar; Deacon Laurence DeCarolis.
Mailing Address: 810 W. Chapel Hill St., 27701.
Res.: 720 Vickers Ave., 27701. Tel: 919-667-1722; Fax: 919-682-7999. Web: www.icdurham.org.
School—Immaculata, 721 Burch Ave., 27701. Tel: 919-682-5847; Fax: 919-956-7073. Dana Corcoran, Prin. Lay Teachers 32; Students 382.
Catechesis/Religious Program—Margie Burton, Youth Min. Students 1,282.

4—ST. MATTHEW (1990) [CEM] Rev. Thanh N. Nguyen.
Rectory—7 Timbercreek Ct., 27712. Tel: 919-471-0658; Fax: 919-479-4848.
Catechesis/Religious Program—Betsy Strauss, D.R.E.; John Toohil, Music Min. Students 126.

EDENTON, CHOWAN CO., ST. ANNE (1858) [CEM] Revs. William L. Pitts; Manuel Segundo Noriega, Parochial Vicar; Deacon Frank Taft Jones III.
Mailing Address: P.O. Box 422, 27932.
Church: 207 N. Broad St., 27932. Tel: 252-482-2617; Fax: 252-482-8702.
Catechesis/Religious Program—Students 34.
Mission—All Souls 917 Main St., Columbia, Tyrrell Co. 27925.

ELIZABETH CITY, PASQUOTANK CO., HOLY FAMILY (1915) Very Rev. Samuel James Buchholz.
Mailing Address: 1453 N. Road St., 27906-1525. Tel: 252-338-2521; Fax: 252-338-4183.
Res.: 1453 N. Road St., 27909. Tel: 252-335-4419.
Catechesis/Religious Program—Sharon Lupton, D.R.E. (Grades K-5); Cathy Terranova, D.R.E. (Grades 6-12); Carl Terranova, Youth Min. Students 93.
Mission—St. Katharine Drexel 154 Maple Rd., P.O. Box 64, Maple, Currituck Co. 27956. Tel: 252-453-6035.

FARMVILLE, PITT CO., ST. ELIZABETH OF HUNGARY (1931) Rev. Joseph J. Yaeger.
Mailing Address: 3447 S. Contentnea St., 27828-1686. Tel: 252-753-4367; Fax: 252-753-4400. Email: stelizabethnc@embarqmail.com. Web: www.dioceseofraleigh.org.
Catechesis/Religious Program—Rita Zalonis, C.R.E. Students 79.

FAYETTEVILLE, CUMBERLAND CO.
1—ST. ANDREW KIM (2000), (Korean), Rev. Seung Hoon Han.
1401 Valencia Dr., 28303. Tel: 910-630-2316; Fax: 910-487-8737.

2—ST. ANN (1939), (African American), Rev. Thomas Malloy, O.S.F.S.
Office: 357 N. Cool Spring St., 28301. Tel: 910-483-3216; Fax: 910-483-4185. Email: info@stanncatholicchurch.org. Web: www.stanncatholicchurch.org.
Res.: 228 Temple Ave., 28301. Tel: 910-483-5871.
School—(Grades PreK-8), 365 N. Cool Spring St., 28301. Tel: 910-483-3902; Fax: 910-483-3195. Email: principal@stanncatholicschool.org. Web: www.stanncatholicschool.org. N. Rene Corders, Prin. Lay Teachers 15; Students 173.
Catechesis/Religious Program—Tel: 910-488-7137; Fax: 910-483-4185. Kathy Flynn, D.R.E. Students 94.

3—ST. ELIZABETH ANN SETON (1981) Rev. John J. Kelly, O.S.F.S.
Res.: 700 Carnegie St., 28311. Tel: 910-488-1797; Fax: 910-488-7116. Web: seachurch.net.
Catechesis/Religious Program—John Bunting, D.R.E. Students 218.

4—ST. PATRICK (1824) Rev. Msgr. Michael P. Shugrue; Rev. Rafael A. Leon-Valencia, Parochial Vicar; Deacon Vincent Joseph Mescall.
Mailing Address: 2844 Village Dr., 28304-3813. Tel: 910-323-2410; Fax: 910-323-3006. Email: churchoffice@stpatnc.org. Web: stpatnc.org.
Res.: 433 Holly Ln., 28305. Tel: 910-484-8253.
School—1620 Marlborough Rd., 28304. Tel: 910-323-1865; Fax: 910-484-1573. Web: stpatrickschoolnc.org. Dr. Eric Westley, Prin. Lay Teachers 15; Students 236.
Catechesis/Religious Program—Tel: 910-323-2410, Ext. 107; Fax: 910-323-3006. Margaret Blanc, D.R.E. Students 402.

FUQUAY-VARINA, WAKE CO., ST. BERNADETTE (1987) [CEM] Revs. Fernando Torres; Robert P. Staley.
Mailing Address: 1005 Wilbon Rd., 27526-9702. Tel: 919-552-8758; Fax: 919-552-1846. Email: office@stbernadettechurch.org. Web: st-bernadettechurch.org.
Catechesis/Religious Program—Tel: 919-552-8758. Mrs. Michele Dexter, D.R.E. Students 740.
Social Outreach Office—Tel: 919-552-2922.

GARNER, WAKE CO., ST. MARY, MOTHER OF THE CHURCH (1966) Revs. Robert T. Schriber; Roger Malonda Nyimi, Parochial Vicar; Deacons Leo Tapler; Ronald Soriano.
Res.: 1008 Vandora Springs Rd., 27529. Tel: 919-772-5777; 919-772-5524 (Office); Fax: 919-772-5534. Email: smgoffice@stmarygarner.org. Web: www.stmarygarner.org.
Catechesis/Religious Program—Tel: 919-772-5199; Fax: 919-772-5534. Email: smgfaith@stmarygarner.org. Students 506.

GOLDSBORO, WAYNE CO., ST. MARY (1889) Rev. Thomas P. Norris, O.S.F.S.; Deacon Webster A. James.
Res.: 1000 N. Jefferson Ave., 27530-3141. Tel: 919-734-5033; Fax: 919-580-0730. Email: office@saintmarygoldsboro.org. Web: www.saintmarygoldsboro.org.
School—1601 Edgerton St., 27530-3181. Tel: 919-735-1931; Fax: 919-735-1917. Email: lynnmagoon@smsgoldsboro.org. Lynn E. Magoon, Prin. Lay Teachers 17; Students 240.
Catechesis/Religious Program—Tel: 919-734-5033, Ext. 22. Email: wjames408@earthlink.net. Students 159.

GREENVILLE, PITT CO.
1—ST. GABRIEL (1936) Rev. Michael A. Butler.
3250 Dickinson Ave., 27834.
Res.: 402 Trey Dr., 27834. Tel: 252-758-1504; Fax: 252-355-6128.
Catechesis/Religious Program—Students 169.

2—ST. PETER'S (1884) Very Rev. Justin Kerber, C.P.; Rev. Edward Wolanski, C.P.
Res.: 2700 E. Fourth St., 27858. Tel: 252-757-3259; Fax: 252-752-1499. Web: www.saintpetercatholicchurch.org.
School—Tel: 252-752-3529; Fax: 252-752-7604. Web: stpeterscatholicschool.com. Joseph A. Nelson, Prin. Lay Teachers 37; Students 556.
Catechesis/Religious Program—Tel: 252-757-3259, Ext. 204. Students 300.

HAMPSTEAD, PENDER CO., ST. JUDE THE APOSTLE (1992) Rev. John G. Durbin.
Mailing Address: 18737 Hwy. 17 N., 28443. Tel: 910-270-1477; Fax: 910-270-1424.
Res.: 557 Osprey Dr., 28443. Tel: 910-270-1689; Fax: 910-270-1424.
Catechesis/Religious Program—Tel: 910-270-1477. Students 130.
Mission—St. Mary, Gate of Heaven P.O. Box 2667, Surf City, Pender Co. 28445.

HAVELOCK, CRAVEN CO., ANNUNCIATION (1953) [CEM] Very Rev. Gregory D. Spencer; Deacon Walter Calabrese.
Mailing Address: 246 E. Main St., 28532-0720. Tel: 252-447-2112; Fax: 252-447-2113. Web: annunciationparish.org.
School—(Grades PreK-8) Tel: 252-447-3137; Fax: 252-447-3138. Mrs. Susan Parks, Prin. Lay Teachers 10; Students 97.
Catechesis/Religious Program—Mrs. Marlene Rink, D.R.E. Students 167.

HENDERSON, VANCE CO., ST. JAMES (1995) [CEM] [JC] Consolidated St. Paul and St. Catherine of Siena, Oxford merged to form St. James. Very Rev. William J. Upah.
Res.: 3275 Hwy. 158 Bypass, 27536. Tel: 252-438-3124; Fax: 252-438-3214.
Catechesis/Religious Program—Students 96.
Mission—St. Joseph Norlina Rd., Warrenton, Warren Co. 27589. Tel: 252-438-3124.

HILLSBOROUGH, ORANGE CO., HOLY FAMILY (1989) Rev. Thomas S. Tully.
Mailing Address: 216 Governor Burke Rd., 27278. Tel: 919-732-1030; Fax: 919-732-7852.
Rectory—2120 Rhonda Rd., 27278. Tel: 919-732-7265.
Catechesis/Religious Program—Students 199.

HOPE MILLS, CUMBERLAND CO., GOOD SHEPHERD (1981) Revs. Thomas R. Davis, Admin.; Thomas J. Gaul, Pastor Emeritus (Retired).
Res.: 5050 Oak St., 28348. Tel: 910-425-1590; Fax: 910-423-9973. Email: gdshprd1@earthlink.net. Web: www.good-shepherd-church.org.
Catechesis/Religious Program—Tel: 910-425-5617. Janice Carnahan, D.R.E. Students 211.
Mission—St. Isidore 8569 Clinton Rd., Stedman, Cumberland Co. 28391. Tel: 910-424-2698.

JACKSONVILLE, ONSLOW CO., SHRINE OF THE INFANT OF PRAGUE, CHURCH OF THE HOLY SPIRIT (1941) Revs. Ernest J. Ruede; Jeffrey Bowker, L.C., Parochial Vicar.
Mailing Address: 205 Chaney Ave., 28540. Tel: 910-347-4196; Fax: 910-347-9338. Email: iop1@ec.rr.com. Web: iopnc.org.
Res.: 330 Mildred Ave., 28540. Tel: 910-347-8881.
School—501 Bordeaux St., 28540. Tel: 910-353-1300; 910-455-0838; Fax: 910-455-0270. Monette Mahoney, Interim Prin. Lay Teachers 16; Religious Male 1; Students 140.
Catechesis/Religious Program—Tel: 910-455-1296. Email: faithdevelopment.iop@gmail.com. Mrs. Anne Mauthe, D.R.E. Students 380.

KINSTON, LENOIR CO., HOLY SPIRIT CATHOLIC CHURCH (1921), (Formerly Holy Trinity-Our Lady of the Atonement) Rev. Bill John Acosta-Escobar.
Mailing Address: P.O. Box 1455, 28503-1455. Tel: 252-523-8898; Fax: 252-527-9495.
Res.: 137 Rae Rd., 28504. Tel: 252-523-4377.
Church: 400 Academy Heights Rd., 28504. Tel: 252-523-8898; Fax: 252-523-9495. Email: holyspirit@suddenlinkmail.com.
Catechesis/Religious Program—Pat Kaspryzk, D.R.E. Students 186.

KITTY HAWK, DARE CO., HOLY REDEEMER BY THE SEA (1937) Rev. William F. Walsh, O.S.F.S.
Mailing Address: P.O. Box 510, 27949. Tel: 252-261-4700; Fax: 252-261-1405. Email: info@obxcatholicparish.org. Web: obxcatholicparish.org.
Office: 301 W. Kitty Hawk Rd., 27949.
Res.: 109 Sunrise View, 27949. Tel: 252-261-2728.
Catechesis/Religious Program—Tel: 252-261-4700; Fax: 252-261-1405. Students 127.
Mission—Holy Trinity by the Sea Catholic Nags Head, Dare Co. 27959. Tel: 252-261-1168.

LAURINBURG, SCOTLAND CO., ST. MARY (1946) [JC] Rev. JaVan Saxon.
Mailing Address: P.O. Box 1148, 28353-1148. Tel: 910-276-4468; Fax: 910-276-9519.
Catechesis/Religious Program—Students 42.

LOUISBURG, FRANKLIN CO., OUR LADY OF THE ROSARY (1999) Rev. Johanes Teguh Raharjo, C.I.C.M., Admin.; Deacon Patrick Gerald McIlmoyle.
Church: 460 Fox Park Rd., 27549. Tel: 919-340-0556; Fax: 919-340-0556.
Catechesis/Religious Program—Students 75.

LUMBERTON, ROBESON CO., ST. FRANCIS DE SALES (1938) Rev. John Gillespie; Deacon Juan Alexander Vicent Martinez.
Mailing Address: 2000 Elizabethtown Rd., P.O. Box 2249, 28358. Tel: 910-739-4723; Fax: 910-739-5443.
Res.: 2000 Elizabethtown Rd., 28358.
Catechesis/Religious Program—Tel: 910-739-4713. Students 136.

MOREHEAD CITY, CARTERET CO., ST. EGBERT (1929) Rev. Douglas J. Smiley; Rev. Msgr. Francis R. Moeslein, Pastor Emeritus (Retired).
Parish Hall—1706 Evans St., 28557. Tel: 252-726-3559; Fax: 252-726-2232.
Res.: 1612 Evans St., 28557. Tel: 252-726-2535.
School—1705 Evans St., 28557. Tel: 252-726-3418; Fax: 252-727-0150. Mr. John J. Donohue, Prin. Lay Teachers 9; Students 81.
Catechesis/Religious Program—Joseph McKenzie, D.R.E. Students 89.

MOUNT OLIVE, DUPLIN CO., MARIA, REINA DE LAS AMERICAS, (Mary, Queen of the Americas) Revs.

Edgar Sepulveda (Colombia); Martin Restrepo.
Mailing Address: P.O. Box 332, Kenansville, 28349.
Res.: 208 Cavenaugh St., Beulaville, 28518.
Church: 636 Whitfield Rd., 28365.
Mission—St. Teresa del Nino Jesus 206 Cavenaugh St., Beulaville, Duplin Co. 28518.

MOUNT OLIVE, WAYNE CO., ST. MARY OF THE ANGELS (1916) [CEM] [JC] Very Rev. James F. Garneau; Deacon Felix Saez Jr.
Mailing Address: P.O. Box 1145, 28365. Tel: 919-658-4023; Fax: 919-658-4023.
Catechesis/Religious Program—Students 110.

NEW BERN, CRAVEN CO., ST. PAUL (1821) [CEM] Rev. Msgr. Gerald L. Lewis, Admin. (Retired); Rev. John Victor Gournas; Deacons Frederick Melvin Fisher Jr.; Michael A. Mahoney; Sisters Monique Dissen, I.H.M., Pastoral Assoc.; Grace Campbell, I.H.M., Pastoral Assoc.
Rectory—3108 Farrior Cir., 28562. Tel: 252-638-4436.
Church: 3005 Country Club Rd., 28562. Tel: 252-638-1984; Fax: 252-638-2144. Email: stpaulcatholicchurch@suddenlinkmail.com. Web: www.stpaulccnewbern.org.
School—St. Paul Catholic School, (Grades PreK-8), 3007 Country Club Rd., 28562. Tel: 252-633-0100; Fax: 252-633-4457. Email: info@stpaulcs.org. Web: stpaulcs.org. Ms. Catherine Warwick, Prin.; Kathleen Fisher, Librarian. Lay Teachers 17; Students 155.
Catechesis/Religious Program—Joy Harsen, D.R.E. (Elementary); Sr. Maria Goretti Timpiero, D.R.E. Students 177.

NEW HILL, WAKE CO., ST. HA-SANG PAUL JUNG (1988) Rev. Chul Ho Lee (Archdiocese of Seoul, Korea).
2340 New Hill Olive Chapel Rd., 27562. Tel: 919-303-6424. Web: www.tkcc.org.
Catechesis/Religious Program—

NEWTON GROVE, SAMPSON CO., OUR LADY OF GUADALUPE (1871) [CEM] Rev. Patrick A. Keane.
Office:—P.O. Box 100, 28366. Tel: 910-594-0287; Fax: 910-594-1749. Email: olog@embarqmail.com.
Res.: 211 Irwin Dr., 28366. Tel: 910-594-0152.
Catechesis/Religious Program—Students 314.

ORIENTAL, PAMLICO CO., SAINT PETER THE FISHERMAN (2000) Unassigned. Mission of St. Paul, New Bern.
Church: 1149 White Farm Rd., 28571. Tel: 252-249-3687; Fax: 252-249-0349. Email: stpeteronc@embarqmail.com.
Catechesis/Religious Program—Students 6.

PINEHURST, MOORE CO., SACRED HEART (1919) Revs. Edward Burch; Gregory Anatuanya, Parochial Vicar.
Mailing Address: P.O. Box 1768, 28370. Tel: 910-295-6550; Fax: 910-255-0299. Email: sacredheart@pinehurst.net. Web: sacredheartpinehurst.org.
Early Childhood Center—P.O. Box 5269, 28374. Tel: 910-295-3514. Stephanie Hinds, Dir.
Catechesis/Religious Program—Tel: 910-295-3072; Fax: 910-255-0299. Mrs. Barbara Kemple, D.R.E. Students 202.
Mission—Saint Juan Diego 6963 Hwy. 705 S., Robbins, Moore Co. 27325. Tel: 910-948-4100; Fax: 910-948-4101. Rev. Rodolfo Gonzalez, Admin.

PLYMOUTH, WASHINGTON CO., ST. JOAN OF ARC (1959) Sr. Arcadia Rivera Gutierrez, D.S.M.G., Pastoral Admin.
Mailing Address: P.O. Box 822, 27962. Tel: 252-793-4052; Fax: 252-793-5315.
506 E. Main St., 27962. Email: stjoanofarcparish@mchsi.com.
Catechesis/Religious Program—Fax: 252-793-5315. Students 66.

RAEFORD, HOKE CO., ST. ELIZABETH OF HUNGARY (1959) Sr. Elizabeth Bullen, I.H.M., Pastoral Admin.
P.O. Box 665, 28376-0665. Tel: 910-875-8803; Fax: 910-875-8802. Email: stelizabethofhungaryraeford@yahoo.com. Web: www.stelizabethofhungary.net.
Catechesis/Religious Program—Students 172.

RED SPRINGS, ROBESON CO., ST. ANDREW Rev. Fernando Melendez, Admin.
Mailing Address: P.O. Box 649, 28377. Tel: 910-843-3440; Fax: 910-843-5700. Email: standrewrs@embarqmail.com.
Res.: 518 S. Main St., 28377. Tel: 910-843-6828.
Church: 301 Mercer Ave., 28377.
Station—Our Lady of Mount Carmel Saint Pauls, 28384.

RIEGELWOOD, COLUMBUS CO., CHRIST THE KING (1964), (Hispanic), Revs. Steven V. Carlson; Marco Antonio Gonzalez-Hernandez, Parochial Vicar.
Mailing Address: 1011 Eastwood Rd., Wilmington, 28403. Tel: 910-392-0720; Fax: 910-392-6777.
Catechesis/Religious Program—Wick Westmoreland, D.R.E. Students 11.

ROANOKE RAPIDS, HALIFAX CO., ST. JOHN THE BAPTIST (1931) [CEM] Rev. Pius S. Wekesa, Admin.
Res.: 71 Dalton Ct., 27870. Tel: 252-537-4667; Fax: 252-535-2076. Email: stjohnbaptist@embarqmail.com.
Catechesis/Religious Program—Teri Bales, D.R.E. Students 66.
Station—Immaculate Conception King St., Halifax, 27839.

ROCKY MOUNT, NASH & EDGECOMBE COS., OUR LADY OF PERPETUAL HELP (1892) Rev. Clyde Timberlake Meares.
Mailing Address: 328 Hammond St., 27804. Tel: 252-972-0452; Fax: 252-972-4780.
Res.: 501 Hammond St., 27804. Tel: 252-972-1949; Fax: 252-972-4780.
School—(Grades PreK-8), 315 Hammond St., 27804. Tel: 252-972-1971; Fax: 252-972-7831. Mrs. Connie Urbanski, Prin. Lay Teachers 12; Students 129.
Catechesis/Religious Program—Tel: 252-972-0498. Dianne Young, D.R.E. Students 155.
Mission—Immaculate Conception 721 Virginia Ave., Nash & Edgecombe Cos. 27804.

ROXBORO, PERSON CO., STS. MARY AND EDWARD (1935) Rev. William H. Rodriguez.
Res.: 611 N. Main St., 27573-5040. Tel: 336-599-4122 (Office); Fax: 336-598-0412.
Catechesis/Religious Program—Students 43.

SANFORD, LEE CO., ST. STEPHEN THE FIRST MARTYR (1932) [CEM] Rev. Msgr. Stephen C. Worsley; Deacons Emilio Mejia; Mark Alan Westrick.
901 N. Franklin Dr., 27330.
Res.: Tel: 919-776-1532. Email: secretaryststephen@earthlink.net. Web: www.ststephensch.net.
Catechesis/Religious Program—Students 307.

SHALLOTTE, BRUNSWICK CO., ST. BRENDAN THE NAVIGATOR (1983) [JC] Revs. Robert F. Ippolito, M.S.; Hector LaChapelle, M.S.; Deacons A. R. McGahran; Thomas Kronyak.
Mailing Address: Box 2984, 28459-9999. Tel: 910-754-8544; Fax: 910-755-6046. Email: brenavigator@atmc.net. Web: saintbrendan-shallotte.org.
Church & Office: 5101 Ocean Hwy. W., 28459.
Catechesis/Religious Program—Tel: 910-754-8544. Students 120.

SILER CITY, CHATHAM CO., ST. JULIA (1961), (Spanish), Rev. James Fukes, O.F.M.Conv.
Mailing Address: 210 Harold Hart Rd., 27344. Tel: 919-742-5584; Fax: 919-742-4917. Web: www.saintjulia.org.
Catechesis/Religious Program—Students 284.

SMITHFIELD, JOHNSTON CO., ST. ANN (1935) See new location under Clayton, NC.

SOUTHERN PINES, MOORE CO., ST. ANTHONY OF PADUA (1895) [CEM] Rev. Msgr. Jeffrey A. Ingham; Deacon Joseph Pius Piyasiri Gabriel.
Mailing Address: P.O. Box 29, 28388-0029. Tel: 910-692-6613; Fax: 910-692-4964.
Rectory—2952 Camp Easter Rd., 28387. Tel: 910-692-9847; Fax: 910-692-4964. Email: office@st-anthony-of-padua.org. Web: www.st-anthony-of-padua.org.
School—(Grades PreK-8), 2922 Camp Easter Rd., 28387-0029. Tel: 910-692-6241; Fax: 910-692-2286. Email: kstepnoski@jp2catholicschool.org. Web: www.jp2catholicschool.org. Dr. Richard Kruska, Prin. Lay Teachers 16; Students 180.
Catechesis/Religious Program—Tel: 910-692-6613. Email: dwake@st-anthony-of-padua.org. Students 196.

SOUTHPORT, BRUNSWICK CO., SACRED HEART (1941) Rev. Trent L. Watts; Patricia Ciemnicki, Dir. Pastoral Svcs.
Mailing Address: 5269 Dosher Cutoff, S.E., 28461. Tel: 910-457-6173; Fax: 910-457-6421.
Res.: 213 Yaupon Dr., 28461. Tel: 910-457-0223.
Catechesis/Religious Program—Tel: 910-457-6173. Patricia Novotny, D.R.E. Students 89.

SWANSBORO, ONSLOW CO., ST. MILDRED (1947) [CEM] Rev. Donald G. Baribeau, M.S.
Res.: 616 Sabiston Dr., 28584-9674. Tel: 910-340-2765; Fax: 910-326-5589. Web: www.stmildred.info. Email: srectory@ec.rr.com.
Catechesis/Religious Program—Tel: 910-326-5589. Francine Sabisch, D.R.E. Students 198.

TARBORO, EDGECOMBE CO., ST. CATHERINE OF SIENA (1897) Rev. Frank M. Raffo.
Res.: 1004 St. David St., 27886. Tel: 252-823-3866; Fax: 252-824-0412.
Catechesis/Religious Program—

WAKE FOREST, WAKE CO., ST. CATHERINE OF SIENA (1940) Revs. Philip M. Tighe; Brendan Joseph Buckler, Parochial Vicar; Deacon Bradley Evans Watkins.
Church: 520 W. Holding Ave., 27587. Tel: 919-570-0070; Fax: 919-570-0071. Web: www.saintcatherinesienawf.org.
School—Christina Preskenis, Prin.
Catechesis/Religious Program—Tel: 919-570-0070, Ext. 108. Email: sgammon@saintcatherinesienawf.org. Susan Gammon, D.R.E. Students 1,178.
Early Childhood Center—Tel: 919-556-4104. Mary Jane Haga, Dir.

WASHINGTON, BEAUFORT CO., MOTHER OF MERCY (1963) Rev. M. Arturo Cabra.
112 W. 9th St., 27889.
Res.: 412 Crown Dr., 27889. Tel: 252-946-1792; Fax: 252-946-1399. Email: office@momchurch.org.
Church: 111 W. Ninth St., 27889. Tel: 252-946-2941.
Catechesis/Religious Program—Tel: 919-946-0769. Dana Lawson, D.R.E. Students 129.

WENDELL, WAKE CO., ST. EUGENE (1948) Revs. Joseph A. Lapauw, C.I.C.M.; Ryan Z. Carnecer, C.I.C.M., Parochial Vicar; Deacon Willie Foggie.
Mailing Address: 608 Lions Club Rd., P.O. Box 188, 27591. Tel: 919-365-7114; Fax: 919-365-9431. Email: steugeneoffice@gmail.com. Web: www.steugeneparish.org.
Catechesis/Religious Program— Trish Clemmer, D.R.E. Students 311.
Mission—Our Lady of the Rosary 460 Fox Park Rd., Louisburg, 27549. Tel: 919-340-0556; Fax: 919-340-0556. Email: olrcatholic@gmail.com.

WHITEVILLE, COLUMBUS CO., SACRED HEART (1938) Very Rev. Marcos Leon-Angulo.
Res.: 302 N. Lee St., 28472. Tel: 910-642-3895; Fax: 910-640-1948.
Catechesis/Religious Program—Students 111.
Mission—Our Lady of the Snows 701 W. Broad St., P.O. Box 1766, Elizabethtown, Bladen Co. 28337-1766. Tel: 910-862-4998; Fax: 910-862-7298. Email: olsnw736@earthlink.net.

WILLIAMSTON, MARTIN CO., HOLY TRINITY (1951) Sr. Kieran Williams, I.H.M., Pastoral Admin.
Mailing Address: P.O. Box 894, 27892-0894. Tel: 252-792-4091; Fax: 252-792-4091.
Church: 3751 Bear Grass Rd., 27892.
Catechesis/Religious Program—Students 57.

WILMINGTON, NEW HANOVER CO.

1—IMMACULATE CONCEPTION (1925) Rev. John E. McGee, O.S.F.S.
Church: 6650 Carolina Beach Rd., 28412. Tel: 910-791-1003; Fax: 910-791-0081.
Catechesis/Religious Program—Students 279.

2—ST. MARK (1978) Revs. Steven V. Carlson; Marco Antonio Gonzalez-Hernandez; Deacon Orlando Perez.
Church & Office: 1011 Eastwood Rd., 28403. Tel: 910-392-0720, Ext. 226; Fax: 910-392-6777. Email: vicar@stmarkcatholicchurch.com. Web: www.stmarkcatholicchurch.com.
School—1013 Eastwood Rd., 28403-1905. Tel: 910-452-2800, Ext. 239; Fax: 910-332-6505. Web: www.stmarkcatholicschool.org. Marguerite DiFulvio, Prin.
Catechesis/Religious Program—Tel: 910-392-0792, Ext. 229. Email: ffy@stmarkcatholicchurch.com. Ms. Anne Doyle, D.R.E. Students 394.
Mission—Christ the King 100 Burns Rd., Riegelwood, Columbus Co. 28456-0155.

3—ST. MARY (1912) Very Rev. Robert J. Kus.
Res.: 412 Ann St., 28401-4592. Tel: 910-762-5491; Fax: 910-762-9664. Email: secretary@thestmaryparish.org. Web: thestmaryparish.org.
School—217 S. 4th, 28401. Fax: 910-772-8034. Lay Teachers 17; Students 240; Pre-K 30.
Catechesis/Religious Program—Students 221.

WILSON, WILSON CO.

1—ST. ALPHONSUS DE LIGUORI, Closed. For sacramental records contact St. Therese, Wilson.

2—CHURCH OF ST. THERESE (1923) Revs. Gregory Lowchy; Paul W. Brant, S.J.; Deacon Michel du Sablon.
Church & Office: 700 Nash St., N.E., 27893-3047. Tel: 252-237-3019; Fax: 252-237-2042. Email: wilsonsttherese@embarqmail.com.
Catechesis/Religious Program—Tel: 252-237-3019. Students 274.

WINDSOR, BERTIE CO., CATHOLIC COMMUNITY OF BERTIE COUNTY (2004) Rev. Michael J. Kerin, G.H.M.
Mailing Address: 403 Belmont St., P.O. Box 1394, 27983. Tel: 252-794-5086. Web: bertienccatholicweb.com.
Catechesis/Religious Program—Deana Orbita, D.R.E. Students 15.

WRIGHTSVILLE BEACH, NEW HANOVER CO., ST. THERESE (1939) Rev. Joseph G. Vetter; Deacons James F. Welch; James McCann; Sr. Catherine Michael Fee, S.S.J., Pastoral Assoc.
209 S. Lumina Ave., 28480.
Res.: Tel: 910-256-2471; Fax: 910-256-2459.
Catechesis/Religious Program—Students 92.

Special Assignment:
Revs.—
Acero, Roman A., Cardinal Gibbons High School, 1401 Edwards Mill Rd., 27607.
Shlesinger, Bernard E., III, 226 Hillsborough St., 27603. Tel: 919-832-6279

On Duty Outside the Diocese:
Rev.—
Fitzgerald, R. Martin, Chap. Major, PSC 2, Box 326, Apo, AP 96264.

Absent on Leave:
Revs.—
Drozdzik, Roch T. (Poland)
Mulroney, Joseph G., J.C.L.
Ospina-Briceno, Walter
Spurr, Michael R.

Retired:
Most Rev.—
Gossman, F. Joseph, D.D., J.C.D., 715 Nazareth St., 27606.
Rev. Msgrs.—
Hadden, Thomas P., 2651 Mellow Field Dr., #107, 27604. Tel: 919-838-6907
Hendrick, Matthew D., 590 Central Dr., Apt. C-5, Southern Pines, 28387.
Keenan, Desmond R., 7901 Hinton Rd., Wake Forest, 27587.
Leach, Phillip, 202-1835 Barclay St., Vancouver BC V6G 1K7 Canada.
Lewis, Gerald L., 3005 Country Club Rd., New Bern, 28562. Tel: 919-376-3911
Moeslein, Francis R., 2106 Joslyn Dr., Morehead City, 26557-9200. Tel: 252-726-3579
Wall, John A., Student Center, 218 Pittsboro St., Chapel Hill, 27516-2738.
Revs.—
Butler, James, 5758 Three Oaks Dr., 27612. Tel: 919-787-3049
Collins, Terrence
Dash, Alan J., 6702 Rushwood Ct., Wilmington, 28405. Tel: 910-452-0547
Diegelman, Robert W.
Dorsel, John F., P.O. Box 1881, Pinehurst, 28374. Tel: 910-295-2085
Gaul, Thomas J., 5407 Gales St., Hope Mills, 28348. Tel: 910-426-3728
Ghisalberti, Giacomo G., P.O. Box 70338, Myrtle Beach, SC 29572.
Grabowski, Eugene M., 116 Sutton Dr., Cape Carteret, 28584. Tel: 252-762-3330
Kelly, John R., 779 Galloway Dr., Fayetteville, 28303. Tel: 910-867-2803
Lawson, Douglas J., 1449 South Shore Dr., Southport, 28461. Tel: 910-845-2353
Maloney, Francis G., 590 Central Ave., Villa F.3, Southern Pines, 28387. Tel: 910-246-2123
Parker, Kenneth, 704 McIntosh Rd., Carthage, 28327. Tel: 910-245-4640
Perry, Francis, P.O. Box 506, La Grange, 28551.
Richardson, John L., 592 Central Dr., Villa F., Southern Pines, 28387. Tel: 910-579-8270
Shea, Robert F., 590 Central Ave., Villa F.4, Southern Pines, 28387. Tel: 910-246-0471
Turner, Richard W., P.O. Box 1039, Spring Hope, 27882. Tel: 252-475-3360
Woodhall, Jonathan A., 317-307 W. Morgan St., 27601-1471. Tel: 919-412-3388

Permanent Deacons:
Alig, Michael Boyd, Sacred Heart Cathedral
Calabrese, Walter, Annunciation, Havelock
Charlesworth, Myles, Our Lady of Lourdes, Raleigh
Cortright, William, St. Elizabeth of Hungary, Raeford
DeCarolis, Lawrence, Immaculate Conception, Durham
du Sablon, Michael, St. Therese, Wilson
Evans, Forest, Holy Family, Hillsborough
Fatica, Gerald, St. Mildred, Swansboro
Feneis, Al, St. Egbert, Morehead City
Fisher, Frederick Melvin, Jr., St. Paul, New Bern
Foggie, Willie, St. Eugene, Wendell
Gabriel, Joseph Pius Piyasiri, St. Anthony of Padua, Southern Pines
Henriquez, Juan "Nay", St. Isidore Mission, Stedman
Hoffert, Daniel, St. Andrew the Apostle, Apex
Hubisz, John
Hunt, William, St. Paul, New Bern
James, Webster A., St. Mary, Goldsboro
Jones, Frank Taft, III, St. Anne, Edenton
Kronyak, Thomas
Lacina, Dick, (Retired)
LaPierre, Joseph, (Unassigned)
Leahy, Michael, Holy Infant, Durham
Lewandowski, Stephen, St. Joseph, Raleigh
Mack, Tom, Holy Infant, Durham
Mancuso, Terry, St. Michael the Archangel, Cary
McGahran, Robert, St. Brendan, Shallotte
McIlmoyle, Patrick Gerald, Our Lady of the Rosary, Louisburg
Meier, Anthony, St. Bernadette, Fuquay-Varina
Mejia, Emiliio, St. Stephen the First Martyr, Sanford
Mescall, Vincent Joseph, St. Patrick, Fayetteville
Mirande, Mike, Sacred Heart, Pinehurst
Pelkey, Patrick Daniel, St. Michael the Archangel, Cary
Porter, Thomas, St. Anthony of Padua, Southern Pines
Price, Robert, (Unassigned)
Rodriguez, Jorge, (Unassigned)
Rzewnicki, Phil, St. Thomas More, Chapel Hill
Saez, Felix, Jr., St. James, Henderson
Sanchez, Michael, St. Luke the Evangelist, Raleigh
Schoebel, James, Ft. Bragg, Fayetteville
Snyder, Patrick, Good Shepherd, Hope Mills
Soriano, Ronald, St. Mary, Mother of the Church, Garner
Stonikinis, George, Holy Family, Elizabeth City
Tapler, Leopold, St. Mary, Garner
Velazco Bonilla, Hector, St. Raphael the Archangel, Raleigh
Vicent Martinez, Juan Alexander, St. Francis de Sales, Lumberton
Waldmann, William, Immaculate Conception, Durham
Walsh, Michael, St. Ann, Clayton
Watkins, Bradley Evans, St. Catherine of Siena, Wake Forest
Welch, James, St. Therese, Wrightsville Beach
Westrick, Mark Alan, St. Stephen the First Martyr, Sanford
Whitfield, Robert, St. Peter the Fisherman, Oriental
Wobser, Don, Holy Redeemer, Kitty Hawk

INSTITUTIONS LOCATED IN THE DIOCESE

[A] HIGH SCHOOLS

RALEIGH. *Cardinal Gibbons High School* (1909) 1401 Edwards Mill Rd., 27607. Tel: 919-834-1625; Fax: 919-834-9771. Email: ajay@cghsnc.org. Web: www.cghsnc.org. Mr. Jason D. Curtis, Prin.; Dale Foushee, Librarian & Media Specialist. Priests 1; Sisters 3; Lay Teachers 76; Students 1,240; Total Faculty & Staff 120.

GREENVILLE. *John Paul II Catholic High School*, 3250A Dickinson Ave., 27834. Tel: 252-565-2175; 252-215-1224. Glenn M. Joyner, Dir. Lay Teachers 12.

[B] HIGH SCHOOLS-PRIVATE

RALEIGH. *St. Thomas More Academy*, 3109 Spring Forest Rd., 27616. Tel: 919-878-7640; Fax: 919-878-7641. Email: admissions@stmacademy.org. Web: www.stmacademy.org. Deacon Bradley Evans Watkins, Headmaster. Deacons 1; Full-time teachers 8; Part-time teachers 4; Students 150.

[C] CHILD CARE CENTERS

RALEIGH. *St. Joseph Pre-School*, 2817 Poole Rd., 27610. Tel: 919-231-4545; Fax: 919-231-9884. Email: mshaughn@nc.rr.com. Mrs. Marjorie Shaughnessy, Dir. Students 18.

St. Raphael Catholic School and Early Childhood Center, 5801 Falls of the Neuse Rd., 27609. Tel: 919-865-5750; Fax: 919-865-5701. Mr. Barry Thomas, Prin.; Carrie Griffith, Exec. Dir. Lay Teachers 24; Students 188.

APEX. *Saint Andrew Early Childhood Center*, 3008 Old Raleigh Rd., 27502. Tel: 919-387-8656; Fax: 919-362-5778. Email: ecc@saintandrew.org. Web: www.saintandrewecc.org; www.saintandrew.org. Ann Graf, Prin. Total Staff 20; Students 115.

CARY. *St. Michael Early Childhood Center* (1983) 804 High House Rd., 27513. Tel: 919-468-6110; Fax: 919-468-6130. Email: mtoscano@stmichaelcary.org. Web: www.stmichaelcary.org. Mrs. Marianna Toscano, Dir. Total Staff 21; Students 160.

[D] GENERAL HOSPITALS

SOUTHERN PINES. *St. Joseph of the Pines*, 100 Gossman Dr., Ste. B, 28387. Tel: 910-246-3100; Fax: 910-246-3187. Email: aholt@sjp.org. Web: www.sjp.org. Ms. Anita L. Holt, Pres. & CEO.
St. Joseph of the Pines, Inc. Bed Capacity 392; Total Staff 300.

[E] CATHOLIC SOCIAL SERVICES

RALEIGH. *Catholic Charities of the Diocese of Raleigh, Inc.*, 715 Nazareth St., 27606-2187. Tel: 919-821-9750; Fax: 919-821-9712. Web: catholiccharitiesraleigh.org. Ms. Kathleen Walsh, M.S.W., A.C.S.W., Diocesan Dir. Total Staff 52; Total Assisted 56,153.

Raleigh Office, 3000 Highwoods Blvd., Ste. 128, 27604. Tel: 919-790-8533; Fax: 919-790-8836. Rick Miller-Haraway, L.C.S.W.

Cape Fear Office, 4006 Princess Pl. Dr., Wilmington, 28405. Tel: 910-251-8130; Fax: 910-251-8491. Linda M. Chance, L.C.S.W.

Piedmont Office, 902 Broad St., P.O. Box 647, Durham, 27702. Tel: 919-286-1964; Fax: 919-286-4001. Susan Gilbertson, L.C.S.W.

Fayetteville Office, 590 Cedar Creek Rd. Ste. 110, Fayetteville, 28312-6097. Tel: 910-424-2020; Fax: 910-424-8435. Lisa E. Perkins, P-L.C.S.W.

New Bern Office, 502 Middle St., P.O. Box 826, New Bern, 28563. Tel: 252-638-2188; Fax: 252-638-2417. Linda McAlister, L.C.S.W.

Tar River Office, 204 E. Arlington Blvd., Ste. L, P.O. Box 8241, Greenville, 27835-8241. Tel: 252-355-5111; Fax: 252-355-1088. Betty Byrnes, L.C.S.W.

Albemarle Office, 123 Market St., Hertford, 27944. Tel: 252-426-7717; Fax: 252-426-9940. Stephanie Harrell, L.C.S.W.

Parish Social Ministry, 715 Nazareth St., 27606-2198. Tel: 919-821-9751; Fax: 919-821-9712. Melissa DuCharme.

[F] MONASTERIES AND RESIDENCE OF PRIESTS AND BROTHERS

RALEIGH. *Dominican Priory* (1994) *Dominican Priory of St. Martin de Porres*, 304 E. Park Dr., P.O. Box 12927, 27605-2927. Tel: 919-833-1893. Web: www.opraleigh.org. Very Rev. Stephen Smith, O.P., J.C.D.; Revs. Richard R. Archer, O.P.; Jude Siciliano, O.P.; Very Rev. Victor E. Laroche, O.P.; Rev. Bertrand E. Ebben, O.P.

Jesuit Community (1996) 5801 Falls of the Neuse Rd., 27609. Tel: 919-865-5700; Fax: 919-865-5701. Web: www.saintraphael.org. Priests 5.
Jesuits in Eastern North Carolina: Revs. Bruce Bavinger, S.J.; Paul W. Brant, S.J.; Raymond J. Donaldson, S.J.; Robert M. Hussey, S.J.; Matthew S. Monnig, S.J.; Michael Proterra, S.J.

BURLINGTON. *Conventual Franciscans, Blessed Sacrament Church*, 1236 Westbrook Ave., Elon, 27244. Tel: 336-446-6753; Fax: 336-227-2896. Email: catholic@netpath.net. Web: www.blessedsacramentnc.org. Revs. Briant Cullinane, O.F.M.Conv.; Paul Gabriel, O.F.M.Conv.; Jacek K. Leszczynski, O.F.M.Conv.; Gerald Waterman, O.F.M.Conv. Total in Residence 4.

PITTSBORO. *Our Lady of Guadalupe Friary*, P.O. Box 1638, 27312. Tel: 919-545-5600; Fax: 919-545-5650. Email: ncfriars@aol.com. Web: www.franciscanseast.org. Revs. James Fukes, O.F.M.Conv.; Joseph Madden, O.F.M.Conv.; Michael Martin, O.F.M.Conv.; Bro. Gregory Sphuler, O.F.M.Conv.

[G] CONVENTS AND RESIDENCES FOR SISTERS

RALEIGH. *Congregation of the Sisters of the Holy Cross*, 2017 Quail Forest Dr., 27609. Tel: 919-876-0741.
Sisters of the Holy Cross, Inc. Sisters 2.
Additional Location: 718 Patriots Pointe Dr., Hillsborough, 27278. Tel: 919-245-1327.

Servants of the Immaculate Heart of Mary, 2912 Anderson Dr., 27608. Tel: 919-861-4640. 103 Locust Ct., Pine Knoll Shores, 28512. Sisters 4.

AHOSKIE. *Sisters of St. Louis--California Region*, 409 W. Church St., 27910. Tel: 919-332-2220. Email: tmssl@yahoo.com. Web: www.St-louis-sisters.org.

CHAPEL HILL. *Sisters, Servants of the Immaculate Heart of Mary*, 1194 Great Ridge Pkwy., 27516. Tel: 919-240-5612 (Home); 919-490-5253 (Office). Email: cgellings@aol.com; ecraig@ihmsisters.org. Web: ihmsisters.org.

DURHAM. *Dominican Congregation of St. Catherine DeRicci* (1880) 711 Mason Rd., 27712-9229. Tel: 919-477-1285; Fax: 919-477-9485. Email: camay711@nc.rr.com. Web: www.raldio.org/avila.html.

Sisters of St. Francis of Philadelphia (1855) 711 Mason Rd., 27712-9229. Tel: 919-477-1285; Fax: 919-477-9485. Email: damian711@nc.rr.com. Web: www.raldioc.org/avila.html.

JACKSONVILLE. *Sisters of St. Ursula* (1606) 600 Windsor Cir., Apt. 206, 28546. Tel: 910-347-4196, Ext. 104; Fax: 910-347-9338. Email: bmcady@aol.com. Mailing Address: 205 Chaney Ave., 28540.

NEW BERN. *St. Paul Convent*, 3003 Country Club Rd., 28562. Tel: 252-637-3726. Total in Residence 3.

RAEFORD. *St. Elizabeth of Hungary Parish House* (1959) 210 W. Elwood Ave., 28376. Tel: 910-904-1251. Email: stelizabethofhungaryraeford@yahoo.com. Web: www.stelizabethofhungary.net.

TARBORO. *Congregation of St. Agnes* (1858) 4934 Howard Ave. Ext., 27886. Tel: 252-823-0540. Email: tcoutreach@tarboronc.com. Web: csasisters.org.

WILLIAMSTON. *Sisters, Servants of the Immaculate Heart of Mary*, P.O. Box 894, 27892. Tel: 252-792-4091; Fax: 252-792-4091. Email: holytrinity2@suddenlink.net.

[H] RETREAT HOUSES

RALEIGH. *Madonna House* (1950) 424 Rose Ln., 27610. Tel: 919-231-4049. Email: madonnahouse@nc.rr.com. Web: www.mv.igs.net/~madonnah. Echo Lewis; Joanne Degidio; Theresa Davis, Dir.

DURHAM. *Avila Retreat Center* (1980) 711 Mason Rd., 27712-9229. Tel: 919-477-1285; Fax: 919-477-9485. Email: damian711@nc.rr.com. Web: www.raldioc.org/avila.html. Sr. Damian Marie Jackson, O.S.F., Dir. Total Staff 8; Total in Residence 2.

[I] COLLEGE CAMPUS MINISTRY CENTERS

RALEIGH. *Doggett Center for Catholic Campus Ministry at Aquinas House* North Carolina State University, 600 Bilyeu St., 27606-2152. Tel: 919-833-9668; Fax: 919-833-1194. Email: fathertony.doggett@gmail.com. Web: www.ccm-raleigh.org. Rev. Anthony DeCandia, Campus Min.

CHAPEL HILL. *Newman Catholic Student Center* University of North Carolina, 218 Pittsboro St., 27516. Tel: 919-929-3730; Fax: 919-929-3778. Web: www.newman-chapelhill.org. Rev. Msgr. John A. Wall (Retired).

DURHAM. *Newman Catholic Student Center Duke University* Box 90974, 27708-0974. Tel: 919-684-8959; Fax: 919-681-8660. Web: www.duke.edu/web/catholic/. Rev. Michael Martin, O.F.M.Conv., Dir.

ELON. *Elon University* (1889) *Catholic Campus Ministry*, Campus Box 2960, 27244-2010. Tel: 336-278-7355; Fax: 336-278-7439. Email: gwaterman@elon.edu. Web: org.elon.edu/ccm. Rev. Gerald Waterman, O.F.M.Conv., Campus Min., Res.: Blessed Sacrament Friary, 514 Parkview Dr., Burlington, 27215.

GREENVILLE. *Newman Catholic Student Center of East Carolina University* (1948) 953 E. 10th St., 27858. Tel: 252-757-1991; Fax: 252-757-1991. Email: ecunewman@gmail.com. Web: www.ecunewmancenter.org. Rev. William G. Quigley, C.I.C.M., Dir. Campus Min.

WILMINGTON. *Newman Catholic Student Center* (1986) *University of North Carolina at Wilmington*, UNC-W Station, P.O. Box 20044, 28407. Tel: 910-792-0507; Fax: 910-792-0507. Email: uncw.ccm@gmail.com. Web: www.newman-uncw.org. Sr. Rosemary G. McNamara, S.U., Dir. & Campus Min.

[J] MISCELLANEOUS

RALEIGH. *Catholic Housing Corporation*, 715 Nazareth St., 27606. Tel: 919-821-9704; Fax: 919-821-9705. Email: elmayan@raldioc.org.

Catholic Parish Outreach, 2013 N. Raleigh Blvd., 27604. Tel: 919-873-0245; Fax: 919-873-0260. Web: www.cporaleigh.org. Total Staff 2; Total Assisted: Avg Per Month 8,100; Total Assisted Annually 97,044.

The Clergy Retirement Plan of Diocese of Raleigh, 715 Nazareth St., 27606. Tel: 919-821-9711; Fax: 919-821-9712. Web: www.dioceseofraleigh.org.

Domicile Property, Inc., 715 Nazareth St., 27606.

Vocations Office, 226 Hillsborough St., 27603. Tel: 919-832-6280; Fax: 919-832-6284. Email: shlesinger@raldioc.org. Web: raleighvocations.org. Very Rev. Bernard (Ned) Shlesinger III, V.F., Dir.

SMITHFIELD. *Short Journey Retreat Center*, 2323 Cleveland Rd., 27577. Tel: 919-934-7463; Fax: 919-934-7464.

SOUTHERN PINES. *St. Joseph of the Pines Retirement Villa*, 590 Central Dr., 28387. Tel: 910-246-3001; Fax: 910-246-3016. Email: nsummers@sjp.org. Nathan Summers, Res. Support & Svcs., Pine Knoll. Total Staff 26; Total in Residence 82.

St. Joseph of the Pines, Inc., 100 Gossman Dr., Suite B, 28387. Tel: 910-246-1000; Fax: 910-246-3187. Email: kcormier@sjp.org. Web: www.sjp.org. *St. Joseph of the Pines, Inc.* Long Term Care Facilities 1; Total Staff 300.

LIFE St. Joseph of the Pines, Inc., 100 Gossman Dr., Ste. B, 28387. Tel: 910-483-4911.

RELIGIOUS INSTITUTES OF MEN REPRESENTED IN THE DIOCESE

For further details refer to the corresponding bracketed number in the Religious Institutes of Men or Women section.

[0865]—*Congregation of Mother Coredemptrix*—C.M.C.
[0650]—*Congregation of the Holy Spirit*—C.S.Sp.
[1000]—*Congregation of the Passion*—C.P.
[0480]—*Conventual Franciscans*—O.F.M.Conv
[0520]—*Franciscan Friars*—O.F.M.
[0530]—*Franciscan Friars of the Atonement*—S.A.
[0570]—*Glenmary Home Missioners*—G.H.M.
[0690]—*Jesuit Fathers and Brothers* (Maryland & New York Provs.)—S.J.
[0720]—*The Missionaries of Our Lady of La Salette*—M.S.
[0860]—*Missionhurst Congregation of the Immaculate Heart of Mary*—C.I.C.M.
[0920]—*Oblates of St. Francis De Sales* (American Prov.)—O.S.F.S.
[0430]—*Order of Preachers (Dominicans)*—O.P.

RELIGIOUS INSTITUTES OF WOMEN REPRESENTED IN THE DIOCESE

[3710]—*Congregation of the Sisters of Saint Agnes*—C.S.A.
[3935]—*Congregation of the Sisters of St. Louis*—S.S.L.
[1920]—*Congregation of the Sisters of the Holy Cross*—C.S.C.
[]—*Daughters of St. Mary of Guadalupe* —D.S.M.G.
[0960]—*Daughters of Wisdom*—D.W.
[1070-17]—*Dominican Sisters*—O.P.
[]—*Sister of the Blessed Sacrament of Nigeria*
[0590]—*Sisters of Charity of Saint Elizabeth N.J.*—S.C.
[0990]—*Sisters of Divine Providence*—C.D.P.
[2520]—*Sisters of Mercy*—R.S.M.
[2990]—*Sisters of Notre Dame* (Chardon, OH)—S.N.D.
[1650]—*Sisters of St. Francis of Philadelphia*—O.S.F.
[3830]—*Sisters of St. Joseph*—S.S.J.
[3910]—*Sisters of St. Joseph of St. Mark*—S.J.S.M.
[1990]—*Sisters of the Holy Names of Jesus and Mary*—S.N.J.M.
[2150]—*Sisters, Servants of the Immaculate Heart of Mary*—I.H.M.
[2160]—*Sisters, Servants of the Immaculate Heart of Mary*—I.H.M.
[2170]—*Sisters, Servants of the Immaculate Heart of Mary*—I.H.M.
[4048]—*Society of Sisters Faithful Companions of Jesus*—F.C.J.
[4040]—*Society of St. Ursula*—S.U.

NECROLOGY

† Keaney, Rev. Msgr. James P., (Retired)—Died Oct. 17, 2011
† Byron, J. Paul, (Retired)—Died March 15, 2011
† Creel, Jesse, (Retired)—Died June 30, 2011

An asterisk (*) denotes an organization that has established tax-exempt status directly with the IRS and is not covered by the USCCB Group Ruling.

Diocese of Rapid City

(Dioecesis Rapidopolitana)

Most Reverend

ROBERT D. GRUSS

Bishop of Rapid City; ordained July 2, 1994; appointed Bishop of Rapid City May 26, 2011; installed July 28, 2011.

Chancery Office: 606 Cathedral Dr., Rapid City, SD 57701. Tel: 605-343-3541; Fax: 605-348-7985.

Email: chancery@diorc.org

Square Miles 43,000.

Formerly the Diocese of Lead.

Erected August 4, 1902; See transferred to Rapid City, August 1, 1930.

Comprises the Counties of Bennett, Butte, Corson, Custer, Dewey, Fall River, Gregory, Haakon, Harding, Jackson, Jones, Lawrence, Lyman, Meade, Mellette, Pennington, Perkins, Stanley, Shannon, Todd, Tripp and Ziebach in the State of South Dakota.

For legal titles of parishes and diocesan institutions, consult the Chancery Office.

STATISTICAL OVERVIEW

Personnel	
Bishop	1
Priests: Diocesan Active in Diocese	28
Priests: Diocesan Active Outside Diocese	1
Priests: Retired, Sick or Absent	8
Number of Diocesan Priests	37
Religious Priests in Diocese	17
Total Priests in Diocese	54
Extern Priests in Diocese	2
Ordinations:	
Diocesan Priests	1
Permanent Deacons in Diocese	27
Total Brothers	4
Total Sisters	39
Parishes	
Parishes	88
With Resident Pastor:	
Resident Diocesan Priests	21
Resident Religious Priests	4
Without Resident Pastor:	
Administered by Priests	63
Missions	29
Pastoral Centers	4
Professional Ministry Personnel:	
Brothers	1
Sisters	6
Lay Ministers	13
Welfare	
Catholic Hospitals	1
Total Assisted	15,918
Residential Care of Children	1
Total Assisted	6
Day Care Centers	1
Total Assisted	40
Specialized Homes	1
Total Assisted	5,820
Special Centers for Social Services	6
Total Assisted	21,297
Other Institutions	1
Educational	
Diocesan Students in Other Seminaries	11
Total Seminarians	11
High Schools, Diocesan and Parish	1
Total Students	235
High Schools, Private	1
Total Students	200
Elementary Schools, Diocesan and Parish	1
Total Students	466
Elementary Schools, Private	1
Total Students	333
Catechesis/Religious Education:	
High School Students	894
Elementary Students	2,944
Total Students under Catholic Instruction	5,083
Teachers in the Diocese:	
Priests	1
Scholastics	2
Sisters	3
Lay Teachers	114
Vital Statistics	
Receptions into the Church:	
Infant Baptism Totals	436
Minor Baptism Totals	62
Adult Baptism Totals	26
Received into Full Communion	65
First Communions	425
Confirmations	306
Marriages:	
Catholic	93
Interfaith	67
Total Marriages	160
Deaths	493
Total Catholic Population	24,075
Total Population	227,211

Former Bishops—Most Revs. JOHN STARIHA, D.D., cons. Oct. 28, 1902; retired March 29, 1909 and named Titular Bishop of Antipatride; died in Laibach, Austria, Nov. 28, 1915; JOSEPH F. BUSCH, D.D., cons. May 19, 1910; transferred to Saint Cloud, MN, Feb. 21, 1915; died May 31, 1953; JOHN J. LAWLER, S.T.D., cons. Titular Bishop of Greater Hermopolis and Auxiliary Bishop of St. Paul, Minnesota, May 19, 1910; transferred to the See of Lead, Jan. 29, 1916; died March 11, 1948; LEO F. DWORSCHAK, D.D., cons. Titular Bishop of Tium and Coadjutor Bishop of Rapid City "cum jure successionis," Aug. 22, 1946; transferred to Fargo, ND, April 10, 1947; WILLIAM T. MCCARTY, C.Ss.R., D.D., appt. Titular Bishop of Anaea and Delegate to the Military Vicar, Jan. 2, 1943; appt. Coadjutor Bishop of Rapid City "cum jure successionis," April 10, 1947; succeeded to March 11, 1948; retired Sept. 17, 1969; appt. Titular Bishop of Rotdon; died Sept. 14, 1972; HAROLD J. DIMMERLING, D.D., appt. Bishop of Rapid City, Sept. 17, 1969; ord. May 2, 1940; cons. Oct. 30, 1969; died Dec. 13, 1987; CHARLES J. CHAPUT, D.D., appt. Bishop of Rapid City, April 11, 1988; appt. Archbishop of Denver, Feb. 18, 1997; BLASE J. CUPICH, ord. Aug. 16, 1975; appt. Bishop of Rapid City July 7, 1998; ord. and installed Sept. 21, 1998; appt. Bishop of Spokane June 30, 2010.

Vicar General—Rev. DANIEL JUELFS, J.C.L.

Vicar General for Temporal Affairs—Rev. STEVEN BIEGLER.

Chancery Office—606 Cathedral Dr., P.O. Box 678, Rapid City, 57709. Tel: 605-343-3541; Fax: 605-348-7985. Email: chancery@diorc.org. Office Hours: Mon.-Fri. 8-5; Address all official business to this office.

Chancellor—MARGARET SIMONSON.

Diocesan Tribunal—606 Cathedral Dr., P.O. Box 678, Rapid City, 57709-0678. Tel: 605-343-3541; Fax: 605-348-7985.

Officialis—Rev. LEO HAUSMANN, J.C.L.

Diocesan Consultors—Revs. GEORGE E. WINZENBURG, S.J.; MICHEL MULLOY; DANIEL JUELFS, J.C.L.; BRIAN LANE; MARK MCCORMICK; STEVEN BIEGLER.

Deaneries—Revs. DAVID G. MATZKO, S.J., Rapid City; TIMOTHY S. HOAG, Spearfish; BRYAN SORENSEN, Martin; BRIAN PATRICK CHRISTENSEN, Timber Lake; GARY ORESHOSKI, Presho; EDWARD G. WITT, S.J., St. Francis Mission.

Presbyteral Council—Rev. BRIAN LANE.

Vicar for Retired Priests—Rev. Msgr. MICHAEL WOSTER, J.C.L.

Permanent Diaconate Program, Sioux Spiritual Center—Revs. PETER J. ETZEL, S.J., Dir.; RONALD S. SEMINARA, S.J., Asst. Dir., 20100 Center Rd., HCR 77, Box 271, Howes, 57748. Tel: 605-985-5906.

Development and Stewardship Program—ROBERT BICKETT, Dir.

Continuing Education of Clergy—Rev. BRIAN CHRISTENSEN, Timer Lake.

Vocation Program—Rev. KEVIN LEE ACHBACH, Dir., Mailing Address: P.O. Box 678, Rapid City, 57709-0678. Tel: 605-343-3541.

Diocesan Finance Manager—SUZANNE LAMBERT.

Diocesan Finance Council—Ms. VICKY COYLE; WAYNE ROE; DAN DUFFY; RAY SMITH; RAY HILLENBRAND; TIMOTHY FROST; Rev. BRIAN LANE; JERRY KROETCH; ROBERT WAGNER; FRANK SHORT; DON STUKEL; PAT BURCHILL.

Holy Childhood Pontifical Association—VERONICA VALANDRA.

Propagation of the Faith—VERONICA VALANDRA.

Catholic Relief Service—VERONICA VALANDRA, 606 Cathedral Dr., Rapid City, 57701-5498.

Native Concerns Office—VERONICA VALANDRA, Dir., 606 Cathedral Dr., Rapid City, 57701. Tel: 605-343-3541.

Director of Ongoing Formation—Rev. BRIAN CHRISTENSEN, Mailing Address: P.O. Box 70, Timber Lake, 57656-0070. Tel: 605-865-3653.

Superintendent of Schools—BARBARA HONEYCUTT.

Director of Rural Life—VACANT.

Office of Family Life—JILL SOWERS-LEGNER, Dir., 606 Cathedral Dr., P.O. Box 678, Rapid City, 57709-0678. Tel: 605-343-3541; Fax: 605-348-7985.

Family Life Sponsored Ministries—

Social Justice—SHEILA LIEN, Chm., 606 Cathedral Dr., Rapid City, 57701.

Retreat Ministry—606 Cathedral Dr., P.O. Box 678, Rapid City, 57709-0678. Tel: 605-343-3541.

Beginning Experience, Separated, Divorced and Widowed Support Group—606 Cathedral Dr., P.O. Box 678, Rapid City, 57709-0678. Tel: 605-343-3541.

Bereavement Ministry—606 Cathedral Dr., P.O. Box 678, Rapid City, 57709-0678. Tel: 605-343-3541.

Natural Family Planning Ministry—606 Cathedral Dr., P.O. Box 678, Rapid City, 57709-0678. Tel: 605-343-3541.

Rachel's Vineyard—Mailing Address: 606 Cathedral Dr., P.O. Box 678, Rapid City, 57709-0678. Tel: 605-343-3541.

Independent Ministries—

Retrouvaille—606 Cathedral Dr., P.O. Box 678, Rapid City, 57709-0678. Tel: 605-343-3541.

Right to Life—Tel: 605-718-5215 (local contact).

Birthright—Tel: 605-343-1732.

Catholic Engaged Encounter—606 Cathedral Dr.,

P.O. Box 678, Rapid City, 57709-0678. Tel: 605-343-3541.

Worldwide Marriage Encounter—606 Cathedral Dr., P.O. Box 678, Rapid City, 57709-0678. Tel: 605-343-3541.

Diocesan Office of Religious Education & Office of Faith Formation—LINDA SEVERNS, Dir., 606 Cathedral Dr., P.O. Box 678, Rapid City, 57709-0678. Tel: 605-343-3541.

Campaign for Human Development—VERONICA VALANDRA, 606 Cathedral Dr., Rapid City, 57701-5498. Tel: 605-343-3541.

Victim Assistance Coordinator—MARYANN TULLY. Tel: 605-209-3418. Email: fredoldford@hughes.net.

West River Catholic Newspaper—LAURIE HALLSTROM, Editor, 606 Cathedral Dr., Rapid City, 57701.

Catholic Youth Commission—PROVATIA PIETILA, Coord., 606 Cathedral Dr., Rapid City, 57701.

Archives—KATHY CORDES.

CLERGY, PARISHES, MISSIONS AND PAROCHIAL SCHOOLS

CITY OF RAPID CITY

(PENNINGTON COUNTY)

1—CATHEDRAL OF OUR LADY OF PERPETUAL HELP (1890) Revs. Michel Mulloy, Rector; Christopher Hathaway, F.S.S.P.; Ed Vanorny; Nathan Sparks; Deacons Tom Lane, (Retired); George Gladfelter, (Retired); Raul Daniel; Greg Palmer. In Res., Rev. James Hoerter.
Church: 520 Cathedral Dr., 57701-5499. Tel: 605-342-0507; Fax: 605-721-5986.
See St. Elizabeth Elementary, Middle School and St. Thomas More High School, Rapid City under Diocesan Catholic School System located in the Institution section.
Catechesis/Religious Program—Students 194.
Chapel—Immaculate Conception, Tel: 605-341-1578.
Mission—St. Michael's Hermosa, Custer Co.

2—BLESSED SACRAMENT (1947) Revs. Brian Lane; Tyler Dennis; Janusz Korban; Deacons Larry Kopriva; James VanLoan.
Res.: 4500 Jackson Blvd., 57702-4999. Tel: 605-342-3336; Fax: 605-341-5668. Email: bsc@blessedsacramentchurch.org. Web: www.blessedsacramentchurch.org.
Catechesis/Religious Program—Students 385.
Mission—Our Lady of Mt. Carmel Keystone, Pennington Co.
Mission—St. Rose of Lima 100 Park Ave., Hill City, Pennington Co. 57745.

3—ST. ISAAC JOGUES (1949), (Native American), Rev. David G. Matzko, S.J.; Deacons James Garnett, (Retired); Luis Usera Sr.; Marlon J. Leneaugh; Leroy DeCory, (Retired).
Res.: 221 Knollwood Dr., P.O. Box 1304, 57709-1304. Tel: 605-343-2165; Fax: 605-343-3257. Email: sij@rushmore.com.
Catechesis/Religious Program—Students 92.
Mother Butler Center—Tel: 605-343-2165; Fax: 605-343-3257. Catechetical and Social Center for Indians.
Mission—Indian Health Service, Sioux San Hospital and Pennington County Jail, Pennington Co.

4—ST. THERESE THE LITTLE FLOWER (1941) [JC], Formerly known as The Church of St. John the Evangelist. Rev. William A. Zandri; Deacon Claude Sauer, (Retired). In Res., Rev. Andrzej Wyrostek.
Res.: 532 Adams St., 57701. Tel: 605-342-1556; Fax: 605-348-6272.
Catechesis/Religious Program—Students 130.

OUTSIDE THE CITY OF RAPID CITY

BELLE FOURCHE, BUTTE CO., ST. PAUL (1905) [JC] Rev. Timothy S. Hoag; Deacon Ray Klein.
Res.: 855 Fifth Ave., 57717-1701. Tel: 605-723-3226; Fax: 605-723-3230. Email: stpauls@rushmore.com.
Catechesis/Religious Program—Students 99.

BISON, PERKINS CO., BLESSED SACRAMENT (1918) [JC], Served from Lemmon.
Catechesis/Religious Program—Sara Stadler, D.R.E. Students 22.

BONESTEEL, GREGORY CO., IMMACULATE CONCEPTION (1906) [CEM] Attended by St. Joseph, Gregory. Rev. Godfrey Muwanga.
Mailing Address: P.O. Box 376, 57317-0376. Tel: 605-654-2204; Fax: 605-654-2204. Email: imconsta@gwtc.net.
Res.: 414 Church Ave., Gregory, 57533. Email: stjoseph@gwtc.net.
Catechesis/Religious Program—Students 11.

BUFFALO, HARDING CO., ST. ANTHONY (1917) [CEM 2] [JC] Rev. John Heying.
Res.: 410 Allison St., P.O. Box 85, 57720-0085. Tel: 605-375-3438.
Catechesis/Religious Program—Students 31.
Mission—St. Agnes Cox, Harding Co.
Mission—St. Isidore Ralph, Harding Co.
Mission—Our Lady of the Prairie Reva, Harding Co.

BURKE, GREGORY CO., SACRED HEART (1905) [CEM 2] [JC] Attended by St. Joseph, Gregory. Rev. Godfrey Muwanga.
Res.: 414 Church Ave., Gregory, 57533. Tel: 605-775-2532.
Catechesis/Religious Program—Students 35.

CLEARFIELD, TRIPP CO., ST. BONIFACE, Closed. For inquiries for parish records contact the chancery.

COLOME, TRIPP CO., ST. ISIDORE (1909) [JC] Attended by Immaculate Conception, Winner. Rev. Msgr. Michael Woster.
Res.: P.O. Box 765, Winner, 57580. Tel: 605-842-3520; Fax: 605-842-3520. Email: parishsec@gwtc.net.
Catechesis/Religious Program—Email: dreic@gwtc.net. Students 22.

CUSTER, CUSTER CO., ST. JOHN THE BAPTIST (1911) [JC] Attended by St. Anthony's, Hot Springs. Rev. Peter Kovarik.
Res.: 449 Harney St., P.O. Box 632, 57730-0632. Tel: 605-673-4426; Fax: 605-673-4426.
Catechesis/Religious Program—Tel: 605-673-4426. Students 25.

DEADWOOD, LAWRENCE CO., ST. AMBROSE (1877) [CEM] Rev. Kerry Prendiville.
Res.: 141 S. Siever St., Lead, 57754. Tel: 605-578-1519. Email: kprendiville@rushmore.com.
Catechesis/Religious Program—Twinned with St. Patrick's, Lead. Students 68.

EAGLE BUTTE, DEWEY CO., ALL SAINTS (1911), (Native American), [JC] Revs. Daniel Juelfs; Matthew Fallgren.
Res.: 138 Spruce St., P.O. Box 110, 57625-0110. Tel: 605-964-3391; Fax: 605-964-3300.
Catechesis/Religious Program—Students 57.
Mission—Immaculate Conception Bridger, Ziebach Co.
Mission—St. Joseph Cherry Creek, Ziebach Co.
Catechesis/Religious Program—Students 2.
Mission—Sacred Heart Dupree, Ziebach Co.
Catechesis/Religious Program—Students 18.
Mission—St. Catherine Promise, Dewey Co.
Mission—Sacred Heart Red Scaffold, Ziebach Co.
Catechesis/Religious Program—Students 7.
Mission—St. Joseph Ridgeview, Dewey Co.
Mission—St. Luke Thunder Butte, Ziebach Co.
Mission—St. Therese White Horse, Dewey Co.

FAIRFAX, GREGORY CO., ST. ANTHONY'S (1904) [CEM] Attended by St. Joseph's, Gregory. Rev. Godfrey Muwanga.
Mailing Address: P.O. Box 186, 57335-0186. Tel: 605-654-2204; Fax: 605-654-2204. Email: imconsta@gwtc.net.
Catechesis/Religious Program—Students 10.

FAITH, MEADE CO., ST. JOSEPH (1917) [CEM] Rev. Marcin Stanislaw Garbacz; Deacon Larry Brown.
Res: P.O. Box 307, 57626-0307. Tel: 605-967-2201; Fax: 605-967-2207.
Catechesis/Religious Program—Students 42.
Mission—St. Anthony Red Owl, Meade Co.
Catechesis/Religious Program—Students 5.
Mission—Our Lady of Victory Plainview, Meade Co.
Mission—St. Joseph Mud Butte, Meade Co.
Catechesis/Religious Program—Students 5.

FORT PIERRE, STANLEY CO., ST. JOHN (1905) [JC] Rev. Mark McCormick.
Res.: 206 W. Main, P.O. Box 670, 57532-0670. Tel: 605-223-2176; Fax: 605-223-2805.
Catechesis/Religious Program—Students 67.

GREGORY, GREGORY CO., ST. JOSEPH (1905) [CEM 3] Rev. Godfrey Muwanga.
Res.: 414 Church Ave., 57533. Tel: 605-835-9290. Email: stjoseph@gwtc.net.
Catechesis/Religious Program—Mary Vale Hall, 411 Church St., 57533. Tel: 605-835-9396. Students 37.

HERMOSA, CUSTER CO., ST. MICHAEL'S, Attended by Our Lady of Perpetual Help Cathedral, Rapid City.

HILL CITY, PENNINGTON CO., ST. ROSE OF LIMA (1898) [JC] Attended by Blessed Sacrament, Rapid City. Rev. Brian Lane; Deacons Frederick G. Tully; Patrick Coy.
Res.: 4500 Jackson Blvd., 57702. Tel: 605-342-3336; Fax: 605-341-5668.
Catechesis/Religious Program—Tel: 605-574-2479. Students 75.

HOT SPRINGS, FALL RIVER CO., ST. ANTHONY OF PADUA (1890) [JC] Rev. Peter Kovarik; Deacon Earl F. Witte, (Retired).
Res.: 501 Jennings Ave., P.O. Box 969, 57747-0969. Tel: 605-745-3393; Fax: 605-745-4303. Email: jmroe@gwtc.net.
Catechesis/Religious Program—Students 27.
Mission—St. James the Apostle 310 3rd Ave., P.O. Box 568, Edgemont, Fall River Co. 57735. Tel: 605-622-7801; Fax: 605-662-7801. Email: stjames@goldenwest.net.
Catechesis/Religious Program—Students 7.

KADOKA, JACKSON CO., OUR LADY OF VICTORY (1908) [JC] Attended by Our Lady of the Sacred Heart, Martin.
Catechesis/Religious Program—Lynn Herber, D.R.E. Students 25.

KENEL, CORSON CO., ASSUMPTION OF THE BLESSED VIRGIN MARY (1879), (Native American), Attended by St. Bernard, McLaughlin.
Catechesis/Religious Program—Twinned with St. Bernard, McLaughlin. Students 23.

KENNEBEC, LYMAN CO., ST. MICHAEL'S (1906) [CEM] Attended by St. Mary, Lower Brule, Mailing Address: P.O. Box 185, Lower Brule, 57548-0185. Tel: 605-473-5335; Fax: 605-473-5453. Email: pastteam@gwtc.net.
Catechesis/Religious Program—Students 22.

KYLE, SHANNON CO., OUR LADY OF SORROWS (1910), (Native American), [CEM 2] Rev. Richard P. Abert, S.J. Served from Holy Rosary Mission, Pine Ridge.
Catechesis/Religious Program—Students 2.
Mission—St. John of the Cross Allen, Bennett Co. Tel: 605-454-6261.
Mission—St. Stephens, (Inactive), Medicine Root, Shannon Co.

LEAD, LAWRENCE CO., ST. PATRICK'S (1878) [CEM] [JC] Rev. Kerry Prendiville. In Res., Rev. Timothy William Castor.
Res.: 141 Siever St., 57754. Tel: 605-584-2002.
Catechesis/Religious Program—Twinned with St. Ambrose, Deadwood. Students 68.

LEMMON, PERKINS CO., ST. MARY'S (1908) [JC] Rev. Tony Grossenburg; Deacon Bill Dustman.
Res.: P.O. Box 210, 57638. Tel: 605-374-3767; Fax: 605-374-3768.
Catechesis/Religious Program—Sara Stadler, D.R.E. Students 45.
Mission—Sacred Heart Morristown, Corson Co.
Catechesis/Religious Program—Students 13.
Mission—Blessed Sacrament Bison, Perkins Co.
Catechesis/Religious Program—Students 22.

LOWER BRULE, LYMAN CO., ST. MARY'S (1923), (Native American), [CEM] Revs. Vincent Suparman, S.C.J.; Joseph R. Dean, S.C.J.; Christianus Hendrick.
Office: P.O. Box 185, 57548. Tel: 605-473-5335; Fax: 605-473-5453.
Catechesis/Religious Program—Students 10.

MANDERSON, SHANNON CO., ST. AGNES (1901), (Native American), [CEM], Mailing Address: P.O. Box 88, 57756. Served by Holy Rosary Mission, Pine Ridge.
Res.: 100 Mission Dr., Pine Ridge, 57770-2100. Tel: 605-867-5491; Fax: 605-867-5874.
Catechesis/Religious Program—Students 4.
Mission—Sacred Heart, (Wounded Knee), (Inactive), P.O. Box 88, Shannon Co. 57756. Tel: 605-867-2267.

MARTIN, BENNETT CO., OUR LADY OF THE SACRED HEART (1918) [CEM] [JC] Rev. Bryan Sorensen; Deacon Calvin Clifford.
Mailing Address: P.O. Box 567, 57551. Tel: 605-685-6232. Email: martin1@gwtc.net.
Catechesis/Religious Program—Tel: 605-685-6274. Students 86.
Mission—Our Lady of Victory Kadoka

MCINTOSH, CORSON CO., ST. BONAVENTURE'S (1913) [CEM] Revs. Ron Garry; John Lule.
Res.: P.O. Box 539, McLaughlin, 57642. Tel: 605-823-4401; Fax: 605-823-2325.
Catechesis/Religious Program—Students 13.

MCLAUGHLIN, CORSON CO., ST. BERNARD (1918) [CEM] Revs. Ron Garry; John Lule.
Res.: P.O. Box 539, 57642. Tel: 605-823-4401; Fax: 605-823-2325. Email: stbern@westriv.com.
Catechesis/Religious Program—Twinned with Assumption of the Blessed Virgin Mary, Kenel., Fax: 605-823-4757. Students 20.
Mission—St. Aloysius Bullhead, Corson Co.
Catechesis/Religious Program—Students 30.
Mission—St. Bede Wakpala, Corson Co.
Mission—Our Lady of the Assumption Parish Kenel, Corson Co.
Catechesis/Religious Program—Students 30.

MIDLAND, HAAKON CO., ST. WILLIAM (1911) Attended by Sacred Heart, Philip., Mailing Address: P.O Box 309, Philip, 57567. Tel: 605-859-2664; Fax: 605-859-2812.
Catechesis/Religious Program—Students 10.

MISSION, TODD CO., ST. THOMAS THE APOSTLE (1933), (Native American), [CEM] Attended by St. Francis, Mission.
Church: 150 Jefferson St., P.O. Box 151, 57555. Tel: 605-856-4618; Fax: 605-856-2273.
Catechesis/Religious Program—Tel: 605-856-2273. Gladys Bordeaux, D.R.E. Students 25.
Mission—St. Peter's P.O. Box 151, Okreek, Todd Co. 57572.

MORRISTOWN, CORSON CO., SACRED HEART (1912) [JC] Attended by St. Mary's, Lemmon., Mailing Address: P.O. Box 210, Lemmon, 57638. Tel: 605-374-3767; Fax: 605-374-3768.
Catechesis/Religious Program—Students 13.

MURDO, JONES CO., ST. MARTIN (1906) [CEM] Attended by Christ the King, Presho. Rev. Gary Oreshoski.
Mailing Address: P.O. Box 399, Presho, 57568. Tel: 605-669-2436; Fax: 605-895-9416.
Catechesis/Religious Program—Tel: 605-895-2534. Students 2.

NEW UNDERWOOD, PENNINGTON CO., ST. JOHN THE EVANGELIST (1921) [JC] Rev. William A. Zandri. Served by St. Therese, Rapid City.
Catechesis/Religious Program—Email: sttherese@rushmore.com. Students 20.

NEWELL, BUTTE CO., ST. MARY STAR OF THE SEA (1910) Attended by St. Francis of Assisi, Sturgis, Mailing Address: 1049 Howard St., Sturgis, 57785-1999. Tel: 605-720-3579.
Catechesis/Religious Program—Students 35.

NORRIS, MELETTE CO., SACRED HEART (1955) [JC] Closed. (Inactive)

OGLALA, SHANNON CO., OUR LADY OF THE SIOUX (1916), (Native American), [CEM] Attended by Holy Rosary Mission, Pine Ridge. David Rooks, Parish Coord.
Res.: P.O. Box 140, 57764. Tel: 605-867-5673; Fax: 605-867-1518.
Catechesis/Religious Program—Students 10.
Mission—St. Bernard, Red Shirt Table
Mission—Our Lady of Good Counsel, No Water (Drywood)

PHILIP, HAAKON CO., SACRED HEART (1907) [JC] Rev. Kevin Lee Achbach.
Res.: 307 W. Elm, P.O. Box 309, 57567. Tel: 605-859-2664.
Catechesis/Religious Program—Students 86.
Mission—St. Mary Milesville, Haakon Co.

PIEDMONT-BLACK HAWK, MEADE CO., OUR LADY OF THE BLACK HILLS (1916) [JC] Rev. Steven Biegler; Deacons Walt Wilson; John Osnes.
Res.: 12365 Sturgis Rd., 57769-2007. Tel: 605-787-5168; Fax: 605-787-4106. Email: olbh@olbh.org. Web: www.olbh.org.
Catechesis/Religious Program—Students 131.

PINE RIDGE, SHANNON CO., SACRED HEART (1890), (Lakota), [JC], Attended from Holy Rosary Mission. J. Charles McGaa, Parish Life Coord.
Res.: P.O. Box 892, 57770. Tel: 605-867-5551; Fax: 605-867-1969. Email: sacredheartpr@gwtc.net.
See Red Cloud Indian School under Holy Rosary, Pine Ridge
Catechesis/Religious Program—Sr. Barbara Ann Bogenschutz, O.P., D.R.E. Students 31.

PORCUPINE, SHANNON CO., CHURCH OF CHRIST THE KING (1901), (Native American), [CEM], Served by Holy Rosary Mission, Pine Ridge.
Res.: 100 Mission Dr., Pine Ridge, 57770-2100. Tel: 605-867-1614; Fax: 605-867-2428.
See Red Cloud Indian School under Holy Rosary, Pine Ridge.
Catechesis/Religious Program—Students 5.
Mission—St. Paul, Sharpes Corner [CEM], (Inactive), P.O. Box 7, Shannon Co. 57772. Tel: 605-867-1614.

PRESHO, LYMAN CO., CHRIST THE KING (1906) [CEM] Rev. Gary Oreshoski.
Res.: P.O. Box 399, 57568-0399. Tel: 605-895-2534; Fax: 605-895-9416.
Catechesis/Religious Program—Students 18.
Mission—St. Anthony of Padua P.O. Box 159, Draper, Jones Co. 57531.

RELIANCE, LYMAN CO., ST. MARY'S (1911) [CEM] Attended by St. Mary's, Lower Brule., Mailing Address: P.O. Box 185, Lower Brule, 57548-0185. Tel: 605-473-5335; Fax: 605-473-5453.
Catechesis/Religious Program—Students 19.

ROSEBUD, TODD CO., ST. BRIDGET, (Native American), Rev. John Hatcher, S.J. Served by St. Francis Mission.
Office: P.O. Box 340, 57570. Tel: 605-747-2496.
Res.: P.O. Box 499, Saint Francis, 57572-0499. Tel: 605-747-2361; Fax: 605-747-5057.
Catechesis/Religious Program—Students 100.

ST. FRANCIS, TODD CO., ST. CHARLES BORROMEO (1886), (Native American), [CEM] Revs. John Hatcher, S.J.; Luis Rodriguez, S.J.; Deacon Ben Black Bear Jr.
Res. & Office: Box 499, 57572. Tel: 605-747-2533; Fax: 605-747-5057.
Catechesis/Religious Program—Tel: 605-747-2567. Betty Young, D.R.E. Students 100.
Mission—St. Agnes Parmelee, Todd Co.
Mission—St. Patrick Spring Creek, Todd Co.

SPEARFISH, LAWRENCE CO., ST. JOSEPH (1907) [JC] Rev. Timothy S. Hoag.
Res.: 844 5th St., 57783-2005. Tel: 605-642-2306; Fax: 605-642-1024. Email: stjosephs@rushmore.com. Web: www.stjoseph-spearfish.com.
Catechesis/Religious Program—Students 234.

STURGIS, MEADE CO., ST. FRANCIS OF ASSISI (1840) [CEM] Rev. Arnold Kari.
Res.: 1049 Howard St., 57785-1999. Tel: 605-720-3579; Fax: 605-720-3579. Email: stfrancis@rushmore.com.
Catechesis/Religious Program—Tel: 605-720-3996. Kristi Lyon, D.R.E. Students 158.

TIMBER LAKE, DEWEY CO., HOLY CROSS (1910) Rev. Brian Patrick Christensen.
Res.: 506 F St., P.O. Box 70, 57656-0070. Tel: 605-865-3653; Fax: 605-865-3653. Email: holycrosschurch57656@gmail.com.
Catechesis/Religious Program—Students 130.
Mission—St. Mary Isabel, Dewey Co.
Mission—Holy Rosary Trail City, Corson Co.

WALL, PENNINGTON CO., ST. PATRICK'S (1917) [JC] Rev. Leo Hausmann.
Res.: P.O. Box 405, 57790-0405. Tel: 605-279-2542.
Catechesis/Religious Program—Students 76.
Mission—St. Margaret Lakeside, Meade Co.
Mission—Holy Rosary Interior, Jackson Co.

WANBLEE, JACKSON CO., SAINT IGNATIUS LOYOLA (1920), (Native American), [CEM 3] [JC 5] Rev. Richard P. Abert, S.J.; Deacon Gerald Bush.
Res.: *Holy Rosary Mission*, 100 Mission Dr., Pine Ridge, 57770. Tel: 605-462-6170.
Catechesis/Religious Program—Students 1.
Mission—St. Henry, (Inactive), Potato Creek, Jackson Co.

WATAUGA, CORSON CO., ST. MICHAEL (1912) [CEM] Attended by St. Bernard, McLaughlin., Mailing Address: P.O. Box 539, McLaughlin, 57642. Tel: 605-823-4401; Fax: 605-823-2325.
Catechesis/Religious Program—Students 13.

WHITE RIVER, MELLETTE CO.

1—ST. IGNATIUS (1899), (Native American), [CEM] [JC] Rev. Edward G. Witt, S.J.
Res.: P.O. Box 1461, Mission, 57555-1461. Tel: 605-856-4018.
Church: P.O. Box 245, 57579-0245.
Catechesis/Religious Program—
Mission—Our Lady of Good Counsel Wood, Melette Co. 57585. Tel: 605-452-3267.

2—SACRED HEART (1919) [JC] Rev. Edward G. Witt, S.J.
Mailing Address: 100 S. McKinley St., P.O. Box 185, 57579-0185.
Catechesis/Religious Program—

WINNER, TRIPP CO., IMMACULATE CONCEPTION (1910) [JC] Rev. Msgr. Michael Woster.
Res.: 302 W. Fourth, P.O. Box 765, 57580. Tel: 605-842-3520; Fax: 605-842-3520.
Catechesis/Religious Program—Email: dreic@gwtc.net. Students 113.
Mission—St. Ann [JC] Keyapaha, Tripp Co.

INDIAN MISSIONS

EAGLE BUTTE, DEWEY CO., CHEYENNE RIVER RESERVATION (1911), (Native American), [CEM 8] [JC 2], Mailing Address: *All Saints*, 138 N. Spruce St., P.O. Box 110, 57625. Tel: 605-964-3391; Fax: 605-964-3300.

LOWER BRULE, LYMAN CO., LOWER BRULE RESERVATION (1895), (Native American), [CEM], See St. Mary's, Lower Brule for details.

PINE RIDGE, SHANNON CO., HOLY ROSARY/RED CLOUD INDIAN SCHOOL INC. (Pine Ridge Reservation) (1888), (Native American), Revs. George E. Winzenburg, S.J.; Richard P. Abert, S.J., Supr.; Stephen J. Sanford, S.J.; Peter J. Klink, S.J.; David G. DeMarco, S.J.; Daniel J. Gannon, S.J.
Mailing Address: 100 Mission Dr., 57770-2100. Tel: 605-867-5491. Web: www.redcloudschool.org.
School—Our Lady of Lourdes Elementary, (Grades K-8), P.O. Box 7, Porcupine, 57772. Tel: 605-967-2801; Fax: 605-867-5874. Theresa Lessert, Prin.; Jordan Foos, Librarian. Sisters 2; Lay Teachers 14; Elementary Students 145.
School—Red Cloud Elementary School, (Grades K-8) Tel: 605-867-5889; Fax: 605-867-2128. Jennifer Sierra, Prin.; Kathleen Siebrasse, Librarian. Sisters 1; Lay Teachers 18; Students 203.
School—Red Cloud High School, (Grades 9-12) Tel: 605-867-1289; Fax: 605-867-2528. Mr. Jim Mattern, Prin. Sisters 1; Lay Teachers 24; High School Students 203.
The Heritage Center—Tel: 605-867-8267; Fax: 605-867-1291. Web: www.redcloudschool.org/museum. Peter Strong, Dir.
Catechesis/Religious Program—Students 203.
Mission—St. Joseph, (Inactive), Cuny Table, Shannon Co.
Mission—Our Lady of Sioux P.O. Box 140, Oglala, Shannon Co. 57764. Tel: 605-867-5673; Fax: 605-867-1518.
Mission—Our Lady of Good Counsel No Water, Shannon Co.
Mission—St. Bernard Red Shirt Table, Shannon Co.

ST. FRANCIS, TODD CO., ST. FRANCIS MISSION/ROSEBUD EDUCATIONAL SOCIETY (1886), (Native American), [CEM], St. Francis Mission and Rosebud Educational Society. Revs. John Hatcher, S.J., Supr. Mission.; Edward G. Witt, S.J.; Deacon Ben Black Bear Jr.
Mailing Address: P.O. Box 499, 57572-0499. Tel: 605-747-2361; Fax: 605-747-5057.
Catechesis/Religious Program—Tel: 605-747-2142. Students 450.
Mission—St. Charles, Todd Co. Tel: 605-747-2533.
Mission—St. Peter Okreek, Todd Co. Tel: 605-747-2362.
Mission—St. Patrick Spring Creek, Todd Co. Tel: 605-747-5319.
Mission—St. Agnes Box 115, Parmelee, Todd Co. 57566. Tel: 605-747-2118.
Mission—St. Bridget P.O. Box 340, Rosebud, Todd Co. 57570. Tel: 605-747-2496.
Mission—St. Ignatius Box 245, White River, Mellette Co. 57579. Tel: 605-259-3381.
Mission—Sacred Heart Box 185, White River, Mellette Co. 57579. Tel: 605-747-2362.
Mission—Our Lady of Good Counsel Wood, Mellette Co. Tel: 605-747-2362.
Mission—Sacred Heart, (Inactive)
Mission—St. Thomas Box 151, Mission, Todd Co. 57555. Tel: 605-856-4618.
Mission—St. Agnes (1927)

STANDING ROCK, CORSON CO., STANDING ROCK RESERVATION (1918) Revs. Ron Garry; John Lule. St. Bernard's Church: P.O. Box 539, McLaughlin, 57642. Tel: 605-823-4401; Fax: 605-823-2325.
Mission—St. Bede Wakpala, Corson Co.
Catechesis/Religious Program—Twinned with St. Aloysius, Bullhead.
Mission—St. Aloysius Bullhead, Corson Co.
Mission—Assumption of the Blessed Virgin Mary Church Kenel, Corson Co.
Mission—St. Michael Watauga, Corson Co.

Chaplains of Public Institutions

ELLSWORTH. *Ellsworth AFB*. Rev. David Reinhart, 28th BW/HC, Ellsworth AFB, 57706.

On Duty Outside the Diocese:
Rev.—
Novotny, Richard

Retired:
Rev. Msgr.—
O'Connell, William, Casa Maria, 12541 N. Hwy. 79, Piedmont, 57769.
Revs.—
Baden, Robert D., Casa Maria, 12541 N. Hwy. 79, Piedmont, 57769.
Cower, D. Craig, 255 Texas St., Westhills Village F211, 57701-7356.
Dahms, Paul, 4001 Derby Ln. #319, 57701.
Deisch, Raymond J., Casa Maria, 12541 N. Hwy. 79, Piedmont, 57769.
Hight, Michael, 416 6th Ave., #3, Wall, 57790.
Scherer, Gerald N., Casa Maria, 12541 N. Hwy. 79, Piedmont, 57769.
Valades, Reuben, 1015 Clarkson Mountain View, Rm. 31, 57702.

Permanent Deacons:
Black Bear, Ben, Jr., St. Francis Mission, St. Francis
Brown, Larry, Faith
Bush, Gerald, Wanblee
Clifford, Calvin, Martin
Condon, Harold, Howes
Coy, Patrick, Sioux Spiritual Center
Curtin, Michael, (Retired), Rapid City
Daniel, Raul, Rapid City
DeCory, Leroy, (Retired), Rapid City
Dustman, Bill, Lemmon
Freece, Tom, Spearfish
Garnet, James W., (Retired), Rapid City
Gladfelter, George, Rapid City
Keller, Paul, Mobridge
Klein, Ray, Belle Fourche
Kopriva, Larry, Rapid City
Lane, Thomas, (Retired), Rapid City
Leneaugh, Marlon, Rapid City
Orthman, Carl, Valley City, ND
Osnes, John, Piedmont
Palmer, Greg, Rapid City
Rath, Vern, (Retired), Spearfish
Sauer, Claude, (Retired), St. Therese, Rapid City
Tully, Frederick G., Hill City
Usera, Luis, Sr., Rapid City
VanLoan, James, Rapid City
Wilson, Walt, Piedmont
Witte, Earl Joseph, (Retired), St. James, Edgemont

INSTITUTIONS LOCATED IN THE DIOCESE

[A] DIOCESAN CATHOLIC SCHOOL SYSTEM

RAPID CITY. *St. Thomas More High School*, 300 Fairmont Blvd., 57701. Tel: 605-343-8484; Fax: 605-343-1315. Email: stm@rccss.net. Web: rccss.net. Wayne Sullivan, Prin.; Jane Holeton, Librarian. Priests 1; Lay Teachers 22; Students 235; Total Staff 45.

St. Elizabeth Elementary and Middle School (Grades PreSchool-8), 431 Oakland, 57701. Tel: 605-348-1477; Fax: 605-342-4367. Colleen Lecy, Prin., PreK - 5th; Keiz Shultz, Prin., 6th - 8th; Jane Holeton, Librarian. Lay Teachers 30; Students 537; Staff 62.

[B] GENERAL HOSPITALS

GREGORY. *Avera McKennan dba Avera Gregory Hospital* 400 Park Ave., 57533-0400. Tel: 605-835-8394; Fax: 605-835-9422. Sponsored by Presentation of the B.V.M. of Aberdeen, SD & Benedictine Sisters of Sacred Heart Monastery, Yankton, SD. Acute Hospital Staffed Beds 25; Nursing Home Beds 47; Total Staff 131; Total Assisted 15,918.

[C] MONASTERIES AND RESIDENCES OF PRIESTS & BROTHERS

HOWES. *Kino Jesuit Community*, 20100 Center Rd., 57748-9505. Tel: 605-985-5906; Fax: 605-985-5908. Priests 6; Brothers 1. In Res. Revs. John Hatcher, S.J., Dir. of Inculturation, Supr.; Peter J. Etzel, S.J.; David G. Matzko, S.J.; Luis Rodriguez, S.J.; Ronald S. Seminara, S.J., Asst. Dir.; Edward G. Witt, S.J.; Bro. Patrick Douglas, S.J.; Thomas Olsen, S.J., Scholastic; Anthony Lusvardi, S.J., Scholastic.

LOWER BRULE. *SCJ Community House*, P.O. Box 185, 57548-0185. Tel: 605-473-5335; 605-473-5315; Fax: 605-473-5453. Email: pastteam@gwtc.net. Revs. Joseph R. Dean, S.C.J.; Vincent Suparman, S.C.J.; Christianus Hendrick. Email: chr.hendrick@gmail.com. Priests 3; Total in Residence 3; Total Staff 1.

PIEDMONT. *Casa Maria Residence for Retired Priests*, 12541 N. Sturgis Rd., 57769. Tel: 605-787-4950. Email: rj@rushmore.com. Ronald Johnsen.

PINE RIDGE. *Jesuit Community of Holy Rosary Mission*, 100 Mission Dr., 57770-2100. Tel: 605-867-5491; Fax: 605-867-1291. Email: rabert@jesuitswisprov.org. Web: www.redcloudschool.org. Revs. Richard P. Abert, S.J., Supr.; David G. DeMarco, S.J.; Daniel J. Gannon, S.J.; Peter J. Klink, S.J.; Stephen J. Sanford, S.J.; George E. Winzenburg, S.J., Pastor & Pres.; Bros. Michael Baranek, S.J.; Bill Foster, S.J.; Michael Zimmerman, S.J.; Luke Hansen, S.J; Brad A. Held, S.J., Scholastics; Michael B. Singhurse, S.J., Scholastics. Priests 6; Brothers 3; Scholastics 3; Total in Residence 12.

[D] CONVENTS AND RESIDENCES FOR SISTERS

RAPID CITY. **Benedictine Convent of St. Martin* (1889) 1851 City Springs Rd., 57702-9613. Tel: 605-343-8011; Fax: 605-399-2723. Email: sryvette_stmartins@knology.net. Web: www.blackhillsbenedictine.com. Sr. Yvette Mallow, O.S.B., Prioress. Motherhouse and Novitiate of the Sisters of St. Benedict. Sisters 25.

PORCUPINE. *Our Lady of Lourdes School Convent*, P.O. Box 7, 57772-0007. Tel: 605-867-1056; Fax: 605-867-5874. Email: sistersusan@yahoo.com. School Sisters of Notre Dame.

[E] MISCELLANEOUS

RAPID CITY. *Benedictine Convent of St. Martin Retirement Trust*, 1851 City Springs Rd., 57702-9613. Tel: 605-343-8011; Fax: 605-399-2723. Web: www.blackhillsbenedictine.com. Sr. Mary Wegher, Trustee & Contact Person.

Catholic Parish Association Contingency Fund, Inc., P.O. Box 678, 57709-0678. Tel: 605-343-3541; Fax: 605-348-7985.

Catholic Social Services, 918 5th St., 57701. Tel: 605-348-6086; Fax: 605-348-1050. Email: css@rapidnet.com. Web: www.catholicsocialservices.com. James Kinyon, Dir.

Priest Retirement and Aid Association/Pension Plan Board, P.O. 539, McLaughlin, 57642-0539. Tel: 605-859-2664. Most Rev. Robert D. Gruss; Rev. Msgr. Michael Woster, J.C.L., Exec. Sec.; Revs. Kerry Prendiville; Marcin Stanislaw Garbacz; Ron Garry, Pres.; Bryan Sorensen.

Western South Dakota Catholic Foundation, Inc., P.O. Box 678, 57709-0678. Tel: 605-343-3541; Fax: 605-348-7985. Email: WSDCF@diorc.org.

EAGLE BUTTE. *Sacred Heart Center*, 121 Landmark St., P.O. Box 2000, 57625-2000. Tel: 605-964-6062; Fax: 605-964-6060. Email: mdonovan@shconline.org. Web: www.shconline.org. Margaret Donovan, Exec. Dir. Total Assisted (Including Informational & Educational Outreach) 6,980; Total Staff 25.

HOWES. *The Diocese of Rapid City Mahpiya na Maka Okogna* Sioux Spiritual Center, 20100 Center Rd., 57748-7703. Tel: 605-985-5906; Fax: 605-985-5908. Email: ssc@gwtc.net. Web: puffin.creighton.edu/jesuit/ssc/. Revs. Peter J. Etzel, S.J., Dir.; Ronald S. Seminara, S.J., Asst. Dir. Total in Residence 2; Total Staff 7.

MANDERSON. *St. Francis Home*, P.O. Box 122, 57756-0122. Tel: 605-455-2077; Fax: 605-455-1680. Email: geraldineosf@aol.com. Sr. Geraldine Clifford, O.S.F., Min. Dir. Sisters of St. Francis Marycrest, Denver, CO., Home for abandoned and abused children (Licensed) 2-18 years of age. 6 children at a time. Personnel 3.

RELIGIOUS INSTITUTES OF MEN REPRESENTED IN THE DIOCESE

For further details refer to the corresponding bracketed number in the Religious Institutes of Men or Women section.

[1130]—*Congregation of the Priests and Brothers of the Sacred Heart*—S.C.J.

[0690]—*Jesuit Fathers and Brothers*—S.J.

[1065]—*Priestly Fraternity of St. Peter*—F.S.S.P.

RELIGIOUS INSTITUTES OF WOMEN REPRESENTED IN THE DIOCESE

[0230]—*Benedictine Sisters of Pontifical Jurisdiction* (Rapid City, SD)—O.S.B.

[3832]—*Congregation of the Sisters of St. Joseph*—C.S.J.

[1076]—*Dominican Sisters of Springfield Illinois*

[2970]—*School Sisters of Notre Dame*—S.S.N.D.

[0660]—*Sisters of Christian Charity* (Wilmette, IL)—S.C.C.

[2560]—*Sisters of Mercy*—R.S.M.

[1630]—*Sisters of St. Francis of Penance and Christian Charity* (Denver, CO)—O.S.F.

[2980]—*Sisters of the Congregation of Notre Dame* (Ridgefield, CT)—C.N.D.

[2390]—*Sisters of the Living Word*—S.L.W.

[3320]—*Sisters of the Presentation of the B.V.M.* (Aberdeen, SD; Dubuque, IA; Fargo, ND)—P.B.V.M.

NECROLOGY

† Fawcett, Brian, Fort Pierce, SD St. John.—Died Oct. 9, 2011

An asterisk (*) denotes an organization that has established tax-exempt status directly with the IRS and is not covered by the USCCB Group Ruling.

Diocese of Reno

(Dioecesis Renensis)

Most Reverend

PHILLIP F. STRALING, D.D.

Bishop Emeritus of Reno; ordained March 19, 1959; appointed Bishop of San Bernardino July 18, 1978; installed November 6, 1978; appointed Bishop of Reno March 21, 1995; installed June 29, 1995; retired June 21, 2005. *Office: 290 S. Arlington Ave., Reno, NV 89501-1713.*

Most Reverend

RANDOLPH R. CALVO, D.D., J.C.D.

Bishop of Reno; ordained May 21, 1977; appointed Bishop of Reno December 23, 2005; ordained and installed February 17, 2006. *Office: 290 S. Arlington Ave., Reno, NV 89501-1713.*

Pastoral Center: 290 S. Arlington Ave., Reno, NV 89501-1713. Tel: 775-329-9274; Fax: 775-348-8619.

Web: www.dioceseofreno.org

Email: donnak@catholicreno.org

Square Miles 70,852.

Erected as the Diocese of Reno by His Holiness Pope Pius XI March 27, 1931. Canonical Erection of the Diocese August 19, 1931; Redesignated Diocese of Reno-Las Vegas by Pope Paul VI, October 13, 1976; Reformed Diocese of Reno by His Holiness Pope John Paul II March 21, 1995.

Comprises the Counties of Carson City, Churchill, Douglas, Elko, Eureka, Humboldt, Lander, Lyon, Mineral, Pershing, Storey, and Washoe.

Patrons of the Diocese: Our Lady of the Snows (August 5); The Holy Family (Sunday in the Octave of Christmas); Established through an Apostolic brief dated August 24, 1933.

Legal Title: "The Roman Catholic Bishop of Reno and His Successors, a Corporation Sole".
For legal titles of parishes and diocesan institutions, consult the Pastoral Center.

STATISTICAL OVERVIEW

Personnel	
Bishop	1
Retired Bishops	1
Priests: Diocesan Active in Diocese	20
Priests: Diocesan Active Outside Diocese	1
Priests: Retired, Sick or Absent	11
Number of Diocesan Priests	32
Religious Priests in Diocese	6
Total Priests in Diocese	38
Extern Priests in Diocese	11
Ordinations:	
Transitional Deacons	2
Permanent Deacons	8
Permanent Deacons in Diocese	30
Total Brothers	3
Total Sisters	27
Parishes	
Parishes	28
With Resident Pastor:	
Resident Diocesan Priests	20
Resident Religious Priests	2
Without Resident Pastor:	
Administered by Priests	3
Administered by Deacons	3
Missions	6
Professional Ministry Personnel:	
Brothers	1
Sisters	10
Lay Ministers	28
Welfare	
Catholic Hospitals	1
Total Assisted	162,796
Day Care Centers	3
Total Assisted	263
Special Centers for Social Services	1
Total Assisted	345,078
Educational	
Diocesan Students in Other Seminaries	6
Total Seminarians	6
High Schools, Diocesan and Parish	1
Total Students	612
Elementary Schools, Diocesan and Parish	4
Total Students	1,103
Catechesis/Religious Education:	
High School Students	1,622
Elementary Students	3,130
Total Students under Catholic Instruction	6,473
Teachers in the Diocese:	
Lay Teachers	108
Vital Statistics	
Receptions into the Church:	
Infant Baptism Totals	1,615
Minor Baptism Totals	177
Adult Baptism Totals	150
Received into Full Communion	501
First Communions	1,667
Confirmations	795
Marriages:	
Catholic	170
Interfaith	51
Total Marriages	221
Deaths	420
Total Catholic Population	109,579
Total Population	689,178

Former Bishops—Most Revs. THOMAS K. GORMAN, D.D., D.Sc.Hist., ord. June 23, 1917; appt. Bishop, April 24, 1931; cons. July 22, 1931; appt. Coadjutor Bishop of Dallas "cum jure successionis," Feb. 8, 1952; succeeded to the See, Aug. 19, 1954; resigned Aug. 27, 1969; died Aug. 16, 1980; ROBERT J. DWYER, D.D., Ph.D., ord. June 11, 1932; appt. May 20, 1952; cons. Aug. 5, 1952; elevated to Archiepiscopal Dignity and promoted to Portland in Oregon, Dec. 14, 1966; resigned Jan. 22, 1974; died March 24, 1976; JOSEPH GREEN, D.D., ord. July 14, 1946; appt. Titular Bishop of Trisipa and Auxiliary of Lansing, June 22, 1962; cons. Aug. 28, 1962; appt. Bishop of Reno, March 10, 1967; installed May 25, 1967; resigned Dec. 6, 1974; died Aug. 31, 1982; NORMAN F. MCFARLAND, D.D., J.C.D., ord. June 15, 1946; appt. Titular Bishop of Bida and Auxiliary of San Francisco, June 5, 1970; ord. Bishop, Sept. 8, 1970; appt. Apostolic Admin. of Reno, Dec. 6, 1974; appt. Bishop of Reno, Feb. 10, 1976; installed March 31, 1976; appt. Bishop of Orange, Dec. 29, 1986; installed Feb. 24, 1987; retired June 30, 1998; died April 16, 2010.; DANIEL F. WALSH, D.D., ord. March 30, 1963; appt. Titular Bishop of Tigia and Auxiliary of San Francisco June 30, 1981; ord. Bishop, Sept. 24, 1981; appt. Bishop of Reno-Las Vegas, June 9, 1987; installed Aug. 6, 1987; appt. first Bishop of the newly established Diocese of Las Vegas, March 21, 1995; installed June 28, 1995; appt. Bishop of Santa Rosa April 11, 2000; installed May 22, 2000; retired June 30, 3011.; PHILLIP F. STRALING, D.D., ord. March 19, 1959; appt. Bishop of San Bernardino July 18, 1978; installed Nov. 6, 1978; appt. Bishop of Reno March 21, 1995; installed June 29, 1995; retired June 21, 2005.

Bishop's Office—Most Rev. RANDOLPH ROQUE CALVO, D.D., J.C.D.

Bishop Emeritus—Most Rev. PHILLIP F. STRALING, D.D.

Secretary—Mrs. DONNA KENNEDY. Tel: 775-326-9428.

Vicar General—Very Rev. CHARLES DURANTE, V.G.

Chancellor—Bro. MATTHEW CUNNINGHAM, F.S.R. Tel: 775-326-9429.

Secretary—MARIAN HULL. Tel: 775-326-9410.

Tribunal—

Judicial Vicar/Officialis—Rev. JOSEPH ABRAHAM, J.C.L.

Adjutant Judicial Vicar—Rev. THOMAS FRANSISCUS, C.Ss.R., J.C.L.

Vicar for Clergy—Rev. JOSEPH ABRAHAM, J.C.L.

Secretary/Notary—PIEDAD GONZALEZ, Sec. Tel: 775-326-9411.

Promoter of Justice—Rev. GEORGE C. WOLF (Retired).

Defenders of the Bond—Revs. GEORGE C. WOLF (Retired); GARY M. LUIZ, C.PP.S., J.C.L.

Judges—Rev. ALBERT M. FOSSELMAN, J.C.L. (Retired); Rev. Msgr. STEPHEN FROST, J.C.L.; Rev. PETER ROMEO, J.C.L.

Advocates—Bro. MATTHEW CUNNINGHAM, F.S.R.; Rev. DAVID SCHUYLER, S.M., S.T.L., J.C.D.

Department of Education—

Superintendent of Catholic Schools—Mrs. KAREN L. BARRERAS. Tel: 775-326-9430.

Diocesan School Board—Most Rev. RANDOLPH ROQUE CALVO, D.D., J.C.D.; Rev. JOHN HEINZ, O.F.M.Conv.; Mrs. KAREN L. BARRERAS; Dr. JOHN ANXO, Pres.; Dr. RANDY PANE, Vice Pres.; Ms. MAUREEN O'MARA, Sec.; Ms. BARBARA HAWN; Ms. LYNN HISTING; Ms. SALLY LOVITT; Ms. LISA LAUGHLIN; Ms. CATHERINE FRENCH; Mr. JIM CARRICO; Mr. JIM CAVILIA.

Office of Faith Formation—Ms. MONIQUE JACOBS, Dir. Tel: 775-326-9439; Mrs. ELAINE MENARDI, Assoc. Dir. Tel: 775-326-9431. Secretaries: LETTY ANGUIANO. Tel: 775-326-9413; BREANNA BALMUT. Tel: 775-326-9434; PAT GIANNOTTI. Tel: 775-326-9441.

Conference Associate—Sr. MAXINE LAVELL, O.S.F. Tel: 775-326-9440.

Office of Faith Formation Resource Center—BREANNA BALMUT, Admin. Tel: 775-326-9434.

Office of Safe Environment—JANE O'CONNOR. Tel: 775-326-9445.

Office of Ethnic Ministries—Mrs. MARIPAZ RAMOS, Dir. Tel: 775-326-9423; MARIA DEL ROCIO ESTEVEZ, Sec. Tel: 775-326-9415.

Archives—Bro. MATTHEW CUNNINGHAM, F.S.R.,

Chancellor. Tel: 775-326-9429; Sr. MAXINE LAVELL, O.S.F. Tel: 775-326-9440.

Curia—Most Rev. RANDOLPH ROQUE CALVO, D.D., J.C.D.; Very Rev. CHARLES DURANTE, V.G., Vicar Gen.; Bro. MATTHEW CUNNINGHAM, F.S.R.; Mrs. KAREN L. BARRERAS; Mr. PETER VOGEL; Ms. MONIQUE JACOBS; Mr. MIKE QUILICI; Mrs. MARIPAZ RAMOS; Mrs. ELAINE MENARDI; Mr. TIM WANNER; Rev. JOSEPH ABRAHAM, J.C.L.

Department of Stewardship and Development—Mr. MICHAEL QUILICI, Chief Devel. Officer. Tel: 775-326-9432. Secretaries: CARMEN GODOY. Tel: 775-326-9433; BRIZEDA GONZALEZ. Tel: 775-326-9444.

Diocesan Communications—Bro. MATTHEW CUNNINGHAM, F.S.R. Tel: 775-326-9429.

Diocesan Board of Consultors—Very Rev. CHARLES DURANTE, V.G.; Revs. THOMAS FRANSISCUS, C.Ss.R., J.C.L.; PAUL MCCOLLUM; ROBERT CHOREY; DANIEL HUSSEY; MICHAEL MAHONE; ANTHONY QUIJANO; VINCE FALLON, SS.CC.; ANTHONY VERCELLONE.

Lists of Deans—Revs. DANIEL HUSSEY; ROBERT CHOREY; THOMAS FRANSISCUS, C.Ss.R., J.C.L.; ANTHONY VERCELLONE.

Finance Office—

Finance Council—Most Rev. RANDOLPH ROQUE CALVO, D.D., J.C.D.; Very Rev. CHARLES DURANTE, V.G.; Ms. VIRGINIA ZORIO; Mr. ED HOUSTON; Mr. BOB ARMSTRONG; Bro. MATTHEW CUNNINGHAM, F.S.R.; Mr. TIM WANNER; Mr. RICHARD KWAPIL; Mrs. DEBBIE GRIFFIN; Mr. DENNIS PRICE; Mr. MIKE QUILICI.

Chief Financial Officer—Mr. TIM WANNER. Tel: 775-326-9420.

Payroll and Employee Benefits Coordinator—JUDIE DAY. Tel: 775-326-9424.

Accountants and Bookkeepers—ANNA HILL. Tel: 775-326-9422; RITA SAN PAOLO-OUEILHE. Tel: 775-326-9435.

Frontier of the Faith—Mailing Address: P.O. Box 10930, Reno, 89510. Tel: 775-326-9433.

Director—Bro. MATTHEW CUNNINGHAM, F.S.R. Tel: 775-326-9429.

Missionary Co-Op—Bro. MATTHEW CUNNINGHAM, F.S.R. Tel: 775-326-9429.

"Northern Nevada Catholic" Newspaper—MAUREEN ANGEL, Editor-in-Chief, 290 S. Arlington, Ste. 200, Reno, 89501-1713. Tel: 775-329-9274; Fax: 775-348-8619. Email: nnc@gbis.com.

Ongoing Formation for Permanent Deacons—Rev. JOSEPH ABRAHAM, J.C.L., Vicar for Clergy.

Our Mother of Sorrows Cemetery—2700 N. Virginia St., Reno, 89503. Tel: 775-323-0133. *Mailing Address: P.O. Box 8505, Reno, 89507*. Fax: 775-323-1229. Email: omos@catholicreno.org. SOPHIA MITCHELL, Oper. Mgr.; Sr. OFELIA ROIBAS, R.F., Counselor.

Presbyteral Council—Very Rev. CHARLES DURANTE, V.G.; Revs. THOMAS FRANSISCUS, C.Ss.R., J.C.L.; PAUL MCCOLLUM; DANIEL HUSSEY; MICHAEL MAHONE; ROBERT CHOREY; ANTHONY QUIJANO; VINCE FALLON, SS.CC.; ANTHONY VERCELLONE; Bro. MATTHEW CUNNINGHAM, F.S.R., Ex Officio & Chancellor.

Priest Personnel Board—Most Rev. RANDOLPH ROQUE CALVO, D.D., J.C.D.; Very Rev. CHARLES DURANTE, V.G.; Revs. MICHAEL MAHONE; ANTHONY VERCELLONE; JOSEPH ABRAHAM, J.C.L.; JORGE HERRERA; Bro. MATTHEW CUNNINGHAM, F.S.R.

Detention Ministry— Carson City Area: Deacon MICHAEL JOHNSON.

Reno Area—Deacon JOSE CASTRO. Tel: 775-322-2255.

Lovelock Prison—Rev. EDGAR VILLANUEVA. Tel: 775-273-2189.

Property Management—Mr. TIM WANNER.

Respect Life Commission—Rev. MARK HANIFAN, Priest Moderator; Ms. JULIANNA JERVIS; Mr. MARK FOXWELL, Chm.; Ms. CONNIE FOXWELL; Mr. EDDIE MONTANUCCI; Ms. LINDA UGALDE, Exec. Sec.; Ms. TONI BERRY; Ms. MELISSA CLEMENT.

Seminary Board—Most Rev. RANDOLPH ROQUE CALVO, D.D., J.C.D.; Very Rev. CHARLES DURANTE, V.G.; Revs. MICHAEL MAHONE; ROBERT CHOREY; JORGE HERRERA; MARGARET GRAHAM; Sr. MARIA AHEARN, O.C.D.

Victims' Advocates—KATHLEEN SHANE. Tel: 775-826-6555; MARILYN JANKA. Tel: 775-753-9543.

Vocations Team—Revs. MICHAEL MAHONE; ROBERT CHOREY; JORGE HERRERA.

Secretary—JACKIE CHAVEZ. Tel: 775-326-9426.

Life, Peace & Justice Commission—Very Rev. CHARLES DURANTE, V.G.; MIDGE BREEDEN; JULIE EHRMAN; JEFF HARDCASTLE; Deacon RUSS BERGIN; ANNABELL HALL; ELLIE HAYS; BARBARA HINSVARK; FRAN MCMILLAN, Co Chair; Rev. WILLIAM NADEAU; LIZ REVILLE; LISA STILLER; Sr. ROSELLI TRIA, O.P.; RITA SLOAN, Exec. Sec.

Liturgy Commission—Rev. ROBERT CHOREY, Chm.; Deacon DONALD KORSON; Ms. CAROL SARA; Ms. MARIA LEMAN; Mrs. GLORIA CASTELLANOS; Ms. SANDY MCGOWEN, Sec.; Mrs. JEAN SOKOL, Exec. Sec.; Mrs. DONNA KENNEDY; Ms. TERI IACONIS; Ms. NINA WEAVER.

CLERGY, PARISHES, MISSIONS AND PAROCHIAL SCHOOLS

CITY OF RENO

(WASHOE COUNTY)

1—ST. THOMAS AQUINAS CATHEDRAL (1907) Revs. Francisco Nahoe, O.F.M.Conv., Rector; Joseph Kim, O.F.M.Cov., Parochial Vicar. In Res., Rev. John Heinz, O.F.M.Conv.
Res.: 310 W. Second St., 89503-5398. Tel: 775-329-2571; Fax: 775-329-2456.
Catechesis/Religious Program—Students 144.

2—ST. ALBERT THE GREAT (1948) Revs. Mark Hanifan; Joseph Infante, Parochial Vicar; Deacons Richard Ramm; Charles Lanham.
Office: 1259 St. Albert's Dr., 89503. Tel: 775-747-0722; Fax: 775-746-3976.
Res.: 3100 Coronado Dr., 89503.
School—(Grades K-8), 1255 St. Albert Dr., 89503. Tel: 775-747-3392; Fax: 775-747-6296. Email: lkane@stalbertcatholicschoolreno.org. Web: www.stalbertcatholicschoolreno.org. Mr. Patrick Perry, Prin.; Loreen Vasquez, Librarian. Lay Teachers 15; Students 302.
St. Albert's Child Development Center—1259 St. Albert Dr., 89503. Tel: 775-747-1617; Fax: 775-746-3976. Kristen Mareno, Dir. Teachers 15; Students 92.
Catechesis/Religious Program—Beth Lujan, D.R.E. (Grades K-6); Trish Garcia, D.R.E. Students 145.

3—OUR LADY OF THE SNOWS (1939) Revs. Anthony Vercellone; Michael Mahone, Parochial Vicar; Deacons David Norman; Brian Callister.
Office: 1138 Wright St., 89509. Tel: 775-323-6894; Fax: 775-323-6749. Email: secretary@olsparish.com. Web: www.olsparish.com.
School—(Grades K-8), 1125 Lander St., 89509. Tel: 775-322-2773; Fax: 775-322-0827. Tim Fuetsch, Prin.; Christine Vikre, Librarian. Full Time 13; Part Time 6; Students 318.
Catechesis/Religious Program—Tel: 775-329-6147; Fax: 775-323-6749. Lauri-Anne Reinhart, D.R.E. Students 265.

4—OUR LADY OF WISDOM (1965) Rev. Vince Fallon, SS.CC.; Linda Wanner, Pastoral Assoc.
Mailing Address: P.O. Box 8879, 89507.
Office: 1101 N. Virginia St., 89503. Tel: 775-322-4336; Fax: 775-322-3616. Email: olwnewmancenter@gbis.com. Web: www.ladyofwisdomnewman.org.
Catechesis/Religious Program—
Children's Liturgy of the Word—, (attend on Sunday morning) Students 20.

5—ST. ROSE OF LIMA (1996) Revs. Larry Morrison; Lorenzo Torrente; Joseph Abraham, Parochial Vicar; Deacon Auguste Lemaire; Jane Lucero, Pastoral Assoc.
Mailing Address: 100 Bishop Manogue Dr., 89511. Tel: 775-851-1874; Fax: 775-851-1727. Email: srl@strosereno.com. Web: www.strosereno.com.
Catechesis/Religious Program—Terry Sheldon-Brown, D.R.E. Students 242.
Mission—Holy Spirit 1025 N. U.S. Hwy. 395, Washoe Valley, Washoe Co. 89704. Tel: 775-849-7764.

6—ST. THERESE CHURCH OF THE LITTLE FLOWER (1947) Revs. Honesto Agustin; Ariel Arias, Parochial Vicar; John Heinz, O.F.M.Conv., Parochial Vicar; Deacons Robert Ruggiero; Ron Klonicke.
Office: 875 E. Plumb Ln., 89502. Tel: 775-322-2255; Fax: 775-322-0196.
Res.: 339 Urban Rd., 89509. Tel: 775-826-6579.
School—(Grades K-8), 1300 Casazza Dr., 89502. Tel: 775-323-2931; Fax: 775-323-2997. Brieanne Thoreson, Prin.; Ms. Jennifer Sweazey, Librarian. Lay Teachers 14; Students 301.
Catechesis/Religious Program—Tel: 775-322-3415. Sr. Carol Bettencourt, S.H.F., D.R.E. Students 691.
Convent—Sisters of Mercy, 660 Casazza Dr., 89502. Tel: 775-322-5966; Fax: 775-322-5265. Sr. Margaret Oates, S.M., Contact Person. Sisters of Mercy, S.M. Sisters 2.

OUTSIDE THE CITY OF RENO

BATTLE MOUNTAIN, LANDER CO., ST. JOHN BOSCO (1940) Rev. Elberto Melendez; Deacon Dennis Cahill; Alicia Rodriguez, Parish Sec.
Mailing Address: P.O. Box 428, 89820.
Office: 394 S. Reese St., 89820.
Res.: 384 S. Reese St., 89820. Tel: 775-635-3450; Fax: 775-635-5729.
Catechesis/Religious Program—Tel: 775-635-2135. Griselda Rangel, D.R.E. Students 106.
Station—Austin 113 Virginia St., Austin, Lander Co. 89310. Tel: 775-635-2576.

CARLIN, ELKO CO., SACRED HEART (1910) Deacon Craig LaGier, Admin. & Parish Life Coord.; Rev. Hermes Binlayo, S.J., Priest Supvr.
Mailing Address: P.O. Box 235, 89822.
Office: 651-3rd St., 89822. Tel: 775-754-6425; Fax: 775-754-2942.
Catechesis/Religious Program—Students 8.

CARSON CITY, CARSON CITY CO.

1—CORPUS CHRISTI (1949) Rev. James Setelik.
Res.: 3597 N. Sunridge Dr., 89705. Tel: 775-267-3200; Fax: 775-267-5692. Email: generaloffice@ccchurchcc.org. Web: www.ccchurchcc.org.
Catechesis/Religious Program—Email: karens@ccchurchcc.org. Karen Smeath, Pastoral Asst. Students 121.

2—ST. TERESA OF AVILA (1858) Very Rev. Charles Durante; Rev. Jesus Ballesteros, Parochial Vicar; Sr. Marie McGloin, S.A., Pastoral Assoc.; Deacons Bob Evans, Pastoral Assoc.; Gilbert Coleman.
Res.: 3000 N. Lompa Ln., 89706. Tel: 775-882-1968; Fax: 775-883-7063.
School—(Grades K-8), 567 S. Richmond Ave., 89703. Tel: 775-882-2079; Fax: 775-882-6135. Mrs. Christine Perdomo, Prin. Lay Teachers 14; Students 182.
St. Teresa Child Development Center—561 Richmond Ave., 89703. Tel: 775-283-0261. Email: jsullivan@stts.org. Ms. Jan Sullivan, Dir. Teachers 6; Students 50.
Catechesis/Religious Program—Tel: 775-882-2130. Kari Anderson, C.R.E. (Grades PreK-5); Mary Ann Randall, C.R.E. (Middle School); Joe Koreski, C.R.E. (High School). Students 485.

DAYTON, LYON CO., ST. ANN (1937) Rev. Thomas Fransiscus, C.Ss.R.; Deacon Roger Porcella.
Mailing Address: 3 Melanie Dr., P.O. Box 309, 89403. Tel: 775-246-7578; Fax: 775-246-7560.
Catechesis/Religious Program—Marna Zachry, D.R.E. Students 100.

ELKO, ELKO CO., ST. JOSEPH'S (1917) Revs. Daniel Hussey; Hermes Binlayo, S.J., Parochial Vicar; Deacons Cecil Gingerich; Franklin Martinez.
Office: 1035 C St., 89801. Tel: 775-738-6432; Fax: 775-738-3356. Email: stjoech@ctnis.com. Web: www.elkonv.com/~stjoech/web.
Catechesis/Religious Program—Tel: 775-738-8770. Cathy Higginbotham, D.R.E. Students 530.
Mission—Our Lady of Guadalupe P.O. Box 200, Jackpot, Elko Co. 89825. Tel: 775-755-2168.

EUREKA, EUREKA CO., ST. BRENDAN'S (1872) Deacon Craig LaGier, Admin.& Parish Life Coord.; Rev. Hermes Binlayo, S.J., Priest Supvr.
Mailing Address: P.O. Box 305, 89316.
Res.: 70 N. O'Neill Ave., 89316. Tel: 775-237-5547.
Catechesis/Religious Program—Nancy Plaskett, D.R.E. Students 14.

FALLON, CHURCHILL CO., ST. PATRICK (1920) Rev. Antonio Quijano Jr.; Deacons Kurt Carlson; Ronald Cherry.
Church & Mailing Address: 850 W. Fourth St., 89406. Tel: 775-423-2846; Fax: 775-423-5210. Email: patricksjoann@cccomm.net.
Catechesis/Religious Program—Students 142.

FERNLEY, LYON CO., ST. ROBERT BELLARMINE (1957) Rev. Robert Chorey; Deacon Ruben Cervantes.
Office: 625 Desert Shadows Ln., 89408. Tel: 775-575-4011; Fax: 775-575-7601. Email: frbob@strobertbellarmine.org. Web: www.strobertbellarmine.org.
Catechesis/Religious Program—Sherry Hall, D.R.E. Students 104.
Mission—St. Joseph the Worker Empire, Washoe Co. 89412.

GARDNERVILLE, DOUGLAS CO., ST. GALL (1917) Revs. Paul McCollum; Nathan Mamo, Parochial Vicar; Deacon Emilio Gonzales.
Office & Mailing Address—1343 Centerville Rd., 89410. Tel: 775-782-2852; Fax: 775-782-2622. Email: church@stgall.org. Web: www.saintgall.org.
Catechesis/Religious Program—Tel: 775-782-3784; Fax: 775-782-3930. Laurie Barnhill, D.R.E. Students 314.

HAWTHORNE, MINERAL CO., OUR LADY OF PERPETUAL HELP (1938) Rev. Jorge Herrera.
Mailing Address: P.O. Box 850, 89415.
Office: 838 A St., 89415. Tel: 775-945-2020; Fax: 775-945-2020. Email: olph@att.net.
Res.: 794 A St., 89415.
Catechesis/Religious Program—Students 9.

INCLINE VILLAGE, WASHOE CO., ST. FRANCIS OF ASSISI (1965) Rev. William Nadeau; Deacon Donald Korson.
Church: 701 Mount Rose Hwy., 89450. Tel: 775-831-8184.
Catechesis/Religious Program—Jodi Clouthier, D.R.E. Students 118.

LOVELOCK, PERSHING CO., ST. JOHN THE BAPTIST (1875) Rev. Edgar Villanueva, Admin.
Mailing Address: P.O. Box 177, 89418-0177.
Res.: 1045 Franklin Ave, 89419-0177. Tel: 775-273-2189; Fax: 775-273-1154.
Church: 1085 Franklin Ave., 89419-0177.
Catechesis/Religious Program—Jennifer Feck, D.R.E.; Lisa Moura, D.R.E. Students 60.

SPARKS, WASHOE CO.
1—HOLY CROSS CATHOLIC COMMUNITY (1967) Rev. Jose Issac; Deacons Antonio Baptista; Jose Castro.
Res.: 1299 Flora Glen Dr., 89434. Email: hccchurch@sbcglobal.net. Web: holycrosssparks.com.
Church: 5650 Vista Blvd., 89436. Tel: 775-358-2544; Fax: 775-626-8281.
Catechesis/Religious Program—Chantal Hendricks, D.R.E. (Grades K-8); Geralyn Grape, D.R.E. (Confirmation). Students 374.
2—IMMACULATE CONCEPTION (1904) Rev. Norman A. King.
Res.: 2900 N. McCarran Blvd., 89431. Tel: 775-358-5977; Fax: 775-359-3951. Web: www.icchurch.net.
Catechesis/Religious Program—Tel: 775-358-5977. Laura Balmut, D.R.E., (Elementary); Pat Giannotti, D.R.E., (High School). Students 291.

STEAD, WASHOE CO., ST. MICHAEL'S (1967) Rev. Thomas Babu Perupayikkad.
Res.: 14075 Mt. Vida St., 89506. Tel: 775-972-7462; Fax: 775-972-9373.
Catechesis/Religious Program—Martha Flores, C.R.E. Students 167.

SUN VALLEY, WASHOE CO., ST. PETER CANISIUS (1976) Rev. Guillermo Arias.
Res.: 225 E. Fifth Ave., 89433. Tel: 775-673-6800; Fax: 775-673-2028.
Catechesis/Religious Program—Tel: 775-673-6867. Jennifer Corral, D.R.E. Students 276.

VIRGINIA CITY, STOREY CO., ST. MARY'S IN THE MOUNTAINS (1862) Rev. Tom Fransiscus, C.Ss.R., Admin.
Mailing Address: P.O. Box 510, 89440. Tel: 775-847-9099; Fax: 775-847-9098. Email: stmarysvc@earthlink.net. Web: dioceseofreno.org/mary-mountains.aspx.

WELLS, ELKO CO., ST. THOMAS AQUINAS Deacon Craig LaGier, Admin. & Parish Life Coord.; Rev. Hermes Binlayo, S.J., Priest Supvr.
Church: 619 Sixth St., P.O. Box 369, 89835. Tel: 775-752-3400; Fax: 775-752-3400.
Catechesis/Religious Program—Students 19.

WINNEMUCCA, HUMBOLDT CO., ST. PAUL (1883) Rev. Jose Sobarzo Guerra.
Res. & Mailing Address: 350 Melarkey St., 89445. Tel: 775-623-2928; Fax: 775-623-6816. Email: stpaul@catholicreno.org.
Catechesis/Religious Program—Students 311.
Mission—St. Alphonsus Paradise Valley, Humboldt Co. 89426.
Mission—Sacred Heart McDermitt, Humboldt Co. 89421.

YERINGTON, LYON CO., HOLY FAMILY (1901) Rev. Jorge Herrera; Deacon Wayne Crooks.
Res.: 103 N. West St., 89447. Tel: 775-463-2882; Fax: 775-463-2162.
Catechesis/Religious Program—Jane Montalbano, D.R.E. Tel: 775-463-4258. Students 65.
Mission—St. John the Baptist Wellington. Hwy. 208, P.O. Box 258, Smith, Lyon Co. 89430. Tel: 775-465-2220; Fax: 775-465-9043.

ZEPHYR COVE, DOUGLAS CO., OUR LADY OF TAHOE (1966) Rev. Oliver Curran.
Mailing Address: P.O. Box 115, 89448. Email: olt@pyramid.net. 1 Elks Point Rd., 89448.
Catechesis/Religious Program—Students 22.

RENO. *Renown Medical Center*, 1155 Mill St., 89502. Rev. Lorenzo Torrente, Chap.
V.A. Sierra Nevada Hospital, 975 Kirman Ave., 89502. Rev. Lorenzo Torrente, Chap.

On Special Assignment:
Revs.—
Legerski, John, Campus Ministry, Bishop Manogue Catholic High School, 110 Bishop Manogue Dr., 89511.
Valmonte, Arturo, Spiritual Care Svcs., St. Mary's Regional Medical Center, 235 W. Sixth St., 89520.

Retired:
Rev. Msgr.—
McFadden, Leo E., 3363 Spring Creek Cir., 89509.
Revs.—
Apassa, Cyril
Avella, William, 64 Jasper Ln., Dayton, 89403.
Bain, John, 2875 Idlewild Dr., 89509.
Corona, John, 1740 Lavender Ct., Minden, 89423.
DeMolen, Richard
Donnelly, Thomas, 430 Snowmass Ct., 89511.
Fosselman, Albert M., J.C.L., Double Diamond/The Meadows, 1162 Tule Dr., 89511.
Hanley, Gerald T., P.O. Box 1767, Carson City, 89702.
Hoffmann, Frank, 917 Torrence St., #20, San Diego, CA 92103.
Simpson, Robert, P.O. Box 50148, Sparks, 89435.
Wolf, George C., P.O. Box 50097, Sparks, 89435.

Permanent Deacons:
Baptista, Antonio, 6717 Magical Dr., Sparks, 89436. Tel: 775-626-2196
Bell, Joseph, 9330 Tomahawk Way, 89506. Tel: 775-972-1596
Bergin, Russ, 125 Guildwood Dr., Sun Valley, 89433. Tel: 775-673-5286
Cahill, Dennis, 435 W. Antelope, Battle Mountain, 89820. Tel: 775-635-0355
Callister, Brian, 3689 Cashill Blvd., 89509.
Cargill, Thomas, 65 Bennington Ct., 89511. Tel: 775-849-1588
Carlson, Kurt, 1888 Ryan Way, Fallon, 89406. Tel: 775-428-2055
Castro, Jose, 1586 Oxford Ave., Sparks, 89434. Tel: 775-358-8518
Cervantes, Ruben, 670 Sage Dr., Fernley, 89408. Tel: 775-575-2134
Cherry, Ronald, 428 N. Taylor St., Fallon, 89406. Tel: 775-423-7537
Coleman, Gilbert, 40 Pine View Ct., 89511. Tel: 775-852-1989
Crooks, Wayne, 5100 Workman Rd., Fallon, 89406. Tel: 775-463-2882
Dangle, Robert, 11380 S. Virginia St., #2921, 89511.
Evans, Robert, 887 Thompson St., Carson City, 89703. Tel: 775-883-2341
Garcia, Joseph, 1715 Teal Dr., Carson City, 89706. Tel: 775-885-2546
Gingerich, Cecil, 158 Country Club Pkwy., Spring Creek, 89815. Tel: 775-753-5142
Gonzales, Emilio, 1185 Sage Ocean Dr., Gardnerville, 89460. Tel: 775-783-8880
Johnson, Michael, 399 Pasture Dr., Carson City, 89701. Tel: 775-885-9782
Klonicke, Ron, 490 Golden Vista, 89506. Tel: 775-971-3258
Korson, Donald, 9345 Oakley St., 89521. Tel: 775-852-3650
LaGier, Craig, P.O. Box 235, Carlin, 89822. Tel: 775-754-6425
Lanham, Charles, 4742 Cougar Creek Tr., 89519.
Lemaire, Auguste, 3060 Socrates Dr., 89512. Tel: 775-786-4657
Martinez, Franklin, 891 Blue Jay Dr., Spring Creek, 89815. Tel: 775-777-1648
McHugh, Daniel, P.O. Box 7172, #174, Stateline, 89449. Tel: 775-588-2080
Norman, David, 3785 Gibraltar Dr., 89509. Tel: 775-826-1314
Porcella, Roger, 986 Ridgeview Dr., Carson City, 89705. Tel: 775-267-5110
Ramm, Richard, 3440 Kalispell Ct., 89523. Tel: 775-787-8839
Ruggiero, Robert L., 1280 Davidson Way, 89509. Tel: 775-337-0735
Schreiner, Dennis, 3365 Lyon Ln., Carson City, 89704. Tel: 775-849-0910

INSTITUTIONS LOCATED IN THE DIOCESE

[A] HIGH SCHOOLS, DIOCESAN

RENO. *Bishop Manogue Catholic High School, a Nevada non-profit corporation*, 110 Bishop Manogue Dr., 89511. Tel: 775-336-6000; Fax: 775-336-6015. Email: tim.jaureguito@bishopmanogue.org. Web: www.bishopmanogue.org. Christopher Whitty, Pres.; Tim Jaureguito, Prin.; Lauren Lacombe, Dean of Students; Rev. John Legerski, Chap.; Marcelino Ugalde, Librarian. Lay Teachers 45; Students 612; Priests 1.

[B] GENERAL HOSPITALS

RENO. *Saint Mary's Foundation*, 520 W. Sixth St., 89503. Tel: 775-770-3020; Fax: 775-770-3545. Email: brent.reed@chw.edu. Brent Reed, Admin. Coord. Total Staff 6.
Saint Mary's Regional Medical Center dba Catholic Healthcare West 235 W. Sixth St., 89520-0108. Tel: 775-770-3038; Fax: 775-770-6151. Email: gary.aldax@chw.edu. Sr. Mary Kieffer, O.P., Dir. Sponsorship. Tel: 775-770-3004. Email: mary.kieffer@chw.edu; Michael Uboldi, Pres. & CEO; Michael Johnson, Vice Pres. Community Health & Mission Integration; Rev. Arturo Valmonte. Sisters of the Third Order of St. Dominic, Congregation of the Most Holy Name (San Rafael, CA). Sisters 3; Bed Capacity 380; Patients Assisted Annually 162,796; Total Staff 2,395.

[C] DAY NURSERIES

RENO. *Holy Child Early Learning Center*, 440 Reno Ave., 89509. Tel: 775-329-2979; Fax: 775-329-8537. Email: holychild@ccsnn.org. Web: ccsnn.org/childdayhome.asp. Rebecca S. Vizina, Dir. Lay Teachers 22; Boys 70; Girls 53.

[D] MONASTERIES AND RESIDENCES FOR PRIESTS AND BROTHERS

RENO. *Brothers of Our Lady of the Holy Rosary Monastery*, 232 Sunnyside Dr., 89503-3510. Tel: 775-747-4441. Email: bros-reno@charter.net. Bros. Philip Napolitano, F.S.R.; Matthew Cunningham, F.S.R., Supr.; Edward Zuber, F.S.R. Brothers 3.

[E] CONVENTS AND RESIDENCES FOR SISTERS

RENO. *St. Mary's Convent (O.P.)*, 411 W. Sixth St., 89503. Tel: 775-323-5196. Sr. Mary Kieffer, O.P., Dir. Sponsorship. Dominican Sisters of San Rafael. Sisters 4.
Sisters of Our Lady of Mount Carmel (OCD), 1950 La Fond Dr., 89509-3099. Tel: 775-323-3236; Fax: 775-322-1532. Email: renocarmel@carmelofreno.net. Web: www.carmelofreno.com. Sr. Claire Sokol, O.C.D., Prioress. Discalced Carmelite Nuns 14.
Sisters of the Holy Family, S.H.F., 6730 S. McCarran Blvd., 89509. Tel: 775-827-5370. Email: carolb@holyfamilysisters.org. Holy Family Sisters. Sisters 2.

SPARKS. *Sisters of St. Philip Neri (R.F.)*, 135 Pascus Pl., 89431. Tel: 775-331-0708; Fax: 775-331-0708. Email: sistersreno@sbcglobal.net. Sr. Ofelia Roibas, R.F., Treas. Sisters 2.

[F] CAMPUS MINISTRY

RENO. *University of Nevada, Newman Community* 1101 N. Virginia St., 89503. Tel: 775-322-4336; Fax: 775-322-3616. Email: olwnewmancenter@gbis.com. Web: ladyofwisdomnewman.org. P.O. Box 8879, 89507. Rev. Vince Fallon, SS.CC. Served by Our Lady of Wisdom.

[G] CATHOLIC CHARITIES OF NORTHERN NEVADA

RENO. *Catholic Charities of Northern Nevada*, P.O. Box 5099, 89513-5099. 500 E. Fourth St., 89512. Tel: 775-322-7073; Fax: 775-322-8197. Email: admin@ccsnn.org. Web: www.ccsnn.org. Mr. Peter Vogel, Dir. Tel: 775-322-7073, Ext. 241.
Adoption Linda Kennedy, Dir. Tel: 775-322-7073, Ext. 231.
Emergency Assistance Rachel Tibbles, Mgr. Tel: 775-322-7073, Ext. 230.
St. Vincent's Food Pantry Scott Cocksley, Mgr. Tel: 775-786-5266.
St. Vincent's Thrift Shop James Baker, Mgr. Tel: 775-322-9824.
Immigration Assistance Tel: 775-322-7073, Ext. 239. Kyle Edgerton, Mgr.
Holy Child Day Early Learning Center, 440 Reno Ave., 89509. Tel: 775-329-2979; Fax: 775-329-8537. Rebecca S. Vizina, Dir.
St. Vincent's Dining Room, P.O. Box 5099, 89513-5099. 325 Valley Rd., 89512. Tel: 775-329-5363. Ray Trevino, Dir.
St. Vincent's Residence, P.O. Box 5099, 89513. 395 Gould St., 89502. Tel: 775-332-2143. Tom Smith, Mgr.

[H] MISCELLANEOUS

RENO. *The Catholic Community Foundation of the Diocese of Reno*, 290 S. Arlington, Ste. 200, 89501-1713. Tel: 775-326-9420; Fax: 775-348-8619. Email: timw@catholicreno.org. Mr. Tim Wanner, CFO.
**Fertility Care Center of Reno, Inc.*, 1281 Terminal Way #114, 89502. Tel: 775-827-5111; Fax: 775-851-2114. Email: juliannajervis@att.net. Ms. Julianna Jervis, Pres.
Nevada Catholic Conference, 290 S. Arlington Ave., Ste. 200, 89501-1713. Tel: 775-684-9029; Fax: 775-265-2074.

RELIGIOUS INSTITUTES OF MEN REPRESENTED IN THE DIOCESE

For further details refer to the corresponding bracketed number in the Religious Institutes of Men or Women section.
[0960]—*Brothers of the Congregation of Our Lady of the Holy Rosary*—F.S.R.
[1140]—*Congregation of the Sacred Hearts of Jesus and Mary*—SS.CC.
[0480]—*Conventual Franciscans* (Cupertino Prov.)—O.F.M.Conv.

[0690]—*Jesuit Fathers*—S.J.
[1070]—*Redemptorist Father* (Denver Prov.)—C.SS.R.
RELIGIOUS INSTITUTES OF WOMEN REPRESENTED IN THE DIOCESE
[0420]—*Discalced Carmelite Nuns*—O.C.D.
[1070-04]—*Dominican Sisters of San Rafael*—O.P.
[1190]—*Franciscan Sisters of the Atonement*—S.A.
[2560]—*Sisters of Mercy of Ireland* (U.S. Prov.)—R.S.M.
[]—*Sisters of St. Francis of Holy Family of Dubuque*—O.S.F.
[]—*Sisters of St. Philip Neri* (Madrid, Spain)—R.F.
[1960]—*Sisters of the Holy Family*—S.H.F.

DIOCESAN CEMETERIES

RENO. *Our Mother of Sorrows Cemetery & Mausoleum*, 2700 N. Virginia St., 89503. P.O. Box 8505, 89507. Tel: 775-323-0133; Fax: 775-323-1229. Email: omos@catholicreno.org. Sophia Mitchell, Opers. Mgr.; Sr. Ofelia Roibas, R.F., Counselor.

NECROLOGY

† Avilla, William, (Retired)—Died Dec. 6, 2010

An asterisk (*) denotes an organization that has established tax-exempt status directly with the IRS and is not covered by the USCCB Group Ruling.

Diocese of Richmond

(Dioecesis Richmondiensis)

Most Reverend

FRANCIS X. DILORENZO

Bishop of Richmond; ordained May 18, 1968; appointed Titular Bishop of Tigia and Auxiliary Bishop of Scranton January 26, 1988; consecrated March 8, 1988; appointed Apostolic Administrator of Honolulu October 12, 1993; succeeded to See November 29, 1994; appointed Bishop of Richmond March 31, 2004; installed May 24, 2004.

Most Reverend

WALTER F. SULLIVAN, D.D.

Bishop Emeritus of Richmond; ordained May 9, 1953; appointed Titular Bishop of Selsey and Auxiliary Bishop of Richmond October 20, 1970; consecrated December 1, 1970; appointed Apostolic Administrator of Richmond April 30, 1973; succeeded to the See, June 6, 1974; resigned September 16, 2003. *Mailing Address: 7800 Carousel Lane, Richmond, VA 23294.*

ESTABLISHED IN 1820.

Square Miles 36,711.

Comprises the State of Virginia, with the exception of the Counties of Arlington, Clarke, Culpeper, Fairfax, Fauquier, Frederick, King George, Lancaster, Loudoun, Madison, Northumberland, Orange, Page, Prince William, Rappahannock, Richmond, Shenandoah, Spottsylvania, Stafford, Warren and Westmoreland.

For legal titles of parishes and diocesan institutions, consult the Chancery Office.

Catholic Diocese of Richmond Pastoral Center: 7800 Carousel Lane, Richmond, VA 23294. Tel: 804-359-5661; Fax: 804-358-9159.

Web: www.richmonddiocese.org

Email: aedwards@richmonddiocese.org

STATISTICAL OVERVIEW

Personnel	
Bishop	1
Retired Bishops	1
Priests: Diocesan Active in Diocese	86
Priests: Diocesan Active Outside Diocese	2
Priests: Retired, Sick or Absent	56
Number of Diocesan Priests	144
Religious Priests in Diocese	25
Total Priests in Diocese	169
Extern Priests in Diocese	38
Ordinations:	
Diocesan Priests	2
Transitional Deacons	4
Permanent Deacons	2
Permanent Deacons in Diocese	86
Total Brothers	7
Total Sisters	160
Parishes	
Parishes	146
With Resident Pastor:	
Resident Diocesan Priests	95
Resident Religious Priests	8
Without Resident Pastor:	
Administered by Priests	40
Administered by Deacons	5
Missions	4
Professional Ministry Personnel:	
Brothers	7
Sisters	160
Lay Ministers	450
Welfare	
Catholic Hospitals	10
Total Assisted	700,000
Homes for the Aged	18
Total Assisted	2,000
Day Care Centers	2
Total Assisted	200
Specialized Homes	2
Special Centers for Social Services	2
Residential Care of Disabled	3
Total Assisted	260
Other Institutions	6
Total Assisted	30,000
Educational	
Diocesan Students in Other Seminaries	14
Total Seminarians	14
High Schools, Diocesan and Parish	5
Total Students	1,747
High Schools, Private	3
Total Students	880
Elementary Schools, Diocesan and Parish	22
Total Students	5,958
Elementary Schools, Private	3
Total Students	1,000
Catechesis/Religious Education:	
High School Students	5,653
Elementary Students	15,259
Total Students under Catholic Instruction	30,511
Teachers in the Diocese:	
Priests	1
Brothers	4
Sisters	18
Lay Teachers	912
Vital Statistics	
Receptions into the Church:	
Infant Baptism Totals	3,088
Minor Baptism Totals	71
Adult Baptism Totals	47
First Communions	3,323
Confirmations	3,688
Marriages:	
Catholic	402
Interfaith	306
Total Marriages	708
Deaths	1,664
Total Catholic Population	231,859
Total Population	4,982,668

Former Bishops—Rt. Revs. PATRICK KELLY, D.D., ord. July 18, 1802; first Bishop; cons. Aug. 24, 1820; transferred to Waterford and Lismore in 1822; died Oct. 8, 1829; RICHARD V. WHELAN, D.D., ord. May 1, 1831; second Bishop; cons. March 21, 1841; transferred to Wheeling, July 23, 1850; died July 7, 1874; JOHN MCGILL, D.D., ord. June 13, 1835; cons. Nov. 10, 1850; died Jan. 14, 1872; His Eminence JAMES CARDINAL GIBBONS, D.D., ord. June 30, 1861; cons. Aug. 16, 1868; Bishop of Adramyttum, and Vicar-Apostolic of North Carolina; transferred to the See of Richmond, July 30, 1872; transferred to the See of Baltimore, Oct. 3, 1877; created Cardinal Priest of S. Maria in Trastevere, June 7, 1886; died March 24, 1921; Rt. Revs. JOHN J. KEANE, D.D., ord. July 2, 1866; cons. Aug. 25, 1878; resigned August, 1888; rector of the Catholic University, Washington, DC; transferred to Archbishopric of Dubuque, July 24, 1900; died June 27, 1918; AUGUSTINE VAN DE VYVER, D.D., ord. July 21, 1870; cons. Oct. 20, 1889; died Oct. 16, 1911; DENIS JOSEPH O'CONNELL, D.D., ord. May 26, 1877; cons. May 3, 1908; Titular Bishop of Sebaste and Auxiliary Bishop of San Francisco; appt. Bishop of Richmond, Jan. 19, 1912; resigned Jan. 15, 1926 and appt. Titular Archbishop of Marianne; died Jan. 1, 1927; Most Revs. ANDREW J. BRENNAN, D.D., ord. December 17, 1904; cons. Titular Bishop of Thapsus and Auxiliary Bishop of Scranton, April 25, 1923; appt. Bishop of Richmond, May 28, 1926; resigned April 14, 1945; appt. Titular Bishop of Telmissus; died May 23, 1956; PETER L. IRETON, D.D., ord. June 20, 1906; appt. Titular Bishop of Cime Coadjutor Bishop and Apostolic Administrator of Richmond, Aug. 3, 1935; cons. Oct. 23, 1935; named Bishop of Richmond, April 14, 1945; named Assistant at the Pontifical Throne, May 21, 1956; died April 27, 1958; JOHN J. RUSSELL, D.D., ord. July 8, 1923; appt. Bishop of Charleston, Jan. 28, 1950; cons. March 14, 1950; appt. Bishop of Richmond, July 3, 1958; retired April 3, 1973; died March 17, 1993; WALTER F. SULLIVAN, D.D. (Retired), ord. May 9, 1953; appt. Titular Bishop of Selsey and Auxiliary Bishop of Richmond Oct. 20, 1970; cons. Dec. 1, 1970; appt. Apostolic Administrator of Richmond April 30, 1973; succeeded to the See, June 6, 1974; resigned Sept. 16, 2003.

Central Administrative Offices

Unless otherwise indicated all Diocesan Offices are located at: *7800 Carousel Ln., Richmond, 23294.* Tel: 804-359-5661; Fax: 804-358-9159.

Vicar General & Moderator of the Curia—Rev. Msgr. MARK RICHARD LANE, V.G., S.T.M., D.Min.

Vicar General—Rev. Msgr. THOMAS F. SHREVE, PA., J.C.L., V.G., 7800 Carousel Ln., Richmond, 23294. Tel: 804-359-5661. Regional Vicars: Rev. Msgrs. WALTER C. BARRETT, Eastern Vicariate. Tel: 757-851-8800; R. FRANCIS MUENCH, J.C.L., Central Vicariate. Tel: 804-359-5661; J. KENNETH RUSH JR., D.Min., Western Vicariate. Tel: 434-846-5245.

Bishop's Administrative Advisory Council—Rev. Msgr. MARK RICHARD LANE, V.G., S.T.M., D.Min., Vicar for Clergy; Rev. MICHAEL G. BOEHLING, Vicar Vocations; Mrs. ANNE C. EDWARDS; Mr. MICHAEL

J. McGee, CFO; Mrs. Dorothy Mahanes, Dir., Office of Human Resources.

Special Assistant and Advisor to the Bishop—Mrs. Anne C. Edwards, 7800 Carousel Ln., Richmond, 23294. Tel: 804-359-5661.

Chancellor—Deacon John H. Thomas, J.D., 7800 Carousel Ln., Richmond, 23294. Tel: 804-355-9155; Fax: 804-359-2810.

Vice Chancellor—Vacant. Tel: 804-359-5661, Ext. 218.

Diocesan Tribunal Central Offices—7800 Carousel Ln., Richmond, 23294. Tel: 804-355-9155; Fax: 804-359-2810.

Judicial Vicar—Rev. Msgr. R. Francis Muench, J.C.L.

Adjutant Judicial Vicar—Rev. Michael M. Duffy, J.C.L.

Tribunal Staff—Vacant, Canonist; Rev. David L. Nott, Instructor.

Judges—Rev. Msgr. J. Kenneth Rush Jr., D.Min.; Revs. Wayne L Ball; Michael M. Duffy, J.C.L.; Kevin J. O'Brien, Ph.D.; Mr. Jeffrey Staab, J.C.L.

Defenders of the Bond—Deacon John H. Thomas, J.D.; Mr. Joseph M. Fitzgerald, J.C.D., J.C.L.

Ecclesiastical Notaries—Mrs. Denise Ryan; Cheryl Gambardella; Mrs. Kathleen M. McIntosh.

Propagation of the Faith—Deacon Robert H. Griffin.

Vicar for the Causes of Saints—Very Rev. J. Scott Duarte, J.C.D.

Vicar for Clergy—Rev. Msgr. Mark Richard Lane, V.G., S.T.M., D.Min. Tel: 804-359-5661.

Associate Director—Deacon Robert D. Ewan.

Deacon Specialist—Deacon Frank Ronald Baskind, Ph.D.

Ethnic and Special Liturgies— Filipino, Hispanic, Korean, Vietnamese; Tridentine Latin Mass, Deaf/ Hearing Impaired. Please refer to the diocesan website for location and schedule.

Vicar for Ecumenism & Ecumenical Affairs—Dr. Dominick D. Hankle. Tel: 757-352-4762. Email: dhankle@gmail.com.

Vicar for Vocations—Rev. Michael G. Boehling.

Diocesan Theologians—Dr. Dominick D. Hankle.

Director of Archives and Museum—Ms. Edith Jeter.

Office of Human Resources—Mrs. Dorothy Mahanes, Dir.; Ms. Maryjane M. Fuller, Asst. Dir.; Ms. Tanya Simmons, Benefits Mgr.; Mrs. Sarah L. Fogler, H.R. Generalist.

Office of Development—Mrs. Margaret Keightley, Exec. Dir. Advancement; Mr. Alex Previtera, Dir. Annual Appeal; Mrs. Terri Quinan, Asst. Dir.

Office of Information Technology—Mr. Rick Woods, Dir.; Ms. Lynn Mooney, Assoc. Dir. Web Svcs. & Database Design; Mr. Christopher G. Myers, Assoc. Dir. Network Admin. & Support; Mr. Brian E. Korte, Network Administrative Support.

Office of Printing—Mr. Norman Howard, Dir.

Office of Pastoral Planning—Mrs. Elizabeth A. Neu, Dir.; Bernadette Snyder, Research Analyst.

Office of Finance—Mr. Michael J. McGee, CFO; Mrs. Sarah W. Rabin, Dir. Finance; Mrs. Aimee W. Chappell, Accounting Mgr.

Parish & School Financial Auditors—Mr. William B. Murphy; Mr. Robert D. Boyle.

Diocesan Housing Corporation—Mr. William B. Murphy, Dir.

Financial Coordinator for Catholic Schools—Mrs. Sandra H. Moore.

Facilities Management—Mr. John W. Murphy Jr., Dir.

Office of Risk Management—Mr. Kurt Hickman, Dir.

Office of Christian Formation—Mrs. Emily Filippi, Dir.; Ms. Sheri Kemp, Assoc. Dir.; Mrs. Bernadette E. Harris, Assoc. Dir.; Mrs. Melanie Coddington, Southwest Region Coord.

Office of Catholic Schools—Mrs. Annette Parsons, Chief Educ. Admin.; Mrs. Francine Conway, Supt.; Ms. Miriam Cotton, M.Ed., Asst. Supt.

Office of Evangelization of Youth & Young Adults—Mr. Michael F. School, Dir.; Mr. Albert Drummond, Assoc. Dir.

Youth Ministry—Ms. Angela Hamrick, Assoc. Dir.

Office of Worship—Deacon Christopher Morash, Dir.

Office for the Hispanic Apostolate—Mr. Erik Manuel Giblin, Co Dir.; Sr. Inmaculada Cuesta, C.M.S., Co Dir.

Office for Black Catholics—Mrs. Pam Harris, Coord.

Office for Catholics with Disabilities—Ms. Wanetta J. Grignol, Dir.

Diocesan Councils and Organizations

Catholic Campaign for Human Development—Mr. Jay Brown, Dir., Office of Justice & Peace.

Catholic Relief Services—Contact: Mr. Jay Brown, Dir., Office of Justice & Peace.

Catholic Daughters of America—State Regent: Ms. Larellei Stellwag, 3118 Wynford Dr., Fairfax, 22031. Tel: 703-208-1092.

Catholic Golden Age—Mr. Thomas Milhausen, 8113 Provincetown Dr., Richmond, 23223. Tel: 804-320-1750.

"Catholic Virginian" (Diocesan Newspaper)—Mr. Stephen S. Neill, Editor, 7800 Carousel Ln., Richmond, 23294. Tel: 804-359-5654; Fax: 804-359-5689; Mrs. Judith Lindfors, Business Mgr. & Circulation Dir.

Council of Catholic Women—Vacant.

Catholic Women's Club—Mrs. Barbara McRae, Pres., 4203 Hermitage Rd., Richmond, 23227. Tel: 804-264-9210.

Cemeteries—Rev. George E. Zahn, Dir. Tel: 804-329-0473.

Council of Priests— See Presbyteral Council.

Catholic Charities—

Commonwealth Catholic Charities—1512 Willow Lawn Dr., Richmond, 23230-0565. Tel: 804-285-5900. Ms. Joanne D. Nattrass, M.B.A., B.S.N., R.N., Exec. Dir.

Office of Justice & Peace— Commonwealth Catholic Charities and provides the office's management support social justice issues within the Diocese of Richmond and global community. OJP works to form collaborative relationships with parishes to promote a comprehensive understanding of Catholic social teaching and its practical application in responsible action for the common good. OJP's focus areas include: Catholic social teaching; respect life; Haiti ministry and global solidarity; migrant ministry and domestic poverty; prison ministry and southwest Virginia ministries. *1512 Willow Lawn Dr., Richmond, 23230.* Tel: 804-285-5900 (Main Office). Web: www.richmonddiocese.org/ojp. Mr. Jay Brown, Dir.

Migrant Ministry— within the Office of Justice & Peace and Commonwealth Catholic Charities works with local parishes to extend the church's pastoral presence to migrant farm workers and their families. The office networks with local agencies to meet the social service needs of migrant farm workers and advocates for social policies to protect and promote their rights. Mr. James R. Albright, Regl. Coord., Mailing Address: P.O. Box 584, Accomac, 23301. Tel: 757-787-7862.

Refugee & Immigration Services—1512 Willow Lawn Dr., Ste. A, Richmond, 23230. Tel: 804-355-4559.

Catholic Charities of Eastern Virginia, Inc.—5361-A Virginia Beach Blvd., Virginia Beach, 23462. Tel: 757-467-7707. Mr. Christopher R. Tan, Exec. Dir.; Mr. Neil McNulty, Pres.

Commission for Ecumenical & Interreligious Affairs—Dr. Dominick D. Hankle, 2161 Mill Crossing Dr., Virginia Beach, 23454. Tel: 757-352-4762.

Finance Council—Contact: Mr. Michael J. McGee, CFO.

Haitian Ministry Commission—Office of Justice & Peace. Tel: 804-359-5661.

Knights of Columbus—State Deputy: Isaias Alba, 9310 Brian Run Ln., Springfield, 22153. Tel: 703-455-6010.

Nocturnal Adoration Society—Rev. James Kauffmann, 300 N. Sheppard St., Richmond, 23220.

Diocesan Pastoral Council—Mrs. Patty Huffman, Exec. Sec.

Diocesan School Board—Michael Borza, Chm., 1805 Keeling Wood Lane, Virginia Beach, 23454.

Presbyteral Council—Rev. Joseph H. Metzger III, Chair.

Propagation of the Faith—Deacon Robert H. Griffin.

Respect Life—Vacant.

Secular Carmelite Communities—

Community of the Holy Spirit—Sunni Cowling, O.C.D.S., Pres., 1211 Mt. Erin Dr., Richmond, 23231.

Community of Our Lady of the Annunciation—Tira Knipsel, O.C.D.S., Pres., 1288 Alanton Dr., Virginia Beach, 23454.

Third Order of the Dominicans—

Lay Fraternity of St. Dominic— St. Thomas Aquinas Chapter Rev. Luke Clark, O.P., Supvr., 401 Alderman Rd., Charlottesville, 22903.

Lay Fraternity of St. Dominic— Church of the Vietnamese Martyrs Rev. Peter Huong Pham, O.P., 12500 Patterson Ave., Richmond, 23238.

Serra Club of Richmond—John Strotmeyer, 1000 Beveridge Rd., Richmond, 23226.

Sowers of Justice—Vacant.

Victim Assistance Coordinators—Ms. Marie Olenych, Mailing Address: Commonwealth Catholic Charities, P.O. Box 6565, Richmond, 23230. Tel: 804-285-5900; William Devlin, Commonwealth Catholic Charities, 820 Campbell Ave., S.W., Roanoke, 24016. Tel: 540-344-5107; Ms. Niki Mello, Commonwealth Catholic Charities, P.O. Box 6565, Richmond, 23230. Tel: 804-285-5900; Mr. Joe New, Contact Person Tidewater Catholic Charities of Eastern Virginia, Inc., 5361-A Virginia Beach Blvd., Virginia Beach, 23462. Tel: 757-467-7707.

Youth Ministry Council—Vacant.

Liturgical Commission—Deacon Christopher Morash, Contact.

Commission for Black Catholic—Ms. Christine Thomas, Chm., 4700 Southmoor Rd., Richmond, 23234.

Building and Renovation Committee—Rev. Msgr. Thomas F. Shreve, PA., J.C.L., V.G., Chm., 11000 Smoketree Dr., Richmond, 23236.

Campus & Young Adult Ministry—Mr. Michael F. School, Contact.

Christian Formation Commission—Mrs. Terry Colville, Chm., 8275 Meadowbridge Rd., Mechanicsville, 23116.

Diocesan Pastoral Planning Commission—Mrs. Elizabeth A. Neu, Contact.

Hispanic Commission—Mr. Benny Malave, Chm., 86 Meredith Way, Newport News, 23606.

Human Resources Commission—Mrs. Dorothy Mahanes, Contact.

Women's Commission—Vacant.

CLERGY, PARISHES, MISSIONS AND PAROCHIAL SCHOOLS

CITY OF RICHMOND

1—Cathedral of the Sacred Heart (1906) [JC] Most Rev. Francis Xavier DiLorenzo; Rev. Patrick Golden, Rector; Deacons J. Brian Bergen; Marshall D. Banks; Mark C. Matte.

Bishop's Office—7800 Carousel Ln., 23294. Tel: 804-359-5661; Fax: 804-358-9159.

Cathedral Office—800 S. Cathedral Pl., 23220-1569. Tel: 804-359-5651; Fax: 804-358-8043. Email: kwalters@richmondcathedral.org. Web: www.richmondcathedral.org.

Church: 18 N. Laurel, 23220.

Catechesis/Religious Program—Students 111.

2—St. Augustine (Chesterfield Co.) (1973) Rev. Msgr. Michael S. Schmied; Deacon Eric Christopher Broughton. In Res., Rev. James Fosnot (Retired).

Res.: 9608 Verlinda Ct., 23237. Tel: 804-778-4842.

Church: 4400 Beulah Rd., 23237. Tel: 804-275-7962; Fax: 804-271-4604. Email: staugustinechurch@hotmail.com. Web: www.staugustineparish.net.

Catechesis/Religious Program—Students 356.

3—Saint Benedict (1911) [JC] Rev. James Kauffmann.

Mailing Address: 206 N. Belmont Ave., 23221.

Res.: 1129 West Ave., 23220. Tel: 804-358-2427; Fax: 804-355-5112.

Church: 300 N. Sheppard St., 23221-2407. Tel: 804-254-8810; Fax: 804-355-5112. Email: info@saintbenedictparish.org. Web: www.saintbenedictparish.org.

School—3100 Grove Ave., 23221. Tel: 804-254-8850; Fax: 804-254-9163. Web: www.saintbenedictschool.org. Mr. Sean M. Cruess, Prin. Lay Teachers 16; Students 181.

Catechesis/Religious Program—Students 136.

4—St. Bridget (Richmond, VA) (1949) Rev. Msgr. William H. Carr; Rev. Brian W. Capuano, Parochial Vicar; Deacons John A. Arkestyn; Robert B. Giovenco.

Church: 6006 Three Chopt Rd., 23226-2730. Tel: 804-282-9511; Fax: 804-285-7227. Email: parishmail@stbridgets.org. Web: www.saintbridgetchurch.org.

School—6011 York Rd., 23226. Tel: 804-288-1994; Fax: 804-288-5730. Email: information@saintbridget.org. Web: www.saintbridget.org. Mr. Raymond E. Honeycutt, Prin. Lay Teachers 35; Students 467.

Catechesis/Religious Program—Students 391.

5—Church of the Epiphany (Chesterfield Co.) (1979) Rev. James E. Gordon; Deacons Richard M. Miech; Belardino Lupini.

Mailing Address: 11000 Smoketree Dr., 23236-3144. Tel: 804-794-0222; Fax: 804-378-2013. Email: epiphany@epiphanychurch.org. Web: www.epiphanychurch.org.

See Regional School St. Edward - Epiphany, Richmond under St. Edward, Richmond for details.

Catechesis/Religious Program—Students 554.

6—Church of the Vietnamese Martyrs (1983), (Vietnamese), Rev. Peter Huong Pham, O.P.

Mailing Address: 12500 Patterson Ave., 23238. Tel: 804-784-5450; Fax: 804-784-9822. Email: vietmartyrsrichmond@hotmail.com.

Catechesis/Religious Program—Students 115.

7—ST. EDWARD THE CONFESSOR (1959) Revs. Donald H. Lemay; James M. Glass, O.S.B., Parochial Vicar; Deacons James D. Greer; Thomas B. Elliott.
Res. & Church: 2700 Dolfield Dr., 23235-2618. Tel: 804-272-2948; Fax: 804-560-3565. Email: stedward@stedwardch.org. Web: www.stedchurch.com.
School—Regional School St. Edward-Epiphany, 10701 Huguenot Rd., 23235. Tel: 804-272-2881; Fax: 804-272-2904. Ms. Georgette M. Richards, Prin. Lay Teachers 34; Students 444.
Catechesis/Religious Program—Students 900.

8—ST. ELIZABETH (1923), (African American), [JC] Rev. Francois G. Babulu.
Mailing Address: 1301 Victor St., 23222-3935. Tel: 804-329-4599; Fax: 804-321-0741.
Church: 2712 Second Ave., 23222-3935. Fax: 804-321-0741. Email: stelizcc@verizon.net. Web: www.stelizabethcc.org.
School—All Saints, 3418 Noble Ave., 23222. Tel: 804-329-7524; Fax: 804-329-4201. Mr. Kenneth Soistman, Prin.
Catechesis/Religious Program—Students 5.

9—HOLY ROSARY (1953), (African American), Rev. David J. Stanfill.
Parish Office & Mailing Address: 3300 "R" St., 23223-0416. Tel: 804-222-1105; Fax: 804-226-2204. Email: office@hrccrichmond.org. Web: hrccrichmond.org.
Res.: 901 Hunters Run Dr., 23223. Tel: 804-343-7111.
Catechesis/Religious Program—Students 45.

10—ST. JOSEPH (1991) Revs. Robert Novokowsky, F.S.S.P.; Rudolf Grega, F.S.S.P., Parochial Vicar.
828 Buford Rd., 23235. Tel: 804-320-4932; Fax: 804-451-1009. Email: secretary@stjosephrichmond.org.
Catechesis/Religious Program—Students 58.

11—ST. KIM TAEGON (1986), (Korean), Rev. Adrian Yu Jin Won.
Mailing Address: 3103 Maury St., 23224-3559. Tel: 804-232-0993; Fax: 804-232-0995.
Church: 3100 Logandale Ave., 23224.
Catechesis/Religious Program—Students 49.

12—ST. MARY (1962) Revs. Michael A. Renninger; James M. Arsenault, Parochial Vicar; Sr. Pat McCarthy, s.f.c.c., Pastoral Assoc.; Rebecca Oxenreider, Parish Social Ministry; Joe Lenich, Music Min.
Mailing Address: 9505 Gayton Rd., 23229-5319. Tel: 804-740-4044; Fax: 804-740-2197. Email: parish@stmarysrichmond.org. Web: www.stmarysrichmond.org.
School—9501 Gayton Rd., 23229. Tel: 804-740-1048; Fax: 804-740-1310. Dr. Thomas D. Dertinger, Prin. Lay Teachers 38; Students 440.
Catechesis/Religious Program— John Sweet, D.R.E. & Youth Min. Students 460.

13—ST. MICHAEL (Glen Allen) (1992) Revs. Daniel O. Brady; James M. Arsenault, Parochial Vicar; Deacons David S. Nemetz; Andrew M. Ferguson; Curtis L. Hornstra; Frank Ronald Baskind.
Mailing Address: 4491 Springfield Rd., Glen Allen, 23060. Tel: 804-527-1037; Fax: 804-527-1039. Email: admin@saint-mikes.org. Web: www.saint-mikes.org.
Catechesis/Religious Program—Tel: 804-527-1037, Ext. 13. Email: pmundy@saint-mikes.org. Students 1,263.

14—OUR LADY OF LOURDES (Henrico Co.) (1944) [JC] Rev. Robert M. Spencer, Canonical Pastor; Deacon Robert H. Griffin, Admin.
Church: 8200 Woodman Rd., 23228-3237. Tel: 804-262-7315; Fax: 804-262-7337. Email: lourdes@ollrichva.org. Web: www.ollrichva.org.
School—8250 Woodman Rd., 23228. Tel: 804-262-1770; Fax: 804-200-6295. Email: ollofice@comcast.net. Web: www.ollschoolric.com. Lucy R. Reilley, Prin. Lay Teachers 27; Students 385.
Catechesis/Religious Program—Tel: 804-262-7317; Fax: 804-262-7337. Email: skemp@ollrichva.org. Students 278.

15—ST. PATRICK (1859) Rev. Wayne L Ball, Admin.
Mailing Address: 213 N. 25th St., 23223-7115. Tel: 804-648-0504; Fax: 804-648-5216. Email: office@saintpatrickchurchhill.org. Web: www.saintpatrickchurchhill.org.

16—ST. PAUL (1921) [CEM] Rev. George E. Zahn; R. Wayne Snellings, Music Min.
Mailing Address: 909 Rennie Ave., 23227. Tel: 804-329-0473; 804-329-5512 (Rectory); Fax: 804-321-6454. Email: churchoffice@saintpaulscc.com.
School—All Saints, 3418 Noble Ave., 23227. Tel: 804-329-7524; Fax: 804-321-1538. Mr. Kenneth Soistman, Prin. Lay Teachers 17; Students 123.
Catechesis/Religious Program—Students 69.

17—ST. PETER (1834) [JC] Rev. Robert A. Brownell.
Mailing Address: 800 E. Grace St., P.O. Box 933, 23219-0933. Tel: 804-643-4315; Fax: 804-783-6120. Email: stpeterchurch2@aol.com.
Res.: 4030 Forest Hill Ave., Apt. 27, 23225. Tel: 804-231-3941. Email: stpeterchurch2@aol.com. Web: www.stpeterchurch1834.org.
Church: 800 E. Grace St., 23219.
Catechesis/Religious Program—Students 6.

18—SACRED HEART (1901) [JC] Rev. Shay W. Auerbach, S.J.
Mailing Address: 1400 Perry St., 23224-2057. In Res., Rev. Robert D. Wiesenbaugh, S.J.
Res.: 1409 Perry St., 23224. Tel: 804-232-2266; Fax: 804-231-7247. Email: sacred.heart.church@comast.net.
Church: 1401 Perry St., 23224. Tel: 804-230-4399, Ext. 301.
Catechesis/Religious Program—Federico Alegria, C.R.E. Students 160.

OUTSIDE THE CITY OF RICHMOND

ABINGDON, WASHINGTON CO., CHRIST THE KING (1983) Rev. Paul Maier; Deacon Richard Cronican.
Res. & Mailing Address: P.O. Box 1201, 24212-1201. Tel: 276-628-2941; Fax: 276-783-7282. Web: www.ctk-abingdon.org.
Church: 822 E. Main St., 24212.
Catechesis/Religious Program—Students 51.

AMELIA, WASHINGTON CO., GOOD SAMARITAN (1980) Rev. Pasquale J. Apuzzo, Admin.; Deacon Edward P. Schmidt.
Mailing Address: P.O. Box 759, 23002. Tel: 804-561-6671. Email: carolhix@tds.net.
Catechesis/Religious Program—Students 10.

AMHERST, AMHERST CO., ST. FRANCIS OF ASSISI (1995) Rev. Daniel L. Kelly.
Mailing Address: 332 S. Main St., P.O. Box 663, 24521. Tel: 434-946-2053. Email: office@stfrancisamherst.org. Web: stfrancisamherst.org.
Catechesis/Religious Program—Students 11.

APPOMATTOX, APPOMATTOX CO., OUR LADY OF PEACE (1982) Rev. James E. Gallagher Jr.
Mailing Address: 2938 Oakleigh Ave., P.O. Box 668, 24522-0668.
Church: Corner of Rte. 631 & Rte. 627, 24522. Tel: 434-352-0104; Fax: 434-352-0104. Email: jimg301@juno.com.
Catechesis/Religious Program—Students 28.

ASHLAND, HANOVER CO., ST. ANN (1892) Rev. Christian J. Haydinger; Deacon Eugene P. Kamper.
Res.: 105 S. Snead St., 23005-1514. Tel: 804-798-5039; Fax: 804-798-5072. Email: office@stannscc.org. Web: www.stannscc.org.
Catechesis/Religious Program—Students 287.

BEDFORD, BEDFORD CO., HOLY NAME OF MARY (1874) Rev. Salvador Anonuevo (Philippines); Deacon Raymond Roderique.
Mailing Address: 1307 Oakwood St., 24523-1613. Tel: 540-586-8988; Fax: 540-587-9080.
Res.: 1531 Newton Cir., 24523. Tel: 540-586-9271. Email: fathersalvadore@gmail.com. Web: holynameofmary.net.
Catechesis/Religious Program—Email: rita.zimmermann@verizon.net. Students 146.

BIG STONE GAP, WISE CO., SACRED HEART (1902) Rev. Timothy A. Drake. In Res., Rev. Leslie Schmidt, G.H.M.
Rectory—1821 Holton Ave. E., 24219-2611. Tel: 276-523-1588; Fax: 276-523-1588. Email: shccbsg@yahoo.com.
Catechesis/Religious Program—Students 5.

BLACKSBURG, MONTGOMERY CO., ST. MARY (1938) Revs. Jeremiusz H. Sojka; John A. Grace, Campus Min., VA Tech.; Deacon Mike Ellerbrock.
Mailing Address: 1205 Old Mill Rd., 24060-3618. Tel: 540-552-1091; Fax: 540-953-2962. Email: officestaff@stmaryblacksburg.org. Web: www.stmarysblacksburg.org.
Res.: 1211 Old Mill Rd., 24060.
Newman Community— 203 Otey St., 24060. Tel: 540-951-0032.
Catechesis/Religious Program—Students 192.

BLACKSTONE, NOTTOWAY CO., IMMACULATE HEART OF MARY (1947) Revs. Anthony W. Morris, C.Ss.R.; Emmanuel Tolosa de Leon, Parochial Vicar; Deacons Emmett R. McLane III, Pastoral Assoc.; Peter J. Menting.
Church & Mailing Address: 903 S. Main St., P.O. Box 266, 23824-0266. Tel: 434-292-5535; Fax: 434-392-6677. Email: cubuff03@gmail.com.
Catechesis/Religious Program—Students 22.

BRISTOL, BRISTOL CO., ST. ANNE (1903) [CEM] Rev. Timothy E. Keeney; Deacon Juan Ibarra.
Mailing Address: 350 Euclid Ave., 24201-4014. Tel: 276-669-8200 (Office Phone); Fax: 276-669-7825. Email: stannes@stannes-bristol.org. Web: www.stannes-bristol.org.
Res.: 922 Chester St., 24201. Tel: 276-466-4776.
School—(Grades PreK-8), 300 Euclid Ave., 24201. Tel: 276-669-0048; Fax: 276-669-3523. Email: schooloffice@stanneschoolbristol.org. Dr. Richard Fenchak, Prin.; Angie Bush, Librarian. Lay Teachers 19; Students 156.
Catechesis/Religious Program—Students 120.

BROOKNEAL, CAMPBELL CO., ST. ELIZABETH OF HUNGARY (1957) Closed. For inquiries for parish records contact the chancery.

BUCKINGHAM, BUCKINGHAM, CO., CHURCH OF THE NATIVITY (1981) [CEM] Revs. Anthony W. Morris, C.Ss.R.; Emmanuel Tolosa de Leon, Parochial Vicar; Deacons Emmett R. McLane III, Pastoral Assoc.; Peter J. Menting.
Mailing Address: 709 Buffalo St., Farmville, 23901.
Church: Rte. 60 E., 23921. Tel: 434-969-3306; Fax: 434-392-6677. Email: centralvacluster@gmail.com.
Catechesis/Religious Program—Students 2.

BUMPASS, LOUISA CO., IMMACULATE CONCEPTION (1876) [CEM] See separate listing. See St. Jude, Mineral.

CAPE CHARLES, NORTHAMPTON CO., ST. CHARLES BORROMEO (1886) [CEM] Rev. J. Michael Breslin; Deacon Donald Donovan.
Mailing Address: 545 Randolph Ave., 23310-3305. Tel: 757-331-1724 (Rectory); 757-331-2040 (Office); Fax: 757-331-4619. Email: saintcharles@verizon.net.
Catechesis/Religious Program—Students 61.

CAROLINE COUNTY, CAROLINE CO., ST. MARY OF THE ANNUNCIATION (1914) [CEM 2] Rev. David L. Nott, Sacramental Min.; Deacon David J. Geary, Admin.
Mailing Address: P.O. Box 396, Ladysmith, 22501.
Office & Church: 10306 Ladysmith Rd., Ladysmith, 22501. Tel: 804-448-9064; Fax: 804-448-5464. Email: office@saintmarycc.org. Web: www.saintmarycc.org.
Catechesis/Religious Program—Students 62.

CHARLOTTESVILLE, ALBEMARLE CO.

1—CHURCH OF THE HOLY COMFORTER (1880) Rev. Dennis McAuliffe.
Res.: 133 Old Fifth Cir., 22902. Tel: 434-293-6867. Web: www.holycomforterparish.org.
Church: 208 E. Jefferson St., 22902-5105. Tel: 434-295-7185; Fax: 434-295-7001.
Catechesis/Religious Program—Tel: 434-295-6559. Email: tritzert@holycomforterparish.org. Students 45.
Mission—St. George's P.O. Box 9, Scottsville, Albemarle Co. 24590. Tel: 434-286-3724.

2—CHURCH OF THE INCARNATION (1976) Revs. Gregory Kandt; Edwin Montanez, Parochial Vicar; Deacons Bernard Taylor; Christopher Morash.
Office: 1465 Incarnation Dr., 22901-1716. Tel: 434-973-4381; Fax: 434-973-1757. Email: office@incarnationparish.org. Web: www.incarnationparish.org.
Res.: 838 Belvedere Blvd., 22901-3201. Tel: 434-978-7544.
School—Charlottesville Catholic School, 1205 Pen Park Rd., 22901. Tel: 434-964-0400; Fax: 434-964-1373. Ms. Susan Dougherty, Prin.
Catechesis/Religious Program—Students 353.

3—ST. THOMAS AQUINAS (1963) [JC] Revs. Luke Clark, O.P.; Joseph A. Scordo, O.P., Parochial Vicar; Steven Paul Alcott, O.P., Parochial Vicar; M. Juan-Diego Brunetta, O.P., Parochial Vicar.
Office: Tel: 434-293-8081; 434-293-6472; Fax: 434-296-1941. Email: susiep@stauva.org. Web: www.stauva.org.
Res.: 308 Alderman Rd., 22903. Tel: 434-977-5658.
Church & Mailing Address: 401 Alderman Rd., 22903.
Catechesis/Religious Program—Email: reled@stauva.org. Students 586.

CHESAPEAKE, CHESAPEAKE CO.

1—ST. MARY (1915) Revs. David W. Cupps; Jaroslaw Nowacki, Parochial Vicar.
Church & Mailing Address: 536 Homestead Rd., 23321. Email: admin@stmarys.hrcoxmail.com. Web: www.clusterparishes.com.
Catechesis/Religious Program—Email: christianformation@clusterparishes.com. Students 65.

2—PRINCE OF PEACE (1975) Rev. Romeo D. Jazmin.
Mailing Address: 621 Cedar Rd., 23322. Tel: 757-547-0356; 757-547-3903; Fax: 757-436-6477. Email: pop.office@popparish.org. Web: www.popparish.org.
Res.: 303 Elberon Ct., 23322. Tel: 757-547-2951.
Catechesis/Religious Program—Students 686.

3—ST. STEPHEN, MARTYR (1997) Rev. Brian M. Rafferty; Deacon Keith A. Fournier.
Mailing Address: 1544 S. Battlefield Blvd., 23322-2041. Tel: 757-421-7416; Fax: 757-421-7488. Email: ssm@ssmrcc.org. Web: ssmrcc.org.
Res.: 1117 Vineyard Dr., 23322. Tel: 757-546-9400.
Catechesis/Religious Program—Tel: 757-204-4565. Students 707.

4—ST. THERESE OF LISIEUX (1954) Rev. Kevin J. O'Brien.
Res.: 321 Saunders Dr., Portsmouth, 23701.
Church: 4137 Portsmouth Blvd., 23321-2127. Tel: 757-488-2553; Fax: 757-465-4086. Email: info@sttheresechesva.org. Web: StThereseChesVA.org.
Catechesis/Religious Program—Students 204.

CHESTERFIELD, CHESTERFIELD CO., ST. GABRIEL (1997) Rev. Pasquale J. Apuzzo.
Office & Mailing Address: 8901 Winterpock Rd., 23832. Tel: 804-639-6712; Fax: 804-639-6591. Email: therese.venti@saintgabriel.org. Web:

www.saintgabriel.org.
Catechesis/Religious Program—Students 288.

CHINCOTEAGUE ISLAND, ACCOMACK CO., ST. ANDREW THE APOSTLE (1965) Rev. Richard Chirichiello, O.S.B.
Res. & Mailing Address: 6319 Mumford St., 23336. Tel: 757-336-5432; Fax: 757-336-3515. Email: standrewtheapostle1@verizon.net.
Church: 6288 Church St., 23336.
Catechesis/Religious Program—Tel: 757-336-1209. Students 27.

CHRISTIANSBURG, MONTGOMERY CO., HOLY SPIRIT CATHOLIC CHURCH (1995) Rev. John Prinelli.
355 Independence Blvd., 24068.
Church: P.O. Box 98, 24068. Tel: 540-921-3547; Fax: 540-921-3547. Email: holyspiritemail@yahoo.com.
Catechesis/Religious Program—

CLARKSVILLE, MECKLENBURG CO., ST. CATHERINE OF SIENA (1947) [CEM] Revs. John C. Kazibwe (Uganda); Charles Ssebalamu (Uganda), Parochial Vicar; Deacon John E. Sadowski.
Mailing Address: P.O. Box 1537, 23927.
Res.: 810 Market St., 23927. Tel: 434-374-5040.
Church: 805 Virginia Ave., 23927. Tel: 434-374-8408; Fax: 434-374-9442. Email: saintcatherines@usa.net. Web: www.stcatherineofsienava.org.
Catechesis/Religious Program—Maureen Bellissimo, D.R.E. Students 30.

CLIFTON FORGE, ALLEGHANY CO., ST. JOSEPH (1889) [CEM] Rev. Stephen McNally.
Mailing Address: 620 Jefferson Ave., 24422-1715. Tel: 540-863-5371. Email: stjoseph@ntelos.net.
Catechesis/Religious Program—Students 7.

CLINTWOOD, DICKENSON CO., ST. JOSEPH (1979) Rev. Timothy A. Drake.
Mailing Address: P.O. Box 1250, 24228-1250. Tel: 276-926-5451. Web: www.clintwoodva.catholicweb.com.
Church: 478 Clintwood Main St., 24228. Email: stanthonys3@verizon.net.
Catechesis/Religious Program—

COLONIAL HEIGHTS, COLONIAL HEIGHTS CO., ST. ANN (1925) [CEM] Rev. Lou Ruoff.
Mailing Address: 17111 Jefferson Davis Hwy., 23834-5396. Tel: 804-526-2548; Fax: 804-526-1922. Email: saintann@verizon.net. Web: www.stanncc.com.
Res.: 2433 Aldridge Ave., 23834.
Catechesis/Religious Program—Tel: 804-526-1860. Students 522.

COLUMBIA, FLUVANNA CO., ST. JOSEPH'S/SHRINE OF ST. KATHARINE DREXEL (1884) Rev. Gerald F. Musuubire.
Mailing Address & Parish House: 28 Cameron St., P.O. Box 808, 23038-0808. Tel: 434-842-3970.
Res.: 15 Dogleg Rd., Palmyra, 22963. Tel: 804-589-5200; Fax: 434-589-4463. Email: pastor@stspeterpaul.org.
Catechesis/Religious Program—5125 Rosewood Tr., 23038. Tel: 434-842-3970. Mr. Christopher Hall, D.R.E. Students 16.

COVINGTON, ALLEGHANY CO., SACRED HEART (1924) Unassigned.
Office: 214 W. Locust St., 24426-1537. Tel: 540-962-6541.
Res.: 220 W. Locust St., 24426-1537. Email: sacredheart24426@yahoo.com.
Catechesis/Religious Program—

CREWE, NOTTOWAY CO., ST. JOHN THE BAPTIST (1939) [CEM] Closed. For inquiries for parish records contact the chancery.

DANVILLE, PITTSYLVANIA CO., SACRED HEART (1878) Rev. Anthony E. Marques.
Mailing Address: 538 Central Blvd., 24541. Tel: 434-792-9456; Fax: 434-792-9463. Email: shc_adm@comcast.net. Web: www.sheartcatholic.com.
Res.: 154 College Ave., 24541. Tel: 434-792-0081.
School—540 Central Blvd., 24541. Tel: 434-793-2656; Fax: 434-793-2658. Email: sacredht@earthlink.net. Web: www.sheartschool-.com. Kimberly W. Meadows, Prin. Lay Teachers 15; Students 183.
Catechesis/Religious Program—Students 145.

DINWIDDIE, DINWIDDIE CO., ST. JOHN (1907) [CEM] Rev. John J. Wagner III; Deacon Matthew C. MacLaughlin.
Mailing Address: 7215 Squirrel Level Rd., Petersburg, 23805-7035. Tel: 804-861-0123; Fax: 804-861-0123. Email: stjohndinwiddie@verizon.net. Web: www.stjohndinwiddie.org.
Church: Squirrel Level Rd. & Flank Rd., 23805.
Catechesis/Religious Program—Students 32.

ELKTON, ROCKINGHAM CO., HOLY INFANT (1951) Rev. Lawrence J. Mullaney Jr.
Mailing Address & Church: 101 W. Marshall Ave., 22827-1221. Tel: 540-298-1341. Email: holy_infant@verizon.net.
Catechesis/Religious Program—Mrs. Connie Youngman, D.R.E. Students 19.

EMPORIA, GREENSVILLE CO., ST. RICHARD (1940) Rev. Columba A. Nnorom.
Mailing Address: P.O. Box 90, Ebony, 23845. Tel: 434-636-7782 (Rectory). Email: SPTAmail@buggs.net.
Catechesis/Religious Program—Desi Maldonado, D.R.E. Students 11.

FARMVILLE, PRINCE EDWARD CO.

1—SACRED HEART Revs. Anthony W. Morris, C.Ss.R.; Emmanuel Tolosa de Leon, Parochial Vicar; Deacons Emmett R. McLane III, Pastoral Assoc.; Peter J. Menting.
2597 Bruceville Rd., Meherrin, 23954. Tel: 434-736-9390; Fax: 434-392-6677.

2—ST. THERESA (1939) Revs. Anthony W. Morris, C.Ss.R.; Emmanuel Tolosa de Leon, Parochial Vicar; Deacons Emmett R. McLane III; Peter J. Menting; Mr. Robert Zupanek, Campus Min. (Longwood University & Hampden-Sydney College).
Mailing Address: 709 Buffalo St., 23901-1109.
Res.: 816 Buffalo St., 23901. Tel: 434-315-0311; 434-392-3934 (Main); Fax: 434-392-6677. Email: sttheresa@embarqmail.com.
Catechesis/Religious Program—Email: sttheresa2@embarqmail.com. Karel Bailey, D.R.E. Students 87.
Longwood University—
Hampden-Sydney College—

FINCASTLE, BOTETOURT CO., CHURCH OF THE TRANSFIGURATION (1989) Rev. Stephen McNally, Admin.
Church & Mailing Address: 7624 Roanoke Rd., 24090. Tel: 540-473-2656; Fax: 540-473-2193. Email: transfigure@ntelos.net. Web: www.churchofthetransfiguration.com.
Catechesis/Religious Program—Students 183.
Mission—St. John the Evangelist (2000) 99 Second St., New Castle, Craig Co. 24127. Tel: 540-864-8686.

FORT MONROE, HAMPTON CO., ST. MARY STAR OF THE SEA (1860) Rev. Msgr. Walter C. Barrett; Rev. Eric J. Ayers; Deacon James Wharry.
Mailing Address: 7 Frank Ln., 23651-1010. Tel: 757-722-9855; 757-722-3138; Fax: 757-726-0083. Email: stmary@starofthesea.hrcoxmail.com. Web: stmarystarofthesea.catholicweb.com.
School—St. Mary Star of the Sea, 14 N. Willard Ave., Hampton, 23663. Tel: 757-723-6358; Fax: 757-723-6544. Sr. Marie Andrea, Prin. Sisters 5; Lay Teachers 13; Students 213.
Catechesis/Religious Program—Tel: 757-722-9855. Email: drestmarys@yahoo.com. Students 31.

FRANKLIN, SOUTHAMPTON CO., ST. JUDE (1948) Rev. Charles A. Saglio.
Mailing Address: 1014 Clay St., 23851-1309. Tel: 757-569-9600; Fax: 757-569-9600 (Call First). Email: st_jude1@verizon.net.
Catechesis/Religious Program—Students 65.
Mission—Infant of Prague Rte. 460, Wakefield, Southampton Co. 23888.

GATE CITY, SCOTT CO., ST. BERNARD (1956) Rev. Roland Hautz, G.H.M.
Mailing Address: 139 Linda St., 24251. Tel: 276-386-9665; Fax: 276-386-3902. Email: rollieh@mounet.com.
Catechesis/Religious Program—Students 5.
Mission—St. Patrick (1946)Tel: 276-386-9665.

GLOUCESTER, GLOUCESTER CO., ST. THERESE, THE LITTLE FLOWER (1939) Rev. James Cowles, Admin.
Church & Mailing Address: 6262 Main St., 23061. Tel: 804-693-5939 (Office); Fax: 804-693-4766. Email: office.1@stthersglo.org. Web: www.sainttheresechurch.info.
Catechesis/Religious Program—Tel: 804-693-5939. Students 95.

HAMPTON, HAMPTON CO.

1—CATHOLIC COMMUNITY OF THE KOREAN MARTYRS (1989), (Korean), Rev. Simon Hyo-Sung Ahn; Deacon Joseph N. Riss.
Mailing Address: 2018 Bay Ave., 23661. Tel: 757-245-4485; 757-245-5513; Fax: 757-246-1277. Email: stroseandkm@gmail.com.
Catechesis/Religious Program—Students 50.

2—IMMACULATE CONCEPTION (1968) Rev. Msgr. Robert M. Perkins.
Res.: 40 Pine Cone Dr., 23669. Tel: 757-826-0050.
Church: 2150 Cunningham Dr., 23666. Tel: 757-826-0393; Fax: 757-825-0855. Email: iccc.hampton@verizon.net. Web: www.icchampton.org.
Catechesis/Religious Program—Students 152.

3—ST. JOSEPH (1955) Rev. Msgr. Walter C. Barrett; Revs. Eric J. Ayers, Parochial Vicar; Oscar Paraiso, Parochial Vicar; Deacon Jose M. Gonzalez.
Mailing Address: 512 Buckroe Ave., 23664.
Res.: 410 Buckroe Ave., 23664-0126. Tel: 757-851-1711.
Church: 414 Buckroe Ave., 23664-0126. Tel: 757-851-8800; Fax: 757-851-1875. Email: parishoffice4@verizon.net.
Catechesis/Religious Program—Students 153.

4—OUR LADY OF VIETNAM CHAPEL (1994), (Vietnamese), Rev. Joseph Phien Nguyen (Vietnam); Deacon James Wharry.
Mailing Address: 1806 Ashland Ave., Norfolk, 23509. Tel: 757-531-7214; 757-232-1424.
Chapel— 1307 LaSalle Ave., 23669.
Catechesis/Religious Program—Peter Khoi Nguyen, D.R.E. Students 65.

5—ST. ROSE OF LIMA (1948) Rev. Simon Hyo-Sung Ahn; Deacon Joseph N. Riss.
Mailing Address: 2114 Bay Ave., 23661. Tel: 757-245-5513; Fax: 757-245-1277. Email: strose@erols.com.
Res.: 2108 Bay Ave., 23661. Tel: 757-245-4485.
Catechesis/Religious Program—Students 3.

HARRISONBURG, ROCKINGHAM CO., BLESSED SACRAMENT (1906) Rev. Thomas E. Mattingly; Deacon Fred C. La Spina, Pastoral Assoc.
Mailing Address & Church: 154 N. Main St., 22802. Tel: 540-434-4341. Web: www.bsccva.com.
Res.: 843 Meadowlark Dr., 22802. Tel: 540-433-3585.
Catechesis/Religious Program—Tel: 540-434-5549. Students 473.

HIGHLAND SPRINGS, HENRICO CO., ST. JOHN THE EVANGELIST (1929) Rev. Wayne L Ball.
Mailing Address: P.O. Box 190, 23075-0190. Tel: 804-737-8028; Fax: 804-328-4683. Email: office@stjohnscatholicchurch.org. Web: www.stjohnscatholicchurch.org.
Res.: 7973 Bear Grass Ln., Mechanicsville, 23111. Tel: 804-677-1854.
Church: 813 W. Nine Mile Rd., 23075.
Catechesis/Religious Program—Email: tylesane@stjohnscatholicchurch.org. Students 97.

HOPEWELL, HAMPTON CO., ST. JAMES CHURCH (1918) Rev. Frank Wiggins.
Mailing Address: 510 W. Poythress St., 23860-2508.
Res.: 102 N. Fifth Ave., 23860.
Church: 500 W. Poythress St., 23860. Tel: 804-458-9223; 804-458-9286 (Evening); Fax: 804-458-1216. Email: st.jameshopewell@verizon.net. Web: www.stjameshopewell.org.
Catechesis/Religious Program—Email: st.jameschristianformation@verizon.net. Students 79.

HOT SPRINGS, BATH CO., THE SHRINE OF THE SACRED HEART (1922) Rev. John McGinnity (Retired).
Mailing Address: 1499 Shady Ln., 24445-0047. Tel: 540-839-2603.
Catechesis/Religious Program—Email: shrine@tds.net. Students 3.

HURT, PITTSYLVANIA CO., ST. VICTORIA (1964) Rev. James E. Gallagher Jr.
Mailing Address: P.O. Box 640, 24563-0640. Tel: 434-324-4824. Email: stviccah@fairpoint.net.
Res.: 305 Victoria Dr., 24563. Fax: 434-324-4824.

JONESVILLE, LEE CO., CHURCH OF THE HOLY SPIRIT (1956) Rev. Timothy A. Drake.
Mailing Address: P.O. Box 923, 24263. Tel: 276-346-0269. Email: stanthonys3@verizon.net.
Church: 384 Eagle Ridge Dr., 24263. Tel: 276-679-2336.
Catechesis/Religious Program—Students 1.

LAKE GASTON, MECKLENBERG CO., ST. PETER THE APOSTLE (1995) Rev. Columba A. Nnorom.
Church: Rte. 903, 31 Ebony Rd., Ebony, 23845. Tel: 434-636-7782; Fax: 434-636-4549. Email: sptamail@buggs.net. Web: www.st-peter-the-apostle.org.
Catechesis/Religious Program—Robert Walker, D.R.E. Students 2.

LEBANON, RUSSELL CO., GOOD SHEPHERD (1959) Rev. Michael J. Herbert.
Mailing Address: P.O. Box 730, 24266-0730. Tel: 276-889-1690; 276-889-0127.
Church: 890 W. Main St., Ste. A, 24266. Email: mjherbert@earthlink.net.
Catechesis/Religious Program—Students 7.

LEXINGTON, ROCKBRIDGE CO., ST. PATRICK (1873) Rev. Joseph A. D'Aurora.
Office & Mailing: 221 W. Nelson St., P.O. Box 725, 24450-0725. Tel: 540-463-3533; Fax: 540-464-3790. Email: officestpats@embarqmail.com. Web: stpatrickslexington.com.
Res.: 225 Denny Ln., 24450-1770. Tel: 540-463-6819.
Church: 219 W. Nelson St., 24450.
Catechesis/Religious Program—Students 103.

LOVINGSTON, NELSON CO., ST. MARY (1979) Rev. Daniel L. Kelly; Deacon Richard J. Nees.
Mailing Address: 9900 Thomas Nelson Hwy., 22949-0735. Tel: 434-263-8509. Email: stmarystfrancischurch@verizon.net. Web: www.stmarycatholicchurch.org.
Catechesis/Religious Program—Tel: 434-263-6923. Students 36.

LYNCHBURG, CAMPBELL CO.

1—HOLY CROSS (1859) [CEM] Rev. Msgr. J. Kenneth Rush Jr. In Res., Rev. James E. Gallagher Jr.
Church & Office Address: 710 Clay St., 24504-2530. Tel: 434-846-5245; Fax: 434-846-7022. Email:

hcrosshome@aol.com. Web: www.holycrosslynchburg.org.
Res.: 2000 Burnt Bridge Rd., 24503. Tel: 434-386-0220.
School—Regional School, (Grades PreK-12), 2125 Langhorne Rd., 24501. Tel: 434-847-5436. Mr. John P. Jones, Prin. Lay Teachers 45; Students 317.
Catechesis/Religious Program—Students 270.

2—ST. THOMAS MORE (1978) Rev. Richard T. Mooney; Deacon Frederick Scarletto.
3015 Roundelay Rd., 24502-2036. Tel: 434-237-5911; Fax: 434-237-8854. Email: info@stmva.com. Web: www.stmva.com.
Catechesis/Religious Program—Tel: 434-237-8852. Email: faithformation@stmva.com. Students 300.

MARION, SMYTH CO., ST. JOHN THE EVANGELIST CHURCH (1974) Rev. Paul Maier; Deacon Juan Ibarra, Hipsanic Ministry.
Church: 124 Park Blvd., 24354. Tel: 276-783-7282; Fax: 276-783-7282.
Catechesis/Religious Program—Students 16.

MARTINSVILLE, HENRY CO., ST. JOSEPH (1949), (Hispanic), Rev. Mark White.
Mailing Address: 2481 Spruce St., 24112. Tel: 276-638-4779; 276-638-1192; Fax: 540-638-2218. Email: stjoeoffice@centurylink.net. Web: www.stjoechurch.net.
Res.: 1810 Spruce St., #117, 24112. Tel: 276-632-5182.
Catechesis/Religious Program—Students 77.

MATHEWS, MATHEWS CO., CHURCH OF FRANCIS DE SALES (1983) [JC] Rev. Robert L. Cummins.
Church: 176 Lover's Ln., 23109. Fax: 804-725-0528. Email: fdschurch@gmail.com. Web: www.churchoffrancisdesales.org.
Catechesis/Religious Program—Students 55.

MECHANICSVILLE, HANOVER CO., CHURCH OF THE REDEEMER (1976) Rev. James J. Begley Jr.; Deacons Christopher Stephen Colville; Chris Malone.
Church & Mailing Address: 8275 Meadowbridge Rd., 23116. Tel: 804-746-4911; Fax: 804-746-8657. Email: sphillips@churchredeemer.org. Web: www.churchredeemer.org.
Res.: 8222 N. Mayfield Ln., 23111. Tel: 804-427-6962.
Catechesis/Religious Program—Tel: 804-746-4911. Mrs. Terry Colville, D.R.E.; Mr. LeRoy Orie Jr., Youth Min.; Mr. Dennis Beeman, D.R.E. (Adult). Students 627.

MIDDLESEX, MIDDLESEX CO., CHURCH OF THE VISITATION (1983) [JC] Rev. Robert L. Cummins.
Mailing Address: P.O. Box 38, Topping, 23169-0038. Tel: 804-758-5160; Fax: 804-758-0676. Email: churchofthevisitation@va.metrocast.net. Web: www.visitationcatholicchurch.org.
Res.: 119 Club Dr., Hartfield, 23071. Tel: 804-776-0676.
Church: 8462 Puller Hwy., Topping, 23169.
Catechesis/Religious Program—Students 15.

MINERAL, LOUISA CO., ST. JUDE (1974) [CEM] Rev. Michael M. Duffy; Deacons Robert M. Esposito; Alfonso Benet.
Rectory—Tel: 540-894-8209. Email: stjudemineral@verizon.net. Web: www.louisacatholics.org.
Church: 1937 Davis Hwy., P.O. Box 40, 23117-0040.
Catechesis/Religious Program—Students 48.
Mission—Immaculate Conception (1876) [CEM] P.O. Box 128, Bumpass, 23024-0128. 1107 Fredericks Hall Rd., Bumpass, 23024-0128. Tel: 540-872-3922 (Office); Fax: 540-872-3726. Email: immaculate1876@verizon.net.
Catechesis/Religious Program—Students 39.

MONETA, BEDFORD CO., RESURRECTION (1984) [CEM] Rev. Salvador Anonuevo (Philippines); Deacon Chris Barrett, Senior Pastoral Assoc.; Joe Day, Business Admin.
Mailing Address: 15353 Moneta Rd., 24121-9804. Tel: 540-297-5530; Fax: 540-297-6316. Email: jday@resurrectioncatholic.org. Web: www.resurrectioncatholic.org.
Catechesis/Religious Program—Students 93.

NEW CASTLE, CRAIG CO., SAINT JOHN THE EVANGELIST MISSION (1997) Rev. Stephen McNally.
99 Second St., 24127. Tel: 540-864-8686. Email: stjohnnewcastle@tds.net.
Catechesis/Religious Program—Students 3.

NEWPORT NEWS, NEWPORT CO.

1—ST. JEROME (1966) Rev. V. Henry M. Diesta.
Mailing Address: 116 Denbigh Blvd., 23608-3333. Tel: 757-877-5021; Fax: 757-898-1437. Email: jeanieaa@stjeromennva.org. Web: www.stjeromennva.org.
Catechesis/Religious Program—Tel: 757-877-3771. Email: margie@stjeromennva.org. Students 459.

2—OUR LADY OF MOUNT CARMEL (1953) Revs. Kenneth E. Wood; Peter Tran; Deacon Bernard H. Taylor.
100 Harpersville Rd., 23601-2324. Tel: 757-595-0385; Fax: 757-599-9285. Email: jhassan@olmc.org. Web: www.olmc.org.
School—Tel: 757-596-2754; Fax: 757-596-1570. Sr. John Paul Myers, O.P., Prin. Sisters of St. Dominic 5; Lay Teachers 47; Students 549.
Catechesis/Religious Program—Tel: 757-595-0385, Ext. 119. Students 445.

3—ST. VINCENT DE PAUL (1881) Rev. Msgr. Walter C. Barrett; Rev. Eric J. Ayers.
Church & Mailing Address: 230 33rd St., P.O. Box 258, 23607. Tel: 757-245-4234; Fax: 757-245-0039. Email: stvdpcc@verizon.net. Web: mysite.verizon.net/stvdpcc.
Catechesis/Religious Program—Students 65.

NORFOLK, NORFOLK CITY CO.

1—BASILICA OF ST. MARY OF THE IMMACULATE CONCEPTION (1791), (African American), [JC] Rev. Ernest Livasia Bulinda, Rector; Deacon Calvin J. Bailey.
Office & Rectory: 1000 Holt St., 23504-4201. Tel: 757-622-4487; Fax: 757-625-7969. Email: admin@stmary.hrcoxmail.com. Web: www.basilicaofsaintmary.org.
Church: 232 Chapel St., 23504.
Catechesis/Religious Program—Students 104.

2—BLESSED SACRAMENT (1921) [CEM] Rev. Joseph H. Metzger III.
Mailing Address: 6400 Newport Ave., 23505-4557. Tel: 757-423-8305; Fax: 757-451-3335. Email: office@blessed-sacrament.com. Web: www.blessed-sacrament.com.
Res.: 110 W. Severn Rd., 23505. Tel: 757-489-9636.
Catechesis/Religious Program—Students 179.

3—CHRIST THE KING (1949) Rev. Matthias Lusembo.
Office & Mailing Address—1803 Columbia Ave., 23509-1298. Tel: 757-622-1120; 757-622-9196; Fax: 757-627-8808. Email: office@christtheking.hrcoxmail.com. Web: www.ctkparish-norfolk.org.
Res.: 1804 Ashland Ave., 23509. Tel: 757-627-1723. Email: brafferty@christtheking.hrcoxmail.com.
School—3401 Tidewater Dr., 23509. Tel: 757-625-4951; Fax: 757-623-5212. Email: info@ctkparish.org. Web: www.ctkparish.org. Mrs. Rachel Chatham, Prin. Lay Teachers 22; Students 290.
Catechesis/Religious Program—Tel: 757-625-0208. Students 155.

4—HOLY TRINITY (1921) [JC] Rev. William Daniel Beeman.
Mailing Address: 155 W. Government Ave., 23503-2905. Tel: 757-480-3433; Fax: 757-480-8749. Email: parish.office@trinitynorfolk.org. Web: www.trinitynorfolk.org.
Catechesis/Religious Program—Students 240.

5—OUR LADY OF LAVANG (1991) [JC] Rev. Joseph Phien Nguyen (Vietnam), Admin.; Deacon James Wharry.
1806 Ashland Ave., 23509-1236.
Church: 409 Compostella Rd., 23509. Tel: 757-232-1424; Fax: 757-351-3648.
Catechesis/Religious Program—Joseph Trinh Tu, D.R.E. Students 45.

6—ST. PIUS X (1955) Rev. Nixon Negparanon (Philippines); Deacon Walker King.
Res.: 1615 Longdale Dr., 23518. Tel: 757-855-3297. Email: stpiusxchurch@piusxparish.org. Web: www.piusxparish.org/church.
School—7800 Halprin Dr., 23518. Tel: 757-588-6171; Fax: 757-587-6580. Email: school@piusxparish.org. Web: www.piusxparish.org. Sr. Linda Taber, I.H.M., Prin. Sisters Servants of the Immaculate Heart of Mary 2; Lay Teachers 17; Students 330.
Catechesis/Religious Program—Email: sbernadette@piusxparish.org. Students 219.

7—SACRED HEART (1894) [CEM] Rev. Daniel N. Klem.
Office: 520 Graydon Ave., 23507-1711. Tel: 757-625-6763; Fax: 757-627-1965. Email: office@sacredheartnorfolk.org. Web: www.sacredheartnorfolk.org.
Catechesis/Religious Program—Students 177.

NORGE, JAMES CITY CO., ST. OLAF, PATRON OF NORWAY (1992) Rev. Peter M. Creed; Deacons Robert R. Thompson; Daniel F. Ferry.
Mailing Address: 104 Norge Ln., 23188-7229. Tel: 757-564-3819; Fax: 757-565-1099. Email: office@stolafchurch.hrcoxmail.com. Web: www.stolaf.cc.
Catechesis/Religious Program—Students 135.

NORTON, WISE CO., ST. ANTHONY (1938) Rev. Timothy A. Drake.
Mailing Address & Church: 1009 Virginia Ave., N.W., 24273-1897. Tel: 276-679-2336. Email: stanthonys3@verizon.net. Web: www.stanthonycatholic.org.
Catechesis/Religious Program—Students 16.
Station—University of Virginia at Wise Wise.

ONLEY, ACCOMACK CO., ST. PETER THE APOSTLE (1942) Rev. Rodrigo Mingollo.
Church & Mailing Address: 25236 Coastal Blvd., P.O. Box 860, 23418-0860. Tel: 757-787-4592; Fax: 757-787-2899. Email: stpeterapostle@verizon.net. Web: www.stpetertheapostle.com.
Catechesis/Religious Program—Students 68.

PALMYRA, FLUVANNA CO., SS. PETER & PAUL (1986) Rev. Gerald F. Musuubire.
Mailing Address: 4309 Thomas Jefferson Pkwy., 22963-9506. Tel: 434-589-5201; Fax: 434-589-4463. Email: office@saintspeterpaul.org. Web: www.saintspeterpaul.org.
Catechesis/Religious Program—Students 177.

PEARISBURG, GILES CO., HOLY FAMILY (1965) Rev. John Prinelli.
Mailing Address: 516 Mason Court Dr., 24134-1832. Tel: 540-921-3547. Email: holyfamilyva@lycos.com.
Catechesis/Religious Program—

PETERSBURG, PRINCE GEORGE CO., ST. JOSEPH (1842) [CEM] Rev. Joseph Morton Biber.
Church, Office & Mailing Address: 151 W. Washington St., P.O. Box 2006, 23804-1306. Tel: 804-733-3115; Fax: 804-862-9931. Email: st_joseph_church@sjcpetersburg.com. Web: www.sjcpetersburg.com.
Res.: 19 Centre Hill Ct., 23803.
School—123 Franklin St., 23803. Tel: 804-732-3931; Fax: 804-732-6479. Pamela K. Hartnett, Prin. Lay Teachers 10; Students 150.
Catechesis/Religious Program—Tel: 804-862-9977. Students 35.

POCAHONTAS, TAZEWELL CO., ST. ELIZABETH (1896) Merged with St. Mary, Richlands, St. Theresa, Tazewell & mission church of St. Joseph, Grundy to form Holy Family Parish, Tazewell.

PORTSMOUTH, PORTSMOUTH CO.

1—CHURCH OF THE HOLY ANGELS (1917) [JC] Revs. David W. Cupps; Jaroslaw Nowacki, Parochial Vicar.
Office: 34 Afton Pkwy., 23702-2739. Tel: 757-485-2142; 757-485-2143; Fax: 757-485-3699. Email: holyangels@juno.com.
Catechesis/Religious Program—Students 81.

2—CHURCH OF THE RESURRECTION (1971) Revs. David W. Cupps; Jaroslaw Nowacki, Parochial Vicar.
Mailing Address: 3501 Cedar Ln., 23703. Tel: 757-484-7335; Fax: 757-484-5857. Email: cthies@reschurch.com.
Res.: 518 High St., 23704. Tel: 757-397-7066.
Catechesis/Religious Program—Students 110.

3—ST. PAUL (1804) [CEM] [JC] Revs. David W. Cupps; Jaroslaw Nowacki, Parochial Vicar.
Office: 518 High St., 23704-3516. Tel: 757-397-7066; Fax: 757-393-4334. Email: stpaulsptown@aol.com. Web: www.stpauls-portsmouth.org.
Church: 522 High St., 23704.
Catechesis/Religious Program—Email: christianformation@clusterparishes.com. Students 139.

POWHATAN, CAMPBELL CO., ST. JOHN NEUMANN (1948) Rev. Walter G. Lewis; Deacons Edward P. Schmidt; Fulton Patrick O'Donnell.
Church: 2480 Batterson Rd., 23139-7513. Tel: 804-598-3754; Fax: 804-598-1467. Email: sjn_general@yahoo.com. Web: www.sjnpowhatan.org.
Catechesis/Religious Program—Students 200.

PRINCE GEORGE COUNTY, PRINCE GEORGE CO., CHURCH OF THE SACRED HEART (1906) [CEM] Rev. Jay Wagner; Deacons Raymond K. Linden; Edward G. Hanzlik; Robert Dennis Baker; James E. Rodgers.
Mailing Address: 9300 Community Ln., Petersburg, 23805-7567. Tel: 804-732-6385; Fax: 804-732-6385. Email: sacredheart1906@verizon.net. Web: www.churchsacredheart.com.
Catechesis/Religious Program—Students 176.

QUINQUE, GREENE COUNTY, SHEPHERD OF THE HILLS (1980) Rev. Lawrence J. Mullaney Jr.
Mailing Address: P.O. Box 83, 22965-0083. Tel: 434-985-3929. Email: infant.shepherdVA@yahoo.com. Web: www.infant-shepherd.com.
Church: Rte. 633, 6562 Amicus Rd., 22965-0083.
Catechesis/Religious Program—Jane Lilly, D.R.E. Students 46.

QUINTON, NEW KENT CO., ST. ELIZABETH ANN SETON (1986) Very Rev. J. Scott Duarte; Deacon William R. Hunt.
Mailing Address & Church: 2631 Pocahontas Tr., 23141-0245. Tel: 804-932-4125; Fax: 804-932-8126. Email: seascatholic@verizon.net. Web: www.seascatholicchurch.org.
Catechesis/Religious Program—Students 33.

RADFORD, MONTGOMERY CO., ST. JUDE (1967) Rev. Kenneth J. Shuping; Deacon Michael J. Ellerbrock.
Mailing Address: 1740 Tyler Rd., Christiansburg, 24073-6154. Tel: 540-639-5341; Fax: 540-639-4738. Email: stjudechurch@juno.com. Web: stjuderadfordva.org.
Res.: 1800 Tyler Rd., Christiansburg, 24073. Tel: 540-731-9541.
Catechesis/Religious Program—Students 117.

RICHLANDS, TAZEWELL CO., ST. MARY (1962) Merged with St. Theresa, Tazewell, St. Elizabeth, Pocahontas & mission church of St. Joseph, Grundy to form Holy Family, Tazewell.

ROANOKE, ROANOKE CO.
1—ST. ANDREW (1890) [JC] Rev. Msgr. Thomas G. Miller; Deacon Mark D. Allison.
Res. & Mailing Address: 631 N. Jefferson St., 24016. Email: jblanchard@standrewsroanoke.org. Web: www.standrewsroanoke.org.
Catechesis/Religious Program—Students 370.
2—ST. GERARD (1946) Rev. Rene R. Castillo; Deacon Stephen O'Connell.
809 Orange Ave., N.W., 24016-1117. Tel: 540-343-7744; Fax: 540-343-3599. Email: mail@stgerard.roacoxmail.com. Web: www.stgerard-roanoke-va.org.
Catechesis/Religious Program—Email: reled@stgerard.roacoxmail.com. Students 103.
3—OUR LADY OF NAZARETH (1914) Rev. Msgr. Joseph P. Lehman.
Mailing Address: 2505 Electric Rd., S.W., 24018-3599. Tel: 540-774-0066 (Office); 540-774-0857 (Res.); Fax: 540-774-2148. Web: www.oln-parish.org. Email: secretary@oln-parish.com.
Catechesis/Religious Program—Tel: 540-774-0773. Email: cf@oln-parish.org. Students 547.
ROCKY MOUNT, FRANKLIN CO., FRANCIS OF ASSISI (1984) Rev. Rene R. Castillo; Mr. Larry A. Fischbach, Senior Pastoral Assoc.
Mailing Address: 15 Glennwood Dr., 24151-2111. Tel: 540-483-9591; Fax: 540-483-5232. Email: francismom@jetbroadband.com. Web: www.francis-of-assisi.org.
Catechesis/Religious Program—Students 90.
ST. PAUL, WISE CO., ST. THERESE (1954) Rev. Michael J. Herbert.
Mailing Address: P.O. Box 56, 24283-0056. Tel: 276-762-5932; Fax: 276-762-5932. Email: mjhebert@earthlink.net.
Catechesis/Religious Program—Students 6.
SALEM, PAGE CO., OUR LADY OF PERPETUAL HELP (1947) Rev. Kevin Lee Segerblom; Deacon Eric M. Surat.
Mailing Address: 314 Turner Rd., 24153-2399. Tel: 540-387-0491; Fax: 540-389-8237. Web: www.olphsalem.org. Email: office@olphsalem.org.
Res.: 1408 Kathryn Ln., 24153. Tel: 540-387-1020.
Catechesis/Religious Program—Email: christianformation@olphsalem.org. Students 162.
SCOTTSVILLE, ALBEMARLE CO., ST. GEORGE (1975) [CEM] Rev. Dennis McAuliffe.
Mailing Address: 7240 Scottsville Rd., P.O. Box 9, 24590-0009. Tel: 434-286-3724. Email: stgeorge604@juno.com.
SMITHFIELD, ISLE OF WIGHT CO., GOOD SHEPHERD (1984) Unassigned.Mailing Address: P.O. Box 840, 23431-0840. Tel: 757-365-0579; Fax: 757-365-4749. Email: goodshepherd-smithfield@verizon.net. Web: goodshepherd-smithfield.org.
Church: 300 Smithfield Blvd., 23430.
Catechesis/Religious Program—Students 150.
SOUTH BOSTON, HALIFAX CO., ST. PASCHAL BAYLON (1953) [JC] Revs. John C. Kazibwe (Uganda); Charles Ssebalamu (Uganda), Parochial Vicar.
Church: 800 John Randolph Blvd., 24592-2943. Tel: 434-572-2285; Fax: 434-572-1725. Email: stpaschalchurch@embarqmail.com.
Catechesis/Religious Program—Students 35.
SOUTH HILL, MECKLENBURG CO., GOOD SHEPHERD (1922) Revs. John C. Kazibwe (Uganda); Nixon Negparanon (Philippines), Parochial Vicar.
Mailing Address: P.O. Box 621, 23970-0621. Tel: 434-447-3622; Fax: 434-447-4729. Email: goodsh23970@earthlink.net.
Church: 1664 N. Mecklenburg Ave., 23970.
Catechesis/Religious Program—Students 18.
STAUNTON, AUGUSTA CO., ST. FRANCIS OF ASSISI (1844) Rev. Joseph Wamala (Uganda); Deacon James Kledzik.
118 N. New St., 24401-3636.
Res.: 126 N. New St., 24401. Tel: 540-886-9121; Fax: 540-885-5743. Email: frwamala@stfrancisparish.org. Web: www.stfrancisparish.org.
Catechesis/Religious Program—Students 184.
SUFFOLK, SUFFOLK CO., ST. MARY OF THE PRESENTATION (1927) Unassigned.
Office: 202 S. Broad St., 23434-5715. Tel: 757-539-5732; Fax: 757-538-0103. Email: office@stmarysuffolk.org. Web: www.stmarysuffolk.org.
Church: 200 S. Broad St., 23434.
Catechesis/Religious Program—Students 84.
TABB, YORK CO., BLESSED KATERI TEKAKWITHA (1986) Rev. Charles J. Faul; Mrs. Elaine Riley, Admin.
Church & Office: 3800 Big Bethel Rd., 23693-3814. Tel: 757-766-3800; Fax: 757-766-1125. Email: elaineriley@stkateri.org. Web: www.stkateri.org.
Catechesis/Religious Program—Web: www.stkateriyouth.org. Mrs. Debra Gausmann, D.R.E. (Grades K-7); Mrs. Patricia Kovac, Youth Min. (Grades 8-12); Mrs. Lori Yankoski. Students 358.
TAPPAHANNOCK, ESSEX CO., ST. TIMOTHY (1972) Rev. Jonathan Goertz.
Mailing Address: 708 N. Church Ln., P.O. Box 129, 22560-0129. Web: www.sttimothysparish.org.
Church: 708 N. Church Ln., 22560. Tel: 804-443-2760; 804-443-2570; Fax: 804-443-2022. Email: sttimothychurch@verizon.net.
Catechesis/Religious Program—Students 62.
TAZEWELL, TAZEWELL CO.
1—HOLY FAMILY PARISH Rev. Burt Sare (Philippines). Church & Mailing Address: 304 Tazewell Ave., 24651. Fax: 276-988-8028. Email: theword1875@verizon.net.
Catechesis/Religious Program—Students 32.
2—ST. THERESA (1980) Merged with St. Mary, Richlands, St. Elizabeth, Pochontas & mission church of St. Joseph, Grundy to form Holy Family, Tazewell.
VIRGINIA BEACH, VIRGINIA BEACH CO., CHURCH OF THE ASCENSION (1972) [CEM] Rev. Charles L. Breindel; Deacon Thomas E. McFeely; Lisa Liedl, Business Mgr.; Diane Nestor, Music Min.; Susan Anders.
Office: 4853 Princess Anne Rd., 23462-4446. Tel: 757-495-1886; Fax: 757-495-1516. Web: www.ascensionvb.org.
Catechesis/Religious Program—Tel: 757-495-1886, Ext. 11. Janet Jones, D.R.E.; Robert Hamrick, Youth Min. Students 501.
VIRGINIA BEACH, VIRGINIA CO.
1—CATHOLIC CHURCH OF ST. MARK (1978) [CEM] Rev. James C. Griffin; Deacons Michael Johnson; John J. Kren.
Mailing Address: 1505 Kempsville Rd., 23464-7210. Tel: 757-479-1010; Fax: 757-479-9453. Email: secretary@stmark-parish.org. Web: www.stmark-parish.org.
Res.: 4901 Whitewood Ln., 23464. Tel: 757-467-4932.
Catechesis/Religious Program—Tel: 757-479-9897; Fax: 757-479-9453. Email: jennifer@stmark-parish.org. Students 425.
2—CHURCH OF THE HOLY APOSTLES (1977), (Anglican-Roman Catholic Congregation of Hampton Roads) Revs. James E. Parke, Co-Pastor; Michael B. Ferguson, Co-Pastor.
Church: 1593 Lynnhaven Pkwy., 23453-2008. Tel: 757-427-0963; Fax: 757-427-9434. Email: admin@holyapostlesvb.org. Web: www.ha-arc.com.
Catechesis/Religious Program—Students 30.
3—ST. GREGORY THE GREAT (1957) Revs. Mario Fulgenzi; Michael Gabler, O.S.B., Parochial Vicar; Cristiano Aparecido Brito, O.S.B., Parochial Vicar; Carol Noona, Music Min.; Janice Sigala, Spanish Min.
Office: 5345 Virginia Beach Blvd., 23462. Tel: 757-497-8330; Fax: 757-490-1492. Email: stgregoryg@aol.com. Web: stgregoryvabeach.org.
School—5343 Virginia Beach Blvd., 23462-1896. Tel: 757-497-1811; Fax: 757-497-7005. Sr. Mary Catherine Chapman, I.H.M., Prin. Lay Teachers 46; Students 711; Religious 4.
Catechesis/Religious Program—Tel: 757-499-4494; Fax: 757-490-1492. Anne Marie Holland, D.R.E. Students 619.
Chapel—Chesapeake, St. Benedict Tridentine Chapel (1992) 521 McCosh St., Chesapeake, 23320. Tel: 757-543-0561.
Catechesis/Religious Program—Students 103.
4—HOLY FAMILY (1977) Rev. Gaudencio G. Pugat, S.V.D.
Parish Center—1279 N. Great Neck Rd., 23454-2117. Tel: 757-481-5702; 757-481-0799; Fax: 757-481-3989. Web: www.holyfamilyvb.org.
Catechesis/Religious Program—Students 569.
5—HOLY SPIRIT (1975) [CEM] Rev. Timothy Kuhneman; Deacon Robert J. Durel.
Office: 1396 Lynnhaven Pkwy., 23453-2710. Tel: 757-468-3600; 757-468-3601; Fax: 757-468-3342. Email: office@holyspiritvb.org. Web: www.holyspiritvb.org.
Res.: 3345 Clubhouse Rd., 23452. Tel: 757-216-2347.
Catechesis/Religious Program—Students 491.
6—ST. JOHN THE APOSTLE CHURCH (1989) Rev. Robert J. Cole (Netherlands Antilles); Deacons Joseph F. Grillo; Vernon Krajeski.
Office & Church: 1968 Sandbridge Rd., 23456. Tel: 757-426-2180; Fax: 757-426-6857. Email: parish@sjavb.org. Web: www.sjavb.org.
School—1968 Sandbridge Rd., 23456. Tel: 757-821-1100; Fax: 757-821-1047. Joseph Badali, Prin. Staff 30; Students 204.
Catechesis/Religious Program—Tel: 757-426-2180; Fax: 757-426-6857. Email: jdomingo@sjavb.org. Students 725.
7—ST. LUKE (1986) Rev. Silvio Kaberia (Kenya); Deacon Lawrence P. Illy, Business Mgr.
Mailing Address: 2304 Salem Rd., 23456-1215. Tel: 757-427-5776; Fax: 757-427-2260. Email: stlukecc@aol.com. Web: www.saintlukecc.com.
Catechesis/Religious Program—Tel: 757-427-5776; Fax: 757-427-2260. Students 204.
8—ST. MATTHEW (1924) Rev. John Adam Abe; Deacons Chris Romero; William J. Blatnik; Darrell G. Wentworth.
Office: 3314 Sandra Ln., 23464-1736. Tel: 757-420-6310; 757-420-6311; Fax: 757-420-7734. Email: st.matthews@saintmatts.net. Web: www.saintmatts.net.
Res.: 1020 Josephine Crescent, 23464. Tel: 757-523-1723.
School—3316 Sandra Ln., 23464. Tel: 757-420-2455; Fax: 757-420-4880. Mr. Louis Goldberg, Prin. Lay Teachers 36; Students 507.
Catechesis/Religious Program—Tel: 757-420-6310; Fax: 757-420-7734. Students 160.
9—ST. NICHOLAS (1963) Rev. Venancio R. Balarote Jr. Office & Church: 712 Little Neck Rd., 23452. Tel: 757-340-7231; Fax: 757-340-2727. Email: stnicholas@stnicholasvb.com. Web: www.stnicholasvb.com.
Res.: 3340 Old Kirkwood Dr., 23452-5807. Tel: 757-498-7834.
Catechesis/Religious Program—Students 279.
10—STAR OF THE SEA (1915) Rev. Esteban DeLeon, S.V.D.
Office: 1404 Pacific Ave., 23451-3439. Tel: 757-428-8547; Fax: 757-428-0788. Web: www.staroftheseaparish.com.
School—309 15th St., 23451. Tel: 757-428-8400; Fax: 757-428-2794. Ms. Cathryn Mary Whisman, Prin. Lay Teachers 24; Students 364.
Catechesis/Religious Program—Tel: 757-428-8547; Fax: 757-428-0788. Students 284.
WAYNESBORO, AUGUSTA CO., ST. JOHN THE EVANGELIST (1946) Rev. Rolo B. Castillo.
Mailing Address: 344 Maple Ave., 22980-4706.
Office: Tel: 540-949-6145; 540-949-6146; Fax: 540-932-8512. Web: www.stjohnevan.com.
Church: 300 Maple Ave., 22980.
Catechesis/Religious Program—Students 214.
WEST POINT, KING WILLIAM CO., OUR LADY OF THE BLESSED SACRAMENT (1918) [CEM 2] Rev. Edgar Cleofe.
Mailing Address: 207 W. Euclid Blvd., 23181.
Church: 3570 King William Ave., 23181. Tel: 804-843-3125; Fax: 804-843-9158. Email: olbs@verizon.net. Web: www.catholic-church.org/olbs.
Catechesis/Religious Program—Students 65.
WILLIAMSBURG, JAMES CITY CO., ST. BEDE (1932) Rev. Msgr. Michael D. McCarron; Rev. John David Ramsey, Parochial Vicar; Deacons Dominic Cerrato; Francis Roettinger.
Res.: 4524 The Foxes, 23188. Tel: 757-220-4233.
Church & Mailing Address: 3686 Ironbound Rd., P.O. Box 5400, 23188. Tel: 757-229-3631; Fax: 757-229-7845. Email: stboffice@bedeva.org. Web: www.bedeva.org.
Catechesis/Religious Program—Students 998.
WOODLAWN, CARROLL CO., ST. JOSEPH'S (1981) Rev. Charles W. Brickner; Deacon Nicholas Mammi, Senior Pastoral Assoc.
Mailing Address: 3579 Carrollton Pike, 24381-3651. Tel: 276-236-7814; Fax: 276-236-4897. Email: sjoffice@embarqmail.com.
Catechesis/Religious Program—Students 78.
Mission—Church of the Risen Lord U.S. 58 and County 625, Stuart, Patrick 24171.
Catechesis/Religious Program—Students 1.
Mission—Church of All Saints 598 Needmore Rd., N.E., Floyd, Floyd Co. 24091.
Catechesis/Religious Program—Students 13.
WYTHEVILLE, WYTHE CO., ST. MARY THE MOTHER OF GOD (1845) [CEM] Rev. Esteban Eugenio D. Antes (Philippines).
Mailing Address: P.O. Box 7, 24382-0007. Tel: 276-228-3104; Fax: 276-228-3322. Email: stmarys10@embarqmail.com.
Church: 370 E. Main St., 24382.
Catechesis/Religious Program—Students 38.
Mission—St. Edward P.O. Box 1670, Pulaski, Davis Co. 24301. Tel: 276-980-6511; Fax: 276-980-6511.
Catechesis/Religious Program—Students 28.
YORKTOWN, YORK CO., ST. JOAN OF ARC (1954) Rev. Michael Joly, Admin.; Deacon Daniel F. Johnson.
Office: 315 Harris Grove Ln., 23692-4014. Tel: 757-898-5570; Fax: 757-898-0737.
111 Tradewinds Dr., 23693.
Catechesis/Religious Program—Tel: 757-898-7190. Students 385.

Chaplains of Public Institutions

RICHMOND. *International Airport*. Rev. Wayne L Ball, Chap.
McGuire VA Medical Center. Vacant. Tel: 804-343-7111.

HAMPTON. *VA Medical Center*, Chaplain Service, Bldg. 69, 23667. Tel: 757-722-9961, Ext. 3600. Rev. Donald J. Cavey.

SALEM. *Salem VA Medical Center*, Tel: 540-982-2463. Revs. Rene R. Castillo, Chap., Jeremiusz H. Sojka, Chap.

Military Chaplains:
Revs.—
Caiazzo, Gregory G.
Dang, Chin Van
Iaucci, Thomas
McGuire, David V.

Sabbatical:
Rev.—
Rule, Steven R.

Unassigned:
Revs.—
Bostwick, John
Cowan, Steven
Kanicki, Philip A.
Murphy, Dennis
Smith, Russell E., S.T.D.
Trinh, Thai Z.

Retired:
Most Rev.—
Sullivan, Walter F., D.D., Bishop Emeritus of Richmond, 3203 Hawthorne Ave., 23222. Tel: 804-329-3653; 804-359-5661. Email: Bishop.Sullivan@richmonddiocese.org
Rev. Msgrs.—
Barton, Raymond A.
Caroluzza, Thomas, 475 Water St., #203, Portsmouth, 23704. Tel: 757-425-4555. Email: caroluzza@aol.com
Frias, Santiago C., 155 W. Government Ave., Norfolk, 23503-2095. Tel: 757-480-3434. Email: fathersanti@aol.com
Michael, Chester P., 2568 Ennis Mountain Rd., Afton, 22920-5626. Tel: 540-456-6626. Email: chesterpmichael@aol.com
Pitt, William L., 3288 Page Ave., Apt. 1112, Virginia Beach, 23451. Tel: 757-481-4629. Email: paterchs@aol.com
Revs.—
Bain, Daniel, 141 Green Turtle Ln., Apt. 8, Charlottesville, 22901. Tel: 434-974-7730
Bond, B. Daniel, 8280 Woodman Rd., 23228. Tel: 804-684-5293. Email: bdaniel.bond@att.net
Carr, James V., 217 Beach 99th St., Rockaway Park, NY 11694. Email: jamesvcarr@earthlink.net
Cervantes, Leo, 664 Burgos St., Cagayan de Oro City 9000, Philippines.
Clark, Joseph L., 1016 Donation Dr., Virginia Beach, 23455. Tel: 757-464-1816. Email: rjlc@cox.net
Condon, William F., 215 N. Power Rd., Unit 132, Mesa, AZ 85205-8462. Email: wcondon@cox.net
DeSouza, Carl, 806 Longstreet Rd., Farmville, 23901. Email: rafiki_757@msn.com
Dinga, William, P.O. Box 226, Bath, ME 04530. Email: williamdinga@verizon.net
Dorgan, John J., 19 8th Ave., Southern Shores, NC 27949-3217. Tel: 252-261-9791. Email: eddiesplace@charter.net
Dorson, James E., 133 Routier Hill, Hot Springs, 24445.
Facura, Joseph C., J.C.L., J.C.L., Blk. 3, St. Gabriel Sub.Div., Koronadal City, South Cotabato 9506 Philippines.
Feusahrens, Frederick J., 909 Rennie Ave., 23227-4808. Email: ltlfred@aol.com
Fosnot, James, 4400 Beulah Rd., 23237. Email: jmfvausa@yahoo.com
French, Robert E., 7501-15G River Rd., Newport News, 23607. Email: ref1963@msn.com
Funk, Virgil C., 12960 S.W. Park Way, Portland, OR 97225. Tel: 503-643-3734
Gallagher, Paul V.
Goodman, Julian
Hamlet, Ralph, 141 Green Turtle Ln., Apt. 10, Charlottesville, 22901-2373. Tel: 434-974-1756
Hickman, J. Stephen
Huan, Joseph Van Tran
Ilano, Jovencio, Ph.B., M.Div., P.O. Box 341293, Arleta, CA 91334.
Kloepfer, John S., P.O. Box 1742, Clarksville, 23927.
Kruc, James, P.O. Box 37116, Philadelphia, PA 19148. Tel: 302-573-3107. Email: frjkruc@comcast.net
La Fratta, William, 19 Shortwood Cir., Palmyra, 22963-2747. Tel: 434-589-0824. Email: lmfluv@gmail.com
Leonard, John E.
Majewski, Joseph B., 1991 Beaverdam Rd., Spring Grove, 23881.
Malabad, Antonio R., 400 Waters Dr. #D-104, Southern Pines, NC 28387.
McEleney, Robert J., 1666 Purdum Mill Rd., Appomattox, 24522-8367. Tel: 434-352-2881. Email: robertjmceleney@yahoo.com
Moran, Edward
Nash, Robert, P.O. Box 1093, Deltaville, 23043-1093.
Natale, Samuel, 236 E. Market St., Long Beach, NY 11561. Email: sammymn@aol.com
Naylor, Ronald J., 100 E. Ocean View Ave., #904, Norfolk, 23503-1634. Tel: 757-587-4185. Email: revron904@cox.net
Ngo, Anthony, 12500 Patterson Ave., 23233-6411. Tel: 804-784-5450
O'Brien, William S., 751 Hillsdale Dr., Charlottesville, 22901. Tel: 757-220-4233; 757-229-3700
Pham, Thuy, 1417 Plantation Lake Cir., Chesapeake, 23320. Email: thuy2005an@yahoo.com
Przywara, Gerald A., 5500 Holly Fork Rd., Barhamsville, 23011.
Quinlan, Thomas J., 4853 Princes Anne Rd., Virginia Beach, 23462. Tel: 757-333-6513. Email: tq777@cox.net
Rademacher, Robert, 100 Compton Rd., Cincinnati, OH 45215.
Ruth, Robert F., P.O. Box 258, Newport News, 23607-0258. Email: robert74@cox.net
Slowik, Joseph S.
Stickle, William, 128 Clipper Ct., Kill Devil Hills, NC 27948-9113. Tel: 252-441-4413
Teslovic, Eugene
Torretto, Joseph

Permanent Deacons:
Allison, Mark D., St. Andrew, Roanoke
Arkesteyn, John Aster, Saint Bridget, Richmond
Bailey, Calvin J., Basilica of Saint Mary of the Immaculate Conception, Norfolk
Baker, Robert Dennis, Church of the Sacred Heart, Petersburg
Banks, Marshall D., Cathedral of The Sacred Heart, Richmond
Barrett, Christopher, Resurrection, Moneta
Baskind, Frank Ronald, Ph.D., St. Michael, Richmond
Benet, Alfonso, St. Jude, Mineral; Immaculate Conception
Bergen, J. Brian, Cathedral of The Sacred Heart, Richmond
Blatnik, William J., Saint Matthew, Virginia Beach
Broughton, Eric Christopher, Saint Augustine, Richmond
Cartwright, Gordon Kenneth, Holy Cross, Lynchburg
Cerrato, Dominic, St. Bede
Colville, Christopher Stephen, Church of the Redeemer, Mechanicsville
Cronican, Richard, Christ the King
Donovan, Donald, St. Charles, Cape Charles
Dowdy, Melvin, Ben Secours-St.Mary's Hospital; Cathedral of the Sacred Heart, Richmond
Durel, Robert J., Ph.D., Church of the Holy Spirit, Virginia Beach
Dwyer, Bruce K., All Saints, Floyd; Risen Lord, Woodlawn; St. Joseph, Woodlawn
Ellerbrock, Michael J., Saint Jude Catholic, Christiansburg; Our Lady Of Perpetual Help, Salem; St. Mary, Blacksburg
Elliott, Thomas B., Saint Edward the Confessor, Richmond
Esposito, Robert M., St. Jude, Mineral; Immaculate Conception
Ewan, Robert D., Pastoral Center
Ferguson, Andrew M., Saint Michael, Richmond
Ferry, Daniel, St. Olaf, Norge
Fournier, Keith A., St. Stephen Martyr
Geary, David J., St. Mary of the Annunciation
Giovenco, Robert B., Saint Bridget, Richmond
Gonzalez, Jose Miguel, St. Joseph, Hampton
Greer, James D., Saint Edward the Confessor, Richmond
Griffin, Robert H., Our Lady of Lourdes, Richmond
Grillo, Joseph F., St. Paul, Virginia Beach; St. John the Apostle, Virginia Beach
Hanzlik, Edward G., Church of the Sacred Heart, Petersburg
Harmeyer, Gary R., Church of the Ascension, Virginia Beach
Hornstra, Curtis L., Saint Michael, Richmond
Hunt, William R., St. Elizabeth Ann Seton
Ibarra, Juan, St. Anne's Catholic Church; St. John, Marion
Illy, Lawrence P., Saint Luke, Virginia Beach
Johnson, Daniel F., Saint Joan of Arc, Yorktown
Johnson, Michael, St. Mark
Kamper, Eugene P., Saint Ann, Ashland
King, Walker P., St. Pius X, Norfolk
Kledzik, James, St. Francis of Assisi, Staunton
Kren, John J., Saint Mark, Virginia Beach
LaSpina, Fred C., Blessed Sacrament Church, Harrisonburg
Linden, Raymond K., Church of the Sacred Heart, Prince George County
Lupini, Belardino, Church of the Epiphany
MacLaughlin, Matthew C., Saint John, Petersburg
Mahefky, Paul, St. Benedict, Richmond
Malone, Christopher M., Church of the Redeemer, Mechanicsville
Mammi, Nicholas, All Saints, Woodlawn; Risen Lord; St. Joseph
Matte, Mark C., Sacred Heart, Richmond
Mavrelli, Louis A., (Retired)
McFeely, Thomas E., Church of the Ascension, Virginia Beach
McLane, Emmett R., III, St. Theresa, Farmville
Menting, Peter J., St. Theresa, Farmville
Miech, Richard, Church of the Epiphany, Richmond
Milkevitch, Joseph J.
Morash, Christopher, Pastoral Center Staff, Incarnation, Charlottesville
Moro, Michael, Church of the Ascension, Virginia Beach
Mullen, Thomas, U of R Campus Ministry
Nees, Richard J., Saint Mary, Lovingston
Nemetz, David S., St. Michael, Richmond
O'Connell, Stephen, Our Lady Of Perpetual Help, Salem
O'Donnell, Fulton Patrick, St. John Neumann
Riss, Joseph N., St. Rose of Lima, Hampton
Roderique, Raymond, Holy Name of Mary
Rodgers, James E., Church of the Sacred Heart
Roettinger, Francis, St. Bede, Williamsburg
Romero, Crisanto D., St. Matthew, Virginia Beach
Sadowski, John E., St. Catherine of Siena, Clarksville
Scarletto, Frederick, St. Thomas More, Lynchburg
Schmidt, Edward P., St. John Neumann, Powhatan; Good Samaritan, Amelia
Surat, Eric M., Our Lady of Perpetual Help, Salem
Surrusco, Richard, Our Lady of Nazareth, Roanoke
Taylor, Bernard H., Incarnation, Charlottesville
Taylor, Bernard F., Our Lady of Mt. Carmel, Newport News
Thomas, John H., J.D., Pastoral Center Staff
Thompson, Robert R., St. Olaf, Norge
Wentworth, Darrell G., Saint Matthew, Virginia Beach
Wharry, James, St. Mary Star of the Sea, Fort Monroe; Our Lady of Lavang

INSTITUTIONS LOCATED IN THE DIOCESE

[A] HIGH SCHOOLS, DIOCESAN

DANVILLE. *Sacred Heart School* (1953) (Grades PreK-9), 540 Central Blvd., 24541. Tel: 434-793-2656; Fax: 434-793-2658. Email: sheartschool@gmail.com. Web: www.sheartschool.com. Kimberly W. Meadows, Prin. Lay Teachers 24; Total Staff 29; Total Enrollment 182.

LYNCHBURG. *Holy Cross Regional School* (1879) (Grades PreK-12), 2125 Langhorne Rd., 24501. Tel: 434-847-5436; 434-847-5464; Fax: 434-847-4156. Email: office@hcrs-va.org. Web: www.hcrs-va.org. Patricia R. Culbreth, Prin. Lay Teachers 26; Students 210.

NEWPORT NEWS. *Peninsula Catholic High School*, (Grades 8-12), 600 Harpersville Rd., 23601. Tel: 757-596-7247; Fax: 757-591-9718. Web: www.peninsulacatholic.com. Francine Gagne, Ed.D., Pres.; Janine C. Franklin, Prin.; Anne Catron, Librarian. Lay Teachers 30; Total Staff 13; Students 309.

ROANOKE. *Roanoke Catholic School*, (Grades PreK-12), 621 N. Jefferson St., 24016-1416. Tel: 540-982-3532; Fax: 540-345-0785. Email: info@roanokecatholic.com. Web: www.roanokecatholic.com. Patrick Patterson, Prin., Head School; Julie Frost, Asst. Prin., Lower School; Kathleen Futrell, Asst. Prin., Upper School; Kurt Axt, Librarian. Lay Teachers 36; Students 466.

VIRGINIA BEACH. *Bishop Sullivan Catholic High School*, 4552 Princess Anne Rd., 23462. Tel: 757-467-2881; Fax: 757-467-0284. Email: priced@chsvb.org. Web: www.chsvb.org. Mr. Dennis W. Price, Prin.; Sue Skoczynski, Asst. Prin.; Dana St. John, Librarian. Lay Teachers 40; Students 426.

[B] HIGH SCHOOLS, PRIVATE

RICHMOND. *Benedictine High School of Richmond, Inc. aka Benedictine College Prep* (1911) 304 N. Sheppard St., 23221. Tel: 804-342-1300; Fax: 804-355-2407. Email: bcpinfo@benedictinecollegeprep.org. Web: www.benedictinecollegeprep.org. Rev. Jesse Grapes, Headmaster; Matthew Hamilton, Librarian. A Military High School in the Charge of the Benedictine Monks. Priests 1; Lay Teachers 23; Students 278.

Saint Gertrude High School (1922) 3215 Stuart Ave., 23221. Tel: 804-358-9114; Fax: 804-355-5682. Email: sghs@saintgertrude.org. Web: www.saintgertrude.org. Mrs. Susan Walker, Pres.; Dr. Judi Lynch, Prin.; Mrs. Peggy Boon, Librarian. Benedictine Sisters 1; Lay Teachers 30; Students 262.

WILLIAMSBURG. *Walsingham Academy*, (Grades PreK-12), 1100 Jamestown Rd., 23185. Tel: 757-229-6026; Fax: 757-259-1401. Email: mjo@walsingham.org. Web: www.walsingham.org. Sr. Mary Jeanne Oesterle, R.S.M., Pres.; Katherine Johnson, Upper School Prin.; Ms. Diane Bialkowski, Lower School Prin.; Steve Delaney, Campus Min.; Annie Gallagher, Religion Coord., Lower School. Private Day School for Boys and Girls. Lay Teachers 68; Administrators 7; Students 547.

[C] ELEMENTARY SCHOOLS, DIOCESAN

RICHMOND. *All Saints Catholic School*, (Grades PreK-8), 3418 Noble Ave., 23222. Tel: 804-329-7524; Fax: 804-329-4201. Email: allsaintsric@juno.com. Web: www.allsaintsric.com. Mr. Kenneth W. Soistman, Prin.; Ms. Gloria J. Smith, Librarian. Lay Teachers 15; Total Staff 27; Total Enrollment 123.

St. Benedict School (1919) (Grades PreK-8), 3100 Grove Ave., 23221. Tel: 804-254-8850; Fax: 804-254-9163. Email: scruess@saintbenedictschool.org. Web: www.SaintBenedictSchool.org. Mr. Sean M. Cruess, Prin.; Tara Hundley, Librarian. Teachers 16; Total Staff 25; Total Enrollment 191.

St. Bridget School, (Grades K-8), 6011 York Rd., 23226. Tel: 804-288-1994; Fax: 804-288-5730. Email: information@saintbridget.org. Web: www.saintbridget.org. Mr. Raymond E. Honeycutt, Prin.; Vicki Hanner, Librarian. Priests 2; Lay Teachers 33; Total Enrollment 454; Total Staff 64.

St. Edward/Epiphany Catholic School (1961) (Grades PreK-8), 10701 W. Huguenot Rd., 23235. Tel: 804-272-2881; Fax: 804-327-0788. Email: jkremzir@seeschool.com. Web: www.seeschool.com. Ms. Georgette M. Richards, Prin.; Helen Lorenz, Librarian. Lay Teachers 50; Total Enrollment 444.

St. Mary's Catholic School (1965) (Grades N-8), 9501 Gayton Rd., 23229. Tel: 804-740-1048; Fax: 804-740-1310. Email: albisese@saintmary.org. Web: www.saintmary.org. Dr. Thomas D. Dertinger, Prin.; Mrs. Kelly Taylor, Librarian. Lay Teachers 32; Students 455.

BLACKSBURG. *St. Mary's Little Angels Preschool* (1988) 1205 Old Mill Rd., 24060-3618. Tel: 540-951-0916; Fax: 540-953-2962. Lesley Lafon, Dir. (Ages 12 mos. to 5 years). Lay Teachers 11; Students 60.

BRISTOL. *St. Anne Catholic School*, (Grades PreK-8), 300 Euclid Ave., 24201. Tel: 276-669-0048; Fax: 276-669-3523. Email: schooloffice@stanneschoolbristol.org. Web: www.stanne-school.org. Dr. Richard Fenchak, Ed.D., Prin.; Mrs. Patricia Johnson, Asst. Prin. Lay Teachers 19; Total Staff 35; Total Enrollment 156.

CHARLOTTESVILLE. *Charlottesville Catholic Elementary School*, (Grades PreK-8), 1205 Pen Park Rd., 22901. Tel: 434-964-0400; Fax: 434-964-1373. Email: info@cvillecatholic.org. Web: www.cvillecatholic.org. Ms. Susan Dougherty, Prin.; Jennifer Ferguson, Librarian. Lay Teachers 45; Aides 8; Students 348.

HAMPTON. *St. Mary Star of the Sea*, (Grades PreK-8), 14 N. Willard Ave., 23663. Tel: 757-723-6358; Fax: 757-723-6544. Email: admin@SaintMaryStaroftheSea.com. Web: www.SaintMaryStaroftheSea.com. Sr. Mary Amata, O.P., Prin.; Mrs. Sandra Stearns, Librarian. Sisters 4; Lay Teachers 18; Total Staff 31; Total Enrollment 192.

NEWPORT NEWS. *Our Lady of Mt Carmel* (1954) (Grades PreK-8), 52 Harpersville Rd., 23601. Tel: 757-596-2754; Fax: 757-596-1570. Email: admissions@olmc-school.com. Web: www.olmc-school.com. Sr. Dominic Quinn, O.P., Prin.; Mrs. Melissa Small, Librarian. Sisters 4; Lay Teachers 23; Total Staff 44; Total Enrollment 361.

NORFOLK. *Christ the King*, (Grades PreK-8), 3401 Tidewater Dr., 23509. Tel: 757-625-4951; Fax: 757-623-5212. Email: info@ctkparish.org. Web: www.ctkparish.org. Mrs. Rachael Chatham, Prin.; Carrie Srodulski, Librarian. Priests 1; Lay Teachers 23; Total Staff 32; Total Enrollment 307.

St. Pius X School, (Grades PreK-8), 7800 Halprin Dr., 23518. Tel: 757-588-6171; Fax: 757-587-6580. Email: school@piusxparish.org. Web: www.stpiusxschoolva.org. Sr. Linda Taber, I.H.M., Prin.; Ms. Katherine Oliver, Technology Teacher. Sisters 3; Lay Teachers 26; Total Staff 39; Total Enrollment 317.

PETERSBURG. *St. Joseph School*, (Grades PreK-8), 123 Franklin St., 23803. Tel: 804-732-3931; Fax: 804-732-6479. Email: school@saintjosephschool.com. Web: www.saintjosephschool.com. Diane Young, Prin.; Teresa Fisher, Librarian. Sisters 2; Lay Teachers 12; Total Staff 25; Total Enrollment 120.

PORTSMOUTH. *Portsmouth Catholic Regional*, 2301 Oregon Ave., 23701. Tel: 757-488-6744; Fax: 757-465-8833. Email: office@pces.hrcoxmail.com; principal@pces.hrcoxmail.com. Web: www.portsmouthcatholic.com. Mary Ellen Paul, Prin.; Mr. Franklin Baker, Librarian. Lay Teachers 17; Total Staff 34; Total Enrollment 162.

POWHATAN. *Blessed Sacrament Huguenot* (1998) (Grades PreK-12), 2501 Academy Rd., 23139. Tel: 804-598-4211; Fax: 804-598-1053. Email: tdeleon@bshknights.org. Web: www.BlessedSacramentHuguenot.com. Dr. Tracy Bonday-deLeon, Chief School Admin.; Mr. Mike Henderson, Dir. Student Affairs & Athletic Dir.; Anne Rodriguez, Librarian. Lay Teachers 32; Students 340.

RICHMOND, HENRICO. *Our Lady of Lourdes School*, (Grades PreK-8), 8250 Woodman Rd., 23228. Tel: 804-262-1770; Fax: 804-200-6295. Email: ollofice@comcast.net. Web: www.ollschoolric.com. Lucy R. Reilley, Prin. Total Staff 35; Total Enrollment 385.

VIRGINIA BEACH. *St. Gregory the Great School* (1964) (Grades PreK-8), 5343 Virginia Beach Blvd., 23462. Tel: 757-497-1811; Fax: 757-497-7005. Email: office@sggsvb.org. Web: www.sggsvb.org. Sr. Mary Catherine Chapman, I.H.M., Ed.D., Prin.; Mrs. Sandy Batkin, Librarian. Priests 3; Sisters 4; Teachers 46; Total Staff 80; Total Enrollment 711.

St. John the Apostle Catholic School (2002) (Grades PreK-8), 1968 Sandbridge Rd., 23456. Tel: 757-821-1100; Fax: 757-821-1047. Email: sja@stjohnsandbridge.org. Web: www.stjohnsandbridge.org. Joseph Badali, Prin. Lay Teachers 21; Total Enrollment 277; Total Staff 13.

St. Matthew School, (Grades PreK-8), 3316 Sandra Ln., 23464. Tel: 757-420-2455; Fax: 757-420-4880. Email: office@smsvb.net. Web: www.smsvb.net. Mr. Louis Goldberg, Prin.; Mrs. Ziegenfuss, Librarian. Lay Teachers 36; Total Enrollment 507; Total Staff 74.

Star of the Sea School (1958) (Grades PreK-8), 309 15th St., 23451. Tel: 757-428-8400; Fax: 757-428-2794. Email: information@sosschool.org. Web: www.sosschool.org. Dr. Cathryn Whisman, Prin.; Barbara Wilhelm, Librarian. Lay Teachers 20; Total Staff 14; Total Enrollment 228.

[D] ELEMENTARY SCHOOLS, PRIVATE

NORFOLK. **Barry Robinson Schools of Norfolk* (2001) P.O. Box 1180, 23501. Tel: 757-440-5500. Charles V. McPhillips, Pres.

St. Patrick Catholic School, (Grades PreK-8), 1000 Bolling Ave., 23508. Tel: 757-440-5500; Fax: 757-440-5200. Email: info@stpcs.org. Web: www.stpcs.org. Mr. Stephen Hammond, Prin.; Mrs. Elizabeth Woodard, Librarian. Lay Teachers 25.

[E] GENERAL HOSPITALS

RICHMOND. *Bon Secours Richmond Health System*, 5875 Bremo Rd., Ste 710, 23226. Tel: 804-281-8330; Fax: 804-282-1243. Email: teri_costner@bshsi.org. Web: www.bonsecours.com. Peter Bernard, CEO. Sisters of Bon Secours. Sisters 2; Bed Capacity 850; Total Staff 3,936; Inpatients 46,918; Outpatients 390,829.

Bon Secours-Richmond Health Care Foundation, 5875 Bremo Rd., Ste. 305, 23226. Tel: 804-287-7700; Fax: 804-287-7316. Terry Mohr, CEO.

Bon Secours-Richmond Community Hospital, 1500 N. 28th St., 23233. Tel: 804-225-1701; Fax: 804-225-1725. Michael D. Robinson, CEO. Bed Capacity 104; Total Staff 260; Inpatients 2,854; Outpatients 46,158.

St. Mary's Hospital Toni R. Ardabell, CEO. Sisters 2; Bed Capacity 391; Total Staff 1,728; Inpatients 21,583; Outpatients 135,436.

Bon Secours Memorial Regional Medical Center, 8260 Atlee Rd., Mechanicsville, 23116. Tel: 804-764-6000; Fax: 804-764-6420. Michael D. Robinson, CEO. Bed Capacity 225; Inpatients 13,555; Outpatients 128,267; Total Staff 1,151.

MIDLOTHIAN. *St. Francis Medical Center (Bon Secours Richmond Health System)*, 13700 St. Francis Blvd., Ste. 100, 23114. Tel: 804-594-7400; Fax: 804-594-7410. Mark M. Gordon, CEO; Peter J. McCourt, Mission Leader. Bed Capacity 130; Total Assisted Annually (Inpatient) 9,127; Total Assisted Annually (Outpatient) 87,990; Total Staff 1,100.

NEWPORT NEWS. *Mary Immaculate Hospital* (1952) 2 Bernardine Dr., 23602-4499. Tel: 757-886-6600; Fax: 757-886-6751. Web: www.bonsecourshamptonroads.com. Patricia Lee Robertson, Exec. Vice Pres. & Admin. Tel: 757-886-6768; Fax: 757-886-6751; Sr. Bernard Marie Magill, O.S.F., M.S., N.A.C.C., Dir. Pastoral Care Dept. The Bernardine Sisters of the Third Order of St. Francis 9; Bed Capacity 110; Inpatients 7,522; Outpatients 88,160; Total Staff 6,773.

Bernardine Franciscan Sisters Foundation, Inc., 2 Bernardine Dr., 23602. Tel: 757-886-6025; Fax: 757-886-6881.

NORFOLK. *Bon Secours De Paul Medical Center, Inc.*, 150 Kingsley Ln., 23505. Tel: 757-889-5000; Fax: 757-889-5837. Web: bonsecourshamptonroads.com. Daniel Duggan, Exec. Vice Pres. & Admin.

Bon Secours DePaul Medical Center

Bon Secours DePaul Health Foundation

Bon Secours Bayley Properties Sisters of Bon Secours., Clinic is connected with hospital. Staff 836; Bed Capacity 110; Inpatients 7,522; Outpatients 88,160.

PORTSMOUTH. *Bon Secours Hampton Roads Health Systems, Inc.*, 3636 High St., 23707-3236. Michael K. Kerner, CEO.

Bon Secours Maryview Medical Center, 3636 High St., 23707. Tel: 757-398-2200; Fax: 757-398-2359. Web: www.bonsecourshamptonroads.com. Joseph M. Oddis, CEO; Richard Chasse, Dir. Pastoral Care; Rita Hickey, Vice Pres. Mission; Rev. Pantaleon O. Manalo, Chap.

Maryview Hospital Sisters of Bon Secours. Bed Capacity 346; Inpatients 1,400; Outpatients 187,915; Total Staff 1,569.

Maryview Behavioral Medicine Center, 3636 High St., 23707. Tel: 757-398-2361; Fax: 757-398-2396. Web: www.BonSecoursHamptonRoads.com. Lucy Rotich, Admin. Bed Capacity 54; Patients Assisted Annually 2,700; Total Staff 65.

[F] ORPHANAGES AND INFANT HOMES

NORFOLK. *St. Mary's Home for Disabled Children*, 6171 Kempsville Cir., 23502. Tel: 757-622-2208; Fax: 757-627-5314. Email: tmaryshome@hamptonroads.com. Web: www.saintmaryshome.org. William C. Giermak, CEO; Terry Lyle, Prin. Long-term care for multiply handicapped children birth to twenty-one years old. Daughters of Wisdom 1; Bed Capacity 92; Lay Teachers 8; Total Staff 239.

[G] CHILD LEARNING CENTERS

RICHMOND. *Sacred Heart Center, Inc.*, 1400 Perry St., 23224. Tel: 804-230-4399; Fax: 804-231-7247. Email: mary_wickham@shcrichmond.org. Mary Wickham, Prog. Dir. Adult Education, Social Services.

NORFOLK. *Christ the King Early Childhood Learning Center*, 3401 Tidewater Dr., 23509. Tel: 757-625-4951; Fax: 757-623-5212. Email: arubino@ctkparish.org. Amy Rubino, Asst. Prin.; Mrs. Rachael Chatham, Prin.; Ms. Dawn Lindey, Librarian. Lay Teachers 4; Early Childhood 60; School-Age Extended Care 75.

VIRGINIA BEACH. *Holy Family Day School*, 1279 N. Great Neck Rd., 23454-2117. Tel: 757-481-1180; Fax: 757-481-3989. Email: dayschoolprincipal@holyfamilyvb.org. Web: www.holyfamilyvb.org. Cynthia Girard, Prin.; Colleen Oates, Bookkeeper. Lay Teachers 6.

[H] HOMES FOR THE AGED

RICHMOND. *St. Francis Home, Inc.*, 65 W. Clopton St., 23225. Tel: 804-231-1043; Fax: 804-231-1065. Email: mpyle@saintfrancishome.com. Mike W. Pyle, Exec. Dir. Bed Capacity 106; Total Assisted Annually 130; Total Staff 54.

St. Joseph's Home for the Aged (1874) 1503 Michaels Rd., Henrico, 23229. Tel: 804-288-6245; Fax: 804-288-8906. Email: msrichmond@littlesistersofthepoor.org. Sr. Paul M. Wilson, L.S.P., Supr. & Admin. Attended by Rev. Matthew Paul Richardson (Chap.), Priest In Res. (Retired) Rev. Paul Gallagher. Little Sisters of the Poor 10; Guests 98; Total Assisted Annually 120; Total Staff 115.

St. Mary Wood's (1986) 1257 Marywood Ln., 23229. Tel: 804-741-8624; Fax: 804-740-7912. Email: stmw@mindsprings.com. Web: stmaryswoods.com. Randy Scott, Admin. Units 118; Independent Units 54; Total Staff 56; Total Assisted 64.

Marywood Apartments, 1261 Marywood Ln., 23229. Tel: 804-740-5567; Fax: 804-740-9016. Email: marywood1@verizon.net. Sonja Shepherd, Property Mgr. Residents 129; Total Staff 7.

Our Lady of Hope Health Center, Inc., 13700 N. Gayton Rd., 23233. Tel: 804-360-1960; Fax: 804-364-0737. Email: brichard@ourladyofhope.com. Web: www.ourladyofhope.com. Becky Richard, Admin. Residents 133; Nursing Home Residents 60; Total Assisted Annually 77; Total Staff 150.

CHARLOTTESVILLE. *Our Lady of Peace*, 751 Hillsdale Dr., 22901. Tel: 434-973-1155; Fax: 434-973-3397. Sara Warden, Exec. Dir. Nursing Bed Capacity 30;

Independent Units 32; Assisted Units 94; Total Occupancy 167; Total Staff 125.

HAMPTON. *Seton Manor*, 215 Marcella Rd., 23666. Tel: 757-827-6512; Fax: 757-827-0132. Email: manager@setonmanor.hrcoxmail.com. Pam Jensen, Mgr. Residents 112; Total Staff 5.

LYNCHBURG. *McGurk House Apartments*, 2425 Tate Springs Rd., 24501. Tel: 434-846-2425; Fax: 434-847-5046. Email: mcgurkhouse@comcast.net. Victoria Johnson, Mgr. Independent Living for adults 62 yrs. or older, or mobility impaired. Apartments 88; Total Staff 5.

NEWPORT NEWS. *St. Francis Nursing Center*, 4 Ridgewood Pkwy., 23602. Tel: 757-886-6500; Fax: 757-886-6539. Web: www.bshsihr.com. Le' Anne Bailey, Admin. Tel: 757-886-6500. Beds 115; Total Assisted 1,582; Total Assisted Annually 108; Total Staff 118.

NORFOLK. *Madonna Home*, 814 W. 37th St., 23508. Tel: 757-623-6662; Fax: 757-623-4966. Charlene Davis, Dir. Total Staff 6; Residents 16; Total Assisted Annually 16.

ROANOKE. *Our Lady of the Valley Retirement Community*, 650 N. Jefferson St., 24016. Tel: 540-345-5111; Fax: 540-985-6561. Web: www.OurLadyoftheValley.com. Ryan J. Koeniger, Admin. Assisted Living Units 86; Skilled Nursing Facility Beds 70.

SUFFOLK. *Bon Secours-Maryview Nursing Care*, 4775 Bridge Rd., 23435. Tel: 757-686-0488; Fax: 757-686-8211. Diana L. Jarrett, Admin. Bed Capacity 120.

Martha W. Davis Cancer Center
Maryview Employee Assistance Program
Maryview MedCare Centers (Urgent Care)
Maryview Wellspring Home Health Agency
Maryview Hospice Program

VIRGINIA BEACH. *Marian Manor* (1988) 5345 Marian Ln., 23462. Tel: 757-456-5018; Fax: 757-497-7561. Web: www.marian-manor.com. Karen Land, Admin. Units 117; Total Assisted Annually 135; Total Staff 90.

Our Lady of Perpetual Help Health Center, Inc., 4560 Princess Anne Rd., 23462-7905. Tel: 757-495-4211; Fax: 757-495-7366. Email: cheineman@ourladyperpetualhelp.com. Web: www.OurLadyPerpetualHelp.com. Bed Capacity 123; Total Assisted Annually 123; Total Staff 165.

Russell House, 900 First Colonial Rd., 23454. Tel: 757-481-0770; Fax: 757-496-0859. Email: russellhouse@erols.com. Eleanor Olsen, Admin. Total Staff 6; Units 119; Residents 126.

Sullivan House, Inc., 2033 General Booth Blvd., 23454. Tel: 757-563-9955; Fax: 757-563-2992. Email: sullivan.house@worldnet.att.net. Cecile Shelton, Mgr. 198 units for very low income elderly.

The Sullivan House, 2033 General Booth Blvd., 23454. Tel: 757-437-0220. Mrs. Joanne Lindauer, Admin.

[I] SERVICES FOR THE DISABLED

LYNCHBURG. *Nott Homes, Inc.*, 3009-3011 Roundelay Rd., 24502. Tel: 434-239-0722; Fax: 434-239-1042. Leslie Ozz, Residential Mgr. Residents 8; Bed Capacity 8; Total Staff 22.

VIRGINIA BEACH. *Assisi House*, P.O. Box 2400, #159, 23450-2400. Tel: 757-450-3671. Email: denibrown@msn.com.

[J] SPECIALIZED SERVICES

RICHMOND. *Commonwealth Catholic Charities* (1923) 1512 Willow Lawn Dr., 23230-0565. Tel: 804-285-5900; Fax: 804-285-9130. Email: agency@cccofva.org. Web: www.cccofva.org. Ms. Joanne D. Nattrass, M.B.A., B.S.N., R.N., Exec. Dir.
Satellite Offices:
918 Harris St., Charlottesville, 22903. Tel: 800-974-4494.

Commonwealth Catholic Charities, 541 Luck Ave., Roanoke, 24016. Tel: 540-342-0411; Fax: 540-342-3307.
507 Park Ave., S.W., Norton, 24273. Tel: 276-679-1195; Fax: 276-679-2719. Total Assisted 24,000.
820 Campbell Ave., S.W., Roanoke, 24016-3536. Tel: 540-342-7561; Fax: 540-344-7513.

St. Francis House, 824 Campbell Ave., S.W., Roanoke, 24016-3536. Tel: 540-345-9090.
1615 Kecoughtan Rd., Hampton, 23661. Tel: 757-247-3600; Fax: 757-247-1070.
827 Commerce St., Petersburg, 23803. 827 Commerce St., Petersburg, 23803. Tel: 804-733-6207; Fax: 804-733-0099.

VIRGINIA BEACH. *Catholic Charities of Eastern Virginia, Inc.*, 5361-A Virginia Beach Blvd., 23462. Tel: 757-456-2366; Fax: 757-456-2367. Email: help@cceva.org. Web: www.cceva.org. Mr. Christopher R. Tan, Exec. Dir.; Mr. Neil McNulty, Pres.
Branch Offices:
4855 Princess Anne Rd., 23462. Tel: 757-467-7707; Fax: 757-495-3206.
1802 Ashland Ave., Norfolk, 23509. Tel: 757-533-5217; Fax: 757-533-9562.
3804 Poplar Hill Rd., Ste. A, Chesapeake, 23321. Tel: 757-484-0703; Fax: 757-484-1096.
12829 Jefferson Ave., Ste. 101, Newport News, 23608. Tel: 757-875-0060; Fax: 757-877-7883.
1315 Jamestown Rd., Ste. 202, Williamsburg, 23185. Tel: 757-253-2847; Fax: 757-253-1296. Total Assisted 12,142.
510 N. Main St., Franklin, 23851. Tel: 757-562-6222; Fax: 757-562-3930.
General Delivery, Belle Haven, 23306. Tel: 757-442-6211; Fax: 757-442-6211.
Other Offices:

Catholic Charities Outreach Center, 5361-A Virginia Beach Blvd., 23462. Tel: 757-490-4931; Fax: 757-456-2367.

[K] MONASTERIES AND RESIDENCES OF PRIESTS AND BROTHERS

RICHMOND. *Mary Mother of the Church Abbey*, 12829 River Rd., 23238-7206. Tel: 804-784-3508; Fax: 804-784-2214. Email: abbeyinfo@richmondmonks.org. Web: www.richmondmonks.org. Very Rev. Luke Travers, O.S.B., Admin.; Revs. Gregory Gresko, O.S.B.; Adrian W. Harmening, O.S.B., Prior; Theophile W. Brown, O.S.B.; Joseph M. Lukyamuzi, O.S.B.; James M. Glass, O.S.B.; Theophile W. Brown, O.S.B.; Mark Purcell, O.S.B.; Bros. David Owen, O.S.B.; Jeffery Williams, O.S.B.; Robert Nguyen, O.S.B.; John Mary Lugemwa, O.S.B. Benedictine Monks. Priests 7; Brothers 4.

WEST POINT. *Missionaries of the Holy Family, General Mission Office-M.S.F., Inc.*, 260 W. Euclid Blvd., P.O. Box 918, 23181. Tel: 804-843-2622; Fax: 804-843-3182. Email: msfinc2@aol.com. Rev. John Brieffies, M.S.F., Pres. & Dir. Priests 1; Total Staff 3; Total Assisted 400.

[L] CONVENTS AND RESIDENCES FOR SISTERS

RICHMOND. *Benedictine Sisters of Virginia, Saint Gertrude Convent*, 6826 Monument Ave., 23226. Tel: 804-282-4136. Web: osbva.org. Email: vocations@osbva.org. Sisters Vicki Ix, O.S.B.; Charlotte Lange, O.S.B. Sisters 4.

Comboni Missionary Sisters, Provincial House, 1307 Lakeside Ave., 23228-4710. Tel: 804-266-2975; 804-262-8827; Fax: 804-264-2906. Email: cmsusaprov@verizon.net. Web: www.combonisrs.com. Sr. Mary Bernadette Hilmer, C.M.S., Delegate. Sisters 22.

BARHAMSVILLE. *Bethlehem Monastery of the Poor Clare Nuns*, 5500 Holly Fork Rd., 23011. Tel: 757-566-1684; Fax: 757-566-1697. Email: mtstfrancis@gmail.com. Web: www.poor-clares.org. Sr. Mary Therese, P.C.C., Abbess. Observing the Primitive Rule of St. Clare, Constitutions of the Poor Clare Federation of Mary Immaculate (strictly cloistered, solemn vows). Solemnly Professed 11; Postulants 2.

CLINTWOOD. *Sisters of the Holy Cross, Inc.*, P.O. Box 835, 24228. Tel: 276-926-4328.

CROZET. *Our Lady of the Angels Monastery* (1987) *Cistercian Nuns of the Strict Observance (Virginia)*, 3365 Monastery Dr., 22932. Tel: 434-823-1452; Fax: 434-823-6379. Email: sisters@olamonastery.org. Web: www.olamonastery.org. Sr. Marion Rissetto, O.C.S.O., Prioress. Professed 10.

NEWPORT NEWS. *Bernardine Sisters of the Third Order of St. Francis*, 6E Ridgewood Pkwy., 23602. Tel: 757-886-6395; Fax: 757-886-6751. Web: www.bfranciscan.org. Sisters 8.

NORFOLK. *Sisters Servants of the Immaculate Heart of Mary* (1845)

St. Pius X Convent, 7813 Halprin Dr., 23518. Tel: 757-587-8657 (Home); 757-588-6171 (School); Fax: 757-587-6580. Email: piusihmva@aol.com (Home). Web: piusxparish.org. Sr. Brenda Query, I.H.M., Supr. Sisters 6.

PORTSMOUTH. *Sisters of Bon Secours* (1824) 412 West Rd., 23707. Tel: 757-397-3869. Email: rita_thomas@bshsi.com. Sr. Rita Thomas, M.S.N., Pres.

ROCKVILLE. *Monastery of the Visitation Monte Maria*, 12221 Bienvenue Rd., 23146. Tel: 804-749-4885; Fax: 804-749-8606. Email: info@visitmontemaria.com. Web: www.visitmontemaria.com. Sr. Mary Paula Zemienieuski, V.H.M., Supr. Visitation Sisters 13.

VIRGINIA BEACH. *Franciscan Sisters of St. Joseph*, 5632 Old Providence Rd., 23464-3367.

Sisters Servants of I.H.M., St. Gregory the Great, 5349 Virginia Beach Blvd., 23462. Tel: 757-497-7517; Fax: 757-497-7005. Email: smaryihm@stgregory.pvt.k12.va.us; stgregsihms@aol.com Convent. Sr. Mary Catherine Chapman, I.H.M., Ed.D., Supr./Prin.

WILLIAMSBURG. *Sisters of Mercy, Walsingham Academy*, 1100 Jamestown Rd., P.O. Box 8702, 23187-8702. Tel: 757-229-2642 (Upper School); 757-229-6026 (Lower School); 757-220-8735 (Convent); Fax: 757-259-1401. Web: www.walsingham.org. Sisters Mary Jeanne Oesterle, R.S.M., Pres.; Berenice Eltz, R.S.M., Coord.; Jean A. Burns, C.S.J., Treas.; Rose Morris, R.S.M, Volunteer. Sisters 4.

[M] RETREAT HOUSES

ABINGDON. *Jubilee House Retreat Center*, 822 E. Main St., 24210-4415. Tel: 276-619-0919; Fax: 276-739-7753. Email: info@jubileeretreat.com. Web: www.jubileeretreat.com.

LYNCHBURG. *Tabor Retreat Center*, 2125 Langhorne Rd., 24501. Tel: 434-846-6475; Fax: 434-846-3047. Email: taborretreat@verizon.net. Web: www.taborretreat.com. Deacon Gordon Kenneth Cartwright.

MONTPELIER. *Shalom House*, P.O. Box 196, 23192. Tel: 804-883-6149; Fax: 804-883-5298. Mary E. Alexander, Dir.

ROANOKE. *Madonna House*, 828 Campbell Ave., S.W., 24016. Tel: 540-343-8464. Web: www.madonnahouse.org. Patricia Lawton, Dir.

SMITHFIELD. *The Well* (1987) 18047 Quiet Way, 23430. Tel: 757-255-2366. Email: staff@thewellretreatcenter.org. Web: www.thewellretreatcenter.org.

[N] MISCELLANEOUS

RICHMOND. *St. Francis Home of Richmond Foundation, Ltd.*, 65 W. Clopten St., 23225. Tel: 804-231-1043; Fax: 804-231-1065. Mike W. Pyle, Exec. Dir. Provides grants to subsidize cost of care for aged, infirm and disabled residents of limited means.

Shroud of Turin Center, Mary Mother of the Church Abbey, 12829 River Rd., 23233. Tel: 804-784-3366; Fax: 804-784-3431. Email: shroud@erols.com. Bryan Walsh, Dir. Provides educational services and conducts historical research into the Shroud of Turin.

CHARLOTTESVILLE. *Saint Anselm Institute for Catholic Thought* (2001) P.O. Box 6432, 22906-6432. Tel: 434-924-6993; Fax: 434-924-3389. Email: info@stanselminstitute.org. Web: www.stanselminstitute.org. Charles A. Kromkowski.

PORTSMOUTH. *Catholic Elementary Education Foundation of Hampton Roads*, 2301 Oregon Ave., 23701. Tel: 757-488-6744; Fax: 757-465-8833. Email: sec@pces.hrcoxmail.com. Mary Ellen Paul, Prin.

ROANOKE. *Catholic Historical Society of the Roanoke Valley* (Museum & Religious Goods), 400 W. Campbell Ave., S.W., 24016-3627. Tel: 540-982-0152; Fax: 540-982-0152. Domenick Centrone, Pres.; Vernon E. Jolley, Vice Pres.; Luisa Perkins, Sec.; John Wagner, Treas.

St. Francis House, Inc (1973) P.O. Box 2215, 24009. Tel: 540-345-9090; Fax: 540-345-9090. Email: joelle.henry@cccofva.org. Joelle Henry, Coord.

VIRGINIA BEACH. *Catholic Charities of Eastern Virginia Foundation*, 5361-A Virginia Beach Blvd., 23462. Tel: 757-456-2366; Fax: 757-456-2367. Web: www.cceva.org. Jessica Lombardi, Exec. Dir.

San Lorenzo Spiritual Center, 4556 Indian River Rd., 23456. Tel: 757-471-8949; Fax: 757-424-1313.

RELIGIOUS INSTITUTES OF MEN REPRESENTED IN THE DIOCESE

For further details refer to the corresponding bracketed number in the Religious Institutes of Men or Women section.

[0200]—*Benedictine Monks* (Latrobe, PA)—O.S.B.

[1350]—*Brothers of St. Francis Xavier*—C.F.X.

[0630]—*Congregation of the Missionaries of the Holy Family*—M.S.F.

[0570]—*The Glenmary Home Missioners*—Glmy.

[0690]—*Jesuits Fathers and Brothers*—S.J.

[0430]—*Order of Preachers (Dominicans)* (Province of St. Joseph)—O.P.

[1070]—*Redemptorist Fathers* (Baltimore Prov.)—C.SS.R.

RELIGIOUS INSTITUTES OF WOMEN REPRESENTED IN THE DIOCESE

[0230]—*Benedictine Sisters of Pontifical Jurisdiction*—O.S.B.

[1810]—*Bernardine Sisters of the Third Order of St. Francis*—O.S.F.

[0670]—*Cistercian Nuns of the Strict Observance*—O.C.S.O.
[0690]—*Comboni Missionary Sisters*—C.M.S.
[0270]—*Congregation of Bon Secours*—C.B.S.
[1070-09]—*Congregation of St. Catherine of Siena, Racine*—O.P.
[1070-07]—*Congregation of St. Cecelia, Nashville*—O.P.
[1070-13]—*Congregation of the Most Holy Rosary, Adrian*—O.P.
[1920]—*Congregation of the Sisters of the Holy Cross*—C.S.C.
[0760]—*Daughters of Charity of St. Vincent de Paul*—D.C.
[0820]—*Daughters of the Holy Spirit*—D.H.S.
[0960]—*Daughters of Wisdom*—D.W.
[1180]—*The Franciscan Sisters*—O.S.F.
[1840]—*Grey Nuns of the Sacred Heart*—G.N.S.H.
[2575]—*Institute of the Sisters of Mercy of the Americas*—R.S.M.
[2340]—*Little Sisters of the Poor*—L.S.P.
[2490]—*Medical Mission Sisters*—S.C.M.M.
[2490]—*Medical Mission Sisters*—M.M.S.
[2480]—*Medical Missionaries of Mary*—M.M.M.
[2790]—*Missionary Servants of the Most Blessed Trinity*—M.S.B.T.
[3760]—*Order of St. Clare*—P.C.C.
[3640]—*Poor Servants of the Mother of God*—S.M.G.
[3465]—*Religious of the Sacred Heart of Mary* (Eastern American Prov.)—R.S.H.M
[2970]—*School Sisters of Notre Dame*—S.S.N.D.
[1070-03]—*Sinsinawa Dominican Congregation of the Most Holy Rosary*—O.P.
[]—*Sisters for Christian Community*—S.F.C.C.
[0500]—*Sisters of Charity of Nazareth*—S.C.N.
[0590]—*Sisters of Charity of St. Elizabeth, Convent Station*—S.C.
[0990]—*Sisters of Divine Providence* (Our Lady of Divine Providence Prov.)—C.D.P.
[2990]—*Sisters of Notre Dame*—S.N.D.
[3000]—*Sisters of Notre Dame de Namur*—S.N.D.deN.
[1530]—*Sisters of St. Francis of the Congregation of Our Lady of Lourdes, Sylvania, Ohio*—O.S.F.
[3840]—*Sisters of St. Joseph of Carondelet*—C.S.J.
[2980]—*Sisters of the Congregation of Notre Dame*—C.N.D.
[1990]—*Sisters of the Holy Names of Jesus and Mary*—S.N.J.M.
[2170]—*Sisters, Servants of the Immaculate Heart of Mary* (Immaculata, PA)—I.H.M.
[4130]—*Ursuline Sisters of the Congregation of Tildonk, Belgium*—O.S.U.
[4190]—*Visitation Nuns*—V.H.M.

DIOCESAN CEMETERIES

RICHMOND. *Holy Cross*, First Ave. & Daniels St., 23222. Tel: 804-321-5936.

Mount Calvary, 1400 S. Randolph St., 23220. Tel: 804-355-5271; Fax: 804-355-5277.

LYNCHBURG. *Holy Cross*, 710 Clay St., 24504. Tel: 434-846-5245; Fax: 434-846-7022.

NORFOLK. *St. Mary's Catholic Cemetery*, 3000 Church St., 23504. Tel: 757-627-2874; Fax: 757-627-0369.

PETERSBURG. *Sacred Heart Cemetery Corporation*, 9300 Community Ln., 23805. Tel: 804-706-6897. Email: dhanzlik@comcast.net.

PORTSMOUTH. *St. Paul's Cemetery Portsmouth Catholic Cemetery Commission*, P.O. Box 155, 23705. Tel: 757-488-1723. 2701 Elm Ave., 23705.

ROANOKE. *St. Andrew Diocesan Cemetery*, 3601 Salem Tpke., N.W., P.O. Box 6616, 24017. Tel: 540-342-9180; Fax: 540-342-9180. Email: standrewscemetery@juno.com.

NECROLOGY

† Chmura, Stanislaw T.—Died Jan. 13, 2011
† Dinges, Anthony, (Retired)—Died Aug. 28, 2011
† Gaughan, Paul, (Retired)—Died April 5, 2011
† Warren, Robert, (Retired)—Died Oct. 5, 2011

An asterisk (*) denotes an organization that has established tax-exempt status directly with the IRS and is not covered by the USCCB Group Ruling.

Diocese of Rochester

(Dioecesis Roffensis)

Most Reverend

MATTHEW H. CLARK, D.D.

Bishop of Rochester; ordained December 19, 1962; appointed Bishop of Rochester April 23, 1979; consecrated May 27, 1979; installed June 26, 1979. *Res.: 1150 Buffalo Rd., Rochester, NY 14624.*

Pastoral Center: 1150 Buffalo Rd., Rochester, NY 14624-1890. Tel: 585-328-3210; 800-388-7177; Fax: 585-328-3149.

Web: www.dor.org

ESTABLISHED MARCH 3, 1868.

Square Miles 7,107.

Comprises the Counties of Cayuga, Chemung, Livingston, Monroe, Ontario, Schuyler, Seneca, Steuben, Tioga, Tompkins, Wayne and Yates in the State of New York.

Legal Title of Diocese: The Diocese of Rochester. For legal titles of parishes and diocesan institutions, consult the Pastoral Center.

STATISTICAL OVERVIEW

Personnel	
Bishop	1
Abbots	2
Retired Abbots	2
Priests: Diocesan Active in Diocese	90
Priests: Diocesan Active Outside Diocese	6
Priests: Retired, Sick or Absent	75
Number of Diocesan Priests	171
Religious Priests in Diocese	44
Total Priests in Diocese	215
Extern Priests in Diocese	23
Ordinations:	
Diocesan Priests	1
Permanent Deacons	4
Permanent Deacons in Diocese	134
Total Brothers	27
Total Sisters	443
Parishes	
Parishes	105
With Resident Pastor:	
Resident Diocesan Priests	60
Resident Religious Priests	3
Without Resident Pastor:	
Administered by Priests	15
Administered by Deacons	7
Administered by Religious Women	8
Administered by Lay People	12
Missions	2
Welfare	
Catholic Hospitals	1
Total Assisted	99,200
Health Care Centers	2
Total Assisted	1,450
Homes for the Aged	4
Total Assisted	1,800
Day Care Centers	1
Total Assisted	175
Specialized Homes	8
Total Assisted	750
Special Centers for Social Services	74
Total Assisted	812,108
Residential Care of Disabled	10
Total Assisted	98
Educational	
Diocesan Students in Other Seminaries	13
Total Seminarians	13
High Schools, Diocesan and Parish	1
Total Students	115
High Schools, Private	5
Total Students	3,018
Elementary Schools, Diocesan and Parish	22
Total Students	4,542
Elementary Schools, Private	3
Total Students	334
Catechesis/Religious Education:	
High School Students	1,502
Elementary Students	11,079
Total Students under Catholic Instruction	20,603
Teachers in the Diocese:	
Priests	2
Sisters	18
Lay Teachers	647
Vital Statistics	
Receptions into the Church:	
Infant Baptism Totals	2,646
Minor Baptism Totals	373
Adult Baptism Totals	198
First Communions	3,057
Confirmations	2,646
Marriages:	
Catholic	689
Interfaith	320
Total Marriages	1,009
Deaths	3,819
Total Catholic Population	311,427
Total Population	1,510,953

Former Bishops—Rt. Rev. BERNARD J. MCQUAID, D.D., ord. Jan. 16, 1848; appt. March 31, 1868; cons. July 12, 1868; died Jan. 18, 1909; Most Revs. THOMAS F. HICKEY, D.D., ord. March 25, 1884; cons. May 24, 1905; succeeded to the See, Jan. 18, 1909; appt. assistant at the Pontifical Throne, May 4, 1925; made Archbishop of the Titular See of Viminacium, Oct. 30, 1928; died Dec. 10, 1940; JOHN FRANCIS O'HERN, D.D., ord. Feb. 17, 1901; appt. Bishop of Rochester, Jan. 4, 1929; cons. March 19, 1929; died May 22, 1933; His Eminence EDWARD CARDINAL MOONEY, D.D., appt. Papal Delegate to India Jan. 1, 1926; cons. Jan. 31, 1926; appt. Apostolic Delegate to Japan Jan. 1, 1931; appt. Bishop of Rochester Jan. 1, 1933; installed Bishop of Rochester Oct. 12, 1933; transferred to Detroit, May 26, 1937; installed Archbishop of Detroit, Aug. 3, 1937; created Cardinal, Feb. 18, 1946; died Oct. 25, 1958; Most Revs. JAMES E. KEARNEY, D.D., ord. Sept. 19, 1908; appt. Bishop of Salt Lake, Utah, July 1, 1932; cons. Oct. 28, 1932; transferred to Rochester, July 31, 1937; installed Nov. 11, 1937; retired Oct. 26, 1966; died Jan. 12, 1977; FULTON J. SHEEN, D.D., ord. Sept. 30, 1919; appt. Titular Bishop of Cesariana and Auxiliary of New York, May 28, 1951; cons. June 11, 1951; appt. to Rochester, Oct. 26, 1966; installed Dec. 15, 1966; resigned Oct. 15, 1969; appt. Titular Archbishop of Newport; died Dec. 9, 1979; JOSEPH L. HOGAN, S.T.D., D.D., ord. June 6, 1942; appt. to Rochester, Oct. 15, 1969; cons. and installed Nov. 28, 1969; retired Nov. 28, 1978; died Aug. 27, 2000.

Pastoral Center Administration

Pastoral Center—1150 Buffalo Rd., Rochester, 14624-1890. Tel: 585-328-3210; 800-388-7177 (Toll Free within Diocese); Fax: 585-328-3149. Web: www.dor.org.

Vicars General—Very Rev. JOSEPH A. HART, S.T.D., V.G.; Rev. JOHN M. MULLIGAN, V.G. (Retired).

Moderator of the Pastoral Center—Very Rev. JOSEPH A. HART, S.T.D., V.G.

Chancellor—Rev. DANIEL J. CONDON, J.C.L.

Judicial Vicar—Rev. LOUIS A. SIRIANNI, J.C.L.

Vice Chancellor and Administrator of the Bishop's Office—Sr. MARY ANN BINSACK, R.S.M.

Secretary to the Bishop—Ms. JOSEPHINE C. CONLON.

Office of the Chancellor and Department of Legal Services

Chancellor and Director of the Department of Legal Services—Rev. DANIEL J. CONDON, J.C.L.

Judicial Vicar—Rev. LOUIS A. SIRIANNI, J.C.L.

Vice Chancellor—Sr. MARY ANN BINSACK, R.S.M.

Administrative Assistant—Ms. LYNN PIERLEONI.

Diocesan Archives—Sr. CONNIE DERBY, R.S.M., Dir. Archival Svcs. Email: archives@dor.org.

Censores Librorum—Very Rev. JOSEPH A. HART, S.T.D., V.G.; Rev. WILLIAM F. LAIRD, J.C.L.; Rev. Msgr. WILLIAM H. SHANNON (Retired); Revs. WILLIAM E. GRAF, D.Min. (Retired); JOSEPH W. MARCOUX, S.T.L.

Tribunal—

Director—EMMETT G. WELLS, J.D., J.C.L.

Judges—Revs. LOUIS A. SIRIANNI, J.C.L., Judicial Vicar; R. RICHARD BRICKLER, Adjutant Judicial Vicar (Retired); Ms. RENEE LISS-SIRACO, J.C.L.; Revs. KEVIN E. MCKENNA, J.C.D.; JOHN M. MULLIGAN, V.G. (Retired); T. PIUS PATHMARAJAH, J.C.L.; Mr. EMMETT G. WELLS, J.D., J.C.L.

Defender of the Bond—Rev. Msgr. GERARD C. KRIEG, J.C.L. (Retired).

Staff—Ms. MARY ELLEN GOVERTS, Case Instructor, Advocate, Notary & Defender of the Bond; Rev. WILLIAM E. GRAF, D.Min., Expert (Retired); Miss ANDREA IMBURGIA, Admin. Asst. & Notary; Deacon JAMES STEIGER, Auditor; Ms. ROSANNE WARNER, Case Instructor, Advocate, Notary & Defender of the Bond.

Consultative Bodies

Bishop's Stewardship Council—Most Rev. MATTHEW HARVEY CLARK, D.D., Pres.; Mr. JEROME HASS, Ph.D., Chm.

College of Consultors—Rev. DANIEL J. CONDON, J.C.L., Contact.

Priest Consultors—Most Rev. MATTHEW HARVEY CLARK, D.D.; Very Rev. JOSEPH A. HART, S.T.D., V.G.; Revs. JOHN M. MULLIGAN, V.G. (Retired); EDWARD L. PALUMBOS; DANIEL J. CONDON, J.C.L.; KEVIN E. MCKENNA, J.C.D.; SCOTT M. KUBINSKI; PAUL J. TOMASSO; ROBERT SCOTT BOURCY.

Priests' Council—Rev. PAUL J. TOMASSO, Chm.

Regional Coordinator—Sr. MARY ANN BINSACK, R.S.M., Liaison.

Catholic Charities—

Catholic Charities of the Diocese of Rochester—1150 Buffalo Rd., Rochester, 14624. Tel: 585-328-3210. JACK BALINSKY, Diocesan Dir.; LINDA STUNDTNER, Chm. Bd. Directors, (Refer to Catholic Charities section under Institutions Located in the Diocese for further listings).

Diocesan Newspapers "Catholic Courier"— "El Mensajero Catolico" Tel: 585-529-9530; 800-600-3628. KAREN FRANZ, Gen. Mgr. & Editor.

Board of Directors—Most Rev. MATTHEW HARVEY CLARK, D.D., Pres.; Very Rev. JOSEPH A. HART, S.T.D., V.G., Vicar Gen. & Vice Pres.; Rev. DANIEL J. CONDON, J.C.L., Sec.; MARY AMATO; DONNA DEDEE; SCOTT BENJAMIN; KARLEE BOLANOS; THOMAS FLYNN; JOANNE GORDON; WILLIAM H. KEDLEY, Treas.; MARY HOLLERAN; MYRTLE FONTENETTE; ROBERT FINNERTY; RICHARD HARE; JAMES REDMOND; SAL DICIACCIO; JILL MORGAN; HELEN MCDERMOTT; TIMOTHY FITZGERALD; Rev. MARK ALAN BREWER; ZORY MARTINEZ-ALLACCO; Rev. JOHN A. FIRPO; DOLORES PASTO-ZIOBRO.

Faith Development Ministry—

Department of Catholic Schools—ANNE WILLKENS LEACH, Supt. Schools. Assistant Superintendents: MARY ELLEN WAGNER, Curriculum & Instruction; Mrs. ANN FRANK, Coord. Assessment & Professional Growth; KATHLEEN GRAY, Business Mgr.; TAMMY SYLVESTER, Dir. Human Resources for Catholic Schools.

Department of Evangelization and Catechesis—Ms. MARIBETH MANCINI, Dir.

AV Resource Librarian—Sr. CONNIE DERBY, R.S.M.

Director of Young Adult and Campus Ministry—Ms. SHANNON LOUGHLIN.

Coordinator of Youth Ministry—LINDA MEHLENBACHER.

Coordinator for Family & Catechist Formation—JONATHAN SCHOTT.

Coordinator for Evangelization and Sacramental Catechesis—MARY DUNDAS.

CYO Administrator—GERI PIETRZAK.

Office of Stewardship and Communications—Mr. DOUG MANDELARO.

Associate Directors of Stewardship and Communications—Mr. MARK J. CLARK; Mr. DAVID KELLY.

Administrative Assistant—LYNN TRELLY.

Department of Financial Services—

Chief Financial Officer—Ms. LISA M. PASSERO.

Administrative Assistant—VACANT.

Director of Financial Services—Ms. MARY ZIARNIAK.

Information Technology—Mr. THOMAS VEEDER, Dir.; Mr. DAVID KILPATRICK, Network Admin. Computer Coordinators: Mr. MARK DARLING; Mr. RICHARD BRAXTON; Ms. BRENDA CHEVALIER; Mr. KIM FAY; Ms. RENATA PARKS; Ms. SAM TURETSKY; Mrs. JOYCE CROOKS, Technical Support Specialist. Catholic Charities Computer Associates: Mr. MICHAEL DABRAMO; Mr. SHAWN MLECZYNSKI.

Buildings and Properties—Mr. ERIC PATCHKE, Mgr.

Controller—KATHLEEN M. MOORE.

Human Resources—Ms MARY F. BAUER, Dir.; Ms. JEAN WOOD, Admin. Asst.

Benefits Administration—Ms. PATRICIA HOSKING, Coord.; Ms. AMY IRISH, Dir. Benefits Planning & Pension Admin.

Clergy Services—Mrs. SANDRA GROCKI, Coord.

Deacon Personnel—Deacon JOHN BRASLEY, Dir. & Contact, Deacon Personnel Board.

Department of Management and Staff Relations—Mrs. BARBARA PEDEVILLE, Dir.

Department of Priest Personnel—Rev. EDWARD L. PALUMBOS, Dir.

Department of Human Resources for Catholic Schools—TAMMY SYLVESTER, Dir.

Ministry to Priests—Rev. WILLIAM E. GRAF, D.Min., Coord. (Retired), Legacy at Fairways, 681 High St., Victor, 14564. Email: graf@dor.org.

Newly Ordained Priests—Revs. PETER C. CLIFFORD; DANIEL TORMEY (Retired).

Pension Committee (Lay and Priests)—Very Rev. JOSEPH A. HART, S.T.D., V.G.; Revs. DANIEL J. CONDON, J.C.L.; EDWARD L. PALUMBOS; THOMAS H. WHEELAND; Ms. PAULA DOLAN; Ms MARY F. BAUER; Ms. AMY IRISH; Ms. LISA M. PASSERO.

Priests' Personnel Board—Rev. EDWARD L. PALUMBOS, Chm.

Priests' Sabbatical Committee—Rev. GEORGE P. HEYMAN.

Office of Seminarians—Rev. JAMES A. SCHWARTZ, Dir., St. Joseph, 43 Gebhardt Rd., Penfield, 14526.

Office of Vocations—Revs. WILLIAM COFFAS, Dir., Becket Hall, 2617 East Ave., Rochester, 14610. Tel: 585-461-2890. Email: fconboy@dor.org; TIMOTHY E. HORAN, Dir.

Office of Vocations Awareness—Ms CAROL DADY, Coord. Vocations Awareness. Tel: 585-328-3210.

Vicar for Religious—Rev. DANIEL J. CONDON, J.C.L.

Parish Support Ministries—Tel: 585-328-3228, Ext. 1337.

Director—Mr. BERNARD GRIZARD.

Secretary—DIANA COLLINS.

Office of Liturgy—VACANT.

Liturgical Commission—Rev. ROBERT J. KENNEDY, Chm.

Office of Pastoral Planning—Mr. BERNARD GRIZARD, Dir. Liaisons: Ms. KAREN RINEFIERD; DIANA COLLINS, Administrative Asst.

Ministry Offices—

Multicultural Services—Mr. BERNARD GRIZARD, Dir.

Office of Health Care Ministry—Ms. DEBORAH HOUSEL, Coord.

Office of Migrant Ministry—Rev. JESUS FLORES, Coord.

Office of Spanish Apostolate—Bro. JUAN LOZADA ROCA, C.S.J.E., Coord.

Urban Subsidy Program—Bro. JUAN LOZADA ROCA, C.S.J.E., Coord.

Office of Ecumenical and Interreligious Services—BERNARD GRIZZARD, Coord.

Jail Ministry Coordinator—Ms. DEBORAH HOUSEL.

Support Ministry Liaison—LYNETTE DEJESUS.

Diocesan Missions—

The Society for the Propagation of the Faith—Rev. ROBERT C. BRADLER, Dir. (Retired), 1150 Buffalo Rd., Rochester, 14624. Tel: 585-436-9200.

World and Diocesan Missions/Mission Awareness—Sr. JANET KORN, R.S.M., Coord.; Ms. JOSEPHINE C. CONLON, Sec. & Bookkeeper.

Specialized Ministries—

Bishop Sheen Ecumenical Housing Foundation—935 East Ave., Ste. 300, Rochester, 14607. Tel: 585-461-4263; Fax: 585-461-5177. Email: sheen@rochester.rr.com. Web: sheenhousing.org. ALLYNN SMITH, Exec. Dir.; ROSEANNE HENNESSEY, Pres. Bd. Directors, Subsidiary: Bloomfield Meadows, Inc.

Clergy Relief Society—Rev. THOMAS H. WHEELAND, Holy Cross Church, 4492 Lake Ave., Rochester, 14617. Tel: 585-663-2244.

Diocesan Building Commission—Mr. ERIC PATCHKE, Contact.

Diocesan Women's Commission—Ms. SHANNON LOUGHLIN, Diocesan Liaison. Leadership Team: SHELLEY FESS; JANE SUTTER BRANDT; JOAN TANNOUS.

Holy Sepulchre Cemetery—Mr. JAMES WEISBECK, Dir. & Asst. Treas., 2461 Lake Ave., Rochester, 14612. Tel: 585-458-4110.

Victim Assistance Coordinator—Mrs. BARBARA PEDEVILLE. Tel: 585-328-3228, Ext. 1215. Email: pedeville@dor.org.

CLERGY, PARISHES, MISSIONS AND PAROCHIAL SCHOOLS

METROPOLITAN ROCHESTER

(MONROE COUNTY)

1—SACRED HEART CATHEDRAL (1910) Revs. Kevin E. McKenna; Edison Tayag, Parochial Vicar; Deacons Lynn W. Kershner; John Giugno. In Res., Most Rev. Matthew Harvey Clark; Rev. John M. Mulligan, Senior Priest (Retired).

The Cathedral Community—, (Holy Rosary, Most Precious Blood, Sacred Heart Cathedral), 296 Flower City Pk., 14615. Tel: 585-254-3221; Fax: 585-254-8970.

Catechesis/Religious Program—

Convent—287 Flower City Pk., 14615. Tel: 716-254-5048.

2—ST. AMBROSE (1921) Merged with St. James, Rochester & St. John the Evangelist, Rochester to form Peace of Christ Roman Catholic Parish of Rochester, NY.

3—ST. ANDREW (1914) Closed. Inquiries for Parish records should contact St. Francis Xavier Cabrini Parish.

4—ST. ANNE (1930) [CEM] Sr. Joan Sobala, S.S.J., Pastoral Admin.; Rev. Gary L. Tyman, Sacramental Min. In Res., Revs. Dennis Bonsignore; James F. Lawlor (Retired).

Res.: 1600 Mt. Hope Ave., 14620-4598. Tel: 585-271-3260; Fax: 585-271-7160.

Catechesis/Religious Program—

5—ST. ANTHONY OF PADUA (1906), (Italian—Vietnamese), Closed. For inquiries for parish records, contact Holy Apostles Church, Rochester, NY.

6—ST. AUGUSTINE (1898) Closed. For inquiries for parish records contact St. Monica, Rochester.

7—BLESSED SACRAMENT (1902) Revs. Robert J. Kennedy; Scott Caton, Parochial Vicar.

Parish—534 Oxford St., 14607.

Res. & Mailing Address: 259 Rutgers St., 14607. Tel: 585-271-7240; Fax: 585-442-7517.

Catechesis/Religious Program—

Convent—247 Rutgers St., 14607. Tel: 585-271-7736.

8—ST. BONIFACE (1860), (German), [CEM] Revs. Robert J. Kennedy; Scott Caton, Parochial Vicar.

Res.: 330 Gregory St., 14620. Tel: 585-473-4271; Fax: 585-256-0868.

Catechesis/Religious Program—

9—ST. BRIDGET (1854) Merged with Immaculate Conception, Rochester to form the parish of Immaculate Conception/St. Bridget, Rochester. For inquiries on records contact Immaculate Conception Parish.

10—ST. CECILIA (1949) [CEM] Merged with Christ the King, St. Margaret Mary, St. Salome & St. Thomas the Apostle, Rochester to form the Parish of Blessed Kateri Tekakwitha, Rochester.

11—ST. CHARLES BORROMEO (1925) Revs. John A. Firpo; Mark Alan Brewer, Parochial Vicar; Deacon Lon Smith. In Res., Rev. Thomas R. Statt (Retired).

Res.: 3003 Dewey Ave., 14616. Tel: 585-663-3230; Fax: 585-663-8055.

Catechesis/Religious Program—

12—CHRIST THE KING (1955) Merged with St. Cecilia, St. Margaret Mary, St. Salome & St. Thomas the Apostle, Rochester to form the Parish of Blessed Kateri Tekakwitha, Rochester.

13—CHURCH OF THE ANNUNCIATION (1917), (Italian), Merged with Our Lady of the Americas, St. Michael's and Our Lady of Perpetual Help to form St. Frances Xavier Cabrini.

14—EMMANUEL CHURCH OF THE DEAF OF THE DIOCESE OF ROCHESTER (1981) Rev. Raymond H. Fleming; Deacon Patrick A. Graybill.

Res.: 34 St. Monica St., 14619. Tel: 585-235-3244; 585-235-1812.

15—ST. FRANCIS ASSISI (1929) Closed. For inquiries for parish records, please contact: Holy Apostles, 7 Austin St., Rochester, NY 14606; Tel: 585-254-7171; Fax: 585-254-5813; Email: rholyapo@dor.org.

16—ST. FRANCIS XAVIER, Closed. All inquiries should be directed to St. Frances Xavier Cabrini Parish

17—ST. GEORGE (1907), (Lithuanian), Rev. Dominic F. Mockevicius, Parochial Admin. (Retired).

Mailing Address: 150 Varinna Dr., 14618. Tel: 585-319-5689.

18—GUARDIAN ANGELS (1960) Revs. Gerald Appleby, Sacramental Min.; Robert L. Beligotti, Sacramental Min.; Deacons Emmanuel Asis; Anthony Caruso; Anthony Mercadel; James Carra; Barbara Swiecki, Pastoral Admin.

Res.: 2061 E. Henrietta Rd., 14623-3999. Tel: 585-334-1412; Fax: 585-334-7145.

19—ST. HELEN (1940), Includes Vietnamese Community. Revs. Michael J. Schramel; Leo Vu Dinh Huyen, C.M.C., Parochial Vicar; James E. Hewes, Parochial Vicar.

Res.: 310 Hinchey Rd., 14624. Tel: 585-235-1210; Fax: 585-235-8018.

Catechesis/Religious Program—

20—HOLY APOSTLES (1884) Rev. Anthony P. Mugavero; Deacons John Crego; Salvador Otero; Nemesio Martinez Vellon.

Parish—530 Lyell Ave., 14606.

Res.: 7 Austin St., 14606. Tel: 585-254-7170; Fax: 585-254-5813.

21—HOLY CROSS (1873) Revs. Thomas H. Wheeland; Frederick F. Eisemann (Retired); John Reif, Parochial Vicar (Retired); Deacon Ed Giblin.

Res.: 4492 Lake Ave., 14612. Tel: 585-663-2244; Fax: 585-865-5379.

School—*Holy Cross School*, (Grades PreK-6), 4488 Lake Ave., 14612. Tel: 585-663-6533. Email: hcdcs@dor.org. Kathleen Dougherty, Prin.

Catechesis/Religious Program—Tel: 585-621-8133.

Convent—4490 Lake Ave., 14612. Tel: 716-663-5351.

22—HOLY FAMILY (1864), (German), Merged with Holy Apostles, Rochester. For inquiries for parish records contact Holy Apostles, Rochester.

23—HOLY GHOST (1875) [CEM] Revs. Michael J. Schramel; James E. Hewes, Parochial Vicar; Deacon David Cadregari.

Res.: 220 Coldwater Rd., 14624. Tel: 585-247-3535; Fax: 585-247-4223.

Catechesis/Religious Program—Tel: 585-426-1289.

24—HOLY NAME OF JESUS (1964) Rev. John F. Gagnier; Deacons Joseph Placious; Richard J. Lombard.

Res.: 15 St. Martin's Way, 14616. Tel: 585-621-4040; Fax: 585-621-6343; 585-621-1339.

Catechesis/Religious Program—Tel: 585-621-6343.

25—HOLY REDEEMER-ST. FRANCIS XAVIER (1867-1888) Merged with Our Lady of the Americas, Our Lady of Mount Carmel, Light of Christ, Our Lady of the Angels & Our Lady of Perpetual Help, Rochester to form the Parish of St. Francis Xavier Cabrini, Rochester.

26—HOLY ROSARY (1889) Merged with Most Precious Blood & Sacred Heart Cathedral, Rochester to form Sacred Heart Cathedral. For inquiries for parish records contact Sacred Heart Cathedral, Rochester.

27—IMMACULATE CONCEPTION (1849) Merged with St. Bridget, Rochester to form the parish of Immaculate Conception/St. Bridget, Rochester.

28—IMMACULATE CONCEPTION/ST. BRIDGET Deacon Mark Bovenzi.

Office: 445 Frederick Douglass St., 14608.

29—St. James (1949) Merged with St. Ambrose, Rochester & St. John the Evangelist, Rochester to form Peace of Christ Roman Catholic Parish of Rochester, NY.

30—St. John the Evangelist (1914) Merged with St. Ambrose, Rochester & St. James, Rochester to form Peace of Christ Roman Catholic Parish of Rochester, NY.
See separate listing under Monroe County School System in the Institution section.

31—St. John the Evangelist (1865) Revs. John V. Forni; T. Pius Pathmarajah; Deacon Paul Virgilio.
Res.: 2400 Ridge Rd., W., 14626. Tel: 585-225-8980; Fax: 585-723-9825.
Catechesis/Religious Program—Tel: 585-225-4200.

32—St. Joseph (1836) Closed. For inquiries for parish records contact Our Lady of Victory.

33—St. Jude the Apostle (1968) Revs. Michael J. Schramel; James E. Hewes, Parochial Vicar; Deacon Patrick M. Shanley.
Res.: 4100 Lyell Rd., 14606. Tel: 585-247-4322; Fax: 585-429-5111.
Catechesis/Religious Program—Tel: 585-247-5275.

34—Kateri Tekakwitha Roman Catholic Parish Revs. Norman C. Tanck, C.S.B.; Joseph A. Trovato, C.S.B., Parochial Vicar; Morgan Rice, C.S.B.; Deacon Walter Toot. In Res., Revs. Peter J. Etlinger, C.S.B.; Jack Rosse; Walter Cushing (Retired); Peter Bayer.
Office: 445 Kings Hwy. S., 14617. Tel: 585-266-1288; Fax: 585-266-1074.
Catechesis/Religious Program—

35—St. Lawrence (1959) Revs. Frank J. Falletta; Peter Enyan-Boadu, Parochial Vicar; Deacons James L. Chatterton; Thomas Beck.
Res.: 1000 N. Greece Rd., 14626. Tel: 585-723-1350; Fax: 585-723-1361.
School—St. Lawrence School, (Grades K-6), 1000 N. Greece Rd., 14626. Tel: 585-225-3870. Email: slawrdcs@dor.org. Susan Sak, Prin.
Catechesis/Religious Program—Tel: 585-225-7320.

36—Light of Christ Roman Catholic Parish, Merged with Our Lady of the Americas, Our Lady of the Angels & Our Lady of Perpetual Help, Rochester to form the Roman Catholic Parish of St. Francis Xavier Cabrini, Rochester.

37—St. Lucy (1912) Closed. For inquiries for parish records contact Immaculate Conception Church.

38—St. Margaret Mary (1929) Merged with St. Cecilia, Christ the King, St. Salome & St. Thomas the Apostle, Rochester to form the Parish of Blessed Kateri Tekakwitha, Rochester.

39—St. Mark (1964) Rev. Louis A. Sirianni; Deacon Frank Pettrone. In Res., Rev. Frederick Bush (Retired).
Res.: 54 Kuhn Rd., 14612. Tel: 585-225-3710; Fax: 585-227-6824.
Catechesis/Religious Program—Tel: 585-227-6824; Fax: 585-225-8910.

40—St. Mary (1834) Revs. Scott Caton, Parochial Vicar; Robert J. Kennedy, Parochial Vicar; Anne-Marie Brogan, Pastoral Assoc.
Res.: 15 St. Mary's Pl., 14607. Tel: 585-232-7142; Fax: 585-232-6289.
Catechesis/Religious Program—

41—St. Michael (1872), (German—Hispanic), Merged with Our Lady of the Americas, Our Lady of the Angels & Our Lady of Perpetual Help, Rochester to form the Roman Catholic Parish of St. Frances Xavier Cabrini, Rochester.

42—St. Monica (1898) Rev. Raymond H. Fleming; Deacon Robert Burke. Cluster of Our Lady of Good Counsel, St. Augustine & Ss. Peter and Paul. Consolidated with St. Monica.
Office: 34 Monica St., 14611. Tel: 585-235-3340; Fax: 585-235-8315.

43—Most Precious Blood (1930) Closed. For inquiries for parish records contact Sacred Heart Cathedral, Rochester.

44—Our Lady of Good Counsel (1928) Closed. for inquiries for parish records contact St. Monica, Rochester.

45—Our Lady of Lourdes (1928) Rev. Gary L. Tyman, Sacramental Min.; Sr. Joan Sobala, S.S.J., Pastoral Admin.
Res.: 150 Varinna Dr., 14618. Tel: 585-473-9656; Fax: 585-271-6472.
School—Seton Catholic School, (Grades PreK-6), 165 Rhinecliff Dr., 14618-1525. Tel: 585-473-6604. Email: setondcs@dor.org. Martin Swenson, Prin.
Catechesis/Religious Program—Tel: 585-244-2361.

46—Our Lady of Mercy (1957) Closed. For inquiries for parish records please see Our Mother of Sorrows, Rochester.

47—Our Lady of Mount Carmel (1909) Merged with Our Lady of the Americas, Light of Christ, Our Lady of the Angels, Our Lady of Perpetual Help, Holy Redeemer, St. Francis Xavier & Corpus Christi, Rochester to form Parish of St. Frances Xavier Cabrini, Rochester.

48—Our Lady of Perpetual Help (1905) Merged with Our Lady of the Americas, Our Lady of the Angels & Light of Christ, Rochester to form the Roman Catholic Parish of St. Francis Xavier Cabrini, Rochester.

49—Our Lady of the Americas of Rochester, NY (1888) Merged with Light of Christ, Our Lady of the Angels & Our Lady of Perpetual Help, Rochester to form the Roman Catholic Parish of St. Francis Xavier Cabrini, Rochester.

50—Our Lady of Victory-St. Joseph (1848) Rev. Ronald A. Antinarelli, K.C.H.S.
Res.: 210 Pleasant St., 14604. Tel: 585-454-2244; Fax: 585-454-2246.

51—Our Lady Queen of Peace (1960) Very Rev. Joseph A. Hart, Sacramental Min.; Rev. William Coffas, Sacramental Min.; Margaret Ostromecki, Pastoral Admin. In Res., Rev. John T. Walsh (Retired).
Parish—601 Edgewood Ave., 14618-4329.
Res.: 18 Viennawood Dr., 14618. Tel: 585-244-3010 (Office); Fax: 585-242-7733 (Office).
Catechesis/Religious Program—

52—Our Mother of Sorrows (1829), (Irish), [CEM] Rev. Alexander H. Bradshaw; Deacon David Cadregari. In Res., Revs. Edwin Metzger (Retired); Winfried Kellner (Retired).
Res.: 5000 Mt. Read Blvd., 14612. Tel: 585-663-5432; Fax: 585-663-7683.
Catechesis/Religious Program—Tel: 585-621-3495.

53—St. Patrick (1832) Closed. (Old Cathedral). Records can be obtained from Holy Apostles, 7 Austin St., Rochester, NY 14608. Tel: 585-254-5813.

54—Peace of Christ Roman Catholic Parish of Rochester, NY Revs. Robert J. Schrader; Brian Kumar Carpenter, Parochial Vicar; Timothy Brown, Parochial Vicar.
Mailing Address: 25 Empire Blvd., 14609. Tel: 585-288-5000; Fax: 585-654-7658. Email: rpeace@dor.org. Web: www.peaceofchristparish.org.
Res.: 549 Humboldt St., 14610. Tel: 585-482-4210.
School—St. John Neumann School, (Grades PreK-6), 31 Empire Blvd., 14609-4335. Tel: 585-255-0580. Email: sjndcs@dor.org. Marie L. Arcuri, Prin.
Catechesis/Religious Program—

55—SS. Peter and Paul (1843) Closed. for inquiries for parish records contact St. Monica, Rochester.

56—St. Philip Neri (1929) Closed. For inquiries for parish records, contact St. Francis Xavier Cabrini Parish.

57—St. Pius Tenth (1954) [CEM] William Rabjohn, Pastoral Admin.; Rev. Michael A. Mayer; Deacon Dennis Lohouse.
Mailing Address: 3010 Chili Ave., 14624.
Res.: 3032 Chili Ave., 14624. Tel: 585-247-2566 (Office); Fax: 585-247-8848.
School—St. Pius X School, (Grades PreK-6), 3000 Chili Ave., 14624-4598. Tel: 585-247-5650. Email: spxdcs@dor.org. Stephen Oberst, Prin.
Catechesis/Religious Program—

58—Roman Catholic Parish of St. Francis Xavier Cabrini Revs. William McGrath, Parochial Vicar; Robert Thomas Werth, Parochial Vicar; Deacons David A. Palma, Pastoral Admin.; Jose Berrios; Benny Dejesus; Jorge Malave; Robert Meyer; Carlos Vargas.
Office: 124 Evergreen St., 14605. Tel: 585-325-4041; Fax: 585-287-5160.

59—St. Salome (1925) Merged with St. Cecilia, St. Margaret Mary, Christ the King & St. Thomas the Apostle, Rochester to form the Parish of Blessed Kateri Tekakwitha, Rochester.

60—St. Stanislaus (1890), (Polish), Rev. Adam Ogorzaly; Deacon Donald Eggleston.
Res. & Mailing: 34 St. Stanislaus St., 14621. Tel: 585-467-3068; Fax: 585-467-3072.
Church: 1124 Hudson Ave., 14621.
Catechesis/Religious Program—

61—St. Theodore (1924) Rev. Stephen Kraus; Deacons Angelo Coccia; Laurence Feasel. In Res., Revs. Paul J. Freemesser (Retired); Walter J. Plominski.
Res.: 168 Spencerport Rd., 14606. Tel: 585-429-6811; Fax: 585-429-7726.
Catechesis/Religious Program—Tel: 585-429-5650.

62—St. Theresa (1927), (Polish), Closed. For inquiries for parish records contact St. Stanislaus, Rochester.

63—St. Thomas More (1953) Very Rev. Joseph A. Hart, Sacramental Min.; Rev. William Coffas, Sacramental Min.; Margaret Ostromecki, Pastoral Admin.; Deacon H. Wilson Johnson.
Res.: 2617 East Ave., 14610. Tel: 585-381-4200; Fax: 585-381-6327.
Catechesis/Religious Program—Tel: 585-381-0470.

64—St. Thomas the Apostle (1922) Merged with St. Cecilia, St. Margaret Mary, St. Salome & Christ the King, Rochester to form the Parish of Blessed Kateri Tekakwitha, Rochester.

OUTSIDE METROPOLITAN ROCHESTER

Addison, Steuben Co.

1—St. Catherine of Siena (1854) [CEM] Merged with St. Joseph, Campbell & St. Stanislaus, Bradford to form the Catholic Parish of Saints Isadore and Maria Torribia, Addison.

2—The Catholic Parish of Saints Isidore and Maria Torribia Rev. Patrick L. Connor, Parochial Admin.
Office: 51 Maple St., 14801. Tel: 607-359-2115; Fax: 607-359-2121.

Apalachin, Tioga Co., St. Margaret Mary (1955) Merged with St. Francis, Catatonk; St. John the Evangelist, Newark Valley; St. Pius the Tenth, Van Etten; and St. James, Waverly to form Blessed Trinity, Owego.

Auburn, Cayuga Co.

1—St. Aloysius, Closed. For inquiries for parish records please see Holy Family, Auburn.

2—St. Alphonsus (1853), (German), [JC] Rev. Louis A. Vasile; Deacon Gregg Lawson.
Parish—85 E. Genesee St., 13021.
Mailing & Res.: 10 S. Lewis St., 13021. Tel: 315-252-7261; Fax: 315-252-7262.
See St. Joseph's School (Auburn), Auburn under Schools Outside Monroe County located in the Institution section.
Catechesis/Religious Program—

3—St. Francis of Assisi (1907), (Italian), [JC] Deacon Gary R. DiLallo, Pastoral Admin.; Revs. Michael Brown, Sacramental Min.; Richard M. Murphy, Sacramental Min. (Retired); Felicjan Sierotowicz.
Res.: 299 Clark St., 13021. Tel: 315-252-7593; Fax: 315-252-2447.
Catechesis/Religious Program—

4—Holy Family (1834) Rev. John Gathenya. In Res., Rev. Ronald E. Gaesser (Retired).
Parish—85 North St., 13021. Tel: 315-252-9576; Fax: 315-255-1506.
School—St. Joseph's School, Tel: 315-253-8327; Fax: 315-253-2401. Kathleen A. Coye, Prin.
Catechesis/Religious Program—

5—St. Hyacinth (1905), (Polish), [JC] Revs. Michael Brown, Sacramental Min.; Richard M. Murphy, Sacramental Min. (Retired). In Res., Revs. Michael R. Brown; Felicjan Sierotowicz; Michael F. Conboy (Retired).
Church & Res.: 61 Pulaski St., 13021. Tel: 315-252-7297; Fax: 315-252-2447.
Church Office: 299 Clark St., 13021.
School—St. Joseph School, Tel: 315-253-8327. A consolidation of the following parishes: Holy Family; Sacred Heart; St. Alphonsus; and St. Hyacinth.
Catechesis/Religious Program—

6—St. Mary (1868), (Irish), Revs. Frank E. Lioi; Joseph Osei Bonsu, Parochial Vicar.
Res.: 15 Clark St., 13021. Tel: 315-252-9545; Fax: 315-252-9546.
School—St. Joseph's, Tel: 315-253-8357. Also serving the parishes of Auburn.
Catechesis/Religious Program—

7—Sacred Heart (1955) [JC] Sr. Chris J. Treichel, O.S.F., Pastoral Admin.; Deacon Nicholas Valvo; Revs. Michael Brown, Sacramental Min.; Felicjan Sierotowicz, Sacramental Min.
Res.: 90 Melrose Rd., 13021. Tel: 315-252-7271; Fax: 315-255-0716.
School—St. Joseph School, 89 E. Genesee St., 13021. Tel: 315-253-8327; Fax: 315-253-2401. Kathleen A. Coye, Prin. A consolidation of the following parishes: Holy Family; Sacred Heart; and St. Alphonsus.
Catechesis/Religious Program—
Mission—St. Ann (1912) Main St., Owasco, Cayuga Co. 13021. Tel: 315-252-7271.

Aurora, Cayuga Co.

1—Good Shepherd Catholic Community, [CEM] Rev. Richard J. Shatzel.
Mailing Address: P.O. Box 296, 13026-0296. Tel: 315-364-7197; Fax: 315-364-7197.
Catechesis/Religious Program—

2—St. Patrick (1858) Closed. For inquiries for parish records contact Good Shepherd Catholic Community, Aurora.

Avon, Livingston Co., St. Agnes (1866) [CEM] Sr. Karen Dietz, S.S.J., Pastoral Admin.; Rev. Michael Upson, Sacramental Min.; Deacon Edward Mathis.
Res.: 108 Prospect St., 14414. Tel: 585-226-2100; Fax: 585-226-6436.
School—(Grades PreK-6), For detailed school information please see Category Schools outside Monroe located in the Institution section.
Catechesis/Religious Program—Michael Drexler, D.R.E.

Bath, Steuben Co., St. Mary (1860) [CEM] Deacon David LaFortune, Pastoral Admin.; Rev. James P. Jaeger, Sacramental Min.
Res.: 32 E. Morris St., 14810. Tel: 607-776-3327; Fax: 607-776-3409.
Catechesis/Religious Program—

BRADFORD, STEUBEN CO., ST. STANISLAUS (1922), (Polish), Merged with St. Joseph, Campbell & St. Catherine, Addison to form the Catholic Parish of Saints Isadore and Maria Torribia, Addison.

BROCKPORT, MONROE CO., NATIVITY OF THE BLESSED VIRGIN MARY (1848) [CEM] Rev. Theodore J. Auble, Parochial Vicar; Charlotte M. Bruney, Pastoral Admin.
Res.: 152 Main St., 14420-1972. Tel: 585-637-4500; Fax: 585-637-4232.
Catechesis/Religious Program—

CALEDONIA, LIVINGSTON CO., ST. COLUMBA (1885) [CEM] Revs. William Endres, Parochial Vicar; Steven W. Lape, Parochial Vicar; Irene Goodwin, Pastoral Admin.; Deacon David Paluskiewicz.
Res.: 198 North St., 14423. Tel: 585-538-2126.
Catechesis/Religious Program—

CANANDAIGUA, ONTARIO CO., ST. MARY (1844) [CEM] Revs. Thomas P. Mull; Dominic Nyamai Munini, Sacramental Min.; Deacon Claude Lester.
Res.: 95 N. Main St., Canadaigua, 14424. Tel: 585-394-1220; Fax: 585-396-3230.
See St. Mary (Canandaigua), Canandaigua under Finger Lakes & Southern Tier Schools located in the Institution section.
Catechesis/Religious Program—

CANISTEO, STEUBEN CO., ST. JOACHIM (1880) Closed. See Our Lady of the Valley, Hornell.

CATO, CAYUGA CO., ST. PATRICK (1875) Merged with St. Joseph, Weedsport and St. John, Port Byron to form Our Lady of the Snow, Weedsport.

CAYUGA, CAYUGA CO., ST. JOSEPH (1870) Closed. For inquiries for parish records contact Good Shepherd Catholic Community, Aurora.

CHURCHVILLE, MONROE CO., ST. VINCENT DE PAUL (1869) [CEM] Revs. William Endres, Parochial Vicar; Steven W. Lape, Parochial Vicar; Irene Goodwin, Pastoral Admin.
Res.: 11 N. Main St., P.O. Box 609, 14428. Tel: 716-293-1400; Fax: 716-293-0531.
Catechesis/Religious Program—

CLIFTON SPRINGS, ONTARIO CO.
1—ST. FELIX (1856) Clustered with St. Francis, Phelps to form St. Felix/St. Francis Parish Cluster, Clifton Springs.
2—ST. FELIX/ST. FRANCIS PARISH CLUSTER (1992) [CEM 2] Rev. Donald J. Curtiss; Deacon Robert Cyrana.
Office:—12 Hibbard Ave., 14432. Tel: 315-548-5331 (St. Francis); 315-462-2961 (St. Felix); Fax: 315-462-3608.
Catechesis/Religious Program—

CLYDE, WAYNE CO., ST. JOHN THE EVANGELIST (1852), (Italian), [CEM] Rev. Augustine Chumo; Deacon Gregory Kiley.
Res.: 114 Sodus St., 14433. Tel: 315-923-3941; Fax: 315-923-3941.
Catechesis/Religious Program—
Mission—St. Patrick (1875) Grand Ave., Savannah, Wayne Co. 13146. Tel: 315-365-3244.

COHOCTON, STEUBEN CO.
1—HOLY FAMILY CATHOLIC COMMUNITY, Merger of St. Mary's, Dansville; St. Joseph's, Wayland; Sacred Heart of Jesus, Perkinsville; and St. Pius V, Cohocton. Church: 35 Maple Ave., Cohocton.
2—ST. PIUS V (1861), (German), Consolidated with St. Joseph's, Wayland; St. Mary's Danville; and Sacred Heart of Jesus, Perkinsville to form Holy Family Catholic Community, Cohocton.

CORNING, STEUBEN CO.
1—ALL SAINTS Rev. Lewis E. Brown, Parochial Vicar (Retired); Deacon Dean Condon, Pastoral Admin.
Mailing Address: 222 Dodge Ave., 14830. Tel: 607-936-4689; Fax: 607-936-0222.
Rectory—15 E. High St., Painted Post, 14870. Tel: 607-962-0422.
School— For detailed school information please see Category Schools outside Monroe located in the Institution section.
2—ST. MARY (1848) Closed. For inquiries for parish records contact All Saints, Corning.
3—ST. PATRICK (1903) Closed. For inquiries for parish records contact All Saints, Corning.
4—ST. VINCENT DE PAUL (1913) Closed. For inquiries for parish records contact All Saints, Corning.

DANSVILLE, LIVINGSTON CO., ST. MARY (1845) Consolidated with St. Joseph's, Wayland; St. Pius V, Cohocton; and Sacred Heart of Jesus, Perkinsville to form Holy Family Catholic Community, Cohocton.

DRYDEN, TOMPKINS CO., HOLY CROSS (1962) Rev. Malachy Nwosu.
Parish—375 S. George Rd., Freeville, 13068. Tel: 607-844-8314; Fax: 607-844-8358.
Catechesis/Religious Program—

EAST BAY, WAYNE CO., ST. JOHN FISHER (1935) Closed. All inquiries for mission records can be made at Blessed Trinity, Wolcott.

EAST BLOOMFIELD, ONTARIO CO., ST. BRIDGET (1850) [CEM] Revs. Thomas P. Mull; Dominic Nyamai Munini, Sacramental Min.; Deacon Claude Lester.
Mailing Address: P.O. Box 248, 14443.
Res.: 15 Church St., 14443. Tel: 585-657-7626; Fax: 585-657-5349.
Catechesis/Religious Program—

EAST ROCHESTER, MONROE CO., ST. JEROME (1905) Rev. William B. Leone. In Res., Rev. William Endres.
Res.: 207 S. Garfield St., 14445. Tel: 585-586-3231; Fax: 585-586-0537.
Catechesis/Religious Program—

ELMIRA HEIGHTS, CHEMUNG CO., ST. CHARLES BORROMEO (1904) Merged with Our Lady of Lourdes, Elmira & St. Casimir, Elmira to form Christ the Redeemer, Elmira.

ELMIRA, CHEMUNG CO.
1—ST. ANTHONY (1908), (Italian), Merged with St. Patrick, Elmira & Sts. Peter & Paul Catholic Parish, Elmira to form Blessed Sacrament Roman Catholic Church of Elmira, NY.
2—BLESSED SACRAMENT ROMAN CATHOLIC CHURCH OF ELMIRA, NY Rev. Richard T. Farrell; Deacons George Welch; Joseph Erway.
Mailing Address: 604 Park Pl., 14901. Tel: 607-733-0300; Fax: 607-733-3606. Email: eeastsid@dor.org. Web: www.elmirablessedsacrament.org.
School—Holy Family Catholic Schools, 421 Fulton St., 14904. Tel: 607-732-3588. Wrie Brink, Prin. Serving the parishes in Elmira.
Catechesis/Religious Program—
3—ST. CASIMIR (1890), (Polish), Merged with Our Lady of Lourdes, Elmira & St. Charles Borromeo, Elmira Heights to form Christ the Redeemer, Elmira.
4—ST. CECILIA OF EASTSIDE CATHOLIC PARISH (1904) Closed. For inquiries for parish records contact Blessed Sacrament, Elmira.
5—CHRIST THE REDEEMER Rev. Scott Kubinski; Deacon Alberto Pacete.
Parish—304 Demarest Pkwy., 14905.
Res.: 120 Fairmont Rd., 14905. Tel: 607-732-6261; Fax: 607-732-7256.
See Holy Family Intermediate, Elmira under Schools Outside Monroe County located in the Institution section.
Catechesis/Religious Program—
6—ST. JOHN THE BAPTIST OF EASTSIDE CATHOLIC PARISH (1866), (German), Closed. For sacramental records contact Blessed Sacrament , Elmira.
7—ST. MARY (1873), (Irish), [CEM] Rev. John A. DeSocio. In Res., Revs. Robert C. MacNamara (Retired); Jeremiah P. Moynihan (Retired).
Res.: 224 Franklin St., 14904. Tel: 607-734-6254; Fax: 607-733-8890.
See Holy Family Primary, Elmira under Schools Outside Monroe County located in the Institution section.
Catechesis/Religious Program—
8—OUR LADY OF LOURDES (1940) Merged with St. Charles Borromeo, Elmira Heights & St. Casimir, Elmira to form Christ the Redeemer, Elmira.
9—ST. PATRICK (1871), (Irish), Merged with St. Anthony, Elmira & Sts. Peter & Paul Catholic Parish, Elmira to form Blessed Sacrament Roman Catholic Church of Elmira, NY.
10—STS. PETER AND PAUL CATHOLIC PARISH (1848) Merged with St. Anthony, Elmira & St. Patrick, Elmira to form Blessed Sacrament Roman Catholic Church of Elmira, NY.

FAIRPORT, MONROE CO.
1—ASSUMPTION OF THE BLESSED VIRGIN MARY (1866) [CEM] Revs. Edward L. Palumbos; John Loncle, Parochial Vicar; Deacons Ronald J. Tocci; Stephen Carroll; Robert Corsaro.
Res.: 20 East Ave., 14450. Tel: 585-388-0040; Fax: 585-388-0248.
Catechesis/Religious Program—Assumption School of Religion
2—CHURCH OF ST. JOHN OF ROCHESTER OF PERINTON, NEW YORK (1962) Rev. Peter C. Clifford; Deacon Thomas J. Cleary. In Res., Rev. James E. Boyle (Retired).
Ministry Bldg.—8 Wickford Way, 14450. Tel: 585-248-5993; Fax: 585-387-0517.
Rectory—18 Wickford Way, 14450.
Catechesis/Religious Program—
3—CHURCH OF THE RESURRECTION (1973) Rev. George P. Heyman, Parochial Vicar; Sr. Joan Cawley, S.S.J., Pastoral Admin.
Res.: 52 Mason Rd., 14450. Tel: 585-223-6686; Fax: 585-223-6958.
Church: 63 Mason Rd., 14450. Tel: 585-223-5500; Fax: 585-223-6958.
Catechesis/Religious Program—

FLEMING, CAYUGA CO., ST. ISAAC JOGUES (1946) Closed. For sacramental records contact Good Shepherd Catholic Community, Aurora, NY.

GENESEO, LIVINGSTON CO.
1—ST. LUKE THE EVANGELIST ROMAN CATHOLIC CHURCH SOCIETY OF LIVINGSTON COUNTY (1854) [CEM] Michael Sauter, Pastoral Admin.; Revs. Edward J. Dillon, Parochial Vicar (Retired); Bernard Dan, Parochial Vicar; Deacon Paul Clement.
Office: 13 North St., 14454. Tel: 585-243-1100; Fax: 585-243-0240.
Catechesis/Religious Program—
2—ST. MARY, Merged with Holy Angels, Nunda, St. Patrick, Mt. Morris & St. Thomas Aquinas, Leicester & St. Mary, Retsof to form St. Luke the Evangelist Roman Catholic Church Society of Livingston County.

GENEVA, ONTARIO CO.
1—ST. FRANCIS DE SALES (1835) [CEM] [JC 2] Merged with St. Stephen, Geneva to form Our Lady of Peace Roman Catholic Church of Geneva, NY.
2—OUR LADY OF PEACE ROMAN CATHOLIC CHURCH OF GENEVA, NY Revs. Paul J. Tomasso; Hoan Dinh, Parochial Vicar; Deacon Kevin Carges.
Mailing Address: 130 Exchange St., 14456. Tel: 315-789-0930; Fax: 315-781-1985. Email: gourladyofpeace@dor.org. Web: www.genevarc.org.
School—St. Francis DeSales/St. Stephen School, (Grades K-8), 17 Elmwood Ave., 14456. Tel: 315-789-1828; Fax: 315-789-9179. Email: sfssdcs@dor.org. Mrs. Elaine Morrow, Prin.
3—ST. STEPHEN (1904) [JC] Merged with St. Francis de Sales, Geneve, NY to form Our Lady of Peace Roman Catholic Church of Geneva, NY.

GROTON, TOMPKINS CO., ST. ANTHONY (1873) [CEM] Rev. Malachy Nwosu; Deacon George Kozak.
Res.: 312 Locke Rd., R.D. 2, 13073. Tel: 607-898-5135; Fax: 607-898-7608.
Catechesis/Religious Program—

HAMLIN, MONROE CO., ST. ELIZABETH ANN SETON (1982) Rev. William V. Spilly; Deacon James Steiger.
Mailing Address: P.O. Box 149, 14464.
Res.: 1634 Lake Rd., P.O. Box 149, 14464. Tel: 585-964-8560; Fax: 585-964-3352.
Catechesis/Religious Program—

HAMMONDSPORT, STEUBEN CO., ST. GABRIEL (1845) [JC] Deacon David LaFortune, Pastoral Admin.; Rev. James P. Jaeger, Parochial Vicar.
Res.: 78 Shethar St., 14840. Tel: 607-569-3501; Fax: 607-569-3226.
Catechesis/Religious Program—

HENRIETTA, MONROE CO., CHURCH OF THE GOOD SHEPHERD (1911) [CEM] Barbara Swiecki, Pastoral Admin.; Revs. Gerald J. Appelby, Sacramental Min. (Retired); Robert L. Beligotti, Sacramental Min.; Deacon Tony Caruso.
Res.: 3318 E. Henrietta Rd., 14467. Tel: 585-334-3518; Fax: 585-334-6015.
Catechesis/Religious Program—

HILTON, MONROE CO., ST. LEO (1884) Rev. Joseph R. Catanise; Deacon William Lenhart.
Res.: 167 Lake Ave., 14468. Tel: 585-392-2710, Ext. 2; Fax: 585-392-9254.
Catechesis/Religious Program—

HONEOYE FALLS, MONROE CO., ST. PAUL OF THE CROSS (1870) [CEM] Sr. Karen Dietz, S.S.J., Pastoral Admin.; Revs. Michael Upson, Sacramental Min.; Richard J. Beligotti, Parochial Vicar; Deacons Gregory Emerton; Peter Dohr; Edward Mathis; Gene Edwards.
Res.: 37 Monroe St., 14472. Tel: 585-624-1443; Fax: 585-624-5169.
Catechesis/Religious Program—

HONEOYE, ONTARIO CO., ST. MARY, OUR LADY OF THE HILLS (1868) [CEM] Rev. John H. Hayes; Deacon John Hoffman.
Parish—8961 Main St., P.O. Box 725, 14471.
Res.: Rte. 20A, Box 725, 14471. Tel: 585-229-5007.
Catechesis/Religious Program—

HORNELL, STEUBEN CO.
1—ST. ANN (1849) [CEM] [JC 2], See Our Lady of the Valley, Hornell.
See St. Ann, Hornell under Schools Outside Monroe County located in the Institution section.
2—ST. IGNATIUS LOYOLA (1931), See Our Lady of the Valley, Hornell.
3—OUR LADY OF THE VALLEY (2004), Merger of St. Ann's, Hornell; St. Joachim, Canisteo; St. Ignatius Loyola, Hornell; St. Mary's, Rexville. Revs. Peter Anglaaere; Paulinus Okpala, Parochial Vicar; Deacon Robert W. McCormick.
Mailing Address: 27 Erie Ave., 14843. Tel: 607-324-5811; Fax: 607-324-0116. Email: ourladyofthevalley@dor.org.
See St. Ann, Hornell under Schools Outside Monroe County located in the Institution section.

HORSEHEADS, CHEMUNG CO., ST. MARY OUR MOTHER (1866) [CEM] Rev. Christopher E. Linsler. In Res., Rev. Joseph Francis Shetui.
Res.: 816 W. Broad St., 14845. Tel: 607-739-3817; Fax: 607-739-5628.
See St. Mary Our Mother (Horseheads), Horseheads under Schools Outside Monroe County located in the Institution section.
Catechesis/Religious Program—

INTERLAKEN, SENECA CO., ST. FRANCIS SOLANUS (1875) Rev. Bartholomew Minson, O.F.M.Cap.
Mailing Address: *c/o Holy Cross Church*, P.O. Box 337, Ovid, 14521.

Office: P.O. Box 337, Ovid, 14521-0337. Tel: 607-869-2261; Fax: 607-869-9825.
St. Fidelis Friary: 7790 County Rd. 153, 14847. Tel: 607-532-4432; Fax: 607-532-9271.
Church: 3660 Orchard St., 14847. Tel: 607-869-2261; Fax: 607-869-9825.

ITHACA, TOMPKINS CO.

1—ST. CATHERINE OF SIENA (1960) Rev. Joseph W. Marcoux.
Res.: 302 St. Catherine Cir., 14850. Tel: 607-257-2493; Fax: 607-257-5901.
Catechesis/Religious Program—

2—IMMACULATE CONCEPTION (1848) [CEM 2] Rev. Leo J. Reinhardt.
Res.: 113 N. Geneva St., 14850. Tel: 607-273-6121; Fax: 607-273-0185.
See Immaculate Conception, Ithaca under Schools Outside Monroe County located in the Institution section.
Catechesis/Religious Program—

KING FERRY, CAYUGA CO., OUR LADY OF THE LAKE, KING FERRY (1868) Closed. For inquiries for parish records contact Good Shepherd Catholic Community, Aurora.

LANSING, ALL SAINTS (1913) Rev. Malachy Nwosu; Deacon George Kozak.
Res.: 347 Ridge Rd., 14882. Tel: 607-533-7344.
Catechesis/Religious Program—

LEICESTER, LIVINGSTON CO., ST. THOMAS AQUINAS (1897) Merged with Holy Angels, Nunda, St. Lucy, Retsof, St. Mary, Geneseo & St. Patrick, Mt. Morris to form St. Luke the Evangelist Roman Catholic Church Society of Livingston County, Geneseo.

LIMA, LIVINGSTON CO., ST. ROSE (1848) [CEM] Sr. Karen Dietz, S.S.J., Pastoral Admin.; Revs. Michael Upson, Sacramental Min.; Richard J. Beligotti, Parochial Vicar; Deacons Gregory Emerton; Peter Dohr.
Mailing Address: P.O. Box 8A, 14485.
Res.: 7553 Corby Rd., Honeoye Falls, 14472.
Church: 1985 Lake Ave., 14485.
Catechesis/Religious Program—

LIVONIA CENTER, LIVINGSTON CO., ST. MICHAEL (1848) Closed. For inquiries for parish records contact St. Mary's, Honeoye.

LIVONIA, LIVINGSTON CO.

1—ST. JOSEPH (1911) Closed. For inquiries for parish records contact St. Matthew Catholic Church Society, Livonia.

2—ST. MATTHEW CATHOLIC CHURCH SOCIETY, [CEM] Merged with St. William, Conesus and St. Joseph, Livonia. Rev. John H. Hayes.
Mailing Address: P.O. Box 77, 14487. Tel: 585-346-3815; Fax: 585-346-9445.
Catechesis/Religious Program—

LYONS, WAYNE CO., ST. MICHAEL (1852), (Italian), Clustered with St. John the Evangelist, Clyde and Mission St. Patrick, Savannah. Rev. Augustine Chumo.
Res.: 3 Holley St., 14489-1505. Tel: 315-946-4182; Fax: 315-946-4736.
Catechesis/Religious Program—

MACEDON, WAYNE CO., ST. PATRICK (1883) [CEM] Merged with St. Gregory, Marion & St. Anne, Palmyra to form the Parish of St. Katharine Drexel, Palmyra.

MARION, WAYNE CO., ST. GREGORY (1914) Merged with St. Anne, Palmyra & St. Patrick, Macedon to form the Parish of St. Katherine Drexel, Palmyra.

MENDON, MONROE CO., ST. CATHERINE OF SIENA (1902) Rev. Robert Scott Bourcy; Deacon Philip Yawman.
Res.: 26 Mendon-Ionia Rd., 14506. Tel: 585-624-4990; Fax: 585-624-4996.
Catechesis/Religious Program—
Convent—15 Mendon-Ionia Rd., 14506. Tel: 716-624-1538.

MONTEZUMA, CAYUGA CO., ST. MICHAEL (1865) Closed. For inquiries for parish records contact Our Lady of the Snows, Weedsport.

MORAVIA, CAYUGA CO., ST. PATRICK (1872) Closed. For inquiries for parish records contact Good Shepherd Catholic Community, Aurora.

MOUNT MORRIS, LIVINGSTON CO., ST. PATRICK (1869) [CEM] Merged with Holy Angels, Nunda, St. Mary, Geneseo, St. Thomas Aquinas, Leicester & St. Mary, Retsof to form St. Luke the Evangelist Roman Catholic Church Society of Livingston County, Geneseo.

NEWARK VALLEY, TIOGA CO., ST. JOHN THE EVANGELIST (1880) Merged with St. Francis of Assisi, Catatonk; St. Margaret Mary, Apalachin; St. Pius the Tenth, Van Etten and St. James, Waverly to form Blessed Trinity, Owego.

NEWARK, WAYNE CO., ST. MICHAEL (1863) Rev. Felix Dalimpuo.
Res.: 401 Main St., 14513. Tel: 315-331-6753; Fax: 315-331-2925.
See St. Michael (Newark), Newark under Schools Outside Monroe County located in the Institution section.
Catechesis/Religious Program—

NORTH CHILI, MONROE CO., ST. CHRISTOPHER (1968) Rev. Robert Gaudio.
Res.: 3350 Union St., P.O. Box 399, 14514. Tel: 585-594-1400.
Catechesis/Religious Program—

NUNDA, LIVINGSTON CO., HOLY ANGELS (1854) Merged with St. Patrick, Mt. Morris, St. Mary, Geneseo, St. Thomas Aquinas, Leicester & St. Lucy, Retsof to form St. Luke the Evangelist Roman Catholic Church Society of Livingston County, Geneseo.

ODESSA, SCHUYLER CO., ST. BENEDICT (1965) Rev. Paul Bonacci, Admin.; Deacons Daniel Pavlina; George Roy.
Mailing Address: c/o St. Mary's of the Lake, P.O. Box 289, Watkins Glen, 14891.
Res.: 1101 1/2 Tenth St., Watkins Glen, 14891. Tel: 607-535-2786; Fax: 607-535-2990.
Church: Speedway, 14869. Tel: 607-594-2226.
Catechesis/Religious Program—

ONTARIO, WAYNE CO.

1—ST. MARY OF THE LAKE (1869) [CEM] Merged with Epiphany, Sodus to form St. Maximilian Kolbe, Ontario.

2—ST. MAXIMILIAN KOLBE Rev. Symon Peter Ntaiyia; Deacon James B. Nail.
Res.: 5823 Walworth Rd., P.O. Box 499, 14519. Tel: 315-524-2611; Fax: 607-524-8353.
Catechesis/Religious Program—

OVID, SENECA CO., HOLY CROSS (1849) [CEM] Rev. Bartholomew Minson, O.F.M.Cap.
7231 Main St., P.O. Box 337, 14521-0337.
St. Fidelis Friary: 7790 County Rd. 153, Interlaken, 14847. Tel: 607-869-2261; Fax: 607-869-9825.
Catechesis/Religious Program—

OWEGO, TIOGA CO.

1—BLESSED TRINITY (2003) Revs. William A. Moorby; Peter Adu-Boahen, Parochial Vicar; Thomas H. Watts, Pastor Emeritus (Retired); Deacons Michael Donovan; Warren Rutan.
Mailing Address: *Blessed Trinity and St. Patrick Parishes*, 300 Main St., 13827. Tel: 607-687-1068; 607-625-3192 (Rectory); Fax: 607-687-8122. Email: blessedtrinity@dor.org.
Res.: 1110 Pennsylvania Ave., Apalachin, 13732.

2—ST. PATRICK (1842) [CEM] Revs. William A. Moorby; Thomas H. Watts, Pastor Emeritus (Retired); Peter Adu-Boahen, Parochial Vicar; Deacons Michael Donovan; Warren Rutan.
Mailing Address: 300 Main St., 13827. Tel: 607-687-1068; Fax: 607-687-8122.
Res.: 1110 Pennsylvania Ave., Apalachin, 13732. Tel: 607-625-3192.
Catechesis/Religious Program—

PAINTED POST, STEUBEN CO., IMMACULATE HEART OF MARY (1952) Closed. For inquiries for parish records contact All Saints, Corning.

PALMYRA, WAYNE CO.

1—ST. ANNE (1850) [CEM] Merged with St. Gregory, Marion & St. Patrick, Macedon to form the Parish of St. Katharine Drexel, Palmyra.

2—THE PARISH OF ST. KATHARINE DREXEL Rev. William F. Laird.
Office: 136 Church St., 14522. Tel: 315-597-4571; Fax: 315-597-5252.

PENFIELD, MONROE CO.

1—HOLY SPIRIT (1965) Rev. P. Frederick Helfrich; Deacon Brian Mahoney.
Parish Address—1355 Hatch Rd., Webster, 14580. Tel: 585-671-5520; Fax: 585-671-7262.
Catechesis/Religious Program—

2—ST. JOSEPH (1860) [CEM] Rev. James A. Schwartz; Deacons Don Germano; Duncan Harris; William Coffey. In Res., Revs. Robert G. Kreckel (Retired); William Amann (Retired).
Parish—43 Gebhardt Rd., 14526.
Res.: 35 Gebhardt Rd., 14526. Tel: 585-586-8089; Fax: 585-586-0674.
School—St. Joseph School, (Grades K-6), 39 Gebhardt Rd., 14526-1398. Tel: 585-586-6968. Email: sjpendcs@dor.org. Sr. Christina Marie Luczynski, C.S.S.F., Prin.
Catechesis/Religious Program—

PENN YAN, YATES CO.

1—ST. MICHAEL (1850) [CEM 2] Merged with St. Januarius, Naples; St. Patrick's, Prattsburg; St. Theresa's Stanley, St. Andrew, Dundee & St. Mary, Rushville to form Our Lady of the Lakes Catholic Community.

2—OUR LADY OF THE LAKES CATHOLIC COMMUNITY, Formed by merge of St. Januarius & Our Lady of the Grapes Shrine, Naples, St. Patrick's, Prattsburg, St. Theresa's Stanley and St. Michael's Penn Yan. Revs. Stanley Kacprzak; Jeffrey Tunnicliff, Parochial Vicar; George Wiant, Sacramental Min. (Retired); Deacons Claude Curtin; Robert Stowell.
Rectory & Mailing Address: 210 Keuka St., 14527. Tel: 585-374-2414; Fax: 585-374-2415.
Church: 180 N. Main St., Naples, 14512.
See St. Michael (Penn Yan), Penn Yan under Schools Outside Monroe County located in the Institution section.
Catechesis/Religious Program—
Mission—St. Mary (1869) Gilbert St., Rushville, Ontario Co. 14561.

PERKINSVILLE, STEUBEN CO., SACRED HEART OF JESUS, Consolidated with St. Joseph's, Wayland; St. Mary's, Dansville; and St. Pius V, Cohocton to form Holy Catholic Community, Cohocton.

PHELPS, ONTARIO CO., ST. FRANCIS (1869) Merged with St. Felix, Clifton Springs to form St. Felix/St. Francis Parish Cluster, Clifton Springs.

PITTSFORD, MONROE CO.

1—CHURCH OF THE TRANSFIGURATION (1983) Rev. Michael Bausch; Deacons Michael Piehler; Patrick DiLaura.
50 W. Bloomfield Rd., 14534. Tel: 585-248-2427; Fax: 585-385-9870.
Catechesis/Religious Program—

2—ST. LOUIS (1911) Rev. Robert P. Ring; Deacon John Payne.
64 S. Main St., 14534. In Res., Rev. Msgr. Gerard C. Krieg (Retired), (Senior Priest); Revs. Raymond Booth (Retired), (Senior Priest); Albert L. Delmonte (Retired).
Res.: 60 S. Main St., 14534. Tel: 585-586-5675; Fax: 585-387-9888.
Saint's Place—46 S. Main St., 14534. Tel: 585-385-6860. Email: saintlady@stlouischurch.org. Web: www.saintsplace.org. Colleen Knauf, Dir.
School—St. Louis School, (Grades PreK-6), 11 Rand Pl., 14534-2084. Tel: 585-586-5200. Email: sisdcs@dor.org.
Catechesis/Religious Program—

RED CREEK, WAYNE CO., ST. THOMAS THE APOSTLE (1882) [CEM] Merged with St. Mary Magdalen, Wolcott & St. Jude Chapel, Fair Haven to form Catholic Community of the Blessed Trinity. For inquiries for parish records contact Blessed Trinity, Wolcott.

REXVILLE, STEUBEN CO., ST. MARY (1845), (Irish), [CEM 4], See Our Lady of the Valley, Hornell.

RUSH, MONROE CO., ST. JOSEPH (1863) Barbara Swiecki, Pastoral Admin.; Revs. Gerald J. Appelby, Sacramental Min. (Retired); Robert L. Beligotti, Sacramental Min.
Res.: 1209 Rush West Rush Rd., 14543-0320. Tel: 585-533-1719.
Catechesis/Religious Program—

SCIPIO CENTER, CAYUGA CO., ST. BERNARD (1867) Closed. For inquiries for parish records contact Good Shepherd Catholic Community, Aurora.

SCOTTSVILLE, MONROE CO., ST. MARY OF THE ASSUMPTION (1853) [CEM] Revs. William Endres, Parochial Vicar; Steven W. Lape, Parochial Vicar; Irene Goodwin, Pastoral Admin.
Res.: 99 Main St., P.O. Box 23, 14546. Tel: 585-889-3100; Fax: 585-889-7806.
Catechesis/Religious Program—

SENECA FALLS, SENECA CO., ST. PATRICK (1831) [CEM] Rev. James Fennessy.
Mailing Address: 25 Center St., Waterloo, 13165.
Res.: 97 W. Bayard St., 13148. Tel: 315-568-5203; Fax: 315-568-6609.
Catechesis/Religious Program—

SHORTSVILLE, ONTARIO CO., ST. DOMINIC (1885) [CEM] Rev. Donald J. Curtiss.
Mailing Address: 12 Hibbard Ave., Clifton Springs, 14432. Tel: 315-462-2961; Fax: 315-462-3608.
Church: 6 Canandaigua St., 14548.
Catechesis/Religious Program—

SODUS, WAYNE CO., EPIPHANY (1922) Merged with St. Mary of the Lake, Ontario to form St. Maximilian Kolbe, Ontario.

SPENCERPORT, MONROE CO., ST. JOHN THE EVANGELIST (1867) [CEM] Rev. Lance M. Gonyo; Deacon David Squilla. In Res., Rev. Daniel F. Holland (Retired).
Parish—55 Martha St., 14559.
Res.: 60 Martha St., 14559. Tel: 585-352-5481; Fax: 585-352-3759.
Catechesis/Religious Program—

STANLEY, ONTARIO CO., ST. THERESA (1875) [CEM] Merged with St. Januarius, Naples; St. Patrick's, PraHsburgh; St. Michaels, Penn Yan; St. Andrews, Dondee & St. Mary's Rushville to form Our Lady of the Lakes Catholic Community.

TRUMANSBURG, TOMPKINS CO., ST. JAMES THE APOSTLE (1857) [CEM] Rev. John Tokaz, O.F.M.Cap.
Res.: 17 Whig St., P.O. Box 709, 14886. Tel: 607-387-6781; Fax: 607-387-3763.
Catechesis/Religious Program—

UNION SPRINGS, CAYUGA CO., ST. MICHAEL'S (1851) Closed. For inquiries for parish records contact Good Shepherd Catholic Community, Aurora.

VAN ETTEN, CHEMUNG CO., ST. PIUS THE TENTH (1954) Merged with St. Francis, Catatonk; St. Margaret Mary, Apalachin; St. John the Evangelist, Newark Valley; and St. James, Waverly to form Blessed Trinity, Owego., Mailing Address: *Blessed Trinity*, 300 Main St., Owego, 13827.

VICTOR, ONTARIO CO., ST. PATRICK (1856), (Irish), [CEM] Rev. Timothy L. Niven.

Res.: 115 Maple Ave., 14564. Tel: 585-924-7111; Fax: 585-742-3296.
Catechesis/Religious Program—

WATERLOO, SENECA CO., ST. MARY (1868) [CEM] Rev. James Fennessy.
25 Center St., 13165.
Res.: 35 Center St., 13165. Tel: 315-539-2944; Fax: 315-539-8841.
Catechesis/Religious Program—

WATKINS GLEN, SCHUYLER CO., ST. MARY OF THE LAKE (1846), (Irish—Italian), [CEM 2] Rev. Paul Bonacci, Admin.; Deacons Daniel Pavlina; George (Rick) Roy.
Parish—905 N. Decatur St., P.O. Box 289, 14891.
Res.: 110 1/2 Tenth St., 14891. Tel: 607-535-2786; Fax: 607-535-2990.
Parish Center—10th St., 14891.
Catechesis/Religious Program—

WAVERLY, TIOGA CO., ST. JAMES (1881) [CEM] Merged with St. Francis of Assisi, Catatonk; St. Margaret Mary, Apalachin; St. John the Evangelist, Newark Valley and St. Pius the Tenth, Van Etten to form Blessed Trinity, Owego.

WAYLAND, STEUBEN CO.
1—HOLY FAMILY CATHOLIC COMMUNITY Revs. Stephen Karani; Michael Twardzik; Deacon Dan Slattery.
Mailing Address: 206 Fremont St., 14572-1298. Tel: 585-728-2228; Fax: 585-728-2232.
Rectory—St. Mary's, 40 Elizabeth St., Dansville, 14437. Tel: 585-335-2700.
Catechesis/Religious Program—
2—ST. JOSEPH'S (1881), (German), Consolidated with St. Pius V, Cohocton; St. Mary's, Dansville; and Sacred Heart of Jesus, Perkinsville to form Holy Family Catholic Community, Cohocton.

WEBSTER, MONROE CO.
1—HOLY TRINITY (1861) [CEM] Rev. Timothy E. Horan.
Res.: 1460 Ridge Rd., 14580. Tel: 585-265-0391; Fax: 585-265-1627.
Catechesis/Religious Program—
2—ST. PAUL (1967) Rev. Paul Gitau; Deacon Mark Robbins.
Res.: 783 Hard Rd., 14580. Tel: 585-671-2112; Fax: 585-787-8907.
Catechesis/Religious Program—
3—ST. RITA (1950) Revs. Charles J. Latus; Bartholomew Amobi, Parochial Vicar; Deacon Raymond Garbach.
Res.: 1008 Maple Dr., 14580. Tel: 585-671-1100; Fax: 585-671-5446.
School—St. Rita School, Webster, (Grades PreK-6), 1008 Maple Dr., 14580. Tel: 585-671-3132. Email: sritadcs@dor.org. Sr. Katherine Ann Rappl, R.S.M., Prin.
Catechesis/Religious Program—

WEEDSPORT, CAYUGA CO.
1—ST. JOHN (1865) Merged with St. Joseph, Weedsport and St. Patrick, Cato to form Our Lady of the Snow, Weedsport.
2—ST. JOSEPH (1854) [CEM] Merged with St. John, Port Byron and St. Patrick, Cato to form Our Lady of the Snow, Weedsport.
3—OUR LADY OF THE SNOW (2005) Rev. William G. Darling.
Mailing Address: 2667 Hamilton St., 13166. Tel: 315-834-6266; Fax: 315-834-6278. Email: wstjosep@dor.org.

WOLCOTT, WAYNE CO.
1—CATHOLIC COMMUNITY OF THE BLESSED TRINITY OF WOLCOTT, NY (2006) Rev. Joseph P. McCaffrey.
11956 Washington St., 14590-1133. Tel: 315-594-9430; Fax: 315-594-9430. 2006 consolidation of St. Thomas the Apostle, Red Creek; St. Mary Magdalene, Wolcott and St. Jude Chapel, Fair Haven.
2—ST. MARY MAGDALENE (1940) Merged with St. Thomas the Apostle, Red Creek & St. Jude Chapel, Fair Haven to form Catholic Community of the Blessed Trinity of Wolcott, NY.

Chaplains of Public Institutions

ITHACA. *Cornell University*, G-22 Anabel Taylor Hall, 14853. Rev. Daniel T. McMullin, Dir.

Health Care Facilities

ROCHESTER. *St. Ann's Home/Heritage*. Rev. Peter T. Bayer, Dir. Spiritual Care.
1500 Portland Ave., 14621. Tel: 585-697-6446. Sheila Kinsky, Pastoral Care Coord. Tel: 585-697-6447, Sr. Livia Ruocco, Pastoral Care Coord. Tel: 585-697-6448.
Highland Hospital. Rev. Dennis Bonsignore, Chap.
1000 South Ave., 14620. Tel: 585-341-6890.
Monroe Community Hospital. Rev. Dennis Bonsignore, Sr. Mary Doran, S.S.J., Co-Chap.
435 E. Henrietta Rd., 14620. Tel: 585-760-6164.
Rochester General Hospital/Via Health. Sr. Margaret Kunder, S.S.J., Chap.
1425 Portland Ave., 14621. Tel: 585-922-5121.
Strong Health System. Revs. William Endres, Dennis Bonsignore.
601 Elmwood Ave., 14642. Tel: 585-275-2187.
Unity Health System, St. Mary's Genesee St. Campus, 14651. Rev. Walter J. Plominski, Sacramental Min., Suzanne Shady, Chap. Tel: 585-368-3268.
89 Genesee St., 14611. Tel: 585-328-3268.
Park Ridge Hospital/Unity Health System, 1555 Long Pond Rd., 14626. Tel: 585-723-7969. Jeanne Marie Jongen, Chap. Tel: 585-723-7969, Carl Coloney, Chap. Tel: 585-723-7318, Megan Hoose, Chap. Tel: 585-723-7967.

AUBURN. *Mercy Health and Rehabilitation Center*. Stephen Ash, Admin. Cayuga Co.
3 St. Anthony St., 13021. Tel: 315-253-0351; Fax: 315-258-3904. Rev. Felicjan Sierotowicz, Chap.

BATH. *Soldiers' Home and Veterans' Hospital*, Tel: 607-664-4402, Ext. 1382. Rev. Marcellinus Uwandu, Chap.

CANANDAIGUA. *Veteran's Hospital*, Tel: 585-394-2000, Ext. 3052. Rev. Martin D. Smith-Sourcier, Chap.

HORNELL. *St. James Mercy Hospital*. Ms. Astuti Bijlefeld, Chap., Deacon Robert W. McCormick. Steuben Co.
411 Canisteo St., 14843. Tel: 607-324-8153.

State Facilities

ROCHESTER. *Finger Lakes DDSO - Rochester Site*, 620 Westfall Rd., 14620. Tel: 585-461-8676.
Rochester Psychiatric Center, 1111 Elmwood Ave., 14620. Tel: 585-473-3230. Deacon Brian McNulty, Chap.

AUBURN. *Auburn Correctional Facility*, 135 State St., P.O. Box 618, 13021. Tel: 315-253-8401, Ext. 4321. Rev. Michael R. Brown, Chap., Deacon John Tomandl.

ELMIRA. *Elmira Correctional Facility, Center and Camp Monterey*, P.O. Box 500, 14902. Tel: 607-734-3901. Rev. Richard T. Farrell, Deacon Michael R. McGuire.
Elmira Psychiatric Center, 100 Washington St., 14901. Tel: 607-737-4991. Deacon Michael Mangione, Chap.

GENESEO. *Finger Lakes DDSO - Geneseo Site*, 3 Park St., 14454-1217. Tel: 585-243-6405.

INDUSTRY. *State Agricultural & Industrial School, Div. of Youth* 14474. Tel: 585-533-2600. Deacon Owen Bowers.

MORAVIA. *Cayuga Correctional*, P.O. Box 1150, 13118. Tel: 315-497-1110, Ext. 4000. Rev. Felicjan Sierotowicz, Sacramental Min., Maureen Collins.

NEWARK. *Finger Lakes DDSO - Newark Site*, 703 E. Maple Ave., 14513. Tel: 315-331-1700.

PINE CITY. *Southport Correctional Facility*, P.O. Box 2000, 14871-2000. Tel: 607-737-0850. Rev. Richard T. Farrell, Chap., Mrs. Theresa Stanley, Chap.

RED CREEK. *Butler Correctional Facility*, P.O. Box 388, 13143. Tel: 315-754-8001. Rev. Felicjan Sierotowicz, Chap.

ROMULUS. *Five Points Correctional Facility*, State Rte. 96, 14541. Tel: 607-869-5111. Rev. P. Paul Brennan, Deacon Gregory Kiley, Chap.

SONYEA. *Livingston Correctional Facility and Seneca Correctional Facility*, Rt. 36, P.O. Box 49, 14556. Tel: 585-658-3710. Rev. Michael R. Brown, Deacons Nemesio Martinez Vellon, Paul Clement.

SONYEA. *Groveland Correctional Facility*, 7000 Sonyea Rd., P.O. Box 50, 14556. Tel: 585-658-2871, Ext. 4807. Rev. Michael R. Brown, Deacon Paul Clement.

WILLARD. *Drug Treatment Center*, 7116 County Rd. 132, P.O. Box 303, 14588-0303. Tel: 607-869-5500, Ext. 4800. Rev. P. Paul Brennan.

County Jail Chaplains

ROCHESTER. *Livingston County Jail*.
4 Court St., Geneseo, 14454. Tel: 585-243-1100.
Monroe County Jail. Rev. Robert Thomas Werth, Sr. Judith Greene, S.S.J., Chap., Deacon Salvador Otero.
Tompkins County Jail. Vacant.
Yates County Jail. Vacant.

On Duty Outside the Diocese:
Revs.—
Bartollotta, Victor W., Jr., 6343 Anita St., Dallas, TX 75214.
Curran, Charles E., 4125 Woodcreek Dr., Dallas, TX 75220.
Fleming, Terence K. (SP), 8426 Brentwood Rd., Largo, FL 33777.
Valenti, Thomas J., Church of St. John the Baptist, 670 Yonkers Ave., Yonkers, 10704.

Military Chaplains:
Revs.—
Van Durme, Patrick, S.T.L., Chap., 307 Laurel Oak Ln., Savannah, GA 31404. U.S. Army
Zygadlo, Mitchell, Chap. Capt., United States Air Force, 356 McDonnell Ave., Biloxi, MS 39531.

Unassigned:
Rev.—
Celso, B. Thomas, 163 Patterson St., Newark, 14513.

Absent on Leave:
Revs.—
Chase, Lee P., S.T.L.
DeBellis, Peter
Della Pietra, Douglas
Manning, Charles T.
Walczak, Melvin

Retired:
Rev. Msgrs.—
Krieg, Gerard C., J.C.L., St. Louis Rectory, 64 S. Main St., Pittsford, 14534.
Shannon, William H., Sisters of St. Joseph, 150 French Rd., 14618.
Revs.—
Amann, William, St. Joseph Rectory, 35 Gebhardt Rd., Penfield, 14526.
Ammering, Bruce F., Sisters of St. Joseph, 150 French Rd., 14618.
Appelby, Gerald J., 130 Southland Dr., 14623.
Barrett, William, 15 Washington St., Mayville, 14757.
Billotte, Philip J., 777 Germania Rd., P.O. Box 135, Frenchville, PA 16836.
Booth, Raymond, 60 S. Main St., Pittsford, 14534.
Boyle, James E., St. John of Rochester, 8 Wickford Way, Fairport, 14450.
Bradler, Robert C., 269 Garford Rd., 14622.
Brennan, Paul P., 345 Waters Edge, Auburn, 13021.
Brickler, R. Richard, 1961 #1 Traditions Pl., Henrietta, 14467.
Burke, James C., 2123 S.E. 5th Ter., Cape Coral, FL 33990.
Bush, Frederick, St. Mark's Rectory, 54 Kuhn Rd., 14612.
Calimeri, Anthony F., Sisters of St. Joseph, 150 French Rd., 14618.
Conboy, Michael F., St. Hyacinth, 299 Clark St., Auburn, 13021.
Connor, Gerald T., McAuley Residence, 1437 Blossom Rd., 14610.
Cosgrove, William, 295 Chestnut Ridge Rd., 14624.
Cushing, Walter F., St. Cecilia's Rectory, 2732 Culver Rd., 14622.
Deckman, Peter, 392 Surrey Hill Way, 14623.
Delmonte, Albert L., St. Louis Rectory, 60 S. Main St., Pittsford, 14534.
Dillon, Edward J., St. Luke the Evangelist, 13 North St., Geneseo, 14454.
Dollen, Bernard, 4477 Buffalo Rd., North Chili, 14514.
Donnelly, William, Chapel Oaks, #1216 1500 Portland Ave., 14621.
Doyle, James, Chapel Oaks #1110, 1550 Portland Ave., 14621.
Eisemann, Frederick F., 151 Sheppler St., 14612.
Erb, Francis J., P.O. Box 96, Painted Post, 14870.
Erdle, Thomas M., The Legacy, 100 McAuley Dr., Apt. 275, 14610.
Falcone, Sebastian, McAuley Residence, 1437 Blossom Rd., 14610.
Fratts, Ralph J., 113 Genesee St., New Hartford, 13413.
Freemesser, Paul J., St. Theodore Rectory, 168 Spencerport Rd., 14606.
Gaesser, Ronald E., Holy Family Rectory, 85 North St., Auburn, 13021.
Golden, Edward, 965 Cherry Ridge Blvd., #306, Webster, 14580.
Gordinier, William J., Sisters of St. Joseph, 150 French Rd., 14610.
Graf, William E., D.Min., 681 High St., Victor, 14564.
Gross, Lawrence F., 7553 Corby Rd., Honeoye Falls, 14472.
Hafner, Gerard, 10452 Clairmont Cir. E., Tamarac, FL 33321-7840.
Holland, Daniel F., St. John the Evangelist Rectory, 55 Martha St., Spencerport, 14559.
Kellner, Winfried, Our Mother of Sorrows Rectory, 5000 Mt. Read Blvd., 14612.
Kiggins, Roy, St. Patrick Rectory, 97 W. Bayard St., Seneca Falls, 13148.
Kreckel, Robert G., St. Joseph's Rectory, 35 Gebhardt Rd., 14626.
Lawlor, James F., St. Thomas More Rectory, 2617 East Ave., 14610.
MacNamara, Robert C., St. Mary Rectory, 224 Franklin St., Elmira, 14904.
Mans, Leo J., Cross Keys Village, 19 Fulton Dr., New Oxford, PA 17350.
McDonald, Elmer J., 6145 Sun Blvd., #505B, St. Petersburg, FL 33715.
McMahon, Gerard J., McAuley Residence, 1437 Blossom Rd., 14610.
Metzger, Edwin, Mother of Sorrows Rectory, 5000

Mt. Read Blvd., 14612.
Michatek, William C., 8286 W. Port Bay Rd., Wolcott, 14590-9447.
Mockevicius, Dominic F., Sisters of St. Joseph, 150 French Rd., 14618.
Moynihan, Jeremiah P., St. Mary, 224 Franklin St., Elmira, 14904.
Mulligan, John M., V.G., The Cathedral Community, 296 Flower City Park, 14615.
Murphy, David M., Sisters of St. Joseph, 150 French Rd., 14618.
Murphy, Kevin P., 5892 Rte 64., Canandaigua, 14424.
Murphy, Richard M., Chiropractic College, Box 800, Seneca Falls, 13148-0800.
Nellis, Thomas F., P.O. Box 849, Honeoye, 14471.
O'Connell, Richard C., McAuley Residence, 1437 Blossom Rd., 14610.
O'Connor, John L., 3351 James Rd., Keuka Park, 14478.
Phillips, John, 150 French Rd., 14618.
Reif, John, Holy Cross Rectory, 4492 Lake Ave., 14612.
Rosse, John, 401 Rogers Pkwy., 14616.
Sasso, Joseph M., 8112 Oatka Tr., LeRoy, 14482.
Smith, Robert, 9306 Blind Sodus Bay Rd., Red Creek, 13143.
Statt, Thomas R., P.O. Box 752, Honeoye, 14471.
Tormey, Daniel, 367 Walker Dr., Canandaigua, 14424.
Tracy, Laurence C., 16 Siebert Pl., 14605.
Ventura, Gennaro J., 74 Pickdale Dr., 14626.
Vogt, Otto J., Sisters of St. Joseph Motherhouse, 150 French Rd., 14618.
Wainwright, Walter L., 1502 Maple Ave., Elmira, 14904.
Walsh, John T., M.Div., Sisters of St. Joseph Motherhouse, 150 French Rd., 14618.
Watts, Thomas H., 126 Washington St., Sayre, PA 18840.
Weis, Eugene R., 1759 W. Schwartz Blvd., Lady Lake, FL 32159-6126.
Wiant, George, 5782 County Rd. 33, Canandaigua, 14424.
Zenkel, Edward B., 4218 East Lake Rd., Livonia, 14487.

Permanent Deacons:
Abballe, Dominic, (Retired)
Almeter, Robert C., Diocese of Syracuse
Aman, Leo, (Retired)
Antenucci, John, (Retired), Outside of Diocese
Arnold, Kenneth, Irondequoit Senior Ministries
Asis, Emmanuel, Rush-Henrietta Catholic Community
Baker, William, (Leave of Absence)
Beck, Thomas, St. Lawrence Church, Greece
Behe, Thomas, (Unassigned)
Berrios, Jose, Parish Support Ministries; St. Francis Xavier Cabrini Parish
Bessette, Eric
Birx, Charles, Diocese of Richmond
Bovenzi, Mark, Immaculate Conception; St. Bridget; Parish Support Ministry
Bowers, Owen F., (Retired)
Brasley, John, Dir. of Deacon Personnel & Deacon Formation
Burke, Robert, St. Monica, Rochester
Cadregari, David, Our Mother of Sorrous, Greece
Carges, Kevin, Our Lady of Peace Parish, Geneva
Carra, James, Rush-Henrietta Catholic Community
Carroll, Stephen, Church of the Assumption, Fairport
Caruso, Anthony, Rush-Henrietta Catholic Community
Casey, Lawrence B., Diocese of Atlanta
Cass, K. Thomas, Archdiocese of NY
Chatterton, James, St. Lawrence, Rochester
Cleary, Thomas J., (Retired)
Clement, Paul F., Groveland Correctional Facility, Sonyea; St. Luke the Evangelist, Geneseo
Coccia, Angelo, St. Theodore & St. Francis House, Rochester
Coffey, William, (Retired)
Colomaio, Robert, St. Gabriel, Hammondsport; St. Mary, Bath
Condon, Dean, All Saints, Corning
Corsaro, Robert, Church of the Assumption, Fairport
Crego, John, Holy Apostles, Rochester
Cunningham, John, Diocese of Palm Beach
Curtin, Claude, Our Lady of the Lakes, Penn Yan
Cyrana, Robert, St. Francis, St. Felix, St. Dominic, Parish Cluster
Dardess, George, Parish Support Ministry
Datz, Ramon, (Retired)
Defendorf, Ray, All Saints Parish, Corning
Dejesus, Benny, St. Frances Xavier Cabrini Parish
DiLallo, Gary R., St. Francis of Assisi, St. Hyacinth, Auburn Parish Cluster
DiLaura, Patrick, Church of the Transfiguration, Pittsford
Dohr, Peter, St. Agnes; St. Paul of the Cross; St. Rose; Industry School
Donahue, Dennis, Good Shepherd Catholic Community, Aurora
Donovan, Michael, Blessed Trinity/St. Patrick, Owego; Lourdes Hospice, Tioga Co.
Dougherty, William P., (Retired)
Douglas, Stanley, (Retired)
Doyle, Gregory J., (Retired)
Driscoll, Thomas, St. Mary's Church-Rochester
Ecker, Thomas R., Bethany House, Rochester; St. Jerome's, East Rochester
Edwards, Eugene L., Jr., (Retired)
Eggleston, Donald, St. Stanislaws Kostka, Rochester
Emerton, Gregory, St. Paul of the Cross, Honeoye Falls; St. Rose, Lima
Erb, John, Our Lady of the Lakes Catholic Community, Penn Yan
Erway, Joseph, Blessed Sacrament, Elmira
Feasel, Laurence, St. Theodore, Gates
Federowicz, Joseph F., (Retired)
Fisher, Christopher, St. Elizabeth Ann Seton, Hamlin
Fitch, James E., (Retired)
Garbach, Raymond, St. Rita, Webster
Germano, Donald, St. Joseph, Penfield
Giblin, Edward, Holy Cross Church, Rochester
Giugno, John M., The Cathedral Community, Rochester
Graff, Stephen, Diocese of Syracuse
Graybill, Patrick A., Emmanuel Church of the Deaf, Rcohester
Haber, Francis, (Retired)
Hankey, James D., All Saints Parish, Corning
Harris, Duncan, St. Joseph, Penfield
Henry, Murray, (Leave of Absence)
Hoerner, Gerard A., (Outside the Diocese)
Hoffman, John, St. Matthew/Livonia; St. Matthew/Honeoye
Holmes, John, Jr., Diocese of St. Augustine
Hudzinski, David, St. Anne/Our Lady of Lourdes, Rochester
Hurley, Daniel R., (Leave of Absence)
Jewell, Thomas, St. John Fisher College, Rochester
Johnson, H. Wilson, St. Thomas More & Our Lady Queen of Peace, Brighton
Kershner, Lynn W., The Cathedral Community, Rochester
Kiley, Gregory, St. Michael/St. John/St. Patrick; Lyons/Clyde/Savannah; Five Points Correctional Facility, Romulus
Kinsky, Daniel M., St. Ann's Community
Kluchko, Thomas J., (Retired)
Kohlmeier, Edward, Blessed Trinity
Kozak, George, Holy Cross, Freeville; St. Anthony, Groton; All Saints, Lansing
LaFortune, David, St. Mary, Bath; St. Gabriel, Hammondsport
Lawson, Gregg K., St. Alphonsus, Auburn
Lebron, Juan, (Outside the Diocese)
Lenhart, William, St. Leo, Hilton
Lester, Claude E., St. Mary's, Canandaigua
Lohouse, Dennis, St. Pius X, Chili
Lombard, Richard J., Holy Apostles, Rochester
Loomis, Roger, (Leave of Absence)
Lyons, Robert, Rush-Henrietta Catholic Community
Mahany, Richard E., (Retired)
Mahoney, Brian, Holy Spirit, Webster
Mahoney, I. Michael, (Diocese of Raleigh)
Malave, Jorge, St. Frances Xavier Cabrini Parish, Rochester
Mangione, Michael, Elmira Psychiatric Hospital
Martinez, Nemesio, Holy Apostles; Parish Support Ministries; Livingston Correctional Facility
Mathis, Edward, St. Agnes, Avon; St. Paul of the Cross; St. Rose
Maune, William D., (Retired), Diocese of Chicago
McCormick, Robert W., St. James Mercy Hospital, Hornell; Our Lady of the Valley, Hornell
McDermott, John, St. Rita's, Webster; Parish Support Ministry
McGuire, Michael R., Elmira Correctional Facility
McNulty, Brian J., Rochester Psychiatric Center
Mercadel, Anthony J., (Retired)
Mercado, Conrado, (Outside the Diocese)
Meyer, Robert, St. Frances Xavier Cabrini
Mielcarek, Raymond, (Retired)
Morin, Kenneth, (Outside the Diocese)
Nail, James B., St. Maximilian, Kolbe, Ontario; Catholic Charities of Wayne County
Nelson, John, Diocese of Rockford
Niche, Peter, St. Patrick's Victor
Otera, Salvador, Holy Apostles Church; Parish Support Ministries;
Pacete, Alberto, Elmira Correctional Facility; Christ the Redeemer, Elmira
Palma, David, St. Frances Xavier Cabrini Parish, Rochester
Paluskiewicz, David L., St. Columba/St. Patrick, Caledonia/Mumford
Pavlina, Daniel, Catholic Community of Schuyler County
Payne, John F. X., St. Louis, Pittsford
Pettrone, Frank, St. Mark, Greece
Piehler, Michael J., Church of the Transfiguration, Pittsford
Placious, Joseph, Holy Name of Jesus, Greece
Robbins, Mark, St. Paul, Webster
Rodriguez, Agenol, Diocese of Orlando
Roy, George, Schuyler Catholic Community
Rutan, Warren, (Retired)
Satori, Paul, St. Mary, Elmira
Scarciotta, Kenneth A., (Retired)
Schmitz, William F., (Retired)
Schrader, Robert, (Retired)
Schrage, Thomas, Nativity of the Blessed Virgin Mary, Brockport
Schuler, Richard, St. Helens Church, Gates
Sciolino, Anthony, Monroe County Jail
Shanley, Patrick M., St. Jude the Apostle, Rochester
Skerrett, Jerry, (Retired)
Slattery, Daniel P., Holy Family Catholic Comm., Southern Livingston & Northern Steuben
Smith, Edward A., St. Felix, Clifton Springs; St. Francis, Phelps; St. Dominic's, Shortsville
Smith, Lon, St. Charles Borromeo, Greece
Spezzano, George, (Retired)
Squilla, David, St. John the Evangelist, Spencerport
Steiger, James P., Tribunal-Pastoral Center, St. Elizabeth Ann Seton, Hamlin
Stowell, Robert, (Retired)
Stratton, W. Craig, Catholic Newman Community, U. of R.; Catholic Chaplaincy U. of R. Medical Center
Sullivan, Timothy, Catholic Charities of Wayne Co.
Tocci, Ronald J., Rochester General Hospital, Rochester
Tomandl, John D., Auburn Correctional, Auburn Hospital
Toot, Walter, Blessed Kater: Tekakwitha Parish, Irondequoit
Uschold, Thomas, St. Christopher, N. Chili
Valvo, Nicholas, Sacred Heart, Auburn
Van Etten, Laurence A., Newman Center, S.U.N.Y Brockport
Vargas, Carlos H., St. Frances Xavier Cabrini Parish, Rochester
Verkon, Ronald, Diocese of Scranton
Virgilio, Paul, St. John the Evangelist, Greece
Welch, George J., St. Joseph's Hospital; Blessed Sacrament, Elmira
Wight, Edward, (Unassigned)
Williams, Daniel, SS. Isidore Maria Torribia Parish
Witulski, James, St. Stanislaus Kostka, Rochester
Yawman, Philip, St. Catherine of Siena, Mendon

INSTITUTIONS LOCATED IN THE DIOCESE

[A] GRADUATE SCHOOL OF THEOLOGY

ROCHESTER. *St. Bernard's School of Theology & Ministry*, 120 French Rd., 14618. Tel: 585-271-3657; Fax: 585-271-2045. Email: akeppler@stbernards.edu. Web: www.stbernards.edu. Dr. Patricia A. Schoelles, S.S.J., Pres.; Sr. Katherine Hanley, C.S.J., Dean at Albany; Rev. George P. Heyman, Dir. Community Education; Ms. Mary Muggleton, Dir. Business Affairs; Dr. Devadasan Premnath, Dean; Ellen Morningstar, Registrar; Rev. Sebastian Falcone (Retired); Laura Smith, Dir. Admissions & Fin. Aid; Laura Hamilton, Dir. Advancement; Deacon John Brasley, Dir. Deacon Formation; Sheila Smyth, Librarian. Priests 1; Sisters 2; Lay Teachers 3; Total Staff 14; Total Enrollment 183.

[B] HIGH SCHOOLS

ROCHESTER. *The Aquinas Institute* (1902) 1127 Dewey Ave., 14613-9989. Tel: 585-254-2020; Fax: 585-254-7401. Email: jknapp@aquinasinstitute.com. Web: www.aquinasinstitute.com. Michael Daley, Pres.; Dennis Sadler, Prin.; Sandy Stevens, Librarian. Lay Teachers 70; Students 956.

Bishop Kearney High School (Coed), 125 Kings

Hwy., 14617-5596. Tel: 585-342-4000; Fax: 585-342-4694. Email: principal@bkhs.org. Web: www.bkhs.org. Thomas O'Niel, Pres.; Julie Locey, Prin.; Andrew Smagin, Vice Prin. Curriculum Instruction; Chris Belmont, Athletic Dir.; Fred Tillinghast, Dir. Admissions; Mary Slifer, Librarian. Sponsored by the Congregation of Christian Brothers in association with the School Sisters of Notre Dame, Wilton Province. Sisters 1; Lay Teachers 35; Students 400.

McQuaid Jesuit High School (1954) 1800 S. Clinton Ave., 14618. Tel: 585-473-1130; Fax: 585-256-6171. Web: www.mcquaid.org. Revs. Brian Frain, S.J., Supr.; James J. Fischer, S.J., Chancellor; Edward F. Salmon, S.J., Pres.; John P. Carriero, S.J.; Joseph DeMaio, O.Carm.; Jack Healy, O.Carm.; Kimberly Hanna, Librarian; Revs. James K. Coughlin, S.J., Prin.; Vincent McDonough, S.J. Jesuit Fathers. Priests 6; Lay Teachers 59; Students 838.

Our Lady of Mercy High School, (Grades 7-12), 1437 Blossom Rd., 14610. Tel: 585-288-7120; Fax: 585-288-7966. Web: www.mercyhs.com. Mr. Terry Quinn, Prin.; Kimberly Rouleau, Librarian. Sisters of Mercy 3; Lay Teachers 56; Students 700.

ELMIRA. *Notre Dame High School* (1955) 1400 Maple Ave., 14904. Tel: 607-734-2267; Fax: 607-737-8903. Email: kellyn@notredamehighschool.com. Web: www.notredamehighschool.com. Sr. Mary Walter Hickey, R.S.M., Pres.; Mr. James Snyder, Prin.; Mrs. Jennifer Roberts-O'Brien, Librarian. Sisters of Mercy 3; Lay Teachers 27; Students 226.

GENEVA. *De Sales High School* (Incorporated under the laws of the State of New York), 90 Pulteney St., 14456. Tel: 315-789-5111; Fax: 315-789-8230. Email: mainoffice@desaleshs.org. Web: www.desaleshs.org. Gerald Macaluso, Prin.; Jack Howard, Librarian. Lay Teachers 11; Students 106.

[C] ELEMENTARY SCHOOLS

ROCHESTER. *Nazareth Elementary School* (1871) 1001 Lake Ave., 14613. Tel: 585-458-3786; Fax: 585-647-8717. Web: nazarethschools.org. Sisters Margaret Mancuso, S.S.J., Prin.; Anna Derouchie, S.S.J., Librarian. Sisters of St. Joseph 7; Lay Teachers 19; Students 211.

[D] MONROE COUNTY CATHOLIC SCHOOLS

ROCHESTER. *Monroe County Catholic Schools*, 1150 Buffalo Rd., 14624. Tel: 585-328-3210; Fax: 585-328-3149. Web: www.dor.org. Sisters 7; Lay Teachers 213; Students 3,093.

Junior High Schools:

Siena Catholic Academy (Grades 7-8), 2617 East Ave., 14610-3111. Tel: 585-381-1220; Fax: 585-381-1223. Email: scadcs@dor.org. Vincent Tata, Prin.

Elementary Schools:

Christ the King School (Grades PreK-6), 445 Kings Hwy. S., 14617-4138. Tel: 585-467-8730; Fax: 585-467-5392. Email: ctkdcs@dor.org. Sr. Kathleen Lurz, S.S.J., Prin.

[E] FINGER LAKES AND SOUTHERN TIER SCHOOLS

AUBURN. *St. Joseph School (Auburn)*, (Grades PreK-8), 89 E. Genesee St., 13021-4161. Tel: 315-253-8327; Fax: 315-253-2401. Web: schools.dor.org/stjoauburn. Kathleen A. Coye, Prin.; Jeri Jervis, Librarian. Lay Teachers 11; Students 144; Preschool 40.

AVON. *St. Agnes*, (Grades PreK-6), 60 Park Pl., 14414-1053. Tel: 585-226-8500; Fax: 585-226-8500 (call first). Email: sagnesdcs@dor.org. Dr. Gerald E. Benjamin, Prin. Lay Teachers 16; Students 140; Preschool 35.

CANANDAIGUA. *St. Mary School (Canandaigua)*, (Grades PreK-8), 16 E. Gibson St., 14424-1310. Tel: 585-394-4300; Fax: 585-394-3954. Email: smcdcs@dor.org. Web: www.stmaryscanandaigua.org. Ms. Ann Marie Deutsch, Prin.; Christine Pohorence, Librarian. Lay Teachers 18; Students 204.

CORNING. *All Saints Academy*, (Grades PreK-8), 158 State St., 14830-2594. Tel: 607-936-9234; Fax: 607-936-1797. Email: asadcs@dor.org. Web: schools.dor.org/allsaints. Rose Ann Ewanyk, Prin.; Aurella Dean, Librarian. Lay Teachers 12; Aides 1; Students 110.

ELMIRA. *Holy Family Elementary*, (Grades N-5), 421 Fulton St., 14904-1709. Tel: 607-732-3588; Fax: 607-732-1850. Email: hfpdcs@dor.org. Web: www.schools.dor.org/holyfamilypri. Lori Brink, Prin.; Roberta Considine, Information Technology Coord. Lay Teachers 19; Students 144; Preschool 42.

Holy Family Middle School (1971) (Grades 7-8), 1010 Davis St., 14901-1013. Tel: 607-734-0336; Fax: 607-734-4977. Email: hfjhdcs@dor.org. Web: schools.org/holyfamilyjh. Francis Devine, Prin.; William Giancoli, Librarian. Lay Teachers 12; Students 80.

GENEVA. *St. Francis Desales/St. Stephen*, (Grades PreK-8), 17 Elmwood Ave., 14456-2299. Tel: 315-789-1828; Fax: 315-789-9179. Email: sfssdcs@dor.org. Web: www.stfrancisststephens.org. Mrs. Elaine Morrow, Prin.; Valerie Venuti, Librarian. Lay Teachers 13; Students 162; Preschool 9.

HORNELL. *St. Ann* (1863) (Grades PreK-6), 27 Erie Ave., 14843-1909. Tel: 607-324-0733; Fax: 607-324-0985. Email: sanndcs@dor.org. Web: www.stannhornell.org. Lisa M. Dirlam, Prin. Lay Teachers 7; Students 60; Preschool 35.

HORSEHEADS. *St. Mary Our Mother (Horseheads)* (1959) (Grades PreK-6), 811 Westlake St., 14845-2099. Tel: 607-739-9157; Fax: 607-739-2532. Email: smomdcs@dor.org. Marilyn Zinn, Prin.; Karen Solometo, Librarian. Lay Teachers 12; Students 118; Preschool 19.

ITHACA. *Immaculate Conception*, (Grades PreK-6), 320 W. Buffalo St., 14850-4193. Tel: 607-273-2707; Fax: 607-272-8456. Email: icdcs@dor.org. Web: schools.dor.org/ic. Diana M. Oravec, Prin. Lay Teachers 10; Students 70; Preschool 33.

OWEGO. *St. Patrick School*, (Grades PreSchool-5), 309 Front St., 13827. Fax: 607-687-4305. Email: spodcs@dor.org. Web: www.stpatrickowego.org. Paula Smith, Prin.; Linda Williams, Librarian. Lay Teachers 7; Students 59; Preschool 36.

PENN YAN. *St. Michael (Penn Yan)* (1884) (Grades PreK-5), 214 Keuka St., 14527-1143. Tel: 315-536-6112; Fax: 315-536-6112. Email: smpydcs@dor.org. Web: stmichaelpennyan.org. David M. Paddock, Prin.; Liz Castner, Librarian. Lay Teachers 6; Students 102; Preschool 22.

[F] HOMES FOR AGED

ROCHESTER. *St. Ann's Home for the Aged*, 1500 Portland Ave., 14621. Tel: 585-697-6000; Fax: 585-342-9585. Email: info@stannscommunity.com. Web: www.stannscommunity.com. Betty Mullin-DiProsa, Pres. & CEO; Rev. Peter T. Bayer, Dir. of Pastoral Care; Sr. Livia Ann Ruocco, R.S.M., Pastoral Care Coord.; Sheila Kinsky, Pastoral Care Coord. Residents 388.

St. Ann's Nursing Home Co., Inc. (The Heritage), 1450 Portland Ave., 14621. Tel: 585-697-6000; Fax: 585-342-9585. Email: info@stannscommunity.com. Web: www.stannscommunity.com. Betty Mullin-Di Prosa, Pres. & CEO; Rev. Peter T. Bayer, Dir. Pastoral Care; Sr. Livia Ann Ruocco, R.S.M., Pastoral Care Coord.; Sheila Kinsky, Pastoral Care Coord. Residents 203.

Chapel Oaks:, 1550 Portland Ave., 14621. Tel: 585-342-3052; Fax: 585-338-3453. Email: info@stannscommunity.com. Web: www.stannscommunity.org. Betty Mullin-DiProsa, Pres. & CEO; Rev. Peter T. Bayer, Dir. of Pastoral Care; Sr. Livia Ann Ruocco, R.S.M., Pastoral Care Coord.; Sheila Kinsky, Pastoral Care Coord.

[G] SPECIALTY HOUSING

ROCHESTER. *Churchville Housing Development Fund, Corp.*, 1136 Buffalo Rd., 14624. Tel: 585-328-3229, Ext. 1305; Fax: 585-529-9525.

Providence - Brown Street Housing Development Fund Corporation, 1150 Buffalo Rd., 14624. Tel: 585-328-3228, Ext. 1305; Fax: 585-529-9525.

Providence Eastgate Development Company, Inc., 1136 Buffalo Rd., 14624. Tel: 585-328-3228, Ext. 1305; Fax: 585-529-9525.

Providence Housing Development Corporation, 1136 Buffalo Rd., 14624. Tel: 585-328-3228, Ext. 1393; Fax: 585-529-9525. Email: mmccullough@dor.org. Web: www.providencehousing.org. Monica C. McCullough, Exec. Dir.; Jack Balinsky, Pres. Bd. of Directors; Helen Bianchi, Dir. Asset Mgmt.; Lori A. Foster, Mktg. & Fundraising Dir.; Fran Haywood, Dir. Finance; Minchin G. Lewis, Sr. Financial Advisor. Mission Statement: To strengthen families & communities by creating & providing access to quality affordable housing enriched by the availability of supportive services. Providence, a not-for-profit corporation affiliated with Catholic Charities of the Diocese of Rochester, develops, finances, & manages housing for individuals & families in the 12 counties of the Diocese of Rochester.

Providence Atwood Park Housing Development Fund Company, Inc., 1136 Buffalo Rd., 14624. Tel: 585-328-3228, Ext. 1393; 585-529-9525. Email: mmccullough@dor.org. Web: www.providencehousing.org. Monica C. McCullough, Pres.

Providence Lyons Housing Development Fund Company, Inc., 1136 Buffalo Rd., 14624. Tel: 585-328-3228, Ext. 1434; Fax: 585-529-9525. Web: www.providencehousing.org. Paul Pickering, Pres.; Monica C. McCullough, Sec.

Providence Medina Housing Development Fund, 1136 Buffalo Rd., 14624. Tel: 585-328-3228, Ext. 1305; Fax: 585-529-9525.

Providence Northstar Housing Development Fund Company, Inc., 1136 Buffalo Rd., 14624. Tel: 585-328-3228, Ext. 1434; Fax: 585-529-9525. Email: mmccullough@dor.org. Web: www.providencehousing.org. Monica C. McCullough, Pres.

Providence Olean Housing Development Fund Company, Inc., 1136 Buffalo Rd., 14624. Tel: 585-328-3228, Ext. 1305; Fax: 585-529-9525.

Providence Olean-Kennedy Housing Development Fund Company, Inc., 1136 Buffalo Rd., 14624. Tel: 585-328-3228, Ext. 1305; Fax: 585-529-9525.

Providence South Plymouth Housing Development Fund Company, 1136 Buffalo Rd., 14624. Tel: 585-328-3228, Ext. 1305; Fax: 585-529-9525.

Providence St. Andrew's Housing Corporation, 1136 Buffalo Rd., 14624. Tel: 585-328-3228, Ext. 1305; Fax: 585-529-9525.

Providence St. Salome Housing Development Fund Company, Inc., 1136 Buffalo Rd., 14624. Tel: 585-328-3228, Ext. 1305; Fax: 585-529-9525.

Providence State Street Housing Development Fund Company, Inc., 1136 Buffalo Rd., 14624. Tel: 585-328-3228, Ext. 1305; Fax: 585-529-9525.

Providence Union Meadows II Housing Development Fund Company, Inc., 1136 Buffalo Rd., 14624. Tel: 585-328-3228, Ext. 1305; Fax: 585-529-9525.

Providence Union Park Housing Development Fund Company, Inc., 1136 Buffalo Rd., 14624. Tel: 585-328-3228, Ext. 1305; Fax: 585-529-9525.

Providence Westside Housing Development Fund Company, Inc., 1136 Buffalo Rd., 14624. Fax: 585-529-9525.

Providence Yates Housing Development Fund Company, Inc., 1136 Buffalo Rd., 14624. Tel: 585-328-3228, Ext. 1434; Fax: 585-529-9525. Email: mmccullough@dor.org. Web: www.providencehousing.org. Paul Pickering, Pres.; Monica C. McCullough, Sec.

Union Meadows Housing Development Fund Company, Inc., 1150 Buffalo Rd., 14624. Tel: 585-328-3228, Ext. 1305.

West Town Village Housing Development Fund Company, Inc., 1150 Buffalo Rd., 14624. Tel: 585-328-3228, Ext. 1305; Fax: 585-529-9525.

[H] CAMPS

LIVONIA. *Camp Stella Maris*, 4395 E. Lake Rd., 14487. Tel: 585-346-2243; Fax: 585-346-6921. Email: info@campstellamaris.org. Web: campstellamaris.org. Christian Nadler, Bd. Pres. Purpose: Residential camping under Catholic auspices, for boys and girls (ages 7-15) of all faiths. Encampment period: Eight weeks during summer (June/July/August). Rental of facility available September-June for family/youth development retreats. ACA accredited.; Day Camp Center for boys and girls (ages 5-12). Encampment period: Eight weeks during June/July/August in conjunction with resident camp. Adventure-Based Learning Experience (ABLE) high and low challenge ropes courses ideal for building trust, confidence, cooperation, teamwork, self-esteem, communication, and leadership skills. Total Staff 8; Summer/Seasonal 140.

Conesus Lake, 4395 E. Lake Rd., 14487. Tel: 585-346-2243; Fax: 585-346-6921. John Quinlivan, Exec. Dir.

[I] GENERAL HOSPITALS

AUBURN. *Mercy Health & Rehabilitation Center Nursing Home Co., Inc.* (1972) 3 St. Anthony St., 13021. Tel: 315-253-0351. Web: www.mercyrehab.net. Sr. Frances Ann Thom, Dir. Mission Svcs. & Spiritual Care; Rev. Felicjan Sierotowicz, Chap.; Stephen Ash, Admin. Sisters of the Third Franciscan Order. Nursing Facility Beds 297.

ELMIRA. **St. Joseph's Health System, Inc.*, 555 E. St. Josephs Blvd., P.O. Box 1512, 14902-1512. Tel: 607-733-6541, Ext. 264; Fax: 607-737-7837. Web: www.stjosephs.org. David P. Sullivan, Pres. & CEO.

St. Joseph's Hospital (1908) 555 St. Josephs Blvd., 14901. Tel: 607-733-6541, Ext. 264; Fax: 607-737-7837. Email: dsullivan@stjosephs.org. Web: www.stjosephs.org. David P. Sullivan, Pres. & CEO. Skilled Nursing Facility. Total Staff 959; Bed Capacity 224; Skilled Nursing Facility 71; Patients Assisted Annually 110,000.

St. Joseph's Hospital Foundation, Inc., 555 E.St. Josephs Blvd., 14901. Tel: 607-737-7004; Fax: 607-271-3418. Anthony J. Cooper, Interim Pres. & CEO.

HORNELL. *St. James Mercy Health System*, 411 Canisteo St., 14843. Tel: 607-324-8000; Fax: 607-324-8115. Email: mlarowe@sjmh.org. Web: www.stjamesmercy.org. Mary LaRowe, Pres. &

CEO. Total Staff 916; Bed Capacity 297; Patients Assisted Annually 226,739.

[J] CATHOLIC CHARITIES

ROCHESTER. *Catholic Charities of the Diocese of Rochester, Inc.*, 1150 Buffalo Rd., 14624. Tel: 585-328-3210; Fax: 585-529-9534. Email: balinsky@dor.org. Web: www.dor.org/charities/index.htm. Jack Balinsky, Diocesan Dir.; Linda Stundtner, Chm. Bd. of Dir.; Jann K. Armantrout, Life Issues Coord.; Ruth Putnam Marchetti, Justice & Peace Coord. for Wayne & Finger Lakes Counties.

Regional Diocesan Administration Tel: 607-734-9748; Fax: 607-734-3764. Anthony T. Barbaro, Assoc. Diocesan Dir. Tel: 607-734-9784; Fax: 607-734-3764; Lee Randall, Dir. Fin. Svcs. Tel: 607-734-9784; Fax: 607-733-3614; Donna L. Rieker, H.R. Dir. Tel: 607-734-9784, Ext. 165; Fax: 607-734-3764; Barbara Poling, Sr. H.R. Dir.

Regional Offices:

Catholic Charities Community Services, 1945 E. Ridge Rd., Ste. 24, 14622. Tel: 585-339-9800; Fax: 585-339-9377. Paul Pickering, Exec. Dir.; Ed Starowicz, Chm. Bd. of Directors; Barbara Poling, Human Resources Dir.; Tracy Boff, AIDS Svcs. Dir.; Kathleen Termine, Devel. Disabilities Svcs. Dir.; Tracy Kraft, Devel. Dir.; Penny Coon, Quality Compliance Dir.; Tracy McNett, Traumatic Brain Injury Dir.

Catholic Family Center, 87 N. Clinton Ave., 14604. Tel: 585-546-7220; Fax: 585-546-6396. Mark Wickham, Pres. & CEO; John M. Pennell, CFO; Mary Anne Townsend, Chm. Bd. of Dir.; Mel Carpino, Senior Vice Pres. Devel. & Mktg.

Departments of Catholic Family Center:

Aging & Adult Services Tel: 585-232-1840; Fax: 585-454-6286. Mary Kanerva, Dept. Dir.

Children, Youth and Family Services Tel: 585-262-7115; Fax: 585-325-3867. Anne Eichas, Dir.

Employee Assistance & Counseling Tel: 585-262-7029; Fax: 585-262-7091. Tina Simson, Dir.

Homeless & Housing Services Tel: 585-423-9590; Fax: 585-262-7006. Lisa Lewis, Dir.

Personalized Recovery Oriented Services Tel: 585-232-1840; Fax: 585-232-8419. Kristie Elias, Assoc. Dir.

Mental Health Tel: 585-262-7034; Fax: 585-423-2201. Peter Roche, Interim Dir.

Office of Social Policy & Research Tel: 585-262-7021; Fax: 585-546-2042. Marvin Mich, Dir.

Refugee Immigration Employment Services Tel: 585-262-7082; Fax: 585-262-7084. Jim Morn, Dir.

Restart Substance Abuse Services Tel: 585-262-7052; Fax: 585-546-2042. Betty Mandly, Dir. Residential Svcs.; Cathy Saresky, Dir. Outpatient Svcs.

Fund Development & Community Relations Tel: 585-262-7020; Fax: 585-262-7166. Mel Carpino, Dir.

Catholic Charities of the Finger Lakes Tel: 315-789-2235; Fax: 315-789-5785. (Serving Yates, Ontario, Seneca, and Cayuga Counties)

Main Office:, 94 Exchange St., Geneva, 14456-2235. Tel: 315-789-2686; Fax: 315-789-5785. Ellen Wayne, Exec. Dir.; Ruth Putnam Marchetti, Dir. Parish Svcs.; L. Trojnor, Dir. Cayuga County Office; Robert McFadden, Bd. Chm. (Satellite Office at: 134 E. Genesee St., Auburn, NY 13021. Tel: 312-262-0018)

Catholic Charities of Wayne County, 1141 E. Union St., Newark, 14513. Tel: 315-331-4867; Fax: 315-331-4918. Carmen Pagano, Bd. Chm.; Timothy Sullivan, Exec. Dir.

College Bound

Community Outreach P. Mares, Contact Person.

Early Intervention I. Rojas, Contact Person.

General Counseling I. Rojas, Contact Person.

Justice & Peace/Parish Social Ministry Support R. Putnam-Marchetti, Contact Person.

LaCasa Transitional Housing P. Mares, Contact Person.

PINS Diversion and Counseling S. VanLiew, Contact Person.

Wolcott Clothing Center

Catholic Charities of Chemung/Schuyler, 215 E. Church St., Elmira, 14901. Tel: 607-734-9784; Fax: 607-734-6588. Bridget Steed, Exec. Dir.; Marie Finnerty, Bd. Chm.; Kathy Dubel, Dir., Justice & Peace. Tel: 607-734-9784, Ext. 135; C. Nogera, Dir., Residential Svcs.; E. Topping, Dir., Agency Youth Svcs.; L. Winters, Devel.; M. McInerny, Contact Person, Property Dept.

Second Place East Homeless Services/Shelter S. Fritz, Dir. Emergency Svcs.

Homeless Intervention Program Samaritan Center T. Parker, Dir., Samaritan Center.

First Time Homebuyer J. Galvin, Contact Person.

Schuyler Services P. Marx, Contact Person.

Catholic Charities of Steuben, 23 Liberty St., Bath, 14810. Tel: 607-734-8085; Fax: 607-776-4092. Laura Opelt, Exec. Dir.; Michael Gabrielle, Bd. Chm.; Lynda Lowin, (Justice & Peace).

Turning Point D. Cherry, Contact Person.

Substance Abuse Services, Prevention and Education J. Bassage, Contact Person.

Kinship Family & Youth Services, 2 Bethesda Dr., Ste. 10, Hornell, 14843. Tel: 607-324-0909; Fax: 607-324-0983. Joseph Weider, Exec. Dir.; Barbara Fairbanks, Pres. Bd. of Dir.

In-Home Family Preservation S.H.A.P.E. M. Duff, Contact Person.

Healthy Families L. Galatio, Contact Person.

Foster Care C. Fitzwater, Contact Person.

Alcoholism Services K. Robards-Smith, Contact Person.

Catholic Charities of Tompkins/Tioga, 324 W. Buffalo St., Ithaca, 14850. Tel: 607-272-5062; Fax: 607-272-4427. Diane DeMoth, Exec. Dir.

Justice and Peace, Tompkins L. Konwinski, Contact Person.

Justice and Peace, Tioga K. Dubel, Contact Person.

Family Empowerment Services T. Miller, Contact Person.

Samaritan Center E. Greenly, Contact Person.

Immigrant Support Services S. Chaffee, Contact Person.

Tioga Outreach A. Klopf, Contact Person.

Food Bank of the Southern Tier, 945 County Rt. 64, Elmira, 14903. Tel: 607-796-6061; Fax: 607-796-6028. Natasha Thompson, Exec. Dir.; Mary Pat Dolan, Bd. Chm.

Catholic Charities of Livingston County, 34 E. State St., Mt. Morris, 14510. Tel: 716-658-4466; Fax: 585-658-2513. Tabitha Brewster, Agency Admin. Departments: Christa Barrows, Faith in Action; Brigit Hurley, Parish Social Ministry; Tabitha Brewster, Asst. Exec. Dir.; Michelle Dourie, Community of Caring; C. Tinney, SSI Case Mgmt.; Wes Kennison, Bd. Chm.

Catholic Charities of the Southern Tier, 215 E. Church St., Elmira, 14901. Tel: 607-734-9784; Fax: 607-734-6588.

[K] MONASTERIES AND RESIDENCES OF PRIESTS AND BROTHERS

ROCHESTER. *Basilian Fathers, Christ the King Church*, 445 Kings Hwy., S., 14617. Tel: 585-266-1288. Very Rev. George T. Smith, Supr.; Rev. Paul F. English, Gen. Councilor.

Basilian Residence, 3497 East Ave., 14618. Tel: 585-586-4600; Fax: 585-385-6383. Revs. Jim Stenberg, C.S.B., Supr.; Joseph M. Lanzalaco, C.S.B.; T. Paul Broadhurst, C.S.B.; Albert W. Cylwicki, C.S.B.; Leo A. Hetzler, C.S.B., Councilor; John R. Lee, C.S.B.; Thomas M. Miller, C.S.B.; John C. Murray, C.S.B.; John A. Poluikis, C.S.B.; Donald J. Lococo, C.S.B., Councilor.

Priests of the Region Serving Elsewhere: Revs. William J. Sheehan, C.S.B., Collegio San Clemente, Via Labicana, 95, 00184, Rome, Italy; George Kosicki, C.S.B., c/o Companions of Christ the Lamb, P.O. Box 12, Paradise, MI 49768. Tel: 906-492-3647; J. Gareth Poupore, C.S.B., 16 Village Trail, Honeoye Falls, 14472; Paul F. O'Connor, C.S.B.

Becket Hall, 2617 East Ave., 14610. Tel: 585-647-6657. Email: beckethall@dor.org. Web: www.dor.org. Rev. William Coffas, Rector. Residence for Pre-Theologate candidates.

Missionaries of the Precious Blood (1815) 1261 Highland Ave., 14620-1873. Tel: 585-461-0318; Fax: 585-461-0318. Email: jcolacino@sjfc.edu. Rev. John A. Colacino, C.PP.S. Tel: 716-461-2750.

Whitefriars Priory, 625 Colebrook Dr., 14617. Tel: 585-266-2560. Revs. Joseph DeMaio, O.Carm.; Jack Healy, O.Carm., Prior & Treas.; Matthew Temple, O.Carm. Total in Residence 3.

INTERLAKEN. *St. Fidelis Friary* (1951) 7790 County Rd. 153, 14847. Tel: 607-532-4423; Fax: 607-532-9271. Rev. Bartholomew Minson, O.F.M.Cap.; Bros. Antonine Lizama, O.F.M.Cap.; Carmine Funaro, O.F.M.Cap.; Revs. John Tokaz, O.F.M.Cap., Guardian; Eugene O'Hara, O.F.M.Cap., Vicar. Capuchin Friars-Province of St. Mary (Order of Friars Minor Capuchin). Priests 3; Brothers 2.

PIFFARD. *Abbey of the Genesee* (1951) 3258 River Rd., 14533. Tel: 585-243-0660. Email: community@geneseeabbey.org. Web: www.geneseeabbey.org. Rt. Revs. John Denburger, O.C.S.O., Abbot; John Eudes Bamberger, O.C.S.O., Retired Abbot (Retired); Revs. Eugene Chung, O.C.S.O.; Francis R. Steger, O.C.S.O.; Marcellus R. Earl, O.C.S.O.; Jerome J. Machar, O.C.S.O.; Robert O. Moore, O.C.S.O.; Stephen Muller, O.C.S.O.; Justin R. Sheehan, O.C.S.O.; Gerard D'Souza, O.C.S.O.; Aelred W. Wentz, O.C.S.O. The Order of Cistercians of the Strict Observance (Trappists). Professed Monks 30; Priests 12; Total in Community (Piffard) 30.

Absent on Leave: Rev. Michael M. Hayden, O.C.S.O.

PINE CITY. *Mount Saviour Monastery* (1950) 231 Monastery Rd., 14871-9787. Tel: 607-734-1688; Fax: 607-734-1689. Email: info@msaviour.org. Web: www.msaviour.org. Rev. James Cronen, O.S.B. Professed Monks 9; Professed Priests 2; Total in Community 11.

[L] CONVENTS AND RESIDENCES FOR SISTERS

ROCHESTER. *Sisters of Mercy of the Americas - New York, Pennsylvania, Pacific West Community*, 1437 Blossom Rd., 14610. Tel: 585-288-2710; Fax: 585-288-2756. Email: nhoff@mercynyppaw.org. Web: www.sistersofmercy.org. Sr. Nancy Hoff, R.S.M, Pres. Professed Sisters & Perpetual Vows 463; Associates 414.

Sisters St. Joseph of Rochester (1854) 150 French Rd., 14618-3822. Tel: 585-641-8100; Fax: 585-641-8524. Email: cong@ssjrochester.org. Web: www.ssjrochester.org. Sr. Mary Louise Mitchell, S.S.J., Congregational Pres.; Rev. Msgr. William H. Shannon, Chap. (Retired); Rev. Bruce F. Ammering, Chap. (Retired). Sisters of St. Joseph of Rochester, Inc. Priests 11; Professed Sisters in Community 258; Total Assisted 72; Total Staff 120.

Spirit House, Inc. (1981) 72 Dorvid Rd., 14617. Tel: 585-544-5698; Fax: 585-266-2611. Email: spirithouse1@juno.com. Web: www.wounded-in-spirit.com. Sr. Mary Ann Ayers, R.S.M., Dir.

ELMIRA. *Monastery of Mary the Queen, Dominican Nuns*, 1310 W. Church St., 14905. Tel: 607-734-9506; Fax: 607-734-1452. Email: mmtqblog@gmail.com. Web: http://monasteryofmarythequeen.op.org. Sr. Miriam Scheel, O.P., Prioress. Solemn Vows 13.

PITTSFORD. *Monastery of Our Lady and St. Joseph Carmelite Monastery*, 1931 W. Jefferson Rd., 14534-1041. Tel: 585-427-7094. Sr. Therese Marie of Jesus Crucified, O.C.D., Prioress. Discalced Carmelite Nuns. Professed Nuns with Solemn Vows 13.

[M] RETREAT HOUSES

ROCHESTER. *Mercy Prayer Center* (1978) 65 Highland Ave., 14620. Tel: 585-473-6893; Fax: 585-473-6414. Email: info@mercyprayercenter.org. Web: www.mercyprayercenter.org. Sponsored by Sisters of Mercy, New York, Pennsylvania, Pacific West Community. Total Staff 6.

CANANDAIGUA. *Notre Dame Retreat House* (1967) 5151 Foster Rd., Box 342, 14424. Tel: 585-394-5700; Fax: 585-394-9215. Web: ndretreat.org. Revs. Michael Sergi, Rector; Thomas Barrett, C.Ss.R.; Paul A. Miller, C.Ss.R.

[N] CAMPUS MINISTRY

ROCHESTER. *Campus Ministry* Pastoral Center, 1150 Buffalo Rd., 14624. Tel: 585-328-3210; Fax: 585-328-3149. Email: loughlin@dor.org. Ms. Shannon Loughlin, Dir. of Young Adult & Campus Ministry.

Catholic Newman Community at the University of Rochester Interfaith Chapel, 320 Wilson Blvd., 14627. Tel: 585-275-4321; Fax: 585-506-0203. Rev. Brian Cool, Dir.; Deacon W. Craig Stratton, Medical Center Outreach; Nathan Drahms, Campus Min.; Sr. Jacqulyn Reichart, R.S.M., Campus Min.

Eastman School of Music Catholic Students Organization Tel: 585-275-4321; Fax: 585-506-0203. Rev. Brian Cool, Contact Person.

Nazareth College of Rochester 4245 East Ave., 14618. Tel: 585-389-2308; Fax: 585-389-2300. Jamie Fazio, Campus Min.

Newman (Catholic Campus) Parish, RIT/NTID Interfaith Center, 40 Lomb Memorial Dr., 14623. Tel: 585-475-5172; Fax: 585-475-5485. Email: mlkcpm@rit.edu. Web: www.rit.edu/~newman/. Mrs. Mary Lou Knapp, Dir.

St. John Fisher College 3690 East Ave., 14618. Tel: 585-385-8368; Fax: 585-385-8129. Rev. Joseph M. Lanzalaco, C.S.B., Dir., Campus Min. Tel: 585-385-8368; Deacon Thomas Jewell, Campus Min.

State University College at Brockport, the Newman Oratory of Brockport 101 Kenyon St., Brockport, 14420. Tel: 585-637-5036; Fax: 585-637-7866. Email: campusminister1@aol.com. Margot Van Etten, Dir. of Campus Ministry; Deacon Lawrence Van Etten, Pastoral Min.

State University College at Geneseo (Geneseo), Newman Catholic Community at the Interfaith Center 11 Franklin St., Geneseo, 14454. Tel: 585-243-1460. Email: sauter@geneseo.edu. Mike Sauter, Dir.; Rev. Edward J. Dillon, Sacramental Min. (Retired).

The Cornell Catholic Community, Inc. (Ithaca) Cornell University, G-22 Anabel Taylor Hall, Ithaca, 14853. Tel: 607-255-4228; Fax: 607-255-7793. Email: catholic@cornell.edu. Rev. Daniel T. McMullin, Dir. & Chap.

The Catholic Community of Ithaca College 100 Muller Chapel, Ithaca College, 953 Danby Rd., Ithaca, 14850. Tel: 607-274-3103; Fax: 607-274-1901. Rev. Carsten Martensen, S.J., Dir.; Stephen Hill, Campus Min.

Elmira College One Park Place, Elmira, 14901. Tel:

607-732-1994. Rev. Richard Farrell, Contact Person.

Hobart and William Smith College c/o Our Lady of Peace, 130 Exchange St., Geneva, 14456. Tel: 315-789-0930. Rev. Paul J. Tomasso. Tel: 315-789-0930. Roman Catholic Community.

Keuka College c/o St. Michael's Church 312 Liberty St., Penn Yan, 14527. Tel: 315-536-7459; Fax: 315-536-6964. Rev. Stanley Kacprzak, Our Lady of the Lakes.

Roberts Wesleyan College c/o St. Christopher Church 2301 Westside Dr., North Chili, 14514. Tel: 585-595-1400. Rev. Robert Gaudio.

Wells College, c/o Good Shepherd Catholic Community Main St., P.O. Box 296, Aurora, 13026-0296. Tel: 315-364-7197. Rev. Richard J. Shatzel.

Monroe Community College 1000 E. Henrietta Rd., 14623. Email: mupson@monroecc.edu.

New York Chiropractic College c/o St. Hyacinth, 63 Pulaski St., Auburn, 13021. Tel: 315-252-7297 (Rectory); 315-568-3124 (College); Fax: 315-568-4893. Rev. Richard M. Murphy (Retired). Priests 14; Total Staff 24; Total Assisted 120,721.

[O] MISCELLANEOUS LISTINGS

ROCHESTER. *Apostleship of Prayer*, Diocesan Pastoral Center, 1150 Buffalo Rd., 14624. Tel: 585-328-3210. Rev. Thomas P. Mull.

Archivist (Diocese of Rochester Archives), 1150 Buffalo Rd., 14624. Tel: 585-328-3210, Ext. 1204; Fax: 585-328-3149. Email: archive@dor.org. Sr. Connie Derby, R.S.M., Dir. of Archives and Records.

Catholic Committee on Scouting, 1150 Buffalo Rd., 14624. Tel: 585-328-3210; Fax: 585-328-3149. Email: lmehlenbacher@dor.org. Web: www.dor.org. Rev. William McGrath.

Catholic Gay & Lesbian Family Ministry, 66 Meadowbrook Rd., 14620. Tel: 585-303-8605. Ms. Karen Rinefierd, Diocesan Liaison.

Communis Fund of the Diocese of Rochester, Inc., 1150 Buffalo Rd., 14624. Tel: 585-328-3228, Ext. 1269.

Daystar For Medically Fragile Infants, Inc., 47 Lochnavar Pkwy., Pittsford, 14534. Tel: 585-385-6287; Fax: 585-383-0033. Web: daystarhome.net. Sr. Eileen Daly, S.S.J., Councilor.

DOR Holding, Inc., 1150 Buffalo Rd., 14624. Tel: 585-328-3228, Ext. 1269; Fax: 585-328-4142.

Dunn Tower Apartments, Inc. (1976) 100 Dunn Tower Dr., 14606. Tel: 585-429-5520; Fax: 585-429-9720. Email: dt1@dunntower.com. Web: www.dunntower.com. Housing for Seniors; Under 62 with Physical or Mobility; Disabled Vets Total Staff 6; Total in Residence 192.

Family Rosary For Peace, Inc. (1950) 7 Austin St., 14606. Tel: 585-254-7170; Fax: 585-254-5813. Email: rholyapo@dor.org. Rev. Paul J. Tomasso, Dir.; Dolores Mary Brien, Sec.

Holy Childhood Association, 1150 Buffalo Rd., 14624. Tel: 585-436-9200; Fax: 585-529-9501. Email: jconlon@dor.org. Web: www.dor.org/missions. Rev. Robert C. Bradler, Dir. (Retired).

St. Joseph's House of Hospitality, 402 South Ave., 14620. Tel: 585-232-3262. Email: cathwork@frontiernet.net. Mailing Address: P.O. Box 31049, 14603. Tel: 585-232-3262. Services provide soup kitchen, personal assistance to the needy, emergency men's housing and social justice advocacy. Total Staff 5; Total Assisted 120.

Magnificat - Rochester, P.O. Box 24787, 14624. Tel: 585-233-8674. Louise Carson, Treas. & Contact.

Marriage Encounter Apostolate (Worldwide), 132 Clay Ave., 14613. Tel: 585-719-9848. Email: jbrasley@dor.org. Web: www.wwme.org. Rev. John Murray, C.S.B.; Deacon John Brasley, Contact Person; Belinda Brasley, Contact Person. Priests 2; Total Staff 18.

Mercy Community Services, Inc. (1980) 142 Webster Ave., 14609. Tel: 585-288-2634; Fax: 585-288-0252. Email: info@mercycommunityservices.org. Web: www.mercycommunityservices.org. Susan Aiello, Pres. & CEO. Supportive Housing for Single Mothers and their Children and primary healthcare for the uninsured. Total Staff 17; Families Assisted 90; Total Assisted 400.

Nativity Preparatory Academy Associates of Rochester Inc, 15 Whalin St., 14620. Tel: 585-271-1630; Fax: 585-271-1633. Email: nativityrochester@frontiernet.net. Web: www.nativityrochester.org. 15 Whalin St., 14620. William M. Carpenter, Bd. Chm. & Contact.

Notre Dame Learning Center, Inc., P.O. Box 77175, 14617. Tel: 585-254-5110; Fax: 585-254-2378. Email: ndlc@frontiernet.net. Web: www.ndlcenter.org. 71 Pkwy., 14608. Sr. Mary Lennon, Treas. Ministry for children and adults by providing educational opportunities in literacy, reading & math to enable them to reach the fullness of their potential & become successful & productive citizens.

St. Peter's Kitchen, Inc, 681 Brown St., P.O. Box 11031, 14611. Tel: 585-235-6511. Email: stpeterskitchen@dor.org. Candice Johnson, Pres.; Bob Stuver, Vice Pres.; Patricia Lorenzen, Prog. Dir. Provide nutritious lunches to men, women, and children in need. In addition there is a clothing closet.

Providence Housing Development Corporation (1994) 1136 Buffalo Rd., 14624. Tel: 585-328-3228, Ext. 1393; Fax: 585-529-9525. Email: mmccullough@dor.org. Web: www.providencehousing.org. Programs offered: Property Management, Shelter & Care for the Homeless, Housing Development and Housing Consultation. Units Developed 841; Units Managed 753.

Providence Rivendell Court Apartments, Inc., 1136 Buffalo Rd., 14624. Tel: 585-328-3228, Ext. 1305; Fax: 585-529-9525. Monica C. McCullough, Pres.

Rochester Catholic Worker Bethany House (1978) 111 Joseph Ave., 14611. Tel: 585-454-4197; Fax: 585-454-4197 *51. Email: rbethan1@rochester.rr.com. Donna Ecker, Contact Person. Total Staff 4.

Sisters of Saint Joseph of Rochester Charitable Trust, c/o Thomas Nientimp, Presiding Trustee, 150 French Rd., 14618. Tel: 585-641-8166; Fax: 585-641-8524. Alicia Pender, Contact Person.

Sisters of Saint Joseph of Rochester Ministry Foundation, Inc. (2004) 150 French Rd., 14618-3822. Tel: 585-641-8125; Fax: 585-641-8524. Web: www.ssjrochester.org. Sr. Barbara Staropoli, S.S.J.

The Diocese of Rochester Lay Employees' Retirement Accumulation Plan, 1150 Buffalo Rd., 14624.

The Diocese of Rochester Priests' Retirement Plan, 1150 Buffalo Rd., 14624.

St. Theodore's Apartment Housing Development Fund Co., Inc. (Dunn Tower II Apts.) (1980) 200 Dunn Tower Dr., 14606. Tel: 585-429-6840; Fax: 585-247-3723. Email: dt2@dunntower.com. Web: www.dunntower.com.

CORNING. *Anawim Community Center*, 122 E. First St., 14830. Tel: 607-936-4965; Fax: 607-936-0207. Email: oxford@anawim.com. Web: www.anawim.com. Revs. Daniel Healy (Philippines), Dir.; Richard M. Rusk, Missions & Vocations Dir. Priests 2; Total in Residence 4; Total Staff 10.

ELMIRA. *Powell Street Housing Development Fund Company, Inc.*, 1700 College Ave., 14901. Tel: 607-734-9784. Anthony T. Barbaro, Contact Person.

FAIRPORT. *Catholic Charismatic Renewal*, 48 South Ave., 14450. Tel: 585-425-7434. Email: don.germano@gmail.com. Deacon Donald Germano, Diocesan Liaison.

GENEVA. *DeSales Institution Foundation Inc.*, 90 Pulteney St., 14456. Tel: 315-789-5111; Fax: 315-789-8230. Web: www.desaleshs.org.

OWEGO. *Owego -Tioga Rural Ministry* (1978) 143 North Ave., 13827. Tel: 607-697-3021; Fax: 607-687-3033. Email: sphilrsm@stny.rr.com. Sr. Phyllis McGuire, R.S.M., Exec. Dir. This ministry serves as a food pantry and an emergency outreach to the poor and elderly of the county. Total Staff 4; Total Assisted 2,496.

SENECA FALLS. *Patrician Fund Trust*, 25 Center St., Waterloo, 13165. Tel: 315-651-4349; Fax: 315-539-8841. Email: sstpatri@dor.org. Web: www.senecafallsonline.com/stpats/. Kimberly Partee.

SPENCERPORT. *Rochester Comitium*, 1522 Nine Mile Point Rd., Penfield, 14526. Tel: 585-266-8087. Ms. Marcy Leonardo, Pres.

RELIGIOUS INSTITUTES OF MEN REPRESENTED IN THE DIOCESE

For further details refer to the corresponding bracketed number in the Religious Institutes of Men or Women section.

[0170]—*Basilian Fathers*—C.S.B.
[0200]—*Benedictine Monks*—O.S.B.
[0470]—*The Capuchin Friars* (Province of St. Mary)—O.F.M.Cap.
[0270]—*Carmelite Fathers and Brothers*—O.Carm.
[0350]—*Cistercians Order of the Strict Observance (Trappists)*—O.C.S.O.
[0310]—*Congregation of Christian Brothers* (Eastern Prov.)—C.F.C.
[1140]—*Congregation of the Sacred Hearts of Jesus and Mary*—SS.CC.
[0480]—*Conventual Franciscans* (Buffalo & Immaculate Conception Provinces)—O.F.M.Conv.
[0520]—*Franciscan Friars* (Assumption B.V.M. Prov.)—O.F.M.
[0690]—*Jesuit Fathers and Brothers* (New York Province)—S.J.
[0610]—*Priests of the Congregation of Holy Cross*—C.S.C.
[1070]—*Redemptorist Fathers* (Baltimore Province)—C.SS.R.
[0760]—*Society of Mary (Marianists)*—S.M.
[1060]—*Society of the Precious Blood*—C.PP.S.
[0560]—*Third Order Regular of Saint Francis*—T.O.R.

RELIGIOUS INSTITUTES OF WOMEN REPRESENTED IN THE DIOCESE

[3110]—*Congregation of Our Lady of the Retreat in the Cenacle*—R.C.
[0760]—*Daughters of Charity of St. Vincent de Paul*—D.C.
[0420]—*Discalced Carmelite Nuns*—O.C.D.
[1050]—*Dominican Contemplative Nuns*—O.P.
[1070-13]—*Dominican Sisters (Adrian, MI)*—O.P.
[1070-05]—*Dominican Sisters (Amityville, NY)*—O.P.
[]—*Franciscan Sisters of Alleghany, New York*—O.S.F.
[2575]—*Institute of the Sisters of Mercy of the Americas* (Rochester, NY)—R.S.M.
[2470]—*Maryknoll Sisters of St. Dominic*—M.M.
[]—*Misioneras Guadalupanas del Espiritu Santo*
[3430]—*Religious Teachers Filippini*—M.P.F.
[2970]—*School Sisters of Notre Dame*—S.S.N.D.
[3950]—*Sisters of Saint Mary of Namur*—S.S.M.N.
[1800]—*Sisters of St. Francis of the Third Order Regular (Williamsville, New York)*—O.S.F.
[3840]—*Sisters of St. Joseph of Carondolet*—C.S.J.
[3830-14]—*Sisters of St. Joseph (Rochester)*—S.S.J.
[3730]—*Sisters of the Order of St. Basil the Great*—O.S.B.M.
[1490]—*Sisters of the Third Franciscan Order*—O.S.F.
[3620]—*Sisters, Servants of Mary Immaculate*—S.S.M.I.
[2160]—*Sisters, Servants of the Immaculate Heart of Mary*—I.H.M.
[4120-04]—*Ursuline Sisters of Cleveland*—O.S.U.

DIOCESAN CEMETERIES

ROCHESTER. *Holy Sepulchre*, 2461 Lake Ave., 14612. Tel: 585-458-4110; Fax: 585-458-3059. Web: www.holysepulchre.org. Email: jim@holysepulchre.org.

REGIONAL CEMETERIES

AUBURN. *St. Joseph's*
CORNING. *St. Mary*
ELMIRA. *SS. Peter and Paul's*
GENEVA. *St. Mary's and St. Patrick's*

NECROLOGY

† Dillon, John D., (Retired)—Died June 2, 2011
† Hoctor, Thomas D., (Retired)—Died March 22, 2011
† Hogan, Michael C., (Retired)—Died Sept. 8, 2011
† Kanka, Robert, (Retired)—Died Oct. 19, 2011
† Lynch, John A., (Retired)—Died June 4, 2011
† Morgan, John A., (Retired)—Died Sept. 5, 2011

Diocese of Rockford

(Dioecesis Rockfordiensis)

Most Reverend

DAVID J. MALLOY

Bishop of Rockford; ordained July 1, 1983; appointed Bishop of Rockford March 20, 2012. *Office: 555 Colman Center Dr., Rockford, IL 61125.*

Most Reverend

THOMAS G. DORAN

Retired Bishop of Rockford; ordained December 20, 1961; appointed Bishop of Rockford April 19, 1994; consecrated and installed June 24, 1994; retired March 20, 2012. *Res.: P.O. Box 7044, Rockford, IL 61125.*

Most Reverend

ARTHUR J. O'NEILL, D.D., V.G.

Retired Bishop of Rockford; ordained March 27, 1943; appointed Bishop of Rockford August 19, 1968; consecrated and installed October 11, 1968; retired April 19, 1994. *Res.: 3330 Maria Linden Dr., Rockford, IL 61114.* Tel: 815-877-7416.

ESTABLISHED SEPTEMBER 23, 1908.

Square Miles 6,457.

Comprises Jo Daviess, Stephenson, Winnebago, Boone, McHenry, Carroll, Ogle, DeKalb, Kane, Whiteside and Lee Counties in the State of Illinois.

For legal titles of parishes and diocesan institutions, consult the Chancery Office.

Diocesan Chancery: 555 Colman Center Dr., P.O. Box 7044, Rockford, IL 61125. Tel: 815-399-4300; Fax: 815-399-5266.

Web: www.rockforddiocese.org

Email: chancery99@aol.com

STATISTICAL OVERVIEW

Personnel	
Bishop	1
Retired Bishops	2
Abbots	1
Retired Abbots	1
Priests: Diocesan Active in Diocese	135
Priests: Diocesan Active Outside Diocese	9
Priests: Diocesan in Foreign Missions	1
Priests: Retired, Sick or Absent	51
Number of Diocesan Priests	196
Religious Priests in Diocese	42
Total Priests in Diocese	238
Extern Priests in Diocese	10
Ordinations:	
Diocesan Priests	7
Transitional Deacons	2
Permanent Deacons in Diocese	145
Total Brothers	11
Total Sisters	95
Parishes	
Parishes	104
With Resident Pastor:	
Resident Diocesan Priests	83
Resident Religious Priests	9
Without Resident Pastor:	
Administered by Priests	12
Administered by Deacons	1
Welfare	
Catholic Hospitals	3
Total Assisted	551,273
Health Care Centers	17
Total Assisted	232,132
Homes for the Aged	7
Total Assisted	3,198
Day Care Centers	1
Total Assisted	36
Special Centers for Social Services	6
Total Assisted	66,574
Educational	
Diocesan Students in Other Seminaries	22
Total Seminarians	22
Colleges and Universities	1
Total Students	132
High Schools, Diocesan and Parish	6
Total Students	3,185
High Schools, Private	2
Total Students	941
Elementary Schools, Diocesan and Parish	40
Total Students	10,441
Catechesis/Religious Education:	
High School Students	4,581
Elementary Students	24,407
Total Students under Catholic Instruction	43,709
Teachers in the Diocese:	
Priests	10
Sisters	10
Lay Teachers	1,029
Vital Statistics	
Receptions into the Church:	
Infant Baptism Totals	5,748
Minor Baptism Totals	150
Adult Baptism Totals	201
Received into Full Communion	307
First Communions	7,011
Confirmations	4,938
Marriages:	
Catholic	784
Interfaith	236
Total Marriages	1,020
Deaths	2,074
Total Catholic Population	461,297
Total Population	1,972,238

Former Bishops—Most Revs. PETER J. MULDOON, D.D., ord. Dec. 18, 1886; cons. Titular Bishop of Tamassus and Auxiliary Bishop of Chicago, July 25, 1901; appt. Bishop of Rockford, Sept. 28, 1908; made Assistant to the Pontifical Throne, June 8, 1921; died Oct. 8, 1927; EDWARD F. HOBAN, S.T.D., ord. July 11, 1903; cons. Titular Bishop of Colonia and Auxiliary Bishop of Chicago, Dec. 21, 1921; appt. Bishop of Rockford, Feb. 10, 1928; appt. Assistant at the Pontifical Throne, Nov. 25, 1937; appt. Titular Bishop of Listra and Coadjutor Bishop of Cleveland, Nov. 16, 1942; succeeded to the See of Cleveland, Nov. 2, 1945; died Sept. 22, 1966; JOHN J. BOYLAN, D.D., Ph.D., ord. July 28, 1915; appt. Nov. 21, 1942; cons. Feb. 17, 1943; died July 19, 1953; RAYMOND P. HILLINGER, D.D., ord. April 2, 1932; appt. Nov. 3, 1953; cons. Dec. 29, 1953; appt. Titular Bishop of Derbe and Auxiliary Bishop of Chicago, June 27, 1956; died Nov. 13, 1971; Rt. Rev. DONALD M. CARROLL, D.D., ord. April 7, 1934; appt. June 27, 1956; resigned Sept. 25, 1956; died Jan. 3, 2002; Most Revs. LORAS T. LANE, D.D., ord. March 19, 1937; appt. Titular Bishop of Bencenna and Auxiliary of Dubuque, May 29, 1951; cons. Aug. 20, 1951; appt. to Rockford, Oct. 11, 1956; died July 22, 1968; ARTHUR J. O'NEILL, D.D., V.G., ord. March 27, 1943; appt. Bishop of Rockford Aug. 19, 1968; cons. and installed Oct. 11, 1968; retired April 19, 1994.; THOMAS G. DORAN, ord. Dec. 20, 1961; appt. Bishop of Rockford April 19, 1994; cons. and installed June 24, 1994; retired March 20, 2012.

Diocesan Chancery—555 Colman Center Dr., P.O. Box 7044, Rockford, 61125. Tel: 815-399-4300; Fax: 815-399-5266. Address all official business to this office. Office Hours: Mon.-Fri. 8:30-12, 1-4:30.

Vicars General—Most Rev. ARTHUR J. O'NEILL, D.D., V.G.; Rev. Msgrs. THOMAS C. BRADY, P.A., V.G., Ph.D. (Retired); ERIC R. BARR, V.G., S.T.L., Mailing Address: P.O. Box 7044, Rockford, 61125. Tel: 815-399-4300; Fax: 815-399-5962; GLENN L. NELSON, V.G., J.C.L., Christ the Teacher Parish, 512 Normal Rd., DeKalb, 60115. Tel: 815-787-7770; Fax: 815-758-2053.

Moderator of the Curia—Rev. Msgr. GLENN L. NELSON, V.G., J.C.L.

Vicar for Clergy and Religious—Very Rev. BRIAN D. GRADY.

Parish Services and Directors—Mr. PATRICK WINN, Dir. Social Svcs., 555 Colman Center Dr., P.O. Box 7044, Rockford, 61125; Rev. JOHN A. SLAMPAK, Dir. Pastoral Svcs., Blessed Sacrament Church, 801 Oak St., North Aurora, 60542; LORRIE GRAMER, Asst. Dir. Pastoral Svcs., Mailing Address: P.O. Box 7044, Rockford, 61125. Tel: 815-399-4300; Fax: 815-399-6303; Mr. JOHN MCGRATH, Dir. Educational Svcs., Catholic Education Office, 555 Colman Center Dr., P.O. Box 7044, Rockford, 61125; Mr. MICHAEL KAGAN, Asst. Dir. Educational Svcs., Catholic Education Office, 555 Colman Center Dr., P.O. Box 7044, Rockford, 61125; Dr. WAYNE LENELL, CPA, Ph.D., Dir. Financial & Admin. Svcs., 555 Colman Center Dr., P.O. Box 7044, Rockford, 61125; Mrs. JODI RIPPON, Asst. Dir. Financial & Admin. Svcs., 555 Colman Center Dr., P.O. Box 7044, Rockford, 61125.

Chancellor—Rev. Msgr. JOHN C. FRITZ.

Vice Chancellor—Rev. MARTINS EMEH, J.C.L.

Bishop's Secretary for Retired Priests—Rev. Msgr. DANIEL J. DEUTSCH, V.F.

Secretary to the Bishop & Diocesan Master of Ceremonies—Rev. Msgr. JOHN C. FRITZ.

Diocesan Tribunal—555 Colman Center Dr., P.O. Box 7044, Rockford, 61125.. Tel: 815-399-4300; Fax: 815-399-4861. Address all official business to this office.

Judicial Vicar—Rev. Msgr. MICHAEL A. KURZ, J.C.L.

Adjunct Judicial Vicar—Rev. Msgr. ARQUIMEDES VALLEJO, J.C.D.

Secretary for Administrative Processes—Rev. Msgr. ROBERT J. SWEENEY.

Promoter of Justice—Rev. Msgr. ARQUIMEDES

VALLEJO, J.C.D.

Defenders of the Bond—Rev. Msgrs. ARQUIMEDES VALLEJO, J.C.D.; MICHAEL A. HACK, J.C.D.

Pro Synodal Judges—Rev. Msgrs. RAYMOND J. WAHL, P.A., J.C.D. (Retired); GLENN L. NELSON, V.G., J.C.L.; THOMAS L. DZIELAK, V.F.; WILLIAM H. SCHWARTZ, P.A., S.T.L.; GERALD P. KOBBEMAN (Retired); Rev. FRANCIS E. MCDONNELL (Retired).

Advocates—Sisters MARGARET ANNE FLOTO, O.S.F.; NADINE MEYER, S.S.N.D.

Experts—Rev. Msgr. THOMAS J. MONAHAN, Ph.D. (Retired); Mr. MICHAEL M. KAGAN, M.A.

Notaries—Mrs. DENISE GEORGE; Mrs. DONNA HAYES.

Diocesan Consultors—Rev. Msgrs. THOMAS C. BRADY, P.A., V.G., Ph.D. (Retired); DANIEL J. HERMES; ERIC R. BARR, V.G., S.T.L.; P. WILLIAM MCDONNELL; JOHN J. MITCHELL (Retired); RAYMOND J. WAHL, P.A., J.C.D. (Retired); DANIEL J. DEUTSCH, V.F.; Revs. DONALD M. AHLES; STEPHEN ST. JULES; Rev. Msgr. STEPHEN J. KNOX, S.T.L.; Rev. GEOFFREY D. WIRTH.

Deans—Rev. Msgrs. DANIEL J. DEUTSCH, V.F., Aurora Deanery; GLENN L. NELSON, V.G., J.C.L., DeKalb Deanery; JOSEPH B. LINSTER, Elgin Deanery; P. WILLIAM MCDONNELL, Freeport Deanery; JAMES W. MCLOUGHLIN, McHenry County Deanery (Retired); GERALD P. KOBBEMAN, Rockford Deanery (Retired); THOMAS L. DZIELAK, V.F., Sterling Deanery.

Diocesan Offices and Directors

Accounting and Data Processing Office—DAN O'MALLEY, Dir. Accounting; ROBERT WHITE, Dir. Information Technology; LORI GLENN, Office Mgr., Mailing Address: P.O. Box 7044, Rockford, 61125. Tel: 815-399-4300; Fax: 815-399-5657.

Catholic Campaign for Human Development—555 Colman Center Dr., P.O. Box 7044, Rockford, 61125. Tel: 815-399-4300; Fax: 815-399-6303.

Catholic Charismatic Renewal Services—Mr. RON BERGMAN, Diocesan Liaison, 1910 Bracknel Blvd., Rockford, 61103. Tel: 815-654-4111.

Catholic Office of the Deaf—Rev. Msgr. GLENN L. NELSON, V.G., J.C.L., Dir., Christ the Teacher Parish, 512 Normal Rd., Dekalb, 60115. Tel: 815-787-7770 (Voice); 815-962-2994 (TTY); Fax: 815-758-2053.

Catholic Relief Services—Mr. THOMAS MCKENNA, 555 Colman Center Dr., P.O. Box 7044, Rockford, 61125. Tel: 815-399-4300; Fax: 815-399-6303.

Catholic Social Services—Mr. PATRICK WINN, Dir.; Dr. VIRGINIA DESJARLAIS, Assoc. Dir., Mailing Address: P.O. Box 7044, Rockford, 61125. Tel: 815-399-4300; Fax: 815-399-6303.

Cemeteries—Rev. Msgrs. THOMAS C. BRADY, P.A., V.G., Ph.D., Exec. Dir. (Retired); JOHN C. FRITZ, Asst. Dir.; Dr. WAYNE LENELL, CPA, Ph.D., Admin.; CAROL GIAMBALVO, Dir., 8616 W. State St., Winnebago, 61088. Tel: 815-965-1450; Fax: 815-965-9632.

Censores Librorum—Rev. Msgr. CHARLES W. MCNAMEE, P.A., J.C.L. (Retired); Rev. FRANCIS E. MCDONNELL (Retired).

Charities—Mr. PATRICK WINN, Dir., 1700 N. Farnsworth Ave., Ste. 18, Aurora, 60505. 566 Dundee Ave., Elgin, 60120. 5215 W. Bull Valley Rd., McHenry, 60050.

Clergy Relief Society, Priests' Retirement Committee—Rev. Msgr. DANIEL J. DEUTSCH, V.F., Exec. Sec., 2300 Main St., Batavia, 60510. Tel: 630-879-4750; Fax: 630-879-9502.

Communications—Mrs. PENNY WIEGERT, Dir., 555 Colman Center Dr., P.O. Box 7044, Rockford, 61125. Tel: 815-399-4300; Fax: 815-399-6225.

Conciliation and Arbitration Council—Mrs. ELLEN LYNCH HARRISON, Exec. Sec., 555 Colman Center Dr., P.O. Box 7044, Rockford, 61125. Tel: 815-399-4300; Fax: 815-399-6168.

Council of Catholic Women, Diocesan—Rev. Msgr. THOMAS L. DZIELAK, V.F., Moderator, 708 10th Ave., Rock Falls, 61071. Tel: 815-625-4508; Mrs. PATRICIA WIGHTMAN, 7605 Kemman Rd., Hebron, 60034. Tel: 630-648-2415.

Cursillo Movement—Rev. ROBERT N. SHERRY, Dir., 5211 W. Bull Valley Rd., McHenry, 60050. Tel: 815-385-5673.

Development Office—Mr. DAVID HOUGAN, Dir., 555 Colman Center Dr., P.O. Box 7044, Rockford, 61125. Tel: 815-399-4300; Fax: 815-399-5657.

Divine Worship, Office for— (and RCIA Resources)-- Rev. JOSEPH P. NAILL, M.A., Dir., 881 N. Mongan, Oregon, 61061. Tel: 815-732-7383; Fax: 815-732-4742.

Ecumenism, Office of—Rev. Msgr. THOMAS L. DZIELAK, V.F., 708 Tenth Ave., Rock Falls, 61071. Tel: 815-625-4508; Fax: 815-625-1569.

Education—Mr. MICHAEL KAGAN, Supt. Schools; Mr. JOHN MCGRATH, Dir., Rel. Educ. & Formation, 555 Colman Center Dr., P.O. Box 7044, Rockford, 61125. Tel: 815-399-4300; Fax: 815-399-6278.

Ethicist for Health Care Issues, Diocesan—Rev. KENNETH P. WASILEWSKI, 565 Standish St., Elgin, 60123. Tel: 847-468-6900; Fax: 847-468-6904.

Family Life—LORRIE GRAMER, Dir., Mailing Address: P.O. Box 7044, Rockford, 61125. Tel: 815-399-4300; Fax: 815-399-6303.

Finance and Administration—Dr. WAYNE LENELL, CPA, Ph.D., Dir. Fin. & Admin. Svcs., 555 Colman Center Dr., P.O. Box 7044, Rockford, 61125. Tel: 815-399-4300; Fax: 815-399-5591.

Hispanic Ministry Offices—Rev. Msgr. ARQUIMEDES VALLEJO, J.C.D., 555 Colman Center Dr., P.O. Box 7044, Rockford, 61125. Tel: 815-399-4300; Fax: 815-399-6303. Offices for Diocese Aurora Deanery: Centro Cristo Rey, 115 State St., Aurora, 60505. DeKalb Deanery: Centro Cuerpo de Cristo, 308 Fisk Ave., Dekalb, 60115. Elgin Deanery: Centro Jesus Resucitado, 90 N. Kennedy Dr., Carpentersville, 60110. Freeport Deanery: Centro Jesus Galileo, 21 Burr Oaks Dr., E., Stockton, 61085. McHenry Deanery: St. Thomas the Apostle, 272 King St., Crystal Lake, 60014. Rockford Deanery: P.O. Box 7044, Rockford, 61125. Sterling Deanery: Centro TU C.A.S.A., 202 W. Sixth St., Sterling, 61081.

Holy Childhood Association—VACANT, Dir., 555 Colman Center Dr., P.O. Box 7044, Rockford, 61125. Tel: 815-399-4300; Fax: 815-399-6278.

Immigration Services—Mrs. JEANNE LINDBERG, Dir., 1536 S. Main St., Rockford, 61102. Tel: 815-399-1709; Fax: 815-399-1731.

Investment and Loan—Dr. WAYNE LENELL, CPA, Ph.D., 555 Colman Center Dr., P.O. Box 7044, Rockford, 61125. Tel: 815-399-4300; Fax: 815-399-5591.

Liturgical Commission, Diocesan—Rev. JOSEPH P. NAILL, M.A., Chm., St. Mary, 881 N. Mongan, Oregon, 61061. Tel: 815-732-7383.

Ministry Formation, Office of—Mr. JOHN MCGRATH, Dir., 555 Colman Center Dr., P.O. Box 7044, Rockford, 61125. Tel: 815-399-4300; Fax: 815-399-6278.

Ministry to Priests Program—Very Rev. BRIAN D. GRADY, Vicar, Clergy Sabbaticals and Diocesan Priests' Retreats, 555 Colman Center Dr., P.O. Box 7044, Rockford, 61125. Tel: 815-399-4300; Fax: 815-399-5962.

Newman-Campus Ministry—Rev. Msgr. GLENN L. NELSON, V.G., J.C.L., 512 Normal Rd., DeKalb, 60115. Tel: 815-787-7770; Fax: 815-758-2053.

Newspaper— "The Observer" Mrs. PENNY WIEGERT, Mng. Editor; Rev. Msgr. ERIC R. BARR, V.G., S.T.L., Assoc. Publisher, 555 Colman Center Dr., P.O. Box 7044, Rockford, 61125. Tel: 815-399-4300; Fax: 815-399-6225.

Permanent Diaconate Program Diocesan—Rev. Msgr. WILLIAM H. SCHWARTZ, P.A., S.T.L., Dir., 555 Colman Center, P.O. Box 7044, Rockford, 61125. Tel: 815-399-4300; Fax: 815-399-6303.

Priests' Eucharistic League—Rev. Msgr. THOMAS J. MONAHAN, Ph.D. (Retired), 4295 Ahlstrand Dr., Rockford, 61101. Tel: 815-282-9972.

Priest Personnel—Very Rev. BRIAN D. GRADY, Vicar, Clergy and Religious, 555 Colman Center Dr., P.O. Box 7044, Rockford, 61125. Tel: 815-399-4300; Fax: 815-399-5962.

Pro-Life Activities, Office of—Mr. MITCH STRIEDL, Dir., 555 Colman Center Dr., P.O. Box 7044, Rockford, 61125. Tel: 815-399-4300; Fax: 815-399-5266.

Propagation of the Faith—Rev. Msgr. ROBERT J. SWEENEY, Dir., 555 Colman Center Dr., P.O. Box 7044, Rockford, 61125. Tel: 815-399-4300; Fax: 815-399-4861.

Property Management Office—Mr. BRIAN HEINKEL, Mailing Address: P.O. Box 7044, Rockford, 61125. Tel: 815-399-4300; Fax: 815-399-5657.

Research and Planning—Dr. MICHAEL CIESLAK, Ph.D., Dir., 555 Colman Center Dr., P.O. Box 7044, Rockford, 61125. Tel: 815-399-4300; Fax: 815-399-6225.

Rural Life Conference—Mr. THOMAS MCKENNA, Dir., 555 Colman Center Dr., P.O. Box 7044, Rockford, 61125. Tel: 815-399-4300; Fax: 815-399-6303.

Scouts—Rev. MATTHEW MCMORROW, 4000 St. Francis Dr., Rockford, 61103. Tel: 815-877-0531; Fax: 815-877-2544.

Diocesan Administration Offices—Mrs. GWEN LASHOCK, Bldg. Mgr., 555 Colman Center Dr., P.O. Box 7044, Rockford, 61125. Tel: 815-399-4300; Fax: 815-399-6303.

Unemployment Insurance Office—JUDITH A. CROSS, Mgr., Mailing Address: P.O. Box 7044, Rockford, 61125. Tel: 815-399-4300; Fax: 815-399-5657.

Victim Assistance Coordinator—JOHN MCCOY, M.S.W. Tel: 815-962-9347. Email: chancery99@aol.com.

Vocations—Rev. CARL E. BEEKMAN, Dir., 555 Colman Center Dr., P.O. Box 7044, Rockford, 61125. Tel: 815-399-4300; Fax: 815-399-6085.

CLERGY, PARISHES, MISSIONS AND PAROCHIAL SCHOOLS

CITY OF ROCKFORD

(WINNEBAGO COUNTY)

1—ST. PETER CATHEDRAL (1922) Revs. Carl E. Beekman, Admin.; Jeremy Trowbridge, Parochial Vicar; Deacons Martin Czerniewski; Ronald Magee; Robert Mitchison.

Res.: 1243 N. Church St., 61103. Tel: 815-965-2765; Fax: 815-965-0743.

School—(Grades PreK-8), 1231 N. Court St., 61103. Tel: 815-963-3620; Fax: 815-963-0551. Mr. James Burns, Prin.; Cindy Buffo, Librarian. Lay Teachers 16; Students 228.

Catechesis/Religious Program—Students 90.

2—ST. ANTHONY OF PADUA (1909), (Italian), Revs. James M. Ciaramitaro, O.F.M.Conv.; Robert Melnick, O.F.M.Conv.; Bro. James Dufresne, O.F.M.Conv.

Res.: 1010 Ferguson St., 61102. Tel: 815-965-2761; Fax: 815-968-2798. Email: sainttonys@aol.com. Web: stanthonyrockford.com.

Catechesis/Religious Program—Tel: 815-965-3448. Email: sttonysdre@aol.com. Students 157.

3—ST. BERNADETTE (1957) Revs. Kenneth Stachyra; Joel Lopez; Deacon Richard Gerdeman; Mary Trapani, Business Mgr.; Joan Wagner, Liturgy & Music Dir. In Res., Rev. Msgr. Philip E. O'Neil (Retired); Rev. Pierre G. Polycarpe.

Res.: 2400 Bell Ave., 61103. Tel: 815-968-0904; Fax: 815-987-9476. Web: www.stbernadette.info.

Church: Rockton Ave. & Bell Ave., 61103. Tel: 815-968-0904; Fax: 815-987-9476.

School—2300 Bell Ave., 61103. Tel: 815-968-2288; Fax: 815-987-9453. Mrs. Elizabeth Heitkamp, Prin. Lay Teachers 18; Students 202.

Catechesis/Religious Program—2300 Bell Ave., 61103. Tel: 815-962-7345. Mrs. Judy Rossato, D.R.E. Students 53.

4—ST. EDWARD (1929) Revs. Lorenzo Gonzalez; Anthony Pantyra; Deacon Lambert Verstynen.

Parish Office—3004 11th St., 61109. Tel: 815-229-0282; Fax: 815-229-8912. Web: www.stedwardrockford.org.

Res.: 3026 11th St., 61109. Tel: 815-398-1249.

School—3020 S. 11th St., 61109. Tel: 815-398-2631; Fax: 815-398-3134. Mrs. Cori Gendron, Prin. Lay Teachers 13; Students 199.

Catechesis/Religious Program—Tel: 815-229-8914. Sandra Dettori, D.R.E. Students 587.

5—HOLY FAMILY (1963) Revs. Edward J. Seisser; David Vogel; Andrew T. Mulcahey; Deacons William Bronzi; Michael Cristoforo.

4401 Highcrest Rd., 61107. Tel: 815-398-4280; Fax: 815-398-4287. Web: www.holyfamilyrockford.org.

School—4407 Highcrest Rd., 61107. Tel: 815-398-5331; Fax: 815-398-5902. Web: www.holyfamilyrockford.org. Mrs. Rebecca Schmitt, Prin. Lay Teachers 29; Students 502.

Catechesis/Religious Program—Julie Schwartz, D.R.E. Students 185.

6—ST. JAMES (1853) [JC] Revs. Dean E. Russell; Joachim B. Tyrtania (Poland); Deacon William Dean.

Res.: 428 N. Second St., 61107. Tel: 815-962-1214; Fax: 815-962-1236.

School—(Grades K-8), 409 N. First St., 61107. Tel: 815-962-8515. Mr. John Fitzsimmons, Prin. Lay Teachers 16; Students 230.

Catechesis/Religious Program—Tel: 815-962-5588. Students 65.

7—ST. MARY ORATORY (1997) Rev. Brian Bovee.

Res.: 517 Elm St., 61102. Tel: 815-965-5971; Fax: 815-965-6029. Email: stmaryrockford@institute-christ-king.org. Web: www.institute-christ-king.org.

8—ST. PATRICK (1919) [JC] Rev. Ricardo Hernandez; Deacon Frank Barone.

Res.: 2505 School St., 61101. Tel: 815-965-9539; Fax: 815-965-0086. Email: stpatrickchurchh@tds.net.

Catechesis/Religious Program—Students 180.

9—SS. PETER AND PAUL (1911), (Hispanic), Rev. Zbigniew Zajchowski, O.F.M.Conv. (Poland).

Res.: 617 Lincoln Ave., 61102. Tel: 815-962-7171; Fax: 815-962-5184. Email: zzajchowski@gmail.

10—ST. RITA (1914) Revs. David A. Peck; Ariel A. Valencia; Deacon William Dall.

Res.: 6254 Valley Knoll Dr., 61109-1898. Tel: 815-398-0853; Fax: 815-397-7499. Web: www.stritarockford.org.

School—6284 Valley Knoll Dr., 61109-1898. Tel: 815-398-3466; Fax: 815-398-6104. Email: schooloffice.strita@gmail.com. Patrick Flanagan,

Prin. Lay Teachers 13; Students 276.
Catechesis/Religious Program—Tel: 815-398-6483; Fax: 815-397-7499. Doug Colloton, C.R.E.; Paul Vogrinc, Coord.Youth Ministry. Students 130.

11—ST. STANISLAUS KOSTKA (1912), (Polish), Rev. Edward Staniukiewicz, O.F.M.Conv.; Deacon James Hudzinski.
Res.: 201 Buckbee St., 61104. Tel: 815-965-3913; Fax: 815-965-3915. Email: margaretb@st-stanislaus.org. Web: www.saint-stanislaus.com.
Catechesis/Religious Program—Students 65.

OUTSIDE THE CITY OF ROCKFORD

ALBANY, WHITESIDE CO., ST. PATRICK (1948) Rev. David M. Austin.
Hwy. 84, 61230. Tel: 815-589-3542; 815-589-4915. Email: icsecretary@mchsi.com. Mailing Address: 703 12th Ave., Fulton, 61252.
Catechesis/Religious Program—

ALGONQUIN, MCHENRY CO., ST. MARGARET MARY (1954) Revs. Piotr Sarnicki, O.F.M.Conv.; Piotr Tymko, O.F.M.Conv.; Darek Barna; Deacons Howard Fischer; Simon Grossmayer; Patrick Maher; Donald Miller; Michael LeRoy; James Woeste.
Parish Office—111 S. Hubbard St., 60102. Tel: 847-658-7625; Fax: 847-658-7882. Web: www.saintmargaretmary.org.
School—(Grades PreK-8), 119 S. Hubbard St., 60102. Tel: 847-658-5313; Fax: 847-854-0501. Mrs. Susan Snyder, Prin. Lay Teachers 22; Students 462.
School—*Polish School*, Tel: 224-436-0321. Students 500.
Catechesis/Religious Program—Jr. High/H.S. R.E. Prog.: 113 S. Hubbard St., 60102. Tel: 847-658-7881; Fax: 847-658-2378. Email: teresa@saintmargaretmary.org. Elementary R.E. Prog.: 119 S. Hubbard St., 60102. Tel: 847-658-9339; Fax: 847-854-0501. Email: enelson@saintmargaretmary.org. Mrs. Ellie Nelson, D.R.E.; Mrs. Teresa Chiappone, D.R.E. (Junior High & High School). Students 1,038.

AMBOY, LEE CO., ST. PATRICK (1857) [CEM] Rev. Msgr. Thomas E. Bales; Deacon Kevin Prunty.
Res.: 32 N. Jones Ave., 61310. Tel: 815-857-2315; Fax: 815-857-3485. Email: office@stpatrickamboy.org. Web: stpatrickamboy.org.
Catechesis/Religious Program—Web: www.stpatrickamboy.org. Students 110.

APPLE RIVER, JO DAVIESS CO., ST. JOSEPH (1868) [CEM] Rev. Max J. Striedl, Parochial Admin.
Mailing Address: *c/o St. Ann*, P.O. Box 665, Warren, 61087. Tel: 815-745-2312; Fax: 815-745-2312. Email: parishes@catholic.org.
Res./Rectory: 410 W. Lena St., Lena, 61048. Tel: 815-369-7810.
Church: 107 Webster St., 61001.
Catechesis/Religious Program— Twinned with St. Ann, Warren. Students 14.

AURORA, KANE CO.

1—ANNUNCIATION OF THE BLESSED VIRGIN MARY (1875) [CEM] Rev. Patrick S. Gillmeyer, O.S.B.; Deacons Harold Poss; Michael Giblin.
Res.: 1820 Church Rd., 60505. Tel: 630-851-1436; Fax: 630-851-2435.
School—1840 Church Rd., 60505. Tel: 630-851-4300; Fax: 630-851-4316. Karen Wollwert, Prin. Lay Teachers 10; Students 256.
Catechesis/Religious Program—Tel: 630-851-4300. Students 178.

2—HOLY ANGELS (1892) Rev. Msgr. Martin G. Heinz; Revs. John Earl; Randy Fronek; Deacons Tim White; Tom Hawksworth; Jim Hall.
Mailing Address: 180 S. Russell Ave., 60506.
Res.: 720 Hardin Ave., 60506-4997. Tel: 630-897-1194; Fax: 630-897-1370.
School—720 Kensington Pl., 60506. Tel: 630-897-3613; Fax: 630-897-8233. Mrs. Tonya Forbes, Prin. Lay Teachers 26; Students 522.
Catechesis/Religious Program—Tel: 630-897-1194, Ext. 26. Email: releducation@holy-angels.org. Rose Gatze, D.R.E.; Mimi Steinwart, D.R.E. Students 175.

3—ST. JOSEPH (1899) Rev. Jerome L. Leake; Deacons Thomas Petit; Norbert Szudarski, Pastoral Assoc.
Mailing Address: 722 High St., P.O. Box 4395, 60507. In Res., Rev. Msgr. Robert J. Willhite (Retired).
Res.: 405 St. Joseph Ave., 60505. Tel: 630-844-3780; Fax: 630-844-1338. Email: stjoe722@sbcglobal.net. Web: www.stjosephaurora.4lpi.com.
School—706 High St., 60505. Tel: 630-844-3781; Fax: 630-844-3656. Ms. Nancy Coughlin, Prin. Lay Teachers 16; Students 180.
Catechesis/Religious Program—Tel: 630-844-3782. Students 61.

4—ST. MARY (1851), (Irish), Rev. Timothy Piasecki.
Res.: 430 E. Downer Pl., 60505-3475. Tel: 630-892-0480; Fax: 630-892-8664.
Catechesis/Religious Program—*Aurora Deanery Center for Religious Education*, 432 E. Downer Pl., 60505. Tel: 630-859-3922; Fax: 630-859-9637. Email: auroraareacenter@sbcglobal.net; stmary432@yahoo.com. Students 150.

5—ST. NICHOLAS (1862), (Hispanic), [CEM] Revs. Andres Salinas; Juan Arciniegas.
Res. & Mailing Address: 308 High St., 60505. Tel: 630-898-8707; Fax: 630-585-6423. Email: stnicholascatholicaurora@yahoo.com.
Catechesis/Religious Program—Tel: 630-898-8707; Fax: 630-585-6423. Mrs. Kathy Jack, D.R.E. Students 702.

6—OUR LADY OF GOOD COUNSEL (1909) Revs. David R. Engbarth; Ruben Herrera, Pastoral Assoc.; Deacons Carlos Navarro; Ray Weaver.
Res.: 620 S. Fifth St., 60505. Tel: 630-851-1100; Fax: 630-851-4069. Email: olgcchurch@aol.com. Web: www.ourladyofgoodcounsel.net.
School—601 Talma St., 60505. Tel: 630-851-4400; Fax: 630-851-8220. Mr. Mick Swanson, Prin. Students 222.
Catechesis/Religious Program—Tel: 630-851-1100; Fax: 630-851-4069. Students 421.

7—ST. PETER (1929) Rev. Antoni Kretowicz (Poland); Deacon Carlos Navarro.
Res.: 925 Sard Ave., 60506. Tel: 630-896-6816; Fax: 630-896-2534. Email: stpeter-aurora@rockforddiocese.org.
School—915 Sard Ave., 60506. Tel: 630-892-1283; Fax: 630-892-4836. Sr. Ann Brummel, O.P., Prin. Sisters 3; Lay Teachers 6; Students 141.
Catechesis/Religious Program—Students 53.

8—ST. RITA OF CASCIA (1927) Revs. Cesar C. Pajarillo; Louis Busemeyer, S.J.
Res.: 750 W. Old Indian Trail Rd., 60506. Tel: 630-892-5918; Fax: 630-892-6273. Web: www.saintritaofcascia.org.
School—770 W. Old Indian Trail Rd., 60506. Tel: 630-892-0020; Fax: 630-892-4236. Ms. Elizabeth Faxon, Prin. Lay Teachers 18; Students 245.
Catechesis/Religious Program—Tel: 630-892-9507. Sr. Rita Mary Phalen, O.S.F., D.R.E. Students 572.

9—SACRED HEART (1861), (Hispanic), [CEM] Rev. Msgr. Arquimedes Vallejo; Rev. William Tunarosa.
Res.: 771 Fulton St., 60505. Tel: 630-898-4165; Fax: 630-898-3940.
Catechesis/Religious Program—771 Fulton St., 60505. Tel: 630-499-4023; Fax: 630-898-3940. Students 232.

10—ST. THERESE OF JESUS (1925) Rev. Michael I. Miller, M.S.C.; Deacons Bruce M. Watermann; Julio Rosado.
Res.: 271 N. Farnsworth Ave., 60505. Tel: 630-898-5422; Fax: 630-898-5327. Email: stthereseaurora@sbcglobal.net. Web: www.sttheresaaurora.41pi.com.
School—255 N. Farnsworth Ave., 60505. Tel: 630-898-0620; Fax: 630-898-3087. Mrs. Annise Hawkinson, Prin. Lay Teachers 7; Students 52.
Catechesis/Religious Program—Tel: 630-898-5422; Fax: 630-898-5327. Students 575.

BATAVIA, KANE CO., HOLY CROSS (1871) [JC] Rev. Msgr. Daniel J. Deutsch; Revs. Keith D. Romke; John R. Evans; Deacons Raymond J. Martin; Larry Motyka; William A. Stankevitz; William L. Jacobson, Business Mgr.; Karen A. Mc Quillan, Early Teen Minister.
2300 Main St., 60510-7625. Tel: 630-879-4750; Fax: 630-879-9502. Email: staff@holycross-batavia.org. Web: www.holycross-batavia.org.
Rectory—
School—Tel: 630-593-5290; Fax: 630-593-5289. Tricia H. Weis, Prin. Students 355.
Catechesis/Religious Program—(2008)Tel: 630-879-4751. Patricia A. Roatch, Children's Minister; Jennifer A. Haviland, Early Teen Youth Minister; Patrick B. Haviland, H.S. Youth Minister. Students 1,436.

BELVIDERE, BOONE CO., ST. JAMES (1886) [CEM] Revs. Brian A. Geary; Diego Ospina; Deacon James D. Olson.
Office: 535 Caswell St., 61008. Tel: 815-547-6397; Fax: 815-547-0607. Web: stjamesbelvidere.org.
Res.: 514 Caswell St., 61008. Tel: 815-547-6397.
School—320 Logan Ave., 61008. Tel: 815-547-7633; Fax: 815-544-2294. Mr. Gregory Wilhelm, Prin. Lay Teachers 13; Students 171.
Catechesis/Religious Program—Tel: 815-544-3698. Judith Cadie, D.R.E. Students 695.

BYRON, OGLE CO., ST. MARY (1895) [CEM] Rev. Howard C. Barch.
.P.O. Box 1070, 61010. Tel: 815-234-7431; Fax: 815-234-2133.
Catechesis/Religious Program—Joetta Hass, C.R.E.; Beth Hildreth, C.R.E. Students 244.

CARPENTERSVILLE, KANE CO., ST. MONICA (1957), (Hispanic), Rev. Josue Lara, Parochial Admin.; Deacon Dennis Garber.
Res.: 90 N. Kennedy Dr., 60110-1695. Tel: 847-428-2646; Fax: 847-428-1021. Email: saintmonica@sbcglobal.net. Web: www.saintmonicacville.org.
Catechesis/Religious Program—Tel: 847-428-7562. Mary Helin, D.R.E. Students 817.

CARY, MCHENRY CO., SS. PETER & PAUL (1904) Revs. Stephen St. Jules; Joseph Jaskierny; Deacons Howard Ganschow II; Michael Boyce; Michael O'Connor.
Res.: 410 N. First St., 60013. Tel: 847-516-2636; Fax: 847-639-3474. Email: info@ssppcary.org. Web: www.peterpaulchurchcary.org.
School—416 N. First St., 60013. Tel: 847-639-3041; Fax: 847-639-5329. Email: dstrzelinski@ssppcary.org. Sr. Katrina Lamkin, O.P., Prin. Dominican Sisters 1; Lay Teachers 25; Students 493.
Catechesis/Religious Program—Tel: 847-639-0414; Fax: 847-639-5329. Email: tzbylut@ssppcary.org. Terri Zbylut, D.R.E. Students 843.

CRYSTAL LAKE, MCHENRY CO.

1—ST. ELIZABETH ANN SETON (1978) Very Rev. Brian D. Grady; Revs. Bernard J. Sehr; Christopher P. Di Tomo; Tricia Westhoven, Business Mgr.
Office: 1023 McHenry Ave., 60014. Tel: 815-459-3033; Fax: 815-459-3040. Email: parish.office@elizabethannseton.org. Web: www.elizabethannseton.org.
Res.: 991 McHenry Ave., 60014. Tel: 815-788-0062.
Catechesis/Religious Program—Tel: 815-459-3096; Fax: 815-459-3040. Vicky Serio, C.R.E.; Denise Ramis, Youth Min. Students 886.

2—ST. THOMAS THE APOSTLE (1881) Rev. Msgr. Daniel J. Hermes; Revs. Akan S. Simon; Rafael Tunarosa; Jerome Koutnik.
Res.: 200 Washington St., 60014. Tel: 815-455-5407; Fax: 815-455-2733.
Pastoral Center—272 King St., 60014. Tel: 815-455-5400; Fax: 815-455-2733.
School—(Grades PreK-8), 265 King St., 60014. Tel: 815-459-0496; Fax: 815-459-0591. Mrs. Deanne Roy, Prin. Lay Teachers 25; Students 367.
Catechesis/Religious Program—Tel: 815-455-9787. Charlotte Kolodzik, D.R.E. Students 1,095.

DEKALB, DEKALB CO.

1—CHRIST THE TEACHER, UNIVERSITY PARISH OF NORTHERN ILLINOIS UNIVERSITY (1963) Rev. Msgr. Glenn L. Nelson, Dir.; Revs. Alejandro del Toro; Matthew J. Camaioni; Deacon James Dombek.
Office: 512 Normal Rd., 60115. Tel: 815-787-7770; Fax: 815-758-2053. Email: parishoffice@newmanniu.org. Web: www.newmanniu.org.
Catechesis/Religious Program—Email: newmanniudre@gmail.com. Web: www.newmanniu.org. Mrs. Cheryl Lehman, D.R.E. Students 380.

2—ST. MARY (1861) [CEM] Revs. Kenneth J. Anderson (CHI); Saul E. Cruz. In Res., Rev. Anthony Vu Khac Long; Deacon Stephen Puscas.
Office: 302 Fisk Ave., 60115. Tel: 815-758-5432; Fax: 815-758-2487. Email: mail@stmarydekalb.org. Web: www.stmarydekalb.org.
Res.: 321 Pine St., 60115. Tel: 815-748-5654.
School—210 Gurler Rd., 60115. Tel: 815-756-7905; Fax: 815-758-1459. Patricia Weis, Prin. Lay Teachers 18; Students 231.
Catechesis/Religious Program—Tel: 815-758-8504. Students 188.

DIXON, LEE CO.

1—ST. ANNE (1928) Rev. Michael E. Morrissey, Admin.
Res.: 1104 N. Brinton Ave., 61021. Tel: 815-288-3131; Fax: 815-288-3139.
School—(Grades PreK-8), 1112 N. Brinton Ave., 61021. Tel: 815-288-5619; Fax: 815-288-5820. Sr. Marcianne Bzdon, S.S.N.D., Prin. Lay Teachers 15; Students 104.
Catechesis/Religious Program—Tel: 815-288-3131; Fax: 815-288-3139. Students 104.
Convent—926 N. Brinton Ave., 61021.

2—ST. PATRICK (1854) Rev. John Gow; Deacons Sam Berard; Terry Wagner.
Office: 612 Highland Ave., 61021. Tel: 815-284-7719; Fax: 815-284-4758. Email: stpatdixon@essexl.com. Web: www.stpatrickdixon.org.
School—*St. Mary Elementary & Junior High*, (Grades PreK-8), 704 S. Peoria Ave., 61021. Tel: 815-284-6986; Fax: 815-284-6905. Email: st_marysschool@comcast.net. Web: www.stmarysdixon.org. Mrs. Jean Spohn, Prin. Lay Teachers 14; Students 217.
Catechesis/Religious Program—Tel: 815-284-2867; Fax: 815-284-4758. Mrs. Molly Smith, D.R.E. Students 55.

DUNDEE, KANE CO., ST. CATHERINE OF SIENA (1912) Revs. Michael G. Lavan, Parochial Admin.; James C. Canova; Deacons William Whitehead Jr.; Steven Fox; Hank Schmalen.
Office: 845 W. Main St., 60118. Tel: 847-426-2217; Fax: 847-426-1130.
School—(Grades PreK-8) Tel: 847-426-4808; Fax: 847-426-0437. Renee Link, Prin. Lay Teachers 16; Students 244.
Catechesis/Religious Program—Roberta Bellock, D.R.E.; Jessica Cranston, Youth Min. Students 671.

Mission—St. Mary [CEM] c/o 845 W. Main St., West Dundee, Kane Co. 60118.

DURAND, WINNEBAGO CO., ST. MARY (1862), (Irish), [CEM 2] Rev. Msgr. Eric R. Barr; Deacons Richard Mulcahey; Steven Pulkrabek.
Mailing Address: 606 W. Main St., 61024. Tel: 815-248-2490; Fax: 815-248-9100.
Catechesis/Religious Program—Students 142.
Mission—St. Patrick [CEM] Irish Grove Rd., Stephenson Co.

EAST DUBUQUE, JO DAVIESS CO., ST. MARY (1868) [JC] Revs. James W. Parker; Michael T. Barry, Parochial Vicar; Deacons Douglas Kremer; Anthony Keppler.
Res.: 170 Montgomery Ave., 61025. Tel: 815-747-3221; Fax: 815-747-3212. Email: stmaryeastdubuque@yahoo.com. Web: www.stmaryedbq.org.
School—701 Rte. 35 N., 61025. Tel: 815-747-3010; Fax: 815-747-6188. Web: www.stmary-ed.org. Mrs. Wendi Kletecka, Prin. Lay Teachers 5; Students 90.
Catechesis/Religious Program—Daisy Bauman, C.R.E. Students 70.

ELBURN, KANE CO., ST. GALL (1870), (Irish), [CEM] Rev. Karl P. Ganss.
Res.: 120 W. Shannon, 60119. Tel: 630-365-6030; Fax: 630-365-5483. Email: parishoffice@stgall.com. Web: www.stgall.com.
Catechesis/Religious Program—Tel: 630-365-9166; Fax: 630-365-9166. Students 270.

ELGIN, KANE CO.

1—ST. JOSEPH (1887), (German—Spanish), Revs. Jesus Dominguez; Leonardo Maldonado; Adalberto Sanchez; Deacon Armando Martinez.
Res.: 272 Division St., 60120. Tel: 847-931-2800; Fax: 847-931-2810.
School—274 Division St., 60120. Tel: 847-931-2804; Fax: 847-931-2811. Mr. Rafael Villagomez, Prin. Lay Teachers 10; Students 196.
Catechesis/Religious Program—Tel: 847-931-2808; 847-931-2800, Ext. 127. Students 1,246.

2—ST. LAURENCE (1929) Rev. Kenneth P. Wasilewski.
Office: 565 Standish St., 60123. Tel: 847-468-6900; Fax: 847-468-6904.
Res.: 226 Orchard St., 60123. Tel: 224-535-8815.
School—(Grades PreK-8), 572 Standish St., 60123. Tel: 847-468-6100; Fax: 847-468-6104. Mrs. Phyllis Jensen, Prin. Lay Teachers 14; Students 179.
Catechesis/Religious Program—Tel: 847-468-6900; Fax: 847-468-6104. Students 159.

3—ST. MARY (1851) Revs. James R. Keenan; Jorge H. Loaiza; David Reese; Deacons Henry Orlik; Loc Nguyen.
Parish Office—397 Fulton St., 60120. Tel: 847-888-2828; Fax: 847-888-2883. Web: www.stmaryelgin.com.
Res.: 390 Fulton St., 60120. Tel: 847-888-0502.
School—(Grades K-8), 103 S. Gifford St., 60120. Tel: 847-695-6609; Fax: 847-695-6623. Mr. Carl Koester, Prin. Lay Teachers 12; Students 211.
Catechesis/Religious Program—Tel: 847-888-2718; Fax: 847-888-2883. Students 179.

4—ST. THOMAS MORE (1959) [JC] Revs. Geoffrey D. Wirth; Kevin M. Butler; Deacons Jack Roder; Gregory Stevens. In Res., Rev. Andrew J. Plesa (Retired).
Office: 215 Thomas More Dr., 60123. Tel: 847-888-1682; Fax: 847-888-3198.
School—1625 W. Highland Ave., 60123. Tel: 847-742-3959; Fax: 847-931-1066. Ms. Margaret Fabrizius, Prin. Lay Teachers 16; Students 271.
Catechesis/Religious Program—Tel: 847-888-4887. Mr. Ron Becker, D.R.E. Students 726.

ELIZABETH, JO DAVIESS CO., ST. MARY (1886) [CEM] Rev. Leonardo M. Jacob.
Res.: 112 E. Washington St., P.O. Box 246, 61028. Tel: 815-858-3422; Fax: 815-858-2622. Email: st_mary@jcwifi.com. Web: www.stmarysch.org.
Catechesis/Religious Program— Norma Schwirtz, D.R.E. Students 27.

FREEPORT, STEPHENSON CO.

1—ST. CATHERINE, Closed. For inquiries for parish records contact the chancery.

2—ST. JOSEPH (1862), (German), [CEM] Rev. Timothy J. Barr.
Res.: 229 W. Washington Pl., 61032. Tel: 815-232-8271; Fax: 815-235-4690. Email: stjosephfreeport@comcast.net.
School—Aquin Elementary School, 202 W. Pleasant St., 61032. Tel: 815-232-6416. Mrs. Kathy Runte, Prin.; Mrs. Diane Potts, Admin. & Prin. Lay Teachers 7; Students 196.
Catechesis/Religious Program—Tel: 815-235-4324. Students 51.

3—ST. MARY (1846) [CEM] Rev. Timothy J. Barr.
704 S. State Ave., 61032.
Office & Res.: 229 W. Washington Place, 61032. Tel: 815-232-8271; Fax: 815-233-0005; 815-235-4690 (Res.).
Catechesis/Religious Program— (Freeport Catholic School System) Students 47.

4—ST. THOMAS AQUINAS (1921) Rev. Msgr. P. William McDonnell; Rev. Arturo O. Mallari; Deacons H. Donald Brunette; Richard Dinneen; Vincent Drees; Michael Jones; Stephen Pospischil.
Res.: 1400 Kiwanis Dr., 61032. Tel: 815-232-3225; Fax: 815-232-3231. Email: stthomas9@frontier.com. Web: www.stthomas-freeport.com.
Catechesis/Religious Program—Tel: 815-232-3225; Fax: 815-232-3231. Marie Dinneen, C.R.E.; Julie Dorsey, C.R.E. Students 95.

FULTON, WHITESIDE CO., IMMACULATE CONCEPTION (1863) Rev. David M. Austin.
Res.: 703 12th Ave., 61252. Tel: 815-589-3542; Fax: 815-589-4915. Email: ICSecretary@mchsi.com.
Catechesis/Religious Program—Students 60.

GALENA, JO DAVIESS CO.

1—ST. MARY (1850), (German), [CEM] Revs. Christopher J. Kuhn; Stanislaw Kos.
Res.: 406 Franklin St., 61036. Tel: 815-777-0134; Fax: 815-776-0138.
Catechesis/Religious Program—Tel: 815-541-2312. Stefanie Karberg, C.R.E. Students 117.

2—ST. MICHAEL (1832), (Irish), [CEM] Rev. Christopher J. Kuhn.
Res.: 227 S. Bench St., 61036. Tel: 815-777-2053; Fax: 815-777-1193.
Catechesis/Religious Program— Cindy Kocol, D.R.E. Students 86.

GENEVA, KANE CO., ST. PETER (1911) [JC] Revs. Martins Emeh; Michael Chernetzki; Deacons Michael Zibrun; Michael Sullivan.
Office: 1891 Kaneville Rd., 60134. Tel: 630-232-0124; Fax: 630-232-9262. Email: writetostpeter@stpetergeneva.org. Web: www.stpeterchurch.com.
Res.: 1771 Kaneville Rd., 60134.
School—(Grades PreK-8), 1881 Kaneville Rd., 60134. Tel: 630-232-0476; Fax: 630-208-5681. Mrs. Roseann Feldmann, Prin. Lay Teachers 25; Students 507.
Catechesis/Religious Program— Miss Nicole Billapando, C.R.E. Students 1,346.

GENOA, DEKALB CO., ST. CATHERINE OF GENOA (1912) [CEM] Rev. Timothy J. Seigel.
Res.: 350 S. Stott St., 60135. Tel: 815-784-2355; Fax: 815-784-2045. Web: www.st-catherine-genoa.org.
Catechesis/Religious Program—Email: alaisa340@atcyber.net. Alaisa Emmens, C.R.E. Students 212.

GILBERTS, KANE CO., ST. MARY'S MISSION OF GILBERTS, [CEM] Revs. Michael G. Lavan, Parochial Admin.; James C. Canova; Deacons William Whitehead Jr.; Steven Fox; Hank Schmalen.
Mailing Address: 845 W. Main St., Dundee, 60118. 10 Matteson Rd., 60136.

HAMPSHIRE, KANE CO., ST. CHARLES BORROMEO (1878) [CEM] Rev. Sylvester A. Nnaso.
Res.: 297 E. Jefferson Ave., 60140-7646. Tel: 847-683-2391; Fax: 847-683-2396. Email: parishoffice@scbparish.org. Web: www.scbparish.org.
School—(Grades PreK-8), 288 E. Jefferson Ave., 60140. Tel: 847-683-3450; Fax: 847-683-3209. Email: scbschool@scbparish.org. Kel Kissamis, Prin. Lay Teachers 14; Students 179.
Catechesis/Religious Program—297 E. Jefferson Ave., 60140. Tel: 847-683-1536. Email: CVincent@scbparish.org. Mrs. Cynthia Vincent, D.R.E. Students 197.

HANOVER, JO DAVIESS CO., ST. JOHN THE EVANGELIST (1925) [JC] Rev. Leonardo M. Jacob.
Res.: 103 Savanna Rd., 61041. Tel: 815-591-2258; Fax: 815-591-3533. Email: st_john@jcwifi.com. Web: www.stjohnsch.org.
Catechesis/Religious Program—Tel: 815-591-2258. Students 19.

HARMON, LEE CO., ST. FLANNEN (1898), (Irish), [CEM] Rev. Msgr. Thomas E. Bales.
Res.: 32 N. Jones Ave., Amboy, 61310. Tel: 815-857-2670; Fax: 815-857-3485. Web: www.stpatrickamboy.org/office.
Catechesis/Religious Program—Tel: 815-857-2670; Fax: 815-857-3485. Twinned with St. Patrick Amboy

HARTLAND, MCHENRY CO., ST. PATRICK (1837) [CEM] Rev. Thomas J. Doyle; Deacons Arthur Holt; Joseph Kayser.
Parish Office—15012 St. Patrick Rd., Woodstock, 60098. Tel: 815-338-7883; Fax: 815-338-5570.
Catechesis/Religious Program—Tel: 815-338-5570.

HARVARD, MCHENRY CO., ST. JOSEPH (1866) [CEM] Rev. Paul C. White; Deacons Anthony Koss; Phillip Emmert.
Res.: 206 E. Front St., 60033. Tel: 815-943-6406; Fax: 815-943-1604. Email: pmc@stjoeharvard.org.
School—(Grades PreK-8), 201 N. Division St., 60033. Tel: 815-943-6933; Fax: 815-943-0549. Email: principal@stjoeharvard.org. Mr. Michael J. Shukis, Prin. Lay Teachers 5; Students 74.
Catechesis/Religious Program—Tel: 815-943-1644; Fax: 815-943-1604. Amber Emmert, D.R.E. Students 117.

HUNTLEY, MCHENRY CO., ST. MARY (1873) [CEM] Rev. Msgr. Stephen J. Knox; Revs. Jonathan Bakkelund; W. Scott DuVall; Deacons Thomas W. O'Brien; Armand Ferrini; Policarpo Jimenez; Anthony Schubert; John A. McPhee; Louis Farinella; George Coltman; Mr. Thomas O'Brien, Pastoral Assoc.
Res. & Mailing Address: 10307 Dundee Rd., 60142. Tel: 847-669-3137; Fax: 847-669-3138. Web: www.stmaryhuntley.org.
Catechesis/Religious Program—Students 1,637.

JOHNSBURG, MCHENRY CO., ST. JOHN THE BAPTIST (1841) [CEM] Rev. Jacek Junak, C.R.; Deacon Jerry Giessinger.
Res.: 2302 W. Church St., 60051. Tel: 815-385-1477; Fax: 815-363-3333.
School—(Grades PreK-8), 2304 W. Church St., 60051. Tel: 815-385-3959; Fax: 815-363-3337. Pamela Dvonch, Prin. Sisters 1; Lay Teachers 10; Students 147.
Catechesis/Religious Program—Tel: 815-385-4870. Charlotte Phillips, D.R.E. Students 316.

LEE, LEE CO., ST. JAMES (1878) [CEM 2] Rev. Bonaventure Okoro (Nigeria).
221 W. Kirke Gate, P.O. Box 100, 60530.
Res.: 321 S. Viking Vie, 60530. Tel: 815-824-2004; 815-824-2053 (Office); Fax: 815-824-2043 (Office). Email: stjames@heartlandcable.com.
Catechesis/Religious Program—Tel: 815-824-2053. Students 57.

LENA, STEPHENSON CO., ST. JOSEPH (1870) [CEM] Rev. Max J. Striedl, Parochial Admin.
Res.: 410 W. Lena St., 61048. Tel: 815-369-2810; Fax: 815-369-9137. Email: stjoseph@aeroinc.net. Students 63.
Catechesis/Religious Program—Tel: 815-369-2810. Teresa Brown, C.R.E. Students 58.

LOVES PARK, WINNEBAGO CO., ST. BRIDGET (1946) Revs. Burt H. Absalon; Brian A. Olsen; Deacons Philip Abel; William Riseley. In Res., Rev. Msgr. Arquimedes Vallejo.
Res.: 600 Clifford Ave., 61111. Tel: 815-633-6311; Fax: 815-633-6314.
School—(Grades PreK-8), 604 Clifford Ave., 61111. Tel: 815-633-8255; Fax: 815-633-5847. Web: www.saint-bridget.org. Mrs. Mary Toldo, Prin.; Mrs. Linda Lynch, Librarian. Religious 1; Lay Teachers 22; Students 386.
Catechesis/Religious Program—Tel: 815-633-4006. Students 27.

MAPLE PARK, DEKALB CO., ST. MARY (1850) [CEM 2] Rev. Dennis M. Morrissy, Parochial Admin.
Res.: 123 S. County Line Rd., 60151-8024. Tel: 815-827-3218.
Novak Center—211 S. County Line Rd., 60151-8024. Tel: 815-827-3205; Fax: 815-827-3062.
Catechesis/Religious Program—Tel: 815-827-3205; Fax: 815-827-3062. Students 93.

MARENGO, MCHENRY CO., SACRED HEART (1902) [CEM] Rev. Richard M. Russo; Deacons Robert Anchor; John O'Leary.
Res.: 323 N. Taylor St., 60152. Tel: 815-568-7878; Fax: 815-568-7929. Email: sacredheart7929@sbcglobal.net. Web: www.sacredheartmarengo.4lpi.com.
Catechesis/Religious Program—Tel: 815-568-6230; Fax: 815-568-7929. Susan Wilkening, C.R.E.; Brenda Ramus, C.R.E. Students 258.

MAYTOWN, LEE CO., ST. PATRICK (1840) [CEM] [JC 2] Rev. Max Lasrado.
Res.: 32 N. Jones Ave., Amboy, 61310. Tel: 815-857-2670; Fax: 815-857-3485. Web: www.stpatrickamboy.org/office.
Catechesis/Religious Program—Students 124.

MCHENRY, MCHENRY CO.

1—CHURCH OF HOLY APOSTLES (1989) [CEM] Revs. Robert N. Sherry; Oscar Cortes; Deacons Joseph Phelan; Curtis Fiedler.
Church: 5211 W. Bull Valley Rd., 60050. Tel: 815-385-5673; Fax: 815-385-6045. Email: hapostles@thechurchofholyapostles.org. Web: www.thechurchofholyapostles.org.
Catechesis/Religious Program—Tel: 815-385-4273. Jeanne Fraser, D.R.E. Students 620.

2—ST. MARY (1894), (German), [CEM] Rev. Robert A. Balog.
Res.: 1401 N. Richmond Rd., 60050. Tel: 815-385-0024; Fax: 815-385-7809. Email: stmarylady@aol.com.
School—Montini-Middle Grades, 1405 N. Richmond Rd., 60050. Tel: 815-385-1022; Fax: 815-363-7536. Mrs. Sheila Murphy, Prin. Consolidated with St. Patrick and Church of Holy Apostles. Lay Teachers 17; Students 221.
Catechesis/Religious Program—1407 N. Richmond Rd., 60050. Tel: 815-385-2135. Mrs. Kimberly Schaefer, D.R.E. Students 60.

3—ST. PATRICK (1840), (Irish), [CEM 2] Rev. Godwin Nsikan-Ubom Asuguo, Parochial Admin.; Jerri-Lynn Welch, Pastoral Assoc.

Res.: 3425 W. Washington St., 60050. Tel: 815-385-0025; Fax: 815-385-0861. Email: parishoffice@stpatrickmchenry.org. Web: www.stpatrickmchenry.org.
School—Montini Catholic School, Tel: 815-385-1022; Fax: 815-363-7536. Mrs. Sheila Murphy, Prin.; Mrs. Marilyn Knapp, Asst. Prin. Lay Teachers 27; Students 377.
Catechesis/Religious Program—Tel: 815-385-2959; Fax: 815-385-0861. Students 178.

MENOMINEE, JO DAVIESS CO., NATIVITY OF THE BLESSED VIRGIN MARY (1864), (German), [CEM] Revs. James W. Parker; Michael T. Barry; Deacons Douglas Kremer; Anthony Keppler.
Res.: 170 Montgomery Ave, East Dubuque, 61025. Fax: 815-747-3212. Email: nativitynativity@hotmail.com. Web: www.nativity-bvm.com.
Church: 15406 W. Creek Valley Rd., East Dubuque, 61025. Tel: 815-747-3670; Fax: 815-747-2050.
Catechesis/Religious Program—

MORRISON, WHITESIDE CO., ST. MARY (1904) Rev. William R. Antillon.
Office: 13320 Garden Plain Rd., 61270. Tel: 815-772-3095 (Rectory); 815-772-4890 (Church Office); Fax: 815-772-4890. Email: stmarymor@frontiernet.net.
Res.: 611 Greenwood Dr., 61270. Tel: 815-772-3095; Fax: 815-772-4890. Email: william_antillon@yahoo.com.
Catechesis/Religious Program—Tel: 815-772-4890. Students 41.

MOUNT CARROLL, CARROLL CO., SS. JOHN AND CATHERINE (1923) Attended by Savanna. Rev. Dennis D. Atto.
Res.: 314 S. Main St., P.O. Box 193, 61053. Tel: 815-244-1835 (Church); Fax: 815-244-1835. Web: www.ssjohncatherinech.org.
Catechesis/Religious Program—Fax: 815-244-1835. Students 30.

NORTH AURORA, KANE CO., BLESSED SACRAMENT CATHOLIC CHURCH (1970) Revs. John A. Slampak; David C. Finn.
Res.: 801 Oak St., 60542-1063. Tel: 630-897-1029; Fax: 630-897-1062. Email: blesacra@sbcglobal.net. Web: http://blessedsacrament-na.org.
Catechesis/Religious Program—Tel: 630-897-4396. Sr. Rose Marie Weber, O.S.F., D.R.E. Students 308.

OREGON, OGLE CO., ST. MARY (1885) [CEM] Rev. Joseph P. Naill.
Res. & Rectory: 303 N. 4th St., 61061. Email: st.marys.rectory@comcast.net. Web: www.st-mary-parish.com.
Catechesis/Religious Program—Tel: 815-732-7383; 815-973-5602; Fax: 815-732-4742. Students 80.

PECATONICA, WINNEBAGO CO., ST. MARY (1872), (Irish—German), [CEM] Rev. Msgr. Robert J. Sweeney; Deacons Warren LaMont; Michael Giambalvo.
Res.: 126 W. Fifth St., P.O. Box 656, 61063. Tel: 815-239-1271; Fax: 815-239-1271.
Catechesis/Religious Program—Students 117.

POLO, OGLE CO., ST. MARY'S (1854) [CEM] [JC] Rev. Louis F. Tosto.
Res.: 211 N. Franklin Ave., 61064. Tel: 815-946-2535; Fax: 815-946-9025. Email: stmary-polo@rockforddiocese.org.
Catechesis/Religious Program—Fax: 815-946-9025. Students 47.

PROPHETSTOWN, WHITESIDE CO., ST. CATHERINE (1917) Rev. Zdzislaw F. Wawryszuk.
Res.: 308 E. Third St., 61277. Tel: 815-537-2077; Fax: 815-537-2077. Email: stcatherine@mchsi.com.
Catechesis/Religious Program—Tel: 815-537-5731. Tani Bauer, C.R.E. Students 12.
Mission—St. Ambrose [JC] P.O Box 746, Erie, Whiteside Co. 61250. Tel: 309-659-2781 (Tuesdays Only); 815-537-2077.
Catechesis/Religious Program—Students 20.

RICHMOND, MCHENRY CO., ST. JOSEPH (1899), (German), [CEM] Rev. Andrew Lewandowski, C.R.; Deacon Albert Dietz.
Res.: 10519 Main St., 60071. Tel: 815-678-7421; Fax: 815-678-6961. Email: saintjosephchurch@gmail.com.
Catechesis/Religious Program—Tel: 815-678-4720. Laura Wisinski, C.R.E. Students 113.

ROCHELLE, OGLE CO., ST. PATRICK (1868) [CEM] Revs. Steven J. Lange; William Vallejo.
Res.: 250 Kelley Dr., 61068. Tel: 815-562-2370; Fax: 815-562-5250. Email: stpats7@gmail.com. Web: www.stpatricks.rochelle.net.
Catechesis/Religious Program—Tel: 815-561-0079. Kalah Williams, D.R.E. Students 275.

ROCK FALLS, WHITESIDE CO., ST. ANDREW (1950) [JC] Rev. Msgr. Thomas L. Dzielak.
Res.: 708 10th Ave., 61071. Tel: 815-625-4508; Fax: 815-625-1569. Email: standrews.church@comcast.net.
School—(Grades PreK-8), 701 11th Ave., 61071. Tel: 815-625-1456; Fax: 815-625-1724. Email: standrewsgrad@comcast.net. Mr. Norb Rozanski, Prin.; Tiffany Clark-Grove, Librarian. Lay Teachers 10; Students 200.
Catechesis/Religious Program—Tel: 815-625-4508. Students 59.

SAINT CHARLES, KANE CO.

1—ST. JOHN NEUMANN (1977) Revs. Richard A. Rosinski; Andrew Skrobutt; Deacons Tom Elms; Paul Iwanski; Ronald Williams.
Res.: 2900 E. Main St., 60174. Tel: 630-377-2797; Fax: 630-377-2834.
Catechesis/Religious Program—Tel: 630-377-2803. Jan Donovan, D.R.E.; Joe Weyers, H.S. Youth Min. Students 927.

2—ST. PATRICK (1851) Rev. Msgr. Joseph B. Linster; Revs. Jorge H. Loaiza; Moises Apostol; Slawomir Zimodro.
Res. & Office: 6N487 Crane Rd., 60175. Tel: 630-338-8000; Fax: 630-338-8008.
Church (downtown): 400 Cedar St., 60174. Church: 6N491 Crane Rd., 60175.
School—Preschool, (Extended Day Care), 118 N. Fifth St., 60174. Tel: 630-338-8200; Fax: 630-338-8208. Sr. Maria I. Garza, Dir. Lay Teachers 3; Students 64.
School—787 Crane Rd, 60175. Tel: 630-338-8100; Fax: 630-338-8108. Mr. Joseph Battisto, Prin. Sisters 2; Lay Teachers 29; Students 529.
Catechesis/Religious Program—Tel: 630-338-8160; Fax: 630-338-8168. Patrice Spirou, D.R.E.; Jerome Ryndak, D.R.E. Students 2,044.

SANDWICH, DEKALB CO., ST. PAUL THE APOSTLE (1910) [CEM] Rev. Andrew C. Hougan.
Mailing Address: 110 N. Eddy St., 60548.
Office & Parish Center: 340 W. Arnold Rd., 60548. Tel: 815-786-9266; Fax: 815-786-2977. Email: stpaulssandwich@aol.com.
Rectory—505 W. Lisbon St., 60548.
Catechesis/Religious Program—Tel: 815-786-2004. Students 174.

SAVANNA, CARROLL CO., ST. JOHN THE BAPTIST (1884) [CEM] Rev. Dennis D. Atto.
Res.: 318 Chicago Ave., 61074. Tel: 815-273-3961; Fax: 815-273-3503. Email: sjboffice@centurylink.net. Web: www.stjohnbaptistch.org.
Catechesis/Religious Program—Students 38.

SCALES MOUND, JO DAVIESS CO., HOLY TRINITY (1863) [CEM 2] Revs. Christopher J. Kuhn; Stanislaw Kos.
Res.: 406 Franklin St., Galena, 61036.
Rectory & Church: 302 Franklin St., 61075. Email: holytrinity@jcwifi.com. Web: www.holytrinitych.us.
Catechesis/Religious Program—Tel: 815-845-2347. Carol Bilgri, C.R.E. Students 35.

SHANNON, CARROLL CO., ST. WENDELIN (1870) [CEM] Rev. Michael J. Bolger.
18 S. Linn St., P.O. Box 23, 61078. Tel: 815-864-2548 (Church); Fax: 815-864-2729.
Catechesis/Religious Program—Students 43.

SOMONAUK, DEKALB CO., ST. JOHN THE BAPTIST (1865) [CEM] Rev. Thomas E. Brantman.
Res.: 320 S. Depot St., Box 276, 60552. Tel: 815-498-2010; Fax: 815-498-2770. Email: stjbsom@mchsi.com.
Catechesis/Religious Program—Tel: 815-498-2627. Students 194.

SOUTH BELOIT, WINNEBAGO CO., ST. PETER (1909) Revs. Nicholas Federspiel; Robert J. McClellan; Deacons Peter Calgaro; Michael Ryan.
Res.: 620 Blackhawk Blvd., 61080. Tel: 815-525-3400; Fax: 815-525-3409.
School—320 Elmwood Ave., 61080. Tel: 779-475-0560; Fax: 779-475-0562. Email: stpeter-sbeloit@rockforddiocese.org. Mr. Edward O'Brien, Prin. Lay Teachers 14; Students 136.
Catechesis/Religious Program—Jeanne Pulkrabek, D.R.E. Students 238.
Mission—Church of the Holy Spirit P.O. Box 478, Roscoe, Winnebago Co. 61073. Tel: 815-623-6930; Fax: 815-623-1890.
Catechesis/Religious Program—Fax: 815-623-1890. Email: religioused@charter.net. Kate Elliott, D.R.E. Students 47.

SPRING GROVE, MCHENRY CO., ST. PETER (1900), (German), [CEM] Rev. Msgr. Joseph F. Jarmoluk.
Church: 2118 Main St., P.O. Box 129, 60081. Tel: 815-675-2288; Fax: 815-675-6774.
Catechesis/Religious Program—Tel: 815-675-2576. Students 227.

STERLING, WHITESIDE CO.

1—ST. MARY (1898) [CEM] Revs. Donald M. Ahles; Juan Ayala; Deacons John Kellen; James Lopez; Larry Zitkus; Jane Olson, Pastoral Assoc.
Res.: 600 Ave. B, 61081. Tel: 815-625-0640; Fax: 815-625-1684.
School—6 W. Sixth St., 61081. Tel: 815-625-2253; Fax: 815-625-8942. Web: www.smsterling.org. Mr. Tom DePasquale, Prin. Lay Teachers 20; Students 200.
Catechesis/Religious Program—6 W. 6th St., 61081. Tel: 815-625-6688; Fax: 815-625-8942. Students 140.

2—SACRED HEART (1870), (German), [CEM] Rev. David C. Finn, Parochial Admin.; Deacon Larry Zitkus.
Res.: 2224 Avenue J, 61081. Tel: 815-625-0631; 815-625-1134; Fax: 815-625-1138. Web: www.sacredheartparish.net.
Catechesis/Religious Program—Fax: 815-625-1138. Students 115.

STOCKTON, JO DAVIESS CO., HOLY CROSS (1893), (German), [CEM] Rev. Dean M. Smith.
223 E. Front Ave., 61085.
Res.: 216 E. Benton Ave., 61085. Tel: 815-947-2545; Fax: 815-947-3705. Email: holycross096@yahoo.com.
Catechesis/Religious Program—Students 66.

SUBLETTE, LEE CO., OUR LADY OF PERPETUAL HELP (1860) [CEM] Rev. Max Lasrado.
Mailing Address: Box 80, 61367. Tel: 815-849-5412; Fax: 815-849-5412.
Church: 201 Locust St., 61367.
Catechesis/Religious Program—Students 40.

SUGAR GROVE, KANE CO., ST. KATHARINE DREXEL PARISH (2008) Rev. Robert W. Jones.
264 Main St., P.O. Box 1189, 60554. Tel: 630-466-0303; Fax: 630-466-0333. Email: stephanie@skdmail.org.
Catechesis/Religious Program—Mrs. Pat Weis, D.R.E. Students 224.

SYCAMORE, DE KALB CO., ST. MARY (1885) [CEM] Rev. Frank John Timar, M.S.C.; Deacon Lee Deatherage.
Res.: 244 Waterman St., 60178. Tel: 815-895-3275; Fax: 815-899-7890. Email: churchofstmary@stmarysycamore.com. Web: www.stmarysycamore.com.
School—(Grades PreK-8), 222 Waterman St., 60178. Tel: 815-895-5215; Fax: 815-895-5295. Email: stmarys@tbcnet.com. Mr. Ross Bubolz, Prin. Lay Teachers 19; Students 237.
Catechesis/Religious Program—322 Waterman St., 60178. Tel: 815-895-3726; Fax: 815-895-4561. Students 527.

TAMPICO, WHITESIDE CO., ST. MARY (1875) [CEM] Rev. Msgr. Thomas L. Dzielak; Deacon William Lemmer.
Res.: 105 Benton St., P.O. Box 159, 61283. Tel: 815-438-5425; Fax: 815-438-5425. Email: heartofmary@thewisp.net. Web: www.saintmarytampico.org.
Catechesis/Religious Program—Students 17.

VIRGIL, KANE CO., SS. PETER AND PAUL (1909) [CEM] Rev. Perfecto L. Vasquez; Deacon Jim Newhouse.
Res.: 5 N. 939 Meredith Rd., 60151. Tel: 630-365-6618; Fax: 630-365-6659. Email: ssppvirgil@aol.com. Web: www.ssppvirgil.org.
Catechesis/Religious Program—Students 62.

WALTON, LEE CO., ST. MARY (1913) [JC] Rev. Msgr. Thomas E. Bales.
Res.: 32 N. Jones Ave., Amboy, 61310. Tel: 815-857-2670; Fax: 815-857-3485.
Catechesis/Religious Program— Twinned with St. Patrick Amboy.

WARREN, JO DAVIESS CO., ST. ANN (1914) [CEM] Rev. Max J. Striedl, Parochial Admin.
P.O. Box 665, 61087. Tel: 815-745-2312; Fax: 815-745-2312. Email: parishes@catholic.org.
Res.: 410 W. Lena St., Lena, 61048. Tel: 815-369-2810; Fax: 815-369-9137. Email: stjoseph@aeroinc.net.
Church: 608 E. Railroad St., 61087.
Catechesis/Religious Program—Students 44.

WEST BROOKLYN, LEE CO., ST. MARY (1889) [CEM] Rev. Max Lasrado.
Mailing Address: 2520 Johnson St., P.O. Box 80, 61378. Tel: 815-849-5412; Fax: 815-849-5412.
Catechesis/Religious Program—Fax: 815-849-5412. Held at Our lady of Perpetual Help, Sublette Students 8.

WONDER LAKE, MCHENRY CO., CHRIST THE KING (1949) [CEM] Rev. Steven M. Sabo.
Res.: 5006 E. Wonder Lake Rd., 60097. Tel: 815-653-2561; Fax: 815-653-9401. Email: ctksecretary@comcast.net.
Catechesis/Religious Program—Tel: 815-653-2581. Mrs. Karen Verr, C.R.E. Students 81.

WOODSTOCK, MCHENRY CO.

1—ST. MARY (1853) [CEM] Rev. Msgr. Aaron R. Brodeski; Rev. Johnson Lopez; Deacons Louis Barone; Hans Rokus; Jim Devona.
Res.: 312 Lincoln Ave., 60098. Tel: 815-338-3377; Fax: 815-338-3497.
School—313 Tryon St., 60098. Tel: 815-338-3598; Fax: 815-338-3408. Frank Shields, Prin. Lay Teachers 24; Students 322.
Catechesis/Religious Program—Tel: 815-338-3413; Fax: 815-334-4391. Mrs. Diane O'Donnell, D.R.E. Students 327.

2—RESURRECTION (1978) Rev. Stephen Glab, C.R.
Mailing Address: 2918 S. Country Club Rd., 60098. Tel: 815-338-7330; Fax: 815-338-7365. Email: office.rcc@hughes.net. Web: www.resurrectioncatholic.net.

Catechesis/Religious Program—Nancy Neumeister, D.R.E. Students 142.

Chaplains of Public Institutions

ELGIN. *Elgin State Hospital*, 750 S. State St., 60123. Vacant.

MOOSEHEART. *School of the Loyal Order of Moose*, 301 Fifth Ave., 60539. Vacant.

SAINT CHARLES. *Illinois State Youth Center*, Chapel of the Immaculate Conception, 60175. Records kept at St. Patrick, St. Charles.

Special Assignment:
Rev. Msgrs.—
Barr, Eric R., V.G., S.T.L., Vicar for Clergy & Religious, 555 Colman Center Dr., P.O. Box 7044, 61125. Tel: 815-399-4300
Fritz, John, S.T.L., Chancellor & Sec. to the Bishop & Diocesan Master of Ceremonies
Kagan, David D., V.G., J.C.L., Vicar Gen., 555 Colman Center Dr., 61125. Tel: 815-399-4300
Kurz, Michael A., J.C.L., Judicial Vicar, Chap., Poor Clare Monastery, 555 Colman Center Dr., P.O. Box 7044, 61125. Tel: 815-399-4300
Nelson, Glenn L., V.G., J.C.L., Vicar Gen. & Moderator of the Curia, 555 Colman Center Dr., P.O. Box 7044, 61125. Tel: 815-399-4300
Schwartz, William H., P.A., S.T.L., Diocesan Dir. of Permanent Deacons
Sweeney, Robert J., Propagation of the Faith, Tribunal, P.O. Box 7044, 61125. Tel: 815-399-4300
Vallejo, Arquimedes, J.C.D., Episcopal Vicar for Hispanic Ministry Tribunal, 555 Colman Center Dr., P.O. Box 7044, 61125. Tel: 815-399-4300
Very Rev.—
Grady, Brian D., Vicar for Clergy, 2000
Revs.—
Beekman, Carl E., Vocations Dir.
Birungyi, George, Chap., St. Joseph Hospital, Elgin
Camacho, Robert, Hispanic Ministry, Freeport Deanery
Cruz, Saul E., Hispanic Ministry, DeKalb, Deanery
Doyle, Thomas J., Asst. Principal, Marian CC High School, Woodstock
Emeh, Martins, J.C.L., Vice Chancellor
Etheredge, F. William, Supt., Aurora CC High School, Aurora
Finn, David C., Superintendent & Prin., Newman High School, Sterling
Fuller, Michael J.K., S.T.D., Mundelein, IL
Lipinski, Paul M., Acting Principal, Boylan CC High School, Rockford
Long, Anthony Vu Khac, Vietnamese Catholic Ministry, St. Mary Parish, 321 Pine St., DeKalb, 60115.
McMorrow, Matthew, Asst. Prin.; Dir. of Rel. Ed., Boylan CC High School, Rockford (Diocesan Scout Chap.)
Naill, Joseph P., M.A. Office of Divine Worship
Peck, David A., Superintendent, St. Edward CC High School, Elgin
Polycarpe, Pierre G., Chap., St. Anthony Hospital, Rockford
Wentink, William R., Chaplain St. Anthony Hospital, St. Anthony Hospital, 5666 E. State St., 61108.

Active Outside the Diocese:
Revs.—
Donahugh, Donald E., Port Arthur, TX
Falcone, Emilio (Retired), United States Air Force
Garrity, Robert M., Ave Maria University, Naples, FL
Kaim, Phillip, United States Air Force
Schuessler, William R., Missions, Peru

Retired:
Rev. Msgrs.—
Brady, Thomas C., P.A., V.G., Ph.D., 16 Country Club Beach, 61103.
Clausen, William J., 747 Tulip Ln., 61107.
Dempsey, Thomas J., 13750 White Oak Rd., Huntley, 60142.
Hoffman, Robert B., 271 Trent Dr., Batavia, 60510.
Kobbeman, Gerald P., 12795 Edgewater Pointe, Winnebago, 61088.
McLoughlin, James W., 11335 Bellflower Ln., Huntley, 60142.
McNamee, Charles W., P.A., J.C.L., Unit 15, 4718 Covey Ridge Ct., Loves Park, 61111.
Mitchell, John J., 250 Spring Cove Dr., Elgin, 60123.
Monahan, Thomas J., Ph.D., 4295 Ahlstrand Dr, 61103.
O'Neil, Philip E., 2323 Rockton Ave., 61103.
Tierney, Michael J., 15 Delbourne Dr., Davis, 61019.
Wahl, Raymond J., P.A., J.C.D., Cor Mariae Center, 3330 Maria Linden Dr., 61114.
Willhite, Robert J., P.O. Box 4395, Aurora, 60507.
Revs.—
Beauvais, David E., P.O. Box 94, Rock City, 61070.
Becker, Anthony J., Oak Ridge Manor, 124 Liberty Ct., Dixon, 61021.
Budden, William A., 4878 Ashelford Dr., Byron, 61010.
Burr, Thomas E., 401 Inverrary #17, Rockport, TX 78382.
Cahill, John W., 13351 Red Alder Ave., Huntley, 60142.
Clapsaddle, Harlan, P.O. Box 7044, 61125.
Collins, William P., Luther Center, 111 W. State St., Apt. 1303, 61101.
DeSalvo, Donald D., 15519 Crystal Acres Dr., Somonauk, 60552.
Echevia, Les Suberi, 987 Stonefield Ln, 61108.
Gillespie, Edward F., 6152 Wingate Dr., Lisle, 60532.
Guagliardo, Salvatore J., Siena on Brendenwood, 4444 Brendenwood Rd., 61107.
Heraty, John T., 11936 Tuliptree Ln, Huntley, 60142.
Hiller, Everett J., 2520 W. Council Hill Rd., Scales Mound, 61075.
Hughes, Edward R., 5455 N. Sheridan Rd., 60640.
Jones, Ronald A., P.O. Box 7044, 61125.
Knott, William P., 15528 W. Sky Hawk Dr., Sun City West, AZ 85375.
Kraemer, John A., 6033 A Sheridan Rd., Apt. 32J, Chicago, 60660.
Kramer, Richard R., 209 W. Shellhammer Rd., P.O Box 130, Harmon, 61042.
Kulak, Joseph F., 1213 Oakdale, Elgin, 60123.
Lewandowski, Theodore V., N1829 William Dr., Waupaca, WI 54981.
Librandi, Michael A., Cor Mariae Center, 3330 Maria Linden Dr., 61114.
Lutz, Joseph L., 136 Lakeside Dr., Apt. 716, St. Charles, 60174.
McDonnell, Francis E., 1801 Ave. G, Sterling, 61081.
McKitrick, James V., N.1555 Shadow Ln., Fontana, WI 53125.
Mullane, Bernard J., P.O. Box 1403, Williams Bay, WI 53191.
Neumann, Aloysius J., 5225 N. Bernard St., Chicago, 60625.
Neville, Thomas, Mohan Health Care Center, 2340 Airport Dr., Columbus, OH 43219.
Peterson, William F., 147 Shadowood Dr., Martinez, GA 30907.
Plesa, Andrew J., 215 Thomas More Dr., Elgin, 60123.
Ratazak, Bernard A., Cor Mariae Center, 3330 Maria Linden Dr., 61114.
Rudden, Matthew T., 6102 Garrett Ln., 61107.
Stringini, John L.
Tranel, Daniel D., 8615 N. Tranel Rd., East Dubuque, 61025.
Urbaniak, Lawrence M., 4210 W. Marshall Ave., Phoenix, AZ 85019.
Vlasz, Melvyn J., Cor Mariae Center, 3330 Maria Linden Dr., 61114.

Permanent Deacons:
Abel, Philip, St. Bridget, Loves Park
Anchor, Robert, Sacred Heart, Marengo
Bach, John, St. Monica, Carpentersville
Badillo, Ignacio, St. Peter, South Beloit
Barone, Frank, St. Patrick, Rockford
Barone, Louis, St. Mary, Woodstock
Berard, Samuel, St. Patrick, Dixon
Bondi, Allen, St. Thomas the Apostle, Crystal Lake
Boyce, Michael, SS. Peter & Paul, Cary
Bracken, Robert, (Retired)
Brandenburg, Robert, (Retired)
Bronzi, William, Holy Family, Rockford
Brunette, Donald J., St. Thomas Aquinas, Freeport
Calgaro, Peter, St. Peter, South Beloit; Church of the Holy Spirit, Roscoe
Callahan, Donald J., (Retired)
Chaplin, Mark, St. Gall, Elburn
Ciochon, Thaddeus, (Retired)
Coltman, George, St. Mary, Huntley
Cooper, Charles, St. Francis by the Sea, Hilton Head, SC
Cristoforo, Michael, Holy Family, Rockford
Czerniewski, Martin, St. Peter Cathedral, Rockford
Dall, William, St. Rita, Rockford
Dean, William, St. James, Rockford
Deatherage, Lee, St. Mary, Sycamore
Demming, Robert, St. Anne, Haines, FL
Devona, James, St. Mary, Woodstock
Dietz, Albert, St. Joseph, Richmond
Dinneen, Richard, St. Thomas Aquinas, Freeport
Dombek, James, Christ the Teacher, DeKalb
Drees, Vincent, St. Thomas Aquinas, Freeport
Duffey, Gregory, St. Peter , Spring Grove
Elms, Thomas, St. John Neumann, St. Charles
Emmert, Phillip, St. Joseph, Harvard
Falcón, Jose, Sacred Heart, Aurora
Farinella, Louis, St. Mary, Huntley
Fast, Randy, St. Francis Assisi, LaQuinta, CA
Felix, Ignacio, St. Rita of Cascia, Aurora
Ferrini, Armand, St. Mary, Huntley
Fiedler, Curtis, Church of Holy Apostles, McHenry
Fischer, Howard, St. Margaret Mary, Algonquin
Fox, Steven, St. Catherine of Siena, Dundee
Frazier, J. Michael, St. Elizabeth, Elizabethtown, TN
Freund, Walter, (Retired)
Gagnon, Charles, St. Elizabeth Ann Seton, Crystal Lake
Ganshow, Howard, SS. Peter & Paul, Cary
Garber, Dennis, St. Monica, Carpentersville
Gartland, William, St. Patrick, St. Charles
Geinosky, Larry, San Juan del Rio, Switzerland, FL
Gerdeman, Richard, St. Bernadette, Rockford
Giambalvo, Michael, St. Mary, Pecatonica
Giblin, Michael, Annunciation B.V.M., Aurora
Giessinger, Jerry, St. John the Baptist, Johnsburg
Goetz, Daniel, Sacred Heart, Newton, IA
Graw, Ronald, St. James, Belvidere
Grossmayer, Simon, St. Margaret Mary, Algonquin
Hainchek, Alex J., (Retired)
Hall, James, Holy Angels, Aurora
Hawksworth, Thomas, Holy Angels, Aurora
Hetzel, Martin, St. Thomas Aquinas, Boulder, CO
Holt, Arthur, (Retired)
Hudzinski, James, St. Stanislaus, Rockford
Iwanski, Paul, St. John Neumann, St. Charles
Jimenez, Policarpo, St. Mary, Huntley
Johnson, William, St. Patrick, St. Charles
Jones, Michael, St. Thomas Aquinas, Freeport
Kayser, Joseph, St. Mary, Woodstock
Kellen, John, St. Mary, Sterling
Keppler, Anthony, St. Mary, East Dubuque
Kocol, Theodore, St. Mary, Galena; Holy Trinity, Scales Mound
Koss, Anthony, St. Joseph, Harvard
Kremer, Douglas, St. Mary, East Dubuque
Kulpin, John, (Retired)
LaMont, Warren R., St. Mary, Pecatonica
Lemmer, William, St. Mary, Tampico
LeRoy, Michael, St. Margaret Mary, Algonquin
Lopez, James, St. Mary, Sterling
Magee, Ronald, (Retired)
Maher, Patrick, St. Margaret Mary, Algonquin
Martin, Raymond J., Holy Cross, Batavia
Martin, Richard, St. Rita of Cascia, Aurora
Martinez, Armando, St. Joseph, Elgin
McNealy, Ken, Our Lady of the Desert, Tucson, AZ
McPhee, John, St. Mary, Huntley
Milano, Robert, St. Anne, Dixon
Miller, Donald, St. Margaret Mary, Algonquin
Mitchison, Robert, Cathedral of St. Peter, Rockford
Morrison, Edward, St. Thomas the Apostle, Crystal Lake
Motyka, Larry, Annunciation, Aurora
Moynihan, Patrick, Haiti
Mulcahey, Richard, St. Mary, Durand
Navarro, Carlos, St. Peter, Aurora; Our Lady of Good Counsel, Aurora
Nelson, John, St. Charles Borromeo, Hampshire
Newhouse, James, SS. Peter & Paul, Virgil
Nguyen, Loc, St. Mary, Elgin
O'Brien, Thomas, St. Mary, Huntley
O'Connor, Michael, SS. Peter & Paul, Cary
O'Leary, Jack, Sacred Heart, Marengo
Olson, James D., St. James, Belvidere
Orlik, Henry, St. Mary, Elgin
Petit, Thomas, St. Joseph, Aurora
Phelan, Joseph, Church of Holy Apostles, McHenry
Plazewski, Robert, St. Lawrence, Elgin
Porter, John, (Retired)
Pospischil, Steven, St. Thomas Aquinas, Freeport
Poss, Harold, Annunciation of the B.V.M., Aurora
Prunty, Kevin, St. Patrick, Amboy
Pulkrabek, Steven, St. Mary, Durand; St. Patrick, Irish Grove
Puscas, Stephen, St. Mary, DeKalb
Raz, Mark, Christ the King, Wonder Lake
Real, Robert, St. Joseph, Elgin
Riseley, William, St. Bridget, Loves Park
Roder, John, St. Thomas More, Elgin
Rokus, Hans, St. Mary, Woodstock
Rosado, Julio, St. Therese of Jesus, Aurora
Ryan, Michael, St. Peter, South Beloit
Ryndak, Jerry, St. Charles Borromeo, Hampshire
Sauceda, John, (Retired)
Schmalen, Hank, St. Catherine of Siena, Dundee
Schubert, Anthony, St. Mary, Huntley
Sims, Fred, St. Patrick, St. Charles
Skrade, Fred, (Retired)
Smith, Daniel
Smits, Robert, St. Patrick, Anadarko, OK
Stankevitz, William A., Holy Cross, Batavia
Statter, Ralph, St. Thomas, Crystal Lake
Stevens, Greg, St. Thomas More, Elgin
Sullivan, Michael, St. Peter, Geneva
Swearingen, Alvin, St. Mary, Morrison

Sweeney, Robert, Holy Family, Rockford
Szudarski, Norbert, St. Joseph, Aurora
Urban, Gregory, St. Mary, Maple Park
Verstynen, Lambert, St. Edward, Rockford
Wagner, Terrence, St. Patrick, Dixon
Watermann, Bruce, St. Therese, Aurora; St. Nicholas, Aurora
Weaver, Raymond, Our Lady of Good Counsel, Aurora
White, Thomas, Holy Angels, Aurora
Whitehead, William, Jr., St. Catherine of Siena, Dundee
Wilbricht, David, (Retired)
Williams, Ronald, St. John Neumann, St. Charles
Woeste, James, St. Margaret Mary, Algonquin
Zibrun, Michael, St. Peter, Geneva
Zitkus, Lawrence, Sacred Heart, St. Mary, Sterling

INSTITUTIONS LOCATED IN THE DIOCESE

[A] SEMINARIES, RELIGIOUS OR SCHOLASTICATES

AURORA. *Marmion Abbey* (1933) 850 Butterfield Rd., 60502. Tel: 630-897-7215; Fax: 630-897-0393. Email: jbrahill@marmion.org. Web: www.marmion.org. Rt. Rev. John Brahill, O.S.B., Abbot; Very Rev. Basil Yender, O.S.B., Prior; Rt. Rev. David J. Cyr, O.S.B. Priests 22; Brothers 8.

[B] HIGH SCHOOLS, DIOCESAN

ROCKFORD. *Boylan Central Catholic High School*, 4000 St. Francis Dr., 61103. Tel: 815-877-0531; Fax: 815-877-2544. Email: boylan@boylan.org. Web: www.boylan.org. Revs. Paul M. Lipinski, Acting Prin.; Matthew McMorrow, Asst. Prin. & D.R.E.; Mr. Dan Appino, Guidance Dir.; Mrs. Mary Gavan, Asst. Prin.; Mr. Dennis Hiemenz, Asst. Prin., Academic Affairs; Jerry Kerrigan, Asst. Prin., Student Affairs; Mr. Christopher Lindstedt, Dean of Students; Mrs. Denise Ethum, Librarian. Priests 4; Lay Teachers 86; Students 1,151.

AURORA. *Aurora Central Catholic High School*, 1255 N. Edgelawn Dr., 60506. Tel: 630-907-0095; Fax: 630-907-1076. Email: fetheredge@auroracentral.com. Web: www.auroracentral.com. Rev. F. William Etheredge, Prin. & Supt.; Mr. Mark Krebs, Asst. Prin.; Mrs. Patricia Griffin, Librarian. Priests 6; School Sisters of St. Francis 1; Lay Teachers 35; Students 560.

ELGIN. *St. Edward Central Catholic High School*, 335 Locust St., 60123. Tel: 847-741-7535; Fax: 847-695-4682. Email: stedward@stedhs.org. Web: www.stedhs.org. Rev. David A. Peck, Supt.; Mr. Rich Thomas, Prin.; Mrs. Susan Doherty, Librarian. Priests 2; Lay Teachers 30; Students 407.

FREEPORT. *Aquin Central Catholic High School*, 1419 S. Galena Ave., 61032. Tel: 815-235-3154; Fax: 815-235-3185. Email: superintendent@aquinschools.org. Web: www.aquinschools.org. Mrs. Kathleen Runte, Prin.; Rev. Michael J. Bolger, Asst. Prin. & Chm. Religious Studies Dept.; Mrs. Connie Gogel, Librarian. Priests 1; Lay Teachers 18; Students 154.

STERLING. *Newman Central Catholic High School* (1915) 1101 W. 23rd St., 61081-9002. Tel: 815-625-0500; Fax: 815-625-8444. Email: aedmondson@newmancchs.org. Web: www.newmancchs.org. Andy Edmondson, Prin.; Inez Vits, Librarian. Priests 1; Lay Teachers 20; Students 261.

WOODSTOCK. *Marian Central Catholic High School* (1959) 1001 McHenry Ave., 60098. Tel: 815-338-4220; Fax: 815-338-4253. Email: tlanders@marian.com. Web: www.marian.com. Mr. Thomas E. Landers, Supt. & Prin.; Rev. Msgr. Aaron R. Brodeski, Spiritual Dir.; Mrs. Mary Ann Martinez, Devel. Dir.; Mr. Charles Maveus, Dean of Students; Rev. Thomas J. Doyle, Asst. Prin.; Mr. Charles Rakers, Dir. Academics & Personnel. Priests 1; Lay Teachers 40; Students 717.

[C] HIGH SCHOOLS, PRIVATE

AURORA. *Marmion Academy*, 1000 Butterfield Rd., 60502. Tel: 630-897-6936; Fax: 630-897-7086. Email: jmilroy@marmion.org. Web: www.marmion.org. Rt. Rev. John Brahill, O.S.B., Abbot & Pres., 850 Butterfield Rd., 60504. Tel: 630-897-1881; Fax: 630-897-0393. Email: jbrahill@marmion.org. Web: www.marmion.org; Dr. James Quaid, Ph.D., Headmaster; Rev. Mario Pedi, O.S.B., Librarian. Day School for Boys. Benedictines (10 Priests, 1 Brother) 11; Lay Teachers 44; Students 513.

Rosary High School (1962) 901 N. Edgelawn Ave., 60506. Tel: 630-896-0831; Fax: 630-896-8372. Email: spbop@rosaryhs.com. Web: www.rosaryhs.com. Sisters Patricia Burke, O.P., Prin.; Bernadette Marie, O.P., Librarian. Sisters of St. Dominic 5; Lay Teachers 38; Girls 428.

[D] GENERAL HOSPITALS

ROCKFORD. *Saint Anthony College of Nursing* (1915) 5658 E. State St., 61108. Tel: 815-395-5091; Fax: 815-395-2275. Email: Terriburch@sacn.edu. Web: www.sacn.edu. Terese A. Burch, Ph.D., R.N., Pres., College. Faculty 32; Undergraduate Students 194; Graduate Students 47; Staff 13.

Saint Anthony Medical Center, 5666 E. State St., 61108. Tel: 815-226-2000; Fax: 815-395-5449. Web: www.osfhealthcare.org. Mailing Address: 1175 St. Francis Ln., East Peoria, 61611. Mr. David Schertz, Pres. & CEO; Rev. William R. Wentink, Chap. & Dir. of Pastoral Care. Sisters of the Third Order of St. Francis 2; Bed Capacity 254; Patients Assisted Annually 461,602; Total Staff 2,417.

AURORA. *Provena Mercy Medical Center*, 1325 N. Highland Ave., 60506. Tel: 630-859-2222. Web: www.provenamercy.com. George Einhorn, R.N., M.H.A., C.P.H.Q., Interim Pres & CEO; Edward J. Hunter, Regl. Vice Pres. Mission Svcs.

Provena Hospitals dba Provena Mercy Medical Center. Licensed Beds 299; Patients Assisted Annually 198,541; Total Staff 1,100.

Center for Diabetic Wellness, 1325 N. Highland Ave., 60506. Tel: 630-897-4000; Fax: 630-897-9032.

Health Institute, 1975 Melissa Ln., 60505. Tel: 630-907-1129; Fax: 630-907-1354.

ELGIN. *Provena Saint Joseph Hospital* (1902) 77 N. Airlite St., 60123. Tel: 847-695-3200; Fax: 847-931-5550. Email: edward.hunter@provena.org. Web: www.provena.org. Eugene J. McMahon, M.D., M.B.A., F.C.A.P., System Sr. Vice Pres., Pres & CEO; Edward J. Hunter, Regl. Vice Pres. Mission Svcs.; Rev. George Birungyi.

Provena Hospitals dba Provena Saint Joseph Hospital. Sisters 2; Licensed Beds 178; Patients Assisted Annually 174,216; Total Staff 1,121.

Provena Saint Joseph Hospital MedCare, 2250 W. Algonquin Rd., Lake in the Hills. Tel: 847-854-5511; Fax: 847-854-5531.

Provena Family Care, Huntley, 12155 Regency Sq. Pkwy., Huntley, 60142. Tel: 847-515-2100; Fax: 847-515-2328.

Provena Family Care, Carpentersville, 2201 Randall Rd., Carpentersville, 60110. Tel: 847-844-7800; Fax: 847-783-0628.

Provena Family Care, Hampshire, 895 S. State St., Ste. 201, Hampshire, 60140. Tel: 847-683-7099; Fax: 847-683-7104.

[E] SCHOOLS FOR EXCEPTIONAL ADOLESCENTS AND ADULTS

FREEPORT. *Provena St. Vincent's Community Living Facility and Supported Living Arrangement*, 659 E. Jefferson St., 61032. Tel: 815-232-6181; Fax: 815-232-6143. Ms. Diane Cushman, Prog. Dir. Patients Assisted Annually 40; Total Staff 13.

[F] HOMES FOR AGED AND ADULT DAY CARE CENTERS

ROCKFORD. *St. Anne Place*, 4444 Brendenwood Rd., 61107. Tel: 815-399-6167; Fax: 815-399-6169. Email: kathleen.russell@provena.org. Web: www.sienaonbrendenwood.org. Kathleen Russell, Exec. Dir. Owned by the Rockford Diocese, managed by Provena Senior Services. Total Staff 40; Total in Residence 120; Apartment Capacity 105; Total Assisted Annually 100.

Provena Cor Mariae Center, 3330 Maria Linden Dr., 61114. Tel: 815-877-7416; Fax: 815-877-4299. Web: www.provena.org/cormariae. Teresa Wester-Peters, Admin.; Rev. Michael A. Librandi, Chap. (Retired).

Provena Senior Services dba Provena Cor Mariae Center. Bed Capacity 162; Total Assisted Annually 500; Total Staff 179.

Provena St. Anne Center, 4405 Highcrest Rd., 61107. Tel: 815-229-1999; Fax: 815-229-1560. Email: janelle.chadwick@provena.org. Web: www.provena.org. Janelle Chadwick, Admin.; Sr. Marie Ange Marcotte, Dir. Pastoral Care.

Provena Senior Services dba Provena St. Anne Center. Bed Capacity 179; Total Assisted Annually 1,000; Total Staff 215.

AURORA. *Provena Fox Knoll*, 421 N. Lake St., 60506. Tel: 630-844-0380; Fax: 630-844-0702. Web: www.provena.org/foxknoll. Carol Ricken, Exec. Dir.

Provena Senior Services dba Provena Fox Knoll. Total Staff 67; Total in Residence 165; Independent Living 87; Assisted Living 77; Total Assisted Annually 120.

Provena McAuley Manor (1985) 400 W. Sullivan Rd., 60506. Tel: 630-859-3700; Fax: 630-264-1862. Web: www.provena.org/mcauley. Sr. Peg Barrett, R.S.M., Dir. Pastoral Care. Bed Capacity 87; Total Staff 120; Total Assisted Annually 570.

Batavia

Assisi Homes-Batavia Apartments, Inc. (1993) 1259 E. Wilson St., Batavia, 60510. Tel: 630-879-3117; Fax: 630-879-0665. Web: www.fm-inc.org. 26 W171 Roosevelt Rd., Wheaton, 60187-0667. Susan M. Dillberg, Contact. Housing Units 290; Residents 639; Staff 9.

ELGIN. *Provena Home Health, Inc. dba Provena Home Care* 799 S. McLean Blvd, 60123. Tel: 847-931-5553; Fax: 847-622-2055. Thomas F. Nehring, Contact Person.

FREEPORT. *Provena St. Joseph Adult Day Center*, 659 E. Jefferson St., 61032. Tel: 815-266-8067; Fax: 815-266-8001. Email: sharon.batten@provenahealth.org. Ms. Sharon Batten, Dir. Total Staff 11; Total Assisted Annually 68; Bed Capacity 55.

Provena St. Joseph Center, 659 E. Jefferson St., 61032. Tel: 815-232-6181; Fax: 815-232-6143. Mary Waters, Dir. Pastoral Care; Ms. Michelle Lindeman, Admin.

Provena Senior Services dba Provena St. Joseph Center. Aged Residents 120; Total Staff 136.

GENEVA. *Provena Geneva Care Center*, 1101 E. State St., 60134. Tel: 630-232-7544; Fax: 630-232-4409. Email: debra.porter@provena.org. Web: www.provena.org/genevacare. Debra Porter, B.S., M.S., L.N.H.A., Admin.; Elena Haas, Dir. Pastoral Care.

Provena Senior Services dba Provena Geneva Care Center. Bed Capacity 107; Total Staff 100; Total Assisted Annually 200.

SAINT CHARLES. *Provena Pine View Care Center*, 611 Allen Ln., 60174. Tel: 630-377-2211; Fax: 630-377-4352. Email: dawnfurman@provena.org. Web: provena.org. Sr. Maureen Becker, Dir. Pastoral Care; Dawn Renee Furman, B.S.N., L.N.H.A., M.S.N., M.B.A., Admin.

Provena Senior Services dba Provena Pine View Care Center. Bed Capacity 120; Total Staff 140; Residents 90; Total Assisted Annually 375.

[G] MONASTERIES AND RESIDENCES OF PRIESTS AND BROTHERS

AURORA. *Marmion Abbey* (1933) 850 Butterfield Rd., 60502. Tel: 630-897-7215; Fax: 630-897-0393. Email: jbrahill@marmion.org. Web: www.marmion.org. Rt. Revs. Gerald Benkert, O.S.B., Abbot Emeritus (Retired); David J. Cyr, O.S.B., Abbot Emeritus; John Brahill, O.S.B., Abbot; Vincent Bataille, O.S.B., Abbot Emeritus; Very Rev. Basil Yender, O.S.B., Prior; Revs. Thomas Bailey, O.S.B.; Michael Burrows, O.S.B.; Rene Otzoy Colaj, O.S.B.; Aaron Devett, O.S.B.; Patrick S. Gillmeyer, O.S.B.; Orlando Perez Gomez, O.S.B.; Philip Kremer, O.S.B.; Juan Francisco Peren Mux, O.S.B.; Mario Pedi, O.S.B.; Frederick Peterson, O.S.B.; Christian Pusateri, O.S.B.; Cristobal Coche Quic, O.S.B.; Charles Reichenbacher, O.S.B.; Joel Rippinger, O.S.B.; Nathanael Roberts, O.S.B.; Bernard Schaefer, O.S.B.; Kenneth Theisen, O.S.B.; Paul Weberg, O.S.B.

Marmion. Priests 23; Brothers 8.

Missionaries of the Sacred Heart Community (1854) 305 S. Lake St., P.O. Box 270, 60507. Tel: 630-892-2371; Fax: 630-892-1678. Email: rfdmsc@misacor-usa.org. Web: www.misacor-usa.org. Very Rev. Raymond Diesbourg, M.S.C., Provincial Supr.; Revs. Peter E. Campbell, M.S.C.; Joseph Gleixner, M.S.C., Asst. Treas.; Michael I. Miller, M.S.C.; Bro. Daniel Rakow, M.S.C.; Revs. John Schweikert, M.S.C.; Frank John Timar, M.S.C.; Norbert B. Weber, M.S.C.; Leon Weisenberger, M.S.C.; Bros. Steve Boland, M.S.C.; James Miller, M.S.C., Local Supr. & Treas.; Joseph Tesar, M.S.C.; Michael Tomcics, M.S.C. Provincial Administrative Office of the Missionaries of the Sacred Heart. Priests 13; Brothers 4.

Priests and Brothers of the Aurora Community Serving Elsewhere:

In Chicago, IL Very Rev. Joseph Jablonski, M.S.C.; Revs. Moo-Chan Benedict Ko, M.S.C.; Hugo Leon Londono, M.S.C.; Dario Moreno, M.S.C., Parochial Vicar; Andrew Torma, M.S.C., Vocation Dir.; Bro. Frank Natale, M.S.C.

MCHENRY. *Villa Desiderata Retreat House*, 3015 N. Bayview Ln., 60051-9641. Tel: 815-385-2264. Bro. Patrick T. Drohan, C.S.V., Facilities Mgr.

[H] CONVENTS AND RESIDENCES FOR SISTERS

ROCKFORD. *The Poor Clares of Rockford* (1916) Corpus Christi Monastery, 2111 S. Main St., 61102-3591. Tel: 815-963-7343; Fax: 815-963-7369. Web:

www.poorclares.org/rockford/. Sr. Mary Dominica Stein, P.C.C., Abbess. Poor Clare Colettines. Cloistered Sisters 18; Extern Sisters 1; Postulants 1.

BATAVIA. *Holy Heart of Mary Novitiate*, 717 N. Batavia Ave., 60510. Tel: 630-879-1296; Fax: 630-879-7831. Email: evelynbv@sbcglobal.net. Web: www.sscm-usa.org. Sr. Evelyn Varboncoeur, S.S.C.M., Supr. & Formation Dir. Servants of the Holy Heart of Mary. Professed Sisters 6.

FREEPORT. *Congregation of the Sisters of the Immaculate Heart of Mary, Mother of Christ-Nigeria* (1937) 1209 S. Walnut St., 61032. Tel: 815-297-8287; Fax: 815-297-1786. Sisters 9.

[I] COMMUNITY SERVICES

ROCKFORD. *St. Elizabeth Catholic Community Center* (1911) 1536 S. Main St., 61102. Tel: 815-969-6526; Fax: 815-969-0541. Email: saintel911@ccrfd.org. Web: www.stelizabeth-rockford.org. Karen Carlson, Dir. Total Staff 14; Total Assisted Annually 49,405.

AURORA. *Public Action to Deliver Shelter, Inc. (PADS)*, 659 S. River St., 60506. Tel: 630-897-2165; Fax: 630-801-9759. Email: info@hesedhouse.org. Web: www.hesedhouse.org. Ryan J. Dowd, M.P.A., J.D., Exec. Dir. Ecumenical advocacy, overnight and transitional shelters and daytime drop-in center for homeless persons. Total Assisted 70,835.

[J] RETREAT HOUSES

ROCKFORD. *Bishop Lane Retreat Center* (1966) 7708 E. McGregor Rd., 61102. Tel: 815-965-5011; Fax: 815-965-5811. Email: bishoplane@rockforddiocese.org. Web: www.blrc.dpsrfd.org. Rev. Victor H. Alcazar, Admin.; Anne Marie Coyle, Mgr.

[K] FOUNDATIONS

ROCKFORD. *Boylan Educational Foundation, Inc.* (1980) 4000 St. Francis Dr., 61103. Tel: 815-877-8008; Fax: 815-877-2544. Email: boylan@boylan.org. Web: www.boylan.org.

The Catholic Foundation for the People of the Diocese of Rockford, 555 Colman Center Dr., P.O. Box 7044, 61125-7044. Tel: 815-399-4300; Fax: 815-399-5657. Email: dhougan@rockforddiocese.org. Web: www.foundationrockford.org. Mr. David Hougan, Exec. Dir.

AURORA. *Aurora Catholic Education Foundation* (1973) P.O. Box 234, 60507. Tel: 630-898-2998; Fax: 630-898-2998.

CRYSTAL LAKE. *St. Thomas the Apostle School Foundation, Inc.*, 272 King St., 60014. Tel: 815-455-5400; Fax: 815-455-2733.

DEKALB. *Newman Center of Northern Illinois University Educational Program*, 512 Normal Rd., 60115. Tel: 815-787-7770; Fax: 815-758-2053. Email: parishoffice@newmanniu.org. Web: www.newmanniu.org.

Newman Center of Northern Illinois University Educational Program and Development Fund, Inc. Total Staff 9.

ELGIN. *St. Edward Central Catholic High School Education Foundation*, 335 Locust St., 60123. Tel: 847-741-7535; Fax: 847-695-4682. Email: Stedward@stedhs.org. Web: www.stedhs.org. Rev. Matthew DeBlock, Foundation Chm.

FREEPORT. *Education Through the 90's Foundation*, 1419 S. Galena Ave., 61032. Tel: 815-235-3154; Fax: 815-235-3185. Email: superintendent@aquinschools.org. Web: www.aquinschools.org. The foundation provides financial support for the Aquin Catholic School System.

Freeport Catholic Education Foundation, 1419 S. Galena Ave., 61032. Tel: 815-235-3154; Fax: 815-235-3185. Email: superintendent@aquinschools.org. Web: www.aquinschools.org. The foundation provides financial support for the Aquin Catholic School System.

STERLING. *Sauk Valley Catholic Education Foundation*, 1101 St. Mary's Rd., 61081. Tel: 815-757-5540. Email: ckromm@whitesideeroe.org. Web: www.whitesideroe.org.

Sauk Valley Area Religious Education Center, 1101 St. Mary Rd., 61081. Tel: 815-626-5570; Fax: 815-626-5570.

SYCAMORE. *St. Mary's Educational Foundation, Ltd.* (1981) 244 Waterman St., 60178. Tel: 815-895-3275, Ext. 707; Fax: 815-899-7890. Email: fjtimar@stmarysycamore.com. Web: www.stmarysycamore.com. Rev. Frank John Timar, M.S.C.

[L] NEWMAN CENTERS

DEKALB. *Newman Foundation for Catholic Students of Northern Illinois University* 512 Normal Rd., 60115. Tel: 815-787-7770; Fax: 815-758-2053. Email: parishoffice@newmanniu.org. Web: www.newmanniu.org. Rev. Msgr. Glenn L. Nelson, V.G., J.C.L., Dir. Campus Ministries; Revs. Alejandro del Toro, S.T.L., Assoc. Campus Ministries; Matthew J. Camaioni, Assoc. Campus Ministries; Leslie Venere, Dir. Music; Denise Sanders, Campus Min./ Dir. H.S. Youth Min.

[M] MISCELLANEOUS

ROCKFORD. *Catholic Office of the Deaf*, 555 Colman Center Dr., P.O. Box 7044, 61125. Tel: 815-399-4300 (Voice); 815-399-8184 (TTY); Fax: 815-399-5266; Tel: 877-215-2219 (V.P.). Email: RockfordHI@aol.com. Web: www.rockforddiocese.org/deafapostle.

Vineyard Books, Gifts & Church Supplies, Highcrest Centre, 1638 N. Alpine Rd., 61107. Tel: 815-398-4030; Fax: 815-398-8477; 800-587-9777. Email: manager@vineyardbooksgifts.com. Web: www.catholicfamilygifts.com; www.catholicbiblestore.com; www.vineyardchurchsupply.com. Chris Weickert, Mgr. Total Staff 9.

AURORA. **Dominican Literacy Center, Aurora* (1993) 260 Vermont Ave., 60505-3100. Tel: 630-898-4636; Fax: 630-898-4636. Email: domlitctr@sbcglobal.net. Web: www.dominicanliteracycenter.org. Sr. Kathleen Ryan, O.P., Dir.

The J. Chevalier Charitable Trust, Old Second National Bank, Trustee, 37 S. River St., 60506-4172. Tel: 630-906-5478; Fax: 630-892-0170. Email: sbeach@02bancorp.com. Web: www.02bancorp.com. Joel Binder, Sr. Vice Pres.

HARVARD. *Magnificat, A Ministry to Catholic Women*, 905 Dewey St., 60033. Tel: 815-546-5063.

SAINT CHARLES. *Cultivation Ministries* (1990) P.O. Box 662, 60174. Tel: 630-513-8222; Fax: 630-549-3031. Email: info@cultivationministries.com. Web: www.cultivationministries.com. Frank Mercadante, Exec. Dir. To cultivate team-based, comprehensive and disciple-making Catholic youth ministries by training, resourcing and supporting adult and student leaders.

Queen of Americas Guild, 345 Kautz Rd., P.O. Box 851, 60174. Tel: 630-584-1822; Fax: 630-587-2200. Email: staff@queenoftheamericasguild.org. Web: www.queenoftheamericasguild.org. His Eminence Raymond Cardinal Burke, D.D., J.C.D., Dir.; Most Rev. Joseph J. Madera, M.Sp.S., D.D., Episcopal Moderator; Mr. Stephen Banaszak, Vice Pres.; Mr. Frank Smoczynski, Pres.; Beverly Smoczynski, Treas. & Dir.

Board of Directors: Rev. George M. Hastrich; Mrs. Ruth Sloan.

SAVANNA. *Mercy Homecare/Hospice*, 1121 N. 5th St., 61074. Tel: 815-273-2628; Fax: 815-273-7025. Email: nocj@mercyhealth.com. Web: www.mercyclinton.com. Joan Noe, B.S.N., M.B.A., Vice Pres. Prof. Srvcs., Admin; Sharon Meister, R.N., M.S.N., Dir.; Sean Williams, CEO. Sponsor: Trinity Health of Novi, Michigan, Catholic Health Ministries.

STERLING. *St. Vincent DePaul Society*, Tel: 815-625-0311; Fax: 815-625-1684. Email: vincent.depaul@att.net. Total Staff 20; Total Assisted 5,400.

St. Mary's Conference, 600 Ave. B, 61081. Tel: 815-625-0640; Fax: 815-625-1684.

STOCKTON. *Christ in the Wilderness* (1980) 7500 S. Randecker Rd., 61085-8922. Tel: 815-947-2476; Fax: 815-947-2476. Email: citw@dishmail.net. Web: www.citwretreat.com. Sr. Julia Marie Bathon, O.S.F., Exec. Dir. Center of Solitude & Prayer.

SYCAMORE. **Lighthouse Catholic Media NFP*, 303 E. State St., 60178. Tel: 847-488-0333; Fax: 815-895-0333. Email: tim@lighthousecatholicmedia.org. Web: www.lighthousecatholicmedia.org. Tim Truckenbrod, Vice Pres. Mktg. & Opers.

RELIGIOUS INSTITUTES OF MEN REPRESENTED IN THE DIOCESE

For further details refer to the corresponding bracketed number in the Religious Institutes of Men or Women section.

[0200]—*Benedictine Monks* (Marmion Abbey, Aurora)—O.S.B.

[1320]—*Clerics of St. Viator*—C.S.V.

[1080]—*Congregation of the Resurrection* (Chicago Prov.)—C.R.

[0480]—*Conventual Franciscans* (St. Bonaventure Province)—O.F.M.Conv

[]—*Institute of Christ the King Sovereign Priest (Provincial House-Italy)*

[1110]—*Missionaries of the Sacred Heart* (U.S. Province)—M.S.C.

[0690]—*Society of Jesus*—S.J.

RELIGIOUS INSTITUTES OF WOMEN REPRESENTED IN THE DIOCESE

[0350]—*Carmelite Sisters (Corpus Christi)*—O.Carm.

[2100]—*Congregation of the Humility of Mary*—C.H.M.

[1920]—*Congregation of the Sisters of the Holy Cross*—C.S.C.

[1710]—*Congregation of the Third Order of St. Francis of Mary Immaculate*—O.S.F.

[]—*Daughters of Mary Help of Christians Salesian Sisters of St. John Bosco*—F.M.A.

[1070-03]—*Dominican Sisters*—O.P.

[1070-10]—*Dominican Sisters*—O.P.

[1070-13]—*Dominican Sisters*—O.P.

[1430]—*Franciscan Sisters of Our Lady of Perpetual Help*—O.S.F.

[1450]—*Franciscan Sisters of the Sacred Heart*—O.S.F.

[]—*Missionaries of the Rosary of Fatima*—M.R.F.

[]—*Passionist Sisters*—C.F.P.

[3760]—*Poor Clare Colettines*—P.C.C.

[2970]—*School Sisters of Notre Dame*—S.S.N.D.

[1680]—*School Sisters of St. Francis*—O.S.F.

[3520]—*Servants of the Holy Heart of Mary*—S.S.C.M.

[0430]—*Sisters of Charity of the Blessed Virgin Mary*—B.V.M.

[2360]—*Sisters of Loretto at the Foot of the Cross*—S.L.

[2575]—*Sisters of Mercy of the Americas* (Chicago, IL)—R.S.M.

[]—*Sisters of St. Francis* (Clinton, IA)—O.S.F.

[1570]—*Sisters of St. Francis of the Holy Family*—O.S.F.

[3930]—*Sisters of St. Joseph of the Third Order of St. Francis*—S.S.J.-T.O.S.F.

[2183]—*Sisters of the Immaculate Heart of Mary Mother of Christ, Nigeria*—I. H. M.

[1770]—*Sisters of the Third Order of St. Francis* (Peoria, Illinois)—O.S.F.

DIOCESAN CEMETERIES

ROCKFORD. *Calvary-St. Mary's/St. James*

AURORA. *Mount Olivet*

BATAVIA. *Geneva-St. Charles Resurrection*

ELGIN. *Mount Hope*

WINNEBAGO. *Calvary*

NECROLOGY

† Kaiser, Joseph W., (Retired)—Died July 15, 2011

† Paddock, Richard W., (Retired)—Died July 20, 2011

An asterisk (*) denotes an organization that has established tax-exempt status directly with the IRS and is not covered by the USCCB Group Ruling.

Diocese of Rockville Centre

(Dioecesis Petropolitana In Insula Longa)

Most Reverend

JAMES J. DALY

Retired Auxiliary Bishop of Rockville Centre; ordained May 22, 1948; appointed Titular Bishop of Castra Nova and Auxiliary to the Bishop of Rockville Centre February 28, 1977; ordained May 9, 1977; retired July 1, 1996.

Most Reverend

EMIL A. WCELA

Retired Auxiliary Bishop of Rockville Centre; ordained June 2, 1956; appointed Titular Bishop of Filaca and Auxiliary Bishop of Rockville Centre October 21, 1988; ordained December 13, 1988; retired April 3, 2007. *Church of St. John the Evangelist, 546 St. John's Pl., Riverhead, NY 11901.* Tel: 631-727-2030.

Most Reverend

WILLIAM FRANCIS MURPHY, S.T.D., L.H.D.

Bishop of Rockville Centre; ordained December 16, 1964; appointed Auxiliary Bishop to the Archbishop of Boston and Titular Bishop of Saia Maggiore, November 21, 1995; consecrated December 27, 1995; appointed Fourth Bishop of Rockville Centre, June 26, 2001; installed September 5, 2001. *Mailing Address: Diocesan Pastoral Center, P.O. Box 9023, Rockville Centre, NY 11571-9023*Email: bishopsoffice@drvc.org.

Pastoral Center: P.O. Box 9023, Rockville Centre, NY 11571-9023. Tel: 516-678-5800; Fax: 516-764-3316.

Web: drvc.org

Most Reverend

JOHN C. DUNNE, D.D.

Auxiliary Bishop of Rockville Centre; ordained June 1, 1963; appointed Titular Bishop of Abercorn and Auxiliary Bishop of Rockville Centre October 21, 1988; ordained December 13, 1988. *Central Vicariate - Diocese of Rockville Centre, P.O. Box 39, Farmingdale, NY 11735-0039.* Tel: 516-249-1700.

Most Reverend

PAUL H. WALSH

Auxiliary Bishop of Rockville Centre; ordained June 9, 1966; appointed Titular Bishop of Abthugni and Auxiliary Bishop of Rockville Centre April 3, 2003; ordained May 29, 2003. *Western Vicariate - Diocese of Rockville Centre, P.O. Box 933, Roosevelt, NY 11575-0933.* Tel: 516-867-6341.

ESTABLISHED APRIL 6, 1957.

Square Miles 1,198.

The Roman Catholic Diocese of Rockville Centre, New York.

Comprises the Counties of Nassau and Suffolk (excepting Fishers Island) in the State of New York.

For legal titles of parishes and diocesan institutions, consult the Chancery Office.

STATISTICAL OVERVIEW

Personnel	
Bishop	1
Auxiliary Bishops	2
Retired Bishops	2
Priests: Diocesan Active in Diocese	220
Priests: Diocesan Active Outside Diocese	8
Priests: Diocesan in Foreign Missions	1
Priests: Retired, Sick or Absent	124
Number of Diocesan Priests	353
Religious Priests in Diocese	64
Total Priests in Diocese	417
Extern Priests in Diocese	89
Ordinations:	
Diocesan Priests	4
Transitional Deacons	4
Permanent Deacons	11
Permanent Deacons in Diocese	278
Total Brothers	77
Total Sisters	1,112
Parishes	
Parishes	133
With Resident Pastor:	
Resident Diocesan Priests	124
Resident Religious Priests	6
Without Resident Pastor:	
Administered by Priests	3
Missions	1
Professional Ministry Personnel:	
Brothers	6
Sisters	84
Lay Ministers	415
Welfare	
Catholic Hospitals	6
Total Assisted	648,401
Health Care Centers	3
Total Assisted	42,287
Homes for the Aged	3
Total Assisted	2,132
Residential Care of Children	3
Total Assisted	877
Specialized Homes	8
Total Assisted	1,625
Special Centers for Social Services	50
Total Assisted	43,167
Residential Care of Disabled	51
Total Assisted	253
Other Institutions	113
Total Assisted	135,955
Educational	
Seminaries, Diocesan	1
Students from This Diocese	14
Students from Other Diocese	32
Diocesan Students in Other Seminaries	3
Total Seminarians	17
Colleges and Universities	1
Total Students	3,037
High Schools, Diocesan and Parish	5
Total Students	4,623
High Schools, Private	5
Total Students	7,705
Elementary Schools, Diocesan and Parish	49
Total Students	17,159
Elementary Schools, Private	4
Total Students	1,337
Non-residential Schools for the Disabled	1
Total Students	98
Catechesis/Religious Education:	
High School Students	2,503
Elementary Students	94,203
Total Students under Catholic Instruction	130,699
Teachers in the Diocese:	
Priests	11
Brothers	38
Sisters	46
Lay Teachers	1,794
Vital Statistics	
Receptions into the Church:	
Infant Baptism Totals	15,720
Adult Baptism Totals	598
Received into Full Communion	318
First Communions	17,123
Confirmations	16,296
Marriages:	
Catholic	4,152
Interfaith	525
Total Marriages	4,677
Deaths	10,108
Total Catholic Population	1,737,498
Total Population	3,527,942

Former Bishops—Most Revs. WALTER P. KELLENBERG, D.D., first Bishop of Rockville Centre; ord. June 2, 1928; appt. Titular Bishop of Joannina and Auxiliary Bishop of New York, Aug. 25, 1953; cons. Oct. 5, 1953; appt. Bishop of Ogdensburg, Jan. 19, 1954; appt. first Bishop of Rockville Centre, April 16, 1957; installed May 27, 1957; retired May 3, 1976; died Jan. 11, 1986; JOHN R. MCGANN, D.D., second Bishop of Rockville Centre; ord. June 3, 1950; appt. Titular Bishop of Morosbisdus and Auxiliary to the Bishop of Rockville Centre, Nov. 12, 1970; cons. Jan. 7, 1971; appt. second Bishop of Rockville Centre, May 3, 1976; installed June 24, 1976; retired Jan. 4, 2000; died Jan. 29, 2002; JAMES T. MCHUGH, S.T.D., third Bishop of Rockville Centre; ord. May 25, 1957; appt. Titular Bishop of Morosbisdo and Auxiliary Bishop of Newark, Nov. 20, 1987; cons. Jan. 25, 1988; appt. Bishop of Camden, May 13, 1989; installed June 20, 1989; appt. Coadjutor Bishop of Rockville Centre, Dec. 7, 1998; installed Feb. 22, 1999; succeeded to the See, Jan. 4, 2000; died Dec. 10, 2000.

Diocesan Bishop—Most Rev. WILLIAM FRANCIS MURPHY, S.T.D., L.H.D.

Auxiliary Bishops—Most Revs. EMIL A. WCELA, D.D., Emeritus; PAUL H. WALSH, D.D.; JOHN C. DUNNE, D.D.; JAMES J. DALY, D.D., Emeritus.

Secretary to the Bishop—Rev. Msgr. ROBERT O. MORRISSEY, M.Div., J.C.D. Tel: 516-678-5800, Ext. 402; Fax: 516-678-3138. Email: rmorrissey@drvc.org.

Vicar General and Moderator of the Curia—Rev. Msgr. ROBERT J. BRENNAN, V.G., P.O. Box 9023, Rockville Centre, 11571-9023. Tel: 516-678-5800, Ext. 622. Email: rbrennan@drvc.org.

Episcopal Vicars—Western Vicariate: Most Rev. PAUL H. WALSH, D.D., Mailing Address: P.O. Box 933, Roosevelt, 11575-0933. Tel: 516-867-6340; Fax: 516-867-6341. Email: phwalsh@drvc.org. Central Vicariate: Most Rev. JOHN C. DUNNE, D.D., Mailing Address: P.O. Box 39, Farmingdale, 11735-0039. Tel: 516-249-1700; Fax: 516-249-1701. Email: dunnejc@worldnet.att.net. Eastern Vicariate: VACANT, Mailing Address: P.O. Box 999, Riverhead, 11901. Tel: 631-727-5376; Fax: 631-727-2326.

Chancery Office—

Co Chancellors—Rev. Msgr. ANDRZEJ ZGLEJSZEWSKI; Sr. LUCY BLYSKAL, C.S.J., J.C.D. Tel: 516-678-5800, Ext. 583. Email: chancellor@drvc.org.

Vice Chancellor—Rev. Msgr. ROBERT O. MORRISSEY, M.Div., J.C.D. Email: rmorrissey@drvc.org.

Cabinet—

Secretary for Diocesan Administration—Mr. KEVIN T. MURPHY. Tel: 516-678-5800, Ext. 543. Email: ktmurphy@drvc.org.

Secretary for Communications—Mr. SEAN P. DOLAN. Tel: 516-678-5800, Ext. 625. Email: rvcinfo@drvc.org.

Secretary for Education—Sr. JOANNE CALLAHAN, O.S.U., M.S., Ph.D. Tel: 516-678-5800, Ext. 548. Email: jcallahan@drvc.org.

Secretary for Faith Formation—Sr. MARY ALICE PIIL, C.S.J., Ph.D. Tel: 516-678-5800, Ext. 512. Email: mapiil@drvc.org.

Secretary for Ministerial Personnel—Rev. Msgr. BRIAN J. MCNAMARA. Tel: 516-678-5800, Ext. 585. Email: bmcnamara@drvc.org.

Secretary for New Evangelization—Bro. JAMES MCVEIGH, O.S.F. Tel: 516-678-5800, Ext. 588. Email: jmcreigh@drvc.org.

Secretary for Social Services—LAURA CASSELL. Tel: 516-733-7013. Email: cassell.laura@catholiccharities.cc.

Secretary for Institutional Advancement—ENES CARNESECCA. Tel: 516-379-5210, Ext. 226. Email: ecarnesecca@drvc.org.

Secretary for General Counsel—Mr. THOMAS RENKER. Tel: 516-678-5800, Ext. 241. Email: trenker@drvc.org.

Secretary to the Bishop—Rev. Msgr. ROBERT O. MORRISSEY, M.Div., J.C.D. Tel: 516-678-5800, Ext. 402. Email: rmorrissey@drvc.org.

Co Chancellors—Rev. Msgr. ANDRZEJ ZGLEJSZEWSKI. Tel: 516-678-5800, Ext. 503. Email: azglejszewski@drvc.org; Sr. LUCY BLYSKAL, C.S.J., J.C.D. Tel: 516-678-5800, Ext. 583. Email: chancellor@drvc.org.

Vicar General—Rev. Msgr. ROBERT J. BRENNAN, V.G. Tel: 516-678-5800, Ext. 622. Email: rbrennan@drvc.org.

Censors of Books—Rt. Rev. Msgr. JOHN A. ALESANDRO, P.A., J.C.D.; Rev. CHARLES CACCAVALE, S.T.L., S.T.D.; Rev. Msgrs. GEORGE P. GRAHAM, J.C.D., Ph.D. (Retired); ROBERT O. MORRISSEY, M.Div., J.C.D.; FRANCIS J. SCHNEIDER, M.Div., J.C.D.; Revs. ROBERT J. SMITH, S.T.L., S.T.D.; PETER I. VACCARI, S.T.L.

Diocesan Tribunal—P.O. Box 9023, Rockville Centre, 11571-9023. Tel: 516-678-5800; Fax: 516-594-1548.

Judicial Vicar—Rev. Msgr. JAMES F. PEREDA, M.Div., M.A., J.C.D. Tel: 516-678-5800, Ext. 565. Email: jpereda@drvc.org.

Adjutant Judicial Vicar—Rev. THOMAS V. ARNAO, M.Div., J.C.D. Tel: 516-678-5800, Ext. 558.

Diocesan Judge—Rev. ERIC R. FASANO, M.Div., J.C.L. Tel: 516-678-5800, Ext. 216.

Defenders of the Bond—Rt. Rev. Msgr. CHARLES A. GUARINO, P.A., M.A., M.Div., J.C.D. (Retired); Deacon THOMAS B. RICH, J.C.L., D.Min. Tel: 516-678-5800, Ext. 559.

Promoter of Justice—Rt. Rev. Msgr. CHARLES A. GUARINO, P.A., M.A., M.Div., J.C.D. (Retired).

Judges for Interdiocesan Tribunal—Rev. Msgr. RICHARD C. BAUHOFF, J.C.D., Ph.D.; Sr. LUCY BLYSKAL, C.S.J., J.C.D.; Rev. Msgrs. THOMAS D. CANDREVA, S.T.L., J.C.D. (Retired); DOMENICK T. GRAZIADIO, M.A.; RICHARD P. KOPINSKI, M.S., M.A.; FRANCIS S. MIDURA, M.Div., M.Ch.A.; THOMAS E. MOLLOY (Retired); ROBERT O. MORRISSEY, M.Div., J.C.D.; JOHN C. NOSSER, M.S., M.Div. (Retired); Rev. JOHN J. TUTONE, M.Div., J.C.D.

Notaries—Sr. RUTH BORGERSEN, R.S.M., M.A.; Mrs. CAROL GATZ; Mrs. MAYRA REYES; Mrs. NANNO E. HAYES; Mrs. HELEN HOWE.

In-Take Secretary—Mrs. NANNO E. HAYES. Tel: 516-678-5800, Ext. 571.

Medical Experts—MARY W. HOULIHAN, Ph.D.; Sr. THOMAS MORE FAHEY, R.G.S., Psy.D.; THOMAS P. DEMARIA, Ph.D.

Coordinator of Post-Annulment Counseling Program—Mrs. BARBARA BUTLER, M.A., L.M.F.T. Tel: 631-754-9765.

Procurator & Advocates—Deacon GEOFFREY ANISANSEL; Mrs. LORRAINE ANISANSEL; Mrs. TERRI BLAKENEY; Mrs. MARIAN BOPP; Sr. RUTH BORGENSEN, R.S.M.; Rev. Msgr. WILLIAM G. BRESLAWSKI; Ms. NOREEN BRITTENHAM; Mrs. BARBARA BUTLER, M.A., L.M.F.T.; Sr. HELEN BYRNE, C.S.J.; Deacons FRANCISCO CALES; JAMES CARROLL; TONY CEDRONE; Mrs. DOLORES CONNORS; Sr. MIRIAM HONORA CORR, C.S.J.; Rev. THOMAS C. COSTA; Deacon FRANK COVE; Sr. EILEEN CURLEY, R.S.M.; Ms. ANITA DOS SANTOS; Rev. LAWRENCE T. DUNCKLEE; Mrs. VALERIE DUNNE; Mr. WILLIAM DWYER; Deacons THOMAS J. EVRARD; ANDREW GARGIULO; RONALD J. GILLETTE; Mr. JOHN E. GLYNN; Rev. THOMAS HAGGERTY; Mrs. NANNO E. HAYES; Dr. JOANNE HEANY-HUNTER; Mr. RICHARD HUMINSKI; Rev. WALTER F. KEDJIERSKI; Sisters BONNIE KELLY, C.S.J.; JANE LYONS, C.I.J.; Rev. JAMES P. MANNION JR.; Rev. Msgr. JAMES M. MCDONALD; Rev. MARTIN MCGEOUGH, C.M.; Deacon JAMES MCQUADE; Ms. ANN MESSINA; Rev. JOSEPH A. MIRRO; Mr. CHRISTOPHER J. MURANO; Deacons CHARLES MUSCARNERA; MONTFORD D. NAYLOR; Rev. CHRISTOPHER NOWAK; Deacon JOHN O'CONNOR; Mrs. MARY ANN O'CONNOR; Deacon THOMAS O'CONNOR; Dr. MARY O'GRADY; Ms. ROSEMARY PADALA; Deacon PHIL PAOLICELLI; Mr. JOSEPH PARADISE; Ms. EILEEN PHILLIPS; Mr. JOHN P. REALI; Deacon GEORGE REICH; Mrs. LINDA REICH; Rev. ROBERT A. ROMEO; Ms. CARMEN RONCAL; Deacons CARL SANFILIPPO; NEIL SQUITIERI; JOHN SULLIVAN; Sr. KATHLEEN T. SULLIVAN, C.S.J.; Rev. Msgr. EDWARD A. SWEENY, M.Div., J.C.D., Ph.D.; Sr. EUGENIA M. TRAVERS, O.P.; Rev. Msgr. EDMOND J. TRENCH (Retired); Sr. PATRICIA TURLEY, C.S.J.; Ms. JULIE VAN NOSTRAND; Rev. MICHAEL A. VETRANO; Sr. ELLEN ZAK, C.S.F.N.; Rev. KENNETH M. ZACH; Rev. Msgr. ANDRZEJ ZGLEJSZEWSKI.

Presbyteral Council—Most Revs. JOHN C. DUNNE, D.D.; PAUL H. WALSH, D.D.; Rev. Msgrs. ROBERT J. BRENNAN, V.G.; WILLIAM G. BRESLAWSKI; Revs. PETER DEVARAJ, S.A.C.; ROBERT J. CLERKIN; Rev. Msgr. JOSEPH DEGROCCO, D.Min.; Rev. ROBERT KUZNIK; Rev. Msgrs. ROBERT O. MORRISSEY, M.Div., J.C.D., Exec. Sec.; STEVEN CAMP; Revs. FRANCIS PIZZARELLI, S.M.M.; GERARD J. GENTLEMAN, M.A., M.Div.; Rev. Msgr. PAUL RAHILLY; Revs. GREGORY J. CAPPUCCINO; GENNARO J. DISPIGNO; GONZALO OAJACA-LOPEZ; MICHAEL A. VETRANO; Rev. Msgrs. THOMAS COOGAN; BRENDAN P. RIORDAN; JOSEPH P. GRANATA; FRANCIS S. MIDURA, M.Div., M.Ch.A.; Rev. MICHAEL J. RIEDER.

College of Consultors—Most Revs. JOHN C. DUNNE, D.D.; PAUL H. WALSH, D.D.; Rev. Msgrs. ROBERT J. BRENNAN, V.G.; WILLIAM G. BRESLAWSKI; JOSEPH DEGROCCO, D.Min.; ROBERT O. MORRISSEY, M.Div., J.C.D.; PAUL RAHILLY; BRENDAN P. RIORDAN.

Deans—Rockville Centre Deanery: Rev. Msgr. WILLIAM E. KOENIG. North Hempstead Deanery: Rev. Msgr. JOHN J. MCCANN. Oyster Bay Deanery: Rev. ROBERT ROMEO. Belmont Deanery: Rev. Msgr. THOMAS J. HAROLD. Hicksville Deanery: Rev. GERARD A. RINGENBACK, M.S.Ed., M.A. Five Towns Deanery: Rev. JOHN J. TUTONE, M.Div., J.C.D. Seaford Deanery: Rev. Msgr. PETER J. PFLOMM. Huntington Deanery: Rev. Msgr. JOHN R. DREASEN. Smithaven Deanery: Rev. ANTHONY M. STANGANELLI. Babylon Deanery: Rev. Msgr. CHRISTOPHER J. HELLER. Islip Deanery: Rev. Msgr. THOMAS COOGAN. North Brookhaven Deanery: Rev. Msgr. WILLIAM A. HANSON. South Brookhaven Deanery: Rev. GENNARO J. DISPIGNO. Peconic Deanery: Rev. JOSEPH A. MIRRO.

Diocesan Offices

Pastoral Center—P.O. Box 9023, Rockville Centre, 11571-9023. Tel: 516-678-5800; Fax: 516-764-3316.

Director of Diocesan Administration—Mr. KEVIN T. MURPHY. Tel: 516-678-5800, Ext. 543. Email: ktmurphy@drvc.org.

Archives—Mrs. JEAN LYNCH, Archivist, Seminary of the Immaculate Conception, 440 W. Neck Rd., Huntington, 11743. Tel: 631-423-0483; Fax: 631-423-7922. Email: archives@drvc.org.

Institutional Advancement—ENES CARNESECCA. Tel: 516-379-5210, Ext. 226. Email: ecarnesecca@drvc.org.

Catholic Ministries Appeal—Mailing Address: P.O. Box 4000, Rockville Centre, 11571. Tel: 516-379-5210, Ext. 210; Fax: 516-379-5043. Email: catholicministries@drvc.org.

Parish Stewardship—200 W. Centennial Ave., Ste. 202, Roosevelt, 11575. Tel: 516-379-4055; Fax: 516-379-3234. Email: stewardship@prodigy.net. Web: www.stewardshipli.org.

Religious & Priest Retirement Fund—Tel: 516-379-5210, Ext. 210; Fax: 516-379-5043. Email: catholicministries@drvc.org.

Catholic Charities—LAURA A. CASSELL, Exec. Dir., 90 Cherry Ln., Hicksville, 11801. Tel: 516-733-7013 See separate listing below.

Cemeteries—Mr. PETER RYAN, Acting Dir., Mailing Address: Catholic Cemeteries, Diocese of Rockville Centre, P.O. Box 182, Westbury, 11590. Tel: 516-334-7990; Fax: 516-334-4383. Email: director@holyroodcemetery.org. Web: www.holyroodcemetery.org; Holy Rood Cemetery, 111 Old Country Rd., Box 182, Westbury, 11590-0182. Tel: 516-334-7990; Fax: 516-334-4383. Holy Sepulchre Cemetery, 3442 Rte. 112, Coram, 11727. Tel: 631-732-3460; Fax: 631-732-3476. Queen of All Saints Cemetery, 115 Wheeler Rd., Central Islip, 11722. Tel: 631-234-8297; Fax: 631-234-8632.

Chaplains (Uniformed)—

Chaplain of the Nassau County Fire Services—Rev. KEVIN M. SMITH St. Dominic, Oyster Bay.

Chaplains of the Nassau County Police Department—Rev. Msgr. THOMAS HARTMAN; Revs. JOSEPH D'ANGELO Sacred Heart, North Merrick.; GERARD GORDON St. Dominic, Oyster Bay.

Chaplains of the Suffolk County Police Department—Revs. SEÁN J. GANN St. Joseph, Kings Park.; BRUCE J. POWERS Sts. Peter and Paul, Manorville.

Consultation Service for Religious Personnel—Sr. MILDRED SCHUBERT, S.C., Exec. Dir., Mailing Address: P.O. Box 467, Rockville Centre, 11571. Tel: 516-678-2135.

Deacons—Deacons JAMES MURPHY, Dir. Deacon Personnel, Seminary of the Immaculate Conception, Office of Deacons, 440 W. Neck Rd., Huntington, 11743. Tel: 631-424-8360, Ext. 177; Fax: 631-424-8361. Email: jmurphy@drvc.org; THOMAS W. CONNOLLY, Dir. Diaconate Formation. Tel: 631-424-8360, Ext. 178. Email: tconnolly@drvc.org.

Ecumenical & Interreligious Affairs—Rev. Msgr. DONALD M. BECKMANN, Dir. Tel: 516-678-5800, Ext. 613; Fax: 516-763-1078.

Education—Sr. JOANNE CALLAHAN, O.S.U., M.S., Ph.D., Supt. Tel: 516-678-5800, Ext. 548; Fax: 516-678-7362. Email: edoffice@drvcschools.org; Dr. STEVEN F. CHEESEMAN, Ed.D., Assoc. Supt. Tel: 516-678-5800, Ext. 546. Email: scheeseman@drvcschools.org; Sr. LORRAINE MCDONALD, O.P., M.S., P.D., Asst. Supt. Elementary Schools. Tel: 516-678-5800, Ext. 545. Email: lmcdonald@drvcschools.org; MAUREEN HANNAN, B.S., M.B.A., Coord. Finances for Elementary Schools. Tel: 516-678-5800, Ext. 225. Email: mhannan@drvc.org; BIAGIO ARPINO, M.S., Ph.D., Asst. Supt. Personnel. Tel: 516-678-5800, Ext. 553. Email: barpino@drvcschools.org; KATHLEEN RAZZETTI, M.S., C.A.S., Asst. Supt. Public Policy, Govt. Programs & Student Svcs. Tel: 516-678-5800, Ext. 550. Email: krazzetti@drvcschools.org; Sr. ANTOINETTE DE AVEIRO, O.P., M.S., Asst. Supt. Elementary Schools. Tel: 516-678-5800, Ext. 277. Email: adeaveiro@drvcschools.org; NORMA WHITLEY, M.A., Asst. Supt. Technology. Tel: 516-678-5800, Ext. 404. Email: nwhitley@drvcschools.org; Dr. ELIZABETH FRANGELLA, Ed.D., Asst. Supt. Curriculum, Instruction & Assessment. Tel: 516-678-5800, Ext. 617. Email: efrangella@drvcschools.org.

Faith Formation—Sr. MARY ALICE PIIL, C.S.J., Ph.D., Dir. Tel: 516-678-5800, Ext. 512; Fax: 516-536-3473. Email: mapiil@drvc.org; ESTELLE PECK, Assoc. Dir. Adult Faith Formation. Tel: 516-678-5800, Ext. 200; Fax: 516-536-3473. Email: epeck@drvc.org; ELLEN ZAFONTE, Assoc. Dir. Children & Youth Formation. Tel: 516-678-5800, Ext. 506; Fax: 516-536-3473. Email: ezafonte@drvc.org; KATHLEEN LOGAN, Dir. Family Ministry. Tel: 516-678-5800, Ext. 202; Fax: 516-536-3473. Email: klogan@drvc.org; JOHN ROMANOWSKY, Assoc. Dir. Media Technology. Tel: 516-678-5800, Ext. 210; Fax: 516-536-3473. Email: jromanowsky@drvc.org; MARY ANN RUSSO, Assoc. Dir. Persons With Disabilities. Tel: 516-678-5800, Ext. 540; Fax: 516-536-3473. Email: marusso@drvc.org.

Temporal Affairs—

Director of Diocesan Administration—Mr. KEVIN T. MURPHY. Tel: 516-678-5800, Ext. 543; Fax: 516-536-6554. Email: ktmurphy@drvc.org.

Chief Financial Officer—THOMAS DOODIAN. Tel: 516-678-5800, Ext. 522. Email: tdoodian@drvc.org.

General Counsel—Mr. THOMAS RENKER. Tel: 516-678-5800, Ext. 241. Email: trenker@drvc.org.

Facilities and Risk Management—Mr. WILLIAM G. CHAPIN, Dir. Tel: 516-678-5800, Ext. 261; Fax: 516-763-2606. Email: wgchapin@drvc.org.

Health Care Apostolate—Catholic Health Services of Long Island, 992 N. Village Ave., Rockville Centre, 11570. Tel: 516-705-3700. Mr. RICHARD J.J. SULLIVAN JR., Exec. Chm. Catholic Health Svcs.; Ms. CATERINA MAKO, 245 Old Country Rd., Melville, 11747. Tel: 631-465-6277; Fax: 631-465-6522 For individual hospitals and other healthcare institutions see separate listings below.

Office of Public Information—Mr. SEAN P. DOLAN, Dir. Tel: 516-678-5800, Ext. 625; Fax: 516-594-0984. Email: rvcinfo@drvc.org.

Immigrant Services—Ms. CARMEN MAQUILON, Dir. Immigrant Svcs. Catholic Charities, 143 Schleigel Blvd., Amityville, 11701. Tel: 631-789-5210; Fax: 631-789-5245.

Ministry to Senior Priests—Rev. Msgr. THOMAS F. MULVANERTY; Bro. PATRICK MURPHY, St. Pius X Residence, 555 Albany Ave., Amityville, 11701.

Office of New Evangelization—Bro. JAMES MCVEIGH, O.S.F., Dir. Tel: 516-678-5800, Ext. 588. Email: jmcveigh@drvc.org.

Catholics of African Ancestry—DARCEL WHITTEN-WILAMOWSKI. Tel: 516-678-5800, Ext. 239.

Campus Ministry—MARIANNE SHERIDAN, Coord. Tel: 516-678-5800, Ext. 615. Email: msheridan@drvc.org.

Haitian-American Apostolate—Rev. EDEN JEAN BAPTISTE, Coord. Tel: 516-678-5800, Ext. 233. Email: ebaptiste@drvc.org.

Hispanic Ministry—Deacon FRANCISCO CALES, Coord. Tel: 516-678-5800, Ext. 618.

Mission Office— Society for the Propagation of the Faith, Holy Childhood Association, Catholic Relief Services, Diocesan Mission in the Dominican Republic, American Home Missions, Secretariat for Latin America. Rev. JOSEPH

McCABE, M.M. Tel: 516-678-5800, Ext. 513.
Youth and Young Adult Ministry—MARIANNE SHERIDAN, Coord. Tel: 516-678-5800, Ext. 615. Email: msheridan@drvc.org.
Renewal Apostolate—Dr. JOHN PALMER. Tel: 516-678-5800, Ext. 408. Email: jpalmer@drvc.org.
Newspaper - "The Long Island Catholic"— (published by the Catholic Press Association of the Diocese of Rockville Centre, Inc.) *200 W. Centennial Ave., Ste. 201, P.O. Box 9000, Roosevelt, 11575*. Tel: 516-594-1000; Fax: 516-594-1092. Web: www.licatholic.org. Email: editor@licatholic.org (editorial); adstlic@licatholic.org (advertisements). RICHARD HINSHAW, Editor.
Office for the Protection of Children & Young People—EILEEN PUGLISI, Dir. Tel: 516-678-5800, Ext. 573; Fax: 516-887-1584. Email: epuglisi@drvc.org.
Clergy Personnel—Rev. Msgr. BRIAN J. MCNAMARA. Tel: 516-678-5800, Ext. 584; Fax: 516-764-3467. Email: bmcnamara@drvc.org.
Priestly Life and Ministry—Rev. Msgr. JAMES P. SWIADER, M.Div., Church of Saint Joseph, 130 Fifth St., Garden City, 11530. Tel: 516-747-3535.
Priests' Personnel Assignment Board—Most Revs. JOHN C. DUNNE, D.D.; PAUL H. WALSH, D.D.; Rev. Msgrs. ROBERT J. BRENNAN, V.G.; BRIAN J. MCNAMARA; Revs. LEE R. DESCOTEAUX; MICHAEL T. MAFFEO; FRANCIS M. NELSON; Rev. Msgr. PETER J. PFLOMM; Revs. PATRICK J. WHITNEY; ROBERT J. SMITH, S.T.L., S.T.D.; Mrs. MADLEN YOUNG, Sec.
Priests' Personnel Policy Board—Rev. Msgr. BRIAN J. MCNAMARA; Rev. BRIAN INGRAM; Rev. Msgrs. THOMAS F. MULVANERTY; FRANCIS J. SCHNEIDER, M.Div., J.C.D.; Rev. ANTHONY M. STANGANELLI; Rev. Msgr. JAMES P. SWIADER, M.Div.
Priests' Retirement Board—Most Rev. JOHN C. DUNNE, D.D., Ex Officio; Rev. Msgrs. BRIAN J. MCNAMARA; THOMAS F. MULVANERTY, Sec. & Ex Officio; RICHARD C. BAUHOFF, J.C.D., Ph.D.; Rev. ROBERT J. CLERKIN; Rev. Msgrs. GEORGE P. GRAHAM, J.C.D., Ph.D. (Retired); JOSEPH K. CURLEY (Retired); Rt. Rev. Msgr. JAMES P. KELLY (Retired); Revs. PETER C. DOOLEY; JOSEPH V. DAVANZO; Rt. Rev. Msgr. EMMET FAGAN.
Prison Ministry and Criminal Justice Affairs—26 S. Saxon Ave., Bay Shore, 11706-8920. Tel: 631-969-0837; Fax: 631-666-5073. Bro. JACK MOYLAN, O.S.F., D.Min., Dir.; SUZANNE D. JONES, Coord. Ministerial Svcs.
Nassau County Correctional Center—100 Carman Ave., East Meadow, 11554-1146. Tel: 516-572-4145; 516-572-3622. Chaplains: Rev. RALPH FERRO; Sr. DOLORES CASTELLANO, C.I.J.; Deacons JOHN H. MCGONIGLE; SCOTT BAKER; MANUEL RAMOS.
Nassau County Juvenile Detention Center—61 Carman Ave., Westbury, 11590. Tel: 516-571-9153. Sr. DOLORES CASTELLANO, C.I.J.; Bro. JACK MOYLAN, O.S.F., D.Min., Chap.
Suffolk County Correctional Facility—100 Center Dr., Riverhead, 11901. Tel: 631-852-2294; 631-852-2728. Chaplains: Sr. MICHELLE BREMER, C.S.F.N.; Deacon CHRIS VIGLIOTTA.
Suffolk County Minimum Security Facility—Mailing Address: P.O. Box 69, Yaphank, 11980. Tel: 631-852-4713. Chaplains: Deacon CHRIS VIGLIOTTA; Sr. MICHELLE BREMER, C.S.F.N.; Deacon RONALD BLASIUS.
Religious—Vicar for Religious: Bro. JAMES MCVEIGH, O.S.F. Tel: 516-678-5800, Ext. 588. Email: jmcveigh@drvc.org; Sr. MARY WALSH, C.S.J. Tel: 516-678-5800, Ext. 589. Email: mwalsh@drvc.org.
Respect Life—ALLISON O'BRIEN, Dir. Tel: 516-678-5800, Ext. 381. Email: aobrien@drvc.org.
Television (Telecare/TV 29)—1200 Glenn Curtiss Blvd., Uniondale, 11553. Tel: 516-538-8700; Fax: 516-489-9701. Email: info@telecaretv.org. Rev. Msgr. JAMES C. VLAUN.
Victim Assistance Coordinator—EILEEN PUGLISI. Tel: 516-678-5800, Ext. 573. Email: epuglisi@drvc.org.
Vocations—Rev. BRIAN P. BARR, Dir., Vocation Office, 440 W. Neck Rd., Huntington, 11743. Tel: 631-242-9888; Fax: 631-242-9889. Email: vocations@drvc.org. Web: www.drvc.org/vocations.
Worship—Rev. Msgr. ANDRZEJ ZGLEJSZEWSKI, Dir. Tel: 516-678-5800, Ext. 503.

Diocesan Organizations

Apostleship of Prayer—Rev. Msgr. JAMES M. MCDONALD, Dir., 505 Willis Ave., Williston Park, 11596. Tel: 516-746-6585; Fax: 516-746-6055.
Catholic Accountants' Guild—Miss MARY R. GOELLER, Contact Person, 155 Garfield Ave., Mineola, 11501. Tel: 516-746-1223.
Catholic Lawyer's Guild—Rev. Msgrs. JAMES F. PEREDA, M.Div., M.A., J.C.D., Diocesan Chap. Tel: 516-678-5800, Ext. 565. Email: jpereda@drvc.org; ROBERT J. BRENNAN, V.G., Nassau County Chap.
Catholic Youth Organization of Nassau and Suffolk—Mr. FRANK SEELY, Exec. Dir.; Ms. MARGARET JOHNSON, Prog. Dir.; Rev. GERARD A. RINGENBACK, M.S.Ed., M.A., Priest Moderator, 20 E. Cherry St., Hicksville, 11801.
Nocturnal Adoration Society—Rev. Msgr. JAMES M. MCDONALD, Dir., 505 Willis Ave., Williston Park, 11596. Tel: 516-746-6585; Fax: 516-746-6055.
Legion of Mary—Rev. Msgr. JAMES M. MCDONALD, Dir., 505 Willis Ave., Williston Park, 11596. Tel: 516-746-6585; Fax: 516-746-6055.
Society of St. Vincent de Paul—JAMES T. DILTS, Exec. Dir., 249 Broadway, Bethpage, 11714. Tel: 516-822-3132; Fax: 516-822-2728.

CLERGY, PARISHES, MISSIONS AND PAROCHIAL SCHOOLS

VILLAGE OF ROCKVILLE CENTRE

(NASSAU COUNTY)

1—ST. AGNES CATHEDRAL (1894) Rev. Msgr. William E. Koenig, Rector; Revs. German Villabon, O.S.A.; Adrian McHugh (Ireland); Deacons Thomas McDaid; Donald Stamm. In Res., Rt. Rev. Msgr. James P. Kelly, Rector Emeritus (Retired); Rev. Msgr. Andrzej Zglejszewski (Poland).
Res.: 29 Quealy Pl., 11570. Tel: 516-766-0205; Fax: 516-763-0745. Email: parishoffice@stagnescathedral.org. Web: www.stagnescathedral.org.
School—70 Clinton Ave., 11570. Tel: 516-678-5550; Fax: 516-678-0437. Sr. Kathleen Carlin, Co-Prin.; Helen Newman, Co-Prin. Sisters of St. Dominic 1; Lay Teachers 48; Students 827.
Catechesis/Religious Program—Tel: 516-678-2306. Dr. Donna Eschenauer, D.R.E. Students 1,435.

2—CAMPUS PARISH OF LONG ISLAND (1972) Rev. Brian P. Barr, Admin. & Dir.
P.O. Box 9023, 11571. Tel: 516-678-5800, Ext. 614; Fax: 516-763-1078.
For details, please refer to Campus Ministries and Newman Centers under the Institution section.

OUTSIDE VILLAGE OF ROCKVILLE CENTRE

AMITYVILLE, SUFFOLK CO., ST. MARTIN OF TOURS (1897) Rev. Richard T. Stelter; Deacons Michael Aprile; Richard Ferri.
Res.: 37 Union Ave., 11701. Tel: 631-264-0124; Fax: 631-264-0139. Email: martours@optonline.net.
School—41 Union Ave., 11701. Tel: 631-264-7166; Fax: 631-264-0136. Web: smtschool.org. Sisters of St. Joseph 1; Lay Teachers 24; Students 403.
Catechesis/Religious Program—Tel: 631-691-1617. Students 221.

BABYLON, SUFFOLK CO., ST. JOSEPH (1877) [CEM] Rev. Msgr. Christopher J. Heller; Revs. Joseph V. Arevalo; Seth N. Arwo-Doqu; Francis A. Samuel, O.C.I.; Deacons Michael J. Leyden; John F. Sullivan; Barry P. Croce; George F. Nealis; Geoffrey R. Anisanel.
Res.: 39 N. Carll Ave., 11702-2701. Tel: 631-669-0068; Fax: 631-669-9175. Email: parishoffice@stjosephsbabylon.org. Web: www.stjosephsbabylon.org.
Catechesis/Religious Program—Tel: 631-587-4717. Claire Moyle, D.R.E. Students 1,313.
Mission— Oak Beach, Suffolk Co. 11702. (Summer)
Mission— West Gilgo Beach, Suffolk Co. 11702. (Summer)

BALDWIN, NASSAU CO., ST. CHRISTOPHER (1915) Rev. Msgr. Steven Camp; Rev. Robert A. Holz; Deacons Charles Muscarnera; Anthony Banno; James Carroll.
Res.: 11 Gale Ave., 11510-3202. Tel: 516-223-0723; Fax: 516-867-5678. Email: info@stchristopherbaldwin.org. Web: www.stchris.com.
School—15 Pershing Blvd., 11510. Tel: 516-223-4404; Fax: 516-223-1409. Anne Lederer, Prin. Sisters of St. Joseph, Brentwood 1; Lay Teachers 20; Students 310.
Catechesis/Religious Program—Tel: 516-223-5813; Fax: 516-223-5609. Mrs. Gail Milne, D.R.E. (Adult & Faith Formation); James Montalbano, Music & Liturgy Dir. Students 771.

BAY SHORE, SUFFOLK CO., ST. PATRICK'S (1883) [CEM] Rev. Msgr. Thomas Coogan; Revs. Stephen J. Pietrowski; Harold J. Noviello; Deacons Joseph Peralta; Frank Keach.
Res.: 9 N. Clinton Ave., 11706. Tel: 631-665-4911; Fax: 631-665-8388.
School—Tel: 631-665-0569; Fax: 631-968-6007. Web: www.spsbayshore.org. Mrs. Roseann Petruccio, Prin. Lay Teachers 22; Students 426.
Catechesis/Religious Program—Tel: 631-665-4914; Fax: 631-665-9009. Students 1,183.

BAYVILLE, NASSAU CO., ST. GERTRUDE'S (1959) Rev. Stephen J. Brigandi.
Res.: 28 School St., 11709. Tel: 516-628-1113; Fax: 516-628-9032.
School—Pre School, Tel: 516-628-3710. Students 30.
Catechesis/Religious Program—Tel: 516-628-2432; Fax: 516-628-0224. Students 328.

BELLMORE, NASSAU CO., ST. BARNABAS THE APOSTLE (1912) Revs. Joseph C. Coschignano; Charles Omotu (Nigeria); Valentine D. Rebello (India); Deacons Bernard Sherlock; Richard Iandoli.
Res.: 2320 Bedford Ave., 11710. Tel: 516-785-0054; Fax: 516-221-7789. Web: www.stbarnabasny.org.
See St. Elizabeth Ann Seton Regional School, Bellmore under Regional Schools located in the Institution section.
Catechesis/Religious Program—Tel: 516-785-0130; Fax: 516-221-0391. Email: stbarnabasocf@yahoo.com. Students 1,900.

BELLPORT, SUFFOLK CO., MARY IMMACULATE (1905) Rev. Gennaro J. DiSpigno.
Res.: 16 Brown's Ln., 11713. Tel: 631-286-0154; Fax: 631-286-2937. Email: pastormib@aol.com. Web: maryimmaculatechurch.net.
See Holy Angels Regional School, Patchogue under Regional Schools located in the Institution section.
Catechesis/Religious Program—Tel: 631-286-3504; Fax: 631-286-2937. Students 440.

BETHPAGE, NASSAU CO., ST. MARTIN OF TOURS (1923) Revs. Patrick Wood, C.Ss.R.; Henry Sattler, C.Ss.R.; James Szobonya, C.Ss.R; Deacons James A. Biggin; Eugene Capobianco; Thomas Hennessy.
Res.: 40 Seaman Ave., 11714. Tel: 516-931-0818; Fax: 516-931-0559.
See St. John Baptist de LaSalle Regional School, Farmingdale under Regional Schools located in the Institution section.
Catechesis/Religious Program—220 Central Ave., 11714. Tel: 516-822-9768; Fax: 516-932-8454. Patricia Ryan, C.R.E.; Laura Leigh Agnese, C.R.E. Students 1,300.

BLUE POINT, SUFFOLK CO., OUR LADY OF THE SNOW (1917) Rev. Edward R. D'Andrea; Sr. Noreen Cleary, S.C., Pastoral Assoc.; Deacons Robert Gronenthal; Frank Hartmann. In Res., Rev. Diarmuid F. McGann (Retired).
Res.: 175 Blue Point Ave., 11715. Tel: 631-363-6385; Fax: 631-363-7394. Email: olsbp@aol.com. Web: www.ourladyofthesnowbluepoint.e-paluch.com.
See Prince of Peace Regional School, Sayville under Regional Schools located in the Institution section.
Catechesis/Religious Program—Tel: 631-363-6394. Students 1,056.

BOHEMIA, SUFFOLK CO., ST. JOHN NEPOMUCENE (1919) [CEM] Revs. Joseph M. Schlafer, Admin.; Kevin W. Gruber; Sr. Phyllis Esposito, C.S.J., Pastoral Assoc.; Deacons James Bohuslaw; Anthony Cusumano; George Reich; Roger Mott.
Res.: 1140 Locust Ave., 11716. Tel: 631-589-0540; Fax: 631-244-8086. Email: stjohnep@optonline.net. Web: mychurchandtown.com.
See Prince of Peace Regional School, Sayville under Regional Schools located in the Institution section.
Catechesis/Religious Program—1150 Locust Ave., 11716. Tel: 631-567-1765. Mrs. Cathy Roberts, D.R.E. Students 1,663.

BRENTWOOD, SUFFOLK CO.

1—ST. ANNE'S (1895) Revs. Francis M. Nelson; Eden Jean Baptiste; Gonzalo Oajaca-Lopez; Deacons Terence A. Rasanen; Thomas R. Samson; John E. Walters; Andres Colpa.
Res.: 88 Second Ave., 11717. Tel: 631-273-8113; Fax: 631-436-7914.
See Our Lady of Providence Regional School, Central Islip under Regional Schools located in the Institution section.
Catechesis/Religious Program—Tel: 631-231-7344. Students 640.

2—ST. LUKE (1965), (Hispanic), [JC] Rev. Msgr. Thomas E. Molloy, Pastor Emeritus, Temp. Admin. (Retired); Deacons Richard A. Luken; Wenceslao Rivera, (Retired); Debby Crustaldo, Office Mgr.
Res.: 266 Wicks Rd., 11717. Tel: 631-273-1110; Fax: 631-951-2779.
See Our Lady of Providence Regional School, Central Islip under Regional Schools located in the Institution section.
Catechesis/Religious Program—Tel: 631-273-4333. Students 600.

BRIDGEHAMPTON, SUFFOLK CO., QUEEN OF THE MOST HOLY ROSARY (1922) Rev. Peter Devaraj, S.A.C.
Catechesis/Religious Program—Tel: 631-537-0156; Fax: 631-537-7116. Sr. Maryann McCarthy, C.S.J., D.R.E. Students 5.

BROOKVILLE, NASSAU CO., ST. PAUL THE APOSTLE (1962) Rev. Robert J. Clerkin.
Res.: 2534 Cedar Swamp Rd., Rte. 107, 11545. Tel: 516-935-1880; Fax: 516-938-3683. Email: stpaulbrookville@aol.com. Web: www.stpaulsbrookville.com.
Catechesis/Religious Program—Tel: 516-938-4530;

Fax: 516-938-4531. Mrs. Louise Shannon, Faith Formation Admin.; Bro. Joseph Bellizzi, S.M., D.R.E. Students 447.

CARLE PLACE, NASSAU CO., CHURCH OF OUR LADY OF HOPE (1987) Rev. Thomas V. Arnao; Deacons John T. Hickey; Thomas B. Rich; Raymond J. Tirelli; Patrick J. Dunphy; Raymond J. Henderson, Music Min.
Church: 534 Broadway, 11514-1712. Tel: 516-334-6288; Fax: 516-997-4622.
School—St. Brigid/ Our Lady of Hope Regional School, 101 Maple Ave., Westbury, 11590. Tel: 516-333-0580; Fax: 516-333-0590.
Catechesis/Religious Program—Tel: 516-334-4781. Tricia Powers, D.R.E. Students 502.

CEDARHURST, NASSAU CO., ST. JOACHIM (1894) Rev. Msgr. Paul Rahilly; Deacons Frank J. Bono; Charles R. Goldburg.
Res.: 614 Central Ave., 11516. Tel: 516-569-1845; Fax: 516-569-0117. Email: joachimrcc@yahoo.com.
Catechesis/Religious Program—Tel: 516-569-2290.

CENTER MORICHES, SUFFOLK CO., ST. JOHN THE EVANGELIST (1898) Revs. Walter F. Kedjierski; John J. Corcoran, Pastor Emeritus (Retired); Robert J. Kline; Felix Akpabio; Deacons Galvin Murphy; John C. Pettorino.
Res.: 25 Ocean Ave., 11934. Tel: 631-878-0009; Fax: 631-874-2466. Email: stjohnch@optonline.net.
See Our Lady, Queen of the Apostles Regional School, Center Moriches under Regional Schools located in the Institution section.
Catechesis/Religious Program—Tel: 631-878-4141. Students 2,050.

CENTEREACH, SUFFOLK CO., ASSUMPTION OF THE BLESSED VIRGIN MARY (1955) Revs. Christopher J. Aridas; Joseph Alenchery (India); Deacon Michael Montelione.
Res.: 20 Chestnut St., 11720. Tel: 631-585-8760; Fax: 631-585-3601. Email: rectory@abvmcentereach.com. Web: www.abvmcentereach.com.
Catechesis/Religious Program—Tel: 631-588-6408. Email: jflynnabvm@optonline.net. Mrs. Jeanne Flynn, D.R.E. Students 1,110.

CENTERPORT, SUFFOLK CO., OUR LADY QUEEN OF MARTYRS (1966) Rev. Msgr. John D. Gilmartin; Sr. Eileen Corcoran, O.P., Pastoral Assoc.; Deacons Christopher Sisinni; Richard Bilella.
Res.: 53 Prospect Rd., 11721. Tel: 631-757-8184; Fax: 631-262-0155. Email: rectory@olqmparish.org. Web: www.olqmparish.org.
See Trinity Regional School, East Northport under Regional Schools located in the Institution section.
Catechesis/Religious Program—Tel: 631-757-0720; Fax: 631-757-3512. Email: olqmre@optonline.net. Ninette Euler, D.R.E.; Angela Sangioardi, Parish Social Ministry. Students 1,178.

CENTRAL ISLIP, SUFFOLK CO., ST. JOHN OF GOD (1904) [CEM] Revs. Christopher Nowak; Romulo Cesar Gomez; Sisters Agnes Claudia Allen, C.S.J., Pastoral Assoc. (Spanish Apostolate); Valerie Scholl, C.S.J., Pastoral Assoc. Admin.; Deacon Ronald J. Gillette, Pastoral Assoc.
Res.: 84 Carleton Ave., 11722. Tel: 631-234-6535; Fax: 631-234-7474. Email: sjogno1@aol.com. Web: stjohnofgodparish.org.
See Our Lady of Providence Regional School, Central Islip under Regional Schools located in the Institution section.
Catechesis/Religious Program—Tel: 631-234-4040. Email: sjogre@verizon.net. Maggie Martin, D.R.E. Students 567.
Parish Outreach—Tel: 631-234-1884. Ana Sullivan, Dir.
Convent—Sisters of St. Joseph, 330 St. John St., 11722. Tel: 631-234-6533. Email: nunsnine@aol.com.

COMMACK, SUFFOLK CO., CHRIST THE KING (1959) Revs. Joseph V. Davanzo; Brian McQuade; Deacons Joseph Marfoglio; Louis Anetrella; Christopher Ferraro, Pastoral Assoc.
Res.: 2 Indian Head Rd., 11725. Tel: 631-864-1623; Fax: 631-864-8891. Email: parishoffice@ctkrcc.org. Web: ctkrcc.org.
See Holy Family Regional School, Commack under Regional Schools located in the Institution section.
Catechesis/Religious Program—Tel: 631-864-3696. Mrs. Margaret Marconi, D.R.E.; Ms. Suzanne Richards, Dir. Adult Faith Formation. Students 1,653.

COPIAGUE, SUFFOLK CO., OUR LADY OF THE ASSUMPTION (1928) Revs. Dariusz Koszyk; Piotr Rozek; Camillo Lugo (Colombia); Deacon Philip Mills Jr.
Res.: 1 Molloy St., 11726. Tel: 631-842-5211; 631-842-5476 (Emergency); Fax: 631-789-5326. Email: assumptioncopia@optonline.net.
Catechesis/Religious Program—Tel: 631-842-3545. Ruth Durago, D.R.E. Students 581.

CORAM, SUFFOLK CO., ST. FRANCES CABRINI (1953) Rev. Donald M. Baier; Deacons Carmen L. Pagnotta; Monte Naylor Jr., (Retired); Peter Acquaro.
Res.: 134 Middle County Rd., 11727. Tel: 631-732-8445; Fax: 631-732-8978. Email: coramcab@aol.com. Web: www.buoy.com/~sfc.
See Holy Angels Regional School, Patchogue under Regional Schools located in the Institution section.
Catechesis/Religious Program—Tel: 631-698-3149. Students 427.

CUTCHOGUE, SUFFOLK CO.

1—OUR LADY OF OSTRABRAMA (1909), (Polish), [JC] Rev. Marian Bicz.
Res.: 3000 Depot Ln., Box 997, 11935. Tel: 631-734-6446; Fax: 631-734-4117.
School—North Fork Regional Catholic School, Cutchogue, Tel: 631-734-5166. See Regional Schools under Institutions Located in the Diocese.
Catechesis/Religious Program—Students 36.

2—SACRED HEART (1901) [CEM] Rev. Msgr. Joseph W. Staudt; Sr. Anne Lynch, R.S.M., Pastoral Assoc.; Deacon Jeffrey Sykes.
Res.: 27905 Main Rd., P.O. Box 926, 11935-0926. Tel: 631-734-6722; Fax: 631-734-7906.
See Our Lady of Mercy Regional School, Cutchogue under Regional Schools located in the Institution section.
Catechesis/Religious Program—Tel: 631-734-2568. Sr. Ann Lynch, D.R.E. Students 387.
Mission—Our Lady of Good Counsel Main Rd., Mattituck, Suffolk Co. 11952.

DAVIS PARK, FIRE ISLAND SUFFOLK CO., MOST PRECIOUS BLOOD (1962), (Summer Mission) Rev. Francis Pizzarelli, S.M.M.
Mailing Address: P.O. Box 358, Port Jefferson, 11777. Tel: 631-928-2377; Fax: 631-473-5210.
Res.: Spindrift Walk, Fire Island, 11728. Tel: 631-597-6525.

DEER PARK, SUFFOLK CO., SS. CYRIL AND METHODIUS (1956) Revs. Lee R. Descoteaux; Dennis Suglia; Caetano F. Costa (India); Francis D. Sang (Vietnam); Richard F. Kammerer; Deacons John F. Fitzpatrick; Charles F. Huber.
Res.: 125 Half Hollow Rd., 11729-4288. Tel: 631-667-4044; Fax: 631-667-6237.
School—Tel: 631-667-6229; Fax: 631-667-0093. Sr. Susan Snyder, C.S.J., Prin. Lay Teachers 21; Students 264; Preschool 36.
Catechesis/Religious Program—Tel: 631-667-6264; Fax: 631-667-7767. Virginia Conzo, D.R.E. Students 1,819.

DIX HILLS, SUFFOLK CO., ST. MATTHEW (1965) Revs. Robert S. Hewes; Lawrence A. Chadwick; Raymond Akpunonu; Deacons James M. McQuade; James Hanly; Carmine DeStefano; Luis Roberto Polanco; Dolores Tiernan, Business Mgr.
Res.: 35 N. Service Rd., 11746. Tel: 631-499-8520; Fax: 631-499-1530. Email: pastor@smrcc.org. Web: smrcc.org.
See Holy Family Regional School, Commack under Regional Schools located in the Institution section.
Catechesis/Religious Program—Tel: 631-499-8521. Mary Donaldson, D.R.E. Students 1,806.

EAST HAMPTON, SUFFOLK CO., MOST HOLY TRINITY (1894) [CEM] Rev. Msgr. Donald M. Hanson.
Mailing Address: 57 Buell Ln., 11937.
Res.: 53 Buell Ln., 11937. Email: pastor@mht-eh.org. Web: mht-eh.org.
Business: 79 Buell Ln., 11937. Tel: 631-324-0134; Fax: 631-329-3552. Email: kbyrnes@mht-eh.org.
Catechesis/Religious Program—44 Meadow Way, 11937. Tel: 631-324-0134, Ext. 730. Email: slieder@mht-eh.org. Suzanne Lieder, D.R.E. Students 253.
Mission—St. Peter the Apostle 286 Main St., Amagansett, Suffolk Co. 11930.

EAST ISLIP, SUFFOLK CO., ST. MARY'S (1898) Revs. Donald E. Babinski; Hugh D. Cannon; Janusz Mocarski; Sr. Pat Tippen, Pastoral Assoc.
Res.: 20 Harrison Ave., 11730. Tel: 631-581-4266; Fax: 631-581-0112. Email: tvanburen@stmaryseastislip.org. Web: www.stmaryseastislip.org.
School—16 Harrison Ave., 11730. Tel: 631-581-4266, Ext. 5; Fax: 631-581-7509. Biagio Arpino, Prin. Lay Teachers 32; Students 428.
Catechesis/Religious Program—Linda Crowley, D.R.E. Students 1,500.

EAST MEADOW, NASSAU CO., ST. RAPHAEL (1941) Revs. Thomas Haggerty; Antony Asir; Cyril Bayim (Nigeria); Deacons Angelo D'Aversa; Victor R. Costa; Joan Heaney-Hunter, Pastoral Assoc.; Dr. Kathleen Andersen, Pastoral Assoc.; Sr. Judy Fay, C.S.J., Parish Social Ministry; Diane Lawlor, Business Mgr.
Res.: 600 Newbridge Rd., 11554. Tel: 516-785-0236; Fax: 516-783-9578. Web: www.straphaelparish.org.
See St. Elizabeth Ann Seton Regional School, Bellmore under Regional Schools located in the Institution section.
Catechesis/Religious Program—Tel: 516-221-9096; Fax: 516-221-9084. Email: raphaelreo@hotmail.com. Sr. Karen Lademann, O.P., Dir. Faith Formation. Students 1,347.

EAST NORTHPORT, SUFFOLK CO., ST. ANTHONY OF PADUA (1951) Rev. Msgr. John R. Dreasen; Revs. Frank M. Grieco; James Calledo (Philippines); Rev. Msgr. John R. Dreasen; Deacon Robert Braun.
Res.: 20 Cheshire Pl., 11731-2591. Tel: 631-261-1077; Fax: 631-757-0572. Email: pastor@saintanthonyofpadua.org. Web: www.saintanthonyofpadua.org.
See Trinity Regional School, East Northport under Regional Schools located in the Institution section.
Catechesis/Religious Program—Tel: 631-261-1306. Mrs. Judith Corbellini, D.R.E.; Mrs. Eileen Schlee, D.R.E.; Mrs. Patricia Seibert, D.R.E. Students 2,033.

EAST PATCHOGUE, SUFFOLK CO., ST. JOSEPH THE WORKER (1955) Revs. John Mellitt, O.F.M.Cap.; Martin Curtin, O.F.M.Cap.; Deacon Albert Pickford. In Res., Rev. William H. Winters, O.F.M.Cap.
Church: 510 Narragansett Ave., 11772. Tel: 631-286-9133; Fax: 631-286-9145. Email: sjw510@gmail.com. Web: www.stjosephtheworkerparish.org.
See Holy Angels Regional School, Patchogue under Regional Schools located in the Institution section.
Catechesis/Religious Program—Tel: 631-286-2550; Fax: 631-286-9145. Mrs. Rita Dlug, D.R.E. Students 510.

EAST ROCKAWAY, NASSAU CO., ST. RAYMOND'S (1909) Rev. Charles Romano; Rev. Msgr. William V. Singleton, Pastor Emeritus (Retired); Rev. Francis X. Eisele; Deacons Richard W. LaRossa, Pastoral Assoc.; Robert C. Campbell; Thomas W. Connolly; Guy Donza, Pastoral Assoc.; Thomas Malone.
Res.: 263 Atlantic Ave., 11518. Tel: 516-593-5000; Fax: 516-887-0554. Email: strayrcc@optonline.net. Web: www.saintraymonds.org.
School—Tel: 516-593-9010; Fax: 516-593-0986. Sr. Ruthanne Gypalo, I.H.M., Prin. Sisters, Servants of the Immaculate Heart of Mary 3; Lay Teachers 23; Students 364.
Catechesis/Religious Program—Tel: 516-593-9075. Email: econtaldisrre@optonline.net. Mrs. Evelyn Contaldi, C.R.E. Students 697.

ELMONT, NASSAU CO.

1—ST. BONIFACE (1852) [CEM] Revs. William J. Gomes; Eddy Julien; Gabriel Miah; Sr. Evelyn Lamoureux, D.W., Human Svcs.; Deacons William Mildeberger; Dominique Silien. In Res., Rev. George Punti (Retired).
Res.: 631 Elmont Rd., 11003. Tel: 516-354-0715; Fax: 516-354-0446.
Catechesis/Religious Program—Tel: 516-437-7112. Nancy Cosgrove, D.R.E. Students 565.

2—ST. VINCENT DE PAUL (1951) Rev. Msgr. Richard M. Figliozzi, Admin.
Mailing Address: 1500 dePaul St., 11003.
Res.: 33 New Hyde Park Rd., Franklin Square, 11010. Tel: 516-352-0146; Fax: 516-326-7427. Email: svdp1500@optonline.net.
Catechesis/Religious Program—St. Catherine School, 990 Holzheimer St., Franklin Square, 11010. Tel: 516-437-2733. Students 85.

FARMINGDALE, NASSAU CO., ST. KILIAN (1896) Rev. Msgr. Michael P. Flynn; Revs. Augustine Fernando (India); Lennard Sabio (Philippines); Stanislaw Wadowski (Poland); Deacons Frank D. Barone; Lucio Cotone; Francis P. Marino; George Owen; Mark Wetzel; Frank Shanley, Business Mgr. In Res., Most Rev. John C. Dunne.
Res.: 485 Conklin St., 11735. Tel: 516-249-0127; Fax: 516-249-7131. Email: info@stkilian.com. Web: www.stkilian.com.
See St. John Baptist de LaSalle Regional School, Farmingdale under Regional Schools located in the Institution section.
Catechesis/Religious Program—Tel: 516-694-0633; Fax: 516-454-8612. Mr. Jon Lindstrom, D.R.E.; Mr. Paul C. Phinney, Music Dir. Students 2,000.
Parish Social Ministry/Outreach—Tel: 516-756-9656. Mrs. Nina Petersen, Dir.

FARMINGVILLE, SUFFOLK CO., CHURCH OF THE RESURRECTION (1988) Rev. Malcolm J. Burns; Deacons James DiGiovanna; Juan Diaz.
Church: 50 Granny Rd., 11738. Tel: 631-696-0232; Fax: 631-696-0271. Email: info@resurrectionrcchurch.org. Web: resurrectionrcchurch.org.
Catechesis/Religious Program—Tel: 631-696-0270, Ext. 25. Email: religioused@resurrectionrcchurch.org. Rosemarie Hayman, D.R.E. Students 550.

FLORAL PARK, NASSAU CO.

1—ST. HEDWIG'S (1902), (Polish), Rev. Piotr Rozek.
Res.: One Depan Ave., 11001. Tel: 516-354-0042; Fax: 516-327-2458. Email: sthedwig@optonline.net.
Catechesis/Religious Program—Students 81.

2—OUR LADY OF VICTORY (1921) Rev. John V. O'Farrell; Rev. Msgr. Charles J. Nosser, Pastor Emeritus (Retired); Revs. John J. McCartney; Ryszard Ficek; Deacon Lawrence P. Mulligan; Jane Parrinelli, Business Mgr.; Eileen Tracy, Youth Min.; Donald Lefante, Dir. Music Ministry & Liturgy.

Res.: 2 Floral Pkwy., 11001-3198. Tel: 516-354-0482; 516-354-0479; Fax: 516-354-7450.
School—2 Bellmore St., 11001. Tel: 516-352-4466; 516-354-2150; Fax: 516-352-2998. Margaret M. Augello, Prin. Lay Teachers 26; Students 459.
Catechesis/Religious Program—Tel: 516-352-0510. Christine Fuchs, D.R.E.; Eileen Tracy, D.R.E. Students 978.

FRANKLIN SQUARE, NASSAU CO., ST. CATHERINE OF SIENNA (1913) Rev. Msgr. Richard M. Figliozzi; Revs. Francis Gnansegaram; Charles Srion; Johnny Mendonca; Deacons Joseph Benincasa; Francisco Gonzalez. In Res., Rev. William D. O'Rourke (Retired).
Res.: 33 New Hyde Park Rd., 11010. Tel: 516-352-0146; Fax: 516-326-7427. Web: stcatherineofsienna.org.
School—990 Holzheimer St., 11010. Tel: 516-437-2733; Fax: 516-437-6073. Web: scsschool.org. Ms. Cecelia Rando, Prin. Lay Teachers 13; Students 193.
Catechesis/Religious Program—Tel: 516-354-4554. Meaghan McKeown, Faith Formation Coord. Students 1,400.

FREEPORT, NASSAU CO., OUR HOLY REDEEMER (1903) Revs. Douglas R. Arcoleo; Humberto E. Contreras (Colombia); Deacons Francisco Cales; Bruce A. Burnham; Cristobal Sanchez, Pastoral Assoc.; Alfonso Martinez, Dir. Parish Human Svcs. In Res., Most Rev. Paul H. Walsh, Aux. Bishop; Rev. Jerome Francis Ackah (Ghana).
Res.: 37 S. Ocean Ave., 11520. Tel: 516-378-0665; Fax: 516-546-1416. Email: ohr1903@aol.com. Web: ohrfreeport.org.
Catechesis/Religious Program—87 Pine St., 11520. Tel: 516-546-1057; Fax: 516-546-0526. Email: reled3@aol.com. Joanne Stuhlinger, D.R.E. Students 430.

GARDEN CITY, NASSAU CO.

1—ST. ANNE (1929) Rev. Msgr. Thomas J. Harold; Rev. Rudy Pesongco; Deacons George Browne; James J. O'Brien; Basil Bliss.
Res.: 35 Dartmouth St., 11530. Tel: 516-352-5904; Fax: 516-352-1360. Web: www.stannesgc.org.
School—25 Dartmouth St., 11530. Tel: 516-352-1205; Fax: 516-352-5969. Dr. William O'Sullivan, Prin. Lay Teachers 28; Students 514.
Catechesis/Religious Program—Tel: 516-488-1032; Fax: 516-352-1360. Lyn Beck, D.R.E. Students 1,261.

2—ST. JOSEPH'S (1901) Rev. Msgr. James P. Swiader; Rev. Gregory Breen; Deacon John J. McKenna; Joseph Cangialosi, Dir. Music & Liturgy; Sr. Louise Cullen, R.S.M., Dir. Stewardship. In Res., Rev. Msgr. Brian J. McNamara.
Res.: 130 Fifth St., 11530. Tel: 516-747-3535; Fax: 516-746-0719.
School—450 Franklin Ave., 11530. Tel: 516-747-2730; Fax: 516-747-2854. Dr. Eileen Kilbride, Prin.; Regina A. Cioffi, Asst. Prin.; Sr. Virginia Maguire, O.P., Dir. Human Svcs. Lay Teachers 27; Students 356.
Catechesis/Religious Program—Tel: 516-741-7787; Fax: 516-741-5049. Susan Mirabella, D.R.E.; Sr. Kathleen Corr, O.P., Dir. Adult Faith Formation. Students 1,471.

GLEN COVE, NASSAU CO.

1—ST. PATRICK'S (1856) [CEM] Very Rev. Dom Stephen Nash, Can.Reg.; Revs. Rolando Ticllasuca, M.R.S.M. (Peru); Martin L. Klein; Mr. Cantalicio Gamarra, Spanish Min.; Deacons Frank Borchardt; Alfredo Mora; Michael Devenney, Business Mgr.; Juan Guilfu; Frances Howlett, Music Min.
Res.: 235 Glen St., 11542. Tel: 516-676-0276; Fax: 516-674-9137. Email: stpatshill@aol.com. Web: www.stpatrickshill.com.
For Hispanic Ministry—Tel: 516-759-6039.
See All Saints Regional Catholic School, Glen Cove under Regional Schools located in the Institution section.
Catechesis/Religious Program—Tel: 516-671-7223. Sr. Teresa Raftery, I.H.M., D.R.E. Students 403.
Convent—Sisters of St. Joseph, 16 Pearsall St., 11542. Tel: 516-671-3963. (Brentwood Congregation) Sisters 2.

2—ST. ROCCO (1937), (Italian), Very Rev. Dom Elias Carr, Can. Reg.
Res.: 18 Third St., 11542. Tel: 516-676-2482; Fax: 516-676-2117. Email: stroccochurch@netzero.net. Web: www.stroccoglencove.com.
See All Saints Regional Catholic School, Glen Cove under Regional Schools located in the Institution section.
Catechesis/Religious Program—Students 343.

GLEN HEAD, NASSAU CO., ST. HYACINTH (1909), (Polish), Rev. Msgr. Richard P. Kopinski; Revs. Joseph P. Kozlowski, Pastor Emeritus (Retired); Piotr Wasek.
Res.: 319 Cedar Swamp Rd., 11545. Tel: 516-676-0361; Fax: 516-674-4728.
See All Saints Regional Catholic School, Glen Cove under Regional Schools located in the Institution section.
Catechesis/Religious Program—Tel: 516-676-0361, Ext. 123. Miss Eileen Meserole, D.R.E. Students 225.

GREAT NECK, NASSAU CO., ST. ALOYSIUS (1876), (Hispanic—Korean), Rev. Msgr. Brendan P. Riordan; Rev. Tu-Jin Paul Kim, C.P., Korean Ministry. Tel: 516-466-8700 (Office); Fax: 516-466-6006. In Res., Rev. Msgr. Alan J. Placa (Retired).
Res.: 592 Middle Neck Rd., 11023. Tel: 516-482-2770; Fax: 516-829-3504. Email: saintals592@aol.com.
Catechesis/Religious Program—Tel: 516-482-5660; Fax: 516-829-4054. Students 359.

GREENLAWN, SUFFOLK CO., ST. FRANCIS OF ASSISI (1966) Rev. Peter Kaczmarek; Rev. Msgrs. Patrick Armshaw, Pastor Emeritus; Robert J. Batule; Deacons Allan Longo; David Campbell; Jean Cantave; James Byrne.
Res.: 29 Northgate Dr., 11740. Tel: 631-757-7435; Fax: 631-757-0469.
See Trinity Regional School, East Northport under Regional Schools located in the Institution section.
Catechesis/Religious Program—Tel: 631-754-6436. Students 575.

GREENPORT, SUFFOLK CO., ST. AGNES (1886), (Hispanic), [CEM] Rev. Thomas P. Murray.
Res.: 523 Front St., 11944. Tel: 631-477-0048; Fax: 631-477-8519. Email: rectory@optonline.net. Web: stagnesgpt.org.
See Our Lady of Mercy Regional School, Cutchogue under Regional Schools located in the Institution section.
Catechesis/Religious Program—Tel: 631-477-1422. Students 246.

HAMPTON BAYS, SUFFOLK CO., ST. ROSALIE'S (1901) Revs. Edward M. Sheridan; Sabbas Rodrigues; Kevin Thompson; Deacons Christopher Ervin, Pastoral Assoc.; Robert Mongillo, Pastoral Assoc. & Business Mgr.
Res.: 31 Montauk Hwy., 11946. Tel: 631-728-9461; Fax: 631-728-2559. Web: www.saintrosalie.com.
See Our Lady of the Hamptons Regional School, Southampton under Regional Schools located in the Institution section.
Catechesis/Religious Program— Eileen McPhelin, Coord. Students 528.
Mission— Montauk Hwy. & Walnut Ave., East Quogue, Suffolk Co. 11946.

HAUPPAUGE, SUFFOLK CO., ST. THOMAS MORE (1967) Rev. Msgr. Francis S. Midura; Deacons Robert Weisz; Edward R. Vigneaux; John S. Rapacki.
Res.: 115 Kings Hwy., 11788-4204. Tel: 631-234-5551; Fax: 631-234-6412. Email: stm73@live.com.
See Holy Family Regional School, Commack under Regional Schools located in the Institution section.
Catechesis/Religious Program—119 Kings Hwy., 11788. Tel: 631-234-0397; Fax: 631-234-1199. Mrs. Mary Ellen Carroll, D.R.E.; Mrs. Patricia Chapin, D.R.E. Students 1,400.

HEMPSTEAD, NASSAU CO.

1—ST. JOHN CHRYSOSTOM MALANKARA MISSION (1999) Rev. Joseph Nedumankuzhiyil (India), Admin.
115 Greenwich St., 11550. Tel: 516-775-1779; Fax: 516-216-5350.

2—ST. LADISLAUS (1915), (Polish), Rev. Piotr Wasek, Admin. In Res., Rev. John Siebor (Retired).
Res.: 18 Richardson Pl., 11550. Tel: 516-489-0368; Fax: 516-292-9193.
See St. Martin de Porres Regional School, Uniondale under Regional Schools located in the Institution section.
Catechesis/Religious Program—

3—OUR LADY OF LORETTO (1870) Rev. Msgr. Pablo M. Rodriguez; Rev. Gerardo Bengochea, S.J.; Sr. Winifred Cunniff, S.C., Pastoral Assoc.; Deacons Jose Roa; Juan Perez.
Res.: 104 Greenwich St., 11550. Tel: 516-489-3675; Fax: 516-485-8371.
See St. Martin de Porres Regional School, Uniondale under Regional Schools located in the Institution section.
Catechesis/Religious Program—Tel: 516-483-3643. Cecilia Bradley, D.R.E. Students 322.

HEWLETT, NASSAU CO., ST. JOSEPH'S (1872) Rev. Thomas Moriarty Jr.; Deacons Thomas Costello; Daniel Otton. In Res., Rev. John Hein (Vietnam) (Retired).
Res.: 1346 Broadway, 11557. Tel: 516-374-0290; Fax: 516-374-2598. Email: joehewlett@aol.com. Web: saintjoseph-hewlett.org.
Catechesis/Religious Program—1355 Noel Ave., 11557. Tel: 516-569-6080; Fax: 516-374-3664. Elizabeth McCaffrey, D.R.E. Students 410.

HICKSVILLE, NASSAU CO.

1—HOLY FAMILY (1951), (Irish—Italian), Revs. Gerard J. Gentleman; Frank Zero; Deacons Joseph G. McNicholas; John H. McGonigle; Ronald Land, Music Dir.; Ms. Donna Grosso, Business Mgr.
17 Fordham Ave., 11801. In Res., Revs. Sebastian Owusa-Mensah; R. Michael Reid.
Res.: 5 Fordham Ave., 11801. Tel: 516-938-3846; Fax: 516-938-6241.
School—Holy Family School, 25 Fordham Ave., 11801. Fax: 516-938-5041. Email: phillin@hfsli.org. Web: hfsli.org. Mrs. MaryAlice Doherty, Prin. Lay Teachers 20; Students 282.
Catechesis/Religious Program—Tel: 516-938-3846, Ext. 320. Mrs. Cathy Weiss, D.R.E. Students 463.
Outreach—Tel: 516-938-3846, Ext. 331. Email: outreach@holyfamilyparishny.org. Sr. Carol Radosti, Coord.

2—ST. IGNATIUS LOYOLA (1859) Revs. James T. Stachacz; Jose Quilcate (Peru); Rev. Msgr. Edward L. Tarrant, Pastor Emeritus (Retired); Mrs. Rosemary Cassese, Pastoral Asst.; Deacon George A. Mais Jr.; Ms. Jennifer Toohey, Music Min.
129 Broadway, 11801. Tel: 516-931-0056; Fax: 516-939-0852. Email: stignatius1859@aol.com. Web: st-ignatius-parish.org. In Res., Rev. Msgr. Donald T. Bennett, Pastor Emeritus (Retired); Rev. Joseph McCabe, M.M.
School—30 E. Cherry St., 11801. Tel: 516-931-0831; Fax: 516-933-6528. Web: www.stignatiushicksville.org. Sisters Mary Ann Noonan, R.S.M., Prin.; Mary F. O'Donnell, O.P., Co-Prin. Lay Teachers 17; Students 228.
Catechesis/Religious Program—Tel: 516-935-6873. Colleen Tuzzolo, C.R.E. Students 475.

3—OUR LADY OF MERCY (1953) Revs. Thomas C. Costa; Richard F. Kammerer; Dariusz Koszyk; Rev. Msgr. James E. Boesel (Retired).
Res.: 500 S. Oyster Bay Rd., 11801. Tel: 516-931-4351; Fax: 516-433-8702. Email: therectory@olmrcc.com. Web: www.ourladyofmercy.org.
School—Tel: 516-433-7040; Fax: 516-433-8286. Email: jdeegan@olmercy.drvc.org. Sr. Mary Joanne Deegan, R.S.M., Prin. Sisters of Mercy 5; Lay Teachers 25; Students 378.
Catechesis/Religious Program—Tel: 516-681-1228; Fax: 516-681-1527. Email: religioused@olmrcc.com. Joanne Kolasa, D.R.E. Students 816.

HOLBROOK, SUFFOLK CO., GOOD SHEPHERD (1970) Rev. Msgr. Thomas L. Spadaro; Revs. Francis Lasrado; Babu Michael; Deacons Robert Hernandez; Thomas O'Connor; Edward Tappin; John Newhall; Mary E. Rieger, Business Mgr.
Res.: 1370 Grundy Ave., 11741. Tel: 631-588-7689; Fax: 631-588-7603. Web: www.goodshepherdonline.com.
See Prince of Peace Regional School, Sayville under Regional Schools located in the Institution section.
Catechesis/Religious Program—Tel: 631-981-3889. Sisters Lillian Delorme, O.P., D.R.E.; Ellen Zak, C.S.F.N., D.R.E.; Jeanne Cook, D.R.E. Students 1,037.

HUNTINGTON STATION, SUFFOLK CO., ST. HUGH OF LINCOLN (1913) Rev. Msgr. Joseph P. Granata; Rev. Michael J. Bartholomew; Deacons Edward W. Billia; Vito B. Taranto; Thomas Reilly; Luis Giraldo.
Res.: 21 E. Ninth St., 11746. Tel: 631-427-0638; Fax: 631-427-1319. Email: rectory@sthugh.org. Web: sthugh.org.
Parish Center—1450 New York Ave., 11746.
See Trinity Regional School, East Northport under Regional Schools located in the Institution section.
Catechesis/Religious Program—Tel: 631-271-6081. Mrs. Helen Schramm, D.R.E. Students 690.

HUNTINGTON, SUFFOLK CO., ST. PATRICK'S (1849) [CEM] Rev. Msgr. John F. Bennett; Revs. Stephen H. Donnelly, Parochial Vicar; Thomas P. Tuite Jr., Parochial Vicar; Deacons William Casey; Dale Bonocore; Louis Consentino. In Res., Rev. Thomas Edamattan (India).
Res.: 400 Main St., 11743-3208. Tel: 631-385-3311; Fax: 631-673-4102. Web: www.stpatrickchurchhunt.org.
School—360 Main St., 11743-3298. Tel: 631-673-5325; Fax: 631-673-4609. Sr. Maureen McDade, Prin.; Mrs. Jean Grasso, Asst. Prin. Sisters 1; Lay Teachers 34; Students 762.
Catechesis/Religious Program—Miss Jill Rowbo, C.R.E. Students 1,437.

INWOOD, NASSAU CO., OUR LADY OF GOOD COUNSEL (1910) Rev. Thomas Moriarty Jr., Admin.; Deacon George Bruck. In Res., Rev. Eric R. Fasano.
Res.: 68 Wanser Ave., 11096. Tel: 516-239-0953; Fax: 516-239-0386.
Catechesis/Religious Program—Tel: 516-239-0662. Sr. Kathryn Slevin, C.S.J., D.R.E. Students 296.

ISLAND PARK, NASSAU CO., SACRED HEART (1938) Rev. John J. Tutone.
Res.: 282 Long Beach Rd., 11558. Tel: 516-432-0655; Fax: 516-897-7567.
Catechesis/Religious Program—Tel: 516-431-7877. Mrs. Carmel Caracciolo, D.R.E. Students 255.

ISLIP TERRACE, SUFFOLK CO., ST. PETER THE APOSTLE (1962) Rev. Anthony Iaconis. In Res., Rev. Christopher Okoli (Nigeria).

Res.: 94 Valley Stream St., 11752. Tel: 631-277-9448. Email: stpeters11752@optonline.
See Our Lady of Providence Regional School, Central Islip under Regional Schools located in the Institution section.
Catechesis/Religious Program—Tel: 631-650-0950. Students 324.

KINGS PARK, SUFFOLK CO., ST. JOSEPH'S (1888) Revs. Seán J. Gann; Francis P. Vattakudiyil; Paul J. Mijas (Poland); Deacons John E. Trodden; Roy Smith. In Res., Rev. Msgr. Alexander F. Manly (Retired).
Parish Center—59 Church St., 11754. Tel: 631-269-6635; Fax: 631-269-7508.
See Holy Family Regional School, Commack under Regional Schools located in the Institution section.
Catechesis/Religious Program—Tel: 631-269-4383. Students 2,020.

LAKE RONKONKOMA, SUFFOLK CO., ST. ELIZABETH ANN SETON (1988) Rev. Msgr. Daniel A. Picciano; Deacons Joseph Maffeo; John Grebe; Bro. Ferdinand Vogrin, Pastoral Assoc.; Lori Marando, Business Mgr.
Res.: 59 Frances Blvd., Holtsville, 11742.
Church: 800 Portion Rd., 11779. Tel: 631-737-4388; Fax: 631-737-4389. Email: steas@optonline.net. Web: www.steas.org.
Catechesis/Religious Program—800 Portion Rd., 11779. Tel: 631-737-8915. Email: mhahnstliz@optonline.net. Mrs. Michele Hahn, D.R.E. Students 1,182.

LEVITTOWN, NASSAU CO., ST. BERNARD (1948) Revs. Gerard A. Ringenback; Christopher M. Costigan; Deacons John Blakeney; James W. Flannery. In Res., Rev. Msgr. George P. Graham (Retired); Revs. Cyprian Osuegbu (Nigeria); Martin J. Hall (Retired).
Res.: 3100 Hempstead Tpke., 11756. Tel: 516-731-4220; Fax: 516-731-4355. Email: parish@stbernardslevittown.org. Web: www.stbernardslevittown.org.
Catechesis/Religious Program—Tel: 516-731-8511; Fax: 516-731-7860. Students 1,227.

LINDENHURST, SUFFOLK CO., OUR LADY OF PERPETUAL HELP (1871) Rev. Anthony M. Trapani; Rev. Msgr. Daniel S. Hamilton, Pastor Emeritus (Retired); Revs. Moise Aime (Haiti); Robert J. Kline; Deacons Frank A. Odin; Douglas Smith; William Crosby.
Res.: 210 S. Wellwood Ave., 11757-4989. Tel: 631-226-7725; Fax: 631-225-9597. Email: olphlindenhurst@gmail.com. Web: www.olphlindenhurst.org.
School—240 S. Wellwood Ave., 11757. Tel: 631-226-0208; Fax: 631-226-4221. Lay Teachers 23; Students 196.
Catechesis/Religious Program—Tel: 631-226-2384. Tom Acemoglu, D.R.E. Students 1,440.

LONG BEACH, NASSAU CO.

1—ST. IGNATIUS MARTYR (1926) Rev. Msgr. Donald M. Beckmann; Rev. Joseph Paul Fernando. In Res., Rev. Msgr. Edward A. Sweeny.
Res.: 721 W. Broadway, 11561. Tel: 516-432-0045; Fax: 516-432-6848. Email: saintignatiusmar@yahoo.com. Web: home.catholicweb.com/stignatiusmartyr/index.cfm.
See Long Beach Regional Catholic School, Long Beach under Regional Schools located in the Institution section.
Catechesis/Religious Program—Tel: 516-432-6788. Pam Shannon, D.R.E. Students 32.
Parish Social Ministry/Outreach—Tel: 516-432-4899. Blanca Cales, Dir.; Sr. Diane Morgan, O.P., Pastoral Assoc.; Deacon Phillip J. Newton.

2—ST. MARY OF THE ISLE (1915) Rev. Msgr. Robert J. Brennan; Rev. Thomas E. Donohoe (Retired); Deacon Nelson Daza; Blanca Cales, Outreach Dir. In Res., Rev. Paschal Onwugbenu.
Res.: 315 E. Walnut St., 11561. Tel: 516-432-0157; Fax: 516-897-0566. Email: stmarylb@gmail.com.
See Long Beach Regional Catholic School, Long Beach under Regional Schools located in the Institution section.
Catechesis/Religious Program—Tel: 516-432-1320. Maryann Specht, D.R.E. Students 279.

LYNBROOK, NASSAU CO., OUR LADY OF PEACE (1941) Rev. Msgr. William G. Breslawski; Deacons Aniello Squitieri; Anthony M. Cedrone; Thomas J. Evrard; Kevin McCormack.
Res.: 25 Fowler Ave., 11563. Tel: 516-599-6414; Fax: 516-596-1847. Email: olprcc@olplynbrook.com.
School—21 Flower Ave., 11563. Tel: 516-593-4884; Fax: 516-593-9861. Email: olpschool@optonline.net. Sisters of Mercy 1; Lay Teachers 19; Students 283.
Catechesis/Religious Program—Tel: 516-593-5150. Email: srgracem@olplynbrook.com. Students 540.

MALVERNE, NASSAU CO., OUR LADY OF LOURDES (1926) Rev. Frank J. Parisi; Deacons Francis X Cove; Richard H. Portvese. In Res., Revs. Richard R. Donovan (Retired); John F. Wymes, M.M. (Retired); Chux Okochi; Anthony Madu.
Res.: 65 Wright Ave., 11565. Tel: 516-599-1269; Fax: 516-887-9517. Email: ollmalvchurch@aol.com.
School—76 Park Blvd., 11565. Tel: 516-599-7328; Fax: 516-599-3813. Mary Carmel Murphy, Prin. Lay Teachers 20; Students 290.
Catechesis/Religious Program—Tel: 516-599-7222; Fax: 516-599-2256. Miss Mary Lasar, D.R.E. Students 371.

MANHASSET, NASSAU CO., ST. MARY'S (1853) Rev. Msgrs. John J. McCann; John J. Skelly, Pastor Emeritus (Retired); Revs. Allan Sikorski; Raphael Soadwah (Ghana); Deacons Charles Kammerer; Frank Bice.
Res.: 1300 Northern Blvd., 11030. Tel: 516-627-0385; Fax: 516-627-6070. Email: information@stmary.ws. Web: stmary.ws.
School—St. Mary's Elementary School, 1340 Northern Blvd., 11030. Tel: 516-627-0184; Fax: 516-627-3795. Web: www.stmary11030.org. (Elementary) Lay Teachers 30; Students 404.
High School—St. Mary's High School, (Coed), 51 Clapham Ave., 11030. Tel: 516-627-2711; Fax: 516-627-3209. Web: www.stmary.ws/highschool. Dominican Sisters 1; Lay Teachers 52; Students 700.
Catechesis/Religious Program—Tel: 516-627-4028; Fax: 516-627-5543. Students 1,168.

MANORHAVEN, NASSAU CO., OUR LADY OF FATIMA (1948) Rev. Steven J. Peterson; Deacon Arthur Candido; Sr. Kathy Somerville, O.P., Parish Social Ministry; Barbara Minerva, Business Mgr.
Res.: 6 Cottonwood Rd., Port Washington, 11050. Tel: 516-767-0781; Fax: 516-767-2981.
Catechesis/Religious Program—Tel: 516-944-8322. Sr. Gerri O'Neil, O.P., D.R.E. Students 126.

MANORVILLE, SUFFOLK CO., STS. PETER & PAUL (1996) Rev. Bruce J. Powers; Deacon Robert Dejewski.
Res.: 781 Wading River Rd., P.O. Box 207, 11949. Tel: 631-369-1273; Fax: 631-369-7141. Email: pmc207@optonline.net. Web: www.saintspeterandpaul.org.
Catechesis/Religious Program—Tel: 631-208-1978. Students 547.

MASSAPEQUA PARK, NASSAU CO., OUR LADY OF LOURDES (1955) Rev. Msgr. James P. Lisante; Revs. Gregory Heinlein; Edward M. Seagriff; Deacon Domenick Valdaro. In Res., Rev. Robert E. Mason (Retired).
Res.: 855 Carmans Rd., 11762. Tel: 516-541-3270; Fax: 516-797-9851. Email: ollmpk@aol.com. Web: www.ollmp.org.
Catechesis/Religious Program—379 Linden St., 11762. Tel: 516-799-5179. Students 485.

MASSAPEQUA, NASSAU CO., ST. ROSE OF LIMA (1952) Revs. Kenneth M. Zach; Bruno Dekrem; Khoa T. Le; Lachlan T. Cameron; Deacons Thomas J. Forbes; Frank J. Flood; Francis B. McGuinness; Dennis R. O'Connor. In Res., Rev. Msgr. Daniel J. Hurley, Pastor Emeritus (Retired).
Res.: 2 Bayview Ave., 11758-7299. Tel: 516-798-4992; Fax: 516-795-7836. Email: michelez@stroseoflimaparish.org. Web: www.stroseoflimaparish.org.
School—4704 Merrick Rd., 11758. Tel: 516-541-1546; Fax: 516-797-0351. Web: www.stroseschool-.net. Sr. Kathleen Gallina, O.P., Prin. Sisters of St. Dominic 1; Lay Teachers 26; Students 419.
Catechesis/Religious Program—Tel: 516-541-1712. Email: religioused@stroseoflimaparish.org. Students 2,890.

MASTIC BEACH, SUFFOLK CO., ST. JUDE (1949) Rev. Gregory Yacyshyn; Deacons Thomas Gillen; Kenneth Geoghan; Mark Herrmann; Joseph Simeone. In Res., Rev. Msgr. John T. Heinlein (Retired).
Res.: 89 Overlook Dr., 11951. Tel: 631-281-5743; Fax: 631-395-5786. Email: rectory@stjudemb.org. Web: stjudemb.org.
See Our Lady, Queen of the Apostles Regional School, Center Moriches under Regional Schools located in the Institution section.
Catechesis/Religious Program—Tel: 631-281-2835. Theresa Amorese, D.R.E. Students 900.
Parish Human Services Center—89 Overlook Dr., 11951. Tel: 631-281-5634.

MEDFORD, SUFFOLK CO., ST. SYLVESTER (1948) Rev. Thomas W. Coby; Deacons George J. Riegger; Frank Rivera; Mary Weiber, Dir. Parish Social Ministry/Outreach. Tel: 631-475-3871.
Res.: 68 Ohio Ave., 11763. Tel: 631-475-4506; Fax: 631-475-1057. Email: parishoffice@stsylvesterli.org. Web: www.stsylvesterli.org.
See Holy Angels Regional School, Patchogue under Regional Schools located in the Institution section.
Catechesis/Religious Program—Tel: 631-475-8191. Frances McMahon, D.R.E. Students 1,200.

MELVILLE, SUFFOLK CO., ST. ELIZABETH (1962) Rev. Msgr. Francis J. Schneider; Deacons Joseph Mercolino, (Retired); John Failla.
Res.: 181 Wolf Hill Rd., 11747. Tel: 631-271-4455; Fax: 631-271-1415.
Church: 175 Wolf Hill Rd., 11747. Email: center@stelizabeth.org. Web: www.stelizabeth.org.
See Trinity Regional School, East Northport under Regional Schools located in the Institution section.
Catechesis/Religious Program—Students 794.

MERRICK, NASSAU CO., CURÉ OF ARS (1926) Revs. Charles N. Mangano; Zachary Callahan (Retired); Josep Augustine Kadungamparambil (India).
Res.: 2323 Merrick Ave., 11566. Tel: 516-623-1400; Fax: 516-623-1107. Web: www.cureofarschurch.net.
See St. Elizabeth Ann Seton Regional School, Bellmore under Regional Schools located in the Institution section.
Catechesis/Religious Program—Tel: 516-623-1400, Ext. 101; Fax: 516-223-7401. Students 980.

MINEOLA, NASSAU CO., CORPUS CHRISTI (1901), (Spanish—Portuguese), Rev. Msgr. Robert J. Coyle; Revs. Tomaz Gomide; Gabriel Miah; Deacons John C. Reinhart, (Retired); Brian J. Mannix. In Res., Rev. Msgr. Edward L. Tarrant (Retired); Revs. Ethel Anarado (Nigeria), Hospital Chap.; Polycarp Nnajiofor (Nigeria), Hospital Chap.
Res.: 155 Garfield Ave., 11501. Tel: 516-746-1223; Fax: 516-294-5311.
Catechesis/Religious Program—Tel: 516-294-0631; Fax: 516-294-0352. Mrs. Susan Anaisclik, D.R.E. Students 504.

MONTAUK, SUFFOLK CO., ST. THERESE OF LISIEUX (1950) Rev. Michael J. Rieder.
Mailing Address: P.O. Box 5027, 11954.
Res.: 67 S. Essex St., P.O. Box 5027, 11954. Tel: 631-668-2200; Fax: 631-668-2384.
Day Care/Nursery School—Tel: 631-668-5353. (2 & 3 years old) Children 43.
Catechesis/Religious Program—Tel: 631-668-2460. Suzanne Lieder, D.R.E. Students 150.

NESCONSET, SUFFOLK CO., CHURCH OF THE HOLY CROSS (1988) Rev. Msgr. James M. McNamara; Deacons Gerard K. Steffens, Pastoral Min.; Owen E. Farley Jr., Pastoral Min.; Mrs. Judith Pickel, Pastoral Assoc.
95 Old Nichols Rd., 11767.
Res.: 85 Old Nichols Rd., 11767. Tel: 631-979-2386; Fax: 631-265-2229. Email: pothc@aol.com; pothc@optonline.net. Web: www.pothc.org.
Catechesis/Religious Program—Tel: 631-265-2200, Ext. 12. Email: hcreled@optonline.net. Ms. Ellen Fox, D.R.E. Students 1,700.

NEW HYDE PARK, NASSAU CO.

1—HOLY SPIRIT (1893) Rev. Joseph E. Nohs. In Res., Rev. Ralph Ferro; Deacon Richard Garcia; Rev. Lachlan T. Cameron.
Res.: 16 S. Sixth St., 11040. Tel: 516-354-0359; Fax: 516-354-2611 (Rectory). Email: holyspchurch@aol.com. Web: www.holyspiritchurch.com.
Catechesis/Religious Program—13 S. 6th St., 11040. Tel: 516-354-2363. Students 540.

2—NOTRE DAME (1941) Revs. William T. Slater; Steven J. Hannafin. In Res., Rev. John Denniston.
Res.: 45 Mayfair Rd., 11040. Tel: 516-352-7203; Fax: 516-326-7988.
School—25 Mayfair Rd., 11040. Tel: 516-354-5618; Fax: 516-354-5373. Mrs. Caryn Durkin Flores, Prin. Sisters of St. Dominic (Amityville) 1; Lay Teachers 33.
Catechesis/Religious Program—25 Mayfair Rd., 11040. Tel: 516-437-5604. Sr. Mary Jane Coleman, R.S.M., D.R.E.

NORTH MERRICK, NASSAU CO., SACRED HEART (1952) Revs. Joseph J. Nixon; Joseph D'Angelo.
Mailing Address: 720 Merrick Ave., 11566. Tel: 516-379-1356; Fax: 516-379-1610. Email: sacredheartnmerrick@hotmail.com. Web: www.hearttoheartparish.org.
School—730 Merrick Ave., 11566. Tel: 516-378-5797; Fax: 516-378-5797. Kerry Kahn, Prin. Sisters of St. Joseph 1; Lay Teachers 21; Students 238.
Catechesis/Religious Program—Tel: 516-868-9406. Sr. Ancilla Keinberger, O.P., D.R.E. Students 650.

NORTHPORT, SUFFOLK CO., ST. PHILIP NERI (1894) [CEM] Rev. Peter C. Dooley; Deacons John F. Burkart; Richard Becker; Sr. Grace Vagnini, C.S.J., Pastoral Assoc. In Res., Rev. Msgr. Thomas J. Colgan (Retired).
Office: 15 Prospect Ave., 11768. Tel: 631-261-2485; Fax: 631-261-2701.
Res.: 344 Main St., 11768. Fax: 631-261-7420.
See Trinity Regional School, East Northport under Regional Schools located in the Institution section.
Catechesis/Religious Program—Tel: 631-261-2485, Ext. 108; Fax: 631-261-2701. Kathleen Reid, D.R.E.; Patricia Merenda, D.R.E. Students 865.

OCEAN BEACH, (FIRE ISLAND) SUFFOLK CO., OUR LADY OF THE MAGNIFICAT (1921) Rev. Msgr. John C. Nosser (Retired).
Mailing Address: P.O. Box 445, 11770. Tel: 631-583-5868.
Catechesis/Religious Program—

OCEANSIDE, NASSAU CO., ST. ANTHONY (1927) Revs. D. James French, S.J.; Donald C. Gannon, S.J.; Daniel A. O'Brien, S.J.; Francis X. Hezel, S.J.; Deacons Michael Monahan; James O'Neill; John O'Connor, Business Mgr.; Anna Maria Sirianni, Parish Outreach Coord. Tel: 516-764-9257; Daniel Gibbons, Dir. Music.

Res.: 110 Anchor Ave., 11572. Tel: 516-764-0048; Fax: 516-282-2525. Email: sareception1@aol.com; saoffice3@aol.com. Web: stanthonyoceanside.org.
Catechesis/Religious Program—Tel: 516-282-2520. Mrs. Rose Dillon, D.R.E.

OYSTER BAY, NASSAU CO., ST. DOMINIC'S (1894) Rev. Kevin M. Smith; Rev. Msgr. Romualdo Sosing; Rev. Dariusz Koszyk.
Res.: 93 Anstice St., 11771. Tel: 516-922-4488; Fax: 516-922-9491. Email: parishoff@stdoms.org. Web: stdoms.org.
School—35 School St., 11771. Tel: 516-922-4233; Fax: 516-624-7613. Email: sdes@stdoms.org. Sisters of the Immaculate Heart of Mary 2; Lay Teachers 14; Students 224.
High School—110 Antice St., 11771. Tel: 516-922-4888; Fax: 516-922-5794. Email: sdhs@stdoms.org. Lay Teachers 31; Students 420.
Catechesis/Religious Program—Tel: 516-922-7788. Email: religioused@stdoms.org. Students 927.

PATCHOGUE, SUFFOLK CO.

1—ST. FRANCIS DE SALES (1888) [CEM] Rev. Thomas J. Pers; Deacons Martin McIndoe; Francisco Diaz-Granados; Mrs. Anne Boyce, Pastoral Assoc.; Gina Crawford, Outreach Coord.
Res.: 7 Amity St., 11772. Tel: 631-475-0161; Fax: 631-475-1481.
See Holy Angels Regional School, Patchogue under Regional Schools located in the Institution section.
Catechesis/Religious Program—Tel: 631-289-4339. Email: sanfraninpatch@hotmail.com. Elaine Heschl, D.R.E. Students 681.

2—OUR LADY OF MT. CARMEL (1925), (Italian), Revs. Michael J. Torpey; Freddy Lozano (Colombia), Brookhaven Hispanic Ministry; Thomas Aidoo, Chap. Stoney Brook Hospital; John Attakruh, Chap. Brookhaven Memorial Hospital; Deacons Joseph Mystkowski; Anthony Graviano; Christine Erhart, Business Mgr.
Res.: 495 New North Ocean Ave., 11772. Tel: 631-475-4739; Fax: 631-447-1030.
See Holy Angels Regional School, Patchogue under Regional Schools located in the Institution section.
Catechesis/Religious Program—Tel: 631-289-7327. Students 670.

PLAINVIEW, NASSAU CO., ST. PIUS X (1955) Rev. Msgr. Domenick T. Graziadio; Linda Curro, Pastoral Assoc.
Res.: One St. Pius Ct., 11803. Tel: 516-938-3956; Fax: 516-433-6138. Email: spxrecty@optonline.net.
See St. John Baptist de LaSalle Regional School, Farmingdale under Regional Schools located in the Institution section.
Catechesis/Religious Program—Tel: 516-822-8348; Fax: 516-938-0001. Students 319.

POINT LOOKOUT, NASSAU CO., OUR LADY OF THE MIRACULOUS MEDAL (1937), (Irish), Rev. Patrick J. Callan.
Res.: 75 Parkside Dr., P.O. Box 20, 11569. Tel: 516-431-2772; Fax: 516-432-8669. Email: olmmc@optonline.net. Web: olmmc.com.
See Long Beach Regional Catholic School, Long Beach under Regional Schools located in the Institution section.
Catechesis/Religious Program—Tel: 516-432-8074. Email: reled@optonline.net. Students 42.

PORT JEFFERSON STATION, SUFFOLK CO.

1—ST. GERARD MAJELLA (1968) Rev. Msgr. William A. Hanson; Deacon Vincent Beckles.
Mailing Address: 300 Terryville Rd., 11776.
Res.: 65 Nadine Ln., 11776. Tel: 631-473-2900; Fax: 631-473-0015. Web: www.stgmajella.org.
See Our Lady of the Wisdom Regional School, Port Jefferson under Regional Schools located in the Institution section.
Catechesis/Religious Program—Tel: 631-928-2550. Marguerite Goglia, D.R.E. Students 1,430.

2—INFANT JESUS (1903) Revs. Patrick M. Riegger; Paul Dolan; Francis Lasrado; Deacons William J. Powers; Richard E. Waldmann; Robert A. Kruse; Kenneth Clifford. In Res., Rev. Martin Bancroft.
Res.: 110 Myrtle Ave., 11777. Tel: 631-473-0165; Fax: 631-331-8094. Web: www.infantjesus.org.
See Our Lady of the Wisdom Regional School, Port Jefferson under Regional Schools located in the Institution section.
Catechesis/Religious Program—Tel: 631-928-0447; Fax: 631-928-2370. Ms. Maryanne Trezza, D.R.E. Students 1,466.

PORT WASHINGTON, NASSAU CO., ST. PETER OF ALCANTARA (1901) Rev. Patrick J. Whitney; Deacon Frank G. D'Angelo.
Res.: 1327 Port Washington Blvd., 11050. Tel: 516-883-6675; Fax: 516-944-7461.
School—Tel: 516-944-3772; Fax: 516-767-8075. Sean O'Connell, Prin. Lay Teachers 28; Students 330.
Catechesis/Religious Program—Tel: 516-883-5584; Fax: 516-767-6194. Students 735.
Convent—1317 Port Washington Blvd., 11050. Tel: 516-767-1282.

RIVERHEAD, SUFFOLK CO.

1—ST. ISIDORE'S (1903), (Polish), [CEM] Rev. Robert Kuznik; Deacon Michael A. Bonocore.
Res.: 622 Pulaski St., 11901. Tel: 631-727-2114; Fax: 631-369-3566. Email: sisidore@optonline.net.
School—515 Marcy Ave., 11901. Tel: 631-727-1650; Fax: 631-727-3945. Email: sljsis@aol.com. Sr. Linda Joseph Chichi, C.S.F.N., Prin. Sisters of the Holy Family of Nazareth 1; Lay Teachers 17; Students 220.
Catechesis/Religious Program—Students 100.

2—ST. JOHN THE EVANGELIST (1861) [CEM] Rev. Thomas W. Coby. In Res., Most Rev. Emil A. Wcela; Deacon John Lovett.
Res.: 546 St. John's Pl., 11901. Tel: 631-727-2030; Fax: 631-369-5228. Email: stjohnriverhead@aol.com.
Catechesis/Religious Program—Tel: 631-727-6774. Students 321.

ROCKY POINT, SUFFOLK CO., ST. ANTHONY OF PADUA (1948) Rev. Richard P. Hoerning; Sr. Josephine Olimpieri, C.S.J., Pastoral Assoc.
Res.: 614 Rte. 25A, 11778. Tel: 631-744-2609; Fax: 631-744-5782. Email: stasrp@optonline.net. Web: www.starockypoint.com.
Catechesis/Religious Program—Tel: 631-821-0872. Sr. Phylis O'Dowd, O.P., D.R.E. Students 1,435.

RONKONKOMA, SUFFOLK CO., ST. JOSEPH'S (1910) Revs. Michael T. Maffeo; Henry Leuthardt; Juniper J. Thomas; Peter T. Liu (Retired); Michael Boyle; Deacons James Altonji; Michael J. DeBellis; Joseph Dougherty, (Retired); Joseph Califano; Michael Devenney; William Dobbins; Frank Dell'Aglio.
Res.: 45 Church St., 11779-3300. Tel: 631-588-8456; Fax: 631-471-2569. Email: info@stjoronk.org. Web: stjoronk.org.
School—25 Church St., 11779. Tel: 631-588-4760; Fax: 631-588-0543. Email: school@stjoronk.org. Leona Arpino, Prin. Lay Teachers 19; Students 258.
Catechesis/Religious Program—35 Church St., 11779. Tel: 631-981-1805; Fax: 631-588-6140. Email: reled@stjoronk.org. Sr. Anne Marie Dean, C.S.J., D.R.E. Students 1,173.

ROOSEVELT, NASSAU CO., QUEEN OF THE MOST HOLY ROSARY (1919) Revs. Joseph Baidoo; Gabriel Muteru (Kenya) (NY); Deacons Clinton Lewis; Thomas Jackson; Mrs. Elena A. Powers, Music Min. In Res., Most Rev. Paul H. Walsh.
Res.: 196 W. Centennial Ave., 11575. Tel: 516-378-1315; Fax: 516-378-5754. Email: qmhr@optonline.net.
Catechesis/Religious Program—200 W. Centennial Ave., 11575. Tel: 516-623-1391; Fax: 516-378-5754. Email: cherylwhite@optonline.net. Cheryl White, D.R.E. Students 98.

ROSLYN, NASSAU CO., ST. MARY'S (1871) Rev. Msgr. John A. Alessandro, Admin.; Deacon Edward M. Case.
Res.: 110 Bryant Ave., 11576. Tel: 516-621-2222; Fax: 516-621-7892.
See All Saints Regional Catholic School, Glen Cove under Regional Schools located in the Institution section.
Catechesis/Religious Program—Tel: 516-621-6798. Nora Toal, C.R.E. Students 406.

SAINT JAMES, SUFFOLK CO., SS. PHILIP AND JAMES (1907) Revs. Anthony M. Stanganelli; Edward H. Koch, Parochial Vicor; Deacons Kenneth Maher; Robert Heschl, (Retired); John Keenan; Gerard Reda; Ronald Blasius. In Res., Rev. James L. Maltese, Hospital Chap.
Res.: 1 Carow Pl., 11780. Tel: 631-584-5454; Fax: 631-862-9675. Email: info@sspj.org. Web: www.sspj.org.
School—(Grades PreK-8) Tel: 631-584-7896; Fax: 631-584-3258. Web: sspjschool.net. Mr. Anthony Giordano, Prin. Lay Teachers 20; Students 255.
Catechesis/Religious Program—Tel: 631-584-3204. Students 1,750.

SAG HARBOR, SUFFOLK CO., ST. ANDREW'S (1859) [CEM] Rev. Peter Devaraj, S.A.C., Admin. In Res., Rev. Andrew P. Blake, Pastor Emeritus (Retired).
Res.: 122 Division St, 11963-3154. Tel: 631-725-0123; Fax: 631-725-3310.
See Stella Maris Regional School, Sag Harbor under Regional Schools located in the Institution section.
Catechesis/Religious Program—Students 125.

SALTAIRE, SUFFOLK CO., OUR LADY STAR OF THE SEA, MISSION CHAPEL, (Summer Mission) Rev. Richard R. Viladesau, Admin.
Res.: 2000 Jackson Ave., Seaford, 11783. Tel: 516-785-1266, Ext. 15.
Church: 310 Pilot Walk, 11706. Tel: 631-583-7613.

SAYVILLE, SUFFOLK CO., ST. LAWRENCE THE MARTYR (1895) [CEM] Revs. Nicholas J. Figliola; Brian Ingram; Deacon Patrick LaBella.
Res.: 27 Handsome Ave., 11782. Tel: 631-589-0042; 631-589-8135; 631-589-3887; Fax: 631-589-5318. Email: office@stlawrencesayville.org. Web: stlawrencesayville.org.
See Prince of Peace Regional School, Sayville under Regional Schools located in the Institution section.
Catechesis/Religious Program—Tel: 631-589-3160. Mrs. Maria Davidson, D.R.E. Students 1,227.

SEA CLIFF, NASSAU CO., ST. BONIFACE MARTYR (1898) Rev. Robert A. Romeo; Deacon Tom Fox; Eileen Krieb, Business Mgr.; Jeff Schneider, Music Dir.
Rectory, Office & Parish Center: 145 Glen Ave., 11579. Tel: 516-676-0676; Fax: 516-674-6742. Email: stbonchurch@gmail.com. Web: saintboniface.org.
Res.: 220 Carpenter Ave., 11579.
See All Saints Regional Catholic School, Glen Cove under Regional Schools located in the Institution section.
Catechesis/Religious Program—Tel: 516-671-0418. Email: stbonccd@gmail.com. Karen Croce, D.R.E.; Chris Mandato, Youth Min. Students 500.

SEAFORD, NASSAU CO.

1—ST. JAMES (1951) Revs. John Derasmo; John David Ryan; Aaron T. Vellaramparampil; Deacons James G. Beirne; Richard Brunner; Allan J. Helmbrecht, Business Mgr.; Jane Lawson, Music Min.
Res.: 80 Hicksville Rd., 11783. Tel: 516-731-3710; Fax: 516-731-4828. Email: stjamesrcchurch@aol.com.
See St. John Baptist de LaSalle Regional School, Farmingdale under Regional Schools located in the Institution section.
Catechesis/Religious Program—Tel: 516-796-2979; Fax: 516-731-4828. Marianne Mirkow, C.R.E.; Julie Labeck, C.R.E. Students 1,648.

2—MARIA REGINA (1954) Rev. Msgr. Peter J. Pflomm; Revs. Allan Arnaud; Stephen Morris; Deacons Gerald F. Whitfield; Andrew Gargiulo; John R. Nuzzi; Paul Neuhedel.
Res.: 3945 Jerusalem Ave., 11783. Tel: 516-798-2415; Fax: 516-798-7493.
School—4045 Jerusalem Ave., 11783. Tel: 516-541-1229; Fax: 516-541-1235. Mrs. Denise Carlin Seck, Prin.; Mrs. Donna DiGiovanna, Asst. Prin. Lay Teachers 27; Students 400.
Catechesis/Religious Program—3945 Jerusalem Ave., 11783. Tel: 516-541-0921; Fax: 516-795-2510. Carol Tannehill, D.R.E. Students 2,010.

3—ST. WILLIAM THE ABBOT (1928) Revs. Robert L. Hayden; Paul F. Butler; Bala Rathinam; Deacons Thomas Buchenberger; John Lynch; Sr. Jo Ann Bouauro, S.C., Pastoral Assoc. In Res., Rev. Richard R. Viladesau.
Res.: 2000 Jackson Ave., 11783. Tel: 516-785-1266; Fax: 516-785-4824. Email: information@stwilliam.org. Web: www.stwilliam.org.
School—2001 Jackson Ave., 11783. Tel: 516-785-6784; Fax: 516-785-2752. Email: aguardino@stwilliamtheabbot.net. Web: www.stwilliamtheabbot.net. Mrs. Anna Guardino, Prin. Lay Teachers 27; Students 586.
Catechesis/Religious Program—Tel: 516-679-9558; Fax: 516-679-1649. Email: reled@stwilliam.org. Mrs. Mary Calabrese, D.R.E. Students 1,378.

SELDEN, SUFFOLK CO., ST. MARGARET OF SCOTLAND (1948) Revs. James L. Wood; Henry W. Reid; Deacons William E. Kogler; Biagio Muratore; Phil Paolicelli; Joseph Scollan; Edward Hayes; Barbara Mahon, Admin.
Res.: 81 College Rd., 11784. Tel: 631-732-3131; Fax: 631-732-8827. Web: saintmargaret.com.
See Holy Angels Regional School, Patchogue under Regional Schools located in the Institution section.
Catechesis/Religious Program—Tel: 631-698-0798. Sharon Orabona, D.R.E.; Eileen Lorio, C.R.E.; Tina Muller, C.R.E.; Marianne Hordt, Youth Min. Students 1,050.

SETAUKET, SUFFOLK CO., ST. JAMES (1949) [CEM] Revs. Robert J. Smith; James P. Mannion Jr. In Res., Rev. John J. Fitzgerald (Retired).
Res.: 429 Rte. 25-A, 11733. Tel: 631-941-4141; Fax: 631-751-6607.
See Our Lady of the Wisdom Regional School, Port Jefferson under Regional Schools located in the Institution section.
Catechesis/Religious Program—Tel: 631-751-7287. Web: www.stjamessetauket.org. Louise DiCarlo, D.R.E. Students 1,694.

SHELTER ISLAND, SUFFOLK CO., OUR LADY OF THE ISLE (1907) [CEM] Revs. Thomas Murray, Admin.; Peter DeSanctis.
Shelter Island Heights, Box 3027, Shelter Island Heights, 11965. Tel: 631-749-0001; Fax: 631-749-4218. Email: oliheights@aol.com.
See Stella Maris Regional School, Sag Harbor under Regional Schools located in the Institution section.
Catechesis/Religious Program—Students 10.

SHOREHAM, SUFFOLK CO., ST. MARK (1973) Revs. Theodore J. Howard; Ivan Gonzalez (El Salvador); Christopher Deh (Ghana); Deacon Patrick Gerace.
Res.: 105 Randall Rd., 11786. Tel: 631-744-2800; Fax: 631-821-1628. Email: stmarksrcc@aol.com.
Catechesis/Religious Program—Tel: 631-821-0550. Email: relform@verizon.net. Mrs. Lynn Fein, D.R.E. Students 1,174.

SMITHTOWN, SUFFOLK CO., ST. PATRICK (1952), (Irish—Italian), [CEM] Rev. Msgr. Ellsworth R. Walden; Revs. David Matthew Regan; Desmond Chilagorom. In Res., Revs. Frederick Hill; Vitalis Abiamiri.
Res.: 280 E. Main St., 11787. Tel: 631-265-2271; Fax: 631-863-1586. Email: rectory@stpatricksmithtown.org.
School—284 E. Main St., 11787. Tel: 631-724-0285; Fax: 631-265-4841. Web: www.sps-smithtown.org. Ms. Rita Anne Swift, Prin. Lay Teachers 27; Students 530.
Catechesis/Religious Program—Tel: 631-724-7454; Fax: 631-265-1250. Email: stpatsrfc@optonline.net. Mrs. Elaina Kedjierski, D.R.E. (Levels 1-4); Peggy Soviero, D.R.E. (Levels 5-8). Students 1,500.

SOUND BEACH, SUFFOLK CO., ST. LOUIS DE MONTFORT (1971) Rev. Charles E. Papa; Rev. Msgr. John A. McGuire, Pastor Emeritus (Retired); Deacons Joseph T. Bartolotto, Pastoral Assoc.; Gary F. Swane; Robert Mullane.
75 New York Ave., 11789-2506. Tel: 631-744-8566; Fax: 631-744-8611. Email: tkretz@sldmrc.org.
See Our Lady of the Wisdom Regional School, Port Jefferson under Regional Schools located in the Institution section.
Catechesis/Religious Program—Tel: 631-744-9515; Fax: 631-821-6089. Email: jmcnamara@sldmrc.org. Mr. John McNamara, D.R.E. Students 1,841.

SOUTHAMPTON, SUFFOLK CO.
1—OUR LADY OF POLAND (1918), (Polish), Rev. Stanley Kondeja; Deacon James Ashe.
Res.: 35 Maple St., 11968. Tel: 631-283-0667; Fax: 631-287-4146.
See Our Lady of the Hamptons Regional School, Southampton under Regional Schools located in the Institution section.
Catechesis/Religious Program—168 Hill St., 11968. Tel: 631-283-0097; Fax: 631-283-3836. Students 20.
2—SACRED HEARTS OF JESUS AND MARY (1896) [CEM] Rev. Msgrs. Jeffrey J. Madley; Edmond J. Trench, Pastor Emeritus (Retired); Deacon John P. Moran. In Res., Rev. Msgr. William J. Gill (Retired).
Res.: 168 Hill St., 11968. Tel: 631-283-0097; Fax: 631-283-3836.
See Our Lady of the Hamptons Regional School, Southampton under Regional Schools located in the Institution section.
Catechesis/Religious Program—Tel: 631-283-0508. Students 350.

SOUTHOLD, SUFFOLK CO., ST. PATRICK'S (1865) [CEM] Rev. Peter J. Garry.
Res.: Main Rd., P.O. Box 1117, 11971-1401. Tel: 631-765-3442; Fax: 631-765-9631. Email: saintpat@optonline.net.
See Our Lady of Mercy Regional School, Cutchogue under Regional Schools located in the Institution section.
Catechesis/Religious Program—Tel: 631-765-2338. Students 290.

SYOSSET, NASSAU CO., ST. EDWARD CONFESSOR (1952) Revs. Thomas M. Fusco; Paul Kenny, S.S.C.; Sr. Jacqueline Walsh, R.S.M., Pastoral Assoc. Tel: 516-921-8030, Ext. 134; Deacons James Murphy; Thomas F. Reilly Jr.; Raymond P. D'Alessio. In Res., Rev. Joseph Fitzgerald.
Res.: 205 Jackson Ave., 11791-4218. Tel: 516-921-8030; Fax: 516-921-4549. Web: www.st-edwards.org.
School—2 Teibrook Ave., 11791. Tel: 516-921-7767; Fax: 516-496-0001. Mrs. Joanne Fitzgerald, Prin. Lay Teachers 17; Students 214.
Catechesis/Religious Program—Tel: 516-921-8030, Ext. 126 (Grades 1-5); 516-921-8030, Ext. 124 (Grades 6-8). Pamela Sanders, D.R.E.; Susan Lawlor, Dir. Parish Social Ministry. Students 1,083.

UNIONDALE, NASSAU CO., ST. MARTHA (1949) Rev. Msgr. Frank J. Caldwell, C.S.W.; Most Rev. Alfonso Cabezas, C.M.; Deacon Trevor S. Mathurin; Sr. Eileen Curley, R.S.M., Pastoral Assoc.
Tel: 516-481-2550, Ext. 302 (Pastor's Office); 516-292-1603 (Parish Outreach).
Res.: 546 Greengrove Ave., 11553. Tel: 516-481-2550, Ext. 302; Fax: 516-564-4552. Email: saintmartha@yahoo.com. Web: www.saintmartha-.org.
See St. Martin de Porres Marianist School, Uniondale under Elementary Schools, Private located in the Institution section.
Catechesis/Religious Program—Tel: 516-481-2550, Ext. 311. Mrs. Marlene Jean-Baptiste, Dir. Parish Social Ministry. Tel: 516-292-1603. Students 335.

VALLEY STREAM, NASSAU CO.
1—BLESSED SACRAMENT (1950) Rev. Peter Dugandzic; Deacon John F. Coughlin.
Res.: 201 N. Central Ave., 11580. Tel: 516-568-1027; Fax: 516-872-1499.
Catechesis/Religious Program—April Carbaugh, Co-ord. Faith Formation. Students 370.
2—HOLY NAME OF MARY (1902) Rev. Msgr. Romualdo Sosing; Rev. Robert W. Ketcham; Deacons James O'Hara; Clyde Ruggieri; Richard F. Raad; Scott Baker. In Res., Rev. Msgr. Edward J. Donnelly (Retired).
Res.: 55 E. Jamaica Ave., 11580. Tel: 516-825-1450; Fax: 516-568-1906. Email: holynamemary@aol.com. Web: www.hnom.org.
School—90 S. Grove St., 11580. Tel: 516-825-4009; Fax: 516-825-2710. Richard A. Mc Mahon, Prin. Lay Teachers 16; Students 340.
Catechesis/Religious Program—90 S. Grove St., 11580. Tel: 516-825-1810; Fax: 516-256-0724. Sr. Emily Masse, O.P., D.R.E. Students 730.
Religious Education—Fax: 516-825-5092. Sr. Margie Kelly, C.S.J., Parish Outreach Dir.; Kevin Faughey, Music Min.; Rosemary Pettei, Dir. Family Ministry.

WADING RIVER, SUFFOLK CO., ST. JOHN BAPTIST (1922) Rev. John J. Barrett; Deacons Frederick Finter; Vincent Pozzolano.
Res.: 1488 North Country Rd., 11792. Tel: 631-929-4339; Fax: 631-929-6961.
Catechesis/Religious Program—Students 670.

WANTAGH, NASSAU CO., ST. FRANCES DE CHANTAL (1952) Revs. Gregory J. Cappuccino; Lito D. Amande; Antonio S. Pascual (Retired); Francisco Gius Garcia (Philippines); Sr. Jocelyn Panzetta, C.I.J.; Deacons Robert O'Donovan; Joseph Torres. In Res., Rev. Msgr. John J. Rowan (Retired).
Res.: 1309 Wantagh Ave., 11793. Tel: 516-785-2333; Fax: 516-826-7645. Web: www.stjanefrances.com.
See St. Elizabeth Ann Seton Regional School, Bellmore under Regional Schools located in the Institution section.
Catechesis/Religious Program—Tel: 516-785-2333, Ext. 205. Ellen Lafonte, D.R.E.; Donna Mugno, Admin. Students 2,228.

WEST BABYLON, SUFFOLK CO., OUR LADY OF GRACE (1962) Rev. Msgr. Vincent Rush; Revs. Gilbert D. Lap; Eugenio Solera (Philippines); Deacons Irwin Saffran; William Austin; Brian Miller; Peter DiGiuseppe.
Res.: 666 Albin Ave., 11704. Tel: 631-587-5185; Fax: 631-587-1427. Email: olograce@ourladyofgrace.net. Web: ourladyofgrace.net.
Catechesis/Religious Program—700 Albin Ave., 11704. Tel: 631-661-9353. Mrs. Barbara McGrellis, Dir. Day Care; Mrs. Susan Martin, D.R.E. Students 1,550.

WEST HEMPSTEAD, NASSAU CO., ST. THOMAS, THE APOSTLE (1931) Rev. Msgr. Francis J. Maniscalco; Revs. Noel Effiong, M.S.P. (Nigeria); Fernando Egargo; Deacons John E. Ford; Edward Cunningham; Jacques Philippeaux; Anthony S. D'Auria.
Res.: 24 Westminster Rd., 11552. Tel: 516-489-8585; Fax: 516-292-2651. Email: stthomasap@optonline.net. Web: stthomasapostle.org.
School—12 Westminster Rd., 11552. Tel: 516-481-9310; Fax: 516-481-8769. Mrs. Christina Teisch, Prin. Sisters 2; Lay Teachers 27; Students 453.
Catechesis/Religious Program—Tel: 516-538-7460. Mrs. Mary Ann Pellegrino, D.R.E.; Eileen Minutoli, D.R.E. Students 570.
Mission—Chapel 876 Hempstead Ave., Nassau Co. 11552. Tel: 516-483-4091.

WEST ISLIP, SUFFOLK CO., OUR LADY OF LOURDES (1956) Revs. Michael A. Vetrano; Robert C. Scheckenback; Stanislaus Chukwube; Deacons Stephen M. Behar; John Teufel; John DeGuardi; Jack Meehan.
Res.: 455 Hunter Ave., 11795. Tel: 631-661-3224; Fax: 631-661-7143.
School—44 Toomey Rd., 11795. Tel: 631-587-7200; Fax: 631-587-4531. Regina A. Cioffi, Prin. Lay Teachers 18; Students 355.
Catechesis/Religious Program—Tel: 631-661-5440; Fax: 631-661-3606. Sisters Diane Liona, D.R.E.; Nancy Campkin, D.R.E. Students 2,600.

WESTBURY, NASSAU CO., ST. BRIGID (1850) Rev. Msgr. Ralph Sommer; Revs. Ronel Charelus, S.M.M.; Gregory Rannazzisi; Jaime Calderon; Deacons Manuel Ramos; Michael Metzdorff; James Morris; Frank Pesce. In Res., Rev. Wismick Jean Charles, S.M.M.
Res.: 75 Post Ave., 11590. Tel: 516-334-0021; Fax: 516-334-0082. Email: parish@saintbrigid.net. Web: www.saintbrigid.net.
School—St. Brigid/ Our Lady of Hope Regional School, 101 Maple Ave., 11590. Tel: 516-333-0580; Fax: 516-333-0590. Paul P. Clagnaz, Prin. School Sisters of Notre Dame 1; Lay Teachers 22; Students 329.
Catechesis/Religious Program—101 Maple Ave., 11590. Tel: 516-333-9434. Sr. Ann Horn, O.P., D.R.E.; Socorro Moreno, D.R.E.; Meg Westfall, D.R.E. Students 781.

WESTHAMPTON BEACH, SUFFOLK CO., IMMACULATE CONCEPTION (1891) Rev. Joseph A. Mirro; Deacon Joseph Byrne; Virginia Mattera, Pastoral Assoc.
Res.: 580 Main Rd., 11978. Tel: 631-288-1423; Fax: 631-288-5498.
See Our Lady, Queen of the Apostles Regional School, Center Moriches under Regional Schools located in the Institution section.
Catechesis/Religious Program—Tel: 631-288-4188; Fax: 631-288-8215. Virginia Mattera, D.R.E. Students 554.

WILLISTON PARK, NASSAU CO., ST. AIDAN'S CHURCH (1928) Rev. Msgrs. James M. McDonald; Robert J. Kirwin, Pastor Emeritus (Retired); Revs. Thomas W. Tassone; Kevin J. Dillon; Deacons Francis J. Love; Salvatore Villani; Joseph F. Connelly. In Res., Rev. Msgr. James C. Vlaun.
Res.: 505 Willis Ave., 11596. Tel: 516-746-6585; Fax: 516-746-6055.
School—(Grades N-3), 525 Willis Ave., 11596. Tel: 516-746-6585, Ext. 9202; Fax: 516-746-8817. Mrs. Patti Serrano, Librarian.
School—(Grades 4-8), 510 Willis Ave., 11596. Tel: 518-747-6585, Ext. 9302; Fax: 516-746-3086. Eileen Oliver, Prin.; Marie-Elaine Galenskas, Asst. Prin. Lay Teachers 35; Students 558.
Catechesis/Religious Program—508 Willis Ave., 11596. Tel: 516-746-6585, Ext. 9404. Mr. James F. Corrigan, D.R.E.; Mrs. Patti Serrano, Librarian. Students 1,250.

WOODBURY, NASSAU CO., HOLY NAME OF JESUS (1962) Revs. Lawrence B. Rafferty; Yong Don Ju (Korea, South), (Spiritual Leader Korean Catholic Apostolate).
Res.: 690 Woodbury Rd., 11797-2504. Tel: 516-921-2334; Fax: 516-682-8161. Email: frrafferty@hnjchurch.net. Web: www.hnjchurch.net.
Catechesis/Religious Program—Students 103.

WYANDANCH, SUFFOLK CO., OUR LADY OF THE MIRACULOUS MEDAL (1932) Rev. William F. Brisotti; Deacon Jules Gagnon.
Res.: 1434 Straight Path, 11798. Tel: 631-643-7568; Fax: 631-643-5935.
Gerald Ryan Outreach Center, Inc.—Tel: 631-643-7591. Noelle Campbell, Dir.; Naycha Florival, Religious Education & Youth Ministry. Tel: 631-643-3364.
Catechesis/Religious Program—Tel: 631-643-3364. Students 240.

Chaplains of Public Institutions

ROCKVILLE CENTRE. *Mercy Medical Center*, 1000 N. Village Ave., 11570. Tel: 516-705-2525. Revs. Anthony Madu, Francis Oranefo (Nigeria), Sisters Mary Alice Aschenbach, C.I.J., Chap., Vice Pres., Pastoral Care, Mary Ellen Eichmann, Chap., Norma Jean Lokcinski, C.I.J., Chap., Eileen Vassallo, Chap.
Good Shepherd Hospice (Nassau), 245 Old Country Rd., Melville, 11747. Tel: 631-465-6300. Rev. Robert Dawley, Chap., Deacon Michael Metzdorff, Dir. Pastoral Care, Sisters Mary Alice Duggin, O.S.U., Chap., Lorraine Leibold, O.P., Chap., Joyce Osgood, O.P., Chap., Pauline T. Lavelle, Chap.

AMITYVILLE. *South Oaks Psychiatric Hospital*, Sunrise Hwy., 11701. Tel: 631-264-4000.

BAY SHORE. *Southside Hospital*, Montauk Hwy., 11706. Tel: 631-968-3000. Revs. Peter J. McCrann, S.M.M., Christopher Okoli (Nigeria).

BETHPAGE. *New Island Hospital, New Island Hospital*, 4295 Hempstead Tpke., 11714. Tel: 631-520-0222. Rev. Hilary Ezenwa.

EAST MEADOW. *Nassau County Police Department*. Rev. Msgr. John A. Alesandro, Revs. Joseph D'Angelo, Gerard Gordon.
Nassau County, Fire Chiefs, Council of. Rev. Kevin M. Smith.
Nassau University Medical Center, 2201 Hempstead Tpke., 11554. Tel: 516-572-3195; 516-572-6069. Sr. Maureen Chase, Dir. Pastoral Care, Revs. Cyprian Osuegbu (Nigeria), Sebastian Owusa-Mensah.

GLEN COVE. *North Shore University Hospital at Glen Cove*, Tel: 516-674-7300. Rev. Frederick Kutubebi.

HUNTINGTON. *Huntington Hospital*, 270 Park Ave., 11743. Tel: 631-351-2000. Rev. Thomas Edamattan (India), Deacon Edward Billia.

LONG BEACH. *Long Beach Memorial Medical Center*, 455 E. Bay Dr., 11561. Rev. Joseph Paul Fernando, Chap.

MANHASSET. *North Shore Univ. Hospital*, 1554 Community Dr., 11030. Tel: 516-562-0100. Revs. Antony Xavier, Benet Uwasomba (Nigeria), Jon Overvold, Dir.
North Hills Hospital, Tel: 516-562-4713.

MELVILLE. *Long Island Developmental Center*, Box 788, 11747. Tel: 516-385-2700. Rev. Malachy Flaherty, O.F.M.Cap.

MINEOLA. *Winthrop Hospital*, First St., 11501. Tel: 516-663-0333. Revs. Polycarp Nnajiofor (Nigeria), Ethel Anarado (Nigeria).
Corpus Christi, 155 Garfield Ave., 11501-2583. Tel: 516-746-1223.

NESCONSET. *Nesconset Nursing Home* 11767. Tel: 516-361-8800. Vacant.

NORTHPORT. *Veteran's Administration Hospital* 1176.

Tel: 631-261-4400, Ext. 7194. Revs. John Malone, David Lazar Mani.

OCEANSIDE. *South Nassau Communities Hospital*, Tel: 516-763-2030. Rev. Jerome Francis Ackah (Ghana), Deacon Charles Muscarnera.

PATCHOGUE. *Brookhaven Hospice*, Tel: 631-687-2960. Deacon Bob Gronenthal, Elaine Kotlowski.

Brookhaven Memorial Hospital, 100 Hospital Rd., 11772. Tel: 631-654-7100. Rev. John Attakruh, James Maloney.

PLAINVIEW. *North Shore Hospital at Plainview*, 888 Old Country Rd., 11083. Tel: 516-681-8900. Rev. Jose Simon Palliparambil (Retired).

St. Pius X: 1 St. Pius Ct., 11803-4023. Tel: 516-938-3959.

PORT JEFFERSON. *St. Charles Hospital, Port Jefferson, New York* 11777. Tel: 631-474-6411. Revs. Samuel Aririatu (Nigeria) (NY), Charles Oppong (Ghana), Deacon Joseph Scollan, Sisters Josefita Rodriguez, O.P., Dir., Pastoral Care, Edith Menegus, O.S.U., Chap.

Maryhaven Center of Hope 11777. Tel: 631-474-3400. Sisters Maryaline Zierle, O.P., Cathy Smith, O.P.

Mather Memorial Hospital 11777. Tel: 631-473-1320, Ext. 4007. Rev. Martin Bancroft.

ROCKVILLE CENTRE. *Catholic Health Services of Long Island*, 992 N. Village Ave., 11570. Tel: 516-705-3700; 631-474-5663. Mary T. O'Neill, Vice Pres. for Spiritual Care & Pastoral Educ., Mrs. Cathy B. Grandjean, Dir. Chaplaincy.

ROSLYN. *St. Francis Hospital* 11576. Revs. Emmanuel Okeiyi, John B. Ephraim, Sisters Minda Castrillo, F.M.M., Elisa Fernando, F.M.M., Mari Garesche, Pauline Gilmore, F.M.M., Dir., Pastoral Care, Thresi Kalloorthottiyil, Claire MacDonald, O.P., Ms. Mary Toole, Mary Ellen Beneivenga, Patricia Tarpinian.

SAYVILLE. *Good Samaritan Nursing Home.* 11782. Tel: 631-244-2400. Sr. Doris Marie Deane, S.C., Chap.

SMITHTOWN. *St. Catherine of Siena Hospital* 11787. Tel: 631-360-2000. Sr. Patricia McDonnell, O.P., Dir., Revs. Frederick Hill, Mark Applewhite, Anselm Okeke, Theresa Maynard, Chap.

280 E. Main St., 11787. Tel: 631-862-3000; 631-979-1292.

STONY BROOK. *L.I. State Veterans' Home*, Tel: 631-444-8737. Rev. Peter O'Rourke.

Stony Brook University Hospital, SUNY at Stony Brook, 11790. Tel: 631-444-8157. Revs. Steve Unger, Dir. Pastoral Care, James L. Maltese, (on call weekends), Patrick Chudi Okafor, Thomas Aidoo, Patrick Okafor, (M T W on-call), Sr. Lynn Queck, Chap., Mrs. Anne Coulehan, Chap.

UNIONDALE. *Holly Patterson Geriatric Center*, 875 Jerusalem Ave., 11553. Tel: 516-572-1500. Rev. R. Michael Reid (Retired).

Res.: *Holy Family*, Hicksville, 11801. Tel: 516-938-3846.

VALLEY STREAM. *Franklin Medical Center Hospital* 11580. Tel: 516-256-6000. Revs. James Barnum, Augustine Okochi, Kathryn Martino, Chap.

Our Lady of Peace, 25 Fowler Ave., Lynbrook, 11563. Tel: 516-399-6414.

WEST BRENTWOOD. *Pilgrim Psychiatric Center*, P.O. Box A, 11717. Tel: 631-761-2828. Rev. Lawrence J. O'Leary (Retired), Sr. Mary Summerville, C.S.J.

WEST ISLIP. *Consolation Nursing Home* 11795. Tel: 631-587-1600. Rev. William R. Logan, Rabbi Kathleen Novick, Deacon Robert Raines, Mrs. Theresa McNally, Chap., Mrs. Peggy Nixdorf, Dir., Pastoral Care, Mrs. Sandra Smith, Chap., Ms. Alycia Zawol, Chap.

Good Samaritan Hospital Medical Center 11795. Tel: 631-376-3000. Revs. Jerome Madumelu, Cletus Nwaogwugwu, Paul Nwobi, Sisters Mona Garrett, D.W., Jean Agnes Geraghty, O.P., Rosemary Jermusryk, O.P., Ellen Moore, O.P., Gertrude O'Brien, D.W., Ann Marie Pierce, O.P., Mary Ann Bonner, Chap., Carmen Springer, Chap., Kevin Stolz, Chap.

Catholic Home Care, 15 Park Ave., Hauppauge, 11749. Tel: 631-929-8200. Mr. Charles Zeiss, Kevin Danaher, Linda Smith, Alex Daszewski.

Prison Ministry

BAY SHORE. *Office of Prison Ministry and Criminal Justice Affairs*, 26 S. Saxon Ave., 11706-8920. Tel: 631-969-0837; Fax: 631-666-5073. Bro. Jack Moylan, O.S.F., D. Min., Dir., Suzanne D. Jones, Coord. of Ministerial Svcs.

EAST MEADOW. *Nassau County Correctional Center*, 100 Carman Ave., 11554-1146. Tel: 516-572-4145. Rev. Ralph Ferro, Sisters Dolores Castellano, C.I.J., Virginia Waters, F.S.P., Deacons John H. McGonigle, Manuel Ramos.

RIVERHEAD. *Suffolk County Correctional Facility*, 100 Center Dr., 11901. Tel: 631-852-2294; 631-852-2728. Sr. Michelle Bremer, C.S.F.N., Deacon Chris Vigliotta.

WESTBURY. *Nassau County Juvenile Detention Center*, 61 Carman Ave., 11590. Tel: 516-571-9153. Bro. Jack Moylan, O.S.F., D.Min., Sr. Dolores Castellano, C.I.J.

YAPHANK. *Suffolk County Minimum Security Facility*, P.O. Box 69, 11980. Tel: 631-852-4713. Sr. Michelle Bremer, C.S.F.N., Deacons Miguel Romero, Chris Vigliotta.

Academic Leave:
Rev.—
Mastrogiacomo, Richard J.

Leave of Absence:
Revs.—
Kennedy, Glenn
Rogers, Paul E.
White, John

Serving Outside the Diocese:
Rev. Msgrs.—
Boccafola, Kenneth
Cervini, John
Revs.—
Blyman, Robert Y.
Denniston, John
McCarthy, John D.
Okochi, Chux
Rowan, Mark P.
Viladesau, Richard R., S.T.D.

Medical Leave:
Rev. Msgr.—
Hayde, Ronald
Revs.—
Bie, Paul R.
Johnston, Jeffrey
Lubrano, Robert

Retired:
Most Revs.—
Daly, James, Diocese of Rockville Centre, P.O. Box 9023, 11571-9023.
Wcela, Emil, Church of St. John the Evangelist, 546 St. John's Pl., Riverhead, 11901.
Rev. Msgrs.—
Ballweg, Lawrence F., 220 Main Blvd. 1C, Boynton Beach, FL 33435.
Bennett, Donald T., Church of St. Ignatius Loyola, 129 Broadway, Hicksville, 11801.
Boesel, James E., Church of Our Lady of Mercy, 500 S. Oyster Bay Rd., Hicksville, 11801.
Brassil, James A., Church of the Sacred Heart, 720 Merrick Ave., North Merrick, 11566.
Candreva, Thomas D., S.T.L., J.C.D., 560 West Broadway #4R, Long Beach, 11561.
Colgan, Thomas J., St. Philip Neri, 15 Prospect Ave., Northport, 11768.
Curley, Joseph K., Assumption of BVM, 20 Chestnut St., Centereach, 11720.
Donnelly, Edward J., 10 Gotham Walk, Breezy Point, 11697.
Fagan, Robert Emmet, M.S.W., Sem. of the Immaculate Conception, 440 W. Neck Rd., Huntington, 11743.
Gaeta, Francis X., St. Pius Residence, 565 Albany Ave., Amityville, 11701.
Gallagher, Thomas G., Church of Maria Regina, 3945 Jerusalem Ave., Seaford, 11783.
Gill, William J., Sacred Hearts of Jesus & Mary, 168 Hill St., Southampton, 11968.
Graham, George P., J.C.D., Ph.D., St. Bernard, 3100 Hempstead Tpke., Levittown, 11756.
Hamilton, Daniel S., Church of Our Lady of Perpetual Help, 210 S. Wellwood Ave., Lindenhurst, 11757.
Heinlein, John T., St. Jude, 89 Overlook Dr., Mastic Beach, 11951.
Hurley, Daniel J., St. Rose of Lima, 2 Bayview Ave., Massapequa, 11758.
Jablonski, William W., St. Vincent de Paul, 1500 De Paul St., Elmont, 11003.
Kane, Thomas S., 4384 Bowspirit Ct. 2D, Fort Myers, FL 33919.
Kirwin, Robert J., St. Aidan, 505 Willis Ave., Williston Park, 11596-1786.
Manly, Alexander F., St. Joseph, 59 Church St., Kings Park, 11754.
Martin, John P., 37 N. Bayview Rd., Southampton, 11968.
McGuire, John A., St. Louis de Montfort, 75 New York Ave., Sound Beach, 11789-0810.
Molloy, Thomas E., St. Francis de Sales, 7 Amity St., Patchogue, 11772.
Murphy, Eugene F., Church of Corpus Christi, 155 Garfield Ave., Mineola, 11501.
Nosser, Charles J., Church of Our Lady of Victory, 2 Floral Parkway, Floral Park, 11001.
Nosser, John C., M.S., M.Div., Church of Our Lady of the Magnificat, P.O. Box 445, Ocean Beach, 11770.
Placa, Alan J., St. Aloysius, 592 Middle Neck Roda, Great Neck, 11023.
Ribaudo, Charles A., 20 Suncrest Dr., Dix Hills, 11746.
Rowan, John J., P.O. Box 1142, Southold, 11971.
Ryan, T. Peter, Our Lady Queen of Martyrs, 53 Prospect Rd., Centerport, 11721.
Saccacio, Robert J., 3102 Bludds Dr. S., Baiting Hollow, 11933.
Savastano, Anthony J., St. Pius X Residence, 1220 Front St., Uniondale, 11553.
Singleton, William V., St. Raymond, 263 Atlantic Ave., East Rockaway, 11518-1117.
Skelly, John J., P.O. Box 5217, Rocky Point, 11778.
Sweeney, Edward A., St. Ignatius Martyr, 721 W. Broadway, Long Beach, 11561.
Tarrant, Edward L., Corpus Christi, 155 Garfield Ave., Mineola, 11501.
Trench, Edmond J., P.O. Box 1503, East Quogue, 11942.
Wawerski, Edward, Church of St. Hedwig, 1 Depan Ave., Floral Park, 11001.
Revs.—
Alarcon, Felix, 207 Oxford House, 21267 Gertrude Ave., Port Charlotte, FL 33952.
Allen, Peter, Diocese of Rockville Center, P.O. Box 9023, 11571.
Benack, Henry I., St. Patrick, 235 Glen St., Glen Cove, 11542-3091.
Blake, Andrew P., St. Andrew, 122 Division St., Sag Harbor, 11963-3154.
Bogert, James, 721 S.W. Lake Court #104, Boynton Beach, FL 33426.
Buckley, Harold P., St. Rose of Lima, Two Bayview Ave., Massapequa, 11758-7299.
Callahan, Zachary, Church of Cure of Ars, 2323 Merrick Ave., Merrick, 11566.
Carmody, James P., 26 Panorama Dr., Binghamton, 13901.
Collins, Edwin J., 24065 Martin Dr., Brooksville, FL 34601.
Connolly, Andrew P., St. Francis de Sales, 7 Amity St., P.O. Box 71, Patchogue, 11772.
Corali, Serafino A., St. Pius X Residence, 1220 Front St., Uniondale, 11553-2097.
Corcoran, John J., St. John the Evangelist, 25 Ocean Ave., Center Moriches, 11934.
D'Souza, Claude J., Church of St. Luke, 2892 S. Congress Ave., Palm Springs, FL 33461.
Dahm, Paul J., 176 Montauk Hwy., Southampton, 11968.
De Vita, James C., 4760-A Greentree Way, Boynton Beach, FL 33436.
Delaney, William I., Maria Regina Residence, 1725 Brentwood Rd., Brentwood, 11717.
Diederich, Donald F., J.C.D., Founders Village Apt. 18 B, 2555 Youngs Ave., Southold, 11971.
Dineros, Santiago A., Church of St. Pius X, One St. Pius X Ct., Plainview, 11803.
Donohue, Thomas E., Church of St. Mary of the Isle, 315 E. Walnut St., Long Beach, 11561.
Donovan, Richard R., Our Lady of Lourdes, 65 Wright Ave., Malverne, 11565.
Drab, John P., St. Pius X Residence, 565 Albany Ave., Amityville, 11701.
Driscoll, Paul G., 16 Croyden Rd., Mineola, 11501.
Fernando, Simon, Suwinda Dummalademoya, Wennappuwa, Sri Lanka.
Filmanski, Francis E., Cypress Club Condominiums, 145 Cypress Club Dr., Apt. 509, Pompano Beach, FL 33060.
Fitzgerald, John J., Church of St. James, 429 Route 25A, East Setauket, 11733.
Gallagher, William G., 9949 Shore Rd., Brooklyn, 11209.
Gartner, Charles A., Our Lady of Mercy, 500 S. Oyster Bay Rd., Hicksville, 11801-3570.
Hagan, Vincent J., Bloomsfield Station, P.O. Box 18 PE Canada.
Hall, Martin J., M.A., St. Bernard, 3100 Hempstead Tpke., Levittown, 11756-1339.
Hannon, James J., St. Pius X Residence, 565 Albany Ave., Amityville, 11701.
Heenan, Michael F., 2021 Bonisle Cir., Palm Beach Gardens, FL 33418.
Hein, John (Vietnam), Church of St. Joseph, 1346 Broadway, Hewlett, 11557.
Kayser, Robert J., Manor Park, 215 Carll's Path, Apt. 4C, Deer Park, 11729.
Kealey, Edward J.
Kohli, Charles F., St. Joseph Guest House, 350 Cuba Hill Rd., Huntington, 11743.
Kottaram, Mathew, Kottarathil House, Grace Hill, Upper Coonoor, Tamilnadu 643102 India.
Kozlowski, Joseph P., St. Hyacinth, 319 Cedar Swamp Rd., Glen Head, 11545-2296.
Liu, Peter T., 2886 Fernley Dr. E. #75, West Palm Beach, FL 33417.
Maloney, Thomas P., Church of St. Joseph, 39 N. Carll Ave., Babylon, 11702.
Mason, Robert E., Church of Our Lady of Lourdes, 855 Carmans Rd., Massapequa Park, 11762.

McCabe, John H., St. Pius X Residence, 1220 Front St., Uniondale, 11553.
McCarthy, Thomas, 215 W. Santa Barbara Rd., Lindenhurst, 11757.
McCarthy, William E., M.M., St. Teresa's Residence, P.O. Box 321, Maryknoll, 10545.
McComiskey, Joseph C., 137 Brookside Dr., Smithtown, 11787.
McGann, Diarmuid F., Church of Our Lady of the Snow, 175 Blue Point Ave., Blue Point, 11715.
McGratty, John J.
McMullen, Francis R., 14415 Capt. John Smith Dr., Accokeek, MD 20607.
Minturn, Joseph, 107 Colonial Pkwy., Manhasset, 11030.
Mitchell, George J., St. Patrick, P.O. Box 1117, Southold, 11971.
Murray, John P., 51 Fox Blvd., Massapequa, 11758.
Newman, Louis I., St. Columba's Rectory, 3327 Glencolum Dr., San Diego, CA 92123.
Nieva, Constantino S., St. Pius X Residence, 1220 Front St., Uniondale, 11553.
Niewczas, Taddeus, 84 Berry St. Apt. 1L, Brooklyn, 11211.
Nuss, Francis B., Church of St. Matthew, 35 N. Service Rd., Dix Hills, 11746.
O'Leary, Lawrence J., Maria Regina Residence, 1725 Brentwood Rd., Brentwood, 11717.
Palliparambil, Jose Simon, St. Pius X Residence, 565 Albany Ave., Amityville, 11701.
Pascual, Antonio S., J.C.L., Church of St. Francis de Chantal, 1309 Wantaugh Ave., Wantagh, 11793.
Pedzik, Vitalis B., 7-8 State St., New York, 10004.
Punti, George, St. Boniface, 631 Elmont Road, Elmont, 11003-4028.
Reid, R. Michael, Church of the Holy Family, Five Fordham Ave., Hicksville, 11801.
Sheehan, Augustine J., 85 Richmond Blvd. 1A, Ronkonkoma, 11779.
Sheridan, Denis J., St. Pius X Residence, 1220 Front St., Uniondale, 11553-2097.
Siebor, John, Church of St. Ladislaus, 18 Richardson Pl., Hempstead, 11550.
Swiatocha, Bruno, 34 Country Club Dr., Shallotte, NC 28470.
Weerasinghe, Felix M. (Sri Lanka), 52 Alles Rd., Negombo, Sri Lanka.
Whelan, Dennis J.
Whelan, John F., 413 Marcellus Rd., Mineola, 11501.
Wilutis, John P., St. Pius X Residence, 1220 Front St., Uniondale, 11553-2097.

Rt. Rev. Msgrs.—
Guarino, Charles A., P.A., M.A., M.Div., J.C.D.
Kelly, James P., St. Agnes Cathedral, 29 Quealy Pl., 11570.

Permanent Deacons:
Acquaro, Peter, St. Frances Cabrini, Coram
Altonji, James F., St. Joseph, Ronkonkoma
Anderson, Thomas, St. Frances de Chantal, Wantagh
Anetrella, Louis, Christ the King, Commack
Anisansel, Geoffrey, St. Joseph, Babylon
Aprile, Michael, St. Martin of Tours, Amityville
Ashe, James C., Our Lady of Poland, Southampton
Austin, William, Our Lady of Grace, West Babylon
Baker, Scott, Holy Name of Mary, Valley Stream
Banno, Anthony, St. Christopher, Baldwin
Barone, Frank D., St. Kilian, Farmingdale
Bartolotto, Joseph T., St. Louis De Montfort, Sound Beach
Becker, Richard, St. Philip Neri, Northport
Beckles, Vincent, St. Gerard Majella, Port Jefferson Station
Bedell, Paul, Campus Ministry, Adelphi University
Behar, Stephen, Mary Immaculate, Bellport
Beirne, James G., St. James, Seaford
Bellevue, Hernst, St. Martha, Uniondale
Benincasa, Joseph, St. Catherine of Sienna, Franklin Square
Bice, Frank, St. Mary, Manhasset
Biggin, James A., St. Martin of Tours, Bethpage
Bilella, Richard, Our Lady Queen of Martyrs, Centerport
Billia, Edward W., St. Hugh of Lincoln, Huntington Station
Blakeney, John, St. Bernard, Levittown
Blasius, Ronald, Ss. Philip & James, St. James
Bliss, Basil, St. Anne, Garden City
Bohuslaw, James, St. John Nepomucene, Bohemia
Bono, Frank J., St. Joachim, Cedarhurst
Bonocore, Dale, St. Patrick, Huntington
Bonocore, Michael A., St. Isadore, Riverhead
Borchardt, Frank, St. Patrick, Glen Cove
Braun, Robert G., St. Anthony of Padua, East Northport
Browne, George J., St. Anne, Garden City
Bruck, George P., Our Lady of Good Counsel, Inwood
Brunner, Richard, St. James, Seaford
Buchenberger, Thomas E., St. William the Abbot, Seaford
Burkart, John F., St. Philip Neri, Northport
Burnham, Bruce A., Our Holy Redeemer, Freeport
Byrne, James, St. Francis of Assisi, Greenlawn
Byrne, Joseph, Immaculate Conception, Westhampton Beach
Cales, Francisco, Our Holy Redeemer, Freeport
Califano, Joseph, St. Joseph, Ronkonkoma
Cameron, Lachlan, Holy Spirit, New Hyde Park
Campbell, David, St. Francis of Assisi, Greenlawn
Campbell, Robert, St. Raymond, East Rockaway
Candido, Arthur, Our Lady of Fatima, Manorhaven
Cantave, Jean, St. Francis of Assisi, Greenlawn
Capobianco, Eugene, St. Martin of Tours, Bethpage
Carroll, James P., St. Christopher, Baldwin
Case, Edward M., St. Mary, Roslyn
Casey, William, St. Patrick, Huntington
Cedrone, Anthony M., Our Lady of Peace, Lynbrook
Cepeda, Jose A., Our Lady of Assumption, Copiague
Chamberlain, Anthony J., St. Anthony, Rocky Point
Choi, Stephen Gil Soo, St. Aloysius, Great Neck
Clifford, Kenneth, Infant Jesus, Port Jefferson
Coleman, Thomas, St. Barnabas the Apostle, Bellmore
Colpa, Andres, St. Anne, Brentwood
Connelly, Joseph F., St. Aidan, Williston Park
Connolly, Thomas, St. Raymond, East Rockaway
Cosentino, Louis, St. Patrick, Huntington
Costa, Victor R., St. Raphael, East Meadow
Costello, Thomas P., St. Joseph, Hewlett
Cotone, Louis, St. Kilian, Farmingdale
Coughlin, John F., Blessed Sacrament, Valley Stream
Cove, Francis K., Our Lady of Lourdes, Malverne
Croce, Barry, St. Joseph, Babylon
Crosby, William, O.L.P.H., Lindenhurst
Cunningham, Edward F., St. Thomas the Apostle, West Hempstead
Cusumano, Anthony P., St. John Nepomucene, Bohemia
D'Alessio, Raymond P., St. Edward Confessor, Syosset
D'Angelo, Frank G., St. Peter of Alcantara, Port Washington
D'Auria, Anthony S., St. Thomas the Apostle, West Hempstead
D'Averse, Angelo D., St. Raphael, East Meadow
Daza, H. Nelson, St. Mary of the Isle, Long Beach
DeBellis, Michael J., St. Joseph, Ronkonkoma
DeGuardi, John P., Our Lady of Lourdes, West Islip
Dejewski, Robert, Ss. Peter & Paul, Manorville
Dell'Aglio, Frank, St. Joseph, Ronkonkoma
DeStefano, Carmine E., St. Matthew, Dix Hills
Devenney, Michael L., St. Joseph, Ronkonkoma
Diaz, Juan, Resurrection, Farmingville
Diaz-Granados, Francisco, St. Francis de Sales, Patchogue
DiGiovanna, James R., Resurrection, Farmingville
DiGiuseppe, Peter A., O.L. Grace, West Babylon
Dobbins, William, St. Joseph, Ronkonkoma
Donza, Gaetano, St. Raymond, East Rockaway
Dougherty, Joseph M., St. Joseph, Ronkonkoma
Dunphy, Patrick J., Our Lady of Hope, Carle Place
Ervin, Christopher, St. Rosalie, Hampton Bays
Evrard, Thomas J., Our Lady of Peace, Lynbrook
Failla, John, St. Elizabeth, Melville
Farley, Owen, Holy Cross, Nesconset
Faulkenberry, Lawrence, Church of the Most Holy Trinity, East Hampton
Ferreiro, Douglas, Holy Spirit, New Hyde Park
Ferri, Richard, St. Martin of Tours, Amityville
Finter, Frederick E., St. John the Baptist, Wading River
Fitzpatrick, John F., Ss. Cyril and Methodius, Deer Park
Flannery, James W., St. Anthony, Oceanside
Flood, Frank J., St. Rose of Lima, Massapequa
Forbes, Thomas J., St. Rose of Lima, Massapequa
Ford, John E., St. Thomas the Apostle, West Hempstead
Fox, Thomas, St. Boniface Martyr, Sea Cliff
Gagnon, Jules O. A., Our Lady of the Miraculaous Medal, Wyandanch
Gargiulo, Andrew T., Maria Regina, Seaford
Gariboldi, Frank, St. John of God, Central Islip
Geoghan, Kenneth, St. Jude, Mastic Beach
Gerace, Patrick C., St. Mark, Shoreham
Gillen, Thomas J., St. Jude's, Mastic Beach
Gillette, Ronald J., St. John of God, Central Islip
Giraldo, Luis D., St. Hugh of Lincoln, Huntington Station
Goldburg, Charles R., St. Joachim, Cederhurst
Gonzalez, Francisco, St. Catherine of Sienna, Franklin Square
Graff, Charles, Our Lady of Grace, West Babylon
Graviano, Anthony, Our Lady of Mount Carmel, Patchogue
Grebe, John, St. Elizabeth Ann Seton, Lake Ronkonkoma
Gronenthal, Robert W., Our Lady of Snow, Blue Point
Guilfu, Juan, St. Patrick, Glen Cove
Hanly, James, St. Matthew, Dix Hills
Hartmann, Frank C., Our Lady of the Snow, Blue Point
Hayes, Edward, St. Margaret of Scotland, Selden
Hennessy, Thomas R., St. Martin of Tours, Bethpage
Hernandez, Robert, Good Shepherd, Holbrook
Herrmann, Mark, St. Jude, Mastic Beach
Heschl, Robert J., Sts. Philip & James, St. James
Hickey, John, Our Lady of Hope, Carle Place
Huber, Charles F., SS. Cyril & Methodius, Deer Park
Iandoli, Richard, St. Barnabas the Apostle, Bellmore
Jackson, Thomas H., Queen of the Most Holy Rosary, Roosevelt
Janiec, Richard, St. Patrick, Smithtown
Kammerer, Charles, St. Mary, Manhasset
Keach, Frank, St. Patrick, Bay Shore
Keenan, John, Sts. Philip & James, St. James
Kogler, William E., St. Margaret of Scotland, Selden
Kolakowski, Theodore, St. Gertrude, Bayville
Kruse, Robert A., Infant Jesus, Port Jefferson
LaBella, Patrick, St. Lawrence the Martyr, Sayville
LaRossa, Richard W., St. Raymond, East Rockaway
Lewis, Clinton, Queen of the Most Holy Rosary, Roosevelt
Leyden, Michael J., St. Joseph, Babylon
Logan, George, Most Holy Trinity, East Hampton
Logsdon, Patrick B., Anthony House, Roosevelt
Longo, Allan D., St. Francis of Assisi, Greenlawn
Love, Francis J., St. Aidan, Williston Park
Lucie, Thomas, Our Lady of Lourdes, West Islip
Luken, Richard A., St. Luke, Brentwood
Lynch, John, St. William the Abbot, Seaford
Lyon, Robert, Mary Immaculate, Bellport
Maffeo, Joseph R., St. Elizabeth Ann Seton, Lake Ronkonkoma
Maggipinto, V. Anthony, SS. Philip and James, St. James
Maher, Kenneth, SS. Philip & James, St. James
Mais, George A., Jr., St. Ignatius Loyola, Hicksville
Malone, Thomas, St. Raymond's, East Rockaway
Mannix, Brian, Corpus Christi, Mineola
Marfoglio, Joseph, Christ the King, Commack
Marino, Francis, St. Kilian, Farmingdale
Mathurin, Trevor S., St. Martha, Uniondale
McCormack, Kevin, Our Lady of Peace, Lynbrook
McDaid, Thomas P., St. Agnes, Rockville Centre
McGauvran, John W., Queen of the Most Holy Rosary, Bridgehampton
McGonigle, John H., Holy Family, Hicksville
McGowan, John, St. Vincent de Paul, Elmont
McGuinness, Francis B., St. Rose of Lima, Massapequa
McIndoe, Martin B., St. Francis de Sales, Patchogue
McKenna, John J., St. Joseph, Garden City
McKenna, Michael A., St. Boniface, Elmont
McLaughlin, James, St. Anthony of Padua, Rocky Point
McNicholas, Joseph G., Holy Family, Hicksville
McQuade, James J., St. Matthew, Dix Hills
Meehan, John J., Our Lady of Lourdes, West Islip
Mercolino, Joseph T., St. Elizabeth, Melville
Metzdorff, Michael C., St. Brigid, Westbury
Mildeberger, William, St. Boniface, Elmont
Miller, Brian, Our Lady of Grace, West Babylon
Mills, Philip, Jr., Our Lady of the Assumption, Copiague
Monahan, Michael, St. Anthony, Oceanside
Mongillo, Robert, St. Rosalie, Hampton Bays
Montelione, Michael, Assumption of BVM, Centereach
Mora, Alfredo, St. Patrick, Glen Cove
Moran, John, Sacred Hearts of Jesus and Mary, Southampton
Morris, James, St. Brigid, Westbury
Mott, Roger P., St. John Nepomucene, Bohemia
Mullane, Robert, St. Louis de Montfort, Sound Beach
Mulligan, Lawrence P., Our Lady of Victory, Floral Park
Murano, James A., Ss. Cyril & Methodius, Deer Park
Muratore, Biagio V., St. Margaret of Scotland, Selden
Murphy, Galvin C., St. John the Evangelist, Center Moriches
Murphy, James, St. Edward the Confessor, Syosset
Muscarnera, Charles, St. Christopher, Baldwin
Mystkowski, Joseph J., Our Lady of Mt. Carmel, Patchogue
Naylor, Montford D., St. Frances Cabrini, Coram
Nealis, George F., St. Joseph, Babylon
Neuhedel, Paul, Maria Regina, Seaford
Newhall, John, Good Shepherd, Holbrook

Newton, Philip, St. Ignatius Martyr, Long Beach
Nuzzi, John, Maria Regina, Seaford
O'Brien, James J., St. Anne, Garden City
O'Connor, Dennis R., St. Rose of Lima, Massapequa
O'Connor, John, St. Anthony, Oceanside
O'Connor, Thomas F., Good Shepherd, Holbrook
O'Donovan, Robert S., St. Frances de Chantal, Wantagh
O'Hara, James, Holy Name of Mary, Valley Stream
O'Neill, James, St. Anthony, Oceanside
Odin, Frank A., Our Lady of Perpetual Help, Lindenhurst
Otton, Daniel, St. Joseph, Hewlett
Owen, George, St. Kilian, Farmingdale
Owens, Thomas F., St. James, Setauket
Padula, Wayne, St. James, Setauket
Pagnotta, Carmen, St. Frances Cabrini, Coram
Paolicelli, Philip, St. Margaret of Scotland, Selden
Pellegrino, Joseph C., St. Christopher, Baldwin
Peralta, Joseph F., St. Patrick, Bay Shore
Perez, Juan, Our Lady of Loretto, Hempstead
Pesce, Frank V., St. Brigid, Westbury
Pettorino, John C., St. John the Evangelist, Center Moriches
Philppeaux, Jacques, St. Thomas the Apostle, West Hempstead
Pickford, Albert, St. Joseph the Worker, East Patchogue
Polanco, Luis Roberto, St. Matthew, Dix Hills
Portuese, Richard, Our Lady of Lourdes, Malverne
Powers, William J., Infant Jesus, Port Jefferson
Pozzolano, Vincent, St. John the Baptist, Wading River
Quinn, Thomas J., St. Rose of Lima, Massapequa
Raad, Richard, Holy Name of Mary, Valley Stream
Ramos, Manuel J., St. Brigid, Westbury
Rasanen, Terence A., St. Anne, Brentwood
Raspacki, John, St. Thomas More, Hauppauge
Reda, Gerard, Ss. Philip & James, St. James
Reich, George F., St. John Nepomucene, Bohemia
Reilly, Thomas, St. Edward the Confessor, Syosset
Reilly, Thomas J., St. Hugh of Lincoln, Huntington Station
Rich, Thomas B., J.C.L., D.Min., Our Lady of Hope, Carle Place
Rieger, John, Our Lady Queen of Martyrs, Centerport
Riegger, George J., St. Sylvester, Medford
Rivera, Franklin, St. Sylvester, Medford
Rivera, Wenceslao, St. Luke, Brentwood
Roa, Jose, Our Lady of Loretto, Hempstead
Romero, Miguel A., St. Anne, Brentwood
Ruggieri, Clyde, Holy Name of Mary, Valley Stream
Saffran, Irwin, Our Lady of Grace, West Babylon
Saint Louis, Evenou, St. Martha, Uniondale
Samson, Thomas R., St. Anne, Brentwood
Sanchez, Cristobal, Our Holy Redeemer, Freeport
Sandberg, Louis C., Queen of the Most Holy Rosary Church, Roosevelt
Sanfilippo, Carl, St. Andrew, Sag Harbor
Schultz, Peter F., St. John the Evangelist, Riverhead
Scollan, Joseph M., St. Margaret of Scotland, Selden
Sheehan, John W., St. Martin of Tours, Amityville
Sherlock, Bernard F., St. Barnabas Apostle, Bellmore
Silien, Dominique, St. Boniface, Elmont
Simeone, Joseph, St. Jude, Mastic Beach
Sisinni, Christopher, Our Lady Queen of Martyrs, Centerport
Smith, Douglas, Our Lady of Perpetual Help, Lindenhurst
Squiteri, Aniello, Our Lady of Peace, Lynbrook
Stamm, Donald, St. Agnes Cathedral, Rockville Centre
Steffens, Gerard K., Holy Cross, Nesconset
Sullivan, John F., St. Joseph, Babylon
Sullivan, Kenneth R., St. Martha, Uniondale
Swane, Gary, St. Louis de Montfort, Sound Beach
Sykes, Jeffrey, Church of the Sacred Heart, Cutchogue
Tappin, Edward, Church of the Good Shepherd, Holbrook
Taranto, Vito, St. Hugh, Huntington Station
Teufel, John G., Our Lady of Lourdes, West Islip
Tirelli, Raymond J., Our Lady of Hope, Carle Place
Torres, Joseph, St. Frances de Chantal, Wantagh
Trodden, John E., St. Joseph, Kings Park
Valdaro, Domenick, Our Lady Lourdes, Massapequa Park
Valdes, Jesus, St. Dominic, Oyster Bay
Vigliotta, Crescenzo T., Suffolk County Correctional Facility, Bay Shore
Vigneaux, Edward, St. Thomas More, Hauppauge
Villani, Salvatore B., St. Aidan, Williston Park
Walaski, Daniel, St. John the Evangelist, Riverhead
Waldmann, Richard E., Infant Jesus, Port Jefferson
Walters, John, St. Anne, Brentwood
Weisz, Robert D., St. Thomas More, Hauppauge
Wetzel, Mark, St. Kilian, Farmingdale
Whitfield, Gerald F., Maria Regina, Seaford
Zirkel, Don, Our Lady of the Miraculous Medal, Wyandanch
Zubrovich, Joseph, Cure of Ars, Merrick

INSTITUTIONS LOCATED IN THE DIOCESE

[A] SEMINARIES, DIOCESAN

HUNTINGTON. *Diocesan Seminary of the Immaculate Conception*, 440 West Neck Rd., 11743. Tel: 631-423-0483; Fax: 631-423-2346. Email: info@icseminary.edu. Most Rev. William Francis Murphy, S.T.D., L.H.D., Chm., Bd. of Governors; Rev. Msgrs. Peter I. Vaccari, S.T.L., Rector & Assoc. Prof. Church History; Robert J. Batule, S.T.L., Assoc. Prof. Systematic Theology; Joseph DeGrocco, D.Min., Dir. Liturgical Formation & Prof. Liturgy; Charles R. Fink, M.Div., Dir. Spiritual Formation; Richard G. Henning, M.A., M.Div., S.T.D., Vice Rector & Prof. of Scripture; Revs. Nicholas A. Zientarski, S.T.L., Dir. Pastoral Formation & Dean of Seminarians; Charles Caccavale, S.T.L., S.T.D., Prof. of Moral Theology; Sr. Mary Louise Brink, S.C., Ph.D., Academic Dean; Elyse B. Hayes, M.L.S., Dir. Library & Information Technologies; Dennis J. Schlosser, B.B.A., Dir. Finance & Operations; Katherine M. Hayes, Ph.D., Prof. of Scripture; Michael Hoonhout, Ph.D., Assoc. Prof. of Systematic Theology. Priests 7; Sisters 1; Lay Professors 2; Support Lay Staff 16; Seminarians 46; M.A. Students 84.

[B] COLLEGES AND UNIVERSITIES

ROCKVILLE CENTRE. *Molloy College* (1955) 1000 Hempstead Ave., P.O. Box 5002, 11571-5002. Tel: 516-678-5000; 888-466-5569; Fax: 516-678-7295. Web: www.molloy.edu. Drew Bogner, Ph.D., Pres.; Linda Albanese, Vice Pres. for Enrollment Management; Valerie Collins, Ph.D., Vice Pres. Academic Affairs & Dean Faculty; Sr. Dorothy Anne Fitzgibbons, O.P., Ed.D., Vice Pres. for Mission; Robert Houlihan, Vice Pres. Student Affairs; Michael McGovern, Vice Pres. Finance & Treas.; Edward J. Thompson, Vice Pres. for Advancement; Robert Paterson, Ph.D., Vice Pres. Information Technology, Planning & Research; Rev. Gabriel Muteru (Kenya) (NY), Chap.; Judith Brink-Drescher, Interim Library Dir. Priests 4; Chaplains 1; Sisters of St. Dominic (Amityville Community) 22; Lay Teachers 612; Students 4,337.

[C] HIGH SCHOOLS, DIOCESAN
NASSAU COUNTY

HICKSVILLE

Holy Trinity Diocesan High School (1966) 98 Cherry Ln., 11801. Tel: 516-433-2900; Fax: 516-433-2827. Email: hths98@holytrinityhs.echalk.com. Web: www.holytrinityhs.org. Mr. Gene Fennell, Prin. Tel: 516-433-2900, Ext. 140; Rev. Joseph Fitzgerald, M.Div., Chap. Sisters 3; Lay Teachers 94; Students 1,395.

SUFFOLK COUNTY

RIVERHEAD

McGann Mercy High School, 1225 Ostrander Ave., 11901. Tel: 631-727-5900; Fax: 631-727-8483; 631-369-7328. Web: www.mcgann-mercy.org. Carl Semmler, Prin.; Mrs. Lisa Navarra, Asst. Prin.; Mr. Charles Bender, Dean of Students. Directed by the Diocese of Rockville Centre/Sisters of Mercy., (Coed) Sisters of Mercy (Mid-Atlantic) 2; Lay Teachers 45; Students 507.

WEST ISLIP

St. John the Baptist, 1170 Montauk Hwy., 11795. Tel: 631-587-8000; Fax: 631-587-8996. Web: www.stjohnsdhs.org. Walter D. Lace, Prin.; Rev. Michael Holzmann, Chap. Priests 1; Sisters 3; Lay Teachers 110; Students 1,700.

[D] HIGH SCHOOLS, PRIVATE

HEMPSTEAD. *Sacred Heart Academy* College preparatory-girls, 47 Cathedral Ave., 11550. Tel: 516-483-7383; Fax: 516-483-1016. Email: sha@sacredheartacademyhempstead.org. Web: www.sacredheartacademyhempstead.org. Sisters Jeanne Marie Ross, C.S.J., Pres.; Joanne Forker, C.S.J., Prin.; Regina Foge, Librarian. Sisters 6; Lay Teachers 85; Students 910.

MINEOLA. *Chaminade High School (Boys)* (1930) Directed by the Society of Mary (Marianists), 340 Jackson Ave., 11501. Tel: 516-742-5555; Fax: 516-742-1989. Email: flyers@chaminade-hs.org. Web: www.chaminade-hs.org. Bros. Thomas J. Cleary, S.M., Pres.; Joseph D. Bellizzi, S.M., Prin.; Mr. Salvatore Trentacoste, Asst. Prin.; Mr. Daniel Petruccio, Dir. of Guidance; John Callinan, Dean of Students; Mr. Michael Ingrassia, Dir. Student Svcs.; Rev. Garrett J. Long, S.M., Chap.; Bro. Peter H. Heiskell, S.M., Dir. of Apostolic Action. Priests 3; Brothers 18; Lay Teachers 55; Students 1,700.

SOUTH HUNTINGTON. *St. Anthony's High School* (1933) College Prep., 275 Wolf Hill Rd., 11747-1394. Tel: 631-271-2020; Fax: 631-547-6820. Email: administration@stanthonyshs.org. Web: www.stanthonyshs.org. Bro. Gary Cregan, O.S.F., Prin. Directed by the Franciscan Brothers of Brooklyn. Priests 1; Brothers 18; Permanent Deacons 1; Intercommunity Sisters 7; Lay Teachers 108; Students 2,400.

SYOSSET. *Our Lady of Mercy Academy* Girls-day students., 815 Convent Rd., 11791-3895. Tel: 516-921-1047; Fax: 516-921-3634. Web: www.olma.org. Sr. Helen Lyons, R.S.M., Co-Prin.; Mrs. Joan Gordon, Co-Prin.; Mrs. Sheila Wilson, Librarian. Directed by the Sisters of Mercy/Mid-Atlantic Community. Sisters of Mercy 3; Sisters of St. Joseph 1; Sisters of St. Dominic 1; Sisters of St. Ursula 1; Lay Teachers 49; Students 540.

UNIONDALE. *Kellenberg Memorial High School* (1987) 1400 Glenn Curtiss Blvd., 11553. Tel: 516-292-0200; Fax: 516-292-0877. Email: brokenneth@kellenberg.org. Web: www.kellenberg.org. Rev. Philip K. Eichner, S.M., Pres.; Bro. Kenneth M. Hoagland, S.M., Prin.; Rev. Albert Bertoni, S.M., Asst. Prin. Guidance; Miss Maria Korzekwinski, Asst. Prin. Latin School; Bro. Roger Poletti, S.M., Asst. Prin. Activities; Rev. Thomas A. Cardone, S.M., Chap.; Mrs. Marina Trentacoste, Dean of Students; Mr. John McCutcheon, Dean of Men; Mr. Bryan Finn, Dir. Apostolic Activities; Mr. John Fechtmann, Athletic Dir.; Mr. John Krumm, Supvr. of Building Maintenance & Landscaping; Bro. Donald Nussbaum, S.M., Suprv. New Construction, Vehicles; Mr. Jim Payne, Supvr. Cleaning Maintenance; Mrs. Catherine Zabrouski, Financial Supvr.; Bro. David Bruner, S.M., Librarian. Directed by the Society of Mary. Priests 4; Brothers 12; Lay Teachers 114; Students 2,553.

[E] REGIONAL SCHOOLS

BELLMORE. *St. Elizabeth Ann Seton Regional School* Tel: 516-785-5709; Fax: 516-785-4468. Email: lag@seas.edrvc.org. Supported by the following parishes: St. Barnabas, Bellmore; St. Raphael, East Meadow; Cure of Ars, Merrick; St. Frances de Chantal, Wantagh. Lay Teachers 29; Students 341.

Bellmore Campus, 2341 Washington Ave., 11710. Tel: 516-785-5709; Fax: 516-785-4468. Leeann Graziose, Prin. Sisters 1; Lay Teachers 31; Students 450.

Wantagh Campus, 1309 Wantagh Ave., Wantagh, 11793. Tel: 516-826-3882; Fax: 516-679-2082. N-K Early Childhood Center Lay Teachers 4; Students 145.

CENTER MORICHES. *Our Lady, Queen of Apostles Regional School*, 2 St. Johns Pl., 11934. Tel: 631-878-1033; Fax: 631-878-1059. Email: sreileen@olqa.edruc.org. Sr. Eileen Martin, S.C., Prin. Supported by the following parishes: St. John Evangelist, Center Moriches; St. Jude, Mastic Beach; Immaculate Conception, Westhampton Beach; Ss. Peter & Paul, Manorville. Sisters 2; Lay Teachers 19; Students 294.

CENTRAL ISLIP. *Our Lady of Providence Regional School* (1992) 82 Carleton Ave., 11722. Tel: 631-234-6324; Fax: 631-234-6360. Email: lfitzpatrick@olprov.org. Web: www.olprov.org. Jo Ann DiNardo, Prin.; Lorena Fitzpatrick, School Sec. Supported by the following parishes: St. Anne, Brentwood; St. Luke, Brentwood; St. John of God, Central Islip; St. Peter the Apostle, Islip Terrace. Sisters 1; Lay Teachers 21; Students 280.

COMMACK. *Holy Family Regional School*, Indian Head Rd., P.O. Box 729, 11725. Tel: 631-543-0202; Fax: 631-543-2818. Email: hfrs@aol.com. Mrs. Constance Jenkins, Prin.; Sr. Dorothy Sconzo, Librarian. Supported by the following parishes: Christ the King, Commack; St. Matthew, Dix Hills; St. Thomas More, Hauppauge; St. Joseph, Kings Park. Sisters 4; Lay Teachers 17; Students 340.

CUTCHOGUE. *Our Lady of Mercy Regional School*, 27685 Main Rd., P.O. Box 970, 11935. Tel: 631-734-5166; Fax: 631-734-4266. Email: olm@olmregional.org; ldelgenio@olmregional.org. Web: www.olmregional.org. Mrs. Lorraine Del Genio, Prin. Supported by the following parishes: Sacred Heart, Cutchogue; Our Lady of Ostrabrama, Cutchogue; St. Agnes, Greenport; and St. Patrick, Southold. Lay Teachers 11; Students 116.

EAST NORTHPORT. *Trinity Regional School*, 1025 Fifth Ave., 11731. Tel: 631-261-5130; Fax: 631-266-5345. Email: tregion@optonline.net. Web: trinityregional.com; trinityregional.org. Miss Jeanne Morcone, Prin.; Mrs. Patricia Ayers, Asst. Prin.; Miss Meghan Finnegan, Librarian. Supported by the following parishes: Our Lady Queen of Martyrs, Centerport; St. Anthony of Padua, East Northport; St. Francis of Assisi, Greenlawn; St. Hugh of Lincoln, Huntington Station; St. Elizabeth, Melville; St. Philip Neri, Northport. Sisters 1; Lay Teachers 32; Students 600.

Satellite campuses exist at:

175 Wolf Hill Rd., Melville, 11747-1340. Tel: 631-549-7450; Fax: 631-549-7464. Email: tregion@optonline.net. Web: trinityregional.com; trinityregional.org. Miss Jeanne Morcone, Prin.

364 Main St., Northport, 11768. Tel: 631-261-8520; Fax: 631-261-8560. Email: tregion@optonline.net. Web: trinityregional.com; trinityregional.org.

FARMINGDALE. *St. John Baptist de LaSalle Regional School*, (Grades N-8) Tel: 516-694-3610; Fax: 516-694-7296. Email: dscotto@lasalleregionalschool.org. Ms. Christine Bendish, Prin.; Michael Ruckdaschel, Librarian. Supported by the following parishes: St. Martin of Tours, Bethpage; St. Kilian, Farmingdale; St. Pius X, Plainview; St. James, Seaford. Lay Teachers 16; Students 222.

GLEN COVE. *All Saints Regional Catholic School*, (Grades N-8), 12 Pearsall Ave., 11542-3052. Tel: 516-676-0762; Fax: 516-676-0660. Web: www.asrcatholic.com. James W. Thompson, Prin.; Marie Diffley, Librarian. Supported by the following parishes: St. Boniface, Sea Cliff; St. Hyacinth, Glen Head; St. Mary, Roslyn; St. Patrick, Glen Cove; St. Rocco, Glen Cove. Lay Teachers 20; Students 297.

LONG BEACH. *Long Beach Catholic Regional School*, (Grades PreK-8), 735 W. Broadway, 11561. Tel: 516-432-8900; Fax: 516-432-3841. Email: lbcatholic@aol.com. Web: lbcrs.org. Mrs. Veronica Danca, Prin. Supported by the following parishes: St. Ignatius, Long Beach; St. Mary of the Isle, Long Beach, and Our Lady of the Miraculous Medal, Point Lookout. Sisters 2; Lay Teachers 25; Students 500.

PATCHOGUE. *Holy Angels Regional School* (1923) (Grades PreK-8), 1 Division St., 11772. Tel: 631-475-0422; Fax: 631-475-2036. Email: mmartinez@holyangelsregional.org. Web: www.holyangelsregional.org. Maria Martinez, Prin.; Sara Noce, Librarian. Supported by the following parishes: Mary Immaculate, Bellport; St. Frances Cabrini, Coram; St. Joseph the Worker, E. Patchogue; St. Sylvester, Medford; Our Lady of Mount Carmel, Patchogue; St. Frances de Sales, Patchogue, and St. Margaret of Scotland, Selden. Lay Teachers 25; Students 336.

PORT JEFFERSON. *Our Lady of Wisdom Regional School*, 114-116 Myrtle Ave., 11777. Tel: 631-473-1211; Fax: 631-473-1064. Email: ninaed@optonline.net. Web: www.ourladyofwisdom.com. Dorothy Onysko, Prin. Supported by the following parishes: Infant Jesus, Port Jefferson; St. Louis de Montfort, Sound Beach; St. James, Setauket; St. Gerard Majella, Port Jefferson Station. Lay Teachers 14; Students 225; Total Staff 25.

SAYVILLE. *Prince of Peace Regional Catholic School* (1992) (Grades N-8), 200 Main St., 11782. Tel: 631-589-3426; Fax: 631-589-4523. Web: www.poprcs.org. Jane F. Harrigan, Prin.; Mrs. Barbara Pellerito, Librarian. Supported by the following parishes: Our Lady of Snow, Blue Point; St. John Nepomucene, Bohemia; Good Shepherd, Holbrook; St. Lawrence, Sayville. Lay Teachers 20; Students 200.

SOUTHAMPTON. *Our Lady of the Hamptons Regional School*, (Grades PreK-8), 160 N. Main St., 11968. Tel: 631-283-9140; Fax: 631-287-3958. Email: sks@hamptons.com. Web: www.olh.org. Nursery and PreK.; Supported by the following parishes: St. Rosalie, Hampton Bays; Our Lady of Poland, Southampton, and Sacred Hearts Jesus Mary, Southampton.

31 Montauk Hwy., Hampton Bays, 11946. Tel: 631-723-3740; Fax: 631-728-2559. Sisters Kathryn Schlueter, C.S.J., Prin.; Virginia Crowley, C.S.J., Asst. Prin.; Linda Robins, Librarian. Sisters 2; Lay Teachers 26; Students 375.

[F] ELEMENTARY SCHOOLS, PRIVATE

FREEPORT. *The De La Salle School* (2001) 87 Pine St., 11520-3615. Tel: 516-379-8660; Fax: 516-379-8806. Email: DeLaSalleLI@hotmail.com. Web: www.delasalleschool.org. Bro. Thomas P. Casey, F.S.C., Exec. Dir.; Kevin Rall, Dean Student Life; Kathleen Boniello, Dean Academics. Brothers 1; Lay Teachers 5; Total Enrollment 66.

MANHASSET. *Our Lady of Grace Montessori School and Center*, (Grades N-2), 29 Shelter Rock Rd., 11030. Tel: 516-365-9832 (School); 516-627-9255 (Center); Fax: 516-365-9329. Sisters Maria Regina Loures, I.H.M., Admin.; Kelly Quinn, Prin. Sisters, Servants of the Immaculate Heart of Mary 2; Lay Teachers 17; Students 190.

OLD WESTBURY. *Holy Child Academy*, (Grades Toddler-8), 25 Store Hill Rd., 11568. Tel: 516-626-9300; Fax: 516-626-7914. Email: cbowen@holychildacademy.org. Web: www.holychildacademy.org. Mr. Michael O'Donoghue, Head of School; Palma Gartland, Div. Head 3, 4, 5 & Campus Min.; Gail Walker, Dir. Curriculum & Professional Devel.; Marie O'Donoghue, ECC Dir. & Div. Head 1 & 2. Lay Teachers 50; Students 211.

UNIONDALE. *St. Martin de Porres Marianist School* (2004) 530 Hempstead Blvd., 11553. Tel: 516-481-3303; Fax: 516-483-4138. Web: www.stmartinmarianist.org. Bro. Kenneth M. Hoagland, S.M., Prin.; Mr. John Holian, Headmaster; Mrs. Andrea Nordquist, Asst. Prin.; Bro. James W. Conway, S.M., Dir. Student Svcs. Brothers 2; Sisters 1; Lay Teachers 20; Students 460.

[G] SPECIALIZED CHILD CARE AGENCIES

NESCONSET. *Cleary Deaf Child Center, Inc.* (1925) 301 Smithtown Blvd., 11767. Tel: 631-588-0530 (Voice and TTY); Fax: 631-588-0016. Email: kmorseon@clearyschool.org. Web: www.clearyschool.org. Mr. Kenneth Morseon, Supt. Directed by Catholic Charities., Day School (Infants thru 21 years). Students 85.

SYOSSET. *MercyFirst* (1894) 525 Convent Rd., 11791-3864. Tel: 516-921-0808; Fax: 516-921-4542. Email: gmccaffery@mercyfirst.org. Web: www.mercyfirst.org. Gerard McCaffery, Pres. & CEO. Under the sponsorship of the Sisters of Mercy., Residential services provided in campus and group home settings, including diagnostic/group emergency foster care, non secure detention, hard to place (JD and clinically intensive), abuse treatment and prevention, mother/child, and OMH programs.; Family Foster Care/Adoption, Aftercare and Prevention Services programs provide services in Nassau, Queens and Brooklyn. Bed Capacity 194; Total Assisted 3,452; Total Staff 547.

WADING RIVER. **Little Flower Children & Family Services of New York* (1929) 2450 N. Wading River Rd., 11792-1402. Tel: 631-929-6200; Fax: 631-929-6121. Web: www.LittleFlowerNY.org. Sr. Rita Wasilewski, C.S.F.N., Supr.; Grace G. Lo Grande, Exec. Dir. & CEO; Kevin Kundmueller, CFO. Sisters of the Holy Family of Nazareth., Affiliated with the Diocese of Brooklyn. Foster care, adoption & post-adoption svcs., intermediate care facilities, residential treatment center, Special Act school district, family day care, family care for MR/DD clients, foster homes for teen mothers & their babies. Therapeutic foster boarding homes. Eldercare Solutions: Counseling for employees of client organizations. Bed Capacity 141; Total Assisted 2,600; Total Staff 525.

[H] CATHOLIC CHARITIES

HICKSVILLE. *Catholic Charities*, 90 Cherry Ln., 11801-6299. Tel: 516-733-7000; Fax: 516-733-7099. Web: www.catholiccharities.cc. Laura A. Cassell, CEO. Tel: 516-733-7013; Paul F. Engelhart, Chief Oper. Officer. Tel: 516-733-7012; Fax: 516-733-7099; Robert J. Manfredi, Dir., IT. Tel: 516-733-7003; Fax: 516-733-7098; John Gonta, Dir., Purchasing & Facilities. Tel: 516-733-7090; Fax: 516-733-7099.

Human Resources, 90 Cherry Lane, 11801-6299. Tel: 516-733-7005; Fax: 516-733-7038. Kristy D'Errico, Dir., Human Resources. Tel: 516-733-7005; Fax: 516-733-7038.

Finance, 90 Cherry Ln., 11801-6299. Tel: 516-733-7015; Fax: 516-733-7099. Edwin M. Kennedy, CFO; Richard Balcom, Dir. Finance.

Mental Health Residences, 333 N. Main St., Freeport, 11520. Tel: 516-634-0012; Fax: 516-634-0017. Howard G. Duff, Prog. Dir., Mental Health Progs.

Regina Maternity Services/Mentoring Tel: 516-223-7888; Fax: 516-223-2752. Kathleen Ryan, Dir. Maternity Svcs.

Regina Maternity Services Corporation, 90 Cherry Ln., 11801.

Chemical Dependency Services, 155 Indian Head Rd., Commack, 11725. Tel: 631-543-6200; Fax: 631-543-6203.

Outpatient Clinics:

Talbot House Alcohol Crisis Center, 30-C Carlough Rd., Bohemia, 11716. Tel: 631-589-4144; Fax: 631-589-3281.

Mental Health Programs, 333 N. Main St., Freeport, 11520. Tel: 516-634-0012, Ext. 126; Fax: 516-634-0017. Howard G. Duff, Dir., Mental Health Svcs.

Dental Services Program, 333 N. Main St., Freeport, 11520. Tel: 516-623-4420; Fax: 516-623-1313. Dr. Fabiola Milford, Dental Dir.

Housing Services (1980) 90 Cherry Ln., 11801-6299. Tel: 516-733-7076; Fax: 516-733-7098. Jay Korth, Dir. Housing & Legal Affairs.

Commodity Supplemental Food Program, 66 N. 19th St., Wyandanch, 11798. Tel: 631-491-4166; Fax: 631-491-4950.

Health Services:

Office for Persons with Disabilities, 147 Schleigel Blvd., Amityville, 11701. Tel: 631-789-5218; Fax: 631-789-3844.

Residential Services, 147 Schleigel Blvd., Amityville, 11701. Tel: 631-665-3434; Fax: 631-665-3586. Diane Ammirati, Dir. Disability Svcs.

Bi-County Alliance of Senior Clubs Tel: 516-733-7051; Fax: 516-733-7099.

Sr. Services Case Management, 333 N. Main St., Freeport, 11520. Tel: 516-771-3410.

Senior Services, 90 Cherry Ln., 11801. Tel: 516-733-7071; Fax: 516-733-7098. Eileen Verity, Dir., Senior Svcs.

Immigrant Services, 143 Schleigel Blvd., Amityville, 11701. Tel: 631-789-5210; Fax: 631-789-5245. Carmen Maquilon, Dir., Immigrant Svcs.

Parish Social Ministry, 90 Cherry Ln., 11801. Tel: 516-733-7059; Fax: 516-733-7098. Jan Jamroz, Prog. Dir., Parish Social Min. Tel: 516-733-7084.

Central Intake & Referral Developers Tel: 516-733-7045; Fax: 516-733-7098.

Development and Communications, 90 Cherry Ln., 11801. Tel: 516-733-7042; Fax: 516-733-7098. Scott A. Stepp, Dir. Devel. & Communications. Tel: 516-733-7042.

Catholic Charities Health Systems Corp. of the Diocese of Rockville Centre, Inc.

Catholic Charities Support Corp.

[I] HOSPITALS

BETHPAGE. **WSNCHS North Inc. dba St. Joseph Hospital* 4295 Hampstead Tpke., 11714. Dr. Aaron Glatt, Pres. & CEO.

[J] CATHOLIC HEALTHCARE APOSTOLATE NASSAU COUNTY

ROCKVILLE CENTRE

Catholic Health Services of Long Island dba Catholic Health System of Long Island, Inc. 992 N. Village Ave., 11570. Tel: 516-705-3700; Fax: 516-705-3730. Web: www.chsli.org.

Catholic Healthcare Network of Long Island, 992 N. Village Ave., 11570. Tel: 516-705-3700; Fax: 516-705-3730. Mr. Richard J.J. Sullivan Jr., Exec. Chair; Sr. Elaine Callahan, Vice Chair; Thomas F. Christman, Treas.; Colleen Blye, Exec. Vice Pres., Fin. & CFO; Joel Yohai, M.D., Exec. Vice Pres. Medical Affairs & CMO; David DeCerbo, Senior Vice Pres. & Gen. Counsel.

Hospitals:

St. Charles Hospital and Rehabilitation Center, 200 Belle Terre Rd., Port Jefferson, 11777. Tel: 631-474-6600; Fax: 631-474-6884. James Caldas, Pres. & CEO; James O'Connor, Exec. Vice Pres.

Catholic Charities Health Systems, 90 Cherry Ln., Hicksville, 11801.

Mercy Medical Center, 1000 N. Village Ave., 11570. Tel: 516-705-2525; Fax: 516-705-1406. Alan D. Guerci, M.D., Pres. & CEO; Dr. Aaron Glatt, Chief Admin. Officer & Senior Vice Pres.

St. Francis Hospital, 100 Port Washington Blvd., Roslyn, 11576. Tel: 516-562-6000; Fax: 516-629-2448. Alan D. Guerci, M.D., Pres. & CEO; Ruth Hennessey, Exec. Vice Pres. & Chief Admin. Officer.

St. Catherine of Siena Medical Center, 50 Rte. 25A, Smithtown, 11787. Tel: 631-862-3000; Fax: 631-862-3105. James Caldas, Pres. & CEO; Dennis Verzi, Exec. Vice. Pres. & Chief Admin. Officer.

Good Samaritan Hospital Medical Center, 1000 Montauk Hwy., West Islip, 11795. Tel: 631-376-4001; Fax: 631-376-4208. James Caldas, Pres. & CEO; Nancy Simmons, Senior Vice Pres. & Chief Admin. Officer.

Nursing Homes and Sub-Acute Care:

Good Shepherd Hospice Foundation, Inc., 245 Old Country Rd., Melville, 11747. Tel: 631-465-6300; Fax: 631-465-6534.

Long Term Care Facilities:

Good Samaritan Nursing Home, 101 Elm St., Sayville, 11782. Tel: 631-244-2400; Fax: 631-244-2405. Terriann Cronin, Admin. Operating under the license of Good Samaritan Hospital Medical Center

St. Catherine of Siena Nursing and Rehabilitation Care Center, 52 Rte. 25A, Smithtown, 11787. Tel: 631-862-3900; Fax: 631-862-3983. Michael Quartararo, Senior Admin. Operating under the license of St. Catherine of Siena Medical Center.

Our Lady of Nursing and Rehabilitative Care Center dba Our Lady of Consolation Nursing and Rehabilitative Care Center 111 Beach Dr., West Islip,

11795. Tel: 631-587-1600; Fax: 631-587-5960. Sr. Marilyn Breen, O.P., Senior Vice Pres.
Hospice and Palliative Care Services:
Good Shepherd Hospice, 245 Old Country Rd., Melville, 11747. Tel: 631-465-6300; Fax: 631-465-6534. Mary Ellen Polit, Chief Admin. Officer; Joseph J. Tomaino, Pres. CEO.
Nursing Sisters Home Care, Inc. dba Catholic Home Care 1150 Portion Rd., Holtsville, 11742. Tel: 631-696-1002; Fax: 631-224-8678. Mary Ellen Polit, Chief Admin. Officer; Joseph J. Tomaino, Pres. & CEO.
Behavioral/Developmentally Disabled Programs:
Maryhaven Center of Hope, Inc., 51 Terryville Rd., Port Jefferson Station, 11776. Tel: 631-474-4120; Fax: 631-474-4110. Lewis Grossman, Pres. & CEO.
Adult Day Services (over age 18): Participants develop skills necessary to obtain employment within an array of community-based options, or within the agency's work center.; Participants receive assistance with learning skills necessary for independent living.; Individuals receive intensive therapeutic services along with increased community integration.
Vocational Training/Supported Work/Sheltered Center formerly Vocational Training/Supported Work/Sheltered Workshop Tel: 631-924-5900; Fax: 631-924-2464.
Day Habilitation Tel: 631-474-4100; Fax: 631-474-4156.
Adult Residential Services: The agency operates a variety of housing alternatives within community-based settings.; Individuals still living at home receive assistance in accessing needed support services.
Adult Residences Tel: 631-474-4100; Fax: 631-474-9014.
Mental Health Services: Staff offer individuals assistance with accessing supports and services, advocacy and individual follow-up.; These day programs work to develop individual skills to improve a person's living, working, learning, and social situations.
Personalized Recovery Oriented Services for People with Psychiatric Disabilities (PROS East & West) formerly Continuing Day Treatment/Intensive Psychiatric Rehabilitation Treatment Tel: 631-727-4044; Fax: 631-727-6531.
Children Services (Ages 5-21): Progressive educational programming for children with developmental disabilities. The school is committed to the IEP diploma recipient and has a specialization in autism.; Provides 24-hour programming for students requiring greater support than can be provided at home.
Maryhaven School Tel: 631-474-3400; Fax: 631-474-4181.
Children's Residences Tel: 631-474-3400; Fax: 631-474-4181.
Maryhaven School, 51 Terryville Rd., Port Jefferson Station, 11776. Tel: 631-474-4120; Fax: 631-474-4110. Robin Dwyer, Div. Dir. Children's Svcs.
**Maryhaven Transportation Services, Inc.*, 51 Terryville Rd., Port Jefferson Station, 11776. Tel: 631-474-4120. Paul Commesso.
Miscellaneous Entities:
CHS Services, Inc., 51 Terryville Rd., Port Jefferson Station, 11776. Tel: 631-474-4120. Mr. James Harden, Pres.
Suffolk Hearing & Speech Center, Inc., 369 E. Main St., East Islip, 11730. Tel: 631-376-4001; Fax: 631-376-4208. A diagnostic and treatment center.
The Samaritan Corporation
St. Charles Corporation
CHS Home Support Services
The St. Francis Research and Educational Corporation
The St. Francis-Mercy Corporation
Siena Village, Inc., 2000 Bishop's Rd., Smithtown, 11787. Tel: 631-360-6000; Fax: 631-360-6006. Kim Parbst, Admin. A low income housing program.
**Wisdom Gardens Housing Development Fund Company, Inc., c/o Maryhaven Center of Hope*, 51 Terryville Rd., Port Jefferson Station, 11776. Tel: 631-474-4120; Fax: 631-474-4110.
The Maryhaven Center of Hope Foundation, 51 Terryville Rd., Port Jefferson Station, 11776. Tel: 631-474-4120; Fax: 631-474-4110. Lewis Grossman, Pres. & CEO.
Siena Retirement Community Realty, LLC, 50 Rte. 25A, Smithtown, 11787. Tel: 631-862-3100; Fax: 631-862-3105.

[K] RESIDENCES FOR AGED

AMITYVILLE. *Dominican Village, Inc.*, 565 Albany Ave., 11701. Tel: 631-842-6091; Fax: 631-842-6131. Email: dv@dominicanvillage.org. Kenneth Ruthinoski, Pres. & CEO; Sr. Mary Casey, Vice Pres. Operations. Housing Units 266; Total Assisted 66; Total Staff 130.

HUNTINGTON. *St. Joseph's Guest Home for the Aged, Inc.*, 350 Cuba Hill Rd., 11743. Tel: 631-368-9528; Fax: 931-266-1015. Email: sjgh350@yahoo.com. Web: www.missionarysistersofstbenedict.org. Sr. M. Joachima Mystkowska, O.S.B., Admin. Missionary Sisters of St. Benedict. Bed Capacity 45; Total Assisted Annually 40; Total Staff 21.

[L] SOCIETY OF ST. VINCENT DE PAUL

BETHPAGE. **Society of St. Vincent de Paul-Central Council* (1833) 249 Broadway, 11714. Tel: 516-822-3132; Fax: 516-822-2728. Email: jdilts@svdprvc.org. Web: svdprvc.org. Rev. Msgr. Patrick Armshaw, Spiritual Dir.; Paul Hodermarsky, Pres.; James T. Dilts, Exec. Dir. & COO. Total Assisted 228,508; Volunteers 1,337; Total Staff 94.

[M] HOME HEALTH SERVICES

HAMPTON BAYS. *Dominican Sisters Family Health Service*, 103-6 W. Montauk Hwy., 11946. Tel: 631-728-0181; Fax: 631-723-0866. Email: pash@dsfhs.org. Web: www.dsfhs.org. Pamella Ash, B.S.N., M.A., Admin. Suffolk Offices.
360 Montauk Hwy., P.O. Box 678, Wainscott, 11975. Tel: 631-537-6759; Fax: 631-537-7187. Web: www.dsfhs.org.
1729A N. Ocean Ave., Medford, 11763. Tel: 631-207-1170; Fax: 631-207-0149. Web: www.dsfhs.org.
DSFHS Special Programs, P.O. Box 1028, 11946. Tel: 631-728-0937; Fax: 631-728-7162. Web: www.dsfhs.org.

[N] MONASTERIES AND RESIDENCES OF PRIESTS AND BROTHERS

AMITYVILLE. *St. Pius X Residence*, 565 Albany Ave., 11701. Tel: 631-608-2622; Fax: 631-608-2624. Rev. Msgr. Thomas F. Mulvanerty, Vicar for Senior Priests; Bro. Patrick Murphy, O.S.F., Pastoral Assoc. for Senior Priests In Res. Rev. Msgrs. Francis X. Gaeta (Retired); William W. Jablonski (Retired); Thomas F. Mulvanerty; Eugene F. Murphy (Retired); Anthony J. Savastano (Retired); John J. Skelly (Retired); Revs. Serafino A. Corali (Retired); Thomas E. Donohoe (Retired); John P. Drab (Retired); Charles A. Gartner (Retired); James J. Hannon (Retired); Robert J. Kayser (Retired); John H. McCabe (Retired); Richard A. Nilsson; Francis B. Nuss (Retired); Jose Simon Palliparambil (Retired); Denis J. Sheridan (Retired); John P. Wilutis (Retired).

BAY SHORE. *Montfort Missionaries*, 26 S. Saxon Ave., 11706. Tel: 631-666-7500; Fax: 631-665-4349. Email: PRETRE@worldnet.att.net. Revs. Roger M. Charest, S.M.M. (Retired); Everett Brown, S.M.M.; Jose Jacob, S.M.M., (Shrine of Our Lady of the Island, Manorville, NY); George J. Werner, S.M.M., Supr., Preaching Team; Francis Pizzarelli, S.M.M., Hope House Ministry; James Manning, S.M.M., Convent Chap.; Peter J. McCrann, S.M.M., Hospital Chap.; Theodore Murphy, S.M.M. (Retired); John Breslin, S.M.M. (Retired); Vincent P. Cunningham, S.M.M. (Retired); Roy Tvrdik, S.M.M., (Dir., Shrine of Our Lady of the Island, Manorville, NY); Bro. Christopher Golla, S.M.M., Hospital Chap. Montfort Spiritual Center and Headquarters of "Montfort Publications" Priests 11; Brothers 1. *Montfort Missionaries - Retreat Center* (1928) 26 S. Saxon Ave., 11706. Tel: 631-666-7500; Fax: 631-666-4349.

GLEN COVE. *St. Josaphat's Monastery, Novitiate and Retreat House*, East Beach Dr., 11542. Tel: 516-671-0545; Fax: 516-676-7465. Email: stjosaphatnvtt@gmail.com. Revs. Athanasius B. Pekar, O.S.B.M.; Leo Goldade, O.S.B.M., Supr. Master of Novices; Theodosius (Roman) Ilnicki, O.S.B.M., Provincial Sec.; Eugene (Andriy) Khdmyn, O.S.B.M., Asst. Master of Novices, Vicar. Basilian Fathers.
Manorville
Shrine of Our Lady of the Island, 258 Eastport Manor Rd., Manorville, 11949. Tel: 631-325-0661; Fax: 631-325-5592. Web: ourladyoftheisland.org. Rev. Roy Tvrdik, S.M.M., Dir.

MINEOLA. *Provincial Residence and Novitiate*, 240 Emory Rd., 11501. Tel: 516-742-5555; Fax: 516-742-1989. Email: tcleary@chaminade-hs.org. Bro. Thomas J. Cleary, S.M., Prov. & Asst. for Educ.; Revs. Garrett J. Long, S.M., Asst. Prov. & Asst. Rel. Life; Thomas A. Cardone, S.M., Councilor; Bros. James W. Conway, S.M., Asst. Temporalities; Timothy S. Driscoll, S.M., Councilor. Society of Mary (Marianists). In Res. Rev. Ernest P. Lorfanfant, S.M.

[O] CONVENTS AND RESIDENCES FOR SISTERS

ROCKVILLE CENTRE. *Congregation of the Infant Jesus* (1905) 984 N. Village Ave., 11570. Tel: 516-823-3808; Fax: 516-594-0412. Email: dwisniewski123@earthlink.net. Web: www.cijnssp.org. Congregation of the Infant Jesus (Nursing Sisters of the Sick Poor). Professed Sisters 50.

AMITYVILLE. *Queen of the Rosary, Motherhouse* (1853) 555 Albany Ave., 11701-1197. Tel: 631-842-6000; Fax: 631-842-0240. Email: prioress@amityop.org. Web: www.amityvilleop.org. Sisters Mary Hughes, O.P., Prioress; Jane Creighton, O.P., Admin.
Sisters of the Order of St. Dominic
Amityville Dominican Sisters, Inc. Sisters of St. Dominic. Total in Residence 112.

BAY SHORE. *New Jerusalem*, 106 N. Penataquit Ave., 11706-6939. Tel: 631-968-8859. Sisters 4.

BLUE POINT. *St. Ursula Center*, 186 Middle Rd., 11715. Tel: 631-363-2422; Fax: 631-363-0319. Email: shoran@tildonkursuline.org. Web: www.tildonkursuline.org. Sandy Horan, Admin. Ursuline Sisters, Congregation of Tildonk.

BRENTWOOD. *Saint Joseph Convent* (1856) Motherhouse, 1725 Brentwood Rd., 11717. Tel: 631-273-4531; Fax: 631-273-1451. Email: rooney@csjbrentwood.org. Web: www.brentwoodcsj.org. Sisters Helen M. Kearney, C.S.J., Pres.; Helen Rooney, C.S.J., Gen. Sec.; Eugenia Calabrese, C.S.J., Gen. Treas.; Virginia Dowd, Community Archivist. Sisters of Saint Joseph Generalate. Sisters 609.
Saint Joseph Novitiate, 1725 Brentwood Rd., 11717. Tel: 631-273-1187; Fax: 631-273-1451. Web: www.brentwoodcsj.org. Sr. Mary Walsh, C.S.J., Dir. Formation.
Maria Regina Residence, Inc. Sisters of St. Joseph, 1725 Brentwood Rd., Bldg. 1, 11717-5589. Tel: 631-299-3000; Fax: 631-952-2378. Email: mrr2007@mariareginaresidence.org. Web: www.mariareginaresidence.org.

FRANKLIN SQUARE. *Spiritual Life Center*, 1031 Mosefan St., 11010. Tel: 516-328-7438. Email: kmurphyop@verizon. Sr. Kathleen Murphy, O.P., Dir. Sisters of St. Dominic. Sisters 2.

HAMPTON BAYS. *St. Joseph's Villa Retreat and Renewal Center*, 81 Lynn Ave., 11946. Tel: 631-728-6074; Fax: 631-273-1451. Email: stjosephvilla@optonline.net. Web: www.csjbrentwoodny.org. Sisters of St. Joseph 2.

HUNTINGTON. *Missionary Sisters of St. Benedict*, 350 Cuba Hill Rd., 11743. Tel: 631-368-9528; Fax: 631-266-1015. Email: mssb350@yahoo.com. Web: www.missionarysistersofstbenedict.org. Sr. M. Matea Mirecka, O.S.B., Supr. Sisters 21.

ISLIP. *Daughters of Wisdom (Administration)*, 385 Ocean Ave., 11751. Tel: 631-277-2660; Fax: 631-277-3274. Email: jrohan@daughtersofwisdom.org. Web: www.daughtersofwisdom.org. Sr. Ann Gray, D.W., Prov. Administration Offices. Sisters 4.

OCEANSIDE. *St. Anthony's Parish House*, 111 Anchor Ave., 11572. Tel: 516-536-3308. Email: oceansideop@verizon.net. Sr. Margaret Sammon, O.P., Contact Person. Sisters of St. Dominic 3.

POINT LOOKOUT. *St. Clare Convent-Franciscan Sisters of Allegany*, 104 Ocean Blvd., P.O. Box 823, 11569. Tel: 718-842-2615; 347-963-4552. Sr. Catherine Moran, O.S.F., Contact Person.
St. Elizabeth Convent-Franciscan Sisters of Allegany, 29 Ocean Blvd., 11569. Tel: 718-842-2615; 347-963-4552. Sr. Catherine Moran, O.S.F., Contact Person.

RONKONKOMA. *Religious of Our Lady of the Retreat in the Cenacle*, 310 Cenacle Rd., 11779-0430. Tel: 631-588-8366; Fax: 631-580-2050. Web: www.cenaclesisters.org.
Cenacle Retreat House Tel: 631-588-8366; Fax: 631-580-2050. Sr. Mary Jane Laffan, Supr.
St. Therese Couderc Community, 312 Cenacle Rd., 11779-2203. Tel: 631-588-8366; Fax: 631-580-2050. Sr. Mary Jane Laffan, Supr.
Maude Adams House, 310 Cencale Rd., 11779. Tel: 631-588-8366; Fax: 631-738-9511. Sr. Mary Spratt, Contact.
Cenacle Sisters at Brentwood (Maria Regina Convent) Tel: 631-273-4500. Sr. Mary Walsh, C.S.J., Contact Person. Sisters 4.

ROOSEVELT. *Oblate Sisters of the Most Holy Redeemer, Mother of Good Counsel Home*, 290 Babylon Tpke., P.O. Box 329, 11575-0329. Tel: 516-223-1013; Fax: 516-223-4254. Email: ossr290@earthlink.net. Sr. Matilde Murillo, O.SS.R., Dir. Mother of Good Counsel Home is a group home for pregnant and parenting teenage mothers and their infants.

SOUND BEACH. *Our Lady of Perpetual Help Convent*, 49 Convent Dr., 11789. Tel: 631-744-2477; Fax: 631-744-2515. Email: sbeachdirector@aol.com. Gayle Walkowiak, Facility Coord. Daughters of Wisdom 23.

[P] RETREAT HOUSES

CENTERPORT. *St. Francis Center, Inc.* (1961) 105 Prospect Rd., P.O. Box 301, 11721. Tel: 631-261-5730; Fax: 631-754-4204. Email: alverniacenterportny@gmail.com. Web: www.alvernia.org. Directed by Franciscan Bros. of Brooklyn.

MANHASSET. *St. Ignatius Jesuit Retreat House,*

Inisfada, 251 Searingtown Rd., 11030. Tel: 516-621-8300; Fax: 516-521-7201. Email: inisfada@inisfada.net. Web: www.inisfada.net. Revs. Damian O. Halligan, S.J.; William P. Walsh, S.J. The Society of Jesus. Sisters 1; Total Staff 3.

PATCHOGUE. *St. Joseph's Prayer Center*, 312 Maple Ave., 11772. Tel: 631-730-6210; Fax: 631-730-6210. Email: stjoepc@optonline.net. Craig W. Nurnberger, Dir.; Rev. James J. Wheeler, S.J., Apostolic Dir. Priests 2; Total Assisted 500; Total Staff 10.

RONKONKOMA. *Cenacle Retreat Center*, 310 Cenacle Rd., P.O. Box 4005, 11779-0430. Tel: 631-588-8366; Fax: 631-738-9511. Email: retreat@cenaclesisters.org. Web: www.cenaclesisters.org. Sr. Margaret Rohde, R.C., Dir. Ministry. Religious of the Cenacle. Ministry Staff 8.

SAG HARBOR. *Cormaria Retreat House* (1949) P.O. Box 1993, 11963. Tel: 631-725-4206; Fax: 631-725-1837. Email: cormaria@aol.com. Web: www.cormaria.org. Sr. Ann Thaddeus Marino, R.S.H.M., Retreat Dir. Directed by the Religious of the Sacred Heart of Mary. Religious of the Sacred Heart of Mary 7; Total Staff 17.

[Q] MISCELLANEOUS

ROCKVILLE CENTRE. **Ecclesia Assurance Company*, P.O. Box 9023, 11571.

Mission Assistance Corporation, P.O. Box 9023, 11571. Tel: 516-678-5800. Mr. Kevin T. Murphy, Dir. Diocesan Admin.

**Tomorrow's Hope Foundation, Inc.*, P.O. Box 9023, 11571. Tel: 516-678-5800. Mr. Kevin T. Murphy, Chancellor for Business Affairs.

Unitas Investment Fund Inc., P.O. Box 9023, 11571-9023. Tel: 516-678-5800. Mr. Kevin T. Murphy, Diocesan Admin.

AMITYVILLE. *Amityville Dominican Sisters, Inc.*, 555 Albany Ave., 11701. Tel: 631-842-6000; Fax: 631-842-0240. Email: prioress@amityop.org. Web: www.amityvilleop.org. Sisters Mary Hughes, O.P., Pres.; Elaine Jahrsdoerfer, O.P., Vice Pres.; Theresa A. Gallagher, O.P., Sec. & Treas.

Benincasa Family Services, Inc., 555 Albany Ave., 11701. Tel: 631-842-6000, Ext. 351; Fax: 631-842-1596. Email: mkbenin555@aol.com. Sr. Margaret A. Krajci, O.P., Contact.

Dominican Sisters Community Support Corp., 555 Albany Ave., 11701. Tel: 631-842-6000; Fax: 631-842-0240. Email: prioress@amityop.org. Web: www.amityvilleop.org. Sisters Mary Hughes, O.P., Pres.; Elaine Jahrsdoerfer, O.P., Vice Pres.; Theresa A. Gallagher, O.P., Sec. & Treas.

Federation of Dominican Sisters, USA Inc., 555 Albany Ave., 11701. Tel: 631-842-6000, Ext. 221; Fax: 631-842-0240. Web: www.amityvilleop.org. Sr. Rose Celeste O'Connell, O.P., Chair.

BAY SHORE. *Pronto of Long Island, Inc.*, 128 Pine Aire Dr., 11706. Tel: 631-231-8290; Fax: 631-231-8390. Email: vhart@prontolongisland.org. Web: www.prontoli.org. Vivian Hart, Exec. Dir.

BRENTWOOD. *Congregation of the Sisters of St. Joseph (1856) Charitable Trust*, Brentwood Rd., 11717-5587. Tel: 631-273-1187; Fax: 631-273-1345. Web: www.brentwoodcsj.org. Sr. Eugenia Calabrese, C.S.J., Treas.

The CSJ Learning Connection for Adult Education, Inc., 1725 Brentwood Rd., 11717. Tel: 631-951-4783; Fax: 631-951-0642. Email: CSJTLC@optonline.net. Sr. Kathleen Carberry, C.S.J., Dir.

Sisters of Saint Joseph Lay Employee Pension Plan Charitable Trust, 1725 Brentwood Rd., 11717. Tel: 631-273-1187; Fax: 631-273-1451. Web: www.brentwoodcsj.org. Sr. Eugenia Calabrese, C.S.J., Trustee.

CENTERPORT. *Mt. Alvernia, Inc.* (1888) 105 Prospect Rd., P.O. Box 301, 11721. Tel: 631-261-5730; Fax: 631-754-4204. Email: alverniacenterportny@gmail.com. Web: www.alvernia.org. Directed by the Franciscan Brothers.

Camp Alvernia Tel: 631-261-5730; Fax: 631-754-4204. Email: info@campalvernia.org. Web: www-.campalvernia.org. Directed by the Franciscan Brothers.

Mt. Alvernia Center for Retreats Tel: 631-261-5730; Fax: 631-754-4204. Email: alverniacenterportny@gmail.com. Web: www.alvernia.org. Directed by the Franciscan Brothers.

FARMINGVILLE. *Religious Computer Systems* (1982) P.O. Box 508, 11738-0508. Tel: 631-732-7270; Fax: 631-732-6591. Email: rcsjane@optimum.net. Web: www.rcswebsite.org. Sr. Jane Muller, O.P. Social Security and computer services for Religious institutions under sponsorship of the Amityville Dominicans

HAMPTON BAYS. *Centro Corazon de Maria, Inc.*, 31 Montauk Hwy. E., 11946. Tel: 631-728-5558; Fax: 631-728-5559.

ISLIP. *Wisdom Charitable Trust*, 385 Ocean Ave., 11751. Tel: 631-277-2660; Fax: 631-277-3274.

NESCONSET. **Cleary Foundation for the Deaf, Inc.*, 301 Smithtown Blvd., 11767-2007.

NEW HYDE PARK. *Sisters of the Imitation of Christ United States Mission, Inc.*, 1653 Highland Ave., 11040. Tel: 516-358-4597.

OAKDALE. *Saint John Baptist De La Salle of New York, Inc.*, P.O. Box 538, 11769. Tel: 401-789-0244; Fax: 401-783-5303. Email: eprecourt@cbc.necoxmail.com. Bro. Edmond Precourt, F.S.C., Provincial.

RIVERHEAD. *Sisters of the Holy Family of Nazareth, Inc.*, 3560 Sound Ave., 11901.

ROOSEVELT. *Friends of Mother of Good Counsel Home, Inc.*, 290 Babylon Tpke., 11575. Tel: 516-223-1013; Fax: 516-223-4254. Email: ossr290@earthlink.net. Sr. Matilde Murillo, O.SS.R., Dir. Bed Capacity 6; Total Assisted Annually 12; Total Staff 3.

Syosset

**Emmaus House Foundation, Inc. dba Harvest Houses* 235 Cold Spring Rd., Syosset, 11791. Tel: 516-496-9796; Fax: 516-496-9796. Sr. Jeanne A. Brendel, O.P., Exec. Dir.

UNIONDALE. *TELECARE of the Diocese of Rockville Centre*, 1200 Glenn Curtiss Blvd., 11553. Tel: 516-538-8700; Fax: 516-489-9701. Email: info@telecaretv.org. Web: www.telecaretv.org. Rev. Msgr. James C. Vlaun, Pres. & CEO; Joseph Perrone, Gen. Mgr.

WESTBURY. *Sisters, Lovers of the Holy Cross, Inc.* (1993) 43 Crown Ln, 11590. Tel: 516-333-9464; Fax: 516-333-9464. Email: sr.theresanguyen@yahoo.com.

St. Theresa Convent, 43 Crown Ln., 11590. Tel: 516-333-9464; Fax: 516-333-9464. Email: srteresanguyen@yahoo.com. Sr. Theresa Nguyen, L.H.C., Pres.

WYANDANCH. *Gerald J. Ryan Outreach Center, Inc.*, 1434 Straight Path, 11798. Tel: 631-643-7591; Fax: 631-643-1871. Email: ryanouthreach@optonline.net. Myrna Salmeron, Hispanic Ministry Coord./Asst. to Dir.; Ivonne Taveras, Support Svcs. Total Assisted 20,150; Volunteers 35; Total Staff 4.

The Opening Word Program, Inc. (1991) 1434 Straight Path, 11798. Tel: 631-643-0541; Fax: 631-643-5935. Email: opword@optonline.net. Sisters Mary Ryan, O.P., Treas.; Leonore Toscano, O.P., Exec. Dir.; Mary Hughes, O.P., Chairperson. Directed by the Sisters of St. Dominic.

RELIGIOUS INSTITUTES OF MEN REPRESENTED IN THE DIOCESE

For further details refer to the corresponding bracketed number in the Religious Institutes of Men or Women section.

[0330]—*Brothers of the Christian Schools*—F.S.C.
[]—*Canons Regular of St. Augustine*—Can.Reg.
[0470]—*The Capuchin Friars* (St. Mary Prov.)—O.F.M.Cap.
[1330]—*Congregation of the Mission-Vincentians* (Eastern Prov.)—C.M.
[1000]—*Congregation of the Passion* (Prov. of St. Paul of the Cross)—C.P.
[0490]—*Franciscan Brothers of Brooklyn*—O.S.F.
[0690]—*Jesuit Fathers and Brothers* (NY Prov.)—S.J.
[0770]—*The Marist Brothers*—F.M.S.
[0800]—*Maryknoll*—M.M.
[0720]—*Missionaries of Our Lady of La Salette*—M.S.
[0870]—*Montfort Missionaries*—S.M.M.
[0430]—*Order of Preachers-Dominicans*—O.P.
[S.A.C.]—*Pallotines*
[1070]—*Redemptorist Fathers*—C.SS.R.
[0760]—*Society of Mary* (Provs. of NY; Meribah)—S.M.

RELIGIOUS INSTITUTES OF WOMEN REPRESENTED IN THE DIOCESE

[]—*Congregation of Notre Dame*—C.N.D.
[3110]—*Congregation of Our Lady of the Retreat in the Cenacle*—R.C.
[2240]—*Congregation of the Infant Jesus*—C.I.J.
[]—*Daughters of Mary* (Haiti)—F.de M.
[0960]—*Daughters of Wisdom*—D.W.
[1070-05]—*Dominican Sisters* (Amityville)—O.P.
[1070-15]—*Dominican Sisters* (Blauvelt)—O.P.
[1070-16]—*Dominican Sisters* (Hope)—O.P.
[1070-11]—*Dominican Sisters* (Sparkill)—O.P.
[1370]—*Franciscan Missionaries of Mary*—F.M.M.
[1180]—*Franciscan Sisters of Allegany, New York*—O.S.F.
[1840]—*Grey Nuns of the Sacred Heart*—G.N.S.H.
[2070]—*Holy Union Sisters*—S.U.S.C.
[2575]—*Institute of the Sisters of Mercy of the Americas* (Mid-Atlantic Community)—R.S.M.
[0210]—*Missionary Benedictine Sisters*—O.S.B.
[]—*Missionary Servants of the Most Blessed Trinity*—M.S.B.T.
[3030]—*Oblate Sisters of M.H. Redeemer*—O.SS.R.
[3465]—*Religious of the Sacred Heart of Mary*—R.S.H.M.
[2970]—*School Sisters of Notre Dame*—S.S.N.D.
[0640]—*Sisters of Charity of St. Vincent de Paul* (Halifax)—S.C.
[0650]—*Sisters of Charity of St. Vincent de Paul, of New York*—S.C.
[0430]—*Sisters of Charity of the Blessed Virgin Mary*—B.V.M.
[2990]—*Sisters of Notre Dame de Namur*—S.N.D.
[3000]—*Sisters of Notre Dame de Namur* (Baltimore & Base Communities Provinces)—S.N.D.deN.
[3830-05]—*Sisters of St. Joseph* (Brentwood, NY)—C.S.J.
[3840]—*Sisters of St. Joseph of Carondelet* (Province of Albany)—C.S.J.
[3830-11]—*Sisters of St. Joseph of Philadelphia*—S.S.J.
[]—*Sisters of the Blessed Koran Martyrs*—S.B.K.M.
[3180]—*Sisters of the Cross and the Passion*—C.P.
[1830]—*Sisters of the Good Shepherd*—R.G.S.
[1970]—*Sisters of the Holy Family of Nazareth*—C.S.F.N.
[]—*Sisters of the Imitation of Christ*—S.I.C.
[2392]—*Sisters, Lovers of the Holy Cross* (Brookville, N.Y.)—L.H.C.
[2160]—*Sisters, Servants of the Immaculate Heart of Mary*—I.H.M.
[4130]—*Ursuline Sisters of the Congregation of Tildonk, Belgium*—O.S.U.

DIOCESAN CEMETERIES

CENTRAL ISLIP. *Queen of All Saints Cemetery*, 115 Wheeler Rd., 11722. Tel: 631-234-8297; Fax: 631-234-8632.

CORAM. *Holy Sepulchre Cemetery*, 3442 Rte. 112, 11727. Tel: 631-732-3460; Fax: 631-732-3476.

WESTBURY. *Cemetery of the Holy Rood*, 111 Old Country Rd., Box 182, 11590-0182. Tel: 516-334-7990; Fax: 516-334-4383.

NECROLOGY

† Rooney, Rev. Msgr. Thaddeus, (Retired)—Died July 25, 2011
† Anderson, Arthur C., (Retired)—Died Oct. 1, 2011
† LeTure, Theodore J., (Retired)—Died July 3, 2011
† Murphy, William T., (Retired)—Died June 7, 2011
† Traynor, John J., (Retired)—Died July 11, 2011

Diocese of Sacramento

(Dioecesis Sacramentensis)

Most Reverend

JAIME SOTO, D.D., M.S.W.

Bishop of Sacramento; ordained June 12, 1982; appointed Auxiliary Bishop of Orange and named Titular Bishop of Segia March 23, 2000; installed May 31, 2000; appointed Coadjutor Bishop of Sacramento October 11, 2007; installed November 18, 2007; Succeeded to the See November 30, 2008. *Diocesan Pastoral Center: Office of the Bishop, 2110 Broadway, Sacramento, CA 95818-2541.* Tel: 916-733-0200; Fax: 916-733-0215.

Most Reverend

WILLIAM K. WEIGAND, D.D.

Retired Bishop of Sacramento; ordained May 25, 1963; appointed Bishop of Salt Lake City September 3, 1980; ordained and installed November 17, 1980; appointed Bishop of Sacramento November 30, 1993; installed January 27, 1994; retired November 30, 2008. *Diocesan Pastoral Center, Office of the Bishop: 2110 Broadway, Sacramento, CA 95818-2541.* Tel: 916-733-0200; Fax: 916-733-0215.

Diocesan Pastoral Center: 2110 Broadway, Sacramento, CA 95818-2541. Tel: 916-733-0100; Fax: 916-733-0195.

Web: www.diocese-sacramento.org

Most Reverend

FRANCIS A. QUINN, D.D., ED.D.

Retired Bishop of Sacramento; ordained June 15, 1946; appointed Titular Bishop of Numana and Auxiliary Bishop of San Francisco April 28, 1978; Episcopal ordination June 29, 1978; appointed Bishop of Sacramento December 18, 1979; retired November 30, 1993. *Office: 2110 Broadway, Sacramento, CA 95818-2541.* Tel: 916-733-0200.

Square Miles 42,597.

Erected by His Holiness, Leo XIII, May 28, 1886.

Comprises the Counties of Amador, Butte, Colusa, El Dorado, Glenn, Lassen, Modoc, Nevada, Placer, Plumas, Sacramento, Shasta, Sierra, Siskiyou, Solano, Sutter, Tehama, Trinity, Yolo and Yuba in the State of California.

Co-Patrons of Diocese: St. Patrick; Our Lady of Guadalupe.

Legal Title: "Roman Catholic Bishop of Sacramento, A Corporation Sole."
For legal titles of parishes and diocesan institutions, consult the Diocesan Pastoral Center.

STATISTICAL OVERVIEW

Personnel	
Bishop	1
Retired Bishops	2
Abbots	1
Retired Abbots	2
Priests: Diocesan Active in Diocese	111
Priests: Diocesan Active Outside Diocese	3
Priests: Retired, Sick or Absent	60
Number of Diocesan Priests	174
Religious Priests in Diocese	70
Total Priests in Diocese	244
Extern Priests in Diocese	32
Ordinations:	
Diocesan Priests	4
Transitional Deacons	3
Permanent Deacons	138
Permanent Deacons in Diocese	143
Total Brothers	12
Total Sisters	169
Parishes	
Parishes	102
With Resident Pastor:	
Resident Diocesan Priests	79
Resident Religious Priests	14
Without Resident Pastor:	
Administered by Priests	12
Missions	44
Pastoral Centers	3
Professional Ministry Personnel:	
Brothers	2
Sisters	19
Lay Ministers	78
Welfare	
Catholic Hospitals	6
Total Assisted	666,574
Homes for the Aged	1
Total Assisted	130
Specialized Homes	1
Total Assisted	214
Special Centers for Social Services	11
Total Assisted	57,400
Educational	
Diocesan Students in Other Seminaries	29
Seminaries, Religious	2
Students Religious	1
Total Seminarians	30
High Schools, Diocesan and Parish	3
Total Students	1,780
High Schools, Private	3
Total Students	2,333
Elementary Schools, Diocesan and Parish	40
Total Students	10,093
Catechesis/Religious Education:	
High School Students	2,492
Elementary Students	24,697
Total Students under Catholic Instruction	41,425
Teachers in the Diocese:	
Priests	9
Sisters	14
Lay Teachers	1,003
Vital Statistics	
Receptions into the Church:	
Infant Baptism Totals	8,987
Minor Baptism Totals	566
Adult Baptism Totals	418
Received into Full Communion	1,296
First Communions	7,030
Confirmations	5,300
Marriages:	
Catholic	985
Interfaith	268
Total Marriages	1,253
Deaths	3,650
Total Catholic Population	979,091
Total Population	3,524,422

Former Bishops—Rt. Revs. EUGENE O'CONNELL, D.D., ord. May 21, 1842; cons. Titular Bishop of Flaviopolis and appt. Vicar Apostolic of Marysville, Feb. 3, 1861; appt. First Bishop of Grass Valley, March 22, 1868; resigned March 17, 1884 and appt. Titular Bishop of Joppa; died Dec. 4, 1891; PATRICK MANOGUE, D.D., ord. Dec. 21, 1861; cons. Titular Bishop of Ceremos, Coadjutor to Bishop O'Connell of Grass Valley, Jan. 16, 1881; succeeded to the See of Grass Valley on Bishop O'Connell's resignation, March 17, 1884; became the first Bishop of Sacramento, May 1886; died Feb. 27, 1895; THOMAS GRACE, D.D., cons. June 16, 1896; died Dec. 27, 1921; PATRICK J. KEANE, D.D., ord. June 20, 1895; cons. Bishop of Samaria, Dec. 14, 1920; appt. to See of Sacramento, March 17, 1922; died Sept. 1, 1928; Most Revs. ROBERT J. ARMSTRONG, D.D., Litt.D., ord. Dec. 10, 1910; cons. March 12, 1929; died Jan. 14, 1957; JOSEPH T. MCGUCKEN, D.D., S.T.D., LL.D., ord. Jan. 16, 1928; cons. Titular Bishop of Sanavo and Auxiliary Bishop of Los Angeles, March 19, 1941; Coadjutor Bishop of Sacramento, Oct. 26, 1955; succeeded to Jan. 14, 1957, as Bishop of Sacramento; promoted to the See of San Francisco, Feb. 21, 1962; died Oct. 6, 1983; ALDEN J. BELL, D.D., M.S.S.W., ord. May 14, 1932; appt. Titular Bishop of Rhodopolis and Auxiliary Bishop of Los Angeles, April 18, 1956; cons. June 4, 1956; appt. Bishop of Sacramento, March 30, 1962; retired March 15, 1979; died Aug. 28, 1982; JOHN S. CUMMINS, D.D., ord. Jan. 24, 1953; appt. Titular Bishop of Lambesi and Auxiliary Bishop of Sacramento, Feb. 26, 1974; cons. May 26, 1974; appt. Bishop of Oakland, May 3, 1977; FRANCIS A. QUINN, D.D., Ed.D., ord. June 15, 1946; appt. Titular Bishop of Numana and Auxiliary Bishop of San Francisco, April 28, 1978; Episcopal Ordination, June 29, 1978; appt. Bishop of Sacramento, Dec. 18, 1979; retired Nov. 30, 1993; ALPHONSE GALLEGOS, O.A.R., D.D., ord. May 24, 1958; appt. Titular Bishop of Sassabe and Auxiliary Bishop of Sacramento, Sept. 1, 1981; cons. Nov. 4, 1981; died Oct. 6, 1991; WILLIAM K. WEIGAND, D.D., ord. May 25, 1963; appt. Bishop of Salt Lake City Sept. 3, 1980; ord. and installed Nov. 17, 1980; appt. Bishop of Sacramento Nov. 30, 1993; installed Jan. 27, 1994; retired Nov. 30, 2008.

Moderator of the Curia—Very Rev. Msgr. JAMES T. MURPHY. Tel: 916-733-0200; Fax: 916-733-0215.

Vicar General—Very Rev. Msgr. JAMES T. MURPHY. Tel: 916-733-0200; Fax: 916-733-0215.

Director of Finance—Mr. THOMAS J. MCNAMARA. Tel: 916-733-0277; Fax: 916-733-0295.

Director of Pastoral Services—KATHY CONNER. Tel: 916-733-0200; Fax: 916-733-0215.

Interim Vicar Episcopal for Clergy—Very Rev. Msgr. JAMES T. MURPHY. Tel: 916-733-0200; Fax: 916-733-0215.

Director of Hispanic Institute—Sr. VIRGINIA ALCALA, S.C.J.C. Tel: 916-733-0123; Fax: 916-733-0195.

Interim Director Permanent Diaconate—Very Rev. Msgr. JAMES T. MURPHY. Tel: 916-733-0244; Fax: 916-733-0224.

Director of Social Services—Very Rev. MICHAEL F. KIERNAN. Tel: 916-733-0253; Fax: 916-733-0224.

Chancellor—KATHY CONNER. Tel: 916-733-0200; Fax: 916-733-0215.

Vice Chancellor and Secretary to the Bishop—Rev. TIMOTHY NONDORF.

Coordinator for Retired Priests—Rev. LIAM J. MAC CARTHY (Retired). Tel: 916-698-1482.

Delegate for Deacons—Deacon LUIGI DEL GAUDIO,

2110 Broadway, Sacramento, 95818-2541. Tel: 916-733-0256; Fax: 916-733-0224.

Vicars Forane—Revs. JOYLE MARTINEZ, (Shasta); REY BERSABAL, (Gold Country); BRIAN ATIENZA, (Mother Lode); MERVIN P. CONCEPCION, (Siskiyou); RENIER C. SIVA, (Ridge); LINO O. OTERO, L.C., (Southern Suburbs); BLAISE R. BERG, S.T.D., (Sutter Buttes); ARNOLD ORTIZ, O.S.J., (West Placer); LORETO BONG ROJAS, (Yolo); MATHEW M. MARANKULAM, (Solano); Very Rev. MICHAEL F. KIERNAN, (City); Rev. EDUINO T. SILVEIRA, (American River).

Diocesan Tribunal— Please direct all requests to the Tribunal. *2110 Broadway, Sacramento, 95818-2541.* Tel: 916-733-0225; Fax: 916-733-0224.

Judicial Vicar—Very Rev. MARK R. RICHARDS, J.C.L.

Adjutant Judicial Vicar—Rev. CESAR R. AGEAS.

Judges—Revs. JOSEPH HUYEN NGUYEN, J.C.L.; CESAR R. AGEAS; VINCENT R. JUAN; LYNDA ROBITAILLE, J.C.D.; Rev. DAVID L. DEIBEL, J.D., J.C.L.

Promoter of Justice—VACANT.

Defenders of the Bond—Revs. VINCENT R. JUAN; CESAR R. AGEAS; DEBORAH A. BARTON, J.C.L.

Approved Advocates—SUSAN BOONE; CAROL LEE; LUCIA BARRON-RODRIGUEZ; YVETTE ESPINOZA.

Notaries—CAROL LEE; SUE BOONE; LUCI GUADARRRAMA; YVETTE ESPINOZA.

College of Consultors—Very Rev. Msgr. JAMES T. MURPHY; Revs. ALDRIN BASARTE; OSCAR GOMEZ-MEDINA; ALBERT O'CONNOR (Retired); Very Rev. MARK R. RICHARDS, J.C.L.

Diocesan Offices and Directors

AIDS, Ministry to—Rev. JOHN J. HEALY, Coord., Mercy General Hospital, 4001 J St., Sacramento, 95819. Tel: 916-453-4753.

Alcoholism Advisory Board—Rev. THOMAS J. MAGUIRE (Retired). Tel: 916-985-2561, Ext. 4206.

Archives—Rev. JOHN E. BOLL, Archivist, 2110 Broadway, Sacramento, 95818-2541. Tel: 916-733-0299; 916-480-2165.

Black Catholic Council—CHARLENE HARRIS, Office: 2110 Broadway, Sacramento, 95818-2541. Tel: 916-733-0160; 916-227-2288; Fax: 916-733-0195.

Building Committee— Direct inquiries to: Mr. THOMAS J. MCNAMARA, Staff, Diocesan Pastoral Center, 2110 Broadway, Sacramento, 95818-2541. Tel: 916-733-0277; Fax: 916-733-0295.

Department of Evangelization and Catechesis—STEPHEN PATTON, Respect Life/NFP Coord.; CARSON WEBER, Assoc. Dir. New Media Evangelization & Catechesis; Deacon ANTONIO RAMIREZ, Coord., Spanish Catechesis; Sr. VIRGINIA ALCALA, S.C.J.C., Asst. Hispanic Catechesis; STEVE PATTON, Project Rachel Coord. Coordinators Deaf Ministry: MARY PHAM; STANLEY SIMONET; KEVIN STASZKOW, Dir. Youth & Young Adult; KARLA MARQUEZ, Youth & Young Adult Coord.

Department of Social Services—Very Rev. MICHAEL F. KIERNAN, Vicar, 2110 Broadway, Sacramento, 95818. Tel: 916-733-0253; Fax: 916-733-0224; LORI ROSENE, Dir. Pendola Center; KATHLEEN BARBER, Admin. Camp Recreation.

Catholic Charities of Sacramento, Inc.—Very Rev. MICHAEL F. KIERNAN, Exec. Dir., 2110 Broadway, Sacramento, 95818. Tel: 916-733-0253; Fax: 916-733-0224.

Communications and Media—BOB DUNNING. Tel: 916-733-0168; Fax: 916-733-0195.

Presbyteral Council—Direct all correspondence to: 2110 Broadway, Sacramento, 95818-2541. Rev. CESAR R. AQEAS. Tel: 916-733-0225; Most Rev. JAIME SOTO, M.S.W.; Revs. JEREMY P. LEATHERBY; BRIAN ATIENZA; JOEL S. GENABIA; Very Rev. MARK R. RICHARDS, J.C.L.; Revs. CHARLES KELLY; JONATHAN B. MOLINA; LINO O. OTERO, L.C.; Very Rev. Msgr. JAMES T. MURPHY; Revs. JESUS T. SORIANO; LUIS IDO URREGO; JOHN P. SULLIVAN (Retired); RICHARD L. PARKS, C.P.; ALDRIN BASARTE; SHERWIN S. COLASTE; CHRISTOPHER FRAZER; OSCAR GOMEZ-MEDINA; RENIER C. SIVA; Very Rev. Msgr. JAMES T. MURPHY; Rev. TIMOTHY NONDORF; Deacon JERRY PAULY.

Development—VACANT, Diocesan Dir., 2110 Broadway, Sacramento, 95818-2541. Tel: 916-733-0266; Fax: 916-733-0295.

Diocesan Pastoral Council— Please direct all inquiries to: KATHY CONNER, Chancellor. Tel: 916-733-0204.

Diocese of Sacramento Priests' Pension Trust—Most Rev. JAIME SOTO, M.S.W., Plan Sponsor. Please direct all inquiries to: Rev. Msgr. MURROUGH C. WALLACE (Retired), St. Theresa Church, 1041 Lyons Ave., South Lake Tahoe, 96150. Tel: 530-544-3533; Fax: 916-544-4662.

Divorced and Separated, Ministry to—Direct inquiries to: Catholic Evangelization & Catechesis, 2110 Broadway, Sacramento, 95818-2541. Tel: 916-733-0123; Fax: 916-733-0195.

Due Process— Direct inquiries to: Very Rev. MARK R. RICHARDS, J.C.L., 2110 Broadway, Sacramento, 95818-2541. Tel: 916-733-0225; Fax: 916-733-0224.

Eastern Catholic Churches—VACANT.

"Ecclesia Dei" Community (Latin Mass)—Rev. MATTHEW MCNEELY, F.S.S.P., Mailing Address: 5461 44th St., Sacramento, 95820. Tel: 916-455-5114; Fax: 916-455-1018.

Ecumenical & Interreligious Affairs—Very Rev. MICHAEL F. KIERNAN, 2110 Broadway, Sacramento, 95818-2541. Tel: 916-733-0253; Fax: 916-733-0224.

Finance Council—Members: Rev. Msgr. T. BRENDAN O'SULLIVAN (Retired); ROBERT GRANUCCI, Esq.; ANNE HECK LONG, CPA; Mr. MICHAEL PROFUMO, CPA; Very Rev. MARK R. RICHARDS, J.C.L.; SUSAN GODWIN; Rev. F. IGNATIUS HARAN (Retired); Mr. LON BURFORD; Mr. MICHAEL HACKARD, Esq.; Rev. Msgr. ROBERT P. WALTON. Ex Officio: Very Rev. Msgr. JAMES T. MURPHY; Mr. THOMAS J. MCNAMARA, Chancery Office, 2110 Broadway, Sacramento, 95818-2541. Tel: 916-733-0277.

Investment Review Committee— Direct inquiries to: Mr. THOMAS J. MCNAMARA, 2110 Broadway, Sacramento, 95818-2541. Tel: 916-733-0277; Fax: 916-733-0295.

Finance Office—Mr. THOMAS J. MCNAMARA, Dir., 2110 Broadway, Sacramento, 95818-2541. Tel: 916-733-0277; Fax: 916-733-0295.

Hispanic Apostolate—Deacon GERMAN TORO, 2110 Broadway, Sacramento, 95818-2541. Tel: 916-733-0177; Fax: 916-733-0195.

Holy Childhood Association—2110 Broadway, Sacramento, 95818-2541. Tel: 916-733-0110; Fax: 916-733-0120.

Hospitals, Diocesan Liaison for Catholic—Rev. JOHN J. HEALY, Mercy General Hospital, 4001 J St., Sacramento, 95819. Tel: 916-453-4753.

Lay Personnel—KATHY CONNER, Mgr., 2110 Broadway, Sacramento, 95818-2541. Tel: 916-733-0200; Fax: 916-733-0215.

Marriage Preparation—STEPHEN PATTON, Assoc. Dir., Evangelization & Catechesis, 2110 Broadway, Sacramento, 95818-2541. Tel: 916-733-0123.

Magazine— "Catholic Herald" Ms. JULIE SLY, Editor, 2110 Broadway, Sacramento, 95818. Tel: 916-733-0170.

Ongoing Education of Clergy—Very Rev. Msgr. JAMES T. MURPHY, Interim Vicar Episcopal for Clergy, 2110 Broadway, Sacramento, 95818. Tel: 916-733-0200.

Permanent Diaconate Office—Very Rev. Msgr. JAMES T. MURPHY, Dir. Delegate for Deacons: Deacon LUIGI DEL GAUDIO, Office, 2110 Broadway, Sacramento, 95818-2541. Tel: 916-733-0244.

Priests' Personnel Board, Diocesan—Please direct all inquiries to: Priest Personnel, Office of the Bishop, 2110 Broadway, Sacramento, 95818. Tel: 916-733-0200. Revs. DANIEL A. LOONEY, Chm.; BLAISE BERG; Very Rev. Msgr. JAMES T. MURPHY; Revs. HUMBERTO GOMEZ; SYLVESTER KWIATKOWSKI; ALBERT O'CONNOR (Retired); JONATHAN B. MOLINA, Chm.; LIAM J. MAC CARTHY (Retired); BENEDICT DELEON; TIMOTHY NONDORF.

Propagation of the Faith—Rev. Msgr. JAMES F. CHURCH, Dir., 2110 Broadway, Sacramento, 95818-2541. Tel: 916-733-0200; Fax: 916-733-0215.

Properties Committee— Please direct all inquiries to: Mr. THOMAS J. MCNAMARA, Staff, 2110 Broadway, Sacramento, 95818-2541. Tel: 916-733-0277.

Radio and Television— (See Communications and Media).

Research and Planning—VACANT.

Respect Life/NFP—STEPHEN PATTON, Diocesan Coord., Catholic Evangelization & Catechesis, 2110 Broadway, Sacramento, 95818-2541. Tel: 916-733-0123.

Schools—Mr. RICK MAYA, Dir. Catholic Schools, 2110 Broadway, Sacramento, 95818-2541. Tel: 916-733-0110; Fax: 916-733-0120.

Pastoral Care Coordinator—CATHI FISHER. Tel: 916-733-0142.

Safe Environment Coordinator—MARY HASTINGS. Tel: 916-733-0227.

Vocations—Rev. FRANCISCO J. HERNANDEZ-GOMEZ.

Worship, Office of—Mrs. SANDRA HOLLAND, Dir., 2110 Broadway, Sacramento, 95818. Tel: 916-733-0221; Fax: 916-733-0295.

Lay Organizations—

Beginning Experience—MARIE ALFUSO, Contact, Mailing Address: P.O. Box 161761, Sacramento, 95816. Tel: 916-835-2282. Web: www.sacramentobe.org. Email: besacramento@yahoo.com.

Catholic Alumni Club—VACANT, Mailing Address: P.O. Box 1777, Carmichael, 95609-1777. Tel: 916-962-6107.

Catholic Daughters of the Americas—

Court Sacramento #172— St. Paul Parish, Florin FRANCIS B. GOMEZ, Regent, 6940 Mirador Way, Sacramento, 95828. Tel: 916-421-0300.

Court Our Lady of the Visitation #1890— St. Philomene Parish, Sacramento VALERIE K. MUNOZ, 5069 Pasadena Ave., Sacramento, 95841.

Court St. Felicitas #1939— St. Lawrence Parish, North Highlands PAT KORF, Regent, 6255 Stagecoach Dr., Sacramento, 95842. Tel: 916-331-4255.

Court Our Lady of Wisdom #2392— St. John Vianney Parish, Rancho Cordova JOAN DUBOIS, Regent, 8313 Pillares Dr., Sacramento, 95827. Tel: 916-363-2847.

Charismatic Renewal—Deacon JERRY PAULY, Assoc. Diocesan Liaison. Tel: 916-452-6866.

Cursillo Movement—Office: 2110 Broadway, Sacramento, 95818-2541. Tel: 916-733-0181.

Daughters of Isabella—KIMBERLY PEREZ, Regent, Mailing Address: P.O. Box 276, Galt, 95632. Tel: 209-745-1389.

Diocesan Council of Catholic Women—Rev. Msgr. EDWARD J. KAVANAGH, Mod. (Retired); DEE TASSINARI, Pres., 6628 Oak Branch Ct., Citrus Heights, 95621. Tel: 916-729-7684.

Italian Catholic Federation—LYNDA COOK, District Pres., Mailing Address: P.O. Box 1780, Sutter Creek, 95685. Tel: 209-267-9235.

Knights of Peter Claver and Ladies Auxiliary—PHILLIP MOSEBY, Grand Knight, Council #175, 6391 Weatherford Way, Sacramento, 95823. Tel: 916-224-7186; LENA N. HALL, Ladies Auxiliary Area Deputy, 559 Rivergate Way, Sacramento, 95831. Tel: 916-392-2796.

Knights of Columbus—JOHN NORWOOD, Northern California Chapter Pres., 1523 Pine Valley Cir., Roseville, 95661. Tel: 916-783-0453.

Legion of Mary—Rev. ALDRIN BASARTE, 1040 39th St., Sacramento, 95816. Tel: 916-452-4136; HOPE HARRINGTON, Pres., 1056 44th St., Sacramento, 95819. Tel: 916-456-1015.

Marriage Encounter Worldwide—Coordinators: EDDY HOOD; ABBY HOOD. Tel: 707-451-9871. Additional Contacts: PAT SWEENEY; DIANE SWEENEY. Tel: 707-447-4481; 866-825-2046. Email: pndsweeney@aol.com. Web: www.lovemoredeeply.org. Hispanic Coordinators: ABEL CARDENAS; YUYU CARDENAS. Tel: 916-606-7849. Web: www.wwme.org.

Scouting, Diocesan Catholic Committee on—Very Rev. MARK R. RICHARDS, J.C.L., Chap., 2110 Broadway, Sacramento, 95818. Tel: 916-733-0200; KEVIN STASZKOW, Contact. Tel: 916-733-0152; Fax: 916-733-0195.

Secular Franciscan Order—

Little Portion Fraternity—KATHLEEN MOLARO, SFO Regl. Sec. Tel: 530-272-1416.

Sacramento-St. Francis of Assisi Parish— Fraternidad De San Juan (Spanish) VACANT.

Secular Order of Discalced Carmelites—JUDY CARLSON, 7056 Rushwood Dr., El Dorado Hills, 95762. Tel: 916-933-6163.

Serra Club of Sacramento—ROBERT LEACH, 2161 Tenstone Loop, Roseville, 95747. Tel: 916-797-0830. Email: rcl1939@gmail.com.

Young Ladies Institute—MARILYN WALTER, Mailing Address: 2605 Zinfandel Dr., Rancho Cordova, 95670. Tel: 916-638-7905; Fax: 916-635-4381.

St. Thomas More Society—HERB BOLZ, Pres. Tel: 530-848-7252. Email: stms.sacramento@yahoo.com. Web: www.sacstms.org.

CLERGY, PARISHES, MISSIONS AND PAROCHIAL SCHOOLS

CITY OF SACRAMENTO

(SACRAMENTO COUNTY)

1—CATHEDRAL OF THE BLESSED SACRAMENT (1889) Most Rev. Jaime Soto; Very Rev. Michael F. Kiernan, Rector; Deacons Don De Haven; Raul Leon; Jorge Usi; John Gisla. Catechetical Center Cathedral Parish Hall conducted by parish CCD and Daughters of Charity of Canossa. In Res., Very Rev. Msgr. James T. Murphy; Very Rev. Mark R. Richards; Rev. Kieran M. McMahon.

Church: 1017 Eleventh St., 95814. Tel: 916-444-3071; Fax: 916-443-2749. Email: blessed@cathedralsacramento.org. Web: www.cathedralsacramento.org.

Catechesis/Religious Program—1949 North Ave., 95838. Tel: 916-444-5364; 916-925-4001; Fax: 916-925-8897. Email: jenny@cathedralsacramento.org. Sr. Jenny Aldeghi, D.R.E. Students 545.

2—ALL HALLOWS (1942) Revs. Oscar Gomez-Medina; Julian Medina, Parochial Vicar; Deacons Tou Moua;

Orin Rovito.
Res.: 5500 13th Ave., 95820. Tel: 916-456-7206; Fax: 916-456-7325.
Church: 5501 13th Ave., 95820.
Catechesis/Religious Program— Twinned with St. Peter Parish, Sacramento. 410 Spanish; 140 English 550.

3—ST. ANNE (1961) Rev. Joseph Huong (Vietnam); Deacons Pedro Manriquez, (Retired); Alani Vivi.
Res.: 7724 24th St., 95832. Tel: 916-422-8380; Fax: 916-422-7538.
Catechesis/Religious Program—Students 150.

4—ST. ANTHONY (1974) Rev. Manuel B. Soria; Rev. Msgr. T. Brendan O'Sullivan, Pastor Emeritus (Retired); Rev. John E. Boll, Pastor Emeritus; Deacons James Healy; Richard Koppes; Michael Crowley.
Res.: 660 Florin Rd., 95831. Tel: 916-428-5678; Fax: 916-428-0312. Email: office@stanthony-sacramento.org. Web: stanthony-sacramento.org.
Catechesis/Religious Program—Tel: 916-392-6362. Students 271.

5—ST. CHARLES BORROMEO (1960), (Spanish), Revs. Jeronimo Marcelo, Parochial Admin.; Brent C. Nall, Parochial Vicar; Eugenio Lopez-Restrepo, Parochial Vicar.
Res.: 7584 Center Pkwy., 95823. Tel: 916-421-5177; Fax: 916-392-4831.
School—7580 Center Pkwy., 95823. Tel: 916-421-6189; Fax: 916-421-3954. Susan Jaftok, Prin. Lay Teachers 17; Students 218.
Catechesis/Religious Program—Tel: 916-421-1063; 916-421-7174. Students 670.

6—DIVINE MERCY (2005) Rev. Soane T. Kaniseli.
2175 Burberry Way, 95835. Tel: 916-256-3134. Email: divinemercy.parish@sbcglobal.net. Web: www.divinemercynatomas.org.
Catechesis/Religious Program—Rev. Octavio Ventura, L.C., D.R.E. Students 326.

7—ST. ELIZABETH (1909), (Portuguese), Revs. Giancarlo Mittempergher, C.S.S. (Italy); Antonio dos Santos, C.S.S. (Brazil), Parochial Vicar.
Res.: 1817 12th St., 95811-6508. Tel: 916-442-2333; Fax: 916-498-0676. Email: stelizportugal@gmail.com. Web: www.stelizabethsac.org.
Catechesis/Religious Program—Students 22.

8—ST. FRANCIS OF ASSISI (1894) Rev. Anthony Garibaldi, O.F.M.; Sr. Margaret Chambers, O.M.C., Pastoral Assoc.; Michael Humphrey, Music Dir.
1066 26th St., 95816. Tel: 916-443-8084; Fax: 916-443-7356. Email: info@stfrancisparish.com. Web: www.stfrancisparish.com. In Res., Rev. Tran Nguyen, O.F.M.; Bros. John Summers, O.F.M. Email: johnsumm@att.net; Mark Schroeder, O.F.M.; Jeff Shackleton, O.F.M.
School—2500 K St., 95816. Tel: 916-442-5494; Fax: 916-442-1390. Web: www.stfranciselem.org. Cheryl Ramirez, Prin. Lay Teachers 15; Students 308.
Catechesis/Religious Program—Combined with Newman Catholic Community. Students 468.
Parish Children's Faith Formation Program—Tel: 916-443-8084, Ext. 112. Email: georgies@stfrancisparish.com. Georgie Saydak, Dir. Youth Faith Formation. Students 160.

9—HOLY SPIRIT (1940) Rev. Daniel A. Looney; Rev. Msgr. Albert G. O'Connor, Pastor Emeritus (Retired); Rev. Charles Brady, Pastor Emeritus (Retired).
Res.: 3159 Land Park Dr., 95818. Tel: 916-443-5442; Fax: 916-446-9015. Email: holyspiritlandpark@sbcglobal.net. Web: www.holyspiritparishsac.org.
School—3920 W. Land Park Dr., 95822. Tel: 916-448-5663; Fax: 916-444-9631. Fran Wise, Prin. Lay Teachers 16; Students 299.
Catechesis/Religious Program—Tel: 916-448-8257. Students 79.
Convent—Sisters of Mercy (Auburn, CA), Tel: 916-448-3578.

10—ST. IGNATIUS OF LOYOLA (1954) Revs. Michael E. Moynahan, S.J.; Gerald P. McCourt, S.J., Parochial Vicar; Thomas G. Piquado, S.J., Parochial Vicar; Arthur J. Wehr, S.J., Parochial Vicar; Deacon Jackson Gualco.
Res.: P.O. Box 254647, 95865-4647. Tel: 916-482-6060; Fax: 916-972-8037.
School—3245 Arden Way, 95825. Tel: 916-488-3907; Fax: 916-488-0569. Patricia Lane, Prin. Lay Teachers 19; Students 380.
Catechesis/Religious Program—Tel: 916-482-9666, Ext. 238; Fax: 916-482-6573. Fatima Avila-Ohlsen, D.R.E. Students 130.
Ignatian Institute for Family Life—Tel: 916-482-9666, Ext. 205.

11—IMMACULATE CONCEPTION (1909) Rev. Isnardo Serrano, C.O.; Deacon Gerald Pauly.
Parish Office—3263 First Ave., 95817. Tel: 916-452-6866; Fax: 916-452-3879. Email: info@icparishsac.com. Web: www.immaculateconceptionsacramento.org.
Catechesis/Religious Program—Students 200.

12—ST. JEONG-HAE ELIZABETH (1993), (Korean), [CEM] Rev. Chundo Her (Korea, North).
Res.: 9354 Kiefer Blvd., 95826. Tel: 916-368-9204; Fax: 916-368-8304. Web: www.sackcc.net.
Catechesis/Religious Program—Students 45.

13—ST. JOSEPH'S (1924) Revs. Luis Ido Urrego (Colombia); Michael Vaughan, Vicar; Sr. Rose Ereba, H.H.C.J., Parish Min.; Deacon Henry Garcia, (Retired).
Res.: 1717 El Monte Ave., 95815. Tel: 916-925-3584; Fax: 916-925-1045. Web: saintjosephsacramento.org.
School—(Grades PreSchool-8), 1718 El Monte Ave., 95815. Tel: 916-925-1465; Fax: 916-925-0963. Mrs. Patricia Peterson, Prin. Filipino Sisters Religious of the Virgin Mary 1; Lay Teachers 8; Students 160.
Catechesis/Religious Program—Tel: 916-925-3485, Ext. 24. Sr. Soledad Castillo, H.R.F., D.R.E. (Spanish); Irene Ogbonna, D.R.E. Students 160.

14—ST. MARIA GORETTI (2007) Rev. Terry A. Fulton; Deacon Raymond Helgeson.
8998 Robins Rd., 95829. Email: pastor@smgcc.net. Web: www.saintmariagoretti.net.
Catechesis/Religious Program—Students 192.

15—ST. MARY (1906) Revs. James Narithookil, C.M.I.; Francis Chirackal, C.M.I., Parochial Vicar; Deacons George Kriske; Luigi Del Gaudio.
Res.: 1333 58th St., 95819. Tel: 916-452-0296; Fax: 916-452-3908. Web: www.stmarys-sacramento.com.
School—1351 58th St., 95819. Tel: 916-452-1100; Fax: 916-453-2750. Web: www.saintmaryschool-.com. Lawrence J. White, Prin. Lay Teachers 16; Aides 6; Students 383.
Catechesis/Religious Program—Tel: 916-452-0296, Ext. 20. Email: rciaoffice_stmarys@comcast.net. Students 50.

16—OUR LADY OF GUADALUPE SHRINE (1958), (Hispanic), Revs. Lino O. Otero, L.C.; Gregory Woodward, L.C., Parochial Vicar.
Mailing Address: 711 T St., 95811. In Res., Revs. Thomas MoyLan, L.C.; Anthony Bailleres, L.C.
Res.: 1909 7th St., 95811. Tel: 916-442-3211; Fax: 916-442-3679.
Catechesis/Religious Program—Tel: 916-446-3500. Students 280.

17—OUR LADY OF LOURDES (1957) Revs. Troy David Powers; Anthony Traynor, Pastor Emeritus (Retired); Pius Amah.
Res.: 1951 North Ave., 95838. Tel: 916-925-5313; Fax: 916-922-0625. Email: ourladyoflourdes@comcast.net.
Catechesis/Religious Program—Tel: 916-925-4001. Students 98.
Convent—Daughters of Charity of Canossa, 1949 North Ave., 95838. Tel: 916-925-4001; Fax: 916-925-8897. Email: fdcc_sac@yahoo.com.

18—ST. PAUL (1958) Revs. Vicente Teneza; Felipe Paraguya (Philippines), Parochial Vicar; Deacons Charles Morrison; Antonio Ramirez.
Res.: 7200 Gardner Ave., P.O. Box 292280, 95829. Tel: 916-381-5200; Fax: 916-381-0332. Email: saintpaulcatholic@comcast.net. Web: www.stpaul-florin.org.
Catechesis/Religious Program—Students 377.

19—ST. PETER (1955) Revs. Oscar Gomez-Medina; Julian Medina; Deacons Tou Moua; Orin Rovito; Orin Rovito.
Mailing Address: *All Hallows Church*, 5500 13th Ave., 95820.
Church: 6210 McMahon Dr., 95824. Tel: 916-456-7206; Fax: 916-456-7325.
Catechesis/Religious Program— Combined with All Hallows, Sacramento
Convent—Sisters Servants of the Blessed Sacrament (Guadalajara, Mexico), 5929 61st St., 95824. Tel: 916-457-0182.

20—ST. PHILOMENE (1948) Revs. Eduino T. Silveira; John K. Hannan, Pastor Emeritus (Retired); Gerald J. Ryle, Pastor Emeritus (Retired); Deacon Charles Cheever; Alan Nissila, Music Dir.
Res.: 2428 Bell St., 95825. Tel: 916-481-6757; Fax: 916-481-1603. Web: www.stphilomene.com.
School—2320 El Camino Ave., 95821. Tel: 916-489-1506; Fax: 916-489-2642. Email: dmosbrucker@stphilomene.org. Web: www.stphilomene.org. Dr. Michele Hamilton, Prin. Lay Teachers 11; Students 123.
Catechesis/Religious Program— Michaela Escobar, Dir. Faith Formation; Tracy Urban, Dir. Faith Formation. Students 830.

21—PRESENTATION OF THE BLESSED VIRGIN MARY (1961) Rev. Jeremy P. Leatherby.
Res.: 4123 Robertson Ave., 95821. Tel: 916-481-7441; Fax: 916-481-2841. Email: barbara@presentationparish.org; amy@presentationparish.org. Web: www.presentationparish.org.
School—3100 Norris Ave., 95821. Tel: 916-482-0351; Fax: 916-482-0377. Lay Teachers 13; Students 215.
Convent—3110 Norris Ave., 95821.
Catechesis/Religious Program—Tel: 916-482-8883; Fax: 916-481-2841. Students 215.

22—ST. ROBERT (1955) Rev. Santiago Raudes.
Res.: 2243 Irvin Way, 95822. Tel: 916-451-1475, Ext. 10; Fax: 916-451-0534. Email: churchst.robert@comcast.net.
School—2251 Irvin Way, 95822. Tel: 916-452-2111; Fax: 916-452-5765. Brian James, Prin. Lay Teachers 10; Students 245.
Catechesis/Religious Program—Cell: 916-730-5869; Fax: 916-454-1747. Students 32.

23—ST. ROSE (1942) Rev. Msgrs. James F. Church, Parochial Admin.; Edward J. Kavanagh, Pastor Emeritus (Retired); Rev. Isnardo Serrano, C.O., Parochial Vicar.
Res.: Oak Park Station, P.O. Box 5037, 95817. Tel: 916-421-1414; Fax: 916-421-0460.
School—St. Patrick Succeed Academy, 5945 Franklin Blvd., 95823. Tel: 916-421-4963; Fax: 916-421-3849. Laura Allen, Prin. Lay Teachers 14; Students 290.
Catechesis/Religious Program—Tel: 916-392-5679. Students 780.

24—SACRED HEART OF JESUS (1926) Rev. Msgr. Robert P. Walton; Deacons Gilbert Parra; William Riehl.
Res.: 1040 39th St., 95816. Tel: 916-452-4136; Fax: 916-457-9361.
School—Sacred Heart, 856 39th St., 95816. Tel: 916-456-1576; Fax: 916-456-4773. Theresa Sparks, Prin. Lay Teachers 13; Students 302.
Catechesis/Religious Program—Tel: 916-454-3640. Kristin Hansen, D.R.E. Students 38.

25—ST. STEPHEN THE FIRST MARTYR PARISH (2002), (Tridentine Latin Mass) Revs. John Lyons, D.M.V., Parochial Vicar; Matthew McNeely, F.S.S.P., Parochial Admin.; Michael Stinson, F.S.S.P., Parochial Vicar.
5461-44th St., 95820. Tel: 916-455-5114; Fax: 916-455-1018. Email: stephenproto@yahoo.com. Web: www.sacfssp.com.
Catechesis/Religious Program—Tel: 916-455-5114; Fax: 916-455-1018. Students 203.

26—VIETNAMESE MARTYRS PARISH (1976), (Vietnamese), Revs. Philip B. Tran, C.M.C.; Charles Pham, C.M.C.; Deacons Anthony Huy Nguyen; Tien Nam Nguyen; An Binh Nguyen.
Res.: 8191 Florin Rd., 95828. Tel: 916-383-4276; Fax: 916-383-4276.
Church: 8181 Florin Rd., 95828.
Catechesis/Religious Program—Students 560.
Mission—St. Dominic 475 E. I St., Benicia, 94510-0756. Tel: 707-747-7220.

OUTSIDE THE CITY OF SACRAMENTO

ALTURAS, MODOC CO., SACRED HEART (1883) Rev. Bernardin Mugabowakigeri.
Res.: 507 E. Fourth St., 96101-3406. Tel: 530-233-2119; Fax: 530-233-2575.
Catechesis/Religious Program—Students 25.
Mission—St. James Bonner St. & Garfield St., Cedarville, Modoc Co. 96104.

ANDERSON, SHASTA CO., SACRED HEART (1949) Rev. Philip J. Wells; Deacons Michael Evans; Anthony Short; Rich Valles.
Res.: 3141 St. Stephen's Dr., 96007. Tel: 530-365-8573; Fax: 530-365-9544. Email: info@sacredheartparish.com. Web: sacredheartparish.com.
Catechesis/Religious Program—Students 65.
Mission—St. Anne 2nd St. & Main St., Cottonwood, Shasta Co. 96022.

AUBURN, PLACER CO.

1—ST. JOSEPH (1861) [CEM] Rev. Brian Atienza; Deacons Richard Cadanesso; Mike Young.
Res.: 1162 Lincoln Way, 95603. Tel: 530-885-2956; Fax: 530-823-6676. Email: stjosephparish@auburncatholic.com. Web: www.auburncatholic.com.
School—11610 Atwood Rd., 95603. Tel: 530-885-4490; Fax: 530-885-0182. Sr. Ann Marie Miller, R.S.M., Prin. Lay Teachers 20; Students 174.
Catechesis/Religious Program— Katie Prust, C.R.E. Students 97.
Mission—St. Joseph of Foresthill (1994) 22200 Foresthill Rd., Foresthill, Placer Co. 95631.
Station— Forest Hill.

2—ST. TERESA OF AVILA PARISH (1994) Rev. Michael A. Carroll.
11600 Atwood Rd., 95603. Email: info@stteresaauburn.com. Web: stteresaauburn.com.
Catechesis/Religious Program—Judy Jones, C.R.E. Students 160.

BENICIA, SOLANO CO., ST. DOMINIC (1854) [CEM] Revs. Michael Hurley, O.P., Parish Admin. & Dominican Superior; LaSalle Sean Hallissey, O.P., Parochial Vicar; John Marie Bingham, O.P., Parochial Vicar; Deacons Ed Lazarek, (Retired); John Flanagan, (Retired); Juvencio Vela.
Mailing Address: P.O. Box 756, 94510-0756. In Res., Rev. Victor Cavalli, O.P. (Retired).
Res. & Church: 475 E. I St., 94510-3427. Tel:

707-747-7220; Fax: 707-745-5642.
School—935 E. 5th St., 94510-3427. Tel: 707-745-1266; Fax: 707-745-1841. Theresa Cullen, Prin. Lay Teachers 22; Students 351.
Catechesis/Religious Program—Students 551.

BURNEY, SHASTA CO., ST. FRANCIS OF ASSISI (1948) Rev. Efren Fergus Garcia Flores.
Mailing Address: 37464 Juniper Ave., P.O. Drawer 160, 96013.
Res. & Church: 37464 Juniper Ave., 96013. Tel: 530-335-2372; Fax: 530-335-2306. Web: www.stfrancisburney.org.
Catechesis/Religious Program—Students 52.
Mission—St. Stephen Hwy. 299, Bieber, Lassen Co. 96009. Students 16.
Mission—Our Lady of the Valley 43434 Main St., Fall River Mills, Shasta Co. 96028. Tel: 530-336-6212. Students 22.

CARMICHAEL, SACRAMENTO CO.

1—ST. JOHN THE EVANGELIST (1960) Revs. Thomas A. Bland; Arthur Najera Jr., Parochial Vicar; Deacons James Weeks, (Retired); Lawrence Niekamp. In Res., Rev. Alban Uba, S.M.M.M. (Nigeria).
Res.: 5751 Locust Ave., 95608. Tel: 916-483-8454; Fax: 916-481-8326. Email: office@sjecarmichael.org. Web: www.sjecarmichael.org.
School—5701 Locust Ave., 95608. Tel: 916-481-8845; Fax: 916-481-1319. Web: www.stjohnev.com. Mrs. Nancy Conroy. Lay Teachers 15; Students 224.
Catechesis/Religious Program—Tel: 916-483-4628. Sr. Hannah O'Donoghue, D.R.E. Students 150.

2—OUR LADY OF THE ASSUMPTION (1952) Revs. Brendan McKeefry; Hector Coria; Deacon Michael Tateishi.
Res.: 5057 Cottage Way, 95608. Tel: 916-481-5115; Fax: 916-481-4026. Email: parish@olaparish.net. Web: www.olaparish.net.
School—2141 Walnut Ave., 95608. Tel: 916-489-8958; Fax: 916-489-3237. Robert Love, Prin. Lay Teachers 23; Students 313.
Catechesis/Religious Program—Tel: 916-488-4626. Kimberly Sax, C.R.E. Students 162.

CHICO, BUTTE CO.

1—ST. JOHN THE BAPTIST (1878) Revs. Blaise R. Berg; J. Michael Baricuatro, Parochial Vicar; Deacons Jesus Padilla Campos; Stephen Schwartz. In Res., Rev. Juan Manuel Ponce.
Res.: 435 Chestnut St., 95928. Tel: 530-343-8741; Fax: 530-345-8602. Email: stjohn33@sbcglobal.net. Web: www.stjohnthebaptistchico.org.
School—Notre Dame Elementary School, (Grades K-8), 435 Hazel St., 95928. Tel: 530-342-2502; Fax: 530-342-6292. Web: www.ndschico.org. Ms. Teresa Sobieralski, Prin. Lay Teachers 13; Students 204.
Catechesis/Religious Program—Students 376.
Mission—St. James [JC] P.O. Box 562, Durham, Butte Co. 95938.

2—OUR DIVINE SAVIOR (1967) Rev. Joel S. Genabia.
Office: 566 E. Lassen Ave., 95973. Tel: 530-343-4248; Fax: 530-343-3538. Email: ourdivines@yahoo.com.
Catechesis/Religious Program—Students 190.

CITRUS HEIGHTS, SACRAMENTO CO., HOLY FAMILY (1949) Revs. Cesar R. Ageas, Parochial Admin. Pro-Tem; Polycarpo (Pol) R. Gumapo.
Res.: 7817 Old Auburn Rd., 95610. Tel: 916-723-2494; Fax: 916-723-0199. Email: holyfamilychurch@surewest.net. Web: parishesonline.com/scripts/hostedsites/org.asp?p=1&ID=17422.
School—Tel: 916-722-7788; Fax: 916-722-5297. Mr. Charles Suarez, Prin. Lay Teachers 9; Students 276.
Preschool—Tel: 916-722-4620; Fax: 916-722-4509. Lucy Eberhardt, Preschool Dir. Tel: 916-722-4620. Lay Teachers 9; Students 58.
Catechesis/Religious Program—Tel: 916-726-7217 (English); 916-721-3292 (Spanish). Bonnie Johnson, D.R.E. (English); Lupita Wandry, D.R.E. (Spanish). Students 293.

CLARKSBURG, YOLO CO., ST. JOSEPH (1893) Rev. Daniel Madigan.
Res. & Church Address: 32890 S. River Rd., 95612. Tel: 916-665-1132; Fax: 916-665-9264.
Catechesis/Religious Program—Students 55.

COLFAX, PLACER CO., ST. DOMINIC (1929) [CEM] Rev. Thomas L. Seabridge.
Mailing Address: 58 E. Oak St., P.O. Box 752, 95713.
Res. & Church: 58 E. Oak St., 95713. Tel: 530-346-2286; Fax: 530-346-8122.
Catechesis/Religious Program—Tel: 530-389-2553; Cell: 530-906-0302; Fax: 530-389-2653. Students 84.

COLUSA, COLUSA CO., OUR LADY OF LOURDES (1870) Rev. Arbel Cabasagan; Deacon Miguel Fernandez.
Parish Office: 745 Ware Ave., 95932. Tel: 530-458-4170; Fax: 530-458-8728. Web: www.ourladyoflourdescolusa.com.
Church: 345 Oak St., 95932.
School—(Grades PreK-8), 741 Ware Ave., 95932. Tel: 530-458-8208; Fax: 530-458-8657. Mrs. Barbara Genera, Prin. Lay Teachers 6; Students 128.
Catechesis/Religious Program—Students 140.
Mission—St. Joseph 1st St. & Center St., Princeton, Colusa Co. 95970.
Station—Our Lady of Sorrows [CEM] [JC] Sycamore.

CORNING, TEHAMA CO., IMMACULATE CONCEPTION (1946) [JC] Rev. Cormac Lacre.
Res.: 814 Solano St., 96021. Tel: 530-824-5879; Fax: 530-824-6534.
Catechesis/Religious Program—Tel: 530-824-4989. Students 80.
Mission—St. Stanislaus 4th St. & D St., Tehama, Tehama Co. 96090.

DAVIS, YOLO CO., ST. JAMES (1912) [JC] Rev. Loreto Bong Rojas; Deacons Paul Taloff, (Retired); Sam Colenzo; Clark Goecker; Joe O'Donnell.
1275 B St., 95616. Tel: 530-756-3636; Fax: 530-756-5342. Web: stjamesdavis.org. In Res., Revs. Richard Boyle, O.S.M.; Innocent Subiza (Rwanda).
School—1215 B St., 95616. Tel: 530-756-3946; Fax: 530-753-9765. Web: www.sjsdavis.com. David Perry, Prin. Lay Teachers 18; Students 309.
Catechesis/Religious Program—Tel: 530-756-3636, Ext. 208. Linda O'Hara, D.R.E. Students 412.
Newman Center— 514 C St., 95616. Tel: 530-753-7393; Fax: 530-753-2794.

DIXON, SOLANO CO., ST. PETER (1877) Rev. Eduardo W. Mendoza, P.E.S.; Deacon Robert H. Ikelman.
105 S. 2nd St., 95620.
Res.: 1510 Folsom Downs Cr., 95620. Tel: 707-678-9424; Fax: 707-678-9432.
Catechesis/Religious Program—Students 400.

DOWNIEVILLE, SIERRA CO., IMMACULATE CONCEPTION (1853) [CEM] [JC] Revs. Sylvester Kwiatkowski; Julito, Parochial Vicar.
Mailing Address: P.O. Box 302, 95936.
Office & Church: Church St., 95936. Tel: 530-289-3102.
Mission—St. Thomas 109 Butte Ave., Sierra City, 96125.

DUNSMUIR, SISKIYOU CO., ST. JOHN THE EVANGELIST (1899) [JC] Rev. Michael Canny.
Church: 5603 Shasta Ave., 96025. Fax: 530-235-4759.
Catechesis/Religious Program—Tel: 530-235-4705; Fax: 530-235-4759. Twinned with St. Anthony, Mt. Shasta. Students 4.

EL DORADO HILLS, EL DORADO CO., HOLY TRINITY (1992) Rev. Msgr. James C. Kidder; Rev. Desmond T. O'Reilly, Parochial Vicar; Deacons Neil Zachary; Robert T. Shauger; James Hopp.
Church: 3111 Tierra de Dios Dr., 95762-8008. Tel: 530-677-3234; Fax: 530-677-3570. Email: holytrinity@holytrinityparish.org. Web: www.holytrinityparish.org.
School—3115 Tierra de Dios Dr., 95762-8008. Tel: 530-677-3591; Fax: 530-350-3032. Email: hts@holytrinityparish.org. Web: www.holytrinityparish.org/school. Mrs. Trisha Uhrhammer, Prin.
Catechesis/Religious Program—Tel: 530-677-3234, Ext. 133. Susie Hahn, D.R.E. Students 781.

ELK GROVE, SACRAMENTO CO.

1—GOOD SHEPHERD CATHOLIC CHURCH (1993) Revs. Leon Juchniewicz; Francis Stevenson, Parochial Vicar.
9539 Racquet Ct., 95758.
Res.: 6808 Kilconnell Dr., 95758. Tel: 916-684-5722; Fax: 916-684-4472. Email: goodshepherdchurch@frontiernet.net.
School—St. Elizabeth Ann Seton Elementary School, Tel: 916-684-7903; Fax: 916-691-4064. Trina Koontz, Prin. Students 318.
Catechesis/Religious Program—Tel: 916-683-2963, Ext. 30. Sr. Maria Concepcion Cambaya, R.V.M., D.R.E. Students 950.

2—ST. JOSEPH (1962) Revs. Rodolfo D. Llamas; Bony Arackal, Parochial Vicar; Deacon Dennis Merino. In Res., Rev. Patrick J. Lee (Retired).
Res.: 9961 Elk Grove-Florin Rd., 95624. Tel: 916-685-3681; Fax: 916-685-7254. Web: www.stjoseph-elkgrove.net.
Catechesis/Religious Program—Tel: 916-685-5636. Students 773.
Mission—St. Vincent de Paul Mission Church 14673 Cantova Way, Rancho Murieta, Sacramento Co. 95683. Tel: 916-354-2403; Fax: 916-354-2406.

FAIR OAKS, SACRAMENTO CO., ST. MEL (1948) Revs. Liam P. McSweeney; Mauricio Hurtado, Parochial Vicar; Deacons David Lehman; Anthony Pescetti.
Res. & Church: 4745 Pennsylvania Ave., P.O. Box 1180, 95628. Tel: 916-967-1229; Fax: 916-967-5659. Web: www.stmelchurch.org.
School—Tel: 916-967-2814; Fax: 916-967-0705. Web: www.stmelschool.org. Janet Nagel, Prin. Lay Teachers 14; Students 250.
Catechesis/Religious Program—Tel: 916-966-4314. Students 214.
Convent—P.O. Box 1180, 95628. Tel: 916-967-9504.

FAIRFIELD, SOLANO CO.

1—HOLY SPIRIT (1950) Revs. Michael Downey; Jovito Rata, Parochial Vicar.
Mailing Address: P.O. Box X, 94533.
Res. & Church: 1050 N. Texas St., 94533. Tel: 707-425-3138; Fax: 707-425-2029. Email: hschurch3138@aol.com. Web: www.holyspiritfairfield.com.
School—(Grades K-8) Tel: 707-422-5016; Fax: 707-422-0874. Sr. Elizabeth Curtis, C.H.F., Prin.; Bonnie Hiris, Librarian. Sisters 2; Lay Teachers 17; Students 346.
Catechesis/Religious Program—Tel: 707-425-9042. Suselia Hernandez, D.R.E. Students 753.
Convent—Sisters of the Holy Faith (Dublin, Ireland), Tel: 707-425-3572.

2—OUR LADY OF MOUNT CARMEL, (1979), (Carmelite Fathers) Revs. David A. Fontaine, O.Carm.; Patrick Gitonga Nyaga, Parochial Vicar; Deacon Phil Verba.
Parish Office—Tel: 707-422-7767; Fax: 707-422-7946.
Res. & Church: 2700 Dover Ave., 94533. Tel: 707-426-3639.
Catechesis/Religious Program—Tel: 707-422-2814. Students 265.

FOLSOM, SACRAMENTO CO., ST. JOHN THE BAPTIST (1857) [CEM] Revs. Rey Bersabal; F. Ignatius Haran, Pastor Emeritus (Retired); Christopher Frazer, Parochial Vicar.
307 Montrose Dr., 95630. Tel: 916-985-2065; Fax: 916-985-7579. Email: office@stjohnsfolsom.org. Web: stjohnsfolsom.org. In Res., Rev. Thomas J. Maguire (Retired).
Res.: 107 Joseph Way, 95630. Tel: 916-351-1939.
School—St. John's-Notre Dame, Tel: 916-985-4129; Fax: 916-985-7958. Web: sjnds.com. Sue Halfman, Prin. Lay Teachers 21; Students 332.
Catechesis/Religious Program—Tel: 916-985-7338. Email: re@stjohnsfolsom.org. Students 1,191.
Station—Folsom State Prison P.O. Box W, Represa, 95671. Tel: 916-985-2561; Fax: 916-351-3070. Deacon William Goeke, Chap.
Station—California State Prison P.O. Box 29, 95671. Tel: 916-985-8610; Fax: 916-985-6425.

FORT JONES, SISKIYOU CO., SACRED HEART (1921) [CEM] Revs. Aldrin Basarte; Glenn Giovanni Jaron, M.S.P. (Philippines).
Res.: 101 Carlock St., P.O. Box 126, 96032-0126. Tel: 530-468-2605; Fax: 530-468-5577.
Catechesis/Religious Program—Students 23.
Mission—St. Mary's Etna. 386 Center St., Etna, Siskiyou Co. 96027.
Mission—All Saints 1321 Indian Creek Rd., Happy Camp, Siskiyou Co. 96093. Tel: 530-493-2657.
Mission—St. Joseph Etna. Sawyer's Bar Rd., Sawyer's Bar, Siskiyou Co. 96027.

GALT, SACRAMENTO CO., ST. CHRISTOPHER (1885) Rev. Robert A. Copsey.
Mailing Address: 950 S. Lincoln Way, 95632.
Res.: P.O. Box 276, 95632. Tel: 209-745-1389; Fax: 209-744-2183. Email: mpolanco_1@sbcglobal.net. Web: www.st-christopherchurch.com.
Catechesis/Religious Program—Tel: 209-745-1389, Ext. 304. Students 300.

GRANITE BAY, PLACER CO., ST. JOSEPH MARELLO (2004) Rev. Arnold Ortiz, O.S.J.; Deacon Dennis Gorsuch.
Mailing Address: P.O. Box 2480, 95746.
Church: 7200 Auburn Folsom Rd., 95746. Tel: 916-786-5001; Fax: 916-786-5011. Email: frarnold@osjoseph.org. Web: stjosephmarello.org.
Catechesis/Religious Program—Cyndee Reed, D.R.E. (Grades 1-5); Mary Maguire, Youth Min. (Grades 6-12). Students 389.

GRASS VALLEY, NEVADA CO., ST. PATRICK (1855) [CEM] Revs. Sylvester Kwiatkowski; Julito R. Orpilla, Parochial Vicar; Deacons James Chatigny, (Retired); Brian Moore, (Retired); Carlos Astesana, (Retired).
Res.: 235 Chapel St., 95945. Tel: 530-273-2347; Fax: 530-272-9681.
School—Mt. St. Mary's Academy, 400 S. Church St., 95945. Tel: 530-273-4694; Fax: 530-273-1724. Edee Wood, Prin. Religious 1; Lay Teachers 9; Students 160.
Catechesis/Religious Program—Tel: 530-273-2336. Karen Burford, Dir. Faith Formation. Students 210.

GRIDLEY, BUTTE CO., SACRED HEART (1926) Rev. Avram E. Brown.
Res. & Church: 1560 Hazel St., 95948. Tel: 530-846-2140; Fax: 530-846-5077. Email: sacredheartgridley@gmail.com.
Catechesis/Religious Program—Students 182.
Mission—Our Lady of Guadalupe 9660 Broadway, Live Oak, Sutter Co. 95953.

IONE, AMADOR CO., SACRED HEART OF JESUS (1932) [JC] Revs. Lawrence J. Beck; Thomas Relihan, Pastor Emeritus (Retired); Roland B. Ramirez, Parochial Vicar.
20 Relihan Dr., 95640. 11361 Prospect Dr., Jackson, 95642.
Rectory—115 Court St., Jackson, 95642. Tel:

209-223-2970.
Catechesis/Religious Program—Students 53.
Station—Mule Creek State Prison P.O. Box 409099, Amador Co. 95640. Tel: 209-274-4911. Rev. Diogo Baptista.

ISLETON, SACRAMENTO CO., ST. THERESE'S (1953) Rev. Andrzej A. Koziczuk.
Res.: 100 4th St., P.O. Box 697, 95641. Tel: 916-777-6871; Fax: 916-777-6871.
Church: 4th St. & Jackson Blvd., 95641.
Catechesis/Religious Program—Students 61.

JACKSON, AMADOR CO., ST. PATRICK'S (1864) [CEM 2] Revs. Lawrence J. Beck; Roland B. Ramirez, Parochial Vicar; Jeannine Crew, Sec.; Deacons Gary Evans; Jaime Garcia.
11361 Prosoect Dr., 95642.
Res.: 115 Court St., 95642. Tel: 209-223-2970; Fax: 209-223-1147. Email: stpat@stpatparish.org. Web: stpatparish.org.
Catechesis/Religious Program—Students 85.
Mission—Our Lady of the Pines Pioneer. 26750 Tiger Creek Rd., Buckhorn, Amador Co. 95666. Tel: 209-295-4909.
Mission—St. Bernard Plug-Emigrant St., Volcano, Amador Co. 95689.
Mission—Amador Catholic Center

KNIGHTS LANDING, YOLO CO., ST. PAUL (1949) [CEM] Rev. Joseph Huyen Van Nquyen, Parochial Admin.; Deacons Antonio Gonzalez; Hermennegildo Valera.
Res.: 222 Sycamore Way, P.O. Box 176, 95645. Tel: 530-735-6478; Fax: 530-735-9498. Email: parishofstpaul@yahoo.com.
Catechetical Center—6th St. & Locust St., 95645.
Catechesis/Religious Program—Students 60.
Mission—St. Agnes 9865 Main St., Zamora, Yolo Co. 95645.

LAKE ALMANOR, PLUMAS CO., OUR LADY OF THE SNOWS (1929) Revs. Geraldo J. Ranin; Mario Valmorida, Parochial Vicar.
Res.: 307 Fifth St., P.O. Box 905, Westwood, 96137. Tel: 530-256-3151; Fax: 530-256-2070. Email: ourladyofthesnows@frontiernet.net.
Church: 220 Clifford Dr., 96137. Tel: 530-259-2200.
Catechesis/Religious Program—Students 4.

LINCOLN, PLACER CO., ST. JOSEPH (1892) [CEM] [JC] Revs. Eric Lofgren; Fernando Meza, Parochial Vicar; Deacons Jesus Rodriguez; Roberto Ruiz.
Res.: 280 Oak Tree Ln., 95648. Tel: 916-645-2102; Fax: 916-645-1422.
Catechesis/Religious Program—Students 500.
Mission—St. Boniface 1028 Marcum Rd., Nicolaus, Sutter Co. 95659. Tel: 916-656-2368.
Mission—St. Daniel 214 Main St., Wheatland, Yuba Co. 95692. Tel: 916-633-0344.
Shrine—Our Lady of Guadalupe 3rd St. & K St., 95648.

MARYSVILLE, YUBA CO., ST. JOSEPH (1852) [CEM] Revs. Godwin Xavier; Juan Perez, Parochial Vicar; Deacons Jesus Munoz; David Perez; Barry Johnson.
Office & Mailing Address: 223 Eighth St., 95901. Email: stjoseph1155@sbcglobal.net.
Res.: 319 Seventh St., 95901. Tel: 530-742-6461; Fax: 530-742-0346.
Catechesis/Religious Program—Students 576.
Mission—Sacred Heart Church P.O. Box 208, Dobbins, Yuba Co. 95953.

MAXWELL, COLUSA CO., SACRED HEART (1881) Revs. Perlito De la Cruz, Admin.; John J. Myles, Pastor Emeritus (Retired).
P.O. Box 1327, Williams, 95987. Tel: 530-473-2432. Email: sh_maxwell@yahoo.com. Web: www.sacredheart-maxwell.org.
Church: P.O. Box 22, 95955.
Office: 627 8th St., Williams, 95987. Fax: 530-473-2440; 530-473-2432.
Mission—Holy Cross 408 Laurel St., Arbuckle, Colusa Co. 95912.
Mission—Church of the Annunciation 617 8th St., Williams, Colusa Co. 95987.
Mission—St. Mary of the Mountain 2nd St. & Geary St., Stonyford, Colusa Co. 95979.
Catechesis/Religious Program—Students 477.

MCCLOUD, SISKIYOU CO., ST. JOSEPH (1933) [JC] Rev. Aldrin Basarte.
Church & Mailing Address: 213 Colombero Dr., P.O. Box 518, 96057. Tel: 530-842-4874; Fax: 530-842-7076.
Res.: 314 4th St., Yreka, 96097. Tel: 530-842-3842.
Catechesis/Religious Program—

MOUNT SHASTA, SISKIYOU CO., ST. ANTHONY (1954) Rev. Michael Canny.
Res. & Church: 507 Pine St., 96067. Tel: 530-926-4477; Fax: 530-926-4234. Email: stanthonyshasta@sbcglobal.net.
Catechesis/Religious Program—Tel: 530-926-3061. Students 53.

NEVADA CITY, NEVADA CO., ST. CANICE (1851) [CEM] Revs. Sylvester Kwiatkowski; Julito R. Orpilla, Parochial Vicar.
Res.: 317 Washington St., 95959. Tel: 530-265-2049; Fax: 530-265-3697. Email: stcanice@sbcglobal.net.
Church: 316 Washington St., 95959.
Catechesis/Religious Program—Students 20.

NORTH HIGHLANDS, SACRAMENTO CO., ST. LAWRENCE THE MARTYR (1955) Rev. Enrique Alvarez; Deacon Donald Galli.
Res.: 4325 Don Julio Blvd., 95660. Tel: 916-332-4777; Fax: 916-332-8325. Web: saintlawrencechurch.org.
Catechesis/Religious Program—Tel: 916-332-4777. Email: drejean2@aol.com. Students 375.

ORANGEVALE, SACRAMENTO CO., DIVINE SAVIOR (1987) Rev. Roman Mueller, S.D.S.
Mailing Address: 9079 Greenback Ln., 95662-4703. Tel: 916-989-7400; Fax: 916-989-7410. Web: www.divinesavior.com. In Res., Rev. Dennis Thiessen, S.D.S.
Res.: 8680 Hickory Leaf Pl., 95662-3444. Tel: 916-989-5425.
Catechesis/Religious Program—Email: sharon@divinesavior.com. Students 267.

ORLAND, GLENN CO., ST. DOMINIC (1919) Rev. Hernando Gomez Amaya (Colombia).
Mailing Address: Box 816, 95963.
Res. & Church: 822 A St., 95963. Tel: 530-865-4550; Fax: 530-865-8451. Email: dominicorland@yahoo.com.
Catechesis/Religious Program—Students 136.
Mission—St. Mary 400 Los Robles, Hamilton City, Glenn Co. 95951.

OROVILLE, BUTTE CO., ST. THOMAS THE APOSTLE (1857) Rev. Roy Doner; Deacons Emmett Pogne; Jesus Venegas; Tom O'Connell.
Res.: 1330 Bird St., 95965. Tel: 530-533-0262; Fax: 530-533-1148.
Rectory—1355 First Ave., 95965. Tel: 530-693-4531.
School—1380 Bird St., 95965. Tel: 530-534-6969; Fax: 530-534-9374. Jim Stefaniak, Prin. Lay Teachers 6; Students 90.
Catechesis/Religious Program—Students 63.

PARADISE, BUTTE CO., ST. THOMAS MORE (1949) Rev. Mieczyslaw "Mitch" Maleszyk.
Res.: 767 Elliott Rd., 95969. Tel: 530-877-4501; Fax: 530-877-5633. Web: www.stmparadise.com.
Catechesis/Religious Program—Tel: 530-514-3892. Students 100.

PLACERVILLE, EL DORADO CO., ST. PATRICK'S (1852) Revs. John Cantwell; Walter Tabios; Deacons Stan S. Rudger; Manuel Ocon.
Res.: 3109 Sacramento St., 95667. Tel: 530-622-0373; Fax: 530-621-7770.
Catechesis/Religious Program—3090 Benham St., 95667. Tel: 530-622-7692. Email: spcff@sbcglobal.net. Students 395.
Mission—St. James 2831 Harkness St., Georgetown, El Dorado Co. 95634. Tel: 530-333-9432.
St. Patrick Ladies Society—
St. Patrick Aid Ministry (S.P.A.M.)—
Mother Teresa Maternity Home—
The Upper Room—1868 Broadway, 95667. Tel: 530-621-7730. Providing hot meals to those in need.
St. James Society—2831 Harkness St., Georgetown, 95634. Tel: 530-333-2292.
Mother Teresa Maternity Home—3122 Sacramento St., 95667. Tel: 530-295-8006. Barbara Goyette, Pres. of Guild. Staff 10; Mothers Served 197.

PORTOLA, PLUMAS CO., HOLY FAMILY (1929) Rev. Renier C. Siva.
Res. & Church: 108 Taylor Ave., 96122. Tel: 530-832-5006; Fax: 530-832-5520. Email: hfport@sbcglobal.net.
Catechesis/Religious Program—Students 65.
Mission—Holy Rosary 614 4th St., Loyalton, Sierra Co. 96118.

QUINCY, PLUMAS CO., ST. JOHN (1947) [JC 6] Revs. Geraldo J. Ranin, Parochial Admin.; Mario Valmorida, Parochial Vicar.
Mailing Address: P.O. Box 510, 95971.
Res. & Church: Hwy. 70 W, 170 Lawrence St., 95971. Tel: 530-283-0890; Fax: 530-283-4204.
Catechesis/Religious Program—Students 25.
Mission—St. Anthony 209 Jesse St., Greenville, Plumas Co. 95947. Tel: 530-284-6882.

RANCHO CORDOVA, SACRAMENTO CO., ST. JOHN VIANNEY (1958) Revs. Charles Kelly; Michael J. Estaris, Parochial Vicar; Deacons Walter Little; David Robinson.
Res.: 10497 Coloma Rd., 95670. Tel: 916-362-1385; Fax: 916-361-8102.
School—10499 Coloma Rd., 95670. Tel: 916-363-4610; Fax: 916-363-3243. Julia Boen, Prin. Lay Teachers 11; Students 220.
Catechesis/Religious Program—Tel: 916-362-3827; 916-368-9410 (Spanish). Students 345.

RED BLUFF, TEHAMA CO., SACRED HEART (1867) [JC] Revs. Joyle Martinez; Francisco Leon Villasenar, Parochial Vicar; Deacon Jack Bullen.
Parish Hall—2355 Monroe Ave., 96080. Tel: 530-527-1351; Fax: 530-529-2586. Email: sacredheartrb@hotmail.com.
School—2255 Monroe Ave., 96080. Tel: 530-527-6727; Fax: 530-527-5026. Email: sacredheart@sacredheartparishschool.org. Web: sacredheartparishschool.org. Mrs. Leslie Trujillo, Prin. Lay Teachers 11; Students 149.
Catechesis/Religious Program—Students 246.

REDDING, SHASTA CO.

1—ST. JOSEPH (1907) [CEM] Revs. George T. Snyder Jr.; John M. Lawrence, Parochial Vicar; Deacons David Gasman; Frank Lopez; Michael Mangas.
Res.: 2040 Walnut Ave., 96001. Tel: 530-243-3463; Fax: 530-243-7999. Email: stjoeparish@sbcglobal.net.
School—2460 Gold St., 96001. Tel: 530-243-2302; Fax: 530-243-2747. Lay Teachers 11; Students 153.
Catechesis/Religious Program—Students 70.
Mission—St. Michael 3440 Shasta Dam Blvd., Shasta Lake City, Shasta Co. 96019.

2—OUR LADY OF MERCY (1980) Revs. Jonathan B. Molina; Uriel Ojeda, Parochial Vicar.
Office: 2600 Shasta View Dr., 96002. Tel: 530-222-3424; Fax: 530-221-5717. Web: ourladyofmercyparish.org.
Catechesis/Religious Program—Tel: 530-222-3424, Ext. 12. Email: renaemagna@ymail.com. Students 137.
Mission—Mary Queen of Peace 30725 Shingletown Ridge Rd., Shingletown, Shasta Co. 96088. Tel: 530-474-1870.

RIO VISTA, SOLANO CO., ST. JOSEPH (1885) [CEM 2] Revs. Sherwin S. Colaste; William K. Walsh, Pastor Emeritus (Retired); Deacon Bill Bolduc.
130 S. 4th St., 94571. Tel: 707-374-2155; 707-374-2607 (Parish Hall); Fax: 707-374-5071. Email: stjosephoffice@frontiernet.net.
Catechesis/Religious Program—Students 70.

ROCKLIN, PLACER CO., SS. PETER AND PAUL (1981) Revs. Stanley Poltorak; Michael J. Dillon, Pastor Emeritus (Retired); Dariusz Malczuk (Poland), Parochial Vicar; Deacon David Haproff; John Gloudeman, Music Coord.
Res. & Church: 4450 Granite Dr., 95677. Tel: 916-624-5827; Fax: 916-624-5924. Email: linda.blincow@sspeter-paul.net. Web: sspeter-paul.net.
Catechesis/Religious Program—Kris Dahla, Faith Formation Coord. (Grades 1-6). Tel: 916-624-5827, Ext. 213; Todd Nelson, Faith Formation Coord. (Grades 7-12). Tel: 916-624-5827, Ext. 214; Jessica Ourada, High School Youth Min. Tel: 916-624-5827, Ext. 203; Darcy Wharton, Adult Faith Formation; Jen Gordon, Faith Formation Asst. Tel: 916-624-5827, Ext. 212. Students 2,129.

ROSEVILLE, PLACER CO.

1—ST. CLARE (1992) [JC] Florence Kurttila, Parish Admin.; Rev. Steven E. Foppiano; Deacons Carl Kube; Richard Driggs; Marintzo Kraljevich.
Res.: 1950 Junction Blvd., 95747. Tel: 916-772-4717; Fax: 916-772-4152. Email: stclare@surewest.net. Web: www.stclare-church.org.
Catechesis/Religious Program— Paula Straszkow, Dir. Faith Formation & Youth Min.; Agnes Soria, Coord. Faith Formation. (Faith Formation) 584.

2—ST. ROSE OF LIMA (1907), (Mexican), Revs. Michael O'Reilly; Michael J. Cormack, Pastor Emeritus (Retired); Michael C. McKeon, Pastor Emeritus (Retired); Orlando Gomez, Parochial Vicar; Joshy Mathew, C.M.I., Parochial Vicar; Deacons Peter M. Silott; Mark Van Hook.
Res.: 508 Marietti Way, 95678. Tel: 916-783-5211; Fax: 916-783-5212.
School—633 Vine Ave., 95678. Tel: 916-782-1161; Fax: 916-782-7862. Suzanne Smolley, Prin. Sisters 1; Lay Teachers 14; Students 305.
Catechesis/Religious Program—Maria Chadburn, Life Teen Dir.; Dona Gentile, D.R.E.; Frida Callejas, D.R.E. (Spanish). Students 417.

SOUTH LAKE TAHOE, EL DORADO CO., ST. THERESA (1951) Rev. Benedict DeLeon; Rev. Msgr. Murrough C. Wallace, Pastor Emeritus (Retired); Rev. John J. Grace, Pastor Emeritus (Retired).
Res.: 1041 Lyons Ave., 96150. Tel: 530-544-3533; Fax: 530-544-4662. Email: sainttheresachurch@yahoo.com. Web: www.tahoecatholic.com.
School—1081 Lyons Ave., 96150. Tel: 530-544-8944; Fax: 530-544-8909. Anne Filce, Prin. Lay Teachers 9; Students 70; Preschool 18.
Catechesis/Religious Program—Tel: 530-544-4788; Fax: 530-544-8909. Students 206.
Mission—Our Lady of the Sierra Camp Sacramento, El Dorado Co.

SUSANVILLE, LASSEN CO., SACRED HEART (1894) Rev. Ambrose Ugwuegbu (Nigeria).
Mailing Address: P.O. Box 430, 96130.
Res. & Church: 120 N. Union St., 96130-3935. Tel: 530-257-3230; Fax: 530-257-9213. Email: sacredheartssv@yahoo.com.
Catechesis/Religious Program—Msgr. Moran Hall, 140 N. Weatherlow St., 96130-3935. Tel: 530-257-8008 (local calls only). Students 65.
Station— Herlong.

SUTTER CREEK, AMADOR CO., IMMACULATE CONCEPTION (1864) [CEM 4] Revs. Lawrence J. Beck; Ronan P. Brennan, Pastor Emeritus (Retired); Roland B. Ramirez, Parochial Vicar; Deacon Ed Pogue.
11361 Prospect Dr., Jackson, 95642. Tel: 209-223-2970; Fax: 209-223-1147. Email: office@suttercreekparish.com. 125 Amelia St., 95685.
Catechesis/Religious Program—Students 58.
Mission—St. Mary of the Mountains 18765 Church St., Plymouth, Amador Co. 95669.

TAHOE CITY, PLACER CO., CORPUS CHRISTI (1961) Rev. Robert E. Brooks.
Mailing Address: P.O. Box 1878, 96145.
Church & Res.: 905 W. Lake Blvd., 96145. Tel: 530-583-4409; Fax: 530-583-1408. Email: secretary@corpuschristi-tahoe.org. Web: www.corpuschristi-tahoe.org.
Catechesis/Religious Program—Tel: 530-581-4637. Email: education@corpuschristi-tahoe.org. Students 25.
Mission—Queen of the Snows 1550 Squaw Valley Rd., Olympic Valley, Placer Co. 96146.
Station—Marie Sluchak Community Park Pine & Wilson Sts., Tahoma.

TRUCKEE, NEVADA CO., ASSUMPTION OF THE BLESSED VIRGIN MARY (1869) Rev. Matthew Blank; Deacon Ray Craig.
Mailing Address: 10930 Alder Dr., 96161. Tel: 530-587-3595; Fax: 530-582-8648. Email: info@assumptiontruckee.com. Web: assumptiontruckee.com.
Catechesis/Religious Program—Students 294.
Mission—Our Lady of the Lake 8363 Steelhead, Kings Beach, Placer Co. 96143.

TULELAKE, SISKIYOU CO., HOLY CROSS (1949) Rev. Mervin P. Concepcion, Admin.
Mailing Address: P.O. Box 266, 96134.
Church: 765 First St., P.O. Box 266, 96134. Tel: 530-667-2727.
Catechesis/Religious Program—Students 46.
Mission—Our Lady of Good Counsel W. 3rd St., Dorris, Siskiyou Co. 96023.

VACAVILLE, SOLANO CO.

1—ST. JOSEPH (1992) [JC] Revs. Mathew M. Marankulam; Vincent P. O'Reilly, Pastor Emeritus; Jose J. Beltran, Parochial Vicar.
Res.: 1791 Marshall Rd., 95687. Tel: 707-447-2354; Fax: 707-447-9322. Web: www.stjoseph-vacaville.org.
School—Notre Dame, 1781 Marshall Rd., 95687. Tel: 707-447-1460; Fax: 707-447-1498. Lay Teachers 15; Students 312.
Catechesis/Religious Program—Students 175.

2—ST. MARY (1947) Revs. Humberto Gomez; Michael McFadden, Pastor Emeritus; Ruel Z. Mesa, Parochial Vicar; Deacons Domingo Cabrera, (Retired); John King; Gilberto Miranda; Felix Lupercio.
Res.: 350 Stinson Ave., 95688. Tel: 707-448-2390; Fax: 707-448-2818. Email: st.maryschurch@sbcglobal.net. Web: www.stmarysvacaville.com.
Catechesis/Religious Program—Tel: 707-446-1881. Students 416.

VALLEJO, SOLANO CO.

1—ST. BASIL (1941) Revs. Alfredo L. Tamayo; Walter Borkowski, Parochial Vicar; Deacons Mike Urick; Errol Kissinger.
Parish Office: 1225 Tuolumne St., 94590. Tel: 707-644-5251; Fax: 707-644-1423. Web: stbasilvallejo.org.
Res.: 1200 Tuolumne St., 94590.
School—1230 Nebraska St., 94590. Tel: 707-642-7629; Fax: 707-642-8635. Mr. Neil Orlina, Prin. Lay Teachers 17; Students 306; Preschool 65.
Catechesis/Religious Program—Tel: 707-644-8309. Students 293.

2—ST. CATHERINE OF SIENA (1964) [CEM] Revs. Jesus T. Soriano; Michael Olszewski (Poland), Parochial Vicar; Deacons Pete Lobo; Rudy David; Bobby Peregrino.
Res. & Mailing Address: 3450 Tennessee St., 94591. Tel: 707-553-1355; Fax: 707-557-6896.
School—(Grades PreK-8), 3460 Tennessee St., 94591. Tel: 707-643-6691; Fax: 707-647-4441. Susan Kealy, Prin. Lay Teachers 25; Students 328.
Catechesis/Religious Program—Tel: 707-647-4445. Students 305.

3—ST. VINCENT FERRER (1855) Revs. Stephen M. Borlang; Martin J. Ramat, Parochial Vicar.
Office & Res.: 816 Santa Clara St., 94590. Tel: 707-644-8396; Fax: 707-644-1330. Email: resource@stvincentferrer.org; fund@stvincentferrer.org. Web: www.stvincentferrer.org. In Res., Revs. Hector Montoya Juarez; Luis V. Resma; Jeffrey F. Henry.
School—420 Florida St., 94590. Tel: 707-642-4311; Fax: 707-642-1329. Web: svfsvallejo.org. Tom Yurkovic, Prin. Lay Teachers 14; Students 357.
Catechesis/Religious Program—Tel: 707-643-0188. Email: ccd@stvincentferrer.org. Students 408.
Chapel—St. Louis Bertrand Chapel 651 Sonoma Blvd., 94590.

WALNUT GROVE, SACRAMENTO CO., ST. ANTHONY (1881) Rev. Andrzej A. Koziczuk.
Res. & Church: 14012 Walnut Ave., 95690. Tel: 916-776-1330.
Catechesis/Religious Program— St. Anthony Parish Hall, Walnut Grove. Students 105.

WEAVERVILLE, TRINITY CO., ST. PATRICK (1853) [CEM] Revs. Derek R. P. LaBranch; Keith E. Canterbury, Pastor Emeritus (Retired).
Res.: P.O. Box 1219, 96093-1219. Tel: 530-623-4383; Fax: 530-623-4383.
Church: 102 Church St., 96093.
Catechesis/Religious Program—Students 14.
Mission—Holy Trinity Hayfork, Trinity Co.
Mission—St. Gilbert Lewiston, Trinity Co.

WEED, SISKIYOU CO., HOLY FAMILY (1933) Rev. Mervin P. Concepcion.
Res.: 1051 N. Davis Ave., 96094. Tel: 530-938-2076; 530-938-4334 (Office); Fax: 530-938-3837.
Catechesis/Religious Program—Tel: 530-459-5124. Students 35.

WEST SACRAMENTO, YOLO CO.

1—HOLY CROSS (1913) Revs. Giancarlo Mittempergher, C.S.S. (Italy); Antonio dos Santos, C.S.S. (Brazil), Parochial Vicar.
Res.: 1321 Anna St., 95605. Tel: 916-371-1211; Fax: 916-371-9277. Email: holycrossws@gmail.com.
School—800 Todhunter Ave., 95605. Tel: 916-371-1313; Fax: 916-371-4193. Email: hcsinformation@yahoo.com. Web: www.holy-cross.ws. Ms. Julieta Mendoza, Prin. Lay Teachers 5; Students 98.
Catechesis/Religious Program—Tel: 916-371-5884. Students 308.

2—OUR LADY OF GRACE (1949) Rev. Nicholas Ho.
Res.: 911 Park Blvd., 95691. Tel: 916-371-4814. Email: olgoffice@wavecable.com.
School—1990 Linden Rd., 95691. Tel: 916-371-9416; Fax: 916-371-1319. Mr. Joshua Rucker, Prin. Lay Teachers 10; Students 247.
Catechesis/Religious Program—Fax: 916-371-4816. Students 259.

WILLOWS, GLENN CO., ST. MONICA (1877) [CEM] Rev. Maurice O'Brien.
Res.: 1129 W. Wood St., 95988. Tel: 530-934-3314.
Catechesis/Religious Program—Tel: 530-934-3293. Students 135.
School—Catechetical School, 1151 W. Wood St., 95988. Tel: 530-934-5916; Fax: 530-934-3205. Students 140.

WINTERS, YOLO CO., ST. ANTHONY (1913) [JC] Rev. Michael J. Hebda; Deacon Alejandro Arroyo.
Mailing Address: 511 Main St., 95694.
Res.: 507 Main St., 95694. Tel: 530-795-2230; Fax: 530-795-5470.
Church: 301 Main St., 95694.
Catechesis/Religious Program—Katy Long, Coord. Faith Formation. Students 253.
Mission—St. Martin 25633 Grafton Rd., Esparto, Yolo Co. 95627. Tel: 530-787-3750.

WOODLAND, YOLO CO., HOLY ROSARY (1870) [CEM] Revs. Francisco Velazquez; Jacob Antonio Caceres, Parochial Vicar; Giovanni Gamas, Parochial Vicar; Deacons Edward Kull; Gonzalo Chavez; Antonio Fernandez; Jose Luis Collazo.
Mailing Address: 503 California St., 95695.
Parish Pastoral Center: 503 California St., 95695. Tel: 530-662-2805; Fax: 530-662-0796. Email: parish@holyrosary.com. Web: www.holyrosary.com. (Corner of Walnut & Court Sts.), Church: 301 Walnut St., 95695.
School—505 California St., 95695. Tel: 530-662-3494; Fax: 530-668-2442. Email: office@hrsaints.com. Web: www.hrsaints.com. Marianne Cates, Prin. Lay Teachers 14; Students 184.
Catechesis/Religious Program—575 California St., 95695. Tel: 530-662-5394 (English); Fax: 530-662-1310; Tel: 530-662-2894 (Spanish). Ana Elizabeth Contreras, Dir. Tel: 530-662-2894; 530-662-5394. Students 596.
Mission—Our Lady of Guadalupe 36670 Sacramento St., Yolo, Yolo Co. 95697. (Not in service)

YREKA, SISKIYOU CO., ST. JOSEPH (1855) Revs. Aldrin Basarte; Glenn Giovanni Jaron, M.S.P. (Philippines), Parochial Vicar.
Res.: 314 Fourth St., 96097. Tel: 530-842-3842; Fax: 530-842-7076.
Catechetical Center—310 Fourth St., 96097. Tel: 530-842-4874.
Catechesis/Religious Program—Tel: 530-842-4874. Students 6.
Mission—Immaculate Conception Hawkinsville, Siskiyou Co.

YUBA CITY, SUTTER CO., ST. ISIDORE (1952) Revs. Miguel Silva; Arlon Vergara, O.S.A., Parochial Vicar.
Res.: 222 Clark Ave., 95991. Tel: 530-673-1573; Fax: 530-673-2512.
School—200 Clark Ave., 95991. Tel: 530-673-2217; Fax: 530-673-3673. Mrs. Karen McDonald, Prin. Lay Teachers 12; Students 214.
Catechesis/Religious Program—Tel: 530-673-1573, Ext. 221. Students 575.

Chaplains of Public Institutions

SACRAMENTO. *Mule Creek State Prison*.
P.O. Box 409099, Ione, 95640. Tel: 209-274-4911. Rev. Diogo Baptista.
Sacramento International Airport. Rev. Soane T. Kaniseli.
Sacramento Juvenile Hall, 9601 Kiefer Blvd., 95827. Tel: 916-875-5083. Vacant, Youth Chap. & Contact Person. Tel: 916-489-3394.
Sutter General Hospital, 2801 L St., 95816. Rev. James P. Sheets.
Sutter Memorial Hospital, 52nd & F Sts., 95819. Tel: 916-454-3333. Rev. James P. Sheets.
University of California, Davis Medical Center, 2315 Stockton Blvd., 95817. Tel: 916-453-2011. Vacant.

ELK GROVE. *Rio Consumnes Correctional Center*, 12500 Bruceville Rd, 95758. Tel: 916-684-2001. Vacant.

FOLSOM. *California State Prison*, Tel: 916-985-8610, Ext. 6025.
P.O. Box 29, Represa, 95671. Deacon Dennis Merino.
Folsom State Prison.
P.O. Box 71, Represa, 95671. Tel: 916-985-2561, Ext. 4206. Rev. Polycarp Ndugbu (Nigeria).

IONE. *Preston California Youth Facility* 95640. Tel: 209-274-8250. Deacon Adolfo Rivera, Chap.

SUSANVILLE. *California Correctional Center*, P.O. Box 790, 96130. Tel: 530-257-2181, Ext. 1180. Rev. Anthony B. Warnakula, C.H.S.P.
High Desert State Prison, P.O. Box 750, 96130. Tel: 916-251-5100, Ext. 6722. Rev. Matthew Vanissery.

VACAVILLE. *California Medical Facility*, P.O. Box 2000, 95688. Tel: 707-448-6841, Ext. 2976. Vacant.
California State Prison, Solano, P.O. Box 4000, 95696. Tel: 707-451-0182, Ext. 5474. Vacant.

Special Assignment:
Revs.—
dos Santos, Antonio, C.S.S. (Brazil), Chap. to Port of West Sacramento, Holy Cross Parish, 1321 Anna St., West Sacramento, 95605. Tel: 916-371-1211
Kaniseli, Soane T., Chap. to Airport, Divine Mercy Parish, 2231 Club Center Dr., 95835. Tel: 916-285-9031
Mittempergher, Giancarlo, C.S.S. (Italy), Chap. to Port of West Sacramento, Holy Cross Parish, 1321 Anna St., West Sacramento, 95605. Tel: 916-371-1211
Ternullo, Joseph P., Chap. to Sheriff Deputies & Firefighters, St. Lawrence, 4325 Don Julio Blvd., North Highlands, 95660. Tel: 916-442-2333

On Duty Outside the Diocese:
Rev.—
Bosque, Peter J.

Absent on Leave:
Revs.—
Nguyen, Charles
Valenzuela, Luciano

Retired and in Senior Ministry:
Rev. Msgrs.—
Kavanagh, Edward J., c/o St. Rose Parish, P.O. Box 5037 - Oak Park Station, 95817.
O'Sullivan, T. Brendan, 84 Shore Line Cir., 95831.
Schons, Gerard, c/o St. Rose Parish, P.O. Box 5037 - Oak Park Station, 95817.
Terra, Russell G., 2040 Walnut Ave., Redding, 96001.
Wallace, Murrough C., P.O. Box 612043, South Lake Tahoe, 96150.
Revs.—
Batch, Thomas A., 9000 Lankin Rd., Live Oak, 95953.
Brady, Charles, 33 Miranda Ct., 95822.
Brennan, Ronan P., 6600 VanMaren Ln., #12A, Citrus Heights, 95621.
Canterbury, Keith E., P.O. Box 2663, Weaverville, 96093.
Carrigan, Thomas C., Clarabricken House, Kilkenny, Co. Clifden Ireland.
Cormack, Michael J., 6600 VanMaren Ln., #2B, Citrus Heights, 95621.
Delahunty, Thomas P., 3247 Sandhurst Ct., Cameron Park, 95682.
Dermody, Thomas, P.O. Box 1151, Brawley, 92227.
Dillon, Michael J., 3700 Argonaut Ave., Rocklin, 95677. Tel: 916-624-1947
Dinelli, William J., Christian Brothers H. S., 4315 Martin Luther King Jr. Blvd., 95820.
Duggan, Nicholas, 6600 VanMaren Ln. #2A, Citrus Heights, 95621.
Grace, John J., 3035 Berkeley Ave., South Lake Tahoe, 96150.

Hall, Rodney, 6600 Van Maren Ln., #3B, Citrus Heights, 95621.
Hall, Sidney, Mercy McMahon Terrace, 3865 J St., 95816.
Hannan, John K., 6600 VanMaren Ln., #5B, Citrus Heights, 95621.
Haran, F. Ignatius, 105 Joseph Way, Folsom, 95630.
Hold, William, 873 Colombine Way, Central Pointe, OR 97502.
Kinane, William P., 6600 Van Maren Ln., #4B, Citrus Heights, 95621.
Lee, Patrick J., c/o Immaculate Conception, 3263 1st Ave., 95817.
Lenehan, Vincent, 8 Glenburren Park, Co. Galway, Ireland.
Macdonald, Colin, 6600 Van Maren Ln. #12-B, Citrus Heights, 95621.
Maguire, Thomas J., 418 Coventry Ct., Folsom, 95630.
McKeon, Michael C., 8020 Walerga Rd., #1162, Antelope, 95843.
McKnight, James, 9 MaLinmore Mews, Dublin Rd., Down BT3585A Ireland.
Moroney, Martin J., 2110 Broadway, 95818.
Myles, John J., Whitegate Keel - Castlemaine, Co. Kerry, Ireland.
O'Connor, Albert
O'Hara, Edward, Lisryan, Longford, Granard Ireland.
O'Kelly, P. Colm, 3109 Tierra de Dios, El Dorado Hills, 95762-8008.
O'Leary, Sean, Bunowen Rd., Louisburgh, Co. Mayo Ireland.
O'Rafferty, Patrick, 6600 VanMaren Ln., #3A, Citrus Heights, 95621.
O'Reilly, Aidan, Virginia, Co. Cavan Ireland.
Ramos, Cipriano, Mercy McMahon Terrace, 3865 J St., 95816.
Relihan, Thomas, c/o Sacred Heart of Jesus Parish, P.O. Box 4, Ione, 95640.
Ricks, Paul
Ryan, Lawrence A., Campus Commons, 22 Cadilac Dr., Apt. 136, 95825.
Schloeder, Paul, 2640 3rd Ave., 95818.
Sullivan, John P., c/o Holy Family Parish, 7817 Old Auburn Rd., Citrus Heights, 95610.
Traynor, Anthony, 6212 Rebel Cir., Citrus Heights, 95621-4720.
Walsh, James B., 14 Castle Demesne, Tralee, Kerry Ireland.
Walsh, William K., 50 River Rd., #30, Rio Vista, 94571.
Wdowiak, Boleslaw, 2404 Ruby Ct., Rocklin, 95677.

Permanent Deacons:
Arroyo, Alejandro, (Retired), St. Anthony, Winters
Astesana, Carlos, (Retired), Immaculate Conception, Downieville
Balduc, Bill, St. Joseph's, Rio Vista
Bullen, Jack, Sacred Heart, Red Bluff; St. Dominic, Orland
Burke, Keith, (Retired)
Burkett, James, Our Divine Savior Parish, Chico
Cabrera, Domingo, (Retired), Divine Mercy, Sacramento
Cadenasso, Richard, St. Joseph, Auburn
Chatigny, James, (Retired), St. Patrick, Grass Valley
Chavez, Gonzalo, Holy Rosary, Woodland
Cheever, Charles, St. Philomene, Sacramento
Colenzo, Sam, St. James, Davis
Collazo, Jose Luis, Holy Rosary, Woodland
Conley, Roger, (Unassigned)
Craig, Ray, Assumption, Truckee
Crowley, Michael, St. Anthony, Sacramento
David, Rudy, St. Catherine of Siena, Vallejo
DeHaven, Donald, (Retired), Cathedral, Sacramento
Del Gaudio, Luigi, St. Mary, Sacramento
Donovan, Michael, (Retired), All Hallows, Sacramento
Driggs, Richard, St. Clare, Roseville
Dufault, Duane, St. Joseph, McCloud; St. Joseph, Yreka
Elias, Raymond, Holy Spirit, Fairfield
Enos, Richard, (Retired), St. Joseph, Yreka
Evans, Gary, St. Patrick, Jackson
Evans, Michael, Sacred Heart, Anderson
Fernandez, Antonio, (Retired), Holy Rosary, Woodland
Fernandez, Miguel, Our Lady of Lourdes, Colusa
Flanagan, John, (Retired), St. Dominic, Benicia
Ford, David, St. Teresa of Avila, Auburn
Galli, Donald, St. Lawrence, N. Highlands
Garcia, Henry, (Retired), St. Joseph, Sacramento
Garcia, Jaime, St. Patrick, Jackson
Gasman, David H., (Retired), St. Joseph, Redding
Gisla, John, Cathedral, Sacramento
Godinez, Rafael, (Retired), St. Joseph, Elk Grove
Goecker, Clark, St. James, Davis; Newman Center, Davis
Goeke, William, St. John the Baptist, Folsom
Gonzalez, Antonio, St. Paul, Knights Landing
Gorsuch, Dennis, St. Joseph Marello, Granite Bay
Gualco, Jack, St. Ignatius of Loyola, Sacramento
Haproff, David, SS. Peter & Paul, Rocklin
Healy, James, (Retired), St. Anthony's, Sacramento
Helgeson, Raymond, St. Maria Goretti, Elk Grove
Hemenway, Raymond, Our Lady of Mercy, Redding
Henning, Patrick, (Retired), St. Mel, Fair Oaks
Hernandez, Jesus, (Unassigned)
Holt, Mark, Holy Family, Citrus Heights
Hopp, James, Holy Trinity, El Dorado Hills
Ikelman, Robert, St. Peter, Dixon
Imrisek, Paul, (Retired), St. Joseph, Elk Grove
Johnson, Barry, St. Joseph, Marysville
Kearns, Patrick, Our Lady of Mercy, Redding
Kim, Byong, Korean Catholic Church, Sacramento
King, John, St. Mary, Vacaville
Kissinger, Errol, St. Basil, Vallejo
Klimecki, Lawrence, Presentation, Sacramento
Koppes, Richard, St. Anthony, Sacramento
Kraljevich, Marintzo, St. Clare, Roseville
Kriske, George, (Retired), St. Mary's, Sacramento
Kube, Carl, St. Clare, Roseville
Kull, Edward, Holy Rosary, Woodland
Layne, Everett H., (Retired), Our Lady of Mercy, Redding
Lazarek, Edward, (Retired), St. Dominic, Benicia
Lehman, David, St. Mel, Fair Oaks
Leon, Raul, Cathedral of the Blessed Sacrament
Link, Robert, (Unassigned)
Little, Walter, St. John Vianney, Rancho Cordova
Lobo, Pete, St. Catherine of Siena, Vallejo
Lopez, Frank, (Retired/Active), St. Joseph, Redding; St. Michael Mission, Shasta
Lupercio, Felix, St. Mary's, Vacaville
Madero, Alejandro, St. Vincent Ferrer, Vallejo
Mangas, Michael, St. Joseph, Redding
Mangoba, Leo, (Retired), St. Vincent Ferrer, Vallejo
Manriquez, Pedro, (Retired), St. Anne, Sacramento
Marchese, Charles, Jr., (Retired), Divine Savior, Orangevale
McFadden, James, Divine Savior, Orangevale
Merino, Dennis, St. Joseph, Elk Grove
Meucci, James, (Retired), Holy Trinity, El Dorado Hills
Miranda, Gilberto, All Hallows, Sacramento; St. Peter, Sacramento
Moore, Brian, (Retired), St. Patrick, Grass Valley
Morales, Rick, Divine Mercy, Sacramento
Morgado, Edwin, Teresa of Avila, Auburn
Morrison, Charles, (Unassigned)
Moua, Tou, St. Peter, Sacramento; All Hallows, Sacramento
Munoz, Jesus, St. Joseph, Marysville
Nguyen, An Binh, Vietnamese Catholic Martyrs, Sacramento
Nguyen, Anthony, Vietnamese Catholic Martyrs, Sacramento
Nguyen, Tien Nam, Vietnamese Martyrs, Sacramento
Niekamp, Lawrence, St. John the Evangelist, Carmichael
O'Connell, Tom, St. Thomas the Apostle, Oroville
O'Donnell, Joseph, St. James, Davis
Ocon, Manuel, St. Patrick, Placerville
Padilla, Jesus, St. John the Baptist, Chico
Parra, Gilbert, Sacred Heart, Sacramento
Pauly, Gerald, Immaculate Conception, Sacramento
Peregrino, Bobby, St. Catherine of Siena, Vallejo
Perez, David, (Retired), St. Joseph's, Marysville
Pescetti, Anthony, St. Mel, Fair Oaks
Pierre, Allen, (Retired), St. Joseph, Elk Grove
Pogue, Edwin, (Retired), Immaculate Conception, Sutter Creek
Pogue, Emmett, St. Thomas the Apostle, Oroville
Quigley, Ned, St. Joseph, Elk Grove
Ramirez, Antonio, St. Paul, Sacramento
Ramirez, Jose, (Unassigned)
Ramirez, Preciliano, St. Robert, Sacramento
Revelo, Jose, St. Catherine of Siena, Vallejo
Rey, Rafael, St. Vincent Ferrer, Vallejo
Reyna, Pedro, Sacred Heart, Maxwell
Rico, Benito, St. Dominic, Orland
Riehl, William, (Retired), Sacred Heart, Sacramento
Robinson, David, St. John Vianney, Rancho Cordova
Rodriguez, Jesus, St. Joseph, Lincoln
Rojo, Ruben, St. Isidore, Yuba City
Rovito, Orin, St. Peter/All Hallows, Sacramento
Rudger, Stanley, St. Patrick, Placerville
Ruiz, Roberto, St. Joseph, Lincoln
Schirmer, Erik, (Unassigned)
Schwartz, Steve, St. John the Baptist, Chico
Shauger, Robert T., Holy Trinity, El Dorado Hills
Sheldon, Lawrence, (Retired), (Unassigned)
Short, Anthony, (Retired), Sacred Heart, Anderson
Silott, Peter, (Retired), St. Rose of Lima, Roseville
Smith, Colby, (Unassigned)
Smith, Edward, Good Shepherd, Elk Grove
Sousa, William, (Retired), Good Shepherd, Elk Grove
Symkowick, Joseph, Newman Catholic Community, Sacramento
Taloff, Paul, (Retired), St. James, Davis
Tateishi, Michael, Our Lady of the Assumption, Carmichael
Tokuno, Doug, Sacred Heart, Gridley
Toro, German, Hispanic Ministry for the Diocese, Sacramento
Urick, Michael, St. Basil, Vallejo
Usi, Jorge, Cathedral of the Blessed Sacrament, Sacramento
Valles, Rich, Sacred Heart, Anderson
Van Hook, Mark, St. Rose of Lima, Roseville
Varela, Hermengildo, St. Paul, Knights Landing
Vela, Juvencio, St. Dominic, Benecia
Venegas, Jesus, St. Thomas, Oroville
Verba, Phil, Jr., Our Lady of Mt. Carmel, Fairfield
Vignery, Eldon, St. Isidore, Yuba City
Vivi, Alani, St. Anne, Sacramento
Weeks, James, (Retired), St. John the Evangelist, Carmichael
Ya, Jacques, All Hallows, Sacramento
Young, Michael, (Retired), St. Joseph, Auburn
Zachary, Neil, Holy Trinity, El Dorado Hills
Zellmer, Gary, St. Thomas More, Paradise

INSTITUTIONS LOCATED IN THE DIOCESE

[A] SEMINARY, RELIGIOUS

LOOMIS. *Mount St. Joseph Novitiate and Seminary* (1964) 6530 Wells Ave., P.O. Box 547, 95650. Tel: 916-652-6336; Fax: 916-652-0620. Email: fphil@osjoseph.org. Web: www.osjoseph.org. Revs. Steven Peterson, O.S.J., Rector; Matthew Spencer, O.S.J., Vocation Dir.; Arnold Ortiz, O.S.J.; Bro. Mathew Chipp, O.S.J. Novitiate of Oblates of St. Joseph. Priests 2; Brothers 1.

VINA. *Abbey of New Clairvaux, Trappist Seminary* (1955) 26240 7th St., P.O. Box 80, 96092. Tel: 530-839-2161; Fax: 530-839-2332. Email: pmschwan@newclairvaux.org. Web: www.newclairvaux.org. Rt. Rev. Paul Mark Schwan, O.C.S.O., Abbot. Priests 8; Brothers 7; Novices 1. In Res. Rt. Revs. Thomas X. Davis, O.C.S.O., J.C.L., Abbot Emeritus; Bernard Johnson, O.C.S.O., J.C.L., Abbot Emeritus; Revs. Anthony R. Bellesorte, O.C.S.O.; Lawrence A. Glaser, O.C.S.O.; Paul Jerome Konkler, O.C.S.O.; Harold K. Meyer, O.C.S.O.; Mark Scott, O.C.S.O., S.S.L., Prof. of Scripture; Bro. Placid Morris, Librarian.

[B] HIGH SCHOOLS, DIOCESAN

SACRAMENTO. *St. Francis High School* (Girls), 5900 Elvas Ave., 95819. Tel: 916-452-3461; Fax: 916-452-1591. Email: sfhsinfo@stfrancishs.org. Web: www.stfrancishs.org. Marion L. Bishop, Pres.; Patrick O'Neill, Prin.; Judy Walker, Librarian. Lay Teachers & Staff 132; Girls 1,114.

RED BLUFF. *Mercy Catholic High School*, 233 Riverside Way, 96080. Tel: 530-527-8313; Fax: 530-527-3058. Email: mercy@mercy-high.org. Web: www.mercy-high.org. Eileen Bauer, Admin. Lay Teachers 3; Students 78.

VALLEJO. *St. Patrick-St. Vincent High School*, 1500 Benicia Rd., 94591. Tel: 707-644-4425; Fax: 707-644-3107. Email: meryan@spsv.org. Web: www.spsv.org. Mary Ellen Ryan, Prin.; Alexa Stoneman, Dir., Library & Technology Svcs. Priests 1; Lay Teachers 43; Students 534.

[C] HIGH SCHOOLS, PRIVATE

SACRAMENTO. *Christian Brothers High School of Sacramento, Inc.* (1876) 4315 Martin Luther King Jr. Blvd., 95820. Tel: 916-733-3600; Fax: 916-733-3624. Web: www.cbhs-sacramento.org. Lorcan P. Barnes, Pres.; Mary Hesser, Prin. Lay Teachers 70; Students 977.

Cristo Rey High School, 6200 McMahon Dr., 95824-3153. Tel: 916-733-2660; Fax: 916-739-1310. Web: www.cristoreysacramento.org. Joanne Castronovo, Prin. Priests 1; Sisters 4; Lay Teachers 11.

Jesuit High School (1963) P.O. Box 254647, 95865-4647. 1200 Jacob Ln., Carmichael, 95608-6024. Tel: 916-482-6060; Fax: 916-482-2310. Web: www.jhssac.org. Revs. Gregory R. Bonfiglio, S.J., Pres.; Michael C. Gilson, S.J., Supr.; Francis G. Hernandez, S.J.; David F. Klein, S.J.; Kevin A. Leidich, S.J.; Charles R. Olsen, S.J.; William K. Stolz, S.J.; Dennis Thiessen, S.D.S.; Bro. Justin DeChance, S.J.; Ms. Brianna Latko, Prin.; Mrs.

Heidi Bleckmann, Librarian; Mr. Phillip Ganir, S.J.; Mr. Julian Climaco, S.J. (Boys) Jesuit Priests 7; Religious 1; Brothers 1; Scholastics 2; Lay Teachers 75; Boys 1,070.

[D] ELEMENTARY SCHOOLS

ELK GROVE. *St. Elizabeth Ann Seton Catholic School* (1999) 9539 Racquet Ct., 95758. Tel: 916-684-7903; Fax: 916-691-4064. Web: www.stelizabetheg.org. Trina Koontz, Prin. Lay Teachers 13; Students 323; Total Staff 36.

[E] DAY NURSERY AND CHILD CARE HOMES

SACRAMENTO. *St. Patrick Children's Home, Inc.*, P.O. Box 5112, 95817. Tel: 916-733-0254; Fax: 916-733-0224. Email: mkiernan@diocese-sacramento.org. Web: www.sphsac.net. Very Rev. Michael F. Kiernan, Exec. Dir.

[F] HOMES FOR SENIOR CITIZENS

SACRAMENTO. *Mercy-McMahon Terrace*, 3865 J St., 95816. Tel: 916-733-6510; Fax: 916-733-6515. Email: mmtcook@comcast.net. Web: www.mercymcmahonterrace.org. Jim Cook, CEO. Mercy Senior Housing, Inc. Licensed Units 118; Total Assisted Annually 132; Total Staff 65.

[G] GENERAL HOSPITALS

SACRAMENTO. *Mercy General Hospital, a dba of Catholic Healthcare West* (1897) 4001 J St., 95819. Tel: 916-453-4545; Fax: 916-453-4587. Web: www.mercygeneral.org. Denny Powell, Pres. Sponsored by Sisters of Mercy of the Americas West Midwest Community. Sisters of Mercy 6; Patients Assisted Annually 171,670; Beds 342; Total Staff 2,267.

CARMICHAEL. *Mercy San Juan Medical Center, a dba of Catholic Healthcare West* (1967) 6501 Coyle Ave., 95608. Tel: 916-537-5000; Fax: 916-537-5111. Web: www.mercysanjuan.org. Brian Ivie, Pres. Sponsored by Sisters of Mercy of the Americas West Midwest Community. Sisters of Mercy 4; Beds 370; Patients Assisted Annually 163,605; Total Staff 2,341.

FOLSOM. *Mercy Hospital of Folsom, a dba of Catholic Healthcare West* (1962) 1650 Creekside Dr., 95630. Tel: 916-983-7400; Fax: 916-983-7406. Web: www.mercyfolsom.org. Don Hudson, Pres. Sponsored by Sisters of Mercy of the Americas West Midwest Community. Sisters of Mercy 1; Bed Capacity 106; Total Staff 693; Patients Assisted Annually 50,792.

MT. SHASTA. *Mercy Medical Center Mt. Shasta, a dba of Catholic Healthcare West* (1938) 914 Pine St., Mount Shasta, 96067. Tel: 530-926-6111; Fax: 530-926-0517. Web: www.mercy.org. Kenneth Platou, Pres. Sponsored by Sisters of Mercy of the Americas West Midwest Community. Sisters 1; Bed Capacity 68; Patients Assisted Annually 58,192; Total Staff 273.

RED BLUFF. *St. Elizabeth Community Hospital, a dba of Catholic Healthcare West* (1906) 2550 Sr. Mary Columba Dr., 96080-4397. Tel: 530-529-8000; Fax: 530-529-8009. Web: www.mercy.org. Jon Halfhide, Pres. Sponsored by Sisters of Mercy of the Americas West Midwest Community. Sisters 1; Bed Capacity 76; Patients Assisted Annually 72,243; Total Staff 451.

REDDING. *Mercy Medical Center Redding, a dba of Catholic Healthcare West* (1944) 2175 Rosaline Ave., 96001. Tel: 530-225-6000; Fax: 530-225-6125. Web: www.mercy.org. Mark Korth, Pres. Sponsored by Sisters of Mercy of the Americas West Midwest Community. Sisters of Mercy 1; Beds 266; Patients Assisted Annually 150,072; Total Staff 1,694.

[H] MONASTERIES AND RESIDENCES OF PRIESTS AND BROTHERS

CARMICHAEL. *Sacramento Jesuit Community* (1963) 1200 Jacob Ln., 95608. Tel: 916-482-6060; Fax: 916-972-8037. Email: mgilson@calprov.org. Web: www.jesuithighschool.org. Revs. Michael C. Gilson, S.J., Supr. Email: mgilson@calprov.org; David F. Klein, S.J.; Kevin A. Leidich, S.J.; Gerald P. McCourt, S.J.; Michael E. Moynahan, S.J.; Charles R. Olsen, S.J.; Thomas G. Piquado, S.J. Email: tpiquado@calprov.org; Arthur J. Wehr, S.J. Email: awehr@calprov.org; David J. Suwalsky, S.J.; Bro. Justin DeChance, S.J.; Mr. Alejandro O. Baez, S.J.; Mr. Julian Climaco, S.J.; Mr. Martin Silva, S.J. (California Prov., Los Gatos) Priests 9; Brothers 1; Scholastics 3.

CITRUS HEIGHTS. *Christ the King Passionist Retreat Center*, 6520 Van Maren Ln., 95621. Tel: 916-725-4720; Fax: 916-725-4812. Email: christtheking@passionist.org. Web: www.passionist.org. Revs. Alfonso San Juan, C.P.; Richard L. Parks, C.P.; James G. Strommer, C.P.; Blaise Czaja, C.P.; John Hilgert, C.P.; Bro. Kurt Wernert, C.P. The Passionists (Chicago, IL)., A community residence for the Passionist priests and brothers who conduct missions and retreats. Priests 5; Brothers 1.

VINA. *Abbey of New Clairvaux, Trappist*, 26240 7th St., P.O. Box 80, 96092. Tel: 530-839-2161; Fax: 530-839-2332. Email: monks@newclairvaux.org. Web: www.newclairvaux.org. Rt. Revs. Paul Mark Schwan, O.C.S.O., Abbot; Thomas X. Davis, O.C.S.O., J.C.L., Abbot Emeritus; Bernard Johnson, O.C.S.O., J.C.L., Abbot Emeritus; Revs. Harold K. Meyer, O.C.S.O.; Lawrence A. Glaser, O.C.S.O.; Paul Jerome Konkler, O.C.S.O.; Anthony R. Bellesorte, O.C.S.O.; Rt. Rev. Mark A. Scott, O.C.S.O. Cistercian Abbey, Cistercians of the Strict Observance. Priests 8; Professed Brothers 13; Novices 1.

WALNUT GROVE. *Monastery of Chau Son Sacramento*, 14080 Leary Rd., P.O. Box 99, 95690. Tel: 916-776-1356; Fax: 916-776-1921. Email: chausonus@gmail.com. Revs. Dominic Hung Tran, Prior; Francis Xavier Phan Bao Luyen; Vincent Nguyen Dinh Hau, Cantor; Francis de Sales Vu Khac Nam; Nicolas Le Quang Thanh; Bros. Matthias Dinh Van Bon; Leo Nguyen Van Tien.

[I] CONVENTS AND RESIDENCES FOR SISTERS

SACRAMENTO. *Canossian Daughters of Charity* (1808) Our Lady of Lourdes Convent, 1949 North Ave., 95838. Tel: 916-925-4001; Fax: 916-925-8897. Email: fdcc_sac@yahoo.com. Web: www.canossiansacramento.wordpress.com. Sisters 5. *Religious of the Institute of the Blessed Virgin Mary*, 3606 Chadsworth Way, 95821. Tel: 916-485-6384; Fax: 916-485-6385. Sisters 3. *Religious of the Institute of the Blessed Virgin Mary*, 9190 Sebastiani Way, 95829. Tel: 916-681-2016; Fax: 916-739-1178. Sisters 1. *Religious of the Institute of the Blessed Virgin Mary*, 3632 Ardmore Rd., 95821. Tel: 916-489-8931. Sisters 1.

Religious of the Virgin Mary, 8804 El Verano Ave., 95626-0444. Tel: 916-992-6318. Sr. Maria Olivia Kingsbury, R.V.M., Admin. Sisters 6.

Religious of the Virgin Mary, 10816 Richert Ln., Elk Grove, 95624. Tel: 916-682-1203. Sr. Maria Concepcion Cambaya, R.V.M., District Supr.

Sister Servants of the Blessed Sacrament (1904, Congregation); (1971, Community) 5929 61st St., 95824. Tel: 916-457-0182; Fax: 916-453-8950. Email: marcelasjs@yahoo.com. Sr. Marcela G. de la Pena, S.J.S., Supr. Sisters 4.

Sisters Catechists of Jesus Crucified (1962) 5712 Muskingham Way, 95823. Tel: 916-395-1875. Email: hermanascjc@aol.com. Sisters 4.

Sisters of the Holy Rosary of Fatima (1952) 1708 U St., 95818. Tel: 916-442-8646; Fax: 916-733-0195. Email: vicentalemus@sbcglobal.net. Sisters 3.

AUBURN. *Sisters of Mercy of the Americas West Midwest Community, Inc.*, 535 Sacramento St., 95603-5699. Tel: 530-887-2000; Fax: 530-887-0789. Email: info@mercywmw.org. Web: www.mercywestmidwest.org. Sisters Judith Frikker, R.S.M., Pres.; Sheila Megley, R.S.M., Treas.; Judith Cannon, R.S.M., Sec.; Kathy Thornton, R.S.M., Leadership Team; Michelle Gorman, R.S.M., Leadership Team; Kim Kinsel, Community Oper. Officer; Carol Kelley, Community Fin. Officer; Sandy Goetzinger-Comer, Dir. Communications. Sisters 740; Associates 536.

FAIRFIELD. *Sisters of the Holy Faith* (1867) Holy Spirit Convent, 1050 N. Texas St., 94533. Tel: 707-425-3572. Email: ecurtis@diocese-sacramento.org. Web: www.hsschool.org. Sisters 2.

GEORGETOWN. *Discalced Carmelite Nuns* (1935) P.O. Box 4210, 95634. Tel: 530-333-1617; Fax: 530-333-1617. Web: www.carmelitemonastery.com. Carmel of the Holy Family and Saint Therese. Sisters 16.

[J] RETREAT HOUSES

SACRAMENTO. *Pendola Center*, 2110 Broadway, 95818-2541. Tel: 916-733-0141; Fax: 916-733-0195. Email: camppendola@diocese-sacramento.org. Web: www.pendola.org. Center located in Sierra-Nevada foothills near Camptonville. Summer camp for boys and girls 6-16. Available for teenage and young adult retreats, school midweek retreats, field trips. Contact: Dir. of Pendola Center.

AUBURN. *Mercy Center Auburn*, 535 Sacramento St., 95603-5699. Tel: 530-887-2019; Fax: 530-887-1154. Email: info@mercycenter.org. Web: www.mercycenter.org. A ministry of the Sisters of Mercy of the Americas West Midwest Community.

LOS GATOS. *Jesuit Retreat Center of the Sierra*, 1001 Boole Rd., Applegate, 95703. Tel: 530-878-2776; Fax: 530-878-1615. Email: jrc@vccr.com. Rev. Charles J. Tilley, S.J., Dir. Tel: 916-482-9666; Kris Holland, Res. Site Dir. Tel: 530-878-2776. Available for retreats and conferences from August 14 to May 15.

[K] CAMPUS MINISTRIES AND NEWMAN CENTERS

SACRAMENTO. *Newman Catholic Community at Sacramento State aka The Newman Club of Sacramento* (1967) Mailing Address: 5900 Newman Ct., 95819-2610. Tel: 916-454-4188; Fax: 916-454-4180. Email: tcortese@sacnewman.org. Web: www.sacnewman.org. Rev. James A. Doogan, S.J., Dir.; Maggie Kawasaki-Murray, M.A., Youth Min.; Tony Cortese, M.A., Campus Min.; Ms. Mary Ann Williams, Business Mgr.

Newman Catholic Student Community @ Davis 514 C St., Davis, 95616. Tel: 530-753-7393; Fax: 530-753-2794. Web: www.davisnewman.org. Deacon Clark Goecker, Dir.; Rev. Innocent Subiza (Rwanda), Chap.; Ellie Wright, Admin. Asst.

St. Thomas Aquinas Newman Center @ Chico 346 Cherry St., Chico, 95928. Tel: 530-342-5182; Fax: 530-342-3016. Email: newmancenterchico@yahoo.com. Web: www.chiconewman.org. Rev. Blaise R. Berg, S.T.D., Dir.

[L] CATHOLIC SOCIAL WELFARE ACTIVITIES

SACRAMENTO. *Catholic Charities of Sacramento, Inc.*, 2110 Broadway, 95818. Tel: 916-733-0253; Fax: 916-733-0224. Email: mkiernan@diocese-sacramento.org. Very Rev. Michael F. Kiernan, Chm. Bd. of Directors & Exec. Dir.

Member Agencies of Catholic Charities of Sacramento, Inc.:

Catholic Social Service of Sacramento, 5890 Newman Ct., 95819-2608. Tel: 916-452-7481; Fax: 916-736-0282. Web: www.csssac.org. Very Rev. Michael F. Kiernan, Chm. Bd. of Dir.; Kurt Chismark, Exec. Dir. Total Staff 3; Total Assisted 675.

Northern Valley Catholic Social Service, 2400 Washington Ave., Redding, 96001. Tel: 530-241-0552; Fax: 530-247-3354. Web: www.nvcss.org. David Gasman, Chm. Bd. of Directors; Don Chapman, Exec. Dir. Total Staff 120; Total Served 16,798.

Catholic Social Service of Solano County, 125 Corporate Pl., Ste. A, Vallejo, 94590. Tel: 707-644-8909; Fax: 707-644-6314. Email: admin@csssolano.org. Web: www.csssolano.org. Ellen McBride, Chm. Bd. of Directors; Kurt Chismark, Exec. Dir. Total Staff 8; Total Assisted 5,500.

Subsidiaries of Catholic Charities of Sacramento:

Sacramento Food Bank and Family Services, 3333 Third Ave., 95817. Tel: 916-456-1980; Fax: 916-451-5920. Web: www.sfbs.org. Patrick McClain, Chm. Bd. of Directors; Blake Young, Exec. Dir. & Pres. Total Staff 40; Total Served 56,104.

Administrative Project of Catholic Charities of Sacramento:

Mother Teresa Maternity Home, 3109 Sacramento St., Placerville, 95667. Tel: 530-295-8006. Barbara Goyette, Chm. Bd. of Directors. Total Staff 4; Total Served 169.

Downtown Senior Outreach Program, 719 J. St., 95814. Tel: 916-733-0253; Fax: 916-733-0224. Elizabeth White, Prog. Dir. Total Staff 2; Total Assisted 100.

Centro Guadalupe, 711 T St., 95811. Tel: 916-443-5367; Fax: 916-443-5845. Elizabeth White, Prog. Dir. Total Staff 3; Total Assisted 5,000.

Mercy Education Resource Center, 6007 Folsom Blvd. #200, 95819. Tel: 916-737-6026; Fax: 916-737-6507. Email: info@mercyeducation.org. Web: www.mercyeducation.org. Sponsored by the Sisters of Mercy West Midwest Community., Provides marriage counseling and individual counseling, psycho-educational assessment for learning disabilities, school counseling, school resource teachers and instructional services, English language services for adults. Total Staff 36; Total Assisted 3,800.

Society of St. Vincent de Paul, Sacramento District Council, Thrift Store: 2275 Watt Ave., 95825. Tel: 916-972-1212; Fax: 916-972-1242. Email: jhallissy@svdp-sacramento.org. Web: svdp-sacramento.org. Office: 608 University Ave., 95825. Tel: 916-649-2214; Fax: 916-649-9241. John P. Hallissy, Pres.

Society St. Vincent de Paul, Sacramento District Council. Tel: 916-649-2214; Fax: 916-649-9241. Email: jhallissy@svdp-sacramento.org. Total Assisted 136,000; Total Staff 12.

MARYSVILLE. *Grand Council, Catholic Ladies Relief Society of the Diocese of Sacramento*, 1324 Los Verjeles, 95901. Tel: 530-743-6022. Charlene Adams, Grand Pres.; Very Rev. Michael F. Kiernan, Grand Chap.

ROSEVILLE. *Society of St. Vincent DePaul* (1983) 503 Giuseppe Ct. #8, 95678. Tel: 916-781-3303 (Office & Food Locker); 916-781-5434 (Thrift Store); Fax: 916-781-8105 (Office Fax). Mr. Tom Stanko, Pres. Emergency Services, Clothing Vouchers, Food Assistance, Dining Room, Thrift Store, Mail

Service. Also free medical clinic on Wednesday mornings 8:30 a.m. to 10:00 a.m. Provide triage and urgent care; no longitudinal care. Total Assisted 24,130.

VALLEJO. *Society of St. Vincent de Paul*, 1225 Tuolumne St., 94590. Tel: 707-644-0376; Fax: 707-644-1423. Benedict Archer, Pres. Total Assisted 3,000.

[M] YOUTH AND YOUNG ADULT MINISTRIES

SACRAMENTO. *Catholic Committee on Scouting*, 2110 Broadway, 95818. Tel: 916-733-0123; Fax: 916-733-0224. Email: mrichards@diocese-sacramento.org. Web: www.oharanetworks.com/dccs.htm. Very Rev. Mark R. Richards, J.C.L., Diocesan Chap.

Department of Evangelization & Catechesis, 2110 Broadway, 95818. Tel: 916-733-0123; Fax: 916-733-0195. Web: www.diocese-sacramento.org. Lori Rosene, Dir., Camp Pendola; Kevin Staszkow, Dir.; Steve Patton, Assoc. Dir., Family & Respect Life Ministries; Carson Weber, Assoc. Dir. New Media Evangelization; Karla Marquez, Coord., Young Adult Ministry; Deacon Antonio Ramirez, Coord. Parish Ministry Support; Kathi Barber, Admin., Camp ReCreation; Stanley Simonet, Deaf Ministry Pastoral Worker; Sr. Virginia Alcala, S.C.J.C., Assoc. Dir., Lay Ministry Formation; Kevin Staszkow, Assoc. Dir., Youth & Young Adults; Jennifer Collins.

[N] MISCELLANEOUS

SACRAMENTO. *California Catholic Conference, Inc.* (1971) 1119 K St., 95814. Tel: 916-313-4000; Fax: 916-313-4066. Web: www.cacatholic.org. Most Revs. Gerald E. Wilkerson, D.D., V.G., Pres.; Jaime Soto, M.S.W., Vice Pres.; Richard J. Garcia, D.D., Sec. & Treas.; Mr. Edward "Ned" E. Dolejsi, Exec. Dir.; Carol Hogan, Dir. Pastoral Projects & Communication; Debbie McDermott, Exec. Asst./Assoc. Dir. Restorative Justice CA Catholic Conference; Mrs. Linda Wanner, Assoc. Dir. Governmental Relations; Stephen J. Pehanich, Senior Dir. Advocacy & Educ. CA Catholic Conference; Barbara Caselli, Office Mgr.

California Conference of Catholic Bishops, 1119 K St., 95814. Tel: 916-313-4000; Fax: 916-313-4066. Web: www.cacatholic.org. Most Revs. Gerald E. Wilkerson, D.D., V.G., Pres.; Jaime Soto, M.S.W., Vice Pres.; Richard J. Garcia, D.D., Sec. & Treas.; Mr. Edward "Ned" E. Dolejsi, Exec. Dir.; Carol Hogan, Dir. Pastoral Projects & Communication; Debbie McDermott, Exec. Asst./Assoc. Dir. Restorative Justice CA Catholic Conference; Mrs. Linda Wanner, Assoc. Dir. Governmental Rels.; Stephen J. Pehanich, Senior Dir. Advocacy & Educ. CA Catholic Conference; Barbara Caselli, Office Mgr.

Catholic Charities of California, Inc. (1987) 1119 K St., 2nd Fl., 95814. Tel: 916-313-4005; Fax: 916-443-4731. Email: smlahey@catholiccharitiesca.org. Web: www.catholiccharitiesca.org. Shannon M. Lahey, Exec. Dir.; Ken Sawa, Pres.; Solomon Belette, Vice Pres.; Rev. Msgr. Gregory Cox, Sec. & Treas.

The Catholic Foundation of the Diocese of Sacramento, Inc., P.O. Box 189656, 95818-9656. Tel: 916-733-0277; Fax: 916-733-0295. Mr. Kelly Brothers, Pres.

Mercy Senior Housing, Inc. dba Mercy McMahon Terrace (1919) 3865 J St., 95816. Tel: 916-733-6510; Fax: 916-733-6515.

The Parochial Fund, Inc., P.O. Box 189666, 95818. Tel: 916-733-0277; Fax: 916-733-0295. Rev. F. Ignatius Haran, Pres. (Retired).

PAX Ministerio Foundation Trust Fund, 2110 Broadway, 95818. Tel: 916-733-0245. Web: www.diocese-sacramento.org. Very Rev. Msgr. James T. Murphy, Interim Dir.

The Preserving Our Past, Building Our Future Foundation of Northern California, Inc., P.O. Box 188617, 95818. Tel: 916-733-0277; Fax: 916-733-0295. Mr. David Krotine Esq., Pres.

Sacramento Catholic Forum (2002) P.O. Box 254848, 95865-4848. Tel: 916-572-3171. Web: www.saccatholicforum.org.

**Stanford Settlement* (1936) 450 W. El Camino Ave., 95833-2299. Tel: 916-927-1303; Fax: 916-922-1694. Email: sisterjeanne@stanfordsettlement.org. Web: www.stanfordsettlement.org. Sr. Jeanne Felion, S.S.S., Exec. Dir. Total Assisted Annually 8,000.

DIXON. *Pro Ecclesia Sancta of California*, 105 S. 2nd St., 95620. Tel: 707-592-1662. F. Carlos Farfan, Pres.

LOOMIS. *Dominican Sisters of Mary, Mother of the Eucharist - Loomis*, 5820 Rocklin Rd., 95650. Tel: 734-994-7437. Email: sjdr@sistersofmary.org. Sr. John Dominic Rasmussen, Treas.

**IHR Educational Broadcasting*, 3256 Penryn Rd., Ste. 100, 95650. Tel: 888-887-7120; Fax: 916-535-0504. Douglas Sherman, Pres.; Kimberly Britz, Admin. Dir.

Spiritus Sanctus Enrichment, 5820 Rocklin Rd., 95650. Tel: 734-994-7437. Email: sjdr@sistersofmary.org. Sr. John Dominic Rasmussen, Treas. Sponsored by Dominican Sisters of Mary, Mother of the Eucharist - Loomis.

RANCHO CORDOVA. *Catholic Healthcare West - Sacramento Office*, 3400 Data Dr., 95670. Tel: 916-851-2000; Fax: 916-851-2727. Web: www.chwhealth.org/sacramento.

Corporate Headquarters, Catholic Healthcare West, 185 Berry St., Ste. 300, San Francisco, 94107. Tel: 415-438-5500; Fax: 415-438-5726.

Holy Trinity Community North America (HTCNA), 4216 Silver Water Way, 95742. Tel: 916-213-9281. Erick Yo, Pres.; Yanliwaty S. Guerzon, Sec.

Mercy Foundation (1954) 3400 Data Dr., 95670. Tel: 916-851-2700; Fax: 916-851-2724. Email: mercyfoundationsac@chw.edu. Web: www.supportmercyfoundation.org.

WOODLAND. *Sociedad Guadalupana de Woodland*, Mailing Address: P.O. Box 1173, 95776. 920 North St., 95695. Tel: 530-662-4025. Email: ncampiz@cal.net. Ms. Luz Elena Campiz, Pres.

RELIGIOUS INSTITUTES OF MEN REPRESENTED IN THE DIOCESE

For further details refer to the corresponding bracketed number in the Religious Institutes of Men or Women section.

[]—*Augustinian Assumptionist Fathers*—A.A.
[0330]—*Brothers of the Christian Schools* (Napa, CA)—F.S.C.
[0270]—*Carmelite Fathers & Brothers* (Barrington, IL)—O.Carm.
[0350]—*Cistercians Order of the Strict Observance-Trappists* (Rome, Italy)—O.C.S.O.
[0370]—*Columban Fathers*—S.S.C.
[]—*Congregation of Mother Coredemptrix*—C.M.C.
[1000]—*Congregation of the Passion* (Chicago, IL)—C.P.
[]—*Crusade of the Holy Spirit*
[0520]—*Franciscan Friars* (Prov. of St. Barbara)—O.F.M.
[]—*Franciscan Order of the Atonement*—S.A.
[]—*Hermits of the Most Blessed Virgin Mary of Mt. Carmel*—H.O.C.
[0690]—*Jesuit Fathers and Brothers* (California Prov., Los Gatos, CA)—S.J.
[0730]—*Legionaries of Christ*—L.C.
[0930]—*Oblates of St. Joseph* (Santa Cruz, CA)—O.S.J.
[]—*Oratorians* (Colombia)
[0950]—*Oratorians*—C.O.
[0430]—*Order of Preachers-Dominicans*—O.P.
[1065]—*Priestly Fraternity of St. Peter*—F.S.S.P.
[1200]—*Society of the Divine Savior* (Milwaukee, WI)—S.D.S.
[]—*Society of the Divine Word*—S.V.D.

RELIGIOUS INSTITUTES OF WOMEN REPRESENTED IN THE DIOCESE

[1940]—*Congregation of the Sisters of the Holy Faith*—C.H.F.
[0730]—*Daughters of Charity of Canossa* (Rome, Italy)—Fd.CC.
[]—*Daughters of Divine Love*
[0820]—*Daughters of the Holy Spirit* (Putnam, CT)—D.H.S.
[0420]—*Discalced Carmelite Nuns*—O.C.D.
[1070-03]—*Dominican Sisters* (Sinsinawa, WI)—O.P.
[1070-04]—*Dominican Sisters* (San Rafael, CA)—O.P.
[]—*Dominican Sisters of Charity of the Presentation of the Blessed Virgin Mary*—O.P.
[]—*Dominican Sisters of Mary, Mother of the Eucharist - Loomis* (Ann Arbor, MI)
[]—*Handmaids of the Holy Child Jesus*—H.H.C.J.
[2370]—*Institute of the Blessed Virgin Mary (Loretto Sisters)*—I.B.V.M.
[2575]—*Institute of the Sisters of Mercy of the Americas*—R.S.M.
[]—*Religious of the Virgin Mary* (Quezon City, Philippines)—R.V.M.
[3499]—*Sister Servants of the Blessed Sacrament*—S.S.B.S.
[]—*Sisters Catechists of Jesus Crucified* (Mexico)—S.J.C.
[]—*Sisters of Mercy* (Omaha)—R.S.M.
[]—*Sisters of Mercy of Cashel* (U.S. Province)—R.S.M.
[4080]—*Sisters of Social Service of Los Angeles, Inc.*—S.S.S.
[1630]—*Sisters of St. Francis of Penance and Christian Charity* (Redwood City, CA)—O.S.F.
[]—*Sisters of St. Joseph of Carondelet*—C.S.J.
[1960]—*Sisters of the Holy Family* (San Jose, CA)—S.H.F.
[]—*Sisters of the Holy Rosary of Fatima* (Salvatierra, Mexico)—H.R.F.
[3680]—*Sisters of the Sacred Hearts of Jesus and Mary* (Essex)—S.H.J.M.
[4110]—*Ursuline Nuns of the Congregation of Paris*—O.S.U.
[]—*Visitation Sisters of Alleppey*—S.V.C.

DIOCESAN CEMETERIES

SACRAMENTO. *Calvary Catholic Cemetery & Mausoleum*, 7101 Verner Ave., 95841. Tel: 916-726-1232; Fax: 916-726-4821.

St. Joseph Catholic Cemetery, 2615 21st St., 95818. Tel: 916-452-4831; Fax: 916-452-1364.

St. Mary's Catholic Cemetery & Mausoleum, 6700 21st Ave., 95820-5981. Tel: 916-452-4831; Fax: 916-452-1364.

COLUSA. *Holy Cross Catholic Cemetery*, 1741 Westscott, 95932. Tel: 916-726-1232; Fax: 916-726-4821.

FAIRFIELD. *St. Alphonsus Catholic Cemetery*, 1801 Union Ave., 94533. Tel: 707-644-5209; Fax: 707-554-4091.

RANCHO MURIETA. *St. Vincent DePaul Catholic Cemetery*, Jackson Hwy., 95683. Tel: 916-452-4831; Fax: 916-452-1364.

RIO VISTA. *St. Joseph Catholic Cemetery*, Hwy. 12, 94571. Tel: 916-452-4831; Fax: 916-452-1364; 707-374-5071.

VALLEJO. *All Souls Catholic Cemetery & Mausoleum*, 550 Glen Cove Rd., 94591. Tel: 707-644-5209; Fax: 707-554-4091.

St. Vincent Cemetery, 550 Glen Cove Rd., 94591. Tel: 707-644-5209; Fax: 707-554-4091.

WOODLAND. *St. Joseph Catholic Cemetery & Mausoleum*, 503 California St., 95695. Tel: 530-662-8645; Fax: 530-662-0796.

NECROLOGY

† O'Neill, Rev. Msgr. Patrick J., (Retired)—Died Oct. 4, 2011
† Phelan, Nicholas, (Retired)—Died Sept. 24, 2011

An asterisk (*) denotes an organization that has established tax-exempt status directly with the IRS and is not covered by the USCCB Group Ruling.

Diocese of Saginaw

(Dioecesis Saginavensis)

Most Reverend

JOSEPH R. CISTONE

Bishop of Saginaw; ordained May 17, 1975; appointed Titular Bishop of Casae Medianae and Auxiliary Bishop of Philadelphia; ordained July 28, 2004; appointed Bishop of Saginaw May 20, 2009; installed July 28, 2009.

Chancery: 5800 Weiss St., Saginaw, MI 48603-2762. Tel: 989-799-7910; Fax: 989-797-6670.

Web: www.saginaw.org

ESTABLISHED FEBRUARY 26, 1938.

Square Miles 6,955.

Comprises the following Counties in the State of Michigan: Arenac, Bay, Clare, Gladwin, Gratiot, Huron, Isabella, Midland, Saginaw, Sanilac and Tuscola.

For legal titles of parishes and diocesan institutions, consult the Chancery Office.

STATISTICAL OVERVIEW

Personnel	
Bishop	1
Priests: Diocesan Active in Diocese	55
Priests: Diocesan Active Outside Diocese	3
Priests: Retired, Sick or Absent	34
Number of Diocesan Priests	92
Religious Priests in Diocese	6
Total Priests in Diocese	98
Extern Priests in Diocese	5
Ordinations:	
Diocesan Priests	4
Transitional Deacons	2
Permanent Deacons	4
Permanent Deacons in Diocese	17
Total Sisters	90
Parishes	
Parishes	105
With Resident Pastor:	
Resident Diocesan Priests	52
Resident Religious Priests	5
Without Resident Pastor:	
Administered by Priests	25
Administered by Deacons	4
Administered by Religious Women	17
Administered by Lay People	2
Professional Ministry Personnel:	
Sisters	18
Lay Ministers	31
Welfare	
Catholic Hospitals	1
Total Assisted	300,590
Health Care Centers	1
Total Assisted	1,406
Homes for the Aged	1
Total Assisted	168
Residential Care of Children	3
Total Assisted	252
Specialized Homes	2
Total Assisted	208
Special Centers for Social Services	7
Total Assisted	13,425
Other Institutions	3
Total Assisted	28,305
Educational	
Diocesan Students in Other Seminaries	6
Total Seminarians	6
High Schools, Diocesan and Parish	3
Total Students	607
Elementary Schools, Diocesan and Parish	17
Total Students	2,676
Catechesis/Religious Education:	
High School Students	1,056
Elementary Students	5,708
Total Students under Catholic Instruction	10,053
Teachers in the Diocese:	
Priests	1
Lay Teachers	215
Vital Statistics	
Receptions into the Church:	
Infant Baptism Totals	805
Minor Baptism Totals	195
Adult Baptism Totals	93
Received into Full Communion	192
First Communions	1,153
Confirmations	1,266
Marriages:	
Catholic	299
Interfaith	149
Total Marriages	448
Deaths	1,470
Total Catholic Population	104,726
Total Population	700,771

Former Bishops—Most Revs. WILLIAM F. MURPHY, J.C.L., LL.D., S.T.D., ord. June 13, 1908; appt. first Bishop of Saginaw, March 17, 1938; cons. May 17, 1938; died Feb. 7, 1950; STEPHEN S. WOZNICKI, D.D., second Bishop; ord. Dec. 22, 1917; appt. Titular Bishop of Pelte and Auxiliary Bishop of Detroit, Dec. 13, 1937; cons. Jan. 25, 1938; transferred to Saginaw, March 28, 1950; Assistant at the Pontifical Throne, Dec. 22, 1967; resigned and transferred to the Titular See of Tiava, Oct. 30, 1968; died Dec. 10, 1968; FRANCIS F. REH, S.T.L., J.C.D., third Bishop; ord. Dec. 8, 1935; appt. Bishop of Charleston, June 4, 1962; cons. June 29, 1962; transferred to the Titular See of Macrinna in Maurentania; Rector Pontifical North American College in Rome, Sept. 5, 1964; transferred to Saginaw, Dec. 18, 1968; installed Feb. 26, 1969; retired April 29, 1980; died Nov. 14, 1994; KENNETH E. UNTENER, ord. June 1, 1963; ord. and installed as Bishop of Saginaw Nov. 24, 1980; died March 27, 2004.; ROBERT J. CARLSON, ord. May 22, 1970; appt. Titular Bishop of Aviocala and Auxiliary Bishop of Saint Paul and Minneapolis Nov. 22, 1983; cons. Jan. 11, 1984; appt. Coadjutor Bishop of Sioux Falls Jan. 13, 1994; Succeeded to the See March 21, 1995; appt. Bishop of Saginaw Dec. 29, 2004; installed Feb. 24, 2005; appt. Archbishop of St. Louis April 21, 2009.

Vicar General—Rev. THOMAS J. MCNAMARA.

Vicar for Priests—Rev. RONALD F. WAGNER, 5800 Weiss St., Saginaw, 48603. Tel: 989-797-6649.

Episcopal Vicars—

Territorial Vicars—Revs. ROBERT PARE; WILLIAM J. GRUDEN; RICHARD BOKINSKIE; JOHN F. COTTER; JAMES E. FALSEY; PETER J. GASPENY; CRAIG L. ALBRECHT; RANDY J. KELLY.

Hispanic Ministries Director—MARIA CEPEDA. Tel: 989-797-6604.

Delegate for Religious—Sr. JANET FULGENZI, O.P., Ph.D., 5800 Weiss St., Saginaw, 48603-2799. Tel: 989-799-7910.

Chancery—5800 Weiss St., Saginaw, 48603-2799. Tel: 989-799-7910; Fax: 989-797-6670.

Chancellor—Sr. MARY JUDITH O'BRIEN, R.S.M., J.D., J.C.D. Tel: 989-797-6620.

Director of Human Resources—CONNIE HUISKENS WOJDA. Tel: 989-797-6687.

Financial and Business Operations—

Chief Financial Officer—DEBRA BIERLEIN. Tel: 989-797-6688.

Director of Accounting Services—NANCY SCHULTZ. Tel: 989-797-6642.

Accounting Assistant—JOSEPHINE MENDOZA. Tel: 989-797-6629.

Catholic Cemeteries—KENNETH GROYA, Dir. Tel: 989-797-6627.

Diocesan Finance Council—SHELLEY STORER, Chm.

Diocesan Building Commission—DAN KOZAKIEWICZ, Chm., 5800 Weiss St., Saginaw, 48603-2799. Tel: 989-799-7910.

Diocesan Investment Committee—JIM PAPAJESEK, Chm.

Inter-Parish Deposit & Loan—ROBERT WOLAK, Chm.

Catholic Services Appeal—ANDREA GASPER, 5800 Weiss St., Saginaw, 48603-2799. Tel: 989-797-6626.

Tribunal—5800 Weiss St., Saginaw, 48603-2799. Tel: 989-797-6623.

Judicial Vicar—Rev. ROBERT J. DELAND. Tel: 989-797-6622.

Tribunal Coordinator—HEIDI KRUPP, J.C.L. Tel: 989-797-6667.

Defenders of the Bond—Sr. VICTORIA VONDENBERGER, R.S.M., J.C.L.; Rev. THOMAS E. SUTTON, J.C.L.

Judges—Rev. ROBERT J. DELAND; Sr. MARY JUDITH O'BRIEN, R.S.M., J.D., J.C.D.; Rev. RICHARD M. FILARY, J.C.L.; HEIDI KRUPP, J.C.L.

Promoter of Justice—Rev. MICHAEL BRADLEY.

Notary—CHRIS WOLAK.

Diocesan Presbyteral Council—Rev. PETER J. GASPENY, Chm., 1503 Kosciuszko Ave., Bay City, 48708-8027. Tel: 989-893-6421.

Diocesan College of Consultors—Revs. ROBERT H. BYRNE; PETER J. GASPENY; FREDERICK J. KAWKA (Retired); THOMAS J. MCNAMARA; WILLIAM J. RUTKOWSKI; RONALD F. WAGNER.

Clergy Personnel Board—Rev. WILLIAM R. TAYLOR, Chm. (Retired), 1525 S. Washington, Saginaw, 48601-2895. Tel: 989-755-8020.

Diocesan Council of Catholic Women—RITA FAITH MAHER, Pres., 3028 McGill St., Marlette, 48453; Rev. CRAIG L. ALBRECHT, Moderator, 4195 Midland St., Box 99, Merrill, 48637-0099.

Office of Communication—ERIN LOOBY CARLSON, 5800 Weiss St., Saginaw, 48603-2799. Tel: 989-797-6630.

Mission Office—Sr. MARGO TAFOYA, M.S.Sp., Dir. for Missions, 5800 Weiss St., Saginaw, 48603-2799. Tel: 989-797-6633.

Education/Formation—Dr. DANIEL OSBORN, S.T.D., Dir. Center for Ministry, 5802 Weiss St., Saginaw, 48603. Tel: 989-797-6662; JOAN M. LAPOINTE, Coord. Lay Formation. Tel: 989-797-6609; PAUL SCHROEDER, Dir. Catechesis. Tel: 989-797-6608; Mr. MARK GRAVELINE, Dir. Youth Ministry &

Vocations. Tel: 989-797-6639; PATRICIA D. PRESTON, Sec. Tel: 989-797-6654.

Bay Area Catholic Schools—MICHAEL J. KNOFF, Dir., 607 E. South Union, Bay City, 48706. Tel: 989-894-8777.

Saginaw Area Catholic Schools—MARY ANN DESCHAINE, Supt. Schools, 5800 Weiss St., Saginaw, 48603. Tel: 989-797-6651; IRENE HENSINGER, Dir. & Prin. Nouvel Catholic Central, 2555 Weineke Rd., Saginaw, 48603. Tel: 989-399-2221; 989-797-6632; Fax: 989-399-2257.

Ecumenism Ministry—Rev. JAMES R. CARLSON, 5800 Weiss St., Saginaw, 48603. Tel: 989-790-5086.

Ministry to Charismatic Renewal—MARGE FOBEAR, Dir., Charismatic Renewal Center, 1110 State St., Bay City, 48706. Tel: 989-684-4640.

Ministry to Priests—Rev. RONALD F. WAGNER, Vicar for Priests. Tel: 989-797-6649.

Roman Catholic Diocese of Saginaw Catholic School Foundation—5800 Weiss St., Saginaw, 48603-2799. Tel: 989-797-6679. VACANT.

Roman Catholic Diocese of Saginaw Inter-Parish Endowment Fund—5800 Weiss St., Saginaw, 48603-2799. ANNETTE M. O'BRIEN, Dir. Office of Stewardship & Planned Giving. Tel: 989-797-6679.

Office of Christian Service—TERRI GRIERSON, Dir. Tel: 989-797-6650; SANDY BUZA, Respect Life Coord. Tel: 989-797-6652.

Marriage and Family Coordinator—MARY ANN CHERRY. Tel: 989-797-6660.

Office of Liturgy—Sr. CHRISTINE GRETKA, C.S.J., Assoc. Liturgical Music. Tel: 989-797-6663.

Organizations and Services—

Diocese of Saginaw Priests' Retirement Association—Rev. ROBERT J. MEISSNER, 2956 E. North Union Rd., Bay City, 48706-9246. Tel: 989-684-1170.

Holy Childhood Association—Sr. MARGO TAFOYA, M.S.Sp., 5800 Weiss St., Saginaw, 48603-2799. Tel: 989-797-6633.

Director of Development—DAN MCKUNE. Tel: 989-797-6624.

Office of Stewardship and Planned Giving—ANNETTE O'BRIEN, 5800 Weiss St., Saginaw, 48603-2799. Tel: 989-797-6679.

Victim Assistance Coordinator—Sr. JANET FULGENZI, O.P., Ph.D. Tel: 989-797-6682. Email: jfulgenzi@dioceseofsaginaw.org.

CLERGY, PARISHES, MISSIONS AND PAROCHIAL SCHOOLS

CITY OF SAGINAW

(SAGINAW COUNTY)

1—CATHEDRAL OF MARY THE ASSUMPTION formerly St. Mary Cathedral (1853) Rev. Thomas J. McNamara, Rector; Most Rev. Joseph R. Cistone; Rev. David Jenuwine, Parochial Vicar.
Res.: 615 Hoyt Ave., 48607. Tel: 989-752-8119; Fax: 989-752-2165.
Convent—Our Lady of the Assumption Convent Religious Sisters of Mercy Sisters 4.
Catechesis/Religious Program—Students 6.
St. Mary Cathedral Parish Inter-Parish Endowment Fund

2—ST. ANDREW Revs. Ronald F. Wagner; Daniel Roa, Parochial Vicar.
Res.: 612 N. Michigan Ave., 48602. Tel: 989-754-0487; Fax: 989-754-0308.
Catechesis/Religious Program—Students 7.

3—ST. ANTHONY OF PADUA, [JC] Rev. Thomas Schmied, O.F.M.Cap.
Res.: 3680 S. Washington Rd., 48601. Tel: 989-752-1971; Fax: 989-752-1441.
Catechesis/Religious Program—Students 31.

4—SS. CASIMIR & ST. GEORGE formerly St. Casimir/St. George [JC] Rev. Reginaldo Salcedo, Admin.
Res.: 2122 S. Jefferson Ave., 48601. Tel: 989-752-6648; Fax: 989-752-6691.
Catechesis/Religious Program—Students 19.

5—ST. GEORGE, [JC] Merged with St. Casimir, Saginaw to form SS. Casimir & St. George, Saginaw.

6—ST. HELEN, [JC] Rev. Ronald Wagner; Joyce DeKarske, Pastoral Assoc.; Rev. Daniel Roa, Parochial Vicar.
Res.: 2445 N. Charles St., 48602. Tel: 989-793-0618; Fax: 989-793-5487.
Catechesis/Religious Program—Students 49.

7—HOLY FAMILY, [CEM] Rev. Ronald F. Wagner, Sacramental Min.; Deacon Roger Pasionek, Pastoral Admin.; Rev. Daniel Roa, Sacramental Min.
Res.: 1525 S. Washington Ave., 48601. Tel: 989-755-8020; Fax: 989-755-7193.
Catechesis/Religious Program—Students 9.

8—HOLY ROSARY, Closed. For inquiries for parish records contact SS. Simon and Jude Parish, Saginaw.

9—ST. JOHN VIANNEY Rev. James R. Carlson.
Church: 6400 McCarty Rd., 48603. Tel: 989-790-5086; Fax: 989-790-1681.
Catechesis/Religious Program—Kathy Bronz, D.R.E.; Jim Rapin, Youth Min. Students 135.

10—ST. JOSEPH Rev. Francis Voris, O.F.M.Cap.
Res.: 936 N. Sixth Ave., 48601. Tel: 989-755-7561; Fax: 989-755-1090.
Catechesis/Religious Program—Students 84.

11—OUR LADY HELP OF CHRISTIANS, Closed. For inquiries for parish records contact SS. Simon and Jude Parish, Saginaw.

12—OUR LADY OF MOUNT CARMEL, Closed. For inquiries for parish records contact SS. Simon and Jude Parish, Saginaw.

13—SS. PETER AND PAUL Rev. John R. Johnson; Catalina Echeverri, Pastoral Assoc.
Res.: 4735 W. Michigan Ave., 48638. Tel: 989-799-5448; Fax: 989-799-1495.
Catechesis/Religious Program—Students 124.

14—ST. RITA, Closed. For inquiries for parish records contact SS. Simon & Jude Parish, Saginaw.

15—SACRED HEART, Closed. For inquiries for parish records contact SS. Simon and Jude Parish, Saginaw.

16—SS. SIMON AND JUDE Rev. John Mancini, O.S.F.S.
Res.: 2395 S. Outer Dr., 48601. Tel: 989-752-7424; Fax: 989-752-0216.
Catechesis/Religious Program—Students 11.

17—ST. STEPHEN Rev. James Heller. In Res., Rev. William R. Taylor (Retired).
Res.: 2711 Mackinaw St., 48602. Tel: 989-799-2334; Fax: 989-793-3611.
School—(Grades Day Care-8) Tel: 989-793-2811; Fax: 989-793-8463. Kristi Long, Prin. Lay Teachers 21; Students 319.
Catechesis/Religious Program—Sharon Wahl, D.R.E. Students 68.
St. Stephen Catholic School Foundation Endowment Fund

18—ST. THOMAS AQUINAS, [JC] Rev. Randy J. Kelly.
Res.: 5376 State Rd., 48603. Tel: 989-799-2460; Fax: 989-799-0207.
School—Bernardine Sisters of Third Order of St. Francis, (Grades PreSchool-8) Sr. Ann de Guise, O.S.F., Prin. (Farmington, MI) Sisters 1; Lay Teachers 25; Students 446.
Catechesis/Religious Program—Jennifer Giddings, Youth Min. Students 108.
St. Thomas Aquinas Catholic School Foundation Endowment Fund

OUTSIDE THE CITY OF SAGINAW

ALBEE, SAGINAW CO., ST. MARY Rev. Todd Arnberg.
Res.: 5661 Fergus Rd., Rte. 2, St. Charles, 48655. Tel: 989-770-4453; Fax: 989-770-5111.
Catechesis/Religious Program—Joy Tanner, D.R.E. Students 36.

ALMA, GRATIOT CO., ST. MARY Deacons Aloysius J. Oliver, Pastoral Admin. Protem; John J. Cremin, Pastoral Assoc.; Rev. Thai Hung Nguyen, Sacramental Min.
Res.: 510 N. Prospect Ave., 48801. Tel: 989-463-5370; Fax: 989-463-1369.
School—(Grades PreSchool-6), 220 W. Downie St., 48801. Tel: 989-463-4579. Lisa Seeley, Prin. Lay Teachers 11; Students 116.
Catechesis/Religious Program—Marilyn Lorenz, D.R.E.; Linda Goodman, Youth Min.; Kathleen Cranna, Youth Min. Students 45.

ARGYLE, SANILAC CO., ST. JOSEPH, [CEM] Rev. Joseph M. Griffin.
Res.: 4960 N. Ubly Rd., 48410. Tel: 989-658-8145; Fax: 989-658-8105.
Mission—St. Ignatius Frieburg, Sanilac Co.
Catechesis/Religious Program—Edith Izydorek, D.R.E. Students 37.

AUGRES, ARENAC CO., ST. MARK Revs. James E. Falsey; Thomas Kowalczyk, Sacramental Min.
Res.: 415 S. Court St., 48703. Tel: 989-876-7925; Fax: 989-876-7778.
Catechesis/Religious Program—Nancy LaLonde, D.R.E. Students 22.

AUBURN, BAY CO., ST. ANTHONY/ST. JOSEPH, Operates jointly with St. Anthony, Fisherville. Rev. Thomas E. Sutton.
Res.: 84 W. Midland Rd., 48611. Tel: 989-662-6861; Fax: 989-662-0064.
Church: 4699 S. 11 Mile Rd., Auburn, Fisherville, 48611.
School—Area School, (Grades PreSchool-5) Terri Duch, Prin. Students 88; Lay Teachers 6.
School—Auburn Area Catholic, Early Childhood Center, (Grades PreSchool-5), 1492 W. Midland Rd., 48611. Tel: 989-662-6481; Fax: 989-662-3391.
Catechesis/Religious Program—Kellie Deming, D.R.E.; Michelle Butterfield, Youth Min. Students 129.

BAD AXE, HURON CO., SACRED HEART, [CEM] Rev. Robert J. Howe; Jan Rapson, Pastoral Assoc.
Res.: 311 Whitelam St., 48413. Tel: 989-269-7729; Fax: 989-269-4010.
Catechesis/Religious Program—Lorraine Keller, D.R.E.; Matt Guza, Youth Min. Students 108.

BANNISTER, GRATIOT CO., ST. CYRIL Revs. Richard Bokinskie; Joseph Marcel Portelli, Parochial Vicar.
Res.: 517 E. Main St., 48807. Tel: 989-862-5270; Fax: 989-862-4534.
Catechesis/Religious Program—Students 45.

BAY CITY, BAY CO.

1—ST. BONIFACE Rev. Dale A. Orlik; Mary Jo Bourdon, Admin.
Res.: 510 N. Lincoln St., 48708. Tel: 989-893-4851; Fax: 989-893-1781.
Catechesis/Religious Program—Diane Seidel, D.R.E. Students 105.
St. Boniface Parish Inter-Parish Endowment Fund

2—ST. HEDWIG Rev. Kevin Kerbawy, Sacramental Min.; Sr. Joann Plumpe, O.P., Pastoral Admin.
Res.: 1504 S. Kiesel St., 48706. Tel: 989-893-1072; Fax: 989-893-4710.
Catechesis/Religious Program—Phyllis Madziar, D.R.E. Students 56.

3—HOLY TRINITY Revs. Robert S. Gohm; Kevin Kerbawy; Nancy Ruh, Pastoral Min.
Res.: 1008 S. Wenona St., 48706. Tel: 989-893-4073; Fax: 989-893-7087.
School—(Grades PreSchool-5) Tel: 989-892-3018. Terrie DeWaele, Prin. Lay Teachers 7; Students 120.
Catechesis/Religious Program—Mary Dierich, D.R.E. Students 155.
Holy Trinity Parish Inter-Parish Endowment Fund

4—ST. HYACINTH, [CEM] Rev. Edward J. Konieczka; Deacon Lee Stilwell, Pastoral Assoc.
Res.: 1515 Cass Ave., 48708. Tel: 989-895-5581; Fax: 989-895-5583.
Catechesis/Religious Program—Susana Roznowski, D.R.E. Students 74.
Convent—912 S. Farragut St., 48708.

5—ST. JAMES (1983) [CEM] Rev. William J. Gruden; Deacon George Keller.
Res.: 710 Columbus Ave., 48708. Tel: 989-893-4693; Fax: 989-893-1504.
School—(Grades PreK-5) Tel: 989-892-4371. Sr. Julie Gatza, S.C., Prin. Sisters of Charity of Cincinnati 2; Lay Teachers 9; Students 143.
Catechesis/Religious Program—Students 62.
Convent—200 S. Farragut St., 48708.

6—ST. JOSEPH Revs. Rick M. Varner, Sacramental Min.; Dale A. Orlik, Sacramental Min.; Sr. Gail Addis, I.H.M., Pastoral Admin.
Res.: 1005 Third St., 48708. Tel: 989-895-5783; Fax: 989-895-8837.
Catechesis/Religious Program—Ruth Neitzel, D.R.E. Students 34.

7—ST. MARIA GORETTI Sr. Virginia Scally, S.N.D.deN., Pastoral Admin.; Rev. George J. Serour, Sacramental Min. (Retired).
Res.: 2872 N. Euclid Ave., 48706. Tel: 989-684-1523; Fax: 989-684-8286.
Catechesis/Religious Program—Barbara Walkley, D.R.E. Students 52.

8—ST. MARY OF THE ASSUMPTION Rev. Craig L. Albrecht.
Res.: 607 E. S. Union St., 48706. Tel: 989-892-6031; Fax: 989-892-4005.
Catechesis/Religious Program—Students 58.
St. Mary Parish Inter-Parish Endowment Fund

9—OUR LADY OF GUADALUPE Rev. Reginaldo Salcedo, Sacramental Min.; Maria Cepeda, Pastoral Admin.
Res.: 1619 Broadway, 48708. Tel: 989-894-0661; Fax: 989-894-0771.
Catechesis/Religious Program—Josefina Ramirez, D.R.E. Students 24.

10—OUR LADY OF THE VISITATION Rev. Stephen Fillion.
Res.: 1106 State St., 48706. Tel: 989-684-5184; Fax: 989-684-5189.
Catechesis/Religious Program—Gerald Hegenauer, D.R.E. Students 4.

11—ST. STANISLAUS KOSTKA Rev. Richard M. Filary; Deacon Stanislaw Kuczyunski; Sr. Beatrice M. Plamondon, C.S.S.F., Pastoral Ministry; Linda Studniarz, Pastoral Ministry.
Res.: 1503 Kosciuszko Ave., 48708. Tel: 989-893-6421; Fax: 989-893-3985.
Catechesis/Religious Program—Jan Musinski, D.R.E. Students 139.

12—ST. VINCENT DE PAUL Rev. Robert J. Meissner; Cathy Converse, Pastoral Min.
Res.: 2956 E. North Union Rd., 48706. Tel: 989-684-1203; Fax: 989-684-4925.
Catechesis/Religious Program—Chris Platko, D.R.E. Students 76.

BEAL CITY, ISABELLA CO., ST. JOSEPH THE WORKER, [CEM] Rev. Patrick M. Jankowiak; Deacon Michael Smith.
Res.: 2163 N. Winn Rd., Mount Pleasant, 48858. Tel: 989-644-2041; Fax: 989-644-2026.

School—(Grades K-6) Tel: 989-644-3970. Mrs. Mary Hauck, Prin. Lay Teachers 8; Students 114.
Catechesis/Religious Program—Barbara Schafer, D.R.E.; Josette Lorence, Youth Min. Students 111.

BEAVER, BAY CO., ST. VALENTINE, [CEM] Rev. Jerzy Dobosz, Admin.; Deacon Michael Arnold, Pastoral Assoc.
Res.: 999 S. 9 Mile Rd., Kawkawlin, 48631. Tel: 989-662-6843; Fax: 989-662-0152.

BIRCH RUN, SAGINAW CO., SACRED HEART Rev. John S. Sarge; Noreen Harkins, Pastoral Assoc.
Res.: 12157 Church St., 48415. Tel: 989-624-9098; Fax: 989-624-9427.
Catechesis/Religious Program—Ginger Scheffler, D.R.E.; Janet Scheffler, Youth Min. Students 119.

BRIDGEPORT, SAGINAW CO.
1—ASSUMPTION OF THE BLESSED VIRGIN MARY Rev. John S. Sarge.
Res.: 7877 Bell Rd., P.O. Box 602, 48722. Tel: 989-777-1200; Fax: 989-777-6280.
Catechesis/Religious Program—Dave Fackler, D.R.E.; Janet Scheffler, Youth Min. Students 55.
2—ST. CHRISTOPHER Rev. John Mancini, O.S.F.S.
Res.: 3945 Williamson Rd., 48601. Tel: 989-777-2091; Fax: 989-777-9691.
Catechesis/Religious Program—Karen Smith, C.R.E. Students 50.

CARO, TUSCOLA CO., SACRED HEART, [CEM] Rev. Dennis H. Kucharczyk.
Res.: 140 Atwood St., 48723. Tel: 989-673-2346; Fax: 989-673-5669.
Catechesis/Religious Program—Lisa Bednarski, D.R.E.; Karen Cody; Ann Reinelt. Students 128.

CARROLLTON, SAGINAW CO.
1—ST. JOHN THE BAPTIST Rev. Ronald J. Dombrowski, Sacramental Min.; Sr. Christine Gretka, S.S.J., Pastoral Admin.
Res.: 3160 Carla Dr., 48604. Tel: 989-753-5103; Fax: 989-753-4943.
Catechesis/Religious Program—Students 21.
2—ST. JOSAPHAT Rev. Ronald J. Dombrowski.
Res.: 469 Shattuck Rd., 48604. Tel: 989-753-2497; Fax: 989-753-2498.
Catechesis/Religious Program—Sr. Janet Pewoski, C.S.J., D.R.E. Students 15.

CASEVILLE, HURON CO., ST. ROCH Rev. Robert Pare.
Res.: 6253 Main St., P.O. Box 1238, 48725. Tel: 989-856-4933; Fax: 989-856-2861.
Catechesis/Religious Program—Elizabeth Weisenbach, C.R.E. Students 32.

CASS CITY, TUSCOLA CO., ST. PANCRATIUS Rev. Paul W. Bala, Sacramental Min. (Retired); Sr. Maria Dina Puddu, M.C., Pastoral Admin.
Res.: 4292 S. Seeger St., 48726. Tel: 989-872-3336; Fax: 989-872-1852.
Catechesis/Religious Program—Mary Shantz, D.R.E. Students 76.

CHESANING, SAGINAW CO., OUR LADY OF PERPETUAL HELP, [CEM] Revs. Richard Bokinskie; Joseph Marcel Portelli, Parochial Vicar; Diane Hunderford, Pastoral Assoc.
Res.: 404 S. Wood, 48616. Tel: 989-845-6894; Fax: 989-845-7787.
Catechesis/Religious Program—Students 133.

CLARE, CLARE CO., ST. CECILIA, [CEM] Revs. William J. Rutkowski; Christian Tabares, Parochial Vicar.
Res.: 106 E. Wheaton Ave., 48617. Tel: 989-386-9862; Fax: 989-386-3550.
School—(Grades PreSchool-6) Kimberly Smith, Prin. Lay Teachers 7; Students 54.
Catechesis/Religious Program—Ann Croskey, D.R.E. Students 39.
St. Cecilia Catholic School Foundation Endowment Fund

COLEMAN, MIDLAND CO., ST. PHILIP NERI Revs. William J. Rutkowski; Christian Tabares, Parochial Vicar; Deacon Frank Alex.
Res.: 5199 W. Shaffer Rd., P.O. Box 512, 48618. Tel: 989-465-1768; Fax: 989-465-6311.
Catechesis/Religious Program—Judie Klimkiewicz, D.R.E. Students 57.
Mission—St. Anne Edenville, Gladwin Co.
Catechesis/Religious Program—Students 52.

CROSWELL, SANILAC CO., ST. PATRICK, [CEM] Rev. Robert Schikora, Admin.
Mailing Address: P.O. Box 399, Lexington, 48450.
Res.: 105 W. Sanborn Ave., 48422-1353. Tel: 810-679-3849; Fax: 810-679-3903.
Catechesis/Religious Program—Christina Lowry, D.R.E. Students 62.

ESSEXVILLE, BAY CO., ST. JOHN THE EVANGELIST Rev. Rick M. Varner, Parochial Admin.; Kathy Madziar, Pastoral Min.
Res.: 614 Pine St., 48732. Tel: 989-894-2701; Fax: 989-894-5558.
School—(Grades PreSchool-5), 619 Main St., 48732. Sue Grzegorczyk, Prin. Lay Teachers 6; Students 88.
Catechesis/Religious Program—Rose Yagiel, D.R.E. Students 129.

FISHERVILLE, BAY CO., ST. ANTHONY/ST. JOSEPH, [CEM], See St. Anthony/St. Joseph, Auburn.

FRANKENMUTH, SAGINAW CO., BLESSED TRINITY Rev. Robert H. Byrne; Kathleen Myles, Pastoral Min.; Senior Deacon Larry Masserang.
Res.: 958 E. Tuscola St., 48734. Tel: 989-652-3259; Fax: 989-652-2206.
Catechesis/Religious Program—Carol Fox, D.R.E. Students 293.

FREELAND, SAGINAW CO., ST. AGNES Rev. Robert J. DeLand.
Res.: 300 Johnson St., 48623. Tel: 989-695-5652; Fax: 989-695-6275.
Catechesis/Religious Program—Andy Troiano, Youth Min. Students 106.

GAGETOWN, TUSCOLA CO., ST. AGATHA Sr. Dorothy Ann Blasko, O.P., Pastoral Admin.; Rev. Paul W. Bala, Sacramental Min. (Retired).
Res.: 4618 South St., Box 139, 48735. Tel: 989-665-9966; Fax: 989-665-9966.
Catechesis/Religious Program—Students 15.

GLADWIN, GLADWIN CO., SACRED HEART Rev. John F. Cotter.
Res.: 300 N. Silverleaf St., 48624. Tel: 989-426-7154; Fax: 989-426-0896.
Catechesis/Religious Program—Students 29.

HARBOR BEACH, HURON CO., OUR LADY OF LAKE HURON, [CEM] Rev. William Spencer.
Res.: 412 S. First St., 48441. Tel: 989-479-3393; Fax: 989-479-3335.
School—(Grades PreK-8), 222 Court St., 48441. Tel: 989-479-3427. David Mausolf, Prin. Lay Teachers 9; Students 100.
Catechesis/Religious Program—Students 62.
Convent—406 S. First St., 48441.

HARRISON, CLARE CO., ST. ATHANASIUS Rev. Noel Rudy, Sacramental Min. (Retired); Sr. Jean T. Baumann, O.S.F., Pastoral Admin.
Res.: 310 S. Broad St., P.O. Box 528, 48625. Tel: 989-539-6232; Fax: 989-539-0129.
Catechesis/Religious Program—Students 23.

HELENA, HURON CO., ST. ANTHONY, [CEM] Rev. William Spencer.
Church: 8239 Helena Rd., Harbor Beach, 48441.
Catechesis/Religious Program—Students 31.

HEMLOCK, SAGINAW CO., ST. MARY, [CEM] Rev. Steven M. Gavit.
Res.: 151 St. Mary's Dr., 48626. Tel: 989-642-5606; Fax: 989-642-5240.
St. Mary Center—245 St. Mary's Dr., 48626.
Catechesis/Religious Program—Sheila Bugbee, D.R.E.; Wally Rohn, D.R.E. Students 80.

ITHACA, GRATIOT CO., ST. PAUL THE APOSTLE Carol Hale, Pastoral Admin.
Res.: 121 N. Union St., 48847. Tel: 989-875-2852; Fax: 989-875-7027.
Catechesis/Religious Program—Teresa Davaloz Cervantes, D.R.E. Students 40.
Mission—St. Martin De Porres Perrinton, Gratiot Co.
Catechesis/Religious Program—Students 38.

KAWKAWLIN, BAY CO., SACRED HEART Rev. Jerzy Dobosz, Admin.
Res.: 2510 Fraser Rd., 48631. Tel: 989-684-1402; Fax: 989-684-0038.
Catechesis/Religious Program—Leoma Bujalski, D.R.E. Students 104.

KINDE, HURON CO., ST. MARY-ST. EDWARD Revs. Andrew Booms; Nathan E. Harburg, Parochial Vicar; Sr. Judy O'Brien, I.H.M., Pastoral Min.
Office: 5083 Park St., 48445.
Res.: 1709 Moeller Rd., P.O. Box 68, 48445. Tel: 989-874-4744; Fax: 989-874-4744.
Catechesis/Religious Program—Sr. Judy O'Brien, I.H.M., D.R.E. Students 82.

LEXINGTON, SANILAC CO., ST. DENIS, [CEM] Rev. Robert Schikora, Parochial Admin.
Res.: 5366 Main St., P.O. Box 399, 48450. Tel: 810-359-5400; Fax: 810-359-5833.
Catechesis/Religious Program—Matthew Tonge, Youth Min. Students 33.

LINWOOD, BAY CO., ST. ANNE Rev. Nicholas F. Coffaro.
Res.: 315 W. Center St., 48634. Tel: 989-697-4443; Fax: 989-697-3630.
School—(Grades PreK-6) Tel: 989-697-3100. Dr. Angela Radlinski, Prin. Lay Teachers 5; Students 52.
Catechesis/Religious Program—Luann Hugo, Youth Min. Students 36.

MAPLE GROVE, SAGINAW CO., ST. MICHAEL, [CEM] Rev. T.J. Fleming.
Res.: 17994 Lincoln Rd., New Lothrop, 48460. Tel: 989-845-7011; Fax: 989-845-4729.
Catechesis/Religious Program—Students 314.

MARLETTE, SANILAC CO., ST. ELIZABETH Rev. Andrzej Boroch.
Res.: 6785 W. Marlette St., 48453. Tel: 989-635-7581; Fax: 989-635-5808.
Catechesis/Religious Program—Roxann Ross, D.R.E.; Rick Tanis, Youth Min. Students 40.

MAYVILLE, TUSCOLA CO., ST. JOSEPH Sr. Riccardina Silvestri, M.C., Pastoral Admin.
315 W. Ohmer Rd., 48744. Tel: 989-843-6565; Fax: 989-683-2556. Mailing Address: 1951 Kingston Rd., Deford, 48729.
Catechesis/Religious Program—Students 40.

MERRILL, SAGINAW CO., SACRED HEART, [CEM] Rev. Craig Carolan, Parochial Admin.
Res.: 419 S. Midland St., P.O. Box 99, 48637. Tel: 989-643-5171; Fax: 989-643-7710.
Catechesis/Religious Program—Students 87.

MIDLAND, MIDLAND CO.
1—ASSUMPTION OF THE BLESSED VIRGIN MARY Rev. Kevin M. Maksym.
Res.: 3516 E. Monroe Rd., 48642. Tel: 989-631-4447; Fax: 989-835-9722.
Catechesis/Religious Program—Betty Zeestraten, D.R.E.; Maria Christie, D.R.E.; Sr. Mary Lou Owczarzak, M.S.Sp., Youth Min. Students 148.
2—BLESSED SACRAMENT Revs. Peter J. Gaspeny; Edwin C. Dwyer, Parochial Vicar; Deacon Michael Jankowiak.
Res.: 3109 Swede Ave., 48642. Tel: 989-835-6777; Fax: 989-835-2451.
School—(Grades PreSchool-5) Lee Ann Berg, Prin. Lay Teachers 8; Students 169.
Catechesis/Religious Program—Janet Martyn, Dir., Faith Formation; Lauree Birchmeier, Youth Min. Students 597.
Blessed Sacrament Parish Inter-Parish Endowment Fund
3—ST. BRIGID Rev. Patrick C. O'Connor.
Res.: 207 Ashman St., 48642. Tel: 989-835-7121; Fax: 989-835-9141.
School—(Grades K-8), 130 W. Larkin St., 48640-6579. Tel: 989-835-9481; Fax: 989-835-9141. Maureen Becker, Prin. Lay Teachers 13; Students 187.
Catechesis/Religious Program—Paula Dachsteiner, Youth Min. Students 101.

MOUNT PLEASANT, ISABELLA CO.
1—ST. MARY UNIVERSITY PARISH Rev. William Prospero, S.J.; Jeremy Priest, Pastoral Assoc.
Res.: 1405 S. Washington St., 48858. Tel: 989-773-3931; Fax: 989-772-2745.
Catechesis/Religious Program—
St. Mary University Parish Inter-Parish Endowment Fund
2—SACRED HEART, [CEM] Rev. Loren M. Kalinowski; Deacons James Damitio; Larry Fussman.
Res.: 302 S. Kinney Ave., 48858. Tel: 989-772-1385; Fax: 989-773-9118.
School—(Grades PreK-12), 200 S. Franklin St., 48858. Dennis Starnes, Prin. Lay Teachers 21; Students 332.
High School—Sacred Heart Academy, (Grades 7-12), 316 E. Michigan Ave., 48858. Tel: 989-772-1457. Dennis Starnes, Prin. Priests 1; Lay Teachers 12; Students 121.
Catechesis/Religious Program—Mary Gagnon, D.R.E. Students 131.

MUNGER, BAY CO., ST. NORBERT Rev. Prentice Tipton Jr.; Sr. Tereska Wozniak, O.P., Pastoral Assoc.
Res.: 126 W. Munger Rd., 48747. Tel: 989-659-2193; Fax: 989-659-3417.
Catechesis/Religious Program—Mary Anne Adams, D.R.E.; Judy Lauria, Youth Min. Students 49.

OAKLEY, SAGINAW CO., ST. MICHAEL, [CEM] Revs. Richard Bokinskie, Sacramental Min.; Joseph Marcel Portelli, Parochial Vicar.
Res.: 509 Parshall St., P.O. Box 75, 48649. Tel: 989-845-3545; Fax: 989-845-5499.
Catechesis/Religious Program—Students 28.

PALMS, SANILAC CO., ST. PATRICK Rev. Peter Nwokoye, Admin.
Res.: 1801 Palms Rd., 48465. Tel: 810-376-4853; Fax: 810-376-4853.
Catechesis/Religious Program—Students 9.

PARISVILLE, HURON CO., ST. MARY Rev. Peter Nwokoye.
Res.: 4190 Parisville Rd., P.O. Box 55, Ruth, 48470. Tel: 989-864-3523; Fax: 989-864-3164.
Catechesis/Religious Program—Brenda Plester, D.R.E. Students 29.

PIGEON, HURON CO., ST. FRANCIS BORGIA, [CEM] Rev. John Weis, Admin.
Res.: 25 Moeller St., 48755. Tel: 989-453-2151; Fax: 989-453-2090.
Catechesis/Religious Program—Linda Oeschger, D.R.E. Students 55.

PINCONNING, BAY CO.
1—ST. MARY, [CEM] Rev. Joseph K. Miller.
Res.: 739 W. Cody-Estey Rd., 48650. Tel: 989-879-5596; Fax: 989-879-6151.
Catechesis/Religious Program—Terry Stevens, D.R.E. Students 33.
Station—St. Agnes, (Closed), 216 E. Fifth St., 48650.
2—ST. MICHAEL Rev. Joseph K. Miller, Sacramental Min.; Deacon Gary Patelski, Pastoral Admin.
Res.: 225 S. Jennings St., 48650. Tel: 989-879-2141; Fax: 989-879-6633.

School—(Grades PreK-8) Tel: 989-879-3063. Melissa Paulik, Prin. Lay Teachers 7; Students 123.
Catechesis/Religious Program—Students 63.
St. Michael Catholic School Foundation Endowment Fund

PINNEBOG, HURON CO., ST. FELIX, [CEM] Rev. Robert Pare.
Res.: 3515 Limerick Rd., Kinde, 48445. Tel: 989-874-5833; Fax: 989-874-6534.
Catechesis/Religious Program—Cynthia Tait, Youth Min. Students 12.

PORT AUSTIN, HURON CO., ST. MICHAEL, [CEM] Revs. Andrew Booms; Nathan E. Harburg, Parochial Vicar.
Res.: 8637 Garfield, P.O. Box 355, 48467. Tel: 989-738-7521; Fax: 989-738-5886.
Parish Center—8661 Independence Ave., P.O. Box 350, 48467.
Catechesis/Religious Program—Students 24.

PORT SANILAC, SANILAC CO., ST. MARY, [CEM] Sr. Maria Inniolata Honma, S.M.D.G., Pastoral Admin.; Rev. Donald Eppenbrock, Sacramental Min. (Retired).
Res.: 7066 W. Main St., P.O. Box 467, 48469. Tel: 810-622-9904; Fax: 810-622-7953.
Catechesis/Religious Program—Maureen O'Mara, D.R.E. Students 35.
Mission—St. John Chrysostom Forestville, Sanilac Co.

RAPSON, HURON CO., ST. JOSEPH, [CEM] Rev. Robert J. Howe.
Res.: 3455 Rapson Rd., Bad Axe, 48413. Tel: 989-269-8084; Fax: 989-269-8084.
Catechesis/Religious Program—Students 39.
Mission—Most Holy Trinity [CEM] Smiths Corners, Huron Co.
Catechesis/Religious Program—Students 35.

REESE, TUSCOLA CO., ST. ELIZABETH, [CEM] Rev. Prentice Tipton Jr.; Sr. Tereska Wozniak, O.P., Pastoral Assoc.
Res.: 12835 E. Washington Rd., P.O. Box 392, 48757. Tel: 989-868-4081; Fax: 989-868-0060.
School—(Grades PreSchool-8) Tel: 989-868-4108. M. Gabriela Marguery Costoya, Prin. Lay Teachers 5; Students 104.
Catechesis/Religious Program—Louis Pierce, D.R.E. Students 14.

ROSEBUSH, ISABELLA CO., ST. HENRY/ ST. CHARLES, [CEM] Revs. William J. Rutowski; Christian Tabares, Parochial Vicar.
Res.: 4079 E. Vernon Rd., 48878. Tel: 989-433-2229; Fax: 989-433-5440.
Catechesis/Religious Program—Erin Zimmer, D.R.E. Students 14.

RUTH, HURON CO., SS. PETER AND PAUL, [CEM] Rev. Peter Nwokoye.
Res.: 7115 E. Atwater Dr., P.O. Box 55, 48470. Tel: 989-864-3649; Fax: 989-864-8600.
Catechesis/Religious Program—Students 38.

RYAN, MIDLAND CO., ST. PATRICK, [CEM] Rev. Craig Carolan.
Res.: 4708 S. Meridian Rd., Merrill, 48637. Tel: 989-643-5652; Fax: 989-643-5505.
Catechesis/Religious Program—Students 23.

ST. CHARLES, SAGINAW CO., IMMACULATE CONCEPTION, [CEM] Rev. Todd Arnberg.
Res.: 708 Sanderson St., 48655. Tel: 989-865-9460; Fax: 989-865-6699.
Catechesis/Religious Program—Joy Tanner, D.R.E. Students 50.

ST. LOUIS, GRATIOT CO., ST. JOSEPH Deacon Aloysius J. Oliver, Parochial Admin. Pro tem; Rev. Thai Hung Nguyen, Sacramental Min.
Office: 605 S. Franklin St., 48880. Tel: 989-681-5080; Fax: 989-681-2887.
Catechesis/Religious Program—Kathy Fairchild, D.R.E.; Linda Goodman, Youth Min. Students 14.

SANDUSKY, SANILAC CO., ST. JOSEPH Rev. Charles Hammond.
Res.: 511 N. Sandusky Rd., P.O. Box 249, 48471. Tel: 810-648-2968; Fax: 810-648-2968.
Catechesis/Religious Program—Christina Lowry, D.R.E. Students 72.
Mission—St. John [CEM] Peck, Sanilac Co.
Catechesis/Religious Program—

SANFORD, MIDLAND CO., ST. AGNES Rev. Daniel Fox, O.F.M.Cap.; Deacon Edward Kebblish.
Res.: 2500 N.W. River Rd., 48657. Tel: 989-687-5657; Fax: 989-687-2450.
Catechesis/Religious Program—Laura Schelbert, D.R.E. Students 94.

SEBEWAING, HURON CO., HOLY FAMILY, [CEM] Rev. John Weis.
Res.: 8370 Unionville Rd., 48759. Tel: 989-883-2746; Fax: 989-883-2810.
Catechesis/Religious Program—Patty Burgett, D.R.E. Students 35.

SHEPHERD, ISABELLA CO., ST. VINCENT DE PAUL, [CEM] Sr. Patricia Warbritton, C.S.J., Pastoral Admin.; Rev. Frederick J. Kawka, Sacramental Min. (Retired); Deacon John Wilberding.
Res.: 168 Wright, 48883. Tel: 989-828-5720; Fax: 989-828-4652.
Catechesis/Religious Program—Karon Van Antwerp Latham, Dir. Faith Formation. Students 57.
Mission—St. Leo [CEM] Winn, Isabella Co.
Catechesis/Religious Program—
Mission—St. Patrick Irishtown, Gratiot Co.
Catechesis/Religious Program—Students 32.

SHIELDS, SAGINAW CO., HOLY SPIRIT Rev. David L. Parsch; Sr. Marie Markel, I.H.M., Pastoral Assoc.
Res.: 1035 N. River Rd., 48609. Tel: 989-781-2457; Fax: 989-781-5518.
Catechesis/Religious Program—Sandy Des Jardins, D.R.E.; Melissa Shields, Youth Min. Students 247.

STANDISH, ARENAC CO., RESURRECTION OF THE LORD, [CEM] Rev. Christopher M. Coman, Parochial Admin.
Res.: W. 423 Cedar St., P.O. Box 306, 48658-0306. Tel: 989-846-9545; Fax: 989-846-9566.
Catechesis/Religious Program—Students 60.
Mission—St. Joseph Alger, Arenac Co. 48610.

UBLY, HURON CO.
1—ST. COLUMBKILLE, [CEM] Rev. Joseph M. Griffin.
Res.: 4470 N. Washington St., 48475. Tel: 989-658-8824; Fax: 989-658-2088.
Church: 3031 McAlpine Rd., Sheridan Twp.
Catechesis/Religious Program—Students 34.
2—ST. JOHN THE EVANGELIST, [CEM] Rev. Joseph M. Griffin.
Res.: 4470 N. Washington St., 48475. Tel: 989-658-8824; Fax: 989-658-2088.
Catechesis/Religious Program—Audean Vatter, D.R.E. Students 84.

VASSAR, TUSCOLA CO., ST. FRANCES XAVIER CABRINI, Unassigned. Sr. Ellen Rinke, I.H.M., Parochial Admin.
Res.: 334 Division St., 48768. Tel: 989-823-2911; Fax: 989-823-2999.
Mission—St. Bernard Millington, Tuscola Co. Closed.
Catechesis/Religious Program—Students 34.

WILMOT, TUSCOLA CO., ST. MICHAEL, [CEM] Sr. Riccardina Silvestri, M.C., Pastoral Admin.
Res.: 1951 Kingston Rd., Deford, 48729. Tel: 989-683-2475; Fax: 989-683-2556.
Catechesis/Religious Program—Students 39.

ZILWAUKEE, SAGINAW CO., ST. MATTHEW Rev. Ronald J. Dombrowski, Sacramental Min.; Sr. Janet Pewoski, C.S.J., Pastoral Admin.
Res.: 511 W. Cornell St., 48604. Tel: 989-755-7336; Fax: 989-755-4228.
Catechesis/Religious Program—Students 22.

Chaplains of Public Institutions

BAY CITY. *Bay Medical Center and Bay Osteopathic Hospital*, 1201 S. Erie, 48706. Vacant.

Outside the Diocese:
Revs.—
Cabrera, Jose, Casa Santa Maria, Via dell'Umilta 30, Rome 00187 Italy.
Friske, Joseph P. (Retired), Burgermeister-Keller Strasse, Munich 81829 Germany.
Heames, Denis M., Casa Santa Maria, Via dell'Umilta 30, Rome 00187 Italy.
Mullet, John, 1200 Seventh Ave., Saint Petersburg, FL 33705.

Retired:
Revs.—
Bala, Paul W.
Balwinski, Gerald E.
Boucher, Edward F.
Ederer, John A.
Eppenbrock, Donald
Fitzpatrick, James M.
Friske, Joseph P.
Gavit, James F., J.C.D.
Janowicz, Barney J.
Jozwiak, Richard
Kawka, Frederick J.
Kowalczyk, Thomas M.
LeFleur, R. Keith
Loos, Frederick C.
Maher, Michael L.
Marceau, Emmett L.
Moeggenberg, Raymond
Pilarski, Chester J.
Roach, Joseph W.
Rudy, Noel
Schabel, Joseph A.
Serour, George J.
Shine, Robert W.
Sierminski, Vernon
Sikorski, Harold R.
Skornia, Bernard L.
Spleet, Julius A.
Streichardt, Wolfgang
Surman, Stanley
Taylor, William R.
Thome, John J.
Vaughn, Mason
Yaroch, Kenneth E.

Permanent Deacons:
Alex, Frank, St. Anne, Edenville; & St. Philip Neri, Coleman
Arnold, Michael, St. Valentine Church, Beaver
Cremin, John J., St. Mary, Alma
Damitio, James, Mt. Pleasant, Sacred Heart
Fussman, Lawrence, Sacred Heart Church, Mount Pleasant
Hudson, Francis W., St. Brigid, Midland
Jankowiak, Michael, Blessed Sacrament, Midland
Kebblish, Edward, St. Agnes, Sanford
Keller, George, St. James, Bay City
Kuczyunski, Stanislaw, Bay City, St. Stanislaws
Masserang, Lawrence, Blessed Trinity, Frankenmuth
Oliver, Aloysius J., St. Brigid, Midland
Pasionek, Roger, Holy Family, Saginaw
Patelski, Gary, Pinconning, St. Michael
Smith, Michael, Beal City, St. Joseph
Stilwell, Lee, St. Hyacinth, Bay City
Wilberding, John, St. Vincent de Paul, Shepherd

INSTITUTIONS LOCATED IN THE DIOCESE

[A] HIGH SCHOOLS, INTER-PAROCHIAL

SAGINAW. *Nouvel Catholic Central High School* (1984) 2555 Wieneke Rd., 48603. Tel: 989-791-4330; Fax: 989-797-6603. Email: ihensinger@sacschools.org. Web: www.sacschools.org. Irene Hensinger, Prin. Lay Teachers 36; Students 343.
Nouvel Catholic Central Educational Foundation Endowment Fund

BAY CITY. *All Saints Central Catholic Middle and High School*, 217 S. Monroe St., 48708. Tel: 989-892-2533; Fax: 989-892-7188. Web: www.bayareacatholicschools.org. John Hoving, Prin.; Brian Campbell, Asst. Prin.; Laura Tacey, Librarian. Lay Teachers 15; Students 264.

[B] ELEMENTARY SCHOOLS

AUBURN. *Auburn Area Catholic Schools*, (Grades PreK-5), East Campus: W. 114 Midland Rd., 48611. Tel: 989-662-6431; Fax: 989-662-3391. Web: www.auburnac.org. Terri Duch, Prin. Lay Teachers 6; Students 88.

[C] CHILDREN'S HOMES

SAGINAW. *Holy Cross Children's Services*, 925 N. River Rd., 48609. Tel: 989-781-2780; Fax: 989-781-5422. Sharon Berkobien, L.M.S.W., Regl. Dir. Residential and community-based treatment programs for troubled youth and families with facilities located throughout the state of Michigan, under the auspices of the Brothers of the Holy Cross at Notre Dame. Includes Specialized Foster Care, Supervised Independent Living and In-Home Treatment. Youths 252.
Queen of Angels Center, 3400 S. Washington, 48601. Tel: 989-755-1971; Fax: 989-755-2780.

[D] GENERAL HOSPITALS

SAGINAW. *St. Mary's of Michigan Medical Center*, 800 S. Washington Ave., 48601-2524. John Graham, CEO; Rev. Osward Munung, A.J., Chap. Daughters of Charity of St. Vincent de Paul, East Central Province, Evansville, IN. Bed Capacity 268; Patients Assisted Annually 300,590.
Field Neurosciences Institute, 800 S. Washington Ave., 48601-2524.

[E] HOMES FOR AGED

SAGINAW. *St. Francis Home of Saginaw* (1953) 915 N. River Rd., 48609. Tel: 989-781-3150; Fax: 989-781-3791. Total Staff 145; Residents 95.

[F] FAMILY SERVICE

SAGINAW. *Catholic Family Service of the Diocese of Saginaw*, Administrative Center: 5800 Weiss St., 48603-2799. Tel: 989-797-6638; Fax: 989-797-7436. Web: www.cfssite.org. Thomas Conklin, L.M.S.W., Exec. Dir.
Adoption Center: 915 Columbus Ave., Bay City, 48708-6690. Tel: 989-892-2504; Fax: 989-892-1923.
Counseling Centers:
Bay City:
915 Columbus Ave., Bay City, 48708. Tel: 989-892-2504; Fax: 989-892-1923.
Mt. Pleasant:
210 Court St., Mount Pleasant, 48858. Tel: 989-773-9328; Fax: 989-773-9803.

Saginaw:
710 N. Michigan Ave., 48602-4372. Tel: 989-753-8336; Fax: 989-753-2582.

[G] CONVENTS AND RESIDENCES FOR SISTERS

SAGINAW. *Franciscan Poor Clare Nuns, O.S.C.* (1991) 4875 Shattuck Rd., 48603-2962. Tel: 989-797-0593. Email: sisters@srsclare.org. Web: www.srsclare.com. Sr. Dianne Doughty, O.S.C., Abbess. Solemnly Professed 4.

Motherhouse and Novitiate of the Mission Sisters of the Holy Spirit (1932) 1030 N. River Rd., 48609. Tel: 989-781-0934. Sr. Margo Tafoya, M.S.Sp., Pres. Sisters 7.

ALMA. *Motherhouse and Novitiate of the Religious Sisters of Mercy* (1973) 1965 Michigan Ave., 48801. Tel: 989-463-6035; Fax: 989-463-5811. Web: www.rsmofalma.org. Sisters Mary McGreevy, R.S.M., Supr. Gen.; Jane Mary Firestone, R.S.M., Vicar Gen. Sisters 19.

[H] MISCELLANEOUS LISTINGS

SAGINAW. **Catholic Community Foundation of Mid-Michigan*, P.O. Box 6883, 48608-6883. Tel: 989-797-6624.

**The Catholic Weekly*, 1520 Court St., P.O. Box 1405, 48605-1405. Tel: 989-793-7661; Fax: 989-793-7663. Email: catholicweekly@sbcglobal.net.

Holy Spirit Sisters Charitable Trust (1988) 1030 N. River Rd., 48609. Tel: 989-781-0934. Sr. Margo Tafoya, M.S.Sp., Pres.

**Little Books of the Diocese of Saginaw, Inc.*, 5802 Weiss St., P.O. Box 6009, 48608-6009. Tel: 989-797-6653; Fax: 989-797-6606. Leona Jones, Operations Mgr.; Catherine Haven, Editor.

**Partnership Center*, 723 Emerson St., 48602-2013. Tel: 989-907-5610. Joshua Gonzales, Dir.

**St. Robert Bellarmine Trust*, 5800 Weiss St., 48603. Tel: 989-797-6642.

Roman Catholic Diocese of Saginaw Inter-Parish Endowment Fund, 5800 Weiss St., 48603-2799. Tel: 989-797-6683. Annette M. O'Brien, Dir., Office of Stewardship & Planned Giving.

ALMA. *Saint Joseph Corporation*, 1965 Michigan Ave., 48801. Tel: 989-463-6035; Fax: 989-463-5811. Sr. Jane Mary Firestone, R.S.M., Pres.

**Sacred Heart Mercy Health Care Center* (1981) 2025 W. Cheesman Rd., 48801. Tel: 989-463-3451; Fax: 989-463-1534. Email: shmhcc@sacredheartmercy.com. Web: www.sacredheartmercy.org. Sr. Mary Patricia Glowski, R.S.M., Admin.

BAY CITY. *Society of St. Vincent de Paul, Bay County Council*, 523 Michigan Ave., 48708. Tel: 989-893-5772. Email: bcsvdp@mail.speednetllc.comFax: 989-893-1201. Mr. Paul Dombrowski, Pres. Member Conferences: Bay City-Holy Trinity, St. Hyacinth, St. James, St. Joseph's, St. Mary, Visitation, St. Vincent de Paul; Essexville-St. John.

PORT SANILAC. *Sisters of Our Mother of Divine Grace, St. Mary-Our Lady of Sorrow Church*, 7066 W. Main St., 48469.

RELIGIOUS INSTITUTES OF MEN REPRESENTED IN THE DIOCESE

For further details refer to the corresponding bracketed number in the Religious Institutes of Men or Women section.

[]—*Apostles of Jesus*—A.J.
[0470]—*The Capuchin Friars* (St. Joseph Prov.)—O.F.M.Cap.
[0920]—*Oblates of St. Francis De Sales*—O.S.F.S.
[0690]—*Society of Jesus*—S.J.

RELIGIOUS INSTITUTES OF WOMEN REPRESENTED IN THE DIOCESE

[1810]—*Bernadine Sisters of Third Order of St. Francis*—O.S.F.
[1150]—*Congregation of St. Joseph*—C.S.J.
[3832]—*Congregation of the Sisters of St. Joseph*—C.S.J.
[0720]—*Consolata Missionary Sisters*—M.C.
[1070-03]—*Dominican Sisters* (Sinsinawa, WI)—O.P.
[1070-13]—*Dominican Sisters* (Adrian, MI)—O.P.
[1070-14]—*Dominican Sisters* (Grand Rapids)—O.P.
[1115]—*Dominican Sisters of Peace*—O.P.
[1170]—*Felician Sisters*—C.S.S.F.
[]—*Franciscan Poor Clare Nuns*—O.S.C.
[2740]—*Mission Sisters of the Holy Spirit*—M.S.Sp.
[2790]—*Missionary Servants of the Most Blessed Trinity*—M.S.B.T.
[3760]—*Order of St. Clare*—O.S.C.
[2519]—*Religious Sisters of Mercy of Alma, Michigan*—R.S.M.
[3560]—*Servants of Jesus*—S.J.
[0440]—*Sisters of Charity of Cincinnati, Ohio*—S.C.
[]—*Sisters of Christian Community*
[2575]—*Sisters of Mercy of the Americas* (Detroit, MI)—R.S.M.
[3000]—*Sisters of Notre Dame de Namur* (Boston, MA; Cincinnati, OH)—S.N.D.deN.
[3260]—*Sisters of the Precious Blood (Dayton, Ohio)*—C.PP.S.
[2150]—*Sisters, Servants of the Immaculate Heart of Mary* (Monroe)—I.H.M.

DIOCESAN CEMETERIES

SAGINAW. *St. Andrew's, Mt. Olivet & Calvary*
BAY CITY. *St. Patrick's, Calvary & St. Stanislaus*
LINWOOD. *St. Anne*
MIDLAND. *Calvary*

NECROLOGY

† Klimas, George H., (Retired)—Died Feb. 14, 2011
† Pashak, Lawrence M., Freeland, MI St. Agnes.—Died Dec. 11, 2010
† Wolf, Michael H., (Retired)—Died Jan. 5, 2011

An asterisk (*) denotes an organization that has established tax-exempt status directly with the IRS and is not covered by the USCCB Group Ruling.

Diocese of St. Augustine

(Dioecesis Sancti Augustini)

Most Reverend

FELIPE DE JESUS ESTEVEZ

Bishop of St. Augustine; ordained May 30, 1970; appointed Titular Bishop of Kearney and Auxiliary Bishop of Miami November 21, 2003; consecrated January 7, 2004; appointed Bishop of Saint Augustine April 27, 2011; installed June 2, 2011. *Office: 11625 Old St. Augustine Rd., Jacksonville, FL 32258.*

Most Reverend

VICTOR BENITO GALEONE

Bishop Emeritus of St. Augustine; ordained December 18, 1960; appointed Bishop of St. Augustine June 26, 2001; ordained August 21, 2001; retired April 27, 2011. *Office: 11625 Old St. Augustine Rd., Jacksonville, FL 32258.*

Catholic Center: 11625 Old St. Augustine Rd., Jacksonville, FL 32258. Tel: 904-262-3200; Fax: 904-262-0698.

Web: www.dosafl.com

Square Miles 11,032.

Florida, east of the Apalachicola River, was erected by Pope Pius IX into a Vicariate-Apostolic in the year 1857, and in 1870 into the Diocese of St. Augustine.

Comprises all of the northeastern Counties of the State of Florida including Alachua, Baker, Bradford, Clay, Columbia, Dixie, Duval, Flagler, Gilchrist, Hamilton, Lafayette, Levy, Nassau, Putnam, St. Johns, Suwannee and Union Counties.

For legal titles of parishes and diocesan institutions, consult the Catholic Center.

STATISTICAL OVERVIEW

Personnel	
Bishop	1
Retired Bishops	2
Priests: Diocesan Active in Diocese	65
Priests: Diocesan Active Outside Diocese	2
Priests: Retired, Sick or Absent	38
Number of Diocesan Priests	105
Religious Priests in Diocese	15
Total Priests in Diocese	120
Extern Priests in Diocese	27
Ordinations:	
Permanent Deacons	15
Permanent Deacons in Diocese	77
Total Brothers	2
Total Sisters	107
Parishes	
Parishes	52
With Resident Pastor:	
Resident Diocesan Priests	46
Resident Religious Priests	6
Without Resident Pastor:	
Administered by Priests	2
Missions	8
Welfare	
Catholic Hospitals	2
Total Assisted	172,738
Homes for the Aged	2
Total Assisted	42,683
Special Centers for Social Services	9
Total Assisted	100,951
Residential Care of Disabled	4
Total Assisted	30
Other Institutions	5
Total Assisted	326
Educational	
Diocesan Students in Other Seminaries	18
Total Seminarians	18
High Schools, Diocesan and Parish	4
Total Students	2,200
Elementary Schools, Diocesan and Parish	27
Total Students	8,036
Non-residential Schools for the Disabled	1
Total Students	113
Catechesis/Religious Education:	
High School Students	1,015
Elementary Students	8,003
Total Students under Catholic Instruction	19,385
Teachers in the Diocese:	
Scholastics	3
Sisters	14
Lay Teachers	661
Vital Statistics	
Receptions into the Church:	
Infant Baptism Totals	1,890
Minor Baptism Totals	224
Adult Baptism Totals	339
Received into Full Communion	430
First Communions	2,256
Confirmations	2,049
Marriages:	
Catholic	351
Interfaith	191
Total Marriages	542
Deaths	1,122
Total Catholic Population	175,215
Total Population	2,013,960

Former Bishops—Most Revs. AUGUSTIN VEROT, S.S., D.D., cons. April 25, 1858; Vicar-Apostolic of Florida; translated to the See of Savannah in July, 1861; appt. Bishop of St. Augustine March, 1870; died June 10, 1876; JOHN MOORE, D.D., cons. May 13, 1877; died July 30, 1901; WILLIAM JOHN KENNY, D.D., ord. Jan. 15, 1879; cons. May 18, 1902; died Oct. 23, 1913; M. J. CURLEY, D.D., cons. June 30, 1914; promoted to See of Baltimore Aug. 10, 1921; died May 16, 1947; PATRICK BARRY, D.D., ord. June 9, 1895; appt. Feb. 22, 1922; cons. May 3, 1922; died Aug. 13, 1940; JOSEPH P. HURLEY, D.D., ord. May 25, 1919; appt. Aug. 16, 1940; cons. Oct. 6, 1940; Received Personal title of Archbishop Aug. 18, 1950; died Oct. 30, 1967; PAUL F. TANNER, D.D., ord. May 30, 1931; appt. Titular Bishop of Lamasba, Oct. 18, 1965; appt. Bishop of Saint Augustine, Feb. 21, 1968; retired April 21, 1979; Remained as Administrator to Dec. 4, 1979; died July 29, 1994; JOHN J. SNYDER, D.D. (Retired), ord. June 9, 1951; appt. Titular Bishop of Forlimpopuli Dec. 19, 1972; cons. Feb. 2, 1973; appt. Bishop of St. Augustine Oct. 2, 1979; installed Dec. 5, 1979; retired Dec. 12, 2000; remained as Administrator to Aug. 21, 2001; VICTOR B. GALEONE, ord. Dec. 18, 1960; appt. Bishop of St. Augustine June 26, 2001; ord. Aug. 21, 2001; retired April 27, 2011.

Catholic Center—11625 Old St. Augustine Rd., Jacksonville, 32258. Tel: 904-262-3200; Fax: 904-262-0698. Office Hours: Mon.-Fri. 9-4:30.

Vicar General—Rev. WILLIAM A. KELLY, V.G.

Chancellor—Rev. MICHAEL P. MORGAN, J.D., J.C.L.

Secretary to the Bishop—NANCY ELLIS.

Secretary to the Chancellor—JUDY T. PINSON.

Episcopal Vicar for Development and Finance—Rev. MICHAEL HOULE, E.V., M.A., M.Ed., M.Div., 11625 Old St. Augustine Rd., Jacksonville, 32258. Tel: 904-262-3200.

Fiscal Office—Ms. CATHERINE MACINA, CPA, Chief Fiscal Officer.

Diocesan Tribunal—11625 Old St. Augustine Rd., Jacksonville, 32258. Tel: 904-262-3200.

Judicial Vicar—Rev. TIMOTHY M. LINDENFELSER, J.C.L.

Associate Judges—Rev. Msgr. DANIEL B. LOGAN; Rev. MICHAEL P. MORGAN, J.D., J.C.L.; KAREN KIGHT, J.C.L.

Defenders of the Bond—Revs. CAESAR RUSSO, M.A., J.C.L., S.T.L.; PETER AKIN-OTIKO.

Promoter of Justice—VACANT; MARY C. SLEEPER, Administrative Asst.

Diocesan Consultors—Rev. DANIEL CODY; Rev. Msgr. VINCENT J. HAUT, V.G., M.S.W., V.F.; Revs. WILLIAM A. KELLY, V.G.; JOSE J. KULATHINAL, C.M.I., V.F.; MICHAEL P. MORGAN, J.D., J.C.L.; THANH T. NGUYEN; MICHAEL PENDERGRAFT, V.F.; MICHAEL S. WILLIAMS.

Diocesan Pastoral Council—ERIN MCGEEVER, Sec., Diocese of St. Augustine Catholic Center, 11625 Old St. Augustine Rd., Jacksonville, 32258. Tel: 904-262-3200; Fax: 904-262-0698.

Presbyteral Council—Most Rev. FELIPE J. ESTEVEZ, Pres.; Revs. THANH T. NGUYEN; ROBERT TRUJILLO, Sec.; EDWARD ROONEY; MICHAEL P. MORGAN, J.D., J.C.L., Treas.; JOSE J. KULATHINAL, C.M.I., V.F.; TIMOTHY R. LOZIER; JOHN R. REYNOLDS; WILLIAM A. KELLY, V.G.; JHON GUARNIZO; TIMOTHY S. CUSICK, Vice Chm.; ALAN BOWER, Vice Chm.; DANIEL CODY; D. TERRENCE MORGAN.

Deans—Revs. THOMAS S. WILLIS, V.F., St. Augustine Deanery; MICHAEL PENDERGRAFT, V.F., Gainesville Deanery; JOSE J. KULATHINAL, C.M.I., V.F., North Jacksonville Deanery; Rev. Msgr. VINCENT J. HAUT, V.G., M.S.W., V.F., South Jacksonville Deanery.

Building Commission—Most Rev. FELIPE J. ESTEVEZ, Chm.; Revs. MICHAEL P. MORGAN, J.D., J.C.L., Chancellor; GUY NOONAN, S.T.D., M.B.A.; WILLIAM A. KELLY, V.G.; Ms. CATHERINE MACINA, CPA, Fiscal Mgr.; Mr. RONALD SCALISI; Mr. JAY

DEMETREE; Mr. MICHAEL COFFEY; Mr. CHARLES DAVID, Dir. Construction & Land Use Mgmt.

Catholic Foundation of Diocese of St. Augustine—Ms. CATHERINE MACINA, CPA, Exec. Dir.; MARY TOOMEY, Chair; Most Rev. FELIPE J. ESTEVEZ, Pres.

Finance Council—Rev. WILLIAM A. KELLY, V.G., Chm., 11625 Old St. Augustine Rd., Jacksonville, 32258. Tel: 904-262-3200.

Insurance Committee, Diocesan—Mr. RON GINDER, Chm., 11625 Old St. Augustine Rd., Jacksonville, 32258. Tel: 904-262-3200.

Diocesan Offices and Directors

Apostleship of the Sea—Deacon GJET BAJRAKTARI, Providence Center, 134 E. Church St., Jacksonville, 32202-3130. Tel: 904-356-3104.

Archives of Diocese—Sr. CATHERINE BITZER, S.S.J., Archivist, Mailing Address: P.O. Box 3506, Saint Augustine, 32085. Tel: 904-823-8707.

Multicultural Ministry—134 E. Church St., Jacksonville, 32202. Tel: 904-353-3243. Ms. ALBA M. OROZCO, Dir. Tel: 904-854-0669; Revs. JHON GUARNIZO, Hispanic Ministry Coord.; JAMES R. BODDIE JR., Black Catholic Commission Coord.

Diocesan Schools and Social Action Appeal—Rev. EDWARD K. ROONEY, Dir. (Retired), 1606 Blanding Blvd., Middleburg, 32068. Tel: 904-282-0439.

Christian Formation—ERIN MCGEEVER, Dir., 11625 Old St. Augustine Rd., Jacksonville, 32258. Tel: 904-262-3200.

Catholic Burse Endowment Fund, Inc.— (Education of Priests), *11625 Old St. Augustine Rd., Jacksonville, 32258*. Tel: 904-262-3200.

Catholic Charities Bureau, Inc.—VACANT, 134 E. Church St., Jacksonville, 32202. Tel: 904-262-3200 See separate listing for more details.

Catholic Relief Services—VACANT, 134 E. Church St., Jacksonville, 32202. Tel: 904-262-3200.

Catholic Women, Council of—Rev. LUKE MCLOUGHLIN, Spiritual Moderator, St. Matthew Church, 1773 Blanding Blvd., Jacksonville, 32210. Tel: 904-388-8698.

Charismatic Renewal—KATHERINE A. PERNINI, Sec., Mailing Address: P.O. Box 13888, Gainesville, 32604. Tel: 352-371-2185.

Hispanic Charismatic Renewal—1720 Hollow Glen Dr., Middleburg, 32068. Tel: 904-505-3043; Cell: 804-304-8709; Fax: 904-628-3771. Rev. RODOLFO GODINEZ, Spiritual Dir.; JAMES CARBONELL, Diocesan Coord.

Civil Institutions—Rev. SLAWOMIR BIELASIEWICZ, Mailing Address: St. Mary Parish, P.O. Box 1120, Macclenny, 32063. Tel: 904-259-6414.

Communications, Office of—KATHLEEN BAGG, Dir., 11624 Old St. Augustine Rd., Jacksonville, 32258. Tel: 904-262-3200.

Continuing Education for Priests—Deacon ROBERT DELUCA, Dir., 12366 Brady Place Blvd., Jacksonville, 32223. Tel: 904-880-2692.

Cursillos de Cristiandad—Revs. JOSE J. KULATHINAL, C.M.I., V.F., Diocesan Spiritual Advisor, St. Matthew, 1773 Blanding Blvd., Jacksonville, 32210. Tel: 904-388-8698; TIMOTHY R. LOZIER, Asst. Diocesan Spiritual Dir., Most Holy Redeemer, 8523 Normany Blvd., Jacksonville, 32221. Tel: 904-786-1192; Mr. PETER LASHER, Rgnl. Coord. Tel: 904-910-6646. Email: petelasher@earthlink.net; BILL FARNSWORTH, Lay Dir. Tel: 904-241-0919.

Diocesan Development Office—11625 Old St. Augustine Rd., Jacksonville, 32258. Tel: 904-262-3200.

Disabilities, Ministry of Persons with—REBECCA ALEMAN, Dir., Mailing Address: Providence Center, 134 E. Church St., Jacksonville, 32202-3130. Tel: 904-356-0810; Fax: 904-358-7302.

Ecumenism and Interfaith—Rev. MICHAEL P. MORGAN, J.D., J.C.L., Chm., 11625 Old St. Augustine Rd., Jacksonville, 32258. Tel: 904-262-3200.

Educational Services—PATRICIA H. BRONSARD, M.S., M.A., Supt. Schools, 11625 Old St. Augustine Rd., Jacksonville, 32258. Tel: 904-262-3200; Rev. MICHAEL HOULE, E.V., M.A., M.Ed., M.Div., Diocesan Dir. Secondary Schools. Tel: 904-398-7545.

Family Life, Diocesan Center for—VACANT, Dir., 2577 Park St., Jacksonville, 32204. Tel: 904-308-7474; Rev. DANIEL CODY, Consultant. Tel: 904-268-5422.

Farmworker Services Program—Ms. OLGA LARA-MOSER, Coord., 234 S. Summit St., Crescent City, 32112. Tel: 386-698-4234.

Florida Catholic Conference—D. MICHAEL MCCARRON, Ph.D., Exec. Dir., 201 W. Park Ave., Tallahassee, 32301-7715. Tel: 850-222-3803.

Holy Childhood Association, The—Deacon BRYAN OTT, Dir., 107A 15th St., Saint Augustine, 32080. Tel: 904-461-5762.

Holy Name Societies—VACANT.

Justice and Peace Commission—Mr. WILLIAM J. TIERNEY, Chm., 11625 Old. St. Augustine Rd., Jacksonville, 32258. Tel: 904-262-3200.

Legalization—Mrs. JULIA CASTRO, Dir., Providence Center, 134 E. Church St., Rm. D-21, Jacksonville, 32202. Tel: 904-354-5904; Fax: 904-356-2092.

Legion of Mary—Rev. JOSE MANIYANGAT, Spiritual Dir., 1649 Kingsley Ave., Orange Park, 32073. Tel: 904-264-0577.

Office of Liturgy—Rev. THOMAS S. WILLIS, V.F., Dir., 11625 Old St. Augustine Rd., Jacksonville, 32258. Tel: 904-262-3200.

Priests' Spirituality Committee—Rev. JOHN M. PHILLIPS, 747 N.W. 43rd St., Gainesville, 32607. Tel: 352-376-5405.

Propagation of the Faith—Deacon BRYAN OTT, Dir., 107A 15th St., Saint Augustine, 32080. Tel: 904-461-5762.

Refugee Resettlement—MICHELLE KAROLAK, Dir., Providence Center, 134 E. Church St., Jacksonville, 32202-3130. Tel: 904-354-4846.

Respect Life—VACANT, Coord., 2577 Park St., Jacksonville, 32204. Tel: 904-308-7474.

Rural Life Director—Rev. MICHAEL PENDERGRAFT, V.F., Mailing Address: 1905 S.W. Epiphany Court, Lake City, 32025. Tel: 386-752-4470.

Scouts—Revs. JAMES R. BODDIE JR., Chap.; EDWARD W. MURPHY, Asst. Chap., Mailing Address: 11625 Old St. Augustine Rd., Jacksonville, 32258. Tel: 904-262-3200.

Seminarians—Rev. REMIGIUSZ BLASZKOWSKI, Dir., 11625 Old St. Augustine Rd., Jacksonville, 32258. Tel: 904-262-3200.

Vicar for Priests—Rev. DONAL P. SULLIVAN, 7190 Hwy. 17 S., Fleming Island, 32003. Tel: 904-284-3811.

Vicar for Deacons—Deacon HENRY ZMUDA, 258 S.W. 132nd Terr., Newberry, 32669.

Episcopal Delegate for Religious—Sr. MAUREEN KELLEY, O.P., 1520 Royal County Dr., Jacksonville, 32221. Tel: 904-381-0605; Fax: 904-786-3801.

Vicar for Senior Priests—Rev. Msgr. EUGENE C. KOHLS, P.A., J.C.D. (Retired), 5201 Atlantic Blvd., #228, Jacksonville, 32207. Tel: 904-348-3983.

Victim Assistance Coordinator—JUDY PINSON. Tel: 904-262-3200. Email: jpinson@dosafl.com.

Vocations—Revs. REMIGIUSZ BLASZKOWSKI, Dir.; DAVID RUCHINSKI, Assoc. Dir., 11625 Old St. Augustine Rd., Jacksonville, 32258. Tel: 904-262-3200.

Youth and Young Adult Ministry—11625 Old St. Augustine Rd., Jacksonville, 32258. Tel: 904-262-3200; Fax: 904-262-0698. ERIN MCGEEVER, Dir.

CLERGY, PARISHES, MISSIONS AND PAROCHIAL SCHOOLS

CITY OF ST. AUGUSTINE

(ST. JOHN'S COUNTY)

1—CATHEDRAL - BASILICA OF ST. AUGUSTINE (1565) [CEM] Revs. Thomas S. Willis; Edward Booth; Deacon Charles Kanaszka.
Res.: 35 Treasury St., 32084. Tel: 904-824-2806; Fax: 904-824-0761. Email: cathparish@gmail.com. Web: www.thefirstparish.org.
School—Cathedral Parish School, (Grades K-8), 259 St. George St., 32084. Tel: 904-824-2861; Fax: 904-829-2059. Email: tdeclemente@cpsschool.org. Web: www.thecathedralparishschool.org. Todd DeClemente, Prin.; Kathleen Poage, Librarian. Lay Teachers 25; Students 275.
Cathedral Parish Early Education Center—10 Sebastian Ave., 32084. Tel: 904-829-2933; Fax: 904-829-9339. Email: valleycpeec@aol.com. Web: www.cpeec.org. Jill Valley, Dir. (Preschool with Before and After School Care) Lay Teachers 14; Students 100.
Catechesis/Religious Program—Tel: 904-824-2806, Ext. 335. Email: cathedralcfp@gmail.com. Students 75.
Mission—St. Benedict the Moor 86 Martin Luther King Ave., St. Johns Co. 32084.

2—ST. ANASTASIA (1988) Rev. D. Terrence Morgan; Deacons Ron Gagne; George Murati; Ken Baechel; William Joyce; Bryan Ott.
Mailing Address: 5205 A1A S., 32080-8006. Email: stanastasiacc@aol.com. Web: stanastasiacc.org.
Res.: 5319 Fifth St., 32080. Tel: 904-471-5364 (Office); Fax: 904-471-7448.
Catechesis/Religious Program—Email: stanastasiaccyg@aol.com. Students 175.

3—MISSION NOMBRE DE DIOS AND SHRINE OF OUR LADY OF LA LECHE (1565) [JC] Eric P. Johnson, Dir.
Office: 27 Ocean Ave., 32084. Tel: 904-824-2809; Fax: 904-829-0819. Email: shrine@missionandshrine.org. Web: www.missionandshrine.org.
Mission Nombre de Dios Museum—101-D San Marco, Saint Augustine, 32084.

4—OUR LADY OF GOOD COUNSEL (2008) [CEM] Rev. Guy Noonan.
5950 State Rd. 16, 32092. Tel: 904-824-8688. Web: www.olgc-church.org.
Church: 5005 Church Rd., 32092-0459. Fax: 904-824-5110. Email: olgcsecretary@gmail.com.
Catechesis/Religious Program—Kathy Garske, C.R.E. Students 157.

5—SAN SEBASTIAN (1968) Revs. John D. Gillespie; Marek Dzien, Parochial Vicar; Deacon James Swanson.
Res.: 1112 State Rd. 16, 32084. Tel: 904-824-6625; Fax: 904-829-0459. Web: sansebastiancatholicchurch.com.
Catechesis/Religious Program—Students 225.

OUTSIDE THE CITY OF ST. AUGUSTINE

ATLANTIC BEACH, DUVAL CO., ST. JOHN THE BAPTIST (1967) Rev. Mark S. Waters.
Mailing Address: P.O. Drawer 330005, 32233. Tel: 904-246-6014; Fax: 904-246-1219.
Catechesis/Religious Program—Carole Fuchs, D.R.E. Students 141.

BRANFORD, SUWANNEE CO., SAN JUAN MISSION (1976) Rev. Sebastian K. George, C.M.I.; Deacon Paul Pettie.
304 S.E. Plant Ave., 32008. Tel: 386-935-2632; Fax: 386-935-4050. Email: sanjuancruz@live.com. Web: sanjuanmission.org.
Catechesis/Religious Program—

BUNNELL, FLAGLER CO., ST. STEPHEN (1957) Rev. John R. Reynolds. Mission Church for St. Elizabeth Ann Seton.
Res.: 2400 E. Hwy. 100, 32110. Tel: 904-445-2246; Fax: 904-445-7808.
Catechesis/Religious Program— Twinned with St. Elizabeth Ann Seton, Palm Coast.

CALLAHAN, NASSAU CO., OUR LADY OF CONSOLATION (1974) Rev. Richard Perko.
Res.: 541668 U.S. Hwy. One, P.O. Box 692, 32011. Tel: 904-879-3662; Fax: 904-879-3677.
Catechesis/Religious Program—Sandy Wilfong, D.R.E. Students 38.

CHIEFLAND, LEVY CO., ST. JOHN THE EVANGELIST (1981), (Hispanic), Rev. Joseph McDonnell.
Mailing Address: P.O. Box 863, 32644.
Res.: 4050 N.W. Alternate 27, 32626. Tel: 352-493-1561 (Rectory); 352-493-9723 (Office); Fax: 352-493-9724 (Office). Email: stjhc@bellsouth.net.
Catechesis/Religious Program—Students 34.
Mission—Holy Cross 18278 S.E. Hwy. 19, Cross City, 32628. Tel: 352-498-5671.

CRESCENT CITY, PUTNAM CO., ST. JOHN THE BAPTIST (1906) [CEM] [JC] Rev. Jhon Guarnizo.
Mailing Address: P.O. Box 908, 32112.
Res.: 2725 Hwy. 17 S., P.O. Box 908, 32112. Tel: 386-698-2055; Fax: 386-698-4146. Email: stjohnbcc@windstream.net. Web: stjohnbaptistcatholicchurch.com.
Catechesis/Religious Program—Students 138.

ELKTON, ST. JOHN CO., ST. AMBROSE (1875), (Minorcan), [CEM] Rev. Timothy M. Lindenfelser; Deacon Ed Wolff.
Res.: 6070 Church Rd., 32033. Tel: 904-692-1366; Fax: 904-692-1136. Email: choffice1@windstream.net. Web: www.saintambrose-church.org.
Catechesis/Religious Program—Email: olgcsareledu@windstream.net. Students 14.

FERNANDINA BEACH, AMELIA ISLAND NASSAU CO., ST. MICHAEL'S (1872) [JC] Rev. Jose Kallukalam (India); Deacon Art Dreadwell; Sr. Bridie Ryan, R.S.M., Pastoral Assoc.
Res.: 505 Broome St., 32034. Tel: 904-261-3472; Fax: 904-321-1901. Email: smjdean@bellsouth.net. Web: www.stmichaelscatholic.com.
School—St. Michael's Academy, (Grades PreK-8), 228 N. 4th St., 32034. Tel: 904-321-2102; Fax: 904-321-2330. Deborah Suddarth, Prin.; Colleen Hodge, Librarian. Students 220.
Catechesis/Religious Program—Students 195.

FLAGLER BEACH, FLAGLER CO., SANTA MARIA DEL MAR (1970) Rev. Alberto Esposito; Deacons Michael Moody; John A. Hartnedy.
Res.: 915 N. Central Ave., P.O. Box 130, 32136. Tel: 386-439-2791; Fax: 386-439-1362. Web: www.smdm-fb.org.
Catechesis/Religious Program—Students 330.

FLEMING ISLAND, CLAY CO., SACRED HEART (1954) [CEM] Revs. Donal Sullivan; Rene Robert, Parochial Vicar.
7190 Hwy. 17 S., 32003. Tel: 904-284-3811; Fax: 904-529-8845. Email: shbulletin3811@bellsouth.net. Web: www.sacredheartgcs.org.
Res.: 1065 Live Oak Ln., 32003. Tel: 904-284-2169.
Catechesis/Religious Program—Tel: 904-284-9983.

Kristin Michler-Belleza, C.R.E. (Elementary); Sandra Curtis, C.R.E. (High School). Students 586.

GAINESVILLE, ALACHUA CO.

1—ST. AUGUSTINE (1923), (Student Center) Revs. David Ruchinski; Jose L. Mesa, S.J. (Dominican Republic), Parochial Vicar; Anthony M. Eseke, Parochial Vicar.
Res.: 1738 W. University Ave., P.O. Box 13888, 32604. Tel: 352-372-3533; Fax: 352-378-9010.
Catechesis/Religious Program—Thomas Rinkoski, D.R.E. & Marraige Min. Students 55.

2—HOLY FAITH (1973) Revs. John M. Phillips; Emmanuel J. Pazhayapurackal, C.M.I. (India); Deacon Michael J. Demers.
Res.: 747 N.W. 43 St., 32607. Tel: 352-376-5405; Fax: 352-375-7568. Web: holyfaithchurch.org.
Catechesis/Religious Program—Tel: 352-376-5405; Fax: 352-375-7568. Dr. Charlotte Chadik, Family Life Dir. Students 271.

3—ST. PATRICK CHURCH (1887) Revs. Roland M. Julien; Dung Quang Bui, Parochial Vicar; Deacon Richard Dugan. In Res., Revs. Robert J. McDermott; Alan Bower.
Res.: 1806 N.W. 21 St., 32605. Tel: 352-372-4641; Fax: 352-376-0575. Email: stpatchurch@bellsouth.net. Web: www.saintpatricksparish.org.
Catechesis/Religious Program—Tel: 352-376-9878, Ext. 60. Brad O'Hara, D.R.E. Students 51.
Mission—St. Philip Neri 1908 Hwy. 301 S., Hawthorne, Alachua Co. 32640. Tel: 352-481-3353.

4—QUEEN OF PEACE (1987) [JC] Revs. Jeffrey A. McGowan; Kazimierz Ligeza.
Church: 10900 S.W. 24th Ave., 32607. Tel: 352-332-6279; Fax: 352-331-7347. Email: office@queenofpeaceparish.org. Web: www.queenofpeaceparish.org.
School—Tel: 352-332-8808. Web: www.qopacademy.org. Sr. Nancy Elder, I.H.M., Prin. Sisters 1; Lay Teachers 41; Students 382.
Catechesis/Religious Program—Tel: 352-332-6279, Ext. 17. Sr. Beatrice Caulson, I.H.M., D.R.E. Students 368.

HIGH SPRINGS, ALACHUA CO., ST. MADELEINE SOPHIE PARISH (1925) Rev. Sebastian K. George, C.M.I.
Mailing Address: 17155 N.W. US Hwy. 441, 32643. Tel: 386-454-2358; Fax: 386-454-4985. Email: stmadeleinecc@windstream.net. Web: www.stmadeleinecatholicchurch.com.
Catechesis/Religious Program—Students 59.
Mission—San Juan 304 S.E. Plant St., Branford, Suwannee Co. 32008. Tel: 386-935-2632; Fax: 386-935-4050.

INTERLACHEN, PUTNAM CO., ST. JOHN (1968) [JC] Rev. Robert L. Napier; Deacon Frederic H. Brown.
Res.: P.O. Box 207, 32148. Tel: 386-684-2528; Fax: 386-684-3819. Email: sjcc1200@aol.com.
Catechesis/Religious Program—Students 20.

JACKSONVILLE BEACH, DUVAL CO., ST. PAUL'S (1930) Revs. William A. Kelly; James Kaniparampil, C.M.I.; Anthony G. Sebra; Deacon Tom Hughes.
Res.: 224 N. Fifth St., 32250. Tel: 904-249-2600; Fax: 904-249-3635.
School—Tel: 904-249-5934; Fax: 904-241-2911. Mrs. Katherine Boice, Prin. Lay Teachers 3; Students 610.
Catechesis/Religious Program—Tel: 904-249-2660; Fax: 904-249-8085. Mary Coleman, D.R.E. Students 556.
Mission—St. Peter 960 Girvin Rd., Duval Co. 32225.

JACKSONVILLE, DUVAL CO.

1—ASSUMPTION (South Jacksonville) (1913) Revs. Frederick R. Parke; Rafal Mazurowski, Parochial Vicar. Email: acidofilny@hotmail.com. In Res., Rev. Donald Lum.
Res.: 2403 Atlantic Blvd., 32207. Tel: 904-398-1963; Fax: 904-398-6115. Email: assumptionchurch@cxp.com. Web: www.assumptioncatholichurch.org.
School—2431 Atlantic Blvd., 32207. Tel: 904-398-1774; Fax: 904-398-6712. Angela Fuller, Prin. Lay Teachers 38; Students 578.
Catechesis/Religious Program—Sr. Therese Ryan, D.R.E. Students 93.

2—BLESSED TRINITY (1957) Rev. Msgr. Vincent J. Haut; Rev. Lam Nguyen, Parochial Vicar.
Res.: 10472 Beach Blvd., 32246. Tel: 904-641-1414; Fax: 904-641-8171. Email: btcc@bellsouth.net. Web: www.btccjax.com.
School—(Grades PreK-8) Tel: 904-641-6458; Fax: 904-645-3762. Email: btschool@comcast.net. Web: www.blessedtrinitycatholicschool.org. Marie Davis, Prin. Students 253.
Catechesis/Religious Program—Tel: 904-646-4320. Email: prep@blessedtrinitycatholicschool.org. Mrs. Aixa Feliciano, D.R.E. Students 174.

3—CHRIST THE KING (1954) Revs. Thanh T. Nguyen; Pawel Duda, Parochial Vicar; Deacon James Scott.
Res.: 742 Arlington Rd. N., 32211. Tel: 904-724-0080; Fax: 904-724-3340. Web: www.ctkcatholic.com.
School—6822 Larkin Rd., 32211. Tel: 904-724-2954; Fax: 904-721-8004. Email: ctks@ctks.org. Stephanie Chinault, Prin. Lay Teachers 23; Teacher Aides 3; Students 288.
Catechesis/Religious Program—Tel: 904-724-9617. Lucille Guzzone, D.R.E. Students 210.

4—CHURCH OF THE CRUCIFIXION (1974), (African American), Rev. Chukwudi Callistus, O. Onwere (Nigeria).
Res.: 3183 W. Edgewood Ave., 32209-2209. Tel: 904-765-5284; Fax: 904-765-1680. Email: crucifixion@comcast.net.
Catechesis/Religious Program—6739 Alaro Rd., 32209. Tel: 904-765-2851. Beatrice Gilliard, D.R.E. Email: crucifixion@comcast.net. Students 7.

5—ST. EPHREM SYRIAC ANTIOCHIAN CATHOLIC CHURCH (1986) Rev. Selwan Sulaiman Taponi (OLD).
Church: 4650 Kernan Blvd. S, 32224. Tel: 904-998-7800; Fax: 904-997-9656.

6—ST. FRANCIS CHOE CHAPEL (1997), (Korean), Rev. Jacobus Seokroul Pork.
Res.: 8051 Rampart Rd., 32244. Tel: 904-573-1833; Fax: 904-519-1004.
Catechesis/Religious Program—Students 6.

7—HOLY FAMILY (1974) Revs. Timothy Cusick; Remek Blaszkowski.
Office: 9800 Baymeadows Rd., 32256. Tel: 904-641-5838; Fax: 904-641-9704. Email: plambardo@holyfamilyjax.com. Web: www.holyfamilyjax.com.
School—9800-3 Baymeadows Rd., 32256. Tel: 904-645-9875; Fax: 904-899-6060. Rosemary Nowotny, Prin. Lay Teachers 29; Students 446.
Catechesis/Religious Program—Maria Petrotta, D.R.E. Students 207.

8—HOLY ROSARY (1921) Rev. Michael Houle.
Res.: 2110 Blue Ave., 32209. Tel: 904-764-3241; Fax: 904-765-4995.
Church: 4731 Norwood Ave., 32206. Email: holyrosaryjax@comcast.net.
School—Sisters of Notre Dame, Tel: 904-764-9032; 904-765-6522; Fax: 904-765-9486. Sr. Dianne Rumschlag, S.N.D., Prin. (Toledo Prov.) Sisters 6; Lay Teachers 12; Students 190.
Catechesis/Religious Program—Students 24.

9—HOLY SPIRIT (1966) Revs. Ananda Prasad Maddineni, M.S.F.S.; Anthony Bonela, M.S.F.S. (India); Deacon Michael J. O'Brien.
Mailing Address: 11665 Fort Caroline Rd., 32225. Email: ltaylor@holyspiritchurchjax.org.
Res.: 11324 Oak Landing Dr., 32225. Tel: 904-641-7244; Fax: 904-641-7266. Email: info@holyspiritchurchjax.org. Web: holyspiritchurchjax.org.
School—(Grades PreK-8) Tel: 904-642-9165; Fax: 904-642-1047. Web: www.hscatholicschool.com. John Luciano, Prin.; Karen Galas, Librarian. Lay Teachers 17; Students 291.
Catechesis/Religious Program—Email: hoovermover1@gmail.com. Debbie Hoover, D.R.E. Students 210.

10—IMMACULATE CONCEPTION (1854) [CEM] [JC] Revs. Edward W. Murphy; Warren Keene; Deacons Robert DeLuca; Miguel Rodriguez.
Res.: 121 E. Duval St., 32202. Tel: 904-359-0331; Fax: 904-356-8133.
Catechesis/Religious Program—Students 98.

11—ST. JOSEPH'S (1883) [CEM] Revs. Daniel Cody; Bernadine Eikhuemelo. In Res., Rev. Bernie Ahern.
Res.: 11730 Old St. Augustine Rd., 32258-2002. Tel: 904-268-5422; Fax: 904-292-0248.
School—11600 Old St. Augustine Rd., 32258. Tel: 904-268-6688; Fax: 904-268-8989. Mrs. Rhonda Rose, Prin. Lay Teachers 32; Students 540.
Catechesis/Religious Program—Tel: 904-880-6404; Fax: 904-880-1559. Dodi Flora, D.R.E. Students 534.

12—MARY QUEEN OF HEAVEN (1988) Rev. Denis O'Shaughnessy; Deacon David A. Williams.
Res.: 9401 Staples Mill Dr., 32244. Tel: 904-647-7641; 904-777-3168 (Office); Fax: 904-777-6772. Email: mqoh@att.net. Web: maryqueenofheaven.org.
Catechesis/Religious Program—Tel: 904-777-3168. Students 97.

13—ST. MATTHEW'S (Lake Shore) (1949) Rev. Jose J. Kulathinal, C.M.I. (India).
Res.: 1773 Blanding Blvd., 32210. Tel: 904-388-8698; Fax: 904-384-1233. Email: stmatthews@stmatthewsjax.com. Web: www.stmatthewsjax.com.
School—Tel: 904-387-4401; Fax: 904-388-4404. Email: stmatthewsoffice@comcast.net. Web: www-.stmatthewscs.org. Mrs. Cathy Tuerk, Prin. Lay Teachers 18; Students 269.
Catechesis/Religious Program—Tel: 904-388-1207. Email: onieshine@aol.com. Onie Lee, D.R.E. Students 166.

14—MOST HOLY REDEEMER (1962) Rev. Timothy R. Lozier.
Res.: 8523 Normandy Blvd., 32221-6701. Tel: 904-786-1192; Fax: 904-786-4224. Email: mhrjax@mhrjax.org. Web: www.mhrjax.org.
Catechesis/Religious Program—Sharon Tomore, D.R.E. Students 90.

15—OUR LADY OF THE ANGELS (1917) [CEM] Closed. Records moved to St. Paul's Parish, 2609 Park St., Jacksonville.

16—ST. PATRICK (1959) Rev. Christopher Liguori; Deacon Vincent Abrahams.
Res.: 1429 Broward Rd., 32218. Tel: 904-768-2593; Fax: 904-768-2251. Email: fatherliguori@hotmail.com. Web: stpatrickjax.org.
School—(Grades PreK-8) Tel: 904-768-6323; Fax: 904-768-2144. Mrs. Mary Margaret Martin, Prin. Lay Teachers 13; Students 179.
Catechesis/Religious Program—Students 174.

17—ST. PAUL'S (1923) Revs. Silverio DiFazio; Manuel Puga.
Res.: 2609 Park St., 32204. Tel: 904-387-2554; Fax: 904-388-6871. Email: stpaulsriverside@gmail.com.
School—Tel: 904-387-2841; Fax: 904-387-1781. Kim Repper, Prin. Lay Teachers 15; Students 179.
Catechesis/Religious Program—Students 46.

18—ST. PIUS THE FIFTH (1919), (African American), Rev. Chukwudi Callistus, O. Onwere (Nigeria).
Res.: 2110 Blue Ave., 32209. Tel: 904-354-1501; Fax: 904-354-7240.
School—1470 W. 13th St., 32209. Tel: 904-354-2613; Fax: 904-356-4522. Email: stpiusvjax@aol.com. Web: www.edline.net/pages/st--pius_school. Sr. Elise Kennedy, S.S.J., Prin. Sisters 2; Lay Teachers 12; Students 181.
Catechesis/Religious Program—Tel: 904-354-1501; Fax: 904-354-7240. Students 20.

19—PRINCE OF PEACE (1970) Rev. Michael J. Larkin.
Res.: 6320 Bennett Rd., 32216. Tel: 904-733-6860; Fax: 904-367-0215.
Catechesis/Religious Program—Tel: 904-733-6011; Fax: 904-367-0215. Email: theresalcurtis@bellsouth.net. Web: www.princeofpeacecatholicchurch.net. Students 70.

20—RESURRECTION (1959) Rev. Jason Trull; Deacons Patrick Goin; Chuck Patterson.
Res.: 3383 University Blvd. N., 32277-2483. Tel: 904-744-0833; Fax: 904-744-7235. Web: www.respar.net.
School—5710 Jack Rd., 32277. Tel: 904-744-1266; Fax: 904-744-5800. Patricia Donahue, Prin. Lay Teachers 16; Students 206.
Catechesis/Religious Program—Tel: 904-744-0833; Fax: 904-744-7235. Students 96.

21—SACRED HEART (1959) Revs. Victor Z. Narivelil, C.M.I. (India); Kiran Kumar Medipalli (India), Parochial Vicar; Deacon Jeffrey P. Burgess. In Res., Rev. Michael P. Morgan.
Res.: 5752 Blanding Blvd., 32244. Tel: 904-771-2152; Fax: 904-573-8816.
School—Tel: 904-771-5800; Fax: 904-771-5323. Marybeth O'Neill, Prin. Lay Teachers 34; Students 444.
Catechesis/Religious Program—Tel: 904-771-5800, Ext. 23; Fax: 904-771-5323. Santa Cochran, C.R.E. Students 196.

22—SAN JOSE (1959) Revs. Gregory J. Fay; Heriberto Vergara, Parochial Vicar; Deacon Paul Consbruck.
Mailing Address: 3619 Toledo Rd., 32217.
School—Tel: 904-733-2313; Fax: 904-731-7169. Mrs. Jan Magiera, Prin. Lay Teachers 28; Students 450.
Catechesis/Religious Program—Tel: 904-733-1630, Ext. 18; Fax: 904-731-4335. Email: dre@sjcatholic.org. Sr. Ambrose Cruise, R.S.M., D.R.E. Students 80; Spanish Students 92.

KEYSTONE HEIGHTS, CLAY CO., ST. WILLIAM (1948) [JC] Rev. Michael S. Williams.
210 Peach St., P.O. Box 721, 32656.
Res.: P.O. Box 721, 32656. Tel: 352-473-4136; Fax: 352-473-4119. Email: stwilliamcatholi@bellsouth.net.
Catechesis/Religious Program—Tel: 352-473-4223. Students 66.

KORONA, FLAGLER CO., ST. MARY (1914) [CEM] Rev. Slawomir S. Podsiedlik, O.C.D.
Mailing Address: 89 St. Mary's Pl., Bunnell, 32110-1537. Tel: 386-437-5098. Email: stmarysfl@bellsouth.net. Web: www.stmaryccfl.org.
Res.: 141 Carmelite Dr., Bunnell, 32110. Tel: 386-437-2910; Fax: 386-437-5125. Email: carmelitefathers@aol.com.
Catechesis/Religious Program—Mary Araya, D.R.E.

LAKE CITY, COLUMBIA CO., EPIPHANY (1965) Revs. Michael Pendergraft; Robert Trujillo, Parochial Vicar.
Res.: 1905 S.W. Epiphany Ct., 32025. Tel: 386-752-4470; Fax: 386-752-4652. Email: epiphanycatholic@bellsouth.net.
School—Tel: 386-752-2320; Fax: 386-752-2364. Email: epiphanyeagles@yahoo.com. Web: epiphanycatholiclakecity.com. Mrs. Rita Klenk, Prin. Lay Teachers 13; Students 76.
Catechesis/Religious Program—Students 75.

LIVE OAK, SUWANNEE CO., ST. FRANCIS XAVIER (1979) Rev. Andrzej Mitera.
Res.: 928 E. Howard St., 32064. Tel: 386-364-1108; Fax: 386-364-1836. Email: stfxoff@comcast.net.
Catechesis/Religious Program—Tel: 386-330-2736. Sherri Ortega, D.R.E. Students 90.
Mission—Our Lady of Guadalupe 137 E. Main St., Mayo, Lafayette Co. 32066.
Mission—St. Therese of the Child Jesus P.O. Box 890, Jasper, Hamilton Co. 32052. Tel: 386-364-1108.

MACCLENNY, BAKER CO., ST. MARY'S (1960) [JC] Rev. Slawomir Bielasiewicz; Deacon Kenneth L. Cochran Sr.
Mailing Address: P.O. Box 1120, 32063.
Res.: 894 Jacqueline Cir., P.O. Box 1120, 32063. Tel: 904-259-6414; Fax: 904-259-9712. Web: www.stmarymacclenny.com.
Catechesis/Religious Program—Angela Boyette, D.R.E. Students 45.
Chaplaincy— Northeast Florida State Hospital, Macclenny; Union Correctional Institute, Raiford; and Florida State Prison, Starke.

MIDDLEBURG, CLAY CO., ST. LUKE (1982) Revs. Andy Blaszkowski, Admin.; Paul Grizzelle-Reid, S.C.J., Parochial Vicar.
1606 Blanding Blvd., 32068. Email: office@stlukesparish.org. Web: www.stlukesparish.org.
Res.: 3392 Aspen Forest Dr., 32068.
Catechesis/Religious Program—Richard Meloche, D.R.E. Students 383.

ORANGE PARK, CLAY CO., ST. CATHERINE'S (1877) Revs. James R. Boddie Jr.; Dennis (Dan) Nelson, Parochial Vicar; Jose Maniyangat, Parochial Vicar.
Res.: 1649 Kingsley Ave., 32073. Tel: 904-264-0577; Fax: 904-264-7999. Email: parish@stcatherinesiena.com. Web: www.stcatherinesiena.com.
Catechesis/Religious Program—Tel: 904-264-2470. Vincent Reilly, Dir. Faith Formation. Students 494.
Mission—Moosehaven Chapel 1700 Park Ave., Clay Co. 32073. Tel: 904-278-1210.

PALATKA, PUTNAM CO., ST. MONICA (1858) [CEM] Rev. Ignatius J. Plathanam, C.M.I. (India).
114 S. 4th St., 32177.
Office:—210 S. 4th St., 32177. Tel: 386-325-9777; Fax: 386-329-1960. Email: stmonicacatholic@bellsouth.net. Web: www.stmonicacatholicchurch.com.
Catechesis/Religious Program— Tracy McKeown, CCF Coord. Students 39.

PALM COAST, FLAGER CO., ST. ELIZABETH ANN SETON (1978) [CEM] Revs. John R. Reynolds; Peter Akin-Otiko; Deacons Perlito (Tom) Alayu; Bob Devereaux.
Res.: 4600 Belle Terre Pkwy., 32164. Tel: 386-445-2246; Fax: 386-445-7808. Email: motherseton@bestnetpc.com. Web: www.stelizabethannseton.org.
Catechesis/Religious Program—Eileen Daley, D.R.E. Email: seasreligioused@aol.com. Students 430.

PONTE VEDRA BEACH, ST. JOHN CO., OUR LADY STAR OF THE SEA (1972) Rev. Msgr. Daniel B. Logan; Rev. Steven Zehler, Parochial Vicar; Deacons Anthony Marini, (Retired); Daniel Scrone.
Mailing Address: 545 Hwy. A1A N., 32082. Tel: 904-285-2698; Fax: 904-285-2502. Email: office@olsspvb.org. Web: www.olsspvb.org.
Preschool—Tel: 904-285-2698, Ext. 2; Fax: 904-273-9740. Email: lsdirector@olsspvb.org. Chris Saliba, Dir.
School—Palmer Catholic Academy, 4889 Palm Valley Rd., 32082. Tel: 904-543-8515; Fax: 904-543-8750. Web: www.palmercatholic.org. Mrs. Linda Earp, Prin.
Catechesis/Religious Program—Tel: 904-285-2698, Ext. 5; Fax: 904-273-0590. Email: dre@olsspvb.org. Dina Voutour, D.R.E. Students 525.

ST. AUGUSTINE SHORES, ST. JOHN CO., CORPUS CHRISTI (1975) [CEM] Rev. William C. Mooney.
Res.: P.O. Box 3064, 32085. Tel: 904-797-4842; Fax: 904-797-2746.
Catechesis/Religious Program—Students 68.

ST. JOHN, ST. JOHN CO., SAN JUAN DEL RIO (1977) Revs. John H. Tetlow; Anthony Ike; Deacons Jeff C. Silvernale; Jerry Turkowski; Stan Boschert.
Res.: 1718 State Rd., No. 13, 32259. Tel: 904-287-0519 (Office); Fax: 904-287-1504. Web: www.sjdrparish.org.
School—1714 State Rd. 13, 32259. Tel: 904-287-8081; Fax: 904-287-4574. Lay Teachers 30; Students 403.
Catechesis/Religious Program—Tel: 904-287-2801. Students 840.

STARKE, BRADFORD CO., ST. EDWARD (1941) Rev. Conrad Cowart.
Res.: 441 N. Temple Ave., 32091-3207. Tel: 904-964-6155; Fax: 904-964-1411. Email: stedsecretary@yahoo.com. Web: www.stedwardstarke.com.
Catechesis/Religious Program—Web: www.stedstarke.com. Students 23.

WILLISTON, LEVY CO., HOLY FAMILY (1970) Rev. Rodolfo Godinez.
Res.: 17353 N.E. 27 A, 32696. Tel: 352-528-2893; Fax: 352-528-6002. Email: holyfamilycathch@earthlink.net. Web: www.holyfamilywilliston.com.
Catechesis/Religious Program—Email: dre.holyfamily@earthlink.net. Students 21.
Mission—St. Anthony the Abbot P.O. Box 1070, Inglis, Levy Co. 34449. Tel: 352-447-4573; Fax: 352-447-4573.

Special Assignment:
Revs.—
Houle, Michael, E.V., M.A., M.Ed., M.Div., Pres., Bishop Kenny High School, P.O. Box 5544, 32247.
McDermott, Robert, Chap., Prison Ministry, Shands Hospital, 500 N. East 16th Ave., Gainesville, 32601.
Palazzolo, Anthony P., 101 Marsh Cove Ln., Ponte Vedra Beach, 32082. Tel: 904-280-5422 Diocese of Mandeville, Jamaica
Young, Dennis M., V.A. Medical Center, 1601 S.W. Archer Rd., Gainesville, 32608-1197.

On Duty Outside the Diocese:
Rev. Msgr.—
Brennan, Keith R., J.C.D., Rector, St. Vincent de Paul Seminary, 10701 S. Military Tr., Boynton Beach, 33436. Tel: 561-732-4424
Rev.—
O'Neal, James E., Active Duty U.S. Army Chaplain Corps

Unassigned:
Revs.—
Camarda, Ronald A.
Ligeza, Jan A.

Absent or Sick Leave:
Revs.—
Brandstrup, Christian
Brault, Gilles
Buchmelter, Brendan
Fisher, Roe
Kerr, Robert
Morse, Michael
Moss, James
Oliver, John
Pollard, John L.
Thompson, Michael
Whitehead, Joseph

Retired:
Rev. Msgrs.—
Conesa, Diego
Danaher, Mortimer, 7843 Fawn Oaks Ct., 32256.
Heslin, James J., P.O. Box 16552, 32245.
Kohls, Eugene C., P.A., J.C.D., 5201 Atlantic Blvd., #228, 32207.
Lenihan, John J., 102 Hammock Circle, 32095.
Revs.—
Besendorfer, Ralph L., J.C.D.
Cody, Thomas
Colasurdo, Peter, 3800 Michael's Landing E., 32224.
Ducci, Alex, Poste Italiane BG Centro, C.P. 127, 24100 Bergamo, Italy.
Dux, John H., 311 Ayers Cir., Summerville, SC 29485.
Finlay, Joseph F.
Florez, Luis, 2201 Glencoe Dr., Orange Park, 32073.
Gagan, Phillip R., 365 Marywood Dr., #4, St. Johns, 32259.
Hochheim, William A., Casa San Pedro, 365 Marywood Dr., #3, St. Johns, 32259.
Maniangat, Joseph
May, James
Meehan, Joseph
Moore, Frederick Thomas
Notarpole, Joseph
O'Flynn, Seamus
Revilla, Francisco, Suecia 100-3-3B, 28022 Madrid, Spain.
Rooney, Edward K.
Sullivan, Thomas K.
Walsh, Flannan J.
Walsh, Thomas P.

INSTITUTIONS LOCATED IN THE DIOCESE

[A] DIOCESAN SCHOOLS

ST. AUGUSTINE. *St. Joseph's Academy, Inc.*, 155 State Rd. 207, 32084. Tel: 904-824-0431; Fax: 904-826-4477. Web: www.sjaweb.org. Rev. Michael Houle, E.V., M.A., M.Ed., M.Div., Pres.; Michael Heubeck, Prin.; Sr. Suzan Foster, S.S.J., Vice Prin.; Mr. Michael Maloney, Athletic Dir. & Dean of Students. Day School. Priests 1; Sisters 2; Lay Teachers 24; Students 260.

GAINESVILLE. *St. Francis Catholic High School, Inc.*, 4100 N.W. 115 Ter., 32606. Tel: 352-376-6545; Fax: 352-248-0418. Email: info@sfchs.org. Web: www.sfchs.org. Ernest D. Herrington Jr., Prin.; Theresa D. Cartell, Librarian. Sisters 2; Lay Teachers 21; Students 242.

JACKSONVILLE. *Bishop John Snyder High School, Inc.*, 5001 Samaritan Way, 32221. Tel: 904-771-1029; Fax: 904-908-8988. Email: davidyazdiya@bishopsnyder.org. Web: www.bishopsnyder.org. Deacon David Yazdiya, Prin. Lay Teachers 33; Students 524; Total Staff 50.
Bishop Kenny High School, Inc. (1952) 1055 Kingman Ave., 32247. Tel: 904-398-7545; Fax: 904-398-5728. Rev. Michael Houle, E.V., M.A., M.Ed., M.Div., Pres.; Mr. Todd Orlando, M.Ed., Prin.; Robert West, M.Ed., Vice Prin. & Athletic Dir.; Mrs. Mary DeSalvo, M.Ed., Vice Prin.; Dave Williams, M.Ed., Dean of Students. Priests 1; Sisters 1; Lay Teachers 93; Students 1,240.
Guardian Catholic Schools, Inc., 4920 Brentwood Ave., 32206. Tel: 904-765-1920; Fax: 904-765-8155. Shariffa A. Spicer, Exec. Dir. This alliance includes the following schools:
Holy Rosary Catholic School (Grades PreK-8), 4920 Brentwood Ave., 32206. Tel: 904-765-6522; Fax: 904-765-9486. Email: principalhrcs@comcast.net. Sr. Dianne Rumschlag, S.N.D., Prin.; April Rice, Librarian/Media Specialist. Sisters 5; Lay Teachers 14; Students 192.
St. Pius Catholic School (Grades PreK-8), 1470 W. 13th St., 32209. Tel: 904-354-2613; Fax: 904-356-4522. Email: kennede@aol.com. Web: www.edline.net/pages/st__pius_school. Sr. Elise Kennedy, S.S.J., Prin.; Michele Rademacher, Librarian. Sisters 4; Lay Teachers 14.

[B] ELEMENTARY SCHOOLS, INTERPAROCHIAL

GAINESVILLE. *St. Patrick School*, 550 N.E. 16th Ave., 32601. Tel: 352-376-9878; Fax: 352-371-6177. Email: info@stpatrickschoolgnv.org. Web: www.stpatrickschoolgnv.org. J. Mark Akerman, Prin. Interparish school composed of students from St. Patrick, Holy Faith & St. Augustine, Gainesville. Lay Teachers 25; Students 305.

MIDDLEBURG. *Annunciation School* (1993) (Grades PreK-8), 1610 Blanding Blvd., 32068. Tel: 904-282-0504; Fax: 904-282-6808. Email: saltieri@annunciationcatholic.org. Web: www.annunciationcatholic.org. Mrs. Susan Altieri, Prin.; Vicki Cowman, Librarian. Interparish school composed of students from Sacred Heart, Green Cove Springs; St. Catherine's, Orange Park; and St. Luke, Middleburg. Lay Teachers 26; Students 430.

[C] CATHOLIC CHARITIES

ST. AUGUSTINE. *Catholic Charities Bureau St. Augustine Regional Office*, 225 W. King St., P.O. Box 543, 32085. Tel: 904-829-6300; Fax: 904-829-0494. Email: info@ccbstaug.org. Web: ccbstaug.org. Rebecca Stringer, COO.

GAINESVILLE. *Catholic Charities Regional Office*, 1701 N.E. 9th St., 32609. Tel: 352-372-0294; Fax: 352-371-3157. Email: coo@catholiccharitiesgainesville.org. Web: www.catholiccharitiesgainesville.org. Karen M. Slevin, Exec. Dir. & COO. Emergency services, counseling, respite care, and adoptions.

JACKSONVILLE. *Catholic Charities Bureau, Inc.*, 134 E. Church St., 32202. Tel: 904-899-5500; Fax: 904-899-5510. Web: www.ccbdosa.org.
Catholic Charities Regional Office (1945) 134 E. Church St., 32202. Tel: 904-354-4846, Ext. 233; Fax: 904-354-4718. Email: lhickey@ccbjax.org. Web: www.ccbjax.org. Laura M. Hickey, COO. Emergency financial assistance for housing/utilities, food pantry, adoption programs, & financial assistance for housing opportunities for persons with AIDS, and refugee resettlement.

LAKE CITY. *Catholic Charities Lake City Regional Office*, 258 N.W. Burk Ave., 32055. Tel: 386-754-9180; Fax: 386-754-5325. Email: cclc@bellsouth.net. Web: www.catholiccharitieslakecity.org. Suzanne Edwards, COO.

[D] SPECIAL APOSTOLATES

ST. AUGUSTINE. *Religious Education for Catholic Deaf and Blind*, 30 Ocean Ave., 32084-2813. Tel: 904-825-4272 (Voice/TDD); Fax: 904-825-4348. Email: religiouseduc90@bellsouth.net. Web: www.catholicdeaf.org. Florida School for the Deaf and Blind. Total Staff 4.

JACKSONVILLE. *L'Arche Harbor House* (1985) 700 Arlington Rd. N., 32211. Tel: 904-721-5992; Fax: 904-721-7143. Email: communityleader@bellsouth.net. Web: larchejacksonville.org. Amy Finn-Schultz, Exec. Dir. & Community Leader. A residential community for adults with developmental disabilities and those who choose to share life with them (assistants). We also have an adult day program called the Rainbow Workshop. Bed Capacity 20; Total Assisted Annually 30; Total Staff 25.

Morning Star School (1956) 725 Mickler Rd., 32211. Tel: 904-721-2144; Fax: 904-721-1040. Email: jmbarnes23@bellsouth.net. Web: www.morningstar-jax.org. Jean Barnes, Prin. A school for exceptional children. Lay Teachers 16; Students 118.

[E] GENERAL HOSPITALS

JACKSONVILLE. *St. Luke's - St. Vincent's HealthCare, Inc. dba St. Luke's Hospital* 4201 Belfort Rd., 32216. Tel: 904-308-4025; 907-308-7300; Fax: 904-308-4072. Web: www.stlukesjax.com. Laurie Teppert, Sr. Vice Pres. & Gen. Counsel. Bed Capacity 313; Total Staff 816; Nurses 362; Outpatients 30,824; Inpatients 9,141.

St. Vincent's Health System, Inc., 1 Shircliff Way, 32204. Tel: 904-308-8446; 904-308-7300; Fax: 904-308-2947. Moody Chisholm, Pres. & CEO. Statistics are reported under St. Vincent's Medical Center, Inc. Bed Capacity 528; Total Staff 4,963; Total Assisted Annually 34,000; Outpatients 147,000; Emergency Room 91,500.

St. Vincent's Medical Center, Inc., One Shircliff Way, P.O. Box 2982, 32204. Tel: 904-308-7300; Fax: 904-308-7326. Web: www.jaxhealth.com. Daughters of Charity of St. Vincent de Paul., Member St. Vincent's Health System, Inc. Nurses 1,001; Total Staff 2,920; Bed Capacity 528; Bassinets 17; Outpatients 143,680; Inpatients 29,058.

St. Vincent's Foundation, Inc. Tel: 904-308-7306; Fax: 904-308-7573.

St. Vincent's Ambulatory Care, Inc. Tel: 904-308-2110; Fax: 904-396-3646.

St. Catherine Laboure Manor, Inc. Tel: 904-308-4702; Fax: 904-308-2987.

[F] HOMES FOR AGING

JACKSONVILLE. *All Saints Catholic Nursing Home & Rehabilitation Center, Inc.*, 5888 Blanding Blvd., 32244. Tel: 904-772-1220; Fax: 904-772-6334. Email: blee@allsaintsnursing.org. Web: www.allsaintsnursing.org. Connie O'Donnell, Admin. Physical Therapy, Speech Therapy, Occupational Therapy Available, Respite Services, Medicare, Medicaid Accepted, VA, inpatient & outpatient rehabilitative services provided. Total Assisted 41,622; Bed Capacity 120; Total Staff 167.

Casa San Pedro, 365 Marywood Dr., St. Johns, 32259. Tel: 904-230-2562; Fax: 904-230-2563. Email: csanpedr@bellsouth.net. Web: www.marywoodcenter.org. Mary Ruth Mustonen.

St. Catherine Laboure Manor, 1750 Stockton St., 32204. Tel: 904-308-4700; Fax: 904-308-2987. Email: mgartlan@jaxhealth.com. Web: www.stvincentshealth.com. Long term health care Skilled Nursing Facility. Bed Capacity 240; Sisters 3; Total Staff 239; Patients Assisted Annually 1,194.

[G] CATHOLIC CHARITIES OFFICE OF HOUSING

JACKSONVILLE. *Jacksonville, Family Housing Management Co.* (1986) 134 E. Church St., 32202. Tel: 904-632-1255; Fax: 904-632-2135. Email: aballard@ccbjax.org. Alma C. Ballard, Exec. Dir.; John Oetjen, Pres.

Jacksonville, Office of Housing Development, 134 E. Church St., 32202. Tel: 904-632-1255; Fax: 904-632-2135. Alma C. Ballard, Exec. Dir.

Hurley Manor Apartments (1984) 3333-35 University Blvd. N., 32277. Tel: 904-744-6022; Fax: 904-744-6037. Email: admin@hurleymanor.org. Lloyd Belson, Pres.; Franceli Gimenez, Mgr. Parent Co., Catholic Charities Housing Association of Jacksonville, Inc.

Barry Manor Apartments (1984) 1000 Husson Ave., Palatka, 32177. Tel: 386-328-5137; Fax: 386-328-5138. Email: barrymanorapt@att.net. Joyce Miller, Pres.; Marilyn Canup, Mgr. Parent Co., Palatka Retirement Villas, Inc.

Providence Center, 134 E. Church St., 32202. Tel: 904-632-1255; Fax: 904-632-2135.

San Jose Manor I (1991) 3630 Galicia Rd., 32217. Tel: 904-739-0555; Fax: 904-739-0559. Email: sjm@sanjosemanor.comcastbiz.net. Janis E. Bebeau, Pres.; Jacqueta Nash, Mgr. (Parent Company: Housing Association of the Diocese of St. Augustine.)

San Jose Manor II (2000) 3622 Galicia Rd., 32217. Tel: 904-739-0555; Fax: 904-739-0559. Email: sjm@sanjosemanor.comcastbiz.net. C. Donald MacLean, Pres.; Jacqueta Nash, Mgr. (Parent Company: San Jose Catholic Housing Assoc., Inc.)

[H] MONASTERIES AND RESIDENCES OF PRIESTS AND BROTHERS

BUNNELL. *Discalced Carmelite Fathers of Florida*, 141 Carmelite Dr., 32110. Tel: 386-437-2910; Fax: 386-437-5125. Email: carmelitefathers@aol.com. Revs. Joseph F. Zawada, O.C.D.; Arthur Chojda, O.C.D., Prior; Slawomir S. Podsiedlik, O.C.D.; Bro. Anthony Gemmato, O.C.D. Total Staff 4.

[I] CONVENTS AND RESIDENCES FOR SISTERS

ST. AUGUSTINE. *Motherhouse of the Sisters of St. Joseph of St. Augustine, Florida*, 241 St. George St., P.O. Box 3506, 32085. Tel: 904-824-1752; Fax: 904-826-0949. Email: ssjfl@bellsouth.net. Web: ssjfl.org. Sr. Jane Stoecker, S.S.J., Gen. Supr. Professed Sisters 72.

The Sisters of St. Joseph Continuing Community Support Trust Fund. Tel: 904-824-1752; Fax: 904-826-0949.

St. Joseph Ministries, P.O. Box 3506, Saint Augustine, 32085.

[J] RETREAT HOUSES

JACKSONVILLE. *Marywood Center for Spirituality and Ministry*, 235 Marywood Dr., St. Johns, 32259. Tel: 904-287-2525; Fax: 904-287-9738. Email: info@marywoodcenter.org. Web: www.marywoodcenter.org. Mr. Charles David, Admin.; Ginger Eddy, Prog. Coord. Total Staff 15.

[K] NEWMAN CENTERS

ST. AUGUSTINE. *Flagler College Newman Center* c/o Cathedral of St. Augustine, 35 Treasury St., 32084. Tel: 904-461-5795. Email: ccfis@juno.com. Rev. Thomas S. Willis, V.F.

[L] MISCELLANEOUS

ST. AUGUSTINE. *St. Augustine House of Prayer & Evangelization Center*, 34 Ocean Ave., 32084. Tel: 904-824-4831.

Sisters of St. Joseph's Architectural Stained Glass, 2745 Industry Center Rd., #6, 32084. Tel: 904-669-5388. Email: liteart@aol.com. Web: www.ssjstainedglass.com. Sr. Diane Couture, S.S.J., Dir.

GAINESVILLE. *The Center for the Study of the Passion of Christ and the Holy Shroud*, 1738 W. University, 32603. Tel: 352-372-3533. Mrs. Gerry DeGraff, Exec. Sec.

Spirit Radio of North Florida, Inc., 500 N.E. 16th Ave., 32601. Tel: 352-372-2191; Fax: 352-376-0575. Email: rolandjulien@hotmail.com. Web: www.spirit-radio.org. Rev. Roland M. Julien, V.F.

JACKSONVILLE. **Association of St. Lawrence Comunita Cenacolo America Inc.*, 1050 Talleyrand Ave., 32206. Tel: 904-353-5353; Fax: 904-353-4707. Albino Aragno, Exec. Dir.

DSA Land, Inc., 11625 Old St. Augustine Rd., 32258.

Florida Catholic Heritage Museum, Inc., 11625 Old St. Augustine Rd., 32258. Tel: 904-262-3200.

Office for the Maryknoll Fathers & Brothers, 3619 Toledo Rd., 32217. Tel: 904-739-1112. Deacon Larry Hart.

RELIGIOUS INSTITUTES OF MEN REPRESENTED IN THE DIOCESE

For further details refer to the corresponding bracketed number in the Religious Institutes of Men or Women section.

[0275]—*Carmelites of Mary Immaculate*—C.M.I.
[1130]—*Congregation of the Priests of the Sacred Heart*—S.C.J.
[0260]—*Discalced Carmelite Friars*—O.C.D.
[0650]—*Holy Ghost Fathers*—C.S.Sp.
[0690]—*Jesuit Fathers and Brothers*—S.J.
[]—*Marist Brothers*—F.M.S.
[0920]—*Oblates of St. Francis de Sales*—M.S.F.S.

RELIGIOUS INSTITUTES OF WOMEN REPRESENTED IN THE DIOCESE

[]—*Carmelite Sisters*—O.Carm.
[0685]—*Claretian Missionary Sisters*—R.M.I.
[3110]—*Congregation of Our Lady of Retreat in the Cenacle*—R.C.
[0760]—*Daughters of Charity of St. Vincent de Paul* (Eastern Prov.)—D.C.
[1070-13]—*Dominican Sisters*—O.P.
[]—*Servant Sisters of the Home of the Mother*—S.S.H.M.
[2170]—*Servants of the Immaculate Heart of Mary*—I.H.M.
[]—*Sisters for Christian Community*—S.F.C.C.
[]—*Sisters of Mercy of Ireland*—R.S.M.
[2575]—*Sisters of Mercy of the Americas*—R.S.M.
[2990]—*Sisters of Notre Dame* (Toledo Prov.)—S.N.D.
[]—*Sisters of St. Francis Xavier*—S.F.X.
[3900]—*Sisters of St. Joseph of St. Augustine, FL*—S.S.J.
[]—*Trinitarian Handmaids of the Divine Word*—T.H.D.W.

DIOCESAN CEMETERIES

ST. AUGUSTINE. *St. Augustine Diocesan Cemeteries* Operates San Lorenzo Cemetery in St. Augustine and St. Mary Cemetery in Bunnell., 1635 U.S. 1 S., 32084. Tel: 904-824-6680; Fax: 904-824-3845. Email: srnicole@nflcemeteries.org. Rev. Timothy M. Lindenfelser, J.C.L., Dir.; Sr. Nicole Cayer, S.S.J., Dir. Family Svcs. Priests 1; Total Staff 6.

NECROLOGY

† Haryasz, Francis S., (Retired)—Died Jan. 9, 2011

An asterisk (*) denotes an organization that has established tax-exempt status directly with the IRS and is not covered by the USCCB Group Ruling.

Diocese of St. Cloud

(Dioecesis S. Clodoaldi)

Most Reverend

JOHN F. KINNEY, D.D., J.C.D.

Bishop of St. Cloud; ordained February 2, 1963; appointed Titular Bishop of Caorle and Auxiliary Bishop of St. Paul and Minneapolis November 16, 1976; consecrated January 25, 1977; appointed Bishop of Bismarck June 28, 1982; installed August 23, 1982; appointed Bishop of St. Cloud May 9, 1995; installed July 6, 1995. *Office: 214 Third Ave. S., P.O. Box 1248, St. Cloud, MN 56302-1248.* Tel: 320-251-2340.

Chancery: 214 Third Ave. S., P.O. Box 1248, St. Cloud, MN 56302. Tel: 320-251-2340; Fax: 320-251-0470.

Web: www.stcdio.org

Square Miles 12,251.

Corporate Title: "The Diocese of St. Cloud."

Erected as the Vicariate of Northern Minnesota, February 12, 1875.

Created as the Diocese of St. Cloud, September 22, 1889.

Comprises the Counties of Stearns, Sherburne, Benton, Morrison, Mille Lacs, Kanabec, Isanti, Pope, Stevens, Traverse, Grant, Douglas, Wilkin, Otter Tail, Todd and Wadena in the State of Minnesota.

For legal titles of parishes and diocesan institutions, consult the Chancery Office.

STATISTICAL OVERVIEW

Personnel	
Bishop	1
Retired Bishops	1
Abbots	1
Priests: Diocesan Active in Diocese	59
Priests: Diocesan Active Outside Diocese	1
Priests: Retired, Sick or Absent	50
Number of Diocesan Priests	110
Religious Priests in Diocese	101
Total Priests in Diocese	211
Extern Priests in Diocese	2
Ordinations:	
Diocesan Priests	2
Transitional Deacons	2
Permanent Deacons	5
Permanent Deacons in Diocese	51
Total Brothers	65
Total Sisters	463
Parishes	
Parishes	132
With Resident Pastor:	
Resident Diocesan Priests	49
Resident Religious Priests	8
Without Resident Pastor:	
Administered by Priests	75
New Parishes Created	1
Closed Parishes	3
Professional Ministry Personnel:	
Sisters	8
Lay Ministers	64
Welfare	
Catholic Hospitals	4
Total Assisted	367,136
Homes for the Aged	12
Total Assisted	1,040
Residential Care of Children	1
Total Assisted	368
Special Centers for Social Services	67
Total Assisted	52,625
Residential Care of Disabled	8
Total Assisted	56
Other Institutions	11
Total Assisted	727
Educational	
Diocesan Students in Other Seminaries	19
Seminaries, Religious	1
Students Religious	1
Total Seminarians	20
Colleges and Universities	2
Total Students	4,096
High Schools, Diocesan and Parish	1
Total Students	650
High Schools, Private	1
Total Students	306
Elementary Schools, Diocesan and Parish	29
Total Students	4,076
Catechesis/Religious Education:	
High School Students	5,263
Elementary Students	10,998
Total Students under Catholic Instruction	25,409
Teachers in the Diocese:	
Priests	24
Brothers	2
Sisters	15
Lay Teachers	751
Vital Statistics	
Receptions into the Church:	
Infant Baptism Totals	1,843
Adult Baptism Totals	44
Received into Full Communion	138
First Communions	2,039
Confirmations	1,819
Marriages:	
Catholic	463
Interfaith	184
Total Marriages	647
Deaths	1,414
Total Catholic Population	142,042
Total Population	559,865

Former Bishops—Rt. Revs. RUPERT SEIDENBUSCH, O.S.B., D.D., ord. June 22, 1853; cons. Bishop of Halia, Vicar-Apostolic of Northern Minnesota, May 30, 1875; resigned Nov. 15, 1888; died June 2, 1895; OTTO ZARDETTI, D.D., ord. Aug. 21, 1870; cons. Oct. 20, 1889; transferred to Bucharest, Romania, and raised to the Archiepiscopal Dignity, Feb. 23, 1894; died May 9, 1902; MARTIN MARTY, O.S.B., D.D., ord. Sept. 14, 1856; cons. Bishop of Tiberias, Feb. 1, 1880; Bishop of Sioux Falls, 1889; transferred to St. Cloud, Jan. 21, 1895; died Sept. 19, 1896; JAMES TROBEC, D.D., ord. Sept. 8, 1865; cons. Bishop of St. Cloud, Sept. 21, 1897; resigned April 15, 1914; appt. Titular Bishop of Lycopolis; died Dec. 14, 1921; Most Revs. JOSEPH F. BUSCH, D.D., ord. July 28, 1889; appt. Bishop of Lead, S. D., April 9, 1910; cons. May 19, 1910; transferred to See of St. Cloud, Jan. 19, 1915; died May 31, 1953; PETER W. BARTHOLOME, D.D., ord. June 12, 1917; appt. Titular Bishop of Lete and Coadjutor Bishop of St. Cloud "cum jure successionis", Dec. 6, 1941; cons. March 3, 1942; succeeded to See May 31, 1953; appt. Assistant at the Pontifical Throne July 23, 1954; resigned Jan. 31, 1968; died June 17, 1982; GEORGE H. SPELTZ, D.D., Ph.D., ord. June 2, 1940; appt. Auxiliary Bishop of Winona and Titular Bishop of Claneus February 13, 1963; cons. March 25, 1963; appt. Coadjutor of St. Cloud April 4, 1966; succeeded Jan. 31, 1968; resigned Jan. 13, 1987; died Feb. 1, 2004; JEROME HANUS, O.S.B., D.D., ord. July 30, 1966; appt. Bishop of St. Cloud, July 6, 1987; ord. and installed Aug. 24, 1987; appt. Coadjutor Archbishop of Dubuque, IA, Aug. 23, 1994.

Chancery—214 Third Ave. S., P.O. Box 1248, St. Cloud, 56302. Tel: 320-251-2340; 320-259-5227 (after hours); Fax: 320-251-0470. Office Hours: Mon.-Fri. 8:30-12 & 1-4:30.

Vicar General—Very Rev. ROBERT ROLFES, J.C.L.

Chancellor—CATHERINE M. COGHLAN.

Assistant Chancellor—Sr. MARY MANDERNACH, O.S.B.

Diocesan Tribunal—305 Seventh Ave. N., St. Cloud, 56303. All marriage cases are to be directed to: The Tribunal, Box 576, St. Cloud, 56302. Tel: 320-251-6557.

Judicial Vicar—Rev. VIRGIL A. HELMIN, J.C.L.

Adjutant Judicial Vicar—Rev. MARVIN ENNEKING, J.C.L.

Promoter Justitiae—Rev. ROBERT C. HARREN, J.C.L.

Defensor Vinculi—Rev. GREGORY LIESER (Retired); Very Rev. ROBERT ROLFES, J.C.L.; Revs. JONATHAN LICARI, O.S.B.; THOMAS OLSON; ROGER KLASSEN, O.S.B.; Deacon JOHN SALCHERT.

Judges—Rev. MARVIN ENNEKING, J.C.L.; Very Rev. ROBERT ROLFES, J.C.L.; Rev. VIRGIL HELMIN, J.C.L.; THERESA A. WYBURN, J.C.L.; Deacon DONALD TZINSKI, J.C.L.

Notaries—Rev. VIRGIL A. HELMIN, J.C.L.; Very Rev. ROBERT ROLFES, J.C.L.; Deacon DONALD TZINSKI, J.C.L.; KARRIE MOLLNER; JENNA VAVRA.

Advocates—Revs. JOSEPH KORF; MARK INNOCENTI; Mrs. DOLORES SALCHERT.

Marriage Counseling—Caritas Family Services, 911 18th St. N., St. Cloud, 56303. Tel: 320-650-1660.

Diocesan Consultors—Very Rev. ROBERT ROLFES, J.C.L.; Revs. KEVIN ANDERSON; TIMOTHY BALTES; JOSEPH FEDERS, O.S.B.; JOSEPH HERZING; MARK STANG; STANLEY WIESER.

Deans—Revs. STEVEN BINSFELD, Alexandria/Morris; STEPHEN BEAUCLAIR, O.S.B., Cold Spring; JOSEPH KORF, Fergus Falls/Wadena; LAUREN GERMANN, Foley/Princeton; KENNETH BRENNY, Little Falls (Retired); MARVIN ENNEKING, J.C.L., Melrose/Sauk Centre; GREGORY LIESER, St. Cloud (Retired).

Diocesan Corporate Board—Most Rev. JOHN F. KINNEY, D.D., J.C.D., Pres.; Very Rev. ROBERT ROLFES, J.C.L., Vice Pres.; Revs. JOSEPH KORF; LAUREN GERMANN, Sec.; CATHERINE M. COGHLAN.

Diocesan Finance Council—Most Rev. JOHN F. KINNEY, D.D., J.C.D.; JOSEPH SPANIOL, Finance Officer; Very Rev. ROBERT ROLFES, J.C.L.; Rev. RONALD WEYRENS; Sr. ARDELLA KVAMME, O.S.B.; JEAN HART; Mr. PETER FUCHSTEINER; MARY KESKE; Mr. JAMES MEGEL; Mr. PAUL PFANNENSTEIN; Mr. RAYMOND SCHULTE; NANCY WHITNEY.

Due Process Service—JANE MARRIN, Dir.

Presbyteral Council—Most Rev. JOHN F. KINNEY, D.D., J.C.D.; Very Rev. ROBERT ROLFES, J.C.L.; Revs. EUGENE DOYLE, Chair; DAVID MACIEJ; ALAN WIELINSKI; ALFRED STANGL (Retired); MICHAEL WOLFBAUER; PETER K. KIRCHNER JR.; JEFFREY D. ETHEN; JOSEPH FEDERS, O.S.B.; GREGORY PAFFEL; RICHARD WALZ, Address correspondence to: Immaculate Conception Church, P.O. Box 426, Becker, 55308.

Pastoral Council—Most Rev. JOHN F. KINNEY, D.D., J.C.D.; PATRICIA LOXTERCAMP, Exec. Sec.; Rev. PETER VANDERWEYST; Bro. WALTER KIEFFER, O.S.B.; Deacon EUGENE KRAMER; PEGGY KOSCIELNIAK; EUGENE FISCHER; EVELYN OTTO;

KATY BLUME; HANNAH VOSS; MONICA SEGURA-SCHWARTZ; Sr. LORETTA DENFELD, O.S.F.; ARLEEN ROELIKE; LINDA CHRISTEN; ABIGAIL NEVILLE; LORI KOHORST; SARAH LACHOWITZER; CATHERINE M. COGHLAN.

Diocesan Offices and Programs

Archives—LOUISE THEISEN, Archivist. Tel: 320-251-2340. Email: ltheisen@gw.stcdio.org.

Boy Scouts—Rev. LEROY SCHEIERL, Dir., 16921 County Rd. 7, N.W., Brandon, 56315.

Catholic Campaign for Human Development—KATHY LANGER, 911 18th St. N., P.O. Box 2390, St. Cloud, 56302. Tel: 320-229-6020.

Campus Ministry—Rev. ANTHONY OELRICH, S.T.L., Newman Center, 396 First Ave. S., St. Cloud, 56301.

Catholic Charities—Mr. STEVEN BRESNAHAN, Exec. Dir., 911 18th St. N., P.O. Box 2390, St. Cloud, 56302. Tel: 320-650-1550; Fax: 320-650-1528 Community Services (Senior Dining, Central Minnesota Foster Grandparent Program, Support and Advocacy for Independent Living, Supported Housing for Youth, In Home Program for Persons with Disabilities); Caritas Family Services (Adoption; Caritas Mental Health Clinic; Emergency Services: Food, Clothing, Financial; Financial Counseling; La Cruz Community Support; Immigration Services; Life Transitions; Pregnancy Counseling; Hope Community Support Program); Housing Services (Housing Management Services and Transitional Housing including Domus Transitional Housing & V.A. Homes); Residential and Day Services (St. Elizabeth's Home, Community Alternative for Handicapped Individuals, Mother Teresa Home, St. Anne's Home, St. Francis Home, St. Luke's Home, Bethany Home, St. Margaret's Home, St. Michael's Home, St. Cloud Children's Home, Intensive Treatment Unit, Young Learners, Day Programs); Social Concerns. Web: www.ccstcloud.org.

Catholic Foundation of the Diocese of St. Cloud—GEORGE SJOGREN, Exec. Dir., 305 7th Ave. N., St. Cloud, 56303. Tel: 320-258-0390.

Catholic Relief Services—Rev. WILLIAM VOS, Dir. (Retired), Mailing Address: 11 Eighth Ave. S., St. Cloud, 56301. Tel: 320-251-1100; Fax: 320-251-2061.

Catholic Women, Council of—Rev. GREGORY LIESER, Moderator (Retired), Mailing Address: 308 3rd St. S., Sauk Rapids, 56379. Tel: 320-250-6390; ARLEEN ROELIKE, Pres., 26483 350th St., Freeport, 56331. Tel: 320-836-2196.

Cemeteries Assumption-Calvary—2341 Roosevelt Rd., St. Cloud, 56301. Tel: 320-251-5511.

Censores Librorum—Rev. ROBERT C. HARREN, J.C.L.; Sr. RENEE DOMEIER, O.S.B.

Clerical Aid Association—Most Rev. JOHN F. KINNEY, D.D., J.C.D., Pres.; Very Rev. ROBERT ROLFES, J.C.L., Sec.; CATHERINE M. COGHLAN. Directors: Revs. VIRGIL R. BRAUN; NICHOLAS LANDSBERGER, S.T.L.; PETER K. KIRCHNER JR.; THOMAS KNOBLACH, Ph.D.; LAURN VIRNIG; DAVID MACIEJ, Address Mail to: The Chancery, P.O. Box 1248, St. Cloud, 56302.

Communications Office— (Radio, Television, Public Information), REBECCA KUROWSKI, Dir., Pastoral Center, Diocese of St. Cloud, 305 N. Seventh Ave., St. Cloud, 56303. Tel: 320-251-0558.

Continuing Formation of Priests—Rev. ANTHONY OELRICH, S.T.L., 305 7th Ave. N., Saint Cloud, 56303. Tel: 320-251-8335.

Development Office—GEORGE SJOGREN, Dir. Stewardship & Devel., 305 7th Ave. N., Ste. 105, St. Cloud, 56303. Tel: 320-258-0390.

Diocesan Education Council—LINDA KAISER, Dir.; Rev. LAUREN GERMANN; Deacon STEPHEN ARNOLD; JOAN KRAUSE; BRENDA KRESKY; DAN HOLLENHORST; KATHY LANGER; MELISSA FOX; ROBERT DOYLE; KATERI MANCINI; KENT SCHMITZ; Mrs. MAYULI BALES; TIMOTHY WELCH; IRENE SCHMIDT; CHRISTINE CODDEN; JANET BRINKMAN.

Office of Catholic Education Ministries—LINDA KAISER, Dir.; DAN HOLLENHORST, School Consultant; VACANT, Consultant for Disabilities & Catechist Formation; TIMOTHY WELCH, Consultant, Educational Technology; KENT SCHMITZ, Consultant for Youth Ministry & Rel. Educ.; BRENDA KRESKY, Consultant for Adult Faith Formation & Ministry Formation Prog.; JULIE TSCHIDA, Receptionist/Sec., Address all correspondence to: Catholic Education Ministries, Pastoral Center, Diocese of St. Cloud, 305 Seventh Ave., N., St. Cloud, 56303. Tel: 320-251-0111.

Diocesan Commission on Ecumenical and Interreligious Affairs—Sr. HELEN ROLFSON, O.S.F., 3402 22nd St. S., Saint Cloud, 56301.

Diocesan Planning Council—JANE MARRIN, Dir.; Deacon MARK BARDER, Planning Consultant; Revs. MICHAEL KELLOGG, Chm.; TIMOTHY BALTES; Very Rev. ROBERT ROLFES, J.C.L.; Revs. EUGENE DOYLE; JONATHAN LICARI, O.S.B.; Deacon STEPHEN PAREJA; Dr. WILLIAM CAHOY; Ms. RITA CLASEMANN; PATRICIA LOXTERCAMP; JAMES KAPSNER; TOM EHLINGER; Sisters JEAN SCHWARTZ, O.S.B.; CLARA STANG, O.S.F.; Mr. STEVEN BRESNAHAN; CATHERINE M. COGHLAN.

Diocesan Priests Pension Plan Trustees—Most Rev. JOHN F. KINNEY, D.D., J.C.D.; Revs. THOMAS OLSON; VIRGIL A. HELMIN, J.C.L.; GERALD MISCHKE (Retired); STANLEY WIESER; PETER VANDERWEYST; RICHARD LEISEN (Retired); Very Rev. ROBERT ROLFES, J.C.L.; CATHERINE M. COGHLAN.

Director of Retired Priests—Very Rev. ROBERT ROLFES, J.C.L.

Health Ministry—Rev. THOMAS KNOBLACH, Ph.D., Consultant for Healthcare Ethics; ANNETTE JESH, Coord. Parish Health.

Holy Childhood Association—Rev. WILLIAM VOS, Dir. (Retired), 11 Eighth Ave., S., St. Cloud, 56301.

Koinonia Program of Central Minnesota—Rev. DAVID MACIEJ, Mailing Address: P.O. Box 38, Lastrup, 56344.

Legion of Decency—Very Rev. ROBERT ROLFES, J.C.L., Mailing Address: P.O. Box 1248, St. Cloud, 56302.

Legion of Mary—Rev. RICHARD LEISEN (Retired), 308 3rd St. S., Sauk Rapids, 56379.

Multicultural Ministry—Mrs. MAYULI BALES, Dir., 305 N. 7th Ave., Saint Cloud, 56303. Tel: 320-529-4614; Rev. FREDDIMIR VILLAVICENCIO.

Office of Marriage and Family—CHRISTINE CODDEN, Dir., 305 N. 7th Ave., Ste. 100, St. Cloud, 56303. Tel: 320-252-4721; Fax: 320-258-7658.

Newspaper "St. Cloud Visitor"—Pastoral Center, Diocese of St. Cloud, 305 N. Seventh Ave., Box 1068, St. Cloud, 56302. Tel: 320-251-3022. JOE TOWALSKI, Editor.

Office of Diaconate—Deacon MARK BARDER, Dir., 305 7th Ave. N., Ste. 100, Saint Cloud, 56303. Tel: 320-203-0554; Fax: 320-258-7658; Rev. BERNARD GRUENES, Vicar for Permanent Deacons (Retired); Deacon THOMAS MCFADDEN, Pres. Diaconal Community, 305 Seventh Ave. N., St. Cloud, 56303. Tel: 320-352-6306.

Personnel Committee—Most Rev. JOHN F. KINNEY, D.D., J.C.D.; Very Rev. ROBERT ROLFES, J.C.L., Dir.; Revs. TIMOTHY BALTES, Chair; LEROY SCHEIERL; SCOTT POGATCHNIK; DONALD WAGNER; ROGER KLASSEN, O.S.B.; Deacon ERNEST KOCIEMBA; JANE MARRIN, Mailing Address: P.O. Box 1248, Saint Cloud, 56302.

Propagation of the Faith—ELIZABETH NEVILLE, 11 8th Ave. S., Saint Cloud, 56301. Tel: 320-251-2061.

Rural Life Program—KATHY LANGER, 911 18th St. N., P.O. Box 2390, Saint Cloud, 56302. Tel: 320-229-6020.

TEC (Central Minnesota TEC) (Together Encountering Christ)—MICHAEL LENTZ, Coord., Mailing Address: P.O. Box 500, Onamia, 56359. Tel: 320-532-3103.

Assistance Coordinator—ROXANNE STORMS. Tel: 320-248-1563.

Vocations—Rev. GREGORY MASTEY, Dir., 305 Seventh Ave. N., Ste. 100, St. Cloud, 56303-3633. Tel: 320-251-5001; Fax: 320-258-7658. Email: gmastey@gw.stcdio.org.

Worship, Office of—ANITA FISCHER, Dir., Pastoral Center, Diocese of St. Cloud, 305 N. Seventh Ave., St. Cloud, 56303. Tel: 320-255-9068.

CLERGY, PARISHES, MISSIONS AND PAROCHIAL SCHOOLS

CITY OF ST. CLOUD

(BENTON, STEARNS, SHERBURNE COUNTIES)

1—ST. MARY'S CATHEDRAL OF ST. CLOUD, [JC] Revs. Anthony Oelrich, Rector; Scott Pogatchnik; Deacons Richard Scheierl; Jeff Kowitz; John Wocken. In Res., Rev. Gerald Mischke (Retired).
Res.: 25 Eighth Ave. S., 56301-4279. Tel: 320-251-1840; Fax: 320-253-5001. Email: office@stmarystcloud.org.
School-See St. Katherine Drexel School, St. Cloud under Inter-Parochial Schools located in the Institution section.
Catechesis/Religious Program—Lisa Neu, D.R.E. Students 177.

2—ST. ANTHONY OF PADUA (1920) Revs. Thomas Knoblach; Matthew Crane.
Office: 2405 1st St. N., 56303. Tel: 320-251-5966; Fax: 320-251-0664.
School-See St. Elizabeth Ann Seton School, St. Cloud under Inter-Parochial Schools located in the Institution section.
Catechesis/Religious Program—2410 1st. St. N., 56303. Virginia Duschner, D.R.E. Students 163.

3—ST. AUGUSTINE (1919) Revs. Anthony Oelrich; Scott Pogatchnik; Deacon Richard Scheierl.
Office: 442 Second St., S.E., 56304. Tel: 320-251-8335; Fax: 320-529-3231. Email: info@staugs.com.
Res.: 25 8th Ave. S., Saint Cloud, 56301. Tel: 320-251-1840.
School-See St. Katharine Drexel School under Inter-Parochial Schools located in the Institution section.
Catechesis/Religious Program—Tel: 320-252-6042; Fax: 320-529-3236. Lisa Neu, D.R.E. Students 145.

4—CHRIST CHURCH (1964), (Newman Center) Revs. Anthony Oelrich; Scott Pogatchnik.
Office: 396 First Ave. S., 56301. Tel: 320-251-3260; Fax: 320-252-3930.
Catechesis/Religious Program—Students 145.

5—HOLY ANGELS, Closed. For inquiries for parish records contact St. Mary's Cathedral, St. Cloud.

6—HOLY SPIRIT (1952) [JC] Revs. Thomas Knoblach; Matthew Crane; Deacon Vernon Schmitz; Sr. Diane Hunker, C.S.J., Pastoral Assoc.
Office: 2405 Walden Way, 56301. Tel: 320-251-3764; Fax: 320-252-5143. Email: hspirit@charterinternet.com. Web: holyspirit-stcloud.com.
School-See St. Elizabeth Ann Seton School, St. Cloud under Inter-Parochial Schools located in the Institution section.
Catechesis/Religious Program—Ginny Duschner, D.R.E. Students 178.

7—ST. JOHN CANTIUS (1901) Revs. Thomas Knoblach; Matthew Crane; Deacons Fred Reker; Frank Ringsmuth.
Office: 1515 Third St. N., 56303. Tel: 320-251-4455; Fax: 320-240-1238. Email: stjohncantius@charter.net.
Catechesis/Religious Program—Ginny Duschner, D.R.E. Students 41.

8—ST. MICHAEL (1970) [CEM] Revs. Vincent Lieser; Matthew Kuhn.
Res.: 1036 Co. Rd. 4, 56303. Tel: 320-251-6923; Fax: 320-202-1104.
School-See Sts. Peter & Paul & Michael, St. Cloud under Inter-Parochial Schools located in the Institution section.
Catechesis/Religious Program—Students 205.

9—ST. PAUL (1946) [JC] Rev. Alan Wielinski; Deacon David Lindmeier.
Office: 1125 11th Ave. N., 56303. Tel: 320-251-4831; Fax: 320-251-2648. Email: general@churchofstpaul.org.
School-See Sts. Peter & Paul & Michael, St. Cloud under Inter-Parochial Schools located in the Institution section.
Catechesis/Religious Program—Geralyn Nathe Evans, D.R.E. Students 152.

10—ST. PETER (1947) [JC] Rev. Alan Wielinski; Deacons William Ritchie; David Lindmeier.
Office: 930 31st Ave. N., 56303. Tel: 320-252-2113; Fax: 320-529-0796. Email: stpeters@charterinternet.com.
School-See Sts. Peter & Paul & Michael, St. Cloud under Inter-Parochial Schools located in the Institution section.
Catechesis/Religious Program—Tel: 320-253-5768. Laura Mullin, D.R.E. Students 153.

OUTSIDE THE CITY OF ST. CLOUD

ALBANY, STEARNS CO., SEVEN DOLORS (1868) [CEM] Rev. Michael Naughton, O.S.B.
Res.: P.O. Box 277, 56307. Tel: 320-845-2705. Email: 7dolors@albanytel.com.
School—Holy Family, (Grades K-6) Tel: 320-845-2011; Fax: 320-845-7380. Email: hfamily@albanytel.com. Bonnie Massmann, Prin. Lay Teachers 8; Students 130.
Catechesis/Religious Program—Tel: 320-845-4335. Sr. Alice Imdieke, O.S.B., D.R.E. Students 366.

ALEXANDRIA, DOUGLAS CO., ST. MARY'S (1882) [CEM] Rev. Steven Binsfeld.
Office: 420 Irving St., P.O. Box 669, 56308. Tel: 320-763-5781; Fax: 320-763-4833. Email: stmary@stmaryalexandria.org.
School—(Grades K-6) Tel: 320-763-5861; Fax: 320-763-7992. Email: stmaryss@stmaryalexandria.org. Troy Sladek, Prin.; Aaron Korynta, Librarian. Lay Teachers 15; Students 209.
Catechesis/Religious Program—Tel: 320-763-9202. Email: stmreled@stmaryalexandria.org. Students 470.

AVON, STEARNS CO., ST. BENEDICT'S (1868) [CEM] Rev. Blane Wasnie, O.S.B.
Church: P.O. Box 98, 56310. Tel: 320-356-7121; Fax: 320-356-9203.
Catechesis/Religious Program—Timothy Stanoch, Dir. Faith Formation. Students 217.

BATTLE LAKE, OTTER TAIL CO., OUR LADY OF THE LAKE

(1953) [CEM] Rev. LeRoy Schik.
Res.: 407 Lake Ave. N., P.O. Box 671, 56515. Tel: 218-864-5619; Fax: 218-864-5747.
Catechesis / Religious Program—Students 110.

BECKER, SHERBUNE CO., IMMACULATE CONCEPTION (1918) [CEM] Rev. Eugene Doyle.
Office: 12100 Sherburne Ave., Box 426, 55308. Tel: 763-261-4242; Fax: 763-261-2242. Email: genedoyle@izoom.net.
Catechesis / Religious Program—Sr. Julie Schleper, O.S.B., D.R.E. Students 336.

BELGRADE, STEARNS CO., ST. FRANCIS DE SALES (1890) [CEM] Rev. Jeffrey D. Ethen.
Office: 541 Martin Ave., P.O. Box 69, 56312. Tel: 320-254-8218; Fax: 320-254-8218.
Catechesis / Religious Program—JoAnn Braegelman, D.R.E. Students 58.

BELLE PRAIRIE, MORRISON CO., HOLY FAMILY (1852) [CEM] Revs. Nicholas Landsberger; Mark Innocenti; Deacon Bruce Geyer.
Office: 18777 Riverwood Dr., Little Falls, 56345. Tel: 320-632-5720. Email: holyfam@fallsnet.com.
Catechesis / Religious Program—Tel: 320-632-5754. Cindy Loidolt, D.R.E. Students 99.

BELLE RIVER, DOUGLAS CO., ST. NICHOLAS (1871) [CEM] Rev. David Jeffrey Petron; Deacon Stanley Hennen.
Res.: P.O. Box F, Osakis, 56360.
Catechesis / Religious Program—Tel: 320-852-7041. Tonya Beulke, D.R.E. Students 57.

BERTHA, TODD CO., ST. JOSEPH (1914) [CEM] Rev. Peter VanderWeyst.
Res.: P.O. Box 158, 56437-0158. Tel: 218-924-2144. Email: stjoseph_bertha@yahoo.com.
Catechesis / Religious Program—Elizebeth Blashack, D.R.E. Students 52.

BIG LAKE, SHERBURNE CO., OUR LADY OF THE LAKE (1958) [CEM] Rev. Eugene Doyle.
Res.: 440 Lake St. N., Box 100, 55309. Tel: 763-263-2863; Fax: 763-263-3187. Email: parish@ourladybiglake.org.
Catechesis / Religious Program—Students 386.

BLUEGRASS, WADENA CO., ST. HUBERT (1908) [CEM] Rev. Arlie Sowada.
Res.: 20 Brown St. N., P.O. Box C, Verndale, 56481. Tel: 218-445-5786; Fax: 218-445-5087.
Catechesis / Religious Program—63215 County Hwy. 68, Wadena, 56482. Tel: 218-631-1836; 218-837-5910; 218-631-1711; Fax: 218-445-5280. Shirley Malone, D.R.E. Students 76.

BLUFFTON, OTTER TAIL CO., ST. JOHN THE BAPTIST (1902) [CEM] Rev. Donald Wagner.
Res.: 310 Main St., P.O. Box 36, 56518. Tel: 218-385-2608; Fax: 218-385-2808.
Catechesis / Religious Program—Students 106.

BOWLUS, MORRISON CO., ST. STANISLAUS KOSTKA, [CEM] Revs. Michael Kellogg; John Odero.
Office: P.O. Box 249, Upsala, 56384. Tel: 320-573-2132; Fax: 320-573-9133.
Res.: P.O. Box 8, 56314. Tel: 320-584-5313.
Catechesis / Religious Program—Amy Trettel, D.R.E. Students 47.

BRAHAM, ISANTI CO., ST. PETER & PAUL (1986) [CEM] Rev. Kevin Anderson; Deacon Thomas Pinataro, Parish Life Coord.
Res.: 1050 Southview Ave., P.O. Box 483, 55006. Tel: 320-396-3105. Email: stspeter_paulchurch@yahoo.com.
Catechesis / Religious Program—Students 100.

BRANDON, DOUGLAS CO., CHURCH OF ST. ANN, [CEM] Rev. LeRoy Scheierl.
Res.: P.O. Box 256, 56315. Tel: 320-834-5095. Email: stanns@gctel.com.
Catechesis / Religious Program— Marilyn Kelly, D.R.E. Students 57.

BRECKENRIDGE, WILKIN CO., ST. MARY OF THE PRESENTATION (1898) [CEM 2] Rev. Kenneth Popp.
Res.: 221 Fourth St. N., 56520-1496. Tel: 218-643-5173; Fax: 218-643-1881.
School—(Grades PreK-8) Tel: 218-643-5443. Linda Johnson, Prin. Lay Teachers 11; Students 113.
Catechesis / Religious Program—Students 127.

BRENNYVILLE, BENTON CO., ST. ELIZABETH OF HUNGARY (1927) [CEM] Rev. Leo Moenkedick.
Mailing Address: P.O. Box 86, Gilman, 56333.
Res.: 16426 125th Ave., N.E., Foley, 56329. Tel: 320-355-2454; Fax: 320-355-2819.
Catechesis / Religious Program—Tel: 320-387-3332. Students 39.

BROOTEN, STEARNS CO., ST. DONATUS (1911) [CEM] Rev. Jeffrey D. Ethen.
Office: 301 Eastern Ave. S., P.O. Box 159, 56316. Tel: 320-346-2431; Fax: 320-346-2431. Email: stdonatus@tds.net.
Catechesis / Religious Program—Tel: 320-346-2431. Audrey Radermacher, C.R.E. Students 46.

BROWERVILLE, TODD CO., CHRIST THE KING (1978) [CEM] Rev. Peter VanderWeyst.
Res.: 720 Main St. N., P.O. Box 83, 56438. Tel: 320-594-2291. Email: ctkparish_school@embarqmail.com.
School—(Grades PreK-6) Tel: 320-594-6114; Fax: 320-594-6313. Paula Becker, Prin. Lay Teachers 4; Students 52.
Catechesis / Religious Program—Beverly Geraets, D.R.E. Tel: 320-594-2441; Glenda Kotula, D.R.E. Tel: 320-594-6524. Students 140.

BROWNS VALLEY, TRAVERSE CO., ST. ANTHONY'S (1896) [CEM] Rev. David Breu.
Church: 122 2nd St. S., Box 359, 56219. Tel: 320-695-2621.
Catechesis / Religious Program—Students 44.

BUCKMAN, MORRISON CO., ST. MICHAEL'S, [CEM] Rev. Gerald Dalseth; Deacon Guy Beck.
Res.: P.O. Box 428, Pierz, 56364. Tel: 320-468-6033; Fax: 320-468-2296.
Catechesis / Religious Program—Tel: 320-468-2640. Students 125.

BUTLER, OTTER TAIL CO., HOLY CROSS (1910) [CEM] Rev. Joseph Herzing.
54216 County Hwy. 148, Menahga, 56464.
Res.: 234 - 2nd Ave. S.W., Perham, 56573. Tel: 218-346-4240.
Catechesis / Religious Program—Mary Peeters, D.R.E.; Glenda Hofland, D.R.E. Students 55.

CAMBRIDGE, ISANTI CO., CHRIST THE KING, [CEM] Rev. James David Hahn; Deacon Eugene Kramer.
Res.: 230 Fern St. N., 55008-1094. Tel: 763-689-1221; Fax: 763-689-8950.
Catechesis / Religious Program—Tel: 763-689-3728. Students 115.

CHOKIO, STEVENS CO., ST. MARY'S (1897) [CEM] Revs. Joseph Vandeberg; Peter VanderWeyst.
Res.: P.O. Box 187, 56221. Tel: 320-324-2680; Fax: 320-324-2732. Email: stmarych@fedtel.net.
Catechesis / Religious Program—Students 53.

CLARISSA, TODD CO., ST. JOSEPH (1896) [CEM] Rev. Peter VanderWeyst.
Res.: Box 83, Browerville, 56438. Tel: 320-594-2291; Fax: 320-594-6313.
Office & Mailing Address: 105 John St. S., P.O. Box 5, 56440. Tel: 218-756-2205; Fax: 218-756-2203. Email: stjoschu@eaglevalleytel.net.
Catechesis / Religious Program—Tel: 218-756-3614. Eileen Uhlenkamp, D.R.E. Students 60.

CLEAR LAKE, SHERBURNE CO., ST. MARCUS (1888) [CEM] Rev. Virgil A. Helmin.
Res.: 8701 Main Ave., P.O. Box 237, 55319. Tel: 320-743-2481; Fax: 320-743-3346. Email: stmarcus@frontiernet.net.
Catechesis / Religious Program—Tel: 320-743-3346. Melissa Fox, D.R.E. Students 153.

COLD SPRING, STEARNS CO., ST. BONIFACE (1878) [CEM] Rev. Cletus Connors, O.S.B.; Deacon Lawrence Sell.
Res.: 501 Main St., 56320. Tel: 320-685-3280; Fax: 320-685-7792.
School—(Grades PreSchool-6) Tel: 320-685-3541. Sr. Sharon Waldoch, S.S.N.D., Prin. Lay Teachers 16; Students 319.
Catechesis / Religious Program—Tel: 320-685-8222, Ext. 103. Karen Neu, Elementary Min. Students 373.

COLLEGEVILLE, STEARNS CO., ST. JOHN THE BAPTIST (1875) [JC] Rev. Jerome Tupa, O.S.B.; Deacon Michael Keable.
Res.: 14241 Fruit Farm Rd., Saint Joseph, 56374. Tel: 320-363-2569.
Catechesis / Religious Program—Julie Ortloff, D.R.E. Students 72.

DENT, OTTER TAIL CO., SACRED HEART (1921) [CEM] Rev. George Michael, V.C.
Res.: 36963 State Hwy. 108, 56528. Tel: 218-758-2700; Fax: 218-758-3861. Email: sacredheart@arvig.net.
Catechesis / Religious Program—Joe Sazama, D.R.E.; Diane Sazama, D.R.E. Students 70.

DONNELLY, STEVENS CO., ST. THERESIA, Closed. For inquiries for parish records contact St. Charles, Herman.

DUELM, BENTON CO., ST. LAWRENCE'S, [CEM] Rev. Virgil Helmin.
Mailing Address: 10915 Duelm Rd., N.E., Foley, 56329.
Res.: P.O. Box 237, Clear Lake, 55319. Tel: 320-968-7502; 320-743-2481.
Catechesis / Religious Program—Tel: 320-968-6595. Betty Pundsack, D.R.E. Students 209.

DUMONT, TRAVERSE CO., ST. PETER'S, Closed. For inquiries for Parish Records contact: Ave Maria, Wheaton. Mailing address: 201 9th St. S., Wheaton, MN 56296.

EDEN VALLEY, STEARNS CO., THE CHURCH OF THE ASSUMPTION (1892) [CEM 2] Rev. Virgil R. Braun.
Res.: P.O. Box 9, 55329. Tel: 320-453-2788.
Catechesis / Religious Program—Tel: 320-453-7388. Sherry Braegelmen, D.R.E.; Sherri Lego, D.R.E. Students 152.

ELBOW LAKE, GRANT CO., ST. OLAF, [CEM] Rev. Ronald Schmelzer; Deacon Joseph Wood.
Res.: 518 E. Division St., 56531. Tel: 218-685-4318.
Catechesis / Religious Program—Students 62.

ELIZABETH, OTTER TAIL CO., ST. ELIZABETH, [CEM] Rev. Stanley Wieser.
Res.: 706 W. Pleasant Ave., 56533. Tel: 218-736-5230.
Catechesis / Religious Program—Tel: 218-739-1140. Jan Dumas, D.R.E. Students 60.

ELK RIVER, SHERBURNE CO., THE CHURCH OF ST. ANDREW (1890) [CEM] Revs. Lauren Germann; John Knopik; Deacon Frederick St. Jean.
Res.: 566 Fourth St., 55330. Tel: 763-441-1483; Fax: 763-441-1485.
School—(Grades K-6), 428 Irving Ave., 55330. Tel: 763-441-2216; Fax: 763-441-1146. Kari Staples, Prin. Sisters 1; Lay Teachers 15; Students 192.
Catechesis / Religious Program—Tel: 763-441-3202. Students 749.

ELMDALE, MORRISON CO., ST. EDWARD'S, [CEM] Revs. Michael Kellogg; John Odero.
Office: P.O. Box 249, Upsala, 56384. Tel: 320-573-2132.
Res.: 8550 State Hwy. 238, Bowlus, 56314. Tel: 320-573-2975.
Catechesis / Religious Program—308 S. Main St., Upsala, 56384. Tel: 320-573-2132. Students 46.

ELROSA, STEARNS CO., SS. PETER AND PAUL (1891) [CEM] Rev. Jeffrey D. Ethen.
Res.: 302 State St., P.O. Box 95, 56325. Tel: 320-697-5541; Fax: 320-254-3239.
Catechesis / Religious Program—Tel: 320-254-8218; Fax: 320-254-8218. Jo Braegelman, D.R.E. Students 58.

FARMING, STEARNS CO., ST. CATHERINE'S (1879) [CEM] Closed. For inquiries for parish records please see St. Martin, MN

FERGUS FALLS, OTTER TAIL CO., OUR LADY OF VICTORY (1881) [CEM] Rev. Gregory Paffel; Deacon Charles Kampa.
Office & Mailing Address: 207 N. Vine St., 56537. Tel: 218-736-2429.
Res.: 407 Lake Ave. N., P.O. Box 671, Battle Lake, 56515. Tel: 218-736-7988; Fax: 218-736-4407. Email: olv@prtel.com.
School—(Grades PreSchool-6), 426 W. Cavour Ave., 56537. Tel: 208-736-6661; Fax: 218-736-6931. Sandy Carpenter, Prin.; Sue Herder, Librarian. Lay Teachers 9; Students 122.
Catechesis / Religious Program—Tel: 218-736-6837. Becky Pyle, D.R.E.; Chastity Soupir, D.R.E. Students 240.

FLENSBURG, MORRISON CO., SACRED HEART, [CEM 2] Rev. Jimmy Joseph, V.C.
Mailing Address: 9406 Church Cir., Little Falls, 56345. Tel: 320-632-6930; Fax: 320-632-5644.
Catechesis / Religious Program—Sheila Gardner, D.R.E. Students 27.

FOLEY, BENTON CO., ST. JOHN'S, [CEM] Rev. Daniel Walz.
Mailing Address: 621 Dewey St., P.O. Box 337, 56329. Tel: 320-968-7913; Fax: 320-968-4424.
Res.: 310 Murphy St., Box 242, 56329. Tel: 320-968-7143.
School—St. John's Area School, (Grades PreSchool-6), P.O. Box 368, 56329. Tel: 320-968-7972; Fax: 320-968-9956. Mary Sabin, Prin.; Michelle Buettner, Librarian. Lay Teachers 8; Students 117.
Catechesis / Religious Program—Fax: 320-968-4424. Sheila Matteson, D.R.E.; Andrea Rahm, D.R.E.; Shannon Schmit, D.R.E. & Youth Min. Students 171.

FORESTON, MILLE LACS CO., ST. LOUIS BERTRAND, [CEM] Rev. James H. Remmerswaal, O.S.C.
Res.: 187 First St. S., P.O. Box 128, 56330. Tel: 320-294-5460; Fax: 320-294-5588. Email: stlouis@jetup.net.
Catechesis / Religious Program—Students 101.

FOXHOME, WILKIN CO., ST. JOSEPH, Closed. For inquiries for parish records contact St. Mary of the Presentation, Breckenridge.

FREEPORT, STEARNS CO., SACRED HEART (1881) [CEM] Rev. Roger Klassen, O.S.B.; Deacon Richard Scherping.
Res.: 106 - 3rd Ave., N.E., P.O. Box 155, 56331-9017. Tel: 320-836-2143; Fax: 320-836-2142. Email: triparish@albanytel.com.
School—(Grades PreSchool-6), 303 2nd St. N.E., P.O. Box 39, 56331. Tel: 320-836-2591; Fax: 320-836-2514. Email: shs@albanytel.com. Sr. Janine Braun, O.S.B., Prin. Lay Teachers 7; Students 90.
Catechesis / Religious Program—Students 53.

GILMAN, BENTON CO., SS. PETER AND PAUL (1872) [CEM] Rev. Leo Moenkedick.
Res.: P.O. Box 86, 56333. Tel: 320-387-2255.
See St. John's School, Foley under Inter-Parochial Schools located in the Institution section.
Catechesis / Religious Program—Tel: 320-387-3332. Students 94.

GLENWOOD, POPE CO., SACRED HEART (1903) [CEM 2] Rev. Peter K. Kirchner Jr.; Deacon Frank Schmainda.
Office: 122 N.W. 1st St., 56334. Email: sheartchurch@gmail.com.
Res.: 105 Franklin St. N., 56334. Tel: 320-634-3813.

Catechesis/Religious Program—Tel: 320-634-4828. Diane Mrnak, D.R.E. Students 165.

GREENWALD, STEARNS CO., ST. ANDREW'S (1924) [CEM] Revs. Marvin Enneking; Omar Guanchez.
Res.: P.O. Box 120, 56335. Tel: 320-987-3160; Fax: 320-987-3306. Email: stjohn1@meltel.net.
School—(Grades K-2) Tel: 320-987-3133. Susan Hennen, Prin. Lay Teachers 2; Students 32.
Catechesis/Religious Program—Tel: 320-352-2783. Ruth Klaphake, D.R.E. Students 21.

GREY EAGLE, TODD CO., ST. JOSEPH'S, [CEM 2] Rev. Ronald Dockendorf.
Res.: 118 Minnesota St., P.O Box 366, 56336. Tel: 320-285-2545; Fax: 320-285-5255.
Catechesis/Religious Program—Students 128.

HARDING, MORRISON CO., HOLY CROSS (1904) [CEM] Rev. David Maciej.
Mailing Address: 29482 243rd St, Pierz, 56364.
Res.: 28520 Church St., P.O. Box 38, Lastrup, 56344. Tel: 320-468-2111.
Catechesis/Religious Program—Students 55.

HENNING, OTTER TAIL CO., CHURCH OF ST. EDWARD OF HENNING (1945) [CEM] Rev. LeRoy Schik.
Res.: 201 Douglas Ave., 56551. Tel: 218-583-2490.
Catechesis/Religious Program—Lyn Andrews, D.R.E. Students 55.

HERMAN, GRANT CO., ST. CHARLES (1913) [CEM] Rev. Ronald Schmelzer.
Res.: P.O. Box 187, Chokio, 56221. Tel: 320-677-2433; Fax: 320-324-2732. Email: stmarych@fedtel.net.
Catechesis/Religious Program—Katy Blume, D.R.E. Students 29.

HILLMAN, MORRISON CO., ST. RITA'S (1920) [CEM] Revs. Jude Verley, O.S.C.; Jerome Schik, O.S.C.; Gregory Poser, O.S.C.
Mailing Address: 16691 371st Ave., 56338. Tel: 320-277-3807. Email: strita@brainerd.net.
Catechesis/Religious Program—Wendy Tretter, Faith Formation Coord.; Carol Wacker, Faith Formation Coord. Students 47.

HOLDINGFORD, STEARNS CO.
1—CHURCH OF ALL SAINTS Rev. Mark Stang; Deacon Jeffrey Fromm.
Res.: P.O. Box 308, 56340. Tel: 320-746-2231; Fax: 320-746-2449.
Catechesis/Religious Program—Students 191.
2—ST. HEDWIG'S, [CEM] Closed. For inquiries for parish records please see Church of All Saints, Holdingford, MN.
3—ST. MARY'S (1883) [CEM] Closed. For inquiries for parish records please see Church of All Saints, Holdingford, MN.

ISANTI, ISANTI CO., ST. ELIZABETH ANN SETON (1976) Rev. Jose Edayadiyil, V.C. (India), Parochial Admin.
Office: 207 County Rd. 23 N.W., 55040. Tel: 763-444-4035; Fax: 763-444-6019.
Res.: 109 Fifth Ave. S., 55040. Tel: 763-444-5226; Fax: 763-444-5226. Email: annseton76@yahoo.co.in.
Catechesis/Religious Program—Mary Mack, D.R.E. Students 173.

JACOB'S PRAIRIE WAKEFIELD TOWNSHIP, STEARNS CO., ST. JAMES, [CEM] Rev. Julius Beckermann, O.S.B.
Res.: 25042 County Rd. 2, Cold Spring, 56320. Tel: 320-685-3479.
Catechesis/Religious Program—Students 27.

KENSINGTON, GRANT CO., OUR LADY OF THE RUNESTONE, [CEM] Rev. Roger Thoennes.
Res.: 25890 110th St., Lowry, 56349-4580. Tel: 320-283-5273; Fax: 320-283-5253.
Catechesis/Religious Program—Students 52.

KENT, WILKIN CO., ST. THOMAS, [CEM] Rev. Kenneth Popp.
P.O. Box 23, 56553. Tel: 218-557-8312.
Catechesis/Religious Program—Christi Hopping, D.R.E. Students 24.

KIMBALL, STEARNS CO., CHURCH OF SAINT ANNE (1919) [CEM] Rev. Thomas Olson.
Res.: 441 Hazel Ave. E., P.O. Box 99, 55353. Tel: 320-398-2229; 320-398-2211 (Office); Fax: 320-398-3860 (Office). Email: sannekim@meltel.net.
Catechesis/Religious Program—Students 120.

LAKE HENRY, STEARNS CO., ST. MARGARET'S, [CEM] Rev. Glenn A. Krystosek; Deacon James Schulzetenberg. In Res., Rev. Walter Bednark (Retired).
Office: 505 Burr St., Paynesville, 56362. Tel: 320-243-4413; Fax: 320-243-4443.
Catechesis/Religious Program—JoAnn Weidner, D.R.E. Students 33.

LAKE RENO, POPE CO., ST. JOHN NEPOMUK, [CEM] Rev. Roger Thoennes.
Res.: 25890 110th St., Lowry, 56349-4580. Tel: 320-283-5273; Fax: 320-283-5253.
Catechesis/Religious Program—Students 44.

LASTRUP, MORRISON CO., ST. JOHN NEPOMUK (1900) [CEM] Rev. David Maciej.
Res.: 28520 Church St., P.O. Box 38, 56344. Tel: 320-468-2111.
Catechesis/Religious Program—Students 79.

LITTLE FALLS, MORRISON CO.
1—ST. MARY, [CEM 3] Rev. Nicholas Landsberger; Deacon Bruce Geyer.
Res.: 305 Fourth St., S.E., 56345. Tel: 320-632-5640; Fax: 320-632-6002. Email: office@stmaryslf.org.
See Mary of Lourdes Elementary and Middle School, Little Falls under Inter-Parochial Schools located in the Institution section.
Catechesis/Religious Program—Tel: 320-632-3911. Brenda Przybilla, D.R.E. Students 177.
2—OUR LADY OF LOURDES (1917) [CEM] Rev. Mark Innocenti; Deacons Bruce Geyer; Craig Korver.
Res.: 208 W. Broadway, 56345. Tel: 320-632-8243; Fax: 320-616-2129.
See Mary of Lourdes Elementary and Middle School, Little Falls under Inter-Parochial Schools located in the Institution section.
Catechesis/Religious Program—Tel: 320-616-9689. Linda Pilarski, D.R.E. Students 313.

LONG PRAIRIE, TODD CO., ST. MARY OF MT. CARMEL (1868) [CEM] [JC] Rev. Richard Walz. In Res., Rev. Mark Willenbring (Retired).
Res.: 409 Central Ave., 56347. Tel: 320-732-2635; Fax: 320-732-2632. Email: stmarylp@embarqmail.com.
School—(Grades PreK-6), Day Care, 425 Central Ave. S, 56347. Tel: 320-732-3478; Fax: 320-732-8023. Email: lpstmarys@embarqmail.com. Brenda Guggelberger, Prin. Lay Teachers 8; Students 89.
Catechesis/Religious Program—Email: smrock@embarqmail.com. Brenda Guggelberger, D.R.E. Students 251.

LUXEMBURG, STEARNS CO., ST. WENDELIN'S (1859) [CEM] Revs. Ralph Zimmerman; Mark Ostendorf.
Office: 22714 State Hwy. 15, 56301. Tel: 320-251-6944. Email: stwencc@mq.com.
School—(Grades PreK-6) Tel: 320-251-9175; Fax: 320-654-9030. Email: stwend@citescape.com. Lynn Rasmussen, Prin. Sisters 1; Lay Teachers 6; Students 62.
Catechesis/Religious Program—Students 77.

MAINE, OTTER TAIL CO., CHURCH OF SAINT JAMES AT MAINE, [CEM] Rev. LeRoy Schik.
Res.: 32009 County Hwy. 74, Underwood, 56586. Tel: 218-495-2184; Fax: 218-495-2185.
Catechesis/Religious Program—Students 52.

MAYHEW LAKE, BENTON CO., ANNUNCIATION (1896) [CEM] Rev. Thomas Becker.
Res.: 9965 Mayhew Lake Rd., N.E., Sauk Rapids, 56379. Tel: 320-252-1729; Fax: 320-393-1729. Email: annunciation@cloudnet.com.
Catechesis/Religious Program—Tel: 320-259-4941. Shirley Scapanski, D.R.E. Students 112.

MEIRE GROVE, STEARNS CO., ST. JOHN'S (1858) [CEM] Revs. Marvin Enneking; Omar Guanchez.
Res.: P.O. Box 120, Greenwald, 56335. Tel: 320-987-3160; Fax: 320-987-3306. Email: stjohn1@meltel.net.
School—(Grades 3-6) Tel: 320-987-3491. Susan Hennen, Prin. Lay Teachers 2; Students 35.
Catechesis/Religious Program—Tel: 320-352-2783. Ruth Klaphake, D.R.E. Students 22.

MELROSE, STEARNS CO., ST. MARY'S (1958) [CEM 2] Revs. Marvin Enneking; Omar Guanchez; Deacons Ernest Kociemba; Stephen Arnold.
Res.: 211-5th Ave. S.E., 56352-1427. Tel: 320-256-4207; Fax: 320-256-4208. Email: stmarys@stmarysmelrose.com.
School—(Grades PreSchool-6), 320 5th S.E., 56352. Tel: 320-256-4257. Email: sms@meltel.net. Robert Doyle, Prin.; Autumn Nelson, Librarian & Media Specialist. Lay Teachers 8; Students 127.
Catechesis/Religious Program—Tel: 320-256-4258. Debra Duclos, D.R.E. Students 335.

MENAHGA, WADENA CO., THE CHURCH OF THE ASSUMPTION OF OUR LADY OF MENAHGA (1953) [CEM 4] Rev. Arlie Sowada.
Mailing Address: P.O. Box C, Verndale, 56481. Tel: 218-445-5786; Fax: 218-445-5087.
Church: 113 Aspen Ave., 56464.
Catechesis/Religious Program—Kathy Olson, D.R.E. Students 29.

MILACA, MILLE LACS CO., ST. MARY'S (1954) [CEM] Rev. James H. Remmerswaal, O.S.C.
Res.: 625 3rd Ave., S.E., 56353. Tel: 320-983-3255; Fax: 320-983-6564. Email: stmary.milaca@frontiernet.net.
Catechesis/Religious Program—Students 113.

MILLERVILLE, DOUGLAS CO., SEVEN DOLORS (1870) [CEM] Rev. LeRoy Scheierl.
Res.: 16921 County Rd. 7, N.W., Brandon, 56315. Tel: 320-876-2240.
Catechesis/Religious Program—Tel: 320-834-7889. Beverly Hanson, D.R.E. Students 44.

MORA, KANABEC CO., ST. MARY'S (1895) [CEM] Rev. Eugene Doyle, Canonical Pastor; Ms. Rita Clasemann, Parish Life Coord.
Res.: 201 Forest Ave. E., 55051. Tel: 320-679-1593; Fax: 320-679-6896.
Catechesis/Religious Program—Sue Grabowski, D.R.E. Students 164.

MORAN, TODD CO., ST. ISIDORE, [CEM] Closed. For inquiries for parish records contact Christ the King, Browerville.

MORRILL, MORRISON CO., ST. JOSEPH'S (1914) [CEM] Rev. Leo Moenkedick.
Res.: 16454 125th Ave., N.E., Foley, 56329. Tel: 320-355-2454.
Catechesis/Religious Program—Students 100.

MORRIS, STEVENS CO., ASSUMPTION OF THE BLESSED VIRGIN MARY, [CEM] Rev. Robert Kieffer.
Mailing Address: 207 E. Third, Box 287, 56267.
Res.: 301 E. Third, Box 287, 56267. Tel: 320-589-3003; Fax: 320-589-1822. Email: assump@info-link.net.
School—(Grades K-6), 411 Colorado Ave., 56267. Tel: 320-589-1704; Fax: 320-589-1703. Jennifer Grammond, Prin. Lay Teachers 7; Students 68.
Catechesis/Religious Program—Lorna Lauringer, C.R.E. Students 125.

MOTLEY, MORRISON CO., ST. MICHAEL'S (1888) [JC] Rev. Joseph Korf; Deacons John Wolak; Robert Shaffer.
Mailing Address: P.O. Box 177, Staples, 56479. Tel: 218-894-2291. Email: sheart@arvig.net.
Catechesis/Religious Program—Tel: 218-352-6782. Students 36.

NEW MUNICH, STEARNS CO., IMMACULATE CONCEPTION (1857) [CEM] Rev. Roger Klassen, O.S.B.; Deacon Richard Scherping.
Res.: 106 3rd Ave., N.E., P.O. Box 155, Freeport, 56331. Tel: 320-836-2143; Fax: 320-836-2142. Email: triparish@albanytel.com.
Church: 650 Main St., P.O. Box 131, 56356-9028.
Catechesis/Religious Program—Rita Revermann, D.R.E. Students 114.

NORTH PRAIRIE, MORRISON CO., HOLY CROSS (1876) [CEM] Rev. Laurn Virnig.
Res.: P.O. Box 258, Royalton, 56373. Tel: 320-584-5484; Fax: 320-584-0028.
Catechesis/Religious Program—Students 30.

OGILVIE, KANABEC CO., ST. KATHRYN'S (1947) [CEM] Rev. Eugene Doyle, Canonical Pastor; Ms. Rita Clasemann, Parish Life Coord.
Res.: 201 Forest Ave. E., Mora, 55051. Tel: 320-679-1593; Fax: 320-679-6896. Email: ritac@stmarysmora.org.
Catechesis/Religious Program—Students 51.

ONAMIA, MILLE LACS CO., THE CHURCH OF THE HOLY CROSS OF ONAMIA (1910) [CEM] Revs. Jude Verley, O.S.C.; Jerome Schik, O.S.C.; Gregory Poser, O.S.C.
Res.: *Crosier Priory of the Holy Cross*, P.O. Box 500, 56359. Tel: 320-532-3122; Fax: 320-532-5222.
Catechesis/Religious Program—Students 30.

OPOLE, STEARNS CO., OUR LADY OF MT. CARMEL (1887) [CEM] Rev. Mark Stang; Deacon Jeffrey Fromm.
Res.: *St. Mary's Rectory*, P.O. Box 308, Holdingford, 56340. Tel: 320-746-2231; Fax: 320-746-2449. Email: fivepoffice@yahoo.com.
Catechesis/Religious Program—Students 100.

OSAKIS, DOUGLAS CO., IMMACULATE CONCEPTION (1899) [CEM] Rev. David Jeffrey Petron; Deacon Stanley Hennen.
Mailing Address: 316 Third Ave. W., P.O. Box F, 56360.
Res.: 306 W. Oak St., P.O. Box F, 56360. Tel: 320-859-2390. Email: iccosakis@arvig.net.
School—*St. Agnes*, (Grades PreSchool-6), 307 4th Ave. W., P.O. Box O, 56360. Tel: 320-859-2130; Fax: 320-859-5850. Kimra Kirksey, Prin.; Pat Pospisil, Prin.; Rosalie Kreemer, Librarian. Lay Teachers 6; Students 51.
Catechesis/Religious Program—Jennifer Wolbeck, D.R.E.; Greta Petrich, D.R.E. Students 108.

PADUA, STEARNS CO., CHURCH OF ST. ANTHONY OF PADUA, Closed. For inquiries for parish records contact St. Donatus Church, Brooten.

PARKERS PRAIRIE, OTTER TAIL CO., CHURCH OF ST. WILLIAM (1951) [CEM] Rev. LeRoy Scheierl.
Res.: 209 W. Soo St., P.O. Box 339, 56361. Tel: 218-338-2761.
Catechesis/Religious Program—Students 86.

PAYNESVILLE, STEARNS CO., ST. LOUIS (1899) [CEM] Rev. Glenn A. Krystosek; Deacon James Schulzetenberg.
Res.: 505 Burr St., 56362. Tel: 320-243-4413; Fax: 320-243-4443. Email: frglenn@saintalm.org.
Catechesis/Religious Program—Hannah Voss, D.R.E. Students 261.

PEARL LAKE, STEARNS CO., HOLY CROSS (1897) [CEM] Revs. Ralph Zimmerman; Mark Ostendorf; Deacon Andrew Kunkel.
Mailing Address: 10651 County Rd. 8, Kimball, 55353. Tel: 320-398-3900.
School—(Grades PreK-6), Day Care, Tel: 320-398-7885; Fax: 320-398-7873. Susan Scipioni, Prin.; Lorraine Gregory, Librarian. Lay Teachers 5; Students 52.
Catechesis/Religious Program—Twinned with Rockville.

PELICAN RAPIDS, OTTER TAIL CO., ST. LEONARD'S (1951) [CEM] Rev. Stanley Wieser; Deacon Joseph Hilber.
Res.: 36 1st Ave. N.E., P.O. Box 378, 56572. Tel: 218-863-5161.
Catechesis/Religious Program—Ann Bergquist, D.R.E. Students 51.

PERHAM, OTTER TAIL CO.
1—ST. HENRY'S (1875) [CEM] Rev. Joseph Herzing.
Res.: 234 2nd Ave S.W., 56573. Tel: 218-346-4240; Fax: 218-346-4235. Email: sthenry@arvig.net.
School—St. Henry Area School, (Grades K-6), 253 2nd St. S.W., 56573. Tel: 218-346-6190; Fax: 218-346-6190. Email: sthenryschool@arvig.net. Jason Smith, Prin. Lay Teachers 8; Students 94.
Catechesis/Religious Program—Tel: 218-346-7030. Students 149.
2—ST. STANISLAUS (1895) [CEM] Closed. For inquiries for parish records contact St. Henry, Perham.

PIERZ, MORRISON CO., ST. JOSEPH'S, [CEM] Rev. Gerald Dalseth; Deacon Guy Beck.
Res.: 68 Main St., P.O. Box 428, 56364. Tel: 320-468-6033; Fax: 320-468-2296.
See Holy Trinity School, Pierz under Inter-Parochial Schools located in the Institution section.
Catechesis/Religious Program—P.O. Box 205, 56364. Tel: 320-468-2640. Students 198.

PRINCETON, MILLE LACS CO.
1—THE CHURCH OF CHRIST OUR LIGHT PRINCETON/ZIMMERMAN, [CEM] Rev. Kevin Anderson; Deacon Mark Barder.
Office: 804 - 7th Ave. S., 55371.
Catechesis/Religious Program—Nancy Patten, D.R.E. Students 485.
2—ST. EDWARD'S (1898) [CEM] Merged With St. Pius X, Zimmerman to form The Church of Christ Our Light Princeton/Zimmerman.

RANDALL, MORRISON CO., ST. JAMES, [CEM] Rev. Jimmy Joseph, V.C.
Mailing Address: P.O. Box 225, 56475.
Catechesis/Religious Program—Students 77.

RICE, BENTON CO., IMMACULATE CONCEPTION (1885) [CEM] Rev. Thomas G. Becker.
Office: 130 First Ave., N.E., P.O. Box 189, 56367. Tel: 320-393-2725; Fax: 320-393-7507.
Catechesis/Religious Program—Tel: 320-393-2826. Pat Spence, D.R.E. Students 145.

RICHMOND, STEARNS CO., SS. PETER AND PAUL (1856) [CEM] Rev. Stephen Beauclair, O.S.B.
Res.: 56 - 1st St. N.E., P.O. Box 69, 56368. Tel: 320-597-2575; Fax: 320-597-5231.
Church: 110 Central Ave. N., 56368.
School—(Grades K-5), 111 Central Ave. N., 56368. Tel: 320-597-2565; Fax: 320-597-4385. Email: jwalz@ssppr.com. Jacqueline Walz, Prin. & Librarian. Lay Teachers 6; Students 60.
Catechesis/Religious Program—Tel: 320-597-3720. Teri Krowka-Ansberry, D.R.E. Students 181.

ROCKVILLE, STEARNS CO., MARY OF THE IMMACULATE CONCEPTION (1911) [CEM] Revs. Ralph Zimmerman; Mark Ostendorf.
Res.: 113 Broadway, P.O. Box 7, 56369. Tel: 320-251-7801. Email: micchurch@mywdo.com.
Catechesis/Religious Program—Students 163.

ROSCOE, STEARNS CO., ST. AGNES, [CEM] Rev. Glenn A. Krystosek; Deacon James Schulzetenberg.
Office: 505 Burr St., Paynesville, 56362. Tel: 320-243-4413; Fax: 320-243-4443. Email: frglenn@saintalm.org.
Catechesis/Religious Program—Students 23.

ROYALTON, MORRISON CO., HOLY TRINITY (1897) [CEM] Rev. Laurn Virnig.
Res.: P.O. Box 258, 56373. Tel: 320-584-5484; Fax: 320-584-0028. Email: htrinity@fallsnet.com.
Catechesis/Religious Program—Students 193.

RUSH LAKE, OTTER TAIL CO., ST. LAWRENCE (1886) [CEM] Rev. George Michael, V.C.
Res.: 46404 County Hwy. 14, Perham, 56573. Tel: 218-346-7729; Fax: 218-346-5946.
Catechesis/Religious Program—Students 52.

ST. ANNA, STEARNS CO., IMMACULATE CONCEPTION, [CEM] Rev. Mark Stang; Deacon Jeffrey Fromm.
Res.: *All Saints Rectory*, P.O. Box 308, Holdingford, 56340. Tel: 320-746-2231; Fax: 320-746-2449. Email: fiveoffice@yahoo.com.
Catechesis/Religious Program—Students 104.

ST. ANTHONY, STEARNS CO., ST. ANTHONY'S (1874) [CEM] Rev. Michael Naughton, O.S.B.
Res.: 24326 Trobec St., Albany, 56307. Tel: 320-845-2416; Fax: 320-845-2414.
Catechesis/Religious Program—Kathy Bushman, D.R.E. Students 68.

ST. AUGUSTA, STEARNS CO., ST. MARY HELP OF CHRISTIANS (1856) [CEM] Very Rev. Robert Rolfes; Deacon Kenneth Rosha.
Res.: 24588 County Rd. 7, 56301. Tel: 320-252-1799; Fax: 320-252-1992.
School—(Grades K-6) Tel: 320-251-3937; Fax: 320-251-3937. Bonnie Van Heel, Prin. Lay Teachers 10; Students 125.
Catechesis/Religious Program—Jan Minke, D.R.E. Students 225.

ST. FRANCIS, STEARNS CO., ST. FRANCIS OF ASSISI, [CEM] Revs. Michael Kellogg; John Odero.
Office: P.O. Box 249, Upsala, 56384. Tel: 320-573-2132.
Res.: 8550 State Hwy. 238, Bowlus, 56314. Tel: 320-573-2975.
Church: 44055 State Hwy. 238, Freeport, 56331.
Catechesis/Religious Program—Jane Keepers, D.R.E. Students 55.

SAINT JOSEPH, STEARNS CO., ST. JOSEPH'S (1856) [CEM] Rev. Joseph Feders, O.S.B.; Deacon Thomas A. Murray.
Res.: 12 W. Minnesota St., 56374. Tel: 320-363-7505; Fax: 320-363-0710. Email: parish@churchstjoseph.org.
School—(Grades PreSchool-6), Day Care, Tel: 320-363-7769; Fax: 320-363-7760. Email: principal@churchstjoseph.org. Karl Terhaar, Prin. Lay Teachers 10; Students 125.
Catechesis/Religious Program—Students 242.

ST. MARTIN, STEARNS CO., ST. MARTIN (1858) [CEM] Rev. Stephen Beauclair, O.S.B.; Deacon Gerald Theis.
Res.: 119 Maine St., Box 290, 56376. Tel: 320-548-3550.
Catechesis/Religious Program—Tel: 320-548-3209. Joan Rothstein, D.R.E. Students 86.

ST. NICHOLAS, STEARNS CO., ST. NICHOLAS (1857) [CEM] Rev. Thomas Olson.
15862 County Rd. 165, Watkins, 55389.
Catechesis/Religious Program—Students 49.

ST. ROSA, STEARNS CO., ST. ROSE OF LIMA (1898) [CEM] Rev. Roger Klassen, O.S.B.; Deacon Richard Scherping. In Res., Rev. Arthur Hoppe (Retired).
Res.: 106-3rd Ave. N.E., Freeport, 56331. Tel: 320-836-2143; Fax: 320-836-2142. Email: triparish@albanytel.com.
Catechesis/Religious Program—Mary Kimman, D.R.E. Students 85.

ST. STEPHEN, STEARNS CO., ST. STEPHEN'S (1871) [CEM] Rev. Robert C. Harren.
Res.: 103 Central Ave. S., 56375. Tel: 320-251-1520.
Catechesis/Religious Program—Tel: 320-251-5066. Sharon Selensky, D.R.E. Students 190.

ST. WENDEL, STEARNS CO., ST. COLUMBKILLE'S, [CEM] Rev. Mark Stang; Deacon Jeffrey Fromm. In Res., Rev. Robert Landsberger (Retired).
Rectory—All Saints, P.O. Box 308, Holdingford, 56340. Tel: 320-746-2231; Fax: 320-746-2449. Email: fiveoffice@yahoo.com.
Catechesis/Religious Program—Students 93.

SARTELL, STEARNS CO., ST. FRANCIS XAVIER (1948) [CEM] Revs. Timothy Baltes; Michael Wolfbauer; Deacons Stephen Pareja; Stephen Yanish.
Res.: 219 - 2nd St. N., P.O. Box 150, 56377. Tel: 320-252-1363; Fax: 320-259-7090.
School—(Grades PreSchool-6) Tel: 320-252-9940. Email: lwilfahrt@stfrancis.sartell.org. Linda Wilfahrt, Prin. Lay Teachers 10; Students 174.
Catechesis/Religious Program—Tel: 320-252-8761. Students 715.

SAUK CENTRE, STEARNS CO.
1—OUR LADY OF THE ANGELS, [CEM] Rev. James Statz; Deacon Lawrence Kaas.
Res.: 211 S. 7th St., 56378-1505. Tel: 320-352-3502; Fax: 320-351-3502. Email: angels@mainstreetcom.com.
Catechesis/Religious Program—Tel: 320-352-5580. Students 120.
2—ST. PAUL'S (1870) [CEM] Rev. Todd Schneider; Deacons Thomas McFadden; Lawrence Kaas.
Res.: 304 Sinclair Lewis Ave., 56378. Tel: 320-352-2196; Fax: 320-351-8475. Email: stpaulschurch@mainstreetcom.com.
See Holy Family School, Sauk Centre under Inter-Parochial Schools located in the Institution section.
Catechesis/Religious Program—220 S. Birch, 56378. Tel: 320-352-5580. Students 200.

SAUK RAPIDS, BENTON CO.
1—ST. PATRICK, [CEM] Rev. Daniel Walz.
Mailing Address: 7286 Duelm Rd., N.E., 56379.
Res.: P.O. Box 337, Foley, 56329. Tel: 320-968-7913.
2—SACRED HEART (1919) [CEM] Rev. Ronald Weyrens; Deacons Carl S. Nord; Joseph Kresky.
Mailing Address: 2875 - 10th Ave. N.E., 56379. Tel: 320-251-8115; Fax: 320-252-0710. Email: parish@sacredheartsaukrapids.org.
See St. Katherine Drexel under Inter-Parochial Schools, St. Cloud for details.
Catechesis/Religious Program—Joan Krause, D.R.E. Students 311.

SEDAN, POPE CO., IMMACULATE CONCEPTION, Closed. For inquiries for parish records contact Sacred Heart, Glenwood.

SOBIESKI, MORRISON CO., ST. STANISLAUS (1884) [CEM] Rev. Jimmy Joseph, V.C.
Res.: 9406 Church Cir., Little Falls, 56345-9803. Tel: 320-632-6930; Fax: 320-632-5644. Email: ststans@littlefalls.net.
Catechesis/Religious Program—Students 44.

SPRING HILL, STEARNS CO., ST. MICHAEL'S (1857) [CEM] Revs. Marvin Enneking; Omar Guanchez. In Res., Rev. Richard McGuire (Retired).
Res.: 211 2nd Ave. N., P.O. Box 120, Greenwald, 56335. Tel: 320-987-3160.
Catechesis/Religious Program—Tel: 320-987-3192. Hortense Walz, D.R.E. Students 55.

STAPLES, TODD CO., SACRED HEART, [JC] Rev. Joseph Korf; Deacons John Wolak; Robert Shaffer.
Res.: 310 Fourth St., N.E., Box 177, 56479. Tel: 218-894-2296; Fax: 218-894-2296. Email: sheart@arvig.net.
School—Sacred Heart Area School, (Grades PreSchool-6), 324 - 4th St. N.E., 56479. Tel: 218-894-2077. James Opelia, Prin. Lay Teachers 8; Students 81.
Catechesis/Religious Program—Tel: 218-894-1095. Students 96.

SWANVILLE, MORRISON CO., ST. JOHN THE BAPTIST, [CEM] Rev. Ronald Dockendorf.
Res.: P.O. Box 366, Grey Eagle, 56336. Tel: 320-285-2545; Fax: 320-547-2578.
Catechesis/Religious Program—P.O. Box 68, 56382. Tel: 320-547-2920. Students 153.

TINTAH, TRAVERSE CO., ST. GALL (1881) [CEM] Rev. Ronald Schmelzer; Deacon Joseph Wood.
Res.: 110 Minnesota Ave., 56583. Tel: 218-369-2188. Email: stgull@runestone.net.
Catechesis/Religious Program—Students 13.

UPSALA, MORRISON CO., ST. MARY, [CEM] Revs. Michael Kellogg; John Odero.
Office: P.O. 249, 56384. Tel: 320-573-2132.
Res.: 8550 State Hwy. 238, Bowlus, 56314. Tel: 320-584-5313; 320-573-2975.
Catechesis/Religious Program—Students 100.

URBANK, OTTER TAIL CO., SACRED HEART (1902) [CEM] Rev. LeRoy Scheierl.
Res.: 60 Central Ave. N., Parkers Prairie, 56361. Tel: 218-267-2661.
Catechesis/Religious Program—Students 38.

VERNDALE, WADENA CO., ST. FREDERICK (1910) [CEM] Rev. Arlie Sowada.
Res.: 20 Brown St. N., P.O. Box C, 56481. Tel: 218-445-5786.
Catechesis/Religious Program—50047 - 171st Ave., 56481. Tel: 218-639-1491; Fax: 218-445-5280. Students 54.

VILLARD, POPE CO., ST. BARTHOLOMEW'S (1883) [CEM] Rev. Peter K. Kirchner Jr.
105 N. Franklin, Glenwood, 56334. Tel: 320-634-3813; Fax: 320-634-0590.
Office: 122 - N.W. 1st St., Glenwood, 56334.
Catechesis/Religious Program—Leonard Heidelberger, D.R.E. Students 24.

VINELAND, MILLE LACS CO., ST. THERESE, [CEM] [JC] Revs. Jerome Schik, O.S.C.; Jude Verley, O.S.C.; Gregory Poser, O.S.C.
Mailing Address: *Crosier Priory of the Holy Cross*, P.O. Box 500, Onamia, 56359. Tel: 320-532-3601; Fax: 320-532-5222.
Catechesis/Religious Program—Students 7.

WADENA, WADENA CO., ST. ANN'S (1895) [CEM] Rev. Donald Wagner; Deacon Gerald Snyder.
Res.: 514 First St., S.E., 56482. Tel: 218-631-1593; Fax: 218-631-7149.
Catechesis/Religious Program—Students 108.

WAHKON, MILLE LACS CO., SACRED HEART, [CEM] Revs. Jude Verley, O.S.C.; Jerome Schik, O.S.C.; Gregory Poser, O.S.C.
Mailing Address: P.O. Box 68, 56386.
Catechesis/Religious Program—Tel: 320-495-3324. Lola Larson, D.R.E. Students 33.

WAITE PARK, STEARNS CO., ST. JOSEPH'S (1916) [CEM] Revs. Vincent Lieser; Matthew Kuhn.
Office: 106 7th Ave. N., 56387. Tel: 320-251-5231; Fax: 320-251-3010. Email: stjosephwp@charterinternet.com.
School—(Grades PreSchool-6), 108 7th Ave. N., 56387. Tel: 320-251-4741, Ext. 1; Fax: 320-230-2161. Kathy Cziok, Prin. Lay Teachers 8; Students 98.
Catechesis/Religious Program—Students 76.

WARD SPRINGS, TODD CO., ST. BERNARD'S, Closed. For inquiries for parish records contact St. Joseph, Grey Eagle.

WEST UNION, TODD CO., ST. ALEXIUS, [CEM] Rev. James Statz.
Church: 11 Oak St., P.O. Box 104, 56389.
Res.: 211 S. 7th St., Sauk Centre, 56378. Tel: 320-352-3502.
Catechesis/Religious Program—Box 4A, 56389. Tel: 320-352-2563; Fax: 320-352-2930. Students 22.

WHEATON, TRAVERSE CO., AVE MARIA, [JC] Rev. Joseph Vandeberg.
Res.: 201 Ninth St. S., 56296. Tel: 320-563-4421.
Catechesis/Religious Program—Barb Tauber, D.R.E. Students 118.

ZIMMERMAN, SHERBURNE CO., ST. PIUS X, [CEM] Merged With St. Edward's, Princeton to form The Church of Christ Our Light Princeton/Zimmerman.

Chaplains of Public Institutions

ST. CLOUD. *Minnesota State Reformatory for Men.* Vacant.
U.S. Veteran's Hospital 56301.

CAMBRIDGE. *Cambridge State School and Hospital* 55008. Vacant.

FERGUS FALLS. *State Hospital Chapel* 56537. Vacant.

Special Assignment:
Revs.—
Belland, David
Holmes, Albert
Kuhn, Aaron J.
Marfori, Antonio
Wittkop, Scott

Retired:
Most Rev.—
Sowada, Alphonse, O.S.C., 308 3rd St. S., Sauk Rapids, 56379.
Rev. Msgr.—
Taufen, Daniel J., S.T.L., 1009 10th Ave. N.E., Sauk Rapids, 56379.
Revs.—
Bednark, Walter, 23189 State Hwy. 4, Paynesville, 56362.
Brenny, Kenneth, P.O. Box 608, Buckman, 56317.
Eccleston, John, 1810 Minnesota Blvd., S.E., Saint Cloud, 56304.
Fehrenbacher, Henry, 1810 Minnesota Blvd., S.E., Saint Cloud, 56304.
Folsom, Paul, 39880 Crane Lake Dr., Battle Lake, 56515.
Gruenes, Bernard, 1001 - 24th Ave. N., Saint Cloud, 56303.
Haupt, Lloyd, 929 Brenda Lee Dr., 56303.
Hoppe, Arthur, 28905 County Rd. 17, Freeport, 56331.
Kahlhamer, Bernard, 525 Roberts St. S. #116, Pierz, 56364.
Kalkman, Richard, 23 Diaz Ave., San Francisco, CA 94132.
Kleinschmidt, Sylvester, 412 First St. S., Apt. 1, Sauk Centre, 56378.
Kraemer, Edwin, 828 Village Ave., Sartell, 56377.
Kroll, Anthony, 308-3rd St. S., #203, Sauk Rapids, 56379.
Landsberger, Robert, 12536 County Rd. 4, Avon, 56310.
Leisen, Leo, 1810 Minnesota Blvd., S.E., Saint Cloud, 56304.
Leisen, Richard, 308-3rd St. S., #107, Sauk Rapids, 56379.
Lieser, Gregory, 308-3rd St. S., Sauk Rapids, 56379.
Ludwig, Alexander, 1423 Melvina Ln., Alexandria, 56308.
Majerus, Daniel, 6007 Royal Breeze, San Antonio, TX 78239.
Marthaler, Andrew, 750 Railroad Ave., Apt. 132, Sauk Centre, 56378.
Maus, Le Roy, 11367 Phoenix Dr., #75, Yuma, AZ 85367.
McGuire, Richard, 102 St. Michael Ave. N., Melrose, 56352.
Mischke, Gerald, 25-8th Ave. S., Saint Cloud, 56301.
Otto, Leo, 12372-92nd Ave., Box 118, Little Falls, 56345.
Pavelis, Harold, Box 88, Concord, CA 94522.
Poncelet, Frank, 10207 1/2 - 230th St. E., Hastings, 55033.
Quade, Alvin, 7807 Emerald Rd., Randall, 56475.
Riedemann, Kenneth, 21398 Alcott Ln., Sauk Centre, 56378.
Rieder, Donald, 1810 Minnesota Blvd., S.E., 56304.
Schefers, Eberhard, 702-2nd Ave., N.E., Saint Joseph, 56374.
Schmitt, Silverius, 5290-175th St., N.W., Royalton, 56373.
Slominski, Leon, 822 10th Ave. N. #4, Sartell, 56377.
Snyers, Peter, 520-1st St. N.E., Sartell, 56377.
Stangl, Alfred, 210 3rd St. S. #303, Saint Cloud, 56301.
Thielman, Kenneth, Park View Center, 125 N. Fifth Ave. W., Melrose, 56352.
Thoennes, James, P.O. Box 1248, Saint Cloud, 56302.
Tomasiewicz, Frank, 308 3rd St. S. #201, Sauk Rapids, 56379.
Torborg, Elmer, 615 1st St. N., #110, Cold Spring, 56320.
Vogel, Arthur, 617 Pinecone Rd., Apt. 308, Sartell, 56377.
Vos, William, 1664 Payton Ct., N.E., Sauk Rapids, 56379.
Wenzel, Timothy, 21949 100th Ave., Randall, 56475.
Wey, Richard, 89 Greenstone Ln., Waite Park, 56387.
Willenbring, Mark, 409 Central Ave., Long Prairie, 56347.
Zimmer, Nicholas, Elmhurst Commons, 400 3rd St., S.W., Apt. 211, Braham, 55006.
Zylla, Paul, 1615-15th Ave., S.E. #251, 56304.

Permanent Deacons:
Anderberg, George, (Retired)
Arnold, Stephen, St. Mary, Melrose
Barder, Mark, Christ Our Light, Princeton/ Zimmerman
Beck, Guy, St. Michael, Buckman; St. Joseph, Pierz
Bobertz, Charles
Clack, James
Curry, Dirck
Dupay, Steven
Fromm, Jeffrey, Holdingford Area Catholic Comm., Opole
Geyer, Bruce, St. Mary, Little Falls; Holy Family, Belle Prairie
Hennen, Stanley, St. Nicholas, Belle River; Immaculate Conception, Osakis
Hilber, Joseph, St. Leonard's, Pelican Rapids; St. Elizabeth, Elizabeth
Kaas, Lawrence, Our Lady of the Angels, Sauk Centre
Kampa, Charles, Our Lady of Victory, Fergus Falls
Keable, Michael, St. John Baptist, Collegeville
Kociemba, Ernest, St. Mary, Melrose
Korver, Craig, Our Lady of Lourdes, Little Falls
Kosiba, Leo, (Retired)
Kowitz, Jeff, St. Mary's, St. Cloud
Kramer, Eugene, Christ the King, Cambridge
Krebs, Brian
Kresky, Joseph, Sacred Heart, Sauk Rapids
Kunkel, Andrew, Holy Cross, Pearl Lake
Lindmeier, David, St. Paul, St. Cloud; St. Peter, St. Cloud
Maltzen, Bruce
McFadden, Thomas, St. Paul's Sauk Centre
Midas, Richard, (Retired)
Murray, Thomas A., St. Joseph, St. Joseph.
Nord, Carl, Sacred Heart, Sauk Rapids
Pareja, Stephen, St. Francis, Sartell
Pinataro, Thomas, Sts. Peter & Paul, Braham
Reker, Fred, St. John Cantius, St. Cloud
Ringsmuth, Frank, St. John Cantius, St. Cloud
Ritchie, William, St. Peter, St. Cloud
Rosha, Kenneth, St. Mary Help of Christian, St. Augusta
Roth, Jerome, (Retired)
Salchert, John, (Retired)
Scheierl, Richard, St. Augustine, St. Cloud; St. Mary, St. Cloud
Scherping, Richard, Sacred Heart, Freeport; Immaculate Conception, New Munich; St. Rose, St. Rosa
Schmainda, Frank, Sacred Heart, Glenwood
Schmitz, Vernon, Holy Spirit, St. Cloud
Schulzetenberg, James, St. Margaret, Lake Henry; St. Louis, Paynesville; St. Agnes, Roscoe
Schwarzbauer, Jerome, (Retired)
Scott, John W., (Retired)
Sell, Lawrence, St. Boniface, Cold Spring
Shaffer, Robert, St. Michael, Motley; Sacred Heart, Staples
Snyder, Gerald, St. Ann, Wadena; St. John, Bluffton
St. Jean, Fred, St. Andrew, Elk River
Steele, Gregory J.
Theis, Gerald, St. Martin, St. Martin
Tzinski, Donald, J.C.L., (Diocesan Tribunal)
Warren, Todd
Wocken, John, St. Mary, St. Cloud; St. Augustine, St. Cloud
Wolak, John, Sacred Heart, Staples; St. Michael, Motley
Wood, Joseph, St. Olaf, Elbow Lake; St. Gall, Tintah
Yanish, Stephen, St. Francis, Sartell
Zenner, Mark

INSTITUTIONS LOCATED IN THE DIOCESE

[A] SEMINARIES, RELIGIOUS OR SCHOLASTICATES

COLLEGEVILLE. *St. John's School of Theology and Seminary*, P.O. Box 7288, 56321. Tel: 320-363-2100; Fax: 320-363-3145. Web: www.csbsju.edu/sot. Rev. Michael Patella, O.S.B., Rector; Dr. William Cahoy, Dean; Sr. Stephanie Weisgrram, O.S.B., Librarian.
St. John's School of Theology and Seminary Priests 4; Sisters 2; Lay Teachers 10; Students 133.

[B] COLLEGES AND UNIVERSITIES

COLLEGEVILLE. *Saint John's University* (1857) (Men), Box 2000, 56321-2000. Tel: 320-363-2011; Fax: 320-363-2504. Email: rknuesel@csbsju.edu. Web: www.csbsju.edu. Rt. Rev. John Klassen, O.S.B., Ph.D., Abbot & Chancellor. Sponsored by the Collegeville Benedictine Monks as a division of the corporate Order of Saint Benedict, Collegeville, MN.; Sponsored Programs: The Hill Museum and Manuscript Library and Saint John's Pottery Studio and The Liturgical Press; The Graduate School of Theology (Coed)/Saint John's Seminary (Men): M.A. in Theology, Liturgical Studies, Liturgical Music, Pastoral Ministry and a Master of Divinity. The Undergraduate College of Liberal Arts and Sciences (Men), in full coordinate academic relation with the College of Saint Benedict, St. Joseph (Women), offers forty departments, ten pre-professional and ten special academic programs. Priests 18; Brothers 12; Sisters 3; Lay Faculty 161; Students 2,016.
Officers Group: Bro. Benedict Leuthner, O.S.B., Corp. Treas.; Rev. Robert Koopmann, O.S.B., Pres.; Dr. William Cahoy, Dean, School of Theology; Mr. Rob Culligan, Vice Pres., Institutional Advancement; Rev. Douglas Mullin, O.S.B., Vice Pres., Student Devel.; Rita Knuesel, Provost Academic Affairs; Jon McGee, Vice Pres. Planning & Public Affairs.
Administrative Group: Rt. Rev. John Klassen, O.S.B., Ph.D., Abbot & Chancellor; Revs. Timothy Backous, O.S.B., Headmaster, Prep School; William Schipper, O.S.B., Dir. Campus Ministry; Columba Stewart, O.S.B., Exec. Dir. Hill Museum & Manuscript Library; Bro. David Klingeman, O.S.B., Archivist; Martha Tomhave Blauvelt, Ph.D., The Michael Blecker Professorship; David Lyngaard, Assoc. Dean, Academic; Margrette Newhouse, The John & Elizabeth Myers Chair in Mgmt.; Mr. Richard Bresnahan, Potter, Saint John's Pottery Studio; Patti Epsky, Exec. Asst. to the Pres.; Dr. Bernard Evans, The Butler Family's Virgil Michel Ecumenical Chair in Rural Social Ministries; Dr. Daniel Rush Finn, The William & Virginia Clemens Chair in Economics & the Liberal Arts; Ms. Julie Gruska, Registrar; Dr. Nicholas P. Hayes, Univ. Chair in Critical Thinking; Mr. Gregory Hoye, Exec. Dir. Communications & Mktg.; Kathy Parker, Dir. Libraries and Media; Mr. James Koenig, Dir. Information Technology Svcs.; Mr. Michael Connolly, Dean of Campus Life; Bernadette W. Suwareh, Dir. Intercultural Center; Mr. Stuart Perry, Dir. Financial Aid; Carol Abell, Dir. Human Resources; Mr. John Young, Assoc. Vice Pres. Devel.

SAINT JOSEPH. *College of Saint Benedict* (1913) (Women), 37 College Ave. S., 56374-2099. Tel: 320-363-5011; Fax: 320-363-5136. Email: rknuesel@csbsju.edu. Web: www.csbsju.edu.
College of Saint Benedict Sisters of the Order of Saint Benedict., Affiliation: Roman Catholic, established for the undergraduate education of women by the Sisters of the Order of Saint Benedict.; Partnership: The College of Saint Benedict is a private, nationally recognized women's, residential, liberal arts, Catholic, Benedictine college, located in St. Joseph, MN joined in a coeducational mission with Saint John's University for men. As the only Catholic all women's Baccalaureate I college, Saint Benedict's is unique in its commitment to gender specific education within a coeducational environment. Sisters 8; Faculty 171; Administrators 168; Students 2,080.
Officers Group: Mary Geller, Vice Pres. Student Devel.; MaryAnn Baenninger, Pres.; Joseph Des Jardins, Vice Provost; Kim Motes, Vice Pres., Inst. Advancement; Susan Palmer, Vice Pres. of Finance & Admin.; Rita Knuesel, Provost, Academic Affairs.
Administrative Group: Jason Kelly, Dir. of Academic Advising/Asst. Dean; Mike Durbin, Dir. Athletic Media Rels.; Mary Geller, Vice Pres. of Student Devel.; Ms. Julie Gruska, Registrar; Mary Harlander-Locke, Assoc. Dir. Career Svcs.; Jane Haugen, Exec. Dir. Fin. Aid; Carol Howe-Veenstra, Dir. Athletics; Greg Hoye, Exec. Dir. Communication & Mktg. Svc.; Kathy Parker, Dir. Libraries & Media; Mr. James Koenig, Dir., Information Technology Svc.; Jon McGee, Vice Pres. Planning & Public Affairs; Diane Hageman, Dir. CSB Media Rels.; Jody Terhaar, Dean of Students; Carol Abell, Dir. Human Resources.

[C] HIGH SCHOOLS, DIOCESAN

ST. CLOUD. *The Cathedral High School*, (Grades 7-12), 312 7th Ave. N., Saint Cloud, 56303. Tel: 320-251-3421; Fax: 320-253-5576. Email: mmullin@chsj23.org. Mr. Michael Mullin, Pres.; Ms. Lynn

Grewing, Prin.; Rev. Michael Wolfbauer, Chap.; Julie Notsch, Librarian. Priests 1; Lay Teachers 43; Students 650.

Cathedral High School Education Foundation, P.O. Box 1579, 56302. Tel: 320-251-3421; Fax: 320-253-5576.

[D] HIGH SCHOOLS, PRIVATE

COLLEGEVILLE. *Saint John's Preparatory School*, (Grades 6-12), College Preparatory., 2280 Water Tower Rd., P.O. Box 4000, 56321. Tel: 320-363-3315; Fax: 320-363-3513. Email: tbackous@sjprep.net. Web: www.sjprep.net. Rev. Timothy Backous, O.S.B., Headmaster; Kathryn Kockler, Prin.; Cindy Peterson, Librarian. Priests 1; Lay Teachers 50; Students 306.

[E] INTER-PAROCHIAL SCHOOLS

ST. CLOUD. *St. Elizabeth Ann Seton School*, (Grades PreK-6), 1615 Eleventh Ave. S., 56301. Tel: 320-251-1988; Fax: 320-229-2149. Email: ttroness@stelizabethannseton.net. Tom Troness, Prin.; Kaye Sauer, Librarian. Consolidation of schools of the following parishes: Holy Spirit, St. Anthony and St. John Cantius, St. Cloud. Lay Teachers 13; Students 200.

St. Katharine Drexel School, (Grades PreK-6), 428 2nd St., S.E., Saint Cloud, 56304. Tel: 320-251-2376; Fax: 320-529-3222. Erin Hatlestad, Prin.; Ruth Steffes, Librarian. Consolidation of schools of the following parishes: St. Mary and St. Augustine, St. Cloud, and Sacred Heart, Sauk Rapids Lay Teachers 18; Students 308.

Sts. Peter, Paul and Michael School, (Grades PreK-3), Primary: 925 30th Ave. N., 56303. Tel: 320-251-4737; Fax: 320-253-7110. Email: sbichler@sppmschools.com. Sharon Bichler, Prin.; Amy O'Neal, Librarian. Serves the following parishes: St. Michael; St. Paul; St. Peter, St. Cloud. Lay Teachers 15; Students 165.

Middle (Grades 4-6), 1215 N. 11th Ave., 56303. Tel: 320-251-5295; Fax: 320-251-7014. Email: sppmmiddle@charterinternet.com. Mary Cheryl Opatz, Teacher & Devel.; Amy O'Neal, Librarian. Lay Teachers 10; Students 105.

FOLEY. *St. John's Area School*, (Grades PreK-6), 215 7th Ave. S., P.O. Box 368, 56329. Tel: 320-968-7972; Fax: 320-968-9956. Email: sjasfm@cloudnet.com. Web: www.cloudnet.com~sjasfm. Mary Sabin, Prin.; Michelle Buettner, Librarian. Consolidation of the following parishes: St. John's, Foley; St. Lawrence, Duelm; St. Elizabeth, Brennyville; St. Joseph, Morrill; SS. Peter and Paul, Gilman; St. Louis, Foreston; St. Patrick of Minden Township Lay Teachers 8; Students 103.

LITTLE FALLS. *Mary of Lourdes School*, (Grades PreK-4), Primary: 307 Fourth St., S.E., 56345. Tel: 320-632-5408; Fax: 320-632-5409. Email: mhbecker@molschool.org. Web: www.molschool.org. Mailing Address: 205 N.W. 3rd St., 56345. Julie Barten, Librarian. Consolidation of following parishes: St. Mary and Our Lady of Lourdes, Little Falls Lay Teachers 15; Students 146; Preschool Students 20.

Middle: (Grades 5-8), 205 N.W. Third St., 56345. Tel: 320-632-6742; Fax: 320-632-3556. Maria Heymans-Becker, Prin. Teachers 12; Students 125.

PIERZ. *Holy Trinity School*, (Grades PreK-6), 80 Edward St. S., Box 427, 56364. Tel: 320-468-6446; Fax: 320-468-6446. Email: dmm@holytrinitypierz.org. Web: holytrinitypierz.org. Debra Meyer-Myrum, Prin.; Kristi Schmidtbauer, Librarian. Consolidation of the following parishes: St. Michael's, Buckman; Holy Cross, Harding; St. John Nepomuk, Lastrup; St. Joseph, Pierz. Lay Teachers 14; Students 181.

SAUK CENTRE. *Holy Family School*, (Grades K-6), 231 Sinclair Lewis Ave., 56378. Tel: 320-352-6535; Fax: 320-352-6537. Email: lynn_peterson@isd743.k12.mn.us. Web: www.holyfamilysc.stclouddiocese.org. Lynn Peterson, Prin.; Patty Dirkes, Librarian. Consolidation of the following parishes: St. Paul's and Our Lady of the Angels, Sauk Centre. Lay Teachers 16; Students 201.

[F] HOMES FOR EMOTIONALLY DISTURBED AND HANDICAPPED

ST. CLOUD. *St. Cloud Children's Home of the Diocese of St. Cloud*, 1726 Seventh Ave. S., 56301. Tel: 320-650-1500; Fax: 320-650-1508. Mr. Steven P. Bresnahan, Exec. Dir.; Tim Lieser, Dir. Residential Day Svcs. Children 78.

St. Elizabeth Home Contact Tim Lieser at Catholic Charities, 306 15th Ave. N., 56303. Tel: 320-240-3350. Email: Tlieser@ccstcloud.org. Mr. Steven P. Bresnahan, Exec. Dir.; Tim Lieser, Dir. Residential Day Svcs. Board and Lodging Home for Functionally Impaired Adults. Residents 18.

St. Francis Home, 1727 Roosevelt Rd., 56301. Tel: 320-251-7630; Fax: 320-240-8097. Mr. Steven P. Bresnahan, Exec. Dir.; Tim Lieser, Dir. Residential Day Svcs. Supervised Living Situation for Persons with Developmental Disabilities. Residents 4.

LaPaz Community Inc., Catholic Charities Housing Services, 530 S. 16th St., 56301. Mailing Address: 157 Roosevelt Rd., Ste. 200, 56301. Mr. Steven P. Bresnahan, Exec. Dir.; Harvey Schmitt, Dir. Housing Svcs. Residents 36.

COLD SPRING. *St. Anne's Home* Contact Catholic Charities, 103 10th Ave. N., 56320. Tel: 320-685-7898; Fax: 320-685-9819. Mr. Steven P. Bresnahan, Exec Dir.; Tim Lieser, Dir. Residential Day Svcs. Supervised Living Situation for Persons with Developmental Disabilities. Residents 4.

Bethany Home Contact Tim Lieser at Catholic Charities, 13 Eighth Ave. S., 56320. Tel: 320-685-7899; Fax: 320-685-9808. Email: tlieser@ccstcloud.org. Mr. Steven P. Bresnahan, Exec Dir.; Tim Lieser, Dir. Residential Day Svcs. Supervised Living Situation for Persons with Developmental Disabilities. Residents 4.

St. Luke's Home Contact Catholic Charities, 411 Eighth Ave. N., 56320. Tel: 320-685-7750. Mr. Steven P. Bresnahan, Exec. Dir.; Tim Lieser, Dir. Residential Day Svcs. Adults with mild to moderate developmental disabilities. Residents 4.

Mother Teresa Home Contact Catholic Charities, 101 Tenth Ave., 56320. Tel: 320-685-8626; Fax: 320-685-8626. Mr. Steven P. Bresnahan, Exec. Dir.; Tim Lieser, Dir. Residential Day Svcs. Supervised Living Situation for Persons with Developmental Disabilities. Residents 4.

FERGUS FALLS. *Catholic Charities Intensive Treatment Unit*, 1010 Maryland Ln., 56537. Tel: 218-739-9325; Fax: 218-739-2242. Mr. Steven Bresnahan, Exec. Dir.; Tim Lieser, Dir. Residential Day Svcs. Capacity 16; Total Served 35.

LITTLE FALLS. *St. Camillus Place*, 1100 S.E. Fourth St., 56345. Tel: 320-631-5020; Fax: 320-631-5025. Lisa Thielman, Dir.; Barbara A. Miller, Admin.; Bea Britz, Chap. Bed Capacity 14.

PAYNESVILLE. *Adult Foster Care for Handicapped Individuals*, 1790 W. Mill St., 56362. Tel: 320-243-3750; Fax: 320-243-3718. Tim Lieser, Dir. Catholic Charities Residential & Day Svcs. Bed Capacity 4.

[G] GENERAL HOSPITALS

ST. CLOUD. *St. Cloud Hospital*, 1406 Sixth Ave. N., 56303. Tel: 320-251-2700; Fax: 320-255-5711. Web: www.stcloudhospital.com. Craig Broman, Pres.; Bret Reuter, Dir. Mission and Spiritual Care; Rev. Roger Botz, O.S.B., Chap. Sisters of St. Benedict 2; Bed Capacity 489; Bassinets 18; Patients Assisted Annually 244,756.

ALBANY. *Albany Area Hospital* (1969) 300 Third Ave., 56307. Tel: 320-845-2121; Fax: 320-845-6127. Web: www.albanyareahospital.com. Nick Brandner, Admin.; Deborah Robinson, Chap. Bed Capacity 16; Patients Assisted Annually 10,000.

BRECKENRIDGE. *St. Francis Medical Center* (1899) 2400 St. Francis Dr., 56520. Tel: 218-643-3000; Fax: 218-643-0850. Email: davidnelson@catholichealth.net. Web: www.sfcare.org. David Nelson, Pres.; Ann Trebsch, Vice Pres. Mission; Rev. Kenneth Popp, Chap. Bed Capacity 25; Patients Assisted Annually 26,000.

LITTLE FALLS. *St. Gabriel's Hospital*, 815 S.E. Second St., 56345. Tel: 320-632-5441; Fax: 320-631-5480. Chad Cooper, Pres. & CEO; Mary Ann Koth, Chap. Licensed Beds 25; Bassinets 10; Patients Assisted Annually 32,814.

[H] HOMES FOR AGED

ST. CLOUD. *St. Benedict's Senior Community* (1978) 1810 Minnesota Blvd., S.E., 56304. Tel: 320-252-0010; Fax: 320-654-2351. Linda Doerr, Exec. Dir.; Sr. Susan Rudolph, O.S.B., Dir. of Pastoral Care & Lay Ecclesial Health Care Min.; Rev. Meinrad Dindorf, O.S.B., Chap.; Debora Galvez, Asst. Lay Ecclesial Min., Health Care Ministry. Corporate Division of the St. Cloud Hospital. Operated under the auspices of the local Catholic Church of St. Cloud.; Care Center managed by St. Benedict's Senior Community. A division of the St. Cloud Hospital. Operated under the auspices of the local Catholic Church of St. Cloud. Residents 170; Short Stay Units - Beds 52.

Benedict Village: 2000 15th Ave., S.E., 56304. Tel: 320-252-4380; Fax: 320-654-2351. Linda Doerr, Exec. Dir.; Robin Theis, Admin., Housing and Community Svcs. Managed by St. Benedict's Senior Community. A Division of the St. Cloud Hospital. Operated under the auspices of the local Catholic Church of St. Cloud. Residents 115.

Benedict Homes (4), 1342 Minnesota Blvd., S.E., 56304. Tel: 320-252-0010. Residential Homes for residents with Alzheimer's. All Benedict Homes are managed by St. Benedict's Senior Community. A division of the St. Cloud Hospital. Operated under the auspices of the local Catholic Church of St. Cloud. Residents 24.

Benedict Court, 1980 15th Ave., S.E., 56304. Tel: 320-252-0010; Fax: 320-654-2351. Linda Doerr, Exec. Dir.; Robin Theis, Admin., Housing and Community Svcs. 39 assisted living apartments; Managed by St. Benedict's Senior Community. A Division of the St. Cloud Hospital. Operated under the auspices of the local Catholic Church of St. Cloud. Residents 40.

Benet Place North, 1420 Minnesota Blvd., S.E., 56304. Tel: 320-252-2557; Fax: 320-654-2351. Subsidized apartments with supportive services for older adults only. Managed by St. Benedict's Senior Community. Tenants 40.

Benet Place South, 1975 15th Ave., S.E., 56304. Tel: 320-529-8700; Fax: 320-654-2351. Tenants 36.

ALBANY. *Mother of Mercy Campus of Care*, Box 676, 56307. Tel: 320-845-2195; Fax: 320-845-7092. Email: jhoefs@momnursinghome.com. John J. Hoefs, Admin. & CEO. Guests 188.

BRECKENRIDGE. *Appletree Court* (1998) 601 Oak St., 56520. Tel: 218-643-0407; Fax: 218-643-0850. Email: jolyndohman@catholichealth.net. Web: sfcare.org. David Nelson, CEO. Residents 20.

St. Francis Home, 2400 St. Francis Dr., 56520. Tel: 218-643-3000; Fax: 218-643-0850. Web: www.sfcare.org. David Nelson, CEO; Rev. Kenneth Popp, Chap. Residents 120.

COLD SPRING. *Assumption Court*, 615 First St. N., 56320. Tel: 320-685-4110; Fax: 320-685-7044. Jan Luthens, Admin.; Rev. Julius Beckermann, O.S.B., Chap. Apartments 59.

Assumption Home (1963) 715 First St. N., 56320. Tel: 320-685-3693; Fax: 320-685-7044. Web: assumptionhome.org. Jan Luthens, Admin.; Rev. Julius Beckermann, O.S.B. Residents 82.

John Paul Apartments, 200 Eighth Ave. N., 56320. Tel: 320-685-4429; Fax: 320-685-7044. Email: jpa@cloudnet.com. Jan Luthens, Admin.; Rev. Julius Beckermann, O.S.B., Chap. Apartments 61.

LITTLE FALLS. *Alverna Apartments*, 300 Eighth Ave., S.E., 56345. Tel: 320-631-5030; Fax: 320-631-5035. Bea Britz, Chap.; Sharon Bauer, Mgr. (An Affiliate of Catholic Health Initiatives) Units 60.

MORA. *Benedictine Living Community of Mora*, 110 N. 7th St., 55051. Tel: 320-679-1411; Fax: 320-679-8350. Dale Thompson, Chm. Bd.; Jack L'Heureux, CEO. Skilled care and assisted living facility.

MORRIS. *West Wind Village*, 1001 Scotts Ave., 56267. Tel: 320-589-1133; Fax: 320-589-7955. Email: solson@wvv.sfhs.org. Deacon Stan Hennen, Pastoral Care. Beds 88.

PARKERS PRAIRIE. *St. William's Living Center* (1963) P.O. Box 30, 56361. Tel: 218-338-4671; Fax: 218-338-5917. Email: pbaer@midwestinfo.net. Paul Baer, Admin. Bed Capacity 63.

[I] MONASTERIES AND RESIDENCES OF PRIESTS AND BROTHERS

ST. CLOUD. *St. Joseph Province of the Vincentian Congregation* St. Joseph Province, Vincentian Congregation, 210 5th Ave., S.E., Saint Cloud, 56304. Tel: 320-229-7759. Revs. Joseph Arackal, V.C., Supr.; Jose Edayadiyil, V.C. (India); Jimmy Joseph, V.C.; George Michael, V.C.

COLLEGEVILLE. *Holy Cross Trust*, 31802 County Rd. 159, 56321.

St. John's Abbey, of the Order of St. Benedict and St. John's University, School of Theology, Seminary, Preparatory School and Novitiate., 31802 Co. Rd. 159, P.O. Box 2015, 56321-2015. Tel: 320-363-2011. Web: saintjohnsabbey.org. Rt. Rev. John Klassen, O.S.B., Ph.D., Abbot & Chancellor; Very Rev. Thomas Andert, O.S.B., Prior; Revs. Jonathan Licari, O.S.B., Subprior; Paul Richards, O.S.B., Dir. Formation; Knute Anderson, O.S.B.; Alexander Andrews, O.S.B.; Timothy Backous, O.S.B., Pres. St. John's Preparatory School; Stephen Beauclair, O.S.B.; Nickolas Becker, O.S.B.; Julius Beckermann, O.S.B.; Luigi Bertocchi, O.S.B.; Michael Bik, O.S.B.; Roger Botz, O.S.B.; Allan Bouley, O.S.B.; Fintan Bromenshenkel, O.S.B.; Jerome Coller, O.S.B.; Corwin Collins, O.S.B.; Cletus Connors, O.S.B.; Alberic Culhane, O.S.B.; Meinrad Dindorf, O.S.B.; Ian Dommer, O.S.B., Univ. Chap.; Daniel Durken, O.S.B.; John Patrick Earls, O.S.B.; Richard Eckroth, O.S.B.; Geoffrey Fecht, O.S.B.; Joseph Feders, O.S.B.; Jonathan Fischer, O.S.B.; Thomas Gillespie, O.S.B.; Nathanael Hauser, O.S.B.; Henry Bryan Hays, O.S.B.; Francis Hoefgen, O.S.B., (Leave of Absence); Eric Hollas, O.S.B.; Roger Kasprick, O.S.B.; Chrysostom Kim, O.S.B.; Roger Klassen, O.S.B.; Robert Koopmann, O.S.B.; John Kulas, O.S.B.; Michael Kwatera, O.S.B.; Dale Launderville, O.S.B.; Donald LeMay, O.S.B.; Matthew Luft, O.S.B; Brennan Maiers, O.S.B.; Luke Mancuso, O.S.B.; J. Patrick McDarby, O.S.B.; Finian McDonald, O.S.B.; Kilian McDonnell, O.S.B.; Eugene J. McGlothlin, O.S.B.;

Rene McGraw, O.S.B.; Gregory Miller, O.S.B.; Dunstan Moorse, O.S.B.; Douglas Mullin, O.S.B.; Michael Naughton, O.S.B.; Michael Patella, O.S.B.; Raymond Pedrizetti, O.S.B.; Robert Pierson, O.S.B.; Martin Rath, O.S.B.; James Reichert, O.S.B.; Anthony Ruff, O.S.B.; Dominic Ruiz, O.S.B.; William Schipper, O.S.B.; Julian Schmiesing, O.S.B.; Francisco Schulte, O.S.B.; Kevin Seasoltz, O.S.B.; Luke Steiner, O.S.B.; Columba Stewart, O.S.B., HMML Dir.; Don Talafous, O.S.B.; Allen Tarlton, O.S.B.; Donald Tauscher, O.S.B.; Gordon Tavis, O.S.B.; Mark Thamert, O.S.B.; Wilfred Theisen, O.S.B.; Hilary Thimmesh, O.S.B.; Simeon J. Thole, O.S.B.; Thomas Thole, O.S.B.; Jerome Tupa, O.S.B.; Blane Wasnie, O.S.B.; Arnold Weber, O.S.B.; Magnus Wenninger, O.S.B.; Hugh Witzmann, O.S.B.; George Wolf, O.S.B. Priests within Diocese 75; Priests Elsewhere 17; Brothers 55; Permanent Deacons 1.

On Special Assignments: Revs. Joel Kelly, O.S.B.; Barnabas Laubach, O.S.B., St. Bernardine Hospital, 2101 N. Waterman Ave., San Bernardino, CA 92404. Tel: 909-883-8711; Daniel Ward, O.S.B., 2613 Woodege Rd., Silver Spring, MD 20906. Tel: 301-933-0447; Fax: 301-589-2897; Cyprian Weaver, O.S.B.

Priests of the Abbey Serving Abroad: Revs. Cyril Gorman, O.S.B.; Peter Kawamura, O.S.B., Holy Trinity Benedictine Monastery, 3110 Fujimi-Fujimi Machi, Nagano Ken 399-0211 Japan. Tel: 011-81-266-62-8770; Fax: 011-81-266-62-8765; Kieran Nolan, O.S.B., Holy Trinity Benedictine Monastery, 3110 Fujimi-Fujimi Machi, Nagano Ken 399-0211 Japan. Tel: 011-81-266-62-8770; Fax: 011-81-266-62-8765; Roman Paur, O.S.B.; William Skudlarek, O.S.B.; Mel Taylor, O.S.B., St. Augustine Monastery, Box N-3940, Nassau, Bahamas. Tel: 242-364-1331; Fax: 242-364-8929; Very Rev. Thomas Wahl, O.S.B., Prior, Holy Trinity Benedictine Monastery, 3110 Fujimi-Fujimi Machi, Nagano Ken 399-0211 Japan. Tel: 011-81-266-62-8770; Fax: 011-81-266-62-8765; Rev. Edward Vebelun, O.S.B., Holy Trinity Benedictine Monastery, 3110 Fujimi-Fujimi Machi, Nagano Ken 399-0211 Japan. Tel: 011-81-266-62-8770; Fax: 011-81-266-62-8765.

ONAMIA. *Crosier Priory* (1922) *Crosier Priory of the Holy Cross*, 104 Crosier Dr. N., P.O. Box 500, 56359. Tel: 320-532-3103; Fax: 320-532-5222. Email: info@crosier.org. Web: www.crosier.org. Very Rev. Kermit Holl, O.S.C., Prior; Revs. Thomas Carkhuff, O.S.C.; John J. Fleischhacker, O.S.C.; David Gallus, O.S.C.; Edward Greiwe, O.S.C.; Clement N. Gustin, O.S.C.; John Hawkins, O.S.C.; Charles Kunkel, O.S.C.; Ernest Martello, O.S.C.; James Moeglein, O.S.C.; Virgil Petermeier, O.S.C.; Eugene D. Plaisted, O.S.C.; Gregory Poser, O.S.C.; James H. Remmerswaal, O.S.C.; Jerome Schik, O.S.C.; Oscar Schoenberg, O.S.C.; Raymond Steffes, O.S.C.; Jude Verley, O.S.C.

Crosier Fathers of Onamia, The National Shrine of St. Odilia is sponsored and maintained by the Crosier Fathers of Onamia Priests in Residence 18; Priests Elsewhere 4; Brothers in Residence 10. Priests Elsewhere: Revs. James Cashman, O.S.C.; Bernard Mischke, O.S.C.; Adrian Piotrowski, O.S.C.; John Vincent, O.S.C.

[J] CONVENTS AND RESIDENCES FOR SISTERS

LITTLE FALLS. *St. Francis Convent* (1891) 116 Eighth Ave., S.E., 56345. Tel: 320-632-2981; Fax: 320-632-6313. Email: info@fslf.org. Web: www.fslf.org. Sr. Beatrice Eichten, O.S.F., Community Min. Motherhouse of Franciscan Sisters of Little Falls, MN. Sisters 68; Total in Community 163.

Franciscan Life Center Sr. Bernice Rieland, O.S.F., Contact Person.

SAINT JOSEPH. *St. Benedict's Monastery* (1857) 104 Chapel Ln., 56374-0220. Tel: 320-363-7100; Fax: 320-363-7130. Email: dmanuel@csbsju.edu. Web: www.sbm.osb.org. Sisters Michaela Hedican, O.S.B., M.A. Theology, Prioress; Elaine Schroeder, O.S.B., Coord. Eucharistic Presiders. Motherhouse and Formation House for Sisters of the Order of Saint Benedict. Sisters 150; Total in Community 280.

SAUK RAPIDS. *St. Clare's Monastery* (1923) Major Papal Cloister, 421 4th St. S., 56379. Tel: 320-251-3556; Fax: 320-203-7052. Sr. Mary Matthew, O.S.C., Abbess. Franciscan Poor Clare Nuns. Cloistered Nuns: Solemn Professed 17; Extern Sisters: Perpetual Professed 1.

[K] RETREAT HOUSES

ST. FRANCIS. *Pacem in Terris Center for Spirituality*, Mailing Address: *Hermitage Retreats*, P.O. Box 418, 55070. Tel: 763-444-6408; Fax: 763-444-9649. Email: alain@paceminterris.org. Shirley Wanchena, Dir.

[L] NEWMAN CENTERS

ST. CLOUD. *Newman Center, Inc.* 396 First Ave. S., 56301. Tel: 320-251-3260; Fax: 320-252-3930. Email: newmancenter@charterinternet.com. Web: scsucatholicorg. Rev. Anthony Oelrich, S.T.L., Admin.

MORRIS. *Newman Catholic Student Center* 306 E. Fourth St., 56267. Tel: 320-589-1947. Email: newman@hometownsolutions.net. Web: www.mrs.umn.edu/~catholic. Scott Crumb, Dir. Campus Ministry.

[M] MISCELLANEOUS

ST. CLOUD. *Affordable Community Housing, Inc.*, P.O. Box 2390, 56303. Tel: 320-229-4576. Harvey Schmitt, Dir. Housing; Mr. Steven P. Bresnahan, Exec. Dir.

Carmelite Hermits of Adoration, Inc. (1986) 1810 Minnesota Blvd. S.E., 56304. Tel: 320-252-0010. Sr. Imelda, Prioress. Sisters 2.

Central Minnesota Residents Encountering Christ (1998) 6667 County Rd. 91 SE, 56304. Tel: 320-251-0098. Email: ccarolt@yahoo.com. Carol Tembreull, Prog. Coord.

Domus Transitional Housing, 17 S. 19 1/2 Ave., 56301. Mr. Steven P. Bresnahan, Exec. Dir.; Harvey Schmitt, Contact Person.

Key Row Community, Inc., 700-790 S. 14th St., 56301. Tel: 320-229-4576. 157 Roosevelt Rd., Ste. 200, 56301. Mr. Steven P. Bresnahan, Exec. Dir.; Harvey Schmitt, Contact Person. Providing low-cost housing to elderly and families in Morris and St. Cloud.

BROWNS VALLEY. **Browns Valley Health Center*, 114 Jefferson St. S., 56219. Tel: 320-695-2165; Fax: 320-695-2166. Email: cward@bvhc.sfhs.org. Capacity 41.

Valley Vista Apartments of Browns Valley Inc., 317 S.W. 2nd Ave., 56219. 157 Roosevelt Rd., Ste. 200, Saint Cloud, 56301.

CAMBRIDGE. *Benedictine Care Centers* (Includes: St. Brigid's at Hi-Park and The Villa at Hi-Park, Red Wing, MN; St. Isidore Health Center of Greenwood Prairie and Green Prairie Place, Plainview, MN.; Benedictine Health Center at Innsbruck, New Brighton, MN; St. Eligius Health Center, Duluth, MN), 1995 E. Rum River Dr. S., 55008. Tel: 763-689-1162; Fax: 763-689-1197. Dale M. Thompson, Pres. & CEO.

Benedictine Health Dimensions, Inc., 1995 E. Rum River Dr., S., 55008. Tel: 763-689-1162; Fax: 763-689-1197. Email: webmaster@bhshealth.org. Web: www.bhshealth.org. Dale M. Thompson, Pres. & CEO.

LITTLE FALLS. *Key Row Little Falls, Inc.*, 905 N.E. 6th Ave., 56345. 157 Roosevelt Rd., Ste. 200, Saint Cloud, 56301. Harvey Schmitt, Dir. Housing & Contact Person.

MELROSE. *Rose Mill Apartments, LLC*, 407 E. 5th St. N., 56352. 157 Roosevelt Rd., Ste. 200, Saint Cloud, 56301. Mr. Steven P. Bresnahan, Exec. Dir.; Harvey Schmitt, Dir. Housing Svcs.

MILACA. *Key Row Milaca, Inc.*, 410 N.W. 4th Ave., 56353. Tel: 320-229-4576; Fax: 320-253-7464. 157 Roosevelt Rd., Ste. 200, Saint Cloud, 56301. Harvey Schmitt, Dir. Housing & Contact Person.

MORRIS. *St. Francis Health Services* (1984) 801 Nevada, Ste. 100, 56267. Tel: 320-589-2004; Fax: 320-589-1270. Email: lhoffman@sfhs.org. Web: www.sfhs.org.

Prairie Community Services (1987) 801 Nevada Ave., P.O. Box 468, 56267. Tel: 320-589-3077; Fax: 320-589-2543. Web: www.pcs.sfhs.org.

Key Row Community, Inc., 151 Sunnyslope Rd., Bldgs. 301, 306, 311, 318, 324, 56267. Tel: 320-589-4661; Fax: 320-589-4661.

ONAMIA. *National Shrine of St. Odilia Crosier Priory of the Holy Cross*, P.O. Box 500, 56359-0500. Tel: 320-532-3103; Fax: 320-532-5222. Email: info@crosier.org. Web: www.crosier.org. Bro. Albert Becker, O.S.C., Contact Person & Dir. Devel. Sponsored and maintained by Crosier Fathers of Onamia.

RICHMOND. *Maple Apartments of Richmond , Inc.*, 488 1st St., N.E., 56368. Tel: 320-229-4576; Fax: 320-253-7464. 157 Roosevelt Rd., Ste. 200, Saint Cloud, 56301. Mr. Steven P. Bresnahan, Exec. Dir.; Harvey Schmitt, Dir. Housing Svcs.

SAINT JOSEPH. *Monastic Interreligious Dialogue*, St. Benedict's Monastery, 104 Chapel Ln., 56374-2020. Tel: 320-363-7187; Fax: 320-363-7173. Email: khoward@csbsju.edu. Web: www.monasticdialog.org. Sr. Katherine Howard, O.S.B., Contact Person.

St. Joseph's Apartment, Inc., 410 W. Minnesota St., 56374. 157 Roosevelt Rd., Ste. 200, 56301. Mr. Steven P. Bresnahan, Exec. Dir.; Harvey Schmitt, Dir. Housing Svcs.

SAUK CENTRE. *Sauk Centre Apts.*, 217 Railroad Ave. Ct., 56378. 157 Roosevelt Rd., Ste. 200, Saint Cloud, 56301. Mr. Steven P. Bresnahan, Exec. Dir.; Harvey Schmitt, Dir. Housing Svcs. & Contact Person.

RELIGIOUS INSTITUTES OF MEN REPRESENTED IN THE DIOCESE

For further details refer to the corresponding bracketed number in the Religious Institutes of Men or Women section.

[0200]—*Benedictine Monks* (Collegeville, MN)—O.S.B.

[0400]—*Canons Regular of the Order of the Holy Cross* (Province of St. Odilia)—O.S.C.

[]—*Vincentian Congregation* (St. Joseph Prov.)—V.C.

RELIGIOUS INSTITUTES OF WOMEN REPRESENTED IN THE DIOCESE

[0230]—*Benedictine Sisters of Pontifical Jurisdiction*—O.S.B.

[1920]—*Congregation of the Sisters of the Holy Cross*—C.S.C.

[1310]—*Franciscan Sisters of Little Falls, Minnesota*—O.S.F.

[3760]—*Order of St. Clare*—O.S.C.

[2970]—*School Sisters of Notre Dame* (Northwestern Prov.)—S.S.N.D.

[1710]—*Sisters of St. Francis of Mary Immaculate*—O.S.F.

NECROLOGY

† Riley, Patrick, (Retired)—Died Dec. 14, 2010

An asterisk (*) denotes an organization that has established tax-exempt status directly with the IRS and is not covered by the USCCB Group Ruling.

Archdiocese of St. Louis

(Archidioecesis S. Ludovici)

Most Reverend

ROBERT JAMES CARLSON

Archbishop of St. Louis; ordained May 22, 1970; appointed Titular Bishop of Aviocala and Auxiliary Bishop of Saint Paul and Minneapolis November 22, 1983; consecrated January 11, 1984; appointed Coadjutor Bishop of Sioux Falls January 13, 1994; Succeeded to the See March 21, 1995; appointed Bishop of Saginaw December 29, 2004; installed February 24, 2005; appointed Archbishop of St. Louis April 21, 2009; installed June 10, 2009. *Office: 20 Archbishop May Dr., St. Louis, MO 63119-5738.*

20 Archbishop May Dr., St. Louis, MO 63119-5738. Tel: 314-792-7005; Fax: 314-792-7710.

Web: www.archstl.org

Email: communication@archstl.org

Most Reverend

EDWARD M. RICE, D.D.

Auxiliary Bishop of Saint Louis; ordained January 3, 1985; appointed Auxiliary Bishop of St. Louis and Titular Bishop of Sufes December 1, 2010; consecrated January 13, 2011. *Office: 20 Archbishop May Dr., St. Louis, MO 63119-5738.* Tel: 314-792-7000.

Most Reverend

ROBERT J. HERMANN, D.D.

Retired Auxiliary Bishop of St. Louis; ordained March 30, 1963; appointed Auxiliary Bishop of St. Louis October 16, 2002; ordained December 12, 2002; retired December 1, 2010. *Office: 20 Archbishop May Dr., St. Louis, MO 63119.*

Square Miles 5,968.

Diocese July 18, 1826; Archdiocese July 20, 1847.

Comprises that portion of the State of Missouri bounded on the north by the northern line of the County of Lincoln; on the west by the western lines of the Counties of Lincoln, Warren, Franklin and Washington; on the south by the southern lines of the Counties of Washington, St. Francois and Perry; on the east by the Mississippi River.

Heavenly Patrons--Saint Louis, King, Saint Vincent de Paul and Saint Rose Philippine Duchesne.

For legal titles of parishes and archdiocesan institutions, consult the Catholic Center.

STATISTICAL OVERVIEW

Personnel	
Archbishops	1
Auxiliary Bishops	1
Retired Bishops	1
Abbots	1
Retired Abbots	2
Priests: Diocesan Active in Diocese	237
Priests: Diocesan Active Outside Diocese	14
Priests: Diocesan in Foreign Missions	4
Priests: Retired, Sick or Absent	93
Number of Diocesan Priests	348
Religious Priests in Diocese	319
Total Priests in Diocese	667
Extern Priests in Diocese	16
Ordinations:	
Diocesan Priests	4
Religious Priests	6
Transitional Deacons	5
Permanent Deacons in Diocese	265
Total Brothers	132
Total Sisters	1,321
Parishes	
Parishes	188
With Resident Pastor:	
Resident Diocesan Priests	153
Resident Religious Priests	22
Without Resident Pastor:	
Administered by Priests	11
Administered by Deacons	2
Missions	8
Welfare	
Catholic Hospitals	9
Total Assisted	2,181,270
Homes for the Aged	12
Total Assisted	2,403
Residential Care of Children	2
Total Assisted	379
Day Care Centers	3
Total Assisted	26,159
Specialized Homes	11
Total Assisted	8,343
Special Centers for Social Services	14
Total Assisted	29,172
Other Institutions	1
Total Assisted	174,885
Educational	
Seminaries, Diocesan	2
Students from This Diocese	39
Students from Other Diocese	68
Diocesan Students in Other Seminaries	3
Seminaries, Religious	2
Students Religious	27
Total Seminarians	69
Colleges and Universities	2
Total Students	16,605
High Schools, Diocesan and Parish	12
Total Students	4,536
High Schools, Private	16
Total Students	8,259
Elementary Schools, Diocesan and Parish	107
Total Students	27,892
Elementary Schools, Private	8
Total Students	2,139
Non-residential Schools for the Disabled	4
Total Students	179
Catechesis/Religious Education:	
High School Students	93
Elementary Students	20,380
Total Students under Catholic Instruction	80,059
Teachers in the Diocese:	
Priests	33
Brothers	21
Sisters	79
Lay Teachers	3,811
Vital Statistics	
Receptions into the Church:	
Infant Baptism Totals	5,454
Minor Baptism Totals	359
Adult Baptism Totals	272
Received into Full Communion	449
First Communions	6,271
Confirmations	6,651
Marriages:	
Catholic	1,278
Interfaith	627
Total Marriages	1,905
Deaths	3,995
Total Catholic Population	524,507
Total Population	2,211,707

Former Bishops—Most Revs. LOUIS WILLIAM VALENTINE DUBOURG, Archbishop of the Cardinalatial See of Besancon; ord. 1788; cons. in Rome, Sept. 24, 1815, Bishop of Louisiana, Upper and Lower, took his first residential seat in St. Louis, Jan. 6, 1818. On July 18, 1826, the Diocese of Louisiana was divided and the Sees of St. Louis and New Orleans erected. Bishop DuBourg having resigned the See of Louisiana, was transferred to the Diocese of Montauban in France, Aug. 13, 1826, and made Archbishop of the Cardinalatial See of Besancon, Feb. 15, 1833, where he died Dec. 12 of the same year; JOSEPH ROSATI, C.M., Bishop of St. Louis; born Jan. 12, 1789 in Lazio, Italy; ord. Feb. 10, 1811; cons. Bishop of the Titular See of Tenagra and constituted Coadjutor of Bishop DuBourg of Louisiana at Donaldsville, LA, March 25, 1824. When the See of Louisiana was divided Bishop Rosati was made Bishop of St. Louis and Administrator of New Orleans. He died while on business in Rome on Sept. 25, 1843; PETER RICHARD KENRICK, D.D., Archbishop of St. Louis; born Aug. 17, 1806 in Dublin, Ireland; ord. March 6, 1832; cons. Nov. 30, 1841, Bishop of Drasa and Coadjutor to Bishop of St. Louis; Succeeded as Bishop Sept. 25, 1843; appt. Archbishop of St. Louis July 12, 1847; retired May 21, 1895; died March 4, 1896; JOHN JOSEPH KAIN, D.D., Archbishop of St. Louis; born May 31, 1841 in Martinsburg, Virginia; ord. July 2, 1866; cons. Bishop of Wheeling, WV on May 23, 1875; Titular Archbishop of Oxyrynchia and Coadjutor "cum jure successionis" of Archbishop of St. Louis, 1893; Administrator of Archdiocese of St. Louis, Dec. 14, 1893; created Archbishop of St. Louis on May 21, 1895; died Oct. 13, 1903; His Eminence JOHN CARDINAL GLENNON, D.D., Archbishop of St. Louis; born June 14, 1862; ord. Dec. 20, 1884; appt. Titular Bishop of Pinara and Coadjutor to the Bishop of Kansas City, March 14, 1896; cons. June 29, 1896; transferred to St. Louis, April 27, 1903, as Coadjutor to the Archbishop of St. Louis "cum jure successionis"; Archbishop of St. Louis, Oct. 13, 1903; Pallium received May 14, 1905; Assistant at the Pontifical Throne, June 21, 1921; created Cardinal Priest, Feb. 18, 1946; died March 9, 1946; JOSEPH CARDINAL RITTER, D.D., Archbishop of St. Louis; born July 20, 1892; ord.

May 30, 1917; appt. Titular Bishop of Hippo, Feb. 3, 1933 and Auxiliary Bishop of Indianapolis; cons. March 28, 1933; appt. Archbishop of Indianapolis, Nov. 11, 1944; appt. Archbishop of St. Louis, July 20, 1946 assistant at the Pontifical Throne, Oct. 5, 1956; created Cardinal, Priest Jan. 16, 1961; died June 10, 1967; JOHN JOSEPH CARDINAL CARBERRY, D.D., S.T.D., J.C.D., Ph.D., Archbishop of St. Louis; born July 31, 1904 in Brooklyn, New York; ord. July 28, 1929; appt. Titular Bishop of Elis and Coadjutor of Lafayette in Indiana, May 3, 1956; cons. July 25, 1956; Succeeded to See, Nov. 20, 1957; transferred to Columbus, Jan. 16, 1965; appt. Archbishop of St. Louis, Feb. 17, 1968; installed March 25, 1968; created Cardinal, April 28, 1969; retired July 31, 1979; died June 17, 1998; Most Rev. JOHN L. MAY, D.D., Archbishop of St. Louis; born March 31, 1922 in Evanston, Illinois; ord. May 3, 1947; appt. Auxiliary Bishop of Chicago, June 21, 1967; cons. Aug. 24, 1967; transferred to Mobile, Oct. 8, 1969; installed as Bishop of Mobile, Dec. 10, 1969; appt. Archbishop of St. Louis, Jan. 29, 1980; installed March 25, 1980; resigned Dec. 9, 1992; died March 24, 1994; His Eminence JUSTIN CARDINAL RIGALI, J.C.D., Archbishop of St. Louis; born April 19, 1935; ord. April 25, 1961; appt. Titular Archbishop of Bolsena, June 8, 1985; cons. Sept. 14, 1985; appointed Archbishop of St. Louis, Jan. 25, 1994; installed March 15, 1994; Pallium received June 29, 1994; transferred to Archdiocese of Philadelphia, July 15, 2003; created Cardinal, Sept. 28, 2003; installed as Archbishop of Philadelphia, Oct. 7, 2003; retired July 19, 2011; RAYMOND L. BURKE, D.D., J.C.D., born June 30, 1948 in Richland Center, Wisconsin; ord. June 29, 1975; appt. to the Residential See of La Crosse Dec. 10, 1994; cons. Jan. 6, 1995; installed as Eighth Bishop of La Crosse Feb. 22, 1995; appt. Archbishop of St. Louis Dec. 2, 2003; installed Jan. 26, 2004; appt. Prefect of the Apostolic Signatura June 27, 2008; created Cardinal Nov. 20, 2010.

Vicars General—Most Revs. EDWARD M. RICE; ROBERT J. HERMANN, D.D. (Retired); Rev. Msgr. MARK S. RIVITUSO, J.C.L., M.C.L., M.A., M.Div.

Office of Child and Youth Protection—Deacon PHILIP R. HENGEN, 20 Archbishop May Dr., St. Louis, 63119. Tel: 314-792-7704.

Chancellor—Ms. NANCY J. WERNER, 20 Archbishop May Dr., St. Louis, 63119. Tel: 314-792-7836; Fax: 314-792-7842.

Chancellor for Canonical Affairs—Rev. Msgr. JEROME D. BILLING, S.T.L., J.C.L., 20 Archbishop May Dr., St. Louis, 63119. Tel: 314-792-7408; Fax: 314-792-7401.

Vice Chancellor for Special Projects—Mrs. JENNIFER STANARD.

Master of Ceremonies—Rev. BRIAN R. FISCHER.

Archdiocesan Master of Ceremonies—Rev. JOSEPH XIU HUI JIANG.

Metropolitan Tribunal—20 Archbishop May Dr., St. Louis, 63119. Tel: 314-792-7400; Fax: 314-792-7401.

Judicial Vicar—Rev. Msgr. JOHN B. SHAMLEFFER, J.C.L., M.C.L., M.A., M.Div.

Adjutant Judicial Vicars—Revs. DENNIS M. DOYLE, J.C.L.; NICHOLAS E. KASTENHOLZ, J.C.L.

Defender of the Bond—Rev. Msgr. JEROME D. BILLING, S.T.L., J.C.L.

Judges—Revs. DENNIS M. DOYLE, J.C.L.; NICHOLAS E. KASTENHOLZ, J.C.L.; Deacon J. GERARD QUINN.

Promoter of Justice—Rev. Msgr. JEROME D. BILLING, S.T.L., J.C.L.

Notaries—Mrs. ANN MERTEN; Mrs. PATRICIA LANASA.

Missouri Appellate Tribunal—20 Archbishop May Dr., St. Louis, 63119. Tel: 314-792-7167.

Judicial Vicar—Rev. JOACHIM CULOTTA, O.P., J.C.D.

Archdiocesan Consultors—Most Rev. ROBERT J. HERMANN, D.D. (Retired); Rev. Msgrs. JOHN B. SHAMLEFFER, J.C.L., M.C.L., M.A., M.Div.; JOHN J. LEYKAM, V.F.; VERNON E. GARDIN, Ph.D.; JOHN J. BRENNELL; MICHAEL DIECKMANN; Rev. JOHN M. SEPER.

Deaneries/Deans—Rev. GARY M. MEIER, V.F., North City - St. Louis; Rev. Msgr. MICHAEL E. TUREK, V.F., South City - St. Louis; Very Revs. JAMES M. MITULSKI, Northeast County; CHARLES E. BURGOON, Northwest County; Rev. Msgrs. JOHN J. LEYKAM, V.F., Southwest County; JAMES T. TELTHORST, V.F., Southeast County; Very Rev. JOSEPH E. WORMEK, V.F., Festus; Rev. Msgrs. TED L. WOJCICKI, Ed.D., V.F., St. Charles; MATTHEW M. MITAS, Washington; Very Rev. ANTHONY A. DATTILO, V.F., Ste. Genevieve.

Chief Financial Officer—Deacon C. FRANK CHAUVIN.

Chief Operating Officer—Dr. DAVID MUECKL, Ph.D.

Archdiocesan Offices and Directors

Archdiocesan Archives—Rev. Msgr. JEROME D. BILLING, S.T.L., J.C.L., Chancellor for Canonical Affairs; AUDREY POWDERLY-NEWCOMER, Archivist, 20 Archbishop May Dr., St. Louis, 63119. Tel: 314-792-7020; Fax: 314-792-7029.

Catholic Family Counseling—MARY CAROLE CURRAN, Exec. Dir., 9200 Watson Rd., G101, Saint Louis, 63126. Tel: 314-544-3800; Fax: 314-843-0552 See MISCELLANEOUS section for more information.

Catholic Family Tuition—20 Archbishop May Dr., St. Louis, 63119.

Annual Catholic Appeal—Mr. BRIAN NIEBRUGGE, Dir., 20 Archbishop May Dr., St. Louis, 63119. Tel: 314-792-7680; Fax: 314-792-7699. See MISCELLANEOUS section for more information.

Catholic Relief Services—Mrs. JENNIFER STANARD, 20 Archbishop May Dr., St. Louis, 63119. Tel: 314-792-7812.

Catholic Cemeteries of St. Louis—Rev. Msgr. DENNIS M. DELANEY, Dir., 5239 W. Florissant Ave., Saint Louis, 63115. Tel: 314-381-1313 See CEMETERIES section for more information.

Central Purchasing—Mr. DARREL KALBFLEISCH, Dir., 20 Archbishop May Dr., St. Louis, 63119. Tel: 314-792-7065; Fax: 314-792-7019.

Charismatic Renewal—Rev. Msgr. EDMUND O. GRIESEDIECK, Dir. (Retired), 10909 St. Henry Lane, Saint Ann, 63074. Tel: 314-427-7786.

Finance Office—20 Archbishop May Dr., St. Louis, 63119-5738. Tel: 314-792-7100.

Catholic Charities—Mr. BRIAN J. O'MALLEY, Pres., 4532 Lindell Blvd., St. Louis, 63108. Tel: 314-367-5500; Fax: 314-367-2982. Web: www.ccstl.org. See MISCELLANEOUS section for more information.

Cardinal Ritter Senior Services—Sr. SUZANNE WESLEY, C.S.J., COO, 7601 Watson Rd., St. Louis, 63119. Tel: 314-961-8000; Fax: 314-961-1934. Email: swesley@ccstl.org. See SERVICES FOR THE ELDERLY section for more information.

Archdiocesan Deaf Ministry—VACANT, Dir., 309 E. Hoffmeister Ave., Saint Louis, 63125. Teletype: 314-727-2747; Tel: 314-631-0691 See MISCELLANEOUS section for more information.

Office of Information Technology—PAUL GILJUM, Dir., 20 Archbishop May Dr., St. Louis, 63119. Tel: 314-792-7570; Fax: 314-792-7579.

Office for Ecumenical & Interreligious Affairs—LAWRENCE J. WELCH, Ph.D., Dir., 20 Archbishop May Dr., St. Louis, 63119. Tel: 314-792-7060; Fax: 314-792-7164.

Office of Consecrated Life—Sr. MARY CHARLES MAYER, R.S.M., Dir., 20 Archbishop May Dr., St. Louis, 63119. Tel: 314-792-7250.

Fleur de Lis—20 Archbishop May Dr., St. Louis, 63119.

Archdiocesan Office of Worship—Rev. Msgr. WILLIAM W. MCCUMBER, M.A.L., 20 Archbishop May Dr., St. Louis, 63119. Tel: 314-792-7230; Fax: 314-792-7019.

Archdiocesan Commission for Sacred Liturgy—Sr. CATHY DOHERTY, S.S.N.D., Chm.

Archdiocesan Commission for Sacred Music—Mr. JEFF BUSH, Chm.

Archdiocesan Commission for Sacred Art and Architecture—Mr. ROBERT BARRINGER, Chm.

Council of Catholic Youth—Rev. Msgr. JOHN J. BORCIC, Exec. Dir., 20 Archbishop May Dr., St. Louis, 63119. Tel: 314-792-7612; Fax: 314-792-7619.

Holy Childhood, Pontifical Association—Rev. Msgr. FRANCIS X. BLOOD, Dir., 20 Archbishop May Dr., St. Louis, 63119. Tel: 314-792-7655; Fax: 314-792-7669.

Holy Name Society—Mr. NICK PFISTER, Archdiocesan Pres., Mailing Address: Holy Name Society, P.O. Box 190435, St. Louis, 63119-6435. Tel: 314-428-9073.

Human Resources—Mr. KEVIN J. LOOS, Mng. Dir., 20 Archbishop May Dr., St. Louis, 63119. Tel: 314-792-7542.

Latin American Apostolate, Archdiocese of St. Louis—Rev. Msgr. FRANCIS X. BLOOD, Dir., 20 Archbishop May Dr., St. Louis, 63119. Tel: 314-792-7655; Fax: 314-792-7669.

The Legion of Mary—336 E. Ripa Ave., Saint Louis, 63125. Spiritual Directors: Revs. DAVID L. WICHLAN; EDWARD J. HILGEMAN (Retired).

Pan y Amor—Rev. Msgr. FRANCIS X. BLOOD, Dir., 20 Archbishop May Dr., St. Louis, 63119. Tel: 314-792-7655; Fax: 314-792-7669.

Archdiocesan Newspaper "The St. Louis Review"—Rev. Msgr. JOSEPH D. PINS, Theological Consultant; TEAK PHILLIPS, Editor, 20 Archbishop May Dr., St. Louis, 63119. Tel: 314-792-7500; Fax: 314-792-7534.

Pastoral Planning, Office of—Mr. JOHN SCHWOB. Tel: 314-792-7237.

Archdiocesan Office of Stewardship & Development—Mr. BRIAN NIEBRUGGE, Exec. Dir., 20 Archbishop May Dr., St. Louis, 63119-5004. Tel: 314-792-7210.

Archdiocesan Planned Giving and Endowment Council— See MISCELLANEOUS section for more information.

Priests' Mutual Benefit/Risk Management—BOB RYAN, Dir.; Mr. FRED J. HUMMEL, Admin., 20 Archbishop May Dr., St. Louis, 63119. Tel: 314-792-7200; Fax: 314-792-7209.

Priests' Purgatorial Society—Rev. Msgr. JEROME D. BILLING, S.T.L., J.C.L., Pres.

Respect Life Apostolate—Mrs. BETH LAUVER, Dir., 20 Archbishop May Dr., St. Louis, 63119. Tel: 314-792-7555; Fax: 314-792-7569.

Project Rachel—20 Archbishop May Dr., St. Louis, 63119.

Regina Cleri—Ms. NANCY BRYANT, Admin., 10 Archbishop May Dr., St. Louis, 63119. Tel: 314-968-2240; Fax: 314-968-1049.

Society for the Propagation of the Faith—Rev. Msgr. FRANCIS X. BLOOD, Dir., 20 Archbishop May Dr., St. Louis, 63119. Tel: 314-792-7655; Fax: 314-792-7669.

Building and Real Estate—THOMAS W. RICHTER, P.E., Dir., 20 Archbishop May Dr., Saint Louis, 63119. Tel: 314-792-7002.

Today and Tomorrow Educational Foundation—Ms. SHARON GERKEN, Exec. Dir., 20 Archbishop May Dr., St. Louis, 63119. Tel: 314-792-7620; Fax: 314-792-7629.

Criminal Justice Ministry—Sr. CARLEEN RECK, S.S.N.D., Dir., 4127 Forest Park Ave., Saint Louis, 63108. Tel: 314-241-8062; Fax: 314-531-6712.

Office of Communications—Mrs. KATHLEEN PESHA, Dir., 20 Archbishop May Dr., St. Louis, 63119. Tel: 314-792-7172.

Office of Marketing—Ms. ELIZABETH WESTHOFF, Dir., 20 Archbishop May Dr., St. Louis, 63119. Tel: 314-792-7635.

Society of St. Vincent de Paul, Council of St. Louis—Rev. JAMES CORMACK, C.M., Spiritual Advisor; Mr. JOSEPH KOMADINA, Pres., 4127 Forest Park Ave., St. Louis, 63108. Tel: 314-521-2183; Fax: 314-531-6712 See MISCELLANEOUS section for more information.

Society of St. Vincent de Paul, Council of the United States--(Territory: United States)—SHEILA K. GILBERT, Natl. Pres.; ROGER T. PLAYWIN, Natl. Exec. Dir., 58 Progress Pkwy., St. Louis, 63043-3706. Tel: 314-576-3993; Fax: 314-576-6755 See MISCELLANEOUS section for more information.

Schools/Catholic Education Office—Mr. GEORGE HENRY, Supt., 4445 Lindell Blvd., Saint Louis, 63108. Tel: 314-792-7300; Fax: 314-792-7399 See SCHOOLS section for more information.

St. Louis Roman Catholic Theological Seminaries, Inc.—Rev. Msgr. JEROME D. BILLING, S.T.L., J.C.L., Sec., 20 Archbishop May Dr., St. Louis, 63119. Tel: 314-633-2261.

Kenrick-Glennon Seminary— (St. Louis Roman Catholic Theological Seminary-Kenrick School of Theology) Rev. JOHN HORN, S.J., Pres. & Rector.

Cardinal Glennon College—Rev. JOHN HORN, S.J., Pres. & Rector, 5200 Glennon Dr., St. Louis, 63119. Tel: 314-792-6100; Fax: 314-792-6500 See SEMINARIES section for more information.

Office of Vocations—Rev. CHRISTOPHER M. MARTIN, Dir., 5200 Glennon Dr., St. Louis, 63119. Tel: 314-792-6460; Fax: 314-792-6502.

Archdiocesan Council of Priests—Rev. JEFFREY G. VOMUND, Chm.

Office of Priests' Personnel and Continuing Formation of Priests—Rev. Msgr. RICHARD E. HANNEKE, Dir., 20 Archbishop May Dr., St. Louis, 63119. Tel: 314-792-7550; Fax: 314-792-7554.

Archdiocesan Office of Urban and Community Affairs—Rev. Msgr. SALVATORE E. POLIZZI, Dir.; LOUIS G. BERRA, Consultor, 6052 Waterman, St. Louis, 63112. Tel: 314-721-6340; Fax: 314-721-1656.

Archdiocesan Office of the Permanent Diaconate—Rev. MICHAEL J. WITT, Dir.; Rev. Msgr. JOHN J. BORCIC, Spiritual Dir. Formation; Deacon CHRISTOPHER M. AST, Assoc. Dir., Deacon Formation; Ms. SUE CURRAN, Sec., 20 Archbishop May Dr., St. Louis, 63119. Tel: 314-633-2530; Fax: 314-633-2539.

Office of Apostolic Services—Mr. GEORGE KERRY, Interim Dir., 20 Archbishop May Dr., St. Louis, 63119-5738. Tel: 314-792-7180; Fax: 314-792-7199.

Blessed John XXIII Center—8300 Morganford Rd., St. Louis, 63123-6815. Tel: 314-633-2600; Fax: 314-633-2529.

Cardinal Rigali Center—STEPHEN LUDWIG, Bldg. Admin., 20 Archbishop May Dr., St. Louis, 63119. Tel: 314-792-7000; Fax: 314-792-7019.

Office of Youth Ministry—Rev. Msgr. JOHN J. BORCIC, Exec. Dir.; Rev. BRIAN R. FISCHER, Part-Time Dir.

Victim Assistance Coordinator—Mrs. CAROL BRESCIA.

CLERGY, PARISHES, MISSIONS AND PAROCHIAL SCHOOLS

CITY OF ST. LOUIS

ST. LOUIS COUNTY

1—CATHEDRAL BASILICA OF SAINT LOUIS (1896) Rev. Msgr. Joseph D. Pins, Rector; Rev. Joseph Xiu Hui Jiang.
4431 Lindell Blvd., 63108. Email: parish@cathedralstl.org. Web: www.cathedralstl.org. In Res., Most Rev. Robert J. Hermann, Auxiliary Bishop (Retired).
School—(Grades PreSchool-8) Tel: 314-373-8250; Fax: 314-373-8289. Sr. Kathleen Donovan, S.S.N.D., Prin. Lay Teachers 10; Students 136.

2—ST. AGATHA PARISH, POLISH ROMAN CATHOLIC CHURCH (1871), (Polish), Rev. Czeslaw Litak.
Mailing Address: 3239 S. Ninth St., Saint Louis, 63118. Tel: 314-772-1603; Fax: 314-772-3979. Email: parishoffice@polishchurchstlouis.org. Web: www.polishchurchstlouis.org.

3—ST. ALBAN ROE (1980) Rev. Msgr. Gregory R. Mikesch; Rev. Mark A. Chrismer; Deacons Mark A. Guilford; Norman Nuelle, (Retired); Frank Vonesh. In Res., Rev. Msgr. William A. Drennan (Retired).
Res.: 2001 Shepard Rd., Wildwood, 63038. Tel: 636-458-2977; Fax: 636-405-1276. Web: www.stalbanroe.org/site.
School—2005 Shepard Rd., Wildwood, 63038. Tel: 636-458-6084. Mary Chrapek, Prin. Religious 3; Lay Teachers 23; Students 495.
Catechesis/Religious Program—Tel: 636-458-2460; Fax: 636-405-3026. Email: slowery@stalbanroe.org. Sarah Lowery, C.R.E. Students 541.

4—ALL SAINTS (1901) Rev. Michael Witt; Deacon Stephen L. Murray.
Res.: 6403 Clemens Ave., University City, 63130. Tel: 314-721-6403; Fax: 314-659-9799. Email: all_saintschurch@sbcglobal.net.
Catechesis/Religious Program—Students 11.

5—ALL SOULS (1906) Rev. Robert W. Burkemper; Deacon Samuel Lee.
Res.: 9550 Tennyson Ave., Overland, 63114. Tel: 314-427-0442; Fax: 314-427-3872.
Catechesis/Religious Program—Students 28.
Convent—9600 Tennyson Ave., Overland, 63114. Tel: 314-427-3413.

6—ST. ALOYSIUS (SPANISH LAKE) (1871) Closed. For inquiries regarding sacramental records, contact the Archdiocesan Archives, 20 Archbishop May Dr., Saint Louis, MO 63119.

7—ST. ALOYSIUS GONZAGA (1892) Closed. For inquiries regarding sacramental records, contact the Archdiocesan Archives, 20 Archbishop May Dr., Saint Louis, MO 63119.

8—ST. ALPHONSUS LIGUORI (1867) Revs. Matthew S. Bonk, C.Ss.R.; The Joseph Pham, C.Ss.R.; Bro. Terrence Burke, C.Ss.R. In Res., Rev. David Polek, C.Ss.R.; Deacons Richard W. Fischer, C.Ss.R.; Kyle Fisher, C.Ss.R.
Res.: 1118 N. Grand Blvd., 63106. Tel: 314-533-0304; Fax: 314-533-4260.
Catechesis/Religious Program—Ms. Donna Lane, D.R.E.

9—ST. AMBROSE (1903) Rev. Msgr. Vincent R. Bommarito; Rev. Jason J. Schumer; Deacons John J. Stoverink; Daniel J. Tracy Sr.
Res.: 5130 Wilson Ave., 63110. Tel: 314-771-1228; Fax: 314-771-0454.
School—(Grades K-8), 5110 Wilson Ave., 63110. Tel: 314-772-1437; Fax: 314-771-4560. Sr. Carol Sansone, A.S.C.J., Prin. Sisters (Apostles of the Sacred Heart of Jesus) 4; Lay Teachers 22; Students 300.
Catechesis/Religious Program—Tel: 314-771-5298. Students 332.

10—ST. ANDREW (1905) Rev. Aaron Arce, O.P., Sacramental Min.; Deacon C. Allen Boedeker, Admin.
Res.: 309 Hoffmeister Ave., 63125-1609. Tel: 314-631-0691; Fax: 314-631-0692.
Catechesis/Religious Program—Mrs. Mary Boedeker, D.R.E. Students 66.
Convent—Sisters of Notre Dame, 232 Hoffmeister Ave., 63125. Tel: 314-631-2010.

11—ST. ANDREW KIM (2001), (Korean), Rev. Park Chi Young, Admin.
Church: 8665 Olive Blvd., University City, 63132. Tel: 314-993-1277; Fax: 314-993-2031.

12—ST. ANGELA MERICI (1962) Rev. Thomas G. Keller; Deacon Ronald S. Le Fors.
Res.: 14005 Davey Dr., Florissant, 63034. Tel: 314-838-6565; Fax: 314-838-6566.
School—(Grades K-8), 3860 N. Hwy. 67, Florissant, 63034. Tel: 314-831-8012. Lay Teachers 17; Students 256.

13—ST. ANN (1856) [CEM] Rev. William G. Kempf.
Res.: 7530 Natural Bridge Rd., Normandy, 63121. Tel: 314-385-5090; Fax: 314-385-6527.
School—(Grades K-8), 7532 Natural Bridge, Normandy, 63121. Tel: 314-381-0113; Fax: 314-381-1367. Mary Jo Reichenbach, Prin. Lay Teachers 13; Students 160.
Catechesis/Religious Program—

14—ST. ANN, MOTHER B.V.M., Closed. For inquiries regarding sacramental records, contact the Archdiocesan Archives, 20 Archbishop May Dr., Saint Louis, MO 63119.

15—ANNUNCIATION (1950) Rev. Robert T. Evans. In Res., Rev. John J. Ghio (Retired).
Res.: 12 W. Glendale Rd., Webster Groves, 63119. Tel: 314-962-5955; Fax: 314-961-0643. Email: parishsecretary@goannunciation.com. Web: www.goannunciation.com.
School—(Grades K-8), 16 W. Glendale, Webster Groves, 63119. Tel: 314-961-7712; Fax: 314-961-2157. Mr. Michael Biggs, Prin. Lay Teachers 14; Students 124.
Catechesis/Religious Program—Email: mkelly-creannunciation@hotmail.com. Students 98.

16—ST. ANSELM (1966) Revs. Gerard Garrigan, O.S.B.; R. Benedict Allin, O.S.B.; Deacons Steven H. Wohlert, Pastoral Assoc.; Charles Durban.
Res.: 530 S. Mason Rd., 63141. Tel: 314-878-2120; Fax: 314-878-2199. Email: parishoffice299@att.net. Web: www.stanselmstl.org.
Catechesis/Religious Program—Students 133.

17—ST. ANTHONY OF PADUA (1863) Revs. Michael Fowler, O.F.M.; Richard Jeske, O.F.M.; Bro. Thomas Smith, O.F.M., Pastoral Assoc.; Lisa Sieve, Bookkeeper.
Res.: 3140 Meramec St., 63118. Tel: 314-353-7470; Fax: 314-655-0573.
Catechesis/Religious Program—Tel: 314-655-0550. Students 38.

18—ASCENSION (1923) Rev. Msgr. Dennis R. Stehly; Rev. Brian E. Hecktor; Deacons C. Frank Chauvin; Robert Keeney; John Marino.
Res.: 230 Santa Maria Dr., Chesterfield, 63005. Tel: 636-532-3304; Fax: 636-532-3518. Web: ascensionchesterfield.org.
Preschool—Ascension Early Childhood Center, 238 Santa Maria Dr., Chesterfield, 63005. Tel: 636-532-3375.
School—(Grades K-8), 238 Santa Maria Dr., Chesterfield, 63005. Tel: 636-532-1151; Fax: 636-532-6502. Mrs. Cathie Wayland, Prin. Lay Teachers 31; Students 390.
Catechesis/Religious Program—Tel: 636-532-1136. Students 670.

19—ASCENSION-ST. PAUL (1995) Closed. For inquiries for sacramental records contact the Archdiocesan Archives, 20 Archbishop May Dr., St. Louis, MO 63119.

20—ASSUMPTION (1839) [CEM] Rev. John M. Seper.
Res.: 4725 Mattis Rd., 63128. Tel: 314-487-7970; Fax: 314-892-5513. Web: www.assumptionstl.org.
School—(Grades K-8) Tel: 314-487-6520; Fax: 314-487-3598. Email: hastenc@assumptionstl.org. Lay Teachers 20; Students 301.
Catechesis/Religious Program—Tel: 314-487-6520, Ext. 2219. Evelyn Tucker, C.R.E. (Adult); Donna Koppy, C.R.E. (Children). Students 205.

21—ST. AUGUSTINE (1992) [JC], Consolidation of St. Barbara, St. Rose of Lima, St. Edward, St. Mark, and Notre Dame de Lourdes (Wellston). Rev. Msgr. Robert J. Gettinger; Deacon Edward R. Grotpeter. 1371 Hamilton Ave., 63112. Tel: 314-385-1934; Fax: 314-385-2949.
Catechesis/Religious Program—Students 214.

22—ST. BARBARA, Closed. For inquiries regarding sacramental records, contact the Archdiocesan Archives, 20 Archbishop May Dr., Saint Louis, MO 63119.

23—ST. BARTHOLOMEW (HAZELWOOD) (1959) Closed. For inquiries regarding sacramental records, contact the Archdiocesan Archives, 20 Archbishop May Dr., Saint Louis, MO 63119.

24—BASILICA OF ST. LOUIS, KING OF FRANCE (1770) Rev. Msgr. Jerome D. Billing; Rev. Richard J. Quirk.
Res.: 209 Walnut St., 63102. Tel: 314-231-3250; Fax: 314-231-4280.

25—ST. BERNADETTE (1947) Rev. Gary J. Faust; Deacon Michael Buckley.
Res.: 68 Sherman Rd., Lemay, 63125. Tel: 314-892-6882; Fax: 314-892-7716. Email: stbrect@mindspring.com.
Catechesis/Religious Program—Tel: 314-892-8379. Students 21.

26—ST. BLAISE (MARYLAND HEIGHTS) (1961) Closed. For inquiries regarding sacramental records, contact the Archdiocesan Archives, 20 Archbishop May Dr., Saint Louis, MO 63119.

27—BLESSED TERESA OF CALCUTTA (2005) Revs. Robert T. Rosebrough; Timothy R. Cook; Deacons Charles R. Davanzo; Ralph Hayes; Allen F. Love.
Mailing Address: 1050 Smith Ave., Ferguson, 63135. Tel: 314-524-0500; Fax: 314-524-0744.
School—150 N. Elizabeth, Ferguson, 63135. Tel: 314-522-3888; Fax: 314-521-3173. Jennifer Stutsman, Prin.
Catechesis/Religious Program—Debbie Davisson, P.S.R. Dir. Students 45.

28—ST. BONIFACE (1859) Closed. For inquiries regarding sacramental records, contact the Archdiocesan Archives, 20 Archbishop May Dr., Saint Louis, MO 63119.

29—ST. BRIDGET OF ERIN (1853) Closed. For inquiries regarding sacramental records, contact the Archdiocesan Archives, 20 Archbishop May Dr., Saint Louis, MO 63119.

30—ST. CASIMIR (HATHAWAY MANOR), Closed. For inquiries regarding sacramental records, contact the Archdiocesan Archives, 20 Archbishop May Dr., Saint Louis, MO 63119.

31—ST. CATHERINE LABOURE (1953) Rev. James Cormack, C.M.; Deacons George Tichacek; John B. Wainscott.
Res.: 9740 Sappington Rd., 63128. Tel: 314-843-3245; Fax: 314-843-3196. Web: www.sclparish.org.
School—(Grades K-8), 9750 Sappington Rd., 63128. Tel: 314-843-2819; Fax: 314-843-7687. Mrs. Peggy Visconti, Prin. Lay Teachers 27; Students 513.
Catechesis/Religious Program—Tel: 314-843-2996. Peggy Brinkmann, D.R.E. Students 243.

32—ST. CATHERINE OF ALEXANDRIA (RIVERVIEW GARDENS) (1921) Closed. For inquiries regarding sacramental records, contact the Archdiocesan Archives, 20 Archbishop May Dr., Saint Louis, MO 63119.

33—ST. CATHERINE OF SIENA (PAGEDALE) (1909) Closed. For inquiries regarding sacramental records, contact the Archdiocesan Archives, 20 Archbishop May Dr., Saint Louis, MO 63119.

34—ST. CECILIA (1906), (Hispanic), Unassigned. In Res., Rev. Randall Soto.
Res.: 5418 Louisiana Ave., 63111. Tel: 314-351-1318; Fax: 314-351-3372.
Church: Eiler & Alaska Ave., 63111.
School—(Grades PreK-8), 906 Eichelberger Ave., 63111. Tel: 314-353-2455; Fax: 314-353-2411. Jim Ford, Prin. Lay Teachers 13; Students 212.
Catechesis/Religious Program—Students 136.

35—CHRIST THE KING (1927) Rev. Timothy M. Foley; Deacon E. Ray Kiely. In Res., Rev. John Jay Hughes (Retired).
Res.: 7316 Balson Ave., University City, 63130. Tel: 314-721-8737; Fax: 314-721-8738.
School—(Grades PreK-8), 7324 Balson Ave., University City, 63130. Tel: 314-725-5855; Fax: 314-725-5981. Mrs. Susan E. Hooker, Prin. Lay Teachers 15; Students 209.

36—CHRIST, PRINCE OF PEACE (1971) Rev. Charles Barthel; Deacon Joseph M. Kennedy.
Res.: 415 Weidman Rd., Manchester, 63011. Tel: 636-391-1307; Fax: 636-391-1319. Email: nzoia@christprinceofpeace.com. Web: www.christprinceofpeace.com.
School—(Grades K-8), 417 Weidman Rd., Manchester, 63011. Tel: 636-394-6840; Fax: 636-394-3860. Web: www.cpopschool.com. Marlise Albert, Prin. Lay Teachers 27; Students 337.
Catechesis/Religious Program—Tel: 636-391-1560. Email: caliperti@christprinceofpeace.com; caroldrecpop239@aol.com. Students 168.

37—ST. CHRISTOPHER (FLORISSANT) (1967) Closed. For inquiries regarding sacramental records, contact the Archdiocesan Archives, 20 Archbishop May Dr., Saint Louis, MO 63119.

38—CHURCH OF THE ANNUNZIATA (1929) Rev. Msgr. John J. Leykam; Rev. John A. Ditenhafer (Retired); Deacon Thomas J. Gottlieb.
Res.: 9305 Clayton Rd., Ladue, 63124. Tel: 314-993-4422; Fax: 314-994-7877.
Catechesis/Religious Program—Students 176.

39—ST. CLARE OF ASSISI (1963) Rev. Msgr. Kevin G. Callahan; Rev. James D. Theby; Deacon W. Alan Whitson. In Res., Rev. Patrick J. Christopher.
Res.: 15642 Clayton Rd., Ellisville, 63011. Tel: 636-394-7307; Fax: 636-394-6264. Email: assisi@swbell.net. Web: saintclareofassisi.org.
School—(Grades K-8), 15668 Clayton Rd., Ellisville, 63011. Tel: 636-227-8654; Fax: 636-394-0359. Mrs. Marie Sinnett, Prin. Lay Teachers 24; Students 428.
Catechesis/Religious Program—Tel: 636-394-4368; Fax: 636-591-0024. Mrs. Jerrie Coughlin, C.R.E. Students 318.

40—ST. CLEMENT (1952) Rev. Msgr. James E. Pieper; Rev. Rodger P. Fleming; Deacon Richard Vehige.
Res.: 1510 Bopp Rd., 63131. Tel: 314-965-0709; Fax: 314-965-1486. Email: saintclementrectory@yahoo.com.
School—(Grades K-8), 1508 Bopp Rd., 63131. Tel:

314-822-1903; Fax: 314-822-8371. Susan Cunningham, Prin. Lay Teachers 36; Students 315.
Catechesis/Religious Program— Mary Alice Helmsing, D.R.E. Students 120.

41—CORPUS CHRISTI (JENNINGS) (1915) Closed. For inquiries regarding sacramental records, contact the Archdiocesan Archives, 20 Archbishop May Dr., Saint Louis, MO 63119.

42—ST. CRONAN (1878) Rev. Gerald J. Kleba.
Res.: 1203 S. Boyle Ave., 63110. Tel: 314-289-9545; Fax: 314-535-1437.
Catechesis/Religious Program—Tel: 314-256-9350. Students 65.

43—CURE' OF ARS (1966) Rev. Msgr. Mark S. Rivituso; Deacons Patrick G. Monahan; Theodore J. Rodis.
Res.: 670 S. Laclede Station Rd., 63119. Tel: 314-962-5883; Fax: 314-968-3554.

44—ST. DISMAS (FLORISSANT) (1956) Closed. For inquiries regarding sacramental records, contact the Archdiocesan Archives, 20 Archbishop May Dr., Saint Louis, MO 63119.

45—ST. DOMINIC SAVIO (1956) Rev. Gerald A. Meier; Deacons James L. Murphy; John W. Beckmann, Pastoral Assoc.; John E. Hivner. In Res., Rev. Michael J. Lydon.
Res.: 6120 Pebble Hill Dr., Affton, 63123. Tel: 314-353-7629; Fax: 314-481-2908.
Church: 7748 MacKenzie Rd., Affton, 63123.
School—(Grades PreK-8) Tel: 314-832-4161; Fax: 314-352-6331. Kathy Wisemann, Prin. Lay Teachers 23; Students 326.
Catechesis/Religious Program—Students 104.

46—ST. EDWARD (1893) Closed. For inquiries regarding sacramental records, contact the Archdiocesan Archives, 20 Archbishop May Dr., Saint Louis, MO 63119.

47—ST. ELIZABETH OF HUNGARY (1956) Rev. Msgr. Timothy P. Cronin; Deacon Robert Snyder.
Res.: 1420 S. Sappington Rd., Crestwood, 63126. Tel: 314-968-0760; Fax: 314-968-8023.
Catechesis/Religious Program—Tel: 314-963-8868. Students 54.
Convent—1406 S. Sappington Rd., Crestwood, 63126. Tel: 314-961-2630.

48—ST. ELIZABETH, MOTHER OF JOHN THE BAPTIST (1891), (African American), Rev. Jeffrey G. Vomund; Deacon Charles M. Allen. In Res., Rev. Arthur J. Cavitt.
Res.: 4330 Shreve Ave., 63115. Tel: 314-381-4145; Fax: 314-381-2212.
School—St. Louis Catholic Academy, 4720 Carter Ave., 63115. Tel: 314-389-0401; Fax: 314-389-7042. Mr. Meke Smith, Prin. Religious 1; Lay Teachers 12; Students 185.

49—EPIPHANY OF OUR LORD (1911) Rev. Thomas C. Miller; Deacon James E. Tetreault.
Res.: 6596 Smiley Ave., 63139. Tel: 314-781-1199; Fax: 314-645-8760.
Catechesis/Religious Program—
Convent—6580 Smiley Ave., Saint Louis, 63139. Tel: 314-647-3610.

50—ST. FERDINAND (1788) Rev. Msgr. A. John Schuler; Rev. William J. Baier; Deacons Joseph C. Kroutil; Peter E. Gounis; James Russell.
Res.: 1765 Charbonier Rd., Florissant, 63031. Tel: 314-837-3165; Fax: 314-837-5799. Email: stferd@juno.com. Web: stferdinand.org.
School—(Grades K-8), 1735 Charbonier Rd., Florissant, 63031. Tel: 314-921-2201; Fax: 314-921-2253. Ursuline Sisters of the Roman Union 1; Lay Teachers 14; Students 251.
Catechesis/Religious Program—Tel: 636-978-3301. Students 120.

51—ST. FRANCES XAVIER CABRINI (JENNINGS) (1965) Closed. For inquiries regarding sacramental records, contact the Archdiocesan Archives, 20 Archbishop May Dr., Saint Louis, MO 63119.

52—ST. FRANCIS OF ASSISI (1927) Revs. Gary M. Gebelein; Nicholas J. Muenks; Deacons George R. Fink; William Sinak; Alan Ecker.
Res.: 4556 Telegraph Rd., 63129. Tel: 314-487-5736; Fax: 314-487-3701. Email: sfaparish@sbcglobal.net. Web: sfastl.org.
School—(Grades K-8), 4550 Telegraph Rd., 63129. Fax: 314-416-7118. Email: sfaschool@sbcglobal.net. Web: sfaschool-stlouis.org. Mr. Gregory Sturgill, Prin. Lay Teachers 21; Students 343.
Catechesis/Religious Program—Tel: 314-487-5736, Ext. 125. Students 154.

53—ST. FRANCIS XAVIER (1841), (College) Revs. Richard O. Buhler, S.J.; James J. Costello, S.J.
3628 Lindell Blvd., 63108. Tel: 314-977-7300; Fax: 314-977-7315. Email: church@slu.edu.
Catechesis/Religious Program—Tel: 314-977-7302. Students 175.

54—ST. GABRIEL THE ARCHANGEL (1934) Revs. Robert J. Samson; Timothy J. Henderson; Bernard J. Schloemer (Retired); Deacons James Volansky; David J. Willis.
Res.: 6303 Nottingham Ave., 63109. Tel: 314-353-6303; Fax: 314-353-7704.
School—4711 Tamm Ave., 63109. Tel: 314-353-1229; Fax: 314-353-6737. Lay Teachers 39; Students 475.
Catechesis/Religious Program—Students 835.

55—ST. GEORGE (1915) Rev. Thomas M. Robertson; Deacon Robert Penberthy.
Res.: 4980 Heege Rd., 63123. Tel: 314-352-3544; Fax: 314-832-6916.
School—Consolidated with St. Dominic Savio, St. Louis, MO.

56—ST. GERARD MAJELLA (1955) Revs. Thomas M. Molini; Thomas C. Bryon; Deacons Timothy Dolan; Donald Denham; Leslie Walrath, Pastoral Assoc.
Res.: 1969 Dougherty Ferry Rd., Kirkwood, 63122. Tel: 314-965-3985; Fax: 314-965-7650.
School—(Grades K-8), 2005 Dougherty Ferry Rd., Kirkwood, 63122. Tel: 314-822-8844; Fax: 314-822-8588. Dr. Jane Koberlein, Prin. Lay Teachers 26; Students 355.
Catechesis/Religious Program—Students 289.

57—GOOD SHEPHERD (FERGUSON) (1958) Closed. For inquiries regarding sacramental records, contact the Archdiocesan Archives, 20 Archbishop May Dr., Saint Louis, MO 63119.

58—ST. GREGORY (ST. ANN) (1942) Closed. For inquiries regarding sacramental records, contact the Archdiocesan Archives, 20 Archbishop May Dr., Saint Louis, MO 63119.

59—SAINT GREGORY THE GREAT AND SAINT AUGUSTINE OF CANTERBURY ORATORY (2007) Rev. Bede Price, O.S.B.
530 S. Mason Rd., Creve Coeur, 63141.
Catechesis/Religious Program—Marilyn Lonigro, D.R.E. Students 36.

60—ST. HEDWIG (1904) Closed. For inquiries regarding sacramental records, contact the Archdiocesan Archives, 20 Archbishop May Dr., Saint Louis, MO 63119.

61—HOLY ANGELS (KINLOCH) (1931), (African American), Closed. For inquiries regarding sacramental records, contact the Archdiocesan Archives, 20 Archbishop May Dr., Saint Louis, MO 63119.

62—HOLY FAMILY (1898) Closed. For inquiries regarding sacramental records, contact the Archdiocesan Archives, 20 Archbishop May Dr., Saint Louis, MO 63119.

63—HOLY GHOST (BERKELEY) (1923) Closed. For inquiries regarding sacramental records, contact the Archdiocesan Archives, 20 Archbishop May Dr., Saint Louis, MO 63119.

64—HOLY GUARDIAN ANGELS (1866) Closed. For inquiries regarding sacramental records, contact the Archdiocesan Archives, 20 Archbishop May Dr., Saint Louis, MO 63119.

65—HOLY INFANT (1954) Revs. Edward J. Stanger; Christopher J. Dunlap; Timothy L. Bannes; Deacon Kenneth C. Clemens Jr.
Res.: 627 Dennison Dr., Ballwin, 63021. Tel: 636-227-7440; Fax: 636-227-4548. Email: rectoryoffice@holyinfantballwin.org. Web: www.holyinfantballwin.org.
School—(Grades K-8) Tel: 636-227-0802; Fax: 636-227-9184. Email: schooloffice@holyinfantschool.org. Web: www.holyinfantschool.org. Sr. Rosario Delaney, R.S.M., Prin. Sisters of Mercy (Meath Mercy Generalate, Ireland) 2; Lay Teachers 43; Students 680.
Catechesis/Religious Program—Email: psroffice@holyinfantballwin.org. Students 529.
Convent—239 Nancy Pl., Ballwin, 63021. Tel: 636-391-1528.

66—HOLY INNOCENTS (1893) Closed. For inquiries regarding sacramental records, contact the Archdiocesan Archives, 20 Archbishop May Dr., Saint Louis, MO 63119.

67—HOLY NAME OF JESUS (2005) Rev. Michael L. Henning; Deacons George Watson; Matthew E. Duban.
Mailing Address: 10235 Ashbrook Dr., Saint Louis, 63137. Tel: 314-868-2310; Fax: 314-868-3919. Email: parishoffice10235@sbcglobal.net. Web: www.archstl.org/parishes/502.shtml.
School—Christ, Light of the Nations, (Grades PreK-8) Tel: 314-741-0400; Fax: 314-653-2531. Email: sr_mary@charter.net. Web: www.christlightofthenations.com.
Catechesis/Religious Program—Students 175.

68—HOLY REDEEMER (1886) Rev. Kenneth A. Brown; Deacon John P. Flanigan Jr.
Res.: 17 Joy Ave., Webster Groves, 63119. Tel: 314-962-0038; Fax: 314-962-2084. Web: www.holyr.org.
School—(Grades K-8), 341 E. Lockwood, Webster Groves, 63119. Tel: 314-962-8989; Fax: 314-962-3560. Wayne Schiefelbein, Prin. Lay Teachers 16; Students 232.
Catechesis/Religious Program—Tel: 314-962-2043. Email: cre@holyr.org. Patricia Maloney, C.R.E. Students 170.

69—HOLY SPIRIT (2004), St. Blaise closed and merged with St. Lawrence, and formed Holy Spirit. Revs. Richard J. Bockskopf; Philip D. Krill; Deacons Eugene Naumann; Charles Georges.
Res.: 3130 Parkwood Ln., Maryland Heights, 63043. Tel: 314-739-0230; Fax: 314-739-0237. Web: www.holyspiritstl.org.
School—(Grades K-8) Tel: 314-739-1934; Fax: 314-739-7703. Lay Teachers 15; Students 154.
Catechesis/Religious Program— Sharon Kaufman, C.R.E. Students 212.

70—HOLY TRINITY (2002) Revs. Paul J. Niemann; Anthony B. Ochoa; Deacon William F. Priesmeyer. In Res., Rev. John J. Wetmore.
Res.: 3500 St. Luke Ln., St. Ann, 63074. Tel: 314-733-1463; Fax: 314-395-1326.
School—(Grades K-8), 10901 St. Henry Ln., St. Ann, 63074. Tel: 314-426-8966; Fax: 314-428-7084. Margaret Ahle, Prin. Students 209.
Catechesis/Religious Program—Students 360.

71—IMMACOLATA (1945) Rev. Msgr. Vernon E. Gardin; Deacons Joseph LaMartina, (Retired); David Osmack. In Res., Rev. Msgr. Vernon E. Gardin.
Church: 8900 Clayton Rd., Richmond Heights, 63117. Tel: 314-991-5700; Fax: 314-991-5700.
School—(Grades K-8), 8910 Clayton Rd., Richmond Heights, 63117. Tel: 314-991-5700, Ext. 302; Fax: 314-991-9354. Web: www.immacolata.org. Mr. Salvatore Latragna, Prin. Lay Teachers 26; Students 268.
Catechesis/Religious Program—Tel: 314-991-5700, Ext. 303. Students 98.

72—IMMACULATE CONCEPTION (1904) [JC] Rev. James C. Gray; Deacons Clyde McEntire; Lawrence L. Clark.
Res.: 2934 Marshall Ave., Maplewood, 63143. Tel: 314-645-3307; Fax: 314-645-0672. Email: icmplwd@sbcglobal.net.
Catechesis/Religious Program—7240 Anna Ave., Maplewood, 63143. Tel: 314-644-6787. Students 65.

73—IMMACULATE CONCEPTION-ST. HENRY (1865) Closed. For inquiries regarding sacramental records, contact the Archdiocesan Archives, 20 Archbishop May Dr., Saint Louis, MO 63119.

74—IMMACULATE HEART OF MARY (1951) Rev. Bradley E. Modde, Admin.
Res.: 4092 Blow St., 63116. Tel: 314-481-7543; Fax: 314-481-6316.
School—(Grades PreK-8), 4070 Blow St., 63116. Tel: 314-832-1678; Fax: 314-832-1627. Web: www.ihm4070.org. Mr. Richard Danzeisen, Prin. Lay Teachers 20; Students 257.

75—INCARNATE WORD (1965) Revs. G. Timothy Vowels; Gerald J. Blessing; James M. Sullivan, Senior Assoc.; Deacon Larry Stallings.
Res.: 13416 Olive Blvd., Chesterfield, 63017. Tel: 314-576-5366; Fax: 314-576-2046. Web: www.incarnate-word.org.
School—(Grades K-8) Tel: 314-576-5366, Ext. 11. C. Michael Welling, Prin. Lay Teachers 23; Students 460.
Catechesis/Religious Program—Tel: 314-576-5366, Ext. 26. John Valenti, D.R.E. Students 325.

76—ST. JAMES THE GREATER (1860), (Irish), Rev. John J. Johnson; Deacon Michael A. Nicolai.
Res.: 6401 Wade Ave., 63139. Tel: 314-645-0167; Fax: 314-645-0168.
School—(Grades K-8), 1360 Tamm Ave., 63139. Tel: 314-647-5244; Fax: 314-647-8237. Ms. Karen Battaglia, Prin. Lay Teachers 19; Students 168.
Catechesis/Religious Program—Students 151.

77—ST. JEROME (BISSELL HILLS) (1952) Closed. For inquiries regarding sacramental records, contact the Archdiocesan Archives, 20 Archbishop May Dr., Saint Louis, MO 63119.

78—ST. JOAN OF ARC (1941) Rev. Msgr. Michael E. Turek; Rev. Nicholas W. Smith; Rev. Msgr. Thomas J. Dempsey (Retired); Deacons Daniel H. Henroid; Terrance Pimmel.
Res.: 5800 Oleatha St., 63139. Tel: 314-832-2838; Fax: 314-352-9350.
School—Tel: 314-752-4171; Fax: 314-351-8562. Mrs. Debra Dabay, Prin. Lay Teachers 15; Students 185.

79—STS. JOHN AND JAMES (FERGUSON) (1882) Closed. For inquiries regarding sacramental records, contact the Archdiocesan Archives, 20 Archbishop May Dr., Saint Louis, MO 63119.

80—ST. JOHN BOSCO (1972) Revs. Gerard R. Welsch; William J. Kester (Retired).
Res.: 12934 Marine Ave., Maryland Heights, 63146. Tel: 314-434-1312; Fax: 314-514-0478.
Catechesis/Religious Program—Tel: 314-878-6492. Students 145.

81—ST. JOHN NEPOMUK CHAPEL (1854) Deacon Michael L. Buckley, Dir.
Res.: 1625 S. 11th St., 63104. Tel: 314-231-0141; Fax: 314-231-0141.

82—ST. JOHN THE APOSTLE AND EVANGELIST (1847) Rev. Msgr. Dennis M. Delaney.
Res.: 15 Plaza Sq., 63103. Tel: 314-421-3467; Fax: 314-588-9544.
Catechesis/Religious Program—Students 3.

83—ST. JOHN THE BAPTIST (1914) Rev. Richard J. Rath.
4200 Delor St., 63116. Tel: 314-353-1255; Fax: 314-752-3154. Email: sjb4200@sbcglobal.net; rectory@sjbstl.org. In Res., Rev. John L. Mayer (Retired).
School—5021 Adkins, 63116. Tel: 314-481-6654; Fax: 314-481-3179. Religious Sisters 2; Lay Teachers 17; Students 170.
Catechesis / Religious Program—4170 Delor, Saint Louis, 63116. Tel: 314-773-3070; Fax: 314-773-3070. Students 131.
South City Deanery PSR at St. John the Baptist Parish—Rev. Leo J. Spezia, Dir.

84—ST. JOSEPH (1904), (Croatian), Rev. Stjepan Pandzic, O.F.M.
Res.: 2112 S. 12th St., 63104. Tel: 314-771-0958; Fax: 314-772-2675.
Catechesis / Religious Program—Students 39.

85—ST. JOSEPH (1865) [CEM] Revs. Thomas J. Santen; Henry K. Purcell; Binu Edathumparambil, M.S.F.S.; Deacons George Miller; Daniel R. Donnelly; Dale J. Follen.
Res.: 567 St. Joseph Ln., Manchester, 63021. Tel: 636-227-5247; Fax: 636-391-8393. Email: info@stjoemanchester.org. Web: stjoemanchester.org.
School—(Grades PreK-8), 555 St. Joseph Ln., Manchester, 63021. Tel: 636-391-1253; Fax: 636-391-1462. Jeannie Dandino, Prin. Lay Teachers 23; Students 354.
Catechesis / Religious Program—Tel: 636-391-1404. Students 473.

86—ST. JOSEPH (1842) Rev. Msgr. John B. Shamleffer; Rev. Thomas J. Schaab, Senior Assoc.; Deacons Albert Williams; Delfin S. Leonardo.
Res.: 106 N. Meramec Ave., Clayton, 63105. Tel: 314-726-1221; Fax: 314-721-5110. Email: pat_stj@hotmail.com. Web: www.stjosephclayton.org.
Catechesis / Religious Program—Tel: 314-727-9059; Fax: 314-727-2271. Mrs. Terri Venneman, D.R.E. Students 193.

87—ST. JUDE (1953) Rev. Joseph L. Parisi.
Res.: 2218 N. Warson Rd., Overland, 63114. Tel: 314-428-2262; Fax: 314-890-2257.
Catechesis / Religious Program—Students 21.

88—ST. JUSTIN MARTYR (1964) Rev. Joseph A. Weber; Deacon Christian H. Winkelmann.
Res.: 11910 Eddie and Park Rd., Sunset Hills, 63126. Tel: 314-843-8482; Fax: 314-843-8507.
School—(Grades K-8), 11914 Eddie and Park Rd., 63126. Tel: 314-843-6447; Fax: 314-843-9257. Mrs. Beth Bartolotta, Prin. Lay Teachers 16; Students 203.
Catechesis / Religious Program—Tel: 314-843-8482, Ext. 3. Elizabeth D. Balbo-Ryan, D.R.E. Students 103.

89—ST. KEVIN (ST. ANN) (1953), (Irish), Closed. For inquiries regarding sacramental records, contact the Archdiocesan Archives, 20 Archbishop May Dr., Saint Louis, MO 63119.

90—ST. LAWRENCE THE MARTYR (BRIDGETON) (1960) Closed. For inquiries regarding sacramental records, contact the Archdiocesan Archives, 20 Archbishop May Dr., Saint Louis, MO 63119.

91—ST. LIBORIUS (1856) Closed. For inquiries regarding sacramental records, contact the Archdiocesan Archives, 20 Archbishop May Dr., Saint Louis, MO 63119.

92—LITTLE FLOWER (1925) Rev. Lawrence A. Herzog; Deacon William G. Weiss.
1264 Arch Terrace, Richmond Heights, 63117. Email: littleflower@little-flower-parish.org. Web: www.little-flower-parish.org.
School—(Grades PreK-8), 1275 Boland Pl., Richmond Heights, 63117. Tel: 314-781-4995; Fax: 314-781-9177. Robert Baird, Prin. Lay Teachers 15; Students 176.

93—ST. LOUISE DE MARILLAC (JENNINGS) (1935) Closed. For inquiries regarding sacramental records, contact the Archdiocesan Archives, 20 Archbishop May Dr., Saint Louis, MO 63119.

94—ST. LUCY (JENNINGS) (1957) Closed. For inquiries regarding sacramental records, contact the Archdiocesan Archives, 20 Archbishop May Dr., Saint Louis, MO. 63119.

95—ST. LUKE THE EVANGELIST (1914) Rev. Msgr. William W. McCumber; Deacon Leonard A. Sisul.
Res.: 7230 Dale Ave., 63117. Tel: 314-644-2144; Fax: 314-644-4624.

96—ST. MARGARET MARY ALACOQUE (1962) Rev. Msgr. Norbert A. Ernst; Rev. Matthew D. Barnard; Rev. Msgr. William J. Leach (Retired); Deacons Andrew Daus; Robert Orr.
4900 Ringer Rd., 63129. Fax: 314-487-4475. Web: www.smmaparish.org.
Res.: 5056 Faust Ct., 63129. Tel: 314-487-2522.
School—(Grades K-8) Tel: 314-487-1666. Lay Teachers 40; Students 491.
Catechesis / Religious Program—Students 235.

97—ST. MARGARET OF SCOTLAND (1899) Rev. Matthew L. O'Toole.
Res.: 3854 Flad Ave., 63110. Tel: 314-776-0363; Fax: 314-776-0364. Web: www.stmargaretstl.org.
School—(Grades PreK-8), 3964 Castleman, 63110. Tel: 314-776-7837; Fax: 314-776-7955. Web: smosschool.org. Lay Teachers 22; Students 315.

98—ST. MARK (2003) Rev. Msgr. Patrick K. Hambrough; Rev. Thomas M. Pastorius.
8300 Morganford Rd., 63123. Tel: 314-743-8600; Fax: 314-743-8618. Web: www.stmarkstl.com. In Res., Rev. Msgr. Charles Forst (Retired).
Rectory—4230 Ripa Ave., Saint Louis, 63125. Tel: 314-743-8620.
School—4220 Ripa Ave., Saint Louis, 63125. Tel: 314-743-8640; Fax: 314-743-8690. Students 170.
Catechesis / Religious Program—Students 75.

99—ST. MARK, EVANGELIST (PAGE & ACADEMY) (1893) Closed. For inquiries regarding sacramental records, contact the Archdiocesan Archives, 20 Archbishop May Dr., Saint Louis, MO 63119.

100—ST. MARTIN DE PORRES (1962) Revs. Ferdinand J. Wesloh; Robert L. Szydlowski, Senior Assoc.; Deacons David Pacino; Edward Bierne.
Res.: 615 Dunn Rd., Hazelwood, 63042-1799. Tel: 314-895-1100; Fax: 314-895-5992.
Knobbe House—627 Undercliff, Hazelwood, 63042.
Catechesis / Religious Program—Students 94.

101—ST. MARTIN OF TOURS (1939) Rev. Charles F. Ferrara; Deacons Edward Fronick; Phillip Warren. In Res., Rev. Msgr. James J. Ramacciotti.
Res.: 610 W. Ripa Ave., Lemay, 63125. Tel: 314-544-5664; Fax: 314-631-3118.
Catechesis / Religious Program—Students 25.

102—ST. MARY (BRIDGETON) (1852) Closed. For inquiries regarding sacramental records, contact the Archdiocesan Archives, 20 Archbishop May Dr., Saint Louis, MO 63119.

103—STS. MARY AND JOSEPH CHAPEL (1821) Rev. Ronald J. Hopmeir, Chap.
Res.: 6304 Minnesota Ave., 63111. Tel: 314-481-6304; Fax: 314-481-6337.
Catechesis / Religious Program—Students 2.

104—ST. MARY MAGDALEN (1919) Rev. Msgr. John J. Borcic; Rev. Leo J. Spezia; Deacons Joseph Iovanna; J. Gerard Quinn.
Res.: 4924 Bancroft Ave., 63109. Tel: 314-352-2111; Fax: 314-481-7661.
Catechesis / Religious Program—Southside Regional Parish School of Religion, 4170 Delor, Saint Louis, 63116. Tel: 314-773-3070. Students 70.

105—ST. MARY MAGDALEN (1912) Rev. John S. Siefert; Deacon Leroy Martin. In Res., Rev. Christopher M. Martin.
Res.: 2618 Brentwood Blvd., Brentwood, 63144. Tel: 314-961-8400; Fax: 314-961-7019.
School—8750 Magdalen Ave., Brentwood, 63144. Tel: 314-961-0149; Fax: 314-961-7208. Email: smmsch@stmmlab.com. Web: stmmlab.com. Amy Sauer, Prin. Lay Teachers 16; Students 157.
Catechesis / Religious Program—Students 100.

106—ST. MARY OF VICTORIES (1843), (Hungarian), Rev. Msgr. John F. McCarthy, Chap.
Res.: 744 S. 3rd St., 63102. Tel: 314-231-8101.

107—MARY, MOTHER OF THE CHURCH (1971) Rev. Msgr. James T. Telthorst; Rev. James J. Byrnes; Deacon Richard Coffman.
Res.: 5901 Kerth Rd., 63128. Tel: 314-894-1373; Fax: 314-894-3801.
Catechesis / Religious Program— Ed Lewandowski, D.R.E. Students 288.

108—MARY, QUEEN OF PEACE (1922) Revs. Robert J. Reiker; Craig T. Holway; Deacon Thomas O. Mulvihill.
Res.: 676 W. Lockwood Blvd., Webster Groves, 63119. Tel: 314-962-2311; Fax: 314-968-9885.
School—(Grades K-8), 680 W. Lockwood Ave., Webster Groves, 63119. Tel: 314-961-2891; Fax: 314-961-7469. Dr. Jerry Kettenbach, Prin. Lay Teachers 38; Students 537.
Catechesis / Religious Program— Leslie Walrath, D.R.E. Students 110.

109—MARY, QUEEN OF THE UNIVERSE (1955) Closed. For inquiries regarding sacramental records, contact the Archdiocesan Archives, 20 Archbishop May Dr., Saint Louis, MO 63119.

110—ST. MATTHEW, APOSTLE (1893), (African American), [CEM] Rev. Mark D. McKenzie, S.J. In Res., Revs. Peter P. Saengthien, S.J.; William J. Hutchison, S.J.
Res.: 2715 N. Sarah St., 63113. Tel: 314-531-6443; Fax: 314-533-7318. Email: stmatthews@sbcglobal.net. Web: www.st-matthew-church.org.
Catechesis / Religious Program—Students 43.

111—ST. MATTHIAS (1959) Rev. Dennis R. Port. In Res., Rev. Eugene P. Selzer (Retired).
Res.: 796 Buckley Rd., 63125. Tel: 314-892-5109; Fax: 314-892-0629. Email: st.matthiasoffice@sbcglobal.net.
Catechesis / Religious Program—Students 84.

112—ST. MICHAEL (1895) Rev. Dennis J. Doyle.
Res.: 7622 Sutherland Ave., Shrewsbury, 63119. Tel: 314-647-5611; Fax: 314-781-9211. Email: rectory@stmike.org. Web: www.stmike.org.
School—(Grades K-8), 7630 Sutherland Ave., 63119. Tel: 314-647-7159; Fax: 314-644-1433. Lay Teachers 12; Students 128.
Catechesis / Religious Program—Students 67.

113—ST. MONICA (1872) [CEM] Rev. Msgr. Dennis E. Doerhoff; Rev. Michael L. Donald, Senior Assoc.; Deacons Robert Birkenmaier; James P. Martin.
Res.: 12136 Olive Blvd., Creve Coeur, 63141-6629. Tel: 314-434-4211; Fax: 314-434-5978.
School—(Grades K-8), 12132 Olive Blvd., Creve Coeur, 63141-6698. Tel: 314-434-2173; Fax: 314-434-7689. Mrs. Kathy Hunt, Prin. Lay Teachers 16; Students 180.
Catechesis / Religious Program—Tel: 314-205-9276. Email: mdoerr@stmonicastl.org. Students 79.

114—MOST BLESSED SACRAMENT (1907) Closed. For inquiries regarding sacramental records, contact the Archdiocesan Archives, 20 Archbishop May Dr., Saint Louis, MO 63119.

115—MOST HOLY NAME OF JESUS (EAST GRAND) (1875) Closed. For inquiries regarding sacramental records, contact the Archdiocesan Archives, 20 Archbishop May Dr., Saint Louis, MO 63119.

116—MOST HOLY ROSARY (1891) Closed. For inquiries regarding sacramental records, contact the Archdiocesan Archives, 20 Archbishop May Dr., Saint Louis, MO 63119.

117—MOST HOLY TRINITY (1848) Rev. Richard H. Creason; Sr. Janice Munier, S.S.N.D., Pastoral Assoc.
Res.: 3519 N. Fourteenth St., 63107-3796. Tel: 314-241-9165; Fax: 314-436-9291.
School—(Grades K-8), 1435 Mallinckrodt St., 63107-3796. Tel: 314-231-9014; Fax: 314-436-9291. Ann Russek, Prin. Lay Teachers 9; Students 146.
Catechesis / Religious Program—Students 80.
Convent—Tel: 314-621-6835.

118—MOST PRECIOUS BLOOD (LEMAY) (1961) Closed. For inquiries regarding sacramental records, contact the Archdiocesan Archives, 20 Archbishop May Dr., Saint Louis, MO 63119.

119—ST. NICHOLAS (1865) Rev. Urey P. Mark, S.V.D.; Deacon Stanley Peterson. In Res., Bro. Larry Camilleri, S.V.D.
Res.: 701 N. 18th St., 63103. Tel: 314-231-2860; Fax: 314-241-9823. Email: stnickcatholic@yahoo.com. Web: snrcc.org.
School—Central Catholic School and Academy, (Grades PreK-8), 1805 Lucas St., 63103. Tel: 314-421-1822. Lay Teachers 40; Students 300.
Catechesis / Religious Program—Students 9.

120—ST. NORBERT (1965) Very Rev. James M. Mitulski; Rev. Eric F. Olsen; Deacons William H. Twellman; David A. Felber.
Res.: 16455 New Halls Ferry Rd., Florissant, 63031. Tel: 314-831-3874; Fax: 314-830-3586. Email: secretary@saintnorbert.com. Web: www.saintnorbert.com.
School—(Grades PreK-8), 16475 New Halls Ferry Rd., Florissant, 63031. Tel: 314-839-0948; Fax: 314-839-3053. Email: school@saintnorbert.com. Mrs. Pam Gilbert, Prin. Lay Teachers 34; Students 462.
Catechesis / Religious Program—Web: home.catholicweb.com/stnpsr. Students 68.

121—NORTH AMERICAN MARTYRS (FLORISSANT) (1955) Closed. For inquiries regarding sacramental records, contact the Archdiocesan Archives, 20 Archbishop May Dr., Saint Louis, MO 63119.

122—NOTRE DAME DE LOURDES (WELLSTON) (1902) Closed. For inquiries regarding sacramental records, contact the Archdiocesan Archives, 20 Archbishop May Dr., Saint Louis, MO 63119.

123—ORATORY OF ST. FRANCIS DE SALES (2005), (Roman Missal of 1962) Rev. Canons Michael K. Wiener, Rector; William E. Avis. Administered by the Institute of Christ the King Sovereign Priest Extraordinary Form of The Roman Rite.
Res.: 2653 Ohio Ave., 63118. Tel: 314-771-3100; Fax: 314-771-3295. Email: sfds@institute-christ-king.org. Web: www.institute-christ-king.org.

124—OUR LADY OF FATIMA (FLORISSANT) (1950) Closed. For inquiries regarding sacramental records, contact the Archdiocesan Archives, 20 Archbishop May Dr., Saint Louis, MO 63119.

125—OUR LADY OF GOOD COUNSEL (BELLEFONTAINE NEIGHBORS) (1951) Closed. For inquiries regarding sacramental records, contact the Archdiocesan Archives, 20 Archbishop May Dr., Saint Louis, MO 63119.

126—OUR LADY OF GUADALUPE (1954), (Hispanic), Rev. John Paul Hopping; Sr. Cathy Doherty, S.S.N.D., Pastoral Assoc.
Res.: 17 Hawkesbury Dr., Saint Louis, 63121. Tel: 314-522-9264; Fax: 314-522-8461.
School—(Grades K-8), 1115 S. Florissant Rd., Ferguson, 63121. Tel: 314-524-1948. Peggy O'Brien, Prin. Lay Teachers 10; Students 173.
Catechesis / Religious Program—Students 83.

127—OUR LADY OF LORETTO (SPANISH LAKE) (1959)

Closed. For inquiries regarding sacramental records, contact the Archdiocesan Archives, 20 Archbishop May Dr., Saint Louis, MO 63119.

128—OUR LADY OF LOURDES (1916) Rev. Carl J. Scheble. In Res., Rev. Nicholas E. Kastenholz.
Res.: 7148 Forsyth Blvd., University City, 63105. Tel: 314-726-6200; 314-726-6201; Fax: 314-726-1602. Email: rectory@ucitylourdes.org. Web: www.ucitylourdes.org.
School—(Grades K-8), 7157 Northmoor Dr., University City, 63105. Tel: 314-726-3352; Fax: 314-726-0503. Lay Teachers 25; Students 260.

129—OUR LADY OF MERCY (HAZELWOOD) (1964) Closed. For inquiries regarding sacramental records, contact the Archdiocesan Archives, 20 Archbishop May Dr., Saint Louis, MO 63119.

130—OUR LADY OF MOUNT CARMEL (1872) Closed. For inquiries regarding sacramental records, contact the Archdiocesan Archives, 20 Archbishop May Dr., Saint Louis, MO 63119.

131—OUR LADY OF PERPETUAL HELP (1873) Closed. For inquiries regarding sacramental records, contact the Archdiocesan Archives, 20 Archbishop May Dr., Saint Louis, MO 63119.

132—OUR LADY OF PROVIDENCE (1954) Rev. David E. Rauch; Deacon David Amelotti. In Res., Rev. Msgr. Francis X. Blood.
Res.: 8866 Pardee Rd., 63123. Tel: 314-843-3570; Fax: 314-843-8033. Email: ladyprov@charter.net. Web: www.olpstl.com.
School—(Grades K-8), 8874 Pardee Rd., 63123. Tel: 314-842-2073; Fax: 314-842-2406. Ms. Clare Ortmeier, Prin. Lay Teachers 14; Students 149.
Catechesis/Religious Program—Students 54.

133—OUR LADY OF SORROWS (1907) Rev. Peter M. Blake; Deacons Robert Wertz; Daniel Skillman. In Res., Rev. Joy Thachil, S.A.C.
Res.: 5020 Rhodes Ave., 63109. Tel: 314-351-1600; Fax: 314-351-1602. Email: olsorrows@sbcglobal.net. Web: www.olsorrows.org.
School—*Our Lady of Sorrows*, 5831 S. Kingshighway Blvd., 63109. Tel: 314-353-1451; Fax: 314-351-8464. Lay Teachers 19; Students 177.
Catechesis/Religious Program—Students 242.

134—OUR LADY OF THE HOLY CROSS (1864) Rev. Donald L. Buhr; Deacon Donald Driscoll.
Res.: 8115 Church Rd., 63147. Tel: 314-381-0323; Fax: 314-381-4828.

135—OUR LADY OF THE PILLAR (1938) Revs. James M. Tobin, S.M.; Thomas French, S.M.; Deacon James R. Powers; Bro. William O'Leary, S.M.
Res.: 401 S. Lindbergh Blvd., 63131. Tel: 314-993-2280; Fax: 314-993-6462.
School—(Grades K-8), 403 S. Lindbergh Blvd., 63131. Tel: 314-993-3353; Fax: 314-993-2172. Franciscan Sisters of Our Lady of Perpetual Help 1; Lay Teachers 19; Students 159.
Catechesis/Religious Program—Students 135.

136—OUR LADY OF THE PRESENTATION (1915) Rev. Mark A. Dolan; Deacon Kevin Carroll.
Res.: 8860 Tudor Ave., Overland, 63114. Tel: 314-427-0486; Fax: 314-423-3020.

137—OUR LADY OF THE ROSARY (2005) Rev. Thomas Haley; Deacon David I. Harpring.
Mailing Address: 11725 Bellefontaine Rd., Saint Louis, 63138. Tel: 314-741-7700; Fax: 314-653-0910. Email: shartig@sbcglobal.net. Web: www.archstl.org.
School—*Christ Light of the Nations*, 1650 Redman Rd., Saint Louis, 63138. Tel: 314-741-0400; Fax: 314-653-2531. Email: st_mary@christlightofthenations.com. Web: www.christlightofthenations.com. Sr. Mary Lawrence, S.S.N.D., Prin. Lay Teachers 15; Students 157.
Catechesis/Religious Program—Sr. Nancy Becker, S.S.N.D., D.R.E.

138—ST. PATRICK (1981) Closed. For inquiries for parish records contact the chancery.

139—ST. PATRICK (UNIVERSITY CITY) (1940) Closed. For inquiries regarding sacramental records, contact the Archdiocesan Archives, 20 Archbishop May Dr., Saint Louis, MO 63119.

140—ST. PAUL (1878) [CEM] Rev. Msgr. Michael Dieckmann; Rev. James A. Holbrook; Deacons John Weatherholt; Paul Crafts.
Res.: 15 Forest Knoll, Fenton, 63026-3105. Tel: 636-343-1234; Fax: 636-343-4809. Web: www.stpaulfenton.org.
School—(Grades PreK-8), 465 New Smizer Mill Rd., Fenton, 63026. Tel: 636-343-4333; Fax: 636-343-1769. Web: www.stpaulfenton.org/school. Lay Teachers 31; Students 370.
Catechesis/Religious Program—Students 350.

141—ST. PAUL THE APOSTLE, Merged to form Ascension-St. Paul, Normandy.

142—ST. PETER (1832) [CEM] Rev. Msgr. John M. Costello; Rev. Michael J. Esswein; Deacon John W. Komotos. In Res., Rev. Msgr. Gregory L. Schmidt (Retired).
Res.: 243 W. Argonne Dr., Kirkwood, 63122. Tel: 314-966-8600; Fax: 314-966-5721.
School—(Grades K-8), 215 N. Clay St., Kirkwood, 63122. Tel: 314-821-0460. Lay Teachers 30; Students 450.
Catechesis/Religious Program—Tel: 314-822-1347. Linda Doyle, C.R.E.; Jan Hartman, C.R.E. Students 380.

143—STS. PETER AND PAUL (1849) Rev. Bruce H. Forman; Deacons Thomas Gorski; Dennis Chitwood.
Res.: 1919 S. 7th St., 63104. Tel: 314-231-9923; Fax: 314-231-7464.

144—ST. PIUS V (1905) Rev. John Rogers Vien.
Res.: 3310 S. Grand Blvd., 63118. Tel: 314-772-1525; Fax: 314-772-5615. Web: www.stpiusv.org.
See St. Frances Cabrini Academy, St. Louis under St. Wenceslaus, St. Louis for details.

145—ST. PIUS X (GLASGOW VILLAGE) (1954) Closed. For inquiries regarding sacramental records, contact the Archdiocesan Archives, 20 Archbishop May Dr., Saint Louis, MO 63119.

146—QUEEN OF ALL SAINTS (1972) Rev. Msgr. Joseph M. Simon; Rev. Eric J. Kunz; Deacons Richard Schellhase; Joseph Wingbermuehle.
Res.: 6603 Christopher Dr., Saint Louis, 63129. Tel: 314-846-8207; Fax: 314-846-0636.
School—(Grades K-8), 6611 Christopher Dr., Saint Louis, 63129. Tel: 314-846-0506; Fax: 314-846-4939. Dr. Catherine Johns, Prin. Students 379.
Catechesis/Religious Program—Tel: 314-846-8126. Ms. Carrie Sallwasser, C.R.E. Students 331.

147—ST. RAPHAEL THE ARCHANGEL (1950) Rev. Msgr. Henry J. Breier; Deacons Gerald Geiser; Roger Kreitler. In Res., Rev. Richard H. Suren (Retired).
Res.: 6047 Bishops Pl., 63109. Tel: 314-352-8100; Fax: 314-353-6603.
School—(Grades K-8), 6000 Jamieson, Saint Louis, 63109. Tel: 314-352-9474; Fax: 314-352-7285. Mr. Peter Abegg, Prin. Lay Teachers 13; Students 157.
Catechesis/Religious Program—Students 175.

148—RESURRECTION OF OUR LORD (1930), (Vietnamese), Revs. Dominic Nguyen, S.V.D.; Dominic Savio Pham, S.V.D.
3900 Meramec St., 63116. Tel: 314-832-7023; Fax: 314-832-7024.
Catechesis/Religious Program—Students 131.

149—ST. RICHARD (1963) Very Rev. Charles E. Burgoon; Deacons John A. Bischof; Ronald Lee Reuther. In Res., Rev. John P. Kennehan.
Res.: 11223 Schuetz Rd., 63146. Tel: 314-432-6224; Fax: 314-432-6030.
School—(Grades K-8), 11211 Schuetz Rd., 63146. Tel: 314-872-3152; Fax: 314-872-0931. Miss Julie Smith, Prin. Lay Teachers 14; Students 107.

150—ST. RITA (1919) Rev. David L. Wichlan.
Res.: 8240 Washington St., 63114. Tel: 314-428-4845; Fax: 314-428-4845.
Catechesis/Religious Program—Students 2.

151—ST. ROCH (1911) Rev. Msgr. Salvatore E. Polizzi. In Res., Rev. Robert T. McDermott.
Res.: 6052 Waterman Blvd., 63112. Tel: 314-721-6340; Fax: 314-721-1656. Web: strochparish.com.
School—(Grades K-8), 6040 Waterman Blvd., 63112. Tel: 314-721-2595. Gloria Openlander, Prin. Lay Teachers 13; Students 204.

152—ST. ROSE OF LIMA (1884) Closed. For inquiries regarding sacramental records, contact the Archdiocesan Archives, 20 Archbishop May Dr., Saint Louis, MO 63119.

153—ST. ROSE PHILIPPINE DUCHESNE Revs. Thomas W. Wyrsch; Joseph Rajpaul Sundararaj.
Mailing Address: 2650 Parker Rd., Florissant, 63033. Tel: 314-837-3410; Fax: 314-837-6628. Web: www.strpdparish.org.
School—3500 St. Catherine, Florissant, 63033. Tel: 314-921-3023; Fax: 314-921-3025. Students 300.
Catechesis/Religious Program—Marie Carter, D.R.E. Students 50.

154—ST. SABINA (1960) Rev. Joseph W. Banden; Deacons Harold A. Strauss; Gerard M. Lauterwasser. In Res., Rev. Eugene P. Brennan (Retired).
Res.: 1365 Harkee Dr., Florissant, 63031. Tel: 314-837-1365; Fax: 314-837-7680.
Catechesis/Religious Program—Tel: 314-837-0146. Students 145.

155—SACRED HEART (1889) Revs. Richard J. Schilli; Lijo Kallarackal, O.S.B.Silv.; Deacons Thomas L. Eultgen; Leo S. Fehner.
Res.: 350 E. Fourth St., Eureka, 63025. Tel: 636-938-5048; Fax: 636-587-2736. Web: www.sacredhearteureka.org.
School—(Grades K-8) Tel: 636-938-4602; Fax: 636-938-5802. Monica Wilson, Prin. Lay Teachers 13; Students 220.
Catechesis/Religious Program—Tel: 636-938-9507. Students 365.

156—SACRED HEART (1866) Rev. Msgr. Mark C. Ullrich; Rev. Robert Dorhauer; Deacons Bruce A. Burkhard; J. John Heithaus.
Res.: 751 N. Jefferson St., Florissant, 63031. Tel: 314-837-3757; Fax: 314-837-8897. Email: rectory@mostsacredheartchurch.org.
School—(Grades K-8), 501 St. Louis St., Florissant, 63031. Tel: 314-831-3372; Fax: 314-831-2844. Lois Vollmer, Prin. Lay Teachers 22; Students 329.
Catechesis/Religious Program—Tel: 314-837-3757, Ext. 221. Students 62.

157—SACRED HEART (1903) [CEM] Revs. Denny M. Schaab; Timothy J. Noelker; Deacons Dave Lemoine; Charles R. Snyder; Thomas E. Forster. In Res., Rev. Robert J. Suit.
Res.: 17 Ann Ave., Valley Park, 63088. Tel: 636-225-5268; Fax: 636-225-6969.
School—(Grades PreK-8), 12 Ann Ave., Valley Park, 63088. Tel: 636-225-3824; Fax: 636-225-8941. Joan Wojciechowski, Prin. Lay Teachers 27; Students 408.
Catechesis/Religious Program—Students 585.

158—ST. SEBASTIAN (GLEN OWEN), Closed. For inquiries regarding sacramental records, contact the Archdiocesan Archives, 20 Archbishop May Dr., Saint Louis, MO 63119.

159—SEVEN HOLY FOUNDERS (1927) Revs. Donald Siple, O.S.M.; Ananda Lourdu Raj Arulsamy, O.S.M.; Eugene M. Smith, O.S.M.; Deacons Charles Lombardo; Joel Lechner, O.S.M.
Office: 6820 Aliceton Ave., Affton, 63123. Tel: 314-638-3938; Fax: 314-638-0613. Web: www.foundersaffton.org.
Church: 6741 Rock Hill Rd., 63123. Tel: 314-631-3938.
School—(Grades K-8), 6737 Rock Hill Rd., 63123. Tel: 314-631-8149; Fax: 314-631-8442. Web: www.shfschool.org. Bro. Joel Lechner, O.S.M., Prin. Lay Teachers 17; Students 232.
Catechesis/Religious Program—Students 120.

160—SHRINE OF ST. JOSEPH (1844) Rev. Dale P. Wunderlich, Rector.
Res.: 1220 N. 11th St., 63106. Tel: 314-231-9407; Fax: 314-231-0802. Web: www.shrineofstjoseph.org.

161—ST. SIMON OF CYRENE (1993) Closed. For inquiries regarding sacramental records, contact the Archdiocesan Archives, 20 Archbishop May Dr., Saint Louis, MO 63119.

162—ST. SIMON THE APOSTLE (1959) Revs. Erich A. Fechner; Anthony R. Yates; Deacons David Camden; Paul F. Stackle. In Res., Rev. Mitchell S. Doyen.
Res.: 11011 Mueller Rd., 63123. Tel: 314-842-3848, Ext. 1; Fax: 314-842-9829. Email: stsimon@sbcglobal.net. Web: www.stsimonchurch.org.
Preschool—11015 Mueller Rd., 63123. Fax: 314-842-4935. Email: simonsaysecc@sbcglobal.net. Web: www.simonsaysecc.com.
School—(Grades K-8), 11019 Mueller Rd., 63123. Tel: 314-842-3848, Ext. 2; Fax: 314-849-6355. Email: slenger@stsimonschool.org. Web: www.stsimonschool.org. Lay Teachers 26; Students 343.
Catechesis/Religious Program—Students 134.

163—STE. GENEVIEVE DU BOIS (1956) Rev. Daniel E. Mosley; Rev. Msgr. John M. Unger; Deacon Donald Heitert, (Retired).
Res.: 1575 N. Woodlawn Ave., Warson Woods, 63122. Tel: 314-966-3780; Fax: 314-966-4687. Email: stegen@sbcglobal.net. Web: www.catholic-forum.com/churches/015stgenevieve/.
School—(Grades K-8) Tel: 314-821-4245; Fax: 314-822-4881. Mrs. Claudia Dougherty, Prin. Lay Teachers 12; Students 152.
Catechesis/Religious Program—Students 70.

164—ST. STEPHEN, PROTOMARTYR (1926) Rev. Ronald J. Hopmeir. In Res., Rev. Msgr. Richard E. Hanneke.
Res.: 3949 Wilmington Ave., 63116. Tel: 314-481-1133; Fax: 314-481-6036.
School—(Grades K-8), 3923 Wilmington Ave., 63116. Tel: 314-752-4700; Fax: 314-752-5165. Meghan Bohac, Prin. Lay Teachers 15; Students 170.
Catechesis/Religious Program—Students 7.

165—STS. TERESA AND BRIDGET (2003) Revs. Gary M. Meier; Cajetan Ihewulezi, C.S.S.P.
3636 N. Market, Saint Louis, 63113. Tel: 314-371-1190; Fax: 314-531-1047. Email: pastor@ststb.org. Web: www.ststb.org.

166—ST. TERESA OF AVILA (1865) Closed. For inquiries regarding sacramental records, contact Sts. Teresa & Bridget Church, 3636 N. Market St., Saint Louis, MO 63113.

167—ST. THOMAS MORE (BEL-RIDGE) (1955) Closed. For inquiries regarding sacramental records, contact the Archdiocesan Archives, 20 Archbishop May Dr., Saint Louis, MO 63119.

168—ST. THOMAS OF AQUIN (1882) Closed. For inquiries regarding sacramental records, contact the Archdiocesan Archives, 20 Archbishop May Dr., Saint Louis, MO 63119.

169—ST. THOMAS THE APOSTLE (FLORISSANT) (1960) Closed. For inquiries regarding sacramental records, contact the Archdiocesan Archives, 20 Archbishop May Dr., Saint Louis, MO 63119.

170—ST. TIMOTHY (1958) Closed. For inquiries regarding sacramental records, contact the Archdiocesan Archives, 20 Archbishop May Dr., Saint

Louis, MO 63119.

171—TRANSFIGURATION (FLORISSANT) (1965) Closed. For inquiries regarding sacramental records, contact the Archdiocesan Archives, 20 Archbishop May Dr., Saint Louis, MO 63119.

172—ST. VINCENT DE PAUL (1841) Rev. Edward F. Murphy, C.M.
Res.: 1408 S. Tenth St., 63104. Tel: 314-231-9328; Fax: 314-621-2232. Email: mail@stvstl.org. Web: www.stvstl.org.
Catechesis/Religious Program—Email: lmertz@stvstl.org. Linda Mertz, D.R.E. Students 30.

173—VISITATION-ST. ANN'S SHRINE (1881) Rev. J. Edward Vogler.
Res.: 4515 Evans Ave., 63113. Tel: 314-535-8804; Fax: 314-531-8486. Email: vizstann@sbcglobal.net. Web: www.vizstann.greatnow.com.

174—ST. WENCESLAUS (1895) Rev. James E. Wuerth, M.S.F.; Deacon George W. Miller.
Res.: 3014 Oregon Ave., 63118. Tel: 314-865-1020; Fax: 314-664-8260.
Catechesis/Religious Program—St. Frances Cabrini Academy, 3022 Oregon Ave., 63118. Tel: 314-776-0883; Fax: 314-776-4912. Students 135.

175—ST. WILLIAM (WOODSON TERRACE) (1953) Closed. For inquiries regarding sacramental records, contact the Archdiocesan Archives, 20 Archbishop May Dr., Saint Louis, MO 63119.

CHURCHES OUTSIDE ST. LOUIS CITY AND ST. LOUIS COUNTY

APPLE CREEK, PERRY CO., ST. JOSEPH (1828) [CEM] [JC 2] Very Rev. Anthony A. Dattilo.
Res.: 138 St. Joseph Ln., 63775. Tel: 573-788-2330; Fax: 573-788-2351.
Catechesis/Religious Program—Tel: 573-547-5246. Students 40.

ARNOLD, JEFFERSON CO.

1—ST. DAVID (1963) Rev. Jeffrey A. Maassen; Deacon Thomas G. Politte.
Res.: 2334 Tenbrook Rd., 63010. Tel: 636-296-5485; Fax: 636-296-8717. Email: stdavid@swbell.com. See Holy Child School, Arnold under Immaculate Conception, Arnold for details.
Catechesis/Religious Program—Students 175.

2—IMMACULATE CONCEPTION (1840) [CEM] Rev. Mark Whitman; Deacon Steven M. Schisler. In Res., Rev. John G. Dempsey (Retired).
Res.: 2300 Church Rd., 63010. Tel: 636-321-0002; Fax: 636-321-0004.
School—Holy Child School, (Grades K-8), Consolidated with St. David, Arnold., Tel: 636-321-0002, Ext. 21; Fax: 636-296-5639. Dr. Robert Cowell, Prin. Lay Teachers 13; Students 169.
Catechesis/Religious Program—Tel: 636-321-0004, Ext. 74. Mary Winkelmann, D.R.E. Students 300.

AUGUSTA, ST. CHARLES CO., IMMACULATE CONCEPTION (1851) [CEM] Rev. Edward L. Heim.
Res.: 5912 S. Hwy. 94, 63332. Tel: 636-482-4455; Fax: 636-228-4529. Email: icaugustamo@hotmail.com. Web: www.rc.net/stlouis/immac.
Catechesis/Religious Program—Students 25.

BELGIQUE, PERRY CO., NATIVITY OF THE BLESSED VIRGIN MARY, Closed. For inquiries regarding sacramental records, contact the Archdiocesan Archives, 20 Archbishop May Dr., Saint Louis, MO 63119.

BERGER, ST. PAUL (1853), (German), [CEM] Rev. John C. Deken.
Res.: 603 Miller St., New Haven, 63068. Tel: 573-237-3372; Fax: 573-237-3372.
Catechesis/Religious Program—Students 7.

BIEHLE, PERRY CO., ST. MAURUS (1870) [CEM] [JC] Very Rev. Anthony A. Dattilo.
Res.: 10198 Hwy. B, Perryville, 63775. Tel: 573-788-2330; 573-547-5246; Fax: 573-788-2351.
Catechesis/Religious Program—Students 36.

BLOOMSDALE, STE. GENEVIEVE CO., ST. AGNES (1835) [CEM] Rev. Clark B. Maes; Deacon James Basler.
Res.: 40 St. Agnes Dr., P.O. Box 124, 63627. Tel: 573-483-2555; Fax: 573-483-9497. Email: stagnes@brick.net.
School—(Grades PreK-8) Tel: 573-483-2506. Patricia A. Kirk, Prin. Sisters of the Most Precious Blood (O'Fallon, MO) 1; Lay Teachers 11; Students 183.
Catechesis/Religious Program—Students 23.

BONNE TERRE, ST. FRANCOIS CO., ST. JOSEPH'S (1872) [CEM] Rev. John H. Schneider; Deacon Mark A. Byington.
Res.: 15 St. Joseph St., 63628. Tel: 573-358-2112; Fax: 573-358-4233.
School—(Grades K-6) Tel: 573-358-5947. Lay Teachers 4; Students 29.
Catechesis/Religious Program—Students 38.
Mission—St. Anne 5425 Brickey Rd., P.O. Box 307, French Village, St. Francois Co. 63036. Tel: 573-358-2112.

BREWER, PERRY CO., CHRIST THE SAVIOR (1907) [CEM] Rev. R. William Rhinehart, C.M.
Res.: 57 Shady Ln., Perryville, 63775. Tel: 573-547-2677; Fax: 573-547-7556. Email: christthesavior57@yahoo.com.
Catechesis/Religious Program—Students 33.

CATAWISSA, FRANKLIN CO., ST. JAMES (1913) [CEM] Rev. Mark S. Bozada.
Res.: 1107 Summit Dr., 63015. Tel: 636-451-4685; Fax: 636-742-4820. Email: simarparr@aol.com.
Mission—St. Patrick [CEM] Hwy. NN & Rock Church Rd., Armagh, Franklin Co. 63015. Tel: 636-257-2227.

CLOVER BOTTOM, FRANKLIN CO., ST. ANN (1883) [CEM] Rev. Richard V. Coerver, Admin.
Res.: 7851 Hwy. YY, Washington, 63090-4050. Tel: 636-239-3222; Fax: 636-390-2849. Email: stann@yhti.net. Web: www.stannschurch.yhti.net.
Catechesis/Religious Program—Students 40.

COFFMAN, STE. GENEVIEVE CO., ST. CATHERINE OF ALEXANDRIA (1929) [CEM] [JC] Attended by River Aux Vases
Res.: 18411 RAV Church Rd., Ste. Genevieve, 63670. Tel: 573-883-2923; Fax: 573-883-9605.
Catechesis/Religious Program—Students 1.

CONCORD HILL, WARREN CO., ST. IGNATIUS LOYOLA (1857) [CEM 3] Rev. Finbarr Dowling, O.S.B.; Deacon Paul J. Hecktor.
Res.: 19127 Mill Rd., Marthasville, 63357-1439. Tel: 636-932-4445; Fax: 636-932-4032.
School—691 Mill Rd., 63357. Tel: 636-932-4444; Fax: 636-932-4479. Email: office@saintignatius.net. Jennifer Fregalette, Prin. Lay Teachers 5; Students 69.

COTTLEVILLE, ST. CHARLES CO., ST. JOSEPH (1873) [CEM] Rev. Msgr. James P. Callahan; Revs. Joseph S. Post; Kevin M. Schroeder; Sr. Nancy Ames, O.P., Pastoral Assoc.; Deacons Michael Piva; Eugene Schaeffer III; Glennon Schultheis.
Res.: 1355 Motherhead Rd., St. Charles, 63304. Tel: 636-441-0055; Fax: 636-926-7341. Email: parish@stjoecot.org.
School—(Grades K-8), 1351 Motherhead Rd., St. Charles, 63304. Fax: 636-441-9932. Email: info@stjoecot.org. Web: www.stjoecot.org. Sr. Maria Christi, O.P., Prin.; Mr. Daniel Mullenschlader, Asst. Prin. Lay Teachers 45; Students 941.
Catechesis/Religious Program—Tel: 636-441-0055, Ext. 300; Fax: 636-926-7341. Mrs. Laura Weinzirl, C.R.E. Tel: 636-441-0055, Ext. 300. Students 1,060.
Convent—1353 Motherhead Rd., St. Charles, 63304. Tel: 636-244-2257.

CRYSTAL CITY, JEFFERSON CO., SACRED HEART (1881) [CEM] Very Rev. Joseph E. Wormek; Deacon Gerard G. Stoverink.
Res.: 555 Bailey Rd., 63019-1798. Tel: 636-937-4662; Fax: 636-931-5507. Email: sh324cc@sbcglobal.net.
Catechesis/Religious Program—Students 149.

DARDENNE PRAIRIE, ST. CHARLES CO., IMMACULATE CONCEPTION (1880) [CEM] Rev. Msgr. Ted L. Wojcicki; Revs. Timothy J. Foy; Nicklaus E. Winker; Deacons Ernie Rohaly; Paul Bast.
Res.: 7701 Hwy. N., 63368. Tel: 636-561-6611; Fax: 636-561-3883. Email: parishoffice@icdparish.org. Web: www.icdparish.org.
School—(Grades K-8) Tel: 636-561-4450; Fax: 636-625-9020. Web: www.icdschool.org. Lay Teachers 56; Students 805.
Catechesis/Religious Program—Tel: 636-561-1974. Email: psr@icdparish.org. Students 1,208.

DE SOTO, JEFFERSON CO., ST. ROSE OF LIMA (1866) [CEM] Rev. Alexander R. Anderson; Deacon Edward J. Boyer.
Res.: 504 S. Third St., 63020. Tel: 636-337-2212; Fax: 636-337-2394.
School—(Grades PreSchool-8), 523 S. 4th St., 63020. Tel: 636-586-3594; 636-337-7855. Imogene Renick, Prin. Lay Teachers 8; Students 90.
Catechesis/Religious Program—Students 127.

DUTZOW, WARREN CO., ST. VINCENT DE PAUL (1856) [CEM] Rev. Eugene G. Robertson.
Res.: 13497 S. Hwy. 94, Marthasville, 63357. Tel: 636-433-2678; Fax: 636-433-2924.
School—13495 S. State Hwy. 94, Marthasville, 63357. Tel: 636-433-2466. Sisters 2; Lay Teachers 6; Students 91.
Catechesis/Religious Program—Students 6.

ELSBERRY, LINCOLN CO., SACRED HEART (1905) Rev. Raymond D. Hager.
Res.: 714 Lincoln St., 63343. Tel: 573-898-2202; Fax: 573-898-2652.
Catechesis/Religious Program—Students 49.

FARMINGTON, ST. FRANCOIS CO., ST. JOSEPH (1890) [JC 2] Revs. Rickey J. Valleroy; James W. Dyer; Deacon Albin A. Gegg.
Res.: 10 N. Long St., 63640. Tel: 573-756-4250; Fax: 573-756-6938. Web: www.stjosephfarmington.com.
School—(Grades K-8), 501 Ste. Genevieve Ave., 63640. Tel: 573-756-6312; Fax: 573-756-0738. Web: www.stjosephfarmington.com. Students 106.
Catechesis/Religious Program—Students 102.

FESTUS, JEFFERSON CO., OUR LADY (1956) Rev. John V. Kerber; Deacon Donald Kintz.
Res.: 1550 St. Mary Ln., 63028-1543. Tel: 636-937-5513; 636-931-4702 (toll-free); Fax: 636-933-2230. Email: olchurch@sbcglobal.net. Web: www.ourladyfestus.org.
School—(Grades K-8), 1599 St. Mary Ln., 63028-1557. Tel: 636-937-5008. Email: ourladyschool@sbcglobal.net. Lay Teachers 20; Students 281.
Catechesis/Religious Program—Students 152.

FLINT HILL, ST. CHARLES CO., ST. THEODORE (1883) [CEM] Rev. Gary L. Vollmer; Deacons Patrick Rankin; Thomas N. Rothermich.
Res.: 5051 Hwy. P, P.O. Box 246, 63346. Tel: 636-332-9269; Fax: 636-639-1385. Email: sttheodore.church@centurytel.net.
School—5059 Hwy. P, Wentzville, 63385. Tel: 636-332-9269, Ext. 4; Fax: 636-327-5115. Email: sttheodore.school@centurytel.net. Lay Teachers 13; Students 204.
Catechesis/Religious Program—Students 20.

GILDEHAUS, FRANKLIN CO., ST. JOHN THE BAPTIST (1839) [CEM] Rev. James R. French.
Res.: 5567 Gildehaus Rd., Villa Ridge, 63089. Tel: 636-583-2488; Fax: 636-583-6114. Email: stjohnsgild@yhti.net.
School—(Grades PreSchool-8) Tel: 636-583-2392. Mrs. Judith Wilson, Prin. Lay Teachers 13; Students 114.
Catechesis/Religious Program—Students 50.

HAWK POINT, LINCOLN CO., ST. MARY (1919) [CEM 2] Rev. Francis F. Koeninger.
Res.: P.O. Box 205, 63349. Tel: 636-338-4331; Fax: 636-338-4007. Email: marysrectory@centurytel.net.
Catechesis/Religious Program—Fax: 636-338-4331. Students 20.

HERCULANEUM, JEFFERSON CO., CHURCH OF THE ASSUMPTION OF B.V.M. (1916) [CEM] Very Rev. Joseph E. Wormek; Deacon Steven D. Baugh.
Res.: 329 Station St., 63048-1328. Tel: 636-475-5305.
Catechesis/Religious Program—Students 8.

HIGH RIDGE, JEFFERSON CO., ST. ANTHONY OF PADUA (1944) Rev. Sebastian Mundackal, O.S.B.
Res.: 3009 High Ridge Blvd., 63049. Tel: 636-677-4868; Fax: 636-677-4868. Email: rusalynesahr@att.net. Web: www.stanthonyhr.org.
Catechesis/Religious Program—Students 91.

HILLSBORO, JEFFERSON CO., CHURCH OF THE GOOD SHEPHERD (1934) [CEM] Rev. Christopher F. Holtmann; Deacons Kenneth A. Henning; Paul A. Martin.
Res.: 703 Third St., 63050-4342. Tel: 636-789-3356; Fax: 636-789-9986. Email: parishsecretary@mygoodshepherd.com. Web: mygoodshepherd.com.
School—(Grades PreK-8), 701 Third St., 63050. Tel: 636-797-2300; Fax: 636-797-2300. Mrs. Julie Connors, Prin. Lay Teachers 10; Students 82.
Catechesis/Religious Program—Students 108.

HOUSE SPRINGS, JEFFERSON CO., OUR LADY, QUEEN OF PEACE (1961) [CEM 2] Revs. Michael G. Murphy; James T. Beighlie, C.M.; Deacons Thomas Gerling; Paul Turek.
Res.: 4696 Notre Dame Ln., 63051. Tel: 636-671-3062; Fax: 636-671-0003.
School—(Grades K-8), 4675 Notre Dame Ln., 63051. Tel: 636-671-0247; Fax: 636-671-0418. Renee Chauvin, Prin. Sisters 1; Lay Teachers 15; Students 149.
Catechesis/Religious Program—Students 180.

IMPERIAL, JEFFERSON CO.

1—ST. JOHN (1869) [CEM] Rev. Steven P. Robeson; Deacons Norbert Gawedzinski; Charles Ryder; Lawrence Nava.
Res.: 4525 Old Hwy. 21, 63052. Tel: 636-296-8061; Fax: 636-296-8067.
Catechesis/Religious Program—Students 122.

2—ST. JOSEPH (1905) [CEM] Revs. John J. Brennell; Anthony J. Gerber; Deacon Brian T. Selsor.
Res.: 6020 Old Antonia Rd., 63052-0968. Tel: 636-464-1013; Fax: 636-461-0411.
School—(Grades K-8), 6024 Old Antonia Rd., 63052. Tel: 636-464-9027; Fax: 636-464-3574. Mary Ellen Smith, Prin. Students 317.
Catechesis/Religious Program—Students 340.

JOSEPHVILLE, ST. CHARLES CO., ST. JOSEPH (1852) [CEM] Rev. Larry T. Huber; Deacon Fielding Harrison.
Res.: 1390 Josephville Rd., Wentzville, 63385. Tel: 636-332-6676; Fax: 636-332-8648.
School—(Grades PreK-8), 1410 Josephville Rd., Wentzville, 63385. Tel: 636-332-5672. Dwight Elmore, Prin. Lay Teachers 8; Students 101.
Catechesis/Religious Program—Trisha Roettger, D.R.E. Students 27.

KRAKOW, FRANKLIN CO., ST. GERTRUDE (1845) [CEM] Rev. Richard V. Coerver; Deacon Charles Gildehaus. In Res., Rev. Bernard J. Wilkins (Retired).
Res.: 6535 Hwy. YY, Washington, 63090. Tel: 636-239-4216; Fax: 636-239-3590. Email: stger@charter.net. Web: www.stgertrudekrakow.org.
School—(Grades K-8), 6520 Hwy. YY, Washington,

63090. Tel: 636-239-2347; Fax: 636-239-3550. Email: stgertrude@primary.net. Mike Newbanks, Prin. Lay Teachers 21; Students 255.
Catechesis/Religious Program—Students 80.

LAKE ST. LOUIS, ST. CHARLES CO., SAINT GIANNA (2006) Rev. Timothy P. Elliott; Deacons Anthony Falbo; Richard R. Moore.
Res.: 8676 Orf Rd., Lake Saint Louis, 63367. Tel: 636-332-0531; Fax: 636-561-1299.

LAWRENCETON, STE. GENEVIEVE CO., ST. LAWRENCE (1872) [CEM] Attended by St. Agnes Rectory. Rev. Clark B. Maes.
8055 State Rt. Y, P.O. Box 124, Bloomsdale, 63627. Tel: 573-483-2555; Fax: 573-483-9497.
Catechesis/Religious Program—Students 13.

LUEBBERING, FRANKLIN CO., ST. FRANCIS OF ASSISI (1874) [CEM] Rev. Vincent R. Nyman, Admin.
Res.: 1000 Luebbering Rd., 63061-3100. Tel: 888-960-1717; Fax: 888-960-1717.
Catechesis/Religious Program—Students 62.

MILLWOOD, LINCOLN CO., ST. ALPHONSUS (1850) [CEM] Rev. Charles P. Tichacek, Admin.
Res.: 29 St. Alphonsus Rd., Silex, 63377. Tel: 573-384-6223; Fax: 573-384-5981.
School—Tel: 573-384-5305. Lay Teachers 5; Students 36.
Catechesis/Religious Program—Students 30.

NEIER, FRANKLIN CO., ST. JOSEPH (1881) [CEM] Rev. Kevin V. Schmittgens.
Res.: 2401 Neier Rd., Union, 63084. Tel: 636-583-2806; Fax: 636-583-0627.
Catechesis/Religious Program—Students 68.

NEW HAVEN, FRANKLIN CO., ASSUMPTION (1892) [CEM] Rev. John C. Deken.
Res.: 603 Miller St., 63068. Tel: 573-237-3372; Fax: 573-237-3372.
Catechesis/Religious Program—Students 107.

NEW MELLE, ST. CHARLES CO., IMMACULATE HEART OF MARY (1945) [CEM] Rev. Richard L. Stoltz; Deacons Lonnie Weishaar; Christopher M. Ast.
Res.: 8 W. Hwy. D, Box 100, 63365-0100. Tel: 636-398-5270; Fax: 636-398-5577. Web: www.ihm-newmelle.org.
Catechesis/Religious Program— Mr. Shawn Mueller, D.R.E. Students 170.

O'FALLON, ST. CHARLES CO.
1—ASSUMPTION (1871) [CEM] Revs. Joseph G. Kempf; Ronald J. Rubbelke; Stephen P. Giljum; Deacons Fred Volansky; Howard Vanbooven. In Res., Rev. Eugene F. Bendel (Retired).
Res.: 403 N. Main St., 63366. Tel: 636-240-3721; Fax: 636-240-3722. Web: www.assumptionbvm.org.
School—(Grades PreK-8), 203 W. Third St., 63366. Tel: 636-240-4474; Fax: 636-240-5795. Lay Teachers 23; Students 510.
Catechesis/Religious Program—Tel: 636-240-1020. Students 565.
2—ST. BARNABAS (1961) Rev. Msgr. Daniel M. Hogan. In Res., Rev. Robert C. Lane.
Res.: 1400 N. Main St., 63366. Tel: 636-240-4556; Fax: 636-978-3358.
Catechesis/Religious Program—Tel: 636-281-3211. Students 50.

OLD MINES, WASHINGTON CO., ST. JOACHIM (1723) [CEM 3] Rev. Theodore X. Pieper.
Res.: 10120 Crest Rd., Cadet, 63630. Tel: 573-438-6181; Fax: 573-438-3685. Email: stjoachimparish@hotmail.com. Web: stjoachimchurch.com.
School—Tel: 573-438-3973; Fax: 573-438-3161. Email: stjoachimschool_63630@yahoo.com. Web: stjoachimschool.com. Joyce Politte, Prin. Lay Teachers 6; Students 73.
Catechesis/Religious Program—Students 25.

OLD MONROE, LINCOLN CO., IMMACULATE CONCEPTION (1867) [CEM] Rev. Philip G. Krahman; Deacon Anthony Trautman.
Res.: 110 Maryknoll Rd., 63369. Tel: 636-661-5002; Fax: 636-661-5002.
School—120 Maryknoll Rd., 63369. Tel: 636-661-5156. Susan Schutz, Prin. Lay Teachers 12; Students 195.
Catechesis/Religious Program—Students 45.

OZORA, STE. GENEVIEVE CO., SACRED HEART (1898) [CEM] Rev. James W. Schaefer.
Res.: 17742 State Rte. N., Saint Mary, 63673. Tel: 573-543-2209; Fax: 573-543-5576.
School—17740 State Rte. N., Saint Mary, 63673. Tel: 573-543-2997. Sr. Agnes Keena, B.V.M., Prin. Sisters of Charity 1; Lay Teachers 2; Students 17.
Catechesis/Religious Program—Students 18.

PACIFIC, FRANKLIN CO., ST. BRIDGET CHURCH (1841) [CEM 2] Rev. John A. Keenoy; Deacon Michael E. Suden. In Res., Rev. Martin J. Mulvihill.
Res.: 111 W. Union St., 63069. Tel: 636-271-3993; Fax: 636-257-6265.
School—Tel: 636-257-4533; Fax: 636-257-2504. Lay Teachers 10; Students 145.
Catechesis/Religious Program—Students 85.

PARK HILLS, ST. FRANCOIS CO., IMMACULATE CONCEPTION (1903) [CEM] [JC] Rev. Mark S. Ebert; Deacon Michael D. Burch.
Res.: 1020 W. Main St., Box 66, 63601-0066. Tel: 573-431-2427; Fax: 573-431-4060.
Catechesis/Religious Program—Students 45.
Mission—St. John (1879) [CEM] [JC] Maple St. & Walnut St., Bismarck, St. Francois Co. 63624.

PERRYVILLE, PERRY CO., ST. VINCENT DE PAUL (1817) [CEM 4] Rev. Milton F. Ryan, C.M.
Res.: 1000 Rosati Court, 63775. Tel: 573-547-4591; Fax: 573-547-4145.
Parish Center—1010 Rosati Ct., 63775.
School—(Grades K-6), 1007 W. St. Joseph St., 63775. Tel: 573-547-6503. Elaine Blair, Prin. Lay Teachers 19; Students 308.
High School—210 S. Water St., 63775. Tel: 573-547-2560. Louise Wibbenmeyer, Prin. Lay Teachers 22; Students 300.
*Catechesis/Religious Program—Parish School of Religion*Email: ldauster@svdepaul.org. Students 235.
Mission—St. Joseph 1701 W. St. Joseph, Highland, Perry Co. 63775. Tel: 314-547-4591.
Mission—St. James c/o St. Vincent De Paul Parish, Crosstown, Perry Co. 63775.

PORT HUDSON, FRANKLIN CO., HOLY FAMILY (1872) [CEM] Rev. James J. Foster.
Res.: 124 Holy Family Church Rd., New Haven, 63068. Tel: 573-459-6441; Fax: 573-459-2257.
Catechesis/Religious Program—Tel: 573-459-6594; 573-764-3292. Students 30.
Mission—St. Gerald 124 Holy Family Church Rd., New Haven, Franklin Co. 63068.

PORTAGE DES SIOUX, ST. CHARLES CO., ST. FRANCIS OF ASSISI (1799), (French—German), [CEM 2] Rev. Robert L. Banken; Deacon Robert Klostermann.
Res.: 1355 Farnham St., P.O. Box 129, 63373. Tel: 636-899-0906; Fax: 636-899-0909.
Mission—Immaculate Conception 14060 Hwy. 94 N., P.O. Box 129, West Alton, 63386.

POTOSI, WASHINGTON CO., ST. JAMES (1829) [CEM 2] Rev. Joseph J. Welschmeyer.
Res.: 201 N. Missouri Ave., 63664. Tel: 573-438-4686; 888-868-8188 (toll-free); Fax: 573-438-2100.
Catechesis/Religious Program—Students 68.

RICHWOODS, WASHINGTON CO., ST. STEPHEN (1841) [CEM] Rev. Robert C. Liss.
Res.: 11514 Hwy. A, P.O. Box 233, 63071-0233. Tel: 573-678-2207; 573-678-2203 (Hall); Fax: 573-678-2380.

RIVER AUX VASES, STE. GENEVIEVE CO., SS. PHILIP AND JAMES (1840) [CEM] Rev. William J. Wigand.
Res.: 18411 RAV Church Rd., Ste. Genevieve, 63670. Tel: 573-883-2923; Fax: 573-883-9605.
Catechesis/Religious Program—Students 32.

ST. CHARLES, ST. CHARLES CO.
1—ST. CHARLES BORROMEO (1792) Rev. John H. Reiker; Rev. Msgr. Donald C. Schramm.
Res.: 601 N. 4th St., 63301. Tel: 636-946-6370; 636-946-1893; Fax: 636-946-5598. Web: borromeoparish.com.
School—(Grades K-8), 431 Decatur, 63301. Tel: 636-946-2713; Fax: 636-946-3096. Web: borromeoschool.com. Sisters of Notre Dame 1; Lay Teachers 23; Students 361.
Catechesis/Religious Program—Tel: 636-946-2916. Students 233.
2—ST. CLETUS (1965) Revs. James J. Benz; Terry J. Borgerding; Deacons Frank Olmsted; Mark McCarthy; Kenneth M. Potzman.
Res.: 2705 Zumbehl Rd., 63301. Tel: 636-946-6327; Fax: 636-946-6466.
School—2721 Zumbehl Rd., 63301. Tel: 636-946-7756; Fax: 636-946-6526. Lay Teachers 21; Students 248.
Catechesis/Religious Program—Tel: 636-946-5936. Students 166.
3—ST. ELIZABETH ANN SETON (1975) Rev. Msgr. Robert P. Jovanovic; Rev. David P. Skillman; Deacons Gerald Hurlbert; Richard Tadlock.
Res.: 2 Seton Ct., 63303. Tel: 636-946-6717; Fax: 636-946-9263. Web: setonscene.org.
School—1 Seton Ct., Saint Charles, 63303. Tel: 636-946-6716; Fax: 636-946-2670. Lay Teachers 20; Students 240.
Catechesis/Religious Program—Tel: 636-669-6706. Web: www.setonscene.org. Nancy Burian, D.R.E. Students 261.
4—STS. JOACHIM AND ANN (1981) Revs. John A. Brockland; Noah A. Waldman; James L. Gahan; Deacons Timothy Schulte; Paul Antor.
Mailing Address: 4112 McClay Rd., 63304. Tel: 636-441-7503; Fax: 636-441-6574.
School—(Grades K-8), 4110 McClay Rd., 63304-7915. Tel: 636-441-4835; Fax: 636-441-9534. Mrs. Debbie Pecher, Prin. Lay Teachers 24; Students 331.
Catechesis/Religious Program—Tel: 314-926-0021. Students 400.
5—ST. PETER (1850) [CEM] Revs. Stephen F. Bauer; Frederick A. Meyer; Deacons John Schiffer; Lawrence R. Boldt. In Res., Rev. Msgr. Raymond A. Hampe (Retired).
Res.: 324 S. Third St., 63301-3413. Tel: 636-946-6641; Fax: 636-946-9789.
School—201 First Capitol Dr., 63301. Tel: 636-947-9669. Lay Teachers 16; Students 160.
Catechesis/Religious Program—Students 62.
6—ST. ROBERT BELLARMINE (1964) Rev. Patrick Ryan; Deacons Joseph C. Meiergerd; Phillip King.
Res.: 1424 First Capitol Dr. S., 63303. Tel: 636-946-6799; Fax: 636-946-0380. Email: strsecretary@sbcglobal.net.
School—St. Elizabeth/St. Robert Regional School, Tel: 636-946-6716; Fax: 636-946-2670. Email: jperry@mysesr.org. Web: www.mysesr.org.
Catechesis/Religious Program—Tel: 636-946-6461. Email: strdre@sbcglobal.net. Students 54.

ST. CLAIR, FRANKLIN CO., ST. CLARE (1916) [CEM] Rev. Robert Knight; Deacon Harvey Dubbs.
Res.: 165 E. Springfield St., 63077. Tel: 636-629-0315; Fax: 636-629-2327.
School—Tel: 636-629-0413. Lay Teachers 8; Students 82.
Catechesis/Religious Program—Students 60.

SAINT MARY, STE. GENEVIEVE CO., IMMACULATE CONCEPTION (1869) [CEM] Rev. Richard C. Kasznel.
Res.: 481 Immaculate Conception Dr., P.O. Box 27, 63673. Tel: 573-543-2536; Fax: 573-543-2536.

ST. PAUL, ST. CHARLES CO., ST. PAUL (1850) [CEM] Rev. Msgr. John J. Hickel; Deacons James J. Litteken; Martin G. Towey; Thomas F. Dehler.
Res.: 1223 Church Rd., 63366. Tel: 636-978-1900, Ext. 240 (Rectory); 636-978-1900, Ext. 221 (Parish Center Offices); Fax: 636-978-1400 (Parish Center Offices).
School—1235 Church Rd., 63366. Tel: 636-978-1900, Ext. 230; Fax: 636-978-1944. Lay Teachers 17; Students 195.
Catechesis/Religious Program—Tel: 636-978-1900, Ext. 222. Students 155.

ST. PETERS, ST. CHARLES CO., ALL SAINTS (1815) [CEM] Revs. Donald R. Wester; Philip G. Krahman; Deacons Gerald Knobbe; Gary Meyerkord.
Res.: 7 McMenamy Rd., 63376. Tel: 636-397-1440; Fax: 636-397-1421. Email: asparish@allsaints-stpeters.org. Web: www.allsaints-stpeters.org.
School—5 McMenamy Rd., Saint Peters, 63376. Tel: 636-397-1477; Fax: 636-970-3735. Rae Ann Kielty, Prin. Religious Teachers 1; Lay Teachers 23; Students 291.
Catechesis/Religious Program—Tel: 636-397-6995. Ms. Marya Pohlmeier, D.R.E. Students 278.

SERENO, PERRY CO., OUR LADY OF VICTORY (1908) [JC] Rev. R. William Rhinehart, C.M.
Res.: 172 PCR 920, Perryville, 63775. Tel: 573-547-6812; Fax: 573-547-1427.
Catechesis/Religious Program—Students 41.

SILVER LAKE, PERRY CO., ST. ROSE OF LIMA (1885) [CEM] Rev. Milton F. Ryan, C.M.
Res.: 1010 Rosati Ct., Perryville, 63775. Tel: 573-547-4591; Fax: 573-547-4145.

STE. GENEVIEVE, STE. GENEVIEVE CO., STE. GENEVIEVE (1759) [CEM] Revs. Dennis C. Schmidt; Gregory S. Klump.
Res.: 49 Du Bourg Pl., 63670. Tel: 573-883-2731; Fax: 573-883-2907.
School—40 N. Fourth St., 63670. Tel: 573-883-2403; Fax: 573-883-7413. Lay Teachers 16; Students 255.
High School—Valle High School, Tel: 573-883-7496; Fax: 573-883-9142. Lay Teachers 16; Students 132.
Catechesis/Religious Program—Students 65.

SULLIVAN, FRANKLIN CO.
1—ST. ANTHONY (1891) [CEM] Rev. Paul E. Telken.
Res.: 201 W. Springfield Ave., 63080. Tel: 573-468-6101; Fax: 573-468-8584.
School—119 W. Springfield Ave., 63080. Tel: 573-468-4423. Joann Kuchler, S.F.C.C., Prin. Lay Teachers 9; Students 90.
Catechesis/Religious Program—Students 43.
2—CHURCH OF THE HOLY MARTYRS OF JAPAN (1879) [CEM 2] Rev. John Patrick Day, C.P., Admin.
Church: 8244 Hwy. AE, 63080-3229. Tel: 573-627-3378; Fax: 573-627-3387.
Catechesis/Religious Program—Students 45.

TIFF, WASHINGTON CO., ST. JOSEPH (1905) [CEM] Rev. Theodore X. Pieper, Admin.
Res.: 10120 Crest Rd., Cadet, 63630. Tel: 573-438-6181; Fax: 573-438-3685.

TROY, LINCOLN CO., SACRED HEART (1891) [CEM] Rev. Thomas Wissler.
Res.: 100 Thompson Dr., 63379. Tel: 636-528-8219; Fax: 636-528-3983. Email: tlwsheart@lincoln.mo.us. Web: sacredhearttroy.org.
School—110 Thompson Dr., 63379. Tel: 636-528-6684; Fax: 636-528-3923. Sr. Jeannette Fennewald, S.S.N.D., Prin. Lay Teachers 13; Students 298.
Catechesis/Religious Program—Students 300.

UNION, FRANKLIN CO., IMMACULATE CONCEPTION (1866) [CEM] Rev. Msgr. Matthew M. Mitas; Deacon Gerald H. Becker.

Res.: 100 N. Washington Ave., 63084. Tel: 636-583-5144; Fax: 636-583-7784.
School—6 W. State St., 63084. Tel: 636-583-2641; Fax: 636-583-3073. Sisters 1; Lay Teachers 21; Students 352.
Catechesis/Religious Program—Students 109.
Convent—111 N. Washington Ave., 63084. Tel: 636-583-2188.

VILLA RIDGE, FRANKLIN CO., ST. MARY OF PERPETUAL HELP (1905) [CEM] Rev. Mark S. Bozada.
Res.: 1587 Hwy. AM, 63089. Tel: 636-451-4685; Fax: 636-742-4820. Email: stmarparr@aol.com.
Catechesis/Religious Program—811 American Inn Rd., 63089. Tel: 636-742-2460. Carolyn Henneken, C.R.E. Students 33.

WARRENTON, WARREN CO., HOLY ROSARY (1868) [CEM] Rev. William C. Thess; Deacon Ray Burle.
Res.: 724 E. Booneslick Rd., 63383. Tel: 636-456-3698, Ext. 1; Fax: 636-456-5560. Email: holyrosary724@earthlink.net. Web: www.holyrosarywarrenton.com.
School—716 Booneslick Rd., 63383. Tel: 636-456-3698, Ext. 2; Fax: 636-456-6181. Email: archstl369@centurytel.net. Web: www.holyrosary-warrenton.net. Mr. Michael Etter, Prin. Permanent Deacons 1; Lay Teachers 8; Students 101.
Catechesis/Religious Program—Students 105.

WASHINGTON, FRANKLIN CO.
1—ST. FRANCIS BORGIA (1834) [CEM] Revs. Andrew J. Sigmund; John W. Mayo; Deacon Leon Noelker. 115 Cedar St., 63090. Email: sfbparish@sfbparish.org. Web: www.sfbparish.org.
Res.: 311 W. 2nd St., 63090. Tel: 636-239-6701; Fax: 636-239-9499.
School—225 Cedar St., 63090. Tel: 636-239-2590; Fax: 636-239-3501. Lay Teachers 25; Students 250.
Catechesis/Religious Program—Students 95.
2—OUR LADY OF LOURDES (1958) Rev. Michael P. Boehm, Admin.; Deacon Richard J. Boland.
Res.: 1014 Madison Ave., 63090-4806. Tel: 636-239-3520; Fax: 636-239-7682. Email: lourdes1014@yahoo.com. Web: ollwashingtonmo.com.
School—950 Madison Ave., 63090. Tel: 636-239-5292; Fax: 636-239-7682. Lay Teachers 13; Students 196.
Catechesis/Religious Program—Students 103.

WEINGARTEN, STE. GENEVIEVE CO., OUR LADY, HELP OF CHRISTIANS (1872) [CEM] Rev. William Wigand.
Res.: 13370 Hwy. 32, Ste. Genevieve, 63670-9402. Tel: 573-883-3796; Fax: 573-883-8871. Email: olhc@isp.com.
Catechesis/Religious Program—Students 31.

WENTZVILLE, ST. CHARLES CO., ST. PATRICK (1905) [CEM] [JC] Rev. Msgr. Patrick J. O'Laughlin; Revs. Donald A. Glastetter; Frank A. D'Amico; Deacons Bernard A. Buckman; Richard Quistorff.
Res.: 405 S. Church St., 63385. Tel: 636-332-9225; Fax: 636-332-6998.
School—701 Church St., 63385. Tel: 636-332-9913; Fax: 636-332-4877. Diane Kelly, Prin. Lay Teachers 26; Students 464.
Catechesis/Religious Program—Tel: 636-332-9036; Fax: 636-332-4877. Students 373.

ZELL, STE. GENEVIEVE CO., ST. JOSEPH (1845) [CEM] Rev. Msgr. Jeffrey N. Knight.
Res.: 11824 Zell Rd., Ste. Genevieve, 63670. Tel: 573-883-3481; Fax: 573-883-7829. Email: stjozell@isp.com.
School—Tel: 573-883-5097. Adorers of the Blood of Christ (Ruma, IL) 2; Lay Teachers 3; Students 16.
Catechesis/Religious Program—Students 110.

Chaplains of Public Institutions

ST. LOUIS. *St. Anthony's Medical Center*, Tel: 314-525-1000. Vacant.
Barnes - Jewish Hospital. Rev. James C. Gray. Tel: 314-747-3000.
Christian Hospital Northeast-Northwest, 11133 Dunn Rd., 63136. Tel: 314-653-5000 (Northeast); 314-953-6000 (Northwest). Vacant.
DePaul Health Center. Rev. Lawrence F. Asma, C.M.
Lambert - St. Louis International Airport. Rev. Eugene P. Brennan (Retired).
St. Mary's Health Center, Tel: 314-768-8000. Vacant.
Mercy Hospital St. Louis, Tel: 314-569-6000. Rev. John P. Kennehan, Deacon Ken Potzman.

ST. CHARLES. *St. Joseph Health Center*, Tel: 636-946-6641. Rev. Msgr. Raymond A. Hampe (Retired). Tel: 636-947-5000.

WASHINGTON. *Mercy Hospital Washington*, Tel: 636-239-8000. Rev. Timothy J. Toohey (Retired).

Special Assignment:
Rev. Msgrs.—
Lyons, William J., S.T.L., North American College, Rome, Faculty
Morris, C. Eugene, Pontifical College Josephinum, 7625 N. High St., Columbus, OH 43235.
Revs.—
Aten, Robert L., 20542 Echo Vlaley Rd., Rocky Mount, 65072. Tel: 573-648-2467
Bene, Philip J., J.C.D., 25 E. 39th St., New York, NY 10016.
Chochol, Ronald C., Chap., Mother of Good Counsel Home, 6825 Natural Bridge Rd., 63121.
Fischer, Brian R., Master of Ceremonies
Heil, John P., S.S.D., Catholic University, 620 Michigan Ave. N.E., DC 20069.
Houser, Michael J., Via Rusticucci 13, Rome 00193 Italy.
Nord, Aaron P., Casa Santa Maria, Via dell'Umilta 30, Rome 00187 Italy.
O'Brien, John J., Via dell'Umilta, 30, Rome 00187 Italy.
O'Connor, Andrew, Chap., Nazareth Living Center, 2 Nazareth Ln., Saint Louis, 63129.
Tillman, Richard J., Bell Fountain Rd., P.O. Box 187, Cadet, 63630.

On Duty Outside the Archdiocese:
Revs.—
Brennan, Lawrence C., Monument, Colorado
Classen, Joseph, Kodiak, AK 99615
Hayden, Patrick T., La Paz, Bolivia
Kopfensteiner, Thomas R., Englewood, CO
Kovalcin, John A., Las Vegas, NV
Means, David A., Chamois, MO
Menner, Robert J., La Paz, Bolivia
Mesa, Luis, Colombia
Michler, James R., La Paz, Bolivia.

Military Chaplains:
Rev. Msgr.—
Butler, Michael T.
Revs.—
Breig, Gary R.
Kirchhoefer, Thomas A.
Ramatowski, Edward F.

On Leave of Absence:
Revs.—
Barnhart, Victor A.
Doherty, Glennon C.
Hederman, Kevin F.
Zacheis, Dennis B.
Zinser, Robert E.

Retired:
Rev. Msgrs.—
Anthony, Paul G., Regina Cleri, 10 Archbishop May Dr., 63119.
Baker, Joseph W., 3200 Southern Aire Pl., 63125.
Buchheit, Jerome J., 3293 Old County Rd., DeSoto, 63020.
Dempsey, Thomas J., St. Joan of Arc, 5800 Oleatha Ave., Saint Louis, 63139.
Dietz, Norbert J., Regina Cleri, 63119.
Drennan, William A., St. Alban Roe Church, 2001 Shephard Rd., Wildwood, 63038.
Forst, Charles J., Saint Mark, 4230 Ripa, 63125.
Griesedieck, Edmund O., Kenrick-Glennon Seminary, 5200 Glennon Dr., 63119.
Hampe, Raymond A., St. Peter, 324 S. Third St., Saint Charles, 63301.
Hanson, James E., 10021 Grouse Rd., Cadet, 63630.
Kennedy, John J., Regina Cleri, 10 Archbishop May Dr., 63119.
Leach, William J.
Lubeley, Richard J., Regina Cleri, 63119.
McCarthy, Robert, St. Agnes Home, 10341 Manchester Rd., 63122.
Overman, Robert F., 4917 Ravenswood Dr. Apt. 357, San Antonio, TX 78227.
Ratermann, David A., Regina Cleri, 10 Archbishop May Dr., 63119.
Reilly, Edward W.
Ronquest, John T., St. Agnes Home, 10341 Manchester Rd., Saint Louis, 63122.
Schmidt, Gregory L., V.F., St. Peter, 243 Argonne Dr., Saint Louis, 63122.
Schneider, Nicholas A., 6333 S. Rosebury Ave. 2W, Clayton, 63105.
Sudekum, Edward J., Regina Cleri, 63119.
Wilkerson, Jerome F., Ph.D., Pope John Paul II Residence for Priests, St. Agnes Home, 10341 Manchester Rd., Saint Louis, 63122.
Woracek, Thomas J., Regina Cleri, 10 Archbishop May Dr., 63119.
Revs.—
Ahrens, William B., Alexian Brothers, 4624 Lansdowne, 63116.
Althoff, Arthur J., Regina Cleri, 10 Archbishop May Dr., 63119.
Argent, Robert W., Regina Cleri, 10 Archbishop May Dr., 63119.
Begley, Thomas M., 404 W. Adams, Apt. A, Saint Louis, 63122.
Bendel, Eugene F., Assumption, 403 N. Main St., O'Fallon, 63366.
Blattner, Joseph H., 72176 Hwy. 2, Moyie Springs, ID 83845.
Blomberg, John F., Regina Cleri, 10 Archbishop May Dr., 63119.
Boisaubin, Robert D., Regina Cleri, 10 Archbishop May Dr., 63119.
Brennan, Eugene P., St. Sabina, 1365 Harkee Dr., Florissant, 63031.
Brennan, George P., 300 N. Fourth St., #501, 63102.
Britt, William J., Regina Cleri, 10 Archbishop May Dr., 63119.
Brunnert, Theodore J., Regina Cleri, 10 Archbishop May Dr., 63119.
Burghoff, Theodore H., Mother of Good Counsel Home, 6825 Natural Bridge Rd., 63121.
Comer, John P., Regina Cleri, 10 Archbishop May Dr., 63119.
Corbett, Robert L., Regina Cleri, 10 Archbishop May Dr., 63119.
Dalton, Donald T., 116 Hancock Ct., Festus, 63028.
Danter, Albert F., St. Agnes Home, 10341 Manchester Rd., Kirkwood, 63122.
Dempsey, John G., Immaculate Conception, 2300 Church Rd., Arnold, 63010.
Ditenhafer, John A., Annunziata Church, 9305 Clayton Rd., 63124.
Edwards, James T., Regina Cleri, 10 Archbishop May Dr., 63119.
Everding, Richard F., Regina Cleri, 10 Archbishop May Dr., 63119.
Fitzgibbon, Edmond J., Regina Cleri, 10 Archbishop May Dr., 63119.
Fleiter, Robert V., Regina Cleri, 10 Archbishop May Dr., 63119.
Forst, Aloysius A., 4141 Germania, Apt. 2B, 63116.
Galovich, George, 100 Aldergate #8, Bonne Terre, 63628.
Geoghegan, John F., St. Agnes Home, 10341 Manchester Rd., Saint Louis, 63122.
Ghio, John J., Annunciation, 12 W. Glendale Rd., Webster Groves, 63119.
Halleman, John L., Pope John Paul II Residence for Priests, St. Agnes Home, 10341 Manchester Rd., 63122.
Hauck, Herbert C., Our Lady of Joy, P.O. Box 1359, Carefree, AZ 85377.
Heimos, Robert L., P.O. Box 85, Gray Summit, 63039.
Heman, Richard J., 9405 Pancho Dr., 63123.
Hilgeman, Edward J., Regina Cleri, 10 Archbishop May Dr., 63119.
Hughes, John Jay, Christ the King Church, 7316 Balson Ave., University City, 63130.
Kersgieter, Paul J., Mother of Good Counsel Home, 6825 Natural Bridge Rd., Saint Louis, 63121.
Kester, William J., St. John Bosco, 12934 Marine Ave., 63146.
Knoll, Urban H., 629 S. Fourth St., St. Charles, 63301.
Koch, Donald J.
Lampert, Robert E., 680 E. Basse Rd., Apt. 426, San Antonio, TX 78209.
Leibrecht, Robert G., Regina Cleri, 10 Archbishop May Dr., 63119.
Lewis, Leo T., 73 Kings Rd., Evergreen, CO 80439.
Mahoney, Kevin J.
Manning, Robert C., 8755 Scarborough Dr., Colorado Springs, CO 80920.
Mannion, Martin K., Regina Cleri, 10 Archbishop May Dr., 63119.
Marshall, James C., The Arbors at Mount Carmel, 720 Jackson St. Apt. 2, St. Charles, 63301.
Marshall, Robert A., St. Agnes Home, 10341 Manchester Rd., 63122.
Mattler, Albert A., Regina Cleri, 10 Archbishop May Dr., 63119.
Mayer, John L., St. John the Baptist, 4200 Delor St., Saint Louis, 63116.
McEntee, John B., Regina Cleri, 10 Archbishop May Dr., 63119.
Mersinger, Norbert A., Our Lady of Good Counsel Home, 6825 Natural Bridge Rd., Saint Louis, 63121.
Molitor, Donald F., 478 Vass Creek Rd., Union, 63084.
Monahan, Joseph R., Mother of Perpetual Help, 7604 Watson Rd., 63119.
Nienhaus, Gerald T., Regina Cleri, 10 Archbishop May Dr., 63119.
Novak, David A., Regina Cleri, 10 Archbishop May Dr., 63119.
Oge, Raymond J., 12134 Lakewood Dr., Sainte Genevieve, 63670.
Rodis, James, 4840 Germania, 63116.
Roedig, Robert L., Regina Cleri, 10 Archbishop May Dr., 63119.
Ruff, Charles R., St. Agnes Home, 10341 Manchester Rd., Saint Louis, 63122.
Ryan, Joseph J., Mother of Perpetual Help, 7604 Watson Rd., 63119.

Sandweg, Michael J., Ph.D., 1364 Haute Loire Dr., Manchester, 63011.
Schloemer, Bernard J., St. Gabriel the Archangel, 6303 Nottingham Ave., 63109.
Selzer, Eugene P., St. Matthias, 796 Buckley Rd., 63125.
Sinz, Eugene R., Regina Cleri, 10 Archbishop May Dr., 63119.
Spielman, Paul J., 6315 Weber Rd., Saint Louis, 63123.
Sullivan, David C., St. Agnes Home, 10341 Manchester, 63122.
Suren, Richard H., St. Raphael The Archangel, 6047 Bishops Pl., 63109.
Thomas, David T., 4445 Lindell Blvd., Saint Louis, 63108.
Toohey, Timothy J., 301 Country Villas Ln., 63090.
Utrup, Eugene E., P.O. Box 260191, 63126.
Voelker, Harold H., Regina Cleri, 10 Archbishop May Dr., 63119.
Walter, David A., Regina Cleri, 10 Archbishop May Dr., 63119.
Wilke, James B., St. Agnes Home, 10341 Manchester, Saint Louis, 63122.
Wilkins, Bernard J., St. Gertrude, 6535 Hwy. YY, 63090.
Winzerling, James L., 12685 Dorsett Rd., #228, Maryland Heights, 63043.
Wolf, Joseph B., St. Agnes Home, 10341 Manchester Rd., Saint Louis, 63122.
Zinzer, Walter W., 3605 Hidden Rd., #B-4, San Antonio, TX 78217.

Permanent Deacons:
Allen, Charles M., St. Elizabeth, Mother of John the Baptist, St. Louis
Amelotti, David, Our Lady of Providence, Grantwood
Antor, Paul, St. Joachim & Ann, St. Charles, MO
Ast, Christopher M., Immaculate Heart of Mary, New Melle
Auer, Edward J., (Retired)
Bachista, Ronald J., (Retired)
Bansbach, Paul, (Retired)
Barbero, Dennis J., St. Rose Philippine Duchesne, Florissant, MO
Basler, James H., St. Agnes, Bloomsdale
Bast, Paul, Immaculate Conception, Dardenne Prairie
Baugh, Steven D., Assumption, Herculaneum
Becker, Gerald H., Immaculate Conception, Union
Beckmann, John W., St. Dominic Savio, Affton
Beirne, Edward R., St. Martin De Porres, Hazelwood
Bernsen, Albert B., (Retired)
Birkenmaier, Robert G., St. Monica, Creve Coeur
Bischof, John A., St. Richard, Creve Coeur
Boedeker, C. Allen, St. Andrew, Lemay
Boland, Richard J., Our Lady of Lourdes, Washington
Bolderson, David A., (Retired), (Temporary Leave of Absence)
Boldt, Lawrence R., St. Peter, St. Charles, MO
Boyer, Edward J., St. Rose of Lima, DeSoto
Broyles, Jimmy D.
Buchek, Bradford M., (Retired), (Temporary Leave of Absence)
Buckley, James Mike, St. Elizabeth Mother of John the Baptist, St. Louis, MO
Buckley, Michael L., St. John Nepomuk Chapel; SSM St. Clare Health Center
Buckman, Bernard A., St. Patrick, Wentzville
Buhr, Thomas A., (Retired)
Burch, Michael D., Immaculate Conception, Park Hills
Burkard, Bruce A., Sacred Heart, Florissant
Burkemper, Thomas B., (Retired)
Burle, Raymond J., Jr., Holy Rosary, Warrenton
Burton, James L., (Retired)
Butler, James R., (Retired)
Byington, Mark A., St. Joseph, Bonne Terre
Camden, David M., St. Simon the Apostle, Green Park
Carroll, Kevin, Our Lady of the Presentation, Overland
Casseau, William U., (Retired)
Chauvin, C. Frank, Ascension, Chesterfield/ Archdiocesan C.F.O.
Chavaux, Paul H., (Retired)
Chitwood, Dennis M., Sts. Peter and Paul, St. Louis
Christ, Walter W., (Retired)
Clark, Lawrence L., Immaculate Conception, Maplewood
Clemens, Kenneth C., Jr., SSM St. Mary Health Center
Coffman, Richard W., Mary, Mother of the Church, Mattese
Conley, Allen M., (Retired)
Coppage, Michael J., Jr., (Leave of Absence)
Crafts, R. Paul, St. Paul, Fenton
Craska, Paul D., St. John Bosco, Creve Coeur
Curtin, John A., Cathedral Basilica of St. Louis
Damato, Larry, (Retired)
Danna, Frank, (Retired)
Darin, John, St. Vincent de Paul, Perryville
Daus, Andrew C., St. Margaret Mary Alacoque, Oakville; CJM - Potosi Correctional Center
Davanzo, Charles R., Blessed Teresa of Calcutta, Ferguson
Dehler, Thomas F., (Retired)
Denham, Donald C., St. Gerard Majella, Kirkwood
Dickerson, Raymond A., (Retired)
Dingman, Edwin H., (Retired)
Dodson, Fred, (Retired)
Dolan, Timothy C., St. Gerard Majella, Kirkwood; SSM St. Clare Health Center
Donnelly, Daniel R., St. Joseph, Manchester
Dorhauer, Jacob W., (Retired)
Driscoll, Donald L., Our Lady of the Holy Cross, St. Louis
Duban, Matthew E., Holy Name of Jesus, Bissell Hills
Dubbs, Harvey, St. Clare, St. Clair
Durban, Charles, St. Anselm, Creve Coeur
Ecker, Alan E., St. Francis of Assisi, Oakville
Ehrhard, Herbert L., (Retired)
Esswein, Leo F., (Retired)
Eultgen, Thomas L., Most Sacred Heart, Eureka
Falbo, Anthony, St. Gianna, Lake St. Louis
Farley, Robert G., Assumption, Mattese
Fehner, Leo S., Most Sacred Heart, Eureka
Felber, David A., St. Norbert, Florissant
Fink, George Russ, St. Francis of Assisi, Oakville
Flanigan, John P., Jr., Holy Redeemer, Webster Groves
Follen, Dale J., St. Joseph, Manchester
Forster, Thomas E., Sacred Heart, Valley Park
Fronick, Edward C., St. Martin of Tours, Lemay
Gawedzinkski, Norbert L., St. John, Imperial
Gearon, William A., (Retired)
Gegg, Albin A., St. Joseph, Farmington
Geiser, Gerald J., St. Raphael the Archangel, St. Louis
Georges, Charles W., Holy Spirit, Maryland Heights
Gerling, Thomas J., Our Lady, Queen of Peace, House Springs; SSM St. Mary's Health Center
Gettemeier, Herbert B., (Retired)
Gildehaus, Charles R., St. Gertrude, Krakow
Gorski, Thomas, Sts. Peter and Paul, St. Louis
Gottlieb, Thomas J., Church of the Annunziata, Ladue
Gounis, Peter E., St. Ferdinand, Florissant
Griffard, James M., (Leave of Absence)
Groner, H. Wayne, Assumption, New Haven; St. Paul, Berger
Grotpeter, Edward R., St. Augustine, St. Louis, MO
Guilford, Mark A., St. Alban Roe, Wildwood
Gunsaullus, Roland J., (Retired)
Haefner, Joseph Tom, St. Anthony, Sullivan
Haehnel, Fred M., St. Charles Borromeo, St. Charles, MO
Harpring, David I., Our Lady of the Rosary, Spanish Lake
Harrison, R. Fielding, (Retired)
Hayes, Ralph, Blessed Teresa of Calcutta, Ferguson
Hecktor, Paul J., St. Ignatius, Concord Hill
Heitert, Donald C., (Retired)
Heithaus, J. John, Sacred Heart, Florissant
Hengen, Philip R., Washington University, Newman Center
Henning, Kenneth A., Church of the Good Shepherd, Hillsboro
Henroid, Daniel H., St. Joan of Arc, St. Louis
Hivner, John W., (Retired)
Holmes, Charles E., (Retired)
Holtmeyer, Gilbert C., (Retired)
Hurlbert, Gerald R., St. Elizabeth Ann Seton, St. Charles
Iovanna, Joseph, St. Mary Magdalen, St. Louis
Janson, Norman F., (Retired)
Johnson, Leslie A., (Retired)
Johnson, William P., St. Rose Philippine Duchesne, Florissant
Kaiser, Roland, (Retired)
Keeney, Robert J., Ascension, Chesterfield
Kelly, Lawrence C., (Retired)
Kennedy, Joseph M., Christ, Prince of Peace, Manchester
Kenney, T. Michael, III, (Retired)
Kiely, Edward Ray, Christ the King, University City
King, Philip, St. Robert Bellarmine, St. Charles
Kintz, Donald, Our Lady, Festus
Klostermann, Robert A., Sr., St. Francis of Assisi, Portage des Sioux
Knobbe, Gerald E., All Saints, St. Peters
Komotos, John W., St. Peter, Kirkwood
Kreitler, Roger A., St. Raphael the Archangel, St. Louis
Krieger, Arnold F., (Retired)
Kroutil, Joseph C., St. Ferdinand, Florissant
Krull, William J., (Retired)
La Martina, Joseph A., (Retired)
Lauterwasser, Gerard M., St. Sabina, Florissant
Le Fors, Ronald S., St. Angela Merici, Flourissant
Lechner, Joel, O.S.M., Seven Holy Founders, Affton
Lee, Samuel, All Souls, Overland
Lemoine, David E., Sacred Heart, Valley Park
Leonardo, Delfin S., St. Joseph, Clayton; Chap., St. John's Mercy Hospital
Litteken, James J., St. Paul, St. Paul
Lombardo, Charles W., Seven Holy Founders, Affton
Love, Allen F., Blessed Teresa of Calcutta, Ferguson
Maranan, Diosdado L., (Retired)
Marino, John, Ascension, Chesterfield
Martin, James P., St. Monica, Creve Coeur; Airport Chaplaincy
Martin, Leroy A., Jr., St. Mary Magdalen, Brentwood; SSM St. Mary's Health Center
Martin, Paul A., Church of the Good Shepherd, Hillsboro
Maxwell, Perez E., (Leave of Absence)
Mayo, Robert J., II, St. Rose Philippine Duchesne, Florissant
McCarthy, Mark J., St. Cletus, St. Charles
McElroy, Donald L., St. Charles Borromeo, St. Charles
McEntire, Clyde W., (Retired)
McGuire, Jerry N., (Retired)
McKee, Paul R., Ph.D., (Retired)
Meere, John F., Ste. Genevieve, Ste. Genevieve
Meiergerd, Joseph C., St. Robert Bellarmine, St. Charles
Meister, William G., Assumption, Mattese
Menard, Louis A., (Retired)
Meyerkord, Gary A., All Saints, St. Peters
Miller, George W., St. Wenceslaus, St. Louis
Miller, George A., St. Joseph, Manchester
Miller, Millard Ray, Cardinal Glennon Children's Hospital
Monahan, Patrick G., Cure of Ars, Shrewsbury
Moore, Richard R., Saint Gianna, Lake St. Louis
Mueller, Frederick J., (Retired)
Mulvihill, Thomas O., Mary, Queen of Peace, Webster Groves
Murphey, James W., Jr., Immaculate Heart of Mary, St. Louis
Murphy, James L., St. Dominic Savio, Affton
Murray, Stephen L., All Saints, University City
Naumann, Eugene J., Holy Spirit, Maryland Heights
Nava, Lawrence, St. John, Imperial
Nesbitt, Frank E., (Retired)
Nicolai, Michael A., St. James the Greater, St. Louis
Noelker, Leon R., St. Francis Borgia, Washington
Nuelle, Norman C., (Retired)
Olmsted, Francis J., St. Cletus, St. Charles; Asst., DeSmet Jesuit High School
Orr, Robert J., St. Margaret Mary Alacoque, Oakville
Osmack, David, Immacolata, Richmond Heights
Pacino, David, St. Martin De Porres, Hazelwood
Penberthy, Robert S., St. George, Gardenville
Peterson, Stanley M., Jr., St. Nicholas, St. Louis
Pimmel, Terrance, St. Joan of Arc, St. Louis
Piva, Michael J., St. Joseph, Cottleville
Politte, Glennon P., Sr., (Retired)
Politte, Stephen A., (Retired)
Politte, Thomas J., St. David, Arnold
Porterfield, Paul D., (Retired)
Potzman, Kenneth M., St. John's Mercy Hospital, St. Cletus, St. Charles
Powers, James R., Ph.D., Our Lady of the Pillar, Saint Louis; Catholic Education Office
Powers, Robert J., (Retired)
Prideaux, Frank W., (Retired)
Priesmeyer, William F., Jr., Holy Trinity, St. Ann
Prives, Gerald J., (Retired)
Quinn, J. Gerard, Judge, Metropolitan Tribunal/St. Mary Magdalen, St. Louis
Quistorff, Richard, St. Patrick, Wentzville
Rankin, Patrick J., St. Theodore, Flint Hill
Renard, Richard L., Diocese of Savannah, GA
Reuther, Ronald Lee, St. Richard, Creve Coeur
Reynoso, Louis J., St. Rita, Vinita Park
Riegel, Robert C., (Retired)
Roberson, Robert L., (Retired)
Rodis, Theodore J., Cure of Ars, Shrewsbury
Rohaly, Ernest G., Immaculate Conception, Dardenne Prairie
Rothermich, Thomas N., St. Theodore, Flint Hill
Ruegg, Walter J., (Retired)
Russell, James W., St. Ferdinand, Florissant
Ryder, Charles T., St. John's Mercy Medical Center; St. John, Imperial
Schaeffer, Eugene W., III, St. Joseph, Cottleville
Schellhase, Richard H., Queen of All Saints, Oakville
Schiffer, John, St. Peter, St. Charles
Schiffman, Donald J., (Retired)

Schisler, Steven M., Immaculate Conception, Arnold
Schmitt, Donald J., (Retired)
Schultheis, Glennon J., St. Joseph, Cottleville; St. Joseph's Health Center
Schultz, Timothy, Sts. Joachim and Ann, St. Charles
Selsor, Brian T., St. Joseph, Imperial
Shannon, John R., (Retired)
Sinak, William S., De Greeff Hospice House; St. Francis of Assisi, Oakville
Sisul, Leonard A., St. Luke the Evangelist, Richmond Heights
Skillman, Daniel, Our Lady of Sorrows, St. Louis
Smith, Randall G., St. John the Baptist, Gildehaus
Snyder, Charles R., Sacred Heart, Valley Park
Snyder, Robert J., St. Elizabeth of Hungary, Crestwood
Stackle, Paul F., St. Simon the Apostle, Green Park
Stallings, Larry J., Incarnate Word, Chesterfield
Stevens, Richard L., St. Anthony of Padua, High Ridge
Stigall, Donald R., (Retired)
Stovall, Dennis K.
Stoverink, Gerard G., Sacred Heart, Crystal City
Stoverink, John J., St. Ambrose, St. Louis
Strauss, Harold A., St. Sabina, Florissant
Streckfuss, Joseph C., (Retired)
Suden, Michael E., D.D.S., St. Bridget, Pacific
Sulze, Joseph W., (Retired)
Sutton, Ronald L., (Retired)
Tadlock, Richard, St. Elizabeth Ann Seton, St. Charles
Tetreault, James E., Epiphany of Our Lord, St. Louis
Tichacek, George A., St. Catherine Laboure, Sappington
Towey, Martin G., Ph.D., St. Paul, St. Paul
Tracy, Daniel J., St. Ambrose, St. Louis
Trautman, Anthony G., Immaculate Conception, Old Monroe
Turek, Paul J., Sr., Our Lady, Queen of Peace, House Springs
Twellman, William H., St. Norbert, Florissant
Van Booven, Howard J., Assumption, O'Fallon
Vaughn, Albert X., (Retired)
Vehige, Richard J., St. Clement of Rome, Des Peres
Volansky, Fred N., Assumption, O'Fallon
Volansky, James M., St. Gabriel the Archangel, St. Louis
Wainscott, John B., St. Catherine Laboure, Sappington
Walbridge, William F., (Retired)
Warren, Phillip C., St. Martin of Tours, Lemay
Watson, George H., Holy Name of Jesus, Bissel Hills
Weatherholt, H. John, St. Paul, Fenton
Weishaar, Lonnie G., Immaculate Heart of Mary, New Melle
Weiss, William G., St. Mary Magdalen, Brentwood
Werner, Norman B., (Retired)
Wertz, Robert E., Our Lady of Sorrows, St. Louis
White, Otis D., (Retired)
Whitson, Alan W., St. Clare of Assisi, Ellisville
Willbrand, Thomas J., (Retired)
Williams, Albert C., St. Joseph, Clayton
Willis, David J., St. Gabriel the Archangel, St. Louis
Wingbermuehle, Joseph, Queen of All Saints, Oakville
Winkelmann, Christian H., St. Justin Martyr, Sunset Hills
Wohlert, Steven H., St. Anselm, Creve Coeur/Permanent Diaconate Office
Wolffer, John Robert, St. John the Baptist, St. Louis, MO
Wussler, Donald A., (Retired)

INSTITUTIONS LOCATED IN THE ARCHDIOCESE

[A] SEMINARIES, ARCHDIOCESAN

ST. LOUIS. *Kenrick-Glennon Seminary* (1818) (St. Louis Roman Catholic Theological Seminary), Tel: 314-792-6100; Fax: 314-792-6500. Web: www.kenrick.edu.

Kenrick School of Theology, 5200 Glennon Dr., 63119. Tel: 314-792-6100; Fax: 314-792-6500. Web: www.kenrick.edu. Revs. John Horn, S.J., Rector & Pres.; John M. Hunthausen, S.J., Spiritual Dir.; Donald E. Henke, Assoc. Academic Dean, Moral Theology; Rev. Msgrs. Edmund O. Griesedieck, Assoc. Spiritual Dir. (Retired); James J. Ramacciotti, Canon Law; Revs. Michael J. Witt, Ph.D., Assoc. Prof. Church History; Dennis M. Doyle, J.C.L., Spiritual Dir./Confessor; Kristian C. Teater, Asst-.Prof. Spiritual Theology; Paul J. Rothschild, Dean Students & Dir. Pastoral Formation; Sr. Catherine Marie Stewart, S.D.S.H., Rel. Educ.; Dr. Daniel Van Slyke, Assoc. Prof. Church History; Dr. Susanne M. Harvath, Ph.D., Prof. Pastoral Counseling; Mary Beth Wittry, Dir. of Music; Dr. John L. Gresham, Dir. Library & Assoc. Academic Dean & Assoc. Prof. Systematic Theology; Dr. Sebastian Mahfood, Assoc. Prof. Intercultural Studies & Coord. Instructional Technology; Dr. Lawrence J. Welch, Ph.D., Prof. Systematic Theology. Priests 14; Sisters 1; Students 98; St. Louis Students 30; Permanent Staff: Priests 14; Lay Staff 19.

Cardinal Glennon College, 5200 Glennon Dr., 63119. Tel: 314-792-6100; Fax: 314-792-6500. Revs. Dennis M. Doyle, J.C.L.; Jason J. Schumer; Dr. Randall Colton, Asst. Prof. Philosophy/Assoc. Academic Dean; Dr. John Doyle, Distinguished Prof. Philosophy. Lay Teachers 3; Students 23; St. Louis Students 19; Permanent Staff: Priests 3; Lay Teachers 3; Kansas City in Kansas 2; Springfield-Cape Girardeau 1; Colorado Springs 1. In Res. Most Rev. Edward M. Rice.

[B] SEMINARIES, RELIGIOUS, OR SCHOLASTICATES

ST. LOUIS. *Aquinas Institute of Theology*, 23 S. Spring St., 63108. Tel: 314-256-8800; Fax: 314-256-8888. Email: info@ai.edu. Web: www.ai.edu. Revs. Richard A. Peddicord, O.P., Pres.; Gregory J. Heille, O.P., Vice Pres. & Academic Dean; Thomas Barbarak, Business Mgr.; Jim Hubbman, Dir. of Mktg.& Communications; David Werthmann, Dir. Admissions; Barbara Maynard, Dir. Inst. Advancement; Julie Quint, Registrar. Priests 9; Sisters 5; Lay Faculty & Admin Staff 9.

Faculty: Revs. Seán Martin; Harry M. Byrne, O.P.; George R. Boudreau, O.P.; Donald Goergen, O.P., Ph.D., S.T.M.; Daniel E. Harris, C.M.; Jose Santiago, O.P.; David Wright, O.P.; Sisters Jean deBlois, C.S.J.; Colleen Mary Mallon, O.P.; Carla Mae Streeter, O.P.; Catherine Vincie, R.S.H.M.; Patricia Walter, O.P.; Kathleen Tehan, Librarian; Ann Garrido; Marian Love; Michael Porterfield; Carolyn Wright.

[C] COLLEGES AND UNIVERSITIES

ST. LOUIS. *Fontbonne University* (1923) 6800 Wydown Blvd., 63105. Tel: 314-862-3456; Fax: 314-889-1451. Email: mjohnson@fontbonne.edu. Web: www.fontbonne.edu. Dennis C. Golden, Ed.D., Pres. Sisters 4; Lay Teachers 81; Students 2,532.

Saint Louis University (1818) Corporate Title: Saint Louis University, One Grand Blvd., St. Louis, Mo 63103, 3634 Verhaegen Hall, Rm 212, Saint Louis, 63108. Tel: 314-977-2222; Fax: 314-977-3874. Email: admitme@slu.edu. Web: www.slu.edu. Mr. John Pruellage, Chm. Bd. of Trustees; Rev. Lawrence H. Biondi, S.J., Pres.; Manoj Patankar, Ph.D., Vice Pres. Academic Affairs. Priests 33; Brothers 4; Sisters 1; Lay Teachers 1,685; Total Staff 3,497; Total Enrollment 14,073.

Vice Presidents: Robert Woodruff, Vice Pres. & CFO; Jeff L. Fowler, Vice Pres. Univ. Advancement; Kathleen B. Brady, Vice Pres. Facilities Mgmt. & Civic Affairs; William R. Kauffman, J.D., Vice Pres. & General Counsel; Kenneth Fleischmann, J.D., Vice Pres. Human Resources; Kent Porterfield, Vice Pres. Student Devel.; Tim Brooks, Vice Pres., Chief Info. Officer; Rev. Paul Stark, S.J., Vice Pres. Mission & Ministry; Raymond C. Tait, Vice Pres. Research; Philip O. Alderson, M.D., Vice Pres., Health Svcs.; Diana Bartelli Carlin, Ph.D., Assoc. Vice Pres., Graduate Educ.; Elizabeth J. Whitt, Ph.D., Assoc. Vice Pres., Undergraduate Educ.

Deans:

Doisy College of Health Sciences Tel: 314-977-8501; Fax: 314-977-4344. Charlotte Brasic Royeen, Ph.D., O.T.R., F.A.O.T.D., Dean.

Arts and Sciences, College of Tel: 314-977-2710; Fax: 314-977-3649. Rev. Michael D. Barber, S.J., Dean.

John Cook School of Business Tel: 314-977-3833; Fax: 314-977-3497. Ellen F. Harshman, J.D., Ph.D., Dean.

Law, School of Tel: 314-977-2800; Fax: 314-977-3333. Annette E. Clark, M.D., J.D., Dean.

Medicine, School of Tel: 314-977-9801; Fax: 314-977-9899. Philip O. Alderson, M.D., Dean.

Nursing, School of Tel: 314-977-8910; Fax: 314-977-8949. Teri A. Murray, Ph.D., R.N., Dean.

Parks College of Engineering, Aviation and Technology Tel: 314-977-8203; Fax: 314-977-8403. Krishnaswamy Ravindra, Ph.D., Interim Dean.

Philosophy and Letters, College of Tel: 314-977-2701; Fax: 314-977-7211. Rev. Michael D. Barber, S.J., Dean.

School for Professional Studies Tel: 314-977-2330; Fax: 314-977-2333. Jennifer Giancola, Ph.D., Dean.

Public Health, School of Tel: 314-977-8100; Fax: 314-977-8150. Edwin Trevathan, M.D., M.P.H., Dean.

College of Education and Public Service Tel: 314-977-3292; Fax: 314-977-3290. Gerald Fowler, Ph.D., J.D., Interim Dean.

Academic Advising and Support Tel: 314-977-2369; Fax: 314-977-1424. Lisa B. Israel, Dir.

Pius XII Memorial Library Tel: 314-977-3102; Fax: 314-977-3108. Gail Staines, Ph.D., Asst. Vice Pres. Univ. Libraries.

Student Educational Services Tel: 314-977-2930; Fax: 314-977-3315. Tim Hercules, Dir.

Madrid Spain Campus Tel: 314-977-8177; Fax: 314-977-1445. Paul A. Vita, Ph.D., Interim Dir.

Other Jesuits Associated with the University: Revs. James H. Baker, S.J.; Michael D. Barber, S.J.; Lawrence H. Biondi, S.J.; Richard Buhler, S.J.; James Costello, S.J.; Anthony C. Daly, S.J.; Denis E. Daly, S.J.; Terrence E. Dempsey, S.J.; John B. Foley, S.J.; Michael D. French, S.J.; James F. Goeke, S.J.; Eugene Grollmes, S.J.; W. Charles Heiser, S.J. (Retired); Donald Highberger, S.J.; John Kavanaugh, S.J.; Thomas E. J. Kelly, S.J. (Retired); Edwin Lisson, S.J.; Michael K. May, S.J.; David V. Meconi, S.J.; Ronald A. Mercier, S.J.; John J. Mueller, S.J.; William P. O'Brien, S.J.; Claude N. Pavur, S.J.; Chris D. Pinne, S.J.; Robert L. Poirier, S.J.; Patrick T. Quinn, S.J.; Frank Reale, S.J.; Albert C. Rotola, S.J.; Mr. Michael D. Rozier, S.J.; Revs. Stephen A. Schoenig, S.J.; James A. Sebesta, S.J.; Gary G. Seibert, S.J.; James M. Short, S.J.; Paul V. Stark, S.J.; James V. Veltrie, S.J.; James K. Voiss, S.J.; Bro. William R. Rehg, S.J.

Pastoral Care Dept. of Saint Louis University Hospital: Sr. Sheila Hammond, R.S.C.J., Pastoral Care Dir.

[D] RELIGIOUS EDUCATION

ST. LOUIS. *Paul VI Institute of Catechetical and Pastoral Studies*, 20 Archbishop May Dr., 63119. Tel: 314-792-7450; Fax: 314-792-7459. Email: paul6@archstl.org. Web: www.archstl.org/paul6. Dr. Edward Hogan, Dir.; Rev. Donald E. Henke, Assoc. Dir.; Dr. John L. Gresham, Curriculum & Technology Coord.; Sisters Catherine Marie Stewart, S.D.S.H., Coord. of Sacramental/Catechetical Retreats; Mary Kathleen Ronan, R.S.M., Coord. of Lay Formation Prog.; Mary L. Beier, Registrar - Business Mgr.; Marisol D. Pfaff, Admin. Asst.- Online Course System Admin. Priests 5; Sisters 4; Lay Teachers 14; Total Enrollment 1,055.

[E] HIGH SCHOOLS, ARCHDIOCESAN

ST. LOUIS. *Bishop DuBourg High School* (1950) 5850 Eichelberger St., 63109. Tel: 314-832-3030; Fax: 314-832-0529. Email: cdandridge@bishopdubourg.org. Web: www.bishopdubourg.org. Mr. Kermit V. Boschert, Pres.; Ms. Bridget Timoney, Prin. A Co-Educational School Staffed by Diocesan Priests, Religious and Lay Teachers. Priests 1; Deacons 1; Lay Teachers 51; Students 575.

Cardinal Ritter College Prep, 701 N. Spring, 63108. Tel: 314-446-5501; Fax: 314-446-5570. Email: chall@archstl.org. Web: info.csd.org/ritter.htm. Leon Henderson, Pres.; Michael R. Blackshear, Prin.; Christine Turland, Librarian. Co-Educational High School Staffed by Religious and Laity. Priests 1; Sisters 1; Lay Teachers 25; Students 315.

Saint Mary's High School (1931) 4701 S. Grand Blvd., 63111. Tel: 314-481-8400; Fax: 314-481-3670. Email: mainoffice@stmaryshs.com. Web: www.stmaryshs.com. Rev. Mitchell S. Doyen, Pres.; Mr. Kevin Hacker, B.A., M.Ed., Prin.; Jake Parent, Librarian. For Boys, Staffed by Brothers of Mary and Archdiocesan Priests. Priests 1; Sisters 1; Lay Teachers 32; Total Enrollment 345.

Rosati-Kain High School (1911) 4389 Lindell Blvd., 63108-2701. Tel: 314-533-8513; Fax: 314-533-1618. Email: rkoffice@rosati-kain.org. Web: www.rosati-kain.org. Sr. Joan Andert, S.S.N.D., Pres.; Mrs. Judy Mohan, Assoc. Prin.; Susan Faron, Librarian. Conducted for Girls by the Archdiocese of St. Louis, the Sisters of St. Joseph and the School Sisters of Notre Dame. Sisters 2; Lay Teachers 32; Girls 400.

Trinity Catholic High School (2002) 1720 Redman Rd., 63138. Tel: 314-741-1333; Fax: 314-741-1335. Email: office@trinitycatholichighschool.org. Web: www.trinitycatholichighschool.org. Ms. Nancy Lydon, Prin.; Mrs. Gail Hoffman, Librarian. Sisters 1; Lay Teachers 29; Students 339.

FESTUS. *St. Pius X High School*, 1030 St. Pius Dr., 63028. Tel: 636-937-3695; 636-931-7488; Fax: 636-931-7487. Email: lancer@stpius.com. Web: stpius.com. Mrs. Karen DeCosty, Prin. A Co-Educational High School Conducted by Diocesan Priests and Lay Faculty. Priests 2; Lay Teachers 23; Students 278.

MANCHESTER. *John F. Kennedy Catholic High School*

(1968) 500 Woods Mill Rd., 63011. Tel: 636-227-5900; Fax: 636-227-0298. Email: admin@kennedycatholic.net. Web: www.kennedycatholic.net. Christine A. Bolesta, Pres.; Mary Hey, Prin.; Shelagh Fant, Librarian. A Co-Educational High School Staffed by Lay Faculty. Priests 1; Lay Teachers 30; Students 365.

O'FALLON. *St. Dominic High School* (1962) 31 St. Dominic Dr., 63366. Tel: 636-240-8303; Fax: 636-240-9884. Email: mainoffice@stdominichs.org. Web: www.stdominichs.org. Sr. Mary H. Bender, S.S.N.D., Pres.; Cathy Fetter, Prin.; Mary Fridley, Librarian. A Co-Educational High School Conducted by Diocesan Priests laymen and laywomen. Priests 1; Sisters 1; Lay Teachers 54; Students 707.

ST. CHARLES. *Duchesne High School*, 2550 Elm St., 63301-1494. Tel: 636-946-6767; Fax: 636-946-6267. Email: tgravemann@duchesne-hs.org. Web: www.duchesne-hs.org. Terry W. Gravemann, Pres.; Frederick Long, Prin.; Rev. James L. Gahan, Campus Min.; Ms. Sharon Ziegler, Librarian. A Co-Educational College Prep High School Conducted by Archdiocesan Priests and Catholic Lay Staff. Under the Auspices of the Catholic Education Office and the Archdiocese of St. Louis. Priests 1; Lay Teachers 44; Students 475.

WASHINGTON. *St. Francis Borgia Regional High School* (1982) 1000 Borgia Dr., 63090. Tel: 636-239-7871; Fax: 636-239-1198. Email: mtraffas@borgia.com. Web: www.borgia.com. Marilyn Traffas, Admin.; Mr. George Wingbermuehle, Prin.; Rebecca Price, Librarian. A Co-Educational High School Staffed by Diocesan Priests and dedicated lay faculty. Priests 1; Sisters 1; Lay Teachers 41; Students 545.

[F] HIGH SCHOOLS, PRIVATE

ST. LOUIS. *Christian Brothers College High School (C.B.C.)* (1850) 1850 De La Salle Dr., 63141. Tel: 314-985-6100; Fax: 314-985-6115. Email: admin@cbchs.org. Web: www.cbchs.org. Rev. Matthew L. O'Toole, Chap.; Mr. Michael F. England, Pres.; Bro. David Poos, F.S.C., Prin. Brothers 3; Lay Teachers 72; Students 860.

Cor Jesu Academy (1956) 10230 Gravois Rd., 63123. Tel: 314-842-1546; Fax: 314-842-6061. Email: principal@corjesu.org. Web: www.corjesu.org. Sisters Barbara Thomas, A.S.C.J., Pres.; Kathleen Mary Coonan, A.S.C.J., Prin. Apostles of the Sacred Heart. Sisters 6; Lay Teachers 51; Students 580.

De Smet Jesuit High School, 233 N. New Ballas Rd., 63141. Tel: 314-567-3500; Fax: 314-567-1519. Web: www.desmet.org. Dr. Gregory A. Densberger, Ph.D., Prin.; Rev. Walter T. Sidney, S.J., Pres. Priests 5; Sisters 2; Scholastics 2; Brothers 1; Lay Teachers 80; Students 964.

St. Elizabeth Academy (1882) 3401 Arsenal St., 63118. Tel: 314-771-5134; Fax: 314-771-3528. Email: ccheak@stelizabethacademy.org. Web: stelizabethacademy.org. Christina R. Cheak, Prin., Head of School. Sisters of the Most Precious Blood. Sisters 3; Lay Teachers 25; Students 215.

Incarnate Word Academy (1932) 2788 Normandy Dr., 63121. Tel: 314-725-5850; Fax: 314-725-2308. Email: rmikolas@iwacademy.org. Web: www.iwacademy.org. Randy Berzon-Mikolas, Ph.D.; Mary T. Maguire, Prin.; Julie Hamilton, Librarian; Sr. Eileen O'Keeffe, C.C.V.I., Mission Integration. Sisters of Charity of Incarnate Word of San Antonio. Lay Teachers 40; Support Staff 14; Students 500.

St. Joseph's Academy (1840) 2307 S. Lindbergh Blvd., 63131. Tel: 314-965-7205; Fax: 314-965-9114. Email: pdunphy@stjosephacademy.org. Web: www.stjosephacademy.org. Sr. Pat Dunphy, C.S.J., Prin. Religious 9; Sisters of St. Joseph of Carondelet 7; Lay Teachers 63; Girls 643.

St. Louis University High School, George H. Backer Memorial, 4970 Oakland Ave., 63110. Tel: 314-531-0330; Fax: 314-534-3441. Web: www.sluh.org. Revs. Thomas W. Cummings, S.J.; Carl J. Heumann, S.J., Supr.; Michael A. Marchlewski, S.J.; James G. Knapp, S.J., Supr.; Ralph D. Houlihan, S.J.; John Lan Tran, S.J. Priests 6; Administrators 6; Lay Teachers 92; Students 1,068.

Notre Dame High School (1934) 320 E. Ripa Ave., 63125. Tel: 314-544-1015; Fax: 314-544-8003. Email: emmem@ndhs.net. Web: www.ndhs.net. Sr. Michelle Emmerich, S.S.N.D., Ed.D., Prin.; Amanda Meehan, Librarian. Sisters 2; Lay Teachers 25; Girls 240.

CREVE COEUR. *Chaminade College Preparatory School Inc.*, 425 S. Lindbergh Blvd., 63131-2799. Tel: 314-993-4400; Fax: 314-993-4403. Email: archstl851@impresso.com. Web: www.chaminademo.com. Rev. Ralph A. Siefert, S.M., Pres.; Dr. Louis Peters, Prin.; James Zolnowski, Librarian. Society of Mary., Residents and Day Students. Priests 2; Brothers 1; Sisters 1; Lay Teachers 62; Students 491.

St. Louis Priory School, 500 S. Mason Rd., 63141-8500. Tel: 314-434-3690; Fax: 314-576-7088. Web: www.priory.org. Very Revs. J. Gregory Mohrman, O.S.B., Prior; M. Paul Kidner, O.S.B.; Revs. Ambrose Bennett, O.S.B.; Michael Brunner, O.S.B., Headmaster; Linus Dolce, O.S.B.; Dominic Lenk, O.S.B.; Bede Price, O.S.B.; Augustine Wetta, O.S.B.; D. Ralph Wright, O.S.B.; Susanne M. Kress, Librarian. Priests 9; Brothers 5; Lay Teachers 47; Students (9-12) 277; Students (7-8) 170.

FRONTENAC. *Villa Duchesne/Oak Hill* (1929) 801 S. Spoede Rd., 63131. Tel: 314-432-2021; Fax: 314-432-0199. Email: vdoh@vdoh.org. Web: www.vdoh.org. Douglas Lowney, Prin. (7-12); Dr. Deborah Steurer, Prin. (PreK-6); Sr. Lucie Nordmann, R.S.C.J., Head of School. Religious of the Sacred Heart., (Girls: PreK-12; Boys: PreK-6) Sisters 4; Lay Teachers 92; High School Students (7-12) 432; Elementary School Students (PreK-6) 248.

KIRKWOOD. *St. John Vianney High School* (1960) 1311 S. Kirkwood Rd., 63122. Tel: 314-965-4853; Fax: 314-965-1950. Email: lkeller@vianney.com. Web: www.vianney.com. Mr. Michael Loyet, Pres.; Mr. Lawrence D. Keller, Prin.; Mr. Gerard Stevison, Librarian. Conducted for Boys by the Society of Mary (Marianists). Priests 1; Brothers 3; Lay Teachers 45; Students 625.

Ursuline Academy (1848) 341 S. Sappington Rd., 63122. Tel: 314-984-2800; Fax: 314-966-3795. Email: treichardt@ursulinestl.org. Web: www.ursulinestl.org. Dr. Tina Reichardt, Pres.; Sr. Mary Ann Dooling, O.S.U., Prin.; Bernyce Christiansen, Librarian. Ursuline Nuns of the Roman Union. Sisters 4; Lay Teachers 47; Students 645.

TOWN AND COUNTRY. *Visitation Academy* (1833) 3020 N. Ballas Rd., 63131. Tel: 314-625-9100; Fax: 314-432-5355. Web: www.visitationacademy.org. Mrs. Rosalie Henry, Head of School; Mrs. Mary Ellen Schraeder, Upper School Prin. (Grades 7-12); Mrs. Margaret Karl, Lower School Prin. (PK-6). Sisters in the Monastery 12; Lay Teachers 70; Students 469; Lower School (PreK-6) 173; Upper School (7-12) 458.

WEBSTER GROVES. *Nerinx Hall High School* (1924) 530 E. Lockwood, 63119. Tel: 314-968-1505; Fax: 314-968-0604. Email: broche@nerinxhs.org. Web: www.nerinxhs.org. Sr. Barbara Roche, S.L., Pres.; Mrs. Jane W. Kosash, Prin.; Dr. Angela F. Zinkl, Assoc. Prin.; Carol Ann K. Winkler, Librarian. Sisters of Loretto at the Foot of the Cross 3; Religious 2; Lay Teachers 61; Students 633.

[G] ELEMENTARY SCHOOLS, PRIVATE

ST. LOUIS. **De La Salle Middle School*, 4145 Kennerly Ave., 63113. Tel: 314-531-9820; Fax: 314-531-4820. Corey M. Quinn, Pres.; Mr. Phil Pusateri, Prin. Lay Teachers 7; Students 62.

Holy Cross Academy, 8874 Pardee Rd., 63123.

Loyola Academy of St. Louis (1994) 3851 Washington Blvd., 63108. Tel: 314-531-9091; Fax: 314-531-3603. Email: eclark@loyolaacademy.org. Web: www.loyolaacademy.org. M. H. Eric Clark, Pres.; Mrs. Katherine Petron, Prin. Religious 1; Lay Teachers 7; Students 70.

Marian Middle School (1999) 4130 Wyoming, 63116. Tel: 314-771-7674; Fax: 314-771-7679. Email: mhermann@mms-stl.org. Web: www.mms-stl.org. Maureen A. Herrmann, Dir.; Ms. Christy Leming, Prin. Lay Teachers 7; Students 75.

CREVE COEUR. *Chaminade College Preparatory*, (Grades 6-12), 425 S. Lindbergh Blvd., 63131. Tel: 314-993-4400; Fax: 314-993-4403. Email: archstl851@impresso.com. Web: www.chaminademo.com. Rev. Ralph A. Siefert, S.M., Pres.; Mr. Michael T. Bander, Prin.; James Zolnowski, Librarian. Society of Mary., (Middle School), Residents and Day Students (Boys) Priests 2; Brothers 1; Lay Teachers 23; Students 292.

FESTUS. *Ursuline Learning Center*, 201 Brierton Ln., 63028. Tel: 636-937-3344. Carolyn Meinhardt, Dir.

FRONTENAC. *Villa Duchesne* (1929) (Grades 7-12), (Girls), 801 S. Spoede Rd., 63131-2699. Tel: 314-432-2021; Fax: 314-432-0199. Email: admissions@vdoh.org. Web: www.vdoh.org. Dr. Deborah Steurer, Prin. (PreK-6); Douglas Lowney, Prin. (7-12); Sr. Lucie Nordmann, R.S.C.J., Head of School. Sisters 4; Lay Teachers 92; Girls & Boys 248.

ST. CHARLES. *Academy of the Sacred Heart* (1818) (Coed), 619 N. 2nd St., 63301. Tel: 636-946-6127; Fax: 636-949-6659. Email: mglavin@ash1818.org. Web: www.ash1818.org. Sr. Maureen Glavin, Head of School; Joanna Collins, Prin. Middle School; Mrs. Marcia Renken, Prin. Lower School. Sisters 7; Lay Teachers 51; Students 538.

TOWN AND COUNTRY. *Visitation Academy* (1833) (Grades PreK-12), 3020 N. Ballas Rd., 63131. Tel: 314-625-9100; Fax: 314-432-5355. Email: swilliams@visitationacademy.org. Web: www.visitationacademy.org. Mrs. Rosalie Henry, Head of School; Mrs. Margaret Karl, Prin. (PreK-6); Mrs. Mary Ellen Schraeder, Prin. (Grades 7-12). Visitation Sisters 1; Lay Teachers 70; Students 173.

[H] DEPARTMENT OF SPECIAL EDUCATION

ST. LOUIS. *Department of Special Education* (1950) 4445 Lindell Blvd., 63108. Tel: 314-792-7320; Fax: 314-792-7325. Email: ktichy@archstl.org. Dr. Karen Tichy, Admin.; Rev. Msgr. Vernon E. Gardin, Ph.D., Spiritual Advisor. Special Education ungraded classrooms at Ascension, and St. John the Baptist. Special Education Schools at Annunziata and the Academy at St. Rose Philippine Duchesne. Special Education Day Care, Preschool and Early Intervention Services at St. Mary's North and St. Mary's South. Special Education Program for children with autism and developmental delays at St. Gemma Center. Special Education services for high school students with disabilities at partner Catholic high schools through St. Joseph's Special Services. Special religious education classes for children and adults with developmental disabilities or major learning disabilities. Psycho-Educational Testing Service. Administrative office for above programs and services. Total Staff 69; Total Number of Students Served 300.

St. Mary's Special Services for Exceptional Children (1952) Administrative Office: 4445 Lindell Blvd., 63108. Tel: 314-792-7320; Fax: 314-792-7325.

St. Mary's Special School for Exceptional Children, Early Intervention services, day care and Preschool for all children (ages 6 weeks-6years), both with developmental delays and typically-developing, in an inclusionary early childhood center.

St. Mary's - North, 1724 Redman Ave., 63138. Tel: 314-653-2591; Fax: 314-653-6811. Web: www.archstl.org/education.

St. Mary's - South, 1045 Union Rd., 63123. Tel: 314-631-8231; Fax: 314-631-0015. Rev. Msgr. Vernon E. Gardin, Ph.D., Exec. Dir.; Dr. Karen Tichy, Admin. Total Staff 42; Total Children Served 175.

CHESTERFIELD. *St. Joseph Institute for the Deaf*, 1809 Clarkson Rd., 63017-5065. Tel: 636-532-3211 (Voice/TTY); Fax: 636-532-4560. Web: www.sjid.org. Deborah S. Wilson, Pres. School for the Deaf; Auditory-oral day school for hearing-impaired children from birth-8th grade. Early intervention therapy for children 0-5; pre- & elementary school offering intense speech & academic prog. Sisters 4; Lay Teachers 20; Personnel 47; Therapists 5; Students 30.

[I] SERVICES FOR THE ELDERLY

ST. LOUIS. *Cardinal Carberry Senior Living Center*, 7601 Watson Rd., 63119. Tel: 314-961-8000; Fax: 314-961-1934. Email: swesley@ccstl.org. Web: www.cardinalritterseniorservices.org. Sr. Suzanne Wesley, C.S.J., CEO.

Cardinal Ritter Senior Services, 7601 Watson Rd., 63119. Tel: 314-961-8000; Fax: 314-961-1934. Email: swesley@ccstl.org. Web: www.cardinalritterseniorservices.org. Sr. Suzanne Wesley, C.S.J., CEO.

Cardinal Ritter Senior Services, Catholic Charities network of agencies provides social services, in home services, residences, adult day care, employment and volunteer services for the elderly. Total Staff 525; Total Housing Units 1,825; Total Clients Served 28,378.

Cardinal Ritter Senior Services - Adult Day Program, 7663 Watson Rd., 63119. Tel: 314-962-7501; Fax: 314-962-7140. Web: www.cardinalritterseniorservices.org.

Cardinal Ritter Institute Residential Services Corporation, 7601 Watson Rd., 63119. Tel: 314-961-8000; Fax: 314-961-4850. Web: www.cardinalritterseniorservices.org. Sr. Suzanne Wesley, C.S.J., CEO. Provides housing mgmt., housing & assisted living facilities for the elderly.

St. Robert Adult Day Program, 1424 First Capitol Dr. S., St. Charles, 63303. Tel: 636-916-3709; Fax: 636-916-3732.

Alexian Court Apartments, 2636 Chippewa St., Saint Louis, 63118. Tel: 314-771-5604; Fax: 314-771-7629. Web: www.alexianbrothers.net.

Alexian Brothers Services, Inc., Sponsored by Alexian Brothers Senior Ministries. Managed by National Church Residence.

St. John Neumann Apartments, Inc., 8424 Lucas & Hunt Rd., 63136. Tel: 314-385-0707; Fax: 314-385-5299. Web: www.cardinalritterseniorservices.org.

St. Joseph Apartments, Inc., 7677 Watson Rd.,

63119. Tel: 314-962-0969; Fax: 314-962-1393. Web: www.cardinalritterseniorservices.org.

St. Patrick Apartments, Inc., 555 Bluff Parks Dr., 63031. Tel: 314-839-3212; Fax: 314-839-7537. Web: www.cardinalritterseniorservices.org.

St. Patrick's Apartments II, Inc., 583 Bluff Parks Dr., Florissant, 63031. Tel: 314-837-4101; Fax: 314-837-4389. Web: www.cardinalritterseniorservices.org.

Holy Infant Apartments, Inc., 7663 Watson Rd., 63119. Tel: 314-962-7878; Fax: 314-962-1393. Web: www.cardinalritterseniorservices.org.

St. Agnes Apartments, Inc., 2840 Wisconsin, 63118. Tel: 314-664-1255; Fax: 314-664-1192. Web: www-.cardinalritterseniorservices.org.

Pope John Paul II Apartments, Inc., 6325 Waterways Dr., 63033. Tel: 314-653-0400, Ext. 294; Fax: 314-653-2840. Web: www.cardinalritterseniorservices.org.

St. Elizabeth Hall, 325 N. Newstead, 63108. Tel: 314-652-9525; Fax: 314-652-8879. Web: www.cardinalritterseniorservices.org.

Du Bourg House, 5890 Eichelberger, 63109. Tel: 314-752-1901; Fax: 314-752-0572. Web: www.cardinalritterseniorservices.org.

Cardinal Carberry Senior Living Center Tel: 314-961-8000; Fax: 314-961-1934. Sr. Suzanne Wesley, C.S.J., CEO.

Our Lady of Life Apartments, Inc., 7655 Watson Rd., 63119. Tel: 314-968-9447; Fax: 314-968-1758. Web: www.cardinalritterseniorservices.org.

Mother of Perpetual Help Residence, Inc., Mother of Perpetual Help Residence, Inc., 7609 Watson Rd., 63119. Tel: 314-918-2260; Fax: 314-961-3061. Web: www.cardinalritterseniorservices.org.

Mary, Queen and Mother Center, 7601 Watson Rd., 63119. Tel: 314-961-8000; Fax: 314-961-1548. Web: www.cardinalritterseniorservices.org.

Holy Angels Apartments I, Inc., 3455 DePaul Ln., Bridgeton, 63044. Tel: 314-298-9505; Fax: 314-298-2414. Web: www.cardinalritterseniorservices.org.

Holy Angels Apartments II, Inc., 3499 DePaul Ln., Bridgeton, 63044. Tel: 314-291-1345; Fax: 314-291-2851. Web: www.cardinalritterseniorservices.org.

St. Clare of Assisi Senior Village, Inc., 409 Warrenton Village Dr., Warrenton, 63383. Tel: 314-298-9505; Fax: 314-298-2414. Web: www.cardinalritterseniorservices.org.

St. William Apartments I, Inc., 1979 Hanley Rd., Dardenne Prairie, 63368. Tel: 636-695-4200.

St. William Apartments II, Inc., 1983 Hanley Rd., Dardenne Prairie, 63368. Tel: 636-379-9990.

Corporate Action for the Care of the Elderly, Inc., 4330 Olive St., Saint Louis, 63108. Tel: 314-533-4770; Fax: 314-533-3226. Sr. Cathy Vetter, C.C.V.I., Pres. Association Composed of Representatives of 14 Religious Communities. Grants offered to assist those who work with the elderly.

St. Elizabeth Adult Day Care Center (1981) 3401 Arsenal St., 63118. Tel: 314-772-5107; Fax: 314-772-3674. Email: sjamiller@juno.com. Web: www.seadcc.org. Sr. John Antonio Miller, C.PP.S., Admin. Conducted by the Sisters of the Most Precious Blood to Provide Day Care for the Elderly and Handicapped.

St. Elizabeth Adult Day Care Center of Florissant (1994) 1831 N. New Florissant Rd., Florissant, 63033. Tel: 314-838-5005; Fax: 314-838-5005.

St. Elizabeth Adult Day Care Center of Overland (1997) 2543 Hood, Overland, 63114. Tel: 314-890-0005; Fax: 314-890-0005. Web: www.seadcc.org.

St. Elizabeth Arnold Adult Day Care Center, 2000 El Lago, Arnold, 63010. Tel: 636-461-0730; Fax: 636-461-0730. Web: www.seadcc.org.

St. Elizabeth Adult Day Care Center - Mapaville, 3825 Plass, Box 105, Mapaville, 63065. Tel: 636-931-7498; Fax: 636-931-7498. Web: www.seadcc.org.

St. Elizabeth Adult Day Care Center - Olivette, 9723 Grandview, Olivette, 63132. Tel: 314-994-9165; Fax: 314-994-9165. Web: www.seadcc.org.

St. Elizabeth Adult Day Care Center - Lemay, 317 Hoffmeister, Lemay, 63125. Tel: 314-638-8850; Fax: 314-638-8850. Web: www.seadcc.org.

St. Elizabeth Adult Day Care Center - Ste. Genevieve, 765 Market St., Sainte Genevieve, 63670. Tel: 573-883-7603; Fax: 573-883-7603. Web: www.seadcc.org.

San Luis Apartments, Inc., 20 Archbishop May Dr., 63119.

[J] GENERAL HOSPITALS

ST. LOUIS. *St. Anthony's Medical Center* (1900) 10010 Kennerly Rd., 63128. Tel: 314-525-1000; Fax: 314-525-4485. Email: sandra-straub@samcstl.org. Web: www.stanthonysmedcenter.com. Sr. Sandra Straub, C.S.J., Dir. Mission Integration; Rev. William Cardy, O.F.M., Chap. Licensed Beds 767; Operating Beds 554; Total Staff 3,846; Full-Time Employees 3,105; Patients Assisted Annually 528,372.

SSM St. Mary's Health Center (1924) 6420 Clayton Rd., 63117. Tel: 314-768-8000; Fax: 314-768-8011. Email: rob_shelton@ssmhc.com. Web: www.stmarys-stlouis.com. Kate Becker, Pres. Member of SSM Health Care Bed Capacity 525; Total Staff 2,030; Patients Assisted Annually 192,282.

BRIDGETON. *SSM De Paul Health Center Foundation* (1828) 12303 De Paul Dr., 63044. Tel: 314-344-6000; Fax: 314-344-6172. Email: patrice_komoroski@ssmhc.com. Web: www.ssmdepaul.com. Pat Komoroski, Pres.; Rev. David Boyle, Chap.; Stephen Robin, Chap.; Charlene Raitt, Chap.; Rev. Glenn Reitz, Chap.; Teresa Roberson-Mullins, Dir. Passtoral Care & Ethics; John Sharp. Member of SSM Health Care.

SSM DePaul Health Center (Operating) Excluding Nursery 476; (Licensed) Excluding Nursery 476; Sisters 1; Patients Assisted Annually 215,344; Staff 2,227.

St. Vincent Division, 12303 De Paul Dr., 63044. Tel: 314-344-6700; 800-426-2083. Pre-Adolescent, Adolescent, Adult & Gero Psychiatric Care and outpatient Chemical Dependency. Operating 98; Licensed 98.

CREVE COEUR. *Mercy Hospital St. Louis* formerly St. John's Mercy Medical Center , 615 S. New Ballas Rd., 63141. Tel: 314-251-6000; Fax: 314-251-4168. Web: www.stjohnsmercy.org. 14528 S. Outer Forty Rd. Ste. 100, Chesterfield, 63017. Jeff Johnston, Pres. & CEO. Conducted by the Sisters of Mercy of the Americas South Central Communty, Inc. merged 7/1/2008., (See Branch Unit under Washington, MO). Sisters 3; Nurses 2,000; Bed Capacity 979; Skilled Nursing 120; Total Staff 5,800; Patients Assisted 711,108.

FENTON. *SSM St. Clare Health Center* (1954) 1015 Bowles Ave., 63026. Tel: 636-496-2500; Fax: 636-496-4901. Timothy Pratt, M.D., Interim Pres. & Chief Medical Officer. Member of SSM Health Care. Sisters 1; Bed Capacity 180; Total Nurses 512; Total Staff 1,117; Total Assisted Annually 103,101.

SSM St. Clare Health Center Foundation, 1015 Bowles Ave., 63026. Tel: 636-496-2515; Fax: 636-496-4901. Email: susan_ell@ssmhc.com. Web: www.ssmstclare.com.

LAKE ST. LOUIS. *SSM St. Joseph Hospital West*, 100 Medical Plaza, Lake Saint Louis, 63367. Tel: 314-625-5200; Fax: 636-755-3876. Web: www.ssmstjoseph.com. Drew Rector, Pres.; Sisters Donna Olson, Pastoral Care; Charlotte Lehman, Pastoral Care. Member of SSM Health Care. Bed Capacity 122; Total Staff 823; Patients Assisted Annually 121,206.

ST. CHARLES. *SSM St. Joseph Health Center*, 300 First Capitol Dr., 63301. Tel: 314-947-5000; Fax: 314-947-5090. Web: www.ssmstjoseph.com. Gaspare Calvaruso, Pres.; David Fitzgerald, Dir. Pastoral Care; Rev. Msgr. Raymond A. Hampe (Retired). Member of SSM Health Care. Sisters 1; Bed Capacity 410; Total Staff 1,590; Patients Assisted Annually 158,863.

WASHINGTON. *Mercy Hospital Washington* formerly St. John's Mercy Hospital (1926) 901 E. 5th St., 63090. Tel: 636-239-8000; Fax: 636-569-6733. Web: www.stjohnsmercy.org/sjmh. Terri McLain, Pres.; Mark Covington, Vice Pres., Mission; Mary Salois, Mgr. Pastoral Svcs.; Rev. Timothy J. Toohey, Chap. (Retired); Sr. Michaelanne Estoup, R.S.M., (Retired); Rev. Tom Haller, Chap. (Protestant). (See Listing Under Creve Coeur, MO). Bed Capacity 187; Total Staff 685; Total Assisted Annually 122,674.

WENTZVILLE. *SSM St. Joseph Health Center - Wentzville*, 500 Medical Dr., 63385. Tel: 636-327-1000; Fax: 636-327-1110. Web: www.ssmstjoseph.com. Gaspare Calvaruso, Pres.; David Fitzgerald, Contact Person. (Member: SSM Health Care) 74; Total Staff 204; Patients Assisted Annually 28,320.

[K] SPECIAL HOSPITALS

ST. LOUIS. *SSM Cardinal Glennon Children's Medical Center* (1956) 1465 S. Grand Blvd., 63104. Tel: 314-577-5610; Fax: 314-268-6468. Email: sherlyn_hailstone@ssmhc.com. Web: www.cardinalglennon.com. Member of SSM Health Care. Sisters 4; Bed Capacity (for Children) 190; Total Staff 1,782; Patients Assisted Annually 174,885.

CREVE COEUR. *SSM Rehab*, 10101 Woodfield Ln., Ste. 100, Exec. Offices, 63132. Tel: 314-768-5300; Fax: 314-768-5355. Web: www.ssmrehab.com. Victoria Horst, Exec. Vice Pres. Rehab. Opers. Member of SSM Health Care; For rehabilitation of pediatrics, adolescents and adults. Bed Capacity: SSM St. Mary's Health Center, St. Louis 80; SSM St. Joseph Health Center, St. Charles 20; Outpatient Locations 24.

[L] PROTECTIVE INSTITUTIONS

Day Care Centers

ST. LOUIS

Guardian Angel Settlement Association, P.O. Box 2055, 63158-0055. Tel: 314-231-3188; Fax: 314-231-8126. Email: efmurphy@guardianangelsettlement.org. Web: www.guardianangelsettlement.org. Rev. Edward F. Murphy, C.M., Exec. Dir. Founded by the Daughters of Charity of St. Vincent de Paul., Child Care Services and Social Services. Priests 2; Total Staff 55; Total Assisted Annually 26,123.

DeSales Child Care Center, 2652 Iowa, 63118. Tel: 314-771-6417; Fax: 314-231-8126.

Gabriel Child Care Center, 818 Cass Ave., 63106. Tel: 314-621-2898; Fax: 314-231-8126.

Guardian Angel at Hosea House, 2635 Gravois Ave., 63118. Tel: 314-773-9027; Fax: 314-773-6140.

Peace for Kids, 4415 Maryland, Saint Louis, 63108. Tel: 314-531-0511, Ext. 104; Fax: 314-531-2954. Email: meversgerd@ccstl.org. Lara Pennington, Exec. Dir.; Sarah Williams, Dir. A child development center providing high quality child development education and care to children 6 weeks to 6 years. Licensed by the State of Missouri and accredited by Counsel of Accreditation (COA) and Missouri Accreditation of Programs for Chldren and Youth (MOA). Students 36.

Sacred Heart Villa (1940) 2108 Macklind Ave., 63110. Tel: 314-771-2224; Fax: 314-771-1262. Web: sacredheartvilla.org. Sr. Jude Ruggeri, A.S.C.J., Exec. Dir. Conducted by the Apostles of the Sacred Heart of Jesus., Full-Time Care From 6:30-5:30 for children 3-5 years old. Total Assisted 120; Total Staff 26.

IMPERIAL

Queen of Apostles Center (1989) 800 Montebello Camp Rd., 63052. Tel: 636-464-0163; Fax: 636-464-0163. Email: rbuttice@yahoo.com. Days of Recollection, conferences and private weekend retreats; children's spirituality classes, spiritual direction. Apostles of the Sacred Heart of Jesus 4; Total Staff 3.

KIRKWOOD

Carmelite Child Development Center, 1111 N. Woodlawn Ave., 63122. Tel: 314-822-0058; Fax: 314-822-3573. Email: vocations@carmelitedcj.org. Web: www.carmelitedcj.org. Ann Cunningham, Dir. Operated by the Carmelite Sisters of the Divine Heart of Jesus. Provides child development, child care and services. Full Day 106; Total Staff 15.

[M] HOMES FOR CHILDREN

ST. LOUIS. *Boys Hope/Girls Hope of St. Louis, Inc.*, 755 S. New Ballas Rd., Ste. 120, 63141. Tel: 314-692-7477; Fax: 314-692-7810. Email: hopestlouis@bhgh.org. Web: www.hopestlouis.org. Michael E. Howard, Exec. Dir. Residential Care for Adolescent Boys and Girls, Troubled by Family Disruptions, who are Capable of College Preparatory High School Work. Ages 10-18. Total Assisted Annually 25; Total Staff 11.

FLORISSANT. *Child Center - Marygrove* (1849) 2705 Mullanphy Ln., 63031. Tel: 314-837-1702; Fax: 314-830-6263. Email: hnegri@ccstl.org. Web: www.childcentermarygrove.org. Sr. Helen Negri, D.C., D.C., L.G.S.W., B.C.C.S.W., CEOWeb: www.marygroveservices.org. Owned and operated under the auspices of Catholic Charities; Residential treatment for emotionally disturbed males and females (ages 6-21). Special education, therapy and medical services. Overnight emergency care: and crisis nursery males and females (Birth-21). Transitional Services, Apartments, Sequoia House and Drury House. Male and Female (ages 17-21). Bed Capacity 132; Total Staff 201; Total Assisted 624.

NORMANDY. *St. Vincent Home for Children* (1850) 7401 Florissant Rd., 63121. Tel: 314-261-6011; Fax: 314-385-1467. Email: lataylor@saintvincenthome.org. Web: www.saintvincenthome.org. Lee Ann Taylor, Exec. Dir.; Jill Kelsey, Dir. Educ./Prin.; Connie Mowery, Dir. Residential.

The German St. Vincent Orphan Association, Chapel of the Sacred Heart. Lay Teachers 4; Teacher Assistants 4; Therapists 2; Interventionists 2; Children 95; Child Care 47; Total Staff 90; Total Assisted 247.

[N] HOMES FOR AGED

ST. LOUIS. *Alexian Brothers Lansdowne Village* (1988) 4624 Lansdowne, 63116. Tel: 314-351-6888; Fax: 314-351-5825. Web: ablv.org. Daniel Stricker, Admin. Bed Capacity 145; Total Assisted Annually 651; Total Staff 155.

Alexian Brothers Sherbrooke Village (1991) 4005 Ripa Ave., 63125. Tel: 314-544-1111; Fax: 314-544-5134. Email: mroth@alexianbrothers.net. Web: alexianbrothers.net. C. Michael Roth, Pres. Total in Residence (Assisted Living) 44; Total Assisted

(Nursing Care) 120; Total Assisted Annually 651; Total Staff 224.

Little Sisters of the Poor, Home for the Aged (1869) 3225 N. Florissant Ave., 63107. Tel: 314-421-6022; Fax: 314-436-9069. Sr. Chantal Peyton, L.S.P., Supr.; Rev. James Beegan, M.S.F., Chap. Sisters 13; Residents 116; Total Assisted 125; Total Staff 125.

Mary, Queen and Mother Center, 7601 Watson Rd., 63119. Tel: 314-961-8000; Fax: 314-961-3580. Email: mbarth@ccstl.org. Web: www.ccstl.org/crss. Mike Barth, Admin. Skilled Nursing Facility.; A part of Cardinal Carberry Living Center Bed Capacity 230; Total Staff 255; Total Assisted Annually 630.

Mother of Good Counsel Home (1932) 6825 Natural Bridge Rd., (St. Louis Co.), 63121. Tel: 314-383-4765; Fax: 314-383-7256. Email: administration@mogch.org. Web: mogch.org. Sr. M. Mikela Meidl, Admin. Conducted by Sisters of St. Francis of the Martyr St. George., Skilled Nursing Facility for Men and Women. Sisters 12; Residents 70; Total Staff 100.

Mother of Perpetual Help Residence, 7609 Watson Rd., 63119. Tel: 314-918-2260; Fax: 314-961-3061. Email: swesley@ccstl.org. Web: www.cardinalrittersenior services.org. Sr. Suzanne Wesley, C.S.J., CEO; Bonnie Sue Hugo, Admin. A part of Cardinal Ritter Senior Services Total Assisted 120; Total Staff 45.

Nazareth Living Center, 2 Nazareth Ln., 63129. Tel: 314-487-3950; Fax: 314-487-8001. Email: lu.westhoff@bhshealth.org. Web: www.nazarethlivingcenter.com. Rev. Andrew O'Connor, Chap.; Lola J. Westhoff, CEO & Admin.; Ronda Griffin, Dir. Assisted Living; Betty Fuller, Dir. Mission & Pastoral Care. Sisters of St. Joseph of Carondelet & Benedictine Health System., Residential and Skilled Nursing Care Facility. Total Staff 310; Total Assisted Skilled 140; Total Assisted Living 150.

Our Lady of Life Apartments, Inc., 7655 Watson Rd., 63119. Tel: 314-968-9447; Fax: 314-968-1758. Web: www.cardinalrittersenior services.org. A part of Cardinal Ritter Senior Services. Total Independent Living Apartments 206; Total Staff 41.

Regina Cleri Residence (1959) 10 Archbishop May Dr., 63119. Tel: 314-968-2240; Fax: 314-968-1049. Email: reginacleri@earthlink.net. Ms. Nancy Bryant, Admin. A Residence for Retired Diocesan Priests of the Archdiocese of St. Louis. Conducted by the Archdiocese of St. Louis. Sisters of the Most Precious Blood (O'Fallon, MO) 2; Franciscan Sisters of Our Lady of Perpetual Help 2; Priests 37; Total Staff 26; Total Assisted Annually 45.

EUREKA. *St. Joseph Hill Infirmary, Inc. dba St. Joseph Hill Infirmary* P.O. Box 550, 63025. Tel: 636-587-3661; Fax: 636-938-6398. Bro. Bernardo Trosa, O.S.F., Admin. A skilled nursing facility conducted by the Franciscan Missionary Brothers of the Sacred Heart of Jesus. Brothers 3; Residents 1; Total Assisted 2; Total Staff 5.

Price Memorial, Forby Rd., P.O. Box 476, 63025. Tel: 636-587-3200; Fax: 636-938-5266. Email: pricesnf@mindspring.com. Bro. John A. Spila, O.S.F., Admin. A skilled nursing facility conducted by the Franciscan Missionary Brothers of St. Joseph's Hill Infirmary. Brothers 3; Residents 120.

KIRKWOOD. *St. Agnes Home for the Elderly*, 10341 Manchester Rd., 63122. Tel: 314-965-7616; Fax: 314-965-3179. Web: www.stagneshome.com. Dianne Strutynski, Admin.; Rev. Msgr. Arthur B. Calkins, Chap.

Carmelite Sisters of the Divine Heart of Jesus of Missouri Sisters 16; Bed Capacity 150; Total Staff 124; Total Assisted Annually 124.

[O] MONASTERIES AND RESIDENCES OF PRIESTS AND BROTHERS

ST. LOUIS. *The Abbey of St. Mary and St. Louis* (1955) 500 S. Mason Rd., 63141-8500. Tel: 314-434-3690; Fax: 314-434-0795. Web: www.priory.org. Rt. Revs. Thomas Frerking, O.S.B., Abbot; J. Luke Rigby, O.S.B. (Retired); Very Revs. Timothy Horner, O.S.B.; J. Gregory Mohrman, O.S.B., Prior; M. Paul Kidner, O.S.B.; Revs. D. Ralph Wright, O.S.B.; R. Benedict Allin, O.S.B.; Finbarr Dowling, O.S.B.; J. Laurence Kriegshauser, O.S.B.; Gerard Garrigan, O.S.B.; Dominic Lenk, O.S.B.; Bede Price, O.S.B.; Augustine Wetta, O.S.B.; Ambrose Bennett, O.S.B.; Michael Brunner, O.S.B., Headmaster; Linus Dolce, O.S.B. Benedictines of the English Congregation. Priests 16; Brother Monks 13; Total Staff 29.

Bellarmine House of Studies, 3737 Westminster Pl., 63108-3407. Tel: 314-652-8862; Fax: 314-535-4597. Revs. Ronald A. Mercier, S.J., Rector; James F. Goeke, S.J., Treas.; Frank Reale, S.J.; David J. Suwalsky, S.J., Min.; James M. Short, S.J.; Bro. William R. Rehg, S.J. Jesuit Residence for Students in the College of Philosophy and Letters of St. Louis University. Priests 5; Brothers 1; Students 27; Total Staff 6.

Congregation of the Resurrection, Seminary House, 4252 W. Pine Blvd., 63108. Tel: 314-652-8814; Fax: 314-371-0675. Rev. Gary Hogan, C.R., Dir. Formation.

De Smet Jesuit High School Community, 330 Emerson Rd., 63141. Tel: 314-567-3500; Fax: 314-567-1519. Email: jcraig@desmet.org. Revs. John V. Craig, S.J., Supr.; John J. Bergin, S.J.; Robert E. Bosken, S.J. (Retired); Michael H. Durso, S.J.; Walter T. Sidney, S.J.; Bro. Donald E. Lee, S.J.; Mr. Vincent A. Giacabazi, S.J.; Mr. Ronald R. O'Dwyer, S.J. Priests 5; Brothers 1; Scholastics 2; Jesuits 8.

St. Dominic Priory, 3407 LaFayette Ave., Saint Louis, 63104. Tel: 314-633-4400; Fax: 314-256-8888. Web: www.op.org/stlouis. Revs. Donald Goergen, O.P., Ph.D., S.T.M., Prior; Aaron Arce, O.P.; James Barnett, O.P.; Vincent W. Bryce, O.P.; Joachim Culotta, O.P., J.C.D.; David L. Delich, O.P., Syndic; Thomas McDermott, O.P.; Jose Santiago, O.P., Subprior; David Wright, O.P., Student Master. Priests 9; Student Brothers 23; Total in Residence 32.

Dominican Community of St. Louis (1982) St. Louis Bertrand Priory - Province of St. Albert the Great., 97 Waterman Pl., 63112-1820. Tel: 314-361-4445; Fax: 314-256-8888. Revs. Harry M. Byrne, O.P., Supr.; Gregory J. Heille, O.P., Business Mgr.; Richard A. Peddicord, O.P. Priests 3.

Dominican Studentate (2010) 3407 Lafayette Ave., 63104. Very Rev. Michael A. Mascari, O.P., Prior Prov.

Franciscan Friary of St. Anthony of Padua (Franciscan Province of the Sacred Heart-Provincial Headquarters), 3140 Meramec St., 63118-4339. Tel: 314-353-7470; Fax: 314-353-0935. Email: provoff@aol.com. Web: www.thefriars.org. Bros. Patrick Darnell, O.F.M., Fraternal Svc.; Patrick Hanrahan, O.F.M.; Christopher Lambert, O.F.M., Province Sec.; Joseph Rogenski, Dir. Franciscan Missionary Union, Holy Land Commissariat & Sec. for Missionary Evangelization; Revs. Andrew Lewandowski, O.F.M., Chap. for Franciscan Sisters of Mary, Charismatic Ministry; John Rausch, O.F.M., Fraternal Svc.; Nathan McNally, O.F.M., Supply Ministry & Fraternal Svc.; Bros. Damian Pfeifer, O.F.M., Fraternal Svc.; William Schulte, O.F.M., Fraternal Svc.; Revs. Alois Gabrus, Health Care & Chap. Maryville Gardens & Fraternal Svc.; William Cardy, O.F.M., Chap. St. Anthony's Hosp. & Supply Ministry; Bernardine Hahn, Chap. Poor Clares; Edwin Albers, O.F.M., Supply Ministry; Edmund Mundwiller, O.F.M., Contemplative & Visual Ministry, 3140 Meramec St., Saint Louis, 63118-4399. Tel: 314-353-7470; Bro. Donald Lachowicz, O.F.M.; Revs. Damien Dougherty, O.F.M., Formation Prog.; Paul VI Institute; Chap. St. Alexius Hospital; Joseph B. Hagen, O.F.M., Supply Ministry, (Semi-Retired); Michael Grawe, O.F.M., Supply Ministry; Richard Jeske, O.F.M., Sr. Assoc.; Thomas Nairn, O.F.M., Sr. Ethicist Catholic Health Assoc. of the US; Friars Charles Reid, O.F.M., Franciscan Devel. Office & Hospice Ministry; Javier Ruiz E. Cadena, O.F.M., St. Anthony Food Pantry & Hispanic Ministry; Rev. William Spencer, O.F.M., Prov. Min.; Bro. Thom Smith, O.F.M., Pastoral Assoc.; Friar James Lammers, O.F.M., Fraternal Svc.; Bro. Pauli Johnson, O.F.M., Fraternal Svc.

The Franciscan Friars of the State of Missouri, Co-sponsor of The Franciscan Action Network Priests 17; Brothers 12.

Military Chaplains: Rev. Richard Bendorf, O.F.M. (Retired), Georgia.

Friars of Sacred Heart Province Serving Abroad: Revs. Jesus Aguirre-Garza, O.F.M., Eglise Catholique, Rue El Iman Ali, Marrakech-Gueliz 40000 Morocco. Tel: 212-0-44-43-05-85; Joseph Tan Doan Nguyen, O.F.M., Teaching in Vietnam, c/o Franciscan Missionary Office, 3140 Meraec St., Saint Louis, 63118; Michael Perry, O.F.M., Gen. Vicar O.F.M. Order Serving in Rome, Italy.; Allan DaCorte, O.F.M., Vice Bursar Gen.; Jeffery Haller, O.F.M., Missionary; Kenneth Capalbo, O.F.M., Teaching in Vietnam; Bro. Donald Lachowich, O.F.M., Teaching in Vietnam.

Ignatius House (1990) 4517 W. Pine Blvd., 63108-2191. Tel: 314-361-6145; Fax: 314-758-7185. Email: dfleming@jesuits-mis.org. Web: www.jesuits-mis.org. Revs. David L. Fleming, S.J., Supr.; Edward K. Burger, S.J., Pastoral Min.; Daniel C. O'Connell, S.J., Writer; Paul C. Pilgram, S.J., Aide in Province Offices; John D. Arnold, S.J., Asst. Treas. Total in Residence 5.

Jesuit Community Corporation at Saint Louis University - Jesuit Hall, 3601 Lindell Blvd., 63108-3393. Tel: 314-633-4400; Fax: 314-633-4404. Email: rghuse@gmail.com. Revs. Ralph G. Huse, S.J.; James H. Baker, S.J.; Peter W. Bayhi, S.J.; Lawrence H. Biondi, S.J.; Robert E. Bosken, S.J. (Retired); Francis C. Brennan, S.J.; Richard O. Buhler, S.J.; J. Richard Burtschi, S.J.; Thomas Joseph Casey, S.J.; Richard Comboy, S.J.; J. David Corrigan, S.J.; James J. Costello, S.J.; Robert T. Costello, S.J.; Richard F. Costigan, S.J.; Donald M. Cunningham, S.J.; Anthony C. Daly, S.J.; Denis E. Daly, S.J.; Carl A. Dehne, S.J.; Terrence E. Dempsey, S.J.; John B. Foley, S.J.; Michael D. French, S.J., Prof., St. Louis Univ.; Eugene E. Grollmes, S.J.; Francis J. Guentner, S.J.; Garth L. Hallett, S.J.; W. Charles Heiser, S.J. (Retired); Donald E. Highberger, S.J., Campus Min., St. Louis Univ.; Thomas J. Hogan, S.J.; John P. Horn, S.J., Rector, Kenrick Seminary; John M. Hunthausen, S.J.; John Kavanaugh, S.J.; Thomas E. J. Kelly, S.J. (Retired); Muthumbi wa Kimani, S.J.; James G. Knapp, S.J., Counsellor, Kenrick Seminary; David L. Koesterer, S.J.; Philip D. Kraus, S.J.; Wilfred L. LaCroix, S.J. (Retired); Gerhardt B. Lehmkuhl, S.J.; Edwin Lisson, S.J.; Edward L. Maginnis, S.J.; L. Gene Martens, S.J.; Michael K. May, S.J.; John L. McCarthy, S.J.; Anthony F. McGinn, S.J., Asst. to Prov.; Frederick G. McLeod, S.J.; David V. Meconi, S.J., Prof.; Thomas J. Melancon, S.J., Dir. Fusz Pavilion; John J. Mueller, S.J.; Francis J. Murphy, S.J.; Walter G. Nesbit, S.J.; James M. O'Leary, S.J.; John W. Padberg, S.J.; Claude N. Pavur, S.J.; Christopher P. Pinne, S.J., Consellor, Law School, St. Louis Univ.; Donald W. Reck, S.J. (Retired); Ralph C. Renner, S.J.; Albert C. Rotola, S.J.; Francis X. Ryan, S.J., Archivist: Missouri Province; Peter F. Ryan, S.J., Counsellor at Kenrick Seminary; James A. Sebesta, S.J.; Anthony J. Short, S.J.; John F. Snyder, S.J.; Paul V. Stark, S.J.; James H. Swetnam, S.J. (Retired); Joseph A. Tetlow, S.J., Writer; William S. Udick, S.J.; John G. Valenta; Curtis E. Van Del, S.J. (Retired); James V. Veltrie, S.J.; Richard J. Vogt, S.J.; Ralph E. Vonderhaar, S.J.; James P. Walsh, S.J.; Martin J. Whealen, S.J. (Retired); Robert F. Weiss, S.J.; Bros. Robert L. Aug, S.J.; Robert C. Snyder; Henry E. Welch, S.J. Priests 73; Brothers 3.

The Jesuits of the Missouri Province, 4511 W. Pine Blvd., 63108-2191. Tel: 314-361-7765; Fax: 314-758-7164. Email: moprov@jesuits-mis.org. Web: www.jesuits-mis.org. Revs. Douglas W. Marcouiller, S.J., Prov.; J. Daniel Daly, S.J., Socius; Mr. Thom Digman, Dir. Advancement; Rev. John F. Armstrong, S.J., Asst. for Formation; Mr. Sean Agniel, Asst. for Secondary and Pre-Secondary Educ.; Rev. Louis J. McCabe, S.J., Asst. for Vocations; David P. Miros, Ph.D., Archivist; Revs. Robert F. Weiss, S.J., Assoc. Dir. of Devel.; Thomas M. Rochford, S.J., Asst. Communications; Brian J. Christopher, S.J., Delegate Social & Intl. Ministries; Daniel P. White, S.J., Asst. for Pastoral & Spiritual Ministries; Kevin L. Cullen, S.J., Treas. & Asst. for Higher Educ.; Barbara Middleton, Asst. for Health Care. Missouri Province of the Society of Jesus. Priests 188; Students in Major Seminary 17; Novices 8; Brothers 15. *Sacred Heart Jesuit Community*, 3900 Westminster Pl., 63108-3902. Revs. John F. Armstrong, S.J.; Michael D. Barber, S.J.; J. Daniel Daly, S.J.; Douglas W. Marcouiller, S.J.; Louis J. McCabe, S.J.; William P. O'Brien, S.J.; Frank Reale, S.J.; Steven A. Schoenig, S.J., Supr.

Lazarist Residence, 13245 Tesson Ferry Rd., 63128-3888. Tel: 314-843-0108; Fax: 314-849-1267. Revs. John F. Clark, C.M., M.A.; Joseph E. Begue, C.M.; Philip J. Coury, C.M.; Martin J. Culligan, C.M. (Retired); Ray Van Dorpe, C.M.; Michael P. Joyce, C.M.; Richard L. Lause, C.M.; Very Rev. James E. Swift, C.M.; Revs. Ignatius M. Melito, C.M.; Lawrence F. Asma, C.M.; Robert J. Brockland, C.M.; Daniel E. Harris, C.M.; William Hartenbach, C.M.; Thomas R. Hinni, C.M.; Paul O. Schneebeck, C.M.; Daniel R. Thiess. Priests 16.

Leo Brown Jesuit Community, 3550 Russell Blvd., 63104. Tel: 314-771-5884; Fax: 314-771-6953. Email: poirierb@jesuits-mis.org. Revs. Robert L. Poirier, S.J., Supr.; Michael D. Barber, S.J.; Roger de la Rosa, S.J.; Peter Lah, S.J.; Gary G. Seibert, S.J.; James K. Voiss, S.J.; Thomas M. Rochford, S.J.; Mr. Michael D. Rozier, S.J. Priests 6; Total in Residence 7.

St. Louis University High School Jesuit Community, #3 Lawn Pl., 63110. Tel: 314-652-5425; Fax: 314-652-7028. Web: sluh.org. Revs. Thomas W. Cummings, S.J., Supr.; Ralph D. Houlihan, S.J.; James G. Knapp, S.J.; Michael A. Marchlewski, S.J.; Carl J. Heumann, S.J.; John Lan Tran, S.J. Priests 5.

Marianist Community, P.O. Box 718, Eureka,

63025. Tel: 636-938-5470; Fax: 636-938-3493. Email: mcmrcc@aol.com. Revs. Jose Ramirez, S.M.; Eugene Sweeney, S.M. (Retired); Bros. James Droste, S.M., Dir.; Joseph Markel, S.M., Dir.; Irwin Wachtel, S.M. Priests 2; Brothers 3.

Marianists, Province of the United States (Society of Mary), 4425 W. Pine, 63108-2301. Tel: 314-533-1207; Fax: 314-533-0778. Email: msolma@sm-usa.org. Web: www.marianist.com. Revs. Martin A. Solma, S.M., Prov.; Paul Marshall, S.M., Asst. Temporalities; William J. Meyer, S.M., Asst. Religious Life; Bros. Edward Brink, S.M., Asst. Educ.Chancellor; Joseph Kamis, S.M., Asst. Prov. Total Staff 28.

Priests of the Province on Special Assignment: Revs. John L. Bakle, S.M., St. Agatha Rectory, 2777 E. Livinstone Ave., Columbus, OH 43209-3039. Tel: 416-237-4689; Paul Donoghue, S.M., 363 Ocean Dr. W., Shippan Pt., Stamford, CT 06902-8222. Tel: 203-324-7889; James Heft, S.M.; Joseph Lynch, S.M.; John A. Melloh, S.M., 1922 Churchill Dr., South Bend, IN 46617-2213. Tel: 574-287-2263; Francis Nakagawa, S.M., 1184 Bishop St., Honolulu, HI 96813-2857. Tel: 808-536-7036; David Paul, S.M.; Bros. William Campbell, S.M.; Frank Gomes, S.M.; Robert Juenemann, S.M.; Robert Metzger, S.M.; Robert Moriarty, S.M.; Rev. Patrick Philbin, S.M., 7734 Santiago Canyon Rd., Orange, CA 92869-1829. Tel: 714-633-2698; Bros. Lawrence Scrivani, S.M.; Edwin Shiras, S.M.; Joseph Spehar, S.M.

Priests of the Province Serving Outside the USA: Rev. Michael R. Reaume, S.M., St. Colmba's, Church Ave., Ballybrack, Dublin Ireland. Tel: 011-353-1285-8301; Fax: 011-353-1235-2789; Bros. James Contadino, S.M., St. Colmba's, Church Ave., Ballybrack, Dublin Ireland. Tel: 011-353-1285-8301; Fax: 011-353-1235-2789; Gerard McAuley, S.M., Dir., St. Colmba's, Church Ave., Ballybrack, Dublin Ireland. Tel: 011-353-1285-8301; Fax: 011-353-1235-2789; Fred Rech, S.M., St. Colmba's, Church Ave., Ballybrack, Dublin Ireland. Tel: 011-353-1285-8301; Fax: 011-353-1235-2789; Edward Violett, S.M., (Rome, Italy).

Priests of the Province Serving in the Missions: Revs. William Christensen, S.M.; Allen DeLong, S.M.; Richard A. Loehrlein, S.M., Chaminade Marianist Community, P.O. Box 100, Karonga, Malawi. Tel: 011-265-1-362334; Michael F. Nartker, S.M., Marianist Novitiate, P.O. Box 210, Limuru 00217 Kenya. Tel: 011-254-066-73158; Bros. Ralph Doorack, S.M. (Peru), Peru; William Farrell, S.M.; Steven Grazulis, S.M.; David Herbold, S.M. (Japan), Japan; William Scholsser, S.M. *Marycliff Marianist Community*, 4000 Hwy. 109, Box 718, Eureka, 63025-0178. Tel: 636-938-5470; Fax: 636-938-3493. Bros. James Droste, S.M.; Joseph Markel, S.M., Dir.; Irwin Wachtel, S.M.; Rev. Jose Ramirez, S.M.; Bro. Leo Slay, S.M. Priests 1; Brothers 4. *Chaminade Community*, 17 Chaminade Dr., Saint Louis, 63141-8421. Tel: 314-997-4336; Fax: 314-997-4762. Revs. Ralph A. Siefert, S.M.; Oscar Vasquez, S.M., dir.; Bros. James Eppy; Andrew Kosmowski. Priests 2; Brothers 2. *Maryland Avenue Marianist Community*, 4528 Maryland Ave., 63108. Tel: 314-367-0390. Bros. Edward Brink, Dir.; Joseph Grieshaber, S.M.; Francis Heyer; James Maus; Robert Resing, S.M.; Kenneth Straubinger; Brian Zampier; Revs. Martin A. Solma, S.M.; Robert Osborne, S.M.; Alvin McMenamy, S.M. Priests 3; Brothers 7. *Marianist Community, Our Lady of the Pillar Parish*, 401 S. Lindbergh Blvd., 63131-2729. Tel: 314-993-2282; Fax: 314-993-6462. Revs. James M. Tobin, S.M., Dir.; Thomas French, S.M.; Bro. William O'Leary, S.M. Priests 3; Brothers 1. *Cure of Ars Marianist Community*, 1311 S. Kirkwood Rd., 63122-7299. Tel: 314-965-0727; Fax: 314-835-1342. Revs. J. Donald Cahill, S.M. (Retired); Timothy Kenney, S.M., Dir.; Joseph Uvietta, S.M.; Bros. Chester Burnog, S.M.; Walter Ebbesmeyer, S.M.; Kenneth Jung; Roy McLoughlin; Melvin Meyer, S.M.; Leonard Rudy, S.M. Priests 3; Brothers 6. *Salve Marianist Community*, 4108 W. Pine Blvd., Saint Louis, 63108-1805. Tel: 314-289-9499. Revs. Paul Marshall, S.M.; William J. Meyer, S.M.; Bros. Joseph Kamis; Thomas Wendorf. Priests 2; Brothers 2.

St. Matthew Jesuit Community, 2715 N. Sarah St., 63113-2940. Tel: 314-531-6443; Fax: 314-533-7318. Email: stmatthews@sbcglobal.net. Web: www.st-matthew-church.org. Revs. Mark D. McKenzie, S.J., Pastor & Supr.; Peter P. Saengthien, S.J.; William J. Hutchison, S.J. Priests 3.

Missionaries of LaSalette, Province of Mary, Mother of the Americas, 4650 S. Broadway, 63111-1398. Tel: 314-353-5000; Fax: 314-353-4582. Web: www.lasalette.org. Rev. Dennis J. Meyer, M.S., Local Supr.

Missionaries of La Salette Corp. of Missouri LaSalette Spirituality Center Tel: 314-353-5000; Fax: 314-353-4582. Kathleen Crawford, Dir.; Rev. James R. Dunphy, M.S.; Bro. Luke D. Bauer, Oblate; Revs. John Nuelle, M.S. (Retired); Richard Lavoie, M.S. *La Salette Novitiate*, 4650 S. Broadway, 63111-1398. Tel: 314-353-5000. Rev. Dennis J. Meyer, M.S., Novitiate Dir. *North American La Salette Mission Center*, 4650 S. Broadway, Saint Louis, 63111-1398. Tel: 314-352-0064; Fax: 314-352-3737. Email: lsmc2@charter.net. Web: www.lsmc.org. Rev. Thomas Vellappallil, M.S.

North American La Salette Mission Center

Redemptorist Fathers (1867) 1118 N. Grand Blvd., 63106. Tel: 314-533-0304; Fax: 314-533-4260. Email: the-rock@saintly.com. Web: www.stalphonsusrock.org. Total Staff 6. In Res. Revs. David Polek, C.Ss.R.; Kyle Fisher, C.Ss.R.; Richard M. Potts, C.Ss.R.; Bro. Terrence Burke, C.Ss.R.; Deacon Richard W. Fischer, C.Ss.R.

Vincentian Residence, 2904 Arsenal St., 63118. Tel: 314-773-7633; Fax: 314-773-0882. Revs. Romain G. Morales, C.M., Supr.; Edward F. Murphy, C.M.; Daniel A. Ricci, C.M.; David G. Nations, C.M.; William Hartenbach, C.M.; Thomas E. Esselman, C.M.; Bro. David P. Goodman, C.M. Priests 5; Brothers 1.

Attached But Not In Residence: Revs. Lawrence F. Asma, C.M.; James T. Beighlie, C.M.; P. Vincent Aherne, C.M., Carlsbad, CA; Philip M. Floersh, C.M., Tucson, AZ.

Vincentian Residence, 2912 Arsenal St., 63118. Tel: 314-771-1869; Fax: 314-771-2410. Bro. David Nations, C.M.; Rev. Thomas E. Esselman, C.M.

White House Retreat Jesuit Community (1922) 7410 Christopher Dr., 63129-5799. Tel: 314-846-2575; Fax: 314-293-0931. Email: whretreat@whretreat.org. Web: www.whretreat.org. (1922) Office: 7410 Christopher Dr., 63129-5799. Tel: 314-416-6400; 800-643-1003; Fax: 314-416-6464. Email: reservations@whretreat.org. Revs. James J. Burshek, S.J., Dir. & Supr.; Richard E. Hadel, S.J., Assoc. Dir.; Eugene C. Renard, S.J., Assoc. Dir.; Leonard E. Kraus, S.J., Assoc. Dir.; Bro. John C. Fava, S.J., Assoc. Dir.

DARDENNE PRAIRIE. *Franciscan Brothers of the Holy Cross St. Charles Friary*, 12 Dardenne Woods Ct., 63368. Tel: 636-561-0589. Email: bdavids61@aol.com. Web: www.franciscanbrothers.net. Bros. David Sarnecki, F.F.S.C., Supr.; Luke Morin, F.F.S.C., Asst. Supr.; Raphael Kreikemeier, F.F.S.C.

DITTMER. *Servants of the Paraclete* (1947) St. Michael's Community, 6476 Eime Rd., 63023. Tel: 636-274-5226; Fax: 636-274-1430. Email: benedictl@yahoo.com. Web: www.theservants.org. Rev. Benedict Livingston, s.P.; Very Rev. Liam Hoare, s.P.; Rev. Edward Rolph, s.P. *Vianney Renewal Center* (1989) 6476 Eime Rd., 63023. Tel: 636-274-5226; Fax: 636-274-1430.

EARTH CITY. *Congregation of the Mission Western Province (Vincentians)*, 13663 Rider Tr. N., 63045-1512. Tel: 314-344-1184; Fax: 314-344-2989. Email: cmstlouis@vincentian.org. Web: www.vincentian.org. Revs. Perry Henry, C.M., Prov.; Mark S. Pranaitis, C.M., Asst. Prov.; Raymond Van Dorpe, C.M., Prov. Treas.

EUREKA. *Franciscan Brothers House of Studies*, 300 Forby Rd., P.O. Box 129, 63025. Tel: 636-938-5539. Bro. John A. Spila, O.S.F., Dir. House of Studies of Franciscan Missionary Brothers of the Sacred Heart of Jesus. Total in Residence 2; Total Staff 1.

HIGH RIDGE. *Society of Our Mother of Peace* (1966) Sons of Our Mother of Peace, Mary the Font Solitude, 6150 Antire Rd., 63049-2135. Tel: 636-677-3235; Fax: 636-677-5284. Email: marythefont@yahoo.com. Rev. Placid Guste, S.M.P., Supr. Gen. Priests 2; Brothers 7; Total in Residence 9; Total Staff 2.

LIGUORI. *Alphonsian Foundation*, One Liguori Dr., 63057-9998. Tel: 636-223-1455; Fax: 636-223-1394. Email: foundation@alfonsiana.edu. Web: www.alfonsiana.edu. Rev. Martin McKeever, C.Ss.R., Pres. Alphonsian Academy. Purpose: to provide public relations and financial support for the Alphonsian Academy of Moral Theology in Rome.

St. Clement Health Care Center (1988) 300 Liguori Dr., 63057. Tel: 636-464-3656; Fax: 636-464-4717. Revs. Theodore L. Lawson, C.Ss.R., Rector & Dir.; Vincent H. Aggeler, C.Ss.R. (Retired); Joseph R. Armshaw, C.Ss.R. (Retired); Albert C. Babin, C.Ss.R.; Charles C. Bueche, C.Ss.R. (Retired); Edward Cosgrove, C.Ss.R.; Joseph Elliot, C.Ss.R. (Retired); M. Durkin Fitzgerald, C.Ss.R. (Retired); Kevin Fraher, C.Ss.R.; Roderick Garvey, C.Ss.R. (Retired); Joseph M. Greenwell, C.Ss.R (Retired); Donald Liberty, C.Ss.R. (Retired); Bruno V. Lischwe, C.Ss.R.; Henry McKeever, C.Ss.R. (Retired); Francis A. Novak, C.Ss.R. (Retired); Henry J. Novak, C.Ss.R.; James J. Nugent, C.Ss.R. (Retired); Eugene M. Oates, C.Ss.R. (Retired); James Patterson, C.Ss.R. (Retired); Gerard J. Pecht, C.Ss.R. (Retired); Michael P. Quinn, C.Ss.R.; George Rassley, C.Ss.R. (Retired); Bros. Raymond Bowersox, C.Ss.R., (Retired); James Burke, C.Ss.R., (Retired); Thomas C. Sanhuber, C.Ss.R., (Retired); Michael Schnittker, C.Ss.R., (Retired); Martin Temple, C.Ss.R., (Retired). The Redemptorists. Total in Residence 35; Total Staff 2.

Liguori Mission House/Redemptorists, Ten Liguori Dr., 63057. Tel: 636-464-6999; Fax: 636-464-6765. Email: vkarls@liguorimissionhouse.org. Revs. Richard Boever, C.Ss.R.; Victor Karls, C.Ss.R., Supr.; Andrew Meiners, C.Ss.R., Vicar; William H. Broker, C.Ss.R.; Joseph Butz, C.Ss.R.; Joseph M. Curalli, C.Ss.R.; Albert J. Castellino, C.Ss.R.; Donnell Kirchner, C.Ss.R.; Rudy Papes, C.Ss.R.; William Parker, C.Ss.R.; Gilbert Enderle, C.Ss.R.; Peter Schavitz, C.Ss.R.; Bros. Paul Yasenak, C.Ss.R.; Robert T. Ruffing, C.Ss.R.; Marvin Hamann, C.Ss.R.; Daniel Korn, C.Ss.R. Priests 11; Brothers 4.

Order of the Most Holy Redeemer, Monastery of the Most Holy Redeemer, Thailand, The Redemptoristine Nuns, 200 Liguori Dr., 63057.

PACIFIC. *Franciscan Missionary Brothers of the Sacred Heart of Jesus*, 265 St. Joseph Rd., 63069. Tel: 636-587-3661; Fax: 636-938-4960. Web: www.franciscancaring.org. Bro. John Spils, O.S.F., Dir. Gen. Generalate of Franciscan Missionary Brothers of the Sacred Heart of Jesus., Apostolate: Price Memorial Nursing Home and St. Joseph's Hill Infirmary/Black Madonna Shrine, Adult Boarding Facility at Camilus Hall Boarding Home, Merkle Knipprath Nursing home, Joliet Diocese and Countryside Villas Retirement Center, Clifton, IL 60927. Professed Brothers 7.

PERRYVILLE. *Congregation of the Mission*, 1701 W. St. Joseph St., 63775-1599. Tel: 573-547-6533; Fax: 573-547-2204. Revs. Alphonse X. Hoernig, C.M.; Oscar Lukefahr, C.M.; Edward J. Mullin, C.M.; John A. Cantore, C.M.; Jerome Fortenberry, C.M.; Thomas A. Grace, C.M.; Charles E. Prost, C.M.; Arthur L. Trapp, C.M.; Robert E. Lamy, C.M.; John F. Gagnepain, C.M.; Philip M. Floersh, C.M.; Robert Wood, C.M.; Patrick V. Harrity, C.M.; J. Dennis Martin, C.M.; Bros. Harvey Goertz, C.M.; Richard A. Hermann, C.M.; Mark Howard Argus, C.M.; Rev. James G. Ward, C.M.; Bros. Paul P. Joseph, C.M.; Thomas Juneman, C.M.; John Mangogna, C.M.; Matthew J. Teel, C.M.; Richard Zoellner, C.M. U.S. Motherhouse of the Congregation of the Mission (Vincentian Fathers, Prov. of the Midwest). Fathers 20; Professed Brothers 7; Total Staff 5.

ROCKY MOUNT. *Contemplative Heart of Mary Hermitage*, 20542 Echo Valley Rd., 65072. Tel: 573-557-2119. Rev. Robert L. Aten.

[P] PERSONAL PRELATURES

KIRKWOOD. *Prelature of the Holy Cross and Opus Dei*, Wespine Study Center, 100 E. Essex Ave., 63122. Tel: 314-821-1608; Fax: 314-821-4722. Email: info@wespine.org. Web: www.opusdei.org. Revs. Michael E. Giesler; John J. Alvarez.

[Q] CONVENTS AND RESIDENCES FOR SISTERS

ST. LOUIS. *Adorers of the Blood of Christ, United States Region*, 4233 Sulphur Ave., 63109. Tel: 314-351-6294; Fax: 314-351-6789. Email: kenileyd@adorers.org. Web: www.adorers.org. Sr. Jan E. Renz, A.S.C., Regl. Leader.

Carmel of St. Joseph (1863) 9150 Clayton Rd., 63124-1898. Tel: 314-993-4394; Fax: 314-993-5039. Email: stlouiscarmel@sbcglobal.net. Sr. Mary Joseph, O.C.D., Prioress. Discalced Carmelites., Chapel of the Precious Blood. Professed 9; Extern Sisters 1; Postulants 2; Novices 2; Total Number of Sisters 14.

Carmelite Religious of Trivandrum, 4172 Delor, 63116. Sr. Vivienne Gemma Mendonca, C.C.R., Contact Person.

Congregation of Mary, Queen, 3811 Westminster Pl., 63108. Tel: 314-371-1294. Email: vocation@trinhvuong.org. Web: www.trinhvuong.org. Sr. Irene Dinh, C.M.R., Local Supr.

Daughters of Charity of St. Vincent de Paul, Province of St. Louise (1910) 4330 Olive St., 63108-2624. Tel: 314-533-3004. Web: www.daughtersofcharity.org. Provincial House for Daughters of Charity of St. Vincent de Paul, Province of St. Louise. *Provincial Offices*, 4330 Olive St., 63108-2622. Tel: 314-533-4770; Fax: 314-561-3226. Email: choelscher@dcwcp.org. Web: www.daughters-of-charity.org.

Daughters of Our Mother of Peace (1966) 8307 Madison Ave., Saint Louis, 63114-6225. Tel: 314-426-7725. Email: smpconvent@yahoo.com. Sr. Maryjoy Lambert, S.M.P., Supr. Sisters 3.

Daughters of St. Paul Convent, 9804 Watson Rd.,

63126. Tel: 314-965-6935; Fax: 314-984-8431. Email: stlouis@pauline.org. Web: www.pauline.org. Sisters 6.

Eucharistic Missionaries of St. Theresa, 12934 Marine Ave., 63146. Tel: 314-434-1312.

Franciscan Sisters of Mary Administration (1872) 3221 McKelvey Rd. - Ste 107, Bridgeton, 63044. Tel: 314-768-1824; Fax: 314-768-1880. Email: rdowling@fsmonline.org. Web: www.fsmonline.org. Sr. Rose Mary Dowling, F.S.M., Pres. Offices of the Franciscan Sisters of Mary. Professed Sisters in Archdiocese 89; In Residence 57; Professed Sisters elsewhere 11.

Franciscan Sisters of Mary Novitiate (1872) 3221 McKelvey Rd. - Ste. 107, Bridgeton, 63044. Tel: 314-768-1828; Fax: 314-768-1880. Email: sschwartz@fsmonline.org. Web: www.fsmonline.org.

Franciscan Sisters of Our Lady of Perpetual Help (1901) 335 S. Kirkwood Rd., 63122. Tel: 314-965-3700; Fax: 314-965-3710. Email: srpauline@fsolph.org. Web: www.franciscansisters-olph.org. Sr. Pauline Schwandt, O.S.F., Min. Gen. Motherhouse and Novitiate of Franciscan Sisters of Our Lady of Perpetual Help. Total in Community 98; Total Staff 6.

Heart of Mary Center, 6220 Westway Pl., 63109-3417. Tel: 314-752-4459. Email: chanelatwellspring@sbcglobal.net. Web: www.dhmna.org. Sr. Nancy Fell, D.H.M., Supr. Daughters of the Heart of Mary 4.

St. Joseph's Convent of Mercy, 611 S. New Ballas Rd., 63141. Tel: 314-569-6800; Fax: 314-215-1920. Email: cacallahan@rsm-stl.org. Sr. Carol Ann Callahan, R.S.M., Coord. Sisters of Mercy of the Americas. Sisters 45.

St. Joseph's Provincial House (1836) 6400 Minnesota Ave., 63111-2899. Tel: 314-481-8800; Fax: 314-481-2366. Email: pclune@csjsl.org. Web: www.csjsl.org. Sisters Helen Flemington, C.S.J., Province Leadership Team; Patricia Giljum, C.S.J., Province Leadership Team; Mary F. Johnson, C.S.J., Province Treas.; Marion Renkens, C.S.J., Admin. Prov. House of the Sisters of St. Joseph of Carondelet. Sisters in Province 356; In Archdiocese 250.

Loretto Center, 590 E. Lockwood, 63119-3217. Tel: 314-968-1887; Fax: 314-968-4887. Sisters 23; Total Staff 16.

Missionaries of Charity, 3629 Cottage Ave., 63113-3539. Tel: 314-533-2777. Sr. M. Annaleah, M.C., Regl. Supr. Missionaries of Charity also in: Peoria, IL; Chicago, IL; Detroit, MI; Memphis, TN; Dallas, TX; Little Rock, AR; Baton Rouge, LA; Lafayette, LA; Jenkins, KY; Atlanta, GA; Charlotte, NC; Gary, IN; Indianapolis, IN., Houston, TX; Minneapolis, MN. Sisters 7; Total Assisted Annually 19,669.

Monastery of St. Clare of the Immaculate Conception, 200 Marycrest Dr., 63129-4813. Tel: 314-846-2618. Sr. Mary Leo Hoffman, O.S.C., Abbess. Poor Clare Nuns. Cloistered Nuns 9.

Mount Grace Convent and Chapel of Perpetual Adoration, 1438 E. Warne Ave., 63107. Tel: 314-381-2654; Fax: 314-381-6756. Email: holyspiritadoration@gmail.com. Web: www.mountgraceconvent.org. P.O. Box 16459, 63125. Tel: 314-381-2654; Fax: 314-381-6756. Sr. Mary Catherine, S.Sp.S.deA.P., Supr. Sister Servants of the Holy Spirit of Perpetual Adoration (Generalate, Bad Driburg, Germany)Attended by Divine Word Fathers. Sisters 23.

1438 E. Warne Ave., 63107-6756. Tel: 314-381-2654; Fax: 314-381-6756.

1438 E. Warne Ave., 63107. Tel: 314-381-2654; Fax: 314-381-6756. Sisters 24.

Religious Sisters of Mercy, 5047 Washington Pl., 63108. Tel: 314-932-7326; Fax: 314-932-7327. Sr. Mary Charles Mayer, R.S.M., Local Supr.

Salesian Missionaries of Mary Immaculate, 798 Buckley Rd., 63125. Tel: 314-416-1778. Sr. Elsy Joyce, S.M.M.I., Supr.

School Sisters of Notre Dame (1895) Sancta Maria in Ripa, 320 E. Ripa Ave., 63125-2897. Tel: 314-544-0455; Fax: 314-544-6754. Email: elleenmbeelman@ssnd-sl.org. Web: www.ssnd.org. Sr. Mary Anne Owens, S.S.N.D., Prov. Leader; Rev. Charles C. Deister, Chap. Motherhouse of the School Sisters of Notre Dame, St. Louis Province. Sisters in Diocese 303.

Interprovincial Novitiate for School Sisters of Notre Dame (1982) 320 E. Ripa, 63125. Tel: 314-633-7082; Fax: 314-633-7077.

Liturgical Fabric Arts (1983) Tel: 314-544-0455; 314-633-7030; Fax: 314-544-6754. Email: josephinessnd@yahoo.com. Web: www.liturgicalfabricarts.com.

Maria Center (1980) Tel: 314-544-6757; 314-633-7050; Fax: 314-633-7052. Email: mariacenter@ssnd-sl.org.

Resource Development (1991) Tel: 314-631-3530; Fax: 314-633-7056. Email: ssndrdo@ssnd-sl.org. Web: www.ssnd-sl.org.

School Sisters of Notre Dame Central Pacific Province, Inc., 320 E. Ripa, Saint Louis, 63125. Sr. Mary Anne Owens, S.S.N.D., Prov. Supr.

Sisters of Good Shepherd Province of Mid North America (1999) 7654 Natural Bridge Rd., 63121. Tel: 314-381-3400; Fax: 314-381-7102. Email: cmassei@gspmna.org. Web: goodshepherdsisters.org. Sr. Mary Catherine Massei, R.G.S., Prov.

Sisters of the Good Shepherd Candidate House, 4116 W. Pine Blvd., 63108. Email: cmcquaid@gspmna.org. Web: www.goodshepherdsisters.org. Sr. Mary Carolyn McQuaid, R.G.S., Contact Person.

Sisters of the Good Shepherd Formation House, 4317 Forest Park Ave., 63108. Tel: 314-533-0834; Fax: 314-652-2305. Email: cmcquaid@gspmna.org. Sr. Mary Carolyn McQuaid, Contact Person. Professed Sisters 2.

Sisters of St. Francis of the Martyr St. George Tel: 314-383-4765; Fax: 314-383-7256. Web: mogch.org.

Mother of Good Counsel Home, 6825 Natural Bridge Rd., 63121. Tel: 314-383-4765; Fax: 314-383-7256. Rev. Ronald C. Chochol, Chap. Sisters 12.

Sisters of the Good Shepherd (1835) 7654 Natural Bridge Rd., 63121. Tel: 314-381-3400; Fax: 314-382-5294. Email: srolgargs@gmail.com. Web: www.goodshepherdsisters.org. Sr. Olga Cristobal, R.G.S., Local Leader. Sisters 16; Total Staff 12.

Sisters of the Good Shepherd Generalate, 7654 Natural Bridge Rd., 63121. Sr. Mary Carolyn McQuaid, R.G.S., Sec.

Society of Helpers (Paris 1856) (St. Louis 1903) 2800 Olive St., Apt 12K, 63103. Tel: 314-535-2622. Email: httngr@peoplepc.com. Web: www.helpers.org. Sr. Patricia A. Hottinger, S.H., Contact.

Society of the Helpers of the Holy Souls., Spiritual Direction, Parish Weeks of Guided Prayer, Visiting homebound and frail elders.

3817 McDonald Ave., 63116. Tel: 314-776-6917. Email: m.funge@worldnett.att.net.

Society of the Sacred Heart, United States Province, Provincial House, 4120 Forest Park Ave., 63108. Tel: 314-652-1500; Fax: 314-534-6800. Email: provincialhouse@rscj.org. Web: www.rscj.org. Sr. Paula Toner, R.S.C.J., Prov. Province Corporations: California Province of the Society of the Sacred Heart, Inc.; Ladies of the Sacred Heart of St. Louis, Missouri; Society of the Sacred Heart, Chicago Province, Inc.; Religious of the Sacred Heart, Washington Province, Inc.; Religious of the Sacred Heart, New York Province, Inc.; Religious of the Sacred Heart in Massachusetts, Inc. Sisters in Archdiocese 30.

BRIDGETON. *Incarnate Word Sisters* (1869) 3393 McKelvey Rd., Apt. 326, 63044. Tel: 314-387-3326. Email: mseeker314@aol.com. Web: www.ccrtsantonio.org. Sisters Bette Bluhm, C.C.V.I., Prov. Coord.; Mary Ann Seeker, C.C.V.I., Contact (Retired). Sisters 24.

Sisters of Divine Providence, 3415 Bridgeland Dr., 63044. Tel: 314-209-9181; Fax: 314-209-9207. Email: srmfranciscdp@hotmail.com. Web: www.divineprovidenceweb.org. Sr. Mary Francis Fletcher, C.D.P., Prov.

Sisters of Divine Providence of Missouri

Sisters of Divine Providence of Missouri Charitable Trust Providence Ministry Corporation. Sisters 35.

CHESTERFIELD. *Missionary Sisters of St. Peter Claver* (1894) 667 Woods Mill Rd. S., P.O. Box 6067, 63006-6067. Tel: 314-469-4932; Fax: 314-469-0869. Email: stl1928@charter.net. Sr. Genevieve Kudlik, Delegate. Sisters 4.

ELLISVILLE. *Passionist Nuns Monastery* (1948) 15700 Clayton Rd., 63011-2300. Tel: 636-527-6867. Sr. Mary Salvador, C.P., Supr. Cloistered Contemplatives. Professed Religious 9.

FLORISSANT. *Contemplative Sisters of the Good Shepherd* (1859) 2711 Mullanphy Ln., 63031. Tel: 314-837-1719; Fax: 314-837-5925. Email: cgsflo@mindspring.com. Web: www.archstl.org. Sr. Sharon Rose Authorson, C.G.S., Supr. Sisters 6.

Pallottine Missionary Sisters-Queen of Apostles Province (Rome 1838) (U.S. 1912) 15270 Old Halls Ferry Rd., 63034-1611. Tel: 314-837-7100; 314-838-5129; Fax: 314-837-1041. Email: srgail@sbcglobal.net. Web: www.pallottinespirit.org. Sr. Gail Borgmeyer, S.A.C., Prov. Provincialate, novitiate & renewal center of the Missionary Sisters of the Catholic Apostolate. Sisters at Provincial House 6; Total Staff 17.

FRONTENAC. *Congregational Office of the Sisters of St. Joseph of Carondelet*, 2311 S. Lindbergh Blvd., 63131. Tel: 314-966-4048; Fax: 314-966-5041. Email: congctroffice@csjcarondelet.org. Web: www.csjcarondelet.org. Sisters Laura Bufano, C.S.J., Congregational Leadership Team; Francine Costello, C.S.J., Congregational Leadership Team; Susan Hames, C.S.J., Congregational Leadership Team; Catherine McNamee, C.S.J., Congregational Leadership Team; Pam Harding, C.S.J., Admin. Asst. Sisters 4.

Religious of the Sacred Heart Convent (1929) Villa Duchesne, 801 S. Spoede Rd., 63131. Tel: 314-432-2021; Fax: 314-432-7713. Email: nghio@rscj.org. Sisters 3.

HIGH RIDGE. *Society of Our Mother of Peace, Daughters of Our Mother of Peace* (1966) Mary the Font Solitude, 6150 Antire Rd., 63049-2135. Tel: 636-677-3235; Fax: 636-677-5284. Email: marythefont@yahoo.com. Web: our-mother-of-peace.org. Sisters Mary Perpetua Spranger, S.M.P., Local Supr.; Anne Marie DeFord, S.M.P., Treas. & Sec. Total in Residence 6.

KIRKWOOD. *Carmelite Sisters of the Divine Heart of Jesus Provincial House and Novitiate* (1891) 10341 Manchester Rd., 63122. Tel: 314-965-7616; Fax: 314-822-3154. Email: vocations@carmelitedcj.org. Web: carmelitedcj.org. Sr. Mary Joseph Heisler, Prov. Supr. The Sisters own and operate two nursing homes and one day care center in their Province. Final Professed 19; Junior Professed 1; Novices 3.

Ursuline Provincialate, 353 S. Sappington Rd., 63122. Tel: 314-821-6884; Fax: 314-821-6888. Email: ursulines@osucentral.org. Web: www.usaosu.org. Sr. Diane Fulgenzi, O.S.U., Prov. Prioress. United States Province of the Ursuline Nuns of the Roman Union. Sisters: In Province 282; In the Archdiocese 24.

Other Locations: *Ursuline Sisters*, 500 Clemens Dr., Florissant, 63033. Tel: 314-839-2803. Sisters 4.

Ursuline Sisters, 105 N. Holmes Ave., 63122. Tel: 314-698-2506. Sisters 4.

Ursuline Sisters, 5821 Sutherland, Saint Louis, 63109. Tel: 314-353-5745. Sisters 4.

Ursuline Sisters, 801 Fairdale Ave., 63119. Tel: 314-968-9591. Sisters 2.

LIGUORI. *Monastery of St. Alphonsus* (1960) 200 Liguori Dr., 63057-9999. Tel: 636-464-1093; Fax: 636-464-9446; 636-464-1073. Email: rednun@redemptoristinenuns.org; prayerrequest@redemptoristinenuns.org. Web: www.redemptoristinenuns.org. Sisters Eleanor Wilkinson, O.Ss.R., Prioress; Mary Supawadee Khamsamran, Solemn Professed; Weena Suttinavin, Solemn Professed. Order of the Most Holy Redeemer (Redemptoristine Nuns). Professed 14.

NORMANDY. *Convent of the Immaculate Heart*, 7626 Natural Bridge Rd., 63121. Tel: 314-383-0300; Fax: 314-383-0337. Email: srmpbrgs@aol.com. Web: www.goodshepherdsisters.org. A residence for aged & infirm Good Shepherd Sisters of the Mid-North America Prov. Total Staff 30; Total in Residence 25.

O'FALLON. *St. Mary's Institute of O'Fallon*, 204 N. Main St., 63366-2299. Tel: 636-240-6010; Fax: 636-272-5031. Email: fraia@cpps-ofallon.org. Web: www.cpps-ofallon.org. Sr. Fran Raia, C.PP.S., Supr. Gen. Motherhouse of the Sisters of the Most Precious Blood., Chapel of St. Joseph. Sisters in Archdiocese 127.

ST. CHARLES. *Franciscan Sisters of Mary* (1872) 320 Jackson St., 63301-3496. Tel: 636-255-0194; Fax: 636-947-5090. Email: inez_kennedy@ssmhc.com.

Religious of the Sacred Heart (1800) 301 Decatur St., 63301-2089. Tel: 636-946-7276; Fax: 636-949-6659. Email: mmmunch@rscj.org. Sisters 6; Religious 6.

ST. LOUIS COUNTY. *Religious of the Sacred Heart*, 13644 Conway Rd., 63141. Tel: 314-434-7687. Email: hpadberg@rscj.org. Sisters 2.

Religious of the Sacred Heart, 541 S. Mason Rd., 63141-8550. Tel: 314-878-6705. Email: lnordmann@rscj.org. Web: www.rscj.org. Sisters 6.

TOWN AND COUNTRY. *Monastery of the Visitation, St. Louis*, 3020 N. Ballas Rd., 63131. Tel: 314-625-9260; Fax: 314-432-5354. Email: srvh@visitationmonastery.org. Web: www.visitationmonastery.org/stlouis. Sr. M. Veronica Haronik, V.H.M., Supr. Residence of Visitation Nuns Living at the Monastery of the Visitation. Sisters 13.

[R] HOMES FOR MEN AND WOMEN

ST. LOUIS. *Cathedral Tower*, 325 N. Newstead Ave., 63108. Tel: 314-367-5500, Ext. 121; Fax: 314-361-5099. Email: tgorski@ccstl.org. Web: www.ccstl.org. Building which houses several agencies of Catholic Charities: Queen of Peace Center; St. Elizabeth Hall; and Peace for Kids, Inc. Residents 150.

Father Dempsey's Hotel, Inc., 3427 Washington Ave., 63103. Tel: 314-535-7221; Fax: 314-535-7289. Email: maboussie@archstl.org. Martie Aboussie, Exec. Dir. Total Staff 4; Total in Residence 77.

Father Jim's Home, 3427 Washington Ave., 63103. Tel: 314-535-7221; Fax: 314-535-7289. Email: maboussie@archstl.org. Martie Aboussie, Exec. Dir. Total Staff 4; Total in Residence 77.

St. Martha's Hall, P.O. Box 4950, 63108. Tel: 314-533-1313; Fax: 314-533-2035. Email: stmarthashall@sbcglobal.net. Web: www.saintmarthas.org. Michelle Schiller-Baker, Exec. Dir. Provides Shelter, Advocacy and Support to Abused Women & their Children. Capacity 24; Total Staff 14; Total Assisted Annually 220.

St. Philippine Home (1996) 1015 Goodfellow Blvd., 63112. Tel: 314-454-1012; Fax: 314-367-7455. Email: cneumann@ccstl.org. Constance S. Neumann, Exec. Dir. Transitional housing for drug affected homeless city women and their children. Bed Capacity 33; Outpatients 20; Total Assisted Annually 96; Total Staff 12.

Queen of Peace Center (1985) 325 N. Newstead Ave., 63108. Tel: 314-531-0511; Fax: 314-531-1458. Email: cneumann@ccstl.org. Constance S. Neumann, Exec. Dir. Comprehensive residential and outpatient behavioral healthcare for addicted women and their children. Specialty in pregnant women, trauma and dually diagnosed. Permanent and transitional housing programs. Licensed by the Department of Mental Health Division of Alcohol and Drug Abuse. Accredited by COA Council on Accreditation. Vouchers 277; Total Staff 113; Total Assisted Annually 1,254.

Rosati Center, 4220-24 N. Grand Ave., 63107. Tel: 314-534-6624; Fax: 314-535-4394. Permanent supportive housing for former homeless single adults. Managed by St. Patrick Center. Total Assisted 30; Studio Apartments 26; Total Staff 8.

Rosati Group Home, Inc., 4218 N. Grand Blvd., 63107. Tel: 314-534-6624; Fax: 314-535-4394. Email: nboland@stpatrickcenter.org. Web: stpatrickcenter.org. Greg Vogelweid, Admin. Group Home for homeless mentally ill adults. Managed by St. Patrick Center. Total Assisted 140; Total Staff 10.

NORMANDY. *Maria Droste Residence* (1979) 7660 Natural Bridge Rd., 63121. Tel: 314-383-5553; Fax: 314-382-1325. Web: goodshepherdsisters.org. Sisters of the Good Shepherd., For Women in Need. Capacity 11; Total Assisted 85; Total Staff 7.

[S] RETREAT HOUSES

ST. LOUIS. *Mercy Center*, 2039 N. Geyer Rd., 63131. Tel: 314-966-4686; Fax: 314-909-4631. Email: dawn.stringfield@mercy.net. Dawn Stringfield, Admin. Operated by the Sisters of Mercy of the Americas, Province St. Louis., Conference and Renewal Ministry.

Mercy Conference and Retreat Center, Sisters of Mercy of the Americas, 2039 N. Geyer Rd., 63131. Tel: 314-966-4686; Fax: 314-909-4631. Dawn Stringfield, Exec. Dir.

White House Retreat (1922) 7400 Christopher Dr., 63129. Tel: 314-416-6400; Fax: 314-416-6464; Tel: 800-643-1003. Email: whretreat@whretreat.org. Web: www.whretreat.org.

Retreat House (1922) 7400 Christopher Dr., 63129. Tel: 314-846-2575. Revs. James J. Burshek, S.J., Dir.; Richard E. Hadel, S.J., Assoc. Dir.; Eugene C. Renard, S.J., Assoc. Dir.; Leonard E. Kraus, S.J., Assoc. Dir.; Bro. John C. Fava, S.J., Assoc. Dir. Total in Residence 6; Total Staff 6.

DITTMER. *Il Ritiro-The Little Retreat* (1981) 7935 St. Francis Ln., P.O. Box 38, 63023. Tel: 636-274-0554 (Toll Free from St. Louis); Fax: 636-274-2380. Email: gpeter@nightowl.net. Revs. Bertin Miller, O.F.M., Exec. Dir.; Michael Crosby, O.F.M., Dir.; Paul Gallagher, Dir.; Bros. Patrick Kendrick, O.F.M.; Pio Jackson, O.F.M. Operated by the Franciscan Friars. Priests 6; Brothers 1; Total in Residence 7; Total Staff 4.

Vianney Renewal Center (1988) 6476 Eime Rd., P.O. Box 130, 63023. Tel: 636-274-5226; Fax: 636-274-1430. Web: www.theservants.org. Very Rev. Liam Hoare, s.P., Paraclete Dir.; Rev. Benedict Livingstone, s.P., Prog. Dir.; Dr. Rob Furey, Ph.D., Clinical Dir. Operated by the Servants of the Paraclete. Total in Residence 24; Total Staff 11.

EUREKA. *Marianist Retreat & Conference Center* (1967) P.O. Box 718, 63025-0718. Tel: 636-938-5390; Fax: 636-938-3493. Email: macmrcc@aol.com. Web: www.mretreat.org. Sr. Paulette Patritti, O.P., Dir.; Rev. Jose Ramirez, S.M. Conducted by the Society of Mary., Center for Formation and Growth in the Christian Life. Total in Residence 8; Total Staff 22.

FLORISSANT. *Pallottine Renewal Center, Inc.* (1969) 15270 Old Halls Ferry Rd., 63034-1611. Tel: 314-837-7100; Fax: 314-837-1041. Email: Pall4@juno.com. Web: www.pallottinerenewal.org. Sisters Helen Ann Collier, C.C.V.I., Vice Pres.; Gail Borgmeyer, S.A.C., Provincial Supr.; Beth Moritz, Dir. Pallottine Missionary Sisters, Queen of Apostles Province. Total in Residence 2; Total Staff 10.

HIGH RIDGE. *Society of Our Mother of Peace at Mary the Font Solitude* (1966) 6150 Antire Rd., 63049-2135. Tel: 636-677-3235; Fax: 636-677-5284. Email: marythefont@yahoo.com. Web: marythefont.org. Sisters Mary Perpetua Spranger, S.M.P., Local Supr.; Anne Marie DeFord, S.M.P., Treas.; Rev. Placid Guste, S.M.P.

PEVELY. *Vision of Peace Ministries* (1977) Abbey Ln., P.O. Box 69, 63070. Tel: 636-475-3697; Fax: 636-475-3697. Email: visofpeace@juno.com. Mrs. Jane Guenther, Treas. Total in Residence 1; Total Staff 1.

WILDWOOD. *La Salle Institute - Retreat and Conference Center* (1886) 2101 Rue De La Salle, 63038-2299. Tel: 636-938-5374; Fax: 636-587-9792. Email: Cblasalle@sbcglobal.net.

Christian Brothers (De La Salle) (1886) Tel: 636-938-6142; Fax: 636-587-9792. Bro. Bill Brynda, Community Dir.; Mr. Michael Sawicki, Pres.; Gerri Schroeder, Retreat Coord. Community 4; Total in Residence 4; Total Staff 11.

[T] NEWMAN CENTERS

ST. LOUIS. *University of Missouri, St. Louis, Catholic Newman Center* (1965) 8200 Natural Bridge Rd., 63121. Tel: 314-385-3455; Fax: 314-385-1523. Email: cnc@cncumsl.org. Web: www.cncumsl.org. Rev. William G. Kempf, Dir.

Washington University Newman Centers, Washington University Newman Chapel, 6352 Forsyth Blvd., 63105-2269. Tel: 314-935-9191, Ext. 213; Fax: 314-727-6053. Email: braun@washucsc.org. Web: www.washucsc.org. Rev. Gary G. Braun, Archdiocesan Dir. of Campus Ministries. Total in Residence 1; Total Staff 15.

[U] ASSOCIATIONS OF THE FAITHFUL

ST. LOUIS. *Oblates of Wisdom Study Center*, P. O. Box 13230, Saint Louis, 63157. Tel: 314-621-2055. Email: jfmccarthy1@sbcglobal.net. Rev. Msgr. John F. McCarthy, Dir. In Res. Rev. Brian W. Harrison, O.S., Scholar.

[V] MISCELLANEOUS

ST. LOUIS. *Alexian Brothers of St. Louis, Inc.* (1972) *Alexian Brothers (Residence)*, 4173 Crescent Dr., Ste. A, 63129. Tel: 314-880-8545; Fax: 314-894-2695.

Alexian Brothers Services, Inc., 4175 Crescent Dr., 63129. Tel: 314-880-8545.

Almost Home (1993) 3200 St. Vincent Ave., 63104-1336. Tel: 314-771-4663; Fax: 314-865-4692. Email: smukhtiar@almosthomestl.org. Web: www.almosthomestl.org. Sheroo Mukhtiar, Exec. Dir. Transitional living program for teenage mothers and their children who are homeless. Members and Children 40; Total Staff 20.

American Academy of FertilityCare Professionals, 11700 Studt Ave., Ste. C, 63141. Tel: 314-991-0327; Fax: 314-692-8097. Email: diane.daly@mercy.net. Web: aafcp.org. Mrs. Diane Daly.

The Angela Foundation for Ursuline Education, 341 S. Sappington Rd., Saint Louis, 63122. Tel: 314-966-7725.

Anna Foundation, c/o Sisters of St. Joseph of Carondelet, St. Louis Province, 6400 Minnesota Ave., Saint Louis, 63111. Tel: 314-481-8800, Ext. 321; Fax: 314-481-2366. Sr. Mary Frances Johnson, C.S.J., Treas. & Contact Person.

Annual Catholic Appeal, 20 Archbishop May Dr., 63119. Tel: 314-792-7680; Fax: 314-792-7229. Email: niebruggeb@archstl.org. Web: www.archstl.org. Mr. Brian Niebrugge, Dir., Annual Catholic Appeal. Staff 5.

Archdiocesan Planned Giving & Endowment Council, 20 Archbishop May Dr., Shrewsbury, 63119. Tel: 314-792-7680; Fax: 314-792-7229. Web: www.archstl.org. Mr. Brian Niebrugge, Exec. Dir. Stewardship & The Annual Catholic Appeal; Mrs. Jeanne Rudolph, Planned Giving Assoc.; Ms. April Esenwah, Planned Giving Assoc.; Mr. Jonathan W. Igoe, Chm.; Mr. John Cleary; Mr. William A. Drennan; David Fairchild; Ms. Rosemary Fairhead; Mr. William Jochens; Mr. Raymond S. Kreienkamp; Mr. Joseph McAuliffe; Mr. Michael F. Niemann; Mr. William P. O'Connor; Mrs. Jill M. Palmquist; Mrs. Carolyn Parmer; Dr. David Shelton, Ed.D.; Mr. Mark Riordan; Ms. Sharon Sanders; Mr. James Schaller; Mr. Charles D. Surdyke; Mr. Richard S. Vest; Mr. Michael Weisbrod.

Archdiocesan Stewardship Education Committee, 20 Archbishop May Dr., 63119. Tel: 314-792-7215; Fax: 314-792-7229. Email: erschen@arstl.org. Web: www.archstl.org/stewardship. Susan Erschen, Dir. Stewardship Education; John Drabik; Matthew Mayer; Mrs. Chris Kern; Don Lapoint; Ms. Dian Valentine; Revs. Erich A. Fechner; James J. Benz; Christopher M. Martin; Rev. Msgr. Gregory R. Mikesch; Karen Schamel; Rev. John R. Vien.

ASC Health, 4233 Sulphur Ave., 63109. Tel: 314-351-6294; Fax: 314-351-6789.

ASC Investment Group Inc., 4233 Sulphur Ave., Saint Louis, 63109. Sr. Jan E. Renz, A.S.C., Pres.

Ascension Health, 4600 Edmundson Rd., 63134. Tel: 314-733-8000; Fax: 314-733-8013. Email: atersigni@ascensionhealth.org. Web: www.ascensionhealth.org. Anthony R. Tersigni, Pres. & C.E.O. Sponsored by Ascension Health Ministries, a public juridic person.

Ascension Health Alliance, 4600 Edmundson Rd., 63134.

Ascension Health-IS, Inc., 4600 Edmundson Rd., 63134. Tel: 314-733-8000; Fax: 314-733-8013. Email: atersigni@ascensionhealth.org. Web: www.ascensionhealth.org. Anthony R. Tersigni, Pres. & CEO.

Aware, Inc. (1973) St. Anthony's Medical Center, 10016 Kennerly Rd., 63128. Tel: 314-525-1622. Karen Molner, Pres.

Birthright, 2525 S. Brentwood Blvd., Ste. 102, 63144. Tel: 314-962-5300; Fax: 314-962-7606. Web: www.birthrightstlouis.org. Ruth A. Bradberry, Admin. Dir. Total Assisted 5,679; Total Staff 25.

Branch Offices:

6680 Chippewa, 63109. Tel: 314-962-3653; Fax: 314-351-4531.

3435-C Bridgeland, Bridgeton, 63044. Tel: 314-298-0945; Fax: 314-298-0813.

205 N. 5th St., St. Charles, 63301. Tel: 636-724-1200; Fax: 636-946-0447.

625 N. Euclid, 63108. Tel: 636-946-4900; Fax: 314-361-0129.

800 N. Tucker Blvd., 63101. Tel: 636-916-4300; Fax: 314-588-1179.

Cardinal Glennon Children's Foundation, 3800 Park Ave., Saint Louis, 63110. Tel: 314-577-5605; Fax: 314-268-6416. Email: info@glennon.org. Web: www.glennon.org. Member of SSM Health Care

Cardinal Ritter General Partner Corporation, 7601 Watson Rd., 63119.

The Caroline Trust (1991) 320 E. Ripa Ave., 63125-2897. Tel: 314-633-7021; Fax: 314-633-7057. Email: lindajansen@ssnd-sl.org. Supports the Religious and Charitable Purposes of the School Sisters of Notre Dame and Provides Support for the Aged, Infirm and Disabled Sisters of the Province.

Carondelet Health System, Inc., 4600 Edmundson Rd., 63134. Tel: 314-733-8000; Fax: 314-733-8013. Email: atersigni@ascensionhealth.org. Anthony R. Tersigni, Pres. & CEO.

Catholic Charities Foundation, 4532 Lindell Blvd., 63108. Tel: 314-367-5500; Fax: 314-367-2982. Web: www.ccstl.org. Mr. Brian J. O'Malley, Pres. A Charitable Fund Established to Support the Activities of Catholic Charities.

Catholic Charities Housing Resource Center, 800 N. Tucker Blvd., Saint Louis, 63101. Tel: 314-802-5440; Fax: 314-802-5408. Email: cchrc@ccstl.org. Web: www.ccstl.org. Karen Wallensak, Dir. A Program of Catholic Charities helping homeless and near-homeless people achieve stability in safe, affordable housing. Total Staff 34; Total Assisted Annually 16,010.

Catholic Charities Parish Social Ministry, 4532 Lindell Blvd., 63108. Tel: 314-367-5500, Ext. 155; Fax: 314-361-5099. Email: rohde@ccstl.org. Web: www.ccstl.org. Recruitment and placement of volunteers serving the agencies and programs of Catholic Charities Federation.

Catholic Charities Service Agency, 4532 Lindell Blvd., 63108-2497.

Catholic Charities Information and Referral Services (Dial Help), 4532 Lindell, 63108. Tel: 314-371-4357 (314-371-HELP).

Catholic Charities Refugee Services, 2840 Wisconsin Ave., 63118-1632. Tel: 314-771-2570; Fax: 314-771-6406. Mary Carroll, Resettlement Dir.

Catholic Charities Southside Center (Vietnamese and Hispanic Programs), 5880 Christy, 63116. Tel: 314-773-6100; 314-664-8990. Courtney Prentis, Dir.

Hispanic Programs Tel: 314-773-6100.

Vietnamese Programs Tel: 314-664-8990.

Catholic Charities Father Tolton Center, 1018 Baden, 63147. Tel: 314-385-3445; Fax: 314-385-4479. Monica Anderson, Dir.

Catholic Charities Jefferson County Center, 110 N. Brierton Ln. at N. 2nd, Crystal City, 63019-1720. Tel: 636-931-5859; Fax: 636-933-5148. P.O. Box 668, Festus, 63028-0668. Donna Thornton, Dir.

Catholic Charities Midtown Center (Including Friends of Moms Program), 1202 S. Boyle Ave., 63110-3814. Tel: 314-534-1180; Fax: 314-534-3727. John Pachak, Dir.

Catholic Charities St. Charles Area Center, 255 Spencer Rd., #202, St. Peters, 63376-1632. Tel:

636-498-2273; Fax: 636-498-0390. Gerry Mazzuca, Dir.

Catholic Charities St. Jane Center, 7005 Ascension Dr., 63121-3427. Tel: 314-383-6539; Fax: 314-383-6591. Jamie Saunders, Dir.

Catholic Family Services (1992) 9200 Watson Rd., G101, 63126. Tel: 314-544-3800; 800-652-8055; Fax: 314-843-0552. Provides residential and social services, professional counseling and health care access to families and communities. Staff 54; Total Assisted Annually 12,599.

Locations:

Catholic Family Service, 311 S. Main #100, O'Fallon, 63366. Tel: 636-281-1990; 877-498-2271; Fax: 636-281-1995.

Catholic Family Services South Office, 9200 Watson Rd., G101, 63126-1528. Tel: 314-544-3800; Fax: 314-843-0552.

Catholic Family Services Schools Partnership Program, 9200 Watson Rd, G101, 63126-1528. Tel: 314-544-3800; Fax: 314-843-0552.

Catholic Family Services/Troy, #140 Professional Pkwy., Troy, 63379. Tel: 636-281-1990; Fax: 636-281-1995.

Language Access Metro Project (LAMP), 8050 Watson, Ste. 340, 63119. Tel: 314-842-0062; Fax: 314-842-1303. Jelena Mujanovic, Dir.

Fatherhood Initiative/Places for Fathers, 1911 N. Taylor Ave., 63113-2601. Tel: 314-535-0017; Fax: 314-535-3155.

Catholic Family Services West County Office, 498 Woods Mill Rd., Manchester, 63011-4144. Tel: 636-391-9966; Fax: 636-394-4678.

Catholic Family Services Franklin County, 102 E. Springfield, Ste 202, Union, 63084-1818. Tel: 636-583-1800; 800-583-8355; Fax: 636-583-0836.

Catholic Family Services Northwest Office, 1385 Harkee Rd., Florissant, 63031. Tel: 314-831-1533; Fax: 314-831-1391.

The Catholic Health Association of the United States, 4455 Woodson Rd., 63134-3797. Tel: 314-427-2500; Fax: 314-427-0029. Web: www.chausa.org. Sr. Carol Keehan, D.C., Pres. & CEO. Established June 24, 1915. Total Staff 74.

Catholic Healthcare Investment Management Company, 4600 Edmundson Rd., Saint Louis, 63134. Joseph R. Impicciche, Contact Person.

Catholic High School Association, Catholic Education Center, 4445 Lindell Blvd., 63108. Tel: 314-792-7300; Fax: 314-792-7399. Email: stlsupt@archstl.org. Web: www.archstl.org/education/. Mr. George Henry, Supt.

Catholic Education Office, Catholic Education Center, 4445 Lindell Blvd., 63108. Tel: 314-792-7300; Fax: 314-792-7399. Email: stlsupt@archstl.org. Web: www.archstl.org/education/. Mr. George Henry, Supt.

Catholic Kolping Society of America, 4035 Keokuk St., 63116. Tel: 314-776-5312. Noreen G. Nutt, Treas.

Catholic Legal Assistance Ministry, 321 N. Spring, Saint Louis, 63108. Tel: 314-977-3993; Fax: 314-977-3334. Email: kenyonm@slu.edu. Ms. Marie Kenyon, J.D., Dir. A Program of Catholic Charities providing legal advocacy and representation in civil matters and immigration for low-income clients.

Catholic Office of Disability Ministry (1980) 20 Archbishop May Dr., 63119. Tel: 314-792-7150; 314-792-7158 (TDD); Fax: 314-792-7199. Email: dministry@archstl.org. Web: www.archstl.org.

Central Bureau of the C.C.V.A., 3835 Westminster Pl., 63108-3472. Tel: 314-371-1653; Fax: 314-371-0889. Email: centbur@sbcglobal.net. Web: www.socialjusticereview.org. Rev. Edward Krause, C.S.C., Dir. & Editor of the Social Justice Review.

St. Charles Lwanga Center (1978) 4746 Carter Ave., Ste. 100, 63115-2238. Tel: 314-367-7929; Fax: 314-367-4134. Email: info@lwangacenter.org. Web: www.archstl.org/lwangacenter/. Rev. Arthur J. Cavitt, Exec. Dir. A spiritual formation Center for leadership in the African American Catholic Community, in the Archdiocese of St. Louis. The Center collaborates with other Christians throughout the United States and provides leadership training for junior high and teenage youth and adult laity. In conjunction with our service to 10 sponsoring parishes, we conduct workshops on the Sacrament of Confirmation, evangelization, coping with grief and loss, marriage preparation, marriage enrichment, days of reflection, pastoral care and retreats. Bible study, consultation services. Total Staff 4.

Chiara Corporation (1995) 3221 McKelvey Rd. Ste 107, Bridgeton, 63044. Tel: 314-768-1817; Fax: 314-768-1803. Email: joshaughnessy@fsmonline.org. Mr. John O'Shaughnessy, Contact Person. Ministries that promote, enhance and provide for the spiritual, religious, physical or mental well-being of members of society in accordance with the religious and charitable purposes of the Franciscan Sisters of Mary.

Collaborative Dominican Novitiate, 4928 Washington Blvd., 63108-1621. Tel: 314-454-0664; Fax: 314-454-3849. Email: kelsner@spdom.org. John Rich, Contact Person; Megan McElroy, O.P., Contact Person.

**Covenant House Missouri*, 2727 N. Kingshighway Blvd., 63113.

CSJ Ministries, 6400 Minnesota Ave., 63111. Tel: 314-481-8800; Fax: 314-481-2366.

Daughters of Charity Foundation (1996) *c/o Ascension Health*, 4600 Edmundson Rd., 63134. Tel: 314-802-2060; Fax: 314-802-2051. Email: jimpicciche@ascensionhealth.org. Web: www.daughtersofcharityfdn.org. Joseph R. Impicciche, Sr. Vice Pres. & Gen. Counsel.

Daughters of Charity Foundation of St. Louis (1995) 231 S. Bemiston, Ste. 735, 63105. Tel: 314-802-2060; Fax: 314-802-2051. Web: www.daughtersofcharityfdn.org. Email: jkuester@docfdn.org. Sr. Joan Kuester, D.C., Exec. Dir.

Daughters of Charity Ministries, Inc., 4330 Olive St., 63108-2624. Tel: 314-533-4770; Fax: 314-561-3226. Web: www.daughtersofcharity.org.

Daughters of Charity National Health System, Inc., 4600 Edmundson Rd., 63134. Tel: 314-733-8000; Fax: 314-733-8013. Email: atersigni@ascensionhealth.org. Anthony R. Tersigni, Pres. & CEO.

Daughters of Charity, Inc., 4330 Olive St., 63108-2622. Tel: 314-533-4770; Fax: 314-561-3226. Web: www.daughtersofcharity.org.

Dismas House of St. Louis, 5025 Cote Brilliante Ave., 63113. Tel: 314-361-2802; Fax: 314-367-0604. John R. Flatley, Exec. Dir. Total in Residence 170; Total Staff 60.

Equestrian Order of the Holy Sepulchre of Jerusalem, 2870 S. Lindbergh Blvd., 63131. Tel: 314-984-5077; Fax: 314-984-9390. Email: nardance@aol.com. Nancy Ross, Sec.

St. Francis de Sales Association (Paris 1872) (St. Louis 1950) 9328 Pine Ave., 63144. Tel: 314-963-9603. Email: ann.wiedl@sbcglobal.net. Ann Doody Wiedl, Contact Person. A call to the laity to live their individual vocation in the spirit of Jesus, using the writings of St. Francis de Sales as a means to see and do God's will and grow in holiness.; Private Universal Association of the Faithful.

The Franciscan Connection (1991) 2903 Cherokee St., 63118. Tel: 314-773-8485; Fax: 314-773-8573. Email: franciscanconnection@thefriars.org. Web: www.franciscanconnection.org. Rev. Lawrence M. Nickels, O.F.M., Exec. Dir.

Franklin County Catholic Church Real Estate Corporation (1834) 20 Archbishop May Dr., 63119. Tel: 314-792-7408; Fax: 314-792-7401. Rev. Msgr. Jerome D. Billing, S.T.L., J.C.L., Contact Person.

Good Shepherd Children & Family Services, 1340 Partridge Ave., Saint Louis, 63130. Tel: 314-854-5700; Fax: 314-854-5747. Email: goodshepinfo@ccstl.org. Peggy Slater, Exec. Dir. A Catholic Charities agency merging the services of Catholic Services for Children & Youth, Father Dunne's Newsboys' Home, Marian Hall Agencies, St. Joseph's Home and Family Support Services, and Villa Maria Center. Provides child welfare services including the foster care, adoption, expectant parent counseling, advocacy and residential services.

Good Shepherd Mission Development Corporation, 7654 Natural Bridge Rd., 63121. Sr. Mary Carolyn McQuaid, R.G.S., Sec.

Good Shepherd Programs, Inc. (1979) 7654 Natural Bridge Rd., 63121. Tel: 314-381-3400; Fax: 314-382-1325. Web: goodshepherdsisters.org. Operates the Maria Droste Residence. Total Staff 6; Total Assisted 77.

Hispanic Ministry of the Archdiocese of St. Louis (1995) 20 Archbishop May Dr., 63119. Tel: 314-792-7890; Fax: 314-792-7898.

Incarnate Word Foundation, Missouri (1997) 5257 Shaw Ave., Ste. 309, 63110. Tel: 314-773-5100; Fax: 314-773-5102. Email: info@iwfdn.org. Web: www.iwfdn.org. Bridget M. Flood, Exec. Dir.

Institute for Theological Encounter with Science & Technology (ITEST), 20 Archbishop May Dr., 63119. Tel: 314-792-7220. Email: mariannepost@archstl.org. Web: www.faithscience.org. Sr. Marianne Postiglione, R.S.M., Assoc. Dir.

Institute of Jesuit Sources (1961) 3601 Lindell Blvd., 63108. Tel: 314-633-4622; Fax: 314-633-4623. Email: ijs@jesuitsources.com. Web: www.jesuitsources.com. Rev. John W. Padberg, S.J., Dir. Priests 5; Total Staff 6.

Intercommunity Housing Association (1993) 1049 N. Clay, Ste. 300, Kirkwood, 63122. Tel: 314-965-4700. Email: donald.schneiber@sbcglobal.net. Web: www.intercommunityhousing.org. Provides safe, affordable housing & supportive svcs. for economically disadvantaged & working poor families in St. Louis; operates Pillar Place Apartments, Compton Place Apartments.

Jefferson County Catholic Church Real Estate Corporation, 4445 Lindell Blvd., 63108. Tel: 314-792-7408; Fax: 314-792-7401. Rev. Msgr. Jerome D. Billing, S.T.L., J.C.L., Contact Person.

The Jesuits of the Missouri Province, Office of Advancement, 4511 W. Pine Blvd., 63108-2191. Tel: 314-361-7765; Fax: 314-758-7163. Email: advancement@jesuits-mis.org. Web: www.jesuits-mis.org. Mr. Thom Digman, Dir.; Rev. Robert F. Weiss, S.J., Assoc. Dir.

The Jesuits of the Missouri Province

Ladies of Charity of St. Catherine Laboure, 12160 Leelaine Dr., 63126. Susan Tumminia, Pres. Affiliate with Ladies of Charity of the United States & the Assoc. of Intl. Charities of St. Vincent de Paul.

Ladies of Charity of St. Vincent-Guardian Angel, Tel: 314-231-9328; Fax: 314-621-2232. Email: stvstl@swbell.net. Affiliate with Ladies of Charity of the United States & the Assoc. of Intl. Charities of St. Vincent de Paul.

St. Vincent's Church: 1408 S. Tenth St., 63104. Tel: 314-231-9328; Fax: 314-621-2232.

Ladies of Charity Service Center, 7500 Natural Bridge Rd., 63121. Tel: 314-383-4207; Fax: 314-383-0605. Phyllis A. Makowski, Pres.

Ladies of Charity Service Center, Ladies of Charity Service Center; Thrift Store & Food Pantry. Total Staff 25; Total Assisted 1,065.

Lincoln County Church Real Estate Corporation, 20 Archbishop May Dr., 63119. Tel: 314-792-7408; Fax: 314-792-7401. Rev. Msgr. Jerome D. Billing, S.T.L., J.C.L., Contact Person.

The St. Louis Archdiocesan Fund, 20 Archbishop May Dr., Shrewsbury, 63119-5738. Tel: 314-792-7129. Email: dfairchi@archstl.org. David Fairchild, Finance Mgr.

St. Louis Area Women Religious Collaborative Ministries (1998) 4330 Olive St., 63108. Tel: 314-770-2627; Fax: 314-533-3226. Email: etpproject@aol.com. Sr. M. Philip Agnew, D.C., Contact Person. Includes English Tutoring Project for Immigrant/Refugee Children and Intercommunity Environmental Council.

St. Louis Catholic Charismatic Renewal, 10909 St. Henry Ln., St. Ann, 63074. Tel: 314-427-7786; Fax: 314-427-7789. Email: janeguenther@archstl.org. Web: www.stlrenewal.org. Rev. Msgr. Edmund O. Griesedieck, Dir. (Retired); Mrs. Jane Guenther, Coord.

Abiding Bible Companion (2001) Tel: 314-725-6527.

Healing & Deliverance Ministry

Magnificat Tel: 314-427-7786; Fax: 314-427-7789.

Theotokos Ministry, 4311 S. Compton, 63111. Tel: 314-351-6061. Center with books & tapes, prayer time, ministry times, retreats for parishes, leaders training, small faith groups, conferences, special events & days of renewal.

Two Alike Tel: 314-427-7786; Fax: 314-427-7789.

St. Louis County Catholic Church Real Estate Corporation, 20 Archbishop May Dr., 63119. Tel: 314-792-7408; Fax: 314-792-7401. Rev. Msgr. Jerome D. Billing, S.T.L., J.C.L., Contact Person.

Mary and Joseph Trust, 3221 McKelvey Rd. Ste 107, Bridgeton, 63044. Tel: 314-768-1817; Fax: 314-768-1803. Email: joshaughnessy@fsmonline.org.

Mary Queen Charitable Trust Fund, La Salette Missionaries, 4650 South Broadway, 63111. Tel: 314-353-5000.

Mercy Foundation for Health Innovation (2003) 14528 S. Outer Forty, Ste. 100, Chesterfield, 63017. Tel: 314-579-6100; Fax: 314-628-3732. Email: michele.giunta@mercy.net. Shannon Sock, Pres.

Mercy Investment Services, Inc., 2039 N. Geyer Rd., 63131.

Midwest Coalition for Responsible Investment, 6400 Minnesota Ave., 63111. Tel: 314-678-0471. Web: www.midwestcri.com.

Missionaries of the Holy Family Retirement Trust Fund, 3014 Oregon Ave., Saint Louis, 63118. Tel: 314-577-6300; Fax: 314-577-6301.

National Catholic Ministry to the Bereaved, P.O. Box 16353, Saint Louis, 63125-0353. Tel: 314-638-2638; Fax: 314-638-2639. Email: NCMBereave@aol.com. Web: www.griefwork.org. Sr. Mary Ann Wachtel, S.F.C.C., Exec. Dir.; Linda Cherek, Pres. N.C.M.B. offers pastoral and spiritual support to the bereaved, caregivers, agencies, dioceses, congregations, and parishes through education and resources for the development of grief support groups and a training program & manual for ministers of consolation. Total Staff 1; Total Assisted 12,000.

National Christian Life Community of the United States of America (CLC) (1540) 3601 Lindell Blvd., 63108-3393. Tel: 713-246-3785. Web: www.clc-usa.org. Mong-Hang Nguyen, Pres. Founded c. 1540 & approved 1584, a public, intl.

assn. of the Faithful of Pontifical Right which builds small Faith-Communities for mission & svc. to the church. It uses the Spiritual Exercises of Saint Ignatius of Loyola as its specific source & characteristic instrument for its spirituality. Membership equally open to primarily Catholic Christian men, women, youth & young adults, clergy, brothers & sisters.

Network of Sacred Heart Schools, Inc., 700 N. Third St., St. Charles, 63301. Tel: 636-724-7003; Fax: 636-724-4049. Email: nshoffice@sofie.org. Web: www.sofie.org. Madeleine Ortman, Dir.

Notre Dame Ministry Corporation (1994) 320 Ripa Ave., 63125. Tel: 314-544-0455; Fax: 314-544-6754. Gail Sneed, Pres.; Anne Rackers, Treas.; Mr. Bernard Huger, Legal Counsel, Asst. Sec.; Sr. Susan Birk, S.S.N.D., Recording Sec. Includes: Notre Dame High School, Notre Dame Preschool.

Our Lady's Inn (1981) 4223 S. Compton, 63111. Tel: 314-351-4590; Fax: 314-351-2119. Email: glee@ourladysinn.org. Web: www.ourladysinn.org. 3607 Hwy. D., Defiance, 63341. Tel: 636-398-5375; Fax: 636-398-5376. Gloria Lee, Contact Person. Residential shelters for pregnant women who have no home, who are being abused, who have no one who cares, and/or who are being pressured to abort their baby. We provide living facilities, food, clothing, counseling, vocational guidance and follow up care. Total Assisted 650; Total Staff 42. 3607 Hwy. D, Defiance, 63341. Tel: 636-398-5375; Fax: 636-398-5376.

St. Patrick Center (1983) 800 N. Tucker, 63101. Tel: 314-802-0700; Fax: 314-802-1981. Email: gvogelweid@stpatrickcenter.org. Web: stpatrickcenter.org. Located in downtown St. Louis, St. Patrick Center provides opportunities for self-sufficiency and dignity to persons who are homeless or at risk of becoming homeless. Individuals achieve permanent, positive changes in their lives through education, affordable housing, sound mental health, employment and financial stability. Total Assisted 8,000; Total Staff 125.

St. Patrick Partnership Center, 800 N. Tucker, 63101.

Pauline Books and Media, 9804 Watson Rd., 63126. Tel: 314-965-3512; 314-965-5273; Fax: 314-821-8401. Email: stlouis@pauline.org. Web: www.pauline.org. Daughters of St. Paul.

Pelletier Trust, a Charitable Trust of the Sisters of the Good Shepherd (1990) 7654 Natural Bridge Rd., 63121. Tel: 314-381-3400; Fax: 314-381-6449.

Perpetual Help Retirement Corporation (2002) 335 S. Kirkwood Rd., 63122. Tel: 314-965-3700; Fax: 314-965-3710. Email: srmaryanne@fsolph.org. Web: www.franciscansisters-olph.org. Established by the Franciscan Sisters of Our Lady of Perpetual Help to Support the Religious and Charitable Purposes of the Franciscan Sisters of Our Lady of Perpetual Help.

Perry County Catholic Church Real Estate Corporation, 20 Archbishop May Dr., 63119. Tel: 314-792-7408; Fax: 314-792-7401. Rev. Msgr. Jerome D. Billing, S.T.L., J.C.L., Contact Person.

Redemptorists of Mattese (1989) 1118 N. Grand Blvd., 63106. Tel: 314-533-0304; Fax: 314-533-4260. Bro. Terrence Burke, C.Ss.R.

Review for Religious, 3601 Lindell Blvd., 63108. Tel: 314-633-4610; Fax: 314-633-4611. Email: reviewrfr@gmail.com. Web: www.reviewforreligious.org. Rev. Michael G. Harter, S.J., Editor. Total Staff 4.

Rosati Center, 4220 N. Grand Ave., 63107.

The Sarah Community, 3221 McKelvey Rd. Ste 107, Bridgeton, 63044. Tel: 314-768-1817; Fax: 314-768-1803. Email: joshaughnessy@fsmonline.org. Purpose: provides retirement housing and services to members of religious congregations and laity. Operates the following: Anna House, a skilled nursing facility; Veronica House, a residential care facility; Naomi House, an independent living facility.

The Sarah Community Foundation, 1100 Bellevue Ave., 63117-1826. Tel: 314-768-1817; Fax: 314-768-1803. Email: joshaughnessy@fsmonline.org. Mr. John O'Shaughnessy, Contact Person.

Seton Institute, Ascension Health, 4600 Edmundson Rd., P.O. Box 45998, 63164. Tel: 314-733-8286; Fax: 314-733-8013. Email: jimpicciche@ascensionhealth.org. Web: www.setoninstitute.org. Joseph R. Impicciche, Senior Vice Pres. & Gen. Counsel, Ascension Health.

Sisters of the Good Shepherd Province of Mid-North America Foundation (2001) 7654 Natural Bridge Rd., 63121. Tel: 314-381-3400; Fax: 314-381-7102. Email: cmcquaid@gspmna.org. Web: goodshepherdsisters.org. Sr. Mary Carolyn McQuaid, R.G.S.

Society Devoted to the Sacred Heart, 9600 Tennyson Ave., Saint Louis, 63114. Tel: 314-429-0526; Fax: 314-429-0794. Email: sdshstl@juno.com. Web: www.sacredheartsisters.com.

Society of St. Vincent de Paul, Council of St. Louis (1845) 100 N. Jefferson Ave., 63103. Tel: 877-238-3228; 314-881-6000; Fax: 314-531-6712. Email: info@svdpstl.org. Web: www.servingthepoor.com. Lay-based volunteer organization which provides both direct aid and program services to all eleven counties of the Archdiocese. Affiliated with 142 parishes; Car donation program which provides cars to those in need; Serves the incarcerated, their families, and victims through a three-fold approach of direct service, public education, and advocacy for systemic change within the judicial and corrections systems; Provides referrals for people seeking work, for those addicted to drugs or alcohol, and for those with emotional problems; Archdiocesan outreach program targeting hunger and utility relief, administered by the Society of St. Vincent de Paul; Provides household resources to members attempting to help needy individuals. Offers low-cost items for sale to the public. Proceeds benefit agency programs and services. Total Assisted 259,021; Total Staff 45; Volunteer Members 2,800.

Vinnie's Auto, 4127 Forest Park Ave., 63108-2808. Tel: 800-240-4225; Fax: 314-531-6712. Email: info@svdpstl.org. Web: www.servingthepoor.org.

Criminal Justice Ministry, 100 N. Jefferson Ave., 63103. Tel: 314-652-8062; Fax: 314-531-6712. Email: info@svdpstl.org. Web: www.servingthepoor.org.

Food and Fuel for Life, 100 N. Jefferson Ave., 63103. Tel: 877-238-3228; 314-881-6000; Fax: 314-531-6712. Email: info@svdpstl.org. Web: www.servingthepoor.org. Mr. Ronald F. Guz, Pres.

St. Vincent de Paul Thrift Store, 4127 Forest Park Ave., 63108. Tel: 314-881-6013; Fax: 314-531-6712. Email: info@svdpstl.org. Provides household resources to members helping needy individuals. Offers low-cost items for sale to the public. Proceeds benefit agency programs and services.

St. Vincent de Paul Thrift Store, 1071 Regency Pkwy., St. Charles, 63303. Tel: 636-946-1700.

**Society of St. Vincent de Paul, National Administration Services, Inc.*, 58 Progress Pkwy., 63043-3706. Tel: 314-576-3993; Fax: 314-576-6755. Email: usacouncil@svdpusa.org. Web: www.svdpusa.org. Roger T. Playwin, Natl. Exec. Dir.; Terry Wilson, Bd. Chair.

**Society of St. Vincent DePaul, National Council of the United States* (1845) 58 Progress Pkwy., 63043-3706. Tel: 314-576-3993; Fax: 314-576-6755. Email: usacouncil@svdpusa.org. Web: www.svdpusa.org. Sheila K. Gilbert, Natl. Pres.; Roger T. Playwin, Natl. Exec. Dir.; Most Rev. John Quinn, Natl. Episcopal Advisor.

SSM Health Businesses, 477 N. Lindbergh, 63141. Tel: 314-994-7800; Fax: 314-994-7900. Email: june_pickett@ssmhc.com. Member of SSM Health Care.

SSM Health Care Corporation, 477 N. Lindbergh, 63141. Tel: 314-994-7800; Fax: 314-994-7782. Email: june_pickett@ssmhc.com. Member of SSM Health Care.

SSM Health Care Portfolio Management Company, 447 N. Lindbergh Blvd., 63141. Tel: 314-994-7800; Fax: 314-994-7900. Email: june_pickett@ssmhc.com. Member of SSM Health Care

SSM Health Care St. Louis, 1173 Corporate Lake Dr., 63132. Tel: 314-989-2000; Fax: 314-989-2400. Web: www.ssmhealth.com. Email: judy_gartland@ssmhc.com. Member of SSM Health Care.

SSM Hospice and Home Care Foundation, 10143 Paget Dr., 63132. Tel: 314-989-2775; Fax: 314-989-2903. Linda Wulf, Foundation Dir.

SSM St. Mary's Health Center Foundation, 6420 Clayton Rd., 63117. Tel: 314-768-8741; Fax: 314-768-7124. Email: lindsey_tischer@ssmhc.com. Web: www.stmarys-stlouis.com. Member of SSM Health Care.

SSM Regional Health Services, 477 N. Lindbergh Blvd., 63141. Tel: 314-994-7800; Fax: 314-994-7900. Email: june_pickett@ssmhc.com. Member of SSM Health Care.

St. Charles County Catholic Church Real Estate Corporation, 20 Archbishop May Dr., 63119. Tel: 314-792-7408; Fax: 314-792-7401. Rev. Msgr. Jerome D. Billing, S.T.L., J.C.L., Contact Person.

St. Francois County Catholic Church Real Estate Corporation, 20 Archbishop May Dr., 63119. Tel: 314-792-7408; Fax: 314-792-7401. Rev. Msgr. Jerome D. Billing, S.T.L., J.C.L., Contact Person.

St. Louis City Catholic Church Real Estate Corporation, 20 Archbishop May Dr., 63119. Tel: 314-792-7408; Fax: 314-792-7401. Rev. Msgr. Jerome D. Billing, S.T.L., J.C.L., Contact Person.

Ste. Genevieve County Catholic Church Real Estate Corporation 20 Archbishop May Dr., 63119. Tel: 314-792-7408; Fax: 314-792-7401. Rev. Msgr. Jerome D. Billing, S.T.L., J.C.L., Contact Person. Priests 1.

Ursuline Sisters Trust Fund, 353 S. Sappington Rd., 63122. Tel: 314-821-6884; Fax: 314-821-6888. Web: www.osucentral.org. Russell F. Weil.

The Vincentian Press Religious Supply, 1405 S. Ninth St., 63104. Tel: 314-421-2834; Fax: 314-421-0684. Rev. Joseph E. Begue, C.M., Dir. Total Staff 2.

Warren County Catholic Church Real Estate Corporation, 20 Archbishop May Dr., 63119. Tel: 314-792-7408; Fax: 314-792-7401. Rev. Msgr. Jerome D. Billing, S.T.L., J.C.L., Contact Person.

Washington County Catholic Church Real Estate Corporation (1821) 20 Archbishop May Dr., 63119. Tel: 314-792-7408; Fax: 314-792-7401. Rev. Msgr. Jerome D. Billing, S.T.L., J.C.L., Contact Person.

We & God Spirituality Center, 3601 Lindell Blvd., Ste. 617, 63108. Tel: 314-633-4630; Fax: 314-633-4404. Email: wgsc@weandgod.org. Web: www.weandgod.org.

**Women for Faith and Family* (1984) P.O. Box 300411, 63130. Tel: 314-863-8385; Fax: 314-863-5858. Email: editor@wf-f.org. Web: www.wf-f.org. Mrs. Helen Hull Hitchcock, Pres.

Young Catholic Musicians, 1919 S. 7th St., Saint Louis, 63104. Tel: 314-962-9260; Fax: 314-231-7464. Email: revycm@charter.net. Mary Smith, Contact Person.

BRIDGETON. *Boys Hope Girls Hope*, 12120 Bridgeton Square Dr., 63044. Tel: 314-298-1250; Fax: 314-298-1251. Email: hope@bhgh.org. Web: www.boyshopegirlshope.org. Paul A. Minorini, Pres. & CEO. A College Preparatory Residential Child Care Agency Serving Abandoned, Abused and Neglected Children. Founded in 1977; With affiliated programs in: Baton Rouge; Chicago; Cincinnati; Denver; Detroit; Nevada; New Orleans; New York; Northeast Ohio; Orange County, CA; Phoenix; Pittsburgh; St. Louis; San Francisco, Baltimore, Kansas City. Total Staff 130; Total Assisted 500.

Room at the Inn formerly Providence Ministry Corporation (1998) 3415 Bridgeland Dr., 63044. Tel: 314-209-9181; Fax: 314-209-9207. Web: www.divineprovidenceweb.org. Sr. Mary Francis Fletcher, C.D.P., Prov.

Sisters of Divine Providence, 3415 Bridgeland Dr., 63044. Tel: 314-209-9181; Fax: 314-209-9207. Email: srmfranciscdp@hotmail.com. Web: www.divineprovidenceweb.org. Sisters Jacklyn Pritchard, C.D.P., Contact Person; Mary Francis Fletcher, C.D.P., Provincial. Sisters 35.

SSM De Paul Health Center, 12303 De Paul Dr., 63044.

SSM DePaul Health Center Foundation, 12303 DePaul Dr., 63044. Tel: 314-344-7003; Fax: 314-344-6172. Email: valerie_stricker@ssmhc.com. Web: www.ssmdepaulfoundation.org. Member of SSM Health Care.

CADET. *Rural Parish Workers of Christ the King* (1942) 15540 Cannon Mines Rd., 63630. Tel: 636-586-5171; Fax: 636-586-5918. Email: rpwck@sbcglobal.net. Web: rpwck.com. Miss Natalie Villmer, Gen. Dir. A Secular Institute of the Archdiocese of St. Louis. Workers 5; Total Assisted 2,500; Total in Residence 4; Total Staff 6.

CHESTERFIELD. *Gateway Academy Incorporated*, 17815 Wild Horse Creek Rd., 63005. Tel: 914-773-1368. Email: jortega@legionaries.org. Web: www.gatewayacademy.org. Rev. Jose Felix Ortega, L.C., Sec. & Treas.

Gateway Educational Foundation, Inc., 17803 Wild Horse Creek Rd., 63005. Tel: 914-773-1368; Fax: 914-773-1438. Rev. Jose Felix Ortega, L.C., Sec. & Treas.

Saint Louis LaSalle Leadership, Inc. (1996) 645 Clovertrail Dr., 63017-2612. Tel: 314-434-8789; Fax: 314-434-8789. Email: stl3i@aol.com. Waldemar E. Bode, Pres.; Gregory M. Gantz, Vice Pres.; John J. Hall, Sec.; Staunton E. Boudreau, Treas.

McAuley Portfolio Management Company, 14528 S. Outer 40, Ste. 100, 63017. Tel: 314-628-3676; Fax: 314-628-3732. Email: philip.wheeler@mercy.net. Mr. Philip Wheeler Sr., Vice Pres. & Gen. Counsel.

Mercy Health formerly Sisters of Mercy Health System 14528 S. Outer Forty, Ste. 100, 63017. Tel: 314-579-6100; Fax: 314-628-3732. Email: michele.giunta@mercy.net. Web: www.mercy.net. Philip Wheeler, Sec.

MHM Support Services, 14528 S. Outer Forty, Ste. 100, 63017. Tel: 314-579-6100; Fax: 314-628-3732. Mr. Philip Wheeler Sr., Senior Vice Pres. & Gen. Counsel.

DARDENNE PRAIRIE. *Saint William Apartments, Inc.*, 1979 Hanley Rd., 63368. Tel: 636-695-4200; Fax: 636-695-4208.

St. William Apartments II, Inc., 1983 Hanley Rd., 63368. Tel: 636-695-4205; Fax: 636-695-4216.

DITTMER. *Our Lady of Victory Charitable Foundation*, 6476 Eime Rd., 63023. Tel: 636-274-5226; Fax: 636-274-1430.

Servants of the Paraclete Missouri Generalate Corporation, 6476 Eime Rd., 63023. Tel: 636-274-5226; Fax: 636-274-1430. Very Revs. David Fitzgerald, s.P., Dir.; Liam Hoare, s.P., Sec.; Revs. Peter Lechner, s.P., Trustee; Benedict Livingstone, s.P., Trustee; Philip Taylor, s.P., Trustee.

EARTH CITY. *Congregation of the Mission International Fund*, 13663 Rider Tr. N., 63045-1512. Tel: 314-344-1184; Fax: 314-344-2989.

Ladies of Charity of the United States of America (1960) 100 N. Jefferson Ave., Saint Louis, 63104. Tel: 314-881-6067; Fax: 314-881-6017. Email: lers@starpower.net. Lucy Ann Saunders, Pres. 2009-2010. LCUSA continues, expands, and improves the charitable works of the local associations of the LCUSA, which number 70.

Lazarist Trust Fund, 13663 Rider Tr. N., 63045-1512. Tel: 314-344-1184; Fax: 314-344-2989.

Vincentian Solidarity Office, Congregation of the Mission Western Province, 13663 River Trail N., 63045.

FESTUS. *TEC Conference (Teens Encounter Christ)*, 114 S. 2nd St., 63028. Tel: 636-933-9233; Fax: 636-933-9531. Ronald Reiter, Exec. Dir.

FLORISSANT. *Child Center Foundation* (1947) 2705 Mullanphy Ln., 63031. Tel: 314-837-1702; Fax: 314-830-6263. Email: hnegri@ccstl.org. Mr. Timothy Drury, Pres., Bd. of Directors. Child Center Foundation provides financial support to the Child Center - Marygrove, a residential and day treatment facility serving severely emotionally disturbed children and their families.

Pope John Paul II Apartments, Inc., 6325 Waterways Dr., 63033. Tel: 314-653-0400; Fax: 314-653-2840. Email: bperrone@ccstl.org. Web: www.ccstl.org/cri/independent.html. Purpose: to provide facilities and services specifically designed to meet the physical, social, spiritual and psychological needs of elderly persons.

KIRKWOOD. *Ursuline Provincialate Foundation, Central Province of the United States*, 353 Sappington Rd., 63122.

LEMAY. *Catholic Deaf Ministry*, 309 Hoffmeister Ave., 63125. Email: vbarnhart@archstl.org. Rev. Victor A. Barnhart, Dir. Provides Services for Deaf and Hearing Impaired Persons.

LIGUORI. *Redemptorist Fathers dba Liguori Publications* One Liguori Dr., 63057. Tel: 636-464-2500; Fax: 636-464-8449. Email: mkessler@liguori.org. Web: www.liguori.org. Rev. Mathew Kessler, C.Ss.R., Pres. & Publisher.

O'FALLON. *Centers for Professional and Pastoral Services*, 204 N. Main St., 63366-2299. Tel: 636-240-6010; Fax: 636-272-5031. Email: fraia@cpps-ofallon.org. Sisters Sandra Barton, C.PP.S., Admin.; Fran Raia, C.PP.S. Sponsored by Sisters of the Most Precious Blood of O'Fallon, MO. Centers 1; Total Assisted 700; Total Staff 5.

Charitable Trust, Sisters of the Most Precious Blood of O'Fallon, MO, 204 N. Main St., 63366-2299. Tel: 636-240-6010; Fax: 636-272-5031. Email: cschnyder@cpps-ofallon.org. Web: www.cpps-ofallon.org. Trust fund for support of retired Sisters of the Most Precious Blood.

St. Dominic Endowment Fund, St. Dominic High School, 31 St. Dominic Dr., 63366. Tel: 314-240-8303; Fax: 314-240-9884. Email: mainoffice@stdominichs.org. Web: www.stdominichs.org. Sr. Mary H. Bender, S.S.N.D., Treas.

PACIFIC. *Providence Trust*, Our Lady of the Angels Monastery, 265 St. Joseph Rd., 63069. Tel: 636-938-5361; Fax: 636-938-4960. Web: www.franciscancaring.org. Purpose: To support the religious and charitable purposes of the Franciscan Missionary Brothers of the Sacred Heart.

PERRYVILLE. *Association of the Miraculous Medal* (1918) 1811 W. Saint Joseph St., 63775. Tel: 573-547-8343; Fax: 573-547-1389. Email: ammfather@amm.org. Web: www.amm.org. Rev. James G. Ward, C.M., Pres.

Catholic Home Study Service, P.O. Box 363, 63775. Email: chss@ldd.net. Web: www.amm.org/chss/chss.asp. Revs. James G. Ward, C.M., Dir.; Oscar Lukefahr, C.M., Dir. Emeritus. Priests 2; Total Staff 5; Total Assisted 12,000.

Offers free correspondence courses on the Catholic Faith.

Ladies of Charity of St. Vincent de Paul Parish, 1010 Rosati Ct., 63775. Tel: 573-547-4591; Fax: 573-547-4145. Email: svdepaul@svdepaul.org. Marilyn R. Schumer, Pres. Affiliate with Ladies of Charity of the United States & the Assoc. of Intl. Charities of St. Vincent de Paul. Total Assisted 4,067.

St. Vincent De Paul Educational Foundation, 1010 A Rosati Ct., 63775. Tel: 573-547-4591; Fax: 573-547-4145. Email: svdepaul@svdepaul.org. Web: www.svdepaul.org. Rev. Milton F. Ryan, C.M., Moderator. Develops, Promotes and Sustains Catholic Education in Perry County.

ST. CHARLES. *Academy of the Sacred Heart of St. Charles, Missouri Endowment Trust Fund* (1818) 619 N. 2nd St., 63301. Tel: 636-946-5632; Fax: 636-949-6659. Email: mglavin@ash1818.org. Web: www.ash1818.org.

Duchesne High School Endowment Fund Inc., 2550 Elm St., 63301. Tel: 636-946-6767; Fax: 636-946-6267. Email: tgravemann@duchesne-hs.org. Web: www.duchesne-hs.org. Terry W. Gravemann, Pres. Receives Bequests and Gifts from Various Donors for the Express Purpose of Aiding and Benefitting Duchesne High School, St. Charles, and by Investment and Use of Such Bequests and Gifts and Income there from Aids and Benefits the High School in Fulfilling its Educational Purposes.

Sts. Joachim and Ann Care Service, 4116 McClay Rd., 63304. Tel: 636-441-1302; Fax: 636-229-4684. Email: mmahan@jacare.org. Web: jacares.org. Miriam Mahan, Exec. Dir.

SSM St. Joseph Foundation, 300 First Capitol Dr., 63301. Tel: 314-947-5612; Fax: 636-947-5676. Web: www.ssmstjosephfoundation.org. Member of SSM Health Care.

Warrenton Senior Village, Inc., Hwy. U & Woolf Rd., Warrenton, 63383.

RELIGIOUS INSTITUTES OF MEN REPRESENTED IN THE ARCHDIOCESE

For further details refer to the corresponding bracketed number in the Religious Institutes of Men or Women section.

[0120]—*Alexian Brothers* (Chicago)—C.F.A.
[0140]—*The Augustinians. (Prov. of Our Mother of Good Counsel)*—O.S.A.
[0200]—*Benedictine Monks. (English, Swiss American Congregation)*—O.S.B.
[]—*Brothers of St. Charles Lwanga*—B.S.C.L.
[0330]—*Brothers of the Christian Schools. (St. Louis Prov.)*—F.S.C.
[0470]—*The Capuchin Friars* (Kansas City, MO)—O.F.M.Cap.
[1330]—*Congregation of the Mission (Midwest Prov.)*—C.M.
[0630]—*Congregation of the Missionaries of the Holy Family* (Europe)—M.S.F.
[1000]—*Congregation of the Passion (Eastern Prov. of Holy Cross)*—C.P.
[1000]—*Congregation of the Passion (Western Prov. of Holy Cross)*—C.P.
[1130]—*Congregation of the Priests of the Sacred Heart*—S.C.J.
[1080]—*Congregation of the Resurrection* (Rome, Italy)—C.R.
[0480]—*Conventual Franciscans. (Our Lady of Consolation Prov.)*—O.F.M.Conv.
[0510]—*Franciscan Brothers of the Holy Cross*—F.F.S.C.
[0520]—*Franciscan Friars. (Croatian Franciscan Commissariat, Sacred Heart Prov.)*—O.F.M.
[0540]—*Franciscan Missionary Brothers of the Sacred Heart of Jesus* (Eureka, MO)—O.S.F.
[]—*Institute of Christ The King Sovereign Priest*
[0690]—*Jesuit Fathers and Brothers* (Missouri Prov.)—S.J.
[0730]—*Legionaries of Christ*—L.C.
[0800]—*Maryknoll*—M.M.
[0720]—*The Missionaries of Our Lady of La Salette*—M.S.
[0870]—*Monfort Missionaries*—S.M.M.
[0430]—*Order of Preachers*—O.P.
[0610]—*Priests of the Congregation of Holy Cross*—C.S.C.
[1070]—*Redemptorist Fathers* (Denver Prov.)—C.SS.R.
[1230]—*Servants of the Paraclete*—s.P.
[1240]—*Servites* (Chicago)—O.S.M.
[0760]—*Society of Mary* (St. Louis Prov.)—S.M.
[0975]—*Society of Our Lady of the Most Holy Trinity*—S.O.L.T.
[0420]—*Society of the Divine Word* (Northern Prov.)—S.V.D.
[]—*Sons of Our Mother*—S.M.P.

RELIGIOUS INSTITUTES OF WOMEN REPRESENTED IN THE ARCHDIOCESE

[0100]—*Adorers of the Blood of Christ* (U.S. Prov.)—A.S.C.
[0130]—*Apostles of the Sacred Heart of Jesus*—A.S.C.J.
[0360]—*Carmelite Sisters of the Divine Heart of Jesus* (Carmel)—D.C.J.
[3110]—*Congregation of Our Lady of the Retreat in the Cenacle*—R.C.
[]—*Congregation of Our Lady of the Rosary*
[]—*Congregation of Our Lady of the Sacred Heart*
[]—*Congregation of St. Catherine of Siena*
[]—*Congregation of the Most Holy Rosary*
[0460]—*Congregation of the Sisters of Charity of the Incarnate Word*—C.C.V.I.
[1730]—*Congregation of the Third order of St. Francis Oldenburg, IN*—O.S.F.
[1830]—*Contemplatives of the Good Shepherd*—C.G.S.
[0760]—*Daughters of Charity of St. Vincent de Paul*—D.C.
[]—*Daughters of Our Mother of Peace*—S.M.P.
[0810]—*Daughters of the Heart of Mary*—D.H.M.
[0420]—*Discalced Carmelite Nuns*—O.C.D.
[1070-19]—*Dominican Sisters* (of Houston, TX)—O.P.
[]—*Eucharist Missionaries of St. Theresa*—M.E.S.T.
[1370]—*Franciscan Missionaries of Mary*—F.M.M.
[1310]—*Franciscan Sisters of Little Falls, Minnesota*—O.S.F.
[1415]—*Franciscan Sisters of Mary*—F.S.M.
[1430]—*Franciscan Sisters of Our Lady of Perpetual Help*—O.S.F.
[]—*Franciscan Sisters, Daughters of the Sacred Hearts of Jesus and Mary*
[2340]—*Little Sisters of the Poor*—L.S.P.
[2490]—*Medical Mission Sisters*—M.M.S.
[2710]—*Missionaries of Charity*—M.C.
[0390]—*Missionary Carmelites of St. Teresa*—C.M.S.T.
[3990]—*Missionary Sisters of St. Peter Claver*—S.S.P.C.
[3760]—*Order of St. Clare*—O.S.C.
[2010]—*Order of the Most Holy Redeemer*—O.SS.R.
[0950]—*Pius Society Daughters of St. Paul*—F.S.P.
[3170]—*Religious of the Passion of Jesus Christ*—C.P.
[3465]—*Religious of the Sacred Heart of Mary*—R.S.H.M.
[]—*Religious Sisters of Mercy* (St. Louis, MO.)—R.S.M.
[2970]—*School Sisters of Notre Dame*—S.S.N.D.
[]—*Sinsinawa Dominican Congregation of the Most Holy Rosary*
[0430]—*Sisters of Charity of the Blessed Virgin Mary*—B.V.M.
[0460]—*Sisters of Charity of the Incarnate Word* (San Antonio, TX)—C.C.V.I.
[0660]—*Sisters of Christian Charity*—S.C.C.
[0990]—*Sisters of Divine Providence*—C.D.P.
[2360]—*Sisters of Loretto at the Foot of the Cross* (St. Louis Prov.)—S.L.
[2570]—*Sisters of Mercy*—R.S.M.
[2580]—*Sisters of Mercy of the Americas*—R.S.M.
[1540]—*Sisters of Saint Francis, Clinton, Iowa*—O.S.F.
[1600]—*Sisters of St. Francis of the Martyr St. George*—F.S.G.M.
[3830]—*Sisters of St. Joseph*—C.S.J.
[1830]—*Sisters of the Good Shepherd*—R.G.S.-C.G.
[3270]—*Sisters of the Most Precious Blood* (O'Fallon, MO)—C.PP.S.
[3150]—*Sisters of the Pallottine Missionary Society*—S.A.C.
[3540]—*Sisters Servants of the Holy Spirit of Perpetual Adoration*—S.Sp.S.deA.
[2150]—*Sisters, Servants of the Immaculate Heart of Mary*—I.H.M.
[1890]—*Society of Helpers of the Holy Souls*—S.H.
[4070]—*Society of the Sacred Heart*—R.S.C.J.
[4110]—*Ursuline Nuns*—O.S.U.
[4190]—*Visitation Nuns*—V.H.M.

ARCHDIOCESAN CEMETERIES

ST. LOUIS. *Calvary*, Business Office: 5239 W. Florissant Ave., 63115. Tel: 314-381-1313; Fax: 314-381-3218.

Location:

Calvary Cemetery, 5239 W. Florissant Ave., 63115.

Sacred Heart Cemetery, Graham Rd., Florissant, 63033.

Saint Ferdinand Cemetery, Graham Rd., Hazelwood, 63042.

Saint Mary Cemetery, 5200 Fee Fee Rd., Hazelwood, 63042.

Saint Peter Cemetery, Geyer at W. Monroe Ave., Kirkwood, 63122.

Cemetery of Our Lady, Lake St. Louis Blvd. & Orf Rd., Lake St. Louis, 63366.

Saint Charles Borromeo Cemetery, Randolph St., St. Charles, 63301.

Ste. Philippine Cemetiere, 4057 Towers Rd., St. Charles, 63304.

Resurrection, Business Office: 6901 Mackenzie Rd., 63123. Tel: 314-352-5300.

Location:

Resurrection Cemetery, 6901 Mackenzie Rd., 63123.

Saints Peter and Paul Cemetery, 7030 Gravois Ave., 63116.

Saint Vincent Cemetery, 1488 Romaine Creek Rd., Fenton, 63026.

Holy Cross Cemetery, 16200 Manchester Rd.,

Ellisville, 63011.

Mount Olive Cemetery, 3906 Mt. Olive Rd., Lemay, 63125.

Ascension Cemetery, 5563 Country Club Rd., Washington, 63090.

NECROLOGY

† Buchheit, Rev. Msgr. Richard A., (Retired)—Died June 29, 2011

† Meyer, Rev. Msgr. Louis F., (Retired)—Died May 14, 2011

† Rau, Rev. Msgr. Donald E., (Retired)—Died July 14, 2011

† Murphy, James E., (Retired)—Died Nov. 29, 2010

† Reilly, F. Joseph, River aux Vases, MO Sts. Philip & James—Died Sept. 22, 2011

An asterisk (*) denotes an organization that has established tax-exempt status directly with the IRS and is not covered by the USCCB Group Ruling.

Archdiocese of St. Paul and Minneapolis

(Archidioecesis Paulopolitana et Minneapolitana)

Most Reverend

JOHN C. NIENSTEDT, S.T.D., D.D.

Archbishop of Saint Paul and Minneapolis; ordained July 27, 1974; appointed Auxiliary Bishop of Detroit June 12, 1996; episcopal ordination July 9, 1996; appointed Bishop of New Ulm June 12, 2001; installed August 6, 2001; appointed Coadjutor Archbishop of Saint Paul and Minneapolis April 24, 2007; succeeded to the See May 2, 2008. *Office: 226 Summit Ave., St. Paul, MN 55102.* Tel: 651-291-4511; Fax: 651-291-4549.

Most Reverend

HARRY J. FLYNN, D.D.

Archbishop Emeritus of Saint Paul and Minneapolis; ordained May 28, 1960; appointed Coadjutor of Lafayette April 19, 1986; episcopal ordination June 24, 1986; appointed Bishop of Lafayette May 13, 1989; appointed Coadjutor Archbishop of Saint Paul and Minneapolis February 22, 1994; succeeded to the See September 8, 1995; retired May 2, 2008. *Office: 226 Summit Ave., St. Paul, MN 55102.* Tel: 651-291-4420; Fax: 651-291-4549.

Chancery: 226 Summit Ave., St. Paul, MN 55102. Tel: 651-291-4400; Fax: 651-290-1629.

Web: www.archspm.org

Email: chancery@archspm.org

Most Reverend

LEE ANTHONY PICHÉ

Auxiliary Bishop of Saint Paul and Minneapolis; ordained May 26, 1984; appointed Auxiliary Bishop of Saint Paul and Minneapolis and Titular Bishop of Tamata May 27, 2009; episcopal ordination June 29, 2009. *Office: 226 Summit Ave., St. Paul, MN 55102.* Tel: 651-291-4521; Fax: 651-290-1637. Email: bishoppiche@archspm.org.

Square Miles 6,187.

Diocese Established, July 19, 1850. Archdiocese Established, May 4, 1888.

Comprises the following twelve Counties of the State of Minnesota: Ramsey, Hennepin, Anoka, Carver, Chisago, Dakota, Goodhue, Le Sueur, Rice, Scott, Washington and Wright.

Corporate Title: The Archdiocese of Saint Paul and Minneapolis.

For legal titles of parishes and archdiocesan institutions, consult the Chancery.

STATISTICAL OVERVIEW

Personnel	
Archbishops	1
Retired Archbishops	1
Auxiliary Bishops	1
Priests: Diocesan Active in Diocese	221
Priests: Diocesan Active Outside Diocese	7
Priests: Diocesan in Foreign Missions	2
Priests: Retired, Sick or Absent	107
Number of Diocesan Priests	337
Religious Priests in Diocese	84
Total Priests in Diocese	421
Extern Priests in Diocese	28
Ordinations:	
Diocesan Priests	5
Transitional Deacons	3
Permanent Deacons in Diocese	214
Total Brothers	46
Total Sisters	643
Parishes	
Parishes	200
With Resident Pastor:	
Resident Diocesan Priests	163
Resident Religious Priests	19
Without Resident Pastor:	
Administered by Priests	17
Completely Vacant	1
Missions	2
Pastoral Centers	4
Closed Parishes	6
Welfare	
Catholic Hospitals	3
Total Assisted	227,315
Health Care Centers	1
Total Assisted	173
Homes for the Aged	19
Total Assisted	27,771
Residential Care of Children	2
Total Assisted	1,099
Day Care Centers	2
Total Assisted	241
Specialized Homes	2
Total Assisted	821
Special Centers for Social Services	2
Total Assisted	37,000
Residential Care of Disabled	3
Total Assisted	12
Educational	
Seminaries, Diocesan	2
Students from This Diocese	69
Students from Other Diocese	31
Diocesan Students in Other Seminaries	2
Seminaries, Religious	1
Students Religious	11
Total Seminarians	82
Colleges and Universities	2
Total Students	16,178
High Schools, Diocesan and Parish	2
Total Students	853
High Schools, Private	10
Total Students	6,370
Elementary Schools, Diocesan and Parish	82
Total Students	21,211
Elementary Schools, Private	5
Total Students	811
Catechesis/Religious Education:	
High School Students	10,285
Elementary Students	29,961
Total Students under Catholic Instruction	85,751
Teachers in the Diocese:	
Priests	5
Brothers	6
Sisters	42
Lay Teachers	2,822
Vital Statistics	
Receptions into the Church:	
Infant Baptism Totals	6,306
Minor Baptism Totals	310
Adult Baptism Totals	180
Received into Full Communion	1,025
First Communions	9,126
Confirmations	7,214
Marriages:	
Catholic	1,053
Interfaith	550
Total Marriages	1,603
Deaths	3,338
Total Catholic Population	825,000
Total Population	2,686,763

Former Bishops—Rt. Rev. JOSEPH CRETIN, D.D., cons. Jan. 26, 1851; died Feb. 22, 1857; Most Revs. THOMAS L. GRACE, O.P., D.D., cons. July 24, 1859; resigned July 31, 1884; named Titular Bishop of Menith, and later, Titular Archbishop of Siunia; died Feb. 22, 1897; JOHN IRELAND, D.D., cons. Dec. 21, 1861; Bishop of Maronea, and Coadjutor to; died Sept. 25, 1918; THOMAS L. GRACE, O.P., D.D., succeeded to the See of St. Paul, July 31, 1884; appt. Archbishop, May 15, 1888; died Sept. 25, 1918; AUSTIN DOWLING, D.D., Archbishop of St. Paul; ord. June 24, 1891; appt. Bishop of Des Moines, Iowa, Jan. 31, 1912; cons. April 25, 1912; Nominated Archbishop of St. Paul, Feb. 1, 1919; died Nov. 29, 1930; JOHN GREGORY MURRAY, S.T.D., ord. April 14, 1900; appt. Titular Bishop of Flavias, Auxiliary to the Bishop of Hartford, Nov. 15, 1919; cons. April 28, 1920; transferred to the Diocese of Portland, May 29, 1925; appt. Archbishop of St. Paul, Oct. 29, 1931; died Oct. 11, 1956; WILLIAM O. BRADY, D.D., Archbishop of St. Paul; ord. Dec. 21, 1923; appt. Bishop of Sioux Falls, June 10, 1939; cons. Aug. 24, 1939; appt. Titular Archbishop of Selymbria and Coadjutor "cum jure successionis" of St. Paul, June 16, 1956; succeeded to See, Oct. 11, 1956; died Oct. 1, 1961; LEO C. BYRNE, D.D. Coadjutor Archbishop "cum jure successionis" of Saint Paul and Minneapolis ord. June 10, 1933; appt. titular Bishop of Sabidia and Auxiliary of St. Louis, May 21, 1954; cons. June 29, 1954; transferred to Wichita, "cum jure successionis" 1961; appt. Apostolic Administrator of Wichita, Feb. 25, 1963; promoted to St. Paul and Minneapolis, Aug. 2, 1967; died Oct. 21, 1974; LEO BINZ, D.D., ord. March 15, 1924; appt. Titular Bishop of Pinara and Coadjutor Bishop of Winona, Nov. 21, 1942; cons. Dec. 21, 1942; Titular Archbishop of Silyum and Coadjutor to the Archbishop of Dubuque "cum jure successionis," Oct. 15, 1949; Archbishop of Dubuque, Dec. 2, 1954; appt. Archbishop of Saint Paul, Dec. 16, 1961; resigned May 21, 1975; died Oct. 9, 1979; JOHN R. ROACH, D.D., Archbishop of St. Paul and Minneapolis; ord. June 8, 1946; appt. Titular Bishop of Cenae and Auxiliary Bishop of St. Paul and Minneapolis, July 12, 1971; cons. Sept. 8, 1971; appt. Archbishop of St. Paul and Minneapolis, May 21, 1975; resigned Sept. 8, 1995; died July 11, 2003; HARRY J. FLYNN, D.D., ord. May 28, 1960; appt. Coadjutor of Lafayette April 19, 1986; cons. June 24, 1986; appt. Bishop of Lafayette May 13, 1989; appt. Coadjutor Archbishop of Saint Paul and Minneapolis Feb. 22, 1994; appt. Archbishop of Saint Paul and Minneapolis Sept. 8, 1995; retired May 2, 2008.

Chancery—226 Summit Ave., St. Paul, 55102. Tel: 651-291-4400; Fax: 651-290-1629.

Office of the Archbishop—Most Rev. JOHN C. NIENSTEDT; Ms. DEB THIELEN, Administrative Asst. to the Archbishop. Tel: 651-291-4511; Fax: 651-291-4549. Email: thielend@archspm.org; Mr. THOMAS SCHULZETENBERG, Administrative Chancellor, 226 Summit Ave., St. Paul, 55102. Tel: 651-290-1644. Email: schulzetenbergt@archspm.org.

Office of the Auxiliary Bishop and Vicar General—Most Rev. LEE ANTHONY PICHE. Email: bishoppiche@archspm.org; Ms. LORNA ANDERSON, Administrative Asst. to the Auxiliary Bishop, 226 Summit Ave., St. Paul, 55102. Tel: 651-291-4521. Email: andersonl@archspm.org.

Office of Vicar General and Moderator of the Curia—Very Rev. PETER A. LAIRD, Vicar Gen. & Moderator of the Curia. Email: vicargeneral@archspm.org; Ms. JENNIFER HALL, Administrative Asst. to the Vicar Gen., 226 Summit Ave., St. Paul, 55102. Tel: 651-291-4430; Fax: 651-290-1629. Email: hallj@archspm.org.

Presbyteral Council—

Executive Director—Rev. ROBERT H. HART, St. Patrick, 3535 72nd St. E., Inver Grove Heights, 55076-2627. Tel: 651-455-6624. Email: bhart@churchofstpatrick.com. Secretary Election Pending: Treasurer: Rev. JOHN L. UBEL, Church of St. Thomas the Apostle, 20000 County Rd. 10, Corcoran, 55340-9501.

Deanery 1—Rev. RALPH W. TALBOT, Church of St. Jude of the Lake, 700 Mahtomedi Ave., Mahtomedi, 55115-1673. Email: frtalbot@stjudeofthelake.org.

Deanery 2—Rev. PATRICK J. HIPWELL, Church of the Nativity, 1900 Wellesley Ave., St. Paul, 55105. Email: frphipwell@nativity-mn.org.

Deanery 3—Rev. JOHN L. UBEL, Church of St. Agnes, 535 Lafond Ave., Saint Paul, 55103-1631. Email: frubel@stagnesschools.org.

Deanery 4—Rev. WILLIAM J. BAER, Church of Transfiguration, 6133 15th St. N., Oakdale, 55128. Tel: 651-738-2646. Email: frbaer@transfigurationmn.org.

Deanery 5—Rev. THOMAS J. WALKER, J.D., Saint Ambrose of Woodbury, 4125 Woodbury Dr., Saint Paul, 55129. Email: tom.walker@saintambroseofwoodbury.org.

Deanery 6—Rev. STAN P. MADER, Mailing Address: Church of Saint Mary, 8433 239th St. E., Hampton, 55031-9766. Email: frstan@stmathias.com.

Deanery 7—Rev. CHRISTOPHER SHOFNER, Church of St. Mary, 165 Waterville Ave. N., Le Center, 56057-1524. Tel: 507-357-6633. Email: fr.chris@hotmail.com.

Deanery 8—VACANT.

Deanery 9—Rev. THEODORE C. CAMPBELL, Church of The Good Shepherd, 145 Jersey Ave. S., Golden Valley, 55426. Tel: 763-544-0416. Email: tccampbell@goodshepherdgv.org.

Deanery 10—Rev. TIMOTHY E. DOLAN, Our Lady of the Lake, 2385 Commerce Blvd., Mound, 55364-1427. Email: tdolan@oll.pvt.k12.mn.us.

Deanery 11—Rev. PETER M. RICHARDS, St. Michael, 11300 Frankfort Pkwy., N.E., Saint Michael, 55376-4550. Tel: 763-497-2745. Email: frrichards@stmcatholicchurch.org.

Deanery 12—Rev. MICHAEL VAN SLOUN, Church of St. Stephen, 525 Jackson St., Anoka, 55303-2353. Tel: 763-421-2471. Email: mvansloun@ststephenchurch.org.

Deanery 13—Rev. JOHN BAUER, Mailing Address: The Basilica of St. Mary, P.O. Box 50010, Minneapolis, 55405-0010. Tel: 612-333-1381. Email: jbauer@mary.org.

Deanery 14—Rev. PAUL C. TREACY, Church of Our Lady of Peace, 5426 12th Ave. S., Minneapolis, 55417. Tel: 612-824-3455. Email: htasto@stampls.org.

Deanery 15—Rev. WILLIAM A. MURTAUGH, The Church of Pax Christi, 12100 Pioneer Tr., Eden Prairie, 55347-4208.

Deanery 16— (Academic) Rev. MICHAEL J. KEATING, Univ. of St. Thomas, 2115 Summit Ave. #55S, St. Paul, 55105-1078. Tel: 651-962-5700. Email: mjkeating@stthomas.edu.

Deanery 17— (Specialized) Rev. STEPHEN J. LACANNE, M.Div., N.A.C.C., St. Joseph Hospital, 45 10th St. E., St. Paul, 55101-2222. Email: sjlacanne@healtheast.org.

Deanery 18— (Retired) Revs. RINALDO B. CUSTODIO (Retired), Leo C. Byrne Residence, 60 S. Mississippi River Blvd., St. Paul, 55105-1052. Tel: 651-699-1233. Email: rbc1962@msn.com; FRANCIS R. KITTOCK (Retired), Leo C. Byrne Residence #230, 60 S. Mississippi River Blvd., St. Paul, 55105-1052. Tel: 651-690-4900. Email: frkit@msn.com.

Appointees—Revs. FERNANDO ORTEGA, Church of St. Stephen, 525 Jackson St., Anoka, 55303-2353. Tel: 763-421-2471. Email: fortega@ststephenchurch.org; CHARLES LACHOWITZER, Church of St. John Neumann, 4030 Pilot Knob Rd., Eagan, 55122-1898. Tel: 651-454-2079. Email: fr.charlie@sjn.org; ROLF R. TOLLEFSON, Church of Saint Hubert, 8201 Main St., Chanhassen, 55317. Email: fatherrolf.tollefson@sthubert.org.

Ex Officio—Most Revs. JOHN C. NIENSTEDT, S.T.D., D.D. Tel: 651-291-4400. Email: thielend@archspm.org; LEE ANTHONY PICHE. Tel: 651-291-4400. Email: pichel@archspm.org; Very Rev. PETER A. LAIRD, 226 Summit Ave., St. Paul, 55102. Tel: 651-291-4403. Email: lairdp@archspm.org.

Archdiocesan Finance Council (AFC)—Mr. BRIAN WENGER, Chm.; Deacon WILLIAM HEIMAN; Rev. JOHN L. UBEL; STEWART W. LAIRD; Mr. MARK MISUKANIS; JACKIE DAYLOR; Mr. THOMAS ABOOD; MARGARET LECLAIR; RICHARD J. PEARSON; DANIEL STATSICK; Mr. THOMAS SKIBA; Most Rev. JOHN C. NIENSTEDT, S.T.D., D.D., Archbishop; Very Rev. PETER A. LAIRD, Vicar Gen. & Moderator of the Curia; Mr. JOHN F. BIERBAUM, CFO; RUTH PORTER, Staff Support, 226 Summit Ave., St. Paul, 55102. Tel: 651-291-4492.

Archdiocesan Catholic Schools Advisory Council—226 Summit Ave., St. Paul, 55105. Mr. JOHN MCMAHON, Chm.

College of Consultors—Revs. DANIEL F. GRIFFITH; ROBERT H. HART, Church of St. Patrick, 3535 72nd St. E., Inver Grove Heights, 55076-2627; PATRICK J. HIPWELL, Church of the Nativity, 1900 Wellesley Ave., St. Paul, 55105; Very Rev. PETER A. LAIRD, 226 Summit Ave., St. Paul, 55102; Revs. JAMES M. PERKL, St. Elizabeth Ann Seton, 2035 15th St. W., Hastings, 55033-9294; THOMAS H. SIEG, St. Michael, 16311 Duluth Ave., S.E., Prior Lake, 55372-2423; PETER J. WILLIAMS, Church of the Maternity of the Blessed Virgin Mary, 1414 Dale St. N., St. Paul, 55117; RALPH W. TALBOT, Church of St. Mary of the Lake, 4690 Bald Eagle Ave., White Bear Lake, 55110; THOMAS J. WALKER, J.D., Saint Ambrose of Woodbury, 4125 Woodbury Dr., Woodbury, 55129-9627; FRANCIS R. KITTOCK (Retired), Leo C. Byrne Residence #228, 60 S. Mississippi River Blvd., St. Paul, 55105-1052.

Archdiocesan Curia

Members of the Corporation—Most Revs. JOHN C. NIENSTEDT, S.T.D., D.D., Archbishop. Tel: 651-291-4511; LEE PICHE, Auxiliary Bishop. Tel: 651-291-4414; Very Rev. PETER A. LAIRD, Vicar Gen. Tel: 651-291-4403; Mr. ANDREW J. EISENZIMMER, J.D., Chancellor. Tel: 651-291-4405; Mr. JOHN F. BIERBAUM, CFO, 226 Summit Ave., St. Paul, 55102. Tel: 651-291-4492.

Board of Directors—Most Revs. JOHN C. NIENSTEDT, S.T.D., D.D., 226 Summit Ave., St. Paul, 55102. Tel: 651-291-4511; LEE PICHE, Auxiliary Bishop, 226 Summit Ave., St. Paul, 55102. Tel: 651-291-4414; Very Rev. PETER A. LAIRD, Vicar Gen., 226 Summit Ave., St. Paul, 55102. Tel: 651-291-4403; Mr. ANDREW J. EISENZIMMER, J.D., Chancellor, 226 Summit Ave., St. Paul, 55102. Tel: 651-291-4405; Mr. JOHN F. BIERBAUM, CFO, 226 Summit Ave., St. Paul, 55102. Tel: 651-291-4492; PETER DALY, M.D., Summit Orthopedics, 17 W. Exchange St., #307, St. Paul, 55102. Tel: 651-968-5200 (office); 651-699-3063 (home); Mr. STEPHEN J. HEMSLEY, United Health Group, 9900 Bren Rd. E., MN 008-T010, Minnetonka, 55343. Tel: 952-936-1308; KAREN RAUENHORST, 1875 Meadowoods Trail, Long Lake, 55356. Tel: 763-473-2344; ROGER SCHERER, 12001 Bass Lake Rd., Plymouth, 55442. Tel: 763-557-9749; THOMAS SCHREIER, 15 Lily Pond Rd., North Oaks, 55127. Tel: 651-483-1781; Rev. PETER C. WITTMAN, Church of St. Mary, 2700 17th Ave. E., Shakopee, 55379-4443. Tel: 952-445-1319.

Chancellor for Civil Affairs—Mr. ANDREW J. EISENZIMMER, J.D., 226 Summit Ave., St. Paul, 55102. Tel: 651-291-4405; Fax: 651-290-1629. Email: eisenzimmera@archspm.org.

Chancellor for Canonical Affairs—Ms. JENNIFER HASELBERGER, J.C.L., Ph.D., 226 Summit Ave., St. Paul, 55102. Tel: 651-291-4437; Fax: 651-290-1629. Email: haselbergerj@archspm.org.

Vice Chancellor—Mr. SEAN MCDONOUGH, 226 Summit Ave., St. Paul, 55102. Tel: 651-291-4406; Fax: 651-290-1629. Email: mcdonoughs@archspm.org.

Protection of Children and Youth Initiative—Ms. SHARON TOMLIN, Coord., 328 Kellogg Blvd. W., St. Paul, 55102. Tel: 651-290-1622. Email: tomlins@archspm.org.

Delegate for Religious—Sr. MARY MADONNA ASHTON, C.S.J., 226 Summit Ave., St. Paul, 55102. Tel: 651-291-4400; Fax: 651-290-1629. Web: www.archspm.org/departments/delegate-religious.

Office of Conciliation—Ms. JENNIFER HASELBERGER, J.C.L., Ph.D., 226 Summit Ave., St. Paul, 55102. Tel: 651-291-4437; Fax: 651-290-1629. Web: www.archspm.org/conciliation.

Archives and Records Management—Ms. HEATHER BLOCK LAWTON, Dir. Tel: 651-251-7721. Email: lawtonh@archspm.org; Mr. STEVEN T. GRANGER, Archivist. Tel: 651-291-4485. Email: archives@archspm.org; Ms. THERESA HARTNETT, Archives/Records Asst. Tel: 651-291-4486. Email: hartnett@archspm.org; Ms. SUSAN STEPKA, Mgr., 226 Summit Ave., St. Paul, 55102. Tel: 651-291-4481. Email: stepkas@archspm.org.

Administration and Financial Services—Mr. JOHN F. BIERBAUM, CFO. Tel: 651-291-4492. Email: bierbaumj@archspm.org; Mr. SCOTT J. DOMEIER, Dir. Accounting Svcs., 226 Summit Ave., St. Paul, 55102. Tel: 651-290-1641. Email: domeiers@archspm.org.

Parish Accounting Service Center—MARY JO JUNGWIRTH, Dir. Parish Oper., 226 Summit Ave., St. Paul, 55102. Tel: 651-291-4439.

Human Resources and Benefits—Ms. NATALIE MCKLIGET, 226 Summit Ave., St. Paul, 55102. Tel: 651-291-4426. Email: mckligetn@archspm.org.

Office of Catholic Schools—Ms. MARTHA FRAUENHEIM, M.Ed., Supt., 328 Kellogg Blvd. W., St. Paul, 55102. Tel: 651-291-4498. Web: www.archspmschools.org. Email: frauenheimm@archspm.org.

Office of Marriage, Family, & Life—Ms. KATHLEEN M. LAIRD, Dir., 328 Kellogg Blvd. W., St. Paul, 55102. Tel: 651-291-4438. Web: www.archspm.org/family.

Worship—Rev. JOHN PAUL ERICKSON, Dir.; Ms. LAURINDA IRWIN, Administrative Asst., 226 Summit Ave., St. Paul, 55102. Tel: 651-251-7727; Fax: 651-290-1629. Email: irwinl@archspm.org. Web: www.archspm.org/worship.

Development and Stewardship—Mr. MICHAEL HALLORAN, Dir., 328 Kellogg Blvd. W., St. Paul, 55102. Tel: 651-290-1610. Web: www.archspm.org/development-stewardship.

Communications—Mr. JAMES ACCURSO, Media & External Rels. Mgr. Tel: 651-291-4480. Email: accursoj@archspm.org; Ms. LISA GIEFER, Web Coord., 226 Summit Ave., St. Paul, 55102. Tel: 651-291-4544. Email: gieferl@archspm.org.

Center for Formation—2260 Summit Ave., St. Paul, 55105-1094. Rev. Msgr. ALOYSIUS R. CALLAGHAN, S.T.L., J.C.D., Dir.

Archdiocesan Vocation Office—Rev. TROY D. PRZYBILLA, Dir., 2260 Summit Ave., St. Paul, 55105. Tel: 651-962-6892. Email: stpaulpriest@10000vocations.org.

Center for Ongoing Clergy Formation—Rev. PETER J. WILLIAMS, Dir.

Archbishop Harry J. Flynn Catechetical Institute—Mr. JEFF CAVINS, Dir.

Institute for Diaconal Formation—Deacon JOSEPH THOMAS MICHALAK JR., Dir.

Parish Services Team—Mr. MARK DITTMAN, Dir., 328 Kellogg Blvd. W., St. Paul, 55102. Tel: 651-291-4512. Email: dittmanm@archspm.org.

Catholic Charities—TIM MARX, CEO, 1200 2nd Ave. S., Minneapolis, 55403. Tel: 612-664-8527. Web: www.cctwincities.org.

Catholic Senior Services—Mr. DANIEL GANNON, Pres., 328 Kellogg Blvd. W., St. Paul, 55102. Tel: 651-500-4380. Email: gannond@archspm.org.

Ecumenical and Interreligious Affairs—Rev. ERICH RUTTEN, M.A., M.Div., University of St. Thomas, 2115 Summit Ave., Mail #5028, St. Paul, 55105-1096. Tel: 651-962-6560. Email: erutten@stthomas.edu.

Center for Mission/Society for the Propagation of the Faith—Deacon MICKEY FRIESEN, Dir., 328 Kellogg Blvd. W., St. Paul, 55102. Tel: 651-291-4445. Web: www.centerformission.org.

Clergy Services and Diaconate—Deacon JOHN EDWARD VOMASTEK, 226 Summit Ave., St. Paul, 55102. Tel: 651-291-4428. Email: vomastekj@archspm.org.

Clergy Review Board—Mr. ANDREW J. EISENZIMMER, J.D., 226 Summit Ave., St. Paul, 55102. Tel: 651-291-4405.

The Saint Paul Seminary School of Divinity—Rev. Msgr. ALOYSIUS R. CALLAGHAN, S.T.L., J.C.D., Rector-Vice Pres., 2260 Summit Ave., St. Paul, 55105. Tel: 651-962-5050. Web: www.stthomas.edu/spssod.

Saint John Vianney Seminary—Rev. MICHAEL C. BECKER, Rector, 2115 Summit Ave., #5024, St. Paul, 55105-1095.

"Catholic Spirit"— (Newspaper) Most Rev. JOHN C. NIENSTEDT, S.T.D., D.D., Publisher; Mr. ROBERT ZYSKOWSKI, Assoc. Publisher, 244 Dayton Ave., St. Paul, 55102. Tel: 651-291-4453. Web: www.thecatholicspirit.com.

Office for Safe Environment—Rev. KEVIN M. MCDONOUGH, Delegate, 226 Summit Ave., St. Paul, 55102. Tel: 651-646-1797. Email: mcdonoughk@archspm.org.

Promotor of Ministerial Standards—Mr. TIM ROURKE,

Dir., 226 Summit Ave., St. Paul, 55102.

Victim Assistance—Ms. GRETA SAWYER, Dir., 328 Kellogg Blvd. W., St. Paul, 55102. Tel: 651-291-4497. Email: sawyerg@archspm.org.

Catholic Cemeteries—Mr. JOHN CHEREK, Dir., 2105 Lexington Ave. S., Mendota Heights, 55120. Tel: 651-228-9991; Fax: 651-228-9995. Web: www.catholic-cemeteries.org.

Censores Librorum—Revs. GEORGE A. WELZBACHER, Church of St. John of St. Paul, 977 5th St., St. Paul, 55106. Tel: 651-771-3690; Fax: 651-771-7919; DAVID W. SMITH (Retired); MARK B. DOSH; Very Rev. JOSEPH R. JOHNSON; Dr. DON J. BRIEL; Dr. CATHERINE CORY; Rev. J. MICHAEL BYRON, S.T.D.; Dr. CHRISTOPHER THOMPSON.

Metropolitan Tribunal—

Judicial Vicar—Very Rev. TIMOTHY CLOUTIER, J.C.L., 328 Kellogg Blvd. W., St. Paul, 55102-1997. Tel: 651-291-4466; Fax: 651-291-4467. Email: tribunal@archspm.org. Web: www.archspm.org/tribunal.

Regional Vicars—Revs. MICHAEL C. SKLUZACEK, Vicar Region 1 (Northeast); CHARLES LACHOWITZER, Vicar Region 2 (South); ROBERT M. SCHWARTZ, Vicar Region 3 (Northwest).

Archdiocesan Council on Catholic Women—Rev. DAVID W. KOHNER, Moderator; Ms. ROSE ANNE HALLGREN, Pres., 328 Kellogg Blvd. W., St. Paul, 55102. Tel: 651-291-4545. Web: www.accwarchspm.org.

Vicar for Latinos—Rev. KEVIN T. KENNEY, Our Lady of Guadalupe, 401 Concord St., Saint Paul, 55107-2475.

Archbishop's Commission on Bio-Medical Ethics—Very Rev. PETER A. LAIRD, Vicar Gen. & Moderator of the Curia, 226 Summit Ave., St. Paul, 55102. Tel: 651-291-4430; Fax: 651-290-1629. Email: vicargeneral@archspm.org.

Commission for Black Catholics—Rev. KEVIN M. MCDONOUGH, Church of St. Peter Claver, 375 N. Oxford, St. Paul, 55102. Tel: 651-646-1797; Fax: 651-647-5394.

Office of Indian Ministry—Rev. MICHAEL TEGEDER, The Church of Gichitwaa Kateri, 3045 Park Ave. S., Minneapolis, 55407. Tel: 612-824-7606.

CLERGY, PARISHES, MISSIONS AND PAROCHIAL SCHOOLS

METROPOLITAN ST. PAUL

(RAMSEY COUNTY)

1—CATHEDRAL OF SAINT PAUL (1850) Very Rev. Joseph R. Johnson, Rector; Rev. John D. Meyer; Deacons James Meyer; Russell Shupe; Phil Stewart.
Res.: 239 Selby Ave., 55102. Tel: 651-228-1766; Fax: 651-228-9942. Email: info@cathedralsaintpaul.org. Web: www.cathedralsaintpaul.org.
Additional Worship Site: Church of St. Vincent—651 Virginia St., Saint Paul, 55103.
Catechesis/Religious Program—Students 71.

2—ST. ADALBERT (1881), (Polish), Rev. Minh Vu. In Res., Rev. Thomas Do Minh Tam (Vietnam).
Office & Res.: 265 Charles Ave., 55103. Tel: 651-228-9002; Fax: 651-225-0902. Email: adalbert@cpinternet.com.
Catechesis/Religious Program—Students 175.

3—ST. AGNES (1887), (German), Rev. John L. Ubel; Deacons Harold Hughesdon; Bernard Pedersen; Nathan Edward Allen.
Office & Res.: 548 Lafond Ave., 55103. Tel: 651-293-1710; Fax: 651-227-4229. Email: rectory@stagnes.net. Web: www.stagnes.net.
School—(Grades K-12), 530 Lafond Ave., 55103. Tel: 651-925-8700; Fax: 651-228-1158. Web: stagnesschools.org. Rev. John L. Ubel, Head of Schools (K-12); Mr. James Morehead, Prin. K-12; Trish Roddy, Librarian. Sisters of Charity of Our Lady, Mother of the Church 4; Lay Teachers 31; Students 532.
Catechesis/Religious Program—Students 41.

4—ST. ANDREW (1895) Merged with Maternity of the Blessed Virgin, St. Paul.

5—ST. ANDREW KIM (1990), (Korean), [JC] Rev. Raymond Won; Deacon Joseph Chang Lee.
Church & Office: 1850 Mississippi River Blvd. S., 55116. Tel: 651-644-1605; Fax: 651-846-4842. Email: mr.korean.catholic@gmail.com.
Catechesis/Religious Program—Fax: 651-644-4908. Students 62.

6—ASSUMPTION (1856), (German), Rev. Stephen R. O'Gara; Deacon Jerome Ciresi.
Church & Office: 51 W. Seventh St., 55102. Tel: 651-224-7536; Fax: 651-224-8514. Web: www.assumptionsp.org.
Catechesis/Religious Program—261 E. 8th St., 55101. Tel: 651-222-2619. Students 78.

7—BLESSED SACRAMENT (1916) Rev. Curtis C. Wehmeyer; Deacon Jeremiah Saladin.
Office: 1801 La Crosse Ave., 55119. Tel: 651-735-3707; Fax: 651-738-6492.
Catechesis/Religious Program—Students 156.
Worship Site: St. Thomas the Apostle—2119 Stillwater Ave., 55119.

8—ST. CASIMIR (1892), (Polish), Rev. William O'Donnell, O.M.I. In Res., Rev. Harry Winter, O.M.I.
Church & Office: 934 E. Geranium Ave., 55106. Tel: 651-774-0365; Fax: 651-774-0508. Email: jferra5591@aol.com. Web: www.stcasimirchurch.org.
Catechesis/Religious Program—Tel: 651-774-0365, Ext. 101. Email: suevanyo@stcasimirchurch.org. Students 42.

9—ST. CECILIA (1912) Rev. J. Michael Byron.
Church & Office: 2357 Bayless Pl., 55114. Tel: 651-644-4502; Fax: 651-647-1445. Email: info@stceciliaspm.org. Web: www.stceciliaspm.org.
Catechesis/Religious Program—Students 36.

10—CHURCH OF ST. BERNARD (1890), (German), Rev. Michael F. Anderson.
Mailing Address: 1160 Woodbridge St., 55117-4491. Tel: 651-488-8535; Fax: 651-489-9203. Email: kserva@churchofstbernard-stp.org. Web: www.stbernardstpaul.org.
Catechesis/Religious Program—Students 26.

11—CHURCH OF LUMEN CHRISTI, (Merger of St. Therese, St. Gregory and St. Leo in 2004.) Rev. Paul F. Feela.
Office: 2055 Bohland Ave., 55116. Tel: 651-698-5581; Fax: 651-698-9526. Web: www.lumenchristicc.org.
See Highland Catholic School, St. Paul under Elementary Schools, Consolidated, Parochial located in the Institution section.
Catechesis/Religious Program—Students 56.

12—ST. COLUMBA (1914) Rev. Hoang D. Nguyen; Deacon Thomas Stiles.
Office: 1327 Lafond Ave., 55104. Tel: 651-645-9179; Fax: 651-645-9170. Web: www.stcolumba.org.
Catechesis/Religious Program—Students 83.

13—ST. FRANCIS DE SALES (1884), (German), Revs. Juan Miguel Betancourt, S.E.M.V.; Luis Curbelo, S.E.M.V.; Daniel Moore, S.E.M.V.; Deacon Steven Maier.
Worship Site: St. James Church—496 View St., 55102.
Office & St. Francis Church: 650 Palace Ave., 55102-3593. Tel: 651-228-1169; Fax: 651-224-7744. St. James Church: 496 View St., 55102.
School—Saint Francis de Sales School dba St. Francis/St. James United School (Grades K-8), 486 View St., 55102. Tel: 651-228-1167; Fax: 651-228-0169. Gail Rappe, Prin. Lay Teachers 9; Students 85.
Catechesis/Religious Program—Shared program with St. James. Students 44.

14—ST. GREGORY THE GREAT (1951) Merged See Lumen Christi Catholic Community, St. Paul for records.

15—HOLY CHILDHOOD (1946) Rev. James G. Wolnik.
Office: 1435 Midway Pkwy., 55108. Tel: 651-644-7495. Web: www.holychildhoodparish.org.
Catechesis/Religious Program—Students 16.

16—HOLY SPIRIT (1936) Rev. Daniel C. Haugan; Deacon Joseph Thomas Michalak Jr.
Office: 515 S. Albert St., Saint Paul, 55116. Tel: 651-698-3353; Fax: 651-698-1605. Web: www.holy-spirit.org.
School—(Grades K-8) Dr. Mary Adrian, Prin.; Mary Wollmering, Librarian. Lay Teachers 26; Students 274.
Catechesis/Religious Program—Tel: 651-698-3353; Fax: 651-698-1605. Students 41.

17—THE IMMACULATE HEART OF MARY (1949) Merged with St. Luke, St. Paul to form St. Thomas More, St. Paul.

18—ST. JAMES (1887) Merged with St. Francis De Sales, St. Paul as of 1/1/2011.

19—ST. JOHN OF ST. PAUL (1886) Rev. George A. Welzbacher.
Office: 977 E. Fifth St., 55106. Tel: 651-771-3690; Fax: 651-771-7919. Email: stjohns@stjstp.org. Web: www.stjstp.org.

20—ST. LEO (1945) Merged See Lumen Christi Catholic Community, St. Paul for records.

21—ST. LOUIS KING OF FRANCE (1868), (French), Revs. Paul F. Morrissey, S.M.; Joseph Hurtuk, S.M.; Paul M. Cabrita, S.M.
Office: 506 Cedar St., 55101-2245. Tel: 651-224-3379; Fax: 651-224-0017. Email: stlouischurch@comcast.net.
Catechesis/Religious Program—See St. Mary's, St. Paul.

22—ST. LUKE (1888) Merged with Immaculate Heart of Mary, St. Paul to form St. Thomas More, St. Paul.

23—ST. MARK (1889) Revs. Humberto Palomino, P.E.S.; Carlos Farfan, P.E.S.; Bros. Adam Keiji Tokashiki, P.E.S.; Alvaro Perez, P.E.S.
Office: 2001 Dayton Ave., 55104. Tel: 651-645-5717; Fax: 651-644-0011. Email: stmarkstpaul@yahoo.com. Web: www.saintmark-mn.org.
School—(Grades K-8), 1983 Dayton Ave., 55104. Tel: 651-644-3380; Fax: 651-644-1923. Molly Whinnery, Prin. Lay Teachers 18; Students 278.
Catechesis/Religious Program—Students 85.

24—ST. MARY (1865) Rev. Biju Mathew, C.F.I.C. In Res., Revs. Anthony Scaria, C.F.I.C.; Benny Mekkat, C.F.I.C.; Bro. Pascal Atanga, C.F.I.C.
Office: 261 E. 8th St., 55101. Tel: 651-222-2619; Fax: 651-224-1190. Email: stmary@lynxuc.com. Web: www.stmarystpaul.parishesonline.com.
Catechesis/Religious Program—Students 21.

25—MATERNITY OF THE BLESSED VIRGIN (1949) Revs. Peter J. Williams; Francis A. Pouliot (Retired); Deacons Dennis Chlebeck; Francis Asenbrenner.
Office & Maternity of the Blessed Virgin Church: 1414 N. Dale St., 55117. Tel: 651-489-8825; Fax: 651-488-4055. Email: info@maternityofmarychurch.org. Web: www.maternityofmarychurch.org.
See Maternity of Mary/St. Andrew School, St. Paul under Elementary Schools, Consolidated, Parochial located in the Institution section.
Catechesis/Religious Program—Tel: 651-489-8825; Fax: 651-488-4055. Students 126.

26—ST. MATTHEW (1886), (German), Rev. Stephen J. Adrian; Deacon John Murphy.
Office: 490 Hall Ave., 55107. Tel: 651-224-9793.
School—(Grades K-8), 497 Humboldt Ave., 55107. Tel: 651-224-6912. Doug Lieser, Prin. Lay Teachers 12; Students 183.
Catechesis/Religious Program—Students 95.

27—THE NATIVITY OF OUR LORD (1922) Revs. Patrick J. Hipwell; Joseph Jerome Bambenek.
Office:—1900 Wellesley Ave., 55105. Tel: 651-696-5401; Fax: 651-696-5458. Email: info@nativity-mn.org. Web: www.nativity-mn.org.
School—(Grades K-8), 1900 Stanford Ave., 55105. Tel: 651-699-1311; Fax: 651-696-5420. Ms. Kate Wollan, Prin.; Judy Cody, Librarian. Lay Teachers 35; Students 764.
Catechesis/Religious Program—Tel: 651-696-5454; Fax: 651-696-5458. Students 120.

28—OUR LADY OF GUADALUPE (1931), (Hispanic), Rev. Kevin T. Kenney.
Center: 401 Concord Street, 55107. Tel: 651-228-0506; Fax: 651-224-5162.
Catechesis/Religious Program—Students 176.

29—ST. PASCAL BAYLON (1946) Rev. J. Anthony Andrade; Deacon Richard Moore.
Office: 1757 Conway St., 55106. Tel: 651-774-1585; Fax: 651-774-9152. Email: church@stpascals.org. Web: www.stpascalbaylon.com.
School—(Grades K-8) Tel: 651-776-0092. Martha Laurent, Prin. Sisters 1; Lay Teachers 14; Students 217.
Catechesis/Religious Program—Students 60.

30—ST. PATRICK (1884) Rev. William O'Donnell, O.M.I.
Office: 1095 De Soto St., 55130. Tel: 651-774-8675; Fax: 651-774-9106.
Catechesis/Religious Program—Tel: 651-776-7686. Students 89.

31—ST. PETER CLAVER (1892), (African American), Rev. Kevin M. McDonough; Deacon Fred L. Johnson.
Office: 375 N. Oxford St., 55104. Tel: 651-646-1797; Fax: 651-647-5341. Email: mcdonoughk@archspm.org. Web: www.stpc.org.
School—(Grades K-8), 1060 W. Central Ave., Saint Paul, 55104. Josie Johnson, Prin.; Helen Stassen, Librarian. Lay Teachers 12; Students 115.
Catechesis/Religious Program—Students 128.

32—SACRED HEART (1881), (German), Rev. Eugene Michel, O.F.M.; Deacon Wayne Wittman. In Res., Bro. Robert Gross, O.F.M.
Office: 840 E. Sixth St., 55106. Tel: 651-776-2741; Fax: 651-776-2759.
Catechesis/Religious Program—Students 69.

33—ST. STANISLAUS (1872), (Czech), Rev. John C. Clay.
Office: 398 Superior St., 55102. Tel: 651-292-0303. Web: www.ststans.org.
Catechesis/Religious Program—395 Superior St., 55102. Tel: 651-292-1913. Students 95.

34—ST. THERESE (1926) Merged See Lumen Christi Catholic Community, St. Paul for records.

35—ST. THOMAS MORE Rev. Joseph E. Weiss, S.J.; Deacons Thomas Dzik; David Ingwell.
Office: Tel: 651-227-7669; Fax: 651-227-0847.
Churches—
East Campus Church—1079 Summit Ave., 55105-2243.
West Campus Church—1550 Summit Ave., 55105.
School—St. Thomas More Catholic School, (Grades K-8), 1065 Summit Ave., 55105. Tel: 651-224-4836; Fax: 651-224-0097. Email: dwitucki@morecommunity.org. Web: www.morecommunity.org. Brian Ragatz, Prin.; Hagdis Tschunko,

Librarian. Sisters 1; Lay Teachers 23; Students 351; Total Staff 24.
Catechesis/Religious Program—Email: mzetvas@luke-acts.org. Students 67.
36—ST. THOMAS THE APOSTLE (1954) Merged with Blessed Sacrament, St. Paul.
37—ST. VINCENT DE PAUL (1888) [CEM] Merged with Cathedral of Saint Paul.

OUTSIDE METROPOLITAN ST. PAUL

COTTAGE GROVE, WASHINGTON CO., CHURCH OF ST. RITA (1966) Rev. Richard A. Banker; Deacons John Nicklay; Steve Koop.
8694 80th St. S., 55016. Tel: 651-459-4596; Fax: 651-459-5364. Email: stritas@saintritas.org. Web: www.saintritas.org.
Catechesis/Religious Program—Students 484.
LITTLE CANADA, RAMSEY CO., ST. JOHN OF LITTLE CANADA (1851) [CEM] Rev. David W. Kohner.
Office: 380 Little Canada Rd., 55117. Tel: 651-484-2708; Fax: 651-484-0567. Email: info@stjohnoflc.org. Web: www.stjohnsoflc.org.
School—Saint John's School of Little Canada, (Grades PreK-8), 2621 McMenemy St., 55117. Tel: 651-484-3038; Fax: 651-481-1355. Mary Kay Rowan, Prin.; Jan Truhler, Librarian. Lay Teachers 15; Students 211.
Catechesis/Religious Program—Tel: 651-484-0048; Fax: 651-288-3233. Students 140.
MAHTOMEDI, WASHINGTON CO., ST. JUDE OF THE LAKE (1939) Rev. Cory J. Rohlfing.
Office: 700 Mathomedi Ave., 55115. Tel: 651-426-3245; Fax: 651-633-3554. Web: www.stjudeofthelake.org.
School—(Grades K-8), 600 Mahtomedi Ave., 55115. Tel: 651-426-2562; Fax: 651-653-3662. Jennifer Cassidy, Prin. Lay Teachers 12; Students 128.
Catechesis/Religious Program—Students 128.
MAPLEWOOD, RAMSEY CO.
1—HOLY REDEEMER (1880), (Italian), Merged See St. Peter, North St. Paul.
2—ST. JEROME (1940) Rev. Cletus Basekela.
Church & Office: 380 Roselawn Ave. E., 55117. Tel: 651-771-1209; Fax: 651-771-3623. Email: mahles@stjerome-church.org. Web: www.stjeromechurch.org.
School—(Grades PreK-8), 384 E. Roselawn Ave., 55117. Tel: 651-771-8494; Fax: 651-771-3466. Laurie Sherman, Prin.; Patti Eckert, Librarian. Sisters 1; Lay Teachers 8; Students 134.
Catechesis/Religious Program—Students 46.
3—PRESENTATION OF THE BLESSED VIRGIN MARY (1946) Rev. Mark A. Huberty; Deacon James Saumweber.
Mailing Address: 1725 Kennard St., 55109. Tel: 651-777-8116; Fax: 651-777-8743. Web: www.presentationofmary.org.
School—(Grades K-8), 1695 Kennard St., 55109. Tel: 651-777-5877; Fax: 651-777-8283. Michael Rogers, Prin.; Nikki Giel, Librarian. Lay Teachers 10; Students 157.
Catechesis/Religious Program—Fax: 651-777-8743. Students 172.
MENDOTA, DAKOTA CO., ST. PETER (1840) [CEM] Rev. Joseph G. Gallatin.
1405 Hwy. 13, 55150. Tel: 651-452-4550; Fax: 651-456-0646. Email: church@stpetersmendota.org. Web: www.stpetersmendota.org.
See Faithful Shepherd Catholic School, Eagan under Elementary Schools, Consolidated, Parochial located in the Institution section.
Catechesis/Religious Program—Tel: 651-452-4550; Fax: 651-456-0646. Students 142.
NEW BRIGHTON, RAMSEY CO., ST. JOHN THE BAPTIST (1906) [CEM] Revs. Michael C. Skluzacek; Michael Johnson, Parochial Vicar; Deacons Gary Schneider; Rodney Palmer.
Office: 835 2nd Ave., N.W., 55112. Tel: 651-633-8333; Fax: 651-633-7404. Email: stjohnnyb@pclink.com. Web: www.stjohnnyb.com.
School—(Grades K-8), 845 2nd Ave., N.W., 55112. Tel: 651-633-1522. Sue Clausen, Prin.; Susan Eilefson, Librarian. Lay Teachers 22; Students 373.
Catechesis/Religious Program—Tel: 651-633-1540; Fax: 651-633-7404. Students 373.
NORTH ST. PAUL, RAMSEY CO., ST. PETER (1888), (Italian), [CEM] Rev. William Deziel, O.S.C.; Deacons Robert Anthony Bisciglia; Gregg Sroder.
2600 N. Margaret St., North Saint Paul, 55109. Tel: 651-777-8304; Fax: 651-777-0497.
School—(Grades PreK-8) Cecilia Crowley, Prin.; Annie Clintsman, Librarian. Lay Teachers 16; Students 242.
Catechesis/Religious Program—Tel: 651-777-1231. Students 242.
OAKDALE, WASHINGTON CO.
1—GUARDIAN ANGELS (1885) [CEM] Rev. Rodger Bauman; Deacon Terry Beer.
Mailing Address: 8260 4th St. N., 55128. Tel: 651-738-2223; Fax: 651-738-2453. Email: ga@guardian-angels.org. Web: www.guardian-angels.org.
Preschool—Email: sdwuznik@guardian-angels.org. Lay Teachers 8; Students 120.
Catechesis/Religious Program—Students 422.
2—TRANSFIGURATION (1939) Rev. William J. Baer; Deacon Glenn Skuta.
Office: 6133 15th St. N., 55128. Tel: 651-738-2646; Fax: 651-501-2230. Web: www.transfigurationmn.org.
School—(Grades K-8), 6135 15th St. N., 55128. Tel: 651-501-2220; Fax: 651-501-2258. Jan Heuman, Prin. Lay Teachers 22; Students 338.
Catechesis/Religious Program—Students 338.
ROSEVILLE, RAMSEY CO.
1—CORPUS CHRISTI (1939) Rev. Francis L. Fried; Deacon Michael Humbert.
Mailing Address: 2131 Fairview Ave., N., 55113-5499. Tel: 651-639-8888; Fax: 651-639-8288. Email: corpus@mninter.net. Web: www.churchofcorpuschristi.org.
Catechesis/Religious Program—Students 95.
2—ST. ROSE OF LIMA (1939) Rev. Robert J. Fitzpatrick; Deacon Donald Hamilton.
Office: 2048 N. Hamline Ave., 55113. Tel: 651-645-9389; Fax: 651-646-4187. Web: saintroseoflima.net.
School—(Grades PreSchool-8), 2072 Hamline Ave. N., 55113. Tel: 651-646-3832; Fax: 651-647-6437. Cressy Epperly, Prin.; Donna Graw, Librarian. Lay Teachers 13; Students 202.
Catechesis/Religious Program—Tel: 651-646-8029; Fax: 651-646-4187. Students 202.
SHOREVIEW, RAMSEY CO., ST. ODILIA (1960) Revs. Phillip J. Rask; Douglas Arthur Louis-Marie Pierce; Deacons Ramon Garcia De Gollardo; Ifeangi John Ochiagha; William Carroll.
3495 N. Victoria St., 55126. Tel: 651-484-6681; Fax: 651-484-0780. Web: www.stodilia.org.
School—(Grades K-8) Tel: 651-484-3364; Fax: 651-415-3395. Mr. Robert Grose, Prin.; Molly Conway, Librarian. Lay Teachers 29; Students 490.
Catechesis/Religious Program—Students 490.
WEST ST. PAUL, DAKOTA CO.
1—ST. JOSEPH (1942) Revs. Michael Creagan; James Lannan; Deacon Jerry Scherkenbach.
Mailing Address: 1154 Seminole Ave., 55118. Tel: 651-457-2781; Fax: 651-451-1272. Web: www.churchofstjoseph.org.
School—(Grades PreSchool-8), 1138 Seminole Ave., 55118. Tel: 651-457-8550; Fax: 651-457-0780. Web: www.stjosephwsp.org. Jane Nordin, Prin.; Sally McNamera, Librarian. Lay Teachers 35; Students 509.
Catechesis/Religious Program—Tel: 651-457-8841. Students 509.
2—ST. MICHAEL (1868) Rev. Michael L. Rudolph.
Church & Office: 337 E. Hurley Ave., 55118. Tel: 651-457-2334; Fax: 651-451-1668.
School—(Grades K-8), 335 Hurley Ave., E., 55118. Tel: 651-457-2510; Fax: 651-457-5049. Maryanna Charley, Prin. Lay Teachers 10; Students 92.
Catechesis/Religious Program—Tel: 651-457-0172. Students 31.
WHITE BEAR LAKE, RAMSEY CO.
1—ST. MARY OF THE LAKE (1881) [CEM] Rev. Ralph W. Talbot.
Office: 4690 Bald Eagle Ave., 55110. Tel: 651-429-7771; Fax: 651-429-9539. Email: contactus@stmarys-wbl.org. Web: www.stmarys-wbl.org.
School—(Grades PreK-8), 4690 Bald Eagle Ave., 55110. Patrick Gallivan, Prin. Lay Teachers 12; Students 242.
Catechesis/Religious Program—Tel: 651-429-8001. Students 242.
2—ST. PIUS X (1954) Rev. Fernando Ortega, Parochial Admin.; Deacon Thomas L. Semlak.
Mailing Address: 3878 Highland Ave., 55110. Tel: 651-429-5337; Fax: 651-429-5339. Email: parish@stpiusx-wbl.org. Web: www.stpiusx-wbl.org.
School—(Grades PreSchool-8) Tel: 651-429-9359; Fax: 651-429-9359. Email: kgroettum@spxhf-wbl.org. Web: www.spxhf-wbl.org. K. Groettum, Prin. Lay Teachers 12; Students 159.
Catechesis/Religious Program—Tel: 651-762-3634. Email: sgutowski@stpiusx-wbl.org. Students 159.
WOODBURY, WASHINGTON CO., SAINT AMBROSE OF WOODBURY (1998) Rev. Thomas J. Walker; Deacon Rip Riordan.
Office: 4125 Woodbury Dr., 55129-9627. Tel: 651-714-1058; Fax: 651-714-9257.
School—(Grades K-8) Tel: 651-768-3000. Matthew Metz, Prin.; Tim Demco, Librarian. Lay Teachers 36; Students 584.
Catechesis/Religious Program—Tel: 651-768-3011. Students 1,167.

METROPOLITAN MINNEAPOLIS

(HENNEPIN COUNTY)
1—ST. ALBERT THE GREAT (1935) Rev. Joseph P. Gillespie, O.P. In Res., Revs. Cornelius A. Kilroy, O.P.; Joseph E. Bidwill, O.P.; James A. Spahn, O.P.; Paul J. Johnson, O.P.; Bros. William E. (Kevin) Carroll, O.P.; Raymond (Steven) Bryce, O.P.
Office: 2836-33rd Ave. S., 55406. Tel: 612-724-3643; Fax: 612-722-9726. Email: info@saintalbertthegreat.org. Web: www.saintalbertthegreat.org.
Res.: 2833 32nd Ave. S., 55406. Tel: 612-724-3644; Fax: 612-724-5057.
Catechesis/Religious Program—Students 61.
2—ALL SAINTS (1916), (Polish), Rev. Eugene W. Tiffany.
Res.: 435 4th St., N.E., 55413. Tel: 612-379-4996.
See Pope John Paul II Catholic School, Minneapolis under Elementary Schools, Consolidated, Parochial located in the Institution section.
Catechesis/Religious Program—See St. Boniface, Minneapolis for details., Tel: 612-379-2761; Fax: 612-676-1532.
3—ST. ANNE (1884) Merged See Church of St. Anne-St. Joseph Hien.
4—ANNUNCIATION (1922) Rev. James R. Himmelsbach; Deacon Joseph Damiani.
Mailing Address: 509 W. 54th St., 55419. Tel: 612-824-0787; Fax: 612-824-8232. Web: www.annunciation.org.
School—(Grades K-8), 525 W. 54th St., 55419-1818. Tel: 612-823-4394; Fax: 612-824-0998. Mary Ann Pearson, Pres.; Sandra Nesvig, Prin.; Carol Skala, Librarian. Lay Teachers 27; Students 412.
Catechesis/Religious Program—Tel: 612-824-9993, Ext. 260. Students 412.
5—ST. ANTHONY OF PADUA (1849) Rev. Glen T. Jenson; Deacon John Belian.
Mailing Address: 804 Second St., N.E., 55413. Tel: 612-379-2324; Fax: 612-379-2325. Email: stanthonychrch@msn.com. Web: www.stanthony-paduampls.org.
See Pope John Paul II Catholic School, Minneapolis under Elementary Schools, Consolidated, Parochial located in the Institution section.
Catechesis/Religious Program—See St. Boniface, Minneapolis for details.
6—ASCENSION (1890) Rev. Michael O'Connell.
Mailing Address: 1723 Bryant Ave. N., 55411. Tel: 612-529-9684; Fax: 612-529-7618.
School—(Grades K-8), 1726 Dupont Ave. N., 55411. Tel: 612-521-3609; Fax: 612-522-3862. Dorwatha Woods, Prin. Lay Teachers 21; Students 245.
Catechesis/Religious Program—Tel: 612-521-7454; Fax: 612-529-3343. Students 104.
7—ST. AUSTIN (1937) Merged with St. Bridget, Minneapolis.
8—THE BASILICA OF ST. MARY CO-CATHEDRAL (1907) Rev. John M. Bauer.
Mailing Address: P.O. Box 50010, 55405-0010.
Office: 88 N. 17th St., 55403-1295. Tel: 612-333-1381; Fax: 612-333-7230. Email: bsm@mary.org. Web: www.mary.org.
Catechesis/Religious Program—Tel: 612-317-3473. Students 256.
9—ST. BONIFACE (1858), (German), Rev. Eugene W. Tiffany, Parochial Admin.
629 Second St., N.E., 55413. Tel: 612-379-2761; Fax: 612-676-1532. Email: boniface1858@usfamily.net. Web: www.stboniface-minneapolis.org.
See Pope John Paul II Catholic School, Minneapolis under Elementary Schools, Consolidated, Parochial located in the Institution section.
Catechesis/Religious Program—This is a shared program with St. Clement, All Saints, St. Hedwig, St. Anthony, Sts Cyril & Methoduis, Minneapolis., Tel: 612-379-2451. Students 61.
10—ST. BRIDGET (1915) Very Rev. Anthony M. Criscitelli, T.O.R.; Deacon Richard Heineman.
3811 Emerson Ave. N., 55412. Tel: 612-529-7779; Fax: 612-529-8451. Email: sbrigid2@juno.com. In Res., Bro. John Kerr, T.O.R.
Additional Worship Site: Church of St. Austin—4050 Upton Ave. N., 55412.
Catechesis/Religious Program—Students 21.
11—ST. CHARLES BORROMEO (1938) Revs. Paul A. LaFontaine; Patrick Thomas Barnes; Deacon Stephen Najarian.
Church, Office & Res.: 2739 Stinson Blvd., St. Anthony, 55418-3124. Tel: 612-781-6529; Fax: 612-787-1170.
School—(Grades K-8), 2727 Stinson Blvd., St. Anthony, 55418-3124. Tel: 612-781-2643; Fax: 612-787-1110. John Hartnett, Prin.; Terry McDonald, Librarian. Lay Teachers 19; Students 289.
Catechesis/Religious Program—Students 289.
12—CHRIST THE KING (1938) [JC] Rev. Dale J. Korogi.
Church & Office: 5029 Zenith Ave. S., 55410. Tel: 612-920-5030; Fax: 612-920-1179. Web: www.ctkm-pls.org.
See Carondelet Catholic School under Elementary Schools, Consolidated, Parochial located in the Institution section
Catechesis/Religious Program—
13—CHURCH OF GICHIWAA KATERI (2008), (Native American), (Quasi-Parish Native American) Rev. Michael Tegeder, Chap.
Church & Office: 3045 Park Ave. S., 55407-1517.

Tel: 612-824-7606; Fax: 612-824-7616.

14—CHURCH OF ST. ANNE - ST. JOSEPH HIEN (1884/1987), (Vietnamese), Revs. Ignatius Nguyen Dai Kinh, C.M.C.; Hilary M. Nhuan Tran, C.M.C.
Office: 2627 Queen Ave. N., 55411. Tel: 612-529-0503; Fax: 612-529-5860.
Catechesis/Religious Program— Recorded at St. Mary's, Minneapolis Students 411.

15—ST. CLEMENT (1902) Rev. Earl C. Simonson.
Res.: 911 24th Ave., N.E., 55418. Tel: 612-789-3533.
See Pope John Paul II Catholic School, Minneapolis under Elementary Schools, Consolidated, Parochial located in the Institution section.
Catechesis/Religious Program—Combined with St. Boniface, Minneapolis.

16—SS. CYRIL & METHODIUS (1891), (Slovak), Rev. Edison Galarza, O.C.C.S.S.; Deacon Clarence Shallbetter.
Mailing Address: 1315 2nd St., N.E., 55413-1905. Tel: 612-379-9736. Email: cyril1891@aol.com.
Catechesis/Religious Program—Students 111.

17—ST. FRANCES CABRINI (1946) Rev. Michael Tegeder, Parochial Admin.; Deacon Mickey Friesen.
Office: 1500 Franklin Ave., S.E., 55414-3697. Tel: 612-339-3023; Fax: 612-339-0734. Email: office@cabrinimn.org. Web: www.cabrinimn.org.
Catechesis/Religious Program—Students 80.

18—ST. HEDWIG (1914), (Polish), Revs. Glen T. Jenson; Donald Schwalm (Retired); Deacon John Belian.
Office: 129 29th Ave., N.E., 55418. Tel: 612-789-4830; Fax: 612-789-1985. Email: sthedwig@msn.com.
See Pope John Paul II Catholic School, Minneapolis under Elementary Schools, Consolidated, Parochial located in the Institution section.
Catechesis/Religious Program—Combined program with St. Boniface. See St. Boniface, Minneapolis for details.

19—ST. HELENA (1913) Rev. Richard R. Villano.
3204 E. 43rd St., 55406. Tel: 612-729-7344.
School—(Grades K-8), 3200 E. 44th St., 55406. Tel: 612-729-9301. Jane Hileman, Prin.; Nancy Rivers, Librarian. Lay Teachers 11; Students 171.
Catechesis/Religious Program—Tel: 612-729-7321. Students 30.

20—HOLY CROSS (1886), (Polish), Revs. Glen T. Jenson; Jan Michalski; Deacon John Belian.
Mailing Address: 1621 University Ave., N.E., 55413. Tel: 612-789-7238; Fax: 612-789-5769. Web: ourholycross.com.
See Pope John Paul II Catholic School, Minneapolis under Elementary Schools, Consolidated, Parochial located in the Institution section.
Catechesis/Religious Program—Tel: 612-789-9168. Students 74.

21—HOLY NAME (1916) Rev. Leo J. Schneider.
Mailing Address: 3637 11th Ave. S., 55407. Tel: 612-724-5465; Fax: 612-724-5466. Web: www.churchoftheholyname.org.
See Risen Christ Catholic School, Minneapolis under Elementary Schools, Consolidated, Parochial located in the Institution section.
Catechesis/Religious Program—Students 34.

22—HOLY ROSARY/SANTO ROSARIO (1878) Rev. James A. Spahn, O.P.
Mailing Address: 2424 18th Ave. S., 55404. Tel: 612-724-3651; Fax: 612-728-8944.
See Risen Christ Catholic School, Minneapolis under Elementary Schools, Consolidated, Parochial located in the Institution section.
Catechesis/Religious Program—Students 410.
Convent—1614 E. 24th St., 55404. Tel: 612-724-2620. Dominican Sisters (Sinsinawa, WI) 6.

23—CHURCH OF THE INCARNATION (1909) Rev. Kevin M. McDonough.
Office: 3817 Pleasant Ave., 55409-1228. Tel: 612-822-2101; Fax: 612-822-7928.
See Risen Christ Catholic School, Minneapolis under Elementary Schools, Consolidated, Parochial located in the Institution section.

24—ST. JOAN OF ARC (1946) Revs. James R. DeBruycker; James Cassidy.
Mailing Address: 4537 3rd Ave. S., 55419. Tel: 612-823-8205; Fax: 612-825-7028.
Catechesis/Religious Program—Students 496.

25—ST. JOSEPH HIEN (1987), (Vietnamese), [JC] Closed. See Church of St. Anne-St. Joseph Hien, Minneapolis.

26—ST. LAWRENCE (1887) Rev. Ivan Tou, C.S.P.
Mailing Address: 1203 5th St., S.E., 55414. Tel: 612-331-7941; Fax: 612-378-1771. Email: parish@umncatholic.org. Web: www.umncatholic.org. In Res., Rev. Robert J. O'Donnell.
Catechesis/Religious Program—Students 28.

27—ST. LEONARD OF PORT MAURICE (1941), (African American), Rev. Stephen J. LaCanne.
Mailing Address: 3949 Clinton Ave S., 55409. Tel: 612-825-5811; Fax: 612-825-5811.

28—ST. OLAF (1941) [JC] Revs. Mark L. Pavlik; A. Michael Sauber.
Office: 215 S. 8th St., 55402. Tel: 612-332-7471; Fax: 612-332-3412. Web: www.saintolaf.org.

29—OUR LADY OF LOURDES (1877), (French), Rev. Charles L. Froehle; Deacon Mike Wurdock.
Office: One Lourdes Pl., 55414. Tel: 612-379-2259; Fax: 612-379-0165. Email: info@ourladyoflourdesmn.com. Web: www.ourladyoflourdesmn.com.
Catechesis/Religious Program—Students 66.

30—OUR LADY OF MOUNT CARMEL (1938), (Italian), Rev. Thomas Margevicius; Deacon Michael D. Powers.
Church & Office: 701 Fillmore St., N.E., 55413. Tel: 612-623-4019; Fax: 612-331-3407. Email: olmc@olmcmpls.org. Web: www.olmcmpls.org.
See Pope John Paul II Catholic School, Minneapolis under Elementary Schools, Consolidated, Parochial located in the Institution section.

31—OUR LADY OF PEACE (1991) Rev. Paul C. Treacy; Deacon Paul Tatone.
Mailing Address: 5425 11th Ave. S., 55417. Tel: 612-824-3455; Fax: 612-823-5102. Email: ourladyofpeace@olpmn.org. Web: www.olpmn.org.
School—(Grades K-8), 5435 11th Ave. S., 55417. Tel: 612-823-8253; Fax: 612-824-7328. Dr. Lori Glynn, Prin.; Danielle Manus-Hoben, Librarian. Lay Teachers 8; Students 147.
Catechesis/Religious Program—Students 127.

32—OUR LADY OF PERPETUAL HELP, Closed. For inquiries for parish records contact the chancery.

33—OUR LADY OF VICTORY (1945) Rev. Terrence M. Hayes.
Office: 5155 Emerson Ave. N., 55430. Tel: 612-529-7788; Fax: 612-529-3343.
Church: 52nd and Fremont Aves., 55430.
Catechesis/Religious Program—Students 88.

34—ST. PHILIP (1906) [CEM] Rev. Michael O'Connell.
Mailing Address: 2507 Bryant Ave. N., 55411. Tel: 612-529-3125; Fax: 612-287-9133. Web: www.churchofstphilip.org.
Catechesis/Religious Program—Students 30.

35—ST. STEPHEN (1885) Rev. Joseph A. Williams; Deacon Luis Rubi.
Mailing Address: 2211 Clinton Ave., 55404. Tel: 612-767-2430; Fax: 612-767-2439. Email: mail@ststevensmpls.org. Web: www.ss-mpls.org.
See Risen Christ Catholic School, Minneapolis under Elementary Schools, Consolidated, Parochial located in the Institution section.
Catechesis/Religious Program—Students 75.

36—ST. THOMAS THE APOSTLE (1908) Rev. Harold J. Tasto.
Office: 2914 W. 44th St., 55410. Tel: 612-922-0041; Fax: 612-922-1921. Email: info@sta-mpls.org. Web: www.sta-mpls.org.
Catechesis/Religious Program—Students 156.

37—VISITATION (1946) Rev. Thomas F. O'Brien.
Church & Office: 4530 Lyndale Ave. S., 55419. Tel: 612-822-3139; Fax: 612-824-3515. Email: visichurch@aol.com. Web: www.visitationchurch.com.
Catechesis/Religious Program—Students 4.

OUTSIDE METROPOLITAN MINNEAPOLIS

BLAINE, ANOKA CO., ST. TIMOTHY'S (1943) Rev. Charles A. Brambilla; Deacons Don Hamilton; Thomas Quayle.
Mailing Address: 707 89th Ave., N.E., 55434. Tel: 763-784-1329; Fax: 763-784-0652. Email: info@churchofsttimothy.com. Web: www.churchofsttimothy.com.
Catechesis/Religious Program—Students 481.

BLOOMINGTON, HENNEPIN CO.

1—ST. BONAVENTURE (1959) Rev. Richard Kaley, O.F.M.Conv.; Deacon Jon Alexander DeLuney.
Mailing Address: 901 E. 90th St., 55420. Tel: 952-854-4733; Fax: 952-851-9690. Email: office@saintbonaventure.org. Web: www.saintbonaventure.org.
Catechesis/Religious Program—Tel: 952-854-4753. Email: faithformation@saintbonaventure.org. Students 165.

2—ST. EDWARD (1967) Revs. Brian J. Fier; James Barry; Deacon James DeShane.
Mailing Address: 9401 Nesbitt Ave. S., 55437. Tel: 952-835-7101; Fax: 952-835-0156. Email: receptionist@stedwardchurch.org. Web: www.stedwardschurch.org.
Catechesis/Religious Program—Students 250.

3—NATIVITY OF THE BLESSED VIRGIN MARY (1949) Rev. Abraham Kochupurackal, C.M.I.; Deacon James McLaughlin.
Office: 9900 Lyndale Ave. S., 55420-4733. Tel: 952-881-8671; Fax: 952-881-8692. Email: nativity@nativitybloomington.org.
School—(Grades K-8), 9901 Bloomington Fwy., 55420. Tel: 952-881-8160; Fax: 952-881-3032. Barbara Castagna, Prin.; Tina Meyer, Librarian. Lay Teachers 21; Students 278.
Catechesis/Religious Program—Students 139.

BROOKLYN CENTER, HENNEPIN CO., ST. ALPHONSUS (1959) Revs. Peter Connolly, C.Ss.R.; Martin Stillmock, C.Ss.R.; Joseph Stenger, C.Ss.R.; William Bueche, C.Ss.R.; Wilfred Lowery, C.Ss.R.; Brian Gilles, C.Ss.R.; Thomas Pham, C.Ss.R.; Steven Nyl, C.Ss.R.; Tuan Nguyen, C.Ss.R.; Deacons David Holst; John Winkelman.
Office: 7025 Halifax Ave. N., 55429. Tel: 763-561-5100; Fax: 763-561-0336. Email: parishoffice@stalsmn.org. Web: www.stalsmn.org.
School—(Grades K-8), 7031 Halifax Ave., N., 55429. Tel: 763-561-5101; Fax: 763-503-3368. Robert Terry, Prin. Lay Teachers 16; Students 223.
Catechesis/Religious Program—4111 71st Ave. N., 55429. Tel: 763-503-3340 (D.R.E.); Fax: 763-560-8634. Students 522.

BROOKLYN PARK, HENNEPIN CO.

1—ST. GERARD MAJELLA (1970) Revs. Bradley C. Baldwin, T.O.R.; Edward J. Sabo, T.O.R.
Office: 9600 Regent Ave. N., 55443. Tel: 763-424-8770; Fax: 763-424-4327. Web: www.st-gerard.org.
Catechesis/Religious Program—Tel: 763-424-8600; Fax: 763-424-4327. Students 544.

2—ST. VINCENT DE PAUL (1855) [CEM] Revs. John Long; Jon Bennet Tran; Deacon Sean Curtan.
Office: 9100 93rd Ave. N., 55445-1407. Tel: 763-425-2210; Fax: 763-425-7898.
School—(Grades K-8) Tel: 763-425-3970; Fax: 763-425-2674. Kathleen O'Hara, Prin.; Kim Lyngen, Librarian. Lay Teachers 26; Students 441.
Catechesis/Religious Program—Students 972.

BURNSVILLE, DAKOTA CO.

1—CHURCH OF THE RISEN SAVIOR (1970) Revs. Thomas Krenik; Stephan Kappler.
Office: 1501 E. County Rd. 42, 55306. Tel: 952-431-5222; Fax: 952-431-5221. Web: www.risensavior.org.
Catechesis/Religious Program—Students 114.

2—MARY, MOTHER OF THE CHURCH (1965) Rev. James C. Zappa Jr.; Deacon Rob Warhol.
Office: 3333 Cliff Rd. E., 55337. Tel: 952-890-0045; Fax: 952-890-0789.
Catechesis/Religious Program—Students 370.

COLUMBIA HEIGHTS, ANOKA CO., IMMACULATE CONCEPTION (1923) Rev. John J. Mitchell; Deacon Larry Palkert.
Office: 4030 Jackson St., N.E., 55421. Tel: 763-788-9062; Fax: 763-788-0202. Email: icchurch@immac-church.org. Web: www.immac-church.org.
School—(Grades K-8), 4030 Jackson St., N.E., 55421. Tel: 763-788-9065; Fax: 763-788-9066. Email: ischool@immac-church.org. Jane Bona, Prin. Sisters of St. Francis 1; Lay Teachers 6; Students 72.
Catechesis/Religious Program—Students 68.

COON RAPIDS, ANOKA CO., CHURCH OF THE EPIPHANY (1964) [CEM] Revs. Dennis Zehrem; Gregory E. Abbott; Alex Bernard Carlson; Deacon Bruce Maltzen.
Mailing Address: 1900 111th Ave., N.W., 55433. Tel: 763-755-1020; Fax: 763-862-4303. Web: www.epiphanymn.org. In Res., Rev. Peter Yakubu Ali.
School—(Grades K-8), 11001 Hanson Blvd. N.W., 55433. Tel: 763-754-1750; Fax: 763-862-4350. Laurie Jennrich, Prin.; Melissa Guenther, Librarian. Sisters 1; Lay Teachers 32; Students 516.
Catechesis/Religious Program—Tel: 763-862-4331; Fax: 763-862-4354. Students 577.

CRYSTAL, HENNEPIN CO., ST. RAPHAEL (1951) Revs. Michael J. Izen; James Herrmann; Deacon Bruce Bowman.
Office: 7301 Bass Lake Rd., 55428. Tel: 763-537-8401; Fax: 763-537-4878.
School—(Grades PreSchool-8) Tel: 763-504-9450; Fax: 763-504-9460. Web: www.srsmn.org. Dorothy Bialke, Prin. Sisters 1; Lay Teachers 12; Students 193.
Catechesis/Religious Program—Tel: 763-537-8401, Ext. 211; Fax: 763-537-4878. Students 154.

EAGAN, DAKOTA CO.

1—ST. JOHN NEUMANN (1977) Revs. Charles V. Lachowitzer; Anthony O'Neill; Deacons Richard Klish; Richard Stevens.
Office: 4030 Pilot Knob Rd., 55122. Tel: 651-454-2079; Fax: 651-454-0860. Web: www.sjn.org.
See Faithful Shepherd Catholic School under Elementary Schools, Consolidated, Parochial located in the Institution section.
Catechesis/Religious Program—Students 1,361.

2—ST. THOMAS BECKET (1989) Rev. Timothy Wozniak; Deacon Bob Kelly.
Office: 4455 S. Robert Tr., 55123. Tel: 651-683-9808 (Parish Center); Fax: 651-683-0361. Email: parish@st.thomasbecket.org. Web: www.st.thomasbecket.org.
See Faithful Shepherd Catholic School under Elementary Schools, Consolidated, Parochial located in the Institution section.
Catechesis/Religious Program—Students 587.

EDEN PRAIRIE, HENNEPIN CO., PAX CHRISTI (1981) Revs. Patrick A. Kennedy; William A. Murtaugh; Deacon Al Schroeder.
Office: 12100 Pioneer Trl., 55347-4208. Tel: 952-941-3150; Fax: 952-941-7942. Email: pax@paxchristi.com. Web: www.paxchristi.com.
Catechesis/Religious Program—Students 809.

EDINA, HENNEPIN CO.
1—OUR LADY OF GRACE (1946) Revs. Robert M. Schwartz; Allan Paul Eilen; Deacon Anthony Pasko. *Additional Worship Site: Most Holy Trinity*—4017 Utica Ave., St. Louis Park, 55416.
5071 Eden Ave., 55436. Tel: 952-929-3317; Fax: 952-929-4612. Web: www.olgparish.org.
School—(Grades K-8), 5051 Eden Ave., 55436-2308. Tel: 952-929-8170; Fax: 952-929-8170. Email: maureentrenary@olgschool.net. Web: www.olgschool-.net. Maureen Trenary, Prin.; Nancy Jackson, Librarian. Lay Teachers 37; Students 676.
Catechesis/Religious Program—Students 356.
2—ST. PATRICK (1857) Rev. Timothy C. Rudolphi.
Office: 6820 St. Patrick's Ln., 55439. Tel: 952-941-3164; Fax: 952-941-7371. Email: office@stpatrick-edina.org. Web: www.stpatrick-edina.org.
Catechesis/Religious Program—Students 488.
FRIDLEY, ANOKA CO., ST. WILLIAM (1963) Rev. Joseph Whalen; Deacon Jim Wagner.
Parish Center—6120 5th St., N.E., 55432. Tel: 763-571-5600; Fax: 763-571-6924.
Catechesis/Religious Program—Students 94.
GOLDEN VALLEY, HENNEPIN CO.
1—GOOD SHEPHERD (1946) [JC] Rev. Theodore C. Campbell.
Mailing Address: 145 Jersey Ave. S., 55426. Tel: 763-544-0416; Fax: 763-544-9896. Email: info@goodshepherdgv.org. Web: www.goodshepherdgv.org.
School—(Grades K-6) Tel: 763-545-4285; Fax: 763-545-1896. Email: contact@gsgvschool.org. Web: www.gsgvschool.org. Tom Zellmer, Prin.; Diane Keefe, Librarian. Lay Teachers 19; Students 329.
Catechesis/Religious Program—Tel: 763-544-0416; Fax: 763-544-0416. Students 56.
2—ST. MARGARET MARY (1946) Rev. Paul Moudry.
Mailing Address: 2323 Zenith Ave., N., 55422. Tel: 763-588-9466; Fax: 763-588-0040. Email: info@smm-gv.org. Web: www.smm-gv.org.
See St. Elizabeth Seton School under Elementary Schools, Consolidated, Parochial located in the Institution section.
Catechesis/Religious Program—Students 70.
HAM LAKE, ANOKA CO., CHURCH OF SAINT PAUL (1981) Rev. Jon Vander Ploeg; Deacon Timothy Zinda.
Office: 1740 Bunker Lake Blvd., N.E., 55304. Tel: 763-757-6910; Fax: 763-757-6920. Email: contact@churchofsaintpaul.com. Web: www.churchofsaintpaul.com.
Catechesis/Religious Program—Tel: 763-757-1148. Students 633.
LINO LAKES, ANOKA CO., ST. JOSEPH OF THE LAKES (1891) [CEM] Rev. Mark J. Underdahl; Deacon Thomas A. Konkel.
Mailing Address: 171 Elm St., 55014. Tel: 651-784-3015; Fax: 651-784-3699. Web: www.saintjosephsparish.org.
Catechesis/Religious Program—Students 806.
NEW HOPE, HENNEPIN CO., ST. JOSEPH (1858) [CEM] Rev. Terrence Rassmussen, Parochial Admin.; Deacon Robert Bramwell.
Church: 8701 36th Ave. N., 55427. Tel: 763-544-3352; Fax: 763-544-3435. Web: www.stjosephparish.com.
Catechesis/Religious Program—Students 391.
PLYMOUTH, HENNEPIN CO., ST. MARY OF THE LAKE (1935) Rev. Curtis F. Lybarger.
Mailing Address: 105 Forestview Ln. N., 55441. Tel: 763-545-1443; Fax: 763-797-0996. Web: www.stmaryofthelakeply.org.
Office: 105 Forestview Ln. N., 55441. Tel: 763-545-1443; Fax: 763-797-0996. Web: www.stmaryofthelakeply.org.
Catechesis/Religious Program—Students 189.
RICHFIELD, HENNEPIN CO.
1—THE CHURCH OF THE ASSUMPTION/LA IGLESIA DE LA ASUNCION (1876) Rev. Charles McCarthy, O.F.M-.Conv.; Deacon Robert Smith.
Mailing Address: 305 E. 77th St., 55423. Tel: 612-866-5019; Fax: 612-866-5274.
School—Blessed Trinity Nicollet & Penn Campus, (Grades PreK-8) Tel: 612-869-5200 (Nicollet); 612-866-6906 (Penn); Fax: 612-869-0277; 612-767-2191. Email: doylek@btcsmn.org. Web: www.btcsm-n.org. Lay Teachers 16; Students 236.
Catechesis/Religious Program—Students 195.
2—ST. PETER (1943) Rev. Gerald Dvorak; Deacon Mark Johanns.
Mailing Address: 6730 Nicollet Ave. S., 55423. Tel: 612-866-5089; Fax: 612-866-5080. Email: ann@btcsmn.org. Web: www.stpetersrichfield.org.
See Blessed Trinity Catholic School of Richfield, Minnesota under Elementary Schools, Consolidated, Parochial located in the Institution section
Catechesis/Religious Program—Students 79.
3—ST. RICHARD (1952) Rev. William F. Martin; Deacon Bob Schnell.
Office:—7540 Penn Ave. S., 55423. Tel: 612-869-2426; Fax: 612-869-0277. Email: secretary@strichards.com. Web: www.strichards.com.
School—Blessed Trinity Catholic School, (Grades PreK-8) Tel: 612-866-6906; Fax: 612-866-5274. Web: www.btcsmn.org. Sue Kerr, Prin.; Jackie Spano, Librarian. Consolidation of Assumption, St. Peter & St. Richard. Lay Teachers 16; Students 263.
Catechesis/Religious Program—Students 92.
ROBBINSDALE, HENNEPIN CO., SACRED HEART (1910) Rev. Bryan J. B. Pedersen; Deacon James Ramsey.
Mailing Address: 4087 W. Broadway, 55422. Tel: 763-537-4561; Fax: 763-537-5426. Web: www.sacredheartrobbinsdale.org.
School—(Grades PreSchool-8), 4050 Hubbard Ave., N., 55422. Tel: 763-537-1329; Fax: 763-537-1486. Web: www.sacredheartschoolrobbinsdale.org. Karen Bursey, Prin.; Sarah Svien, Librarian. Lay Teachers 14; Students 231.
Catechesis/Religious Program—Students 138.
ST. LOUIS PARK, HENNEPIN CO.
1—HOLY FAMILY (1926) Rev. Thomas W. Dufner.
Mailing Address: 5900 W. Lake St., 55416. Tel: 952-929-0113; Fax: 952-915-1474. Web: www.hfcmn.org.
School—5925 W. Lake St., 55416-2019. Tel: 952-925-5298; Fax: 952-925-5298. Email: acoone@hfamn.org. Web: www.hfamn.org. Ann Coone, Prin. Lay Teachers 10; Students 201.
Catechesis/Religious Program—Students 127.
2—MOST HOLY TRINITY (1943) Merged with Our Lady of Grace, Edina.

OUTSIDE TWIN-CITY METROPOLITAN AREA

ALBERTVILLE, WRIGHT CO., ST. ALBERT (1902) [CEM] Rev. Xavier Thelakkatt (India); Deacon John Wallin.
Mailing Address: P.O. Box 127, 55301. Tel: 763-497-2474; Fax: 763-497-7678. Web: www.stalbertschurch.org.
Office: 11400 57th St. N.E., 55301-0127.
Catechesis/Religious Program—Students 220.
ANNANDALE, WRIGHT CO., ST. IGNATIUS (1882) [CEM] Rev. Victor Valencia.
Mailing Address: P.O. Box 126, 55302. Tel: 320-274-8828; Fax: 320-274-3961.
Church: 35 Birch St., E., 55302-0126. Web: www.stignatiusmc.com.
Catechesis/Religious Program—Tel: 320-274-8828, Ext. 24; Fax: 320-274-3961. Students 207.
ANOKA, ANOKA CO., ST. STEPHEN (1856) [CEM] Revs. Michael Van Sloun; Kevin P. Magner; Nathan LaLiberte; Deacons Peter Bednarczyk; Dominic Ehrmantraut; Charles Waugh; Ramon Garcia Degollado.
Office:—525 Jackson St., 55303. Tel: 763-421-2471; Fax: 763-421-4230. Web: www.ststephenchurch.org.
School—(Grades PreSchool-8), 506 Jackson St., 55303. Tel: 763-421-3236; Fax: 763-712-7433. Rebecca Gustafson, Prin. Lay Teachers 24; Students 392.
Catechesis/Religious Program—Students 9.
BAYPORT, WASHINGTON CO., ST. CHARLES (1943) [CEM] [JC] Rev. Mark R. Juettner; Deacon Roger B. Carlson.
Mailing Address: 409 N. 3rd St., 55003. Tel: 651-439-4511; Fax: 651-430-9717. Email: parishoffice@stcharlesbayport.org. Web: www.stcharlesbayport.org.
See St. Croix Catholic School, Stillwater under Elementary Schools, Consolidated, Parochial located in the Institution section.
Catechesis/Religious Program—Tel: 651-439-7142; Fax: 651-439-7705. Web: www.scuff.org. Students 34.
BELLE CREEK, GOODHUE CO., ST. COLUMBKILL (1860) [JC] Rev. Bruce Peterson; Deacon Paul Tschann.
Mailing Address: 36483 Co. 47 Blvd., Goodhue, 55027. Tel: 651-258-4307.
Catechesis/Religious Program—Combined program with Holy Trinity. Students 139.
BELLE PLAINE, SCOTT CO., OUR LADY OF THE PRAIRIE (1972) [CEM 2] Rev. Michael C. Kaluza; Deacon Robert Raleigh.
Office: 215 N. Chestnut St., 56011. Tel: 952-873-6564; Fax: 952-873-6717.
School—(Grades K-6) Daniel Gardner, Prin. Lay Teachers 4; Students 40.
Catechesis/Religious Program—Students 173.
BELLECHESTER, GOODHUE CO., ST. MARY (1859) [CEM] Rev. Bruce Peterson.
Mailing Address: 221 Chester Ave., 55027. Tel: 651-923-4305.
Catechesis/Religious Program—Students 45.
BUFFALO, WRIGHT CO., ST. FRANCIS XAVIER (1888) [CEM 2] Rev. David R. Hennen; Deacon Sherman H. Otto.
Parish Office—223 - 19th Street N.W., 55313-5042. Tel: 763-684-0075; Fax: 763-684-4771. Web: www.stfxb.org.
School—(Grades K-8), 219 19th St., N.W., 55313-5042. Tel: 763-684-0075, Ext. 200. Kim Zumbusch, Prin.; Pat Miller, Librarian. Lay Teachers 18; Students 223.
Catechesis/Religious Program—Tel: 763-684-0075, Ext. 105. Students 467.
CANNON FALLS, GOODHUE CO., ST. PIUS V (1856) [CEM] Rev. Jay K. Kythe.
Office: 410 W. Colvill Ave., P.O. Box 367, 55009-0367. Tel: 507-263-2578; Fax: 507-263-8005. Email: stpiusvcf@fronteirnet.net. Web: stpiusvcf.org.
Catechesis/Religious Program—Students 173.
CARVER, CARVER CO., ST. NICHOLAS (1868) [CEM 2] Rev. Thomas Joseph.
Mailing Address: 412 W. Fourth St., Box 133, 55315. Tel: 952-448-2345; Fax: 952-368-0502.
Catechesis/Religious Program—Tel: 952-448-6181. Students 75.
CEDAR LAKE, SCOTT CO., ST. PATRICK OF CEDAR LAKE TOWNSHIP (1856) [CEM] Rev. Orlando G. Tatel.
Office: 24425 Old Hwy. 13 Blvd., Cedar Lake Twp., Jordan, 55352. Tel: 952-492-6276; Fax: 952-492-6290.
Catechesis/Religious Program—Tel: 952-492-6290. Students 151.
Mission—St. Catherine of Spring Lake Township (1865) [CEM] 220th St. E., Spring Lake, Itasca Co. 56680. Tel: 952-447-2180.
CEDAR, ANOKA CO., ST. PATRICK (1894) [CEM] Rev. David Blume; Deacon George Stahl.
Mailing Address: 19921 Nightingale St., N.W., Oak Grove, 55011-9204. Tel: 763-753-2011; Fax: 763-753-9803. Email: stpats@st-patricks.org. Web: www.st-patricks.org.
Catechesis/Religious Program—Students 813.
CENTERVILLE, ANOKA CO., ST. GENEVIEVE (1854) [CEM] Rev. Thomas P. Fitzgerald; Deacon Daniel D. Kirchoffner.
Mailing Address: 7087 Goiffon Rd., 55038. Tel: 651-429-7937; Fax: 651-653-0071. Email: stgens@usfamily.net. Web: www.stgen.org.
Catechesis/Religious Program—Tel: 612-426-1818. Students 227.
CHANHASSEN, CARVER CO., ST. HUBERT (1865), (German), [CEM] Revs. Rolf R. Tollefson; Paul Basil Kubista; Deacons Timothy Helmeke; Jim McDonald.
Office: 8201 Main St., 55317. Tel: 952-934-9106; Fax: 952-934-8209. Web: www.sthubert.org.
School—(Grades K-8) Tel: 952-934-6003; Fax: 952-906-1229. Mary Roles, Prin. Lay Teachers 43; Students 679.
Catechesis/Religious Program—Students 1,080.
CHASKA, CARVER CO., GUARDIAN ANGELS (1858) [CEM] Rev. Douglas Ebert; Deacon James William Bauhs.
Office: 215 W. 2nd St., 55318. Tel: 952-227-4000; Fax: 952-227-4051. Web: www.gachaska.org.
School—(Grades K-8) Tel: 952-227-4010; Fax: 952-227-4050. Amy Gallus, Prin. Lay Teachers 10; Students 135.
Catechesis/Religious Program—Tel: 952-227-4007. Students 191.
CLEARWATER, WRIGHT CO., ST. LUKE (1870) [CEM] Rev. Steven B. Hoffman; Deacon Peter G. Bellavance.
Church, Office & Mailing Address: 17545 Huber Ave. N.W., 55320-0249. Tel: 320-558-2124; Fax: 320-558-2875.
Catechesis/Religious Program—Students 127.
CLEVELAND, LE SUEUR CO., CHURCH OF THE NATIVITY OF THE BLESSED VIRGIN MARY (1865) [CEM] Rev. Dennis J. Backer.
200 W. Main, 56017. Tel: 507-243-3166; Fax: 507-243-3849.
Catechesis/Religious Program—Students 75.
COATES, DAKOTA CO., ST. AGATHA (1870) [CEM] Rev. Richard J. Mahoney (Retired).
Office: 3700 160th St., E., MN 55068. Tel: 651-689-0660; Fax: 651-696-1972.
Catechesis/Religious Program—Students 27.
COLOGNE, CARVER CO., ST. BERNARD (1859) [CEM] Rev. Martin Shallbetter.
Church & Office: 212 Church St. E., 55322. Tel: 952-466-2031; Fax: 952-466-3319. Email: parishinfo@st-bernard-cologne.org. Web: www.st-bernard-cologne.org.
School—(Grades PreSchool-6), 300 Church St. E., 55322. Tel: 952-466-5917. Email: schoolinfo@st-bernard-cologne.org. Sr. Jancy Nedumkallel, Prin. Religious 2; Lay Teachers 4; Students 52.
Catechesis/Religious Program—Students 39.
Convent—Franciscan Clarist Congregation, 214 Church St., 55320. Tel: 952-466-5620.
CORCORAN, HENNEPIN CO., ST. THOMAS THE APOSTLE (1896) [CEM 4] [JC 4] Revs. John Gallas; Scott M. Carl.
Office: 20,000 County Rd. 10, 55340. Tel: 763-420-2385; Fax: 763-420-4710. Email: office@churchofstthomas.org. Web: www.churchofstthomas.org.
Catechesis/Religious Program—Students 219.
DAYTON, HENNEPIN CO., ST. JOHN THE BAPTIST (1862) [CEM 2] Rev. Xavier Thelakkatt (India); Deacon John Wallin.
Mailing Address: 18380 Columbus St., 55327. Tel: 763-428-2828; Fax: 763-428-6462. Email:

sjbchurch@yahoo.com. Web: www.stjohnsdayton.org. Office: 18380 Columbus St., 55327. Tel: 763-428-2828; Fax: 763-428-6462.
Catechesis/Religious Program—Students 57.

DEEPHAVEN, HENNEPIN CO., ST. THERESE (1946) Rev. Douglas E. Dandurand; Deacon Joseph Smith.
Office: 18323 Minnetonka Blvd., 55391. Tel: 952-473-4422; Fax: 952-261-0585. Email: parish@st-therese.org. Web: www.st-therese.org.
School—(Grades K-8), 18325 Minnetonka Blvd., 55391. Tel: 952-473-4355; Fax: 952-261-0630. Lauren Caton, Prin.; Lin Mulhern, Librarian. Sisters 3; Lay Teachers 9; Students 140.
Catechesis/Religious Program—Students 305.

DELANO, WRIGHT CO.
1—ST. JOSEPH (1902), (Polish), [CEM] Rev. Paul A. Kammen; Deacons Joseph Kittok; Michael Dewitte.
Mailing Address: 401 N. River St., P.O. Box 470, 55328-0470. Tel: 763-972-2077; Fax: 763-972-6177. Web: www.delanocatholic.com.
Church: 401 N. River St., P.O. Box 470, 55328-0470. Tel: 763-972-2077; Fax: 763-972-6177. Web: www.delanocatholic.com.
Catechesis/Religious Program—
2—ST. MARY OF CZESTOCHOWA (1884) [CEM] Rev. Thomas J. Balluff.
Mailing Address: 1867 95th St., S.E., 55328. Tel: 952-955-1139. Web: www.stboniface-stmary.org.
Catechesis/Religious Program—Students 40.
3—ST. PETER (1865), (German), [CEM 2] Rev. Paul A. Kammen; Deacon Michael Dewitte.
Offices: 204 S. River St., P.O. Box 470, 55328. Tel: 763-972-2077; Fax: 763-972-6177. Email: dcc@delanocatholic.com. Web: www.delanocatholic.com.
School—St. Peter School, (Grades K-6) Tel: 763-972-2528; Fax: 763-972-6177. Nicole Belpedio, Prin. Combined with St. Joseph, Delano Lay Teachers 7; Students 82.
Catechesis/Religious Program—Students 279.

ELYSIAN, LE SUEUR CO., ST. ANDREW (1894) Rev. Michael W. Ince.
Church: Box 261, 56028. Tel: 507-267-4928; Fax: 507-362-4339.
Catechesis/Religious Program—Students 50.

EXCELSIOR, HENNEPIN CO., ST. JOHN THE BAPTIST (1903) [CEM] Rev. Mark B. Dosh.
Mailing Address: 680 Mill St., 55331-3272. Tel: 952-474-8868; Fax: 952-474-5962. Web: www.stjohns-excelsior.org.
School—(Grades PreK-8) Tel: 952-474-5812; Fax: 952-401-8778. Email: kchapman@stjohns-excelsior.org. Nancy Ronhovde, Prin. Lay Teachers 9; Students 99.
Catechesis/Religious Program—Students 117.

FARIBAULT, RICE CO.
1—DIVINE MERCY CATHOLIC CHURCH (2002) [CEM 2] Revs. J. Kevin Finnegan; Erik Carl Martin Lundgren; Deacon Steven Moses.
Office: 4 Second Ave., S.W., 55021-6029. Tel: 507-334-2266; Fax: 507-334-3895. Web: www.divinemercycatholics.org.
Church: 139 Mercy Dr., 55021.
See Divine Mercy Catholic School of Faribault, Faribault under Elementary Schools, Consolidated, Parochial located in the Institution section.
Catechesis/Religious Program—Tel: 507-334-2266, Ext. 20. Email: stvoh@divinemercycatholics.org. Students 194.
2—IMMACULATE CONCEPTION (1856) Merged with Sacred Heart and St. Lawrence, Faribault to form Divine Mercy Catholic Church, Faribault.
3—ST. LAWRENCE (1869), (German), Merged with Sacred Heart and Immaculate Conception, Faribault to form Divine Mercy Catholic Church, Faribault.
4—SACRED HEART, (French—German), Merged with St. Lawrence and Immaculate Conception, Faribault to form Divine Mercy Catholic Church, Faribault.

FARMINGTON, DAKOTA CO., ST. MICHAEL (1854) [CEM] Rev. Dennis Thompson.
Mailing Address: 22120 Denmark Ave., 55024. Tel: 651-463-3360; Fax: 651-463-2339. Email: info@stmichael-farmington.org. Web: www.stmichael-farmington.org.
Catechesis/Religious Program—Students 570.

FOREST LAKE, WASHINGTON CO., ST. PETER (1904) [CEM] Revs. Donald E. DeGrood; Mark J. Joppa; Deacons Gary Houle; Ralph L'Allier; Terrence Moravec.
Mailing Address: 1250 S. Shore Dr., 55025. Tel: 651-982-2200; Fax: 651-982-2220. Web: www.stpeterfl.org.
School—(Grades K-6) Tel: 651-982-2215; Fax: 651-982-2230. Web: www.schools.stpeterfl.org. Ann Laird, Prin. Lay Teachers 48; Students 267.
Catechesis/Religious Program—Tel: 651-982-2235. Students 625.

FRANCONIA, CHISAGO CO., THE CHURCH OF SAINT FRANCIS XAVIER OF FRANCONIA Rev. Frank J. Wampach.
25293 Redwing Ave., 55084-0234. Tel: 651-465-7345.
Catechesis/Religious Program—Students 35.

GOODHUE, GOODHUE CO., THE CHURCH OF THE HOLY TRINITY Rev. Bruce Peterson.
308 4th St. N., 55027. Tel: 651-923-4472.
Catechesis/Religious Program—Students 116.

HAMEL, HENNEPIN CO., ST. ANNE (1879) [CEM] Revs. Corey T. Belden; Scott M. Carl.
Mailing Address: 200 Hamel Rd., Box 256, 55340-0256. Tel: 763-478-6644; Fax: 763-478-9141. Email: office@saintannehamel.org. Web: www.saintannehamel.org.
Catechesis/Religious Program—Students 119.

HAMPTON, DAKOTA CO., ST. MATHIAS (1900) [CEM] Rev. Stan P. Mader.
Office: 23315 Northfield Blvd., 55031. Tel: 651-437-9030; Fax: 651-437-3427. Email: parishoffice@stmathias.com. Web: www.stmathias.com.
Catechesis/Religious Program—Tel: 651-480-1795. Students 82.

HANCOCK TOWNSHIP, CARVER CO., ASSUMPTION, Closed. For inquiries for parish records contact the chancery.

HASSAN TOWNSHIP, HENNEPIN CO., ST. WALBURGA (1857) Merged For inquiries for parish records please see Mary Queen of Peace, Rogers.

HASTINGS, DAKOTA CO., ST. ELIZABETH ANN SETON (1987) [CEM] [JC] Revs. James M. Perkl; Cole Kracke.
Office: 2035 W. Fifteenth St., 55033. Tel: 651-437-4254; Fax: 651-438-2948. Web: www.seasparish.org.
School—(Grades PreSchool-8), 600 Tyler St., 55033. Tel: 651-437-3098; Fax: 651-438-3377. Jill Moes, Prin.; Meghan Moynihan, Librarian. Lay Teachers 21; Students 296; Preschool 54.
Catechesis/Religious Program—Tel: 651-437-9191. Students 426.

HAZELWOOD, RICE CO., ANNUNCIATION (1863) [CEM] Rev. Thomas Rayar.
Office: 4996 Hazelwood Ave., Northfield, 55057-4255. Tel: 952-652-2625.
Catechesis/Religious Program—Students 24.

HEIDELBERG, LE SUEUR CO., ST. SCHOLASTICA (1856) [CEM] Merged with St. Wenceslaus, New Prague.

HOPKINS, HENNEPIN CO.
1—ST. JOHN THE EVANGELIST (1950) Rev. James C. Liekhus; Deacons Darrel Thomas Branch; James Murphy.
Mailing Address: 6 Interlachen Rd., 55343. Tel: 952-935-5536; Fax: 952-938-2724. Email: receptionistchurch@stjohnhopkins.org. Web: www.stjohnshopkins.org.
School—(Grades K-6), 1503 Boyce St., 55343. Tel: 952-935-7782. Email: tnelson@stjohnhopkins.org. Kathleen Segna, Prin. Lay Teachers 8; Students 107.
Catechesis/Religious Program—Students 119.
2—ST. JOSEPH'S (1922) [CEM] Rev. James C. Liekhus.
Mailing Address: 1310 Main St., 55343. Tel: 952-935-0111; Fax: 952-935-4539. Email: parishoffice@stjoeshopkins.org. Web: www.stjoeshopkins.org.
Office: 1310 Main St., 55343. Tel: 952-935-0111; Fax: 952-935-4539. Email: parishoffice@stjoeshopkins.org. Web: www.stjoeshopkins.org.
Catechesis/Religious Program—Tel: 952-935-7004; 952-935-5059. Students 65.

HUGO, WASHINGTON CO., ST. JOHN THE BAPTIST (1902) [CEM] Rev. Jonathan P. Shelley.
Mailing Address: 14383 N. Forest Blvd., 55038. Tel: 651-429-9170; Fax: 651-429-3190. Web: www.stjohnhugo.org.
Catechesis/Religious Program—Tel: 651-762-4676. Students 93.

INVER GROVE HEIGHTS, DAKOTA CO., CHURCH OF ST. PATRICK (1856) [CEM] Rev. Robert H. Hart; Deacon John Edward Vomastek.
Mailing Address: 3535 72nd St., E., 55076. Tel: 651-455-6624; Fax: 651-455-8984. Web: www.churchofstpatrick.com.
Office: 3535 72nd St. E., 55076. Tel: 651-455-6624; Fax: 651-455-8984. Email: tlevi@churchofstpatrick.com. Web: www.churchofstpatrick.com.
Catechesis/Religious Program—Students 272.

JORDAN, SCOTT CO., ST. JOHN THE BAPTIST (1858) [CEM] [JC] Rev. Timothy J. Yanta; Deacon Gary Hoffman.
Mailing Address: 313 E. 2nd St., 55352. Tel: 952-492-2640; Fax: 952-492-5683. Web: www.stjohnthebaptistjordan.org.
School—(Grades PreSchool-6), 215 Broadway St. N., 55352. Tel: 952-492-2030; Fax: 952-492-3211. Email: bonita.jungels@stjohynschool/jordan.org. Bonita Jungels, Prin.; Sue Colling, Librarian. Lay Teachers 6; Students 114.
Catechesis/Religious Program—Tel: 952-492-5827. Email: cburnell@frontiernet.net. Students 245.

KENYON, GOODHUE CO., ST. MICHAEL (1944) [CEM] Revs. Kevin Finnegan; Erik Carl Martin Lundgren; Deacon Newell McGee.
Church & Office: 108 Bullis St., 55946. Tel: 507-789-6120; Fax: 507-789-6120 (Call first.).
Catechesis/Religious Program—Students 50.

KILKENNY, LE SUEUR CO., ST. CANICE (1858) [CEM] Rev. George Kallumkalkudy, C.M.I.
Mailing Address: 183 W. Maple St. W., Box 37, 56052. Tel: 507-595-2561. Email: stcanice@frontiernet.net.
Catechesis/Religious Program—Students 39.

LAKE ST. CROIX BEACH, WASHINGTON CO., ST. FRANCIS OF ASSISI (1938) Rev. Jerome F. Keiser.
Mailing Address: 16770 13th St., S., Lakeland, 55043. Tel: 651-436-7817; Fax: 651-436-6524. Web: www.catholic-church.org/st-francis.
Catechesis/Religious Program—Students 216.

LAKEVILLE, DAKOTA CO., ALL SAINTS (1877) [CEM] Revs. Thomas Wilson; Jonathan Kelly; Deacons James Marschall; George Nugent.
Mailing Address: 19795 Holyoke Ave., 55044. Tel: 952-469-4481; Fax: 952-469-5752. Web: www.allsaintschurch.com.
School—(Grades K-8) Tel: 952-469-3332; Fax: 952-469-4484. Karen Meskill, Prin.; Martha Johnson, Librarian. Lay Teachers 20; Students 358.
Catechesis/Religious Program—Tel: 952-469-6461. Students 1,087.

LE CENTER, LE SUEUR CO., ST. MARY (1899) [CEM] Rev. Christopher Shofner.
Mailing Address: 165 N. Waterville Ave., 56057. Tel: 507-357-4838; Fax: 507-357-4838.
Catechesis/Religious Program—

LE SUEUR, LE SUEUR CO., ST. ANNE (1852) [CEM 2] Rev. George J. Grafsky.
Worship Site: Church of St. Thomas of Derrynane—31525 181st St., New Prague, 56071-4474.
St. Anne Church: 211 N. 3rd St., 56058. Tel: 507-665-3811; Fax: 507-665-3811.
School—(Grades K-5) Tel: 507-665-2489; Fax: 507-665-6186. Adam Bemmels, Prin.; Norma Nuessmeier, Librarian. Clergy 1; Lay Teachers 2; Students 48.
Catechesis/Religious Program—Tel: 507-665-2995. Students 87.

LEXINGTON, LE SUEUR CO., ST. JOSEPH (1903) [CEM] Merged with St. Wenceslaus, New Prague.

LINDSTROM, CHISAGO CO., ST. BRIDGET OF SWEDEN (1948) Rev. Mark H. Wehmann.
Mailing Address: P.O. Box 754, 55045.
Church & Office: 13060 Lake Blvd., 55045. Tel: 651-257-2474; Fax: 651-257-1498. Web: www.stbridgetofsweden.org.
Catechesis/Religious Program—Students 269.

LONG LAKE, HENNEPIN CO., ST. GEORGE (1917) [CEM] Rev. Ralph Huar.
Mailing Address: 133 N. Brown Rd., 55356-9560. Tel: 952-473-1247; Fax: 952-404-0129.
Church & Office: Tel: 952-476-0170; Fax: 952-404-0129. Email: stgeorge@msn.com. Web: www.stgeorgelonglake.org.
Catechesis/Religious Program—Students 46.

LONSDALE, RICE CO., IMMACULATE CONCEPTION (1903) [CEM 2] Rev. Thomas E. McCabe; Deacon Thomas P. Michaud.
P.O. Box 169, 55046-0169. Tel: 507-744-2829.
See Holy Cross LNMV Catholic School, Lonsdale under Elementary Schools, Consolidated, Parochial located in the Institution section.
Catechesis/Religious Program—Students 3.

LORETTO, HENNEPIN CO., SS. PETER AND PAUL (1867) [CEM] Revs. John Gallas; Scott M. Carl; Deacon Darrel Courrier.
Mailing Address: P.O. Box 96, 55357. Tel: 763-479-0535; Fax: 763-479-4383.
Church & Office: 145 Railway St., E., 55357. Web: www.cspap.org.
Catechesis/Religious Program—Tel: 763-479-2810. Students 128.

MAPLE GROVE, HENNEPIN CO., ST. JOSEPH THE WORKER (1870) Revs. Michael Sullivan; Donald J. Piche; Deacon Kevin O'Connor.
Mailing Address: 7180 Hemlock Ln., 55369. Tel: 763-425-6505; Fax: 763-425-6587. Web: www.sjtw.net.
Catechesis/Religious Program—Students 843.

MAPLE LAKE, WRIGHT CO., ST. TIMOTHY (1882) [CEM 3] Deacons Ron Freeman; Michael Medley.
Mailing Address: 8 Oak Ave., N., 55358. Tel: 320-963-3726; Fax: 320-963-2008. Web: www.churchofsttimothy.org.
School—(Grades K-6) Tel: 320-963-3417; Fax: 320-963-8804. Mike O'Malley, Prin. Lay Teachers 8; Students 132.
Catechesis/Religious Program—Students 215.

MARYSBURG, LESUEUR CO. , IMMACULATE CONCEPTION OF MARYSBURG (1857) [CEM] Rev. Dennis J. Backer.
Mailing Address: 27528 Patrick St., Madison Lake, 56063. Tel: 507-243-3166.

Catechesis/Religious Program—Fax: 507-243-3849. Students 35.

MARYSTOWN, SCOTT CO., ST. MARY OF THE PURIFICATION (1855) [CEM] Revs. Peter C. Wittman; Thomas Boedy, S.J.; Thomas Merrill, O.F.M.Conv.; Deacon William Heiman.
15850 Marystown Rd., Shakopee, 55379-9341. Tel: 952-445-2647; Fax: 952-403-9330. Web: www.stmary-purification.org.
See Shakopee Area Catholic School, Shakopee under Elementary Schools, Consolidated, Parochial located in the Institution section.
Catechesis/Religious Program—Shakopee Area Religious Education (SARE), 2700 17th Ave. W., Shakopee, 55379. Tel: 952-445-3387, Ext. 145; Fax: 952-445-7256. Students 45.

MEDINA, HENNEPIN CO., HOLY NAME OF JESUS (1865) [CEM] Revs. Stephen D. Ulrick; Joseph-Quoc T. Vuong; Deacons Joe Wierschem; Sam Catapano; Dennis Hanson.
Church & Office: 155 County Rd., 24, 55340. Tel: 763-473-7901; Fax: 763-745-3488. Email: info@hnoj.org. Web: www.hnoj.org.
School—(Grades K-6) Tel: 763-473-3675; Fax: 763-745-3499. Email: mmoch@hnoj.org. Web: www.hnoj.org/school. Mike Moch, Prin.; Kim Prodahl, Librarian; Jill Reiner, Librarian. Lay Teachers 22; Students 343.
Catechesis/Religious Program—Students 963.

MIESVILLE, DAKOTA CO., ST. JOSEPH (1873) [CEM] Rev. Jay K. Kythe.
Office: 23955 Nicolai Ave. E., 55033-9650. Tel: 651-437-3526.
Catechesis/Religious Program—Students 115.

MINNETONKA, HENNEPIN CO., IMMACULATE HEART OF MARY (1946) Rev. David T. Ostrowski.
Church & Office: 13505 Excelsior Blvd., 55345. Tel: 952-935-1432; Fax: 952-935-0474.
School—Tel: 952-935-2031; Fax: 952-935-2031. Email: principal@ihms.org. Web: www.ihms.org. Cheri Gardner, Prin. Lay Teachers 22; Students 234.
Catechesis/Religious Program—Tel: 952-935-7077. Students 168.

MONTGOMERY, LE SUEUR CO., MOST HOLY REDEEMER (1881) [CEM 2] Rev. George Kallumkalkudy, C.M.I.
Mailing Address: 206 Vine Ave., W., 56069. Tel: 507-364-7981; Fax: 507-364-8660. Email: hredeemer@frontiernet.net. Web: www.hredeemerparish.org.
School—(Grades PreSchool-8), 205 Vine Ave., W., 56069. Tel: 507-364-7383; Fax: 507-364-5964. Email: mymgmurop@frontiernet.net. Mindy Reeder, Prin. Lay Teachers 7; Students 75.
Catechesis/Religious Program—Students 123.

MONTICELLO, WRIGHT CO., ST. HENRY (1904) [CEM] Rev. Tony VanderLoop.
Office:—1001 E. 7th St., 55362. Tel: 763-295-2402; Fax: 763-295-6333.
Catechesis/Religious Program—Tel: 763-271-3079. Students 519.

MOUND, HENNEPIN CO., OUR LADY OF THE LAKE (1909) [CEM] Rev. Timothy E. Dolan.
Church & Office: 2385 Commerce Blvd., 55364. Tel: 952-472-1284; Fax: 952-472-1216. Web: ourladyofthelake.com.
Preschool—Tel: 952-472-1284, Ext. 142; Fax: 952-472-9152. Email: mrosenberg@oll.pvt.k12.mn.us. Students 70.
School—(Grades PreK-8) Tel: 952-472-1284, Ext. 151. Ellen Feuling, Prin.; Beth Randklev, Librarian. Sisters 10; Lay Teachers 12; Students 129.
Catechesis/Religious Program—Tel: 952-472-1284, Ext. 144; Fax: 952-472-1216. Students 224.

NEW MARKET, SCOTT CO., SAINT NICKOLAUS (1893) [CEM] Rev. James F. Adams.
Church & Office: 51 Church St., 55054. Tel: 952-461-2403; Fax: 952-461-2423.
See Holy Cross LNMV Catholic School, Lonsdale under Elementary Schools, Consolidated, Parochial located in the Institution section.
Catechesis/Religious Program—Students 233.

NEW PRAGUE, SCOTT CO., ST. WENCESLAUS (1857) [CEM] Revs. Kevin I. Clinton; David A. Barrett; Deacon Robert Wagner.
Mailing Address: 215 Main St. E., 56071-1837. Tel: 952-758-3225; Fax: 952-758-2960. Web: www.saintwenceslaus.org.
Worship Sites—
St. John Campus—
St. Scholastica Campus—
School—(Grades K-8), 227 Main St. E., 56071. Tel: 952-758-3133; Fax: 952-758-2958. Kimberly Doyle, Prin.; Marcia Pleiss, Librarian. Lay Teachers 16; Students 251.
Catechesis/Religious Program—Tel: 952-758-2276. Students 370.

NEW TRIER, DAKOTA CO., ST. MARY (1856) [CEM] Rev. Stan P. Mader.
Church & Office: 8433 239th St. E., 55031. Tel: 651-437-5546. Web: www.stmarysnewtrier.com.
Catechesis/Religious Program—Students 48.

NORTH BRANCH, CHISAGO CO., ST. GREGORY THE GREAT (1874) [CEM] Rev. Mark Shane Wasinger; Deacon Michael Martin Jr.
Church & Office: 38725 Forest Blvd., P.O. Box 609, 55056. Tel: 651-674-4056; 651-674-4274 (Rectory); Fax: 651-277-4563. Email: info@stgregorynb.org. Web: www.stgregorynb.org.
Catechesis/Religious Program—Tel: 651-277-4563. Students 272.

NORTHFIELD, RICE CO., ST. DOMINIC (1869) [CEM] Rev. Dennis Dempsey; Deacon Len Gruber.
Office & Mailing Address: 216 N. Spring St., 55057-1431. Tel: 507-645-8816; Fax: 507-645-8818. Email: secretary@churchofstdominic.org. Web: www.churchofstdominic.org.
School—(Grades K-8) Tel: 507-650-0680; Fax: 507-645-8818. Vicki Kalina Marvin, Prin. Lay Teachers 11; Students 157.
Catechesis/Religious Program—Students 288.

NORWOOD, CARVER CO., ASCENSION (1859) [CEM 2] Rev. Martin Shallbetter.
Mailing Address: 323 Reform St., N., 55368. Tel: 952-467-3351. Web: www.ascensionnya.org.
Catechesis/Religious Program—Students 139.

PINE ISLAND, GOODHUE CO., ST. MICHAEL (1878) [CEM] Rev. Randal J. Kasel.
Mailing Address: 451 5th St., S.W., 55963-0368. Tel: 507-356-4280; Fax: 507-356-2080. Web: www.stmichaels-pineisland.4lpi.com.
Catechesis/Religious Program—Tel: 507-356-4280. Students 67.

PRIOR LAKE, SCOTT CO., ST. MICHAEL (1912) [CEM 2] Rev. Thomas H. Sieg; Deacon Richard Roy.
Mailing Address: 16311 Duluth Ave., S.E., 55372. Tel: 952-447-2491; Fax: 952-447-2489. Email: info@stmichael-pl.org. Web: www.stmichael-pl.org.
School—(Grades PreSchool-8), 16280 Duluth Ave., S.E., 55372. Tel: 952-447-2124; Fax: 952-447-2132 (Primary); 952-447-2348 (Middle School). Email: haycraft@saintmpl.org. Patrick Fox, Prin.; Debra Meidl, Librarian. Lay Teachers 23; Students 433.
Catechesis/Religious Program—Tel: 612-447-2486; Fax: 612-447-2489. Students 860.

RAMSEY, ANOKA CO., ST. KATHARINE DREXEL (2004), (Quasi-Parish) Rev. Paul A. Jaroszeski; Deacon Randall J. Bauer.
Office & Church: 7101 143rd Ave., N.W., Ste. G, 55303. Tel: 763-323-4424; Fax: 763-323-7040. Email: info@stkdcc.org. Web: www.stkdcc.org.
Catechesis/Religious Program—Students 155.

RED WING, GOODHUE CO., CHURCH OF ST. JOSEPH (1865) [CEM] Rev. Thomas M. Kommers.
Church & Office: 426 8th St., W., 55066. Tel: 651-388-1133; Fax: 651-388-5294.
Catechesis/Religious Program—Tel: 651-388-6000.

ROGERS, HENNEPIN CO.
1—ST. MARTIN (1912) Merged For inquiries for parish records contact The Catholic Church of Mary Queen of Peace, Rogers.
2—THE CATHOLIC CHURCH OF MARY QUEEN OF PEACE, Merged in Jan. 2003. Rev. Mark D. Moriarty; Deacon Michael Patrick Nevin.
Worship Sites—
St. Martin Church—21304 Church St., 55374. Tel: 763-428-2585; Fax: 763-428-3460. Email: mqpchurchoffice@yahoo.com.
St. Walburga Church—12020 Fletcher Ln., 55374.
School—(Grades PreSchool-8), 21201 Church Ave., 55374. Tel: 763-428-2355; Fax: 763-428-2062. Web: www.mqpcatholicschool.org. Heidi Van De Berg, Prin.; Shirley Khoshnevis, Librarian. Lay Teachers 11; Students 125.
Catechesis/Religious Program—Students 392.

ROSEMOUNT, DAKOTA CO., ST. JOSEPH (1865) [CEM 2] Rev. Paul Jarvis; Deacon Stephen Boatwright.
Mailing Address: 13900 Biscayne Ave., 55068. Tel: 651-423-4402; Fax: 651-423-6616. Web: www.stjosephcommunity.org.
School—(Grades K-8) Tel: 651-423-1658. Thomas Joseph, Prin.; Paula Krekelberg, Librarian. Sisters 1; Lay Teachers 11; Students 216.
Catechesis/Religious Program—Students 605.

RUSH CITY, CHISAGO CO., SACRED HEART (1870) [CEM] Rev. Edwin Savundra.
Mailing Address: 415 W. 5th St., 55069. Tel: 320-358-4370. Email: sacredheart@g.com. Web: www.sacredheartrushcity.org.
Catechesis/Religious Program—Students 63.

ST. BENEDICT, SCOTT CO., ST. BENEDICT, [CEM] [JC] Merged with St. Wenceslaus, New Prague.

ST. BONIFACIUS, HENNEPIN CO., ST. BONIFACE (1859) [CEM] Rev. Thomas J. Balluff.
Church & Office: 4025 Main St., 55375. Tel: 952-446-1054; Fax: 952-446-1158. Email: stbonifaceoffice@mchsi.com. Web: www.stboniface-stmary.org.
Catechesis/Religious Program—Students 67.

ST. MICHAEL, WRIGHT CO., ST. MICHAEL (1857) [CEM 2] Revs. Peter M. Richards; Nathaniel Rene Francis Meyers; Deacons Maynard Warne; Greg J. Steele; Donald Becker.
Mailing Address: 11300 Frankfort Pkwy., N.E., 55376. Tel: 763-497-2745; Fax: 763-497-5273. Web: www.stmcatholicchurch.org.
School—(Grades K-6), 14 Main St. N., Saint Michael, 55376. Tel: 763-497-3887; Fax: 763-497-9159. Jenny Haller, Prin.; Sharon House, Librarian. Lay Teachers 22; Students 351.
Catechesis/Religious Program—Students 590.

ST. PAUL PARK, WASHINGTON CO., ST. THOMAS AQUINAS (1884) [CEM] Rev. Gregory L. Esty; Deacon James T. Price.
Mailing Address: 920 Holley Ave., 55071. Tel: 651-459-2131; Fax: 651-459-8756.
Catechesis/Religious Program—Students 93.

ST. THOMAS, LE SUEUR CO., ST. THOMAS (1858) Merged with St. Anne, Le Sueur.

SAVAGE, SCOTT CO., ST. JOHN THE BAPTIST (1854) [CEM] Rev. Michael Tix; Deacons Robert Scott Durham; Jerry Little.
Mailing Address: 4625 W. 125th St., 55378-1357. Tel: 952-890-9465; Fax: 952-890-3006. Web: www.stjohns-savage.org.
School—(Grades PreK-8), 12508 Lynn Ave. S., 55378. Tel: 952-890-6604; Fax: 952-890-9481. Mike Smalley, Prin.; Jean Algren, Librarian. Lay Teachers 36; Students 502.
Catechesis/Religious Program—Tel: 952-890-9434; Fax: 952-890-9481.

SHAKOPEE, SCOTT CO.
1—CHURCH OF ST. MARY (1865) [CEM] [JC] Revs. Peter C. Wittman; Thomas Boedy, S.J.; Thomas Merrill, O.F.M.Conv.
Office: 2700 17th Ave. E., 55379. Tel: 952-445-1319; Fax: 952-445-0511.
Church: 535 S. Lewis St., 55379.
See Shakopee Area Catholic School, Shakopee under Elementary Schools, Consolidated, Parochial located in the Institution section.
2—ST. MARK (1856), (German), [JC 2] Revs. Peter C. Wittman; Thomas Boedy, S.J.; Thomas Merrill, O.F.M.Conv.; Deacon James Pufahl. In Res., Rev. Thomas Boedy, S.J.
Church & Office: 350 S. Atwood St., 55379-1238. Tel: 952-445-1229; Fax: 952-445-9639. Email: stmarkshakopee@usfamily.net. Web: www.stmark-shakopee.com.

SHARON TOWNSHIP, LE SUEUR CO., CHURCH OF ST. HENRY (1859) [CEM] Rev. Christopher Shofner.
165 N. Waterville, 56058. Tel: 507-357-4838.
Catechesis/Religious Program—Combined with St. Mary, Le Center.

SHIELDSVILLE, RICE CO., ST. PATRICK (1856) [CEM] Revs. Kevin Finnegan; Erik Carl Martin Lundgren; Deacon Steven Moses.
Church & Office: 7525 Dodd Rd., 55021. Tel: 507-334-6002; Fax: 507-334-1960. Email: spshieldsville@quest.net.
Catechesis/Religious Program—Students 65.

SOUTH ST. PAUL, DAKOTA CO.
1—ST. AUGUSTINE (1896) Merged with Holy Trinity, South St. Paul.
2—HOLY TRINITY (1918) Rev. John P. Echert.
Mailing Address: 749 6th Ave. S., 55075. Tel: 651-455-1302 (Office); Fax: 651-455-7600.
School—(Grades K-8), 745 6th Ave. S., 55075. Tel: 651-455-8557; Fax: 651-455-9696. Dan Gleason, Prin. Lay Teachers 8; Students 133.
Catechesis/Religious Program—Tel: 651-455-6004; Fax: 651-455-7600. Students 100.
Worship Site: St. Augustine—408 Third St., N., South St Paul, 55075.
3—ST. JOHN VIANNEY (1946) [CEM] Rev. Terry P. Beeson; Deacon Scott Wright.
Church & Office: 789 17th Ave. N., 55075. Tel: 651-451-1863; Fax: 651-451-1864. Email: sjvssp@comcast.net. Web: www.sjvssp.org.
School—(Grades K-8), 1815 Bromley St., 55075. Tel: 651-451-8395. Patrick Gannon, Prin.; Pepper Wolf, Librarian. Lay Teachers 9; Students 74.
Catechesis/Religious Program—Students 144.

STILLWATER, WASHINGTON CO.
1—ST. MARY (1865), (German), [JC] Revs. Michael J. Miller; Brian T. Lynch.
Mailing Address: 423 S. Fifth St., 55082. Tel: 651-439-1270; Fax: 651-439-7045. Web: www.stmarystillwater.org. In Res., Rev. Robert L. Valit (Retired).
See St. Croix Catholic School, Stillwater under Elementary Schools, Consolidated, Parochial located in the Institution section.
2—ST. MICHAEL (1853) [JC] Revs. Michael J. Miller; Brian T. Lynch; Deacons Roger Carlson; Guy Glover.
Church & Office: 611 S. Third St., 55082-4908. Tel: 651-439-4400; Fax: 651-430-3271. Web: www.stillwatercatholics.org.
See St. Croix Catholic School, Stillwater under Elementary Schools, Consolidated, Parochial located in the Institution section.

TAYLORS FALLS, CHISAGO CO., ST. JOSEPH'S (1873)

[CEM] [JC] Rev. Frank J. Wampach.
Church & Office: 490 Bench St., 55084. Tel: 651-465-7345; Fax: 651-465-6683. Email: sjtaylorsfalls@yahoo.com. Web: www.stjosephtaylorsfalls.org.
Catechesis/Religious Program—Students 74.

UNION HILL, LE SUEUR CO., ST. JOHN THE EVANGELIST, [CEM] Merged with St. Wenceslaus, New Prague.

VERMILLION, DAKOTA CO., ST. JOHN THE BAPTIST (1881) [CEM] Rev. Stan P. Mader.
Church & Office: 106 W. Main St., 55085. Tel: 651-437-5652; Fax: 651-437-5652.
School—(Grades PreSchool-5), 111 W. Main St., 55085. Tel: 651-437-2644; Fax: 651-437-9006. Email: stjohnscverm@bevcomm.net. Web: www.stjohns-vermillion.com. Sr. Tresa Margaret, Prin.; Sandy Bauer, Librarian. Franciscan Clarist Sisters 3; Lay Teachers 4; Students 99.
Catechesis/Religious Program—Email: stjohnsc@bevcomm.net. Students 50.

VESELI, RICE CO., MOST HOLY TRINITY (1874) [CEM 2] Rev. John G. Lapensky.
Mailing Address: 4939 Washington St., 55046. Tel: 507-744-2823; Fax: 507-744-2823.
See Holy Cross LNMV Catholic School, Lonsdale under Elementary Schools, Consolidated, Parochial located in the Institution section.
Catechesis/Religious Program—Students 62.

VICTORIA, CARVER CO., ST. VICTORIA (1856) [CEM] Rev. Robert L. White; Deacon Ray Ortman.
Mailing Address: 8228 Victoria Dr., 55386. Tel: 952-443-2661; Fax: 952-443-3866. Web: www.stvictoria.net.
Catechesis/Religious Program—Tel: 952-443-3536. Students 490.

WACONIA, CARVER CO., ST. JOSEPH (1859) [CEM] Rev. Lawrence R. Blake.
Mailing Address: 41 E. 1st St., 55387. Tel: 952-442-2384; Fax: 952-442-3719. Email: churchoffice@stjosephwaconia.org. Web: www.stjosephwaconia.org.
School—(Grades PreSchool-8) Tel: 952-442-4500. Email: schooloffice@stjosephwaconia.org. Donna Woodard, Headmaster; Jeff Lenzmeier, Prin.; Jenny Linn, Librarian. Lay Teachers 11; Students 205.
Catechesis/Religious Program—Students 398.

WATERTOWN, CARVER CO., IMMACULATE CONCEPTION (1863) [CEM] Rev. Joseph Fink.
Church & Office: 109 Angel Ave., N.W., P.O. Box 548, 55388. Tel: 952-955-1458; Fax: 952-955-1777.

WATERVILLE, LE SUEUR CO., HOLY TRINITY (1892) [CEM] Rev. Michael W. Ince.
Church & Office: 506 Common St., 56096. Tel: 507-362-4311; Fax: 507-362-4339. Email: holyt7@frontiernet.net.
Catechesis/Religious Program—Tel: 507-362-8396. Students 63.

WAVERLY, WRIGHT CO., ST. MARY (1884) [CEM] [JC 3] Rev. Kenneth L. O'Hotto.
Church & Office: 607 Maple Ave., 55390. Tel: 763-658-4319; Fax: 763-658-3519.
Catechesis/Religious Program—Tel: 763-658-4118. Students 127.

WAYZATA, HENNEPIN CO., ST. BARTHOLOMEW (1916) Rev. Michael A. Reding; Deacon Richard P. Witucki.
Office & Church: 630 E. Wayzata Blvd., 55391. Tel: 952-473-6601; Fax: 952-473-0980. Email: stbarts@st-barts.org. Web: www.st-barts.org.
School—(Grades PreK-6) Tel: 952-473-6189; Fax: 952-745-4598. Lynn Volkenant, Prin. Lay Teachers 13; Students 163.
Catechesis/Religious Program—Students 248.

ZUMBROTA, GOODHUE CO., ST. PAUL (1900) [CEM] [JC] Rev. Randal J. Kasel.
749 S. Main St., 55992-1608. Tel: 507-732-5324. Email: stpauls@hcinet.net. Web: www.stpaul-zumbrota.4lpi.com.
Catechesis/Religious Program—Students 81.

Chaplains of Public Institutions

ST. PAUL. *Children's Hospital*. Rev. Michael G. Monogue.
HealthEast, Inc. & HealthEast Hospice. Rev. Stephen J. LaCanne, M.Div., N.A.C.C., Contact Person.
St. Joseph's Hospital, Tel: 651-232-3611 (Spiritual Care Dept.). Revs. Stephen J. LaCanne, M.Div., N.A.C.C., Dir. Spiritual Care, Jonathan Fischer, O.S.B.
Ramsey County Correctional Facilities. Served by Jesuit Novitiate
Regions Medical Center. Revs. Ronald Harrer, O.M.I., Antony Skaria, C.F.I.C.
United Hospitals, Inc. Rev. Michael G. Monogue.

MINNEAPOLIS. *Abbot-Northwestern Hospital*, 3617 38th Ave. S., 55066. Rev. John Hofstede.
Fairview University Medical Center. Revs. Joseph Whalen, Jacob Yali (Nigeria).
Hennepin County Medical Center, 2421 Third Ave. S., 55404. Rev. Benny Mekkatt Varghese, C.F.I.C.
Minneapolis Children's Hospital, 3617 38th Ave. S., 55406. Rev. John Hofstede.
Veterans Administration Medical Center. Rev. Damien Schill.

EDINA. *Fairview-Southdale Hospital*. Rev. Jerry Fehn.

COON RAPIDS. *Mercy Hospital*. Rev. Peter Yakubu Ali.

FARIBAULT. *Faribault State School and Hospital*. Attended by Divine Mercy Catholic Church

GOLDEN VALLEY. *North Memorial Hospital*. Revs. James T. Livingston, Jules Omba Omalanga.

HASTINGS. *Regina Medical Center*. Rev. Robert J. Altier.

LINO LAKES. *Minnesota Correctional Facility*. Vacant. 1121 E. 46th St., 55407.

MAPLEWOOD. *St. John's Hospital*, 1575 Beam Ave., 55109. Rev. Leo J. Schneider. (Lutheran)

NEW HOPE. *St. Therese Care Center & Residence*, 8000 Bass Lake Rd., 55428. Rev. Matthew Ehmke, Chap.

SHAKOPEE. *Women's State Reformatory*. Vacant. Attended by St. Mark's, Shakopee

ST. LOUIS PARK. *Methodist Hospital*. Rev. Jerry Fehn.

STILLWATER. *Minnesota State Prison*. Vacant.

Special Assignment:
Very Rev.—
Beaudet, Christopher J., J.C.D.
Revs.—
Conlin, Daniel C., J.C.D.
Gjengdahl, Nels H., Chap., Saint Thomas Academy
Gorman, James
Krenik, Michael J.
Lepak, Roy C. (Retired), Hermit, Cotton, MN
Morin, Timothy
Wenthe, Christopher T.

On Duty Outside the Archdiocese:
Revs.—
Burns, James P., Boston College
Campbell, Shane A., Serving in Diocese of Bismarck
Norris, Timothy L., Venezuelan Mission, Diocese of Ciudad Guayana
O'Connell, Marvin R. (Retired), University of Notre Dame, IN
Schaffer, Gregory J., El Buen Pastor Parroquia San Francisco de Asis, Apartado 22, Puerto Ordaz, Estado Bolivar 8015 Venezuela.
Snyder, Larry J., Catholic Charities, U.S.A.

Military Chaplains:
Revs.—
Magnuson, Sean R.
Thiesen, Eugene

Graduate Studies:
Revs.—
Bodin, Daniel J. Catholic University of America
Floeder, John P., Pontifical John Paul II Institute, Washington, DC

Retired:
Rev. Msgrs.—
Baumgaertner, William L., 60 S. Mississippi River Blvd., #16, 55105.
Boxleitner, J. Jerome, 1001 E. 46th St., 55407.
Lavin, James M., 330 Exchange St., 55102.
Moudry, Richard P., 11113 Hyland Ter., Eden Prairie, 55344.
Srnec, Stanley J., 60 S. Mississippi River Blvd., 55105.
Revs.—
Abbott, Eugene J., 330 Exchange Pl., 55102.
Ardolf, Paul C., Ascension, 323 Reform St. N., Norwood Young America, 55368-9706. Tel: 952-467-3351
Arms, Michael M., 34257 Urbans Point Rd., Crosslake, 56442-2731. Tel: 218-692-3190
Backmann, Albert P., 1304 Medicine Lake Dr. W. #222, Plymouth, 55441.
Beckman, Martin A., P.O. Box 1751, Minnetonka, 55345.
Berg, Richard V., 60 S. Mississippi River Blvd., Apt. 319, 55105.
Bowers, Ronald J., J.C.D., 3500 Oasis Springs Rd., N.E., Rio Rancho, NM 87144-2583. Tel: 505-896-0331. Email: frjab@cableone.net
Brandes, John F., 629-2nd St. N.E., 55413-1905.
Bury, Harold J., 60 S. Mississippi River Blvd., Apt. 318, 55105.
Carroll, Roger, 60 S. Mississippi River Blvd., Apt. 317, 55105.
Clubb, Ronald E., S.T.P., 60 S. Mississippi River Blvd., 55105.
Colon, Vincent A., 15125 Derby Cir., Rosemount, 55068.
Custodio, Rinaldo B., Leo C. Byrne Residence, 60 Mississippi River Blvd. S., 55105. Tel: 651-699-1233. Email: rbc1962@msn.com
Dahlheimer, Ronald W., 139 N. Vinegar Hill Ln., Kilkenny, 56052.
Dittberner, Jerome M., S.T.D., St. Paul Seminary, 2260 Summit Ave., Mail #5010, 55105. Tel: 651-962-8487. Email: jmdittberner@stthomas.edu
Dobihal, Robert F., 60 S. Mississippi River Blvd., Apt. 119, 55116.
Doffing, Gordon M., 5820 E. Marlin St., Mesa, AZ 85215.
Dolan, Leo A., 330 Exchange Pl. S., 55102.
Donahue, John G., 1454 60th St., Somerset, WI 54025.
Dufresne, Oliver J., 200 Earl St., 55106. Tel: 651-771-1798
Endres, Gilbert J., 60 S. Mississippi River Blvd., Saint Paul, 55116.
Erlander, Michael, 60 S. Mississippi River Blvd., 55105.
Evenson, Dennis D., 235 W. Cottage Ave., 55117-4407. Tel: 651-488-1566. Email: deGuadalupe@juno.com
Fitzpatrick, John P., 642 Monn Ave., Vadnais Heights, 55127.
Fleming, Martin M.P., 383 Portland Ave., 55102.
Forliti, John E., 1130 N. Oxford St., Saint Paul, 55103.
Friberg, Daniel, 2021 Wentworth, South St. Paul, 55075.
Gamber, William K., 105 Concord St. N., Fergus Falls, 56537.
Garvey, Thomas J., 2327 27th Ave. S., #3, 55406. Tel: 612-378-2214. Email: garvey57@gmail.com
Goman, Ralph J., 1011 Feltl Ct., #732, Hopkins, 55343. Email: 0615retired@comcast.net
Grieman, Gerald G., 264 Ashurst Dr., Phoenix, AZ.
Griffin, Patrick E., 4334 4th Ave. S., 55409. Email: pgriffin@q.com
Gutierrez, Jose, 60 S. Mississippi River Blvd., 55105.
Hackenmueller, Jerome B.
Hamel, Robert F., 225 Frank St., 55106.
Hazel, Robert L., 3501 Xenium Ln. N., Apt. 377, Plymouth, 55441. Email: rhazel100@yahoo.com
Hessian, Roger J., 27595 Navaho Ave., Belle Plaine, 56011-8216. Tel: 507-665-4205
Holl, James E., 86 Wilkin St., 55102.
Hubbard, Lawrence E., 1181 Edgcumbe Rd., #101, 55105. Email: l.hubbard@usfamily.net
Hunstiger, Thomas, 1920 Graham Ave., #103, Saint Paul, 55116.
Janski, Jerome J., 10419 El Captain Cir., Sun City, AZ 85351.
Jenniges, Leonard J., 700 3rd Ave., N.W., Sleepy Eye, 56085-1099.
Jude, Robert J., P.O. Box 127, Maple Lake, 55358.
Keane, Robert E., 3059 W. Fuller St., 55417.
Keefe, Gerald E., 2919 Randolph St., N.E., 55418.
Keller, Lawrence E., 1212 Larpenteur Ave. E., Saint Paul, 55109-4335. Tel: 651-771-3223
Kenney, William J., 5545 Nolan Ave. N., Oak Park Heights, 55082.
Kinney, George R., Leo C. Byrne Residence, 60 S.Mississippi River Blvd., 55105. Email: gkinney313@gmail.com
Kittock, Francis R., 60 S. Mississippi River Blvd., Apt. 228, 55102.
Kivel, Joseph G., 1870 Randolph Ave., 55105.
Klaers, Marvin J., 300 Hoosac St., Waterville, 56096.
Kovalik, George J., 5520 Bryant Ave. N., Brooklyn Center, 55430.
Lachner, Anton, 330 Exchange St., 55102.
LaVan, Kenneth G., 1657 Granada N., Apt. 105, Oakdale, 55128.
Lepak, Roy C., 8830 Strand Lake Rd. N., Cotton, 55724.
Ludescher, Kenneth F., 1901 DeSoto St. N., Maplewood, 55117.
Mahon, Ambrose J., 1010 Coventry Pl., Edina, 55435.
Mahoney, Richard J., 60 S. Mississippi River Blvd., Apt. 315, 55105.
Maslowski, Stanley J., P.O. Box 28338, Saint Paul, 55128. Email: smaslowski@guardian-angels.org
McCauley, David, 200 Wilkin St. #210, 55102.
McDonough, Thomas R., 1111 Elway St., #202, Saint Paul, 55116. Tel: 651-699-3527
Meyer, Frederick C., 413 Turril St., #3, Le Sueur, 56058. Tel: 507-665-2998
Monaghan, Robert T., 4334 Bloomington Ave. S., 55407. Tel: 612-822-2101; Fax: 612-822-7928. Email: rtmmpls2003@yahoo.com
Monsour, Raymond G., 16991 Koppy Ln., Avon, 56310. Tel: 320-356-1039. Email: raimundo@mywdo.com
Nolan, Timothy F., P.O. Box 691, Saint Francis, 55070.
Notebaart, James C., 667 5th St. E., 55106. Tel: 612-824-7616 Work; 651-776-7988 Home
Nygaard, Robert C., 6451 207th Ave. N., Wyoming, 55092.
O'Connell, Marvin R., P.O. Box 303, Notre Dame, IN 46556.

O'Rourke, Bryan A., 3740 W. Santa Rosalia Dr., 212, Los Angeles, CA 90008.
Parkos, John F., 1480 Applewood Ct. W., #103, Roseville, 55113.
Paron, William J., 1503 Prosperity Ln., Waconia, 55387-4705. Tel: 952-688-7586. Email: gailjohnson1@peoplepc.com
Pierre, Kenneth J., 894 Hoyt Ave., 55117.
Pierre, Roger P., 1670 Legacy Pwy. E., Maplewood, 55109.
Pouliot, Eugene A., 10902 Quebec Ave. S., Bloomington, 55438-2388. Email: poul44@comcast.net
Pouliot, Francis A., Leo C. Byrne Residence, 60 Mississippi River Blvd. S., 55105-1052. Tel: 651-489-8825 Work; 651-699-6446 Home. Email: stplfrancis@aol.com
Power, J. Timothy, 14218 Chestnut Dr., Eden Prairie, 55347.
Reidy, James E., 60 S. Mississippi River Blvd., Apt. 124, 55105.
Riley, John F., 60 S. Mississippi River Blvd., 55105.
Roach, Francis J., 2132 Bard Ct., P.O. Box 1064, Faribault, 55021.
Roedel, Richard P., Kingsway Retirement Living, 815 W. Main St., #202, Belle Plaine, 56011. Tel: 952-873-5745
Ryan, Patrick J., 2122 N. Twin Lakes St., Saint Croix Falls, WI 54024-7810. Tel: 715-483-1730
Schoenberger, James T., 60 S. Mississippi River Blvd., Apt. 312, 55105.
Siebenaler, John M., 256 Summit Point Dr., Hastings, 55033.
Siebenaler, Leonard, 109 Northwest Ct., Cannon Falls, 55009.
Siebenaler, Martin, 122 Farm St., Hastings, 55033.
Sipe, Robert J., 34351 Sipe Rd., Grand Rapids, 55744.
Skrypek, Gregory A., 51 7th St. W., 55102.
Sledz, Stanley V., 2353 Springside Dr., Maplewood, 55119. Tel: 651-501-0771. Email: revsvps@comcast.net
Slusser, Michael S., Leo C. Byrne Residence, 60 S. Mississippi River Blvd., 55105.
Smith, David W., 2115 Summit Ave., Mail #4137, 55105. Tel: 651-962-5325. Email: dwsmith@stthomas.edu
Sochacki, Walter L., 8008 Bass Lake Rd., #727, New Hope, 55428-3118. Tel: 651-216-6466
Stolzman, William F., Leo C. Byrne Residence, 60 S. Mississippi River Blvd., 55105. Email: wfstolzman@gmail.com
Stromberg, James S., 60 S. Mississippi River Blvd., 55105.
Tibesar, Leo J.
Valit, Robert L., 423 5th St., 55082.
Welch, Gregory T., 181 Edgecumbe Rd., #1402, 55105.
Wertin, George P., 3901 Drew Ave. S., 55410. Tel: 612-922-0460. Email: george@wertinmail.com
Whittier, William O., 2801 Flag Ave. N., New Hope, 55427.
Wolter, Richard J., 60 S. Mississippi River Blvd., Apt. 117, 55105.

Permanent Deacons:
Allen, Nathan Edward, St. Agnes, Saint Paul
Asenbrenner, Francis, (Retired)
Babcock, George H., (Retired)
Barrett, Ervin F., (Retired)
Barrett, Thomas F., (Retired)
Bauer, Randall J., St. Katharine Drexel, Ramsey
Bauhs, James William, Guardian Angels, Chaska
Beck, William E., (Retired)
Becker, Donald L., St. Michael, St. Michael
Bednarczyk, Peter, St. Stephen, Anoka
Beer, Terry, Guardian Angels
Belian, John, St. Anthony, St. Hedwig & Holy Cross, Minneapolis; Health East-St. Joseph Hospital
Bellavance, Peter G., St. Luke, Clearwater
Berghoff, William J., (Retired)
Bernard, Charles V., (Retired)
Bisciglia, Robert Anthony, St. Peter, North Saint Paul
Boatwright, Stephen, St. Joseph, Rosemount
Boisclair, A. Richard, On Leave of Absence
Bowen, Bruce LeDell, St. Raphael, Crystal
Bramwell, Robert, St. Joseph, New Hope
Branch, Darrel Thomas, St. John the Evangelist, Hopkins
Carlson, Roger B., Michaels, Stillwater
Carroll, William, (Archdiocese of Mexico City) St. Odilia, Shoreview
Catapano, Salvatore, Holy Name of Jesus
Chlebeck, Dennis, Maternity of Mary, St. Paul
Christensen, Harlan L., Assigned to further education
Ciresi, Jerome D., Assumption, St. Paul
Clasen, James, On loan to Diocese of Winona
Courrier, Darrel, On loan Archdiocese of Dubuque
Crowley, John, St. Lawrence, Minneapolis
Curtan, Sean, St. Vincent de Paul, Brooklyn Park
D'Heilly, Peter, (Retired)
Damiani, Joseph, Annunication, Minneapolis
DeLuney, Jon Alexander, St. Bonaventure, Bloomington
DeShane, James, St. Edward, Bloomington
Devine, Gerald L., Calix Ministry
Dewitte, Michael, Delano Catholic Community, Delano
Dolan, Thomas E., (Retired)
Dols, Bernard R., (Retired)
Dornfeld, Willard, (Retired)
Downie, Kevin Michael, St. Paul, Zumbrota
Durham, Robert Scott, St. John the Baptist, Savage
Dzik, Thomas W., St. Thomas More
Ehrmantraut, Dominic, St. Stephen, Anoka
Erpenbach, William L., (Retired)
Evans, Patrick, St. Joseph, Red Wing
Feffer, Edward F., (Retired)
Fidler, Donald, Marion Center, St. Paul
Flood, John J., (Retired)
Fredrick, Mark, On loan to Diocese of Knoxville
Freeman, Ronald, St. Timothy, Maple Lake
Friesen, Michael, St. Francis Cabrini, Minneapolis
Garcia Degollado, Ramon, Hispanic Ministry-St. Odilia, Shoreview; St. Stephen, Anoka
Glover, Guy, St. Michael/St. Mary, Stillwater
Gregory, Gabriel, (Retired)
Gruber, Leonard L., St. Dominic, Northfield
Hamilton, Don, St. Rose of Lima, Roseville; St. Timothy, Blaine
Hanson, Dennis, Holy Name, Wayzata
Harrer, Timothy, St. Mary of the Lake, Medicine Lake
Haselhuhn, Walter, (Retired)
Hathaway, Donald F., (Diocese of Knoxville)
Heiman, William, St. Mary, Shakopee; St. Mary of the Purification, Shakopee
Heineman, Richard, St. Bridget, Minneapolis
Helmeke, Timothy, St. Hubert, Chanhassen
Hepp, James E., (Retired)
Herzog, Jack, (Retired)
Hoffman, Gary, St. John the Baptist, Jordan
Holst, David, St. Alphonsus, Brooklyn Park, MN
Houle, Gary J., St. Peter, Forest Lake
Huber, James, On Leave of Absence
Huberty, Peter J., (Retired)
Hughesdon, Harold, St. Agnes, St. Paul
Huibregtse, David, (Retired)
Humbert, Michael, Corpus Christi, Roseville
Ingwell, David, St. Thomas More, St. Paul
Janes, Edward, (Retired)
Jaques, Martin, On Leave
Jents, Kevin, (Retired)
Johanns, Mark, St. Peter, Richfield
Johnson, Fred, St. Peter Claver, St. Paul
Kasbohm, Thomas F., (Retired)
Kelly, Robert, St. Thomas Becket
Kenney, Joseph G., (Retired)
Keyes, Thomas, St. John's Hospital, Maplewood
Kirchoffner, Daniel D., St. Genevieve, Centerville
Kittok, Joseph, St. Joseph, Delano
Klish, Richard, St. John Neumann, Eagan
Kocemba, Russell, Our Lady of the Lake, Mound
Konkel, Thomas A., St. Joseph, Lino Lakes
Koop, Steven E., St. Rita, Cottage Grove
Kuebler, Myon, On Loan to Tuscon
L'Allier, Ralph, St. Peter, Forest Lake
Langlois, Thomas, (Retired)
Lawinger, Lawrence William, Good Shepherd, Golden Valley
Lee, Joseph Chang
Little, Gerald, St. John the Baptist, Savage
Lo, Va Thai, (Retired)
Maier, Steven, St. Francis de Sales; St. Paul
Maltzen, Bruce, Epiphany, Coon Rapids
Mangan, John T., (Retired)
Mann, George A., (Retired)
Marshall, James, All Saints, Lakeville
Martin, Michael, Jr., St. Gregory, North Branch; MN Correctional Facility, Rush City
Masla, John, (Retired)
McDonald, James F., St. Hubert, Chanhassen
McGee, Newell, St. Michael, Pine Island; MN Correctional Facility, Faribault
McLaughlin, James, (Retired)
McPherson, Joseph T., (Retired)
Medley, Michael, St. Timothy Maple Lake
Medlicott, James V., (Retired)
Meyer, James, Cathedral of St. Paul, St. Paul
Michalak, Joseph Thomas, Jr., Holy Spirit, Saint Paul
Michaud, Thomas P., (Retired)
Michaud, Thomas P., Jr., Immaculate Conception, Lonsdale
Moore, Richard, St. Thomas the Apostle
Moravec, Terry, St. Peter, Forest Lake
Moses, Steven, Divine Mercy Catholic, Fairbault
Murphy, John W., Jr., St. John's, Hopkins
Murphy, John L., St. Matthew, St. Paul
Najarian, Stephen, St. Charles Borromeo, Minneapolis
Neumann, Dennis J., (Retired)
Nevin, Michael Patrick, Mary, Queen of Peace, Rogers
Nicklay, John, St. Rita, Cottage Grove
Nugent, George J., All Saints, Lakeville
O'Connor, Kevin, St. Joseph, Maple Grove
O'Connor, Robert, (Retired)
Ochiagha, Ifeangi John, St. Odilia, Shoreview
Ortman, Raymond, St. Victoria, Victoria
Otto, Sherman H., St. Francis Xavier, Buffalo
Palkert, Lawrence, Immaculate Conception, Columbia Heights
Palmer, Rodney, St. John the Baptist, New Brighton
Pashby, Richard E., (Retired)
Pasko, Anthony, Our Lady of Grace, Edina
Pederson, Bernard A., St. Agnes, St. Paul
Pendergast, Donald, (Retired)
Powers, Michael, Our Lady of Mt. Carmel, Minneapolis
Price, James T., St. Thomas Aquinas, Saint Paul Park
Pufahl, James, St. Mark's, Shakopee
Quayle, Thomas, St. John the Baptist, New Brighton
Raleigh, Robert, Our Lady of the Prairie, Belle Plaine; Minnesota Correctional Facility
Ramsey, James, Ph.D., Sacred Heart, Robbinsdale
Reed, John A., Diocese of Duluth
Riordan, William, St. Ambrose, Woodbury
Rollings, Virgil, (Retired)
Roy, Richard, St. Michael, Prior Lake
Rubi, Luis, St. Stephen, Minneapolis; Hennepin County Home School
Rudolphi, Byron W., Jr., (Retired)
Saladin, Jeremiah, Blessed Sacrament & St. Thomas, St. Paul
Saumweber, James, On Leave
Scherer, Terrance P., On Leave of Absence
Scherkenbach, Gerald A., M.A., St. Joseph, West Saint Paul
Schmitz, Joseph, (Retired)
Schneider, Frank J., (Retired)
Schneider, Gary, St. Timothy, Blaine; Unity Hospital, Fridley; Mercy Hospital, Coon Rapids
Schnell, Robert, St. Richard's, Richfield
Schramer, Joseph J., (Retired)
Schroeder, Allan, (Retired)
Schroeder, Alphonse, Pax Christi, Eden Prairie
Seaton, James B., (Retired)
Semlak, Thomas L., St. Pius X, White Bear Lake
Shallbetter, Clarence, Sts. Cyril & Methodius
Shambour, Leonard, (Retired)
Shupe, Russell, Cathedral, St. Paul
Skuta, Glenn, Transfiguration, Annadale
Smisek, Ronald Michael, Holy Trinity/St. Augustine, South Saint Paul
Smith, James, (Retired)
Smith, Joseph, St. Therese, Deephaven
Smith, Robert B., Assumption, Richfield
Sroder, Gregory, St. Peter, North St. Paul
Stahl, George, St. Peter, Oak Grove
Steele, Greg J., St. Michael, Saint Michael (on loan from St. Cloud)
Stevens, Richard, St. John Neuman, Eagan
Stewart, Phillip, Cathedral of St. Paul, St. Paul
Stiles, Thomas G., St. Columba, St. Paul
Stromen, Sherman, (Retired)
Swirtz, Lawrence, (Retired)
Tangney, Francis J., (Retired)
Tatone, Paul M., Our Lady of Peace, Minneapolis
Thell, Frank J., Washington County Sheriff's Dept.
Thornton, James, (Retired)
Tift, J. Neil, On Loan
Timmerman, Dale, (Retired)
Tschann, Paul, Holy Trinity, Goodhue
Umphress, William G., (Retired)
Urbanski, Roger G., (Retired)
Valdez, Carl R., Sagrado Corazon de Jesus, Minneapolis
Vomastek, John Edward, St. Patrick, Inver Grove Heights
Wagner, James M., St. William's, Fridley
Wagner, Robert C., St. Wenceslaus, New Prague
Wallin, John, St. Albert, Albertville; St. John, Dayton
Warhol, Robert W., Mary, Mother of the Church, Burnsville
Warne, Maynard E., St. Michael, St. Michael
Waugh, Charles, St. Stephen, Anoka
Weiland, John D., Immaculate Heart of Mary, Minnetonka
Wesley, R. Daniel, (Retired)
Wierschem, Joseph G., Holy Name, Medina
Winkelman, John W., St. Alphonsus, Brooklyn Center
Winn, Michael, (Retired)
Winninger, Thomas, St. Olaf, Minneapolis

Wittman, Wayne C., Sacred Heart, St. Paul
Witucki, Richard P., St. Bartholomew, Wayzata
Woznick, Greg, St. Henry, Monticello
Wright, Scott, St. John Vianney, South St. Paul
Wurdock, Mike, Our Lady of Lourdes
Yang, Naokao, St. Vincent de Paul, St. Paul
Yekaldo, Fred, (Retired)
Zinda, Timothy, St. Paul's, Ham Lake; Ramsey County Corrections

INSTITUTIONS LOCATED IN THE ARCHDIOCESE

[A] SEMINARIES, ARCHDIOCESAN

ST. PAUL. *St. John Vianney Seminary*, 2115 Summit Ave., #5024, 55105. Tel: 651-962-6825; Fax: 651-962-6835. Email: sjv@stthomas.edu. Web: www.vianney.net. Rev. Michael C. Becker, Rector & Pres. Priests 7; Students 137; Total Staff 6.
Spiritual Directors & Counselors: Revs. John Acrea; Paul Gitter; Carlos Farfan, P.E.S.; Mr. John Daniewicz, Dir. Academic Formation; Revs. Sebastien Bakatu; John J. Bauer; Carlos Farfan, P.E.S.

The Saint Paul Seminary (1894) School of Divinity of the University of St. Thomas, 2260 Summit Ave., 55105. Tel: 651-962-5050; Fax: 651-962-5790. Email: sann8730@stthomas.edu. Web: www.stthomas.edu/sod. Rev. Msgr. Aloysius R. Callaghan, S.T.L., J.C.D., Rector & Vice Pres.; Revs. Andrew H. Cozzens, S.T.D.; J. Michael Byron, S.T.D.; Thomas Margevicius, S.T.L., Dir., Worship; Thomas Fisch, Ph.D.; Kenneth D. Synder, Ph.D.; Charlotte Berres, Ph.D., Assoc. Dir. Pastoral Formation; David Jenkins, D.Mus., Dir. Liturgical Music; Sisters Paul Therese Saiko, S.S.N.D., M.A.; Katarina Schuth, O.S.F., Ph.D.; Revs. Allen Kuss (BIS), Interim Dir. Pastoral Formation; Scott M. Carl, S.S.L.; Jeffrey H. Huard, Dir., Spiritual Formation; John A. Klockeman, Assoc.Dir. Spiritual Formation; Christopher Thompson, Ph.D., Academic Dean; Rev. Robert H. Pish, Vice Rector; Stephen A. Hipp, S.T.D.; Deborah Savage, Ph.D.; Christian D. Washburn, Ph.D.; Revs. Juan Miguel Betancourt, S.E.M.V.; John P. Floeder (On Study Leave); Mr. N. Curtis LeMay, Dir., Archbishop John Ireland Memorial Library.

The Saint Paul Seminary M.Div./Seminarians 100; School of Divinity 74; Priests 11; Sisters 3; Lay Staff 12; Total Staff 26; Students 174.

[B] SEMINARIES, RELIGIOUS, OR SCHOLASTICATES

ST. PAUL. *Jesuit Novitiate*, 1035 Summit Ave., 55105-3034. Tel: 651-224-5593; Fax: 651-224-4734. Revs. Christopher J. Manahan, S.J., Supr. & Socius; Thomas J. Pipp, S.J., Novice Dir.; Charles Rodrigues, S.J., Socius. Priests 3; Total Staff 3; Novices 11.

[C] COLLEGES AND UNIVERSITIES

ST. PAUL. *St. Catherine University* (1905) 2004 Randolph Ave., 55105. Tel: 651-690-6000; Fax: 651-690-8752. Email: admissions@stkate.edu. Web: www.stkate.edu. Andrea J. Lee, Ph.D., IHM Vice Pres.; Colleen Hegranes, Sr. Vice Pres.; Stacy Jacobson, Exec. Asst. to the Pres. & Sec.; Brian Bruess, Ph.D., Vice Pres. Enrollment Mgmt. & Student Affairs; Tom Rooney, Vice Pres. Finance & Admin., CEO & Treas.; Marjorie Mathison Hance, Vice Pres. External Rels.; Alan Silva, Ph.D., Vice Pres. & Dean School of Humanities A&S and College for Women; Penelope Moyers, Dean Henrietta Schnoll School of Health; MaryAnn Janosik, Dean, The School of Professional Studies and The Graduate College; Paula King, Dean, The School of Business and Leadership; Barbra Shank, Ph.D., Dean School of Social Work; Curt Galloway, M.A., Dean Student Affairs; Tone Blechert, M.A., Assoc. Dean Health Profession & Two-Yr. Prog.; Sr. Amata Miller, I.H.M., Ph.D., Dir. Myser Initiative on Catholic Identity; Carol Johnson, Librarian. Sisters of St. Joseph of Carondelet 4; Lay Teachers 322; Total Staff 468; Students 5,327.

University of St. Thomas (1885) 2115 Summit Ave., 55105. Tel: 651-962-5000; Fax: 651-962-6504. Web: www.stthomas.edu. Rev. Dennis J. Dease, Pres.; Susan Huber, Exec. Vice Pres. & Chief Academic Officer; Dr. Susan Alexander, Exec. Advisor to the Pres; Dr. Terence Langan, Interim Dean of the College of Arts & Sciences; Dr. Joseph Kreitzer, Assoc. Vice Pres. Academic Affairs; Jane W. Canney, Vice Pres. Students Affairs; Rev. John M. Malone, Vice Pres. for Mission; Dr. Mark Dienhart, Exec. Vice Pres. & Chief Oper. Officer; Christopher Puto, Ph.D., Dean College of Business; Ms. Karen Lange, Dean of Student Life; Dr. Donald Weinkauf, Dean, School of Engrg.; Dr. Samuel Levy, Vice Pres. Information Resources & Technologies; Mr. Doug Hennes, Vice Pres. Univ. & Govt. Rels.; Mr. Thomas Mengler, J.D., Dean School of Law; Rev. Msgr. Aloysius R. Callaghan, S.T.L., J.C.D., Vice Pres. & Rector of St. Paul Seminary School of Divinity; Dr. Christopher Thompson, Dean St. Paul Seminary School of Divinity; Dr. Bruce Kramer, Dean, College of Applied Professional Studies; Dr. Barbara Shank, Dean School of Social Work; Revs. J. Michael Byron, S.T.D., Asst. Prof. of Systematic Theology, School of Divinity; Andrew H. Cozzens, S.T.D., Instructor, Sacramental Theology; Erich Rutten, M.A., M.Div., Dir. Campus Ministry; Jan Michael Joncas, Assoc. Prof. Theology, Catholic Studies; Thomas Margevicius, S.T.L., Instructor, Sacramental Theology & Liturgy Dir. of Worship; Steven J. McMichael, O.F.M.Cap., Asst. Prof. Theology; Michael J. Keating, Asst. Prof. Catholic Studies; Hugo L. Montero, Campus Ministry, Instructor Theology; David W. Smith, Prof. Theology (Retired); Dwight Reginald Whitt, O.P., Prof. Law; Jean Pierre Bongila, Asst. Prof., Leadership, Policy & Admin.; John Acrea, Spiritual Dir., St. John Vianney Seminary; John A. Klockeman, Formator Spiritual Dir., St. John Vianney Seminary; Michael C. Becker, Rector, St. John Vianney Seminary; Paul Gitter, St. John Vianney Seminary; Scott M. Carl, S.S.L., School of Divinity; Jeffrey H. Huard, School of Divinity; Robert H. Pish, Vice Rector, School of Divinity; Sebastien Bakatu, St. John Vianney Seminary; John J. Bauer, St. John Vianney Seminary; Daniel F. Griffith, Adjunct Prof. Priests 15; Sisters 3; Lay Teachers 862; Students 10,851; Total Faculty & Staff 1,972.

MINNEAPOLIS. *University of St. Thomas*, 1000 La Salle Ave., 55403.

[D] HIGH SCHOOLS, ARCHDIOCESAN

MENDOTA HEIGHTS. *The Saint Thomas Academy*, (Grades 7-12), (Boys), 949 Mendota Heights Rd., 55120-1496. Web: www.cadets.com. Mike Sjoberg, Prin.; Thomas Mich, B.A., M.A., Ph.D., Headmaster; Christina Lindstrom, Librarian. Clergy 2; Lay Teachers 61; Total Staff 63; Students 559.

[E] HIGH SCHOOLS, PRIVATE

ST. PAUL. *Cretin-Derham Hall*, 550 S. Albert St., 55116. Tel: 651-690-2443; Fax: 651-696-3394. Email: rengler@c-dh.org. Web: www.c-dh.org. Richard Engler, Pres. & Prin.; Kathleen Roy, Librarian. Co-Sponsors: Brothers of the Christian Schools and Sisters of St. Joseph of Carondelet. Brothers 3; Lay Teachers 98; Students 1,322; Total Staff 168.

MINNEAPOLIS. *Cristo Rey Jesuit High School - Twin Cities*, 2924 - 4th Ave. S, 55408. Tel: 612-545-9700. Jeb Myers, Prin.; Rev. Timothy T. Manatt, S.J., Pres. & Headmaster; Mariah Snyder, Librarian. Clergy 2; Brothers 1; Lay Teachers 21; Students 280; Total Staff 22.

DeLaSalle High School, One DeLaSalle Dr., 55401. Tel: 612-676-7600; Fax: 612-676-7691. Email: principal@delasalle.com. Web: www.delasalle.com. Barry C. Lieske, A.F.S.C., Prin.; Rev. Patrick Thomas Barnes, Chap.; Judith Roggow, Librarian. Clergy 1; Brothers 2; Lay Teachers 35; Students 637.

Totino-Grace High School, 1350 Gardena Ave., N.E., Fridley, 55432-5899. Tel: 763-571-9116; Fax: 763-571-9118. Email: julie.michels@totinograce.org. Web: www.totinograce.org. Dr. William Hudson, Pres.; Julie Michels, Prin.; Christie Burke, Librarian. Brothers 1; Lay Teachers 60; Students 805; Total Staff 130.

FARIBAULT. *Bethlehem Academy*, (Grades 7-12), 105 Third Ave. S.W., 55021. Tel: 507-334-3948; Fax: 507-334-3949. Email: slangfeldt@bacards.org. Web: www.bacards.org. Sherri Langfeldt, Prin. Lay Teachers 20; Students 300; Total Staff 38.

MAPLEWOOD. *Hill-Murray School*, (Grades 7-12), 2625 Larpenteur Ave. E., 55109-5098. Tel: 651-777-1376; Fax: 651-748-2444. Email: spaul@hill-murray.org. Web: www.hill-murray.org. Dr. Susan Paul, Pres.; David Meyer, Prin.; Jane Rolnick, Librarian; Rev. James Lannan, Chap. Lay Teachers 59; Students 765; Total Staff 99.

MENDOTA HEIGHTS. *Convent of the Visitation School* (1873) (Grades PreK-12), 2455 Visitation Dr., 55120. Tel: 651-683-1700; Fax: 651-454-7144. Email: phealy@vischool.org. Web: www.visitation.net. Dr. Dawn Nichols, Head of School; Patty Healy Janssen, Dir. Enrollment; Michelle Mechtel, Dir. Lower School; Curt Zander, Dir. Middle School; Renee Genereux, Dir. Upper School; Tracy Joyce, Librarian Lower School; Harriet Spira, Librarian Middle & Upper School; Rev. Anthony O'Neill, Chap. Grades P-6 are co-ed classes. Day School for Girls grades 7-12. Sisters 1; Lay Teachers 48; Total Faculty 49; Students 567; Total Staff 69.

RICHFIELD. *Academy of Holy Angels*, 6600 Nicollet Ave. S., 55423-2498. Tel: 612-798-2600; Fax: 612-798-2610. Email: tshipley@academyofholyangels.org. Web: www.academyofholyangels.org. Thomas Shipley, Pres.; Heidi Foley, Prin.; Sheila Brennan, Media Dir. Priests 1; Lay Teachers 56; Students 708; Total Staff 110; Faculty 56.

ST. LOUIS PARK. *Benilde-St. Margaret's School* (1907) (Grades 7-12), 2501 Hwy. 100 S., 55416. Email: sskinner@bsmschool.org. Web: www.bsmschool.org. Dr. Sue Skinner, Prin.; Dr. Bob Tift, Pres. & Headmaster; Lynn Bottge, Librarian. Sisters 1; Lay Teachers 92; Students 920; Total Staff 93.

VICTORIA. *Holy Family Catholic High School* (2000) 8101 Kochia Ln., 55386. Tel: 952-443-4659; Fax: 952-443-1822. Email: communications@hfchs.org. Web: www.hfchs.org. Scott Lutz, Chm.; Mary Steiner, Vice Chm.; Tim Collins, Sec.; Kathleen Brown, Pres. & Prin; Kari Lenzmeier, Librarian. Lay Teachers 47; Students 550; Total Staff 68.

[F] ELEMENTARY SCHOOLS, CONSOLIDATED, PAROCHIAL

ST. PAUL. *Highland Catholic School*, (Grades PreK-8), 2017 Bohland Ave., 55116. Tel: 651-690-2477; Fax: 651-699-1869. Email: jschmidt@highlandcatholic.org. Web: www.highlandcatholic.org. Jane Schmidt, Prin.; Helen Stasson, Librarian. Serving the parishes of Lumen Christi Catholic Community. Lay Teachers 30; Students 457; Total Staff 56.

Maternity of Mary/St. Andrew School (1953) (Grades PreSchool-8), 592 Arlington Ave. W., 55117. Tel: 651-489-1459; Fax: 651-489-3560. Email: principal@mmsaschool.org. Web: www.mmsaschool.org. Athena Novack, Prin.; Beth Sullivan, Librarian. Serving the parishes in the Como Park neighborhood Sisters 1; Lay Teachers 16; Students 215; Total Staff 23.

MINNEAPOLIS. *Carondelet Catholic School*, (Grades K-8) Tel: 612-927-8673; 612-920-9075; Fax: 612-927-7426. Sue Kerr, Prin.; Sandy Knauff, Librarian. Cooperative program with St. Thomas the Apostle, Minneapolis. Lay Teachers 29; Students 441.

Pope John Paul II Catholic School, (Grades K-8), 1630 Fourth St, N.E., 55413. Tel: 612-789-8851; Fax: 612-789-8773. Web: www.popejohnpaul2ne.org. Debra King, Prin. Serving the parishes of St. Cyril & Methodius, Holy Cross, St. Anthony, All Saints, Our Lady of Lourdes, St. Hedwig, St. Clement, St. Boniface, Our Lady of Mt. Carmel and St. Lawrence. Lay Teachers 10; Students 146; Total Staff 25.

Risen Christ Catholic School (1993) (Grades K-8), 1120 E. 37th St., 55407. Tel: 612-822-5329; Fax: 612-729-2336. Email: info@risenchristschool.org. Web: risenchristschool.org. Helen Dahlman, Pres.; Liz Ramsey, Prin.; Fran Rusciano Murnane, Dir. Advancement. Founded by the parishes of Holy Name, Holy Rosary, Incarnation, St. Albert the Great and St. Stephen. Lay Teachers 21; Students 332; Total Staff 39.

EAGAN. *Faithful Shepherd Catholic School*, (Grades K-8), 3355 Columbia Dr., 55121. Tel: 651-406-4747; Fax: 651-406-4743. Email: info@fscsmn.org. Web: www.fscsmn.org. Rev. Joseph G. Gallatin, Canonical Admin.; John Boone, Exec. Dir.; Terese Shimshock, Prin.; Deb DeSteno, Librarian. Serving the parishes of St. Peter, St. John Neumann and St. Thomas Becket. Lay Teachers 35; Total Staff 55; Total Enrollment 557.

FARIBAULT. *Divine Mercy Catholic School*, (Grades PreK-6), 15 S.W. Third Ave., 55021. Tel: 507-334-7706; Fax: 507-332-2669. Email: bseidel@dmcs.cc; pjohnson@dmcs.cc. Web: www.dmcs.cc. Mr. Robert Seidel, Prin.; Peggy Johnson, Sec. & Scrip Coord. Serving the parish of Divine Mercy Catholic Church. Lay Teachers 18; Students 281; Total Staff 29.

PLYMOUTH. **Cedarcrest Academy*, 12325 Hwy. 55, P.O. Box 46255, 55446.

RICHFIELD. *Blessed Trinity Catholic School of Richfield, Minnesota* (1994) (Grades PreK-8), 6720 Nicollet Ave., 55423. Tel: 612-866-5200; Fax: 612-767-2191. Email: kerrs@btcsmn.org. Web: www.btcsmn.org. Patrick O'Keefe, Prin. Serving the parishes of Assumption, St. Peter's and St. Richard's. Lay Teachers 21; Students 370; Total Staff 48.

SHAKOPEE. *Shakopee Area Catholic Education Consolidation, Inc.* (1895) (Grades PreK-8), 2700 17th Ave. E., 55379. Tel: 952-445-3387; Fax: 952-445-7256. Email: dlee@sacsschools.org. Web: www.sacsschools.org. Diane M. Lee, Pres.; Scott

Breimhorst, Prin.; Bruce Doyle, Dean of Students; Sandy Greening, Librarian. Serving the parishes of St. Mark, St. Mary, St. Mary of the Purification. Lay Teachers 47; Students 861; Total Staff 92.

STILLWATER. *St. Croix Catholic School*, (Grades PreSchool-8), 621 S. Third St., 55082. Tel: 651-439-5581; Fax: 651-439-8360. Email: srmaryjuliana@stccs.com. Web: www.stcroixcatholic.com. Rev. Michael J. Miller, Canonical Admin.; Sr. Mary Juliana, Prin.; Jenny Koenning, Librarian. Serving the parishes of St. Charles, Bayport; St. Mary, Stillwater; St. Michael, Stillwater. Sisters 4; Lay Teachers 26; Students 415; Total Staff 30.

WEBSTER. *Holy Cross Catholic School*, (Grades PreSchool-8), 6100 37th St. W., 55088. Tel: 952-652-6100; Fax: 952-652-6102. Email: lisar@holycrossschool.net. Web: www.holycrossschool.net. Lisa Reicherlt, Prin.; Rev. Thomas E. McCabe, Canonical Admin. Serving the parishes of Lonsdale, New Market and Veseli. Lay Teachers 15; Students 220; Total Staff 30.

[G] GENERAL HOSPITALS

ST. PAUL. **HealthEast St. Joseph's Hospital* (1853) 45 W. 10th St., 55102. Tel: 651-232-4144; Fax: 651-232-3518. Email: sjcriger@healtheast.org. Sara Criger, CEO & Vice Pres.; Revs. Stephen J. LaCanne, M.Div., N.A.C.C., Dir., Spiritual Care. Tel: 651-232-3060; Fax: 651-232-4155; Jonathan Fischer, O.S.B. Priests 2; Bed Capacity 425; Lay Staff 1,216; Total Staff 1,600; Total Assisted 17,000.

St. Mary's Health Clinics (1992) 1884 Randolph Ave., 55105-1700. Tel: 651-287-7700; Fax: 651-690-7075. Email: bdickie@stmarysclinics.org. Web: www.stmaryshealthclinics.org. Barbara L. Dickie, Exec. Dir. Neighborhood Clinics 8; Park Nicollet Clinics 11; Patients Visist Annually 14,260; Total Staff 18; Lay Staff 16; Sisters 2.

HASTINGS. *Regina Medical Center*, 1175 Nininger Rd., 55033. Tel: 651-480-4100; Fax: 651-480-4212. Email: kochendorferp@reginamedical.org. Web: www.reginamedical.org. Ty Erickson, CEO; Rev. Robert J. Altier, Chap.; Sr. LaVonne Schackman; Mary Salm, Dir. Pastoral Care; Joanne Peters, Contact. A part of Regina Healthcare. Patients Assisted Annually 46,983; Total Staff 495; Bed Capacity 57.

SHAKOPEE. *St. Francis Regional Medical Center* (1938) 1455 St. Francis Ave., 55379-3380. Tel: 952-428-2401; Fax: 952-428-2656. Web: www.stfrancis-shakopee.com. Mike Baumgartner, M.S.A., CEO & Pres.; Diana Robertson, Chap. & Mgr. Spiritual Care Dept. Sponsored by Sisters of St. Benedict, Duluth, MN. Nurses 251; Bed Capacity 93; Patients Assisted Annually 114,645; Total Staff 771.

[H] SPECIAL HOSPITALS AND SANATORIA FOR INVALIDS

ST. PAUL. *Our Lady of Peace Home* (1941) 2076 St. Anthony Ave., 55104-5096. Tel: 651-646-2797; Fax: 651-646-7884. Web: www.franciscancare.org. Franciscan Health Community Nursing Sisters 4; Bed Capacity 40; Patients Assisted Annually 173; Total Staff 40.

[I] HOMES FOR AGED

ST. PAUL. *Bethany Convent for Retired Sisters*, 1884 Randolph, 55105. Tel: 651-696-2500; Fax: 651-696-2501. Email: bcarlson@csjstpaul.org. Sisters Lillian Waldera, C.S.J., M.A., Community Living Coord.; George Ann Bohl, C.S.J., B.A., Asst. Community Living Coord.; Kevin Bopp, C.S.J., Assoc. Community Living Coord. Sisters of St. Joseph of Carondelet, St. Paul Province. Bed Capacity 160; Lay Staff 120; Total in Residence 100.

Franciscan Health Community (1936) 2076 St. Anthony Ave., Saint Paul, 55104. Tel: 651-646-2797; Fax: 651-789-0690. Email: ceo@fhcare.org. Web: www.franciscancare.org. Joseph Stanislav, Pres. & CEO. Total Assisted Annually 490; Total Staff 90.

Holy Family Residence, 330 Exchange St. S., 55102. Tel: 651-227-0336; Fax: 651-227-7321. Email: msstpaul@littlesistersofthepoor.org. Web: www.littlesistersofthepoor.org. Sr. Theresa Robertson, Supr., Admin. & Pres. Little Sisters of the Poor 11; Aged Residents 73; Apartments 32; Bed Capacity 73; Total Staff (All Facilities) 103; Total Assisted Annually 116.

MINNEAPOLIS. *Benedictine Health Center of Minneapolis*, 618 E. 17th St, 55404. Tel: 612-879-2800. Mr. David Brennan, Admin. & CEO.

HASTINGS. *Regina Retirement Center*, 1175 Nininger Rd., 55033. Tel: 651-480-4100; Fax: 651-480-6801. Email: kochendorferp@reginamedical.org. Web: www.reginamedical.org. Rev. Robert J. Altier, Resident Chap. Total Assisted Annually 349; Total Staff 168; Bed Capacity 190.

Regina Medical Center Tel: 651-480-4100; Fax: 651-480-6801. A part of Regina Healthcare. Number under care 181; Nursing Care 61; Assisted Living 129; Total Staff 168.

SHAKOPEE. *St. Gertrude's Health and Rehabilitation Center*, 1850 Sarazin St., 55379. Tel: 952-233-4400; Fax: 952-233-4476. Web: www.stgertrudesshakopee.org. Lee Larson, CEO & Admin.; Bill Wermerskirchen, Chairperson; Kevin Rymanowski, Treas. Bed Capacity 115; Total Staff 183; Total Assisted Annually 26,500.

The Gardens at St. Gertrudes Assisted Living

[J] MONASTERIES AND RESIDENCES OF PRIESTS AND BROTHERS

ST. PAUL. *Congregation of the Sons of the Immaculate Conception*, 261 8th St. E., 55101. Tel: 651-222-2619; Fax: 651-224-1190. Revs. Biju Mathew, C.F.I.C., Supr. & Pastor; Antony Skaria, C.F.I.C., Chap.; Benny Mekkatt Varghese, C.F.I.C., Chap.

Oblate Residence, 104 N. Mississippi River Blvd., 55104-2374. Tel: 651-645-3560; Fax: 651-645-3704. Bro. Anthony Szklarski, O.M.I., Dir. of House In Res. Revs. Ronald Harrer, O.M.I.; Robert Morin, O.M.I.; John E. Pilaczynski, O.M.I.

Sacred Heart Friary, 840 6th St. E., 55106-4543. Tel: 651-776-2741; Fax: 651-776-2759. Revs. Eugene Michel, O.F.M.; Raymond Rickels, O.F.M.; Bro. Robert Gross, O.F.M.

MINNEAPOLIS. *St. Albert the Great Priory*, 2833 32nd Ave. S., 55406. Tel: 612-724-3644; Fax: 612-724-5057. Email: dommpls@comcast.net. Revs. James A. Spahn, O.P., Prior; Joseph E. Bidwill, O.P.; Paul J. Johnson, O.P., Lector; Cornelius A. Kilroy, O.P.; Joseph P. Gillespie, O.P.; Bros. William E. (Kevin) Carroll, O.P.; Raymond (Steven) Bryce, O.P. Order of Preachers (Dominicans). Province of St. Albert the Great. Total in Residence 7.

St. Bridget Friary, 3811 Emerson Ave. N., 55412-2038. Tel: 612-529-2526; Fax: 612-529-8451. Web: www.franciscanfriarstor.com. Very Rev. Anthony M. Criscitelli, T.O.R., Pastor & Econome; Bros. John Kerr, T.O.R., Pastoral Min. & Local Min., St. Bridget Parish; David Liedl, T.O.R., Student. Third Order Regular of St. Francis, Province of the Immaculate Conception. Priests 1; Brothers 2.

St. Gerard Friary (1990) 9600 Regent Ave. N., Brooklyn Park, 55443-1499. Tel: 763-425-7659; 763-424-8770. Revs. Bradley C. Baldwin, T.O.R., B.A., M.Div., Pastor; Edward J. Sabo, T.O.R., B.A., M.M.Ed., Parocial Vicar.

Markoe House Jesuit Community, 2900 11th Ave. S. 1017-1019, 55407-5171. Revs. Philip F. Dreckman, S.J.; Charles Sim Teck Kim, S.J.; Leon F. Klimczyk, S.J.; Matthew L. Linn, S.J.; Charles Sim, S.J. *Pro Ecclesia Sancta Residence SEMV Residence*

Paulist Fathers, 1203 5th St., S.E., 55414. Tel: 612-331-7941; Fax: 612-378-1771. Email: parish@umncatholic.org. Web: www.umncatholic.org. Revs. Ivan Tou, C.S.P., Pastor & Dir.; Robert J. O'Donnell. Total in Residence 2.

BLOOMINGTON. *St. Bonaventure Friary*, 901 E. 90th St., 55420. Tel: 952-854-4731. Revs. Richard Kaley, O.F.M.Conv., Guardian; Charles McCarthy, O.F.M.Conv.; Bro. Jeffrey Hines, O.F.M.Conv.

Maryknoll Fathers and Brothers, Catholic Foreign Mission Society of America (1911) P.O. Box 20626, 55420. Tel: 952-884-1024. Email: minneapolis@maryknoll.org. Web: www.maryknoll.org. Mr. Gregory Darr, Dir.; Rev. Edward M. Doughtery, Supr. Gen.; Bette Jane Baxter.

BROOKLYN CENTER. *Redemptorist Fathers of Hennepin County*, 7025 Halifax Ave. N., 55429-1394. Tel: 763-561-5100; Fax: 763-561-0336. Revs. William Bueche, C.Ss.R., Parochial Vicar; Brian Gilles, C.Ss.R., Parochial Vicar; Peter Connolly, C.Ss.R., Parochial Vicar; Tuan Nguyen, C.Ss.R., Parochial Vicar; Steven Nyl, C.Ss.R., Parochial Vicar; Wilfred Lowery, C.Ss.R., Parochial Vicar; Thomas Pham, C.Ss.R., Parochial Vicar; Joseph Stenger, C.Ss.R., Parochial Vicar; Martin Stillmock, C.Ss.R., Parochial Vicar.

LAKE ELMO. *Carmelite Hermitage of the Blessed Virgin Mary* (1987) 8249 De Montreville Tr. N., 55042-9545. Tel: 651-779-7351. Email: carmelus@earthlink.net. Web: www.decorcarmeli.com. Revs. Patrick Peter Peach, O.Carm.; John M. Burns, O.Carm., Prior; Joseph V. Vaccaro, O.Carm. Carmel of the Blessed Virgin Mary. Priests 3; Brothers 5.

PRIOR LAKE. *St. Joseph Cupertino Friary*, 16385 St. Francis Ln., 55372. Tel: 952-447-2182. Bro. Bob Roddy, O.F.M.Conv., Vicar; Revs. Steven McMichael, O.F.M.Conv., Guardian; Jude Rochford, O.F.M.Conv.; James Van Dorn, O.F.M.Conv.; Juniper Cummings, O.F.M.Conv.; Thomas Merrill, O.F.M.Conv.

[K] CONVENTS AND RESIDENCES FOR SISTERS

ST. PAUL. *Contemplative Sisters of the Good Shepherd*, 5391 Nolan Ln., Oak Park Heights, 55082-6493. Tel: 651-275-5492; Fax: 651-482-5242. Email: cgsstpaul@gmail.com. Sr. Beverly Hedgecoth, Coord. Sisters 5.

Franciscan Sisters of St. Paul (1863) Franciscan Regional Center, 1388 Prior Ave. S., 55116. Tel: 651-690-1501; Fax: 651-690-2509. Email: spfranci@askmotherrose.org. Web: www.askmotherrose.org. Sr. Mary Lucy Scheffler, O.S.F., Supr. Sisters 8.

St. Mary's Mission House (1894) 265 Century Ave., 55125. Tel: 651-738-9704; Fax: 651-738-9704. Email: sspcdelegateoffice@usfamily.net. Web: www.clavermissionarysisters.org. Sr. Genevieve Kudlik, S.S.P.C., Supr. Missionary Sisters of St. Peter Claver. Sisters 8.

Monastery of the Visitation (1873) 2455 Visitation Dr., Mendota Heights, 55120. Tel: 651-683-1700; Fax: 651-454-0602. Sisters Mary Denise Villaume, V.H.M., Supr.; Brigid Marie Keefe, Sec. Visitation Nuns 9.

St. Paul's Monastery, 2675 Benet Rd., 55109-4808. Tel: 651-777-8181; Fax: 651-773-5124. Email: srlucia@stpaulsmonastery.org. Web: www.osb.org/spm. Sisters Lucia Schwickerath, O.S.B., Prioress; Linda Soler, O.S.B., Subprioress. Benedictine Sisters of Pontifical Jurisdiction. Sisters 44.

Sisters of St. Joseph of Carondelet (1851) 1884 Randolph Ave., 55105-1700. Tel: 651-690-7000; Fax: 651-690-7039. Web: www.csjstpaul.org. Sisters of Province 260; Total Staff 186.

Province Leadership Team: Carondelet Center; St. Joseph School of Music; Editorial Development Associates; Good Ground Press; St. Mary's Health Clinics; Youth & Family Center, Inc.; Sisters of St. Joseph of Carondelet Ministries Foundation, St. Paul Province; Learning in Style; Women at the Well; Adult Literacy; St. Catherine University; Minnesota Center for Health Care Ethics; Wisdom Ways: A Resource Center for Spirituality; St. Joseph Worker Program; Sarah's, an Oasis for Women; Celeste's Dream; Dwelling in the Woods; CSJ Ministry Collaborative. Sisters Katherine Rossini, C.S.J.; Margaret Gillespie, C.S.J.; Jean Wincek, C.S.J.

MINNEAPOLIS. *St. Clare's Monastery of the Infant Jesus*, 8650 Russell Ave. S., 55431-1998. Tel: 952-881-4766. Email: fgosc@juno.com. Web: www.poorclaresminneapolis.org. Sr. Frances Getchell, O.S.C., Abbess. Franciscan Poor Clare Nuns. Professed Nuns 11.

Visitation Monastery of Minneapolis, 1527 Fremont Ave. N., 55411. Tel: 612-521-6113; Fax: 612-521-4020. Email: vmonastery@aol.com. Web: www.visitationmonasteryminneapolis.org. Sr. Karen Mohan, V.H.M., Supr. Sisters 6.

DEEPHAVEN. *Franciscan Clarist Congregation, F.C.C.*, Vimala Province, Convent of St. Therese House, 17931 Minnetonka Blvd., 55391-3322. Tel: 952-473-4771. Email: srtresamargret@yahoo.com. Sr. Tresa Margaret, Prin. & Regl. Supr. Total in Residence 15.

LAKE ELMO. *Carmel of Our Lady of Divine Providence* (1952) 8251 De Montreville Tr. N., 55042-9547. Tel: 651-777-3882. Sr. Rose of the Sacred Heart, O.C.D., Prioress; Rev. John M. Burns, O.Carm., Chap. Discalced Carmelite Nuns. Professed 12.

[L] SECULAR INSTITUTES

ST. PAUL. *Missionaries of the Kingship of Christ*, 8951 Thomas Ln., Woodbury, 55125. Tel: 651-501-3640. Email: woodburyjane@aol.com. Web: www.simrc.org. Secular Institute of Pontifical Right for women and men founded in Italy in 1919.

[M] RETREAT HOUSES AND CENTERS OF SPIRITUALITY

ST. PAUL. *Benedictine Center - St. Paul's Monastery*, 2675 Benet Rd., 55109. Tel: 651-777-7251; Fax: 651-773-5124. Email: benedictinecenter@stpaulsmonastery.org. Web: www.stpaulsmonastery.org. Sam Rahberg, Dir. Total Staff 1.

Loyola, 389 N. Oxford St., 55104. Tel: 651-641-0008; Fax: 651-641-0554. Email: loyolasrr.@comcast.net. Web: www.loyolaspiritualitycenter.org. Tom Allen, Spiritual Dir.; David Rothstein, Spiritual Dir.; Sheila Laughton, Spiritual Dir.; Barbara Leonard, Spiritual Dir.; Kay VanderVort, M.A., Spiritual Dir.; Sisters Joanne Dehmer, S.S.N.D., M.A., Spiritual Dir.; Elizabeth Kerwin, C.S.J., Spiritual Dir.; Nancy Loyd, Spiritual Dir. Total Staff 10.

Maryhill (1790) 1988 Summit Ave., 55105. Tel: 651-696-2970. Email: maryhill1988@aol.com. Web:

www.dhmna.org. Daughters of the Heart of Mary 5; Total in Residence 1; Total Staff 1.

BUFFALO. *Christ the King Retreat Center* (1952) 621 First Ave. S., 55313. Tel: 763-682-1394; Fax: 763-682-3453. Email: christtheking@kingshouse.com. Web: www.kingshouse.com. Revs. Aloysius Svobodny, O.M.I.; Raymond R. Kirtz, O.M.I.; Louis Studer, O.M.I., Dir.; James Deegan, O.M.I.; Lon Konold, O.M.I.; Gari Ruthenberg, O.M.I.; Bro. Daniel Bozek, O.M.I. Priests 6; Brothers 1; Total in Residence 7; Lay Staff 31; Total Staff 38.

FRONTENAC. *Villa Maria Retreat and Conference Center*, 29847 County 2 Blvd., 55026. Tel: 651-345-4582; Fax: 651-345-3457. Email: info@villamariaretreats.org. Web: villamariaretreats.org. Rhonda McKim, Interim Exec. Dir. Total Served Annually 4,598.

LAKE ELMO. *Jesuit Retreat House* (1948) 8243 Demontreville Tr. N., 55042-9545. Tel: 651-777-1311; Fax: 651-777-1312. Revs. Edward S. Sthokal, S.J., Asst.; Patrick M. McCorkell, S.J., Office Dir. Total in Residence 2; Total Staff 10.

MARINE ON ST. CROIX. *Christian Brothers Retreat Center*, 15525 St. Croix Tr. N., 55047. Tel: 651-433-2486; Fax: 651-433-5755. Email: dunrovin@dunrovin.org. Web: www.dunrovin.org. Jerome Meeds, Pres. Total in Residence 9; Total Staff 18; Total Assisted 3,332; Bed Capacity 65.

PRIOR LAKE. *Franciscan Retreats* (1956) 16385 Saint Francis Ln., 55372. Tel: 952-447-2182; Fax: 952-447-2170. Email: director@franciscanretreats.net. Web: www.franciscanretreats.net. Revs. Steven McMichael, O.F.M.Conv., Guardian; James Van Dorn, O.F.M.Conv., Assoc. Dir.; Bro. Bob Roddy, O.F.M.Conv., Retreat Dir.; Rev. Juniper Cummings, O.F.M.Conv., Sacramental Min. Priests 3; Brothers 1; Lay Staff 6; Staff 9; People Served 1,700. In Res. Revs. Thomas Merrill, O.F.M.Conv.; Robert Showers, O.F.M.Conv.

[N] HOMES FOR DISABLED

ST. PAUL. *Our House of Minnesota, Inc. I* (1975) 1846 Dayton Ave., 55104. Tel: 651-644-6650; Fax: 651-646-1104. Bed Capacity 6; Staff 21; Mentally Handicapped Adults 6; Total Assisted 6.
Office: Tel: 615-646-1104; Fax: 615-646-1104. Dennis Holman, Admin.

Our House of Minnesota, Inc. II (1975) 1846 Portland, 55104. Tel: 651-644-2411; Fax: 651-646-1104. Bed Capacity 6; Staff 21; Mentally Handicapped Adults 6; Total Assisted Annually 6.
Office: Tel: 615-646-1104; Fax: 615-646-1104. Dennis Holman, Admin.

[O] ASSOCIATIONS OF THE FAITHFUL

ST. PAUL. *The Companions of Christ* (1992) 2137 Marshall Ave., 55104. Tel: 651-642-5933. Email: contact@companionsofchrist.org. Web: www.CompanionsOfChrist.org. Rev. Jon Vander Ploeg, Supr. Total Membership 13.

Franciscan Brothers of Peace, Queen of Peace Friary, 1289 Lafond Ave., 55104-2035. Tel: 651-646-8586; Fax: 651-646-9083. Email: franciscan@brothersofpeace.org. Web: www.brothersofpeace.org. Bros. Paul O'Donnell, F.B.P., Guardian Overall; Joseph Katzmarek, F.B.P., Vicar; Conrad Richardson, F.B.P., Vocation Dir.; James Voeller, F.B.P.; John Mary Kaspari, F.B.P.; Pio King, F.B.P.; Seraphim Wirth, F.B.P.; Maximilian Connolly, F.B.P. Total in Residence 8; Total Staff 1.

WEST ST. PAUL. *Community of Christ the Redeemer*, 110 Crusader Ave. W., 55118. Tel: 651-451-6123; Fax: 651-453-0810. Email: info@ccredeemer.org. Web: www.ccredeemer.org. Dr. James C. Kolar, Pres.

[P] PUBLIC ASSOCIATION OF THE FAITHFUL

ST. PAUL. *Franciscan Brothers of Peace*, Queen of Peace Friary, 1289 Lafond Ave., 55104-2035. Tel: 651-646-8586; Fax: 651-646-9083. Web: www.brothersofpeace.org. Bros. Paul O'Donnell, F.B.P., Guardian Overall; Conrad Richardson, F.B.P., Vocation Dir.; Joseph Katzmarek, F.B.P., QPF House Guardian, Vicar; John Mary Kaspari, F.B.P.; Pio King, F.B.P.; Maximilian Connolly, F.B.P., Novice; James Voeller, F.B.P.; Seraphim Wirth, F.B.P.

[Q] CAMPS AND COMMUNITY CENTERS

MCGREGOR. *Catholic Youth Camps, Inc.*, Administrative Offices: 2131 Fairview Ave. N., #200, Roseville, 55113. Tel: 651-636-1645; Fax: 651-628-9323. Email: office@cycamp.org. Web: www.cycamp.org. Camp location: 19590 520th Ln., 55760. Tel: 218-426-3383. Natalie King, Exec. Dir.; Rev. Robert C. Nygaard, Pres., Bd. Dirs. (Retired); John Breon, Chm. & Vice Pres., Bd. Dirs. Total Assisted 650; Total Staff 20.

[R] NEWMAN CENTERS

MINNEAPOLIS. *Newman Center at St. Lawrence* 1203 5th St., S.E., 55414. Tel: 612-331-7941; Fax: 612-378-1771. Email: parish@umncatholic.org. Web: www.umncatholic.org. Revs. Ivan Tou, C.S.P.; Robert J. O'Donnell. Total Staff 3.

[S] MISCELLANEOUS LISTINGS

ST. PAUL. *Aim Higher Minnesota Foundation*, 226 Summit Ave., 55102.

**Catholic Community Foundation*, One Water St. W., Ste. 200, Saint Paul, 55107. Tel: 651-389-0300; Fax: 651-389-0650. Email: info@ccf-mn.org. Web: www.ccf-mn.org. Dr. Marilou Eldred, Pres.

Christian Brothers Youth Home (1983) 1540 Lincoln Ave., 55105. Tel: 651-699-0736. Bro. Michael Lee Anderson, F.S.C., Dir.; Mr. Bob Paradise, Pres. Brothers 1; Bed Capacity 5; Total Assisted 6; Total Staff 1.

Common Bond Communities, 328 Kellogg Blvd. W., 55102. Tel: 651-291-1750; Fax: 651-291-1003. Web: www.commonbond.org. Mr. Paul Fate, Pres. & CEO.

Francophone African Chaplaincy, 226 Summit Ave., 55102. Rev. Jules Omba Omalanga, Chap.

Friends of Catholic Urban Schools (FOCUS), 375 N. Oxford St., 55104. Tel: 651-646-1797; Fax: 651-647-1797. Web: www.focustwincities.org. Thomas McCarver, Exec. Dir.

Growing in Faith Capital Campaign, 226 Summit Ave., 55102. Tel: 651-290-1610; Fax: 651-290-1609.

**Minnesota Catholic Education Association*, 475 University Ave., 55103-1996. Tel: 651-227-8777; Fax: 651-227-2675. Email: pnoll@mncc.org. Web: www.mncc.org. Dr. Peter Noll, Exec. Dir.

Minnesota Conference of Catholic Bishops, 475 University Ave. W., Ste. B, 55103. Tel: 651-227-8777; Fax: 651-227-2675. Email: info@mncc.org. Web: www.mncc.org. Jason Adkins, Exec. Dir.; Dr. Peter A. Noll, Dir. Educ. The M.C.C. is a Minnesota Corporation, the purpose of which is to promote the general welfare of the people of the State of Minnesota. All Catholic Bishops of the State of Minnesota constitute Ex Officio the Board of Directors. Total Staff 7.

Nativity of Our Lord Endowment Fund, 1900 Wellesley Ave., 55105. Tel: 651-696-5401; Fax: 651-696-5458. Email: info@nativity-mn.org. Web: www.nativity-mn.org. Laura Barr, Admin. Total Assisted 5,000.

Oblate Media and Communication Corporation, 104 N. Mississippi River Blvd., 55104. Tel: 651-645-3560. Rev. William Antone, O.M.I., Provincial, U.S. Province.

Sisters of St. Joseph of Carondelet Ministries Foundation, St. Paul Province, 1884 Randolph Ave., 55105. Tel: 651-690-7026; Fax: 651-690-7039. Email: rscorpio@csjministriesfoundation.org. Web: www.csjministriesfoundation.org. Ralph Scorpio, Exec. Dir.

WomanWell, 1784 La Crosse Ave., 55119-4808. Tel: 651-739-7953; Fax: 651-739-7475. Email: seeking@WomanWell.org. Web: www.womanwell.org. Sr. Delmarie Gibney, F.S.P.A., Dir. Sisters 3; Bed Capacity 13; Total Staff 3; Total Assisted 3,600.

MINNEAPOLIS. *Catholic Eldercare, Inc.* (1982) 817 Main St., N.E., 55413. Tel: 612-379-1370; Fax: 612-362-2486. Email: ksmyth@catholiceldercare.org. Web: www.catholiceldercare.org. Dan Johnson, Pres. & CEO. Total Assisted 439; Total Staff 340.

Skilled Nursing Facility Tel: 612-379-1370; Fax: 612-379-2486. Web: www.catholiceldercare.org. Bed Capacity 150; Lay Staff 272; Total Staff 272; Total Assisted 375.

Main Street Lodge Assisted Living, 909 Main St., N.E., 55413. Tel: 612-362-2450; Fax: 612-362-2449. Web: www.catholiceldercare.org. Units 51; Sisters 1; Lay Staff 19; Total Staff 20; Total Assisted 64.

Catholic Eldercare By Day Tel: 612-362-2405; Fax: 612-362-2401. Web: www.catholiceldercare.org. Assisted 95; Lay Staff 7; Staff 7.

Catholic Eldercare, Inc., 1101 on Main Apartments, 1101 Main St., NE, 55413. Tel: 612-378-8814; Fax: 612-378-4725. Web: www.1101onmain.com. Units 50; Staff 11.

River Village East Assisted Living, 2919 Randolph St. N.E., 55418. Tel: 612-605-2500; Fax: 612-605-2404. Web: www.catholiceldercare.org. Units 70; Sisters 1; Lay Staff 39; Total Staff 40; Total Assisted 80.

Cristo Rey Corporate Internship Program - Twin Cities, 2924 - 4th Ave. S., 55408. Tel: 612-545-9703. Meg Brudney, Exec. Dir.; Rev. Timothy T. Manatt, S.J., Pres.

The Islander Foundation, 1 De La Salle Dr., 55401. Tel: 612-676-7603. Douge M. Schildgen, Devel. Mgr. Coord.; Jill Stricker, Sec.

Queen Anne Communities, 2627 Queen Ave., 55411. Tel: 612-529-0503; Fax: 612-529-5860. Rev. Ignatius Nguyen Dai Kinh, C.M.C.

Sagrado Corazon de Jesus, 3800 Pleasant Ave., 55409. Tel: 612-874-7169; Fax: 612-870-0408. Email: sagradocorazonl@msn.com. Rev. Kevin M. McDonough, Pres.; Bradley Capouch, Vice Pres.; Deacon Carl Valdez, Sec.; Victor Guillen, Treas.

Twin Cities Catholic Alumni Club (1958) P.O. Box 581321, 55458-1321. Tel: 651-603-1412. Carl Berstrom, Club Pres. Members 75.

Youth and Family Center Inc. (1986) 4405 E. Lake St., 55406. Tel: 612-722-9612. Sisters Martha Merriman, C.S.J., Dir.; Betty Wurm, C.S.J., Dir. Counseling Center. Total Assisted 25; Total Staff 2.

HASTINGS. *Regina Foundation*, 1175 Nininger Rd., 55033. Tel: 651-480-4104; Fax: 651-480-6801. Email: kochendorferp@reginamedical.org. Web: www.reginamedical.org. Ty Erickson, CEO; Pam Kochendorfer, Corp. Sec.

Regina Healthcare, Inc., 1175 Nininger Rd., 55033. Tel: 651-480-4104; Fax: 651-480-6801. Email: kochendorferp@reginamedical.org. Web: www.reginamedical.org. Stewart W. Laird, Pres. & Chair; Pam Kochendorfer, Corp. Sec.

INVER GROVE HEIGHTS. *Catholic Finance Corporation* (2000) 5826 Blackshire Path, 55076. Tel: 651-389-1070; Fax: 651-389-1071. Email: info@catholicfinance.org. Web: www.catholicfinance.org. Alan J. Erickson, Mng. Dir.; Amanda Ellefson, Mgr. Office Operations.

MAPLEWOOD. *The Hill-Murray Foundation*, 2625 Larpenteur Ave. E., 55109. Tel: 651-777-1376. Dr. Susan Paul, Pres.

Maple Tree Monastery Childcare Center, 2625 Benet Rd., 55109. Tel: 651-770-0766. Email: jschlauch2@aol.com. Sisters Lucia Schwickerath, O.S.B., Prioress - St. Paul Monastery; Jeron Osterfeld, Bd. Pres. Religious Board 3; Lay Staff 25; Bd. Members 6; Total Assisted 74; Total Staff 25.

To Encounter Christ of the Archdiocese of St. Paul-Minneapolis, Minnesota, Inc., (Twin Cities TEC): 1725 Kennard St., Ste. 201, 55109. Tel: 651-281-0085; Fax: 866-600-2748. Email: retreats@twincitiestec.org. Web: www.twincitiestec.org. Gretchen Sonnen, Prog. Dir. Total Assisted 2,500; Total Staff 3.

NEW PRAGUE. *First Avenue Properties of New Prague*, 215 Main St. E, 56071. Tel: 952-758-3920. David B. Bruzek, Pres.

OSSEO. *Benedictine Senior Living at Steeple Pointe*, 625 Central Ave., 55369. Tel: 763-425-4440; Fax: 763-391-0747. Email: stephanie.ritter@bhshealth.org. Stephanie Ritter, Housing & Svcs. Dir. Bedrooms 59; Lay Staff 37; Total Assisted 100.

STILLWATER. *St. Croix Valley Faith Formation*, 218 E. Willard St., 55082. Tel: 651-351-3175. Eileen Douglass, Dir. Faith Formation.

WEST ST. PAUL. *NET Ministries, Inc.*, 110 Crusader Ave. W., 55118-4427. Tel: 651-450-6833; Fax: 651-450-9984. Email: ministry@netusa.org. Web: www.netusa.org. Mr. Mark Berchem, Exec. Dir. Total Staff 49.

Saint Paul's Outreach, Inc., 110 Crusader Ave. W., 55118. Tel: 651-451-6114; Fax: 651-453-0810. Email: info@spoweb.org. Web: www.spoweb.org. Mr. Gordon C. DeMarais, Exec. Dir.; Very Rev. Peter A. Laird, Bd. Pres. Total Staff 45.

RELIGIOUS INSTITUTES OF MEN REPRESENTED IN THE ARCHDIOCESE

For further details refer to the corresponding bracketed number in the Religious Institutes of Men or Women section.

[0200]—*Benedictine Monks* (St. John's Abbey)—O.S.B.

[0330]—*Brothers of the Christian Schools* (Midwest Prov.)—F.S.C.

[0470]—*The Capuchin Fathers* (Prov. of St. Joseph)—O.F.M.Cap.

[0270]—*Carmelite Fathers and Brothers*—O.Carm.

[]—*Carmelite Hermitage of the Blessed Virgin Mary*—O.Carm.

[]—*Carmelites of Mary Immaculate* (Sacred Heart Province); (Kerala, India)—C.M.I.

[]—*Congregation of the Mother Co-Redemptrix* (Carthage, MO)—C.M.C.

[]—*Congregation of the Sons of the Immaculate Conception* (Woodbridge, Ontario)—C.F.I.C.

[0480]—*Conventual Franciscans* (Prov. of Our Lady of Consolation)—O.F.M.Conv.

[0520]—*Franciscan Friars* (St. Louis); (Prov. of Sacred Heart)—O.F.M.

[0690]—*Jesuit Fathers and Brothers*—S.J.

[0780]—*Marist Fathers* (American Prov.)—S.M.

[0800]—*Maryknoll*—M.M.

[]—*Misioneros Oblatos de los Sagrados Corazones* (Ecuador)—O.C.C.S.S.

[]—*Oblates of Mary Immaculate* (Washington, DC)—O.M.I.

[0430]—*Order of Preachers (Dominicans)* (Prov. of St. Albert the Great)—O.P.
[1030]—*Paulist Fathers*—C.S.P.
[]—*Pro Ecclesia Sancta* (Peru)—P.E.S.
[1070]—*Redemptorist Fathers* (St. Louis Prov.)—C.SS.R.
[]—*Servants of the Holy Eucharist of the Blessed Virgin Mary* (Puerto Rico)—S.E.M.V.
[]—*Society of Christ* (Lombard, IL)—S.CH.
[1060]—*Society of the Precious Blood* (Cincinnati Prov.)—C.PP.S.
[0560]—*Third Order Regular of St. Francis* (Prov. of the Immaculate Conception)—T.O.R.
[]—*Vincentian Congregation* (India)—V.C.

RELIGIOUS INSTITUTES OF WOMEN REPRESENTED IN THE ARCHDIOCESE

[0230]—*Benedictine Sisters of Pontifical Jurisdiction* St. Paul, St. Joseph, Duluth, MN; Watertown, SD)—O.S.B.
[]—*Congregation of Our Lady of Sion* (Toronto, ON)—N.D.S.
[]—*Congregation of the Most Holy Rosary* (Sinsinawa, WI)
[3710]—*Congregation of the Sisters of St. Agnes*—C.S.A.
[3832]—*Congregation of the Sisters of St. Joseph* (Created from merger of several C.S.J. Provinces)—C.S.J.
[1780]—*Congregation of the Sisters of the Third Order of St. Francis of Perpetual Adoration* (Eastern Region)—F.S.P.A.
[]—*Contemplative Sisters of the Good Shepherd*—C.G.S.
[0810]—*Daughters of the Heart of Mary*—D.H.M.
[0420]—*Discalced Carmelite Nuns*—O.C.D.
[1070-03]—*Dominican Sisters* Congregation of the Most Holy Rosary (Sinsinawa, WI)—O.P.
[]—*Dominican Sisters Congregation of St. Cecilia* (Nashville, TN)
[]—*Franciscan Clarist Congregation* (Deephaven, MN)—F.C.C.
[1310]—*Franciscan Sisters of Little Falls, Minnesota*—O.S.F.
[1485]—*Franciscan Sisters of St. Paul, MN*—O.S.F.
[]—*Guadalupan Sisters* (Congregacion de Hermanas de La Salle); (Mexico)—H.G.S.
[]—*Immaculate Heart of Mary Mother of Christ* (Nigeria)—I.H.M.
[2575]—*Institute of the Sisters of Mercy of the Americas* (West/Midwest Community; Omaha, NE)—R.S.M.
[2340]—*Little Sisters of the Poor*—L.S.P.
[]—*Missionaries of Charity* (St. Louis, MO)—M.C.
[3990]—*Missionary Sisters of St. Peter Claver*—S.S.P.C.
[3760]—*Order of St. Clare*—O.S.C.
[2970]—*School Sisters of Notre Dame*—S.S.N.D.
[1680]—*Schools Sisters of St. Francis*—O.S.F.
[3590]—*Servants of Mary (Servite Sisters)*—O.S.M.
[]—*Sisters of Charity of our Lady, Mother of the Church* (Baltic, CT)—S.C.M.C.
[0520]—*Sisters of Charity of Our Lady, Mother of Mercy*—S.C.M.M.
[0430]—*Sisters of Charity of the Blessed Virgin Mary*—B.V.M.
[]—*Sisters of Providence of St. Mary-of-the-Woods* (Indiana)—S.P.
[1530]—*Sisters of St. Francis of the Congregation of Our Lady of Lourdes, Sylvania, Ohio*—O.S.F.
[1570]—*Sisters of St. Francis of the Holy Family* (Dubuque, IA)—O.S.F.
[3840]—*Sisters of St. Joseph of Carondelet*—C.S.J.
[3930]—*Sisters of St. Joseph of the Third Order of St. Francis*—S.S.J.-T.O.S.F.
[1830]—*The Sisters of the Good Shepherd*—R.G.S.
[]—*Sisters of the Living Word* (Arlington Heights, IL)—S.L.W.
[3320]—*Sisters of the Presentation of the B.V.M.* (Dubuque, IA; Aberdeen, SD)—P.B.V.M.
[1720]—*Sisters of the Third Order Regular of St. Francis of the Congregation of Our Lady of Lourdes* (Rochester, MN)—O.S.F.
[2150]—*Sisters, Servants of the Immaculate Heart of Mary* (Monroe, MI)—I.H.M.
[4190]—*Visitation Nuns*—V.H.M.

ARCHDIOCESAN CEMETERIES

ST. PAUL. *Calvery*
The Catholic Cemeteries, 2105 Lexington Ave., S., Mendota Heights, 55120. Tel: 651-228-9991; Fax: 651-228-9995. Web: www.catholic-cemeteries.org. John Cherek, Dir.

MINNEAPOLIS. *St. Anthony & St. Mary*

MENDOTA HEIGHTS. *Resurrection*

NEW HOPE. *Assumption & Gethsemane*

PARISH CEMETERIES

ALBERTVILLE. *St. Albert Cemetery*, P.O. Box 127, 55301.

ANNANDALE. *St. Ignatius Cemetery*, P.O. Box 126, 55302. Tel: 320-274-8828; Fax: 320-274-3961.

ANOKA. *Calvary Cemetery*, 525 Jackson St., 55303. Tel: 763-421-2471; Fax: 263-421-4230.

BAYPORT. *St. Michael Cemetery*, 409 Third St., 55003.

BELLE PLAINE. *Sacred Heart Cemetery*, 212 N. Chestnut, 56011.
Saint Peter and Paul Cemetery, 212 N. Chestnut, 56011.

BELLECHESTER. *St. Mary Cemetery*, 221 Chester Ave., Bellchester, 55027.

BUFFALO. *St. Mark's Cemetery*, Mailing Address: 223 19th St. N.W., 55313. Tel: 763-684-0075, Ext. 100; Fax: 763-684-4771. 3370 Edmonson Ave. N.E., 55313. Web: www.stfxb.org/parish/cemeteries.html.
Saint Francis Xavier Cemetery, Mailing Address: 223 19th St. N.W., 55313. Tel: 763-684-0075, Ext. 100; Fax: 763-684-4771. 1300 Barton Ave. N.W., 55313. Web: www.stfxb.org/parish/cemeteries.html.

CANNON FALLS. *St. Pius V Cemetery*, Mailing Address: P.O. Box 367, 55009-0367. 410 W. Colvill St., 55009.

CARVER. *St. Nicholas Cemetery*, 412 W. 4th St., 55315. Tel: 952-448-2345; Fax: 952-368-0502.

CENTERVILLE. *St. Genevieve Cemetery*, 7087 Goiffon St., 55038.

CHANHASSEN. *St. Hubert Cemetery*, 381 W. 78th St., 55317. Tel: 952-934-9106; Fax: 952-934-8209.

CHASKA. *Guardian Angels Cemetery*, 215 W. 2nd St., 55318.

CLEARWATER. *St. Luke Cemetery*, P.O. Box 249, 55320.

CLEVELAND. *Calgary Cemetery*, P.O. Box 187, 56017.

COATES. *Saint Agatha of Vermillion Cemetery*, 3700 160th St. E., 55068. Tel: 641-437-3226.

COLOGNE. *St. Bernard Cemetery*, 212 Church St. E., 55322.

COON RAPIDS. *Epiphany Cemetery*, 1900 111th Ave. N.W., 55433. Tel: 763-755-1020; Fax: 763-862-4303.

CORCORAN. *St. Jean de Chantel Cemetery*, 20000 County Rd. 10, 55340.
Old St. Thomas Cemetery, 20000 County Rd. 10, 55340.
St. Patrick's Cemetery, 20000 County Rd. 10, 55340.
St. Thomas the Apostle Cemetery, 20000 County Rd. 10, 55340.

DAYTON. *St. John the Baptist Cemetery*, 18380 Columbus St., 55327.
Old St. John the Baptist Cemetery, 18380 Columbus St., 55327.

DELANO. *Calvary Cemetery*, P.O. Box 470, 55328.
St. Joseph Cemetery, P.O. Box 470, 55328.
St. Mary of Czestochowa Cemetery, 1867 95th St. S.E., 55328.
St. Peter Cemetery, P.O. Box 470, 55328.

EXCELSIOR. *Resurrection Cemetery*, 680 Mill St., 55331.

FARIBAULT. *Calvary Cemetery*, 4 Second Ave. S.W., 55021.
St. Lawrence Cemetery, 4 Second Ave. S.W., 55021.
St. Patrick Shieldsville Cemetery, 7525 Dodd Rd., 55021. Tel: 507-334-6002; Fax: 507-334-1960.

FARMINGTON. *St. Michael Cemetery*, 22120 Denmark Ave., 55024.

FOREST LAKE. *Calvary Cemetery*, 1250 S. Shore Dr., 55025. Tel: 651-982-2200.

FRANCONIA TOWNSHIP. *St. Francis Xavier Cemetery*, Mailing Address: P.O. Box 234, Taylors Falls, 55084. 25267 Redwing Ave., Shafer, 55074. Tel: 651-465-7345.

HAMEL. *St. Anne Cemetery*, P.O. Box 256, 55340. Tel: 763-478-6644; Fax: 763-478-9141.

HAMPTON. *St. Mary Cemetery*, 8433 239th St. E., 55031. Tel: 651-437-5546.
St. Mathias Cemetery, 23315 Northfield Blvd., 55031. Tel: 651-437-9030; Fax: 651-437-3427.

HASTINGS. *St. Elizabeth Ann Seton Cemetery*, 2035 W. 15th St., 55033.

HOPKINS. *St. Margaret's Cemetery*, 1310 Main St., 55343. Tel: 952-935-0111; Fax: 952-935-4539.

HUGO. *St. John the Baptist Cemetery*, 14383 Forest Blvd. N., 55038.

INVER GROVE HEIGHTS. *St. Patrick Cemetery*, 3535 72nd St. E., 55076.

JORDAN. *St. John the Baptist Cemetery*, 313 E. 2nd St., 55352.
Saint Catherine Cemetery
Saint Patrick Cemetery, 24425 Old Hwy. Blvd., 55352.

KENYON. *St. Edwards of Richland*, 108 Bullis St., 55946.

KILKENNY. *St. Canice Cemetery*, P.O. Box 38, 56052.

LAKEVILLE. *All Saints Cemetery*, 19795 Holyoke Ave., 55044.

LE CENTER. *St. Mary's Calvary Cemetery*, 165 N. Waterville Ave., 56057.

LE SUEUR. *St. Anne*, 217 N. 3rd St., 56058.
Calvary Cemetery, 217 N. 3rd St., 56058.

LINO LAKES. *St. Joseph Cemetery*, 171 Elm St., 55014.

LITTLE CANADA. *St. John's Church of Little Canada Cemetery*, Office & Mailing Address: 380 Little Canada Rd., 55117. Tel: 651-484-0480; Fax: 651-484-0567. Cemetery: 460 Little Canada Rd. E., 55117.

LONG LAKE. *St. George Cemetery*, 133 N. Brown Rd., 55356.

LONSDALE. *Calvary Cemetery*, P.O. Box 169, 55046. Tel: 507-744-2829; Fax: 507-744-2826.

LORETTO. *Sts. Peter and Paul Cemetery*, P.O. Box 96, 55357.

MADISON LAKE. *Marysburg Cemetery*, 27528 Patrick St., 56063.

MAPLE LAKE. *St. Timothy Cemetery*, 8 Oak Ave. N., 55358.

MENDOTA. *St. Peter Cemetery*, P.O. Box 50679, 55150.

MIESVILLE. *St. Joseph Cemetery*, 23955 Nicolai Ave. E., St. Joseph, 56374.

MINNEAPOLIS. *St. Joan of Arc Memorial Garden*, 4537 3rd Ave. S., 55419. Tel: 612-823-8205; Fax: 612-825-7028.

MONTGOMERY. *Calvary Cemetery*, 206 Vine Ave. W., 56069.
St. John's Cemetery, 206 Vine Ave. W., 56069.

MONTICELLO. *St. Henry Cemetery*, Parish Office & Mailing Address: 1001 7th St. E., 55362. Tel: 763-295-2402; Fax: 763-295-6333. 3630 90th St. N.E., 55362.

MOUND. *Our Lady of the Lake Cemetery*, 2385 Commerce Blvd., 55364.

NEW BRIGHTON. *St. John the Baptist Cemetery*, 835 2nd Ave. N.W., 55112. Tel: 651-633-8333.

NEW MARKET. *St. Nicholas Cemetery*, P.O. Box 9, Elko/New Market, 55020. Tel: 952-461-2403; Fax: 952-461-2423.

NEW PRAGUE. *St. Benedict Cemetery*, 20087 Hub Dr., 56071.
St. John the Evangelist Cemetery, 20687 Hub Dr., 56071.
St. Joseph Cemetery, 31525 181st Ave., 56071.
St. Scholastica Cemetery, 31525 181st Ave., 56071.
St. Thomas Cemetery, 31525 181st Ave., 56071.
St. Wenceslaus Cemetery, 215 E. Main St., 56071.

NORTH BRANCH. *St. Joseph Cemetery*, P.O. Box 609, 55056. Tel: 651-674-4056.

NORTH SAINT PAUL. *St. Mary's Cemetery*, 2590 Margaret St. N., 55109.

NORTHFIELD. *Annunciation of Hazelwood Cemetery*, 4996 Hazelwood Ave., 55057. Tel: 952-652-2625.
Calvary Cemetery, 216 Spring St. N., 55057.

NORWOOD. *Ascension Cemetery*, 319 Reform St. N., 55368.
St. Patrick's Cemetery, 319 Reform St. N., 55368.

OAK GROVE. *St. Patrick of Cedar Creek Cemetery*, 19921 Nightingale St. N.W., 55011.

OAKDALE. *Guardian Angels Cemetery*, 8260 4th St. N., 55128.

OSSEO. *St. Vincent de Paul Cemetery*, 8601 93rd Ave. N., 55369.

PINE ISLAND. *St. Michael Cemetery*, 451 5th St. S.W., 55963.

PLYMOUTH. *St. Joseph Cemetery*, Mailing Address: 8701 36th Ave. N., New Hope, 55427. 13015 Rockford Rd., 55441. Tel: 763-544-3352; Fax: 763-544-3435.

PRIOR LAKE. *St. Michael Cemetery*, 16311 Duluth Ave. S.E., 55372.

RED WING. *Calvary Cemetery*, 426 W. 8th St., 55066.

RICHFIELD. *Assumption Cemetery*, 305 E. 77th St., 55423.

ROGERS. *St. Martin Cemetery*, 12020 Fletcher Ln., 55374.
St. Walburga Cemetery, 12020 Fletcher Ln., 55374.

ROSEMOUNT. *St. Agatha Cemetery*, 3700 160th St. E., 55068. Tel: 651-437-3226; Fax: 651-437-8400.
St. Joseph Cemetery, 13900 Biscayne Ave., 55068.

RUSH CITY. *Calvary Cemetery*, P.O. Box 45, 55069. Tel: 320-358-4370; Fax: 866-779-1580.

SAVAGE. *St. John the Baptist Cemetery*, 4625 W. 125th St., 55378. Tel: 952-890-9465; Fax: 952-890-3006.

SHAKOPEE. *Catholic Cemeteries of Shakopee, Minnesota, Inc.*, 350 S. Atwood St., 55379. Tel: 952-445-1229; Fax: 952-445-9639. A corporation formed by the Church of St. Mark and the Church of St. Mary, both of Shakopee, to consolidate separate cemeteries.
St. Mary of the Purification Cemetery, 15850 Marystown Rd., 55379.

ST. BONIFACIUS. *St. Boniface Cemetery*, P.O. Box 68, 55375. Tel: 952-446-1054; Fax: 952-446-1158.

ST. MICHAEL. *St. Michael Catholic Church*, 11300 Frankfort Pkwy N.E., 55376. Tel: 763-497-2745.

ST. PAUL PARK. *St. Thomas Aquinas Cemetery*, 920 Holley Ave., 55071.

VERMILLION. *St. John the Baptist Cemetery*, P.O. Box 8, 55085. Tel: 651-437-9030; Fax: 651-437-3427.

VESELI. *St. John's Cemetery*, 4939 Washington N., 55046.

Most Holy Trinity, 4939 Washington N., 55046. Tel: 507-744-2823; Fax: 507-744-4463.

VICTORIA. *St. Victoria Cemetery*, 8228 Victoria Dr., 55386. Tel: 952-443-2661.

WACONIA. *St. Joseph Cemetery*, 41 E. 1st St., 55387.

WATERTOWN. *Immaculate Conception Cemetery*, P.O. Box 548, 55388.

WATERVILLE. *Calgary Cemetery*, 506 Common St., 56096.

WAVERLY. *St. Mary Cemetery*, P.O. Box 278, 55390.

WAYZATA. *Holy Name of Jesus Cemetery*, 155 County Rd. 24, 55391.

WHITE BEAR LAKE. *St. Mary of the Lake Cemetery*, 4741 Bald Eagle Ave., 55110.

ZUMBROTA. *St. Paul Cemetery*, 749 Main St., 55992. Tel: 507-732-5324; Fax: 507-732-5347.

NECROLOGY

† Antus, Lawrence, (Retired)—Died May 24, 2011
† Fenton, Jerry F., (Retired)—Died Nov. 17, 2011
† Gannon, Joseph, (Retired)—Died July 20, 2011
† Hogan, Richard, (On Duty Outside Archdiocese)—Died June 14, 2011
† Klein, Bernard, (Retired)—Died May 4, 2011
† Moorman, Raymond J., (Retired)—Died July 17, 2011
† Reiser, Bernard A., (Retired)—Died Dec. 27, 2011

An asterisk (*) denotes an organization that has established tax-exempt status directly with the IRS and is not covered by the USCCB Group Ruling.

Diocese of St. Petersburg

(Dioecesis Sancti Petri in Florida)

Most Reverend

ROBERT N. LYNCH

Fourth Bishop of St. Petersburg; ordained May 13, 1978; appointed Fourth Bishop of St. Petersburg December 5, 1995; consecrated and installed January 26, 1996. *Office: P.O. Box 40200, St. Petersburg, FL 33743-0200.*

Pastoral Center: P.O. Box 40200, St. Petersburg, FL 33743-0200. Tel: 727-344-1611; Fax: 727-345-2143.

Web: www.dioceseofstpete.org

Email: communicate@dosp.org

ESTABLISHED JUNE 17, 1968.

Square Miles 3,177.

Comprises the Counties of Citrus, Hernando, Hillsborough, Pasco and Pinellas in the State of Florida.

For legal titles of parishes and diocesan institutions, consult the Pastoral Center.

STATISTICAL OVERVIEW

Personnel	
Bishop	1
Retired Bishops	1
Abbots	1
Priests: Diocesan Active in Diocese	83
Priests: Diocesan Active Outside Diocese	4
Priests: Diocesan in Foreign Missions	2
Priests: Retired, Sick or Absent	59
Number of Diocesan Priests	148
Religious Priests in Diocese	116
Total Priests in Diocese	264
Extern Priests in Diocese	77
Ordinations:	
Transitional Deacons	2
Permanent Deacons	6
Permanent Deacons in Diocese	123
Total Brothers	38
Total Sisters	178
Parishes	
Parishes	74
With Resident Pastor:	
Resident Diocesan Priests	58
Resident Religious Priests	12
Without Resident Pastor:	
Administered by Priests	4
Missions	7
Professional Ministry Personnel:	
Brothers	1
Sisters	60
Welfare	
Catholic Hospitals	2
Total Assisted	355,000
Health Care Centers	7
Total Assisted	35,000
Homes for the Aged	10
Total Assisted	830
Day Care Centers	16
Total Assisted	1,205
Specialized Homes	5
Total Assisted	139
Special Centers for Social Services	65
Total Assisted	25,000
Educational	
Diocesan Students in Other Seminaries	34
Total Seminarians	34
Colleges and Universities	1
Total Students	15,564
High Schools, Diocesan and Parish	4
Total Students	1,850
High Schools, Private	2
Total Students	1,095
Elementary Schools, Diocesan and Parish	26
Total Students	7,336
Elementary Schools, Private	2
Total Students	877
Non-residential Schools for the Disabled	2
Total Students	104
Catechesis/Religious Education:	
High School Students	2,153
Elementary Students	17,146
Total Students under Catholic Instruction	46,159
Teachers in the Diocese:	
Priests	8
Scholastics	3
Brothers	3
Sisters	13
Lay Teachers	813
Vital Statistics	
Receptions into the Church:	
Infant Baptism Totals	3,676
Minor Baptism Totals	280
Adult Baptism Totals	384
Received into Full Communion	372
First Communions	4,653
Confirmations	3,742
Marriages:	
Catholic	620
Interfaith	302
Total Marriages	922
Deaths	3,641
Total Catholic Population	432,209
Total Population	2,924,479

Former Bishops—Most Revs. CHARLES B. MCLAUGHLIN, D.D., ord. June 6, 1941; appt. Titular Bishop of Risinium and Auxiliary of Raleigh, Jan. 13, 1964; appt. First Bishop of St. Petersburg, May 8, 1968; installed June 17, 1968; died in Office, Dec. 14, 1978; W. THOMAS LARKIN, D.D., ord. May 15, 1947; Second Bishop of St. Petersburg; appt. April 24, 1979; ord. Bishop, May 27, 1979; installed June 28, 1979; retired Nov. 28, 1988; died Nov. 4, 2006.; JOHN C. FAVALORA, D.D., S.T.L., Third Bishop of St. Petersburg; ord. Dec. 20, 1961; appt. Bishop of Alexandria, June 16, 1986; ord. and installed July 29, 1986; appt. Third Bishop of St. Petersburg, March 7, 1989; installed May 16, 1989; appt. third Archbishop of Miami Nov. 3, 1994; installed Dec. 20, 1994; retired April 20, 2010.

Diocesan Offices

Pastoral Center—6363 Ninth Ave. N., St. Petersburg, 33710. Tel: 727-344-1611; Fax: 727-345-2143. *Mailing Address: P.O. Box 40200, St. Petersburg, 33743-0200.*

Tribunal—6363 Ninth Ave. N, Saint Petersburg, 33710. Tel: 727-341-6858; 727-341-6859; Fax: 727-374-0206. Address all Rogatory commissions and matrimonial matters to the Tribunal.

WBVM 90.5 FM, Inc.—717 S. Dale Mabry Hwy., Tampa, 33609. Tel: 813-289-8040.

Office of the Bishop

Office of the Bishop—Most Rev. ROBERT N. LYNCH; Mrs. ANGELICA "VIVI" IGLESIAS, Exec. Sec. to Bishop Lynch & Notary.

Diocesan Curia

Vicar General—Rev. Msgr. ROBERT F. MORRIS, V.G.; Mrs. ANGELICA "VIVI" IGLESIAS, Exec. Sec. & Notary.

Moderator of the Curia—Rev. Msgr. ROBERT F. MORRIS, V.G.

Chancellor—Mrs. JOAN G. MORGAN, Chancellor & Notary; Mrs. MARIA T. GONZALEZ, Exec. Sec.; Mrs. LISA MOBLEY, Archivist & Notary.

Vice Chancellor—Deacon RICK WELLS, J.C.L., Notary.

Victim Assistance Coordinator—Ms. MARTI ZEITZ, M.A., 1213 16th St. N., St. Petersburg, 33705. Tel: 866-407-4505 (Toll Free). Email: mzeitz@ccdosp.org.

Secretary for Administration—Mrs. ELIZABETH DEPTULA.

Secretary for Priest Personnel—Rev. LEONARD PIOTROWSKI.

Secretary of Christian Formation—Rev. Msgr. ROBERT F. MORRIS, V.G.

Secretary of Christian Service—Mr. FRANK V. MURPHY III.

The Tribunal—

Judicial Vicar—Very Rev. RONALD AUBIN, J.C.L.

Coordinator of Tribunal Services—Mr. DAVID RIDENOUR, J.D., J.C.L.

Tribunal Staff—

Judges—Rev. Msgr. ROBERT C. GIBBONS, J.C.L.; Very Rev. RONALD AUBIN, J.C.L.; Rev. FRANCIS MUTEESASIRA LUBOWA, J.C.L.; Deacon RICK WELLS, J.C.L.; Very Rev. JOSEPH L. WATERS, V.F., J.C.L.; Mr. DAVID RIDENOUR, J.D., J.C.L.

Promoter of Justice—Rev. Msgr. DACIAN DEE, J.C.D. (Retired).

Defenders of the Bond—Rev. Msgr. DACIAN DEE, J.C.D. (Retired); Rev. WILLIAM J. SWENGROS, J.C.D.

Auditor—KAZ MIELCAREK, Ph.D.

Notaries—Mrs. MARY SUE OLIVER; Ms. ANA RIVERA; Mrs. KIM PACANA.

College of Consultors—Rev. Msgrs. ROBERT F. MORRIS, V.G.; ROBERT C. GIBBONS, J.C.L.; Very Rev. RONALD AUBIN, J.C.L.; Revs. ARTHUR PROULX, V.F.; JOHN TAPP; JAMES B. JOHNSON, V.F.; CRAIG MORLEY.

Vocations Office—Revs. JOHN BLUM, Dir.; CARL J. MELCHIOR JR., Assoc. Dir.; Mrs. HEIDI VARLEY, Sec.

Permanent Diaconate Office—Rev. RALPH J. ARGENTINO, Dir.; Deacons JAMES GREVENITES, Asst. Dir.; JOHN ALVAREZ, Dir. Formation; PETER ANDRE, Supervision of Practicums; Mrs. SUE HUERTAS, Administrative Asst.

Vicar for Religious—Sr. MARLENE WEIDENBORNER, O.S.F., Dir.

Department of Christian Formation

Department of Christian Formation—Rev. Msgr. ROBERT F. MORRIS, V.G.

Sea, Apostleship of the—

Tampa Port Ministry-Seafarers Center—1912 Eastport Dr., Tampa, 33610. Tel: 813-234-8693;

Fax: 813-238-5060. Deacon MAXIMO MONTAYRE, Chap.

Charismatic Renewal—

*English—*DOTTIE VINSON, Dir. Tel: 813-961-3675. Email: tandyvinson@msn.com.

*Spanish Speaking Spiritual Moderator—*Rev. Msgr. ANTONIO DIEZ (Retired), 6819 Krycul Ave., P.O. Box 418, Riverview, 33568. Tel: 813-677-2175; MARIA RODRIGUEZ, Pres., Commission, 17306 Hubers Ct., Odessa, 33556. Email: bythespiritonly@aol.com.

*Cursillo, English—*Rev. ANGELUS MIGLIORE, T.O.R., Cursillo, English & Spiritual Advisor, St. Patrick Parish, 4518 S. Manhattan Ave., Tampa, 33611. Tel: 813-839-5337; JAY TAYLOR, Lay Dir. Email: jct1013@verizon.net.

*Cursillo, Spanish—*Rev. RAFAEL E. MARTOS, Spiritual Advisor, St. Clement. Tel: 813-759-2721; NYDIA VIZCARRONDO, Directora Laica. Tel: 727-942-6606.

*Ecumenical and Inter-Religious Affairs—*Rev. ROBERT J. SCHNEIDER, Dir., Espiritu Santo Church, 2405 Philippe Pkwy., Safety Harbor, 34695. Tel: 727-726-8477; Deacon JAMES GREVENITES, Asst. Dir., St. Raphael Church, 1376 Snell Isle Blvd., N.E., Saint Petersburg, 33704. Tel: 727-821-7989.

*Lay Pastoral Ministry Institute—*Tel: 727-344-1611. DALE BROWN, Dir.; ELAINE THELAN, Coord. Mentors.

*Multicultural Ministry—*Mrs. ANGELINA KARPINSKI, Assoc. Dir.; Ms. ANYELY GARCIA, Sec.

*Our Lady of Good Counsel Camp—*Rev. JAMES B. JOHNSON, V.F., Dir., 8888 E. Gobbler Dr., Floral City, 34436. Tel: 352-726-2198. Email: goodcounselcamp@aol.com.

*Propagation of the Faith—*Rev. PAUL KOCHU, Dir.; Mrs. CAROLYN MARHEFKA, Sec.

*Worship, Office of—*Rev. JOHN TAPP, Sec. Worship; Mr. DOUGLAS REATINI, Dir.; Ms. KATHY PROEFKE, Assoc. Dir.

*Catholic Schools Office—*Mr. ALBERTO VAZQUEZ-MATOS, Supt.; Mrs. HELEN S. MARSTON, M.S., Deputy Supt.; Mrs. KAY RIZZO, MAT, CAS, District Supt.-Northern; Mr. CHRISTOPHER WIAND, M.Ed., District Supt.-Pinellas; Mr. ADAM JENKINS, Asst. Supt. Educ. Programs; Dr. KRISTY SWOL, Ed.D., District Supt.-Hillsborough. Secretaries: Mrs. LISA BAGGETT; Mrs. DEBRA KLEINBERGER.

*Evangelization and Lifelong Faith Formation—*Mr. BRIAN A. LEMOI, Dir.; Mrs. KATHY FILIPPELLI, Assoc. Dir. Catechist Certification; Mrs. DIANE KLEDZIK, Assoc. Dir. Adult Faith Formation; Mr. RYAN PHELAN, Assoc. Dir. Youth & Young Adult Ministry.

Father William F. Balfe Memorial Library—Located at: Bishop McLaughlin High School, 13651 Hays Rd., Spring Hill, 34610.

*Scouting Office, Girls—*Rev. Msgr. ANTON DECHERING, Dir., 1600 54th Ave. S., St. Petersburg, 33712. Tel: 727-867-3663; JOSEPHINE MAESTAS, Diocesan Chair. Tel: 813-748-3043.

*Scouting Office, Boys—*Rev. TIMOTHY CUMMINGS, Diocesan Chap. Tel: 727-733-8305; Mr. MICHAEL KOSIBA, Diocesan Chm. Tel: 813-839-4644; Mr. MACK ZEWALK, Vice Chm. Tel: 813-620-9112.

Department of Christian Service

*Secretary of Christian Service—*Mr. FRANK V. MURPHY III.

*Communications Office—*Mr. FRANK V. MURPHY III, Dir.; Ms. MARIA MERTENS, Web Editor; Mrs. MARIA T. GONZALEZ, Sec.

*Diocesan Radio - WBVM 90.5 FM—*Mr. JOHN MORRIS, Station Mgr., Mailing Address: 717 S. Dale Mabry Hwy., Tampa, 33609. Tel: 813-289-8040; 800-223-9286 (800-223-WBVM); Fax: 813-282-3580.

*Prison and Jail Ministry—*Deacon PETER ANDRE, Dir.; Mrs. HEIDI SUMNER, Sec. Tel: 727-344-1611, Ext. 414; 727-344-1611, Ext. 415.

*Life Ministry—*Mrs. SABRINA BURTON-SCHULTZ, Dir. Tel: 727-344-1611, Ext. 325.

*Parish Ministry Support—*Deacon PETER BURNS, Dir. Tel: 727-344-1611, Ext. 325.

Department of Administration

*Department of Administration—*Mrs. ELIZABETH DEPTULA, Sec. for Admin.; Mr. PAUL A. WARD JR., Exec. Dir., Finance Office.

*Calvary Catholic Cemetery and Miserere Guild—*Rev. RALPH J. ARGENTINO, Dir. Cemeteries.

*Finance and Accounting—*Mr. PAUL A. WARD JR., Exec. Dir.; Ms. LISA CAMPBELL, Controller; Mr. MICHAEL AKERS, Dir. Parish & School Accounting; Mrs. CAROL PILARSKI, Technology Coord.

*Diocesan Finance Council—*Rev. JOSEPH A. PELLEGRINO; Very Rev. RICHARD JANKOWSKI, V.F.; Mr. NEIL J. RAUENHORST; Mr. ROBERT S. FISHER; Mr. MICHAEL CARRERE; Mr. GREG KIELER; Mr. EMIL MARQUARDT; Ms. RETIA McADORY; Mrs. NANCY RIDENOUR; Mr. JOSEPH WHITE; Mrs. ELIZABETH DEPTULA; Mr. FRANK V. MURPHY III; Mr. GERALD P. GIGLIA.

*Insurance and Risk Management—*Mr. RICARDO OSORIO, Dir.; VALERIE BURNS, Admin. Asst.

*Real Estate and Plannning—*Mr. STEVE B. ZIENTEK, Real Estate Planning Mgr.

*Information Technology—*Mr. MARK MOFFITT, Dir.; Ms. CHRISTINE DANDARAW, Training Coord.; Mr. SCOTT SHARLOW, Computer Tech. & Network Admin.; Mr. RAY MILLER, Enterprise Information Analyst.

*Office of Construction Management—*Mr. RICK KOLHOFF, Exec. Dir.; Mr. BRIAN LAVERTY, Project Mgr.; Mrs. KATHLEEN FIXTER, Sec.

*Human Resources—*Mr. CHRIS RAJK, Exec. Dir.; Mr. ANDRE GLAUDE, Safe Environment Mgr.; Mrs. JOYCE VELENO, Admin. Asst.; Mrs. MONITA BONCZEK, Coord. Employee Benefits; Mrs. CHARLOTTE MYERS, Payroll Mgr.

*Internal Services Administration—*Ms. MARY SHEALY, Dir.

*Office of Stewardship and Development—*VACANT. Parish Resource Specialist: Ms. JEANNE SMITH.

*The Catholic Foundation—*Mr. JONATHON JONES, Dir.; Mrs. TERRI RICK, Sec.

Pastoral Offices and Consultative Bodies to the Diocesan Curia

Presbyteral Council—

*Executive Committee—*Most Rev. ROBERT N. LYNCH, Pres.; Rev. Msgrs. ROBERT F. MORRIS, V.G.; ROBERT C. GIBBONS, J.C.L., Chm.; Very Rev. RONALD AUBIN, J.C.L.; Revs. LEONARD PLAZEWSKI, Sec.; LEONARD PIOTROWSKI.

*Vicars Forane—*Very Revs. MICHAEL ROBERT CORMIER, V.F., Northern Deanery; DANIEL R. KAYAJAN, C.S.C., V.F., East Central Deanery; KENNETH MALLEY, V.F., North Central Deanery; JOHN McEVOY, V.F., Southeast Deanery; MICHAEL T. O'BRIEN, V.F., Southwest Deanery; MICHAEL R. SMITH, V.F., Northern Deanery; MICHAEL SUSZYNSKI, V.F., South Central Deanery; GREGG TOTTLE, V.F., Central Deanery; JOSEPH L. WATERS, V.F., J.C.L., Southern Deanery.

*Elected Pastors—*Rev. Msgr. ROBERT C. GIBBONS, J.C.L.; Revs. JOSEPH A. PELLEGRINO; ROBERT CADRECHA; GARY DOWSEY; PAUL PECCHIE; DAVID TOUPS.

*Elected Parochial Vicars—*Revs. TIMOTHY CUMMINGS; CARL J. MELCHIOR JR.; JOSEPH MUSCO; LEONARD PLAZEWSKI; DOMINIC CORONA; CARLOS ROJAS; ALLAN TUPA.

*Appointed Members—*Revs. JAMES B. JOHNSON, V.F.; CRAIG MORLEY; ARTHUR PROULX, V.F.; JOHN TAPP.

*Personnel Board—*Very Rev. ERIC HUNTER, V.F.; Revs. JAMES B. JOHNSON, V.F.; JOSEPH A. PELLEGRINO; Rev. Msgr. ROBERT F. MORRIS, V.G.; Rev. JOHN BLUM; Very Rev. KENNETH MALLEY, V.F.; Rev. LEONARD PIOTROWSKI.

*Incardination Committee—*Very Revs. JOHN A. D'ANTONIO, V.F.; DENNIS E. HUGHES, V.F.; Rev. Msgr. PATRICK IRWIN; Rev. GILBERTO QUINTERO. Ex Officio: Rev. Msgr. ROBERT F. MORRIS, V.G.; Rev. LEONARD PIOTROWSKI.

Diocesan Legal Counsel— DiVito & Higham, P.A. Mr. JOSEPH A. DIVITO; FREDERICK A. HIGHAM JR., 4514 Central Ave., St. Petersburg, 33711-1041. Tel: 727-321-1201; Fax: 727-321-5181.

*Diocesan Pastoral Council—*Mrs. JOAN VALLAR, Chm.

*Diocesan Review Board—*Mrs. SUE BRETT, Chm. Tel: 727-384-0730; Fax: 727-344-4060.

Organizations Serving the Diocese

Pension Plan For Employees of the Entities of the Diocese of St. Petersburg—

Pension Plan Administrator—Gabriel, Roeder, Smith & Co., One E. Broward Blvd., Ste. 505, Fort Lauderdale, 33301-1872. Tel: 954-527-1616; Fax: 954-525-0083.

Catholic Charities, Diocese of St. Petersburg, Inc.—

Central Services—1213 16th St., N., St. Petersburg, 33705. Tel: 727-893-1314; Fax: 727-893-1307. Web: www.ccdosp.org. Mr. FRANK V. MURPHY III, Pres.; SHEILA LOPEZ, COO.

Pious Foundations

Catholic Education Foundation, Inc.—6363 Ninth Ave. N., St. Petersburg, 33710. Tel: 727-344-1611. *Mailing Address: P.O. Box 40200, St. Petersburg, 33743-0200.*

Emmaus Foundation, Inc.—dba Catholic Foundation of the Diocese of St. Petersburg 6363 Ninth Ave. N., St. Petersburg, 33710. Tel: 727-344-1611. *Mailing Address: P.O. Box 40200, St. Petersburg, 33743-0200.*

Organizations of the Catholic Faithful

*Catholic Daughters of America—*Ms. JOANNE TOMASSI, Natl. Regent, Manasquan, NJ; Ms. DELIA SUNNELL, State Regent. Tel: 813-714-9685. Email: dlsunn@verizon.net; National Office. Tel: 212-877-3041.

*Diocesan Council of Catholic Women—*Very Rev. JOHN McEVOY, V.F., Diocesan Moderator. Tel: 727-526-5783.

*Family of St. Jerome, "Familian Sancti Hieronymi"—*Mr. JAN G. HALISKY, P.A., Praeses Generalis, 507 S. Prospect Ave., Clearwater, 33756.

*Knights of Columbus—*Rev. PAUL HERVEY, Diocesan Chap. (Retired). Tel: 813-634-2328.

Knights of Peter Claver— St. Peter Claver, Tampa Council #379 Grand Knight CONRAD JOHNSON. Tel: 813-835-0529. Web: kofpc.org (National); kpc379.org (Local).

Knights of Peter Claver Ladies Auxiliary— St. Peter Claver, Tampa Court #379 Grand Lady YVONNE NELLUM. Tel: 813-681-3010. Web: kofpc.org (National); kpc379.org (Local).

Society of St. Vincent de Paul—

**Central Council of St. Petersburg Diocese, 4556 Manhattan Ave., Ste. A, Tampa, 33611.* Tel: 813-831-5100. Very Rev. JOHN McEVOY, V.F., Spiritual Advisor. Tel: 813-645-1302; Mr. MARVIN ROPERT, Pres.

**Hernando Citrus St. Vincent de Paul Society District Council.* Mr. RON LEGER. Tel: 352-688-1511.

**West Hillsborough District Council.* Ms. NANCY JONES, Pres. Tel: 813-251-8678.

**East Hillsborough District Council.* Ms. CAROLYN CHISANO, Pres. Tel: 813-643-2466.

**Pasco District Council.* Ms. PAT DWYER. Tel: 813-944-0447.

**South Pinellas District Council.* Mr. PATRICK SULLIVAN, Pres. Tel: 727-867-9452; MICHAEL J. RAPOSA, Exec. Dir.

**Upper Pinellas District Council.* Mr. JAMES CAMPBELL, Pres. Tel: 727-712-3828.

CLERGY, PARISHES, MISSIONS AND PAROCHIAL SCHOOLS

CITY OF ST. PETERSBURG

(PINELLAS COUNTY)

ST. PETERSBURG

1—CATHEDRAL OF ST. JUDE THE APOSTLE (1950) Very Rev. Joseph L. Waters, Rector; Rev. Kenneth Breen, O.de.M. In Res., Rev. Msgr. Robert F. Morris.

Res.: 5815 Fifth Ave. N., Saint Petersburg, 33710. Tel: 727-347-9702; Fax: 727-343-8370.

School—(Grades PreSchool-8) Tel: 727-347-8622; Fax: 727-343-0305. Mrs. Kelly Wiand, Interim Prin.; Barbara Ervin, Librarian. Lay Teachers 20; Students 337.

*Catechesis/Religious Program—*Tel: 727-347-9702; Fax: 727-343-8370. Students 176.

2—BLESSED TRINITY (1960) Rev. Msgr. Anton Dechering; Rev. J. Frederick McGuire (CIN); Sr. Jean Barrett, O.S.F., Pastoral Assoc.; Deacon Lionel Roberts; Robert Dudley, Contemporary Choir Dir.

Res.: 1600 54th Ave. S., 33712. Tel: 727-867-3663; Fax: 727-864-2679.

See St. Paul Interparochial School, St. Petersburg under Elementary Schools, Interparochial located in the Institution section.

*Catechesis/Religious Program—*Tel: 727-867-3663; Fax: 727-864-2679. Ellen Voegele, Dir. Faith Formation. Students 45.

3—HOLY CROSS (1965) Very Rev. John A. D'Antonio; Rev. Raphael Kilumanga; Deacon Richard Nagle Jr.

Res.: 7851 54th Ave. N., 33709. Tel: 727-546-3315; 727-541-2242; Fax: 727-547-2005.

*Catechesis/Religious Program—*Tel: 727-546-9654; Fax: 727-547-2005. Students 188.

4—HOLY FAMILY (1956) Revs. John Tapp; Paul Mangiafico; Deacons Michael Columbus; Peter Andre, Admin.; Ted Fahrendorf.

Res.: 200 78th Ave., N.E., 33702-4416. Tel: 727-526-5783; Fax: 727-521-2545. Email: holyfamily33702@yahoo.com. Web: www.holyfamilystpete.com.

School—Holy Family Early Childhood Center, 200 78th Ave. N.E., Saint Petersburg, 33702. Tel: 727-525-8489. Nina Meyers, Dir. PreK 2-PreK 4 Teachers 10; Students 75.

School—(Grades K-8), 250 78th Ave., N.E., 33702-4416. Tel: 727-526-8194; Fax: 727-527-6567. Web: www.holyfamily-school.com. Sr. Florence Ann Marino, I.H.M., Prin.; Mrs. Mary Karbowsky, Librarian. Sisters 1; Lay Teachers 14; Students 183.

*Catechesis/Religious Program—*Tel: 727-526-5783, Ext. 21; Fax: 727-521-2545. Linda Johnston, Dir.

Faith Formation. Students 159.

5—ST. JOSEPH (1926) Rev. John H. Gerth, Parochial Admin. (Pro Temp).
Mailing Address: 2025-22 Ave. S., 33712. Tel: 727-822-2153; Fax: 727-823-5820. Email: stjosephstpete@tampabay.rr.com. Web: stjosephstpete.org.
Preschool—Immaculate Conception, 2100 26 Ave. S., 33712. Tel: 727-822-2156; Fax: 727-553-9133. Lay Teachers 18; Students 142.
Catechesis/Religious Program—Students 20.

6—ST. MARY OUR LADY OF GRACE (1921) Revs. Cletus M. Watson, T.O.R.; Damian Amantia, T.O.R.; Julio Rivero, T.O.R.; Deacon John Fox.
Res.: 515 Fourth St. S., 33701. Tel: 727-896-2191; Fax: 727-895-6279. Email: info@stmaryolg.org. Web: www.stmaryolg.org.
Catechesis/Religious Program—Students 26.

7—ST. PAUL (1929) Rev. Msgr. Robert C. Gibbons; Rev. Babu Gangolu, S.A.C.
Res.: 1800 12th St. N., 33704. Tel: 727-822-3481; Fax: 727-822-1754. Web: stpaulstpete.com.
See St. Paul Catholic School, St. Petersburg under Elementary Schools, Interparochial located in the Institution section.
See St. Paul Children's Center under Pre Schools and Day Care Centers located in the Institution section.
Catechesis/Religious Program—Tel: 727-822-3481; Fax: 727-822-1754. Students 93.
Mission—The Mercy of God Polish Mission 1358 20th Ave. N., Pinellas Co. 33704. Tel: 727-823-6997; Fax: 727-821-8242. Rev. Janusz Burzawa.

8—ST. RAPHAEL (1961) Rev. Timothy H. Sherwood; Rev. Msgr. J. Bernard Caverly, Pastor Emeritus (Retired); Rev. Dominic Corona, Parochial Vicar; Deacon James Grevenites, Business Mgr. In Res., Rev. Jose G. Gonzalez (Retired).
Res.: 1376 Snell Isle Blvd., N.E., 33704. Tel: 727-821-7989; Fax: 727-896-9619. Web: www.st-raphaels.com.
School—(Grades PreK-8) Tel: 727-821-9663; Fax: 727-502-9594. Web: www.straphaelschool.net. Ms. Valerie Wostbrock, Prin.; Jane Venzke, Librarian. Lay Teachers 24; Students 225.
Catechesis/Religious Program—Tel: 727-821-0155. Lynn Edmonds, D.R.E. Students 260.

9—TRANSFIGURATION (1959) Rev. Edward Wal.
Church: 4000 43rd St. N., 33714. Tel: 727-525-0262; Fax: 727-526-7794. Email: parishadmin@transfigparish.org. Web: transfigparish.org.
Transfiguration Early Childhood Center—, (Ages 2-5), *Lower Pinellas Deanery*, 4300 43rd St., N., Saint Petersburg, 33714. Tel: 727-527-2880. Ms. Amy Lounsbury, Dir.
Catechesis/Religious Program—Email: religioused@transfigparish.org. Sue Sharlow, D.R.E. Students 124.

OUTSIDE THE CITY OF ST. PETERSBURG

BEVERLY HILLS, CITRUS CO., OUR LADY OF GRACE (1964) Rev. Msgr. Avelino R. Garcia; Rev. Francis Muteesasira Lubowa.
Res.: 6 Roosevelt Blvd., 34465. Tel: 352-746-2144; Fax: 352-746-6892. Email: olgbh@earthlink.net. Web: www.ourladyofgracefl.catholicweb.com.
See Pope John Paul II, Lecanto under Elementary Schools, Interparochial located in the Institution section.
Catechesis/Religious Program—Tel: 352-746-2144; Fax: 352-746-6892. Clara Makoid, D.R.E. Students 62.

BRANDON, HILLSBOROUGH CO., CHURCH OF THE NATIVITY (1960) [JC] Rev. Arthur Proulx; Rev. Msgr. James C. Lara, Pastor Emeritus (Retired); Rev. Carlos Rojas; Deacons Mark Taylor; Luis Zayas. In Res., Rev. Msgr. John A. Cippel (Retired).
Church: 705 E. Brandon Blvd., 33511. Tel: 813-681-4608; Fax: 813-653-9482. Web: www.nativitycatholicchurch.org.
Res.: 805 Westbrook, 33511. Tel: 813-684-0256.
School—(Grades PreK-8) Tel: 813-689-3395; Fax: 813-681-5406. Web: www.nativitycatholicschool.org. Dr. Bernadette Kunnen, Prin.; Sue Winter, Librarian. Lay Teachers 33; Students 750.
Catechesis/Religious Program—Tel: 813-689-9101; Fax: 813-684-1880. Vicki Hawkins, D.R.E. Students 1,032.

BROOKSVILLE, HERNANDO CO., ST. ANTHONY THE ABBOT (1892) Rev. Craig Morley; Deacons Manuel Carreiro; Michael Ruffner.
Res.: 20428 Cortez Blvd., 34601-5601. Tel: 352-796-2096; Fax: 352-796-7144. Email: parishoffice@stantchurch.org. Web: www.stantchurch.org.
See Notre Dame Interparochial School, Spring Hill under Elementary Schools, Interparochial located in the Institution section.
Catechesis/Religious Program—Tel: 352-796-2096; Fax: 352-796-7144. Email: faithformation@stantchurch.org. Mrs. Miriam Melfy, Dir. Faith Formation. Students 161.

CITRUS SPRINGS, CITRUS CO., ST. ELIZABETH ANN SETON (1976) Rev. Eric Peters; Rev. Msgr. George Cummings, Pastor Emeritus (Retired).
Office & Mailing Address: 1460 W. St. Elizabeth Pl., 34434. Tel: 352-489-4889; Fax: 352-489-4770. Email: steas@tampabay.rr.com. Web: stelizabeth-citrussprings.parishesonline.com.
See Pope John Paul II, Lecanto under Elementary Schools, Interparochial located in the Institution section.
Catechesis/Religious Program—Tel: 352-489-4889. Students 100.

CLEARWATER, PINELLAS CO.

1—ALL SAINTS (1987) Rev. Callist N. Nyambo; Deacons Jack Lyons; Thomas Shiel.
Office: 2801 Curlew Rd., 33761. Tel: 727-789-1025; Fax: 727-784-8025. Email: allsaintsclearwater@verizon.net. Web: allsaints-northpinellas.org.
See Guardian Angels Interparochial School, Clearwater under Elementary Schools, Interparochial located in the Institution section.
Catechesis/Religious Program—Tel: 727-789-1025; Fax: 727-784-8025. Students 102.

2—ST. BRENDAN (1978) Very Rev. Eric Hunter; Rev. Msgrs. Michael F. Devine, Pastor Emeritus (Retired); Edward Mulligan, Pastor Emeritus (Retired); Deacon William Gorman.
Res.: 245 Dory Passage, 33767. Tel: 727-443-5485; Fax: 727-442-5896. Email: stbrendan@tampabay.rr.com. Web: www.stbrendan-catholic.org.
See St. Cecelia Interparochial School, Clearwater under Elementary Schools, Interparochial located in the Institution section.
Catechesis/Religious Program—

3—ST. CATHERINE OF SIENA (1976) Rev. Msgr. Robert Morris; Revs. Carl J. Melchior Jr.; John J. Marino, O.F.M.; Sisters Kathleen Beatty, S.S.J., Pastoral Assoc.; Marie Cella, S.S.J., Pastoral Assoc.; Deacons Barry Wallace; Frederick Kunder.
Res.: 1955 S. Belcher Rd., 33764. Tel: 727-531-7721; Fax: 727-531-7723. Web: www.scosparish.org.
See St. Cecelia Interparochial School, Clearwater under Elementary Schools, Interparochial located in the Institution section.
Catechesis/Religious Program—Tel: 727-531-7721; Fax: 727-531-7723. Michelle Szczepanski, Dir. Faith Formation; Amy Simmons, D.R.E. Students 205.

4—ST. CECELIA (1924) Rev. Msgrs. Patrick Irwin; Aiden Foynes, Pastor Emeritus (Retired); Revs. Gilberto Quintero; Thomas Madden; Deacons Peter Andre; Eusebio Torres. In Res., Rev. Patrick Kennedy (Retired).
Office: 820 Jasmine Way, 33756. Tel: 727-447-3494; Fax: 727-442-4810. Email: office@stceceliachurch.org. Web: www.stceceliachurch.org.
See St. Cecelia Interparochial School, Clearwater under Elementary Schools, Interparochial located in the Institution section.
Catechesis/Religious Program—Email: dre@stceceliachurch.org. Mary Russell, D.R.E. Students 504.

5—LIGHT OF CHRIST (1966) Rev. Jacob Monteleone; Deacons James Hassett; James Gibson.
Res.: 2176 Marilyn St., 33765. Tel: 727-441-4545; Fax: 727-441-8771. Email: locchurch@ij.net.
See St. Cecelia Interparochial School, Clearwater under Elementary Schools, Interparochial located in the Institution section.
Pre-School—Tel: 727-442-4797; Fax: 727-441-8771. Mrs. Rebecca Daschbach, Dir. Lay Teachers 8; Students 80.
Catechesis/Religious Program—Tel: 727-442-7081. Debra Barry, C.R.E. Students 169.

6—ST. MICHAEL THE ARCHANGEL (1981) Very Rev. Gregg Tottle; Rev. Ted Costello; Sisters Therese Carolan, Pastoral Assoc.; Therese Dugan, S.N.D., Pastoral Assoc.
2281 State Rd. 580, 33763. Tel: 727-797-2375; Fax: 727-791-8287. Email: smaclw@verizon.net.
Catechesis/Religious Program—Mrs. Katie White, D.R.E. Students 287.

CRYSTAL RIVER, CITRUS CO., ST. BENEDICT (1953) Rev. Ryszard Stradomski.
Mailing Address: 455 S. Suncoast Blvd., 34429. Tel: 352-795-4478; 352-795-4479. Email: stbens@tampabay.rr.com. Web: stbenedictcrystalriver.org.
See Pope John Paul II, Lecanto under Elementary Schools, Interparochial located in the Institution section.
Catechesis/Religious Program—Tel: 352-795-4479; Fax: 352-795-3108. Students 87.
Daystar—6751 W. Gulf to Lake Hwy., 34429. Tel: 352-795-8668.

DADE CITY, PASCO CO.

1—ST. RITA (1912), (Hispanic), Very Rev. Daniel R. Kayajan, C.S.C.; Rev. William Persia, C.S.C.
Office & Mailing Address: 14404 14th St., 33523. Tel: 352-567-2894; Fax: 352-567-2777. Web: www.stritaparish.org.
See St. Anthony Interparochial School, San Antonio under Elementary Schools, Interparochial located in the Institution section.
Catechesis/Religious Program—Sisters Silvia Vivas, M.D.M.L., D.R.E.; Martha Flores, M.D.M.L., D.R.E. Students 474.

2—SACRED HEART (1888) [CEM] Rev. John C. Murphy; Deacons William Connors; David Cardona.
Res.: 32145 St. Joe Rd., 33525. Tel: 352-588-3641; Fax: 352-588-5299. Email: shcdadecity@embarqmail.com.
See St. Anthony Interparochial School, San Antonio under Elementary Schools, Interparochial located in the Institution section.
Catechesis/Religious Program—Tel: 352-588-3641; Fax: 352-588-5299. Students 102.
Sacred Heart Child Care Center—32245 St. Joe Rd., 33525. Tel: 352-588-4060; Fax: 352-588-4871. Email: shecctw@embarqmail.com. Mrs. Toni Watkins.

DUNEDIN, PINELLAS CO., OUR LADY OF LOURDES (1959) Revs. Gary Dowsey; Jose Colina.
Res.: 750 San Salvador Dr., 34698. Tel: 727-733-3606; Fax: 727-733-8305. Email: ourlady@gate.net. Web: ourladydunedin.org.
School—730 San Salvador Dr., 34698. Tel: 727-733-3776; Fax: 727-733-3776. Kathy Bogataj, Prin.; Tracy Maclean, Librarian. Lay Teachers 18; Students 203.
Catechesis/Religious Program—Tel: 813-733-0872; Fax: 813-733-8305. Email: faithformation@ourladydunedin.org. Americo Menendez, D.R.E. & Youth Min. Students 217.

GULFPORT, PINELLAS CO., MOST HOLY NAME OF JESUS (1960) Rev. James Ruhlin, Parochial Admin.; Deacon Glenn Pickart; Geraldine Bowine, Office Mgr.
Res.: 5800 15th Ave. S., 33707. Tel: 727-347-9989; Fax: 727-343-6420. Email: parishoffice@mostholyname.org. Web: mostholyname.org.
Catechesis/Religious Program—Tel: 727-347-9989; Fax: 727-343-6420. Email: dre@mostholyname.org. Fran Marinari, D.R.E.; Brianna Sims, Youth Min. Students 94.
Mission—St. Casimir Lithuanian Mission Office: 555 68th Ave., St. Pete Beach, Pinellas Co. 33706. Tel: 727-367-2408; 727-368-0523 (English). Rev. Bernardas Talaisis.

HOLIDAY, PASCO CO., ST. VINCENT DE PAUL (1969) Revs. Michael Arkins, S.S.S.; Thomas Fitzgerald, S.S.S.; Deacons Frank Longo; James Keough.
Res.: 4843 Mile Stretch Dr., 34690. Tel: 727-938-1974; Fax: 727-938-1975. Web: svdp4843.org.
See Bishop Larkin Interparochial School, Port Richey under Elementary Schools, Interparochial located in the Institution section.
Catechesis/Religious Program—Tel: 727-938-1001. Email: svdpfaithformation@yahoo.com. Jane Etzel, D.R.E. Students 145.

HOMOSASSA, CITRUS CO., ST. THOMAS THE APOSTLE (1987) Rev. Ronald Marecki; Deacon Eric Makoid; Susan Pistone, Office Admin.
Church: 7040 S. Suncoast Blvd., 34446. Tel: 352-628-7000; Fax: 352-628-4723. Web: home.catholicweb.com/sthomashomosassa.
Res.: 18 Beverly Ct., 34446. Tel: 352-503-6260.
See Pope John Paul II, Lecanto under Elementary Schools, Interparochial located in the Institution section.
Catechesis/Religious Program—Email: reled60@embarqmail.com. Sharon Bassing, D.R.E. Students 55.

HUDSON, PASCO CO., ST. MICHAEL THE ARCHANGEL (1971) Revs. Henry J. Riffle; Seamus Collins, O.P.; Jose Tejada; Deacon Robert Simpson.
Res.: 8014 State Rd. #52, 34667. Tel: 727-868-5276; Fax: 727-862-9187. Email: office@saintmichaelchurch.org. Web: www.saintmichaelchurch.org.
Catechesis/Religious Program—Tel: 727-819-5131. Mary Alber, Dir. Faith Formation. Students 293.

INDIAN ROCKS BEACH, PINELLAS CO., ST. JEROME (1956) Rev. Msgr. Brendan Muldoon; Rev. Frans Berkhout; Sisters Lucia Brady, O.S.C., Pastoral Assoc.; Phyllis Shaughnessy, O.S.C., Pastoral Asst.; Thomas Kurt, Dir. Music Min.
Mailing Address: P.O. Box 100, 33785. Email: sjcc@tampabay.rr.com. Web: stjeromeonline.org.
Res.: 10895 Hamlin Blvd., Largo, 33774. Tel: 727-595-4610; Fax: 727-596-6792.
Early Childhood Center—Tel: 727-596-9491; Fax: 727-596-8953. Denise Roach, Dir.
Catechesis/Religious Program—Tel: 727-595-3100. Web: stjeromeonline.org. Tamara Gildea, D.R.E. Students 225.

INVERNESS, CITRUS CO., OUR LADY OF FATIMA (1955) Revs. James B. Johnson; Charles Leke.
Mailing Address: 550 U.S. Hwy. 41 S., 34450. Tel: 352-726-1670; Fax: 352-344-8384. Web:

home.catholicweb.com/ladyofatima.
Res.: 518 Desota Ave., 34450. Tel: 352-726-1670.
See Pope John Paul II, Lecanto under Elementary Schools, Interparochial located in the Institution section.
Catechesis/Religious Program—Rebecca Pound, D.R.E.; Annette Tremante, D.R.E. Students 172.

LAND O'LAKES, PASCO CO., OUR LADY OF THE ROSARY (1952) Very Rev. Ronald Aubin; Rev. Rene Tapel; Deacons Augustin Ortiz; Kenneth Anderson; Dennis Snyder.
P.O. Box 1229, 34639. Email: office@ladyrosary.org. Web: www.ladyrosary.org.
Res.: 2348 Collier Pkwy., Land O Lakes, 34639. Tel: 813-949-4565; Fax: 813-948-1981. Email: office@ladyrosary.org. Web: ladyrosary.org.
See Most Holy Redeemer Interparochial School, Tampa under Elementary Schools, Interparochial located in the Institution section.
Catechesis/Religious Program—Tel: 813-949-2699; Fax: 813-948-1981. Email: religioused@ladyrosary.org. Constance Whittington, C.R.E. Students 1,331.

LARGO, PINELLAS CO.

1—ST. MATTHEW (1985) Rev. Patrick M. Rebel; Deacons Bernard Braun, (Retired); Anthony Kijonka, (Retired); Rick Wells.
Mailing Address: P.O. Box 10097, 33773-0097. Email: info@stmat.org. Web: www.stmat.org.
Office: 9111 90th Ave. N., 33777. Tel: 727-393-1288; Fax: 727-398-2683.
Catechesis/Religious Program—Tel: 727-393-1288, Ext. 207. Regina Dougherty, D.R.E. Students 105.
Mission—Holy Martyrs of Vietnam 9099 90th Ave. N., Pinellas Co. 33777. Tel: 727-397-7906. Rev. Joseph Thai Tran.

2—ST. PATRICK (1958) Revs. Paul Pecchie; Claudius Mpuya; Deacons Richard Brady; Ken Spaulding.
Res.: 2121 16th Ave., S.W., 33770. Tel: 727-584-2318; Fax: 727-586-5413. Email: stpat2000@aol.com. Web: www.stpatrick-largo.com.
School—1501 Trotter Rd., 33770. Tel: 727-581-4865; Fax: 727-581-7842. Sr. Veronica Visceglia, S.S.N.D., Prin. Lay Teachers 17; Students 180.
Catechesis/Religious Program—Joseph Blum, D.R.E.; Sr. Kathleen Luger, D.R.E. Students 85.

LECANTO, CITRUS CO., ST. SCHOLASTICA CHURCH (1987) Very Rev. Michael R. Smith; Rev. Thomas Spillett; Deacons Terrence E. Knox; Stephen Sablone; Robert Smith.
Res. & Church: 4301 W. Homosassa Trail, 34461. Tel: 352-746-9422; Fax: 352-746-2335. Email: lboyer@stscholastica.org. Web: stscholastica.org.
See Pope John Paul II, Lecanto under Elementary Schools, Interparochial located in the Institution section.
Catechesis/Religious Program—Tel: 352-746-9422; Fax: 352-746-2335. Alexander Groppe, D.R.E. Students 104.

LUTZ, HILLSBOROUGH CO., ST. TIMOTHY (1985) Very Rev. Kenneth Malley; Rev. Sojan Punakkattu; Deacons Peter Burns; Jerry L. Crall.
Res.: 17512 Lakeshore Rd., 33558-4802. Fax: 813-961-9429. Email: parishmanager@sainttims.org. Web: www.sainttims.org.
See Most Holy Redeemer Interparochial School, Tampa under Elementary Schools, Interparochial located in the Institution section.
Catechesis/Religious Program—Tel: 813-961-1716. Judy Anderson, Youth Min.; Jean Gadoury, Dir. Faith Formation. Students 849.

MASARYKTOWN, PASCO CO., ST. MARY, OUR LADY OF SORROWS (1931) Rev. James A. Bucaria.
Mailing Address: 18810 U.S. Hwy. 41, 34604. Tel: 352-796-2792; Fax: 352-544-0398. Email: sacerdos@bellsouth.net. Web: www.saintmary-ols.com.
See Notre Dame Interparochial School, Spring Hill under Elementary Schools, Interparochial located in the Institution section.
Catechesis/Religious Program—Mary Ann Martin, D.R.E. Students 6.

NEW PORT RICHEY, PASCO CO.

1—OUR LADY QUEEN OF PEACE (1913) Revs. Sebastian Earthedath, M.S.T.; Joseph Kalarickal, M.S.T.; Saji James, M.S.T.; Deacons Roger F. Lind; Juan Valentin.
Res.: 5340 High St., 34652. Tel: 727-849-7521; Fax: 727-849-4814. Email: office@ladyqueenofpeace.org. Web: ladyqueenofpeacenpr.org.
See Bishop Larkin Interparochial School, Port Richey under Elementary Schools, Interparochial located in the Institution section.
Catechesis/Religious Program—Tel: 727-842-9396; Fax: 727-841-6601. Patricia A. Mahoney, D.R.E. Students 148.

2—ST. THOMAS AQUINAS (1980) Revs. Michael Lydon; George Varkey, M.S.T.
Res.: 8320 Old C.R. #54, 34653-6415. Tel: 727-372-8600; Fax: 727-376-7204. Email: sta@stanpr.org. Web: www.stanpr.org.
St. Thomas Early Childhood Development Center—Tel: 727-376-2330; Fax: 727-372-5712. Email: staecc@aol.com.
See Bishop Larkin Interparochial School, Port Richey under Elementary Schools, Interparochial located in the Institution section.
Catechesis/Religious Program—Email: sta_faith@yahoo.com. Philip Coit, D.R.E. Students 319.

PALM HARBOR, PINELLAS CO., ST. LUKE THE EVANGELIST (1985) Revs. Paul Kochu; Jose Thomas; Deacons Joe Reid, Pastoral Assoc.; Cesar Fernando Quinones.
Res.: 2757 Alderman Rd., 34684. Tel: 727-786-3648; Fax: 727-789-9556. Email: stlukepalmharbor@gmail.com. Web: www.stlukepalmharbor.org.
St. Luke Early Childhood Center—Tel: 727-787-2914; Fax: 727-786-8648. Email: stlecc@gte.net.
See Guardian Angels Interparochial School, Clearwater under Elementary Schools, Interparochial located in the Institution section.
Catechesis/Religious Program—Tel: 727-787-2845; Fax: 727-786-8648. Students 271.

PINELLAS PARK, PINELLAS CO., SACRED HEART (1910) Revs. Anthony Coppola; Tom Tobin; Deacons L. Roger Cartier; David Sirrianna.
Church: 7809 46th Way, 33781. Tel: 727-541-4447; Fax: 727-541-2073. Email: office@sacredheartcatholic.org.
School—7951 46th Way N., 33781. Tel: 727-544-1106; Fax: 727-548-9606. Mr. Andy Shannon, Prin. Religious 1; Lay Teachers 16; Students 143.
Catechesis/Religious Program—Email: religiouseducation@sacredheartcatholic.org. Marion Gawlowicz, D.R.E. Students 56.

PLANT CITY, HILLSBOROUGH CO., ST. CLEMENT (1912) Revs. Thomas Anastasia; Rafael E. Martos; Rev. Msgr. Cesar Petilla; Deacons Manuel Santiago; Neil Legner; Kevin Orth.
Church & Mailing Address: 1104 N. Alexander St., 33563. Tel: 813-752-8251; Fax: 813-759-2721; 813-764-8019. Email: info@stclementpc.org. Web: www.stclementpc.org.
St. Clement Early Childhood Center—, (Ages 3-5), Tel: 813-754-1237. Maureen Ringley, Dir.
Catechesis/Religious Program—Cathy Rosales, C.R.E. Students 566.

PORT RICHEY, PASCO CO., ST. JAMES THE APOSTLE (1984) Very Rev. Michael Robert Cormier; Deacons Daniel McCarthy; James Minary.
Res.: 8400 Monarch Dr., 34668. Tel: 727-869-3130; Fax: 727-869-8886.
See Bishop Larkin Interparochial School, Port Richey under Elementary Schools, Interparochial located in the Institution section.
Catechesis/Religious Program—Email: faith.formation@stjamesportrichey.org. Barbara Ferreris, D.R.E. Students 252.

RIDGE MANOR, HERNANDO CO., ST. ANNE (1960) Rev. John S. Hays; Deacon Robert Mintz.
4142 Treiman Blvd., Hwy. 301, 33523. Email: stanne@embarqmail.com.
Res.: 35135 Whispering Oaks Blvd., 33523. Tel: 352-583-2550; Fax: 352-583-0300.
Catechesis/Religious Program—Sr. Patricia Saunders, O.P., D.R.E. Students 13.

RIVERVIEW, HILLSBOROUGH CO., RESURRECTION (1983) Rev. Eugeniusz Gancarz.
Mailing Address: P.O. Box 418, 33568.
Res.: 6819 Krycul Ave., 33578. Tel: 813-677-2175; Fax: 813-671-7844.
Resurrection Early Childhood Center—, (Ages 3-4), Tel: 813-672-0077. Ivonne Roldan-Cortes, Dir.
Catechesis/Religious Program—Tina Ver Pault, D.R.E. Students 225.

RUSKIN, HILLSBOROUGH CO., ST. ANNE (1956) Very Rev. John McEvoy; Deacons Dale Bacik; Edward Smith; Linda Parkansky, Min. & Liturgy Coord.
Office: 106 11th Ave., N.E., 33570-3625. Tel: 813-645-1714; Fax: 813-645-5570. Email: office@saintanneruskin.org. Web: www.saintanneruskin.org.
Catechesis/Religious Program—Email: office@saintanneruskin.org. Mrs. Cindy Cyman, Dir. Faith Formation. Students 370.

ST. PETE BEACH, PINELLAS CO., ST. JOHN VIANNEY (1948) Revs. John Blum; Allan Tupa; Dermot Dunne; Deacon Joseph Grote.
Church: 445 82nd Ave., 33706. Tel: 727-360-1147; Fax: 727-367-4418 (Office).
School—500 84th Ave., 33706. Tel: 727-360-1113; Fax: 727-367-8734. Email: cjudson@sjvcc.org. Web: www.sjvcs.org. Jillian Hudson, Prin. Lay Teachers 16; Students 235.
Catechesis/Religious Program—Tel: 727-360-1147, Ext. 201; Fax: 727-367-4418. Students 98.

SAFETY HARBOR, PINELLAS CO., ESPIRITU SANTO (1960) Revs. Robert J. Schneider; Joseph Musco; Sr. Paulamarie Lacy, S.N.D., Dir. Liturgical Ministries; Deacons Vincent Alterio, Parish Admin.; Dominic P. Friscia.
Office: 2405 Philippe Pkwy., 34695. Tel: 727-726-8477; Fax: 727-799-2062. Web: www.espiritusanto.cc.
See Espiritu Santo Catholic School, Safety Harbor under Elementary Schools, Interparochial located in the Institution section.
Catechesis/Religious Program—Tel: 727-812-4656; Fax: 727-812-4658. Students 664.

SAN ANTONIO, PASCO CO., ST. ANTHONY OF PADUA (1883) [CEM] Rev. Edwin Palka; Deacons Michael Arno; Irvin Lau; Mrs. Sandra Lau, Music Min.
Res.: 12144 Joe Herrmann Dr., P.O. Box 875, 33576. Tel: 352-588-3081; Fax: 352-588-5070. Email: church@saopcc.com.
See St. Anthony Interparochial School, San Antonio under Elementary Schools, Interparochial located in the Institution section.
Catechesis/Religious Program—Tel: 352-588-3081; Fax: 352-588-5070. Students 70.

SEFFNER, HILLSBOROUGH CO., ST. FRANCIS OF ASSISI (1987) Revs. Martin Madavana, I.C.; Christopher Fitzgerald, I.C., Pastor Emeritus (Retired); Michael O'Neill, I.C.; Deacons Jerome Thomas; Richard Beaudry.
Res.: 4450 C.R. 579, 33584. Tel: 813-681-9115; Fax: 813-689-4148.
Catechesis/Religious Program—Students 170.

SEMINOLE, PINELLAS CO.

1—BLESSED SACRAMENT (1959) Revs. James Gordon, I.C.; G. Richard Pilger, I.C.
Res.: 11565 66th Ave. N., 33772. Tel: 727-391-4661. Email: office@blessedsacramentonline.org.
School—11501 66th Ave. N., 33772. Tel: 727-391-4660; Fax: 727-391-5638. Web: www.bsschool.org. Cindy Yevich, Prin. Lay Teachers 13; Students 155.
Catechesis/Religious Program—Tel: 727-391-4661; Fax: 727-391-5638. Students 156.

2—ST. JUSTIN MARTYR (1987) Very Rev. Michael T. O'Brien.
Mailing Address: 10851 Ridge Rd., 33778. Web: www.stjustinmartyr.net.
Catechesis/Religious Program—Tel: 727-397-3312, Ext. 307; Fax: 727-392-6653. Walt Smith, D.R.E. Students 93.

SPRING HILL, HERNANDO CO.

1—ST. FRANCES XAVIER CABRINI (1980) Very Rev. Richard Jankowski; Rev. Krzysztof Gazdowicz; Deacon James Leonard.
Mailing Address: 5030 Mariner Blvd., 34609. Tel: 352-683-9666; Fax: 352-688-2660. Email: frontdesk@stfrances.org. Web: www.stfrances.org.
In Res., Rev. Andrew Beaudoin, S.S.S.; Deacons Roland Desjardins; Gregorio Lugo; Edward Smith; Robert "Bob" Anderson; Scott Conway.
See Notre Dame Interparochial School, Spring Hill under Elementary Schools, Interparochial located in the Institution section.
Catechesis/Religious Program—Tel: 352-686-9954, Ext. 201. Sherri Collinsworth, D.R.E. Students 720.

2—SAINT JOAN OF ARC (1988) Rev. Raymond F. O'Neill; Deacon Lee Hinderscheid.
Res.: 13485 Spring Hill Dr., 34609. Tel: 352-688-0663; Fax: 352-686-7937. Email: jchrchca@campabay.rr.com. Web: home.catholiweb.com/stjoanspringhill.fl.
See Notre Dame Interparochial School, Spring Hill under Elementary Schools, Interparochial located in the Institution section.
Catechesis/Religious Program—Tel: 352-688-0663; Fax: 352-686-7937. Donna Greco, D.R.E. Students 224.

3—ST. THERESA (1968) Revs. James McAteer, I.C.; Edison Bernavas, I.C.; Deacons Jose Rios; James McMahon.
Res.: 1107 Commercial Way, 34606. Tel: 352-683-2849; Fax: 352-683-3437. Email: sttheresa.office@bellsouth.net.
See Notre Dame Interparochial School, Spring Hill under Elementary Schools, Interparochial located in the Institution section.
Catechesis/Religious Program—Dorothy Siegrist, D.R.E. Students 167.

SUN CITY CENTER, HILLSBOROUGH CO., PRINCE OF PEACE (1970) Revs. Joel Kovanis; Augustine Mailadiyil; Deacon Matthew Shirina; Maureen Vilcheck, Business Mgr.
Mailing Address: 702 Valley Forge Blvd., 33573-5353. Tel: 813-634-2328; Fax: 813-633-6670. Web: www.popcc.org.
Res.: 1002 Fordham Dr., 33573. Tel: 813-634-2328.
Catechesis/Religious Program—Email: pat@popcc.org. Students 77.
Mission—Our Lady of Guadalupe Mission (1989) 16650 U.S. 301 S., Wimauma, Hillsborough 33598. Tel: 813-633-2384; Fax: 813-642-9047. Rev. Demetrio Lorden.

TAMPA, HILLSBOROUGH CO.

1—BLESSED SACRAMENT (1959) Rev. Kazimierz Domek.
Res.: 1205 Windermere Way, 33619-4601. Tel: 813-626-2984; Fax: 813-626-2842. Email:

office@blessedsacramentcatholic.org.
Church: 7001 12th Ave. S., 33619-4601.
Catechesis/Religious Program—Students 109.

2—CHRIST THE KING (1941) Rev. David Toups.
Res.: 821 S. Dale Mabry Hwy., 33609. Tel: 813-876-5841; Fax: 813-873-2426. Web: www.ctk-tampa.org.
School—3809 Morrison Ave., 33629. Tel: 813-876-8770; Fax: 813-879-0315. Web: www.cks-school.org. Gerard Carrier, Prin. Lay Teachers 40; Students 495.
Catechesis/Religious Program—Tel: 813-870-2509. William W. Woodward, D.R.E. Students 513.

3—EPIPHANY OF OUR LORD (1963) Revs. Ignatius Tuoc; Pierre A Dorvil, S.M.M.; Deacon Maximo E. Montayre.
Mailing Address: P.O. Box 11246, 33680. Tel: 813-234-8693; Fax: 813-238-5060. Email: epiphany_tampa2@yahoo.com.
Res.: 2510 E. Hanna Ave., 33610. Tel: 813-234-8693; Fax: 813-238-5060.
Catechesis/Religious Program—Tel: 813-238-1751. Students 120.
Mission—St. Joseph Vietnamese Mission 2510 E. Hanna Ave., Hillsborough Co. 33610. Tel: 813-238-8693.
Mission—Immaculate Conception Haitian Catholic Mission 2510 E. Hanna Ave., Hillsborough Co. 33610. Tel: 813-234-8693; Fax: 813-238-5060.

4—INCARNATION (1962) Very Rev. Michael Suszynski; Revs. Diego Ossa; Philip Dac Clement; Deacons Frank Julian; Joseph Krzanowski; Pablo Maldonado.
Res.: 5124 Gateway Dr., 33615. Tel: 813-885-7861; Fax: 813-884-3624. Email: irenemartz@tampabay.rr.com. Web: icctampa.org.
School—5111 Webb Rd., 33615. Tel: 813-884-4502; Fax: 813-885-3734. Email: icsmmood@icstampa.org. Web: icstampa.org. Mr. Michael Zelenka, Prin. Lay Teachers 28; Students 316.
Catechesis/Religious Program—(Grades PreK-5) Carmen Cayon, D.R.E. Students 476.

5—ST. JOSEPH (1896) Rev. Vladimir Dziadek.
Mailing Address: P.O. Box 4298, 33677. Email: stjoecctpa@tampabay.rr.com.
Res.: 3012 Cherry St., 33607. Tel: 813-877-5729; Fax: 813-877-5720.
School—St. Joseph Catholic School, (Grades 3-8) Tel: 813-879-7720; Fax: 813-873-0804. Web: www-.stjosephcatholicschooltampa.org. Brenda Budd, Prin.; Mrs. Claudia Dyer, Librarian. Daughters of Mary Help of Christians (Paterson, NJ) 2; Lay Teachers 15; Students 212.
Catechesis/Religious Program—Students 91.

6—ST. LAWRENCE (1959) Very Rev. Thomas Morgan; Rev. Msgr. Laurence E. Higgins, Pastor Emeritus (Retired); Rev. Dayan Machado; Deacons Gregory Lambert; Julio Vazquez; Crispin Stout. In Res., Rev. Edward C. Keating, O.F.M. (Retired).
Res. and Mailing: 5225 N. Himes Ave., 33614. Tel: 813-875-4040; Fax: 813-876-0491. Email: office@stlawrence.org. Web: www.stlawrence.org.
School—Tel: 813-879-5090; Fax: 813-879-6886. Therese Hernandez, Prin. Lay Teachers 40; Students 585.
Catechesis/Religious Program—Tel: 813-875-4040, Ext. 206; Fax: 813-876-0491. Students 220.

7—ST. MARK THE EVANGELIST (1996) Rev. David DeJulio; Deacons Scott Paine; Jose Moronta.
Church: 9724 Cross Creek Blvd., 33647-2594. Tel: 813-907-7746, Ext. 307; Fax: 813-907-7556. Email: frdavid@stmarktampa.org. Web: www.stmarktampa.org.
Catechesis/Religious Program—Tel: 813-907-7746, Ext. 308; Fax: 813-907-7556. Email: faithformation@stmarktampa.org. Mrs. Claudia Garcia, D.R.E. Students 1,161.

8—ST. MARY (1966) Revs. Jude Vera; Wayne C. Genereux, O.de.M.; Deacons John Iadanza; James Maniz. In Res., Rev. Ramon Hernandez (Retired).
Church: 15520 North Blvd., 33613. Tel: 813-961-1061; Fax: 813-961-3782. Email: office@stmarytampa.org. Web: www.stmarytampa.org.
Res.: 15304 Stonecreek Ln., 33613.
See Most Holy Redeemer Interparochial School, Tampa under Elementary Schools, Interparochial located in the Institution section.
Catechesis/Religious Program—Tel: 813-963-2079; Fax: 813-968-7218. Students 222.
Mission—Santa Maria 14004 N. 15th St., 33613-3554. Tel: 813-910-3575.

9—MARY HELP OF CHRISTIANS (1966) Revs. Bruce Craig, S.D.B.; Joseph Hyue Chong, S.D.B.; Deacon Edmond Anctil.
Tel: 813-626-7588; Fax: 813-626-5882. Email: goodshepherd6410@aol.com; mhcparishtampa@gmail.com.
Res.: 6400 E. Chelsea St., 33610.
Catechesis/Religious Program—Tel: 813-626-9991 (Sundays). Students 42.

10—MOST HOLY REDEEMER (1937) Revs. John C. Aurilia, O.F.M.Cap.; Alfonso D. Pagliara, O.F.M-.Cap.; Anthony Giudice, O.F.M.Cap.; Peter Nicosia, O.F.M.Cap.; Bro. Miguel Ramirez, O.F.M.Cap.
Res.: 10110 Central Ave., N., 33612-7402. Tel: 813-933-2859; Fax: 813-932-6153. Email: mhroffice@aol.com.
See Most Holy Redeemer Interparochial School, Tampa under Elementary Schools, Interparochial located in the Institution section.
Catechesis/Religious Program—Students 85.

11—OUR LADY OF PERPETUAL HELP (1890), (Hispanic—Haitian), [JC] Revs. Thomas A. Stokes, S.M.; Raymond Coolong, S.M.
Res.: 1711 11th Ave., 33605. Tel: 813-248-5701; Fax: 813-241-4128.
Catechesis/Religious Program—Students 63.

12—ST. PATRICK (1958) [JC] Revs. Angelus Migliore, T.O.R.; Stanley Holland, T.O.R., Parochial Vicar; Mr. Francis (Buzz) Bruno, Operations Mgr.; Deacon James Ben Hooks.
Parish Office—4518 S. Manhattan Ave., 33611. Tel: 813-839-5337; Fax: 813-831-2778. Web: www.stpatricktampa.org.
Catechesis/Religious Program—Students 90.

13—ST. PAUL (1963) Revs. Leonard Piotrowski; J. Glenn Diaz; Timothy Cummings; Deacons Greg Kovalesky, Pastoral Assoc.; John Alvarez; Carlos Celaya; Ron Rojas; Winston McDonald; Raymond Dever.
Mailing Address: 12708 N. Dale Mabry, 33618. Tel: 813-961-3023; Fax: 813-962-8780. Web: www.stpaul-church.com.
See Most Holy Redeemer Interparochial School, Tampa under Elementary Schools, Interparochial located in the Institution section.
Catechesis/Religious Program—Tel: 813-264-3309; Fax: 813-962-8780. Sue Sferra, D.R.E. Students 830.

14—ST. PETER CLAVER (1893), (African American), Rev. Hugh Chikawe; Deacon William Mahood.
1203 N. Nebraska Ave., 33602-3044. Tel: 813-223-7098. Email: stpeterclaver@gmail.com. Web: spc.catholicweb.com.
Res.: 3708 N. 12th St., 33603. Fax: 813-223-6520.
School—(Grades PreK-8), 1401 Governor St., 33602-3044. Tel: 813-224-0865; Fax: 813-223-6726. Sr. Maria Goretti Babatunde, Prin. Lay Teachers 14; Students 103.
Catechesis/Religious Program—Students 20.

15—SACRED HEART (1860) Revs. George C. Corrigan, O.F.M.; Zachary Elliott, O.F.M.; Sean O'Brien, O.F.M.; Bro. Juan Turcios, O.F.M.; Larry Cabrera, Business Mgr.; Sean Fitzsimmons-Brown, Dir. Liturgical Ministries.
Mailing Address: P.O. Box 1524, 33601. Tel: 813-229-1595; Fax: 813-221-2350. Web: sacredheartfla.org.
School—3515 N. Florida Ave., 33603. Tel: 813-229-0618; Fax: 813-223-7667. Mr. Kenneth Hitchcock, Prin. Lay Teachers 16; Students 108.
Catechesis/Religious Program—Students 160.

TARPON SPRINGS, PINELLAS CO., ST. IGNATIUS OF ANTIOCH (1889) Revs. Joseph A. Pellegrino; Mathew Moothasseril; Kevin Molloy; Deacons Samuel Moschetto; John Edgerton.
Mailing Address: P.O. Box 1306, 34688-1306. Email: kcreamer@ignatius.net. Web: st.ignatius.net.
Res.: 715 E. Orange St., 34689. Tel: 727-937-4050; Fax: 727-943-0676. Email: kcreamer@ignatius.net. Web: st.ignatius.net.
See Guardian Angels Interparochial School, Clearwater under Elementary Schools, Interparochial located in the Institution section.
St. Ignatius Early Childhood Center— (1984)Tel: 727-937-4050, Ext. 225; Fax: 727-722-9000. Web: stignatiusecc.org. Nancy Gorby, Dir.
Catechesis/Religious Program—Tel: 727-937-4050, Ext. 223; Fax: 727-942-2331. Matthew Moothasseril, Dir. Faith Formation. Students 910.

TEMPLE TERRACE, HILLSBOROUGH CO., CORPUS CHRISTI (1958) Revs. Robert Cadrecha; Erwin Belgica; Deacon David Lesieur.
Mailing Address: 9715 N. 56th St., 33617. Tel: 813-988-1593; Fax: 813-985-3583. Web: www.spiritualhome.org.
School—Tel: 813-988-1722; Fax: 813-989-2665. Web: www.corpuschristicatholicschool.org. Carmen Caltigirone, Prin. Lay Teachers 16; Students 233.
Catechesis/Religious Program—Lily Hughson, D.R.E. Students 401.

TRINITY, PASCO, CO., ST. PETER THE APOSTLE CATHOLIC CHURCH IN TRINITY, INC. (2008) Very Rev. Dennis E. Hughes.
10710 S.R. 54, Ste. 101, 34655. Tel: 727-264-8968; Fax: 727-264-8969. Email: dhughes54@tampabay.rr.com.
Catechesis/Religious Program—Kevin Hansat, D.R.E. Students 74.

VALRICO, HILLSBOROUGH CO., ST. STEPHEN (1987) Revs. William J. Swengros; Jose George; Emery Longanga; Deacons Daniel Gratkowski; Richard Zeitler.
Church: 5049 Bell Shoals Rd., 33594. Tel: 813-689-4900; Fax: 813-689-7492. Web: www.ststephencatholic.org.
School—(Grades PreK-8), 10424 St. Stephen Cir., Riverview, 33569. Tel: 813-741-9203; Fax: 813-741-9622. Ms. Therese Jackson, Prin. Lay Teachers 52; Students 346.
Catechesis/Religious Program—10424 St. Stephen Cir., Riverview, 33569. Tel: 813-671-4434; Fax: 813-671-2994. Kelly Goudreau, D.R.E. Students 1,186.

ZEPHYRHILLS, PASCO CO., ST. JOSEPH CATHOLIC CHURCH (1912) Revs. Mathew K. Abraham, A.L.C.P.; Theobold Weria, A.L.C.P.; Deacon Neil Huiskens; Mrs. Theresa H. Miner, Business Admin. Email: thminer@stjoezhills.org.
Church: 5316 11th St., 33542. Tel: 813-782-2813; Fax: 813-788-1036. Email: info@stjoezhills.org. Web: www.stjosephzephyrhills.org.
See St. Anthony Interparochial School, San Antonio under Elementary Schools, Interparochial located in the Institution section.
Catechesis/Religious Program—Tel: 813-788-2510. Sr. Kathleen Lyons, S.N.D., D.R.E. Students 80.

On Duty Outside the Diocese:
Revs.—
McDonagh, Donat Michael
Morris, Michael J.
Muhr, Michael
Scott, Philip
Wilson, Bill
Young, Robert

Retired:
Rev. Msgrs.—
Balthazar, Norman
Bumpus, Harold
Caverly, J. Bernard
Cippel, John A.
Cooke, Colman M., Ph.D.
Cummings, George
Daly, Desmond, V.F.
Dee, Dacian, J.C.D.
Devine, Michael F.
Diez, Antonio
DuBois, William
Earner, Thomas
Foynes, Aiden
Higgins, Laurence E., P.A.
Lara, James C.
McCahon, Joseph F.
Mullen, Austin
Mulligan, Edward
Neff, John
Revs.—
Colgan, John
Cottrell, James
Dauss, Francis
Dionne, Francis
Estibalez, Inocencio
Gonzalez, Jose G.
Goudreau, Paul
Hernandez, Ramon
Hervey, Paul
Kane, John
Kennedy, Patrick
Lamp, Edward
Lawlor, Brendan
Lettre, Raymond
Mahony, John
Morton, Vincent
Sanchez, Felix
Villemaire, Arthur

Permanent Deacons:
Alterio, Vincent
Alvarez, John
Anctil, Edmond
Anderson, Kenneth
Anderson, Robert "Bob"
Andre, Peter
Arno, Michael
Bacik, Dale
Beaudry, Richard
Bevvino, Frank, (On Duty Outside of Diocese)
Brady, Richard
Braun, Bernard
Buckley, John J.
Burns, Peter
Cardona, David
Carreiro, Manuel
Cartier, Roger L.
Celaya, Carlos
Columbus, Michael
Connelly, Bartley
Connors, William
Conway, Scott
Crall, Jerry

Desjardins, Roland
Dever, Raymond
Diaz, William
Dodenhoff, Edward
Dunphy, Melvin
Edgerton, John
Evans, Forrest, (On Duty Outside the Diocese)
Fahrendorf, Ted
Fox, John
Friscia, Dominic
Garcia, Luis
Gibson, James
Gorman, William
Gould, Stanley, (On Duty Outside the Diocese)
Gratkowski, Daniel
Grevenites, James
Grote, Joseph
Haber, Paul
Hassett, James
Hecht, Lowell, (On Duty Outside the Diocese)
Hinderscheid, Lee
Hooks, James Ben
Huiskens, Nell
Hunt, Samuel
Iadanza, John
Julian, Frank
Kennedy, James
Keough, James J.
Kijonka, Anthony
Knox, Terrence
Koppenaal, John, (On Duty Outside the Diocese)
Kovalesky, Gregory
Krzanowski, Joseph
Kunder, Frederick
Kurylowicz, Stephen
Lambert, Gregory
Lamothe, Allan
Lau, Irvin
Legner, Neil
Leonard, James
Lesieur, David
Lind, Roger F.
Longo, Frank
Lugo, Gregorio
Lyons, John
Mahood, William
Makoid, Eric
Maldonado, Pablo
McCarthy, Daniel E.
McDonald, Winston
McGory, Gerald
McMahon, James
Minary, James
Mintz, Robert
Moniz, John
Montayre, Maximo
Moronta, Jose
Moschetto, Samuel
Nagle, Richard, Jr.
Nova, Leocadio
Orth, Kevin
Ortiz, Augustin
Paine, Scott
Pese, Howard
Pickart, Glenn
Pignataro, Angelo
Polcari, Joseph
Postadan, Romulo
Quiles, Rafael
Quinones, Cesar Fernando
Reid, Joseph
Rios, Jose
Roberts, Lionel
Rodriguez, Manuel
Rojas, Ronald
Rosa, Abraham
Ruffner, Michael
Sablone, Stephen
Santiago, Manuel
Shiel, Thomas
Shirina, Matthew
Simpson, Robert C.
Sirrianna, David
Smith, Edward
Smith, Edward
Smith, Robert
Snyder, Dennis
Solorzano, Jose
Sparks, Robert
Spaulding, Ken
Stahl, Raymond
Stout, Crispin
Taylor, Mark, M.D.
Thomas, Jerome
Tibbets, Albert
Torres, Eusebio
Valentin, Juan E.
Vance, Ronald
Varner, David
Vasquez, Julio
Wallace, Barry
Wells, Rick, J.C.L.
White, Gerard
Zayas, Luis
Zeitler, Richard

INSTITUTIONS LOCATED IN THE DIOCESE

[A] COLLEGES

SAINT LEO. *Saint Leo University, Office of Assessment and Institutional Research*, MC 2004, P.O. Box 6665, 33574-6665. Tel: 352-588-8657; 352-588-8894; Fax: 352-588-8917. Email: eileen.dunbar@saintleo.edu. Web: www.saintleo.edu. Dr. Arthur F. Kirk Jr., Pres.; Revs. Stephan Brown, S.V.D., Dir. of Univ. Ministry. Email: stephan.brown@saintleo.edu; Anthony Kissel, Ph.D., S.T.D., Dept. Chm. Philosophy & Religion & Dir. Graduate Theology; Sr. Mary Dorothy Neuhofer, O.S.B., Prof. & Archivist; Rev. Michael Cooper, S.J., S.T.D., Asst. Prof. Religion.
Saint Leo University, Inc.
Saint Leo University Educational Fund, Inc., An Independent and Catholic Coeducational Liberal Arts University Priests 3; Sisters 1; Lay Teachers 214; Total Enrollment 15,564.

[B] HIGH SCHOOLS, DIOCESAN

ST. PETERSBURG. *St. Petersburg Catholic High School, Inc.*, 6333 Ninth Ave. N., 33710. Tel: 727-344-4065; Fax: 727-343-9311. Email: info@spchs.org. Web: spchs.org. Rev. Michael Conway, S.D.B., Pres.; Mr. John McMahon, Prin.; Mrs. Kathleen King, Asst. Prin.; Mrs. Lori Wright, Media Center Coord.; Mr. Mike Moran, Asst. Dir. Athletics; Mr. Nick Vandewalle, Dean of Students; Mr. Stephen McEntegart, Coord. of Youth Ministry; Mr. John Gerdes, Athletic Dir. Salesians of St. John Bosco (New Rochelle, NY) 5; Sisters of the Third Franciscan Order (Syracuse, NY) 1; School Sisters of Notre Dame 1; Lay Teachers 27; Students 462.

CLEARWATER. *Clearwater Central Catholic High School, Inc.* (1962) 2750 Haines Bayshore Rd., 33760. Tel: 727-531-1449; Fax: 727-535-7034. Email: jdeputy@ccchs.org. Web: www.ccchs.org. John Venturella, Pres.; James Deputy, Prin.; Cyndi Kibby, Media Specialist; Karen Johnson, Media Specialist. Lay Teachers 28; Students 466.

SPRING HILL. *Bishop McLaughlin Catholic High School, Inc.* (2003) 13651 Hays Rd., 34610. Tel: 727-857-2600; Fax: 727-857-2610. Email: rmckendrick@bmchs.com. Web: bmchs.com. Sarah M. Regan, Prin.; Linda Haynie, Media Specialist. Lay Teachers 25; Students 257.

TAMPA. *Tampa Catholic High School, Inc.* (1962) 4630 N. Rome Ave., 33603. Tel: 813-870-0860; Fax: 813-877-9136. Email: jlynch@tampacatholic.org. Web: www.tampacatholic.org. Mr. Thomas Reidy, Prin.; Michael Gregory, Librarian. Congregation of Christian Brothers (New Rochelle, NY) 3; Lay Teachers 56; Students 685.

[C] HIGH SCHOOLS, PRIVATE

TAMPA. *Academy of the Holy Names High School* (1881) 3319 Bayshore Blvd., 33629. Tel: 813-839-5371; Fax: 813-839-3924. Email: ehumphries@holynamestpa.org. Web: www.holynamestpa.org. Mr. Arthur Raimo, Pres.; Mrs. Camille Jowanna, Prin. High School; Ms. Bridgid Fishman, Prin. Elementary; Mrs. Emily Swiger, Dir. Media Svcs.
Academy of the Holy Names of Florida, Inc. Sisters of the Holy Name of Jesus and Mary (U.S. Ontario Province) 6; Lay Teachers 90; Students 362.

Jesuit High School, 4701 N. Himes Ave., 33614. Tel: 813-877-5344; Fax: 813-872-1853. Web: www.jesuittampa.org. Revs. Douglas Hypolite, S.J., Rector; Richard C. Hermes (S.J.), Chap. & Pres.; Barry Neuburger, Prin.; Ted Beil, Librarian.
Jesuit High School of Tampa, Inc., FKA
St. Louis Catholic, Benevolent and Educational Association, Inc.
Jesuit High School Foundation, Inc. Priests 3; Scholastics 3; Lay Teachers 54; Students 720.

[D] ELEMENTARY SCHOOLS, INTERPAROCHIAL

ST. PETERSBURG. *St. Paul School* (Early Childhood Care Program-K-8), 1900 12th St. N., 33704. Tel: 727-823-6144; Fax: 727-896-0609. Email: efulham@sp1930.org. Web: www.sp1930.org. Elizabeth Fulham, Prin.; Sr. Joan Carberry, Asst. Prin. & Librarian; Mary Becker, Librarian. Serving Blessed Trinity and St. Paul. Sisters 1; Lay Teachers 21; Students 325.

CLEARWATER. *St. Cecelia Interparochial School*, (Grades PreK-8), 1350 Court St., 33756. Tel: 727-461-1200; Fax: 727-446-9140. Email: scsoffice@st-cecelia.org. Web: www.st-cecelia.org. Ms. Mary Beth Scanlon, Prin.; Barbara Bailey, Librarian; Sheila Dale, Contact Person & Admin. Asst. Serving Light of Christ, St. Brendan, St. Catherine of Siena and St. Cecelia. Lay Teachers 31; Students 471.

Guardian Angels Catholic School, (Grades PreK-8), 2270 Evans Rd., 33763. Tel: 727-799-6724; Fax: 727-724-9018. Email: cmalinski@gacsfl.com. Web: www.gacsfl.com. Cindy Malinski, Prin. & Contact Person; Wanda Pejka, Librarian. Serving All Saints, St. Ignatius, St. Luke and St. Michael the Archangel. Sisters 1; Lay Teachers 22; Students 281.

LECANTO. *Pope John Paul II Catholic School*, 4341 W. Homosassa Tr., 34461. Tel: 352-746-2020; Fax: 352-746-3448. Email: lwhitaker@pjp2.net. Web: www.pjp2.net. Dr. Lou Whitaker, Prin.; Lisa Nalepa, Admin. Coord. & Contact Person. Serving Our Lady of Fatima, Our Lady of Grace, St. Benedict, St. Elizabeth Ann Seton, St. Scholastica and St. Thomas the Apostle. Lay Teachers 20; Students 196.

PINELLAS PARK. *Sacred Heart Interparochial School*, (Grades PreK-8), 7951 46th Way N., 33781. Tel: 727-544-1106; Fax: 727-541-2073. Email: principal@sacredheartcatholic.org. Mr. Andy Shannon, Prin. Religious 1; Lay Teachers 17; Students 142.

PORT RICHEY. *Bishop Larkin Interparochial School*, (Grades PreK-8), 8408 Monarch Dr., 34668. Tel: 727-862-6981; Fax: 727-869-9893. Email: office@bishoplarkin.org. Sr. Regina Ozuzu, H.H.C.J., Prin.; Mary S. Barzelay, Librarian. Serving Our Lady Queen of Peace, St. James, St. Michael the Archangel, St. Thomas Aquinas, St. Vincent de Paul and St. Peter the Apostle. Lay Teachers 19; Sisters 2; Students 260.

RIVERVIEW. *St. Stephen Catholic School* (2001) 3-6, Extended Day; 3 yrs. to 8th grade, 10424 Saint Stephen Cir., 33569. Tel: 813-741-9203; Fax: 813-741-9622. Email: tjackson@ststephencatholic.org. Web: www.ststephencatholicschool.org. Ms. Therese Jackson, Prin. Lay Teachers 25; Students 408.

SAFETY HARBOR. *Espiritu Santo Catholic School* (2001) (Grades PreK-8), Formerly Espiritu Santo Early Childhood Center., 2405A Philippe Pkwy., 34695-2047. Tel: 727-812-4650; Fax: 727-812-4658. Email: mpenn@escschool.org. Margaret Penn, Prin.; Kathleen Sheehan, Librarian. Lay Teachers 35; Students 455.

SAN ANTONIO. *St. Anthony Interparochial Catholic School* (1884) (Grades K-8), 32902 Saint Anthony Way, P.O. Box 847, 33576-0847. Tel: 352-588-3041; Fax: 352-588-3142. Email: salice@stanthonyschoolfl.org. Web: www.stanthonyschoolfl.org. Sr. Alice Ottapurackal, F.S.S.E., Prin.; Betty Will, Librarian. Serving Sacred Heart, St. Anthony, St. Joseph and St. Rita, St. Mark's, St. Anne's, St. Anthony, Brooksville. Sisters 3; Lay Teachers 12; Students 163.

SPRING HILL. *Notre Dame Catholic School*, (Grades PreK-8), 1095 Commercial Way, 34606. Tel: 352-683-0755; Fax: 352-683-3924. Email: notredame@ndischool.org. Web: www.ndischool.org. Dr. Lou Whitaker, Prin.; Barbara Williams, Librarian. Serving St. Anne, St. Anthony, St. Frances Xavier Cabrini, St. Joan of Arc, St. Mary and St. Theresa. Lay Administrators 2; Lay Teachers 17; Students 165.

TAMPA. *Most Holy Redeemer Interparochial School* (1954) (Grades K-8), 302 E. Linebaugh Ave., 33612. Tel: 813-933-4750; Fax: 813-933-3181. Email: office@mhr-tampa.org. Web: www.mhr-tampa.org. Mr. Thom Laux, Prin.; Dr. Jo Ann Quinn, Asst. Prin.; Mary Anderson, Librarian. Serving Most Holy Redeemer, Our Lady of the Rosary, St. Mary, St. Paul, St. Timothy and St. Mark. Lay Teachers 19; Students 247.

[E] ELEMENTARY SCHOOLS, PRIVATE

TAMPA. *Academy of the Holy Names* (1881) (Grades PreK-12), 3319 Bayshore Blvd., 33629. Tel: 813-839-5371; Fax: 813-839-7103. Email: webmaster@holynamestpa.org. Web: www.holynamestpa.org. Mr. Arthur Fishman, Pres.; Ms. Bridgid Fishman, Prin. Elementary School; Mrs. Camille Jowanna, Prin. High School; Ms. Emily Swiger, Dir. Media Svcs.
Academy of the Holy Names of Florida, Inc.
Academy of the Holy Names Foundation, Inc. Sisters of the Holy Names of Jesus and Mary (U.S.-Ontario Provinces) 5; Lay Teachers 90; Students 800.

Villa Madonna School, (Grades 3-8), (Early Childhood Care Program-3-8), 315 W. Columbus

Dr., 33602. Tel: 813-229-1322; Fax: 813-223-4812. Web: www.edline.net/pages/vms; villamadonnaschool.com. Sr. Danielle Gonzalez, F.M.A., Prin.; Mrs. Vicki Fabiano, Librarian. Email: vfabians@villamadonnaschool.com.

Salesian Sisters of Tampa, Inc. Daughters of Mary Help of Christians 5; Lay Teachers 31; Students 448.

[F] PRESCHOOLS AND DAY CARE CENTERS

ST. PETERSBURG. *Immaculate Conception Early Childhood Center* (1970) Ages 2-5, Extended Care., Lower Pinellas Deanery, 2100 26th Ave. S., 33712. Tel: 727-822-2156; Fax: 727-553-9133. Email: icrita@tampabay.rr.com. Roberta Bell, Dir. & Contact Person; Rev. John Gerth. Lay Teachers 18; Children 142; Total Staff 25.

St Paul Children's Center, 1800 12th St. N., 33704. Tel: 727-822-3481; Fax: 727-822-1754. Email: toni@stpaulstpete.com. Ms. Toni Johnston, Dir. 2 months through 2 yrs.

CLEARWATER. *Light of Christ (Early Childhood Center)* (1985) Ages 2-5, Extended Care., Upper Pinellas Deanery, 2176 Marilyn St., 33765. Tel: 727-442-4797; Fax: 727-489-1903. Email: locecc@ij.net. Mrs. Rebecca Daschbach, Preschool Dir. Lay Teachers 10; Students 78.

DADE CITY. *Sacred Heart Early Childhood Center* Infant-PreK, Extended Care., Pasco Deanery, 32245 Saint Joe Rd., 33525. Tel: 352-588-4060; Fax: 352-588-4871. Email: shecctw@embargmail.com. Mrs. Toni Watkins, Dir. & Admin. Lay Teachers 28; Children 180.

LAND O'LAKES. *Our Lady of the Rosary Early Childhood Center - Mary's House - ECC*, 2348 Collier Pkwy., P.O. Box 1229, Land O Lakes, 34639. Tel: 813-949-4565. Corrine Ertl, Admin.; Very Rev. Ronald Aubin, J.C.L. Lay Teachers 12; Students 165.

LARGO. *St. Jerome Early Childhood Center* (1990) Ages 2-4., 10895 Hamlin Blvd., 33774. Tel: 727-596-9491; Fax: 727-596-8953. Email: sjecc@tampabay.rr.com. Web: stjeromeearlychildhoodcenter.org. Denise Roach, Dir.; Rev. Msgr. Brendan Muldoon. Lay Teachers 4; Total Staff 11; Children 80.

LUTZ. *St. Timothy Catholic Early Childhood Learning Center*, 17512 Lakeshore Rd., 33558. Tel: 813-960-4857; Fax: 813-961-9429. Email: daisy.cintron@sainttims.org. Web: www.sainttims.org. Ms. Daisy Cintron, M.Ed., Dir.; Very Rev. Kenneth Malley, V.F. Lay Teachers 5; Students 90.

NEW PORT RICHEY. *St. Thomas Aquinas Early Childhood Center*, 8320 Old CR 54, 34653. Tel: 727-376-2330; Fax: 727-376-2330. Email: staecc@aol.com. Mrs. Cindy McKallip, Dir.; Rev. Michael Lydon; Pamela Bruno, Sec. Lay Teachers 5; Assistants 5; Children 100.

PALM HARBOR. *St. Luke Early Childhood Center* Ages 2-4, Extended Care., 2757 Alderman Rd., 34684. Tel: 727-787-2914; Fax: 727-786-8648. Email: stlecc@verizon.net. Christi Stanziani, Dir.; Rev. Paul Kochu. Lay Teachers 2; Children 108.

TAMPA. *St. Paul Child Enrichment* (1981) Ages 3-4., 12708 N. Dale Mabry Hwy., 33618-2802. Tel: 813-264-3314; Fax: 813-962-8780. Email: maguiar@stpaulchurch.com. Mrs. Martha Aguiar, Dir.; Rev. Leonard Piotrowski. Lay Teachers 14; Children 104.

TARPON SPRINGS. *St. Ignatius Early Childhood Center* Ages 2-5., 725 E. Orange St., 34689-1306. Tel: 727-937-5427; Fax: 727-722-9000. Email: ngorby@ignatius.net. Web: www.siecc.net. Nancy Gorby, Dir.; Rev. Joseph A. Pellegrino. Teachers 14; Children 120.

[G] SCHOOLS FOR EXCEPTIONAL CHILDREN

PINELLAS PARK. *Morning Star Catholic School - Pinellas Park, Inc.* (1969) 4661 80th Ave. N., 33781. Tel: 813-544-6036; Fax: 813-546-9058. Email: mschool2@tampabay.rr.com. Web: www.morningstarschool.org. Mrs. Susan Conza, Prin. Lay Teachers 6; Students 30.

TAMPA. *Morning Star Catholic School - Tampa, Inc.* (1958) 210 E. Linebaugh Ave., 33612. Tel: 813-935-0232; 813-932-2321; Fax: 813-932-2321. Email: edaly@morningstartampa.org. Web: www.morningstartampa.org. Eileen Daly, Prin.; Leslie Maggio, Librarian. Lay Teachers 12; Students 72.

[H] SCHOOLS FOR THEOLOGICAL AND SPIRITUAL TRAINING

ST. PETERSBURG. *Father William F. Balfe Memorial Library*, 1365 Hays Rd., Spring Hill, 34610. Rev. Msgr. Robert Morris, V.G., Exec. Dir. Diocesan Library

CLEARWATER. *The Cenacle of Our Lady of Divine Providence* School of Spirituality., 702 S. Bayview Ave., 33759. Tel: 727-724-9505; Fax: 727-724-9421. Email: cenacleofourlady@aol.com. Web: www.divineprovidence.org. Ronald W. Novotny, S.T.L., Ph.D., Dir. & Contact Person. Lay Teachers 2; Total Staff 9; Total Enrollment 125.

[I] CATHOLIC CHARITIES

ST. PETERSBURG. *Catholic Charities, Diocese of St. Petersburg, Inc.* Tel: 727-893-1313; Fax: 727-893-1307. Email: catholic.charities@ccdosp.org. Web: www.ccdosp.org. Mr. Frank V. Murphy III, Pres.; Sheila Lopez, COO. Personnel 95.

Jeff Forbes Center - Administrative Offices, 1213 16th St. N., 33705. Tel: 727-893-1313; Fax: 727-893-1307. Email: catholiccharities@ccdosp.org. Web: www.ccdosp.org.

Services Provided Life Ministry: Elder: Respite Programs for Caregivers of Memory Loss Clients, Parish based Volunteer Support. Family Services: Family Support & Case Management, Life Skills Education, Counseling, Resettlement & Immigration Assistance, Mobile Medical Unit for Farm Workers, Pregnancy & Parenting Support.; Shelter Ministry: HIV Services: Permanent & Transitional Housing & Voucher Program.Farm Worker Services: Full Service for Migrant Farm Workers including 122 apartments. Homeless Services: Prevention, Housing Counseling, Respite, Emergency, Permanent & Transitional Housing. Elder: HUD 202 Very Low-Income Senior Housing, HUD 202 Service Co-ordination. Affordable Housing: Homebuyer Education & Housing Counseling & Foreclosure Prevention.Email: catholic.charities@cdosp.org. Web: www.ccdosp.org.

Catholic Charities Community Development Corp., 1213 16th St. N., 33705. Tel: 727-893-1313; Fax: 727-893-1307. Email: cccdc@ccdosp.org. Web: www.ccdosp.org. Mr. Frank V. Murphy III, Pres.

[J] GENERAL HOSPITALS

ST. PETERSBURG. *St. Anthony's Hospital, Inc.*, 1200 7th Ave. N., 33705. Tel: 727-825-1103; Fax: 727-825-1223. Web: www.stanthonys.com. Email: john.mullet@baycare.org. Rev. John Mullet, M.Div., M.A., Dir. Pastoral Care; Rev. Al Hall, Chap. (Baptist); Rev. Mardie Chapman, Chap. (United Church of Christ); Revs. Jose Furtado, Chap.; Jerome Massimino, O.F.M., Chap.; Mr. Robert Sherman, Dir. Foundation; Sisters Mary McNally, O.S.F., Mission Integration, Vice Pres.; Margaret Foley, O.S.F., Chap.

St. Anthony's Hospital, Inc.

St. Anthony's Ancillary Services, Inc.

St. Anthony's Professional Buildings and Services, Inc.

St. Anthony's Health Care Foundation, Inc. Franciscan Sisters of Allegany.

TAMPA. *St. Joseph's Hospital, Inc.* (1934) 3001 W. Martin Luther King Blvd., 33607. Tel: 813-870-4020; Fax: 813-870-4639. Email: sisterpat.shirley@baycare.org. Web: www.sjbhealth.org. P.O. Box 4227, 33677. Tel: 813-870-4000; Fax: 813-870-4639. Revs. Kenneth Gerth, M.C.C.J., Chap.; Carmen Caban, Chap.; Marilyn Cummings, Chap.; George Francis, Chap.; Sabrina Mc Gavock, Chap.; John Aransi, Chap.; Denis Kitenge (Congo), Chap.; Tina Imperato, Chap.; Gail Radu, Chap.; Revs. Bernard Smith, Chap.; George Maliekal, Chap.; Molly Mary Darnet, Chap.; Bev Shives, Chap.; Jan Hoyt, Pastoral Care Educ.

St. Joseph's Hospital, Inc.

St. Joseph's Ancillary Services, Inc.

St. Joseph's Community Care, Inc.

St. Joseph's Enterprises, Inc.

St. Joseph's Health Care Center, Inc.

St. Joseph's Hospital of Tampa Foundation, Inc.

St. Joseph's Specialty Services, Inc.

John Knox Village of Tampa Bay, Inc.

Franciscan Properties, Inc.

San Damiano Enterprises, Inc. Franciscan Sisters of Allegany. Inpatient Admissions 50,015; Emergency Room Visits 169,230; Outpatient Visits 198,037; Pastoral Care Volunteers 18; Eucharistic Ministers 70; Bed Capacity 881; Physicians 1,200; Total Assisted Annually 188,107; Total Staff 4,893.

[K] RETIREMENT AND HEALTH CARE CENTERS

ST. PETERSBURG. *Bon Secours St. Petersburg Home Care Services Inc.*, 11001 Roosevelt Blvd, Ste. 1000, Saint Petersburg, 33716. Tel: 727-577-7990; Fax: 727-576-6138. Email: janet_keller@bshsi.com. Web: www.bonsecoursstpete.org. Karen Reich, Exec. Vice Pres. Sisters of Bon Secours, (Serves Pinellas & Pasco Counties)

**Bon Secours-Maria Manor Nursing Care Center, Inc.*, 10300 Fourth St. N., 33716. Tel: 727-576-1025; Fax: 727-576-1447. Email: janet_ford@bshsi.org. Web: www.bonsecourstpete.org. Karen Reich, Exec. Vice Pres.; Janet Keller, Admin. Sisters of Bon Secours. Bed Capacity 274; Residents Year Round 260; Total Assisted Annually 360; Total Staff 400.

CLEARWATER. *La Clinica Guadalupana, Inc.* (1995) 1000 Lakeview Rd., Unit 4, 33756. Tel: 727-462-5424; Fax: 727-462-8117. Dr. Jay E. Carpenter, M.D., Pres. Total Assisted Annually 3,500; Staff 1.

[L] RETIREMENT HOUSING

ST. PETERSBURG. *Blessed Trinity Housing, Inc. dba Trinity House* 5701 16th St. S., 33705. Tel: 727-865-7590; Fax: 727-867-1701. Email: trinityhousemgr@spm.net. Nanci Huffer, Mgr. Residents 76; Total Staff 4.

St. Clement Housing, Inc., 6363 9th Ave., N., P.O. Box 40200, 33743-0200. Rev. Thomas Anastasia, Contact Person.

Holy Cross Housing dba Casa Santa Cruz 7825 54th Ave. N., 33709. Tel: 727-541-2631; Fax: 727-547-6741. Email: sjacobs@ccdosp.org. Mr. Joseph A. DiVito, Registered Agent. Total Staff 5; Total in Residence 76.

CLEARWATER. *St. Michael's Housing, Inc. dba Casa Miguel* (1984) 2285 State Rd. #580, 33763. Tel: 727-797-8551. Email: jlungaro@ccdosp.org. Mrs. JoAnn Lungaro, Admin. Independent Living. Total Staff 5; Residents 82.

HUDSON. *Bethlehem Housing, Inc. dba Bethlehem House* 8010 State Rd. 52, 34667. Tel: 727-819-2861; Fax: 727-869-2781. Email: bethlehem.house@verizon.net. Virginia Seamster, Mgr. Residents 60; Total Staff 3.

TAMPA. *Blessed Sacrament Housing, Inc. dba Blessed Sacrament Manor* 6801 12th Ave. S., 33619. Tel: 813-620-0221; Fax: 813-620-0473. Email: cgallo@ccdosp.org. Mr. Frank Murphy, Pres. Clients 74; Total Staff 2.

Christ the King Housing, Inc. dba Kings Arms 4125 N. Lincoln Ave., 33607. Tel: 813-873-0234; Fax: 813-871-2061. Email: k.arms@verizon.net. Jesus Arias, Mgr. Total Staff 4; Total in Residence 90.

Christ the King Housing, Inc. dba Kings Manor 2946 W. Columbus Dr., 33607. Tel: 813-875-0139; Fax: 813-876-2182. Email: browen@ccdosp.org. Betsy Rowen, Admin. Residents 115; Total Staff 5.

Epiphany Housing of Tampa, Inc. dba Epiphany Arms 2508 E. Hanna Ave., 33610. Tel: 813-232-2693; Fax: 813-232-2984. Email: epiphanyarms@carteretmgmt.com. Total Staff 12; Residents 78.

St. Lawrence Housing, Inc., 5225 N. Himes Ave., 33614-6623. Tel: 813-875-4040; Fax: 813-876-0491. Very Rev. Thomas Morgan, V.F., Pres.

St. Lawrence Housing II, Inc., c/o 5225 N. Himes Ave., 33614. Tel: 813-875-4040; Fax: 813-876-0491. Very Rev. Thomas Morgan, V.F.

St. Patrick's Housing Corporation dba Patrician Arms 4516 S. Manhattan Ave., 33611. Tel: 813-835-8227; Fax: 813-835-7918. Email: blendstrom@ccdosp.org. Total Staff 6; Total in Residence 82.

St. Patrick's Housing Corporation II, 4516 S. Manhattan Ave., 33611. Tel: 727-430-1767.

[M] SENIOR CENTERS

LARGO. *Bethlehem Centre, Inc.*, 10895 Hamlin Blvd., 33774. Tel: 727-596-9394; Fax: 727-596-6792. Lois Wisuri, Dir. & Contact. Senior Center offering programs in Fitness, Exercise, Social, Educational, Music, Art, Computers, and Religious Nature on Tuesday, Wednesday, and Friday. Hot luncheon is available on Tuesday and Friday (Oct.-April). Total Staff 1; Total Assisted Per Week 100.

[N] MONASTERIES AND RESIDENCES OF PRIESTS AND BROTHERS

ST. PETERSBURG. *St. Anthony Friary* Franciscan Residence and Retirement Community., 357 Second St. N., 33701. Tel: 727-822-7917; Fax: 727-821-8067. Email: saf@tampabay.rr.com. Revs. Roy Gasnick, O.F.M. (Retired); Mario Di Lella, O.F.M. (Retired); Gerald M. Dolan, O.F.M. (Retired); Louis V. Iasiello, O.F.M.; Venant Lalonde, O.F.M. (Retired); John J. Marino, O.F.M.; Venard Murphy, O.F.M. (Retired); James F. Toal, O.F.M., Guardian; Thomas K. Murphy, O.F.M.; John Anglin, O.F.M.; Martin Bednar, O.F.M.; Roderic Petrie, O.F.M.; Alexander A. DiLella, O.F.M.; Edward J. Dillon, O.F.M. (Retired); Emeric Szlezak, O.F.M. (Retired); Alexius J. Mulrenan, O.F.M. (Retired); Alexis P. Morris, O.F.M. (Retired); James Jones, O.F.M. (Retired); Clement Comesky, O.F.M.; Roch A. Coogan, O.F.M. (Retired); Alfonso Guzman, O.F.M.; Joseph Hertel, O.F.M.; Leonard Lencewicz, O.F.M.; Jerome Massimino, O.F.M.; Bernerd Splawski, O.F.M.; Stan Widomski, O.F.M.; Bros. Paul J. Chelus, O.F.M.; Michael Madden, O.F.M.; Paul Santoro, O.F.M.; Valerian Vaverchack, O.F.M., (Retired). Total in Residence 30; Total Staff 9.

Missionaries of Africa (1868) 5757 Seventh Ave. N., 33710. Tel: 727-343-1001; Fax: 727-343-4395. Email: mafrica@tampabay.rr.com. Revs. Richard Archambault, M.Afr., Office Coord.; Joseph Elmo Hebert, M.Afr., Coord. (Retired); John Joseph Braun, M.Afr. (Retired); Roger Bisson, M.Afr. (Retired); Youville Labonte, M.Afr. (Retired); Joseph Kay, M.Afr. (Retired); James Heintz, M.Afr.; Richard Paul Roy, M.Afr. (Retired); Bro. Martin Chapper, M.Afr. (Retired). Priests 7; Brothers 2.

St. Peter Nolasco Residence (1984) 5650 Seventh Ave. N., 33710-7112. Tel: 727-345-4766; Fax: 727-347-5345. Email: wayne@orderofmercy.org. Revs. Kenneth Breen, O.de.M., Local Supr.; Oscar Kozyra, O.de.M.; Michael E. Perry, O.de.M.
Fathers of Our Lady of Mercy, Inc. Total Staff 3; Total in Residence 3.

CLEARWATER BEACH. *St. Paul Friary*, 50 Somerset St., 33767-1543. Tel: 727-443-7351; Fax: 727-462-0150. Rev. Edmund Ansaloni, O.F.M., Vicar; Bros. Kenneth Ghastin, O.F.M.; Mark Brown, O.F.M.; Juniper O'Connor, O.F.M.

PINELLAS PARK. *Priests of the Sacred Heart*, 6701 82nd Ave. N., 33781. Tel: 727-541-2661; Fax: 727-547-0408. Most Rev. Joseph Potocnack, S.C.J. (Retired); Revs. Thomas Burns, S.C.J.; Frank Burshnick, S.C.J.; Joseph Doscher, S.C.J. (Retired); Ralph Intranuovo, S.C.J.; Steve Pujdak, S.C.J., House Treas.; Gregory Speck, S.C.J., Assoc. Coord.; Leonard Tadyszak, S.C.J. (Retired); Raymond Vega, S.C.J. (Retired); Charles Yost, S.C.J. (Retired); Bros. Benedict Humpfer, S.C.J., Coord.; Gabriel Kersting, S.C.J., (Retired). Total Staff 2; Total in Residence 12.

SAINT LEO. *St. Leo Abbey* (1889) P.O. Box 2350, 33574. Tel: 352-588-8624; Fax: 352-588-5217. Web: www.saintleoabbey.org. Rt. Rev. Isaac Camacho, O.S.B., Abbot; Revs. Damian DuQuesnay, O.S.B.; James Hoge, O.S.B.; Andrew Metzger, O.S.B.; Paul Romfh, O.S.B.; David Steinwachs, O.S.B., Prior; Robert Velten, O.S.B. Priests 7; Brothers 18; Internal Oblates 1; Novices & Juniors 2.

ST. PETE BEACH. *Franciscan Friary*, 555 - 68th Ave., 33706. Tel: 727-367-2408. Rev. Bernardas Talaisis.

SEMINOLE. *Capuchin Franciscan Residence*, 7171 128th St. N., 33776. Tel: 727-397-0011; Fax: 727-392-7183. Web: www.capuchin.org. Rev. Gregory Reisert, O.F.M.Cap., Admin.

TAMPA. *Salesians of Don Bosco, Mary Help of Christians Center*, 6400 E. Chelsea St., 33610. Tel: 813-626-6191; Fax: 813-621-5251. Web: www.mhctampa.org. Rev. Dennis Donovan, S.D.B., Contact Person.

[O] CONVENTS AND RESIDENCES FOR SISTERS

ST. PETERSBURG. *St. Anthony Hospital Convent*, 1332 7th Ave. N., 33705-1409. Tel: 727-498-8709; 727-954-3980 (Sr. Rose). Email: berose1026@gmail.com. Sr. Rose Bernhardt, O.S.F., Contact & Local Min. Franciscan Sisters of Allegany (Allegany, NY). Total in Residence 6.

SAINT LEO. *Holy Name Monastery* (1889) 33201 State Hwy. 52, 33574-2450. Tel: 352-588-8320; Fax: 352-588-8319. Email: holyname@saintleo.edu. Web: www.floridabenedictines.com. P.O. Box 2450, 33574-2450. Sr. Mary Clare Neuhofer, O.S.B., Prioress.
Benedictine Sisters of Florida, Motherhouse and Novitiate of the Benedictine Sisters of Florida. Professed Sisters 16.

TAMPA. *St. Clare Convent*, Franciscan Sisters of Allegany, Attn: Brenda Johnson: 2924 W. Curtis St., 33614-7102. Tel: 813-870-4272; Fax: 813-414-9074. Franciscan Sisters of Allegany (Allegany, NY).

St. Elizabeth Convent, 3000 N. Perry Ave., 33603-5345. Tel: 813-229-1978; Fax: 813-228-9066. Email: st.e3000@juno.com. Web: www.alleganyfranciscans.org. Franciscan Sisters of Allegany. Total Staff 7; Total in Residence 10.

Franciscan Convent, 3006 Perry Ave., 33603-5345. Tel: 813-229-2492; Fax: 813-228-0748. Email: sranniel@aol.com. Franciscan Sisters of Allegany. Total in Residence 4.

Surfside Condos - Franciscan Sisters of Allegany, NY, 15462 Gulf Blvd., #1003, Madeira Beach, 33708. Tel: 727-898-9501. Email: joanc1230@tampabay.rr.com.

Villa Madonna Convent, 2611 N. Massachusetts Ave., 33602. Tel: 813-229-1322, Ext. 393; Fax: 813-223-4812. Email: helenegodin24@aol.com. Web: www.villamadonnaschool.com. Daughters of Mary Help of Christians (Haledon, NJ). Total Staff 5; Total in Residence 8.

[P] RETREAT CENTERS

CLEARWATER. *Retreat Ministry of the Marian Servants of Divine Providence*, 702 S. Bayview Ave., 33759. Tel: 727-799-4003; Fax: 727-724-9421. Email: msretreats@aol.com. Web: www.divineprovidence.org. Adrienne Novotny, Contact Person.

LUTZ. *Bethany Center, Inc.*, 18150 Bethany Center Dr., 33558. Tel: 813-960-6300; Fax: 813-960-6303. Web: www.bethanycenterfl.org. Rev. John B. Lipscomb, Spiritual Dir.

SAINT LEO. *Saint Leo Abbey Retreat Center* (1975) 33601 State Rd. 52, P.O. Box 2350, 33574-2350. Tel: 352-588-8184; Fax: 352-588-5217. Email: wellofjacob@hotmail.com. Web: www.saintleoabbey.org. Bro. Jacob Tippett, Guest Master. Total Staff 4.

TAMPA. *Franciscan Center, Retreat House*, 3010 N. Perry Ave., 33603-5345. Tel: 813-229-2695; Fax: 813-228-0748. Email: info@franciscancentertampa.org. Web: www.franciscancentertampa.org. Sr. Catherine Cahill, O.S.F., Dir.; Christina Strain, Admin.; Maureen R. Connors, Ph.D., Co-Dir. Progs.; Carol Mitchell, Ph.D., Co-Dir. Progs.; Karen Davies-Chaieb, Admin. Asst.; Scott Taylor, Dir. Mktg & Communications. Franciscan Sisters of Allegany. Total Staff 12.

Mary Help of Christians Center (1928) 6400 E. Chelsea St., 33610-5628. Tel: 813-626-6191; Fax: 813-621-5251. Web: www.mhctampa.org. Revs. Paul Bedard, S.D.B.; Michael Chubirko, S.D.B.; Joseph Hyue Chong, S.D.B.; Bruce Craig, S.D.B.; Dennis Donovan, S.D.B., Dir.; Sidney Figlia, S.D.B.; John Masiello, S.D.B.; Paul Chuong Nguyen, S.D.B.; Jeremiah Reen, S.D.B.; Bros. Joseph Ackroyd, S.D.B.; Jerome B. Cincotta, S.D.B.; Kevin Connolly, S.D.B.; David Iovacchini, S.D.B.; George Marquis, S.D.B.; Xavier F. Verrett, S.D.B.

[Q] PRIVATE ASSOCIATIONS OF THE CHRISTIAN FAITHFUL

CLEARWATER. *Community of the Marian Servants of Divine Providence* (1981) 711 S. Bayview Ave., 33759. Tel: 727-797-7412; Fax: 727-726-1631. Email: marianservants@juno.com. Web: www.divineprovidence.org. Diane F. Brown, Dir.

Our Lady of Divine Providence House of Prayer Tel: 727-797-7412; Fax: 727-726-1631. Email: marianservant@juno.com.

[R] SUMMER CAMPS

ST. PETERSBURG. *Our Lady of Good Counsel Camp* (1948) 8888 E. Gobbler Dr., Floral City, 34436. Tel: 352-726-2198; Fax: 352-726-3212. Email: goodcounselcamp@aol.com. Web: goodcounselcamp.catholicweb.com. Rev. James B. Johnson, V.F., Dir.
Our Lady of Fatima Church: 550 U.S. Hwy. 41 S., Inverness, 34450. Tel: 352-726-1910; Fax: 352-344-8384.

TAMPA. *Mary Help of Christians Camp* 6400 Chelsea St., 33610. Tel: 813-626-6191; Fax: 813-626-5251. Web: www.mhctampa.org. Rev. Dennis Donovan, S.D.B., Contact Person.

[S] CAMPUS MINISTRY

ST. PETERSBURG. *Eckerd College - Catholic Campus Ministry* c/o 5650 7th Ave. N., 33710-7112. Tel: 727-864-8470; Fax: 727-864-8040. Rev. Oscar Kozyra, O.de.M., Chap. Total in Residence 1.

TAMPA. *Catholic Student Center, University of South Florida* (1967) 13005 N. 50th St., Temple Terrace, 33617-1022. Tel: 813-988-3727; Fax: 813-988-3727. Email: director@catholicusf.org. Web: www.catholicusf.org. Rev. Alan Weber, Dir.

University of Tampa - Catholic Student Organization c/o University of Tampa, 401 W. Kennedy Blvd., 33606. Tel: 813-229-1595; Fax: 813-221-2350.

[T] MISCELLANEOUS

ST. PETERSBURG. *Catholic Charities Community Dev. Corp.*, 1213 16th St. N., 33705. Tel: 727-893-1313; Fax: 727-893-1307. Web: www.ccdosp.org. Mr. Frank V. Murphy III, Pres.

Catholic Charities Housing, Inc., 1213 16th St. N., 33705. Tel: 727-893-1314, Ext. 202; Fax: 727-893-1307. Email: housing@ccdosp.org. Web: www.ccdosp.org. Mr. Frank V. Murphy III, Pres.

Magnificat Inc., Lower Pinellas Deanery Chapter of the Diocese of St. Petersburg, Florida, 3228 13th St. N., Saint Petersburg, 33704. Tel: 727-825-0418. Email: magnificatofstpetersburg@verizon.net.

Partners with Haiti, Inc., 1800 12th St., N., Saint Petersburg, 33704. Tel: 727-822-3481; Fax: 727-822-1754. Rev. Msgr. Robert C. Gibbons, J.C.L.

Pastoral Center, 6363 9th Ave N., 33710. For detailed information on the following listings contact the Chancery Office.
Allegany Community Out Reach Grant Fund, Inc.
Catholic Charities - Alicia Arms, Inc.
Catholic Charities - Arbor Villas, Inc.
Catholic Charities - Fountain View, Inc.
Catholic Charities Housing, Inc.
Catholic Charities - Sand Dollar, Inc.
Catholic Education Foundation, Inc.
Catholic Media Ministry, Inc.
Christopher Assurance, Inc.
The Congregation of the Sisters of St. Clare (Florida), Inc., 625 Court St. 2nd Fl., Clearwater, 33756.
Allegany Franciscan Ministries, Inc.
Regis Manor, Inc.
WBVM, 90.5 FM, Inc., Clearwater.
Catholic Charities Community Development, Corp.
Catholic Charities Foundation of Tampa Bay, Inc.
The Greater Tampa Catholic Lawyers Guild, Inc., P.O. Box 1816, Tampa, 33601.
Franciscan Center of Tampa, FL, Inc., 3010 Perry Ave., Tampa, 33603. Tel: 813-229-2695; Fax: 813-228-0748.
Savings and Loan Trust
Employee Benefit Trust

The Salesian Society of St. Petersburg, Inc., 6470 13th Ave., N., 33710. Tel: 727-374-0224. Rev. Michael J. Conway, S.D.B, Contact Person.

Transfiguration Housing, Inc., 4000 43rd St. N., 33714.

BELLAIR. *Mantle of Mary, Inc.*, 845 Indian Rocks Rd., Belleair, 33756. Tel: 727-446-0939. Email: mpublishing2@tampabay.rr.com; info@mantlepublishing.com. Web: www.mantlepublishing.com. Carol Marquardt, Pres., Founder.

CLEARWATER. *Allegany Franciscan Ministries, Inc.* (1997) 33920 U.S. Hwy 19, #269, Palm Harbor, 34684. Tel: 727-507-9668; Fax: 727-507-8557. Email: eboyle@afmfl.org. Web: www.afmfl.org. Total Staff 7.

OLDSMAR. **Living His Life Abundantly International, Inc.*, 325 Scarlet Blvd., 34677-3019. Tel: 813-854-1518; 800-558-5452; Fax: 813-891-1267. Email: info@lhla.org. Web: www.lhla.org. Johnnette S. Benkovic, Pres.

TAMPA. **Help Brings Hope for Haiti, Inc.*, 3816 Morrison Ave., 33629. Tel: 813-832-4244. Email: hbhh123@gmail.com. Web: www.hbhh.org. Patricia M. Eddy, Board Chair & Founder.

Tampa Magnificat, 3301 Bayshore Blvd., #1004, 33629. Tel: 813-831-7522. Eleanor Gonzalez, Coord.

VALRICO. **Knanya Catholic Congress of Central Florida, Inc.*, 2620 Washington, 33594. Tel: 813-681-6189; Fax: 813-230-8031. Email: jillikal@aol.com.

RELIGIOUS INSTITUTES OF MEN REPRESENTED IN THE DIOCESE

For further details refer to the corresponding bracketed number in the Religious Institutes of Men or Women section.

[]—*Apostles of Jesus*—A.J.
[0380]—*Comboni Missionaries of the Sacred Heart* (Verona)—M.C.C.J.
[0310]—*Congregation of Christian Brothers* (New Rochelle, NY)—C.F.C.
[0220]—*Congregation of the Blessed Sacrament* (Cleveland, OH)—S.S.S.
[1330]—*Congregation of the Missions* (Madrid, Spain)—C.M.
[0520]—*Franciscan Friars* (New York, NY; Dublin, Ireland)—O.F.M.
[]—*Franciscan Province of Our Lady of Guadalupe*—O.F.M
[]—*Holy Spirit Fathers*—A.L.C.P.
[0300]—*Institute of Charity* (Peoria, IL)—I.C.
[0780]—*Marist Brothers* (New York, NY)—F.M.S.
[0780]—*Marist Fathers* (Washington, D.C.)—S.M.
[0800]—*Maryknoll Brothers*—M.M.
[0850]—*Missionaries of Africa* (Washington, DC)—M.Afr.
[0380]—*Missionary Society of St. Thomas the Apostle*—M.S.T.
[0870]—*Montford Missionaries*—SMM
[0350]—*Order of Cistercians of the Strict Observance* Spencer, MA—O.C.S.O.
[0470]—*Order of Friar Minor Capuchin* (White Plains, NY; Union City, NJ)—O.F.M.Cap.
[0970]—*Order of Our Lady of Mercy* (Cleveland, OH)—O.deM.
[0430]—*Order of Preachers (Dominicans)* (Dublin, Ireland)—O.P.
[0200]—*Order of St. Benedict* (St. Leo, FL)—O.S.B.
[0610]—*Priests of the Congregation of the Holy Cross* (Bridgeport, CT)—C.S.C.
[1130]—*Sacred Heart Fathers and Brothers* (Hales Corner, WI)—S.C.J.

[1190]—*Salesians of St. John Bosco* (New Rochelle, NY)—S.D.B.

[]—*Scarboro Foreign Missions* (Scarboro, Ontario, Canada)—S.F.M.

[0690]—*Society of Jesus* (New Orleans, LA; Chicago, IL; Boston, MA)—S.J.

[0990]—*Society of the Catholic Apostolate*—S.A.C.

[1200]—*Society of the Divine Savior* (Milwaukee, WI)—S.D.S.

[0420]—*Society of the Divine Word* (Waukegen, IL.)—S.V.D.

[0560]—*Third Order Regular of Saint Francis* (Pittsburgh, PA; Etlers, PA)—T.O.R.

RELIGIOUS INSTITUTES OF WOMEN REPRESENTED IN THE DIOCESE

[]—*African Benedictine Sisters of St. Agnes*

[0230]—*Benedictine Sisters of Florida* (St. Leo, FL)—O.S.B.

[1010]—*Congregation of Divine Providence* (San Antonio, TX)—C.D.P.

[3110]—*Congregation of Our Lady of Retreat in the Cenacle* (Lake Ronkonkoma, NY)—R.C.

[0850]—*Daughters of Mary Help of Christians* (Haledon, NJ)—F.M.A.

[0960]—*Daughters of Wisdom* (Islip, NY)—D.W.

[1070-13]—*Dominican Sisters* (Adrian, MI)—O.P.

[1070-11]—*Dominican Sisters of Our Lady of the Rosary* (Sparkill, NY)—O.P.

[1370]—*Franciscan Missionaries of Mary* (Bronx, NY)—F.M.M.

[1180]—*Franciscan Sisters of Allegany, New York*—O.S.F.

[1430]—*Franciscan Sisters of Our Lady of Perpetual Help* (St. Louis, MO)—O.S.F.

[1460]—*Franciscan Sisters of St. Elizabeth* (Parsippany, NJ)—F.S.S.E.

[3760]—*Fransiscan Poor Clare* (New Orleans, LA)—O.S.C.

[1260]—*Handmaids of the Holy Child Jesus* (Nigeria)—H.H.C.J.

[]—*Hermanas Franciscanas deLa Imaculada*—H.F.I.

[]—*Hermit: Consecrated Virgin* (St. Petersburg, FL)—HER.C.V.

[2577]—*Institute of the Sisters of Mercy of the Americas* (Cumberland, RI)—R.S.M.

[2392]—*Lovers of the Holy Cross Sisters* (Ho Chi Minh City, Vietnam)—L.H.C.

[2420]—*Marist Missionary Sisters (Missionary Sisters of the Society of Mary)*—S.M.S.M.

[2490]—*Medical Mission Sisters* (Philadelphia, PA)—M.M.S.

[]—*Missionaries of Our Lady of Light*—M.D.M.L.

[D]—*Our Lady of Kilimanjaro* (Tanzania, Africa)—C.D.N.K.

[3760P]—*Poor Clare Sisters* (Evansville, IN)—O.S.C.

[3760-P]—*Poor Clare Sisters* (New Orleans, LA)—O.S.C.

[2970]—*School Sisters of Notre Dame* (Baltimore, MD; Chicago, IL; Wilton Prov.)—S.S.N.D.

[1680]—*School Sisters of St. Francis* (Milwaukee, WI)—S.S.S.F.

[3590]—*Servants of Mary (Servite Sisters)* (Ladysmith, WI)—O.S.M.

[1070-03]—*Sinsinawa Dominicans* (Sinsinawa, WI)—O.P.

[0440]—*Sisters of Charity of Cincinnati* (Mt. St. Joseph, OH)—S.C.

[0500]—*Sisters of Charity of Nazareth* (Nazareth, KY)—S.C.N.

[0590]—*Sisters of Charity of Saint Elizabeth* (Convent Station, NJ)—S.C.

[1930]—*Sisters of Holy Cross* (Montreal, Canada)—C.S.C

[2575]—*Sisters of Mercy of The Americas* (Chicago, IL; Buffalo, NY)—R.S.M.

[2990]—*Sisters of Notre Dame* (Chardon, OH)—S.N.D.

[3360]—*Sisters of Providence* (St. Mary of the Woods, IN)—S.P.

[1490]—*Sisters of Saint Francis of the Neuman Communities* (Syracuse)—O.S.F.

[3893]—*Sisters of Saint Joseph of Chestnut Hill, Philadelphia*—S.S.J.

[]—*Sisters of St. Anne Bangalore*—S.A.B.

[3730]—*Sisters of St. Basil the Great* (Uniontown, PA)—O.S.B.M.

[0230]—*Sisters of St. Benedict of Beech Grove, IN*—O.S.B.

[3750]—*Sisters of St. Chretienne* (Wrentham, MA)—S.S.Ch.

[3770]—*Sisters of St. Clare* (Dublin, Ireland)—O.S.C.

[1710]—*Sisters of St. Francis of Mary Immaculate* (Joliet, IL)—O.S.F.

[1630]—*Sisters of St. Francis of Penance and Christian Charity* (Stella Niagara, NY)—O.S.F.

[1570]—*Sisters of St. Francis of the Holy Family* (Dubuque, IA)—O.S.F.

[3900]—*Sisters of St. Joseph* (St. Augustine, FL)—S.S.J.

[3893]—*Sisters of St. Joseph* (Chestnut Hill, PA)—S.S.J.

[3930]—*Sisters of St. Joseph, Third Order of St. Francis*—S.S.J.-T.O.S.F.

[]—*Sisters of St. Michael the Archangel* (Toronto, Canada)—S.S.M.A.

[1920]—*Sisters of the Holy Cross* (Notre Dame, IN)—C.S.C.

[1930]—*Sisters of the Holy Cross* (Montreal, Quebec, Canada)—C.S.C.

[1990]—*Sisters of the Holy Names of Jesus and Mary* (Albany, NY)—S.N.J.M.

[2160]—*Sisters, Servants of the Immaculate Heart of Mary* (Scranton, PA)—I.H.M.

[4190]—*Visitation of Holy Mary* (Wheeling, WV)—V.H.M.

DIOCESAN CEMETERIES

CLEARWATER. *Miserere Guild, Inc. dba Calvary Catholic Cemetery* 5233 118th Ave. N., 33760. Tel: 727-572-4355; Fax: 727-592-9241. Rev. Ralph J. Argentino, Dir.

ST. PETERSBURG. *Holy Cross Catholic Cemetery, Inc.*, 6363 Ninth Ave. N., 33713.

NECROLOGY

† Rozycki, George, Zephyrhills, FL St. Joseph—Died June 27, 2011

An asterisk (*) denotes an organization that has established tax-exempt status directly with the IRS and is not covered by the USCCB Group Ruling.

Diocese of Salina

(Dioecesis Salinensis)

Most Reverend

EDWARD J. WEISENBURGER

Bishop of Salina; ordained December 19, 1987; appointed Bishop of Salina February 6, 2012; ordained May 1, 2012. *103 N. Ninth, P.O. Box 980, Salina, KS 67402-0980.* Tel: 785-827-8746.

Most Reverend

GEORGE K. FITZSIMONS, D.D.

Retired Bishop of Salina; ordained March 18, 1961; appointed Titular Bishop of Pertusa and Auxiliary Bishop of Kansas City-St. Joseph May 27, 1975; Episcopal ordination July 3, 1975; appointed Bishop of Salina March 22, 1984; installed May 29, 1984; retired October 21, 2004. *Mailing Address: P.O. Box 980, Salina, KS 67402-0980.*

Chancery Office: 103 N. Ninth, P.O. Box 980, Salina, KS 67402-0980. Tel: 785-827-8746; Fax: 785-827-6133.

Email: chancery@salinadiocese.org

Web: www.salinadiocese.org

Square Miles 26,685.

Formerly Diocese of Concordia.

Established August 2, 1887.

See transferred to Salina December 23, 1944.

(New boundaries established by Apostolic Letters dated July 1, 1897).

Bounded on the west by Colorado, on the north by Nebraska, on the east by the east lines of Washington, Riley, Geary and Dickinson Counties, and on the south by the south lines of Dickinson, Saline, Ellsworth, Russell, Ellis, Trego, Gove, Logan and Wallace Counties in the State of Kansas.

For legal titles of parishes and diocesan institutions, consult the Chancery Office.

STATISTICAL OVERVIEW

Personnel	
Bishop	1
Retired Bishops	1
Priests: Diocesan Active in Diocese	39
Priests: Diocesan Active Outside Diocese	1
Priests: Retired, Sick or Absent	19
Number of Diocesan Priests	59
Religious Priests in Diocese	16
Total Priests in Diocese	75
Extern Priests in Diocese	3
Ordinations:	
Diocesan Priests	1
Transitional Deacons	2
Permanent Deacons in Diocese	7
Total Brothers	1
Total Sisters	140
Parishes	
Parishes	86
With Resident Pastor:	
Resident Diocesan Priests	34
Resident Religious Priests	6
Without Resident Pastor:	
Administered by Priests	41
Administered by Religious Women	1
Administered by Lay People	4
Professional Ministry Personnel:	
Sisters	9
Lay Ministers	33
Welfare	
Homes for the Aged	5
Total Assisted	409
Educational	
Diocesan Students in Other Seminaries	15
Total Seminarians	15
High Schools, Diocesan and Parish	5
Total Students	656
Elementary Schools, Diocesan and Parish	11
Total Students	2,142
Catechesis/Religious Education:	
High School Students	1,667
Elementary Students	4,011
Total Students under Catholic Instruction	8,491
Teachers in the Diocese:	
Priests	4
Sisters	1
Lay Teachers	229
Vital Statistics	
Receptions into the Church:	
Infant Baptism Totals	838
Minor Baptism Totals	64
Adult Baptism Totals	66
Received into Full Communion	134
First Communions	914
Confirmations	572
Marriages:	
Catholic	167
Interfaith	136
Total Marriages	303
Deaths	637
Total Catholic Population	42,765
Total Population	315,983

Former Bishops—Rt. Revs. RICHARD SCANNELL, D.D., cons. in Nashville, Tenn., Nov. 30, 1887; transferred to Omaha, Jan. 30, 1891; died Jan. 8, 1916; JOHN J. HENNESSY, D.D. Apostolic Administrator, 1891-98, Bishop of Wichita; THADDEUS BUTLER, D.D., Bishop-elect; died July 17, 1897; JOHN F. CUNNINGHAM, D.D., cons. Sept. 21, 1898; died June 23, 1919; Most Revs. FRANCIS J. TIEF, D.D., cons. March 30, 1921; retired and appointed Titular Bishop of Nisa, June 11, 1938; died Sept. 22, 1965; FRANK A. THILL, D.D., cons. Oct. 28, 1938; transferred to Salina, Dec. 23, 1944; died May 21, 1957; FREDERICK W. FREKING, D.D., J.C.D., cons. Nov. 30, 1957; transferred to LaCrosse, Dec. 30, 1964; CYRIL J. VOGEL, D.D., ord. Bishop, June 17, 1965; died Oct. 4, 1979; DANIEL W. KUCERA, O.S.B., Ph.D., D.D., ord. May 26, 1949; appt. Titular Bishop of Natchez and Auxiliary Bishop of Joliet, June 6, 1977; cons. July 21, 1977; appt. Bishop of Salina, March 11, 1980; installed May 7, 1980; transferred to Archbishop of Archdiocese of Dubuque, Feb. 23, 1984; retired Oct. 16, 1995; GEORGE K. FITZSIMONS, D.D. (Retired), ord. March 18, 1961; appt. Titular Bishop of Pertusa and Auxiliary Bishop of Kansas City-St. Joseph May 27, 1975; Episcopal ord. July 3, 1975; appt. Bishop of Salina March 22, 1984; installed May 29, 1984; retired Oct. 21, 2004; PAUL S. COAKLEY, ord. May 21, 1983; appt. Bishop of Salina Oct. 21, 2004; ord. and installed Dec. 28, 2004; appt. Archbishop of Oklahoma City Dec. 16, 2010; installed Feb. 11, 2011.

Chancery Office—103 N. Ninth, P.O. Box 980, Salina, 67402-0980. Tel: 785-827-8746; Fax: 785-827-6133.

Diocesan Administrator—Rev. BARRY BRINKMAN, J.C.L.

Moderator of the Curia—Rev. RANDALL WEBER, J.C.L., Res.: 118 N. 9th, Salina, 67401.

Chancellor—Rev. BARRY BRINKMAN, J.C.L., Mailing Address: P.O. Box 980, Salina, 67402-0980.

Diocesan Finance Officer—Rev. JEROME L. MORGAN; JENNIFER HOOD, Asst. Finance Officer & Business Mgr., Mailing Address: P.O. Box 980, Salina, 67402-0980.

Diocesan Tribunal—103 N. Ninth, P.O. Box 980, Salina, 67402-0980. Tel: 785-827-8746; Fax: 785-827-6133.

Judicial Vicar-Officialis—Rev. KENNETH P. LOHRMEYER, J.C.L.

Associate Judges—Revs. KENNETH P. LOHRMEYER, J.C.L.; BARRY BRINKMAN, J.C.L.

Defender of the Bond—Rev. Msgr. JAMES E. HAKE, J.C.L.

Auditor-Notary—SUSAN OTTLEY.

Promoter of Justice and Guardian—Rev. DANIEL L. SCHEETZ, J.C.L. (Retired).

Procurator and Advocate—Rev. RANDALL WEBER, J.C.L.

Diocesan Finance Council—Rev. JEROME L. MORGAN; BILL BECKMEYER; JOHN GRAHAM; JENNIFER HOOD; ROBERT SCHMIDT; JAN MARKS; CHUCK HEIDRICK; JOHN O. FARMER; STEVE BROWN; Mr. SHAWN D. CRAWFORD, Ph.D.; TIM WERTH; SYNDI LAREZ.

College of Consultors—Rev. Msgr. JAMES E. HAKE, J.C.L.; Revs. ALLEN SCHEER; JARETT KONRADE; NORBERT DLABAL; JEROME L. MORGAN; KERRY NINEMIRE; JOSEPH KIEFFER; CHARLES STEIER; RANDALL WEBER, J.C.L.

Personnel Board—Rev. KEVIN WEBER; Rev. Msgr. JAMES E. HAKE, J.C.L., Ex Officio; Revs. BARRY BRINKMAN, J.C.L., Chancellor, Ex Officio; RANDALL WEBER, J.C.L., Ex Officio; KERRY NINEMIRE; ALLEN SCHEER; DONALD D. ZIMMERMAN; DONALD F. PFANNENSTIEL.

Office of Priestly Vocations—Rev. JARETT KONRADE, Dir.

Diocesan Offices and Directors

Art and Architecture Commission—Rev. JEROME L. MORGAN, Chm.; Rev. Msgr. JAMES E. HAKE, J.C.L., Vice Chm.; Revs. FRANK COADY; DONALD D. ZIMMERMAN; KEVIN WEBER; RANDALL WEBER, J.C.L.; Mr. CHARLES BOSTER; JENNIFER HOOD.

Priests' Continuing Formation Committee—Revs. KERRY NINEMIRE, Chm.; NICHOLAS PARKER; BENJAMIN SAW; JARETT KONRADE. Ex Officio: Rev. Msgr. JAMES E. HAKE, J.C.L.; Rev. RANDALL WEBER, J.C.L.

Catholic Charities Board—Dr. KAREN S. HAUSER, Ed.D., CEO; Revs. CARLOS RUIZ-SANTOS; DANA CLARK; NORMAN KELLY, Pres.; KATIE PLATTEN,

Vice Pres.; Mr. SHAWN D. CRAWFORD, Ph.D., Advisor; KAREN SPLICHAL; KIM HOELTING; Deacon LARRY ERPELDING; GARY SCHMEIDLER; ROBERT BUTTS, Sec.; GERALD HUNTER; LEON BOOR, Treas.; MARY JO BOOR; VICTOR LYCZAK; MARY LYCZAK; Rev. BARRY BRINKMAN, J.C.L., Diocesan Admin.

Catholic Charities of Salina, Inc.—Dr. KAREN S. HAUSER, Ed.D., CEO; CARLISLE BERGQUIST, M.A., L.C.M.F.T., Counseling; SUE BROUGHTON, L.C.M.F.T., Adoption; CECILIA SMITH, Finance Clerk; LIZ DEL REAL, Office Mgr.; KELCEY SMITH, Americorp Member; CHERYL WALTERS, Emergency Asst. Coord.; SHEILA MARCOTTE, Counseling Sec., 425 W. Iron, P.O. Box 1366, Salina, 67401. Tel: 785-825-0208; 888-468-6909; Fax: 785-826-9708. Email: ccharsal@salhelp.org. Web: www.catholiccharitiessalina.org.

Immigration—JUAN TORRES, Immigration Consultant; MARIBEL PANUCO, Hispanic Svcs. Coord., 425 W. Iron, P.O. Box 1366, Salina, 67401. Tel: 785-825-0208; 888-468-6909; Fax: 785-826-9708. Email: ccharsal@salhelp.org. Web: www.catholiccharitiessalina.org.

Catholic Charities Outreach Office - Hays—CHRISTINE M. HARDMAN, Office Mgr.; KELLI LEGLEITER, L.S.C.S.W., Adoption; Rev. WILLIAM J. SURMEIER, PsyD., L.C.P.C., Counseling, 2707 Vine, #17, P.O. Box 811, Hays, 67601. Tel: 785-625-2644; 877-625-2644; Fax: 785-625-6497. Email: cchaysof@sbcglobal.net.

Catholic Charities Outreach Office - Manhattan—GERRI WYBO ZIMMERLING, M.A., Dir. Marriage for Keeps & Fatherhood; JANELLE MURRAY, Administrative Asst., 323 Poyntz, Ste. 102, Manhattan, 66502. Tel: 785-323-0644. Email: ccmanhattan@flinthills.com.

Catholic Charities - Concordia—VACANT, 520 Washington, Ste. D, Concordia, 66901. Tel: 785-243-4167.

Catholic Community Annual Appeal—Mailing Address: P.O. Box 980, Salina, 67402-0980. Fax: 785-827-6133.

Office of Catholic Formation—Sr. BARBARA ELLEN APACELLER, C.S.J., Dir., 103 N. Ninth, P.O. Box 825, Salina, 67402. Tel: 785-827-8746; Fax: 785-827-6133.

Coordinator of Office of Catholic Formation—Sr. BARBARA ELLEN APACELLER, C.S.J. Email: barbcsj@salinadiocese.org.

Director of Religious Education—Sr. BARBARA ELLEN APACELLER, C.S.J. Email: barbcsj@salinadiocese.org.

Superintendent of Schools—Dr. NICK COMPAGNONE. Email: ministry@salinadiocese.org. Web: www.salinadiocese.com.

Consultant for Religious Education & Media—(Grades K-8), JULIE BILSON. Email: avlibrary@salinadiocese.org.

Consultant for Religious Education— (Grades 9-12), Sr. BARBARA ELLEN APACELLER, C.S.J.

Director Adult Faith Formation—Rev. FRANK COADY. Email: liturgy@salinadiocese.org.

Office of Deacons—Rev. FRANK COADY, Dir., Mailing Address: P.O. Box 980, Salina, 67402. Email: liturgy@salinadiocese.org.

Audiovisual—JULIE BILSON. Email: avlibrary@salinadiocese.org.

Office of Family Life—REG KONRADE, Co Dir. Email: familylife@salinadiocese.org; JAN KONRADE, Co Dir.; SHEILA MARCOTTE, Exec. Sec., 103 N. 9th St., P.O. Box 980, Salina, 67402-0980. Tel: 785-827-8746; Fax: 785-827-6133. Email: familylife2@salinadiocese.org.

Office of New Evangelization—Deacon MARK ROBERTI, Mailing Address: P.O. Box 908, Salina, 67402-0980.

Catholic Youth Organization and Youth Ministry—Sr. BARBARA ELLEN APACELLER, C.S.J., Mailing Address: P.O. Box 980, Salina, 67402.

Office of Communications—Rev. RANDALL WEBER, J.C.L., Mailing Address: P.O. Box 980, Salina, 67402.

Cursillo—Rev. DAMIAN RICHARDS, Spiritual Dir., St. Boniface Church, Box 87, Tipton, 67485. Tel: 785-373-4455; ANITA HORINEK, Contact Person, 1980 County Rd. 13, Colby, 67701. Tel: 785-586-2255.

Holy Childhood, Pontifical Association—Rev. STEVEN HEINA, Dir., Mailing Address: P.O. Box 980, Salina, 67402.

Office of Liturgy—Rev. FRANK COADY, Dir., Mailing Address: P.O. Box 980, Salina, 67402. Tel: 785-827-8746; Fax: 785-827-6133. Email: liturgy@salinadiocese.org.

Newspaper— The Register of the Roman Catholic Diocese of Salina, Inc. DOUG WELLER, Editor; JENNIFER HOOD, Business Mgr. Email: newspaper1@salinadiocese.org; Mailing Address: P.O. Box 1038, Salina, 67402.

Propagation of the Faith—Rev. STEVEN HEINA, Dir., Mailing Address: P.O. Box 980, Salina, 67402. Tel: 785-827-8746.

Rural Life Conference—Rev. ALLEN SCHEER, Dir., Mailing Address: Sacred Heart Cathedral, 118 N. 9th, Salina, 67401. Tel: 785-823-7221; Fax: 785-820-8063. Email: rurallifecommission@hotmail.com.

Salina Diocesan Clergy Health and Retirement Association, Inc.—Board of Trustees: VACANT, Pres., 103 N. Ninth, P.O. Box 980, Salina, 67402-0980; Revs. LARRY LETOURNEAU; NORBERT DLABAL; ALVIN WERTH (Retired); LARRY GRENNAN; KEVIN WEBER; DONALD F. PFANNENSTIEL; Mr. SHAWN D. CRAWFORD, Ph.D. Ex Officio: Revs. JEROME L. MORGAN; BARRY BRINKMAN, J.C.L.; RANDALL WEBER, J.C.L.; JENNIFER HOOD.

Salina Diocesan Council of Catholic Women (S.D.CC.W.)—Rev. DAMIAN RICHARDS, Moderator, St. Boniface, Box 87, Tipton, 67485.

Boy Scouts—Rev. JARETT KONRADE, 230 E. Cloud, Salina, 67401.

Girl Scouts—Sr. BARBARA ELLEN, C.S.J., Dir., Mailing Address: P.O. Box 825, Salina, 67402-0825.

Office of Priestly Vocations—Rev. JARETT KONRADE, Dir.

Lay Review Board-Diocesan Committee Regarding Alleged Cases of Child Sexual Abuse—Rev. BARRY BRINKMAN, J.C.L.; Mrs. JOYCE RATCLIFF, Chm.; Mrs. NANCY MAIN; Dr. GEORGE JERKOVICH; Mrs. ANNE KRESIN, Victim Assistance Coord.; Mrs. MONICA WOOLSONCROFT; Mr. GUY STEIER; Mr. BILL FAERBER. Consultors: Revs. JEROME L. MORGAN; WILLIAM J. SURMEIER, PsyD., L.C.P.C.; Rev. Msgr. JAMES E. HAKE, J.C.L., Ex Officio Member; Rev. RANDALL WEBER, J.C.L.

Victim Assistance Coordinator—Mrs. ANNE KRESIN, P.O. Box 2984, Salina, 67402. Tel: 785-825-0865. Email: reportabuse@salinadiocese.org.

Respect Life—

Moderator—Rev. HENRY BAXA, St. Andrew's Church, 311 S. Buckeye, Box 429, Abilene, 67410. Tel: 785-263-1570. Email: frhenry@eaglecom.net. Coordinators: Mr. GIL OTTER; Mrs. CAROL OTTER, 509 N. 1st St., Norton, 67654. Tel: 785-877-5423. Email: caotter@ruraltel.net.

Office of Stewardship & Development—Mr. SHAWN D. CRAWFORD, Ph.D., Dir.; SYNDI LAREZ, Asst. Dir., Chancery Office: P.O. Box 980, Salina, 67402-0980. Email: development@salinadiocese.org.

Office of Hispanic Ministry—Rev. CARLOS RUIZ-SANTOS, Moderator.

Office of Ecumenical and Interreligious Affairs—Rev. RANDALL WEBER, J.C.L., Dir.

Office of Information Technology—Mr. JEFF EASTER, Dir.

CLERGY, PARISHES, MISSIONS AND PAROCHIAL SCHOOLS

CITY OF SALINA

(SALINE COUNTY)

1—SACRED HEART CATHEDRAL PARISH (1876) [JC] Revs. Allen Scheer, Rector; Carlos Ruiz-Santos; Sisters Carmella Thibault, C.S.J., Pastoral Assoc.; Carolyn Juenemann, C.S.J., Pastoral Assoc. In Res., Rev. Randall Weber.
Church: 118 N. Ninth St., 67401. Tel: 785-823-7221; Fax: 785-820-8063.
Catechesis/Religious Program—Nancy Jaquay, D.R.E. & R.C.I.A. Students 560.

2—ST. ELIZABETH ANN SETON PARISH (1982) [JC] Rev. Frank Coady, Priest Supvr.; Sr. Rose Walters, C.S.A., Parish Life Coord.
Res.: 1000 Burr Oak Ln., 67401. Tel: 785-825-5282; Fax: 785-825-1140. Email: stelizabethsalina@ruraltel.net. Web: www.stelizabethsalina.com.
Rectory—1061 Burr Oak Ln., 67401.
Catechesis/Religious Program—Melanie Melander, D.R.E.; Lucy Larson, D.R.E. Students 119.

3—ST. MARY QUEEN OF THE UNIVERSE PARISH (1959) [JC] Revs. Kerry Ninemire; Peter O'Donnell, Parochial Vicar.
Office: 230 E. Cloud St., 67401. Tel: 785-827-5575; Fax: 785-827-8997.
Rectory—324 Albert, 67401.
School—(Grades PreK-6), 304 E. Cloud St., 67401. Tel: 785-827-4200; Fax: 785-827-7765. Dr. Nick Compagnone, Prin. Lay Teachers 29; Students 389.
Catechesis/Religious Program—Nancy Sherffius, D.R.E. Students 227.

OUTSIDE THE CITY OF SALINA

ABILENE, DICKINSON CO., ST. ANDREW PARISH (1874) [CEM] Rev. Henry Baxa; Deacon Terry Chaput.
Rectory—201 S.W. 4th. Tel: 785-263-7094.
Church: 311 S. Buckeye Ave., P.O. Box 429, 67410. Tel: 785-263-1570; Fax: 785-263-3570.
School—(Grades PreK-5) Tel: 785-263-2453. Christina Bacon, Prin. Lay Teachers 5; Students 70.
Catechesis/Religious Program—Tel: 785-263-1570. Joanna Picking, C.R.E. Students 111.

ANGELUS, SHERIDAN CO., ST. PAUL PARISH (1887), (German), [CEM] Attended by St. Joseph Parish, Oakley. Rev. Michael Elanjimattathil, C.M.I. (India).
Mailing Address: *c/o St. Joseph Parish*, 625 Freeman Ave., Oakley, 67748. Email: stpaul@st-tel.net.
Church: Tel: 785-824-3221; Fax: 785-824-3215.
Catechesis/Religious Program—Students 25.

ANTONINO, ELLIS CO., OUR LADY HELP OF CHRISTIANS PARISH (1905) Attended by St. Joseph, Hays. Rev. Earl Befort, O.F.M.Cap.
Mailing Address: *c/o St. Joseph Parish*, 215 W. 13th, Hays, 67601. Tel: 785-628-9214; Fax: 785-625-7394.

ATWOOD, RAWLINS CO., SACRED HEART PARISH (1879) [CEM] [JC 3] Rev. Nicholas Parker.
Res.: 508 N. Railroad Ave., 67730. Tel: 785-626-3335; Fax: 785-626-3431. Email: church508@yahoo.com.
Catechesis/Religious Program—Loretta A. Studer, Office Mgr./D.R.E. Students 22.

AURORA, CLOUD CO., ST. PETER PARISH (1880) [JC] Attended by St. John the Baptist Parish, Clyde. Rev. Larry Letourneau.
P.O. Box 9, 67417.
Catechesis/Religious Program—Students 9.

BEARDSLEY, RAWLINS CO., ST. JOHN NEPOMUCENE PARISH (1910), (Czech), [CEM] Rev. Nicholas Parker.
Mailing Address: *c/o Sacred Heart Parish*, 508 N. Railroad Ave., Atwood, 67730. Tel: 785-626-3335; Fax: 785-626-3431.
Church: Atwood, 67730.
Catechesis/Religious Program—Students 20.

BELLEVILLE, REPUBLIC CO., ST. EDWARD PARISH (1901) [CEM] Rev. Barry Brinkman, Parochial Admin.
Res.: 1827 Q St., P.O. Box 99, 66935. Tel: 785-527-5559. Email: stedward6810@nckcn.com.
Catechesis/Religious Program—Sacred Hearts Center, 1813 Q St., 66935. Tel: 785-527-5819. Steve Heiman, D.R.E. Students 87.

BELOIT, MITCHELL CO., ST. JOHN THE BAPTIST PARISH (1869) [CEM] Revs. Joseph Kieffer; Charles K. Awotwi, Parochial Vicar.
Office: 622 E. Main, 67420. Email: sjparish@nckcn.com. Web: www.nckcn.com/homepage/stjohns/parish.htm.
Res.: 701 E. Court St., 67420. Tel: 785-738-2851; Fax: 785-738-3410.
School—(Grades PreK-5) Tel: 785-738-3941; Fax: 785-738-3703. Web: gostj.com. Sharon Kresin, Librarian. Lay Teachers 10; Students 79.
High School—(Grades 6-12) Tel: 785-738-2942; Fax: 785-738-4462. Marcy Kee, Prin. (K-12). Lay Teachers 11; Students 64.
Catechesis/Religious Program— Gale Liesemeyer, D.R.E.; Jennifer Hewitt, D.R.E. Students 62.

BIRD CITY, CHEYENNE CO., ST. JOSEPH PARISH (1911) [JC] Attended by St. Francis Parish, St. Francis. Rev. Roger K. Meitl.
Mailing Address: *c/o St. Francis Parish*, 625 River St., P.O. Box 1170, St. Francis, 67756. Tel: 785-332-2680.
Church: 67731.
Catechesis/Religious Program—Rose Hengen, D.R.E. Students 10.

BROOKVILLE, SALINE CO., ST. JOSEPH PARISH (1884) [CEM] Attended by St. Patrick Parish, Lincoln. Rev. Msgr. James E. Hake.
Mailing Address: *c/o St. Patrick Parish*, 206 N. 5th, P.O. Box 327, Lincoln, 67455. Tel: 785-524-4823.
Church: 67425.
Catechesis/Religious Program—Students 8.

CATHARINE, ELLIS CO., ST. CATHERINE PARISH (1892), (German), [CEM 2] Rev. Earl Befort, O.F.M.Cap., Priest Supvr.; Glenda Schuetz, Parish Life Coord.
Mailing Address: 1681 St. Joseph St., P.O. Box 18, 67627-0018. Tel: 785-625-5091; Fax: 785-625-5091. Email: stonehill@ruraltel.net.
Catechesis/Religious Program—Ann Schmidt, C.R.E. Students 13.

CAWKER CITY, MITCHELL CO., SAINTS PETER AND PAUL PARISH (1878), (German), [CEM] Attended by St. Boniface Parish, Tipton. Rev. Damian Richards.
c/o St. Boniface Parish, 308 Gambrinus, P.O. Box 87, Tipton, 67485-0087.
Church: Tel: 785-781-4319; 785-373-4455.
Catechesis/Religious Program—1202 Holly, 67430. Tel: 785-781-4835. Lisa La Rocque, D.R.E. Students 22.

CHAPMAN, DICKINSON CO., ST. MICHAEL PARISH (1883) [CEM] Rev. Henry Baxa, Priest Supvr.; Marita Campbell, Parish Life Coord.
Res.: 210 E. 6th St., P.O. Box 217, 67431-0217. Tel: 785-922-6509. Email: smichael-chapman@sbcglobal.net. Web:

smchapmanparish.org.
Catechesis/Religious Program—Tel: 785-922-6509. Laurie McLaughlin, D.R.E. Students 41.

CLAY CENTER, CLAY CO., SAINTS PETER AND PAUL PARISH (1879) [CEM] Rev. Lawrence E. Grennan.
Res.: 730 Court St., 67432. Tel: 785-632-5011; Fax: 785-632-3914. Email: sspp@eaglecom.net. Web: www.claycentercatholics.parishesonline.com.
Catechesis/Religious Program—Tel: 785-632-3204. Cyndy Schwensen, D.R.E. Students 97.

CLIFTON, WASHINGTON CO., ST. MARY PARISH, (French—German), [CEM] Attended by St. John the Baptist Parish, Clyde. Rev. Larry Letourneau.
Mailing Address: *c/o St. John the Baptist*, 204 N. High, Clyde, 66938. Tel: 785-446-3474. Email: stjohn@nckcn.com.
Catechesis/Religious Program—Tel: 785-348-5404. Therese Leiszler, D.R.E. Students 35.

CLYDE, CLOUD CO., ST. JOHN THE BAPTIST PARISH (1880), (French—German), [CEM] Rev. Larry Letourneau; Brenda Koch, Pastoral Asst.
Res.: 204 N. High, 66938. Tel: 785-446-3474. Email: stjohn@nckcn.com.
Catechesis/Religious Program—Nicole Francis, C.R.E. Students 89.

COLBY, THOMAS CO., SACRED HEART PARISH (1886) [CEM] Rev. Dana Clark.
Res.: 585 N. French Ave., 67701. Tel: 785-462-2179. Web: www.sacredheartcolby.com.
School—(Grades PreK-5) Tel: 785-460-2813; Fax: 785-460-9688. Mr. David Evert, Prin. Lay Teachers 13; Students 160.
Catechesis/Religious Program—Fax: 785-460-6613. Students 169.

COLLYER, TREGO CO., ST. MICHAEL PARISH (1893), (German), [CEM] [JC] Attended by Christ the King Parish, WaKeeney, Mailing Address: Ainsie Ave., Box 174, 67631.
Catechesis/Religious Program—Laura Walt, D.R.E. Students 3.

CONCORDIA, CLOUD CO., OUR LADY OF PERPETUAL HELP PARISH (1887), (French), [CEM 2] Rev. Barry Brinkman.
Office: 307 E. Fifth, P.O. Box 608, 66901. Tel: 785-243-1099; Fax: 785-243-1939.
Res.: 420 Kansas, P.O. Box 608, 66901. Tel: 785-243-4658. Email: conolph@yahoo.com. Web: www.concordiacatholicchurch.com.
Catechesis/Religious Program—Tel: 785-243-1410. Laura Jo Meyer, D.R.E. Students 173.

CUBA, REPUBLIC CO., ST. ISIDORE PARISH (1873), (Czech), [CEM] Attended by St. Edward Parish, Belleville. Rev. Barry Brinkman, Parochial Admin.
Mailing Address: *c/o St. Edward Parish*, P.O. Box 99, Belleville, 66935.
Catechesis/Religious Program—

DAMAR, ROOKS CO., ST. JOSEPH PARISH (1912), (French), [CEM] Attended by Immaculate Heart of Mary Parish, Hill City. Rev. Henry Saw Lone.
Mailing Address: 100 N. Main, P.O. Box 68, 67632. Tel: 785-839-4343.
Catechesis/Religious Program—Tel: 785-737-4341. Monte Keller, D.R.E. Students 40.

DELPHOS, OTTAWA CO., ST. PAUL PARISH, [CEM] Merged Canonically merged with Immaculate Conception Parish, Minneapolis.

DORRANCE, RUSSELL CO., ST. JOSEPH PARISH (1902), (German—Irish), [CEM] Attended by St. Wenceslaus Parish, Wilson. Rev. Jarett Konrade, Parochial Admin.
Mailing Address: *c/o St. Wenceslaus Parish*, P.O. Box 528, Wilson, 67490. Tel: 785-658-3361.

DOWNS, OSBORNE CO., ST. MARY PARISH (1903) Attended by St. Aloysius Gonzaga Parish, Osborne. Rev. Damian Richards.
Mailing Address: *c/o St. Aloysius Gonzaga Parish*, P.O. Box 267, Osborne, 67473-0267.
Res.: 308 Gambrinus, Tipton, 67485.
Church: 1312 Prentiss, 67437. Tel: 785-454-3551.
Catechesis/Religious Program—Students 23.

ELLIS, ELLIS CO., ST. MARY PARISH (1870) [CEM] Rev. Richard Daise, Parochial Admin.; Sr. Doris M. Flax, C.S.J., Pastoral Assoc.
703 Monroe, 67637-2231.
Church: 603 Monroe, 67637. Tel: 785-726-4696. Email: stmary@gbta.net. Web: www.stmarysofellis.org/church.
School—(Grades K-6), 605 Monroe St., 67637. Tel: 785-726-3185; Fax: 785-726-3166. James Moeder, Prin.; Pamela Newton, Librarian. Lay Teachers 11; Students 116.
Catechesis/Religious Program—April Pfeifer, C.R.E. Students 74.

ELLSWORTH, ELLSWORTH CO., ST. BERNARD PARISH (1909) Rev. Steven Heina.
Res.: 911 Kansas St., 67439. Tel: 785-472-3136; Fax: 785-472-3593. Email: stbernards@att.net.
Catechesis/Religious Program—Students 64.

ELMO, DICKINSON CO., ST. COLUMBA PARISH, [CEM] Attended by St. John the Evangelist Parish, Herington. Rev. Mark Wesely.
c/o St. John the Evangelist Parish, 712 N. Broadway, Herington, 67449. Tel: 785-258-2013.
Catechesis/Religious Program—

ESBON, JEWELL CO., SACRED HEART PARISH (1887) [CEM] Attended by St. Theresa Parish, Mankato. Rev. George Chalbhagam, C.M.I. (India).
Mailing Address: *c/o St. Theresa Parish*, P.O. Box 265, Mankato, 66956. Fax: 785-378-3913.
Church: Tel: 785-378-3939. Email: stheresa@nckcn.com.
Catechesis/Religious Program—Students 15.

FORT RILEY, GEARY CO., FORT RILEY CATHOLIC COMMUNITY, Attended by Archdiocese for the Military Services. Rev. Orlando R. Fuller, Chap.
Chapel—Morris Hill Chapel Bldg 5315, 66442.

GLASCO, CLOUD CO., ST. MARY PARISH (1878) [CEM] Attended by Immaculate Conception, Minneapolis, KS Rev. Kenneth P. Lohrmeyer, Parochial Admin.
Mailing Address: *c/o Immaculate Conception*, P.O. Box 167, Minneapolis, 67467. Tel: 785-392-2079.
Church: 301 E. First St., P.O. Box 554, 67445. Tel: 785-392-2079 (Minneapolis).
Catechesis/Religious Program—Peggy Forshee, D.R.E. Students 9.

GOODLAND, SHERMAN CO., OUR LADY OF PERPETUAL HELP PARISH (1887) Rev. Norbert Dlabal; Sr. Barbara Berthiaume, C.S.J., Pastoral Assoc.
Church: 307 W. 13th, 67735. Tel: 785-890-7205; Fax: 785-890-7205.
Catechesis/Religious Program—Michael Gerber, C.R.E. (Grade School). Students 116.

GORHAM, RUSSELL CO., ST. MARY HELP OF CHRISTIANS PARISH (1894) [CEM] Rev. William J. Surmeier.
Res.: 135 - 3rd St., Box 135, 67640. Tel: 785-637-5241. Email: st_marys@gorhamtel.com.
Catechesis/Religious Program—Tonya Murphy, D.R.E.; Pam Nowak, D.R.E. Students 17.

GRAINFIELD, GOVE CO., ST. AGNES PARISH (1910), (German), [JC] Attended by Sacred Heart Parish, Park. Rev. James Maruthukunnel Thomas, C.M.I.
Mailing Address: *c/o Sacred Heart Parish*, P.O. Box 78, Park, 67751-0078. Tel: 785-673-4684.
Catechesis/Religious Program—Kim Wildeman, D.R.E. Students 40.

GREENLEAF, WASHINGTON CO., SACRED HEART PARISH (1890) [CEM] Attended by St. John the Baptist, Hanover. Rev. David Metz.
Mailing Address: *c/o St. John the Baptist*, 114 S. Church St., P.O. Box 395, Hanover, 66945. Tel: 785-337-2342.
Catechesis/Religious Program—Students 20.

GRINNELL, GOVE CO., IMMACULATE CONCEPTION OF THE BLESSED VIRIGN MARY PARISH (1896), (German), [CEM] Attended by Sacred Heart, Park. Rev. James Maruthukunnel Thomas, C.M.I.
Church & Mailing Address: 308 Monroe, P.O. Box 69, 67738. Tel: 785-824-3221; 785-673-4684; Fax: 785-824-3215.
Catechesis/Religious Program—Tel: 785-824-3215. Christy Mense, C.R.E. Students 16.

GYPSUM, SALINE CO., ST. PATRICK PARISH, Attended by Immaculate Conception of the Blessed Mary Parish, Solomon. Rev. John Wolesky, Priest Supvr.; Daylene Tracy, Parish Life Coord.
c/o Immaculate Conception of the Blessed Virgin Mary Parish, 3599 N. Field Rd., P.O. Box 337, Solomon, 67480-0337.
Catechesis/Religious Program—Students 7.

HANOVER, WASHINGTON CO., ST. JOHN THE BAPTIST PARISH (1868), (Bohemian), [CEM] Rev. David Metz.
Res.: 114 S. Church St., Box 395, 66945. Tel: 785-337-2342.
School—Tel: 785-337-2368. Timothy Rundle, Prin. Lay Teachers 7; Students 95.
Catechesis/Religious Program—Students 29.

HAYS, ELLIS CO.

1—IMMACULATE HEART OF MARY PARISH (1967) [JC] Revs. Kevin Weber; Joshua Werth, Parochial Vicar.
Res.: 1805 Vine, 67601. Tel: 785-625-7339; Fax: 785-625-7643. Web: www.ihm-church.com.
Catechesis/Religious Program—Rick Binder, Youth Dir.; Annette Hammeke, D.R.E. Students 340.

2—ST. JOSEPH PARISH (1876) [JC] Revs. Michael Scully, O.F.M.Cap.; Barnabas Eichor, O.F.M.Cap., Parochial Vicar; Canice Froelich, O.F.M.Cap.; Felix Petrovsky, O.F.M.Cap.; Jane Vanek, Pastoral Assoc.
Res.: 210 W. 13th St., P.O. Drawer 1000, 67601. Tel: 785-625-7356; Fax: 785-625-7394. Email: stjoseph@ruraltel.net. Web: www.stj-church.com.
See Holy Family Grade School, Hays under Grade Schools, Inter-Parochial located in the Institution section.
See Thomas More Prep Marian High School, Hays under High Schools Inter-Parochial located in the Institution section.
Catechesis/Religious Program—Martha A. Brungardt, D.R.E. Students 80.

3—ST. NICHOLAS OF MYRA PARISH (1983) Rev. Daryl Olmstead.
Office & Mailing Address: 2901 E. 13th, 67601. Tel: 785-628-1446; Fax: 785-623-4207.
Catechesis/Religious Program— Kathy Volker, C.R.E. Students 186.

HERINGTON, DICKINSON CO., ST. JOHN THE EVANGELIST PARISH, [CEM] Rev. Mark Wesely.
Res.: 712 N. Broadway, 67449. Tel: 785-258-2013.
Catechesis/Religious Program—Kathleen Walter, D.R.E.; Annetta Vasholtz, Dir. Youth Ministry. Students 78.

HERNDON, RAWLINS CO., ASSUMPTION OF MARY PARISH (1880), (German), [CEM] Attended by Sacred Heart Parish, Atwood. Rev. Nicholas Parker.
Mailing Address: *c/o Sacred Heart Parish*, 508 N. Railroad Ave., Atwood, 67730. Tel: 785-626-3335; Fax: 785-626-3431.
Church: P.O. Box 247, 67739.
Catechesis/Religious Program—Students 7.

HILL CITY, GRAHAM CO., IMMACULATE HEART OF MARY PARISH (1958) Rev. Henry Saw Lone.
Res.: 110 N. 10th Ave., 67642. Tel: 785-421-2535. Email: ihmhc@ruraltel.net.
Catechesis/Religious Program—Tel: 785-421-2819. Joyce Gosselin, D.R.E. Students 67.
Mission—St. Joseph Parish 107 N. Oak, Damar, Rooks Co. 67632. Tel: 785-839-4343. Email: sjdamar@ruraltel.net.

HOLYROOD, ELLSWORTH CO., ST. MARY PARISH (1886) Attended by St. Wenceslaus Parish, Wilson. Rev. Jarett Konrade, Parochial Admin.
Mailing Address: *c/o St. Wenceslaus Parish*, Box 528, Wilson, 67490. Tel: 785-658-3361.
Catechesis/Religious Program—Students 27.

HOPE, DICKINSON CO., ST. PHILLIP PARISH, Attended by St. John Parish, Herington. Rev. Mark Wesely.
Mailing Address: *c/o St. John Parish*, 712 N. Broadway, Herington, 67449. Tel: 785-258-2013.
Church: 67451. Tel: 785-366-7353.
Catechesis/Religious Program—Students 15.

HOXIE, SHERIDAN CO., ST. FRANCES CABRINI PARISH (1948) [CEM] Rev. B. Thomas Mangat, C.M.I. (India).
Res.: 924 N. 17th, Box 38, 67740. Tel: 785-675-3300. Email: sfrances@ruraltel.net.
Catechesis/Religious Program—Ellen Weiner, Rel. Educ. Coord.; Amanda Tremblay, Youth Min. Coord. & Parish Spiritual Life. Twinned with St. Martin's, Seguin, Hoxie, KS. Students 80.

JAMESTOWN, CLOUD CO., ST. MARY'S (1873) Closed. For sacramental records contact Our Lady of Perpetual Help, Concordia.

JUNCTION CITY, GEARY CO., ST. FRANCIS XAVIER PARISH (1867) [CEM] Rev. Aloysius Brungardt.
Res.: 218 N. Washington, P.O. Box 399, 66441. Tel: 785-238-2998; Fax: 785-238-4731.
School—(Grades PreK-12), 200 N. Washington St., 66441. Tel: 785-238-2841; Fax: 785-238-5021. Web: www.saintxrams.org. Lori Balderrama, Co-Prin. (Elementary and High School); Russell Swisher, Vice-Prin. (Elementary and High School); Deborah Nohler, Librarian. Lay Teachers 12; Students 73.
Jr. High School— Lay Teachers 10; Students 73.
Catechesis/Religious Program—Tel: 785-238-2841; Fax: 785-238-5021. Students 226.

KANOPOLIS, ELLSWORTH CO., ST. IGNATIUS LOYOLA PARISH (1947), (Mexican), [JC] Attended by St. Bernard Parish, Ellsworth. Rev. Steven Heina.
Mailing Address: *c/o St. Bernard Parish*, 911 Kansas, Ellsworth, 67439. Tel: 785-472-3136.
Church: Tel: 785-472-4628.
Catechesis/Religious Program—127 N. Missouri, 67454. Students 12.

LEOVILLE, DECATUR CO., IMMACULATE CONCEPTION OF THE BLESSED VIRGIN MARY PARISH (1885) [CEM] Attended by Sacred Heart Parish, Oberlin. Rev. Mark Berland.
c/o Sacred Heart Parish, 210 E. Washington, Oberlin, 67749. Tel: 785-475-3103.
Catechesis/Religious Program—Stephanie Ritter, D.R.E. Students 21.

LINCOLN, LINCOLN CO., ST. PATRICK PARISH (1870) [CEM 2] Rev. Msgr. James E. Hake.
Res.: 206 N. Fifth, Box 327, 67455. Tel: 785-524-4823. Email: stpat327@att.net.
Catechesis/Religious Program—Tel: 785-524-3043. Dora Schroeder, D.R.E. Students 68.

LOGAN, PHILLIPS CO., ST. JOHN PARISH (1878) [CEM] Attended by Saints Philip & James Parish, Philipsburg. Rev. Benjamin Saw (Burma).
Mailing Address: P.O. Box 128, 67646. Tel: 785-689-4299. Email: stjohn1@ruraltel.net.
Catechesis/Religious Program—Tel: 785-689-4299. Terra Brown, D.R.E. Students 28.

MANHATTAN, RILEY CO.

1—ST. ISIDORE CATHOLIC STUDENT CENTER PARISH (1963) Rev. Keith Weber.
Res.: 711 Denison Ave., 66502. Tel: 785-539-7496; Fax: 785-539-0220. Email: stisidores@stisidores.com. Web: www.stisidores.com.

2—SEVEN DOLORS OF THE BLESSED VIRGIN MARY PARISH (1880) Rev. Joseph Popelka. In Res., Rev. Merlin Kieffer (Retired).

Res.: 731 Pierre St., 66502. Tel: 785-565-5000; Fax: 785-565-5003. Email: seven_dolors@sbcglobal.net. Web: www.sevendolors.com.
Rectory—624 Pierre St., 66502.
Catechesis/Religious Program—Bettina Boller, D.R.E.; Maria McAnerney, D.R.E. & Dir. Youth Ministry. Students 132.

3—ST. THOMAS MORE PARISH (1981) Rev. Donald D. Zimmerman; Wayne Talbot, Pastoral Assoc.
Church Office: 2900 Kimball Ave., 66502. Tel: 785-776-5151; Fax: 785-776-5219. Email: stm@stmmanhattan.com. Web: stmmanhattan.com.
Catechesis/Religious Program— Sherry Watts, D.R.E.; Mark Ellner, D.R.E.; Braudi Petitjean, D.R.E.; Rick Smith, Youth Min. Students 400.

MANKATO, JEWELL CO., ST. THERESA PARISH (1949) [CEM] Rev. George Chalbhagam, C.M.I. (India).
Res.: 422 N. Commercial, Box 265, 66956-0265. Tel: 785-378-3939; Fax: 785-378-3913. Email: stheresa@nckcn.com.
Catechesis/Religious Program—Students 19.

MILTONVALE, CLOUD CO., ST. ANTHONY PARISH (1910) Attended by Saints Peter and Paul Parish, Clay Center. Rev. Lawrence E. Grennan.
Mailing Address: *c/o Saints Peter and Paul Parish*, 730 Court St., Clay Center, 67432. Tel: 785-632-5011; Fax: 785-632-3914.
Church: Tel: 785-427-2263.

MINNEAPOLIS, OTTAWA CO., IMMACULATE CONCEPTION OF THE BLESSED VIRGIN MARY PARISH Rev. Kenneth P. Lohrmeyer.
Mailing Address: Box 167, 67467.
Res.: 216 Cherry St., Box 167, 67467. Tel: 785-392-2079 (Parish House); 785-392-2013 (Church Hall).
Catechesis/Religious Program—Students 54.

MORROWVILLE, WASHINGTON CO., SAINTS PETER AND PAUL PARISH (1887) [CEM] Merged Canonically merged with St. Augustine's Parish, Washington. Rev. David Metz.
c/o St. Augustine Parish, 410 B St., Washington, 66968. Tel: 785-325-2346.

MUNDEN, REPUBLIC CO., ST. GEORGE PARISH (1887), (Czech), [CEM] Attended by St. Edward Parish, Belleville. Rev. Barry Brinkman, Parochial Admin.
Mailing Address: *c/o St. Edward Parish*, P.O. Box 99, Belleville, 66935.
Catechesis/Religious Program—Steve Heiman, D.R.E. Students 8.

MUNJOR, ELLIS CO., ST. FRANCIS OF ASSISI PARISH (1876) [CEM] Rev. Daryl Olmstead; Mrs. Lilly Binder, Pastoral Assoc.
Church: 883 Moscow, 67601. Tel: 785-625-5314. Email: st_francis_church@hotmail.com.
Catechesis/Religious Program—Kolleen Dome, C.R.E. Students 12.

NEW ALMELO, NORTON CO., ST. JOSEPH PARISH (1874) [CEM] Attended by St. Francis of Assisi Parish, Norton. Rev. Vincent Thu Laing.
Res. & Mailing Address: 28035 St. John St., 67645-9742. Tel: 785-567-4875; Fax: 785-567-4261.
Catechesis/Religious Program—Gayle James, D.R.E. Students 23.

NORTON, NORTON CO., ST. FRANCIS OF ASSISI PARISH (1878) Rev. Vincent Thu Laing.
Res.: 108 S. Wabash, Box 148, 67654. Tel: 785-877-2234; Fax: 785-874-4096. Email: stfranci@ruraltel.net.
Catechesis/Religious Program—Pam Engelbert, D.R.E. Students 106.
Mission—St. Joseph's Church 28035 St. John St., New Almelo, Norton Co. 67652. Tel: 785-567-4875. Email: stjosephcc@ruraltel.net.

OAKLEY, LOGAN CO., ST. JOSEPH PARISH (1890) [CEM] Rev. Michael Elanjimattathil, C.M.I. (India).
Res.: 625 Freeman Ave., 67748. Tel: 785-671-3828; Fax: 785-671-3828. Email: parish@sjoakley.org. Web: www.sjoakley.org.
School—(Grades K-5), 725 Freeman Ave., 67748. Tel: 785-671-4451; Fax: 785-671-3919. Michael Kuhlman, Prin.; Theresa Blair, Librarian. Priests 1; Lay Teachers 8; Students 57.
Catechesis/Religious Program—St. Joseph Parish Annex Barbara Hemmert, D.R.E.; Bradley Joseph, D.R.E. Students 97.

OBERLIN, DECATUR CO., SACRED HEART PARISH (1888) [JC] Rev. Mark Berland.
Res.: 210 E. Washington, 67749. Tel: 785-475-3103.
Catechesis/Religious Program—Megan Carter, D.R.E.; Jennifer Juenemann, D.R.E. Students 35.

OGDEN, RILEY CO., ST. PATRICK PARISH (1859) [CEM] Attended by Seven Dolors of the Blessed Virgin Mary Parish, Manhattan. Rev. Joseph Popelka; Deacon John Bloomfield.
Mailing Address: *c/o Seven Dolors of the Blessed Virgin Mary Parish*, 731 Pierre, Manhattan, 66502.
In Res., Most Rev. George K. Fitzsimons, Bishop Emeritus (Retired).
Res.: P.O. Box A, 66517. Tel: 785-565-5090.

OSBORNE, OSBORNE CO., ST. ALOYSIUS GONZAGA PARISH (1881) [CEM] Rev. Damian Richards.
Mailing Address: 203 N. Elm, 67473. Tel: 785-346-5582. Email: stal@ruraltel.net.
Res.: 308 Gambrinus, Tipton, 67485. Tel: 785-373-4455.
Catechesis/Religious Program—Brenda Henke, D.R.E. Students 54.
Mission—St. Mary's 1312 Prentice, Downs, Osborne Co. 67437. Tel: 785-454-3551.

PARK, GOVE CO., SACRED HEART PARISH (1898), (German), [CEM] Rev. James Maruthukunnel Thomas, C.M.I.
Res.: 202 S. Cottonwood, P.O. Box 78, 67751. Tel: 785-673-4684; Fax: 785-673-4248. Email: shcpark@ruraltel.net.
Catechesis/Religious Program—Donna Garrett, D.R.E. Tel: 785-673-4315. Students 46.

PFEIFER, ELLIS CO., HOLY CROSS, Closed. For sacramental records contact St. Fidelis, Victoria.

PHILLIPSBURG, PHILLIPS CO., SAINTS PHILIP AND JAMES PARISH (1875) Rev. Benjamin Saw (Burma).
Res.: 690 S. 7th, 67661. Tel: 785-543-5577; 785-543-5367. Email: sspjchurch@sbcglobal.net.
Catechesis/Religious Program—Kim Ellen Berger, D.R.E. Students 75.
Mission—St. John the Evangelist Logan, Phillips Co. Tel: 785-689-4299.

PLAINVILLE, ROOKS CO., SACRED HEART PARISH (1890) [CEM] Rev. Galen Long.
Church: 206 N. Washington, P.O. Box 100, 67663. Tel: 785-434-4658; Fax: 785-434-2480. Email: sacredheartchurch@ruraltel.net. Web: sacredheartplainville.org.
School—Tel: 785-434-2157. Carol Parker, Prin. Lay Teachers 8; Students 85.
Catechesis/Religious Program—Kathryn Owings, C.R.E. Students 99.

RUSSELL, RUSSELL CO., ST. MARY QUEEN OF ANGELS PARISH formerly St. Mary Queen of the Angels Parish (1886) [CEM] Rev. Charles Steier.
Church & Office: 415 S. Windsor St., 67665.
Rectory & Mailing Address: 28 N. Kansas St., 67665. Tel: 785-483-2871; Fax: 785-483-2871 (Call First).
Catechesis/Religious Program—Tel: 785-483-2871. Bonita Ney, D.R.E. Students 116.

ST. FRANCIS, CHEYENNE CO., ST. FRANCIS OF ASSISI PARISH (1912), (German), [JC] Rev. Roger K. Meitl.
Res.: 625 S. River St., P.O. Box 1170, 67756. Tel: 785-332-2680. Email: sfrancath@att.net.
Catechesis/Religious Program—Myra Douthit, D.R.E. Students 30.
Mission—St. Joseph's 203 N. Bird, Bird City, Cheyenne Co. 67731. Tel: 785-734-2287.

SCHOENCHEN, ELLIS CO., ST. ANTHONY PARISH (1877) [CEM] Attended by St. Joseph Parish, Hays. Rev. Earl Befort, O.F.M.Cap.
Res.: 215 W. 13th, Hays, 67601. Tel: 785-628-9214; Fax: 785-625-7394.

SEGUIN, SHERIDAN CO., ST. MARTIN PARISH (1910) [CEM] Attended by St. Frances Cabrini Parish, Hoxie. Religious education twinned with St. Francis Cabrini, Hoxie, KS. Rev. B. Thomas Mangat, C.M.I. (India).
Mailing Address: *c/o St. Francis Cabrini Parish*, 924 N. 17th St., P.O. Box 38, Hoxie, 67740. Tel: 785-675-3300.

SELDEN, SHERIDAN CO., SACRED HEART PARISH (1906) [CEM] Rev. Mark Berland.
Res.: 205 S. Missouri, P.O. Box 57, 67757. Tel: 785-386-4496.
Catechesis/Religious Program—Dolores Juenemann, D.R.E. Students 33.

SHARON SPRINGS, WALLACE CO., HOLY GHOST PARISH (1907), (German), Attended by Our Lady of Perpetual Help Parish, Goodland. Rev. Norbert Dlabal.
Mailing Address: *c/o Our Lady of Perpetual Help Parish*, 307 W. 13th, Goodland, 67735.
Res.: 403 N. Main St., 67758. Tel: 785-852-4984.
Catechesis/Religious Program—Mrs. Barbara Bussen, D.R.E. (Grade & High School). Students 76.

SMITH CENTER , SMITH CO., ST. MARY PARISH (1959) Attended by St. Theresa Parish, Mankato. Rev. George Chalbhagam, C.M.I. (India).
403 W. Hwy. 6, Box 263, 66967. Tel: 785-282-6888.
Catechesis/Religious Program—Mrs. Stacey Rempe, D.R.E. Students 43.

SOLOMON, DICKINSON CO., IMMACULATE CONCEPTION OF THE BLESSED VIRGIN MARY PARISH (1886) [CEM] Rev. John Wolesky, Priest Supvr.; Daylene Tracy, Parish Life Coord.
Res.: 3599 N. Field Rd., P.O. Box 337, 67480. Tel: 785-655-2221; Fax: 785-655-2221.
Catechesis/Religious Program—Marcia Ryan, D.R.E. Students 16.
Mission—St. Patricks Gypsum, Saline Co. 67448.

STOCKTON, ROOKS CO., ST. THOMAS PARISH (1878), (German), [CEM] Attended by Sacred Heart Parish, Plainville. Rev. Galen Long.
Mailing Address: *c/o Sacred Heart Parish*, 206 N. Washington, P.O. Box 100, Plainville, 67663-0100.
Res.: 722 Main, 67669. Tel: 785-425-6656. Web: sacredheartplainville.org.
Catechesis/Religious Program—Jessica Billinger, C.R.E. Students 56.

TIPTON, MITCHELL CO., ST. BONIFACE PARISH (1874) [CEM] Rev. Damian Richards.
Res.: 308 Gambrinus, P.O. Box 87, 67485. Tel: 785-373-4455.
High School—Tel: 785-373-5635. Gary Hake, Prin. Priests 1; Lay Teachers 8; Students 14.
Catechesis/Religious Program—Lori Schmitt, D.R.E. Students 40.
Mission—SS. Peter & Paul 1202 Holly, P.O. Box 25, Cawker City, Mitchell Co. 67430.

VICTORIA, ELLIS CO., ST. FIDELIS PARISH (1876), (German—Russian), [CEM] Revs. Jeff Ernst, O.F.M.Cap., Parochial Admin.; Earl Meyer, O.F.M.Cap.
Church Office: 601 10th St., 67671. Tel: 785-735-2777; Fax: 785-735-2779.
Res.: 900 Cathedral Ave., 67671. Tel: 785-735-2777; 785-735-9456; Fax: 785-735-9455. Email: fidelis@ruraltel.net. Web: www.stfidelischurch.com.
Catechesis/Religious Program—Tel: 785-735-9244; Fax: 785-735-2779. Email: sfreled@ruraltel.net. Shirley Brungardt, D.R.E. Students 201.

VINCENT, ELLIS CO., ST. BONIFACE PARISH (1904), (German—Russian), [CEM] Attended by St. Fidelis Parish, Victoria. Rev. Jeff Ernst, O.F.M.Cap., Parochial Admin.
c/o St. Fidelis Parish, 601 10th St., Victoria, 67671. Tel: 785-735-2777; 785-735-9456; Fax: 785-735-2779.
Catechesis/Religious Program—Students 23.

WAKEENEY, TREGO CO., CHRIST THE KING PARISH (1933) [CEM] Rev. Donald F. Pfannenstiel, Parochial Admin.
Res.: 412 N. Ninth St., 67672. Tel: 785-743-2330.
Catechesis/Religious Program—Tel: 785-743-2339. Verna Flax, D.R.E. Students 103.
Mission—St. Michael c/o 412 N. 9th, Wa Keeney, Trego Co. 67672.

WALKER, ELLIS CO., ST. ANN PARISH (1904), (German—Russian), [CEM] Attended by St. Fidelis Parish, Victoria. Rev. Jeff Ernst, O.F.M.Cap., Parochial Admin.
Mailing Address: *c/o St. Fidelis Parish*, 601 10th St., Victoria, 67671. Tel: 785-735-2777; Fax: 785-735-2779.
Catechesis/Religious Program— Attended by St. Fidelis, Victoria. Students 5.

WASHINGTON, WASHINGTON CO., ST. AUGUSTINE PARISH (1946) [JC] Rev. David Metz.
Res.: 410 B St., 66968. Tel: 785-325-2346; Fax: 785-325-3147.
Catechesis/Religious Program—Twinned with SS. Peter & Paul, Morrowville, Washington, KS., and Sacred Heart, Greenleaf. Cristi Gilliam, C.R.E. Students 76.

WILSON, ELLSWORTH CO., ST. WENCESLAUS PARISH (1882), (Czech), [CEM] Rev. Jarett Konrade, Parochial Admin.
Res.: P.O. Box 528, 67490. Tel: 785-658-3361; Fax: 785-658-3364. Email: swchurch@wtciweb.com.
Catechesis/Religious Program—Tel: 785-658-2341. Students 42.
Mission—St. Joseph P.O. Box 528, Dorrance, Russell Co. 67490.
Mission—St. Mary Parish Holyrood, Ellsworth Co. 67450.

On Duty Outside the Diocese:
Rev.—
Montoya, Francisco, Archdiocese of Morelia in Mexico

Retired:
Most Rev.—
Fitzsimons, George K., P.O. Box 980, 67402-0980.
Revs.—
Colucci, Bennett, 900 Cathedral Ave., Victoria, 67671-9782.
Conrad, Simon, O.F.M.Cap., St. Fidelis Friary, 900 Cathedral Ave., Victoria, 67671.
Dallen, James, W. 818 21st Ave., Spokane, WA 99203.
Flax, Myron, O.F.M.Cap., St. Fidelis Friary, 900 Cathedral Ave., Victoria, 67671.
Gibson, Beryl, 501 3rd St., Phillipsburg, 67661.
Grennan, James, 403 Barton St., Russell, 67665.
Hoover, James, 13th and Washington, P.O. Box 279, Concordia, 66901.
Hough, Roger, 1902 W. 139th St., Leawood, 66224-4567. Tel: 785-346-5582
Kieffer, Merlin, 618 Pierre, Manhattan, 66502.
Kramer, Carl, St. John's Inc., 701 7th St., Victoria, 67671.
Long, Melvin, P.O. Box 4350, Palm Springs, CA 92263-4350.

Mattas, Louis, Assisted Living Center, 6550 E. 45th St. N., Apt. 108, Bel Aire, 67226.
McCarthy, Donald, 1203 Holly, Cawker City, 67430.
Metro, LeRoy, 137 N. 9th, 67401.
Moeder, August L., 217 Grant, P.O. Box 74, Quinter, 67752.
Moeder, John, 1414 N. Kuney St., P.O. Box 265, Abilene, 67410.
Pierce, Larry E., P.O. Box 237, Oakley, 67748.
Posey, Thaddeus J., O.F.M.Cap., St. Fidelis Friary, 900 Cathedral Ave., Victoria, 67671.
Scheetz, Daniel L., J.C.L., 312 E. 3rd, Ellsworth, 67439.
Scheetz, Joseph, 510 Easter Ave., WaKeeney, 67672.
Torrez, Basil, P.O. Box 214, Collyer, 67631.
Werth, Alvin, 501 W. 37th, #11, Hays, 67601.
Werth, Loren J., 1725 Winne Dr., Manhattan, 66502.

INSTITUTIONS LOCATED IN THE DIOCESE

[A] HIGH SCHOOLS, INTER-PAROCHIAL

SALINA. *Sacred Heart Junior-Senior High School* (1908) 234 E. Cloud, 67401. Tel: 785-827-4422; Fax: 785-827-8648. Email: heart@sacredheartknights.org. Web: www.sacredheartknights.org. John Krajicek, Prin.; Rev. Peter O'Donnell, Chap.; Susan Goodman, Librarian. Sisters 1; Lay Teachers 18; Students 250.

HAYS. *Thomas More Prep-Marian* (1908) 1701 Hall, 67601. Tel: 785-625-6577; Fax: 785-625-3912. Email: dewitt@tmp-m.org. Web: www.tmp-m.org. Rev. Fred Gatschet; William DeWitt, Prin.

Thomas More Prep-Marian High Inc., Four-year Catholic High School, with college preparatory programs conducted by the local Catholic parishes; residency programs for boys and girls; special program for candidates for Priesthood and Religious Life. Priests 2; Lay Teachers 28; Students 245; Total Staff 30.

Endowment Foundation of Thomas More Prep-Marian, Inc. Galen Romme, Pres.

Thomas More Prep-Marian Alumni Assoc., 1701 Hall, 67601. Rev. Earl Befort, O.F.M.Cap., Chap.

[B] GRADE SCHOOLS, INTER-PAROCHIAL

HAYS. *Holy Family Elementary Grade School*, (Grades PreSchool-6), 1800 Milner, 67601-3796. Tel: 785-625-3131; Fax: 785-625-2098. Email: jsimon@hfehays.org. Web: www.hfehays.org. Jana Simon, Prin.; Janice Collins, Librarian. Lay Teachers 22; Students 363.

MAHATTAN. *Manhattan Catholic Schools*, (Grades K-8), 306 S. Juliette Ave., Manhattan, 66502-6297. Tel: 785-565-5050; Fax: 785-565-5055. Email: lroggenkamp@manhattancatholicschools.org. Web: www.manhattancatholicschools.org. Linda R. Roggenkamp, Prin.; Lisa Herkenrath, Librarian. Lay Teachers 22; Students 252.

[C] HOMES FOR AGED

HAYS. *St. John's Inc.*, 2403 Canterbury, 67601. Tel: 785-625-0077; Fax: 785-625-4760. Web: www.via-christi.org/villages. David Karlin, CEO.

St. John's Victoria, 701 Seventh St., Victoria, 67671. Tel: 785-735-2208; Fax: 785-735-2270. Email: david_karlin@via-christi.org. Web: www.via-christi.org. Rev. Harvey Dinkel, O.F.M.Cap., M.A., M.S., Chap.; David Karlin, CEO. Total Staff 145; Skilled Nursing Beds 90.

St. John's Assisted Living, 2225 Canterbury, 67601. Tel: 785-628-8742; Fax: 785-625-3973. Email: david_karlin@via-christi.org. Web: www.via-christi.org. Theresa Thomas, Exec. Dir. Assisted Living Units 57; Total Staff 44.

St. John's Hays, 2401 Canterbury, 67601. Tel: 785-628-3241; Fax: 785-628-3310. Joe Hess, Chairperson; Renee Davison, Exec. Dir; Rev. Harvey Dinkel, O.F.M.Cap., M.A., M.S., Chap. Total Staff 140; Skilled Nursing Beds 60.

MANHATTAN. *Via Christi Village Manhattan, Inc.* (1990) Owned & operated by the Via Christi Health System of Wichita., 2800 Willow Grove Rd., 66502. Tel: 785-539-7671; Fax: 785-539-9125. Email: amyboller@viachristi.org. Web: www.viachristi.org/villages. Amy Boller, CEO. Total Staff 165; Skilled Nursing 96; Assisted Living 36; Independent Living 8.

[D] MONASTERIES AND RESIDENCES OF PRIESTS AND BROTHERS

HAYS. *St. Joseph's Friary* (1876) 215 W. 13th St., 67601. Tel: 785-628-9214; Fax: 785-625-7394. Revs. Earl Befort, O.F.M.Cap.; Earl Meyer, O.F.M.Cap.; Canice Froelich, O.F.M.Cap. Priests 4; Total Staff 6.

VICTORIA. *St. Fidelis Friary* 67671. Tel: 785-735-9456; Fax: 785-735-9455. Revs. Jeff Ernst, O.F.M.Cap., Guardian; Harvey Dinkel, O.F.M.Cap., M.A., M.S.; Bennett Collucci, O.F.M.Cap.; Myron Flax, O.F.M.Cap. (Retired); Thaddeus J. Posey, O.F.M.Cap. (Retired); Simon Conrad, O.F.M.Cap. (Retired); Bro. Joseph McGlynn, O.F.M.Cap. Total in Residence 8.

[E] CONVENTS AND RESIDENCES FOR SISTERS

Concordia

Sisters of St. Joseph of Concordia, 215 Court St., P.O. Box 279, Concordia, 66901. Tel: 785-243-2149; Fax: 785-243-4741. Email: csjcenter@sbcglobal.net. Web: www.csjkansas.org. Sr. Marcia Allen, C.S.J., Pres., Nazareth Motherhouse for the Sisters of St. Joseph; Contact Person; Rev. James Hoover, Chap. (Retired). Professed Sisters 140; Total in Community 140.

[F] RETREAT CENTERS

CONCORDIA. *Manna House of Prayer*, 323 E. Fifth St., Box 675, 66901. Tel: 785-243-4428; Fax: 785-243-4321. Email: mannahse@mannahouse.org. Web: www.mannahouse.org. Sr. Betty Suther, C.S.J., Admin. Total Staff 10; Total in Residence 8.

VICTORIA. *Capuchin Center for Spiritual Life*, 900 Cathedral Ave., 67671. Tel: 785-735-9393; Fax: 785-735-9455. Email: ccsl@ruraltel.net. Rev. Earl Meyer, O.F.M.Cap., Dir.

[G] CAMPUS MINISTRY

HAYS. *Comeau Catholic Campus Center* Office: 506 W. Sixth, 67601. Tel: 785-625-7396. Email: comeauccc@yahoo.com. Rev. Fred Gatschet, Chap. Total Staff 2.

MANHATTAN. *St. Isidore's Catholic Student Center* , Kansas State University., 711 Denison Ave., 66502. Tel: 785-539-7496. Email: stisidores@stisidores.com. Web: www.stisidores.com. Total Staff 4; Total in Residence 1. In Res. Rev. Keith Weber, Chap.

[H] MISCELLANEOUS

SALINA. *St. Joseph Annex, Inc.*, 401 W. Iron, P.O. Box 980, 67401. Tel: 785-827-8746; Fax: 785-827-6133. Rev. Jerome L. Morgan.

Marymount Memorial Educational Trust Fund, P.O. Box 980, 67402-0980. Tel: 785-827-8746; Fax: 785-827-6133. Email: chancery@salinadiocese.org.

The Register of the Roman Catholic Diocese of Salina, Inc., 103 N. Ninth St., P.O. Box 980, 67402-0980.

Roman Catholic Diocese of Salina Deposit and Loan Inc., 103 N. Ninth St., P.O. Box 980, 67401. Tel: 785-827-8746; Fax: 785-827-6133. Email: chancery@salinadiocese.org.

Roman Catholic Diocese of Salina St. Joseph Fund, Inc., P.O. Box 980, 67402-0980.

Sacred Heart Junior-Senior Endowment Fund, Inc., 234 E. Cloud, 67401-6436. Tel: 785-825-4011; Fax: 785-827-8648. Email: melissaa@sacredheartknights.org. Web: www.sacredheartknights.org. Melissa Anderson, Special Events Coord.

Salina Catholic Diocese Education Endowment, Inc., 103 N. Ninth St., P.O. Box 980, 67402-0980. Tel: 785-827-8746; Fax: 785-827-6133. Email: chancery@salinadiocese.org.

Salina Catholic Diocese Gift & Annuity Fund, Inc., 103 N. Ninth St., P.O. Box 980, 67402-0980. Tel: 785-827-8746; Fax: 785-827-6133. Email: chancery@salinadiocese.org.

Salina Catholic Diocese Seminary Burses, Inc., 103 N. Ninth St., P.O. Box 980, 67402-0980. Tel: 785-827-8746; Fax: 785-827-6133. Email: chancery@salinadiocese.org.

Salina Diocesan Clergy Health and Retirement Association, Inc., Diocese of Salina, P.O. Box 980, 67402-0980. Tel: 785-827-8746; Fax: 785-827-6133.

The Serra Club of Salina, Kansas, 103 N. Ninth, P.O. Box 980, 67402-0980.

CONCORDIA. *Nazareth Convent & Academy Corporation, Administration Offices*, 215 Court St., P.O. Box 279, 66901. Tel: 785-243-2149; Fax: 785-243-4741. Email: csjcenter@sbcglobal.net. Web: www.csjkansas.org. Sr. Marcia Allen, C.S.J., Pres., Nazareth Motherhouse for the Sisters of St. Joseph; Contact Person; Rev. James Hoover, Chap. (Retired).

Neighborhood Initiatives, Inc., 215 Court St., P.O. Box 279, 66901. Tel: 785-243-2149; Fax: 785-243-4741.

RELIGIOUS INSTITUTES OF MEN REPRESENTED IN THE DIOCESE

For further details refer to the corresponding bracketed number in the Religious Institutes of Men or Women section.

[0470]—*The Capuchin Friars* (Province of Mid-America)—O.F.M.Cap.

[0275]—*Carmelites of Mary Immaculate* (Provincial House - Kerala, India)—C.M.I.

RELIGIOUS INSTITUTES OF WOMEN REPRESENTED IN THE DIOCESE

[3710]—*Congregation of the Sisters of Saint Agnes*—C.S.A.

[3832]—*Congregation of the Sisters of St. Joseph*—C.S.J.

[1115]—*Dominican Sisters of Peace*—O.P.

[]—*Missionaries of the Eucharistic Heart of Christ the King*

[3830-15]—*Sisters of St. Joseph*—C.S.J.

NECROLOGY

(No Deaths)

An asterisk (*) denotes an organization that has established tax-exempt status directly with the IRS and is not covered by the USCCB Group Ruling.

Diocese of Salt Lake City

(Dioecesis Civitatis Lacus Salsi)

Most Reverend

JOHN C. WESTER

Bishop of Salt Lake City; ordained May 15, 1976; appointed Bishop of Salt Lake City January 8, 2007; installed March 14, 2007. *Office: 27 C St., Salt Lake City, UT 84103-2397.* Tel: 801-328-8641, Ext. 304; Fax: 801-328-0324.

Diocesan Offices and Organizations: 27 C St., Salt Lake City, UT 84103-2397. Tel: 801-328-8641; Fax: 801-328-9680.

Web: www.dioslc.org

ESTABLISHED AS A VICARIATE-APOSTOLIC ON NOV. 23, 1886.

Square Miles 84,990.

Erected a Diocese on January 27, 1891.

Originally comprised all Utah and the Counties of Eureka, Lander, Lincoln, White Pine, Nye, Elko and Clark in the State of Nevada. By Apostolic Constitution dated March 27, 1931, the Nevada section was separated from the Salt Lake Diocese and incorporated in the Reno Diocese. The name was changed to Diocese of Salt Lake City on March 31, 1951.

Comprises the State of Utah.

Patron of the Diocese of Salt Lake City: St. Mary Magdalene.

For legal titles of parishes and diocesan institutions, consult the Chancery Office.

STATISTICAL OVERVIEW

Personnel	
Bishop	1
Abbots	1
Retired Abbots	3
Priests: Diocesan Active in Diocese	42
Priests: Diocesan Active Outside Diocese	1
Priests: Retired, Sick or Absent	13
Number of Diocesan Priests	56
Religious Priests in Diocese	12
Total Priests in Diocese	68
Extern Priests in Diocese	7
Permanent Deacons in Diocese	76
Total Brothers	9
Total Sisters	35
Parishes	
Parishes	48
With Resident Pastor:	
Resident Diocesan Priests	37
Resident Religious Priests	7
Without Resident Pastor:	
Administered by Priests	2
Administered by Deacons	1
Administered by Lay People	1
Missions	19
Professional Ministry Personnel:	
Brothers	9
Sisters	35
Lay Ministers	33
Welfare	
Day Care Centers	16
Total Assisted	564
Special Centers for Social Services	3
Total Assisted	542,500
Educational	
Diocesan Students in Other Seminaries	6
Seminaries, Religious	3
Total Seminarians	6
High Schools, Diocesan and Parish	3
Total Students	1,728
Elementary Schools, Diocesan and Parish	13
Total Students	3,693
Catechesis/Religious Education:	
High School Students	2,033
Elementary Students	8,170
Total Students under Catholic Instruction	15,630
Teachers in the Diocese:	
Scholastics	1
Sisters	1
Lay Teachers	526
Vital Statistics	
Receptions into the Church:	
Infant Baptism Totals	3,278
Minor Baptism Totals	483
Adult Baptism Totals	284
Received into Full Communion	506
First Communions	3,404
Confirmations	2,228
Marriages:	
Catholic	415
Interfaith	114
Total Marriages	529
Deaths	576
Total Catholic Population	270,000
Total Population	2,763,885

Former Bishops—Rt. Revs. LAWRENCE SCANLAN, D.D., ord. June 24, 1868; appt. Vicar-Apostolic of Utah, Jan. 25, 1887; cons. Titular Bishop of Larandum, June 29, 1887; named first Bishop of Salt Lake, Jan. 30, 1891; died May 10, 1915; JOSEPH S. GLASS, C.M., D.D., LL.D., ord. Aug. 15, 1897; cons. Aug. 24, 1915; died Jan. 26, 1926; JOHN J. MITTY, D.D., ord. Dec. 22, 1906; cons. Sept. 8, 1926; made Coadjutor Archbishop of San Francisco, cum jure successionis, Feb. 4, 1932; Titular Archbishop of Egina; succeeded to the See, March 5, 1935; died Oct. 15, 1961; Most Revs. JAMES E. KEARNEY, D.D., ord. Sept. 19, 1908; appt. July 4, 1932; cons. Oct. 28, 1932; appt. Bishop of Rochester, July 31, 1937; installed Nov. 11, 1937; died Jan. 12, 1977; LEO J. STECK, D.D., ord. June 8, 1924; appt. Auxiliary Bishop of Salt Lake, March 3, 1948; cons. Titular Bishop of Ilium, May 20, 1948; died June 19, 1950; DUANE G. HUNT, D.D., LL.D., ord. June 27, 1920; appt. Aug. 6, 1937; cons. Oct. 28, 1937; appt. assistant at the Pontifical Throne; appt. May 25, 1946; died March 31, 1960; JOSEPH LENNOX FEDERAL, D.D., ord. Dec. 8, 1934; appt. Auxiliary Bishop of Salt Lake City, Feb. 5, 1951; cons. April 11, 1951; made Coadjutor Bishop of Salt Lake City, May 8, 1958; succeeded to the See, March 31, 1960; retired April 22, 1980; died Aug. 31, 2000; WILLIAM KEITH WEIGAND, D.D., ord. May 25, 1963; appt. Sept. 3, 1980; ord. Bishop, Nov. 17, 1980; transferred to the See of Sacramento; installed Jan. 27, 1994; GEORGE H. NIEDERAUER, Ph.D., ord. April 30, 1962; appt. Bishop of Salt Lake City Nov. 3, 1994; ord. Jan. 25, 1995; appt. Archbishop of San Francisco Dec. 15, 2005; installed Feb. 15, 2006.

Diocesan Pastoral Center—27 C St., Salt Lake City, 84103-2397. Tel: 801-328-8641; Fax: 801-328-9680.

Office of the Bishop—SHIRLEY MARES, Exec. Asst.

Administrative Assistant to the Bishop—Rev. Msgr. J. TERRENCE FITZGERALD, P.A. (Retired).

Vicar General, Vicar for Clergy and Moderator of the Curia—Rev. Msgr. COLIN F. BIRCUMSHAW. Tel: 801-328-8641; DEBRA ALIRES, Sec. Tel: 801-328-8641, Ext. 317.

Chancellor—Deacon SILVIO MAYO. Tel: 801-328-8641, Ext. 315; DEBRA ALIRES, Sec. Tel: 801-328-8641, Ext. 317.

Vice Chancellor—Rev. LANGES J. SILVA, J.C.D. Tel: 801-328-8641, Ext. 312.

Diocesan Offices

Apostleship of Prayer—Rev. Msgr. MATTHEW O. WIXTED, Dir. (Retired).

Archives—GARY TOPPING, Ph.D., Dir. Tel: 801-328-8641, Ext. 346.

Campus Ministry—VACANT. Tel: 801-328-8641, Ext. 313.

Catholic Community Services—KEVIN J. POTTS, Pres.; BRADFORD R. DRAKE, Exec. Dir., 745 E. 300 S., Salt Lake City, 84102. Tel: 801-977-9119, Ext. 1222; Fax: 801-977-8227.

Catholic Foundation of Utah—ARMANDO LUJAN, Pres.; JENNIFER L. CARROLL, Exec. Dir. Tel: 801-328-8641, Ext. 306.

Catholic Relief Services—Deacon SILVIO MAYO. Tel: 801-328-8641, Ext. 315.

Catholic Schools Offices—Sr. CATHERINE KAMPHAUS, C.S.C., Supt. Tel: 801-328-8641, Ext. 330; PAM PERRI, Sec. Tel: 801-328-8641, Ext. 329.

Cemetery--Mount Calvary—JOHN CURTICE, Dir.; OLIVIA SAGASTUME, Sec. Tel: 801-355-2476; Fax: 801-328-3294.

Chancery—Deacon SILVIO MAYO, Chancellor. Tel: 801-328-8641, Ext. 315; DEBRA ALIRES, Sec. Tel: 801-328-8641, Ext. 317.

College of Consultors—Rev. Msgrs. COLIN F. BIRCUMSHAW; ROBERT R. SERVATIUS; ROBERT J. BUSSEN; TERENCE M. MOORE, Ph.D.; JOSEPH M. MAYO; J. TERRENCE FITZGERALD, P.A. (Retired); Revs. HERNANDO DIAZ; FRANCISCO PIRES; JAVIER G. VIRGEN.

Communications Media Office—COLLEEN GUDREAU. Tel: 801-328-8641, Ext. 344.

Deans—Revs. CARL SCHLICHTE, O.P., Salt Lake Deanery; HERNANDO DIAZ, Southwestern Deanery; MARTIN DIAZ, Wasatch Deanery; DONALD E. HOPE, Eastern Deanery; KENNETH L. VIALPANDO, Northern Deanery.

Permanent Diaconate—Deacon FORREST GRAY, Dir. Tel: 801-328-8641, Ext. 327.

Diaconate Formation—Rev. ELEAZAR SILVA. Tel: 801-328-8941.

Diocesan Stewardship and Development—SHANNON LEE, Dir. Tel: 801-328-8641, Ext. 328.

Diocesan Office for Persons with Disabilities—DOLORES LOPEZ. Tel: 801-328-8641, Ext. 333.

Diocesan Pastoral Council—Deacon JACK CLARK, Pres.; VACANT, Staff Liaison.

Ecumenical Commission—Rev. Msgr. JOSEPH M. MAYO; Rev. LANGES J. SILVA, J.C.D.

Engaged Encounter—FRANK PEDROZA; JOANNA PEDROZA. Tel: 801-486-9828.

Family Life-Natural Family Planning—VEOLA MARTINEZ-BURCHETT. Tel: 801-328-8641, Ext. 324.

Finance Council—Most Rev. JOHN C. WESTER; Rev. Msgr. COLIN F. BIRCUMSHAW; MARY KAY GRIFFIN, CPA; DAVE SIMPSON; KATHIE BROWN ROBERTS, Esq.; MICHAEL LEE; NANCY ESSARY; Ms. JOAN LOFFREDO, CPA, Staff Liaison; LANDELL FROERER.

Finance Office—Ms. JOAN LOFFREDO, CPA, CFO. Tel: 801-328-8641, Ext. 309; DEBRA CANDELARIA, Sec. Tel: 801-328-8641, Ext. 310.

Government Liaison—JEAN HILL. Tel: 801-328-8641, Ext. 336.

Hispanic Ministry—MARIA-CRUZ GRAY, Dir. Tel: 801-328-8641, Ext. 361; SANDRA MAXWELL, Sec. Tel:

801-328-8641, Ext. 332; MARYLIN ACOSTA, Sec. Tel: 801-328-8641, Ext. 338.

Hispanic Affairs—Rev. JAVIER G. VIRGEN, Episcopal Vicar. Tel: 801-328-8641, Ext. 358; Deacon RICARDO ARIAS, Sec. Tel: 801-328-8641, Ext. 398.

Holy Childhood Association—Deacon SILVIO MAYO, Dir. Tel: 801-328-8641, Ext. 315.

Liturgy Office—RUTH DILLON, Dir. Tel: 801-328-8641, Ext. 363.

Liturgical Commission—Rev. SAMUEL DINSDALE. Tel: 801-487-1000.

Correctional Institution Ministry—Rev. JAMES E. BLAINE, Dir. Utah State Prison, Mailing Address: P.O. Box 142, American Fork, 84003. Tel: 801-756-7771; ILLA WRIGHT, Coord. Ministry for Salt Lake Valley Detention Center, Decker Lake, Wasatch Youth Center and Adult Detention Complex 3357 Enterada Ave., West Valley City, 84119. Tel: 801-969-5617; Rev. RICHARD T. SHERMAN Central Utah Correctional Facility, Gunnison, UT.Tel: 435-896-5593.

Board For Ongoing Formation of Priests— Clergy Continuing Education, Most Rev. JOHN C. WESTER; Rev. Msgr. COLIN F. BIRCUMSHAW; Rev. JAVIER G. VIRGEN, Chm. Team: Revs. MARTIN DIAZ; OSCAR MARTINEZ; ROBERT T. MORIARTY, J.C.L.; KENNETH L. VIALPANDO; ANDRZEJ SKRZYPIEC; SAMUEL DINSDALE.

Native American Ministry—DOLORES LOPEZ. Tel: 801-328-8641, Ext. 333.

Newspaper— "Intermountain Catholic" MARIE MISCHEL, Editor. Tel: 801-328-8641, Ext. 340; CHRISTINE YOUNG, Assoc. Editor. Tel: 801-328-8641, Ext. 341; ARTHUR HEREDIA, Business Mgr. Tel: 801-328-8641, Ext. 356; CATHERINE PAIZ, Advertising Rep. & Mktg. Dir. Tel: 801-328-8641, Ext. 339; BARBARA S. LEE, Staff Writer. Tel: 801-328-8641, Ext. 365; LAURA VALLEJO, Staff Writer. Tel: 801-328-8641, Ext. 351; JENNIFER SPARKS, Graphic Designer. Tel: 801-328-8641, Ext. 342.

Peace and Justice Commission—JEAN HILL, Dir. Tel: 801-328-8641, Ext. 336.

Presbyteral Council—Rev. Msgr. TERENCE M. MOORE, Ph.D., Pres.; Revs. DONALD E. HOPE, Pres.; MARTIN DIAZ, Vice Pres.; ROBERT T. MORIARITY, Sec.

Priests' Mutual Benefit Society (Retirement)—Board of Directors: Most Rev. JOHN C. WESTER, Chm.; Rev. Msgrs. COLIN F. BIRCUMSHAW, Pres.; JOSEPH M. MAYO; TERENCE M. MOORE, Ph.D., Sec. & Treas.; ROBERT R. SERVATIUS; Revs. FRANCISCO PIRES; KENNETH L. VIALPANDO; Ms. JOAN LOFFREDO, CPA.

Priests' Personnel Board—Most Rev. JOHN C. WESTER; Rev. Msgrs. COLIN F. BIRCUMSHAW; JOSEPH M. MAYO; Revs. JAVIER G. VIRGEN; LANGES J. SILVA, J.C.D.; ANDRZEJ SKRZYPIEC; KENNETH L. VIALPANDO; DONALD E. HOPE.

Real Estate Office—MICHAEL LEE, Dir. Tel: 801-328-8641, Ext. 364.

Religious Education—SUSAN NORTHWAY, Dir. Tel: 801-328-8641, Ext. 326.

Sisters' Council—Executive Team: Sisters GENEVRA ROLF, C.S.C., Episcopal Liaison for Women Rel.; KATHLEEN MORONEY, C.S.C., Pres.; MARY ZENZEN, O.S.B., Vice Pres.; CECILIA VAN ZANDT, D.C., Treas.; DANILE KNIGHT, O.S.B., Sec.

Society for the Propagation of the Faith—Deacon SILVIO MAYO, Dir. Tel: 801-328-8641, Ext. 315.

Pastoral Operations—MICHAEL LEE, Dir. Tel: 801-328-8641, Ext. 364.

Special Needs Program Scholarship Assistance—Sr. STELLA MARIE ZAHNER, D.C. Tel: 801-328-8641, Ext. 334.

Tribunal—

Judicial Vicar—Rev. LANGES J. SILVA, J.C.D. Tel: 801-328-8641, Ext. 312.

Secretary and Notary—VIOLA SMITH. Tel: 801-328-8641, Ext. 316.

Promoter of Justice—Rev. Msgr. J. TERRENCE FITZGERALD, P.A. (Retired).

Defenders of the Bond—Rev. Msgrs. ROBERT R. SERVATIUS; JOSEPH M. MAYO; Mrs. DEBORAH BARTON, J.C.L.

Judges—Revs. LANGES J. SILVA, J.C.D.; DAVID H. SCHULYER, S.M.; Mr. ROBERT J. FLUMMERFELT, J.C.L.; Dr. KELLY O'DONNELL, J.C.D.

Victim Assistance Coordinator and Safe Environment—COLLEEN GUDREAU. Tel: 801-328-8641, Ext. 344. Email: colleengudreau@dioslc.org.

Vocation Office—Rev. JAVIER G. VIRGEN, Dir. Tel: 801-328-8641, Ext. 358; Deacon RICARDO ARIES, Assoc. Dir. Tel: 801-328-8641, Ext. 398.

Youth and Young Adult Ministry—VACANT. Tel: 801-328-8641, Ext. 313.

CLERGY, PARISHES, MISSIONS AND PAROCHIAL SCHOOLS

SALT LAKE CITY

(SALT LAKE COUNTY)

1—CATHEDRAL OF THE MADELEINE LLC 202 (1866) Rev. Msgr. Joseph M. Mayo; Rev. Eleazar Silva; Deacons Lynn R. Johnson; Silvio Mayo; Scott Dodge; Drew Peterson; Armando Solorzano. In Res., Rev. Langes J. Silva.
Res.: 331 E. S. Temple St., 84111. Tel: 801-328-8941; Fax: 801-364-6504. Web: www.saltlakecathedral.org.
School—Madeleine Choir School, 205 E. 1st Ave., 84103. Tel: 801-323-9850; Fax: 801-323-0581. Ms. Jill Baillie, Prin. Priests 1; Lay Teachers 26; Students 252.
Catechesis/Religious Program—Fax: 801-364-6504. Students 198.
Good Samaritan Program—Laurel Dokos Griffith, Prog. Dir. Number Served 135,000.

2—SAINT AMBROSE LLC 214 (1948) Revs. Andrzej Skrzypiec; Jerome Kim, Parochial Vicar; Deacons John Bash; George Reade.
Res.: 2315 Redondo Ave., 84108. Tel: 801-485-5610; Fax: 801-484-3642. Email: paroff@xmission.com. Web: www.stambroseslc.com.
School—J. E. Cosgriff Memorial School, (Grades PreK-8), 2335 Redondo Ave., 84108. Tel: 801-486-3197; Fax: 801-484-8270. Mrs. Elizabeth Hunt, Prin.; Linda Paoletti, Librarian. Lay Teachers 25; Preschool 81; Students 303.
Catechesis/Religious Program—Tel: 801-485-9324; Fax: 801-484-1065. Students 137.

3—SAINT ANN LLC 215 (1917) Rev. Michael R. Sciumbato; Deacon Mansueto Flaim.
Res.: 2119 S. 400 E., 84115-2872. Tel: 801-487-1000; Fax: 801-487-1416.
School—(Grades PreSchool-8), 430 E. 2100 S., 84105. Tel: 801-486-0741; Fax: 801-486-0742. Kathleen McMahon, Prin.; Mary T. Sena, Librarian. Lay Teachers 18; Students 260.
Catechesis/Religious Program—Tel: 801-261-5943; Fax: 801-261-5903 (Call first). Email: slavole9@msn.com. Students 67.

4—SAINT CATHERINE OF SIENA LLC 218 (1981) Revs. Carl Schlichte, O.P.; Peter Do, O.P.
Res.: 170 S. University, 84102. Tel: 801-359-6066; Fax: 801-359-4547.
Catechesis/Religious Program—

5—OUR LADY OF GUADALUPE LLC 208 (1944), (Hispanic), Rev. Oscar Martinez; Deacon Mario A. Rodriguez.
Res.: 323 Argyle Ct., 84116.
Church: 715 W. 300 N., 84116. Tel: 801-364-2019; Fax: 801-359-2678.
Catechesis/Religious Program—Linda Martinez, D.R.E. & Coord. Students 716.

6—OUR LADY OF LOURDES LLC 211 (1913) [CEM] Rev. J. J. Schwall; Deacon Lowell Palm.
Res.: 1085 E. 700 S. St., 84102. Tel: 801-322-3330; Fax: 801-363-6007.
School—(Grades PreK-8), 1065 E. 700 S. St., 84102. Tel: 801-364-5624; Fax: 801-364-0925. Louise Herman, Prin. Lay Teachers 13; Students 237.
Catechesis/Religious Program—Tel: 801-322-3330; Fax: 801-363-6007. Students 15.

7—OUR LADY OF PERPETUAL HELP LLC 261 (1994), (Vietnamese), (Vietnamese Parish) Rev. Dominic Thuy Dang Ha.
Mailing Address: P.O. Box 18306, 84118-0306. Tel: 801-968-8981.
Church & Res.: 5415 S. 4360 W., 84118. Tel: 801-968-8981.
Catechesis/Religious Program—Students 170.

8—SAINT PATRICK LLC 241 (1892) Rev. Lourduraj Gally Gregory; Deacon Sefo A. Manu.
Mailing Address: 1058 W. 400 S., 84104-1261.
Res.: 1072 W. 400 S., 84104-1261. Tel: 801-596-7233; Fax: 801-363-3743.
Catechesis/Religious Program—Students 72.

9—SACRED HEART LLC 210 (1917) Rev. Eugenio Yarce.
Res.: 948 S. 2nd East St., 84111. Tel: 801-363-8632; Fax: 801-363-1539. Email: sacredheart.slc@hotmail.com.
Catechesis/Religious Program—174 E. 900 S., 84111. Students 333.

10—SAINT THOMAS MORE CATHOLIC CHURCH LLC 248 (1981) Revs. David L. Van Massenhove; Paul J. McCarthy, S.J.; Deacon Mark E. Solak. In Res., Rev. Anastasius Iwuoha.
Res. & Parish Center: 3015 E. Creek Rd., Sandy, 84093-6575. Tel: 801-942-5285 (Office); 801-942-7678 (Rectory); Fax: 801-942-5287. Email: stm@stmore.com. Web: stmutah.org.
Catechesis/Religious Program—Tel: 801-942-5285. Students 246.

11—SAINT VINCENT DE PAUL LLC 250 (1925) Rev. Msgr. M. Francis Mannion; Deacons John Kranz; David Osman.
Res.: 1375 E. Spring Ln., 84117. Tel: 801-272-9216; Fax: 801-273-1156.
School—(Grades PreK-8), 1385 E. Spring Ln., 84117. Tel: 801-277-6702; Fax: 801-424-0450. Mark Longe, Prin. Lay Teachers 20; Students 280.
Catechesis/Religious Program—Tel: 801-527-2037. Students 120.

SUBURBAN SALT LAKE CITY

1—BLESSED SACRAMENT LLC 201 (1972) Rev. Msgr. Robert R. Servatius; Deacons Russell Langner; Marcel Soklaski; Sharon Jackson, Pastoral Assoc.
Res.: 9757 S. 1700 E., Sandy, 84092. Tel: 801-571-5517 (Office); 801-576-1644 (Rectory); Fax: 801-676-0900. Web: blessedsacramentsandy.parishesonline.com.
School—(Grades PreSchool-8), 1745 E. 9800 S., Sandy, 84092. Tel: 801-572-5311; Fax: 801-572-0251. Email: tnielsen@blessedsacschool.org. Web: www.blessedsacschool.org. Mr. Matt Devoll, Prin.; Mr. John Nuttall, Librarian. Lay Teachers 20; Students 276.
Catechesis/Religious Program—1745 E. 9800 S., Sandy, 84092. Tel: 801-571-2071. Email: rcatlin@blessedsacschool.org. Lisa Johnson, D.R.E. Students 106.
Station—Our Lady of the Snows Alta. Tel: 801-742-2889.

2—SAINT FRANCIS XAVIER LLC 222 (1955) Revs. Robert T. Moriarty; Joseph S. Frez; Deacon Douglas C. Biediger.
Res.: 4501 W. 5215 S., Kearns, 84118. Tel: 801-968-2123; Fax: 801-966-1639.
See St. Francis Xavier Regional School, Kearns under Elementary Schools, Regional located in the Institution section.
Catechesis/Religious Program—Tel: 801-968-2123, Ext. 153. Students 700.

3—IMMACULATE CONCEPTION LLC 206 (1890) Rev. Dennis Ruane, Sacramental Min.
Mailing Address: 112 W. State Hwy., P.O. Box 151, Copperton, 84006.
Res.: 8892 W. State Hwy., P.O. Box 151, Copperton, 84006. Tel: 801-569-2706.
Catechesis/Religious Program—Students 19.

4—SAINT JOSEPH THE WORKER LLC 232 (1964) Rev. Patrick F. Carley, Admin.
Res.: 7405 S. Redwood Rd., P.O. Box 98, West Jordan, 84084. Tel: 801-255-8902; Fax: 801-561-4062. Email: stjoseph-wj@hotmail.com. Web: www.stjoseph-wj.org.
Catechesis/Religious Program—Tel: 801-251-1236. Students 160.

5—SAINT JUDE (1975), (Maronite), [CEM] Chorbishop William J. Leser, Temporary Admin.
Res.: 4893 Wasatch St., Murray, 84107. Tel: 801-268-2820. Email: stjudechurch@stinger.net.
Catechesis/Religious Program—Fax: 801-268-4404. Students 19.

6—SAINT MARTIN DE PORRES LLC 236 (1982) Rev. Jan Bednarz.
Mailing Address: 4976 Valois Cir., Taylorsville, 84118. Tel: 801-968-2369.
Church: 4914 S. 2200 W., Taylorsville, 84118.
Catechesis/Religious Program—Students 41.

7—OUR LADY OF LOURDES LLC 209 (1916) [CEM] Rev. John Norman.
Res.: 2840 S. 9000 W., P.O. Box 38, Magna, 84044. Tel: 801-508-1598; Fax: 801-250-7027.
Catechesis/Religious Program—8585 W. 3010 S., Magna, 84044. Tel: 801-250-6052. Students 121.

8—SAINTS PETER AND PAUL LLC 243 (1972) Revs. Omar Ontiveros; Roberto H. Montoro Sasia, Pastoral Assoc.; Dennis Reily, O.P., Pastoral Assoc.; Deacons Eugene Farrell; Sunday S. Espinoza; George J. Sluga.
Res. & Mailing Address: 3580 W. 3650 S., West Valley City, 84119.
Catechesis/Religious Program—Tel: 801-966-5111, Ext. 202; Fax: 801-966-2114. Students 493.

9—SAINT THERESE OF THE CHILD JESUS LLC 246 (1925), (Spanish), Revs. Martin Diaz; Denis Reilly, O.P., Parochial Vicar; Deacons Stanley L. Stott; Meliton Sanchez.
Office: 7832 S. Allen St., Midvale, 84047. Tel: 801-255-3721; Fax: 801-255-4516. Email: stthereses@yahoo.com. Web: www.stthererse.org.
Res.: 7860 S. Allen St., Midvale, 84047. Tel: 801-561-6015. 612 Lennox St., Midvale, 84047. Tel: 801-568-3650.
Catechesis/Religious Program—Tel: 801-561-2495. Students 594.

OUTSIDE SALT LAKE CITY

AMERICAN FORK, UTAH CO., SAINT PETER LLC 242 (1969) Rev. James E. Blaine.
634 N. 600 E., 84003. Email: stpeters6@yahoo.com. Web: www.stpetersamericanfork.parishesonline.com.
Catechesis/Religious Program—Tel: 801-756-2747. Students 130.
Station—Eagle Mountain

BOUNTIFUL, DAVIS CO., SAINT OLAF LLC 239 (1944) Rev. Raynato Rodillas, S.V.D.; Deacons Dan Essary; Manuel Trujillo.
Res.: 276 E. 1700 S., 84010. Tel: 801-295-3621; Fax: 801-295-8261.
School—(Grades K-8), 1793 S. Orchard Dr., 84010. Tel: 801-295-5341; Fax: 801-295-5915. Lay Teachers 13; Students 148.
Catechesis/Religious Program—Students 112.

BRIGHAM CITY, BOX ELDER CO., SAINT HENRY LLC 225 (1950) Rev. Patrick Reuse, S.J.; Deacons Kary Meyersick; Andy Hunnel.
Res.: 380 S. 2nd E., P.O. Box 872, 84302. Tel: 435-723-2941; Fax: 435-723-1215. Email: sthenrys@comast.net.
Catechesis/Religious Program—Tel: 435-723-1215. Students 85.
Mission—Santa Ana 760 W. 600 N., Tremonton, Box Elder Co. 84337.

CEDAR CITY, IRON CO., CHRIST THE KING LLC 203 (1934) [JC] Rev. Msgr. Robert J. Bussen; Rev. Jose Fidel Barrera; Deacon Denny Davies; Sr. Yvonne Hatt, C.S.C.
Mailing Address: 690 S. Cove Dr., 84720.
Res.: 680 S. Cove Dr., 84720. Tel: 435-586-8298; Fax: 435-865-5960.
Catechesis/Religious Program—Students 110.
Mission—St. Gertrude Panguitch, 84759.
Mission—St. Sylvester Escalante, Garfield Co. 84726.
Station—St. Dominic
Station— Duck Creek Village, Kane Co. 84762.

CENTRAL VALLEY, SEVIER CO., SAINT ELIZABETH LLC 220 (1947) Rev. Richard T. Sherman.
Mailing Address: 815 N. SR 110, 84754.
Res.: 76 S. 200 W., Richfield, 84701. Tel: 435-896-8734; Fax: 435-896-8734.
Catechesis/Religious Program—Students 160.
Mission—St. Anthony of the Desert North on Sandcreek Rd., Torrey, Wayne Co. 84775. Tel: 435-425-3319.
Mission—St. Jude 160 E. Center St., Ephraim, Sanpete Co. 84627. Tel: 435-283-6242.
Mission—San Juan Diego Mission 25 W. Center St., Gunnison, Sanpete Co. 84634.
Station—Central Utah Correctional Facility [JC] Gunnison. Tel: 801-528-6000; Fax: 801-528-6259.

DRAPER, SALT LAKE CO., SAINT JOHN THE BAPTIST LLC 252 (1999) Rev. Msgr. Terence M. Moore; Deacons Paul Graham; Dale R. Dillon.
300 E. 11800 S., 84020. Tel: 801-984-7101; Fax: 801-984-7114.
School—Tel: 801-984-7100; Fax: 801-984-7122.
Catechesis/Religious Program—Tel: 801-984-7101; Fax: 801-984-7114. Students 585.

EAST CARBON, CARBON CO., GOOD SHEPHERD LLC 204 (1947) Rev. Donald E. Hope, Pastoral Admin.
Res.: P.O. Box 99, 84520. Tel: 435-888-3306.
Catechesis/Religious Program—Students 16.
Mission—St. Michael 140 N. Long St., Green River, Emery Co. 84525. Tel: 435-637-1846.

EUREKA, JUAB CO., SAINT PATRICK LLC 257 (1885) Rev. Joseph S. Rooney, S.J.
Res.: P.O. Box 387, Payson, 84651. Tel: 801-465-4782. Email: sanandres@qwestoffice.net.
Catechesis/Religious Program—Students 1.

HELPER, CARBON CO., SAINT ANTHONY OF PADUA CATHOLIC CHURCH LLC 216 (1944) [JC] Rev. Donald E. Hope.
Res.: 5 S. Main, 84526-1533. Tel: 435-472-5661; Fax: 435-472-5661. Email: santhony@emerytelcom.net. Web: www.stanthony-helper.org.
Catechesis/Religious Program—Tel: 435-472-8367; Fax: 435-472-8367. Students 37.

HUNTSVILLE, WEBER CO., SAINT FLORENCE CATHOLIC COMMUNITY LLC 254 (1990) Rev. Charles T. Cummins, Admin.
Mailing Address: 514-24th St., Ogden, 84401-1594. Tel: 801-399-9531.
Church: 6461 E. Hwy. 39, 84317. Tel: 801-745-5673.
Catechesis/Religious Program—Students 59.

KANAB, KANE CO., SAINT CHRISTOPHER LLC 219 (1953) Deacon Denny Davies, Pastoral Admin.
Res.: 39 W. 200 S., 84741. Tel: 435-644-3414 (Office).
Catechesis/Religious Program—

LAYTON, DAVIS CO., SAINT ROSE OF LIMA LLC 245 (1948) Rev. Clarence J. Sandoval; Deacons Willis Bassett; John C. Weis.
Mailing Address: P.O. Box 557, 84041. 210 S. Chapel St., 84041. Tel: 801-544-4269; Fax: 801-593-0808.
Res.: 321 Whitesides St., 84041. Tel: 801-546-2541. Email: church@stroseut.org. Web: www.stroseoflimacatholic.net.
Catechesis/Religious Program—Tel: 801-544-5425. Students 372.

LOGAN, CACHE CO., SAINT THOMAS AQUINAS LLC 247 (1941) Rev. Francisco Pires; Deacon Jim Miller.
Res.: 573 E. 2050 N., North Logan, 84341. Tel: 435-753-6724.
Church: 725 S. 250 E., Hyde Park, 84318. Tel: 435-752-1478; Fax: 435-792-3792. Email: stthomas2006@gmail.com. Web: www.stthomaslogan.org.
Catechesis/Religious Program—Tel: 435-752-1478. Students 451.
Mission—Utah State University St. Jerome Newman Center, 795 N. 800 E., Cache Co. 84321. Tel: 435-753-7670.

MILFORD, BEAVER CO., SAINT BRIDGET LLC 217 (1948) Rev. Hernando Diaz.
Mailing Address: 210 S. 1st W., P.O. Box 785, 84751.
Res.: 96 S. Center, P.O. Box 924, Delta, 84624. Tel: 435-864-3710.
Catechesis/Religious Program—Students 60.
Mission—St. John Bosco P.O. Box 924, Delta, Millard Co. 84624. Tel: 435-864-3710.
Mission—Holy Family P.O. Box 292, Fillmore, Millard Co. 84631. Tel: 435-743-4275.

MOAB, GRAND CO., SAINT PIUS X LLC 244 (1955) Rev. William F. Wheaton; Deacon Richard H. Klein.
Res.: 122 W. 400 N., P.O. Box 636, 84532. Tel: 435-259-5211; Fax: 435-259-3984. Email: piusx@frontiernet.net.
Catechesis/Religious Program—Students 16.
Mission—Sacred Heart Hwy. 46/Main, LaSal, San Juan Co. 84530.

MONTICELLO, SAN JUAN CO., SAINT JOSEPH LLC 229 (1935) [JC] Rev. William F. Wheaton; Deacon Thomas P. Corrao.
Res. & Mailing Address: 365 S. Main, P.O. Box 518, 84535. Tel: 435-587-2322.
Catechesis/Religious Program—Students 46.
Station— Blanding.

OGDEN, WEBER CO.

1—HOLY FAMILY LLC 205 (1979) Rev. Patrick H. Elliott.
Res. & Office: 1100 E. 5550 S., 84403. Tel: 801-479-1112; Fax: 801-479-1126. Web: holyfamilycatholicchurch.org.
Catechesis/Religious Program—Students 133.

2—SAINT JAMES THE JUST LLC 226 (1966) Rev. Erik J. Richtsteig; Deacons Herschel Hester; Robert W. Bambrick.
Res.: 495 N. Harrison Blvd., 84404. Tel: 801-782-5393; Fax: 801-782-9559.
Catechesis/Religious Program—Tel: 801-782-7372; Fax: 801-479-4909. Email: stjames_dre@comcast.net. Students 195.

3—SAINT JOSEPH LLC 230 (1875) Revs. Kenneth L. Vialpando; Jose Alberto Barrera; Charles T. Cummins; Deacons John Conniff; Anthony J. Lopez; Keith W. Norrell; Honorio Moreno.
Res.: 514 24th St., 84401. Tel: 801-399-5627; Fax: 801-399-5918.
See St. Joseph Regional School, Ogden under Elementary Schools, Regional located in the Institution section.
Catechesis/Religious Program—Tel: 801-621-3602; Fax: 801-621-3602. Email: reprogram3602@msn.com. Students 565.
Mission—St. Florence 6481 E. Hwy. 39, Huntsville, Weber Co. 84317. Tel: 801-745-5673.

4—SAINT MARY LLC 237 (1957) Rev. Gustavo Vidal; Deacons Jack Clark; Steve Neveraski; Ken Murphy.
Mailing Address: 4050 S. 3900 W., West Haven, 84401. Tel: 801-621-7961; Fax: 801-394-1244.
Catechesis/Religious Program—Tel: 801-621-2274. Students 400.

OREM, UTAH CO., ST. FRANCIS OF ASSISI LLC 221 (1892) [CEM] Revs. David J. Bittmenn; Jose Gregorio Rausseo Gomez, Parochial Vicar; Deacon Moises Ruiz.
Mailing Address: 65 E. 500 N., 84057-4030. Email: oremstfrancis@lycos.com.
Res.: 1661 N. 500 E., 84057-4030. Tel: 801-221-1307.
Catechesis/Religious Program—Tel: 801-221-0750, Ext. 16; Fax: 801-221-0759. Students 551.
Mission—Mission San Isidro Elberta, Utah Co. 84626.

PARK CITY, SUMMIT CO., SAINT MARY OF THE ASSUMPTION LLC 238 (1881) Revs. Stanislaw Herba; Marco T. Lopez; Deacons Tom Tosti; Robert H. Hardy.
Res.: 1505 W. White Pine Canyon Rd., 84060. Tel: 435-649-9676; Fax: 435-658-0067. Web: www.stmarysparkcity.com.
Catechesis/Religious Program—Students 493.
Mission—St. Lawrence 1st West Center, Heber City, Wasatch Co. 84032. Tel: 435-654-4035; Fax: 435-654-4035.

PAYSON, UTAH CO., SAN ANDRES LLC 212 (1986) Rev. Joseph S. Rooney, S.J.
Church & Mailing Address: 315 E. 100 N., P.O. Box 387, 84651. Fax: 801-465-7729. Email: sanandres@qwestoffice.net.
Catechesis/Religious Program—Students 82.

PRICE, CARBON CO., NOTRE DAME DE LOURDES LLC 207 (1918) Rev. Donald E. Hope.
185 N. Carbon Ave., 84501.
Res.: 205 N. Carbon Ave., 84501. Tel: 435-636-8124; Fax: 435-637-6338. Web: www.notredamechurch.com.
Catechesis/Religious Program—Tel: 435-637-6338; 435-630-0815. Students 142.
Mission—San Rafael 1716 S. Hwy. 10, Huntington, Emery Co. 84528. Tel: 435-687-2116; Fax: 435-384-3215.

RIVERTON, SALT LAKE CO., SAINT ANDREW CATHOLIC CHURCH LLC 233 (2006) Rev. John Evans, O.P.; Deacon Michael E. Bulson.
11835 S. 3600 W., 84065. Tel: 801-984-7500; Fax: 801-254-1142. Email: standrew@catholicweb.com. Web: www.standrewriverton.com.
Catechesis/Religious Program—Students 154.

ROOSEVELT, DUCHESNE CO., SAINT HELEN LLC 224 (1940) [CEM] Rev. Albert Kileo, A.L.C.P.
Res.: 433 E. 200 N., P.O. Box 415, 84066. Tel: 435-722-2975; Fax: 435-722-0525.
Catechesis/Religious Program—Tel: 435-722-0525. Students 35.
Mission—Holy Spirit Duchesne, Duchesne Co.
Mission—Blessed Kateri Tekakwitha Fort Duchesne, Uintah Co. Tel: 435-722-4734.

ST. GEORGE, WASHINGTON CO., ST. GEORGE LLC 223 (1955) Revs. Oscar M. Picos; Tai Nguyen, Parochial Vicar; Deacons Rigoberto Aquirre; Jack Gorman; Rogaciano Tellez; Mark A. Bourget Sr.; Willie Folkes.
Mailing Address: 259 W. 200 N., P.O. Box 188, 84771. Tel: 435-688-1948 (Giftshop); 435-673-2604 (Office); Fax: 435-688-2704. Email: st_george_catholic@hotmail.com. Web: www.saintgeorgecatholics.com.
Res.: 289 W. 200 N., 84770. Tel: 435-673-7354.
Catechesis/Religious Program—Bishop Scanlan Bldg., 157 N. 200 W. Tel: 435-673-6701; Fax: 435-688-2704. Students 496.
Mission—San Pablo Beryl, Iron Co. 84714. Saturdays 6pm
Station—Zion National Park, Tel: 435-772-3256. (Lodge); Saturdays 6pm
Station—Saint Paul Catholic Center 171 S. Main, Hurricane, 84737. Tel: 435-635-9186. Every Sunday 10:00am

TOOELE, TOOELE CO., ST. MARGUERITE LLC 235 (1910) Rev. Samuel Dinsdale; Deacon Rick Huffman.
Res.: 15 S. 7th St., 84074. Tel: 435-882-3860; Fax: 435-882-3866. Email: stmarg@stmarguerites.org.
School—(Grades PreK-8) Tel: 435-882-0081. Web: stmargschool.org. Marcella Burden, Prin. Faculty 13; Students 160.
Catechesis/Religious Program—Students 132.

VERNAL, UINTAH CO., SAINT JAMES THE GREATER LLC 227 (1923) [JC] Revs. Albert Kileo, A.L.C.P.; Beda Msaki, A.L.C.P.
Res.: 138 N. 100 West St., 84078. Tel: 435-789-3016; Fax: 435-789-5774.
Catechesis/Religious Program—Tel: 435-789-3034. Students 80.

WENDOVER, TOOELE CO., SAN FELIPE LLC 251 (2000), (Spanish), Rev. German Umaña, Admin.
Res.: 606 E. Aria Blvd., P.O. Box 1270, 84083. Tel: 435-665-2339.
Catechesis/Religious Program—Students 190.

Chaplains of Public Institutions

SALT LAKE CITY. *Adult Detention Complex*, Tel: 801-743-5500.
County Youth Detention Center, Tel: 801-261-2060.
Decker Lake Youth Detention Center, Tel: 801-954-9200. Illa Wright. Tel: 801-969-5617.
Veterans Administration Hospital, 500 Foothill Dr., 84113. Tel: 801-582-1565. Rev. Lourduraj Gally Gregory.
Wasatch Youth Center, Tel: 801-265-5860.

DRAPER. *Utah State Prison*, P.O. Box 142, American Fork, 84003. Tel: 801-576-7827. Rev. James E. Blaine. Tel: 801-576-7485.

GUNNISON. *Central Utah Correctional Facility*, Tel: 435-528-6000. Rev. Richard T. Sherman. Tel: 435-896-5539.

On Duty Outside the Diocese:
Rev.—
Gaeta, David R., 1225 E. Bennington St., Boston, MA 02128.

Retired:
Rev. Msgrs.—
Bonnell, Victor G.
Davich, George
Daz, Rudolph A.
Fitzgerald, J. Terrence, P.A.
Sweeney, Lawrence P.
Winterer, Michael J.
Wixted, Matthew O.
Revs.—
Curnutte, William G.
Fogarty, James

Govorchin, Vincent
Hart, John B.
Rodriguez, Reyes G.
Semple, James

Permanent Deacons:
Aquirre, Rigoberto, St. George, St. George
Arias, Ricardo, Office of Hispanic Affairs
Bambrick, Robert W., St. James, Ogden
Bash, John, St. Ambrose, Salt Lake City
Bassett, Willis, St. Rose of Lima, Layton
Biediger, Douglas C., St. Francis Xavier, Kearns
Bourget, Mark A., Sr., St. George, St. George
Bulson, Michael E., St. Andrew, Riverton
Clark, Jack, St. Mary, West Haven
Conniff, John, St. Joseph, Ogden
Cormier, Joe H., (Out of Diocese)
Corrao, Thomas P., St. Pius X, Moab
Cummings, Owen, Mount Angel Seminary, Oregon
Davies, Denny, Christ the King, Cedar City
Dillon, Dale R., St. John the Baptist, Draper & St. Peter, American Fork
Dodge, Scott, Cathedral, Salt Lake City
Espinoza, Sunday S., St. Peter & Paul, St. Peter, American Fork
Essary, Dan, St. Olaf, Bountiful
Farrell, Eugene, Sts. Peter and Paul, West Valley
Flaim, Mansueto, St. Ann, Salt Lake City
Folkes, Willie, St. George, St. George
Garcia, James D., (Retired)
Glodowski, Robert J., (On Duty Outside the Diocese)
Gorman, Jack, St.George, St. George
Graham, Paul, St. John the Baptist, Draper
Gray, Forrest, Diaconate Dir.
Hardy, Robert H., St. Mary of the Assumption, Park City
Hester, Herschel, St. James, Ogden
Huber, Roger, (On Duty Outside the Diocese)
Huffman, Rick, St. Marguerite, Tooele
Hunnel, Dwayne A., St. Henry, Brigham City
Januszewski, William A., (On Duty Outside the Diocese)
Johansson, Otto, Christus St. Joseph Villa, Salt Lake City
Johnson, Lynn R., Cathedral, Salt Lake City
Keyser, John, St. Catherine of Siena, Salt Lake City
Kirts, Steven W., St. Thomas More, Sandy
Klein, Richard H., St. Pius X, Moab
Kranz, John, St. Vincent de Paul, Murray
Langner, Russell, Blessed Sacrament, Sandy
Lopez, Anthony J., St. Joseph, Ogden
Manu, Sefo A., St. Patrick, Salt Lake City
Martin, Billy, Blessed Sacrament, Sandy
Mayo, Silvio, Chancellor, Cathedral of the Madeleine, Salt Lake
McElfresh, James L., (Retired)
Merino, Reynaldo Q., (On Duty Outside the Diocese)
Meyersick, Karl E., St. Henry, Brigham City
Miller, James P., St. Thomas Aquinas, Hyde Park
Moreno, Honorio, St. Joseph, Ogden
Mota, Hector, Jail Ministry, Guadalupe
Murphy, Kenneth W., St. Mary, West Haven
Neveraski, Steve, St. Mary, Ogden
Norrell, Keith W., St. Joseph, Ogden
Osman, David, St. Vincent de Paul, Murray
Palm, Lowell, Our Lady of Lourdes, Salt Lake City
Petersen, Drew M., Jr., Cathedral of the Madeleine, Salt Lake City
Reade, George, St. Ambrose, Salt Lake City
Rodgers, Thomas A., Christ Prince of Peace, Hill AFB
Rodriguez, Mario A., Our Lady of Guadalupe, Salt Lake City
Ruiz, Moises, St. Francis of Assisi, Orem
Salaz, Rubel J., St. Francis Xavier, Kearns
Sanchez, Mel J., St. Theresa, Midvale
Sluga, George J., St. Peter & Paul, West Valley City
Smith, Douglas B., Holy Family, Ogden; St. Joseph Catholic High School, Ogden
Soklaski, Marcel, Blessed Sacrament, Sandy
Solak, Mark E., St. Thomas More, Sandy
Solorzano, Armando, Cathedral of the Medeleine, Salt Lake City
Spencer, Noel, (On Duty Outside the Diocese)
Stewart, Thomas J., (On Duty Outside the Diocese)
Stott, Stanley L., St. Therese, Midvale
Tellez, Rogaciano, St. George, St. George
Thaeler, John S., Holy Family, Ogden
Toro, German A., Sacramento, CA
Tosti, Tom, St. Mary, Park City
Trudell, William J., Christ the King, Cedar City
Trujillo, Manuel, St. Rose of Lima, Layton, UT
Velez, Manuel
Waiss, Terrance, St. Florence Mission, Huntsville
Weis, John C., (Retired)

INSTITUTIONS LOCATED IN THE DIOCESE

[A] SEMINARIES, RELIGIOUS, OR SCHOLASTICATES

HUNTSVILLE. *Abbey of Our Lady of the Holy Trinity*, 1250 S. 9500 E., 84317. Tel: 801-745-3784; Fax: 801-745-6430. Email: hta@xmission.com. Web: www.xmission.com/~hta. Revs. David Altman, O.C.S.O.; Charles J. Cummings, O.C.S.O., Novice Master. Priests 8; Brothers 7; Oblates 1.

[B] HIGH SCHOOLS, DIOCESAN

SALT LAKE CITY. *Judge Memorial Catholic High School* (1921) 650 S. 1100 E., 84102. Tel: 801-363-8895; Fax: 801-236-2923. Web: www.judgememorial.com. J. Richard Bartman, Prin.; Linda Bult, Librarian. Day School. (Coed) Lay Teachers 69; Students 719; Total Staff 30.

DRAPER. *Juan Diego Catholic High School, Skaggs Catholic Center, LLC* (1999) 300 E. 11800 S., 84020. Tel: 801-984-7650; Fax: 801-984-7601. Email: drgaleycolosimo@skaggscatholiccenter.org. Web: www.jdchs.org. Dr. Gabriel Colosimo, Prin.; Jan Duane, Librarian. Faculty 58; Total Staff 95; Total Enrollment 819.

OGDEN. *St. Joseph Catholic High School*, 1790 Lake St., 84401. Tel: 801-394-1515; Fax: 801-394-6428. Email: hscampusoffice@stjosephutah.com. Web: www.stjosephutah.com. Norman Allred, Prin.; Terri Sousa, Librarian. Lay Teachers 22; Total Staff 29; Students 193.

[C] ELEMENTARY SCHOOLS, REGIONAL

KEARNS. *St. Francis Xavier Regional School*, (Grades PreSchool-8), 4501 W. 5215 S., 84118. Tel: 801-966-1571; Fax: 801-966-1659. Email: preeder@stfrancisxavier.org. Web: stfrancisxavierschool.org. Patricia Reeder, Prin.; Mrs. Kathleen Kilby, Librarian. Lay Teachers 17; Students 278.

OGDEN. *St. Joseph Catholic Elementary School* (1877) (Grades PreSchool-8), 2980 Quincy Ave., 84403. Tel: 801-393-6051; Fax: 801-393-6086. Email: nessary@stjosephutah.com. Web: www.stjosephutah.com/es. Rev. Kenneth L. Vialpando; Nancy Essary, Prin.; Paige Laubacher, Librarian. Lay Teachers 31; Total Staff 39; Students 402.

[D] FOUNDATIONS

SALT LAKE CITY. *Catholic Foundation of Utah* (1984) 27 C St., 84103. Tel: 801-328-8641, Ext. 306; Fax: 801-355-5904. Email: jennifer.carroll@dioslc.org. Web: www.catholicfoundationofutah.org. Jennifer L. Carroll, Exec. Dir.; Armando Lujan, Pres.

OGDEN. *St. Benedict's Foundation* (1994) 6000 S., 1075 E., 84405-4945. Tel: 801-479-1800; Fax: 801-479-4997. Email: stbenedictsfd@mbmutah.org. Web: www.mbmutah.org. Yvonne Coiner, Exec. Dir.; Gary Francis, Chm. Bd. Dir.

[E] MONASTERIES AND RESIDENCES OF PRIESTS AND BROTHERS

HUNTSVILLE. *Abbey of Our Lady of the Holy Trinity of the Order of Cistercians* (1947) 1250 S. 9500 E., 84317. Tel: 801-745-3784; Fax: 801-745-6430. Email: hta@xmission.com. Web: www.xmission.com/~hta. Revs. Alan Hohl, O.C.S.O.; David Altman, O.C.S.O., Abbot; Rt. Rev. Casimir Bernas, O.C.S.O.; Revs. Patrick Boyle, O.C.S.O.; Charles J. Cummings, O.C.S.O., Novice Master; Leander Dosch, O.C.S.O.; Malachy Flaherty, O.C.S.O.

Abbey of Our Lady of the Holy Trinity of the Order of Cistercians of the Strict Observance Priests 8; Brothers 7; Oblates 1; Total in Community 16. Residing Elsewhere: Rev. Gregory Santos, O.C.S.O.

[F] CONVENTS, MONASTERIES AND RESIDENCES FOR SISTERS

SALT LAKE CITY. **Carmel of the Immaculate Heart of Mary Monastery* (1952) 5714 Holladay Blvd., 84121. Tel: 801-277-6075; Fax: 801-277-4263. Email: carmelslc@xmission.com. Web: www.carmelslc.org. Sr. Maureen Goodwin, O.C.D., Prioress. Professed Cloistered Sisters 8.

Our Lady of Lourdes Convent, 675 S. 1100 E., 84102. Tel: 801-583-1204. Sisters of the Holy Cross 3.

DRAPER. *Congregation of the Sisters of the Holy Cross, Vivian Skaggs Armstrong Convent* (1998) 554 E. 11800 S., 84020. Tel: 801-501-8349; Fax: 801-254-1142. Email: celinedounies@sjbelementary.org; karlamckinnie@standrewut.org.

Sisters of the Holy Cross, Inc. Sisters 2.

MURRAY. *Sisters of the Holy Cross Convent*, 1238 W. Bullion St., 84123. Tel: 801-313-9611.

Sisters of the Holy Cross, Inc. Sisters 2.

OGDEN. *Mount Benedict Convent* (1994) 6000 S. 1075 E., 84405-4945. Tel: 801-479-6030; Fax: 801-479-4997. Email: mbmutah@mbmutah.org. Web: www.mbmutah.org. Sisters of St. Benedict 6.

PARK CITY. *Congregation of the Sisters of the Holy Cross*, 3221 Homestead Rd., 84098. Tel: 435-655-7980.

Sisters of the Holy Cross, Inc. Sisters 3.

[G] NEWMAN CENTERS

SALT LAKE CITY. *University of Utah, Newman Center* , (St. Catherine of Siena University Parish), 170 S. University, 84102. Tel: 801-359-6066; Fax: 801-359-4547. Web: www.unewman.org. Revs. Carl Schlichte, O.P.; Peter Do, O.P. Total Students in Residence 4; Total Staff 3.

EPHRAIM. *St. Jude Catholic Center* 160 E. Center, 84627. Tel: 435-896-8527. Rev. Richard T. Sherman.

OGDEN. *Weber State University, Newman Center* 3738 Custer Ave., 84403. Tel: 801-399-9531. Rev. Charles T. Cummins, Dir. Total in Residence 1; Total Staff 1.

[H] CATHOLIC SOCIAL SERVICES

SALT LAKE CITY. *Catholic Community Services of Utah*, 745 E. 300 S., 84102. Tel: 801-977-9119; Fax: 801-977-8227; 801-977-9224. Web: www.ccsutah.org. Kevin J. Potts, Board Pres.; Bradford R. Drake, Exec. Dir. Total Assisted 400,000; Meals served at the St. Vincent de Paul Center 253,396; Total Staff 70.

Catholic Community Services Basic Needs Services - Ogden, 2504 F. Ave., Ogden, 84401. Tel: 801-394-5944; Fax: 801-621-8468. Mailing Address: 2504 F Ave., Ogden, 84401.

Treatment Services - St. Mary's Home for Men, 745 E. 300 S., 84102. Tel: 801-328-1894; Fax: 801-328-1895. Residential Substance Abuse Treatment for Adult Males.

Basic Needs Services - Salt Lake St. Vincent de Paul Dining Hall, 437 W. 200 S., 84104. Tel: 801-363-7710; Fax: 801-595-8532.

Basic Needs Services - Salt Lake Bishop K. Weigand Day Center, 437 W. 200 S., 84104. Tel: 801-363-7710; Fax: 801-595-8532.

Refugee Resettlement, 745 E. 300 S., 84102. Tel: 801-977-9119; Fax: 801-977-9224.

Holy Cross Ministries, 860 E. 4500 S., Ste. 204, 84107. Tel: 801-261-3440; Fax: 801-261-3390. Email: sbrennan@hcmutah.org. Web: www.holycrossministries.org. Sr. Suzanne Brennan, C.S.C. Outreach Program, Health Education, English as a Second Language (ESL), Seniors, Children, Women, Immigration Legal Services, Bi-Lingual Counseling, Parish Health, Afterschool, School Readiness & Summer Programs. Total Staff 35; Total Assisted Annually 7,500.

[I] MISCELLANEOUS

SALT LAKE CITY. *Catholic Diocese of Salt Lake City Capital Development Corporation*, 27 C St., 84103.

Catholic Diocese of Salt Lake City Real Estate Corporation, 27 C St., 84103.

Ministries of the Catholic Diocese of Salt Lake City LLC, 27 C St., 84103.

DRAPER. *Skaggs Catholic Center LLC*, 300 E. 11800 S., 84020.

OGDEN. *Give Me A Chance, Inc.*, 2620 Washington Blvd., 84401-3614.

RELIGIOUS INSTITUTES OF MEN REPRESENTED IN THE DIOCESE

For further details refer to the corresponding bracketed number in the Religious Institutes of Men or Women section.

[]—*Apostolic Life Community Priests in the Opus Spiritus Sanctu*—A.L.C.P.

[]—*Clerical Society of the Most Holy Trinity of Mininac*—S.S.T.

[0220]—*Congregation of the Blessed Sacrament*—S.S.S.

[0690]—*Jesuit Fathers* (California Prov.)—S.J.

[0690]—*Jesuit Fathers* (NY Prov.)—S.J.

[0350]—*Order of Cistercians of the Strict Observance (Trappists)*—O.C.S.O.

[0430]—*Order of Preachers (Dominicans)* (Western Province)—O.P.

[0420]—*Society of the Divine Word*—S.V.D.

RELIGIOUS INSTITUTES OF WOMEN REPRESENTED IN THE DIOCESE

[0230]—*Benedictine Sisters of Pontifical Jurisdiction*—O.S.B.

[1920]—*Congregation of the Sisters of the Holy Cross*—C.S.C.

[0760]—*Daughters of Charity of St. Vincent de Paul*

(Province of the West)—D.C.
[0420]—*Discalced Carmelite Nuns*—O.C.D.
[1190]—*Franciscan Sisters of the Atonement*—S.A.
[3130]—*Our Lady of Victory Missionary Sisters*—O.L.V.M.
[]—*Sisters for Christian Community*—S.F.C.C.

DIOCESAN CEMETERIES

SALT LAKE CITY. *Mount Calvary Catholic*, Office, 275 U St., 84103. Tel: 801-355-2476. John Curtice, Dir.

NECROLOGY

† Pellegrino, Rev. Msgr. Francis B., (Retired)—Died June 11, 2011
† Pollock, Rev. Msgr. Robert C., (Retired)—Died Dec. 2, 2010

An asterisk (*) denotes an organization that has established tax-exempt status directly with the IRS and is not covered by the USCCB Group Ruling.

Diocese of San Angelo

(Dioecesis Angeliana)

Most Reverend

MICHAEL D. PFEIFER, O.M.I.

Bishop of San Angelo; ordained December 21, 1964; consecrated and installed Bishop of San Angelo July 26, 1985. *Res.: P.O. Box 1829, San Angelo, TX 76902.*

ESTABLISHED OCTOBER 16, 1961.

Square Miles 37,433.

Comprises 29 Counties in the State of Texas as follows: Andrews, Brown, Callahan, Coke, Coleman, Concho, Crane, Crockett, Ector, Glasscock, Howard, Irion, Kimble, McCulloch, Martin, Menard, Midland, Mitchell, Nolan, Pecos, Reagan, Runnells, Schleicher, Sterling, Sutton, Taylor, Terrell, Tom Green and Upton.

For legal title of parishes and diocesan institutions, consult the Chancery Office.

The Chancery: P.O. Box 1829, San Angelo, TX 76902. Tel: 325-651-7500; Fax: 325-651-6688.

Web: www.san-angelo-diocese.org

Email: mdpomi@aol.com

STATISTICAL OVERVIEW

Personnel	
Retired Archbishops	1
Priests: Diocesan Active in Diocese	41
Priests: Diocesan Active Outside Diocese	5
Priests: Retired, Sick or Absent	5
Number of Diocesan Priests	51
Religious Priests in Diocese	11
Total Priests in Diocese	62
Ordinations:	
Diocesan Priests	2
Permanent Deacons in Diocese	87
Total Sisters	22
Parishes	
Parishes	47
With Resident Pastor:	
Resident Diocesan Priests	34
Resident Religious Priests	3
Without Resident Pastor:	
Administered by Priests	3
Administered by Deacons	2
Missions	22
Professional Ministry Personnel:	
Sisters	22
Educational	
Diocesan Students in Other Seminaries	13
Total Seminarians	13
Elementary Schools, Diocesan and Parish	3
Total Students	705
Catechesis/Religious Education:	
High School Students	4,203
Elementary Students	7,013
Total Students under Catholic Instruction	11,934
Teachers in the Diocese:	
Lay Teachers	54
Vital Statistics	
Receptions into the Church:	
Infant Baptism Totals	1,810
Minor Baptism Totals	84
Adult Baptism Totals	224
Received into Full Communion	157
First Communions	1,751
Confirmations	1,288
Marriages:	
Catholic	282
Interfaith	67
Total Marriages	349
Deaths	854
Total Catholic Population	84,555
Total Population	831,998

Former Bishops—Most Revs. THOMAS J. DRURY, D.D., LL.D., ord. June 2, 1935; appt. Oct. 16, 1961; cons. and installed Jan. 24, 1962; transferred to Corpus Christi, July 19, 1965; died July 22, 1992; THOMAS TSCHOEPE, D.D., ord. May 30, 1943; appt. Bishop Jan. 12, 1966; cons. March 9, 1966; transferred to Dallas, Aug. 27, 1969; died Jan. 24, 2009; STEPHEN A. LEVEN, D.D., ord. June 10, 1928; cons. Feb. 8, 1956, Auxiliary of San Antonio; appt. to San Angelo Oct. 22, 1969; retired April 16, 1979; died June 28, 1983; JOSEPH A. FIORENZA, ord. May 29, 1954; appt. Sept. 4, 1979; ord. and installed Oct. 25, 1979; transferred to Galveston-Houston, Dec. 18, 1984.

Vicar General—Rev. Msgr. LARRY J. DROLL, B.A., M.A., J.C.L.

Chancery Office—804 Ford, San Angelo, 76905. Tel: 325-651-7500; Fax: 325-651-6688. *Mailing Address: Box 1829, San Angelo, 76902.* Office Hours: Mon.-Fri. 9-5.

Chancellor—Mr. MICHAEL WYSE.

Diocesan Tribunal—Mailing Address: P.O. Box 1829, San Angelo, 76902.

Judicial Vicar—Rev. TOM BARLEY, M.S.W., M.B.A., M.Div., J.C.L., Mailing Address: P.O. Box 1829, San Angelo, 76902.

Judges—Rev. Msgr. MAURICE VOITY, S.T.L., S.T.M.; Mr. TOM BURKE, S.T.B., M.C.L., J.C.L., Tribunal Judge.

Promoter Justitiae—Rev. Msgr. JAMES A. PLAGENS, S.T.B., M.A.

Defensores Vinculi—Rev. Msgr. LARRY J. DROLL, B.A., M.A., J.C.L.; Revs. CHARLES C. GREENWELL, Ed.D.; MARK WOODRUFF, B.A.

Diocesan Consultors—Rev. Msgr. LARRY J. DROLL, B.A., M.A., J.C.L.; Revs. HUBERT WADE; BARRY L. MCLEAN; Rev. Msgrs. ROBERT BUSH; FREDERICK NAWARSKAS; Rev. TOM BARLEY, M.S.W., M.B.A., M.Div., J.C.L.

Priests' Personnel Board—Rev. Msgr. LARRY J. DROLL, B.A., M.A., J.C.L., Chm.; Rev. BERNARD L. GULLY; Rev. Msgr. FREDERICK NAWARSKAS; Rev. JOSEPH CHOUTAPALLI; Mr. MICHAEL WYSE, Ex Officio.

Presbyteral Council—Rev. TOM BARLEY, M.S.W., M.B.A., M.Div., J.C.L.; Rev. Msgr. LARRY J. DROLL, B.A., M.A., J.C.L.; Mr. MICHAEL WYSE; Revs. HUBERT WADE, Chm.; BERNARD L. GULLY; THOMAS MANIMALA; BARRY L. MCLEAN; SANTIAGO D. UDAYAR, Ed.D.; Rev. Msgrs. ROBERT BUSH; FREDERICK NAWARSKAS.

Vicar for Women Religious—Sr. MALACHY GRIFFIN, O.P.

Diocesan Offices and Directors

Diocesan Finance Officer—REGINA BODIFORD.

Director of Seminarians—Rev. HUBERT WADE.

Campaign for Human Development—Mr. MICHAEL WYSE.

Catholic Relief Services—MICHAEL R. WYSE.

Catholic University, Friends of—VACANT.

Communications Office—Mr. JIMMY PATTERSON.

Continuing Education of the Clergy—Rev. BARRY L. MCLEAN.

Cursillos de Cristiandad—Rev. BERNARD L. GULLY.

Deans—Revs. JOSEPH CHOUTAPALLI, San Angelo Deanery; BERNARD L. GULLY, Midland-Odessa Deanery; Rev. Msgr. FREDERICK NAWARSKAS, Abilene Deanery.

Diocesan Liturgical Commission—Rev. EDWARD T. DE LEON, O.M.I.

Holy Childhood, Pontifical Association—Miss MARY SUE BREWER.

Pastor Review Board—Rev. Msgr. FREDERICK NAWARSKAS.

Newspaper— "West Texas Angelus" Mr. JIMMY PATTERSON, Editor.

Office of Education and Formation—Sr. HILDA MAROTTA, O.S.F.

Permanent Deacon Director—Deacon TIM GRAHAM.

Prison Ministry Coordinator—Sr. ESTELA TOVAR, C.D.P.

Permanent Deacon Formation—Deacon TIM GRAHAM.

Pro-Life—Mr. JERRY MICHAEL PETERS.

Priests' Pension Plan—Rev. Msgr. LARRY J. DROLL, B.A., M.A., J.C.L. Board of Directors: Rev. HUBERT WADE, Chm.; Rev. Msgrs. LARRY J. DROLL, B.A., M.A., J.C.L., Sec.; MAURICE VOITY, S.T.L., S.T.M.; Revs. BARRY L. MCLEAN; MARK WOODRUFF, B.A.

Propagation of the Faith—Mr. MICHAEL WYSE.

Rural Life—Deacon CHARLIE EVANS, Dir.

Schools—Sr. ELIZABETH ANN SWARTZ, S.S.N.D., Supt.

Victim Assistance Coordinator—Mrs. LORI HINES. Tel: 325-651-7500.

Vocations—Rev. BARRY L. MCLEAN, Dir.

CLERGY, PARISHES, MISSIONS AND PAROCHIAL SCHOOLS

CITY OF SAN ANGELO

(TOM GREEN COUNTY)

1—CATHEDRAL OF THE SACRED HEART (1884) Rev. Msgr. Maurice Voity, Rector; Deacons Steven Zimmerman; Franciso Aguirre. In Res., Rev. Tom Barley.

Office: 19 S. Oakes St., 76903-5929. Tel: 325-658-6567; Fax: 325-659-0588. Email: shcsanangelo@hotmail.com.

School—Angelo Catholic School, Sacred Heart Campus, (Grades 2-6) Tel: 325-655-3325; Fax: 325-655-1286. Mrs. Lucy Thomas, Prin. Lay Teachers 13; Students 105.

Catechesis/Religious Program—Students 280.

Sacred Heart Cathedral-Parish Educational Endowment Fund, Inc.—Tel: 915-658-6567.

2—HOLY ANGELS (1961) Rev. Charles C. Greenwell; Deacons Harry J. Pelto Sr.; Federico Medina Jr.;

Walter Hammons II.
Parish Office: 2202 Rutgers Ave., 76904. Tel: 325-949-3308; 325-944-8967; Fax: 325-944-8967.
Church: 2309 A & M Ave., 76904.
School—Angelo Catholic School, (Grades PreK-1), 2315 A & M Ave., 76904. Tel: 325-949-1747; Fax: 325-942-1547. Mrs. Lucy Thomas, Prin. Holy Angels Campus Lay Teachers 4; Students 55.
Catechesis/Religious Program—Tel: 325-942-8192; Fax: 325-944-3633. Mrs. Lori Hines, D.R.E. (Grades PreK-12). Students 253.

3—ST. JOSEPH (1942), (Hispanic), Rev. Emilio Sosa; Deacons Ray Ramirez; Claudio Sanchez.
Res.: 301 W. 17th, 76903. Tel: 325-653-5006; Fax: 325-659-2795.
Catechesis/Religious Program—Mara Hernandez, C.R.E. Students 414.

4—ST. MARGARET (1967) Rev. Joseph Choutapalli (India).
Office: 2619 Era St., 76905. Tel: 325-651-4633; Fax: 325-651-4366.
Catechesis/Religious Program—Muriel Emerson, C.R.E. (CYM). Tel: 325-450-6971; Michael Scammel, C.R.E. (Elementary & High School). Students 30.

5—ST. MARY'S (1930), (Hispanic), Rev. David Herrera; Deacons Roy Ibarra; Michael Lopez; Marc Mata; Mario Torres.
Res.: 7 West Ave. N., 76903. Tel: 325-655-6278; Fax: 325-655-1524. Email: saintmarychurch.office@verizon.net.
Catechesis/Religious Program—Tel: 325-665-1976; Fax: 325-665-1524. Minnie Ibarra, C.R.E. Students 677.

OUTSIDE THE CITY OF SAN ANGELO

ABILENE, TAYLOR CO.

1—ST. FRANCIS OF ASSISI (1906), (Hispanic), Rev. Bhaskar Morugui; Deacons Marc P. Main; Jose Sanchez, (Retired).
Office: 826 Cottonwood St., 79601. Tel: 325-672-6695; Fax: 325-670-0129. Email: saintfrancisabilene@yahoo.com. Web: stfrancisabilene.com.
Catechesis/Religious Program—Students 192.

2—HOLY FAMILY (1976) Rev. Msgr. Frederick Nawarskas; Deacons Paul Klein; Gerald Schwalb; Charles Lambert; Gary Rhodes; Daniel Vaughan.
Res.: 5410 Buffalo Gap Rd., P.O. Box 5970, 79606. Tel: 325-692-1820; Fax: 325-698-5131. Email: mail@holyfamilyabilene.org. Web: www.holyfamilyabilene.org.
Catechesis/Religious Program—Dr. Robert Moore, D.R.E.; Sr. Xavier Jujjuvarapu, C.S.A., C.R.E.; Mrs. Penny Pope, Coord. Youth Min. Students 346.

3—SACRED HEART (1891) Rev. Msgr. Robert Bush; Deacons Arturo Casarez; Dwain Hennessey; Jesse Vasquez.
Res.: 837 Jeanette St., 79602-2410. Tel: 325-677-7951; Fax: 325-677-7710.
Catechesis/Religious Program—Tel: 325-673-0697. Dunn Clement, C.R.E. Students 228.
Mission—Sts. Joachim and Ann [CEM] N. 1st St. & Cherry St., Clyde, Callahan Co. 79510. Deacon Peter Ballaro.
Oratory—Sacred Heart Perpetual Adoration Chapel 1541 S. 8th St., 79602.

4—ST. VINCENT PALLOTTI (1963), (Mexican-American), Rev. Terence V. Brenon.
Res.: 2525 Westview Dr., 79603-2138. Tel: 325-672-1794 (Office); Fax: 325-672-8780. Email: office@stvincent-pallotti.org. Web: www.stvincent-pallotti.org.
Catechesis/Religious Program—Students 259.
Mission—Our Mother of Mercy 1300 S. Locust, P.O. Box 206, Merkel, Taylor Co. 79536. Tel: 325-928-5239; Fax: 325-928-3739.

ANDREWS, ANDREWS CO., OUR LADY OF LOURDES (1958) Rev. Joey Faylona.
Res.: 201 N.E. Ave. K, 79714. Tel: 432-523-4215; Fax: 432-523-5070. Email: ollandrews@valornet.com.
Catechesis/Religious Program—Marilyn Heman, D.R.E. Students 479.

BALLINGER, RUNNELS CO., ST. MARY STAR OF THE SEA (1885) Rev. Hubert Wade; Deacons Henry Martinez; David Workman.
Res.: 608 N. 6th St., 76821-4836. Tel: 325-365-2687; Fax: 325-365-9986.
Catechesis/Religious Program—Caroline Toliver, D.R.E. Students 115.
Mission—St. James 215 N. Washington, Bronte, Coke Co. 76933.
Mission—Our Lady of Guadalupe 601 W. 10th, Robert Lee, Coke Co. 76945.

BIG LAKE, REAGAN CO., ST. MARGARET OF CORTONA (1949) [JC] Rev. Isidore Ochiabuto.
Res.: 107 E. 1st. St., 76932. Tel: 325-884-2645; Fax: 325-884-3070.
Church & Office: 100 N. Mississippi St., 76932.
Catechesis/Religious Program—Mercy Navarez, C.R.E. Students 142.
Mission—St. Thomas 110 Hwy. 67, Rankin, 79778.
Mission—St. Francis 500 S. Blanton, Iraan, Pecos Co. 79744.

BIG SPRING, HOWARD CO.

1—HOLY TRINITY PARISH Rev. Bernard L. Gully.
Mailing Address: P.O. Box 951, 79721.
Res.: 610 S. Main St., 79721. Tel: 432-714-4930; Fax: 432-714-4932. Email: htcch@crcom.net.
Catechesis/Religious Program—Tel: 432-263-0648. Richard Light, D.R.E.; Laurie Barraza, C.R.E.; Adrian Saldivar, C.R.E. Students 320.

2—IMMACULATE HEART OF MARY (1961) Consolidated with St. Thomas and Sacred Heart, Big Spring to form Holy Trinity Parish, Big Spring.

3—SACRED HEART (1948), (Hispanic), Consolidated with St. Thomas and Immaculate Heart of Mary, Big Spring to form Holy Trinity Parish, Big Spring.

4—ST. THOMAS (1887), (Hispanic), Consolidated with Sacred Heart and Immaculate Heart of Mary, Big Spring to form Holy Trinity Parish, Big Spring.

BRADY, MCCULLOCH CO., ST. PATRICK'S (1876) [JC] Rev. Hilary A. Ihedioha.
Mailing Address: P.O. Box 1188, 76825.
Rectory—201 S. Pecan St., 76825.
Church: 406 S. Bridge, 76825. Tel: 325-597-2324; Fax: 325-597-2991.
Catechesis/Religious Program—Delma Nuncio, C.R.E. (K-5); Tina Selvera, C.R.E. (6-12). Students 95.
Mission—St. Francis Xavier Melvin, McCullogh Co.

BROWNWOOD, BROWN CO., ST. MARY'S (1896), (Hispanic), [JC] Rev. Francis Njoku (Africa); Deacons John Specht; William Brady.
Office: 1101 Booker St., 76801. Email: stmarysbwd@hotmail.com.
Res.: 1105 Main Ave., 76801. Tel: 325-646-7455; Fax: 325-646-6643.
Catechesis/Religious Program— Karen Mosqueda, C.R.E. (K-5); Brent Fanning, C.R.E. (6-12); Beatrice Fanning, C.R.E. (6-12); Amelia Martinez, Sec. Students 258.

CARLSBAD, TOM GREEN CO., ST. THERESE OF THE CHILD JESUS (1957) Rev. Joseph Choutapalli (India).
Mailing Address: P.O. Box 416, 76934-0416. Tel: 325-465-8062; Fax: 325-465-4472.
Catechesis/Religious Program—Students 12.
Station—San Angelo State-Supported Living Center, Tel: 915-465-4391.

COLEMAN, COLEMAN CO., SACRED HEART (1892), (Anglo—Hispanic), Rev. Romanus Arinze Akamike (Nigeria).
Mailing Address: 303 E. College, 76834. Tel: 325-625-5773; Fax: 325-625-3320. Email: scrdhrt@web-access.net. Web: www.web-access.net/~scrdhrt.
Catechesis/Religious Program—201 San Saba, 76834. Fax: 325-625-3320. Students 93.

COLORADO CITY, MITCHELL CO., ST. ANN'S (1943), (Hispanic), [JC] Rev. Michael Udegbunam (Nigeria).
Res.: 107 E. 21st St., 79512. Tel: 325-728-3252; Fax: 325-728-3266. Email: ann-joseph@att.net.
Catechesis/Religious Program—Tel: 325-728-5865. Students 107.
Mission—St. Joseph (1924) 403 S. Hinson, Loraine, Mitchell Co. 79532.

CRANE, CRANE CO., GOOD SHEPHERD (1943) Rev. Laurent Mvondo; Deacons Julio Carrasco; Apolonio Gutierrez; Felix Segura.
Res.: 1109 S. Virginia St., P.O. Box 1294, 79731. Tel: 432-558-7497. Email: abmvondo@yahoo.com.
Church & Mailing Address: 810 S. Virginia St., P.O. Box 1294, 79731. Tel: 432-558-2718; Fax: 432-558-7917. Email: gcatholic@att.net.
Catechesis/Religious Program— Teresa Figueroa, C.R.E. Students 200.
Mission—St. Isidore 4614 S. Frank, Coyanosa, Pecos Co. Tel: 432-652-8216; Fax: 432-652-3875.
Mission—Our Lady of Lourdes 103 Merrill Ave., Imperial, Pecos Co.

EDEN, CONCHO CO., ST. CHARLES (1927), (Mexican—German), [JC] Rev. Joseph Ogbonna; Deacons Leroy Beach; Joe Lopez.
P.O. Box 575, 76837.
Res.: 802 S. Main, P.O. Box 575, 76837. Tel: 325-869-8311; Fax: 325-869-5396.
Rectory—
Catechesis/Religious Program—Tel: 325-869-2891. Students 40.
Mission—Our Lady of Guadalupe P.O. Box 123, Millersview, Concho Co. 76862. Tel: 915-483-5426.

ELDORADO, SCHLEICHER CO., OUR LADY OF GUADALUPE (1924), (Hispanic), [CEM] [JC] Rev. Joseph Vathalloor, C.M.I.; Deacons Michael Kahlig; Victor Belman.
Res.: P.O. Box 211, 76936. Tel: 325-853-2663; Fax: 325-853-3638.
Catechesis/Religious Program—Tel: 325-853-3366. Sylvia Belman, C.R.E.; Rosie Diaz, D.R.E. Students 93.
Mission—Immaculate Conception P.O. Box 36, Knickerbocker, Tom Green Co. 76939. Tel: 325-944-2820.
Mission—St. Peter's 324 N. Commerce, P.O. Box 471, Mertzon, Irion Co. 76941. Tel: 325-835-2000. Deacon Michael Kahlig.

FORT STOCKTON, PECOS CO.

1—ST. AGNES (1953), (Hispanic), [CEM] [JC] Revs. Quirino H. Cornejo; Mamachan Joseph, C.M.I., Parochial Vicar; Deacon Reuben Reyes, RCIA Coord.; Alicia Salcido, Sec. Asst.
Mailing Address: 4094 N. Hwy. 18, P.O. Box 1488, 79735. Tel: 432-336-5027; 432-336-2724; Fax: 432-336-6668.
Catechesis/Religious Program—twinned with St. Joseph's Connie Villarreal, D.R.E. Students 469.

2—ST. JOSEPH'S (1875), (Hispanic), [CEM] [JC] Revs. Quirino H. Cornejo; Mamachan Joseph, C.M.I., Parochial Vicar; Deacons Reuben Reyes; Luis Villarreal; Daniel Holguin Jr.
Mailing Address: P.O. Box 1488, 79735.
Res.: 113 S. Sage, 79735. Tel: 432-336-2057; Fax: 432-336-6668.
Catechesis/Religious Program—Tel: 432-336-5027. Connie Villarreal, D.R.E. Students 469.
Mission—St. James 209 E. Hackberry, P.O. Box 526, Sanderson, 79848. Tel: 432-345-2354; Fax: 432-345-2354.

JUNCTION, KIMBLE CO., ST. THERESA OF THE CHILD JESUS (1959) [JC] Revs. George Thirumangalam, C.M.I.; Knick Knickerbocker, Sacramental Min., P.O. Box 129, London, 76854; Deacon James T. Graham.
Res.: South 7th & Oak St., P.O. Box 486, 76849. Tel: 325-446-3393; Fax: 325-446-4803. Email: st.theresachurch@verizon.net.
Catechesis/Religious Program—Students 40.

MCCAMEY, UPTON CO., SACRED HEART (1935) Rev. Laurent Mvondo; Deacons Julio Carrasco; Felix Segura; Apolonio Gutierrez.
Res.: 710 Burleson St., Box 1320, 79752. Tel: 432-652-8216; Fax: 432-652-3875. Email: blm@apex2000.net.
Catechesis/Religious Program—Tel: 432-652-8810. Students 86.
Mission—St. Isidore 4614 S. Frank, Coyanosa, Pecos Co. 79730.
Mission—Our Lady of Lourdes 103 Merrille Ave., Imperial, Pecos Co. 79743.

MENARD, MENARD CO., SACRED HEART (1873) [JC] Rev. George Thirumangalam, C.M.I.
Office: 609 Ellis St., P.O. Box 788, 76859. Tel: 325-396-4906; Fax: 325-396-2076. Email: sacredheartchurch1@verizon.net.
Catechesis/Religious Program—Tel: 325-396-4906; Fax: 325-396-2076. Stella Flutsch, C.R.E. (Elementary). Tel: 325-396-5116. Students 14.

MIDLAND, MIDLAND CO.

1—ST. ANN'S (1896) Rev. Msgrs. Larry J. Droll; James A. Plagens, Senior Priest; Rev. Yesuratnam Mulakaleti; Steve Pepper, Business Mgr.
Mailing Address: 1906 W. Texas Ave., 79701-6564. Tel: 432-682-6303; Fax: 432-684-4528. Web: www.st-anns.us.
Res.: 1910 W. Indiana Ave., 79701-6951. Tel: 432-682-3218.
School—(Grades PreK-8), 2000 W. Texas Ave., 79701. Tel: 432-684-4563; Fax: 432-687-2468. Ms. Joan Wilmes, Prin.; Ms. Stephanie Masterson Guss, Librarian. Lay Teachers 32; Students 341.
Catechesis/Religious Program—Tel: 432-682-6304. Carol Ann Hunt, D.R.E.; Leonor Spencer, C.R.E.; Alison Pope, Youth Min. Students 435.

2—OUR LADY OF GUADALUPE (1960), (Hispanic), Rev. Edward T. de Leon, O.M.I.; Deacons Jesse Guajardo; Victor Lopez; Robert Moreno; Jesus Napoles; Ricardo Torres.
P.O. Box 7, 79702.
Res.: 1401 E. Garden Ln., P.O. Box 7, 79702. Tel: 432-682-2581; Fax: 432-682-9364. Email: guadalupe@olgmidland.com. Web: www.olgmidland.com.
Catechesis/Religious Program—Sisters Regina C. Javier, O.N.D., D.R.E. (Elem.); Isabel Tadeo, O.N.D., Dir. Adult Faith Formation. Students 160.

3—OUR LADY OF SAN JUAN DE LOS LAGOS (1984), (Hispanic), Rev. Frank Chavez.
Res.: 1100 Camp St., 79701. Tel: 432-570-0952; Fax: 432-687-5082. Email: sanmiguelarcangel@sbcglobal.net.
Catechesis/Religious Program—Tel: 432-620-9546. Elsa Lujan, D.R.E. Students 240.

4—ST. STEPHEN'S (1982) Rev. Msgr. James P. Bridges; Revs. Gilbert Rodriguez; Joseph Prem Thumma; Deacons Fidel Saldivar; Luis Mata Sr.; Ignacio Villa; Leonard Hendon Jr.
Res. & Mailing Address: 4601 Neely Ave., 79707. Tel: 432-520-7394; Fax: 432-520-7395.
Rectory—2410 Wydewood, 79707.
Catechesis/Religious Program—Students 816.

MILES, RUNNELS CO., ST. THOMAS (1962) [JC] Rev. Ariel R. Lagunilla.
Res.: P.O. Box 306, 76861. Tel: 325-468-3171; Fax: 325-468-2146. Email: st.thomas_miles@wcc.net.

Catechesis/Religious Program—Tel: 915-468-2665. Students 11.

ODESSA, ECTOR CO.

1—ST. ANTHONY (1948), (Hispanic), Revs. Serafin P. Avenido Jr. (Philippines); Patrick Akpanobong; Deacons Bonifacio Rodriguez, (Retired); Alex Sosa; Flavio Franco; Paul Hinojos.
1321 W. Monahans St., 79763.
Office: 907 S. Dixie Blvd., 79761. Tel: 432-337-2213; Fax: 432-333-3631. Email: jucpps@sbcglobal.net.
Catechesis/Religious Program—twinned with St. Joseph, Tel: 915-337-0241. Sisters Elizabeth P. Villegas, O.N.D., D.R.E.; Esperanza Razura, A.S.C., Dir. Adult Formation.

2—ST. ELIZABETH ANN SETON (1982) Revs. Mark Woodruff; Thomas Manimala, Parochial Vicar; Steven D. Rojo, Bus. Manager; Victoria Detiveaux, Sec.
Office: 7601 N. Grandview Ave., 79765-3401. Tel: 432-367-4657; Fax: 432-367-0700. Email: seas@nts-online.net. Web: setonparishodessa.org.
Catechesis/Religious Program—Tel: 432-367-4668. Maria Isela Carrasco, C.R.E. (Elementary); Carlos Garcia, C.R.E. (Jr. & Sr. High School). Students 700.
Mission—Our Lady of San Juan 905 Edgeport, Ector Co. 79765. Tel: 432-362-2017; Fax: 432-362-2017.
Catechesis/Religious Program—Delfina M. Hernandez, C.R.E.; JoAnn Acosta, Sec. Students 70.

3—HOLY REDEEMER (1961), (Hispanic), Revs. Bernardito Getigan; Arturo P. Pestin, O.P.; Deacons Ignacio Cisneros; Antonio Gonzales.
Res.: 2633 Conover, 79763. Tel: 432-580-4295; Fax: 432-332-6631. Email: hrcc@clearwire.net.
Catechesis/Religious Program—Tel: 432-332-9231. Anita T. Diaz, C.R.E. Students 837.

4—ST. JOSEPH (1948), (Hispanic), Revs. Serafin P. Avenido Jr. (Philippines); Patrick Akpanobong; Deacons Flavio Franco; Paul Hinojos; Alex Sosa; Bonifacio Rodriguez, (Retired).
Res.: 1321 W. Monahans, 79763. Tel: 432-337-1093; Fax: 432-333-3631. Email: jucpps@sbcglobal.net.
Catechesis/Religious Program—Tel: 432-334-6478. Sisters Elizabeth P. Villegas, O.N.D., D.R.E.; Esperanza Razura, A.S.C., Dir. Adult Formation. Students 849.
Mission—St. Martin de Porres 2821 E. Hammett, Ector Co. 79766. Tel: 432-337-2213.

5—ST. MARY'S (1938) [CEM] Rev. Santiago D. Udayar.
Res.: 612 E. 18th St., 79761. Tel: 432-332-5334; Fax: 432-332-1844.
School—(Grades PreK-6), 1703 N. Adams, 79761. Tel: 432-337-6052; Fax: 432-337-6052. Web: smccsodessa.org. Bethany McKee Alexander, Prin.; Mayra Canales, Librarian. Sisters 1; Lay Teachers 14; Students 204.
Catechesis/Religious Program—Tel: 432-332-1154. Rose Mendez, C.R.E. (K-6); Monica Ramirez, C.R.E. (7-12). Students 528.

OLFEN, RUNNELS CO., ST. BONIFACE (1901) [CEM] Rev. Ariel R. Lagunilla.
Res.: 1118 CR 234, P.O. Box 96, Rowena, 76875-0096. Tel: 325-442-2893; Fax: 325-442-4602.
Church: 1118 County Rd. 234, Rowena, 76875. Tel: 325-442-2893; Fax: 325-442-2893.
Catechesis/Religious Program—Students 29.

OZONA, CROCKETT CO., OUR LADY OF PERPETUAL HELP (1929), (Hispanic), Rev. Nilo Nalugon (Philippines).
Res.: 227 Martinez St., P.O. Box 1069, 76943. Tel: 325-392-3353; Fax: 325-392-3720.
Catechesis/Religious Program—Margaret Longoria, C.R.E. (Elementary); Adrian Tijerina, C.R.E. (High School); Lilia Tijerina, C.R.E. (High School); Michelle Ramos, C.R.E. (Jr. High); Ashlee Ramos, Sec. Students 196.
Mission—Good Shepherd Sheffield, Pecos Co.

ROWENA, RUNNELS CO., ST. JOSEPH'S (1906), (German—Czech), [CEM] Rev. Ariel R. Lagunilla.
Res.: 501 Bennie St., P.O. Box 96, 76875. Tel: 325-442-3521; Fax: 325-442-4602. Email: stjosephcatholic@verizon.net. Web: www.stjosephrowenatx.com.
Catechesis/Religious Program—Charles Frerich, D.R.E. Students 93.

ST. LAWRENCE, GLASSCOCK CO., ST. LAWRENCE (1948), (German), [CEM] Rev. Arockiaraj Gali.
Res.: 2400 FM 2401, Garden City, 79739. Tel: 432-397-2300; Fax: 432-397-2777.
Catechesis/Religious Program—Tel: 432-397-2777. Linda Jones, D.R.E. Students 160.
Mission—St. Thomas Midkiff, Upton Co. Tel: 432-535-2266.
Mission—St. Paschal Baylona P.O. Box 271, Sterling City, Sterling Co. 76951-0271.

SANDERSON, TERRELL CO., ST. JAMES (1916), (Hispanic), Rev. Quirino H. Cornejo.
Res.: 209 E. Hackberry, 79848. Tel: 432-345-2354; Fax: 432-345-2354.
Catechesis/Religious Program—Students 31.

SONORA, SUTTON CO., ST. ANN'S (1927), (Hispanic), Rev. Lionel Fernando.
Office: 311 W. Plum St., P.O. Box 1397, 76950-1397. Tel: 325-387-2278; Fax: 915-387-2797. Email: stannsec@verizon.net.
Res.: 105 Oakwood, Box 1397, 76950. Tel: 325-387-5966.
Catechesis/Religious Program—Students 152.

STANTON, MARTIN CO., ST. JOSEPH'S (1881), (Mexican-American), Rev. Msgr. Timothy Schwertner, Sacramental Min.; Deacons Ernie Sanchez, (Retired); Mike Medina; Clemente Villa, Pastoral Coord.
Res.: 405 N. Convent St., P.O. Box 846, 79782-0846. Tel: 432-756-3743; Fax: 432-756-3756. Email: clemby1@yahoo.com.
Catechesis/Religious Program—Tel: 432-756-3743. Students 182.
Mission—St. Isidore [CEM] Lenorah, Martin Co.
Catechesis/Religious Program—Students 23.

SWEETWATER, NOLAN CO.

1—HOLY FAMILY (1885), (Hispanic), Deacon W. W. Butler.
Mailing Address: P.O. Box 847, 79556.
Res.: 507 Crane St., 79556. Tel: 325-235-2694; Fax: 325-235-3483.
Catechesis/Religious Program—consolidated with Immaculate Heart., 511 W. Alabama, 79556. Tel: 325-235-3318; Fax: 325-235-0258.

2—IMMACULATE HEART OF MARY (1962), (Hispanic), Deacon W. W. Butler.
511 W. Alabama, 79556.
Res.: 507 Crane St., 79556. Tel: 915-235-3318 (Office); Fax: 915-235-0258.
Catechesis/Religious Program—Students 213.
Mission—St. Albert the Great 205 Laurel St., Roscoe, Nolan Co. 79545.

WALL, TOM GREEN CO., ST. AMBROSE (1941) [CEM] Rev. Chinnapureddy Pagidela; Deacons Allan Lange; Daniel Shannahan.
Res.: 8602 Loop 570, P.O. Box 228, 76957. Tel: 325-651-7551; Fax: 325-651-6605. Email: saint_ambrose@zipnet.us. Web: www.saint-ambrose.org.
Catechesis/Religious Program—Dolores Gully, C.R.E.; Kenneth Baker, C.R.E.; Sharon Morris, C.R.E.; Berni Halfmann, C.R.E.; Sylvia Chappa, C.R.E. Students 279.
Mission—Holy Family 18370 Bledsoe Rd., Mereta, Tom Green Co. 76940. Tel: 325-468-3101.

WINTERS, RUNNELS CO., OUR LADY OF MT. CARMEL (1962), (Hispanic), Rev. Romanus Arinze Akamike (Nigeria).
Res.: 119 W. College, 79567. Tel: 325-754-4626; Fax: 325-754-4015.
Catechesis/Religious Program—Tel: 325-754-5436; 325-754-5011. Marianne Woffenden, D.R.E.; Rene Woffenden, Youth Dir. Students 46.

Military Chaplains:
Revs.—
Covos, Ruben, 312 Cabell, Biloxi, MS 39531.
Hicks, Steven, 74822 Twilight Dr., Twentynine Palms, CA 92277.

Retired:
Rev. Msgrs.—
Frey, Francis, 5708 Stockbridge Ct., Mc Donald, PA 15057-3549. Tel: 412-221-2628
Zientek, Benedict, P.O. Box 2447, Brenham, 77834.
Revs.—
Kennelly, Stephen (Ireland), Lislaughtin, Ballylongford, Co. Kerry, Ireland.
Regan, Richard J., 1001 Society Hill Blvd., Cherry Hill, NJ 08003. Tel: 432-264-2936
Scanlan, Cornelius, 802 Ford, 76905. Tel: 839-317-1786

Permanent Deacons:
Aguirre, Franciso, Sacred Heart Cathedral, San Angelo
Arguello, Juan, Sacred Heart, Big Spring
Ballaro, Peter, Sts. Joachim & Ann Mission, Clyde
Beach, Leroy, Our Lady of Guadalupe, Millersview
Belman, Victor, Our Lady of Guadalupe, Eldorado
Brady, Bill, St. Mary, Brownwood
Butler, Bill, Holy Family, Sweetwater
Camacho, Isaac, Holy Family, Abilene
Camarillo, Alfred, St. Mary, Odessa
Carrasco, Julio, Good Shepherd, Crane
Casarez, Art, Sacred Heart, Abilene
Cisneros, Ignacio, Holy Redeemer, Odessa
Crochet, Larry, Austin
Duenes, Jerry, Holy Trinity, Big Spring
Evans, Charlie, St. Patrick, Brady
Fernandez, Abel, Our Lady of Grace, Goodfellow AFB
Franco, Flabio, St. Joseph, Odessa
Giovannitti, Thomas, (On Duty Outside the Diocese)
Gonzales, Antonio, Holy Redeemer, Odessa
Gonzalez, Antero, St. Margaret, San Angelo
Graham, Tim, St. Theresa, Junction
Guajardo, Jesse, Our Lady of Guadalupe, Midland
Gutierrez, Apolonio, Good Shepherd, Crane
Hammons, Walter, II, Holy Angels, San Angelo
Hendon, Leonard, Jr., St. Stephen, Midland
Hennessey, Dwain, Sacred Heart, Abilene
Hernandez, Andres, St. Agnes, Ft. Stockton
Hinojos, Paul, St. Joseph, Odessa
Holguin, Daniel, Jr., St. Joseph, Fort Stockton
Ibarra, Roy, St. Mary, San Angelo
Kahlig, Michael, St. Peter, Mertzon
Kenny, Mike, Holy Family, Abilene
Klein, Paul, Holy Family, Abilene
Lambert, Charles, Holy Family, Abilene
LaMonica, Michael, Our Lady of San Juan, Midland
Lange, Allan, St. Ambrose, Wall
Lange, Stanley, St. Thomas, Miles
Leibrecht, Robert, St. Stephen, Midland
Lopez, Joseph, St. Philip's, Eola
Lopez, Miguel, St. Mary, San Angelo
Lopez, Victor, Our Lady of Guadalupe, Midland
Luevano, Manuel, St. Elizabeth, Odessa
Main, Marc P., St. Francis, Abilene
Martinez, Enrique, St. James, Bronte
Mata, Luis, Sr., Our Lady of Guadalupe, Midland
Mata, Marc, St. Mary, San Angelo
Medina, Federico, Jr., Holy Angels, San Angelo
Medina, Mike, St. Joseph, Stanton
Mendez, Hector, St. Mary, Odessa
Moreno, Robert, Our Lady of Guadalupe, Midland
Napoles, Jesus, Our Lady of Guadalupe, Midland
Neff, Alan, St. Elizabeth Ann Seton, Odessa
Nunez, Reynaldo, Sacred Heart, Coleman
Ortiz, Jesse, St. Mary, Odessa
Pelto, Harry J., Sr., Holy Angels, San Angelo
Pena, Daniel, (On Duty Outside the Diocese)
Perez, Alex, Our Lady of San Juan, Midland
Primera, Salvador, St. Elizabeth Ann Seton, Midland
Ramirez, Reinaldo, St. Joseph, San Angelo
Ramirez, Victor, St. Vincent, Abilene
Reyes, Reuben, St. Joseph's, Fort Stockton; St. Agnes, Fort Stockton
Rhodes, Gary, Holy Family, Abilene
Rodriguez, Bonifacio (Barney), St. Anthony's, Odessa
Salazar, Lorenzo, St. Stephen, Midland
Saldivar, Fidel, St. Stephen, Midland
Sanchez, Claudio, St. Joseph, San Angelo
Sanchez, Ernie, St. Joseph, Stanton
Sanchez, Pedro, St. Francis, Abilene
Schwalb, Gerald, Holy Family, Abilene
Segura, Felix, Good Shepherd, Crane
Selvera, Robert, St. Patrick, Brady
Shannahan, Daniel, St. Ambrose, Wall
Smith, Raymond, (On Duty Outside the Diocese)
Sosa, Alex, St. Anthony, Odessa
Sotelo, Sador, Our Lady of San Juan, Midland
Specht, John, St. Mary, Brownwood
Torres, Mario, St. Mary, San Angelo
Torres, Ricardo
Trevino, Jerry, Sacred Heart, San Angelo
Vasquez, Jesse, Sacred Heart, Abilene
Vaughan, Daniel, Holy Family, Abilene
Villa, Clemente, Jr., St. Joseph, Stanton
Villa, Ignacio, Our Lady of San Juan, Midland
Villarreal, Luis, St. Agnes, Fort Stockton
Workman, David, St. Mary, Ballinger
Yanez, Horacio, St. Thomas, Big Spring
Zimmerman, Steven, Sacred Heart Cathedral, San Angelo

INSTITUTIONS LOCATED IN THE DIOCESE

[A] MONASTERIES AND RESIDENCES OF PRIESTS & BROTHERS

CHRISTOVAL. *Hermits of the Blessed Virgin Mary of Mount Carmel* (1991) P.O. Box 337, 76935-0337. Tel: 325-896-2249; Fax: 325-896-2265. Email: stellamaris@carmelitehermits.org. Web: www.CarmeliteHermits.org. Rev. Fabian Maria Rosette, O.Carm., Prior. Mt. Carmel Hermitage Hermits 7.

[B] CONVENTS AND RESIDENCES FOR SISTERS

SAN ANGELO. *School Sisters of St. Francis*, 110 Crestwood Dr., 76905. Tel: 325-651-2403. Sr. Hilda Marotta, O.S.F., Contact Person.

ABILENE. *Congregation of Divine Providence*, P.O. Box 5970, 79608. Tel: 325-698-2367; Fax: 325-698-5131.

CHRISTOVAL. *Carmelite Nuns of the Ancient*

Observance (1989) *Monastery of Our Lady of Grace*, 6202 CO Rd. 339, 76935-3023. Tel: 325-853-1722; Fax: 325-853-1722. Email: desertcarmel@carmelnet.org. Web: carmelnet.org/christoval/christoval.htm. Sr. Mary Grace Erl, O.Carm., Vicar Prioress.

MIDLAND. *Oblates of Notre Dame* (1991) 1400 Garden Ln., 79701. Tel: 432-684-8318; Fax: 432-682-9364. Sisters Regina C. Javier, O.N.D., D.R.E., Elementary; Virginia Isabel Tadeo, O.N.D., Dir., Adult Faith Formation.

ODESSA. *Oblates of Notre Dame*, 907 S. Dixie Blvd., 79761. Tel: 432-337-2213; Fax: 432-333-3631. Email: rcjond@sbcglobal.net. Sr. Elizabeth P. Villegas, O.N.D., D.R.E.

[C] ST. VINCENT DE PAUL SOCIETY

SAN ANGELO. *Catholic Outreach Services*, 410 N. Chadbourne, 76903. Tel: 915-658-4124; Fax: 915-481-0315. Email: cos.margie@verizon.net. Thrift Store Social Services. Total Assisted Annually 5,000; Total Staff 30.

ABILENE. *St. Vincent De Paul Society*, 1241 Walnut, 79601. Tel: 915-677-6871. Total Assisted 12,000; Total Staff 4.

St. Vincent De Paul Thrift Store

BIG SPRING. *St. Vincent De Paul Society* Food Distribution., P.O. Box 951, 79720. Tel: 432-267-4124; Fax: 432-267-7844. Email: ihmch@crcom.net. Families 1,280; People 2,296.

MIDLAND. *St. Vincent De Paul Society* (1985) 1906 W. Texas Ave., 79701. Tel: 432-684-3887. P.O. Box 711, 79702. Priests 3.

ODESSA. *Catholic Charities Community Services Odessa, Inc.*, 2500 Andrews Hwy., 79761. Tel: 432-332-1387; 432-332-2398. Faye Rodriguez, Dir.

STANTON. *St. Vincent De Paul Society*, P.O. Box 846, 79782. Tel: 432-756-3743; Fax: 432-756-3756. Deacon Clemente Villa Jr., Pastoral Coord.; Rev. Msgr. Timothy Schwertner, Sacramental Min.

[D] CAMPUS MINISTRY

SAN ANGELO. *Catholic Newman Center* 2451 Dena Dr., 76904. Tel: 325-949-8033. Email: newmancenter2010@gmail.com. Sr. Kathleen Kudlac, O.S.F., Campus Min. Total Staff 1.

[E] MISCELLANEOUS

SAN ANGELO. *The Catholic Charitable Foundation for the Roman Catholic Diocese of San Angelo*, 804 Ford St., 76905.

Christ the King Retreat Center, 802 Ford, 76905. Tel: 325-651-5352; 325-651-5358; Fax: 325-651-5667. Email: ckrc@zipnet.us. Total Staff 20.

Franciscan Resource Center, 133 W. Concho, Ste. 108, 76903. Tel: 325-651-2403.

RELIGIOUS INSTITUTES OF MEN REPRESENTED IN THE DIOCESE

For further details refer to the corresponding bracketed number in the Religious Institutes of Men or Women section.

[0910]—*Oblates of Mary Immaculate* (Southern American Prov.)—O.M.I.

[]—*Order of Preachers (Dominicans)* (Philippines)—O.P.

[1060]—*Society of the Precious Blood* (Kansas City Prov.)—C.PP.S.

RELIGIOUS INSTITUTES OF WOMEN REPRESENTED IN THE DIOCESE

[0320]—*Carmelite Nuns of the Ancient Observance*—O.Carm.

[]—*Catechetical Sisters of Arogyamathal* (India)—C.S.A.

[1010]—*Congregation of Divine Providence of San Antonio, Texas*—C.D.P.

[1070-03]—*Dominican Sisters, Sinsinawa*—O.P.

[2960]—*Oblates of Notre Dame*—O.N.D.

[]—*Oblates of Notre Dame* (Midland, TX)

[]—*Oblates of Notre Dame, Philippines*

[1680]—*School Sisters of St. Francis*—O.S.F.

[0990]—*Sisters of Divine Providence*—C.D.P.

[1570]—*Sisters of St. Francis of the Holy Family*—O.S.F.

NECROLOGY

(No Deaths)

An asterisk (*) denotes an organization that has established tax-exempt status directly with the IRS and is not covered by the USCCB Group Ruling.

Archdiocese of San Antonio

(Archidioecesis Sancti Antonii)

Most Reverend

GUSTAVO GARCIA-SILLER, M.Sp.S.

Archbishop of San Antonio; ordained June 22, 1984; appointed Auxiliary Bishop of Chicago and Titular See of Esco January 24, 2003; consecrated March 19, 2003; appointed Archbishop of San Antonio October 14, 2010; installed November 23, 2010; pallium conferred June 20, 2011. *Pastoral Center, P.O. Box 28410, San Antonio, TX 78228-0410.* Tel: 210-734-2620; 210-734-1664; Fax: 210-734-0231.

Pastoral Center: 2718 W. Woodlawn Ave., P.O. Box 28410, San Antonio, TX 78228-0410. Tel: 210-734-2620; Fax: 210-734-0231.

Web: www.archdiosa.org

Email: administrator@archdiosa.org

Most Reverend

OSCAR CANTÚ

Auxiliary Bishop of San Antonio and Former Apostolic Administrator of San Antonio; ordained May 21, 1994; appointed Auxiliary Bishop of San Antonio and Titular Bishop of Dardanus April 10, 2008; ordained June 2, 2008; appointed Apostolic Administrator of San Antonio May 26, 2010; resigned Apostolic Administrator October 14, 2010. *Pastoral Center: P.O. Box 28410, San Antonio, TX 78228-0410.* Tel: 210-734-2620; Fax: 210-734-0708. Email: oscar.cantu@archsa.org.

Most Reverend

PATRICK F. FLORES, D.D.

Retired Archbishop of San Antonio; ordained May 26, 1956; appointed Titular Bishop of Italica and Auxiliary of San Antonio March 18, 1970; consecrated May 5, 1970; appointed Bishop of El Paso April 4, 1978; installed May 29, 1978; promoted Archiepiscopal See of San Antonio August 28, 1979; installed October 13, 1979; Pallium conferred May 25, 1982; retired December 29, 2004. *Res.: Padua Place, 80 Peter Baque Rd., San Antonio, TX 78209.* Tel: 210-826-7721.

Most Reverend

BERNARD F. POPP, D.D.

Retired Auxiliary Bishop of San Antonio; ordained February 24, 1943; appointed Titular Bishop of Capsus and Auxiliary Bishop of San Antonio June 7, 1983; consecrated July 25, 1983; retired March 23, 1993. *Res.: Padua Place, 80 Peter Baque Rd., San Antonio, TX 78209.* Tel: 210-826-7721.

Most Reverend

THOMAS J. FLANAGAN, D.D.

Retired Auxiliary Bishop of San Antonio; ordained June 10, 1956; appointed Auxiliary Bishop of San Antonio and Titular Bishop of Bavagaliana January 15, 1998; consecrated February 16, 1998; retired December 15, 2005. *Res.: Oblate Madonna House, 5722 Blanco Rd., San Antonio, TX 78216-6615.* Tel: 210-734-2620; 210-734-1610. *Mailing Address: P.O. Box 28410, San Antonio, TX 78228-0410.*

Established August 28, 1874.

Square Miles 23,180.

Created an Archbishopric, August 3, 1926.

The San Antonio Archdiocese comprises Atascosa, Bandera, Bexar, Comal, Edwards, Frio, Gillespie, Gonzales, Guadalupe, Karnes, Kendall, Kerr, Kinney, McMullen (that part of McMullen County north of the Nueces River), Medina, Real, Uvalde, Val Verde and Wilson.

For legal titles of parishes and archdiocesan institutions, consult the Pastoral Center.

STATISTICAL OVERVIEW

Personnel	
Archbishops	1
Retired Archbishops	1
Auxiliary Bishops	1
Retired Bishops	2
Priests: Diocesan Active in Diocese	100
Priests: Diocesan Active Outside Diocese	8
Priests: Retired, Sick or Absent	44
Number of Diocesan Priests	152
Religious Priests in Diocese	179
Total Priests in Diocese	331
Extern Priests in Diocese	43
Ordinations:	
Religious Priests	1
Transitional Deacons	1
Permanent Deacons	18
Permanent Deacons in Diocese	359
Total Brothers	85
Total Sisters	702
Parishes	
Parishes	139
With Resident Pastor:	
Resident Diocesan Priests	91
Resident Religious Priests	42
Without Resident Pastor:	
Administered by Priests	6
Missions	34
Professional Ministry Personnel:	
Brothers	5
Sisters	19
Lay Ministers	134
Welfare	
Catholic Hospitals	5
Total Assisted	400,000
Health Care Centers	5
Total Assisted	37,800
Homes for the Aged	8
Total Assisted	714
Residential Care of Children	3
Total Assisted	469
Day Care Centers	10
Total Assisted	977
Specialized Homes	3
Total Assisted	267
Special Centers for Social Services	8
Total Assisted	12,828
Other Institutions	1
Total Assisted	80
Educational	
Seminaries, Diocesan	2
Students from This Diocese	22
Students from Other Diocese	69
Seminaries, Religious	6
Students Religious	28
Total Seminarians	50
Colleges and Universities	5
Total Students	15,498
High Schools, Diocesan and Parish	5
Total Students	1,283
High Schools, Private	6
Total Students	2,402
Elementary Schools, Diocesan and Parish	30
Total Students	8,101
Elementary Schools, Private	7
Total Students	1,561
Catechesis/Religious Education:	
High School Students	10,511
Elementary Students	29,769
Total Students under Catholic Instruction	69,175
Teachers in the Diocese:	
Priests	34
Brothers	20
Sisters	51
Lay Teachers	1,595
Vital Statistics	
Receptions into the Church:	
Infant Baptism Totals	8,772
Minor Baptism Totals	858
Adult Baptism Totals	392
Received into Full Communion	1,337
First Communions	9,206
Confirmations	6,457
Marriages:	
Catholic	1,608
Interfaith	309
Total Marriages	1,917
Deaths	4,540
Total Catholic Population	716,269
Total Population	2,363,714

Former Bishops—Rt. Revs. Anthony Dominic Pellicer, D.D., ord. Aug. 15, 1850; cons. Dec. 8, 1874; died April 14, 1880; John C. Neraz, D.D., ord. Feb. 19, 1854; cons. May 8, 1881; died Nov. 15, 1894; John Anthony Forest, D.D., ord. April 12, 1863; cons. Oct. 28, 1895; died March 11, 1911; Most Revs. John W. Shaw, D.D., Coadjutor Bishop of San Antonio; appt. Feb. 7, 1910; cons. Titular Bishop of Castabala, April 14, 1910; succeeded to the See of San Antonio, March 11, 1911; made assistant at the Pontifical Throne, Sept., 1916; promoted to the See of New Orleans, Jan. 25, 1918; died Nov. 2, 1934; Arthur Jerome Drossaerts, D.D., LL.D., Bishop of San Antonio; appt. July 18, 1918; cons. Dec. 8, 1918; named Archbishop, Aug. 3, 1926; pallium conferred February 16, 1927; assistant at the Pontifical Throne, Aug. 19, 1934; died Sept. 8, 1940; Robert E. Lucey, S.T.D., Bishop of Amarillo; appt. Feb. 10, 1934; cons. May 1, 1934; promoted to the Archiepiscopal See of San Antonio, Jan. 23, 1941; assistant to Pontifical Throne April 1959; retired June 4, 1969; died Aug. 1, 1977; Francis J. Furey, Titular Bishop of Temnus and Auxiliary of Philadelphia; appt. Aug. 24, 1960; cons. Dec. 22, 1960; promoted to Coadjutor and Apostolic Administrator "sede plena" of San Diego, July 25, 1963; succeeded March 6, 1966; promoted to Archiepiscopal See of San Antonio, June 4, 1969; Pallium conferred, Dec. 15, 1969; died April 23, 1979; Patrick F. Flores, D.D. (Retired), ord. May 26, 1956; appt. Titular Bishop of Italica and Auxiliary of San Antonio March 18, 1970; cons. May 5, 1970; appt. Bishop of El Paso April 4, 1978; installed May 29, 1978; promoted Archiepiscopal See of San Antonio Aug. 28, 1979; installed Oct. 13, 1979; retired Dec. 29, 2004; Jose H. Gomez, S.T.D., ord. Aug. 15, 1978; appt. Auxiliary Bishop of Denver and Titular See of Belali Jan. 23, 2001; ord. March 26, 2001; appt. Archbishop of San Antonio Dec. 29, 2004; installed Feb. 15, 2005; Pallium conferred June 29, 2005; appt. Coadjutor Archbishop of Los Angeles April 6, 2010.

Vicars General—Most Revs. Thomas J. Flanagan, D.D., V.G. (Retired); Oscar Cantú, D.D., S.T.L., S.T.D., V.G., Mailing Address: P.O. Box 28410, San Antonio, 78228-0410. Tel: 210-734-2620; Fax: 210-734-1670.

Office of Victim Assistance and Safe Environment—Mr. Steve Martinez, L.C.S.W., L. S.O.T.P., Dir.. Email: smartinez@archsa.org; Tracie B. Enriquez, M.B.A., C.P.M., Assoc. Dir.. Email: tracie.enriquez@archsa.org; Norma

ALVARADO, Admin. Asst., St. Paul Community Center, 1201 Donaldson, San Antonio, 78228. Tel: 210-734-7786; 877-700-1888 (Toll Free). Email: ovase@archsa.org.

Moderator of the Curia & Director of Administration—Rev. MARTIN J. LEOPOLD. Tel: 210-734-1674.

Pastoral Center—2718 W. Woodlawn Ave., P.O. Box 28410, San Antonio, 78228-0410. Tel: 210-734-2620; Fax: 210-734-0231. Office Hours: Mon.-Fri. 8:30-5.

Chancellor—Rev. Msgr. TERENCE NOLAN, J.C.L. Tel: 210-734-1676.

Archives—Bro. EDWARD J. LOCH, S.M., Archivist, Mailing Address: P.O. Box 28410, San Antonio, 78228-0410. Tel: 210-734-2620; 210-734-1609. Email: eloch@archsa.org.

Baptismal Records Office—Mrs. MARGARET PEREZ, Mailing Address: P.O. Box 28410, San Antonio, 78228-0410. Tel: 210-734-2620; 210-734-1647. Email: mperez@archsa.org.

Administrative Assistant to the Archbishop—Rev. MARTIN J. LEOPOLD. Tel: 210-734-1674. Email: mleopold@archsa.org.

Office of the Archbishop—Rev. JONATHAN W. FELUX, Personal Sec. to Archbishop; Mrs. LIDIA ROMAN, Sec. to the Archbishop. Email: lidia.roman@archsa.org.

College of Consultors—Most Revs. BERNARD F. POPP, D.D. (Retired); THOMAS J. FLANAGAN, D.D., V.G. (Retired); OSCAR CANTÚ, D.D., S.T.L., S.T.D., V.G.; Rev. Msgrs. LAWRENCE J. STUEBBEN (Retired); TERENCE NOLAN, J.C.L.; THOMAS MURPHY (Retired); Very Rev. Msgr. CARLOS DAVALOS, V.U.; Rev. Msgrs. JAMES JANISH; FRANCISZEK KURZAJ; MICHAEL J. BOULETTE, V.F.; Rev. DAVID GARCIA.

Deans—In Metropolitan Area: Very Rev. Msgr. CARLOS DAVALOS, V.U., North; Very Revs. KEVIN FAUSZ, C.M., V.U., Central; CHRISTIAN A. JANSON, S.M., V.U., Northwest; EDUARDO D. MORALES, V.U., Northeast; FIDELE O. DIKETE, V.U., Western; LENIN NAFFATE, V.U., Southwest; JOHN J. FLANAGAN, V.U., Southeast; Very Rev. Msgr. PATRICK J. RAGSDALE, V.U., North Central. In Rural Area: Very Rev. GRZEGORZ SAWICKI, S.D.S., V.F., Floresville; Rev. Msgr. MICHAEL J. BOULETTE, V.F., Fredericksburg; Very Revs. WALLIS J. STILES, V.F., Hondo; GILBERTO VALLEJO, V.F., Pleasanton; CAMILLO BOTELLO JR., M.S.F., V.F., Seguin; JAMES FISCHLER, C.I.C.M., V.F., Uvalde.

Vicar for Clergy—Rev. TONY VILANO, Pastoral Center. Tel: 210-734-2620, Ext. 1672. Email: tony.vilano@archsa.org.

Vicar for Retired Priests—Rev. Msgr. JOHN WAGNER (Retired), Casa De Padres, 8520 Cross Mountain Trail #202, San Antonio, 78255. Tel: 210-698-0175.

Archdiocesan Presbyteral Council—Most Revs. BERNARD F. POPP, D.D. (Retired); THOMAS J. FLANAGAN, D.D., V.G. (Retired); OSCAR CANTÚ, D.D., S.T.L., S.T.D., V.G.; Rev. Msgrs. TERENCE NOLAN, J.C.L.; JOHN WAGNER (Retired); Very Rev. Msgr. MICHAEL YARBROUGH, At Large Chm.; Very Revs. KEVIN FAUSZ, C.M., V.U.; CHRISTIAN A. JANSON, S.M., V.U.; EDUARDO D. MORALES, V.U.; CAMILLO BOTELLO JR., M.S.F., V.F.; JOHN J. FLANAGAN, V.U.; Revs. MARTIN J. LEOPOLD; TONY VILANO; Very Revs. FIDELE O. DIKETE, V.U.; GRZEGORZ SAWICKI, S.D.S., V.F.; Very Rev. Msgr. PATRICK J. RAGSDALE, V.U.; Very Revs. WALLIS J. STILES, V.F.; GILBERTO VALLEJO, V.F.; LENIN NAFFATE, V.U.; Rev. Msgr. MICHAEL J. BOULETTE, V.F.; Very Rev. Msgr. CARLOS DAVALOS, V.U.; Rev. Msgrs. JAMES JANISH, At Large; FRANCISZEK KURZAJ, At Large; Very Rev. JAMES FISCHLER, C.I.C.M., V.F.; Revs. DAVID GARCIA, At Large; ROBERT E. WRIGHT, O.M.I., Ph.D., Education.

Women's Commission—Mrs. CHRIS ALDERETE, Chm., 1602 Hillcrest Dr., E., San Antonio, 78228.

Archdiocesan Tribunal—Mailing Address: P.O. Box 28410, San Antonio, 78228-0410. Tel: 210-734-2620, Ext. 1135; 210-734-1696.

Judicial Vicar—Rev. Msgr. TERENCE NOLAN, J.C.L.

Assistant Director—Ms. MARGARITA M. GONZALEZ.

Judges—Rev. Msgrs. TERENCE NOLAN, J.C.L.; JAMES HENKE (Retired); JAMES JANISH; Rev. EMMET CAROLAN.

Defenders of the Bond—Rev. Msgr. KEVIN E. RYAN; Rev. PAUL CLEARY; Rev. Msgr. THOMAS MURPHY (Retired).

Approved Advocates—Mrs. ADRIANA FERRARO SEAWRIGHT; Sr. MARY DOLORES DOYLE, C.C.V.I.

Notaries—Ms. MARGARITA M. GONZALEZ; Ms. SYLVIA FALCON; Ms. THERESA VALLEJO; Mrs. LORETTA REYES; Mrs. IRENE KING.

Interdiocesan Appellate Court—Mailing Address: P.O. Box 28410, San Antonio, 78228-0410. Tel: 210-736-9444; 210-734-2620, Ext. 1147; 210-734-1608.

Moderator—Most Rev. GUSTAVO GARCIA-SILLER, M.Sp.S.

Judicial Vicar—VACANT.

Adjutant Judicial Vicar—Rev. Msgr. LESLIE A. VANCE, J.C.L. (Retired).

Judges—Revs. JACK HOPKA, J.C.L.; WARREN A. BROWN III, O.M.I., J.C.D.; Rev. Msgr. ALBERT HUBERTUS (Retired); Revs. DAVID MARIA A. JAEGER, O.F.M., J.C.D.; JOHN M. MAKOTHAKAT, Ph.D., S.T.D., J.C.D. (Retired).

Defenders of the Bond—Revs. ANH Q. TRAN, J.C.L.; JAMES A. KOTARA; MATTHEW C. IWUJI, J.C.D.; TIMOTHY A. GOLLOB; RENE ANGEL, J.C.L.; RICHARD B. WILLIAMS, O.P., J.D.; EDWARD RODEN-LUCERO, J.C.L.; MICHAEL P. COLWELL, J.C.L.; Mr. CARLOS VENEGAS, J.C.L.; Ms. LAURA L. LEFAVE, J.C.L.

Promoter Justitiae—Ms. DENISE J. DOYLE, J.C.D., Ph.D.

Notaries—Mrs. LUANN HARTNETT; Mrs. DONNA MILLS.

Due Process: Councils of Conciliation and Arbitration—Chancery Office, 2718 W. Woodlawn Ave., San Antonio, 78228-5195. Tel: 210-734-2620.

Diocesan Administration

Administrative Services Department—Rev. MARTIN J. LEOPOLD, Dir., Mailing Address: P.O. Box 28410, San Antonio, 78228-0410. Tel: 210-734-2620; 210-734-1674.

Archdiocesan Chief Financial Officer—Mr. RUBEN HINOJOSA, Mailing Address: P.O. Box 28410, San Antonio, 78228-0410. Tel: 210-734-2620, Ext. 1309; 210-734-1605; Fax: 210-734-2774. Email: ruben.hinojosa@archsa.org.

Archdiocesan Controller—Mrs. DELIA THOMAS, Mailing Address: 2718 W. Woodlawn, San Antonio, 78228. Tel: 210-734-2620, Ext. 1333; 210-734-1677; Fax: 210-734-2774. Email: delia.thomas@archsa.org.

Archdiocesan Office of Stewardship and Development—VACANT, Dir., Mailing Address: P.O. Box 28410, San Antonio, 78228-0410. Tel: 210-734-2620; Fax: 210-734-0231.

Office of Construction, Real Estate and Facilities Management—ROBERT B. HOLBROOK, Mgr., Mailing Address: 2718 W. Woodlawn, San Antonio, 78228. Tel: 210-734-1942; 210-630-7495. Email: robert.holbrook@archsa.org.

Office of Risk Management—Mr. HAL HENRY, Dir., Mailing Address: 2718 W. Woodlawn, San Antonio, 78228. Tel: 210-431-3465; 800-831-9107 (Toll Free); Fax: 210-431-7742. Email: hal.henry@archsa.org.

Archdiocesan Finance Council—Mrs. LISA SIMS; Ms. RACHEL BENAVIDES; Mr. BRUCE HAAN; Mrs. SYLVIA GUTIERREZ; Mr. DAVID KVAPIL; Mr. MIKE WROB; Mr. RAY STRAUCH; Mr. MEL SHRADER; Mrs. JENNIFER ROTHE; Mr. EDWARD ADAM, Chm.; Mr. ALTON PETSCH.

Archdiocesan Debt Review Committee—Mr. CURTIS HEINEN; Mrs. DELIA THOMAS, Chm.; Mr. LOUIS SANCHEZ; Mrs. NANCY DOUCETTE.

Building Board—Mr. MARIO MEDINA; Mr. JIM RODRIGUEZ; Mr. DAN CERNA; Mr. STEVE PERSYN; Mr. BENNETT R. FEINSILBER.

Lay Pension Plan Committee—Mr. CHRIS MCGUIRE; Mrs. MARGARET O'BRIEN; Mrs. DELIA THOMAS; Mrs. VICTORIA ESPARZA; Rev. MARTIN J. LEOPOLD; Mr. RUBEN HINOJOSA, Mailing Address: P.O. Box 28410, San Antonio, 78228-0410. Tel: 210-734-2620, Ext. 1309; 210-734-1905. Email: ruben.hinojosa@archsa.org.

Archdiocesan Cemeteries Office—Mr. RUBEN HINOJOSA; Mr. ROBERT CORNEJO, Exec. Dir., 746 Castroville Rd., San Antonio, 78207. Tel: 210-432-2303.

Information Technology—Mailing Address: 2718 W. Woodlawn, San Antonio, 78228. Mr. JOHN TROLLINGER. Tel: 210-734-2620, Ext. 1320; ALFONSO REBELLOSO. Tel: 210-734-2620, Ext. 1265; MARY ROSE CASTILLO. Tel: 210-734-2620, Ext. 1183.

Pension Office—LYDIA WASHINGTON. Tel: 210-734-2620, Ext. 1140. Email: lydia.washington@archsa.org.

Human Resources—Mrs. VICTORIA ESPARZA, Mailing Address: 2718 W. Woodlawn, San Antonio, 78228. Tel: 210-734-2620, Ext. 1324. Email: victoria.esparza@archsa.org.

Annual Appeal, Grants—LUCY HERRERA, Mailing Address: 2718 W. Woodlawn, San Antonio, 78228. Tel: 210-734-2620, Ext. 1223. Email: lucy.herrera@archsa.org.

Hope for the Future— Tuition Assistance and School Grants. JULIE SEGUIN, Dir. Tel: 210-734-2620, Ext. 1219. Email: julie.seguin@archsa.org; ANN MARIE COMMINOS, Assoc. Dir., 2718 W. Woodlawn, San Antonio, 78228. Tel: 210-734-1907; 210-734-1943. Email: annmarie.comminos@archsa.org.

Catholic Community Foundation—Mr. JEFF JUNG, Pres. Tel: 210-734-2620, Ext. 1241; Mr. ED BENNINGER. Tel: 210-734-2620, Ext. 1189.

Parish and School Accounting—Mrs. CHANA FINCH. Tel: 210-734-2620, Ext. 1245. Email: chana.finch@archsa.org.

Mail Room—MARIA HINOJOSA. Tel: 210-734-2620; 210-734-1631; Fax: 210-734-0231.

Print Service Center—Ms. WILLA GARIBAY. Tel: 210-734-2620, Ext. 1501.

Department for Pastoral Services—ROSIO GONZALEZ, L.M.S.W., Dir., Mailing Address: 2718 W. Woodlawn, P.O. Box 28410, San Antonio, 78228-0410. Tel: 210-734-2620, Ext. 1212.

Archdiocesan Catechetical-Religious Education Center—Ms. GLORIA ZAPIAIN, Dir., Mailing Address: 2718 W. Woodlawn, P.O. Box 28410, San Antonio, 78228-0410. Tel: 210-734-2620. Email: gloria.zapiain@archsa.org.

Office of Youth Ministry—JOAN MARTINEZ, Dir., Mailing Address: 2718 W. Woodlawn, P.O. Box 28410, San Antonio, 78228-0410. Tel: 210-734-2620, Ext. 1119.

Catholic Committee on Scouting (Boys)—Mr. RICH MAZZARA, Assoc. Dir., 2718 W. Woodlawn, P.O. Box 28410, San Antonio, 78228. Tel: 210-734-2620, Ext. 1115.

Catholic Committee on Girl Scouting—Mrs. BARBARA COVERTINO, Assoc. Dir., 2718 W. Woodlawn, P.O. Box 28410, San Antonio, 78228. Tel: 210-734-2620, Ext. 1157.

Office of Young Adult/Catholic Campus Ministry (Newman Apostolate)—Catholic Student Center, San Antonio College, 312 W. Courtland, San Antonio, 78212. Tel: 210-736-3752. Sr. THERESE SAN MIGUEL, O.S.F., Coord., St. Anthony Catholic Student Center at U.T.S.A., 14523 Roadrunner Way, San Antonio, 78249. Tel: 210-699-9594. St. Philip College. Palo Alto College. SAC, UTSA, UTSA Downtown, Texas A&M Extension, Northwest Vista, Texas Lutheran University, Schreiner University, Kerrville, Trinity, UT Health Science Center, S.W. Texas Junior College-Uvalde.

The Pontifical Mission Societies - Missions Awareness Office— (Holy Childhood Pontifical Assn.; Propagation of the Faith). MARY WISNIEWSKI, Dir., Mailing Address: 2718 W. Woodlawn, P.O. Box 28410, San Antonio, 78228-0410. Tel: 210-734-2620, Ext. 1144.

Office of Worship—Rev. HELIODORO LUCATERO, Dir., Mailing Address: 2718 W. Woodlawn, P.O. Box 28410, San Antonio, 78228-0410. Tel: 210-734-2620, Ext. 1238.

Office of Marriage, Family Life and NFP—Mr. JAKE SAMOUR, Dir., Mailing Address: 2718 W. Woodlawn, P.O. Box 28410, San Antonio, 78228-0410. Tel: 210-734-2610, Ext. 1214. Email: jake.samour@archsa.org.

Office of Christian Initiation (RCIA)—Mr. MARCO ROMAN, Ph.D., Dir., Mailing Address: 2718 W. Woodlawn, P.O. Box 28410, San Antonio, 78228-0410. Tel: 210-734-2620, Ext. 1250.

Office for Evangelization—Miss MARTHA FERNANDEZ-SARDINA, Dir., Mailing Address: 2718 W. Woodlawn, P.O. Box 28410, San Antonio, 78228-0410. Tel: 210-734-1668; 210-734-1990. Email: mfernandez-sardina@archsa.org.

Office of Life, Justice and Peace—VACANT, Mailing Address: 2718 W. Woodlawn, P.O. Box 28410, San Antonio, 78228-0410. Tel: 210-734-2620, Ext. 1212.

Future Evangelization Program for the Missions with Archbishop Gustavo Garcia-Siller—Rev. DAVID GARCIA, Dir.

Department of Formation—Mr. MARCO ROMAN, Ph.D., Dir., Mailing Address: P.O. Box 28410, San Antonio, 78228-0410. Tel: 210-734-2620; 210-734-1911. Email: marco.roman@archsa.org.

Office of Catholic Schools—

Superintendent—Ms. PATRICIA DAVIS, Mailing Address: P.O. Box 28410, San Antonio, 78228-0410. Tel: 210-734-2620; 210-734-1657. Web: sacatholicschools.org. Email: patricia.davis@archsa.org.

Associate Superintendent for Professional Development, Recruitment—Mrs. JOANN GAWLIK.

Associate Superintendent for Curriculum and Government Programs—BEVERLY LEJESKI.

Director of School Finance—Mr. DAVID NIXON.

Department of Clergy and Consecrated Life—Rev. TONY VILANO, Dir. & Vicar for Clergy, Mailing Address: P.O. Box 28410, San Antonio, 78228-0410. Tel: 210-734-2620; 210-734-1672.

Priests Personnel Board—Most Revs. OSCAR CANTÚ, D.D., S.T.L., S.T.D., V.G.; THOMAS J. FLANAGAN, D.D., V.G., Dir. (Retired); BERNARD F. POPP, D.D. (Retired); Rev. MARTIN J. LEOPOLD; Very Rev. Msgr. CARLOS DAVALOS, V.U.; Very Revs. CHRISTIAN A. JANSON, S.M., V.U.; KEVIN FAUSZ, C.M., V.U.; EDUARDO D. MORALES, V.U.; FIDELE O. DIKETE, V.U.; LENIN NAFFATE, V.U.; JOHN J. FLANAGAN, V.U.; Very Rev. Msgr. PATRICK J. RAGSDALE, V.U.; Very Rev. GRZEGORZ SAWICKI, S.D.S., V.F.; Rev. Msgr. MICHAEL J. BOULETTE, V.F.; Very Revs. WALLIS J. STILES, V.F.; GILBERTO

VALLEJO, V.F.; CAMILLO BOTELLO JR., M.S.F., V.F.; JAMES FISCHLER, C.I.C.M., V.F.

Permanent Diaconate Program—Very Rev. Msgr. PATRICK J. RAGSDALE, V.U., Dir., 2718 W. Woodlawn, San Antonio, 78228. Tel: 210-734-2620; Fax: 210-734-0231.

Vocation Office—Rev. ALEX PEREIDA, Dir.; Sr. JANE MARIE GAWLICK, C.S.S.F., Assoc. Dir., 2600 W. Woodlawn Ave., San Antonio, 78228-5196. Tel: 210-735-0553.

Office for Religious—Sr. MARY TERESA CULLEN, C.S.B., Dir., Mailing Address: P.O. Box 28410, San Antonio, 78228-0410. Tel: 210-734-2620; 210-734-1907.

Ecumenical Relations—Rev. MARTIN J. LEOPOLD.

Vicar for Retired Priests—Rev. Msgr. JOHN WAGNER (Retired), Casa De Padres, 8520 Cross Mountain Trail, San Antonio, 78255. Tel: 210-698-8682.

Department of Assumption-St. John's Seminary—Rev. JEFFERY PEHL, Rector & Pres., 2600 W. Woodlawn, San Antonio, 78228-5196. Tel: 210-734-5137.

Business Office—Mr. JOSE CASTANEDA, Admin. Coord. Tel: 210-734-5137.

Development Coordinator—VACANT.

Department of Communications—Deacon PAT RODGERS, Dir., 2718 W. Woodlawn, San Antonio, 78228. Tel: 210-734-1610; Fax: 210-734-2939. Email: pat.rodgers@archsa.org; SONIA ANGUIANO, Administrative Asst. Tel: 210-734-1988. Email: sonia.anguiano@archsa.org.

Catholic Television of San Antonio (CTSA), Channel 15—Deacon PAT RODGERS, 2718 W. Woodlawn, San Antonio, 78228. Tel: 210-734-2620, Ext. 1109; 210-734-1610; Fax: 210-734-2939.

Today's Catholic Newspaper—Mr. JORDAN MC MORROUGH, Editor, 2718 W. Woodlawn, San Antonio, 78228. Tel: 210-734-2620; Fax: 210-734-2939.

Department of Social and Community Services—Mr. STEVE SALDANA, Dir., 202 W. French, San Antonio, 78212. Tel: 210-222-1294; Fax: 210-227-0217.

Catholic Counseling and Consultation Center—Mr. HOWARD KRAVITZ, O.P.A., M.A., N.C.C., L.P.C.-S., Mng. Dir.; Sr. GERI KLINE, O.P., L.P.C., N.C.C., Clinical Dir., 7711 Madonna Dr., San Antonio, 78213. Tel: 210-377-1133; Fax: 210-377-1230.

Deaf and Hard of Hearing Ministry—Rev. THOMAS COUGHLIN, O.P.Miss., Dir., Dominican Missionaries for the Deaf Apostolate, 143 Honeysuckle Ln., San Antonio, 78213. Tel: 210-627-6303. Office: St. Leo, 4401 S. Flores St., San Antonio, 78214. Tel: 210-533-9108.

Ministry to Persons with Disabilities—Sr. JO-MICHELE SIERRA, S.S.C.J., 7112 Hagy Circle, San Antonio, 78216. Tel: 210-872-8794.

Bexar County Detention Ministries—Sr. TERESA CARTER, C.S.B. Tel: 210-299-4540; Rev. CARL SCHINDLER, C.Ss.R.; Bro. CHARLES FUCIK, C.Ss.R., 503 San Pedro, San Antonio, 78212. Tel: 210-299-4540; Sr. KATHLEEN EGGERING, S.S.N.D., Juvenile Detention, Cindi Kreir Correctional Center, 3621 Farm Rd., San Antonio, 78223. Tel: 210-335-1754.

Criminal Justice Ministry—Deacon ROBERT J. LEIBRECHT, Church of the Good Shepherd, P.O. Box 929, Schertz, 78154. Tel: 210-658-4350; Fax: 210-658-6188. Email: leibrecht@sbcglobal.net.

St. Peter and Joseph's Home— (See Protective Institutions)

Seton Home— (See Protective Institutions)

Catholic Charities, Archdiocese of San Antonio, Inc.—Mr. STEVEN SALDANA, Pres., 202 W. French, San Antonio, 78212-5818. Tel: 210-222-1294; Fax: 210-227-0217.

Refugee Services—PAULA WALKER, 202 W. French, San Antonio, 78212-5818. Tel: 210-222-1294; Fax: 210-242-3174.

Immigration Services—LINDA BRANDMILLER, 2903 W. Salinas St., San Antonio, 78207. Tel: 210-433-3256; Fax: 210-433-0851.

Director of Development—Ms. PAMELA RAINES. Tel: 210-222-1294.

Diocesan Offices And Directors

Archdiocesan Council of Catholic Women—MARGARET TRACY, 7145 Webwood Way, San Antonio, 78250. Tel: 210-647-8728; Rev. WILLIAM MCNAMARA, Spiritual Moderator, Mailing Address: P.O. Box 248, Elmendorf, 78112-0248. Tel: 210-635-8539.

Catholic Center for Charismatic Renewal—Most Rev. THOMAS J. FLANAGAN, D.D., V.G., Dir., Liaison (Retired); ROSBEL HERNANDEZ, 1707 S. Flores, San Antonio, 78204. Tel: 210-226-7545; Fax: 210-212-9330. Email: info@cccr.net.

Catholic Lawyers Guild—Rev. Msgr. TERENCE NOLAN, J.C.L., Spiritual Moderator, Mailing Address: P.O. Box 28410, San Antonio, 78228-0410. Tel: 210-734-2620.

Catholic Physicians Guild—Rev. JOHN A. LEIES, S.M., S.T.D., 520 Fordham Ln., San Antonio, 78228. Tel: 210-436-3227; WILLIAM P. MUELLER M.D., M.D., Pres., 2701 Babcock Rd., Ste. A, San Antonio, 78229.

Censores Librorum—VACANT.

Movimiento de Apostolado Familiar & Marriage Encounter (Rural)—Rev. JOSEPH G. RASKY, S.M., 1403 N. St. Marys, San Antonio, 78215. Tel: 210-225-1360.

Movimiento Familiar Cristano (Urban)—Presidents: MANUEL GUERRA; CRUCITA GUERRA, 117 Stonewall, San Antonio, 78214. Tel: 210-924-1890. Email: mguerra45@juno.com.

Black Catholic Apostolate—Mrs. CAROL WHITE, 1819 Nevada, San Antonio, 78203. Tel: 210-532-5358.

Cursillo Movement (Spanish)—VACANT, Spiritual Advisor; RUDY RAMIREZ, Lay Dir., 602 Urban Loop, San Antonio, 78207. Tel: 210-492-8788.

Cursillos of Christianity of the Archdiocese of San Antonio—Rev. EINER OCHOA, Spiritual Advisor (Retired); ANN J. HALL, Dir.; VERONICA TREVINO, Treas., Mailing Address: P.O. Box 5152, San Antonio, 78201. Tel: 210-492-8788.

Ecumenical Affairs—Rev. MARTIN J. LEOPOLD.

Holy Childhood, Pontifical Association—MARY WISNIEWSKI, Mailing Address: P.O. Box 28410, San Antonio, 78228-0410. Tel: 210-734-2620; 210-734-1913.

Holy Name Society—Mr. JOSE CUELLAR, Mailing Address: P.O. Box 54, Adkins, 78101. Tel: 210-649-1997.

Pre-Seminary Program—VACANT.

Priests Eucharistic League—Most Rev. THOMAS J. FLANAGAN, D.D., V.G., Dir. (Retired), Mailing Address: P.O. Box 28410, San Antonio, 78228-0410. Tel: 210-734-2620.

Propagation of the Faith—MARY WISNIEWSKI, Mailing Address: P.O. Box 28410, San Antonio, 78228-0410.

Retreats, Men—Rev. ROCKY GRIMARD, O.M.I., Dir., Oblate Renewal Center, 127 Oblate Dr., San Antonio, 78216. Tel: 210-349-4173.

Respect Life Program—VACANT.

CLERGY, PARISHES, MISSIONS AND PAROCHIAL SCHOOLS

CITY OF SAN ANTONIO

1—CATHEDRAL OF SAN FERNANDO (1731), (Hispanic), Revs. Tony Vilano, Rector; Jose Ramon Perez-Martinez, Parochial Vicar; Rolando Rivera, Parochial Vicar; Edvin Rodriguez, Parochial Vicar; Deacons Doroteo E. Pedroza; Pedro Garza; Ismael Casanova; Pedro G. Nanez.
Res. & Mailing Address: 231 W. Commerce, 78205. Tel: 210-227-1297; Fax: 210-271-0149.
Catechesis/Religious Program—Students 157.
Mission—San Francesco di Paola (Italian) 205 Piazza Italia, Bexar Co. 78207. Tel: 210-227-0548; Fax: 210-226-5086. P.O. Box 7783, 78207-7783. Rev. Anton Quang Dinh Van, Admin.

2—ST. AGNES (1923), (Hispanic), Revs. Jaime Renteria Torres, M.N.M.; Mauricio Gomez-Sosa.
Office: 814 Ruiz St., 78207. Tel: 210-227-8258; Fax: 210-212-7757.
Res.: 804 Ruiz St., 78207.
Catechesis/Religious Program—Yolanda Vargas, D.R.E. Students 208.

3—ST. ALPHONSUS (1925), (Hispanic), Rev. Horacio Florez Coicedo, Admin.; Sr. Adele Massaro, Pastoral Assoc.; Deacons Trinidad Gutierrez; Roy Y. Muñoz Jr.
Res.: 2004 Chihuahua St., 78207. Tel: 210-433-9365; Fax: 210-433-9365.
Catechesis/Religious Program—Tel: 210-432-3176. Students 127.

4—ST. ANN (1912), (Hispanic), Rev. N. James Rutkowski, Admin.
Res.: 210 St. Ann St., 78201. Tel: 210-734-6687; 210-734-6688; Fax: 210-738-1755.
Catechesis/Religious Program—Tel: 210-734-6687, Ext. 225. Sr. Blanca Hinojosa, H.C.G., D.R.E. Students 286.

5—ST. ANTHONY MARY CLARET (1988) Rev. Jan Piotr Klak; Deacons Jesse C. Galvan; Angel Arredondo; Jerome P. Kozar.
Res.: 6150 Roft Rd., 78253. Tel: 210-688-9033; Fax: 210-688-3575. Email: saclaret@saclaret.com.
Catechesis/Religious Program—Catherine Prochko, D.R.E. Students 1,063.

6—ST. ANTHONY OF PADUA (1957) Rev. Kevin Shananhan, M.S.C.; Deacons Gilbert Wiessler; William I. Simmonds; Joe Borrego.
Res.: 102 Lorenz Rd., 78209. Tel: 210-824-1743; Fax: 210-824-3283. Email: marcia@stanthonydepadua.org.
Catechesis/Religious Program—Students 405.

7—BASILICA OF THE NATIONAL SHRINE OF THE LITTLE FLOWER, OUR LADY OF MT. CARMEL AND ST. THERESE PARISH (1926), (Hispanic), Discalced Carmelite Fathers. Revs. Luis Gerardo Belmonte, O.C.D.; James A. Curiel, O.C.D.; Marion J. Bui, O.C.D.; Gregory Ross, O.C.D.; Deacons Antonio G. Rodriguez; Jimmy Garza. In Res., Revs. Luis J. Castaneda, O.C.D.; Bonaventure Sauer, O.C.D.
Office & Mailing Address: 824 Kentucky Ave., 78201. Tel: 210-735-9126; Fax: 210-735-1389.
Res.: 906 Kentucky Ave., 78201-6097. Tel: 210-735-9127; Fax: 210-738-0818.
School—(Grades PreK-8), 905 Kentucky Ave., 78201. Tel: 210-732-9207; Fax: 210-732-3214. Web: www.littleflowerschool.net. Carmen R. Alicardi, Prin.; Cecilia Garibay, Librarian. Sisters of the Holy Spirit 1; Lay Teachers 19; Students 288.
Catechesis/Religious Program—Tel: 210-734-4893. Rita Beltran, D.R.E. Students 306.

8—ST. BENEDICT (1958), (Polish—Hispanic), Rev. Edward Bernal; Deacon James Raso.
Res.: 4535 Lord Rd., 78220. Tel: 210-648-0123; Fax: 210-648-1722.
Catechesis/Religious Program—Tel: 210-648-4632. Students 140.

9—BLESSED SACRAMENT (1956) Rev. John O'Donoghue; Deacons Joe Fertitta; Joseph Jorgensen; Frank Martinez.
Office: 600 Oblate Dr., 78216. Tel: 210-824-7231; Fax: 210-824-4293.
School—(Grades K-8) Tel: 210-824-3381; Fax: 210-826-6146. Mr. Michael Fierro, Prin.; Kathy Garza, Librarian. Lay Teachers 21; Students 264; Day Care 65.
Catechesis/Religious Program—Students 176.

10—ST. BONAVENTURE (1959), (Hispanic), Rev. Celso Tabalanza, C.I.C.M.; Deacons Fidel Hinojosa; Amador Gonzalez; Luis L. Arredondo.
Res.: 1918 Palo Alto Rd., 78211. Tel: 210-922-1685; Fax: 210-922-7821.
Catechesis/Religious Program—Tel: 210-922-1882. Mrs. Diane Guerra, D.R.E. Students 632.

11—ST. BRIGID (1972) Rev. Stuart Juleen; Deacons Thomas Billimek; Paul Heye; Juan Espinosa; Harold DeCuir; Donald V. Bradley Jr.; Ernest Roy Amo; Patrick Frisina.
Mailing Address: 6907 Kitchener St., 78240.
Res.: 6903 Kitchener St., 78240. Tel: 210-696-0896; Fax: 210-696-7319.
Catechesis/Religious Program—Renee Kuntz, D.R.E. Students 603.

12—ST. CECILIA (1919), (Hispanic), Rev. Ruben Garcia, O.C.D.; Deacons Ricardo Villarreal; Richard Hobbs.
Res.: 125 W. Whittier St., 78210-2897. Tel: 210-533-7109; Fax: 210-532-2599.
School—(Grades PreK-8) Tel: 210-534-2711; Fax: 210-533-8284. Mrs. Mary I. Crow, Prin.; Sr. Margie Vinlik, Librarian. Sisters 3; Lay Teachers 14; Students 134.
Catechesis/Religious Program—Mrs. Limba Reyes, D.R.E. Students 153.
Mission—Purisima Concepcion 807 Mission Rd., Bexar Co. 78210. Revs. David Garcia, Admin.; N. James Rutkowski; Deacon Raymond F. Jiminez.

13—CHRIST THE KING (1928), (Hispanic), Rev. Lawrence Mattingly, O.F.M.Conv.; Laura Cardenas, Admin.
Res.: 2623 Perez St., 78207. Tel: 210-433-6301; Fax: 210-435-2736.
Catechesis/Religious Program—Tel: 210-433-3640. Lily Landeros, D.R.E. Students 126.

14—ST. CLARE (1959), (Hispanic), Rev. Msgr. Lambert S. Bily; Deacon Gilbert M. Maldonado.
Res.: 7701 Somerset Rd., 78211. Tel: 210-924-5252.
Catechesis/Religious Program—Tel: 210-922-6458. Maria Delores M. Marek, D.R.E. Students 110.

15—DIVINE PROVIDENCE (1981), (Hispanic), Rev. Jean-Marie Mvumbi Phongo, C.I.C.M. (Congo); Deacon Ricardo DeLaGarza.
Church: 5667 Old Pearsall Rd., 78242-2335. Tel: 210-623-3970; Fax: 210-623-3978.
Catechesis/Religious Program—Tel: 210-623-3971. Diana Garza-Valdez, D.R.E. Students 338.

16—ST. DOMINIC (1971) Rev. Eric Ritter; Deacons Bert Stewart; Ree Stockton; Scott Imburgia; Leonard Cortina.
Res.: 5919 Ingram Rd., 78228. Tel: 210-435-6211; Fax: 210-435-1732.
Catechesis/Religious Program—Sr. Dympna Clark, S.H.Sp., D.R.E. Students 354.

17—ST. ELIZABETH ANN SETON (1961) Rev. Msgr. Conor McGrath.
Res.: 8500 Cross Mountain Tr., 78255. Tel: 210-698-1941; Fax: 210-698-1983.
Catechesis/Religious Program—Dina S. Elva, Coord. Faith Formation. Students 565.

18—ST. FRANCIS OF ASSISI (1980) Revs. Lawrence J. Christian; James K. Seiwert, Parochial Vicar; Sr. Rose Kruppa, C.D.P., Pastoral Assoc.; Deacons Tom Franklin, (Retired); Brian Clayton; Patrick F.

Frisina; Michael Portele; Eugene A. Festa, (Retired).
Office & Mailing Address: 4201 De Zavala Rd., 78249-2000. Tel: 210-492-4600; Fax: 210-492-8128.
Res.: 14219 Golden Woods, 78249. Tel: 210-492-3266.
Catechesis/Religious Program—Anthony Deosdade, D.R.E. Students 529.

19—ST. GABRIEL (1958), (Hispanic), Rev. Richard Pena.
Res.: 747 S.W. 39th St., 78237. Tel: 210-433-3689; Fax: 210-433-0546.
Catechesis/Religious Program—Tel: 210-433-3354. Virginia Ibarra, D.R.E. Students 220.

20—ST. GERARD MAJELLA (1911) Rev. James E. Shea, C.Ss.R.; Deacon Jose L. Ocampo; Rick McLaughlin, Music Dir. In Res., Revs. Francis Han Pham, C.Ss.R.; Monroe Perrier, C.Ss.R., Supr.; Alton Carr, C.Ss.R.
Church Office: 1523 Iowa St., 78203. Tel: 210-533-0161 (Church Office); Fax: 210-533-0558.
Res.: 1617 Iowa St., 78203.
Catechesis/Religious Program—Students 22.

21—ST. GREGORY'S (1955) Rev. Msgr. Michael B. O'Gorman (Ireland); Robert Martinez, Pastoral Assoc.; Deacon Fred Campos Jr.
Res.: 700 Dewhurst, 78213. Tel: 210-342-5271; Fax: 210-342-0542.
School—(Grades PreK-8) Tel: 210-342-0281; Fax: 210-308-7177. Martha Gomez, Prin.; Joyce Greenlee, Librarian. Lay Teachers 41; Students 597.
Catechesis/Religious Program—Tel: 210-342-3826. Gloria Silva, C.R.E. Students 305.

22—ST. HELENA (1974) Rev. Msgr. Leo M. Dolan; Deacon Paul Gustowski; Laura Yzaguirre, Pastoral Assoc.
Office: 14714 Edgemont, 78247. Tel: 210-653-3316; Fax: 210-653-2702.
Res.: 14527 Angora, 78247. Tel: 210-653-3850.
Catechesis/Religious Program—Tel: 210-653-3316; Fax: 210-653-2702. Corrie Solis, D.R.E. Students 360.

23—ST. HENRY (1904), (Hispanic), Rev. Msgr. Emil J. Wesselsky; Deacon Ruben Peter Olivares.
Res.: 1619 S. Flores St., 78204. Tel: 210-225-6877; Fax: 210-212-5802.
Catechesis/Religious Program—Tel: 210-227-1585. Sr. Virginia Clara Ruiz, H.C.G., D.R.E. Students 412.

24—HOLY FAMILY (1963), (Hispanic), Rev. Emmet Carolan; Deacons Manuel Carranza; Pedro Castillo.
Res.: 152 Florencia, 78228-5899. Tel: 210-433-8216; Fax: 210-433-0090.
Catechesis/Religious Program—Tel: 210-433-8216 (Ext 17 or 23). Ester Mango, C.R.E. Students 206.

25—HOLY NAME (1961), (Polish—Hispanic), Rev. Arkadiusz Szyda; Deacon Reynaldo Hinojosa Sr.
Res.: 3814 Nash Blvd., 78223. Tel: 210-333-5020; Fax: 210-333-5021.
School—(Grades PreK-8) Tel: 210-333-7356; Fax: 210-333-7642. Mr. Chad Mills, Prin. Lay Teachers 13; Students 230.
Catechesis/Religious Program—Tel: 210-333-5020; Fax: 210-333-5021. Cathy Kelley, D.R.E. Students 342.

26—HOLY REDEEMER (1901), (African American), [CEM] Very Rev. Kevin Fausz, C.M.
Res.: 1819 Nevada, 78203. Tel: 210-532-5358.
Catechesis/Religious Program—Students 59.

27—HOLY ROSARY (1948), (Hispanic), Very Rev. Christian A. Janson, S.M.; Bro. Richard Schrader, S.M., Pastoral Assoc.; Deacons Felipe Barajas; Richard B. Salazar.
Res.: 159 Camino Santa Maria, 78228. Tel: 210-433-3241; Fax: 210-433-2133.
Catechesis/Religious Program—Debi Garza, C.R.E. Students 118.

28—HOLY SPIRIT (1964) Revs. Carlos B. Velazquez; Mike Horan, Parochial Vicar; Deacons Jesse Greer, (Retired); Patrick Cunningham; William Peche; Evan Wittig.
Res.: 758 W. Ramsey Rd., 78216. Tel: 210-341-1395; Fax: 210-341-8438.
School—(Grades PreK-8), 770 W. Ramsey Rd., 78216. Tel: 210-349-1169; Fax: 210-349-1247. Jennifer Marg, Prin. Lay Teachers 29; Students 459.
Catechesis/Religious Program—Tel: 210-341-1397; Fax: 210-341-2287. Students 684.

29—HOLY TRINITY (1987) Very Rev. Msgr. Michael Yarbrough; Rev. Martin Garcia Avila, Parochial Vicar; Deacons Jerry Micek; Chris Laskowski; Guy LoTruco; Oscar Perez.
Office: 20523 Huebner Rd., 78258-3915.
Res.: 18018 Crystal Knoll, 78258. Tel: 210-497-4200; Fax: 210-497-4285.
Catechesis/Religious Program—Tel: 210-497-4145; Fax: 210-497-3041. Kristen Casas, C.R.E.; Eric Mejia, Asst. C.R.E. Students 1,419.

30—IMMACULATE CONCEPTION (1933), (Hispanic), Rev. William Collins, M.S.C.; Deacons Jose Hernandez; Marcos Criado.
Res.: 314 Merida St., 78207. Tel: 210-225-2986; Fax: 210-225-2987.
Catechesis/Religious Program—Herlinda Barrentos, D.R.E. Students 120.

31—IMMACULATE HEART OF MARY (1912), (Hispanic), Revs. Ignacio A. Blanco, C.M.F.; Paschal C. Amagba, C.M.F.; Deacons Jorge Bonilla-Valentin; Alfonso Cervantes. In Res., Revs. Stephen K. Sherwood, C.M.F.; Luis Dussan, C.M.F. (Retired).
Res.: 617 S. Santa Rosa Blvd., 78204. Tel: 210-226-8268; 210-472-2160 (Res.); Fax: 210-226-2412.
Catechesis/Religious Program—Tel: 210-224-8829. Alfonso Cervantes, D.R.E. Students 122.

32—ST. JAMES THE APOSTLE (1954), (Hispanic), Revs. Plutarco Belanggoy, C.I.C.M.; Archie Tacay, C.I.C.M., Parochial Vicar; Deacons Jesse P. Alcala; Ernest Huizar; Charlie Von Allmen.
Res.: 907 W. Theo Ave., 78225. Tel: 210-922-2136; Fax: 210-923-0940.
School—(Grades PreK-8) Tel: 210-924-1201; Fax: 210-924-0201. Sr. Ignacia Carrillo, F.M.A., Prin. Daughters of Mary Help of Christians 3; Lay Teachers 16; Students 227.
Catechesis/Religious Program—Tel: 210-922-4061. Mary Toscano, D.R.E. Students 461.

33—ST. JOHN BERCHMANS (1910), (Hispanic), Rev. Rudy T. Carrola Jr.; Deacons Jose G. Diaz; Francisco Sandoval; Jesus Rodriguez; Mrs. Evangeline Clor, Librarian.
Res.: 1147 Cupples Rd., 78226. Tel: 210-434-3247; Fax: 210-432-0431.
School—(Grades PreK-8) Tel: 210-433-0411; Fax: 210-433-2335. Mrs. Beverly Abbott, Prin. (PreK 3-8) Lay Teachers 23; Students 357.
Catechesis/Religious Program—Tel: 210-433-2121; Fax: 210-432-0431. Ms. Rosalinda Rodriguez, D.R.E. Students 185.

34—ST. JOHN NEUMANN (1977) Rev. Octavio A. Muguerza, Admin. Pro-Tem.
Mailing Address: 6680 Crestway Dr., 78239. Tel: 210-654-1643; Fax: 210-654-8031.
Catechesis/Religious Program—Tel: 210-654-3707. Students 340.

35—ST. JOHN THE EVANGELIST (1956) Rev. Martin J. Leopold. In Res., Rev. Raymond Schuster.
Office: 4603 St. John's Way, 78212. Tel: 210-738-2201; Fax: 210-738-0599.
Catechesis/Religious Program—Patricia J. Pollack, D.R.E. Students 175.

36—ST. JOSEPH (Downtown) (1868) [CEM] Rev. Mario Marzocchi, S.S.S.
Res.: 623 E. Commerce St., 78205. Tel: 210-227-0126; Fax: 210-227-7690.
Catechesis/Religious Program—Students 60.

37—ST. JOSEPH (South San) (1935), (Hispanic), Very Rev. Lenin Naffate (Mexico); Deacon Genaro Herrera.
Res.: 535 New Laredo Hwy., 78211-1900. Tel: 210-924-4383; Fax: 210-928-9020. Email: church@stjosephsouthsan.org.
Catechesis/Religious Program—Tel: 210-924-4383. Students 180.

38—ST. JUDE (1954), (Hispanic), Rev. Roney M. Cardoso, O.S.A.; Deacon Bartolo Ramos.
Res.: 130 S. San Augustine Ave., 78237. Tel: 210-432-8044; Fax: 210-432-1760.
Catechesis/Religious Program—Tel: 210-438-0392; Fax: 210-433-3959. Students 325.
Mission—Santa Maria Goretti, Bexar Co.

39—ST. LAWRENCE (1959), (Hispanic), Rev. Tu T. Nguyen; Deacons Alois Keller, (Retired); Ernesto Leal, (Retired); Arturo Garcia; Richard Gonzales; Ricardo Medina.
Res.: 236 E. Petaluma, 78221. Tel: 210-924-4401; Fax: 210-924-4075.
Catechesis/Religious Program—Tel: 210-924-6470. Guadalupe G. Bernal, D.R.E. Students 401.

40—ST. LEO (1919), (Hispanic), Rev. Frank Macias; Deacons Gerald Gonzalez; Tom Torrez; Lupe Sielski, Pastoral Assoc.
Office: 4401 S. Flores, 78214. Tel: 210-533-9108; Fax: 210-533-0643. Email: stleochurch@sbcglobal.net.
Res.: 148 W. Hafer, 78214.
School—(Grades PreK-8), 119 Octavia Pl., 78214. Tel: 210-532-3166; Fax: 210-532-5997. Carol Johnson, Prin.; Yanara Cruz, Librarian. Lay Teachers 13; Students 182.
Catechesis/Religious Program—Teresa Sanchez, D.R.E.; Diana Rodriguez, Youth Min. Students 370.
Deaf Community—Rev. Thomas Coughlin, O.P-.Miss.; Deacon Robert M. Caldwell Jr.

41—ST. LEONARD'S (1966), (Hispanic), Revs. David Gutierrez, T.O.R. (Mexico); Juan Carlos Bello, T.O.R.; Deacons Carlos Salinas, (Retired); Rey Ybarra.
Res.: 8510 S. Zarzamora, 78224-2099. Tel: 210-924-6000; Fax: 210-924-5552.
Catechesis/Religious Program—Tel: 210-924-6000, Ext. 19. Students 294.

42—ST. LUKE (1959) Revs. James P. Barlow; Jesus G. Anguiano-Rivera, Parochial Vicar.
Office: 4603 Manitou, 78228-1889. Tel: 210-433-2777; Fax: 210-433-2778.
Res.: 6014 Horizon, 78228. Tel: 210-436-9777.
School—(Grades PreK-8) Tel: 210-434-2011; Fax: 210-432-2419. Marcella Salazar, Prin.; Carolyn Lomas, Librarian. Lay Teachers 34; Students 519.
Catechesis/Religious Program—Rick Olivarez, C.R.E.; Gloria Clayton, Faith Formation Dir. Students 524.

43—ST. MARGARET MARY (1955), (Hispanic), Rev. Norman Ermis; Deacons Gerardo Mechler; Zeke Moczygemba; Jose Almanza, (Retired); Gabriel J. Rosas; Francisco Lafuente.
Res.: 1314 Fair Ave., 78223. Tel: 210-532-6309; Fax: 210-532-6333. Email: stmargaretmary@yahoo.com.
School—(Grades K-8), 1202 Fair Ave., 78223. Tel: 210-534-6137; Fax: 210-534-2225. Mr. Ramon Guerra, Prin. (PreK 3-8) Felician Sisters 1; Lay Teachers 10; Students 154.
Catechesis/Religious Program— Ofelia Fuentes Valdez, Faith Formation Dir. Students 256.
Mission—St. Catherine 2202 Hicks, Bexar Co. 78210.

44—ST. MARK THE EVANGELIST (1976) Rev. Msgr. Kevin E. Ryan; Dorothea G. Hamlin, Pastoral Admin.; Shane Hamilton, Devel. Dir.; Catherine Lopez, Pastoral Assoc.; Deacons Steven Marques; Gilbert S. Hernandez; Raul Adam; David R. Seguin.
Res.: 1602 Thousand Oaks Dr., 78232-2398. Tel: 210-494-1606; 210-494-1607; Fax: 210-494-4957.
Catechesis/Religious Program—Tel: 210-494-7434. Theresa Crow, D.R.E. (Elem.); Cindy Hamilton, D.R.E. (High School); Dorothy Godines, D.R.E. (High School). Students 1,016.

45—ST. MARTIN DE PORRES (1964), (Hispanic), Rev. Gilbert Obin, C.I.C.M.; Deacons Jose Menchaca; Anthony Patlan; Benito Resendiz; Jesus Lucio Jr.
Res.: 1730 Dahlgreen Ave., 78237. Tel: 210-432-5203; Fax: 210-436-1187.
Catechesis/Religious Program—Tel: 210-436-2071. Students 315.

46—ST. MARY (1852) [CEM] Rev. John J. Gordon, O.M.I.
Res.: 202 N. St. Mary's St., 78205. Tel: 210-226-8381; Fax: 210-226-8440.

47—ST. MARY MAGDALEN (1940), (Hispanic), Revs. Joseph Mary Marshall, S.M.; William H. Combs; Deacon Gerald Campa. In Res., Revs. George T. Montague, S.M.; Robert E. Hogan.
Office: 1710 Clower St., 78201. Tel: 210-735-5269; Fax: 210-738-0698.
Res.: 1701 Alametos St., 78201. Tel: 210-734-6727.
School—(Grades PreK-8), 1700 Clower St., 78201. Tel: 210-735-1381; Fax: 210-735-2406. Miguel Mejia, Prin.; Roberta Gujardo, Librarian. Brothers 1; Sisters 3; Lay Teachers 9; Students 190.
Catechesis/Religious Program—Tel: 210-735-5284. Linda Froboese, D.R.E. Students 572.

48—ST. MATTHEW'S (1968) Revs. Dennis Arechiga; James L. Empereur, S.J., Parochial Vicar; Valentine Gallegos Jr., Parochial Vicar; Deacons Tom Fox; Wilbur Hoelscher; Norman Kutschenreuter; Keith Werner, (Retired); Ernesto Garza, (Retired); Anton Svatek, (Retired); James Exparza, (Retired); Rafael Lara; Pedro Luz Cuellar; Gabriel N. Mendiola; Michael F. Nealis; Roberto Rios; Anthony Rivera.
Res.: 10703 Wurzbach Rd., 78230. Tel: 210-478-5000; Fax: 210-696-8858.
School—(Grades PreK-8) Tel: 210-478-5099; Fax: 210-696-7624. Alvin Caro, Prin.; Diane Michaud, Librarian. Lay Teachers 40; Students 739.
Catechesis/Religious Program—Fax: 210-696-8858. Sr. Therese Gleitz, D.R.E. Students 1,035.

49—ST. MICHAEL (1866), (Hispanic), [CEM] Rev. Heliodoro Lucatero.
Res.: 418 Indiana, 78210. Tel: 210-532-3707; Fax: 210-532-3707.
Catechesis/Religious Program—Students 118.

50—OUR LADY OF GOOD COUNSEL (1952), (Hispanic), Very Rev. Fidele O. Dikete.
Res.: 1204 Castroville Rd., 78237. Tel: 210-432-0873; Fax: 210-432-7576.
Catechesis/Religious Program—Tel: 210-432-6430. Students 145.

51—OUR LADY OF GRACE (1938) Rev. Msgr. Lawrence Walsh; Rev. Jonathan W. Felux, Parochial Vicar; Deacon Frank Gallardo.
Res.: 223 E. Summit Ave., 78212. Tel: 210-734-7285; Fax: 210-734-8334.
Catechesis/Religious Program—Students 246.

52—OUR LADY OF GUADALUPE (1911), (Hispanic), Revs. Ronald Gonzales, S.J.; James Marshall, S.J.; Bro. Alexander Gussio, S.J.; Deacons Robert Galvan; Carlos Sandoval; Ruben Felan.
Res.: 1321 El Paso St., 78207. Tel: 210-226-4064; Fax: 210-226-4973.
Catechesis/Religious Program—Jacqueline Walters, D.R.E. Students 102.

53—OUR LADY OF PERPETUAL HELP (1913), (Hispanic), Rev. Daniel Cisneros.
Res.: 618 S. Grimes St., 78203. Tel: 210-532-7031;

Fax: 201-532-7031.
Catechesis / Religious Program—Tel: 210-534-7193. Students 180.

54—OUR LADY OF SORROWS (1915), (Hispanic), Rev. Thaddeus Tabak, S.D.S.; Deacon Jesse Fraga. In Res., Rev. Marian Piekarczyk, S.D.S., Dir. Polish Catholic Mission & Army Chap.
Res.: 3107 N. St. Mary's St., 78212. Tel: 210-732-6295; 210-736-6719 (Polish); Fax: 210-732-9249.
Catechesis / Religious Program—Students 97.

55—OUR LADY OF THE ANGELS (1947), (Hispanic), Rev. James Hynes (Peru); Deacons Albert Ramirez; Jose F. Moreno.
Res.: 1214 Stonewall St., 78211. Tel: 210-924-6591; Fax: 210-924-6593.
Catechesis / Religious Program—Tel: 210-924-8046. Alicia Q. Gutierrez, D.R.E. Students 277.

56—OUR LADY OF THE ATONEMENT CATHOLIC CHURCH (1983), (A Personal Parish for the Anglican Use). Revs. Christopher G. Phillips; Jeffery Wade Moore; Deacons James P. Orr, Business Mgr.; Michael D'Agostino; Mr. Edmund G. Murray, Music Dir.; Mrs. Chalon Murray, Asst. Dir. Music.
Res.: 8015 Shady Hollow Ln., 78255. Tel: 210-695-3332.
Church: 15415 Red Robin Rd., 78255. Tel: 210-695-2944; Fax: 210-695-9679.
School—The Atonement Academy, (Grades PreK-12) Tel: 210-695-2240. Mr. Ralph Johnston, Prin.; Mrs. Deborah Divis, Librarian. Priests 2; Religious 1; Lay Teachers 39; Students 547.
Catechesis / Religious Program—Deacon James P. Orr, D.R.E. Students 27.
Convent—The Poor Clares of Perpetual Adoration, Tel: 210-621-5560. Sr. Grace Marie, Supr. Sisters 5.

57—ST. PATRICK (1895), (Hispanic), Rev. Andre Kazadi, C.I.C.M.; Deacon Juan Jose Delgado.
Res.: 1114 Willow St., 78208. Tel: 210-226-5223; Fax: 210-227-8616.
Catechesis / Religious Program—Students 196.

58—ST. PAUL (1954), (Hispanic), Rev. Msgr. Franciszek Kurzaj; Deacons Daniel Muriada, (Retired); Agustin Arismendez; Pedro Patlan; Albert Sanchez.
Res.: 350 Sutton Dr., 78228-3168. Tel: 210-733-7152; Fax: 210-733-0929.
School—(Grades K-8), 307 John Adams, 78228. Tel: 210-732-2741; Fax: 210-732-7702. Mrs. Sandra Sanchez, Prin. Lay Teachers 17; Students 192.
Ministry & Service Office—1201 Donaldson, 78228. Tel: 210-732-8735; Fax: 210-732-6279. Deacon Pedro Patlan, Coord.
Community Center—Tel: 210-736-0055; Fax: 210-738-9600. Mary Davila, Dir.
Learning Center—Tel: 210-738-8715; Fax: 210-738-8403. Marisa Morales, Dir. (Daycare) Children 99.
Catechesis / Religious Program—Yolanda Gutierrez, D.R.E. Students 257.

59—ST. PETER PRINCE OF THE APOSTLES (1923) Very Rev. Eduardo D. Morales; Becky Finley, Admin.; Deacons John Dunn, (Retired); Richard De Hoyos.
Office & Res.: 111 Barilla Pl., 78209. Tel: 210-822-3367; Fax: 210-828-5826.
School—(Grades PreK-8), 112 Marcia Pl., 78209. Tel: 210-824-3171; Fax: 210-822-4504. Ann Lauder, Prin. (PreK 3-8) Lay Teachers 20; Students 279.
Catechesis / Religious Program—Tel: 210-822-1605. Alma Small, D.R.E. Students 149.

60—ST. PHILIP OF JESUS (1914), (Hispanic), Rev. Steven A. Gamez; Deacons Jose Sanchez; Gilbert C. De La Portilla; Myron Benavides.
Res.: 131 Bank St., 78204. Tel: 210-226-5024; Fax: 210-226-9005.
School—(Grades PreK-8), 134 E. Lambert St., 78204. Tel: 210-222-2872; Fax: 210-229-1829. Ana Maria De La Portilla, Prin.; Sr. Irene Arredondo, Librarian. Lay Teachers 15; Aides 2; Students 118.
Catechesis / Religious Program—Tel: 210-225-6622. Sr. Oralia Arzola, M.C.M., D.R.E. Students 308.

61—ST. PIUS X (1957) Rev. Francis McHugh (Ireland); Deacons Eugene Townsend; Daniel T. McShane.
Office: 3303 Urban Crest, 78209. Tel: 210-824-0139; Fax: 210-829-5125.
School—(Grades PreK-8), 7734 Robin Rest Dr., 78209. Tel: 210-824-6431; Fax: 210-824-7454. Mr. Tom Deming, Prin.; Kathy Gray, Librarian. Lay Teachers 21; Students 281.
Catechesis / Religious Program—Humberto Hernandez, Youth Min. Students 227.

62—PRINCE OF PEACE (1980) Rev. Msgr. Patrick Cronin; Deacons Agripino Sanabria; Art Marin; Robert G. Correa; Louis P. Bernal; Heriberto "Eddie" Limas; Wayne Archer; Timothy McCarthy.
Res.: 7893 N. Grissom Rd., 78251. Tel: 210-681-8330; Fax: 210-681-2286.
Catechesis / Religious Program—Tel: 210-681-5063. Students 1,089.

63—RESURRECTION OF THE LORD (1981) Rev. Msgr. Adolfo Valdivia; Deacons Richard Gomez; George Salazar Sr.
Office & Mailing Address: 7990 W. Military Dr., 78227. Tel: 210-675-1470; Fax: 210-675-8203.
Res.: 7151 Cypress Grove, 78227.
Catechesis / Religious Program—Students 445.

64—ST. ROSE OF LIMA (1981) Rev. Msgr. Juan Alfaro; Rev. Virgil Elizondo; Deacons Rey Jasso; Antonio Lira; Chester Ostaszewski; Robert Espinosa; Francisco D. Garcia II.
Res.: 9883 Marbach Rd., 78245. Tel: 210-675-1920; Fax: 210-675-6067.
Catechesis / Religious Program—Students 878.

65—SACRED HEART (1899), (Hispanic), Revs. Walter O. D'heedene, C.I.C.M. (Belgium); Roy Quiogue, C.I.C.M.; Deacons Valentin Gallegos; Rudy Rodriguez.
Res.: 2114 W. Houston St., 78207-3496. Tel: 210-227-5059; Fax: 210-227-6209. Email: sacredheartsa@hotmail.com.
Catechesis / Religious Program—Tel: 210-227-9763. Sr. Juanita Ramirez, M.J.M.J., D.R.E. Students 256.

66—SAN FRANCISCO DE LA ESPADA (1731), (Hispanic), Revs. Herbert Jones, O.F.M.; Lawrence Brummer, O.F.M.
Res.: 10040 Espada Rd., 78214. Tel: 210-627-2064; Fax: 210-627-2059.
Catechesis / Religious Program—Tel: 210-627-2962. Students 153.
Mission—St. Frances Cabrini 1606 San Casimiro, Bexar Co. 78214.

67—SAN JOSE Y SAN MIGUEL (1720), (Hispanic), Revs. J. Antonio Posadas, O.F.M.; Nicholas Baxter, O.F.M.; Deacons Santiago Rodriguez; Frank J. "Chip" Perry III; Mike R. Munoz. In Res., Revs. Charles Gunti, O.F.M.; Edward Boren, O.F.M.
Res.: 701 E. Pyron Ave., 78214. Tel: 210-922-0543; Fax: 210-932-2271.
Catechesis / Religious Program—Tel: 210-923-8681. Joyce Broussard, D.R.E. Students 189.

68—SAN JUAN CAPISTRANO (1731), (Hispanic), Rev. James Gerard Galvin (Scotland), Admin. Pro-Tem.
Mailing Address: P.O. Box 14308, 78214-0308.
Res.: 9101 Graf Rd., 78214.
Church: 78214. Tel: 210-534-3161; Fax: 210-534-2426.
Catechesis / Religious Program—Students 112.
Mission—St. Ann Southton, Bexar Co.

69—SAN JUAN DE LOS LAGOS SHRINE (1952), (Hispanic), Revs. Richard R. Hall, O.M.I.; Ricardo V. Guerra, O.M.I.; Deacons Albert Salinas; Robert Cruz.
Res.: 2918 El Paso St., 78207. Tel: 210-432-5153; Fax: 210-433-9526.
Catechesis / Religious Program—Tel: 210-433-2411. Students 184.

70—SANTO NINO DE CEBU (1993), (Filipino), Revs. Martin Parayno, O.S.B. (Philippines); Anthony Maria Mendoza, O.S.B. (Philippines); Deacons Arsenio Reyes Jr.; Wallace Daniel Kearns; Mrs. Belma De la Cruz, Parish Council Chair. Tel: 830-426-8984.
Mailing Address: 5655 Rigsby Ave., 78222. Tel: 210-648-1705; Fax: 210-648-5365.
Catechesis / Religious Program—Students 98.

71—SHRINE OF ST. PADRE PIO OF PIETRELCINA (2001) Very Rev. Msgr. Patrick J. Ragsdale; Deacons Kevin Kanter; Richard F. Neville Jr.; John Patrick McGarrity; Hipolito Huerta; Joseph Hilbert.
Mailing Address: PMB 611, 20770 Hwy 281 N., Ste. 108, 78258-7500.
Catechesis / Religious Program—Laurie Mielke, D.R.E. Students 456.
Shrine—Shrine of St. Padre Pio 3843 Bulverde Pkwy., 78259. Tel: 210-497-6101; Fax: 210-497-2956.

72—ST. STEPHEN (1965), (Hispanic), Rev. Luis Ruiz.
Res.: 2127 S. Zarzamora St., 78207. Tel: 210-224-8474; Fax: 210-224-8474.
Catechesis / Religious Program—Tel: 210-224-7116. Beatrice Martinez, C.R.E. Students 50.

73—ST. THOMAS MORE (1964) Rev. James A. Kotara; Deacons Jerome Ciarrocchi, (Retired); Paul Charron; Roberto Rosas; Timothy M. Tate Sr.
Res.: 4411 Moana, 78218. Tel: 210-655-5070; Fax: 210-655-8446.
School—(Grades PreK-8), 4427 Moana, 78218. Tel: 210-655-2882; Fax: 210-655-9603. Mirella Kennedy, Prin. Lay Teachers 12; Students 130.
Catechesis / Religious Program—Tel: 210-654-6824. Students 250.

74—ST. TIMOTHY'S (1953), (Hispanic), Rev. Michael DeGerolami; Deacons Rudy Medrano; Antonio Caballero.
Res.: 1515 Saltillo St., 78207. Tel: 210-434-2391; Fax: 210-434-4828.
Catechesis / Religious Program—Patricia Ramos, D.R.E. Students 80.

75—VIETNAMESE MARTYRS CATHOLIC CENTER (1976) Rev. Francis Han Pham, C.Ss.R.
Center—1240 Holbrook, 78218. Tel: 210-646-0726; Fax: 210-533-0558.
Catechesis / Religious Program—Students 70.

76—ST. VINCENT DE PAUL (1961) Rev. Agustin Estrada Fernandez, Admin. Pro Tem; Deacon Apolonio Eduardo Garcia.
Res.: 4222 S.W. Loop 410, 78227-4495. Tel: 210-674-1200; Fax: 210-674-1640.
Catechesis / Religious Program—Tel: 210-674-4291. Lucille O'Barr, C.R.E. Students 428.

OUTSIDE THE CITY OF SAN ANTONIO

BANDERA, BANDERA CO., ST. STANISLAUS (1855), (Polish), [CEM] [JC] Revs. Stanislaw Oleksy, S.D.S.; Gabriel Kamienski, S.D.S., Parochical Vicar; Deacon Robert J. Stein.
Res.: Box 757, 78003-0757. Tel: 830-460-4712; Fax: 830-796-7641.
Catechesis / Religious Program—Tel: 830-796-3573. Elouise Mangold, C.R.E. Students 180.
Mission—St. Victor's Chapel 10514 Park Rd. 37, Lakehills, Bandera Co. 78063. Tel: 830-751-2557.

BOERNE, KENDALL CO., ST. PETER THE APOSTLE (1866), (German), Rev. Anthony O. Cummins; Deacon Paul Rayburg; Mary Ann Hawn, Pastoral Assoc.
Mailing Address: 202 W. Kronkosky St., 78006. Tel: 830-816-2233; Fax: 830-249-6175.
Catechesis / Religious Program—Julia Cortez, D.R.E.; Laura Balderama Contreras, D.R.E.; Sharon Mecke, D.R.E.; Michelle Pechacek, D.R.E. Students 546.

BRACKETTVILLE, KINNEY CO., ST. MARY MAGDALEN (1875) [CEM] Rev. Pius Ezeigbo; Deacons James Bader; Joseph E. Goebel.
Res.: Box 95, 78832. Tel: 830-563-2487; Fax: 830-563-3088.
Catechesis / Religious Program—Students 136.
Mission—St. Blaise Spofford Junction, Kinney Co.

CANYON LAKE, COMAL CO., ST. THOMAS THE APOSTLE (1967) Rev. Msgr. Marvin G. Doerfler; Deacon Paul Hunsucker.
Res.: 180 St. Thomas Dr., 78133-4131. Tel: 830-964-3497; Fax: 830-964-2574.
Catechesis / Religious Program—Christine Hanly, D.R.E./C.R.E. Students 99.

CASTROVILLE, MEDINA CO., ST. LOUIS (1844), (Alsatian), [CEM] Rev. James Conway; Deacons Gene Ebner; Archibald Henson; George White, (Retired).
Res.: 610 Madrid, 78009. Tel: 830-931-2826; Fax: 830-931-9016.
School—(Grades PreK-5) Tel: 830-931-3544; Fax: 830-931-0155. Mr. Larry Dorsey-Spitz, Prin. Lay Teachers 8; Students 137.
Catechesis / Religious Program—Tel: 830-931-2556; Fax: 830-931-2826. Deborah Ruiz, D.R.E. Students 431.
Mission—St. Francis of Assisi (Medina Lake Chapel) Mico, Medina Co.

CESTOHOWA, KARNES CO., NATIVITY OF THE BLESSED VIRGIN MARY (1873), (Polish), [CEM] Rev. Andrzej Waszczenko, S.D.S.
Res.: 300 FM 3191 Cestohowa, Falls City, 78113. Tel: 830-745-2633; Fax: 830-745-9004.
Catechesis / Religious Program—Students 39.

CHARLOTTE, ATASCOSA CO., ST. ROSE OF LIMA (1909), (Hispanic), Rev. Jesus Camacho, Admin. Pro Tem.
Mailing Address: P.O. Box 69, 78011. Tel: 830-277-1242; Fax: 830-274-1700.
Catechesis / Religious Program—Tel: 830-274-1841. Rosa Juarez, D.R.E. Students 53.
Mission—St. Joseph 703 Congress St., P.O. Box 297, Tilden, McMullen Co. 78072. Tel: 361-274-3374.

COMFORT, KENDALL CO., SACRED HEART (1949) Rev. James Cashin.
Mailing Address: P.O. Box 599, 78013-0599. Tel: 830-995-3708.
Church: 510 Broadway, 78013. Tel: 830-995-3708; Fax: 830-995-2952.
Res.: 104 Daniel St., 78013. Tel: 830-995-3501.
Catechesis / Religious Program—Students 131.

CONVERSE, BEXAR CO., ST. MONICA (1959) Revs. Alejandro del Bosque, L.C.; Mauricio Lopez; Deacon Gaspar Gomez.
Res.: 501 North St., P.O. Box 1209, 78109. Tel: 210-658-3816; Fax: 210-566-3821.
School—(Grades Day Care-8) Tel: 210-658-6701; Fax: 210-658-6945. Joann M. Wood, Prin.; Margaret Fischer, Librarian. Lay Teachers 22; Students 510; Day Care 191.
Catechesis / Religious Program—Tel: 210-658-7920. Janice Van Slambrouck, D.R.E. Students 580.

D'HANIS, MEDINA CO., HOLY CROSS (1847), (Hispanic), [CEM] Very Rev. Wallis J. Stiles.
Res.: P.O. Box 426, 78850. Tel: 830-363-7268; Fax: 830-363-7269 (Call before faxing).
Catechesis / Religious Program—Students 133.
Mission—Immaculate Heart of Mary Yancey, Medina Co.

DEL RIO, VAL VERDE CO.

1—ST. JOSEPH'S (1927) [CEM] Rev. Henry Clay Hunt III; Deacons Filomeno Salazar, (Retired); Efrain Santana; Raymundo Mendoza; Ronnie Van Dyke, (Retired).
Res.: 510 Wernett St., P.O. Box 1429, 78841-1429.

Tel: 830-775-4753; Fax: 830-774-7128.
Catechesis/Religious Program—Tel: 830-775-5200. Esther G. Cardenas, D.R.E.; Mr. Evaristo Patino, Coord.; Mrs. Blanca Patino, Coord. Students 636.
2—OUR LADY OF GUADALUPE (1906), (Hispanic), Revs. Salvador Diaz-Llamas, M.N.M.; Javier Uribe Guzman, M.N.M.; Deacons Elieser Hernandez; Adrian Falcon; Juan Padilla.
Office: 505 Cuellar St., 78840.
Res.: 509 Garza St., 78840. Tel: 830-775-3713; Fax: 830-775-9161.
Catechesis/Religious Program—Tel: 830-775-2178. Students 300.
Mission—San Juan Diego Chapel 523 Jeffery Dr., V V Park Estates, Valverde Co. 78840.
3—SACRED HEART (1895) [CEM] Very Rev. James Fischler, C.I.C.M.; Deacons John C. Graf, (Retired); Robert C. Kusenberger; David B. Scarbo; Roger Rodriguez, (Retired).
Mailing Address: P.O. Box 1503, 78841-1503.
Office: 307 E. Losoya, 78840. Tel: 830-775-2143; Fax: 830-775-9902.
Res.: 411 Spring St., 78840. Tel: 830-775-4240.
School—(Grades PreK-8), 209 E. Greenwood, 78840. Tel: 830-775-3274; Fax: 830-774-2800. Mrs. Aurora Guerra, Prin. Lay Teachers 21; Students 201.
Catechesis/Religious Program—Students 183.
Mission—Mary, Queen of the Universe Comstock, Valverde Co.

DEVINE, MEDINA CO., ST. JOSEPH'S (1897) [CEM] Rev. Robert Ploch (Poland).
Res.: 108 S. Washington Dr., 78016. Tel: 830-663-2244; Fax: 830-665-4400.
Catechesis/Religious Program—Students 291.
Mission—St. Augustine Moore, Frio Co. 78057.
Mission—Our Lady of Mt. Carmel Bigfoot, Frio Co. 78005.

DILLEY, FRIO CO., ST. JOSEPH'S (1899), (Hispanic), Rev. Jose Antonio Villanueva; Deacons Bernard Carroll; Salvador Tijerina.
Res.: 114 E. Frio, P.O. Box N, 78017. Tel: 830-965-1926; 830-965-2080 (Office); Fax: 830-965-2080 (Call first).
Catechesis/Religious Program—Steve Lozano, D.R.E. Students 140.
Mission—St. Mary, Frio Co.

ELMENDORF, BEXAR CO., ST. ANTHONY (1896) [CEM] Rev. William McNamara; Deacon John K. Miller.
Mailing Address: P.O. Box 248, 78112.
Res.: 16505 Killowatt Rd., 78112. Tel: 210-635-8539; Fax: 210-635-8644.
Catechesis/Religious Program—Tel: 210-635-8570. Mary Jo Johnson, D.R.E. Students 184.
Mission—Our Lady of Perpetual Help [CEM] Saspamco, Bexar Co.

FALLS CITY, KARNES CO., HOLY TRINITY (1902), (Polish), [CEM] Very Rev. Grzegorz Sawicki, S.D.S. (Poland); Deacon Stanley Kolodzie, (Retired).
Mailing Address: Box 158, 78113. Tel: 830-254-3539; Fax: 830-254-3530.
Res.: 211 W. Meyer St., 78113.
Catechesis/Religious Program—Mary Waitrek, D.R.E. Students 143.

FLORESVILLE, WILSON CO., SACRED HEART (1882) [CEM] Rev. Phillip D. Henning; Deacons Scott Donaho; Doroteo Chavarria; Ralph E. Guerra; Juan A. Bosquez; Frank Castellano.
Res.: 1009 Trail St., 78114. Tel: 830-393-6117; 830-216-7706 (Metro); Fax: 830-393-9071.
School—(Grades 3-5), 1007 Trail St., 78114. Tel: 830-393-2117; Fax: 830-393-6968. Patty Barber, Prin. Lay Teachers 5; Students 55.
Catechesis/Religious Program—Students 413.

FREDERICKSBURG, GILLESPIE CO., ST. MARY'S (1846), (German), [CEM] Rev. Msgr. Enda McKenna; Deacons Gregorio Martinez Jr.; Francisco De La Torre; Patrick Klein; James Bacon, (Retired); Ken Knopp, (Retired).
Mailing Address: 307 W. Main, 78624.
Res.: 309 W. San Antonio St., 78624. Tel: 830-997-9523; Fax: 830-997-1037.
Church: 306 W. San Antonio St., 78624.
School—(Grades PreK-8) Tel: 830-997-3914; Fax: 830-997-2382. Billy Pahl, Prin.; Theresa Walch, Librarian. Lay Teachers 25; Students 301.
Catechesis/Religious Program—Tel: 830-997-9523; Fax: 830-997-1037. Students 451.
Mission—Our Lady of Guadalupe, Gillespie Co.

GONZALES, GONZALES CO., ST. JAMES (1885) [CEM] Rev. Paul A. Raaz; Deacons Alfonso Moreno; Terrence Brennan; John Klapuch.
Res.: 417 N. College St., 78629. Tel: 830-672-2945; Fax: 830-672-1058.
Catechesis/Religious Program—Tel: 830-672-6291. Mrs. Patricia Brennan, D.R.E. Students 528.
Mission—Sacred Heart 426 St. John, Gonzales Co. 78629. Rev. Paul A. Raaz.
Mission—St. Patrick U.S. Hwy. 90 A, Waelder, Gonzales Co. 78959.
Station—Texan Nursing and Rehab, Tel: 830-672-2867.
Station—Hill Country Nursing and Rehab, Tel: 830-672-2887.

HARPER, GILLESPIE CO., ST. ANTHONY'S (1908) [CEM] Rev. Michael E. Peinemann, Admin.; Deacons Curtis Klein; Dennis Link.
Mailing Address: P.O. Box 309, 78631. Tel: 830-864-4026; Fax: 830-864-4379.
Res.: 163 N. Third St., 78631.
Catechesis/Religious Program—Students 34.

HELOTES, BEXAR CO., OUR LADY OF GUADALUPE (1942) [CEM] Very Rev. Msgr. Carlos Davalos; Rev. Cesar Betancourt; Deacons Daniel D. Quaderer; William Thornberry; Joaquin Varela; Peter Gutierrez; Anthony Ludolph; Ernest G. Zepeda; Larry Edwards; Laura Garcia Brill, Pastoral Assoc.
Res.: 13715 Riggs Rd., 78023. Tel: 210-695-8791; Fax: 210-695-9957.
Catechesis/Religious Program—Danna Peaks-Sullivan, D.R.E.; Jon Lamers, Youth Min. (H.S.); Lisa Pena, Youth Min. (Middle School); Ana Alvarado, Youth Min.; Nancy Baize, Youth Min. (Elementary). Students 497.

HOBSON, KARNES CO., ST. BONIFACE (1901), (German—Polish), [CEM] Very Rev. Grzegorz Sawicki, S.D.S. (Poland).
Res.: 358 CR 220, 78117. Tel: 830-780-3559.
Catechesis/Religious Program—Students 34.

HONDO, MEDINA CO., ST. JOHN THE EVANGELIST (1892) [CEM] Rev. Kenneth M. Dakin; Deacons Richard Edminson; John Schoellman; Vangie Pimentel, Admin.
Mailing Address: 2102 Ave. J, 78861. Tel: 830-426-3260; Fax: 830-426-3339.
Catechesis/Religious Program—Tel: 830-741-2513. Sylvia Fernandez, D.R.E. Students 470.

JOURDANTON, ATASCOSA CO., ST. MATTHEW'S (1912) [CEM] Rev. Kazimierz Oleksy, S.D.S.; Deacon Eusebio Guevara.
Mailing Address: P.O. Box 670, 78026.
Res.: 1608 Campbell Ave., 78026. Tel: 830-769-3687; Fax: 830-769-2861.
Catechesis/Religious Program—Students 181.
Mission—St. Ignatius 101 W. Ave. F, Christine, Atascosa Co. 78012.

KARNES CITY, KARNES CO., ST. CORNELIUS (1917) Rev. Stanislaw P. Marciniak.
Res.: 605 E. Calvert St., 78118. Tel: 830-780-3947; Fax: 830-780-3948.
Catechesis/Religious Program—Tel: 830-780-3949. Vivian Janysek, D.R.E. Students 141.
Mission—St. Elizabeth Fashing, Atascosa Co.

KENEDY, KARNES CO., OUR LADY QUEEN OF PEACE (1959) [CEM] Rev. Norbert H. Herman (Poland).
Mailing Address: P.O. Box 89, 78119.
Res.: One Notre Dame Pl., 78119. Tel: 830-583-2417; Fax: 830-583-2410.
Catechesis/Religious Program—Tel: 830-583-2247. Ms. Diana Martinez, C.R.E. Students 110.

KERRVILLE, KERR CO., NOTRE DAME (1889) Rev. Msgr. Michael J. Boulette, Admin. Pro Tem; Rev. Alberto Colin; Deacons Daniel Arriaga; Charles Domingues; Juan A. Martinez; Sonny Kaufhold.
Mailing Address: 909 Main St., 78028.
Res.: 959 Main St., 78028. Tel: 830-257-5961; Fax: 830-895-9771.
School—(Grades PreK-8), 907 Main St., 78028. Tel: 830-257-6707; Fax: 830-792-4370. Ms. Sandra Trujillo-Garcia, Prin. Lay Teachers 20; Students 115.
Catechesis/Religious Program—Tel: 830-896-4233. Students 430.

KIRBY, BEXAR CO., ST. JOAN OF ARC (1971) Rev. Jose Francisco Puente; Deacons John Buchanan, (Retired); Robert Galan Jr.; Gilbert P. Rivera; John X. Huttinger; Wilfredo (Todd) Dapilmoto.
Res.: 2829 Ackermann Rd., 78219-2100. Tel: 210-661-5277; Fax: 210-661-5735.
Catechesis/Religious Program—Tel: 210-661-2220. Students 355.

KOSCIUSZKO, WILSON CO., ST. ANN'S (1898), (Polish), [CEM] Rev. Andrew Waszczenko.
Res.: 8161 FM 541-E, Stockdale, 78160-6554. Tel: 830-745-2541; Fax: 830-745-2434.
Catechesis/Religious Program—Students 39.

LA VERNIA, WILSON CO., ST. ANN (1917) [CEM] Rev. Canon Stanislaw Fiuk (Poland); Deacons Israel Bocanegra; Wesley Rist; Jack Karam.
Res.: 14151 U.S. Hwy. 87 W., 78121. Tel: 830-779-3131; Fax: 830-779-1749.
Catechesis/Religious Program—Tel: 830-253-8124. Marie Gerlich, D.R.E. Students 425.

LACOSTE, MEDINA CO., OUR LADY OF GRACE (1911) [CEM] Rev. Paul Cleary; Deacon Joseph C. Boland.
Mailing address: P.O. Box 39, 78039.
Res.: 15825 Bexar St., 78039. Tel: 830-985-3357 (Office); 830-985-3346 (Rectory); Fax: 830-985-3400.
Catechesis/Religious Program—Tel: 830-985-3355. Mr. Jesse Mendoza, D.R.E. Students 222.
Mission—St. John Vianney 12703 Cinco de Mayo, Bexar Co. 78252.

LOSOYA, BEXAR CO., EL CARMEN CATHOLIC CHURCH (1813), (Hispanic), [CEM], (Our Lady of Mt. Carmel) Rev. Carl R. Maurer.
Res.: 18555 Leal Rd. (Losoya), 78221. Tel: 210-626-2333; Fax: 210-626-1874.
Catechesis/Religious Program—Maria Celia Aldrich, D.R.E. Students 192.

LYTLE, ATASCOSA CO., ST. ANDREW (1904) [CEM] Rev. Romeo D. Olivares, C.I.C.M.
Res.: P.O. Box 326, 78052. Tel: 830-709-9896 (Rectory/Res); 830-709-4287 (Office); Fax: 830-709-0069.
Catechesis/Religious Program—Students 281.
Mission—St. John Bosco Natalia, Medina Co.
Mission—Immaculate Conception P.O. Box 326, Coal Mine, Atascosa Co. 78052.

MACDONA, BEXAR CO., OUR LADY QUEEN OF HEAVEN (1994), (Hispanic), Rev. Msgr. James Janish.
Mailing Address: P.O. Box 94, 78054-0094. Tel: 210-622-3282.
Res.: 11150 Macdona-LaCoste Rd., Atascosa, 78002. Tel: 210-622-9477; Fax: 210-622-0877.
Catechesis/Religious Program—Betty Arredondo, D.R.E. Students 149.

MARTINEZ, BEXAR CO., ST. JEROME (1925) [CEM] Very Rev. John J. Flanagan.
Res.: 7955 Real Rd., 78263. Tel: 210-648-2694; Fax: 210-648-3690.
Catechesis/Religious Program—Tel: 210-260-3489. Sandra Dorsey, D.R.E. Students 205.

NEW BRAUNFELS, COMAL CO.
1—HOLY FAMILY (1964) Rev. Ignatius Himawan, M.S.F.; Deacons Raymond Ybarra; Cayetano Morales.
Res.: 245 S. Hidalgo, 78130. Tel: 830-609-5320; Fax: 830-609-5322.
Catechesis/Religious Program—Tel: 210-608-9615. Angie Kiesling, Rel. Coord. Students 276.
2—OUR LADY OF PERPETUAL HELP (1926) Very Rev. Camillo Botello Jr., M.S.F., Admin. Pro Tem; Deacon Ralph Brock.
Res.: 138 W. Austin St., 78130. Tel: 830-625-3534; Fax: 830-625-3566.
Catechesis/Religious Program—Tel: 830-629-4506. Students 102.
Mission—St. John 210 House St., Comal Co. 78130.
3—SS. PETER AND PAUL (1845) [CEM 2] Rev. Anthony Pesek; Deacons Fred Fey; Ben Wehman; Frank Fikac; William Schroeder; Robert Gorman; Beck E. Knox; Rusty W. Brandt; John Schwartze.
Res.: 386 N. Castell St., 78130. Tel: 830-625-4531; Fax: 830-606-5461.
School—(Grades PreK-8), 198 W. Bridge St., 78130. Tel: 830-625-4531, Ext. 3; Fax: 830-606-6916. Robert J. Whitworth Jr., Prin.; Kathy Foegelle, Librarian. Lay Teachers 25; Students 304.
Catechesis/Religious Program—386 N. Castell, 78130. Tel: 830-625-4531, Ext. 201. Bill Smith, D.R.E. Students 1,042.
Mission—St. Joseph Comal, Comal Co.

NIXON, GONZALES CO., ST. JOSEPH'S (1915) [CEM] Rev. Alfonso Gioppato, O.M.I.; Deacon John Moreno.
Res.: 207 S. Washington Ave., 78140-2920. Tel: 830-582-1127.
Catechesis/Religious Program—Students 105.

PANNA MARIA, KARNES CO., IMMACULATE CONCEPTION OF THE BLESSED VIRGIN MARY (1854), (Polish), [CEM] Rev. Mariusz Lazarek.
Res.: P.O. Box 9, 78144. Tel: 830-780-2748; Fax: 830-780-2334.
Catechesis/Religious Program—Tel: 830-745-2021. Students 55.
Mission—St. Helena Helena, Karnes Co.

PEARSALL, FRIO CO., IMMACULATE HEART OF MARY (1891) [CEM] [JC] Rev. Andrew Kafara (Poland); Deacon Marcus Salazar.
Res.: 422 W. Brazos, P.O. Box AK, 78061. Tel: 830-334-2382; Fax: 830-334-4046.
Catechesis/Religious Program—Tel: 830-334-4046. Students 215.

PLEASANTON, ATASCOSA CO.
1—ST. ANDREW (1913), (Hispanic), [CEM] [JC 3] Very Rev. Gilberto Vallejo; Deacon Bennie Garcia Jr.
Res.: 626 Market St., 78064-2747. Tel: 830-569-3356; 830-281-4902 (Metro); Fax: 830-569-1158.
Catechesis/Religious Program—Elizabeth Lyons, D.R.E. Students 385.
Mission—Sacred Heart Campbell and St. Francis St., Campbellton, Atascosa Co. 78008.
2—ST. LUKE-LOIRE (1859) Rev. Stefan Wiera; Deacon Jose Guadalupe Trevino.
Res.: 3930 FM 536, 78064. Tel: 830-393-6021; Fax: 830-216-4286.
Catechesis/Religious Program—Students 89.
Mission—Our Lady of Guadalupe [CEM] [JC 2] 170 Hackberry St., Leming, Loire Co. 78050.

POTEET, ATASCOSA CO., ST. PHILIP BENIZI (1897), (Hispanic), [CEM] Rev. Albert Lelo, C.I.C.M.
Res.: P.O. Box 348, 78065. Tel: 830-742-3796; 830-742-8985 (Metro); Fax: 830-742-8853.
Catechesis/Religious Program—Rudy Gonzales,

D.R.E. Students 229.

POTH, WILSON CO., BLESSED SACRAMENT (1910) [CEM] Rev. Grzegorz Szewczyk, S.D.S. (Poland); Deacon Alan Crosby.
Mailing Address: P.O. Box 339, 78147.
Res.: 488 W. Westmeyer, 78147. Tel: 830-484-3302; Fax: 830-484-2903.
Catechesis/Religious Program—Tel: 830-484-3303. Students 251.

ROCKSPRINGS, EDWARDS CO., SACRED HEART OF MARY (1900), (Hispanic), [JC] Rev. Sady Nelson Santana, Admin.
Res.: P.O. Box 887, 78880. Tel: 830-683-2165; Fax: 830-683-6165.
Catechesis/Religious Program—Students 91.
Mission—St. Mary Magdalen P.O. Box 610, Camp Wood, Real Co. 78833. Tel: 830-597-5165.
Mission—St. Raymond of Pennafort P.O. Box 989, Leakey, Real Co. 78873. Tel: 830-232-5852. Deacons Ruben Navarro; Warren Seymour.

RUNGE, KARNES CO., ST. ANTHONY'S (1901), (Polish), [CEM 2] Rev. Norbert H. Herman (Poland).
Mailing Address: P.O. Box 188, 78151.
Res.: 101 W. Arenoso St., 78151. Tel: 830-239-4146; Fax: 830-239-4146.
Catechesis/Religious Program—Pablo Nunez, C.R.E. Students 97.

ST. HEDWIG, BEXAR CO., ANNUNCIATION OF THE BLESSED VIRGIN MARY (1855), (Polish), [CEM] Rev. Boleslaw Zadora, S.D.S.
Res.: P.O. Box 100, 78152. Tel: 210-667-1232; Fax: 210-667-9088.
Catechesis/Religious Program—Students 113.

SABINAL, UVALDE CO., ST. PATRICK'S (1884) [CEM] Rev. Antonio X. Hernandez.
Res.: Box 117, 78881. Tel: 830-988-2255; Fax: 830-988-2255.
Catechesis/Religious Program—Students 57.
Mission—St. Joseph Knippa, Uvalde Co.
Mission—St. Mary Vanderpool, Bandera Co.

SCHERTZ, GUADALUPE CO., CHURCH OF THE GOOD SHEPHERD (1972) Rev. Edward A. Pavlicek Jr.; Rev. Msgr. Roger P. Robbins, Parochial Vicar; Cathy Wilkes, Admin.; Deacons John J. Gorman; Paul La Combe, (Retired); George Vick Jr., (Retired); Harvey Balcer; Elmer Fernandez; Robert J. Leibrecht.
Res.: P.O. Box 929, 78154. Tel: 210-658-4350; Fax: 210-658-7051.
Catechesis/Religious Program—Tel: 210-658-6188. Mrs. Geri Grimm, D.R.E.; Mrs. Jean Smith, D.R.E. Students 430.
Mission—Immaculate Conception 213 N. Barnett St., Marion, Guadalupe Co. 78124.

SEGUIN, GUADALUPE CO.

1—ST. JAMES (1873) [CEM] Rev. Msgr. Dennis Darilek; Very Rev. Gregory J. Nevlud; Bruce Peterson, Pastoral Admin.
Res.: 510 S. Camp St., 78155. Tel: 830-379-1796; Fax: 830-379-1797.
School—(Grades PreK-8), 507 S. Camp St., 78155. Tel: 830-379-2878; Fax: 830-379-2878. Deanna Sanchez, Prin.; Kathy Matalik, Librarian. Lay Teachers 13; Students 198.
Catechesis/Religious Program—Tel: 830-379-7689. Antonia Hernandez, D.R.E.; Chachi Diaz, Youth Min. Students 119.

2—OUR LADY OF GUADALUPE (1908), (Hispanic), [CEM] Revs. David Tonary, M.S.F.; Jack Kilburg, M.S.F.; Francois Rakotovoavy, M.S.F., Parochial Vicar; Deacon Nick Carillo; Bro. Rolland Kapsner, M.S.F.
Res.: 409 W. Krezdorn, 78155-4429. Tel: 830-379-4338; Fax: 830-303-1002.
Catechesis/Religious Program—Tel: 830-379-2818. Glenda Moreno, D.R.E. Students 471.
Mission—St. Joseph 5093 Redwood Rd., Redwood, Guadalupe Co. 78666.

SELMA, BEXAR CO., OUR LADY OF PERPETUAL HELP (1897), (German), [CEM] Revs. Jose Luis De la Rosa; Gonzalo E. Razo Meza; Deacons Edward F. Courtney; Louis Heimer.
Res.: 16075 N. Evans Rd., 78154-3824. Tel: 210-651-6913; Fax: 210-651-5272.
School—(Grades PreK-8) Tel: 210-651-6811; Fax: 210-651-5516. Ms. Jacqueline S. Palermo, Prin.; Christine Martinez, Librarian. Sisters 1; Lay Teachers 36; Students 422.
Catechesis/Religious Program—Vilma Vasquez de Torres, D.R.E.; Suzy Krisak, D.R.E. Students 932.

SMILEY, GONZALES CO., ST. PHILIP BENIZI (1963), (Hispanic), Rev. Alfonso Gioppato, O.M.I.; Deacons Frank Rojas, Pastoral Admin. (Retired); John J. Moreno.
Res.: P.O. Box 32, 78159-0032. Tel: 830-587-6258.
Catechesis/Religious Program—Students 40.

SOMERSET, BEXAR CO., ST. MARY'S (1920), (Hispanic), [CEM] Rev. Rolando Rivera, Admin.; Deacon Robert Cruz.
Mailing Address: Box 295, 78069.
Res.: 19711 N. Dixon St., 78069. Tel: 830-701-3123.
Catechesis/Religious Program—Mrs. Sylvia Cruz, D.R.E. Students 180.

SPRING BRANCH, COMAL CO. (HONEY CREEK), ST. JOSEPH (1876) [CEM] Rev. Jimmy David Drennan; Deacons James Legendre, (Retired); Ken Nickel.
Res.: 25781 Hwy. 46 W., 78070-3613. Tel: 830-980-2268; Fax: 830-980-3184.
Catechesis/Religious Program—Nita Kaminski, D.R.E. Students 515.

STOCKDALE, WILSON CO., ST. MARY (1895) [CEM] Rev. Dennis Jarzombek; Deacon Benjamin Gimenez.
Box 535, 78160.
Res.: 1201 W. St. Mary St., 78160. Tel: 830-996-3415; Fax: 830-996-3415.
Catechesis/Religious Program—Students 102.

STONEWALL, GILLESPIE CO., ST. FRANCIS XAVIER (1945), (German—Hispanic), [CEM] Rev. James A. Harnan, M.S.C.
Res.: 400 St. Francis St., P.O. Box 209, 78671-3717. Tel: 830-644-2368; Fax: 830-644-2068.
Catechesis/Religious Program—Students 40.

UVALDE, UVALDE CO., SACRED HEART (1883), (Hispanic), [CEM] Rev. Wieslaw Iwaniec; Deacons Hector V. Garcia; Antonio Hinojosa; Fortunato Hinojosa, (Retired); Gilbert Salazar; Daniel A. Ibarra; Federico Flores.
Res.: 408 Fort Clark St., 78801. Tel: 830-278-3448; Fax: 830-278-2835.
School—(Grades PreK-6) Tel: 830-278-2661; Fax: 830-279-0634. Olivia Talavera, Prin.; Guadalupe Rodriguez, Librarian. Lay Teachers 10; Students 112.
Catechesis/Religious Program—Tel: 830-278-4846. Linda Milam, D.R.E. Students 900.

VON ORMY, BEXAR CO.

1—ST. PETER THE FISHERMAN (1990), (Hispanic), Rev. Miguel Arango-Medina (Colombia); Deacons Richard Wells; Ernesto Bravo.
Office: 17534 N. State Hwy. 16, 78073. Tel: 830-276-8778; 830-276-4985 (Res.); Fax: 830-276-8778.
Catechesis/Religious Program—Students 93.

2—SACRED HEART (1935), (Hispanic), Rev. Msgr. James Janish; Deacons Carlos Rodriguez; Larry Contreras.
Mailing Address: P.O. Box 722, 78073-0722. Tel: 210-622-3457.
Res.: 11150 Macdonna-LaCoste Rd., Atascosa, 78002. Tel: 210-622-9477; Fax: 210-622-0877.
Catechesis/Religious Program—Annalisa Aguirre, D.R.E. Students 151.

KOREAN APOSTOLATE

BOERNE, KENDALL CO., KOREAN MARTYRS CATHOLIC CHURCH (1982), (Korean), Rev. Jea Ho Song.
Res.: 7655 Curres Creek, 78015. Tel: 210-698-3877.

OLD SPANISH MISSIONS

SAN ANTONIO, BEXAR CO., OLD SPANISH MISSIONS *aka Las Misiones* Rev. David Garcia.
Mailing Address: *c/o Pastoral Center*, P.O. Box 28410, 78228.
Purisima Concepcion—807 Mission Rd., 78210. Mailing Address: 125 Whittier St., 78210. Revs. David Garcia, Admin.; N. James Rutkowski.
San Francisco de la Espada—10040 Espada Rd., 78214.
San Juan Capistrano—9101 Graf Rd., 78214.
San Jose—701 E. Pyron Rd., 78214.

Chaplains of Public Institutions

SAN ANTONIO. *Audie Murphy VA Hospital*, 7400 Merton Minter Blvd., 78229. Tel: 210-617-5308. Vacant.
Baptist Memorial Hospital, 111 Dallas St., 78205. Tel: 210-222-8431. Mrs. Pat Sammis.
Brooke Army Medical Center, Tel: 210-916-1105; 210-916-2172; Fax: 210-916-1169. Rev. James E. Schellenberg, D.Min. Tel: 210-916-4141 (After 4:30 pm & weekends).
Res.: 3851 Roger Brooke Blvd., Bldg. 3600, Fort Sam Houston, 78234. Tel: 210-916-4141 (After 4:30pm & Weekends).
St. Luke's Baptist Hospital; University Hospital, 4502 Medical Dr., 78229. Tel: 210-680-2635 (Res.). Rev. Nicholas Brown, S.C.J.
Methodist Hospital, 7700 Floyd Curl, 78229. Tel: 210-692-4030. Revs. Marian Piekarczyk, S.D.S., Joseph Determan, O.P.
San Antonio State Hospital, 6711 S. New Braunfels, 78223. Tel: 210-532-8811. Vacant.
Santa Rosa Hospital System, 519 W. Houston, 78207. Tel: 210-704-2021. Revs. Guillermo Casipong, C.I.C.M., Roy Quiogue, C.I.C.M.
Southwest General Hospital, Tel: 210-921-2000. Deacon Leon Mueller.

KERRVILLE. *Veterans' Administration Hospital*, Tel: 830-896-2020. Sr. Jane McKenzie, O.S.F.

KENEDY. *Texas State Prison System-Connley Unit*, HC 67 Box 115, 78119. Rev. Shaji (Joseph) Varghse, C.C.

Special Assignment:
Revs.—
Dymowski, Thomas H., O.SS.T., Chap., Incarnate Word University, Trinitarian House, 401 Squires Row, 78213. Tel: 210-781-4945
Foster, John Mary, F.J., 1346-A Hueco Springs LP, New Braunfels, 78132. Tel: 830-629-5042
Pillari, Moses de Jesus, 1346-A Hueco Springs Loop, New Braunfels, 78132. Tel: 830-629-5042

On Duty Outside the Archdiocese:
Revs.—
Mannion, Patrick John (Retired), Ireland
Martinez, Manuel, Providence Memorial Hospital, Dept. Spiritual Care, 2001 N. Oregon St., El Paso, 79902.
Pogorelc, Anthony J., S.S., Washington, DC.

Military Chaplains:
Revs.—
Eke, Rafael E. (Nigeria), U.S. Army
Gonzalez, George G., Chap. Major, 4707 Winged Foot Way, Columbus, GA 31909-8006.
Hernandez, Alfred Ricardo, Col. Catholic Chap., 9028 Privilege Point, Converse, 78109. Tel: 210-566-3523
Nee, Eugene O., PSC 50 Box 667, APO, AE 09494.
Tellez, Jairo A., Major, U.S.A.F., Air Police CMR 480, Box 3029, APO, AE 09128.

On Sabbatical:
Rev.—
Maxwell, Palmer

On Leave:
Revs.—
Duran, Jorge
Hernandez, Antonio X.
Kammerer, James
Ruiz, Enrique
Sandoval, Luis
Sieczynski, Jerzey

Retired:
Most Revs.—
Flores, Patrick F., D.D., 80 Peter Baque Rd., 78209. Tel: 210-826-7721
Flanagan, Thomas J., D.D., Oblate Madonna House, 5722 Blanco Rd., 78216-6615.
Popp, Bernard F., D.D., 80 Peter Baque Rd., 78209. Tel: 210-826-7721
Yanta, John W., D.D., 5015 Bayonne, 78228.
Rev. Msgrs.—
Brosnan, Dermot, 80 Peter Baque Rd., 78209. Tel: 210-826-7721
Brosnan, Liam P., 2006 Steves Ave., 78210. Tel: 210-534-7426
Fater, Douglas, 619 Birdsong S., 78258.
Fecher, Vincent, 80 Peter Baque Rd., 78209. Tel: 210-826-7721
Flanagan, Patrick J., 3843 Barrington #204A, 78217. Tel: 210-599-4900
French, Thomas A., 4707 Broadway, 78209. Tel: 210-822-0385
Garcia, Raymond, 80 Peter Baque Rd., 78209. Tel: 210-826-7721
Goertz, Alois J., 8520 Cross Mountain Tr., #100, 78255. Tel: 210-698-9067
Henke, James, 11929 FM 340, Shiner, 77984.
Hubertus, Albert, 8520 Cross Mountain Tr., #4, 78255. Tel: 210-698-8682
Marron, Patrick L., P.O. Box 206, Fischer, 78623-9998.
Martinez, Leo, 80 Peter Baque Rd., 78209. Tel: 210-826-7721
Matocha, John L., 4130 S. Alemeda St., Corpus Christi, 78411-1529.
McManus, Michael, 8520 Cross Mt. Tr., #1102, 78255.
McSwiggan, Thomas, 630 W. Woodlawn, 78212.
Murphy, Thomas, Casa de Padres, 8520 Cross Mountain Tr., 78255.
O'Callaghan, Eugene, 386 N. Castell, New Braunfels, 78130. Tel: 830-606-5461
Palmer, Thomas, 80 Peter Baque Rd., 78209. Tel: 210-826-7721
Petsch, Joseph, Casa de Padres, 8520 Cross Mountain Tr., #702, 78255. Tel: 210-698-7055
Rihn, Roy, 8520 Cross Mountain Tr., #301, 78255. Tel: 210-698-0287
Smith, Sherrill, Padua Place, 80 Peter Baque Rd., 78209. Tel: 210-826-7721
Stuebben, Lawrence J., Casa de Padres, 8520 Cross Mountain Tr., 78255. Tel: 210-288-0988
Vance, Leslie A., J.C.L., 8520 Cross Mountain Tr. #1302, 78255.
Wagner, John A., 8520 Cross Mountain Tr., #202, 78255. Tel: 210-698-1332
Revs.—
Avau, Felix A., C.I.C.M., P.O. Box 1824, Poteet,

78065. Tel: 210-225-0150
Benonis, Richard (PH), P.O. Box 668, Camp Wood, 78833. Tel: 830-597-2230
Dillane, Maurice, Ireland
Ebarb, Walter, 18866 Stoneoak Pkwy., Ste. 103-64, 78258.
Haby, Gerald, S.M., 1403 N. St. Mary's St., 78215.
Heitkamp, Samuel, 764 Fredricksburg Rd., New Braunfels, 78130-6014. Tel: 830-632-5490
Johnston, Robert F., 837 Village Sq., Palm Springs, CA 92262. Tel: 760-322-3236
Kaczkowski, Conrad J., S.M., Ph.D., 5903 Babcock Rd., #1606, 78240. Tel: 210-475-3588
Lampert, Robert E., 4707 Broadway, #180, 78209. Tel: 210-829-8381
Makothakat, John M., Ph.D., S.T.D., J.C.D., 285 Oblate Dr., 78216. Tel: 210-341-1366
Mannion, Patrick John, , Galway Ireland.
Martin, Harry
McKenna, Peter, 123 Trillium, 78213. Tel: 210-366-2188
Mushalla, Walter, P.O. Box 467, Somerset, 78069.
O'Callaghan, Patrick, 630 W. Woodlawn Ave., 78202. Tel: 210-736-3177
Ochoa, Einer, 5825 Elmwood Rd., San Bernardino, CA 92404.
Rubaj, Leon B., Casa de Padres, 8520 Cross Mountain Tr., 78255.
Uribe-Guzman, Francisco J., M.N.M., Our Lady of Guadalupe, 505 Cueller St., Del Rio, 78840. Tel: 830-775-3713
Verboomen, Willy, C.I.C.M., Padua Place, 80 Peter Baque Rd., #11, 78209. Tel: 210-826-7721
Zumaya, David, Mexico

Permanent Deacons:
Abat, Jacques, Our Lady of Perpetual Help, Selma
Adam, Raul, St. Mark the Evangelist, San Antonio
Alcala, Jesse, St. James, San Antonio
Almanza, Jose M., St. Margaret Mary, San Antonio
Alvarado, Thomas, (Retired)
Amo, Ernest Roy, St. Brigid, San Antonio
Anaya, Vacillo, St. John Neumann, San Antonio
Archer, Wayne, Prince of Peace, San Antonio
Arismendez, Agustin, St. Paul, San Antonio
Arredondo, Luis L., St. Bonaventure, San Antonio
Arriaga, Dan, Notre Dame, Kerrville
Bacon, James, St. Mary's, Fredericksburg
Bader, James W., St. Mary Magdalen, Brackettville
Baker, Robert L., (Retired), Thurmont, MD
Balcer, Harvey J., Good Shepherd, Schertz
Barajas, Felipe, Holy Rosary, San Antonio
Behling, James, St. Stanislaus, Bandera
Beinke, George, St. James, Seguin
Bellg, Bruce, (Unassigned)
Benavides, Myron, St. Philip of Jesus, San Antonio
Benigno, Pasquale, St. Louis, Castroville
Berg, Jim, (Unassigned)
Bernal, Louis P., Prince of Peace, San Antonio
Billimek, Thomas E., St. Brigid, San Antonio
Bocanegra, Israel, St. Ann, La Vernia
Boland, Joseph C., Our Lady of Grace, La Coste
Bonilla-Valentin, Jorge, Immaculate Heart of Mary, San Antonio
Borrego, Joe T., St. Anthony of Padua, San Antonio
Bosquez, Juan A., Sacred Heart, Floresville
Bowlin, William R., (Unassigned)
Bozek, Edwin J., Jr., Shrine of St. Padre Pio, San Antonio
Bradley, Donald V., St. Brigid, San Antonio
Brandt, Rusty W., SS. Peter & Paul, New Braunfels
Bravo, Ernesto G., St. Peter the Fisherman, Von Ormy
Brennan, Terrence, St. James, Gonzales
Brock, Ralph, Our Lady of Perpetual Help, New Braunfels
Brumley, Denson C., St. Leonard, San Antonio
Buchanan, John, (Retired)
Burkart, David, Sacred Heart, Comfort
Caballero, Antonio, St. Timothy, San Antonio
Caldwell, Robert M., Jr., St. Leo, San Antonio
Callaway, George, Jr., (Retired)
Camero, A. C., Our Lady of Guadalupe & Jail Ministry, San Antonio
Campa, Gerard, St. Mary Magdalen, San Antonio
Campos, Fred, Jr., St. Gregory the Great, San Antonio
Carranza, Manuel G., Jr., Holy Family, San Antonio
Carrillo, Nick L., Our Lady of Guadalupe, Seguin
Carrizales, Manuel, Immaculate Heart of Mary, Pearsall
Carroll, Bernard, St. Joseph, Dilley
Casanova, Ismael G., St. Margaret Mary, San Antonio
Castellano, Frank V., St. Gabriel, San Antonio
Castillo, Pedro C., Holy Family, San Antonio
Cena, Librado, (Retired), St. John Berchmans, San Antonio
Cervantes, Alfonso, Immaculate Heart of Mary, San Antonio
Charron, Paul, St. Thomas More, San Antonio
Chavarria, Doroteo, Sacred Heart, Floresville
Chavez, Hugo V., St. Luke, San Antonio
Ciarrochi, Jerome, (Retired)
Clancey, Patrick, (On Leave)
Clayton, Brian J., St. Francis of Assisi, San Antonio
Colley, Earl M., Cameron, TX
Contreras, Larry, Sacred Heart, Vonormy
Coronado, Richard T., Annunciation of B.V.M., St. Hedwig
Correa, Robert G., Prince of Peace, San Antonio
Cortinaz, Leonard T., St. Dominic, San Antonio
Courtney, Edward F., Our Lady of Perpetual Help, Selma, TX
Criado, Marcos, Immaculate Conception, San Antonio
Crosby, Alan, Blessed Sacrament, Poth
Cruz, Robert, San Juan de los Lagos, San Antonio
Cruz, Roberto, St. Mary's, Somerset
Cuellar, Pedro Luz, St. Matthew, San Antonio
Cunningham, W. Patrick, Holy Spirit, San Antonio
D'Agostino, Michael, Our Lady of the Atonement, San Antonio
Dapilmoto, Wilfredo M., St. Joan of Arc, Kirby
De Hoyos, Richard, St. Peter Prince, San Antonio
De La Portilla, Gilbert C., St. Philip, San Antonio
De la Torre, Francisco, St. Mary, Fredericksburg
DeCuir, Harold, St. Brigid, San Antonio
DeLaGarza, Gustavo, (On Leave)
DeLaGarza, Ricardo, Divine Providence, San Antonio
DeLeon, Joseph L., (Diocese of Harrisburg, PA)
Delgado, Juan Jose, St. Patrick, San Antonio
Diaz, Jose G., St. John Berchmans, San Antonio
Dillard, Henry, (On Leave)
Dirksen, Kenneth, Sacred Heart, Uvalde
Domingues, Charles, Notre Dame, Kerrville
Donaho, Scott, Jr., Sacred Heart, Floresville
Donias, Justo, (Unassigned)
Ebner, Eugene, St. Louis, Castroville
Edminson, Richard, St. John Evangelist, Hondo
Edwards, Larry, Our Lady of Guadalupe, Helotes
Elliot, Robert R., St. James, Seguin
Enriquez, Marcos, (On Leave)
Espinosa, Jose R., (On Leave)
Espinosa, Juan, St. Brigid, San Antonio
Espinosa, Robert, St. Rose of Lima, San Antonio
Estrada, Melchor, (Unassigned)
Exparza, James, St. Elizabeth Ann Seton, San Antonio
Falcon, Adrian, Our Lady of Guadalupe, Del Rio
Felan, Ruben, Our Lady of Guadalupe, San Antonio
Ferguson, Edward T., St. Francis Xavier, Stonewall
Fernandez, Elmer, Good Shepherd, Schertz
Fertitta, J. V., Sr., Blessed Sacrament, San Antonio
Festa, Eugene A., St. Francis of Assisi, San Antonio
Fey, Fred, Sts. Peter & Paul, New Braunfels
Fikac, Frank J., Sts. Peter & Paul, New Braunfels
Flores, Federico, Sacred Heart, Uvalde
Fox, Thomas J., St. Matthew's, San Antonio
Fraga, Jesse, Our Lady of Sorrows, San Antonio
Franklin, Thomas M., St. Francis of Assisi, San Antonio
Friesenhahn, Clifford, (Retired), Our Lady of Perpetual Help, Selma
Frisina, Patrick, St. Brigid, San Antonio
Galan, Robert, Jr., St. Joan of Arc, Kirby
Gallardo, Frank, Our Lady of Grace, San Antonio
Gallegos, Valentine, Sacred Heart, San Antonio
Galvan, Jesse C., St. Anthony Mary Claret, San Antonio
Galvan, Robert, (Retired)
Garcia, Apolonio Eduardo, St. Vincent de Paul, San Antonio
Garcia, Arturo, St. Lawrence, San Antonio
Garcia, Bennie, St. Andrew, Pleasanton
Garcia, Francisco D., II, St. Rose of Lima, San Antonio
Garcia, Hector, Sacred Heart, Uvalde
Garcia, Julio, III, San Fernando Cathedral, San Antonio
Garcia, Roberto, (On Leave)
Garcia, Victor, St. James, Seguin
Garza, Albert G., (Retired), Cathedral of San Fernando, San Antonio
Garza, Ernesto, St. Matthew, San Antonio
Garza, Jimmy, Basilica of the Little Flower, San Antonio
Garza, Lionel, Jr., (Retired)
Garza, Pedro F., San Fernando Cathedral, San Antonio
Garza, Robert M., St. Luke, San Antonio
Gimenez, Benjamin, St. Mary's, Stockdale
Goebel, Joseph E., St. Mary Magdalen, Brackettville
Gomez, Gaspar, St. Monica, Converse
Gomez, Richard, Resurrection of the Lord, San Antonio
Gonzalez, Amador, St. Bonaventure
Gonzalez, Gerald, St. Leo, San Antonio
Gonzalez, Richard, St. Luke, San Antonio
Gordon, Ralph, (Unassigned)
Gorman, John J., Good Shepherd, Schertz
Gorman, Robert, SS. Peter & Paul, New Braunfels
Gorton, Everett D., (Retired), Shrine of St. Padre Pio, San Antonio
Graf, John E., (Retired)
Greer, Jesse R., (Retired), Church of the Holy Spirit, San Antonio
Guerra, Ralph E., Sacred Heart, Floresville
Guevara, Eusebio, St. Matthew's, Jourdanton
Gustowski, Paul, St. Helena's, San Antonio
Gutierrez, Pedro, Our Lady of Guadalupe, Helotes
Gutierrez, Ramon, (On Leave)
Gutierrez, Trinidad, St. Alphonsus, San Antonio
Hansbauer, Eugene, St. Luke, San Antonio
Heimer, Louis H., Our Lady of Perpetual Help, Selma
Henson, Archibald, St. Louis, Castroville
Herbert, David L., (Retired), Sacred Heart, Von Ormy
Hernandez, Elieser, Our Lady of Guadalupe, Del Rio
Hernandez, Gilbert S., St. Mark the Evangelist, San Antonio
Hernandez, Jose D., St. Lawrence, San Antonio
Herrera, Genaro M., St. Joseph's (South San), San Antonio
Herrera, Ramon, (On Leave)
Hewson, Jim H., St. Francis Assisi, San Antonio
Heye, Paul F., St. Brigid, San Antonio
Hilbert, Joseph, Shrine of St. Padre Pio, San Antonio
Hinojosa, Antonio, Sacred Heart, Uvalde
Hinojosa, Fidel, St. Bonaventure, San Antonio
Hinojosa, Fortunato, (Retired)
Hinojosa, Reynaldo G., Sr., Our Lady of the Atonement, San Antonio
Hobbs, John R., St. Cecilia, San Antonio
Hoelscher, Wilbur L., St. Matthew's, San Antonio
Houle, Thomas W., Prince of Peace, Altus, OK
Houlihan, Timothy, Our Lady of Guadalupe, Helotes, TX
Huerta, Hipolito, Shrine of St. Padre Pio, San Antonio
Huizar, Ernest, St. James, San Antonio
Hunsucker, Paul, St. Thomas the Apostle, Canyon Lake
Huttinger, John X., St. Joan of Arc, Kirby
Ibarra, Daniel A., Sacred Heart, Uvalde
Ibarra, Robert Paiz, St. Leo the Great, San Antonio
Imburgia, Scott, St. Dominic, San Antonio
Jasso, Reynaldo, St. Rose of Lima, San Antonio
Jimenez, Edward G., Jr., St. Jerome, San Antonio
Jiminez, Raymond F., Mission Concepcion, San Antonio
Jorgensen, J. D., Blessed Sacrament, San Antonio
Kanter, Kevin, St. Padre Pio of Pietrelcina, San Antonio
Karam, Jack, St. Mary's, Stockdale
Kattengell, Leon E., (On Leave)
Kaufold, Harold "Sonny", Notre Dame, Kerrville
Kearns, W. Daniel, Senyor Santo Nino de Cebu, San Antonio
Keller, Alois, Jr., (Retired)
King, Charles D., St. Anthony Mary Claret, San Antonio
Klalpuch, John, St. James, Gonzales
Klein, Curtis, St. Anthony, Harper
Klein, Patrick, St. Mary, Fredricksburg
Knopp, Kenneth P., (Retired)
Knox, Beck E., SS. Peter & Paul, New Braunfels
Kolodzie, Stanley, (Retired)
Kozar, Jerome P., St. Anthony Mary Claret, San Antonio
Kusenberger, Robert, Sacred Heart, Del Rio
Kutschenreuter, Norman, St. Matthew's, San Antonio
La Combe, Paul B., (Retired), Good Shepherd, Schertz
Lafuente, Francisco, St. Margaret Mary, San Antonio
Lammons, Charles, St. Jerome, San Antonio
Lara, Rafael, St. Matthew, San Antonio
Laskowski, Norbert C., Holy Trinity, San Antonio
Lauer, Donald E., (Retired), St. Monica, Converse
Leal, Ernesto T., (Retired)
Legendre, James F., (Retired), St. Joseph, Honey Creek, Spring Branch
Leibrecht, Robert J., Good Shepherd, Schertz
Lewis, Brian Anthony, St. Vincent de Paul, San Antonio
Limas, Heriberto "Eddie", Prince of Peace, San Antonio
Limones, Manuel R., St. Joseph, Del Rio
Link, John Dennis, St. Anthony, Harper
Lira, Antonio, St. Rose of Lima, San Antonio
Lira, Rodolfo, Toledo, OH
Longoria, Leobardo, (Retired)
LoTurco, Guy S., Holy Trinity, San Antonio
Lucio, Jesus, Jr., St. Martin de Porres, San Antonio
Ludolph, Anthony, Our Lady of Guadalupe, Helotes

Maldonado, Gilbert M., St. Clare, San Antonio
Marin, Arturo, Prince of Peace, San Antonio
Marques, Steven J., St. Mark the Evangelist, San Antonio
Martinez, Frank, Blessed Sacrament, San Antonio
Martinez, Gregorio, Jr., St. Mary, San Antonio
Martinez, John, (Unassigned)
Martinez, Jose Angel, St. Andrew, Lytle
Martinez, Juan A., Notre Dame, Kerrville
McCarthy, Timothy, Prince of Peace, San Antonio
McGarrity, John Patrick, St. Padre Pio, San Antonio
McShane, Daniel T., St. Pius X, San Antonio
Mechler, Gerardo A., St. Margaret Mary, San Antonio
Medina, Ricardo, St. Lawrence, San Antonio
Medrano, Rudy C., St. Timothy, San Antonio
Menchaca, Jose, St. Martin De Porres, San Antonio
Mendez, Ernest, SS. Peter and Paul, New Braunfels
Mendiola, Gabriel, St. Matthew, San Antonio
Mendoza, Raymundo V., St. Joseph, Del Rio
Merino, Reynaldo Q., Our Lady of Grace, San Antonio
Meyers, Joseph L., (Retired)
Micek, Jerome, Holy Trinity, San Antonio
Michel, John A., St. Pius X, San Antonio
Miller, John K., St. Anthony, Elmendorf
Miller, Mark C., St. Francis Assisi, Harrisburg, PA
Miller, Myles, St. Monica, Cameron
Moczygemba, Zafirin, St. Margaret Mary, San Antonio
Morales, Cayetano, Holy Family, New Braunfels
Moreno, Alfonso, Sacred Heart, Gonzales
Moreno, John J., St. Philip's, Smiley & Nixon
Moreno, Jose F., Our Lady of Angels, San Antonio
Mueller, Leon, (Retired)
Munoz, Mike R., Mission San Jose, San Antonio
Munoz, Roy Y., St. Alphonsus, San Antonio
Muraida, Daniel, St. Paul's, San Antonio
Nanez, Pedro G., San Fernando Cathedral, San Antonio
Navarro, Ruben W., St. Raymond Pennafort, Leakey
Nealis, Michael F., St. Matthew, San Antonio
Nelson, Robert W., (Retired)
Nichols, Jackey Don, St. Luke, San Antonio
Nickel, Kenneth F., St. Joseph, Honey Creek & Spring Branch
Novian, Donald, (On Leave)
Ocampo, Jose L., St. Gerard, San Antonio
Olivares, Jesse, (Unassigned)
Olivares, Peter, St. Henry, San Antonio
Orr, James, Our Lady of Atonement, San Antonio
Ostaszewski, Chester R., St. Rose of Lima, San Antonio
Padilla, Juan R., O.L., Guadalupe, Del Rio
Patlan, Antonio, St. Martin de Porres, San Antonio
Patlan, Pedro, St. Paul, San Antonio
Peche, William, Holy Spirit, San Antonio
Pedroza, Doroteo E., San Fernando, San Antonio
Perez, Julio T., (Diocese of San Angelo)
Perez, Miguel, Jr., St. Joseph, Devine
Perez, Oscar, Holy Trinity, San Antonio
Perry, Frank J. "Chip", III, San Jose Mission, San Antonio
Pope, Charles F., Sr., St. Clare, San Antonio
Portele, Michael, St. Francis of Assisi, San Antonio
Prevott, Raymond, (Retired)
Quaderer, Daniel D., Our Lady of Guadalupe, Helotes
Ramirez, Albert, Our Lady of Angels, San Antonio
Ramirez, Victor, (Retired)
Ramos, Bartolo, St. Jude, San Antonio
Raso, James, St. Benedict, San Antonio
Rayburg, Paul M., St. Peter, Boerne
Resendiz, Benito, St. Martin de Porres, San Antonio
Reyes, Arsenio, Jr., Santo Nino de Cebu, San Antonio
Richard, Joseph, (On Leave)
Riojas, Francisco, St. Philip, Smiley & Nixon
Rios, Roberto, St. Matthew, San Antonio
Rist, Wesley Raymond, St. Ann, La Vernia
Rivera, Antonio, St. Matthew, San Antonio
Rivera, Gilbert, St. Joan of Arc, Kirby
Rodriguez, Antonio G., Basilica of Little Flower, San Antonio
Rodriguez, Carlos, Sacred Heart, Von Ormy
Rodriguez, Jesus, St. John Berchmans, San Antonio
Rodriguez, Roger, Sacred Heart, Del Rio, TX
Rodriguez, Rudolph, Sacred Heart, San Antonio
Rodriguez, Santiago, San Jose Mission, San Antonio
Rosas, Gabriel J., St. Margaret Mary, San Antonio
Rosas, Roberto, St. Thomas More, San Antonio
Ruiz, Roberto R., Espada Mission, San Antonio
Salazar, Filomeno, St. Joseph, Del Rio
Salazar, George, Sr., Resurrection of the Lord, San Antonio
Salazar, Gilberto, Sacred Heart, Uvalde
Salazar, Marcus, Immaculate Heart of Mary, Pearsall
Salazar, Richard B., Holy Rosary, San Antonio
Salinas, Alberto, San Juan DeLos Lagos, San Antonio
Salinas, Carlos, (Retired)
Sanabria, Agripino, Prince of Peace, San Antonio
Sanchez, Albert, St. Paul, San Antonio
Sanchez, Jose H., St. Philip of Jesus, San Antonio
Sandoval, Carlos, Our Lady of Guadalupe, San Antonio
Sandoval, Jose F., St. John Berchmans, San Antonio
Santana, Efrain, St. Joseph, Del Rio
Scarbo, David B., Sacred Heart, Del Rio
Schoellman, John J., St. John Evangelist, Hondo
Schroeder, William, SS. Peter and Paul, New Braunfels
Schwartze, John, SS. Peter & Paul, New Braunfels
Seguin, David R., St. Mark the Evangelist, San Antonio
Sekinger, Eugene E., Mc Allen, TX
Seymour, Warren V., (Retired)
Shockley, Gordon F., (Retired)
Shoemake, William, (Diocese of San Angelo)
Simmonds, William I., St. Anthony of Padua, San Antonio
Stein, Robert J., St. Stanislaus, Bandera
Stenstrom, James, St. Peter the Apostle, Boerne
Stewart, Wilbert, St. Dominic, San Antonio
Stockton, Ree, St. Dominic, San Antonio
Stokes, Leslie, (Diocese of Phoenix)
Suniga, Jose A., St. Patrick, San Antonio
Svatek, Anton, (Retired)
Tamez, Javier, (On Leave)
Tate, Timothy M., Sr., St. Thomas More, San Antonio
Telfer, James, (On Leave)
Terry, Frank, (Retired)
Thayer, Robert, Annunciation, St. Hedwig
Thornberry, William, Our Lady of Guadalupe, Helotes
Tijerina, Salvador, St. Joseph, Dilley
Torres, George R., St. Joseph, Devine
Torres, Thomas, San Jose Mission, San Antonio
Townsend, Eugene, St. Pius X, San Antonio
Trevino, Jose S., St. Luke Loire, Pleasanton
Trujillo, Jose M., (Diocese of San Angelo)
Uriegas, Gonzalo, (Retired)
Valdez, Oscar J., St. Luke, San Antonio
Van Dyke, Ronnie, St. Joseph, Del Rio
Varela, Joaquin, Our Lady of Guadalupe, Helotes
Vick, George, Jr., (Retired)
Villanueva, Luis, St. Joseph, Devine
Villareal, Ricardo, St. Cecilia, San Antonio
Von Allmen, Charles, St. James, San Antonio
Wasniewski, Michael S., (Unassigned)
Wehman, Ben, Sts. Peter and Paul, New Braunfels
Weissler, Gilbert, St. Anthony of Padua, San Antonio
Wells, Richard, St. Peter The Fisherman, Von Ormy
Werner, Keith N., (Retired), St. Matthew, San Antonio
White, George, (Retired)
Wittig, Evan, Holy Spirit, San Antonio
Ybarra, Hermengildo Rey, St. Leonard, San Antonio
Ybarra, Raymond, Holy Family, New Braunfels
Zamora, David, St. Mary Magdalen, San Antonio
Zapata, Thomas, (On Leave)
Zepeda, Ernest G., Our Lady of Guadalupe, Helotes

INSTITUTIONS LOCATED IN THE ARCHDIOCESE

[A] SEMINARIES, ARCHDIOCESAN

SAN ANTONIO. *Assumption Seminary aka Assumption-St. John's Seminary* 2600 W. Woodlawn Ave., P.O. Box 28240, 78228. Tel: 210-734-5137; Fax: 210-734-2324. Web: www.assumptionseminary.org. Revs. Jeffery Pehl, Rector/Pres.; John Collet, O.M.I., Spiritual Dir.; James S. Tucker, S.S., Dir. Spirituality; Mrs. Amy Zuberbueler, Dir. Music; Chris Stravitsch, M.A., Dir. Collegians & Admissions; Revs. Arnold Ibarra, Vice Rector; Michael E. Peinemann, Formation Faculty; Antonio Ortiz, Formation Faculty; Alex Pereida, Vocation Dir. of Seminarians; Jonathan W. Felux, Dir.; Virgil Elizondo, Vice Rector; Martin L. Elsner, S.J., Spiritual Dir.; Jose Ramon Perez-Martinez, Formation; Augustin Estrada, Formation.

The Seminary of the Assumption of the Blessed Virgin Mary-St. John of San Antonio, TX Priests 11; Sisters 2; Seminarians 91; Domestic Dept.: Josephine Sisters (Mexico City, Mexico) 14; Lay Staff 3.

Diaconate Program, Pastoral Center, P.O. Box 28410, 78228-0410. Tel: 210-734-2620; Fax: 210-734-1626. Email: diacprog@swbell.net. Rev. Msgr. Patrick Ragsdale, V.U., Dir.

[B] SEMINARIES, RELIGIOUS OR SCHOLASTICATES

SAN ANTONIO. *Congregation of Holy Cross - Formation Community* (1989) Bro. Charles Andersen Residence, 320 Brahan Blvd., 78215-1020. Tel: 210-223-9117. Bro. Michael Winslow, C.S.C., B.A., M.A., Dir. Brothers 3.

Dominican Missionaries for the Deaf Apostolate House of Studies, 143 Honeysuckle Ln., 78213-2527. Tel: 210-627-6303. Web: dominicanmissionaries.org. Rev. Thomas Coughlin, O.P.Miss., Prior Gen.; Bro. Erick Kumana, O.P.Miss., Subprior. Seminarians 5; Postulants 3; Novices 4.

George Sexton House of Studies (Theology), 314 E. King's Hwy., 78212. Tel: 210-735-7318; Fax: 210-734-3150. Revs. James F. Allen, O.M.I.; Raul Salas, O.M.I.; Paul Waldie, O.M.I. Missionary Oblates of Mary Immaculate, United States Province. Scholastic Brothers 13.

MSF Formation Community, 3126 W. Ashby Pl., 78228. Tel: 210-344-9145; Fax: 210-344-9146. Web: www.catholic-forum.com/msf. Rev. James Wasser, M.S.F., Dir. of Formation. Priests 1; Brothers 1.

San Antonio de Padua Friary (Franciscan Friars), 318 Oblate Dr., 78216-6632. Tel: 210-377-2518. Email: jcrofm@ymail.com. Web: www.olgofm.org. Rev. Jack Clark Robinson, O.F.M., Dir. Formation. Priests 2; Brothers 1; Seminarians 4.

San Damiano Friary, Prenovitiate House of Formation, 1104 Kentucky Ave., 78201. Tel: 210-734-4962. Revs. Martin Day, O.F.M.Conv.; Lawrence Mattingly, O.F.M.Conv.; Gary W. Johnson, O.F.M.Conv.; Phillip Ley, O.F.M.Conv.; Bro. Timothy Unser, O.F.M.Conv. Conventual Franciscan Friars. Pre-Novitiates 4; Professed 5; Post Novitiates 3.

[C] COLLEGES AND UNIVERSITIES

SAN ANTONIO. *St. Mary's University of San Antonio, Texas* (1852) One Camino Santa Maria, 78228-8572. Tel: 210-436-3722; Fax: 210-431-2226; 210-431-6864 (Alumni Relations). Email: ccotrell@stmarytx.edu. Web: www.stmarytx.edu. Dr. Charles Cotrell, Pres.; Rev. Rudy Vela, S.M., Vice Pres. Mission & Identity; Dr. Andre Hampton, J.D., Interim Vice Pres. Academic Affairs; Rebeckah J. Day, Vice Pres. Admin. & Finance; Mrs. Katherine Sisoian, Vice Pres. Student Devel.; Mrs. Suzanne Petrusch, Vice Pres. Enrollment Mgmt.; Dr. Janet Dizinno, Ph.D., Dean School of Humanities & Social Sciences; Rocky Kettering, Ed.D., Vice Pres. Univ. Advancement; Dr. Tanja Singh, D.B.A., Interim Dean, Bill Greehey School of Business; Dr. Winston Erevelles, Ph.D., Dean School of Science, Engineering and Technology; Dr. Henry Flores, Dean Graduate School; Mr. Charles Cantu, LL.M., Dean School of Law; Chad Bridwell, Dir. Admissions; Dr. H. Palmer Hall, Ph.D., Dir. Louis J. Blume Academic Library; Christopher Cantu, Marianist Leadership; Robert Hu, Dir. Law Library; Dr. Grace Walle, F.M.I., Chap. Law School; Revs. Norbert C. Brockman, S.M.; Conrad J. Kaczkowski, S.M., Ph.D. (Retired); John A. Leies, S.M., S.T.D.; George T. Montague, S.M.; W. Franz Schorp, S.M.; Richard Wosman, S.M.; Charles Stander, S.M. Conducted by the Society of Mary., (Coed) Priests 5; Brothers 4; Sisters 1; Lay Teachers 357; Students 4,188.

The Mexican American Catholic College (1972) 3115 W. Ashby Pl., 78228-5104. Tel: 210-732-2156; 886-893-6222; Fax: 210-732-9072. Web: www.maccsa.org. Most Rev. Oscar Cantu, S.T.D., Chm.; Arturo Chavez, Ph.D., Pres. & CEO; Juanita Garcia, Librarian. The Mexican American Catholic College (MACC)'s mission is to empower and educate leaders for service in a culturally diverse Church and society by offering a bi-literate, multicultural formation program that can lead to a BA and MA degree in Pastoral Ministry. MACC offers a holistic program that integrates the four elements of ministry formation — the human, spiritual, intellectual and pastoral dimensions; MACC has been a leader in higher education since 1972, providing excellent courses that are accepted for credit by many accredited institutions. The Continuing Education courses and workshops continue to prepare leaders for service in Hispanic and Multicultural communities; The Mexican American Catholic College sponsors a Ministry Formation Program with Hispanic Ministry for the 21st Century, Hispanic Pastoral Ministry, and Language Studies which is accredited by the United States Conference of Catholic Bishops Commission on

Certification and Accreditation, 3211 S. Lake Dr., Ste. 317, St. Francis, WI 53235 (414-486-0139). Religious 4; Lay Teachers 24; Staff 20; Students 50.

Oblate School of Theology (1903) (Coed) (Graduate Theology), 285 Oblate Dr., 78216-6693. Tel: 210-341-1366; Fax: 210-341-4519. Email: info@ost.edu. Web: www.ost.edu. Rev. Ronald Rolheiser, O.M.I., Pres.; Dr. Scott Woodward, Dean, Vice Pres. Academic Affairs; Mrs. Rose A. Marden, M.T.S., M.Div., Continuing Educ. Assoc. Dean; Mr. James Oberhausen, Dir. Admissions, Registrar; Mr. Morris Lim, Dir. Physical Plant; Mr. Rene Espinosa, Vice Pres. Finance & Human Resources; Ms. Elva Barba, Admin. Asst. Pres. Conducted by the Missionary Oblates of Mary Immaculate. Priests 19; Sisters 6; Brothers 1; Lay Professors 8; Students 191.

Faculty: Revs. Ken Hannon, O.M.I., Ph.D.; Jan Piotr Klak, Ph.L., S.T.L.; John M. Makothakat, Ph.D., S.T.D., J.C.D. (Retired); Vicente Louwagie, O.M.I., Dir. Ministry to Ministers & Intl. Priests Prog. Tel: 210-349-9928; Francis Kelly Nemeck, O.M.I., S.S.D.; Leopoldo G. Perez, O.M.I., S.T.D., M.Div., Asst. Prof. Moral Theology; Joseph LaBelle, O.M.I., S.T.D., Dir. M.A. Sp. Prog.; Stephen K. Sherwood, C.M.F., S.T.D.; Rocky Grimard, O.M.I., Dir. Opers.; Robert E. Wright, O.M.I., Ph.D., Co-Dir. M. Div. Prog.; Sisters Maria Cimperman, O.S.U., Ph.D.; Sarah Ann Sharkey, O.P., Ph.D.; Mrs. Bonnie Le Melle Abadie, Dir. Lay Ministry; Mrs. Rita Velasquez, Asst. Dir. Lay Ministry; Mrs. Sally T. Gomez-Jung, M.T.S., M.A., Dir. T.F.E.; Sisters Susan Pontz, S.S.C.M., IT Dir.; Laura Gonzalez, S.S.C.J., Asst. Dir. Ministry to Ministers; Dr. Ronald Quillo, Th.D., Dir. M.A.(TH) Prog.; Dr. Ed Alcott; Rev. John Markey, O.M.I., Ph.D., Dir.; Dr. Greg Zuschlag, Ph.D., M.A., Dir.; Renata Furst, Asst. Prof. Sacramental Scripture; Sr. Linda Gibler, O.P., Assoc. Academic Dean.

**Our Lady of the Lake University*, 411 S.W. 24th, 78207-4689. Tel: 210-434-6711; Fax: 210-438-9496. Email: pollt@lake.ollusa.edu. Web: www.ollusa.edu. Dr. Tessa Martinez Pollack, Ph.D., Pres.; David C. Estes, Ph.D., Exec. Vice Pres.; Gloria Urrabazo, Vice Pres. Mission & Ministry; Allen R. Klaus, B.B.A., Vice Pres. Finance & Facilities; Michael E. Acosta, Vice Pres. Enrollment; Daniel J. Yoxall, Vice Pres. Inst. Advancement; Mrs. Susan Schleicher, Communications; Helen J. Streubert, Ed.D., Vice Pres. Academic Affairs; Judith Larson, Dean Library. Sponsored by Congregation of Divine Providence. Sisters 4; Lay Teachers 234; Students 2,614.

Campus Ministry Team: Sr. Joyce Detzel, C.D.P., Dir.

The United Colleges of San Antonio (A Consortium of Catholic Colleges in San Antonio), 285 Oblate Dr., 78216. Tel: 210-341-1366; Fax: 210-341-4519. Rev. Ronald Rolheiser, O.M.I.; Charles L. Cotrell, Ph.D.; Dr. Louis Agnese Jr., Ph.D.; Dr. Tessa Martinez Pollack, Ph.D.

University of the Incarnate Word, 4301 Broadway, 78209. Tel: 210-829-6000; Fax: 210-829-3901. Email: douge@uiwtx.edu. Web: www.uiw.edu. Dr. Louis J. Agnese Jr., Ph.D., Pres.; Sr. Kathleen Coughlin, C.C.V.I., Vice Pres. Inst. Advancement; Douglas B. Endsley, M.B.A., C.P.A., Vice Pres. Fin. & Technology; Dr. David Jurenovich, Ph.D., Vice Pres. Enrollment & Student Svcs.; Kevin B. Vichcales, Ph.D., Dean, Graduate Studies & Research; Marcos Fragojo, Vice Pres. Intl. Programs; Dr. Denise Doyle, Ph.D., Provost; Dr. Renee Moore, Ph.D., Dean Campus Life; Andrea Cyterski-Acosta, Dean of Enrollment; Annette Thompson, Dir. Human Resources; Dr. Shawn Daly, Ph.D., Dean, HEB School of Business Admin.; Dr. Arcelia Johnson-Fannin, Ph.D., Dean Feik School of Pharmacy; Elisabeth F. Villarreal, Dir. Campus Min.; Sr. Eilish Ryan, Th.D., Chm. Pastoral Institute; Dr. Bobbye Fry, Ed.D., Registrar; Dr. Robert Connelly, Ph.D., Dean, College of Humanities, Arts & Social Sciences; Dr. Glenn E. James, Ph.D., Dean, School of Math, Science & Engineering; Dr. Kathleen Light, Ph.D., Dean, School of Nursing & Health Professionals; Dr. Cheryl Anderson, Dean, Library Svcs.; Edith Cogdell, C.P.A., Comptroller; Dr. Cyndi Wilson Porter, Vice Pres. Extended Academic Programs; Vincent Porter, Dean, School of Extended Studies; Rita Russ, Dean, Virtual Univ.; Dr. Andrew Buzzelli, Interim Dean of Optometry; Dan Ochoa, Dean, Univ. Preparatory Programs; Sharon Welkey, Dean, School of Media & Design. Priests 2; Charity of the Incarnate Word 3; Lay Faculty 231; Students 7,708.

[D] HIGH SCHOOLS, ARCHDIOCESAN

SAN ANTONIO. *Antonian College Preparatory High School*, 6425 West Ave., 78213. Tel: 210-344-9265; Fax: 210-344-9267. Email: gsaenz@Antonian.org. Web: Antonian.org. Mr. Gilbert L. Saenz, Prin.; Rev. John G. Castro, O.M.I.; Marlene Graham, Librarian. (Coed) Priests 1; Deacons 1; Lay Teachers 50; Students 762.

St. Gerard Catholic High School, 521 S. New Braunfels Ave., 78203. Tel: 210-533-8061; Fax: 210-533-3697. Email: beebee.rodriguez@stgerardsa.org. Web: www.stgerardsa.org. Very Rev. Kevin Fausz, C.M., V.U., Admin.; Maurice Abadie, Dir. Devel. & Alumni; Peter Rivera, Prin.; Blanca Gonzalez, Librarian. Sisters 3; Lay Teachers 11; Students 114.

NEW BRAUNFELS. *John Paul II High School*, 6720 FM 482, 78132. Tel: 830-643-0802; Fax: 830-643-0806. Web: www.johnpaul2chs.org. Andrew Iliff, Prin. Staff 16; Students 100.

[E] HIGH SCHOOLS, REGIONAL

KERRVILLE. *Our Lady of the Hills Regional Catholic High School* (2002) 235 Peterson Farm Rd., 78028. Tel: 830-895-0501; Fax: 830-895-3470. Email: olh@ourladyofthehills.org. Web: www.ourladyofthehills.org. Mrs. Therese Schwarz, Prin.; Lynette Jackson, Librarian. Lay Teachers 18; Total Enrollment 107.

[F] HIGH SCHOOLS, PRIVATE

SAN ANTONIO. *St. Anthony Catholic High School*, 3200 McCullough Ave., 78212-3099. Tel: 210-832-5600; 210-832-5603; Fax: 210-832-5615. Email: rjescobe@uiwtx.edu. Web: www.sachs.org. Rene Escobedo, Prin.; Rev. Carl Frisch; Douglas B. Endsley, M.B.A., C.P.A., Vice Pres. Business & Finance; Debra Bryant, Librarian. Priests 1; Sisters 1; Lay Teachers 34; Students 430.

Central Catholic High School, 1403 N. St. Mary's St., 78215-1785. Tel: 210-225-6794; Fax: 210-227-9353. Email: admissions@cchs-satx.org. Web: www.cchs-satx.org. Bro. Peter Pontolillo, S.M., Pres.; Mr. Edward Ybarra, Prin.; Revs. Donald Cowie, S.M.; Patrick McDaid, S.M.; B.J. Schanzer, Librarian. Priests 2; Brothers 6; Deacons 1; Lay Teachers 44; Students 556.

Healy Murphy Center, Inc., 618 Live Oak St., 78202. Tel: 210-223-2944; Fax: 210-224-1033. Email: dwatson@healymurphy.org. Douglas J. Watson, Exec. Dir.; Janie Whiteley, Prin.; Gene Brown, Librarian. Day School for High School Students. Provides an alternative to the Regular School System. Sisters 3; Lay Teachers 17; Counselors 2; Nurses 1; On Campus Clinic: Nurses 1; Students 300; Childhood Development Department: Ages 6 wks - 5 yrs 110.

Holy Cross of San Antonio, (Grades 6-12), 426 N. San Felipe, 78228. Tel: 210-433-9395; Fax: 210-433-1666. Email: SAHCMAN@hotmail.com. Web: www.holycross-sa.org. Bro. Stanley Culotta, C.S.C., Pres.; Henry Galindo, Prin.; Mrs. Karen Braeuler, Librarian. Brothers of Holy Cross. Brothers 2; Lay Teachers 32; Students 430.

Incarnate Word High School, 727 E. Hildebrand Ave., 78212-2598. Tel: 210-829-3100; Fax: 210-829-3120. Web: www.incarnatewordhs.org. B.J. Nelsen, Prin.; Michiko Tonegawa, Librarian. Sisters 2; Brothers 1; Lay Teachers 43; Students 514.

Providence Catholic School, (Grades 6-12), 1215 N. St. Mary's St., 78215-1737. Tel: 210-224-6651; Fax: 210-224-6214. Web: www.providencehs.net. Ms. Alicia Garcia, Prin.; Charlene Ibrom, Academic Vice Prin.; Stella Gonzalez, Librarian. Sisters 4; Lay Teachers 38; Students 372.

[G] ELEMENTARY SCHOOLS, PRIVATE

SAN ANTONIO. *St. Anthony's School*, (Grades PreK-8), 205 W. Huisache St., 78212. Tel: 210-732-8801; Fax: 210-732-5968. Email: pramirez@stanthonysa.org. Web: www.stanthonysa.org. Patricia Ramirez, Prin.; Rev. Patrick Guidon, O.M.I.; Laurie Packard, M.L.S., Librarian. Priests 1; Lay Teachers 49; Students 399.

St. John Bosco School (1944) (Grades K-8), 5630 W. Commerce St., 78237. Tel: 210-432-8011; Fax: 866-214-8083. Email: fmasuojbc@aol.com. Sr. Rosann Ruiz, F.M.A., Pres.; Mrs. Roxanne LeBlanc, Prin.; Linda Gonzales, Librarian. Institute of the Daughters of Mary Help of Christians (Salesian Sisters of St. John Bosco)., Day School. Sisters 10; Lay Teachers 14; Students 277.

St. John Bosco Child Development Center Mrs. Sandra Guerrero, Dir. Staff 18; Students 75.

Mount Sacred Heart School, Inc., (Grades PreK-8), 619 Mount Sacred Heart Rd., 78216. Tel: 210-342-6711; Fax: 210-342-4032. Email: mcasto@msheagles.com. Web: www.mountsacredheart.com. Ms. Maria V. Casto, Prin.; Shantel Ramirez, Librarian. Sisters 2; Lay Teachers 30; Students 421.

**Rolling Hills Academy, Inc.* (1996) (Grades PreK-8), 21240 Gathering Oak, 78260. Tel: 210-497-0323; Fax: 210-497-5192. Email: info@rhacademy.org. Rick McCormick, Prin.; Revs. Jose Felix Ortega, L.C.; Javier Fayos, L.C.; Carmel Chapline, Librarian. Priests 1; Lay Teachers 19; Students 215.

PLEASANTON. *Our Lady of Grace Academy*, (Grades PreK-3), 626 Market St., 78064. Tel: 830-569-8073; Fax: 830-569-8073. Margie Coleman, Prin. Staff 8; Students 49.

[H] GENERAL HOSPITALS

SAN ANTONIO. *Christus Santa Rosa Children's Hospital*, 333 N. Santa Rosa Blvd., 78207. Tel: 210-704-2011; Fax: 210-704-3632. Email: marcy.doderer@christushealth.org. Web: www.christussantarosa.org. Marcela Doderer, Regl. Vice Pres. & Admin. Owned and operated by Christus, Santa Rosa Health Care Corp. Licensed Beds 196; Total Staff 852; Patients Assisted Annually 5,983.

Christus Santa Rosa Health Care Corporation, 333 N. Santa Rosa Blvd., 78207. Tel: 210-704-2011; Fax: 210-704-3632. Web: www.christussantarosa.org. Patrick Carrier, Pres. & CEO; Rosario Perez, Mission, Integration, Outreach; Mary Davis, Dir. Pastoral Ministry; Revs. Guillermo Casipong, C.I.C.M.; Roy Quiogue, C.I.C.M.; Victor LaRoche, O.P. Health related activities Priests 3; Sisters 3; Staff 4,300; Bed Capacity 1,128; Patients Assisted Annually 400,000.

Christus Santa Rosa Hospital - Alamo Heights, 403 Treeline Park Dr., 78209.

Christus Santa Rosa Hospital-City Centre, 333 N. Santa Rosa Blvd., 78207. Tel: 210-704-2011; Fax: 210-704-3632. Web: www.christussantarosa.org. Gerry Rodriguez, Interim Regl. Vice Pres. & Admin. Owned and operated by Christus, Santa Rosa Health Care Corp. Licensed Beds 419; Patients Assisted Annually 69,000; Total Staff 1,135.

Christus Santa Rosa Hospital, Westover Hills Owned & operated by Christus Santa Rosa Health Care Corp., 11212 Hwy. 151, 78251. Tel: 210-703-8000. Jeff Bourgeois, Vice Pres. & Admin. Bed Capacity 150; Staff 350.

Christus Santa Rosa Hospital-Medical Center, 2827 Babcock Rd., 78229. Tel: 210-705-6300; Fax: 210-705-6094. Email: reza.kaleel@ChristusHealth.org. Web: www.christussantarosa.org. Reza Kaleel, Regl. Vice Pres. & Admin. Bed Capacity 178; Staff 560; Patients Assisted Annually 39,000.

Christus Santa Rosa Rehabilitation Hospital (Part of CRSH - Medical Center), 2827 Babcock, 78229. Tel: 210-705-6100; Fax: 210-705-6028. Owned and operated by Christus Health, Santa Rosa Health Care Corp. Bed Capacity 35; Staff 120; Patients Assisted Annually 9,300.

San Fernando Health Care Centre of San Antonio, 2718 W. Woodlawn, 78228. Tel: 210-734-2620. Rev. Martin J. Leopold, Contact Person.

NEW BRAUNFELS. *Christus Santa Rosa Hospital-New Braunfels*, 600 N. Union Ave., 78130. Tel: 830-606-9111. Web: www.christussantarosa.org. Jim Wesson, Regl. Vice Pres. & Admin. Owned and operated by Christus, Santa Rosa Health Care Corp. Licensed Beds 112; Patients Assisted Annually 6,138; Total Staff 537.

[I] PROTECTIVE INSTITUTIONS

SAN ANTONIO. *Father Flanagan's Boys' Town of San Antonio*, 503 Urban Loop, 78204. Tel: 210-271-1010; Fax: 210-271-3333. Email: janie.cook@boystown.org. Web: www.boystown.org. Ms. Janie Cook, Pres. Total Staff 49; Bed Capacity 61; Children Under Care 722.

Residential Center: Foster Family Service Homes, 8400, 8401, 8402, 8405, 8406 Flanagan St., 78249. Tel: 210-271-1010; Fax: 210-271-3333. (For Children under 18) Staff 25; Bed Capacity 30; Children Served 64.

Family Preservation Services: In Home Family Services, Common Sense Parenting, 503 Urban Loop, 78204. Tel: 210-271-1010; Fax: 210-271-3333. Staff 16; Families Assisted 800.

St. Peter & St. Joseph Childrens' Home (1891) 919 Mission Rd., 78210. Tel: 210-533-1203; Fax: 210-533-6199. Web: www.stpjhome.org. James Castro, Exec. Dir. House Parent Staff 100; Administrative & Support Staff 40; Bed Capacity 143; Children Under Care (Ages Infant-17) 143; Total Assisted 425.

Seton Home, 1115 Mission Rd., 78210. Tel: 210-533-3504; Fax: 210-533-3467. Email: margretstarkey@setonhomesa.org. Web: www.setonhomesa.org. Margret Starkey, Pres. & CEO. Bed Capacity 80; Total Assisted 170; Total Staff 89.

Visitation House Ministries, 945 W. Huisache, 78201. Tel: 210-735-6910; Fax: 210-738-8794. Web: www.vhmin.org. Sr. Cynthia Stacy, C.C.V.I., Dir. Operated by the Sisters of Charity of the Incarnate Word of San Antonio, TX., A nonprofit corporation chartered under the laws of the State of Texas; Provides a two year transitional housing program for homeless women and children and learning center for women. Total Assisted 47; Staff 5; Capacity 20.

BOERNE. *Childrens' Inn*, 216 W. Highland Dr., 78006. Tel: 830-249-9456; Fax: 830-249-3327. Email: children@gvtc.com. Sr. Kathleen Kean, S.S.J., Co-Dir.; Marilyn Haider, Co-Dir. Provides foster care for children with special needs in a holistic setting. Total Assisted 7.

[J] DAY CARE CENTERS AND KINDERGARTENS

SAN ANTONIO. *St. Anthony Day Care Learning Center; Infant and Toddler Center*, 1707 Centennial Blvd., 78211. Tel: 210-924-4443; Fax: 210-924-4469. Email: salc@satx.rr.com. Sisters Mary Ann Domagalski, M.S.S.A., Admin.; Lucelia Sanchez, M.S.S.A., Dir. Sisters 2; Lay Staff 22; Children 140.

Blessed Sacrament Academy, (Grades Day Care-PreSchool), 1135 Mission Rd., 78210. Tel: 210-532-4731; Fax: 210-534-2882. Email: odilia@sbcglobal.net. Web: blessedsacramentacademy.org. Sr. M. Odilia Korenek, I.W.B.S., Exec. Dir.

Child Development Center Tel: 210-532-5363; Fax: 210-532-2149. Carol Silva, Dir. Sisters of the Incarnate Word and Blessed Sacrament 1; Lay Teachers 25; Students 195; Support Staff 10.

Blessed Sacrament Learning Center, 227 Keller St., 78204. Tel: 210-223-5013; Fax: 210-444-0779. Email: sistermusict@yahoo.com. Sr. Teresa Gomez, H.M.S.S., Dir. Mercedarian Sisters of the Blessed Sacrament. Sisters 2; Lay Staff 2; Children 30.

Carmelite Learning Center, 2006 Martin Luther King Dr., 78203. Tel: 210-533-0651; Fax: 210-533-3910. Email: smf3964@yahoo.com. Sr. Maria Faustina, D.C.J., Dir. Attended from St. Patrick's Church. Carmelite Sisters of the Divine Heart of Jesus 5; Lay Staff 9; Day Care 80.

Immaculate Conception Kindergarten and Nursery, 2407 W. Travis St., 78207. Tel: 210-226-3934; Fax: 210-226-3934. Sr. Maria Del Carmen Sanchez, A.P.G., Dir. Sisters 4; Lay Staff 10; Kindergarten & Nursery Children 52.

[K] HOMES FOR AGED

SAN ANTONIO. *Casa De Padres*, 8520 Cross Mountain Tr. #100, 78255. Tel: 210-698-0175; Fax: 210-698-5138. Email: jengberg@gvtc.com. Mrs. Jeannine Engberg, Dir. Tel: 210-698-0175; 830-981-9192; Rev. Msgrs. Alois J. Goertz (Retired). Tel: 210-698-9067 No. 402; Roy Rihn (Retired). Tel: 210-698-0287 No. 301; Albert Hubertus (Retired). Tel: 210-698-8682 No. 1101; Joseph Petsch (Retired). Tel: 210-698-7055 No. 702; John Wagner (Retired). Tel: 210-698-1332 No. 202; Lawrence Steuben (Retired). Tel: 210-288-0988 No. 201; Leslie A. Vance, J.C.L. (Retired), No. 1302; Michael McManus (Retired), No. 1102; Thomas Murphy (Retired), No. 1301; Rev. Leon B. Rubaj (Retired), No. 1202. Home for retired Priests of San Antonio. Bed Capacity 18; Total Assisted Annually 12; Staff 3. In Res. Rev. Msgr. Terence Nolan, J.C.L. Tel: 201-698-0349 No. 701.

St. Francis Nursing Home and Boarding Home for the Aged, 630 W. Woodlawn, 78212. Tel: 210-736-3177; Fax: 210-738-2221. Sisters Helen Haladyna, S.O.L.S., Pres. of Corp.; Agnes Bochenek, S.O.L.S., Admin. Seraphic Sisters of Our Lady of Sorrows., Home for the Aged and Convalescents. Sisters 11; Bed Capacity 143; Total Staff 150; Total Assisted 155.

Incarnate Word Retirement Community, 4707 Broadway, 78209. Tel: 210-829-7561; Fax: 210-828-0020. Email: steve.fuller@iwretire.org. Web: www.IwRetire.org. Mr. Steven E. Fuller, Exec. Dir.; Rev. Msgr. Thomas A. French (Retired). For lay persons also. Total in Residence 315; Staff 200; Bed Capacity 299; Outreach Program 850.

Marianist Residence: Skilled Nursing, 520 Fordham Ln., 78228-4800. Tel: 210-436-3771 (Nurses' Station); Fax: 210-431-4240. Email: lkaehler@stmarytx.edu. Bros. Lester Kaehler, S.M., Dir.; James Jaeckle, S.M., Sub Dir., Health Care Oper.; Revs. Paul Ryan, S.M. Tel: 210-436-3766; August Biehl, S.M.; Joseph A. Tarrillion, S.M., D.Min.; Michael Barber, S.M.; Eugene Sweeny, S.M. Home for Infirm Marianist Brothers and Priests. Infirm Priests 5; Infirm Brothers 22; Total Assisted 28; Total Staff 43.

McCullough Hall Nursing Center, Inc. (1992) (Incorporated 2003) 603 S.W. 24th St., 78207-4696. Tel: 210-435-7711; Fax: 210-433-6600. Email: mtheus@mchall.org. Michelle Theus, Admin. Bed Capacity 51; Staff 56; Total Assisted 65.

Oblate Madonna Residence, 5722 Blanco Rd., 78216. Tel: 210-341-2350; Fax: 210-340-3732. Email: roblatemadonna@satx.rr.com. Rev. Msgr. Stanley Petru; Revs. Michael Levy, O.M.I., Dir.; Charles Banks, O.M.I.; Gerard Barrett, O.M.I.; Richard Beck, O.M.I.; Rolland Bennett, O.M.I.; Ronald Carignan, O.M.I.; William Dubuisson, O.M.I.; Matias Felipe, O.M.I.; Jose Gago, O.M.I.; Jan Heemrood, O.M.I., S.S.L.; Richard A. Houlahan, O.M.I.; Henri Janssen, O.M.I.; Donald J. Joyce, O.M.I., M.Div.; Adolph Kaler, O.M.I.; Charles Krzewinski, O.M.I., Supr.; John McGrath, O.M.I.; Clarence Menard, O.M.I.; James Miller, O.M.I.; Galeb Mokarzel, O.M.I.; Roberto Pena, O.M.I.; Francis Pfeifer, O.M.I.; George Protopapas, O.M.I.; Charles Sellars, O.M.I.; Richard Sheehan, O.M.I.; John Sokolski, O.M.I.; Francis Montalbano, O.M.I.; Robert Vreteau, O.M.I.; Gerald Weber, O.M.I.; Bros. Benjamin Juarez, O.M.I.; Valmond LeClerc, O.M.I. Missionary Oblates of Mary Immaculate., Home for retired Priests and Brothers. Bishops 1; Monsignors 1; Priests 27; Brothers 2; Total Staff 33; Assisted Living 10; Bed Capacity 38. In Res. Most Rev. Thomas J. Flanagan, D.D., V.G. (Retired).

Padua Place, 80 Peter Baque Rd., 78209. Tel: 210-826-7721; Fax: 210-824-4554. Email: paduaplace@missionaryservants.org. Sr. Rose Mary Martinez, M.S.S.A., Admin. Home for infirm and retired Priests and Brothers. Bishops 2; Priests 10; Brothers 1; Bed Capacity 17; Total Assisted Annually 17. In Res. Most Rev. Patrick F. Flores, D.D.; Rev. Msgrs. Dermot Brosnan (Retired); Vincent Fecher (Retired); Leonel Martinez; Thomas Palmer (Retired); Most Rev. Bernard F. Popp, D.D. (Retired); Rev. Msgrs. Ramon V. Garcia; Sherrill Smith (Retired); Revs. John P. Buzga (E) (Retired); Leonard H. Kelly, M.S.F.; Willy Verboomen, C.I.C.M. (Retired).

KENEDY. *John Paul II Nursing Home*, 209 S. 3rd St., 78119. Tel: 830-583-9841; Fax: 830-583-9458. Krystiana Sadlo, Admin. Seraphic Sisters of Our Lady of Sorrows 5; Residents 64; Independent Living 13; Total Staff 75.

[L] MONASTERIES AND RESIDENCES OF PRIESTS AND BROTHERS

SAN ANTONIO. *Casa Maria Marianist Community*, St. Mary's University, One Camino Santa Maria, #18, 78228-8518. Tel: 210-436-3066; Fax: 210-431-4216. Rev. William Behringer, S.M.; Bros. Michael Sullivan, S.M. Tel: 210-436-3258; Dennis Bautista, S.M. Tel: 210-436-3775; Brian Halderman, S.M., Dir. Tel: 210-436-3239; Brandon Alana, S.M.

Casa Pasionista Guadalupe, 700 Waverly, 78201-6138. Tel: 210-736-5228; Fax: 210-737-6549. Email: cbarron@passionist.org. Web: www.passionist.org. Rev. Clemente Barron, C.P.

Casa San Juan Marianist Community, 1701 Alametos, 78201. Tel: 210-734-6727; Fax: 210-738-0698. Email: GMontague@stmarytx.edu. Revs. George T. Montague, S.M., Dir.; Joseph Mary Marshall, S.M.

Central Catholic Marianist Community, 1403 N. St. Mary's St., 78215-1785. Tel: 210-225-1112; Fax: 210-227-9353. Email: jimburk@cchs-satx.org. Revs. Donald Cowie, S.M.; Joseph G. Rasky, S.M.; Gerald Haby, S.M. (Retired); Bro. James Burkholder, Dir. Priests 3; Brothers 5.

De Mazenod House (Faculty Residence), 7707 Madonna Dr., 78216. Tel: 210-349-8572; Fax: 210-349-8572. Revs. Warren A. Brown III, O.M.I., J.C.D.; Ken Hannon, O.M.I., Ph.D., Supr.; Raymond John Marek, O.M.I., D.Min.; Joseph LaBelle, O.M.I., S.T.D.; David Kalert, O.M.I., S.T.L., Ph.L., M.S.Ed. Missionary Oblates of Mary Immaculate. Priests 6.

Discalced Carmelite Fathers of San Antonio, 906 Kentucky Ave., 78201-6097. Tel: 210-735-9127; Fax: 210-738-0818. Web: www.littleflowerbasilica.org. Revs. Marion J. Bui, O.C.D.; Luis J. Castaneda, O.C.D.; James A. Curiel, O.C.D.; Luis G. Belmonte Luna, O.C.D.; Gregory Ross, O.C.D.; Bonaventure Sauer, O.C.D. Priests 6; Brothers 3.

Dominican Priory of San Juan Macias, 2226 W. Gramercy, 78201. Tel: 210-233-9272. Revs. Wayne A. Cavalier, O.P., M.A.; Joseph Determan, O.P., 5622 Evers Rd., #3501, 78238. Tel: 210-680-2806; Luis Roberto Aguilar, O.P.; Ramon Gonzalez, O.P.; John J. Markey, O.P.; Gustavo Montanez, O.P. Priests 5.

Holy Cross Community, 426 N. San Felipe St., 78228. Tel: 210-434-9100; Fax: 210-433-1666. Email: SAHCMAN@hotmail.com. Web: www.holycross-sa.org. Rev. Lawrence A. LeVasseur, C.S.C.; Bro. Stanley Culotta, C.S.C., Dir. Priests 1; Brothers 2. *Bro. Charles Andersen Residence*, 320 Brahan Blvd., 78215. Tel: 210-223-9117; Fax: 210-223-2081. Bro. Michael Winslow, C.S.C., B.A., M.A., Dir. Brothers 2.

Holy Rosary Marianist Community, 159 Camino Santa Maria, 78228-4997. Tel: 210-433-6137; Fax: 210-433-2133. Email: cjanson@swbell.net. Very Rev. Christian A. Janson, S.M., V.U.; Bros. Richard Schrader, S.M.; Richard Thompson, S.M., Dir.; Michael Galvin, S.M.

Hospital Ministry House, 6111 Walking Gait, 78240. Tel: 210-437-0147. Rev. Nicholas Brown, S.C.J.

Joseph Gerard House, 222 Oblate Dr., 78216. Tel: 210-377-3462. Revs. Robert E. Wright, O.M.I., Ph.D. Tel: 210-348-0545; Jaime del Rosario, O.M.I.

Ligustrum Marianist Community, 253 W. Ligustrum Dr., 78228-4020. Tel: 210-433-9114; Fax: 210-433-9124. Email: rvela3@stmarytx.edu. Bro. Thomas Suda, S.M., Dir.; Revs. Rudy Vela, S.M.; Bernard Lee, S.M.

Marianist Residence, St. Mary's University, 520 Fordham Ave., 78228-4800. Tel: 210-436-3745; Fax: 210-431-4240. Email: lkaehler@stmarytx.edu. Bro. Lester Kaehler, S.M., Dir. Tel: 210-436-3745; Revs. Norbert Brockman, S.M.; John A. Leies, S.M., S.T.D. Tel: 210-436-3227; John J. Manahan, S.M.; Paul Neumann, S.M.; Gerald Pleva, S.M.; W. Franz Schorp, S.M. Tel: 210-431-2259. Priests 6; Brothers 36.

Marianist Vocation Ministry, One Camino Santa Maria, 78228-8556. Tel: 210-431-2193; Fax: 210-436-3724. Email: gtrautman@sm-usa.org. Web: marianist.com/vocations. Sr. Gretchen Trautman, F.M.I., Dir.

Missionaries of the Sacred Heart Sectional Headquarters of the Irish Province for California and Southern States., 123 W. Laurel St., 78212-4667. Tel: 210-226-5514; Fax: 210-226-5725. Email: magnoliamsc@sbcglobal.net. Revs. William Collins, M.S.C., Supr.; James Dudley, M.S.C.; James A. Harnan, M.S.C.; Jeremiah McCarthy, M.S.C.; Michael O'Brien, M.S.C.; Patrick O'Connor, M.S.C.; Patrick O'Shea, M.S.C.; Stephen White, M.S.C. *Religious Activities Office*, 3700 N. Capitol St. N.W., Washington, DC 20317. Tel: 202-882-1888.

Missionary Oblates of Mary Immaculate, Southwest Area Office, 327 Oblate Dr., 78216-6602. Tel: 210-349-1475; Fax: 210-349-7411. Email: swarea@omiusa.org. Web: www.omiusa.org. Rev. Arthur Flores, O.M.I., Southwest Area Councilor. *Oblate Vocation Office*, 327 Oblate Dr., 78216-6602. Tel: 210-349-1475; 800-358-4394; Fax: 210-349-7411. Email: vocations@omiusa.org. Rev. Charles Banks, O.M.I., Province Vicar for Vocations. 214 Oblate Dr., 78216-6630. Revs. Hugo Van Den Bussche, O.M.I. Tel: 210-348-9045; John G. Castro, O.M.I. 218 Oblate Dr., 78216-6630. Rev. Ronald Rolheiser, O.M.I. Tel: 210-342-3492; Bro. Paul Hoemeke, O.M.I. 222 Oblate Dr., 78216. Rev. Robert E. Wright, O.M.I., Ph.D. Tel: 210-377-3462.

Oblate Benson Residence (Southwest Area), 334 W. Kings Hwy., 78212. Tel: 210-732-5162. Rev. Pat Guidon, O.M.I. Tel: 210-267-8565. Missionary Oblates of Mary Immaculate - Southwest Area. Priests 1.

Redemptorists of Texas-San Antonio #1, 1617 Iowa St., 78203. Tel: 210-313-6669; Fax: 210-533-0558. Email: monper@satx.rr.com. Revs. James E. Shea, C.Ss.R., Supr., 1523 Iowa St., 78203; Robert A. Ruhnke, C.Ss.R. Fax: 210-534-1280; Carl Schindler, C.Ss.R.; Francis Han Pham, C.Ss.R., 1523 Iowa St., 78203; Alton Carr, C.Ss.R., 1523 Iowa St., 78203; Monroe Perrier, C.Ss.R.; Nghia Cao, C.Ss.R.; Bro. Charles Fucik, C.Ss.R. (Province of Denver)

San Damiano Friary, 1104 Kentucky Ave., 78201. Tel: 210-734-4962. Revs. Martin Day, O.F.M.Conv.; Philip Ley, O.F.M.Conv.; Lawrence Mattingly, O.F.M.Conv.; Gary W. Johnson, O.F.M.Conv.; Bro. Tim Unser, O.F.M.Conv. Conventual Franciscan Friars.

Trinitarian Residence, 401 Squires Row, 78213. Tel: 210-781-4945. Rev. Thomas Dymowski, O.SS.T.

Woodlawn Marianist Community, 3303 W. Woodlawn Ave., 78228. Tel: 210-436-0182; Fax: 210-436-0188. Email: rwosmansm@wosman.com. Revs. Charles Stander, S.M.; Patrick McDaid, S.M. Priests 2; Brothers 4.

FALLS CITY. *Salvatorian Fathers Community of Texas*, 211 W. Meyer St., P.O. Box 158, 78113. Tel: 830-254-3539; Fax: 830-254-3530. Very Rev. Grzegorz Sawicki, S.D.S., V.F. (Poland), Supr.; Revs. Grzegorz Szewczyk, S.D.S. (Poland); Stanislaw Oleksy, S.D.S.; Krzystof Bugno, S.D.S.; Eugeniusz Grytner, S.D.S.; Gabriel Kamienski, S.D.S.; Josef Musiol, S.D.S.; Kazimierz Oleksy, S.D.S.; Marian Piekarczyk, S.D.S.; Andrzej Waszczenko, S.D.S.; Thaddeus Tabak, S.D.S.; Boleslaw Zadora, S.D.S.; Dariusz Ziebowicz, S.D.S.

[M] CONVENTS AND RESIDENCES FOR SISTERS

SAN ANTONIO. *St. Anthony Convent*, 100 Peter Baque Rd., 78209. Tel: 210-824-4553; Fax: 210-824-4554. Web: missionaryservants.org. Sr. Mary Ann Domagalski, M.S.S.A., Supr. Motherhouse and

Novitiate of the Missionary Servants of St. Anthony; St. Anthony Retreat Center; St. Anthony Learning Center; Padua Place. Sisters 3.

Blessed Sacrament Convent, 227 Keller St., 78204. Tel: 210-223-5013; Fax: 210-444-0779. Email: teresitap@sbcglobal.net. Sr. Rosario Vega, H.M.S.S., Supr. Mercedarian Sisters of the Blessed Sacrament. Sisters 8.

Blessed Sacrament and Incarnate Word Convent, 1135 Mission Rd., 78210. Tel: 210-534-8005; Fax: 210-534-2882. Email: odilia@sbcglobal.net. Sr. M. Odilia Korenek, I.W.B.S., Supr. Sisters of the Incarnate Word and Blessed Sacrament. Sisters 10.

St. Brigid's Convent, 5118 Loma Linda Dr., 78201. Tel: 210-733-0701; 210-738-1721; Fax: 210-785-2820. Email: brigidines@sbcglobal.net. Web: www.brigidine.org.au. Sr. Anne Drea, C.S.B., Regl. Coord. Regional House.; Address matters connected with congregation to the Regl. Coord. Sisters 15.

Brigid's Place A day retreat center.

Carmelite Convent, 2006 Martin Luther King Dr., 78203. Tel: 210-533-0651; Fax: 210-533-3910. Email: smf3694@yahoo.com. Sr. Luz Divina Medina, D.C.J., Supr. Carmelite Sisters of the Divine Heart of Jesus. Sisters 5.

Convent of the Sisters of the Holy Spirit and Mary Immaculate, 300 Yucca St., 78203. Tel: 210-533-5149; Fax: 210-533-3434. Email: holyspirit@shsp.org. Web: www.shsp.org. Sr. Miriam Mitchell, S.H.Sp., Gen. Supr. Motherhouse of the Sisters of the Holy Spirit and Mary Immaculate. Sisters 46.

Cordi-Marian Missionary Sisters, Cordi-Marian Villa, 11624 FM 471, #501, 78253. Tel: 210-798-8220; 210-688-3099; Fax: 210-798-8225. Email: info@cordi-marian.org. Web: cordi-marian.org. Sisters Matilda Jaime, M.C.M., B.A., Prov. Supr.; Christine Romo, M.C.M., Local Supr.; Celina Martin, M.C.M., Retreat Center; Rev. Christopher Udeani, C.M.F., Chap. Convent, Provincial House, Retirement and Retreat Center. Sisters 33.

Cordi-Marian Missionary Sisters Convent Formation House (1921) 2902 Morales St., 78207. Tel: 210-433-5064; Fax: 210-433-5064. Email: mcmoralia@aol.com. Sisters Virginia Hernandez, M.C.M., Supr. & Formation Provider; Oralia Arzola, M.C.M. Sisters 3; Novices 1.

Daughters of Charity Convent, 3026 Golden Ave., 78211. Tel: 210-927-2795. Sr. Lucretia Burns, D.C., Supr. Daughters of Charity of St. Vincent de Paul. Sisters 5.

Eucharistic Franciscan Missionary Sisters, 558 Cumberland, 78204. Tel: 210-224-7993. Sr. Maria Guadalupe Villasenor, M.E.F., Supr. Sisters 4.

Generalate of the Congregation of Divine Providence, 515 S.W. 24th St., 78207. Tel: 210-434-1866; Fax: 210-568-1050. Email: generalate@cdptexas.org. Web: www.cdptexas.org. Sr. Ann Petrus, C.D.P., Supr. Gen. Sisters 5.

Sophia Women's Learning Center Ida Ayala, Dir.

Mobile Ministry Sr. Bernadette Bezner, C.D.P., Dir. Sisters 2.

Hermanas Catequistas Guadalupanas Convent, 4110 S. Flores St., 78214. Tel: 210-532-9344; Fax: 210-532-9344. Sr. Maria Marta Ruiz, H.C.G., Supr. Sisters 14.

Hermanas Josefinas, 2622 W. Summit Ave., 78228. Tel: 210-737-0584; Fax: 210-737-0584. Sr. Crispina Paraguirre, Regl. Delegate.

Casa Santa Maria de Guadalupe, 2622 W. Summit Ave., 78228. Tel: 210-737-0584; Fax: 210-737-0584. Sisters 4.

Communidad de la Asuncion, 3203 W. Ashby Pl., 78228. Tel: 210-734-0039. Sisters 9.

Casa San Jose (Retired Sisters), 402 John Adams Dr., 78228. Tel: 210-732-1973. Sisters 11.

Incarnate Word Generalate (1869) 4503 Broadway, 78209-6297. Tel: 210-828-2224; Fax: 210-828-9741. Email: yolanda.tarango@amormeus.org. Web: www.amormeus.org. Sr. Yolanda Tarango, C.C.V.I., Congregation Leader. General Administration of the Congregation of Sisters of Charity of the Incarnate Word. Total in Congregation 377; Total in U.S. Province 192.

Headwaters Coalition (San Antonio Headwaters Coalition, Inc.), 4503 Broadway, 78209. Tel: 210-828-2224; Fax: 210-828-9741. Web: www.headwaterscoalition.org. Helen Ballew, Exec. Dir.

Womens Global Connection, 4106 Bretton Ridge, 78217. Tel: 210-653-7492. Email: dorthy.ettling@sbcglobal.net. Web: www.womensglobalconnection.org. Sr. Dorthy Ettling, C.C.V.I., Dir.

Incarnate Word Retirement Community Inc., U.S. Province, 4707 Broadway, 78209-6215. Tel: 210-829-7561 (Retirement Center); Fax: 210-828-0020. Email: steve.fuller@iwretire.org. Web: www.iwretire.org. Mr. Steven Fuller, CEO; Thelma Martinez, Admin. Extended Care; Sr. Margaret Kelly, Asst. Coord. Extended Care; Alma Cosme, Dir. Community Relations; Rev. Msgr. Thomas A. French (Retired). Total in Residence 80.

Institute of the Daughters of Mary Help of Christians, Province of Mary Immaculate, 6019 Buena Vista St., 78237-1700. Tel: 210-432-0089; 210-432-0090; Fax: 210-432-4016. Email: pkingfma@gmail.com. Web: www.salesiansisterswest.org. Sr. Patricia King, F.M.A., Prov. Supr. Salesian Sisters of St. John Bosco.

St. James Convent, 402 Nunes, 78225. Tel: 210-533-9659; Fax: 210-924-0201. Email: fmasuojames@gmail.com. Sr. Mary Link, F.M.A., Supr. Daughters of Mary Help of Christians (Salesian Sisters of St. John Bosco). Sisters 4.

St. John Bosco Convent, 5630 W. Commerce St., 78237. Tel: 210-432-8011; Fax: 866-214-8083. Email: fmasuojbc@stjohnbosco-satx.org. Sr. Rosann Ruiz, F.M.A., Supr. Daughters of Mary Help of Christians. Sisters 10.

St. Joseph's Convent - S.S.N.D., 2372 W. Southcross, 78211-1898. Tel: 210-923-2364; Fax: 210-924-2229. Email: dsiebenmorgen@yahoo.com. Sr. Dolores Marie Siebenmorgen, Coord. Sisters 4.

Marianist Sisters Residence, 235 Ligustrum Dr., 78228. Tel: 210-433-5501; Fax: 210-433-0300. Email: trautmanfmi@yahoo.com. Web: www.marianistsisters.org. Sisters Gretchen Trautman, F.M.I., Prov.; Lavon Kampf, F.M.I., Dir. of Sisters. Centralhouse of the Congregation of the Daughters of Mary Immaculate. Marianist Sisters, (Community Dayton, OH). Sisters 16.

McCullough Hall Nursing Center, Inc., 603 S.W. 24th St., 78207-4696. Tel: 210-435-7711; Fax: 210-433-6600. Michelle Theus, Admin. Sisters 45; Lay Persons 6; Total Assisted 73; Staff 75.

Missionary Catechists of Divine Providence Central House and Admin. Offices, St. Andrew's Convent, 2318 Castroville Rd., 78237. Tel: 210-432-0113; Fax: 210-432-1709. Email: mainoffice-mcdp@yahoo.com. Sr. Carmen M. Sanchez, M.C.D.P., Supr. Gen. Sisters 38.

Missionary Sisters of Our Lady of Perpetual Help (M.P.S.), 427 Rigsby, 78210. Tel: 210-532-3546. Sr. Rosamaria Benavides, M.P.S., Contact Person. Sisters 3.

Monastery of St. Michael the Archangel, 17503 La Cantera Pkwy., Ste. 104-505, 78257. Tel: 210-368-9581.

Monastery of the Discalced Carmelite Nuns, 6301 Culebra Rd., 78238-4909. Tel: 210-680-1834; Fax: 210-680-3106. Email: saocdnun21@sbcglobal.net. Web: www.carmelsanantonio.org. Sr. Therese Leonard, O.C.D., Prioress. Sisters 9.

Our Lady of the Lake Convent Center, 515 S.W. 24th St., 78207. Tel: 210-434-1866; Fax: 210-431-9965. Sisters of Divine Providence., Home for retired Sisters of Divine Providence. Professed Sisters 52.

O.L.L. Convent Home for retired Sisters of Divine Providence Sisters Frances Lorene Lange, C.D.P., Coord.; Cathy Parent, C.D.P., Coord.; Patrice Sullivan, C.D.P., Coord.; Madeline Zimmerer, C.D.P., Coord.

Our Lady of Victory Missionary Sisters, 2101 Vera Cruz, Apt. 113, 78207-6727. Tel: 210-433-3296. Sr. M. Adele Massaro, O.L.V.M.

Presentation Province Center, P.O. Box 100785, 78201-8785. Tel: 210-979-8879; Fax: 210-979-5582. Email: unionpresprov@aol.com. Web: www.pbvmunion.org. Sr. Antonio Heaphy, P.B.V.M., Provincial Leader Province Admin. of U.S. Province. Congregation: Union of Sisters of the Presentation of the Blessed Virgin Mary Total in U.S. Province 63.

Presentation Sisters, 8931 Callaghan Rd., 78230-4570. Tel: 210-342-2503; Fax: 210-349-4772. Email: pbvmsat@juno.com. Web: www.pbvm.org. Sr. Finbar O'Driscoll, P.B.V.M., Supr. Residence of the Community of the Union of the Sisters of the Presentation of the B.V.M. Sisters 12.

Presentation Sisters, 415 Arbor Pl., 78207. Tel: 210-223-4916. Email: pbvmsisters@yahoo.com. Web: www.pbvmunion.org. Congregation: Union of Sisters of the Presentation of the Blessed Virgin Mary Sisters 3.

Provincial Offices of the Sisters of the Sacred Heart of Jesus of St. Jacut, 11931 Radium St., 78216-2714. Tel: 210-344-7203; Fax: 210-341-0721. Email: crsscj@yahoo.com. Sr. Cecilia Rodriguez, S.S.C.J., Prov. Sisters 38.

Convent: St. Joseph Community, 1014 Spent Wing, 78213. Tel: 210-375-2914. Sisters 4. 818 Firefly, 78216. Tel: 210-349-6689. Sisters 4.

Convent: Sacred Heart Community, 7112 Hagy Cir., 78216. Tel: 210-340-0249. Sisters 3.

Convent: Holy Spirit Convent, 10802 Silhouette Dr., 78216. Sisters 7.

Convent: Casa Ste. Emile, 302 Harriet Dr., 78216. Tel: 210-822-9844. Sisters 5.

Convent: Santa Maria Community, 10803 Silhouette Dr., 78216. Tel: 210-340-1872. Sisters 6.

Convent: Beth Rachamim Community, 1203 Viewridge, 78213. Tel: 210-308-0257. Sisters 3.

Religious of Mary Immaculate Convent, 719 Augusta St., 78215. Tel: 210-226-0025; Fax: 210-226-3305. Email: villamarmi@yahoo.com. Web: www.religiosasdemariainmaculada.org. Sr. Martha Ochoa, R.M.I., Local Supr. Religious of Mary Immaculate Sisters. Sisters 7.

School Sisters of Notre Dame, 3415 W. Woodlawn, 78228. Tel: 210-435-3234. Sisters Suzanne Menshek, S.S.N.D., Correspondent; Barbara Masch, S.S.N.D., Co-Correspondent. Sisters 3.

Seraphic Sisters of Our Lady of Sorrows Convent, 621 W. Woodlawn Ave., 78212. Tel: 210-734-3364. Sr. Inez Smietana, S.O.L., Supr.; Rev. Stanislaw Pieczara, S.D.S, Chap. Sisters 7.

The Sisters of Perpetual Adoration Convent, 2403 W. Travis St., 78207. Tel: 210-227-5546; Fax: 210-226-3934. Sr. Maria Concepcion Quesada-Aguirre, A.P.G., Supr. Sisters 9.

St. Teresa's Convent, 138 Fair Ave., 78223-1014. Tel: 210-533-5330; Fax: 210-533-2532. Email: judyroxstj@yahoo.com. Web: www.teresians.org. Sr. Amelia Ibarra, S.T.J., Coord. Society of St. Teresa of Jesus 9.

Ursuline Residence, 3810 Portsmouth Dr., 78223. Tel: 210-333-2907; Fax: 210-333-2907. Sr. Diane Fulgenzi, O.S.U., Prioress. Sisters 3.

Ursuline Convent, 3807 Southport, 78223. Tel: 210-333-4213; 210-333-2907; Fax: 210-333-2907. Sisters 2.

BOERNE. *St. Scholastica Monastery*, 416 W. Highland, 78006. Tel: 830-249-2645; 830-816-8504; Fax: 830-249-1365. Email: benstrs@ktc.com. Web: www.boernebenedictines.com. Sr. Bernadine Reyes, O.S.B., Prioress. Congregation of Benedictine Sisters, Monastery, and Novitiate. Sisters 17.

UVALDE. *Society of St. Teresa of Jesus* (Teresian Sisters), 466 Encino, 78801. Tel: 830-278-6724; Fax: 830-278-5170. Email: stjsendin@yahoo.com. Web: teresians.org. Sr. Angeles Sendin, S.T.J., Coord. Sisters 3.

[N] RETREAT HOUSES

SAN ANTONIO. *Oblate Renewal Center*, Mailing Address: 5700 Blanco Rd., 78216-6615. Tel: 210-349-4173; Fax: 210-349-4281. Email: orc@ost.edu. Web: www.ost.edu/oblate_renewal_center.htm. Revs. Rocky Grimard, O.M.I., Dir.; William E. Zapalac, O.M.I.; Sisters Theresa O'Toole, S.H.Sp.; Susan Hazenski, SS.C.M., Hospitality Dir.

BOERNE. *Omega Retreat Center* (1982) 216 W. Highland Dr., 78006. Tel: 830-816-8470 (San Antonio); 830-249-3894 (Boerne); Fax: 830-249-3327. Email: omegactr@gvtc.com. Web: www.boernebenedictines.com. Mr. Andrew Anderson, Dir.

CASTROVILLE. *Moye Retreat Center*, 600 London, 78009. Tel: 830-931-2233; Fax: 830-931-2227. Web: www.moyecenter.org. Email: moyecenter@cdptexas.org. Linda Follis, Exec. Dir. Under the direction of the Sisters of Divine Providence., Center for Retreats, Renewal, and Conferences. Sisters 2.

[O] CATHOLIC CHARITABLE ORGANIZATIONS AND CLINICS

SAN ANTONIO. *Catholic Charities, Archdiocese of San Antonio Inc.* Crisis intervention/emergency assistance; pregnancy/parenting education and support services; transitional housing for homeless, pregnant women; mental health services; senior volunteer services; guardianship services; money management services; immigration and refugee services; community voicemail program; community center providing social services; volunteer income tax assistance; military family relief services. Anti-traffican services, doula summer programs for seniors, Teleton Navideno.

Administration, 202 W. French Pl., 78212. Tel: 210-222-1294; Fax: 210-227-0217. Email: info@ccaosa.org. Web: www.ccaosa.org. Mr. Steve Saldana, Pres. & CEO.

Office: 202 W. French, 78212. Tel: 210-222-1294; Fax: 210-227-0217.

Immigration Services Programs, 2903 W. Salinas St., 78207. Tel: 210-433-3256; Fax: 210-433-0851.

Crisis Intervention Program, 1801 W. Durango, 78207. Tel: 210-226-6178; Fax: 210-226-9188.

Refugee Services, 202 W. French, 78212. Tel: 210-222-1294; Fax: 210-242-3174.

Guadalupe Home for Homeless Pregnant Women, 1223 S. Trinity St., 78207. Tel: 210-476-0707; Fax: 210-224-7388.

San Antonio Birth Doulas, 1223 S. Trinity, 78207. Tel: 210-222-0988; Fax: 210-223-3980. Email: doulas@ccaosa.org.

Catholic Counseling and Consultation Center, 7711

Madonna, 78216. Tel: 210-377-1133; Fax: 210-377-1230. Rev. N. James Rutkowski, S.T.L., Clinical Dir. See Curia Section - Department of Social & Community Services.

Guadalupe Community Center, 1801 W. Durango, 78207. Tel: 210-226-6178; Fax: 210-226-9188.

Teleton Navideno, 202 W. French, 78212. Tel: 210-222-1294; Fax: 210-227-0217. Ms. Pamela Raines, Dir. Christmas Telethon-Branch of Catholic Charities Archdiocese of San Antonio, Inc.

Daughters of Charity Services of San Antonio, 7607 Somerset Rd., 78211. Tel: 210-334-2300; Fax: 210-922-0332. Email: larry.mejia@dcssa.org. Web: www.dcssa.org. Mr. Larry Mejia, Pres. & CEO, Daughters of Charity Svcs.

This corporation operates centers at four locations:

De Paul Family Center, 7607 Somerset, 78211. Tel: 210-334-2311; Fax: 210-922-1728. Sisters 5.

El Carmen Wellness Center, 18555-1 Leal Rd., 78221. Tel: 210-626-1745.

La Mision Family Health Care, 19780 U.S. Hwy. 281 S., 78221. Tel: 210-626-0600; Fax: 210-626-1174.

De Paul Childrens' Center, 3050 Golden Ave., 78211. Tel: 210-334-2311; Fax: 210-334-2344. Sisters 5.

[P] NEWMAN CENTERS

SAN ANTONIO. *St. Anthony Catholic Student Center at U.T.S.A. 1604 Campus* 14523 Roadrunner Way, 78249. Tel: 210-699-9594; Fax: 210-699-9572. Rev. Ramon Gonzalez, O.P., Coord.

Our Lady of Guadalupe Center at San Antonio College, 312 W. Courtland Pl., 78212. Tel: 210-736-3752. Sr. Therese San Miguel, O.S.F., Dir.

[Q] FOUNDATIONS, ENDOWMENTS AND TRUSTS

SAN ANTONIO. *The Archbishop Charity Fund*, Mailing Address: P.O. Box 28410, 78228. Tel: 210-734-2620; Fax: 210-734-0708.

Archbishop Flores Charity Fund, Mailing Address: P.O. Box 28410, 78228. Tel: 210-734-2620; Fax: 210-734-0708.

Archdiocesan Designated Catholic Schools Endowment Fund, 2718 W. Woodlawn, 78228. Tel: 210-734-2620.

Archdiocesan Endowment Fund, Mailing Address: P.O. Box 28410, 78228-0410. Tel: 210-734-2620; Fax: 210-734-0708. Most Rev. Gustavo Garcia-Siller, M.Sp.S.

Archdiocese of San Antonio Endowment Fund for Parishes, School and Ministries, 2718 W. Woodlawn, 78228. Tel: 210-734-2620. Rev. Msgr. Lawrence J. Stuebben (Retired).

Assumption Seminary Endowment Fund, Mailing Address: P.O. Box 28410, 78228-0410. Tel: 210-734-2620; Fax: 210-734-0708. Most Rev. Gustavo Garcia-Siller, M.Sp.S.

Casa de Padres Endowment Fund, Mailing Address: P.O. Box 28410, 78228-0410. Tel: 210-734-2620; Fax: 210-734-0708. Most Rev. Gustavo Garcia-Siller, M.Sp.S.

The Catholic Community Foundation for the Roman Catholic Church of the Archdiocese of San Antonio, 2718 W. Woodlawn Ave., 78228. Tel: 210-734-1910. Mr. Jeff Jung, Pres.

Friends of Santa Rosa Foundation dba Friends of Christus Santa Rosa Foundation 333 N. Santa Rosa Blvd., 78207. Tel: 210-704-2541; Fax: 210-704-2384. Web: www.christussantarosa.org. Linda O'Brien, Vice Pres. & Chief Devel. Office.

Historical Centre Foundation (2000)Mailing Address: P.O. Box 831-078, 78283-1078. Tel: 210-576-1365; Fax: 210-576-1367. Email: hcfed@sfcathedral.org. Web: www.sfcathedral.org. Amelia G. Nieto, C.F.R.E. Exec. Dir.; Rev. Tony Vilano.

Holy Spirit Sisters' Trust, 300 Yucca St., 78203. Tel: 210-533-8142; Fax: 210-533-3434. Email: holyspirit@shsp.org. Sr. Miriam Mitchell, S.H.Sp., Pres. Sisters of the Holy Spirit.

Mary Jane Ihle Clark Endowment Fund for Ministry to Persons with Disabilities, 2718 W. Woodlawn, 78228. Tel: 210-734-2620; Fax: 210-734-0231. Rev. Msgr. Lawrence J. Stuebben (Retired).

National Foundation for Mexican-American Vocations, 2600 W. Woodlawn, 78228. Tel: 210-735-0553; Fax: 210-734-4942. Web: savocations.org. Rev. Alex Pereida, Vocation Office. A nonprofit organization to financially help Mexican American Seminarians.

Providence Trust, 515 S.W. 24th St., 78207. Tel: 210-434-1866; Fax: 210-431-9965. Sisters Ramona Bezner, C.D.P., Trustee; Diane Heinrich, C.D.P., Trustee; Anita Brenk, C.D.P., Trustee. Congregation of Divine Providence, Inc. Charitable Trust.

San Antonio Catholic Worker Community Housing Trust of 1992, 622 Nolan St., 78202. Tel: 210-533-5149. Email: pvance@ost.edu. Paul Vance, Pres.

Seton Home Endowment Fund, Mailing Address: P.O. Box 28410, 78228-0410. Tel: 210-734-2620; Fax: 210-734-0708. Most Rev. Gustavo Garcia-Siller, M.Sp.S.

BOERNE. *Benedictine Sisters Charitable Trust One*, 416 W. Highland Dr., 78006. Tel: 210-219-5514; Fax: 210-348-6745. Email: srmika2010@gmail.com. Sr. Susan Mika, O.S.B., Trustee.

Benedictine Sisters Charitable Trust Two, 416 W. Highland, 78006. Tel: 830-816-8504; Fax: 830-249-1365. Sr. Sylvia Ahr, O.S.B., Trustee.

[R] SHRINES

SAN ANTONIO. *Basilica of the National Shrine of the Little Flower* 1715 N. Zarzamora, 78201. Tel: 210-735-9127; Fax: 210-738-0818. Web: www.littleflowerbasilica.org. Mailing Address: 824 Kentucky Ave., 78201.

Oblate Lourdes Grotto Shrine of the Southwest, Tepeyac de San Antonio 5712 Blanco Rd., 78216. Tel: 210-342-9864; Fax: 210-342-7144. Email: omsa@oblatemissions.org. Web: www.oblatemissions.org. Revs. Saturnino Lajo, O.M.I., Ministries Dir.; Leopoldo G. Perez, O.M.I., S.T.D., M.Div., Grotto Dir.

Our Lady of Czestochowa Grotto Shrine and Convent, 138 Beethoven St., 78210. Tel: 210-337-8193 (Convent). Sr. Elza Lyszczarz, S.O.L.S., Supr.; Rev. Stanislaw Pieczara, S.D.S, Chap. Seraphic Franciscan Sisters of Our Lady of Sorrows. Sisters 5.

[S] MISCELLANEOUS

SAN ANTONIO. *Acts Missions, c/o Oblate School of Theology*, 285 Oblate Dr., 78216. Tel: 210-342-1077; Fax: 866-541-9261. Email: acts@ost.edu. Web: www.actsmissions.org. Mr. Tom Peterson, Outreach Dir.

**The Alexander House Apostolate*, 1343 Alpine Pond, 78260. P.O. Box 59-2107, 78259-2107. Tel: 210-376-1967; Fax: 210-490-8869. Email: info@thealexanderhouse.org. Web: www.thealexanderhouse.org. Gregory Alexander, Co-Founder & Dir.; Julie Alexander, Co-Founder & Dir.

Archdiocesan Union of Holy Name Societies, P.O. Box 54, Adkins, 78101. Tel: 210-649-1977.

Brothers of the Beloved Disciple A private association of the faithful., 1701 Alametos, 78201. Tel: 210-734-6727; Fax: 210-738-0698. Email: GMontague@stmarytx.edu. Web: www.brothersofthebeloveddisciple.org. Revs. George T. Montague, S.M.; Robert E. Hogan, M.A., B.B.D.; Joseph Mary Marshall, S.M.; William H. Combs, B.B.D.

Catholic Association of Latino Leaders, Inc., Pastoral Center - Archdiocese of San Antonio, 2718 W. Woodlawn Ave., 78228. Tel: 210-734-1653; Fax: 210-734-0708. Web: www.call-usa.org. Robert Aguirre, Dir. & Treas.

Catholic Cemeteries of the Archdiocese of San Antonio, 746 Castroville Rd., 78237. Tel: 210-438-8134; Fax: 210-438-8128. Mr. Robert Cornejo, Gen. Mgr.

Catholic Physicians Guild, c/o The Rehabilitation Group P.A., 2701 Babcock Rd., Ste. A, 78229. William P. Mueller M.D., M.D., Pres. Tel: 210-614-3225.

Catholic Television of San Antonio, P.O. Box 28410, 78228-0410. Tel: 210-734-1610; Fax: 210-734-2939. Email: pat.rodgers@archsa.org. 2718 W. Woodlawn, 78228.

Christus Continuing Care dba Christus Homecare 4241 Woodcock Dr., Ste. A-100, 78228. Tel: 210-785-5401; Fax: 210-785-5490. Email: christopher.karam@ChristusHealth.org. Web: www.christushomecare.org.

Christus Santa Rosa Family Health Center, 333 N. Santa Rosa, 78207. Tel: 210-704-2535; Fax: 210-704-2545. Email: todd.thames@christushealth.org. Web: www.christussantarosa.org. Dr. Todd Thames, M.D., Dir. Family Health Ctr.

2829 Babcock Rd. #236 C, 78229.

Cordi-Marian Education Center (2003) 2902 Morales St., 78207. Tel: 210-433-5064; Fax: 210-798-8225. Email: mjaime@cordi-marian.org. Sr. Matilda Jaime, M.C.M., B.A., Dir.

Daughters of Mary Help Development Office, 6019 Buena Vista St., 78237-1700. Tel: 210-431-4999; Fax: 210-431-0944. Email: sswdevelopment@sbcglobal.net. Web: salesiansisterswest.org. Esmeralda Castillo, Dir. Promotes the apostolic works of both the Daughters of Mary Help of Christians (Salesian Sisters) and VIDES-USA (Volunteers International for Development, Education, and Service).

Deaf Ministry of San Antonio, Mailing Address: 4401 S. Flores, 78214. Tel: 210-533-9108. Email: sanantoniodeafministry@yahoo.com. Revs. Thomas Coughlin, O.P.Miss., Dir.; Fernando Solomon, O.P.Miss.; Sharon Inclan.

Eucharistic Adoration of San Antonio, Inc., Mailing Address: P.O. Box 691006, 78269-1006. Tel: 210-558-8802; Cell: 210-724-5842; Fax: 512-366-9787. Email: adore24@aol.com; sanctusangelicus@yahoo.com. Web: www.adore24.org. Mary Therese Corcoran, Pres. & Exec. Dir.

**Family Lifeworks, Inc.*, 215 Switch Oak, 78230. Tel: 210-386-6943; Fax: 210-479-7152. Web: www.familylifeworks.net. Graciela Urruchua, Mgr.

Federation of Catholic Parent Teacher Clubs of the Archdiocese of San Antonio, c/o Catholic Schools Office, 2718 W. Woodlawn, 78228. Tel: 210-734-2620. Web: www.archdiosa.org. Priscilla Gonzaba, Pres.

Friends of St. Clare, 2718 W. Woodlawn, 78228. Tel: 210-924-5252. Hector Guzman, Pres.

The Good Shepherd Network of Catholic Schools, Inc., 2718 W. Woodlawn Ave., 78228-0410. Tel: 210-734-2620; Fax: 210-734-0231.

**La Promesa Foundation aka Guadalupe Radio Network* 3308 Broadway, Ste. 401, 78209. Tel: 830-388-3009 (Spanish); 210-579-9844; Fax: 210-821-5052. Web: www.grnonline.com.

Ladies of Charity of El Carmen, 18555 Leal Rd., 78221. Tel: 210-626-1432. Rev. Carl R. Maurer, Admin.

Madonna Neighborhood Center, 1906 Castroville Rd., 78237. Tel: 210-432-2374; Fax: 210-432-2389. Email: normafunari@flash.net. Norma J. Funari, Dir. Casework, Day Care, After School Care, Social Services, Adult & Youth Socialization Programs. Emergency Food Pantry, Clothing, Furniture, Noon Meal, Summer Recreation, Sports.

Marian Center of San Antonio, Mailing Address: P.O. Box 831001, 78283-1001. Tel: 210-225-6279; Fax: 210-225-0044. Email: mariancenterofsa@hotmail.com. Ms. Therese H. Palacios, Pres.

Marian Community of Reconciliation Societies of Apostolic Life, 2715 Marlborough Dr., 78230. Tel: 210-541-0635. Email: mcrsanantonio@fraternasusa.org. Web: www.fraternas.org. Alejandra Corrales, Supr.

Mary Help Network (ADMA), 6019 Buena Vista St., 78237. Tel: 210-432-1919; 210-432-0804; Fax: 210-436-7719. Email: v.adma@vides.us. Sr. Rachel Crotti, F.M.A., Dir.

MCSP, Inc. dba Youth Sports, Inc. 2718 W. Woodlawn, 78228. Tel: 210-734-1944; Fax: 210-734-2774. James Trimboli, Special Projects Mgr.

Merced Housing Texas, 212 W. Laurel St., 78212. Tel: 210-281-0234; Fax: 210-281-0238. Email: merced@mercedhousingtexas.org. Web: www.mercedhousingtexas.org. Susan R. Sheeran, Pres. Founded by a consortium of religious orders to provide quality, affordable, service enriched housing for the economically poor, to strengthen families and promote healthy communities.

St. Monica's Guild (1929) 6515 Broadway, 78209. Tel: 210-828-9266; Fax: 210-824-6110. Mrs. Celeste Barron, Contact Person. A social, civic, and charitable group.

Oblate Missions, 323 Oblate Dr., 78216-6629. Tel: 210-736-1685; Fax: 210-736-1314. Email: omsa@oblatemissions.org. Web: www.oblatemissions.org. Mailing Address: P.O. Box 659432, 78265-9432. Revs. Arthur Flores, O.M.I.; Saturnino Lajo, O.M.I., Chap., Dir.

Office of Youth Ministry, Mailing Address: 2718 W. Woodlawn, 78228. Tel: 210-734-1625; Fax: 210-734-0231. Email: oym@archsa.org. Web: www.archsa.org/oym. Joan Martinez, Dir.

Parents Academy, 1135 Mission Rd., 78210. Tel: 210-532-0894; Fax: 210-532-6698. Sr. M. Odilia Korenek, I.W.B.S., Dir. & Supr.; Katherine Lozano, Prin. Lay Teachers 3; Support Staff 5; Students 300.

Pilgrim Center of Hope - Evangelization Center (1993) 7680 Joe Newton, 78251. Tel: 210-521-3377; Fax: 210-521-0288. Web: www.pilgrimcenterofhope.org. Deacon Tom Fox, Dir.; Mrs. Mary Jane Fox, Co-Dir.

Polish American Priest Association (P.A.P.A.), 5035 Bernadine, 78220. Tel: 210-648-1991. Rev. Eric Orzech, Pres.

Project Rachel of San Antonio, 9862 Lorene Ln., Ste. 108, 78216. Tel: 210-342-4673; 210-722-4213 (Spanish); (800) 651-HOPE; Fax: 210-341-1572. Email: rachel@anewchoice.org. Web: www.anewchoice.org; www.projectrachelsanantonio.org. Mary Ann Parks, Dir. Total Assisted 886; Staff 2.

Religious of Mary Immaculate (Pontifical), Villa Maria, 719 Augusta St., 78215. Tel: 210-226-0025; Fax: 210-226-3305. Email: villamarmi@yahoo.com. Web: www.religiosasdemariainmaculada.org. Sr. Martha Ochoa, Local Supr. Apostolic Work: Counseling & guidance of young women of good moral conduct of any race or religion. Sisters 8; Girls 70.

San Antonio Community Law Center, 322 W. Woodlawn Ave., 78212. Tel: 210-271-9595; Fax: 210-734-4410. Email: sacommunitylawcenter@

netzero.net. Bro. William Dooling, C.S.C., Attorney. Provides legal assistance to the working poor, children, and underserved.

San Antonio Inter-Community Finance Office, 11931 Radium Dr., 78216. Tel: 210-341-8884; Fax: 210-341-0721. Email: kmoylan@saifo.com. Kimberly Moylan, Accounting Business Mgr.

San Antonio Rolling Hills, Inc., 21240 Gathering Oak, 78260. Tel: 210-497-0323; Fax: 210-497-5192. Rev. Jose Felix Ortega, L.C., Contact Person.

Servants of Jesus and Mary, S.A., 5734 Quail Canyon, 78249. Tel: 210-691-0684. Web: www.servantsofjesusandmary.ning.com. Milagros Abellera, Pres.

Socially Responsible Investment Coalition, Mailing Address: P.O. Box 90238, 78209. Tel: 210-344-6778. Email: info@sric-south.org. Web: www.sric-south.org. Sr. Susan Mika, O.S.B., Exec. Dir.

Today's Catholic Newspaper, Mailing Address: P.O. Box 28410, 78228-0410. 2718 W. Woodlawn Ave., 78228. Tel: 210-734-2620; Fax: 210-734-2939. Email: tcpaper@archsa.org. Web: www.satodayscatholic.org. Most Rev. Gustavo Garcia-Siller, M.Sp.S., Publisher; Mr. Jordan B. McMorrough, Editor. Official Catholic newspaper of the Archdiocese of San Antonio.

The World Apostolate of Fatima, 719 Wayside, 78213. Tel: 210-344-9810. Rev. Mauricio Lopez, Moderator.

BOERNE. *Benedictine Ministries Corporation*, 416 Highland Dr., 78006. Tel: 830-428-0002; Fax: 830-249-7064. Email: reyesosb@gvtc.com. Web: www.boernebenedictines.com. Sr. Michael Brandt, O.S.B., Pres.

INGRAM. *St. Peter Upon the Water, A Center For Spiritual Direction and Formation*, Mailing Address: P.O. Box 509, 78025-0509. Tel: 830-367-5959; Fax: 830-367-3774. Email: frmike@stpeteruponthewater.org. 234 Indian Creek Rd., 78025. Rev. Msgr. Michael J. Boulette, V.F., Dir.

MOUNTAIN HOME. *Tecaboca - A Marianist Center For Spiritual Renewal*, 5045 Junction Hwy. 27, 78058. Tel: 830-866-3425; Fax: 830-866-3781. Email: director@tecaboca.com. Web: www.tecaboca.com. Kay Tally-Foos, Exec. Dir. Operated by the Society of Mary, Province of the U.S.A., Texas Catholic Boy's Camp (mid-June to mid-August).

RELIGIOUS INSTITUTES OF MEN REPRESENTED IN THE ARCHDIOCESE

For further details refer to the corresponding bracketed number in the Religious Institutes of Men or Women section.

[0140]—*The Augustinians* (Prov. of Castile)—O.S.A.
[0200]—*Benedictine Monks*—O.S.B.
[0600]—*Brothers of the Congregation of Holy Cross*—C.S.C.
[0360]—*Claretian Missionaries* (Western Prov.)—C.M.F.
[0310]—*Congregation of Christian Brothers*—C.F.C.
[0220]—*Congregation of the Blessed Sacrament*—S.S.S.
[1330]—*Congregation of the Mission*—C.M.
[0630]—*Congregation of the Missionaries of the Holy Family*—M.S.F.
[1000]—*Congregation of the Passion*—C.P.
[1130]—*Congregation of the Priests of the Sacred Heart*—S.C.J.
[0480]—*Conventual Franciscans*—O.F.M.Conv.
[0260]—*Discalced Carmelite Fathers*—O.C.D.
[]—*Dominican Missionaries*—O.P.Miss.
[0520]—*Franciscan Friars* (Sacred Heart Prov.; Our Lady of Guadalupe Prov.)—O.F.M.
[0690]—*Jesuit Fathers and Brothers* (New Orleans Prov.)—S.J.
[0730]—*Legionaries of Christ*—L.C.
[]—*Missionaries of the Nativity of Mary* (Mexico)—M.N.M.
[1110]—*Missionaries of the Sacred Heart*—M.S.C.
[0860]—*Missionhurst Congregation of the Immaculate Heart of Mary*—C.I.C.M.
[0910]—*Oblates of Mary Immaculate*—O.M.I.
[0430]—*Order of Preachers (Dominican)* (New Orleans Prov.)—O.P.
[1310]—*Order of The Holy Trinity*—O.SS.T.
[0610]—*Priests of the Congregation of Holy Cross*—C.S.C.
[1070]—*Redemptorist Fathers*—C.SS.R.
[0760]—*Society of Mary (Marianists)*—S.M.
[1290]—*Society of St. Sulphice*—S.S.
[1200]—*Society of the Divine Savior*—S.D.S.
[0560]—*Third Order Regular of St. Francis*—T.O.R.

RELIGIOUS INSTITUTES OF WOMEN REPRESENTED IN THE ARCHDIOCESE

[0100]—*Adorers of the Blood of Christ*—A.S.C.
[0230]—*Benedictine Sisters of the Pontifical Jurisdiction*—O.S.B.
[1810]—*Bernardine Sisters of the Third Order of St. Francis*—O.S.F.
[]—*Caritas Christi*—C.C.
[]—*Carmelitas del Sagrado Corazon*—O.C.D.
[0360]—*Carmelite Sisters of the Divine Heart of Jesus*—Carmel.D.C.J.
[0460]—*Congregation of Sisters of Charity of the Incarnate Word*—C.C.V.I.
[3735]—*Congregation of St. Brigid*—C.S.B.
[0870]—*Congregation of the Daughters of Mary Immaculate (Marianist Sisters)*—F.M.I.
[2200]—*Congregation of the Incarnate Word and Blessed Sacrament*—I.W.B.S.
[0725]—*Cordi-Marian Sisters*—M.C.M.
[0760]—*Daughters of Charity of St. Vincent de Paul*—D.C.
[0850]—*Daughters of Mary Help of Christians*—F.M.A.
[]—*Daughters of Mary Mother of Mercy*—D.M.M.M
[0420]—*Discalced Carmelite Nuns*—O.C.D.
[1070-13]—*Dominican Adrian MI*—O.P.
[1070-03]—*Dominican Sinsinawa WI*—O.P.
[1070-19]—*Dominican Sisters*—O.P.
[1115]—*Dominican Sisters of Peace*—O.P.
[1150]—*Eucharistic Franciscan Missionary Sisters*—M.E.F.
[1170]—*Felician Sisters*—C.S.S.F.
[1900]—*Hermanas Catequistas Guadalupanas*—H.C.G.
[1910]—*Hermanas Josefinas*—H.J.
[2590]—*Hermanas Mercedarias Del Santisimo Sacramento*—H.M.S.S.
[]—*Marian Community of Reconciliation*—M.C.R.
[2470]—*Maryknoll*—M.M.
[]—*Misionarios Del Nino De Salud*—M.N.J.S.
[2770]—*Missionaries of Jesus, Mary and Joseph*—M.J.M.J.
[2690]—*Missionary Catechists of Divine Providence, San Antonio, Texas*—M.C.D.P.
[2890]—*Missionary Servants of St. Anthony*—M.S.S.A.
[]—*Missionary Sisters of Mary Immaculate*—M.S.M.I.
[]—*Missionary Sisters of Our Lady of Perpetual Help*—M.P.S.
[]—*Oblate Missionaries of Mary Immaculate*—O.M.M.I.
[]—*Oblates of Notre Dame* (Philippines)—O.N.D.
[3130]—*Our Lady of Victory Missionary Sisters*—O.L.V.M.
[]—*Pax Christi Institute*—P.C.I.
[]—*Poor Clares of Perpetual Adoration*—P.C.P.A.
[3460]—*Religious of Mary Immaculate*—R.M.I.
[2540]—*Religious Sisters of Mercy*—R.S.M.
[1570]—*St. Francis of Assisi Holy Family* (Dubuque IA)—O.S.F.
[2970]—*School Sisters of Notre Dame*—S.S.N.D.
[1690]—*School Sisters of the Third Order of St. Francis*—O.S.F.
[]—*Seraphic Franciscan Sisters of Our Lady of Sorrows* (Poland)—O.L.S.
[]—*Sisters for Christian Community*—S.F.C.C.
[0430]—*Sisters of Charity of the Blessed Virgin Mary* (Dubuque, IA)—B.V.M.
[1010]—*Sisters of Divine Providence of San Antonio, Texas*—C.D.P.
[3195]—*Sisters of Perpetual Adoration*—A.P.G.
[3360]—*Sisters of Providence St. Mary of the Woods*—S.P.
[3740]—*Sisters of St. Casimir of Chicago*—S.C.C.
[3780]—*Sisters of St. Cyril and Methodius*—S.S.C.M.
[1640]—*Sisters of St. Francis of Perpetual Adoration*
[1570]—*Sisters of St. Francis of the Holy Family*—O.S.F.
[3840]—*Sisters of St. Joseph of Carondolet*—C.S.J.
[1960]—*Sisters of the Holy Family*—S.H.F.
[2050]—*Sisters of the Holy Spirit and Mary Immaculate*—S.H.Sp.
[3320]—*Sisters of the Presentation of the B.V.M.*—P.B.V.M.
[3670]—*Sisters of the Sacred Heart of Jesus*—S.S.C.J.
[2150]—*Sisters, Servants of the Immaculate Heart of Mary*—I.H.M.
[4020]—*Society of St. Theresa of Jesus*—S.T.J.
[4110]—*Ursuline Nuns (Roman Union)*—O.S.U.
[4120-04]—*Ursuline Sisters of Cleveland OH*—O.S.U.

ARCHDIOCESAN CEMETERIES

SAN ANTONIO. *Holy Cross*, 17501 Nacogdoches, 78266. Tel: 210-651-6011; Fax: 210-651-5241. Mailing Address: 746 Castroville Rd., 78237.

San Fernando No. 1, 1100 S. Colorado, 78207. Tel: 210-432-2303; Fax: 210-432-3254. Mailing Address: 746 Castroville Rd., 78237.

San Fernando No. 2, 746 Castroville Rd., 78237. Tel: 210-432-2303; Fax: 210-432-3254.

San Fernando No. 3 (Roselawn), 2500 Frio City Rd., 78226. Tel: 210-432-2364; Fax: 210-432-4346. Mailing Address: 1735 Cupples Rd., 78226-1297.

PRIVATE RELIGIOUS ORDER CEMETERY

SAN ANTONIO. *Resurrection Cemetery*, 11624 FM 471 #501, 78253. Tel: 210-798-8220; Fax: 210-798-8225. Email: resurrection@cordi-marian.org. Richard Ruiz, Gen. Mgr.

NECROLOGY

† Lopez, Rev. Msgr. Joseph A., San Antonio, TX Assumption Seminary.—Died May 28, 2011
† De La Garza, Jose Gerardo, (Retired)—Died July 7, 2011
† Hoelscher, James, (Retired)—Died May 28, 2011
† Vigil, Edwin, San Antonio, TX St. John the Evangelist.—Died Feb. 27, 2011

An asterisk (*) denotes an organization that has established tax-exempt status directly with the IRS and is not covered by the USCCB Group Ruling.

Diocese of San Bernardino

Most Reverend

GERALD R. BARNES

Bishop of San Bernardino; ordained December 20, 1975; appointed Titular Bishop of Montefiascone and Auxiliary of San Bernardino January 28, 1992; ordained March 18, 1992; succeeded to the See, December 28, 1995; installed as Second Bishop of San Bernardino March 12, 1996. *Office: 1201 E. Highland Ave., San Bernardino, CA 92404-4641.*

Most Reverend

RUTILIO DEL RIEGO

Auxiliary Bishop of San Bernardino; ordained June 5, 1965; appointed Titular Bishop of Daimlaig and Auxiliary Bishop of San Bernardino July 26, 2005; ordained September 20, 2005. *Office: 1201 E. Highland Ave., San Bernardino, CA 92404-4641.*

ESTABLISHED NOVEMBER 6, 1978.

Square Miles 27,293.

Comprises the Counties of San Bernardino and Riverside.

Legal Title: The Roman Catholic Bishop of San Bernardino, a Corporation Sole (Churches, Rectories, Halls, Catechetical Centers, etc.).

Diocesan Pastoral Center: 1201 E. Highland Ave., San Bernardino, CA 92404-4641. Tel: 909-475-5300; Fax: 909-475-5155.

Web: www.sbdiocese.org

Email: sbdiocese@sbdiocese.org

STATISTICAL OVERVIEW

Personnel	
Bishop	1
Auxiliary Bishops	1
Retired Abbots	1
Priests: Diocesan Active in Diocese	55
Priests: Diocesan Active Outside Diocese	2
Priests: Retired, Sick or Absent	55
Number of Diocesan Priests	112
Religious Priests in Diocese	114
Total Priests in Diocese	226
Extern Priests in Diocese	37
Ordinations:	
Diocesan Priests	5
Religious Priests	1
Permanent Deacons	6
Permanent Deacons in Diocese	113
Total Brothers	19
Total Sisters	145
Parishes	
Parishes	93
With Resident Pastor:	
Resident Diocesan Priests	29
Resident Religious Priests	32
Without Resident Pastor:	
Administered by Priests	19
Administered by Deacons	2
Administered by Religious Women	4
Administered by Lay People	7
Missions	6
Pastoral Centers	5
Professional Ministry Personnel:	
Brothers	1
Sisters	29
Lay Ministers	166
Welfare	
Catholic Hospitals	2
Total Assisted	291,325
Health Care Centers	1
Total Assisted	1,200
Homes for the Aged	2
Total Assisted	156
Specialized Homes	1
Total Assisted	26
Special Centers for Social Services	4
Total Assisted	52,412
Educational	
Seminaries, Diocesan	1
Students from This Diocese	15
Diocesan Students in Other Seminaries	27
Total Seminarians	42
High Schools, Diocesan and Parish	2
Total Students	878
High Schools, Private	1
Total Students	483
Elementary Schools, Diocesan and Parish	25
Total Students	5,682
Elementary Schools, Private	1
Total Students	510
Catechesis/Religious Education:	
High School Students	15,423
Elementary Students	32,568
Total Students under Catholic Instruction	55,586
Teachers in the Diocese:	
Priests	1
Sisters	10
Lay Teachers	392
Vital Statistics	
Receptions into the Church:	
Infant Baptism Totals	10,479
Minor Baptism Totals	942
Adult Baptism Totals	361
Received into Full Communion	507
First Communions	15,546
Confirmations	8,022
Marriages:	
Catholic	1,571
Interfaith	182
Total Marriages	1,753
Deaths	2,633
Total Catholic Population	929,467
Total Population	4,224,851

Former Bishop—Most Rev. PHILLIP F. STRALING, D.D., ord. March 19, 1959; appt. Bishop of San Bernardino July 18, 1978; cons. Nov. 16, 1978; transferred to See of Reno, June 29, 1995.

Diocesan Pastoral Center—1201 E. Highland Ave., San Bernardino, 92404-4641. Tel: 909-475-5300; Fax: 909-475-5155. Office Hours: Mon.-Fri. 8:30-4:30.

All correspondence should be addressed to the Diocesan Pastoral Center unless otherwise noted.

Office of the Bishops—Email: bishopsoffice@sbdiocese.org.

Executive Office Administrator to the Bishop—EDNA PRECIADO. Tel: 909-475-5113; Fax: 909-475-5109. Email: epreciado@sbdiocese.org.

Office Administrator—LILIANA B. MENDEZ-CHAVEZ. Tel: 909-475-5117; Fax: 909-475-5109. Email: lmendez-chavez@sbdiocese.org.

Episcopal Master of Ceremonies/Special Assistant to the Bishop—Mr. RICHARD C. HERBST. Tel: 909-475-5124; Fax: 909-475-5139. Email: rherbst@sbdiocese.org.

Office of the Vicar General/Moderator of the Curia—Very Rev. Msgr. GERARD M. LOPEZ, S.T.L., V.G. Tel: 909-475-5120; Fax: 909-475-5109. Email: glopez@sbdiocese.org.

Office Administrator—YOLANDA LEAR. Tel: 909-475-5123; Fax: 909-475-5109. Email: ylear@sbdiocese.org.

Coordinator of Victim Assistance Ministry—Sr. ROSALINE O'CONNOR, R.S.M. Tel: 909-855-2296; Fax: 909-475-5109. Email: roconnor@sbdiocese.org.

Office of Episcopal Vicars—Riverside Episcopal Region: Most Rev. RUTILIO J. DEL RIEGO, D.D., V.G. Riverside Pastoral Region: Very Rev. Msgr. THOMAS M. WALLACE, E.V. San Bernardino Pastoral Region: Very Rev. ROMEO N. SELECCION, M.S., E.V.

Office Administrator—CYNTHIA ORTEGA. Tel: 909-475-5107; Fax: 909-475-5109. Email: cortega@sbdiocese.org.

Vicars Forane—Hemet: Very Rev. THOMAS J. BURDICK, V.F. Tel: 951-698-8180. High Desert: Very Rev. SANTOS L. ORTEGA, V.F. Tel: 760-244-9180. Low Desert: Very Rev. DENNIS L. LEGASPY, V.F. Tel: 760-329-8794. Riverside: Very Rev. GENEROSO T. SABIO, M.S.C., V.F. Tel: 951-781-9855. San Bernardino: Very Rev. LEONARD D. DEPASQUALE, I.M.C., V.F. Tel: 909-884-0104. West End: Very Rev. ANTHONY C. DAO, O.P., V.F. Tel: 909-626-7278.

Chief Financial Officer—Ms. LAURA J. CLARK. Tel: 909-475-5150; Fax: 909-475-5156.

Office of the Chancellor—Ms. THERESA D. MONTMINY. Tel: 909-475-5100; Fax: 909-475-5109. Email: officeofthechancellor@sbdiocese.org.

Office Administrator—MARTHA DE JIMENEZ. Tel: 909-475-5104; Fax: 909-475-5109. Email: mdejimenez@sbdiocese.org.

Archives/Records Management—PETER BRADLEY, Archivist. Tel: 909-475-5399; Fax: 909-475-5109. Email: pbradley@sbdiocese.org.

Statistical Researcher and Archival Assistant—ANGELA VALENCIA. Tel: 909-475-5143; Fax: 909-475-5109. Email: avalencia@sbdiocese.org.

Development Office—Tel: 909-475-5460; Fax: 909-475-5155. Email: development@sbdiocese.org. Ms. THERESA D. MONTMINY, Interim Dir.

Office of Human Resources—Tel: 909-475-5170; Fax: 909-475-5189. Email: humanresources@sbdiocese.org. VIRGINIA TURNER, Dir. Tel: 909-475-5172. Email: vturner@sbdiocese.org.

Diocesan Office of Child and Youth Protection—Tel: 909-475-5125; Fax: 909-475-5126. Sr. CATHY WHITE, S.P., Dir. Tel: 909-475-5127; Fax: 909-475-5126. Email: cwhite@sbdiocese.org.

Emergency Operations Collaborative—ANN MARIE GALLANT, Dir. Tel: 909-475-5440; Fax: 909-475-5109. Email: agallant@sbdiocese.org.

Vice Chancellor, Apostolic and Ethnic Affairs—MARIA ECHEVERRIA. Tel: 909-475-5140; Fax: 909-475-5343. Email: mecheverria@sbdiocese.org.

Administrative Assistant—MIRYAM CACHU. Tel: 909-475-5142; Fax: 909-475-5343. Email: mcachu@sbdiocese.org.

Vice Chancellor, Ecclesial Services—Deacon F. MICHAEL JELLEY. Tel: 909-475-5119; Fax: 909-475-5164. Email: mjelley@sbdiocese.org.

Administrative Assistant—NORMA VERDUGO. Tel: 909-475-5160; Fax: 909-475-5164.

Legal Counsel—WILFRID C. LEMANN, Fullerton, Lemann, Schaefer and Dominick LLP, 215 N. "D" St., San Bernardino, 92401-1701. Tel: 909-889-3691; Fax: 909-888-5119.

Office of Canonical Services (Tribunal)—Tel: 909-475-5320; Fax: 909-475-5330. Email: canonicalservices@sbdiocese.org.

Judicial Vicar—Very Rev. DAVID ANDEL, J.C.L., J.V. Email: dandel@sbdiocese.

Director—VACANT.

Defender of the Bond—Rev. Msgr. ROBERT E. LAWRENCE, J.C.L. (Retired).

Promoter of Justice—VACANT.

Judges—Rev. Msgr. DONALD S. WEBBER, J.C.L. (Retired); Very Rev. DAVID ANDEL, J.C.L., J.V.; Rev. Msgr. PHILIP A. BEHAN, J.C.L.; Rev. GEORGE GONZALES (Retired); Deacon SCOTT HUNSICKER, J.C.L.; Ms. MARLA V. PRUNEDA, J.C.L.

Canonical Administrative Assistant—GINA GRADIAS-PENMAN. Email: ggradias@sbdiocese.org.

Canonical Auditor / Consultant—VACANT.

Diocesan Notaries—GINA GRADIAS-PENMAN. Email: ggradias@sbdiocese.org; IRENE MARTINEZ. Email: imartinez@sbdiocese.org.

Canonical Secretary—JARELI JACOBO. Email: jjacobo@sbdiocese.org.

Assessor—VACANT.

Office of Worship—Tel: 909-475-5335; Fax: 909-475-5334. Email: worship@sbdiocese.org. Sr. MARILU COVANI, S.P., Dir. Tel: 909-475-5336. Email: mcovani@sbdiocese.org.

Bishop's Advisors and Advisory Boards

College of Consultors—Most Revs. GERALD R. BARNES, D.D.; RUTILIO J. DEL RIEGO, D.D., V.G.; Very Rev. Msgrs. GERARD M. LOPEZ, S.T.L., V.G.; THOMAS M. WALLACE, E.V.; Very Rev. ROMEO N. SELECCION, M.S., E.V.; Rev. ROBERT L. MILLER (Retired); Very Rev. DAVID ANDEL, J.C.L., J.V.; Revs. JACK BARKER, K.C.H.S.; JAMES MCLAUGHLIN.

Diocesan Curia—Most Revs. GERALD R. BARNES, D.D.; RUTILIO J. DEL RIEGO, D.D., V.G.; Very Rev. Msgrs. GERARD M. LOPEZ, S.T.L., V.G.; THOMAS M. WALLACE, E.V.; Very Rev. ROMEO N. SELECCION, M.S., E.V.; Ms. THERESA D. MONTMINY; Deacon F. MICHAEL JELLEY; Ms. MARIA ECHEVERRIA; Ms. LAURA J. CLARK; Sr. SARA M. KANE, C.S.J.; JEANETTE ARNQUIST; Mr. JOHN H. ANDREWS, B.A.; Mr. THEODORE FURLOW; Very Rev. DAVID ANDEL, J.C.L., J.V.

Presbyteral Council—Most Rev. GERALD R. BARNES, D.D., Pres. Ex Officio Member: Most Rev. RUTILIO J. DEL RIEGO, D.D., V.G., Auxiliary Bishop; Very Rev. Msgrs. GERARD M. LOPEZ, S.T.L., V.G.; THOMAS M. WALLACE, E.V.; Very Rev. ROMEO N. SELECCION, M.S., E.V. Appointed Members: Very Revs. GENEROSO T. SABIO, M.S.C., V.F.; THOMAS J. BURDICK, V.F.; LEONARD D. DEPASQUALE, I.M.C., V.F.; SANTOS L. ORTEGA, V.F.; DENNIS L. LEGASPI; ANTHONY C. DAO, O.P., V.F., Vice Chm.; Revs. ELISEO HERNANDEZ, C.O.R.C.; JORGE A. GARCIA; BENEDICT C. NWACHUKWU. Elected At-Large Members: Revs. TIMOTHY F. KEPPEL, C.R., Interim Vice Chair; ERIK L. ESPARZA; TRONG JOSEPH NGUYEN, S.V.D.; Very Rev. DAVID ANDEL, J.C.L., J.V.; Revs. HOWARD A. LINCOLN; JOHN S. VIEIRA. Elected Members: Revs. ROBERT J. ERICKSON (Retired); MANUEL CARDOZA; RAFAEL PARTIDA; JOHN F. WAGNER.

Council for Consecrated Life—Most Rev. GERALD R. BARNES, D.D.; Very Rev. GENEROSO T. SABIO, M.S.C., V.F.; Sisters MARY FRANCES COLEMAN, R.S.M.; MARY ANN SCHEPERS, O.S.B.; Bro. ANTHONY SCULLY, O.H.; Sisters PATRICIA PHILLIPS, S.H.C.J.; MARIA CARLOS, E.I.N.; MARY JANE KENNEY, S.M.S.M.; JUDINE JACOBS, S.M.I.C.

Ministerial Personnel and Placement Board—Ex Officio: Most Revs. GERALD R. BARNES, D.D.; RUTILIO J. DEL RIEGO, D.D., V.G.; Very Rev. Msgrs. GERARD M. LOPEZ, S.T.L., V.G.; THOMAS M. WALLACE, E.V.; Very Rev. ROMEO N. SELECCION, M.S., E.V.; Deacon F. MICHAEL JELLEY. Elected Members: Deacon STEPHEN SEREMBE; Ms. KIRSTEN R. THORSTAD; Revs. JEROME OCHETTI; JOHN S. VIEIRA; RAFAEL A. PARTIDA; Rev. Msgr. PHILIP A. BEHAN, J.C.L. Appointed: JOYCE DRAKE.

Bishop's Advisory Commissions—

Commission on the Status of Women in Church and Society—URSULA HINKSON, Chm., 1201 E. Highland Ave., San Bernardino, 92404-4641. Tel: 909-475-5153.

Commission for Ministry with Families of Gay and Lesbian Catholics—VACANT.

Diocesan Liturgical Commission—Sr. SARA MICHAEL KING, C.S.J., St. Mary of the Valley, 7495 Church St., Yucca Valley, 92284-3247. Tel: 760-365-2287.

Ecumenical Office—Rev. GREGORY ELDER, Chm., St. Martha Church, 37200 Whitewood Rd., Murrieta, 92563. Tel: 951-698-8180; Fax: 951-698-7353.

Bishop's Advisory Committees—

Diocesan Building Committee—Tel: 909-475-5310. Email: building@sbdiocese.org. Ms. SUSANNA HUGHES, 6860 Abel Stearns Ave., Riverside, 92509. Tel: 951-906-8409.

Diocesan Review Committee—Mr. GERARDO J. LOPEZ, Chm., 4873 Laurel Ridge Dr., Riverside, 92509. Tel: 951-955-5475.

Finance Council—Ms. LAURA J. CLARK, CFO. Tel: 909-475-5150; Fax: 909-475-5457; Mr. BRUCE SATZGER, Interim Chm.

Budget Committee—Mr. BRUCE SATZGER, Chm.

Catholic Foundation Trustees—VACANT, Chm.

Financial Review Committee—VACANT.

Investment Committee—Mr. MICHAEL VANDERPOOL, Chm.

Diocesan Departments

Department of Catholic Communications—Tel: 909-475-5420; Fax: 909-475-5357. Mr. JOHN H. ANDREWS, B.A., Dept. Dir. Tel: 909-475-5421; Fax: 909-475-5357.

Information Services—Tel: 909-475-5400; Fax: 909-475-5357. Email: informationservices@sbdiocese.org. DALE JONASSON, M.S., Office Dir. Tel: 909-475-5400. Email: djonasson@sbdiocese.org; ALFRED VELASQUEZ, Oper. Mgr. Tel: 909-475-5405. Email: avelasquez@sbdiocese.org.

Media Relations—Mr. JOHN H. ANDREWS, B.A., Dept. Dir. Tel: 909-475-5421; Fax: 909-475-5357.

Caritas Telecommunications—Tel: 909-475-5350; Fax: 909-475-5357. Email: caritas@sbdiocese.org. Mr. JOHN H. ANDREWS, B.A., Dept. Dir. Tel: 909-475-5420; Fax: 909-475-5357.

Ministry of Life, Dignity and Justice—JEANETTE ARNQUIST, Dept. Dir. Tel: 909-475-5478; Fax: 909-475-5473. Email: jarnquist@sbdiocese.org.

Office of Social Concerns—Tel: 909-475-5465; Fax: 909-475-5473. Mr. VERNE SCHWEIGER, Dir. Tel: 909-475-5468; Fax: 909-475-5473. Email: vschweiger@sbdiocese.org.

Office of Restorative Justice—Tel: 909-475-5474; Fax: 909-475-5473. Sr. SUE REIF, O.S.F., Dir. Email: sreif@sbdiocese.org.

Catholic Campaign for Human Development—Mr. VERNE SCHWEIGER, Dir. Tel: 909-475-5468; Fax: 909-475-5473. Email: vschweiger@sbdiocese.org.

Pro Life Catholic Ministries—Tel: 909-475-5350; Fax: 909-475-5473. Email: prolifecathmins@sbdiocese.org. MARIE WIDMANN, Office Dir. Tel: 909-475-5351. Email: mwidmann@sbdiocese.org.

Department of Ecclesial Services—Tel: 909-475-5160; Fax: 909-475-5164. Deacon F. MICHAEL JELLEY, Vice Chancellor & Dept. Dir. Tel: 909-475-5119; Fax: 909-475-5109. Email: mjelley@sbdiocese.org.

Administrative Assistant—NORMA VERDUGO. Tel: 909-475-5160. Email: nverdugo@sbdiocese.org.

Office of Continuing Formation of Priests—Dr. MICHAEL DOWNEY, Office Dir. Tel: 909-475-5459; Fax: 909-475-5164. Email: mdowney@sbdiocese.org.

Office of the Vicar for Priests—Tel: 909-475-5459; Fax: 909-475-5343. Email: vicar-for-priests@sbdiocese.org. Very Rev. PATRICK J. O'HAGAN, SS.CC., V.F. Tel: 909-475-5455; Fax: 909-475-5164. Email: pohagan@sbdiocese.org.

Office of Vicar for Retired Priests—Sr. MARY FRANCES COLEMAN, R.S.M., Interim Dir. Tel: 909-475-5342; Fax: 909-475-5343. Email: mfcoleman@sbdiocese.org. Administrative Assistant: NORMA VERDUGO. Tel: 909-475-5160. Email: nverdugo@sbdiocese.org.

Office for Consecrated Life—Tel: 909-475-5345; Fax: 909-475-5343. Email: religious@sbdiocese.org. Sr. MARY FRANCES COLEMAN, R.S.M., Office Dir. Tel: 909-475-5342; Fax: 909-475-5343. Email: mfcoleman@sbdiocese.org.

Office of Permanent Diaconate Formation—Tel: 909-475-5162; Fax: 909-475-5343. Email: diaconate@sbdiocese.org. Deacon EDWARD CLARK, Dir. Email: eclark@sbdiocese.org.

Office of Seminarians—Rev. JOSE A. SANZ, D.L.P., Office Dir., 12725 Oriole Ave., Grand Terrace, 92313. Tel: 909-783-0260; Fax: 909-783-0223.

Office of Vocations—Tel: 909-783-1305; Fax: 909-783-0223. Email: vocations@sbdiocese.org. Sr. SARAH SHREWSBURY, O.S.C., Office Dir. Email: sshrewsbury@sbdiocese.org.

Blessed Junipero Serra House of Formation—12725 Oriole Ave., Grand Terrace, 92313. Tel: 909-783-0260; Fax: 909-783-0223. Revs. JOSE A. SANZ, D.L.P., Rector; JUAN L. GARCIA, D.L.P., Spiritual Dir.

Department of Educational Services—Tel: 909-475-5450; Fax: 909-475-5155. Email: educationalservices@sbdiocese.org. Sr. SARA M. KANE, C.S.J., Dept. Dir. Tel: 909-475-5340. Email: skane@sbdiocese.org; MARCELLA RUIZ, Dept. Office Admin. Tel: 909-475-5450. Email: mruiz@sbdiocese.org.

Office of Charismatic Renewal—1201 E. Highland Ave., San Bernardino, 92404-4641. Tel: 909-475-5365; Fax: 909-475-5369. Email: crc@sbdiocese.org. MARINA CARRION, Office Dir. Tel: 909-475-5366. Email: mcarrion@sbdiocese.org.

Ministry Formation Institute—Tel: 909-475-5375; Fax: 909-475-5379. Email: mfi@sbdiocese.org. JOYCE DRAKE, Dir. Tel: 909-475-5381. Email: jdrake@sbdiocese.org.

Ministry With Youth Office—1201 E. Highland Ave., San Bernardino, 92404-4641. Tel: 909-475-5165; Fax: 909-475-5398. Email: ministrywithyouth@sbdiocese.org. KATHERINE JA-EUN CHO, Dir. Tel: 909-475-5166; Cell: 909-938-5405. Email: kcho@sbdiocese.org.

Office of Campus Ministry—1201 E. Highland Ave., San Bernardino, 92404. Tel: 909-475-5451; Fax: 909-475-5155. LUZ LARA, Campus Min., University of Redlands. Tel: 909-793-2469; Fax: 909-475-5155. Email: llara@sbdiocese.org; Sr. PESIO IOSEFO, S.P., Campus Min., Cal State Univ., San Bernardino. Tel: 909-537-7337; Fax: 909-475-5155. Email: miosefo@sbdiocese.org.

Office of Catholic Schools—Tel: 909-475-5437; Fax: 909-475-5477. Email: catholicschools@sbdiocese.org. PATRICIA VESELY, Supt. Email: pvesely@sbdiocese.org; Sr. LINDA NICHOLSON, C.S.J., Assoc. Supt. Curriculum & Instruction. Tel: 909-475-5437. Email: lnicholson@sbdiocese.org; AUSTIN CONLEY III, Dir. Advancement for Catholic Schools. Tel: 909-475-5437. Email: aconley@sbdiocese.org.

Office of Catechetical Ministry—Tel: 909-475-5452; Fax: 909-475-5457. Email: catechetical@sbdiocese.org. MARIA COVARRUBIAS, Office Dir. Email: mcovarrubias@sbdiocese.org.

Office of Small Faith Communities—Tel: 909-475-5195; Fax: 909-475-5155. Email: smallfaithcommunities@sbdiocese.org. STEVE VALENZUELA, Office Dir. Tel: 909-475-5197. Email: svalenzuela@sbdiocese.org.

Department of Financial Affairs—Tel: 909-475-5150; Fax: 909-475-5156. Email: financialaffairs@sbdiocese.org. Ms. LAURA J. CLARK, CFO & Dept. Dir. Tel: 909-475-5150. Email: lclark@sbdiocese.org; GLORIA SANTOS, Exec. Sec. Tel: 909-475-5150. Email: gloriasantos@sbdiocese.org.

Accounting Services—Tel: 909-475-5480; Fax: 909-475-5489. Email: accounting@sbdiocese.org. PEGGY KOSTER, Office Dir. Tel: 909-475-5482. Email: pkoster@sbdiocese.org.

Catholic Mutual Insurance Group—2724 N. Waterman Ave., Ste. J, San Bernardino, 92404. Tel: 909-886-6001; Fax: 909-883-9311. Email: wanchales@catholicmutual.org. TAMARA BRINKERHOFF, Claims & Risk Mgr. Email: tbrinkerhoff@catholicmutual.org.

Office of Payroll Services—Tel: 909-475-5188; Fax: 909-475-5183. Email: payroll@sbdiocese.org. TRANG PHAM, C.P.P., Office Dir. Tel: 909-475-5182. Email: tpham@sbdiocese.org.

Office of Parish Assistance—Tel: 909-475-5490; Fax: 909-475-5307. Email: parishassistance@sbdiocese.org. Web: www.sbdiocese.org/parish-assistance.htm. CAROLINE BEATTY, Dir. Tel: 909-475-5492. Email: cbeatty@sbdiocese.org.

Department of Pastoral and Ethnic Ministries—MARIA ECHEVERRIA, Vice Chancellor & Dept. Dir. Tel: 909-475-5141; Fax: 909-475-5109. Email: mecheverria@sbdiocese.org.

Administrative Assistant—MIRYAM CACHU. Tel: 909-475-5140; Fax: 909-475-5343. Email: mcachu@sbdiocese.org.

Asian-Pacific Islander Ministry—Tel: 909-475-5348; Fax: 909-475-5364. Sr. MARIA JENNIFER NGUYEN, L.H.C., Dir. Tel: 909-475-5348; Fax: 909-475-5364. Email: mjnguyen@sbdiocese.org.

The following ministries can be contacted through

the Office of Asian/Pacific Islander Ministry:
Chamorro Ministry—
Filipino Ministry—
Indonesian Ministry—
Korean Ministry—
Vietnamese Ministry—
Tongan Ministry—
Ministry to Catholics of African Decent—Tel: 909-475-5194; Fax: 909-475-5155. DAVID C. OKONKWO, Dir. Email: dokonkwo@sbdiocese.org.
Commission and Assembly for Catholics of African Descent—
Nigerian Igbo Ministry—
The Ministry of Hispanic Affairs—Tel: 909-475-5362; Fax: 909-475-5364. Email: hispanicaffairs@sbdiocese.org. Web: hispanicaffairs.sbdiocese.cc. PETRA ALEXANDER, Dir. Tel: 909-475-5363. Email: palexander@sbdiocese.org.
Native American Ministry—Rev. EARL HENLEY, M.S.C., Chap. & Pastor, 23600 Soboba Rd., P.O. Box 1027, San Jacinto, 92581. Tel: 951-654-2086; Fax: 951-654-2086 (Call First). Email: ehenley@sbdiocese.org.
Mission Office of the Diocese of San Bernardino—Mailing Address: P.O. Box 1416, San Bernardino, 92402-1416. Tel: 909-475-5130; Fax: 909-475-5135. Email: mission@sbdiocese.org. Web: missions.sbdiocese.cc. Rev. RENO AIARDI, I.M.C., Dir. Tel: 909-475-5131. Email: raiardi@sbdiocese.org.
Marriage Ministry— Please contact the office of Maria Echeverria, Vice Chancellor for all Marriage Ministries.
Engaged Encounter (English)—
Engaged Encounter (Spanish)—
Marriage Encounter (English)—
Marriage Encounter (Spanish)—
Marriage Enrichment—
Retrouvaille Coordinators—
Apostolic Organizations in the Diocese— Please contact the office of Maria Echeverria, Vice Chancellor for all lay organizations.
Catholic Committee on Scouting—
Catholic Daughters of America—
Catholic Men's Fellowship—
Council of Catholic Women—
Couples for Christ—
Cursillo—
English Movement—
Filipino Movement—
Korean Movement—
Spanish Movement—
Vietnamese Movement—
Desert Refuge for Peace Officers—
El Shaddai—
Equestrian Order of the Holy Sepulchre of Jerusalem—
Escuela de Evangelizacion Nazareth (E.D.E.N.)—
Fellowship of Catholic Christian Women (FCCW)—
Italian Catholic Federation—
Jovenes Para Cristo—
Knights of Columbus—
Knights of Malta—
Knights of Peter Claver—
Ladies Auxiliary, Knights of Peter Claver—
Magnificat—
Movimiento Familiar Cristoano—
Serra International—
Society of St. Vincent de Paul—
Su Misericordia—
Talleres de Oracion y Vida—
World Apostolate of Fatima (Blue Army)-San Bernardino Division—
Department of Planning—Tel: 909-475-5146; Fax: 909-475-5144. Email: pastoralplanning@sbdiocese.org. Mr. THEODORE FURLOW, Dept. Dir. Tel: 909-475-5147; Fax: 909-475-5144. Email: tfurlow@sbdiocese.org.
Office of Construction and Real Estate—Tel: 909-475-5310; Fax: 909-475-5319. Email: ocre@sbdiocese.org. DAVID MEIER, Dir. Tel: 909-475-5305. Email: dmeier@sbdiocese.org; JUDY A. JUAREZ-FLORES, Opers. Mgr. Tel: 909-475-5313. Email: jjuareaflores@sbdiocese.org.
Office of Pastoral Planning—Tel: 909-475-5146; Fax: 909-475-5109. Email: pastoralplanning@sbdiocese.org. Web: www.futureofhope.org. Mr. TED FURLOW, Office Dir. Tel: 909-475-5147; Fax: 909-475-5744. Email: tfurlow@sbdiocese.org.

CLERGY, PARISHES, MISSIONS AND PAROCHIAL SCHOOLS

CITY OF SAN BERNARDINO

(SAN BERNARDINO COUNTY)

1—OUR LADY OF THE ROSARY CATHEDRAL (1927) Revs. Alan Jenkins, S.V.D.; Hieu Trong Nguyen, S.V.D., Parochial Vicar; Deacons Michael F. Jelley; Thomas Dewhirst.
Office, Church & Mailing Address: 265 W. 25th St., 92405-3799. Tel: 909-883-8991; Fax: 909-882-2061. Email: olrosary.sb@sbdiocese.org. Web: http://ourladyoftherosarycathedral.catholicweb.com. Church: 2525 Arrowhead Ave., 92405-3799.
School—Holy Rosary Academy, (Grades PreSchool-8), 2620 N. Arrowhead Ave., 92405. Tel: 909-886-1088; Fax: 909-475-5263. Email: holyrosary.ocs@sbdiocese.org. Web: www.holyrosaryacademyandpreschool.org. Ms. Cheryll Austin, Prin. Lay Teachers 7; Total Staff 17; Students 156.
Catechesis/Religious Program—Ms. Monica Havins, D.R.E. Students 365.

2—ST. ANTHONY (1948) Rev. Zbigniew Fraszczak, S.V.D.; Deacons Nelson Glass; Mario Gutierrez.
Office: 1640 Western Ave., 92411-1300. Tel: 909-887-3810; Fax: 909-880-0982. Email: stanthony.sb@sbdiocese.org.
Catechesis/Religious Program—Tel: 909-887-3210. Amparo Martinez, C.R.E. (Spanish). Students 431.

3—ST. BERNARDINE (1862) Very Rev. Leonard D. DePasquale, I.M.C., Admin.
Office: 531 N. F. St., 92410-3109. Tel: 909-884-0104; Fax: 909-885-4634. Email: stbernardine.sb@sbdiocese.org.
Catechesis/Religious Program—Rosie Aguirre, D.R.E. Students 299.

4—OUR LADY OF GUADALUPE (1925), (Hispanic), Revs. Francisco J. Sebastian, C.O.R.C.; Jorge Luis Rodriguez Pina, C.O.R.C., Parochial Vicar; Deacon Dan Taylor.
Office: 1430 W. 5th St., 92411. Tel: 909-888-0044; Fax: 909-888-4428. Email: olg.sb@sbdiocese.org.
Catechesis/Religious Program—Mrs. Andrea Villa, C.R.E. (Spanish); Ms. Olga Saenz, C.R.E. (English). Students 574.

5—OUR LADY OF HOPE CATHOLIC COMMUNITY, INC. (2006) Very Rev. Romeo N. Seleccion, M.S., Priest Mod.; Revs. Miguel R. Ceja, Priest Min.; Scott C. Nguyen, Parochial Vicar; Sr. Maureen Chicoine, R.S.C.J., Pastoral Coord.
Mailing Address: P.O. Box 3860, 92413-3860.
Office: 6885 Del Rosa Ave., 92404. Tel: 909-884-6375; Fax: 909-884-8976. Email: ourladyofhope.sb@sbdiocese.org.
Del Rosa Avenue Worship Site—6885 Del Rosa Ave., 92404.
Valencia Avenue Worship Site—1000 Valencia Ave., 92410. Tel: 909-885-0948.
Catechesis/Religious Program—Ms. Luz Hernandez, C.R.E. - Valencia; Ms. Laura Aguilar, C.R.E. - Del Rosa; Sr. Mary Tin Nguyen, L.H.C., C.R.E. - Del Rosa (Vietnamese). Students 1,032.

6—OUR LADY OF THE ASSUMPTION (1954) Rev. Henry M. Sseriiso, I.M.C., Admin.; Deacon Daniel O'Camb.
Office: 796 W. 48th St., 92407-3594. Tel: 909-882-2931; Fax: 909-883-4851. Email: olassumption.sb@sbdiocese.org.
School—Our Lady of the Assumption School, (Grades K-8) Tel: 909-881-2416. Email: ourladyofassumption@sbdiocese.org. Ms. Sue Long, Prin. Lay Teachers 10; Students 225; Total Staff 6.
Catechesis/Religious Program—Sr. Maura Redington, R.S.M., D.R.E. Students 360.

OUTSIDE THE CITY OF SAN BERNARDINO

ADELANTO, SAN BERNARDINO CO., CHRIST THE GOOD SHEPHERD (1962) Rev. Mario V. Ramirez, M.S.C.
Mailing Address: P.O. Box 577, 92301-0577.
Office: 17900 Jonathan St., 92301-1731. Tel: 760-246-7083; Fax: 760-246-4603. Email: christthegoodshepherd.adelanto@sbdiocese.org.
Catechesis/Religious Program—Students 204.

ALTA LOMA, SAN BERNARDINO CO., ST. PETER & ST. PAUL (1970) Rev. Patrick V. Kirsch; Deacon Donnie Geaga.
Office: 9135 Banyan St., 91737-2338. Tel: 909-987-9312; Fax: 909-890-9404. Email: stpeterstpaul.altaloma@sbdiocese.org. Web: www.stpeterstpaul.com.
School—St. Peter and St. Paul School, (Preschool), Tel: 909-987-7908; Fax: 909-987-6779. Ms. Patricia Ferrer, Prin. Lay Teachers 2; Students 107.
Catechesis/Religious Program—Tel: 909-980-9423. Ms. Maegan Frazier, C.R.E. Students 914.

ANZA, RIVERSIDE CO., SACRED HEART (1988) Rev. Hilary Fischer, M.S.C., Admin.
Mailing Address: P.O. Box 390118, 92539-0118.
Office: 56250 Hwy. 371, 92539. Tel: 951-763-5636; Fax: 951-763-0236. Email: sacredheart.anza@sbdiocese.org.
Catechesis/Religious Program—Students 47.

APPLE VALLEY, SAN BERNARDINO CO., OUR LADY OF THE DESERT (1974) Rev. Timothy F. Keppel, C.R.; Deacon Simon Pimentel. In Res., Rev. Henry A. Ruszel, C.R. (Retired).
Office: 18386 Corwin Rd., 92307-2328. Tel: 760-242-4427; Fax: 760-242-1195. Email: oldesert.applevalley@sbdiocese.org. Web: ourladyofthedesert92307.parishworld.net.
Catechesis/Religious Program—Tel: 760-242-5819. Students 369.

BARSTOW, SAN BERNARDINO CO., ST. JOSEPH (1914) Revs. Eliseo Hernandez, C.O.R.C.; Jose C. Mendez, C.O.R.C., Parochial Vicar; Deacons Donald Burgett; Margarito Saenz.
Office: 505 E. Mountain View Ave., 92311-2924. Tel: 760-256-6818; Fax: 760-256-8307. Email: stjoseph.barstow@sbdiocese.org.
Catechesis/Religious Program—Students 259.
Mission—Our Lady of the Desert 57457 Hwy. 127, Baker, San Bernardino Co. 92309. Tel: 760-733-4308.

BEAUMONT, RIVERSIDE CO., BLESSED KATERI TEKAKWITHA CATHOLIC COMMUNITY, INC. (2006) Revs. Trong Joseph Nguyen, S.V.D.; Demetrio I. Aguilar, S.V.D., Parochial Vicar; Deebar Yonas, S.V.D., Parochial Vicar; Jesus Zamarripa, S.V.D., Parochial Vicar; Deacon Mark Hodnick.
Office: 1234 Palm Ave., 92223. Tel: 951-845-2849; Fax: 951-849-8698. Email: blessedkateritekakwitha.banning@sbdiocese.org.
Catechesis/Religious Program—Tel: 951-849-1897. Ms. Irene Rodrigues, D.R.E. Students 370.

BIG BEAR LAKE, SAN BERNARDINO CO., ST. JOSEPH (1931) Rev. Ikechukwu Eliseus Uju (Nigeria), Admin.; Deacons Ralph Partida Jr.; James Webber.
Mailing Address: P.O. Box 1709, 92315-1709.
Office: 42242 N. Shore Dr., 92315-1709. Tel: 909-866-3030; Fax: 909-866-5087. Email: stjoseph.bigbear@sbdiocese.org.
Catechesis/Religious Program—Tel: 909-938-1781. Students 78.

BLOOMINGTON, SAN BERNARDINO CO., ST. CHARLES BORROMEO (1939), (Hispanic), Rev. Richard A. Humphrys.
Mailing Address: P.O. Box 248, 92316-0248.
Office: 11342 Spruce Ave., 92316-3400. Tel: 909-877-0792; Fax: 909-877-4304. Email: stcharlesborromeoblo@sbdiocese.org.
Catechesis/Religious Program—Tel: 909-421-1494. Ms. Socorro Olivas, D.R.E. Students 349.

BLYTHE, RIVERSIDE CO., ST. JOAN OF ARC (1920) Rev. Henry Licznerski, C.R.; Deacon Hikyung (H.K.) Han.
Office: 875 E. Chanslorway, 92225. Tel: 760-922-3261; Fax: 760-922-5279. Email: stjooanofarcinblythe@hotmail.de.
Catechesis/Religious Program—Tel: 760-922-8934. Ms. Norma Castillo, D.R.E. Students 305.

CATHEDRAL CITY, RIVERSIDE CO., ST. LOUIS (1948) Revs. Michael N. Maher, SS.CC.; Omar Martinez, O.P., Parochial Vicar; Roberto A. Barco, Parochial Vicar.
Office: 68633 C St., 92234-1817. Tel: 760-328-2398; Fax: 760-770-4598. Email: stlouis.cathedralcity@sbdiocese.org.
Catechesis/Religious Program— Raquel Nunez, C.R.E. Students 591.

CHINO HILLS, SAN BERNARDINO CO., ST. PAUL THE APOSTLE (1986) Revs. Michael J. Gilsenan, SS.CC.; Thomas Mullen, SS.CC, Parochial Vicar; Deacon Pat Martinez.
Office: 14085 Peyton Dr., 91709-1610. Tel: 909-465-5503; Fax: 909-465-1683. Email: stpaultheapostle.chinohills@sbdiocese.org. Web: www.stpacc.org.
School—St. Paul the Apostle Little Tots, (Grades PreSchool) Ms. Christina Stutzman, Dir. Lay Teachers 4; Students 30.
Catechesis/Religious Program—Mr. Jeanie Kiefer, D.R.E. Students 2,412.

CHINO, SAN BERNARDINO CO.

1—ST. MARGARET MARY (1947) Revs. Peter Bosque, Admin.; Gabriel Vargas, Parochial Vicar. In Res., Rev. Eugene Eburuche, S.M.M.M.
Office: 12686 Central Ave., 91710. Tel: 909-591-7400; Fax: 909-461-4548. Email: smmary.chino@sbdiocese.org. Web: www.stmargaretmaryparishchino.org.
School—St. Margaret Mary School, (Grades PreSchool-8), 12664 Central Ave., 91710. Tel: 909-591-8419; Fax: 909-591-6960. Web: www.stmargaretmaryschool.org. Ms. Joan Blank, Prin.; Sr. Kathleen Cleary, O.S.F., Librarian. Religious 1; Lay Teachers 15; Students 317; Total Staff 31.
Catechesis/Religious Program—Tel: 909-591-7408. Students 721.

2—OUR LADY OF GUADALUPE (1902), (Hispanic), Rev. Robert Guerrero, Admin.; Deacon Anthony Brenes-Rios.
Office: 5048 D St., 91710. Tel: 909-591-9402; Fax: 909-591-9404. Email: olg.chino@sbdiocese.org.
Catechesis/Religious Program—Tel: 909-628-3615. Students 723.

COACHELLA, RIVERSIDE CO., OUR LADY OF SOLEDAD (1923), (Hispanic), Revs. Victor R. Santiago-Mateo; Nicholas J. Barille, S.T., Parochial Vicar; Rigoberto Chavez, S.T., Parochial Vicar; Deacons Miguel

Badena; Jose Israel Garcia; Sergio Vazquez. In Res., Rev. Allen D. Rodriguez, S.T.
Office: 52-525 Oasis Palm Ave., 92236-3047. Tel: 760-398-5577, Ext. 21; Fax: 760-398-1783. Email: olsoledad.coachella@sbdiocese.org.
Catechesis/Religious Program—Mrs. Dorothy Cordova, D.R.E. Students 443.
Mission—San Felipe de Jesus 67-305 Hwy. 86, Thermal, Riverside Co. 92274.
Mission—Sacred Heart of Mary & Jesus Torres-Martinez Indian Reservation, Thermal, Riverside Co. 92274.

COLTON, SAN BERNARDINO CO.
1—IMMACULATE CONCEPTION (1943) Revs. Benedict C. Nwachukwu, Admin.; Minh Nguyen, Parochial Vicar; Deacon Leonard Castanon. In Res., Rev. Michael Fredericks.
Office: 1106 N. La Cadena Dr., 92324. Tel: 909-825-5110; Fax: 909-825-0912. Email: immaculateconception.colton@sbdiocese.org.
Catechesis/Religious Program—Tel: 909-825-4685. Lorenzo Rangel, D.R.E. Students 580.
2—SAN SALVADOR (1852), (Hispanic), Revs. Benedict C. Nwachukwu, Admin.; Minh Nguyen, Parochial Vicar; Deacon Robert Amador.
Mailing Address: 178 W. K St., 92324-3446.
Office: 7th & L Sts., 92324. Tel: 909-825-3481; Fax: 909-825-4473. Email: sansalvador.colton@sbdiocese.org. Web: www.coltoncatholic.net.
Catechesis/Religious Program—Lorenzo Rangel, D.R.E. Students 200.

CORONA, RIVERSIDE CO.
1—CORPUS CHRISTI (1994) Rev. Gerald C. De Luney.
Office: 3760 McKinley St., 92879-1956. Tel: 951-272-9043; Fax: 951-272-6821. Email: corpuschristi.corona@sbdiocese.org.
Catechesis/Religious Program—Tel: 951-272-9043, Ext. 11. Ms. Maria V. Sell, C.R.E. Students 1,286.
2—ST. EDWARD (1896) Revs. Jose Varela, C.O.R.C.; Josué Arellano-Reynoso, C.O.R.C., Parochial Vicar; Deacon Paul Von Ins.
Office & Church: 605 W. Fifth St., 92882-2199. Tel: 951-549-6000, Ext. 200; Fax: 951-549-6009. Email: stedwards.corona@sbdiocese.org. Web: http://stedward92882.parishworld.net.
School—St. Edward School, (Grades PreSchool-8), 500 S. Merrill St., 92882. Tel: 951-737-2530; Fax: 951-737-1074. Mrs. Leilani Lister, Prin.; Ms. Heidi Morgan, Librarian. Lay Teachers 19; Students 399.
Catechesis/Religious Program—Tel: 951-549-6000, Ext. 203. Students 765.
3—ST. MARY MAGDALENE (1989) Rev. Vincent Au, C.M.C.; Deacon Jose Armando Hernandez.
Office: 8540 Weirick Rd., 92883-4995. Tel: 951-277-1801; Fax: 951-277-2104. Email: stmarymagdalene.corona@sbdiocese.org. Web: www.smmcorona.com.
Catechesis/Religious Program—Margaret Miller, C.R.E. (English); Lourdes Chumacero, C.R.E. (Spanish). Students 29.
4—ST. MATTHEW (1973) Rev. Neil Fuller, S.V.D.
Office: 2140 W. Ontario Ave., 92882-5651. Tel: 951-737-1621; Fax: 951-737-9715. Email: stmatthew.corona@sbdiocese.org. Web: www.stmatthewcorona.com.
Catechesis/Religious Program—Isaura Cera, D.R.E. Students 882.

CRESTLINE, SAN BERNARDINO CO., ST. FRANCES XAVIER CABRINI (1946) Rev. Tom Burns, M.S.C.; Deacon Rick Bassford.
Mailing Address: P.O. Box 3817, 92325-3817.
Office: 23079 Crest Forest Dr., 92325-3817. Tel: 909-338-2303; Fax: 909-338-2383. Email: stfrancesxaviercabrini.crestline@sbdiocese.org. Web: www.stfrancesxaviercabrini.org.
Catechesis/Religious Program—Mrs. Dawn Turner, D.R.E. Students 32.

DESERT HOT SPRINGS, RIVERSIDE CO., ST. ELIZABETH OF HUNGARY (1946) Very Rev. Dennis L. Legaspi (Philippines); Deacon Gerald Campbell.
Office: 66-700 Pierson Blvd., 92240-3740. Tel: 760-329-8794; Fax: 760-329-6760. Email: stelizabethofhungary.dhs@sbdiocese.org. Web: stelizabethofhungarydhs.catholicweb.com.
Catechesis/Religious Program—Tel: 760-251-9268. Students 319.

FONTANA, SAN BERNARDINO CO.
1—BLESSED JOHN XXIII CATHOLIC COMMUNITY, INC. (2006) Rev. Rafael A. Partida; Deacon Abel Zamora.
Office: 7650 Tamarind Ave., 92336. Tel: 909-822-4732; Fax: 909-822-0620. Email: blessedjohnxxiii.fontana@sbdiocese.org.
School—Resurrection Academy, 17434 Miller Ave., 92336. Tel: 909-822-4431; Fax: 909-822-0617. Email: resurrection.ocs@sbdiocese.org. Web: www.sites.google.com/site/resurrectioncatholicfontan. Madeleine Thomas, Prin. Lay Teachers 12; Students 202.
Catechesis/Religious Program—Tel: 909-822-4040. Mrs. Guadalupe Huerta, D.R.E. Students 1,038.
2—ST. GEORGE (1954) Rev. Gerardo Mendoza.
Office: 17895 San Bernardino Ave., 92335-6155. Tel: 909-877-1531; Fax: 909-877-6531. Email: stgeorge.fontana@sbdiocese.org.
Catechesis/Religious Program—Tel: 909-877-3935. Maria Ramirez, C.R.E. Students 322.
3—ST. JOSEPH (1930) Revs. Guillermo Martinez Flores, M.S.P.; Efrain Villalobos-Cuellar, M.S.P., Parochial Vicar; Deacon Michael Juback.
Office: 17080 Arrow Blvd., 92335-3807. Tel: 909-822-0566; Fax: 909-829-1739. Email: stjoseph.fontana@sbdiocese.org.
Catechesis/Religious Program—Tel: 909-822-3411. Students 357.
4—ST. MARY (1939) Rev. Gerard O'Shaughnessy, S.S.C.
Mailing Address: 16548 Jurupa Ave., 92337-7452.
In Res., Rev. Bernard E. Toal, S.S.C. (Retired).
Office: 16550 Jurupa Ave., 92337-7452. Tel: 909-822-5670, Ext. 0; Fax: 909-357-4688. Email: stmary.fontana@sbdiocese.org.
Catechesis/Religious Program—Tel: 909-822-5670, Ext. 222. Students 204.

FRENCH VALLEY, RIVERSIDE CO., BLESSED TERESA OF CALCUTTA CATHOLIC COMMUNITY, INC. (2006) Very Rev. Thomas J. Burdick; Deacon Manuel Robles.
Office & Mailing Address: 31579 Vinters Pointe Ct., 92596. Tel: 951-325-7707; Fax: 951-325-2306. Email: blessedteresaofcalcutta.winchester@sbdiocese.org.
Worship Site: Winchester Rd. & Briggs Rd., 92596.
Catechesis/Religious Program—Students 530.

GRAND TERRACE, SAN BERNARDINO CO., CHRIST THE REDEEMER (1981) Very Rev. Romeo N. Seleccion, M.S., Priest Mod.; Mr. Jose Crespo, Pastoral Coord.
Office: 12745 Oriole Ave., 92313-6133. Tel: 909-783-3811; Fax: 909-783-4689. Email: christtheredeemer.grandterrace@sbdiocese.org.
Catechesis/Religious Program—Tel: 909-783-3800. Kay Kendal, C.R.E. Students 172.

GUASTI, SAN BERNARDINO CO., SAN SECONDO D'ASTI (1926), (Italian), Rev. Louis N. Marx.
Mailing Address: P.O. Box 1056, 91743-1056.
Office: 250 N. Turner Ave., Ontario, 91764. Tel: 909-390-0011; Fax: 909-390-9919. Email: sansecondodasti.guasti@sbdiocese.org. Web: www.sansecondodasti.com.
Catechesis/Religious Program—Tel: 909-390-6364. Mrs. Alma Zendejas, D.R.E. Students 416.

HEMET, RIVERSIDE CO.
1—HOLY SPIRIT (1991) Very Rev. Msgr. Thomas M. Wallace, Priest Moderator; Deacons Fernando Vera; Glen Harmon; Ms. Joyce Fritchel, Pastoral Coord.
Mailing Address: P.O. Box 5268, 92544.
Office: 26340 Soboba St., 92544. Tel: 909-927-8544; Fax: 909-927-8546. Email: holyspirit.hemet@sbdiocese.org. Web: www.holyspirithemet.org.
Catechesis/Religious Program—Students 215.
2—OUR LADY OF THE VALLEY (1946) Revs. Wayne Epperley, C.S.Sp., Admin.; Joseph L. Deniger, C.S.Sp., Parochial Vicar.
Office: 780 S. State St., 92543-7163. Tel: 951-929-6131; Fax: 951-929-8009. Email: olvhemet@sbdiocese.org.
Catechesis/Religious Program—Tel: 951-658-7436. Mr. Gustavo Lermus, D.R.E. Students 523.

HESPERIA, SAN BERNARDINO CO., HOLY FAMILY (1963) Very Rev. Santos L. Ortega; Revs. John Fahnestock, M.S.C., Parochial Vicar; Rigoberto Sanchez-Maya, Parochial Vicar; Deacon Scott Hunsicker.
Office: 9974 I Ave., 92345. Tel: 760-244-9180; Fax: 760-244-1959. Email: holyfamily.hesperia@sbdiocese.org. Web: www.hfchesperia.org.
Catechesis/Religious Program—Tel: 760-244-5423. Ms. Rose Esparza, D.R.E. Students 1,088.

HIGHLAND, SAN BERNARDINO CO., ST. ADELAIDE (1956) Rev. Pierre L. Deglaire, C.S.Sp. In Res., Rev. Jose G. Jaramillo, M.G.
Office: 27457 E. Baseline, 92346-3206. Tel: 909-862-8669; Fax: 909-862-1603. Email: stadelaide.highland@sbdiocese.org.
School—St. Adelaide Academy, (Grades PreK-8), 27487 E. Base Line Rd., 92346. Tel: 909-862-5851; Fax: 909-862-2877. Email: stadelaide.ocs@sbdiocese.org. Web: www.stadelaideacademy.org. Mr. Greg Blanco, Prin. Lay Teachers 10; Students 196.
Catechesis/Religious Program—Tel: 909-862-8184. Ms. Nadine Scharnott-Morales, D.R.E. Students 578.
Mission—St. John Bosco 28991 Merris St., East Highlands, San Bernardino Co. 92346. Tel: 909-425-0931.

IDYLLWILD, RIVERSIDE CO., QUEEN OF ANGELS (1942) Rev. Charles E. Miller.
Mailing Address: P.O. Box 1106, 92549-1106.
Office: 54525 N. Circle Dr., 92549-1106. Tel: 951-659-2708; Fax: 951-659-0208. Email: queenofangels.idyllwild@sbdiocese.org.
Catechesis/Religious Program—Ms. Cathy Regalado, D.R.E. Students 26.

INDIO, RIVERSIDE CO., OUR LADY OF PERPETUAL HELP (1937) Very Rev. Msgr. Thomas M. Wallace, Priest Mod.; Revs. Luis Guido, Priest Min.; Hector Miguel Corona, M.Sp.S., Priest Min.; Laura Lopez, Pastoral Coord.; Deacon Brijido Rodriguez.
Mailing Address: 45299 Deglet Noor St., 92201.
Office: 82500 Bliss St., 92201. Tel: 760-347-3507; Fax: 760-347-8367. Email: olph.indio@sbdiocese.org.
School—Our Lady of Perpetual Help School, (Grades PreK-8), 82-470 Bliss St., 92201. Tel: 760-347-3786; Fax: 760-347-7207. Email: olphindio.ocs@sbdiocese.org. Web: www.olphschoolindio.com. Ms. Diane Arias, Prin. Lay Teachers 11; Students 246.
Catechesis/Religious Program—Tel: 760-347-0594. Yolanda Nieves, D.R.E. Students 655.

JOSHUA TREE, SAN BERNARDINO CO., ST. CHRISTOPHER OF THE DESERT (1961) [JC] Closed. Sacramental records at St. Mary of the Valley, Yucca Valley.

LA QUINTA, RIVERSIDE CO., ST. FRANCIS OF ASSISI (1974) Rev. James McLaughlin; Deacons Pablo Benavides; Randy Fast.
Office: 47-225 Washington St., 92253. Tel: 760-564-1255; Fax: 760-564-0763. Email: stfrancisofassisi.laquinta@sbdiocese.org. Web: www.stfrancislq.org.
Catechesis/Religious Program—Tel: 760-564-1255, Ext. 208. Students 483.

LAKE ARROWHEAD, SAN BERNARDINO CO., OUR LADY OF THE LAKE (1938) Rev. Leonard Kryzwda, C.R.
Mailing Address: P.O. Box 1929, 92352-1929.
Church & Office: 27627 Rim of the World Dr., 92352. Tel: 909-337-2333; Fax: 909-337-5041. Email: ollake.lakearrowhead@sbdiocese.org.
Catechesis/Religious Program—Tel: 909-337-2333, Ext. 140. Gia Brown, D.R.E. Students 184.

LENWOOD, SAN BERNARDINO CO., ST. PHILIP NERI (1979) Revs. Eliseo Hernandez, C.O.R.C.; Jose C. Mendez, C.O.R.C., Parochial Vicar.
Office, Church & Mailing Address: 25333 Third St., 92311. Tel: 760-253-5412; Fax: 760-253-3191. Email: stphilipnericc@verizon.net.
Catechesis/Religious Program—Mr. John Salazar, D.R.E. Twinned with St. Joseph, Barstow. Students 25.

LOMA LINDA, SAN BERNARDINO CO., ST. JOSEPH THE WORKER (1944) Rev. Msgr. Philip A. Behan; Deacons William Shalhoub; Victor Barrion.
Office: 10816 Mt. View Ave., 92354. Tel: 909-796-2605; Fax: 909-796-0755. Email: stjosephtheworker.lomalinda@sbdiocese.org. Web: www.stjosephlomalinda.org.
Catechesis/Religious Program—Tel: 909-796-4308; Fax: 909-796-4308. Caridad Santiago, D.R.E. Students 139.

LUCERNE VALLEY, SAN BERNARDINO CO., ST. PAUL (1963) Rev. Timothy F. Keppel, C.R.
Mailing Address: P.O. Box 588, 92356.
8973 Mesa Rd., 92356. Tel: 760-248-7410; Fax: 760-248-2559. Email: stpaul.lucernevalley@sbdiocese.org.
Catechesis/Religious Program—Betty Curnett, C.R.E.

MECCA, RIVERSIDE CO., SANCTUARY OF OUR LADY OF GUADALUPE (1964), (Hispanic), Rev. Francisco Javier Escobar Felix, Admin.; Deacon Miguel Badena.
Mailing Address: P.O. Box 218, 92254.
Office: 65-100 Dale Kiler Rd., 92254. Tel: 760-396-2717, Ext. 110; Fax: 760-396-0047. Email: olgshrine.mecca@sbdiocese.org.
Catechesis/Religious Program—Tel: 760-396-2717, Ext. 112. Ms. Maribel Lopez, D.R.E. Students 509.

MONTCLAIR, SAN BERNARDINO CO., OUR LADY OF LOURDES (1955) Very Rev. Anthony C. Dao, O.P., Admin.; Rev. Mark Bertelli, Parochial Vicar; Deacon Donald Norris.
Office: 10191 Central Ave., 91763-3801. Tel: 909-626-7278; Fax: 909-626-0562. Email: ollourdes.montclair@sbdiocese.org.
School—Our Lady of Lourdes School, (Grades PreK-8), 5303 Orchard St., 91763. Tel: 909-621-4418; Fax: 909-625-5034. Email: ourladyoflourdes.ocs@sbdiocese.org. Web: www.ollschool.com. Beverly Diaz De Leon, Prin. Lay Teachers 9; Students 174.
Catechesis/Religious Program—Tel: 909-626-0318. Mrs. Yoselin Romero, D.R.E. Students 772.

MORENO VALLEY, RIVERSIDE CO.
1—ST. CHRISTOPHER (1957) Rev. Joven T. Junio, M.S.
Office: 25075 Cottonwood Ave., 92553-0397. Tel: 951-924-1968, Ext. 101; Fax: 951-247-6477. Email: stchristopher.morenovalley@sbdiocese.org. Web: www.stchristophermv.org.
School—St. Christopher Preschool, (Grades PreSchool) Tel: 951-924-1968. Email: stchristopher.ocs@sbdiocese.org. Rebecca Reynoso, Prin. Lay Teachers 1; Students 42.
Catechesis/Religious Program— Ms. Teresita Felix, D.R.E. (Spanish); Ms. Jessica Mejia-Lara, C.R.E. (English). Students 1,327.

2—ST. PATRICK (1989) Very Rev. Msgr. Thomas M. Wallace, Priest Moderator; Rev. Arlan G. Intal, M.S., Priest Min.; Deacons Richard Heames, Pastoral Coord.; Austin Kilbourn; Ricardo Uribe.
Office: 10915 Pigeon Pass Rd., 92557. Tel: 951-485-6673; Fax: 909-485-3834. Email: stpatrick.morenovalley@sbdiocese.org. Web: stpatrick92557.parishworld.net.
Rectory—22589 Mountain View Rd., 92557.
Catechesis/Religious Program—Tel: 951-485-6673, Ext. 113. Christina Robbins, C.R.E.; Ms. Graciela Gutierrez, C.R.E. (Spanish). Students 876.

MURRIETA, RIVERSIDE CO., ST. MARTHA (1992) Revs. Jack Barker; Gregory Elder, Parochial Vicar; Joseph T. Ellison, Parochial Vicar; Fabian Reynalte, Parochial Vicar.
Office: 37200 Whitewood Rd., 92563-5040. Tel: 951-698-8180; Fax: 951-698-7353. Email: stmartha.murrieta@sbdiocese.org.
Catechesis/Religious Program—Tel: 951-698-1528; Fax: 951-698-5546. Annette Wester, D.R.E. Students 144.

NEEDLES, SAN BERNARDINO CO., ST. ANN (1887) Rev. Amaro Saumell III.
Mailing Address: P.O. Box 190, 92363-0190.
Office: 218 D St., 92363. Tel: 760-326-2721; Fax: 760-326-3068. Email: stann.needles@sbdiocese.org. Web: http://home.catholicweb.com/saintanncatholicchurch.
Catechesis/Religious Program—Elaine Blake, D.R.E. Students 65.

NORCO, RIVERSIDE CO.

1—ST. ANDREW KIM KOREAN COMMUNITY (1989) Rev. Young Seung J. Han; Deacons Paul Ahan; John Kim.
Church: 4110 Corona Ave., 92860.
Office: 4750 Challen Ave., Riverside, 92503. Tel: 951-352-4900; Fax: 951-352-4900. Email: stkimdaekonandrew.norco@sbdiocese.org.
Catechesis/Religious Program—Ms. Scholastica Hong, D.R.E. Students 65.

2—ST. MEL (1959) Revs. Declan Fogarty, O.S.A., Admin.; Emmanuel Ukaegbu-Onuoha, Parochial Vicar; Deacon Joe Vela.
Mailing Address: P.O. Box 700, 92860-0700.
Office: 4140 Corona Ave., 92860. Tel: 951-737-7144; Fax: 951-735-8332. Email: stmel.norco@sbdiocese.org.
Catechesis/Religious Program—Tel: 951-737-8140. Emily Guilherme, D.R.E. Students 596.

ONTARIO, SAN BERNARDINO CO.

1—ST. ELIZABETH ANN SETON (1980) Revs. John S. Vieira; Augustine I. Obasi, Parochial Vicar.
Office: 2713 S. Grove Ave., 91761-6931. Tel: 909-947-2956, Ext. 15; Fax: 909-923-2946. Email: stelizabethannseton.ontario@sbdiocese.org. Web: www.seascc-ont.org.
Catechesis/Religious Program—Tel: 909-947-2956, Ext. 27. Ms. Armida Duran, D.R.E. Students 575.

2—ST. GEORGE (1905) Revs. Michael L. Sturn; Abel E. Balbi (Argentina), Parochial Vicar; Deacon Christopher Carroll. In Res., Rev. Msgr. Timothy F. Lawlor (Retired).
Office: 505 N. Palm Ave., 91762. Tel: 909-983-2637, Ext. 101; Fax: 909-395-9707. Email: stgeorge.ontario@sbdiocese.org.
School—St. George School, (Grades PreK-8), 322 W. D St., 91762. Tel: 909-984-9123; Fax: 909-984-0921. Peter Horton, Prin. Lay Teachers 9; Students 285.
Catechesis/Religious Program—Tel: 909-460-1578. Ms. Katherine Martinez, D.R.E. (English); Sr. Mary Faith Tin, L.H.C., D.R.E. (Vietnamese). Students 138.

3—OUR LADY OF GUADALUPE (1948), (Hispanic), Rev. Pavol Sochulak, S.V.D.
Office: 710 S. Sultana Ave., 91761-2554. Tel: 909-986-6154; Fax: 909-984-1541. Email: olg.ontario@sbdiocese.org.
Catechesis/Religious Program—Tel: 909-983-2904. Sr. Guadalupe Flores, D.R.E. Students 503.

PALM DESERT, RIVERSIDE CO.

1—CHRIST OF THE DESERT (1928), (Newman Center) Rev. Howard A. Lincoln.
Office: 73441 Fred Waring Dr., 92260-2286. Tel: 760-346-0089; Fax: 760-340-2245. Email: christofthedesert@sacredheartpalmdesert.com. Web: www.sacredheartpalmdesert.com.
Catechesis/Religious Program—Combined with Sacred Heart, Palm Desert.

2—SACRED HEART (1956) Rev. Howard A. Lincoln; Deacon Fernando Heredia.
Office: 43-775 Deep Canyon Rd., 92260-3164. Tel: 760-346-6502; Fax: 760-773-4873. Email: sacredheart.pd@sbdiocese.org. Web: www.sacredheartpalmdesert.com.
School—Sacred Heart School, (Grades PreSchool-8) Tel: 760-346-3513; Fax: 760-773-0673. Alan Bruzzio, Prin. Religious Teachers 1; Lay Teachers 25; Students 620.
Catechesis/Religious Program—Tel: 760-346-6502. Ms. Silvia Ramirez, D.R.E. Students 725.

PALM SPRINGS, RIVERSIDE CO.

1—OUR LADY OF GUADALUPE (1912), (Cahuilla Indian), Revs. John P. Kavcak, M.S.C.; David K. Foxen, M.S.C., Parochial Vicar.
Mailing Address: P.O. Box 1947, 92263-1947.
204 S. Calle El Segundo, 92263-1947. Tel: 760-325-5809; Fax: 760-325-2049. Email: olg.palmsprings@sbdiocese.org. Web: ourladyofguadalupe92263.parishworld.net.

2—OUR LADY OF SOLITUDE (1928), (Hispanic), [JC] Revs. John P. Kavcak, M.S.C.; David K. Foxen, M.S.C., Parochial Vicar; Deacon John Skora.
Office: 151 W. Alejo Rd., 92262-5666. Tel: 760-325-3816; Fax: 760-325-5316. Email: olsolitude.ps@sbdiocese.org. Web: ourladyofsolitude92262.parishworld.net.
Catechesis/Religious Program—Students 329.

3—ST. THERESA (1948) Very Rev. Msgr. Thomas M. Wallace, Priest Mod.; Rev. Walter Downs, M.S.C., Priest Min.; Sr. Diane Smith, Pastoral Coord. In Res., Rev. Ron L. Rusk.
Office: 2800 E. Ramon Rd., 92264-7996. Tel: 760-323-2669; Fax: 760-322-8581. Email: parishoffice.sttheresa.ps@sbdiocese.org. Web: www.sttheresaps.com.
School—St. Theresa School, (Grades PreK-8), 455 S. Compadre, 92262-7996. Tel: 760-327-4919; Fax: 760-327-4429. Email: sttheresa.ocs@sbdiocese.org. Web: www.stsps.org. Cheryl Corey, Prin. Lay Teachers 15; Students 302.
Catechesis/Religious Program—Tel: 760-323-4351 (English). Ms. Catherine Knox, D.R.E. Students 600.

PERRIS, RIVERSIDE CO., ST. JAMES (1907) Revs. Edmund Gomez; Peter Phan, Parochial Vicar.
Office: 269 W. Third St., 92570-2073. Tel: 951-657-2380; Fax: 951-943-7290. Email: stjamesperris@sbdiocese.org. Web: stjames92570.googlepages.com.
School—St. James School, (Grades K-8), 250 W. Third St., 92570-2005. Tel: 951-657-5226; Fax: 951-657-1793. Email: stjames.ocs@sbdiocese.org. Sr. Sylvia Parkes, R.S.M., Prin. Lay Teachers 9; Students 157.
Catechesis/Religious Program—Tel: 951-940-5219; Fax: 951-940-5192. Students 1,137.
Convent—230 W. B St., 92570. Tel: 951-657-4050.

PHELAN, SAN BERNARDINO CO., BLESSED JUNIPERO SERRA (1989) Rev. Frank T. Dicristina.
Mailing Address: P.O. Box 292570, 92329-2570.
Office: 8820 Sheep Creek Rd., 92371. Tel: 760-868-4342; Fax: 760-868-2171. Email: blessedjuniperoserra.phelan@sbdiocese.org. Web: www.blessedjuniperoserra.org.
Catechesis/Religious Program—Tel: 760-868-4342, Ext. 42. Students 134.

RANCHO CUCAMONGA, SAN BERNARDINO CO.

1—OUR LADY OF MOUNT CARMEL (1905) Very Rev. Romeo N. Seleccion, M.S., Priest Moderator; Rev. Franklin Cubas-Ramirez, S.M., Priest Min.; Deacon Luis Sanchez; Ms. Josefina Herrera, Pastoral Coord.
Office: 10079 Eighth St., 91730. Tel: 909-987-2717, Ext. 20; Fax: 909-987-3818. Email: olmtcarmel.rc@sbdiocese.org.
Catechesis/Religious Program—Tel: 909-987-2717, Ext. 21. Ms. Esthela Garcia, D.R.E. Students 408.

2—SACRED HEART (1953) Very Rev. Romeo N. Seleccion, M.S., Priest Moderator; Revs. Cletus Imo (Nigeria), Priest Min.; Erik L. Esparza, Priest Min.; Deacon Edward Clark; Dr. Peter Newburn, Pastoral Coord. In Res., Rev. Edward J. Molumby, S.T.
Office: 12704 Foothill Blvd., 91739-9795. Fax: 909-899-3229. Email: sacredheart.rc@sbdiocese.org. Web: www.sacredheartrc.com.
School—Sacred Heart School, (Grades K-8), 12676 Foothill Blvd., 91739. Tel: 909-899-1049; Fax: 909-899-0413. Ms. Trenna Meins, Prin. Lay Teachers 28; Students 603.
Catechesis/Religious Program—Students 1,224.

REDLANDS, SAN BERNARDINO CO., THE HOLY NAME OF JESUS CATHOLIC COMMUNITY, INC. (2006) Very Rev. Romeo N. Seleccion, M.S., Priest Moderator; Rev. Msgr. Cesar E. Encinares (Philippines), Priest Min.; Rev. Oscar Reynoso, Priest Min.; Sr. Mary Garascia, C.P.P.S., Pastoral Coord.; Deacon Michael Bellinder. In Res., Rev. Jorge A. Garcia.
Office: 115 W. Olive Ave., 92373-5245. Tel: 909-793-2469; Fax: 909-335-1719. Email: theholynameofjesus.redlands@sbdiocese.org. Web: www.theholynameofjesus.org.
Columbia Street Worship Site—1214 Columbia St., 92373-5245.
Olive Avenue Worship Site—115 W. Olive Ave., 92374.
School—Sacred Heart Academy, (Grades PreSchool-8), 215 S. Eureka St., 92373. Tel: 909-792-3958; Fax: 909-792-7292. Sr. Angela C. Williams, Prin. Lay Teachers 23; Students 279.
Catechesis/Religious Program—Tel: 909-798-4167; Fax: 909-335-1719. Karen Grozak, D.R.E. Students 511.

RIALTO, SAN BERNARDINO CO., ST. CATHERINE OF SIENA (1949) Revs. Stephen C. Porter; Albert R. Utzig, S.S.C., Parochial Vicar; Deacons Gonzalo Sotelo; Eric Vilchis.
Office: 339 N. Sycamore Ave., 92376-5943. Tel: 909-875-1360, Ext. 100; Fax: 909-875-2822. Email: stcatherineofsiena.rialto@sbdiocese.org. Web: stcatherineofsiena92376.parishworld.net.
School—St. Catherine of Siena School, (Grades PreSchool-8), 335 N. Sycamore Ave., 92376. Tel: 909-875-7821; Fax: 909-875-7948. Email: cougars_1956@yahoo.com. Web: www.stcatherinerialto.com. Enrique Landin, Prin. Lay Teachers 9; Students 200.
Catechesis/Religious Program—Tel: 909-875-1360, Ext. 122. Ms. Terry Moriarty, D.R.E. Students 735.

RIVERSIDE, RIVERSIDE CO.

1—ST. ANDREW NEWMAN CENTER (1971), Serving Riverside Community College & University of California at Riverside. Revs. Raymond Finerty, O.P.; Michael A. Amabisco, O.P., Parochial Vicar.
Office: 105 W. Big Springs Rd., 92507-4737. Tel: 909-682-8751; Fax: 909-682-3513. Email: newman.riv@sbdiocese.org. Web: newmancenter92507.parishworld.net.
Catechesis/Religious Program—Tel: 951-682-8751, Ext. 13. Frances Hodgkinson, D.R.E. Students 184.

2—ST. ANTHONY OF PADUA (1923) Rev. Adrian Ochoa-Lugo, O.de.M., Admin.; Deacon Carlos Rosado.
Office: 3074 Madison St., 92504-4478. Tel: 951-352-8393; Fax: 951-352-8816. Email: stanthony.riv@sbdiocese.org.
Catechesis/Religious Program—Tel: 951-785-4908. Ms. Lily Gonzalez, D.R.E. Students 283.

3—ST. CATHERINE OF ALEXANDRIA (1946) Very Rev. Generoso T. Sabio, M.S.C.; Rev. Arturo P. Mateo, M.S.C., Parochial Vicar; Deacons John DeGano; Donald Tillitson. In Res., Rev. Adrianus Budhi, M.S.C.
Office & Mailing Address: *(Ministry Center)*, 7005 Brockton Ave., 92506. Tel: 951-781-9855; Fax: 951-683-4114. Email: stcatherineofalexandria.riv@sbdiocese.org. Web: www.stcofa.org.
Church: 3680 Arlington Ave., 92506.
School—Sr. Catherine of Alexandria School, (Grades PreK-8), 7025 Brockton Ave., 92506. Tel: 951-684-1091; Fax: 951-684-4936. Rick Howick, Prin. Religious Teachers 1; Lay Teachers 16; Students 333.
Catechesis/Religious Program—Tel: 951-781-9855, Ext. 25; Fax: 951-781-3061. Ms. Olivia Garcia, D.R.E. Students 664.

4—ST. FRANCIS DE SALES (1886) Revs. Reno Aiardi, I.M.C., Admin.; Louis Abdoo, I.M.C., Parochial Vicar.
Office: 4268 Lime St., 92501-3868. Tel: 951-686-4004; Fax: 951-686-3948. Email: stfrancisdesales.riv@sbdiocese.org. Web: www.stfrancisdesales-riverside.com.
School—St. Francis de Sales School, (Grades PreSchool-8), 4205 Mulberry St., 92501. Tel: 951-683-5083; Fax: 951-683-0249. Ms. Kathy Kothlow, Prin. Religious Teachers 1; Lay Teachers 9; Students 246.
Catechesis/Religious Program—Tel: 951-534-0929. Ms. Toni Bastian, D.R.E. (English); Ms. Consuelo Grajeda, D.R.E. (Spanish). Students 404.

5—ST. JOHN THE EVANGELIST (1956) Revs. Saul Garcia Avila, M.S.P.; J. Asuncion F. Hernandez-Barron, Parochial Vicar.
Office: 3980 Opal St., 92509-7297. Tel: 951-684-6864; Fax: 909-684-3115. Email: stjohntheevangelist.riv@sbdiocese.org.
Catechesis/Religious Program—Tel: 909-686-5181. Lorraine Pittman, D.R.E. Students 558.
Mission—Our Lady of Guadalupe 2518 Hall Ave., Riverside Co. 92509. Tel: 909-788-1464.

6—OUR LADY OF GUADALUPE SHRINE (1929), (Hispanic), Rev. Alfonso Duran-Ortega, O.de M.
Office: 2858 Ninth St., 92507-4957. Tel: 951-684-0279; Fax: 951-684-0390. Email: olgshrine.riv@sbdiocese.org.
Catechesis/Religious Program—Tel: 951-683-1123. Maria Elena Alba. Students 58.

7—OUR LADY OF PERPETUAL HELP (1955) Very Rev. Msgr. Thomas M. Wallace, Priest Mod.; Revs. Charles A. Patron, Priest Min.; Rogelio Gonzalez-Alba, Priest Min.; Timothy T. Do, Priest Minister; Deacon Nam Bui; Dr. Sara Elder, Pastoral Coord.
Office: 5250 Central Ave., 92504-1825. Tel: 951-689-8921, Ext. 20; Fax: 951-689-3619. Email: olph.riv@sbdiocese.org. Web: olphriv.wordpress.com/.
Rectory—6390 Lionel Ct., 92504.
School—Our Lady of Perpetual Help School, (Grades PreSchool-8), 6866 Streeter Ave., 92504-2299. Tel: 951-689-2125; Fax: 951-689-9354. Mrs. Ann R. Meier, Prin. Lay Teachers 12; Students 250.

Catechesis/Religious Program—Tel: 909-689-9821, Ext. 23. Mrs. Mary Fisher, C.R.E. (English); Ms. Eva Jaimes, C.R.E. (Spanish); Sr. Hang Le, C.R.E. (Vietnamese). Students 658.

8—QUEEN OF ANGELS (1949) Revs. Miguel A. Ruiz, S.V.D.; Arul Pragasam Irudayaraj, S.V.D., Parochial Vicar; Deacon James A. Neufell.
Office: 4824 Jones Ave., 92505-1432. Tel: 951-689-3674, Ext. 101; Fax: 951-687-6146. Email: queenofangelsriv@sbdiocese.org. Web: http://qofar.e-pauluch.com.
Catechesis/Religious Program—Tel: 951-687-3674, Ext. 121. Mariana Flores, D.R.E. Students 551.

9—SACRED HEART (1945) Rev. Martin S. Rodriguez, C.O.R.C., Admin.; Deacon John Barna.
Office: 9935 Mission Blvd., 92509. Tel: 951-685-5058; Fax: 951-685-1056. Email: sacredheart.riv@sbdiocese.org. Web: www.parishesonline.com/sacredheartriv.
Catechesis/Religious Program—Tel: 951-685-8510. Maria Ornales, D.R.E. Students 600.

10—ST. THOMAS THE APOSTLE (1903) Rev. Joseph F. Felker.
Office: 3774 Jackson St., 92503-4359. Tel: 951-689-1131; Fax: 909-354-7402. Email: stthomastheapostel.riv@sbdiocese.org. Web: www.stthomasriverside.com.
School—St. Thomas the Apostle School, (Grades K-8), 9136 Magnolia Ave., 92503. Tel: 951-689-1981; Fax: 951-689-1985. Cathy Thompson, Prin. Lay Teachers 9; Students 210.
Catechesis/Religious Program—Tel: 951-689-7980. Ms. Lynn S. Zupan, C.R.E. Students 408.

RUNNING SPRINGS, SAN BERNARDINO CO., ST. ANNE IN THE MOUNTAINS (1963) Rev. Leonard Kryzwda, C.R.
Mailing Address: P.O. Box 2400, 92382-2400.
Office: 30480 Fredalba Rd., 92382. Tel: 909-867-2832; Fax: 909-867-2832. Email: stanne.runningsprings@sbdiocese.org. Web: www.mountaincatholic.org.
Catechesis/Religious Program—Combined with Our Lady of the Lake, Lake Arrowhead.

SAN JACINTO, RIVERSIDE CO., ST. ANTHONY (1890) Rev. Cristobal Subosa, F.I.M., Admin.
Office: 630 S. Santa Fe Ave., 92583-4012. Tel: 951-654-7911; Fax: 951-654-2309. Email: stanthony.sjc@sbdiocese.org.
School—St. Hyacinth Academy, (Grades K-8), 275 S. Victoria Ave., 92583. Tel: 951-654-2013; Fax: 951-654-5644. Email: sha.ocs@sbdiocese.org. Web: www.shaeagles.org. Ladonna Lambert, Prin. Lay Teachers 12; Students 238.
Catechesis/Religious Program—Sr. Nina Achacoso, C.R.E. (English); Ana Melgar, C.R.E. (Spanish). Students 598.

SOBOBA INDIAN RESERVATION, RIVERSIDE CO., ST. JOSEPH MISSION (1888), (Native American), Rev. Earl Henley, M.S.C.
Mailing Address: *Soboda Indian Reservation*, P.O. Box 1027, San Jacinto, 92581-1027.
Office: 23600 Soboba Rd., San Jacinto, 92583. Tel: 951-654-2086; Fax: 951-654-2086. Email: stjoseph.sanjacinto@sbdiocese.org.
Catechesis/Religious Program—Students 64.
Chapel—Our Lady of the Snows Chapel Cahuilla Indian Reservation, Cahuilla.
Chapel—St. Theresa Chapel Santa Rosa Indian Reservation, Santa Rosa. Tel: 909-659-2708.
Chapel—St. Mary Chapel Morongo Indian Reservation (11231 Mission Rd.), Banning, 92220.
Chapel—St. Michael Chapel Pechanga Indian Reservation, Temecula, 92592.
Chapel—Sacred Hearts of Mary & Jesus Chapel Torres-Martinez Indian Reservation, Thermal, 92274.

SUN CITY, RIVERSIDE CO., ST. VINCENT FERRER (1965) Rev. Antonio Das Neves; Deacon Patrick Necerato.
Office: 27931 Murrieta Rd., 92586-2320. Tel: 951-679-4531; Fax: 951-679-7521. Email: stvincentferrer@sbdiocese.org. Web: mystvincentferrer.com.
Catechesis/Religious Program—Tel: 951-672-4019. Mary Wedeking, D.R.E. Students 843.

TEMECULA, RIVERSIDE CO., ST. CATHERINE OF ALEXANDRIA (1979) Revs. John F. Wagner; Manuel Cardoza, Parochial Vicar; Deacons John Barth; Jose Ibarra; James Kincaid; Dennis Malkowski.
Office: 41875 C St., 92592-3029. Tel: 951-676-4403; Fax: 951-695-6659. Email: stcatherineofalexandria.temecula@sbdiocese.org. Web: stcatherineofalexandria.net.
Catechesis/Religious Program—Tel: 951-695-6656. Letha Heylmun, C.R.E.; Ms. Mary Histzeman, C.R.E. Students 1,207.

TRONA, SAN BERNARDINO CO., ST. MADELEINE SOPHIE BARAT (1936) Rev. Eliseo Hernandez, C.O.R.C. All sacramental records located at St. Joseph, Barstow.
Office & Mailing Address: 505 E. Mountain View Rd., Barstow, 92311. Tel: 760-256-6818; Fax: 760-256-8307. Email: stmadeleinesophiebarat.trona@sbdiocese.org; stjoseph.barstow@sbdiocese.com.
Church: 83395 Trona Rd., 93562.
Catechesis/Religious Program—Students 16.

TWENTYNINE PALMS, SAN BERNARDINO CO., BLESSED SACRAMENT (1940) Rev. Gerald Vidad (Philippines), Admin.
Office: 6785 Sage Ave., 92277-9227. Tel: 760-367-3343; Fax: 760-367-0543. Email: blessedsacrament.29palms@sbdiocese.org.
Catechesis/Religious Program—Laurette Hill, D.R.E. Students 66.

UPLAND, SAN BERNARDINO CO.

1—ST. ANTHONY (1974) Very Rev. Romeo N. Seleccion, M.S., Priest Moderator; Rev. Patrick A. Brennan, O.S.A., Priest Min.; Deacons Stephen Serembe, Pastoral Coord.; Robert Beidle.
Mailing Address: P.O. Box 608, 91785.
Office: 2110 N. San Antonio Ave., 91784. Tel: 909-958-2803; Fax: 909-982-8643. Email: st.anthony1@netscape.com.
Catechesis/Religious Program—Ms. Lori Muniz, D.R.E. Students 349.

2—ST. JOSEPH (1922) Revs. Jerome Ochetti; Tong Ba Nguyen, Parochial Vicar; George S. Fernandes, Parochial Vicar; Deacon Greg Moore.
Office: 877 N. Campus Ave., 91786-3930. Tel: 909-981-8110; Fax: 909-982-8991 1. Email: stjoseph.upland@sbdiocese.org. Web: www.stjosephupland.org.
School—St. Joseph School, (Grades PreSchool-8), 905 N. Campus Ave., 91786. Tel: 909-920-5185; Fax: 909-920-5190. Sr. Mary Kelly, P.B.V.M., Prin. Religious Teachers 3; Lay Teachers 13; Students 334.
Catechesis/Religious Program—Tel: 909-981-8110, Ext. 29. Debbi Aud, D.R.E. Students 422.
Convent—Sisters of the Presentation of the Blessed Virgin Mary (P.B.V.M.), 925 N. Campus Ave., 91786. Tel: 909-982-2686.

VICTORVILLE, SAN BERNARDINO CO.

1—HOLY INNOCENTS (1991) Rev. Patrick Travers, SS.CC, Admin.; Deacons William Shellem; Marcial Ampuero.
Office: 13230 El Evado Rd., 92392. Tel: 760-955-6010; Fax: 760-955-2100. Email: holyinnocents.victorville@sbdiocese.org. Web: holyinnocents92392.parishworld.net.
Catechesis/Religious Program—Tel: 769-955-2100. Students 943.

2—ST. JOAN OF ARC (1922) Rev. Ciro Libanati; Deacon Manual Gomez.
Office: 15512 Sixth St., 92395-3209. Tel: 760-245-7674; Fax: 760-245-7077. Email: stjoanofarc.victorville@sbdiocese.org.
Catechesis/Religious Program—Tel: 760-245-4904. Ms. Alicia Lombardo, C.R.E. Students 692.

WILDOMAR, RIVERSIDE CO., ST. FRANCES OF ROME (1887) Rev. Mark E. Kotlarczyk; Deacons Rigoberto Ruano; Joseph Franco.
Office: 21591 Lemon St., 92595-8410. Tel: 951-674-6881, Ext. 222; Fax: 951-674-6443. Email: sfrancesofrome.wildomar@sbdiocese.org.
School—St. Frances of Rome Preschool, Tel: 951-471-5144; Fax: 951-471-5154. Catherine Beck, Prin. Lay Teachers 1; Students 30.
Catechesis/Religious Program—Tel: 951-674-6881, Ext. 224. Sr. Angelita Bacleon, M.S.M., D.R.E. Students 798.

WRIGHTWOOD, SAN BERNARDINO CO., OUR LADY OF THE SNOWS (1946) Rev. Frank T. Dicristina.
Office: 975 Lark, 92397. Tel: 760-868-4342; Fax: 760-868-2171. Email: olsnows.phelan@sbdiocese.org. Web: www.our-lady-of-the-snows.org.
Catechesis/Religious Program—Tel: 760-868-4342, Ext. 42. Rita Evens, C.R.E. Students 24.

YUCAIPA, SAN BERNARDINO CO., ST. FRANCES XAVIER CABRINI (1948) Very Revs. Romeo N. Seleccion, M.S., Priest Moderator; David Andel, Priest Min.; Ms. Kirsten R. Thorstad, Pastoral Coord.; Deacons Peter S. Bond; Daniel D. Hudec.
Office: 12687 California St., 92399-4405. Tel: 909-797-2533; Fax: 909-790-5803. Email: stfrancesxaviercabrini.yucaipa@sbdiocese.org. Web: www.stfrancesxcabrinichurch.org.
Catechesis/Religious Program—Linda Ornelas, D.R.E. Students 497.

YUCCA VALLEY, SAN BERNARDINO CO., ST. MARY OF THE VALLEY (1953) Very Rev. Msgr. Thomas M. Wallace, Priest Moderator; Sr. Sara Michael King, C.S.J., Pastoral Coord.; Deacon Glenn Miller.
Office: 7495 Church St., 92284-3247. Tel: 760-365-2287, Ext. 221; Fax: 760-369-0622. Email: stmaryofthevalley.yuccavalley@sbdiocese.org. Web: www.saintmaryofthevalley.org.
Catechesis/Religious Program—Tel: 760-365-2287. Students 158.

Chaplains of Public Institutions

SAN BERNARDINO. *St. Bernardine Medical Center*. 2101 N. Waterman Ave., 92404. Tel: 909-883-8711; Fax: 909-881-4546. Rev. Msgr. Antonio Sudario (Philippines), Rev. Joel Kelley, O.S.B.
Patton State Hospital, 3102 E. Highland Ave., Patton, 92369. Tel: 909-425-7429. Revs. Edmond "Ned" G. O'Donnell, Ignatius H. Rodrigues (Retired).

APPLE VALLEY. *St. Mary Medical Center*, 18300 Hwy. 18, 92307-0404. Tel: 760-242-2311. Rev. Peter Gelfer, O.H.

BLYTHE. *Chuckawalla Valley State Prison*, P.O. Box 2289, 92226. Tel: 760-922-5300, Ext. 644. Deacon Hakyung (HK) Han.

CHINO. *California Institute for Men*, P.O. Box 128, 91710. Tel: 909-782-7455. Rev. Eugene Eburuche, S.M.M.M.

COLTON. *Arrowhead Regional Medical Center*, 400 N. Pepper, 92324. Tel: 909-580-1000. Rev. Miguel A. Urrea.

CORONA. *California Institute for Women*, 16756 Chino-Corona Rd., Frontera, 91720. Tel: 909-597-1771. Vacant.

FONTANA. *Kaiser Permanente Hospital*, 9961 Sierra Ave., 92335. Tel: 909-829-5850. Rev. Javier Gonzales-Cabrera.

LOMA LINDA. *Jerry L. Pettis Memorial Veterans Hospital*, 11201 Benton Sr., 92357. Tel: 909-825-7084, Ext. 310. Rev. Leonard Mestos.
Loma Linda University Medical Center, 11234 Anderson St., 92354. Tel: 909-558-4000, Ext. 44367. Revs. Jorge A. Garcia, John Gunningham, Stanley I. Onwuegbule.

MORENO VALLEY. *Riverside County Regional Medical Center*, 56520 Cactus Ave., 92555. Tel: 951-486-4334. Rev. Celestine Mbanu (Nigeria).

NORCO. *California Rehabilitation Center*, Western & Fifth Sts., P.O. Box 1841, 91760. Tel: 909-737-2683, Ext. 4305. Vacant.

RIVERSIDE. *Riverside Community Hospital*, 4445 Magnolia Ave., 92501. Tel: 909-788-3000. Rev. Adrianus Budhi, M.S.C.

VICTORVILLE. *Federal Corrections Institute*, 13777 Air Expwy. Blvd., 92394. Tel: 760-530-5000, Ext. 5400. Rev. Innocent Emechete.

Special or Other Diocesan Assignment:
Revs.—
Barry, Michael, SS.CC., Mary's Mercy Center
Jaramillo, Jose G., M.G., San Bernardino Region Korean Chap.
Nguyen, Matthias Huy Chuong, C.M.C., Chap., Shrine of the Presentation
Rodriguez, Allen D., S.T., Chap., Valley Missionary Program

On Duty Outside The Diocese:
Rev.—
Lowe, Frank E.

On Sabbatical:
Rev.—
Tran, Luc Nghi

On Leave of Absence:
Very Revs.—
Lama, Michael, V.F.
Lander, Mark C., V.F.
Revs.—
Borba, Joseph
Granillo, Paul C., J.C.L.
Hindman, John
Monzon-Balagat, Arturo J.

Retired:
Rev. Msgrs.—
Battle, Lawrence, 73450 Country Club Dr. #190, Palm Desert, 92260.
Corciulo, Cosimo, 316 Mount Shasta Dr., Norco, 92860.
Lawlor, Timothy F., Diocesan Pastoral Center, 1201 E. Highland Ave., 92401.
Lawrence, Robert E., J.C.L., 1300 Cypress Point Dr., Banning, 92220.
Ryan, John, 934 N. Dearborn, Redlands, 92374.
Webber, Donald S., J.C.L., 26634 Amhurst Ct., Sun City, 92586.
Revs.—
Baseford, Paul, 485 Foxenwood Dr., Santa Maria, 93455.
Benjamin, John J., 19184 Palo Verde Dr., Apple Valley, 92308.
Brinn, Adrian J., 6086 Pebble Beach, Banning, 92220.
Buchanan, Robert E., Diocesan Pastoral Center, 1201 E. Highland Ave., 92404.
Cardoza, Edward, 21267 George Brown, Riverside, 92518.
Casey, Donald A., 546 Reliance Ave., Henderson, NV 89009.
Chavez, Arturo, 26071 St. Mary, Sun City, 92586.
Cima, Jose, 23505 Evening Snow, Moreno Valley, 92557.

Connor, Vincent, 23277 Sand Canyon Cir., Corona, 92883.
Devine, Charles F., P.O. Box 3021, Idyllwild, 92549.
DiLeo, Anthony, 43981 Northgate Ave., Temecula, 92592.
Domas, John R., 5801 Sun Lake Blvd. Apt. 205, Banning, 92220.
Donat, Robert J., 5412 Calle de Arboles, Torrance, 90505.
Erickson, Robert J., P.O. Box 460, Rim Forest, 92378.
Gaglia, Fred R., 3250 W. 46th Ave., Denver, CO 80211.
Gillespie, Thomas, 1100 E. Ocean Blvd. #2, Long Beach, 90802.
Gonzales, George, c/o Vina de Lestonnac Retreat Center, 39300 De Portola Rd., Temecula, 92592.
Gorman, John, Nazareth House, 6333 Rancho Mission Rd., San Diego, 92108.
Grajek, Lawrence, P.O. Box 2077, Big Bear City, 92314.
Guillen-Santoyo, Patricio, 2002 S. Magnolia Ave., Ontario, 91762.
Kiefer, William J., 27920 Niagara Ct., Sun City, 92586.
Kopec, Chester C., O.P., 4320 Columbia Ave., Riverside, 92501.
Kurilec, Robert E., 7743 Grundy St., Pensacola, FL 32507.
Leahy, Maurice J., St. Barnabas Church, Chicago, IL 60643.
McGuiness, Edward J., 4667 Braemar Pl. #210, Riverside, 92513.
McNally, Michael R., P.O. Box 3802, 92413.
Miller, Robert L., Diocesan Pastoral Center, 1201 E. Highland Ave., 92404.
Moore, James, c/o St. Catherine of Siena, 339 N. Sycamore Ave., Rialto, 92376.
O'Donnell, Edmond "Ned", P.O. Box 1405, Upland, 91786.
Rasquinha, G. Ignatius, St. Michael's of Morongo Valley, Inc., 9466 Navajo Trail, Morongo Valley, 92256.
Rodrigues, Ignatius H., 1728 N. Forest Oaks Dr., Beaumont, 92223.
Rogan, Brian, 819 Sherwood St., Redlands, 92373.
Schultz, Charles F., Jr., S.T.D., Diocesan Pastoral Center, 1201 E. Highland Ave., 92404.
Speno, Eugene, 43-120 Rutledge Way, Palm Desert, 92260.
Tomkins, Robert J., Diocesan Pastoral Center, 1201 E. Highland Ave., 92404.
Walters, Vincent, Plymouth Tower, Rm. 415-416, 3401 Lemon St., Riverside, 92501.

Permanent Deacons:
Acosta, Joseph, (Retired)
Aguilera, Santo, Hesperia
Ahan, Paul, Norco
Alaniz, Frank, (Retired)
Amador, Robert, Colton
Ampuero, Marcial, Victorville
Ayala, Luis, Indio
Badena, Miguel, Coachella
Barna, John, Rancho Cucamonga
Barrion, Victor, Loma Linda
Bassford, Rick, Crestline
Beidle, Robert, Upland
Bellinder, Michael, Redlands
Benavides, Pablo, La Quinta
Bond, Peter S., Yucaipa
Brannick, Tom, (Retired)
Bui, Nam, Riverside
Burgett, Donald, (Retired)
Burris, Bud, (Retired)
Campbell, Gerald, (Retired)
Cardenas, Roberto, Rancho Cucamonga
Carroll, Christopher, Ontario
Castanon, Leonard, Colton
Clark, Ed, Rancho Cucamonga
Clinton, Jack, (Retired), Upland
Cover, Richard, (Retired)
Cruz, Michael, Riverside
DeGano, John, Riverside
Dewhirst, Thomas, San Bernardino
Filipek, Marlin, (Retired)
Franco, Joseph, Wildomar
Garcia, Jose Israel, Coachella
Geaga, Donnie, Alta Loma
Glass, Nelson, Fontana/Rialto
Gonzalez, Victor, (Inactive)
Gutierrez, Mario, San Bernardino
Han, Hikyung (H.K.), Blythe
Henke, Jack, (Retired)
Heredia, Fernando, Palm Desert
Hernandez, Armando, Corona
Hodnick, Mark, Beaumont
Hoy, Wayne, (Retired)
Hudec, Daniel D., Yucaipa
Hunsicker, Scott, J.C.L., Hesperia
Ibarra, Jose, Temecula
Jelley, Michael F., San Bernardino
Juback, Michael, Fontana
Keough, Bill, (Retired)
Kilbourn, Austin, Moreno Valley
Kim, John, M.D., Norco
Kincaid, James, Temecula
Luevano, Armando, Beaumont
Malkowski, Dennis, Temecula
Marino, Joseph, Moreno Valley
Martinez, Pat, Chino Hills
Miller, Glenn, Yucca Valley
Mirci, Philip, (Inactive)
Moore, Greg, Upland
Morales, Carlos, Moreno Valley
Moralez, Tony, Chino Hills
Necerato, Patrick, Sun City
Neufell, James A., (Retired)
Norris, Donald, Montclair
O'Camb, Daniel, San Bernardino
Olivas, Manuel, (Retired)
Partida, Ralph, Jr., Big Bear
Phillips, Robert, (Retired)
Ramirez, Efren, Temecula
Rehaume, Ronald J., (Retired)
Rodriguez, Brijido, Indio
Rosado, Carlos, Riverside
Ruano, Rigoberto, Wildomar
Saenz, Margo, (Retired)
Salinas, Arcadio, Jr., (Retired)
Sanchez, Luis, Rancho Cucamonga
Sanchez, Samuel, (Retired)
Sepulveda, Ralph, (Retired)
Serembe, Stephen
Shalhoub, William J., Loma Linda
Shellem, William, Victorville
Simoni, Frank, (Retired)
Skora, John, Palm Springs
Sotelo, Gonzalo, Rialto
Taylor, Daniel, San Bernardino
Tillitson, Donald, Riverside
Uribe, Ricardo, Moreno Valley
Vasquez, Sergio, Coachella
Vela, Joe, Norco
Vera, Fernando, Hemet
Vilchis, Eric, Rialto
Von Ins, Paul, Corona
Weber, James, Big Bear Lake
Ybarra, Rudy, (Retired), Riverside
Zamora, Abel, Fontana

INSTITUTIONS LOCATED IN THE DIOCESE

[A] SEMINARIES, RELIGIOUS OR SCHOLASTICATES

GRAND TERRACE. *Blessed Junipero Serra House of Formation* (1985) 12725 Oriole Ave., 92313. Tel: 909-783-0260; Fax: 909-783-0223. Revs. Juan L. Garcia, D.L.P., Spiritual Dir.; Jose A. Sanz, D.L.P., Rector. Priests 2; Sisters 2; Seminarians 15; Lay Persons 1.

[B] HIGH SCHOOLS, DIOCESAN

SAN BERNARDINO. *Aquinas High School* (Coed), 2772 N. Sterling Ave., 92404. Tel: 909-886-4659; Fax: 909-886-7717. Email: Aquinas@Aquinashs.net. Web: www.aquinashs.net. Christopher Barrows, Prin.; Dr. James Brennan, Pres. Priests 2; Sisters 2; Lay Teachers 28; Students 363.

RIVERSIDE. *Notre Dame High School* (Coed), 7085 Brockton Ave., 92506. Tel: 951-275-5896; Fax: 951-781-9020. Email: jsalley@ndhsriverside.org. Web: ndhsriverside.org. Dr. Jo Dean Salley, Prin.; Mrs. Lydia Dashkovitz, Librarian. Priests 1; Lay Teachers 30; Students 515.

[C] HIGH SCHOOLS, PRIVATE

PALM DESERT. **Xavier College Preparatory High School*, 34-200 Cook St., 92211. Tel: 760-601-3900; Fax: 760-601-3901. Email: calling@xavierprep.org. Web: xavierprep.org. Mr. Chris Alling, Prin. Lay Teachers 41; Students 483.

[D] ELEMENTARY SCHOOLS, PRIVATE

TEMECULA. *Saint Jeanne de Lestonnac School*, (Grades PreSchool-8), 32650 Avenida Lestonnac, 92592. Tel: 951-587-2505; Fax: 951-587-2515. Email: sjdls@sjdls.com. Web: www.sjdls.com. Ms. Kristen Mora, Prin. Sisters 5; Staff 50; Students 510.

[E] HOMES FOR SENIOR CITIZENS

SAN BERNARDINO. *St. Bernardine Plaza*, 550 W. Fifth St., 92401. Tel: 909-888-0153; Fax: 909-381-1589. Email: stbern2@la.twcbc.com. Dee Moyes, Resident Mgr. Total Staff 5; Units 150.

PALM DESERT. *La Paz Villas*, 43555 Deep Canyon Rd., 92211. Mailing Address: *Sacred Heart Parish*, 43775 Deep Canyon Rd., 92211. Tel: 760-346-6502; Fax: 760-773-4873. Email: dpelletier@sacredheartpalmdesert.com. Dorothy Pelletier, Contact Person. Units 6.

[F] GENERAL HOSPITALS AND CLINICS

SAN BERNARDINO. *St. Bernardine Medical Center* a dba of Catholic Healthcare West, 2101 N. Waterman Ave., 92404. Tel: 909-883-8711; Fax: 909-881-4531. Email: sbmcf@chw.edu. Web: www.stbernardinemedctr.org. Steve Barron, Pres. & CEO. Bed Capacity 463; Total Assisted Annually 141,325; Total Staff 1,652.

St. Bernardine Medical Center Foundation, 2101 N. Waterman Ave., 92404. Tel: 909-883-8711. Patricia A. Davis, Pres. Foundation.

APPLE VALLEY. *St. Mary Medical Center*, 18300 Hwy. 18, 92307. Tel: 760-242-2311; Fax: 760-242-2994. Web: stmaryapplevalley.com. John Perring-Mulligan, Ph.D., Vice Pres., Mission Integration. Bed Capacity 205; Total Assisted Annually 150,000; Total Staff 1,634.

St. Joseph Health System, Orange. Tel: 714-347-7500. Sisters 3; Bed Capacity 205.

St. Mary Medical Center Auxiliary Tel: 760-242-2311; Fax: 760-242-9750.

St. Mary Medical Center Foundation Tel: 760-242-2311; Fax: 760-242-9750. Bed Capacity 205; Patients Assisted Annually 150,000; Total Staff 1,634.

[G] ALCOHOL AND DRUG REHABILITATION CENTERS

VICTORVILLE. *St. John of God Health Care Services*, 13333 Palmdale Rd., P.O. Box 2457, 92393. Tel: 760-241-4917; Fax: 760-241-8911. Email: admin@sjghcs.org. Santiago Lopez, Admin. & Exec. Dir. Sponsored by the Brothers of St. John of God., Alcohol & Drug Rehabilitation Program. Brothers 1; Total Staff 29; Bed Capacity 77; Patients Assisted Annually 1,200.

[H] CATHOLIC SOCIAL SERVICE ORGANIZATIONS

SAN BERNARDINO. *Catholic Charities San Bernardino / Riverside, Administration Office*, 1450 N. D St., 92405. Tel: 909-388-1239; Fax: 909-384-1130. Email: info@ccsbriv.org. Web: www.ccsbriv.org. Ken F. Sawa, M.S.W., L.C.S.W., CEO, Exec. Vice Pres.; Douglas House, M.S., CFO; Joyce Leon, M.P.A., Dir. of Accounting.

**Mary's Mercy Center, Inc.*, 641 Roberds Ave., P.O. Box 7563, 92411. Tel: 909-889-2558; Fax: 909-386-7704. Email: mmcinc@msn.com. Web: marysmercycenter.org. Michael J. Hein, Vice Pres.

INDIO. **Martha's Village & Kitchen, Inc.*, 83-791 Date Ave., 92201. Tel: 760-347-4741; Fax: 760-347-9551. Email: patricia.cruise@neighbor.org. Web: www.marthasvillage.org. Blair Amidei, Charitable Giving Dir. Tel: 760-347-4741, Ext. 302; John Wolohan, Exec. Dir. Tel: 760-347-4741, Ext. 304. A member of Father Joe's Villages. Total Staff 55.

[I] MONASTERIES AND RESIDENCES OF PRIESTS AND BROTHERS

APPLE VALLEY. *Congregation of the Resurrection, CR*, 18386 Corwin Rd., 92307. Tel: 760-242-4427; Fax: 760-242-1195. Revs. Timothy F. Keppel, C.R.; Richard McGee, C.R. (Retired); Charles Messler, C.R.; Henry A. Ruszel, C.R. (Retired). P.O. Box 1929, Lake Arrowhead, 92359. Tel: 909-337-2333; Fax: 909-337-5041. Rev. Leonard Krzywda, C.R. 875 E. Chanslorway, Blythe, 92225. Tel: 760-922-3261; Fax: 760-922-5279. Rev. Henry Licznerski, C.R.

Hospitaller Brothers of St. John of God, O.H., P.O. Box 1664, 92307. Tel: 760-242-6560. Bros. Anthony Scully, O.H., Prior; Paul Hanson, O.H.; Ignatius Sudal, O.H.; Andre Archuletta, O.H.; Gabriel Monarch. Brothers 6.

CHINO HILLS. *Congregation of the Sacred Hearts of Jesus & Mary, SS.CC.*, Western U.S. Province, St. Paul the Apostle Rectory, 14085 Peyton Dr., 91709. Tel: 909-465-5503; Fax: 909-465-1683. Very Rev. Patrick J. O'Hagan, SS.CC., V.F., Pastor; Revs. Michael J. Gilsenan, SS.CC., Pastor; Tom Mullen, SS.CC., Parochial Vicar.

CORONA. *Confraternity of Operarios Del Reino De Cristo, C.O.R.C.*, 605 W. 5th St., 92882. Tel: 951-549-6000; Fax: 951-549-6009. Revs. J. Trinidad Hernandez, C.O.R.C., Regl. Dir., (Mexico); Josue Arellano, C.O.R.C.; Eliseo Hernandez, C.O.R.C.; Jorge Luis Rodriguez Pina, C.O.R.C.; Martin S. Rodriguez, C.O.R.C.; Jose Varela, C.O.R.C.; Jose Cruz Mendez Garcia, C.O.R.C.; Francisco Javier Esteban Salinas, C.O.R.C.

Congregation of the Mother Co-Redemptrix, C.M.C., 1775 S. Main St., 91720-4961. Tel: 909-739-0462;

Fax: 951-479-0002. Email: dtmedancon@gmail.com. Web: www.medangcon.net. Revs. John Mary Vu Cao, C.M.C.; Felix Mary Luan Viet Dinh, C.M.C.; Andrew Mary Sang Linh Do, C.M.C.; Michael Mary Mai Tran, C.M.C. Shrine of Presentation (Den Thanh Me Dang Con).

GRAND TERRACE. *Diocesan Laborer Priests, DLP, Blessed Juniper Serra House of Formation*, 12725 Oriole Ave., 92313. Tel: 909-783-0260; Fax: 909-783-0223. Revs. Jose A. Sanz, D.L.P., Dir. of Seminarians; Juan L. Garcia, D.L.P., Spiritual Dir.

HEMET. *Congregation of the Holy Spirit*, Casa Laval Retirement Community, 309 E. Whitter Ave., P.O. Box 3509, 92546-3509. Tel: 951-658-2241; Fax: 909-765-3137. Email: spiritan@pc.net. Web: www.spiritan.org. Revs. George Healy, C.S.Sp., Acting Supr. (Retired); Joseph B. Gaglioni, C.S.Sp. (Retired); Francis Kichak, C.S.Sp. (Retired); Albert McKnight, C.S.Sp. (Retired).

LUCERNE VALLEY. *The Cistercian Congregation of the Holy Family, St. Joseph Monastery*, 21010 Lucerne Valley Cutoff, P.O. Box 960, 92356-0960. Tel: 714-625-9466. Email: saintjoseph.ocist@yahoo.com. Rev. M. Anthony Hanh Si Pham, O.Cist., Supr.; Rt. Rev. M. John Lam Dinh Vuong, O.Cist., Abbot (Retired); Revs. M. Justin Cong Huu Ho, O.Cist.; M. Timothy Qui Van Than, O.Cist.; Bros. M. Peter-Binh Quynh Dang Pham, O.Cist.; M. Matthew-Gam Phong Hoai Nguyen, O.Cist.; M. Francis of Assisi Phu Quoc Nguyen, O.Cist.; Bonaventure Dong Van Pham, O.Cist.

MORENO VALLEY. *Missionaries of Our Lady of La Salette, MS*, 25075 Cottonwood Ave., 92553. Tel: 951-924-1968; Fax: 951-247-6477. Very Rev. Romeo N. Seleccion, M.S.; Revs. Frederick A. Costales, M.S.; Arlan Intal, M.S.; Joven T. Junio, M.S.; Arnel Macabio, M.S.; Maurice Cardinal, M.S.

REDLANDS. *Discalced Carmelites, OCD*, P.O. Box 446, 92373. Tel: 909-792-1047; Fax: 909-798-3497. Email: elcarmelorh@gmail.com. Web: www.elcarmelo.org. Revs. Adam Gregory Gonzales, O.C.D., Vicar Prov.; Matthew Williams, O.C.D., Prov.; James Zakowicz, O.C.D.; Mark Kissner, O.C.D.

RIVERSIDE. *Divine Word Seminary, Western Province - Society of the Divine Word, S.V.D.*, 11316 Cypress Ave., 92505. Tel: 951-689-4858; Fax: 951-785-0327. Email: dwrc05@cs.com. Revs. Briccio Tamoro, S.V.D., Provincial Supr.; Jose Rodriguez Goopio, S.V.D., Rector & Dir. Retreat Center; William J. Caffrey, S.V.D.; Donald O'Connor, S.V.D.; Ky Ngoc Dinh, S.V.D.; Gerard O'Dougherty, S.V.D.; Ignacio Estrada, S.V.D.; Robert Fisher, S.V.D.; Paul Prince Appiah-Kubi, S.V.D.; John A. Niessen, S.V.D.; Ponciano Ramos, S.V.D.; Paul Lester Schmidt, S.V.D.; Joseph P. Scott, S.V.D.; Sony Sebastian, S.V.D.; Duy John Tran, S.V.D.; John Tran, S.V.D.; Long Nguyen, S.V.D.; Bros. Bernard Dorade, S.V.D.; Andrew Hotchkiss, S.V.D.; Steve Kerekes, S.V.D.; Vinh Trinh, S.V.D.; Daniel Yunck, S.V.D.

30823 Mission St., Highland, 92346-6345. Revs. Joseph P. Scott, S.V.D.; Sony Sebastian, S.V.D.

St. Vincent Ferrer House Dominican Priests and Brothers, Western Province, OP, 872 Spruce St., 92507. Tel: 951-784-0160. Revs. Raymond Finerty, O.P.; Michael Augustine Amabisco, O.P.; Lawrence Farrell, O.P. Dominicans.

[J] CONVENTS AND RESIDENCES FOR SISTERS

APPLE VALLEY. *Sisters of St. Joseph of Orange, C.S.J.O*, 18810 Munsee Rd., 92307. Tel: 760-242-7644. Sisters 2.

BIG BEAR LAKE. *Society Devoted to the Sacred Heart, S.D.S.H.*, 896 Cienega Rd., P.O. Box 1795, 92315. Tel: 909-866-5696; Fax: 909-866-5650. Email: sdshbb@verizon.net. Sisters 4.

CALIMESA. *Missionary Sisters of the Immaculate Conception* (SMIC), 1271 Nugget Ct., 92320. Fax: 909-795-8128. Email: judinefran@aol.com. Sisters Judine Jacobs, S.M.I.C., Volunteer, Carol's Kitchen; Blessed Kateri Tekakawitha Church; Cabazon Community Center; Banning Community Center.; Frances Karovic, S.M.I.C., Coord., Parish Health Ministry at Blessed Kateri Tekakwitha Church. Sisters (Madonna of Desert Community) 2.

REDLANDS. *Sisters of Mercy, U.S. Province, U. S. Province, Provincial House*, 1075 Bermuda Dr., 92374. Tel: 909-798-4747; Fax: 909-798-5300. Email: roconnor-sm@sbdiocese.org. Web: www.sistersofmercy.ie. Sr. Rosaline O'Connor, R.S.M., Prov. Total in Residence 4; Total in U.S. Province 78.

TEMECULA. *Congregation of Kkottongnae Sisters of Jesus* (CKSJ), 37885 Hwy. 79 S., 92592. Tel: 951-302-3400; Fax: 951-302-3400. Email: tmclkkot@hotmail.com.

Sisters of the Company of Mary Our Lady, Convent, 39300 De Portola Rd., 92592. Tel: 951-302-2800; Fax: 951-491-0686. Email: hruvalcaba@sjdls.com. Web: www.lestonnac.org. Sr. Henrietta Ruvalcaba, O.D.N., Admin./Teacher. Sisters 13.

Vina de Lestonnac Ministry Center-Convent, 39300 De Portola Rd., 92592. Tel: 951-302-2800; Fax: 951-491-0686. Email: vinaodn@verizon.net. Web: www.companyofmary.us. Sr. Elvira Rios, O.D.N., Prov. Sec. Total in Residence 13.

[K] DIOCESAN CORPORATIONS

SAN BERNARDINO. *Blessed Junipero Serra House of Formation, Inc.*, 1201 E. Highland Ave., 92404. Tel: 909-475-5150; Fax: 909-475-5156. Email: lclark@sbdiocese.org. Ms. Laura J. Clark, CFO.

The Catholic Foundation, 1201 E. Highland Ave., 92404. Tel: 909-475-5150; Fax: 909-475-5156. Email: lclark@sbdiocese.org. Ms. Laura J. Clark, CFO.

Diocesan Development Fund, Inc., 1201 E. Highland Ave., 92404. Tel: 909-475-5150; Fax: 909-475-5156. Email: lclark@sbdiocese.org. Ms. Laura J. Clark, CFO.

Diocese of San Bernardino Cemetery Corp., Inc., 1201 E. Highland Ave., 92404. Tel: 909-475-5150; Fax: 909-457-5156. Email: cemeteries@sbdiocese.org. Ms. Laura J. Clark, CFO.

Diocese of San Bernardino Education & Welfare Corporation, 1201 E. Highland Ave., 92404-4641. Tel: 909-475-5150; Fax: 909-457-5156. Email: lclark@sbdiocese.org. Ms. Laura J. Clark, CFO.

Diocese of San Bernardino Land Development Corporation, 1201 E. Highland Ave., 92404. Tel: 909-475-5150; Fax: 909-475-5156. Email: lclark@sbdiocese.org. Ms. Laura J. Clark, CFO.

SAN JACINTO. *Kateri Tekakwitha Fund*, P.O. Box 302, 92581-0302. Tel: 951-654-7899; Fax: 951-654-2086. Sr. Marianna Torrano, R.S.C.J., Sec. & CFO.

[L] CAMPS & RETREATS

BIG BEAR LAKE. *Sacred Heart Retreat Camp*, 896 Cienega Rd., P.O. Box 1795, 92315. Tel: 909-866-5696; Fax: 909-866-5650. Email: sacredheart.retreatcamp@verizon.net. Web: www.sacredheartretreatcamp.com. Total in Residence 4; Total Staff 12.

REDLANDS. *El Carmelo Retreat House*, 926 E. Highland Ave., P.O. Box 446, 92373. Tel: 909-792-1047; Fax: 909-798-3497. Email: elcarmelorh@gmail.com. Web: www.elcarmelo.org. Revs. Adam Gregory Gonzales, O.C.D., Supr.; Mark Kissner, O.C.D.; Matthew Williams, O.C.D.; James Zakowicz, O.C.D. Priests 4; Sisters 4; Total in Residence 8; Total Staff 17.

RIVERSIDE. *Divine Word - Seminary - Divine Word Retreat Center*, 11316 Cypress Ave., 92505. Tel: 951-689-2961; Fax: 909-785-0327. Email: jsgp1247@yahoo.com.

RUNNING SPRINGS. *St. Anne in the Mountains Retreat Center*, P.O. Box 2400, 92382. Tel: 909-867-2832; Fax: 909-867-2832. Email: stanneinthemountains@verizon.net. Web: www.mountaincatholic.org. Terri MacDonald, Contact Person.

TEMECULA. *Vina de Lestonnac Ministry Center - Retreat*, 39300 De Portoal Rd., 92592. Tel: 951-302-5571; Fax: 951-302-2830.

Lestonnac Chalet, 24719 San Moritz Dr., Crestline, 92325. Tel: 714-541-3125.

[M] NEWMAN CENTERS

SAN BERNARDINO. *California State University San Bernardino Newman Center* 1201 E. Highland Ave., 92404. Tel: 909-537-7337; Fax: 909-475-5155; Cell: 909-965-9714. Email: miosefo@sbdiocese.org. Web: sites.google.com/site/csusbcatholicnewmanclub. Sr. Maria Asopesio Iosefo, S.M.S.M.

University of Redlands Newman Center 1201 E. Highland Ave., 92404. Tel: 909-793-2469, Ext. 36; Fax: 909-475-5155; Cell: 909-816-4164. Email: llara@sbdiocese.org. Web: sites.google.com/site/redlandsnewman. Luz Lara.

RIVERSIDE. *St. Andrew Newman Center* 105 W. Big Springs Rd., 92507. Tel: 951-682-8751; Fax: 951-682-3513. Email: catholictucr@earthlink.net. Revs. Raymond Finerty, O.P., Dir.; Michael A. Amabisco, O.P., Assoc. Dir. Email: frmaaop@gmail.com. Serving Riverside Community College and University of California at Riverside.

[N] MISCELLANEOUS

SAN BERNARDINO. **Caritas Telecommunications*, 1201 E. Highland Ave., 92404. Tel: 909-475-5107; Fax: 909-475-5109. Email: jandrews@sbdiocese.org. Web: www.sbdiocese.org. Mr. John H. Andrews, B.A., Dir.

Ministerio Biblico Verbo Divino (MBVD), Mailing Address: P.O. Box 1610, 92402. 555 N. E St., 92401. Tel: 909-383-1610; Fax: 909-383-4987. Web: www.verbodivino.org. Rev. Joseph Scott, Pres. & Contact Person.

**Wordnet, Inc.*, 532 N. "D" St., 92401-1304. Tel: 909-383-4333; Fax: 909-383-4347. Email: exdir@wordnet.tv. Web: wordnet.tv. Rev. Michael Manning, S.V.D., Pres.; Sr. Patricia Phillips, S.H.C.J., Exec. Dir.; Rev. Sony Sebastian, S.V.D., Exec. Producer; Bro. Stephen Pardy, S.V.D., Devel. Dir.; Sr. Jeanne Harris, O.P., Communications Dir. Brothers 1; Priests 2; Lay Staff 2; Sisters 2.

[O] CLOSED OR MERGED PARISHES

ALBERHILL. *Blessed Sacrament Parish* Closed 1965. For sacramental records, contact Diocesan Archives.

AMBOY. *St. Raymond Parish* Closed 1970. For sacramental records, contact Diocesan Archives.

BANNING. *Precious Blood* (1890) Closed 2006. For sacramental records, contact Blessed Kateri Tekakwitha, Tel: 951-849-2434.

BEAUMONT. *Sacred Heart Parish* Closed 1965. For sacramental records, contact Blessed Kateri Tekakwitha, Tel: 951-849-2434.

San Gorgonio (1908) Closed 2006. For sacramental records, contact Blessed Kateri Tekakwitha, Tel: 951-849-2434.

EAGLE MOUNTAIN. *St. Augustine* Closed 2001. For sacramental records, contact Diocesan Archives.

FONTANA. *Church of the Resurrection* (1953) Closed 2006. For sacramental records, contact Blessed John XXIII, Tel: 909-822-4732.

HIGHGROVE. *Our Lady of Guadalupe* Closed 1981. For sacramental records, contact Christ the Redeemer, Tel: 909-475-5399.

JOSHUA TREE. *St. Christopher of the Desert* Closed 1961. For sacramental records, contact St. Mary of the Valley Parish, Tel: 760-365-2287

LUDLOW. *St. Michael Parish* Closed 1962. For sacramental records, contact Diocesan Archives.

ORO GRANDE. *St. Cecilia Parish* Closed 1975. For sacramental records, contact St. Joan of Arc, Victorville, Tel: 760-245-7674.

REDLANDS. *St. Mary* (1941) Closed 2006. For sacramental records, contact The Holy Name of Jesus, Tel: 909-793-2469.

Sacred Heart (1894) Closed 2006. For sacramental records, contact The Holy Name of Jesus, Tel: 909-793-2469.

RIALTO. *St. Thomas More* (1961) Closed 2006. For sacramental records, contact Blessed John XXIII, Tel: 909-822-4732.

RIVERSIDE. *St. Ignatius Parish* Closed 1972. For sacramental records, contact Our Lady of Guadalupe Shrine, Tel: 951-684-0279.

SAN BERNARDINO. *St. Anne* (1938) Closed 2006. For sacramental records, contact Our Lady of Hope, Tel: 909-884-6375.

Christ the King (1934) Closed 2006. For sacramental records, contact Our Lady of Hope, Tel: 909-884-6375.

Our Lady of Fatima (1952) Closed 2006. For sacramental records, contact Our Lady of Hope, Tel: 909-884-6375.

St. Theresa Parish Closed 1992. For sacramental records, contact Diocesan Archives.

THOUSAND PALMS. *St. Philip the Apostle* (1991) Closed 2007. For sacramental records, contact Diocesan Archives.

RELIGIOUS INSTITUTUES OF MEN REPRESENTED IN THE DIOCESE

For further details refer to the corresponding bracketed number in the Religious Institutes of Men or Women section.

[0140]—*Augustinians*—O.S.A.

[]—*Byzatine Brothers of St. Francis*—B.B.S.F.

[0470]—*Capuchin Franciscan Friars*—O.F.M.Cap.

[0360]—*Claretian Missionaries (Western Province)*—C.M.F.

[]—*Confraternity of Operarios del Reino de Cristo*—C.O.R.C.

[0533]—*Congregation of Franciscan Friars of the Immaculate*—F.I.

[]—*Congregation of Mother Coredemptrix*—C.M.C.

[1130]—*Congregation of the Priests of the Sacred Heart*—S.C.J.

[0650]—*Congregation of the Holy Spirit*—C.S.Sp.

[1080]—*Congregation of the Resurrection*—C.R.

[1140]—*Congregation of the Sacred Hearts of Jesus and Mary* (Western Prov.)—SS.CC.

[0390]—*Consolata Missionaries*—I.M.C.

[]—*Diocesan Laborer Priests*—D.L.P.

[0260]—*Discalced Carmelite Friars* (Western Prov.)—O.C.D.

[]—*Guadalupe Missioners*—M.G.

[0670]—*Hospitaller Brothers of St. John of God*—O.H.

[0780]—*Marist Fathers*—S.M.

[]—*Misioneros Servidores de la Palabra*—M.S.P.
[0660]—*Missionaries of the Holy Spirit*—M.Sp.S.
[0720]—*Missionaries of Our Lady of La Salette*—M.S.
[1110]—*Missionaries of the Sacred Heart*—M.S.C.
[]—*Missionaries of the Sacred Heart* (Philippines)—M.S.C.
[0840]—*Missionary Servants of the Most Holy Trinity*—S.T.
[0520]—*National Fraternity of the Secular Franciscan Order, U.S.A.*
[0340]—*Order of Cistercians*—O.Cist.
[0970]—*Order of Our Lady of Mercy*—O.de.M.
[0430]—*Order of Preachers (Dominican)* Southern Province—O.P.
[0430]—*Order of Preachers (Dominican)* (Western Province)—O.P.
[0200]—*Order of St. Benedict* (MN)—O.S.B.
[0370]—*Society of St. Columbian*—S.S.C.
[0420]—*Society of the Divine Word* (Western Prov.)—S.V.D.
[]—*Sons of Mary Mother of Mercy*—S.M.M.M.

RELIGIOUS INSTITUTES OF WOMEN REPRESENTED IN THE DIOCESE

[2020]—*Community of the Holy Spirit*—C.H.S.
[]—*Congregation of Kkottongnae Sisters of Jesus*—C.K.S.J.
[3260]—*Congregation of Sisters of the Precious Blood*—C.PP.S.
[]—*Congregation of the Sacred Heart*—S.H.
[2549]—*Congregation of the Sisters of Mercy* (U.S. Prov.)—R.S.M.
[3935]—*Congregation of the Sisters of St. Louis, Juilly-Monaghan*—S.S.L.
[0790]—*Daughters of Divine Charity* (Akron, OH)—F.D.C.
[0880]—*Daughters of Mary and Joseph*—D.M.J.
[]—*Daughters of Mary Mother of Mercy*—D.M.M.M.
[1070-13]—*Dominican Sisters* (Adrian)—O.P.
[1070-19]—*Dominican Sisters* (Houston)—O.P.
[1070-15]—*Dominican Sisters* (Blauvelt)—O.P.
[1070-30]—*Dominican Sisters* (Oakford, South Africa)—O.P.
[1070-12]—*Dominican Sisters of Mission San Jose*—O.P.
[]—*Esclavas De La Inmaculata Nina*—E.I.N.
[]—*Franciscan Sisters of the Heart of Jesus* Pakistan—C.J.H.
[]—*Hermanas Evangelizadoras Eucaristicas de los Pobres*—E.E.P.
[2390]—*Lovers of the Holy Cross*—L.H.C.
[2420]—*Marist Missionary Sisters*—S.M.S.M.
[]—*Misioneras Servidoras de la Palabra* Mexico—H.M.S.P.
[2800]—*Missionaries of the Sacred Heart of Jesus (Hiltrup)*—M.S.C.
[]—*Missionary Sisters of Mary*—M.S.M.
[2760]—*Missionary Sisters of the Immaculate Conception of the Mother of God*—S.M.I.C.
[]—*Oblates of Santa Marta*—O.S.M.
[3130]—*Our Lady of Victory Missionary Sisters*—O.L.V.M.
[4070]—*Religious of the Sacred Heart*—R.S.C.J.
[3465]—*Religious of the Sacred Heart of Mary*—R.S.H.M.
[1680]—*School Sisters of St. Francis* Milwaukee—O.S.F.
[]—*Sisters for Christian Community*—S.F.C.C.
[]—*Sisters of Charity of the Incarnate Word*—CCVI
[3360]—*Sisters of Providence of St. Mary of-the-Woods*—S.P.
[1540]—*Sisters of Saint Francis* Clinton, Iowa—O.S.F.
[3770]—*Sisters of St. Clare*—O.S.C.
[3840]—*Sisters of St. Joseph of Carondolet*—C.S.J.
[3830-03]—*Sisters of St. Joseph of Orange*—C.S.J.
[3890]—*Sisters of St. Joseph of Peace*—C.S.J.P.
[0700]—*Sisters of the Company of Mary Our Lady*—O.D.N.
[1990]—*Sisters of the Holy Names of Jesus and Mary*—S.N.J.M.
[1720]—*Sisters of the Third Order Regular of St. Francis of the Congregation of Our Lady of Lourdes* (Rochester)—O.S.F.
[4050]—*Society Devoted to the Sacred Heart*—S.D.S.H.
[4060]—*Society of the Holy Child*—S.H.C.J.
[3320]—*Union of Sisters of the Presentation of the B.V.M.* (U.S. Province)—P.B.V.M.

DIOCESAN CEMETERIES

SAN BERNARDINO. *Our Lady Queen of Peace Catholic Cemetery*, Mailing Address: 1201 E. Highland Ave., 92404-4641. Tel: 909-475-5133; Fax: 909-475-5138. 3510 Washington St., Colton, 92324. Tel: 909-796-9351.

NECROLOGY

† McGuinness, Gerard J., (Retired)—Died Dec. 21, 2011
† O'Day, Michael, (Retired)—Died March 11, 2011

An asterisk (*) denotes an organization that has established tax-exempt status directly with the IRS and is not covered by the USCCB Group Ruling.

Diocese of San Diego

(Dioecesis Sancti Didaci)

Most Reverend

ROBERT H. BROM, D.D.

Bishop of San Diego; ordained December 18, 1963; appointed Bishop of Duluth March 25, 1983; consecrated and installed May 23, 1983; appointed Coadjutor Bishop of San Diego April 22, 1989; appointed Bishop of San Diego July 10, 1990. *Office: P.O. Box 85728, San Diego, CA 92186-5728.* Tel: 858-490-8200.

Most Reverend

CIRILO FLORES

Coadjutor Bishop of San Diego; ordained June 8, 1991; appointed Auxiliary Bishop of Orange January 5, 2009; ordained March 19, 2009; appointed Coadjutor Bishop of San Diego January 4, 2012. *Mailing Address: Office, P.O. Box 85728, San Diego, CA 92186-5728.* Tel: 858-490-8200.

Pastoral Center: P.O. Box 85728, San Diego, CA 92186-5728. Tel: 858-490-8200; Fax: 858-490-8272.

Web: www.diocese-sdiego.org

Email: scallaha@diocese-sdiego.org

ESTABLISHED JULY 11, 1936.

Square Miles 8,852.

Comprises the Counties of Imperial and San Diego in the State of California.

Legal Titles: The Roman Catholic Bishop of San Diego, a Corporation Sole--(Churches, Rectories, Halls, Catechetical Centers, etc.) Diocese of San Diego.
For legal titles of parishes and diocesan institutions, consult the Diocesan Office.

STATISTICAL OVERVIEW

Personnel	
Bishop	2
Retired Bishops	1
Abbots	1
Priests: Diocesan Active in Diocese	105
Priests: Diocesan Active Outside Diocese	4
Priests: Retired, Sick or Absent	57
Number of Diocesan Priests	166
Religious Priests in Diocese	85
Total Priests in Diocese	251
Extern Priests in Diocese	57
Ordinations:	
Religious Priests	1
Permanent Deacons	4
Permanent Deacons in Diocese	171
Total Brothers	17
Total Sisters	246
Parishes	
Parishes	98
With Resident Pastor:	
Resident Diocesan Priests	84
Resident Religious Priests	10
Without Resident Pastor:	
Administered by Priests	3
Administered by Lay People	1
Missions	13
Closed Parishes	1
Professional Ministry Personnel:	
Brothers	17
Sisters	246
Lay Ministers	195
Welfare	
Catholic Hospitals	2
Total Assisted	89,114
Homes for the Aged	3
Total Assisted	264
Day Care Centers	1
Total Assisted	170
Specialized Homes	3
Total Assisted	3,555
Special Centers for Social Services	7
Total Assisted	147,798
Residential Care of Disabled	1
Total Assisted	70
Educational	
Diocesan Students in Other Seminaries	6
Total Seminarians	6
Colleges and Universities	2
Total Students	8,484
High Schools, Diocesan and Parish	3
Total Students	2,684
High Schools, Private	3
Total Students	1,494
Elementary Schools, Diocesan and Parish	44
Total Students	14,254
Elementary Schools, Private	3
Total Students	884
Non-residential Schools for the Disabled	1
Total Students	390
Catechesis/Religious Education:	
High School Students	7,892
Elementary Students	16,234
Total Students under Catholic Instruction	52,322
Teachers in the Diocese:	
Priests	8
Sisters	22
Lay Teachers	1,087
Vital Statistics	
Receptions into the Church:	
Infant Baptism Totals	9,447
Minor Baptism Totals	730
Adult Baptism Totals	481
Received into Full Communion	852
First Communions	9,212
Confirmations	5,172
Marriages:	
Catholic	1,534
Interfaith	315
Total Marriages	1,849
Deaths	2,760
Total Catholic Population	982,183
Total Population	3,124,081

Former Bishops—Most Revs. CHARLES F. BUDDY, D.D., S.T.D., Ph.D., ord. Sept. 19, 1914; appt. First Bishop of San Diego, Oct. 31, 1936; cons. Dec. 21, 1936; named Asst. at Pontifical Throne, Jan. 12, 1964; died March 6, 1966; FRANCIS J. FUREY, D.D., Ph.D., LL.D., ord. March 15, 1930; appt. Auxiliary Bishop of Philadelphia, Aug. 24, 1960; cons. Dec. 22, 1960; succeeded to the See of San Diego, March 6, 1966; translated to Archbishop of San Antonio, June 4, 1969; died April 23, 1979; LEO T. MAHER, D.D., Bishop of San Diego; ord. Dec. 18, 1943; First Bishop of Santa Rosa; appt. Feb. 21, 1962; cons. April 5, 1962; translated to San Diego, Aug. 27, 1969; retired July 10, 1990; died Feb. 23, 1991.

Pastoral Center—3888 Paducah Dr., San Diego, 92117. Mailing Address: P.O. Box 85728, San Diego, 92186-5728. Tel: 858-490-8200; Fax: 858-490-8272. Office Hours: Mon.-Fri. 8:30-4:30.

Vicar General—Very Rev. Msgr. STEVEN F. CALLAHAN, J.C.L. Tel: 858-490-8310.

Chancellor—RODRIGO VALDIVIA, J.C.L. Tel: 858-490-8310.

Judicial Vicar—Very Rev. Msgr. STEVEN F. CALLAHAN, J.C.L.

Diocesan Tribunal

Adjutant Judicial Vicar—Rev. EDWARD P. MCNULTY, J.C.L.

Promoter of Justice—Rev. DAVID N. CROISETIERE.

Defenders of the Bond—KELLY BEAURIVAGE, J.C.D.; Rev. Msgr. DANIEL J. DILLABOUGH.

Diocesan Judges—RODRIGO VALDIVIA, J.C.L.; Rev. Msgr. MARK A. CAMPBELL, J.C.L.

Tribunal Auditors—Deacons RAYMOND ARNOLD; ROBERT FITZMORRIS.

Notaries—CONNIE NOEL; LETICIA MENDOZA.

Diocesan Offices and Directors

Archivist—Contact: Chancellor's Office. Tel: 858-490-8208.

Catholic Charities—Sr. RAYMONDA DUVALL, C.H.S., Exec. Dir., 349 Cedar St., San Diego, 92101. Tel: 619-231-2828.

Cemetery Committee—Very Rev. Msgr. DENNIS MIKULANIS, Dir., Holy Cross Cemetery, 4470 Hilltop Dr., San Diego, 92102. Tel: 619-264-3127.

Censores Librorum—Very Rev. Msgr. RICHARD DUNCANSON, S.T.D.; BERNADEANE CARR, S.T.L.

Child and Youth Protection—RODRIGO VALDIVIA, J.C.L. Tel: 858-490-8310.

Civil Affairs—MARIA C. ROBERTS, Esq. Tel: 858-490-8277.

Spiritual Direction for Candidates and Priests—Rev. WILLIAM DILLARD. Tel: 619-291-5042.

Information Technology—MATTHEW DOLAN, Dir. Tel: 858-490-8329.

Construction Services—DANIEL RANCOURT, Dir. Tel: 858-490-8215.

Ecumenical and Interreligious Affairs—Very Rev. Msgr. DENNIS MIKULANIS, Vicar, 17252 Bernardo Center Dr., Rancho Bernardo, 92128-2086. Tel: 858-487-4314.

Evangelization & Catechetical Ministry—MARYJO WAGGONER, Dir. Tel: 858-490-8232.

Institute for Adult Education and Formation for Ministry—BERNADEANE CARR, S.T.L., Dir. Tel: 858-490-8212.

Schools—STEVAN LAAPERI, Dir. Tel: 858-490-8240; Sr.

BREEGE BOYLE, S.S.L., Assoc. Dir. Tel: 858-490-8240; PATRICIA BANNON, Assoc. Dir. Tel: 858-490-8244.

Media Center—Tel: 858-490-8230.

Youth Ministry—GERARDO ROJAS, Dir. Tel: 858-490-8260.

Young Adult Ministry—CARRIE GIEBEL, Dir. Tel: 858-490-8261.

Finance—Mr. MICHAEL WEST, Dir. Tel: 858-490-8277; SHIRLEY PAJANOR, Controller. Tel: 858-490-8207.

Human Resources—ROBERTA ESPINOSA, Dir. Tel: 858-490-8282.

Liturgy and Spirituality—Rev. EARL EGGLESTON, Dir. Tel: 858-490-8290.

Marriage and Family Life—MARGARET SKIANO, Dir. Tel: 858-490-8295.

Missions—Rev. JOSEPH MILLER, S.V.D., Dir.; Sr. EVA RODRIGUEZ, Assoc. Dir. Tel: 858-490-8250.

Cultural Diversity—RODRIGO VALDIVIA, J.C.L., Dir. Tel: 858-490-8306.

Parish Administration—ROBERTA ESPINOSA, Dir. Tel: 858-490-8284.

Permanent Diaconate—Sr. CARLOTTA DI LORENZO, C.S.J., Dir.; JOSE ERNESTO GONZALEZ, Assoc. Tel: 858-490-8239.

Priests—Rev. MICHAEL MURPHY, Dir., 655 C Ave., Coronado, 92118-3167. Tel: 619-437-4846; Fax: 619-437-1572.

Priestly Formation -- St. Francis Center—Rev. MATTHEW D. SPAHR, Dir. Tel: 619-291-7446; Fax: 619-291-7011.

Social Ministry—KENT PETERS, Dir. Tel: 858-490-8324; Deacon JAMES WALSH, Asst. Dir. Tel: 858-490-8375; LINDA ARREOLA, Asst. Dir. Tel: 858-490-8323.

"Southern Cross"-(Diocesan Newspaper)—Rev. CHARLES FULD, Editor (Retired). Tel: 858-490-8279.

Spiritual Direction for Candidates and Priests—Rev. WILLIAM DILLARD, Dir. Tel: 619-291-5042.

Priestly Vocations—Rev. ANTHONY SAROKI, Dir. Tel: 619-291-7446.

Women Religious—Sr. JEANETTE LUCINIO, S.P., Dir. Tel: 858-490-8289.

Vocations to the Priesthood and Consecrated Life—Sr. AURORA LOPEZ-ORNELAS, S.J.S., Dir. Tel: 858-490-8346.

Advisory Bodies

Clergy Personnel Board—Very Rev. Msgr. STEVEN F. CALLAHAN, J.C.L., Chm. Tel: 858-490-8310; Revs. EDWARD P. MCNULTY, J.C.L.; MICHAEL PHAM; Very Rev. JAMES N. POULSEN; Revs. RONALD J. BUCHMILLER; MICHAEL A. CUNNANE (Retired); PETER ESCALANTE; PETER MCGUINE; PATRICK J. MURPHY.

College of Consultors—Rev. Msgrs. DANIEL J. DILLABOUGH; HENRY F. FAWCETT (Retired); Very Rev. Msgr. STEVEN F. CALLAHAN, J.C.L.; Rev. MATTHEW D. SPAHR; Very Rev. BRUCE J. ORSBORN; Rev. Msgr. MARK A. CAMPBELL, J.C.L.

Diocesan Pastoral Council—Most Rev. ROBERT H. BROM, D.D., Ex Officio.

Finance Council—Most Rev. ROBERT H. BROM, D.D., Chm.; Mr. FRED BARANOWSKI; Mr. THOMAS BLAKE; JEAN BONK; Very Rev. Msgr. STEVEN F. CALLAHAN, J.C.L.; Dr. CONSTANCE CARROLL; Mrs. SUSAN CARTER; Rev. Msgr. DANIEL J. DILLABOUGH; Mr. PETER KRUSE; Mr. MICHAEL MAHER; Mr. MARK LINDSAY; Mr. BRIAN RILEY; Rev. ANTHONY SAROKI; Mr. LAWRENCE SHEA; Mr. RICHARD WOLTMAN.

Presbyteral Council—Most Rev. ROBERT H. BROM, D.D.; Rev. JOHN PROCTOR JR., Special Works; Very Rev. Msgr. STEVEN F. CALLAHAN, J.C.L.; Rev. RONALD J. BUCHMILLER, El Cajon Deanery; Very Rev. BRUCE J. ORSBORN; Revs. MICHAEL MURPHY; MATTHEW D. SPAHR; WILLIAM M. PETRUSKA, Military Liaison; Very Rev. EDDIE RUIZ, El Centro Deanery; Revs. EDWARD P. MCNULTY, J.C.L.; JAMES BAHASH; Rev. Msgrs. MARK A. CAMPBELL, J.C.L.; DANIEL J. DILLABOUGH; Revs. MANUEL EDIZA; PETER ESCALANTE; Rev. Msgr. HENRY F. FAWCETT (Retired); Revs. STEVEN LARION; RAYMOND G. O'DONNELL; MICHAEL RATAJCZAK; RICHARD L. PEROZICH.

Vicars Forane—Very Revs. BRUCE J. ORSBORN, Cathedral; JAMES N. POULSEN, El Cajon; Very Rev. Msgr. LAWRENCE M. PURCELL, S.T.D., Oceanside; Very Revs. EDDIE RUIZ, El Centro; JOHN P. DOLAN, South Bay; Very Rev. Msgrs. RICHARD DUNCANSON, S.T.D., Mission; DENNIS MIKULANIS, Escondido.

Miscellaneous

Apostleship of the Sea—Deacon SAM MARTINEZ. Tel: 619-702-4703; Rev. JAMES BOYD, Chap. Tel: 858-292-1822.

Hispanic Charismatic Renewal Center (Carismatica Hispana)—JOSE MACIAS, Coord. Tel: 619-423-2474.

Cursillo—Spiritual Advisors: Deacon CHARLES FRICE; PATRICK O'BRIEN, Lay Dir.

Filipino—LUZ MONTEMAYER, Lay Dir.; Rev. DIONISIO MACALINTAL, Spiritual Advisor; Deacon SAM MARTINEZ, Assoc. Spiritual Advisor. Tel: 619-267-0074.

Hispanic—CUCA ANGULO, Pres. Secretariat. Tel: 619-823-3119; Rev. ANDRES RIVERO, O.F.M., Spiritual Advisor. Tel: 619-232-6681.

Vietnamese—Deacon SALVADOR LOI D. HOANG, Spiritual Dir.; JOSEPH DINH Q. DAO, Lay Dir. Tel: 858-689-1128.

Holy Childhood Association—Sr. EVA LUCIA RODRIGUEZ, Assoc. Dir., Mailing Address: P.O. Box 82386, San Diego, 92138-2386. Tel: 858-490-8250.

Propagation of the Faith—Rev. JOSEPH MILLER, S.V.D., Dir., Mailing Address: P.O. Box 82386, San Diego, 92186-2386. Tel: 858-490-8250.

Victim Assistance Coordinator—Very Rev. Msgr. STEVEN F. CALLAHAN, J.C.L.: 858-490-8310.

CLERGY, PARISHES, MISSIONS AND PAROCHIAL SCHOOLS

CITY OF SAN DIEGO

(SAN DIEGO COUNTY)

1—SAINT JOSEPH CATHEDRAL CATHOLIC PARISH (1874) Rev. Peter Escalante.
Res.: 1535 Third Ave., 92101-3192. Tel: 619-239-0229; Fax: 619-239-3788.
Catechesis/Religious Program—Students 117.

2—ASCENSION CATHOLIC PARISH (1980) Rev. Anthony Saroki; Deacon Jim Scull.
11292 Clairemont Mesa Blvd., 92124. Tel: 858-279-2735; Fax: 858-279-1023.
St. Columba Rectory: 3327 Glencolum Dr., 92123.
Catechesis/Religious Program—Tel: 858-279-2752. Students 222.

3—BLESSED SACRAMENT CATHOLIC PARISH (1938) Very Rev. Bruce J. Orsborn; Rev. Agustin Opalalic; Deacons A. Anthony Albers; Herbert Kelsey. In Res., Revs. Jerry Hamperzonian (PSC); James Burson, C.J.M.
Res.: 4540 El Cerrito Dr., 92115. Tel: 619-582-5722; Fax: 619-582-2505. Email: jyin@blessedsacrament-sd.org. Web: www.blessedsacrament-sd.org.
School—(Grades PreK-8), 4551 56th St., 92115. Tel: 619-582-3862; Fax: 619-265-9310. Ms. Theodora Furtado, Prin.; Sharon Gaskin, Preschool Prin. Tel: 619-582-3862, Ext. 260. Lay Teachers 20; Students 221.
Catechesis/Religious Program—Tel: 619-582-4633. Students 65.
Mission—SDSU Newman Center 5855 Hardy Ave., San Diego Co. 92115. Tel: 619-583-9181; Fax: 619-583-8925.

4—CHRIST THE KING CATHOLIC PARISH (1938) Rev. Tommie Jennings; Deacons Harry Guess Jr.; Jose Luis Del Rio.
Church: 29 N. 32nd St., 92102. Tel: 619-231-8906; Fax: 619-238-7060. Email: ctksango@sbcglobal.net.
Catechesis/Religious Program—Students 157.

5—GOOD SHEPHERD CATHOLIC PARISH (1970) Revs. Michael Robinson; Phien Van Pham; Deacon Jaime Aquino. In Res., Rev. Richard Huston (Retired).
Res.: 8200 Gold Coast Dr., 92126-3699. Tel: 858-271-0207; Fax: 858-271-0748.
School—(Grades K-8), 8180 Gold Coast Dr., 92126. Tel: 858-693-1522; Fax: 858-271-3439. Email: gsoffice@san.rr.com. Web: www.gscs-online.org. Mrs. Chris Corpora, Prin.; Geraldine Gorga, Librarian. Lay Teachers 15; Students 232.
Catechesis/Religious Program—Tel: 858-271-8769. Students 1,925.

6—HOLY FAMILY CATHOLIC PARISH (1942) Rev. Michael Pham; Deacon Frank Santoyo.
Res.: 1957 Coolidge St., 92111-7098. Tel: 858-277-0404; Fax: 858-279-6414. Email: hfchurch@san.rr.com. Web: holyfamilysd.catholicweb.com.
Preschool—Kathie Morgen, Dir.
School—(Grades PreSchool-8) Tel: 858-277-0222; Fax: 858-277-0224. Email: hschool1@san.rr.com. Mr. Daniel O'Neal, Prin. Lay Teachers 14; Students 187.
Catechesis/Religious Program—Tel: 858-268-0557. Students 350.

7—HOLY SPIRIT CATHOLIC PARISH (1952) Rev. Msgr. Roger A. Lechner; Rev. Doan Van Lai; Deacon Marvin Threatt. In Res., Rev. Lawrence Agi.
Res.: 2725-55th St., 92105-5094. Tel: 619-262-2435; Fax: 619-262-8718. Web: www.holyspiritsd.org.
Catechesis/Religious Program—Tel: 619-263-9307. Students 742.

8—THE IMMACULATA CATHOLIC PARISH (1958) Rev. Matthew D. Spahr.
St. Francis Center: 1667 Santa Paula Dr., 92111. Tel: 619-291-7446; Fax: 619-291-7011. Web: www.theimmaculata.org.
Catechesis/Religious Program—Tel: 619-574-5702; Fax: 619-574-5703. Students 188.

9—IMMACULATE CONCEPTION CATHOLIC PARISH (1849) [CEM] Rev. Justin Langille; Deacon Robert H. Fitzmorris.
Res.: 2540 San Diego Ave., 92110-2840. Tel: 619-295-4148; Fax: 619-295-4141. Web: www.ic-sandiego.org.
Catechesis/Religious Program—Students 33.

10—ST. JEROME (1985) Closed. For inquiries for parish records contact the chancery.

11—ST. MAXIMILIAN KOLBE MISSION (1971), (Polish), Rev. Jerszy Frydrych, S.Ch.
1735 Grand Ave., 92109.
Res.: 8585 La Mesa Blvd., La Mesa, 91941. Tel: 858-272-7655; Fax: 619-668-0028.
Catechesis/Religious Program—Tel: 619-668-0485. Students 23.

12—MISSION SAN DIEGO DE ALCALA CATHOLIC PARISH (1769), (California's First Mission) Rev. Msgr. Richard F. Duncanson; Rev. William A. Springer; Deacons H. William Vasquez Jr.; Ernest Grosso.
Res.: 10818 San Diego Mission Rd., 92108-2429. Tel: 619-283-7319; Fax: 619-283-7762. Web: www.missionsandiego.com.
Catechesis/Religious Program—Tel: 619-624-0900; Fax: 619-624-0019. Students 270.

13—OUR LADY OF ANGELS CATHOLIC PARISH (1906) Rev. Earl Eggleston.
Res.: 656 24th St., 92102-2911. Tel: 619-239-1231; Fax: 619-234-5520. Email: ourladyofangels@cox.net.
Catechesis/Religious Program—Sr. Gloria Galvan, D.R.E. Students 581.

14—OUR LADY OF GUADALUPE CATHOLIC PARISH SAN DIEGO (1919) Revs. Robert Fambrini, S.J.; Richard Brown, S.J.; William Ameche, S.J.
Res.: 1770 Kearny Ave., 92113-1128. Tel: 619-233-3838; Fax: 619-233-3252.
School—Our Lady's School, (Grades K-8), 650 24th St., 92102. Tel: 619-233-8888; Fax: 619-501-2951. Peter Hickey, Prin. Please see Our Lady's School under Our Lady of Guadalupe. Lay Teachers 16; Students 231.
Catechesis/Religious Program—Tel: 619-233-3838; Fax: 619-233-3252. Students 404.

15—OUR LADY OF MT. CARMEL CATHOLIC PARISH SAN DIEGO (1976) Rev. Patrick J. Murphy; Deacons Noel Rivera; Manny Porciuncula; Juan Faus; Robert Holgren.
Res.: 13541 Stoney Creek Rd., 92129. Tel: 858-566-3550; 858-484-1070; Fax: 858-484-6157. Email: ourlady@olmc-sandiego.org. Web: www.olmc-sandiego.org.
Catechesis/Religious Program—Students 532.

16—OUR LADY OF REFUGE CATHOLIC PARISH (1977) Rev. David N. Croisetiere.
Res.: 4226 Jewell St., 92109. Tel: 858-274-9670; Fax: 858-274-7486.
Catechesis/Religious Program—Tel: 858-274-2959. Vicky Jimenez, D.R.E. Students 91.

17—OUR LADY OF THE ROSARY CATHOLIC PARISH (1925), (Italian), Revs. Joseph Tabigue, C.R.S.P.; Louis M. Solcia, C.R.S.P.
Res.: 1629 Columbia St., 92101. Tel: 619-234-4820; Fax: 619-234-3559. Web: www.olrsd.org.
Catechesis/Religious Program—Tel: 619-234-4820; Fax: 619-234-3445. Esther Leuzzi, D.R.E. Students 125.

18—OUR LADY OF THE SACRED HEART CATHOLIC PARISH (1911) Revs. Duong Nguyen, S.V.D.; Jesus Zamarripa, S.V.D. In Res., Rev. Raymundus Wea, S.V.D.
Church: 4177 Marlborough Ave., 92105-1412. Tel: 619-280-0515; Fax: 619-280-0517. Email: ourladyofsacred@hotmail.com.
Preschool—Tel: 619-284-0124. Enid Dixon, Dir.
School—(Grades PreK-8), 4106 42nd St., 92105. Tel: 619-284-1715; Fax: 619-284-8332. Ms. Christine Haddad, Prin.; Mary Hutchings, Librarian. Lay Teachers 14; Students 172.
Catechesis/Religious Program—Tel: 619-283-9262. Ms. Ada Padilla, D.R.E. Students 559.

19—OUR MOTHER OF CONFIDENCE CATHOLIC PARISH (1964) Rev. Msgr. Mark A. Campbell; Deacon William Klopchin; Sr. Angela Therse Merami, Pastoral Assoc.
Church: 3131 Governor Dr., 92122. Tel: 858-453-0222; Fax: 858-453-2547. Email: omcchurch@san.rr.com. Web: www.omoc.org.
Catechesis/Religious Program—Tel: 858-453-3554. Ian Mascarenhas, D.R.E. Students 263.

20—SACRED HEART CATHOLIC PARISH SAN DIEGO (1911) Rev. Ronald Hebert; Deacons Giles Schmitt; Mark Wieczorek.
Church: 4776 Saratoga Ave., 92107-9990. Tel: 619-224-2746; Fax: 619-224-0459. Web: www.sacredheartob.org.
Preschool— Gabriela Vieira, Dir.
School—(Grades PreK-8), 4895 Saratoga Ave., 92107. Tel: 619-222-7252; Fax: 619-222-2836. Web:

www.s-h-a.org. Mr. Jeff Saavedra, Prin. Lay Teachers 13; Students 171.
Catechesis/Religious Program—Tel: 619-223-4594. Cathleen Hornsby, D.R.E. Students 124.

21—SAINT AGNES CATHOLIC PARISH (1908) Rev. Edward P. McNulty.
Res.: 1140 Evergreen St., 92106. Tel: 619-223-2200; Fax: 619-223-7568.
Catechesis/Religious Program—Tel: 619-223-9748; Fax: 619-223-4725. Students 102.

22—SAINT ANNE CATHOLIC PARISH (2008) Revs. Carl Gismondi, F.S.S.P.; Dennis Gordon, F.S.S.P.; Joel Kiefer.
2337 Irving Ave., 92113. Tel: 619-239-8253.
Catechesis/Religious Program—Students 90.

23—SAINT BRIGID CATHOLIC PARISH (1940) Very Rev. Msgr. Steven F. Callahan; Rev. Msgr. Sean Murray, Pastor Emeritus (Retired); Rev. Emilio C. Tozzi; Deacon Michael Daniels.
Church & Res.: 4735 Cass St., 92109-2698. Tel: 858-483-3030; Fax: 858-483-7131.
Catechesis/Religious Program—Tel: 858-483-3032. Sr. Hilda McDonagh, R.S.M., D.R.E.; Grant Milbrand, Youth Min. Tel: 858-682-8888; Carrie Giebel, Young Adult Min. Tel: 858-483-3416. Students 230.

24—SAINT CATHERINE LABOURE CATHOLIC PARISH (1964) Rev. Msgr. Patrick J. Mullarkey.
Mailing Address: 4124 Mt. Abraham Ave., 92111.
In Res., Revs. Joseph Miller, S.V.D.; Dennis Flynn, S.V.D.
Res.: 4038 Mt. Abraham Ave., 92111. Tel: 858-277-3133; Fax: 858-277-9181. Email: stcl@sbcglobal.net.
Catechesis/Religious Program—Tel: 858-279-0587; Fax: 858-277-9181. Sandra Welch, D.R.E. Students 188.

25—SAINT CHARLES BORROMEO CATHOLIC PARISH (1946) Rev. William A. Kernan.
Res.: 2802 Cadiz St., 92110-4813. Tel: 619-225-8157; Fax: 619-225-2288. Web: www.stcharlesborromeo.us.
School—(Grades PreK-8) Tel: 619-223-8271; Fax: 619-223-2695. Thomas Mamara, Prin. Lay Teachers 12; Students 184.
School—Preschool, (Grades PreSchool) Tel: 619-758-0903. Karen Snedden, Dir. Lay Teachers 3; Students 38.
Catechesis/Religious Program—Students 100.

26—SAINT CHARLES CATHOLIC PARISH (1946) Revs. James Bahash; Arnold Tadena; Deacons Howard Mick Dennison; Ken Montoya; Sam Martinez, (Retired); Raul Hernandez. In Res., Rev. Burt Boudoin.
Res.: 990 Saturn Blvd., 92154. Tel: 619-423-0242; Fax: 619-423-1966. Web: www.saintcharles.org.
School—(Grades K-8), 929 18th St., 92154. Tel: 619-423-3701; Fax: 619-423-5331. Mr. Steve Stutz, Prin.; Sr. Elizabeth Wekall, Librarian. Sisters of Mercy 1; Lay Teachers 13; Students 237.
Catechesis/Religious Program—Tel: 619-575-2240. Students 746.

27—SAINT COLUMBA CATHOLIC PARISH (1955) Revs. Mario Elias; Chol-Min Ahn, Assoc. Pastor & Korean Chap.; Deacon H. William Vasquez Jr.
Res.: 3327 Glencolum Dr., 92123. Tel: 858-277-3863; Fax: 858-277-3883. Web: www.stcolumbasandiego.com.
Preschool—Tel: 858-279-0161. Trish Gilsdorf, Dir.
School—(Grades PreK-8) Tel: 858-279-1882; Fax: 858-279-1653. Mrs. Geraldine Nau, Prin. Lay Teachers 12; Students 237.
Catechesis/Religious Program—Tel: 858-277-3861. Students 123.

28—SAINT DIDACUS CATHOLIC PARISH (1926) Rev. Michael Sinor; Deacon Peter Nguyen.
Church: 4772 Felton St., 92116. Tel: 619-284-3472; Fax: 619-284-3484. Email: stdidacusparish@pacbell.net. Web: www.stdidacus.com.
Preschool—Tel: 619-284-8730, Ext. 307. Rose Witt, Dir.
School—(Grades PreSchool-8), 4630 34th St., 92116. Tel: 619-284-8730; Fax: 619-284-1764. Mrs. Elizabeth LaCosta, Prin.; Celeste Dueber, Librarian. Lay Teachers 14; Students 276.
Catechesis/Religious Program— Elena Platas, D.R.E. Students 254.

29—SAINT GREGORY THE GREAT CATHOLIC PARISH (1985) Rev. Nicholas P. Clavin; Deacons L. Ferris Bell, (Retired); Ronald H. Diem.
Mailing Address: 11451 Blue Cypress Dr., 92131. Tel: 858-653-3540; Fax: 858-653-3550. Email: information@stgg.org. Web: www.stgg.org.
School—St. Gregory the Great Catholic School, (Grades K-6), 15315 Stonebridge Pkwy., 92131. Tel: 858-397-1290; Fax: 858-397-1294. Web: www-.stggcs.org. Maeve O'Connell, Prin. Lay Teachers 13; Students 145.
Catechesis/Religious Program—Tel: 858-653-3594. Lay Teachers 2; Students 968.

30—SAINT JOHN THE EVANGELIST CATHOLIC PARISH SAN DIEGO (1913) Revs. William Dillard; Eugene Sta. Ana; Deacon Robert Booth. In Res., Rev. Tommie Jennings.
Res.: 1638 Polk Ave., 92103. Tel: 619-291-1660; Fax: 619-291-4597. Email: sjesd@sbcglobal.net. Web: sje-sd.e-paluch.com.

31—SAINT JUDE SHRINE OF THE WEST CATHOLIC PARISH (1946) [CEM] Revs. Pedro Rivera; Alexis Davila; Deacons Manuel Nunez; Manuel Rodriguez.
Res.: 1129 South 38th St., 92113-3210. Tel: 619-264-2195; Fax: 619-264-8528. Web: www.stjudesd.com.
St. Jude's Child Care and Development Center—3751 Boston Ave., 92113. Tel: 619-264-8256; Fax: 619-264-2793.
St. Jude's Senior Nutrition Program—Tel: 619-264-4771; Fax: 619-264-0797.
Catechesis/Religious Program—Tel: 619-264-4795. Rosa Murguia, D.R.E. Students 761.

32—SAINT MARY MAGDALENE CATHOLIC PARISH (1953) Rev. Stephen P. McCall; Rev. Msgr. John A. Dickie, Pastor Emeritus (Retired); Deacon Ralph Skiano. In Res., Rev. Anthony C. May (Retired).
Church: 1945 Illion St., 92110. Tel: 619-276-1041; Fax: 619-276-0144.
Preschool—Tel: 619-276-6545, Ext. 226. Valerie Grove, Dir.
School—(Grades PreK-8) Tel: 619-276-6545; Fax: 619-276-5359. Donna Wittouck, Prin. Lay Teachers 30; Students 606.
Catechesis/Religious Program—Tel: 619-276-1248. Kristine Bacich, D.R.E. Students 165.

33—SAINT MICHAEL CATHOLIC PARISH SAN DIEGO (1957) Revs. Manuel Ediza; Bernardo Ranoa (Philippines); Marcelino Bandico; Deacons Carl Shelton; Severo Santas Jr.
Church: 2643 Homedale St., 92139. Tel: 619-470-1977; Fax: 619-470-6357.
Preschool—Tel: 619-472-5437; Fax: 619-470-5231. Miss Lucy Zumarrano, Dir.
School—(Grades PreSchool-8), 2637 Homedale St., 92139. Tel: 619-470-4880; Fax: 619-267-9397. Mrs. Evelyn Urbitzando, Prin.; Diana Gonsalves, Librarian. Lay Teachers 14; Students 171.
Catechesis/Religious Program—Tel: 619-470-2291; Fax: 619-267-9397. Ms. Barbara Kearns, D.R.E. Students 487.

34—SAINT PATRICK CATHOLIC PARISH SAN DIEGO (1921) Rev. Michael McFadden, O.S.A.
Church & Parish Center Office: 3585 30th St., 92104. Tel: 619-295-2157.
School—(Grades K-8) Tel: 619-297-1314; Fax: 619-297-3346. Mr. Daniel O'Neal, Prin. Lay Teachers 13; Students 191.
Catechesis/Religious Program—Students 214.
Chapel—St. Augustine 3266 Nutmeg St., 92104-5151. Tel: 619-282-2028; Fax: 619-282-2233. Jim Horne, Prin.

35—SAINT RITA CATHOLIC PARISH (1941) Revs. Armando P. Escurel; Joseph Viet Hoang.
Church: 5124 Churchward St., 92114-3797. Tel: 619-264-3165; Fax: 619-264-2907.
Preschool—Tel: 619-264-8831. Vicky Torres, Dir.
School—(Grades PreK-8), 5165 Imperial Ave., 92114. Tel: 619-264-0109. Amber Johnson, Prin.; Ruberta Castro, Librarian. Lay Teachers 14; Students 202.
Catechesis/Religious Program—Tel: 619-264-4399. Sr. Margaret Castro, D.R.E. Students 333.

36—SAINT THERESE CATHOLIC PARISH (1956) Very Rev. Bruce J. Orsborn; Revs. William Stevenson; Daniel Nganga; Deacon Robert Ekhaml.
Res.: 6016 Camino Rico, 92120-3099. Tel: 619-582-3716; Fax: 619-582-2535. Web: www.stthereseparish.org.
Preschool—Tel: 619-583-1493. Barbara Paddock, Dir.
School—St. Therese Academy, (Grades PreSchool-8), 6046 Camino Rico, 92120. Tel: 619-583-6270; Fax: 619-583-5721. Mark Sperrazzo, Prin. Sisters 2; Lay Teachers 18; Students 346.
Catechesis/Religious Program—Tel: 619-582-2585. Students 273.

37—SAINT THERESE OF CARMEL CATHOLIC PARISH (1985) Rev. Nicholas Dempsey; Deacon John Fanelle.
Church: 4355 Del Mar Trails Rd., 92130-2296. Tel: 858-481-3232; Fax: 858-481-3289. Email: parishoffice@sttheresecarmel.org. Web: www.sttheresecarmel.org.
Catechesis/Religious Program—Jessica Firsching, Coord. Faith Formation; Cort Peters, D.R.E.; Nina Baumgardner, Youth Ministry. Students 550.

38—SAINT VINCENT DE PAUL CATHOLIC PARISH (1910) Revs. William Dillard; Eugene Sta. Ana.
Church: 4077 Ibis St., 92103-1899. Tel: 619-299-3881; Fax: 619-299-9509. Web: www.vincentcatholic.org.
Preschool—Tel: 619-296-2261. Denise Blaha, Dir.
School—(Grades K-8) Tel: 619-296-2222; Fax: 619-296-2763. Web: www.svscatholic.org. Sr. Kathleen Walsh, R.S.M., Prin. Sisters of Mercy 2; Lay Teachers 13; Students 220.
Catechesis/Religious Program—Tel: 619-299-3880. Students 80.

39—SAN RAFAEL CATHOLIC PARISH (1974) Very Rev. Msgr. Dennis Mikulanis; Rev. Msgr. Lloyd Bourgeois, Pastor Emeritus (Retired); Deacons Leonard Vaillancourt, Pastoral Assoc.; Ward Thompson, Business Mgr.; Bernard Yeatts.
Church: 17252 Bernardo Center, 92128. Tel: 858-487-4314; Fax: 858-487-1498. Email: office@sanrafaelparish.org. Web: www.sanrafael-sandiego.myownparish.com.
Catechesis/Religious Program—Tel: 858-487-0491. Sisters Laura Abat, O.S.F., D.R.E.; Michele McQueeney, O.S.F., D.R.E. Students 571.

OUTSIDE THE CITY OF SAN DIEGO

ALPINE, SAN DIEGO CO., QUEEN OF ANGELS CATHOLIC PARISH (1950) Rev. Chris Kintanar; Deacon John A. Snyder.
2569 Victoria Dr., 91901-3662. Tel: 619-445-2145; Fax: 619-445-9682. Email: parish@queenofangels.org. Web: www.queenofangels.org.
Catechesis/Religious Program—Students 205.

BONITA, SAN DIEGO CO., CORPUS CHRISTI CATHOLIC PARISH (1984) Rev. Patrick J. Mulcahy; Deacons James H. Hitch; Guillermo Jiron; Wil Hollowell.
Church: 450 Corral Canyon Rd., 91902-4072. Tel: 619-482-3954; Fax: 619-482-7236. Web: www.corpuschristicatholic.org.
Preschool—Leanna Zarzar Prelle, Dir.
Catechesis/Religious Program—Tel: 619-482-3953; Fax: 619-482-7236. Michael Wickham, D.R.E. Students 1,150.

BORREGO SPRINGS, SAN DIEGO CO., SAINT RICHARD CATHOLIC PARISH (1954) [CEM] Rev. Nemesio Sungcad.
Res.: 611 Church Ln., P.O. Box 1128, 92004-1128. Tel: 760-767-5701; Fax: 760-748-0215.
Catechesis/Religious Program—Students 65.
Mission— 3389 Sea View Ave., Salton Sea Beach, Riverside Co. 92274.

BRAWLEY, IMPERIAL CO.

1—OUR LADY OF PERPETUAL HELP CATHOLIC PARISH BRAWLEY (1956) Rev. Jorge Moreno.
Res.: 1250 B St., P.O. Box 1283, 92227. Tel: 760-344-2226; Fax: 760-344-1557.
Catechesis/Religious Program—Tel: 760-344-5787; 760-344-1557. Julia Garcia, D.R.E. Students 131.

2—SACRED HEART CATHOLIC PARISH BRAWLEY (1908) Very Rev. Eddie Ruiz; Rev. Alexander Aquino; Deacon Donald L. Spinney.
Church: 402 S. Imperial Ave., 92227. Tel: 760-344-3171; Fax: 760-344-3174.
Preschool—Anna Salgado, Dir.
School—(Grades PreK-8), 428 S. Imperial Ave., 92227. Tel: 760-344-2662; Fax: 760-344-1910. Brian Barrett, Prin. Lay Teachers 7; Students 109.
Catechesis/Religious Program—Carol Sassie, C.R.E.; Alicia Rangel, C.R.E. Students 87.

3—SAINT MARGARET MARY CATHOLIC PARISH (1934) Very Rev. Eddie Ruiz; Rev. Alexander Aquino.
Res.: 620 S. Cesar Chavez St., 92227. Tel: 760-344-3571; Fax: 760-344-3598. Email: smmbrawley@yahoo.com.
Catechesis/Religious Program—Tel: 760-344-6515; Fax: 760-344-7598. Students 350.

CALEXICO, IMPERIAL CO., OUR LADY OF GUADALUPE CATHOLIC PARISH CALEXICO (1907), (Mexican), Rev. Gerardo Fernandez; Deacon Refugio Gonzalez.
Res.: 124 E. Fifth St., 92231. Tel: 760-357-1822; Fax: 760-357-0115.
Preschool—Jazel Gonzalez, Dir.
School—Our Lady of Guadalupe Academy, (Grades PreSchool-8), 535 Rockwood Ave., 92231. Tel: 760-357-1986; Fax: 760-357-3282. Sr. Maria Elvia Gonzalez, S.J.S., Prin.; Silvia Chavarin, Librarian. Lay Teachers 24; Students 556.
Catechesis/Religious Program— Samuel Salazar, Faith Formation Dir. Students 465.

CALIPATRIA, IMPERIAL CO., SAINT PATRICK CATHOLIC PARISH CALIPATRIA (1919) Rev. Emilio A. Magana.
Res.: 133 E. Church St., P.O. Box 238, 92233. Tel: 760-348-2733; Fax: 760-348-7070.
Catechesis/Religious Program—Tel: 760-348-2454. Students 85.
Mission—Immaculate Heart of Mary P.O. Box 238, 92233. 19 Sixth St., Niland, 92257. Tel: 760-359-0464.

CARLSBAD, SAN DIEGO CO.

1—SAINT ELIZABETH SETON CATHOLIC PARISH (1977) Rev. Donald E. Coleman; Deacons Henry Chia; Dale Fickes.
Res.: 6628 Santa Isabel St., 92009-5148. Tel: 760-438-3393; Fax: 760-438-7739. Web: www.stelizabeth-seton.org.
Catechesis/Religious Program—Tel: 760-438-3438. Email: reled-ses@stelizabeth-seton.org. Larry Broding, D.R.E. Students 738.

2—SAINT PATRICK CATHOLIC PARISH CARLSBAD (1943) Revs. William F. Rowland, C.J.M.; Ricardo

Chinchilla, C.J.M.; Deacons Michael Frazee; Gerald McClellan Jr.; Edward Moser.
Church: 3821 Adams St., 92008-0249. Tel: 760-729-2866; Fax: 760-434-3325. Web: www.stpatrickcarlsbad.com.
School—(Grades K-8), 3820 Pio Pico, 92008. Tel: 760-729-1333; Fax: 760-729-4643. Web: www.stpaddys.org. Mary Beth Clark, Prin.; Denise Nelson, Prin.; Anette Latassa, Librarian. Lay Teachers 26; Students 466.
Catechesis/Religious Program—Tel: 760-729-8442. Students 850.

CAMPO, SAN DIEGO CO., SAINT ADELAIDE OF BURGUNDY CATHOLIC PARISH Rev. Ignatius Dibeashi.
1347 Dewey Pl., P.O. Box 369, 91906. Tel: 619-478-1017.
Catechesis/Religious Program—Students 12.
Mission—St. Mary Magdalene 44686 Calexico Ave., Jacumba, San Diego Co. 91934.

CHULA VISTA, SAN DIEGO CO.

1—MATER DEI CATHOLIC PARISH (2004) Rev. Jovencio D. Ricafort.
P.O. Box 212047, 91921. Tel: 619-656-3735. Email: parish@materdeicv.org. Web: www.materdeicv.org.
Catechesis/Religious Program—Tel: 619-656-3740; Fax: 619-656-2939. Email: rep@materdeicv.org. Students 630.

2—MOST PRECIOUS BLOOD CATHOLIC PARISH (1957) Revs. Paul Nourie, O.M.I.; Joseph Ferraioli, O.M.I.; Deacons Daniel Parra; Rolando Bongatt; Ruben Pelina; Sr. Sanjuana Mora, C.V.I., Hispanic Ministry.
Church: 1245 4th Ave., 91911-3012. Tel: 619-422-2100; Fax: 619-422-1375. Email: churchmpb@attglobal.net. Web: www.preciousbloodchurch.com.
Catechesis/Religious Program—Tel: 619-422-2159. Sr. Camille Crabbe, C.V.I., D.R.E. Students 545.

3—OUR LADY OF GUADALUPE CATHOLIC PARISH CHULA VISTA (1945) Rev. Jose Luis Muro; Deacon Margarito Lozoya.
Church: 345 Anita St., 91911-4198. Tel: 619-422-3977; Fax: 619-422-1056.
Catechesis/Religious Program—Tel: 619-422-1887. Students 450.

4—SAINT PIUS X CATHOLIC PARISH CHULA VISTA (1955) Rev. Luke Jauregui; Rev. Msgr. Donald R. Kulleck, Pastor Emeritus (Retired); Rev. Edwin Tutor; Deacons Glenn Vecchitto; Daniel Prado; Peter Johnson.
Church: 1120 Cuyamaca Ave., 91911-3506. Tel: 619-420-9193; Fax: 619-420-9353. Email: office@saintpiusx.org. Web: www.saintpiusx.org.
Preschool—Maria Lira, Dir.
School—(Grades K-8), 37 E. Emerson, 91911. Tel: 619-422-2015; Fax: 619-422-0048. Eileen Hanson, Prin. Lay Teachers 13; Students 284.
Catechesis/Religious Program—Tel: 619-420-9193 ext. 104/105; Fax: 619-427-0015. Dora Castenada, D.R.E. Students 420.

5—SAINT ROSE OF LIMA CATHOLIC PARISH (1913) Very Rev. John P. Dolan; Rev. Jacob Bertrand; Deacons Gerardo Marquez; Gregory Smyth; Charles Frice. In Res., Rev. Mario Vesga (Retired).
Church: 293 H St., 91910-4703. Tel: 619-427-0230; Fax: 619-427-5786.
Preschool—278 Alvarado St., Unit 2, 91910. Glenda Martinez, Dir.
School—(Grades PreK-8), 278 Alvarado, Unit B, 91910. Tel: 619-422-1121; Fax: 619-422-8007. Web: www.strosecv.com. Mrs. Maria Tollefson, Prin. Religious 1; Lay Teachers 12; Students 328.
Catechesis/Religious Program—Tel: 619-426-6717. Sisters Patricia Weldon, D.R.E.; Joan King, O.S.B., D.R.E. Students 670.

CORONADO, SAN DIEGO CO., SACRED HEART CATHOLIC PARISH CORONADO (1897) Rev. Michael F. Murphy; Deacons Robert E. Griffin Jr.; Kevin Murray; Frank Osgood.
655 C Ave., 92118-2229. Tel: 619-435-3167; Fax: 619-437-1572. Web: www.sacredheartcor.org. In Res., Rev. Msgrs. Jeremiah O'Sullivan, Pastor Emeritus (Retired); Donal C. Sheehan (Retired).
Res.: 672 B Ave., 92118-2229. Tel: 619-435-3167; Fax: 619-437-1572.
School—(Grades K-8), 706 C Ave., 92118. Tel: 619-437-4431; Fax: 619-437-1473. Web: www.sacredheartcoronado.org. Mr. Peter Harris, Prin. Lay Teachers 9; Students 243.
Catechesis/Religious Program—Tel: 619-435-3167, Ext. 302. Students 197.

DESCANSO, SAN DIEGO CO., OUR LADY OF LIGHT CATHOLIC PARISH (1935) Rev. Gerald F. Palcheck.
Res.: 9136 Riverside Dr., 91916. Tel: 619-445-3620; Fax: 619-445-4972.
Catechesis/Religious Program—Eileen Briese, D.R.E. Students 11.

EL CAJON, SAN DIEGO CO.

1—THE CHURCH OF SAINT LUKE CATHOLIC PARISH (1985) Rev. Ronald Cochran; Deacons Dennie C. Nickell; Allan Williams.
Church: 1980 Hillsdale Rd., 92019. Tel: 619-442-1697; Fax: 619-442-2293. Email: parishoffice@thechurchofstluke.org. Web: www.thechurchofstluke.org.
Catechesis/Religious Program—Tel: 619-442-2515. Debbie Stenovec, D.R.E. (K-5); Jane Alfano, D.R.E. (6-12). Students 239.

2—HOLY TRINITY CATHOLIC PARISH (1903) Revs. Brian Hayes; Alfredo Heyrosa; Deacon Louis Rocha.
Church: 405 Ballard St., 92019-2123. Tel: 619-444-9425; Fax: 619-444-9426. Web: www.holytrinityelcajon.org.
Preschool—Tel: 619-444-1052. Rita McClurg, Dir.
School—(Grades PreK-8) Tel: 619-444-7529; Fax: 619-444-3721. Web: holytrinityschool.mswin.net. Francine Wright, Prin. Lay Teachers 18; Students 307.
Catechesis/Religious Program—Email: admin@holytrinityelcajon.org. Students 442.

3—OUR LADY OF GRACE CATHOLIC PARISH (1954) Revs. Michael J. Gallagher; Enrique Fuentes, O.C.D.; Sr. Alyce Waters, Pastoral Assoc.; Deacons George Shea; Raymond Arnold, (Retired); William Korty; Ron Allen. In Res., Rev. Omer LeBlanc, C.J.M.
Church: 2766 Navajo Rd., 92020-2183. Tel: 619-469-0133; Fax: 619-469-0575. Web: www.olg-church.org.
School—(Grades K-8) Tel: 619-466-0055; Fax: 619-466-8994. Web: www.olg.org. Mrs. Susan Hause, Prin. Lay Teachers 17; Students 287.
Catechesis/Religious Program—Tel: 619-466-5656. Students 340.

4—SAINT KIERAN CATHOLIC PARISH (1958) Rev. Ben Davison; Deacon D. Frank Reilly.
Office: 1510 Greenfield Dr., 92021-3511. Tel: 619-588-6881; Fax: 619-588-5274. Email: secretary@stkierans.sdcoxmail.com. Web: www.stkierans.org.
Preschool—Debbie Edelbrock, Dir.
School—(Grades PreSchool-8), 1347 Camillo Way, 92021. Tel: 619-588-6398; Fax: 619-588-6382. Mrs. Patricia Provo, Prin. Sisters 2; Lay Teachers 9; Students 120.
Catechesis/Religious Program—Students 50.

5—SAINT LOUISE DE MARILLAC CATHOLIC PARISH (1944) Rev. Scott A. Burnia.
Church: 2005 Crest Dr., 92021-4309. Tel: 619-444-3076; Fax: 619-440-1325.
Catechesis/Religious Program—Students 10.

EL CENTRO, IMPERIAL CO.

1—OUR LADY OF GUADALUPE CATHOLIC PARISH EL CENTRO (1946), (Mexican), Revs. Ruben Valenzuela; Jose Alfredo Moreno; Deacon Domingo Enriquez.
Church: 153 E. Brighton Ave., 92243. Tel: 760-352-5535; Fax: 760-352-8003.
Catechesis/Religious Program—Tel: 760-352-5554. Sr. Flavia Arellano, C.V.I., D.R.E.; Blanca Barela, Youth Min. Students 560.
Mission—Sacred Heart 40 E. Main, Heber, Imperial Co. 92249.

2—SAINT MARY CATHOLIC PARISH EL CENTRO (1907) [JC] Rev. Edward Horning.
Church: 795 LaBrucherie, 92243. Tel: 760-352-4211; Fax: 760-352-7397.
Preschool—Norma Grady, Dir.
School—(Grades PreSchool-8), 700 S. Waterman Ave. Tel: 760-352-7285; Fax: 760-352-9727. Sr. Katia Chavez, Prin. Sister Servants of the Blessed Sacrament 2; Lay Teachers 16; Students 214.
Catechesis/Religious Program—Tel: 760-353-8260 (K-8); 760-353-7280 (9-12). Students 276.

ENCINITAS, SAN DIEGO CO., SAINT JOHN THE EVANGELIST CATHOLIC PARISH ENCINITAS (1946) Revs. Brian Corcoran; Joseph Freeman.
Church: 1001 Encinitas Blvd., 92024-2828. Tel: 760-753-6254; Fax: 760-753-7118. Email: admin@stjohnencinitas.org.
Preschool—Megan Breesee, Dir.
School—(Grades PreSchool-8), 1003 Encinitas Blvd., 92024. Tel: 760-944-8227; Fax: 760-944-8939. Mr. Dan Schuh, Prin. Lay Teachers 32; Students 541.
Catechesis/Religious Program—Tel: 760-436-0664. Students 570.

ESCONDIDO, SAN DIEGO CO.

1—CHURCH OF ST. TIMOTHY CATHOLIC PARISH (1985) Rev. Fernando Ramirez; Deacons J. Michael Early; John Depner.
Church and Administration Center: 2960 Canyon Rd., 92025-7402. Tel: 760-489-1200; Fax: 760-489-2731. Web: www.sttimothychurch.com.
Catechesis/Religious Program—Tel: 760-489-0482. Christopher O'Donnell, D.R.E. Students 219.

2—CHURCH OF THE RESURRECTION CATHOLIC PARISH (1970) [JC] Revs. Kenneth Del Priore; Eduardo Bernardino; Deacons Mitch Rennix; Edwin Gonzales Montoya; Michael Partida; Christine Whitten, Pastoral Assoc.; Deacon Agustin Castro.
Church: 1445 Conway Dr., 92027. Tel: 760-747-2322; Fax: 760-747-7079. Web: www.resurrectionchurch.org.
Catechesis/Religious Program— Debbie Nehring, C.R.E. Tel: 760-747-2322, Ext. 111. Students 634.
Comunidad Hispana—Fax: 760-747-7090.

3—SAINT MARY CATHOLIC PARISH ESCONDIDO (1890) Revs. Richard L. Perozich; Gerald Kasule, C.S.Sp.; David Sereno; Deacons Amador Duran; James Kostick.
Church: 1160 S. Broadway Ave., 92025-5815. Tel: 760-745-1611; Fax: 760-745-1238. Email: pastor@stmary.sdcoxmail.com.
Preschool—Darlene Karnes-Versteegh, Dir.
School—(Grades PreSchool-8), 130 E. 13th Ave. Tel: 760-743-3431; Fax: 760-743-6808. Web: www.stmesc.org. Mrs. Cynthia Ashbury, Prin.; Irene Preuss, Librarian. Lay Teachers 11; Students 250.
Catechesis/Religious Program—130 E. 13th Ave., 92025. Tel: 760-745-8255; Fax: 760-745-8337. Sharon Twilliger, D.R.E. Students 1,500.

FALLBROOK, SAN DIEGO CO., SAINT PETER THE APOSTLE CATHOLIC PARISH (1946) Revs. Ramon Marrufo; Manuel Villarreal.
Church: 450 S. Stage Coach Ln., 92028. Tel: 760-728-7034; Fax: 760-723-4050. Web: www.stpeterscc.org.
Preschool—Amber Ostgaad, Dir.
School—St. Peter's Catholic School, (Grades PreK-8) Tel: 760-728-6961; Fax: 760-723-8973. Web: www.spacschool.com. Linda McCotter, Prin. Lay Teachers 14; Students 141.
Catechesis/Religious Program—Students 611.

HOLTVILLE, IMPERIAL CO., SAINT JOSEPH CATHOLIC PARISH HOLTVILLE (1911) Rev. George Decasa.
Church: 560 Maple Ave., 92250. Tel: 760-356-2147; Fax: 760-356-1985. Email: saint_josephchurch@yahoo.com.
Catechesis/Religious Program—Tel: 760-356-5738. Rocio Ramirez, D.R.E. Students 167.

IMPERIAL, IMPERIAL CO., SAINT ANTHONY OF PADUA CATHOLIC PARISH IMPERIAL (1948) Rev. Reynaldo Roque, Admin.
Church: 210 W. Seventh St., 92251. Tel: 760-355-1347; Fax: 760-355-1226. Web: www.stanparish.org.
Catechesis/Religious Program—Tel: 760-355-1304. Maria Fugett, Dir. Child Ministry. Students 230.

JACUMBA, SAN DIEGO CO., ST. MARY MAGDALENE (1947) See separate listing. A mission of St. Adelaide of Burgundy, Campo.

JAMUL, SAN DIEGO CO., SAINT PIUS X CATHOLIC PARISH JAMUL (1956) Rev. Victor Maristela; Deacons John Trumble; John Turcich.
Res.: 14107 Lyons Valley Rd., P.O. Box 369, 91935-0369. Tel: 619-669-0085; Fax: 619-669-0087.
Catechesis/Religious Program—Tel: 619-669-0086. Students 65.

JULIAN, SAN DIEGO CO., SAINT ELIZABETH OF HUNGARY CATHOLIC PARISH (1949) Rev. Cecilio Moraga.
Res.: 2814 B St., P.O. Box 366, 92036-0366. Tel: 760-765-0613; Fax: 760-765-0552.
Catechesis/Religious Program—Students 35.

LA JOLLA, SAN DIEGO CO.

1—ALL HALLOWS CATHOLIC PARISH (1959) Rev. Raymond G. O'Donnell; Deacon Joseph Wood.
Res.: 6602 La Jolla Scenic Dr. S., 92037-5799. Tel: 858-459-2975; Fax: 858-459-9712. Web: www.allhallows.com.
School—(Grades K-8), 2390 Nautilus, 92037. Tel: 858-459-6074; Fax: 858-459-4602. Mrs. Jill Platt, Dir.; Rafy Holland, Librarian. Lay Teachers 18; Aides 5; Students 233.
Catechesis/Religious Program—Karen Downs, D.R.E. Students 105.

2—MARY, STAR OF THE SEA CATHOLIC PARISH (1906) Rev. James Rafferty.
Office: 7669 Girard Ave., 92037.
Church: 7713 Girard Ave., 92037-4480. Tel: 858-454-2631; Fax: 858-454-5968. Email: marystarofthesea@san.rr.com.
School—Stella Maris Academy, (Grades K-8), 7654 Herschel Ave., 92037. Tel: 858-454-2461; Fax: 858-454-4913. Web: www.stellamarisacademy.org. Patricia Lowell, Prin. Lay Teachers 15; Students 200.
Catechesis/Religious Program—Tel: 858-551-8359. Donna Widmer, D.R.E.; Martin Magana, D.R.E. Students 156.

LA MESA, SAN DIEGO CO., SAINT MARTIN OF TOURS CATHOLIC PARISH (1921) Very Rev. James N. Poulsen. In Res., Rev. Msgr. Patrick J. O'Neill (Retired).
Res.: 7710 El Cajon Blvd., 91942-6932. Tel: 619-465-5334; Fax: 619-465-7297. Email: stmartinch@juno.com. Web: www.stmartinoftoursparish.org.
Preschool—7714 El Cajon Blvd. Tel: 619-698-8462.
School—(Grades PreSchool-8), 7708 El Cajon Blvd., 91942-6932. Tel: 619-466-3241; Fax: 619-466-0285. Web: www.stmartinacademy.org. Antoinette Dimuzio, Prin.; Sr. Charlene Del Bianco, C.S.J., Librarian. Lay Teachers 18; Students 261.
Catechesis/Religious Program—Tel: 619-698-8434. Christine Davis, D.R.E. Students 111.

LAKESIDE, SAN DIEGO CO.

1—BLESSED KATERI TEKAKWITHA (1982) [CEM] [JC 3]

Rev. Michael X Tran, Chap.; Deacon Bill Clarke; Edward Nolan, Pastoral Coord.
Res.: 1054 Barona Rd., 92040-1502. Tel: 619-443-3412; Fax: 619-443-3018. Email: bktparish@aol.com.
Catechesis/Religious Program—Tel: 619-445-8333. Josephine Whaley, D.R.E. Students 84.
Mission—Assumption of BVM
Mission—Nativity of BVM Alpine, San Diego Co.
Mission—Immaculate Conception of BVM El Cajon, San Diego Co.

2—OUR LADY OF PERPETUAL HELP CATHOLIC PARISH LAKESIDE (1947) Revs. Ronald J. Buchmiller; Joseph Khuyen Van Lai; Deacons Dennis O'Neil; Mark Silva; Patrick Root.
Res.: 13208 Lakeshore Dr., 92040. Tel: 619-443-1412; Fax: 619-443-1733. Email: rectory@olphchurch.org. Web: www.olphchurch.org.
School—(Grades PreSchool-8) Tel: 619-443-1440; Fax: 619-443-1714. Web: olphcatholicschool.com. Susan Silvia, Prin.; Pat Garcia, Librarian. Lay Teachers 12; Students 141.
Catechesis/Religious Program—Tel: 619-443-1477. Lisa Hutchenson, D.R.E. Students 220.

LEMON GROVE, SAN DIEGO CO., SAINT JOHN OF THE CROSS CATHOLIC PARISH (1939) Revs. Peter Navarra; Steven Larion; Hignio Garcia; Deacons Juan Francisco Santoyo; Martin Villafana; James Robert Stanley.
Res.: 8086 Broadway, 91945-2598. Tel: 619-466-3209; Fax: 619-466-9276. Web: www.st-johnofthecross.org.
Preschool—Tel: 619-466-8624, Ext. 103. Sr. Gloria Medina, Dir.
School—(Grades PreK-8), 8175 Lemon Grove Way, 91945. Tel: 619-466-8624; Fax: 619-466-3732. Web: www.stjohncross.org/sindex.htm. Sr. Marilupe Mier Y Teran, H.M.S.S., Prin.; Mrs. Rosa Olea, Librarian. Lay Teachers 32; Students 589.
Catechesis/Religious Program—Tel: 619-461-2681. Karen Dey, D.R.E. Students 739.
Convent—8171 Lemon Grove Way, 91945. Tel: 619-460-4271. Sisters of Mercy of the Blessed Sacrament 5.

NATIONAL CITY, SAN DIEGO CO.

1—SAINT ANTHONY OF PADUA CATHOLIC PARISH NATIONAL CITY (1910), (Mexican), Rev. Jose Edmundo Zarate-Suarez; Deacon Braulio Gutierrez.
410 W. 18th St., 91950. Email: stanthonyofpadua@sbcglobal.net.
Res.: 1816 Harding Ave., 91950. Tel: 619-477-4520; Fax: 619-477-8708.
Catechesis/Religious Program—Martha Mendoza, D.R.E. Students 376.

2—SAINT MARY CATHOLIC PARISH NATIONAL CITY (1926) Revs. Dionisio Macalintal; Danilo Valdepenas (Philippines).
Mailing Address: 426 E. Seventh St., 91950-2322. Tel: 619-474-1501; Fax: 619-474-1502.
Catechesis/Religious Program—Tel: 619-474-5777; Fax: 619-474-5777. Pilar Ignacio, D.R.E. Students 301.

NILAND, IMPERIAL CO., IMMACULATE HEART OF MARY, See separate listing. No longer a parish; now a mission of St. Patrick, Calipatria.

OCEANSIDE, SAN DIEGO CO.

1—MISSION SAN LUIS REY CATHOLIC PARISH (1798) Revs. Charles Talley, O.F.M.; Luiz Guzman, O.F.M.; Adrian Peelo, O.F.M.
Res.: 4070 Mission Ave., 92057-6497. Tel: 760-757-3250; Fax: 760-757-3299. Web: www.sanluisreyparish.org.
Old Mission Montessori Preschool—Tel: 760-757-3232. Wanda King, Dir.
Catechesis/Religious Program—Tel: 760-547-0716. Students 732.
Mission—Mission San Luis Rey De Francia 4050 Mission Ave., San Diego Co. 92057. Tel: 760-757-3651; Fax: 760-757-4613.

2—SAINT MARGARET CATHOLIC PARISH (1977) Rev. Cavana Wallace.
Res.: 4300 Oceanside Blvd., 92056-2999. Tel: 760-941-5560; Fax: 760-941-1857. Web: www.oceanside4christ.com.
Catechesis/Religious Program—Students 222.

3—SAINT MARY, STAR OF THE SEA CATHOLIC PARISH (1937) Rev. Michael Diaz.
Res.: 609 Pier View Way, 92054-2861. Tel: 760-722-1688; Fax: 760-722-2653. Web: www.stmarystars.org.
Preschool—Debbie Shapiro, Dir.
School—(Grades PreSchool-8), 515 Wisconsin Ave., 92054. Tel: 760-722-7259; Fax: 760-722-0862. Alan J. Hicks, Prin. Lay Teachers 20; Students 370.
Catechesis/Religious Program—Students 380.

4—SAINT THOMAS MORE CATHOLIC PARISH (1985) Rev. Michael Ratajczak; Deacon Thomas A. Goeltz.
Church & Mailing Address: 1450 S. Melrose Dr., 92056. Tel: 760-758-4100; Fax: 760-758-4165.
Res.: 4703 Majorca Way, 92056.
Catechesis/Religious Program—Students 238.

PALA, SAN DIEGO CO., MISSION SAN ANTONIO DE PALA CATHOLIC PARISH (1816) Revs. Reynaldo Manahan; Herman Manuel, S.V.D.
Res.: 3015 Mission Rd., P.O. Box 70, 92059-0070. Tel: 760-742-3317; Fax: 760-742-3040. Web: www.missionsanantonio.org.
Catechesis/Religious Program—Tel: 760-742-3317, Ext. 112. Students 175.
Chapel—Rincon Indian Reservation, St. Bartholomew
Chapel—La Jolla Indian Reservation, Our Lady of Refuge
Chapel—Pauma Indian Reservation, St. James

POWAY, SAN DIEGO CO.

1—SAINT GABRIEL CATHOLIC PARISH (1973) Rev. Michel Froidurot; Deacon Robert Troy. In Res., Rev. Harold Tindall (Retired).
Church: 13734 Twin Peaks Rd., 92064. Tel: 858-748-5348; Fax: 858-748-5764. Email: office@saintgabrielschurch.com. Web: www.saintgabrielschurch.com.
Catechesis/Religious Program—Tel: 858-748-7475. Mary Romag, D.R.E. Students 427.

2—SAINT MICHAEL CATHOLIC PARISH POWAY (1959) Rev. Msgrs. Neal T. Dolan; Joseph L. Finnerty, Pastor Emeritus (Retired); Rev. Melchisedech Monreal; Deacon John Charron.
Church: 15546 Pomerado Rd., 92064-2404. Tel: 858-487-4755; Fax: 858-487-5937. Web: www.stmichaelschurch-poway.org.
Preschool—Elizabeth Joseph, Dir.
School—(Grades PreSchool-8), 15542 Pomerado Rd., 92064. Tel: 858-485-1303; Fax: 858-485-5059. Kathleen Mock, Prin. Sisters of Mercy of Sligo 1; Lay Teachers 44; Students 584.
Catechesis/Religious Program—Tel: 858-485-1392; 858-485-9500. Kelli Salceda, D.R.E. Students 832.

RAMONA, SAN DIEGO CO., IMMACULATE HEART OF MARY CATHOLIC PARISH (1947) Rev. Andres Ramos, Admin.; Deacon Andre Escobedo.
Church: 537 E St., 92065. Tel: 760-789-0583; Fax: 760-789-3875. Email: ihmramona@parishmail.com. Web: www.ihmramona.parishesonline.com.
Catechesis/Religious Program—Tel: 760-789-6151. Students 18.

RANCHO SANTA FE, SAN DIEGO CO., CHURCH OF THE NATIVITY CATHOLIC PARISH (1985) Very Rev. Msgr. Lawrence M. Purcell.
Mailing Address: P.O. Box 8770, 92067-8770. Web: www.nativitycatholic.org.
Church: 6309 El Apajo Rd., 92067. Tel: 858-756-1911; Fax: 858-756-9562. Email: lmpurcell@nativitycatholic.org.
School—(Grades K-8), 6309 El Apajo Rd., P.O. Box 9180, 92067. Tel: 858-756-6763; Fax: 858-756-9128. Email: office@nativitycatholic.org. Mrs. Margaret Heveron, Prin. Students 180.
Catechesis/Religious Program— Mrs. Patti Smiley, D.R.E.; Mike James, Youth Min. Students 330.

SAN MARCOS, SAN DIEGO CO., SAINT MARK CATHOLIC PARISH (1963) [CEM] Revs. George Dunkley; Silverio Espenilla; Dickens Remy, C.I.C.M.; Deacons Frank Mercardante; Dennis Sullivan; David Bennett; Agustin Castro.
Church: 1147 Discovery St., 92078-1313. Tel: 760-744-1540; Fax: 760-744-3828. Email: office@stmarksrcc.org.
Catechesis/Religious Program—Tel: 760-744-1130. Students 1,000.
Mission— 2557 Sarver Ln., San Diego Co. 92069.

SAN YSIDRO, SAN DIEGO CO., OUR LADY OF MT. CARMEL CATHOLIC PARISH SAN YSIDRO (1927) Revs. Jose Castillo; Jose Whittingham; Deacons Jose Luis Medina; Raul Gonzalez.
Church: 2020 Alaquinas Dr., 92173-2107. Tel: 619-428-1415; Fax: 619-428-5626.
School—(Grades PreK-8), 4141 Beyer Blvd., 92173-2133. Tel: 619-428-2091; Fax: 619-428-8324. Sr. Ana Rosa Aceves, Prin.; Ma. Eugenia Villareal, Librarian. Sisters of the Most Blessed Sacrament 3; Lay Teachers 11; Students 311.
Catechesis/Religious Program—109 Seaward Ave., 92173. Tel: 619-428-3686. Students 462.

SANTA YSABEL, SAN DIEGO CO., SANTA YSABEL INDIAN MISSION CATHOLIC PARISH (1818) [CEM] Rev. Cecilio Moraga.
Res.: 23013 Hwy. 79, P.O. Box 129, 92070-1010. Tel: 760-765-0810; Fax: 760-765-3494. Email: missionsantaysabel@yahoo.com.
Mission—St. Francis of Assisi Hwy. 79 & Stage Rd., Warner Springs, San Diego Co. 92086.
Catechesis/Religious Program—Students 28.

SANTEE, SAN DIEGO CO., GUARDIAN ANGELS CATHOLIC PARISH (1962) Revs. Kevin P. Casey, S.J., Admin.; Michael A. Cunnane, Pastor Emeritus (Retired); Deacons Louis Principe; Richard Melrose.
Preschool—Tel: 619-448-1213, Ext. 314. Joyce Kemp, Dir.
Church: 9310 Dalehurst Rd., 92071-1010. Tel: 619-448-1213; Fax: 619-448-2980. Email: par.sec@ga.sdcoxmail.com. Web: www.guardianangelssantee.org.
Catechesis/Religious Program—9310 Dalehurst, 92071. Tel: 619-448-1213, Ext. 312. Sr. Mary Potter, R.S.M., D.R.E. Students 322.

SOLANA BEACH, SAN DIEGO CO., SAINT JAMES CATHOLIC PARISH (1911) Revs. John Howard, C.J.M.; A. Ernesto Torres, C.J.M.; Deacons Joseph R. Santen; Peter Hodsdon; Albert P. Graff; Laura Millerick, Dir.
Preschool—
School—St. James Academy, (Grades K-8), 623 S. Nardo Ave., 92075. Tel: 858-755-1777; Fax: 858-755-3124. Kathy Dunn, Prin. Lay Teachers 13; Students 239.
Catechesis/Religious Program—Tel: 858-755-2545, Ext. 106; Fax: 858-755-3845. Robert Kidd, D.R.E.; Lee Santen, D.R.E. Students 280.
Mission—St. Leo 936 Genevieve, San Diego Co. 92075. Tel: 858-481-6788; Fax: 858-481-5832. Sr. Zita Toto, O.L.C., Coord.
Catechesis/Religious Program—Vicente Leal, D.R.E. (Spanish). Students 195.

SPRING VALLEY, SAN DIEGO CO., SANTA SOPHIA CATHOLIC PARISH (1956) Rev. Peter McGuine.
Res.: 9800 San Juan St., 91977. Tel: 619-463-6629; Fax: 619-463-8101. Web: www.santasophia.org.
Preschool—Victoria Simanek, Dir.
School—(Grades PreSchool-8), 9806 San Juan St. Tel: 619-463-0488; Fax: 619-668-5469. Karen Laaperi, Prin., ssaklaaperi@hotmail.com. Lay Teachers 8; Aides 7; Students 273.
Catechesis/Religious Program—Tel: 619-463-6011; Fax: 619-668-5458. Bernadette Padlo, D.R.E. Students 220.

VALLEY CENTER, SAN DIEGO CO., SAINT STEPHEN CATHOLIC PARISH (1981) Rev. Elmer Mandac, Admin.; Deacons Charles Embury; Gilbert Salinas.
Church: 31020 Cole Grade Rd., P.O. Box 1015, 92082-1015. Tel: 760-749-3324; Fax: 760-749-6684.
Catechesis/Religious Program—Tel: 760-749-3352; Fax: 760-749-6608. Ellen MacPhee, D.R.E. Students 410.

VISTA, SAN DIEGO CO., SAINT FRANCIS OF ASSISI CATHOLIC PARISH (1941) Revs. Edward Kaicher; Peter Vu Lam; Efrain Bautista; Deacons Loi Hoang; Ronald Arnold; Pedro Enciso; Miguel Enriquez; Robert Mueller; Manny Robles.
Church: 525 W. Vista Way, 92083-5974. Tel: 760-945-8000; Fax: 760-945-8036. Email: info@stfrancis-vista.org. Web: www.stfrancis-vista.org.
Preschool—Tel: 760-630-7964. Jennifer Paino, Dir.
School—(Grades PreSchool-8) Tel: 760-630-7960; Fax: 760-726-2910. Email: info@sfs-vista.org. Web: www.sfs-vista.org. Brian Wheeler, Prin.; Mrs. Kay O'Connell, Librarian. Lay Teachers 17; Students 307.
Catechesis/Religious Program—Tel: 760-945-8010. Susan Ferraris, D.R.E. Students 862.

WESTMORLAND, IMPERIAL CO., SAINT JOSEPH CATHOLIC PARISH WESTMORLAND (1939), Administered by St. Anthony of Padua, Imperial., Mailing Address: P.O. Box 627, 92281. Tel: 760-351-1961; Fax: 760-344-3721.
Res.: 300 N. Center St., 92281.
Catechesis/Religious Program—Students 25.

WINTERHAVEN, IMPERIAL CO., SAINT THOMAS INDIAN MISSION CATHOLIC PARISH (1780) Rev. Duncan W. Monohan.
Res.: 350 Picacho Rd., P.O. Box 1176, 92283-1176. Tel: 760-572-0283. Email: stommisin@aol.com.
Catechesis/Religious Program—Students 27.

Chaplains of Public Institutions
Hospitals

SAN DIEGO. *Children's Hospital*, Tel: 858-541-3475. Rev. Raymundus Wea, S.V.D.
Scripps Hospital, Tel: 858-457-4123. Rev. Thomas Thompson, Chap.
Scripps Mercy Hospital, Tel: 619-260-7020. Revs. Lawrence Agi, James Schorr, Chap.
Sharp Memorial Hospital, Tel: 858-541-3475. Rev. Raymundus Wea, S.V.D.
UCSD Medical Center, Tel: 619-543-6737. Rev. David Leon, Chap.

CHULA VISTA. *Scripps Mercy Hospital*, 435 H St., 91910. Tel: 619-691-7251; Fax: 619-691-7522. Web: www.scrippshealth.org. Mark Weber, Chap. Bed Capacity 183; Total Staff 872; Patients Assisted Annually 9,592.

LA JOLLA. *Thornton Hospital*. Rev. Thomas Thompson, Chap. Tel: 858-657-7000.
Veterans Administration Hospital, Tel: 858-552-8585. Rev. B. Jeffrey Blangiardi, S.J.

OCEANSIDE. *Tri City Hospital*, 4002 Vista Way, 92049. Tel: 760-724-8411. Rev. Peter Vu Lam, Chap.

Retirement Homes

SAN DIEGO. *Nazareth House*, 6333 Rancho Mission Rd., 92108. Tel: 619-563-0480. Rev. David Leon, Chap.

LA MESA. *Little Flower Haven*, 8585 La Mesa Blvd., 91941. Tel: 619-466-3163. Rev. David Leon.

Detention Ministries

SAN DIEGO. *East Mesa Detention Facility*, 446 Alta Rd., 92158. Tel: 619-423-0567. Doris Argoud, Chap. Tel: 619-423-0567.

Geo West Regional Detention Facility. Contact: Office for Social Ministry, (858) 490-8375., Tel: 619-232-9221.

George F. Bailey Detention Facility. Contact: Office for Social Ministry, Tel: 858-490-8375, Tel: 619-661-2620.

Kearny Mesa Juvenile Detention Facility. Contact: Office for Social Ministry, (858) 490-8375., Tel: 858-694-4500.

Metropolitan Correction Center, Tel: 619-232-4311. Rev. Edgar Serrano, Chap. Tel: 619-232-4311, Ext. 1463.

R.J. Donovan Correctional Facility. Rev. Romeo Supnet, O.S.A. Tel: 619-661-6500, Ext. 6632.

San Diego Central Jail, Tel: 619-615-2737. Tom Erpelding, Chap. Tel: 619-696-6526.

San Diego Correction Facility, Federal. Contact: Office for Social Ministry, Tel: (858) 490-8375., Tel: 619-661-9119.

BRAWLEY. *Calipatria State Prison*, Tel: 760-348-7000. Deacon Michael Heidenreich. Tel: 769-348-7000, Ext. 6439.

CHULA VISTA. *South Bay Detention Facility*. Contact: Office for Social Ministry, Tel: (858) 490-8375., Tel: 619-691-4810. Vacant.

EL CENTRO. *El Centro Juvenile Hall*, 324 Applestill Rd., 92243. Refugio Hernandez. Tel: 760-622-8898.

Imperial County Jail, 328 Applestill Rd., 92243. Tel: 760-339-6369. Refugio Hernandez. Tel: 760-339-6367.

IMPERIAL. *Centinela State Prison*, Tel: 760-337-7900. Rev. Luis Valenciano. Tel: 760-337-7900, Ext. 6372.

SANTEE. *Las Colinas Women's Detention Facility*, 9000 Cottonwood Rd., 92071. Tel: 858-490-8375 (Office for Social Ministry).

VISTA. *Vista Detention Facility*, 325 Melrose Dr., Ste. 200, 92083. Jim Hamilton, Chap. Tel: 760-757-9865.

State Conservation Camps

SAN DIEGO. *Rainbow Conservation Camp*, 8215 Rainbow Heights Rd., Fallbrook, 92028. Tel: 760-728-7034. Cliff Sumrall, Chap. Tel: 760-451-5095.

Ports

SAN DIEGO. *Port of San Diego*, 1760 Water St., 92101. Tel: 619-702-4703. Deacon Sam Martinez, Rev. James Boyd, Chap. Tel: 858-292-1822.

San Diego Airport, 2802 Cadiz St., 92110-4813. Tel: 619-225-8157. Rev. William A. Kernan.

On Duty Outside the Diocese:

Revs.—

Conwill, Giles, Xavier University, LA
Haider, Craig
Stanonik, Anthony
White, Robert

Military Chaplains:

Rev.—

Merris, Christopher

Unassigned:

Rev.—

Rodriguez, Henry, Jr.

Retired:

Most Rev.—

Chavez, Gilbert E., D.D.

Rev. Msgrs.—

Bolger, William
Bourgeois, Lloyd
Brockhaus, Edward
Carroll, Joseph A.
Chylewski, Anthony
Clark, Dennis R.
Coughlan, Michael J.
Creighton, Edward
Cuddihy, William
Dickie, John A.
Elliott, William
Fawcett, Henry F.
Finnerty, Joseph L.
Florek, Frederick J.
Fox, Patrick
Giesing, Anthony
Hanley, Andrew W.
Harnett, Timothy
Kirk, Raymond
Kulleck, Donald R.
Lyng, Edward F.
Murray, Sean
O'Donoghue, James P.
O'Neill, Patrick J.
O'Sullivan, Jeremiah
Pattison, W. Francis
Portman, John R.
Prendergast, Thomas
Sheehan, Donal C.
Shipley, William

Revs.—

Byrne, George
Chase, Maurice
Collier, Joseph
Cunnane, Michael A.
Dunn, Stephen
Fischer, Eugene
Fuld, Charles
Gold, William
Holland, Kilian
Huston, Richard
May, Anthony C.
McGray, James
Mooney, William
Nesbitt, John B.
O'Connor, Dennis
Ortiz, Michael
Palmitessa, Paul
Penko, Francis
Quinn, John T.
Rapp, Bernard A.
Ryland, Raymond
Salada, Urbano
Salca, Louis
Sostrich, John L.
Thompson, J. Noel
Tindall, Harold
Vesga, Mario

Permanent Deacons:

Albers, A. Anthony, Blessed Sacrament, San Diego
Allen, Ronald, Our Lady of Grace, El Cajon
Amicone, Nicholas, Bakersfield, CA
Aquino, Jaime, Good Shepherd, San Diego
Arismendez, Joe, (Retired), St. Anthony of Padua, National City
Arnold, Raymond, Our Lady of Grace, El Cajon
Arnold, Ronald, St. Francis of Assisi, Vista
Beatty, Lewis, St. Mary Star of the Sea, Oceanside
Beiner, Robert, St. John the Evangelist, Encinitas
Bell, L. Ferris, (Retired), San Diego
Bennet, David, St. Mark, San Marcos
Bongatt, Rolando, Most Precious Blood, Chula Vista
Booth, Robert, St. John the Evangelist, San Diego
Bucon, Mark, Mary Star of the Sea, La Jolla
Byrne, Patrick J., Jr., Immaculate Heart of Mary, Ramona
Carpizo, Magno, (Retired), Good Shepherd, San Diego
Casabosch, Miguel, Chula Vista, CA
Castro, Agustin, Resurrection, Escondido
Charron, John, St. Michael, Poway
Chia, Henry, (Retired), Carlsbad
Clarke, William G., Blessed Kateri Tekakwitha, Lakeside
Collins, Michael, Nampa, ID
Cooper, James, Morro Bay, CA
Corrao, Jack P., (Retired), San Diego
Daniels, Michael, St. Brigid, San Diego
Davidson, Paul, Oceanside
Dean, Bennett, (Retired), Aguanga, CA
Del Rio, Jose, Christ the King, San Diego
Delano, Joseph, (Retired), Chula Vista
Dennison, Howard Mick, (Retired), St. Charles, San Diego
Depner, John, St. Timothy, Escondido
DePozo, Daniel, Henderson, NV
Diem, Ronald H., St. Gregory the Great, San Diego
Donarski, Conrad, Camp Pendleton, Oceanside
Duran, Amador, St. Mary, Escondido
Early, John Michael, (Retired), St. Timothy, Escondido
Ekhaml, Robert T., St. Therese, San Diego
Ellis, John A., Baker, LA
Embury, Charles, St. Stephen, Valley Center
Enciso, Pedro, (Retired), St. Francis of Assisi, Vista
Enriquez, Domingo, Our Lady of Guadalupe, El Centro
Enriquez, Miguel, St. Francis of Assisi, Vista
Escobedo, Andre, Immaculate Heart of Mary, Ramona
Fanelle, John, St. Therese of Carmel, San Diego
Faus, Juan, Our Lady of Mt. Carmel, San Diego
Fickes, Dale, St. Elizabeth Seton, Carlsbad
Finn, Kenneth, (Retired), Escondido
Fish, Michael, St. Gabriel, Poway
Fitzmorris, Robert H., Immaculate Conception, San Diego
Frazee, Michael, St. Patrick, Carlsbad
Frice, Charles, St. Rose of Lima, Chula Vista
Gasparovic, Anthony L., (Retired), Lakeside
Goeltz, Thomas A., St. Thomas More, Oceanside
Gonzalez, Raul, Our Lady of Mt. Carmel, San Ysidro
Gonzalez, Refugio, Our Lady of Guadalupe, Calexico
Graff, Albert P., (Retired), La Jolla
Griffin, Robert E., Jr., Sacred Heart, Coronado
Grosso, Ernest, Mission San Diego de Alcala, San Diego
Guess, Harry, Jr., Christ the King, San Diego
Gullotta, Daniel, Lakeside, MT
Gutierrez, Braulio, St. Anthony of Padua, National City
Hardick, Richard, St. Augustine High School, San Diego
Hernandez, Raul, St. Charles, San Diego
Hess, Arnold, (Retired), Colorado Springs, CO
Hitch, James, Corpus Christi, Bonita
Hoang, Loi, St. Francis of Assisi, Vista
Hodsdon, Peter, St. James, Solana Beach
Holgren, Robert, Our Lady of Mt. Carmel, San Diego
Hollowell, Christopher Wil, Corpus Christi, Bonita
Hunt, Samuel, (Retired), Homosassa, FL
Jiron, Guillermo, Corpus Christi, Bonita
Johnson, Peter, St. Pius X, Chula Vista
Keeley, James, (Retired), San Diego
Kelsey, Herbert, Blessed Sacrament, San Diego
Klopchin, William, (Retired), Our Mother of Confidence, San Diego
Korty, William, Our Lady of Grace, El Cajon
Kostick, James, (Retired), St. Mary, Escondido
Kutler, Harold, (Retired), Oceanside
Leach, David, (Retired), Carlsbad
Lewandowski, Daniel, (Retired), Spring Valley
Lozoya, Margarito, (Retired), Our Lady of Guadalupe, Chula Vista
Mackey, Robert, (Retired), Anaheim Hills, CA
Magana, Gustavo, San Diego
Maria, Michael, St. Therese, San Diego
Marquez, Gerardo, St. Rose of Lima, Chula Vista
Martinez, Seodello A., (Retired), San Diego
Mather, Richard, (Retired), Oceanside
McClellan, Gerald, Jr., St. Patrick, Carlsbad
McDaniel, Alvin, Hemet, CA
Medina, Jose Luis, Our Lady of Mt. Carmel, San Ysidro
Melrose, Richard, Guardian Angels, Santee
Mercardante, Frank, St. Mark, San Marcos
Miller, James, Logan, UT
Montoya, Edwin Gonzales, Resurrection, Escondido
Montoya, Kenneth, St. Charles, San Diego
Moser, Edward, St. Patrick, Carlsbad
Mueller, Robert, St. Francis of Assisi, Vista
Murray, Kevin, Sacred Heart, Coronado
Nguyen, Peter, St. Didacus, San Diego
Nickell, Dennie, St. Luke, El Cajon
Nunez, Manuel, St. Jude Shrine of the West, San Diego
O'Neil, Dennis, Our Lady of Perpetual Help, Lakeside
O'Riordan, Stephen, Our Lady of the Rosary, San Diego
Osgood, Franklin B., Sacred Heart, Coronado
Parra, Daniel, Most Precious Blood, Chula Vista
Partida, Michael, Resurrection, Escondido
Pelina, Ruben, Most Precious Blood, Chula Vista
Perez, Dominador, St. Mary of the Sea, Oceanside
Pollock, William, (Retired), San Diego
Porciuncula, Manuel, Our Lady of Mt. Carmel, San Diego
Powers, Daniel, Republic, MI
Prado, Daniel, St. Pius X, Chula Vista
Principe, Louis, (Retired), Lakeside
Reilly, Frank, St. Kieran, El Cajon
Rennix, Mitchell, Resurrection, Escondido
Rivera, Noel, Our Lady of Mt. Carmel, San Diego
Robbins, Ralph, (Retired), San Marcos
Robles, Manuel, San Bernadino, CA
Rocha, Louis, Holy Trinity, El Cajon
Rodriguez, Manuel, St. Jude Shrine of the West, San Diego
Root, Patrick, Our Lady of Perpetual Help, Lakeside
Roy, James, Klamath Falls, OR
Salinas, Gilbert, St. Stephen, Valley Center
Sanderville, Richard, San Diego
Santen, Joseph R., St. James, Solana Beach
Santiago, Nicholas M., Tucson, AZ
Santos, Severo, St. Michael, San Diego
Santoyo, Juan Francisco, St. John of the Cross, Lemon Grove
Schmitt, Giles V., (Retired), San Diego
Scull, James, Ascension, San Diego
Shea, George, (Retired), El Cajon
Shelton, Carl, (Retired), St. Michael, San Diego
Shockley, Gordon E., (Retired), San Antonio, TX
Silvia, Mark, Our Lady of Perpetual Help, Lakeside
Skiano, Ralph, St. Mary Magdalene, San Diego
Skupnik, Raymond, Seal Beach, CA
Smyth, Gregory, St. Rose of Lima, Chula Vista
Snyder, John A., Queen of Angels, Alpine
Spinney, Donald L., Sacred Heart, Brawley
Stanley, James, St. John of the Cross, Lemon Grove
Sullivan, Dennis, St. Mark, San Marcos
Swingle, Fred, Mater Dei, Chula Vista

Thompson, Ward, San Rafael, San Diego
Threatt, Marvin, Holy Spirit, San Diego
Treadwell, Timothy, St. Martin of Tours, La Mesa
Troy, Robert, St. Gabriel, Poway
Trumble, John, (Retired), St. Pius X, Jamul
Turcich, John, St. Pius X, Jamul
Vaillancourt, Leonard, San Rafael, San Diego
Valdes, Arturo, Mission San Diego de Alcala, San Diego
Vargas, Jim, Mary Star of the Sea, La Jolla
Vasquez, H. William, Jr., Mission San Diego de Alcala, San Diego
Vecchitto, Glenn, St. Pius X, Chula Vista
Villafana, Martin, (Retired), St. John of the Cross, Lemon Grove
Walling, Robert K., (Retired), Bend, OR
Walsh, James, Nativity, San Diego
Warren, David, St. Joesph Cathedral, San Diego
Wieczorek, Mark, Sacred Heart, San Diego
Williams, Warren, St. Luke, El Cajon
Wood, Joseph, (Retired), La Jolla
Woznicki, Walter, (Retired), La Mesa
Yeatts, Bernard, San Rafael, San Diego

INSTITUTIONS LOCATED IN THE DIOCESE

[A] SEMINARIES, DIOCESAN

SAN DIEGO. *St. Francis De Sales Center*, 1667 Santa Paula Dr., 92111. Tel: 619-291-7446; Fax: 619-291-7011. Email: eceliceo@diocese-sdiego.org. Web: www.diocese-sdiego.org. Revs. William Dillard, Spiritual Dir.; Matthew D. Spahr, Dir. of Priestly Formations; Anthony Saroki, Dir. Priestly Vocations. For priests and priestly formation. Priests 3; Students 6.

[B] COLLEGES AND UNIVERSITIES

SAN DIEGO. **John Paul the Great Catholic University*, 10174 Old Grove Rd., Ste. 200, 92131. Tel: 858-653-6740; Fax: 858-653-3791. Email: info@jpcatholic.com. Web: www.jpcatholic.com. Derry (Jeremiah) Connolly, Ph.D., Pres.; Dominic Iocco, Provost; Melanie Quinn, Librarian. Priests 2; Lay Teachers 26.

University of San Diego (1949) 5998 Alcala Park, 92110-2492. Tel: 619-260-4600. Web: www.sandiego.edu. Dr. Mary E. Lyons, Pres.; Dr. Julie H. Sullivan, Vice Pres. & Provost; Rev. Msgr. Daniel J. Dillabough, Vice Pres. Mission & Ministry; Ms. Carmen M. Vazquez, Vice Pres. Student Affairs; Dr. Mary Boyd, Dean College of Arts & Sciences; Dr. David Pyke, Dean School of Business Admin.; Dr. Paula Cordeiro, Dean School of Leadership & Education Sciences; Dr. Stephen Ferruolo, Dean School of Law; Dr. Sally B. Hardin, Dean Hahn School of Nursing & Health Science; Dr. Timothy O'Malley, Vice Pres. Univ. Rels. Priests 2; Sisters 3; Lay Teachers 388; Total University Full-Time Faculty 393; Law Students 1,084; Undergraduate Students 5,493; Graduate Students 1,740.

University Ministers: Michael Lovette-Colyer, Dir. Univ., Min.; Elizabeth Coyle, Assoc. Univ. Min.; Amy Gualtieri, Sacristan; Mary Kruer, Assoc. Univ. Min.; Maria Gaughan, Assoc. Univ. Min.; Andrew McMillin, Assoc. Univ. Min.; Rev. Owen Mullen, Univ. Chap.; Mark Peters, Asst. Dir. Univ. Min.; Sr. Virginia Rodee, R.S.C.J., Asst. Vice Pres. for Mission; Annette Welsh, Assoc. Univ. Min.; Rev. Michael White, C.S.Sp., Univ. Chap.; Erin Bishop, Assoc. Univ. Min.

Faculty: Revs. William Headley, Admin.; Dennis Krouse; Ron Pachence (Retired); Sisters Mary Hotz; Terri Monroe, R.S.C.J.; Anice Callahan, R.S.C.J.; Maria Pascuzzi, C.S.J.

Msgr. John Portman Chair of Roman Catholic Systematic Theology Tel: 619-260-7844; Fax: 619-260-2260. Web: www.sandiego.edu/theo.

Center for Catholic Thought and Culture Dr. Gerald Mannion, Dir. Tel: 619-260-7936.

Center for the Study of Latino/Latina Catholicism Tel: 619-260-4525; Fax: 619-260-2260. Web: www.sandiego.edu/theo/latino-cath. Dr. Orlando Espin, Dir.

Center for Christian Spirituality Tel: 619-260-4784; Fax: 619-260-7905. Rev. John Keller, O.S.A., Dir.

Pastoral Care and Counseling Program Tel: 619-260-4784; Fax: 619-260-7905.

[C] HIGH SCHOOLS, PRIVATE

SAN DIEGO. *Academy of Our Lady of Peace* (1882) 4860 Oregon St., 92116. Tel: 619-297-2266; Fax: 619-297-2473. Email: jhampel@aolp.org. Web: www.aolp.org. Sr. Dolores Anchondo, C.S.J., Prin.; Deanna Buhr, Librarian. (Girls) Sisters of St. Joseph of Carondelet 2; Lay Teachers 48; Students 750.

St. Augustine High School (1922) 3266 Nutmeg St., 92104-5199. Tel: 619-282-2184; Fax: 619-282-1203. Email: kevenson@sahs.org. Web: www.sahs.org. James Horne, Prin.; Edwin Hearn, Pres.; Revs. Robert W. Gavotto, O.S.A., Chap. Campus Ministry; Alvin Paligutan, O.S.A.; Deacon Richard Hardick; Craig da Luz, Librarian; Rev. Kirk Davis, O.S.A. Conducted by The Augustinians., (Boys); (For information concerning the monastery see separate listing under Monasteries). Priests 3; Deacons 1; Lay Teachers 48; Students 732.

SAN MARCOS. *Saint Joseph Academy* (Co-Ed), 500 Las Flores Dr., 92078. Tel: 760-305-8505; Fax: 760-305-8466; 760-305-8466. Web: www.saintjosephacademy.org. Mr. Michael Dominguez, Prin. Lay Teachers 16.

[D] HIGH SCHOOLS, DIOCESAN

SAN DIEGO. *Cathedral Catholic High School*, 5555 Del Mar Heights Rd., 92130. Tel: 858-523-4000; Fax: 858-523-4073. Web: www.cathedralcatholic.org. Mr. James Tschann, Pres.; Mr. Michael Deely, Prin.; Mrs. Anne Egan, Dir., Curriculum. Priests 3; Sisters 1; Lay Teachers 93; Students 1,730.

CALEXICO. *Vincent Memorial High*, 525 W. Sheridan, 92231. Tel: 760-357-3461; Fax: 760-357-0902. Email: vmchs@aol.com. Web: vmchs.com. Sisters Lilia M. Barba, S.J.S., Prin.; Lilia Vega, Librarian. (Coed). Conducted by Sisters Servants of the Blessed Sacrament. Sisters 3; Lay Teachers 18; Students 269.

CHULA VISTA. *Mater Dei Catholic High School*, 1615 Mater Dei Dr., 91913. Tel: 619-423-2121; Fax: 619-423-6910. Email: kchudy@materdeicatholic.org. Web: www.materdeicatholic.org. Mr. George E. Milke, Prin.; Mr. Thomas Clayton Beecher, Pres. (Coed) Lay Teachers 49; Students 685.

[E] ELEMENTARY SCHOOLS PRIVATE

SAN DIEGO. *Nativity Prep Academy*, (Grades 6-8), 2755 55th St., 92105.

Nazareth School, (Grades PreSchool-8), 10728 San Diego Mission Rd., 92108. Tel: 619-641-7987; Fax: 619-280-4652. Dr. Colleen Mauricio, Prin.; Mrs. Nora Smyth, Librarian; Georgina Barragan, Dir., Preschool. Tel: 619-641-7954. Sisters 1; Lay Teachers 17; Students 326.

Notre Dame Academy, (Grades PreSchool-8), 4345 Del Mar Trails Rd., 92130. Tel: 858-509-2300; Fax: 858-509-5915. Web: www.ndacademy.com. Sr. Marie Pascale, U.S.S.C., Prin.; Ursula Segura, Dir., Preschool. Tel: 858-509-2300. Sisters 3; Lay Teachers 37; Students 455.

SAN MARCOS. *St. Joseph Academy*, (Grades K-12), (Co-Ed), 500 Las Flores Dr., 92078. Tel: 760-305-8505; Fax: 760-305-8466. Web: www.saintjosephacademy.org. Mr. Michael Dominguez, Prin. Lay Teachers 15; Enrollment 274.

[F] SPECIAL SCHOOLS

SAN DIEGO. *Mater Dei Language Academy/Juan Diego Adult Center*, 938 18th St., 92154. Tel: 619-621-5711. Email: storrez@mariancatholic.org. Sylvia Torrez, Dir.

EL CAJON. *St. Madeleine Sophie's Center*, 2119 E. Madison Ave., 92019-1111. Tel: 619-442-5129; Fax: 619-442-9651. Email: dturner@stmsc.org. Web: www.stmsc.org. Debra Emerson, Exec. Dir. Lay Teachers 125; Enrollment 390.

OCEANSIDE. *Old Mission Montessori School*, (Grades PreK-8), 4070 Mission Ave., 92057. Tel: 760-757-3232; Fax: 760-721-0305. Email: office@omms.org. Wanda King, Prin.; Elisabeth Bush, Librarian. Lay Teachers 18.

[G] PROTECTIVE INSTITUTIONS

SPRING VALLEY. *Noah Homes* (1983) 12526 Campo Rd., 91978. Tel: 619-660-6200; Fax: 619-660-1481. Email: m.nocon@noahhomes.org. Web: www.noahhomes.org. Molly Nocon, Chief Exec. Dir. Total Assisted Annually 70; Total Staff 60.

[H] HOSPITALS

SAN DIEGO. *Scripps Mercy Hospital* (1890) 4077 Fifth Ave., 92103. Tel: 619-294-8111; Fax: 619-686-3530. Web: www.scrippshealth.org. Tom Gammiere, CEO; Andrew Santos III, Dir. Mission Integration; Revs. James Schorr; Lawrence Agi; Michael Harkay, Chap.; Ann Albrecht, Chap.; Sr. Mary Gallagher, R.S.M., Mgr. Spiritual Care; Rev. Gerald Swanson, Chap. (Baptist). Bed Capacity 519; Total Staff 2,000; Patients Assisted Annually 208,176.

Scripps Mercy Chula Vista, 435 H St., Chula Vista, 91910. Tel: 619-691-7000. Mark Weber, B.C.C., Chap.; Sr. Pauline Dibb, C.S.Sp., Chap. Bed Capacity 700; Staff 3,075; Patients Assisted Annually 21,214.

[I] HOMES FOR SENIOR CITIZENS

SAN DIEGO. *Cathedral Plaza*, 1551 Third Ave., 92101. Tel: 619-234-0093; Fax: 619-234-5168. Bobbi Pentchev, Resident Mgr.; John Adams, Supvr. Maintenance.

Cathedral Plaza Development Corp., A California Nonprofit Corporation Apartments 222; In Residence 253; Total Staff 6; Total Assisted 172.

Guadalupe Plaza, 4142 42nd St., 92105. Tel: 619-584-2414; Fax: 619-584-2886. Marie Creveling, Resident Mgr.

Guadalupe Plaza Development Corp., A California Nonprofit Corporation Apartments 126; In Residence 142.

St. John's Plaza, 8150 Broadway, Lemon Grove, 91945. Tel: 619-466-5354; Fax: 619-466-6643. Email: stjohnsplaza@sjp.sdcoxmail.com. Malinda Himango, Resident Mgr.

Calexico Plaza Development Corp., A California Nonprofit Corporation Residences 99; Total in Residence 97; Total Staff 2.

Nazareth House Retirement Home, 6333 Rancho Mission Rd., 92108. Tel: 619-563-0480; Fax: 619-624-9215. Sr. Margaret Spence, C.S.N., Admin. Retired Priests Residential and Assisted Living Capacity 139; Priests 15; Sisters of Nazareth of San Diego 6.

LA MESA. *Little Flower Haven*, 8585 La Mesa Blvd., 91942. Tel: 619-466-3163; Fax: 619-466-9642. Email: littleflwrhaven@yahoo.com. Sr. Maria Elena Romero, D.C.J.; Rev. David Leon, Chap. Total Staff 26; Aged Residents 45; Bed Capacity 60.

[J] MONASTERIES AND RESIDENCES OF PRIESTS AND BROTHERS

SAN DIEGO. *Augustinian Community* (1922) 3266 Nutmeg St., 92104. Tel: 619-282-2028; Fax: 619-282-2233. Revs. Thomas W. Behan, O.S.A.; Jerome F. Bevilacqua, O.S.A.; Kirk Davis, O.S.A.; Robert W. Gavotto, O.S.A., Chap.; James E. Hannan, O.S.A.; Patrick J. Keane, O.S.A.; John D. Keller, O.S.A., Prior; Alvin Paligutan, O.S.A.; Harry M. Neely, O.S.A. *Augustinian Provincialate* (1981) 1605 28th St., 92102-1417. Tel: 619-235-0247; Fax: 619-231-2814. Very Rev. Gary Sanders, O.S.A., Prov.

Austin House (1981) 1605 28th St., 92102-1417. Tel: 619-233-9141. Revs. Michael McFadden, O.S.A.; Gary C. Rye, O.S.A.; Deacon Richard Hardick. Total in Residence 3. *Office of the Provincial* Tel: 619-235-0247; Fax: 619-231-2814. Email: osa-west@sbcglobal.net. Web: www.osa-west.org. Very Rev. Gary Sanders, O.S.A., Prior Prov. Tel: 619-235-0247; Fax: 619-231-2814.

Holy Trinity Hermitage-Augustinian Community, 2725 55th St., 92105. Tel: 619-262-9685. A contemplative retreat setting that only accommodates 8 people.

Monica House - Augustinian Community, 1621 28th St., 92102-1417. Tel: 619-338-9268. Very Rev. Gary Sanders, O.S.A. Total in Residence 6.

OCEANSIDE. *Old Mission San Luis Rey* (1798) 4050 Mission Ave., 92057-6402. Tel: 760-757-3651; Fax: 760-757-4613. Email: frdavid@sanluisrey.org. Web: www.sanluisrey.org. Revs. David Gaa, O.F.M., Exec. Dir.; Thomas Herbst, O.F.M.; Andres Rivero, O.F.M.; Laurence Dolan, O.F.M., Guardian; Michael Dallmeier, O.F.M. Franciscan Friars. Priests 8.

Prince of Peace Abbey, 650 Benet Hill Rd., 92058-1253. Tel: 760-967-4200; Fax: 760-967-8711. Email: princeabby@aol.com. Web: www.princeofpeaceabbey.org. Rt. Rev. Charles Wright, O.S.B., Abbot; Revs. Sharbel Ewen, O.S.B., Prior; Basil Mattingly, O.S.B.; Herbert Palmer, O.S.B.; Michael Pham, O.S.B.; Paul Farrelly, O.S.B.; Stephanos Pedrano, O.S.B.; Bros. Peter Aslin, O.S.B.; Timothy Balk, O.S.B., Bro. Oblate; Joseph Black, O.S.B.; Anselm Clark, O.S.B.; Blaise Heuke, O.S.B.; Benedict Menezes, O.S.B.; Raphael Meyer, O.S.B.; Mario Quizon, O.S.B.; Daniel Sokol, O.S.B.; Meinrad Taylor, O.S.B.; David Cobos, O.S.B.; Noel Greenawalt, O.S.B.; Philip Poutous, O.S.B.; Gabriel Stern, O.S.B.; Emmanuel Tran, O.S.B.; Damien Evangelista, O.S.B.; Bede Clark, O.S.B. Benedictine Fathers. Priests 7; Brothers 16; Oblates 1.

SOLANA BEACH. *The Eudists, Congregation of Jesus and Mary*, 744 Sonrisa St., 92075-2407. Rev. John Howard, C.J.M., American Regl. Supr. Tel: 858-755-2545, Ext. 104 (Office).

[K] CONVENTS AND RESIDENCES FOR SISTERS

SAN DIEGO. *Carmelite Monastery of San Diego, California* (Discalced); Cloistered Contemplative Nuns, 5158 Hawley Blvd., 92116-1934. Tel: 619-280-5425; Fax: 619-280-3775. Email: carmelsd@sbcglobal.net. Web: www.carmelsandiego.com. Sr. Ancilla Murray, O.C.D., Prioress. Sisters 14.

Congregation of the Sisters of Nazareth, 6333 Rancho Mission Rd., 92108. Tel: 619-563-0480; Fax: 619-624-9215. Email: superior@nazarethhousesd.org. Sisters 6.

Daughters of Divine Charity, 6036 Camino Rico, 92120. Tel: 619-287-1320. Sisters 3.

Daughters of St. Paul (1915) 5945 Balboa Ave., 92111. Tel: 858-565-9181; Fax: 858-565-9295. Sr. Frances Obrovac, F.S.P., Contact Person.

Dominican Sisters of Adrian, 640 Camino de la Reina #1117, 92117. Tel: 619-255-4238. Email: kclausen2@cox.net. Sisters 6.

Maryknoll Sisters, 10210 San Diego Mission Rd., #10, 92108. Tel: 619-684-5576. Sisters 1.

Missionaries of Charity (1950) 3877 Boston Ave., 92113-3218. Tel: 619-263-9566. Sr. Mary Ann Tang Wing, M.C., Major Supr. Sisters 12.

Religious of Jesus and Mary, 1318 Pequena St., 92154. Tel: 619-690-0242; Fax: 619-690-0257. Email: rosy1510@aol.com. Sr. Rosemary Nicholson, R.J.M., Regl. Supr. Sisters 3.

Religious of Jesus and Mary, 1510 Third Ave., 92101. Tel: 619-234-0556. Email: rosy1510@aol.com. Sisters 5.

School Sisters of Notre Dame, 1997 Magdalene Way, 92110. Tel: 619-276-5830. Email: jweisma1@san.rr.com. Sisters 4.

Sisters de L'Union-Chretienne de Saint Chammound, 4345 Del Mar Trails Rd., 92130. Tel: 858-509-2300. Sr. Marie Pascale Clisson, U.C.S.C., Contact Person. Sisters 3.

Sisters of Loretto (1812) 440 San Antonio Ave. #6, 92106. Tel: 619-224-2341.

Sisters of Mercy of the Americas (West-Midwest), 2560 C St. #32, 92102. Tel: 619-296-4272. Sisters 11.

Sisters of Mercy US Province (1831) 10726 Caminito Cascara, 92108. Tel: 619-284-1027; Fax: 619-284-1027. Email: smjobreen@att.net. Sisters 11.

Sisters of Social Service, 3525 Third Ave., 92103-4908. Tel: 619-295-1896. Sisters 4.

Sisters of St. Francis (Philadelphia) (1855) 6333 Rancho Mission Rd., 92108. Tel: 619-563-0480.

Sisters of St. Joseph Brentwood, NY, 3611 Utah St., 92104. Tel: 619-294-9324.

Sisters of St. Joseph of Carondelet, 4860 Oregon St., 92116. Tel: 619-295-2887; Fax: 619-297-2473. Email: doan@aolp.org. Sisters 2.

Sisters of St. Joseph of Peace, 2880 Caulfield Dr., 92154. Tel: 619-423-7360. Sisters 3.

Sisters of St. Louis, 5824 Kantor Ct., 92122. Tel: 858-490-8240. Email: bboyle@diocese-sdiego.org. Web: www.st-louis-sisters.org.

Society of the Holy Child Jesus, 6243 Caminito Telmo, 92111. Tel: 619-231-7788. Sisters 4.

Trinitarians of Mary, 6702 Del Cerro Blvd., 92120. Tel: 619-667-3742. Sr. Lillie Diaz, T.M., Major Supr. Sisters 6.

BONITA. *Sister Servants of the Blessed Sacrament* (1904) 3173 Winnetka Dr., 91902. Tel: 619-267-0720; Fax: 619-267-0920. Email: sup@sjsusprovince.sdcoxmail.com. Sr. Maria Paz Uribe, S.J.S., Provincial Supr. Sisters 22.

CALEXICO. *Sister Servants of the Blessed Sacrament*, 536 Rockwood, 92231. Tel: 760-357-1046; Fax: 760-357-3282. Email: sjsclx@aol.com. Sisters 23.

CHULA VISTA. *Benedictine Sisters of Glendora* (1956) 236 Alvarado, 91910-3610. Tel: 619-422-3610; Fax: 619-427-5786. Email: jokingosb@strosecv.com. Sisters 2.

Franciscan Missionaries of Our Lady of Peace (1941) 575 E. St. #20, 91910. Tel: 619-691-9008; Fax: 619-425-7514. Email: marumfp@hotmail.com. Sisters 2.

Medical Mission Sisters (Western Office), 440 Vista Way, 91910-4930. Tel: 619-426-5561; Fax: 619-426-5561. Web: www.medicalmissionsisters.org.

Society of Catholic Medical Missionaries, Inc. 440 Vista Way, 91910-4930. Tel: 619-426-5561. Sisters 2. 8150 Broadway, Lemon Grove, 91945. Tel: 619-697-7331; 619-464-8221; 619-697-7331. Sisters 3.

Religious of the Incarnate Word (1625) 153 Rainier Ct., 91911. Tel: 619-420-0231; Fax: 619-691-5939. Email: ccrabbe@hotmail.com. Sisters (Chula Vista) 6; Sisters (El Centro) 5.

EL CENTRO. *Our Lady of Victory Missionary Sisters*, 142 E. Octillo Dr., 92243. Tel: 760-352-1263. Sisters 3.

FALLBROOK. *Hermanas del Corazon de Jesus Sacramentado*, 133 Alvarado Ct., 92028. Tel: 760-645-3372; Fax: 760-645-3372. Email: hcjsfbrk@aol.com. Sr. Maria del Carmen Torres Vega, H.C.J.S., Major Supr. Sisters 4.

LA MESA. *Carmelite Sisters of the Divine Heart of Jesus*, 8585 La Mesa Blvd., 91941. Tel: 619-466-3163; Fax: 619-462-8261. Sisters Mary Alice Prieto, Local Supr. Tel: 619-466-3163; Fax: 619-466-9642; M. Carmela, Contact Person. Sisters 8; Novices 4.

LEMON GROVE. *Mercedarian Sisters of the Blessed Sacrament*, 8171 Lemon Grove Way, 91945. Tel: 619-460-4271; Fax: 619-460-1060. Email: smarilup@stjohncross.org. Sisters 5.

PALA. *Sisters of the Precious Blood* (1833) 10734 Hwy. 76, 92059. Sisters 1.

SAN YSIDRO. *Dominican Sisters, Tacoma WA*, 1879 Via Las Tonadas, 92173. Tel: 619-428-1629. Sisters 3.

Medical Missionaries of Mary, P.O. Box 431134, 92143-1134. Tel: 619-690-9237; Fax: 619-428-9551. Web: www.mmmusa.org.

Sisters Servants of the Blessed Sacrament, 333 W. Park Ave., 92173. Tel: 619-207-0333; Fax: 619-428-8324. Email: sanysidrosjs@yahoo.com.mx. Sisters 7.

SPRING VALLEY. *Community of the Holy Spirit* (1970) 275 S. Worthington St., #109, 91977. Tel: 619-434-8529. Email: jwagenbrenner@cox.net. Sr. Joanne Wagenbrenner, C.H.S., M.A., M.S., CFO. Sisters 8.

Sisters of St. Joseph of Orange, 10771 Del Rio Rd., 91978. Tel: 619-670-9663; Fax: 619-670-6554. Sisters 2.

VISTA. *Sisters of St. Clare (O.S.C.)*, 1171 Via Santa Paulo, 92081. Tel: 760-295-0611. Email: madfitz1@cox.net.

[L] SOCIAL SERVICES

SAN DIEGO. *Catholic Charities*, 349 Cedar St., 92101. Tel: 619-231-2828; Fax: 619-234-2272. Email: srmduvall@ccdsd.org. Web: www.ccdsd.org. Sr. RayMonda DuVall, C.H.S., Exec. Dir.; Dr. Robert Moser, Ph.D., Deputy Dir. Counseling Services.; Homeless Women's Services.

Emergency Services (Main Office) Tel: 619-231-2828; Fax: 619-234-2272.

Clinical Services Tel: 619-231-2828; Fax: 619-234-2272. Patricia Petterson, Ph.D., Dir.

Pregnancy and Adoption Tel: 619-231-2828; Fax: 619-234-2272. Patricia Petterson, Ph.D., Dir.

Immigrant Services--San Diego Tel: 619-287-9454; Fax: 619-234-2272. Dr. Robert Moser, Ph.D., Dir.

La Posada de Guadalupe de Carlsbad Tel: 760-929-2322; Fax: 760-929-8712. Eduardo Presciado, Dir.

El Centro--Imperial County Services, 250 W. Orange, El Centro, 92243. Tel: 760-353-6822; Fax: 760-353-0120.

House of Hope--El Centro-Imperial County Tel: 760-352-1182; Fax: 760-352-5492.

Our Lady of Guadalupe Shelter-Calexico-Imperial County Tel: 760-357-0894; Fax: 760-357-0895.

Rachel's Women's Center--San Diego, 92101. Tel: 619-236-9074.

The Tomorrow Project Tel: 619-230-1151. Martha Ranson, Dir.

Joan of Arc Residence, 1510 Third Ave., 92101. Tel: 619-239-2663. Email: rosy1510@aol.com. Sr. Rosemary Nicholson, R.J.M., Admin. Residence for Employed Young Women and College Students 21-60 Years. Religious 5; Permanent Residents 60; Capacity 71.

**S.V.D.P. Management Inc.*, 3350 E St., 92102. Tel: 619-446-2100; Fax: 619-446-2129. Web: fatherjoesvillages.org. Sr. Patricia Cruise, S.C., Dir. Owns and manages the property for St. Vincent de Paul Village, Inc.; Fr. Joe's Villages; Toussaint Youth Villages in San Diego, and Natl. Aids Foundation. Total Staff 85.

**St. Vincent de Paul Village* (1950) 3350 E St., 92102-3332. Tel: 619-446-2100; Fax: 619-446-2129. Web: www.neighbor.org. Sr. Patricia Cruise, S.C., Pres. Total Staff 271; Total Assisted Annually 162,540.

Joan Kroc Homeless Center (1987) 1501 Imperial Ave., 92101. Tel: 619-446-2100; Fax: 619-446-2129. Web: www.neighbor.org. Mary Case, Vice Pres. Housing for families & single women (326).

Bishop Maher Men's Center (1989) 1501 Imperial Ave., 92101. Tel: 619-446-2100; Fax: 619-446-2129. Web: www.neighbor.org. Single men's center - 150 residents.

Child Development Center, 1506 Commercial St., 92101. 150 units transitional housing, 64 units of low income affordable housing.

National Aids Foundation dba Josue Homes 3350 E St., 92102. Tel: 619-466-4827; Fax: 619-446-2129. Web: www.neighbor.org. Housing for persons with AIDS (38).

Paul Mirabile Center--Mirabile Housing Inc. (1994) 1501 Imperial Ave., 92101. Tel: 619-446-2100; Fax: 619-446-2129. Emergency housing for 270 men & 80 women; free dining room (4000 meals daily).

Toussaint Youth Villages, 1404-5th St., 92101. Tel: 619-687-1080; Fax: 619-446-2129. Web: www.neighbor.org. Residential for 35 homeless teens.

Thrift Stores (1950) 815 33rd St., 92102. Tel: 619-446-2711; Fax: 619-446-2129. Keith MacKay, Vice Pres.

Village Place, 32-17th St., 92101. Tel: 619-446-2100; Fax: 619-446-2129. 54 units - low to moderate income apartments.

Villa Harvey Mandel, 72-17th St., 92101. Tel: 619-446-2100; Fax: 619-446-2129. 95 units - Low to moderate income apts.

16th and Market, 640 16th St., 92102. 137 low income units.

Boulevard Apts., 3137 El Cajon Blvd., 92104. 42 low income units.

Padre Luis Jayme International Outreach, 3350 E St., 92101. Tel: 619-446-2100; Fax: 619-446-2129. Providing assistance to colonias, prison ministries and orphanages; earthquakes and flood relief in Mexico. Total Assisted Annually 6,450; Staff 4.

[M] RETREATS

SAN DIEGO. *Spiritual Ministry Center* (1987) 4822 Del Mar Ave., 92107-3407. Tel: 619-224-9444. Email: spiritmin@rscj.org. Web: www.spiritmin.org.

Whispering Winds Catholic Conference Center (1978) 8186 Commercial St., La Mesa, 91942-2926. Tel: 619-464-1479; Fax: 619-464-4491. Email: office@whisperingwinds.org. Web: www.whisperingwinds.org. Facility: 17606 Harrison Park Rd., Julian, 92036. Martin Rosales, Exec. Dir.; Don Kojis, Co-Founder/Community Rels. Purpose: Serve over 7,000 guests each year for 6th grade camp, retreats, family camp, Confirmation, RCIA, family reunions, leadership training and parish meetings.

DESCANSO. *Camp Oliver*, P.O. Box 206, 91916. Tel: 619-445-5945; Fax: 619-445-3326. Email: director@campoliver.com. Web: www.campoliver.com. Lia Morales, Exec. Dir. Summer Resident Camp for Girls & Boys, ages 6-16. Owned by Sisters of Social Service. (June-Aug.; Available Sept.-June for rental groups).

OCEANSIDE. *Old Mission San Luis Rey Retreat*, 4050 Mission Ave., 92057-6402. Tel: 760-757-3659, Ext. 146; Fax: 760-757-4613. Email: maureen@sanluisrey.org. Web: www.sanluisrey.org. Rev. David Gaa, O.F.M., Exec. Dir.; Ms. Maureen Sullivan, Dir., Retreat Center.

Prince of Peace Retreat Center, 650 Benet Hill Rd., 92058-1253. Tel: 760-967-4200; 760-967-4200, Ext. 248; Fax: 760-967-8711. Email: princeabby@aol.com. Web: www.princeofpeaceabbey.org. Bro. Benedict Menezes, O.S.B., Guest Master. Benedictine Fathers-Benet Hill. Priests 6; Brothers 20.

[N] NEWMAN CENTERS

SAN DIEGO. *Newman Center - SDSU* 5855 Hardy Ave., 92115. Tel: 619-583-9181; Fax: 619-583-8925. Email: office@sdsucatholic.org. Very Rev. Bruce J. Orsborn, Dir.; Mr. Michael McIntyre, Asst. Dir.

University of California at San Diego (Campus Ministry) 4321 Eastgate Mall, 92121-2102. Tel: 858-452-1957 (Office); Fax: 858-452-1985. Email: cathcom@ucsd.edu. Web: www.cathcom-ucsd.org. Rev. John Paul Forte, O.P., Dir.

[O] MISCELLANEOUS

SAN DIEGO. *The Bellesini Foundation* Funding for the education of members of the Order of St. Augustine., 1605 28th St., 92104. Tel: 619-235-0247; Fax: 619-231-2814. Rev. Gregory Heidenblut, O.S.A., Contact Person.

Catholic Committee on Scouting, 3350 E St., 92102. Tel: 619-446-2116; Fax: 619-446-2129. Rev. Msgr. Joseph A. Carroll, Scout Chap. (Retired); Mike McNelly, Chm.; Jim Freed, Coord. Tel: 619-687-1024.

Catholic Secondary Education - Diocese of San Diego, Incorporated (2003) P.O. Box 85728, 92186. Tel: 858-490-8301; Fax: 858-490-8272.

Christ Child Society, 5418 Baja Dr., 92115. Tel: 619-287-9021. Rev. Bernardo Ranoa (Philippines), Spiritual Advisor; Kathleen Israel, Pres.

Magnificat (Central) San Diego Chapter, 5592 Gala Ave., 92120. Tel: 619-583-3389. Rev. Louis M. Solcia, C.R.S.P., Spiritual Advisor; Barbara Faucher, Coord.

Mercy Hospital Foundation, San Diego, 4077 Fifth Ave., 92103. Tel: 619-686-3836; Fax: 619-293-0095. Email: braunwarth.mary@scrippshealth.org. Web: www.scrippsfoundation.org. Mary Braunwarth, Senior Dir., Devel.

Nazareth School of San Diego, Inc., 10728 San Diego Mission Rd., 92108. Tel: 619-641-7987; Fax: 619-280-4652.

Pauline Books & Media, 5945B Balboa Ave., 92111. Tel: 858-565-9181; Fax: 858-565-9295. Email: sandiego@pauline.org. Web: www.pauline.org. Sr. Karen Hamm, F.S.P., Supvr. Daughters of St. Paul. Sisters 2.

The Sisters of Nazareth of San Diego Real Estate Holdings, Inc., 6333 Rancho Mission Rd., 92108. Tel: 619-563-0480; Fax: 619-624-9215.

**Spirit Ministries*, 2725 - 55th St., 92105. Tel: 619-262-9685; Fax: 619-262-8718. Email: spiritministries@cox.net. Rev. Jerome F. Bevilacqua, O.S.A., Spiritual Dir.; Sarah I. McTimmonds, Admin. Asst.

The Tagaste Foundation Funding for the support, care and maintenance of the Order of St. Augustine., 1605 28th St., 92104. Tel: 619-235-0247; Fax: 619-231-2814. Rev. Gregory Heidenblut, O.S.A., Contact Person.

EL CAJON. **Catholic Answers, Inc.*, 2020 Gillespie Way, 92020. Tel: 619-387-7200; Fax: 619-387-0042. Email: publications@catholic.com. Web: www.catholic.com. Karl Keating, Pres.

Kraemer Endowment Foundation, Inc (1992) 2119 E. Madison Ave., 92019-1111. Tel: 619-844-0211; Fax: 619-442-9611. Email: cynkatia@aol.com. Web: www.stmsc.org.

ESCONDIDO. **Benedictus*, 8975-76 Lawrence Welk Dr., 92026. Tel: 760-751-8541; Fax: 760-751-8505. Email: bendictus1@aol.com. Web: www.stdismas.org. Deacon Kenneth J. Finn, Contact Person.

POWAY. *The Genesis Initiative* Supports development movie, television and education iniatives., P.O. Box 612, 92074. Tel: 858-748-3348. Martha Lyles, Contact Person; Dick Lyles, Contact Person.

SAN YSIDRO. *The Mother Teresa of Calcutta Center*, 524 W. Calle Primera, Ste. 1005N, 92173. Tel: 619-662-1484; Fax: 619-662-1268. Web: www.motherteresa.org.

VALLEY CENTER. *San Diego North County Magnificat - Our Lady of Guadalupe Chapter*, 13747 Little Pond Rd., 92082. Tel: 760-749-3457. Rev. Frank Nouza, Chap.; Rosemary Geiger, Coord.

RELIGIOUS INSTITUTES OF MEN REPRESENTED IN THE DIOCESE

For further details refer to the corresponding bracketed number in the Religious Institutes of Men or Women section.

[0140]—*The Augustinians*—O.S.A.
[0200]—*Benedictine Monks*—O.S.B.
[0270]—*Carmelite Fathers*—O.Carm.
[0160]—*Clerics Regular of St. Paul*—C.R.S.P.
[0450]—*Congregation of Jesus and Mary*—C.J.M.
[0650]—*Congregation of the Holy Spirit*—C.S.Sp.
[0860]—*Congregation of the Immaculate Heart of Mary*—C.I.C.M.
[1330]—*Congregation of the Mission*—C.M.
[1130]—*Congregation of the Priests of the Sacred Heart*—S.C.J.
[0520]—*Franciscan Friars*—O.F.M.
[0690]—*Jesuit Fathers and Brothers*—S.J.
[]—*Miles Christi*—M.C.
[]—*Missionaries of Charity Fathers*—M.C.
[]—*Missionaries of Guadalupe*—M.G.
[0840]—*Missionary Servants of the Most Holy Trinity*—S.T.
[0910]—*Oblates of Mary Immaculate*—O.M.I.
[0940]—*Oblates of the Virgin Mary*—O.M.V.
[0260]—*Order of Discalced Carmelites*—O.C.D.
[0430]—*Order of Preachers (Dominicans)*—O.P.
[1030]—*Paulist Fathers*—C.S.P.
[1065]—*Priestly Fraternity of St. Peter*—F.S.S.P.
[0610]—*Priests of the Congregation of the Holy Cross*—C.S.C.
[1260]—*Society of Christ*—S.Ch.
[0370]—*Society of St. Columban*—S.S.C.
[0420]—*Society of the Divine Word*—S.V.D.

RELIGIOUS INSTITUTES OF WOMEN REPRESENTED IN THE DIOCESE

[0230]—*Benedictine Sisters of Pontifical Jurisdiction* (Glendora, CA; St. Joseph, MN)—O.S.B.
[0360]—*Carmelite Sisters of the Divine Heart of Jesus*—Carmel.D.C.
[2020]—*Community of the Holy Spirit*—C.H.S.
[3242]—*Congregation of the Sisters of Nazareth*—C.S.N.
[0790]—*Daughters of Divine Charity*—F.D.C.
[0880]—*Daughters of Mary and Joseph*—D.M.J.
[0420]—*Discalced Carmelite Nuns*—O.C.D.
[1070-03]—*Dominican Sisters*—O.P.
[1070-13]—*Dominican Sisters*—O.P.
[1070-20]—*Dominican Sisters*—O.P.
[1070-11]—*Dominican Sisters*—O.P.
[]—*Franciscan Missionaries of Our Lady of Peace*—M.F.P.
[1845]—*Guadalupan Missionaries of the Holy Spirit*—M.G.Sp.S.
[]—*Hermanas del Corazon de Jesus Sacramentado*—H.C.J.S.
[]—*Immaculate Heart Community*—I.H.M.
[2390]—*Lovers of the Holy Cross*—L.H.C.
[2470]—*Maryknoll Sisters of St. Dominic*—M.M.
[2490]—*Medical Mission Sisters*—M.M.S.
[2480]—*Medical Missionaries of Mary*—M.M.M.
[2590]—*Mercedarian Sisters of the Blessed Sacrament*—H.M.S.S.
[2710]—*Missionaries of Charity*—M.C.
[]—*Missionary Sisters of the Society of Mary*—S.M.S.M.
[3070]—*North American Unions of Sisters of Our Lady of Charity*—N.A.U.-O.L.C.
[3130]—*Our Lady of Victory Missionary Sisters*—O.L.V.M.
[0950]—*Pious Society Daughters of St. Paul*—F.S.P.
[3450]—*Religious of Jesus and Mary*—R.J.M.
[3449]—*Religious of the Incarnate Word*—C.V.I.
[2970]—*School Sisters of Notre Dame*—S.S.N.D.
[]—*Sisters de L'Union-Chretienne de Saint Chaumond*—U.C.S.C.
[0520]—*Sisters of Charity of Our Lady, Mother of Mercy*—S.C.M.M.
[2360]—*Sisters of Loretto At the Foot of the Cross*—S.L.
[2549]—*Sisters of Mercy of Ireland & U.S. Province*—R.S.M.
[2575]—*Sisters of Mercy of The Americas* (West-Midwest)—R.S.M.
[3360]—*Sisters of Providence*—S.P.
[1540]—*Sisters of Saint Francis, Clinton, Iowa*—O.S.F.
[4080]—*Sisters of Social Service of Los Angeles, Inc.*—S.S.S.
[3770]—*Sisters of St. Clare*—O.S.C.
[1705]—*The Sisters of St. Francis of Assisi*—O.S.F.
[1650]—*Sisters of St. Francis of Philadelphia*—O.S.F.
[3830-03]—*Sisters of St. Joseph* (Orange)—C.S.J.
[3830-05]—*Sisters of St. Joseph* (Brentwood, NY)—C.S.J.
[3840]—*Sisters of St. Joseph of Carondelet* (Los Angeles, CA; St. Louis, MO)—C.S.J.
[3890]—*Sisters of St. Joseph of Peace* (Bellevue, WA)—C.S.J.P.
[3935]—*Sisters of St. Louis*—S.S.L.
[1960]—*Sisters of the Holy Family*—S.H.F.
[3260]—*Sisters of the Precious Blood (Dayton, Ohio)*—C.PP.S.
[3499]—*Sisters Servants of the Blessed Sacrament*—S.J.S.
[4060]—*Society of the Holy Child Jesus*—S.H.C.J.
[4070]—*Society of the Sacred Heart*—R.S.C.J.
[]—*Trinitarians of Mary*—T.M.
[4120-04]—*Ursuline Sisters*—O.S.U.

DIOCESAN CEMETERIES

PALA INDIAN MISSIONS. 6 separate Indian burial grounds.

SAN LUIS REY. *Mission San Luis Rey*

SANTA YSABEL INDIAN MISSIONS. 15 separate Indian burial grounds.

NECROLOGY

† Moloney, Rev. Msgr. Alphonsus, (Retired)—Died June 17, 2011
† Vidra, Rev. Msgr. Thomas, (Retired)—Died Jan. 30, 2011
† Caldwell, James V., (Retired)—Died Sept. 18, 2011
† Flynn, Edward R., (Retired)—Died July 16, 2011

An asterisk (*) denotes an organization that has established tax-exempt status directly with the IRS and is not covered by the USCCB Group Ruling.

Archdiocese of San Francisco

(Archidioecesis Sancti Francisci)

Most Reverend

GEORGE H. NIEDERAUER

Archbishop of San Francisco; ordained April 30, 1962; appointed Bishop of Salt Lake City November 3, 1994; Episcopal ordination January 25, 1995; appointed Archbishop of San Francisco December 15, 2005; installed as Archbishop February 15, 2006. *Office: One Peter Yorke Way, San Francisco, CA 94109-6602.*

The Chancery Office: One Peter Yorke Way, San Francisco, CA 94109-6602. Tel: 415-614-5500; Fax: 415-614-5555.

Web: www.sfarchdiocese.org

Email: info@sfarchdiocese.org

His Eminence

WILLIAM J. LEVADA, S.T.D.

Prefect, Congregation for the Doctrine of the Faith; Archbishop Emeritus of San Francisco; ordained December 20, 1961; appointed Titular Bishop of Capri and Auxiliary Bishop of Los Angeles March 29, 1983; Episcopal ordination May 12, 1983; appointed Archbishop of Portland in Oregon July 1, 1986; installed as Archbishop of Portland in Oregon September 21, 1986; appointed Coadjutor Archbishop of San Francisco August 17, 1995; succeeded to See December 27, 1995; appointed Prefect of the Congregation for the Doctrine of the Faith May 13, 2005; departed San Francisco August 15, 2005; Created Cardinal March 24, 2006. *Office: Congregazione perla Dottrina della Fede, Palazzo del S. Uffizio, Vatican City State 00120.*

Most Reverend

JOHN R. QUINN

Archbishop Emeritus of San Francisco; ordained July 19, 1953; appointed Auxiliary Bishop of San Diego and Titular Bishop of Thisiduo October 21, 1967; Episcopal ordination December 12, 1967; transferred to Oklahoma City and Tulsa November 18, 1971; appointed as Archbishop of the Archdiocese of Oklahoma City on February 6, 1973; appointed Archbishop of San Francisco February 22, 1977; installed as Archbishop of San Francisco April 26, 1977; resigned December 27, 1995. *Res.: 2140 Santa Cruz Ave., A103, Menlo Park, CA 94025.* Tel: 650-233-8280; Fax: 650-233-8286. *Office: 1100 Woodside Rd., Redwood City, CA 94061.* Tel: 650-780-9078.

Most Reverend

IGNATIUS WANG, J.C.D.

Retired Auxiliary Bishop of San Francisco; ordained July 4, 1959; appointed Titular Bishop of Sitipa and Auxiliary Bishop of San Francisco December 13, 2002; installed January 30, 2003; retired May 16, 2009. *Holy Name of Jesus Church, 1555 39th Ave., San Francisco, CA 94122.*

Most Reverend

WILLIAM J. JUSTICE

Auxiliary Bishop of San Francisco; ordained May 17, 1968; appointed Titular Bishop of Mathara in Proconsulari and Auxiliary Bishop of San Francisco April 10, 2008; ordained May 28, 2008. *Office: One Peter Yorke Way, San Francisco, CA 94109-6602.*

Most Reverend

ROBERT W. McELROY

Auxiliary Bishop of San Francisco; ordained April 12, 1980; appointed Titular Bishop of Gemellae in Byzacena and Auxiliary Bishop of San Francisco July 6, 2010; ordained September 7, 2010. *Office: One Peter Yorke Way, San Francisco, CA 94109-6602.*

ESTABLISHED JULY 29, 1853.

Square Miles 1,016.

Code Address: Roman, San Francisco.

Comprises the Counties of San Francisco, San Mateo and Marin in the State of California.

Patrons of the Archdiocese of San Francisco: St. Francis of Assisi, October 4; St. Patrick, March 17.

Legal Title: The Roman Catholic Archbishop of San Francisco, a Corporation Sole.
For legal titles of parishes and archdiocesan institutions, consult the Chancery Office.

STATISTICAL OVERVIEW

Personnel	
Archbishops	1
Retired Archbishops	2
Auxiliary Bishops	2
Retired Bishops	3
Priests: Diocesan Active in Diocese	109
Priests: Diocesan Active Outside Diocese	6
Priests: Diocesan in Foreign Missions	1
Priests: Retired, Sick or Absent	90
Number of Diocesan Priests	206
Religious Priests in Diocese	168
Total Priests in Diocese	374
Extern Priests in Diocese	76
Ordinations:	
Diocesan Priests	1
Religious Priests	3
Transitional Deacons	1
Permanent Deacons in Diocese	75
Total Brothers	38
Total Sisters	744
Parishes	
Parishes	91
With Resident Pastor:	
Resident Diocesan Priests	74
Resident Religious Priests	17
Without Resident Pastor:	
Administered by Priests	1
Missions	11
Pastoral Centers	22
Professional Ministry Personnel:	
Brothers	13
Sisters	23
Lay Ministers	124
Welfare	
Catholic Hospitals	3
Total Assisted	384,811
Health Care Centers	4
Total Assisted	51,224
Homes for the Aged	2
Total Assisted	82
Residential Care of Children	1
Total Assisted	80
Day Care Centers	3
Total Assisted	345
Specialized Homes	4
Total Assisted	81
Special Centers for Social Services	5
Total Assisted	4,334
Other Institutions	17
Total Assisted	28,622
Educational	
Seminaries, Diocesan	1
Students from This Diocese	17
Students from Other Diocese	90
Diocesan Students in Other Seminaries	3
Seminaries, Religious	1
Total Seminarians	20
Colleges and Universities	3
Total Students	13,782
High Schools, Diocesan and Parish	4
Total Students	3,432
High Schools, Private	10
Total Students	7,848
Elementary Schools, Diocesan and Parish	51
Total Students	14,362
Elementary Schools, Private	8
Total Students	16,568
Catechesis/Religious Education:	
High School Students	1,980
Elementary Students	11,704
Total Students under Catholic Instruction	69,696
Teachers in the Diocese:	
Priests	7
Brothers	5
Sisters	44
Lay Teachers	1,649
Vital Statistics	
Receptions into the Church:	
Infant Baptism Totals	6,062
Minor Baptism Totals	436
Adult Baptism Totals	231
Received into Full Communion	350
First Communions	5,080
Confirmations	3,490
Marriages:	
Catholic	846
Interfaith	224
Total Marriages	1,070
Deaths	2,339
Total Catholic Population	432,163
Total Population	1,761,000

Former Bishops—Rt. Rev. FRANCISCO GARCIA DIEGO Y MORENO, O.F.M., ord. 1808; cons. Bishop of both Californias, Oct. 4, 1840; died in Santa Barbara, April 30, 1846; Most Revs. JOSEPH SADOC ALEMANY, O.P., D.D., cons. Bishop of Monterey, June 30, 1850; appt. first Archbishop of San Francisco, July 29, 1853; resigned and appt. Titular Archbishop of Pelusio, Dec. 28, 1884; died in Valencia, Spain, April 14, 1888; PATRICK WILLIAM RIORDAN, D.D., cons. Titular Archbishop of Cabasa and appt. Coadjutor Archbishop of San Francisco cum jure successionis Sept. 16, 1883; succeeded to Dec. 28, 1884; died in San Francisco, Dec. 27, 1914; GEORGE MONTGOMERY, D.D., cons. Titular Bishop of Tmui and appt. Coadjutor Bishop of Monterey and Los Angeles cum jure successionis April 8, 1894; succeeded to May 6, 1896; appt. Titular Archbishop of Osimo and

Coadjutor Archbishop of San Francisco cum jure successionis March 27, 1903; died in San Francisco, Jan. 10, 1907; EDWARD J. HANNA, D.D., cons. Titular Bishop of Titopolis and appt. Auxiliary Bishop of San Francisco Dec. 4, 1912; appt. Archbishop of San Francisco, June 1, 1915; resigned and appt. Titular Archbishop of Gortyna, March 2, 1935; died July 10, 1944; JOHN JOSEPH MITTY, D.D., cons. Bishop of Salt Lake City, June 21, 1926; appt. Coadjutor Archbishop of San Francisco cum jure successionis, Jan. 29, 1932; succeeded to March 2, 1935; died Oct. 15, 1961; JOSEPH T. MCGUCKEN, S.T.D., appt. Auxiliary of Los Angeles, Feb. 4, 1941; cons. Titular Bishop of Sanavo March 19, 1941; appt. Coadjutor Bishop of Sacramento cum jure successionis, Oct. 26, 1955; succeeded to Jan. 14, 1957; appt. Archbishop of San Francisco, Feb. 21, 1962; appt. Assistant at the Pontifical Throne, March 19, 1966; retired Feb. 22, 1977; died Oct. 26, 1983; JOHN R. QUINN, D.D. (Retired), appt. Auxiliary Bishop of San Diego, Oct. 21, 1967; cons. Titular Bishop of Thisiduo, Dec. 12, 1967; transferred to Oklahoma City and Tulsa, Nov. 18, 1971; appt. Archbishop of the Archdiocese of Oklahoma City, Feb. 6, 1973; appt. Archbishop of San Francisco, April 26, 1977; resigned Dec. 27, 1995; WILLIAM J. LEVADA, S.T.D., ord. Dec. 20, 1961; appt. Titular Bishop of Capri and Auxiliary Bishop of Los Angeles March 29, 1983; Episcopal ord. May 12, 1983; appt. Archbishop of Portland in Oregon July 1, 1986; installed as Archbishop of Portland in Oregon Sept. 21, 1986; appt. Coadjutor Archbishop of San Francisco Aug. 17, 1995; succeeded to See Dec. 27, 1995; appt. Prefect of Doctrine of the Faith May 13, 2005; created Cardinal March 24, 2006.

Chancery and Pastoral Center—One Peter Yorke Way, San Francisco, 94109-6602. Tel: 415-614-5500; Fax: 415-614-5555. Open Mon.-Fri. All applications for dispensations, faculties, etc., and all correspondence should be addressed: Chancery and Pastoral Center.

Office of the Archbishop—

Archbishop—Most Rev. GEORGE H. NIEDERAUER, D.D., Ph.D.

Executive Assistant to the Archbishop—LAUREL MILLER. Tel: 415-614-5605; Fax: 415-614-5601.

Auxiliary Bishops—Most Revs. WILLIAM J. JUSTICE, Vicar for Clergy; ROBERT W. MCELROY, Vicar for Parish Life & Devel. Tel: 415-614-5611; Fax: 415-614-5613.

Manager, Office of the Auxiliary Bishops, Office of the Vicar for Clergy, Office of the Vicar for Parish Life & Devel.—ANNABELLE C.A. GROH. Tel: 415-614-5612; Fax: 415-614-5613. Email: groha@sfarchdiocese.org. Administrative Assistants: KATYA ALCARAZ. Tel: 415-614-5614. Email: alcarazk@sfarchdiocese.org; CINDY GAMMER. Tel: 415-614-5679 (Vicar for Clergy); 415-614-5616 (Office Vicar for Parish Life & Devel.). Email: gammerc@sfarchdiocese.org.

Office of the Permanent Diaconate—Deacon LEON KORTENKAMP. Tel: 415-614-5531; Fax: 415-614-5555.

Office of Diaconate Formation—Deacon RICHARD FOLEY. Tel: 415-614-5615; Fax: 415-614-5555.

Office of Vocations—Rev. DAVID A. GHIORSO. Tel: 415-614-5683.

Episcopal Vicar for the Spanish Speaking—Rev. MOISES AGUDO. Tel: 415-614-5591.

Episcopal Vicar for Filipinos—Rev. EUGENE D. TUNGOL. Tel: 415-751-0450.

Office for Women Religious—Sr. ROSINA CONROTTO, P.B.V.M., Dir. Tel: 415-614-5535.

Chancellor—Rev. Msgr. C. MICHAEL PADAZINSKI, J.C.D. Tel: 415-614-5619; Fax: 415-614-5696.

College of Consultors—Most Revs. GEORGE H. NIEDERAUER, D.D., Ph.D.; WILLIAM J. JUSTICE; ROBERT W. MCELROY; Rev. Msgrs. MICHAEL D. HARRIMAN; C. MICHAEL PADAZINSKI, J.C.D.; JOHN J. TALESFORE; JAMES T. TARANTINO; Revs. JOHN A. BALLEZA; DAVID A. GHIORSO; RENE ITURBE, S.M.; RAYMUND M. REYES; EUGENE D. TUNGOL.

Deans—Revs. RAYMUND M. REYES, Deanery 1; CHARITO E. SUAN, Deanery 2; Rev. Msgr. JOHN J. TALESFORE, Deanery 3; Revs. RENE J. ITUBE, Deanery 4; MARIO P. FARANA, Deanery 5; MARK V. TAHENY, Deanery 6; CYRIL O'SULLIVAN, Deanery 7; RENE R. RAMOSO, Deanery 8; CHARLES I. PUTHOTA, Ph.D., Deanery 9; ANTHONY E. MCGUIRE, Deanery 10; Rev. Msgr. STEVEN D. OTELLINI, Deanery 11.

Council of Priests—Rev. JOHN A. BALLEZA, Chm.

Archdiocesan Pastoral Council—Mr. PATRICK CODY.

Censor Librorum—Rev. Msgr. WARREN HOLLERAN, S.T.D.

Apostleship of the Sea—Rev. Msgr. MICHAEL D. HARRIMAN, Chap.

Moderator of the Curia and Vicar for Administration—Rev. Msgr. JAMES T. TARANTINO.

Manager, Office of Vicar for Administration—TERA ENGLISH. Tel: 415-614-5589.

Director of the Office of Child and Youth Protection—Deacon JOHN H. NORRIS. Tel: 415-614-5504; Fax: 415-614-5658.

Safe Environment Coordinator—TWYLA POWERS. Tel: 415-614-5576; Fax: 415-614-5658.

Victim Assistance Coordinator—BARBARA ELORDI. Tel: 415-614-5506; Fax: 415-614-5658. Email: elordib@sfarchdiocese.org.

Director of Finance/Chief Finance Officer—Mr. RICHARD P. HANNON. Tel: 415-614-5510.

Office of Development—Mr. MICHAEL O'LEARY, Dir.; Mr. DON RODRIGUES, Assoc. Dir. Tel: 415-614-5581.

Development Associate—FLORIAN ROMERO. Tel: 415-614-5580.

Archdiocesan Legal Office—Mr. JACK M. HAMMEL, Esq.; Mr. LARRY JANNUZZI, Esq. Legal Secretary: KATYA ALCARAZ. Tel: 415-614-5623.

Office of the Propagation of the Faith—GENEVIEVE ELIZONDO, Dir. Tel: 415-614-5673.

Holy Childhood Association Coordinator—Rev. MANUEL J. MEJIA, M.M.

Building and Administrative Services—JOSE LEON, Bldg. Facilities Mgr.; THOMAS HUIJTS. Tel: 415-614-5532.

For Real Estate please contact Real Property Support Corporation (RPSC). Tel: 415-292-0800.

Office of Human Resources—Mr. CARL FEIL, Dir. Tel: 415-614-5541; Mr. PATRICK SCHMIDT, Assoc. Dir. Tel: 415-614-5538; Mr. MARK MOLINA, Benefits Mgr. Tel: 415-614-5539; SUZANNE NAZARIO, Human Resources Coord. Tel: 415-614-5540.

Catholic Cemeteries—MONICA WILLIAMS, Mailing Address: P.O. Box 1577, Colma, 94014. Tel: 650-756-2060; Fax: 650-757-0752. Email: mjwilliams@holycrosscemeteries.com; moreinfo@holycrosscemeteries.com.

Archdiocesan Archives—Deacon JEFFREY BURNS, Ph.D., Dir. Tel: 650-328-6502.

Office of Ecumenism and Interreligious Affairs—VACANT.

Metropolitan Tribunal and Office of Canonical Affairs—

San Francisco Metropolitan Tribunal—One Peter Yorke Way, San Francisco, 94109-6602. Tel: 415-614-5690; Fax: 415-614-5696.

Judicial Vicar and Director—Rev. Msgr. C. MICHAEL PADAZINSKI, J.C.D.

Promoter of Justice—Rev. THUAN V. HOANG, J.C.L.

Defenders of the Bond—Revs. THUAN V. HOANG, J.C.L.; STEPHEN A. MERIWETHER, J.C.L.; DIANE L. BARR, J.C.D.; ROBERT W. GRAFFIO, J.C.L.

Judges—Rev. Msgr. C. MICHAEL PADAZINSKI, J.C.D., V.G.; Rev. ANGEL N. QUITALIG, J.C.L.; ROBERT J.B. FLUMMERFELT, J.C.L.; ROBERT W. GRAFFIO, J.C.L.; KRYSTYNA AMBORSKI, J.C.D.

Tribunal Auditors—JOANN NORRIS; REINA PARADA; JAN SCHACHERN.

Notaries and Secretaries to the Tribunal—REINA A. PARADA; CAROL KUMAGAI.

Archbishop's Cabinet—Most Revs. GEORGE H. NIEDERAUER, D.D., Ph.D.; WILLIAM J. JUSTICE; Rev. Msgrs. C. MICHAEL PADAZINSKI, J.C.D.; JAMES T. TARANTINO; Deacon JOHN H. NORRIS; Ms. MAUREEN HUNTINGTON; GEORGE WESOLEK.

Department of Pastoral Ministry and Office of Evangelization—Deacon JOHN H. NORRIS, Dir. Tel: 415-614-5504; Fax: 415-614-5658. Email: norrisj@sfarchdiocese.org.

Director, Ministry to Spanish Speaking—Mrs. CECILIA ARIAS-RIVAS. Tel: 415-614-5573; Fax: 415-614-5658.

Office of Ethnic Ministries—Sr. MARIA HSU, F.d.C.C., Dir. Tel: 415-614-5575. Email: hsum@sfarchdiocese.org; ELLA TSANG, Administrative Asst. Tel: 415-614-5574.

African American Ministry—Rev. KENNETH M. WESTRAY, St. Vincent de Paul Church, 2320 Green St., San Francisco, 94123. Tel: 415-922-1010.

Chinese Ministry—Sr. MARIA HSU, F.d.C.C. Tel: 415-614-5575. Email: hsum@sfarchdiocese.org.

Japanese Mission—Rev. ERIC FREED, St. Benedict Parish at St. Francis Xavier Church, 1801 Octavia St., San Francisco, 94109. Tel: 415-567-9855.

Arab-American Catholic Ministry—Rev. Msgr. LABIB KOBTI, St. Thomas More Church, 1300 Junipero Serra Blvd., San Francisco, 94132. Tel: 415-452-9634.

Polish, Croatian, Slovenian Mission—Rev. TADEUSZ RUSNAK, S.Ch., Nativity Church, 240 Fell St., San Francisco, 94102. Tel: 415-252-5799. Email: trusnak@comcast.net.

Korean Catholic Ministry—Rev. VINCENT KANG-GUN LEE, St. Michael Korean Church, 32 Broad St., San Francisco, 94112. Tel: 415-333-1194; Fax: 415-333-1196.

Tongan Ministry—Rev. SIONE MALAKAI KATOA, St. Timothy Church, 1515 Dolan Ave., San Mateo, 94401. Tel: 650-342-2470; Fax: 650-342-8156.

Vietnamese Catholic Ministry—Rev. TE VAN NGUYEN, St. Brendan Church, 29 Rockaway Ave., San Francisco, 94127. Tel: 415-681-4225.

Brazilian Ministry—VACANT.

Burmese Ministry—Rev. FRANCIS THAN HTUN, St. Finn Barr Church, San Francisco, 94112. Tel: 415-333-3627.

Filipino Ministry—Rev. EUGENE D. TUNGOL, Church of the Epiphany, 827 Vienna St., San Francisco, 94112. Tel: 415-333-7630.

Hispanic Ministry—Rev. MOISES AGUDO, St. Charles Borromeo Church, 713 S. Van Ness, San Francisco, 94110. Tel: 415-824-1700; Mrs. CECILIA ARIAS-RIVAS. Tel: 415-614-5573. Email: ariasrivasc@sfarchdiocese.org.

Haitian Ministry—Mr. PIERRE LABOSSIERE, 2822 55th Ave., Oakland, 94605. Email: pierrelabossiere@hotmail.com.

Indonesian Ministry—Mr. BENJAMIN LIEN. Cell: 408-221-9262.

Irish Ministry—Rev. BRENDAN MCBRIDE, Coord., St. Philip the Apostle Parish, 725 Diamond St., San Francisco, 94114. Tel: 415-282-0141.

Italian Ministry—Rev. Msgr. BRUNO PESCHIERA, Coord. Catholic Ministry, 101 W. Avalon Dr., Pacifica, 94044. Tel: 650-355-8377; CONSTANCE MERTES, 1550 44th Ave., San Francisco, 94122. Tel: 415-759-1422.

Native American Ministry—SACHEEN LITTLEFEATHER, Coord., San Francisco Kateri Tekawitha Prayer Circle, P.O. Box 150346, San Rafael, 94915. Tel: 415-485-5950.

Igbo Nigerian Ministry—Rev. CHARLES ONUBUGO, Our Lady of the Pillar, 400 Church St., Half Moon Bay, 94019. Tel: 650-726-4674.

Samoan Ministry—JOANNA ILAOA, Contact, Mailing Address: 17 Cypress Lane, Daly City, 94014. Email: joanna_ilaoa@yahoo.com; MAYA SUISALA. Tel: 866-964-7584, Ext. 20715. Email: maya_suisala@ssa.gov.

Office of Religious Education and Youth Ministry—Sr. CELESTE ARBUCKLE, S.S.S., Dir. Tel: 415-614-5652. Email: arbucklec@sfarchdiocese.org; JANET FORTUNA, Coord. Special Needs. Tel: 415-614-5655. Email: fortunaj@sfarchdiocese.org; Sr. GRACIELA MARTINEZ, O.S.F., Assoc. Dir. Hispanic Ministry & Rel. Educ. Tel: 415-614-5653. Email: martinezg@sfarchdiocese.org; Ms. ANELITA REYES, Assoc. Dir. Catechetical Ministries. Tel: 415-614-5651. Email: reyesa@sfarchdiocese.org; VIVIAN CLAUSING, Assoc. Dir. Youth Ministry & Catechetics. Tel: 415-614-5654. Email: clausingv@sfarchdiocese.org.

Ministry of Consolation—BARBARA ELORDI. Tel: 415-614-5506; Fax: 415-614-5658. Email: elordib@sfarchdiocese.org.

Office of Worship—LAURA BERTONE, Interim Dir. Tel: 415-614-5586. Email: bertonel@sfarchdiocese.org.

Department of Catholic Schools—Ms. MAUREEN HUNTINGTON, Supt.; Ms. ANNETTE BROWN, Asst. Supt. Planning & Finance; Mr. BRET E. ALLEN, Assoc. Supt. Educational & Professional Leadership; Dr. NINA RUSSO, Assoc. Supt. Curriculum/School Improvement; Mrs. JANET SUZIO, Asst. Supt. Faith Formation & Rel. Instruction.

Archdiocesan Board of Education—Most Rev. GEORGE H. NIEDERAUER, D.D., Ph.D.; Dr. BRUCE COVILLE; Mr. STEPHEN FORNER; Mrs. JOAN HIGGINS; Deacon JAMES SHEA; Mrs. CYLYN CRUZ-MONTERO; Mr. PAUL HANCE; Dr. CAROL HARRISON-WONG; Mrs. EVALYNNA HO; Mr. JOE HOUK; Mrs. MAUREEN LUNDY; Dr. MARIA MANUEL; Mr. DAVID MAJOR; Ms. ANNE KEARNEY, Vice Chair; Mr. VINCENT RIENER, Vice Chair; Mr. FRED TOTAH; Mr. KENNETH J. WILLERS; Rev. KENNETH M. WEARE; Mr. ROB AVESON; Mr. SCOTT BUSE; Revs. BRIAN L. COSTELLO; KENNETH M. WESTRAY, Chm.

The Roman Catholic Welfare Corporation of San Francisco— (dissolved April 1, 2008)

Department of Communications and Public Policy—GEORGE WESOLEK, Dir.

Archdiocesan Publication: "Catholic San Francisco"—Most Rev. GEORGE H. NIEDERAUER, D.D., Ph.D., Publisher; GEORGE WESOLEK, Assoc. Publisher; RICK DELVECCHIO, Editor & Gen. Mgr.

Office of Public Policy and Social Concerns—Tel: 415-614-5570. Web: www.sflifeandjustice.org. GEORGE WESOLEK, Dir. Tel: 415-614-5571; Fax: 415-614-5568. Email: wesolekg@sfarchdiocese.org.

Administrative Assistant—VERONICA RAMIREZ. Tel: 415-614-5570.

Restorative Justice—JULIO ESCOBAR, Prog. Coord. Tel: 415-614-5638. Email: escobarj@sfarchdiocese.org.

Catholic Campaign for Human Development—GEORGE WESOLEK, Dir. Tel: 415-614-5571. Email: wesolekg@sfarchdiocese.org. Parish Outreach

and Organizing: PATRICIA RIBEIRO, Coord. Tel: 415-614-5572; 415-852-0023. Email: ribeirop@sfarchdiocese.org.
Respect Life—VICKI EVANS, Prog. Coord. Tel: 415-614-5533. Email: evansv@sfarchdiocese.org.
Project Rachel— (Post Abortion Counseling) MARY ANN SCHWAB, Prog. Coord. Tel: 415-614-5567; 415-717-6428.
Project Gabriel—FREDI D'ALESSIO, Prog. Coord.. Email: sfgabrielproject@gmail.com.
The Catholic Campaign to end the Use of Death Penalty—CATHERINE HUSTON, Prog. Coord. Tel: 415-614-5570; 650-344-2676. Email: sflifeandjustice@earthlink.net.
Catholic Relief Services—GEORGE WESOLEK, Dir. Tel: 415-614-5571. Email: wesolekg@sfarchdiocese.org.

CLERGY, PARISHES, MISSIONS AND PAROCHIAL SCHOOLS

CITY OF SAN FRANCISCO

(SAN FRANCISCO COUNTY)

1—CATHEDRAL OF ST. MARY (ASSUMPTION) (1891) Rev. Msgr. John J. Talesfore; Rev. Francisco J. Gamez; Deacons Peter I. Boulware; R. Christoph Sandoval. In Res., Most Rev. William J. Justice; Rev. Msgr. C. Michael Padazinski.
Cathedral Office—1111 Gough St., 94109. Tel: 415-567-2020; Fax: 415-567-2040. Email: mmkeon@stmarycathedralsf.org. Web: www.stmarycathedralsf.org.
Catechesis/Religious Program—Students 75.

2—ST. AGNES (1893) Rev. Raymond Allender. In Res., Revs. Frank C. Buckley, S.J.; Radmar Jao.
Res.: 1025 Masonic Ave., 94117. Tel: 415-487-8560; Fax: 415-487-8575. Web: www.saintagnessf.com.
Catechesis/Religious Program—Sr. Janet Chau, R.S.M., D.R.E. Students 46.

3—ALL HALLOWS CHAPEL OF OUR LADY OF LOURDES (1886) Closed. For sacramental records please contact Our Lady of Lourdes, San Francisco.
Chapel—Our Lady of Lourdes

4—ST. ANNE (1904) Revs. Raymund M. Reyes; Marvin P. Felipe, S.D.B. (Philippines); Deacon John Dupre. In Res., Most Rev. Daniel F. Walsh (SR), Bishop Emeritus, Diocese of Santa Rosa; Rev. Francisco Bagadiong (Retired).
Res.: 850 Judah St., 94122. Tel: 415-665-1600; Fax: 415-665-1603. Web: www.stanne-sf.org.
School—1320 14th Ave., 94122. Tel: 415-664-7977; Fax: 415-661-6904. Web: www.stanne.com. Thomas C. White, Prin. Sisters 2; Lay Teachers 27; Students 433.
Catechesis/Religious Program—Tel: 415-665-1600, Ext. 38; Fax: 415-665-1603. Students 57.

5—ST. ANTHONY OF PADUA (1893) Revs. James L. Garcia; Guglielmo Lauriola, O.F.M.
Res.: 3215 Cesar Chavez St., 94110. Tel: 415-647-2704; Fax: 415-647-7282. Email: sanantonio1893@yahoo.com.
Chapel—Immaculate Conception Chapel 3255 Folsom St., 94110. Tel: 415-824-1762; Fax: 415-824-0129.
School—St. Anthony-Immaculate Conception, (Grades K-8), 299 Precita Ave., 94110. Tel: 415-648-2008; Fax: 415-648-1825. Mr. Dennis Ruggiero, Prin. Lay Teachers 8; Students 170.
Catechesis/Religious Program—Tel: 415-641-2704; Fax: 415-647-7286. Students 125.

6—ST. BENEDICT PARISH AT ST. FRANCIS XAVIER CHURCH (1913), (Japanese), (Founded 1962 for Deaf and Hearing Impaired). Rev. Paul Zirimenya, Chap. In Res., Rev. Ghislain C. Bazikila.
Res.: 1801 Octavia, 94109. Tel: 415-567-9855; 415-567-0438 (TDD); 866-896-0968 (Video Phone); Fax: 415-567-0916. Email: info@sfdeafcatholics.org. Web: www.sfdeafcatholics.org.
Catechesis/Religious Program—Students 12.

7—ST. BONIFACE (1860), (German), Revs. Thomas J. King, O.F.M.; John S. Hardin, O.F.M.; Thomas B. West, O.F.M.; John Luat Nguyen, O.F.M. In Res., Revs. Arturo Lopez, O.F.M.; Hoang T. Trinh, O.F.M.; Bros. Peter Boegel, O.F.M.; Javier Diaz, O.F.M.; John Kiesler, O.F.M.; Diadacus Clavel, O.F.M.; Dennis O. Duffy, O.F.M.; Joseph Sury, O.F.M.; Robert Valentine, O.F.M.
Res.: 133 Golden Gate Ave., 94102. Tel: 415-863-0111; Fax: 415-863-7602. Email: info@saintbonifacesf.org. Web: www.stbonifacesf.org.
Catechesis/Religious Program—

8—ST. BRENDAN (1929) Revs. Daniel Nascimento; Michael F. Quinn; Te Van Nguyen.
Res.: 29 Rockaway Ave., 94127. Tel: 415-681-4225; Fax: 415-681-3976. Email: navigator@stbrendanparish.org. Web: www.stbrendanparish.org.
School—(Grades K-8), 940 Laguna Honda Blvd., 94127-1239. Tel: 415-731-2665; Fax: 415-731-7207. Email: sbs@stbrendansf.com. Web: www.stbrendansf.com. Mrs. Carol Grewal, Prin.; Jan Donovan, Asst. Prin.; Ruth Nelson, Librarian. Lay Teachers 23; Students 330.
Catechesis/Religious Program—Sr. Catherine Cappello, Fd.CC., Pastoral Assoc. Students 14.

9—ST. BRIGID (1863) Closed. For sacramental records please contact St. Vincent de Paul, San Francisco.

10—ST. CECILIA (1917) Rev. Msgr. Michael D. Harriman; Rev. Lodovico Joseph Landi. In Res., Rev. Msgrs. Maurice M. McCormick (Retired); Floro B. Arcamo (Retired).
Res.: 2555 17th Ave., 94116. Tel: 415-664-8481; Fax: 415-661-2957.
School—660 Vicente St., 94116. Tel: 415-731-8400; Fax: 415-731-5686. Email: office@stceciliaschool.org. Web: www.stceciliaschool.org. Sr. Marilyn Miller, S.N.J.M., Prin.. Email: mmiller@stceciliaschool.org. Sisters of the Holy Names of Jesus and Mary 4; Lay Teachers 24; Students 600.
Catechesis/Religious Program—Students 85.

11—ST. CHARLES BORROMEO (1887) Revs. Moises Agudo; Gabriel Flores. In Res., Rev. John H. Wadeson.
Res.: 713 S. Van Ness Ave., 94110. Tel: 415-824-1700; Fax: 415-824-0844. Email: sancarlosborromeo@sbcglobal.net.
School—3250 18th St., 94110. Tel: 415-861-7652; Fax: 415-861-0221. Sr. Nelia Pernecia, O.P., Prin. Dominican Sisters of the Most Holy Rosary (Philippines) 6; Lay Teachers 10; Students 315.
Catechesis/Religious Program—Students 219.

12—CHURCH OF THE EPIPHANY (1914) Revs. Eugene D. Tungol; Erick E. Arauz; Deacons Ding Viray; Ramon Zamora. In Res., Revs. Rolando A. Caverte (Retired); Aquino Padilla (Retired).
Res. & Rectory: 827 Vienna St., 94112. Tel: 415-333-7630; Fax: 415-333-1803. Web: www.epiphanysf.org.
School—600 Italy Ave., 94112. Tel: 415-337-4030; Fax: 415-337-8583. Diane Elkins, Prin. Lay Teachers 23; Students 527.
Catechesis/Religious Program—Tel: 415-333-7630, Ext. 15. Students 221.

13—CORPUS CHRISTI (1898) Revs. Leo A. Baysinger, S.D.B.; Aloysius J. Pestun, S.D.B.; Jose Lucero, S.D.B. In Res., Rev. Edward Liptak, S.D.B.
Res.: 62 Santa Rosa Ave., 94112. Tel: 415-585-2991; Fax: 415-230-5450.
Catechesis/Religious Program—Sr. Elizabeth Villanueva, F.M.A., D.R.E. Students 138.

14—ST. DOMINIC (1873) Revs. Xavier M. Lavagetto, O.P.; Garry J. Cappleman, O.P.; Stephen Maria Lopez, O.P.; Deacons Fred Swanson, (Retired); Charles McNeil; Michael F. Curran. In Res., Revs. Patrick L. LaBelle, O.P., Prior; Felix F. Cassidy, O.P.; Anthony R. Rosevear, O.P., Novice Master; Allen Robert Duston, O.P., Dir., Shrine of St. Jude; Paschal D. Salisbury, O.P.; Anselm Ramelow, O.P.; Bro. Gregory R. Lira, O.P.
Res.: 2390 Bush St., 94115. Tel: 415-567-7824; Fax: 415-567-1608. Email: info@stdominics.org. Web: www.stdominics.org.
Catechesis/Religious Program—Students 102.

15—ST. EDWARD (1916) Closed. For sacramental records please contact St. Dominic, San Francisco.

16—ST. ELIZABETH (1912) Revs. Charito E. Suan; Elias M. Salomon.
Res.: 449 Holyoke Ave., 94134. Tel: 415-468-0820; Fax: 415-468-1457.
Catechesis/Religious Program—Tel: 415-468-0423. Students 64.

17—ST. EMYDIUS (1913) Rev. William J. Brady. In Res., Rev. David M. Pettingill (Retired).
Res.: 286 Ashton Ave., 94112. Tel: 415-587-7066; Fax: 415-587-6690. Email: stemydius@sbcglobal.net.
Catechesis/Religious Program—

18—ST. FINN BARR (1926) [CEM] Revs. Jose M. Corral; Francis Than Htun, Parochial Vicar. In Res., Rev. John Paul A. Otanwa.
Res.: 415 Edna St., 94112. Tel: 415-333-3627; Fax: 415-333-4090. Email: stfinnbarr@yahoo.com.
School—419 Hearst Ave., 94112. Tel: 415-333-1800; Fax: 415-452-0177. Web: www.stfinnbarr.org. Mele Sablan, Prin. Lay Teachers 14; Students 205.
Catechesis/Religious Program—Students 43.

19—ST. FRANCIS OF ASSISI, NATIONAL SHRINE (1849) Very Rev. Gregory Coiro, O.F.M.Cap., Rector.
610 Vallejo St., 94133. Tel: 415-986-4557; Fax: 415-544-9814. Email: info@shrinesf.org. In Res., Rev. Msgr. James T. Tarantino.

20—ST. GABRIEL (1941) Revs. Thomas M. Hamilton; Joseph F. Previtali; Deacon Thomas Reardon. In Res., Rev. Paul Zirimenya.
Res.: 2535 40th Ave., 94116. Tel: 415-731-6161; Fax: 415-731-1270. Web: www.rc.net/sanfrancisco/stgabriel.
School—2550 41st Ave., 94116. Tel: 415-566-0314; Fax: 415-566-3223. Email: office@stgabrielsf.com. Web: www.stgabrielsf.com. Sr. M. Pauline Borghello, R.S.M., Prin. Lay Teachers 24; Students 520.
Catechesis/Religious Program—Students 107.

21—HOLY CROSS (1887), (Korean), Closed. For inquiries for parish records contact the chancery.

22—HOLY FAMILY CHINESE MISSION *aka St. Mary's Chinese Catholic Center--1903)* (1921), (Chinese), Rev. Daniel E. McCotter, C.S.P.; Deacon Simon Tsui, Pastoral Assoc. & Teahouse Ministry.
Res.: 660 California St., 94108. Tel: 415-288-3835; Fax: 415-929-4698. Email: danielcsp@aol.com. Web: stmaryschinese.org.
School—St. Mary School & Chinese Catholic Center, 836 Kearny St., 94108. Tel: 415-929-4690; Fax: 415-929-4699. Web: www.stmaryschinese.org. Nancy Fiebelkorn, Prin.; Ms. Lisa Tom French, Exec. Dir. Sisters 1; Lay Teachers 13; Students 100.
School—Chinese Language School, 838 Kearny St., 94108. Tel: 415-929-4694. Stephen Woon Wah Tang, Prin. - St. Mary's Language School; Bill Chang, Vice Prin. Teachers 10; Elementary Students 300; High School Students 10.
Holy Family Association—Tel: 415-929-4696; Fax: 415-929-4698. Juliana Chung, Chair.
Catechesis/Religious Program—Tel: 415-929-4690. Nancy Fiebelkorn, D.R.E. Students 6.

23—HOLY NAME OF JESUS (1925) Revs. Arnold Zamora; Nicasio G. Paloso. In Res., Most Rev. Ignatius C. Wang; Deacon Michael Doherty.
Res.: 3240 Lawton St., 94122. Tel: 415-664-8590; Fax: 415-664-9007. Email: hnparishsecretary@gmail.com. Web: holyname-sf.org.
School—1560 40th Ave., 94122. Tel: 415-731-4077; Fax: 415-731-3328. Email: office@holynameschool.com. Web: www.holynamesf.com. Judy Cosmos, Prin. Sisters 1; Lay Teachers 16; Students 350.
Catechesis/Religious Program—Students 46.

24—ST. IGNATIUS (1855) Revs. Charles R. Gagan, S.J.; Albert A. Grosskopf, S.J.; James R. Blaettler, S.J.; John A. Coleman.
Res.: 650 Parker Ave., 94118. Tel: 415-422-2188; Fax: 415-387-1867. Web: www.stignatiussf.org.
Catechesis/Religious Program—Tel: 415-422-2195. Email: faloon@usfca.edu. Web: www.stignatiussf.org (click Parish Programs). Dan Faloon, D.R.E. Students 235.

25—ST. JAMES (1888) Rev. Jerome P. Foley.
Res.: 1086 Guerrero St., 94110. Tel: 415-824-4232; Fax: 415-824-0605. Email: stjmscath@aol.com.
School—321 Fair Oaks St., 94110. Tel: 415-647-8972; Fax: 415-647-0166. Web: www.saintjamessf.org. Sr. Mary S. Vasquez, O.P., Prin. Lay Teachers 11; Students 144.
Catechesis/Religious Program—Tel: 415-824-4233. Students 78.
Mission—Dominican Sisters of Mission San Jose 1212 Guerrero St., San Francisco Co. 94110. Tel: 415-648-7460.

26—ST. JOHN OF GOD (1967) Rev. Methodius S. Kiwale, A.L.C.P. (Tanzania).
Res. & Church: 1290 Fifth Ave., 94122. Tel: 415-566-5610; Fax: 415-566-5073. Email: StJohnofGod-SF@sbcglobal.net. Web: www.sjog.net.
Catechesis/Religious Program—Students 15.

27—ST. JOHN THE EVANGELIST (1893) Revs. Jose Pelagio A. Padit (Philippines); Antonio G. Petilla (Retired).
Res.: 19 St. Mary's Ave., 94112-1098. Tel: 415-334-4646; Fax: 415-334-0891.
Parish Center—98 Bosworth St., 94112. Email: saintjohnevangelist@yahoo.com.
School—925 Chenery St., 94131. Tel: 415-584-8383; Fax: 415-584-8359. Web: www.stjohnseagle.com. Sr. Shirley Garibaldi, O.S.U., Prin. Lay Teachers 13; Students 283.
Catechesis/Religious Program—Tel: 415-334-4646, Ext. 104. Ms. Maria Figueroa, D.R.E. Students 76.

28—ST. JOSEPH (1861) Closed. For sacramental records please contact St. Patrick, San Francisco.

29—ST. KEVIN (1922) Rev. Emilio S. Reyes Jr., S.V.D.
Res.: 704 Cortland Ave., 94110. Tel: 415-648-5751; Fax: 415-648-4441.
Catechesis/Religious Program—Tel: 415-282-0277.

30—ST. MICHAEL KOREAN CATHOLIC CHURCH (1898), (Korean), Rev. Vincent Kang-Gun Lee.
Res.: 32 Broad St., 94112. Tel: 415-333-1194; Fax: 415-333-1196. Email: stmichael_info@yahoo.com. Web: cafe.naver.com/sfstmichael.
Catechesis/Religious Program—Email: stmichael_info@yahoo.com. Mr. Kitae Lee, Youth Min. Students 38.

31—MISSION DOLORES BASILICA (1776) [CEM], (San Francisco de Asis), Revs. Arturo L. Albano; William C. Nicholas; Deacon Vicente Cervantes.
Res.: 3321 16th St., 94114. Tel: 415-621-8203; Fax: 415-621-2294. Email: parish@missiondolores.org.
Catechesis/Religious Program—Maria

Rosales-Uribe, D.R.E. Students 61.
32—ST. MONICA (1911) Rev. John L. Greene. In Res., Rev. Msgr. Fred A. Bitanga (Retired); Rev. Lawrence Gould, S.A.C.
Res.: 470 24th Ave., 94121. Tel: 415-751-5275; Fax: 415-751-0440. Email: monicarectory@sbcglobal.net.
School—5950 Geary Blvd., 94121. Tel: 415-751-9564; Fax: 415-751-0781. Email: office@stmonicasf.org. Web: stmonicasf.org. Lay Teachers 11; Students 166.
Catechesis/Religious Program—(Combined with St. Thomas the Apostle, San Francisco)
33—MOST HOLY REDEEMER (1900) Rev. Stephen A. Meriwether. In Res., Revs. James Picket (Retired); William W. Young (Retired).
Res.: 100 Diamond St., 94114-2414. Tel: 415-863-6259; Fax: 415-552-8786. Email: mhr-admin@mhr.org. Web: www.mhr.org.
Catechesis/Religious Program—
34—NATIVITY (1902), (Polish—Croatian), Rev. Tadeusz Rusnak, S.Ch.
Res.: 245 Linden St., 94102. Tel: 415-252-5799; Fax: 415-252-5799.
Catechesis/Religious Program—
35—NOTRE DAME DES VICTOIRES (1856), (French), Revs. Rene Iturbe, S.M.; Etienne Siffert, S.M.; Dennis Steik, S.M., Parochial Vicar.
Res.: 566 Bush St., 94108. Tel: 415-397-0113; Fax: 415-397-3217. Email: ndveglise@ndvsf.org. Web: ndvsf.org.
School—(Grades K-8), 659 Pine St., 94108. Tel: 415-421-0069; Fax: 415-421-1440. Email: office@ndvsf.org. Mary K. Ghisolfo, Prin. Lay Teachers 21; Students 285.
Catechesis/Religious Program—Tel: 415-397-0113; Fax: 415-397-3217. Email: ndveglise@ndvsf.org.
36—OLD ST. MARY'S CATHEDRAL (1854) Revs. Daniel E. McCotter, C.S.P.; Peter G. Shea, C.S.P.; Bartholomew K. Landry, C.S.P. In Res., Revs. Richard Chilson, C.S.P. (Retired); Thomas J. Dove, C.S.P. (Retired); George R. Fitzgerald, C.S.P.; Vincent P. Manalo, C.S.P.; Thomas F. Foley; Terrance Ryan.
Res.: 660 California St., 94108. Tel: 415-288-3800; Fax: 415-288-3838. Web: www.oldsaintmarys.org.
37—OUR LADY OF FATIMA BYZANTINE CATHOLIC CHURCH (1954) Rev. John L. Greene; Deacon Kyrril Bruce E. Pagacz.
Res.: 101 20th Ave., 94121-1398. Tel: 415-752-2052. Web: www.byzantinecatholic.org.
38—OUR LADY OF GUADALUPE, Closed. For sacramental records please contact SS. Peter and Paul, San Francisco.
39—OUR LADY OF LOURDES (1942) Rev. Daniel E. Carter. Email: dancrter@aol.com.
Res.: 1715 Oakdale Ave., 94124. Tel: 415-285-3377; Fax: 415-285-2191. Email: ollsanfran@aol.com.
Catechesis/Religious Program— Joint program with St. Paul of the Shipwreck. Students 75.
Mission—All Hallows Chapel 1440 Newhall St., San Francisco Co. 94124. Tel: 415-285-3377; Fax: 415-285-2191. Email: ollsanfran@aol.com.
40—ST. PATRICK (1851) Revs. Eduardo Dura; Calixto A. Pablo. In Res., Rev. Edward Phelan (Retired).
Res.: 756 Mission St., 94103. Tel: 415-421-3730; Fax: 415-512-9730.
Catechesis/Religious Program—Estrellita Perez, D.R.E.; Nanette Murata, D.R.E. Students 80.
41—ST. PAUL (1880) Rev. Mario P. Farana.
Res.: 221 Valley St., 94131. Tel: 415-648-7538; Fax: 415-648-4740.
St. Paul Littlest Angel Pre-School—Tel: 415-824-5437; Fax: 415-824-5430. Email: littlestangelpreschool@gmail.com. Ms. Peg Kayser, Prin. Students 42.
School—St. Paul, 1690 Church St., 94131. Tel: 415-648-2055; Fax: 415-648-1920. Mr. Daniel Dean, Prin. Lay Teachers 9; Students 235.
Catechesis/Religious Program—Tel: 415-826-4484. Dorothy Vigna, D.R.E. Students 89.
Convent—Novitiate of the Missionaries of Charity, 312 29th St., 94131. Tel: 415-647-1889.
42—ST. PAUL OF THE SHIPWRECK (1915) Rev. Paul Gawlowski, O.F.M.Conv.; Deacon Larry Chatmon; Sr. Eva Camberos, M.F.P., Pastoral Assoc.
Mailing Address: 1122 Jamestown Ave., 94124. In Res., Bros. Mark Folger, O.F.M.Conv.; George Cherrie, O.F.M.Conv.
Res.: 3350 Jennings St., 94124. Tel: 415-468-3434; Fax: 415-468-1400. Email: spswoffice@aol.com. Web: www.stpauloftheshipwreck.org.
Catechesis/Religious Program—Students 73.
43—ST. PETER (1867) Revs. J. Manuel Estrada; John T. Jimenez; Deacon David Gamarra.
Res.: 1200 Florida St., 94110. Tel: 415-282-1652; Fax: 415-282-6097. Email: stpeterparish@yahoo.com.
School—1266 Florida St., 94110. Tel: 415-647-8662; Fax: 415-647-4618. Vicki Butler, Prin. Sisters 3; Lay Teachers 12; Students 361.
Catechesis/Religious Program—Tel: 415-282-1176. Students 270.
44—SS. PETER AND PAUL (1884), (Italian), Revs. John Itzaina, S.D.B.; Harold Danielson, S.D.B.; Deacon Thien Nguyen, S.D.B. In Res., Revs. Austin Conterno, S.D.B.; Paul Maniscalco, S.D.B. (Retired); Mario A. Rosso, S.D.B.; Salvatore H. Giacomini, S.D.B.; Armand Oliveri, S.D.B.
Res.: 666 Filbert St., 94133. Tel: 415-421-0809; Fax: 415-421-0217. Email: gibbons@stspeterpaul.san-francisco.ca.us. Web: www.stspeterpaul.san-francisco.ca.us/church.
School—632 Filbert St., 94133. Tel: 415-421-5219; Fax: 415-421-1831. Dr. Lisa Haris, Prin. Salesian Sisters 5; Lay Teachers 22; Students 250.
Catechesis/Religious Program—
45—ST. PHILIP THE APOSTLE (1910) Rev. Anthony La Torre; Rio Stefanus, Opers. Mgr. & Accountant. In Res., Revs. Brendan McBride (Ireland); Rory E. Murphy.
Res.: 725 Diamond St., 94114. Tel: 415-282-0141; Fax: 415-282-8962. Email: rectory@saintphilipparish.org.
School—665 Elizabeth St., 94114. Tel: 415-824-8467; Fax: 415-282-5746. Email: remy.everett@saintphilipparish.org. Web: www.saintphilipschool.org. Remy Everett, Prin. Lay Teachers 14; Students 240.
Catechesis/Religious Program—Students 20.
46—SACRED HEART (1885) Closed. For inquiries for parish records contact the chancery.
47—STAR OF THE SEA (1894) Revs. Brian L. Costello; Vincent Musaby Imana. In Res., Rev. Benedict Chang (Retired).
Res.: 4420 Geary Blvd., 94118. Tel: 415-751-0450; Fax: 415-386-5651. Email: starparish@sbcglobal.net. Web: www.staroftheseasf.com.
School—360 Ninth Ave., 94118. Tel: 415-221-8558; Fax: 415-221-7118. Web: www.starofthesea.com. Terrence Hanley, Prin. Lay Teachers 19; Students 233.
Catechesis/Religious Program—Tel: 415-713-5624.
48—ST. STEPHEN (1950) Rev. Paul F. Warren; Deacons Gary West; Dan Rosen. In Res., Revs. Leonard J. Calegari (Retired); Edward K. Murray.
Office: 451 Eucalyptus Dr., 94132. Tel: 415-681-2444; Fax: 415-681-7843. Email: info@saintstephensf.org. Web: www.saintstephensf.org.
Res.: 601 Eucalyptus Dr., 94132. Tel: 415-681-2707.
School—401 Eucalyptus Dr., 94132. Tel: 415-664-8331; Fax: 415-242-5608. Web: ststephenschools-f.org. Mrs. Sharon McCarthy Allen, Prin. Lay Teachers 19; Students 323.
Catechesis/Religious Program—Veronica Wong, D.R.E. Students 47.
49—ST. TERESA (1880) Revs. Michael A. Greenwell, O.Carm.; Michael E. Kwiecien, O.Carm.; Deacon Charles Allen Jr.; Sr. Maureen O'Brien, B.V.M., Pastoral Assoc.
Res.: 390 Missouri St., 94107. Tel: 415-285-5272; Fax: 415-285-8510. Email: info@stteresasf.org. Web: stteresasf.org.
Catechesis/Religious Program—Students 17.
50—ST. THOMAS MORE (1950) Rev. Msgr. Labib Kobti; Revs. Andrew R. Johnson; Youssef Keikati; Deacon Khaled Abu-Alshaer.
Res.: 1300 Junipero Serra Blvd., 94132. Tel: 415-452-9634; Fax: 415-452-9653. Email: stmchurch2002@aol.com. Web: www.stmchurch.com.
Catechesis/Religious Program—Students 14.
51—ST. THOMAS THE APOSTLE (1922) Rev. John J. Sakowski.
Res.: 3835 Balboa St., 94121. Tel: 415-387-5545; Fax: 415-221-0868. Email: stthomasapostlechurchsf@gmail.com.
School—3801 Balboa St., 94121. Tel: 415-221-2711; Fax: 415-221-8611. Judy Borelli, Prin. Lay Teachers 23; Students 265.
Catechesis/Religious Program—Sr. Noreen O'Connor, C.S.J., D.R.E. Students 35.
52—ST. VINCENT DE PAUL (1901) Revs. Kenneth M. Westray; J. Michael Strange, S.S. In Res., Most Rev. Robert W. McElroy.
Res.: 2320 Green St., 94123. Tel: 415-922-1010; Fax: 415-922-7203. Web: svdpsf.org.
School—2350 Green St., 94123. Tel: 415-346-5505; Fax: 415-346-0970. Web: www.svdpsf.org. Mrs. Eileen Murphy Vigo, Prin. Lay Teachers 34; Students 268.
53—VISITACION, CHURCH OF THE (1907) Revs. Thuan V. Hoang; Jose Eduardo Mendoza. In Res., Rev. Victorio R. Balagapo (Retired).
Res.: 655 Sunnydale Ave., 94134. Tel: 415-494-5517; Fax: 415-494-5513. Email: info@visitacionchurch.org. Web: www.visitacionchurch.org.
School—Our Lady of the Visitacion, 785 Sunnydale Ave., 94134. Tel: 415-239-7840; Fax: 415-239-2559. Sr. Maxie O'Rourke, Prin. Daughters of Charity of St. Vincent de Paul 4; Lay Teachers 16; Students 200.
Catechesis/Religious Program—
Mission—Our Lady of Guadalupe 285 Alvarado St., Brisbane, San Mateo Co. 94005. Tel: 415-467-9727.

OUTSIDE THE CITY OF SAN FRANCISCO

BELMONT, SAN MATEO CO.
1—IMMACULATE HEART OF MARY (1947) Revs. Stephen H. Howell; Arsenio G. Cirera (Philippines); Deacons Steven Hackett; Henry Jacquemet.
Res.: 1040 Alameda de las Pulgas, 94002. Tel: 650-593-6157; Fax: 650-593-1665. Email: office@ihmbelmont.org. Web: www.ihmbelmont.org.
School—1000 Alameda de las Pulgas, 94002. Tel: 650-593-4265; Fax: 650-593-4342. Email: ihmoffice@ihmschoolbelmont.org. Web: www.ihmschoolbelmont.org. Hannah C. Everhart, Prin. Lay Teachers 12; Students 286.
Catechesis/Religious Program—Mrs. Kathy O'Connor-Grosshauser, C.R.E. Students 270.
2—ST. MARK (1965) Rev. Al Furtado, C.S.Sp. In Res., Rev. Edward A. Bohnert.
Res.: 325 Marine View Ave., 94002. Tel: 650-591-5937; Fax: 650-591-7645. Email: st_markschurch@yahoo.com. Web: www.saintmarks.us.
Catechesis/Religious Program—Email: sm.faithform@yahoo.com. Students 87.
BURLINGAME, SAN MATEO CO.
1—ST. CATHERINE OF SIENA (1908) Revs. John A. Ryan; Clifford Martin; Deacon Roy Twitty.
Res.: 1310 Bayswater Ave., 94010. Tel: 650-344-6884; Fax: 650-344-1022. Email: stcsiena@yahoo.com. Web: www.stcsiena.org.
School—1300 Bayswater Ave., 94010. Tel: 650-344-7176; Fax: 650-344-7426. Email: office@stcatherineofsiena.net. Web: www.stcos.com. Sr. Antonella Manca, M.S.C., Prin. Missionary Sisters of the "Sacro Costato" 4; Lay Teachers 20; Students 312.
Catechesis/Religious Program—Email: silvia@stcsiena.org. Students 148.
2—OUR LADY OF ANGELS (1926) Revs. Michael Mahoney, O.F.M.Cap.; Flavian Welstead, O.F.M.Cap.; Brian McKenna, O.F.M.Cap.; Michael James O'Shea, O.F.M.
Res.: 1721 Hillside Dr., 94010. Tel: 650-347-7768; Fax: 650-347-3550. Email: parishoffice@olaparish.org. Web: www.olaparish.org.
School—1328 Cabrillo Ave., 94010. Tel: 650-343-9200; Fax: 650-343-5260. Patricia Bordin, Co-Prin.; Judy O'Rourke, Co-Prin. Lay Teachers 19; Religious Teachers 1; Students 318.
Preschool—1341 Cortez Ave., 94010. Tel: 650-343-3115. Email: olapreschool@yahoo.com. Lysette Cukor, Dir.; Daniel Martin, Site Supvr. Lay Teachers 7; Students 76.
Catechesis/Religious Program—Tel: 650-347-3671. Ms. Johna Maychrowitz, D.R.E.; Teresita Santiago, Youth Min. & Dir. Confirmation. Tel: 650-343-5809. Students 470.
COLMA, SAN MATEO CO., HOLY ANGELS (1914) Revs. Manuel Curso; Manuel D. Igrobay Jr.; Deacons Lernito Prudenciado; Juan Ruiz.
Res.: 107 San Pedro Rd., 94014. Tel: 650-755-0478; Fax: 650-755-7653. Email: holyangels755@hotmail.com. Web: www.holyangelschurchcolma.com.
School—20 Reiner St., 94014. Tel: 650-755-0220; Fax: 650-755-0258. Email: holyangls@aol.com. Web: www.holyangelscolma.com. Sisters 6; Lay Teachers 20; Students 223.
Catechesis/Religious Program—Tel: 650-992-5539. Email: holyangelsccd@hotmail.com. Sr. Anita Torres, P.B.V.M., C.R.E. Students 262.
DALY CITY, SAN MATEO CO.
1—ST. ANDREW (1968), (Filipino), Revs. Alex L. Legaspi; Bonifacio G. Espeleta (Philippines).
Church: 1571 Southgate Ave., 94015. Tel: 650-756-3223; Fax: 650-756-0251.
Rectory—One Ridgefield Ave., 94015. Tel: 650-756-3222; Fax: 650-756-0251.
Catechesis/Religious Program—Tel: 650-991-2937. Michele Bussey, D.R.E. Students 208.
2—OUR LADY OF MERCY (Westlake) (1954) Revs. Domingo Orimaco; Teodoro P. Magpayo (Philippines); Deacon Michael J. Ghiorso. In Res., Rev. Joseph Palathingal, Chap.
Res.: One Elmwood Dr., 94015. Tel: 650-755-2727; Fax: 650-755-6704. Web: www.olmcath.org.
School—7 Elmwood Dr., 94015. Tel: 650-756-3395; Fax: 650-756-5872. Web: www.olmbulldogs.org. Kathleen M. Garcia, Prin.; Sr. Virgie Barcelona, R.V.M., Pastoral Assoc. Lay Teachers 23; Students 409.
Catechesis/Religious Program—Tel: 650-992-5769; Fax: 650-756-3457. Web: www.olmcath.org. Sr. Fe P. Bigwas, R.V.M., D.R.E. Students 175.
Convent—Religious of the Virgin Mary, Our Lady of Mercy, 15 Elmwood Dr., 94015. Tel: 650-992-5769; Fax: 650-756-3457. Email: bigwasfe@yahoo.com.
3—OUR LADY OF PERPETUAL HELP (1925) Revs. Augusto E. Villote; Dwight Dennis G. Barlaan; Deacon William Bruening.
Res.: 60 Wellington Ave., 94014. Tel: 650-755-9786;

Fax: 650-756-2268. Web: www.olphparishdc.org.
School—80 Wellington Ave., 94014. Tel: 650-755-4438; Fax: 650-755-7366. William Kovacich, Prin. Religious 1; Lay Teachers 8; Students 240.
Catechesis/Religious Program—Tel: 650-755-4010. Email: padre_ba@yahoo.com. Students 204.

EAST PALO ALTO, SAN MATEO CO., ST. FRANCIS OF ASSISI (1951) Rev. Lawrence C. Goode; Deacons Louis Dixon; Benjamin Koloamatangi. In Res., Rev. John R. Coleman (Retired).
Res.: 1425 Bay Rd., 94303. Tel: 650-322-2152; Fax: 650-322-7319. Email: sfofassisi@sbcglobal.net.
Catechesis/Religious Program—Tel: 650-325-6236; Fax: 650-322-7319. Students 520.

FAIRFAX, MARIN CO., ST. RITA (1930) Rev. Kenneth M. Weare; Deacon Peter Kehrlein.
Res.: 100 Marinda Dr., 94930. Tel: 415-456-4815; Fax: 415-456-3677. Email: saintritafairfax@att.net.
School—102 Marinda Dr., 94930. Tel: 415-456-1003; Fax: 415-456-7946. Web: www.strita.edu. Mrs. Carol Arritola, Prin. Lay Teachers 12; Students 174.
Catechesis/Religious Program—Email: mrsbennettstutor@gmail.com. Students 42.

FOSTER CITY, SAN MATEO CO., ST. LUKE (1970) Rev. Jonathan Paala; Deacons Mar Tano; Paul Lucia. 1111 Beach Park Blvd., 94404. Web: www.saintlukefc.org.
Res.: 1388 Halibut St., 94404. Tel: 650-345-6660; Fax: 650-345-8167. Web: www.saintlukefc.org.
Catechesis/Religious Program—Tel: 650-574-9191; Fax: 650-573-7409. Students 258.

GREENBRAE, MARIN CO., ST. SEBASTIAN (1951) Revs. Mark V. Taheny; Paul E. Perry; Deacon William Turrentine.
Res.: 373 Bon Air Rd., 94904. Tel: 415-461-0704; Fax: 415-461-2018.
Catechesis/Religious Program—Students 66.

HALF MOON BAY, SAN MATEO CO., OUR LADY OF THE PILLAR (1868) [CEM] Revs. Fernando Rogelio Velasco; Charles S. Fermeglia; Deacons John Sequeira, Parish Mgr.; John McGhee; Virgil Capetti. In Res, Rev. Charles Onubogu (Nigeria).
Res.: 400 Church St., 94019. Tel: 650-726-4674; Fax: 650-726-0980. Email: info@ourladyofthepillar.org. Web: www.ourladyofthepillar.org.
Catechesis/Religious Program—Tel: 650-726-5587. Students 900.
Mission—St. Anthony [CEM]
Mission—Our Lady of Refuge 146 Sears Ranch Rd., La Honda, San Mateo Co. 94060. Tel: 650-747-9555; Fax: 650-747-0419.

LAGUNITAS, MARIN CO., ST. CECILIA (1937) Rev. Cyril O'Sullivan.
Mailing Address: Box 289, 94938. Email: stcecilia.lagunitas@yahoo.com. Web: www.stcecilia-lagunitas.org.
Rectory—450 West Cintura Ave., 94938. Tel: 415-488-9799; Fax: 415-488-9809. Web: www.stcecilia-lagunitas.org.
Catechesis/Religious Program—Students 21.
Mission—St. Mary (1867) Town Square, Nicasio, Marin Co. 94946. Tel: 415-488-9799; Fax: 415-488-9809. Email: stmary.nicasio@yahoo.com. Web: stmary-nicasio.org.

LARKSPUR, MARIN CO., ST. PATRICK (1915) Rev. Lawrence Vadakkan (India).
Res.: 114 King St., 94939. Tel: 415-924-0600; Fax: 415-924-3617.
School—120 King St., 94939. Tel: 415-924-0501; Fax: 415-924-3544. Linda Kinkade, Prin. Lay Teachers 19; Students 229.
Catechesis/Religious Program—Tel: 415-924-3719. Students 168.

MENLO PARK, SAN MATEO CO.

1—ST. ANTHONY (1951) Revs. Fabio E. Medina; Nam J. Kim, S.S.; Alberto R. Cuevas.
Res.: 3500 Middlefield Rd., 94025. Tel: 650-366-4692; Fax: 650-366-4135. Email: saintanthonycatholicparish@live.com.
Catechesis/Religious Program—Tel: 650-365-6071. Asusena Chavez, D.R.E. Students 540.
Mission—San Jose Obrero 400 Heller St., Redwood City, San Mateo Co. 94063.

2—THE CHURCH OF THE NATIVITY (1877) Rev. Msgr. Steven D. Otellini; Rev. John Mary Chung; Deacon Dominick Peloso.
Res.: 210 Oak Grove Ave., 94025. Tel: 650-323-7914; Fax: 650-323-3231. Email: nativityparish@sbcglobal.net. Web: www.nativitymenlo.org.
School—1250 Laurel St., 94025. Tel: 650-325-7304; Fax: 650-325-3841. Email: info@nativityschool.com. Web: www.nativityschool.com. Lay Teachers 12; Students 270.
Catechesis/Religious Program—Tel: 650-327-2319. Mrs. Monica Hickam, D.R.E. Students 93.

3—ST. DENIS (1853; Restored 1961) Rev. Jose Shaji; Sr. Mary de Chantal, R.S.M., Pastoral Assoc. In Res., Rev. Msgrs. Jose A. Rodriguez (Retired); John F. Rodriguez (Retired).
Res.: 2250 Avy Ave., 94025. Tel: 650-854-5976; Fax: 650-854-3754. Web: www.stdenisparish.org.
Mission—Our Lady of the Wayside (1902) 930 Portola Rd., Portola Valley, San Mateo Co. 94028. Tel: 650-851-5085; Fax: 650-851-1019. In Res., Rev. Msgr. Jose A. Rodriguez (Retired).
Catechesis/Religious Program—Tel: 650-854-1081. Rosemary Lyon, D.R.E. Students 250.

4—ST. RAYMOND (1950) Revs. Edward S. Inyanwachi (Nigeria); Gregory P. Haake, C.S.C.
Office: 1100 Santa Cruz Ave., 94025. Tel: 650-323-1755; Fax: 650-561-3755.
Res.: 1231 Arbor Rd., 94025.
School—1211 Arbor Rd., 94025. Tel: 650-322-2312; Fax: 650-322-2910. Sr. Ann Bernard O'Shea, C.S.J., Prin. Sisters 6; Lay Teachers 17; Students 245.
Catechesis/Religious Program—Kristen Quinlan, D.R.E. Students 90.

MILL VALLEY, MARIN CO., OUR LADY OF MT. CARMEL (1910) Rev. Patrick T. Michaels; Mr. Michael L. Morison, Pastoral Assoc.
Res.: 3 Oakdale Ave., 94941. Tel: 415-388-4190; Fax: 415-388-4197. Email: officeolmc@gmail.com. Web: www.mountcarmelmv.org.
Catechesis/Religious Program—17 Buena Vista, 94941. Tel: 415-388-1008; Fax: 415-388-4297. Email: olmcmv@gmail.com. Students 160.

MILLBRAE, SAN MATEO CO., ST. DUNSTAN (1940) Revs. Diarmid Casey, C.S.Sp.; Joseph Glynn, C.S.Sp.; Patrick Donovan, C.S.Sp.
Res.: 1133 Broadway, 94030. Tel: 650-697-4730; 650-697-4736; Fax: 650-697-5203. Email: secretary@saintdunstanchurch.org. Web: www.saintdunstanchurch.org.
School—1150 Magnolia Ave., 94030. Tel: 650-697-8119; Fax: 650-697-9295. Bruce Colville, Prin. Lay Teachers 14; Students 279.
Catechesis/Religious Program—Tel: 650-697-7451. Sherre Leone, D.R.E. Students 137.

NOVATO, MARIN CO.

1—ST. ANTHONY OF PADUA (1968) Revs. Robert Kevin White; William H. Thornton; Deacons Joseph Brumbaugh; Joseph Borg; Kendric Vattuone, Youth Min. & Coord. Confirmation.
Res.: 1000 Cambridge St., 94947. Tel: 415-883-2177; Fax: 415-883-4049.
Catechesis/Religious Program—Tel: 415-883-9000. Email: religious-education@saint-anthonys.com. Judith Ann Ross, C.R.E. (Grades 1-6). Students 277.

2—OUR LADY OF LORETTO (1892) Rev. William H. McCain; Patrick Reeder; Sr. Jeanette Lombardi, O.S.U., Pastoral Assoc.
Res.: 1806 Novato Blvd., 94947. Tel: 415-897-2171; Fax: 415-897-8251. Email: erin@ollnovato.org. Web: www.ollnovato.org.
School—1811 Virginia Ave., 94945. Tel: 415-892-8621; Fax: 415-892-9631. Mrs. Annette Olinger, Prin. Lay Teachers 12; Students 229.
Catechesis/Religious Program—Tel: 415-897-6714. Amy Bjorklund Reeder, D.R.E.; Victoria Birnberg, D.R.E. Students 230.

OLEMA, MARIN CO., SACRED HEART (1867) [CEM] Rev. Honesto D. Gile.
Mailing Address: P.O. Box 70, 94950. Tel: 415-663-1139; Fax: 415-663-9660.
Res.: 10189 State Route # 1, 94950.
Catechesis/Religious Program—Students 48.
Mission—St. Mary Magdalene 16 Horseshoe Hill, Bolinas, Marin Co. 94924.

PACIFICA, SAN MATEO CO.

1—GOOD SHEPHERD (1951) Rev. Jesus G. Labor; Sr. Carol Fleitz, S.N.J.M., Pastoral Assoc.; Deacons Emmanual R. Santillan; Ben Salvan; James H. Haug.
Res.: 901 Oceana Blvd., 94044. Tel: 650-355-2593; Fax: 650-355-1832. Email: good.shepherd.pac@sbcglobal.net. Web: gschurchca.org.
School—909 Oceana Blvd., 94044. Tel: 650-359-4544; Fax: 650-359-4558. Email: goodsheppac@hotmail.com. Andreina Gualco, Prin. Lay Teachers 13; Students 205.
Catechesis/Religious Program—Tel: 650-355-4214; Fax: 650-355-1832. Email: gsrel@sbcglobal.net. Students 93.

2—ST. PETER (1956) Rev. Mark G. Mazza; Deacons Thomas Reardon; Peter Solan.
Res.: 700 Oddstad Blvd., 94044. Tel: 650-359-6313; Fax: 650-359-2262. Email: stpeterpacifica@comcast.net. Web: www.stpeterspacifica.org.
Catechesis/Religious Program—Tel: 650-359-5000. Mrs. Elizabeth Neopolitan, D.R.E. Students 185.

PORTOLA VALLEY, SAN MATEO CO., OUR LADY OF THE WAYSIDE (1941) See separate listing. See St. Denis, Menlo Park. Rev. Msgrs. Jose A. Rodriguez (Retired); John F. Rodriguez (Retired).

REDWOOD CITY, SAN MATEO CO.

1—ST. MATTHIAS (1961) Rev. Craig W. Forner; Deacon George A. Salinger.
Res.: 1685 Cordilleras Rd., 94062. Tel: 650-366-9544; Fax: 650-366-4817. Web: www.stmatthiasparish.org.
St. Matthias Preschool—533 Canyon Rd., 94062. Tel: 650-367-1320; Fax: 650-366-1049. Web: www.stmatthiasparish.org. Students 90.
Catechesis/Religious Program—Email: cff@stmatthiasparish.org. Students 160.

2—OUR LADY OF MOUNT CARMEL (1887) Revs. Ulysses L. D'Aquila; Peter Linyong Zhai, S.V.D., Parochial Vicar; Deacon Thomas J. Boyle.
Res.: 347 Grand St., 94062.
Parish Center—Mailing Address: 300 Fulton St., 94062. Tel: 650-366-3802; Fax: 650-366-1421. Email: parish@mountcarmel.org. Web: www.mountcarmel.org.
School—301 Grand St., 94062. Tel: 650-366-6127; Fax: 650-366-0902. Lay Teachers 16; Students 286.
Catechesis/Religious Program—Tel: 650-368-8237. Students 310.

3—ST. PIUS (1951) Revs. Paul J. Rossi; Wade E. Bjerke. In Res., Revs. Kevin Kennedy; Gerald D. Coleman, S.S.
Res.: 1100 Woodside Rd., 94061. Tel: 650-361-1411; Fax: 650-369-3641. Email: parish@pius.org. Web: www.pius.org.
School—Tel: 650-368-8327; Fax: 650-368-7031. Email: administration@stpiusschool.org. Web: stpiusschool.org. Rita Carroll, Prin. Lay Teachers 16; Students 295.
Catechesis/Religious Program—Fax: 650-369-3641. Web: www.pius.org. Maria Cornell, C.R.E. Students 146.

ROSS, MARIN CO., ST. ANSELM (1907) Revs. Cornelius J. Healy; Warlito F. Namo; Deacons Bernard O'Halloran; Edward Cunningham.
Mailing Address: P.O. Box 1061, 94957.
Res.: 97 Shady Ln. & Bolinas Ave., P.O. Box 1061, 94957-1061. Tel: 415-453-2342; Fax: 415-453-8713. Email: info@saintanselm.org. Web: www.saintanselm.org.
School—40 Belle Ave., San Anselmo, 94960. Tel: 415-454-8667; Fax: 415-454-4730. Email: stanselmsschool@comcast.net. Web: stanselmschool.com. Cheryl Giurlani, Prin. Lay Teachers 23; Students 270.
Catechesis/Religious Program—Tel: 415-453-2342. Tom Kavanaugh, D.R.E. Students 180.

SAN BRUNO, SAN MATEO CO.

1—ST. BRUNO (1912) Revs. Michael Brillantes; Rafael DeAvila; Deacons Ramon De La Rosa; Joseph Lavulo.
Res.: 555 San Bruno Ave. W., 94066. Tel: 650-588-2121; Fax: 650-588-6087. Web: saintbrunos.org.
Catechesis/Religious Program—Tel: 650-588-2121, Ext. 14. Kacey Carey, D.R.E. (Spanish). Students 370.

2—ST. ROBERT (1958) Revs. Roberto A. Andrey; Michael J. Konopik; Deacons Rusty Duffey; John Meyer. In Res., Rev. Vincent D. Ring (Retired).
Res.: 1380 Crystal Springs Rd., 94066. Tel: 650-589-2800; Fax: 650-588-9628. Web: www.saintroberts.org.
School—345 Oak Ave., 94066. Tel: 650-583-5065; Fax: 650-583-1418. Margo Wright, Prin. Lay Teachers 14; Students 316.
Catechesis/Religious Program—Tel: 650-588-0477. Students 335.

SAN CARLOS, SAN MATEO CO., ST. CHARLES (1928) Revs. David A. Ghiorso; Piers M. Lahey; Deacon Michael Murphy. In Res., Rev. Thomas D. Moran (Retired).
Res.: 880 Tamarack Ave., 94070. Tel: 650-591-7349; Fax: 650-637-1968. Email: parishoffice@stcharlesparish.org. Web: www.stcharlesparish.org.
School—850 Tamarack Ave., 94070. Tel: 650-593-1629; Fax: 650-593-9723. Email: stcharlesschoolsc@stcharlesschoolsc.org. Web: stcharlesschoolsc.org. Maureen Grazioli, Prin. Lay Teachers 16; Students 305.
Catechesis/Religious Program—Nancy Farrant, D.R.E. Students 400.

SAN MATEO, SAN MATEO CO.

1—ST. BARTHOLOMEW (1955) Revs. Michael J. Healy; Dominador F. Corrales (Philippines); Deacon John Sequeira. In. Res., Rev. Peter McDonald (Retired).
Res.: 300 Alameda de las Pulgas, 94402. Tel: 650-347-0701; Fax: 650-347-2429. Email: stbarts@barts.org. Web: www.barts.org.
Rectory—600 Columbia Dr., 94402.
Catechesis/Religious Program—Joanne Ferretti, D.R.E. Students 340.

2—ST. GREGORY (1941) Revs. Paul Arnoult; David A. Schunk; Deacons Fred Iskander; Stephen Fox. In Res., Rev. Msgr. Edward P. McTaggart (Retired); Rev. Joseph A. Bradley (Retired).
Res.: 2715 Hacienda St., 94403. Tel: 650-345-8506; Fax: 650-345-9329.
School—2701 Hacienda St., 94403. Tel: 650-573-0111; Fax: 650-573-6548. Mr. Tom Dooher, Prin. Lay Teachers 15; Students 322.

Catechesis/Religious Program—2715 Hacienda St., 94403. Tel: 650-574-8716. Students 413.

3—ST. MATTHEW (1863) Revs. Anthony E. McGuire; William J. Ahlbach; Juan M. Lopez; Dominic Savio Lee; Deacons James Shea; Rafeal Brown.
Res.: One Notre Dame Ave., 94402. Tel: 650-344-7622; Fax: 650-344-4830. Web: www.stmatthew-parish.org.
School—910 S. El Camino Real, 94402. Tel: 650-343-1373; Fax: 650-343-2046. Email: info@stmatthewcath.org. Web: www.stmatthew-cath.org. Mrs. Beverly Viotti, Prin. Lay Teachers 21; Students 605.
Catechesis/Religious Program—Students 411.

4—ST. TIMOTHY (1954) Revs. Francis Mark P. Garbo; Marlon M. Verduzco-Peregrino (Mexico); Sione Malakai Katoa (Tonga); Deacons Angel Aguilar; Nicolas Rodriguez; Faiva Po'oi.
Res.: 1515 Dolan Ave., 94401. Tel: 650-342-2468; Fax: 650-342-8156. Web: www.sttims.us.
School—Tel: 650-342-6567; Fax: 650-342-5913. Web: www.sttimothyschool.org. Ms. Monica Miller, Prin. Lay Teachers 17.
Catechesis/Religious Program—Tel: 650-579-0901; Fax: 650-342-8156. Students 250.

SAN RAFAEL, MARIN CO.

1—BLESSED SACRAMENT (1951) Closed. For sacramental records please contact St. Isabella, San Rafael.

2—ST. ISABELLA (Terra Linda) (1961) [CEM] Revs. V. Mark Reburiano; Alner Nambatac (Philippines); Deacons Jerry Friedman, (Retired); James Myers. Mailing Address: P.O. Box 6166, 94903. In Res., Rev. Feliciano Mofan.
Res.: One Trinity Way, 94903. Tel: 415-479-1560; Fax: 415-479-8303. Email: office@stisabellasparish.org. Web: www.stisabellasparish.org.
School—P.O. Box 6188, 94903. Tel: 415-479-3727; Fax: 415-479-9961. Email: akalayjian@stisabellaschool.org. Web: www.stisabellaschool.org. Ann Kalayjian, Prin. Lay Teachers 16; Students 246.
Catechesis/Religious Program—Email: mike@stisabellasparish.org. Web: www.stisabellasparish.org. Mike Mangini, D.R.E. Students 318.

3—ST. RAPHAEL (1817) Revs. John A. Balleza; Ngoan V. Phan; Santos Rodriguez; Deacon Eugene B. Smith.
Res.: 1104 Fifth Ave., 94901. Tel: 415-454-8141; Fax: 415-454-8193. Web: www.saintraphael.com.
School—1100 Fifth Ave., 94901. Tel: 415-454-4455; Fax: 415-454-5927. Lydia Collins, Prin. Lay Teachers 16; Students 150.
Catechesis/Religious Program—Tel: 415-459-7331; Fax: 415-454-8193. Students 350.
Mission—St. Sylvester 1115 Point San Pedro Rd., Marin Co. 94901.
Station—San Quentin State Prison San Quentin, NM. Tel: 415-456-8161.

4—ST. SYLVESTER (1961) Closed. For sacramental records please contact St. Raphael, San Rafael.

SAUSALITO, MARIN CO., ST. MARY STAR OF THE SEA (1881) Rev. Thomas M. Parenti. In Res., Revs. Robert P. Cipriano (Retired); Eugene F. Duggan, Pastor Emeritus (Retired).
Res.: 180 Harrison Ave., 94965. Tel: 415-332-1765; Fax: 415-332-4962. Email: starofthesea@starofthesea.us. Web: www.starofthesea.us.
Catechesis/Religious Program—Christine Reich, D.R.E. Elementary Students 15.

SOUTH SAN FRANCISCO, SAN MATEO CO.

1—ALL SOULS (1913) Revs. Agnel De Heredia; W. Paul O'Dell.
Res.: 315 Walnut Ave., 94080. Tel: 650-871-8944; Fax: 650-871-5806. Email: info@allsoulschurchssf.org. Web: www.allsoulschurchssf.org.
School—479 Miller Ave., 94080. Tel: 650-583-3562; Fax: 650-952-1167. Mr. Vincent Riener, Prin. Lay Teachers 14; Students 260.
Catechesis/Religious Program—Tel: 650-873-5356. Miguel Balboa, D.R.E. Students 371.

2—ST. AUGUSTINE (1970) Revs. Rene R. Ramoso; Luello N. Palacpac (Philippines); Deacons Frank Almeida; Robert Bertolani. In Res., Rev. Msgr. Juan Alarcon (Retired).
Res.: 3700 Callan Blvd., 94080. Tel: 650-873-2282; Fax: 650-873-1356. Email: staugustinessf@aol.com.
Catechesis/Religious Program—Tel: 650-873-2878. Email: staugustinessf@aol.com. Sr. Nona Barairo, S.F.C.C., D.R.E. Students 554.

3—MATER DOLOROSA (1961) Rev. Roland De la Rosa; Deacon Alex Aragon. In Res., Rev. Angel N. Quitalig (Philippines).
Res.: 307 Willow Ave., 94080. Tel: 650-583-4131; Fax: 650-616-9066. Email: frances@mdssf.org. Web: mdssf.org.
Catechesis/Religious Program—Tel: 650-588-8175. Email: rachael@mdssf.org. Rachael Smit, D.R.E. Students 115.

4—ST. VERONICA (1951) Revs. Charles Puthota; Linh Tien Nguyen; Deacons Roger Beaudry; Joseph LeBlanc. In Res., Rev. Joseph R. Walsh (Retired).
Res.: 434 Alida Way, 94080. Tel: 650-588-1455; Fax: 650-588-1481. Email: churchoffice@stveronicassf.com. Web: www.stveronicassf.com.
School—Tel: 650-589-3909; Fax: 650-589-2826. Kathryn Lucchesi, Prin. Lay Teachers 20; Students 303.
Catechesis/Religious Program—Email: reled@stveronicassf.com. Students 321.

TIBURON, MARIN CO., ST. HILARY (1951) Revs. William E. Brown; Matthew B. Link, C.PP.S.
Res.: 761 Hilary Dr., 94920-1498. Tel: 415-435-1122; Fax: 415-435-1862. Web: www.sthilary.org.
School—765 Hilary Dr., 94920. Tel: 415-435-2224; Fax: 415-435-5895. Web: www.sainthilaryschool.org. Mr. Charles Hayes, Prin. Lay Teachers 30; Students 250.
Catechesis/Religious Program—Tel: 415-435-1639. Lisa Veto, D.R.E. Students 117.

TOMALES, MARIN CO., CHURCH OF THE ASSUMPTION (1860) [CEM] Rev. Shouraiah Pudota (India).
Res. & Mailing: 26825 Shoreline Hwy., P.O. Box 82, 94971-0082. Tel: 707-878-2208; Fax: 707-878-9422. Email: coatomales@yahoo.com.
Catechesis/Religious Program—
Mission—St. Helen (1902) Marshall. P.O. Box 82, Marin Co. 94971-0082.

WOODSIDE, SAN MATEO CO., ST. MARCELLA MISSION, Closed. For sacramental records please contact St. Denis, Menlo Park.

Chaplains of Public Institutions

SAN FRANCISCO. *St. Anne's Home*. Rev. Martin R. Muruli, Chap.
St. Francis Hospital. Franciscans from St. Boniface Parish.
Kaiser Hospital San Francisco. Rev. Michael E. Kwiecien, O.Carm.
Knights of Malta. The Sovereign Military Order of Malta (Western U.S.A. Association of the Sovereign Military Hospitaller Order of St. John of Jerusalem of Rhodes and of Malta--a Nonprofit Corporation). Rev. Msgr. Steven D. Otellini, Rev. John P. Kavanaugh (Retired).
Laguna Honda Home. Rev. Te Van Nguyen, Sr. Elizabeth Johnson, f.d.C.C.
St. Mary's Medical Center. Revs. Michael A. Greenwell, O.Carm., Edward K. Murray.
San Francisco Fire Department. Rev. John L. Greene.
San Francisco General Hospital. Rev. Bruce J. Lery, S.M.
San Francisco Police Department. Rev. Michael J. Healy.
San Francisco State Univ., Newman Center. Rev. Msgr. Labib Kobti.
Serra Club of San Francisco (Downtown). Rev. David A. Ghiorso.
Serra Club of San Francisco (Golden Gate). Rev. Msgr. Edward P. McTaggart (Retired).
St. Thomas More Society. (Legal). Rev. Msgr. Labib Kobti.
Veterans' Hospital. Rev. Lawrence Gould, S.A.C., San Francisco.
Young Ladies' Institute. Rev. Thomas M. Hamilton, Grand. Chap.

DALY CITY. *Seton Hospital*. Revs. Rory E. Murphy, Joseph Palathingal.

MARIN. *Serra Club of Marin*. Rev. Ngoan V. Phan.

REDWOOD CITY. *Sequoia Hospital*. Rev. Kevin Kennedy, Chap.

SAN MATEO. *Serra Club of San Mateo*. Vacant.
Sheriff's Honor Camp and Medium Security Facility. Served by Archdiocese and St. Vincent de Paul volunteers, San Mateo District Council.

SAN QUENTIN. *California State Prison*, Tel: 415-454-1460. Rev. George T. Williams, S.J., Chap.

On Special Assignment:
Rev. Msgrs.—
Padazinski, C. Michael, J.C.D., Chancellor & Judicial Vicar
Tarantino, James T., Moderator of Curia & Vicar for Admin.
Very Revs.—
Agudo, Moises, Vicar for Spanish-Speaking
Tungol, Eugene, Vicar for Filipinos
Revs.—
Ghiorso, David A., Dir., Vocations, President, Marin Catholic High School, Kentfield & St. Vincent School for Boys, San Rafael
Hoang, Thuan V., J.C.L., Tribunal
Johnson, Andrew R., Office, Devel.
Quitalig, Angel N., J.C.L. (Philippines), Tribunal

On Duty Outside the Archdiocese:
Rev. Msgrs.—
Lopes, Steven J., S.T.L., Secretary to the Prefect of the Congregation for the Doctrine of Faith, Vatican
Piechota, Lech, Particular Secretary to Cardinal Bertone, Vatican
Revs.—
Escalante, Augustin, Laredo, TX
Fredericks, James L., Faculty, Loyola-Marymount Univ., Los Angeles
Hagan, James, Mexico
McElligott, Thomas J., St. Mary College, Moraga, Diocese of Oakland

---

Sabbatical:
Rev.—
Nguyen, Toan X., Catholic Theological Union

Absent on Leave:
Revs.—
Keohane, Daniel T.
Leach, Jerome
Myers, William
Trainor, Henry J. (Retired)
Walsh, Milton T.

Retired:
Most Rev.—
Quinn, John R., D.D.
Rev. Msgrs.—
Arcamo, Floro B.
Bitanga, Fred A.
Foudy, John T.
Holleran, J. Warren, S.T.D.
Keane, James P.
Knapp, Richard
McCormick, Maurice M.
McKay, James P.
McTaggart, Edward P.
O'Connor, John J.
O'Malley, James E.
Pernia, John R.
Rodriguez, John F., Madrid, Spain.
Rodriguez, Jose A.
Schlitt, Harry G.
Sullivan, Joseph P.
Revs.—
Aylward, James W.
Bain, Richard C.
Balagapo, Victorio R.
Bradley, Joseph A.
Bravo, Joseph
Brennan, Bernard F.
Burns, Thomas J.
Calegari, Leonard J.
Caverte, Rolando A.
Chang, Benedict
Chung, Anthony
Cipriano, Robert P.
Cloherty, John J.
Coleman, John K.
Conley, John P.
D'Angelo, Donald S.
Davenport, Clement A.
Davies, Steven E.
Decker, Raymond G.
Deitch, Richard S.
Duggan, Eugene F.
Filice, Francis P.
Finegan, Lawrence J.
Gaffey, Kevin P.
Glogowski, John F.
Gordon, Joseph A.
Greenlaw, Martin F.
Horan, Terence J.
Ingels, Gregory G.
Jocson, Salvador
Kavanaugh, John P.
Kaylor, Lee
Livingstone, James W.
MacDonald, James H.
Madden, J. Thomas
Maguire, Daniel J.
Marini, Joseph J.
McCormick, Kieran J.
McDonald, Peter
McDonnell, Donald C.
Moran, Thomas D.
Morris, James H.
Murray, Francis K.
Namocatcat, Felix S.
O'Connell, Joseph A.
O'Connell, William A.
O'Donnell, Hugh
O'Neill, John J.
O'Rourke, P. Gerard
Padilla, Aquino
Petilla, Antonio G.
Pettingill, David M.
Pham, Joseph Hung
Phelan, Edward
Piro, Frank R.
Quinn, William P.

Raimondi, Michele A.
Richard, Joseph E.
Riley, Miles O'Brien
Ring, John K.
Ring, Vincent D.
Rodriguez, Guillermo
Schipper, Carl A.
Seagrave, Thomas L.
Shipp, Edmund N.
Sigaran, Mamerto
Smith, Wilton S.
Thomas, George L.
Ullery, Kirk J.
Walsh, Joseph R.
Wang, Ignatius C., J.C.D.
Ward, John J.
Young, William W.
Zohlen, Ray

Permanent Deacons:
Abu-Alshaer, Khaled, St. Thomas More, San Francisco
Aguilar, Angel, St. Timothy, San Mateo
Allen, Charles, St. Teresa, San Francisco
Aragon, Alex, Mater Dolorosa, South San Francisco
Ayalin, Romeo P., Phoenix, AZ
Bacon, Nate, Guatemala
Beaudry, Roger, St. Veronica, South San Francisco
Bertolani, Bob, St. Augustine, San Francisco
Bettencourt, John, Palm Springs
Borg, Joe, (Retired), St. Anthony of Padua, Novato
Boulware, Peter I., St. Mary's Cathedral, San Francisco
Boyle, Tom, Our Lady of Mount Carmel, Redwood City
Bromberger, Brian, San Francisco
Brown, Rafeal, St. Matthew, San Mateo
Bruening, Bill, Our Lady of Perpetual Help, Daly City
Brumbaugh, Joe, St. Anthony of Padua, Novato
Buenavista, Tom, Pensicola
Cancilla, Charles, American Canyon, CA
Capetti, Virgil, Our Lady of the Pillar, Half Moon Bay
Carpenter, John W., New Orleans, LA
Cervantes, Vicente, Mission Dolores Basilica, San Francisco
Chatmon, Larry, St. Paul of the Shipwreck, San Francisco
Cunningham, Ed, St. Anselm, San Anselmo
Curran, Michael, St. Dominic, San Francisco
DeLaRosa, Ramon, St. Bruno, San Bruno
Dixon, Louis, St. Francis of Assisi, East Palo Alto
Doherty, Michael, Holy Name of Jesus, San Francisco
Duffey, Rusty, St. Robert, San Bruno
Dupre, John, St. Anne, San Francisco
Enos, Richard, Yreka
Foley, Richard, Diaconate Formation Office; St. Matthias
Fox, Stephen, St. Gregory, San Mateo
Friedman, Jerome, Nazareth House, San Rafael
Gamarra, David, St. Peter, San Francisco
Garcia, Julio, Nicaragua
Ghiorso, Michael J., Our Lady of Mercy, Daly City
Grant, Richard, Tulsa, OK
Hackett, Steven, Immaculate Heart of Mary, Belmont
Hall, J. Bruce, Tiburon
Haug, James H., Church of the Good Shepherd, Pacifica
Iskander, Fred, St. Gregory, San Mateo
Jacquemet, Hank, Immaculate Heart of Mary, Belmont
Kahn, Bob, Albany, OR
Kehrlein, Peter, St. Rita, Fairfax
Koloamatangi, Benjamin, St. Francis of Assisi Church, East Palo Alto
Kortenkamp, Leon, Diaconate Office
Lavulo, Joe, St. Bruno, San Bruno
LeBlanc, Joe, St. Veronica, South San Francisco
Lucia, Paul, St. Luke, Foster City
McGhee, John, Our Lady of Pillar, Half Moon Bay; Our Lady of Refuge, La Honda; St. Anthony Mission, Pescadero
McNeil, Chuck, St. Dominic, San Francisco
Meyer, John, St. Robert, San Bruno
Michaelson, Steven, Paso Robles, CA
Mitchell, William, (Retired), Our Lady of Loretto, Novato
Murphy, Michael, St. Charles, San Carlos
Myers, Jim, St. Isabella, San Rafael
O'Halloran, Bernard, St. Anselm, San Anselmo
Ocon, Manuel, Sacramento
Pagacz, Kyrril Bruce, Our Lady of Fatima Byzantine Catholic Church, San Francisco
Paulino, Antonio, St. Anthony of Padua, San Francisco
Pelimiano, Pete, Diaconate Office
Peloso, Dominick, Nativity, Menlo Park
Po'oi, Faiva, St. Timothy, San Mateo
Prudenciado, Lernito, Holy Angels, Colma
Reardon, Thomas, St. Peter, Pacifica
Rittenhouse, John H., (On Leave)
Rodriguez, Nicolas, St. Timothy, San Mateo
Rosen, Dan, St. Stephen, San Francisco
Ruiz, Juan, Holy Angels, Colma
Salinger, George A., St. Matthias, Redwood City
Salvan, Benjamin, Church of the Good Shepherd, Pacifica
Sandoval, R. Christoph, St. Mary's Cathedral, San Francisco
Santillan, Noel, Church of the Good Shepherd, Pacifica
Sequeira, John, St. Bartholomew, San Mateo; Our Lady of the Pillar, Half Moon Bay
Sevilla, Wilfredo, Corpus Christi, San Francisco
Shea, James, St. Matthew, San Matteo
Simon, Tsui, Holy Family, San Francisco
Smith, Eugene B., St. Raphael, San Raphael
Solan, Peter, St. Peter, Pacifica
Solano, Jose, St. Paul, San Francisco
Sondergaard, Gerald, Albuquerque
Swanson, Fred, St. Dominic, San Francisco
Tano, Mar, St. Luke, Foster City
Turrentine, Bill, St. Sebastian, Kentfield
Twitty, Roy, St. Catherine of Sienna, Burlingame
Viray, Ding, Epiphany, San Francisco
West, Gary, St. Stephen, San Francisco
Young, Mike, Sacramento
Zamora, Ramon, Epiphany, San Francisco

INSTITUTIONS LOCATED IN THE ARCHDIOCESE

[A] SEMINARIES, ARCHDIOCESAN

MENLO PARK. *St. Patrick Seminary and University* (1898) Major Seminary of the Archdiocese of San Francisco, under the direction of the Society of St. Sulpice., 320 Middlefield Rd., 94025. Tel: 650-325-5621; 650-321-5655 (Library); Fax: 650-322-0997. Email: info@stpatricksseminary.org. Web: www.stpatricksseminary.org. Most Rev. George H. Niederauer, D.D., Ph.D., Chancellor.

(1891, 1944): The Roman Catholic Seminary of San Francisco Priests 16; Religious 2; Lay Teachers 13; Students 104.

Officers of the Administration: Revs. James L. McKearney, S.S., S.T.D., Vice Chancellor, Pres, & Rector; Gladstone H. Stevens, S.S., S.T.L., Ph.D., Vice Rector & Academic Dean; Vincent D. Bui, S.S., J.C.L., Dean of Students.

Resident Faculty: Revs. Michael J. Miller; Frederick J. Cwiekowski, S.S., S.T.D., Prof. Emeritus; Eugene J. Konkel, S.S., S.T.L.; John S. Kselman, S.S., Ph.D., Assoc. Prof.; James L. McKearney, S.S., S.T.D., Pres., Rector & Vice Chancellor; Jaime E. Robledo; Jose Antonio Rubio, S.T.D., Asst. Prof./Dir. Liturgy; George E. Schultze, S.J., Ph.D., Asst. Prof.; Gladstone H. Stevens, S.S., S.T.L., Ph.D., Vice Rector/Academic Dean; Noel de Lira, Instructor; Paul A. Maillet, S.S., M.Div., Asst. Prof.; Christy Arockiaraj, Instructor.

Non-Resident Faculty and Staff: Dr. Charles W. James, S.T.D., Assoc. Prof.; Revs. Andrews Amir, M.A., Ph.D., Assoc. Prof. & Dir. Spiritual Life Prog.; Howard P. Bleichner, Assoc. Prof.; Mrs. Nuria Ortiz, Registrar & Asst. to Academic Dean & to Vice Rector & Instructor; Sr. Armanda Santos, F.S.P.; Ms. Jennifer Morris, Dir. Business Finance; Dr. Michael Neri, Ph.D., Prof. (On Sabbatical); Dr. Ruth Ohm, Asst.Prof. Sacred Scripture; Dr. Margaret M. Turek, S.T.D., Assoc. Prof.; Mr. Barry Del Buono, Dir. Devel.; Ms. Anne Grycz, Co-Dir. Pastoral Year; Ms. Lauren John, Librarian; Mrs. Monica Haupt, Language Instructor; Ms. Rebecca Linquist, Instructor ESL.

Vatican II Institute for Clergy Formation (1972) 320 Middlefield Rd., 94025. Tel: 650-325-9122; Fax: 650-325-6765. Web: www.stpatrickseminary.org. Rev. James E. Myers, S.S., M.Div., Dir.

St. Joseph's-St. Patrick's College Alumni Association, St. Patrick's Seminary, 320 Middlefield Rd., 94025. Tel: 650-591-3492; Fax: 650-654-3503. Email: murpur@aol.com. Web: www.saintjosephscollege.ws. Mr. James P. Murphy, Contact.

[B] SEMINARIES, RELIGIOUS OR SCHOLASTICATES

SAN FRANCISCO. *Capuchin Franciscan Order San Buenaventura Friary*, 750 Anza St., 94118. Tel: 415-387-7005; Fax: 415-831-5902. Revs. Christopher Kearney, O.F.M.Cap., Archivist; Martin Haggins, O.F.M.Cap, Hospital Chap.; Quoc Nguyen, O.F.M.Cap., Hospital Chap.; Alan Wilson, O.F.M.Cap, Hospital Chap. & Guardian; Very Rev. Gregory Coiro, O.F.M.Cap., Rector, The National Shrine of St. Francis Assisi; Bro. Mark Ortega, O.F.M.Cap., (Retired). Priests 5; Brothers 1.

[C] COLLEGES AND UNIVERSITIES

SAN FRANCISCO. **University of San Francisco* Established 1855; Chartered by State, 1859., 2130 Fulton St., 94117-1080. Tel: 415-422-5555; Fax: 415-422-2303. Web: www.usfca.edu. Rev. Stephen A. Privett, S.J., Pres.; Dr. Jennifer E. Turpin, Provost & Academic Vice Pres.; Rev. John Lo Schiavo, S.J., Chancellor; George B. Alterbary, Interim Vice Pres., Dev.; Mr. Charles E. Cross, Vice Pres., Business & Finance; Mr. David F. Macmillan, Vice Pres., Communications; Dr. Peter Novak, Vice Provost Student Devel.; Mr. Jeffrey S. Brand, Dean, School of Law; Dr. Walter H. Gmelch, Dean, School of Educ.; Mr. Tyrone H. Cannon, Dean, University Library; Dr. Elizabeth J. Johnson, Vice Provost & Dean Academic & Enrollment Svcs.; Dr. Judith F. Karshmer, Dean, School of Nursing; Dr. Marcelo Camperi, Dean, College of Arts & Sciences; Dr. Michael J. Webber, Interim Dean, School of Mgmt. Jesuit Fathers. Priests 7; Sisters 1; Lay Faculty 386; Students 9,585.

BELMONT. *Notre Dame de Namur University* (1851) 1500 Ralston Ave., 94002. Tel: 650-508-3500; Fax: 650-508-3660. Email: cchu@ndnu.edu. Web: www.ndnu.edu. Dr. Judith Maxwell Greig, Pres.; Dr. Diana Demetrulias, Provost; Ruth Briesemeister, Librarian. Sisters of Notre Dame de Namur. Sisters 2; Lay Faculty 196; Students 1,967.

SAN RAFAEL. *Dominican University of California*, 50 Acacia Ave., 94901-2298. Tel: 415-457-4440; Fax: 415-485-3205. Email: enroll@dominican.edu. Web: www.dominican.edu. Dr. Mary R. Marcy, Pres.; Dr. Luis Calingo, Exec. Vice Pres./Chief Academic Officer; Rev. Robert Haberman, Dir., Campus Ministry; Alan Schut, Dir. Cataloging & Collections; Gary Gorka, Exec. Dir. Library. Resident and non-resident students. Priests 1; Sisters 5; Lay Teachers 425; Students 2,230.

[D] HIGH SCHOOLS, ARCHDIOCESAN

SAN FRANCISCO. *Archbishop Riordan High School (Boys)* (1949) 175 Phelan Ave., 94112. Tel: 415-586-8200, Ext. 216; Fax: 415-587-1310. Email: rkovacich@riordanhs.org. Web: www.riordanhs.org. Patrick Daly, Pres.; Kevin Asbra, Prin. Sisters 1; Lay Teachers 42; Students 573.

Sacred Heart Cathedral Preparatory (Coed) (1852) 1055 Ellis St., 94109. Tel: 415-775-6626; Fax: 415-931-6941. Email: margaret.baptista@shcp.edu. Web: shcp.edu. John Scudder, M.A., Pres.; Gary Cannon, M.Div., Prin.; Judy Scudder, Librarian. Sponsored by Daughters of Charity and Christian Brothers. Brothers 3; Sisters 2; Lay Teachers 107; Students 1,257.

KENTFIELD. *Marin Catholic College Preparatory (Coed)*, 675 Sir Francis Drake Blvd., 94904. Tel: 415-464-3800; Fax: 415-461-7161. Web: www.marincatholic.org. Email: tnavone@marincatholic.org. Tim Navone, Pres.; Mr. Chris Valdez, Prin.; Rev. Msgr. Robert T. Sheeran, S.T.D., Dir., Mission & Ministry; Mrs. Carol Teller, Librarian & Media Specialist. Priests 1; Sisters 3; Lay Teachers 62; Students 714.

SAN MATEO. *Junipero Serra High School (Boys)*, 451 W. 20th Ave., 94403-1385. Tel: 650-345-8207; Fax: 650-573-6638. Email: padres@serrahs.com. Web: www.serrahs.com. Mr. Lars Lund, Pres.; Mr. Barry Thornton, Prin.; Rev. Joseph A. Bradley, Chap. (Retired); Susan Cordes, Librarian. Lay Teachers 65; Students 1,000.

[E] HIGH SCHOOLS, PRIVATE

SAN FRANCISCO. *St. Ignatius College Preparatory (Coed)*, 2001 37th Ave., 94116-1165. Tel: 415-731-7500; Fax: 415-682-5081. Email: info@siprep.org. Web: www.siprep.org. Rev. Robert T. Walsh, S.J., Pres.; Mr. Patrick Ruff, Prin.; Revs. Anthony P. Sauer, S.J.; Thomas Allender, S.J., (In Residence); Michael J. Kotlanger, S.J.; Thomas H. O'Neill, S.J.; James V. Schaukowitch, S.J.; Donald B. Sharp, S.J., S.T.D. (Retired), (In Residence); A. Francis Stiegeler, S.J.; Bros. Douglas E. Draper, S.J.; Arthur W. Lee, S.J.; John E. Maloney, S.J., (In Residence); Andrew Q. Nguyen, S.J.; Michelle Levine, Dean Students; William Gotch, Dean Students; Nnekay FitzClarke. Priests 5; Seminarians 2; Brothers 2; Lay Teachers 106; Students 1,446.

Immaculate Conception Academy, (Girls) (1883) 3625 24th St., 94110. Tel: 415-824-2052; Fax: 415-821-4677. Email: ica@icacademy.org. Web: www.icacademy.org. Sr. Diane Aruda, O.P., Pres.;

Lisa Graham, Prin. Sisters 4; Lay Teachers 24; Students 243.

Mercy High School (Girls) (1952) 3250 19th Ave., 94132. Tel: 415-334-0525; Fax: 415-334-9726. Email: dmccrea@mercyhs.org. Web: www.mercyhs.org. Dorothy McCrea, Ed.D., Prin.; Rev. Gregory McGivern (Ireland), Chap.; Nancy Schaal, Librarian. Priests 1; Sisters 2; Lay Teachers 31; Students 442.

Schools of the Sacred Heart, Convent of the Sacred Heart High School (Girls) (1887) 2222 Broadway, 94115. Tel: 415-563-2900; Fax: 415-929-0553. Email: heart@sacredsf.org. Web: www.sacredsf.org. Gordon Sharafinski, Dir.; Andrea Shurley, Head; Cynthia Velante, Librarian. Lay Teachers 28; Students 181.

Schools of the Sacred Heart, Stuart Hall High School (2000) (Boys), 1715 Octavia St., 94109. Tel: 415-345-5811; Fax: 415-931-9161. Email: donna.morgan@sacredsf.org. Web: www.sacredsf.org. Gordon Sharafinski, Dir.; Friar Anthony Farrell, Head; Amanda Walker, Librarian. Lay Teachers 22; Students 147.

ATHERTON. *Sacred Heart Schools, Atherton dba Sacred Heart Schools, Preparatory* (1898) 150 Valparaiso, 94027. Tel: 650-322-1866; Fax: 650-327-7011. Web: www.shschools.org. Mr. Richard Dioli, Dir. Schools; Dr. James Everitt, Prin.; Bettie Bohler, Librarian. Religious of the Sacred Heart. Lay Teachers 75; Students 577.

BELMONT. *Notre Dame High School (Girls)*, 1540 Ralston Ave., 94002. Tel: 650-595-1913; Fax: 650-595-2116. Email: rgleason@ndhsb.org. Web: www.ndhsb.org. Ms. Rita Gleason, Prin.; Rev. Stephen H. Howell; Claudia Sarconi, Librarian. Priests 1; Sisters 1; Lay Teachers 45; Students 450.

BURLINGAME. *Mercy High School (Girls)*, 2750 Adeline Dr., 94010-5597. Tel: 650-343-3631; Fax: 650-343-2316. Web: www.mercyhsb.com. Laura M. Held, Pres.; Lisa Tortorich, M.A., Prin. Lay Teachers 42; Students 482.

PORTOLA VALLEY. *Woodside Priory School* (Coed, Boarding)., 302 Portola Rd., 94028. Tel: 650-851-8221; Fax: 650-851-2839. Email: mmager@ prioryca.org. Web: www.prioryca.org. Mr. Tim Molak, Head of School; Peter Reinhardt, Librarian.

Benedictine Fathers of the Priory, Inc. Priests 1; Brothers 1; Lay Teachers 52; Students 350.

SAN ANSELMO. *San Domenico School*, (Grades PreK-12) Mrs. Alyce Brownridge, High School Div. Head; Mrs. Carole Chase, Primary School Div. Head; Mrs. Cecily Stock, Middle School Div. Head; Mr. Scott Fletcher, Librarian. (Grades PreK-8, Coed; Grades 9-12, Girls. Boarding and Day Students.); See separate listing under Elementary Schools, Private in the Institution section. Full-time 66.

[F] ELEMENTARY SCHOOLS, ARCHDIOCESAN

SAN FRANCISCO. *St. Brigid Elementary School* (1888) (Grades K-8), 2250 Franklin St., 94109. Tel: 415-673-4523; Fax: 415-674-4187. Email: office@ saintbrigidsf.org. Web: www.saintbrigidsf.org. Sr. Angeles Marin, Prin. Sisters 3; Lay Teachers 15; Students 260.

St. Thomas More School (1954) (Grades PreSchool-8), 50 Thomas More Way, 94132. Tel: 415-337-0100; Fax: 415-333-2564. Email: office@ stthomasmoreschool.org. Web: www.stthomasmoreschool.org. Marie Fitzpatrick, Prin.; Patricia Pinnick, Librarian. Lay Teachers 17; Students 296; Preschool 36.

[G] ELEMENTARY SCHOOLS, PRIVATE

SAN FRANCISCO. *DeMarillac Academy of San Francisco*, 175 Golden Gate Ave., 94102. Tel: 415-552-5220; Fax: 415-520-6969. Email: mike_daniels@demarillac.org. Web: www.demarillac.org. Michael Daniels, Pres. & CEO; Susan Smith, Prin.; Alicia Tapia, Librarian. Co-sponsored by Daughters of Charity and De La Salle Christian Brothers. Lay Teachers 10; Students 118.

Mission Dolores Academy, 3371 16th St., 94114. Tel: 415-346-9500; Fax: 415-346-8001. Email: nicolem@mdasf.org. Robert LaLanne, Chair, Bd. Regents; Nicole McAuliffe, Dir., Advancement; Dan Stovz, Librarian. Sisters 2; Lay Teachers 12.

Schools of the Sacred Heart, Convent of the Sacred Heart Elementary School (1887) (Grades K-8), (Girls), 2222 Broadway St., 94115. Tel: 415-563-2900; Fax: 415-563-0438. Email: heart@ sacredsf.org. Web: www.sacredsf.org. Gordon Sharafinski, Dir.; Sr. Anne Wachter, R.S.C.J., Head; Tevis Jones, Librarian. Sisters 1; Lay Teachers 45; Students 350.

Schools of the Sacred Heart, Stuart Hall For Boys, (Grades K-8), (Boys), 2222 Broadway St., 94115. Tel: 415-563-2900; Fax: 415-292-3165. Email: heart@sacredsf.org. Web: www.sacredsf.org. Gordon Sharafinski, Dir.; Jaime Dominguez, Headmaster; Tevis Jones, Librarian. Schools of the Sacred Heart. Lay Teachers 46; Students 338.

ATHERTON. *Sacred Heart Schools, Atherton dba Sacred Heart Schools Pre-K thru Middle School* (1906) (Grades PreK-8), (St. Joseph's School, Lower and Middle), 150 Valparaiso, 94027. Tel: 650-322-9931; Fax: 650-322-7656. Web: www.shschools.org. Mr. Richard Dioli, Dir. Schools; Mrs. Cee Salberg, Prin. (Grades PreK-K); Bridget Collins, Prin. (Grades 1-8); Joan Eagleson, Librarian. Lay Teachers 77; Students 523.

BELMONT. *Notre Dame Elementary School*, 1200 Notre Dame Ave., 94002. Tel: 650-591-2209; Fax: 650-591-4798. Email: dgreggans@NDE.org. Web: NDE.org. Dr. J. Traynor, Prin.; Sr. Catherine Davis, Librarian. Sisters 3; Lay Teachers 13; Students 206.

SAN ANSELMO. *San Domenico School*, (Grades PreK-12), (Grades PreK-8, Coed; Grades 9-12, Girls; Boarding & Day Students), 1500 Butterfield Rd., 94960-1099. Tel: 415-258-1900; Fax: 415-258-1901. Email: dbehrs@sandomenico.org. Web: www.sandomenico.org. David G. Behrs, Ph.D., Head of School; Mrs. Cecily Stock, Asst. Head of School & Middle School Div. Head (Grades 6-8); Carole Chase, Primary School Div. Head (Grades PreK-5); Mrs. Alyce Brownridge, High School Div. Head (Grades 9-12); Mr. Scott Fletcher, Librarian. Lay Teachers 54; Students 573.

[H] ST. VINCENT DE PAUL SOCIETY

SAN MATEO. **The Society of St. Vincent de Paul, Particular Council of San Mateo County, Inc.* (1931) Main Office, St. Vincent de Paul Society., 50 N. B St., 94401-3917. Tel: 650-373-0622; Fax: 650-343-9495. Email: lmmoriarty@svdp-sanmateoco.org. Web: www.svdp-sanmateoco.org. Lawrence Nejasmich, Pres.; Lorraine Moriarty, Exec. Dir. Total Assisted 41,600; Meals Served 100,000.

Thrift Stores:

40 North B St., 94401. Tel: 650-347-5101; Fax: 650-244-0543.

344 Grand Ave., South San Francisco, 94080. Tel: 650-589-8445; Fax: 650-244-0543. 1600 El Camino Real, San Bruno, 94066.

6256 Mision St., Daly City, 94014. Tel: 650-992-9271; Fax: 650-244-0543.

2406 El Camino Real, Redwood City, 94063. Tel: 650-366-6367; Fax: 650-244-0543.

Donation Pickups:

San Mateo County, San Francisco County, Santa Clara County Tel: 650-871-6844; Fax: 650-244-0543.

SVdP's Catherine's Center, 50 N. "B" St., 94401. Tel: 650-246-1520; Fax: 650-343-9495. Safe, supportive housing program for women previously incarcerated.

Vehicle Donation Program Tel: 800-937-7837; Fax: 415-977-1070. Web: www.yes-svdp.org.

SVdP's Restorative Justice Ministry, 50 N. B St., 94401. Tel: 650-366-9847; Fax: 650-343-9495.

SVdP's Peninsula Family Resource Center (PFRC) Tel: 650-343-4403 Helpline Number; Fax: 650-343-9495.

SVdP's San Mateo Homeless Help Center, 50 N. B St., 94401. Tel: 650-343-9251; Fax: 650-343-9495 Mon.-Fri. 10am-12noon.

SVdP's North County Homeless Help Center, 344 Grand Ave., South San Francisco, 94080. Tel: 650-589-9039; Fax: 650-244-0543 Mon.-Fri.: 10a.m.-noon; Sat.: 10-11a.m..

SVdP's South County Homeless Help Center, 2600 Middlefield Rd., Redwood City, 94063. Tel: 650-343-4403 Mon.-Fri. 1pm-2pm.

SVdP's Youth-Service Learning Opportunities Tel: 650-589-9039; Fax: 650-244-0543.

SAN RAFAEL. **St. Vincent de Paul Society Marin County District Council* (1946) 820 B St., P.O. Box 150527, 94915. Tel: 415-454-3303; Fax: 415-454-3406. Email: svdpmarin@vinnies.org. Web: vinnies.org. Susan Daniloff, Pres.; Steven R. Boyer, Exec. Dir. Staff 15; Total Assisted 9,000; Meals Served 2,000,000.

Affordable Housing (1992) 822 B St., 94901. Tel: 415-454-3303; Fax: 415-454-3406.

Free Dining Room (1981) 820 B St., 94901. Tel: 415-454-0366; Fax: 415-454-3406.

Emergency Help Desk (1992) 822 B. St., 94915. Tel: 415-454-3303; Fax: 415-454-3406.

Thrift Store Pickups Tel: 800-584-1579.

Vehicle Donations Tel: 415-258-5226.

Vehicle Sales & Distribution Tel: 415-258-5226.

[I] DAY NURSERIES

SAN FRANCISCO. *Holy Family Day Home* (1900) 299 Dolores St., 94103. Tel: 415-861-5361; Fax: 415-703-0125. Email: admin@holyfamilydayhome.org. Web: www.holyfamilydayhome.org. Donna M. Cahill, Exec. Dir.

Holy Family Day Homes of San Francisco Religious 1; Lay Staff 50; Capacity 150.

[J] GENERAL HOSPITALS

SAN FRANCISCO. *St. Mary's Medical Center*, 450 Stanyan St., 94117. Tel: 415-668-1000; Fax: 415-750-4893. Web: www.stmarysmedicalcenter.org. Anna Cheung, Pres.; Revs. Edward K. Murray, Chap.; Michael A. Greenwell, O.Carm. Sponsored by Sisters of Mercy of the Americas West Midwest Community. Sisters 9; Bed Capacity 403; Total Staff 1,192; Patients Assisted Annually 139,471.

St. Mary's Medical Center Foundation, 450 Stanyan St., 94117-1079. Tel: 415-750-5790; Fax: 415-750-8132. Web: www.stmarysmedicalcenter.org. Margine Sako, Exec. Dir.

DALY CITY. *Seton Medical Center*, 1900 Sullivan Ave., 94015-2229. Tel: 650-992-4000; Fax: 650-991-6024. Web: www.setonmedicalcenter.org. Lorraine P. Auerbach, Pres. & CEO; Revs. Rory E. Murphy, Dir. Spiritual Care; Joseph Palathingal. Daughters of Charity of St. Vincent de Paul Province of the West., Member of Daughters of Charity Health System. Daughters of Charity 1; Bed Capacity 357; Total Staff 1,080; Patients Assisted Annually 203,000.

Seton Medical Center Foundation Tel: 650-991-6464; Fax: 650-991-6098. Web: www.setonfoundation-.org.

San Francisco Heart Institute Tel: 650-991-6712; Fax: 650-755-7315. Web: www.sfhi.com. Colman Ryan, M.D., Exec. Dir.

MOSS BEACH. *Seton Medical Center Coastside*, 600 Marine Blvd., 94038. Tel: 650-563-7100; Fax: 650-563-7129. Web: www.setonmedicalcenter.org. Lorraine P. Auerbach, Interim Pres. & CEO; Judy Cook, R.N., B.S.N., M.P.A., C.P.H.Q., Admin. Dir. Daughters of Charity of St. Vincent de Paul, Province of the West., Member of Daughters of Charity Health System. Religious 1; Patients Assisted Daily 116; Total Staff 163; Bed Capacity: Skilled Nursing 116.

[K] SENIOR CITIZEN RESIDENCES

SAN FRANCISCO. *Alexis Apartments of St. Patrick's Parish* (1973) 390 Clementina St., 94103-4138. Tel: 415-495-3690; Fax: 415-495-3629. Email: alexis@sco.net.

756 Mission St., 94103. Tel: 415-421-3730; Fax: 415-512-9730. Tessa Reed, Property Mgr. Residents 258.

Home for the Aged of the Little Sisters of the Poor, St. Anne's Home, 300 Lake St., 94118. Tel: 415-751-6510; Fax: 415-751-1423. Email: mslspsf@ hotmail.com. Sr. Margaret Lennon, L.S.P., Supr.; Rev. Martin R. Muruli, Chap. Religious 10; Residents 87. In Res. Revs. Heribert Duquet, M.E.P. (Retired); Thomas Hayes, O.P. (Retired).

Madonna Senior Center and Residence, 350 Golden Gate Ave., 94102. Tel: 415-592-2864; Fax: 415-928-5867. Email: ckoger@stanthonysf.org. Web: www.stanthonysf.org. Cathy Koger, Mgr. Nonprofit residence for women over 60 of low income. Total in Residence 51; Bed Capacity 51; Total Assisted Annually 56; Total Staff 13.

Mercy Housing California Holding Company (1982) 333 Baker St., 94117. Tel: 415-931-2325; Fax: 415-931-7206. Email: larmstrong@mercyhousing.org. Web: www.mercyhousing.org. The purpose of this corporation is to develop, construct, own, and operate housing for low and very low income seniors. Units 159; Bed Capacity 159; Total Assisted Annually 300; Staff 5.

SAN RAFAEL. *Nazareth House of San Rafael, Inc.*, 245 Nova Albion Way, 94903. Tel: 415-479-8282; Fax: 415-479-3878. Email: alice@nazarethhousesr.com. Web: www.sistersofnazareth.com. Sr. Catherine Rea, C.S.N., Supr.; Rev. Msgr. Joseph P. Sullivan, Chap. (Retired). Sisters of Nazareth 8; Bed Capacity 146; Residents 135; Total Staff 82. In Res. Rev. Msgrs. Richard Knapp (Retired); James E. O'Malley (Retired); Revs. Bernard F. Brennan (Retired); Francis P. Filice (Retired); Joseph A. O'Connell (Retired); Hugh O'Donnell (Retired); Wilton S. Smith (Retired).

[L] RESIDENTIAL GROUP HOMES

SAN FRANCISCO. *The Good Shepherd Gracenter* (1986) 1310 Bacon St., 94134. Tel: 415-337-1938; Fax: 415-586-0355. Email: inquiry@gsgracenter.org. Web: www.gsgracenter.org. Residential. Sisters 2; Lay Staff 9; Residence Capacity 12; Total Assisted 34.

Mount St. Joseph-St. Elizabeth (1976) 100 Masonic Ave., 94118. Tel: 415-567-8370; Fax: 415-292-5531. Email: sisterestela@msjse.org. Web: www.msjse.org. Sr. Estela Morales, D.C., Exec. Dir. Successor Corporation to Mount St. Joseph

Home for Girls and St. Elizabeth Infant Hospital. DBA: Epiphany Center Sisters 2; Lay Staff 48; Total Assisted 250.

Epiphany Center for Families in Recovery Tel: 415-567-8370; Fax: 415-346-2356. 1. Comprehensive residential drug treatment with parenting, life skills, and health education groups.; 2. Epiphany In-Home Services for Families at Risk. Families Served 76; Families Served by In-Home Services 113; Individuals Assisted 250.

[M] RETREAT HOUSES

BURLINGAME. *Sisters of Mercy of the Americas West Midwest Community, Inc. Mercy Retreat and Conference Center of Burlingame*, 2300 Adeline Dr., 94010. Tel: 650-340-7474; Fax: 650-340-1299. Web: mercy-center.org; mercywmw.org. Suzanne M. Buckley, Dir.; Constance Quirk, Reservations. Overnight Capacity 90; Daytime Capacity 300; Staff 12.

MENLO PARK. *Vallombrosa Center* (1946) 250 Oak Grove Ave., 94025. Tel: 650-325-5614; Fax: 650-325-0908. Web: www.vallombrosa.org. Kathryn Gray, Interim Dir.

Vallombrosa Center, Conference and Retreat Center of the Archdiocese of San Francisco Priests 1; Staff 5; Daytime Served 120; Overnight Served 100.

SAN RAFAEL. *Santa Sabina Center* (1939) 25 Magnolia, 94901. Tel: 415-457-7727; Fax: 415-457-2310. Email: info@santasabinacenter.org. Web: www.santasabinacenter.org. Sr. Margaret Diener, O.P., Dir. Dominican Sisters Retreat and Conference Center.

[N] MONASTERIES AND RESIDENCES OF PRIESTS AND BROTHERS

SAN FRANCISCO. *St. Dominic Priory* (1876) 2390 Bush St., 94115-3124. Tel: 415-567-7824; Fax: 415-931-3360; 415-567-1608 (Parish). Web: www.stdominics.org. Revs. Xavier M. Lavagetto, O.P., Pastor & Sub-Prior; Anthony R. Rosevear, O.P., Novice Master & Vicar; Garry J. Cappleman, O.P., Parochial Vicar; Felix F. Cassidy, O.P.; Allen Dunston, O.P.; Thomas Hayes, O.P. (Retired); Very Rev. Patrick LaBelle, O.P., Prior; Revs. Stephen Maria Lopez, O.P., Parochial Vicar; Anselm Ramelow, O.P.; Paschal D. Salisbury, O.P.; Bro. Gregory R. Lira, O.P. Priests 10; Brothers 1; Novices 8.

Jesuit Community at St. Ignatius College Preparatory, 2001 37th Ave., 94116-1165. Tel: 415-731-7500; Fax: 415-682-5003. Email: postmaster@siprep.org. Web: www.siprep.org. Rev. Robert T. Walsh, S.J., Pres.; Mr. Patrick Ruff, Prin.; Revs. Thomas Allender, S.J.; Robert F. Curran, S.J.; Joseph D. Fessio, S.J.; Michael J. Kotlanger, S.J.; Thomas H. O'Neill, S.J., Supr.; Anthony P. Sauer, S.J.; James V. Schaukowitch, S.J.; Donald B. Sharp, S.J., S.T.D. (Retired); A. Francis Stiegeler, S.J.; Bros. Daniel C. Corona, S.J.; Douglas E. Draper, S.J.; Arthur W. Lee, S.J.; John E. Maloney, S.J.; Andrew Q. Nguyen, S.J., Seminarian; Andrew A. Rodriguez, S.J., Seminarian. Priests 11; Brothers 3; Seminarians 1.

Loyola House Jesuit Community (Corporate Title: Jesuit Community at University of San Francisco), 2600 Turk Blvd., 94118-4347. Tel: 415-422-4200; Fax: 415-422-5651. Web: www.usfca.edu/jesuit. Revs. Arturo Araujo, S.J., Assoc. Prof., Art & Architecture; James R. Blaettler, S.J., Assoc. Pastor, St. Ignatius Church; House Consultor; Mario J. Prietto, S.J., (Sabbatical); Geoffrey R. Dillon, S.J., Prof., Educ./Dept.; Chair of Teacher Educ.; Project Dir. Learn Belize; Charles R. Gagan, S.J., Pastor, St. Ignatius Church; Albert A. Grosskopf, S.J., Assoc. Pastor, St. Ignatius Church; Stephen Katsouros, S.J., Dir., ICEL, School of Educ.; R. Daniel Kendall, S.J., Prof., Theology; John P. Koeplin, S.J., Assoc. Prof., SOBAM; House Consultor, Rector; John J. Lo Schiavo, S.J., Chancellor; Thomas M. Lucas, S.J., Assoc. Prof., Fine & Performing Arts; Gerdenio S. Manuel, S.J., Prof., Pscyhology; Sean D. Michaelson, S.J., Dir. St. Ignatius Institute; Chair, English Dept.; Stephen A. Privett, S.J., Pres., Univ. of San Francisco; Dennis C. Recio, S.J., Asst. Prof., English; Donal Godfrey, S.J., Exec. Dir. Univ. Ministry; Roger de la Rosa, S.J., Asst. Prof. Chemistry, Campus Ministry; House Minister; Matthew J. Motyka, S.J., Prof. Romance Languages; John A. Coleman, Assoc. Pastor St. Ignatius Church; James R. Stormes, S.J., Visiting Prof.; Bros. Jim Holub, S.J.; John Keck, S.J., House Sub-minister; Rev. M. Joseph Savariappan, S.J., Graduate Student School of Educ. Priests 19; Brothers 2.

Marist Center of the West Society of Mary, U.S. Province (Marist), 625 Pine St., 94108-3210. Tel: 415-398-3543; Fax: 415-781-4937. Revs. Francis Springer, S.M. (Retired); Edward C. Blee, S.M. (Retired); Patrick J. Coyle, S.M. (Retired); Phillip d'Auby, S.M. (Retired); Robert E. Fahey, S.M. (Retired); Bruce J. Lery, S.M., Chap., SF Gen. Hospital; Bros. John A. Hunt, S.M.; Patrick Souza, S.M., Admin.; Joseph Grima, S.M., (Retired). Priests 6; Brothers 3.

Paris Foreign Mission Society Residence (1948) 930 Ashbury St., 94117. Tel: 415-664-6747; Fax: 415-564-5335. Revs. Jacques R. Didier, M.E.P., Dir.; Heribert Duquet, M.E.P. (Retired). Priests 2.

Salesian Provincial Residence, 1100 Franklin St., 94109. Tel: 415-441-7144; Fax: 415-441-7155. Email: suosec@aol.com. Revs. Timothy Ploch, S.D.B., Prov.; Thomas Prendiville, S.D.B., Vice Prov.; Jerry Wertz, S.D.B.; Joseph Farias, S.D.B. Priests 6. In Res. Revs. Larry Lorenzoni, S.D.B. (Retired); Laurence Byrne, S.D.B. (Retired); Richard Presenti, S.D.B.; Robert Delis, S.D.B., Navy Chap.; Bro. Lawrence King, S.D.B., Archivist.

San Buenaventura Friary, 750 Anza St., 94118. Tel: 415-387-7005; Fax: 415-831-5902. Residence of Capuchin Provincial House, Burlingame, CA.

Verbum Dei Missionary Fraternity (1969) 3373 19th St., 94110. Tel: 415-282-3005. Email: sanfrancisco@verbumdeiusa.org. Web: www.verbumdeiusa.org. Convent for missionary sisters. Sisters 19.

BURLINGAME. *Capuchin Provincial House* (1991) 1345 Cortez Ave., 94010. Tel: 650-342-1489; Fax: 650-342-5664. Email: ofmcap@aol.com. Web: www.olacapuchins.org. Revs. Matthew G. Elshoff, O.F.M.Cap., Prov.; James Stump, O.F.M.Cap., Hospital Chap.; Donal Burke, O.F.M.Cap., Devel. Dir.; Richard Lopes, O.F.M.Cap., Hospital Chap.; Eugene M. Ludwig, O.F.M.Cap.; Camillus MacRory, O.F.M.Cap. (Retired); Bertram Mulligan, O.F.M.Cap. (Retired); Miguel Angel Ortiz, O.F.M.Cap., Prov. Sec.; Fintan Whelan, O.F.M.Cap.; Bro. Alexander Escalera, O.F.M.Cap., Hospital Chap. *Capuchin Franciscan Seminarians Foundation*, 1345 Cortez Ave., 94010. Tel: 650-344-8321; Fax: 650-342-5664. Email: ofmcap@aol.com. Ms. Judy Steele, Contact Person. *Capuchin Franciscan Endowment Fund*, 1345 Cortez Ave., 94010. Tel: 650-344-8321; Fax: 650-342-5664. Ms. Judy Steele, Contact Person. *Capuchin Franciscan Mission Foundation*, 1345 Cortez Ave., 94010. Tel: 650-344-8321; Fax: 650-342-5664. Ms. Judy Steele, Contact Person. *Capuchin Franciscan Foundation for Retired Friars*, 1345 Cortez Ave., 94010. Tel: 650-344-8321; Fax: 650-342-5664. Ms. Judy Steele, Contact Person.

PORTOLA VALLEY. *Woodside Priory*, 302 Portola Rd., 94028. Tel: 650-851-8220; Fax: 650-851-2839. Email: mmager@prioryca.org. Web: www.prioryca.org. Very Rev. Martin J. Mager, O.S.B., Supr.; Revs. Pius L. Horvath, O.S.B.; Maurus B. Nemeth, O.S.B.; Bro. Edward Englund, O.S.B.

Benedictine Fathers of the Priory, Inc. Priests 3; Brothers 1.

[O] CONVENTS AND RESIDENCES FOR SISTERS

SAN FRANCISCO. *Carmelite Monastery of Cristo Rey, Discalced Carmelite Nuns* (1927) 721 Parker Ave., 94118-4227. Tel: 415-387-2640. Email: community@cmcrnuns.org. Professed Nuns 16; Novices 2.

Franciscan Missionaries of Our Lady of Peace (1941) *Our Lady of Guadalupe Convent* (1989) 46 Harrington St., 94112. Tel: 415-587-3729; Fax: 415-587-3729. Email: strhilda@gmail.com. Sr. Hilda Sandoval, M.F.P., Supr.

Mercy Place (Sisters of Mercy-Burlingame), 826 30th Ave., 94121-3522. Tel: 415-876-4303. Sisters 3; Candidates 1.

Monastery of Perpetual Adoration, Nuns of Perpetual Adoration, 771 Ashbury St., 94117. Tel: 415-566-2743; Fax: 415-564-4469. Email: mpador@aol.com. Sr. Rosalba Vargas, A.P., Supr. Cloistered Nuns 12.

Sisters of Social Service, 1850 Ulloa St., 94116. Tel: 415-681-9219. Web: www.socialservicesisters.org. Sisters 4.

Sisters of St. Francis - Mt. Alverno Marian Residence, 1330 Brewster Ave., Redwood City, 94062-1312. Tel: 650-369-1725; Fax: 650-369-0845. Email: blohm@sndden.org. Claire Blohm, Chief Fin. Officer.

Sisters of St. Joseph of Orange, 478 12th Ave., 94118-2904. Tel: 415-387-2493; Fax: 415-387-2493. Email: jmrmmcsj@sbcglobal.net.

Sisters of St. Joseph of Orange (1912) 1737 Silliman St., 94134. Tel: 415-585-0159; Fax: 415-585-0159. Email: csjsf@comcast.net. Sisters 2.

Sisters of the Good Shepherd (1932) 1310 Bacon St., 94134. Tel: 415-586-2822; Fax: 415-586-0355. Email: b.beasley@earthlink.net. Sisters 8.

Sisters of the Holy Family, 331 Anza St., Apt. 307A, 94118. Tel: 415-221-6097. Sisters 2.

Sisters of the Presentation San Francisco (1854 - CA; 1775 - Ireland) 281 Masonic Ave., 94118-4416. Tel: 415-422-5001; Fax: 415-422-5026. Email: syu@pbvmsf.org. Web: www.presentationsisterssf.org. Sr. Stephanie Still, P.B.V.M., M.A., Pres. Sisters in Archdiocese 56; Total in Congregation 90.

Verbum Dei Missionary Fraternity (1963) (Institute of Consecrated Life, Rome, Italy), 3373 19th St., 94110. Tel: 415-282-4979; Fax: 415-282-3005. Email: sanfrancisco@verbumdeiusa.org. Web: www.verbumdeiusa.org. Sr. Julia D. E. Prinz, V.D.M.F., Supr. Prayer and ministry of the Word, working with youth, young adults & adults.

ATHERTON. *Religious of the Sacred Heart Oakwood*, 140 Valparaiso Ave., 94027-4403. Tel: 650-323-8343; Fax: 650-326-2251. Sr. Clare Pratt, R.S.C.J., Community Dir. Infirmary for elderly Religious of the Sacred Heart. Sisters 59.

BURLINGAME. *Sisters of Mercy of the Americas West Midwest Community, Inc.* (As of July 1, 2008 the Sisters of Mercy of the Americas Regional Communities of Auburn, CA; Burlingame, CA; Cedar Rapids IA; Chicago, IL; Detroit, MI & Omaha, NE, merged to create Sisters of Mercy of the Americas West Midwest Community, Inc.), 2300 Adeline Dr., 94010-5599. Tel: 650-340-7410; Fax: 650-347-2550. Email: info@mercywmw.org. Web: www.mercywestmidwest.org. Sisters Judith Frikker, R.S.M., Pres.; Sheila Megley, R.S.M., Treas.; Judith Cannon, R.S.M., Leadership Team; Kathy Thornton, R.S.M., Leadership Team; Michelle Gorman, R.S.M., Sec.; Kim Kinsel, Community Oper. Officer; Carol Kelley, Community Fin. Officer; Sandy Goetzinger-Comer, Dir. Communications. Sisters 740; Associates 536.

DALY CITY. *Daughters of Charity of St. Vincent de Paul* (1633) 2000 Sullivan Ave., 94015-2202. Tel: 650-991-6715; Fax: 650-991-6055. Email: docsmc@sbcglobal.net. Sr. Camille Cuadra, Supr.

Quinhon Missionary Sisters of the Holy Cross (1988 - USA; 1926 - Vietnam) 298 Southgate Ave., 94015. Tel: 650-755-7231. Email: sistersmtgqndc@yahoo.org; josephinedao3@yahoo.com. Sisters Josephine Dao Vu, Nurse (Presentation Sisters); Catherine Huong Nguyen, Student; Angeline Tran, PreK Teacher; Mary Rose Trong Dau, Student. Sisters 4.

Religious of the Virgin Mary, Our Lady of Mercy Convent, 15 Elmwood Dr., 94015. Tel: 650-992-5769; Fax: 650-755-3457. Email: bigwasfe@yahoo.com. Sisters Fe P. Bigwas, R.V.M.; Virginia Barcelona, R.V.M.

MENLO PARK. *Corpus Christi Monastery* (1921) 215 Oak Grove Ave., 94025-3272. Tel: 650-322-1801; Fax: 650-322-6816. Email: nunsmenlo@comcast.net. Web: www.nunsmenlo.org. Sr. Mary Assumpta Rufo, O.P., Prioress. Nuns of the Order of Preachers. Cloistered Religious 13; Extern Sisters 1.

PACIFICA. *Missionaries of Charity* (1982) (India), 164 Milagra Dr., 94044. Tel: 650-355-3091. Sisters 8.

Noviciate (1982) 312 29th St., 94131. Tel: 415-647-1889. Sisters 4; Novices 39.

Queen of Peace (1984) 55 Sadowa St., 94112. Tel: 415-586-3449. Sisters 5.

REDWOOD CITY. *Daughters of St. Paul*, 3079 Oak Knoll Dr., 94062. Tel: 650-368-3184; Fax: 650-368-3189. Email: sanfrancisco@paulinemedia.com. Web: www.pauline.org. Sr. Armanda Santos, F.S.P., Supr. Sisters 5.

Santa Chiara Community, 5 Paddington Ct., Belmont, 94002. Tel: 650-593-3010; Fax: 650-593-3350. Email: norberta2@juno.com. Sr. Maureen Sinnott, Liaison. Sisters of St. Francis. Sisters 5.

SAN RAFAEL. *Carmelite Monastery of the Mother of God, Discalced Carmelite Nuns*, 530 Blackstone Dr., 94903. Tel: 415-479-6872; Fax: 415-491-4964. Email: sram@motherofgodcarmel.org. Sr. Anna Marie Vanni, O.C.D., Prioress. Sisters 5.

Dominican Sisters of San Rafael Generalate & Convent (1850) 1520 Grand Ave., 94901-2236. Tel: 415-453-8303; Fax: 415-453-8367. Email: maureenmcinerney@sanrafaelop.org. Web: sanrafaelop.org. Sr. Maureen McInerney, O.P., Prioress Gen. Total in Community 111; Total in Archdiocese 83.

Dominican Convent, 1540 Grand Ave., 94901-2236. Tel: 415-454-9221. Sisters 20.

Jane d'Aza Convent, 60 Locust Ave., 94901-2237. Tel: 415-453-4784. Sisters 7.

Our Lady of Lourdes Convent, 77 Locust Ave., 94901-2237. Tel: 415-457-3171. Sisters 28.

Our Lady of Mt. Carmel Convent, 34 Buena Vista Ave., Mill Valley, 94941-1232. Tel: 415-389-0328. Marin Catholic High School Sisters in Residence 5.

San Domenico Convent, 1500 Butterfield Rd., San Anselmo, 94960-1057. Tel: 415-453-9172. Sisters 6.

St. Margaret Convent, 40 Locust Ave., 94901-2237. Tel: 415-458-2952. Sisters 6.

St. Dominic Convent, 2517 Pine St., 94115-2609. Tel: 415-567-8282; Fax: 415-776-7384. Sisters 7.

St. Rose Convent, 2515 Pine St., 94115-2609. Tel: 415-441-2685. Sisters 7.

[P] CATHOLIC CHARITIES CYO

San Francisco. *Catholic Charities CYO of the Archdiocese of San Francisco*, Dorothy Cartahena, Contact.

Administrative Office, 180 Howard St., Ste. 100, 94105. Tel: 415-972-1200; Fax: 415-972-1201. Email: moreinfo@cccyo.org. Web: www.cccyo.org. Jeffrey V. Bialik, Exec. Dir.; Keith Spindle, Dir. Fin.; Margie Shurgot, Devel. & Communications; Tere Brown, Dir., Prog. & Svcs.; Kent Eagleson, Dir. St. Vincent's Svcs.; Jennifer Bilyk Makokha, Dir. Human Resources; Jane Ferguson Flout, Dir. Parish Partnerships.

Board of Directors: Most Rev. George H. Niederauer, D.D., Ph.D., Chm.; Deborah Dasovich, Pres.; Mark Okashima, Treas.; Carlos Alvarez, Sec.; Nicholas Andrade; Dr. Luis Calingo; Katie Cardinal; Sr. M. Ellene Egan, R.S.M.; Herbert W. Foedisch Jr.; Rev. Charles R. Gagan, S.J.; Cecilia Herbert; John A. Knight; Simon Manning; Maura A. Markus; James McCabe; Sharon McCarthy-Allen; Kathleen McEligot; Robert P. McGrath; Ann Gray Miller; Nanette Miller; Steve Molinelli; Katherine Munter; D. Paul Regan; William Ring; Rita Semel; Timothy Alan Simon; Maureen O'Brien Sullivan; Dr. Pierre Theodore; Rev. Kenneth M. Weare.

Behavioral Health Care and Senior Services:

Counseling Services:

SF Counseling Services, 2559 40th Ave., 94116. Tel: 415-564-7882; Fax: 415-731-1270. Email: dross@cccyo.org. Web: www.cccyo.org. Dave Ross, Ph.D., Dir.

Marin Counseling Services, St. Vincent's School for Boys, One St. Vincent Dr., San Rafael, 94903. Tel: 415-507-4244; Fax: 415-491-0532. Email: lbuntain@cccyo.org. Web: www.cccyo.org. Laurie Buntain, M.F.T., Prog. Dir.

San Mateo Counseling Services, 36 37th Ave., San Mateo, 94403. Tel: 650-295-2160; Fax: 650-286-1141. Email: dross@cccyo.org. Web: www.cccyo.org. Dave Ross, Ph.D., Dir.

Senior Services:

Edith Witt Senior Community, 66 Ninth St., 94103. Tel: 415-863-1141; Fax: 415-861-2873. Chris Callandrillo, Dir.

OMI Senior Center and Homecare Services, 65 Beverly St., 94132. Tel: 415-334-5550; Fax: 415-334-5554. Email: pclement@cccyo.org. Web: www.cccyo.org. Patty Clement-Cihak, Prog. Dir.

San Carlos Adult Day Support, 787 Walnut St., San Carlos, 94070. Tel: 650-592-9325; Fax: 650-592-2316. Email: nkeegan@cccyo.org. Web: www.cccyo.org. Nancy Keegan, Prog. Dir.

San Francisco Adult Day Services/Alzheimer's Day Care Resource Center, 50 Broad St., 94112. Tel: 415-452-3500; Fax: 415-452-3505. Email: pclement@cccyo.org. Web: www.cccyo.org. Patty Clement-Cihak, Prog. Dir.

Children & Family Services:

Canal Family Support Program, Pickelweed Community Center, 50 Canal St., San Rafael, 94901. Tel: 415-454-8596; Fax: 415-485-3185. Email: cgarcia@cccyo.org. Web: www.cccyo.org. Carlos Garcia, Prog. Dir.

10th & Mission Support Services, 1390 Mission St., 94103. Tel: 415-863-1141; Fax: 415-861-2873. Email: ccallandrillo@cccyo.org. Web: www.cccyo.org. Chris Callandrillo, Prog. Dir.

Maureen & Craig Sullivan Youth Services, 801 Jessie St., 94103. Tel: 415-863-1141; Fax: 415-863-1114. Email: lrossi@cccyo.org. Web: www.cccyo.org. Lilliana Rossi, Ph.D., Prog. Dir.

Homelessness Prevention Programs, 180 Howard St., Ste. 100, 94105. Tel: 415-972-1310; Fax: 415-972-1201. Jose Cartagena, Dir.

Family Services:

Refugee & Immigrant Services, 180 Howard St., Ste. 100, 94105. Tel: 415-972-1311; Fax: 415-972-1350. Email: cmartinez@cccyo.org. Web: www.cccyo.org. Christopher Martinez, Prog. Dir.

Information and Referral, 180 Howard St., Ste. 100, 94105. Tel: 415-972-1200; Fax: 415-972-1201. Email: mramirezportal@cccyo.org. Web: www.cccyo.org. Melissa Ramirez Portal, Admin.

Rita da Cascia, 1652 Eddy St., #8, 94115. Tel: 415-202-0941; Fax: 415-202-0937. Email: ehammerle@cccyo.org. Web: www.cccyo.org. Ellen Hammerle, Ph.D., Prog. Dir.

St. Joseph's Family Center, 899 Guerrero St., 94110. Tel: 415-550-4478; Fax: 415-550-4479. Email: kerickson@cccyo.org. Web: www.cccyo.org. Karen Erickson, L.C.S.W., Prog. Dir.

Treasure Island Child Development Center, 850 Avenue D, Bldg. 502, 94130. Tel: 415-834-0602; Fax: 415-834-0612. Email: ngoncalves@cccyo.org. Nella Goncalves, Prog. Dir.

Treasure Island Supportive Housing, P.O. Box 78037, 94107. Tel: 415-743-0017; Fax: 415-834-0612. Email: ngoncalves@cccyo.org. Web: www.cccyo.org. Nella Goncalves, Prog. Dir.

Youth Residential Services:

St. Vincent's School for Boys, One St. Vincent Dr., San Rafael, 94903. Tel: 415-507-2000; Fax: 415-491-0842. Email: dgallagher@cccyo.org. Web: www.cccyo.org. Dan Gallagher, Prog. Dir.

San Francisco Boys' and Girls' Home, 823 Euclid Ave., 94118. Tel: 415-221-3443; Fax: 415-387-1627. Email: sdouglas@cccyo.org. Web: www.cccyo.org. Scheron Douglas, Prog. Dir.

Assisted Housing and Health Services:

Derek Silva Community, 20 Franklin St., 94102. Tel: 415-553-8700; Fax: 415-575-3739. Email: kfauteux@cccyo.org. Web: www.cccyo.org. Kevin Fauteux, Ph.D., M.S.N., Acting Prog. Dir.

Assisted Housing & Health Programs, 180 Howard St., Suite 100, 94105. Tel: 415-972-1344; Fax: 415-972-1339. Email: gsimmons@cccyo.org. Web: www.cccyo.org. George Simmons, Prog. Dir.

Leland House, 141 Leland Ave., 94134. Tel: 415-405-2000; Fax: 415-337-1137. Email: kcunz@cccyo.org. Web: www.cccyo.org. Kevin Cunz, Prog. Dir.

Peter Claver Community, 1340 Golden Gate, 94115. Tel: 415-749-3800; Fax: 415-569-3153. Email: scerreta@cccyo.org. Web: www.cccyo.org. Sally Cerreta, Prog. Dir.

Catholic Youth Organization Programs:

CYO Athletics:

CYO Athletics - San Francisco, 180 Howard St., Ste. 100, 94105. Tel: 415-972-1253; Fax: 415-972-1279. Email: cjohnson@cccyo.org. Web: www.cccyo.org. Courtney Johnson-Clendinen, Prog. Dir.

CYO Athletics - Marin, One St. Vincent Dr., San Rafael, 94903. Tel: 415-507-2000; Fax: 415-491-0842. Email: sfarbstein@cccyo.org. Web: www.cccyo.org. Steve Farbstein, Mgr.

CYO Outdoor Programs:

CYO Camp/Outdoor Environmental Education, 2136 Bohemian Hwy., Occidental, 95465. Tel: 707-874-0200; Fax: 707-874-0230. Email: jwillford@cccyo.org. Web: www.cyocamp.org. Jim Willford, Exec. Dir.

CYO Transportation Services:

699 Serramonte Blvd., Ste. 210, Daly City, 94015. Tel: 650-757-2110; Fax: 650-758-1425. Email: mrea@cccyo.org. Web: www.cccyo.org. Marty Rea, Gen. Mgr.

CYO Retreat Center:

Facility Manager, 2136 Bohemian Hwy., Occidental, 95465. Tel: 707-874-0200; Fax: 707-874-0230. Email: jwillford@cccyo.org. Web: www.cccyo.org. Jim Willford, Exec. Dir.

St. Vincent's Services:

St. Vincent's Foster Family, One St. Vincent Dr., San Rafael, 94903. Tel: 415-507-4387; Fax: 415-491-0842. Email: mchesnut@cccyo.org. Web: www.cccyo.org. Megan Chesnut, Prog. Dir.

Administration, 180 Howard St., Ste. 100, 94105. Tel: 415-972-1230; Fax: 415-972-1339. Email: dcartahena@cccyo.org. Web: www.cccyo.org. Dorothy Carthahena, Exec. Asst.

[Q] NEWMAN CENTERS

San Francisco. *Catholic Student Association of UCSF* (1967) 1290 Fifth Ave., 94122-2649. Tel: 415-566-5610; Fax: 415-566-5073. Email: stjohnofgod-sf@sbcglobal.net. Web: www.sjog.net.

Newman Center, San Francisco State University St. Thomas More Church, 1300 Junipero Serra Blvd., 94132-2913. Tel: 415-452-9634; Fax: 415-452-9653. Email: stmchurch2002@aol.com. Web: www.STMChurch.com. Rev. Msgr. Labib Kobti; Elvira Garcia, Admin. Office Mgr.

[R] PERSONAL PRELATURES

San Francisco. *Prelature of the Holy Cross and Opus Dei* (1982) 765 14th Ave., 94118. Tel: 415-386-0431; Fax: 415-752-7177. Web: www.opusdei.org. Rev. Msgr. James A. Kelly; Revs. Torlach C. Delargy; James Velez. Priests 3; Total Staff 45; Total Assisted 200.

Menlough Study Center, 1160 Santa Cruz Ave., Menlo Park, 94025. Tel: 650-327-1675.

[S] MISCELLANEOUS LISTINGS

San Francisco. *Alliance of Mission District Catholic Schools (AMDCS)*, One Peter York Way, 94109. Tel: 415-614-5660; Fax: 415-614-5664. Email: dcs@sfarchdiocese.org. Ms. Maureen Huntington, Supt. Catholic Schools.

St. Anthony Foundation (1950) 150 Golden Gate Ave., 94102. Tel: 415-241-2600; Fax: 415-440-7770. Email: info@stanthonysf.org. Web: www.stanthonysf.org. Shari Roeseler, Exec. Dir.; Sr. Andrea Tierbok, O.S.F., Chap.; Rev. Thomas B. West, O.F.M., Chap. A nonprofit, charitable corporation assisting the homeless and low-income. Priests 1; Staff 145.

Archdiocesan Council of Catholic Women, One Peter Yorke Way, 94109-6602. Tel: 415-614-5500; Fax: 415-353-5555. Kathryn Parish-Reese, Pres.; Rev. Msgr. Edward P. McTaggart, Moderator (Retired).

The Archdiocese of San Francisco Parish and School Juridic Persons Real Property Support Corporation, 1301 Post St., Ste. 102, 94109. Tel: 415-292-0800; Fax: 415-292-0805.

The Archdiocese of San Francisco Parish, School and Cemetery Juridic Persons Capital Assets Support Corporation, 1301 Post St., Ste. 103, 94109-6667. Tel: 415-292-3600; Fax: 415-292-3603.

St. Benedict Center for Deaf and Hearing Impaired at St. Francis Xavier Church, 1801 Octavia, 94109. Tel: 415-567-9855; 415-567-0438 (TDD); 866-896-0968 (Video Phone); Fax: 415-567-0916. Email: info@sfdeafcatholics.org. Web: www.sfdeafcatholics.org.

Masses for the Deaf & Hard of Hearing., Tel: 415-567-9855 (Video Phone); Fax: 415-567-0916. Email: info@sfdeafcatholics.org. Rev. Paul Zirimenya, Chap.

California Handicapables, Inc. (1965) 1274 30th Ave., 94122. Tel: 415-566-2331. Miss Nadine Calligiuri, Founder; Jack O'Keeffe. To give shut-ins and handicapped people of all faiths an opportunity for monthly Mass, lunch and general fellowship. We generally meet the third Saturday of every month at St. Mary's Cathedral, San Francisco. Please call for more information.

Caritas Business Services, 203 Redwood Shores Pkwy., Redwood City, 94065. Tel: 650-551-6601; Fax: 650-551-6532. Email: wahidchoudhury@dochs.org. Web: www.dochs.org. Wahid Choudhury, Controller.

Catholic Charismatic Movement (1982) One Peter Yorke Way, 94109. Tel: 415-614-5500; Fax: 415-614-5522. Web: sfspirit.com. Revs. Raymund M. Reyes, Liaison; Jose M. Corral, Liaison to Spanish Speaking; Ernie von Emster, Asst. Liaison, Anglo Charismatics.

Catholic Kolping Society (1887) 440 Taraval St., 94116. Tel: 415-661-8305. Hubert Brinkmann, Pres.; Catherine Vennemeyer, Treas.

Catholic Scouting, Tel: 415-614-5652; Fax: 415-614-5658.

Catholics for Truth & Justice (1991) P.O. Box 26756, 94126-0756. Tel: 415-982-0920; Fax: 415-982-0921. Rev. Msgr. Harry G. Schlitt (Retired).

The Christopher Missions Foundation, 100 Portola Dr., #7, 94131. Tel: 415-875-9862; Fax: 415-391-2310. Rory Desmond, Exec. Dir.

Congregation of the Holy Family of Blessed Mariam Thresia, India, 3112 Turk Blvd., 94118. Tel: 415-666-3237. Email: chfsfo@yahoo.com. Web: www.blessedmariamthresia.org.

Daughters of Carmel (Congregation of Putri Karmel) St. Cecilia Convent, 2550-18th Ave., 94116. Tel: 415-242-4625. Sr. Mary Jacinta, P.Karm., Pres.

Equestrian Order of the Holy Sepulchre of Jerusalem - Northwest Lieutenancy, 26 Lagoon Vista Rd., Tiburon, 94920. Tel: 415-789-1049; Fax: 415-789-1049. Mary Ellen Hoffman, Sec.

Father Raphael Piperni Charitable Trust, 1100 Franklin St., 94109. Tel: 415-441-7144; Fax: 415-441-7155. Email: suosec@aol.com. (The FRPC (R) Trust)

Italian Catholic Federation, St. Brendan Church, 29 Rockaway, 94127. Tel: 415-681-4225; Fax: 415-681-3976. Rev. Michael F. Quinn, San Francisco District Chapter Chap.

Legion of Mary (1921) 1425 Bay Rd., East Palo Alto, 94303. Tel: 650-322-2152; Fax: 650-322-7319. Email: sfofassisi@sbcglobal.net. Rev. Lawrence C. Goode, Spiritual Dir., San Francisco Senatus.

St. Mary's Medical Center Foundation, 450 Stanyan St., 94117-1079. Tel: 415-750-4828; Fax: 415-668-4531.

The Megan Furth Memorial Fund, 3371 16th St., 94114. Tel: 415-346-9500; Fax: 415-346-8001. Nicole McAuliffe, Pres.

**Mercy Housing California*, 1360 Mission St., Suite 300, 94103. Tel: 415-355-7100; Fax: 415-355-7101. Email: VAgostino@mercyhousing.org. Web: www.mercyhousing.org. Housing development for low-income families, elderly, and singles.

Mercy Family Plaza, c/o Mercy Housing California, 1360 Mission St., Suite 300, 94103. Tel: 415-355-7100; Fax: 415-355-7101. Thirty-six affordable units for families.

M.H.R. AIDS Support Group, 100 Diamond St., 94114-2414. Tel: 415-863-1581; Fax: 415-552-8786. Email: mhr@mhr-asg.com. Web: www.mhr-asg.com.

**The Ordinary Mutual, RRG*, P.O. Box 191867, 94119-4002. Tel: 415-536-8440; Fax: 415-536-4002. Email: dennis_o'hara@ajg.com. Dennis O'Hara, Underwriting Mgr.; Randolph E. Steiner, Pres. A Risk Retention Group Corporation, incorporated in Vermont, serving the Dioceses of Tucson, Fresno, Monterey, Oakland, Orange, Sacramento,

Santa Rosa, and Stockton, and the Archdioceses of Los Angeles and San Francisco.

St. Paul High School Alumnae Assoc., 221 Valley St., 94131. Tel: 415-648-7538. Email: sphsalumnae@yahoo.com. Sr. Maureen O'Brien, B.V.M., Mod. Not-for-profit charitable outreach.

Pauline Books & Media, 2640 Broadway, Redwood City, 94063. Tel: 650-369-4230; Fax: 650-369-4390. Email: redwood@paulinemedia.com. Web: www.pauline.org. Sr. Armanda Santos, F.S.P., Supr. Daughters of St. Paul. Sisters 4.

Philip Rinaldi Charitable Trust, 1100 Franklin St., 94109. Tel: 415-441-7144; Fax: 415-441-7155. Email: suosec@aol.com. For the care of needy youth and for the formation needs of Salesians of St. John Bosco.

The Ricci Institute for Chinese-Western Cultural History at the Center for the Pacific Rim, University of San Francisco, 2130 Fulton St., 94117-1080. Tel: 415-422-6401; Fax: 415-422-2291. Email: ricci@usfca.edu. Web: www.usfca.edu/ricci. Xiaoxin Wu, Ed.D., Dir.; Mark Mir, Research Fellow & Chinese Library Cataloguer; May Lee, Prog. Asst.

St. Rose Corporation, 2501 Pine St., 94115. Tel: 415-440-9568; Fax: 415-440-9568. Email: lasop@sanrafaelop.org.
Officers of the Board: Sr. Lois Silva, O.P., Pres.; Thomas Bertelsen Jr., CFO & Sec.; Sr. Catherine Murray, O.P., Dir.; Jack R. Bertges, Dir.; Sr. Anne Bertain, O.P., Dir.; Rosario Bacon Billingsley, Dir.; Jeffrey K. Mori, Dir.; Cathy Murphy, Dir.; Sr. Lorna Walsh, S.H.J.M., Dir.

Shrine of St. Jude Thaddeus P.O. Box 15368, 94115-0368. Tel: 415-931-5919; Fax: 415-593-0350. Email: info@stjude-shrine.org. Web: www.stjude-shrine.org. Rev. Allen Robert Duston, O.P., Rector; Stedman Matthew, Chief Admin. Officer; Rosa Pinto, Office Mgr.

Sisters of the Presentation Community Support Trust Fund, 2340 Turk Blvd., 94118. Tel: 415-422-5001. Email: sstill@pbvmsf.org. Mailing Address: 2340 Turk Blvd., 94118. Tel: 415-722-9577. Email: pampbvm@aol.com. Sisters Pamela Chiesa, P.B.V.M., M.A., M.B.A., Trustee, Chairperson; Patricia Boss, O.P., Trustee; Patricia Anne Cloherty, P.B.V.M., Trustee; Rev. John P. Koeplin, S.J., Trustee; Sr. Giovanna Campanella, P.B.V.M., Trustee; Nanette Miller, Trustee; Kathy Atkinson, Trustee. Trust used for the religious and charitable needs of the Sisters of the Presentation of the Blessed Virgin Mary.

BURLINGAME. *Music at Kohl Mansion, Inc.*, 2750 Adeline Dr., 94010. Tel: 650-762-1130; Fax: 650-343-8464. Email: director@musicatkohl.org. Web: www.musicatkohl.org. To develop and promote public knowledge and appreciation of musical arts by sponsoring chamber music concerts and other public performances of music, as well as music education activities.

DALY CITY. *Association of Catholic Student Councils*, 86 Cityview Dr., 94014-3400. Tel: 415-584-9877; Fax: 415-584-9877. Email: tacsc@tacsc.org. Web: www.tacsc.org. Marilyn Thickett, Exec. Dir.

Vincentian Service Corps West, 25 San Fernando Way, Suite B, 94015-2065. Tel: 650-991-6465; Fax: 650-991-3905. Email: vscwest@dochs.org. Web: www.vscorps.org. Kathie Bassett, Contact Person. Tel: 650-991-6490; Fax: 650-991-3905; Sisters Camille Cuadra, D.C., Exec. Dir.; Sharon McCarthy, D.C., Chairperson; James Comstock, M.A., Sec. & Treas.

REDWOOD CITY. *The Catholic Worker Community* (1975) 545 Cassia St., 94063. Tel: 650-366-4415. Lawrence P. Purcell, Dir. A foster home for teenagers.

**St. Francis Center of Redwood City*, 151 Buckingham Ave., 94063. Tel: 650-365-7829; Fax: 650-365-7829. Email: SChristina@aol.com. Web: www.stfrancisrwc.org. Sr. Christina Heltsley, O.P., Exec. Dir.

SAN RAFAEL. **Center Interfaith Housing*, 164 N. San Pedro Rd., 94903. Tel: 415-492-9340; Fax: 415-492-1340.

Mission Holding Corporation (1995) 1520 Grand Ave., 94901-2236. Tel: 415-453-8303; Fax: 415-453-8367. Email: maureenmcinerney@sanrafaelop.org. Web: sanrafaelop.org.
Governing Board: Sisters Maureen McInerney, O.P.; Carla Kovack, O.P.; Patricia Boss, O.P.; Susan Allbritton, O.P.; Patricia Farrell, O.P.

The Sisters of Nazareth of San Rafael Real Estate Holdings, Inc., 245 Nova Albion Way, 94903. Tel: 415-479-8282; Fax: 415-479-6413.

Sisters of the Third Order of St. Dominic Support Charitable Trust Fund, 1520 Grand Ave., 94901-2236. Tel: 415-453-8303; Fax: 415-453-8367. Email: maureenmcinerney@sanrafaelop.org. Web: sanrafaelop.org. Sisters Patricia Boss, O.P., Staff; Maureen McInerney, O.P., Trustee; Lois Silva, O.P., Trustee; Cathryn deBack, O.P.; Mr. Thomas Bertelsen, Staff; John R. Burgis, Trustee; Marcia A. Fitzgerald, Trustee; Eugene F. Lynch, Trustee; Sr. Imelda Maurer, C.D.P., Trustee; Patricia Weir Robertson, Trustee.

Sisters of the Third Order of St. Dominic, Congregation of the Most Holy Name, Support Charitable Trust Fund, Trust used for the religious and charitable needs of the Sisters of the Third Order of St. Dominic, Congregation of the Most Holy Name.

SOUTH SAN FRANCISCO. *The Contemplatives of Saint Joseph*, 377 Willow Ave., 94080-1446. Tel: 650-995-3660; Fax: 650-871-1685. Email: cosj@att.net. Rev. Vito J. Perrone. A private preparatory religious association of the Archdiocese of San Francisco.

[T] CLOSED INSTITUTIONS

SAN FRANCISCO. *All Hallows Church* For sacramental records please contact Our Lady of Lourdes, 1715 Oakdale Ave., San Francisco 94124, Tel: 415-285-3377; Fax: 415-285-2191.

St. Brigid Church For sacramental records please contact St. Vincent de Paul, 2320 Green St., San Francisco 94123, Tel: 415-992-1010; Fax: 415-922-7203.

St. Edward the Confessor Church For sacramental records please contact St. Dominic, 2390 Bush St., San Francisco, 94115, Tel: 415-567-7854; Fax: 415-567-1608.

St. Francis of Assisi Church For sacramental records please contact SS. Peter and Paul, 666 Filbert St., San Francisco, 94133, Tel: 415-421-0809; Fax: 415-421-0217.

Holy Cross Korean Church For sacramental records please contact Chancery Office, One Peter Yorke Way, San Francisco, 94109, Tel: 415-614-5500; Fax: 415-614-5555.

Immaculate Conception Church For sacramental records please contact St. Anthony of Padua, 3215 Cesar Chavez St., San Francisco, 94110, Tel: 415-647-2704; Fax: 415-647-7282.

St. Joseph Church For sacramental records please contact St. Patrick, 756 Mission St., San Francisco, 94103, Tel: 415-421-0547; 512-9730.

Our Lady of Guadalupe Church For sacramental records please contact SS. Peter and Paul, 666 Filbert St., San Francisco, 94133, Tel: 415-421-0809; Fax: 415-421-0217.

Sacred Heart Church For sacramental records please contact the Chancery Office, One Peter Yorke Way, San Francisco, 94109.

SAN RAFAEL. *Blessed Sacrament Church* For sacramental records please contact St. Isabella, One Trinity Way, San Rafael, 94901, Tel: 415-479-1560; Fax: 415-479-8303.

St. Sylvester Church For sacramental records please contact St. Raphael, 1104 Fifth Ave., San Rafael, 94901, Tel: 415-453-2314; Fax: 415-453-5402.

WOODSIDE. *St. Marcella Mission* For sacramental records please contact St. Denis, 2250 Avy Ave., Menlo Park, 94025, Tel: 650-854-5976; Fax: 650-854-3754.

RELIGIOUS INSTITUTES OF MEN REPRESENTED IN THE ARCHDIOCESE

For further details refer to the corresponding bracketed number in the Religious Institutes of Men or Women section.

[]—*Apostolic Life Community of Priests* Moshe, Tanzania
[0200]—*Benedictine Monks* (Hungary)—O.S.B.
[0330]—*Brothers of the Christian Schools* (Prov. of San Francisco)—F.S.C.
[0470]—*The Capuchin Franciscans* (Irish Prov.)—O.F.M.Cap.
[0310]—*Congregation of Christian Brothers*—C.F.C.
[0480]—*Conventual Franciscans*—O.F.M.Conv
[0520]—*Franciscan Friars* (Santa Barbara Prov.)—O.F.M.
[0650]—*Holy Ghost Fathers*—C.S.Sp.
[0690]—*Jesuit Fathers and Brothers* (California Prov.)—S.J.
[0780]—*Marist Fathers and Brothers* (United States Prov.)—S.M.
[0800]—*Maryknoll*—M.M.
[]—*Order of Carmelites*—O.Carm.
[0430]—*Order of Preachers (Dominicans)* (Western Prov.)—O.P.
[0897]—*Paris Foreign Mission Society*—M.E.P.
[1030]—*Paulist Fathers*—C.S.P.
[1190]—*Salesian Don Bosco*—S.D.B.
[1260]—*Society of Christ* (Chicago Prov.)—S.Chr.
[]—*Society of St. Paul* (Philippine-Macau Prov.)
[1290]—*Society of the Priests of Saint Sulpice* (American Prov.)—S.S.P.

RELIGIOUS INSTITUTES OF WOMEN REPRESENTED IN THE ARCHDIOCESE

[1310]—*Congregation of the Franciscan Sisters of Little Falls, MN*
[]—*Congregation of the Holy Family of Blessed Mariam Thresia, India*
[3242]—*Congregation of the Sisters of Nazareth*—C.S.N.
[]—*Daughters of Carmel* (Putri Karmel)
[0730]—*Daughters of Charity of Canossa*—F.D.C.C.
[0760]—*Daughters of Charity of St. Vincent de Paul* (Prov. of the West)—D.C.
[0880]—*Daughters of Mary and Joseph*—D.M.J
[0850]—*Daughters of Mary Help of Christians*—F.M.A.
[0420]—*Discalced Carmelite Nuns*—O.C.D.
[1050]—*Dominican Contemplative Nuns*—O.P.
[1070-13]—*Dominican Sisters*—O.P.
[1070-19]—*Dominican Sisters of Houston*—O.S.F.
[1070-04]—*Dominican Sisters of San Rafael*—O.P.
[]—*Dominican Sisters of the Philippines*
[]—*Franciscan Missionaries, Our Lady of Peace*—M.F.P.
[]—*Las Hermanas Misioneras*—M.S.C.Gpe.
[2340]—*Little Sisters of the Poor*—L.S.P.
[2390]—*Lovers of the Holy Cross Sisters*—L.H.C.
[2710]—*Missionary Sisters of Charity*—M.C.
[]—*Missionary Sisters of the Sacred Side*—M.S.C.
[3190]—*Nuns of the Perpetual Adoration of the Blessed Sacrament*—A.P.
[]—*Oblates Sisters of Jesus the Priest*—O.S.J.
[0950]—*Pious Society Daughters of St. Paul*—F.S.P.
[]—*Religious of the Sacred Heart of Jesus*—R.S.C.J.
[3465]—*Religious of the Sacred Heart of Mary*—R.S.H.M.
[]—*Religious of the Virgin Mary*—R.V.M.
[0430]—*Sisters of Charity of the Blessed Virgin Mary*—B.V.M.
[2575]—*Sisters of Mercy of the Americas* West Midwest Community. (Omaha, NE)—R.S.M.
[3000]—*Sisters of Notre Dame de Namur* (Prov. of CA)—S.N.D.deN.
[4080]—*Sisters of Social Service of Los Angeles, Inc.*—S.S.S.
[]—*Sisters of St. Dominic of Mission San Jose*—O.P.
[1630]—*Sisters of St. Francis of Penance and Christian Charity*—O.S.F.
[3840]—*Sisters of St. Joseph of Carondelet* (Los Angeles Prov.)—C.S.J.
[3930-03]—*Sisters of St. Joseph of Orange*—C.S.J.O.
[1830]—*The Sisters of the Good Shepherd*—R.G.S.
[1960]—*Sisters of the Holy Family* (San Francisco, CA)—S.H.F.
[1990]—*Sisters of the Holy Names of Jesus and Mary* (Provs. of CA; Oregon; Washington)—S.N.J.M.
[2130]—*Sisters of the Immaculate Conception* (Prov. of Madrid)—R.C.M.
[3320]—*Sisters of the Presentation of the B.V.M.*—P.B.V.M.
[1890]—*Society of Helpers*—H.H.S.
[3330]—*Union Sisters of the Presentation of the Blessed Virgin Mary*—P.B.V.M.
[4110]—*Ursuline Nuns (Roman Union)*—O.S.U.
[]—*Verbum Dei Missionary Fraternity*

ARCHDIOCESAN CEMETERIES AND MAUSOLEUMS

SAN FRANCISCO. *Holy Cross Cemetery and Mausoleum*, P.O. Box 1577, Colma, 94014. Tel: 650-756-2060; Fax: 650-757-0752. Email: moreinfo@holycrosscemeteries.com.

MENLO PARK. *Holy Cross*, P.O. Box 1577, Colma, 94014. Tel: 650-323-6375; Fax: 650-757-0752. Email: moreinfo@holycrosscemeteries.com.

SAN RAFAEL. *Mount Olivet*, P.O. Box 4368, 94903. Email: moreinfo@holycrosscemeteries.com.

NECROLOGY

† Bitangjol, Albert P., (Retired)—Died May 7, 2011
† Knapp, William L., (Retired)—Died March 20, 2011
† Shore, Zachary J., (Retired)—Died July 23, 2011

An asterisk (*) denotes an organization that has established tax-exempt status directly with the IRS and is not covered by the USCCB Group Ruling.

Diocese of San Jose in California

(Dioecesis Sancti Josephi in California)

Most Reverend

PATRICK J. MCGRATH, D.D., J.C.D.

Bishop of San Jose; ordained June 7, 1970; appointed Auxiliary Bishop of San Francisco and Titular Bishop of Allegheny December 6, 1988; Episcopal ordination January 25, 1989; appointed Coadjutor Bishop of San Jose June 29, 1998; succeeded to See November 27, 1999.

Diocese of San Jose: 1150 N. First St., Ste. 100, San Jose, CA 95112. Tel: 408-983-0100; Fax: 408-983-0295.

Web: www.dsj.org

Email: chancellor@dsj.org

Most Reverend

THOMAS A. DALY

Auxiliary Bishop of San Jose; ordained May 9, 1987; appointed Auxiliary Bishop of San Jose and Titular Bishop of Tabalta March 16, 2011; Episcopal ordination May 25, 2011.

Most Reverend

PIERRE DUMAINE, D.D., PH.D.

Bishop Emeritus of San Jose; ordained June 15, 1957; appointed Auxiliary Bishop of San Francisco and Titular Bishop of Sarda April 28, 1978; Episcopal ordination June 29, 1978; appointed Bishop of San Jose January 27, 1981; installed as Bishop of San Jose March 18, 1981; retired November 27, 1999. *Chancery Office: Diocese of San Jose, 1150 N. First St., Ste. 100, San Jose, CA 95112.*

ESTABLISHED JANUARY 27, 1981.

Square Miles 1,300.

The Diocese of San Jose comprises the County of Santa Clara in the State of California.

Patrons of the Diocese of San Jose: St. Joseph, Husband of Mary, March 19; St. Clare of Assisi, August 11.

Legal Title: The Roman Catholic Bishop of San Jose, a Corporation Sole.
For legal titles of parishes and diocesan institutions, consult the Chancery Office.

STATISTICAL OVERVIEW

Personnel	
Bishop	1
Auxiliary Bishops	1
Retired Bishops	1
Priests: Diocesan Active in Diocese	112
Priests: Diocesan Active Outside Diocese	26
Priests: Diocesan in Foreign Missions	5
Priests: Retired, Sick or Absent	39
Number of Diocesan Priests	182
Religious Priests in Diocese	195
Total Priests in Diocese	377
Extern Priests in Diocese	8
Ordinations:	
Diocesan Priests	3
Transitional Deacons	1
Permanent Deacons in Diocese	28
Total Brothers	52
Total Sisters	308
Parishes	
Parishes	50
With Resident Pastor:	
Resident Diocesan Priests	43
Resident Religious Priests	6
Without Resident Pastor:	
Administered by Lay People	1
Missions	2
Pastoral Centers	4
New Parishes Created	1
Professional Ministry Personnel:	
Brothers	1
Sisters	16
Lay Ministers	91
Welfare	
Catholic Hospitals	2
Total Assisted	215,000
Health Care Centers	1
Total Assisted	100
Homes for the Aged	1
Total Assisted	140
Day Care Centers	1
Total Assisted	101
Special Centers for Social Services	1
Total Assisted	50,000
Educational	
Diocesan Students in Other Seminaries	16
Total Seminarians	16
Colleges and Universities	1
Total Students	8,490
High Schools, Diocesan and Parish	2
Total Students	3,294
High Schools, Private	4
Total Students	3,419
Elementary Schools, Diocesan and Parish	28
Total Students	9,340
Elementary Schools, Private	2
Total Students	349
Catechesis/Religious Education:	
High School Students	2,335
Elementary Students	14,409
Total Students under Catholic Instruction	41,652
Teachers in the Diocese:	
Priests	4
Brothers	3
Sisters	20
Lay Teachers	1,007
Vital Statistics	
Receptions into the Church:	
Infant Baptism Totals	7,255
Minor Baptism Totals	294
Adult Baptism Totals	263
Received into Full Communion	282
First Communions	5,929
Confirmations	3,302
Marriages:	
Catholic	719
Interfaith	228
Total Marriages	947
Deaths	1,398
Total Catholic Population	585,000
Total Population	1,879,700

Former Bishop—Most Rev. PIERRE DUMAINE, D.D., Ph.D. (Retired), ord. June 15, 1957; appt. Auxiliary Bishop of San Francisco and Titular Bishop of Sarda, April 28, 1978; Episcopal ordination June 29, 1978; appt. Bishop of San Jose Jan. 27, 1981; installed as Bishop of San Jose March 18, 1981; retired Nov. 27, 1999.

Diocese of San Jose—1150 N. First St., Ste. 100, San Jose, 95112. Tel: 408-983-0100; Fax: 408-983-0295. Web: www.dsj.org.

Vicar General and Moderator of the Curia—Rev. Msgr. FRANCIS V. CILIA, V.G. Tel: 408-983-0154; Fax: 408-983-0242.

Vicar General, Office for Special Projects—Very Rev. BRENDAN MCGUIRE, V.G. Tel: 408-983-0198; Fax: 408-983-0121.

Lay Retirement Board—Rev. Msgr. FRANCIS V. CILIA, V.G., Ex Officio; JOSEPH BAUER; SARAH BOSKOVICH; MARTIN CHARGIN; STEVE DUFFY; JOE GUERRA; MARY LYONS; ROSALIE MARTY; ROBERT SERVENTI, Ex Officio; CHARLES TULLY; PATRICIA WEIS, Ex Officio.

Chancellor—LINDA BEARIE. Tel: 408-983-0160; Fax: 408-983-0203.

Vicar for Clergy—Rev. Msgr. FRANCIS V. CILIA, V.G. Tel: 408-983-0154; Fax: 408-983-0242.

Judicial Vicar—Rev. ANDRES C. LIGOT, J.C.D.

Delegate to Religious—Sr. ROSALIE PIZZO, S.N.D.deN. Tel: 408-983-0123; Fax: 408-983-0121.

Director, Office of Stewardship & Development—WILLIAM MATTHEWS. Tel: 408-983-0244; Fax: 408-983-0290.

Bishop's Cabinet—Most Revs. PATRICK JOSEPH MCGRATH, D.D., J.C.D.; THOMAS A. DALY; Rev. Msgr. FRANCIS V. CILIA, V.G.; Very Rev. BRENDAN MCGUIRE, V.G.; LINDA BEARIE; ROBERT SERVENTI.

College of Consultors—Most Rev. THOMAS A. DALY; Rev. Msgrs. FRANCIS V. CILIA, V.G.; J. PATRICK BROWNE; Revs. MARK ARNZEN; THUC SI HO; Very Rev. BRENDAN MCGUIRE, V.G.; Rev. Msgr. WILFREDO S. MANRIQUE, J.C.L.; Revs. RICK RODONI; LUIS VARGAS.

Council of Priests—Most Revs. PATRICK JOSEPH MCGRATH, D.D., J.C.D., Ex Officio; THOMAS A. DALY; Revs. MARK ARNZEN, Chm.; JOSEPH BENEDICT, S.T.D.; Rev. Msgr. FRANCIS V. CILIA, V.G., Ex Officio; Revs. ENGELBERTO GAMMAD, J.C.D.; MARK GAZZINGAN; Rev. Msgr. MICHAEL D. HENDRICKSON; Revs. KEVIN P. JOYCE; JOSEPH KIM; Very Rev. BRENDAN MCGUIRE, V.G.; Revs. ANDREW V. NGUYEN; ERNESTO ORCI; WALTER SUAREZ.

Council of Religious—Sr. ROSALIE PIZZO, S.N.D.deN, Chm.; Bro. WILLIAM BOLTS, S.M.; Sisters DIVINA CAABAY, A.R.; ANA MARIA DE JESUS CARRIO, S.S.V.M.; ROSHEEN GLENNON, C.S.J.; MARIA GRIEGO, S.J.; Bro. CHARLES MUSCAT, C.S.; Sr. GEMMA NEUNZLING, O.P.; Rev. CHRISTOPHER NGUYEN, S.J.; Sisters KATIE QUINN, D.C.; MARY MARGARET TAPANG, P.D.D.M.; Rev. GEORGE WANSER, S.J.

Deans—Revs. JOSEPH BENEDICT, S.T.D., Deanery 2; MARCELO JAVIER NAVARRO, I.V.E., Deanery 3; FRANCISCO MIRAMONTES, Deanery 4; CHRISTOPHER BRANSFIELD, Deanery 5; EUGENE P. O'DONNELL, Deanery 6; CHRISTOPHER BENNETT, Deanery 7.

Ecumenical and Interreligious Affairs—Rev. JOSE ANTONIO RUBIO, S.T.D., Dir. & Delegate to Eastern Rite Churches.

Chinese Catholic Community—Revs. CARLOS ALBERTO OLIVERA, Pastor; PETER KIN CHUNG SUI, S.J., Part-time Chap.

Catholic Charities— Catholic Charities of Santa Clara

County GREGORY R. KEPFERLE, CEO.
Propagation of the Faith-Holy Childhood Association-Catholic Relief Service—LINDA BATTON, Dir. Tel: 408-983-0158.
Roman Catholic Welfare Corporation—Most Revs. PATRICK JOSEPH MCGRATH, D.D., J.C.D., Pres.; THOMAS A. DALY; Rev. Msgr. FRANCIS V. CILIA, V.G., Vice Pres.; LINDA BEARIE, Sec.; ROBERT SERVENTI, Treas.; KATHERINE ALMAZOL.
Roman Catholic Seminary Corporation—Most Revs. PATRICK JOSEPH MCGRATH, D.D., J.C.D., Pres.; THOMAS A. DALY; Rev. Msgr. FRANCIS V. CILIA, V.G., Vice Pres.; LINDA BEARIE, Sec.; ROBERT SERVENTI, Treas.
"The Valley Catholic" (Diocesan Newspaper)—ROBERTA WARD, Editor; RACQUEL BROWN, Business Mgr., Diocese of San Jose, 1150 N. First St., Ste. 100, San Jose, 95112. Tel: 408-983-0262.
Diocesan Tribunal—Diocese of San Jose, 1150 N. First St., Ste. 100, San Jose, 95112. Tel: 408-983-0219.
Judicial Vicar—Rev. ANDRES C. LIGOT, J.C.D.
Adjutant Judicial Vicar—Rev. ENGELBERTO GAMMAD, J.C.D.
Judges—Revs. ENGELBERTO GAMMAD, J.C.D.; SAJU JOSEPH, J.C.L.; Rev. Msgr. WILFREDO S. MANRIQUE, J.C.L.; Sr. MARIE GERTRUDE ROLDAN, C.S.J., J.C.L.
Defender of the Bond—Rev. ROBERT E. HAYES, J.C.L.
Case Instructor—Sr. MICHELE MANGAN, O.S.F. Tel: 408-983-0224.
Administrative Assistant and Notary—Sr. SOFIA BERRONES, M.C.D.P. Tel: 408-983-0219.
Finance Office—ROBERT SERVENTI, CFO; JOHN HOFFMAN, Controller; IAN ABELL, Dir. Facilities; LUPE MONCIVAIS WARREN, Risk Mgr.; RON ROSS, Facilities Inspector & Coord.; TERESA CONVILLE, Compliance Officer.
Finance Council—MICHAEL HOPE, Chm.; MICHAEL BLACH; GEORGE DELUCCHI; STEVE DUFFY; NANCY ERBA; TONY FADELLI; TROY JONES; EUGENE TOOMEY; DONALD WAITE.
Building Committee—Rev. Msgr. FRANCIS V. CILIA, V.G.; Rev. CHRISTOPHER BRANSFIELD; IAN ABELL; PAMELA ANDERSON-BRULE; DAN BROWN; JAMES E. KOEPF; MARK LAUBACH; ROSANNA LERMA; PATRICK PFEIFFER; ROBERT SERVENTI; RICH SIMPSON.
Stewardship & Development Office—WILLIAM MATTHEWS, Dir. Tel: 408-983-0244; Fax: 408-983-0290.
Department of Cemeteries—WILLIAM SOUSAE, Dir. Tel: 650-428-3730.
Office of the Vicar for Clergy—Rev. Msgr. FRANCIS V. CILIA, V.G., Episcopal Vicar for Clergy. Tel: 408-983-0154.
Associate for Deacon Life—Deacon DONALD SIFFERMAN.
Diocesan Clergy Personnel Board—Most Revs. PATRICK JOSEPH MCGRATH, D.D., J.C.D., Ex Officio; THOMAS A. DALY; Rev. Msgr. FRANCIS V. CILIA, V.G., Chm.; Revs. PAUL DUONG; ENGELBERTO GAMMAD, J.C.D.; Rev. Msgr. JOSEPH J. MILANI (Retired); Revs. JOHN PONCINI; FRANCISCO RIOS; DANIEL C. URCIA, Ed.D.; KATHY SCHLOSSER; LUPITA VITAL.
Ongoing Formation of Clergy—Rev. Msgr. FRANCIS V. CILIA, V.G., Ex Officio; Revs. MARK ARNZEN, Chm.; THIERRY GERIS; ROBERT E. HAYES, J.C.L., Emeritus; PETER LOI HUYNH; EDUARDO OBERO; LAWRENCE J. PERCELL; JOHN PONCINI, Ex Officio; Deacons RICK HAECKEL; DONALD SIFFERMAN; KATHERINE ALMAZOL; Sr. MARY LANGE, S.H.F.; SANDY MORY.
Priests' Retirement Board—Rev. Msgrs. J. PATRICK BROWNE, Chm.; FRANCIS V. CILIA, V.G., Ex Officio; ROBERT SERVENTI, Ex Officio; Revs. MICHAEL CARSON; STEVEN P. BROWN; STEPHEN PERATA (Retired); MATTHEW D. STANLEY; JAMES NIELSEN.
Vocation Office—Rev. JOHN PONCINI, Dir. Tel: 408-983-0255.
Deacon Formation—Rev. JOSEPH BENEDICT, S.T.D., Dir. Tel: 408-983-0256; Deacon PHILIP FLOWERS, Dir. Deacon Life.
Department of the Chancellor—LINDA BEARIE, Chancellor. Tel: 408-983-0160.
Diocesan Archives and Records Management—BAYNE BENTLEY, 396 Martin Ave., Santa Clara, 95050. Tel: 408-970-9474.
Human Resources Office—PATRICIA WEIS, Dir. Tel: 408-983-0149.
Education Department—KATHERINE ALMAZOL, Supt. of Schools; NANCY DOYLE, Asst. Supt. of Schools.
Office for Parish Services—Tel: 408-983-0125. Most Rev. THOMAS A. DALY.
Director for Catechetics—WENDY SCHERBART. Tel: 408-983-0138.
Director for Hispanic Apostolate—LUPITA VITAL. Tel: 408-983-0133.
Director for Hispanic Youth and Young Adults—LUPITA VITAL. Tel: 408-983-0133.
Director for Youth and Young Adult Ministry—JOHN RINALDO. Tel: 408-983-0135.
Missions Office—LINDA BATTON, Dir. Tel: 408-983-0158.
Director of Liturgy—DIANA MACALINTAL. Tel: 408-983-0136.
Director of Social Ministries—LINDA BATTON. Tel: 408-983-0158; ANDREA GIOVANNONI, Assoc. Tel: 408-983-0134.
Detention Ministry—Sr. MARYANN CANTLON, C.S.J. Tel: 408-983-0131.
Human Concerns Commission—LINDA BATTON, Liaison. Tel: 408-983-0158.
Liturgical Commission—DIANA MACALINTAL, Liaison. Tel: 408-983-0136.
Pastoral Resource Committee for Ministry to Gay and Lesbian Catholics—Rev. G. ROBERT LEGER. Tel: 408-245-5554.
Respect Life Program—LINDA BATTON, Liaison. Tel: 408-983-0158.
Office for Evangelization—LINDA BATTON, Dir. Tel: 408-983-0158.
Institute for Leadership in Ministry—LINDA CUNHA-RICCHIO, Dir. Tel: 408-983-0111.
Office for the Protection of Children and Vulnerable Adults—ENRIQUE FLORES. Tel: 408-983-0113; 408-983-0141 (Emergency Line); Fax: 408-983-0147.
Victim Assistance Coordinator—ENRIQUE FLORES. Tel: 408-983-0141 (Emergency Line); Fax: 408-983-0147.

CLERGY, PARISHES, MISSIONS AND PAROCHIAL SCHOOLS

CITY OF SAN JOSE

1—CATHEDRAL BASILICA OF ST. JOSEPH (1849), (Hispanic—Latino), (Mexican National Church) Rev. Msgr. J. Patrick Browne; Revs. Gerardo Menchaca; Tadeusz Terembula, S.V.D. (Poland).
Res. & Church: 80 S. Market St., 95113. Tel: 408-283-8100; Fax: 408-283-8110.
Catechesis/Religious Program—Susan Olsen, D.R.E. Students 223.

2—ST. ANTHONY (1982) Rev. Lawrence Hendel; Joann Maier, Pastoral Assoc.
Mailing Address: 20101 McKean Rd., 95120. Tel: 408-997-4800.
Old Church: 21800 Bertram Rd., 95120.
Catechesis/Religious Program—Tel: 408-997-4808; Fax: 408-997-4801. Students 107.

3—ST. BROTHER ALBERT CHMIELOWSKI POLISH CATHOLIC PASTORAL MISSION (1986), (Polish), Rev. Andrzej Salapata, S.Ch. (Poland). In Res., Rev. Edward Mroczynski, S.Ch.
Res.: 10250 Clayton Rd., 95127-4336. Tel: 408-251-8490; Fax: 408-251-8960.
Catechesis/Religious Program—Students 56.

4—CHRIST THE KING (1997) Revs. Jeronimo Gutierrez; Paul Duong.
Res.: 75 Cyclamen St., 95111.
Church: 5284 Monterey Rd., 95111. Tel: 408-362-9958; Fax: 408-362-9695.
Catechesis/Religious Program—Students 234.

5—ST. CHRISTOPHER (1951) Rev. Msgr. Wilfredo S. Manrique; Revs. Andrew C. Nguyen; David Mercer; Deacon Pedro B. Perez.
Office: 2278 Booksin Ave., 95125. Tel: 408-269-2226; Fax: 408-269-2784.
School—(Grades K-8) Tel: 408-723-7223; Fax: 408-978-5458. Anne Ivie, Prin.; Dana Polini, Librarian. Sisters of the Presentation 2; Lay Teachers 36; Students 614.
Catechesis/Religious Program—Tel: 408-264-8764. Sr. Felicia Gross, O.S.F., D.R.E. Students 566.

6—CHURCH OF THE TRANSFIGURATION (1965) Rev. Walter M. McMahon; Deacon Steve Herrera.
Mailing Address: 4325 Jarvis Ave., 95118. Tel: 408-823-3522; Fax: 408-266-2745.
Catechesis/Religious Program—Tel: 408-264-3600, Ext. 5. Paula Ramos, Pastoral Assoc. Students 45.

7—FIVE WOUNDS PORTUGUESE NATIONAL CHURCH (1914), (Portuguese), Rev. Msgr. J. Patrick Browne, Admin.; Revs. Antonio Jose dos Reis (Brazil); James O. Kafor (Nigeria).
Res.: 1375 E. Santa Clara St., 95116. Tel: 408-292-2123; Fax: 408-292-0201.
Catechesis/Religious Program—Tel: 408-293-3938; Fax: 408-293-0431. Joseph Khanh Bui, D.R.E. Students 199.

8—ST. FRANCES CABRINI (1955) Revs. Lieu Vu; Robert Kiefer.
Res.: 15333 Woodard Rd., 95124. Tel: 408-879-1120; Fax: 408-377-3587.
School—(Grades PreSchool-8), 15325 Woodard Rd., 95124. Tel: 408-377-6545; Fax: 408-377-8491. Gail Cirone, Prin. Sisters 1; Lay Teachers 29; Students 653.
Catechesis/Religious Program—Tel: 408-377-2111; Fax: 408-377-3587. Students 110.

9—ST. FRANCIS OF ASSISI (1997) Revs. Eugene P. O'Donnell; That Son Nguyen; Normandy Segovia; Deacons Willy Agbayani, Pastoral Admin.; Andrzej Sobczyk; Sal Alvarez.
Res.: 5111 San Felipe Rd., 95135. Tel: 408-223-1562; Fax: 408-223-1759.
Catechesis/Religious Program—Students 436.

10—HOLY CROSS (1906), (Italian), Revs. Firmo Mantovani, C.S.; Gildardo Blanco.
Res.: 580 E. Jackson St., 95112. Tel: 408-294-2440; Fax: 408-294-8609.
Catechesis/Religious Program—Tel: 408-294-1310; Fax: 408-294-8609. Bro. Charles Muscat, C.S., D.R.E. Students 263.

11—HOLY FAMILY (1905) Revs. Hao Dinh; Tito Jesus Cartagenas Jr.
Office: 4848 Pearl Ave., 95136. Tel: 408-265-4040; Fax: 408-978-9979.
School—(Grades K-8), 4850 Pearl Ave., 95136. Tel: 408-978-0290; Fax: 408-978-0290. Gail Harrell, Prin.; Laurie Brant, Librarian. Lay Teachers 26; Students 458.
Catechesis/Religious Program—Tel: 408-265-5374. Katy Anderson, Dir. Faith Formation. Students 301.

12—HOLY SPIRIT (1963) Very Rev. Brendan McGuire; Rev. Joseph Kim; Penny Warne, Pastoral Assoc.
Church: 1200 Redmond Ave., 95120. Tel: 408-997-5101; Fax: 408-997-5102.
School—(Grades PreSchool-8), 1198 Redmond Ave., 95120. Tel: 408-268-0794; Fax: 408-268-5281. Peggy Krewson, Prin.; Rosemary Van Lare, Librarian. Lay Teachers 31; Students 569.
Catechesis/Religious Program—Tel: 408-997-5115. Merry Reardon, D.R.E. Students 419.

13—ST. JOHN VIANNEY (1952) Revs. Anthony J. Mancuso; Steve Kim. In Res., Rev. James K. Graham (NTN).
Rectory—4609 Alum Rock Ave., 95127.
Church: 4601 Hyland Ave., 95127. Tel: 408-258-7832 (Office); Fax: 408-258-6152 (Office).
School—(Grades K-8) Tel: 408-258-7677; Fax: 408-258-5997. Sr. Michele Anne Murphy, P.B.V.M., Prin.; Tudy Johnson, Librarian. Sisters of the Presentation of the B.V.M. 2; Lay Teachers 27; Students 511.
Catechesis/Religious Program—Tel: 408-258-7832, Ext. 24; Fax: 408-272-1045. Linda Rokita, D.R.E. Students 449.

14—ST. JULIE BILLIART (1974) Revs. Jon Pedigo; Peter Luc Phan.
Res.: 366 St. Julie Dr., 95119. Tel: 408-629-3030; Fax: 408-629-3343.
Catechesis/Religious Program—Tel: 408-629-3030, Ext. 102. Yolanda Toulet, Dir. Faith Formation. Students 580.

15—ST. LEO THE GREAT (1923) Revs. Marcelo Javier Navarro, I.V.E.; Andrey Garcia. In Res., Rev. Matthew Koo (Retired).
Res.: 88 Race St., 95126. Tel: 408-293-3503; Fax: 408-293-3516.
School—(Grades K-8) Tel: 408-293-4846. Marie Bordeleau, Prin.; Mary Barber, Librarian. Lay Teachers 14; Students 297.
Catechesis/Religious Program—Sr. Mary of the Incarnation Creeden, S.S.V.M., D.R.E. Students 257.

16—ST. MARIA GORETTI (1961) Rev. Steven P. Brown; Rev. Msgr. Dominic Dinh Do; Revs. Roberto Gomez; Michael Gazzingan; Deacon Joseph Nhut Ho.
Res.: 2980 Senter Rd., 95111. Tel: 408-363-2300; Fax: 408-363-2305.
Catechesis/Religious Program—Tel: 408-363-2300, Ext. 23. Maureen Ickes, D.R.E. Students 690.
Mission—Santee Mission 1382 Tami Lee Dr. #4, Santa Clara Co. 95122. Tel: 408-292-7610.

17—ST. MARTIN OF TOURS (1914) Revs. Christopher Bransfield; Abraham Antony (India).
Res.: 200 O'Connor Dr., 95128. Tel: 408-294-8953; Fax: 408-294-2624.
School—(Grades K-8), 300 O'Connor Dr., 95128. Tel: 408-287-3630; Fax: 408-287-4313. Karen DeMonner, Prin.; Trish Divis, Librarian. Lay Teachers 19; Students 324.
Catechesis/Religious Program—Tel: 408-289-9608. Liz Schoenwetter, D.R.E. Students 144.

18—ST. MARY OF THE ASSUMPTION (1975), (Croatian), (Croatian Mission) Revs. Drago Gveric, O.F.M.; Ante Juric, O.F.M.
Res.: 901 Lincoln Ave., 95126. Tel: 408-279-0279; Fax: 408-292-5868.
Catechesis/Religious Program—Students 60.
Croatian Franciscan Fathers Corporation—Tel: 408-279-0279; Fax: 408-292-5868.
Franciscan Fathers—Tel: 408-276-0279; Fax: 408-292-5868.

19—MOST HOLY TRINITY (1961) Revs. Eduardo

Samaniego, S.J.; George Wanser, S.J.; Chu Ngo, S.J.; Doanh "John" Nguyen, S.J.; Gerald Robinson, S.J.
Res.: 2040 Nassau Dr., 95122. Tel: 408-729-0101; Fax: 408-258-4131.
School—(Grades K-8) Tel: 408-729-3431; Fax: 408-272-4945. Dorothy Suarez, Prin.; Sue Roy, Librarian. Sisters 1; Lay Teachers 12; Students 253.
Catechesis/Religious Program—Clara Morales, D.R.E. Students 143.

20—OUR LADY OF GUADALUPE (1962), (Hispanic), Revs. Javier Reyes, O.F.M.; Edgar Magana, O.F.M.
Office: 2020 E. San Antonio St., 95116. Tel: 408-926-9207; Fax: 408-258-8249.
Catechesis/Religious Program—Tel: 408-926-9287. Connie Torres, D.R.E. Students 636.

21—PASTOR OF OUR LADY OF REFUGE Rev. Brendan P. McGuire.
2165 Lucretia Ave., 95122. Tel: 408-997-5101.

22—ST. PATRICK (1871), (Vietnamese), Revs. Peter Loi Huynh; Tan Nguyen; Paolo Gobbo (Italy); Andrew V. Nguyen; Deacon Tho Le.
Res.: 389 E. Santa Clara St., 95113. Tel: 408-294-8120; Fax: 408-291-6277.
Vietnamese Ministry—Tel: 408-291-6280; Fax: 408-291-6289.
School—(Grades K-8), 51 N. 9th St., 95112. Tel: 408-283-5858; Fax: 408-283-5852. Olga Islas, Prin.; Ms. M. Delgado, Librarian. Sponsored by the Daughters of Charity. Lay Teachers 11; Students 236.
Catechesis/Religious Program—Tel: 408-291-6270 (Vietnamese); Fax: 408-291-6289 (Vietnamese). Kim Oanh Le, D.R.E. (Vietnamese). Students 2,610.

23—QUEEN OF APOSTLES (1960) Revs. Michael Carson; Angelo David; Deacon Brian McKenna.
Res.: 4911 Moorpark Ave., 95129. Tel: 408-253-7560; Fax: 408-253-9530.
School—(Grades K-8), 4950 Mitty Way, 95129. Tel: 408-252-3659; Fax: 408-873-2645. Martin Chargin, Prin.; Joan Rehbock, Librarian. Lay Teachers 18; Students 294.
Catechesis/Religious Program—Tel: 408-255-9950; Fax: 408-253-9530. Patricia Sarria, D.R.E. Students 204.

24—SACRED HEART OF JESUS (1920), (Hispanic), Revs. Walter Suarez Lopez; Andres Parra.
Res.: 325 Willow St., 95110. Tel: 408-292-0146; Fax: 408-292-0172.
Catechesis/Religious Program—Tel: 408-292-0146, Ext. 202; Fax: 408-292-0172. Students 109.

25—SANTA TERESA (1967) Rev. Christopher Bennett. In Res., Rev. William Pegnam (Retired).
Res.: 794 Calero Ave., 95123. Tel: 408-629-7777; Fax: 408-629-5260.
Catechesis/Religious Program—Fax: 408-629-5260. Students 107.

26—ST. THOMAS OF CANTERBURY (1967) Rev. Mark Catalana.
Res.: 1522 McCoy Ave., 95130. Tel: 408-378-1595; Fax: 408-378-1215.
Catechesis/Religious Program—Tel: 408-364-8840. Sherry Scott, Catechetical Coord. Students 74.

27—ST. VICTOR (1961) Rev. Msgr. Michael D. Hendrickson; Revs. Stephen Perata, Pastor Emeritus (Retired); Jonathan Cuarto; Paul Cuong Phan; Deacon Hon Nguyen.
Rectory—3108 Sierra Rd., 95132. Tel: 408-251-7055; Fax: 408-251-5528.
School—(Grades K-8), 3150 Sierra Rd., 95132. Tel: 408-251-1740; Fax: 408-251-1492. Patricia Wolf, Prin.; Joan Passalaqua, Librarian. Lay Teachers 17; Students 288.
Catechesis/Religious Program—Tel: 408-251-0154; Fax: 408-251-5528. Angela Giampaoli, D.R.E. Students 261.

OUTSIDE THE CITY OF SAN JOSE

ALVISO, SANTA CLARA CO., OUR LADY, STAR OF THE SEA (1984) Rev. Francisco Miramontes.
Mailing Address: P.O. Box 426, 95002-0426.
Res.: 1385 Michigan Ave., 95002-0426. Tel: 408-263-2121; Fax: 408-263-1182.
Catechesis/Religious Program—Students 99.

CAMPBELL, SANTA CLARA CO., ST. LUCY (1947) Revs. Kevin P. Joyce; Joselito Page.
Res.: 2350 Winchester Blvd., 95008. Tel: 408-378-2464; Fax: 408-378-5548.
School—(Grades K-8), 76 Kennedy Ave., 95008. Tel: 408-871-8023; Fax: 408-378-4945. Jennifer Martin, Prin.; Mary Casey, Librarian. Lay Teachers 17; Students 311.
Catechesis/Religious Program—Tel: 408-379-5900; Fax: 408-378-5548. Janet Ang, D.R.E. Students 487.

CUPERTINO, SANTA CLARA CO., ST. JOSEPH OF CUPERTINO (1913) Revs. Gregory C. Kimm; Vincent Pineda, Parochial Vicar; W. Donald Morgan, Parochial Vicar. In Res., Rev. Msgr. Joseph J. Milani, Pastor Emeritus (Retired).
Res.: 10110 N. De Anza Blvd., 95014. Tel: 408-252-7653; Fax: 408-252-5263.
School—(Grades PreK-8), 10120 N. DeAnza Blvd., 95014. Tel: 408-252-6441; Fax: 408-252-9771. Mary Lyons, Prin.; Barbara Hill, Librarian. Sisters 2; Lay Teachers 13; Students 351.
Catechesis/Religious Program—Tel: 408-252-7653, Ext. 60. Tam Tran, D.R.E. Students 228.

GILROY, SANTA CLARA CO., ST. MARY (1865) [CEM] Revs. Daniel Derry; Hugo Marcelo Rojas (Argentina); Noel Sanvicente (Philippines); Deacon Pat Allen; Hilda Porcella, Pastoral Assoc.
Res.: 11 First St., 95020. Tel: 408-847-5151; Fax: 408-847-4851.
School—(Grades K-8), 7900 Church St., 95020-4499. Tel: 408-842-2827; Fax: 408-847-7679. Christa Hanson, Prin. Sisters 1; Lay Teachers 16; Students 296.
Catechesis/Religious Program—7950 Church St., 95020. Tel: 408-847-2652; Fax: 408-847-4851. Barbara Zarka, D.R.E. Students 1,235.

LOS ALTOS, SANTA CLARA CO.

1—ST. NICHOLAS (1947) Revs. Lawrence P. Percell; Vincent Tinh Dang.
Res.: 473 Lincoln Ave., 94022. Tel: 650-948-2158; Fax: 408-948-2056.
School—(Grades K-8), 12816 S. El Monte Ave., Los Altos Hills, 94022. Tel: 650-941-4056. Matt Komar, Prin.; Mary O'Shea, Librarian. Lay Teachers 15; Students 245.
Catechesis/Religious Program—Tel: 650-941-7672; Fax: 650-917-9872. Ginny Hinkle, D.R.E. Students 273.

2—ST. SIMON (1955) Revs. V. Warwick James; Mark Gazzingan; Anthony Nguyen. In Res., Rev. Michael J. Burns (Retired).
Res.: 1860 Grant Rd., 94024. Tel: 650-967-8311; Fax: 650-967-8876.
School—(Grades PreK-8), 1840 Grant Rd., 94024. Tel: 650-968-9952; Fax: 650-988-9308. Mr. Steve Clossick, Prin.; Patti Bo, Librarian. Lay Teachers 31; Students 529.
Catechesis/Religious Program—Tel: 650-967-8311, Ext. 32. Sr. Kathleen Hanley, R.S.M., D.R.E. Students 360.

3—ST. WILLIAM (1959) Rev. Joseph Benedict; Kathy Schlosser, Pastoral Assoc.
Res.: 611 S. El Monte Ave., 94022-4058. Tel: 650-559-2080; Fax: 650-968-8508.
Catechesis/Religious Program—Tel: 650-941-7672. Ginny Hinkle, D.R.E. Students 55.

LOS GATOS, SANTA CLARA CO., ST. MARY OF THE IMMACULATE CONCEPTION (1912) Revs. Rick Rodoni; Truyen Nguyen. In Res., Rev. Saju Joseph.
Res.: 219 Bean Ave., 95030. Tel: 408-354-3726; Fax: 408-354-9302.
School—(Grades K-8), 30 Lyndon Ave., 95030. Tel: 408-354-3944; Fax: 408-395-9151. Sr. Nicki Thomas, S.N.J.M., Prin.; Sheila Chavez, Librarian. Sisters of the Holy Names of Jesus and Mary 2; Lay Teachers 20; Students 291.
Catechesis/Religious Program—Tel: 408-354-4061; Fax: 408-354-9302. Terri Trotter, D.R.E. Students 514.

MILPITAS, SANTA CLARA CO.

1—ST. ELIZABETH (1968) Revs. Justin Le; Estanislao Mikalonis (Argentina).
Res.: 750 Sequoia Dr., 95035. Tel: 408-262-8100; Fax: 408-946-8703.
Catechesis/Religious Program—Tel: 408-263-1995. Sr. Aqueda Poblete, C.H.S., D.R.E. Students 374.

2—ST. JOHN THE BAPTIST (1877) Rev. Ritche Bueza.
Res.: 279 S. Main St., 95035. Tel: 408-262-2546; Fax: 408-263-2564.
School—(Grades PreSchool-8), 360 S. Abel St., 95035. Tel: 408-262-8110; Fax: 408-262-0814. Judy Perkowski, Prin.; Jaclyn George, Librarian. Augustinian Recollect Sisters 2; Lay Teachers 10; Students 223.
Catechesis/Religious Program—Tel: 408-262-3955; Fax: 408-262-7726. Sr. Susan Marie Alconcher, B.V.M., D.R.E. Students 249.

MORGAN HILL, SANTA CLARA CO., ST. CATHERINE OF ALEXANDRIA (1909) Revs. Mark Arnzen; Alexander Affonso; Hector Basanez; Deacons Erik Haeckel; Philip Flowers.
Res.: 17400 Peak Ave., 95037. Tel: 408-779-3959; Fax: 408-779-0289.
School—(Grades K-8), 17500 Peak Ave., 95037. Tel: 408-779-9950; Fax: 408-779-9928. Fabienne Esparza, Prin.; Catherine Graham, Vice Prin. Lay Teachers 13; Students 315.
Catechesis/Religious Program—Tel: 408-779-9604. Deepu Kochuparambil, Youth Dir. Students 723.

MOUNTAIN VIEW, SANTA CLARA CO.

1—ST. ATHANASIUS (1959) Rev. Oscar Tabujara; Deacon Leonel Mancilla. In Res., Rev. Athanasius Kikoba (Uganda).
Res.: 160 N. Rengstorff Ave., 94043. Tel: 650-961-8600; Fax: 650-968-5633.
Catechesis/Religious Program—Tel: 650-961-8611, Ext. 111; Fax: 650-968-5633. Victor Valdez, D.R.E. Students 204.

2—ST. JOSEPH (1901) Revs. Luis Vargas; Robert B. Moran. In Res., Rev. Timothy Kidney (Retired).
Res.: 582 Hope St., 94041. Tel: 650-967-3831; Fax: 650-691-1522.
School—(Grades K-8), 1120 Miramonte Ave., 94040. Tel: 650-967-1839; Fax: 650-691-1530. Stephanie Mirenda-Knight, Prin.; Carmen Ayers, Librarian. Lay Teachers 17; Students 217.
Catechesis/Religious Program—Tel: 650-691-1525. Erica Underwood, Faith Formation. Students 107.

PALO ALTO, SANTA CLARA CO.

1—ST. ALBERT THE GREAT (1961) Merged with St. Thomas Aquinas Parish.

2—OUR LADY OF THE ROSARY (1959) Merged with St. Thomas Aquinas Parish.

3—ST. THOMAS AQUINAS (1901) Revs. Matthew D. Stanley; Randy Valenton; Peter Seimas; Deacon Daniel Hernandez.
Office: 3290 Middlefield Rd., 94306. Tel: 650-494-2496; Fax: 650-494-3780.
School—St. Elizabeth Seton Catholic Community School, (Grades K-8), 1095 Channing Ave., 94301. Tel: 650-326-9004; Fax: 650-326-2949. Evelyn Rosa, Prin.; Neiva Perez, Librarian. Sponsored by the Daughters of Charity. Sisters 2; Lay Teachers 13; Students 265.
Catechesis/Religious Program—Tel: 650-494-2496, Ext. 25; Fax: 650-494-3780. Susan Clingsmith, D.R.E. Students 463.

SANTA CLARA, SANTA CLARA CO.

1—CHINESE CATHOLIC COMMUNITY (1983), (Chinese), Revs. Carlos Alberto Olivera; Peter Kin Chung Siu, S.J.; Matthew Koo, Chap. (Retired).
725 Washington St., 95050-4966. Tel: 408-983-0211; Fax: 408-983-0212.
Catechesis/Religious Program—Students 129.

2—ST. CLARE (1777) Revs. George Aranha; Norman Segovia. In Res., Rev. Carlos Alberto Olivera.
Church & Mailing Address: 725 Washington St., 95050. Tel: 408-248-7786; Fax: 408-248-8150.
School—(Grades K-8) Tel: 408-246-6797; Fax: 408-246-6726. Madeline Rader, Prin. Sisters 1; Lay Teachers 14; Students 301.
Catechesis/Religious Program—Tel: 408-248-7786; Fax: 408-248-8150. Sonia Delgado, D.R.E. Students 49.

3—ST. JUSTIN (1951) Dorothy Carlson, Min. Parish Life; Revs. Edsil Ortiz, O.F.M.; George Mancha; Joseph Bauer, Pastoral Assoc. In Res., Rev. Joseph Prendergast, C.S.Sp. (Retired).
Res.: 2655 Homestead Rd., 95051. Tel: 408-296-1193; Fax: 408-244-9437.
School—(Grades K-8) Tel: 408-248-1094; Fax: 408-248-0691. Kimberly Shields, Prin. Lay Teachers 15; Students 308.
Catechesis/Religious Program—Fax: 408-244-9437. Tracy Sevigny, D.R.E. Students 207.

4—ST. LAWRENCE, THE MARTYR (1959) Revs. Thuc Si Ho; Ernesto Orci.
Res.: 1971 Saint Lawrence Dr., 95051. Tel: 408-296-3000; Fax: 408-296-3100.
School—(Grades PreSchool-5), 1977 St. Lawrence Dr., 95051. Tel: 408-296-2260; Fax: 408-296-1068. Philip Dolan, Prin.; Suzanne Hunter, Librarian. Lay Teachers 9; Students 223.
School—(Grades 6-8) Tel: 408-296-2260. Philip Dolan, Prin.; Suzanne Hunter, Librarian. Lay Teachers 7; Students 113.
School—(Grades 9-12), 2000 Lawrence Ct., 95051. Tel: 408-296-3013; Fax: 408-296-3794. Christie Filios, Prin. Sisters 1; Lay Teachers 21; Students 237.
Catechesis/Religious Program—Tel: 408-296-0208; Fax: 408-296-3100. Jennie de la Cerda, C.R.E. Students 171.

5—ORATORY OF OUR MOTHER OF PERPETUAL HELP (2004), (Forma Extraordinaria) Revs. Canon Henry Fragelli, Rector; Pedro Ottonello, O.A.D., Chaplain. 1298 Homestead Rd., 95050. Tel: 408-580-6548.

6—OUR LADY OF PEACE (1961) Revs. Jose Giunta, I.V.E. (Argentina); Samuel Leonard, I.V.E.; Gerardus Hauwert, I.V.E.
Res.: 2800 Mission College Blvd., 95054. Tel: 408-988-4585; Fax: 408-988-0679.
Catechesis/Religious Program—Tel: 408-988-7543; Fax: 408-980-9436. Students 788.

SARATOGA, SANTA CLARA CO.

1—CHURCH OF THE ASCENSION (1964) Rev. Jose Galang. In Res., Rev. Andres C. Ligot.
Res.: 12033 Miller Ave., 95070. Tel: 408-725-3939.
Catechesis/Religious Program—Tel: 408-725-3930; Fax: 408-725-3932. Ann Liebmann, D.R.E. Students 119.

2—SACRED HEART (1951) Rev. Gary Thomas; Deacon Donald Sifferman.
Res.: 13716 Saratoga Ave., 95070. Tel: 408-867-3634; Fax: 408-867-5339.
Rectory—13724 Saratoga Ave., 95070.
School—(Grades PreSchool-8), 13718 Saratoga Ave., 95070. Tel: 408-867-9241; Fax: 408-867-9242. Tom Pulchny, Prin. Lay Teachers 15; Students 220.

Pre-School—Lay Teachers 5; Students 18.
Catechesis/Religious Program—Tel: 408-867-1530. Patrick DeLorenzo, Dir. Faith Formation. Students 178.

STANFORD, SANTA CLARA CO., CATHOLIC COMMUNITY AT STANFORD (1997) Revs. Nathan Castle, O.P.; Isaiah Molano, O.P.
Mailing Address: P.O. Box 20301, 94309. Tel: 650-725-0080; Fax: 650-723-6797.
Catechesis/Religious Program—

SUNNYVALE, SANTA CLARA CO.

1—CHURCH OF THE RESURRECTION (1963) Revs. G. Robert Leger; Allen Navarro. In Res., Rev. Joseph N. Vanthu (Retired).
Res. & Church: 725 Cascade Dr., 94087. Tel: 408-245-5554; Fax: 408-245-5589.
School—(Grades PreSchool-8), 1395 Hollenbeck Ave., 94087. Tel: 408-245-4571; Fax: 408-733-7301. Jacqueline T. Wright, Prin. Sisters 3; Lay Teachers 14; Students 226.
Catechesis/Religious Program—Tel: 408-746-0172. Students 81.

2—ST. CYPRIAN (1961) Rev. Arturo Yabes.
Res.: 1133 W. Washington Ave., 94086. Tel: 408-739-8506; Fax: 408-739-2815.
School—(Grades PreK-8), 195 Leota Ave., 94086. Tel: 408-738-3444; Fax: 408-733-3730. Priscilla Murphy, Interim Prin. Lay Teachers 13; Students 193.
Catechesis/Religious Program—Tel: 408-739-1669. Porty Nevarez, D.R.E. Students 89.

3—HOLY KOREAN MARTYRS (2005), (Korean), Rev. Matthias Seon Ki Hwang.
Res.: 531 E. Weddell Dr., 94089-2162. Tel: 408-734-9721; Fax: 408-734-9723.
Catechesis/Religious Program—Tel: 408-225-9272. Richard Il-Young Hong, D.R.E. Students 287.

4—ST. MARTIN (1916) Revs. Jose Antonio Medina; Martin Abrego. In Res., Rev. Ed Samy (Retired).
Res.: 590 Central Ave., 94086. Tel: 408-736-3725; Fax: 408-736-4968.
School—(Grades PreSchool-8), 597 Central Ave., 94086. Tel: 408-736-5534. Sharon Lydon, Prin. Lay Teachers 11; Students 197.
Catechesis/Religious Program—593 Central Ave., 94086. Tel: 408-736-3725. Judy Kelch, D.R.E. Students 195.

Chaplains of Public Institutions

SAN JOSE. *Catholic Scouting*. Rev. Paul A. Soukup, S.J. Tel: 408-554-4124.
Detention Ministry for Juveniles. Rev. Daniel C. Urcia, Ed.D. Tel: 408-983-0144.
Notre Dame Club of San Jose/Silicon Valley. Very Rev. Brendan McGuire, V.G.
Santa Clara County Jail. Rev. Daniel C. Urcia, Ed.D.
Santa Clara County Sheriffs Dept. Rev. Paul Weisbeck (Retired).
Santa Clara County Women's Facility. Sr. Maryann Cantlon, C.S.J.
Santa Clara Valley Medical Center. Rev. Eugene J. Corbett, S.J.

STANFORD. *Stanford Medical Center*. Rev. John Hester. Tel: 650-723-4000.

Special Assignment:
Rev. Msgr.—
Cilia, Francis V., V.G., Vicar Gen., Moderator of the Curia & Vicar for Clergy
Very Rev.—
McGuire, Brendan, V.G., Vicar General
Revs.—
Benedict, Joseph, S.T.D., Dir. Permanent Deacon Formation
Brocato, Robert S., Missionary Assignment - Diocese of Montego Bay, Jamaica
Dinh, Hao, Vicar for Vietnamese Ministry
Gammad, Engelberto, J.C.D., Tribunal - Adjutant Judicial Vicar
Hayes, Robert E., J.C.L., Tribunal Ministry, Defender of the Bond
Joseph, Saju, J.C.L., Tribunal
Ligot, Andres C., J.C.D., Judicial Vicar, Vicar Filipino Min.
Nguyen, Hien Minh, J.C.D., Sabbatical
Ovando, Sergio, Assigned Study, Rome
Poncini, John, Dir. Vocations
Rubio, Jose Antonio, S.T.D., Dir. Ecumenical & Interreligious Affairs & Delegate Eastern Rite Churches, Faculty, St. Patrick Seminary & Univ.
Suarez, Walter, Vicar for Hispanic Min.
Urcia, Daniel C., Ed.D., Restorative Justice
Vanthu, Joseph N., Dir. Vietnamese Catholic Center (Retired)

On Duty Outside the Diocese:
Revs.—
Brocato, Robert S., Diocese of Montego Bay, Jamaica, WI
Ovando, Sergio, Rome, Italy
Rich, Joseph, Newport Beach, CA
Saso, Michael (Retired), Macau

On Leave of Absence:
Revs.—
Arnone, Alan
Browne, Dennis
Day, Michael
Delgado, Joseph
Gray, Robert
Hernandez, Enrico
Keulman, Kenneth P.
Lagututta, Nunzio J.
Marx, Robert
Nabbefeld, Grant
Pereira, Anthony
Rojas, Roberto (Argentina)
Smith, Brian
Sullivan, Mervyn

Absent on Sick Leave:
Revs.—
Bonsor, Jack
Neary, Mark

Retired:
Most Rev.—
DuMaine, R. Pierre
Rev. Msgrs.—
Andre, Ludwig
Boyle, Eugene
Coleman, John
Larkin, Alexander C.
Lenane, William
Milani, Joseph J.
Mitchell, Michael J.
Sandersfeld, John
Sullivan, Terrence J.
Walsh, James
Revs.—
Balthazar, Ayala
Burns, Michael J.
Davis, Terrence
Kidney, Timothy
Kilcoyne, Patrick
Koo, Matthew
Largente, Laurent
Leininger, William
Lopez, Abel, J.C.L.
Manding, Benito O.
Passalacqua, Robert
Pegnam, William
Perata, Stephen
Re, Angelo
Samy, Ed
Saso, Michael
Shea, Thomas
Tinh, Joseph Nguyen
Traverso, Leonard
Vanthu, Joseph N.
Weisbeck, Paul

Permanent Deacons:
Agbayani, Willy, Restorative Justice, Liturgical Min., St. Francis of Assisi
Allen, Pat, St. Mary, Gilroy
Alvarez, Joseph, St. John Vianney
Alvarez, Salvador, St. Francis of Assisi
Chavez, Eloy, Our Lady of Guadalupe
Collins, Harry, Restorative Justice
Doyle, James, St. Cyprian
Flowers, Philip, St. Catherine
Haeckel, Eric, St. Catherine
Hanson, Ron, St. Joseph of Cupertino, Santa Clara Univ.
Hernandez, Daniel, St. Thomas Aquinas
Herrera, Steven, Transfiguration
Ho, Joseph Nhut, St. Maria Goretti
Hoang, The, Christ the King
Huynh, Joseph N., St. Patrick
Le, Tho, St. Patrick
Magat, Melchor, St. Victor
Mancilla, Leonel, St. Athanasius
McKenna, Brian, Queen of Apostles
Mendoza, Raul, St. John Vianney
Nguyen, Hon, St. Victor
Nojadera, Bernard V., USCCB, Washington, DC
Perez, Vicente, Most Holy Trinity
Pham, Anthony, Restorative Justice, Liturgical Min., St. Maria Goretti
Sifferman, Donald, Sacred Heart, Saratoga; Children's Hospital, Stanford
Sobezyk, Andrzej, St. Francis of Assisi
Tran, Dung Quoc, St. Martin
Vu, John, St. Elizabeth

INSTITUTIONS LOCATED IN THE DIOCESE

[A] SHRINES

SANTA CLARA. *Shrine of Our Lady of Peace* 2800 Mission College Blvd., 95054. Tel: 408-988-4585; Fax: 408-988-0679. Rev. Jose Giunta, I.V.E. (Argentina), Dir.
Our Lady of Peace Gift Shop Tel: 408-980-9825; Fax: 408-988-2488.

[B] COLLEGES AND UNIVERSITIES

SANTA CLARA. *Santa Clara University*, 500 El Camino Real, 95053-0001. Tel: 408-554-4000; Fax: 408-554-2700. Email: username@scu.edu. Web: www.scu.edu. Elizabeth Salzer, Librarian. Society of Jesus., Mission Santa Clara. Founded in 1777. University established in 1851 and chartered by the State in 1855. Priest Teachers 47; Brothers 2; Scholastics 1; Sisters 3; Lay Teachers 400; Students 8,490.
Administrators: Revs. Michael E. Engh, S.J., Pres.; Kevin F. Burke, S.J., Dean Jesuit School Theology; Dr. Godfrey Mungal, Dean School of Engineering; Dr. Donald J. Polden, Dean School of Law; S. Andrew Starbird, Dean Leavey School of Business Admin.; Dr. Robert Gunsalys, Vice Pres. Univ. Rels.; Mr. Robert Warren, Vice Pres. Finance Admin.; Dr. W. Atom Yee, Dean College of Arts & Sciences.
Jesuit Community, 500 El Camino Real, 95053-1600. Tel: 408-554-4124; Fax: 408-554-4795. Rev. Michael A. Zampelli, S.J., Rector Jesuit Community; Very Rev. Michael D. Weiler, S.J.; Revs. Jeffrey C. Baerwald, S.J.; Samuel Bellino, S.J.; Luis F. Calero, S.J.; Matthew E. Carnes, S.J.; Christopher M. Cartwright, S.J.; Michael T. T. Castori, S.J.; Paul G. Crowley, S.J.; William F. Donnelly, S.J.; James W. Felt, S.J., Prof. Emeritus; Andrew J. Garavel, S.J.; Paul J. Goda, S.J.; Carl H. Hayn, S.J., Prof. Emeritus; Arthur F. Liebscher, S.J.; Paul P. Mariani, S.J.; Francis X. McAloon, S.J.; Michael C. McCarthy, S.J.; Very Rev. John P. McGarry, S.J.; Revs. Gerald L. McKevitt, S.J.; John P. Mossi, S.J.; Alfred E. Naucke, S.J.; Chi V. Ngo, S.J.; Thao N. Nguyen, S.J.; Peter Pabst, S.J.; Dennis R. Parnell, S.J.; Charles T. Phipps, S.J., Min./Contact; Mark A. Ravizza, S.J.; James W. Reites, S.J.; William J. Rewak, S.J.; Theodore J. Rynes, S.J.; Nicky Santos, S.J.; Peter Kin Chung Siu, S.J.; Francis R. Smith, S.J.; Dennis C. Smolarski, S.J.; Paul A. Soukup, S.J.; Salvatore A. Tassone, S.J.; Charles Tilly, S.J.; Frederick P. Tollini, S.J.; Manh D. Tran, S.J.; John P. Treacy, S.J.; Fidelis Udahemuka, S.J.; Tennant C. Wright, S.J.; Bros. Thomas C. Bracco, S.J., Asst. Min.; James Siwicki, S.J.; Mr. Elias Puentes, S.J., Scholastic & Seminarian.
Jesuit Community at Santa Clara University, Inc. Priests 43; Brothers 2.

[C] HIGH SCHOOLS, DIOCESAN

SAN JOSE. *Archbishop Mitty High School* (Coed), 5000 Mitty Ave., 95129. Tel: 408-252-6610; Fax: 408-252-6967. Email: brosnan@mitty.com. Web: www.mitty.com. Mr. Timothy Brosnan, Prin.; Billy King, Librarian. Lay Teachers 104; Students 1,678; Total Staff 165.

SANTA CLARA. *Saint Lawrence Academy*, 2000 Lawrence Ct., 95051. Tel: 408-296-3013; Fax: 408-296-3794. Email: cfilios@saintlawrence.org. Web: www.saintlawrenceacademy.org. Christie Filios, Prin.; Lorianne Ventura, Asst. Prin. College Prep Coed. Sisters 1; Lay Teachers 25; Students 237; Total Staff 29.

[D] HIGH SCHOOLS, PRIVATE

SAN JOSE. *Bellarmine College Preparatory*, 960 W. Hedding St., 95126. Tel: 408-294-9224; Fax: 408-294-1894. Web: www.bcp.org. Chris Meyercord, Prin.; Ann Weber, Librarian; Revs. Christopher Nguyen, S.J., Supr. & Contact; Peter M.Q. Chu, S.J.; Richard E. Cobb, S.J.; Edwin B. Harris, S.J.; William Kelley, S.J.; Robert B. Mathewson, S.J.; Michael Moodie, S.J.; Paul G. Sheridan, S.J.; Robert J. Shinney, S.J.; Gerald T. Wade, S.J., Chancellor; Mr. Erick Berrelleza, S.J. Society of Jesus. Priests 4; Brothers 2; Lay Teachers 105; Students 1,616.

Notre Dame High School, 596 S. Second St., 95112. Tel: 408-294-1113; Fax: 408-293-9779. Web: www.ndsj.org. Mary Beth Riley, Prin.; Amy Huang, Librarian. Sisters of Notre Dame de Namur. Lay Teachers 53; Total Staff 76; Students 630.

Presentation High School, 2281 Plummer Ave., 95125. Tel: 408-264-1664; Fax: 408-266-7333. Web: www.Pres-Net.com. Mary Miller, Prin.; Rev. Rick Rodoni, Chap.; Katy Lemon, Librarian. Sisters of the Presentation. Lay Teachers 66; Students 819; Total Staff 96.

MORGAN HILL. *South County Catholic High School*, 17190 Monterey Rd., Ste. 202, 95037. Tel: 408-776-1017. George Chiala, Pres.

MOUNTAIN VIEW. *St. Francis High School*, 1885 Miramonte Ave., 94040. Tel: 650-968-1213; Fax: 650-968-3241. Email: kemakley@sfhs.com. Web: www.sfhs.com. Mr. Kevin Makley, Pres.; Mr. Simon Raines, Dir. Activities; Mrs. Patricia Tennant, Prin.; Ann Lane, Librarian. Brothers of Holy Cross. Brothers 1; Lay Teachers 107; Students 1,733; Total Staff 151.

[E] MIDDLE SCHOOLS, PRIVATE

SAN JOSE. *Sacred Heart Nativity School*, (Grades 6-8), 310 Edwards, 95110. Tel: 408-993-1293; Fax: 408-993-0675. Email: shnativity@shnativity.org. Web: www.shnativity.org. Rev. Peter Pabst, S.J., Pres.; Kevin Eagleson, Graduate Support Dir.; Jeffrey Cunjak, Co-Prin.; Bridgit McGarry, Co-Prin. Priests 1; Lay Teachers 23; Students 130; Total Staff 28.

CAMPBELL. *Canyon Heights Academy, Inc.*, (Grades PreSchool-8), 775 Waldo Rd., 95008. Tel: 408-370-6727; Fax: 408-370-7147. Email: wpparker@chamail.net. Web: www.canyonheightsacademy.com. W. Paul Parker, Prin. Lay Teachers 16; Students 219.

[F] THE CATHOLIC CHARITIES OF THE DIOCESE OF SAN JOSE

SAN JOSE. *Catholic Charities of Santa Clara County*, 2625 Zanker Rd., 95134. Tel: 408-468-0100; Fax: 408-944-0275. Web: www.catholiccharitiesscc.org. Gregory R. Kepferle, CEO; Margaret Williams, CAO & CFO; Deborah Baker, Human Resources; Ruben Solorio, Parish & Community Rels.; Marilou Cristina, Div. Dir. Older Adult Svcs.; Stephen Hicken, Interim Div. Dir. Economic Dev. Svcs.; Kenneth Bazile, Div. Dir. Children, Youth & Family; Kitty Mason, Div. Dir., Behavioral Health Svcs.; Magi Young, Chief Devel. Officer; Marnie Regen, Assoc. Devel. Dir.; Terrie Iacino, Dir. Community Dev. & Advocacy; Robin Reynolds, Dir. of Communications.

Service Divisions:
Community Dev. & Advocacy
Economic Development Svcs.
Older Adult Svcs.
Behavioral Health Svcs.
Children, Youth & Family Dev.

Community Development & Advocacy
Step Up Silicon Valley Tel: 408-468-0100.
Handicapables Program Tel: 408-468-0100.

Economic Development Services
Asylee Program Tel: 408-468-0100.
Citizenship Services - South County Tel: 408-914-8337.
Employment Services Tel: 408-468-0100.
Financial Education Services Tel: 408-468-0100.
Free Tax Preparation Tel: 408-325-5241.
Focus for Work Tel: 408-468-0100.
Housing Search and Stabilization Tel: 408-468-0100.
Immigration Legal Services Tel: 408-468-0100.
Refugee Foster Care Tel: 408-468-0100.
Refugee Resettlement Tel: 408-468-0100.

Older Adult Services
Day Break Adult Day Care/Caregiver Support Tel: 408-270-4900.
Day Break In-Home Care Tel: 408-468-0100.
Long Term Care Ombudsman Tel: 408-944-0567.
Senior Nutrition Program Tel: 408-468-0100.
Eastside Neighborhood Center Nutrition Tel: 408-251-0215.
John XXIII Multi-Service Center Nutrition Tel: 408-282-8607.
Gilroy Nutrition Tel: 408-846-0428.
Eastside Neighborhood Center Tel: 408-251-0215.
John XXIII Multi-Service Center Tel: 408-282-8600.

Behavioural Health Services
Adult Mental Health Services Tel: 408-295-5288.
CalWORKs Tel: 408-325-5230.
Children and Family Services Tel: 408-468-0100.
Golden Gateway Tel: 408-295-5288.
Homeless Veteran's Program Tel: 408-295-5288.
OASIS (Older Adult Services) Tel: 408-295-5288.
Supportive Housing Tel: 408-468-0100.

Children, Youth & Family Development
CORAL (Communities Organizing Resources to Advance Learning) Tel: 408-283-6150.
El Toro Youth Center Tel: 408-779-6002.
FA'ATASI Tel: 408-938-6731.
First 5 Tel: 408-283-6150.
Franklin McKinley's Children's Initiative Tel: 408-283-6150.
Justice Empowerment Svcs. Tel: 408-468-0100.
Intervention Services Tel: 408-938-6731.
Kinship Resource Center Tel: 408-200-0980.
LEAP Project (Leadership, Ethnic, & Academic Pride) Tel: 408-283-6150.
Peer Educators Tel: 408-823-6150.
Probation Suport Services Tel: 408-295-5288.
Raising A Reader Tel: 408-283-6150.
Successful Parents' Project Tel: 408-283-6150.
The Summit League Tech Lab Tel: 408-938-6731.
Washington United Youth Center Tel: 408-938-6731.
Young Women's Empowerment Tel: 408-938-6731.

[G] DAY CARE CENTERS

SAN JOSE. *St. Elizabeth's Day Home*, 950 St. Elizabeth Dr., 95126. Tel: 408-295-3456; Fax: 408-295-5917. Email: info@stelizabethdayhom.org. Web: www.stelizabethsdayhome.org. Diana Ballesteros, Exec. Dir. Lay Staff 25; Children 101.

[H] GENERAL HOSPITALS

SAN JOSE. *O'Connor Hospital*, 2105 Forest Ave., 95128. Tel: 408-947-2500; Fax: 408-995-0117. Web: www.oconnorhospital.org. James F. Dover, CEO; Rev. Robert McKay, Ph.D. (South Africa), Dir. Chap. Svcs.; Ms. Elsamma James, Staff Chap.; Mr. Raymond Dougherty, Staff Chap.; Rev. Sharon Kim, Staff Chap.

O'Connor Hospital, Sponsored by Daughters of Charity Health System. Total Staff 1,538; Bed Capacity 358; Patients Assisted Annually 150,000.

O'Connor Foundation, 2105 Forest Ave., 95128. Tel: 408-947-2717; Fax: 408-947-2649. Toni Harper, CEO Foundation.

GILROY. *Saint Louise Regional Hospital*, Admin. Office, 9400 No Name Uno, 95020. Tel: 408-848-2000; Fax: 408-842-2155. Email: joanneallen@dochs.org. Web: www.dochs.org. Sr. Paula Baker, P.B.V.M., Vice Pres. Mission Integration; Joanne Allen, Pres. & CEO. Sponsored by Daughters of Charity Health System. Sisters 3; Total Staff 539; Bed Capacity 93; Patients Assisted Annually 64,141.

[I] SPECIAL SANATORIUMS AND HOSPITALS

SARATOGA. *Our Lady of Fatima Villa*, 20400 Saratoga-Los Gatos Rd., 95070. Tel: 408-741-2950; Fax: 408-741-4930. Web: www.fatimavilla.org. Bella Mahoney, Pres. & CEO; Sr. Susan Snyder, O.P., Prioress. Sponsored by Dominican Sisters of St. Catherine of Siena of Kenosha, Inc., Provides skilled nursing rehabilitation services and assisted living facility for aged women and men. Sisters 1; Residents 100; Total Staff 94.

[J] HOTEL, SENIOR CITIZENS RESIDENCE

SAN JOSE. *Giovanni Center, Inc.*, 85 S. Fifth St., 95112. Tel: 408-288-7436; Fax: 408-288-7264. Email: jeannedarc@jsco.net. Francisco Solis, Property Mgr. A California nonprofit charitable, public-benefit, housing project for low-income elderly. Sponsored by the Roman Catholic Bishop of San Jose, a corporation sole. Lay Staff 3; Residents 30.

Jeanne d'Arc Manor, 85 S. Fifth St., 95112. Tel: 408-288-7421; Fax: 408-288-7264. Email: jeannedarc@jsco.net. Francisco Solis, Property Mgr. Housing project for low-income elderly and disabled. Sponsored by the Roman Catholic Bishop of San Jose, A Corporation Sole. Lay Staff 10; Residents 110; Units 87.

[K] HOMES FOR THE AGED

MOUNTAIN VIEW. *Villa Siena*, 1855 Miramonte Ave., 94040. Tel: 650-961-6484; Fax: 650-961-6254. Email: cbernard@villa-siena.org. Web: www.villa-siena.org. Mrs. Corine Bernard, Exec. Dir.; Sr. Judith Lynn Gardenhire, Pres. & Bd. Chm. Daughters of Charity of St. Vincent de Paul., Residential Care and Skilled Nursing Facility. Professed Sisters 3; Residents 77; In Nursing Care 20; Nursing Staff 30; Total Staff 65.

[L] RETREATS

LOS ALTOS. *Jesuit Retreat Center of Los Altos*, 300 Manresa Way, 94022. Tel: 650-917-4000; Fax: 650-948-0640. Email: retreat@jrclosaltos.org. Web: www.jrclosaltos.org. Revs. James Flynn, Supr.; Kevin Ballard, S.J., Retreat Dir.; Bernard J. Bush, S.J.; Robert J. Fabing, S.J.; Joseph J. Fice, S.J.; Joseph Specht, S.J.; Duc Vu, S.J.; Bro. Thomas J. Koller, S.J. Priests 7; Brothers 1.

LOS GATOS. *Presentation Center*, 19480 Bear Creek Rd., 95033-9519. Tel: 408-354-2346; Fax: 408-354-5226. Web: www.presentationcenter.org. Anna M. O'Connor, Exec. Dir. & Contact. Retreat and Conference Center. Religious 4; Lay People 3; Capacity 200; Staff 20.

Villa Holy Names, P.O. Box 907, 95031-0907. Tel: 408-354-1730; Fax: 408-354-8305. Email: jmvillalg@yahoo.com. Sr. Kathryn Ondreyco, S.N.J.M. Total Staff 1.

[M] MONASTERIES AND RESIDENCES OF PRIESTS AND BROTHERS

SAN JOSE. *Carmelite Monastery, Novitiate*, P.O. Box 3420, 95156-3420. Tel: 408-251-1361; Fax: 408-251-1854. Revs. James Geoghegan, O.C.D,; Thomas Koller, O.C.D., Postulant Master; Donald Kinney, O.C.D.; Patrick Sugrue, O.C.D.; Richard Mandoli, O.C.D.

CUPERTINO. *The Marianist Center*, 22683 Alcalde Rd., 95014. Tel: 408-207-4800; Fax: 408-253-3466. Revs. Joseph Hartzler, S.M.; Joseph Stefanelli, S.M.; Raymond Malley, S.M.; Lawrence Mann, S.M.; William O'Connell, S.M.; Daniel Triulzi, S.M.; Stephen Tutas, S.M.; Bros. William Bolts, S.M.; James Christiana, S.M.; Thomas Deasy, S.M.; Charles Ehrenfeld, S.M.; Paul Fennelly, S.M.; Eugene Frank, S.M.; Howard Hughes, S.M.; James Leahy, S.M.; Patrick McMahon, S.M.; Stanley Murakami, S.M., Sub-Dir.; Joseph Nu'uanu, S.M.; John Samaha, S.M.; Frank Spaeth, S.M.; Robert Wade, S.M. Marianist Center. Priests 7; Brothers 14; Total in Residence 22. *The Alcalde House*, 22683 Alcalde Rd., 95014-3903. Tel: 408-207-4808; Fax: 408-253-3466. Rev. David Schuyler, S.M., Community Dir.; Bro. John Haster, S.M. Priests 1; Brothers 1; Total in Residence 2. *The Bordeaux House*, 22683 Alcalde Rd., 95014. P.O. Box 1775, 95015-1775. Tel: 408-207-4800; Fax: 408-253-3466. Rev. John McEnhill, S.M.; Bros. John Schlund, S.M.; Vincent Wayer, S.M. Priests 1; Brothers 2; Total in Residence 3. Living In Other Residences: Bro. Robert Juenemann, S.M., San Jose.

LOS ALTOS. *Maryknoll*, 23000 Cristo Rey Dr., 94024. Tel: 650-967-3822; Fax: 650-965-3473. Maryknoll Residence for Priests and Brothers. Priests 22; Brothers 8. In Res. Revs. Donald Allen, M.M.; William M. Boteler, M.M.; Bernard P. Byrne, M.M.; Robert J. Carleton, M.M.; Thomas E. Danaher, S.M.; Clyde F. Davis, M.M.; Marvin Deutsch, M.M.; Thomas F. Donnelly, M.M.; John F. Felago, M.M.; Arthur J. Dwyer, M.M.; Joseph A. Klecha, M.M.; Joseph W. Kowalczyk, M.M.; Carmen G. LaMazza, M.M.; Richard G. Laszewski, M.M.; Donald P. McQuade, M.M.; Charles A. Murray, M.M.; Joseph C. Nerino, M.M.; Edward J. Quinn, M.M.; James Roth, M.M.; Philip F. Sheerin, M.M.; James S. Stefaniak, M.M.; John J. Vinsko, M.M.; Bros. Luke R. Baldwin, M.M.; Casimir Brezinski, M.M.; Duane S. Crockett, M.M.; Joseph Dowling, M.M.; Venard Ruane, M.M.; Leo Shedy, M.M.; Cyril L. Vellicig, M.M.

LOS GATOS. *California Province of the Society of Jesus, Jesuit Provincial Office*, P.O. Box 519, 95031-0519. Tel: 408-884-1600; Fax: 408-884-1601. Email: calprovsj@calprov.org. Web: www.jesuitscalifornia.org. Very Rev. Michael D. Weiler, S.J., Regl. Prov.; Revs. Alfred E. Naucke, S.J., Exec. Asst. & Contact; Chi V. Ngo, S.J., Formation Dir.; Dennis R. Parnell, S.J., Treas.

Sacred Heart Jesuit Center, Provincial Office, P.O. Box 519, 95031. Tel: 408-884-1700; Fax: 408-884-1701. Revs. John Privett, S.J., Supr. & Contact; James R. Hanley, S.J., Asst. Supr.; Joseph T. Angilella, S.J.; George K. Aziz, S.J.; Philip C. Blake, S.J.; John A. Brady, S.J.; William F. Breault, S.J.; Francis J. Buckley, S.J.; Michael J. Buckley, S.J.; Peter Burns, S.J.; Bernard J. Bush, S.J.; William F. Cain, S.J.; Mario L. Capitolo, S.J.; Paul F. Capitolo, S.J.; George A. Carroll, S.J.; William Carroll, S.J.; Bernard F. Cassidy, S.J.; Gilbert M. Chacon, S.J.; John W. Clark, S.J.; Ronald C. Clemo, S.J.; Eugene J. Corbett, S.J.; Richard T. Coz, S.J.; Andrew C. Dachauer, S.J.; Raymond A. Devlin, S.J.; Ralph J. Drendel, S.J.; John F. Dullea, S.J.; Robert John Egan, S.J.; Carlo A. Farina, S.J.; Thomas P. Finsterbach, S.J.; David T. Fisher, S.J.; John J. Flynn, S.J.; John L. Flynn, S.J.; Thomas W. Foster, S.J.; Reynold J. Gatto, S.J.; John I. Geiszel, S.J.; Robert E. Griffin, S.J.; Francis G. Hernandez, S.J.; Leo J. Hombach, S.J.; Carroll J. Keating, S.J.; George V. Kennard, S.J.; George J. Koch, S.J.; Gerald J. Lentz, S.J.; Candido Lim, S.J.; Jerold W. Lindner, S.J.; Andrew F. Maginnis, S.J.; James P. McCauley, S.J.; Robert McDevitt, S.J.; Lorenzo J. Palafox, S.J.; Louis A. Peinado, S.J.; Camille J. Prat, S.J.; Jamie J. Rasura, S.J.; Thomas J. Reilly, S.J.; Anton J. Renna, S.J.; Norbert J. Rigali, S.J.; Anastacio S. Rivera, S.J.; Martin I. Rock, S.J.; F. Warren Schoeppe, S.J.; William K. Stolz, S.J.; Robert R. Taheny, S.J.; Peter J. Togni, S.J.; Richard P. Vaughn, S.J.; Silvano P. Votto, S.J.; Carlton E. Whitten, S.J.; William J. Wood, S.J.; Warren J. Wright, S.J.; Bros. William C. Farrington, S.J.; John E. Keck, S.J.; Charles J. Onorato, S.J.; Daniel J. Peterson, S.J.; Theodore C. Rohrer, S.J.; Leonard J. Sullivan, S.J.

California Province of the Society of Jesus dba

Sacred Heart Jesuit Center Priests 65; Brothers 6.

SANTA CLARA. *Casa San Inigo, Jesuit Residence*, 1075 Benton St., 95050-4801. Tel: 408-200-1150; Fax: 408-200-1151. Rev. Charles J. Tilley, S.J., Community Coord.; Very Rev. Michael D. Weiler, S.J.; Revs. Francis X. McAloon, S.J.; Chi V. Ngo, S.J.; Peter Pabst, S.J. Priests 5.

Jesuit Community Please see listing under Santa Clara University, located under Colleges and Universities., 500 El Camino Real, 95053. Tel: 408-554-4124; Fax: 408-554-4795.

SARATOGA. *St. Patrick's Missionary Society* (St. Patrick Fathers), 19536 Eric Dr., 95070. Tel: 408-253-3135; Fax: 408-253-5433. Email: spsca@spms.org. Web: www.stpatrickfathers.org. Rev. Michael Moore, S.P.S., Dir. of Promotion. Priests 1.

[N] CONVENTS AND RESIDENCES FOR SISTERS

SAN JOSE. *Community of the Holy Spirit*, 1275 Naglee Ave., 95126. Tel: 408-275-1710. Sr. Jolene M. Schmitz, C.H.S., Contact.

Daughters of Charity of St. Vincent de Paul, O'Connor Sisters Home, 350 O'Connor Dr., 95128. Tel: 408-289-9215. Email: sistersocon@yahoo.com. Sisters 8.

Eucharistic Missionaries of the Most Holy Trinity, 815 S. Daniel Way, 95128. Tel: 408-243-3157; Fax: 408-243-3157. Sr. Teresita Garcia, M.E.S.S.T., Supr. Sisters 4.

La Salle Sisters, 3867 Silver Creek Rd., 95121-1969. Tel: 408-238-9351; Fax: 408-258-4870. Email: nutulasan@yahoo.com. Web: saigon.com/-vietedu. Sr. Ann Olivia Thanh Vu, L.S.S., Contact Person. Sisters 12.

Pious Disciples of the Divine Master, 2076 Lincoln Ave., 95125. Tel: 408-265-8105; Fax: 408-265-8105. Email: sddmsjca@aol.com. Web: www.pddm.us. Sr. Fede Tanno, P.D.D.M., Supr. Sisters 3.

Quinhon Missionary Sisters of the Holy Cross, 1393 Crailford Ct., 95121. Tel: 408-362-0148. Sr. Josefa Ngoc Nguyen, L.H.C., Regl. Supr. & Local Contact. Sisters 3.

Sinsinawa Dominican Congregation of the Most Holy Rosary, 2024 McDaniel Ave., #2, 95128. Tel: 408-298-4050. Sr. Virginia Pfluger, O.P., Local Contact.

Sisters of the Holy Family, P.O. Box 3248, Fremont, 94539. Tel: 510-624-4500; Fax: 510-624-4550. *St. Elizabeth's Day Home Day Care Center* Children 117.

CONCORD. *Sisters of St. Joseph of Carondelet*, 1133 Winston Dr., 94518. Tel: 925-686-9697. Web: www.csjla.org/membersonly. Sr. Mary Ann Martin, Contact Person (Los Angeles Prov.). Sisters 5.

CUPERTINO. *Blessed Virgin Missionaries of Carmel (B.V.M.C.)*, 10130 N. De Anza Blvd., 95014. Tel: 408-257-1022; Fax: 408-257-3272. Sr. Gloria P. Solis, B.V.M.C., Supr. Sisters 3.

Intercommunity Convent, 10351 S. Blaney Ave., 95014-3122. Tel: 408-725-0898; 408-252-9696; Fax: 408-252-4848. Email: insyte@comcast.net.

LOS ALTOS HILLS. *Daughters of Charity of St. Vincent de Paul, Seton Provincialate*, 26000 Altamont Rd., 94022. Tel: 650-941-4490; Fax: 650-949-8883. Email: docpsec@aol.com. Web: www.daughtersofcharity.com. Rev. Andrew E. Bellisario, C.M., Dir. Sisters 51; Total in Province 122; Total in Diocese 51.

Immaculate Heart Monastery of the Poor Clares, 28210 Natoma Rd., 94022-3320. Tel: 650-948-2947. Sr. Maura Heinen, P.C.C., Abbess. Sisters 17.

LOS GATOS. *Sisters of the Holy Names of Jesus & Mary*, P.O. Box 907, 95031-0907. Tel: 408-395-2868; Fax: 408-354-8305. Email: kondreyco@snjmuson.org. Web: www.snjmusontario.org. Sisters Mary Ellen Holohan, S.N.J.M., Prov. Supr. & Contact; Mariellen Blaser, S.N.J.M., Leadership Team; Jane Hibbard, S.N.J.M., Leadership Team; Kathleen Hilton, S.N.J.M., Leadership Team; Marcia Fridgen, S.N.J.M., Vice Pres. Sisters of the Holy Names of Jesus and Mary US-Ontario Province., Other sisters reside in communities in Santa Clara, Los Gatos, San Jose, Cupertino, and Sunnyvale. *Convent of the Holy Names*, P.O. Box 1906, 95031. Tel: 408-354-1730; Fax: 408-395-6447. Ms. Dayna Hurst, Admin.; Sr. Molly Neville, S.N.J.M., Community Life Coord., Siena. Total in Convent 60.

MILPITAS. *Congregation of the Augustinian Recollect Sisters*, 307 Moretti Ln., 95035. Tel: 408-262-3536; Fax: 408-263-2564. Email: clairediane10@hotmail.com. Web: www.augustinianrecollect.org.ph. Sr. Maria Divina N. Caabay, A.R., Contact Person.

Sisters of Mercy of Americas (Burlingame), 186 Beresford Ct. #F303, 95035. Tel: 650-340-7400; Fax: 650-347-2550. Email: mjvanbommel@att.net. Sr. Maria Juanita Van Bommel, R.S.M., Local Contact. Sisters 10.

REDWOOD CITY. *Sisters of St. Francis of Penance and of Christian Charity*, P.O. Box 1028, 94064. Tel: 650-369-1725; Fax: 650-369-0845. Web: www.stfrancisprovince.org. Sr. Patricia Rayburn, O.S.F., Prov. Min. Sisters 3.

SANTA CLARA. *Carmelite Monastery of the Infant Jesus, Discalced Carmelite Nuns*, 1000 Lincoln St., 95050. Tel: 408-296-8412; Fax: 408-248-4846. Email: santaclaracarmel@aol.com. Web: www.members.aol.com/santaclaracarmel. Sr. Irene Soos, O.C.D., Prioress. Sisters 14.

Dominican Sisters of San Rafael Congregation of the Most Holy Name, 1156 Santa Clara St., #11, 95050. Tel: 408-554-6431. Sr. Francine McCarthy, O.P., Contact Person.

Institute of the Servants of the Lord and the Virgin of Matara, 2800 Mission College Blvd., 95054. Tel: 408-988-4160. Email: c.ourladyofpeace@servidoras.org. Web: www.ssvmusa.org. Sisters 8.

Sisters of Charity of the Blessed Virgin Mary, 1220 Tasman Dr. #303, Sunnyvale, 94089. Tel: 408-744-9143. Web: www.bvmcong.org. Sr. Bette Gambonini, B.V.M., Contact. Sisters 5.

Society of the Sacred Heart, 2665 S. Dr., #120, 95051. Tel: 408-247-0322. Email: jmontalvo@rscj.org. Web: www.sofie.org/rscj/. Sr. Josefina Montalvo, R.S.C.J., Contact.

[O] MISCELLANEOUS LISTINGS

SAN JOSE. *Caritas Housing Corporation*, 1400 Parkmoor Ave., Ste. 190, 95126. Tel: 408-550-8300; Fax: 408-550-8339. Email: info@charitieshousing.org. Web: www.charitieshousing.org. Dan Wu, Exec. Dir.

The Catholic Foundation of Santa Clara County, 777 N. First St., Ste. 740, 95112. Tel: 408-995-5219; Fax: 408-995-5865. Email: info@cfoscc.org. Web: www.cfoscc.org. Mary Quilici Aumack, Exec. Dir.

Charities Housing Development Corporation of Santa Clara County, 1400 Parkmoor Ave., Ste. 190, 95126. Tel: 408-550-8300; Fax: 408-550-8339. Email: info@charitieshousing.org. Web: www.charitieshousing.org. Dan Wu, Exec. Dir. Total Staff 52.

Christ Child Society of San Jose, 20577 Manor Dr., Saratoga, 95070. Tel: 408-725-0605. Email: frtatar@pacbell.net. Raffaela Tatar, Pres.

Hope Charities Housing Corporation, 1400 Parkmoor Ave., Ste. 190, 95126. Tel: 408-550-8300; Fax: 408-550-8339. Email: info@charitieshousing.org. Web: www.charitieshousing.org. Dan Wu, Exec. Dir.

San Antonio Charities, 1400 Parkmoor Ave., Ste. 190, 95126. Tel: 408-550-8300; Fax: 408-550-8339. Email: info@charitieshousing.org. Web: www.charitieshousing.org. Dan Wu, Exec. Dir.

San Jose Cathedral Foundation (A nonprofit, charitable, public-benefit California corporation.), 80 S. Market St., 95113. Tel: 408-283-8100, Ext. 2210; Fax: 408-283-8110. Email: atranchina@dsj.org. Web: www.stjosephcathedral.org. Rev. Msgr. J. Patrick Browne, Exec. Dir.

San Jose English Cursillo, P.O. Box 6648, 95150. Tel: 408-629-2928. Email: sanjosecursillo@yahoo.com. Web: www.sanjosecursillo.org. Mr. Kevin F. Eck, Lay Dir.

San Tomas/Charities Housing Corporation, 1400 Parkmoor Ave., Ste. 190, 95126. Tel: 408-550-8300; Fax: 408-550-8339. Email: info@charitieshousing.org. Web: www.charitieshousing.org. Dan Wu, Exec. Dir.

Sierra Vista I/Charities Housing Corporation, 1400 Parkmoor Ave., Ste. 190, 95126. Tel: 408-550-8300; Fax: 408-550-8339. Email: info@charitieshousing.org. Web: www.charitieshousing.org. Dan Wu, Exec. Dir.

Society of St. Vincent de Paul, District Council of Santa Clara County, P.O. Box 5579, 95150. Tel: 408-249-2853. Email: info@svdp.org. Web: www.svdp.org. Peter Wasserberger, Pres. Total Assisted 70,000; Total Staff 1.

Stoney Pine Charities Housing Corporation, 1400 Parkmoor Ave., Ste. 190, 95126. Tel: 408-550-8300; Fax: 408-550-8339. Email: info@charitieshousing.org. Web: www.charitieshousing.org. Dan Wu, Exec. Dir.

Sunset Charities Housing Corporation, 1400 Parkmoor Ave., Ste. 190, 95126. Tel: 408-550-8300; Fax: 408-550-8339. Email: info@charitieshousing.org. Web: www.charitieshousing.org. Dan Wu, Exec. Dir.

Vietnamese Catholic Center, 2849 S. White Rd., 95148. Tel: 408-983-0175. Email: vcc@dsj.org. Web: www.dsj.org. Mailing Address: 2849 S. White Rd., 95148. Rev. Joseph N. Vanthu, Dir. (Retired).

Vietnamese Youth and Culture Association, La Salle Vietnam House, 1103 Maxey Ct., 95132. Tel: 408-926-4665; Fax: 408-926-4665. Email: valery@stmarys-ca.edu. Web: www.lasan.org. Bros. Valery Nguyen Van An, F.S.C., Dir.; Joseph Phan Huu Phuong, F.S.C., Prin.; Simon Hoang Thai, F.S.C., Librarian. Brothers of the Christian Schools (San Francisco Prov.).

CUPERTINO. *St. Joseph Cupertino Retirement Residence*, 10130 N. DeAnza Blvd., 95014. Tel: 408-257-1022; Fax: 408-257-3272. Rev. Msgr. Joseph J. Milani, Dir. (Retired). Priests 3; Total Staff 3.

EAST PALO ALTO. *Rosalie Rendu Inc.*, 1760 Bay Rd. #24, 94303. Tel: 650-949-8868; Fax: 650-949-8864. Mailing Address: 26000 Altamont Rd., Los Altos Hills, 94022.

GILROY. *Saint Louise Regional Hospital Foundation*, 9400 No Name Uno, 95020. Tel: 408-779-4510; Fax: 408-782-0231. Email: micheleaverill@dochs.org. Web: www.saintlouisehospital.org.

LOS ALTOS. *Jesuit Institute for Family Life*, 300 Manresa Way, 94022. Tel: 650-948-4854; Fax: 650-948-0640. Web: www.elretiro.org. Rev. Robert J. Fabing, S.J., Dir.

LOS ALTOS HILLS. *Daughters of Charity Health System*, 26000 Altamont Rd., 94022. Tel: 650-917-4500; Fax: 650-941-6309. Web: www.dochs.org. Mike Stuart, CFO; Robert Issai, Pres. & CEO.

Daughters of Charity Ministry Services Corporation, 26000 Altamont Rd., 94022-4317. Tel: 650-949-8868; Fax: 650-949-8864.

DCHS Medical Foundation, 26000 Altamont Rd., 94022. Tel: 650-917-4500; Fax: 650-941-6309. Web: www.dochs.org. Robynn Van Patten, Contact Person.

Vincentian Marian Youth, 26000 Altamont Rd., 94022. Tel: 650-941-4490; Fax: 650-949-8883. Sr. Marjory Ann Baez, D.C., Visitatrix.

LOS GATOS. *California Jesuit Missions*, P.O. Box 519, 95031-0068. Tel: 408-884-1612; Fax: 408-884-1601. Web: www.jesuits.org. Rev. Theodore Gabrielli, S.J., Dir.

Jesuit Seminary Association, P.O. Box 68, 95031-0068. Tel: 408-884-1647; Fax: 408-884-1631. Rev. John P. Mossi, S.J., Advancement Office Mgr.

MENLO PARK. *Roman Catholic Comm. Corp. dba Catholic Telemedia Network* 324 Middlefield Rd., 94025. Tel: 650-326-7850; Fax: 650-326-4605. Email: ronald@ctnba.org. Most Revs. Patrick Joseph McGrath, D.D., J.C.D., Chm.; Salvatore J. Cordileone (WDC), Vice Chm.; Ronald J. Loiacono, Exec. Dir.

Roman Catholic Communications Corp. of the Bay Area

MORGAN HILL. *Learning and Loving Education Center*, 16890 Church St., #16, 95037. Tel: 408-776-1196. Email: edctr@earthlink.net. Web: www.learningandloving.org. Sr. Patricia Davis, Exec. Dir.

Serra International Region 11, District 31, 14535 Shadowlane Ct., 95037. Tel: 650-520-3657. Marjorie Fiala, Dist. 31 Gov.

MOUNTAIN VIEW. *Villa Siena Foundation*, 1855 Miramonte Ave., 94040. Tel: 650-961-6484; Fax: 650-961-6254. Email: foundation@villa-siena.org. Mrs. Corine Bernard, Exec. Dir.

SANTA CLARA. *Alexian Brothers of San Jose*, c/o 1150 N. First St., Ste. 100, 95112. Tel: 847-385-7147; Fax: 847-483-7036. Melissa Kulik, Contact Person.

Catholic Professionals, P.O. Box 6346, 95150. Tel: 408-491-9229. Email: info@sjcatholicprofessionals.com. Web: sjcatholicprofessionals.org. Rev. Justin Le, Chap.; Michael Wentz, Pres.

Hand of Help Christian Service Program, 1150 N. First St., Ste. 100, 95112. Tel: 408-983-0158; Fax: 520-720-4004. Email: serve@theriver.com. Web: www.handofhelp.info.

Jesuit Volunteer Corps., P.O. Box 459, 95050. Tel: 408-241-4200; Fax: 408-241-4201.

Roman Catholic Seminary Corporation of San Jose, 1150 N. First St., Ste. 100, 95112. Tel: 408-983-0154; Fax: 408-983-0242. Email: cilia@dsj.org. Rev. Msgr. Francis V. Cilia, V.G., Vice Pres. & Contact Person.

The Roman Catholic Welfare Corporation of San Jose, 1150 N. First St., Ste. 100, 95112. Tel: 408-983-0168; Fax: 408-983-0296. Email: serventi@dsj.org. Robert Serventi, Contact Person.

SARATOGA. *Our Lady of Fatima Villa Foundation*, 20400 Saratoga-Los Gatos Rd., 95070. Tel: 408-741-2950; Fax: 408-741-4930. Email: bmahoney@fatimavilla.org. Web: www.fatimavilla.org. Bella Mahoney, Pres., CEO & Admin.

RELIGIOUS INSTITUTES OF MEN REPRESENTED IN THE DIOCESE

For further details refer to the corresponding bracketed number in the Religious Institutes of Men or Women section.

[0330]—*Brothers of the Christian Schools*—F.S.C.

[0600]—*Brothers of the Congregation of the Holy Cross (Southwest Province)*—C.S.C.

[]—*Congregation of the Mission - Vincentians*—C.M.

[0260]—*Discalced Carmelite Friars*—O.C.D.

[]—*Franciscan Friars* (Croatia)—O.F.M.

[0650]—*Holy Ghost Fathers*—C.S.Sp.

[0305]—*Institute of Christ the King Sovereign Priest*

[]—*Institute of Incarnate Word* (Argentina)—I.V.E.

[0690]—*Jesuit Fathers and Brothers (Society of Jesus)* (California Prov.)—S.J.

[]—*Legionaries of Christ*—L.C.

[0760]—*Marianists (Society of Mary)*—S.M.

[0800]—*Maryknoll (Catholic Foreign Mission Society of America, Inc.)*—M.M.

[1210]—*Missionaries of St. Charles - Scalabrinians (Province of St. John Baptist)*—C.S.

[]—*Order of Discalced Augustinian Friars*—O.A.D.

[]—*Order of Friars Minor (Capuchin Franciscans)*—O.F.M.Cap.

[0520]—*Order of Friars Minor (Province of St. Barbara)*—O.F.M.

[0430]—*Order of Preachers (Province of the Most Holy Name of Jesus-Western Dominican Province)*—O.P.

[1260]—*Society of Christ (Society of Christ for Polonia)*—S.Ch.

[]—*Society of the Divine Word*—S.V.D.

[1170]—*St. Patrick's Missionary Society*—S.P.S.

RELIGIOUS INSTITUTES OF WOMEN REPRESENTED IN THE DIOCESE

[]—*Adrian Dominican Sisters*—O.P.

[]—*Blessed Virgin Missionaries of Carmel*—B.V.M.C.

[]—*Caritas Sisters of Miyazaki*—C.S.M.

[2020]—*Community of the Holy Spirit*—C.H.S.

[]—*Congregation of the Augustinian Recollects*—A.R.

[1070-12]—*Congregation of the Queen of the Holy Rosary (Dominican Sisters)*—O.P.

[0760]—*Daughters of Charity of St. Vincent De Paul*—D.C.

[0420]—*Discalced Carmelite Nuns*—O.C.D.

[1070-19]—*Dominican Sisters of Houston, Texas (Congregation of the Sacred Heart)*—O.P.

[1070-30]—*Dominican Sisters of Oakford*—O.P.

[]—*Dominican Sisters of San Rafael*—O.P.

[]—*Dominican Sisters of St. Rose of Lima*—O.P.

[]—*Eucharistic Missionaries of the Most Holy Trinity* (Mexico)—M.E.S.S.T.

[]—*Franciscan Hospitalier Sisters of the Immaculate Conception*—F.H.IC.

[]—*Franciscans of Our Lady of the Poor*—F.L.P.

[]—*Institute of the Servants of the Lord and the Virgin of Matara*—S.S.V.M.

[]—*LaSalle Sisters* (Vietnam)—L.S.

[2470]—*Maryknoll Sisters of St. Dominic*—M.M.

[]—*Missionary Catechists of Divine Providence*—M.C.D.P.

[3760]—*Order of St. Clare (Immaculate Heart Monastery of Poor Clares)*—P.C.C.

[0980]—*Pious Disciples of the Divine Master*—P.D.D.M.

[]—*Quinhon Missionary Sisters of the Holy Cross* (Vietnam)—L.H.C.

[1070-03]—*Sinsinawa Dominican Congregation of the Most Holy Rosary*—O.P.

[0430]—*Sisters of Charity of the Blessed Virgin Mary*—B.V.M.

[2516]—*Sisters of Mercy (Ireland)*—R.S.M.

[2570]—*Sisters of Mercy of the Americas (Regional Community of Burlingame)*—R.S.M.

[]—*Sisters of Notre Dame de Namur*—S.N.D.deN.

[3840]—*Sisters of St. Joseph of Carondelet (Province of Los Angeles)*—C.S.J.

[3840]—*Sisters of St. Joseph of Carondelet (Province of St. Louis)*—C.S.J.

[1990]—*Sisters of the Holy Names of Jesus and Mary (California Province)*—S.N.J.M.

[3320]—*Sisters of the Presentation of the Blessed Virgin Mary*—P.B.V.M.

[1630]—*Sisters of the Third Order of Saint Francis of Penance and Christian Charity*—O.S.F.

[4070]—*Society of the Sacred Heart*—R.S.C.J.

[]—*Ursuline Roman Union*—O.S.U.

DIOCESAN CEMETERIES AND MAUSOLEUMS

SAN JOSE. *Calvary Catholic Cemetery*, 2650 Madden Ave., 95116. Tel: 408-258-2940; Fax: 408-258-5614. Mr. William Sousae, Dir. (Santa Clara Co.)

LOS ALTOS. *Gate of Heaven*, 22555 Cristo Rey Dr., 94024. Tel: 650-428-3730; Fax: 650-428-3733. William Sousae, Dir.

NECROLOGY

† Maher, Raymond, (Retired)—Died June 11, 2011

An asterisk (*) denotes an organization that has established tax-exempt status directly with the IRS and is not covered by the USCCB Group Ruling.

Archdiocese of Santa Fe

(Archidioecesis Sanctae Fidei)

Most Reverend

MICHAEL J. SHEEHAN, S.T.L., J.C.D.

Archbishop of Santa Fe; ordained July 12, 1964; consecrated and installed as First Bishop of Lubbock June 17, 1983; appointed Apostolic Administrator of Santa Fe April 6, 1993; installed as Eleventh Archbishop of Santa Fe September 21, 1993. *Res.: Catholic Center, 4000 St. Joseph Pl., N.W., Albuquerque, NM 87120.*

Archdiocese of Santa Fe Catholic Center: 4000 St. Joseph Pl., N.W., Albuquerque, NM 87120. Tel: 505-831-8100.

ESTABLISHED IN 1850.

Square Miles 61,142.

Created an Archbishopric in 1875.

Solemnly consecrated to the Immaculate Heart of Mary on October 7, 1945.

Comprises the Counties of Colfax, Curry, DeBaca, Guadalupe, Harding, Los Alamos, Mora, Quay, Roosevelt, San Miguel, Santa Fe, Socorro, Taos, Torrance and Union with a part of Bernalillo, Sandoval, Rio Arriba and Valencia Counties.

Patron of the Archdiocese: St. Francis of Assisi.

For legal titles of parishes and archdiocesan institutions, consult the Chancery Office.

STATISTICAL OVERVIEW

Personnel	
Archbishops	1
Retired Archbishops	1
Retired Bishops	1
Abbots	1
Priests: Diocesan Active in Diocese	84
Priests: Diocesan Active Outside Diocese	1
Priests: Retired, Sick or Absent	54
Number of Diocesan Priests	139
Religious Priests in Diocese	77
Total Priests in Diocese	216
Extern Priests in Diocese	22
Ordinations:	
Religious Priests	1
Transitional Deacons	2
Permanent Deacons	13
Permanent Deacons in Diocese	223
Total Brothers	55
Total Sisters	159
Parishes	
Parishes	92
With Resident Pastor:	
Resident Diocesan Priests	71
Resident Religious Priests	15
Without Resident Pastor:	
Administered by Deacons	2
Administered by Religious Women	3
Administered by Lay People	1
Missions	217
Pastoral Centers	4
Professional Ministry Personnel:	
Brothers	2
Sisters	31
Lay Ministers	90
Welfare	
Catholic Hospitals	1
Total Assisted	561,700
Health Care Centers	1
Total Assisted	2,000
Homes for the Aged	1
Total Assisted	25
Day Care Centers	1
Total Assisted	105
Specialized Homes	2
Total Assisted	2,000
Special Centers for Social Services	5
Total Assisted	384,250
Residential Care of Disabled	1
Total Assisted	16
Educational	
Diocesan Students in Other Seminaries	27
Total Seminarians	27
Colleges and Universities	1
Total Students	206
High Schools, Diocesan and Parish	1
Total Students	816
High Schools, Private	1
Total Students	709
Elementary Schools, Diocesan and Parish	15
Total Students	3,356
Catechesis/Religious Education:	
High School Students	4,018
Elementary Students	14,709
Total Students under Catholic Instruction	23,841
Teachers in the Diocese:	
Priests	1
Brothers	1
Sisters	7
Lay Teachers	393
Vital Statistics	
Receptions into the Church:	
Infant Baptism Totals	4,541
Minor Baptism Totals	302
Adult Baptism Totals	202
Received into Full Communion	235
First Communions	4,933
Confirmations	3,196
Marriages:	
Catholic	805
Interfaith	126
Total Marriages	931
Deaths	2,943
Total Catholic Population	319,467
Total Population	1,378,842

Former Archbishops—Most Revs. J. B. LAMY, cons. Nov. 24, 1850; created first Archbishop, 1875; resigned July 18, 1885; died Feb. 13, 1888; J. B. SALPOINTE, D.D., cons. Bishop of Doryla and Vicar Apostolic of Arizona, June 20, 1869; appt. Coadjutor of Santa Fe "cum jure successionis", April, 22, 1884; promoted to the Titular Archiepiscopal See of Anazarba, Oct. 11 of same year; succeeded to the See of Santa Fe, July 18, 1885; resigned Jan. 7, 1894 Titular Archbishop of Tomi; died July 15, 1898; P. L. CHAPELLE, cons. Nov. 1, 1891; Archbishop of Santa Fe, Jan. 7, 1894; transferred to New Orleans, Dec. 1, 1897; died Aug. 9, 1905; PETER BOURGADE, D.D., cons. May 1, 1885 Bishop of Thaumacum and Vic. Ap. of Arizona; Bishop of Tucson, May 8, 1897; transferred to Santa Fe, Jan. 7, 1899; died May 17, 1908; J. B. PITAVAL, D.D., cons. Titular Bishop of Sora and Auxiliary of Santa Fe, July 25, 1902; promoted to the See of Santa Fe, Jan. 3, 1909; resigned Feb., 1918; appt. Titular Archbishop of Amida, July 29, 1918; died May 23, 1928; ALBERT T. DAEGER, O.F.M., D.D., cons. May 7, 1919; died Dec. 2, 1932; RUDOLPH ALOYSIUS GERKEN, D.D., cons. Bishop of Amarillo, April 26, 1927; appt. Archbishop of Santa Fe, June 2, 1933; installed as Archbishop of Santa Fe, Aug. 23, 1933; died March 2, 1943; EDWIN V. BYRNE, D.D., cons. Bishop of Ponce, P.R.; transferred to Diocese of San Juan, P.R.; promoted to Archbishop of Santa Fe, June 15, 1943; died July 25, 1963; JAMES P. DAVIS, D.D., cons. Bishop of San Juan, P.R., Oct. 6, 1943; promoted to Archbishop, April 30, 1960; transferred to Archdiocese of Santa Fe, Jan. 3, 1964; retired Oct. 1974; died March 4, 1988; ROBERT F. SANCHEZ, cons. 10th Archbishop of Santa Fe, July 25, 1974; resigned April 6, 1993; died Jan. 20, 2012.

All offices are located at the Archdiocese of Santa Fe Catholic Center, 4000 St. Joseph Pl., N.W., Albuquerque, NM 87120. Tel: 505-831-8100, unless otherwise indicated.

Office of the Archbishop

Vicar-General—Rev. Msgr. LAMBERT J. LUNA, V.G., 5901 St. Joseph Dr., N.W., Albuquerque, 87120.

Secretary to the Archbishop—Ms. DOLORES CORDOVA. Tel: 505-831-8120.

Office of the Chancellor

Chancellor—Very Rev. JOHN CANNON. Tel: 505-831-8158.

Archivist and Artistic Patrimony—Mrs. MARINA OCHOA, 213 Cathedral Pl., Santa Fe, 87501. Tel: 505-983-3811.

Attorney for the Archdiocese—Mr. JUAN L. FLORES, 302 8th St., N.W., Ste. 200, Albuquerque, 87103. Tel: 505-938-7770; Fax: 505-938-7781.

Communications-Media—Mrs. CELINE RADIGAN, Dir. Tel: 505-831-8180.

Ecumenical Commission and Interreligious Affairs—Rev. Msgr. RICHARD OLONA, Dir., 4000 St. Joseph Pl., N.W., Albuquerque, 87120. Tel: 505-831-8243; Fax: 505-831-8206.

Madonna Retreat and Conference Center—ESTHER-MARIE NAGIEL, Dir., 4040 St. Joseph Pl., N.W., Albuquerque, 87120. Tel: 505-831-8196.

Newspaper, Archdiocesan "People of God"—Most Rev. MICHAEL JARBOE SHEEHAN, S.T.L., J.C.D., Publisher; Mrs. CELINE RADIGAN, Editor, 4000 St. Joseph Pl., N.W., Albuquerque, 87120. Tel: 505-831-8180.

Parish Bulletin Service, "The Catholic Communicator"—JENNY CHILSON, Mailing Address: P.O. Box 93244, Albuquerque, 87199-3244. Tel: 505-856-0333; Fax: 505-822-5589.

Human Resources—Ms. CATHY SALCIDO, Dir. Tel: 505-831-8130.

Immaculate Heart of Mary Retreat and Conference Center—Mr. JEFF SNODGRASS, Dir. Tel: 505-988-1975.

Canonical Services Division

Judicial Vicar—Rev. DENNIS M. GARCIA, J.C.L. Tel: 505-831-8177.

College of Consultors—Most Rev. MICHAEL JARBOE SHEEHAN, S.T.L., J.C.D.; Rev. Msgr. LAMBERT J. LUNA, V.G.; Very Rev. JOHN CANNON, Chancellor; Rev. ADAM LEE ORTEGA Y ORTIZ; Rev. Msgr. FRANCIS EGGERT; Revs. WILLIAM E. YOUNG JR.; JOHN C. DANIEL; LARRY R. BRITO; Rev. Msgr. RICHARD OLONA.

Council of Men and Women Religious—VACANT.

Holy Childhood Association— See Mission Office Svcs.

Mission Office—Rev. ARKAD BICZAK Dir. Propagation of the Faith; Holy Childhood; Catholic Relief Svcs. John XXIII Catholic Community, 4831 Tramway Ridge Dr., N.E., Albuquerque, 87111. Tel: 505-293-0088.

Office of Religious—Very Rev. JOHN CANNON, Vicar for Rel., 4000 St. Joseph Pl., N.W., Albuquerque, 87120. Tel: 505-831-8158; Fax: 505-831-8115. Email: jcannon@archdiosf.org.

Pastoral Planning—MICHELLE MONTEZ, Dir., 4000 St.

Joseph Pl., N.W., Albuquerque, 87120. Tel: 505-831-8221; Fax: 505-831-8206. Email: planning@archdiosf.org.

Permanent Diaconate Program—Deacon STEPHEN S. RANGEL, Dir., 4000 St. Joseph Pl., N.W., Albuquerque, 87120. Tel: 505-831-8229.

Pilgrimage for Vocations—Very Rev. EDMUND SAVILLA, Dir., Ascension Parish, 2150 Raymac Rd., S.W., Albuquerque, 87105. Tel: 505-877-8550.

Presbyteral Council of the Archdiocese of Santa Fe—Most Rev. MICHAEL JARBOE SHEEHAN, S.T.L., J.C.D., Pres. (Ex Officio); Rev. Msgr. LAMBERT J. LUNA, V.G., Vicar Gen. (Ex Officio Member); Very Rev. JOHN CANNON, Chancellor (Ex Officio Member); Revs. EDWARD C. DOMME, Chm.; CLEMENT NIGGEL, Vice Chm. (At Large); JOHN B. TRAMBLEY, Sec. (At Large); TIMOTHY A. MARTINEZ, At Large Member; Very Rev. GABRIEL PAREDES, J.C.L., At Large Member; Revs. LARRY R. BRITO, At Large; OSCAR COELHO, At Large; Very Rev. DANIEL M. BALIZAN, Member; Revs. VITUS EZEIRUAKU; HYGINUS CHUKS ANUTA; Very Rev. DOUGLAS J. MITCHELL, Member; Rev. Msgrs. JEROME MARTINEZ Y ALIRE, J.C.L., Member; DOUGLAS A. RAUN, Member; Very Rev. BENNETT J. VOORHIES, Member; Revs. MICHAEL DEPALMA; KEVIN W. NIEHOFF, O.P.; CLARENCE MAES; Rev. Msgr. FRANCIS EGGERT; Revs. THOMAS MAYEFSKE (Retired); RAFAEL GARCIA, S.J., Delegate for Relg.

Propagation of the Faith— See Mission Office.

Vicars Forane (Deans)—Rev. Msgrs. JEROME MARTINEZ Y ALIRE, J.C.L., Santa Fe Deanery; DOUGLAS A. RAUN, Albuquerque-Deanery A; Very Revs. BENNETT J. VOORHIES, Albuquerque-Deanery B; GABRIEL PAREDES, J.C.L., Albuquerque-Deanery C; DOUGLAS J. MITCHELL, Southwest Deanery; Rev. VITUS EZEIRUAKU, Northwest Deanery; Very Rev. DANIEL M. BALIZAN, Northeast Deanery; Rev. HYGINUS CHUKS ANUTA, Southeast Deanery.

Tribunal—Tel: 505-831-8177.

Judicial Vicar—Rev. DENNIS M. GARCIA, J.C.L.

Adjutant Judicial Vicar—Rev. KEVIN W. NIEHOFF, O.P.

Promoter of Justice—Rev. Msgr. JEROME MARTINEZ Y ALIRE, J.C.L.

Defenders of the Bond—Very Rev. GABRIEL PAREDES, J.C.L.; Revs. STEPHEN SCHULTZ; SOTERO SENA; KURT BURNETT, J.C.L.

Associate Judges—Rev. RONALD J. BOWERS, J.C.D. (Retired); Deacons HARRY BEARE; GEORGE SANDOVAL; MARY ANN ECKLUND.

Notaries—Mr. JOSEPH SINICO; Ms. LOUELLEN N. MARTINEZ.

Delegate for Matrimonial Dispensations—Rev. DENNIS M. GARCIA, J.C.L.

Appeal Court—Tel: 505-831-8177.

Vocations—Rev. MICHAEL DEPALMA, Dir. Tel: 505-831-8143; Mr. ROBERT MARTINEZ, Asst. Dir.

Finance Division

Executive Director of Finance—Mr. TONY SALGADO, CPA. Tel: 505-831-8132.

Annual Catholic Appeal Foundation— Archdiocesan Annual Appeal Program, Dr. DOLORES SOKOL, Ph.D., Exec. Dir. Tel: 505-831-8155.

The Catholic Foundation of the Archdiocese of Santa Fe—MARY P. DUNN, Exec. Dir., 4333 Pan American Frwy., N.E., Ste. D, Albuquerque, 87107. Tel: 505-872-2901; Fax: 505-872-2905 Nonprofit corporation for financial support of Archdiocese of Santa Fe.

Finance Council—Most Rev. MICHAEL JARBOE SHEEHAN, S.T.L., J.C.D., Pres.; Mr. TIM SHEEHAN, Chm.; Very Rev. JOHN CANNON, Chancellor; Rev. Msgr. LAMBERT J. LUNA, V.G., Vicar Gen.; Rev. EDWARD C. DOMME; Mr. GIG BRUMMEL; Mrs. VIRGINIA SCHROEDER; Mr. TONY SALGADO, CPA, Exec. Dir. Finance; Ms. JENNIFER CANTRELL, CPA; Mr. WILLIAM F. RASKOB III.

Property Managers and Construction Contract Coord.—Mr. JOHN HUCHMALA. Tel: 505-831-8136.

Pastoral Ministries

Executive Director—DANIEL MCGILL, 4000 St. Joseph Pl., N.W., Albuquerque, 87120. Tel: 505-831-8151.

Catholic Campaign for Human Development—ANNE AVELLONE, Coord., 4000 St. Joseph Pl., N.W., Albuquerque, 87120. Tel: 505-831-8167.

Catholic Committee on Scouting— (Boy Scouts and Girl Scouts) FRED UNSWORTH, Chm.; Deacon DAVID LITTLE, Spiritual Advisor.

Catholic Schools Office—SUSAN M. MURPHY, M.A., Supt. Tel: 505-831-8173.

Catholic Charities—JAMES GANNON, Dir., 6001 Marble, N.E., Albuquerque, 87110. Tel: 505-724-4670.

Cursillo Movement—Deacon ANDRES CARRILLO, Spiritual Dir.

Ministry to the Disabled—Deacon STEPHEN S. RANGEL, Dir. Tel: 505-831-8229.

Ministry to the Deaf—Mrs. ARDITH MONTANO, Coord. Tel: 505-831-8174.

Evangelization—MICHELLE MONTEZ, Dir. Tel: 505-831-8221.

Formation for Christian Service—Deacon KEITH DAVIS, Dir. Tel: 505-831-8187.

Hospital Ministry—Deacon STEPHEN S. RANGEL, Coord. Tel: 505-831-8229.

Prison & Detention Ministry—Deacon STEPHEN S. RANGEL, Dir. Tel: 505-831-8229; Sr. JOSEFINA PERALTA, Fd.CC., Coord. Prison & Jail Ministry; Mr. CARL KOESTNER, Coord. Threshold Prog.

Archdiocesan Network for Catholic Legislative Advocacy—ANNE AVELLONE. Tel: 505-831-8167.

Liturgical Commission—Most Rev. MICHAEL JARBOE SHEEHAN, S.T.L., J.C.D., Pres.; Ms. BARBARA GUENTHER, Chm., 4000 St. Joseph Pl., N.W., Albuquerque, 87120. Tel: 505-831-8194.

Marriage and Family Life Office—Mrs. REMEDIOS (HEDDY) LONG, Dir. Tel: 505-831-8117.

Ministry to Spanish Speaking—Deacon JUAN BARAJAS, Dir. Tel: 505-831-8152.

African American Ministry—Ms. BRENDA DABNEY. Tel: 505-831-8167.

Native American Ministry—Deacon JOE HERRERA JR., Coord. Tel: 505-228-2757.

Newman Centers—

ALBQ: Aquinas Newman Center—Rev. DANIEL C. DAVIS, O.P., Dir., Univ. of New Mexico, 1815 Lomas Rd., N.E., Albuquerque, 87106. Tel: 505-247-1095.

LAS VEGAS: Newman Center—Rev. GEORGE SALAZAR, Coord., Highlands University, 811 Sixth St., Las Vegas, 87701. Tel: 505-425-9295.

PORTALES: St. Thomas Moore Newman Center—Rev. JAMES MCGOWAN, Chap., Mailing Address: Eastern New Mexico University, P.O. Box 2253, Portales, 88130. Tel: 505-356-5615.

SANTA FE—VACANT.

SOCORRO: St. Patrick Newman Center—Deacon NICHOLAS KELLER, 801 School of Mines Rd., Socorro, 87801. Tel: 575-838-2084.

Office of Worship—LINDA KREHMEIER, Dir. Tel: 505-831-8194.

RCIA—LINDA KREHMEIER. Tel: 505-831-8194.

Religious Education—MARIA E. CRUZ-CORDOBA, Dir. Tel: 505-831-8127. 4000 St. Joseph Pl., N.W., Albuquerque, 87120. Tel: 505-831-8128.

Schools of Lay Ministry Formation—

Albuquerque Deanery A,B,C, "Emmaus Journey"—Deacon FRANK LUCERO, 4000 St. Joseph Pl., N.W., Albuquerque, 87120. Tel: 505-831-8151.

Northwest Deanery—JOANNE DUPONT-SANDOVAL, Coord., Mailing Address: P.O. Box 429, Truchas, 87578. Tel: 505-689-2404.

Santa Fe Deanery— (Jornada de Fe) JUANITA MONTOYA, Coord., 2727 Calle Cedro, Santa Fe, 87505. Tel: 505-471-6489.

Spanish School of Ministry—Deacon JUAN BARAJAS, Dir.; ROCIO GONZALEZ, Coord. Albuquerque Area. Tel: 505-831-8147; ANGIE KOLASH, Coord. Santa Fe Area. Tel: 505-831-8152.

St. Vincent de Paul Council—Deacon SANTOS ABEYTA, Spiritual Dir., Mailing Address: Holy Family Parish, P.O. Box 12127, Albuquerque, 87195. Tel: 505-842-5426.

Social Justice—ANNE AVELLONE. Tel: 505-831-8167.

Youth and Young Adult Ministry—BERNADETTE JARAMILLO, Dir. Tel: 505-831-8145.

Ministry Resource Center—Deacon KEITH DAVIS, Dir. Tel: 505-831-8187.

Victim Assistance Coordinator—ANNETTE M. KLIMKA. Tel: 505-831-8159. Email: aklimka@archdiosf.org.

CLERGY, PARISHES, MISSIONS AND PAROCHIAL SCHOOLS

CITY OF SANTA FE

(SANTA FE COUNTY)

1—THE CATHEDRAL BASILICA OF ST. FRANCIS OF ASSISI (1610) [CEM] Rev. Msgr. Jerome Martinez y Alire, Rector; Rev. John B. Trambley, Assoc. Rector; Deacons William Kollasch; Juan Martinez. In Res., Rev. Msgr. Robert S. Calles (ELP) (Retired).
Res.: 131 Cathedral Pl., P.O. Box 2127, 87504. Tel: 505-982-5619; Fax: 505-989-1952. Email: sfcathedral@cbsfa.org. Web: www.cbsfa.org.
Catechesis/Religious Program—Tel: 505-982-3625; 505-820-3429. Sisters Josephine Macias, C.D.P., D.R.E.; Phyllis Stowell, S.C.L., D.R.E. Students 180.

2—ST. ANNE'S (1942) [JC] Rev. Leo W. Ortiz; Deacons Enrique M. Montoya; Andy Dimas.
Res.: 511 Alicia, 87501. Tel: 505-983-4430; Fax: 505-983-7483.
Catechesis/Religious Program—Students 187.

3—CRISTO REY (1940) [JC] Rev. Msgr. Jerome Martinez y Alire, Canonical Pastor; Deacon Thomas Van Valkenburgh, Parish Life Coord.
Office & Church: 1120 Canyon Rd., 87501. Tel: 505-983-8528; Fax: 505-992-6836. Email: cristorey@qwestoffice.net. Web: www.cristoreysantafe.parishesonline.com.
Mission—Our Lady of Guadalupe La Canada de los Alamos, Santa Fe Co. 87501.
Catechesis/Religious Program— Elementary Grades Twinned with Cathedral Basilica.

4—ST. JOHN THE BAPTIST (1953) Rev. Nathan Libaire; Deacons Andres Carrillo; Joe Garcia, Coord. Faith Formation.
Res.: 1301 Osage Ave., 87505. Tel: 505-983-5034; Fax: 505-983-1861. Email: stjohns@qwestoffice.net. Web: stjohn-sf.org.
Catechesis/Religious Program—Students 141.

5—OUR LADY OF GUADALUPE (1882), (Hispanic), [CEM] [JC] Rev. Tien-Tri Nguyen; Deacons Carlos F. Pacheco, (Retired); Gilbert Valdez, Pastoral Assoc.; Jose Luis Burrola, Pastoral Assoc.; Thomas Stith, Pastoral Assoc.
Res.: 417 Agua Fria St., 87501. Tel: 505-983-8868; Fax: 505-983-4304.
Catechesis/Religious Program—Tel: 505-988-3336. Martha Jasso, C.R.E. Students 474.
Mission—San Ysidro P.O. Box 65, Tesuque, Santa Fe Co. 87574. Tel: 505-984-2930.
Mission—Our Lady of Sorrows Rio en Medio, Santa Fe Co. Tel: 505-982-5588.

6—SAN ISIDRO (1835), (Hispanic), [CEM 2] Rev. Franklin D. Pretto; Deacons Michael Salazar; Michael Siegel; Anthony Trujillo; Martin Gallegos Jr.
Res.: 3552 Agua Fria St., 87507. Tel: 505-471-0710. Email: sanisidro4@gmail.com.
Catechesis/Religious Program—Tel: 505-920-0569. Sr. Juanita Gonzalez, D.R.E. Tel: 505-471-6385 (Home). Students 416.
Mission—San Jose La Cienega, Santa Fe Co.

7—SANTA MARIA DE LA PAZ CATHOLIC COMMUNITY (1990) Revs. Adam Lee Ortega y Ortiz; Jim Wolff (Canada); Earl Rohleder (EVN) (Retired); Paul H. Lujan, Business Mgr.; Sisters Colleen Shanahan, O.S.F., Family Life Dir.; Felipa Lara, M.C.S.H., Dir. Spanish Speaking Ministry; Maria de Jesus Becerril, M.C.S.H.; Deacons Juan M. Rodriguez, (Retired); Manuel Montoya; Eloy Gallegos; John Cordova.
Res.: 11 College Ave., 87508. Tel: 505-438-9410; Fax: 505-473-1602. Email: smdlp@smdlp.org. Web: www.smdlp.org.
Catechesis/Religious Program—Mrs. Patricia Lopez, D.R.E. Students 412.

OUTSIDE THE CITY OF SANTA FE

ABIQUIU, RIO ARRIBA CO., ST. THOMAS APOSTLE (1745), (Hispanic), [CEM 5] Rev. James Marshall.
Res.: P.O. Box 117, 87510. Tel: 505-685-4462; Fax: 505-685-4209. Email: stthomas@valornet.com.
Catechesis/Religious Program—Tel: 505-685-4462 (All Missions). Agapita Lopez, D.R.E.; Juan Chavez, D.R.E.; Crystal Gallegos, D.R.E. Students 95.
Mission— Canones, Rio Arriba Co.
Mission— Medanales, Rio Arriba Co.
Mission— Youngsville, Rio Arriba Co.
Mission— Coyote, Rio Arriba Co.
Mission— Mesa de Poleo, Rio Arriba Co.
Mission— Capulin, Rio Arriba Co.
Mission— Gallina, Rio Arriba Co.

ALBUQUERQUE, BERNALILLO CO.

1—ST. ANNE (1929) Rev. Irby C. Nichols; Deacons Tibo Chavez, Emeritus; Paul LeFebre; Juan Barajas; Benjamin Maes, Admin./ Dir. Music & Liturgy.
Res.: 1400 Arenal Rd., S.W., 87105. Tel: 505-877-3121; Fax: 505-877-0084. Email: stannes@lobo.net.
Catechesis/Religious Program—Tel: 505-877-0581. Jose Marcos Romero, D.R.E.; Brenda Romero, D.R.E. Students 204.
Mission—Morada de San Jose 2100 La Vega Rd., S.W., Bernalillo Co. 87105.

2—ANNUNCIATION (1959) Very Rev. Bennett J. Voorhies; Rev. June N. Ramos, Parochial Vicar; Deacons Harry Gogan; Victor J. Bachechi; Kevin Maloney; Robert Morrow; Lawrence Anthony Rivera. In Res., Rev. James Sampson, s.P.
Office & Res.: 2532 Vermont, N.E., 87110. Tel: 505-298-7553; 505-293-5462 (Res.); Fax: 505-294-7418. Email: contact@annunciationparishabq.org. Web: annunciationparishabq.org.
School—(Grades PreK-8), 2610 Utah N.E., 87110. Tel: 505-299-6783; Fax: 505-299-2182. Mrs. Cindy Shields, Prin. Sisters 1; Lay Teachers 30; Students

434.
Catechesis/Religious Program—Tel: 505-296-0411. Sr. Grace De Paoli, Fd.C.C., D.R.E. Students 104.

3—ASCENSION (1962) [CEM 2] Very Rev. Edmund Savilla; Deacons Bill Hoefler; Manuel Toquinto; Leon Jones.
Res.: 2150 Raymac Rd., S.W., 87105. Tel: 505-877-8550; Fax: 508-877-8508. Email: ascensionparish1@yahoo.com.
Catechesis/Religious Program—Tel: 505-877-8144. Anna Villegas, D.R.E.; Linda Sepulveda, D.R.E. Students 100.

4—ST. CHARLES BORROMEO (1934) [JC] Rev. Jerome D. Mueller, O.F.M.; Deacons William "Bill" Barry; Paul Dung Van Nguyen.
Res.: 1818 Coal Pl., S.E., 87106. Tel: 505-242-3462; Fax: 505-247-1292. Email: office@stcharlesbabq.org.
School—(Grades K-8) Tel: 505-243-5788; Fax: 505-764-8842. Mrs. Vivian LaValley, Prin. Lay Teachers 23; Students 240.
Catechesis/Religious Program—Tel: 505-247-1094, Ext. 15. Students 102.

5—ST. EDWIN (1965), (Hispanic), Rev. William E. Sanchez.
Res.: 2105 Barcelona Rd. S.W., 87105. Tel: 505-877-9118; Fax: 505-877-6810. Email: sechurch1@qwestoffice.net.
Catechesis/Religious Program—Tel: 505-877-2967. Students 40.

6—ST. FRANCIS XAVIER (1928), (Hispanic), [JC] Very Rev. Gabriel Paredes, Canonical Pastor; Deacon Leroy Sanchez, Parish Life Coord. Tel: 505-994-4187.
Mailing Address: 820 Broadway, S.E., 87102.
Res.: 3458 Stony Meadows Cir., N.E., Rio Rancho, 87144.
Catechesis/Religious Program—Tel: 505-243-5201; Fax: 505-243-1179. Students 170.

7—HOLY FAMILY (1953), (Hispanic), Rev. Gerald Steinmetz, O.F.M.; Bro. Andres Hernandez, Pastoral Assoc./C.R.E./Dir. Liturgy; Deacons Santos Abeyta; Eddie Blea. In Res., Rev. Richard Rohr, O.F.M.; Bro. Bart Wolff, O.F.M.
Res.: 562 Atrisco Dr., S.W., P.O. Box 12127, 87195. Tel: 505-842-5426; Fax: 505-842-9767. Email: holyfamilychurch@qwestoffice.net.
Catechesis/Religious Program—Tel: 505-842-5448; Fax: 505-842-5410. Email: religiousprogram@qwestoffice.net. Karen Mitchell, D.R.E. Students 332.

8—HOLY GHOST (1953) Rev. Mark A. Schultz; Deacons Ubaldo Chavez, (Retired); Ricardo Chavez; Faustin Archuleta.
Res.: 833-B Arizona Ave., S.E., 87108. Tel: 505-265-5957; Fax: 505-265-5958. Email: hgparish2@aol.com.
School—(Grades K-8), (Elementary), 6201 Ross S.E., 87108. Tel: 505-256-1563; Fax: 505-262-9635. Email: hgschool964@aol.com. Web: www.holyghost-catholicschool.com. Dr. Noreen Copeland, Prin.; Christa Sena, Librarian. Sisters 2; Lay Teachers 18; Students 218.
Catechesis/Religious Program—Tel: 505-265-1975 (Spanish); 505-255-7798 (English). Email: hgengcat@aol.com (English); hghispanicmin@aol.com (Spanish). Marlene Torres, D.R.E. & Hispanic Min.; Theresa Montoya, D.R.E. English Program. Students 180.

9—IMMACULATE CONCEPTION (1883), (Hispanic), Revs. Rafael Garcia, S.J.; Richard W. McGowan, S.J.; Leo V. Leise, S.J.; Deacon George Sandoval. In Res., Revs. Joseph Vanderholt, S.J.; Oren W. Key, S.J.; J. Patrick Hough, S.J.
Res.: 619 Copper Ave., N.W., 87102. Tel: 505-247-4271; Fax: 505-243-0402.
School—St. Mary, (Grades K-8), 224 Seventh St., 87102. Tel: 505-242-6271; Fax: 505-242-4837. Sr. Marianella Domenici, S.C., Prin. Sisters 2; Lay Teachers 37; Students 530.
Catechesis/Religious Program—Tel: 505-247-2555. Students 165.

10—ST. JOHN THE APOSTLE (1984), (John XXIII Catholic Community) Rev. Arkad Biczak; Deacons John Russo; Alex Trujillo, (Retired); Earl Meyrick; Clara Maestas, Business Mgr.
4831 Tramway Ridge Dr., N.E., 87111. Tel: 505-293-0088; Fax: 505-293-7276. Web: www.johnxxiiic-c.org. In Res., Rev. Charles T. Doughterty, C.P.
Res.: 4749 Danube Dr., N.E., 87111. Tel: 505-291-8858.
Catechesis/Religious Program—Tel: 505-293-7756. Bernadette Downie, D.R.E. Students 198.

11—SAINT JOSEPH ON THE RIO GRANDE (1986) Rev. Msgr. Lambert J. Luna; Deacons Don Bruckner; Jerry Hietpas; Bert Dohle; George Miller; Sr. Kathleen Hurley, O.S.F., Pastoral Assoc.
Office: 5901 St. Joseph Dr., N.W., 87120. Tel: 505-839-7952; Fax: 505-839-7955. Email: jwar@sjrgparish.org.
Catechesis/Religious Program—Tel: 505-244-2154; Fax: 505-833-1920. Students 422.

12—ST. JUDE THADDEUS (1968) Rev. John C. Daniel; Deacons Frank Lucero; Robert Aragon.
Mailing Address: P.O. Box 67710, 87193. Tel: 505-898-0826 (Church); 505-897-0391 (Res.); Fax: 505-792-9810. Email: stjude@stjudenm.org.
Catechesis/Religious Program—Students 770.

13—NATIVITY OF THE BLESSED VIRGIN MARY (1936) [CEM] [JC 2] Rev. Juan Mendez; Deacons Leonard Martinez; Juan Ortiz; Michael Illerbrun; Ralph Vigil.
Res.: 9502 Fourth St., N.W., 87114. Tel: 505-898-5253; Fax: 505-898-0496. Web: www.n-bvm.org.
School—(Grades PreK-K) Nancy A. Suedkamp, Prin. Religious Sisters 1; Students 14.
Catechesis/Religious Program—Michael Illebrun, D.R.E. Students 86.
Mission—Our Lady of Mount Carmel 7807 Edith, Bernalillo Co. 87114.

14—OUR LADY OF FATIMA (1949) [JC] Rev. Msgr. Francis Eggert; Deacons Keith Davis, (Diocese of Phoenix); Thomas Jones; Sandy Hall. In Res., Rev. Aloysius Abaneke (Nigeria).
Office: 4020 Lomas, N.E., 87110. Tel: 505-265-5868; Fax: 505-268-0680.
School—(Grades PreK-8) Tel: 505-255-6391; Fax: 505-268-3279. Tim Whalen, Prin. Lay Teachers 16; Students (K-5) 93; Students (6-8) 46; Students (PreK) 10.
Catechesis/Religious Program—Students 62.

15—OUR LADY OF GUADALUPE (1954), (Hispanic), Rev. Joe Vigil; Deacons Manuel Facio; George W. Valverde; Manuel Cabrera; Jim Garcia, Business Mgr.
Res.: 1860 Griegos, N.W., 87107. Tel: 505-345-4596; Fax: 505-342-2984.
Catechesis/Religious Program—Tel: 505-344-7153. Tracielle Downs, D.R.E.; Jesus Casas, D.R.E. (Hispanic Community). Students 206.

16—OUR LADY OF LAVANG (1986), (Vietnamese), [JC] Rev. Tin Mahn Bui.
Church: 1015 Chelwood Park N.E., 87112. Tel: 505-275-3079.
Catechesis/Religious Program—Students 169.

17—OUR LADY OF MOST HOLY ROSARY (1950), (Hispanic), Revs. Joel P. Garner, O.Praem.; Binu Joseph Pazhayaveetil, O.Praem (India), Parochial Vicar; Deacons Harry Beare; Frank Perez; Gene Tuma; James Beaudette; Joe Herrera Jr.; Joseph Silva; Dr. Christina Spahn, Pastoral Assoc.; Ms. Barbara Guenther, Pastoral Assoc.; Don Conklin, Pastoral Assoc.; Lourdes Garza, Coord., Spanish Speaking Ministries.
Office:—5415 Fortuna Rd., N.W., 87105. Tel: 505-836-5011; Fax: 505-836-7562.
Santa Maria de la Vid Priory: 5825 Coors S.W., 87121. Tel: 505-873-4399; Fax: 505-873-4667.
Catechesis/Religious Program—Tel: 505-831-2525. Sr. Evangeline Salazar, O.S.B., D.R.E.; Michelle Montez, Youth Min.; Louise Nielsen, Dir., Adult Faith Formation. Students 640.

18—OUR LADY OF THE ASSUMPTION (1954) Revs. Edward C. Domme; Michael Cimino, Parochial Vicar; Deacons Jim Delgado; Jack Granato; Maurice Graff.
Office & Mailing Address: 811 Guaymas Pl., N.E., 87108-2331. Tel: 505-256-9818; 505-256-9877; Fax: 505-256-3131.
Res.: 8030 Fruit Ave., N.E., 87108-2324. Tel: 505-255-5727.
School—(Grades PreK-8), 817 Guaymas Pl., N.E., 87108-2331. Tel: 505-256-3167; Fax: 505-232-0282. Robert M. Kaiser, Prin.; Karen Gibbs, Librarian. Lay Teachers 18; Students 174.
Catechesis/Religious Program—Jason Rodarte, D.R.E. Students 195.

19—PRINCE OF PEACE CATHOLIC COMMUNITY (2000) Rev. Michael J. Shea; Deacon Steve Fraker, Pastoral Assoc.
Office:—12500 Carmel Ave., N.E., 87122. Tel: 505-856-7657; Fax: 505-856-2560. Email: mailpop@comcast.net. Web: www.popabq.org.
Catechesis/Religious Program—Tel: 505-797-9115. Robert Shields, Catechetical Leader. Students 190.

20—QUEEN OF ANGELS NATIVE AMERICAN CENTER AND ARCHDIOCESAN SHRINE TO KATERI TEKAKWITHA (1952), (Native American), Rev. Emeric Nordmeyer, O.F.M.
Office: 1100 Indian School Rd., N.W., P.O. Box 6881, 87197. Tel: 505-243-0835.
Catechesis/Religious Program—
Chapel—Queen of Angels Chapel 87197-6881.

21—QUEEN OF HEAVEN (1952) Rev. William E. Young Jr.; Deacons Ruben Barela; Larry Cleveland; Pilar Garcia; Dan Lopez; Donna Duran, Admin. In Res., Rev. Jonas Romea.
Office: 5311 Phoenix, N.E., 87110. Tel: 505-881-1772; Fax: 505-883-5222.
School—(Grades PreK-8), 5303 Phoenix Ave., N.E., 87110. Tel: 505-881-2484; Fax: 505-837-1123. Virginia Guitard, Prin. Lay Teachers 15; Students 174.
Catechesis/Religious Program— Donna Duran, D.R.E. Students 280.

22—RISEN SAVIOR CATHOLIC COMMUNITY (1979) Rev. Msgr. Richard Olona; Rev. Jerome Plotkowski; Deacons Mark Bussemeier, Pastoral Assoc.; Kenn Sinatra, (Retired); Merce Villareal, (Retired); Manuel Garcia; Ken Trujillo; Dan Sheehan.
Church: 7701 Wyoming, N.E., 87109. Tel: 505-821-1571; Fax: 505-857-0065. Web: www.risensaviorcc.org.
Catechesis/Religious Program—Gerry Wood, D.R.E. (Adults); Jennifer Murphy-Dye, D.R.E. (Adults); Denise Sinatra, D.R.E. (Children); Angela Holt, D.R.E. (Youth). Students 639.

23—SACRED HEART (1903) [JC] Rev. Clarence Maes; Deacons Robert Vigil; Edgar L. Torres Sr.
Res.: 412 Stover Ave., S.W., 87102. Tel: 505-242-0561; Fax: 505-243-7857. Email: sacredheartnm@comcast.net.
Catechesis/Religious Program—Students 50.

24—SAN FELIPE DE NERI (1706), (Hispanic), Revs. Dennis M. Garcia; Thomas Noesen, O.P., Parochial Vicar; Deacons Jose Lucero; Maurice Menke; Tom Perez; James Carbajal.
Mailing Address: P.O. Box 7007, 87194.
Res.: 2005 Plaza N.W. Old Town, 87104. Tel: 505-243-4628; Fax: 505-224-9495. Web: www.sanfelipedeneri.org.
School—(Grades PreK-8), 2000 Lomas Blvd., N.W., 87104. Tel: 505-242-2411; Fax: 505-242-7355. Nancy A. Suedkamp, Prin. Lay Teachers 17; Students 219.
Catechesis/Religious Program—Matthew K. Gill, D.R.E. Students 134.
Mission—San Jose de los Duranes 2110 Los Luceros Rd., N.W., Bernalillo Co. 87104.

25—SAN IGNACIO (1916), (Hispanic), Rev. Dennis M. Garcia, Canonical Pastor; Sr. Annette Lucero, O.P., Parish Life Coord.
Res.: 1226 Walter, N.E., 87102. Tel: 505-243-4287; Fax: 505-243-7346.
Catechesis/Religious Program—Students 26.

26—SAN JOSE (1938) [CEM] Very Rev. Gabriel Paredes; Deacons Hector Aguirre; Gregorio Henderson.
Res.: 2401 Broadway, S.E., 87102-5009. Tel: 505-242-3658; Fax: 505-248-0810. Email: sanjoseparish@msn.com.
Catechesis/Religious Program— Sr. Mariza Lopez, Fd.C.C., D.R.E., Spanish; Mirna Davila, D.R.E., Spanish; Sr. Connie Martinez, Fd.CC., D.R.E., English. Students 705.

27—SANGRE DE CRISTO (1972) Rev. Johnny Lee Chavez; Deacons Rudolph Baca; Lloyd Martinez; Paul Ortwerth.
Res.: 8901 Candelaria, N.E., 87112. Tel: 505-293-2327; Fax: 505-292-0590.
Catechesis/Religious Program—Tel: 505-293-2328. Students 74.

28—SANTUARIO SAN MARTIN DE PORRES (1979), (Hispanic), Rev. Leo L. Padget; Deacons Cresencio Salinas; Oscar Marquez; Constantino Avalos-Sanchez.
Res.: 8321 Camino San Martin, S.W., 87121. Tel: 505-836-4676; Fax: 505-836-3253. Email: sanmartin31@aol.com.
Catechesis/Religious Program—Tel: 505-352-2571. Leslie Farias, D.R.E.; Lourdes Ceballos, Catechetical Leader (Spanish Program); Victoriano Ceballos. Students 593.

29—SHRINE OF ST. BERNADETTE (1959) Rev. Timothy A. Martinez; Deacons Alfred McLane; Byron Wicker; Joe Santana; Terry Palmer; Gregory Archunde.
Res.: 11509 Indian School Rd. NE., 87112-3163. Tel: 505-298-7557; Fax: 505-271-8467. Email: stbernacc@aol.com. Web: www.shrineofstbernadette.com.
Catechesis/Religious Program—Students 432.

30—ST. THERESE OF THE INFANT/JESUS SHRINE OF THE LITTLE FLOWER (1947), (Shrine Dedicated 1955) Rev. Vincent P. Chavez; Deacons Patrick Cooney, (Retired); Michael Wesley; Raul Talavera.
Res.: 300 Mildred, N.W., 87107. Tel: 505-344-8050; 505-344-2884. Email: sttheresechurch@yahoo.com. Web: www.littleflowerabq.org.
School—(Grades PreK-8), 311 Shropshire N.W., 87107. Tel: 505-344-4479; Fax: 505-345-6210. Donna Illerbrun, Prin. Lay Teachers 14; Students 137.
Catechesis/Religious Program—Tel: 505-344-7643; Fax: 505-345-3248. Students 193.

31—ST. THOMAS AQUINAS UNIVERSITY PARISH (1950), (Serving the University of New Mexico) Revs. Daniel C. Davis, O.P., Parish Admin.; Richard Litzau, O.P., Parochial Vicar; Bro. Gabriel Dault, O.P., Campus Min.; Steve Herrera, Liturgy Dir.; Deacons Bruce Eklund; Donald Contreras. In Res., Revs. George J.D. Reynolds., O.P.; Kevin W. Niehoff, O.P.; Matthew T.D. Strabala, O.P.; Thomas Noesen, O.P.
Res.: 1815 Las Lomas Rd., N.E., 87106-3803. Tel: 505-247-1094; Fax: 505-247-2933. Web: www.aquinasnm.org.
Catechesis/Religious Program—Tel: 505-247-1094, Ext. 226. Kyle Kemp, Dir. Faith Formation. Students 130.

ANTON CHICO, GUADALUPE CO., SAN JOSE (1857), (Hispanic), [CEM] [JC 5] Rev. Simeon Frank Wimmershoff, O.F.M., Canonical Pastor; Lugardita Romo, Pastoral Assoc.
Res.: 1081 Iglesia Rd., Box 99, 87711. Tel: 575-427-1164.
Catechesis/Religious Program—Tel: 505-427-4114. Students 26.
Mission— Dilia, Guadalupe Co.
Mission— Dahlia, Guadalupe Co.
Mission— Tecolotito, San Miguel Co.
Mission—Sangre de Cristo (1834)

ARROYO SECO, TAOS CO., LA SANTISIMA TRINIDAD (1834), (Spanish), [CEM] [JC 4] Rev. Kevin Iwuoha (Nigeria); Deacon Romolo Arellano.
Res.: 498 Hwy. 150, Box 189, 87514. Tel: 575-776-2273; Fax: 575-776-1543. Email: trinityparish@taosnet.com.
Catechesis/Religious Program—Students 110.
Mission—Nuestra Senora de Dolores Upper Plaza, Arroyo Hondo, Taos Co. 87513.
Mission—San Antonio de Padua Valdez Plaza, Valdez, Taos Co. 87580.
Mission—Santo Nino de Atocha Santo Nino Rd., Las Colonias, Taos Co. 87529.
Mission—San Cristobal San Cristobal, Taos Co.

BELEN, VALENCIA CO., OUR LADY OF BELEN (1793) [CEM] [JC] Revs. Stephen Schultz; Bijoy Francis Valayil, O.Praem., Parochial Vicar; Deacons Felix Barela; Michael Montoya; Robert Sanchez; Manuel Trujillo; Rudy Zamora.
Res.: 101-A N. 10th St., 87002. Tel: 505-864-8043.
School—(Grades PreK-8) Tel: 505-864-0484; Fax: 505-864-2414. Jennifer Mason, Prin. Lay Teachers 12; Students 136.
Catechesis/Religious Program—Tel: 505-864-7869. Therese Salazar, D.R.E. Students 433.
Mission— Los Chavez, Valencia Co.
Mission— Jarales, Valencia Co.
Mission— Pueblitos, Valencia Co.
Mission— Bosque, Valencia Co.

BERNALILLO, SANDOVAL CO., OUR LADY OF SORROWS (1699), (Indian—Hispanic), [CEM 2] Rev. Stephen Imbarrato; Deacons Jose de Jesus Cervantes; Gonzalo Calderon.
Office & Res.: 301 Camino Del Pueblo, P.O. Box 607, 87004. Tel: 505-867-5252; Fax: 505-867-0267.
Catechesis/Religious Program—Patsy Garcia, D.R.E. Students 529.
Mission— 43 San Antonio, Placitas, Sandoval Co. 87043.
Mission— 1416 Hwy. 313, Algodones, Sandoval Co. 87001.
Mission— 300 Parrot Blvd., Sandia Indian Pueblo, Sandoval Co. 87004.

CERRILLOS, SANTA FE CO., ST. JOSEPH (1850) [CEM 4] Very Rev. Francis Malley.
Res.: Box 98, 87010. Tel: 505-471-1562; Fax: 505-438-6584. Email: stjoseph@cnsp.com.
Catechesis/Religious Program—Students 20.
Mission— Golden, Santa Fe Co.
Mission— Galisteo, Santa Fe Co.

CHAMA, RIO ARRIBA CO., ST. PATRICK (1964), (Hispanic—Anglo), [JC] Rev. Joel O. Bugas.
Res.: 352 Pine St., Hwy. 29, P.O. Box 36, 87520-0036. Tel: 575-756-2926; Fax: 575-756-2926. Email: stpats@windstream.net.
Catechesis/Religious Program—Students 110.
Mission—Santo Nino Hwy. 84 & State Rd. 310, Cebolla, Rio Arriba Co. 87518.
Mission—San Juan Nepumoceno County Rd. 295, Canjilon, Rio Arriba Co. 87515.

CHIMAYO, RIO ARRIBA CO., HOLY FAMILY (1955), (Hispanic), [CEM] [JC 2] Revs. Julio Gonzalez, S.F.; Casimiro Roca, S.F.; James Suntum, S.F.; Ron Carrillo, S.F., Parochial Vicar.
Res.: P.O. Box 235, 87522. Tel: 505-351-4360; Fax: 505-351-4698. Email: holyfamily@cybermesa.com. Web: www.holychimayo.us.
Catechesis/Religious Program—Students 70.
Mission—Holy Rosary Truchas, Rio Arriba Co.
Mission—San Jose de Gracia Trampas, Taos Co.
Mission—Santo Domingo Cundiyo, Rio Arriba Co.
Mission—San Antonio Cordova, Rio Arriba Co.
Mission—Sagrado Corazon Rio Chiquito, Rio Arriba Co.
Mission—Santo Tomas Ojo Sarco, Rio Arriba Co.
Mission—San Miguel Archangel El Valle, Taos Co.
Shrine—El Santuario Shrine El Santuario, Santa Fe Co.

CIMARRON, COLFAX CO., IMMACULATE CONCEPTION CHURCH (1864), (Hispanic—Mexican), [JC] Rev. Emmanuel Izuka (Nigeria).
Res.: 440 W. 18th St., 87714-9705. Tel: 575-376-2553; Fax: 575-376-2553.
Catechesis/Religious Program—Mrs. Tori Vigil, C.R.E. Students 53.
Mission—St. Mel 200 Willow Creek, Eagle Nest, Colfax Co. 87718. Tel: 575-377-1937.
Mission—Holy Angels P.O. Box 73, Angel Fire, 87710.
Mission—St. Anthony Black Lake, Colfax Co.

CLAYTON, UNION CO., ST. FRANCIS XAVIER (1937) [JC] Rev. Glenn Jones; Deacon P. Louis Montoya.
Res.: 115 N. First St., 88415. Tel: 575-374-9500; Fax: 575-374-8897. Email: stfrancisxavier@plateautel.net.
Catechesis/Religious Program—Students 100.
Mission—Our Lady of Guadalupe Des Moines, Union Co.
Mission—St. Joseph Folsom, Union Co.
Mission—Sacred Heart Moses, Union Co.
Mission—Holy Trinity Hayden, Quay Co.

CLOVIS, CURRY CO.

1—OUR LADY OF GUADALUPE (1945) [CEM 2] [JC 2] Rev. Sotero Sena; Deacons Bob Pullings; Daniel Chavez.
Res.: 108 Davis St., 88101. Tel: 575-763-4445; Fax: 575-763-0261.
Catechesis/Religious Program—Tel: 575-762-7343. Sally Romero, D.R.E. (Grades K-6); David Briseno, D.R.E. (Grade 7-12); Margaret Briseno, D.R.E. (Grades 7-12). Students 305.
Mission— Box 122, Texico, Curry Co. 88135.

2—SACRED HEART (1908) Rev. Carlos Chavez; Deacons Juan A. Rodriguez; Michael A. Rowley.
Res.: 921 Merriwether St., 88101. Tel: 575-763-6947; Fax: 575-762-5557.
Catechesis/Religious Program—Students 221.
Mission— Melrose, Curry Co. 88124.

CORRALES, SANDOVAL CO., SAN YSIDRO (1966) [CEM] Rev. Michael DePalma; Deacon Steve Rangel.
Res.: 5015 Corrales Rd., Box 182, 87048. Tel: 505-898-1779; Fax: 505-897-6967.
Catechesis/Religious Program—Tel: 505-899-0276. Ken Cantwell, D.R.E. Students 132.

DIXON, RIO ARRIBA CO., ST. ANTHONY (1929) [CEM 3] Rev. Vitus Ezeiruaku (Nigeria); Deacon Jerome Romero.
Res.: 1114 Private Dr. #5, P.O. Box 39, 87527-0039. Tel: 505-579-4389; Fax: 505-579-0084. Email: standixon@valornet.com. Web: www.stanthonydixon.parishesonline.com.
Catechesis/Religious Program—Students 37.
Mission—Nuestra Senora de Guadalupe Velarde, Rio Arriba Co.
Mission—Nuestra Senora de los Dolores Pilar, Taos Co.
Mission—San Jose Lyden, Rio Arriba Co.

EL RITO, RIO ARRIBA CO., SAN JUAN NEPOMUCENO (1832), (Spanish), [CEM] [JC 9] Rev. James Marshall.
Res.: P.O. Box 7, 87530. Tel: 575-581-4714.
Catechesis/Religious Program—Students 35.
Mission— Gen. Del., La Madera, Rio Arriba Co. 87539.
Mission— Gen. Del., Las Tablas, Taos Co. 87539.
Mission— Gen. Del., Ojo Caliente, Rio Arriba Co. 87549.
Mission— Gen. Del., Petaca, Taos Co. 87539.
Mission— Gen. Del., Servilleta, Taos Co. 87539.
Mission— Gen. Del., Vallecitos, Rio Arriba Co. 87581.
Mission— Gen. Del., Canon de Vallecitos, Rio Arriba Co. 87581.
Mission— Gen. Del., Tres Piedras, Taos Co. 87579.
Mission— P.O. Box 7, Placitas, Rio Arriba Co. 87530.

ESPANOLA, RIO ARRIBA CO.

1—SACRED HEART (1950), (Hispanic), [CEM 2] Rev. Oscar Coelho; Deacon Diego Herrera.
Mailing Address: P.O. Box 69, 87532.
Res.: 908 Calle Rosario, 87532. Tel: 505-753-4225; Fax: 505-753-1282. Email: sacredheart@windstream.com.
Catechesis/Religious Program—Students 113.
Mission— Hernandez, Rio Arriba Co.
Mission— El Guache, Rio Arriba Co.
Mission— Guachupanque, Rio Arriba Co.
Mission— El Duende, Rio Arriba Co.

2—TEWA MISSIONS (2000) Rev. Larry R. Brito, Canonical Pastor; Deacon Gregory Aguilar.
Mailing Address: P.O. Box 1075, Ohkay Owingeh, 87566. Tel: 505-747-8220.
Catechesis/Religious Program—Sr. Patrick Marie Dempsey, S.B.S., D.R.E. Students 105.

FORT SUMNER, DE BACA CO., ST. ANTHONY OF PADUA formerly St. Anthony (1958), (Hispanic), [CEM] Rev. Simeon Frank Wimmershoff, O.F.M., Canonical Pastor; Sr. Phyllis Supancheck, O.P., Parish Life Coord.; Deacon Edward Sena.
Church & Mailing Address: 443 W. Richard Ave., P.O. Box 370, 88119. Tel: 575-355-2320; Fax: 575-355-2320.
Catechesis/Religious Program—Students 24.

ISLETA, PUEBLO BERNALILLO CO., ST. AUGUSTINE (1613), (Native American), [CEM] Rev. George Pavamkott, O.Praem.
Res.: P.O. Box 849, 87022. Tel: 505-869-3398; Fax: 505-869-2447.
Catechesis/Religious Program—Students 65.

JEMEZ PUEBLO, SANDOVAL CO., SAN DIEGO INDIAN MISSIONS (1608), (Native American—Spanish), [CEM] [JC 4] Rev. Paul Juniet, O.F.M.; Bro. Ricardo Garcia, O.F.M.; Sr. Karen M Kuta, O.S.F.
Res.: 475 Mission Rd., P.O. Box 79, 87024. Tel: 575-834-7300; Fax: 575-834-7060.
Catechesis/Religious Program—Students 85.
Mission— Canon, Sandoval Co.
Mission— Ponderosa, Sandoval Co.
Mission— San Ysidro, Sandoval Co.
Mission— Santa Ana, Sandoval Co.
Mission— Zia, Sandoval Co.

JEMEZ SPRINGS, SANDOVAL CO., OUR LADY OF THE ASSUMPTION (1947) [CEM] Very Rev. David T. Fitzgerald, s.P.; Rev. Gregory McCormick, s.P., Admin.
Mailing Address: P.O. Box 10, 87025.
Res.: Tel: 575-829-3586; Fax: 575-829-3706. Email: servants@theservants.org.
Catechesis/Religious Program—

LA JOYA, SOCORRO CO., OUR LADY OF SORROWS (1830), (Spanish), [CEM 6] Rev. Peter Hung Nguyen, S.O.L.T.; Deacon Alfred Edwin Esquibel.
Mailing Address: 19 Calle de la Iglesia, P.O. Box 32, 87028. Tel: 505-864-4461; 505-861-3522 (Rectory); Fax: 505-864-4461. Email: parishoffice@olslajoya.nm.org.
Catechesis/Religious Program—Students 50.
Mission—San Antonio Abeytas, Socorro Co.
Mission—San Jose Contreras, Socorro Co.
Mission—San Isidro Las Nutrias, Socorro Co.
Mission—San Juan Veguita, Socorro Co.
Mission—San Antonio Sabinal, Socorro Co.
Mission—San Antonio (Uppertown) Las Vegas, 87701.

LAS VEGAS, SAN MIGUEL CO.

1—IMMACULATE CONCEPTION (1885) [CEM] Rev. George Salazar.
Res.: 811 Sixth St., 87701. Tel: 505-425-7791; 505-425-6942; Fax: 505-425-6991. Email: icchurch2000@yahoo.com.
Catechesis/Religious Program—Tel: 505-454-0685. Rita Garcia, D.R.E. Students 256.
Mission—Los Vigiles (Our Lady of Refuge) 811 6th, San Miguel Co. 87701.

2—OUR LADY OF SORROWS CHURCH (1851), (Hispanic), [CEM 2] [JC 2] Rev. C. John Brasher; Deacons Jose Leroy Martinez; Reyes L. Sanchez.
Res.: 403 Valencia St., 87701. Tel: 505-454-1469; Fax: 505-425-0949.
Catechesis/Religious Program—Tel: 505-425-6823. Beverly Maestas, D.R.E. Students 200.
Mission—Our Lady of Guadalupe HC 68, Box 11, Sapello, San Miguel Co. 87745. Tel: 505-425-8084.
Mission—San Isidro HC 32, Box 26, Trujillo, San Miguel Co. 87701. Tel: 505-641-5367.
Mission—Holy Family Garita. Box 1020, Variadero, San Miguel Co. 88421. Tel: 505-641-5339.
Mission—Santo Nino HC 69, Box 4, Rociada Abajo, San Miguel Co. 87742. Tel: 505-425-8251.
Mission—Santo Nino Montezuma. El Porvenir Rte., Box 63, Gallinas, San Miguel Co. 87731. Tel: 505-425-6015.
Chapel—Christ the King 2609 Encino St., 87701. Tel: 505-425-6894.
Chapel—San Jose Hot Springs.
Chapel—San Antonio Box 90, El Porvenir, 87731. Tel: 505-425-8010.
Chapel—San Ignacio HC 68, Box 15, Sapello, 87745. Tel: 505-425-3092; 505-454-1139.
Chapel—Our Lady of Sorrows Anton Chico Rte., Box 39, 87701. Tel: 505-421-5599.
Chapel—San Geronimo Mineral Hill Rte., Box 310, 87701. Tel: 505-425-3011.
Chapel—San Antonio P.O. Box 85, 87701. Tel: 505-425-3405.
Chapel—Lourdes
Chapel—San Jose HC 69, Box 12A, Rociada, 87742. Tel: 505-425-2809.
Chapel—San Rafael c/o Al Sanchez Jr., General Delivery, Trementina, 88439. Tel: 505-641-5384.
Chapel—Santo Nino de Atocha Anton Chico Rte., Box 20, 87701. Tel: 505-425-8014.
Chapel—Ojitos Frios
Chapel—Manuelitas
Chapel—Santo Nino, Tel: 505-454-0409.

LOS ALAMOS, LOS ALAMOS CO., IMMACULATE HEART OF MARY (1946) Rev. John F. Carney; Deacons Ray Alcouffe; Michael Irving; John Krepps; Gerald Langner; Donato Lucero, Pastoral Assoc.; James O'Hara; John Sutton; Roberto Villareal; Miracle Miller, Business Mgr.; Greg Smithhisler, Music Min. & Liturgy Dir.
Mailing Address: 3700 Canyon Rd., 87544. Tel: 505-662-6193.
Res.: 3694 Canyon Rd., 87544. Tel: 505-662-6921; Fax: 505-662-5191. Web: www.ihmcc.org.
Catechesis/Religious Program—3580 Canyon Rd., 87544. Tel: 505-662-7773. Caren Stevens, D.R.E.; Eric Horne, Youth Dir. & Adult Formation. Students 450.
Mission—St. Joseph 196 Meadow, White Rock, Los Alamos Co. 87544. Tel: 505-672-1270.

LOS LUNAS, VALENCIA CO., SAN CLEMENTE (1961) [CEM 2] [JC] Very Rev. Douglas J. Mitchell; Deacons Jim Snell, Business Mgr.; Robert Burkhard; Paul Baca; Mark Leonard; Sr. Lucille Martinez, O.L.V.M., Mission Life Coord.; Brenda Sais, Family Life Coord.
Res.: P.O. Box 147, 87031. Tel: 505-865-7385; Fax: 505-865-8323. Email: sanclemente@qwestoffice.net. Web: www.sanclementeparish.org.
Catechesis/Religious Program—Tel: 505-865-9370. Students 327.
Mission—San Antonio Los Lentes, Valencia Co.
Mission—San Juan Diego P.O. Box 3320, 87031. Tel: 505-866-0443.

LOS OJOS, RIO ARRIBA CO., SAN JOSE (1883), (Hispanic), [CEM] [JC 2] Rev. Joel O. Bugas.
Res.: Box 6, 87551. Tel: 575-588-7473; Fax: 575-588-7239. Email: sjsncc@windstream.net.
Catechesis/Religious Program— Twinned with Santo Nino, Tierra Amarilla. Students 21.
Station— Ensenada.
Station— La Puente.
Station— Plaza Blanca.

MORA, MORA CO., ST. GERTRUDE (1851), (Hispanic), [CEM] [JC 9] Revs. John McHugh, S.O.L.T.; James Sanchez, S.O.L.T., Parochial Vicar; Deacons Reynaldo Cordova; Cristobal "Eloy" Roybal.
Res.: 1 Church Plaza, P.O. Box 599, 87732. Tel: 505-387-2336; Fax: 575-387-5786.
Catechesis/Religious Program—Deacon Eloy Roybal, D.R.E. Students 182.
Mission— Le Doux, Mora Co.
Mission— El Carmen, Mora Co.
Mission— Lucero, Mora Co.
Mission— Santiago-Talco, Mora Co.
Mission— Ojo Feliz, Mora Co.
Mission— Buenavista, Mora Co.
Mission— Golondrinas, Mora Co.
Mission— Rainsville, Mora Co.
Mission— Chacon, Mora Co.
Mission— Holman, Mora Co.
Mission— Cleveland, Mora Co.
Mission— Guadalupita, Mora Co.
Mission— Monte Aplanado, Mora Co.
Mission— Turquillo, Mora Co.
Mission— La Cueva, Mora Co.
Mission— Canoncito, Mora Co.

MORIARTY, TORRANCE CO., ESTANCIA VALLEY CATHOLIC PARISH (1972) [CEM 3] Revs. Robert Lancaster; Lawrence Merta, Parochial Vicar; Deacons Juan S. Lucero; Don Cupps.
Res.: 1400 B 3rd St., S., P.O. Box 129, 87035. Tel: 505-832-6655; Fax: 505-832-6057. Email: parishoffice@estanciavalleycatholicch.org. Web: www.estanciavalleycatholicch.org.
Catechesis/Religious Program—Email: formation@estanciavalleycatholicch.org. Dorothy Ipiotis, D.R.E.; Jonathan Ipiotis, Dir. Youth Min. Students 230.
Mission—Sts. Peter & Paul 101 S. Ninth St., Estancia, Torrance Co. 87016.
Mission—San Antonio 8566 Hwy. 55 W., Tajique, 87016.
Mission—St. Elizabeth Ann Seton 85 Hwy. 344, Edgewood, 87015.

MOUNTAINAIR, TORRANCE CO., ST. ALICE (1946), (Hispanic), [CEM 5] [JC] Rev. Fernando A. Saenz.
Res.: 206 Roosevelt St., P.O. Box 206, 87036. Tel: 505-847-2264; Fax: 505-847-0146. Email: stalicemtn@q.com.
Catechesis/Religious Program—Deacon Charles E. Schwenn, D.R.E. Students 85.
Mission— Abo, Torrance Co.
Mission— Punta de Agua, Torrance Co.
Mission— Manzano, Torrance Co.
Mission— Torreon, Torrance Co.
Mission— Willard, Torrance Co.

PECOS, SAN MIGUEL CO., ST. ANTHONY OF PADUA (1862) [CEM 5] Rev. Vincent Dominguez.
Res.: HC 74 Box 23, 87552. Tel: 505-757-6345; Fax: 505-757-6377. Email: saintanthonys@wildblue.net.
Catechesis/Religious Program—Tel: 505-757-6305. Students 137.
Mission— Canoncito, Santa Fe Co.
Mission— Las Colonias, San Miguel Co.
Mission— Glorieta, Santa Fe Co.
Mission— Rowe, San Miguel Co.
Mission— El Macho, San Miguel Co.

PENA BLANCA, SANDOVAL CO., NUESTRA SENORA DE GUADALUPE (1877), (Hispanic—Native American), [CEM 3] Revs. Berard Doerger, O.F.M., Parochial Vicar; Hilaire Valiquette, O.F.M., Admin.; Deacons Albert Arquero; Joe Segura; Gerald Chavez.
Res.: Hwy. 22, House #816, P.O. Box 1270, 87041. Tel: 505-465-2226; Fax: 505-465-1336.
Catechesis/Religious Program—Students 160.
Mission—St. Bonaventure, Indian Pueblo, Cochiti, Sandoval Co.
Mission—San Felipe, Indian Pueblo, San Felipe, Sandoval Co.
Mission—Santo Domingo, Indian Pueblo, Santo Domingo, Sandoval Co.
Mission—Santa Barbara Sile, Sandoval Co.
Mission—San Miguel La Bajada, Sandoval Co.

PENASCO, TAOS CO., SAN ANTONIO DE PADUA (1866) [CEM] Rev. Vitus Ezeiruaku (Nigeria); Deacon Jerome Romero.
Res.: 14079 N. Hwy. 75, P.O. Box 460, 87553-0460. Tel: 575-587-2111 (Office); 575-587-0399 (Res.); Fax: 575-587-2188.
Catechesis/Religious Program—Tel: 575-587-2216. Joyce Kilgore, D.R.E. Students 117.
Mission—Santa Cruz Mission Chamisal, Taos Co.
Mission—Sagrado Corazon Mission Rio Lucio, Taos Co.
Mission—Nuestra Senora de los Dolores Mission Vadito, Taos Co.
Mission—San Lorenzo Mission Picuris Indian Pueblo, Taos Co.
Mission—San Juan Nepomuceno Mission Llano San Juan, Taos Co.
Mission—Nuestra Senora de la Asuncion Mission Placita, Taos Co.
Mission—Santa Barbara Mission Rodarte, Taos Co.

PERALTA, VALENCIA CO., OUR LADY OF GUADALUPE (1970), (Hispanic), [CEM] Rev. Hoi Tran; Deacon Edward Espinosa.
Mailing Address: P.O. Box 10, 87042.
Res.: 3674 Hwy. 47, 87042. Tel: 505-869-2189; Fax: 505-869-5850. Email: ologper@aol.com. Web: home.flash.net/~gdc/olog/.
Catechesis/Religious Program—Tel: 505-869-6993; Fax: 505-869-6996. Karen Morgan, Faith Formation Coord. Students 195.
Mission—Sangre de Cristo Valencia, Valencia Co. Tel: 505-866-7254.
Station—Valencia

POJOAQUE, SANTA FE CO., N.S. DE GUADALUPE DEL VALLE DE POJOAQUE (1959), (Spanish—Native American), [CEM 2] Rev. Jose Flavio Santillanes; Deacons John Archuleta; Pedro Garcia; Daniel Valdez; Reuben Roybal.
Res.: 9 Grazing Elk Dr., 87506-7140. Tel: 505-455-2472; Fax: 505-455-3849.
Catechesis/Religious Program—Tel: 505-455-2267. Donna Martinez, D.R.E. Students 165.
Mission— Nambe, Santa Fe Co.
Mission— El Rancho, Santa Fe Co.
Mission— Nambe Indian Pueblo, Santa Fe Co.

PORTALES, ROOSEVELT CO., ST. HELEN (1952) Rev. James McGowan; Deacon Roberto Herrera.
Res.: 1600 S. Avenue O, 88130. Tel: 575-356-4241; Fax: 575-359-1721. Email: sthelenofportales@yahoo.com.
Catechesis/Religious Program—Sylvia Baca, D.R.E. Students 200.
Mission—Thomas More Center P.O. Box 2253, Roosevelt Co. 88130.

QUESTA, TAOS CO., ST. ANTHONY (1841) [CEM 6] Rev. Andrew Ifele; Deacons Marcus J. Rael; Jose Leroy Lucero.
Mailing Address: Box 200, 87556.
Res.: 10 Church Plaza, 87556. Tel: 575-586-0470; 575-586-0471; Fax: 575-586-1755. Email: sanantoniodelrio@qwestoffice.net.
Catechesis/Religious Program—Parish Center: 2453 St. Hwy 522, 87556. Tel: 575-586-2155. Students 180.
Mission— Cerro, Taos Co.
Mission— Red River, Taos Co.
Mission— Costilla, Taos Co.
Mission— Amalia, Taos Co.

RANCHOS DE TAOS, TAOS CO., SAN FRANCISCO DE ASIS (1936), (Hispanic), [CEM] Rev. Dino Candelaria; Deacon Pat Delozier.
Res.: P.O. Box 72, 87557-0072. Tel: 575-758-2754; Fax: 575-751-3923. Email: saintfrancis@kitcarson.net.
Catechesis/Religious Program—Students 144.
Mission—N.S. de San Juan de Los Lagos Talpa, Taos Co.
Mission—N.S. del Carmel Llano Quemado, Taos Co.
Mission—San Isidro Los Cordovas, Taos Co.

RATON, COLFAX CO., ST. PATRICK/ST. JOSEPH (1891) [CEM] [JC] Very Rev. Daniel M. Balizan; Deacon Thomas Alderette.
Res.: 105 Buena Vista St., Box 278, 87740. Tel: 575-445-9763; Fax: 575-445-7026. Email: stspatjoe@bacavalley.com.
Catechesis/Religious Program—104 Buena Vista St., 87740. Tel: 575-445-9563. Louise Ortiz, D.R.E. Students 185.
Mission—St. Vincent de Paul P.O. Box 698, Maxwell, 87728.

RIBERA, SAN MIGUEL CO., SAN MIGUEL DEL VADO (1804), (Hispanic—Native American), [CEM] [JC 7] Rev. Thomas Kayammakal (India).
Res.: P.O. Box 507, 87560. Tel: 575-421-2405; 575-421-2780 (Office); Fax: 575-421-2779. Email: sanmiguel@plateautel.net.
Catechesis/Religious Program—Students 46.
Mission— [CEM] [JC] San Isidro Norte, San Miguel Co.
Mission— [CEM] [JC] San Jose, San Miguel Co.
Mission— [CEM] [JC] San Juan, San Miguel Co.
Mission— [CEM] [JC] Santa Rita, San Miguel Co.
Mission—San Antonio de Padua [CEM] [JC] El Pueblo, San Miguel Co.
Mission— [CEM] [JC] La Lagunita, San Miguel Co.
Mission— [CEM] [JC] San Isidro Sur, San Miguel Co.

RIO RANCHO, SANDOVAL CO.

1—CHURCH OF THE INCARNATION (2003) Rev. Rick Zerwas; Deacons George Meyerson; Norbert Archibeque; Jerome Paszkiewicz.
Mailing Address: 2309 Monterey Rd., NE, 87144. Tel: 505-771-8331. Web: ccincarnation.org.
Catechesis/Religious Program—Mary Margaret Baca, D.R.E. Students 198.

2—ST. THOMAS AQUINAS (1974) Rev. Msgr. Douglas A. Raun; Revs. Scott Mansfield, Parochial Vicar; Fernando A. Saenz, Parochial Vicar; Jeffrey T. Whorton, Parochial Vicar; Deacons Rodger Ayers; James Baca; Thomas Burns; Kenneth Hill; David Little; David Russell; Frank Smith. In Res., Rev. Ronald G. Stone.
Res.: 1502 Sara Rd., S.E., 87124. Tel: 505-892-1511; Fax: 505-891-3044.
School—(Grades K-8), 1100 Hood Rd., S.E., 87124. Tel: 505-892-3221; Fax: 505-892-3350. Sr. Anne Louise Abascal, M.P.F., Prin. Religious 2; Lay Teachers 24; Students 408.
Catechesis/Religious Program—Tel: 505-892-1497. Students 1,217.
Mission—St. John Vianney 1000 26th Ave., N.E., Sandoval Co. 87144.

ROY, HARDING CO., HOLY FAMILY-ST. JOSEPH (1918), (Hispanic), [CEM 4] Rev. Paul Nkumbi (Uganda).
Res.: P.O. Box 37, 87743. Tel: 575-485-9633; Fax: 575-485-9633. Email: holyfamilyroy@yahoo.com.
Catechesis/Religious Program—Students 8.
Mission— Bueyeros, Harding Co.
Mission— Gallegos, Harding Co.
Mission— Sabinoso, San Miguel Co.

SAN JUAN PUEBLO, RIO ARRIBA CO. (INDIAN PUEBLO), SAN JUAN BAUTISTA (1598) Revs. Larry R. Brito; Denis Kaggwa (Uganda), Parochial Vicar; Deacons John Bird; Eloy E. Martinez; Michael Salazar.
Res.: 185 Popaye Ave., P.O. Box 1075, Ohkay Owingeh Pueblo, 87566. Tel: 505-852-4179; Fax: 505-852-9719. Email: sjparish@cybermesa.com.
Catechesis/Religious Program—Tel: 505-852-2270; Fax: 505-852-9719. Savanna Trujillo, D.R.E. Students 217.
Mission— Alcalde, Rio Arriba Co.
Mission— Chamita, Rio Arriba Co.
Mission— El Guique, Rio Arriba Co.
Mission— Ranchitos, Rio Arriba Co.
Mission— [CEM] Estaca, Rio Arriba Co.
Shrine—Our Lady of Lourdes, Pilgrimage shrine.

SANTA CRUZ, SANTA FE CO., HOLY CROSS (1695), (Hispanic), [CEM] Revs. Javier Gutierrez, S.F.; Jose Maria Blanch, S.F., Parochial Vicar; John Plans, S.F., Parochial Vicar.
Res.: 124 S. McCurdy Rd., P.O. Box 1228, 87567-1228. Tel: 505-753-3345; Fax: 505-753-3233. Email: holycrosschurch@windstream.net.
School—(Grades K-6), P.O. Box 1260, 87567-1260. Tel: 505-753-4644; Fax: 505-753-7401. Mrs. Terry Ann Lopez, Prin.; Kathy Lujan, Librarian. Sisters 1; Lay Teachers 13; Students 134.
Catechesis/Religious Program—Tel: 505-753-4567; Fax: 505-753-7401. Betty Andrade, D.R.E. (Elementary); Salomon Velasquez, D.R.E. (Junior & Senior High); Sunny Velasquez, D.R.E. (Junior & Senior High). Students 375.

SANTA ROSA, GUADALUPE CO., ST. ROSE OF LIMA (1907), (Hispanic), [CEM] Rev. Joseph Thomas Kanavalil, C.M.I.; Deacons Arsenio C. Sanchez; Marvin M. Marquez.
Res.: 439 Third St., 88435. Tel: 575-472-3724; Fax: 575-472-4724.
Catechesis/Religious Program—Tel: 505-472-3992. Barbara Perea Sena, D.R.E.; Sr. Ann Kaufmann, D.R.E. Students 275.
Mission— Puerto de Luna, Guadalupe Co.
Mission— San Ignacio, Guadalupe Co.
Mission— Borica, Guadalupe Co.
Mission— Cuervo, Guadalupe Co.
Mission— Colonias, Guadalupe Co.
Mission— Pintada, Guadalupe Co.
Mission— Milagro, Guadalupe Co.

SOCORRO, SOCORRO CO., SAN MIGUEL (1615), (Native American—Hispanic), [CEM 8] [JC] Rev. Andrew J. Pavlak; Deacons Miguel Ybarra; Robert Jiron; Nicholas Keller.
Res.: 403 El Camino Real, N.W., 87801. Tel: 575-835-2891; Fax: 575-835-1620.
Catechesis/Religious Program—Bernadette Zamora, D.R.E. Students 204.
Mission— Lemitar, Socorro Co.

Mission— Polvadera, Socorro Co.
Mission— Luis Lopez, Socorro Co.
Mission— San Antonio, Socorro Co.
Mission— Alamillo, Socorro Co.
Mission— Magdalena, Socorro Co.
Mission— Kelly, Socorro Co.
Mission— Riley, Socorro Co.

SPRINGER, COLFAX CO., ST. JOSEPH (1882), (Hispanic), [JC] Rev. Emmanuel Izuka (Nigeria); Deacon Edward Olona.
Res.: 605 Fifth St., P.O. Box 516, 87747. Tel: 575-483-2775; Fax: 575-483-2518. Email: stjosephicc@hotmail.com.
Catechesis/Religious Program—Diane Alderette, D.R.E. Students 3.
Mission— Palo Blanco, Colfax Co.
Mission— Tinaja, Colfax Co.

TAOS, TAOS CO., NUESTRA SENORA DE GUADALUPE (1801), (Spanish), [CEM] Rev. Clement Niggel; Deacons Donald Martinez; Jerry Quintana, Business Mgr.; Tillie Suazo.
Res.: 205 Don Fernando St., 87571. Tel: 575-779-1248; Fax: 575-758-2745.
Catechesis/Religious Program—Tel: 575-776-4764. Students 133.
Mission—St. Jerome Taos Pueblo, Taos Co. 87571.
Chapel—El Prado, St. Theresa
Chapel—Canon, Our Lady of Sorrows
Chapel—Ranchitos, Immaculate Conception
Chapel—La Loma, San Antonio

TIERRA AMARILLA, RIO ARRIBA CO., SANTO NINO (1966), (Hispanic), [JC] Rev. Joel O. Bugas.
Mailing Address: Box 160, 87575.
Catechesis/Religious Program—Tel: 575-588-7473. Twinned with San Jose, Los Ojos. Students 25.

TIJERAS, BERNALILLO CO., HOLY CHILD (1962) [CEM 9] [JC 2] Rev. Mark E. Granito; Deacon Larry Carmony.
Res.: 19 Camino de Santo Nino, Box 130, 87059. Tel: 505-281-2297; Fax: 505-281-0355. Email: holychildparish@aol.com. Web: members.aol.com/holychildparish.
School—Holy Child Catholic School, Tel: 505-281-3077; Fax: 505-281-3744. Jim Grogan, Prin. Lay Teachers 6; Students 42.
Catechesis/Religious Program—Students 230.
Mission—Holy Child Carnuel, Bernalillo Co.
Mission—San Juan de Nepumoceno Chilili, Bernalillo Co.
Mission—San Isidro Escobosa, Bernalillo Co.
Mission— San Antonio, Bernalillo Co.
Mission—San Isidro Sedillo, Bernalillo Co.
Mission— Canoncito, Bernalillo Co.
Mission—, Bernalillo Co.
Mission—Senor de Mapimi San Antonito.

TOME, VALENCIA CO., IMMACULATE CONCEPTION (1739), (Spanish), [CEM] Rev. Jose A. Hernandez.
Res.: 7 Church Loop, P.O. Box 100, 87060-0100. Tel: 505-866-9201; Fax: 505-865-7622. Web: icchurchtome.org.
Catechesis/Religious Program—7 Church Loop, Juan Diego Hall. Tel: 505-865-4220. Martha Sanchez, D.R.E. Students 153.
Mission— State Hwy. 304 S., Casa Colorada, Valencia Co. 87002.

TUCUMCARI, QUAY CO., ST. ANNE (1910) [JC] Rev. Hyginus Chuks Anuta (Nigeria); Deacons Robert Welch; Raphael (Ray) P. Aragon.
Res.: 306 W. High St., 88401. Tel: 575-461-2515; Fax: 575-461-3058.
Catechesis/Religious Program—Tel: 575-461-3568. Nancy Arias, D.R.E. Students 193.
Mission—San Antonio Logan, Quay Co.
Mission—Sacred Heart Nara Visa, Quay Co.
Mission—Our Lady of Guadalupe San Jon, Quay Co.

VAUGHN, GUADALUPE CO., ST. MARY (1936), (Hispanic), [JC] Rev. Simeon Frank Wimmershoff, O.F.M.
Res.: P.O. Box 276, 88353. Tel: 575-584-2954.
Catechesis/Religious Program—Students 42.
Mission— Encino, Torrance Co.
Mission— Duran, Torrance Co.
Mission— Pastura, Guadalupe Co.
Mission— Pinos Wells, Torrance Co.

VILLANUEVA, SAN MIGUEL, OUR LADY OF GUADALUPE (1830), (Hispanic), [CEM 6] Rev. Thomas Kayammakal (India), Canonical Pastor.
Mailing Address: P.O. Box 39, 87583. Tel: 575-421-2548; Fax: 575-421-2548. In Res., Sr. Elena L. Carney, O.L.V.M., Parish Life Coord.
Catechesis/Religious Program—Students 53.
Mission— Sena, San Miguel Co.
Mission— Cerrito, San Miguel Co.
Mission— Gonzales Ranch, San Miguel Co.
Mission— Leyba, San Miguel Co.
Mission— Aurora, San Miguel Co.

WAGON MOUND, MORA CO., SANTA CLARA (1882), (Hispanic), [CEM] Rev. Paul Nkumbi (Uganda); Deacon Charlie Duran.
Res.: P.O. Box 186, 87752. Tel: 575-666-2478; Fax: 575-666-2478.
Catechesis/Religious Program—Students 12.
Mission— Ocate, Mora Co.
Mission— Los Hueros, Mora Co.
Mission— Los Le Febres, Mora Co.
Mission— Watrous, Mora Co.

PILGRIMAGE SHRINES

ALBUQUERQUE
SHRINE—SHRINE OF ST. BERNADETTE 11509 Indian School Rd. NE., 87112.

CHIMAYO, SANTUARIO DE CHIMAYO, Attended by Holy Family, Chimayo. , 87522.

Priests Serving Private and Public Institutions

SANTA FE. *Hospital*. Deacon Steve Rangel, Dir. Outreach.
New Mexico State Penitentiary. Deacon Andy Carillo.
St. Vincent's Hospital. Rev. Terrence P. Brennan, Chap.

ALBUQUERQUE. *Lovelace Hospital*. Deacon Andy Chavez.
Presbyterian Hospital. Revs. Robert E. Campbell, O.Praem., Ronald G. Stone, Westside Hospitals.
Prison Ministry. Deacon Steve Rangel, Dir. Outreach, Sr. Josefina Peralta, Fd.CC., Coord.
University Hospital. Revs. Aloysius Abaneke (Nigeria), Steve Sanchez.

LAS VEGAS. *State Hospital*. Rev. George Salazar. Attended by Immaculate Conception Parish.

LOS LUNAS. *Correctional Facility (State)*. Deacon Lorenzo Castillo.

On Duty Outside the Archdiocese:
Revs.—
Phillipson, David
Steenson, Jeffery N., University of St. Thomas, Houston, TX.

Retired:
Rev. Msgrs.—
Calles, Robert S. (ELP)
Gomez, Leo, (Gallup Diocese)
Lucero, Leo
Salas, Sipio
Revs.—
Amiro, Raymond M.
Aragon, Ramon
Bolman, Anthony P.
Bowers, Ronald J., J.C.D., (Archdiocese of St. Paul & Minneapolis)
Brand, Fred
Brown, Charles
Chavez, Patrick J.
Conway, John
Coughlan, Robert
DeFazio, Vincent G.
Duffy, Patrick
Falbo, Samuel
Furfaro, Virgil
Garcia, Millan
Hendren, Lucian
Hickman, J. Stephen
Jakobiak, Arthur
Jaramillo, Luis
Johnson, Gerald
Kapitz, Donald
LaVoie, Joseph
Martinez, Vidal
Mayefske, Thomas J. (GB)
Mondragon, Antonio
Moore, Augustine J., Ph.D.
Moore, James
Podvin, Albert J.
Prieto, Frank
Rivera, Guadalupe
Romero, Anthony E.
Rubio-Boitel, Fernando
Schulz, Ronald (PMB)
Shedlock, John
Starkey, Donald
Vance, James L.
Zotter, Thomas A.

Permanent Deacons:
Abeyta, Santos, Holy Family, Albuquerque
Adams, Alton, St. Alice, Mountainair
Aguilar, Gregory, Santa Clara Pueblo, Tewa Missions
Aguirre, Hector, San Jose, Albuquerque
Alcouffe, Raymond, Immaculate Heart of Mary, Los Alamos
Alderette, Thomas, St. Joseph-St. Patrick, Raton
Allen, Charles, (Outside the Archdiocese)
Aragon, Raphael (Ray) P., St. Anne, Tucumcari
Aragon, Robert, St. Jude Thaddeus, Albuquerque
Archibeque, Norbert, Church of the Incarnation, Rio Rancho
Archuleta, Faustin, Holy Ghost, Albuquerque
Archuleta, John, Nuestra Senora de Guadalupe, Pojoaque
Archunde, Gregory, St. Bernadette Parish and Shrine, Albuquerque
Arellano, Romolo, La Santisima Trinidad, Arroyo Seco
Arquero, Albert, Our Lady of Guadalupe, Pena Blanca
Avalos-Sanchez, Constantino, Santuario de San Martin de Porres, Albuquerque
Avitia, Hector, San Clemente, Los Lunas
Ayala, Jose, St. Francis Xavier, Albuquerque
Ayers, Roger, St. Thomas, Rio Rancho
Baca, James, (Retired)
Baca, Paul, San Clemente, Los Lunas
Baca, Rudolph, Sangre de Cristo, Albuquerque
Baca, Thomas, (Outside the Archdiocese)
Baca, Tomas, (Outside the Archdiocese)
Bachechi, Victor, Annunciation, Albuquerque
Bailey, Aston, (Retired)
Barajas, Juan, St. Anne, Albuquerque; Dir. of Hispanic Ministry; Assoc. Dir., Diaconate Program
Barela, Felix, Our Lady of Belen, Belen
Barela, Ruben, Queen of Heaven, Albuquerque
Barry, William, St. Charles, Albuquerque
Beare, Harry, Holy Rosary, Albuquerque
Beaudette, James, Holy Rosary, Albuquerque
Bird, John, St. John the Baptist, Ohkay Owingeh Pueblo
Blea, Edward, Holy Family, Albuquerque
Broussard, Peter, (On Duty Outside the Archdiocese)
Bruckner, Donald G., St. Joseph on the Rio Grande, Albuquerque
Burkhard, Robert, San Clemente, Los Lunas
Burns, Thomas, St. Thomas, Rio Rancho
Burrola, Jose Luis, Our Lady of Guadalupe, Santa Fe
Bussemeier, Mark, Risen Savior, Albuquerque
Cabrera, Juan, Our Lady of Guadalupe, Albuquerque
Calderon, Gonzalo, Our Lady of Sorrows, Bernalillo
Campos, Peter, Immaculate Conception, Las Vegas, New Mexico
Carbajal, James, San Felipe De Neri, Albuquerque
Carmony, Larry, Holy Child, Tijeras
Carrillo, Andres, St. John the Baptist, Santa Fe
Casaus, Luis, (Retired)
Castillo, Lorenzo, Immaculate Conception, Tome
Centenera, Leandro, Prince of Peace, Albuquerque
Cervantes, Jose de Jesus, Our Lady of Sorrows, Bernalillo
Chavez, Andy, (Retired)
Chavez, Daniel, Our Lady of Guadalupe, Clovis
Chavez, Ernest, Immaculate Conception, Las Vegas
Chavez, Gerald, Our Lady of Guadalupe, Pena Blanca
Chavez, Ricardo, Holy Ghost, Albuquerque
Chavez, Tiburcio, (Retired)
Chavez, Ubaldo, Holy Ghost, Albuquerque
Cleveland, Larry, Queen of Heaven, Albuquerque
Contreras, Donald, Aquinas Newman Center, Albuquerque
Contreras, Robert, (Retired)
Cooney, Patrick, (Retired)
Cordova, John, Santa Maria De La Paz, Santa Fe
Cordova, Raynaldo A., (Retired), St. Gertrude the Great, Mora
Cullen, Charles, Prince of Peace, Albuquerque
Cupps, Donald, Estancia Valley Catholic Church, Moriarty
Davis, Keith, Our Lady of Fatima, Albuquerque
Delgado, James P., Our Lady of the Assumption, Albuquerque
DeLozier, Patrick, San Francisco de Asis, Ranchos De Taos
Dimas, Juan (Andy), St. Anne, Santa Fe
Dohle, Albert, St. Joseph, Albuquerque
Duran, Charles, Santa Clara, Wagon Mound
Eklund, Bruce, St. Thomas Aquinas Newman Center, Albuquerque
Escandon, Jose, Our Lady of Fatima, Albuquerque
Espinosa, Edward, Our Lady of Guadalupe, Peralta
Esquibel, A. Edwin, Our Lady of Sorrows, La Joya
Facio, Manuel, Our Lady of Guadalupe, Albuquerque
Fraker, Steven, Prince of Peace, Albuquerque
Gagnon, Fabian, Pastoral Care, Sandia Health System, Albuquerque
Gallegos, Eloy, Santa Maria de la Paz, Santa Fe
Gallegos, Manuel A., (Retired)
Gallegos, Martin, Jr., San Isidro - San Jose, Santa Fe
Garcia, Joseph, St. John the Baptist, Santa Fe
Garcia, Manuel, Risen Savior, Albuquerque
Garcia, Nestor, St. Anne, Albuquerque
Garcia, Pedro, Nuestra Senora de Guadalupe, Pojoaque
Garcia, Pilar, Queen of Heaven, Albuquerque

Gogan, Harry L., Annunciation, Albuquerque
Graff, Maurice, Our Lady of Assumption, Albuquerque
Grajeda, Raul, (On Leave)
Granato, John, Our Lady of the Assumption, Albuquerque
Greivel, Rene, St. Joseph on the Rio Grande, Albuquerque
Hackett, Hugh, (Retired), Our Lady of Fatima, Albuquerque
Hall, Sandy, Our Lady of Fatima, Albuquerque
Henderson, Gregorio, San Jose, Albuquerque
Herrera, Diego A., Sacred Heart, Espanola
Herrera, Joseph, Holy Rosary, Albuquerque
Herrera, Roberto, St. Helen, Portales
Hietpas, Gerald M., St. Joseph on the Rio Grande, Albuquerque
Hill, Kenneth, St. Thomas, Rio Rancho
Hoefler, William C., Ascension, Albuquerque
Illerbrun, Michael, Nativity of the Blessed Virgin Mary, Albuquerque
Irving, Michael, Immaculate Heart of Mary, Los Alamos, NM
Jiron, Robert, San Miguel, Socorro
Johnson, Charles V., (Retired)
Jones, Leon, Church of the Ascension, Albuquerque
Jones, Thomas E., Our Lady of Fatima, Albuquerque
Keller, Nicholas, San Miguel, Socorro
Kollasch, William, St. Francis Cathedral Basilica, Santa Fe
Krepps, John, Immaculate Heart of Mary, Los Alamos, NM
LeFebre, Paul, St. Anne, Albuquerque
Lente, Michael, St. Charles Borromeo, Albuquerque
Leonard, Mark, San Clemente, Los Lunas, NM
Lewis, James R. "Bob", San Felipe de Neri, Albuquerque
Little, David, St. Thomas, Rio Rancho
Lopez, Demetrio, Queen of Heaven, Albuquerque
Lopez, Jose O., Holy Family, Chimayo
Lucero, Charles, (Retired)
Lucero, Donato, Immaculate Heart of Mary, Los Alamos
Lucero, Frank, St. Jude Thaddeus, Albuquerque
Lucero, Jose E., San Felipe de Neri, Albuquerque
Lucero, Juan S., Estancia Valley Parish, Moriarty
Lucero, Leroy, St. Anthony, Questa
Maloney, Kevin, Annunciation, Albuquerque
Marquez, Mark Marvin, St. Rose of Lima, Santa Rosa
Marquez, Oscar, San Martin De Porres, Albuquerque
Martinez, Donald J., Our Lady of Guadalupe, Taos
Martinez, Eloy, St. John the Baptist, Ohkay Owingeh Pueblo
Martinez, Jose Leroy, Our Lady of Sorrows, Las Vegas
Martinez, Juan R., St. Francis Cathedral, Santa Fe
Martinez, Juan G., San Miguel, Ribera
Martinez, Leonard, Nativity, Albuquerque
Martinez, Lloyd, Sangre de Cristo, Albuquerque
McLane, Alfred, St. Bernadette, Albuquerque
Medina, Jesus, St. Francis Xavier, Albuquerque
Menke, Maurice, San Felipe, Albuquerque
Meyerson, George, Incarnation, Rio Rancho
Meyrick, Earl, (Retired)
Miller, George, St. Joseph on the Rio Grande, Albuquerque
Mishler, Richard, (Outside the Archdiocese)
Montoya, Enrique M., St. Anne, Santa Fe
Montoya, Filberto "Manny", Santa Maria, Santa Fe
Montoya, Manuel, Our Lady of Guadalupe, Albuquerque
Montoya, P. Louis, St. Francis Xavier, Clayton
Morrow, Robert, Our Lady of the Annunciation, Albuquerque
Nguyen, Dung (Paul), St. Charles, Albuquerque
O'Hara, James, Immaculate Heart of Mary, Los Alamos, NM
O'Hare, John J., (Outside the Archdiocese)
Olona, Edward, St. Joseph, Springer
Ortiz, Juan, Nativity of the Blessed Virgin Mary, Albuquerque
Ortwerth, Paul, Sangre de Cristo, Albuquerque
Pacheco, Carlos Felix, (Retired)
Pacheco, Charles, (Retired)
Padilla, Enrique, Prince of Peace, Albuquerque
Palmer, Terry, St. Bernadette, Albuquerque
Paszkiewicz, Jerome, Church of the Incarnation, Rio Rancho
Perez, Frank, Holy Rosary, Albuquerque
Perez, Tomas, San Felipe de Neri, Albuquerque
Porto, Tony, (Retired)
Pullings, Harold, Our Lady of Guadalupe, Clovis
Quintana, Jerry, Our Lady of Guadalupe, Taos
Rael, Felimon, St. Mel's Mission, Eagle Nest
Rael, Marcus, St. Anthony, Questa
Rangel, Stephen S., San Ysidro, Corrales; Dir. of Permanent Diaconate
Rasinski, John, Our Lady of the Sandias, Kirtland, AFB
Rivera, Lawrence Anthony, Our Lady of the Annunciation, Albuquerque, NM
Rodriguez, Juan, (Retired)
Rodriguez, Juan A., Sacred Heart, Clovis
Rodriguez, Randall, Holy Child, Tijeras
Romero, Jerome, San Antonio de Padua, Penasco
Roseborough, Donald, (On Leave)
Rowley, Michael, Sacred Heart, Clovis
Roybal, Christobal, St. Gertrude, Mora
Roybal, Reuben, Nuestra Senora de Guadalupe, Pojoaque
Roybal, Richard, St. Anthony, Pecos
Russell, Robert Davis, St. Thomas Aquinas, Rio Rancho, NM
Russo, John L., John XXIII Catholic Community, Albuquerque
Salazar, Michael, San Isidro, San Jose, Santa Fe, NJ
Salazar, Miguel, St. John the Baptist, Ohkay Owingeh Pueblo
Salazar, Phillip, (Outside the Archdiocese)
Salazar, Samuel, (On Leave)
Salinas, Cresencio, San Martin De Porres, Albuquerque
Sanchez, Arsenio, St. Rose of Lima, Santa Rosa
Sanchez, Leroy, St. Thomas, Rio Rancho
Sanchez, Norbert C., (Retired)
Sanchez, Reyes, Our Lady of Sorrows, Las Vegas
Sanchez, Robert, Our Lady of Belen, Belen
Sandoval, George, Immaculate Conception, Albuquerque
Santana, Joe, St. Bernadette, Albuquerque
Santistevan, Peter, (Retired)
Schwenn, Charles E., St. Alice, Mountainair
Sedillo, Michael, Immaculate Conception, Cimarron
Segura, Jose, Our Lady of Guadalupe, Pena Blanca
Sena, Edward, St. Anthony of Padua, Fort Sumner
Sheehan, Dan, Risen Savior, Albuquerque
Siegel, Michael, San Isidro/San Jose, Santa Fe
Silva, Joseph, Holy Rosary, Albuquerque
Sinatra, Kenneth, Risen Savior, Albuquerque
Smith, Frank, St. Thomas, Rio Rancho
Snell, Jimmie, San Clemente, Los Lunas; Dir. of Diaconate Formation
Stith, Thomas, Our Lady of Guadalupe, Santa Fe
Sutton, John, Immaculate Heart of Mary, Los Alamos, NM
Talavera, Raul, St. Therese, Albuquerque
Toliver, Jeffrey, (On Leave)
Toquinto, Jesus, Ascension, Albuquerque
Torres, Edgar L., Sr., Sacred Heart, Albuquerque
Trujillo, Alex, (Retired)
Trujillo, Anthony, San Isidro - San Jose, Santa Fe
Trujillo, Kenneth, Risen Savior, Albuquerque
Trujillo, Manuel, Our Lady of Belen, Belen, NM
Tuma, Eugene, (Retired)
Valdez, Gilbert, Our Lady of Guadalupe, Santa Fe
Valdez, Jose, Nuestra Senora de Guadalupe, Pojoaque
Valkenburgh, Thomas Van, Cristo Rey, Santa Fe
Valverde, George W., Our Lady of Guadalupe, Albuquerque
Valverde, Gilbert, (Retired)
Vigil, Ralph, Nativity of the Blessed Virgin Mary, Albuquerque
Vigil, Robert, Sacred Heart, Albuquerque
Villareal, Merce A., Risen Savior, Albuquerque
Villarreal, Robert, Immaculate Heart of Mary, Los Alamos
Welch, Robert, St. Anne, Tucumcari
Wesley, Michael, St. Therese, Albuquerque
Wicker, Byron, St. Bernadette, Albuquerque
Ybarra, Miguel, San Miguel, Socorro
Zamora, Rudy R., Our Lady of Belen, Belen

INSTITUTIONS LOCATED IN THE ARCHDIOCESE

[A] SEMINARIES, RELIGIOUS OR SCHOLASTICATES

SANTA FE. *Sangre de Cristo Center* (1962) 410 State Rd. 592, 87506-0070. Tel: 505-983-7291; Fax: 505-983-6963. Email: sangre@newmexico.com. Web: www.sangredecristo.org. Bros. Vincent Pelletier, F.S.C., Dir.; Paul Kelly, C.S.C., Dir. Fin.; Dennis Galvin, FSC, Assoc. Dir.; Sisters Janet Franklin, C.S.J., Assoc. Dir.; Susan Kusz, S.N.D., Assoc. Dir. Program of refoundation for religious and priests, under the administration of the Christian Brothers. Participants 60 annually. Brothers 3; Sisters 2; Lay Persons 3; Total Staff 8.

[B] HIGH SCHOOLS, ARCHDIOCESAN AND PAROCHIAL

ALBUQUERQUE. *St. Pius X High School*, (Grades 8-12), 5301 St. Joseph Dr., N.W., 87120. Tel: 505-831-8400; Fax: 505-831-8413. Web: www.saintpiusx.com. Barbara Rothweiler, Prin.; Rev. Anthony G. Maes, O.Praem. Priests 1; Sisters 1; Deacons 1; Lay Teachers 70; Students 814.

[C] HIGH SCHOOLS, PRIVATE

SANTA FE. *St. Michael's High School*, (Grades 7-12), (Coed Day School), 100 Siringo Rd., 87505. Tel: 505-983-7353; Fax: 505-982-8722. Email: mainoffice@stmikes.k12.nm.us. Web: www.stmichaelshs.org. Sam Govea, Prin. Brothers of the Christian Schools 1; Lay Teachers 49; Students 707.

[D] ELEMENTARY REGIONAL SCHOOL

SANTA FE. *Santo Nino Regional Catholic School*, (Grades PreK-6), 23 College Ave., 87508. Tel: 505-424-1766; Fax: 505-473-1441. Email: snrcs@santonino.k12.nm.us. Web: www.santoninoregional.org. Theresa Vaisa, Prin. Lay Teachers 26; Students 347.

[E] SPECIAL HOSPITALS AND SANATORIA FOR INVALIDS

SANTA FE. *Villa Therese Catholic Clinic*, 219 Cathedral Pl., 87501. Tel: 505-983-8561; Fax: 505-982-7863. Email: vtcc@cnsp.com. Total Staff 5; Total Assisted Annually 2,000.

[F] SHELTER CARE HOMES

ALBUQUERQUE. *Good Shepherd Center, Inc.*, 218 Iron St., S.W., P.O. Box 749, 87103. Tel: 505-243-2527; Fax: 505-247-2207. Curits Marks, Pres. Direct Service Agency for the Homeless. Total Assisted 220,000; Total Staff 9.

Marie Amadea Shelter for Unwed Mothers (Alternative to Abortion), P.O. Box 708, 87103. Tel: 505-242-1516; Fax: 505-243-0402. Mrs. Dorothy Wickens, Dir. Home for unwed expectant women. Total Staff 1.

[G] CARE HOMES FOR PHYSICALLY AND MENTALLY HANDICAPPED

ALBUQUERQUE. *Casa Angelica* (1967) 5629 Isleta Blvd., S.W., 87105. Tel: 505-877-5763; Fax: 505-873-2786. Email: lturner@casaangelica.org. Web: www.casaangelica.org. The Daughters of Charity of Canossa., Home for developmentally disabled children and young adults. Sisters 1; Residents 16; Lay Staff 54; Total Assisted 16; Total Staff 55.

[H] MONASTERIES AND RESIDENCES OF PRIESTS AND BROTHERS

ABIQUIU. *Monastery of Christ in the Desert* (1964) 87510. Tel: 801-545-8567; Fax: 419-831-9113. Email: cidguestmaster@christdesert.us. Web: www.christdesert.org. Rt. Rev. Philip Lawrence, O.S.B., Abbot; Revs. Christian Leisy, O.S.B., Business Mgr.; Bernard Cranor, O.S.B.; Luis Regalado, O.S.B.; Odon Nguyen, O.S.B.; Francisco Alanis Rios, Prior; Joseph Gabriel Cusimano, O.S.B., Prior; Andrew Nguyen, O.S.B.; Augustine Seiker, O.S.B. Subiaco Congregation. In Res. Rev. Frederick Brand.

ALBUQUERQUE. *Little Brothers of the Good Shepherd, Villa Mathias-Foundation House*, 901 Bro. Mathias Pl., N.W., P.O. Box 389, 87103. Tel: 505-243-4238; Fax: 505-764-9721. Brothers 7; Total Staff 1.

Santa Maria de la Vid Priory, 5825 Coors Blvd., S.W., 87121-6700. Tel: 505-873-4399; Fax: 505-873-4667. Email: norbertines@norbertinecommunity.org. Web: www.norbertinecommunity.org. Revs. Joel P. Garner, O.Praem., Prior & Vocation Dir.; Eugene Gries, O.Praem.; Nicholas E. Nirschl, O.Praem.; Robert E. Campbell, O.Praem.; Francis W. Dorff, O.Praem.; Anthony G. Maes, O.Praem.; Bijoy Francis Valayil, O.Praem.; George Pavamkott, O.Praem.; Binu Joseph Pazhayaveetil, O.Praem (India); Bro. Dennis Butler. Canons Regular of Premontre (Norbertine Community)., Sponsor of the Hermitage Retreat and the Norbertine Library. Priests 11; Brothers 1.

The Province of Our Lady of Guadalupe formerly Curia Juan Diego (1985) 1204 Stinson, S.W., 87121-3440. Tel: 505-831-9199; Fax: 505-573-5584. Email: ofmprovsec@aol.com. Web: www.olgofm.org. Very Rev. Larry C. Dunham, O.F.M., (Sabbatical); Revs. Gino Correa, O.F.M., Provincial Min.; Don Billiard, O.F.M., Treas.; Bros. Duane Torisky, O.F.M., Sec./Notary Province; Bruce Michalek, O.F.M., Devel. Dir.; George Ward, O.F.M.; Revs. Timon Cook, O.F.M. (Retired); Cecil Kleber, O.F.M.; Gonzalo Moreno, O.F.M., Province

Vocation Dir.; Pio O'Connor, O.F.M.; Bros. Richardo Garcia, O.F.M.; Efren Quintero, O.F.M.; Jose Rodriguez, O.F.M.; Mark Schornack, O.F.M.; Bart Wolff, O.F.M.; Gordon Boykin, O.F.M.; Revs. Salvador Aragon, O.F.M.; Wayne Gibbeaut, O.F.M.; Emeric Nordmeyer, O.F.M.; Diego Mazon, O.F.M.; Ulric Pax, O.F.M.; Richard Rohr, O.F.M.; Chrysostom Partee, O.F.M.; Ramon Smith, O.F.M.; Gerald Steinmetz, O.F.M.; Hilaire Valiquette, O.F.M.

Franciscan Indian Missions

Franciscan Mission Center

The Province of Our Lady of Guadalupe of the Order of Friars Minor, Inc.

Southwest Franciscan Missions Priests 38; Brothers 16.

JEMEZ SPRINGS. *Our Lady of Lourdes*, P.O. Box 10, 87025-0010. Tel: 505-829-3004; Fax: 505-829-3706. Email: servants@theservants.org. Web: www.theservants.org. Very Rev. David T. Fitzgerald, s.P.; Revs. Gregory McCormick, s.P., Supr. & Father Servant; James Sampson, s.P.; Paul Valley, s.P.; Bro. John Paul Pelletier, s.P. Priests 4; Brothers 3. *Formation House* Tel: 505-829-3720; Fax: 505-829-3706.

PECOS. *Our Lady of Guadalupe Abbey*, P.O. Box 1080, 87552-1080. Tel: 505-757-6415; Fax: 505-757-2285. Email: guestmaster@pecosmonastery.org. Web: www.pecosmonastery.org. Revs. Symeon Galazka; Sam Dennis, O.S.B.; Aidan Gore, O.S.B.; Colman Heffern, O.S.B.; Robert Lussier, O.S.B.; Bros. John M. Davies, O.S.B.; James M. Marron, O.S.B.; Todd Barvinek, O.S.B.; Sean Keatin, O.S.B. (Olivetan Benedictine Monks) Priests 4; Brothers 4.

[I] CONVENTS AND RESIDENCES FOR SISTERS

SANTA FE. *Discalced Carmelite Monastery* (1945) 49 Mount Carmel Rd., 87505-0352. Tel: 505-983-7232. Sr. Rose Teresa, O.C.D., Prioress; Revs. Ricardo Russo, O.F.M., Chap.; Robert Lussier, O.S.B. Solemn Professed Nuns 6; Extern Sisters 2.

ALBUQUERQUE. *Cristo Rey Provincial House*, 5625 Isleta Blvd., S.W., 87105. Tel: 505-873-2854; Fax: 505-873-0678. Email: fdccalb@aol.com. Web: www.canossiansisters.org. Sr. Anne Bosio, Prov. Supr. Canossian Daughters of Charity. Sisters 13.

JEMEZ SPRINGS. *Cor Jesu Monastery* (1947) Motherhouse and Novitiate of the Handmaids of the Precious Blood., 87025. Tel: 575-829-3906; Fax: 575-829-3423. Sr. Marietta, H.P.B., Mother Prioress. Perpetually Professed Sisters 19.

RIO RANCHO. *Felician Sisters*, 4210 Meadowlark Ln., S.E., 87124-1021. Tel: 505-892-8862; Fax: 505-891-3893. Web: www.feliciansna.org. Sr. Mary Christopher Moore, C.S.S.F., Provincial Min. Assumption of the Blessed Virgin Mary. Residents 24; Professed Sisters of Province 44; Total Assisted Per Month 6,000; Total Staff 32. In Res. Rev. Salvador Aragon, O.F.M.; Bro. Gerald Grantner, O.F.M.

[J] RETREAT HOUSES

SANTA FE. *Immaculate Heart of Mary Retreat and Conference Center*, 50 Mount Carmel Rd., 87505. Tel: 505-988-1975; Fax: 505-988-3963. Email: jsnodgrass@archdiosf.org. Mr. Jeff Snodgrass, Dir.

ALBUQUERQUE. *Madonna Retreat and Conference Center*, 4040 St. Joseph Pl., N.W., 87120. Tel: 505-831-8196; Fax: 505-831-8103. Email: madonnacenter@archdiosf.org. Web: www.archdiocesesantafe.org. Esther-Marie Nagiel, Dir. Total in Residence 2; Total Staff 3.

The Spiritual Renewal Center, Inc., 6400 Coors Blvd., N.W., 87120. Tel: 505-877-4211; Fax: 505-890-4110. Email: david@src-nm.org. Web: www.src-nm.org. P.O. Box 67860, 87193. Dominican Sisters (Elkins Park, PA)., Center for Retreats. Total Staff 3.

PECOS. *Our Lady of Guadalupe Olivetan Benedictine Abbey*, P.O. Box 1080, 87552. Tel: 505-757-6415; Fax: 505-757-2285. Email: guestmaster@pecosmonastery.org. Web: www.pecosmonastery.org.

[K] NEWMAN CENTERS

ALBUQUERQUE. *St. Thomas Aquinas (Newman Center) University Parish* (1950) 1815 Las Lomas Rd., N.E., 87106. Tel: 505-247-1094; Fax: 505-247-2933. Email: newmancenter@aquinasnm.org. Web: www.aquinasnm.org. Revs. Richard Litzau, O.P., Parochial Vicar; Daniel C. Davis, O.P., Parish Admin.; Deacons Donald Contreras; Bruce Eklund; Bro. Gabriel Dault, O.P., Campus Minister; Steve Herrera, Liturgy Dir.; Kyle Kemp, Rel. Formation Dir. Priests 2; Deacons 2; Total in Residence 5; Total Staff 13. In Res. Revs. Kevin W. Niehoff, O.P.; Tom Noesen, O.P.; George J.D. Reynolds, O.P.; Matthew T.D. Strabala, O.P.

LAS VEGAS. *Highlands University Newman Center* Mailing Address: 811 - 6th St., 87701. Tel: 505-425-7791; Fax: 505-425-6991. Email: icchurch2000@yahoo.com. Attended by Immaculate Conception Parish, Las Vegas.

PORTALES. *University Catholic Center - St. Thomas More Chapel* E.N.M.U., P.O. Box 2253, 88130. Tel: 575-356-4241; Fax: 575-359-1721. Rev. James McGowan, Chap. Total Staff 1.

SOCORRO. *St. Patrick Newman Center* 801 School of Mines Rd., 87801. Tel: 575-835-8650. Deacon Nicholas Keller, Dir.

[L] MISCELLANEOUS LISTINGS

SANTA FE. *St. Michael's High School Foundation*, 100 Siringo Rd., P.O. Box 22563, 87505. Tel: 505-988-2264; Fax: 505-955-8921. Tim Vigil, Pres.

ALBUQUERQUE. *Annual Catholic Appeal Foundation of the Archdiocese of Santa Fe*, 4000 St. Joseph Pl., N.W., 87120. Tel: 505-831-8258; Fax: 505-831-8111. Email: aca@archdiosf.org. Web: www.archdiosf.org.

Anselm Weber Fund, P.O. Box 12315, 87195-0315. Tel: 505-877-6394. Email: frfriars@comcast.net. Rev. Don Billiard, O.F.M., Corp. Treas.

Archbishop's School Fund, 4000 St. Joseph Pl., N.W., 87120. Tel: 505-831-8120; Fax: 505-831-8101. Email: dc@archdiosf.org. Carol Zonski, Pres.

Archdiocesan Priests Retirement Fund, Inc., 5024 4th St., N.W., 87107. Tel: 505-343-9924; Fax: 505-343-1463.

**St. Bernadette Institute of Sacred Art* (1993) P.O. Box 8249, 87198. Tel: 505-265-9126; Fax: 505-266-4678. Email: sbi@nmia.com. Web: www.stbernadetteinstitute.com. Dan Paulos, Dir. Sponsors and supports Catholic art and artists.

Brothers of the Good Shepherd Inc. of New Mexico, 901 Brother Mathias Pl., N.W., P.O. Box 389, 87102-7103. Tel: 505-243-4238; Fax: 505-764-9721. Web: www.lbgs.org. Brothers 7; Total Staff 1.

Caritas Deus Inc., P.O. Box 749, 87103. Tel: 505-243-2527; Fax: 505-247-2207. Property management nonprofit corporation.

Catholic Charismatic Center (1978) 1412 Fifth St., N.W., 87102. Tel: 505-247-0398; Fax: 505-843-9147. Email: sistermagdalena@netzero.net. Web: www.asfccc.org. Total in Residence 2; Total Staff 5.

The Catholic Foundation of the Archdiocese of Santa Fe (1991) 4333 Pan American Fwy., N.E., Suite D, 87107. Tel: 505-872-2901; Fax: 505-872-2905. Email: mary@thecatholicfoundation.org. Web: www.thecatholicfoundation.org. Mary P. Dunn, Exec. Dir. Total Staff 5.

Center for Action and Contemplation, P.O. Box 12464, 87195. Tel: 505-242-9588; Fax: 505-242-9518. Email: info@cacradicalgrace.org. Web: cacradicalgrace.org. Rev. Richard Rohr, O.F.M., Founder & Director; Stephen Picha, Exec. Dir. Total in Residence 1; Total Staff 25.

Charity Unlimited, Inc., P.O. Box 389, 87103. Tel: 505-243-4238; Fax: 505-764-9721. Property management nonprofit corporation.

Dominican Ecclesial Institute (D.E.I.) (1996) 1815 Las Lomas, N.E., 87106. Tel: 505-243-0525; Fax: 505-243-0005. Email: info@d-e-i.org. Web: www.d-e-i.org. Kyle Kemp, Exec. Dir. Total Staff 1.

Fraternidad Piadosa de Nuestro Padre Jesus Nazareno, 4000 St. Joseph Pl., N.W., 87120. Tel: 505-259-0254; 505-345-7397.

Good Shepherd Center, Inc. of New Mexico, 218 Iron St., S.W., P.O. Box 749, 87103. Tel: 505-243-2527; Fax: 505-247-2207. Total Staff 6; Total Assisted 190,000.

St. Joseph Community Health Foundation, 300 Central Ave. S.W., Ste. 3000-W, 87102. Tel: 505-924-8005. Web: www.stjosephnm.org.

St. Joseph Fertility Care Center (1976) 4000 St. Joseph Pl., N.W., Lourdes Hall, #130, 87120. Tel: 505-831-8222; Fax: 505-831-8223. Email: angelgarcia@fertilitycare.net. Angelique N. Garcia, Pres. & Dir.

Norbertine Community of New Mexico, Inc., 5825 Coors Blvd., N.W., 87121-6700. Tel: 505-873-4399; Fax: 505-873-4667. Email: norbertines@norbertinecommunity.org. Web: www.norbertinecommunity.org. Rev. Joel P. Garner, O.Praem., Prior. Total in Residence 15; Total Staff 4.

St. Pius X High School Foundation, Inc., 5301 St. Joseph Dr., N.W., 87120. Tel: 505-831-8423; Fax: 505-831-8438. Email: scross@spx.k12.nm.us. Web: www.saintpiusx.com. Barbara Rothweiler, Prin. Nonprofit corporation for the financial support of St. Pius X High School.

Roger Huser Fund, P.O. Box 12315, 87195-0315. Tel: 505-877-6394. Rev. Don Billiard, O.F.M., Corp. Treas.

Santo Nino Children's Foundation for Catholic Education, LLC, 4000 St. Joseph Pl., N.W., 87120. Tel: 505-831-8132; Fax: 505-831-8113.

SPX Towers, 5301 St. Joseph's Pl., N.W., 87120. Tel: 505-884-1309; Fax: 505-889-2720. Allen Jackson, Contact Person. To generate funds for use as financial aid for economically disadvantaged children to attend St. Pius X High School.

Villa Mathias Inc., P.O. Box 389, 87103. Tel: 505-243-4238; Fax: 505-764-9721.

JEMEZ SPRINGS. *EDSA Charitable Trust*, P.O. Box 10, 87025. Tel: 575-829-3586. Email: manilasp@aol.com. Rev. Paul Valley, s.P.

Fitzgerald Charitable Trust, P.O. Box 10, 87025. Tel: 575-829-3586; Fax: 575-829-3706. Web: www.theservants.org. Rev. Paul Valley, s.P.

RIO RANCHO. *St. Felix Pantry, Inc.*, 4020 Barbara Loop S.E., 87124-1023. Tel: 505-891-8075. P.O. Box 44274, 87174. Sr. M. Edna Pearl Esquibel, C.S.S.F., Pres. Total Assisted Per Month 3,400; Total Staff 50.

RELIGIOUS INSTITUTES OF MEN REPRESENTED IN THE ARCHDIOCESE

For further details refer to the corresponding bracketed number in the Religious Institutes of Men or Women section.

[0170]—*Basilian Fathers* (Houston, TX)—C.S.B.

[0200]—*Benedictine Monks* (Our Lady of Guadalupe Abbey, Pecos; Abbey of Christ in the Desert, Abiquiu)—O.S.B.

[0330]—*Brothers of the Christian Schools* (Baltimore, Midwest & De La Salle Provinces)—F.S.C.

[0580]—*Brothers of the Good Shepherd* (Albuquerque, NM)—B.G.S.

[0900]—*Canons Regular of Premontre* (Norbertine Fathers and Brothers of De Pere, Wisconsin)—O.Praem.

[0520]—*Franciscan Friars* (Our Lady of Guadalupe, St. John the Baptist & St. Barbara Provinces)—O.F.M.

[0535]—*Franciscan Friars of the Renewal* (Bronx, NY)—C.F.R.

[0430]—*Order of Preachers-Dominicans* (St. Albert the Great Province)—O.P.

[1230]—*Servants of the Paraclete* (Jemez Springs, NM)—s.P.

[0690]—*Society of Jesus* (New Orleans Prov., Missouri Prov.)—S.J.

[0975]—*Society of Our Lady of the Most Holy Trinity* (Robstown, TX)—S.O.L.T.

[0640]—*Sons of the Holy Family* (Silver Spring, MD)—S.F.

RELIGIOUS INSTITUTES OF WOMEN REPRESENTED IN THE ARCHDIOCESE

[0200]—*Benedictine Sisters* (Pecos and Abiquiu, NM)—O.S.B.

[0230]—*Benedictine Sisters* (Colorado Springs, CO)—O.S.B.

[0730]—*Canossian Daughters of Charity* (Albuquerque, NM)—Fd.C.C.

[2410]—*Congregation of the Marianites of the Holy Cross* (New Orleans, LA)—M.S.C.

[3832]—*Congregation of the Sisters of St. Joseph*—C.S.J.

[1780]—*Congregation of the Sisters of the Third Order of St. Francis of Perpetual Adoration* (La Crosse, WI)—F.S.P.A.

[0420]—*Discalced Carmelite Nuns* (Santa Fe, NM)—O.C.D.

[0965]—*Disciples of the Lord Jesus Christ* (Prayer Town, TX)—D.L.J.C.

[1070-03]—*Dominican Sisters* (Sinsinawa, WI)—O.P.

[1070-09]—*Dominican Sisters* (Racine, WI)—O.P.

[1070-14]—*Dominican Sisters* (Grand Rapids, MI)—O.P.

[1070-17]—*Dominican Sisters* (Elkins Park, PA)—O.P.

[1070-13]—*Dominican Sisters* (Adrian, MI)—O.P.

[1115]—*Dominican Sisters of Peace* (Columbus, OH)—O.P.

[1170]—*Felician Sisters* (Congregation of Sisters of St. Felix of Cantalice)—C.S.S.F.

[1310]—*Franciscan Sisters* (Little Falls, MN)—O.S.F.

[1430]—*Franciscan Sisters of Our Lady of Perpetual Help* (St. Louis, MO)—O.S.F.

[1860]—*Handmaids of the Precious Blood* (Jemez Springs, NM)—H.P.B.

[2470]—*Maryknoll Sisters of St. Dominic* (Maryknoll, NY)—M.M.

[]—*Missionary Catechists of the Sacred Heart of Jesus and Mary* (Victoria, TX)—M.C.S.H.

[2760]—*Missionary Sisters of the Immaculate Conception of the Mother of God* (Paterson, NJ)—S.M.I.C.

[3130]—*Our Lady of Victory Missionary Sisters* (Huntington, IN)—O.L.V.M.

[3430]—*Religious Teachers Filippine* (St. Lucy Filippine Province, Morristown, NJ)—M.P.F.

[]—*Sisters for Christian Community*—S.F.C.C.

[0440]—*Sisters of Charity of Cincinnati, Ohio* (Mt. St. Joseph, OH)—S.C.

[0480]—*Sisters of Charity of Leavenworth, Kansas*—S.C.L.

[0990]—*Sisters of Divine Providence* (Allison Park, PA)—C.D.P.

[1805]—*Sisters of St. Francis of the Neumann Communities* (Syracuse, NY)—O.S.F.

[2360]—*Sisters of Loretto at the Foot of the Cross* (Denver, CO)—S.L.

[2575]—*Sisters of Mercy of the Americas* (Omaha, NE)—R.S.M.

[2990]—*Sisters of Notre Dame* (Toledo, OH)—S.N.D.

[0230]—*Sisters of Pontifical Jurisdiction* (Colorado Springs, CO)—O.S.B.

[1705]—*The Sisters of St. Francis of Assisi* (Milwaukee, WI)—O.S.F.

[1630]—*Sisters of St. Francis of Penance and Christian Charity* (Sacred Heart & Holy Name Provinces, Stella Niagara, NY)—O.S.F.

[1640]—*Sisters of St. Francis of Perpetual Adoration* (St. Joseph Province, Colorado Springs, CO)—O.S.F.

[3830-01]—*Sisters of St. Joseph* (Boston, MA)—C.S.J.

[0260]—*Sisters of the Blessed Sacrament for Indians and Colored People* (Bensalem, PA)—S.B.S

[1720]—*Sisters of the Third Order Regular of St. Francis of the Congregation of Our Lady of Lourdes* (Rochester, MN)—O.S.F.

[2150-60]—*Sisters, Servants of the Immaculate Heart of Mary* (Scranton, PA)—I.H.M.

[3105]—*Society of Our Lady of the Most Holy Trinity* (Skidmore, TX)—S.O.L.T.

[4120]—*Ursuline Nuns, of the Congregation of Paris* (Maple Mount, KY)—O.S.U.

ARCHDIOCESAN CEMETERIES

ALBUQUERQUE. *Catholic Cemetery Association*, 4000 St. Joseph Pl., N.W., 87120. Tel: 505-831-8100. Leah DeTommaso, Exec. Dir. Tel: 505-248-1532. Diocesan Cemeteries, Rosario (Santa Fe), Mt. Calvary (Albuquerque) and Gate of Heaven (Albuquerque).

NECROLOGY

✠ Sanchez, Most Rev. Robert F., Retired Archbishop of Santa Fe.—Died Jan. 20, 2012

† Sanchez, Stephen A., Albuquerque, NM Our Lady of Fatima—Died April 5, 2011

An asterisk (*) denotes an organization that has established tax-exempt status directly with the IRS and is not covered by the USCCB Group Ruling.

Diocese of Santa Rosa in California

(Dioecesis Sanctae Rosae in California)

Most Reverend

ROBERT FRANCIS VASA

Bishop of Santa Rosa in California; ordained May 22, 1976; appointed Bishop of Baker November 19, 1999; consecrated and installed January 26, 2000; appointed Coadjutor Bishop of Santa Rosa in California January 24, 2011; installed March 6, 2011; succeeded June 30, 2011.

Most Reverend

DANIEL F. WALSH, D.D.

Retired Bishop of Santa Rosa in California; ordained March 30, 1963; appointed Titular Bishop of Tigia and Auxiliary of San Francisco September 24, 1981; appointed Bishop of Reno-Las Vegas June 9, 1987; installed August 6, 1987; appointed Bishop of Las Vegas March 21, 1995; installed June 28, 1995; appointed Bishop of Santa Rosa in California on April 4, 2000; installed May 22, 2000; retired June 30, 2011.

Chancery Office: 985 Airway Ct., Santa Rosa, CA 95403. Tel: 707-545-7610; Fax: 707-542-9702. *Mailing Address: P.O. Box 1297, Santa Rosa, CA 95402-1297*

Web: www.srdiocese.org

ESTABLISHED FEBRUARY 21, 1962.

Square Miles 11,711.

Comprises six Counties in the State of California-viz., Del Norte, Humboldt, Lake, Mendocino, Napa and Sonoma.

Legal Titles: "The Roman Catholic Bishop of Santa Rosa, a Corporation Sole" and "The Roman Catholic Welfare Corporation of Santa Rosa."
For legal titles of parishes and diocesan institutions, consult the Chancery Office.

STATISTICAL OVERVIEW

Personnel	
Bishop	1
Retired Bishops	1
Priests: Diocesan Active in Diocese	51
Priests: Diocesan Active Outside Diocese	2
Priests: Retired, Sick or Absent	23
Number of Diocesan Priests	76
Religious Priests in Diocese	10
Total Priests in Diocese	86
Extern Priests in Diocese	11
Ordinations:	
Transitional Deacons	1
Permanent Deacons in Diocese	31
Total Brothers	25
Total Sisters	36
Parishes	
Parishes	42
With Resident Pastor:	
Resident Diocesan Priests	40
Resident Religious Priests	1
Without Resident Pastor:	
Administered by Religious Women	1
Missions	18
Pastoral Centers	8
Professional Ministry Personnel:	
Sisters	1
Lay Ministers	28
Welfare	
Catholic Hospitals	5
Total Assisted	547,807
Homes for the Aged	1
Total Assisted	52
Residential Care of Children	1
Total Assisted	119
Special Centers for Social Services	7
Total Assisted	30,000
Educational	
Diocesan Students in Other Seminaries	5
Total Seminarians	5
High Schools, Diocesan and Parish	2
Total Students	1,015
High Schools, Private	3
Total Students	928
Elementary Schools, Diocesan and Parish	10
Total Students	2,446
Elementary Schools, Private	2
Total Students	127
Catechesis/Religious Education:	
High School Students	1,400
Elementary Students	4,936
Total Students under Catholic Instruction	10,857
Teachers in the Diocese:	
Priests	1
Sisters	3
Lay Teachers	288
Vital Statistics	
Receptions into the Church:	
Infant Baptism Totals	3,017
Minor Baptism Totals	85
Adult Baptism Totals	100
Received into Full Communion	73
First Communions	2,421
Confirmations	1,106
Marriages:	
Catholic	354
Interfaith	102
Total Marriages	456
Deaths	805
Total Catholic Population	174,357
Total Population	891,101

Former Bishops—Most Revs. LEO T. MAHER, D.D., ord. Dec. 18, 1943; appt. First Bishop of Santa Rosa, Feb. 21, 1962; cons. April 5, 1962; translated San Diego, Aug. 27, 1969; died Feb. 23, 1991; MARK J. HURLEY, D.D., Ph.D., J.C.B., LL.D., ord. Sept. 23, 1944; appt. Titular Bishop of Thunusuda and Auxiliary of San Francisco, Oct. 12, 1967; cons. Jan. 4, 1968; translated Santa Rosa, Nov. 9, 1969; appt. member of the Vatican Secretariat for Non-Believers, consultor to the Congregation for Catholic Education; resigned as Bishop of Santa Rosa, April 15, 1986; died Feb. 5, 2001; JOHN T. STEINBOCK, D.D., ord. May 1, 1963; Titular Bishop of Midila and Auxiliary Bishop of Orange; appt. May 29, 1984; translated Santa Rosa, March 31, 1987; translated Fresno, Nov. 25, 1991; died Dec. 5, 2010; G. PATRICK ZIEMANN, D.D., ord. April 29, 1967; appt. Titular Bishop of Obba and Auxiliary Bishop of Los Angeles, Dec. 29, 1986; ord. Bishop, Feb. 23, 1987; appt. Bishop of Santa Rosa, July 14, 1992; resigned as Bishop of Santa Rosa, July 21, 1999; died Oct. 22, 2009.; DANIEL F. WALSH, D.D., ord. March 30, 1963; appt. Titular Bishop of Tigia and Auxiliary of San Francisco Sept. 24, 1981; appt. Bishop of Reno-Las Vegas June 9, 1987; installed Aug. 6, 1987; appt. Bishop of Las Vegas March 21, 1995; installed June 28, 1995; appt. Bishop of Santa Rosa in California on April 4, 2000; installed May 22, 2000; retired June 30, 2011.

Chancery Office—985 Airway Court, Santa Rosa, 95403. Tel: 707-545-7610; Fax: 707-542-9702. *Mailing Address: P.O. Box 1297, Santa Rosa, 95402-1297*. Office Hours: Mon.-Fri. 8:30-4:30; All applications for dispensations, faculties, etc., and all correspondence should be addressed to the Chancery Office.

Vicar General—Rev. Msgr. JAMES E. PULSKAMP, V.G.

Deans—Revs. MANUEL CHAVEZ, Napa; ANGELITO PERIES, Sonoma-North; FRANK EPPERSON, Mendocino-Lake; MICHAEL W. CLONEY, Humboldt-Del Norte.

Chancellor—Rev. Msgr. JAMES E. PULSKAMP, V.G.

Director of Clergy Personnel—Rev. Msgr. JAMES E. PULSKAMP, V.G.

Vicar for Priests—Rev. Msgr. DANIEL P. WHELTON, J.C.L.

Diocesan Finance Officer—Deacon MICHAEL URICK.

Secretary to the Bishop—PAM HAWKINS. Tel: 707-566-3325; Fax: 707-566-3310.

Diocesan Tribunal—Mailing Address: P.O. Box 1297, Santa Rosa, 95402-1297. Tel: 707-566-3370; Fax: 707-566-3385.

Judicial Vicar—Rev. Msgr. DANIEL P. WHELTON, J.C.L.

Adjutant Judicial Vicar—Rev. FERGAL MCGUINNESS, J.C.L.

Promoter of Justice—Rev. Msgr. JOHN J. BRENKLE, J.C.D.

Defender of the Bond—Rev. DAVID SHAW.

Diocesan Judges—Rev. Msgrs. JOHN J. BRENKLE, J.C.D.; JAMES P. GAFFEY (Retired); DANIEL P. WHELTON, J.C.L.; Revs. JOHN S. CREWS, Ed.D.; ABEL MENA, J.C.L.; FERGAL MCGUINNESS, J.C.L.

Advocates—Rev. WILLIAM P. DONAHUE; Deacon RAY NOLL, Ph.D.; ANN LYNCH.

Auditor—Sr. ROSE MARY KUKLOK, O.S.B.

Notaries—Rev. Msgr. JAMES E. PULSKAMP, V.G.; PAM HAWKINS.

Board of Consultors—Rev. Msgrs. JAMES E. PULSKAMP, V.G.; DANIEL P. WHELTON, J.C.L.; Revs. MANUEL CHAVEZ; MICHAEL W. CLONEY; FRANK EPPERSON; ANGELITO PERIES.

Priests' Council—Rev. Msgrs. JAMES E. PULSKAMP, V.G.; DANIEL P. WHELTON, J.C.L.; Revs. MANUEL CHAVEZ; GORDON KALIL; ANGELITO PERIES; MICHAEL W. CLONEY; FRANK EPPERSON; SEAN ROGERS; DAVID SHAW; OSCAR DIAZ.

Finance Committee—Rev. DAVID SHAW; Rev. Msgr. JAMES E. PULSKAMP, V.G.; Deacon FRANCIS DAHL;

JANET HAGGEN; ROBERT FISH; PAUL LESAGE; MARY LEITTEM-THOMAS; HEDY MONTOYA; JOHN MOYNIER; GEORGE ORTIZ; RICK ROSA; JOHN SCHULTZ; GENE SENESTRARO.

Diocesan Building Committee—Rev. Msgr. JAMES E. PULSKAMP, V.G.; ANTHONY BATTAGLIA; LOWELL ALLEN; ED RONCHELLI; JOHN SCHULTZ.

Diocesan Communications Committee—DEIRDRE FRONTCZAK, Chm.; GARY MOORE; VALERIE PRESTEN; KEVIN CONNOLLY.

Review Board—Rev. Msgr. JAMES E. PULSKAMP, V.G.; Hon. JOHN GALLAGHER; CATHY HUGHES, M.F.T.; BOB MCKEEVER; LIN WEBER. Consultants: DAN GALVIN II, Esq.; JULIE SPARACIO, Dir. Office for the Protection of Children & Youth.

Diocesan Offices and Directors

Archivist—Rev. Msgr. JAMES E. PULSKAMP, V.G., 985 Airway Ct., Santa Rosa, 95403. Tel: 707-566-3312. Mailing Address: P.O. Box 1297, Santa Rosa, 95402-1297.

Director of the Office for the Protection of Children and Youth—JULIE SPARACIO, 985 Airway Ct., Santa Rosa, 95403. Tel: 707-566-3308. Mailing Address: P.O. Box 1297, Santa Rosa, 95402-1297.

Attorney for the Diocese—DANIEL J. GALVIN III, Shapiro, Galvin, Shapiro, Piasta & Moran, 640 Third St., Santa Rosa, 95401. Tel: 707-544-5858; Fax: 707-544-6702.

Boy Scouts—STANLEY CORDERO, 985 Airway Ct., Santa Rosa, 95403. Tel: 707-566-3343; Fax: 707-566-3320.

Catholic Charities, Central Administrative Office—CHUCK FERNANDEZ, Exec. Dir., 987 Airway Ct., Santa Rosa, 95403. Tel: 707-528-8712; Fax: 707-575-4910. Mailing Address: P.O. Box 4900, Santa Rosa, 95402-4900.

Catholic Community Foundation—Rev. DAVID SHAW, Dir., 985 Airway Ct., Santa Rosa, 95403. Tel: 707-545-2311; 707-566-3357; Fax: 707-566-3310. Mailing Address: P.O. Box 1297, Santa Rosa, 95402-1297.

Catholic Youth Organization—KATHY DONLEY, Liaison, Office, 985 Airway Ct., Santa Rosa, 95403. Tel: 707-566-3349. Mailing Address: P.O. Box 1297, Santa Rosa, 95402-1297.

Cemeteries—Rev. Msgr. GERARD FAHEY, Dir., 2930 Bennett Valley Rd., P.O. Box 2098, Santa Rosa, 95405. Tel: 707-546-6290; Fax: 707-546-2773.

Clergy Formation—Rev. MICHAELRAJ PHILOMINSAMY, 985 Airway Ct., Santa Rosa, 95403. Tel: 707-545-7610; Fax: 707-542-9702.

Clergy Personnel Committee—Rev. Msgr. JAMES E. PULSKAMP, V.G.; Revs. FRANK EPPERSON; GERARD GORMLEY; RAUL LEMUS; MICHAELRAJ PHILOMINSAMY; ANGELITO PERIES; Deacon JAMES CARR.

Communications—DEIRDRE FRONTCZAK, Dir., 985 Airway Ct., Santa Rosa, 95403. Tel: 707-566-3302; Fax: 707-546-4239. Mailing Address: P.O. Box 1297, Santa Rosa, 95402-1297.

Custodian of Records—Rev. Msgr. JAMES E. PULSKAMP, V.G., 985 Airway Ct., Santa Rosa, 95403. Tel: 707-566-3312. Mailing Address: P.O. Box 1297, Santa Rosa, 95402-1297.

Catholic Restorative Justice Ministries—24A Ursuline Rd., Santa Rosa, 95403. Tel: 707-544-9080; Fax: 707-544-9081. JOHN STORM, Dir.

Development—DEBBIE DRAGO, Mailing Address: P.O. Box 1297, Santa Rosa, 95402. Tel: 707-566-3344.

Disabled—Chancery Office, 985 Airway Ct., Santa Rosa, 95403. Tel: 707-545-7610. *Mailing Address: P.O. Box 1297, Santa Rosa, 95402.*

Ecumenical and Interreligious Affairs—Rev. THOMAS W. DEVEREAUX, Mailing Address: P.O. Box 549, Cloverdale, 95425. Tel: 707-894-2535; Fax: 707-894-9603.

Hispanic Ministry—Rev. OSCAR DIAZ, Dir., Mailing Address: 150 St. Joseph Way, Cotati, 94931. Tel: 707-795-4807; Fax: 707-795-7851.

Cursillos De Cristiandad—Mailing Address: P.O. Box 1297, Santa Rosa, 95402. Tel: 707-545-7610.

Movimiento Familiar Cristiano—Mailing Address: P.O. Box 1297, Santa Rosa, 95402. Tel: 707-545-7610.

Renovacion Carismatica Catolica—Rev. CARLOS ORTEGA, Dir., Mailing Address: St. John the Baptist Church, 208 Matheson St., Healdsburg, 95448. Tel: 707-433-5536; Fax: 707-433-1813.

National Council of Catholic Women—Mailing Address: P.O. Box 1297, Santa Rosa, 95402. Tel: 707-545-7610.

Newspaper— "North Coast Catholic" DEIRDRE FRONTCZAK, Editor, Mailing Address: P.O. Box 1297, Santa Rosa, 95402-1297. Tel: 707-566-3302; Fax: 707-546-4239.

Parish Priest Consultors—Rev. Msgr. GERARD J. BRADY; Revs. OSCAR DIAZ; MICHAELRAJ PHILOMINSAMY; MICHAEL M. KELLY.

Permanent Diaconate—Deacon JAMES CARR, Dir., Mailing Address: P.O. Box 1297, Santa Rosa, 95402-1297.

Pontifical Association of Holy Childhood—GARY MOORE; JEANNE MOORE, Mailing Address: P.O. Box 1297, Santa Rosa, 95402-1297. Tel: 707-762-2367.

Propagation of the Faith—GARY MOORE; JEANNE MOORE, Mailing Address: P.O. Box 1297, Santa Rosa, 95402-1297. Tel: 707-762-2367.

Religious Education—Sr. OLIVE MURPHY, R.S.M., Dir., 985 Airway Ct., Santa Rosa, 95403. Tel: 707-566-3366; Fax: 707-566-3320. Mailing Address: P.O. Box 11574, Santa Rosa, 95406.

Respect Life—Mailing Address: P.O. Box 1297, Santa Rosa, 95402. Tel: 707-545-7610; Fax: 707-542-9702. Dr. JOHN COLLINS, Dir.

Schools—Dr. JOHN COLLINS, Supt. of Schools, Office, 985 Airway Ct., Santa Rosa, 95403. Tel: 707-566-3311. Mailing Address: P.O. Box 6654, Santa Rosa, 95406.

Youth Ministry—STANLEY CORDERO, Dir., Mailing Address: P.O. Box 1297, Santa Rosa, 95402. Tel: 707-566-3343; Fax: 707-566-3320.

Vocations—Revs. THOMAS K. DIAZ, Dir., Mailing Address: P.O. Box 1297, Santa Rosa, 95402. Tel: 707-566-3395; Fax: 707-542-9702; MANUEL CHAVEZ, Mailing Address: 901 Washington St., Calistoga, 94515. Tel: 707-942-6894; Fax: 707-942-1091; Sr. OLIVE MURPHY, R.S.M., Rel. Life, 985 Airway Ct., Santa Rosa, 95403. Tel: 707-566-3366; Fax: 707-566-3320.

CLERGY, PARISHES, MISSIONS AND PAROCHIAL SCHOOLS

CITY OF SANTA ROSA

(SONOMA COUNTY)

1—CATHEDRAL OF ST. EUGENE (1950) [CEM] Rev. Msgr. James E. Pulskamp; Rev. Fergal McGuinness; Deacon Michael Heinzelman. In Res., Rev. Alvin M. Villaruel.
Res.: 2323 Montgomery Dr., 95405. Tel: 707-542-6984; Fax: 707-542-1621.
School—(Grades PreSchool-8), 300 Farmers Ln., 95405. Tel: 707-545-7252; Fax: 707-545-2594. Mrs. Barbara Gasparini, Prin.; Cindy Kirk, Librarian. Lay Teachers 14; Students 340.
Catechesis/Religious Program—Tel: 707-542-1525. Diane Drew, D.R.E. Students 155.

2—HOLY SPIRIT (1964) Revs. Thomas K. Diaz; Luis M. Penalosa; Deacon Jim Hercher.
Res.: 1244 St. Francis Rd., 95409. Tel: 707-539-4495; Fax: 707-539-3343.
Catechesis/Religious Program—Bernard Ciernick. Students 72.

3—RESURRECTION (1967) Revs. David Shaw; Jose Gonzalez; Deacon Stephen Ellis.
Res.: 303 Stony Point Rd., 95401. Tel: 707-544-7272; Fax: 707-544-2901.
Catechesis/Religious Program—Tel: 707-544-0708. Betty Kovanis, D.R.E. Students 600.

4—ST. ROSE OF LIMA (1877) Revs. Denis A. O'Sullivan; Andrew Metcalf; Mario Valencia.
Res.: 398 10th St., 95401. Tel: 707-542-6448; Fax: 707-542-3359.
School—(Grades PreSchool-8), 4300 Old Redwood Hwy., 95403. Tel: 707-545-0379; Fax: 707-545-7150. Kathy Ryan, Prin.; Carla Flaherty, Librarian. Lay Teachers 15; Students 331.
Catechesis/Religious Program—Tel: 707-542-3080; Fax: 707-542-3359. Ann McGee, C.R.E. Students 413.

5—STAR OF THE VALLEY (1981) Rev. Thomas K. Diaz; Rev. Msgr. Gerard Fahey, Pastor Emeritus; Rev. Luis M. Penalosa. In Res., Rev. Patrick J. Leslie (SAC).
Parish Center—495 White Oak Dr., 95409. Tel: 707-539-6262; Fax: 707-539-8620.

OUTSIDE CITY OF SANTA ROSA

AMERICAN CANYON, NAPA CO., HOLY FAMILY (1994) Rev. Frederick K.A. Kutubebi, Admin.; Deacon Michael Simmons.
Res.: 402 Donaldson Way, 94503. Tel: 707-645-9331; Fax: 707-731-1637.
Catechesis/Religious Program— Carol Strausborger, D.R.E. Students 106.

ARCATA, HUMBOLDT CO., ST. MARY'S (1883) [CEM] Rev. Gerard Gormley; Deacon John Gai.
Res.: 1690 Janes Rd., 95521. Tel: 707-822-7696; Fax: 707-822-6931.
School—(Grades PreSchool-8), 1730 Janes Rd., 95521. Tel: 707-822-3877; Fax: 707-822-8912. James Monge, Prin. Lay Teachers 5; Students 35.
Catechesis/Religious Program—Tel: 707-822-7696. Patricia Heavilin, D.R.E. Students 43.
Mission—St. Joseph Blue Lake.

BOYES HOT SPRINGS, SONOMA CO., ST. LEO (1966) Rev. Jojo Puthussery, M.F. (India).
Res.: 601 W. Agua Caliente Rd., Sonoma, 95476. Tel: 707-996-8422; Fax: 707-996-3984.
Church: P.O. Box 666, 95416.
Catechesis/Religious Program—Tel: 707-996-7503; Fax: 707-996-3984. Rosa Chavez, C.R.E. Students 281.

CALISTOGA, NAPA CO., OUR LADY OF PERPETUAL HELP (1915) Rev. Manuel Chavez.
Res.: 901 Washington St., 94515. Tel: 707-942-6894; Fax: 707-942-1091.

CLEARLAKE, LAKE CO., OUR LADY, QUEEN OF PEACE (1967) Rev. Mario Laguros (Philippines), Admin.; Deacon Ruben De Los Santos.
Res.: 14405 Uhl Ave., P.O. Box 6226, 95422. Tel: 707-994-6618; Fax: 707-994-2223.
Catechesis/Religious Program—Students 75.
Mission—Queen of the Rosary Lucerne, 95458.

CLOVERDALE, SONOMA CO., ST. PETER'S (1917) Rev. Thomas W. Devereaux.
Res.: 491 S. Franklin St., P.O. Box 549, 95425. Tel: 707-894-2535; Fax: 707-894-9603.
Catechesis/Religious Program—Fax: 707-894-9603. Students 53.
Mission—Our Lady of Mt. Carmel Asti.

COTATI, SONOMA CO., ST. JOSEPH (1913) Rev. Oscar Diaz; Deacons Jesus Fernandez; W. Everett Woodruff. In Res., Rev. Msgr. Daniel P. Whelton.
Res.: 150 St. Joseph Way, 94931-4117. Tel: 707-795-4807; Fax: 707-795-7851.
Catechesis/Religious Program—Tel: 707-795-7678; Fax: 707-795-7851. Students 330.

CRESCENT CITY, DEL NORTE CO., ST. JOSEPH (1869) [CEM] Rev. Abel Mena.
Mailing Address: 440 Third St., 95531.
Res.: 319 E St., 95531. Tel: 707-465-1762; Fax: 707-465-1763.
Catechesis/Religious Program—Students 79.
Mission—St. Robert and Ann Klamath.

EUREKA, HUMBOLDT CO.

1—ST. BERNARD (1864) [CEM] Rev. Eric Freed; Deacons Frank Weber; Phillip Salazar.
Res.: 615 H St., 95501. Tel: 707-442-6466; Fax: 707-443-0914.
Catechesis/Religious Program—115 Henderson St., 95501. Students 20.
Mission—St. Joseph 201 Henderson St., 95501.

2—SACRED HEART (1963) Rev. Ismael Mora; Deacons Anthony Viegas; Steven Justus.
Res.: 2085 Myrtle Ave., 95501. Tel: 707-443-8429; Fax: 707-443-8420.
Catechesis/Religious Program—Lupe Barrett, C.R.E. Students 95.

FERNDALE, HUMBOLDT CO., CHURCH OF THE ASSUMPTION (1878) [CEM] Rev. Robert L. Benjamin.
Res.: 546 Berding St., P.O. Box 1097, 95536. Tel: 707-786-9551.
Catechesis/Religious Program—Students 13.
Mission—St. Patrick Petrolia.

FORT BRAGG, MENDOCINO CO., OUR LADY OF GOOD COUNSEL (1890) Rev. Michaelraj Philominsamy.
Res.: 255 S. Harold St., 95437. Tel: 707-964-0229; Fax: 707-222-4340.
Catechesis/Religious Program—Tel: 707-964-9072. Judy Williams, D.R.E. Students 74.
Mission—St. Elizabeth Seton Philo.

FORTUNA, HUMBOLDT CO., ST. JOSEPH (1909) [CEM] Rev. Ramon Pons; Deacons Thomas Silva; Francisco Nunez.
Res.: 2312 Newburg Rd., P.O. Box 430, 95540. Tel: 707-725-1148; Fax: 707-725-1149.
Catechesis/Religious Program—2292 Newburg Rd., 95540. Tel: 707-725-1216. Students 96.
Mission—St. Patrick Loleta.

GARBERVILLE, HUMBOLDT CO., OUR LADY OF THE REDWOODS (1950) Rev. Gary Sumpter, Admin.
Mailing Address: P.O. Box 115, 95542.
Res.: 515 Maple Ln., 95542. Tel: 707-923-7864; Fax: 707-723-7864.

GUERNEVILLE, SONOMA CO., ST. ELIZABETH (1916) Rev. Ray Rioux.
Res.: 14095 Woodland Dr., 95446-9553. Tel: 707-869-2107; Fax: 707-869-2044.
Mission—St. Catherine Monte Rio.
Mission—St. Colman Cazadero.

HEALDSBURG, SONOMA CO., ST. JOHN THE BAPTIST (1884) Revs. Walter Rogina; Carlos Ortega. In Res., Rev. Francis Gayam (India).
Res.: 208 Matheson St., 95448. Tel: 707-433-5536; Fax: 707-433-1813.
School—(Grades PreSchool-8), 217 Fitch St., 95448. Tel: 707-433-2758; Fax: 707-433-0353. Donna Garcia, Prin. Lay Teachers 14; Students 265.
Catechesis/Religious Program—Students 166.

HOOPA, HUMBOLDT CO., BLESSED KATERI TEKAKWITHA MISSION (1955) Sr. Patricia Carson, R.S.M., Dir.; Deacon Ken Bond.
Res.: Pine Creek Rd. & Kateri Ln., P.O. Box 429, 95546. Tel: 530-625-4415; Fax: 530-625-4530.

Catechesis/Religious Program—Students 4.
Tekakwitha Center—P.O. Box 845, 95546. Tel: 530-625-4739. Sr. Patricia Carson, R.S.M., Dir.
LAKEPORT, LAKE CO., ST. MARY IMMACULATE (1871) [CEM] Rev. Ron Serban.
Res.: 801 N. Main St., 95453. Tel: 707-263-4401; Fax: 707-263-6325.
Catechesis/Religious Program—Students 92.
Mission—St. Peter [CEM] Kelseyville.
MCKINLEYVILLE, HUMBOLDT COUNTY, CHRIST THE KING (1967) Rev. Michael W. Cloney; Deacon Robert Shell.
Res.: 1951 McKinleyville Ave., P.O. Box 2367, 95519. Tel: 707-839-2911; Fax: 707-839-9823.
Catechesis/Religious Program—Denise Dolan, C.R.E. Students 43.
Mission—Holy Trinity Trinidad.
MENDOCINO, MENDOCINO CO., ST. ANTHONY (1864) [CEM] Rev. Louis J. Nichols (SY).
Res.: 10700 Lansing St., P.O. Box 665, 95460. Tel: 707-937-5808; Fax: 707-937-2406.
Mission—Blessed Sacrament Elk.
MIDDLETOWN, LAKE CO., ST. JOSEPH (1894) Rev. James McSweeney.
Res.: P.O. Box 1350, 95461. Tel: 707-987-3676; Fax: 707-987-2792.
Catechesis/Religious Program—Students 31.
Mission—Our Lady of the Lake Loch Lomond.
Station—Our Lady of the Pines Forest Lake.
NAPA, NAPA CO.
1—ST. APOLLINARIS (1957) Revs. William P. Donahue; Dominic Malai (Kenya); Deacons Francis Dahl; Joel Momsen.
Res.: 3700 Lassen St., 94558. Tel: 707-257-2555; Fax: 707-224-5400.
School—(Grades K-8) Tel: 707-224-6525. Connie Howard, Prin. Sisters 1; Lay Teachers 18; Students 260.
Catechesis/Religious Program—Tel: 707-255-7200; Fax: 707-255-0797. Sr. Peggy Cruise, S.M., D.R.E. Students 375.
2—ST. JOHN THE BAPTIST (1858) Revs. Gordon Kalil; Francisco Blandon (Nicaragua).
Res.: 960 Caymus St., 94559. Tel: 707-226-9379; Fax: 707-254-9262.
School—(Grades K-8), 983 Napa St., 94559. Tel: 707-224-8388; Fax: 707-224-0236. Nancy Jordan, Prin. Sisters 1; Lay Teachers 11; Students 216.
Catechesis/Religious Program—Tel: 707-255-3533. Celine Ford, C.R.E. (English); Eustolia Valasquez, C.R.E. (Spanish); Teresa Olguin, C.R.E. (Spanish); Kimberly McFadden, Coord. Faith Formation (Youth & Adult). Students 539.
Station—State Hospital, St. Luke's Chapel Imola.
3—ST. THOMAS AQUINAS (1964) Rev. Msgr. Gerard J. Brady.
Res.: 2725 Elm St., 94558-6029. Tel: 707-255-2949; Fax: 707-255-2439.
Catechesis/Religious Program—Students 110.
OCCIDENTAL, SONOMA CO., ST. PHILIP (1903) Rev. Loren Allen.
Res.: 3730 Bohemian Hwy., P.O. Box 339, 95465. Tel: 707-874-3812; Fax: 707-874-9201.
Catechesis/Religious Program—Students 22.
Mission—St. Teresa [CEM] Bodega.
PETALUMA, SONOMA CO.
1—ST. JAMES (1964) Revs. Michael A. Culligan; Boniface Nzomo (Kenya); Deacon Ray Noll.
Res.: 125 Sonoma Mt. Pkwy., 94954. Tel: 707-762-4256; Fax: 707-762-4044.
Catechesis/Religious Program—Tel: 707-762-9063. Students 422.
2—ST. VINCENT DE PAUL (1857) Revs. Gary Lombardi; Sean Rogers; Deacons James Carr; John Norris.
Res.: 35 Liberty St., 94952. Tel: 707-762-4278; Fax: 707-763-8188.
School—(Grades K-8), Howard & Union Sts., 94952. Tel: 707-762-6426; Fax: 707-762-6791. Susan Roffmann, Prin. Lay Teachers 16; Students 289.
High School—849 Keokuk, P.O. Box 517, 94953. Tel: 707-763-1032; Fax: 707-763-9448. John Walker, Prin. Lay Teachers 32; Students 355.
Catechesis/Religious Program—Rose Marie Woodruff, D.R.E.; Abraham Solar, D.R.E.; Louise Martin, Coord. Youth Min. Students 622.
POINT ARENA, MENDOCINO CO., ST. ALOYSIUS (1889) [CEM] Rev. Balaswamy Govindu (India), Admin.
Res.: P.O. Box 66, 95468. Tel: 707-884-4920.
Mission—Mary, Star of the Sea Gualala.
ROHNERT PARK, SONOMA CO., ST. ELIZABETH SETON (1981) Rev. John Griffin.
Res.: 4595 Snyder Ln., 94928. Tel: 707-585-3708; Fax: 707-585-1201.
Catechesis/Religious Program—Tel: 707-585-8821; Fax: 707-585-1202. Alicia Slaugh, D.R.E. Students 68.
SAINT HELENA, NAPA CO., ST. HELENA (1887) [CEM] Rev. Msgr. John J. Brenkle; Rev. Eliseo Avendano.
Res.: 1340 Tainter St., 94574. Tel: 707-963-1228; Fax: 707-963-2894.
School—(Grades K-8), 1255 Oak Ave., 94574. Tel: 707-963-4677; Fax: 707-963-4659. Jim Ritchie, Prin. Lay Teachers 6; Students 83.
Catechesis/Religious Program—Lisa Hinz, D.R.E.; Ilona Falvy, Youth Min. Students 162.
SCOTIA, HUMBOLDT CO., ST. PATRICK (1905) Rev. Gary Sumpter, Admin.
Res.: 418 Church St., P.O. Box 98, 95565. Tel: 707-764-5446; Fax: 707-764-5446.
Catechesis/Religious Program—G. Dillard, D.R.E. Students 4.
SEBASTOPOL, SONOMA CO., ST. SEBASTIAN (1898) Rev. Raul Lemus; Deacon Juventino Vera. In Res., Rev. Msgr. William Hynes (Retired).
Res.: 7983 Covert Ln., 95472. Tel: 707-823-2208; Fax: 707-823-1098.
Catechesis/Religious Program—Tel: 707-823-2208, Ext. 204. Mary McQuown, D.R.E. Students 113.
SONOMA, SONOMA CO., ST. FRANCIS SOLANO (1878) [CEM] Revs. Michael M. Kelly; Adam Kotas.
Res.: 469 Third St., W., 95476. Tel: 707-996-6759; Fax: 707-996-2027.
School—(Grades K-8), 342 W. Napa St., 95476. Tel: 707-996-4994; Fax: 707-996-2662. Debbie Picard, Prin.; Lara Shoop, Librarian. Lay Teachers 23; Students 235.
Catechesis/Religious Program—Tel: 707-996-6994. Catherine Sawicki, D.R.E. Students 357.
UKIAH, MENDOCINO CO., ST. MARY OF THE ANGELS (1887) Revs. Frank Epperson; David Villalobos.
Res.: 900 S. Oak St., 95482. Tel: 707-462-1431; Fax: 707-462-2879.
School—(Grades K-8), 991 S. Dora St., 95482. Tel: 707-462-3888; Fax: 707-462-6014. Mary Leittem-Thomas, Prin. Lay Teachers 16; Students 223.
Catechesis/Religious Program—Christine Hester, D.R.E. Students 347.
Mission—St. Francis Mission Hopland.
WILLITS, MENDOCINO CO., ST. ANTHONY OF PADUA (1903) Rev. Tekle Dini (Ethiopia).
Res.: 61 W. San Francisco Ave., 95490. Tel: 707-459-2252.
Mission—Our Lady, Queen of Peace [CEM] Covelo, Mendocino Co.
WINDSOR, SONOMA CO., OUR LADY OF GUADALUPE (1969) Revs. Angelito Peries; Eric Arroyo (Mexico).
Mailing Address: 8400 Old Redwood Hwy., 95492. Tel: 707-837-8962; Fax: 707-837-9157.
Catechesis/Religious Program—Carole Pforsich, D.R.E. Students 370.
YOUNTVILLE, NAPA CO., ST. JOAN OF ARC (1920) Rev. Robert Blake; Deacon Charles Cancilla.
Res.: 6404 Washington St., Box 2009, 94599. Tel: 707-944-2461; Fax: 707-944-2202.
Catechesis/Religious Program—Lilia Manzo, D.R.E. Students 110.
Mission—Holy Family Rutherford.

Chaplains Of Public Institutions

ELDRIDGE. *Sonoma Developmental Center.* Rev. Patrick J. Leslie (SAC), Chap.
IMOLA. *Napa State Hospital* 94558. Revs. James Lantsberger, O.M.I., Chap., Robert Castro, Chap.
PETALUMA. *U.S. Coast Guard Training Center.*
YOUNTVILLE. *Veterans Administration Home.* Vacant.

Special Assignment:
Rev.—
Diaz De Leon, Juan Ramon

Unassigned:
Revs.—
McCormick, John
Talcott, Peter

On Duty Outside the Diocese:
Revs.—
Baptista, Diego
Boettcher, John

On Leave:
Rev. Msgr.—
Keys, Thomas J.
Revs.—
Hernandez, Apolinar
MacPherson, Stephen E.C.
McAllister, Alex

Retired:
Rev. Msgrs.—
Alzugaray, Joseph
Gaffey, James P.
Hynes, William
Revs.—
Bernard, Andre
Bohner, Allan G.
Canny, Stephen
Coddaire, Louis
Healy, John
Ittiyappara, Mathew
Logan, Gary
Martin, John J.
McIntyre, Justin
Ryan, Philip
Sheehy, Wilfred
Stephenson, Patrick
Thomas, Jerald

Permanent Deacons:
Begin, Kenneth, (Retired)
Bond, Ken, Arcata
Cancilla, Charles, Yountville
Carr, James, Petaluma
Dahl, Francis, Napa
De Los Santos, Ruben, Clearlake
Ellis, Stephen, Santa Rosa
Fernandez, Jesus, Cotati
Gai, John, Aracata
Heinzelman, Michael, Santa Rosa
Hercher, Jim, Santa Rosa
Jacobs, Jeff, (Ministry Outside the Diocese)
Justus, Steven, Eureka
Lemos, Armando, (Retired)
Martin, Harry, Cloverdale
Momsen, Joel, Napa
Moody, William, Palm Court, FL
Noll, Ray, Ph.D., Petaluma
Norris, John, Petaluma
Nunez, Francisco, Fortuna
Olsen, Joseph, Rohnert Park
Ramirez, Arturo, Chehalis, WA
Robinson, David, Turlock
Salazar, Phillip, Eureka
Shell, Robert, McKinleyville
Silva, Thomas, Fortuna
Simmons, Michael, American Canyon
Vera, Juventino, Sebastopol
Viegas, Anthony, Eureka
Weber, Frank, Eureka
Woodruff, W. Everett, Cotati

INSTITUTIONS LOCATED IN THE DIOCESE

[A] SEMINARIES, RELIGIOUS, OR SCHOLASTICATES

NAPA. *Mont La Salle Novitiate*, 4405 Redwood Rd., 94558. Tel: 707-252-0222; Fax: 707-252-3731. Email: novitiate@dlsi.org. Web: www.delasalle.org. Brothers of the Christian Schools.

[B] HIGH SCHOOLS, DIOCESAN

SANTA ROSA. *Cardinal Newman High School*, 50 Ursuline Rd., 95403. Tel: 707-546-6470; Fax: 707-544-8502. Email: info@cardinalnewman.org. Web: cardinalnewman.org. Mike Truesdell, Pres. & CEO; Graham Rutherford, Prin.; Rev. Alvin M. Villaruel; Molly Bone, Librarian. Priests 1; Lay Teachers 48; Students 680.

[C] HIGH SCHOOLS, PRIVATE

SANTA ROSA
NAPA. *Justin-Siena High School*, 4026 Maher St., 94558. Tel: 707-255-0950; Fax: 707-255-0334. Email: robertj@justin-siena.org. Web: justin-siena.org. Robert Jordan, Pres. & CEO; Noel Laird Hesser, Prin.; Robert Bailey, Vice Prin.; Heidi Harrison, Vice Prin. Sisters 1; Lay Teachers 40; Students 645.
**Justin-Siena High School Corporation, Inc.*
**Justin-Siena High School Foundation, Inc.*

[D] SCHOOLS, PRIVATE

EUREKA. **St. Bernard's Catholic School*, (Grades PreSchool-12), 222 Dollison St., 95501. Tel: 707-443-2735; Fax: 707-443-4723. Email: daly@saintbernards.us. David Sharp, Pres.; Craig Brown, Dean of Students; Paul Shanahan, Dean of Academics; Nicole Matas, Librarian. Lay Teachers 30; Students 314.

[E] CATHOLIC CHARITIES

SANTA ROSA. *Catholic Charities of the Diocese of Santa Rosa*, P.O. Box 4900, 95402. Tel: 707-528-8712; Fax: 707-575-4910. Email: info@srcharities.org. Web: srcharities.org.
ADMINISTRATIVE SERVICES CENTER:, 987 Airway Ct., 95403. Tel: 707-528-8712; Fax: 707-575-4910. Chuck Fernandez, Exec. Dir.; Sharon K. McCarty, Dir. Human Resources & Admin. Svcs.; Albert Kovanis, Dir. Accounting & Finance; Betsy Timm, Mgr.; Kristin Berger, Dir. of Advancement & Fundraising.
REGIONAL OFFICES:, 1248 Hayes St., Napa,

94558. Tel: 707-224-4403; Fax: 707-224-2889.

Lake County:

Rural Food Project Tel: 707-987-8139; Fax: 707-987-8139. Hedy Montoya, Prog. Mgr.

Napa County:

Hale Nalu, c/o 1219 Jefferson St., Ste. 2, Napa, 94558. Tel: 707-224-4403; Fax: 707-224-2889.

Rainbow House, 1027 Jefferson and 1219 Jefferson St., Ste. 2, Napa, 94559. Tel: 707-224-4403; Fax: 707-224-2889.

Alzheimer's Respite/Resource Center, 987 Airway Ct., 95403. Tel: 707-528-8712; Fax: 707-575-4910. P.O. Box 4900, 95402. Michele Osmon, Prog. Mgr.

Family Support Center, 465 A St., 95401. Tel: 707-542-5426; Fax: 707-542-3148. P.O. Box 4900, 95402. Jennielynn Holmes, Prog. Mgr.

Homeless Services Center/Project Nightingale at Brookwood/Samuel L. Jones Hall, 600 Morgan St., 95401. Tel: 707-525-0226; Fax: 707-545-1920. P.O. Box 4900, 95402. Nick Baker, Prog. Mgr.

Housing Counseling, 465 A St., 95401. Tel: 707-575-0215; Fax: 707-578-5210. P.O. Box 4900, 95402. Jennielynn Holmes, Prog. Mgr.

Immigration and Resettlement Services, 987 Airway Ct., 95403. Tel: 707-578-6000; Fax: 707-575-4910. P.O. Box 4900, 95401. Ashley Patel, Prog. Coord.

Parish/Community Services, 987 Airway Ct., 95403. Tel: 707-528-8712; Fax: 707-575-4910. P.O. Box 4900, 95402. Michele Osmon, Mgr.

Coach 2 Career, 465 A St., 95401. Tel: 707-575-0215; Fax: 707-578-5210. P.O. Box 4900, 95402. Jennielynn Holmes, Prog. Mgr.

Transitional Housing, 465 A St., 95401. Tel: 707-575-0215; Fax: 707-578-5210. Jennielynn Holmes, Prog. Mgr.

I'm Home Alone, 987 Airway Ct., 95403. Tel: 707-528-8712; Fax: 707-575-4910. Michele Osmon, Prog. Mgr.

[F] GENERAL HOSPITALS

SANTA ROSA. *Santa Rosa Memorial Hospital*, 1165 Montgomery Dr., 95405. Tel: 707-546-3210; Fax: 707-547-4685. Email: katy.hillenmeyer@stjoe.org. Web: www.stjosephhealth.org. Rev. Francis Gayam (India), Priest Chap.; Kevin A. Klockenga, Pres. & CEO. Sisters of St. Joseph of Orange Corporation. Sisters 1; Employees 1,717; Bed Capacity 278; Patients Assisted Annually 19,092.

EUREKA. *St. Joseph Hospital of Eureka*, 2700 Dolbeer St., 95501. Tel: 707-445-8121; Fax: 707-269-3897. Web: www.stjosepheureka.org. Joseph Mark, Pres. & CEO; Ken Meece, Dir. of Spiritual Health. Sisters of St. Joseph of Orange. Bed Capacity 189; Sisters 3; Employees 1,392; Patients Assisted Annually 209,834.

FORTUNA. *Redwood Memorial Hospital*, 3300 Renner Dr., 95540. Tel: 707-725-3361; Fax: 707-725-7212. Web: www.redwoodmemorial.org. Joe Mark, Pres. & CEO. Sisters of St. Joseph of Orange. Total Staff 212; Bed Capacity 25; Patients Assisted Annually 44,049.

NAPA. *Queen of the Valley Medical Center*, 1000 Trancas St., 94558. Tel: 707-252-4411; Fax: 707-257-4173. Web: www.thequeen.org. Walt Mickens, Pres. & CEO; Kathleen Timm, Dir. of Mission Svcs. & Spiritual Care; Revs. Frederick K.A. Kutubebi, Priest Chap.; Alan Wagner, S.D.S., Priest Chap.; Rev. Jim Warnock, Staff Chap. (Lutheran Min.). Sisters of St. Joseph of Orange, California. Priests 2; Sisters 3; Lay Staff 1,446; Bed Capacity 192; Patients Assisted Annually 216,134.

PETALUMA. *Petaluma Valley Hospital*, 400 N. McDowell Blvd., 94954. Tel: 707-778-1111; Fax: 707-778-9117. Web: www.stjosephhealth.org. Jane Read, R.N., Vice Pres. Opers. Sisters of St. Joseph of Orange. Lay Staff 562; Bed Capacity 80; Patients Assisted Annually 58,698.

[G] RESIDENTIAL TREATMENT CENTERS

SONOMA. *Hanna Boys Center*, P.O. Box 100, 95476. Tel: 707-996-6767; Fax: 707-996-4742. Web: www.hannacenter.org. Dennis Crandall, Prin.; Revs. John S. Crews, Ed.D., Exec. Dir.; Gregory Klaas.

Hanna Boys Center, For underprivileged and pre-delinquent boys, ages 13 to 18 years. Priests 2; Total Staff 110; Students 119.

[H] HOMES FOR SENIOR CITIZENS

SANTA ROSA. **Vigil Light Apartments (The Vigil Light, Inc.)*, 1945 Long Dr., 95405. Tel: 707-544-2810; Fax: 707-544-1219. Email: vigillightapts@sbcglobal.net. Sr. Sharon Fritsch, C.S.J., Mgr. Sisters 1; Residents 52.

[I] CAMPS AND COMMUNITY CENTERS

DUNCAN MILLS. *St. Joseph Camp*, 22776 Moscow Rd., P.O. Box 198, 95430-0198. Tel: 707-865-1942; Fax: 707-865-1025. Bro. Michael Saggau, F.S.C., Dir. Tel: 707-865-9304. Brothers of the Christian Schools.

MIDDLETOWN. *Camp Salesian, Office, Salesian Provincial Office*, 1100 Franklin St., San Francisco, 94109. Tel: 415-441-7144; Fax: 415-441-7155. Conducted by the Salesians of St. John Bosco.

[J] NEWMAN CENTERS

ARCATA. *Newman Community, Humboldt State University* 700 Union St., 95521. Tel: 707-822-6057; Fax: 707-822-6057. Email: newmanct@humboldt1.com. Web: www.humboldt.edu. Rev. Eric Freed; Deacon Kenneth M. Bond.

PENNGROVE. *Newman Hall, Sonoma State University, Intercollegiate Catholic Ministries* 1798 E. Cotati Ave., 94951. Tel: 707-794-7957; Fax: 707-794-7957. Rev. Chinh Nguyen.

[K] HOUSES OF PRAYER AND RETREAT HOUSES

SANTA ROSA. *Angela Center*, 535 Angela Dr., 95403. Tel: 707-528-8578; Fax: 707-528-0144. Email: angelacenter@juno.com. Web: www.angelacenter.com. Sisters Christine Van Swearingen, O.S.U., Dir.; Dianne Baumunk, O.S.U., Prog. Dir.

Cardinal Newman Retreat Center, 24 Ursuline Rd., 95403. Tel: 707-546-6470, Ext. 105.

The Santa Rosa Spiritual Enrichment Center, 360 Farmers Ln., 95405. Tel: 707-546-1781; Fax: 707-546-1781. Email: antoniaK@sonic.net. Sr. Antonia Killian, R.S.M., Dir.

NAPA. *Christian Brothers Retreat and Conference Center*, 4401 Redwood Rd., P.O. Box 3720, 94558. Tel: 707-252-3810; 707-252-3811; 707-252-3899; Fax: 707-252-3818. Email: confctr@dlsi.org. Web: www.christianbrosretreat.com. Mary Jane Hagan, Conference Center Mgr.

OAKVILLE. *Carmelite House of Prayer*, P.O. Box 347, 94562. Tel: 707-944-2454; Fax: 707-944-8533. Email: ocdoakville@gmail.com. Rev. Gerald Werner, O.C.D., Dir.

[L] MONASTERIES AND RESIDENCES FOR PRIESTS AND BROTHERS

NAPA. *De La Salle Institute/Provincial Office*, 4401 Redwood Rd., 94558-9708. Tel: 707-252-0222; Fax: 707-252-0407. Email: bbrowne@dlsi.org. Web: www.delasalle.org. P.O. Box 3720, 94558-0372. Bro. Donald Johanson, F.S.C., Provincial. Brothers of the Christian Schools. *Lasallian Education Corporation* Tel: 707-252-3844; Fax: 707-252-0407. *District of San Francisco Christian Brothers Charitable Trust* Tel: 707-252-0222; Fax: 707-252-7046. *Lasallian Education Fund*, 100 Shoreline Hwy., Ste. 386, Mill Valley, 94941. Tel: 415-332-3471; Fax: 415-332-3962.

Holy Family Community, 4405 Redwood Rd., 94558-9708. Tel: 707-252-3857; 707-252-3787; Fax: 707-252-3866. Email: JRiordan@dlsi.org. Web: www.delasalle.org. Bro. James Riordan, F.S.C., Dir. Brothers of the Christian Schools. Brothers 16.

Provincialate Community, 4403 Redwood Rd., 94558. Tel: 707-252-0802; Fax: 707-252-7046. Email: rmoratto@dlsi.org. Bro. Donald Johanson, F.S.C., Prov.; James Joost, F.S.C., Prov. Asst.; Bro. Richard Moratto, F.S.C., Dir.; Rev. David L. Deibel, Chap. Brothers of the Christian Schools. Priests 1; Brothers 8.

OAKVILLE. *Carmelite House of Prayer*, P.O. Box 347, 94562. Tel: 707-944-2454; 707-944-2460; Fax: 707-944-8533. Email: ocdoakville@gmail.com. Revs. Gerald Werner, O.C.D., Supr.; Michael Buckley, O.C.D.; David Costello, O.C.D.; Charles Garrity, O.C.D.; Mark Kristy, O.C.D.; Bros. Roger Larre, O.C.D.; Mark Moran, O.C.D. Discalced Carmelite Friars. Priests 5; Brothers 2.

[M] CONVENTS AND RESIDENCES FOR SISTERS

SANTA ROSA. *Provincialate of Ursuline Nuns*, 639 Angela Dr., 95403. Tel: 707-545-6811; Fax: 707-528-0114. Email: stister2@aol.com. Web: www.ursulinewest.com. Sisters Margaret Johnson, O.S.U., Co-Prov. Tel: 208-301-0293; Shirley Ann Garibaldi, O.S.U., Co-Prov. Tel: 650-346-9897. Ursulines of the Roman Union - Western Province.

NAPA. *St. Apollinaris Convent*, 3700 Lassen St., P.O. Box 3012, 94558. Tel: 707-255-2185. Congregation of the Sisters of Mercy - The United States Province. Sisters 2.

Queen of the Valley Convent, 74 Catania Ln., 94558. Tel: 707-255-6169. Web: www.sistersofstjosephoforange.org. Sisters St. Joseph of Orange. Sisters 4.

SEBASTOPOL. *Sisters of Christ the King*, 1520 Santa Maria Way, 95472. Sr. Mary Minette, S.C.K., Supr. Sisters of Christ the King.

WHITETHORN. *Our Lady of the Redwoods Abbey*, 18104 Briceland-Thorn Rd., 95589. Tel: 707-986-7419; Fax: 707-986-1176. Web: www.redwoodsabbey.org. Sr. Kathleen De Vico, O.C.S.O., Abbess; Rev. Maurice Flood, O.C.S.O., Chap. Cistercian Nuns of the Strict Observance. Priests 1; Sisters 10.

WINDSOR. *Ursuline Residence*, 9248 Lakewood Dr., 95492. Tel: 707-838-4232; Fax: 707-528-0114. Email: cvs535@aol.com. Web: www.ursulinewest.com. Ursuline Nuns. Sisters 1.

[N] MISCELLANEOUS

SANTA ROSA. **Angela Merici and John Henry Newman Foundation, Inc.*, 50 Ursuline Rd., 95403. Tel: 707-546-6470; Fax: 707-544-8502.

**Catholic Community Foundation*, P.O. Box 1297, 95402. Tel: 707-544-7272; Fax: 707-566-3310. Rev. David Shaw, Exec. Dir.

Vietnamese Martyrs Community, 2652 Stony Point Rd., 95407. Tel: 707-546-6436.

NAPA. **Life Legal Defense Foundation*, P.O. Box 2105, 94558. Tel: 707-224-6675; Fax: 707-224-6676. Email: info@lldf.org. Web: lldf.org. Mary Riley, Dir.

SAINT HELENA. **The Nurturing Network*, 1733 Fir Hill Dr., 94574. Tel: 707-963-3393 (Headquarters); 509-493-4026 (Administrative Office); Fax: 509-493-4027. Email: mary@nurturingnetwork.org. Web: www.nurturingnetwork.org. Mary Cunningham Agee, Pres.; Ann Granger, Dir. Communications.

RELIGIOUS INSTITUTES OF MEN REPRESENTED IN THE DIOCESE

For further details refer to the corresponding bracketed number in the Religious Institutes of Men or Women section.

[0330]—*Brothers of the Christian Schools* (San Francisco Prov.)—F.S.C.

[0350]—*Cistercian Order of the Strict Observance*—O.C.S.O.

[0260]—*Discalced Carmelite Friars* (Anglo-Irish Prov.)—O.C.D.

[]—*Missionaries of Faith*—M.F.

[0910]—*Oblates of Mary Immaculate*—O.M.I.

[1200]—*Society of the Divine Savior*—S.D.S.

RELIGIOUS INSTITUTES OF WOMEN REPRESENTED IN THE DIOCESE

[0670]—*Cistercian Nuns of the Strict Observance*—O.C.S.O.

[3110]—*Congregation of Our Lady of Retreat in the Cenacle*—R.C.

[1070-04]—*Dominican Sisters*—O.P.

[2575]—*Institute of the Sisters of Mercy of the Americas*—R.S.M.

[]—*Marian Sisters of Santa Rosa*—M.S.S.R.

[0440]—*Sisters of Charity of Cincinnati* (Cincinnati, Ohio)—S.C.

[0430]—*Sisters of Charity of the Blessed Virgin Mary* (Dubuque, IA)—B.V.M.

[]—*Sisters of Christ the King*—S.C.K.

[4090]—*Sisters of Social Service*—S.S.S.

[0230]—*Sisters of St. Benedict*—O.S.B.

[3740]—*Sisters of St. Casimir*—S.S.C.

[1570]—*Sisters of St. Francis* (Dubuque, IA)—O.S.F.

[3830-03]—*Sisters of St. Joseph*—C.S.J.

[3840]—*Sisters of St. Joseph of Carondelet*—C.S.J.

[3320]—*Sisters of the Presentation of the B.V.M.*—P.B.V.M.

[4110]—*Ursuline Nuns* (Western Prov.)—O.S.U.

DIOCESAN CEMETERIES

SANTA ROSA. *Calvary Catholic*

PETALUMA. *Calvary Catholic*

SAINT HELENA. *Holy Cross*

SONOMA. *St. Francis Solano*

NECROLOGY

† O'Sullivan, Timothy J.—Died March 5, 2011

Diocese of Savannah

(Dioecesis Savannensis)

Most Reverend
GREGORY J. HARTMAYER, O.F.M.CONV.

Bishop of Savannah; ordained May 5, 1979; appointed Bishop of Savannah July 19, 2011; installed October 18, 2011. *Catholic Pastoral Center, 601 E. Liberty St., Savannah, GA 31401-5196.*

Most Reverend
J. KEVIN BOLAND, D.D.

Bishop Emeritus of Savannah; ordained June 14, 1959; appointed Bishop of Savannah February 7, 1995; ordained and installed April 18, 1995; retired July 19, 2011.

Chancery: Catholic Pastoral Center, 601 E. Liberty St., Savannah, GA 31401-5196. Tel: 912-201-4100; Fax: 912-201-4101.

Web: www.dioceseofsavannah.org

Email: communications@diosav.org

Most Reverend
RAYMOND W. LESSARD, D.D.

Retired Bishop of Savannah; ordained December 16, 1956; appointed March 5, 1973; consecrated and installed April 27, 1973; retired February 7, 1995. *Catholic Pastoral Center, 601 E. Liberty St., Savannah, GA 31401-5196.* Tel: 912-201-4100.

Square Miles 37,038.

Established as Diocese of Savannah July 19, 1850. Name changed to Diocese of Savannah-Atlanta Jan. 5, 1937; Redesignated Nov. 8, 1956.

Comprises 90 Counties in the southern part of the State of Georgia.

Patrons of the Diocese: I. St. John the Baptist; II. Our Lady of Perpetual Help. This diocese was solemnly consecrated to the Sacred Heart of Jesus, May 7, 1872, and on Dec. 8, 1943, it was solemnly consecrated to the Immaculate Heart of Mary.

For legal titles of parishes and diocesan institutions, consult the Chancery.

STATISTICAL OVERVIEW

Personnel	
Bishop	1
Retired Bishops	2
Priests: Diocesan Active in Diocese	57
Priests: Diocesan Active Outside Diocese	5
Priests: Retired, Sick or Absent	20
Number of Diocesan Priests	82
Religious Priests in Diocese	25
Total Priests in Diocese	107
Extern Priests in Diocese	13
Ordinations:	
Diocesan Priests	2
Transitional Deacons	1
Permanent Deacons in Diocese	58
Total Brothers	2
Total Sisters	84
Parishes	
Parishes	55
With Resident Pastor:	
Resident Diocesan Priests	38
Resident Religious Priests	15
Without Resident Pastor:	
Administered by Priests	2
Missions	24
Pastoral Centers	15
Professional Ministry Personnel:	
Lay Ministers	35
Welfare	
Catholic Hospitals	1
Total Assisted	200,000
Special Centers for Social Services	15
Total Assisted	28,000
Educational	
Diocesan Students in Other Seminaries	13
Total Seminarians	13
High Schools, Diocesan and Parish	2
Total Students	446
High Schools, Private	3
Total Students	1,016
Elementary Schools, Diocesan and Parish	15
Total Students	3,720
Catechesis/Religious Education:	
High School Students	896
Elementary Students	4,557
Total Students under Catholic Instruction	10,648
Teachers in the Diocese:	
Priests	4
Brothers	1
Sisters	12
Lay Teachers	545
Vital Statistics	
Receptions into the Church:	
Infant Baptism Totals	1,710
Minor Baptism Totals	185
Adult Baptism Totals	154
Received into Full Communion	297
First Communions	1,642
Confirmations	1,396
Marriages:	
Catholic	256
Interfaith	158
Total Marriages	414
Deaths	580
Total Catholic Population	87,718
Total Population	2,884,000

Former Bishops—Rt. Revs. FRANCIS X. GARTLAND, D.D., first bishop; cons. Nov. 10, 1850; died Sept. 20, 1854; JOHN BARRY, D.D., second bishop; cons. Aug. 2, 1857; died Nov. 21, 1859; AUGUSTIN VEROT, S.S., D.D., cons. April 25, 1858; Vic. Ap. of Florida; transferred to Savannah, July 14, 1861; returned to Florida as first Bishop of St. Augustine, 1870; died June 10, 1876; His Eminence IGNATIUS CARDINAL PERSICO, D.D., transferred to this See March 11, 1870; resigned 1872; created Cardinal Jan. 16, 1893; died Dec. 7, 1895; Rt. Revs. W. H. GROSS, C.Ss.R., D.D., cons. April 27, 1873; promoted to Oregon 1885; died Nov. 14, 1898; THOMAS A. BECKER, D.D., cons. Bishop of Wilmington, Aug. 16, 1868; transferred to Savannah, March 26, 1886; died July 29, 1899; BENJAMIN J. KEILEY, D.D., cons. June 3, 1900; resigned Feb. 13, 1922; appt. Titular Bishop of Scillium, March 24, 1922; died June 17, 1925; Most Revs. MICHAEL J. KEYES, S.M., D.D., appt. July 8, 1922; cons. Oct. 18, 1922; resigned Sept. 23, 1935; appt. Titular Bishop of Areopolis and Assistant at the Pontifical Throne; died July 31, 1959; GERALD P. O'HARA, D.D., J.U.D., appt. Titular Bishop of Heliopolis and Auxiliary Bishop of Philadelphia, April 26, 1929; cons. May 20, 1929; transferred to See of Savannah, Nov. 16, 1935; received personal title of Archbishop July 12, 1950; appt. Apostolic Nuncio to Ireland, 1951; appt. Apostolic Delegate to Great Britain, 1954; resigned Nov. 11, 1959; died July 16, 1963; THOMAS J. MCDONOUGH, D.D., J.C.D., appt. Titular Bishop of Thaenae and Auxiliary Bishop of St. Augustine, March 10, 1947; cons. April 30, 1947; transferred to Savannah, Jan. 2, 1957; succeeded to See, March 2, 1960; promoted to Archbishop of Louisville, March 1, 1967; resigned Sept. 29, 1981; died Aug. 4, 1998; GERARD L. FREY, D.D., appt. May 31, 1967; cons. Aug. 8, 1967; transferred to Bishop of Lafayette, Nov. 7, 1972; retired May 13, 1989; RAYMOND W. LESSARD, D.D., S.T.D., J.C.L. (Retired), appt. March 5, 1973; cons. April 27, 1973; resigned Feb. 7, 1995; J. KEVIN BOLAND, ord. June 14, 1959; appt. Bishop of Savannah Feb. 7, 1995; ord. and installed April 18, 1995; retired July 19, 2011.

Chancellor—Rev. DANIEL F. FIRMIN, J.C.L. Tel: 912-201-4110.

Vicars General—Rev. Msgrs. JOHN A. KENNEALLY, V.G., V.F.; WILLIAM O. O'NEILL, V.G., Catholic Pastoral Center, 601 E. Liberty St., Savannah, 31401-5196. Tel: 912-201-4126.

Chancery—Catholic Pastoral Center, 601 E. Liberty St., Savannah, 31401-5196. Tel: 912-201-4100; Fax: 912-201-4101. Rev. DANIEL F. FIRMIN, J.C.L., Chancellor. Tel: 912-201-4110; Fax: 912-201-4081.

Director Child and Youth Protection Services—Mr. STEPHEN B. WILLIAMS. Tel: 912-201-4073.

Director of Finance—Mr. LAWRENCE P. SAUNDERS, Catholic Pastoral Center, 601 E. Liberty St., Savannah, 31401-5196. Tel: 912-201-4123; Fax: 912-201-4101.

Diocesan Tribunal—Catholic Pastoral Center, 601 E. Liberty St., Savannah, 31401-5196. Tel: 912-201-4134; Fax: 912-201-4099.

Officialis—Rev. JEREMIAH J. MCCARTHY, J.C.L., J.V.

Director of the Tribunal—VACANT.

Tribunal Judges—Rev. JEREMIAH J. MCCARTHY, J.C.L., J.V.; Rev. Msgr. FRANCIS J. NELSON, J.C.L.; Rev. DANIEL F. FIRMIN, J.C.L.

Defender of the Bond—Rev. J. GERARD SCHRECK, J.C.D., V.F.

Case Assessors & Notaries—CAROLE BARRAS; MARIA G. RAMOS; BERNADINE REGO; GILLIAN BROWN.

Promoter of Justice—Rev. THOMAS HEALY.

Censor Librorum—Rev. DOUGLAS K. CLARK, S.T.L.

Archivist—GILLIAN BROWN, Catholic Pastoral Center, 601 E. Liberty St., Savannah, 31401-5196. Tel: 912-201-4070.

Legal Counsel—Mr. JOSEPH P. BRENNAN, Catholic Pastoral Center, 601 E. Liberty St., Savannah, 31401-5196. Tel: 912-201-4100.

Finance Council—Mr. S. SCOTT VOYNICH, Chm.; Most Rev. GREGORY J. HARTMAYER, O.F.M.Conv.; Rev. Msgr. JOHN A. KENNEALLY, V.G., V.F.; Rev. BRIAN R. LABURT; Mr. ROBERT W. SCHIVERA; Mr. EUGENE F. MCMANUS JR.; Ms. CELESTE C. SHEAROUSE; Dr. KENNETH L. STANLEY; Mrs. KAY FORD; Dr. FRANCIS

P. ROSSITER JR.; Mr. CLARENCE A. DAVIS; Mr. DONALD THOMPSON. Staff: Mr. LAWRENCE P. SAUNDERS; Mr. JOSEPH P. BRENNAN; Rev. DANIEL F. FIRMIN, J.C.L.

Investment Committee—Most Rev. GREGORY J. HARTMAYER, O.F.M.Conv.; Dr. KENNETH L. STANLEY, Chm.; Mr. EUGENE F. MCMANUS JR.

Clergy Personnel—Rev. Msgr. JOHN A. KENNEALLY, V.G., V.F.

Human Resources Director—Mrs. JO ANN GREEN.

Deans—

Savannah Deanery—Rev. Msgr. P. JAMES COSTIGAN, V.F., Mailing Address: P.O. Box 30859, Savannah, 31410-0859. Tel: 912-897-5156.

Augusta Deanery—Rev. GERALD RAGAN, V.F., 1420 Monte Sano Ave., Augusta, 30904-5394. Tel: 706-733-6627.

Albany Deanery—Rev. FINBARR P. STANTON, V.F., 421 Edgewood Ln., Albany, 31707-3910. Tel: 229-439-2302.

Columbus Deanery—Rev. J. GERARD SCHRECK, J.C.D., V.F., 2000 Kay Cir., Columbus, 31907-3229. Tel: 706-561-8678.

Macon Deanery—Rev. Msgr. FRED J. NIJEM, V.F., 251 S. Davis Dr., Warner Robins, 31088. Tel: 478-923-0124.

Statesboro Deanery—Rev. BRETT A. BRENNAN, V.F., 221 John Paul Ave., Statesboro, 30458-5076. Tel: 912-681-6726.

Valdosta-Brunswick Deanery—Rev. Msgr. JOHN A. KENNEALLY, V.G., V.F., 2300 Frederica Rd., Saint Simons Island, 31522-1965. Tel: 912-265-3249.

College of Consultors—Rev. Msgr. JOHN A. KENNEALLY, V.G., V.F.; Revs. DOUGLAS K. CLARK, S.T.L.; JEREMIAH J. MCCARTHY, J.C.L., J.V.; Rev. Msgr. FRANCIS J. NELSON, J.C.L.; Rev. GERALD RAGAN, V.F.

Presbyteral Council—Revs. J. GERARD SCHRECK, J.C.D., V.F.; JUSTIN R. FERGUSON; MICHAEL J. KAVANAUGH.

Diocesan Offices and Directors

Office of Child and Youth Protection—Mr. STEPHEN B. WILLIAMS, Dir., 601 E. Liberty St., Savannah, 31401. Tel: 912-201-4073. Email: sbwilliams@diosav.org.

Newspaper— "The Southern Cross" MICHAEL JOHNSON, Editor, Catholic Pastoral Center, 601 E. Liberty St., Savannah, 31401-5196. Tel: 912-201-4054; Fax: 912-201-4101. Email: editor@diosav.org; Printing Office, 601 E. 6th St., Waynesboro, 30830. Tel: 706-554-7888.

Director of Communications—Mrs. BARBARA KING, Catholic Pastoral Center, 601 E. Liberty St., Savannah, 31401-5196. Tel: 912-201-4052; Fax: 912-201-4101. Email: communications@diosav.org.

Superintendent of Schools—Sr. ROSE MARY COLLINS, S.S.J., Catholic Pastoral Center, 601 E. Liberty St., Savannah, 31401-5196. Tel: 912-201-4100; Fax: 912-201-4101. Email: rmcollins@diosav.org.

Director of African American Ministry—Rev. ROBERT E. CHANEY, Catholic Pastoral Center, 601 E. Liberty St., Savannah, 31401-5196. Tel: 912-201-4100; Fax: 912-201-4101. Email: af-am-ministry@diosav.org.

Director of Catholic Social Services—VACANT, 601 E. Liberty St., Savannah, 31401-5196. Tel: 912-201-4068; Fax: 912-201-4101.

Director of Family Life—Sr. PATRICIA BROWN, S.S.M.N., Catholic Pastoral Center, 601 E. Liberty St., Savannah, 31401-5196. Tel: 912-201-4058. Email: familylife@diosav.org.

Director of Hispanic/Migrant Ministry—VACANT.

Director of Permanent Diaconate—Deacon GEORGE H. FOSTER, 4568 Betty's Branch Way, Evans, 30809. Tel: 706-651-8989; Fax: 706-651-0370.

Director of Faith Formation—Ms. ANN PINCKNEY, Catholic Pastoral Center, 601 E. Liberty St., Savannah, 31401-5196. Tel: 912-201-4041; Fax: 912-201-4101. Email: apinckney@diosav.org.

Director of Stewardship and Development—Mr. JOSEPH STONG, Catholic Pastoral Center, 601 E. Liberty St., Savannah, 31401-5196. Tel: 912-201-4050.

Director of the Catholic Foundation of South Georgia—Mr. LIAM J. O'CONNOR, Catholic Pastoral Center, 601 E. Liberty St., Savannah, 31401-5196. Tel: 912-201-4061.

Vicar for Religious—Sr. CAMILLE COLLINI, C.S.J., Catholic Pastoral Center, 601 E. Liberty St., Savannah, 31401-5196. Tel: 912-201-4113.

Director of Vocations—Rev. MARK N. VAN ALSTINE, 211 N. Pinetree Blvd., Thomasville, 31792. Tel: 229-226-3624. 221 E. Harris St., Savannah, 31401. Tel: 912-233-4709. Email: padre_van@yahoo.com.

Director of Youth Ministry—Mr. DON BOUCHER, 601 E. Liberty St., Savannah, 31401-5196. Tel: 912-201-4057.

Apostleship of the Sea—Rev. RICHARD YOUNG, 912 E. 35th St., Savannah, 31401. Tel: 912-236-4547; Deacon MICHAEL WRIGHT, O.F.M.Conv., 729 Union St., Brunswick, 31520-8018. Tel: 912-265-3249.

Campaign for Human Development—VACANT.

Catholic Cemetery Advisory Board—Board Members: JOHN E. JAUGSTETTER, Ph.D.; Mr. JOE COUNIHAN, 601 E. Liberty St., Savannah, 31401-5196. Tel: 912-201-4100; Mr. THOMAS I. BRUNSON, 1030 Fisher St., Savannah, 31410. Tel: 912-897-3611; Mr. LAWRENCE P. SAUNDERS; Mr. WALTER E. PAIGE, Staff.

Catholic Relief Services—Rev. DANIEL F. FIRMIN, J.C.L., Dir., Catholic Pastoral Center, 601 E. Liberty St., Savannah, 31401-5196. Tel: 912-201-4110.

Council of Catholic Women—Mrs. YVETTE D. CARR, Pres., 332 Oakview Rd., Rincon, 31326. Tel: 912-754-4007.

Diocesan Worship Commission—Rev. DOUGLAS K. CLARK, S.T.L., Chm. & Pastor, Our Lady of Lourdes, 501 S. Coastal Hwy. (GA Hwy. 25), Port Wentworth, 31407. Tel: 912-964-0219 (Office); Fax: 912-966-1476. Email: dkclark@diosav.org; Mailing Address: P.O. Box 4056, Port Wentworth, 31407-4056.

Diocesan Scout Chairman—Ms. MEGHAN LOWE, Catholic Pastoral Center, 601 E. Liberty St., Savannah, 31401-5196. Tel: 912-201-4049.

Ecumenism and Interreligious Affairs—Rev. MICHAEL J. KAVANAUGH, Dir., Mailing Address: 4074 Chambers Rd., Macon, 31206. Tel: 912-788-6386; Fax: 478-788-2837. Email: mjkavanaug@aol.com.

Georgia Catholic Conference—FRANCIS J. MULCAHY, Esq., Exec. Sec., Ste. 440, 100 N. Point Center E., Alpharetta, 30022-8261. Tel: 770-521-8799; Fax: 770-521-6337.

Mission Cooperative Appeal—Rev. DANIEL F. FIRMIN, J.C.L., Catholic Pastoral Center, 601 E. Liberty St., Savannah, 31401-5196. Tel: 912-201-4110; Fax: 912-201-4081.

Propagation of the Faith—Ms. ANN PINCKNEY, Catholic Pastoral Center, 601 E. Liberty St., Savannah, 31401-5196. Tel: 912-201-4041; Fax: 912-201-4101. Email: apinckney@diosav.org.

Victim Assistance Coordinator—ROSEMARY DOWNING. Cell: 912-657-1534.

CLERGY, PARISHES, MISSIONS AND PAROCHIAL SCHOOLS

CITY OF SAVANNAH

(CHATHAM COUNTY)

1—CATHEDRAL OF ST. JOHN THE BAPTIST (1873) Rev. Msgr. William O. O'Neill; Revs. Daniel F. Firmin; Christopher Ortega, Parochial Vicar; Bro. Robert Sokolowski, S.M., Pastoral Assoc.; Deacon Dewain Smith.
Res.: 222 E. Harris St., 31401-4699. Tel: 912-233-4709; Fax: 912-233-8229.

2—ST. BENEDICT THE MOOR (1874), (African American), Rev. Christian A. Alimaji, M.S.P.
Res.: 556 E. Gordon St., 31401. Tel: 912-232-7147; Fax: 912-238-0184. Email: stbenedict@bellsouth.net.
School—Notre Dame Academy, (Grades 1-6) Tel: 912-232-5473; Fax: 912-232-3352. Email: ndaacademy@bellsouth.net. Mrs. Carole Foran, Prin. Lay Teachers 9; Sisters 1; Students 79.

3—ST. FRANCES XAVIER CABRINI (1968) Rev. Msgr. Francis J. Nelson; Rev. John C. Markham, Parochial Vicar.
Res.: 11500 Middleground Rd., 31419. Tel: 912-925-4725; Fax: 912-925-1379.
School—Tel: 912-925-6249; Fax: 912-925-5661. Web: www.cabrini-sav.org. Ms. Carrie Jane Williamson, Prin. Lay Teachers 10; Students 106.

4—ST. JAMES (1956) Revs. Mark J. Ross; David A. Koetter.
Res.: 8412 Whitfield Ave., 31406-6198. Tel: 912-355-1523; Fax: 912-353-7226. Email: general@stjamessav.com.
School—Tel: 912-355-3132; Fax: 912-355-1996. Web: www.sjcssavannahga.org. Sr. Lisa A. Golden, I.H.M., Prin. Sisters 4; Lay Teachers 30; Students 345.
Mission—Our Lady of Good Hope Isle of Hope, Chatham Co.

5—MOST BLESSED SACRAMENT (1920) Revs. Jeremiah J. McCarthy; Adam J. Kasela, Parochial Vicar.
Res.: 909 E. Victory Dr., 31405-2499. Tel: 912-356-6980; Fax: 912-692-0010. Email: parish@mbschurch.org. Web: www.mbschurch.org.
School—Tel: 912-356-6987; Fax: 912-356-6988. Email: info@bss-savannah.org. Web: bss-savannah.org. Mrs. Lynn Brown, Prin. Lay Teachers 40; Students 428.

6—MOST PURE HEART OF MARY (1907) Closed. For inquiries for parish records contact the chancery.

7—STS. PETER AND PAUL (1980), (Vietnamese), Rev. Kim Son Nguyen.
Res.: 3115 Victory Dr., 31404-4598. Tel: 912-354-4014.

8—ST. PETER THE APOSTLE CHURCH (1993) Rev. Msgr. P. James Costigan; Rev. John Tran, Parochial Vicar.
Mailing Address: 7020 Concord Rd., P.O. Box 30859, 31410.
Res.: 302 Bryson Dr., 31410. Tel: 912-897-5156; Fax: 912-897-7924.
School—Tel: 912-897-5224; Fax: 912-897-0801. Sr. Roberta Thoen, S.S.M.N., Prin. Lay Teachers 25; Sisters 3; Students 259.

9—RESURRECTION OF OUR LORD (2000) Rev. Robert E. Chaney.
112 Fell St., 31415-1828. Tel: 912-232-5258.

10—SACRED HEART OF JESUS (1880) Revs. John J. Lyons; Richard Young.
Res.: 102 E. 57th St., 31405-3326. Tel: 912-232-0792; Fax: 912-236-0065. Email: sacredheartchurc@bellsouth.net. Web: www.sacredheartsavannah.org.

OUTSIDE THE CITY OF SAVANNAH

ALBANY, DOUGHERTY CO., ST. TERESA (1875) Revs. Finbarr P. Stanton; Stephen Pontzer, Parochial Vicar; Deacon John C. Dallas.
Res.: 421 Edgewood Ln., 31707. Tel: 229-432-0891; 229-439-2302 (Office); Fax: 229-439-0516. Email: stteresaschurchalb@yahoo.com.
School—417 Edgewood Ln., 31707-3991. Tel: 229-436-0134; Fax: 229-436-0135. Mrs. Mary Lou Gamache, Prin. Lay Teachers 12; Students 160.

AMERICUS, SUMTER CO., ST. MARY (1891) Rev. Martino Ba Thong Nguyen.
Res.: 332 S. Lee St., 31709-3916. Tel: 229-924-3495; Fax: 229-924-7124.

AUGUSTA, RICHMOND CO.

1—CHURCH OF THE MOST HOLY TRINITY (1810) Revs. Jacek Szuster; Michael Lubinsky; Deacons Elmore J. Butler; Kent Plowman.
Mailing Address: P.O. Box 2446, 30903-2446. Tel: 706-722-4944; Fax: 706-722-7774.
Res.: 303 Broad St., 30901. Tel: 706-724-4367.
School—Immaculate Conception School, Tel: 706-722-9964; Fax: 706-722-9994. Jonathan Pike, Prin. Lay Teachers 10; Students 132.

2—ST. JOSEPH (1954) Revs. Thomas Healy; Cheol Hyun Jung; Matthew Ericksen, Parochial Vicar; Deacons Gregory L. Bernard; Reinaldo Morales; James Lloyd.
Res.: 2607 Lumpkin Rd., 30906-3222. Tel: 706-798-1920; Fax: 706-798-8594.

3—ST. MARY ON THE HILL (1917) Revs. Gerald Ragan; Scott Winchel, Parochial Vicar; Deacons Don McArdle; Brian Goodman; Albert J. Sullivan Jr.; Kenneth R. Maleck; Richard Lucus Renard. In Res., Rev. Charles Hughes, G.H.M. (Retired).
Res.: 1420 Monte Sano Ave., 30904-5394. Tel: 706-733-6627; Fax: 706-733-4887. Email: smoth@knology.net. Web: www.stmaryonthehill.org.
School—1220 Monte Sano Ave., 30904-5394. Tel: 706-733-6193; Fax: 706-737-7985. Mr. Joseph McBride, Prin. Lay Teachers 32; Students 439.
Chapel—Trinity Hospital, Tel: 706-481-7000; Fax: 706-481-7850.
Chapel—Aquinas Chapel, Tel: 706-736-5516; Fax: 706-736-2678.
Chapel—Adoration Chapel

BAINBRIDGE, DECATUR CO., ST. JOSEPH'S (1887) Rev. Rudy V. Breunig, S.T.
Res.: 822 Ramsay St., P.O. Box 192, 39818-0192. Tel: 229-243-9146. Email: stjoebainbridge@hotmail.com.
Mission—Church of the Incarnation 5541 Hwy. 91, Donalsonville, Seminole Co. 31745.

BLAKELY, EARLY CO., HOLY FAMILY (1965) Rev. Joel S. Bladt, S.T.
Mailing Address: Box 425, 39823-0425. In Res., Rev. Victor Seidel, S.T. (Retired).
Res.: 533 Arlington Ave., P.O. Box 425, 39823. Tel: 229-723-3339.
Mission—St. Luke P.O. Box 491, Cuthbert, Randolph Co. 39840.

BRUNSWICK , GLYNN CO., ST. FRANCIS XAVIER (1884) Revs. Charles Henkle, O.F.M.Conv.; Leo Kennedy, O.F.M.Conv.; Wilfrid Logsdon, O.F.M.Conv.; Cletus Pifher, O.F.M.Conv.; Deacons Michael Murphy; Ntungwa Maasha.
Office & Church: 405 Howe St., 31520-7526. Tel: 912-265-3249; Fax: 912-265-6797.
Friary: 729 Union St., 31520-8018. Tel: 912-554-8922.
School—1121 Union St., 31520. Tel: 912-265-9470; Fax: 912-265-9950. Ms. Erin Mary Finn, Prin. Lay Teachers 28; Students 234.

Catechesis/Religious Program—Christian Formation Center, 1116 Richmond St., 31520. Tel: 912-264-6805; Fax: 912-264-6885. Students 143.
Mission—Nativity of Our Lady 1000 N. Way St., Darien, McIntosh Co. 31305.

CLAXTON, EVANS CO., ST. CHRISTOPHER (1958) Rev. Robert Poandl; Sr. Janet Fischer, F.S.P.A., Pastoral Assoc.
Res.: 400 S. River St., 30417-2150. Tel: 912-739-3913.
Convent—Franciscan Sisters of Perpetual Adoration, 402 S. River St., 30417. Tel: 912-739-2275.
Mission—Holy Cross Pembroke, Bryan Co. 30417.
Mission—Our Lady of Guadalupe Sand Hill.

COLUMBUS, MUSCOGEE CO.

1—ST. ANNE (1961) Revs. J. Gerard Schreck; Mariusz K. Fuks, Parochial Vicar; Deacons Robert Hermann; Edgar L. Ensley Jr.; Mrs. Margo Truett, Pastoral Assoc.
Mailing Address: 2000 Kay Cir., 31907-3229. Tel: 706-561-8678; Fax: 706-568-0179.
Res.: 3544 Trinity Dr., 31907-3229. Tel: 706-561-8678; Fax: 706-565-4845.
School—St. Anne-Pacelli Catholic School, 2020 Kay Cir., 31907. Tel: 706-561-8232; Fax: 706-563-0211. Ms. Danni Harris, Pres.; Ms. Gayla Arrington, Prin. (Grades Pre-K - 8); Ms. Kristin Turner, Prin. (Grades 9-12). Lay Teachers 44; Students 495.
Chapel—Mercy Chapel

2—ST. BENEDICT THE MOOR (1958), (African American), Rev. Donatus C. Mgbeajuo, M.S.P.
Church: 2930 Thomas St., 31906-0714. Tel: 706-323-1749; Fax: 706-324-2641. Email: stbenedict07@bellsouth.net.
Res.: 2939 9th St., 31906. Tel: 706-323-8300; Fax: 706-324-2641.

3—HOLY FAMILY (1835) [JC] Rev. Frank Patterson.
Res.: 320 12th St., 31901-2454. Tel: 706-323-6908; Fax: 706-323-2043. Email: holyfamily706@bellsouth.net. Web: holyfamilycolumbus.e-paluch.com.
Catechesis/Religious Program—Students 144.
St. Vincent de Paul—Mrs. Frances Cummings, Dir.

4—OUR LADY OF LOURDES (1958) Rev. Brian R. LaBurt.
Res.: 1953 Torch Hill Rd., 31903. Tel: 706-689-5720; Fax: 706-507-9479.
School—1973 Torch Hill Rd., 31903. Tel: 706-689-5644; Fax: 706-689-0671. Diana Hankins, Prin. Lay Teachers 10; Students 74.
Mission—St. Mary Magdalen 232 S. Broad St., Buena Vista, Marion Co. 31803.

CORDELE, CRISP CO., ST. THERESA (1931) Rev. Robert A. Cushing.
Res.: 807 Third St. S., 31015-1705. Tel: 229-273-3446.
Mission—St. Michael 718 N. Dooly St., P.O. Box 685, Montezuma, Macon Co. 31063-1507.

DOUGLAS, COFFEE CO., ST. PAUL'S (1938) Rev. Raymond G. Levreault; Bertha Capetillo, Pastoral Assoc.
Mailing Address: 4178 U.S. Hwy. 441 S., 31533-5732. Email: saintpaul@windstream.net.
Res.: 623 Briarwood Rd., 31533. Tel: 912-384-8212; Fax: 912-385-8515.
Mission—St. William 807 S. Merrimac, Fitzgerald, Ben Hill Co. 31750-0801.
Mission—Holy Family Willacoochee, Atkinson Co.

DUBLIN, LAURENS CO., IMMACULATE CONCEPTION (1911) Rev. Richard J. Hart.
Res.: 204 N. Church St., 31021-6152. Tel: 478-272-0266. Email: iccdublin@bellsouth.net. Web: immaculate-conception-church.net.
Mission—St. William 301 S. Smith St., Sandersville, Washington Co. 31082. Tel: 478-552-3352.

EASTMAN, DODGE CO., ST. MARK (1989) Rev. Anthony Mbanefo, M.S.P.; Domonica (Mecca) Gibbs, Pastoral Asst.
Mailing Address: P.O. Box 4304, 31023-4241. Tel: 478-374-0238; Fax: 478-374-4454. Email: holyredeemer@windstream.net.

GROVETOWN, COLUMBIA CO., ST. TERESA OF AVILA (1968) Revs. Walter Y. (Mike) Ingram; Michael E. Roverse, Parochial Vicar; Justin R. Ferguson, Parochial Vicar; Deacons William L. Johnson; Kerry C. Diver; Joseph S. Soparas.
Res.: 4921 Columbia Rd., 30813-5237. Tel: 706-854-7824; Fax: 706-863-5001.
Catechesis/Religious Program—Tel: 706-863-0252. Students 575.

HAZLEHURST, JEFF DAVIS CO., GOOD SHEPHERD (1967) Rev. Rafael A. Estrada.
Mailing Address: c/o P.O. Box 330, Baxley, 31515-0330. Tel: 912-366-0238. Email: elbuenpastor40@bellsouth.net.
Mission—St. Rose of Lima N. City Circle Rd., Baxley, Appling Co. 31513.
Mission—St. Raymond c/o P.O. Box 330, Baxley, Appling Co. 31515.

HINESVILLE, LIBERTY CO., ST. STEPHEN, FIRST MARTYR (1980) Rev. Thomas J. Murphy.
Res.: 399 Woodland Ave., 31313-2719. Tel: 912-876-4364; 912-876-4368 (Rectory); Fax: 912-876-3150. Email: sscc399@clds.net.
Mission—St. Jude 911 N. Downing Musgrove, Glennville, Tattnall Co. 30427-0772. Tel: 912-654-1908.

JESUP, WAYNE CO., ST. JOSEPH (1964) Rev. Keith O'Neill, O.F.M.Conv., Admin.
Res.: 1055 E. Plum St., 31546-4012. Tel: 912-427-8276.

KATHLEEN, HOUSTON CO., ST. PATRICK (1969) Rev. Nicholas Mansell; Deacons Ralph H. McAtee; Ken Hutnick; James Roberge.
Res. & Church: 2410 GA Hwy. 127, 31047-2820. Tel: 478-987-4213; Fax: 478-988-3759. Email: saintpat@windstream.net. Web: stpatrickga.catholicweb.com.
Mission—St. Juliana 804 Martin Luther King Blvd. (US 341), P.O. Box 1022, Fort Valley, Peach Co. 31030.

LAKELAND, LANIER CO., QUEEN OF PEACE (1941) Rev. Fredy A. Angel.
Res.: 1706 S. Hutchinson Ave., Adel, 31620. Tel: 229-896-7319; Fax: 229-896-1275. Email: church@queenofpeaceparish.com.
Mission—St. Mary Nashville, Berrien Co.
Mission—St. Margaret Mary Adel, Cook Co.

MACON, BIBB CO.

1—HOLY SPIRIT (1968) Rev. Michael J. Kavanaugh.
Res.: 4074 Chambers Rd., 31206-4702. Tel: 478-788-6683. Email: pastor@holyspiritmacon.org.
Parish Center—4074 Chambers Rd., 31206-4702. Tel: 478-788-6386; Fax: 478-788-2837.

2—ST. JOSEPH (1841) Revs. Allan J. McDonald; Dawid Kwiatkowski, Parochial Vicar; Deacons Donald R. Coates; Thomas J. Eden.
Res.: 830 Poplar St., 31201-2093. Tel: 478-745-1631; Fax: 478-745-2254. Email: church@st-joseph.cc. Web: www.stjosephmacon.com.
School—905 High St., 31201. Tel: 478-742-0636; Fax: 478-746-7685. Dr. Kaye Hlavaty, Prin. Lay Teachers 29; Students 311.

3—ST. PETER CLAVER (1915) Rev. Daniel Ter Melaba (Nigeria).
Res.: 131 Ward St., 31204-3193. Tel: 478-743-1454; Fax: 478-743-9868. Email: stpeterclaver@cbi.magcoxmail.com. Web: stpeterclaverchurch.org.
School—133 Ward St., 31204-3193. Tel: 478-743-3985; Fax: 478-743-0054. Email: info@spcschool.com. Sr. Margaret Mary Scally, Prin. Sisters 1; Lay Teachers 14; Students 173.

MCRAE, TELFAIR CO., HOLY REDEEMER (1968) Rev. Anthony Mbanefo, M.S.P.
17 Telfair Ave., 31055-1625. Tel: 229-868-2002. Email: holyredeemer@windstream.net.

MOULTRIE, COLQUITT CO., IMMACULATE CONCEPTION (1978) Rev. Eric R. Filmer; Deacon Richard F. Fetterman.
Res.: 202 Hillcrest Ave., 31768. Tel: 229-985-6550; Fax: 229-217-4970. Email: icmoult@moultriega.net. Web: www.moultriegacatholic.org.
Mission—St. John Vianney P.O. Box 391, Camilla, Mitchell Co. 31730-0391. Tel: 229-336-8685.

PINE MOUNTAIN, HARRIS CO., CHRIST THE KING CHURCH (2006) Rev. John R. Madden.
Mailing Address: P.O. Box 899, 31822.
Res.: 6740 Hwy. 354, 31822. Tel: 706-663-0090; Fax: 706-663-0091. Email: ctkpinemountain@att.net.

PORT WENTWORTH, CHATHAM CO., OUR LADY OF LOURDES (1940) Rev. Douglas K. Clark; Sr. Georgette Cunniff, M.F.I.C., Pastoral Assoc.
Res.: 501 S. Coastal Hwy., (GA Hwy. 25), 31407-4056. Tel: 912-964-0219; Fax: 912-966-1476. Email: dclark5735@aol.com.

RICHMOND HILL, BRYAN CO., ST. ANNE (1955) Rev. Joseph A. Smith; Deacons Paul Gutting; Ray Moreau.
10550 Ford Ave., 31324.
Res.: P.O. Box 648, 31324-0601. Tel: 912-756-3338.

SPRINGFIELD, EFFINGHAM CO., ST. BONIFACE CHURCH (1987) Rev. Wes Lamb.
1952 GA Hwy. 21 S., 31329-5207. Tel: 912-754-7473; Fax: 912-754-1201. Email: pastor@sbcatholic.com; parishoffice@sbcatholic.com.

ST. MARYS, CAMDEN CO., OUR LADY STAR OF THE SEA (1969) Rev. Gabriel Cummings; Deacon William H. Wilson.
Res.: P.O. Box 6900, 31558. Tel: 912-882-4718; Fax: 912-882-5845. Email: olssgc@tds.net. Web: www.ourladystaronline.org.
Mission—St. Francis of Assisi P.O. Box 487, Folkston, Charlton Co. 31537-0151. Tel: 912-496-3627. Email: carter47@windstream.net.

ST. SIMONS ISLAND, GLYNN CO., ST. WILLIAM (1968) Rev. Msgr. John A. Kenneally; Deacon George F. Ruehling III.
Res. & Mailing Address: 2300 Frederica Rd., 31522-1965. Tel: 912-638-2647; Fax: 912-638-7577. Email: stwilliamschurch@bellsouth.net.

STATESBORO, BULLOCH CO., ST. MATTHEW (1944) Rev. Brett A. Brannen.
Res.: 221 John Paul Ave., 30458-5016. Tel: 912-681-6726; Fax: 912-681-6727.

SWAINSBORO, EMANUEL CO., HOLY TRINITY (1957) Rev. John T. Brown, G.H.M.; Sr. Mary Bordelon, C.D.P., Pastoral Coord.
Res.: 928 W. Main St., 30401-5502. Tel: 478-237-8722; Fax: 478-237-8722.
Mission—Holy Family P.O. Box 231, Metter, Candler Co. 30439-0231. Tel: 912-685-5811. Email: jbrown@glenmary.org.

SYLVANIA, SCREVEN CO., OUR LADY OF THE ASSUMPTION (1957) Rev. Louis Lussier, O.S.Cam.; Sr. Mary Ellen Barrette, G.H.M., Pastoral Assoc.
Res.: 118 Ridgecrest Dr., 30467-1840. Tel: 912-564-2312.
Mission—St. Bernadette P.O. Box 616, Millen, Jenkins Co. 30442-0501. Tel: 478-982-1445.
Chapel—Bay Branch, St. Joseph

THOMASVILLE, THOMAS CO., ST. AUGUSTINE (1936) Rev. Mark N. Van Alstine; Deacons Howard G. Halladay; David Wendell; John Blaha.
Res.: 211 N. Pinetree Blvd., 31792-3973. Tel: 229-226-3624; Fax: 229-226-8808. Email: catholic@rose.net.
Mission—St. Elizabeth Ann Seton 11th Ave. N.W., Cairo, Grady Co. 31728-4007. Tel: 229-377-6996.

THUNDERBOLT, CHATHAM CO., NATIVITY OF OUR LORD, Closed. For inquiries for parish records contact the chancery.

TIFTON, TIFT CO., OUR DIVINE SAVIOUR (1953) Rev. Alfonso Gutierrez; Deacon J. Brian Bergeron.
Res.: 1205 Love Ave., P.O. Box 212, 31793-0201. Tel: 229-382-3170; Fax: 229-382-7611. Email: ods@friendlycity.net.
Rectory—2001 N. Central Ave., 31794.
Mission—St. Ann 9007 U.S. Hwy. 82 E., Alapaha, Berrien Co. 31622. Tel: 229-382-4600. Email: ODS@friendlycity.net.

TYBEE ISLAND, CHATHAM CO., ST. MICHAEL (1891) Rev. Thomas J. Peyton; Deacon Fretwell G. Crider, (Retired); Sr. Barbara Shimkus, R.S.M., Pastoral Assoc.
Res.: 802 Lovell Ave., 31328. Tel: 912-786-4505; Fax: 912-786-4166.

VALDOSTA, LOWNDES CO., ST. JOHN THE EVANGELIST (1927) Revs. Daniel P. O'Connell; Luis Fonseca, Parochial Vicar; Deacons David Lasseter; Columbus Carter; Peter Faulkenhausen; George Heise. In Res., Rev. Msgr. Marvin LeFrois (Retired).
Church Office: 800 Gornto Rd., 31602-1699. Tel: 229-244-2430; Fax: 229-244-5352.
Res.: 2404 Berkley Dr., 31602-1699. Tel: 229-244-9920. Email: stjohns@stjohnevang.org. Web: www.stjohnevang.org.
Newman Center— 412 Baytree Rd., 31602. Tel: 229-247-6707.
School—St. John Catholic School, Tel: 229-244-2556; 229-244-0050 (Convent); Fax: 229-244-0865. Melanie Lasseter, Prin. Sisters 1; Lay Teachers 23; Students 216.
Mission—St. Jose Twin Lakes, Lowndes Co.

VIDALIA, TOOMBS CO., SACRED HEART (1967) Rev. Benjamin Dallas; Deacon Joseph P. Claroni.
Mailing Address: P.O. Box 1086, 30475.
Res.: 3119 E. North St., 30474.
Mission—St. Andrew the Apostle 138 Industrial Blvd., Reidsville, 30453. Tel: 912-537-7709; Fax: 912-537-4691. Email: sacredheartvidalia@gmail.com.

WARNER ROBINS, HOUSTON CO., SACRED HEART (1945) Rev. Msgr. Fred J. Nijem; Rev. Pablo Migone, Parochial Vicar; Deacon James A. Hunt.
Mailing Address: 251 S. Davis Dr., 31099-5052. Tel: 478-923-0124; Fax: 478-328-3078. Email: sacredheart@cbi.mgacoxmail.com.
School—Sacred Heart School formerly Sisters of Presentation Tel: 912-923-9668; Fax: 912-923-5822. Mrs. Staci Erwin, Prin. Students 200.

WAYCROSS, WARE CO., ST. JOSEPH'S (1960) Rev. Paul A. O'Connell.
Res.: 2011 Darling Ave., 31501-1846. Tel: 912-283-7700; Fax: 912-283-1944. Email: sjcwaycross@att.net.

WAYNESBORO, BURKE CO., SACRED HEART (1961) Rev. Patrick A. Otor, Parochial Admin.
Res.: 115 S. Liberty St., P.O. Box 1100, 30830-4548. Tel: 706-554-2535; Fax: 706-554-2570. Email: sacredheartwaynes@att.net.
Mission—St. Joan of Arc P.O. Box 175, Louisville, Jefferson Co. Tel: 478-625-3433.

Special Assignment:
Revs.—
Fisher, Albert, Chap., St. Joseph/Candler Hospital
Madden, John J., S.J., Chap., St. Joseph/Candler Hospital
Markham, John C., Memorial Medical Center & Candler General Hospital
Ryan, Timothy K., 1310 Primrose Dr., Roswell, 30076. Tel: 404-667-1313; Fax: 404-667-6305

On Duty Outside the Diocese:
Rev. Msgr.—
Schreck, Christopher J., S.T.B., S.S.L., Ph.D., S.T.D., Pontifical College Josephinum, 7625 N. High St., Columbus, OH 43235-1498. Tel: 614-885-5585
Revs.—
Johnson, John R.
Pachence, Ronald A., University of San Diego, 5998 Alcala Park, San Diego, CA 92110. Tel: 619-260-4784

Military Chaplains:
Rev.—
Quang, John, U.S.N.

Retired:
Most Revs.—
Boland, Kevin J., D.D., Catholic Pastoral Center, 601 E. Liberty St., 31401-5196. Tel: 912-201-4100
Lessard, Raymond W., D.D., S.T.D., J.C.L., St. Vincent DePaul Seminary, 10701 S. Military Tr., Boynton Beach, FL 33436-4899. Tel: 561-732-4424
Rev. Msgrs.—
Cuddy, John J., 830 Poplar St., Macon, 31201. Tel: 478-464-0731
LeFrois, Marvin, 800 Gornto Rd., Valdosta, 31602-1699. Tel: 912-253-0041
Lucree, Lawrence A., V.F., 332 S. Lee St., Americus, 31709. Tel: 229-924-3495
Revs.—
Brick, Paul T., S.D.S., 727 3rd Ave., Columbus, 31901.
Cerrone, Michael J., 18816 119th Ave., S.E., Yelm, WA 98597. Tel: 972-358-9833
Drozd, Henry J. (LAR), P.O. Box 42063, 31409-1409. Tel: 912-353-8297
Frank, Edward R., 1420 Monte Sano Ave., Augusta, 30904. Tel: 706-738-5623
Gergel, Stephen J., 116 Lake Manor Dr., Kingsland, 31548-5639. Tel: 912-576-2716
Gorny, Edward V., G.H.M., P.O. Box 116, Claxton, 30417-0116. Tel: 912-739-7254
Greenway, George G., 220 Villager Dr., Saint Simons Island, 31522-5331. Tel: 912-634-6272
Hand, Robert T.
Higgins, Francis C., 2117 E. 41st St., 31404. Tel: 912-236-9267
Holloway, James, 500 Ocean Blvd., #7, Saint Simons Island, 31522. Tel: 912-634-2171
Hughes, Charles, G.H.M., 2504 McDowell St., Augusta, 30904. Tel: 706-667-6685
Keohane, Donal, St. Martin of Tours, 11967 Sunset Blvd., Los Angeles, CA 90049. Tel: 310-476-7403
Kumbalaprampil, Xavier, Ponel, P.O. Elamakkara, DT. Ernakulam 682026 India. Tel: 91-484-234-9268
Minch, Richard, 112 Katie Dr., Rincon, 31326. Tel: 912-826-0783
O'Brien, Patrick, 103 Winchester Dr., 31410. Tel: 912-898-7504
O'Keeffe, Michael, Blessed Trinity Church, 5 S.E. 17th St., Ocala, FL 34471.
Peterson, William, G.H.M., 147 Shadowwood Dr., Martinez, 30907-4509. Tel: 706-860-4738
Roxas, Rodolfo P., Chap., 11705 Mercy Blvd., 31419-1791. Tel: 912-819-3464
Seidel, Victor, S.T., P.O. Box 396, Cuthbert, 39840. Tel: 229-310-0094
Smith, Michael H., V.F., 22 Greenwood Ave., Statesboro, 30458. Tel: 229-891-6080
Szufel, Adam, 11 Atrium Dr., Warner Robins, 31088-5694. Tel: 478-328-6481; Fax: 478-328-3876. Email: ASzufel@aol.com

Permanent Deacons:
Andruzzi, Louis J., St. Jude, Glennville
Arcand, Dennis A.
Bergeron, J. Brian, Our Divine Saviour, Tifton
Bernard, Gregory L., St. Joseph's, Augusta
Blaha, John D., St. Augustine, Thomasville
Brown, Raymond E., Queen of Peace, Lakeland
Burns, James, St. John the Evangelist Church, Valdosta
Butler, Elmore J., Holy Trinity, Augusta
Carter, Columbus, Jr., St. John the Evangelist, Valdosta
Castillo, Tirso A., Immaculate Conception, Dublin
Clark, Gerald R., St. Frances Cabrini, Savannah
Claroni, Joseph B., Sacred Heart, Vidalia
Coates, Donald R., St. Joseph, Macon
Crider, Fretwell G., (Retired)
Dallas, John C., St. Teresa, Albany
Daly, Michael F., (Retired)
Diver, Kerry C., St. Teresa of Avila, Grovetown
Eden, Thomas J., St. Joseph, Macon
Ensley, Edgar L., Jr., St. Anne, Columbus
Falkenhausen, Peter H., III, St. John the Evangelist, Valdosta
Fetterman, Richard F., Immaculate Conception, Moultrie
Foster, George H., St. Michael, Fort Gordon
Goodman, Brian, St. Mary on the Hill, Augusta
Gutting, Paul, St. Anne Church, Richmond Hill
Guyer, Lawrence A., St. William, St. Simons Island
Halbur, Richard A., St. Stephen, First Martyr, Hinesville
Halladay, Howard G., St. Augustine, Thomasville
Hayden, David V., St. Peter Claver, Macon
Herrmann, Robert, St. Anne, Columbus
Hubbard, James B., St. Peter Claver, Macon
Hunt, James A., Sacred Heart, Warner Robins
Hutnick, Kenneth P., St. Juliana, Ft. Valley
Johnson, William L., St. Teresa of Avila, Grovetown
Kriegel, David L., St. Michael, Fort Gordon
Lasseter, R. David, St. John the Evangelist, Valdosta
Leslie, Cedric T., St. Peter Claver, Macon
Lloyd, James F., St. Joseph, Augusta
Maasha, Ntungwa, St. Francis Xavier, Brunswick
Maleck, Kenneth R., St. Mary on the Hill, Augusta
Marchek, Michael V., St. Michael's, Fort Gordon
McArdle, Donald R., St. Mary on the Hill, Augusta
McAtee, Ralph H., St. Patrick, Kathleen
McGrath, Michael J., St. Matthew, Statesboro
Mongan, Patrick F.
Morales-Morales, Reinaldo, St. Joseph, Augusta
Moreau, Ray, St. Anne, Richmond Hill
Murphy, Michael, St. Francis Xavier, Brunswick
Plowman, Kenneth M., Most Holy Trinity, Augusta
Quillen, John R., St. Anne, Columbus
Renard, Richard Lucus, St. Mary on the Hill, Augusta
Roberge, James D., Jr., St. Patrick, Kathleen
Ruehling, George F., III, 702 Cedar St., St. Simons Island, 31522-1259.
Smith, Dewain E., Cathedral of St. John the Baptist, Savannah
Soparas, Joseph S., St. Teresa of Avila, Grovetown
Sullivan, Albert J., Jr., St. Mary on the Hill, Augusta
Wendell, David, St. Augustine, Thomasville
Wilson, William H., St. Francis of Assisi, Folkston

INSTITUTIONS LOCATED IN THE DIOCESE

[A] HIGH SCHOOLS, DIOCESAN

AUGUSTA. *Aquinas High School*, 1920 Highland Ave., 30904-5305. Tel: 706-736-5516; Fax: 706-736-2678. Email: cpaul@aquinashigh.org. Web: www.aquinashigh.org. Mrs. Christine Paul, Prin.; Ms. Shannon Williams, Asst. Prin. Lay Teachers 27; Students 261.

COLUMBUS. *St. Anne/Pacelli Catholic School*, 2020 Kay Cir., 31907. Tel: 706-561-8232; Fax: 706-563-0211. Email: dannih@sasphs.net; kturner@sasphs.net. Web: www.pacelli.net. Ms. Gayla Arrington, Prin.; Ms. Kristin Turner, Prin.; Rev. J. Gerard Schreck, J.C.D., V.F., Diocesan Moderator. Lay Teachers 44; Students 529.

[B] HIGH SCHOOLS, PRIVATE

SAVANNAH. *Benedictine Military School*, 6502 Seawright Dr., 31406-2752. Tel: 912-644-7000; Fax: 912-356-3527. Email: deborah.antosca@bcsav.net. Web: www.thebc400.com. Rev. Frank Ziemkiewicz, Headmaster; Dr. Deborah Antosca, Prin.; Revs. Ronald P. Gatman, O.S.B.; Anthony P. Wesolowski, O.S.B.; Jeffrey S. Nyardy, O.S.B.; Bro. Timothy J. Brown, O.S.B. Secondary school conducted by the Dependent Priory of Benedictine Monks of St. Vincent Archabbey, Latrobe, PA. Brothers 1; Lay Teachers 27; Boys 304.

St. Vincent's Academy, 207 E. Liberty St., 31401-3577. Tel: 912-236-5508; Fax: 912-236-7877. Email: maryanne.hogan@savga.net. Web: www.stvincentsacademy.com. Mrs. Mary Anne Hogan, Prin.; Susan Barrett, Librarian. Sisters of Mercy of the Americas. Sisters 7; Lay Teachers 41; Girls 275.

MACON. *Mount de Sales Academy*, (Grades 6-12), 851 Orange St., 31201. Tel: 478-751-3240; Fax: 478-751-3241. Email: mfranklin@mountdesales.net. Web: www.mountdesales.net. Mr. David Held, Pres.; Dr. Michael Franklin, Prin. (Upper). Sisters of Mercy of the Americas. Lay Teachers 72; Students 656.

[C] SERVICES TO FAMILIES

MACON. *Nazareth Life Ministries*, 538 Orange St., 31201-2073. Tel: 478-746-9803; Fax: 478-745-0847. Web: faministries.org. Sr. Elizabeth Greim, Exec. Dir. Pregnancy Services for birth parents/families/newborn, education & direct services.

[D] MONASTERIES AND RESIDENCES OF PRIESTS

SAVANNAH. *The Benedictine Priory*, 6502 Seawright Dr., 31406. Tel: 912-356-3520; Fax: 912-356-3527. Web: thebc400.net. Email: frank.ziemkiewicz@bcsav.net. Revs. Frank Ziemkiewicz, Prior; Anthony P. Wesolowski, O.S.B.; Ronald P. Gatman, O.S.B.; Bro. Timothy Brown, O.S.B. Dependent Priory of St. Vincent Archabbey, Latrobe, PA.

[E] CONVENTS AND RESIDENCES FOR SISTERS

SAVANNAH. *Carmelite Monastery* (1958) 11 W. Back St., 31419-3219. Tel: 912-925-8505; Fax: 912-925-0797. Email: olconfidence@yahoo.com. Sr. Mary Elizabeth Angaine, Contact Person. Professed Nuns 2; Novices 3.

Mercy Convent, 11801 McAuley Dr., 31419-1709. Tel: 912-925-3800; Fax: 912-925-3823. Email: mercy_convent@comcast.net. Ms. Maureen Shumard, Admin. Retired Sisters of Mercy. Sisters 9.

[F] NEWMAN CENTERS

MACON. *Mercer University, Wesleyan College Newman Center* c/o St. Joseph Church, 830 Poplar St., 31201-2093. Tel: 478-745-1631. Email: tex@st-joseph.cc. Web: www.sjcyouth.org. Christina Cambre, Campus Min.

STATESBORO. *St. Matthew Newman Center at Georgia Southern University* 221 John Paul Ave., 30458-5016. Tel: 912-681-6726, Ext. 204; Fax: 912-681-6727.

VALDOSTA. *Valdosta State College Newman Center* 800 Gornto Rd., 31602. Tel: 229-247-6707. Bethany Brogdon, Campus Min.

[G] MISCELLANEOUS

SAVANNAH. *The Catholic Foundation of South Georgia*, 601 E. Liberty St., 31401-5196. Tel: 912-201-4100; Fax: 912-201-4101. Email: loconnor@diosav.org. Web: www.catholicfdn-southga.org. Jack Markley, Chm., Bd. Trustees; Mr. Liam J. O'Connor, Exec. Dir.

Catholic Social Services, 601 E. Liberty St., 31401-5196. Tel: 912-201-4068; Fax: 912-201-4101. Email: catholicsocialservices@diosav.org. Web: www.diosav.org/socialservices.

Mercy Properties Georgia, Inc. (1998) 1826 Florence St., 31415. Tel: 912-401-0008; Fax: 912-401-0012. Email: rhaddock@mercyhousing.org. Web: www.mercyhousing.org. Eugene P. Walker Jr., Pres.; John Corcoran, Vice Pres.

Social Apostolate of Savannah, 502 E. Liberty St., P.O. Box 8703, 31412. Tel: 912-233-1877; Fax: 912-651-3638. Email: socapsa@aol.com. Sr. Julie Franchi, M.F.I.C., Dir.

ALBANY. *St. Clare's Evangelization-Community Center*, 2005 Martin Luther King Dr., P.O. Box 4123, 31706-4123. Tel: 912-883-2566; Fax: 912-883-9116. Sr. Maura Molloy, M.F.I.C., Dir.

Neighbors in Need, 2005 Martin Luther King Dr., P.O. Box 3032, 31706-3001. Tel: 229-883-2872; Fax: 229-883-9116. Sr. Maura Molloy, M.F.I.C., Dir.

AUGUSTA. *Alleluia Catholic Fellowship*, 2110 Richards St., P.O. Box 6805, 30916-6805. Tel: 706-798-1882; Fax: 706-560-2759. Dan Almeter, Moderator.

Catholic Social Services, 811 12th St., 30901-2749. Tel: 706-722-4390; Fax: 706-722-4758. Web: www.cssaugusta.com. Sr. Janet Roddy, M.F.I.C., Dir.

BRUNSWICK. *Society of St. Vincent de Paul (Glynn County)*, 1217 Newcastle St., 31520-7534. Tel: 912-262-6027; Fax: 912-265-6797. Donald A. Heinecke, Pres.

CLAXTON. *Clothesbasket*, 402 S. River St., 30417-2150. Tel: 912-739-2275. Email: jfischer0@bellsouth.net. Sr. Janet Fischer, F.S.P.A., Dir.

COLUMBUS. *St. Anne Community Outreach*, 1820 Box Rd., 31907-3254. Tel: 706-568-1592; Fax: 706-568-1699. Mrs. Donna Bushaw, Dir.

St. Benedict Social Concerns, 2935 Ninth St., 31907. Tel: 706-232-8300; Fax: 706-324-2641. Mrs. Helen Linton, Dir.

Holy Family Church-St. Vincent DePaul Society (Independent Conference), 320 12th St., 31901-2454. Tel: 706-322-0098; Fax: 706-327-8191. Email: holyfamily706@bellsouth.net. Web: holyfamilycolumbus.e-paluch.com. Mrs. Frances Cummings, Dir.

Holy Family Soup Kitchen-Lunch Program formerly Holy Family Soup Kitchen 320 12th St., 31901-2454. Tel: 706-322-0098; Fax: 706-327-8191. Email: holyfamily706@bellsouth.net. Web: holyfamilycolumbus.e-paluch.com. Mrs. Frances Cummings, Dir.

Our Lady of Lourdes, 1953 Torch Hill Rd., 31903. Tel: 706-689-5720; Fax: 706-507-9479. Email: lourdesoffice21@gmail.com. Rev. Brian R. LaBurt. Outreach Parish Social Ministry

MILLEN. *Catholic Thrift Shop*, 562 Perkins Rd., 30442. Tel: 478-982-8361. Sr. Mary Ellen Barrette, G.H.M., Dir.

VALDOSTA. *St. Francis Center* (1975) P.O. Box 1331, 31603. Tel: 229-242-8656; Fax: 229-244-2752. Rev. Daniel P. O'Connell, Interim Dir.

WARNER ROBINS. *Sacred Heart Christian Service Center*, 251 S. Davis Dr., 31088. Tel: 478-929-3897; Fax: 478-328-3078. Email: sacredheart@cbi.mgacoxmail.com. Web: www.sacredheartwr.com. Mr. Roberto Martinez-Perez, Dir.

RELIGIOUS INSTITUTES OF MEN REPRESENTED IN THE DIOCESE

For further details refer to the corresponding bracketed number in the Religious Institutes of Men or Women section.

[0200]—*Benedictine Monks* (St. Vincent Archabbey)—O.S.B.

[0240]—*Camillian Fathers & Brothers*—O.S.Cam.

[0480]—*Conventual Franciscans* (Provs. of Our Lady of Consolation & St. Anthony of Padua)—O.F.M.Conv

[0570]—*Glenmary Home Missioners* (Glendale, OH)—G.H.M

[0690]—*Jesuit Fathers & Brothers*—S.J.

[0854]—*Missionaries of St. Paul*—M.S.P.

[0840]—*Missionary Servants of Most Holy Trinity* (Dublin)—S.T.

[0780]—*Society of Mary*—S.M.

[1200]—*Society of the Divine Savior* (American Prov.)—S.D.S.

RELIGIOUS INSTITUTES OF WOMEN REPRESENTED IN THE DIOCESE

[1780]—*Congregation of the Sisters of the Third Order of St. Francis of Perpetual Adoration*—F.S.P.A.

[0760]—*Daughters of Charity of St. Vincent De Paul* (Emmitsburg, MD)—D.C.

[0420]—*Discalced Carmelite Nuns*—O.C.D.

[]—*Dominican Sisters*—O.P.

[1370]—*Franciscan Missionaries of Mary*—F.M.M.

[2080]—*Home Mission Sisters of America*—G.H.M.S.

[2690]—*Missionary Catechists of Divine Providence*—M.C.D.P.

[1360]—*Missionary Franciscan Sisters of the Immaculate Conception*—M.F.I.C.

[3230]—*Poor Handmaids of Jesus Christ* (Indiana)—P.H.J.C.

[]—*Sisters for Christian Community*—S.F.C.C.

[]—*Sisters of Divine Providence* (San Antonio, TX)—C.D.P.

[2575]—*Sisters of Mercy of the Americas* (Baltimore, Burlingame, Erie)—R.S.M.

[3950]—*Sisters of Saint Mary of Namur*—S.S.M.N.

[3893]—*Sisters of St. Joseph* (Chestnut Hill, PA)—S.S.J.

[3840]—*Sisters of St. Joseph of Carondelet* (St. Louis, MO)—C.S.J.

[2170]—*Sisters, Servants of the Immaculate Heart of Mary*—I.H.M.

DIOCESAN CEMETERIES

SAVANNAH. *Catholic Cemetery and Properties, Catholic Pastoral Center*, 601 E. Liberty St., 31401-5196. Tel: 912-201-4100. Mr. Lawrence P. Saunders, Diocesan Fin. Officer.

AUGUSTA. *Catholic Cemetery*
Church of the Most Holy Trinity: 720 Telfair St., P.O. Box 2446, 30903. Tel: 706-722-4944; Fax: 706-722-7774.

DOUGLAS. *St. Paul's*, c/o 523 Ward St. E., 31533-0309. Tel: 912-384-3560.

SYLVANIA. *Catholic Cemetery*
Our Lady of the Assumption: 121 Ridgecrest Dr., 30467. Tel: 912-564-2312.

WILLACOOCHEE. *Catholic Cemetery* Rev. Raymond G. Levreault.

NECROLOGY

† Girardeau, Robert A., Americus, GA St. Mary.—Died March 20, 2011

An asterisk (*) denotes an organization that has established tax-exempt status directly with the IRS and is not covered by the USCCB Group Ruling.

Diocese of Scranton

(Dioecesis Scrantonensis)

Most Reverend

JOSEPH C. BAMBERA

Bishop of Scranton; ordained November 5, 1983; appointed Bishop of Scranton February 23, 2010; installed April 26, 2010.

Most Reverend

JOSEPH F. MARTINO, D.D., HIST. E.D.

Bishop Emeritus of Scranton; ordained December 18, 1970; appointed Titular Bishop of Cellae in Mauretania and Auxiliary Bishop of Philadelphia January 24, 1996; consecrated March 11, 1996; appointed Bishop of Scranton July 25, 2003; resigned August 31, 2009. *Res.: Regina Coeli Residence for Priests, 685 York Rd., Warminster, PA 18974.* Tel: 267-608-8557.

Most Reverend

JAMES C. TIMLIN, D.D.

Bishop Emeritus of Scranton; ordained July 16, 1951; appointed Titular Bishop of Gunugo and Auxiliary Bishop of Scranton August 3, 1976; consecrated September 21, 1976; succeeded to See of Scranton April 24, 1984; installed June 7, 1984; resigned July 25, 2003. *Res.: Villa St. Joseph, 1600 Green Ridge St., Dunmore, PA 18509.* Tel: 570-343-6170.

Chancery Office: 300 Wyoming Ave., Scranton, PA 18503. Tel: 570-207-2216; Fax: 570-207-2236.

Web: www.dioceseofscranton.org

Most Reverend

JOHN M. DOUGHERTY, D.D.

Auxiliary Bishop Emeritus of Scranton; ordained June 15, 1957; appointed Titular Bishop of Sufetula and Auxiliary Bishop of Scranton February 7, 1995; Episcopal ordination received March 7, 1995; resigned August 31, 2009. *Office: 300 Wyoming Ave., Scranton, PA 18503.* Tel: 570-558-4309.

ESTABLISHED MARCH 3, 1868.

Square Miles 8,847.

Comprises the Counties of Luzerne, Lackawanna, Bradford, Susquehanna, Wayne, Tioga, Sullivan, Wyoming, Lycoming, Pike and Monroe in Pennsylvania.

For legal titles of parishes and diocesan institutions, consult the Chancery Office.

STATISTICAL OVERVIEW

Personnel	
Bishop	1
Retired Bishops	3
Priests: Diocesan Active in Diocese	150
Priests: Diocesan Active Outside Diocese	25
Priests: Retired, Sick or Absent	105
Number of Diocesan Priests	280
Religious Priests in Diocese	60
Total Priests in Diocese	340
Extern Priests in Diocese	15
Ordinations:	
Diocesan Priests	1
Transitional Deacons	2
Permanent Deacons	7
Permanent Deacons in Diocese	71
Total Brothers	7
Total Sisters	488
Parishes	
Parishes	108
With Resident Pastor:	
Resident Diocesan Priests	99
Resident Religious Priests	5
Without Resident Pastor:	
Administered by Priests	4
Missions	18
New Parishes Created	10
Closed Parishes	22
Professional Ministry Personnel:	
Brothers	5
Sisters	45
Lay Ministers	35
Welfare	
Catholic Hospitals	4
Total Assisted	639,244
Health Care Centers	2
Total Assisted	297,982
Homes for the Aged	4
Total Assisted	532
Residential Care of Children	5
Total Assisted	698
Day Care Centers	9
Total Assisted	419
Specialized Homes	9
Total Assisted	1,598
Special Centers for Social Services	13
Total Assisted	209,834
Residential Care of Disabled	1
Total Assisted	151
Educational	
Diocesan Students in Other Seminaries	16
Total Seminarians	16
Colleges and Universities	4
Total Students	14,503
High Schools, Diocesan and Parish	4
Total Students	1,460
High Schools, Private	1
Total Students	838
Elementary Schools, Diocesan and Parish	16
Total Students	4,725
Non-residential Schools for the Disabled	1
Total Students	27
Catechesis/Religious Education:	
High School Students	4,790
Elementary Students	23,100
Total Students under Catholic Instruction	49,459
Teachers in the Diocese:	
Priests	3
Sisters	21
Lay Teachers	312
Vital Statistics	
Receptions into the Church:	
Infant Baptism Totals	2,827
Adult Baptism Totals	87
Received into Full Communion	122
First Communions	3,422
Confirmations	3,776
Marriages:	
Catholic	704
Interfaith	219
Total Marriages	923
Deaths	5,428
Total Catholic Population	293,061
Total Population	1,120,162

Former Bishops—Rt. Revs. WILLIAM O'HARA, D.D., ord. Dec. 21, 1842; First Bishop; cons. July 12, 1868; died Feb. 3, 1899; MICHAEL J. HOBAN, D.D., ord. May 22, 1880; Second Bishop; cons. Coadjutor, March 22, 1896; succeeded to See, Feb. 3, 1899; died Nov. 13, 1926; Most Revs. THOMAS C. O'REILLY, D.D., Third Bishop; ord. June 4, 1898; elected Dec. 19, 1927,; cons. Feb. 16, 1928; installed March 8, 1928; died March 25, 1938; WILLIAM J. HAFEY, D.D., Fourth Bishop; ord. June 16, 1914; appt. First Bishop of Raleigh, April 6, 1925; cons. June 24, 1925; transferred to Scranton as Coadjutor cum jure successionis and Apostolic Administrator, Oct. 2, 1937; succeeded to See, March 25, 1938; died May 12, 1954; JEROME D. HANNAN, D.D., Fifth Bishop; ord. May 22, 1921; appt. August 17, 1954; cons. Sept. 21, 1954; died Dec. 15, 1965; J. CARROLL M. MCCORMICK, D.D., Sixth Bishop; ord. July 10, 1932; appt. Titular Bishop of Ruspae and Auxiliary of Philadelphia, Jan. 11, 1947; cons. April 23, 1947; appt. Bishop of Altoona-Johnstown, June 25, 1960; transferred to the See of Scranton, March 4, 1966; installed May 25, 1966; retired Feb. 15, 1983; died Nov. 2, 1996; JOHN J. O'CONNOR, D.D., Seventh Bishop; ord. Dec. 15, 1945; appt. Titular Bishop of Cuzola and Auxiliary Bishop to the Military Vicar April 24, 1979; cons. May 27, 1979; appt. Bishop of Scranton, May 10, 1983; installed June 29, 1983; transferred to the See of New York, Jan. 31, 1984; died May 3, 2000; JAMES C. TIMLIN, D.D. (Retired), Eighth Bishop; ord. July 16, 1951; appt. Titular Bishop of Gunugo and Auxiliary Bishop of Scranton Aug. 3, 1976; cons. Sept. 21, 1976; succeeded to See of Scranton April 24, 1984; installed June 7, 1984; resigned July 25, 2003; JOSEPH F. MARTINO, D.D., Hist. E.D. (Retired), Ninth Bishop; ord. Dec. 18, 1970; appt. Titular Bishop of Cellae in Mauretania and Auxiliary Bishop of Philadelphia Jan. 24, 1996; cons. March 11, 1996; appt. Bishop of Scranton July 25, 2003; resigned Aug. 31, 2009.

Vicars General—Revs. PHILIP A. ALTAVILLA, V.G.; BRIAN J.W. CLARKE, J.C.L., V.G.

Chancery Office—300 Wyoming Ave., Scranton, 18503-1279. Tel: 570-207-2216; Fax: 570-207-2236.

Moderator of the Curia—Rev. PHILIP A. ALTAVILLA, V.G.

Regional Episcopal Vicars—VACANT, Northern Pastoral Region; Revs. GLENN E. MCCREARY, V.E., Western Pastoral Region. Tel: 570-546-3900; JOHN C. LAMBERT, V.E., Eastern Pastoral Region. Tel: 570-788-1997; JOHN V. POLEDNAK, V.E., Southern Pastoral Region. Tel: 570-650-0954.

Chancellor and Chief Operating Officer—TERESA OSBORNE. Tel: 570-207-2216; Fax: 570-207-2236.

Vice Chancellor—VACANT.

Diocesan Financial Office—ROBERT J. MILLER, Dir. Tel: 570-207-2237.

Diocesan Tribunal—300 Wyoming Ave., Scranton, 18503-1279. Tel: 570-207-2246; Fax: 570-207-2274. Direct all inquiries concerning marriage nullity, dispensations and permissions to this office.

Episcopal Vicar for Administrative Canonical Processes & Judicial Vicar—Rev. Msgr. ANTHONY J. GENEROSE, V.E., J.C.L.

Chief Canonical Counsel—Rev. BRIAN J.W. CLARKE, J.C.L., V.G.

Coordinator—JOSEPH V. FOX.

Judges—Rev. Msgr. PATRICK J. PRATICO, J.C.D.; Rev. THOMAS J. PETRO, J.C.L.; CHARLES J. REID, J.D., J.C.L.; LINDA E. PRICE, J.C.L.

Defenders of the Bond—Rev. Msgr. JOHN H. LOUIS, S.T.L., J.C.D. (Retired); Rev. JAMES J. WALSH, J.C.L.

Promoter of Justice—Rev. FRANCIS J. MARINI, J.D., J.C.O.D.

Auditor—JOSEPH V. FOX.

Procurator/Advocates—JOSEPH V. FOX; Rev. PHILIP A. ALTAVILLA, V.G.

Psychological Expert—JOSEPH A. BARRETT, Ph.D.

Notaries—ANN WALSH; JOSETTE JORDAN; PATRICIA VANCOSKY.

Diocesan Finance Council—Revs. BRIAN J.W. CLARKE, J.C.L., V.G.; PHILIP A. ALTAVILLA, V.G.; THOMAS D. MCLAUGHLIN; RICHARD J. POLMOUNTER; JOHN H. GRAHAM; JAMES E. O'BRIEN JR., Esq.; Mr. FRANK PELLEGRINO; CARLON E. PREATE; KATIE LAMBERT; ROBERT J. MILLER; JASON MORRISON; TERESA OSBORNE; Sr. THERESE O'ROURKE, I.H.M.

Diocesan Consultors—Rev. Msgrs. JOHN A. BERGAMO, J.C.L.; WILLIAM J. FELDCAMP; DAVID L. TRESSLER; Revs. MARTIN M. BOYLAN; RICHARD E. CZACHOR; JOHN M. LAPERA; RICHARD J. POLMOUNTER; ROBERT J. SIMON.

Ex Officio—Revs. PHILIP A. ALTAVILLA, V.G.; BRIAN J.W. CLARKE, J.C.L., V.G.; JOHN V. POLEDNAK, V.E.

Diocesan Pastoral Council— Contact: VACANT, 300 Wyoming Ave., Scranton, 18503-1279. Tel: 570-207-2216.

Deans—Rev. Msgrs. JOHN J. BENDIK, Northern Luzerne; DAVID L. TRESSLER, Mid-Valley/Lackawanna; Revs. MICHAEL J. PICCOLA, V.F., Southern Luzerne; ANDREW S. HVOZDOVIC, Bradford/Sullivan/Susquehanna/Wyoming; SHANE L. KIRBY, S.T.L., Lycoming/Tioga; JAMES J. PAISLEY, V.F., Western Luzerne; THOMAS D. MCLAUGHLIN, Monroe; Rev. Msgr. WILLIAM J. FELDCAMP, Dunmore; Revs. WILLIAM J. KARLE, Wilkes-Barre; AUGUST A. RICCIARDI, Wayne/Pike; SAMUEL J. FERRETTI, Scranton.

Presbyteral Council—Rev. Msgrs. THOMAS V. BANICK; JOHN J. BENDIK; JOHN A. BERGAMO, J.C.L.; WILLIAM J. FELDCAMP; DONALD A. MCANDREWS (Retired); JAMES J. MCGARRY; DAVID L. TRESSLER; Revs. PATRICK L. ALBERT; RICHARD W. BECK; MARTIN M. BOYLAN; RICHARD E. CZACHOR; JOHN A. DORIS; JOSEPH J. EVANKO; PAUL C. FONTANELLA; LOUIS T. KAMINSKI; SHANE L. KIRBY, S.T.L.; PATRICK J. MCLAUGHLIN; THOMAS D. MCLAUGHLIN; RICHARD J. POLMOUNTER; ROBERT J. SIMON; BRIAN F. VAN FOSSEN; DONALD J. WILLIAMS. Ex Officio: Revs. BRIAN J.W. CLARKE, J.C.L., V.G.; PHILIP A. ALTAVILLA, V.G.; JOHN C. LAMBERT, V.E.; GLENN E. MCCREARY, V.E.; THOMAS M. MULDOWNEY, V.E.; JOHN V. POLEDNAK, V.E.; JOHN M. LAPERA.

Diocesan Building Commission— All plans for building should be sent to Chancery Office, *300 Wyoming Ave., Scranton, 18503-1279*. Rev. JOSEPH A. GRESKIEWICZ; AL BROCAVICH; JAMES DEVERS; JOHN POCIUS; THOMAS CONSIDINE. Ex Officio: TERESA OSBORNE; ROBERT J. MILLER; Mr. FRANK M. SEMANSKI.

Episcopal Vicar for Clergy—Rev. THOMAS M. MULDOWNEY, V.E., 300 Wyoming Ave., Scranton, 18503-1279. Tel: 570-207-2269.

Diocesan Offices and Directors

Blue Army of Our Lady of Fatima—Rev. PAUL A. MCDONNELL, O.S.J., Spiritual Dir. Tel: 570-654-7542; VACANT, Chap.; Mr. ALBERT R. MUTO, Pres. Tel: 570-489-9572.

Catholic Campaign for Human Development—DAVID CLARKE, Dir., 400 Wyoming Ave., Scranton, 18503. Tel: 570-207-2213, Ext. 1130.

Campus Ministry—Sr. CATHERINE ANN GILVARY, I.H.M., Dir., Mailing Address: 400 Wyoming Ave., Scranton, 18503. Tel: 570-207-2213, Ext. 1106.

Catholic Charismatic Renewal—Rev. AUGUST A. RICCIARDI, Spiritual Moderator; ROBERT VALIANTE, Liaison to Bishop & Conference Coord., Mailing Address: P.O. Box 3306, Scranton, 18505. Tel: 570-344-2214.

Catholic Relief Services—TERESA OSBORNE, Chancellor, 300 Wyoming Ave., Scranton, 18503-1279. Tel: 570-207-2216.

Catholic Social Services—Rev. Msgr. JOSEPH P. KELLY, V.E., Sec. for Catholic Human Svcs. & Exec. Dir., 33 E. Northampton St., Wilkes-Barre, 18701. Tel: 570-822-7118; Fax: 570-829-7781.

Lackawanna County—

Scranton Office—Sr. JANET JEFFERS, I.H.M., Exec. Dir., 516 Fig St., Scranton, 18505-1753. Tel: 570-207-2283; Fax: 570-207-2206. Res.: 409-411 Olive St., Scranton, 18509. Tel: 570-342-1295; Fax: 570-341-6623; Mr. STEPHEN R. NOCILLA, M.A., Diocesan Dir. Housing & Residential Svcs. *Residential Housing, 409-411 Olive St., Scranton, 18509*. Tel: 570-342-1295.

Carbondale Office—Sr. ROSE GREGORIO, I.H.M., Caseworker, 80 Terrace St., Carbondale, 18407. Tel: 570-282-0460.

Luzerne County—

Wyoming Valley Office—RONALD G. EVANS, Exec. Dir., 33 E. Northampton St., Wilkes-Barre, 18701. Tel: 570-822-7118; Fax: 570-829-7781.

Hazleton Office—Mr. NEIL OBERTO, M.A., Exec. Dir., 214 W. Walnut St., Hazleton, 18201. Tel: 570-455-1521; Fax: 570-455-2707.

Lycoming County—

Williamsport Office—Mr. BERNARD MAKOS, L.S.W., Case Worker, 2110 Linn St., Williamsport, 17701. Tel: 570-322-4220.

Monroe County—

Stroudsburg Office—VACANT, Exec. Dir., 724 Phillips St., Ste. A, Stroudsburg, 18360. Tel: 570-476-6460.

Pike County—

Milford Office—ERIN BUSTELOS, 10 Buist Rd., Ste. 202, Milford, 18337. Tel: 570-296-1054.

Tioga County—

Mansfield Office—Mr. BERNARD MAKOS, L.S.W., 3892 Lambs Creek Rd., Mansfield, 16933. Tel: 570-662-7788; Fax: 570-662-7337.

Wayne County—

Honesdale Office—Mr. MIKE CIPILEWSKI, Case Worker, 100 Fourth St., Honesdale, 18431. Tel: 570-253-1777.

Natural Family Planning Coordinator—BRENDAN MURPHY, Dir. Family Life, Marriage Prep. & Adult Formation, 400 Wyoming Ave., Scranton, 18503. Tel: 570-207-2213, Ext. 1133.

Cemeteries—KEVIN BECK, Dir., 1708 Oram St., Scranton, 18504. Tel: 570-207-2209.

Censor Librorum—Rev. CHARLES P. CONNOR, c/o 300 Wyoming Ave., Scranton, 18503. Tel: 570-207-2216.

Cursillo Movement—Rev. PHILLIP J. SLADICKA, Spiritual Moderator, Queen of the Apostles Parish, 715 Hawthorne St., Avoca, 18641. Tel: 570-457-3412.

Diocesan Commission on Ethics for Catholic Health Care Facilities—VACANT.

Diocesan Commission on Ecumenism and Inter-Faith Matters—Rev. PHILIP A. ALTAVILLA, V.G., Diocesan Dir., St. Peter's Cathedral Parish, 315 Wyoming Ave., Scranton, 18503. Tel: 570-344-7231.

Diocesan Facilities Manager—Mr. FRANK M. SEMANSKI, 300 Wyoming Ave., Scranton, 18503. Tel: 570-207-2232; Fax: 570-207-2273.

Diocesan Historian—Rev. CHARLES P. CONNOR, c/o Chancery Office, 300 Wyoming Ave., Scranton, 18503. Tel: 570-207-2216.

Diocesan Office for Communications—Mr. WILLIAM R. GENELLO, Exec. Dir., 300 Wyoming Ave., Scranton, 18503-1272. Tel: 570-207-2219; 800-246-0288; Fax: 570-207-2281.

Diocesan Compliance Officer—Ms. GAIL FROMM, 300 Wyoming Ave., Scranton, 18503. Tel: 570-207-2214; Fax: 570-207-2273.

Diocesan Office of Development—JASON MORRISON, Diocesan Sec., 300 Wyoming Ave., Scranton, 18503-1279. Tel: 570-207-2250; Fax: 570-207-1835.

Diocesan Appeal Office—JASON MORRISON, Dir., 300 Wyoming Ave., Scranton, 18503-1279. Tel: 570-207-2250; Fax: 570-207-1835.

Diocese of Scranton Catholic Community Foundation—JASON MORRISON, Dir., 300 Wyoming Ave., Scranton, 18503-1279. Tel: 570-207-2250; Fax: 570-207-1835.

Diocese of Scranton Scholarship Foundation—JASON MORRISON, Dir., 300 Wyoming Ave., Scranton, 18503-1279. Tel: 570-207-2250; Fax: 570-207-1835.

Diocesan Office of Ecumenism—Rev. PHILIP A. ALTAVILLA, V.G., Dir., St. Peter's Cathedral Parish, 315 Wyoming Ave., Scranton, 18503. Tel: 570-344-7231.

Diocesan Office for Parish Life—Rev. JOHN M. LAPERA, Interim Sec.; Rev. Msgr. DALE R. RUPERT, Dir., Office for Divine Worship. Tel: 570-558-4303; SARAH MOUNTAIN, Youth & Young Adult Ministry Dir.; CHRISTOPHER TIGUE, Dir, C.Y.O.; BRENDAN MURPHY, Family Life Dir.; DAVID CLARKE, Social Concerns/Pro-Life Dir., 400 Wyoming Ave., Scranton, 18503-1279. Tel: 570-207-2213.

Fatima Renewal Center—SARAH MOUNTAIN, Prog. Dir., 1000 Seminary Rd., Dalton, 18414. Tel: 570-563-8510.

Ministry for Persons with Disabilities—Sr. MARY BETH MAKUCH, SS.C.M., Dir., 400 Wyoming Ave., Scranton, 18503-1272. Tel: 570-207-2213.

Ministry with Deaf and Hard of Hearing—Sr. MARY BETH MAKUCH, SS.C.M., Dir.; Rev. JOSEPH G. ELSTON, Chap., 300 Wyoming Ave., Scranton, 18503-1272. Tel: 570-207-2213.

Diocesan Pro-Life Office—DAVID CLARKE, Diocesan Dir., 400 Wyoming Ave., Scranton, 18503-1279. Tel: 570-207-2213.

Pastoral Formation Institute—MARY ANNE MALONE, Dir., 400 Wyoming Ave., Scranton, 18503. Tel: 570-207-2213.

Religious Education—MARY ANNE MALONE, Dir., 400 Wyoming Ave., Scranton, 18503-1272. Tel: 570-207-2213.

Property & Risk Management Office—Mr. FRANK M. SEMANSKI, Sec., 300 Wyoming Ave., Scranton, 18503. Tel: 570-207-2232; Fax: 570-558-4302; Mr. ED CARLIN, Property Assets Dir., 300 Wyoming Ave., Scranton, 18503. Tel: 570-207-2237, Ext. 1029; THOMAS CONSIDINE, Risk Mgmt. Dir. Tel: 570-558-4310.

Consecrated Life Office—Sr. MARY BETH MAKUCH, SS.C.M., Delegate. Tel: 570-207-2213, Ext. 1101.

Hispanic Ministry Outreach—Rev. Msgr. JOSEPH P. KELLY, V.E., Episcopal Vicar, Catholic Social Services, 33 E. Northampton St., Wilkes Barre, 18701. Tel: 570-822-7118; Sr. JACQUELINE SERVICK, I.H.M.; ALEJANDRA MARROQUIN, St. John Neumann Parish, 633 Orchard St., Scranton, 18505. Tel: 570-558-0848; Revs. JOHN C. RUTH, Coord. Hispanic Min. Lackawanna County, St. John Neumann Parish, 633 Orchard St., Scranton, 18505. Tel: 570-558-0848; 570-961-2297; JOSEPH R. KOPACZ, Coord. Hispanic Min. Monroe County, c/o Most Holy Trinity Parish, 27 Fairview Ave., Mount Pocono, 18344. Tel: 570-839-7138; ALBERT BELLANTONIO, Mailing Address: c/o Most Holy Trinity Parish, 27 Fairview Ave., Mount Pocono, 18344. Tel: 570-839-7138; Sr. JOEL MARIE SHEEHE, I.H.M., Mailing Address: c/o Most Holy Trinity Parish, 27 Fairview Ave., Mount Pocono, 18344. Tel: 570-839-7138; Rev. VICTOR LEON, O.S.J., c/o Annunciation Parish, 122 S. Wyoming St., Hazleton, 18201. Tel: 570-454-0212.

Holy Childhood Association—Deacon EDWARD T. KELLY, Dir.; MIRIAM HEVERLINE, Mission Educ. Coord., 300 Wyoming Ave., Scranton, 18503-1279. Tel: 570-207-2259; Fax: 570-207-2268.

Holy Name Society—VACANT, Spiritual Advisor.

Legion of Mary—Rev. DAVID W. CRAMER, Spiritual Dir., Mailing Address: St. Lawrence Rectory, 380 Franklin St., P.O. Box 592, Great Bend, 18821. Tel: 570-267-1366.

Liturgical Commission—VACANT.

Marriage Encounter—VACANT, Spiritual Advisor. Contact: DIANE ZINDELL; ED ZINDELL, 14 Evergreen Dr., Jermyn, 18433. Tel: 570-876-1610.

D.C.C.M.—VACANT, Spiritual Moderator. Contact: DAVID CLARKE, Dir. Social Concerns. Tel: 570-207-2213, Ext. 1130.

D.C.C.W.—VACANT, Spiritual Moderator. Contact: DAVID CLARKE, Dir. Social Concerns. Tel: 570-207-2213, Ext. 1130.

Newspaper— "The Catholic Light" Mr. WILLIAM R. GENELLO, Editor, 300 Wyoming Ave., Scranton, 18503-1279. Tel: 570-207-2229; 570-207-2272; Fax: 570-207-2271.

Office of Pastoral Planning—Rev. JOHN M. LAPERA, Diocesan Sec. Pastoral Planning (Called to Holiness and Mission).Tel: 570-207-1452; Fax: 570-207-1833.

Diocesan Television Station-CTV—Mr. WILLIAM R. GENELLO, Exec. Dir.; JAMES BRENNAN, Mgr., 400 Wyoming Ave., Scranton, 18503-1272. Tel: 570-207-2219; Fax: 570-207-2281.

Permanent Diaconate Office—Rev. Msgr. DAVID A. BOHR, S.T.D., Diocesan Sec. for Clergy Formation & Dir. Continuing Education for Priests, 300 Wyoming Ave., Scranton, 18503. Tel: 570-207-2269.

Pilgrimages—Rev. ANDREW S. HVOZDOVIC, Diocesan Dir., Epiphany Parish, 304 S. Elmer Ave., Sayre, 18840. Tel: 570-888-9641.

Priests' Purgatorial Society—Rev. THOMAS M. MULDOWNEY, V.E., Sec. & Episcopal Vicar for Clergy, 300 Wyoming Ave., Scranton, 18503-1279. Tel: 570-207-2269.

Priests' Retirement Advisory Board—Revs. JAMES R. NASH; WILLIAM B. HEALEY (Retired); JOSEPH R. KOPACZ; ANDREW R. SINNOTT; JAMES R. BURKE; TERESA OSBORNE; ROBERT J. MILLER.

Propagation of the Faith—Deacon EDWARD T. KELLY, Dir.; MIRIAM HEVERLINE, Mission Educ. Coord., 300 Wyoming Ave., Scranton, 18503-1279. Tel: 570-207-2259; Fax: 570-207-2268. Email: miriam-heverline@dioceseofscranton.org.

Retirement Fund for Religious—Sr. MARY BETH MAKUCH, SS.C.M., Delegate for Consecrated Life, 400 Wyoming Ave., Scranton, 18503. Tel: 570-207-2213, Ext. 1101.

Schools—Rev. JOHN C. LAMBERT, V.E., Episcopal Vicar for School Planning. Tel: 570-788-1997; KATHLEEN P. HANLON, Diocesan Sec., Catholic Schools & Supt. of Schools. Tel: 570-207-2251; Mrs. MARY C. TIGUE, Asst. Supt. Schools, 300 Wyoming Ave., Scranton, 18503. Tel: 570-207-2251; PATRICK CAWLEY, Asst. Supt. Govt. Programs. Tel: 570-207-2235.

Regional School Systems—

Holy Cross Regional School System of the Diocese of Scranton, Inc.—VACANT.

Holy Redeemer Regional School System of the Diocese of Scranton, Inc.—VACANT.

Notre Dame Regional School System of the Diocese of Scranton, Inc.—VACANT.

Saint John Neumann Regional School System of the Diocese of Scranton, Inc.—Mrs. SUSAN KAISER, System Dir., 901 Penn St., Williamsport, 17701. Tel: 570-323-9953. Mailing Address: c/o 300 Wyoming Ave., Scranton, 18503.

Scouts of America—Rev. PHILIP A. ALTAVILLA, V.G.,

Chap., St. Peter's Cathedral Parish, 315 Wyoming Ave., Scranton, 18503. Tel: 570-344-7231.

Victim Assistance Coordinator—JOAN L. HOLMES. Tel: 570-344-5216. Email: jholmes1723@comcast.net.

VIRTUS—Ms. GAIL FROMM, Safe Environment Prog. Coord., 300 Wyoming Ave., Scranton, 18503. Tel: 570-207-2214; Fax: 570-207-2273.

Diocesan Office for Continuing Education for Clergy—Rev. Msgr. DAVID A. BOHR, S.T.D., Dir., 300 Wyoming Ave., Scranton, 18503. Tel: 570-207-2269.

Diocesan Office for Clergy Formation—Rev. Msgr. DAVID A. BOHR, S.T.D. Tel: 570-207-2269.

Vocations—Rev. JAMES A. RAFFERTY, S.T.L., Dir. Vocations & Seminarians, 300 Wyoming Ave., Scranton, 18503. Tel: 570-207-2216, Ext. 1013.

CLERGY, PARISHES, MISSIONS AND PAROCHIAL SCHOOLS

CITY OF SCRANTON

(LACKAWANNA COUNTY)

1—ST. PETER'S CATHEDRAL (1853), Linked with Holy Family, Scranton. Rev. Philip A. Altavilla; Deacon Edward R. Shoener. In Res., Most Rev. Joseph C. Bambera; Revs. Brian J.T. Clarke; Thomas M. Muldowney; Brian J.W. Clarke.
Res.: 315 Wyoming Ave., 18503. Tel: 570-344-7231; Fax: 570-344-4749. Email: info@stpeterscathedral.org.
Convent—333 Wyoming, 18503. Tel: 570-344-9725.

2—ST. ANN'S BASILICA PARISH (1901) Revs. Francis Landry, C.P.; Joseph R. Jones, C.P.
Res.: 1250 St. Ann St., 18504. Tel: 570-342-5166; Fax: 570-348-3750.
Catechesis/Religious Program—Tel: 570-344-8408. Katherine Stocki, D.R.E. Students 160.

3—ST. ANTHONY OF PADUA (1913), (Italian), Closed. For inquiries for parish records please see Holy Rosary, Scranton. (part of Mary Mother of God Parish, Scranton).

4—ST. CLARE (1967), Restructured with St. Paul Scranton. Rev. Msgr. William J. Feldcamp.
c/o 1510 Penn Ave., 18509. Tel: 570-961-1549; Fax: 570-961-0335. In Res., Rev. Eric L. Bergman.

5—ST. DAVID'S (1946) Closed. For all inquiries see St. Patrick's, Scranton.

6—DIVINE MERCY (1875) [CEM], Restructured with Immaculate Conception, St. John the Baptist, Taylor; St. Mary Czestochowa, Moosic & St. Joseph, Minooka. Rev. Francis L. Pauselli.
Res.: 312 Davis St., 18505. Tel: 570-344-1724; Fax: 570-344-1787.
Catechesis/Religious Program—Brittain Banull, D.R.E. Students 250.

7—ST. FRANCIS OF ASSISI (1920), (Italian), Consolidated - additional worship site of St. Paul of the Cross Parish. Rev. Scott P. Sterowski.
c/o 1217 Prospect Ave., 18505. Tel: 570-343-6420; Fax: 570-343-3664.
Catechesis/Religious Program—Mary Ann Lucchi, D.R.E. Students 96.

8—HOLY FAMILY (1891) [CEM] Closed. For inquiries for parish records please see St. Peter's Cathedral, Scranton

9—HOLY NAME OF JESUS (1938) Closed. Additional woship site of St. John Neumann, Scranton.

10—HOLY ROSARY (1871) Closed. Restructured with St. Joseph, Scranton and St. Anthony of Padua, Scranton, both now closed. Worship site of Mary, Mother of God Parish, Scranton.

11—IMMACULATE CONCEPTION (1967), Restructured with Christ the King, Dunmore, closed. Rev. Patrick J. McLaughlin; Deacon J. Patrick McDonald. In Res., Rev. Joseph F. Sica.
Res.: 801 Taylor Ave., 18510. Tel: 570-961-5211; Fax: 570-961-0878.
Catechesis/Religious Program—Sandy Czyzyk, D.R.E. Students 256.

12—ST. JOHN THE EVANGELIST (1886) Closed. For inquiries for parish records please contact St. Paul of the Cross Parish, Scranton.

13—ST. JOSEPH'S (1894), (Lithuanian), [CEM] Closed. See Mary, Mother of God Parish, Scranton for sacramental records.

14—ST. JOSEPH'S (1875) [CEM] Merged Restructured with Immaculate Conception & St. Mary of Czestochowa, Greenwood. For inquiries for parish records please contact Divine Mercy, Scranton.

15—ST. LUCY'S (1901), (Italian), Merged with SS. Peter & Paul, Scranton. Rev. Samuel J. Ferretti; Deacon Steven J. Napoli.
Res.: 949 Scranton St., 18504. Tel: 570-347-9421; Fax: 570-341-8252. Web: stlucy-church.org.
Catechesis/Religious Program—Students 66.

16—ST. MARY CZESTOCHOWA (1904), (Polish), [CEM] Closed. For inquiries for parish records, contact Divine Mercy, Scranton.

17—ST. MARY OF THE ASSUMPTION (1854), (German), [CEM 2] Closed. For inquiries for parish records, please see St. John Neumann, Scranton.

18—MARY, MOTHER OF GOD PARISH Rev. Cyril D. Edwards.
316 William St., 18508. Tel: 570-342-4881; Fax: 570-342-4881.

19—ST. MICHAEL'S (1914), (Lithuanian), Rev. Jose Zepeda, F.S.S.P.; Deacon Gregory Zepeda.
Res.: 1703 Jackson St., 18504. Tel: 570-961-1205; Fax: 570-961-2284. Email: stmichael@epix.net. Web: www.saintmichaelsrcc.org.

20—NATIVITY OF OUR LORD, Merged Restructured with Holy Name of Jesus, Scranton & St. Mary of the Assumption, Scranton. Primary worship site of Saint John Neumann. Inquiries for parish records, please contact Saint John Neumann, Scranton.

21—ST. PATRICK'S (1870) Rev. Martin M. Boylan. Restructured with St. David, Scranton, closed. In Res., Revs. Stephen A. Krawontka; Gregory T. Villaescusa.
Res.: 1403 Jackson St., 18504. Tel: 570-344-2679; 570-343-4353; Fax: 570-343-2835. Email: stpatrick-scr@yahoo.com.
Catechesis/Religious Program—Robin Lipik, D.R.E. Students 308.
Chapel—Scranton, Immaculate Heart of Mary 1605 Oram St., 18504.

22—SAINT PAUL OF THE CROSS, SCRANTON (1885), (Polish), [CEM], Merged with St. John the Evangelist, St. Francis of Assisi, Scranton & Sacred Hearts of Jesus and Mary, Scranton. Rev. Scott P. Sterowski.
1149 Providence Rd., 18505.
1217 Prospect Ave., 18505. Tel: 570-343-6420; Fax: 570-343-3664.
Catechesis/Religious Program—Students 7.
Worship Site: St. Francis of Assisi—

23—ST. PAUL'S (1887), Restructured with St. Clare, Scranton. Rev. Msgr. William J. Feldcamp. In Res., Rev. Msgr. Michael J. Delaney; Revs. Brian F. Van Fossen; James A. Rafferty.
Res.: 1510 Penn Ave., 18509. Tel: 570-961-1549; Fax: 570-961-0335.
Catechesis/Religious Program—Jeanne Evans, D.R.E. Students 175.

24—SS. PETER AND PAUL (1910), (Polish), [CEM], Restructured with St. Lucy, Scranton. Rev. Samuel J. Ferretti.
Res.: 1309 W. Locust St., 18504. Tel: 570-343-7015; Fax: 570-343-7023. Email: ssppscr@verizon.net.
Catechesis/Religious Program—Christina Wasko, D.R.E. Students 23.

25—SACRED HEARTS OF JESUS AND MARY, Merged with St. John the Evangelist & St. Francis of Assisi, Scranton. See Saint Paul of the Cross, Scranton.

26—SAINT JOHN NEUMANN, SCRANTON (1903), Reconstructed with Holy Name of Jesus, St. Mary of the Assumption, Scranton & Nativity of Our Lord, Scranton. Revs. Michael Bryant; John C. Ruth; Deacon Joseph Donovan. In Res., Rev. William B. Pickard.
Res.: 633 Orchard St., 18505. Tel: 570-344-6159; Fax: 570-207-4932.
Catechesis/Religious Program—Maria Revesz, D.R.E. Students 165.

27—ST. VINCENT DE PAUL (1925) Closed. For inquiries for parish records contact the chancery. Merged with St. Joseph, Scranton & St. Anthony of Padua, Scranton.

OUTSIDE THE CITY OF SCRANTON

ARCHBALD, LACKAWANNA CO.

1—CHRIST THE KING PARISH Rev. Christopher S. Sahd.
429 Church St., 18403. Tel: 570-876-1701.

2—ST. THOMAS AQUINAS (1858) [CEM], Restructured with St. Mary of Czestochowa, Eynon. Primary worship site of Christ the King Parish, Archbald. Rev. Christopher S. Sahd; Deacon Edward T. Kelly. In Res., Most Rev. John M. Dougherty (Retired).
Res.: 429 Church St., 18403. Tel: 570-876-1701; Fax: 570-876-3617. Email: st.tom@comcast.net.
Catechesis/Religious Program—Ellen Nielsen, D.R.E.; Maria Tomassoni, D.R.E. Combined with St. Mary of Czestochowa, Eynon. Students 53.

ASHLEY, LUZERNE CO.

1—HOLY ROSARY (1900), (Slovak), Closed. For inquiries for parish records please see St. Leo's, Ashley.

2—ST. LEO'S (1887) Rev. Thomas J. O'Malley.
Res.: 33 Manhattan St., 18706. Tel: 570-825-6669; Fax: 570-825-3055.
Catechesis/Religious Program—Michele Casey, D.R.E. Students 162.

ATHENS, BRADFORD CO., ST. JOSEPH (1852) Closed. following merger with St. John the Evangelist, South Waverly. For inquiries for parish records, contact Epiphany, Sayre.

AVOCA, LUZERNE CO.

1—ST. MARY'S (1871) [CEM] Rev. Phillip J. Sladicka. Worship site of Queen of the Apostles Parish, Avoca.
Res.: 715 Hawthorne St., 18641. Tel: 570-457-3412; Fax: 570-457-2483. Email: stmarysavoca@verizon.net.
Catechesis/Religious Program—Deborah Yuschovitz, D.R.E. Students 104.

2—SS. PETER AND PAUL (1909), (Polish), [CEM] Closed. For inquiries for parish records please see Queen of the Apostles, Avoca.

3—QUEEN OF THE APOSTLES PARISH Rev. Phillip J. Sladicka.
715 Hawthorne St., 18641. Tel: 570-457-3412.

BASTRESS, LYCOMING CO., IMMACULATE CONCEPTION OF THE BLESSED VIRGIN MARY (1847), (German), [CEM] Rev. Bert S. Kozen. Restructured with St. Luke, Jersey Shore.
Res.: 5973 Jacks Hollow Rd., Williamsport, 17702. Tel: 570-745-3301.
Catechesis/Religious Program—Students 125.
Convent—Mother of the Eucharist, 6100 Jacks Hollow Rd., Williamsport, 17702. Tel: 570-745-3334. Sr. Joan May, C.N., Guardian.

BEAR CREEK , LUZERNE CO.

1—ST. CHRISTOPHER (1962) Closed. Merged with Holy Saviour, Wilkes-Barre.

2—ST. ELIZABETH (1938) Rev. William J. Karle.
5700 Bear Creek Blvd., P.O. Box 25, 18602. Tel: 570-472-3061.
Catechesis/Religious Program—Michael Grourke, D.R.E. Students 75.
Mission—St. Mark Thornhurst, Luzerne Co.

BENTLEY CREEK, BRADFORD CO., ST. ANN'S (1843) [CEM] Closed. Restructured with Epiphany, Sayre. For inquiries for parish records please see Epiphany, Sayre.

BLAKESLEE, MONROE CO., CHRIST THE KING (1976) Closed. For inquiries for parish records please see St. Maximilian Kolbe, Pocono Pines.

BLOSSBURG, TIOGA CO.

1—ST. JOHN NEUMANN, Closed. For inquiries for parish records, please see Holy Child, Mansfield.

2—ST. MARY'S (1874), (Polish), [CEM 3] Closed. For inquiries for parish records contact Holy Child, Mansfield. Worship site for Holy Child Parish, Mansfield.

BRODHEADSVILLE, MONROE CO., OUR LADY QUEEN OF PEACE (1968) Revs. Michael F. Quinnan; Sean G. Carpenter; Deacon Robert A. O'Connor Jr.
Res.: Box 38, 18322. Tel: 610-681-6137; Fax: 610-681-6139.
Catechesis/Religious Program—Jacqueline Douglas, D.R.E. Students 731.

CANADENSIS, MONROE CO., ST. BERNADETTE (1967), Linked with St. Mary of the Mount, Mt. Pocono, and St. Ann, Tobyhanna. Worship site of Most Holy Trinity Parish, Mt. Pocono. Revs. Joseph R. Kopacz; Gregory F. Loughney; Deacon Ronald P. Verkon.
Mailing Address: 27 Fairview Ave., Mount Pocono, 18344.
Res.: Rte. 390, 18325. Tel: 570-839-7138; Fax: 570-839-7708.
Catechesis/Religious Program—Dorothy Lewis, D.R.E. Students 121.
Mission—Our Lady of Fatima, Closed., State Park, Promised Land, Monroe Co.

CANTON, BRADFORD CO., ST. MICHAEL (1853) [CEM] Rev. Michael S. McCormick; Deacon William H. Graham.
Parish Office: 106 N. Washington St., 17724.
Res.: 24 N. Washington St., 17724. Tel: 570-673-5253; Fax: 570-673-5630.
Catechesis/Religious Program—Deacon William H. Graham, D.R.E. Students 51.
Mission—St. John Nepomucene [CEM] Troy, Bradford Co. Tel: 570-297-4405.
Mission—St. Aloysius Ralston, Lycoming Co.

CARBONDALE, LACKAWANNA CO.

1—OUR LADY OF MT. CARMEL (1882), (Italian), [CEM] Rev. Russell E. Motsay.
Res.: 15 Fallbrook St., 18407. Tel: 570-282-5172.
Catechesis/Religious Program—Students 59.

2—ST. ROSE OF LIMA (1832) [CEM 2], Linked with St. Michael, Simpson. Rev. Msgr. David L. Tressler; Rev. John C. O'Bell; Deacon Edward Casey.
Res.: 6 N. Church St., 18407. Tel: 570-282-2991; Fax: 570-282-7580.
Catechesis/Religious Program—Patricia Dragwa, D.R.E. (Gr. 1-4); Kathryn Yaklic, D.R.E. (Gr. 5-8). Students 395.

CARVERTON, LUZERNE CO., ST. FRANCES CABRINI (1947) Rev. Vincent H. Dang. In Res., Rev. Donald J. Williams.
Res.: 585 Mt. Olivet Rd., Kingston Twp., Wyoming, 18644-9333. Tel: 570-696-3737; Fax: 570-696-3737.
Catechesis/Religious Program—Students 60.

Mission—Blessed Sacrament, Closed., Centermoreland, Luzerne Co.

CLARKS GREEN, LACKAWANNA CO., ST. GREGORY (1974) Rev. John M. Lapera; Deacon Robert P. Sheils Jr.
Res.: 330 N. Abington Rd., 18411. Tel: 570-587-4808; Fax: 570-586-4515. Email: churchofstgreg@yahoo.com.
Catechesis/Religious Program—Joanne Judge, D.R.E. Students 603.

CLARKS SUMMIT, LACKAWANNA CO., OUR LADY OF THE SNOWS (1911) Rev. Msgr. James J. McGarry; Deacon Leo L. Lynn.
Res.: 301 S. State St., 18411. Tel: 570-586-1741; Fax: 570-586-2504. Email: ols2@epix.net.
Catechesis/Religious Program—Nettie Goldate, D.R.E. Students 1,330.
Mission—St. Benedict Newton, Lackawanna Co.

CONYNGHAM, LUZERNE CO., ST. JOHN BOSCO (1964) Rev. John C. Lambert; Deacon Maurice J. Cerasaro Jr. In Res., Rev. Connell A. McHugh.
Res.: 2 Charles Ave., P.O. Box 919, 18219. Tel: 570-788-1997; Fax: 570-788-6667.
Church: 573 State Rte. 93.
Catechesis/Religious Program—Robert Rock, D.R.E.; Carrie Grandzol, D.R.E. Students 454.

DALLAS, LUZERNE CO., GATE OF HEAVEN (1951), Linked with Our Lady of Victory, Harveys Lake. Rev. Daniel A. Toomey; Deacon Thomas M. Cesarini.
Res.: 40 Machell Ave., 18612. Tel: 570-675-2121; Fax: 570-675-7143. Email: goh@epix.net.
Catechesis/Religious Program—Tel: 570-675-6488. Sonya Cesarini, D.R.E. Students 310.

DALTON, LACKAWANNA CO., OUR LADY OF THE ABINGTONS (1967), Linked with St. Patrick, Nicholson. Rev. Edward L. Michelini.
Res.: 700 W. Main St., 18414. Tel: 570-563-1622; Fax: 570-563-0988.
Catechesis/Religious Program—Jacque Petherick, D.R.E. Students 80.

DICKSON CITY, LACKAWANNA CO.

1—ST. THOMAS THE APOSTLE, Closed. For inquiries for parish records please see Visitation of the Blessed Virgin Mary.

2—VISITATION OF THE BLESSED VIRGIN MARY (1890), (Polish), [CEM], Merged with St. Thomas the Apostle, Dickson City. Rev. Msgr. Patrick J. Pratico; Deacon Jan F. Mroz. In Res., Rev. Joseph C. Rusin (Retired).
Res.: 1090 Carmalt St., 18519. Tel: 570-489-2091; Fax: 570-489-0349.
Catechesis/Religious Program—Marie Piela, D.R.E. Students 142.

DORRANCE, LUZERNE CO., OUR LADY HELP OF CHRISTIANS (1948), (Polish), [CEM], Linked with St. Jude, Mountaintop. Rev. Joseph J. Evanko.
Res.: 3529 St. Mary's Rd. (Dorrance), Wapwallopen, 18660-1901. Tel: 570-868-5855; Fax: 570-868-5876.
Catechesis/Religious Program—Mrs. Patricia Heller, D.R.E. Students 104.

DRUMS, LUZERNE CO., CHURCH OF THE GOOD SHEPHERD (1940) Rev. Connell A. McHugh.
Res.: 87 S. Hunter Hwy., 18222. Tel: 570-788-3141; Fax: 570-788-2916. Email: gsch@ptd.net.
Catechesis/Religious Program—Judy Whitaker, D.R.E. Students 176.

DUNMORE, LACKAWANNA CO.

1—ALL SAINTS (1905), (Slovak), Closed. Merged with Our Lady of Mount Carmel, Dunmore.

2—SS. ANTHONY & ROCCO PARISH, (Italian), Rev. David P. Cappelloni; Deacon Carmine Mendicino.
Res.: 303 Smith St., 18512. Tel: 570-344-1209; Fax: 570-344-1200.
Catechesis/Religious Program—Sr. Donna Cerminaro, M.P.F., D.R.E. Students 192.
Convent—Religious Teachers Filippini, 118 Kurtz St., 18510. Tel: 570-343-1422; Fax: 570-346-3099.

3—ST. ANTHONY OF PADUA (1894), (Italian), Closed. Restructured with St. Rocco, Dunmore to form SS. Anthony & Rocco, Dunmore. Also parish worship site for SS. Anthony & Rocco.

4—ST. CASIMIR, (Polish), Closed. Merged with Our Lady of Mount Carmel, Dunmore.

5—CHRIST THE KING (1949) Closed. For inquiries for parish records please see Immaculate Conception Parish, Scranton.

6—ST. MARY OF MOUNT CARMEL, Merged with All Saints and St. Casimir, Dunmore. See Our Lady of Mount Carmel Parish, Dunmore.

7—OUR LADY OF MOUNT CARMEL PARISH (1856) [CEM 2], (Merged with All Saints and St. Casimir, Dunmore.) Rev. John A. Doris.
Res.: 322 Chestnut St., 18512. Tel: 570-346-7429; Fax: 570-346-0523.
Catechesis/Religious Program—Lisa Murphy, C.C.D. Coord.; Eileen Murphy, C.C.D. Coord.; Cathy Walsh, C.C.D. Coord. Students 338.

8—ST. ROCCO'S (1905), (Italian), Merged with St. Anthony of Padua, Dunmore to form SS. Anthony & Rocco, Dunmore. Additional worship site for SS. Anthony & Rocco.

DUPONT, LUZERNE CO., SACRED HEART OF JESUS (1902), (Polish), [CEM] Rev. Joseph D. Verespy.
Res.: 215 Lackawanna Ave., 18641. Tel: 570-654-3713; Fax: 570-654-7952.
Catechesis/Religious Program—Elaine Starinski, D.R.E. Students 80.

DURYEA, LUZERNE CO.

1—HOLY ROSARY (1893), (Polish), See separate listing. See Nativity of Our Lord Parish, Duryea. Also worship site for Nativity of Our Lord Parish.

2—ST. JOSEPH (1909), (Lithuanian), [CEM] Closed. following merger with Sacred Heart of Jesus, Duryea. For inquiries for parish records, contact Nativity of Our Lord Parish, Duryea.

3—NATIVITY OF OUR LORD PARISH (1893), (Polish), [CEM] Rev. Charles W. Rokosz.
Res.: 127 Stephenson St., 18642. Tel: 570-457-3502; Fax: 570-457-3341. Email: holyrosaryrcc@aol.com.
Catechesis/Religious Program—Judy Lambert, D.R.E. Students 130.

4—SACRED HEART OF JESUS (1889), (German), Merged with Nativity of Our Lord Parish, Duryea in 2003. Additional worship site for Nativity of Our Lord Parish, Duryea. Rev. Charles W. Rokosz.
Res.: 529 Stephenson St., 18642. Tel: 570-457-3502; Fax: 570-451-3341.
Catechesis/Religious Program—Judy Lambert, D.R.E. Total Enrollment 87.

DUSHORE, SULLIVAN CO.

1—ST. BASIL THE GREAT (1838) See separate listing. See Immaculate Heart of Mary, Dushore. Parish worship site for Immaculate Heart of Mary Parish.

2—IMMACULATE HEART OF MARY PARISH (1838) [CEM] Rev. Joseph R. Hornick; Deacon Joseph Roinick.
Res.: 101 Churchill St., P.O. Box 307, 18614-0307. Tel: 570-928-8865; Fax: 570-928-7972. Email: stbasilnfrancis@epix.net.
Catechesis/Religious Program—Carol Roinick, D.R.E. Students 148.
Mission—St. Francis Xavier, Overton.; Closed. For inquiries for parish records please contact St. Basil the Great.
Mission—Sacred Heart, Laporte.; Closed. For inquiries for parish records please contact St. Basil the Great.
Mission—St. Francis of Assisi, (additional worship site), Eagles Mere, Sullivan Co.
Mission—St. Francis of Assisi, (additional worship site), Mildred, Sullivan Co.
Shrine—S. Philip and James Church-St. John Neumann Shrine, (additional worship site), Sugar Ridge.
St. Basil the Great—

EAST STROUDSBURG, MONROE CO.

1—ST. JOHN (1986) Rev. Jeffrey J. Walsh; Deacon Thomas J. Dello Russo.
Mailing Address: 5171 Milford Rd., 18301. Tel: 570-223-9144; Fax: 570-223-9146. Email: stjohnch@ptd.net.
Catechesis/Religious Program—Tel: 570-223-0888. Mary Foglio, C.R.E. Students 389.

2—ST. MATTHEW (1902) Rev. Msgr. John A. Bergamo; Rev. Augustine Lourduswami (India); Deacons Svetko Jurjevic; Jose Oscar Langlois.
Res.: 200 Brodhead Ave., 18301. Tel: 570-421-2342; Fax: 570-421-8414.
Catechesis/Religious Program—Tel: 570-421-0113. Lisa Hoey, D.R.E. Students 383.

ELKLAND, TIOGA CO., ST. THOMAS THE APOSTLE (1907) Rev. John M. Kita.
Res.: 111 First St., 16920. Tel: 814-258-5121; Fax: 814-258-5122.
Catechesis/Religious Program—Michelle Whalen, D.R.E. Students 4.
Mission—St. Catherine 106 Lincoln St., Westfield, Tioga Co. 16950.

ELMHURST, LACKAWANNA CO., ST. EULALIA (1950) Rev. Msgr. John J. Jordan. In Res., Rev. Peter D. Menghini.
Res.: 214 Blue Shutters Rd., Roaring Brook Twp., 18444. Tel: 570-842-7656; Fax: 570-842-7193. Email: steulaliachurch@aol.com.
Catechesis/Religious Program—Elizabeth Strasburger, D.R.E. Students 340.

EXETER, LUZERNE CO.

1—ST. ANTHONY OF PADUA (1928), (Italian), Closed. For inquiries for parish records contact the chancery. Parish worship site for Saint Barbara Parish, Exeter.

2—SAINT BARBARA PARISH Very Rev. Philip V. Massetti, O.S.J.
Res.: 28 Memorial Ave., 18643. Tel: 570-654-2103.

3—ST. CECILIA (1900) [CEM], Additional worship site for Saint Barbara Parish, Exeter. Rev. Msgr. John J. Bendik, Admin.; Deacon William A. Dervinis.
Res.: 1700 Wyoming Ave., 18643. Tel: 570-654-2133; Fax: 570-654-3449.
Catechesis/Religious Program—Students 126.

4—ST. JOHN THE BAPTIST (1898), (Polish), Closed. Contact Saint Barbara Parish, Exeter for parish record inquiries.

EYNON, LACKAWANNA CO.

1—ST. MARY OF CZESTOCHOWA (1915), (Polish), Merged with St. Mary of Vilna, Eynon; Restructured with St. Thomas Aquinas, Archbald. Rev. Christopher S. Sahd; Deacon Edward T. Kelly.
Mailing Address: *c/o Christ the King*, 429 Church St., Archbald, 18403. In Res., Most Rev. John M. Dougherty (Retired).
Res.: 417 Main St., 18403. Tel: 570-876-2223.
Catechesis/Religious Program—Students 87.

2—ST. MARY OF VILNA, (Lithuanian), Closed. For inquiries for parish records, contact St. Mary of Czestochowa, Eynon.

FAIRMOUNT SPRINGS, LUZERNE CO., ST. MARTHA (1966), Restructured with St. Mary, Our Lady of Perpetual Help, Mocanaqua. (All records at Our Lady of Mt. Carmel, Lake Silkworth.); Linked with Corpus Christi, Glen Lyon.; Consolidated with Holy Spirit Parish, Mocanaqua. Also additional worship site for Holy Spirit, Mocanaqua. Rev. Msgr. Anthony J. Generose.
Mailing Address: c/o 150 Main St., Mocanaqua, 18655.
Church: 260 Bonnieville Rd., Stillwater, 17878. Tel: 570-542-4157; Fax: 570-542-4158. Email: stmarychurch@frontier.net.
Catechesis/Religious Program—Kathleen Czeck, D.R.E. Students 29.

FOREST CITY, SUSQUEHANNA CO.

1—ASCENSION PARISH Rev. Patrick L. Albert.
612 Hudson St., 18421. Tel: 570-785-3838.

2—ST. JOSEPH (1904), (Slovenian), Merged with Sacred Heart of Jesus, Forest City. Worship site for Ascension Parish, Forest City.

3—SACRED HEART OF JESUS (1904), (Polish), Merged with St. Agnes, Forest City; Restructured with St. Katharine Drexel, Pleasant Mount. Rev. Patrick L. Albert.
Res.: 612 Hudson St., 18421. Tel: 570-785-3838; Fax: 570-785-3713.

FREELAND, LUZERNE CO.

1—ST. ANTHONY, Closed. For inquiries for parish records please see Our Lady of the Immaculate Conception, Freeland.

2—ST. CASIMIR, Closed. For inquiries for parish records please see Our Lady of the Immaculate Conception, Freeland.

3—ST. JOHN NEPOMUCENE, Closed. For inquiries for parish records please see Our Lady of the Immaculate Conception, Freeland.

4—OUR LADY OF THE IMMACULATE CONCEPTION (1862) [CEM] Rev. J. Duane Gavitt; Deacon Cyril J. Kowalchick.
Office: 898 Centre St., 18224. Tel: 570-636-3035; Fax: 570-636-1743.
Catechesis/Religious Program—Safko Centre, Chestnut St., 18224. Tel: 570-636-3698. Students 134.

FRIENDSVILLE, SUSQUEHANNA CO.

1—SAINT BRIGID PARISH Rev. Casimir M. Stanis.
17 Cottage St., P.O. Box 75, 18818. Tel: 570-553-2288.
Worship Sites—
St. Francis Xavier, Friendsville—
Mission—St. Augustine Silver Lake, Susquehanna Co.

2—ST. FRANCIS XAVIER (1831) [CEM 3], Merged with St. Thomas the Apostle, Little Meadows and restructured with St. Joseph, St. Joseph. Worship site for Saint Brigid Parish, Friendsville. Rev. Casimir M. Stanis; Deacon Kenneth S. Brennan.
Res.: 17 Cottage St., P.O. Box 75, 18818. Tel: 570-553-2288; Fax: 570-553-2975. Email: stxc@epix.net.
Catechesis/Religious Program—Susie Reichlen, D.R.E. Students 75.
Mission—St. Patrick, Closed., Irish Hill, Rte. 3033, Middletown, Susquehanna Co.

3—ST. JOSEPH (1829) [CEM 2] [JC] Closed. For inquiries for parish records please see Saint Brigid Parish, Friendsville.

GLEN LYON, LUZERNE CO.

1—ST. ADALBERT, Merged with Corpus Christi, Glen Lyon. For parish records please contact Holy Spirit Parish, Mocanaqua.

2—CORPUS CHRISTI (2001), (Merging of St. Adalbert, St. Denis & St. Michael's, Glen Lyon & St. Mary's, Wanamie. For inquiries for parish records, contact Corpus Christi.); Linked with Holy Spirit, Mocanaqua. Rev. Msgr. Anthony J. Generose.
Res.: 43 W. Main St., 18617. Tel: 570-736-6372; Fax: 570-736-6232.
Parish Office: 31 S. Market St., 18617.
Catechesis/Religious Program—Ann Marie O'Donnell, D.R.E. Students 90.

3—ST. DENIS, Merged with Corpus Christi, Glen Lyon.

4—ST. MARY (Wanamie) (1906), (Lithuanian), Closed. For inquiries for parish records, contact Corpus Christi, Glen Lyon.

5—ST. MICHAEL, Merged with Corpus Christi, Glen Lyon.

GOULDSBORO, WAYNE CO., ST. RITA (1975) Rev. Alfred J. Vito, Admin.
Res.: P.O. Box 537, 18424. Tel: 570-842-4995; Fax: 570-842-5429.
Catechesis/Religious Program—Students 100.
Mission—St. Anthony of Padua Newfoundland, Wayne Co.

GREAT BEND, SUSQUEHANNA CO., ST. LAWRENCE (1872) [CEM], Linked with St. Martin of Tours, Jackson; St. John the Evangelist, Susquehanna. Revs. David W. Cramer; Alfhones Perikala (India).
Res.: 380 Franklin St., P.O. Box 592, 18821. Tel: 570-267-1366; Fax: 570-267-1367.
Catechesis/Religious Program—Students 72.
Mission—St. John the Apostle [CEM], Closed., New Milford, Susquehanna Co.

HANOVER TOWNSHIP, WASHINGTON CO., EXALTATION OF THE HOLY CROSS (1917), (Polish), [CEM], Linked with St. Casimir, closed and St. Robert Bellarmine, Wilkes Barre. Revs. Kevin P. Mulhern; Joseph K. Polanki (India).
Res.: 420 Main Rd., 18706-6094. Tel: 570-823-6242; Fax: 570-829-4732. Email: exhc@aol.com.
Catechesis/Religious Program—Students 75.

HARDING-FALLS, LUZERNE CO., CHURCH OF THE HOLY REDEEMER (1952), Linked with Corpus Christi, West Pittston.
Res.: 2435 State Rte. 92, Falls, 18615. In Res., Rev. James J. Alco (Retired).
Catechesis/Religious Program—Kathy Justave, D.R.E. Students 102.

HARLEIGH, LUZERNE CO., SACRED HEART OF JESUS (1903) Closed. For inquiries for parish records please see Queen of Heaven Parish, Hazleton.

HARVEYS LAKE, LUZERNE CO., OUR LADY OF VICTORY (1969), Linked with Gate of Heaven, Dallas. Rev. Daniel A. Toomey.
Res.: R.R. #1, Box 309, 18618. Tel: 570-639-1535; Fax: 570-639-1294. Email: olvhl309@aol.com.
Catechesis/Religious Program—Maureen Devine, D.R.E. Students 111.

HAWLEY, WAYNE CO., BLESSED VIRGIN MARY, QUEEN OF PEACE (1852) [CEM] Revs. Richard W. Beck; Joseph B. Pudota (India); Deacon Matthew G. Lorent.
Res.: 314 Chestnut Ave., 18428. Tel: 570-226-3183; Fax: 570-226-2126.
Catechesis/Religious Program—Tel: 570-226-2955. Marie Ribeiro, D.R.E. Students 245.
Mission—St. Veronica Lake Wallenpaupack, Pike Co.

HAZLETON, LUZERNE CO.

1—ANNUNCIATION, HAZLETON (1855) [CEM] Revs. Gregory T. Finn, O.S.J.; Johnson Kochuparambil, O.S.J.; Victor Leon, O.S.J.; Deacon Bernardino Velez.
Res.: 122 S. Wyoming St., 18201. Tel: 570-454-0212; Fax: 570-459-5187.
Catechesis/Religious Program—Students 299.
Worship Site: St. Gabriel—

2—CHURCH OF THE MOST PRECIOUS BLOOD (1885), (Italian), Rev. Louis A. Grippe; Deacon Louis Smolinsky.
Res.: 131 E. Fourth St., 18201. Tel: 570-454-8714; Fax: 570-454-8754.
Catechesis/Religious Program—Tel: 570-454-5916. Sr. Ursula Bower, D.R.E. Students 284.
Convent—221 E. Fourth St., 18201.

3—SS. CYRIL & METHODIUS, HAZLETON (1882), (Slovak), [CEM], Linked with St. Stanislaus, Hazleton. Rev. Michael J. Piccola; Deacon Leonard G. Kassick.
Res.: P.O. Box 2099, 18201. Tel: 570-454-0881; Fax: 570-454-1285.
Catechesis/Religious Program—Zelda Ondish, D.R.E. Students 73.
Mission—St. Ladislaus, Closed.

4—ST. GABRIEL, Merged Restructured with Our Lady of Mount Carmel, Hazelton, (now closed. Worship site of Annunciation, Hazelton.

5—HOLY ROSARY (1916), (Italian), Rev. Patrick J. Genello.
Res.: 240 S. Poplar St., 18201. Tel: 570-454-6693.
Catechesis/Religious Program—Christine LaMonica, D.R.E. Students 350.

6—HOLY TRINITY (1887), (German), [CEM 2] Closed. For inquiries for parish records contact the chancery.

7—HOLY TRINITY (1907), (Slovak), [CEM] Closed. Restructured with Our Lady of Mt. Carmel (Tyrolese), Hazleton. For inquiries for parish records please see SS. Cyril & Methodius, Hazleton.

8—ST. JOSEPH (1882), (Slovak), [CEM] Consolidated Restructured with St. Stanislaus, Hazleton. For inquiries for parish record please contact SS. Cyril & Methodius, Hazleton. Worship site for SS. Cyril & Methodius, Hazleton.

9—OUR LADY OF GRACE (1910), (Italian), [CEM] Closed. Worship site for Queen of Heaven, Hazelton. For inquiries for parish records please contact Queen of Heaven, Hazelton.

10—OUR LADY OF MOUNT CARMEL (1905), (Tyrolese), Closed. Merged with Holy Trinity (Slovak), Hazleton (now closed). For inquiries for parish records please see SS. Cyril & Methodius Parish, Hazleton.

11—SS. PETER AND PAUL (1887), (Lithuanian), Closed. For inquiries for parish records please see Holy Name of Jesus Parish, West Hazleton.

12—QUEEN OF HEAVEN, HAZLETON (1910), (Italian), [CEM], Restructured with Sacred Heart of Jesus, Harleigh; St. Mary, Lattimer & St. Nazarius, Pardeesville (all closed). Rev. Thomas A. Cappelloni; Deacon Robert A. Roman.
Res.: 750 N. Vine St., 18201. Tel: 570-454-8797; Fax: 570-454-1922.
Catechesis/Religious Program—Students 125.

13—ST. STANISLAUS (1893), (Polish), [CEM], Restructured with St. Joseph (Slovak), Hazleton. Consolidation - linked with SS. Cyril & Methodius, Hazleton. Rev. Michael J. Piccola.
Res.: 652 Carson St., 18201-4423. Tel: 570-454-0662; Fax: 570-454-0662.
Catechesis/Religious Program—Carol Baran, D.R.E. Students 31.

HONESDALE, WAYNE CO., ST. JOHN THE EVANGELIST (1842) [CEM 3], Restructured with St. Joseph, White Mills, closed. Revs. William J.P. Langan; Mariadas Bekala (India); Deacon Mark S. Jennings.
Office: 414 Church St., 18431. Tel: 570-253-4561; Fax: 570-253-1058.
Catechesis/Religious Program—Valeria Latona, D.R.E. Students 319.
Mission—St. Joseph, (additional worship site), Rileyville, Wayne Co.
Mission—St. Bernard, Beach Lake
Chapel—Honesdale, St. Mary Magdalene (1853), (additional worship site)

HUDSON, LUZERNE CO., ST. JOSEPH'S (1889), (Polish), [CEM] Closed. Merged with Sacred Heart, Plains & Restructured with SS Peter and Paul, Plains.

HUGHESTOWN, LUZERNE CO., BLESSED SACRAMENT (1945) Closed. Restructured with St. Mary, Help of Christians, Pittston. For inquiries for parish records please see Our Lady of the Eucharist Parish, Pittston.

INKERMAN, LUZERNE CO., ST. MARK (1900) Closed. For inquiries for parish records please contact St. Maria Goretti, Laflin.

JACKSON, SUSQUEHANNA CO., ST. MARTIN OF TOURS (1940), Linked with St. Lawrence, Great Bend & St. John the Evangelist, Susquehanna. Revs. David W. Cramer; Alfhones Perikala (India).
Mailing Address: 15 E. Church St., Susquehanna, 18847. Tel: 570-853-4634; Fax: 570-853-3356.
Catechesis/Religious Program—Charlene Kempa, D.R.E. Students 40.
Convent—Capuchin Sisters of Nazareth, 8175 State Rte. 492, 18825. Tel: 570-756-2205.
Mission—St. Paul Starrucca, Wayne Co.

JERMYN, LACKAWANNA CO.

1—SACRED HEART OF MARY (1889) [CEM] Consolidated Restructured with Sacred Heart of Jesus, Mayfield. For inquiries for parish records please contact Sacred Hearts of Jesus & Mary, Jermyn.

2—SACRED HEARTS OF JESUS & MARY, JERMYN (1889) [CEM], Restructured with Sacred Heart of Jesus, Mayfield. Rev. Msgr. Dale R. Rupert, Admin.; Deacon Patrick J. Massino.
Res.: 624 Madison Ave., 18433-1697. Tel: 570-876-1061; Fax: 570-876-2493. Email: sachmary@verizon.net.
Catechesis/Religious Program—Students 133.

JERSEY SHORE, LYCOMING CO., ST. LUKE (1902), (Restructured with Immaculate Conception of the Blessed Virgin Mary, Bastress). Rev. Bert S. Kozen.
Mailing Address: c/o Immaculate Conception, 5973 Jacks Hollow Rd., Williamsport, 17702.
Res.: 118 Kendall Ave., 17740. Tel: 570-745-3301; Fax: 570-745-3361.
Catechesis/Religious Program—Students 98.

JESSUP, LACKAWANNA CO.

1—ST. JAMES (1899) [CEM] Closed. Worship site of Queen of Angels Parish, Jessup.

2—ST. MARY'S ASSUMPTION (1904), (Italian), [CEM], Restructured with St. James, Jessup. Worship site for Queen of Angels Parish, Jessup., Mailing Address: c/o 605 Church St., 18434.
Res.: 516 Third Ave., 18434. Tel: 570-489-2252.
Catechesis/Religious Program—Angela Muchal, D.R.E. Students 166.

3—QUEEN OF ANGELS PARISH Rev. Gerard M. McGlone.
Res.: 605 Church St., 18434. Tel: 570-489-2252; Fax: 570-489-2527.
Catechesis/Religious Program—Mary Kay McHale, D.R.E. Students 268.
Worship Sites—
St. James, Jessup—
St. Mary's Assumption, Jessup—
St. Michael—322 First Ave., 18434.

KINGSTON, LUZERNE CO.

1—ST. HEDWIG (1901), (Polish), [CEM] Closed. For inquiries for parish records please see St. Ignatius Loyola, Kingston.

2—ST. IGNATIUS LOYOLA, KINGSTON (1885) [CEM] Consolidated with St. Mary's Annunciation, Kingston. Revs. John V. Polednak; Gregory W. Kelly; Gregory T. Villaescusa; Deacon John E. O'Connor.
Res.: 339 N. Maple Ave., 18704. Tel: 570-288-6446; Fax: 570-288-0463.
Catechesis/Religious Program—Carmella Faust, D.R.E. Students 272.
Chapel—St. Ann's, (additional worship site), Tel: 570-288-5919.

3—ST. MARY'S ANNUNCIATION (1902), (Lithuanian), Closed. For inquiries for parish records, please see St. Ignatius Loyola, Kingston.

LAFLIN, LUZERNE CO., ST. MARIA GORETTI (1967) Rev. Msgr. Neil J. Van Loon.
Res.: 42 Redwood Dr., 18702. Tel: 570-655-8956; Fax: 570-655-1746. Email: 42redwood@comcast.net.
Catechesis/Religious Program—Students 206.

LAKE ARIEL, WAYNE CO., ST. THOMAS MORE (1941) [CEM] Rev. Michael E. Finn.
Mailing Address: Box 188, 18436. Tel: 570-698-5584; Fax: 570-698-8468. Email: stthomasstmary@echoes.net.
Catechesis/Religious Program—Tel: 570-698-7150. Marian Menapace, D.R.E. Students 165.
Mission—St. Mary Ledgedale, Wayne Co.

LAKE SILKWORTH, LUZERNE CO., OUR LADY OF MOUNT CARMEL (1923) [CEM] Rev. Richard E. Fox.
Res.: 2011 State Rte. 29, Hunlock Creek, 18621-4303. Tel: 570-477-5040; Fax: 570-477-3040. Email: olmcpastoralcent@aol.com.
Catechesis/Religious Program—Elaine Herceg, D.R.E. Students 115.

LAKE WINOLA, WYOMING CO., ST. MARY OF THE LAKE (1986), Linked with Nativity B.V.M., Tunkhannock. Rev. Richard J. Polmounter; Deacon Raymond A. Pieretti.
Mailing Address: *c/o Nativity of Blessed Virgin Mary*, P.O. Box 186, Tunkhannock, 18657.
Res.: 99 E. Tioga St., Tunkhannock, 18657. Tel: 570-836-3275; Fax: 570-836-4268.
Catechesis/Religious Program—Genieve Sinker, D.R.E. Students 95.

LARKSVILLE, LUZERNE CO., ST. ANTHONY OF PADUA (1908) Closed. For inquiries for parish records please see St. John the Baptist, Plymouth.

LATTIMER, LUZERNE CO.

1—ST. MARY'S LATTIMER, (Italian), Closed. Merged with St. Nazarius, Pardeesville (now closed). Restructured with Our Lady of Grace, Hazleton & Sacred Heart of Jesus, Harleigh. For inquiries for parish records please contact Queen of Heaven (Hazelton).

2—QUEEN OF HEAVEN (HAZLETON) (1903), (Italian), Closed. For inquiries for parish records contact the chancery.

LITTLE MEADOWS, SUSQUEHANNA CO., ST. THOMAS THE APOSTLE (1887) Closed. For inquiries for parish records please see Saint Brigid Parish, Friendsville.

LORDS VALLEY, PIKE CO., ST. JOHN NEUMANN (1976), Linked with St. Ann, Shohola. Rev. Thomas J. Major; Deacons John Nash; Henry J. Ernst.
Res.: 705 Rte. 739, 18428. Tel: 570-775-6791; Fax: 570-775-1527.
Catechesis/Religious Program—Patricia Ohman, D.R.E. Students 50.
Mission—Good Shepherd Blooming Grove.

LUZERNE, LUZERNE CO.

1—ST. ANN'S (1924), (Lithuanian), Closed. For inquiries for parish records please see Holy Family, Luzerne.

2—HOLY FAMILY (1999) Rev. Michael J. Zipay; Deacon John B. Ziegler.
Res.: 574 Bennett St., 18709. Tel: 570-287-6600; Fax: 570-283-0706.
Catechesis/Religious Program—Diane Janoski, D.R.E. Students 246.

3—ST. JOHN NEPOMUCENE (1907), (Slovak), Closed. For inquiries for parish records please see Holy Family, Luzerne.

4—SACRED HEART CHURCH (1893), (German), Closed. For inquiries for parish records contact Holy Family, Luzerne.

MANSFIELD, TIOGA CO., HOLY CHILD (1953), (Restructured with St. John Neumann, Blossburg) Rev. Jacek J. Bialkowski.
Res.: 237 S. Main St., 16933. Tel: 570-662-3568; Fax: 570-662-2113. Email: holychild@ptd.net.
Catechesis/Religious Program—Students 83.
Mission—St. Mary, Closed., Center St., Tioga, Tioga Co. 16946.

MATAMORAS, PIKE CO., ST. JOSEPH (1892) Rev. August A. Ricciardi.
Res.: 309 Ave. F, 18336. Tel: 570-491-2618; Fax: 570-491-4404.
Catechesis/Religious Program—Cristin Cavallaro, D.R.E. Students 150.
Mission—Holy Family Cemetery Rd., Mill Rift, Pike Co. 18340.

MAYFIELD, LACKAWANNA CO., SACRED HEART OF JESUS (1904), (Polish), [CEM] Closed. For inquiries for parish records please see Sacred Hearts of Jesus & Mary, Jermyn.

MESHOPPEN, WYOMING CO., ST. JOACHIM (1873) [CEM], (Restructured with St. Mary's Assumption, Wyalusing) Rev. Joseph J. Manarchuck.
Mailing Address: *Our Lady of Perpetual Help Parish*, 245 State St., Wyalusing, 18853.
Res.: P.O. Box 67, 18630. Tel: 570-746-1006; Fax: 570-746-0389.
Catechesis/Religious Program—Valerie Trowbridge, D.R.E. Students 82.
Mission—St. Bonaventure [CEM], Closed.

MILDRED, SULLIVAN CO., ST. FRANCIS OF ASSISI (1894) Merged with St. Basil, Dushore, closed. For inquiries for parish records, contact Immaculate Heart of Mary, Dushore.
Catechesis/Religious Program—Students 82.
Mission—St. Francis of Assisi Eagles Mere, Sullivan Co.
Mission—Sacred Heart, Closed.

MILFORD, PIKE CO.

1—ST. PATRICK (1946) Unassigned.
Res.: 111 E. High St., P.O. Box W, 18337. Tel: 570-296-7451; Fax: 570-296-7451.
Catechesis/Religious Program—Students 168.

2—ST. VINCENT DE PAUL (1976) Rev. Paul M. Mullen; Deacons Joseph A. LaCorte; Donald F. O'Brien; Joseph A. D'Aiello; Brian Drury.
Res.: 101 St. Vincent Dr., 18337-9672. Tel: 570-686-4545; Fax: 800-565-1762. Email: stvoff@ptd.net.
Catechesis/Religious Program—Tel: 570-686-3493. Students 465.

MOCANAQUA, LUZERNE CO.

1—ASCENSION OF THE LORD, (Slovak), Closed. For Parish records & information see St. Mary, Our Lady of Perpetual Help., Mailing Address: c/o 150 Main St., 18655.

2—ST. MARY, OUR LADY OF PERPETUAL HELP (1904), (Polish), [CEM], Restructured with St. Martha, Fairmount Springs. Rev. Msgr. Anthony J. Generose; Rev. Thumma Savari. Worship site for Holy Spirit Parish, Mocanaqua.
Res.: 150 Main St., 18655. Tel: 570-542-4157; Fax: 570-542-4158.
Catechesis/Religious Program—Tel: 570-542-4878. Students 24.

MONTDALE, LACKAWANNA CO.

1—CORPUS CHRISTI (1942) Consolidated Linked with St. Pius, Royal. Worship site for St. John Vianney Parish, Montdale (Scott Twp.). For inquiries for parish records please contact St. John Vianney, Montdale.

2—ST. JOHN VIANNEY (1942), Linked with St. Pius, Royal - consolidated, now known as St. John Vianney Parish. Rev. Michael J. Kirwin; Deacon Edwin L. Salva Sr.
Res.: 704 Montdale Rd., Scott Twp., 18447. Tel: 570-254-9502; Fax: 570-254-6233.
Catechesis/Religious Program—Students 205.

MONTOURSVILLE, LYCOMING CO., OUR LADY OF LOURDES (1942) Rev. John K. Manno.
Res.: 800 Mulberry St., 17754. Tel: 570-368-8598; Fax: 570-368-2912.
Catechesis/Religious Program—Barbara Burchanowski, D.R.E. Students 156.

MONTROSE, SUSQUEHANNA CO., HOLY NAME OF MARY (1898) [CEM] Rev. Gerard F. Safko.
Res.: 278 S. Main St., 18801. Tel: 570-278-1504; Fax: 570-278-4751.
Catechesis/Religious Program—Francesca Calafut, D.R.E. Students 220.

MOSCOW, LACKAWANNA CO., ST. CATHERINE OF SIENA (1861) Rev. Robert J. Simon; Deacon John J. Franceschelli.
Res.: P.O. Box 250, 18444. Tel: 570-842-4561; Fax: 570-842-6648.
Catechesis/Religious Program—Tel: 570-848-2158. Students 356.

MOUNT POCONO, MONROE CO.

1—ST. MARY OF THE MOUNT (1909) Closed. Linked with St. Bernadette, Canadensis and St. Ann, Tobyhana. Now a worship site for Most Holy Trinity Parish, Mount Pocono.

2—MOST HOLY TRINITY PARISH Revs. Joseph R. Kopacz; Gregory F. Loughney.
Res.: 27 Fairview Ave., 18344. Tel: 570-839-7138; Fax: 570-839-7139.
Catechesis/Religious Program—Mary Lou Dumas, D.R.E. Students 173.

MOUNTAIN TOP, LUZERNE CO., ST. JUDE (1953), Linked with Our Lady Help of Christians, Dorrance. Revs. Joseph J. Evanko; Gerald W. Shantillo; Deacons Eugene J. Kovatch; James T. Atherton.
Res.: 420 S. Mountain Blvd., 18707. Tel: 570-474-6315; Fax: 570-474-0775.
Catechesis/Religious Program—Pamela Urbanski, Youth Min. Students 550.

MUNCY, LYCOMING CO., RESURRECTION (1941) Rev. Glenn E. McCreary.
Res.: 75 Musser Ln., 17756. Tel: 570-546-3900; Fax: 570-546-0322.
Catechesis/Religious Program—Jennifer Frye, D.R.E. Students 138.

NANTICOKE, LUZERNE CO.

1—SAINT FAUSTINA KOWALSKA PARISH (1894), (Polish), [CEM], Merged with St. Stanislaus & Holy Child, Nanticoke & Restructured with St. Mary of Czestochowa, Nanticoke. Rev. James R. Nash; Deacons Thaddeus Wadus; Florian G. Gyza.
Res.: 520 S. Hanover St., 18634-2799. Tel: 570-735-4833; Fax: 570-735-2281.
Catechesis/Religious Program—Students 159.

2—ST. FRANCIS OF ASSISI (1872) [CEM] Closed. For inquiries for parish records please see Saint Faustina Kowalska Parish, Nanticoke.

3—HOLY CHILD (1942), (Polish), Closed. For inquiries for parish records please see Saint Faustina Kowalska Parish, Nanticoke.

4—HOLY TRINITY (1894) See separate listing. See Saint Faustina Kowalska Parish, Nanticoke. Also worship site for Saint Faustina Kowalska Parish, Nanticoke.

5—ST. JOSEPH (1888) [CEM] Closed. For inquiries for parish records please see Saint Faustina Kowalska Parish, Nanticoke.

6—ST. MARY OF CZESTOCHOWA (1901), (Polish), [CEM], Restructured with Holy Trinity, Holy Child, St. Stanislaus, St. Joseph, St. Mary of Czestochowa, Nanticoke. Now part of St. Faustina Kowalska, Nanticoke. Rev. James R. Nash.
Mailing Address: *c/o Saint Faustina Kowalska Parish*, 520 S. Hanover St., 18634.
Res.: 1030 S. Hanover St., 18634.
Catechesis/Religious Program—Tel: 570-735-0313; Fax: 570-735-2123. Sr. Ursula Yerns, D.R.E. Students 17.

7—ST. STANISLAUS (1875), (Polish), [CEM] Closed. For inquiries for parish records see Saint Faustina Kowalska Parish, Nanticoke.

NICHOLSON, WYOMING CO., ST. PATRICK (1888) [CEM], Linked with Our Lady of the Abingtons, Dalton. Rev. Edward L. Michelini; Deacon Paul J. Brojack.
Res.: 205 Main St., P.O. Box 309, 18446. Tel: 570-942-6602; Fax: 570-942-5029.
Catechesis/Religious Program—Mary Smarkusky, D.R.E. Students 78.

OLD FORGE, LACKAWANNA CO.

1—ST. LAWRENCE O'TOOLE (1895) Closed. Worship site for Prince of Peace, Old Forge.

2—ST. MARY (1897), (Italian), Closed. Worship site for Prince of Peace Parish, Old Forge.

3—ST. MICHAEL (1905), (Polish), Closed. For inquiries for parish records please see Prince of Peace Parish, Old Forge.

4—PRINCE OF PEACE PARISH, OLD FORGE (1895) Revs. Louis T. Kaminski; Ronald J. Hughes.
Res.: 123 Grace St., 18518. Tel: 570-457-5900; Fax: 570-457-5896.
Catechesis/Religious Program—Students 200.

5—ST. STANISLAUS, Closed. For inquiries for parish records please see Prince of Peace Parish, Old Forge.

OLYPHANT, LACKAWANNA CO.

1—HOLY CROSS PARISH (1875) [CEM], Merged with Holy Ghost (Slovak), Olyphant and St. Michael the Archangel, Olyphant. Linked with Blessed Sacrament, Throop. Revs. James P. Dougher, Admin.; Nalazala Irudayaraj.
Res.: 200 Delaware Ave., 18447. Tel: 570-489-0752; Fax: 570-489-0225.
Catechesis/Religious Program—Total combined with St. Michael the Archangel & Holy Ghost, Tel: 570-489-2023. Michelle O'Brien, D.R.E. Students 220.

2—HOLY GHOST (1888), (Slovak), Closed. For inquiries for parish records see Holy Cross Parish, Olyphant.

3—ST. MICHAEL THE ARCHANGEL (1909), (Polish), [CEM] Closed. For inquiries for parish records see Holy Cross Parish, Olyphant.

4—ST. PATRICK (1875) Closed. For inquiries for parish records please see Holy Cross Parish, Olyphant. Also worship site for Holy Cross Parish.

PARDEESVILLE, LUZERNE CO., ST. NAZARIUS (1966), (Italian), Closed. For inquiries for parish records please see Queen of Heaven Parish, Hazleton.

PECKVILLE, LACKAWANNA CO., SACRED HEART OF JESUS (1946) Rev. Msgr. Peter P. Madus.
Res.: 1101 Willow St., 18452. Tel: 570-383-3244; Fax: 570-383-8697.
Catechesis/Religious Program—Tel: 570-383-2777. Gayle Castellani, D.R.E. Students 221.

PITTSTON, LUZERNE CO.

1—ST. CASIMIR'S (1890), (Lithuanian), Closed. For inquiries for parish records please see St. John the Evangelist, Pittston.

2—ST. JOHN THE BAPTIST (1892), (Slovak), [CEM 2] Closed. For inquiries for parish records please see St. John the Evangelist, Pittston.

3—ST. JOHN THE EVANGELIST (1854) [CEM], Merged with St. Casimir and St. Joseph, Pittston (all closed). Restructured with St. John the Baptist, Pittston (now closed). Rev. Msgr. John J. Bendik; Rev. Richard J. Cirba; Deacons James G. Corteggerone; David E. Marx. In Res., Rev. Hugh H. McGroarty.
Res.: 35 William St., 18640. Tel: 570-654-0053; Fax: 570-654-3751. Email: angelsofsje@aol.com. Web: www.parishcommunity.com.
Catechesis/Religious Program—Mary Catherine Petroziello, D.R.E. Students 190.

4—ST. JOSEPH (1909), (Polish), Closed. For inquiries for parish records please see St. John the Evangelist, Pittston.

5—ST. JOSEPH MARELLO PARISH Rev. Joseph D. Sibilano, O.S.J., Admin.
237 William St., 18640. Tel: 570-654-6902.

6—ST. MARY'S ASSUMPTION (1863), (German), Closed. For inquiries for parish records please see Our Lday of the Eucharist Parish, Pittston.

7—ST. MARY, HELP OF CHRISTIANS (1851) [CEM] Closed. Worship site of Our Lady of the Eucharist Parish, Pittston.

8—OUR LADY OF MT. CARMEL (1904), (Italian), [CEM], Linked with St. Rocco, Pittston and part of St. Joseph Marello Parish, Pittston. Parish worship site of St. Joseph Marello Parish.

9—OUR LADY OF THE EUCHARIST PARISH Rev. Thomas J. Maloney.
Res.: 535 N. Main St., 18640. Tel: 570-654-0263; Fax: 570-654-0195.
Catechesis/Religious Program—Students 66.

10—ST. ROCCO (1919), (Italian), [CEM], Linked with Our Lady of Mt. Carmel, Pittston. Worship site for St. Joseph Marello Parish, Pittston.

PLAINS, LUZERNE CO.

1—SS. PETER AND PAUL (1898), (Polish), [CEM] Consolidated Revs. Joseph A. Greskiewicz; John T. Albosta.
Res.: 13 Hudson Rd., 18705. Tel: 570-825-6663; Fax: 570-823-4556.
Catechesis/Religious Program—Sandra Holena, D.R.E. Students 146.

2—SACRED HEART (1883) Closed. Merged with St. Joseph's, Hudson & Restructured with SS. Peter and Paul, Plains.

PLEASANT MOUNT, WAYNE CO.

1—ST. JAMES (1887), For inquiries for parish records please see St. Katharine Drexel, Pleasant Mount. Worship site for St. Katharine Drexel, Pleasant Mount.

2—ST. KATHARINE DREXEL PARISH (1887), Restructured with Sacred Heart of Jesus, St. Joseph, Forest City & St. Juliana, Rock Lake. Linked with Ascension Parish, Forest City. Rev. Patrick L. Albert.
P.O. Box 53, 18453.
Office: *c/o Sacred Heart Rectory*, 612 Hudson St., Forest City, 18421.
Catechesis/Religious Program—Students 4.
Mission—St. Cecilia, Closed.
Mission—Assumption of the B.V.M., Closed.

PLYMOUTH, LUZERNE CO.

1—ALL SAINTS (1885) [CEM 3], Merged with St Vincent de Paul, Plymouth. Rev. Robert J. Kelleher; Deacon Joseph F. DeVizia. In Res., Rev. Msgr. Joseph P. Kelly.
Office: 66 Willow St., 18651. Tel: 570-779-5323; Fax: 570-779-4921.
Catechesis/Religious Program—Helen Cebula, D.R.E. Students 305.

2—ST. JOHN THE BAPTIST (1899), (Polish), Merged with St. Anthony of Padua, Larksville and SS. Cyril and Methodius, Edwardsville. Rev. Gerald J. Gurka.

3—ST. STEPHEN (1886), (Slovak), Closed. For Parish records see All Saints, Plymouth.

4—ST. VINCENT DE PAUL (1872) [CEM] Closed. For Parish records see All Saints, Plymouth.

POCONO PINES, MONROE CO.

1—ST. MAXIMILIAN KOLBE (1985) Merged with Christ the King, Blakeslee (closed) and consolidated to become St. Maximilian Kolbe Parish. Rev. John B. Boyle; Deacon Frank Gisoldi.
Res.: 5112 Pocono Crest Rd., P.O. Box O, 18350. Tel: 570-646-6424; Fax: 570-646-1047.
Catechesis/Religious Program—Lynnette Smith, D.R.E. Students 134.

2—OUR LADY OF THE LAKE (1985) Merged with Christ the King, Blakeslee, closed. For inquiries for parish records please contact St. Maximilian Kolbe, Pocono Pines. Worship site for St. Maximilian Kolbe Parish, Pocono Pines.

ROCK LAKE, WAYNE CO., ST. JULIANA (1838) Merged with St. Katharine Drexel, Pleasant Mount & restructured with Sacred Heart, & St. Joseph, Forest City. For inquiries for parish records, see St. Katharine Drexel, Pleasant Mount.

ROYAL, SUSQUEHANNA CO., ST. PIUS X (1967), Linked with Corpus Christi, Montdale. Consolidated, now known as St. John Vianney Parish. Rev. Michael J.

Kirwin; Deacon Edwin L. Salva Sr.
Res.: Rte. 106, Clifford, 18413.
Office: *c/o St. John Vianney Parish*, 704 Montdale Rd., Scott Twp., 18447. Tel: 570-254-9502; Fax: 570-254-6233.
Catechesis/Religious Program—Students 64.

SAYRE, BRADFORD CO., EPIPHANY PARISH (1888), Restructured with St. Ann, Bentley Creek (closed). Linked with St. John, South Waverly (closed) & St. Joseph, Athens (closed). Revs. Andrew S. Hvozdovic; Bryan B. Wright.
Res.: 304 S. Elmer Ave., 18840. Tel: 570-888-9641; Fax: 570-888-2608.
Catechesis/Religious Program—Students 147.

SHAVERTOWN, LUZERNE CO., ST. THERESE (1926) Rev. James J. Paisley.
Res.: 64 Davis St., 18708. Tel: 570-696-1144; Fax: 570-696-1210.
Catechesis/Religious Program—Denise Murphy, D.R.E. Students 576.

SHOHOLA, PIKE CO., ST. ANN'S (1928) [CEM], Linked with St. John Neumann, Lords Valley. Rev. Thomas J. Major; Deacon Glenn J. Biagi.
Mailing Address: 125 Richardson Ave., 18458.
Res.: 123 Richardson Ave., 18458. Tel: 570-832-4275.
Catechesis/Religious Program—Mary Bajda, D.R.E. Students 89.
Mission—St. Mary of the Assumption Lackawaxen, Pike Co.
Mission—Sacred Heart of Jesus Greeley, Pike Co.

SIMPSON, LACKAWANNA CO., ST. MICHAEL (1903) [CEM] Consolidated with St. Rose of Lima Parish, Carbondale., 6 N. Church St., Carbondale, 18407.
Res.: 46 Midland St., 18407.

SOUTH WAVERLY, BRADFORD CO., ST. JOHN THE EVANGELIST (1902) Closed. For inquiries for parish records please see Epiphany Parish, Sayre.

SOUTH WILLIAMSPORT, LYCOMING CO., ST. LAWRENCE (1931), linked with St. Boniface, Williamsport. Rev. Msgr. Stephen D. McGough.
Parish Office: 326 Washington Blvd., Williamsport, 17701. Tel: 570-326-1544; Fax: 570-326-6746.
Res.: 821 W. Central Ave., Williamsport, 17702.
Catechesis/Religious Program—Students 171.

STROUDSBURG, MONROE CO., ST. LUKE (1968) Revs. Thomas D. McLaughlin; Carmen J. Perry; Deacon Thomas W. Hogan Jr.
Office: 818 Main St., 18360. Tel: 570-421-9097; 570-421-9863; Fax: 570-421-6015.
Res.: 906 Main St., 18360. Tel: 570-421-8479; Fax: 570-421-6015.
Catechesis/Religious Program—Scott Fabian, D.R.E. Students 503.

SUGAR NOTCH, LUZERNE CO.
1—HOLY FAMILY PARISH (1901) [CEM], Consolidation. Rev. Joseph R. Kakareka.
Office: 828 Main St., 18706. Tel: 570-822-8983; Fax: 570-822-6016.
Catechesis/Religious Program—Mary Anne Malone, D.R.E. Students 80.
2—SS. PETER AND PAUL CHAPEL (1847), (Lithuanian), Closed. For inquiries for parish records please see Holy Family Parish, Sugar Notch.

SUSQUEHANNA, SUSQUEHANNA CO., ST. JOHN THE EVANGELIST (1847) [CEM], Linked with St. Lawrence, Great Bend & St. Martin of Tours, Jackson. Revs. David W. Cramer; Alfhones Perikala (India).
Res.: 15 E. Church St., 18847. Tel: 570-853-4634; Fax: 570-853-3356.
Catechesis/Religious Program—Victoria Mulligan, D.R.E. Students 100.

SWOYERSVILLE, LUZERNE CO.
1—HOLY NAME OF JESUS (1905) Merged with St. Mary of Czestochowa, Swoyersville.
2—HOLY NAME/ST. MARY'S, [CEM], Linked with Holy Trinity, Swoyersville. Revs. Joseph J. Pisaneschi; Edward P. Lyman; Deacon George Mochin Jr.
Mailing Address: *c/o Holy Trinity*, 116 Hughes St., 18704.
Office: 283 Shoemaker St., 18704. Tel: 570-287-2139; Fax: 570-287-6474.
Catechesis/Religious Program—Students 78.
3—HOLY TRINITY (1895), (Slovak), [CEM], Linked with Holy Name/St. Mary, Swoyersville. Revs. Joseph J. Pisaneschi; Edward P. Lyman; Deacon George Mochin Jr.
Res.: 116 Hughes St., 18704. Tel: 570-287-6624; Fax: 570-287-4704.
Catechesis/Religious Program—Margaret Semanek, D.R.E. Students 102.
4—ST. MARY OF CZESTOCHOWA (1909) Merged with Holy Name of Jesus, Swoyersville.

TANNERSVILLE, MONROE CO., OUR LADY OF VICTORY (1968) Rev. Richard E. Czachor; Deacon Ralph E. Weichand.
Res.: Cherry Lane Rd., P.O. Box 195, 18372. Tel: 570-629-4572; Fax: 570-629-5325.
Catechesis/Religious Program—Students 385.

TAYLOR, LACKAWANNA CO.
1—IMMACULATE CONCEPTION (1898) Closed. Now part of Divine Mercy Parish, Scranton., 312 Davis St., 18505.
2—ST. JOHN THE BAPTIST (1904), (Slovak), Closed. Now part of Divine Mercy Parish, Scranton., 312 Davis St., 18505.

THROOP, LACKAWANNA CO.
1—ST. ANTHONY, Consolidated Now a part of Blessed Sacrament Parish, Throop. Linked with Holy Cross, Olyphant. Worship site for Blessed Sacrament Parish, Throop.
2—BLESSED SACRAMENT PARISH (1911), (Polish), [CEM], Merged with St. Bridget's and St. John the Baptist, Throop. Linked with Holy Cross, Olyphant. Revs. James P. Dougher; Nalazala Irudayaraj.
Church & Office: 215 Rebecca St., 18519. Tel: 570-489-1963; Fax: 570-489-3291.
Catechesis/Religious Program—Students 84.
3—ST. BRIDGET'S (1916) Closed. For inquiries for parish records please see Blessed Sacrament Parish, Throop.
4—ST. JOHN THE BAPTIST (1905), (Slovak), [CEM] Closed. For inquiries for parish records please contact Blessed Sacrament Parish, Throop.

TOBYHANNA, MONROE CO., ST. ANN (1923) [CEM 2], Linked with St. Mary of the Mount, Mount Pocono & St. Bernadette, Canadensis. Worship site for Most Holy Trinity Parish, Mount Pocono. Revs. Joseph R. Kopacz; Gregory F. Loughney.
Mailing Address: 27 Fairview Ave., Mount Pocono, 18344. In Res., Rev. Albert Bellantonio, Coord. Hispanic Ministry, Monroe Co.
Res.: Main St., P.O. Box 188, 18466-0188. Tel: 570-839-7138; Fax: 570-839-7708.
Catechesis/Religious Program—Students 674.

TOWANDA, BRADFORD CO., SS. PETER AND PAUL (1841) [CEM 3] Rev. Thomas J. Petro.
Res.: 106 Third St., 18848. Tel: 570-265-2113; Fax: 570-265-2114.
Catechesis/Religious Program—Anne Leone, D.R.E. Students 36.
Mission—Immaculate Conception, Closed.

TUNKHANNOCK, WYOMING CO., NATIVITY OF BLESSED VIRGIN MARY (1884) [CEM 2], Linked with St. Mary of the Lake, Lake Winola. Rev. Richard J. Polmounter; Deacon Raymond A. Pieretti.
Res.: 99 E. Tioga St., P.O. Box 186, 18657-0186. Tel: 570-836-3275; Fax: 570-836-4268.
Catechesis/Religious Program—Judy Boyanowski, D.R.E. Students 230.

WAYMART, WAYNE CO., ST. MARY (1915) [CEM] Rev. Joseph S. Sitko.
Res.: P.O. Box 160, 18472. Tel: 570-488-6440; Fax: 570-488-7440.
Catechesis/Religious Program—Carol Opalka, D.R.E. Students 100.
Mission—St. Patrick, Closed.

WELLSBORO, TIOGA CO., ST. PETER'S (1879) [CEM 2] Rev. John J. Chmil.
Res.: 38 Central Ave., 16901. Tel: 570-724-3371; Fax: 570-724-6322.
Catechesis/Religious Program—Patti Mitchell, D.R.E. Students 186.
Mission—Sacred Heart, Closed.

WEST HAZLETON, LUZERNE CO.
1—ST. FRANCIS OF ASSISI (1940) Closed. For inquiries for parish records please see Holy Name of Jesus Parish, West Hazleton.
2—HOLY NAME OF JESUS PARISH Rev. Peter J. O'Rourke. In Res., Rev. Msgr. Arthur J. Kaschenbach (Retired).
Res.: 213 W. Green St., 18202. Tel: 570-454-3933; Fax: 570-454-8326.
Catechesis/Religious Program—Susan Houseknecht, D.R.E. Students 85.
3—TRANSFIGURATION (1907), (Polish), [CEM] Closed. For inquiries for parish records please see Holy Name of Jesus Parish, West Hazleton. Worship site for Holy Name of Jesus Parish, West Hezleton.

WEST PITTSTON, LUZERNE CO.
1—CORPUS CHRISTI PARISH (1910), Linked with Holy Redeemer, Harding-Falls. Rev. Msgr. John J. Sempa; Rev. Arbogaste Satoun; Joyce Cecconi, Pastoral Assoc.; Deacon Peter J. Hoegen.
Res.: 605 Luzerne Ave., 18643. Tel: 570-654-2753; Fax: 570-654-9244.
Catechesis/Religious Program—Students 124.
2—IMMACULATE CONCEPTION (1910) Closed. For inquiries for parish records please see Corpus Christi Parish, West Pittston. Worship site for Corpus Christi Parish, West Pittston.

WEST WYOMING, LUZERNE CO.
1—SAINT MONICA PARISH (1953) Rev. Leo J. McKernan; Deacon William G. Jenkins.
Res.: 363 W. 8th St., 18644. Tel: 570-693-1991; Fax: 570-693-1399.
Catechesis/Religious Program—Students 132.
2—OUR LADY OF SORROWS (1953) Closed. For inquiries for parish records please see Saint Monica Parish, West Wyoming. Worship site for Saint Monica Parish, West Wyoming.

WESTON, LUZERNE CO., SACRED HEART (1888) [CEM] Rev. Patrick D. McDowell.
Res.: 554 Main St., P.O. Box A, 18256. Tel: 570-384-4121; Fax: 570-384-3976.
Catechesis/Religious Program—Students 85.

WHITE HAVEN, LUZERNE CO., ST. PATRICK (1874) [CEM] Rev. John F. McHale.
Office: 411 Allegheny St., 18661.
Res.: 521 Northumberland St., 18661. Tel: 570-443-9944; Fax: 570-443-9777.
Catechesis/Religious Program—Linda Kistler, D.R.E. Students 125.
Station—White Haven Center, Tel: 570-453-9564.

WHITE MILLS, WAYNE CO., ST. JOSEPH (1968) Closed. For inquiries for parish records please contact St. John the Evangelist, Honesdale.

WILKES-BARRE, LUZERNE CO.
1—ST. ALOYSISUS (1899) Closed. For inquiries for parish records please contact St. Robert Bellarmine, Wilkes-Barre. Worship site for St. Robert Bellarmine, Wilkes-Barre.
2—ST. ANDRE BESSETTE PARISH Revs. Kenneth M. Seegar; Michael J. Kloton.
Office: 666 N. Main St., 18705. Tel: 570-823-4988; Fax: 570-823-5932.
Res.: 54 Hillard St., Wilkes Barre, 18702. Tel: 570-822-1186; Fax: 570-822-1074.
Catechesis/Religious Program—Joyce Cecconi, D.R.E. Students 22.
3—ST. ANDREW PARISH (1920), Linked with St. Boniface, Wilkes-Barre (now closed). Rev. James E. McGahagan; Deacon Francis J. Bradigan. In Res., Rev. James J. Walsh.
Res.: 316 Parrish St., 18702. Tel: 570-823-1948; Fax: 570-823-3177.
Catechesis/Religious Program—Marian Fadden, D.R.E. Students 45.
4—ST. BENEDICT PARISH (1882) Rev. Joseph A. Kearney.
Res.: 155 Austin Ave., 18705. Tel: 570-822-8871; Fax: 570-823-7866.
Catechesis/Religious Program—Cathy Riccetti, D.R.E. Students 140.
5—BLESSED SACRAMENT (1917) [CEM] Closed. For inquiries for parish records please see St. Benedict Parish, Wilkes-Barre.
6—ST. BONIFACE (1896), (German), Closed. For inquiries for parish records please contact St. Andrew Parish, Wilkes-Barre.
7—ST. CASIMIR (1889), (Lithuanian), [CEM] Closed. For inquiries for parish records please coantact St. Robert Bellarmine Parish, Wilkes-Barre.
8—ST. DOMINIC (1882) Closed. For inquiries for parish records please contact St. Benedict Parish, Wilkes Barre. Worship site for St. Benedict Parish, Wilkes-Barre.
9—ST. FRANCIS OF ASSISI (1913), (Lithuanian), Closed. For inquiries for parish records please contact St. Benedict Parish, Wilkes-Barre.
10—HOLY ROSARY (1906), (Italian), Closed. For inquiries for parish records please see St. Andrew Parish, Wilkes-Barre.
11—HOLY SAVIOUR (1895) Closed. For inquiries for parish records please contact St. Andre Bessette Parish, Wilkes-Barre. Worship site for St. Andre Bessette Parish, Wilkes-Barre.
12—HOLY TRINITY (1893), (Lithuanian), [CEM 2] Closed. For inquiries for parish records please see Our Lady of Hope Parish, Wilkes-Barre.
13—ST. JOHN THE BAPTIST (1924), (Slovak), Closed. For inquiries for parish records see St. Benedict, Wilkes Barre.
14—ST. JOHN THE EVANGELIST (1927) Merged with Sacred Heart of Jesus, Wilkes-Barre.
15—ST. JOSEPH (Georgetown) (1898) Closed. For inquiries for parish records please see Our Lady of Hope Parish, Wilkes-Barre.
16—ST. JOSEPH (1927), (Slovak), Closed. For inquiries for parish records please contact Our Lady of Fatima Parish, Wilkes-Barre.
17—ST. MARY OF THE IMMACULATE CONCEPTION (1845) [CEM] Closed. For inquiries for parish records please contact Our Lady of Fatima Parish, Wilkes-Barre. Worship site for Our Lady of Fatima Parish, Wilkes-Barre.
18—ST. MARY OF THE IMMACULATE CONCEPTION-ST. JOSEPH PARISH (1845) [CEM] Closed. For inquiries for parish records please contact Our Lady of Fatima Parish, Wilkes-Barre.
19—MATERNITY OF THE BLESSED VIRGIN MARY (1885), (Polish), [CEM 2] Closed. For inquiries for parish records please contact Our Lady of Hope Parish, Wilkes-Barre. Worship site for Our Lady of Hope Parish, Wilkes-Barre.
20—ST. NICHOLAS (1856), (German), [CEM 2] Rev. Msgr. Joseph G. Rauscher; Revs. John J. Victoria; Fidel Ticona, C.S.C.
Res.: 226 S. Washington St., 18701-2897. Tel: 570-823-7736; Fax: 570-823-0256.
Catechesis/Religious Program—Mr. James McDermott, D.R.E. Students 562.
21—OUR LADY OF FATIMA PARISH Rev. Msgr. Thomas V. Banick; Deacon Leo R. Thompson.

Catechesis / Religious Program—Sr. Dolores M. Banick, I.H.M., D.R.E. Students 94.
Res.: 134 S. Washington St., P.O. Box 348, 18703-0348. Tel: 570-823-4168; Fax: 570-822-3477.
22—OUR LADY OF HOPE PARISH (1885), (Polish), [CEM 2], Linked with St. Joseph, Wilkes-Barre Township, now closed. Rev. John S. Terry. In Res., Rev. Richard G. Ghezzi.
Res.: 40 Park Ave., 18702. Tel: 570-824-7832; Fax: 570-822-0765.
Catechesis / Religious Program—Frances Jacobs, D.R.E. Students 45.
23—ST. PATRICK (1920) Closed. For inquiries for parish records please contact St. Andrew, Wilkes-Barre. Worship site for St. Andrew Parish, Wilkes-Barre.
24—ST. ROBERT BELLARMINE PARISH (1899), Linked with Exaltation of the Holy Cross, Hanover Twp. Revs. Kevin P. Mulhern; Joseph K. Polanki (India); Deacon Raymond J. Lenahan.
Res.: 143 W. Division St., 18706. Tel: 570-823-3791; Fax: 570-826-0233.
Catechesis / Religious Program—Lynn Sklanny, D.R.E. Students 204.
25—SACRED HEART-ST. JOHN (1896) [CEM] Closed. For inquiries for parish records please contact St. Andre Bessette Parish, Wilkes-Barre.
26—ST. STANISLAUS KOSTKA (1908), (Polish), [CEM] Closed. Worship site for St. Andre Bessette4 Parish, Wilkes-Barre.
27—ST. THERESE (1929) Closed. For inquiries for parish records please contact Our Lady of Fatima Parish, Wilkes-Barre.

WILLIAMSPORT, LYCOMING CO.
1—ST. ANN (1959) Rev. Paul C. Fontanella; Deacon Stephen Frye.
Res.: 1220 Northway Rd., 17701. Tel: 570-322-5935; Fax: 570-322-2451.
Catechesis / Religious Program—Marianne DePasqua, D.R.E. Students 150.
Mission—Assumption of the B.V.M. Cascade, Lycoming Co.
2—ANNUNCIATION, Closed. Worship site for St. Joseph the Worker Parish, Williamsport.
3—ASCENSION (1907), Worship site for St. Joseph the Worker Parish, Williamsport., 2111 Linn St., 17701. Tel: 570-323-9456.
4—ST. BONIFACE (1853), (German), Linked with St. Lawrence, South Williamsport. Rev. Msgr. Stephen D. McGough.
Res.: 326 Washington Blvd., 17701. Tel: 570-326-1544; Fax: 570-326-6746.
5—HOLY ROSARY (1915), (Polish), Closed. For inquiries for parish records please contact St. Joseph the Worker, Williamsport.
6—ST. JOSEPH THE WORKER (1865) [CEM] Revs. Shane L. Kirby; David W. Bechtel; Deacon J. Morris Smith.
Office: 711 W. Edwin St., 17701. Tel: 570-323-9456; Fax: 570-323-3728.
Rectory—635 Hepburn St., 17701.
Catechesis / Religious Program—Tel: 570-323-3799. James Foran, D.R.E. Students 477.
7—MATER DOLOROSA (1908), (Italian), Closed. Worship site for St. Joseph the Worker Parish, Williamsport.

WYALUSING, BRADFORD CO.
1—ST. MARY OF THE ASSUMPTION (1950), Linked with St. Joachim, Meshoppen. Worship site for Our Lady of Perpetual Help.
2—OUR LADY OF PERPETUAL HELP PARISH Rev. Joseph J. Manarchuck.
Office & Mailing Address: 245 State St., 18853. Tel: 570-746-1006; 570-746-0389; Fax: 570-746-1852.
Catechesis / Religious Program—Cathy Hagadon, D.R.E. Students 46.
Mission—St. Anthony, Closed.

WYOMING, LUZERNE CO.
1—ST. JOSEPH'S (1914), (Polish), [CEM] Closed. For inquiries for parish records please contact Saint Monica Parish, West Wyoming. Also worship site for Saint Monica Parish, West Wyoming.

Chaplains of Public Institutions

DALLAS. *State Correctional Institution* 18612. Tel: 570-675-1101. Deacon Steve Napoli.

EAST STROUDSBURG. *East Stroudsburg State University*, 200 Prospect St., 18301. Tel: 570-422-3525; Fax: 570-422-3410. Vacant, Dir.

LA PLUME. *Keystone College*. Rev. Msgr. James J. McGarry.
Clarks Summit. Tel: 570-586-1741.

MUNCY. *Muncy Prison*, Tel: 570-546-3900. Rev. Glenn E. McCreary, V.E., Chap.
Rectory—Resurrection, 75 Musser Lane, 17756.

WILKES-BARRE. *Geisinger Wyoming Valley Hospital*, Tel: 570-822-9561. Rev. Joseph A. Kearney.
Rectory—St. Benedict, 155 Austin Ave., 18705.

WILLIAMSPORT. *Lycoming College*, 700 College Pl., Box 149, 17701. Tel: 570-321-4111. Sr. Catherine Ann Gilvary, I.H.M., Campus Min.

On Special or Other Diocesan Assignment:
Rev. Msgr.—
Grimalia, Vincent J., Chap., St Luke's Villa, 80 East Northampton St., Wilkes Barre, 18701. Tel: 570-826-1031
Revs.—
Bergman, Eric L., Chap., St. Thomas More Society of St. Clare Church, c/o 2301 N. Washington Ave., 18509. Tel: 570-343-0634
Elston, Joseph G., Chap. Ministry for the Deaf, 909 Grove St., Avoca, 18641.
Finn, Edward S. (Retired), 421 Layton Rd., Equinunk, 18417. Tel: 570-224-4380
Yaszcz, Thomas A., Chap., 52 W. Grove St., Nanticoke, 18634. Tel: 570-735-5447

On Duty Outside the Diocese:
Rev. Msgrs.—
Quinn, Joseph G., J.D., J.C.L., Vice Pres. Univ. Misson & Min., Fordham University, 441 E. Fordham Rd., Bronx, NY 10458. Tel: 718-817-3012
Rossi, Walter R., Rector, Basilica of the National Shrine of the Immaculate Conception, 400 Michigan Ave., N.E., Washington, DC 20017. Tel: 202-526-8300
Revs.—
Comellas, Wilfredo T., Chapel of the Blessed Sacrament, P.O. Box 587, Gibson, LA 70356.
Connor, Charles P., Mount St. Mary's Seminary, 16300 Old Emmitsburg Rd., Emmitsburg, MD 21727.
Doherty, Daniel J., S.S., Society of St. Sulpice, St. Mary's Seminary & University, 5400 Roland Ave., Baltimore, MD 21210. Tel: 410-864-4005
Gabuzda, Richard J. (OM), Dir., Institute for Priestly Formation, 302 N. 22nd St., #802, Omaha, NE 68178. Tel: 402-546-6384
Gregoris, Nicholas L., 333 Pearl St., Apt. 15F, New York, NY 10038.
Loch, Killian (Kev), O.S.B., Saint Vincent Archabbey, 300 Fraser Purchase Rd., Latrobe, 15650.
Melnick, John E., Society of St. Augustine, c/o St. Mary-St. Anthony Parish, 615 N. 7th St., Kansas City, KS 66101. Tel: 913-371-1408
Munkelt, Richard A., St. Anthony of Padua Church, 1360 Pleasant Valley Way, West Orange, NJ 07052. Tel: 201-319-1765
O'Connor, Dominic E., 27 Cavendish Rd. E. - The Park, Nottingham N67-1BB England.
Pilon, Jean-Pierre G., The Watergate, 1534 Pioneer, Sudbury ON P3G 1A8 Canada. Tel: 705-523-1437
Reichlen, Gregory A., Casa Santa Maria, Via dell Umilta, 30, Rome 00187 Italy.
Sarnecki, Thomas G., Bay Pines Vet's Hospital, 10036 63rd Ave. N. Bldg. 5, Unit 18, Saint Petersburg, FL 33708. Tel: 727-946-0875
Terrera, C. Bernardo, Chapelle St. Augustin, Avenue de Bethusy 78, Lausanne 1012 Switzerland.
Walsh, John A., P.O. Box 1665, Minneola, FL 34755. Tel: 407-438-0990
Washington, Christopher T., S.T.L., Secretariat of State of The Holy See, Villa Stritch, Via Della Nocetta 63, Rome 00164 Italy. Tel: 011-39-06-66135336

Military Chaplains:
Revs.—
Dormer, David J., Chap. Major, U.S. Army, P.O. Box 4554, Fort Eustis, VA 23604. Tel: 570-441-7496
Fullerton, Daniel, Chap., USN, c/o 201 Woods Ln., Erin, NY 14838.
Hochreiter, Robert S., Chap., Col., U.S.A.F., 2270 White House Cove, Newport News, VA 23602. Tel: 757-874-8602
Kelly, Brian F., Chap., Cap., U.S.N., 7183 Willett Cir., Carlsbad, CA 92011. Tel: 858-577-1333
Petruska, William M., Cap., U.S.N., 4421 Collwood Ln., San Diego, CA 92115-2015. Tel: 619-795-8485

Unassigned or Leave of Absence:
Revs.—
Alco, James J. (Retired)
Balczeniuk, Mark G.
Betts, David R.
Clay, Christopher R.
Ensey, Eric S.
Gibson, Robert J.
Harris, Michael B.
Hawley, Gerard L.
Honhart, Mark A.
Hudak, Thomas R.
Kilpatrick, Andrew W.
Kulik, Francis J.
Kurash, Stanley J.
Kurovsky, Andrew
Kutch, Joseph P.
Leonard, Albert P.
Marchetti, Michael H.
Paulish, W. Jeffrey
Roberts, Marshall M.
Shoback, Thomas P.
Sinnott, Thomas G.
Sokolowski, Thomas J. (Retired)
Tetherow, Gabriel Francis
Timchak, Robert M.
Wysocki, Joseph A.
Young, Vincent J.
Ziebacz, Wieslaw M.

Retired:
Most Revs.—
Dougherty, John M., D.D., Christ the King Parish, 429 Church St., Archbald, 18403. Tel: 570-876-3331 Auxiliary Bishop Emeritus of Scranton
Martino, Joseph F., D.D., Hist. E.D., Regina Coeli Res. For Priest, 685 YOrk Rd., Warminster, 18974. Tel: 267-608-8557 Bishop Emeritus of Scranton
Timlin, James C., D.D., Villa St. Joseph, 1600 Green Ridge St., 18509. Tel: 570-343-6170 Bishop Emeritus of Scranton
Rev. Msgrs.—
Beeda, Francis J., Little Flower Manor, 200 S. Meade St., Rm. 204, Wilkes Barre, 18702. Tel: 570-822-3554
Clarke, James T., St. Therese Residence, 260 S. Meade St., Wilkes Barre, 18702. Tel: 570-823-6131
Conlan, F. Allan, Ph.D., 1101 Tennyson Close, Moosic, 18507. Tel: 570-344-1396
Demuth, George R., Holy Family Pavilion, 2510 Adams Ave., Apt. 303, 18509-1597. Tel: 570-344-3719
Esseff, John A., Villa St. Joseph, 1600 Green Ridge St., Dunmore, 18509. Tel: 570-941-0986
Gajewski, Chester A., Villa St. Joseph, Dunmore, 18509. Tel: 570-347-1851
Gray, Philip A., Villa St. Joseph, 1600 Green Ridge St., Dunmore, 18509. Tel: 570-344-0897
Kulik, Alexander T., Villa St. Joseph, 1600 Green Ridge St., 18509. Tel: 570-341-8881
Louis, John H., S.T.L., J.C.D., Villa St. Joseph, 1600 Green Ridge St., Dunmore, 18509. Tel: 570-207-2961
McAndrews, Donald A., Villa St. Joseph, 1600 Green Ridge St., 18509. Tel: 570-207-5586
Penkala, Edmund S., Villa St. Joseph, Dunmore, 18509. Tel: 570-344-6288
Piorkowski, Stanley W., Villa St. Joseph, Dunmore, 18509. Tel: 570-343-1184
Purcell, Paul J., Green Ridge Healthcare Ctr., 2741 Boulevard Ave., 18509. Tel: 570-963-9453
Siconolfi, Constantine V., 207 Karen Dr., 18505. Tel: 570-343-1001
Ward, William P., Villa St. Joseph, 1600 Green Ridge St., Dunmore, 18509. Tel: 570-341-1558
Yarrish, Bernard E., S.T.L., St. Therese Residence, 260 S. Meade St., Wilkes-Barre, 18702. Tel: 570-208-5371
Revs.—
Adonizio, Joseph J., 154 Rock St., Pittston, 18640. Tel: 570-654-8032
Blake, William B., Villa St. Joseph, 1600 Green Ridge St., Dunmore, 18509. Tel: 570-344-7136
Boles, Joseph M., Villa St. Joseph, Dunmore, 18509. Tel: 570-343-4791
Brogus, Albert G., 43 St. James St., Plains, 18705.
Brozena, Joseph M., 602 Sibley Ave., Old Forge, 18518.
Butcavage, Leonard M., Rear 661 Alter St., Hazleton, 18201. Tel: 570-582-4836
Campbell, William D., Villa St. Joseph, 1600 Green Ridge St., Dunmore, 18509. Tel: 570-344-7865
Carr, Eugene R., P.O. Box 1063, Killington, VT 05751. Tel: 802-422-3589
Casey, John W., St. Luke's Villa, 80 E. Northhampton St., Wilkes Barre, 18701. Tel: 570-826-1031
Cipriano, Joseph F., Villa St. Joseph, 1600 Green Ridge St., Dunmore, 18509. Tel: 570-961-0328
Cortese, Patrick S., 1007 Strawberry Ln., Hazle Township, 18202. Tel: 570-459-5929
Culnane, William R., Villa St. Joseph, 1600 Green Ridge St., 18509-2197. Tel: 570-343-4791
Cummings, Charles J., P.O. Box 3271, 17701. Tel: 570-220-2070
Deviney, Raymond L., 1030 S. Hanover St., Nanticoke, 18634. Tel: 570-735-4833
Fanucci, Santino J., Villa St. Joseph, 1600 Green Ridge St., Dunmore, 18509. Tel: 570-498-7091
Finn, Edward S., 421 Layton Rd., Equinunk, 18417. Tel: 570-224-4380
Flynn, William J., S.S., Villa St. Joseph, 1600 Green Ridge St., Dunmore, 18509. Tel: 570-344-4495
Gaiardo, Martin J., Mulberry Tower, 499 Mulberry St., Apt. 1216, 18503. Tel: 570-347-4826

Gallia, Andrew R., 620 Clark St., Rear, Old Forge, 18518. Tel: 570-457-3423

Gunning, Eugene L., May-Oct.: 35 Nevin Rd., P.O. Box J, Newfoundland, 18445. Nov.-April: 5631 Midnight Pass Rd., Apt. #1007, Sarasota, FL 34242. Tel: 570-881-2368

Hazzouri, Alex J., Villa St. Joseph, Dunmore, 18509. Tel: 570-343-2859

Healey, William B., Villa St. Joseph, 1600 Green Ridge St., Dunmore, 18509. Tel: 570-343-0239

Herhenrerder, Peter V., 54 Lincoln Ave., Carbondale, 18407. Tel: 570-282-0304

Horanzy, Joseph M., Villa St. Joseph, 1600 Green Ridge St., Dunmore, 18509. Tel: 570-479-0446

Jeffrey, George A., Villa St. Joseph, 1600 Green Ridge St., Dunmore, 18509. Tel: 570-814-2745

Kilpatrick, John J., Villa St. Joseph, 1600 Green Ridge St., Dunmore, 18509. Tel: 570-344-2154

Kizis, Kenneth G., Villa St. Joseph, 1600 Green Ridge St., Dunmore, 18509. Tel: 570-344-2142

Langan, Vincent F., St. John the Evangelist Rectory (Res), 85 Division St., South Waverly, 18840-2847. Tel: 570-888-2123

Lewis, Harry J., St. Therese Residence, 260 S. Meade St., Wilkes-Barre, 18702. Tel: 570-823-6131

Litcheck, Michael P., Oblates of St. Joseph Seminary, 1880 Hwy. 315, Pittston, 18640.

Masakowski, Edward M., Cedar Village, 3 Bluebird Ct., Wilkes-Barre, 18706.

Mattey, Joseph J., Villa St. Joseph, 1600 Green Ridge St., Dunmore, 18509. Tel: 570-344-1074

Matz, Joseph A., Saint Mary Manor, 701 Lansdale Ave., Lansdale, 19446. Tel: 215-368-0900

Motsay, Joseph R., 1930 Seeneytown Rd., Dover, DE 19904. Tel: 302-423-5383

Obaza, Theodore L., Two Joseph Ln., Wilkes Barre, 18702. Tel: 570-822-1473

Oldfield, Albert E., St. Therese Residence, 260 S. Meade St., Wilkes Barre, 18702.

Olszewski, Daniel D., 74 Pinewood Dr., Laflin, 18702. Tel: 570-655-2165

Orloski, Joseph F., St. Mary's Villa Residence, Rm 214, ONe Pioneer Pl., Moscow, 18444. Tel: 570-842-5274

Ostrowski, Joseph C., St. Mary's Villa Campus, 516 St. Mary's Villa Rd., Elmhurst Twp., 18444. Tel: 570-842-7621

Rable, Cyril J., Villa St. Joseph, 1600 Green Ridge St., Dunmore, 18509. Tel: 570-344-2113

Rafferty, Michael J., Villa St. Joseph, 1600 Green Ridge St., 18509. Tel: 570-961-3723

Rusin, Joseph C., Visitation of B.V.M., 1090 Carmalt St., Dickson City, 18519. Tel: 570-489-2091

Scott, Edward R., Villa St. Joseph, 1600 Green Ridge St., 18509. Tel: 570-941-0452

Skiba, Walter F., 1414 Schlager St., 18504. Tel: 570-963-7556

Skitzki, Francis P., St. Therese Residence, 260 S. Meade St., Wilkes-Barre, 18702.

Sokolowski, Thomas J., Villa St. Joseph, 1600 Green Ridge St., Dunmore, 18509. Tel: 570-313-1764

Turi, John J., 3182 Hemlock Farms, Lords Valley, 18428. Tel: 570-775-8874

Urban, Anthony M., 635 Church St., Swoyersville, 18704. Tel: 570-283-1763

Weber, Joseph O., Holy Family Pavilion, Apt. 114, 2510 Adams Ave., 18509. Tel: 570-348-3535

Yenkevich, Daniel J., 846 Gibbons St., 18505. Tel: 570-961-0196

Zapotocki, Henry E., P.O. Box 847, Tannersville, 18372. Tel: 570-629-1235

Zavacki, Richard A., 255 Church St. Apt. 15, Kingston, 18704. Tel: 570-283-0660

Zawadzki, Victor C., 5 O'Donnell St., Wilkes-Barre, 18702. Tel: 570-819-1629

INSTITUTIONS LOCATED IN THE DIOCESE

[A] SEMINARIES, RELIGIOUS

PITTSTON. *St. Joseph's Oblate Seminary*, 1880 Hwy. 315, 18640. Tel: 570-654-7542; Fax: 570-654-8621. Email: osjseminary@comcast.net. Revs. Paul A. McDonnell, O.S.J., Rector, Vocation Dir. & 1st Councilor; Joseph D. Sibilano, O.S.J., 2nd Councilor & Prov. Treas.; Daniel L. Schwebs, O.S.J., Vice Rector; Alvaro De Oliveira, O.S.J., Dir. Portugese Community.

[B] COLLEGES AND UNIVERSITIES

SCRANTON. *Marywood University* 18509. Tel: 570-348-6211; Fax: 570-340-6014. Email: annemunley@marywood.edu. Web: www.marywood.edu. Sr. Anne Munley, I.H.M., Pres.; Dr. Alan Levine, Vice Pres. Academic Affairs; Dr. Clayton N. Pheasant, Vice Pres. Univ. Advancement; Dr. Raymond P. Heath, Vice Pres. Student Life; Dr. Michael A. Foley, Dean, College of Liberal Arts & Sciences; Dr. Mary Anne Fedrick, Dean, College of Education & Human Devel.; Dr. Diane Keller, Assoc. Prof.; Dr. Lloyd L. Lyter, Interim Dean, College of Health and Human Svcs.; Collier B. Parker, Dean, Insalaco College of Creative & Performing Arts; Rosemary Burger, Registrar; Ann Boland-Chase, M.A., Vice Pres. Enrollment Mgmt.; Dr. Ellen Boylan, Dir., Inst. Research & Assessment; Ms. Catherine Hanson Schappert, Dir., Library Svcs.; Mr. Gregory Keane Hunt, Dean, School Architecture. Sisters, Servants of the Immaculate Heart of Mary. Sisters 16; Lay Teachers 147; Students 3,403.

The University of Scranton (Society of Jesus), 18510. Tel: 570-941-7400; Fax: 570-941-4097. Email: info@scranton.edu. Web: www.scranton.edu. Rev. Kevin P. Quinn, S.J., Pres.; Dr. Harold W. Baillie, Provost & Vice Pres. for Academic Affairs; Dr. Joseph H. Dreisbach, Assoc. Provost, Academic Affairs; Dr. Steven Jones, Assoc. Provost, Community Engagement & Mission; Ms. Patricia Day, Vice Pres. Human Resources; Mr. Patrick F. Leahy, Vice Pres. Univ. Rels.; Mr. Edward J. Steinmetz, Vice Pres., Finance & Treas.; Mr. Gerald C. Zaboski, Vice Pres. Alumni & Public Rels.; Mr. Jerome P. DeSanto, Chief Information Officer & Vice Pres. for Planning; Dr. Brian Conniff, Dean, College of Arts & Sciences; Dr. Michael Mensah, Dean, Kania School of Mgmt.; Dr. W. Jeffrey Welsh, Dean, College Graduate & Continuing Educ.; Ms. Helen Stager, Registrar; Dr. Debra A. Pellegrino, Dean, Panuska College of Professional Studies; Dr. Thomas Smith, Dir. Counseling Center; Dr. Vincent Carilli, Vice Pres., Student Affairs; Anitra Mcshea, Dean, Students; Mr. Charles E. Kratz, Dean, Library; Robert B. Farrell Esq., Sec. of the Univ. & Gen. Counsel; Revs. John J. Begley, S.J., Prof., Theology; I. Michael Bellafiore, S.J., Prof. Theology; Timothy J. Cadigan, S.J., Prof., Biology; Richard G. Malloy, S.J., Vice Pres. Univ. Ministries; Henry B. Haske, S.J., Pastoral Min.; Herbert B. Keller, S.J., Pres., Scranton Prep; William Lamm, S.J., Pastoral Min.; John W. Lange, S.J., Pastoral Min.; John J. Levko, S.J., Prof., Mathematics; Francis J. MacEntee, S.J., Prof. Emeritus, Biology; Leonard A. Martin, S.J., St. Mary's Byzantine Catholic Church, Scranton.; Bernard R. McIlhenny, S.J., Min. Jesuit Community; Ronald H. McKinney, S.J., Prof., Philosophy; J. Patrick Mohr, S.J., Prof., Philosophy; G. Donald Pantle, S.J., Prof., German & Spanish; Thomas Roach, S.J., Rector; Angelo J. Rizzo, S.J., Scholastic, Instructor, Scranton Preparatory School, Scranton.; Revs. Thomas F. Sable, S.J., Prof., Theology; Daniel Sweeny, S.J., Prof. Political Science; Joseph N. Tylenda, S.J., Chap., Marian Convent; Sr. Carol Tropiano, R.S.M., Univ. Minister. Priests 20; Students 6,135.

DALLAS. *Misericordia University* 18612. Tel: 570-674-6400; Fax: 570-675-2441. Web: www.misericordia.edu. Conference for Mercy Higher Education Mid-Atlantic Region Division, Dallas, PA. Sisters Teaching 2; Students 2,358.

Administration: Michael A. MacDowell, Ed.D., Pres.; Mr. John Risboskin, Vice Pres. of Finance & Admin.; Rev. Donald J. Williams, Chap.; Dr. Mari King, Vice Pres. of Academic Affairs; Ms. Susan Helwig, Vice Pres. Institutional Advancement; Sr. Jean Messaros, R.S.M., Vice Pres. Student Affairs; Mrs. Jane Dessoye, M.S., Enrollment Mgr.; Mr. Edward Lahart, M.S., Registrar; Bernadette Rushmer, Dir., Career Svcs.; Ms. Jacqueline Ghormoz, M.S., Dir. Counseling Svcs.; Mr. Val Apanovich, Dir. Information Technology; Dr. John Sumansky, Chief Information & Planning Officer; Barbara Burd, Dir., Library Svcs.; Ms. Kathleen A. Foley, B.S., M.S., Asst. Vice Pres. Student Affairs; Mr. Ronald Hromisin, C.P.A., Controller; Mr. James Roberts, Dir. Mktg. & Public Rels.

WILKES-BARRE. **King's College* 18711. Tel: 570-208-5900; Fax: 570-208-9049. Web: www.kings.edu. Priests 8; Brothers 4; Lay Teachers 130; Students 2,604.

Officers of the College: Rev. John J. Ryan, C.S.C., Pres.; Dr. Nicholas A. Holodick, Vice Pres. Academic Affairs; Dr. Lisa Marie McCauley, Vice Pres. Business Affairs & Treas.; Ms. Janet Mercincavage, Vice Pres. Student Affairs; Frederick A. Pettit, E.S.Q., Vice Pres. Institutional Advancement; Rev. Richard C. Hockman, C.S.C., College Chap. & Dir. Campus Ministry; Barry H. Wiliams, J.D., C.P.A., Dean, William J. McGowan School of Business; Mr. Paul J. Moran, Exec. Dir. Information and Instructional Technology Svcs.; Ms. Michelle Lawrence-Schmude, Dir., College Mktg. & Advertising; Mr. Daniel T. Cebrick, Registrar; Ms. Theresa E. DeKay, Dir. Counseling Ctr.; Mr. James J. Anderson, Dir. Admissions Holy Cross Community Revs. Genaro P. Aguilar, C.S.C., College Counselor; Thomas F. Carten, C.S.C., College Media; Anthony R. Grasso, C.S.C., Prof. English, Assoc. Vice Pres. Academic Affairs & Dean of Faculty; Richard C. Hockman, C.S.C., Dir. Campus Min.; Daniel J. Issing, C.S.C., Asst. Prof. Theology; Charles J. Kociolek, C.S.C., Assoc. Dir. Academic Advisement; Thomas J. O'Hara, C.S.C., Ph.D., Prof. of Political Science; John J. Ryan, C.S.C., Pres.; Bros. Jerome Donnelly, C.S.C., Dir. Student Success & Retention; Stephen J. LaMendola, C.S.C., Academic Liason, Educ. Dept.; James H. Miller, C.S.C., Assoc. Prof. Theatre; George C. Schmitz, C.S.C., B.A., M.A., Dir. Community Outreach; John R. Kratz, Dir. Academic Advisement In Res. Revs. Joseph J. Long, C.S.C. (Retired); Fidel Ticona, C.S.C., Hispanic Min.

[C] HIGH SCHOOLS, DIOCESAN

SCRANTON. *Holy Cross High School*, 501 E. Drinker St., Dunmore, 18512. Tel: 570-346-7541; 570-346-7542; Fax: 570-348-1070. Rev. Msgr. David L. Tressler, Admin.; Rev. Brian J.T. Clarke, J.C.L., Chap.; Mr. Benjamin Tolerico, Acting Prin. Priests 3; Sisters 4; Lay Teachers 35.

EAST STROUDSBURG. *Notre Dame Jr./Sr. High School*, (Grades 7-12), (member of the Notre Dame Regional School System of the Diocese of Scranton, Inc.), 60 Spangenburg Ave., 18301. Tel: 570-421-0466; Fax: 570-476-0629. Rev. Msgr. John A. Bergamo, J.C.L., Chap. & D.R.E.; Mr. Jeffrey N. Lyons, Prin.; Mrs. Patricia Burke, Librarian. Priests 1; Lay Teachers 33.

WILKES-BARRE. *Holy Redeemer High School*, (Grades 9-12), (member of the Holy Redeemer Regional School System of the Diocese of Scranton, Inc.), 159 S. Pennsylvania Blvd., 18701. Tel: 570-829-2424; Fax: 570-829-4412. Rev. Joseph G. Elston, Chap.; Anita Sirak, Prin.; Mary Francis Selecky, Librarian. Priests 1; Sisters 5; Lay Teachers 40.

WILLIAMSPORT. *Saint John Neumann Regional Academy High School Campus*, (Grades 7-12), (member of the Saint John Neumann Regional School System of the Diocese of Scranton, Inc.), 901 Penn St., 17701. Tel: 570-323-9953; Fax: 570-321-7146. Ms. Denise Tobin, Prin.; Rev. David W. Bechtel, Chap. & D.R.E.

[D] HIGH SCHOOLS, PRIVATE

SCRANTON. **Scranton Preparatory School*, 1000 Wyoming Ave., 18509. Tel: 570-941-7737; Fax: 570-941-6118. Email: pmarx@scrantonprep.com. Web: www.scrantonprep.com. Rev. Herbert B. Keller, S.J., Pres.; Patrick J. Marx, Prin.; Kathleen Dooley, Librarian. Society of Jesus. Priests 2; Jesuit Scholastic 1; Lay Teachers 63; Students 855.

Faculty: Rev. Henry B. Haske, S.J.; Angelo J. Rizzo, S.J., Jesuit Scholastic.

ELMHURST TOWNSHIP. *St. Gregory's Academy* (1993) 135 St. Gregory's Pl., Elmhurst Twp., 18444. Tel: 570-842-8112; Fax: 570-842-4513. Email: sga@saintgregorysacademy.com. Revs. Anthony Sumich, F.S.S.P., Chap.; Simon Harkins, F.S.S.P., Asst. Chap. Priestly Fraternity of St. Peter. Priests 2; Lay Teachers 12; Students 64.

[E] DIOCESAN ELEMENTARY SCHOOLS

SCRANTON. *All Saints Academy*, (Grades PreK-8), (member of the Holy Cross Regional School System of the Diocese of Scranton, Inc.), 1425 Jackson St., 18504. Tel: 570-343-8114; Fax: 570-343-0378. Mrs. Michele Long, Prin.; Sr. Jeanne McAuliffe, I.H.M., Librarian. Sisters 2; Lay Teachers 23.

Saint Clare/Saint Paul Elementary School (Main Campus), (Grades 3-8), (member of the Holy Cross Regional School System of the Diocese of Scranton, Inc.), 1527 Penn Ave., 18509. Tel: 570-343-7880; 570-343-4485; Fax: 570-343-0069. Mrs. Elizabeth Murray, Prin.

Saint Clare/Saint Paul Elementary School (Primary Campus), (Grades PreK-2), (member of the Holy Cross Regional School System of the Diocese of Scranton, Inc.), 2215 N. Washington Ave., 18509. Tel: 570-343-2790; Fax: 570-343-4905. Mrs. Elizabeth Murray, Prin.

CLARKS GREEN. *Our Lady of Peace Elementary School*, (Grades K-8), (member of the Holy Cross Regional School System of the Diocese of Scranton, Inc.), 410 N. Abington Rd., 18411. Tel: 570-587-4152; Fax: 570-586-5393. Mrs. Jane M. Quinn, Prin.; Mrs. Carol Harrison, Librarian.

CRESCO. *Monsignor McHugh Elementary School*, (Grades PreK-8), (member of the Notre Dame Regional School System of the Diocese of Scranton, Inc.), 212 Rte. 390, 18326. Tel: 570-595-7463; Fax: 570-595-9639. Nicole Romano, Prin.

DUNMORE. *Saint Mary of Mount Carmel Elementary School*, (Grades PreK-8), (member of the Holy

Cross Regional School System of the Diocese of Scranton, Inc.), 325 Chestnut St., 18512. Tel: 570-346-4429; 570-346-4560; Fax: 570-346-3016. Mr. Joseph Triano, Prin.

DURYEA. *Holy Rosary Elementary School*, (Grades PreK-8), (member of the Holy Redeemer Regional School System of the Diocese of Scranton, Inc.), 125 Stephenson St., 18642. Tel: 570-457-2553; Fax: 570-457-3537. Ms. Kathleen Gilmartin, Prin.

EAST STROUDSBURG. *Notre Dame Elementary School*, (Grades PreK-6), (member of the Notre Dame Regional School System of the Diocese of Scranton, Inc.), 60 Spangenburg Ave., 18301. Tel: 570-421-3651; Fax: 570-422-6935. Sr. Mary Alice Kane, I.H.M., Prin.; Mrs. Barbara Camlet, Librarian. Sisters 5; Lay Teachers 12.

EXETER. *Wyoming Area Catholic Elementary School*, (Grades PreK-8), (member of the Holy Redeemer Regional School System of the Diocese of Scranton, Inc.), 1690 Wyoming Ave., 18643. Tel: 570-654-7982; 570-655-8082; Fax: 570-654-0605. Christopher Tigue, Prin.

HAZLETON. *Holy Family Academy*, (Grades PreK-8), (member of the Holy Redeemer Regional School System of the Diocese of Scranton, Inc.), 601 N. Laurel St., 18201. Tel: 570-455-9431; Fax: 570-455-2847. Mr. Stan Pavlick, Prin.

JESSUP. *La Salle Academy (Jessup Campus)*, (Grades 4-8), (member of the Holy Cross Regional School System of the Diocese of Scranton, Inc.), 309 First Ave., 18434. Tel: 570-489-2010; Fax: 570-489-3887. Mrs. Ellen M. Murphy, Prin.

LaSalle Academy (Dickson City Campus), (Grades PreK-3), (member of the Holy Cross Regional School System of the Diocese of Scranton, Inc.), 625 Dundaff St., Dickson City, 18519. Tel: 570-489-0061; Fax: 570-489-0157. Mrs. Ellen M. Murphy, Prin.

KINGSTON. *Good Shepherd Academy*, (Grades PreK-8), (member of the Holy Redeemer Regional School System of the Diocese of Scranton, Inc.), 316 N. Maple Ave., 18704. Tel: 570-718-4724; Fax: 570-718-4725. Mr. James A. Jones, Prin.; Mrs. Mary Jane Kozick, Asst. Prin.

MOUNTAINTOP. *Saint Jude Elementary School*, (Grades PreK-8), (member of the Holy Redeemer Regional School System of the Diocese of Scranton, Inc.), 422 S. Mountain Blvd., Mountain Top, 18707. Tel: 570-474-5803; Fax: 570-403-6159. Mrs. Jeanne M. Rossi, Prin.

SAYRE. *Epiphany Elementary School*, (Grades PreK-8), (member of the Holy Cross Regional School System of the Diocese of Scranton, Inc.), 627 Stevenson St., 18840. Tel: 570-888-5802; Fax: 570-888-2362. Sr. Kathleen Kelly, I.H.M., Prin.

TOWANDA. *Saint Agnes Elementary School*, (Grades PreK-6), (member of the Holy Cross Regional School System of the Diocese of Scranton, Inc.), 102 Third St., 18848. Tel: 570-265-6803; Fax: 570-265-3065. Mrs. Kathleen DeWan, Prin.; Karen Troup, Librarian. Lay Teachers 10.

WILKES-BARRE. *Saint Nicholas/Saint Mary Elementary School*, (Grades PreK-8), (member of the Holy Redeemer Regional School System of the Diocese of Scranton, Inc.), 242 S. Washington St., 18701. Tel: 570-823-8089; Fax: 570-823-1402. Sr. Mary Catherine Slattery, S.C.C., Prin. Sisters 3; Lay Teachers 19.

WILLIAMSPORT. *Saint John Neumann Regional Academy*, (Grades PreK-6), (member of the Saint John Newmann Regional School System of the Diocese of Scranton, Inc.), 710 Franklin St., 17701. Tel: 570-326-3738; 570-326-7385. Mrs. Susan Kaiser, Prin.

[F] PRESCHOOLS AND CHILD CARE CENTERS

SCRANTON. *Domiano Early Childhood Center* Marywood University, 2300 Adams Ave., 18509. Tel: 570-340-6085. Sr. Marilyn Muro, I.H.M., Dir.

CLARKS GREEN. *St. Gregory Early Childhood Center*, 330 N. Abington Rd., Clarks Summit, 18411. Tel: 570-587-4808; Fax: 570-586-4515. Rev. John M. Lapera, Dir. Priests 1; Lay Teachers 4.

MILFORD. *St. Vincent de Paul Preschool*, 101 St. Vincent Dr., 18337-9672. Tel: 570-686-1867; 570-686-4545; Fax: 800-565-1762. Denise Spinetta, Dir.

MOSCOW. *St. Catherine Preschool* (1985) Church St., P.O. Box 250, 18444. Tel: 570-848-1258. Lisa Sgobba, Dir.

MUNCY. *St. John Neumann Early Childhood Center*, 75 Musser Ln., 17756. Tel: 570-546-5272; Fax: 570-546-0322. Danielle Mc Fadden, Dir.

[G] RENEWAL CENTERS

CRESCO. *The Immaculate Heart of Mary Spiritual Renewal Center*, 236 Rte. 390, 18326. Tel: 570-595-7548; 570-595-7549; Fax: 570-595-9698. Email: ihmcresco@yahoo.com. Web: ihm.marywood.edu. Sr. Anne Mary Boslett, I.H.M., Dir.

DALTON. *Fatima Renewal Center*, 1000 Seminary Rd., 18414. Tel: 570-563-8500; Fax: 570-563-1857. Email: fatima@dioceseofscranton.org. Web: www.dioceseofscranton.org/fatima. Sarah Mountain, Prog. Coord. Total Staff 10.

NANTICOKE. *Holy Family Spiritual Renewal Center* (1996) 151 Old Newport St., 18634-1300. Tel: 570-735-2599; Fax: 570-735-2599. Email: mlhudak@verizon.net. Martin J. Hudak, Co-Dir.; Louise V. Hudak, Co-Dir. Total Staff 2; Total Assisted 4.

[H] GENERAL HOSPITALS

CARBONDALE. *Marian Community Hospital*, 100 Lincoln Ave., 18407. Tel: 570-281-1000; Fax: 570-282-7177. Email: mariad@marianhospital.org. Web: www.mariancommunityhospital.org. Mary Theresa Vautrinot, Pres. & CEO. Sisters, Servants of the Immaculate Heart of Mary. Component of Maxis Health System, Member Catholic Health East. Sisters 4; Bed Capacity 35; Patients Assisted Annually 68,915.

Maxis Foundation, 100 Lincoln Ave., 18407. Tel: 570-281-1002; Fax: 570-281-7177. Web: www.mariancommunityhospital.org. Mary Theresa Vautrinot, Pres. & CEO.

Maxis Medical Services, 100 Lincoln Ave., 18407. Tel: 570-281-1315; Fax: 570-281-1256. Web: www.mariancommunityhospital.org. Mary Theresa Vautrinot, Pres. & CEO. Patients Assisted Annually 12,056.

MUNCY. *Muncy Valley Hospital*, 215 E. Water St., 17756. Tel: 570-546-8282; Fax: 570-546-4150. Web: www.susquehannahealth.org. Christine Ballard, Pres.; Sr. Sharon Hartman, S.C.C., Chap. Capacity 158; Patients Assisted Annually 106,621.

WILLIAMSPORT. *Divine Providence Hospital of the Sisters of Christian Charity*, 1100 Grampian Blvd., 17701. Tel: 570-320-7833; Fax: 570-320-7820. Email: apaul@susquehannahealth.org. Web: www.susquehannahealth.org. Ronald Reynolds, Pres.; Rev. Fidelis Ekemgba, Chap.; Sisters Christina Marie Cables, S.C.C., Coord.; Ann Marie Paul, S.C.C, Dir. of Mission Integration. Bed Capacity 70; Patients Assisted Annually 226,324; Total Staff 439.

Sisters of Christian Charity Healthcare Corporation, 1100 Grampian Blvd., 17701. Tel: 570-320-7833; Fax: 570-320-7820. Email: apaul@susquehannahealth.org. Web: www.susquehannahealth.org.

[I] SPECIAL HOSPITALS

SCRANTON. *St. Joseph's Center* (1888) 2010 Adams Ave., 18509. Tel: 570-342-8379; Fax: 570-342-6080. Web: www.stjosephscenter.org. Sr. Maryalice Jacquinot, I.H.M., Pres. & CEO; Rev. William B. Pickard, Chap. Priests 1; Bed Capacity 147; Patients Assisted Annually 155; Total Staff 535.

[J] SPECIAL EDUCATION SCHOOLS

SCRANTON. *Lourdesmont* (1889) 1327 Wyoming Ave., 18509. Tel: 570-702-8360; Fax: 570-702-8621. Email: msherman@lourdesmont.org. Web: www.lourdesmont.org. Judy Neri, COO; John A. Antognoli, Ed.D., CEO.

Good Shepherd Youth & Family Services of NEPA Sisters of the Good Shepherd 3; Total Staff 60; Total Assisted 300.

[K] HOMES FOR AGED

SCRANTON. *Home for Aged of the Little Sisters of the Poor, Holy Family Residence* (1907) 2500 Adams Ave., 18509. Tel: 570-343-4065; Fax: 570-346-1196. Sr. Maureen Weiss, L.S.P., Pres.; Rev. E. Francis Kelly, Chap. Little Sisters of the Poor 9; Aged Residents 52; Residents in Independent Living Apartments 23.

DALLAS. *Mercy Center Nursing Unit, Inc.*, Lake St., Box 370, 18612. Tel: 570-675-2131; Fax: 570-674-7606. Web: www.mcnu.org. Sr. Sara Sweeney, R.S.M., Admin.; Sheila Heck, Dir. of Nursing; Rev. John J. Kulavich, Chap. Total Staff 155; Total Assisted 200; Bed Capacity 140.

MOSCOW. *St. Mary's Villa Nursing Home* (1962) 516 St. Mary's Villa Rd., Elmhurst Twp., 18444. Tel: 570-842-7621; Fax: 570-842-2953. Email: lkanarr@stmarysvilla.com. Linda Kanarr, CEO/Admin.; Rev. Peter D. Menghini, Chap. A member of Covenant Health Systems, Tewksbury, MA Residents 112; Total Staff 200; Total Assisted 65; Bed Capacity 112.

St. Mary's Villa Residence (1999) One Pioneer Pl., 18444. Tel: 570-842-5274; Fax: 570-842-3472. Joanne Mazak, Admin.; Rev. Peter D. Menghini, Chap. Residents 64; Total Staff 45.

WILKES-BARRE. *Little Flower Manor of the Diocese of Scranton*, 200 S. Meade St., 18702. Tel: 570-823-6131; Fax: 570-823-5171. Andrew Durako, COO; Rev. Richard G. Ghezzi, Chap. Conducted by the Carmelite Sisters for the Aged and Infirm. Sisters 5; Aged Residents 133; Total Staff 230.

St. Therese Residence, 260 S. Meade St., 18702. Tel: 570-823-6131; Fax: 570-208-0143. Brenda Casciano, Admin.; Rev. Richard G. Ghezzi, Chap. Conducted by the Carmelite Sisters for the Aged and Infirm. Residents 60; Total Staff 41.

Saint Luke's Villa, 80 E. Northampton St., 18701. Tel: 570-826-1031. Rev. Msgr. Vincent J. Grimalia, Chap.

[L] MONASTERIES AND RESIDENCES OF PRIESTS AND BROTHERS

SCRANTON. *Saint Ann's Passionist Monastery* (1909) 1233 St. Ann St., 18504. Tel: 570-347-5691; Fax: 570-347-9387. Email: jimpep@aol.com. Very Rev. James Price, C.P., Rector; Revs. Francis Landry, C.P., Asst. Rector; Vincent Boney, C.P.; Brendan Breen, C.P.; Edward Buchheit, C.P.; Richard Burke, C.P.; Malcolm Cornwell, C.P.; Edward Deviny, C.P.; Brice Edwards, C.P.; Roger Elliott, C.P.; Lee Havey, C.P.; Joseph R. Jones, C.P.; Clement Kasinskas, C.P.; Earl Keating, C.P.; Sebastian Kolinovsky, C.P.; Cassian J. Yuhaus, C.P.; Bros. Joseph Rogers, C.P.; Daniel Turner, C.P. Sponsorship: Congregation of the Passion.

ELMHURST. *Priestly Fraternity of St. Peter (F.S.S.P.), North American District Headquarters* (1991) *Priestly Fraternity of St. Peter*, 119 Griffin Rd., Elmhurst Twp., 18444. Tel: 570-842-4000; Fax: 570-842-4001. Email: info@fssp.com. Web: www.fssp.com. Revs. Jose Zepeda, F.S.S.P., St. Michael's, Scranton; Eric Flood, F.S.S.P., Dist. Supr.; Gregory Pendergraft, F.S.S.P., Dir. Devel.; Anthony Sumich, F.S.S.P., Chap. St. Gregory's Academy, Elmhurst; Simon Harkins, F.S.S.P., Asst. Chap., St. Gregory's Academy, Elmhurst; Carl N. Gismondi, F.S.S.P., District Bursar. Priests 79; Seminarians 77.

LACEYVILLE. *Franciscan Missionary Hermits of St. Joseph* (1998) 85 Joseph Dr., 18623. Tel: 570-869-2918. Rev. Pio Mandato, F.M.H.J.

PITTSTON. *Our Lady of Sorrows Province of the Oblates of St. Joseph*, 1880 Hwy. 315, 18640. Tel: 570-654-7542; Fax: 570-654-8621. Very Rev. Philip Massetti, O.S.J., Prov. Supr.; Revs. Joseph D. Sibilano, O.S.J., Prov. Treas.; Paul A. McDonnell, O.S.J., Rector, Vocation Dir. & 1st Councilor. Priests 11; Temporary Professed 1.

[M] DIOCESAN RESIDENCE FOR RETIRED PRIESTS

DUNMORE. *Villa St. Joseph*, 1600 Green Ridge St., 18509. Tel: 570-343-4791. Rev. Msgr. David A. Bohr, S.T.D., Rector. Tel: 570-343-4791; Fax: 570-343-3040 In Res. Most Rev. James C. Timlin, D.D. (Retired); Rev. Msgrs. John A. Esseff (Retired). Tel: 570-499-9044; Chester A. Gajewski (Retired). Tel: 570-347-1851; Philip A. Gray (Retired). Tel: 570-344-0897; Alexander T. Kulik (Retired). Tel: 570-341-8881; John H. Louis, S.T.L., J.C.D. (Retired). Tel: 570-207-2961; Donald A. McAndrews (Retired). Tel: 570-207-5586; Edmund S. Penkala (Retired). Tel: 570-344-6288; Stanley W. Piorkowski (Retired). Tel: 570-343-1184; William P. Ward (Retired). Tel: 570-341-1558; Revs. William B. Blake (Retired). Tel: 570-344-7136; Joseph M. Boles (Retired). Tel: 570-343-4791; William D. Campbell (Retired). Tel: 570-344-7865; Joseph F. Cipriano (Retired). Tel: 570-961-0328; William R. Culnane (Retired). Tel: 570-343-4791; Leo P. Cummings. Tel: 570-961-1815; Santino J. Fanucci (Retired). Tel: 570-498-7091; William J. Flynn, S.S. (Retired). Tel: 570-344-4495; Alex J. Hazzouri (Retired). Tel: 570-343-2859; William B. Healey (Retired). Tel: 570-343-0239; Joseph M. Horanzy (Retired). Tel: 570-479-0446; George A. Jeffrey (Retired). Tel: 570-814-2745; John J. Kilpatrick (Retired). Tel: 570-344-2154; Kenneth G. Kizis (Retired). Tel: 570-344-2142; Joseph J. Mattey (Retired). Tel: 570-343-4791; Cyril J. Rable. Tel: 570-344-2113; Michael J. Rafferty (Retired). Tel: 570-961-3723; Edward R. Scott (Retired). Tel: 570-941-0452; Thomas J. Sokolowski (Retired). Tel: 570-343-4791.

[N] CONVENTS AND RESIDENCES FOR SISTERS

SCRANTON. *Immaculate Heart of Mary Center* (1971) 2300 Adams Ave., 18509. Tel: 570-342-6850; Fax: 570-346-5439. Email: communications@sistersofihm.org. Web: www.sistersofihm.org. Sisters Therese O'Rourke, I.H.M., Pres. Tel: 570-346-5425; Ellen Maroney, I.H.M., Vice Pres. & Councilor Missioning & Community Life; Ellen Carney, I.H.M., Councilor, Temporal Resources; Deborah Worlinsky, Business Mgr. Tel: 570-346-5406; Sisters Francine Fasolka, I.H.M., Dir. Communications. Tel: 570-346-5404; Ann Marie O'Brien, I.H.M., Dir. Coord. Missioning Resources.

Tel: 570-346-5401; Kathryn Kurdziel, I.H.M., Dir. Candidates & Novices. Tel: 570-346-5414; Ruth Harkins, I.H.M., Dir. Vocations. Tel: 570-346-5413; Ann Monica Baker, I.H.M., Dir. Devel. Tel: 570-346-5431. Sisters, Servants of the Immaculate Heart of Mary. Professed Sisters 449.

Councilors, Missioning & Community Life: Sisters Christine Koellhoffer, I.H.M., Councilor, Spiritual Devel.; Rosemary Goulet, I.H.M., Councilor, Missioning & Community Life; Mary Mark Lowery, I.M.H., I.H.M. Center Admin. Tel: 570-346-5408; Jean Louise Bachetti, I.H.M., Dir. Associates. Tel: 570-963-2480.

Pascucci Family Our Lady of Peace Residence, 2300 Adams Ave., 18509. Tel: 570-346-5423; Fax: 570-346-5418. Sisters Mary Kathleen Faliskie, I.H.M., Asst. Admin. Tel: 570-346-5422; Jean Coughlin, I.H.M., Admin. Tel: 570-346-5421; Eleanor Mary Marconi, I.H.M., Asst. Admin. Tel: 570-346-5424; Rev. Joseph N. Tylenda, S.J., Chap. Sisters, Servants of the Immaculate Heart of Mary 104.

DALLAS. *Sisters of Mercy of the Americas, Mid-Atlantic Community*, 199 Lake St., 18612-0369. Tel: 570-675-2048; Fax: 570-675-9051. Web: www.mercymidatlantic.org. Sr. Christine McCann, R.S.M., Pres. Sisters 1,041.

TUNKHANNOCK. *Capuchin Sisters of Nazareth, Mother of God Convent*, 215 Wellwood Dr., 18657. Tel: 570-836-2737. Sr. Theresa May, Supr.

[O] RETREAT HOUSES

MOUNT POCONO. *Villa Our Lady Retreat House*, HC 1, Box 41, Meadowside Dr., 18344-9714. Tel: 570-839-7217; Fax: 570-839-7553. Email: sbona@ptd.net. Web: www.villaourladyretreathouse.com. Sr. M. Bonaventa Radzai, O.S.F., Supr. & Admin. Bernardine Sisters 7.

SOUTH ABINGTON TOWNSHIP. *St. Gabriel's Retreat Center*, 631 Griffin Pond Rd., 18411. Tel: 570-586-4957; Fax: 570-587-3314. Email: kporter@epix.net.

Religious of the Passion of Jesus Christ; Passionist Nuns (Contemplative).

[P] CAMPS AND COMMUNITY CENTERS

TUNKHANNOCK. *Camp St. Andrew* (1940) 524 Stark Rd., P.O. Box 679, 18657. Tel: 570-836-2975. Off-Season Mailing Address: 33 E. Northampton St., Wilkes Barre, 18701. Tel: 570-822-7118, Ext. 306; Fax: 570-829-7781. Rev. Msgr. Joseph P. Kelly, V.E., Exec. Dir. Regular Camp, Basketball Clinics 800.

WILKES-BARRE. *Catholic Youth Center*, 36 S. Washington St., 18701. Tel: 570-823-6121; Fax: 570-823-0175. Email: wvcyc@epix.net. Rev. John S. Terry, Dir.; Mr. Mark Soprano, Acting Exec. Dir.

[Q] MISCELLANEOUS LISTINGS

SCRANTON. *African Sisters Education Collaborative(ASEC)* (2006) *Marywood University*, 2300 Adams Ave., 18509. Tel: 570-340-6068. Email: jwakahiv@marywood.edu. Web: www.marywood.edu/asec/. Sr. Jane Wakahiv, L.S.O.S.F., Contact Person & Exec. Dir.

**Aid to the Church in Russia*, 300 Wyoming Ave., 18503-1279. Tel: 570-207-2216; Fax: 570-207-2236. Teresa Osborne, Dir., Scranton Office.

St. Ann's Foundation, 1239 St. Ann's St., 18504. Tel: 570-347-5691; Fax: 570-347-9387. Very Rev. James Price, C.P., Exec. Dir.

St. Anthony's Haven, 409-411 Olive St., 18509. Tel: 570-342-1295, Ext. 204; Fax: 570-342-0985. Email: ghallinan@cssresidential.org. Men's & Women's Shelter.

St. James Manor, 600 Wyoming Ave., 18509. Tel: 570-342-1295, Ext. 202; Fax: 570-342-0985. Supportive Housing Program.

St. Francis of Assisi Kitchen, 500 Penn Ave., 18509. Tel: 570-342-5556; Fax: 570-963-8832. Web: www.stfranciskitchen.com. Rev. Msgr. Joseph P. Kelly, V.E., Dir.

Friends of the Poor (1984) *Jackson Terrace*, 148 Meridian St., 18504. Tel: 570-348-4428; Fax: 570-207-1516. Mailing Address: 2300 Adams Ave., 18509. Sr. Ann Walsh, I.H.M., CEO.

The Guild Studio Religious Store, 400 Wyoming Ave., 18503. Tel: 800-367-6610; 570-342-8246; Fax: 570-342-5940. Email: guild01@aol.com. Trish Morrow, Gen. Mgr.

I.H.M. Congregation Charitable Trust (1986) 2300 Adams Ave., 18509. Tel: 570-342-6850; Fax: 570-346-5439. Email: carneye@sistersofihm.org. Web: www.carneyesistersofihm.org. Congregation of the Sisters, Servants of the Immaculate Heart of Mary.

Ministry for Religious Research and Consultancy (1984) 1233 St. Ann St., 18504. Tel: 570-586-9099; Fax: 570-586-9203. Email: cyuhaus@aol.com. Rev. Cassian J. Yuhaus, C.P., Exec. Dir.

VMR Charitable Trust (Vehicle Management for Religious) (1992) Tel: 570-586-9099; Fax: 570-586-9203.

DALLAS. *Mercy Consultation Center of Dallas*, 3560 Memorial Hwy., P.O. Box 370, 18612. Tel: 570-675-2284; Fax: 570-675-4390.

Studio I (1979) *Mercy Center*, Box 370, 18612. Tel: 570-675-1865; 570-674-3281; 570-675-2131; Fax: 570-674-5658. Email: srkiel@aol.com. Web: www.mercymall.com. Sr. Regina Kiel, R.S.M., Designer & Artist. Designing and handcrafting fine original custom jewelry and sculpture. Workshops in jewelry making using the lost wax casting technique: A. Couples - make their own wedding bands/engagement rings. B. All ages interested in learning the art of jewelry making.

NANTICOKE. *People of God Community of Northeastern PA* (1984) 151 Old Newport St., 18634-1300. Tel: 570-735-2599; Fax: 570-735-2679. Email: jimmyg@epix.net. James Gialanella, Pres.

PITTSTON. *The Gabriel House*, 13 William St., 18640. Tel: 570-602-9796; Fax: 570-602-8396. Email: bkuprionas@csswb.org. Anne Marie McCawley, Project Dir. Transitional housing facility for women and women with young children.

WILKES-BARRE. *Project REMAIN*, 215 High St., Apt. 100, 18701. Tel: 570-829-5373. Sr. Mary Glennon, R.S.M., Dir. Service for the elderly and the needy residents in the High Rises.

Project Remain Outreach to the Elderly dba John B. McGlynn Center Boulevard Townhomes, 72 Midland Ct., 18702. Tel: 570-824-8891; Fax: 570-970-1079. Sr. Miriam Francis Stadulis, R.S.M., Dir. Outreach to low income families in the housing projects.

St. Vincent De Paul Kitchen, 39 E. Jackson St., 18701. Tel: 570-829-7796; Fax: 570-208-9182. Email: amccawley@csswb.org. Thomas P. Cherry, Exec. Dir.; Anne Marie McCawley, Project Dir.

RELIGIOUS INSTITUTES OF MEN REPRESENTED IN THE DIOCESE

For further details refer to the corresponding bracketed number in the Religious Institutes of Men or Women section.

[1000]—*Congregation of the Passion* (Union City, NJ)—C.P.

[0690]—*Jesuit Fathers and Brothers* (Maryland Prov.)—S.J.

[0930]—*Oblates of St. Joseph* (Asti, Italy)—O.S.J.

[1065]—*Priestly Fraternity of St. Peter*—F.S.S.P.

[0610]—*Priests of the Congregation of Holy Cross* (Wilkes-Barre, PA)—C.S.C.

[1290]—*Society of the Priests of St. Sulpice*—S.S.

RELIGIOUS INSTITUTES OF WOMEN REPRESENTED IN THE DIOCESE

[1810]—*Bernardine Sisters of the Third Order of St. Francis*—O.S.F.

[0330]—*Carmelite Sisters of the Aged and Infirm*—O.Carm.

[2980]—*Congregation of Notre Dame*—C.N.D.

[0890]—*Daughters of Our Lady of Mercy*—D.M.

[]—*Dominican Sisters of Sparkhill*

[2575]—*Institute of the Sisters of Mercy of the Americas*—R.S.M.

[]—*Little Sisters of St. Francis*—L.S.O.F.

[2340]—*Little Sisters of the Poor*—P.S.D.P.

[3240]—*Poor Sisters of Jesus Crucified and the Sorrowful Mother*—C.J.C.

[3170]—*Religious of the Passion of Jesus Christ*—C.P.

[3430]—*Religious Teachers Filippini*—M.P.F.

[0660]—*Sisters of Christian Charity*—S.C.C.

[3780]—*Sisters of Saints Cyril and Methodius*—SS.C.M.

[3840]—*Sisters of St. Joseph of Carondelet*—C.S.J.

[1830]—*Sisters of the Good Shepherd*—R.G.S.

[2160]—*Sisters, Servants of the Immaculate Heart of Mary*—I.H.M.

[]—*Union Sisters of the Presentation of the Blessed Virgin Mary* (Ireland)—P.B.V.M.

DIOCESAN CEMETERIES

SCRANTON. *Cathedral*, 1708 Oram St., 18504. Tel: 570-347-9251; Fax: 570-347-4354.

Diocesan Cemeteries Office, 1708 Oram St., 18504. Tel: 570-207-2209; Fax: 570-347-4354. Kevin Beck, Dir.

CARVERTON. *Mount Olivet*, 612 Mt. Olivet Rd., 18644. Tel: 570-696-3636; Fax: 570-696-4705. P.O. Box 4257, Wyoming, 18644.

DRUMS. *Calvary*, Rte. 309, 49 S. Hunter Hwy., P.O. Box 485, 18222. Tel: 570-788-2150; Fax: 570-708-2938.

MOSCOW. *St. Catherine*, Main St., Rte. 435, P.O. Box 114, 18444. Tel: 570-842-8411; Fax: 570-842-8406.

OLD FORGE. *Holy Cross*, Oak & Keyser Ave., 18518. Tel: 570-347-9251; Fax: 570-347-4354. c/o 1708 Oram St., 18504.

WILLIAMSPORT. *Resurrection*, 4323 Lycoming Mall Dr., P.O. Box 12, Montoursville, 17754. Tel: 570-368-2727; Fax: 570-368-2727.

NECROLOGY

† Donovan, Rev. Msgr. William L., (Retired)—Died July 2, 2011

† O'Neill, Rev. Msgr. Kevin P., (Retired)—Died May 17, 2011

† Barrett, Edward F., (Retired)—Died July 22, 2011

† Bochinski, Mark J., (Retired)—Died Jan. 6, 2011

† Flynn, Thomas A., (Retired)—Died Nov. 21, 2011

† Krafchak, John S., (Retired)—Died April 20, 2011

† McCawley, William J.—Died Aug. 3, 2011

† Mullally, Gerald F., Milford, PA St. Patrick—Died Dec. 14, 2011

An asterisk (*) denotes an organization that has established tax-exempt status directly with the IRS and is not covered by the USCCB Group Ruling.

Archdiocese of Seattle

Archidioecesis Seattlensis

Most Reverend

ALEXANDER J. BRUNETT, PH.D.

Archbishop Emeritus of Seattle; ordained July 13, 1958; appointed Bishop of Helena April 19, 1994; consecrated and installed July 6, 1994; appointed Archbishop of Seattle October 28, 1997; installed December 18, 1997; retired September 16, 2010. *Office: 710 9th Ave., Seattle, WA 98104.* Tel: 206-382-4886; Fax: 206-382-3495.

Most Reverend

RAYMOND G. HUNTHAUSEN

Archbishop Emeritus of Seattle; ordained June 1, 1946; appointed Bishop of Helena, Montana July 8, 1962; consecrated August 30, 1962; appointed Archbishop of Seattle February 25, 1975; installed May 22, 1975; retired August 21, 1991. *Office: 710 9th Ave., Seattle, WA 98104.* Tel: 206-382-4886; Fax: 206-382-3495.

Most Reverend

JAMES PETER SARTAIN, D.D., S.T.L.

Archbishop of Seattle; ordained July 15, 1978; appointed Bishop of Little Rock January 4, 2000; consecrated and installed March 6, 2000; appointed Bishop of Joliet May 16, 2006; installed June 27, 2006; appointed Archbishop of Seattle September 16, 2010; installed December 1, 2010. *Chancery: 710 9th Ave., Seattle, WA 98104.* Tel: 206-382-4886; Fax: 206-382-3495.

Chancery Office: 710 9th Ave., Seattle, WA 98104. Tel: 206-382-4560; Fax: 206-382-4840.

Web: www.seattlearchdiocese.org

Email: info@seattlearch.org

Most Reverend

EUSEBIO L. ELIZONDO

Auxiliary Bishop of Seattle; ordained August 18, 1984; appointed Auxiliary Bishop of Seattle and Titular Bishop of Acholla May 12, 2005; ordained June 6, 2005. *Office: 710 9th Ave., Seattle, WA 98104.* Tel: 206-274-3112.

Square Miles 28,731.

Established May 31, 1850. Name Changed to Seattle, September 11, 1907.

Created Archdiocese, June 23, 1951.

Comprises the Counties of Clallam, Clark, Cowlitz, Grays Harbor, Island, Jefferson, King, Kitsap, Lewis, Mason, Pacific, Pierce, San Juan, Skagit, Skamania, Snohomish, Thurston, Wahkiakum and Whatcom in the State of Washington.

Legal Title: "Corporation of the Catholic Archbishop of Seattle."

For legal titles of parishes and archdiocesan institutions, consult The Chancery.

STATISTICAL OVERVIEW

Personnel	
Archbishops	1
Retired Archbishops	2
Auxiliary Bishops	1
Abbots	1
Retired Abbots	1
Priests: Diocesan Active in Diocese	122
Priests: Diocesan Active Outside Diocese	2
Priests: Retired, Sick or Absent	75
Number of Diocesan Priests	199
Religious Priests in Diocese	87
Total Priests in Diocese	286
Extern Priests in Diocese	31
Ordinations:	
Diocesan Priests	5
Religious Priests	1
Transitional Deacons	1
Permanent Deacons in Diocese	110
Total Brothers	19
Total Sisters	369
Parishes	
Parishes	147
With Resident Pastor:	
Resident Diocesan Priests	105
Resident Religious Priests	12
Without Resident Pastor:	
Administered by Priests	24
Administered by Lay People	6
Missions	27
Pastoral Centers	6
Professional Ministry Personnel:	
Brothers	5
Sisters	29
Lay Ministers	636
Welfare	
Catholic Hospitals	11
Total Assisted	2,273,059
Health Care Centers	2
Total Assisted	12,800
Homes for the Aged	18
Total Assisted	8,091
Residential Care of Children	221
Total Assisted	505
Day Care Centers	3
Total Assisted	443
Specialized Homes	7
Total Assisted	477
Special Centers for Social Services	126
Total Assisted	52,146
Educational	
Diocesan Students in Other Seminaries	28
Total Seminarians	28
Colleges and Universities	2
Total Students	9,566
High Schools, Diocesan and Parish	5
Total Students	2,429
High Schools, Private	6
Total Students	3,659
Elementary Schools, Diocesan and Parish	57
Total Students	15,654
Elementary Schools, Private	5
Total Students	1,102
Catechesis/Religious Education:	
High School Students	5,800
Elementary Students	26,500
Total Students under Catholic Instruction	64,738
Teachers in the Diocese:	
Priests	11
Brothers	8
Sisters	25
Lay Teachers	1,646
Vital Statistics	
Receptions into the Church:	
Infant Baptism Totals	6,633
Minor Baptism Totals	712
Adult Baptism Totals	449
Received into Full Communion	522
First Communions	6,488
Confirmations	3,869
Marriages:	
Catholic	816
Interfaith	495
Total Marriages	1,311
Deaths	2,662
Total Catholic Population	580,000
Total Population	5,262,350

Former Bishops—Rt. Revs. A. M. A. BLANCHET, cons. Bishop of Walla Walla, Sept. 27, 1846; transferred to Nesqually, May 31, 1850; resigned 1879; made Bishop of Ibora; died Feb. 25, 1887; AEGIDIUS JUNGER, D.D., cons. Oct. 28, 1879; died Dec. 26, 1895; Most Revs. EDWARD JOHN O'DEA, D.D., cons. Bishop of Nesqually, Sept. 8, 1896; See transferred to Seattle, Sept. 11, 1907; died Dec. 25, 1932; GERALD SHAUGHNESSY, S.M., S.T.D., appt. Bishop of Seattle July 1, 1933; cons. Sept. 19, 1933; died May 18, 1950; THOMAS A. CONNOLLY, D.D., cons. Aug. 24, 1939; succeeded, May 18, 1950; retired Feb. 25, 1975; died April 18, 1991; RAYMOND G. HUNTHAUSEN, D.D. (Retired), ord. June 1, 1946; appt. Bishop of Helena, Montana, July 8, 1962; cons. Aug. 30, 1962; appt. Archbishop of Seattle, Feb. 25, 1975; installed May 22, 1975; retired Aug. 21, 1991; THOMAS J. MURPHY, D.D., S.T.D., ord. April 12, 1958; appt. Bishop of Great Falls, July 5, 1978; appt. Coadjutor Archbishop of Seattle, May 26, 1987; succeeded to See Aug. 21, 1991; died June 26, 1997; ALEXANDER J. BRUNETT, Ph.D., D.D., ord. July 13, 1958; appt. Bishop of Helena, Montana April 19, 1994; cons. July 6, 1994; appt. Archbishop of Seattle Oct. 28, 1997; installed Dec. 18, 1997; retired Sept. 16, 2010.

Chancery Office—Office of the Archbishop, 710 9th Ave., Seattle, 98104. Tel: 206-382-4886; Fax: 206-382-3495.

Vicar General—Most Rev. EUSEBIO ELIZONDO, M.Sp.S., J.C.D., 710 9th Ave., Seattle, 98104. Tel: 206-274-3112.

Chancellor—Ms. MARY E. SANTI, J.C.L., 710 9th Ave., Seattle, 98104. Tel: 206-264-2089; Fax: 206-274-3110.

Executive Assistant to the Archbishop—Ms. ANGELA KISON. Tel: 206-382-4525.

Presbyteral Council—Most Rev. EUSEBIO ELIZONDO, M.Sp.S., J.C.D.; Very Revs. JAMES D. PICTON, J.D., J.C.L.; BRYAN L. HERSEY; JAMES P. COYNE; ARMANDO S. PEREZ; JOHN C. MADIGAN; JAMES E. LEE; ANTHONY E. BAWYN, J.C.D.; Revs. RAYMOND CLEAVELAND; STEVEN SALLIS, Council Chm.; KURT NAGEL; Very Revs. KHANH D. NGUYEN; MATTHEW L. O'LEARY; Rev. MICHAEL J. MCDERMOTT; Very Revs. DEREK J. LAPPE; DAVID T. MULHOLLAND; Revs. TUAN NGUYEN; HANS M. OLSON; PAUL M. WECKERT, O.S.B.; TIMOTHY SAUER; PATRICK J. HOWELL, S.J.; THOMAS L. VANDENBERG (Retired).

College of Consultors—Revs. TUAN NGUYEN; MICHAEL J. MCDERMOTT; HANS M. OLSON; TIMOTHY SAUER; PAUL A. MAGNANO, Ph.D.; STEVEN SALLIS; KURT NAGEL; THOMAS L. VANDENBERG (Retired).

Deans—Very Revs. KHANH D. NGUYEN, Northern; BRYAN L. HERSEY, Snohomish; DEREK J. LAPPE, Olympic; Rev. RAYMOND CLEAVELAND, North Seattle; Very Revs. JAMES D. PICTON, J.D., J.C.L., Eastside; JOHN C. MADIGAN, South Seattle; JAMES P. COYNE, South King; MATTHEW L. O'LEARY, Pierce; JAMES E. LEE, South Sound; ARMANDO S. PEREZ, Southern.

Metropolitan Tribunal

Judicial Vicar—Very Rev. ANTHONY E. BAWYN, J.C.D., 710 9th Ave., Seattle, 98104. Tel: 206-382-4830; Fax: 206-382-2071.

Adjunct Judicial Vicar—Rev. PAUL R. PLUTH, J.C.L.

Judges—Very Rev. ANTHONY E. BAWYN, J.C.D.; Rev. JAMES EBLEN, S.T.L., Ph.D. (Retired); Deacon JOHN LARUSSA; Rev. PAUL R. PLUTH, J.C.L.; Sr. CAROLYN A. ROEBER, O.P., J.C.L.; JAMES L. BROOKS, M.Ed.; Ms. LYNDA ROBITAILLE, J.C.D.

Defenders of the Bond—Most Rev. EUSEBIO ELIZONDO, M.Sp.S., J.C.D.; Sr. BEVERLY K. DUNN, S.P., J.C.D.; KAREN S. GIFFIN, M.Min.

Notaries—VALERIE BLESENER; CHRISTINA MACHNIK; LIGIA MAHONEY.

Archdiocesan Offices and Directors

Accounting Services—NAN SEVERNS, Controller, 710 9th Ave., Seattle, 98104. Tel: 206-382-4377; Fax: 206-903-4624. Assistant Controllers: TOM GRECHIS. Tel: 206-382-4287; MARY JO GILLIS. Tel: 206-382-4849.

Administration and Finance, Office of—VACANT, Dir., 710 9th Ave., Seattle, 98104. Tel: 206-382-4529; Fax: 206-274-3199.

African/African American/Black and Native American Ministry Services—Mr. PHILIP TRAN, Dir., 710 9th Ave., Seattle, 98104. Tel: 206-382-4828; 800-465-6862 (Toll Free); Fax: 206-382-2069.

Archdiocesan Building Commission—Mr. EDWARD FOSTER, Staff; Mr. BILL LEHTINEN, Chm., 710 9th Ave., Seattle, 98109. Tel: 206-382-4851; Fax: 206-382-4266.

Archdiocesan Finance Council—VACANT, Finance Officer; Mr. LOU DELL'OSSO, Chm., 710 9th Ave., Seattle, 98104. Tel: 206-382-4529; Fax: 206-274-3199.

Archdiocesan Housing Authority—Mr. MICHAEL REICHERT, Pres., 100 23rd Ave. S., Seattle, 98144-2302. Tel: 206-328-5696; 800-499-5979 (Toll Free); Fax: 206-328-5699.

Archdiocesan Liturgical Commission—Ms. CAROLYN LASSEK, Chm., 710 9th Ave., Seattle, 98104. Tel: 206-382-4878; Fax: 206-903-4612.

Archdiocesan Women's Commission—Mr. JIM THOMAS, Staff, 710 9th Ave., Seattle, 98104. Tel: 206-382-4268; Fax: 206-264-2084.

Archives and Information Services—Mr. SETH DALBY, 710 9th Ave., Seattle, 98104. Tel: 206-382-4352; Fax: 206-382-4840.

Asian Pacific American Ministry Services—Mr. PHILIP TRAN, Dir., 710 9th Ave., Seattle, 98104. Tel: 206-382-4509, Ext. 4828; 800-465-6862, Ext. 4828 (Toll Free); Fax: 206-382-2069.

Associated Catholic Cemeteries—Mr. RICHARD PETERSON, Dir., 710 9th Ave., Seattle, 98104. Tel: 206-522-0996; Fax: 206-525-9628.

Benefits Services—Ms. GERALYN MIRANTE-MARLEY, Dir., 710 9th Ave., Seattle, 98104. Tel: 206-382-4286; Fax: 206-382-3493.

Campaign for Human Development—Mr. J. L. DROUHARD, Dir., 710 9th Ave., Seattle, 98104. Tel: 206-382-4869; Fax: 206-382-3487.

Campus Ministry—Mr. SHAWN MADDEN, Dir., 710 9th Ave., Seattle, 98104. Tel: 206-382-4831; Fax: 206-903-4627.

Catholic Community Services of Western Washington—Mr. MICHAEL REICHERT, Pres., 100 23rd Ave. S., Seattle, 98144-2302. Tel: 206-328-5696; 800-499-5979 (Toll Free); 206-328-5646 (TTY); Fax: 206-328-5699.

Catholic Faith Formation, Office of—Dr. MARY CROSS, Dir., 710 9th Ave., Seattle, 98104. Tel: 206-382-4835; Fax: 206-264-2084.

Catholic Relief Services—Mr. J.L. DROUHARD, Dir., 710 9th Ave., Seattle, 98104. Tel: 206-382-4580; 800-869-7028 (Toll Free); Fax: 206-382-3487.

Catholic Schools Department—Mr. TOM LORD, Interim Supt. Catholic Schools, 710 9th Ave., Seattle, 98104. Tel: 206-382-4861; 800-473-5651 (Toll Free); Fax: 206-654-4651.

Catholic Youth Organization—Mr. SHAWN MADDEN, Dir., 710 9th Ave., Seattle, 98104. Tel: 206-382-4831; Fax: 206-903-4627.

Censor Librorum—Rev. MICHAEL RASCHKO, Ph.D.

Chancery Operations—Mr. DENNIS J. O'LEARY, Exec. Dir. Chancery, 710 9th Ave., Seattle, 98104. Tel: 206-382-4289; Fax: 206-382-4583.

Communications, Office of—Mr. GREG MAGNONI, Dir., 710 9th Ave., Seattle, 98104. Tel: 206-382-4862; 800-473-5641 (Toll Free); Fax: 206-382-3487.

Newspaper "The Catholic Northwest Progress"—Mr. GREG MAGNONI, Assoc. Publisher. Tel: 206-382-4850; 800-473-5641; Fax: 206-382-3487.

Criminal Justice Ministry Services—Ms. ERICA COHEN MOORE, 710 9th Ave., Seattle, 98104. Tel: 206-382-4852; Fax: 206-654-4654.

Cultural and Ethnic Faith Formation—Mr. JOSE RAMIREZ-LOMELI, Dir., 710 9th Ave., Seattle, 98104. Tel: 206-654-4644; 800-950-4970 (Toll Free); Fax: 206-264-2084.

Deacon Services—Deacon ROY HARRINGTON, Assoc. Dir. Deacons, 710 9th Ave., Seattle, 98104. Tel: 206-382-1477; Fax: 206-654-4654.

Disability Ministry Services—Mr. PHILIP TRAN, 710 9th Ave., Seattle, 98104. Tel: 206-382-4509, Ext. 4828; Fax: 206-654-4654.

Due Process—Very Rev. ANTHONY E. BAWYN, J.C.D., Contact, 710 9th Ave., Seattle, 98104. Tel: 800-950-4965 (Toll Free); 206-382-3484.

Ecumenical and Interfaith Commission—Sr. JOYCE M. COX, B.V.M., Dir. Relg. Communities & Ecumenism, 710 9th Ave., Seattle, 98104. Tel: 206-382-4829; 800-406-6613 (Toll Free); Fax: 206-382-4840.

Hispanic/Latino Ministry Services—Mr. ISAAC GOVEA, Dir., 710 9th Ave., Seattle, 98104. Tel: 206-382-4825; 800-465-6862, Ext. 4825 (Toll Free); Fax: 206-382-2069.

Holy Childhood Association—Mr. J.L. DROUHARD, Dir., 710 9th Ave., Seattle, 98104. Tel: 206-382-4850; 800-869-7028 (Toll Free); Fax: 206-382-3487.

Human Resources—Ms. MARY E. SANTI, J.C.L., Dir., 710 9th Ave., Seattle, 98104. Tel: 206-382-4570; 800-261-4749 (Toll Free); Fax: 206-382-4267.

Information Technology & Services—Mr. HOWARD CHANG, 710 9th Ave., Seattle, 98104. Tel: 206-382-4282; Fax: 206-382-4840.

Justice and Peace Ministry Resources—Dr. MARY CROSS, Dir., 710 9th Ave., Seattle, 98104. Tel: 206-382-4268; 800-950-4970 (Toll Free); Fax: 206-264-2084.

Koreans, Ministry to—Revs. JUNKOO YEO, Pastor, St. Andrew Kim Personal Parish, 11700 1st Ave., N.E., Seattle, 98125. Tel: 206-362-2278; 206-362-2492; HENRY SUNG GEE CHOI, Pastor, St. Paul Chong Hasang Personal Parish, 1316 62nd Ave. E., Fife, 98424. Tel: 253-896-4489.

Lay Ecclesial Ministry—Dr. MARY CROSS, Dir., 710 9th Ave., Seattle, 98104. Tel: 206-382-4268; 800-950-4970 (Toll Free); Fax: 206-264-2084.

Parish Leadership Ministry Services—LEIGH STRINGFELLOW, Assoc. Dir., 710 9th Ave., Seattle, 98104. Tel: 206-382-4256; 800-465-6862 (Toll Free); Fax: 206-382-2069.

Library Media Center—Ms. LISA HILLYARD, 710 9th Ave., Seattle, 98104. Tel: 206-382-4883; 800-869-7027 (Toll Free); Fax: 206-382-3487.

Liturgy—Ms. CAROLYN LASSEK, 710 9th Ave., Seattle, 98104. Tel: 206-382-4878; 800-473-5657 (Toll Free); Fax: 206-903-4612.

Missions—Mr. J. L. DROUHARD, Dir., 710 9th Ave., Seattle, 98104. Tel: 206-382-4580; 800-869-7028 (Toll Free); Fax: 206-382-3487.

Native American Ministry Services—Mr. PHILIP TRAN, 710 9th Ave., Seattle, 98104. Tel: 206-382-4828; 800-465-6862 (Toll Free); Fax: 206-382-2069.

Parish and School Faith Formation—Dr. ANNE FREDERICK, Ed.D., Dir., 710 9th Ave., Seattle, 98104. Tel: 206-903-4614; 800-950-4970 (Toll Free); Fax: 206-264-2084.

Parish Financial Services—Mr. ED WILLIAMS, Dir., 710 9th Ave., Seattle, 98104. Tel: 206-382-7316; 800-768-7986 (Toll Free); Fax: 206-382-4279.

Parish Stewardship—Mr. SCOTT BADER, Dir., 710 9th Ave., Seattle, 98104. Tel: 206-903-4619; 866-381-2033 (Toll Free); Fax: 206-903-4610.

Pastoral Care of the Sick & Dying Ministry Services—Mr. PHILIP TRAN, 710 9th Ave., Seattle, 98104. Tel: 206-382-4828; 800-465-6862 (Toll Free); Fax: 206-654-4654.

Pastoral Planning and Research—Mr. DENNIS J. O'LEARY, Dir. Tel: 206-382-4832; 800-327-5295 (Toll Free); Fax: 206-274-3161; Ms. MARY BETH CELIO, Dir. Research, 710 9th Ave., Seattle, 98104. Tel: 206-382-4272.

Planned Giving—Ms. JOANNE STROM, Dir., 710 9th Ave., Seattle, 98104. Tel: 206-903-4621; 800-752-5902 (Toll Free); Fax: 206-903-4610.

Polish Speaking, Ministry to—Revs. EUGENIUSZ BOLDA, S.Ch., Pastor, Sts. Peter and Paul Parish, 3422 Portland Ave., Tacoma, 98404. Tel: 206-272-5232; STANISLAW MICHALEK, S.Ch., Pastor, St. Margaret of Scotland Parish, 3221 14th Ave. W., Seattle, 98119. Tel: 206-282-1804.

Catholic Archdiocese of Seattle Clergy Medical Plan Veba Trust—Most Rev. J. PETER SARTAIN, D.D., S.T.L.; Very Rev. ANTHONY E. BAWYN, J.C.D., Chm. Trustees; Ms. GERALYN MIRANTE-MARLEY, Benefits Dir. Tel: 206-382-4286.

Priests' Pension Plan—Most Rev. J. PETER SARTAIN, D.D., S.T.L.; Very Rev. ANTHONY E. BAWYN, J.C.D., Chm. Trustees; Ms. GERALYN MIRANTE-MARLEY, Benefits Dir. Tel: 206-382-4286.

Propagation of the Faith, Society for the—Mr. J.L. DROUHARD, Dir., 710 9th Ave., Seattle, 98104. Tel: 206-382-4580; 800-869-7028 (Toll Free); Fax: 206-382-3487.

Society for St. Peter the Apostle—Mr. J. L. DROUHARD, Dir., 710 9th Ave., Seattle, 98104. Tel: 206-382-4580; 800-869-7028 (Toll Free); Fax: 206-382-3487.

Property and Construction Services—Mr. EDWARD FOSTER, Dir., 710 9th Ave., Seattle, 98104. Tel: 206-382-4851; 800-809-4923 (Toll Free); Fax: 206-382-4266.

Religious Communities—Sr. JOYCE M. COX, B.V.M., Dir., 710 9th Ave., Seattle, 98104. Tel: 206-382-4829; 800-406-6613 (Toll Free); Fax: 206-382-4840.

Samoan, Ministry to—Rev. TUAN NGUYEN, 7025 S. Park Ave., Tacoma, 98408. Tel: 253-472-1360.

Seminarian Services—Rev. BRYAN DOLEJSI, Dir., 710 9th Ave., Seattle, 98104. Tel: 206-382-4595; 800-809-4919; Fax: 206-654-4654.

Stewardship and Development Department—Mr. RICK FERSCH, Exec. Dir., 710 9th Ave., Seattle, 98104. Tel: 206-903-4620; Fax: 206-903-4610.

Theological Resources—Revs. JAMES EBLEN, S.T.L., Ph.D. (Retired), 131 Bellevue Ave. E., #203, Seattle, 98102-5566. Tel: 206-296-5339. Seattle University, 900 Broadway, Seattle, 98122; MICHAEL RASCHKO, Ph.D., 1614 Summit Ave., #502, Seattle, 98122. Tel: 206-296-5311. Seattle University, 900 Broadway, Seattle, 98122.

Vicar for Clergy, Office of—Very Rev. DAVID T. MULHOLLAND, 710 9th Ave., Seattle, 98104. Tel: 206-382-7317; 800-809-4919 (Toll Free); Fax: 206-654-4654.

Pastoral Outreach Coordinator—Ms. DENISE AUBUCHON. Tel: 206-382-4592; 800-446-7762 (Toll Free). Email: hotline@seattlearch.org.

Vietnamese, Ministry to—Rev. THANH X. DAO, Pastor, Vietnamese Martyrs Personal Parish, 1230 E. Fir St., Seattle, 98122. Tel: 206-325-5626; Fax: 206-324-5849.

Vocations—Rev. BRYAN DOLEJSI, Dir., 710 9th Ave., Seattle, 98104. Tel: 206-387-4595; Fax: 206-654-4654.

Youth and Young Adult Ministry, Office of—Mr. SHAWN MADDEN, Dir., 710 9th Ave., Seattle, 98104. Tel: 206-382-4562; 800-950-4963; Fax: 206-903-4627.

CLERGY, PARISHES, MISSIONS AND PAROCHIAL SCHOOLS

CITY OF SEATTLE

(KING COUNTY)

1—ST. JAMES CATHEDRAL (1904) Very Rev. Michael G. Ryan. In Res., Rev. David A. Brant (Retired).
Res.: 804 Ninth Ave., 98104. Tel: 206-622-3559; Fax: 206-622-5303.
Station—St. Ignatius Chapel Seattle University, 901 12th St., 98122.

2—ST. ALPHONSUS (1901) Rev. Danilo Abalon, S.O.L.T., Admin.
Res.: 5816 15th Ave., N.W., 98107. Tel: 206-784-6464; Fax: 206-789-5709.
School—(Grades PreSchool-8) Tel: 206-782-4363. Maureen Reid, Prin. Lay Teachers 16; Students 200.
Catechesis/Religious Program—Students 40.

3—ST. ANDREW KIM PERSONAL PARISH Revs. Junkoo Yeo; Donghoon Kim, Parochial Vicar; Deacon Duk Kim.
11700 1st Ave. N.E., 98125-4714. Tel: 206-362-2278; Fax: 206-362-2492.
Catechesis/Religious Program—Students 217.

4—ST. ANNE (1908) Revs. John Bowman, Parochial Vicar; Steven Sallis, Priest Moderator; Mr. Ron Ryan, Pastoral Coord.
Res.: 1411 1st Ave. W., 98119. Tel: 206-282-0223; Fax: 206-217-9541.
School—(Grades PreSchool-8), 101 W. Lee St., 98119. Tel: 206-282-3538; Fax: 206-284-4191. Mary Sherman, Prin. Lay Teachers 19; Students 260.

5—ASSUMPTION (1924) Rev. Oliver Duggan.
Office: 6201 33rd Ave. N.E., 98115. Tel: 206-522-7674; Fax: 206-522-6308.
School—(Grades K-8), 6220 32nd Ave., N.E., 98115-7233. Tel: 206-524-7452; Fax: 206-524-6757. Kathi Hand, Prin.; Laurel Throssell, Librarian. Lay Teachers 28; Students 540.
Catechesis/Religious Program—Students 80.

6—ST. BENEDICT (1906) Rev. Steven Sallis.
Mailing Address: 1805 N. 49th St., 98103.
Res.: 1700 N. 49th St., 98103. Tel: 206-632-0843; Fax: 206-632-2167. Web: www.stbens.net.

School—(Grades PreK-8), 4811 Wallingford Ave. N., 98103. Tel: 206-633-3375; Fax: 206-632-3236. Mr. Brian Anderson, Prin.; Susan Lisi, Librarian. Lay Teachers 24; Students 225.
Catechesis/Religious Program—Students 90.

7—ST. BERNADETTE (1958) Rev. Michael H. Wright.
Res.: 861 S.W. 126th St., 98146. Tel: 206-242-7370; Fax: 206-242-7371. Web: www.saintbernadette.net.
School—(Grades PreK-8), 1028 S.W. 128th St., 98146. Tel: 206-244-4934; Fax: 206-244-4943. Robert Rutledge, Prin. Lay Teachers 13; Students 240.
Catechesis/Religious Program—Students 133.

8—BLESSED SACRAMENT (1908) Revs. Daniel Syverstad, O.P.; Raphael Mary Salzillo, O.P., Asst. Dir. Newman Center; Jordan Bradshaw, O.P., Dir. Newman Center; Christopher Fadok, O.P., Parochial Vicar; Boniface Willard, O.P., Parochial Vicar. In Res., Revs. Augustine Hartman, O.P.; James Thompson, O.P.
Res.: 5041 Ninth Ave., N.E., 98105. Tel: 206-547-3020; Fax: 206-547-6371.
Catechesis/Religious Program—Web: www.blessedsacrament.org. Students 127.

9—ST. BRIDGET (1968) [CEM] Rev. Timothy Sauer; Deacon Dennis T. Duffell.
Res.: 4900 N.E. 50th St., 98105. Tel: 206-523-8787; Fax: 206-528-7511. Web: www.stbridgetchurch.org.
Catechesis/Religious Program—Tel: 206-523-9760. Students 28.

10—ST. CATHERINE OF SIENA (1929) Very Rev. Anthony E. Bawyn, Parochial Vicar; Rev. Oliver Duggan, Moderator; Victoria Ries, Pastoral Coord.
Res.: 814 N.E. 85th, 98115. Tel: 206-524-8800.
School—(Grades PreSchool-8), 8524 8th Ave. N.E., 98115. Tel: 206-525-0581; Fax: 206-985-0253. Kris Brown, Prin.; Margaret Hartley, Librarian. Lay Teachers 17; Students 249.
Catechesis/Religious Program—Students 80.

11—CHRIST OUR HOPE PERSONAL PARISH (2009) Rev. Paul A. Magnano; Deacons Samuel Basta; Terrance Marcell; Lawrence McDonald.
710 9th Ave., 98104. 1902 2nd Ave., 98101.
Mission—Plymouth Congregational Church Chapel 1217 6th Ave., 98101.

12—CHRIST THE KING (1930) Rev. Raymond Cleaveland.
Res.: 405 N. 117th St., 98133. Tel: 206-362-1545; Fax: 206-364-8325.
School—(Grades PreSchool-8), 415 N. 117th St., 98133. Tel: 206-364-6890. Anne Brand, Prin. Lay Teachers 16; Students 175.
Catechesis/Religious Program—Students 289.

13—ST. EDWARD (1906) Revs. Felino Paulino; Robert J. Kenny, Parochial Vicar.
Mailing Address: 4212 S. Mead St., 98118. Tel: 205-722-7888; Fax: 206-722-7895. Web: www.stedwardparish.net.
Res.: 4213 S. Orcas, 98118.
School—(Grades PreK-8), 4200 S. Mead St., 98118. Tel: 206-725-1774; Fax: 206-725-4569. Mary Lundeen, Prin. Sisters 1; Lay Teachers 9; Students 164.
Catechesis/Religious Program—Students 67.

14—ST. FRANCIS OF ASSISI (1929) Rev. Richard K. Hayatsu; Deacon Lloyd Snider.
Res.: 15236 21st Ave., S.W., 98166. Tel: 206-242-4575; Fax: 206-242-1957.
School—(Grades K-8), P.O. Box 870, Seahurst, 98062. Tel: 206-243-5690; Fax: 206-433-8593. Sheila Keaton, Prin. Lay Teachers 33; Students 472.
Catechesis/Religious Program—Students 180.

15—ST. GEORGE (1903) Revs. Felino Paulino; Robert J. Kenny; Deacon Sagato Pele.
Res.: 5306 13th Ave. S., 98108. Tel: 206-762-7744; Fax: 206-762-4207.
School—(Grades PreSchool-8), 5117 13th Ave. S., 98108. Tel: 206-762-0656; Fax: 206-763-3220. Monica Wingard, Prin. Lay Teachers 15; Students 250.
Catechesis/Religious Program—Students 45.

16—HOLY FAMILY (1921) Rev. Horacio Yanez; Deacons Ted Wiese; Abel Magaña.
Res.: 9622 20th Ave., S.W., 98106. Tel: 206-767-6220; Fax: 206-767-0374. Web: www.hfseattle.org.
School—(Grades PreSchool-8), 9615 20th Ave. S.W., 98106. Tel: 206-767-6640; Fax: 206-767-9466. Francis Cantwell, Prin. Lay Teachers 15; Students 137.
Catechesis/Religious Program—Students 240.

17—HOLY ROSARY (1907) Very Rev. John C. Madigan.
Res.: 4139 42nd Ave., S.W., 98116. Tel: 206-935-8353; Fax: 206-935-4303.
School—(Grades PreK-8), 4142 42nd Ave., S.W., 98116. Tel: 206-937-7255; Fax: 206-937-2610. Web: www.holyrosaryws.org. Michael Cantu, Prin.; Sue Harris, Librarian. Lay Teachers 30; Preschool 30; Students 494.
Catechesis/Religious Program—Tel: 206-937-1488, Ext. 203. Students 93.

18—IMMACULATE CONCEPTION (1891) Rev. Fabian MacDonald, Priest Admin.; Deacons Joseph Connor; Frederic Cordova. In Res., Rev. Jaime Tolang (Retired).
Res.: 820 18th Ave., 98122. Tel: 206-322-5970; Fax: 206-322-9417.
Catechesis/Religious Program—Students 19.

19—ST. JOHN THE EVANGELIST (1917) Rev. Crispin Okoth.
Office: 121 N. 80th St., 98103. Tel: 206-782-2810; Fax: 206-782-0242.
School—(Grades PreK-8), 120 N. 79th St., 98103. Tel: 206-783-0337; Fax: 206-706-2704. Web: www.stjohnsea.org. Bernadette O'Leary, Prin.; Sherry Grandorf, Librarian. Lay Teachers 30; Students 520.
Catechesis/Religious Program—Students 50.

20—ST. JOSEPH (1907) Rev. John Whitney, S.J.; Deacon Stephen Wodzanowski, Pastoral Assoc.
Res.: 732 18th Ave. E., 98112. Tel: 206-324-2522; Fax: 206-329-5698. Web: www.stjosephparish.org.
School—(Grades K-8), 700 18th Ave. E., 98112. Tel: 206-329-3260; Fax: 206-324-7773. George Hofbauer, Prin. Sisters 1; Lay Teachers 42; Students 625.
Catechesis/Religious Program—Students 125.

21—ST. MARGARET OF SCOTLAND (1910) Rev. Stanislaw Michalek, S.Ch., Admin.
Res.: 3221 14th Ave. W., 98119. Tel: 206-282-1804; Fax: 206-282-6461.
Catechesis/Religious Program—Students 106.

22—ST. MARY (1899) Revs. Anthony J. Haycock, Senior Priest (Retired); Felino Paulino, Moderator; Tricia Wittmann-Todd, Pastoral Coord.
Res.: 611 20th Ave. S., 98144. Tel: 206-324-7100; Fax: 206-329-4596. Web: www.stmarysseattle.org.
Catechesis/Religious Program—Students 134.

23—ST. MATTHEW (1954) Rev. Gerald Burns, Priest Admin.
Mailing Address: 1240 N.E. 127th St., 98125.
Res.: 405 N. 117th St., 98133-8609. Tel: 206-363-6767; Fax: 206-362-4863.
School—(Grades PreK-8), 1230 N.E. 127th St., 98125. Tel: 206-362-2785; Fax: 206-440-9476. Lillian Zadra, Prin. Lay Teachers 13; Students 217.
Catechesis/Religious Program—Students 41.

24—NORTH AMERICAN MARTYRS PERSONAL QUASI-PARISH (2008) Rev. Gerard Saguto, F.S.S.P. 5901 8th Ave., N.W., 98107. Tel: 206-297-1571. Web: www.northamericanmartyrs.org.

25—OUR LADY OF FATIMA (1952) Rev. James Johnson Jr. In Res., Rev. Robert Evanson; Very Rev. David T. Mulholland.
Res.: 3218 W. Barrett, 98199. Tel: 206-283-1456; Fax: 206-283-5788. Web: www.olfatima.org.
School—(Grades K-8), 3301 W. Dravus St., 98199. Tel: 206-283-7031; Fax: 206-352-4588. Susan Burdett, Prin.; Mary Van Tassell, Librarian. Lay Teachers 20; Students 287.
Catechesis/Religious Program—Tel: 206-352-4586. Students 244.

26—OUR LADY OF GUADALUPE (1960) Rev. John Walmesley.
Res.: 7000-35th Ave., S.W., 98126. Tel: 206-935-0358; Fax: 206-935-1230. Web: www.olgseattle.org.
School—(Grades PreK-8), 3401 S.W. Myrtle, 98126. Tel: 206-935-0651; Fax: 206-938-3695. Web: www.guadalupe-school.org. Kristin Dixon, Prin.; Loretta Kramer, Librarian. Lay Teachers 19; Students 253.
Catechesis/Religious Program—Students 310.

27—OUR LADY OF LOURDES (1892) Rev. Gerald L. Mayovsky.
Office: P.O. Box 68340, 98168-1525. Tel: 206-762-3343; Fax: 206-762-3343.
Catechesis/Religious Program—Students 190.

28—OUR LADY OF MOUNT VIRGIN (1911) Very Rev. John C. Madigan, Priest Moderator; Revs. Clarence Edward Jones, C.O., Parochial Vicar; Patrick J. Twohy, S.J., Parochial Vicar (Native American Community); Deacons Joua Pao Yang, Pastoral Assoc. (Lao Community); Joseph Yuen, (Chinese Community); Charlene P. Collora, Pastoral Coord.
Res.: 1531 Bradner Pl. S., 98144. Tel: 206-324-8521; Fax: 206-324-0405.
Catechesis/Religious Program—Students 38.

29—OUR LADY OF THE LAKE (1929) Rev. Timothy Clark, Priest Admin. In Res., Very Rev. Anthony E. Bawyn.
Res.: 8900 35th Ave., N.E., 98115. Tel: 206-523-6776; Fax: 206-524-0848. Web: www.ollseattle.org.
School—(Grades K-8), 3520 N.E. 89th St., 98115. Tel: 206-525-9980; Fax: 206-523-2858. Vince McGovern, Prin.; Carol Jez, Librarian. Lay Teachers 17; Students 199.
Catechesis/Religious Program—Students 127.

30—ST. PATRICK (1918) Rev. Patrick S. Clark.
Res.: 2702 Broadway E., 98102. Tel: 206-329-2960; Fax: 206-329-2961. Web: www.stpatsseattle.org.
Catechesis/Religious Program—Students 45.

31—ST. PAUL (1953) Revs. Felino Paulino; Robert J. Kenny, Parochial Vicar.
Parish Office—5600 S. Ryan St., 98178. Tel: 206-725-2050; Fax: 206-725-7476.
School—(Grades PreSchool-8), 10001 57th Ave. S., 98178. Tel: 206-725-0780; Fax: 206-722-5732. Lay Teachers 15; Students 215.
Catechesis/Religious Program—Students 40.

32—ST. PETER (1931) Rev. Paul A. Magnano, Priest Mod.; Linda Lopez-Liang, Pastoral Coord.
Res.: 2807 15th Ave. S., 98144. Tel: 206-324-2290; Fax: 206-324-4020.
Catechesis/Religious Program—Students 56.

33—SACRED HEART OF JESUS (1889) Revs. Binh Ta, C.Ss.R.; Mark Scheffler, C.Ss.R., Parochial Vicar. In Res., Revs. Lyle Konen, C.Ss.R.; William Cleary, C.Ss.R.; Raymond Maiser, C.Ss.R.; William Peterson, C.Ss.R.; Timothy Watson, C.Ss.R.
Res.: 205 2nd Ave. N., 98109. Tel: 206-284-4680; Fax: 206-284-3161. Web: www.sacredheartseattle.com.

34—ST. THERESE (1926) Rev. Stephen Okumu, Priest Admin.; Deacon Gregory McNabb.
Res.: 3416 E. Marion St., 98122. Tel: 206-325-2711; Fax: 206-329-8373. Web: www.sainttheresеparish.org.
School—(Grades PreK-8), 900-35th Ave., 98122. Tel: 206-324-0460; Fax: 206-324-8464. Mrs. Theresa Haremann, Prin. Lay Teachers 10; Students 135.
Catechesis/Religious Program—Students 114.

35—VIETNAMESE MARTYRS PERSONAL PARISH Rev. Thanh X. Dao; Deacon Mau Nguyen.
1230 E. Fir St., 98122-5425. Tel: 206-325-5626; Fax: 206-324-5849.

OUTSIDE THE CITY OF SEATTLE

ABERDEEN, GRAYS HARBOR CO.

1—ST. MARY (1885) Revs. Dennis E. Robb; Paul J. Brunet, Parochial Vicar.
Res.: 306 E. Third St., 98520. Tel: 360-532-8300; Fax: 360-538-9987.
School—(Grades PreSchool-8), 518 N. H St., 98520. Tel: 360-532-1230; Fax: 360-532-1209. Kathleen Beyer, Prin. Lay Teachers 15; Students 164.
Catechesis/Religious Program—Tel: 360-532-8300, Ext. 110. Students 158.
Mission—St. Paul P.O. Box 332, Westport, Grays Harbor Co. 98585.

2—SS. PETER AND PAUL (1907), (Polish), Revs. Dennis E. Robb; Paul J. Brunet, Parochial Vicar.
Res.: 811 W. !st St., 98520. Tel: 360-532-8300; Fax: 360-538-9987.

ANACORTES, SKAGIT CO., ST. MARY (1910) Rev. Vu Phong Tran.
Res.: 4001 St. Mary's Dr., 98221. Tel: 360-293-2101; Fax: 360-293-8556. Web: www.stmaryanacortes.org; www.faithonfire.org.
Catechesis/Religious Program—Tel: 360-293-6882. Students 84.

ARLINGTON, SNOHOMISH CO., IMMACULATE CONCEPTION (1890) Rev. James Dalton.
Res.: 1200 E. Fifth, P.O. Box 69, 98223. Tel: 360-435-8565; Fax: 360-435-9732. Web: www.icp-sjvm.org.
Catechesis/Religious Program—Tel: 360-435-8565, Ext. 13. Students 157.
Mission—St. John Mary Vianney 1150 Riddle St., Darrington, Snohomish Co. 98241.

AUBURN, KING CO., HOLY FAMILY (1904) Rev. Timothy McKenna.
Res.: 505 17th St., S.E., 98002. Tel: 253-833-5130; Fax: 253-833-3421.
School—(Grades PreK-8), 505 17th St., S.E., 98002. Tel: 253-833-8688; Fax: 253-833-9311. Daniel Hill, Prin. Lay Teachers 15; Students 196.
Catechesis/Religious Program—Students 382.

BAINBRIDGE ISLAND, KITSAP CO., ST. CECILIA (1950) Rev. Emmett H. Carroll, S.J.
Church: 1310 Madison Ave. N., 98110. Tel: 206-842-3594; Fax: 206-842-6988. Web: www.saintcparish.org.
Catechesis/Religious Program—Tel: 206-842-3594, Ext. 102. Students 95.

BATTLE GROUND, CLARK CO., SACRED HEART (1877) [CEM] Rev. Paul M. Weckert, O.S.B.; Deacons Jack Roscoe; Carl Anderson.
Mailing Address: 1603 N. Parkway Ave., P.O. Box 38, 98604. Tel: 360-687-4515; Fax: 360-687-3322. Web: www.sacredheartbg.org.
Catechesis/Religious Program—Tel: 360-687-4515; Fax: 360-687-3322. Students 144.
Mission—St. Joseph the Worker 200 W. Jones St., Yacolt, Clark Co. 98675.
Mission—St. Mary of Guadalupe (1888) [CEM] 1520 N. 65th Ave., Ridgefield, Clark Co. 98642. Tel: 360-887-8194.

BELLEVUE, KING CO.

1—ST. LOUISE (1960) Revs. Thomas Belleque; Milhton Scarpetta Molina, Parochial Vicar; Deacons William Haines Jr.; Samuel Basta.
Res.: 141 156th Ave., S.E., 98007. Tel: 425-747-4450; Fax: 425-644-3678.
School—(Grades K-8), 133 156th Ave., S.E., 98007. Tel: 425-746-4220; Fax: 425-644-3294. Web: www.stlouiseschool.org. Dan Fitzpatrick, Prin.; Mary Carson, Librarian. Lay Teachers 31; Students 437.
Catechesis/Religious Program—Tel: 425-747-4450,

Ext. 55. Students 450.

2—St. Madeleine Sophie (1968) Very Rev. James D. Picton; Deacon William Taube.
Res.: 4400 130th Pl. S.E., 98006-2014. Tel: 425-747-6770; Fax: 425-747-6349.
School—(Grades PreK-8) Tel: 425-747-6770, Ext. 202; Fax: 425-747-1825. Dan Sherman, Prin. Lay Teachers 17; Students 200.
Catechesis/Religious Program—Tel: 425-747-6770, Ext. 124. Students 350.

3—Sacred Heart (1946) Rev. Patrick Ritter.
Res.: 9460 N.E. 14th St., 98004. Tel: 425-454-9536; Fax: 425-450-3909. Web: www.sacredheart.org.
School—(Grades K-8), 9450 N.E. 14th St., 98004. Tel: 425-451-1773; Fax: 425-450-3918. David Burroughs, Prin. Lay Teachers 29; Students 376.
Catechesis/Religious Program—Tel: 425-451-1775. Students 218.

Bellingham, Whatcom Co.

1—Assumption (1889) Rev. K. Scott Connolly; Deacon Lawrence Kheriaty.
Office: 2116 Cornwall Ave., 98225.
Res.: 1111 14th St., 98225. Tel: 360-733-1380; Fax: 360-733-5644. Web: www.assumption.org.
School—(Grades PreSchool-8) Tel: 360-733-6133; Fax: 360-647-4372. Web: www.school.assumption-.org. Ms. Monica Des Jarlais, Prin. Lay Teachers 14; Students 237.
Catechesis/Religious Program—Students 203.

2—Sacred Heart (1905) [JC] Rev. Qui-Thac Nguyen.
Res.: 1111 14th St., 98225. Tel: 360-734-2850; Fax: 360-734-0947.
Catechesis/Religious Program—Students 130.
Station—Newman Campus Ministry 714 N. Garden St., 98225. Tel: 360-410-0218.

Black Diamond, King Co., St. Barbara (1912) Rev. David H. Young.
Res.: 32416 6th Ave., P.O. Box 189, 98010. Tel: 360-886-2229. Web: www.stbarbarachurch.org.
Catechesis/Religious Program—Students 230.

Bothell, King Co., St. Brendan (1949) Very Rev. James Northrop; Deacon Eamon Parsons.
Res.: 10051 N.E. 195th St., 98011-2931. Tel: 425-483-9400; Fax: 425-486-9735. Web: www.saintbrendan.org.
School—(Grades K-8), 10049 N.E. 195th St., 98011. Tel: 425-483-8300; Fax: 425-483-2839. Chris Lunn, Prin.; Carl Carlson, Librarian. Lay Teachers 16; Students 235.
Catechesis/Religious Program—Students 290.

Bothell, Snohomish Co., St. Elizabeth Ann Seton (1983) Revs. Edgar Sanchez, M.Sp.S.; Jorge Gomez del Valle, M.Sp.S., Parochial Vicar; Jose Ugalde, M.Sp.S., Parochial Vicar.
Res.: P.O. Box 12429, Mill Creek, 98082-0429. Tel: 425-481-0303; Fax: 425-485-8510.
Catechesis/Religious Program—Tel: 425-481-9358. Mavis Kalbrener, D.R.E. Students 758.

Bremerton, Kitsap Co.

1—Holy Trinity (1964) Rev. Jack Buckalew.
Mailing Address: P.O. Box 910, Tracyton, 98393.
Res.: 4215 Pine Rd., 98310. Tel: 360-377-7674; Fax: 360-377-6181.
Catechesis/Religious Program—Tel: 360-479-9525. Students 264.

2—Our Lady, Star of the Sea (1902) Very Rev. Derek J. Lappe; Deacon William Hamlin.
Office: 1513-6th St., 98337. Tel: 360-479-3777; Fax: 360-479-1468. Web: www.staroftheseа.net.
School—1516-5th St., 98337. Tel: 360-373-5162. Jeanette Wolfe, Prin. Lay Teachers 11; Students 200.
Catechesis/Religious Program—Students 178.

Buckley, Pierce Co., St. Aloysius (1892) Rev. John J. Ludvik.
Res.: 211 W. Mason Ave., 98321. Tel: 360-829-6515; Fax: 360-829-5190.
Catechesis/Religious Program—Tel: 360-829-9958. Students 54.
Mission—Our Lady of Lourdes (1894) [CEM] Wilkeson, Pierce Co.

Burlington, Skagit Co., St. Charles (1885) Revs. Martin Bourke; Juan Carlos Saenz; Thomas McMichael, Parochial Vicar; Deacons Phil Meyer; Antonio Cavazos.
Res.: 935 Peterson Rd., 98233. Tel: 360-757-0128; Fax: 360-757-0418.
Catechesis/Religious Program—Students 113.

Camas, Clark Co., St. Thomas Aquinas (1870) [CEM] Rev. Matthew T. Oakland, Priest Admin.
Res.: 324 N.E. Oak, 98607. Tel: 360-834-2126; Fax: 360-834-5106. Web: www.st-thomascamas.org.
Catechesis/Religious Program—Tel: 360-834-2126, Ext. 2. Students 287.
Mission—Our Lady Star of the Sea P.O. Box 901, Stevenson, Skamania Co. 98648. Tel: 509-427-8478; Fax: 509-427-8478. Deacon William Townsend.

Castle Rock, Cowlitz Co., St. Mary (1976) Rev. Mel Strazicich, Priest Admin.
Mailing Address: P.O. Box 960, 98611-0960.
Church: 120 Powell Rd., 98611-0960. Tel: 360-274-7404; Fax: 360-274-7328.
Catechesis/Religious Program—Students 35.

Centralia, Lewis Co., St. Mary (1910) Revs. Timothy W. Ilgen; Armando V. Red, Parochial Vicar.
Res.: 225 N. Washington Ave., 98531. Tel: 360-736-4356; Fax: 360-807-0758.
Catechesis/Religious Program—Tel: 360-736-3470. Students 110.

Chehalis, Lewis Co., St. Joseph (1888) Revs. Timothy W. Ilgen; Armando V. Red, Parochial Vicar; Deacon Loren Lane.
Mailing Address: 157 S.W. 6th St., 98532.
Res.: 682 S.W. Cascade Ave., 98532. Tel: 360-748-4953; Fax: 360-748-3149. Web: www.wlpcatholic.org.
School—(Grades PreSchool-8), 123 S.W. 6th St., 98532. Tel: 360-748-0961; Fax: 360-748-8502. Lay Teachers 7; Students 123.
Catechesis/Religious Program—Students 50.

Covington, King Co., St. John the Baptist (1990) Very Rev. James P. Coyne; Deacon Ted Childs.
Church: 25810 156th Ave., S.E., 98042. Tel: 253-630-0701; Fax: 253-630-3174. Web: www.sjtbcc.org.
Catechesis/Religious Program—Students 414.

Des Moines, King Co., St. Philomena (1927) Revs. Stephen Woodland, Priest Admin.; Gilberto Mora Tapia, Parochial Vicar.
Res.: 1790 S. 222nd St., 98198. Tel: 206-878-8709; Fax: 206-824-3480.
School—(Grades K-8), 1815 S. 220th, 98198. Tel: 206-824-4051; Fax: 206-878-8646. Lay Teachers 12; Students 225.
Catechesis/Religious Program—Tel: 206-824-5582. Students 247.

Duvall, King Co., Holy Innocents (1914) Revs. David Rogerson; William Heric.
P.O. Box 850, 98019. Tel: 425-788-1400.
Catechesis/Religious Program—Jennie Caldwell, D.R.E. Students 115.

Edmonds, Snohomish Co., Holy Rosary (1940) Rev. Kenneth Haydock.
Res.: 760 Aloha St., P.O. Box 206, 98020-0206. Tel: 425-778-3122; Fax: 425-672-4909. Web: www.holyrosaryedmonds.org.
School—(Grades PreSchool-8), 770 Aloha St., P.O. Box 206, 98020. Tel: 425-778-3197; Fax: 425-771-8144. Dr. Kathy Carr, Prin.; Carlotta Rojas, Librarian. Sisters 1; Lay Teachers 19; Students 260.
Catechesis/Religious Program—Tel: 425-778-3122. Students 201.

Elma, Grays Harbor Co., St. Joseph (1890) [CEM] Rev. Byron Dichey; Deacon Frank Hawkins.
Res.: 510 W. Waldrip St., P.O. Box 3027, 98541. Tel: 360-482-3190; Fax: 360-482-3107.
Catechesis/Religious Program—Tel: 360-495-3415. Students 24.
Mission—St. John Broadway and Church St., Montesano, Grays Harbor Co. 98563.

Enumclaw, King Co., Sacred Heart of Jesus (1888) [CEM] Rev. Anthony K.A. Davis, Priest Admin.
Res.: 1614 Farrelly St., 98022. Tel: 360-825-3759; Fax: 360-825-6832. Web: www.sacredheartenumclaw.com.
Catechesis/Religious Program—Tel: 360-825-2333. Students 242.
Station—Crystal Mountain, Crystal Mountain Chapel

Everett, Snohomish Co.

1—Immaculate Conception (1904) Very Rev. Bryan L. Hersey; Rev. Sylvain Cibangu, Parochial Vicar; Deacon Matt Zuanich.
Mailing Address: 2619 Cedar St., 98201.
Res.: 2509 Hoyt Ave., 98201. Tel: 425-349-7014; Fax: 425-349-7015. Web: www.ic-olph.org.
Church: 2501 Hoyt Ave., 98201.
School—(Grades PreSchool-8), 2508 Hoyt Ave., 98201. Tel: 425-349-7777; Fax: 425-349-7048. Donna Ramos, Prin. Lay Teachers 19; Students 227.
Catechesis/Religious Program—Students 208.

2—St. Mary Magdalen (1957) Revs. Hans M. Olson; Michael Wagner; Deacon David P. Alcorta.
Res.: 8517 7th Ave., S.E., 98208. Tel: 425-353-1211; Fax: 425-348-0458. Web: www.smmparish.org.
School—(Grades PreSchool-8), 8615 7th Ave., S.E., 98208. Tel: 425-353-7559; Fax: 425-356-2687. Web: www.stmarym.org. Bruce J. Stewart, Prin. Lay Teachers 26; Students 408.
Catechesis/Religious Program—Students 198.
Mission—St. John 829 3rd St., Mukilteo, Snohomish Co. 98275.

3—Our Lady of Perpetual Help (1891) [CEM] Very Rev. Bryan L. Hersey; Rev. Sylvain Cibangu, Parochial Vicar; Deacon Matt Zuanich.
Mailing Address: 2619 Cedar St., 98201. Tel: 425-349-7014; Fax: 425-349-7015.
Res.: 2509 Hoyt Ave., 98201.
Church: 2617 Cedar St., 98201.
Catechesis/Religious Program—Students 232.

Federal Way, King & Pierce Cos., St. Theresa (1924) Revs. Richard K. Hayatsu, Priest Moderator; Leonardo Pestano, Parochial Vicar; Linda M. DeMarce, Pastoral Coord.
Res.: 3939 S.W. 331st, 98023. Tel: 253-838-5924; Fax: 253-838-0300.
Catechesis/Religious Program—Students 280.

Federal Way, King Co., St. Vincent De Paul (1961) Revs. William McKee; Thomas R. Park, Parochial Vicar; Deacons Delbert Hoover; Juan Lezcano.
Res.: 30525 8th Ave. S., 98003. Tel: 253-839-2320; Fax: 253-839-1819.
School—(Grades K-8), 30527 8th Ave. S., 98003. Tel: 253-839-3532; Fax: 253-946-1247. Wanda Stewart, Prin.; Urdene Rickard, Librarian. Lay Teachers 17; Students 255.
Catechesis/Religious Program—Students 353.

Ferndale, Whatcom Co., St. Joseph (1893) Very Rev. Khanh D. Nguyen.
Res.: 5781 Hendrickson Ave., 98248. Tel: 360-384-3651; Fax: 360-384-1879.
Catechesis/Religious Program—Tel: 360-384-8818. Students 250.
Mission—St. Anne Blaine, Whatcom Co. 98230.
Mission—St. Joachim (Indian Reservation) Bellingham. Kwina & Lummi Shore Rds., Bellingham, Whatcom Co. 98226.

Fife, Pierce Co.

1—St. Martin of Tours (1947) Rev. Gary Weisenberger.
Res.: 2303-54th Ave. E., 98424. Tel: 253-922-7882; Fax: 253-922-2068.
School—All Saints at St. Martin of Tours, (Grades K-8), 2323 54th Ave. E., 98424. Tel: 253-922-5360; Fax: 253-922-6746. Web: www.allsaintspuyallup.org. Stephen Morissette, Prin.
Catechesis/Religious Program—Tel: 253-922-6858. Students 75.

2—St. Paul Chong Hasang Personal Parish Revs. Henry Sung Gee Choi; Won Bong Voo, Parochial Vicar.
1316 62nd Ave., 98424-1312. Tel: 253-896-4489; Fax: 253-896-9468.

Forks, Clallam Co., St. Anne Parish (1930) Unassigned.
Res.: 511-5th Ave., P.O. Box 2359, 98331. Tel: 360-374-9184.
Catechesis/Religious Program—Tel: 360-374-6405. Students 34.
Mission—St. Thomas the Apostle Clallam Bay, Clallam Co. Tel: 360-963-2556.

Friday Harbor, San Juan Co., St. Francis (1860) [CEM] Rev. Hung Nguyen.
Mailing Address: 425 Price St., P.O. Box 1489, 98250. In Res., Rev. Raymond Heffernan (Retired).
Res.: 370 Marguerite St., P.O. Box 1489, 98250. Tel: 360-378-6603 (Rectory); 360-378-2910 (Office); Fax: 360-378-1843.
Catechesis/Religious Program—Students 17.
Station—St. Francis-Eastsound 956 N. Beach Rd., Eastsound, 98245.
Station—St. Francis: Lopez Island Community, Center Church Davis Bay Rd., Lopez Island.
Station—Our Lady of Good Voyage Chapel Roche Harbor, WA. Lay Ministers 2.

Gig Harbor, Pierce Co., St. Nicholas (1931) Rev. J. Lawrence Bailey; Deacons John Ricciardi; Patrick Kelley.
Mailing Address: 3510 Rosedale St., 98335-1818.
Res.: 3504 Coho St., 98335. Tel: 253-851-8850; Fax: 253-851-8823.
School—(Grades PreK-8), 3555 Edwards St., 98335. Tel: 253-858-7632; Fax: 253-858-1597. Michelle Corey, Prin. Lay Teachers 14; Students 132.
Catechesis/Religious Program—Tel: 253-851-9040. Students 220.

Hoquiam, Grays Harbor Co., Our Lady of Good Help (1906) Revs. Dennis E. Robb; Paul J. Brunet, Parochial Vicar.
Mailing Address: 306 E. 3rd St., Aberdeen, 98520.
611 2nd St., 98550.
Res.: 208 L St., 98550. Tel: 360-532-8300; Fax: 360-538-9987.
Mission—Our Lady of the Olympics

Issaquah, King Co., St. Joseph (1962) Rev. Todd O. Strange, Priest Admin.; Deacons Patrick Moynihan; Jack Bleile.
Res.: 220 Mt. Park Blvd., S.W., P.O. Box 200, 98027. Tel: 425-392-5516; Fax: 425-392-2722. Web: www.sjcissaquah.org.
School—Issaquah Campus, (Grades PreK-4) Tel: 425-313-9129; Fax: 425-313-7296. Peg Johnston, Prin. Lay Teachers 27; Students 355.
School—Snoqualmie Campus, (Grades PreSchool-3), 38645 S.E. Newton St., Snoqualmie, 98065. Tel: 425-888-9130. Peg Johnston, Prin.
Catechesis/Religious Program—Marge Barnette, D.R.E. Students 375.

Kelso, Cowlitz Co., Immaculate Heart of Mary (1910) Rev. Mel Strazicich, Priest Admin.
Res.: 2200 Allen St., 98626. Tel: 360-423-3650; Fax: 360-423-4165.
Catechesis/Religious Program—Fax: 360-423-4165. Students 15.

KENT, KING CO., HOLY SPIRIT PARISH (1890) [CEM] Rev. Vincent Pastro.
Mailing Address: 310 3rd Ave. S., 98032.
327 2nd Ave. S., 98032. Tel: 253-859-0444; Fax: 253-859-5974. Web: www.holyspiritkent.org.
Catechesis/Religious Program—Students 247.

KIRKLAND, KING CO.
1—HOLY FAMILY (1915) Rev. Kurt Nagel.
Res.: 7045 120th Ave., N.E., 98033. Tel: 425-822-0295; Fax: 425-827-0648. Web: www.hfkparish.org.
School—(Grades PreSchool-8), 7300 120th Ave. N.E., 98033. Tel: 425-827-0444; Fax: 425-827-0150. Web: www.hfkschool.org. Jacqueline Degel, Prin.; Anne Redmon, Librarian. Lay Teachers 21; Students 265.
Catechesis/Religious Program—Students 463.
2—ST. JOHN MARY VIANNEY (1971) Rev. Ramon Santa Cruz.
Mailing Address: 12600 84th Ave., N.E., 98034.
Res.: 12614 84th Ave., N.E., 98034. Tel: 425-823-0787; Fax: 425-814-2115. Web: www.sjvkirkland.org.
Catechesis/Religious Program—Students 200.

LA CONNER, SKAGIT CO., SACRED HEART (1875) Revs. Martin Bourke; Juan Carlos Saenz, Parochial Vicar; Thomas McMichael, Parochial Vicar; Deacon Philip Myer.
Res.: P.O. Box 757, 98257-0757. Tel: 360-466-3967; Fax: 360-466-3942.
Catechesis/Religious Program—Students 57.

LACEY, THURSTON CO., SACRED HEART OF JESUS (1923) Rev. J. Patrick McDermott; Deacons Terry Barber; Ronald San Nicolas; Ms. Ferrell Gilson, Pastoral Assoc. Admin.
Res.: P.O. Box 3805, 98509-3805. Tel: 360-491-0890; Fax: 360-456-1028. Web: www.sacredheartlacey.com.
Catechesis/Religious Program—Students 427.

LAKE STEVENS, SNOHOMISH CO., HOLY CROSS PARISH (2004) Rev. Joseph DeFolco.
P.O. Box 746, 98258. Tel: 360-691-2636. Email: administrator@holy-cross-parish.com. Web: www.holy-cross-parish.com.
Catechesis/Religious Program—Lee Ann Balbirona, D.R.E. Students 110.

LAKEWOOD, PIERCE CO.
1—ST. FRANCES CABRINI (1952) Rev. Peter Mactutis; Deacon George Mounce III.
Res.: 5505 108th St., S.W., 98499. Tel: 253-588-2141; Fax: 253-582-5351. Web: www.cabrini.us.
School—(Grades PreSchool-8), 5621 108th St., S.W., 98499. Tel: 253-584-3850. Stephanie Van Leuven, Prin. Lay Teachers 15; Students 238.
Catechesis/Religious Program—Students 266.
2—ST. JOHN BOSCO (1968) Rev. Oliver Lee Hightower; Deacon Daniel Allen. In Res., Rev. Charles G. Crosse (Retired).
Res.: 10508 112 St., S.W., 98498. Tel: 253-582-1028; Fax: 253-584-0633. Web: www.stjbosco.org.
Catechesis/Religious Program—Students 163.
Mission—Immaculate Conception Nisqually & Main, Steilacoom, Pierce Co. 98388.

LANGLEY, ISLAND CO., ST. HUBERT (1938) Rev. Richard J. Spicer; Deacon Lawrence Jesmer.
Mailing Address: P.O. Box 388, 98260-0388.
Res.: 815 Saratoga Rd., 98260. Tel: 360-221-5030; Fax: 360-221-2011. Web: www.sthubertchurch.org.
Catechesis/Religious Program—Students 43.

LONGVIEW, COWLITZ CO., ST. ROSE DE VITERBO (1928) Rev. Cal Christiansen, Priest Admin.; Deacon Fred Johnson.
Res.: 701 26th Ave., 98632. Tel: 360-425-4660; Fax: 360-577-5820. Web: www.stroselongview.catholicweb.com.
School—(Grades PreSchool-8), 720 26th Ave., 98632. Tel: 360-577-6760; Fax: 360-577-3689. Web: www.strose-school.org. Rosemary Griggs, Prin.; Marie O'Leary, Librarian. Lay Teachers 17; Students 147.
Catechesis/Religious Program—Tel: 360-577-7346. Students 223.
Mission—St. Catherine Cathlamet. 400 Columbia St., Cathlamet, Wahkiakum Co. 98612. Tel: 360-795-8725.

LYNDEN, WHATCOM CO., ST. JOSEPH (1897) Rev. Emilio Gonzalez.
Res.: 205 Twelfth St., 98264. Tel: 360-354-2334; Fax: 360-354-5889.
Catechesis/Religious Program—Students 153.
Mission—St. Peter [CEM 3] 6210 Mt. Baker Hwy., Deming, Whatcom Co. 98244.

LYNNWOOD, SNOHOMISH CO., ST. THOMAS MORE (1962) Revs. Francis Thumbi, Priest Admin.; Ward B. Oakshott, Senior Priest (Retired).
Mailing Address: 6511-176th, S.W., 98037.
Res.: 17414 64th Ave. W., 98037. Tel: 425-743-2929; Fax: 425-743-3652. Web: www.stmp.org.
School—(Grades PreSchool-8) Tel: 425-743-4242; Fax: 425-745-8367. Teresa Fewel, Prin.; Tessa Watters, Librarian. Sisters 1; Lay Teachers 15; Students 246.
Catechesis/Religious Program—Students 195.

MARYSVILLE, SNOHOMISH CO., ST. MARY (1888) [CEM] Rev. Mark A. Guzman, Priest Admin.; Deacons Jack Magnuson, (Retired); Antonio Cavazos, Pastoral Assoc. Hispanic Ministry.
Res.: 4200 88th St., N.E., 98270. Tel: 360-653-9400; Fax: 360-658-7439. Web: www.stmary-stanne.org.
Catechesis/Religious Program—Tel: 360-658-9400, Ext. 103 (Youth); 360-653-9400, Ext. 104 (Elementary). Students 400.
Mission—Tulalip Indian Reservation, St. Anne 7213 Totem Beach Rd., Tulalip, Snohomish Co. 98271. 4200 88th St. N.E., 98270.

MERCER ISLAND, KING CO., ST. MONICA (1958) Revs. Patrick Freitag; Negusse Fesseha Keleta (Eritrea); Deacons Jack Warfield; Larry McDonald.
Res.: 4301 88th Ave., S.E., 98040. Tel: 206-232-2900; Fax: 206-232-7875. Web: www.stmonica.cc.
School—(Grades K-8), 4320 87th, S.E., 98040. Tel: 206-232-5432; Fax: 206-275-2874. Mrs. Pamela Dellino, Prin. Lay Teachers 19; Students 245.
Catechesis/Religious Program—Tel: 206-232-9829; Fax: 206-232-3321. Students 176.

MONROE, SNOHOMISH CO., ST. MARY OF THE VALLEY (1902) Rev. Phillip A. Bloom.
Mailing Address: P.O. Box 279, 98272-0279.
Res.: 601 W. Columbia, 98272-1210. Tel: 360-794-8945; Fax: 360-805-0201.
Catechesis/Religious Program—Students 119.

MORTON, LEWIS CO., SACRED HEART (1922) Rev. Roger J. Smith.
Res.: 277 7th St., P.O. Box 880, 98356. Tel: 360-496-5456; Fax: 360-496-5458.
Catechesis/Religious Program—Students 12.
Mission—St. Yves [CEM] Harmony, Lewis Co. Fax: 360-496-5658.
Station— Packwood.

MOUNT VERNON, SKAGIT CO., IMMACULATE CONCEPTION (1899) Revs. Martin Bourke; Juan Carlos Saenz; Thomas McMichael, Parochial Vicar.
Office: 215 N. 15th St., 98273. Tel: 360-336-6622; Fax: 360-336-5203. Web: www.svcc.us.
School—Immaculate Conception Regional School, (Grades PreSchool-8), 1321 E. Division St., 98273. Tel: 360-428-3912; Fax: 360-424-8838. Web: www.l-crsweb.org. Kathleen Cartee, Prin. Lay Teachers 19; Students 293.
Catechesis/Religious Program—Regla Wilson, D.R.E. (Hispanic). Students 191.
Skagit Valley Catholic Churches—215 N. 15th St., 98273. Tel: 360-336-6622; Fax: 360-336-5203. Email: pastor@svcc.us. Web: www.svcc.us. Rev. Martin Bourke.

MOUNTLAKE TERRACE, SNOHOMISH CO., ST. PIUS X (1955) Revs. Sean P. Fox; Ronald Knudsen, Parochial Vicar.
Res.: 22301 58th Ave. W., 98043. Tel: 425-775-7545; Fax: 425-778-0413.
School—(Grades PreSchool-8), 22105 58th W., 98043. Tel: 425-778-9861; Fax: 425-776-2663. Web: www.stpx.org. Mrs. Ruth Foisy, Prin. Lay Teachers 10; Students 114.
Catechesis/Religious Program—Students 117.

OAK HARBOR, ISLAND CO., ST. AUGUSTINE (1939) Rev. Philip Raether.
Mailing Address: 185 N. Oak Harbor St., P.O. Box 1319, 98277.
Res.: 180 N.W. 1st Ave., 98277. Tel: 360-675-2303; Fax: 360-675-9490.
Catechesis/Religious Program—Tel: 360-675-2303, Ext. 25. Students 172.
Mission—St. Mary 207 N. Main, P.O. Box 1443, Coupeville, Island Co. 98239. Tel: 360-678-6536.

OCEAN SHORES, GRAYS HARBOR CO., ST. JEROME (1969) Revs. Dennis E. Robb; Paul J. Brunet, Parochial Vicar.
Mailing Address: 306 E. Third St., Aberdeen, 98520. In Res., Rev. Stephen Roman (Retired).
Res.: 15 Patrick Way, 98569. Tel: 360-532-8300; Fax: 360-538-9987.
Catechesis/Religious Program—Students 55.

OLYMPIA, THURSTON CO., ST. MICHAEL (1848) [CEM] Very Rev. James E. Lee; Rev. Dwight P. Lewis, Parochial Vicar; Deacon Robert Rensel.
Res.: 1208 11th Ave., S.E., P.O. Box 766, 98507. Tel: 360-754-4667; Fax: 360-754-0628. Web: www.saintmichaelparish.org.
School—(Grades K-8), 1204 11th Ave., S.E., 98501. Tel: 360-754-5131; Fax: 360-753-6090. Web: www-.stmikesolympia.org. Jack Nelson, Prin. Lay Teachers 16; Students 277.
Catechesis/Religious Program—P.O. Box 766, 98507. Students 614.

PE ELL, LEWIS CO., ST. JOSEPH (1894) [CEM 2] Revs. Timothy W. Ilgen; Armando V. Red, Parochial Vicar.
Res.: 417 N. Main, P.O. Box 235, 98572. Tel: 360-291-3434; Fax: 360-291-3434.
Catechesis/Religious Program—Students 24.
Mission—Holy Family State Hwy. 6, Frances, Pacific Co. 98572.

PORT ANGELES, CLALLAM CO., QUEEN OF ANGELS (1891) Rev. Thomas Nathe; Deacons Peter Flatley; Richard Labrecque.
Res.: 209 W. 11th St., 98362. Tel: 360-452-2351; Fax: 360-452-1447. Web: www.olypen.com/qofa.
School—(Grades PreSchool-8), 1007 S. Oak, 98362. Tel: 360-457-6903; Fax: 360-457-6866. Web: www.olypen.com/qofaschool. Mike Juhas, Prin.; Ceci Kimball, Librarian. Lay Teachers 14; Students 135.
Catechesis/Religious Program—Students 80.

PORT ORCHARD, KITSAP CO., ST. GABRIEL (1942) Very Rev. Phuong V. Hoang.
Res.: 1150 Mitchell Ave., 98366-4416. Tel: 360-876-2762; Fax: 360-876-6085.
Catechesis/Religious Program—Tel: 360-876-2834. Students 376.
Mission—Prince of Peace (1970) N.E. 1171 Sand Hill Rd., P.O. Box 517, Belfair, Mason Co. 98528. Tel: 360-275-8760; Fax: 360-275-4418.
Catechesis/Religious Program—Students 61.

PORT TOWNSEND, JEFFERSON CO., ST. MARY STAR OF THE SEA (1859) [CEM] Rev. L. John Topel, S.J.; Deacon Bill Swanson.
Res.: 1335 Blaine St., 98368. Tel: 360-385-3700; Fax: 360-379-1989. Web: www.stmaryss.com.
Catechesis/Religious Program—Tel: 360-385-1662. Students 50.

POULSBO, KITSAP CO., ST. OLAF (1968) Rev. David L. Mayovsky; Deacons Carlton Moyer; James Decker.
Res.: 18943 Caldart Ave., N.E., 98370. Tel: 360-779-4291.
Catechesis/Religious Program—Students 98.
Mission—St. Peter 910 South St., Suquamish, Kitsap Co. 98392.

PUYALLUP, PIERCE CO.
1—ALL SAINTS (1899) Revs. Richard McCallister; Justin D. McCreedy, O.S.B.; Deacons Michael McGillicuddy; Eric Paige.
Office: 204 6th Ave., S.W., 98371. Tel: 253-845-7521; Fax: 253-845-3105.
School—(Grades PreSchool-8), 504 2nd, S.W., 98371. Tel: 253-845-5025; Fax: 253-435-9841. Web: www.allsaintspuyallup.org. Stephen Morissette, Prin. Lay Teachers 23; Students 451.
Catechesis/Religious Program—Students 258.
2—HOLY DISCIPLES (1996) Very Rev. Matthew L. O'Leary.
Res.: 10425 187th St. E., 98374. Tel: 253-875-6630; Fax: 253-846-9535.
Catechesis/Religious Program—Web: www.holydisciples.org. Students 395.
Mission—Our Lady of Good Counsel 229 Antonie Ave. N., Eatonville, Pierce Co. 98328. Tel: 360-832-6363. Web: www.ourladyofgoodcounseleatonville.org. Deacon Rodney McGuire.

RAYMOND, PACIFIC CO., ST. LAWRENCE (1904) Rev. Paul A. Kaech.
1112 Blake St., P.O. Box 31, 98577. Tel: 360-942-3000; Fax: 360-942-3000.
Catechesis/Religious Program—Students 53.

REDMOND, KING CO., ST. JUDE (1978) [CEM] Revs. David Rogerson; William Heric, Parochial Vicar.
Res.: 10526 166th Ave., N.E., 98052. Tel: 425-883-7685; Fax: 425-881-2207.
Catechesis/Religious Program—Students 320.

RENTON, KING CO.
1—ST. ANTHONY (1901) Very Rev. Gary Zender; Rev. Bryan A. Ochs, Parochial Vicar; Deacons Richard Combs, (Retired); Teodoro Rodriguez.
Res.: 314 S. 4th St., 98057. Tel: 425-255-3132; Fax: 425-271-4729. Web: www.st-anthony.cc.
School—(Grades K-8), 336 Shattuck Ave. S., 98057. Tel: 425-255-0059; Fax: 425-235-6555. Web: www.sasr.org. Mr. Roger Gallagher, Prin.; Trisha Swindal, Librarian. Sisters 1; Lay Teachers 30; Students 517.
Catechesis/Religious Program—Students 460.
2—ST. STEPHEN THE MARTYR (1966) Revs. Edward Goodwin White; Brian Snyder, Parochial Vicar; Deacon Marshall Denby.
Res.: 13055 S.E. 192nd St., 98058. Tel: 253-631-1940.
Catechesis/Religious Program—Tel: 253-631-6175. (adults included) 989.

SAMMAMISH, KING CO., MARY, QUEEN OF PEACE (1987) Rev. Kevin F.X. Duggan.
Res.: 1121 228th Ave., S.E., 98075. Tel: 425-391-1178; Fax: 425-391-3797. Web: www.mqp.org.
Catechesis/Religious Program—Students 665.

SEAVIEW, PACIFIC CO., ST. MARY (1965) Rev. Paul A. Kaech; Deacon E. Jerome Sadler.
Res.: P.O. Box 274, 98644. Tel: 360-642-2002; Fax: 360-642-7100.
Catechesis/Religious Program—Students 7.
Station— McGowan.

SEDRO-WOOLLEY, SKAGIT CO., IMMACULATE HEART OF MARY (1890) Revs. Martin Bourke; Thomas McMichael, Parochial Vicar; Paul Grala, S.O.L.T., Parochial Vicar; Juan Carlos Saenz, Parochial Vicar; Deacon Phil Meyer.
Office:—719 Ferry St., Sedro Woolley, 98284. Tel: 360-855-0077; Fax: 360-855-2282.
Catechesis/Religious Program—Students 54.
Mission—St. Catherine 239 Limestone, Concrete,

Skagit Co. 98237.

SEQUIM, CLALLAM CO., ST. JOSEPH (1916) Rev. Thomas Nathe.
Res.: 121 E. Maple, P.O. Box 1209, 98382. Tel: 360-683-6076; Fax: 360-683-4674.
Catechesis/Religious Program—Students 90.

SHELTON, MASON CO., ST. EDWARD (1892) [JC] Rev. Ronald Belisle; Deacons Michael Samuel; William Batstone.
Res.: 601 W. C St., P.O. Box 758, 98584. Tel: 360-426-6134; Fax: 360-426-6231. Web: www.saintedwardshelton.org.
Catechesis/Religious Program—Students 201.

SHORELINE, KING CO.
1—ST. LUKE (1955) Rev. Robert Camuso.
Res.: 322 N. 175th St., 98133. Tel: 206-546-2451; Fax: 206-546-0328. Web: www.stlukecp.org.
School—(Grades K-8), 17533 St. Luke Pl. N., 98133. Tel: 206-542-1133; Fax: 206-546-8693. Mr. Christopher Sharp, Prin.; Jennifer Feucht, Librarian. Lay Teachers 20; Students 365.
Catechesis/Religious Program—Students 120.
2—ST. MARK (1954) Rev. William R. Harris.
Res.: 18033 15th Pl., N.E., 98155. Tel: 206-364-7900; Fax: 206-367-3919. Web: www.stmarkshoreline.org.
School—(Grades K-8) Tel: 206-364-1633. Web: www.stmss.org. Kathryn Palmquist-Keck, Prin. Lay Teachers 16; Students 198.
Catechesis/Religious Program—Students 110.

SNOHOMISH, SNOHOMISH CO., ST. MICHAEL (1886) Revs. Joseph DeFolco; Emmanuel Iweh, Parochial Vicar; Deacons Ed White; Gene Vanderzanden.
Res.: 1512 Pine Ave., 98290. Tel: 360-568-0821; Fax: 360-568-6426.
Catechesis/Religious Program—Students 100.

SNOQUALMIE, KING CO., OUR LADY OF SORROWS (1929) Rev. R. Roy C. Baroma, Priest Admin.
Mailing Address: P.O. Box 909, 98065.
Church: 39025 S.E. Alpha St., 98065.
Res.: 39025 S.E. Beta St., P.O Box 909, 98065. Tel: 425-888-2974; Fax: 425-888-7098. Web: www.olos.org.
Catechesis/Religious Program—Students 130.
Mission—St. Anthony P.O. Box 175, Carnation, King Co. 98014. Tel: 425-333-4930; Fax: 425-333-5001.
Station—St. Bernard's Chapel Snoqualmie Summit. Tel: 425-434-6287.

STANWOOD, SNOHOMISH CO., ST. CECILIA (1908) Rev. Christopher Larocca, O.C.D., Admin.
Res.: 26900 78th Ave., N.W., P.O. Box 1002, 98292. Tel: 360-629-3737; Fax: 360-629-6127. Web: www.home.catholicweb.com/saintcecelia.
Catechesis/Religious Program—Tel: 360-629-4425. Students 142.

SUMNER, PIERCE CO., ST. ANDREW (1921) Rev. Jack D. Shrum, Priest Admin.
Office: 1401 Valley Ave. E., 98390. Tel: 253-863-2253; Fax: 253-863-3567.
Church: 1401 Valley Ave, 98390.
Catechesis/Religious Program—Students 981.
Mission—SS. Cosmas and Damian 213 W. Leber St., P.O. Box 215, Orting, Pierce Co. 98360. Tel: 360-893-3154. Email: sscp@tmis.org.

SWINOMISH, ST. PAUL (1867), (Native American), Rev. Vu P. Tran.
17456 Pioneer Pkwy. Rd., 98257. Tel: 360-466-5737; Fax: 360-466-4039. Mailing Address: P.O. Box 2100, La Conner, 98257.

TACOMA, PIERCE CO.
1—ST. ANN (1924) Revs. Tuan Nguyen; Francisco J. Cancino, Parochial Vicar.
Res.: 7025 S. Park Ave., 98408. Tel: 253-472-1360; Fax: 253-475-6335. Web: www.catholic-tacoma.org.
Catechesis/Religious Program—Tel: 253-472-1360. Students 68.
2—ST. CHARLES BORROMEO (1956) Revs. Michael J. McDermott; Bradley R. Hagelin, Parochial Vicar.
Res.: 7112 S. 12th St., 98465. Tel: 253-564-5185; Fax: 253-565-0936. Web: www.saintcharlesb.org.
School—(Grades PreK-8) Patrick Feist, Prin.; Mrs. Kim Hart, Librarian. Lay Teachers 32; Students 519.
Catechesis/Religious Program—Tel: 253-564-5185, Ext. 3036. Jodi Clark, D.R.E. Students 189.
3—HOLY CROSS (1915) Rev. John J. Renggli.
Res.: 5510 N. 44th St., 98407. Tel: 253-759-3368; Fax: 253-759-6126.
Catechesis/Religious Program—Tel: 253-759-3491. Students 37.
4—HOLY ROSARY (1891) Rev. Jacob M. Maurer, Priest Admin.
Res.: 424 S. 30th St., 98402. Tel: 253-383-4549; Fax: 253-383-4540.
School—(Grades K-7), 504 S. 30th, 98402. Tel: 253-272-7012; Fax: 253-404-1804. Dr. Timothy Uhl, Prin. Lay Teachers 12; Students 115.
5—ST. JOHN OF THE WOODS (1924) Revs. Tuan Nguyen; Francisco J. Cancino, Parochial Vicar.
7001 S. Park Ave., 98408.
Res.: 9903 24th Ave., E., 98445. Tel: 253-537-8551; Fax: 253-537-0459. Web: www.catholic-tacoma.org.
Catechesis/Religious Program—Tel: 253-531-7110. Students 68.
6—ST. JOSEPH (1911), (Slovak), Rev. Jacob M. Maurer, Priest Admin.
Res.: 608 S. 34th St., 98418. Tel: 253-472-2489; Fax: 253-473-1201.
7—ST. LEO THE GREAT (1879) Revs. Stephen C. Lantry, S.J.; James Harbaugh, S.J., Parochial Vicar; Patrick J. Twohy, S.J., Parochial Vicar; Deacons Michael Riggio; David Rapp.
Res.: 710 S. 13th St., 98405. Tel: 253-272-5136; Fax: 253-272-6285.
Catechesis/Religious Program—Students 165.
8—OUR LADY, QUEEN OF HEAVEN (1893) Rev. John J. Wilkie.
Parish Office—14601 A St. S., 98444. Tel: 253-537-3252; Fax: 253-536-2662. Web: www.ourladyqueenofheaven.org.
Catechesis/Religious Program—Students 225.
9—ST. PATRICK (1891) Rev. Seamus Laverty.
Res.: 1001 N. J St., 98403. Tel: 253-383-2783; Fax: 253-627-5396. Web: www.stpats-tacoma.org.
School—(Grades PreSchool-8), 1112 N. G St., 98403. Tel: 253-272-2297; Fax: 253-383-2003. Mr. Chase Nordlund, Prin. Sisters 1; Lay Teachers 26; Students 440.
Catechesis/Religious Program—Students 175.
10—SS. PETER & PAUL (1892), (Polish), Rev. Eugeniusz Bolda, S.Ch.
Res.: 3422 Portland Ave., 98404. Tel: 253-272-5232; Fax: 253-627-7848.
11—ST. RITA OF CASCIA (1922), (Italian), Rev. Eugene P. Delmore, S.J.
Res.: 1403 S. Ainsworth, 98405. Tel: 253-627-1208; Fax: 253-627-4851. Web: www.stritatacoma.org.
Catechesis/Religious Program—Students 16.
12—SACRED HEART (1912) Revs. Tuan Nguyen; Francisco J. Cancino, Parochial Vicar; Deacon Mauricio Anaya.
Res.: 4520 McKinley Ave., 98404. Tel: 253-472-7738; Fax: 253-475-0071.
Catechesis/Religious Program—Students 240.
13—VISITATION (1892) Rev. Nicholas F. Wichert, Priest Admin.
Res.: 3314 S. 58th St., 98409. Tel: 253-473-4960; Fax: 253-474-8378.
School—(Grades PreSchool-8), 3306 S. 58th St., 98409. Tel: 253-474-6424; Fax: 253-474-6718. Web: www.visitationschool.net. Sheila Harrison, Prin. Lay Teachers 13; Students 134.
Catechesis/Religious Program—Students 89.

TOLEDO, LEWIS CO., ST. FRANCIS XAVIER (1838) [CEM] Revs. Timothy W. Ilgen; Armando V. Red, Parochial Vicar; Deacon Clay Hartzell.
Res.: 139 Spencer Rd., 98591. Tel: 360-864-4126; Fax: 360-864-4130. Web: www.toledotel.com/~stfrancis.
Catechesis/Religious Program—Students 29.

TUKWILA, KING CO., ST. THOMAS (1912) Rev. Gerald L. Mayovsky.
Res.: 4415 S. 140th St., 98168. Tel: 206-242-5501; Fax: 206-244-9387.
Catechesis/Religious Program—Tel: 206-242-8189. Students 90.

VANCOUVER, CLARK CO.
1—HOLY REDEEMER (2000) Rev. Joseph P. Mitchell.
Mailing Address: P.O. Box 871417, 98687-1417. Tel: 360-885-7780; Fax: 360-944-7560.
Church: 17010 N.E. Ninth St., 98684. Tel: 360-885-7780, Ext. 11. Web: www.holyredeemervanc.org.
Catechesis/Religious Program—Students 369.
2—ST. JAMES (1836) [CEM] Rev. Dominic D. Hahn.
Res.: 218 W. 12th St., 98660. Tel: 360-693-3052; Fax: 360-693-3077. Web: www.saintjames-parish.com.
Catechesis/Religious Program—Students 102.
3—ST. JOHN THE EVANGELIST (1868) [CEM] Very Rev. Armando S. Perez; Deacon Adolfo Carbajal.
Res.: 8701 N.E. 119 St., 98662. Tel: 360-573-3325; Fax: 360-573-3344.
Catechesis/Religious Program—Students 464.
4—ST. JOSEPH (1952) Revs. Gary F. Lazzeroni; Joseph F. Altenhofen, Parochial Vicar.
Mailing Address: 6600 Highland Dr., 98661. Tel: 360-696-4407; Fax: 360-696-3959.
Church: 400 S. Andresen Rd., 98661. Web: www.stjoevan.org.
School—(Grades K-8), 6500 Highland Dr., 98661. Tel: 360-696-2586; Fax: 360-696-0977. Web: www.stjoevanschool.org. Lesley Harrison, Prin.; Stacie Hunt, Librarian. Lay Teachers 24; Students 403.
Catechesis/Religious Program—Students 331.
5—OUR LADY OF LOURDES (1958) Rev. Michael Radermacher.
Res.: 5007 N.W. Franklin St., 98663. Tel: 360-695-1366; Fax: 360-695-0610.
School—(Grades PreSchool-8), 4701 N.W. Franklin St., 98663. Tel: 360-696-2301; Fax: 360-696-6700. Ms. Diane Cronin, Prin.; Beth Anderson, Librarian. Lay Teachers 37; Students 361.
Catechesis/Religious Program—Students 205.

VASHON, KING CO., ST. JOHN VIANNEY (1964) Rev. Marc L. Powell, Admin.
Mailing Address: P.O. Box 308, 98070. Tel: 206-567-4149; Fax: 206-567-4198.
Church: 16100 115th Ave. S.W., 98070. Tel: 206-567-5736.
Catechesis/Religious Program—Constance Walker, Asst. Faith Formation (Level 1). Students 67.
Chapel—St. Patrick 26100 99th Ave., S.W., Dockton, 98070.

WINLOCK, LEWIS CO., SACRED HEART (1909) [CEM] Revs. Timothy W. Ilgen; Armando V. Red, Parochial Vicar; Deacons Clay Hartzell; Artruro Ramirez.
Res.: 216 N.W. Arden, P.O. Box 69, 98596. Tel: 360-864-4126; Fax: 360-864-4130.
Catechesis/Religious Program—Students 26.

WOODINVILLE, KING CO., BLESSED TERESA OF CALCUTTA (2004) Rev. Frank Schuster.
13632 N.E. 177th PL., 98072. Tel: 425-806-8096. Web: www.blessedteresa.org.

WOODLAND, COWLITZ CO., ST. PHILIP (1950) [CEM] Rev. Gerald Woodman.
Res.: 430 Bozarth, Box 2169, 98674. Tel: 360-225-8308; Fax: 360-225-8866.
Catechesis/Religious Program—Students 127.
Mission—St. Joseph 136 S. 4th St., Kalama, Cowlitz Co. 98625.

YELM, THURSTON CO., ST. COLUMBAN (1960) Rev. Duc Cong Nguyen, Priest Admin.
Res.: 506 1st St. S., 98597. Tel: 360-458-3031; Fax: 360-458-4094.
Mission—St. Peter Sussex & Keithan St., P.O. Box 744, Tenino, Thurston Co. 98589. Tel: 360-264-2124; Fax: 360-264-2666.
Catechesis/Religious Program—Tel: 360-458-2360. Students 154.

Chaplains of Public Institutions

SEATTLE. *Federal Detention Center*. Rev. Timothy Watson, C.Ss.R., Chap.
Immigration & Customs Enforcement. Rev. Salvador Delgadillo.
King County Jail. Rev. Lyle Konen, C.Ss.R., Chap., Shannon O'Donnell, Pastoral Care Min.
U.S. Public Health Hospital. Attended by St. Peter Church, Seattle.
Veterans Administration Medical Center. Rev. David Mani, Chap.

ABERDEEN. *Stafford Creek Correction Center*. Lori Maki, Pastoral Care Min.

BUCKLEY. *Rainier School*. Vacant.

CLALLAM BAY. *Clallam Bay Correction Center*. Deacon Peter Flatley, Chap.

EVERETT. *Snohomish County Jail*. Revs. Jay DeFolco, Chap., Emmanuel Iweh, Chap.

FORKS. *Clearwater / Olympic Correction Center*. Deacon Peter Flatley.

GIG HARBOR. *Washington Corrections Center for Women*. Mary Rutter, Pastoral Care Min.

KENT. *Regional Justice Center*. Rev. Richard Gallagher, Catholic Chap. (Retired), Mary Rutter, Pastoral Care Min.

LITTLE ROCK. *Cedar Creek Correction Center*. Vacant.

MONROE. *Monroe Correctional Complex*. Rev. Lyle Konen, C.Ss.R., Pastoral Care Min.
Minimum Security Unit. Rev. Lyle Konen, C.Ss.R., Pastoral Min.
Special Offenders Center. Rev. Lyle Konen, C.Ss.R., Pastoral Min.
Twin Rivers Correction Center.
Washington State Reformatory. Rev. Lyle Konen, C.Ss.R., Pastoral Care Min. Part of Monroe Correctional Complex.

ORTING. *U.S. Soldiers' Home*. Attended by St. Andrew Church, Sumner.

PORT ORCHARD. *First Hills Hospital*Revs. Robert Evanson, c/o 3307 W. Dravus St., 98199, Donald Perea, c/o 7000 35th Ave. S.W., 98126.
Washington Veterans Home Hospital. Vacant. Attended by St. Gabriel Church, Port Orchard.

SHELTON. *Washington Corrections Center*, P.O. Box 900, 98584. Deacon Robert Rensel, Pastoral Care Min.

SNOQUALMIE. *Echo Glen Children's Center*. Mr. Joseph Cotton, Pastoral Care Minister.

TACOMA. *Remann Hall*. John Boylan, Pastoral Care Min.
Veterans Admin. Medical Center. Rev. Leo R. Rimmele, O.S.B.

VANCOUVER. *Larch Correction Center*. Deacon Jack Roscoe.
Veterans Administration Hospital. Attended from Archdiocese of Portland in Oregon.
Washington State School for the Blind. Attended from St. James Church, Vancouver.
Washington State School for the Deaf. Attended from St. John Church, Vancouver.

Special Assignment:
Very Revs.—
Bawyn, Anthony E., J.C.D., Judicial Vicar, 710 9th Ave., 98104.
Mulholland, David T., Vicar for Clergy, 710 9th Ave., 98104.
Revs.—
Dolejsi, Bryan, Dir. Vocations, 710 9th Ave., 98104.
Eblen, James, S.T.L., Ph.D. (Retired), Theologian, 710 9th Ave., 98104.
Johnson, James, Special Asst. to the Archbishop, 710 9th Ave., 98104.
Pluth, Paul R., J.C.L., Adjunct Judicial Vicar, 710 9th Ave., 98104.
Raschko, Michael, Ph.D., Theologian, 1614 Summit, #602, 98122.

On Duty Outside the Archdiocese:
Revs.—
Larrivee, Leo J., S.S., c/o 710 9th Ave., 98104.
Rowan, Stephen C., Ph.D., 5000 N. Willamete Blvd., Portland, OR 97203-5743.

Retired:
Revs.—
Angelovic, Michael, 424 N. 85th St., #410, 98103.
Basso, Richard, 6909 Weedin Pl., N.E. #B202, 98115.
Batterberry, Michael J., 1801 93rd St., #02, 98108.
Boyle, James, 2333 58th Ave. E., #6, Fife, 98424.
Brant, David A., 804 9th Ave., 98104.
Bulger, John, 54 Mitchell St., Pittson, PA 18640.
Chirico, Peter, S.S., 603 Maiden Choice Ln., Baltimore, MD 21228.
Cloquet, Victor, P.O. Box 1232, Allyn, 98524-1232.
Connole, Marlin J., 2863 Sundance Cir. E., Palm Springs, CA 92262.
Crosse, Charles G., 10508 112th St., SW, Lakewood, 98498.
Dell, Robert, 1535 29th Ave. S., 98144-3803.
Domandich, Anthony, 12717 S.E. Forest, 98683.
Douglas, Gordon W., 3212 40th Ave. W., 98199.
Eblen, James, S.T.L., Ph.D., 131 Bellevue Ave. E. #203, 98102.
Gallagher, Richard, 4707S.W. Dashpoint Rd. Unit E3 Federal Way, Federal Way, 98023.
Gallagher, William E., Providence Mt. St. Vincent, 4831 35th Ave. S.W., Rm. 100, 98126.
Godley, Patrick, 14950 W. Mountain View Blvd., Surprise, AZ 85374.
Hart, Brian, 1022 N.E. Knight Ct., Bremerton, 98311.
Haycock, Anthony J., St. Mary, 611 20th Ave., 98144.
Heneghan, Jarlath, Knock, Claremorris, County Mayo, Ireland.
Horan, John, Providence Mount St. Vincent, 4831 35th Ave. S.W. Rm. 321, 98126.
Jennings, John A., 4700 Dash Point Rd., #E2, Federal Way, 98023.
Jonientz, Bernard, 375 Union Ave. S.E., #B, Renton, 98059.
Koehler, John, 1002 NJ St., Tacoma, 98403.
Kramis, Joseph, 2009 Walker Park Rd., Shelton, 98584.
Lane, William, 4700 S.W. Dash Point Rd. #E1, Federal Way, 98023.
Larson, Jan, 321 S.E. Orchard Dr., #11, North Bend, 98045.
Lovett, Gerald F., 4700 S.W. Dash Point Rd. #G3, Federal Way, 98023.
McCloskey, Lester, 502 43rd Ave. S.E. 14B, Puyallup, 98374.
McEnnis, Thomas, 9151 Greenway Rd., Peoria, AZ 85381.
McGovern, Brian J., 1210 15th Ave. E., #338, 98112.
McLaughlin, John, 1930 S.E. Oakview Dr., Chehalis, 98532.
McMullan, John, 6703 Pampus Dr., Orlando, FL 32819.
Mien, Francis, 1230 E. First St., 98122.
Moran, Kevin, 3425 S. 176th St., #252, 98188.
Morelli, Gary, 3727 101st Way N.E., Kirkland, 98033.
Naumes, Matthew, 8818 East G St., Tacoma, 98445.
O'Brien, Patrick, 2303 54th Ave. E., Fife, 98424-1918.
O'Brien, Roger, 7328 196th St., S.W., #203, Lynnwood, 98036.
O'Callaghan, Thomas, P.O. Box 346, Suquamish, 98392.
O'Neil, Michael, 908 E. Empire Cir., Mesa, AZ 85208.
O'Neill, Patrick G., 16351 W. Labarynth Ln., Surprise, AZ 85374.
Oakshott, Ward B., 11051 15th Ave. N.E. #230, 98125.
Palluck, M. Charles, 35229 S.E. Kinsey St., #203, Snoqualmie, 98065.
Parle, Richard, 301 E. Wallace-Kneeland Blvd., Ste. 224-321, Shelton, 98584.
Peterson, C. Vincent, 9433 Olympus Beach Rd. N.E., Bainbridge Island, 98110.
Petosa, Joseph, 17117 40th Ave. W., Lynnwood, 98037.
Phelan, Thomas, 4700 S.W. Dash Point #G2, Federal Way, Federal Way, 98023.
Quinn, Thomas, Lislea, Aclave Po, Sligo Ireland.
Rink, George, 1828 S.W. 318th Pl., Unit D, Federal Way, 98023.
Roman, Stephen, St. Jerome Church, P.O. Box 190, Ocean Shores, 98569.
Ryan, Michael J., 55 William St. S. #408, Palm Desert, CA 98057.
Slate, William, P.O. Box 4556 Federal Way, Kent, 98063.
Stehly, Mark, 692 Panorama Blvd., Sequim, 98382.
Suss, Thomas J., 13047 W. Blue Sky Dr., Sun City, AZ 85375.
Szeman, Stephen J., 4814 N.E. 5th Ct., Renton, 98059.
Tolang, Jaime, Immaculate Conception, 820 18th Ave., 98122.
Ton, Anthony, 3708 N.E. 40th Ave., 98661.
Tran, Phuong D., 7111 Beverly Ln., Everett, 98203.
Treacy, William, Camp Brotherhood, 24880 Brotherhood Rd., Mount Vernon, 98274.
Vandenberg, Thomas L., 31080 9th Ave. S., Federal Way, 98003.
Ward, Richard J., St. James Cathedral, 804 9th Ave., 98104.
Williams, James, J.C.L., 14423 4th CRT St., 98168.

Permanent Deacons:
Anderson, David, S.J.
Aikin, Scott
Alcorta, David P.
Alexander, Richard
Allen, Daniel
Amlag, John
Anaya, Mauricio
Anderson, Carl
Barber, Terry
Basta, Samuel
Batstone, William
Bemis, James
Benedict, Nathan
Bleile, Jack
Carbajal, Adolfo
Cavazos, Antonio
Childs, Ted
Chin, Kwok
Combs, Richard
Connor, Joseph
Cordova, Frederick
Cummins, Donald
Decker, James
Denby, Marshall
Duffell, Dennis T.
Dunne, Joseph
Eckert, William
Edtl, Leland
Farrell, Daniel
Flatley, Peter
Fraczek, Henry
Gorman, Lawrence
Graddon, Gerald
Greer, Jeffrey
Haines, William, Jr.
Hamlin, William
Hanika, Donald
Harrington, Roy
Hartzell, Clay
Hawkins, F. Thomas
Henn, William
Hoover, Delbert
Jesmer, Lawrence
Johnson, Frederick
Jones, David
Kelley, Patrick
Kheriaty, Lawrence
Kim, Duk
Konold, Paul
Kreilkamp, Ben
La Russa, John
Labrecque, Richard
Lane, Loren
Lezcano, Juan
Magaña, Abel
Magnuson, Jack
Maher, Dean
Marcell, Terrance
McDonald, Lawrence
McGillicuddy, Michael
McGlone, Stephen
McGuire, Rodney
McNabb, Joseph, III
Miller, Gene
Mounce, George, III
Moyer, Carlton
Moynihan, Patrick
Murdy, Don
Myer, Philip
Nguyen, Phillip
O'Loane, Philip
Olsen, David
Olsen, Richard
Paige, Eric
Pardo, Anselmo
Parsons, Eamon D.
Pele, Sagato
Pellegrino, Joseph
Pentony, Michael J.
Peterson, George
Ramirez, Artruro
Rapp, David
Rensel, Robert
Ricciardi, John
Riggio, Michael
Rodriguez, Teodoro
Roscoe, John
Rupno, Robert
Sadler, E. Jerome
Samuel, Michael
San Nicolas, Ronald
Shriver, Joseph
Smith, Carl
Snider, Lloyd
Stenson, Mark
Stromberg, Alton
Swanson, Carl
Tanasse, William
Taube, William
Teskey, Michael
Townsend, William
Tuifua, Asipeli
Vanderzanden, Gene
Warfield, T. Jackson
White, Edward, Sr.
Wiese, Theodore
Wilson, Howard
Wodzanowski, Stephen
Yang, Joua Pao
Yuen, Joseph
Zellmer, Gary
Zuanich, Matthew

INSTITUTIONS LOCATED IN THE ARCHDIOCESE

[A] COLLEGES AND UNIVERSITIES

SEATTLE. *Seattle University*, 901 12th Ave., 98122-1090. Tel: 206-296-6000; Fax: 206-296-6200. Web: www.seattleu.edu. Revs. Stephen V. Sundborg, S.J., Pres.; David Anderson, S.J.; Michael S. Bayard, S.J., Dir. Campus Ministry; Hugh P. Duffy, S.J.; Peter B. Ely, S.J., Vice Pres. Mission Ministry; John F. Foster, S.J.; Patrick Kelly, S.J.; David J. Leigh, S.J.; Patrick J. Howell, S.J.; Michael M. Kelliher, S.J.; Fernando Alvarez Lara, S.J.; Thomas R.E. Murphy, S.J.; Patrick B. O'Leary, S.J.; Ignatius F. Ohno, S.J.; Mr. Matthew Pyrc, S.J.; Revs. James B. Reichmann, S.J.; Josef V. Venker, S.J.; Eric J. Watson, S.J.; Mr. Jason Welle, S.J. Priests 19; Sisters 2; Lay Teachers 728; Students 7,817.

LACEY. *Saint Martin's University* (1895) 5000 Abbey Way, S.E., 98503. Tel: 360-491-4700; Fax: 360-459-4124. Email: admissions@stmartin.edu. Web: www.stmartin.edu. Roy F. Hayndericks, Ph.D., Pres.; Joseph D. Bessie, Ph.D., Provost & Vice Pres. Academic Affairs; Revs. Benedict L. Auer, O.S.B.; Bede Classick, O.S.B., Treas.; Killian Malvey, O.S.B., Faculty, English & Religious Studies; Gerard D. Kirsch, O.S.B., Faculty, History; George J. Seidel, O.S.B.; Bros. Luke Devine, O.S.B., Assoc. Campus Min.; Boniface Lazzari, O.S.B., Faculty, Spanish; Aelred Woodard, O.S.B., Faculty, Religious Studies. Order of St. Benedict Master's Comprehensive University., Resident and non-resident students. Priests 5; Brothers 3; Lay Teachers 70; Students 1,700.

[B] HIGH SCHOOLS, ARCHDIOCESAN

SEATTLE. *Bishop Blanchet High School* (1954) (Coed), 8200 Wallingford Ave. N., 98103. Tel: 206-527-7731; Fax: 206-527-7712. Email: principal@bishopblanchet.org. Web: www.bishopblanchet.org. Kristine Brynildsen-Smith, Ed.D., Prin.; Rev. Armando Guzman; Judy Baumgartner, Librarian. Priests 1; Sisters 1; Lay Teachers 68; Students 991.

O'Dea High School (1923) (Boys), 802 Terry Ave., 98104-1238. Tel: 206-622-6596; Fax: 206-340-4110.

Email: kwalczak@odea.org. Web: www.odea.org. Bro. Karl J. Walczak, C.F.C., Prin.; Lawrence Kight, Librarian. Conducted by the Congregation of Christian Brothers. Brothers 5; Lay Teachers 32; Students 425.

Pope John Paul II High School, P.O. Box 3248, Lacey, 98509-3248. Tel: 360-438-7600; Fax: 360-438-7607. Web: www.popejp2hs.org. 5608 Pacific Ave. S.E., Lacey, 98503. Ronald E. Edwards, Prin.

BURIEN. *John F. Kennedy Catholic High School* (1966) (Coed), 140 S. 140th, 98168. Tel: 206-246-0500; Fax: 206-242-0831. Email: info@kennedyhs.org. Web: www.kennedyhs.org. Mr. Michael L. Prato, Prin.; Rev. Bryan Dolejsi; Ms. Kay Crane, Librarian. Priests 1; Lay Teachers 78; Students 860.

VANCOUVER. *St. Elizabeth Ann Seton Catholic High School*, 811 N.E. 112th Ave., #200, 98684. Tel: 360-258-1932; Fax: 360-258-1936. Ed Little, Prin. & Pres. Full Time Teachers 8.

[C] HIGH SCHOOLS, PRIVATE

SEATTLE. *Holy Names Academy* (1880) (Girls), 728 21st Ave. E., 98112. Tel: 206-323-4272; Fax: 206-323-5254. Email: eswift@holynames-sea.org. Web: www.holynames-sea.org. Ms. Elizabeth Swift, Prin.; Sr. Ann Cornelia Sullivan, S.N.J.M., Librarian. Congregation of the Sisters of the Holy Names of Jesus and Mary. Sisters 6; Lay Teachers 49; Students 665.

Seattle Preparatory School (1891) (Coed), 2400-11th Ave. E., 98102. Tel: 206-324-0400; Fax: 206-323-6509. Email: mbarmore@seaprep.org. Web: www.seaprep.org. Mr. Kent Hickey, Pres.; Dr. Matt Barmore, Prin.; Janice Abe, Librarian. Priests 4; Lay Teachers 69; Students 704.

BELLEVUE. *Forest Ridge School of the Sacred Heart* (1907) (Grades 5-12), (Girls), 4800 139th Ave., S.E., 98006. Tel: 425-641-0700; Fax: 425-643-3881. Email: markpi@forestridge.org. Web: www.forestridge.org. Mr. Mark Pienotti, Head of School; Carola Wittman, High School Dir.; Julie Grasseschi, Middle School Dir.; Joanne Boerth, Librarian. Religious of the Sacred Heart 3; Lay Teachers 62; Students 393.

EVERETT. *Archbishop Thomas J. Murphy High School* (Coed), 12911 39th Ave., S.E., 98208-6159. Tel: 425-379-6363; Fax: 425-385-2875. Web: www.am-hs.org. Dr. Robert Graby, Pres.; Fran Ennis, Prin.; Deborah Hitchcock, Librarian. Lay Teachers 40; Students 467.

SAMMAMISH, KING CO. *Eastside Catholic School* (Coed), 232 228th Ave., S.E., 98074. Tel: 425-295-3000; Fax: 425-392-5160. Web: www.eastsidecatholic.org. Sr. Mary Tracy, Pres.; Steve Schmutz, High School Prin.; Polly Skinner, Middle School Prin. Priests 1; Lay Teachers 67; Students 854.

TACOMA. *Bellarmine Preparatory School* (1928) (Coed), 2300 S. Washington, 98405. Tel: 253-752-7701; Fax: 253-761-3505. Web: www.bellarmineprep.org. Rev. John Fuchs, S.J., Supr.; Mr. Jack Peterson, Pres.; Chris Gavin, Prin.; Revs. Gerard E. Chapdelaine, S.J., Chap.; Frederick P. Mayovsky, S.J., Devel. Officer; Sr. Georgia Yianakulls, S.N.J.M., Librarian. Sponsored by the Oregon Province of the Society of Jesus., Board of Directors: 3 members of the Jesuit order and 16 others. Priests 4; Sisters 1; Lay Teachers 64; Students 1,015. In Res. Revs. Kenneth W. Baher, S.J.; Vincent Beuzer, S.J.; William Bichsel, S.J.; Gerard E. Chapdelaine, S.J.; Eugene P. Delmore, S.J.; Aaron Engebretson, S.J.; James Harbaugh, S.J.; Matthew Holland, S.J.; Stephen C. Lantry, S.J.; Frederick P. Mayovsky, S.J.; Joseph O. McGowan, S.J.; Carmine J. Sacco, S.J.; Charles Schmitz, S.J.

[D] ELEMENTARY SCHOOLS, PRIVATE

SEATTLE. *Villa Academy*, (Grades PreK-8), (Coed), 5001 N.E. 50th St., 98105. Tel: 206-524-8885; Fax: 206-523-7131. Email: jmilroy@thevilla.org. Web: www.thevilla.org. John K. Milroy, Head of School; Karen Strand, Librarian. Lay Teachers 36; Students 369.

CAMAS. *Pacific Crest Academy*, (Grades PreK-8), 324 N.E. Oak St., P.O. Box 1031, 98607-1031. Tel: 360-834-9913; Fax: 360-834-9926. Web: www.pacificcrestacademy.org. Tamar Parker, Prin. Lay Teachers 11; Students 114.

LACEY. *Holy Family School*, (Grades PreK-8), 2606 Carpenter Rd., S.E., P.O. Box 3700, 98509. Tel: 360-491-7060; Fax: 360-456-3725. Email: office@holyfamilylacey.com. Web: holyfamilylacey.com. David Stone, Prin. Lay Teachers 12; Students 102.

[E] CATHOLIC COMMUNITY SERVICES OF THE ARCHDIOCESE OF SEATTLE

SEATTLE. *Association for Catholic Childhood*, 100 23rd Ave. S., 98144. Tel: 206-328-5973; Fax: 206-328-5699. Email: acc@ccsww.org. Web: www.forthechildrenww.org.

Catholic Charities Foundation of Western Washington, 100 23rd Ave., S., 98144-2302. Tel: 206-328-5696; Fax: 206-328-5699. Mr. Michael Reichert, Pres.

Catholic Community Services of Western Washington, 100 23rd Ave. S., 98144-2302. Tel: 206-328-5696; Fax: 206-328-5699. Email: info@ccsww.org. Web: www.ccsww.org. Michael L. Reichert, Pres.

Whatcom Family Center, 1133 Railroad Ave., Ste. 100, Bellingham, 98225-5054. Tel: 360-676-2164; Fax: 360-676-2144. Kathy McNaughton, Regl. COO & Clinical Dir.

Hope House, 207 Kentucky St., Bellingham, 98225. Tel: 360-676-2164.

Skagit Family Center, 160 Cascade Pl., Ste 201, Burlington, 98233-3126. Tel: 360-856-3065; Fax: 360-676-2144.

Snohomish Family Center, 1918 Everett Ave., Everett, 98201-3607. Tel: 425-257-2111; Fax: 425-257-2120. Vicki Howell, Regional COO.

King County Family Centers & Randolph Carter Family and Learning Center, 100 23rd Ave. S., 98144-2302. Tel: 206-323-6336; Fax: 206-324-4835. Bill Hallerman, Vice Pres. & Agency Dir.

Aloha Inn, 1911 Aurora Ave. N., 98109. Tel: 206-283-6070.

First Nations Housing and Recovery Project, 610 Terry Ave., 98104-2011. Tel: 206-268-0880.

Lazarus Day Center, 416 2nd Ave. Ext. S., 98104-2876. Tel: 206-323-6341; Fax: 206-623-6191.

Martin Luther King. Jr., Day Home Center, 1855 S. Lane St., 98144-2907. Tel: 206-328-5670; Fax: 206-325-5922. Susan Vaughn, Chief Regl. Opers. Total Staff 17; Total Assisted 75.

Mary McClinton Center, 304 28th Ave. S., 98144. Tel: 206-328-4815.

Matt Talbot Center, 2313 3rd Ave., 98121. Tel: 206-256-9865.

Monica's Village Place I Programs, 140 23rd Ave. S., 98144. Tel: 206-323-7130.

Monica's Village Place II, 1400 E. Spruce St., 98122. Tel: 206-322-0450.

Sacred Heart Shelter, 232 Warren Ave. N., 98109-4815. Tel: 206-285-7489; Fax: 206-285-9556.

Solanus Casey Center, 1008 James St., 98104-2118. Tel: 206-223-0907.

St. Martin de Porres Shelter, 1561 Alaskan Way S., 98134. Tel: 206-323-6341; Fax: 206-328-5666.

University District Youth Center, 4516 15th Ave. N.E., 98105. Tel: 206-526-2992.

Women's Wellness Center, 1900 2nd Ave., 98101-1102. Tel: 206-256-0665.

East King County Family Center, 875 140th Ave. N.E., Ste. 205, Bellevue, 98005. Tel: 425-213-1963; Fax: 425-213-1068.

Harrington House, 875 140th Ave. N.E., Ste. 205, Bellevue, 98005. Tel: 425-643-1434; Fax: 425-643-2179.

South King County Family Center, 1229 W. Smith St., P.O. Box 398, Kent, 98035. Tel: 253-854-0077; Fax: 253-850-2503.

Katherine's House, P.O. Box 398, Kent, 98035. Tel: 253-856-7716.

Rita's House, P.O. Box 398, Kent, 98035. Tel: 253-883-5271.

Catholic Community Services Southwest Family Centers & Tahoma Family Center, 1323 S. Yakima Ave., Tacoma, 98405-4457. Tel: 253-383-3697; Fax: 253-572-3193. Denny Hunthausen, Vice Pres. & Agency Dir.

Guadalupe Vista Programs, 1305 S. "G" St., Tacoma, 98405. Tel: 253-272-1171; Fax: 253-272-2643.

Nativity House, 2304 S. Jefferson, Tacoma, 98402. Tel: 253-272-5266.

Phoenix Housing Network, 7050 S. "G" St., Tacoma, 98408-5507. Tel: 253-471-5340; Fax: 253-471-5343.

Tacoma Avenue Shelter, 1142 Ct. "E", Tacoma, 98405-2002. Tel: 253-572-0131.

Tahoma Indian Center, 1556 Market St., Tacoma, 98402. Tel: 253-593-2707; Fax: 253-593-2608.

Kitsap Family Center, 645 4th St., Ste. 202A, Bremerton, 98337-4102. Tel: 360-405-0072.

Benedict House, 250 S. Cambrian Ave., Bremerton, 98312. Tel: 360-405-9486.

St. Olaf Child Care Center, 18943 Caldart Ave., Poulsbo, 98370. Tel: 360-779-5791; Fax: 360-598-5888.

Thurston County Family Center, 604 Devoe St. S.E., Olympia, 98501. Tel: 360-586-2960; Fax: 360-586-0968. Gary Sandwick, Dir.

St. Mike's Tikes Early Learning Center, 1208 11th Ave. S.E., Olympia, 98501. Tel: 360-586-1585; Fax: 360-586-1584.

Drexel House, 604 Devoe St., S.E., Olympia, 98501. Tel: 360-753-3340.

Volunteer Chore Services, 129 Decatur St., Olympia, 98502-5220. Tel: 360-586-2960.

Grays Harbor Family Center, 3rd & "H" Sts., Aberdeen, 98520-0284. Tel: 360-586-2960; Fax: 360-637-9016.

Grays Harbor Youth Shelter, 111 E. 4th St.; Aberdeen, 98520. Tel: 360-589-3259.

Clark/Skamania Family Center, 9300 N.E. Oakview Dr., Ste A., Vancouver, 98662-6157. Tel: 360-567-2211.

Cowlitz/Wahkiakum Family Center, 676 26th Ave., Longview, 98632-1816. Tel: 360-577-2200; Fax: 360-577-2205.

Chemical Dependency Treatment System Northwest/Catholic Community Services Recovery Center-Bellingham, 515 Lakeview Dr., Bellingham, 98225. Tel: 360-676-2187; Fax: 360-676-2762. Will Rice, Chemical Dependency System Dir.

CCS Recovery Center - Everett, 2610 Wetmore Ave., Everett, 98201. Tel: 425-258-5270; Fax: 425-258-5270.

CCS Recovery Center - Marysville, 1227 2nd St., Marysville, 98270. Tel: 360-651-2366; Fax: 360-653-3119.

Family Preservation System/Northend Family Preservation System, 5410 N. 44th St., Tacoma, 98407-3715. Tel: 253-759-9544. Mary Stone Smith, Vice Pres. & System Dir.

Bremerton Family Preservation System, 285 5th St., Ste. 2, Bremerton, 98337-1804. Tel: 360-792-2020.

Olympia Family Preservation System, 148 N.W. Rogers St., Olympia, 98502. Tel: 360-586-0967.

Catholic Community Services Long Term Care System, 1323 Yakima Ave., Tacoma, 98405-4457. Tel: 877-870-1582; Fax: 253-272-6356. Peter Nazzal, Vice Pres. & Long Term Care System Dir.

Long-Term Care System - Aberdeen, 36 E. 3rd St., Aberdeen, 98520. Tel: 360-637-8784.

Long-Term Care System - Bellingham, 110 E. Chestnut St., Bellingham, 98225-4396. Tel: 800-219-0335.

Long-Term Care System - Bremerton, 285 5th St., Ste. 3, Bremerton, 98337-1804. Tel: 800-642-8019.

Long-Term Care System - Chehalis, 1570 N. Bishop Rd., Chehalis, 98532-0152. Tel: 800-642-8021.

Long-Term Care System - Everett, 1001 N. Broadway, Ste. A-11 & 12, Everett, 98201. Tel: 800-562-4663.

Long-Term Care System - Kent, 1225 W. Smith St., Kent, 98032. Tel: 800-722-3479.

Long-Term Care System - Lakewood, 5705 Main St., S.W., Lakewood, 98499. Tel: 253-722-5070; Fax: 253-589-0272.

Long-Term Care System - Olympia, 129 Decatur St., Olympia, 98502-5220. Tel: 800-316-6454.

Long-Term Care System - Port Angeles, 701 E. Front St., Port Angeles, 98362. Tel: 360-417-5420; Fax: 360-417-5434. Carol Krula, Contact Person.

Long-Term Care System - Shelton, 1716 Olympic Hwy. N., Shelton, 98584. Tel: 800-642-8026.

Long-Term Care System - Vancouver, 7409 Hazel Dell Ave., Ste. 112, Vancouver, 98665. Tel: 360-213-1023; 360-213-1024.

Kitsap Family Center Counseling, Foster Grandparents and Volunteer Chore Services, 654 4th St., Ste. 202A, Bremerton, 98337. Tel: 866-246-3642; Fax: 360-377-5088.

Vancouver Family Center, 9300 N.E. Oakview Dr., Ste. A-1, Vancouver, 98662. Tel: 360-567-2211; Fax: 360-213-2402.

Longview Family Center, 676 26th Ave., Longview, 98632. Tel: 360-577-2200; Fax: 360-577-2205.

Community Kitchen, 505 E. 5th St. S.E., Olympia, 98501. Tel: 360-349-2808.

St. Martin's Programs, 1561 Alaskan Way S., 98134. Tel: 206-323-6341; Fax: 206-328-5666.

Catholic Immigration Services, 4250 S. Mead St., 98118. Tel: 206-725-2090; Fax: 206-725-9046.

First Nations Women's Housing and Recovery Program, 12794 78th Ave. S., 98178. Tel: 206-268-0880.

First Nations Housing and Recovery Program, 610 Terry Ave., 98104-2011. Tel: 206-268-0880.

Hospitality Kitchen, 1323 S. Yakima Ave., Tacoma, 98405. Tel: 253-502-2696.

[F] CATHOLIC HOUSING SERVICES OF THE ARCHDIOCESE OF SEATTLE

SEATTLE. *Archdiocesan Housing Authority dba Catholic Housing Services of Western Washington* 100 23rd Ave. S., 98144. Tel: 206-328-5731; Fax: 206-328-5743. Michael L. Reichert, Pres.; John R. Hickman, Vice Pres. & Dir., Fin. & Opers.

Chancery Place Apartments, 910 Marion St., Ste. 105, 98104. Tel: 206-343-9415; Fax: 206-343-0680. Total Apartments 84; Total Staff 5.

Coming Home Program, 1902 2nd Ave., 98101. Tel: 206-956-9562; Fax: 206-956-9561.

Dorothy Day House, 106 Bell St., 98121. Tel: 206-374-4364; Fax: 206-374-8611.

Frederic Ozanam House, 801 9th Ave., 98104. Tel:

206-441-4606; Fax: 206-441-5764.
Josephinum Apartments, 1902 2nd Ave., 98101. Tel: 206-448-8500; Fax: 206-956-9561.
Katharine's Place, 3512 S. Juneau St., 98118. Tel: 206-722-0717; Fax: 206-722-3534.
Noel House at Bakhita Gardens, 118 Bell St., 98121. Tel: 206-441-3210; Fax: 206-441-0350.
Parke Studios, 1902 2nd Ave., 98101. Tel: 206-448-8500; Fax: 206-956-9561.
Rose of Lima at Bakhita Gardens, 118 Bell St., 98121. Tel: 206-456-3100; Fax: 206-456-3487.
Santa Teresita del Nino Jesus, 2427 Holden St., 98106. Tel: 206-767-2005; Fax: 206-767-1967.
Spruce Park Apartments, 155 21st Ave., 98122. Tel: 206-322-0450; Fax: 206-328-6637. Staff 3; Assisted 125.
St. Martin's on Westlake, 2008 Westlake Ave., 98121. Tel: 206-340-0410; Fax: 206-682-8843. Total Staff 10; Bed Capacity 53; Total Assisted Annually 63.
Traugott Terrace Services, 2317 3rd Ave., 98121. Tel: 206-267-3023; Fax: 206-267-3027.
Village Spirit Center for Community Change and Healing, 100 23rd Ave. S., 98144. Tel: 206-328-5709; Fax: 206-328-5978.
Wintonia Apartments, 1431 Minor Ave., 98101. Tel: 206-467-1878; Fax: 206-467-7679.
Women's Referral Center, 2030 3rd Ave., 98121. Tel: 206-441-3210; Fax: 206-441-0350.
Champion House, 1800 145th Pl., S.E., Bellevue, 98007. Tel: 425-644-4344; Fax: 425-644-9867. Total Staff 22; Total Assisted 8.
Maurice G. Elbert House, 16000 N.E. 8th St., Bellevue, 98008. Tel: 425-747-5111; Fax: 425-641-3141. Total Assisted Annually 49; Total Staff 4.
Max Hale Center, 285 5th St., Ste 1, Bremerton, 98337. Tel: 360-792-2117; Fax: 460-478-6993.
Franciscan Apartments, 15237 21st Ave., S.W., Burien, 98166. Tel: 206-431-8001; Fax: 206-431-1254. Total Units 38; Total Staff 3; Total Assisted 42.
Tumwater Apartments, 5701 6th Ave., S.W., Tumwater, 98501. Tel: 360-352-4321; Fax: 360-352-3557. Units 50; Total Staff 3.
Kincaid Housing/Kincaid Court Apartments, 6210 Parker Rd. E., Sumner, 98390-2645. Tel: 253-863-8818; Fax: 253-826-1006. John R. Hickman, Dir. Finance & Opers.
Pioneer Court Housing/Pioneer Court Apartments, 507 W. Stewart Ave. #104, Puyallup, 98371-9402. Tel: 253-848-0874; Fax: 253-826-1006. John R. Hickman, Sec. & Vice Pres.
Sunrise Court Housing/Sunrise Court Apartments, 110 140th St. S., Tacoma, 98444-6931. Tel: 253-537-2429; Fax: 253-536-7148. John R. Hickman, Sec. & Vice Pres.
Redmond Elderly Housing Association/Emma McRedmond Manor, 7960-169th Ave, N.E., Redmond, 98053. Tel: 425-869-2424; Fax: 425-558-5526. John R. Hickman, Sec. & Vice Pres.
AHA-Pierce County Association/Norm Fournier Court, 112 127th St. S., Tacoma, 98444-5000. Tel: 253-531-5087; Fax: 253-536-7148. John R. Hickman, Sec. & Vice Pres.
Halcyon Foundation, 1200 134th Ave., N.E., Bellevue, 98005. Tel: 425-644-4344; Fax: 425-644-9867. John R. Hickman, Sec. & Vice Pres.

[G] CHILD CARE SERVICES

SEATTLE. *Providence Mt. St. Vincent Child Care*, 4831 35th Ave., S.W., 98126-2799. Tel: 206-938-6784; Fax: 206-938-8999.

[H] HOSPITALS AND HEALTH CARE SYSTEMS

SEATTLE. *Providence Health & Services*, 1801 Lind Ave. S.W., Renton, 98057-9016. Tel: 425-525-3355; Fax: 425-525-5038. Email: jeff.rogers@providence.org. Jeffrey W. Rogers, Sec.
Providence Health System-California Tel: 425-525-3355; Fax: 425-525-5038.
Providence Health & Services-Oregon Tel: 425-525-3355; Fax: 425-525-5038.
Providence Health & Services-Washington Tel: 425-525-3355; Fax: 425-525-5038.
BELLEVUE. *Sisters of St. Joseph of Peace, PeaceHealth, System Office*, 14432 S.E. Eastgate Way, Ste. 300, 98007-6412. Tel: 425-747-1711; Fax: 425-649-3825. Alan Yordy, Pres. & CEO.
BELLINGHAM. *Peace Health St. Joseph Medical Center*, 2901 Squalicum Pkwy., 98225. Tel: 360-734-5400; Fax: 360-738-6393. Web: www.peacehealth.org. Nancy Steiger, CEO & CMO; Chris Phillips, Dir. Mission and Community Outreach. Sisters of St. Joseph of Peace and PeaceHealth. Sisters 1; Bed Capacity 253; Patients Assisted Annually 160,302; Total Staff 2,700.
CENTRALIA. *Providence Centralia Hospital*, 914 S. Scheuber Rd., 98531. Tel: 360-736-2803; Fax: 360-330-8614. Web: www.providence.org.
Providence Health System dba Providence Centralia Hospital Bed Capacity 191; Patients Assisted Annually 279,155; Total Staff 690.
EVERETT. *Providence General Foundation*, 916 Pacific Ave., 98201. Tel: 425-258-7500; Fax: 425-258-7142. Randy Petty, Exec. Dir.
Providence Regional Medical Center Everett, 1321 Colby Ave., 98206. Tel: 425-261-2000; Fax: 425-261-4051. Web: www.providence.org/everett/. David Brooks, CEO; Tim Serban, Dir. Mission Integration & Spiritual Care. Bed Capacity 468; Patients Assisted Annually 268,023; Total Staff 2,669.
FEDERAL WAY. *St. Francis Hospital of Federal Way*, 34515 9th Ave. S. (M.S. 21-01), 98003-6761. Tel: 253-835-8100 King County; 253-944-8100 Pierce County; Fax: 253-952-7988. Web: www.fhshealth.org. Tony McLean, Pres. Sisters of St. Francis of Philadelphia. Bed Capacity 110; Patients Assisted Annually 92,058; Total Staff 810.
GIG HARBOR. *St. Anthony Hospital*, 11567 Canterwood Blvd., N.W., 98332. Tel: 253-857-1431. Carde Peet, Pres.; Dianna Kielian, Senior Vice Pres. Mission.
LAKEWOOD. *St. Clare Hospital*, 11315 Bridgeport Way, S.W. (M.S. 41-01), 98499. Tel: 253-588-1711; Fax: 253-512-2833. Web: www.fhshealth.org. Kathy Bressler, Pres.; Dianna Kielian, Senior Vice Pres., Mission. Sisters of St. Francis of Philadelphia. Bed Capacity 106; Patients Assisted Annually 94,489; Total Staff 705.
LONGVIEW. *PeaceHealth, St. John Medical Center*, 1615 Delaware St., P.O. Box 3002, 98632. Tel: 360-414-2000; Fax: 360-414-7550. Web: www.peacehealth.org. Sisters of St. Joseph of Peace and PeaceHealth. Bed Capacity 346; Patients Assisted Annually 226,716; Total Staff 1,559.
OLYMPIA. *Providence St. Peter Hospital*, 413 Lilly Rd., N.E., 98506-5166. Tel: 360-491-9480; Fax: 360-493-7268. Medrice Coluccio, Chief Exec.
Sisters of Providence - Mother Joseph Province Bed Capacity 390; Patients Assisted Annually 322,100; Total Staff 2,396.
Providence St. Peter Foundation, 413 Lilly Rd., N.E., 98506-5116. Tel: 360-493-7980; Fax: 360-493-4631. Sr. Anita Butler, S.P., Contact Person; Nancy Riordan, Exec. Dir., Foundation.
TACOMA. *Catholic Pastoral Care-Hospital Tacoma Ministry*, 1001 N. "J" St., 98403. Tel: 253-383-3496; Fax: 253-756-0290. Email: pcdeanery@juno.com. Rev. Justin D. McCreedy, O.S.B., Chap.
Franciscan Health System, 1145 Broadway Plaza, Ste. 1200 (MS07-00), 98402. Tel: 253-680-4000; Fax: 253-680-4056. Dianna Kielian, Contact Person.
St. Joseph Medical Center, 1717 S. J St., P.O. Box 2197, 98405-2197. Tel: 253-426-4101; Fax: 253-426-6880. Web: www.fhshealth.org. Syd Bersante, CEO; Rev. Dennis Sevilla. Sisters of St. Francis of Philadelphia. Patients Assisted Annually 483,869; Total Staff 3,180.

[I] NURSING HOMES

SEATTLE. *Providence Mount St. Vincent*, 4831 35th Ave., S.W., 98126. Tel: 206-937-3700; Fax: 206-938-8999. Email: charlene.boyd@providence.org. Web: www.providence.org/themount. Tom Mitchell, Admin.
Sisters of Providence - Mother Joseph Province Sisters 3; Bed Capacity 215; Apartments 109; Total Assisted Annually 750; Total Staff 500.
Providence Mt. St. Vincent Foundation, 4831 35th Ave., S.W., 98126. Tel: 206-938-8994; Fax: 206-938-8999. Email: cscollins@providence.org. Pat Welch, Bd.Pres.; Molly Swain, Exec. Dir.
ISSAQUAH. *Providence Marianwood*, 3725 Providence Point Dr., S.E., 98029. Tel: 425-391-2800; Fax: 425-391-5440. Web: www.providencemarianwood.org. Sisters of Providence Health System. Bed Capacity 120; Total Assisted Annually 450; Total Staff 175.
Providence Marianwood Foundation, 3725 Providence Point Dr., S.E., 98029. Tel: 425-391-2895. Sr. Anita Butler, S.P., Contact Person; Cindy Sharek, Foundation Dir.
OLYMPIA. *Providence Mother Joseph Care Center*, 3333 Ensign Rd., N.E., 98506. Tel: 360-493-4900; Fax: 360-493-4000. Rev. David Bates, M.Div., Chap.; Kate Gormally, Admin. Total Staff 210; Patients Assisted Annually 900.

[J] HOSPICES

EVERETT. *Providence Hospice and Home Care of Snohomish County*, 2731 Wetmore Ave., #500, 98201. Tel: 425-261-4800; Fax: 425-261-4725. Web: www.providence.org/phhc. Served 5,717; Total Staff 223.
Providence Hospice & Home Care of Snohomish Co. Foundation, 2731 Wetmore Ave., #500, 98201. Tel: 425-261-4805; Fax: 425-261-4850. Email: cwittren@providence.org. Connie Wittren, Devel. Dir.
OLYMPIA. *Providence Sound HomeCare and Hospice*, 3432 South Bay Rd. N.E., 98506. Tel: 800-869-7062; 360-459-8311; Fax: 360-493-4657. Web: www.providence.org. Lisa Rodriguez, COO Home Health. Total Staff 208; Patients Assisted Annually 6,800.

[K] RESIDENCES FOR ELDERLY, DISABLED, OR LOW INCOME

SEATTLE. *Heritage House at The Market*, 1533 Western Ave., 98101. Tel: 206-382-4119; Fax: 206-382-0201. Email: charlene.nichols@providence.org. Total Assisted 64; Total Staff 40.
Providence ElderPlace, 4515 Martin Luther King Jr. Way S., 98118. Tel: 206-320-5325; Fax: 206-320-5326. Email: ellen.garcia@providence.org. Web: www.providence.org/long_term_care/elderplace. Ellen Garcia, Exec. Dir.
Providence Mount St. Vincent, 4831 35th Ave. S., 98126. Tel: 206-937-3700; Fax: 206-938-8999. Email: thomas.mitchell@providence.org. Web: www.providence.org/themount. Jennifer Paquette, Dir. of Spiritual Care. Total Assisted 750; Residents 319; Bed Capacity 335; Total Staff 500.
Providence Peter Claver House, 7101 38th Ave. S., 98118. Tel: 206-721-6265; Fax: 206-721-1327. Email: duong.nguyen@providence.org. Duong Nguyen, Housing Dir. Units 79; Total Assisted Annually 79; Total Staff 5.
Providence Vincent House, 1423 First Ave., 98101. Tel: 206-682-9307; Fax: 206-682-0548. Total Staff 4; Residents 61.
CENTRALIA. *Providence Blanchet House*, 1700 Providence Ln., 98531. Tel: 360-330-8748; Fax: 360-330-8795.
Providence Rossi House, 1700 Providence Ln., 98531. Tel: 360-330-8748; Fax: 360-330-8795.
CHEHALIS. *Providence Place*, 350 S.E. Washington Ave., 98532. Tel: 360-740-8389; Fax: 360-740-6504. Residents 60.
OLYMPIA. *Providence of St. Francis*, 3415 12th Ave., 98506. Tel: 360-493-5700; Fax: 360-493-5801.
Sunshine House, 413 N. Lilly Rd., 98506-5166. Tel: 360-493-7900; Fax: 360-493-5569. Email: ed.micas@providence.org. Web: www.providence.org/swsa/patient_resources/sunshine.htm.
Providence Health System, WA Total Staff 8; Total Assisted 95,000.

[L] SOCIAL SERVICES

SEATTLE. **L'Arche Noah Sealth of Seattle*, P.O. Box 22023, 98122-0023. Tel: 206-325-9434; Fax: 206-568-0367. Email: info@larcheseattle.org. Web: www.larcheseattle.org.
Providence Regina House, 8201 10th Ave. S. #6, 98108. Tel: 206-763-9204; Fax: 206-633-3525. Paige Collins, Mgr.
Sojourner Place, 5071 8th Ave., N.E., 98105. Tel: 206-545-4200; Fax: 206-633-3525. Sisters of Providence - Mother Joseph Province. Staff 4; Residents 11.
MONTESANO. *Archdiocesan Council of Catholic Women-Southern Deanery*, P.O. Box 535, Port Angeles, 98362. Tel: 360-249-2633. Email: eehig@lightstream.net. Edith Higginbothaan, Pres.
PORT ANGELES. *Archdiocesan Council for Catholic Women-Western Deanery*, P.O. Box 535, 98362. Tel: 360-461-0642. Patricia Pitsch, Pres.
Archdiocesan Council of Catholic Women, Northern Deanery, P.O. Box 535, 98362. Donna Rose, Pres.
RENTON. *Archdiocesan Council for Catholic Women-Central Deanery*, 17016 129th Ave., S.E., 98058. Tel: 425-226-6207.

[M] MONASTERIES AND RESIDENCES OF PRIESTS AND BROTHERS

SEATTLE. *Arrupe Jesuit Community at Seattle University*, 924 East Cherry St., 98122-4341. Tel: 206-296-6340; Fax: 206-296-6399. In Res. Revs. Patrick J. Howell, S.J., Seattle Univ. Rector; Stephen V. Sundborg, S.J., Seattle University Pres.; David Anderson, S.J.; Fernando Alvarez Lara, S.J.; Michael S. Bayard, S.J., Dir. Campus Ministry; Emmett H. Carroll, S.J.; Hugh P. Duffy, S.J.; Robert J. Egan, S.J.; Peter B. Ely, S.J., Vice Pres. Mission & Ministry; John F. Foster, S.J.; Ronald R. Funke, S.J.; Jean Baptiste Ganza, S.J.; Robert Grimm, S.J.; Michael M. Kelliher, S.J.; Patrick Kelly, S.J.; David J. Leigh, S.J.; Thomas R.E. Murphy, S.J.; Ignatius F. Ohno, S.J.; Patrick B. O'Leary, S.J.; James B. Reichmann, S.J.; L. John Topel, S.J.; James Taiviet Tran, S.J.; Patrick J. Twohy, S.J.; Josef V. Venker, S.J.; Eric J. Watson, S.J.; William M. Watson, S.J.; Mr. Lorenzo Herman, S.J., Scholastic; Mr. Matthew Pyrc, S.J., Scholastic; Mr. Jason Welle, S.J., Scholastic.
Congregation of Christian Brothers (Irish Christian Brothers), 1021 Columbia St., 98104-2018. Tel:

206-622-2639; Fax: 206-340-4110. Bros. John E. Dornbos; John Hugh Greenan, C.F.C., Community Leader; D. Thomas LeJeune, C.F.C.; G. Gregory Lindeman, C.F.C.; Patrick D. McCormack; John Austin Pettit, C.F.C.; Karl J. Walczak, C.F.C., Prin. Brothers 7.

Jesuit House, Seattle, 621 17th Ave. E., 98112. Tel: 206-324-7496. Revs. John C. Bentz, S.J., Supr.; Richard P. Magner, S.J.; Joseph P. Carver, S.J.; Mr. Juan P. Manufo del Toro, S.J.; Mr. Edwin Martinez, S.J.; Revs. John Rashford, S.J.; Joseph Nguyen, S.J.; John O'Leary, S.J.; John Whitney, S.J.

Maryknoll Fathers & Brothers, 958-16th Ave. E., 98112. Tel: 206-322-8831; Fax: 206-324-6909. Email: mklseatl@maryknoll.org. Web: www.maryknoll.org. Bro. W. Timothy Raible, M.M., Regl. Dir.

The Redemptionist Society of Washington, 205 2nd Ave. N., 98109. Tel: 206-284-4680; Fax: 203-284-3161. Email: info@sacredheartseattle.com. Revs. William Cleary, C.Ss.R.; Lyle Konen, C.Ss.R.; Raymond Maiser, C.Ss.R.; William Peterson, C.Ss.R.; Mark Scheffler, C.Ss.R.; Binh Ta, C.Ss.R.

LACEY. *St. Martin's Abbey*, 5000 Abbey Way, S.E., 98503-7500. Tel: 360-491-4700; 360-438-4440 (Abbot); Fax: 360-438-4441. Email: thabbot@stmartin.edu. Web: www.stmartin.edu. Rt. Rev. Neal G. Roth, O.S.B., Abbot; Very Rev. Alfred J. Hulscher, O.S.B., Prior, Treas. & Dir. Fiscal Affairs; Revs. Bede Classick, O.S.B., Treas., St. Martin Univ.; Thaddaeus R. Arledge, O.S.B.; Benedict L. Auer, O.S.B.; Edward R. Receconi, O.S.B.; Urban C. Feucht; Gerard D. Kirsch, O.S.B., Formation Dir.; Timothy J. Lamm, O.S.B.; Killian Malvey, O.S.B.; Justin D. McCreedy, O.S.B.; Very Rev. Clement Pangratz, O.S.B., Subprior; Revs. John Scott, O.S.B.; George J. Seidel, O.S.B.; Peter Tynan, O.S.B.; Paul M. Weckert, O.S.B.; Bros. Mark Bonneville, O.S.B.; Luke Devine, O.S.B.; Edmund Ebbers, O.S.B.; Boniface Lazzari, O.S.B.; Ramon Newell, O.S.B.; Bede Nicol, O.S.B.; Theodore Vavrek, O.S.B.; Lawrence Vogel, O.S.B.; Nicolaus G. Wilson, O.S.B.; Aelred Woodard, O.S.B. Order of St. Benedict, University, and Novitiate. Priests 17; Brothers 10.

[N] CONVENTS AND RESIDENCES FOR SISTERS

SEATTLE. *St. Joseph's Residence*, 4800 37th Ave., S.W., 98126. Tel: 206-937-4600; Fax: 206-923-4001 (8:30am-8:30pm). Email: jacqueline.fernandes@providence.org. Sr. Jacqueline Fernandes, S.P., Supr. & Admin. Sisters of Providence 28; Dominican Sisters of Tacoma 15; Sisters (Daughters of Mary) 2; Sisters (Carmelites) 2; Dominican Sisters of Adrian 2.

Lovers of the Holy Cross of Go Vap - St. Bernadette Convent, 1022 S.W. 128th St., 98146. Tel: 206-275-2283. Sr. Theresa Rose Tran, Supr.

Sisters of St. Joseph of Peace, 1104 21st Ave. E., 98112. Tel: 206-324-1529. Web: csjp.org. Sisters 3.

Sisters of St. Joseph of Peace, Our Lady Province, Charitable Trust, 1663 Killarney Way, P.O. Box 248, Bellevue, 98009-0248. Tel: 425-451-1770; Fax: 425-462-9760. Web: www.csjp.org. Sr. Margaret Byrne, C.S.J.P., Congregation Leader.

BELLEVUE. *St. Mary's Residence and Novitiate*, P.O. Box 1763, 98009. 1663 Killarney Way, 98004. Tel: 425-451-1833; Fax: 425-462-9760. Web: www.csjp-olp.org. Sr. Judy Johnson, C.S.J.P., Admin. Sisters of St. Joseph of Peace 30.

St. Mary's Western U.S.Office for Sisters of St. Joseph of Peace, 1663 Killarney Way, Box 248, 98009-0248. Tel: 425-467-5400; Fax: 425-462-9760. Email: lhanson@csjp-olp.org. Web: www.csjp.org. Sr. Margaret Byrne, C.S.J.P., Congregational Leader. Sisters of St. Joseph of Peace.

LACEY. *St. Placid Priory*, 500 College St., N.E., 98516. Tel: 360-438-1771; Fax: 360-438-9236. Email: stplacid@stplacid.org. Web: www.stplacid.org. Sr. Maureen O'Larey, O.S.B., Prioress. Includes The Priory Spirituality Center and The Priory Store. Sisters of St. Benedict 15.

RENTON. *Sisters of Providence, Mother Joseph Province*, 1801 Lind Ave. S.W., #9016, 98057-9016. Tel: 425-525-3355; Fax: 425-525-3984. Web: www.sistersofprovidence.net. Sr. Karin Dufault, S.P., Prov. Supr.

Providence Archives, 4800 37th Ave. S.W., 98126-2793. Tel: 206-937-4600; Fax: 206-923-4001. Email: archives@providence.org. Web: www.providence.org/phs/archives. Loretta Greene, Archivist; Peter Schmid, Visual Resources Archivist.

Sisters of Providence Retirement Trust, 1801 Lind Ave. S.W., #9016, 98057. Tel: 425-525-3729. Email: jennifer.hall@providence.org. Sr. Anita Butler, S.P., Chair & Contact Person.

SHAW ISLAND. *Our Lady of the Rock Priory* (Cloistered), P.O. Box 425, 98286. Tel: 360-468-2321; Fax: 360-468-2319. Web: www.rockisland.com/~mhildegard. Sr. Therese Critchley, O.S.B., Supr. Benedictine Nuns. Professed Nuns 8.

SHORELINE. *St. Joseph's Carmelite Monastery*, 2215 N.E. 147th, 98155. Tel: 206-363-7150; Fax: 206-365-7335. Email: seattlecarm@comcast.net. Sr. Maria Valla, O.C.D., Prioress. Discalced Carmelites 8; In Formation 2.

TACOMA. *III Order of St. Dominic*, Tacoma Dominican Center, 935 Fawcett Ave. S., 98402. Tel: 253-272-9688; Fax: 253-272-8790. Email: dominicans@tacomaop.org. Web: www.tacomaop.org. Sr. Sharon Casey, O.P., Pres. (Congregation of St. Thomas Aquinas), Sisters of Saint Dominic of Tacoma Charitable Trust - Tacoma Dominican Center.

Sister of St. Francis of Philadelphia, St. Ann Retirement Convent, 6602 S. Alaska St., 98408. Tel: 253-474-8319; 253-475-0791; Fax: 253-474-0734. Email: saintann@worldnet.att.net. *Serra House*, 6602 S. Alaska St., 98408. Tel: 253-474-8026. *Hermitage Place*, 6602 S. Alaska St., 98408. Tel: 253-474-9803. *Olympus House*, 6602 S. Alaska St., 98408. Tel: 253-474-8573. *Marian House*, 6802 47th St. W., 98466. Tel: 253-564-1816. *St. Marguerite Convent*, 4019 S. Thompson, 98408. Tel: 253-472-9702.

[O] RETREAT HOUSES, CONFERENCE CENTERS AND CAMPS

SEATTLE. *Camp Don Bosco*, 710 9th Ave., 98104. Tel: 206-382-4562 Contact CYO:. Email: cyo@seattlearch.org. Web: www.camping.seattleoyyam.org.

Camp Gallagher, c/o 710 9th Ave., 98104. Email: cyo@seattlearch.org. Web: www.camping.seattleoyyam.org.

Camp Hamilton, 710 9th Ave., 98104. Tel: 206-382-4562. Email: cyo@seattlearch.org. Web: www.camping.seattleoyyam.org.

RA KHOI Foundation, 710 9th Ave., 98104. Tel: 206-274-3120.

FEDERAL WAY. *The Archbishop Alex J. Brunett Retreat and Faith Formation Center at the Palisades*, 4700 S.W. Dash Point Rd., #100, 98023. Tel: 253-927-9621 (Tacoma); 206-748-7991 (Seattle); Fax: 206-382-3482. Email: palisades@seattlearch.org. Web: www.seattlearchdiocese.org/palisades. David Jones, Dir.

LONGBRANCH. *Far-A-Way Retreat House*, 6505 Cliff Ave. Rd., 98351. Tel: 253-884-9331. Mailing Address: 4700 S.W. Dash Point Rd., #100, Federal Way, 98023. Tel: 206-748-7991; Fax: 206-382-3482. Email: faraway@seattlearch.org. Web: www.seattlearchdiocese.org/faraway.

[P] CAMPUS MINISTRY

SEATTLE. *Saint Martin's College (Lacey)* 5000 Abbey Way., S.E., Lacey, 98503-7500. Tel: 360-491-4700. Email: leysters@stmartin.edu. Susan Leyster, Dir. Campus Ministry.

Seattle University Campus Ministry 901 12th Ave., P.O. Box 222000, 98122-1090. Tel: 206-296-6075; Fax: 206-296-6097. Email: campusministry@seattleu.edu. Web: www.seattleu.edu/campusministry/.

University of Washington, Catholic Newman Center 4502 20th Ave., N.E., 98105. Tel: 206-527-5072. Web: www.uwnewman.org. Rev. Jordan Bradshaw, O.P., Chap.

Western Washington University (Bellingham) 714 A. N. Garden St., Bellingham, 98225. Tel: 360-410-0218. Web: http://westerncatholic.org. Rev. Qui-Thac Nguyen, Chap. Catholic Campus Ministry.

TACOMA. *Pacific Lutheran University Catholic Student Ministry* 12180 Park Ave. S., 98447. Tel: 253-531-6900. Email: catholic@plu.edu.

University of Puget Sound Catholic Campus Fellowship 1500 N. Warner St., 98416. Tel: 253-879-3374. Email: ccm@ups.edu.

[Q] MISCELLANEOUS

SEATTLE. *Catholic Seamen's Club*, 2330 1st Ave., 98121. Tel: 206-441-4773; Fax: 206-441-8059. Email: office@catholicseafarercenter.org. Rev. Anthony J. Haycock, Chap. (Retired). Total Assisted 6,083.

Sea-Tac Airport Tel: 206-441-4773. Deacon Michael Riggio.

St. Mary Church: 611 20th Ave. S., 98144. Tel: 206-324-7100, Ext. 14.

Cursillo Movement, P.O. Box 68803, 98168-0803. Tel: 425-466-6808. Jose Blakely, Dir.

The Food Bank at St. Mary's, 611 20th Ave. S., 98144. Tel: 206-324-7100, Ext. 21; Fax: 206-329-4596. Email: alison@thefbsm.org.

St. Francis House, 169 12th Ave., 98122. Tel: 206-621-0945; Fax: 206-621-0945. Email: st.francis@live.com. Kathleen McKay, Dir. Third Order of St. Francis.

Fulcrum Foundation, 710 9th Ave., 98104. Tel: 206-748-7988; Fax: 206-219-5810. Email: joew@fulcrumfoundation.org. Web: www.fulcrumfoundation.org. Mr. Joe Womac, Exec. Dir.

Intercommunity Housing Ferndale, 2505 3rd Ave., Ste. 204, 98121. Tel: 206-838-5700; Fax: 206-838-5705. Email: intercommunity@mercyhousing.org. Web: www.mercyhousing.org.

**Intercommunity Peace & Justice Center*, 1216 N.E. 65th St., 98115. Tel: 206-223-1138; Fax: 206-223-1139. Email: ipjc@ipjc.org. Web: www.ipjc.org. Sr. Linda Haydock, S.N.J.M., Exec. Dir.

**Mercy Housing Northwest*, 2505 3rd Ave., Ste. 204, 98121. Tel: 206-838-5700; Fax: 206-838-5705. Email: intercommunity@mercyhousing.org. Web: www.mercyhousing.org. Paul Chiocco, Contact Person.

South Seattle Catholic Schools, 4212 S. Mead, 98118. Tel: 206-722-7888; Fax: 206-722-7895.

Sterling Senior Housing, 2505 Third Ave., Ste. 204, 98121. Tel: 206-838-5700. Paul Chiocco, Contact Person.

Washington State Catholic Conference, 710 9th Ave., 98104. Tel: 206-301-0556; Fax: 206-301-0558. Email: wscc@thewscc.org. Sr. Sharon Park, O.P., Exec. Dir.

EDMONDS. *Edmonds Dominicans, Holy Angels Alumnae Assoc.*, 942 N.W. 60th, 98107. Tel: 206-782-1181; 206-546-6561; Fax: 206-789-2498.

TACOMA. *Pierce County Deanery*, 1001 N. J St., 98403. Tel: 253-383-3496; Fax: 253-756-0290. Email: pcdeanery@juno.com. Tom O'Brien-Wilson, Admin.

RELIGIOUS INSTITUTES OF MEN REPRESENTED IN THE ARCHDIOCESE

For further details refer to the corresponding bracketed number in the Religious Institutes of Men or Women section.

[0200]—*Benedictine Monks* (Olympia, WA)—O.S.B.

[0310]—*Congregation of Christian Brothers* (Western U.S.)—C.F.C.

[0260]—*Discalced Carmelite Fathers and Brothers* (Western Prov.)—O.C.D.

[0690]—*Jesuit The Society of Jesus* (Oregon Province)—S.J.

[0800]—*Maryknoll*—M.M.

[]—*Missionaries of the Holy Spirit*—H.Sp.S.

[0430]—*Order of Preachers (Dominicans)* (San Francisco, CA)—O.P.

[1070]—*Redemptorist Fathers* (Denver Province)—C.SS.R.

[1250]—*Society of Christ* (American-Canadian Prov.)—S.Ch.

RELIGIOUS INSTITUTES OF WOMEN REPRESENTED IN THE ARCHDIOCESE

[]—*Adrian Dominican Sisters*—O.P.

[0180]—*Benedictine Nuns of the Primitive Observance*—O.S.B.

[]—*Blessed Sacrament Sisters of Charity*—B.S.S.C.

[]—*Carmelite Sisters of Our Lady - Carm.*—O.L.

[]—*Congregation of Divine Providence, TX*—C.D.P.

[]—*Congregation of the Sisters of the Holy Cross*—C.S.C.

[]—*Daughters of Mary*—D.M.

[0420]—*Discalced Carmelite Nuns of the order of Our Blessed Lady of Mount Carmel*—O.C.D.

[1070-19]—*Dominican Sisters* (Sinsinawa)—O.P.

[1115]—*Dominican Sisters of Peace*—O.P.

[]—*Franciscan Sisters of Perpetual Adoration*

[]—*Missionary Sisters of the Rosary of Fatima*—M.R.F.

[2860]—*Missionary Sisters of the Sacred Heart*—M.S.C.

[2970]—*School Sisters of Notre Dame*—S.S.N.D.

[0430]—*Sisters of Charity of the Blessed Virgin Mary*—B.V.M.

[]—*Sisters of Mercy of the Americas*—R.S.M.

[3000]—*Sisters of Notre Dame De Namur*—S.N.D.deN.

[]—*Sisters of Our Lady of Perpetual Help*—S.O.L.P.H.

[]—*Sisters of Our Lady of the Most Holy Trinity*—S.O.L.T.

[3350]—*Sisters of Providence*—S.P.

[]—*Sisters of Social Services*—S.S.S.

[]—*Sisters of St. Benedict, St. Placid Priory*—O.S.B.

[]—*Sisters of St. Dominic, Congregation of St. Thomas Aquinas*—O.P.

[]—*Sisters of St. Francis of Penance and Christian Charity*—O.S.F.

[1650]—*Sisters of St. Francis of Philadelphia*—O.S.F.

[3840]—*Sisters of St. Joseph of Carondelet* (California Prov.)—C.S.J.

[3890]—*Sisters of St. Joseph of Peace*—C.S.J.P.

[1990]—*Sisters of the Holy Names of Jesus and Mary* (U.S. & Ontario Province)—S.N.J.M.

[]—*Society of the Sacred Heart*—R.S.C.J.

[]—*Sisters of the Lovers of the Holy Cross of Go Vap of*

Vietnam—L.H.C.

ARCHDIOCESAN CEMETERIES

Associated Catholic Cemeteries: Central Office 910 Marion, 98104. Tel: 206-382-9281

SEATTLE

Calvary Cemetery, 5041 35th Ave., N.E., 98105. Tel: 206-522-0996; Fax: 206-525-9628.

FEDERAL WAY

Gethsemane Cemetery, 37600 Pacific Hwy. S., 98003. Tel: 253-838-2240; Fax: 253-874-5910.

KENT

St. Patrick Cemetery, 20400 Orillia Rd., 98032. Tel: 253-838-2240; Fax: 253-874-5910. c/o 37600 Pacific Hwy., S., Federal Way, 98003.

SHORELINE

Holyrood Cemetery, 205 N.E. 205th St., 98155. Tel: 206-363-8404; Fax: 206-363-7039.

NECROLOGY

† Mallahan, James, (Retired)—Died July 29, 2011
† O'Hogan, Patrick, Forks, WA St. Anne—Died Aug. 29, 2011
† O'Neil, Patrick, (Retired)—Died Aug. 22, 2011
† O'Shea, Joseph, (Retired)—Died Jan. 28, 2011
† Wallace, Philip, (Retired)—Died Aug. 25, 2011
† Vacant

An asterisk (*) denotes an organization that has established tax-exempt status directly with the IRS and is not covered by the USCCB Group Ruling.

Diocese of Shreveport

(Dioecesis Sreveportuensis in Louisiana)

Most Reverend

MICHAEL G. DUCA, J.C.L.

Bishop of Shreveport; ordained April 29, 1978; appointed Bishop of Shreveport April 1, 2008; ordained May 19, 2008. *Chancery Office: 3500 Fairfield Ave., Shreveport, LA 71104.* Email: bishopsoffice@dioshpt.org.

Most Reverend

WILLIAM B. FRIEND, D.D.

Retired Bishop of Shreveport; ordained May 7, 1959; appointed Titular Bishop of Pomaria and Auxiliary Bishop of Alexandria-Shreveport August 31, 1979; ordained Bishop October 30, 1979; appointed Bishop of Alexandria-Shreveport November 23, 1982; installed January 11, 1983; appointed Bishop of Shreveport June 16, 1986; retired December 20, 2006. *3575 Broken Woods Dr. #301, Coral Springs, FL 33065.* Tel: 954-344-6194.

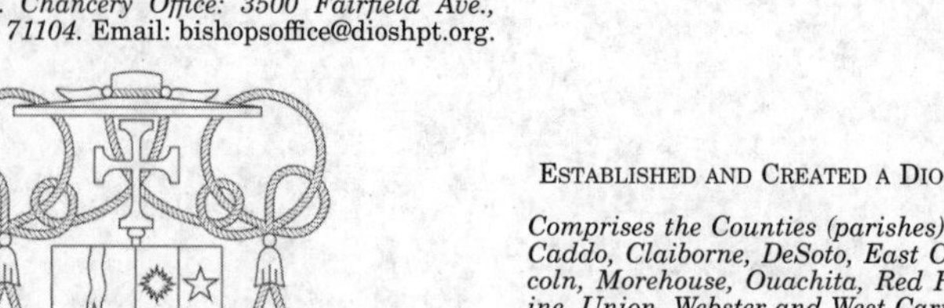

ESTABLISHED AND CREATED A DIOCESE JUNE 16, 1986.

Comprises the Counties (parishes) of Bienville, Bossier, Caddo, Claiborne, DeSoto, East Carroll, Jackson, Lincoln, Morehouse, Ouachita, Red River, Richland, Sabine, Union, Webster and West Carroll.

For legal titles of parishes and diocesan institutions, consult the Chancery Office.

Chancery Office: 3500 Fairfield Ave., Shreveport, LA 71104. Tel: 318-868-4441; Fax: 318-868-4469.

Web: www.dioshpt.org

STATISTICAL OVERVIEW

Personnel	
Bishop	1
Retired Bishops	1
Priests: Diocesan Active in Diocese	24
Priests: Diocesan Active Outside Diocese	1
Priests: Retired, Sick or Absent	8
Number of Diocesan Priests	33
Religious Priests in Diocese	14
Total Priests in Diocese	47
Extern Priests in Diocese	4
Permanent Deacons in Diocese	20
Total Brothers	5
Total Sisters	33
Parishes	
Parishes	27
With Resident Pastor:	
Resident Diocesan Priests	16
Resident Religious Priests	8
Without Resident Pastor:	
Administered by Priests	3
Missions	13
Professional Ministry Personnel:	
Sisters	1
Lay Ministers	9
Welfare	
Health Care Centers	3
Total Assisted	431,518
Homes for the Aged	1
Total Assisted	190
Day Care Centers	2
Total Assisted	148
Special Centers for Social Services	22
Total Assisted	45,132
Other Institutions	2
Total Assisted	1,079
Educational	
Diocesan Students in Other Seminaries	4
Total Seminarians	4
High Schools, Diocesan and Parish	2
Total Students	683
Elementary Schools, Diocesan and Parish	4
Total Students	1,245
Catechesis/Religious Education:	
High School Students	445
Elementary Students	1,760
Total Students under Catholic Instruction	4,137
Teachers in the Diocese:	
Sisters	1
Lay Teachers	130
Vital Statistics	
Receptions into the Church:	
Infant Baptism Totals	512
Minor Baptism Totals	43
Adult Baptism Totals	48
Received into Full Communion	151
First Communions	530
Confirmations	440
Marriages:	
Catholic	92
Interfaith	56
Total Marriages	148
Deaths	373
Total Catholic Population	40,991
Total Population	812,200

Former Bishop—Most Rev. WILLIAM B. FRIEND, ord. May 7, 1959; appt. Titular Bishop of Pomaria and Auxiliary Bishop of Alexandria-Shreveport Aug. 31, 1979; ord. Bishop Oct. 30, 1979; appt. Bishop of Alexandria-Shreveport Nov. 23, 1982; installed Jan. 11, 1983; appt. Bishop of Shreveport June 16, 1986; retired Dec. 20, 2006.

Vicar General and Moderator of the Curia—Very Rev. ROTHELL PRICE, J.C.L., V.G.

Vicars Forane—Very Rev. Msgr. EARL V. PROVENZA, V.F., Western Deanery; Very Revs. FRANK COENS, O.F.M., V.F., Eastern Deanery; TIMOTHY C. HURD, V.F., Southern Deanery.

Chancery Office—Catholic Center, 3500 Fairfield Ave., Shreveport, 71104. Tel: 318-868-4441; Fax: 318-868-4469. Email: chancellorsoffice@dioshpt.org.

Chancellor—Mrs. CHRISTINE RIVERS.

Diocesan Tribunal—3500 Fairfield Ave., Shreveport, 71104. Tel: 318-868-4441; Fax: 318-219-7286.

Judicial Vicar—Very Rev. PETER B. MANGUM, J.C.L., J.V.

Adjutant Judicial Vicar—Very Rev. ROTHELL PRICE, J.C.L., V.G.

Director of the Tribunal—Sr. MARILYN R. VASSALLO, C.S.J., J.C.L. Email: mvassallo@dioshpt.org.

Moderator of the Tribunal—RICOLE WILLIAMS. Email: rwilliam@dioshpt.org.

Secretary—ANN GOELDEN. Email: agoelden@dioshpt.org.

Judges—Very Rev. PETER B. MANGUM, J.C.L., J.V.; Rev. Msgr. FRANZ GRAEF, S.T.D. (Retired); Rev. DAVID T. RICHTER, J.C.L.; Very Rev. ROTHELL PRICE, J.C.L., V.G.; Sr. MARILYN R. VASSALLO, C.S.J., J.C.L.

Defenders of the Bond—Rev. PHILIP F. MICHIELS; Sr. LYNN MCKENZIE, O.S.B.

Promoter of Justice—Sr. LYNN MCKENZIE, O.S.B.

Advocates—Revs. KARL J. DAIGLE; RICHARD J. LOMBARD; Very Rev. TIMOTHY C. HURD, V.F.; Rev. MARK A. WATSON; Deacons TIMOTHY COTITA; CLARY NASH; WILLIAM ROCHE; MICHAEL STRAUB; MICHAEL SULLIVAN.

Notaries—RICOLE WILLIAMS. Email: rwilliam@dioshpt.org; ANN GOELDEN. Email: agoelden@dioshpt.org.

Corporate Council—Most Rev. MICHAEL GERARD DUCA, J.C.L., Bishop; Very Rev. ROTHELL PRICE, J.C.L., V.G.; Mrs. CHRISTINE RIVERS.

College of Consultors—Very Rev. Msgr. EARL V. PROVENZA, V.F.; Very Rev. ROTHELL PRICE, J.C.L., V.G.; Rev. DAVID T. RICHTER, J.C.L.; Very Revs. TIMOTHY C. HURD, V.F.; PETER B. MANGUM, J.C.L., J.V.; Revs. JOSEPH PUTHUPPALLY, V.F.; PHILIP F. MICHIELS; LAVERNE (PIKE) THOMAS; MARK A. WATSON.

Presbyteral Council—Very Rev. PETER B. MANGUM, J.C.L., J.V., Chm.; Revs. PHILIP F. MICHIELS; LAVERNE (PIKE) THOMAS; MARK A. WATSON.

Ex Officio Members—Very Rev. TIMOTHY C. HURD, V.F.; Very Rev. Msgr. EARL V. PROVENZA, V.F.; Very Revs. FRANK COENS, O.F.M., V.F.; ROTHELL PRICE, J.C.L., V.G.

Finance Council—Most Rev. MICHAEL GERARD DUCA, J.C.L., Bishop; Very Rev. ROTHELL PRICE, J.C.L., V.G., Ex Officio; M. VAUGHN ANTLEY; Mrs. CHRISTINE RIVERS, Ex Officio; REGINALD W. ABRAMS; NONA DAILEY; LAWRENCE W. PETTIETTE JR.; MARGARET GREEN; GLENN KINSEY; TOMMY COCKRELL; MATTHEW J. COUVILLION; ELIZABETH PIERRE.

Priests' Retirement Board—Revs. MARK FRANKLIN; CHARLES GLORIOSO; RICHARD NORSWORTHY; Mr. PAUL SKLAR; Revs. JAMES R. MCLELLAND; JOSEPH A. MARTINA JR.; Mr. DOMINIC MAINIERO.

The Catholic Foundation of North-Central Louisiana, Inc.— Contact the Catholic Center for information. Tel: 318-868-4441; Fax: 318-868-4469.

Diocesan Offices and Directors

Black Catholic Commission—Very Rev. ROTHELL PRICE, J.C.L., V.G., Chap., Catholic Center, 3500 Fairfield Ave., Shreveport, 71104. Tel: 318-868-4441; Fax: 318-868-4469.

Business Affairs—Mrs. JILL BRANIFF, CPA, Catholic Center, 3500 Fairfield Ave., Shreveport, 71104. Tel: 318-868-4441; Fax: 318-868-4609.

Campaign for Human Development—Very Rev. ROTHELL PRICE, J.C.L., V.G., Address Communications to: Catholic Center, 3500 Fairfield Ave., Shreveport, 71104. Tel: 318-868-4441; Fax: 318-868-4469.

Campus Ministry— (See Youth and Young Adult Ministry)

Catechetics—VACANT (Address communications to the Chancellor) Catholic Center, 3500 Fairfield Ave.,

Shreveport, 71104. Tel: 318-868-4441; Fax: 318-868-4469.

Catholic Charities—Mrs. JEAN DRESLEY, Exec. Dir., Catholic Charities, 331 E. 71st St., Shreveport, 71106. Tel: 318-865-0200; Fax: 318-865-0230.

Catholic Relief Services—Very Rev. ROTHELL PRICE, J.C.L., V.G., Catholic Center, 3500 Fairfield Ave., Shreveport, 71104. Tel: 318-868-4441; Fax: 318-868-4469.

Cemeteries—Mrs. JILL BRANIFF, CPA, Catholic Center, 3500 Fairfield Ave., Shreveport, 71104. Tel: 318-868-4441; Fax: 318-868-4609.

Censor of Books—Rev. Msgr. FRANZ GRAEF, S.T.D. (Retired).

Church Vocations—Rev. DAVID T. RICHTER, J.C.L., Dir., 3500 Fairfield Ave., Shreveport, 71104. Tel: 318-868-4441; Fax: 318-868-4578.

Church Vocations Board & Vocations Office—Revs. DAVID T. RICHTER, J.C.L., Dir. Diocesan Vocations Office & Ex Officio; CHARLES GLORIOSO; KARL J. DAIGLE; Mr. E. B. POLSON; Dr. ROBERT KENT DEAN; Very Rev. ROTHELL PRICE, J.C.L., V.G., Ex Officio; Rev. MARK A. WATSON; Judge D. MILTON MOORE; Deacon CLARY NASH.

Clergy Continuing Formation Director—Rev. LAVERNE (PIKE) THOMAS.

Communications—Mr. JOHN MARK WILLCOX, Dir., 3500 Fairfield Ave., Shreveport, 71104. Tel: 318-868-4441; Fax: 318-868-4609.

Development Director—Mr. JOHN MARK WILLCOX, Catholic Center, 3500 Fairfield Ave., Shreveport, 71104. Tel: 318-868-4441; Fax: 318-868-4609.

Diocesan Publications—Mrs. JESSICA RINAUDO, Editor, Catholic Center, 3500 Fairfield Ave., Shreveport, 71104. Tel: 318-868-4441; Fax: 318-868-4609.

Ecumenism and Interreligious Affairs—Rev. Msgr. J. CARSON LACAZE, Cathedral of St. John Berchmans, 939 Jordan St., Shreveport, 71101. Tel: 318-221-5296.

Facility Manager, Catholic Center—Mr. EDWARD HYDRO, Catholic Center, 3500 Fairfield Ave., Shreveport, 71104. Tel: 318-868-4441; Fax: 318-868-4605.

Fairview House (Residence for Clergy)—1000 Fairview, Shreveport, 71104. Tel: 318-868-4441; Fax: 318-868-4605.

Greco Institute—Rev. PATRICK J. MADDEN, Ph.D., Dir., Catholic Center, 3500 Fairfield Ave., Shreveport, 71104. Tel: 318-868-4441; Fax: 318-868-4456.

Hispanic Ministry and Immigration Services—Mrs. ROSALBA QUIROZ, Dir., Catholic Center, 3500 Fairfield Ave., Shreveport, 71104. Tel: 318-868-4441; Fax: 318-868-4578; Rev. ALOYS JOST, O.F.M., Hispanic Ministry - Eastern Deanery, Res.: St. Thomas Aquinas Friary, 810 Carey Ave., Ruston, 71270.

Holy Childhood—Sr. CAROL SHIVELY, O.S.U., Contact Person, Catholic Center, 3500 Fairfield Ave., Shreveport, 71104. Tel: 318-868-4441; Fax: 318-868-5057.

Human Resources—Deacon MICHAEL STRAUB, Dir., Catholic Center, 3500 Fairfield Ave., Shreveport, 71104. Tel: 318-868-4441; Fax: 318-868-4609.

Information Systems Management—Ms. PATRICIA PILLORS, Dir., Catholic Center, 3500 Fairfield Ave., Shreveport, 71104. Tel: 318-868-4441; Fax: 318-219-2316.

Jail-Prison Ministry—VACANT.

Diocesan Liturgy Commission—MICHAEL KENNEY; JOHN GUERRIERO; CATHY COBB; Revs. PHILIP F. MICHIELS; LAVERNE (PIKE) THOMAS; CAROLE MOON; Very Revs. TIMOTHY C. HURD, V.F.; PETER B. MANGUM, J.C.L., J.V.; JUSTIN WARD; Mrs. DIANNE RACHAL, Ex Officio.

Master of Ceremonies, Diocese of Shreveport—Rev. LAVERNE (PIKE) THOMAS.

Mission Director—Very Rev. ROTHELL PRICE, J.C.L., V.G., Catholic Center, 3500 Fairfield Ave., Shreveport, 71104. Tel: 318-868-4441; Fax: 318-868-4469.

Mission Effectiveness—Mr. RANDY G. TILLER, Dir., Catholic Center, 3500 Fairfield Ave., Shreveport, 71104. Tel: 318-868-4441; Fax: 318-868-4469.

Permanent Deacon Formation Program—Deacon CLARY NASH, Dir., Catholic Center, 3500 Fairfield Ave., Shreveport, 71104. Tel: 318-868-4441; Fax: 318-868-4578.

Propagation of the Faith—Very Rev. ROTHELL PRICE, J.C.L., V.G., Catholic Center, 3500 Fairfield Ave., Shreveport, 71104. Tel: 318-868-4441; Fax: 318-868-4469.

Religious Education—VACANT Contact: Chancellor Catholic Center, 3500 Fairfield Ave., Shreveport, 71104. Tel: 318-868-4441; Fax: 318-868-4469.

Resource Center (Library)—Mrs. DEBORAH SMITH, Library Technician, Catholic Center, 3500 Fairfield Ave., Shreveport, 71104. Tel: 318-868-4441; Fax: 318-868-4605.

Schools—Sisters CAROL SHIVELY, O.S.U., Supt.; ANN MIDDLEBROOKS, S.E.C., Assoc. Supt., Catholic Center, 3500 Fairfield Ave., Shreveport, 71104. Tel: 318-868-4441; Fax: 318-868-5057.

Child Nutrition Program—3500 Fairfield Ave., Shreveport, 71104. Tel: 318-868-4441; Fax: 318-868-5057.

Catholic Scouting— contact the Office of the Vicar General. *Catholic Center, 3500 Fairfield Ave., Shreveport, 71104.* Tel: 318-868-4441; Fax: 318-868-4469.

St. Vincent de Paul Society—Ms. DOTYE STANFORD, Contact Person, Mailing Address: P.O. Box 3911, Shreveport, 71133-3911. Tel: 318-865-7807.

Victim Assistance Coordinator—Ms. GLENNDA LAWSON. Tel: 318-294-1031.

Worship—Mrs. DIANNE RACHAL, Dir., Catholic Center, 3500 Fairfield Ave., Shreveport, 71105. Tel: 318-868-4441; Fax: 318-868-4578.

Youth and Young Adult Ministry—Mr. JOHN VINING, Dir., Catholic Center, 3500 Fairfield Ave., Shreveport, 71104. Tel: 318-868-4441; Fax: 318-868-4578.

CLERGY, PARISHES, MISSIONS AND PAROCHIAL SCHOOLS

CITY OF SHREVEPORT

(CADDO PARISH)

1—ST. JOHN BERCHMANS CATHEDRAL (1902) Very Rev. Peter B. Mangum, Rector; Rev. Msgr. J. Carson LaCaze, Parochial Vicar; Deacon John Basco.
Office: 939 Jordan St., 71101-4391. Tel: 318-221-5296; Fax: 318-221-8076.
School—(Grades PreK-8), 947 Jordan St., 71101. Tel: 318-221-6005; Fax: 318-425-0648. Mrs. Jo Cazes, Prin.; Judy Polhemus, Librarian. Lay Teachers 17; Students 263.
Catechesis/Religious Program—Students 52.

2—ST. ELIZABETH ANN SETON (1984) Rev. Philip F. Michiels; Deacon Homer Tucker.
Res.: 522 E. Flournoy-Lucas Rd., 71115-3802. Tel: 318-798-1887; Fax: 318-797-7302.
Catechesis/Religious Program—Students 203.

3—HOLY TRINITY (1856) Very Rev. Msgr. Earl V. Provenza; Deacon Jorge Martinez; Martha Martinez, Lay Ecclesial Min.
Res.: 315 Marshall St., P.O. Box 144, 71161-0144. Tel: 318-221-5990; Fax: 318-221-3545.
Catechesis/Religious Program—Students 23.

4—ST. JOSEPH (1949) Revs. Karl J. Daigle; Thomas Elavunkal, C.M.I. (India); Richard J. Lombard; Deacons Bruce Pistorius; William Roche.
Res.: 211 Atlantic Ave., 71105. Tel: 318-865-3581; Fax: 318-865-5125.
School—(Grades PreK-8), 1210 Anniston Ave., 71105. Tel: 318-865-3585; Fax: 318-868-1859. Mrs. Susan J. Belanger, Prin.; Ms. Nia Mitchell, Asst. Prin.; Rebecca Matschek, Librarian. Lay Teachers 28; Students 499.
Catechesis/Religious Program—Students 250.

5—ST. MARY OF THE PINES (1973) Revs. Francis Kamau, F.M.H. (Kenya); Michael Thang'wa, F.M.H. (Kenya); Deacons Clary Nash, Community Coord., Sacred Heart; Thomas Latiolais.
Res.: 1050 Bert Kouns Industrial Loop, 71118-3499. Tel: 318-687-5121 Church Office; 318-687-1818 Rectory; Fax: 318-687-5124.
Catechesis/Religious Program—Students 228.
Mission—Sacred Heart of Jesus Mailing Address: P.O. Box 19467, 71149-0467.
Church: 4736 Lyba St., 71109. Tel: 318-635-2121; Fax: 318-635-5226.

6—OUR LADY OF THE BLESSED SACRAMENT (1923), (African American), Rev. Andre McGrath, O.F.M.; Deacon Harold Dean.
Res.: 1558 Buena Vista St., 71101-2448. Tel: 318-222-3790; Fax: 318-222-3793.
Catechesis/Religious Program—Students 7.

7—OUR LADY OF THE HOLY ROSARY (1952) Closed. For inquiries for parish records contact the chancery.

8—ST. PIUS X (1955) Rev. Joseph Kallookalam, C.M.I. (India); Deacon Jeff Chapman; Susan R. Lanier, Pastoral Assoc.
Res.: 4300 N. Market St., 71107-2953. Tel: 318-222-2165.
Child Development Center—Tel: 318-425-2192; Fax: 318-675-0132. Students 95.
Catechesis/Religious Program—Students 88.

9—ST. THERESA, Consolidated with St. John Berchmans Cathedral.

OUTSIDE THE CITY OF SHREVEPORT

BASTROP, MOREHOUSE PARISH

1—ST. JOSEPH (1943) [CEM] Rev. Richard Norsworthy.
Res.: 217 Harrington Ave., 71220. Tel: 318-281-4327.
Catechesis/Religious Program—Students 8.

2—OUR LADY HELP OF CHRISTIANS, Consolidated with St. Joseph, Bastrop.

BOSSIER CITY, BOSSIER PARISH

1—CHRIST THE KING (1939) Revs. Charles Glorioso; Rigoberto Betancurt. In Res., Rev. Joseph Howard Jr.
Res.: 425 McCormick St., 71111-4692. Tel: 318-221-0238; Fax: 318-425-0011.
Catechesis/Religious Program—Students 60.

2—ST. JUDE (1964) Revs. LaVerne (Pike) Thomas; Jean Bosco Uwamungu (Rwanda); Deacons Larry Craig Mills; W. Freeman Ligon.
Res. & Mailing Address: 3800 Viking Dr., 71111-7403. Tel: 318-746-2508; Fax: 318-742-4526.
Catechesis/Religious Program—Students 282.
Mission—Mary, Queen of Heaven 1659 Palmetto Rd., Benton, Bossier Parish 71006. Tel: 318-742-2508.

3—MARY, QUEEN OF PEACE (1999) Rev. Joseph Ampatt Chacko; Deacon Michael Straub.
Res.: 2101 Hope St, 71112. Tel: 318-752-5971; Fax: 318-752-5973.
Church & Mailing Address: 7738 Barksdale Blvd, 71112.
Catechesis/Religious Program—Students 98.
Mission—St. George 3076 Hwy. 155, Coushatta, Red River Parish 71019-0937. Tel: 318-752-5971; Fax: 318-752-5973.

GRAMBLING, LINCOLN PARISH, ST. BENEDICT THE BLACK (1966), (African American), Rev. Patrick J. Madden.
Res.: 471 Main St., 71245-3088. Tel: 318-247-6734; Fax: 318-247-6288.
Catechesis/Religious Program—Students 8.

HODGE, JACKSON PARISH, ST. LUCY (1935) [CEM] Rev. Patrick J. Madden; Deacon Terry Walsworth, Pastoral Admin.; Alece Walsworth, Lay Ecclesial Min.
Res.: 1104 S. 2nd St., P.O. Box 100, 71247-0100. Tel: 318-259-2326; Fax: 318-259-2326 (Call first.).
Catechesis/Religious Program—(Grades PreK-2) Students 21.

LAKE PROVIDENCE, EAST CARROLL PARISH, ST. PATRICK (1870) [CEM] Rev. Mark A. Watson.
Res.: 207 Scarborough St., P.O. Box 351, 71254-0351. Tel: 318-559-1276; Fax: 318-559-7733.
Catechesis/Religious Program—Students 25.

MANSFIELD, DESOTO PARISH, ST. JOSEPH (1907) [CEM 4] Rev. Edmund A. (Larry) Niehoff.
Res.: 305 Jefferson St., P.O. Box 760, 71052-0760. Tel: 318-872-1158.
Catechesis/Religious Program—Fax: 318-872-1161. Students 35.
Mission—St. Ann's Chapel 2260 Hwy. 171, Stonewall, DeSoto Parish 71078.

MANY, SABINE PARISH, ST. JOHN THE BAPTIST (1871) [CEM] Rev. Joseph A. Martina Jr.; Deacon Michael Sullivan.
Res.: 1130 E. San Antonio Ave., 71449-3226. Tel: 318-256-5680; 318-256-5689; Fax: 318-256-9177.
Catechesis/Religious Program—Students 79.
Mission—St. Terence 1130 E. San Antonio Ave., Hwys. 191 & 476, Sabine Parish 71449. Tel: 318-586-7444.

MINDEN, WEBSTER PARISH, ST. PAUL (1942) Rev. Mark Franklin.
Mailing Address: P.O. Box 799, 71058-0799. Tel: 318-377-5364; Fax: 318-377-5394.
Catechesis/Religious Program—Tel: 318-377-5364. Students 35.
Mission—Blessed Sacrament 2688 Military Rd., Ringgold, Bienville Parish 71068.
Mission—St. Margaret 600 E. 2nd St., Homer, Claiborne Parish 71040.
Mission—Sacred Heart 304 Gaisser St., Springhill, Webster Parish 71075.

MONROE, OUACHITA PARISH

1—JESUS THE GOOD SHEPHERD (1958) Revs. David T. Richter; Matthew Tyler Long; Deacon Timothy Cotita. In Res., Rev. Msgr. Edmund J. Moore (Retired).
Office: 2510 Emerson St., 71201-2699. Tel: 318-325-7549; Fax: 318-322-6969.
Priest's Residence—800 Marquette St., 71201. Tel: 318-325-6956.
School—(Grades PreK-6), 900 Good Shepherd Ln., 71201. Tel: 318-325-8569; Fax: 318-325-9730. Lisa Patrick, Prin.; Mary Jo Norris, Librarian. Lay Teachers 21; Students 334.
Catechesis/Religious Program—Students 73.

2—ST. JOSEPH (1956) Closed. For inquiries for parish records contact the chancery.

3—LITTLE FLOWER OF JESUS (1940), (African American), Rev. Adrian Fischer, O.F.M.; Bro. Roch Pfeifer, O.F.M.; Deacon Verdine Williams.
Res.: 616 S. 16th St., 71201. Tel: 318-324-9706.
Church Office: 600 S. 16th St., 71201. Tel: 318-322-1224; Fax: 318-322-1261.

School—(Grades PreSchool), 610 S. 16th St., 71201. Tel: 318-322-7379. Mrs. Deborah S. Marshall, Dir. Preschool. Lay Teachers 12; Students 53.
Catechesis/Religious Program—Students 30.

4—ST. MATTHEW (1851) [CEM] Revs. Joseph Puthuppally; Thomas Lijo, C.M.I. (India).
Res.: 121 Jackson St., 71201. Tel: 318-323-8878; 318-323-8879; Fax: 318-323-2537.
Catechesis/Religious Program—Students 56.

5—OUR LADY OF FATIMA (1952) [JC] Revs. Sebastian Kallarackal, C.M.I. (India); Job Edathinatt Scaria, C.M.I. (India).
Church: 3205 Concordia, P.O. Box 4136, 71201-4136. Tel: 318-325-7595; Fax: 318-325-8544.
Rectory—207 Sheridan, 71201.
School—(Grades PreK-6), 3202 Franklin St., 71201. Tel: 318-387-1851; Fax: 318-387-7593. Mrs. Donna Eichhorn, Prin. Lay Teachers 13; Students 149.
Catechesis/Religious Program—Tel: 318-325-7596. Students 4.
Mission—St. Lawrence 357 Swartz School Rd., Swartz, Ouachita Parish 71281. Tel: 318-343-1618.

OAK GROVE, WEST CARROLL PARISH, SACRED HEART (1947) Rev. Mark A. Watson.
Church: 201 Purvis St., P.O. Box 419, 71263-0419. Tel: 318-428-2683.
Catechesis/Religious Program—Students 21.

RAMBIN, DESOTO PARISH, ST. MARY, Consolidated with St. Joseph, Mansfield.

RAYVILLE, RICHLAND PARISH, SACRED HEART (1920) Rev. Philip Pazhayakari, C.M.I.
Res. & Mailing Address: 716 Francis St., 71269. Tel: 318-728-2445; Fax: 318-728-0009.
Catechesis/Religious Program—Tel: 318-728-2445. Students 4.
Mission—St. Theresa 420 Main St., Delhi, Richland Parish 71232. Tel: 318-728-2445.

RUSTON, LINCOLN PARISH, ST. THOMAS AQUINAS (1941) Revs. Frank Folino, O.F.M.; Blane O'Neill, O.F.M.; Deacons John J. Serio; Oscar Hannibal; Bro. Michael Ward, O.F.M.
Res.: 810 Carey Ave., 71270-4915. Tel: 318-255-2870; Fax: 318-254-8319.
Catechesis/Religious Program—Tel: 318-251-2142. Students 145.

VIVIAN, CADDO PARISH, ST. CLEMENT (1945) Rev. James R. McLelland.
Office: 819 N. Pine, 71082-3354. Tel: 318-375-2789; Fax: 318-375-3571.
Catechesis/Religious Program—Students 13.

WEST MONROE, OUACHITA PARISH, ST. PASCHAL (1940) [CEM] Very Rev. Frank Coens, O.F.M.
Res.: 711 N. Seventh St., 71291-4211. Tel: 318-323-1631; Fax: 318-361-0527.
Catechesis/Religious Program—Students 115.
Mission—Our Lady of Perpetual Help 600 Water St., Farmerville, Union Parish 71241. Tel: 318-368-9239.

ZWOLLE, SABINE PARISH, ST. JOSEPH (1881) [CEM 3] Very Rev. Timothy C. Hurd.
Res.: 307 Hammond St., P.O. Box 8, 71486-0008. Tel: 318-645-6155; 318-645-9198 (Rectory); Fax: 318-645-9852.
Catechesis/Religious Program—Students 286.
Mission—St. Ann [CEM] 5272 Hwy. 482, Noble, Sabine Parish 71462.

Chaplains of Public Institutions

SHREVEPORT. *Overton Brooks Veteran's Administration Medical Center*, 510 E. Stoner Ave., 71101. Rev. Philip F. Michiels, Chap. Emergencies, St. Elizabeth Ann Seton Church, 522 E. Flournoy Lucas Rd., 71115. Tel: 318-798-1887.

On Sabbatical:
Rev. Zacharias Prakuzhy, C.M.I. (India).

Retired:
Rev. Msgrs.—
Clayton, Murray
Graef, Franz, S.T.D.
Moore, Edmund J.
Revs.—
Ebarb, Walter E.
Kennedy, John D.
McMullen, Roger
Scully, Patrick A.
Williams, Kenneth

Permanent Deacons:
Ainsworth, Burton
Basco, John
Chapman, Jeff
Cotita, Timothy
Dean, Harold
Hannibal, Oscar
Latiolais, Thomas
Ligon, Freeman
Martinez, Jorge
Mills, Larry Craig
Morris, Ronald J., (Retired)
Nash, Clary
Pistorius, Bruce
Roche, William
Serio, John J.
Straub, Michael
Sullivan, Michael
Tucker, Homer
Walsworth, Terry
Williams, Verdine

INSTITUTIONS LOCATED IN THE DIOCESE

[A] HIGH SCHOOLS, DIOCESAN

SHREVEPORT. *Loyola College Prep*, (Grades 7-12), 921 Jordan St., 71101-4390. Tel: 318-221-2675; Fax: 318-226-6334. Email: flyers@loyolaprep.org. Web: www.loyolaprep.org. Mr. Frank Israel, Prin.; Very Rev. Peter B. Mangum, J.C.L., J.V., Chap.; Ms. Stephanie Smith, Librarian. Lay Teachers 26; Students 447.

MONROE. *St. Frederick High School*, (Grades 7-12), 3300 Westminster, 71201-3299. Tel: 318-323-9636; Fax: 318-323-7456. Email: warriors@stfrederickhigh.org. Web: www.stfrederickhigh.org. Lisa Patrick, Prin.; Melissa Shepard, Librarian. Lay Teachers 26; Students 236.

[B] GENERAL HOSPITALS

SHREVEPORT. *CHRISTUS Health Northern Louisiana dba CHRISTUS Schumpert Health System* (1907) One St. Mary Pl., P.O. Box 21976, 71120-1976. Tel: 318-681-4500; Fax: 318-681-4177 (Admin.). Web: christusschumpert.org. Revs. Thomas John Vadakemuriyil, C.M.I. (India), Chap.; James R. McLelland, Chap.; Stephen F. Wright, Pres. & CEO; Sr. Jaya Xavier, S.D., Chap.; Mary Preziosi, Chap. Operated by Christus Health. Sisters 7; Bed Capacity 611; Patients Assisted Annually 218,244; Total Staff 1,511.

CHRISTUS Schumpert Bossier, 2105 Airline Dr., Bossier City, 71111. Tel: 318-848-8000; Fax: 318-848-8440. Stephen F. Wright, Pres. & CEO. (Sub. of Christus Schumpert Health System).

CHRISTUS Schumpert Highland, 1453 E. Bert Kouns Industrial Loop, 71105. Tel: 318-681-5000; Fax: 318-681-5475. Jason Rounds, Admin.; Rev. James R. McLelland, Chap.; Sr. Jaya Xavier, S.D., Chap. (Sub. of Christus Schumpert Health System).

COUSHATTA. *CHRISTUS Coushatta Health Care Center*, 1635 Marvel St., 71019. Tel: 318-932-2000; Fax: 318-932-2198. Karen Mixon, Admin. CHRISTUS Health Central Louisiana. Bed Capacity 25; Total Staff 157.

MONROE. *St. Francis Medical Center*, P.O. Box 1901, 71210-1901. Tel: 318-966-4000; Fax: 318-966-4142. Web: www.stfran.com. Louis H. Bremer Jr., FACHE, Pres. & CEO; Sabrina Ramsey, Vice Pres. Physician Rels.; Revs. Philip Chacko Theempalangattu (India), Chap.; James Dominic Thekkemury (India), Chap. Franciscan Missionaries of Our Lady 2; Bed Capacity 551; Patients Assisted Annually 208,774; Total Staff 2,148; Hospice & Ancillary Care 458,549.

[C] HOMES FOR AGED

MONROE. *CHRISTUS St. Joseph Home*, 2301 Sterlington Rd., P.O. Box 6057, 71211-6057. Tel: 318-323-3426; Fax: 318-387-7157. Larry N. Tucker, CEO. Operated by CHRISTUS Health Monroe. Licensed Capacity Nursing Care 130; Assisted Living Apartments 60; Sisters 2; Total Staff 150.

[D] SPECIAL CENTERS FOR SOCIAL SERVICES & ASSISTANCE

SHREVEPORT. *St. Catherine Community Center*, 7109 Henderson Ave., 71106-7109. Tel: 318-865-9817; Fax: 318-869-2549. Web: www.rc.net/shreveport/stcatherine. 3500 Fairfield Ave., 71104. Afterschool Enrichment, Summer Day Camp, Parenting, Arts, Anger Management, Computers, Teen Mom Mentoring. Total Assisted 601; Total Staff 7.

LAKE PROVIDENCE. **LCWR Region V Lake Providence Collaborative Ministries*, 106 Ingram St., 71254. Tel: 318-559-3747. Sr. Bernadette Barrett, S.H.Sp., Chap. Learning programs for youth, employment skills development, adult literacy, and senior citizen programs. Jail ministry. Staff 1.

[E] CONVENTS AND RESIDENCES FOR SISTERS

SHREVEPORT. *Motherhouse of the Daughters of the Cross in America*, 411 E. Flournoy-Lucas Rd., 71115-3901. Tel: 318-797-0887; Fax: 318-797-7102. Email: dcsrs@bayou.com. Sr. Maria Smith, Pres. Sisters 3.

[F] NEWMAN CENTERS

GRAMBLING. *Student Center* 471 Main St., 71245-3088. Tel: 318-247-6734 (Office); Fax: 318-247-6288. David Ponton, Campus Min.; Youlia Rabon, Campus Min.

MONROE. *Catholic Campus Ministry at the University of Louisiana at Monroe* , (formerly Northeast Louisiana University), 911 University Ave., P.O. Box 7250, 71211-7250. Tel: 318-343-4897; Fax: 318-343-4812. Revs. Sebastian Kallarackal, C.M.I. (India); Job Edathinatt Scaria, C.M.I. (India), Campus Min.; Deacon Timothy Cotita, Assoc. Campus Min.; Margaret Horne, Business Admin.

RUSTON. *E. Donn Piatt Catholic Student Center at Louisiana Tech University* 600 S. Thornton St., 71270-4946. Tel: 318-251-0793; Fax: 318-254-8319. Email: acts@latech.edu. Web: www.stac-acts.com. Rev. Frank Folino, O.F.M.; Bro. Michael Ward, O.F.M., Campus Min.

[G] MISCELLANEOUS

SHREVEPORT. *Magnificat-Nowela Chapter*, 4686 Hwy. 71, 71107. Tel: 318-222-0007. Sandy Chapman, Coord.

RELIGIOUS INSTITUTES OF MEN REPRESENTED IN THE DIOCESE

For further details refer to the corresponding bracketed number in the Religious Institutes of Men or Women section.

[0275]—*Carmelites of Mary Immaculate (India)*—C.M.I.

[0520]—*Franciscan Friars* (Sacred Heart Prov.)—O.F.M.

[0520]—*Franciscan Friars* (Prov. of St. John the Baptist)—O.F.M.

[]—*Franciscan Missionaries of Hope* (Kenya)—FMH

RELIGIOUS INSTITUTES OF WOMEN REPRESENTED IN THE DIOCESE

[1070-14]—*Congregation of Our Lady of the Sacred Heart (Dominican)*—O.P.

[0470]—*Congregation of the Sisters of Charity of the Incarnate Word, Houston, Texas*—C.C.V.I.

[0770]—*Daughters of the Cross*—D.C.

[1380]—*Franciscan Missionaries of Our Lady*—O.S.F.

[1430]—*Franciscan Sisters of Our Lady of Perpetual Help*—O.S.F.

[3120]—*Sisters of Our Lady of Sorrows*—O.L.S.

[3840]—*Sisters of St. Joseph of Carondelet*—C.S.J.

[]—*Sisters of the Destitute* India

[]—*Sisters of the Eucharistic Covenant*—S.E.C.

[2050]—*Sisters of the Holy Spirit and Mary Immaculate*—S.H.Sp.

[4120-03]—*Ursuline Nuns of the Congregation of Paris*—O.S.U.

DIOCESAN CEMETERIES

SHREVEPORT. *St. Joseph, Catholic Center*, 3500 Fairfield Ave., 71104. Tel: 318-868-4441; Fax: 318-868-4609. Mrs. Jill Braniff, CPA, Contact Person.

NECROLOGY

(No Deaths)

Diocese of Sioux City

(Dioecesis Siopolitana)

Most Reverend

R. WALKER NICKLESS

Bishop of Sioux City; ordained August 4, 1973; appointed Bishop of Sioux City November 10, 2005; Episcopal ordination January 20, 2006. *Chancery: Administrative Offices, 1821 Jackson St., P.O. Box 3379, Sioux City, IA 51102-3379.* Tel: 712-255-7933; Fax: 712-233-7598.

Most Reverend

LAWRENCE D. SOENS, D.D.

Bishop Emeritus of Sioux City; ordained May 6, 1950; appointed Bishop of Sioux City June 15, 1983; consecrated and installed August 17, 1983; retired November 28, 1998. *Mailing Address: P.O. Box 3379, Sioux City, IA 51102-3379.* Fax: 712-233-7598.

ESTABLISHED JANUARY 15, 1902.

Square Miles 14,518.

Corporate Title: "The Diocese of Sioux City."

Comprises 24 Counties in the northwest part of Iowa, west of Winnebago, Hancock, Wright, Hamilton and Story Counties, and north of Harrison, Shelby, Audubon, Guthrie and Dallas Counties.

For legal titles of parishes and diocesan institutions, consult the Chancery.

Chancery: Administrative Offices, 1821 Jackson St., P.O. Box 3379, Sioux City, IA 51102-3379. Tel: 712-255-7933; Fax: 712-233-7598.

Web: www.scdiocese.org

Email: bishopnickless@scdiocese.org

STATISTICAL OVERVIEW

Personnel	
Bishop	1
Retired Bishops	1
Priests: Diocesan Active in Diocese	67
Priests: Diocesan Active Outside Diocese	2
Priests: Retired, Sick or Absent	69
Number of Diocesan Priests	138
Total Priests in Diocese	138
Extern Priests in Diocese	1
Ordinations:	
Transitional Deacons	1
Permanent Deacons in Diocese	41
Total Sisters	62
Parishes	
Parishes	112
With Resident Pastor:	
Resident Diocesan Priests	54
Without Resident Pastor:	
Administered by Priests	58
Closed Parishes	1
Professional Ministry Personnel:	
Sisters	9
Lay Ministers	24
Welfare	
Catholic Hospitals	3
Total Assisted	262,262
Homes for the Aged	3
Total Assisted	330
Special Centers for Social Services	5
Total Assisted	4,321
Educational	
Diocesan Students in Other Seminaries	19
Students Religious	1
Total Seminarians	20
Colleges and Universities	1
Total Students	1,185
High Schools, Diocesan and Parish	8
Total Students	1,685
Elementary Schools, Diocesan and Parish	17
Total Students	4,533
Catechesis/Religious Education:	
High School Students	2,653
Elementary Students	6,697
Total Students under Catholic Instruction	16,773
Teachers in the Diocese:	
Priests	5
Sisters	8
Lay Teachers	566
Vital Statistics	
Receptions into the Church:	
Infant Baptism Totals	1,217
Minor Baptism Totals	238
Adult Baptism Totals	75
Received into Full Communion	264
First Communions	1,443
Confirmations	1,366
Marriages:	
Catholic	271
Interfaith	194
Total Marriages	465
Deaths	1,124
Total Catholic Population	98,901
Total Population	459,279

Former Bishops—Most Revs. PHILIP J. GARRIGAN, D.D., ord. June 11, 1870; appt. March 21, 1902; cons. May 25, 1902; died Oct. 14, 1919; EDMOND HEELAN, D.D., ord. June 24, 1890; cons. April 8, 1919; died Sept. 20, 1948; JOSEPH M. MUELLER, D.D., ord. June 14, 1919; cons. Oct. 16, 1947; died Aug. 9, 1981; FRANK H. GRETEMAN, D.D., ord. Dec. 8, 1932; appt. Titular Bishop of Vissalsa April 14, 1965; cons. May 26, 1965; appt. Bishop of Sioux City Oct. 20, 1970; installed Dec. 9, 1970; retired Aug. 17, 1983; died March 21, 1987; LAWRENCE D. SOENS, D.D. (Retired), ord. May 6, 1950; appt. Bishop of Sioux City June 15, 1983; installed Aug. 17, 1983; retired Nov. 28, 1998; DANIEL N. DINARDO, D.D., ord. July 16, 1977; appt. Coadjutor Bishop of Sioux City Aug. 19, 1997; Episcopal ord. Oct. 7, 1997; appt. Bishop of Sioux City Nov. 28, 1998; appt. Coadjutor Bishop of Galveston-Houston Jan. 16, 2004; installed March 26, 2004; appt. Coadjutor Archbishop Dec. 29, 2004; created Cardinal Priest Nov. 24, 2007.

Vicar General—Rev. Msgr. R. MARK DUCHAINE, V.G., J.C.L., Mailing Address: P.O. Box 3379, Sioux City, 51102-3379.

Chancery—Administrative Offices, 1821 Jackson St., P.O. Box 3379, Sioux City, 51102-3379. Tel: 712-255-7933; Fax: 712-233-7598.

Chancellor—Deacon DAVID A. LOPEZ, Ph.D., Mailing Address: P.O. Box 3379, Sioux City, 51102. Tel: 712-233-7512.

Vice Chancellor—Rev. MARK J. STOLL, J.C.L., Immaculate Conception Church, 419 Jones St., P.O. Box 802, Moville, 51039. Tel: 712-233-7537.

Diocesan Tribunal— Address all prenuptial files and marriage nullity process materials to: *P.O. Box 3379, Sioux City, 51102-3379.* Tel: 712-233-7533; Fax: 712-233-7588.

Judicial Vicar—Rev. Msgr. R. MARK DUCHAINE, V.G., J.C.L., 1821 Jackson St., P.O. Box 3379, Sioux City, 51102-3379.

Adjutant Judicial Vicar—Rev. MICHAEL J. ERPELDING, J.C.L.

Promoter of Justice—Rev. Msgr. RICHARD E. ZENK, J.C.D. (Retired).

Defenders of the Bond—Rev. Msgrs. RICHARD E. ZENK, J.C.D. (Retired); MICHAEL D. SERNETT, J.C.D., V.G.

Judges—Rev. Msgr. R. MARK DUCHAINE, V.G., J.C.L.; Rev. MICHAEL J. ERPELDING, J.C.L.; Rev. Msgrs. MICHAEL D. SERNETT, J.C.D., V.G.; ROGER J. AUGUSTINE, V.G. (Retired); Revs. PAUL-LOUIS ARTS, M.S. (Retired); JEROME P. COSGROVE, M.S. (Retired); Ms. ANNE KIRBY, J.C.L.; Mr. EUGENE J. ULSES, J.C.L.

Notary—TERRI NIEDERGESES.

Diocesan Finance Council—Most Rev. R. WALKER NICKLESS, Pres.; Rev. Msgr. R. MARK DUCHAINE, V.G., J.C.L. Directors: Rev. ROGER J. LINNAN; Mr. JEFFREY R. MOHRHAUSER; Mr. RICHARD MONTGOMERY; Mr. RANDY KRAMER; Dr. MICHAEL JUNG; Mr. JAMES COSGROVE; Ms. KAREN WALDSCHMITT; Ms. MARY SWANSON; Mrs. DIANE DONNELLY; Mr. ROYCE RANNIGER.

Diocesan Legal Counsel—Mr. MIKE ELLWANGER, (Rawlings, Nieland, Probasco, Killinger, Ellwanger, Jacobs, Mohrhauser, Law Firm, Sioux City). Refer all legal matters to The Chancery.

Presbyteral Council—Most Rev. R. WALKER NICKLESS; Rev. Msgr. R. MARK DUCHAINE, V.G., J.C.L.; Very Rev. RICHARD D. BALL, V.F.; Very Rev. Msgr. KEVIN C. MCCOY, S.T.D., V.F.; Very Revs. EDWARD M. GIRRES, V.F.; ARMAND J. BERTRAND, V.F.; TIMOTHY R. SCHOTT, V.F.; MERLIN J. SCHRAD, V.F., Pres.; Revs. CRAIG A. COLLISON; STEVEN W. BRODERSEN; RANDY L. SCHON; TIMOTHY A. FRIEDRICHSEN; BRIAN C. HUGHES; ROGER J. LINNAN; JOHN J. MCGUIRK; BRADLEY C. PELZEL; JEREMY J. WIND; JEROME P. COSGROVE, M.S. (Retired); BRENT C. LINGLE; JOHN M. THOMAS (Retired).

Diocesan Consultors—Most Rev. R. WALKER NICKLESS; Rev. Msgr. R. MARK DUCHAINE, V.G., J.C.L.; Very Revs. MERLIN J. SCHRAD, V.F.; RICHARD D. BALL, V.F.; Revs. JOHN M. THOMAS (Retired); BRADLEY C.

PELZEL; BRIAN C. HUGHES.

Deans—Very Revs. RICHARD D. BALL, V.F., Northwest Deanery; EDWARD M. GIRRES, V.F., Northeast Deanery; MERLIN J. SCHRAD, V.F., Southwest Deanery; Very Rev. Msgr. KEVIN C. MCCOY, S.T.D., V.F., Southeast Deanery; Very Revs. TIMOTHY R. SCHOTT, V.F., South Central Deanery; ARMAND J. BERTRAND, V.F., Central Deanery.

Diocesan Offices and Directors

Board of Education—Most Rev. R. WALKER NICKLESS; Revs. PATRICK WALSH; TERRY A. RODER; Mr. MARK THOMSEN; Rev. TIMOTHY A. JOHNSON; Sr. RUTH SCHOCK, O.S.F.; Mr. JAMES SCHALL; Mr. DAN RYAN; Mrs. KATHEE FROEHLICH; Mrs. LORIE A. NUSSBAUM; Mrs. BARB THOMPSON.

Building Commission—Revs. BRIAN C. HUGHES; BRENT C. LINGLE; Mr. BRAD MOLLET; Mr. THOMAS VOGT; Mr. CLETE WINDSCHITL.

Catholic School Foundation of the Diocese of Sioux City—Mr. ROYCE RANNIGER; Mrs. DIANE DONNELLY; Mr. DAN RYAN; Ms. GRACE IVEY; Mrs. KRISTIE ARLT; Most Rev. R. WALKER NICKLESS, Pres., 1821 Jackson St., Sioux City, 51105; Mr. ALLEN WILLETT, Chm.; Mr. JAMES BRIDE; Rev. Msgr. R. MARK DUCHAINE, V.G., J.C.L.; Mrs. MICHELLE PUETZ; Mr. RICK KNEIP; Rev. BRUCE A. LAWLER; Mr. MIKE HURLBURT.

Archives—DANIEL P. BURNS, 1821 Jackson St., P.O. Box 3379, Sioux City, 51102-3379. Tel: 712-233-7525.

Catholic Youth Organization—Rev. RANDY L. SCHON, Sacred Heart Church, 915 12 St., Boone, 50036-2295.

Censor Librorum—VACANT.

Catholic Charities—Mr. JERRY EATON, Dir., 1601 Military Rd., Sioux City, 51103. Tel: 712-252-4547. Algona Office: 715 E. North, Algona, 50511. Tel: 515-295-8840. Carroll Office: 409 1/2 W. 7th St., P.O. Box 13, Carroll, 51401. Tel: 712-792-9597. Fort Dodge Office: 1200 3rd Ave., N.W. #1, Fort Dodge, 50501. Tel: 515-576-4156. Spencer Office: 1111 4th Ave. W, Box 1124, Spencer, 51301. Tel: 712-580-4320. Storm Lake Office: 1709 Richland St., Storm Lake, 50588.

Continuing Education for Priests—Rev. GERALD F. FEIERFEIL, Dir. (Retired), Marian Hall, 1122 Grandview Blvd., Apt. 6, Sioux City, 51103.

Council of Catholic Women—Rev. JAMES J. TIGGES, Moderator, St. Mary Church, 311 4th St. N., Humboldt, 50548-1647. Tel: 515-332-2856.

Department of Formation and Ministry—Mr. DAN RYAN, Exec. Dir. & Supt.; Deacons DAVID A. LOPEZ, Ph.D., Dir. Deacon Formation; TIMOTHY MURPHY, Dir., Deacon Personnel, 1607 N. West St., Carroll, 51401-1498. Tel: 712-792-0513; Mr. SEAN MARTIN, Rel. Educ. & Family Life; Rev. BRENT C. LINGLE, Office of Worship; Ms. KARMEN BOWER, Family Life; Ms. GRACE ZAVALA, Diocesan Coord., Office of Hispanic Ministry.

Episcopal Representative for Religious—Sr. ROSALIE ERDMANN, S.L.W., 3636 Glen Oaks Blvd., Apt. 16, Sioux City, 51104-1564. Tel: 712-258-2579.

Holy Childhood Association—Rev. Msgr. RICHARD E. ZENK, J.C.D., Dir. (Retired), Mailing Address: P.O. Box 3379, Sioux City, 51102-3379.

Liturgy Commission—Rev. WILLIAM J. VIT JR.; Mr. MATTHEW GEERLINGS.

Office of "The Catholic Globe"—Ms. RENEE WEBB, Editor, 1825 Jackson St., P.O. Box 5079, Sioux City, 51102-5079. Tel: 712-255-2550 Editorial Office; Circulation.

Office of Catholic Education—Mr. DAN RYAN, Supt., 1821 Jackson, P.O. Box 3379, Sioux City, 51102-3379. Tel: 712-233-7589.

Priests' Personnel Board—Most Rev. R. WALKER NICKLESS, Chm.; Rev. Msgr. R. MARK DUCHAINE, V.G., J.C.L., Bishop's Liaison; Very Rev. Msgr. KEVIN C. MCCOY, S.T.D., V.F.; Revs. DANIEL M. GREVING; BRUCE A. LAWLER; Rev. Msgr. KENNETH A. SEIFRIED (Retired).

Priests' Pension Plan - Board of Trustees—Most Rev. R. WALKER NICKLESS, Chm.; Rev. Msgrs. ROGER J. AUGUSTINE, V.G. (Retired); R. MARK DUCHAINE, V.G., J.C.L.; Revs. THOMAS J. TOPF (Retired); GARY B. SNYDER; BRUCE A. LAWLER; Deacon RICHARD L. BILLINGS, Chm.; Mr. ALLEN REYNOLDS; Mr. DAVID FLATTERY; Mr. THOMAS P. GRIMSLEY; Mrs. MARGARET FUENTES; Mrs. DIANE DONNELLY; Mr. JEFFREY R. MOHRHAUSER; Mr. ROYCE RANNIGER.

Propagation of the Faith, Association of the Holy Childhood, Catholic Students' Mission Crusade—Rev. Msgr. RICHARD E. ZENK, J.C.D., Dir. (Retired), 1821 Jackson St., P.O. Box 3379, Sioux City, 51102-3379.

Office of Communications—Mrs. KRISTIE ARLT, Dir., Mailing Address: P.O. Box 3379, Sioux City, 51102-3379.

Rural Life Conference—VACANT.

St. Joseph Education Society— (Diocesan Seminarian Board). Rev. WILLIAM J. VIT JR., 1000 Douglas St., Sioux City, 51105-1399. Tel: 712-255-1637.

Victim Assistance Coordinator—ANGIE MACK, Mercy Child Advocacy Center. Tel: 712-279-5610; 866-435-4397 (Toll Free). Email: macka@mercyhealth.com.

Safe Environment Coordinator—COLLEEN SULSBERGER. Tel: 712-233-7517. Email: colleens@scdiocese.org.

Vocations—Rev. BRADLEY C. PELZEL, P.O. Box 3379, Sioux City, 51102. Tel: 712-233-7523; 712-255-3577.

CLERGY, PARISHES, MISSIONS AND PAROCHIAL SCHOOLS

CITY OF SIOUX CITY

(WOODBURY COUNTY)

1—CATHEDRAL OF THE EPIPHANY (1867) Revs. William J. Vit Jr., Rector; Brent C. Lingle; Hieu Nguyen; Deacon David A. Lopez.
Res.: 1000 Douglas St., 51105-1399. Tel: 712-255-1637; Fax: 712-255-4194. Web: www.sccathedral.org.
See Bishop Heelan Catholic Schools under Inter-Parochial Schools located in the Institution section.
Catechesis/Religious Program—Students 464.

2—BLESSED SACRAMENT (1922) Very Rev. Merlin J. Schrad; Rev. Msgr. Roger J. Augustine, Senior Priest (Retired); Deacons John Heffernan, (Retired); Fred Karpuk; Richard Billings; Terry McElroy, Dir. Opers.
Res.: 3012 Jackson St., 51104-2799. Tel: 712-277-2949; Fax: 712-277-2963. Email: hegstromt@bishopheelan.org. Web: www.blessedsac.com.
See Bishop Heelan Catholic Schools under Inter-Parochial Schools located in the Institution section.
Catechesis/Religious Program—Tel: 712-277-4739, Ext. 15; Fax: 712-258-3698. Email: drewalshp@bishopheelan.org. Patricia Walsh, D.R.E.; Ann Schultz, Liturgy Director. Students 132.

3—ST. BONIFACE (1887), (German), [JC] Rev. Michael J. Erpelding; Deacon James Sands. In Res., Rev. Richard A. Sitzmann (Retired).
Res.: 703 W. Fifth St., 51103-3799. Tel: 712-255-3577; Fax: 712-279-0751.
See Bishop Heelan Catholic Schools under Inter-Parochial Schools located in the Institution section.
Catechesis/Religious Program—709 Iowa St., 51105. Tel: 712-258-4962; Fax: 712-258-7101. Students 64.

4—ST. CASIMIR (1915), (Lithuanian), Closed. For inquiries for parish records contact the chancery.

5—ST. FRANCIS OF ASSISI (1907), (Polish), Closed. For inquiries for parish records contact the chancery.

6—IMMACULATE CONCEPTION (1905) [JC] Rev. Daniel C. Guenther.
Res.: 1212 Morningside Ave., 51106. Tel: 712-276-4821; Fax: 712-276-1321. Email: icchurch@cableone.net.
See Bishop Heelan Catholic Schools under Inter-Parochial Schools located in the Institution section.
Catechesis/Religious Program—Tel: 712-276-4571; Fax: 712-276-1321. Students 161.

7—ST. JOSEPH (1887) [JC] Rev. Michael J. Erpelding; Deacons Ronald Pietz; Bruce Chartier. In Res., Rev. Bradley C. Pelzel.
Res.: 1112 Eighth St., 51105-1899. Tel: 712-258-3813; Fax: 712-255-4018.
Catechesis/Religious Program—Twinned with St. Boniface., Tel: 712-258-4962. Students 15.

8—ST. MICHAEL (1906) [JC] Rev. Gary B. Snyder; Sr. Jean Ann Rausch, F.S.P.A., Pastoral Min.; Deacons Larry Sitzman; William Berger, (Retired).
Office and Res.: 2223 Indian Hills Dr., 51104-1605. Tel: 712-239-2411; Fax: 712-239-4710.
See Bishop Heelan Catholic Schools under Inter-Parochial Schools located in the Institution section.
Catechesis/Religious Program—Tel: 712-239-2411. Students 218.

9—NATIVITY OF OUR LORD JESUS CHRIST (1966) Rev. Steven J. McLoud; Deacon Michael J. Hand.
Res.: 4242 Natalia Way, 51106-4099. Tel: 712-276-3022; Fax: 712-274-2703.
See Bishop Heelan Catholic Schools under Inter-Parochial Schools located in the Institution section.
Catechesis/Religious Program—Tel: 712-274-0497. Students 372.

10—SACRED HEART (1907) [JC] Rev. Craig A. Collison; Deacon Mark Wyant.
Res.: 5000 Military Rd., 51103-1564. Tel: 712-233-1652; Fax: 712-255-3056. Email: collisonc@bishopheelan.org. Web: www.sacredheart-siouxcity.com.
See Bishop Heelan Catholic Schools under Inter-Parochial Schools located in the Institution section.
Catechesis/Religious Program—Students 206.

OUTSIDE SIOUX CITY

AKRON, PLYMOUTH CO., ST. PATRICK (1888) [CEM] Rev. Roger J. Linnan; Deacon Richard Port.
Res.: 650 Dakota St., P.O. Box 317, 51001-0317. Tel: 712-568-3292.
Catechesis/Religious Program—Students 70.

ALGONA, KOSSUTH CO., ST. CECELIA (1880) [CEM] Very Rev. Edward M. Girres; Deacon Bill Black.
Res.: P.O. Box 633, 50511-0633. Tel: 515-295-3435; Fax: 515-295-9290. Email: scecelia@netamumail.com.
School—Seton Elementary, Tel: 515-295-3509; Fax: 515-295-7739. Email: seton@garrigan.put.k12.us. Web: www.garrigan.unlimitedweb.net. Consolidation of St. Cecelia, Algona, St. Benedict & St. Joseph, Wesley; St. Joseph, Bode. Presentation Sisters 1; Lay Teachers 25; Students 207.
Catechesis/Religious Program—Students 145.

ALTON, SIOUX CO., ST. MARY'S (1870), (German), [CEM] Rev. Paul F. Eisele.
Res.: 609 10th St., 51003. Tel: 712-756-4224; Fax: 712-756-4431.
School—Spalding Catholic, (Grades 3-6) Tel: 712-756-4532; Fax: 712-756-4532. Judy Stokesbury, Librarian. Consolidation of Alton, Hospers and Granville. Lay Teachers 4; Students 46.
Catechesis/Religious Program— Cluster of St. Mary, St. Anthony's, and St. Joseph's. Students 60.

ANTHON, WOODBURY CO., ST. JOSEPH'S (1890) [CEM] Rev. Terry A. Roder.
Res.: 404 E. Randolph St., P.O. Box 285, 51004-0285. Tel: 712-373-5573; 712-883-2406; Fax: 712-883-2458.
Catechesis/Religious Program—Tel: 712-373-5573. Students 52.

ARCADIA, CARROLL CO., ST. JOHN THE BAPTIST (1875), (German), [CEM] Rev. Joseph A. Dillinger.
Res.: 206 2nd Ave., P.O. Box 39, Breda, 51436-0039. Tel: 712-689-2595.
Catechesis/Religious Program—Students 18.

ARMSTRONG, EMMET CO., ST. MARY'S (1892) [CEM] [JC] Rev. John M. Thomas, Admin. (Retired).
Office: 404 Fifth Ave., P.O. Box 437, 50514-9301. Tel: 712-864-3160.
Catechesis/Religious Program—Tel: 712-380-2548. Students 23.

ASHTON, OSCEOLA CO., ST. MARY'S CATHOLIC CHURCH (1880) [CEM] Rev. John A. Vakulskas Jr.
Res.: P.O. Box 157, 51232-0157. Tel: 712-724-6411.
Catechesis/Religious Program—722 8th Ave., Sibley, 51249. Tel: 712-754-2739. Christy Funk, D.R.E. Students 12.

AUBURN, SAC CO., ST. MARY'S (1893), (German), [JC] Rev. Lynn Bruch.
Res.: 301 E. 4th St., P.O. Box 221, 51433. Tel: 712-688-2845.
Catechesis/Religious Program—Students 58.

BANCROFT, KOSSUTH CO., ST. JOHN THE BAPTIST'S (1891) [CEM] [JC] Rev. John M. Thomas, Admin. (Retired); Deacon Philip Doocy.
Res.: 204 S. Summit Ave., P.O. Box 195, 50517-0195. Tel: 515-885-2462; Fax: 515-885-2424. Web: www.stjohnbancroft.com.
School—St. John's Elementary School, Tel: 515-885-2580; Fax: 515-885-2402. Ms. Jackie Rahe, Prin. Lay Teachers 6; Students 23.
Catechesis/Religious Program— Lori Geitzenauer, D.R.E. Students 133.

BARNUM, WEBSTER CO., ST. JOSEPH'S (1891) [CEM] Closed. For inquiries for parish records contact Holy Trinity Parish of Webster County, Fort Dodge.

BODE, KOSSUTH CO., ST. JOSEPH'S (1876) [CEM] Rev. Victor Ramaeker.
Res.: 603 3rd St., Whittemore, 50598. Tel: 515-884-2618.
Catechesis/Religious Program—Tel: 515-295-3435. Students 4.

BOONE, BOONE CO., SACRED HEART (1868) [CEM] Rev. Randy L. Schon; Deacons David Brown; Darwin Messerly.
Res.: 915 12th St., 50036-2295. Tel: 515-432-1971. Email: shsecretary@mchsi.com. Web: www.sacredhrt.org.
Catechesis/Religious Program—Tel: 515-432-2884; Fax: 515-432-1975. Email: sh-youth@mchsi.com. Students 191.

BREDA, CARROLL CO., ST. BERNARD'S (1880) [CEM] Rev. Joseph A. Dillinger.
Res.: 206 N. 2nd St., P.O. Box 39, 51436-0031. Tel: 712-673-2351; Fax: 712-673-2351.
Parish is a member of the consolidated K-12 Kuemper Catholic School System, Carroll, IA. Please refer to Kuemper Catholic School System under Inter-Parochial Schools in the Institution section.
Catechesis/Religious Program—Tel: 712-792-0513. Students 55.

CARROLL, CARROLL CO.

1—HOLY SPIRIT (1964) [JC], SS. Peter/Paul, and St. Joseph, Carroll merged to form Holy Spirit, Carroll. Revs. Timothy A. Johnson; Timothy J. Boekelman; Deacons Edward Miller; Greg Sampson.
Res.: 421 E. Bluff St., 51401-3099. Tel: 712-792-4386; Fax: 712-792-8038. Email: hsparish@mchsi.com. Web: www.holyspiritcarroll.org.
School—(Grades K-12) Tel: 712-792-3313; Fax: 712-792-8073. Parish is a member of the consolidated K-12 Kuemper Catholic School System, Carroll, IA. Please refer to Kuemper Catholic School System under Inter-Parochial Schools in the Institution section.
Catechesis/Religious Program—Tel: 712-792-0513; Fax: 712-792-9245. Deacon Timothy Murphy, D.R.E. Shared with St. Lawrence & surrounding parishes. Students 368.

2—ST. LAWRENCE (1914) [JC] Very Rev. Timothy R. Schott; Deacon Tim Murphy.
Res.: 1607 N. West St., 51401-1498. Tel: 712-792-9244; Fax: 712-792-9245.
Parish is a member of the consolidated K-12 Kuemper Catholic School System, Carroll, IA. Please refer to Keumper Catholic School System under Inter-Parochial Schools in the Institution section.
Catechesis/Religious Program—Tel: 712-792-0513. Shared with Holy Spirit and surrounding parishes. Students 75.

CHARTER OAK, CRAWFORD CO., ST. BONIFACE (1883), (German—Irish), [CEM] Revs. Paul Kelly; Timothy A. Friedrichsen, Parochial Vicar.
Res.: P.O. Box 280, Denison, 51442. Tel: 712-674-3329.
Mission—St. Mary's [CEM] Box 317, Ute, Monona Co. 51528.
Catechesis/Religious Program—Students 48.

CHEROKEE, CHEROKEE CO., IMMACULATE CONCEPTION (1870) [CEM] Very Rev. Armand J. Bertrand; Deacon Leroy Rupp.
Res.: 709 W. Cedar St., P.O. Box 658, 51012-0658. Tel: 712-225-4606.
Catechesis/Religious Program—7th & Willow, 51012. Tel: 712-225-4466. Students 120.

CHURDAN, GREENE CO., ST. COLUMBKILLE (1886), (German—Irish), [CEM] Rev. Donald C. Ries.
Res.: 807 Head St., P.O. Box 128, 50050-0128. Tel: 515-389-3625; Fax: 515-389-3797. Web: www.geocities.com/st_columbkilleparish.
Catechesis/Religious Program—Tel: 515-389-3714. Email: gnhcarey@wccta.net. Students 42.

CLARE, WEBSTER CO., ST. MATTHEW'S (1886) [CEM] Closed. For inquiries for parish records contact Holy Trinity Parish of Webster County, Fort Dodge.

COON RAPIDS, CARROLL CO., ANNUNCIATION (1891) [CEM] Rev. Andrew W. Hoffmann; Deacons Louis Meiners; Gary Schon.
Res.: 702 Elm St., P.O. Box 76, 50058-0076. Tel: 712-999-2823; Fax: 712-999-2823. Email: anchurch@longlines.com.
Catechesis/Religious Program—(Linked with St. Joseph, Dedham & St. Elizabeth Seton, Glidden), Tel: 712-999-5235. Students 118.
Mission—St. Elizabeth Seton 6th & Dakota, Glidden, 51443. P.O. Box 76, 50058-0076.

DANBURY, WOODBURY CO., ST. MARY'S (1897), (German), [CEM] Rev. Terry A. Roder.
Res.: 604 Peach St., 51019-5028. Tel: 712-883-2406; Fax: 712-883-2458.
School—Danbury Elementary, (Grades PreK-6) Tel: 712-883-2244; Fax: 712-883-2024. Kristi Liechti, Prin. Priests 1; Lay Teachers 5; Students 34.
Catechesis/Religious Program—Students 27.

DAYTON, WEBSTER CO., CHRIST THE KING (1950) [CEM] Closed. For inquiries for parish records contact Holy Trinity Parish of Webster County, Fort Dodge.

DEDHAM, CARROLL CO., ST. JOSEPH'S (1892) [CEM] Rev. Andrew W. Hoffmann; Deacons Louis Meiners; Gary Schon.
Res.: P.O. Box 47, 51440-0047. Tel: 712-683-5744. Email: stjoes@iowatelecom.net.
School—Kuemper Catholic School System, Tel: 712-792-3596; Fax: 712-792-3365. Web: www.kuemper-.org. Consolidation of Dedham, Willey Elementary, Holy Spirit and St. Lawrence.
Catechesis/Religious Program—(Linked with Annunciation, Coon Rapids & St. Elizabeth, Glidden) Students 30.

DENISON, CRAWFORD CO., ST. ROSE OF LIMA (1872) [CEM] Revs. Paul Kelly; Timothy A. Friedrichsen.
Res.: 916 2nd Ave. S., P.O. Box 280, 51442-0280. Tel: 712-263-2152; Fax: 712-263-2153.
School—Tel: 712-263-5408; Fax: 712-263-2153. Lay Teachers 8; Students 50.
Catechesis/Religious Program—Tel: 712-263-5408. Students 127.

DOW CITY, CRAWFORD CO., ST. MARYS (1947), (German—Irish), Revs. Paul Kelly; Timothy A. Friedrichsen, Parochial Vicar.
Res.: P.O. Box 280, Denison, 51442. Tel: 712-674-3329.
Catechesis/Religious Program—Students 50.

DUNCOMBE, WEBSTER CO., ST. JOSEPH'S (1880) [CEM] Closed. For inquiries for parish records contact Holy Trinity Parish of Webster County, Fort Dodge.

EARLY, SAC CO., SACRED HEART (1882) [CEM] Rev. John J. McGuirk; Deacon B. (Butch) Stone.
Res.: 600 S. 12th St., Sac City, 50583-2506. Tel: 712-273-5482; Fax: 712-273-5798. Email: shchurch@frontiernet.net. Web: www.sacredheartearly.org.
Catechesis/Religious Program—Tel: 712-273-5577. Students 29.

EMMETSBURG, PALO ALTO CO.

1—HOLY FAMILY (1856), (Irish), [CEM] Rev. Clement W. Currans.
Res.: 2001 S. Broadway, P.O. Box 322, 50536-0322. Tel: 712-852-3187; Fax: 712-852-4406. Email: holyfamily@iowatelecom.net. Web: www.iowatelecom.net/~holyfamily.
School—Emmetsburg Catholic School, (Grades PreK-8) Tel: 712-852-3464; Fax: 712-852-3464. Email: jhyslop@emmetsburg-catholic.pvt.k12.ia.us. Mrs. Jean Hyslop, Prin. Lay Teachers 11; Students 92.
Catechesis/Religious Program—Tel: 712-852-3187. Students 72.

2—ST. THOMAS, Closed. For sacramental records contact Holy Family, Emmetsburg.

ESTHERVILLE, EMMET CO., ST. PATRICK'S (1891) [CEM] Rev. Msgr. Michael D. Sernett.
Res.: 903 Central Ave., P.O. Box 383, 51334-0383. Tel: 712-362-5851; Fax: 712-362-5852. Email: dawnstpats@mchsi.com.
Catechesis/Religious Program—Duhigg Center, 902 Central Ave., P.O. Box 383, 51334. Tel: 712-362-4172. Students 179.

FONDA, POCAHONTAS CO., OUR LADY OF GOOD COUNSEL (1884) [CEM] Rev. Siby Punnoose (India), Admin.; Deacon Eldon Sullivan.
Res.: P.O. Box 339, 50540-0339. Tel: 712-288-6480; Fax: 712-288-6480. Email: olgc@ncn.net.
Catechesis/Religious Program—Students 73.

FORT DODGE, WEBSTER CO.

1—CORPUS CHRISTI (1856) [JC] Closed. For inquiries for parish records contact Holy Trinity Parish of Webster County, Fort Dodge.

2—HOLY ROSARY (1946) [JC] Closed. For inquiries for parish records contact Holy Trinity Parish of Webster County, Fort Dodge.

3—HOLY TRINITY PARISH OF WEBSTER COUNTY (2006) Very Rev. Msgr. Kevin C. McCoy; Revs. Shane Deman; Sunny Dominic (India).
Office: 2220 4th Ave. N., 50501. Tel: 515-573-3616; Fax: 515-955-8473.
See St. Edmond Catholic School, Inc., Fort Dodge under Inter-Parochial Schools located in the Institution Section.
Catechesis/Religious Program—Students 136.

4—SACRED HEART (1897) [JC] Closed. For inquiries for parish records contact Holy Trinity Parish of Webster County, Fort Dodge.

GILMORE CITY, POCAHONTAS CO., ST. JOHN'S (1889) [CEM] Rev. James J. Tigges.
Res.: 311 4th St. N., Humboldt, 50548. Tel: 515-332-2856 (St. Mary's-Humboldt); Fax: 515-332-1487. Email: stmhbt@goldfieldaccess.net.
Catechesis/Religious Program—Tel: 515-332-2784. Students 4.

GRAETTINGER, PALO ALTO CO., IMMACULATE CONCEPTION (1891) [CEM] Rev. Msgr. Michael D. Sernett.
Res.: 903 Central Ave., P.O. Box 383, Estherville, 51334. Tel: 712-362-5851; Fax: 712-362-5852. Email: icc@rvtc.net.
Catechesis/Religious Program—503 W. Olive St., 51342. Tel: 712-859-3482. Students 73.

GRAND JUNCTION, GREENE CO., ST. BRIGID'S (1873), (Irish), [CEM] Rev. Donald C. Ries.
Res.: 503 N. Chestnut, Jefferson, 50129. Tel: 515-738-2684; Fax: 515-386-3672.
Catechesis/Religious Program—St. Brigid Parish Center, 602 Hager St. E., 50107. Tel: 515-738-2254. Students 22.

GRANVILLE, SIOUX CO., ST. JOSEPH (1886) [CEM] Very Rev. Richard D. Ball.
Res.: 528 Elm St., P.O. Box 127, 51022-0127. Tel: 712-727-3551.
School—Spalding Catholic Schools, Tel: 712-727-3451; Fax: 712-727-3455. Mrs. Lisa Hamerlinck, Prin. (Spalding Catholic Grades K-12); Judy Stokesberry, Librarian. Consolidation of Alton, Hospers and Granville. Lay Teachers 16; Students 101.
Catechesis/Religious Program—Tel: 712-752-8784. Pilgrim cluster held at St. Mary's, Alton. Students 9.

HALBUR, CARROLL CO., ST. AUGUSTINE'S (1904) [CEM] Rev. Steven W. Brodersen.
Res.: P.O. Box 13, 51444-0013. Tel: 712-658-2464. Parish is a member of the consolidated K-12 Kuemper Catholic School System, Carroll, IA. Please refer to Keumper Catholic School System under Inter-Parochial Schools in the Institution section.
Catechesis/Religious Program—Tel: 712-792-0513 (Carroll); 712-653-2131 (Manning). Students 51.

HAWARDEN, SIOUX CO., ST. MARY'S (1887) [JC] Rev. Roger J. Linnan.
Res.: 1125 Avenue L., P.O. Box 271, 51023-0271. Tel: 712-551-1501.
Catechesis/Religious Program—Tel: 712-551-2526. Students 173.

HOLSTEIN, IDA CO., OUR LADY OF GOOD COUNSEL (1884) [CEM] Rev. David Hemann; Deacon Mike Stover, Pastoral Min. In Res., Rev. Msgr. Kenneth A. Seifried (Retired).
Office: 513 Mueller St., 51025. Tel: 712-368-4755.
Catechesis/Religious Program—Tel: 712-368-2504. Students 54.

HORNICK, WOODBURY CO., ST. PHILIP'S (1900) Closed. For inquiries for parish records contact the chancery.

HOSPERS, SIOUX CO., ST. ANTHONY'S (1877) [CEM] Rev. Paul F. Eisele.
506 Elm, P.O. Box 86, 51238-0086. Tel: 712-752-8784. Email: stacc@nethtc.net.
Res.: *c/o St. Mary*, 609 10th St., Alton, 51003. Tel: 712-756-4224. Email: fatherpaul@midlands.net.
School—Spalding Elementary, (Grades K-3) Tel: 712-752-8286. Judy Stokesberry, Librarian. Consolidation of Alton, Hospers and Granville. Lay Teachers 4; Students 42.

HUMBOLDT, HUMBOLDT CO., ST. MARY'S (1878) [CEM] Rev. James J. Tigges.
Res.: 311 Fourth St. N., 50548-1647. Tel: 515-332-2856; Fax: 515-332-1487. Email: stmhbt2@goldfieldaccess.net.
School—Tel: 515-332-2134. Mrs. Cindy Edge, Prin. Lay Teachers 13; Students 212.
Catechesis/Religious Program—Tel: 515-332-2784. Students 99.

IDA GROVE, IDA CO., SACRED HEART (1878) [CEM] Rev. David Hemann.
Res.: 800 N. Main, P.O. Box 244, 51445-1297. Tel: 712-364-2718. Email: igrectory@frontiernet.net. Web: fatherdavid.net.
Catechesis/Religious Program—Tel: 712-364-3628. Students 139.

JEFFERSON, GREENE CO., ST. JOSEPH'S (1875) Rev. Donald C. Ries.
Res.: 503 N. Chestnut St., 50129-1507. Tel: 515-386-2638; Fax: 515-386-3672. Email: joejeff@netins.net. Web: www.catholicweb.com/greenecounty.
Catechesis/Religious Program—501 N. Locust, 50129. Tel: 515-386-4010. Students 115.
Mission—St. Brigid [CEM] 602 Hager, Grand Junction, Greene Co. 50107. Tel: 515-738-2254.

KINGSLEY, PLYMOUTH CO., ST. MICHAEL'S (1888) [CEM] Rev. Mark J. Stoll.
Res.: 403 Jones St., P.O. Box 802, Moville, 51039-0802. Tel: 712-378-2722; Fax: 712-873-3931. Email: icmoville@wiatel.net. Web: www.icmoville.catholicweb.com.
Catechesis/Religious Program—Tel: 712-873-3644. Students 118.

LAKE CITY, CALHOUN CO., ST. MARY'S (1894) [CEM] [JC] Rev. Lynn Bruch.
Res.: 205 N. Lloyd St., P.O. Box 131, 51449-0131. Tel: 712-464-3395; Fax: 712-464-7669.
Catechesis/Religious Program—Students 86.

LARCHWOOD, LYON CO., ST. MARY (1898), (German—Dutch), [JC] Rev. Jeffrey Schleisman; Deacon Jeff Gallagher.
Res.: 1413 Holder St., P.O. Box 37, 51241-0037. Tel: 712-477-2273; Fax: 712-477-2162. Email: amen1030@yahoo.com. Web: www.holymarycluster.wetpaint.com.
Catechesis/Religious Program—Students 126.

LAURENS, POCAHONTAS CO., SACRED HEART (1893) [CEM] Rev. John J. Gerald (India).
Res.: 708 Thomas St., P.O. Box 450, Sioux Rapids, 50585. Tel: 712-841-4596.
Catechesis/Religious Program—Tel: 712-289-6481. Students 33.

LE MARS, PLYMOUTH CO.

1—ST. JAMES (1883) [JC] Rev. Matthew A. Hewitt.
Res.: 109 Sixth Ave., S.W., 51031-3434. Tel: 712-546-5201; Fax: 712-546-8696. Email: saintjameslm@frontiernet.net.
School—Gehlen Catholic Elementary, (Grades PreK-8) Tel: 712-546-4181. Mrs. Lorie A. Nussbaum, Prin. Lay Teachers 21; Students 306.
High School—Gehlen Catholic High School, Tel: 712-546-4181. Lay Teachers 22; Students 153.
Catechesis/Religious Program—20 6th Ave. N.E., 51031. Tel: 712-546-5223. Students 234.

2—ST. JOSEPH'S (1875), (German), [CEM] [JC] Rev. Kevin M. Richter.
Res.: 35 6th Ave. N.E., 51031. Tel: 712-546-4813;

Fax: 712-546-8346. Email: stjoelm@frontiernet.net.
School—Gehlen Catholic School, 709 Plymouth St., S.E., 51031. Tel: 712-546-4181; Fax: 712-546-8696. Email: 1.hatting@gehlencatholic.com. Jeff Alesch, Prin. Students 545.
St. Joseph Endowment Fund—20 6th Ave. N.E., 51031.
Catechesis/Religious Program—Tel: 712-546-5223; Fax: 712-546-8346. Email: faithfor@frontier.net. Sr. Jeanette Homan, D.R.E. Students 157.

LEDYARD, KOSSUTH CO., SACRED HEART (1887) [CEM] [JC] Rev. John M. Thomas (Retired).
Mailing Address: P.O. Box 126, 50556-0067. Tel: 515-646-2525.
Res.: 204 S. Summit Ave., P.O. Box 195, Bancroft, 50517. Tel: 515-885-2462; Fax: 515-885-2424.
Catechesis/Religious Program— Twinned with St. John's, Bancroft. Students 9.

LIDDERDALE, CARROLL CO., HOLY FAMILY (1914), (German), [CEM] Very Rev. Timothy R. Schott; Deacon Timothy Murphy.
Res.: P.O. Box 160, 51452-0160. Tel: 712-822-5522.
Parish is a member of newly consolidated K-12 Kuemper Catholic School System, Carroll, IA. Please refer to Keumper Catholic School System under Inter-Parochial Schools in the Institution section.
Catechesis/Religious Program—Tel: 712-792-0513. Students 6.
Mission—St. Elizabeth Seton Church Glidden, Carroll Co. Tel: 712-659-3051.

LIVERMORE, HUMBOLDT CO., SACRED HEART (1881) [CEM] Rev. James J. Tigges.
Res.: 311 4th St. N, Humboldt, 50548-1647. Tel: 515-679-4279.
Catechesis/Religious Program—Tel: 515-379-2508. Students 27.

LOHRVILLE, CALHOUN CO., ST. JOSEPH'S (1885), (Irish), [CEM] Rev. Lynn Bruch.
Res.: 205 N. Lloyd St., P.O. Box 131, Lake City, 51449. Tel: 712-464-3395; Fax: 712-464-7669.
Catechesis/Religious Program—Students 25.

MADRID, BOONE CO., ST. MALACHY'S (1923) [JC] Rev. James A. Bruch.
Res.: 207 Gerald St., 50156-1464. Tel: 515-795-2731; Fax: 515-795-2731. Email: stmalachys@iowatelecom.net.
Church: 405 Gerald St., 50156. Tel: 515-795-2613.
Catechesis/Religious Program—Students 197.

MALLARD, PALO ALTO CO., ST. MARY'S (1889) [CEM] Rev. Thomas J. Hart.
Mailing Address: P.O. Box 16, West Bend, 50597.
Res.: 206 1st Ave., N.W., West Bend, 50597. Fax: 515-887-3334.
Catechesis/Religious Program—Tel: 515-887-3333; Fax: 515-887-3334. Students 14.

MANILLA, CRAWFORD CO., SACRED HEART (1887) [CEM] Rev. Robert W. Gralapp.
Res.: 269 6th St., P.O. Box 339, Manning, 51454-0339. Tel: 712-654-9511.
Church: 537 3rd Ave., 51454.
Catechesis/Religious Program—Students 62.

MANNING, CARROLL CO., SACRED HEART (1916), (German), [CEM] Rev. Robert W. Gralapp.
Res.: 203 Sue St., 51455-1399. Tel: 712-655-3804; Fax: 712-655-9476.
Catechesis/Religious Program—Tel: 712-655-2933. Students 139.

MANSON, CALHOUN CO., ST. THOMAS (1885) [CEM 2] Rev. Richard S. Ries (Retired); Deacon Robert Lenz.
Res.: P.O. Box 99, 50563-0099. Tel: 712-469-3743; Fax: 712-469-3066.
Catechesis/Religious Program—Tel: 712-469-3334. Students 144.

MAPLE RIVER, CARROLL CO., ST. FRANCIS OF ASSISI (1904), (German), [CEM] Closed. For inquiries for parish records contact Our Lady of Mt. Carmel parish in Mt. Carmel, IA.

MAPLETON, MONONA CO., ST. MARY'S (1894) [CEM 2] Rev. Brian J. Danner; Deacon Ray Rosburg.
Mailing Address: 703 Heisler St., 51034.
Catechesis/Religious Program—Tel: 712-882-1780. Students 47.

MARCUS, CHEROKEE CO., HOLY NAME (1877) [CEM] Very Rev. Armand J. Bertrand; Deacon Jerry Bertrand.
Res.: 709 W. Cedar, P.O. Box 658, Cherokee, 51012-0658. Tel: 712-376-2628.
Catechesis/Religious Program—Tel: 712-376-2625. Students 122.

MARYHILL, CHEROKEE CO., VISITATION OF THE B.V.M. (1895) [CEM] Closed. for inquiries for Parish records please contact Immaculate Conception, Cherokee.

MERRILL, PLYMOUTH CO., ASSUMPTION CHURCH (1890) [CEM 2] Rev. Daniel M. Greving.
Mailing Address: 527 Center St., P.O. Box 175, 51038.
Church: 527 Center St., 51038. Tel: 712-938-2236.
Catechesis/Religious Program—Students 26.
Mission—St. Joseph at Ellendale 23533 K22, Plymouth Co. 51038.
Catechesis/Religious Program—Students 32.

MILFORD, DICKINSON CO., ST. JOSEPH'S (1884) [CEM] Rev. Thomas J. Flanagan.
1305 Okoboji Ave., 51351-1232.
Res.: 1413 Okoboji Ave., 51351. Tel: 712-338-2172; Fax: 712-338-2191.
Catechesis/Religious Program—Students 179.

MOORLAND, WEBSTER CO., OUR LADY OF GOOD COUNSEL (1902) [CEM] Closed. For inquiries for parish records contact Holy Trinity Parish of Webster County, Fort Dodge.

MOUNT CARMEL, CARROLL CO., OUR LADY OF MT. CARMEL (1869), (German), [CEM] Rev. Joseph A. Dillinger.
Res.: 206 2nd Ave., Breda, 51436. Tel: 712-673-2351.
Parish is a member of newly consolidated K-12 Kuemper Catholic School System, Carroll, IA. Please refer to Kuemper Catholic School System under Inter-Parochial Schools in the Institution section.
Catechesis/Religious Program—Tel: 712-792-9244. Students 39.

MOVILLE, WOODBURY CO., IMMACULATE CONCEPTION (1892) Rev. Mark J. Stoll.
Office: 419 Jones St., P.O. Box 802, 51039-0802. Tel: 712-873-3644; Fax: 712-873-3931. Email: icmoville@wiatel.net. Web: www.icmoville.catholicweb.com.
Res.: 403 Jones St., P.O. Box 802, 51039-0802. Tel: 712-873-3745.
Catechesis/Religious Program—Tel: 712-873-3644. Students 34.

NEPTUNE, PLYMOUTH CO., ST. JOSEPH (Hinton) (1884), (German), [CEM] Closed. For inquiries for parish records please contact Assumption Church, Merrill.

ODEBOLT, SAC CO., ST. MARTIN'S (1877) [CEM] Rev. David Hemann.
Res.: 400 Hansen Blvd., P.O. Box 500, 51458-0500. Tel: 712-668-2690.
Rectory—Sacred Heart, 200 N. Main, Ida Grove, 51445.
Catechesis/Religious Program—Students 83.

OGDEN, BOONE CO., ST. JOHN'S (1896) [CEM] Rev. James A. Bruch.
Res.: 801 W. Division St., 50212-0810. Tel: 515-275-2580; Fax: 515-275-2580. Email: stjohnogden@hotmail.com. Web: www.stjohnogden.org.
Catechesis/Religious Program—Tel: 515-275-4095. Students 68.

ONAWA, MONONA CO., ST. JOHN (1900) Rev. Patrick J. O'Kane; Deacons Thomas Morgan; Joseph Scurlock.
Res.: 1009 13th St., 51040-1508. Tel: 712-423-2656; Fax: 712-423-1040. Email: stjohnparishhall@msn.com.
Catechesis/Religious Program—Tel: 712-423-1004. Students 98.
Mission—St. Bernard Blencoe, Monona Co.

OYENS, PLYMOUTH CO., ST. CATHERINE'S (1900) [CEM] Rev. William A. McCarthy; Deacon Rick Roder.
Res.: P.O. Box 509, Remsen, 51050. Tel: 712-786-1437.
School—St. Catherine-St. Mary's Elementary, Tel: 712-786-2764. Email: smparish@midlands.net. (Oyens-Remsen) Lay Teachers 6; Students 49.
Catechesis/Religious Program—121 E. Fourth St., Remsen, 51050. Tel: 712-786-1160. Students 18.

POCAHONTAS, POCAHONTAS CO., CHURCH OF THE RESURRECTION (1973) [CEM] Rev. Paul D. Bormann.
Res.: 21 S.W. 3rd St., 50574-0157. Tel: 712-335-3242.
School—Pocahontas Catholic Elementary, Tel: 712-335-3603; Fax: 712-335-3603. Email: pokycath@ncn.net. Maureen Lenz, Prin. Lay Teachers 7; Students 77.
Catechesis/Religious Program—Students 47.

POMEROY, CALHOUN CO., ST. MARY'S (1881) [CEM] Rev. Richard S. Ries (Retired); Deacon Robert Lenz.
Mailing Address: P.O. Box 99, Manson, 50563-0099.
Res.: 1076 8th St., Manson, 50563. Tel: 712-469-3743; Fax: 712-469-3066.
Catechesis/Religious Program—Tel: 712-468-2248. Students 16.

REMSEN, PLYMOUTH CO., ST. MARY'S (1885) [CEM] Rev. William A. McCarthy.
Res.: 121 E. 4th St., Box #509, 51050. Tel: 712-786-1437; Fax: 712-786-1444. Email: smparish@midlands.net. Web: www.smparishinfo.org.
School—St. Catherine-St. Mary's Elementary, Tel: 712-786-1160; Fax: 712-786-1167. Ms. Elizabeth Gibney, Prin.; Ms. Mary Riedemann, Librarian. (Oyens-Remsen) Lay Teachers 11; Students 165. See St. Mary's High School, Remsen under Inter-Parochial Schools located in the Institution Section.
Catechesis/Religious Program—Tel: 712-786-2889; Fax: 712-786-1167. Students 99.

ROCK RAPIDS, LYON CO., HOLY NAME (1871), (Irish), [CEM] Rev. Jeffrey Schleisman.
Res.: 1108 S. Carroll St., 51246-9529. Tel: 712-472-3248; Fax: 712-472-3189. Email: holynamerr@yahoo.com. Web: www.holmarycluster.webs.com.
Catechesis/Religious Program—Students 55.

ROCK VALLEY, SIOUX CO., ST. MARY'S (1895) [CEM] Rev. Douglas M. Klein.
Res.: 1821 14th St., 51247-0098. Tel: 712-476-2060. Email: smrv@hickorytech.net. Web: www.trinitycluster.org.
Catechesis/Religious Program—Students 122.

ROCKWELL CITY, CALHOUN CO., ST. FRANCIS OF ASSISI (1899), (German), [CEM] Rev. Richard S. Ries (Retired).
Res.: 744 Main St., 50579-1399. Tel: 712-297-8263; Fax: 712-297-8330. Web: www.thomasfrancismary.com.
Catechesis/Religious Program—Tel: 712-297-5116. Students 70.

ROLFE, POCAHONTAS CO., ST. MARGARET'S (1895) [CEM] Rev. Paul D. Bormann.
Res.: 21 S.W. 3rd St., Pocahontas, 50574. Tel: 712-335-3242.
Catechesis/Religious Program—Tel: 712-848-3301. Janet Crowe, D.R.E. Students 23.

ROSELLE, CARROLL CO., HOLY ANGELS (1874) [CEM] Rev. Steven W. Brodersen.
Res.: Box 13, Halbur, 51444-0013. Tel: 712-658-2464; Fax: 712-658-2464.
Parish is a member of the consolidated K-12 Kuemper Catholic School System, Carroll, IA. Please refer to Keumper Catholic School System under Inter-Parochial Schools in the Institution section.
Catechesis/Religious Program—Tel: 712-792-0513 (Carroll); 712-653-2131 (Manning). Students 25.

ROYAL, CLAY CO., ST. LOUIS (1923) Rev. John J. Gerald (India).
Res.: 300 1st Ave., P.O. Box 49, 51357. Tel: 712-933-2667. Email: stlouis@royaltelco.net.
Catechesis/Religious Program—Fax: 712-933-2356. Students 36.

RUTHVEN, PALO ALTO CO., SACRED HEART (1888) [CEM] Rev. Clement W. Currans.
Church: P.O. Box 400, 51358-0400. Tel: 712-837-5240.
Catechesis/Religious Program—Students 25.
Mission—Sacred Heart, Tel: 712-852-3187.

ST. BENEDICT, KOSSUTH CO., ST. BENEDICT'S (1877) [CEM] Rev. Peter Duc Hung Nguyen.
Res.: P.O. Box 38, Wesley, 50483. Tel: 515-679-4279. Email: stjwesley@msn.com.
School—Seton Elementary, Tel: 515-295-3509; Fax: 515-295-7739. Consolidation of St. Cecelia, Algona, St. Benedict and St. Joseph, Wesley. Seton Students 13; Bishop Garrigan Students 10.
Catechesis/Religious Program—St. Patrick's Church, 139 3rd St., S.E., Britt, 50423. Tel: 641-843-3073. Students 8.

SAC CITY, SAC CO., ST. MARY'S (1892), (German—Irish), [CEM] Rev. John J. McGuirk; Deacon B. (Butch) Stone.
Res.: 600 S. 12th St., 50583. Tel: 712-662-7240.
Catechesis/Religious Program—Fax: 712-662-7240. Students 104.

SALIX, WOODBURY CO., ST. JOSEPH'S (1869) [CEM] [JC] Rev. Patrick J. O'Kane.
Res.: 1009 13th. St., Onawa, 51040-1508. Tel: 712-946-5635.
Catechesis/Religious Program—Students 92.

SANBORN, O'BRIEN CO., ST. CECILIA'S (1882) [CEM] Rev. Timothy J. Hogan.
Res.: 310 E. 4th St., P.O. Box 555, 51248. Tel: 712-930-3423.
Catechesis/Religious Program—Tel: 712-928-2626. Nancy Williams, D.R.E. (Grades K-8). Students 81.
Mission—St. Joseph's, Tel: 712-728-2626.

SCHALLER, SAC CO., ST. JOSEPH'S (1891) [CEM] Revs. Bruce A. Lawler; Jeremy J. Wind; Deacon Mark Prosser.
Res.: P.O. Box 457, 51053-0457. Tel: 712-275-4238. Email: stjoseph@evertek.net.
Catechesis/Religious Program—Students 36.

SCRANTON, GREENE CO., ST. PAUL'S (1926) Rev. Donald C. Ries.
403 State St., 51462-8419.
Res. & Mailing Address: 807 Head St., P.O. Box 128, Churdan, 50050. Tel: 515-389-3625 (Church); Fax: 515-389-3797. Email: stcolumbkille@live.com. Web: www.st-paul-catholic-church.org.
Catechesis/Religious Program—Tel: 515-386-4010; Fax: 515-386-3672. Email: ssduffy@yahoo.com. Web: www.stjosephjefferson.net. Students 16.

SHELDON, O'BRIEN CO., ST. PATRICK'S (1873), (Irish), [CEM] Rev. Allan A. Reicks.
Res.: 310 10th St., 51201-1530. Tel: 712-324-3220; Fax: 712-324-3559.
School—1020 4th Ave., 51201. Tel: 712-324-3181. Lay Teachers 11; Students 85.
Catechesis/Religious Program—Tel: 712-724-6513. Students 92.

SIBLEY, OSCEOLA CO., ST. ANDREW'S (1896) [CEM]

Rev. John A. Vakulskas Jr.
Res.: 716 Eighth St., 51249-0130. Tel: 712-754-2739. Email: standrewsibley@hickorytech.net. Web: www.hwy60catholiccluster.org.
Catechesis/Religious Program—(Clustered with St. Mary, Ashton) Students 81.

SIOUX CENTER, SIOUX CO., CHRIST THE KING (2010) Rev. Douglas M. Klein.
501 2nd Ave. S.W., 51250.
Res.: 1821 14th St., Rock Valley, 51247-0098. Tel: 712-476-2060; Fax: 712-476-9074. Email: smrv@hickorytech.net. Web: www.trinitycluster.org.
Catechesis/Religious Program—Tel: 712-722-3011. Students 90.

SIOUX RAPIDS, BUENA VISTA CO., ST. JOSEPH (1886) [CEM] Rev. John J. Gerald (India); Deacon Ken Lindquist.
Res.: 708 Thomas St., P.O. Box 450, 50585-0450. Tel: 712-283-2765.
Catechesis/Religious Program—Students 28.

SPENCER, CLAY CO., SACRED HEART (1883) Rev. William A. Schreiber.
Res.: 1111 4th Ave. W., P.O. Box 817, 51301-0817. Tel: 712-262-3047; Fax: 712-262-4067. Email: spncrsh@juno.com. Web: www.spencersacredheart.com.
School—Tel: 712-262-6428. Mr. Ron Olberding, Prin. Lay Teachers 13; Students 201.
Catechesis/Religious Program—Tel: 712-262-4486. Students 256.

SPIRIT LAKE, DICKINSON CO., ST. MARY'S (1914) [CEM] Rev. Brian C. Hughes.
Res.: 1005 Hill Ave., P.O. Box 354, 51360-0354. Tel: 712-336-1742; Fax: 712-336-1013.
Catechesis/Religious Program—Tel: 712-336-1742. Students 209.

STORM LAKE, BUENA VISTA CO., ST. MARY'S (1872) [CEM] Revs. Bruce A. Lawler; Jeremy J. Wind, Parochial Vicar; Deacon Mark Prosser.
Res.: Third & Seneca Sts., P.O. Box 1106, 50588-1106. Tel: 712-732-3110; Fax: 712-732-8173. Email: parish@stormlakecatholic.com. Web: www.stormlakecatholic.com.
School—Elementary & High School, Tel: 712-732-1856 (Elementary); 712-732-4166 (High School); Fax: 712-732-4590. Email: bmach@stormlakecatholic.com. Web: www.stmarys-storm.pvt.k12.ia.us. Bev Mach, Elementary Prin.; Erv Rowlands, High School Prin. Lay Teachers 34; Students 277; Preschool 39.
Catechesis/Religious Program—Tel: 712-732-4585, Ext. 114. Email: sbenningfield@stormlakecatholic.com. Web: www-.stormlakecatholic.com. Students 248.

STRUBLE, PLYMOUTH CO., ST. JOSEPH'S (1903) [CEM 2] Rev. Daniel M. Greving.
Mailing Address: P.O. Box 175, Merrill, 51038. Tel: 712-938-2236.
Catechesis/Religious Program—Tel: 712-546-5223. Students 22.

SUTHERLAND, O'BRIEN CO., SACRED HEART (1883) [CEM] Rev. Timothy J. Hogan.
Res.: P.O. Box 555, Sanborn, 51248. Tel: 712-930-3423.
Catechesis/Religious Program—Tel: 712-928-2626. Students 62.
Mission—St. Anthony of Padua [CEM] Primghar.

TEMPLETON, CARROLL CO., SACRED HEART (1882) [CEM] Rev. Steven W. Brodersen.
Res.: Box 13, Halbur, 51444. Tel: 712-658-2464; Fax: 712-658-2464.
Parish is a member of the consolidated K-12 Kuemper Catholic School System, Carroll, IA. Please refer to Kuemper Catholic School System under Inter-Parochial Schools in the Institution section.
Catechesis/Religious Program—Tel: 712-792-0513 (Carroll); 712-653-2131 (Manning). Students 11.

VAIL, CRAWFORD CO., ST. ANN'S (1878) [CEM] Revs. Paul Kelly; Timothy A. Friedrichsen.
Res.: 916 2nd Ave. S., P.O. Box 280, Denison, 51442. Tel: 712-263-2152.
See Kuemper Catholic School System, Carroll under Inter-Parochial Schools located in the Institution section.
Catechesis/Religious Program—Students 42.

VARINA, POCAHONTAS CO., ST. COLUMBKILLE'S (1882) [CEM] Rev. Siby Punnoose (India); Deacon Eldon Sullivan.
Res.: Box 339, Fonda, 50540-0339. Tel: 712-288-6480; Fax: 712-288-4465. Email: olgc@iowatelecom.net.
Catechesis/Religious Program—Students 9.

WALL LAKE, SAC CO., ST. JOSEPH'S (1878), (German), Rev. John J. McGuirk; Deacon B. (Butch) Stone.
Res.: 600 S. 12th St., Sac City, 50583. Tel: 712-830-3869.
Catechesis/Religious Program—Tel: 712-664-2910. Students 166.

WESLEY, KOSSUTH CO., ST. JOSEPH'S (1891) [CEM] Rev. Peter Duc Hung Nguyen.
Res.: 403 East St., S., P.O. Box 38, 50483-0038. Tel: 515-679-4279 (Residence); 515-679-4135 (Parish Hall). Email: stjwesley@msn.com.
School—Seton Elementary, (Grades K-6) Tel: 515-295-3509. Consolidation of St. Cecelia, Algona; St. Benedict & St. Joseph, Wesley; St. Michael's, Whittemore; St. Joseph, Bode. Students 6.
High School—Bishop Garrigan High School, (Grades 7-12) Tel: 515-295-3521; Fax: 515-295-7739. Students 20.
Catechesis/Religious Program—Students 15.

WEST BEND, PALO ALTO CO., SS. PETER AND PAUL (1888) [CEM] Rev. Thomas J. Hart; Deacon Gerald Streit.
Res.: P.O. Box 16, 50597-0316. Tel: 515-887-3333; Fax: 515-887-3334.
Catechesis/Religious Program—Students 67.

WHITTEMORE, KOSSUTH CO., ST. MICHAEL'S (1889) [CEM] Rev. Victor Ramaeker; Deacon Joseph Straub, (Retired).
Res.: P.O. Box 337, 50598-0337. Tel: 515-884-2669; Fax: 515-884-2618. Email: stmwhitt@ncn.net.
Catechesis/Religious Program— See separate listing at St. Cecelia, Algona. Students 21.

WILLEY, CARROLL CO., ST. MARY'S (1882) [CEM] Revs. Timothy A. Johnson; Timothy J. Boekelman.
Rectory—421 E. Bluff, Carroll, 51401.
Res.: 205 Olympic Ave., Carroll, 51401. Tel: 712-792-4386; Fax: 712-792-8038. Email: shellyschreck@gmail.com. Web: www.stmaryswilley-.com.
Please see Kuemper Catholic School System under Inter-Parochial Schools located in the Institution Section
Catechesis/Religious Program—Tel: 712-792-4386. Students 11.

WOODWARD, BOONE CO., ST. JOHN OF GOD (1965), (State Hospital and School) Rev. James A. Bruch.
Res.: 207 Gerald St., Madrid, 50156-1464. Tel: 515-795-2731; Fax: 515-795-2731.

Chaplains of Public Institutions

SIOUX CITY. *Mercy Medical Center*. Rev. Richard A. Sitzmann (Retired).
CARROLL. *St. Anthony Regional Hospital*. Revs. Timothy J. Boekelman, Timothy A. Johnson.
CHEROKEE. *State Mental Health Institute*. Vacant.
FORT DODGE. *Marian Village*. Vacant.
Trinity Regional Hospital. Sr. M. Gertrude Keefe, R.S.M.
ROCKWELL CITY. *Calhoun County State Reformatory, Minimum Security for Men*. Rev. Richard S. Ries (Retired).
WOODWARD. *Woodward State Hospital and School*. Rev. James A. Bruch.

On Duty Outside the Diocese:
Revs.—
Barrett, Miles J., 103 Shady Side Ln., New Bern, NC 28562.
Kurzak, John F., 9210 Jole Cove, San Antonio, TX 78239. Tel: 210-650-3238

Retired:
Rev. Msgrs.—
Augustine, Roger J., V.G., 3012 Jackson St., 51104.
Donahoe, Thomas, 916 3 Williams Dr., Fort Dodge, 50501. Tel: 515-573-8612
Hood, Mervin J., 629 Central Ave., #609, Fort Dodge. Tel: 515-576-3268
Lyon, Gerald F., Marian Hall, 1122 Grandview Blvd., 51105. Tel: 712-258-2033
Ruba, Nicholas J., 403 Cleveland Ct., Remsen, 51050. Tel: 712-786-2719
Seifried, Kenneth A.
Zenk, Richard E., J.C.D.
Ziegmann, Leonard M., P.O. Box 3379, 51102-3379.
Revs.—
Adams, Edmond F., 8 Johnson Pl., Fort Dodge, 50501. Tel: 515-955-4859
Arts, Paul-Louis, M.S., 149 Stoney Point Drive, Storm Lake, 50588-7713.
Boes, Clair L., 744 Main St, Rockwell City, 50579. Tel: 712-261-1557
Boes, Marvin, 55 W. Clifton Ave., Apt. 303, 51104. Tel: 712-277-2046
Brown, Robert P., S.T.L.
Burns, Laurence J., V.F., 1122 Grandview Blvd., Apt. 2, 51103.
Cain, John F., 1410 W. 4th St., Apt. B, Spencer, 51301.
Cosgrove, Jerome P., M.S., 1122 Grandview Blvd., Apt. 6, 51103.
Degen, Jerome A., Marian Village, 2320 6th Ave. N. Apt. 105, Fort Dodge, 50501. Tel: 515-295-3329
Devine, William B., 1703 W. 25th St., Apt. 212, 51103. Tel: 712-234-0857
Fangman, James E., 1847 Highland Pkwy., Saint Paul, MN 55116.
Fangman, Robert M., 904 Amy Cir., Carroll, 51401.
Feierfeil, Gerald F.
Fransco, Peter J., 1803 Bruce St., Ruthven, 51358. Tel: 712-837-4323
Friedman, Cecil H., 1703 E. Lucas St., Algona, 50511. Tel: 515-295-5403
Geelan, Thomas E., 1806 Rolling St., Ruthven, 51358.
Grendler, Albert O., P.O. Box 34, Okoboji, 51355-0034.
Hartz, Gerald A., 10913 Alexander Falls Ave., Bakersfield, CA 93312. Tel: 661-587-4282
Kielbasa, Richard, Marian Village, 2320 6th Ave., N., Apt. F3, Fort Dodge, 50501. Tel: 515-955-8990
Kollasch, Merle F., 1023 Hwy 169, Bode, 50519-7031.
Koster, Dale F., W. St., Apt. 8, P.O. Box 264, Auburn, 51433.
Leiting, Robert L., 421 S. Clark St., #116, Carroll, 51401. Tel: 712-792-3358
Lynch, Daniel C., 407 S. 13th St., Sac City, 50583.
Macke, Richard J., 100 Circle Dr., Lake City, 51449.
McAlpin, James C., 916 Williams Dr., Apt. 4, Fort Dodge, 50501.
McAlpine, Harry D., 1108 S. Carroll, Rock Rapids, 51246-2060. Tel: 712-472-2840
McCarty, Lawrence L., V.F., 5157 Lakside Ln., Manson, 50563-7014.
McCormick, James D., P.O. Box 187, Auburn, 51433-0187.
McCoy, Alfred E., P.O. Box 114, 51102. Tel: 712-279-5461
Meinen, Dennis W., 1701 W. 25th St., 51103-1705.
Murray, Eugene, P.O. Box 163, Marcus, 51035.
Nemmers, Francis J., P.O. Box 244, Bancroft, 50517-0244. Tel: 515-885-0212
Nooney, P. Joseph, 2320 6th Ave. N., Apt. F3, Fort Dodge, 50501. Tel: 515-576-5567
Pick, Anthony
Reiff, Dale E.
Remmes, Richard R., P.O. Box 20, Arcadia, 51430. Tel: 712-689-2744
Ries, Richard S., P.O. Box 99, Manson, 50563.
Schimmer, Robert J., 1103 Council Oaks Dr., Apt. B, 51109.
Sefcik, Dennis L., 53133 210 St., Pocahontas, 50574.
Seuntjens, LeRoy L., 1122 Grandview Blvd., Apt. 1, 51103.
Sitzmann, Eugene E., 975 540th St., Cherokee, 51012-7151. Tel: 712-225-2131
Sitzmann, Richard A., 703 W. 5th St., 51103.
Slaven, Donald J., J.C.L., 1707 W. 25th St., Apt. 405, 51103.
Smith, James R.
Stapenhorst, Verne P., P.O. Box 457, Overton, NV 89040.
Thiele, Robert A., 101 N. Earl, Lake City, 51449. Tel: 712-464-8024
Thomas, John M., 310 N. Main St., Algona, 50511.
Tiedeman, Edmund H., 310 N. Main St., Fonda, 50540.
Topf, Thomas J., 1122 Grandview Blvd., Apt. 8, 51103.
Waite, Patrick J., 5682 Tulane St., San Diego, CA 92122-3244.
Walding, Eugene F., 1707 W. 25th St., Apt. 409, 51103-1799.
Wieling, Raymond P., 3015 Chicago Ave., 51106-1259. Tel: 712-276-7065
Wingert, D. William, 110 W. Maple Dr., Hartley, 51346-7606. Tel: 712-728-9911
Wingert, Gerald R., 216 W. Nebraska, Algona, 50511-2608. Tel: 515-295-3123
Zensen, Gerald F., 2 Sunrise Ave., Mapleton, 51034.

Permanent Deacons:
Berger, William J., (Retired)
Bertrand, Gerald L., Holy Name, Marcus
Billings, Richard, Blessed Sacrament, Sioux City
Black, William, St. Cecelia, Algona
Brown, David, Sacred Heart, Boone
Chartier, Bruce, St. Joseph, Sioux City
Doocy, Philip F., St. John the Baptist, Bancroft
Forrest, Ronald M., (Retired)
Gallagher, Jeffrey F., Holy Name, Rock Rapids
Hand, Michael J., Church of the Nativity, Sioux City
Heffernan, John J., (Retired)
Karpuk, Fred P., Blessed Sacrament Church, Sioux City
Kunecke, Donald L., (Unassigned)
Lenz, Robert D., St. Mary's Church, Pomeroy
Lindquist, Ken, St. Joseph, Sioux Rapids
Lopez, David A., Cathedral of the Epiphany, Sioux City
MacDonald, W. B., (Retired)
Meiners, Louis, St. Joseph, Dedham
Messerly, Darwin, Sacred Heart, Boone
Miller, Ed, Holy Spirit, Carroll
Morgan, Tom, St. John's, Onawa
Murphy, Tim, St. Lawrence, Carroll

Pietz, Ronald C., St. Joseph Church, Sioux City
Port, Richard, St. Patrick, Akron
Portz, Ray, St. Patrick, Sheldon
Prosser, Mark, St. Mary, Storm Lake
Roder, Rick, St. Mary, Remsen
Rosburg, Ray, St. Mary, Mapleton
Rupp, J. LeRoy, Immaculate Conception Church, Cherokee
Sampson, Gregory, Holy Spirit, Carroll
Sands, James H., St. Boniface, Sioux City
Schon, Gary, St. Elizabeth Seton, Glidden
Scurlock, Joseph, (Retired)
Sitzman, Larry K., St. Michael's Church, Sioux City
Stone, Byron, St. Joseph, Wall Lake
Stover, Michael, Sacred Heart, Ida Grove
Straub, Joseph J., (Retired)
Streit, Gerald B., Sts. Peter & Paul Church, West Bend
Sullivan, Eldon, Our Lady of Good Counsel, Fonda
Wyant, Mark, Sacred Heart Church, Sioux City

INSTITUTIONS LOCATED IN THE DIOCESE

[A] COLLEGES AND UNIVERSITIES

SIOUX CITY. *Briar Cliff University*, 3303 Rebecca St., P.O. Box 2100, 51104-2100. Tel: 712-279-5200; Fax: 712-279-5410. Web: www.briarcliff.edu. Bev Wharton, Pres.; Deidre Engel, Registrar; Sharisue Wilcoxon, Vice Pres. Enrollment Mgmt.; Rev. Bradley C. Pelzel; Debora Robertson, Librarian. Sisters of St. Francis of the Holy Family of Dubuque, Iowa., Liberal Arts University. Sisters 7; Lay Teachers 61; Lay Administrators & Staff 95; Students 1,185.

[B] INTER-PAROCHIAL SCHOOLS

SIOUX CITY. *Bishop Heelan Catholic Schools*, (Grades PreK-12), 1018 Grandview Blvd., 51103. Tel: 712-252-1350; Fax: 712-252-9086. Email: walsh@bishopheelan.org. Web: www.bishopheelan.org. Rev. Patrick Walsh, Pres. Serving the parishes of Nativity, Immaculate Conception, Cathedral, St. Boniface, St. Joseph, Blessed Sacrament, Sacred Heart, St. Michael. Priests 1; Sisters 1; Lay Teachers 125; Students 1,631; Total Staff 46.

Bishop Heelan High School, 1021 Douglas St., 51104. Tel: 712-252-0573; Fax: 712-252-4897. Web: www.bishopheelan.org. Mr. Chris Bork, Prin.; Sr. Colane Recker, Librarian. Priests 1; Lay Teachers 45; Students 517.

Holy Cross School-Blessed Sacrament Center, 3030 Jackson St., 51104. Tel: 712-277-4739; Fax: 712-258-3698. Michael Sweeney, Prin.; Pam Wilmes, Librarian. Consolidated with St. Michael. Lay Teachers 28; Students 267.

St. Michael (Grades PreK-2), 4105 Harrison, 51108. Tel: 712-239-1090; Fax: 712-239-8546. Web: www.bishopheelan.org. Michael Sweeney, Prin.; Pam Wilmes, Librarian. Consolidated with Blessed Sacrament. Lay Teachers 13; Students 131.

Sacred Heart (Grades K-8), 5010 Military Rd., 51103. Tel: 712-233-1624; Fax: 712-233-1469. Email: ferrieb@bishopheelan.org. Web: www.bishopheelan.org. Brenda Ferrie, Prin.; Julie Walding, Librarian. Lay Teachers 25; Students 326; Total Staff 52.

Mater Dei School Immaculate Conception Center (Grades PreK-5), 3719 Ridge Ave., 51106. Tel: 712-276-6216; Fax: 712-274-1221. Web: www.bishopheelan.org. Ms. Mary Fischer, Prin.; Mrs. Vicky Samuelson, Librarian. Lay Teachers 20; Students 235.

Mater Dei School Nativity Center (Grades 6-8), 4243 Natalia Way, 51106-4099. Tel: 712-274-0268; Fax: 712-274-0377. Email: fischerm@bishopheelan.org. Web: www.bishopheelan.org. Ms. Mary Fischer, Prin. Consolidated with Immaculate Conception Parish. Lay Teachers 11; Total Enrollment 131.

ALGONA. *Bishop Garrigan Catholic High School*, 1224 N. McCoy St., 50511. Tel: 515-295-3521; Fax: 515-295-7739. Email: millerl@garrigan.pvt.k12.ia.us. Web: www.garrigan.unlimitedweb.net. Mr. Eugene Meister, Pres.; Mr. Lynn Miller, Prin. Serving the parishes at Algona, St. Benedict, Bode, Wesley, and Whittemore. Priests 1; Sisters 1; Deacons 1; Lay Teachers 18; Students 172.

CARROLL. *Kuemper Catholic School System*, 116 S. East St., 51401. Tel: 712-792-3313; Fax: 712-792-8073. Email: vrhenkenius@kuemper.org. Web: www.kuemper.org. Mr. Vern Henkenius, Pres. Grades PreK-12 Lay Teachers 85; Students 1,068.

Holy Spirit Center (Grades PreK-5), 201 S. Clark St., 51401. Tel: 712-792-3610; Fax: 712-792-8072. Ted Garringer, Prin.

St. Angela Center (Grades 4-5), 116 N. East St., 51401. Tel: 712-792-8071. Ted Garringer, Prin.

St. Lawrence Center (Grades 6-8), 1519 N. West St., 51401. Tel: 712-792-2123; Fax: 712-792-3365. Mr. Earl Schiltz, Prin.

Kuemper Catholic High School, 109 S. Clark St., 51401. Tel: 712-792-3596. Mrs. Penny Miller, Prin.

FORT DODGE. *St. Edmond Catholic Schools, Inc.*, (Grades K-12), 2220 4th Ave. N., 50501. Tel: 515-955-6077; Fax: 515-955-8473. Web: www.st-edmund.pvt.k12.ia.us. Dr. James T. Barry, Pres.; John Howard, Prin.; Linda Mitchell, Prin.; Mr. Thomas Miklo, Dir. Devel. Lay Teachers 57; Students 875.

GRANVILLE. *Spalding Catholic Schools, Inc.* 51022. Tel: 712-727-3451; Fax: 712-727-3455. Email: lhamerlinck@spaldingcatholic.org. Web: www.spaldingcatholic.org. Very Rev. Richard D. Ball, V.F.; Mrs. Lisa Hamerlinck, Prin. Serving the parishes of Granville; Alton and Hospers. Priests 2; Lay Teachers 16; Students 101.

LE MARS. *Gehlen Catholic School* (1875) 709 Plymouth St. N.E., 51031. Tel: 712-546-4181; Fax: 712-546-9384. Email: l_niebuhr@gehlencatholic.com. Web: www.gehlencatholic.com. Rev. Kevin M. Richter, Pres.; Jeff Alesch, Prin. (7-12); Mrs. Lorie A. Nussbaum, Prin. (PreK-6); Lisa Niebuhr, Devel. Dir.; Melinda Scheitler, Business Mgr.; Pat Beitelspacher, Librarian. Lay Teachers 38; Students 444.

REMSEN. *St. Mary's High School*, 523 Madison, 51050. Tel: 712-786-1433; Fax: 712-786-2499. Web: www.remsenstmarys.org. John Hughes, Prin.; Ms. Linda Loutsch, Librarian. Priests 1; Lay Teachers 12; Students 67.

STORM LAKE. *St. Mary's School*, (Grades PreK-12), 50588. Tel: 712-732-4166; Fax: 712-732-4590. Email: bmach@stormlakecatholic.com. Bev Mach, Prin. (PreK-6); Erv Rowlands, Prin. (7-12). Serving St. Mary's. Lay Teachers 32; Students 323.

[C] GENERAL HOSPITALS

SIOUX CITY. *Mercy Medical Center - Sioux City*, 801 Fifth St., 51101. Tel: 712-279-2010; Fax: 712-279-2494. Email: spencerj@mercyhealth.com. Web: www.mercysiouxcity.com. Robert Peebles, Pres. & CEO; Rev. Richard A. Sitzmann, Chap. (Retired); Rev. Dennis Grohn, Lutheran Chap.; Rev. B. J. Van Kalsbeek, Reformed Presbyterian Chap.; Maria Baker, Chap.; Rev. Dennis W. Meinen, Chap. (Retired). Trinity Health, Catholic Health Ministries Sisters 1; Total Staff 1,507; Bed Capacity 464; Patients Assisted Annually 154,903.

CARROLL. *St. Anthony Regional Hospital*, 311 S. Clark St., P.O. Box 628, 51401. Tel: 712-792-3581; Fax: 712-792-2124. Email: garyr@stanthonyhospital.org. Web: www.StAnthonyHospital.org. Gary P. Riedmann, Pres.; Revs. Timothy A. Johnson; Timothy J. Boekelman. Bed Capacity 99; Patients Assisted Annually 71,473; Total Staff 621.

ESTHERVILLE. *Avera Holy Family Health*, 826 N. Eighth St., 51334. Tel: 712-362-2631; Fax: 712-362-2636. Email: info@avera-holyfamily.org. Web: www.avera-holyfamily.org. Sisters of the Presentation of the B.V.M. (Aberdeen, SD) & Benedictine Sisters of Sacred Heart Monastery, (Yanton, SD). Bed Capacity 25; Patients Assisted Annually 35,886; Total Staff 135.

Holy Family Hospital Foundation. Tel: 712-362-2631; Fax: 712-362-2636.

[D] HOMES FOR THE AGED

SIOUX CITY. *Holy Spirit Retirement Home*, 1701 W. 25th St., 51103. Tel: 712-252-2726. Patrick J. Tomscha, Admin.; Rev. Dennis W. Meinen (Retired). Total in Residence 150; Total Assisted 35; Total Staff 140.

CARROLL. *St. Anthony Nursing Home* (1963) 406 E. Anthony St., 51401. Tel: 712-792-3581; Fax: 712-792-8288. Email: stanthony@netins.net. Gary Riedmann, Admin.; Peg Scheidt, Dir. Pastoral Care. Residents 79; Total Staff 68.

FORT DODGE. *The Marian Home*, 2400 Sixth Ave. N., 50501. Tel: 515-576-1138; Fax: 515-576-5099. Email: ehalverson@marianhome.com. Web: www.marianhome.com. Eric Halverson, Admin. Guests 97; Total in Residence 181; Total Staff 125.

[E] CONVENTS AND RESIDENCES FOR SISTERS

SIOUX CITY. *Monastery of the Discalced Carmelite Nuns*, 2901 S. Cecelia St., 51106-3299. Tel: 712-276-1680; Fax: 712-276-5966. Email: carmelsc@msn.com. Web: www.carmelsc.org. Mother Joseph of Jesus, O.C.D., Prioress. Solemn Professed 7.

[F] SECULAR INSTITUTES

CARROLL. *Opus Spiritus Sancti* (1950) 301 E. 4th St., Auburn, 51433. Tel: 712-790-1749. Rev. James D. McCormick, Regl. Coord. Community Activities & Member Secular Institute of Priests (Retired).

[G] MISCELLANEOUS

SIOUX CITY. *The Catholic Schools Foundation of the Diocese of Sioux City* (1968) 1821 Jackson St., 51105. Tel: 712-255-7933; Fax: 712-233-7598. Email: danr@scdiocese.org. Web: www.scdiocese.org.

Holy Spirit Retirement Home Foundation, Inc., 1701 W. 25th St., 51103. Tel: 712-252-2726; Fax: 712-293-1953. Most Rev. R. Walker Nickless, Dir.; Patrick J. Tomscha, Dir.; Martha Burchard, Pres.

Monsignor Lafferty Tuition Foundation, 1821 Jackson St., 51105. Tel: 712-255-7933. Email: danr@scdiocese.org. Web: scdiocese.org. Mr. Dan Ryan, Contact Person & Supt. Schools.

ALGONA. *Friends of Garrigan High School, Inc.*, Garrigan High School, 1224 N. McCoy, 50511. Tel: 515-295-3521.

CARROLL. *Kuemper Catholic School Foundation, Inc.* (1985) 116 S. East St., 51401. Tel: 712-792-3313; Fax: 712-792-8073. Web: www.kuemper.org. John Steffes, Pres.

Orchard View, Inc., 421 S. Clark St., 51401. Tel: 712-792-2042; Fax: 712-792-2124. Email: esmith@stanthonyhospital.org. Web: www.StAnthonyHospital.org. Gary P. Riedmann, Admin. Franciscan Sisters of Perpetual Adoration. Total in Residence 51.

FORT DODGE. *Saint Edmond Catholic Schools Foundation*, 2220 4th Ave. N., 50501. Tel: 515-955-6077; Fax: 515-955-8473. Email: frkevin@fdcatholic.com. Web: www.st-edmond.pvt.k12.ia.us. Very Rev. Msgr. Kevin C. McCoy, S.T.D., V.F., Interim Pres.; Linda Mitchell, Prin.; Tom Miklo, Devel. Dir.; Tim Hancock, Business Mgr.

Holy Trinity Parish Cemetery Improvement Society, 2220 4th Ave N., 50501. Tel: 515-573-3616; Fax: 515-955-8473. Very Rev. Msgr. Kevin C. McCoy, S.T.D., V.F., Contact Person.

Holy Trinity Parish Foundation of Webster County, 2220 4th Ave N., 50501. Tel: 515-573-3616; Fax: 515-955-8473. Email: fdcatholic@fdcatholic.com. Very Rev. Msgr. Kevin C. McCoy, S.T.D., V.F.

The Marian Home Foundation, 2400 6th Ave. N., 50501. Tel: 515-576-1138; Fax: 515-576-5099. Email: ehalverson@marianhome.com.

GRANVILLE. *Spalding Catholic Schools Foundation, Inc.*, 609 Broad St., P.O. Box 168, 51022. Dan Goebel, Contact Person.

STORM LAKE. *St. Mary's Foundation of Storm Lake, Iowa*, 320 Seneca St., P.O. Box 1106, 50588. Tel: 712-732-3110; Fax: 712-732-8173. Email: smalumni@iw.net. Web: www.stormlakecatholic.com. Rev. Bruce A. Lawler.

WEST BEND. *Grotto of the Redemption*, P.O. Box 376, 50597. Tel: 515-887-2371; Fax: 515-887-2372. Email: info@westbendgrotto.com. Web: www.westbendgrotto.com.

RELIGIOUS INSTITUTES OF WOMEN REPRESENTED IN THE DIOCESE

For further details refer to the corresponding bracketed number in the Religious Institutes of Men or Women section.

[1780]—*Congregation of the Sisters of the Third Order of St. Francis of Perpetual Adoration* (Central Prov.)—F.S.P.A.

[0420]—*Discalced Carmelite Nuns*—O.C.D.

[]—*Opus Spiritus Sancti*—O.S.S.

[1680]—*School Sisters of St. Francis*—S.S.S.F.

[]—*Sisters For Christian Community*—S.F.C.C.

[0430]—*Sisters of Charity of the Blessed Virgin Mary*—B.V.M.

[2575]—*Sisters of Mercy of the Americas* (Cedar Rapids Regional Community)—R.S.M.

[2575]—*Sisters of Mercy of the Union in USA Comm.* Cedar Rapids—O.S.F.

[1570]—*Sisters of St. Francis of the Holy Family*—O.S.F.

[1540]—*Sisters of St. Francis, Clinton, IA*—O.S.F.

[2350]—*Sisters of the Living Word*—S.L.W.

[3320]—*Sisters of the Presentation of the B.V.M.* Dubuque, IA & Aberdeen, SD—P.B.V.M.

[]—*Sisters of the Society of Our Lady of the Most Holy Trinity*

[1720]—*Sisters of the Third Order Regular of St. Francis of the Congregation of Our Lady of Lourdes*—O.S.F.

DIOCESAN CEMETERIES

SIOUX CITY. *Calvary*, Office: 1821 Jackson St., P.O. Box 3379, 51102-3379. Tel: 712-233-7511; Fax: 712-233-7598.

LEMARS. *Calvary Cemetery*, 20 6th Ave. N.E., 51031. Tel: 712-546-5223; Fax: 712-546-8346. Janeen Reuter, Contact Person.

NECROLOGY

† Condon, Robert M., (Retired)—Died July 24, 2011
† Fisch, Gerald M., (Retired)—Died June 22, 2011
† Riesberg, Leo L., (Retired)—Died March 18, 2011
† Smith, Donald R., (Retired)—Died Feb. 22, 2011

An asterisk (*) denotes an organization that has established tax-exempt status directly with the IRS and is not covered by the USCCB Group Ruling.

Diocese of Sioux Falls

(Dioecesis Siouxormensis)

Most Reverend

PAUL J. SWAIN

Bishop of Sioux Falls; ordained to priesthood May 27, 1988, Diocese of Madison; appointed Bishop of Sioux Falls August 31, 2006; Episcopal ordination October 26, 2006. *Chancery Office: 523 N. Duluth Ave., Sioux Falls, SD 57104.*

Chancery Office: 523 N. Duluth Ave., Sioux Falls, SD 57104. Tel: 605-334-9861; Fax: 605-334-2092.

Web: sfcatholic.org

Email: malthoff@sfcatholic.org

ESTABLISHED NOVEMBER 12, 1889.

Square Miles 35,091.

Comprises that part of the State of South Dakota East of the Missouri River.

For legal titles of parishes and diocesan institutions, consult the Chancery Office.

STATISTICAL OVERVIEW

Personnel	
Bishop	1
Abbots	1
Retired Abbots	2
Priests: Diocesan Active in Diocese	86
Priests: Diocesan Active Outside Diocese	2
Priests: Retired, Sick or Absent	34
Number of Diocesan Priests	122
Religious Priests in Diocese	28
Total Priests in Diocese	150
Ordinations:	
Diocesan Priests	5
Transitional Deacons	3
Permanent Deacons in Diocese	35
Total Brothers	9
Total Sisters	247
Parishes	
Parishes	146
With Resident Pastor:	
Resident Diocesan Priests	70
Resident Religious Priests	7
Without Resident Pastor:	
Administered by Priests	63
Administered by Deacons	1
Administered by Professed Religious Men	1
Completely Vacant	4
Pastoral Centers	3
Closed Parishes	4
Professional Ministry Personnel:	
Brothers	1
Sisters	7
Lay Ministers	46
Welfare	
Catholic Hospitals	11
Total Assisted	750,000
Homes for the Aged	9
Special Centers for Social Services	10
Total Assisted	52,000
Educational	
Diocesan Students in Other Seminaries	22
Total Seminarians	22
Colleges and Universities	2
Total Students	1,937
High Schools, Diocesan and Parish	3
Total Students	988
Elementary Schools, Diocesan and Parish	21
Total Students	4,056
Elementary Schools, Private	1
Total Students	228
Catechesis/Religious Education:	
High School Students	4,291
Elementary Students	7,353
Total Students under Catholic Instruction	18,875
Teachers in the Diocese:	
Scholastics	1
Sisters	3
Lay Teachers	339
Vital Statistics	
Receptions into the Church:	
Infant Baptism Totals	1,430
Received into Full Communion	278
First Communions	1,539
Confirmations	1,655
Marriages:	
Catholic	277
Interfaith	233
Total Marriages	510
Deaths	1,017
Total Catholic Population	120,204
Total Population	569,926

Former Bishops—Rt. Revs. MARTIN MARTY, O.S.B., D.D., ord. Sept. 14, 1856; appt. Bishop of Tiberias, Aug. 8, 1879; appt. Vicar Apostolic of Dakota, Aug. 12, 1879; consecrated Feb. 1, 1880; Bishop of Sioux Falls, 1889; transferred to St. Cloud, MN, 1894; died Sept. 19, 1896; THOMAS O'GORMAN, D.D., ord. Nov. 5, 1865; appt. Jan. 24, 1896; consecrated April 19, 1896; died Sept. 18, 1921; Most Revs. BERNARD J. MAHONEY, D.D., ord. Feb. 27, 1904; appt. May 22, 1922; consecrated June 29, 1922; died March 20, 1939; WILLIAM O. BRADY, S.T.D., D.D., appt. Bishop of Sioux Falls, June 10, 1939; consecrated Aug. 24, 1939; appt. Coadjutor of St. Paul, June 21, 1956; succeeded to the See, Oct. 11, 1956; died Oct. 1, 1961; LAMBERT A. HOCH, D.D., ord. May 30, 1928; Bishop of Bismarck; appt. Jan. 23, 1952; consecrated March 25, 1952; transferred to Sioux Falls, Nov. 27, 1956; retired June 13, 1978; died June 27, 1990; PAUL V. DUDLEY, D.D., ord. June 2, 1951; ord. Auxiliary Bishop of Archdiocese of St. Paul/ Minneapolis, Jan. 25, 1977; appt. Bishop of Sioux Falls Sept. 26, 1978; installed Dec. 13, 1978; retired March 21, 1995; died Nov. 20, 2006; ROBERT J. CARLSON, ord. May 22, 1970; appt. Titular Bishop of Aviocala and Auxiliary Bishop of Saint Paul and Minneapolis Nov. 22, 1983; cons. Jan. 11, 1984; appt. Coadjutor Bishop of Sioux Falls Jan. 13, 1994; Succeeded to the See March 21, 1995; appt. Bishop of Saginaw Dec. 29, 2004; appt. Archbishop of St. Louis April 21, 2009.

Office of the Bishop—Most Rev. PAUL J. SWAIN.

Vicar General—Rev. CHARLES L. CIMPL, 523 N. Duluth Ave., Sioux Falls, 57104.

Episcopal Vicar for Clergy—Rev. GREGORY TSCHAKERT, J.C.L.

Chancery Office—523 N. Duluth Ave., Sioux Falls, 57104. Tel: 605-334-9861; Fax: 605-334-2092. Refer all official business to this address.

Chancellor—Mr. MATTHEW ALTHOFF, 523 N. Duluth Ave., Sioux Falls, 57104. Tel: 605-988-3704.

Vice Chancellors—Mr. JEROME KLEIN. Tel: 605-988-3745; Rev. JAMES E. MASON. Tel: 605-988-3749. 523 N. Duluth Ave., Sioux Falls, 57104.

Vocations—Rev. PAUL A. RUTTEN, 523 N. Duluth Ave., Sioux Falls, 57104. Tel: 605-988-3772.

Deacon Formation—Deacon ROGER R. HEIDT, 523 N. Duluth Ave., Sioux Falls, 57104. Tel: 605-988-3715.

Marriage Tribunal—523 N. Duluth Ave., Sioux Falls, 57104. Tel: 605-988-3757.

Judicial Vicar—Rev. GREGORY TSCHAKERT, J.C.L.

Tribunal Judges—Revs. AL KRZYZOPOLSKI (Retired); RODNEY FARKE; KENNETH J. KOSTER; JOHN LANTSBERGER; CHARLES L. CIMPL; GARY TERNES, J.C.L.; SCOTT TRAYNOR, J.C.L.; Deacon WILLIAM FRANKMAN.

Defenders of the Matrimonial Bond—Rev. GREGORY TSCHAKERT, J.C.L.; Sr. LYNN MARIE WELBIG, J.C.L., Ph.D.; Rev. JAMES FRIEDRICH.

Director of Matrimonial Tribunal—Sr. LYNN MARIE WELBIG, J.C.L., Ph.D.

Auditors—Deacon WILLIAM FRANKMAN; Sr. KATHLEEN BIERNE, P.B.V.M., J.C.L.; Miss HEIDI EVERS.

Notary of Matrimonial Tribunal—Ms. VICKIE BEACH, Ecclesiastical Notary.

Master of Ceremonies—NATHAN KNUTSON.

Office of Legal Counsel—Co Directors: TRAVIS BENSON, J.D.; KELLY BENSON, J.D.

Office of Planning—Deacon ROGER R. HEIDT.

Safe Environment—RENEE LEACH, Coord.

Administration and Parish Services—

Delegate and Finance Officer—Mr. MICHAEL BANNWARTH, 523 N. Duluth Ave., Sioux Falls, 57104. Tel: 605-988-3759; Fax: 605-988-3746.

Information Technology—DAWN WOLF, Dir.

Human Resources—TWILA ROMAN, Dir.

Cemeteries and Property Management—Deacon ROGER R. HEIDT.

Catholic Education and Faith Formation—

Catholic Schools—Mrs. KATIE MELLOR, Dir., 523 N. Duluth, Sioux Falls, 57104. Tel: 605-988-3761.

Adult Faith Formation—Dr. CHRISTOPHER BURGWALD, S.T.D., Dir., 523 N. Duluth Ave., Sioux Falls, 57104. Tel: 605-988-3766.

Children Faith Formation—Ms. JEAN LORANG, Dir., 523 N. Duluth Ave., Sioux Falls, 57104. Tel: 605-988-3767.

Youth Ministry and Catechesis—Mr. ERIC GALLAGHER, Dir., 523 N. Duluth Ave., Sioux Falls, 57104. Tel: 605-988-3767.

Marian Apostolate—Rev. Msgr. CHARLES MANGAN, J.C.L.

Communications and Social Ministries—

Delegate and Vice Chancellor—Mr. JEROME KLEIN, 523 N. Duluth Ave., Sioux Falls, 57104. Tel: 605-988-3789.

Catholic Family Services—Mr. JEROME KLEIN, Dir.; Dr. MARCIE MORAN, Clinical Dir., 523 N. Duluth Ave., Sioux Falls, 57104. Tel: 605-988-3745.

Communications Office - "Bishop's Bulletin"—Rev. MICHAEL GRIFFIN, Bishop's Bulletin Exec. Editor; Mr. GENE YOUNG, Bishop's Bulletin Mng. Editor, 523 N. Duluth Ave., Sioux Falls, 57104. Tel: 605-988-3789.

Marriage, Family and Respect Life—Co Directors: TRAVIS BENSON, J.D.; KELLY BENSON, J.D., 523

N. Duluth Ave., Sioux Falls, 57104. Tel: 605-988-3755.
Stewardship—Mr. KEVIN MILES, Dir., 523 N. Duluth Ave., Sioux Falls, 57104. Tel: 605-988-3725.
Parish and Diocesan Advancement—
Delegate and President of the Catholic Foundation for Eastern South Dakota—MARK CONZEMIUS, 523 N. Duluth Ave., Sioux Falls, 57104. Tel: 605-988-3788.
Operations, Catholic Family Sharing Appeal—Mrs. MELINDA NORTH, Vice Pres. & Dir. Catholic Family Sharing Appeal.
Planned Giving—BETTE THEOBALD, Vice Pres.
Diocesan Consultors—Revs. CHARLES L. CIMPL; DAVID A. DESMOND; DAVID KROGMAN; JAMES E. MASON; GREGORY TSCHAKERT, J.C.L.; MICHAEL WENSING.
Consilium Administrationis— Most Rev. Bishop, Vicar General, Chancellor.
Presbyteral Council—Revs. CHARLES L. CIMPL; JEROME RANEK; DAVID A. DESMOND; BRIAN SIMON; DAVID KROGMAN; JAMES E. MASON; SCOTT TRAYNOR, J.C.L.; CHESTER MURTHA; DEWAYNE KAYSER; RODNEY FARKE; GREGORY TSCHAKERT, J.C.L.

Diocesan Offices and Directors

Apostleship of Prayer—Mailing Address: 523 N. Duluth Ave., Sioux Falls, 57105.
Building Commission—Mr. MATTHEW ALTHOFF, Chancellor; Mr. MICHAEL BANNWARTH, Finance Officer, Catholic Chancery Office, 523 N. Duluth Ave., Sioux Falls, 57104.
Social Outreach—Mr. JEROME KLEIN, 523 N. Duluth Ave., Sioux Falls, 57104. Tel: 605-988-3745.
Censor Librorum—Dr. CHRISTOPHER BURGWALD, S.T.L., 523 N. Duluth Ave., Sioux Falls, 57104.
Cursillo—Rev. RODNEY FARKE, 1700 8th St. S., Brookings, 57006.
Diocesan Archivist—Mr. MATTHEW ALTHOFF, Chancellor, 523 N. Duluth Ave., Sioux Falls, 57104. Tel: 605-334-9804.
Ecumenical Commission—VACANT.
Worldwide Marriage Encounter—Rev. JAMES M. JOYCE (Retired), 900 E. 14th St., Apt. 112, Sioux Falls, 57104. Tel: 605-978-1592.
Newman Apostolate—VACANT.
Permanent Diaconate Council—Deacon JOSEPH GRAVES, 1008 Palmer Pl., Mitchell, 57301. Tel: 605-996-7997.
Personnel Board—Revs. CHARLES L. CIMPL, Vicar Gen.; MICHAEL GRIFFIN; ROBERT V. KRANTZ; JOHN LANTSBERGER; ANDREW SWIETOCHOWSKI; J. JOSEPH HOLZHAUSER; JOSEPH VOGEL; MARK LICHTER.
Propagation of the Faith—Rev. JEROME RANEK, Dir., Mailing Address: St. Mary of Mercy Parish, P.O. Box 158, Alexandria, 57311.
Search—523 N. Duluth Ave., Sioux Falls, 57104. Tel: 605-334-9861.
Spanish-Speaking Apostolate—Rev. JOHN HELMUELLER, 105 S. Bates St., Flandreau, 57028-1809. Tel: 605-997-2610.
Teens Encounter Christ—523 N. Duluth Ave., Sioux Falls, 57104. Tel: 605-334-9861.
Victim Assistance Coordinator—Ms. JEAN LORANG. Tel: 605-334-9861. Email: jlorang@sfcatholic.org.

CLERGY, PARISHES, MISSIONS AND PAROCHIAL SCHOOLS

CITY OF SIOUX FALLS

(MINNEHAHA COUNTY)

1—ST. JOSEPH CATHEDRAL (1880) [JC] Revs. Thomas Fitzpatrick; Russell Homic, Parochial Vicar.
Res.: 521 Duluth Ave., 57104. Tel: 605-336-7390; Fax: 605-330-0416. Email: cathedral@sfcatholic.org. Web: www.cathedralofstjosephsiouxfalls.parishesonline.com.
Catechesis/Religious Program—Students 93.

2—CHRIST THE KING (1949) Rev. Richard Fox; Deacons Leon Cantin, (Retired); James Boorman. In Res., Rev. James Zimmer.
Res.: 1501 W. 26th St., 57105. Tel: 605-332-5477; Fax: 605-332-0552. Web: www.ctkparish-sf.org.
See Christ the King Elementary School, Sioux Falls under Inter-Parochial Schools located in the Institution section.
Catechesis/Religious Program—Students 102.

3—HOLY SPIRIT (1988) Revs. James P. Morgan; Jonathan Venner, Parochial Vicar; Deacon Thomas R. Bates.
Res.: 4008 Lisanne, 57103. Tel: 605-371-2320; Fax: 605-371-1957.
Church: 3601 E. Dudley Ln., 57103.
Catechesis/Religious Program—Students 557.

4—ST. JOSEPHINE BAKHITA CATHOLIC CHURCH (2004) Rev. Elias Rinaldo Gamboriko, A.J. (Sudan).
Mailing Address: 521 N. Duluth Ave., 57104. Tel: 605-336-7390.

5—ST. KATHARINE DREXEL CATHOLIC CHURCH (2004) Rev. Joseph Vogel.
Mailing Address: 1800 S. Katie Ste. 1, 57106.
Church: Email: church.stkatharinedrexel@midconetwork.com. Web: www.stkatharinedrexelsfsd.org.
Catechesis/Religious Program—Students 245.

6—ST. LAMBERT (1958) Revs. James E. Mason; Paul Stephen King; Deacon Roger R. Heidt.
Res.: 3901 E. 16th St., 57103. Tel: 605-336-8808; Fax: 605-339-4389. Email: st.lambert.parish@sfcss.org. Web: www.stlambert-parish.org.
See St. Lambert Elementary, Sioux Falls under Inter-Parochial Schools located in the Institution section.
Catechesis/Religious Program—Tel: 605-338-4728. Students 229.

7—ST. MARY (1947) Revs. David Krogman; Jeffrey Thomas Norfolk; Deacon Henry Knapp.
Res.: 2109 S. Fifth Ave., 57105. Tel: 605-332-6391; Fax: 605-338-2953. Web: www.stmarysf.org.
See St. Mary, Sioux Falls under Inter-Parochial Schools located in the Institution section.
Catechesis/Religious Program—Tel: 605-334-1912. Students 120.

8—ST. MICHAEL (1979) [JC] Revs. Charles L. Cimpl; Daniel Lee Moris; Deacon John P. Devlin.
Res.: 1600 S. Marion Rd., 57106. Tel: 605-361-1600; Fax: 605-361-4350.
See St. Michael Elementary School, Sioux Falls under Inter-Parochial Schools located in the Institution section.
Catechesis/Religious Program—Tel: 605-361-1317. Students 508.

9—OUR LADY OF GUADALUPE (1996) [JC] Revs. Thomas Fitzpatrick, Admin.; David Garza.
Res.: 1220 E. 8th St., 57103-1702. Tel: 605-338-8126; Fax: 605-338-0419. Email: olg@msn.com.
Catechesis/Religious Program—Students 167.

10—ST. THERESE (1917) Rev. David Stevens; Deacon Michael Conrads.
Res.: 1301 N. Dubuque Ave., 57110-6450. Tel: 605-338-2433; Fax: 605-339-2203.
Catechesis/Religious Program—Students 185.

OUTSIDE THE CITY OF SIOUX FALLS

ABERDEEN, BROWN CO.

1—ST. MARY, [CEM] Revs. J. Joseph Holzhauser; Jordan Samson, Parochial Vicar; Deacon Peter Mehlaff.
Res.: 409 2nd Ave., N.E., 57401. Tel: 605-229-4422; Fax: 605-226-4908.
School— See separate listing under Inter-Parochial Schools in the Institution section.
Catechesis/Religious Program—Students 145.

2—SACRED HEART (1882) [CEM] Revs. Shane D. Stevens; Shaun Thomas Haggerty; Deacon Richard Kelley.
Res.: 409 3rd. Ave., S.E., 57401. Tel: 605-225-7065; Fax: 605-226-5992. Email: alacher@parishmail.com. Web: parishesonline.com.
Church: 502 2nd Ave., S.E., 57401.
See Roncalli Schools, Aberdeen under Inter-Parochial Schools located in the Institution section.
Catechesis/Religious Program—Tel: 605-225-7065; Fax: 605-226-5992. Students 229.

ALEXANDRIA, HANSON CO., ST. MARY OF MERCY (1880) [CEM] Rev. Jerome Ranek.
Res.: 220 W. 5th St., P.O. Box 158, 57311. Tel: 605-239-4833; Fax: 605-239-4578 (call). Email: maryofmercy@triotel.net. Web: stamryofmercyalexandria.parishesonline.com.
Catechesis/Religious Program—Students 122.

ARLINGTON, KINGSBURY CO., ST. JOHN THE EVANGELIST (1907), Served from DeSmet., Mailing Address: 301 S. Main St., 57212. Tel: 605-854-3564; Fax: 605-854-9961.
Catechesis/Religious Program—Students 46.

ARMOUR, DOUGLAS CO., ST. PAUL THE APOSTLE (1886) Rev. Cathal Gallagher, S.S.C.
Res.: 206 1st St., 57313. Tel: 605-724-2191; Fax: 605-724-2121.
Catechesis/Religious Program—Tel: 605-724-2121. Students 53.

ARTESIAN, SANBORN CO., ST. CHARLES (1908) [JC] Attended by St. Wilfrid, Woonsocket., Mailing Address: Box 266, Woonsocket, 57385. Tel: 605-796-4666; Fax: 605-796-4666.
Catechesis/Religious Program—Students 14.

AURORA, BROOKINGS CO., ST. WILLIAM (1881) [CEM] Deacon Edwin Gruhot, Admin.
Mailing Address: 1647 Edgewater Dr., Lake Benton, MN 56149. Tel: 507-368-9406.
Catechesis/Religious Program—Students 8.

BERESFORD, UNION CO., ST. TERESA OF AVILA (1885) [CEM] Rev. Mark Axtmann.
Res.: 901 S. Third, P.O. Box 472, 57004. Tel: 605-763-2028 (Church); 605-763-5159 (Rectory). Email: markaxtmann@hotmail.com.
Catechesis/Religious Program—Students 110.

BIG BEND, HUGHES CO., ST. CATHERINE (1950) [CEM] Attended by Fort Thompson., Mailing Address: Box 47, Fort Thompson, 57339. Tel: 605-245-2350.
Catechesis/Religious Program—Students 35.

BIG STONE CITY, GRANT CO., ST. CHARLES (1882) [CEM] Rev. Daniel Wolfgram.
Res.: 106 3rd Ave., P.O. Box 68, 57216. Tel: 605-862-8319; Fax: 605-862-8319.
Catechesis/Religious Program—Students 30.

BOWDLE, EDMUNDS CO., ST. AUGUSTINE (1894) [CEM] Rev. DeWayne Kayser.
Mailing Address: 3023 S. 3rd St., Box 310, 57428. Tel: 605-285-6466; Fax: 605-285-6160.
Catechesis/Religious Program—Students 36.

BRANDON, MINNEHAHA CO., RISEN SAVIOR (1979) [JC] Rev. Terry Weber.
Res.: 312 9th Ave. N., 57005.
Church: 301 N. Splitrock Blvd., P.O. Box 80, 57005-0080. Tel: 605-582-8535 (Rectory); 605-582-6902 (Church); Fax: 605-582-3993.
Catechesis/Religious Program—Tel: 605-582-2292. Students 339.

BRIDGEWATER, MCCOOK CO., ST. STEPHEN (1883) [CEM] Rev. Paul Offerman.
Res.: Box 49, 57319. Tel: 605-729-2505. Email: stephen123@unitelsd.com.
Catechesis/Religious Program—Students 38.

BRITTON, MARSHALL CO., ST. JOHN DE BRITTO (1888) [JC] Unassigned.
Res.: 812 8th St., P.O. Box 108, 57430. Tel: 605-448-5379; Fax: 605-448-5388.
Catechesis/Religious Program—Students 34.

BROOKINGS, BROOKINGS CO., ST. THOMAS MORE (1904) [CEM] Rev. Rodney Farke.
Res.: 1700 8th St. S., 57006. Tel: 605-692-4361; Fax: 605-692-6176. Email: vicki@stmbrookings.org. Web: www.stthomasbrookings.parishesonline.com.
Catechesis/Religious Program—Tel: 605-692-6941. Students 592.

BRYANT, HAMLIN CO., ST. MARY (1881) [CEM] Attended by St. Michael, Clark., 110 N. Idaho St., Clark, 57225.
Catechesis/Religious Program—Students 32.

CANTON, LINCOLN CO., ST. DOMINIC Rev. Paul Pathiyamoola.
Mailing Address: 800 E. Walnut, 57013.
Res.: 809 E. Walnut, 57013. Tel: 605-764-5640; Fax: 605-764-3085.
Catechesis/Religious Program—Students 84.

CASTLEWOOD, HAMLIN CO., ST. JOHN (1885) [JC] Attended by Kranzburg., Mailing Address: Box 166, Kranzburg, 57245. Tel: 605-886-9166; Fax: 605-886-2715.
Catechesis/Religious Program—Students 50.

CENTERVILLE, TURNER CO., GOOD SHEPHERD (1888) [JC] Attended by Beresford., Mailing Address: P.O. Box 98, 57014. Tel: 605-563-2220.
Catechesis/Religious Program—Students 42.

CHAMBERLAIN, BRULE CO., ST. JAMES (1891) [JC] Rev. Guy Blair, S.C.J; Deacon Alfred Bud Jetty.
Res.: 400 S. Main, 57325. Tel: 605-734-6122; Fax: 605-734-6729. Email: sjchamofc@parishmail.com. Web: www.stjameschamberlain.com.
Catechesis/Religious Program—Tel: 605-734-6122; Fax: 605-734-6729. Students 120.

CLARK, CLARK CO., ST. MICHAEL (1887) [CEM] Rev. John Short.
Res.: 110 N. Idaho St., 57225. Tel: 605-532-3855; Fax: 605-532-3855.
Catechesis/Religious Program—112 N. Idaho St., 57225. Tel: 605-532-3776. Students 38.

CLEAR LAKE, DEUEL CO., ST. MARY (1900) Unassigned.
Res.: 408 Third St. W., Box 589, 57226. Tel: 605-874-2080; Fax: 605-874-1333.
Catechesis/Religious Program—Students 75.

COLMAN, MOODY CO., ST. PETER (1905) [CEM] Attended by SS. Simon & Jude, Flandreau., *c/o Ss. Simon & Jude*, 105 S. Bates St., Flandreau, 57028. Tel: 605-997-2610; Fax: 605-573-2080.
Catechesis/Religious Program—Students 67.

DAKOTA DUNES, UNION CO., BLESSED TERESA OF CALCUTTA CATHOLIC CHURCH (1999) Rev. Robert Edward Lacey; Deacon Joseph Twidwell.
Church: 995 Sioux Point Rd., 57049. Tel: 605-235-1942; Fax: 605-235-1492. Email: bteresa1@longlines.com.
Catechesis/Religious Program—Students 108.

DANTE, CHARLES MIX CO., ASSUMPTION B.V.M. (1909) [CEM] Rev. Richard Baumberger.
Mailing Address: P.O. Box 63736, Wagner, 57380. Tel: 605-384-5155.
Catechesis/Religious Program—Students 75.

DE SMET, KINGSBURY CO., ST. THOMAS AQUINAS (1901) [CEM] Rev. Greg Frankman.
Res.: 514 3rd St., Box 15, 57231. Tel: 605-854-3564; Fax: 605-854-9961.
Catechesis/Religious Program—Students 87.

DELL RAPIDS, MINNEHAHA CO., ST. MARY'S (1898) [CEM] Revs. Gregory Tschakert; Anthony Urban, Parochial Vicar.
Res.: 608 E. 8th St., 57022. Tel: 605-428-3390; Fax: 605-428-5304.
School—(Grades PreK-6) Tel: 605-428-3459. Lay Teachers 8; Students 143.
School—(Grades 7-12) Tel: 605-428-5591; Fax: 605-428-5377. Lay Teachers 7; Students 90.
Catechesis/Religious Program—Tel: 605-428-3597. Students 226.

DIMOCK, HUTCHINSON CO., SS. PETER AND PAUL (1885) [CEM] Rev. Dana Robert Christensen.
Res.: 146 W. 1st St., 57331. Tel: 605-928-3883. Email: sppaulpd@hotmail.com.
Catechesis/Religious Program—Students 56.

DUNCAN, BUFFALO CO., ST. PLACIDUS (1887) [CEM] Attended by Woonsocket., P.O. Box 266, Woonsocket, 57385. Tel: 605-293-3484.
Church: HCR 3, Box 17, Gann Valley, 57341.
Catechesis/Religious Program—Students 10.

EDEN, MARSHALL CO., SACRED HEART (1917) [CEM] Unassigned.
Res.: Box 15, 57232. Tel: 605-486-4702; Fax: 605-486-4772. Email: sheden@venturecomm.net.
Catechesis/Religious Program—Students 26.

ELK POINT, UNION CO., ST. JOSEPH (1901) [CEM] Attended by St. Peter, Jefferson., 605 E. Main St., Box 340, 57025. Tel: 605-356-2693; Fax: 605-356-3284. Email: stjoseph@iw.net. Web: www.parishesonline.com.
Catechesis/Religious Program—Students 174.

ELKTON, BROOKINGS CO., OUR LADY OF GOOD COUNSEL (1879) [CEM] Attended by Flandreau., Mailing Address: 105 S. Bates, Flandreau, 57028. Tel: 605-997-2610; Fax: 605-573-2080.
Res.: Box E, 57026. Tel: 605-542-8221; Fax: 605-542-8221.
Catechesis/Religious Program—Students 58.

EMERY, HANSON CO., ST. MARTIN (1884) [CEM] Attended by St. Mary of Mercy, Alexandria.
Res.: 342 3rd Ave., Box 312, 57332. Tel: 605-449-4374. Web: www.stmartinemery.parishesonline.com.
Catechesis/Religious Program—Students 79.

EPIPHANY, HANSON CO., CHURCH OF THE EPIPHANY (1896) [CEM] Attended by Howard., Mailing Address: Box 100, Howard, 57349.
Catechesis/Religious Program—Students 40.

ESTELLINE, HAMLIN CO., ST. FRANCIS DE SALES (1884) [CEM] Attended by Clear Lake.
Res.: P.O. Box 589, Clear Lake, 57226. Tel: 605-873-2254; Fax: 605-874-1333.
Catechesis/Religious Program—Tel: 605-874-2080. Students 32.

ETHAN, DAVISON CO., HOLY TRINITY (1889) [CEM] Attended by Dimock., 146 W. 1st St., Dimock, 57331. Tel: 605-928-3883.
Catechesis/Religious Program—Tel: 605-227-4361. Nicole Nuegebauer, D.R.E. Students 41.

EUREKA, MCPHERSON CO., ST. JOSEPH (1896) Attended by Herreid., Mailing Address: P.O. Box 37, Herreid, 57632. Tel: 605-284-5190.
Church: 602 2nd St., 57437.
Catechesis/Religious Program—Students 43.

FARMER, HANSON CO., ST. PETER (1889) Closed. For inquiries for parish records contact the chancery.

FAULKTON, FAULK CO., ST. THOMAS THE APOSTLE (1903) [CEM] Rev. Joji Itukulapati (India); Deacon Arvid Holsing.
Res.: 206 10th Ave. S., P.O. Box 394, 57438. Tel: 605-598-6590; Fax: 605-598-6745. Email: stthomas@venturecomm.net.
Church: 1013 Court St., 57438.
Catechesis/Religious Program—Kelly Bowar, D.R.E. Students 75.

FLANDREAU, MOODY CO., SS. SIMON AND JUDE (1882) [CEM] Rev. John Helmueller.
Res.: 105 S. Bates, 57028. Tel: 605-997-2610; Fax: 605-573-2080.
Catechesis/Religious Program—Students 103.

FLORENCE, CODINGTON CO., BLESSED SACRAMENT (1889) [CEM] Rev. Douglas Binsfeld.
Res.: Box 6, 57235. Tel: 605-758-2271; Fax: 605-758-2113.
Catechesis/Religious Program—Students 50.

FORT THOMPSON, BUFFALO CO., ST. JOSEPH (1889) [CEM] Revs. Joseph Dean, S.C.J.; Vincent Suparman, S.C.J.; Christianus Hendrick, S.C.J.; Deacon Steven A. McLaughlin.
Mailing Address: Box 47, 57339. Tel: 605-245-2350. In Res., Rev. Bernard Rosinski, S.C.J. (Retired).
Catechesis/Religious Program—Students 80.

GARRETSON, MINNEHAHA CO., ST. ROSE OF LIMA (1898) [CEM] Rev. Kenneth Bain; Deacon Donald Wagner.
Res.: Drawer O, 57030. Tel: 605-594-3750; Fax: 605-594-2017.
Catechesis/Religious Program—Students 122.

GARY, DEUEL CO., ST. PETER (1900) Attended by Clear Lake., 408 3rd St. W., Box 589, Clear Lake, 57226. Tel: 605-874-2080; Fax: 605-874-1333.
Catechesis/Religious Program—Students 12.

GEDDES, CHARLES MIX CO., ST. ANN (1902) [CEM] [JC] Attended by Platte., Mailing Address: P.O. Box 137, 57342. Tel: 605-337-3710; 605-337-9717; Fax: 605-337-9717. In Res., Rev. Roger Geditz (Retired).
Catechesis/Religious Program—Students 18.

GETTYSBURG, POTTER CO., SACRED HEART (1905) [CEM] Rev. Jerome Kopel.
Res.: 203 E. Garfield Ave., Box 285, 57442. Tel: 605-765-2161.
Catechesis/Religious Program—Tel: 605-765-2359. Students 75.

GRENVILLE, DAY CO., ST. JOSEPH (1885) [CEM] Attended by Eden.
Res.: Box 191, 57239. Tel: 605-486-4655; 605-486-4702 (Eden).
Catechesis/Religious Program—Students 15.

GROTON, BROWN CO., ST. ELIZABETH ANN SETON (1883), (formerly St. John the Baptist). Rev. Michael D. Kelly.
Res.: 803 1st St. N., P.O. Box 407, 57445. Tel: 605-397-8448; Fax: 605-397-8632.
Catechesis/Religious Program—Students 102.

GROVER, CODINGTON CO., ST. PETER (1901) Attended by Blessed Sacrament, Florence., Mailing Address: P.O. Box 6, Florence, 57235. Tel: 605-758-2271; Fax: 605-758-2113.
Catechesis/Religious Program—Students 7.

HARROLD, HUGHES CO., ST. JOHN THE EVANGELIST, [CEM] Attended by Highmore., Mailing Address: Box 457, Highmore, 57345. Tel: 605-852-2733; Fax: 605-852-2076.
Catechesis/Religious Program—Students 13.

HARTFORD, MINNEHAHA CO., ST. GEORGE (1882) [CEM] Rev. David A. Desmond.
408 S. Western Ave., Box 577, 57033. Tel: 605-528-3902; Fax: 605-528-3924. Email: stgeorgehartford@yahoo.com.
Res.: 300 W. Mickelson, 57033.
Catechesis/Religious Program—St. George Center, 408 S. Western Ave., 57033. Students 223.

HECLA, BROWN CO., ST. ANTHONY OF PADUA (1904) [JC] Unassigned.Mailing Address: Box 108, Britton, 57430. Tel: 605-448-5379; Fax: 605-528-3902.

HENRY, CODINGTON CO., ST. HENRY Rev. Douglas Binsfeld.
Mailing Address: 605 4th St., P.O. Box 73, 57243. Tel: 605-758-2271.
Catechesis/Religious Program—Students 41.

HERREID, CAMPBELL CO., ST. MICHAEL (1895) [CEM] Rev. Thomas Clement.
Res.: 106 2nd Ave. W., Box 37, 57632. Tel: 605-437-2614; Fax: 605-437-2505. Email: stmichaels@valleytel.net.
Catechesis/Religious Program—Students 36.

HIGHMORE, HYDE CO., ST. MARY (1906) [CEM] Rev. Paul Nereparampil, C.M.I. (India).
Res.: Box 457, 57345. Tel: 605-852-2733; Fax: 605-852-2076.
Catechesis/Religious Program—Students 52.

HOSMER, EDMUNDS CO., HOLY TRINITY (1912) [CEM] Attended by Bowdle.
Res.: P.O. Box 310, Bowdle, 57428. Tel: 605-285-6466.
Catechesis/Religious Program—Students 6.

HOVEN, POTTER CO., ST. ANTHONY OF PADUA (1887) [CEM] Rev. Kevin Doyle.
Res.: 546 Main St., Box 98, 57450. Tel: 605-948-2451; Fax: 605-948-2245. Web: www.stanthonyshoven.com.
Catechesis/Religious Program—Students 62.

HOWARD, MINER CO., ST. AGATHA (1882) [CEM] Rev. Paul Josten.
Res.: Box 100, 57349. Tel: 605-772-5564; Fax: 605-772-5179. Students 80.
Catechesis/Religious Program—Students 65.

HUMBOLDT, MINNEHAHA CO., ST. ANN (1912) [CEM] Rev. Robert V. Krantz; Sr. Jane Schoenfelder, O.S.B.
Res.: 204 S. Jefferson, P.O. Box 195, 57035. Tel: 605-363-3330; Fax: 605-363-3856.
Catechesis/Religious Program—Students 82.

HUNTIMER, MINNEHAHA CO., ST. JOSEPH THE WORKMAN (1889) [CEM] Rev. Kenneth Bain.
Mailing Address: 520 Center Ave., P.O. Box O, Garretson, 57030. Tel: 605-594-3750.
Church: 46408 245th St., Colton, 57018.
Catechesis/Religious Program—Students 74.

HURON, BEADLE CO., HOLY TRINITY (1999) [CEM] Rev. Terence Anderson.
Mailing Address: 425 21st St. S.W., 57350.
Res.: 425 20th St., S.W., 57350. Tel: 605-352-2203; Fax: 605-353-0889. Email: hthuron@hur.midco.net. Web: www.holytrinityhuron.parishesonline.com.
School—Tel: 605-352-9344; Fax: 605-352-0889. Lay Teachers 10; Students 156.
Catechesis/Religious Program—Tel: 605-352-2237. Students 185.

IDYLWILDE, TURNER CO., ST. BONIFACE (1885) [CEM] Attended by St. George, Scotland., P.O. Box 449, Scotland, 57059.
Res.: Tel: 605-583-4318; Fax: 605-583-4457.
Catechesis/Religious Program—Students 44.

IPSWICH, EDMUNDS CO., HOLY CROSS (1886) [CEM] Rev. Randy Phillips.
Res.: 20 6th St., Box 67, 57451. Tel: 605-426-6967; Fax: 605-426-6588.
School—13 6th St., P.O. Box 324, 57451. Tel: 605-426-6222. Lay Teachers 5; Students 27.
Catechesis/Religious Program—Students 61.

IROQUOIS, KINGSBURY CO., ST. PAUL (1914) [CEM] Attended by St. Thomas Aquinas, De Smet., Mailing Address: 100 Sullivan St., E., Box 15, 57353. Tel: 605-854-3564; Fax: 605-854-9961.
Catechesis/Religious Program—Students 14.

JEFFERSON, UNION CO., ST. PETER (1867) [CEM] Rev. David Roehrich.
Res.: 400 Main St., P.O. Box 188, 57038-0188. Tel: 605-966-5716; Fax: 605-966-5492. Email: stpeter@longlines.com.
Preschool—P.O. Box 98, 57038-0098. Tel: 605-966-5746. Students 21.
Catechesis/Religious Program— (Combined with St. Joseph, Elk Point) Students 52.

KIMBALL, BRULE CO., ST. MARGARET (1884) [CEM] Rev. Andrew Swietochowski.
Res.: 417 S. Elm., Box 137, 57355. Tel: 605-778-6420. Web: www.stmargarets.midstatesd.net.
Preschool—Teachers 2; Students 27.
Catechesis/Religious Program—Tel: 605-778-6487. Students 108.

KRANZBURG, CODINGTON CO., HOLY ROSARY (1879) [CEM] Rev. Kenneth J. Koster.
Res.: 202 Minnesota Ave. N.E., Box 166, 57245. Tel: 605-886-3344; Fax: 605-886-2715.
School—(Grades K-6) Tel: 605-886-8114. Lay Teachers 4; Students 29.
Catechesis/Religious Program—Students 89.

LAKE ANDES, CHARLES MIX CO., ST. MARK (1904) [CEM] Bro. Martin Zatsick, T.O.R., Admin.
Res.: 251 3rd Ave., N., Box 250, 57356. Tel: 605-487-7300.
Catechesis/Religious Program—Tel: 605-487-7056. Students 29.

LAKE CITY, MARSHALL CO., ST. JOSEPH (1919) [CEM] Attended by Eden., Mailing Address: Box 15, Eden, 57232. Tel: 605-486-4702; Fax: 605-486-4772.

LENNOX, LINCOLN CO., ST. MAGDALEN, [CEM] Attended by St. Dominic, Canton., Mailing Address: Box 136, 57039. Tel: 605-647-2187. Email: stmagdalens@iw.net. Web: stmagdalenlennox.parishesonline.com.
Catechesis/Religious Program—Students 123.

LEOLA, MCPHERSON CO., OUR LADY OF PERPETUAL HELP (1891) [CEM] Attended by Holy Cross, Ipswich.
Res.: P.O. Box 67, Ipswich, 57451. Tel: 605-426-6967; Fax: 605-426-6588.
Catechesis/Religious Program—Students 26.

LESTERVILLE, YANKTON CO., ST. JOHN THE BAPTIST (1904) [CEM] Attended by St. Wenceslaus, Tabor., Mailing Address: 205 N. Lidice, Tabor, 57063. Tel: 605-463-2336; Fax: 605-463-2518.
Catechesis/Religious Program—Students 27.

MADISON, LAKE CO., ST. THOMAS AQUINAS (1881) [CEM] Rev. Robert B. Vinslauski.
Res.: 217 N.W. Fourth St., 57042. Tel: 605-256-2304; Fax: 605-256-9252.
School—Tel: 605-256-4419. Lay Teachers 11; Students 95.
Catechesis/Religious Program—Students 118.

MARION, TURNER CO., OUR LADY OF PERPETUAL HELP (1880) [CEM] Attended by St. Christina, P.O. Box 610, Parker, SD 57053-0610. Rev. Hal L. Barber (Retired).
Res.: 306 E. State St., 57043. Tel: 605-648-3928. P.O. Box 610, Parker, 57053-4983.
Catechesis/Religious Program—Students 11.

MARTY, CHARLES MIX CO., ST. PAUL'S CHURCH (1913), (Native American), [CEM] Rev. David Tickerhoof, T.O.R.; Sr. Miriam Shindelar, O.S.B.S., Admin.
Res.: 102 Church Dr., P.O. Box 266, 57361. Tel: 605-384-3234; Fax: 605-384-3575. Email: stpaulsparish@hcinet.net.
Catechesis/Religious Program—Students 6.

MAYFIELD, YANKTON CO., ST. COLUMBA (1902) [CEM] Unassigned. Attended by St. George, Scotland SD., P.O. Box 449, Scotland, 57059. Tel: 605-583-4318.
Catechesis/Religious Program—Students 23.

MELLETTE, SPINK CO., ALL SAINTS (1944) [CEM] Attended by St. Bernard, Redfield., Mailing Address: Box 46, 57461. Tel: 605-887-3414.
Catechesis/Religious Program—Students 51.

MILBANK, GRANT CO., ST. LAWRENCE (1882) [CEM] Rev. Gary K. DeRouchey.
Church/Office: 113 S. 6th St., 57252.
Res.: 101 S. 6th St., 57252.
School—Tel: 605-432-5673. Lay Teachers 9; Students 135.
Catechesis/Religious Program—Tel: 605-432-5353. Students 170.

MILLER, HAND CO., ST. ANN (1884) [CEM] Rev. Chester Murtha.

Res.: 709 E. 4th, P.O. Box 198, 57362. Tel: 605-853-2207; Fax: 605-853-3037. Email: stann1962@mncomm.com.
Catechesis/Religious Program—Tel: 605-853-2735. Students 95.

MITCHELL, DAVISON CO.
1—HOLY FAMILY (1880) [JC] Rev. Larry Regynski; Deacon Joseph Graves.
Res.: 222 N. Kimball St., 57301. Tel: 605-996-3639; Fax: 605-996-3937. Email: holyfamily@mitchelltelecom.net.
Catechesis/Religious Program—1510 W. Elm, 57301. Tel: 605-996-3842. Students 203.
2—HOLY SPIRIT (1962) Rev. Michael Schneider.
Res.: 1401 W. Cedar Ave., 57301. Tel: 605-996-7424; Fax: 605-990-3401. Email: holyspirit@mitchelltelecom.net.
Catechesis/Religious Program—See Holy Family for details., Tel: 605-996-3842. Students 132.

MOBRIDGE, WALWORTH CO., ST. JOSEPH (1912) [JC] Rev. William Hamak.
Res.: 220 6th St., W., 57601. Tel: 605-845-2100. Email: stjoe@westriv.com.
Preschool—Lay Teachers 1; Students 22.
Catechesis/Religious Program—Students 113.

MONTROSE, MCCOOK CO., ST. PATRICK (1904) [CEM] Rev. Robert V. Krantz.
211 S. Church, P.O. Box 158, 57048. Tel: 605-363-5068; Fax: 605-363-3856. Email: stpatmontrose@siouxvalley.net.
Catechesis/Religious Program—Students 118.

MOUNT VERNON, DAVISON CO., ST. MICHAEL (1900) Attended by Plankinton., Mailing Address: Box 430, Plankinton, 57368. Tel: 605-942-7125.
Catechesis/Religious Program—Students 42.

NEW EFFINGTON, ROBERTS CO., SACRED HEART (1913) Attended by Rosholt., Mailing Address: P.O. Box 45, Rosholt, 57260. Tel: 605-537-4583.
Catechesis/Religious Program—Students 3.

ONAKA, FAULK CO., ST. JOHN THE BAPTIST (1906) [CEM] Attended by St. Anthony of Padua, Hoven., Mailing Address: P.O. Box 98, Hoven, 57450. Tel: 605-948-2451; Fax: 605-948-2245.
Catechesis/Religious Program—Students 1.

ONIDA, SULLY CO., ST. PIUS X (1959) [CEM] Attended by Sacred Heart, Gettysburg., Mailing Address: 102 6th St., P.O. Box 13, 57564. Tel: 605-258-2336. Email: stpiusx@venturecomm.net.
Catechesis/Religious Program—Students 52.

ORIENT, FAULK CO., ST. JOSEPH (1884) Attended by Faulkton., 17985 354th Ave., 57467. Tel: 605-598-6590. P.O. Box 394, Faulkton, 57438.
Catechesis/Religious Program—Students 20.

PARKER, TURNER CO., ST. CHRISTINA (1881) [CEM] Rev. Hal L. Barber (Retired).
Mailing Address: P.O. Box 610, 57053. Email: stchristina@iw.net. Web: www.stchristinaparker.parishesonline.com.
Res.: Maple St., Box 116, Tea, 57064. Tel: 605-498-5449; Fax: 605-498-2110.
Catechesis/Religious Program—Students 57.

PARKSTON, HUTCHINSON CO., SACRED HEART (1887) [CEM 2] Rev. John Rader; Deacon Barry Wagner.
Res.: Box 460, 57366. Tel: 605-928-3676; Fax: 605-928-3862.
Catechesis/Religious Program—Students 169.

PIERRE, HUGHES CO.
1—BLESSED KATERI TEKAKWITHA
Church & Office: 2815 E. Sully, 57501.
2—SS. PETER AND PAUL (1882) [CEM] Revs. Michael Griffin; Kristopher Cowles, Parochial Vicar.
Res.: 304 N. Euclid, 57501. Tel: 605-224-2483; Fax: 605-224-1483.
School—Tel: 605-224-7185; Fax: 605-224-1014. Benedictine Sisters 2; Lay Teachers 9; Students 148.
Catechesis/Religious Program—Students 300.

PLANKINTON, AURORA CO., ST. JOHN Rev. Msgr. Stephen Barnett.
Res.: Box 430, 57368. Tel: 605-942-7125. Email: sbarnett@siouxvalley.net. Web: www.stjohnplankinton.parishesonline.com.
Catechesis/Religious Program—Teachers 80.

PLATTE, CHARLES MIX CO., ST. PETER THE APOSTLE (1904) [CEM] Rev. Jesudas Thaliyan, C.M.I. (India).
Res.: 317 Ohio Ave., 57369. Tel: 605-337-3710; 605-337-2465; Fax: 605-337-9717.
Catechesis/Religious Program—Students 35.

POLO, HAND CO., ST. LIBORIUS (1904) [CEM] Attended by Miller., Mailing Address: 709 E. 4th, P.O. Box 198, Miller, 57362.
Catechesis/Religious Program—Students 13.

PUKWANA, BRULE CO., ST. ANTHONY (1891) Attended by St. James., 400 S. Main, Chamberlain, 57325. Tel: 605-734-6122; Fax: 605-734-6729.
Catechesis/Religious Program—Students 8.

RAMONA, LAKE CO., ST. WILLIAM OF VERCELLI (1899) Attended by St. Agatha, Howard., Mailing Address: Box 100, Howard, 57349. Tel: 605-772-5564; Fax: 605-772-5179.
Catechesis/Religious Program—Students 9.

REDFIELD, SPINK CO., ST. BERNARD (1884) [CEM] Rev. Christopher Hughes.
Res.: 213 E. 6th Ave., 57469-1249. Tel: 605-472-2500. Email: sbernard@abe.midco.net.
Catechesis/Religious Program—Tel: 605-472-1482. Students 188.

REVILLO, GRANT CO., ANNUNCIATION (1889) [CEM] Attended by St. Lawrence, Milbank.
Res.: P.O. Box 128, 57259.
Catechesis/Religious Program—Students 13.

ROSCOE, EDMUNDS CO., ST. THOMAS APOSTLE (1906) [JC], Attended by Bowdle.
Res.: 605 N. Andrew St., P.O. Box 310, 57471. Tel: 605-285-6466.
Catechesis/Religious Program—Students 48.

ROSHOLT, ROBERTS CO., ST. JOHN THE BAPTIST (1911) [CEM] Rev. Dennis Deis, O.M.I.
Res.: 218 W. Dakota St., Box 45, 57260. Tel: 605-537-4583.
Catechesis/Religious Program—Students 56.

SALEM, MCCOOK CO., ST. MARY (1885) [CEM] Rev. Martin E. Lawrence.
Res. & Church: 340 N. Idaho, Box 308, 57058. Tel: 605-425-2600; Fax: 605-425-3310. Email: stmaryadm@triotel.net. Web: www.salemcatholic.org.
School—Tel: 605-425-2607. Lay Teachers 7; Students 68.
Catechesis/Religious Program—Students 106.

SCOTLAND, BON HOMME CO., ST. GEORGE (1906) [CEM] Rev. Mathew Vazhappilly, C.M.I. (India).
Res.: Box 449, 57059. Tel: 605-583-4318; Fax: 605-583-4457.
Catechesis/Religious Program—Tel: 605-583-4696. Students 36.

SELBY, WALWORTH CO., ST. ANTHONY (1900) Attended by Herreid., Mailing Address: 7209 5th Ave., P.O. Box 231, 57472. Tel: 605-649-6338; Fax: 605-437-2505.
Catechesis/Religious Program—Students 31.

SENECA, FAULK CO., ST. BONIFACE (1903) Attended by St. Thomas the Apostle, Faulkton., Mailing Address: P.O. Box 394, Faulkton, 57438-0094. Tel: 605-598-6590.
Catechesis/Religious Program—Students 15.

SIGEL, YANKTON CO., ST. AGNES (1885) [CEM] Unassigned.29882 N. E. Jim River Rd., Mission Hill, 57046.
Catechesis/Religious Program—Students 16.

SISSETON, ROBERTS CO.
1—ST. CATHERINE (1962) [CEM 2] Revs. Norman Volk, O.M.I.; Anthony Dummer, O.M.I.
Office: 120 E. Chestnut, 57262. Tel: 605-698-7414; Fax: 605-698-7236.
Catechesis/Religious Program— (Combined with St. Peter, Sisseton). Students 21.
2—ST. PETER (1899) [CEM] Revs. Norman Volk, O.M.I.; Anthony Dummer, O.M.I.
Office: 120 E. Chestnut, 57262. Tel: 605-698-7414; Fax: 605-698-7236.
Catechesis/Religious Program—Students 74.

SPENCER-FARMER, MCCOOK CO., ST. JOHN NEUMANN (1999) Attended by Bridgewater., Mailing Address: P.O. Box 49, Bridgewater, 57319. Tel: 605-729-2814.
Catechesis/Religious Program—Parish Center, 620 Cordo St., 57374. Tel: 605-246-2391. Students 24.

SPRINGFIELD, BON HOMME CO., ST. VINCENT, Attended by Tyndall., Mailing Address: P.O. Box 130, 57062-0130. Tel: 605-589-3504.
Catechesis/Religious Program—Students 11.

STEPHAN, HYDE CO., IMMACULATE CONCEPTION (1886) [CEM] [JC] Attended by Ft. Thompson. Revs. Joseph Dean, S.C.J.; Bernard Rosinski, S.C.J. (Retired); Christianus Hendrick, S.C.J.
Mailing Address: P.O. Box 185, Lower Brule, 57548. Tel: 605-852-2215.
Catechesis/Religious Program—Students 27.

STICKNEY, AURORA CO., ST. MARY (1908) [CEM] Attended by Armour., Mailing Address: 206 1st St., Armour, 57313. Tel: 605-724-2191; Fax: 605-724-2121.
Catechesis/Religious Program—Students 17.

TABOR, BON HOMME CO., ST. WENCESLAUS (1872) [CEM] Rev. Joseph Puthenkulathil (India).
Res.: 205 N. Lidice St., 57063-2005. Tel: 605-463-2336; Fax: 605-463-2518.
Catechesis/Religious Program—Students 75.

TEA, LINCOLN CO., ST. NICHOLAS (1905) [JC] Rev. Kevin O'Dell.
Church & Res.: 140 W. Brian St., P.O. Box 116, 57064. Tel: 605-498-5449. Email: sharon.st.nicholas@midconetwork.com. Web: www.stnicholastea.parishesonline.com.
Catechesis/Religious Program—Students 142.

TRIPP, HUTCHINSON CO., HOLY ROSARY, Attended by Parkston., Mailing Address: P.O. Box 358, 57376-0358. Tel: 605-928-3676.
Catechesis/Religious Program—Students 11.

TURTON, SPINK CO., ST. JOSEPH (1888) [CEM] [JC], Mailing Address: P.O. Box 127, 57477.
Catechesis/Religious Program—Students 14.

TYNDALL, BON HOMME CO., ST. LEO (1890) [CEM] Rev. Joseph Forcelle.
Res.: 100 E. 20th Ave., Box 47, 57066. Tel: 605-589-3504; Fax: 605-589-3392.
Catechesis/Religious Program—Students 120.
Station—Springfield Correctional Facility Springfield. Tel: 605-369-2201.

VEBLEN, MARSHALL CO., ST. JOHN NEPOMUCENE (1907) [CEM] Attended by Catholic Community, Sisseton., 120 Chestnut St. E., Sisseton, 57262-1428. Tel: 605-698-7414; Fax: 605-698-7236.
Catechesis/Religious Program—Students 9.

VERMILLION, CLAY CO., ST. AGNES (1860) [CEM 2] [JC] Rev. John Fischer.
Res.: 416 Walker St., 57069. Tel: 605-624-4478 (Church); 605-624-1995 (Rectory); Fax: 605-624-4479. Email: saintagneschurch@msn.com. Web: www.stagnesvermillian.parishesonline.com.
School—(Grades K-5), 909 E. Lewis St., 57069. Tel: 605-624-4144; Fax: 605-624-6239. Lay Teachers 7; Students 141.
Catechesis/Religious Program—Students 170.

WAGNER, CHARLES MIX CO., ST. JOHN THE BAPTIST (1903) [CEM] Rev. Richard Baumberger; Deacon Albert J. Kocer, (Retired).
Res.: Box 637, 57380. Tel: 605-384-5518; Fax: 605-384-5518.
Catechesis/Religious Program—Tel: 605-384-5157. Students 85.

WAKONDA, CLAY CO., ST. PATRICK (1904) [CEM 2] Attended by Newman Center, Vermillion. Rev. Scott Traynor.
320 Cherry St., Vermillion, 57069. Tel: 605-624-2697.
Catechesis/Religious Program—Tel: 605-267-2676; Fax: 605-624-4145. Students 32.

WATERTOWN, CODINGTON CO.
1—HOLY NAME (1955) [JC] Rev. John Lantsberger.
Res.: 1009 Skyline Dr., 57201. Tel: 605-886-2628; Fax: 605-886-2142.
Catechesis/Religious Program—Tel: 605-886-3368; Fax: 605-886-2141. Students 338.
2—IMMACULATE CONCEPTION (1887) [CEM] Rev. Michael Wensing.
103 Third St., S.E., 57201.
Res.: 309 Second Ave., S.E., 57201. Tel: 605-886-4049; Fax: 605-882-2911.
School—Tel: 605-886-3883; Fax: 605-886-0199. Lay Teachers 17; Students 209.
Catechesis/Religious Program—Tel: 605-886-2772; Fax: 605-886-0199. Students 437.

WAUBAY, DAY CO., IMMACULATE CONCEPTION (1894) [CEM] Attended by Webster., Mailing Address: 1101 E. 1st St., Webster, 57274. Tel: 605-345-3447; Fax: 605-345-4871.
Catechesis/Religious Program—Students 28.

WAVERLY, CODINGTON CO., ST. JOSEPH (1889) [CEM] Attended by Kranzburg., Mailing Address: 202 Minnesota Ave., Box 166, Kranzburg, 57245. Tel: 605-886-9166; Fax: 605-886-2715.
Catechesis/Religious Program—Students 36.

WEBSTER, DAY CO., CHRIST THE KING (1884) [CEM] Rev. David Axtmann.
Res.: 1101 E. 1st St., 57274. Tel: 605-345-3447; Fax: 605-345-4871. Email: ctkparish@abe.midco.net.
Catechesis/Religious Program—Students 136.

WESSINGTON SPRINGS, JERAULD CO., ST. JOSEPH (1906) [JC] Rev. James Friedrich.
Mailing Address: P.O. Box 266, Woonsocket, 57385. Tel: 605-539-9569; Fax: 605-539-9569.
Church: 510 N. Wallace St., 57382.
Catechesis/Religious Program—Students 51.

WESSINGTON, BEADLE CO., ST. JOSEPH, Attended by Miller., Mailing Address: P.O. Box 198, Miller, 57362-0198. Tel: 605-853-2207; Fax: 605-853-3037. Email: stann1962@mncomm.com.
Catechesis/Religious Program—Students 32.

WESTPORT, BROWN CO., SACRED HEART OF WESTPORT (1889) [CEM] Rev. Thomas Anderson.
P.O. Box 87, 57481. Tel: 605-226-3713.
Catechesis/Religious Program—Students 56.

WHITE LAKE, AURORA CO., ST. PETER (1883) [CEM] Attended by Kimball Deacon James M. Hayes.
Res.: 101 S. Ellis, Box 277, 57383. Tel: 605-249-2700.
Catechesis/Religious Program—Students 74.

WHITE, BROOKINGS CO., ST. PAUL (1898) [JC] Rev. Andrew Dickinson.
Mailing Address: Box 96, 57276. Tel: 605-692-9461.

WILMOT, ROBERTS CO., ST. MARY (1886) [CEM] Rev. John McMullen, O.S.B.
Res.: *Blue Cloud Abbey*, P.O. Box 98, Marvin, 57251.
Church: Box 204, 57279. Tel: 605-938-4289; Fax: 605-398-9201.
Catechesis/Religious Program—Students 60.

WOONSOCKET, SANBORN CO., ST. WILFRID (1884) [CEM] Rev. James Friedrich.
Res.: 203 N. 2nd Ave., Box 266, 57385. Tel: 605-796-4666; Fax: 605-796-4666.
Catechesis/Religious Program—Students 60.

WORTHING, LINCOLN CO., ST. EDWARD (1908) [CEM] Attended by St. Dominic, Canton., 800 E. Walnut,

Canton, 57013. Tel: 605-764-5640; Fax: 605-764-3085.

YANKTON, YANKTON CO.

1—ST. BENEDICT (1993) [JC] Rev. Ken Lulf; Deacon Ronald Kachena.
Res.: 1500 St. Benedict Dr., 57078. Tel: 605-664-6214; Fax: 605-664-2305.
Catechesis/Religious Program—1500 St. Benedict Dr., 57078. Tel: 605-665-6214. Students 186.

2—SACRED HEART (1871) [CEM] Revs. Mark Lichter; Daniel H. Smith; Deacon Stillman W. Slason.
Res.: 509 Capitol St., 57078. Tel: 605-665-3655; Fax: 605-665-6768.
School—Tel: 605-665-5841; Fax: 605-668-9787. Sisters 1; Lay Teachers 15; Students 330.
Catechesis/Religious Program—Students 238.

Chaplains of Public Institutions

SIOUX FALLS. *South Dakota State Penitentiary & Minnehaha County Correctional Centers.* Revs. Gary Ternes, J.C.L., A.W. Ramos.
Veteran's Hospital. Rev. Mark Axtmann.

FLANDREAU. *Government Indian School.* Attended by SS. Simon & Jude, Flandreau

SPRINGFIELD. *Mike Durfee Correctional Facility.* Attended by St. Leo, Tyndall

YANKTON. *Federal Prison Camp.* Rev. Lawrence J. Marbach (Retired).
Mickelson Center for the Neurosciences. Deacon Stillman Slassen.

Retired:
Rev. Msgrs.—
Andraschko, James, 3701 E. Peony Pl., 57103.
Burian, Ed, 1021 Avenue K, Hawarden, IA 51023.
Doyle, James Michael, 2913 Ridgeview Way, 57105.
Hermann, Carlton P., 505 Burgess Rd., 57078-1819.
Mahowald, Richard J., P.A., Laurel Oaks #205, 4510 S. Prince of Peace Pl., 57103.
McPhee, Marvin (DEN), 1417 W. Ash Ave., Mitchell, 57301.
Wagner, Joseph, 3920 Barrington St., San Antonio, TX 78217.
Revs.—
Barber, Hal L., St. Christina, P.O. Box 610, Parker, 57053.
Brady, John, 509 Broadway, 57078.
Bream, James I., 4915 S. Glenview Rd., 57108.
Duman, Charles J., 500 S. Ohlman St., Mitchell, 57301.
Friedrich, Lawrence, 4500 S. Prince of Peace Pl., #A-9, 57103.
Geditz, Roger, P.O. Box 136, Geddes, 57342.
Holtzman, Jerome, 77 Paradise Dr., Watertown, 57201.
Imberi, Anthony, 25216 - 481st Ave., Garretson, 57030.
Imming, Donald, 30 Walker St., Vermillion, 57069.
Janes, David A., 1003 N. Dakota St., #8, Aberdeen, 57401.
Johnson, Doug, 930 W. 7th St., Apt. 3, 57104.
Joyce, James M., 4500 Prince of Peace Pl., Apt. 32, 57103.
Kayser, Leonard, 302 Greenview Dr., #4, 57078-1445.
Krzyzopolski, Al, 4700 S. Cliff Ave., #210, 57103.
Lantz, Gary, S.C.J., Rockford Apts. #3, 104 Cliffs Dr., P.O. Box 6, Chamberlain, 57325-0006.
Marbach, Lawrence J., 617 Maple St., 57078-3823.
Mardian, Pius, 4510 Prince of Peace Pl., #120, 57103.
Meier, Denis, 8728 Benet Pl., 100 28th Ave, S.E. # 212, Watertown, 57201.
Opem, Anthony, 300 Courtyard Dr., #313, Dakota Dunes, 57049.
Osborn, William, P.O. Box 132, Colman, 57017.
Pierce, Edward J., 1108 W. 57th St., #203B, 57108.
Rasmussen, John, 3708 S. Willow Ave., #104, 57105.
Riedman, John, 501 North Buckboard Dr., Kerrville, TX 78028.
Thury, Gerald, 27121 408th Ave., Dimock, 57331.

Permanent Deacons:
Barry, James T. "Tim", Ed.D., (Out of Diocese)
Bates, Thomas R., Holy Spirit, Sioux Falls
Boorman, James, Christ the King, Sioux Falls
Cantin, Leon, (Retired)
Cheskie, Pete, (Out of Diocese)
Conrads, Michael, St. Therese, Sioux Falls
Counter, Ralph, (Retired)
Devlin, John P., St. Michael, Sioux Falls
Frankman, William, Marriage Tribunal
Graves, Joseph, Holy Family, Mitchell
Gruhot, Edward, St. William, Aurora
Hayes, James M., St. Peter, White Lake
Heidt, Roger, Chancery Office; St. Lambert, Sioux Falls
Holsing, Arvid, St. Thomas the Apostle, Faulkton
Huntington, Michael, O'Gorman Junior High School, Sioux Falls
Jetty, Alfred "Bud", Native American Ministry, Chamberlain
Kachena, Ronald, St. Benedict, Yankton
Knapp, Henry J., St. Mary's, Sioux Falls
Kocer, Albert, (Retired), Wagner
McLaughlin, Steven A., Lower Brule Team Ministry, Fort Thompson
Mehlhaff, Peter, St. Mary, Aberdeen
Oliver, Edward B., (Retired), Canton
Pardew, Harold, St. Teresa of Avila, Beresford; Good Shepherd, Centerville
Slason, Stillman W., Sacred Heart, Yankton
Twidwell, Joseph, Blessed Teresa of Calcutta, Dakota Dunes
Vogel, Thomas, (Retired), Wakonda
Wagner, Barry, Sacred Heart, Parkston
Wagner, Donald, St. Rose of Lima, Garretson
Walden, James I., (Retired), Sioux Falls
Wambach, Micheal A., Christ the King, Webster
Wathen, Jerome F., (Retired), Sioux Falls

INSTITUTIONS LOCATED IN THE DIOCESE

[A] COLLEGES AND UNIVERSITIES

ABERDEEN. *Presentation College* (1951) 1500 N. Main St., 57401. Tel: 605-225-1634; Fax: 605-229-8330. Email: lorraine.hale@presentation.edu. Web: www.presentation.edu. Ms. Virginia Tobin, Interim Pres.; Rev. Joseph Sheehan, O.Carm., Chap. Sisters of the Presentation of the B.V.M., Campuses also located at Eagle Butte, SD & Fairmont, MN Priests 1; Sisters 1; Lay Teachers 50; Students 731.

YANKTON. *Mount Marty College*, 1105 W. 8th St., 57078. Tel: 800-658-4552; Fax: 605-668-1357. Web: www.mtmc.edu. Joseph Benoit, Pres.; Sandra Brown, Librarian. Benedictine Sisters. Sisters 7; Lay Teachers 45; Students 1,219.
Mount Marty College - Watertown Campus, 1225 Arrow Ave., P.O. Box 1385, Watertown, 57201. Tel: 605-886-6777; Fax: 605-882-6347. Email: mmcwatwn@dailypost.com. Linda Schurmann, Dir. Conducted by Benedictine Sisters.

[B] EDUCATION CENTERS, PRIVATE

CHAMBERLAIN. *St. Joseph Indian School*, P.O. Box 89, 57325. Tel: 605-234-3300; Fax: 605-234-3480. Web: www.stjo.org. Rev. Stephen Huffstetter, S.C.J.; Kathleen Donohue, Prin.; Judy Houska, Librarian. Priests 3; Lay Teachers 24; Students 200.

[C] INTER-PAROCHIAL SCHOOLS

SIOUX FALLS. *Sioux Falls Catholic School System*, (Grades PreK-12), 3100 W. 41st St., 57105. Tel: 605-336-6241; Fax: 605-373-1035. Email: tlorang@sfcss.org. Web: sfcss.org. Dr. Thomas Lorang, Supt.
O'Gorman High School, 3201 S. Kiwanis Ave., 57105. Tel: 605-336-3644; Fax: 605-336-9272. Kyle Groos, Prin.; Rev. David A. Desmond, Chap. Priests 1; Sisters 1; Lay Teachers 49; Students 749.
O'Gorman Catholic Junior High (Grades 7-8), 3100 W. 41st St., 57105. Tel: 605-988-0546; Fax: 605-336-9839. Wade Charron, Prin. Lay Teachers 22; Students 351.
St. Mary Elementary (Grades PreK-6), 2001 S. 5th Ave., 57105. Tel: 605-334-9881; Fax: 605-334-9224. Courtney Tielke, Prin. Lay Teachers 22; Students 381.
Holy Spirit Elementary (Grades PreK-6), 3601 E. Dudley Ln., 57103. Tel: 605-371-1481; Fax: 605-371-1483. Carol Loeffelholz, Prin. Lay Teachers 17; Students 416.
Christ the King Elementary School (Grades PreK-6), 1801 S. Lake Ave., 57105. Tel: 605-338-5103; Fax: 605-335-1231. Vickie Venhuizen, Prin. Lay Teachers 9; Students 124.
St. Lambert Elementary School (Grades PreK-6), 1000 S. Bahnson Ave., 57103. Tel: 605-338-7042; Fax: 605-336-8727. Barbara Lockwood, Prin. Lay Teachers 22; Students 239.
St. Michael Elementary School (Grades PreK-6), 1600 S. Marion Rd., 57106. Tel: 605-361-0021; Fax: 605-361-0094. Lisa Huemoeller, Prin. Lay Teachers 20; Students 311.
St. Katherine Drexel Elementary (Grades PreK-4), 1800 S. Katie Ave., Ste. 2, 57106. Tel: 605-275-6994. Katie Kerkvliet, Prin. Lay Teachers 6; Students 118.

ABERDEEN. *Aberdeen Catholic Schools Education Office*, 1400 N. Dakota St., S.E., 57401. Tel: 605-226-2100; Fax: 605-226-0616. Email: vickiehaiar@aberdeenroncalli.org. Web: www.aberdeenroncalli.org. James Hamburge, Pres.
Roncalli Primary School (Grades PreK-2), 419 N.E. 1st. Ave., 57401. Tel: 605-225-3460. Laura Wieck, Prin. Lay Teachers 13; Students 169.
Roncalli Elementary School (Grades 3-6), 501 S.E. 3rd. Ave., 57401. Tel: 605-229-4100; Fax: 605-229-4101. Brenda Mitzel, Prin. (Elementary) Lay Teachers 14; Students 156.
Roncalli High School (Grades 7-12), 1400 N. Dakota St., 57401. Tel: 605-225-7440; Fax: 605-226-0616. Web: www.aberdeenroncalli.org. Peggy Cox, Prin.; Cathy McNeary, Librarian. Priests 2; Lay Teachers 24; Students 259.

MITCHELL. *John Paul II School*, (Grades PreK-6), 1510 W. Elm St., 57301. Tel: 605-996-0378; Fax: 605-995-0378. Mrs. Michelle Ommen, Prin. Lay Teachers 13; Total Enrollment 226.

YANKTON. *Sacred Heart School*, (Grades PreK-8), 1500 St. Benedict Dr., Ste. 200, 57078-6884. Tel: 605-665-5841; Fax: 605-260-3400. Email: regan.manning@k12.sd.us. Web: www.shs.k12.sd.us. Regan Manning, Prin. Sisters 1; Lay Teachers 27; Total Enrollment 390.

[D] GENERAL HOSPITALS

SIOUX FALLS. *Avera McKennan*, 1325 S. Cliff Ave., P.O. Box 5045, 57117-5045. Tel: 605-322-8000; Fax: 605-322-7822. Web: www.averamckennan.org. David L. Kapaska, D.O., M.B.A., Pres. & CEO; Rev. David Krogman. Sponsored by Sisters of the Presentation of the B.V.M. of Aberdeen, S.D., and Benedictine Sisters of Sacred Heart Monastery, Yankton, S.D. Sisters of the Presentation of the B.V.M. (Aberdeen, SD) 4; Bed Capacity 505; Total Staff 3,558; Patients Assisted Annually 227,000.
Avera McKennan aka Prince of Peace 4500 Prince of Peace, 57103. Tel: 605-322-5600; Fax: 605-322-5622. Justin Hinker, Admin. Skilled Nursing Care Units 90; Assisted Living 36; Total Staff 185.
Avera McKennan dba Avera Behavioral Health Center 57117. Tel: 605-322-8000; Fax: 605-322-4009. Sponsored by Sisters of the Presentation of the B.V.M. of Aberdeen, S.D. and Benedictine Sisters of Sacred Heart Monastery, Yankton, S.D. Staffed Beds 110; Total Staff 236.

ABERDEEN. *Avera St. Luke's*, 305 S. State St., 57401. Tel: 605-622-5000; Fax: 605-622-5127. Web: www.averastlukes.org. Ron Jacobson, Regl. Pres.; Rev. Charles Emezie (Nigeria), Chap.; Elizabeth Guiliani, Vice Pres. Mission. Sponsored by Sisters of the Presentation of the B.V.M. of Aberdeen, SD, and Benedictine Sisters of Sacred Heart Monastery, Yankton, SD. Presentation Sisters of the B.V.M. (Aberdeen, SD) 1; Bed Capacity 130; Bassinets 20; Total Assisted Annually 285,767; Total Staff 1,314.
Avera St. Luke's dba Avera Mother Joseph Manor Retirement Community 1002 N. Jay St., 57401. Tel: 605-622-5850; Fax: 605-622-5851. Email: tom.snyder@averastlukes.org. Tom Snyder, Admin.; Rev. Charles Emezie (Nigeria). Adult Day Care, Community Outreach, Respite Care, Health Screening Clinics, and Family Support Council. Residents 81; Units for Apartment Living 58; Assisted Living Beds 34; Total Staff 142.

DELL RAPIDS. *Avera McKennan dba Dells Area Health Center* 909 N. Iowa Ave., 57022. Tel: 605-428-5431; Fax: 605-428-3906. Lindsay Leischner, Admin. Acute Care Beds 23; Staff 80.

DE SMET. *Avera Queen of Peace aka Avera De Smet Memorial Hospital* 306 Prairie Ave., S.W., P.O. Box 160, 57231. Tel: 605-854-3329; Fax: 605-854-3161. Janice Schardin, Admin. Bed Capacity 17; Staff 34; Total Assisted Annually 10,545.

EUREKA. *Avera St. Luke's dba Avera Eureka Health Care Center* 202 J Ave., P.O. Box 40, 57437. Tel: 605-284-2145; Fax: 605-284-2011. Web: www.averastlukes.org. Carmen Weber, Admin. Sponsored by Sisters of Presentation of the B.V.M of Aberdeen, SD & Benedictine Sisters of Sacred Heart Monastery, Yankton, SD. Nursing Home Beds 56; Total Staff 74.

GETTYSBURG. *Gettysburg Medical Center*, 606 E. Garfield, 57442. Tel: 605-765-2488; Fax: 605-765-2704. Mark C. Schmidt, Exec. Dir. Bed Capacity 50; Critical Access Hospital 10; Residential Living Units 12.

MILBANK. *Avera McKennan dba Milbank Area Hospital Avera* 901 E. Virgil Ave., 57252. Tel: 605-432-4538; Fax: 605-432-5412. Natalie Gauer, Admin. Bed Capacity 25; Staff 65.

MITCHELL. *Avera Queen of Peace*, 525 N. Foster, 57301. Tel: 605-995-2000; Fax: 605-995-2441. Email: tom.rasmusson@avera.org. Web: www.averaqueenofpeace.org. Sponsored by Sisters of the Presentation of the B.V.M.,

Aberdeen, SD, and Benedictine Sisters of Sacred Heart Monastery, Yankton, SD. Sisters 2; Bed Capacity 120; Staff 531; Patients Assisted Annually 67,195.

Avera Queen of Peace dba Avera Brady Health & Rehabilitation, Avera Brady Assisted Living 500 S. Ohlman, 57301. Tel: 605-996-7701; Fax: 605-995-6134. Mrs. Veronnica Smith, Admin. Sponsored by Sisters of the Presentation of the B.V.M., Aberdeen, SD, and Benedictine Sisters of Sacred Heart Monastery, Yankton, SD. Sisters 1; Skilled Nursing Care Units 84; Assisted Living 30; Total Staff 132.

Avera Queen of Peace dba Bishop Hoch Villa 500 S. Ohlman St., 57301. Tel: 605-996-7701; Fax: 605-995-6134. Units for Congregate Living 6; Additional Senior Units 2.

PARKSTON. *St. Benedict Health Center dba Avera St. Benedict Health Center* 401 W. Glynn Dr., 57366. Tel: 605-928-3311; Fax: 605-928-7368. Email: gale.walker@averastbenedict.org. Web: www.averastbenedict.org. Gale N. Walker, Pres. & CEO. Benedictine Sisters (Yankton, SD) 2; Bed Capacity 100; Total Assisted Annually 26,893; Total Staff 215.

PIERRE. *St. Mary's Foundation*, 800 E. Dakota, 57501. Tel: 605-224-3451; Fax: 605-224-3459. Email: ellenlee@catholichealth.net. Ellen J. Lee, Exec. Dir.

St. Mary's Healthcare Center of Pierre, South Dakota, 800 E. Dakota Ave., 57501. Tel: 605-224-3173; Fax: 605-224-3426. Email: karengallagher@catholichealth.net. Karen Gallagher, Exec. Dir., Mission Integration. Includes: Maryhouse Residential Nursing Facility and Parkwood Retirement Apartments. Sisters 1; Bed Capacity 60; Total Assisted Annually 48,557; Staff 475.

TYNDALL. *St. Michael's Hospital*, 410 W. 16th Ave., 57066. Tel: 605-589-3341; Fax: 605-589-3288. Email: cdeurmier@avera.org. Carol Deurmier, CEO. Bed Capacity 25; Total Assisted Annually 6,971; Total Staff 87.

WESSINGTON SPRINGS. *Avera Queen of Peace dba Avera Weskota Memorial Medical Center* 604 First St., N.E., 57382. Tel: 605-539-1201; Fax: 605-539-4580. Gaea Blue, Admin. Bed Capacity 23; Staff 38.

YANKTON. *Sacred Heart Health Services dba Avera Sacred Heart Hospital* 501 Summit, 57078. Tel: 605-668-8000; Fax: 605-665-0170. Pamela Rezac, Pres. & CEO. Sponsored by Sisters of the Presentation of the B.V.M. of Aberdeen, S.D. and Benedictine Sisters of Sacred Heart Monastery, Yankton, S.D. Sisters 3; Bed Capacity 144; Total Staff 633.

Sacred Heart Health Services dba Avera Sister James Nursing Homes 2111 W. 11th, 57078. Tel: 605-668-8900; Fax: 605-668-8939. Total Bed Capacity for facilities at 2111 W. 11th St. 114; LTC Beds 172; Total Staff 182.

Sacred Heart Health Services dba Avera Yankton Care Center 1212 W. Eighth St., 57078. Tel: 605-668-8800; Fax: 605-668-8815. Sponsored by Sisters of the Presentation of the B.V.M. of Aberdeen, S.D. and Benedictine Sisters of Sacred Heart Monastery, Yankton, S.D. Sisters 1; Bed Capacity 73; Total Staff 92.

[E] HOMES FOR AGED

MILBANK. *St. William Care Center*, 100 S. 9th St., 57252. Tel: 605-432-5811; Fax: 605-432-3187. Conducted by Daughters of St. Mary of Providence, Milbank. Total Staff 100; Bed Capacity 66.

Angela Hall Tel: 605-432-3171; Fax: 605-432-3187. Assisted Living Center Sisters 4.

SISSETON. *Tekakwitha Nursing Center, Inc. dba Tekakwitha Living Center* (sub. of Benedictine Health System), 6 E. Chestnut, 57262. Tel: 605-698-7693; Fax: 605-698-3091. Email: jim.cornelius@bhshealth.org. James P. Cornelius, Admin. (Owned and operated by: Benedictine Health System) Bed Capacity 70; Total Assisted Annually 180; Total Staff 105.

Rainbow Daycare Center Tel: 605-698-3257; Fax: 605-698-3091.

[F] MONASTERIES AND RESIDENCES OF PRIESTS AND BROTHERS

MARVIN. *Blue Cloud Abbey*, 46561 147th St., P.O. Box 98, 57251-0098. Tel: 605-398-9200; Fax: 605-398-9201. Email: abbey@bluecloud.org. Web: www.bluecloud.org. Rt. Revs. Thomas Hillenbrand, Retired Abbot; Alan Berndt, O.S.B., Retired Abbot; Denis Quinkert, O.S.B., Abbot; Revs. John McMullen, O.S.B.; Cletus Miller, O.S.B.; Odilo Burkhardt, O.S.B.; Bernardine Ness, O.S.B.; Christopher Uehlein, O.S.B.; Pedro Choc, O.S.B.; Matthew Kowalski, O.S.B.; Carlos Antonio Pop, O.S.B.; Michael Peterson, O.S.B.; Bro. Benet Tvedten, O.S.B., Prior. Priests 15; Brothers 19.

[G] CONVENTS AND RESIDENCES FOR SISTERS

SIOUX FALLS. *Adoration Sisters of the Blessed Sacrament*, 521 N. Duluth Ave., 57104. Tel: 605-336-2374; Fax: 605-357-7290. Email: adoratrices@msn.com. Sr. Angelica Morales Rendon, A.P., Supr. Sisters 8; Novices 3.

ABERDEEN. *Presentation Convent*, 1500 N. 2nd St., 57401. Tel: 605-229-8419; Fax: 605-229-8412. Email: pdonelan@presentationsisters.org. Web: www.presentationsisters.org. Sr. Pam Donelan, Pres. Motherhouse and Novitiate of the Sisters of the Presentation of the B.V.M. Final Professed Sisters 95.

ALEXANDRIA. *Monastery of Our Mother of Mercy and St. Joseph Discalced Carmelite Nuns*, 221 5th St. W., P.O. Box 67, 57311-0067. Tel: 605-239-4382; Fax: 605-239-4676. Sr. Marie Therese of the Child Jesus, O.C.D., Prioress.

Discalced Carmelite Nuns of Alexandria, South Dakota, Inc. Solemnly Professed Sisters 11; First Professed 3; Novices 3.

MARTY. *Motherhouse Oblate Sisters of the Blessed Sacrament*Sr. Inez Jetty, O.S.B.S., Community Leader. *St. Sylvester's Convent*, 103 Church Dr., P.O. Box 217, 57361-0217. Tel: 605-384-3305; Fax: 605-384-3575. Email: osbs@cme.com. Professed Sisters 6.

MITCHELL. *Sisters of St. Francis of Our Lady of Guadalupe*, 1417 W. Ash, 57301. Tel: 605-996-1410. Email: sistersofstfrancis@mit.midco.net. Sr. M. Loretta Von Rueden, Sister Leader. Private Association of the Faithful. Professed Sisters 3.

WATERTOWN. *Mother of God Monastery*, 110 28th Ave., S.E., 57201-8419. Tel: 605-882-6633; Fax: 605-882-6658. Email: prioress@dailypost.com. Web: watertownbenedictines.org. Sr. Marlene Minnaert, O.S.B., Prioress. Motherhouse and Novitiate of Benedictine Sisters. Sisters 53.

YANKTON. *Sacred Heart Monastery*, 1005 W. Eighth St., 57078-3389. Tel: 605-668-6000; Fax: 605-668-6153. Web: yanktonbenedictines.org. Sr. Penny Bingham, O.S.B., Prioress. Motherhouse and Novitiate of the Benedictine Sisters. Sisters 108.

[H] NEWMAN CENTERS

ABERDEEN. *St. Thomas Aquinas Newman Center* Email: nsunewman@nvc.net. Rev. Thomas Anderson.

Northern State University 310 15th Ave., S.E., 57401. Tel: 605-229-1011; Fax: 605-226-3274. Michala Heller, Campus Min. & Dir.

BROOKINGS. *Pius XII Student Center* Box 730, University Station, 57006. Tel: 605-692-9461; Fax: 605-692-9461. Email: ccpoffice@brookings.net. Web: www.piusxiinewman.com. Rev. Andrew Dickinson.

MADISON. *Dakota State University Newman Club Office* , Attended by St. Thomas Parish, Madison., 217 N.W. 4th St., 57042. Tel: 606-256-4135. Email: kris.larson@dsu.edu.

VERMILLION. *St. Thomas More Catholic Newman Center* Email: newmanpc@usd.edu.

University of South Dakota 320 E. Cherry St., 57069. Tel: 605-624-2697; Fax: 605-624-4145. Rev. Scott Traynor, J.C.L.

[I] MISCELLANEOUS LISTINGS

SIOUX FALLS. *Avera Health*, 3900 W. Avera Dr., 57108-5721. Tel: 605-322-4700; Fax: 605-322-4799. Email: contactus@avera.org. Web: www.avera.org. Sponsored by the Sisters of the Presentation of the B.V.M., Aberdeen, SD, and the Benedictine Sisters of Sacred Heart Monastery, Yankton, SD.

The Berakhah House, 523 N. Duluth, 57104. Tel: 605-334-9861; Fax: 605-334-2092.

The Catholic Foundation for Eastern South Dakota, 523 N. Duluth Ave., 57104. Tel: 605-988-3788; Fax: 605-988-3746. Email: mconzemi@sfcatholic.org. Web: www.sfcatholic.org. Mark Conzemius, Pres.

City of Sioux Falls Catholic Schools Property Corporation, 523 N. Duluth Ave., 57104. Tel: 605-988-3759; Fax: 604-334-2092. Email: mbannwar@sfcatholic.org. Web: www.sfcatholic.org.

Community Outreach, 231 N. Weber Ave., 57103. Tel: 605-331-3935; Fax: 605-336-8924. Email: info@thecommunityoutreach.org. Angela Hyde, Dir. Total Staff 5; Total Families Assisted Annually 3,350.

St. Francis House, 1301 E. Austin St., 57103. Tel: 605-334-3879; Fax: 605-575-3999. Email: director@stfrancishouse.com. Julie Becker, Exec. Dir. Bed Capacity 39.

Good Shepherd Center, 300 N. Main Ave., 57104. Tel: 605-332-3176; Fax: 605-977-4807. Maria Krell, Dir. Total Staff 3; Total Assisted Annually 20,000.

Holy Spirit School Permanent Trust, 3601 E. Dudley Ln., 57103. Tel: 605-371-2320; Fax: 605-371-1957. Email: holyspiritsf@holyspiritsf.org. Rev. James P. Morgan, Trustee.

St. Joseph Catholic Housing, Inc., Catholic Chancery Office, 523 N. Duluth Ave., 57104. Tel: 605-334-9861; Fax: 605-988-3746. Email: mbannwar@SFCatholic.org.

Kateri Indian Center, 300 N. Main Ave., 57104. Tel: 605-335-3321; Fax: 605-977-4807. Total Staff 2; Total Assisted Annually 31,611.

Little Flower of Jesus School Foundation, Inc., 901 N. Tahoe Tr., 57110-5779. Tel: 605-338-2433; Fax: 605-339-2203.

St. Matthew Stewardship, Inc., 523 N. Duluth Ave., 57104. Tel: 605-988-3759; Fax: 605-988-3746. Email: mbannwar@sfcatholic.org. Web: www.sfcatholic.org.

Pension Plan for Priests of the Diocese of Sioux Falls, 523 N. Duluth Ave., 57104. Tel: 605-334-9861; Fax: 605-334-2092. Web: www.sfcatholic.org.

Sioux Falls Catholic School Foundation, 3100 W. 41st St., 57105. Tel: 605-575-3364; Fax: 605-988-0581. Email: mkaten@sfcss.org. Web: sfcss.org. Total Staff 2.

The South Dakota Catholic Broadcasting Corporation, 523 N. Duluth Ave., 57104.

ABERDEEN. *The Presentation Sisters Heritage Trust*, 1500 North Second, 57401. Tel: 605-229-8419; Fax: 605-229-8412. Email: pdonelan@presentationsisters.org. Web: www.presentationsisters.org. Sr. Pam Donelan, P.B.V.M., Contact Person. Sponsored by: Sisters of the Presentation of the Blessed Virgin Mary of Aberdeen, South Dakota.

**Roncalli Foundation*, 1400 N. Dakota St., 57401.

IRENE. *Broom Tree Retreat and Conference Center*, Mailing Address: 523 N. Duluth, 57104. 29827 446th St., 57039. Tel: 605-263-1040; Fax: 605-263-1043.

MARVIN. *Blue Cloud Abbey Retirement Trust*, P.O. Box 98, 57251-0098. Tel: 605-398-9200; Fax: 605-398-9201. Email: mcmullen@tnics.com. Rev. John McMullen, O.S.B., Treas.

Asociacion Benedictina de Coban Resurrection Priory Dependent on Blue Cloud Abbey., P.O. Box 98, 57251-0098. Tel: 605-398-9200; Fax: 605-398-9201. Rev. John McMullen, O.S.B., Treas.

MITCHELL. *Mitchell Foundation for Catholic Education*, 1510 W. Elm, 57301. Tel: 605-999-9127; Fax: 605-995-0378. Nicole Fuhrer, Dir. Devel.

SISSETON. *Tekakwitha Housing Corp.*, Mailing Address: 711 Veteran's Ave., 57262. Tel: 605-698-7693; Fax: 605-698-3091.

Tekakwitha Indian Mission, Inc., 120 E. Chestnut, 57262. Tel: 605-698-7414; Fax: 605-698-7236.

WATERTOWN. *St. Ann's Corporation*, 100 28th Ave. S.E., 57201. Tel: 605-886-9177; Fax: 605-882-3193. Mary Beth Grape, Admin.

Benet Place (Independent Senior Apartments), 100 28th Ave., S.E., 57201. Tel: 605-886-9177; Fax: 605-882-3193. Units 36; Staff 13.

Benet Place Assisted Living, 90 28th Ave., S.E., 57201. Tel: 605-882-8555; Fax: 605-882-8556. Units 16; Staff 8.

The Benedictine Sisters Foundation of Watertown, 110 28th Ave., S.E., #8, 57201. Tel: 605-882-6633; Fax: 605-882-6658. Email: prioress@dailypost.com. Web: watertownbenedictines.org.

Holy Name Foundation, Inc., 1009 Skyline Dr., 57201. Tel: 605-886-2628; Fax: 605-886-2142.

Immaculate Conception School Foundation, Inc., 309 2nd Ave., S.E., 57201. Tel: 605-886-3883; Fax: 605-886-0199.

Retirement Trust, Mother of God Monastery, 110 28th Ave., S.E., 57201. Tel: 605-882-6633; Fax: 605-882-6658. Email: prioress@dailypost.com. Web: watertownbenedictines.org.

YANKTON. *Benedictine Center, Inc.*, 1005 W. 8th, 57078. Tel: 605-668-6000; Fax: 605-668-6153.

Benedictine Health Foundation, Inc., 1000 W. 4th, Ste. 14, 57078. Tel: 605-668-8310; Fax: 605-665-0170. Email: BHF@SHHServices.com. Kelly Kathol, Exec. Dir.

The House of Mary Shrine, Inc., Lewis & Clark Lake, Box 455, 57078-0455. Tel: 605-668-0121. Jean Weller, Pres. Bd. of Directors.

Yankton Catholic Community Development Office, 509 Capital St., 57078. Tel: 605-665-4585; Fax: 605-665-4585. Email: yccdo@yanktoncatholic.org.

RELIGIOUS INSTITUTES OF MEN REPRESENTED IN THE DIOCESE

For further details refer to the corresponding bracketed number in the Religious Institutes of Men or Women section.

[]—*Apostles of Jesus* (Sudan)

[0200]—*Benedictine Monks* (Aurora, IL; Marvin, SD)—O.S.B.

[]—*Carmelite* (India)

[1130]—*Congregation of the Priests of the Sacred Heart* (Hales Corners, WI)—S.C.J.

[0910]—*Oblates of Mary Immaculate* (Central Prov.)—O.M.I.

[0560]—*Third Order Regular of Saint Francis* (Loretto, PA)—T.O.R.

[1335]—*Vincentian Congregation* (India)—V.C.

RELIGIOUS INSTITUTES OF WOMEN REPRESENTED IN THE DIOCESE

[0230]—*Benedictine Sisters of Pontifical Jurisdiction* (Yankton, Watertown, SD)—O.S.B.

[0940]—*Daughters of St. Mary of Providence*—D.S.M.P.

[0420]—*Discalced Carmelite Nuns of the Monastery of Our Mother of Mercy* (Alexandria, SD)—O.C.D.

[3010]—*Oblate Sisters of the Blessed Sacrament*—O.S.B.S.

[3130]—*Our Lady of Victory Missionary Sisters*—O.L.V.M.

[]—*Perpetual Adoration Sisters of the Blessed Sacrament*—A.P.

[2970]—*School Sisters of Notre Dame* (Mankato Prov.)—S.S.N.D.

[2630]—*Sisters of Mercy of the Holy Cross*—S.C.S.C.

[3000]—*Sisters of Notre Dame de Namur*—S.N.D.deN.

[1030]—*Sisters of the Divine Savior*—S.D.S.

[3320]—*Sisters of the Presentation of the B.V.M.*—P.B.V.M.

[1720]—*Sisters of the Third Order Regular of St. Francis of the Congregation of Our Lady of Lourdes*—O.S.F.

INTER-PAROCHIAL CEMETERIES

SIOUX FALLS. *St. Michael*, 3001 N. Cliff, 57104. Tel: 605-338-3376; Fax: 605-338-4270.

NECROLOGY

† Connolly, Thomas, (Retired)—Died Feb. 25, 2011

† Ortmeier, Richard J., (Retired)—Died June 26, 2011

An asterisk (*) denotes an organization that has established tax-exempt status directly with the IRS and is not covered by the USCCB Group Ruling.

Diocese of Spokane

(Dioecesis Spokanensis)

Most Reverend

BLASE J. CUPICH

Bishop of Spokane; ordained August 16, 1975; appointed Bishop of Rapid City July 7, 1998; ordained and installed September 21, 1998; appointed Bishop of Spokane June 30, 2010; installed September 3, 2010. *Office: W. 1023 Riverside Ave., P.O. Box 1453, Spokane, WA 99210-1453.*

Most Reverend

WILLIAM S. SKYLSTAD, D.D.

Bishop Emeritus of Spokane and Apostolic Administrator of Baker; ordained May 21, 1960; appointed Bishop of Yakima February 22, 1977; consecrated and installed May 12, 1977; Transferred to Spokane April 17, 1990; succeeded to the See April 27, 1990; retired June 30, 2010; appointed Apostolic Administrator of Baker January 24, 2011.

Catholic Pastoral Center: W. 1023 Riverside Ave., P.O. Box 1453, Spokane, WA 99210-1453. Tel: 509-358-7300.

Web: www.dioceseofspokane.org

Email: chancellor@dioceseofspokane.org

ESTABLISHED DECEMBER 17, 1913.

Square Miles 24,356.

Solemnly consecrated to the Immaculate Heart of Mary on December 8, 1948.

Corporate Title: "The Catholic Bishop of Spokane, a Corporation Sole."

Comprises the following Counties in the State of Washington: Okanogan, Ferry, Stevens, Pend Oreille, Lincoln, Spokane, Adams, Whitman, Franklin, Walla Walla, Columbia, Garfield and Asotin.

For legal titles of parishes and diocesan institutions, consult the Catholic Pastoral Center.

STATISTICAL OVERVIEW

Personnel	
Bishop	1
Retired Bishops	1
Retired Abbots	1
Priests: Diocesan Active in Diocese	51
Priests: Diocesan Active Outside Diocese	5
Priests: Diocesan in Foreign Missions	1
Priests: Retired, Sick or Absent	24
Number of Diocesan Priests	81
Religious Priests in Diocese	72
Total Priests in Diocese	153
Extern Priests in Diocese	3
Ordinations:	
Diocesan Priests	4
Permanent Deacons in Diocese	48
Total Brothers	7
Total Sisters	156
Parishes	
Parishes	58
With Resident Pastor:	
Resident Diocesan Priests	39
Resident Religious Priests	3
Without Resident Pastor:	
Administered by Priests	16
Missions	21
Professional Ministry Personnel:	
Sisters	1
Lay Ministers	32
Welfare	
Catholic Hospitals	6
Total Assisted	373,143
Homes for the Aged	2
Total Assisted	703
Residential Care of Children	1
Total Assisted	31
Day Care Centers	1
Total Assisted	182
Specialized Homes	3
Total Assisted	1,027
Special Centers for Social Services	17
Total Assisted	222,244
Residential Care of Disabled	2
Total Assisted	24
Other Institutions	13
Total Assisted	2,282
Educational	
Seminaries, Diocesan	1
Students from This Diocese	5
Students from Other Diocese	8
Diocesan Students in Other Seminaries	8
Total Seminarians	13
Colleges and Universities	1
Total Students	7,701
High Schools, Diocesan and Parish	1
Total Students	114
High Schools, Private	2
Total Students	1,070
Elementary Schools, Diocesan and Parish	14
Total Students	3,343
Catechesis/Religious Education:	
High School Students	763
Elementary Students	2,846
Total Students under Catholic Instruction	15,850
Teachers in the Diocese:	
Lay Teachers	225
Vital Statistics	
Receptions into the Church:	
Infant Baptism Totals	1,391
Minor Baptism Totals	135
Adult Baptism Totals	94
Received into Full Communion	147
First Communions	1,783
Confirmations	1,850
Marriages:	
Catholic	201
Interfaith	110
Total Marriages	311
Deaths	577
Total Catholic Population	106,003
Total Population	815,409

Former Bishops—Most Revs. A. F. SCHINNER, D.D., cons. Bishop of Superior, July 25, 1905; resigned from that See, Jan. 15, 1913; appt. first Bishop of Spokane, March 18, 1914; resigned Dec. 17, 1925, and made Titular Bishop of Sala; died Feb. 7, 1937; CHARLES D. WHITE, D.D., ord. Sept. 24, 1910; appt. Dec. 20, 1926; cons. Feb. 24, 1927; died Sept. 25, 1955; BERNARD J. TOPEL, D.D., Ph.D., appt. Coadjutor Bishop Aug. 9, 1955; cons. Sept. 21, 1955; succeeded to the See Sept. 25, 1955; retired April 11, 1978; died Oct. 22, 1986; LAWRENCE H. WELSH, D.D., ord. May 26, 1962; appt. Bishop of Spokane Nov. 7, 1978; cons. and installed Dec. 14, 1978; resigned April 17, 1990; appt. Auxiliary of St. Paul-Minneapolis, Nov. 5, 1991; died Jan. 13, 1999; WILLIAM S. SKYLSTAD, D.D., ord. May 21, 1960; appt. Bishop of Yakima February 22, 1977; cons. and installed May 12, 1977; transferred to Spokane April 17, 1990; succeeded to the See April 27, 1990; retired June 30, 2010.

Vicar General—Rev. STEVE DUBLINSKI, Mailing Address: P.O. Box 1453, Spokane, 99210-1453. Tel: 509-358-7303. Email: sdublinski@dioceseofspokane.org.

Catholic Pastoral Center—*W. 1023 Riverside Ave., P.O. Box 1453, Spokane, 99210-1453.* Tel: 509-358-7300; Fax: 509-358-7302. Email: chancellor@dioceseofspokane.org. Office Hours: Mon.-Fri. 8:30-4.

Moderator of the Curia—Rev. MICHAEL SAVELESKY, Ph.D., Mailing Address: P.O. Box 1453, Spokane, 99210-1453. Tel: 509-358-7303. Email: msavelesky@dioceseofspokane.org.

Chancellor—Rev. MARK PAUTLER, J.C.L., Mailing Address: P.O. Box 1453, Spokane, 99210-1453. Tel: 509-358-7339. Email: mpautler@dioceseofspokane.org.

Archivist—Dr. ANTHONY CLARK, Ph.D.; Rev. THOMAS C. CASWELL (Retired), Mailing Address: P.O. Box 1453, Spokane, 99210-1453. Tel: 509-358-7349. Email: aclark@dioceseofspokane.org. Tues. 9-12.

Diocesan Tribunal—*W. 1023 Riverside Ave., P.O. Box 1453, Spokane, 99210-1453.* Tel: 509-358-7336; Fax: 509-693-3313. Email: tribunal@dioceseofspokane.org.

Judicial Vicar—Rev. MARK PAUTLER, J.C.L.

Defenders of the Bond—Rev. Msgr. JOHN M. STEINER; Rev. JOSE LUIS MILLAN; Rev. Msgr. WILLIAM VAN OMMEREN (Retired).

Secretary—KRISTINA SICILIA.

Diocesan Presbyteral Council—Members: Revs. JOSEPH BELL; MICHAEL BLACKBURN, O.F.M.; RICHARD CASE, S.J.; THOMAS C. CASWELL (Retired); STEVE DUBLINSKI, (Ex Officio); AL GRASHER; TIMOTHY HAYS, Consultor; PATRICK KERST, Consultor; Rt. Rev. ADRIAN PARCHER, O.S.B.; Rev. MATTHEW LARSEN, Consultor; Rev. Msgr. PEDRO RAMIREZ, Consultor (Retired); Revs. MICHAEL J. SAVELESKY, Consultor; TYRONE J. SCHAFF; LUCAS E. TOMSON; ROBERT D. TURNER; STEVEN WERNER, Consultor.

Diocesan Pastoral Council—Most Rev. BLASE J. CUPICH; Rev. STEVE DUBLINSKI, Ex Officio; Mrs. MARY LOU BENTLEY; Sr. JANYCE BOUTA, S.N.J.M.; Mr. LEO LAPKE; BETTY HEENEY; JACK HEENEY; Mr. DON KELLY; PAULA BACON; MARY DRUFFEL; DAVE KISHEL; DOREEN KISHEL; JOYCE MAYER; DENNY PENNA; LUCY STANZYK; JANICE STRIPES.

Diocesan Offices and Directors

Diocesan Business Affairs—Rev. MICHAEL SAVELESKY,

Ph.D., Mailing Address: P.O. Box 1453, Spokane, 99210-1453. Email: msavelesky@dioceseofspokane.org; 1023 W. Riverside Ave., Spokane, 99201. Tel: 509-358-7333; Fax: 509-358-7302.

Fiscal Services Office—MERRILIN FULTON, Mailing Address: P.O. Box 1453, Spokane, 99210-1453. Tel: 509-358-7320. Email: mfulton@dioceseofspokane.org.

Development Office—Mr. CHRIS SMITH, Mailing Address: P.O. Box 1453, Spokane, 99210-1453. Tel: 509-358-4280. Email: csmith@dioceseofspokane.org.

Computer Department—MARY GREEN, Mailing Address: P.O. Box 1453, Spokane, 99210-1453. Tel: 509-358-7346. Email: mgreen@dioceseofspokane.org.

Catholic Schools—Dr. DUANE SCHAFER, Ph.D., Supt., Mailing Address: Office of Education, P.O. Box 1453, Spokane, 99210-1453. Tel: 509-358-7330. Email: dschafer@dioceseofspokane.org.

Faith Formation—Mailing Address: Moderator of the Curia, P.O. Box 1453, Spokane, 99210. Tel: 509-358-7333. Email: msavelesky@dioceseofspokane.org.

Communications Office—Deacon ERIC MEISFJORD, Dir. & Editor, Mailing Address: P.O. Box 1453, Spokane, 99210-1453. Tel: 509-358-7340. Email: emeisfjord@dioceseofspokane.org; NANCY LOBERG, Advertising Mgr. Tel: 509-358-7343. Email: nloberg@dioceseofspokane.org.

Charismatic Renewal—Rev. DANIEL WETZLER (Retired), 1541 E. Cromwell Dr., Coeur d'Alene, ID 83815. Tel: 509-990-6000. Email: dwetzler@dioceseofspokane.org.

Ecumenical Relations—Rev. PATRICK HARTIN, 429 E. Sharp, Spokane, 99202. Tel: 509-313-7102. Email: phartin@dioceseofspokane.org.

Spanish Speaking Apostolates—VACANT.

Vietnamese Apostolate— Vietnamese Catholic Community of the Diocese of Spokane, Rev. JOACHIM L. HIEN, St. Anthony's Parish, 2320 N. Cedar, Spokane, 99205. Tel: 509-327-1162; Fax: 509-328-8728. Email: johien@dioceseofspokane.org.

Vocation Director—Rev. DARRIN CONNALL, 429 E. Sharp Ave., Spokane, 99202-1837. Tel: 509-326-3761. Email: bws@gonzaga.edu.

Diocesan Liturgical Commission—Rev. STEVE DUBLINSKI, Mailing Address: P.O. Box 1453, Spokane, 99210-1453. Tel: 509-358-7303. Email: sdublinski@dioceseofspokane.org.

Director of Deacon Formation—Rev. MICHAEL J. SAVELESKY, Mailing Address: P.O. Box 1453, Spokane, 99210-1453. Tel: 509-358-7333. Email: msavelesky@dioceseofspokane.org.

Director of Deacons—Deacon JOHN SICILIA, Mailing Address: St. Charles Parish, P.O. Box 1453, Spokane, 99210-1453. Tel: 509-327-9573. Email: jsicilia@dioceseofspokane.org.

Deacon Council—Deacon DOUG BANKS, Mailing Address: P.O. Box 1453, Spokane, 99210-1453. Tel: 509-468-3811, Ext. 315.

Catholic Committee on Scouting—Deacon STEVE PRAWDZIK, Chap., 11828 S. Player Dr., Spokane, 99223-9524. Tel: 509-448-8934.

Bishop White Seminary—Rev. STEVEN L. DUBLINSKI, V.G., Rector & Dir. Seminarians, 429 E. Sharp Ave., Spokane, 99202. Tel: 509-326-3255. Web: bishopwhiteseminary.org.

Social Ministries/Catholic Charities Diocesan Director—ROB MCCANN, Exec. Dir. Catholic Charities, Mailing Address: P.O. Box 2253, Spokane, 99210. Tel: 509-358-4250. Email: rmccann@ccspokane.org.

Censor Liborum—Rev. MICHAEL J. SAVELESKY, Assumption of the Blessed Virgin Parish, 3624 W. Indian Trail Rd., Spokane, 99208-4794. Tel: 509-358-7333. Email: msavelesky@dioceseofspokane.org; Mailing Address: P.O. Box 1453, Spokane, 99210-1453.

Continuing Education of Priests—Rev. PATRICK KERST, St. Patrick Parish, 408 W. Poplar, Walla Walla, 99362. Tel: 509-525-1602. Email: pkerst@dioceseofspokane.org.

Detention Ministry—Rev. MIGUEL MEJIA, Coord., Mailing Address: P.O. Box 1453, Spokane, 99210-1453. Tel: 509-358-7315. Email: mmejia@dioceseofspokane.org.

Director of Cemeteries—JAMES G. FALKNER, Mailing Address: P.O. Box 18006, Spokane, 99228-0006. Tel: 509-467-5496. Email: info@cathcem.org. Web: www.cathcem.org.

Immaculate Heart Retreat Center—Deacon JOHN RUSCHEINSKY, Dir., 6910 S. Ben Burr Rd., Spokane, 99223. Tel: 509-448-1224. Web: www.ihrc.net. Email: ihrc@ihrc.net.

Society for the Propagation of the Faith—Mr. CHRIS SMITH, W. 1023 Riverside Ave., P.O. Box 1453, Spokane, 99210. Tel: 509-358-4280. Email: csmith@dioceseofspokane.org.

Victims Assistance Coordinator—ROBERTA SMITH, Mailing Address: P.O. Box 1453, Spokane, 99210-1453. Tel: 509-353-0442. Email: rsmith@dioceseofspokane.org.

CLERGY, PARISHES, MISSIONS AND PAROCHIAL SCHOOLS

CITY OF SPOKANE

(SPOKANE COUNTY)

1—CATHEDRAL OF OUR LADY OF LOURDES (1881) Revs. Darrin Connall; Jeffrey Lewis, Parochial Vicar. In Res., Rev. Jose Luis Hernandez.
Res.: 1115 W. Riverside Ave., 99201. Tel: 509-358-4290; Fax: 509-358-4277. Web: www.spokanecathedral.com.
Catechesis/Religious Program—Tel: 509-358-4293.

2—ST. ALOYSIUS (1890) Rev. Richard Case, S.J.; Mr. Donald Weber, Parish Admin.
Res.: 330 E. Boone Ave., 99202. Tel: 509-313-5896; Fax: 509-313-5892. Email: stals@gonzaga.edu. Web: stalschurch.org.
School—(Grades PreK-8), 611 E. Mission Ave., 99202. Tel: 509-489-7825; Fax: 509-487-0975. Kerrie Rowland, Prin.
Montessori Education Center—Tel: 509-489-7825. Marta Schollenberger, Dir. Lay Teachers 16; Students 284.
Catechesis/Religious Program—Sr. Marianne Therese Wilkinson, S.N.J.M., D.R.E. Students 70.

3—ST. ANN (1902) Rev. Patrick Baraza; Craig Bartmess, Parish Admin.
Mailing Address: 2120 E. First Ave., 99202.
Church: 2116 E. First Ave., 99202. Tel: 509-535-3031. Email: info@stannsspokane.org.

4—ST. ANTHONY (1909) Rev. Joachim L. Hien.
Res.: 2320 N. Cedar St., 99205. Tel: 509-327-1162; Fax: 509-328-8728.
See Trinity School, Spokane under Interparochial Grade Schools located in the Institution section.
Educare Center— Lay Teachers 4; Students 43.
Catechesis/Religious Program—Mary Scripture-Smith, D.R.E.; Allen Peterson, D.R.E. Students 7.

5—ASSUMPTION OF THE BLESSED VIRGIN MARY (1958) Revs. Michael J. Savelesky; Sean Raftis, Parochial Vicar; Deacon Kelly Stewart.
Office: 3624 W. Indian Trail Rd., 99208. Tel: 509-326-0144; Fax: 509-326-0538.
School—(Grades PreK-8), 3618 W. Indian Trail Rd., 99208. Tel: 509-328-1115; Fax: 509-328-7872. Carmen Himenes, Prin.; Valerie Sonderen, Librarian. Lay Teachers 12; Students 162.
Catechesis/Religious Program—Emily Klein, D.R.E. Students 64.

6—ST. AUGUSTINE (1914) Rev. Robert J. McNeese; Deacons Scott Brockway; Ken Dunlap.
Res.: 428 W. 19th Ave., 99203. Tel: 509-747-4421. Email: staugustine@dioceseofspokane.org. Web: staugustinespokane.catholicweb.com.
School—Cataldo Catholic Interparochial, (Grades PreK-8), 455 W 18th Ave., 99203. Tel: 509-624-8759; Fax: 509-624-8763. Web: www.cataloo.org. Stephanie Johnson, Prin. Lay Teachers 23; Students 338.
Catechesis/Religious Program—Tel: 509-747-7972. Susan C. Harmon, D.R.E.; Jeanette Benson, Youth Min. Students 130.

7—ST. CHARLES (1950) Rev. Thomas Connolly; Deacon John F. Sicilia.
Res.: 4515 N. Alberta St., 99205. Tel: 509-327-9573; Fax: 509-325-9353.
School—(Grades PreK-8) Tel: 509-327-9575; Fax: 509-325-9353. George Bonuccelli, Prin. Religious 3; Lay Teachers 13; Students 225.
Catechesis/Religious Program—Students 19.

8—ST. FRANCIS OF ASSISI (1915) Revs. Michael Blackburn, O.F.M.; Alberic Smith, O.F.M.
Res.: 1104 W. Heroy Ave., 99205. Tel: 509-325-1321; Fax: 509-325-0927.
Catechesis/Religious Program—Tammie Fabien, D.R.E. Students 35.

9—ST. FRANCIS XAVIER (1906) Rev. Eugene Tracy; Deacon Gary Veale.
Mailing Address: 5021 N. Nelson St., 99217-6161.
Office:—545 E. Providence, 99207-1899. Tel: 509-487-1325.

10—ST. JOHN VIANNEY (1949) Revs. Joseph Bell; Charles Skok (Retired).
Mailing Address: P.O. Box 141125, Spokane Valley, 99214-1125.
Office: 503 N. Walnut Rd., 99206. Tel: 509-926-5428; Fax: 509-922-5282. Email: admin@sjvchurch.org. Web: www.sjvchurch.org.
School—(Grades PreK-8), 501 N. Walnut Rd., 99206. Tel: 509-926-7987; Fax: 509-891-9030. Web: st.johnvianney.com. Sonia Flores-Davis, Prin. Lay Teachers 11; Students 231.
Catechesis/Religious Program—Tel: 509-926-5553. Rita Crosby, D.R.E. Students 49.

11—ST. JOSEPH (1890) Rev. Jose Luis Hernandez; Sr. Irene Knopes, S.N.J.M., Parish Admin.
Res.: 1503 W. Dean Ave., 99201. Tel: 509-328-4841; Fax: 509-328-4841.
See Trinity School, Spokane under Interparochial Grade Schools located in the Institution section.
Catechesis/Religious Program—Gail Wallace, D.R.E. Students 30.

12—ST. MARY (1913) Revs. Victor M. Blazovich; Matthew Larsen; Deacon Mike Miller.
Res.: 304 S. Adams Rd., Spokane Valley, 99216. Tel: 509-928-3210; Fax: 509-928-3215. Web: stmaryspokane.org.
School—(Grades PreK-8), 14601 E. 4th Ave., 99216. Tel: 509-924-4300. Laurie Nauditt, Prin. Lay Teachers 14; Students 262.
Catechesis/Religious Program—Tel: 509-926-9559; Fax: 509-926-9550. Cecilia Conklin, Coord. Students 120.

13—MARY QUEEN (1957) Rev. Paul Vevik; Deacon Donald Whitney.
Res.: 3423 E. Carlisle Ave., 99217-7208. Tel: 509-483-4384; Fax: 509-483-0127.

14—OUR LADY OF FATIMA (1956) Rev. Tyrone J. Schaff; Deacon John Byrne.
Office:—1517 E. 33rd Ave., 99203. Tel: 509-747-7213; Fax: 509-747-7217. Web: fatimaspokane.com.
School—All Saints Catholic School, (Grades 5-8) Tel: 509-624-5712; Fax: 509-624-7752. Ms. Kathy Hicks, Prin.; Paul Coffey, Librarian. Lay Teachers 12; Students 204.
Catechesis/Religious Program—Joan Leeds, D.R.E. Students 22.

15—OUR LADY OF THE LAKE (2002) Rev. Timothy R. Clancy, S.J.; Deacons George Lukach; Jack Crandall.
Mailing Address: P.O. Box 447, Nine Mile Falls, 99026. Tel: 509-276-7532. Web: maroni.com/olotl.
Catechesis/Religious Program—Lucille Simmons, D.R.E. Students 16.

16—ST. PASCHAL (1916) Rev. W. Roy Floch.
Mailing Address: P.O. Box 11128, 99211-1128. Tel: 509-924-5090. Web: stpaschal.net.
Educare Center—Tel: 509-922-7616. Mrs. Mary Jo Paschall, Dir. Lay Teachers 2; Students 90.
Catechesis/Religious Program—Students 7.

17—ST. PATRICK (1893) Rev. Kenneth T. St. Hilaire.
Res.: 5021 N. Nelson St., 99217-6161. Tel: 509-487-1325; Fax: 509-368-7323.
School—(Grades PreK-8) Tel: 509-487-2830; Fax: 509-487-3101. Julie Simmons, Prin. Lay Teachers 6; Students 95.
Catechesis/Religious Program—Barry Schoedel, Children's Formation Dir. Students 41.
Convent—5008 N. Lacey St., 99217.

18—ST. PETER (1956) Revs. Michael (Brian) Mee, O.S.B.; George Haspedis (Retired).
Res. & Mailing Address: 3520 E. 18th Ave., 99223-3814. Tel: 509-534-2227; Fax: 509-534-2227. Email: stpeterspokane@yahoo.com.
School—All Saints Interparochial, (Grades PreK-4), 3510 E. 18th Ave., 99223. Tel: 509-534-1098; Fax: 509-534-1529. Web: allsaintsspokane.org. Ms. Kathy Hicks, Prin. Lay Teachers 22; Students 245.
Catechesis/Religious Program—Frank Ciccarello, D.R.E.; Katherine Dumais, Dir. Youth Ministry. Students 80.

19—SACRED HEART (1911) Rev. Mark Pautler; Ron Eberley, Pastoral Min.
Res.: 219 E. Rockwood Blvd., 99202. Tel: 509-747-5810; Fax: 509-747-5033. Email: shparish@qwestoffice.net. Web: home.catholicweb.com/sacredheartparishspokane.
Catechesis/Religious Program—Janet Maucione, D.R.E.; Jeanette Benson, Youth Min. Students 31.

20—ST. THOMAS MORE (1957) Rev. Msgr. Pedro Ramirez-Alejos; Rev. Jason Hiner, Parochial Vicar.
Res.: 505 W. St. Thomas More Way, 99208. Tel: 509-466-0220; Fax: 509-466-0220. Web: thomasmorespokane.org.
School—(Grades PreSchool-8), 515 W. St. Thomas Way, 99208. Tel: 509-466-3811 (Option 2). Deacon Doug Banks, Prin.; Shelley Budig, Librarian. Lay Teachers 11; Students 267; Educare Enrollment 110.
Catechesis/Religious Program—Kate Bradley, D.R.E. Students 95.

OUTSIDE THE CITY OF SPOKANE

BREWSTER, OKANOGAN CO., SACRED HEART (1958) Rev. Matthew Nicks.
Res.: P.O. Box 548, 98812. Tel: 509-689-2931. Email: shbrewster@dioceseofspokane.org.
Catechesis/Religious Program—Students 50.

CHENEY, SPOKANE CO., ST. ROSE OF LIMA (1881) Rev. Miguel Mejia; Deacon Gonzalo "Chalo" Martinez.
Res.: 460 N. Fifth St., 99004. Tel: 509-235-6229.

Web: home.catholicweb.com/stroseoflima.
Catechesis/Religious Program—Tel: 509-235-9330; Fax: 509-559-5188. Sr. Sharon Bongiorno, F.S.P.A., Coord. Students 13.

CHEWELAH, STEVENS CO., ST. MARY OF THE ROSARY (1885) [CEM] Rev. Vincent Van Dao Nguyen.
Res.: 3081 5th Ave., Valley, 99181. Tel: 509-937-2452. Web: smr.catholicweb.com.
Church: 502 E. Main St., P.O. Box 26, 99109. Tel: 509-935-8028.
Catechesis/Religious Program—Tel: 509-935-6367. Students 30.

CLARKSTON, ASOTIN CO., HOLY FAMILY (1914) [CEM] Rev. Richard Root.
Res.: 1344 Highland Ave., 99403. Tel: 509-758-6102. Email: holyfamily@qwestoffice.net.
Church: 917 Chestnut St., 99403.
School—(Grades K-6) Tel: 509-758-6621; Fax: 509-758-7025. Mrs. Maribeth Richardson, Prin. Lay Teachers 7; Students 96.
Educare Preschool—Tel: 509-758-2737. Students 26.
Catechesis/Religious Program—Students 47.

CLAYTON, STEVENS CO., ST. JOSEPH, Closed. For inquiries for parish records contact the chancery.

COLBERT, SPOKANE CO., ST. JOSEPH (1910) Rev. Timothy Hays; Deacon Joe Schroeder.
Rectory—4305 E. Park Lane Rd., Mead, 99021.
Office: 3720 E. Colbert Rd., 99005. Tel: 509-466-4991; Fax: 509-466-4992. Email: stjoseph@cet.com. Web: stjosephcolbert.org.
Catechesis/Religious Program—Sr. Kathleen Reynolds, C.C.V.I., D.R.E. Students 156.

COLFAX, WHITMAN CO., ST. PATRICK (1878) Rt. Rev. Adrian Parcher, O.S.B.
Res.: 1018 S. Main St., 99111. Tel: 509-397-3921.
Catechesis/Religious Program—Linda Marler, D.R.E. Students 57.

COLTON, WHITMAN CO., ST. GALL (1893) [CEM] Rev. Joseph Sullivan.
Res.: P.O. Box 108, 99113. Tel: 509-229-3548.
School—Guardian Angel-St. Boniface Interparochial, (Grades K-8) Tel: 509-299-3579. Lori Becker, Prin. Lay Teachers 3; Students 20.
See Guardian Angel-St. Boniface School, Colton under Interparochial Grade Schools located in the Institution section.
Catechesis/Religious Program—Pat Doumit, D.R.E. Students 20.

COLVILLE, STEVENS CO., IMMACULATE CONCEPTION (1861) Revs. Steven Werner; Kevin Oiland, Parochial Vicar.
Res.: 320 N. Maple St., 99114. Tel: 509-684-6223; Fax: 509-684-8084.
Catechesis/Religious Program—Dolores Cline, D.R.E. Students 53.

CONNELL, FRANKLIN CO., ST. VINCENT (1964) Rev. Pedro Bautista-Peráza.
Res.: P.O. Box 1030, 99326. Tel: 509-234-2262; Fax: 509-234-2262.
Catechesis/Religious Program—Maria Pena, D.R.E. Students 187.

COULEE DAM, OKANOGAN CO., ST. BENEDICT, Closed. For sacramental records, contact St. Henry's, Grand Coulee (Diocese of Yakima).

CURLEW, FERRY CO., ST. PATRICK (1907) Unassigned.
Res.: 756 S. Portland St., P.O. Box 333, Republic, 99166. Tel: 509-775-3935.

CUSICK, KALISPEL INDIAN RESERVATION, OUR LADY OF SORROWS Rev. Edward Marier.
Res.: 612 W. First St., Box C, Newport, 99156. Tel: 509-447-4231.

DAVENPORT, LINCOLN CO., IMMACULATE CONCEPTION (1893) [CEM] Rev. Patrick MacMahon.
Res.: 1310 Adams, 99122. Tel: 509-725-1761.

DAYTON, COLUMBIA CO., ST. JOSEPH (1890) Rev. Robert D. Turner.
112 S. First St., 99328-0003.
Church: P.O. Box 3, 99328-1307. Tel: 509-382-2311. Web: rc.net/spokane/stjoseph.
Catechesis/Religious Program—Jeannie Lyonnais, D.R.E. Students 12.

DEER PARK, SPOKANE CO., ST. MARY PRESENTATION (1912) [CEM] Rev. Al Grasher; Deacon Richard Skok.
Res.: 602 E. 6th St., P.O. Box 749, 99006. Tel: 509-276-2948. Web: stmarypresentation.org.
Catechesis/Religious Program—Cathy Chase, D.R.E. Students 31.

ELTOPIA, FRANKLIN CO., ST. PAUL (1964) Rev. Pedro Bautista-Peráza.
Res.: 14181 Glade North Rd., 99330. Tel: 509-297-4371. Email: stpaultheapostle@dioceseofspokane.org.
Catechesis/Religious Program—Sharaon Gamache, D.R.E.; Angie Manteroia, D.R.E.; Cheryl Knight, D.R.E. Students 65.
Mission—San Juan Diego Rd. 170 #7200, Basin City, 99343. Tel: 509-234-2262.

FORD, STEVENS CO., ST. PHILIP BENIZI (1912) Rev. Mark Hoelsken, S.J.
Indian-Spokane Reservation—P.O. Box 214, Wellpinit, 99040. Tel: 509-258-7233.

HARRINGTON, LINCOLN CO., ST. FRANCIS OF ASSISI (1906) Rev. Patrick MacMahon.
Res.: P.O. Box 166, 99134. Tel: 509-253-4310.

INCHELIUM, FERRY CO., ST. MICHAEL'S MISSION Revs. Jake Morton, S.J.; Robert J. Jones, S.J.; Joseph Schmert, Admin.; Deacon Alvin Toulou, (Retired).
Res.: P.O. Box 122, 99138. Tel: 509-722-4592. Web: stmichaelsmission.org.

IONE, PEND OREILLE CO., ST. BERNARD Revs. Steven Werner; Kevin Oiland, Parochial Vicar.
Mailing Address: Box 731, 99139. Tel: 509-447-4231.
Res.: 444 E. 4th, Colville, 99114. Tel: 509-446-2651.

KELLER, FERRY CO., ST. ROSE OF LIMA Rev. Jake Morton, S.J.
Res.: P.O. Box 70, Nespelem, 99155. 323 Edmonds, Omak, 98841-6401.

KETTLE FALLS, STEVENS CO., SACRED HEART OF JESUS (1906) Revs. Steven Werner; Kevin Oiland, Parochial Vicar.
Mailing Address: 320 N. Maple St., Colville, 99114. Tel: 509-684-6223; Fax: 509-684-8084.

LACROSSE, WHITMAN CO., ST. JOSEPH (1906) Rt. Rev. Adrian Parcher, O.S.B.
St. Patrick Parish: 1018 S. Main St., Colfax, 99111. Tel: 509-397-3921.
Catechesis/Religious Program—Students 6.

LIND, ADAMS CO., ST. AMBROSE (1920) Rev. Msgr. John Steiner, Admin. (Retired); Rev. Daniel Wetzler (Retired).
Mailing Address: 404 E. Fifth Ave., Ritzville, 99169. Tel: 509-659-0437.

MEDICAL LAKE, SPOKANE CO., ST. ANNE (1889) Rev. John P. Krier (GF).
Res.: 708 E. Lake St., P.O. Box 125, 99022. Tel: 509-123-1459; Fax: 509-351-3217. Email: stanne99022@hotmail.com; stannes@hotmail.com; jpbarkly@msn.com.

METALINE FALLS, PEND OREILLE CO., ST. JOSEPH (1950) Revs. Steven Werner; Kevin Oiland, Parochial Vicar.
Mailing Address: P.O. Box 417, 99153. Tel: 509-446-2651.
Res.: 320 N. Maple St., Colville, 99114. Tel: 509-684-6223. Email: icp@qwestoffice.net.
Catechesis/Religious Program—Erin Kinney, D.R.E. Students 15.

NESPELEM, OKANOGAN CO., SACRED HEART MISSION (1915) [CEM] Rev. Jake Morton, S.J.
Res.: 209 9th St., P.O. Box 70, 99155. Tel: 509-634-4249; Fax: 509-634-4249.
Catechesis/Religious Program—Nancy Armstrong-Montes, D.R.E. Students 25.

NEWPORT, PEND OREILLE CO., ST. ANTHONY (1908) Rev. Edward Marier.
Res.: 612 W. First St., P.O. Box C, 99156. Tel: 509-447-4231. Web: bojja.org.
Catechesis/Religious Program—John Westover, D.R.E.; Peggy Westover, D.R.E. Students 6.

NORTHPORT, STEVENS CO., PURE HEART OF MARY (1898) Revs. Steven Werner; Kevin Oiland, Parochial Vicar.
Mailing Address: 320 N. Maple St., Colville, 99114. 720 South St., P.O. Box 29, 99157.

OAKESDALE, WHITMAN CO., ST. CATHERINE OF ALEXANDRIA Rev. Jose Luis Hernandez.
Mailing Address: P.O. Box 8, Rosalia, 99170.
Res.: 1115 W. Riverside Ave., 99201. Tel: 509-358-4290.

ODESSA, LINCOLN CO., ST. JOSEPH (1905) Rev. Michael L. Ishida.
Res. & Mailing Address: P.O. Box 106, Wilbur, 99185. Tel: 509-647-2380.

OKANOGAN-OMAK, OKANOGAN CO., OUR LADY OF THE VALLEY (1976) Rev. Lucas E. Tomson.
Res.: 2511 Elmway, 98840. Tel: 509-422-5049.
Catechesis/Religious Program—Suzanne Craig, D.R.E. Students 50.

OMAK, OKANOGAN CO.
1—ST. JOSEPH (1945) Rev. Jake Morton, S.J.; Bro. Fred Mercy, S.J., Pastoral Assoc.
Res.: 323 Edmonds St., 98841-9661. Tel: 509-826-6401. Email: jemorton@hotmail.com.
2—ST. MARY MISSION, [CEM] Bro. Fred Mercy, S.J.
Res.: 25 Mission Rd., 98841. Tel: 509-826-6401.

OROVILLE, OKANOGAN CO., IMMACULATE CONCEPTION (1898) Rev. David Kuttner.
Mailing Address: P.O. Box 308, 98844.
Res.: 1715 Main St., P.O. Box 308, 98844. Tel: 509-476-2110; Fax: 509-476-2110. Web: rc.net/spokane/ichr.
Catechesis/Religious Program—Barbara Reed, D.R.E. Students 22.

OTHELLO, ADAMS CO., SACRED HEART (1956) Rev. Alejandro Zepeda; Deacons Antonio Beraza; Magdaleno Casillas; Joel Pruneda; Jesse Rodelo.
Res.: 616 E. Juniper St., 99344. Tel: 509-488-5653; Fax: 509-488-5654. Web: rc.net/spokane/sacredheart/sacredheart/welcome.
Catechesis/Religious Program—Anna Salmeron, D.R.E. Students 405.

OTIS ORCHARDS, SPOKANE CO., ST. JOSEPH (1892) Rev. Mike Kwiatkowski; Deacon Tom Heafey.
Mailing Address: 4521 N. Arden Rd., 99027-9358.
Res.: 1879 N. Holl Blvd., Liberty Lake, 99016. Tel: 509-926-7133; Fax: 509-926-9454. Web: stjoeparish.org.
Catechesis/Religious Program—Teresa McCann, D.R.E. Students 170.

PASCO, FRANKLIN CO., ST. PATRICK (1909) Revs. Daniel Barnett; Lutakome Nsubuga, Parochial Vicar; Deacons Victor Ortega; Luis Ramos; Abraham Valdovinos; Antonio Rodriguez; Gary Franz; Robert Kalinowski; Juanita Contreras, Pastoral Assoc. In Res., Rev. John G. Birk (Retired).
Res.: 1320 W. Henry, 99301. Tel: 509-547-8841; Fax: 509-547-3604. Email: dbarnett@dioceseofspokane.org.
School—(Grades PreK-8), 1016 N. 14th Ave., 99301. Tel: 509-547-7261; Fax: 509-547-2604. Suzanne Siekawitch, Prin. Lay Teachers 33; Students 245; Educare Enrollment 63.
Catechesis/Religious Program—Peggy DeBord, D.R.E.; Maria Aguirre, D.R.E.; Maricela Rodriguez, D.R.E. (Grades 6-12). Students 1,100.

POMEROY, GARFIELD CO., HOLY ROSARY (1878) [CEM] Rev. Robert D. Turner.
Res.: 634 High St., 99347. Tel: 509-843-3801; 509-843-1110. Web: rc.net/spokane/holyrosary.
Catechesis/Religious Program—Mary Flerschinger, D.R.E. Students 35.

PULLMAN, WHITMAN CO., SACRED HEART (1913) Rev. Jose Luis Millan.
Office: 440 N.E. Ash St., 99163. Tel: 509-332-5312; Fax: 509-332-4402. Email: sacredheartpullman@frontier.com. Web: www.sacredheartpullman.org.
Catechesis/Religious Program—Tel: 509-332-4402. Theresa Paul, D.R.E. Students 103.

REARDAN, LINCOLN CO., ST. MICHAEL (1907) Rev. Patrick MacMahon.
Mailing Address: 1310 Adams St., Davenport, 99122. Tel: 509-725-1761.

REPUBLIC, FERRY CO., IMMACULATE CONCEPTION (1898) Unassigned.
Res.: 756 S. Portland, P.O. Box 333, 99166. Tel: 509-775-3935. Email: repcach@cabletv.com.
Catechesis/Religious Program—Students 7.

RITZVILLE, ADAMS CO., ST. AGNES (1915) Rev. Msgr. John Steiner, Admin. (Retired); Rev. Daniel Wetzler (Retired).
Res.: 404 E. Fifth Ave., 99169. Tel: 509-659-0437.

ROCKFORD, SPOKANE CO., ST. JOSEPH (1901) Rev. Msgr. William Van Ommeren (Retired).
c/o Immaculate Heart Retreat Center, 6910 Ben Burr Rd., 99223-1819.

ROSALIA, WHITMAN CO., HOLY ROSARY (1892) Rev. Jose Luis Hernandez.
Mailing Address: 601 N. Plaza Ave., P.O. Box 8, 99170.
Res.: 1115 W. Riverside Ave., 99201. Tel: 509-358-4290.

SAINT JOHN, WHITMAN CO., OUR LADY OF PERPETUAL HELP (1960) Rev. Jose Luis Hernandez.
Mailing Address: 401 W. Liberty, 99171.
Res.: 1115 W. Riverside Ave., 99201. Tel: 509-358-4290.

SPRAGUE, LINCOLN CO., MARY QUEEN OF HEAVEN (1885) [CEM] Rev. John Krier.
Mailing Address: P.O. Box 129, 99032. Tel: 509-263-5434.

SPRINGDALE, STEVENS CO., SACRED HEART (1911) Rev. Vincent Van Dao Nguyen.
Res.: 3081 Fifth Ave., Valley, 99181. Tel: 509-937-2452.
Catechesis/Religious Program—

TEKOA, WHITMAN CO., SACRED HEART (1893) [CEM] Rev. Jose Luis Hernandez.
Mailing Address: P.O. Box 8, Rosalia, 99170.
Res.: 1115 W. Riverside Ave., 99201. Tel: 509-358-4290.
Catechesis/Religious Program—Joe Heffron, Co-ord.; Mary Heffron, Coord. Students 32.

TONASKET, OKANOGAN CO., HOLY ROSARY Rev. David Kuttner.
Res. & Mailing Address: P.O. Box 308, Oroville, 98844. Tel: 509-476-2110; Fax: 509-476-2110. Web: rc.net/spokane/ichr.
Catechesis/Religious Program—Students 35.

TWISP, OKANOGAN CO., ST. GENEVIEVE (1907) Rev. Matthew Nicks.
Res.: P.O. Box 6, 98856. Tel: 509-997-4201.
Catechesis/Religious Program—Leah Kominak, Rel. Educ. Coord. Students 10.

UNIONTOWN, WHITMAN CO., ST. BONIFACE (1882) [CEM] Rev. Joseph Sullivan.
Res.: P.O. Box 108, Colton, 99113. Tel: 509-229-3548.
See Guardian Angel-St. Boniface School, Colton under Interparochial Grade Schools located in the Institution section.

USK, PEND OREILLE CO., ST. JUDE (1941) Rev. Edward Marier.
Res.: 612 W. First St., P.O. Box C, Newport, 99156. Tel: 509-447-4231. Web: bojja.org.
VALLEY, STEVENS CO., HOLY GHOST (1914) Rev. Vincent Van Dao Nguyen.
Res.: 3081 Fifth Ave., 99181. Tel: 509-937-2452.
Catechesis/Religious Program—Tel: 509-935-6367. Theresa Carr, D.R.E.
Station—St. Joseph Jump-off Joe, Stevens Co., St. Joseph.
WAITSBURG, WALLA WALLA CO., ST. MARK (1888) Rev. Robert D. Turner.
Mailing Address: P.O. Box 0003, Dayton, 99328-0003. Office: 112 S. 1st St., Dayton, 99328-0003. Tel: 509-382-2311. Web: rc.net/spokane/stjoseph.
Catechesis/Religious Program—Students 4.
WALLA WALLA, WALLA WALLA CO.
1—ASSUMPTION OF THE BLESSED VIRGIN MARY (1953) Revs. Patrick Kerst; Miguel Angel Gusatvo Ruiz Juarez, Parochial Vicar; Jeffrey Core, Parochial Vicar; Tyler Smedley, Parochial Vicar; Deacon Jim Barrow.
Res.: 2098 E. Alder St., 99362. Tel: 509-525-8163; Fax: 509-529-7849.
See Walla Walla Catholic School System, Walla Walla under High Schools, Interparochial located in the Institution section.
2—ST. FRANCIS OF ASSISI (1915) Revs. Patrick Kerst; Miguel Angel Gusatvo Ruiz Juarez, Parochial Vicar; Jeffrey Core, Parochial Vicar; Tyler Smedley, Parochial Vicar; Deacon Jim Barrow.
Res.: 722 W. Alder St., 99362. Tel: 509-525-1663; Fax: 509-529-7849.
Catechesis/Religious Program—
3—ST. PATRICK (1859) Revs. Patrick Kerst; Miguel Angel Gusatvo Ruiz Juarez, Parochial Vicar; Jeffrey Core, Parochial Vicar; Tyler Smedley, Parochial Vicar; Deacons Olegario Reyes; James Barrow.
Office & Res.: 408 W. Poplar St., 99362. Tel: 509-525-1602; Fax: 509-529-7849.
Catechesis/Religious Program—Susan Logsdon, D.R.E. (Eng.). Tel: 509-529-5141; Carmen Garcia, D.R.E. (Hispanic). Students 200.
WASHTUNCA, ADAMS CO., HOLY TRINITY (1967) Closed-.Mailing Address: 404 E. 5th, Ritzville, 99169-1608. For inquiries for parish records contact St. Paul, Eltopia.
WELLPINIT, STEVENS CO., SACRED HEART (1943) [CEM] Rev. Mark Hoelsken, S.J.
Indian-Spokane Reservation—P.O. Box 214, 99040. Tel: 509-258-7233. Email: frjackoleary@aol.com.
WESTEND, STEVENS CO., OUR LADY OF LOURDES (1938) Rev. Mark Hoelsken, S.J.
Indian-Spokane Reservation—P.O. Box 214, Wellpinit, 99040. Tel: 509-258-7233.
WILBUR, LINCOLN CO., SACRED HEART (1900) Rev. Michael L. Ishida.
Res.: P.O. Box 106, 99185. Tel: 509-647-2380.
Catechesis/Religious Program—

Chaplains of Public Institutions

WALLA WALLA. *Washington State Penitentiary*. Served by priests of Walla Walla.

Special Ministry:
Revs.—
Maldonado, Fernando, Our Lady of Lourdes Health Center, Pasco
Obisike, Bonaventure, Holy Family Hospital, Spokane
Venneri, Michael D., Sacred Heart Medical Center, Spokane

On Duty Outside the Diocese:
Revs.—
Baronti, David, Diocese of Solola, Guatemala
Lucatero, Heliodoro, San Antonio, Texas
Peak, James, US Army
Pitstick, Rory, Mt. Angel Seminary, St. Benedict, OR
Poole, Richard, US Air Force

Retired:
Rev. Msgrs.—
Bach, Frank J., 1306 N. Blake Rd., Unit B, 99216-1149.
Pearson, Robert A., 1115 W. Riverside Ave., 99201.
Ribble, James M., Ph.D., 3204 W. Grandview Ave., 99204.
Steiner, John, 221 E. Rockwood Blvd., #302, 99202.
Van Ommeren, William, Immaculate Heart Retreat, 6910 S. Ben Burr Rd., 99203-1899.
Revs.—
Birk, John, 520 N. 4th St., Pasco, 99301.
Caswell, Thomas C., 3534 W. Wellesley, 99205.
Dugan, William M., 272 Kennedy St., No. 48, Chula Vista, CA 92011.
Eis, Charles R., 9202 Irvington Ave., San Diego, CA 92123-3129.
Haspedis, George, 3916 S. Alder Cir., 99228-7300.
Hullings, Clifford, 3110 E. Chattaroy Rd., No. 43, Chattaroy, 99003.
Kuhns, James, 1627 E. 33rd, 99203.
Lorge, Felix P., 12011 S. Player Dr., 99223.
O'Brien, John P., P.O. Box 1808, Santa Rosa, CA 95402.
Sand, John, 1344 Mishaw Ave., Clarkston, 99403-2977.
Skok, Charles, 935 W. Glass #301, 99205.
Westbrook, J. Severyn, 221 E. Rockwood Blvd., No. 318, 99202.
Wetzler, Daniel, 1541 E. Cromwell Dr., Coeur d'Alene, ID 83815.
Wietensteiner, Joseph M., P.O. Box 8087, 99203.

Permanent Deacons:
Back, Jack, St. Aloysius, Spokane; Prison Ministry
Banks, Douglas, St. Thomas More, Spokane
Barrow, Jim, St. Francis & St. Patrick, Walla Walla
Bentley, Donald, St. Joseph, Rockfort
Beraza, Antonio, Sacred Heart, Othello
Blaine, Jim, (Retired)
Breier, Michael, (Retired)
Brockway, Scott, St. Augustine, Spokane
Byrne, John, Our Lady of Fatima, Spokane
Casillas, Magdaleno, Sacred Heart, Othello
Crandall, John, Our Lady of the Lake, Tum Tum
Crow, John, (On Leave of Absence)
Dalecki, Robert, (On Leave of Absence)
Dudinsky, David, St. Francis of Assisi, Spokane
Dunlap, Kenneth, St. Augustine, Spokane
Fosmire, Charles, (On Leave)
Franz, Gary, St. Patrick, Pasco
Heafy, Thomas, St. Joseph, Otis Orchards
Kalinowski, Robert, (Retired)
King, Bob, St. Anne, Medical Lake
Lukach, George, Our Lady of the Lake, Tum Tum
Mackin, Francis, Sitka, AK
Malone, Richard, (Retired)
Martinez, Gonzalo "Chalo", St. Rose of Lima, Cheney
Meisfjord, Eric
Miller, Michael D., M.B.A., St. Mary, Spokane
Murphy, James E., (Retired)
Ortega, Victor, St. Patrick, Pasco
Phelps, Andrew, (Retired)
Polensky, Hugh, (On Leave of Absence)
Prawdzik, Steve
Pruneda, Joel, Sacred Heart, Othello
Ramos, Luis, St. Patrick, Pasco
Reyes, Olegario, St. Patrick, Walla Walla
Reyna, Romiro, St. Vincent, Connell
Riherd, John, (On Leave)
Ritchie, Dan, (Retired)
Rodelo, Jesus, Sacred Heart, Othello
Rodriguez, Antonio, St. Patrick, Pasco
Ruscheinsky, John, Immaculate Heart Retreat Center, Spokane
Sando, William, (Retired)
Schaefer, Edward, (On Leave)
Schroeder, Joe, St. Joseph, Colbert
Sicilia, John F., St. Charles, Spokane
Skok, Richard, (Retired)
Stewart, Kelly, Assumption, Spokane
Toulou, Alvin, (Retired)
Valdovines, Abraham, St. Patrick, Pasco
Veale, Gary, St. Francis Xavier, Spokane
Whitney, Donald, Mary Queen, Spokane

INSTITUTIONS LOCATED IN THE DIOCESE

[A] SEMINARIES, DIOCESAN

SPOKANE. *Bishop White Seminary*, E. 429 Sharp Ave., 99202. Tel: 509-313-7100; Fax: 509-313-7101. Email: bws@gonzaga.edu; sdbulinski@dioceseofspokane.org. Web: www.bishopwhiteseminary.org. Revs. Patrick Hartin, Spiritual Dir.; Steve Dublinski. Students 13.

[B] COLLEGES AND UNIVERSITIES

SPOKANE. *Gonzaga University* 99258. Tel: 509-323-6814; Fax: 509-323-6086. Email: cumlauder@gonzaga.edu. Revs. John Apel, S.J.; Donald R. Cadden, S.J.; J. Alfred Carroll, S.J.; Frank Case, S.J.; Richard Case, S.J.; Timothy R. Clancy, S.J.; Scott Coble, S.J.; Michael J. Connolly, S.J.; Joseph Conwell, S.J.; James R. Conyard, S.J.; Michael L. Cook, S.J.; Frank B. Costello, S.J. (Retired); Bernard J. Coughlin, S.J.; Tom Gallagher, S.J.; Gerald R. Gordon, S.J. (Retired); William C. Hausmann, S.J.; Craig Hightower, S.J.; Kenneth R. Krall, S.J.; Stephen R. Kuder, S.J.; Robert Lyons, S.J.; Michael W. Maher, S.J.; James N. Meehan, S.J.; Alfred Morisette, S.J.; George O. Morris, S.J.; John Navone, S.J.; Armand Nigro, S.J.; Louis Renner, S.J.; William F. Ryan, S.J.; Fredric Schlatter, S.J.; Michael Schultheis, S.J.; M. Delmar Skillingstad, S.J.; Dat Tran, S.J.; Bernard J. Tyrrell, S.J.; Gary D. Uhlenkott, S.J.; Anthony P. Via, S.J.; J. Kevin Waters, S.J.; Bro. Stephen J. Souza, S.J. College of Arts and Sciences, and Schools of Law, Engineering, Education, Business Administration, Graduate School. Professional Studies Education conducted by the Fathers of the Society of Jesus. Priests 16; Sisters 2; Lay Teachers 401; Students 7,874.
The Ministry Institute (at Gonzaga University) , E. 405 Sinto Ave., 99202-1849. Tel: 509-313-5765; Fax: 509-313-5766. Email: bartletts@gonzaga.edu. Shonna Bartlett, Prog. Dir.; Diane Imes, Admin. Dir.; Nathaniel Greene, Exec. Dir. Priests 3; Sisters 6; Lay Teachers 2; Full-Time Enrollment 22.

[C] HIGH SCHOOLS, INTERPAROCHIAL

WALLA WALLA. *Walla Walla Catholic School System*, (Grades PreK-12), E. 919 Sumach, 99362. Tel: 509-525-3030; Fax: 509-527-0361. Email: jlesko@wallawallacatholicschools.com. Web: wallawallacatholicschools.net. John Lesko, Prin.; Lynne Kuntz, Asst. Prin. Priests 1; Lay Teachers 23; Students: Elementary 224; High School 114.

[D] HIGH SCHOOLS, PRIVATE

SPOKANE. *Gonzaga Preparatory School*, E. 1224 Euclid Ave., 99207. Tel: 509-483-8511; Fax: 509-483-3124. Email: afalkner@gprep.com. Web: www.gprep.com. Mr. Al Falkner, Pres.; Revs. Kevin Connell, S.J., Prin.; Greg Vance, S.J.; Connie Robinson, Librarian. Priests 3; Lay Teachers 62; Students 905.
PASCO. *Tri Cities Prep, A Catholic High School*, 9612 St. Thomas Dr., 99301. Tel: 509-546-2465; Fax: 509-546-2490. Email: tcprep@tcprep.org. Arlene Jones, Prin.; Steve Potter, Pres. Lay Teachers 15; Students 162.

[E] INTERPAROCHIAL GRADE SCHOOLS

SPOKANE. *All Saints Middle Bldg.*, (Grades 5-8), E. 1428 33rd Ave., 99203. Tel: 509-624-5712; Fax: 509-624-7752. Email: khicks@dioceseofspokane.org. Web: allstaintsspokane.org. Ms. Kathy Hicks, Prin.
All Saints Primary (Grades PreK-4), E. 3510 18th Ave., 99223. Tel: 509-534-1098, Ext. 215; Fax: 509-534-1529. Email: khicks@dioceaseofspokane.org. Ms. Kathy Hicks, Prin. Serving St. Peter, St. Ann, and Our Lady of Fatima Parishes. Lay Teachers 25; Students 435.
Cataldo Catholic School, (Grades PreK-8), 455 W. 18th Ave., 99203. Tel: 509-624-8759; Fax: 509-624-8763. Email: office@cataldo.org. Web: www.cataldo.org. Stephanie Johnson, Prin. Serving St. Augustine, Sacred Heart, and Our Lady of Lourdes Parishes. Lay Teachers 18; Students 329.
Trinity School, (Grades PreK-8), W. 1306 Montgomery Ave., 99205. Tel: 509-327-9369; Fax: 509-328-4128. Email: trinity@dioceseofspokane.org. Mrs. Sandra Nokes, Prin.; Ms. Nancy Likarish, Librarian. Serving St. Anthony and St. Joseph Parishes. Lay Teachers 7; Students 172.
COLTON. *Guardian Angel-St. Boniface School*, (Grades K-8), 306 Steptoe, P.O. Box 48, 99113. Tel: 509-229-3579. Email: gasbschool@colton-wa.com. Web: gasbschool.org. Lori Becker, Prin.; Holly Meyer, Librarian. Serving St. Gall and St. Boniface Parishes. Lay Teachers 3; Students 20.
WALLA WALLA. *Assumption Elementary School*, (Grades PreK-5), E. 2066 Alder St., 99362. Tel: 509-525-9283; Fax: 509-527-0848. Email: jlesko@wallawallacatholicschools.com. John Lesko, Prin.; Lynne Kuntz, Asst. Prin. Serving Assumption, St. Francis of Assisi, and St. Patrick Parishes. Priests 1; Lay Teachers 11; Students 223; High School 114.
Walla Walla Catholic School System, (Grades K-12), See listing under High Schools, Interparochial. John Lesko, Prin.; Lynne Kuntz, Asst. Prin.

[F] GENERAL HOSPITALS

SPOKANE. *Providence Holy Family Hospital (Providence Health & Services-Washington)*, N. 5633 Lidgerwood St., 99208. Tel: 509-482-0111; Fax: 509-482-2456. Web: www.holy-family.org. P.O. Box 2555, 99220. Ms. Kathy Romano, CEO. Chaplains 1; Total Staff 1,156; Bed Capacity 272; Total Assisted Annually 9,086.
Providence Sacred Heart Medical Center & Children's Hospital (Providence Health & Services-Washington), W. 101 Eighth Ave., TAF-C9, 99220. Tel: 509-474-3131; Fax: 509-474-3153. P.O. Box 2555, 99220. Ms. Elaine Couture,

CEO; Rev. Michael D. Venneri, Chap. Chaplains 12; Total Staff 3,559; Bed Capacity 644; Patients Assisted Annually 154,353.

CHEWELAH. *Providence St. Joseph's Hospital (of Chewelah) (Providence Health & Services-Washington)*, 982 E. Columbia Ave., Colville, 99114. Tel: 509-935-8211; Fax: 509-935-5257. Email: pamela.borders@providence.org. Web: www2.providence.org/chewelah. Robert Campbell, Chief Exec.; Michele Sakurai, Mgr., Pastoral Care. Bed Capacity 25; Patients Assisted Annually 20,250; Total Staff 200.

COLVILLE. *Providence Mount Carmel Hospital (Providence Health & Services-Washington)*, 982 E. Columbia, 99114. Tel: 509-685-5483; Fax: 509-685-2080. Email: lori.johanson-fogle@providence.org. Web: wwwz.providence.org/colville. Robert Campbell, Chief Exec. Total Staff 270; Bed Capacity 25; Patients Assisted Annually 32,207.

PASCO. *Lourdes Medical Center*, 520 Fourth Ave., P.O. Box 2568, 99301-2568. Tel: 509-547-7704; 509-543-2483, Ext. 2483; Fax: 509-546-2291. John Serle, Pres. & CEO. Sisters of St. Joseph of Carondelet 2; Total Staff 800; Bed Capacity 127; Patients Assisted Annually 147,893.

WALLA WALLA. *St. Mary Medical Center (Providence Health & Services-Washington)*, 401 W. Poplar St., 99362. Tel: 509-525-3320; Fax: 509-522-5509. Web: www.smmc.com. Steve Burdick, Pres. Sisters of Providence. Total Staff 1,005; Bed Capacity 141; Patients Assisted Annually 154,007.

[G] PROTECTIVE INSTITUTIONS
(Catholic Social Service)

SPOKANE

St. Anne's Children's Family Center, 25 W. 5th, 99204. Tel: 509-232-1111; Fax: 509-232-1118 (Child-care Center). Lee Williams, Dir. For children 1 month through 6 years of age. Staff 35.

Bernadette Place, Mailing Address: P.O. Box 2253, 99210-2253. Tel: 509-326-0547. 925 N. A St., #2, 99210-2253. This complex houses twelve developmentally delayed women; 6 units of affordable housing for persons with disabilities and special needs.

Office:, 12 E. Fifth Ave., P.O. Box 2253, 99210-2253. Tel: 509-358-4250.

Catholic Charities, Inc., 12 E. Fifth Ave., P.O. Box 2253, 99210-2253. Tel: 509-358-4250; Fax: 509-358-4259. Email: sgross@ccspokane.org. Web: www-.catholiccharitiesspokane.org. Robert J. McCann, Ph.D., Exec. Dir. Personnel 260.

Holy Family Adult Day Center (Providence Health & Services-Washington), 6018 N. Astor, 99208. Tel: 509-482-2475; Fax: 509-482-2490. Web: www.hfadc.org. Mr. Jim Lippold, Exec. Dir. Purpose: to provide adult day health programs, including rehab & nursing, to the elderly and disabled.

House of Charity, 32 W. Pacific, P.O. Box 2253, 99210-2253. Tel: 509-624-7821; Fax: 509-742-3463. Email: emccarron@ccspokane.org. Web: catholiccharitiesspokane.org. Ed McCarron, Dir. Housing for homeless men. Total Assisted 75,902.

St. Joseph's Counseling Center dba St. Joseph Family Center N. 1016 Superior St., 99202-2059. Tel: 509-483-6495; Fax: 509-483-1541. Email: sjfc@sjfconline.org. Web: www.sjfconline.org. Sr. Pat Millen, O.S.F., M.Ed., Exec. Dir., St. Joseph Family Center. Bed Capacity 18; Total Assisted Annually 5,587; Total Staff 32.

St. Margaret's Shelter, P.O. Box 2253, 99210-2253. Tel: 509-624-9788; Fax: 509-624-1461. Nadine Van Stone, Dir. Emergency and transitional shelter for women & children. Total Staff 8; Total Assisted Annually 123.

Miryam's House, 1805 W. 9th St., 99204. Tel: 509-747-9222; Fax: 509-747-7261. Email: dcritchlow@help4women.com. Web: www.help4women.com. Transitional housing residential program and supportive services for women in transition. Total Staff 12; Total Assisted 70.

Morning Star Boys' Ranch, P.O. Box 8087, 99203. Tel: 509-448-1411; Fax: 509-448-1413. Email: msbr@msbranch.org. Web: morningstarboysranch.org. John Hindman, Exec. Dir.; Mr. Daniel J. Kuhlmann, Finance Dir. Total Staff 39; Children in Residence 13; Total Assisted 25.

Spokane St. Vincent de Paul Social Services Center, P.O. Box 2906, 99220-2906. Tel: 509-323-9014 (Social Svc.); Fax: 509-535-2493. Mike Cain, Pres. *St. Vincent de Paul Social Service Office and Main Store St. Business Office* Total Assisted 74,101.

Summit View, P.O. Box 2253, 99210-2253. 820 N. Summit Blvd., 99201. Tel: 509-327-9524. Email: measton@ccspokane.org. Mark Easton, Property Mgr. 27 units of housing for families.

Transitional Living Center, 3128 N. Hemlock, 99205. Tel: 509-325-2959; 509-328-6702; Fax: 509-325-8319. Email: ktalbott@help4women.org. Web: www.help4women.org. Housing for homeless women & children. Bed Capacity 16; Total Assisted Annually 75; Total Staff 7.

Transitional Programs for Women, 3104 W. Fort George Wright Dr., 99224. Tel: 509-328-6702; Fax: 509-325-9877. Email: dmaurer@help4women.org. Web: www.help4women.org. Bed Capacity 50; Total Assisted Annually 1,500; Total Staff 42.

Women's Hearth, 920 W. Second Ave., 99201. Tel: 509-456-3531; Fax: 509-456-3531. Web: www.help4women.org. Rev. Edie A. Rice-Sauer, Prog. Dir. & Contact Person. A safe place for women at risk. Total Assisted Annually 1,500; Total Staff 10.

CHEWELAH

Providence DominiCare, 110 S. Third St. E., P.O. Box 1070, 99109. Tel: 509-935-4925; Fax: 509-935-4082. Email: joan.sisco@providence.org. Web: www.providence.org. Joan Sisco, Exec. Dir. A home care/personal care service in Stevens, Pierce & Pend Oreille Counties. Total Assisted Annually 7,550; Total Staff 30; Hours of Home-Care Service 2,900.

CLARKSTON

Lewis and Clark District Council of St. Vincent de Paul, Office: 604 Second St., 99403. Tel: 509-758-7061; Fax: 509-758-9545.

Stores:

609 Third St., 99403. Tel: 509-758-7061; Fax: 509-758-9545.

3138 5th St., Lewiston, ID 83501. Tel: 208-746-7860.

COLVILLE

The Rhodena, 525 S. Main, 99114. Tel: 509-684-5671; Fax: 509-358-4259. Email: cpaige@ccspokane.org. A six unit affordable housing complex for families living in Colville, WA.

DAYTON

Project Timothy: Christian Service Center, 247 E. Main St., 99328. Tel: 509-382-2943. Sponsored by St. Joseph's & St. Mark's Churches. Total Assisted 4,550.

St. Vincent de Paul Store, 247 E. Main, 99328. Tel: 509-382-4146. Lydia C. Buettner, Treas.; Lynn Feeney, Mgr.

PASCO

St. Vincent de Paul Store, 1120 W. Sylvester, 99301. Tel: 509-547-2341; Fax: 509-547-7804. Cynthia Martinez, Mgr.

WALLA WALLA

Catholic Charities Walla Walla, 408 W. Poplar, 99362. Tel: 509-525-0572; Fax: 509-525-0576. Email: tmeliah@ccspokane.org. Tim Meliah, Dir.

St. Vincent de Paul Store, 308 W. Main St., 99362. Tel: 509-525-3903 (Store); 509-529-6778 (Office); Fax: 509-525-3903. Raymond Lane, Society Pres.; Julie Smith, Mgr.

[H] SENIOR CITIZEN HOUSING

SPOKANE. *Cathedral Plaza Apartments*, W. 1120 Sprague Ave., 99201. Tel: 509-747-6777. Email: rcoonse@ccspokane.org. Capacity 150; Staff 5.

The Delaney, W. 242 Riverside Ave., 99201. Tel: 509-747-5081. Email: delaney@ccspokane.org. Capacity 84.

Fahy Garden Apartments, W. 1411 Dean Ave., 99201. Tel: 509-326-6759; Fax: 509-323-5205. Email: fahys@ccspokane.org. Capacity 54.

Fahy West Apartments, W. 1523 Dean Ave., 99201. Tel: 509-326-6759; Fax: 509-323-5205. Email: fahys@ccspokane.org. Capacity 32.

The O'Malley Apartments, E. 707 Mission Ave., 99201. Tel: 509-487-1150. Email: omalley@ccspokane.org. Tandra Melville, Property Mgr. Capacity 99; Total Assisted Annually 101; Staff 5.

Rockwood Lane, E. 221 Rockwood Blvd., 99202. Tel: 509-838-3200; Fax: 509-838-1688. Email: jmcnally@ccspokane.org. Jeannette McNally, Property Mgr. Capacity 104.

Senior Service - Senior Nutrition, P.O. Box 2253, 99210-2253. Tel: 509-459-6175.

CLARKSTON. *Austen Manor*, 1222 Chestnut St., 99403. Tel: 509-751-9640; Fax: 509-751-9610. Email: austenmanor@ccspokane.org. D.J. Joepino, Prop. Mgr. Total Staff 2; Capacity 29.

PULLMAN. *Pioneer Square*, 220 S. E. Kamiaken, 99163. Tel: 509-332-1106; Fax: 509-332-2516. Email: pioneersquare@ccspokane.org. Capacity 45; Total Staff 4.

WALLA WALLA. *Garden Court/Mike Foye*, 420 W. Alder St., 99362. Tel: 509-529-4706. Email: sperez-garcia@ccspokane.org. Sara Perez-Garcia, Property Mgr. Capacity 25.

Mike Foye Apartments, 420 W. Alder St., #13, 99362. Tel: 509-529-4706. Email: ghouston@ccspokane.org. Web: www.catholiccharitiesspokane.org. Bed Capacity 53; Total Assisted Annually 25; Staff 3.

[I] HOMES FOR AGED

SPOKANE. *Emilie Court Assisted Living (Providence Health & Services-Washington)*, 34 E. 8th Ave., 99202-1202. Tel: 509-474-2550; Fax: 509-474-2618. Email: charlene.longworth@providence.org. Charlene Longworth, Dir. Bed Capacity 60; Total Staff 40; Total Assisted Annually 58.

Providence St. Joseph Care Center (Providence Health & Services-Washington) (A Non-profit Corporation), E. 17 Eighth Ave., 99202. Tel: 509-474-5678; Fax: 509-455-4020. P.O. Box 2555, 99220. Robert Hellrigel, CEO. Sisters of Providence-Mother Joseph Province. Bed Capacity 162.

[J] MONASTERIES AND RESIDENCES OF PRIESTS AND BROTHERS

SPOKANE. *Regis Community*, N. 1107 Astor St., 99202. Tel: 509-328-4220; Fax: 509-313-6086. Revs. Paul M. Cochran, S.J., Supr.; Robert L. Fitts, S.J., Asst. to the Supvr.; Arnold R. Beezer, S.J. (Retired); Leo D. Davis; Thomas R. Garvin, S.J. (Retired); Robert A. Goebel, S.J. (Retired); Henry G. Hargreaves, S.J.; Thomas F. Healy, S.J.; James Jacobson, S.J.; Robert J. Jones, S.J.; Leon Kapfer, S.J.; John J. Kindall, S.J.; Philip Lucid, S.J. (Retired); John P. McBride, S.J.; Neill R. Meany, S.J.; John J. Morse, S.J.; Joseph L. Obersinner, S.J.; Robert F. Rekofke, S.J. (Retired); Edmund J. Robinson, S.J. (Retired); Roberto B. Saenz, S.J. (Retired); Robert J. Schlim, S.J.; Joseph Shirey, S.J.; Joseph L. Showalter (Retired); Gerald G. Steckler, S.J.; J. Patrick Stewart, S.J.; Thomas Williams, S.J.; Charles A. Wollesen, S.J.; Bros. Michael J. Bennett, S.J.; Patrick M. Flannigan, S.J.; James J. Lee, S.J.; Michael Richards.

[K] CONVENTS AND RESIDENCES FOR SISTERS

SPOKANE. *Convent of the Holy Names*, 2911 W. Fort George Wright Dr., 99224. Tel: 509-328-4310; Fax: 509-328-9824. Email: mafarley@snjmwa.org. Sr. Mary Ann Farley, S.N.J.M., Convent Community Dir. Sisters of the Holy Names of Jesus and Mary (U.S. Ontario Province). Professed Sisters 42.

Holy Names Foundation, 2911 W. Fort George Wright Dr., 99224. Tel: 509-328-7470; Fax: 509-328-9824. Support for educational activities of Sisters of the Holy Names of Jesus and Mary.

Holy Spirit Community, 3319 E. 57th Ave. #310, 99223-7047. Tel: 509-448-6431. Email: Roy2815@msn.com. Margaret Breitenbach, Pres.

Monastery of St. Clare, 4419 N. Hawthorne St., 99205-1399. Tel: 509-327-4479; Fax: 509-327-5171. Sr. Rita Louise McLean, O.S.C., Abbess. Papal Enclosure Novitiate. Professed Cloistered Nuns 5; Poor Clare Nuns, Solemn Vows 5.

Mount St. Joseph Retirement residence and community., 12 W. Ninth Ave., 99204-2394. Tel: 509-474-2300; Fax: 509-474-2355. Laurie Crane, Gen. Mgr.; Sr. Sue Orlowski, Supr. Sisters of Providence, Mother Joseph, Province.

Sisters of Providence Novitiate, 1016 N. Superior St., #4, 99202-2096. Tel: 509-487-7644; Fax: 509-489-0964. Sr. Margaret Botch, S.P., Novitiate Dir.

NEWPORT. *Carmelite Sisters of Mary*, 2892 Hwy. 211, 99156. Tel: 509-292-0978. Sr. Leslie L. Lund, Prioress. Sisters 2; Hermitages 6.

[L] ASSOCIATIONS OF THE FAITHFUL

SPOKANE. *Sisters of Mary, Mother of the Church*, 6910 S. Ben Burr Rd., 99223. Tel: 509-448-9890; Fax: 509-448-1623. Web: www.sistersofmarymotherofthechurch.org. Sisters Kathryn Joseph, S.M.M.C., Supr.; Marybeth, S.M.M.C., Business Mgr. Members 10.

[M] RETREAT HOUSES

SPOKANE. *Immaculate Heart Retreat Center*, 6910 S. Ben Burr Rd., 99223. Tel: 509-448-1224; Fax: 509-448-1623. Email: ihrc@ihrc.net. Web: www.ihrc.net. Deacon John Ruscheinsky, Exec. Dir.; Rev. Msgr. William Van Ommeren (Retired).

KAIROS House of Prayer, 1714 W. Stearns Rd., 99208. Tel: 509-466-2187. Sr. M. Florence Leone Poch, O.S.F., Coord.; Rita Beaulieu. Provides a place called to a prayerful, reflective environment for people of all faiths. Spiritual accompaniment is available.

Spiritual Exercise in Everyday Life (SEEL), 330 E. Boone, 99202. Tel: 509-313-5898; Fax: 509-313-5892. Email: seel-spokane@comcast.net. Diana Stoffregen, Dir.

TUM TUM. *House of the Lord Retreat Center, Inc., Corporate Office*, 17115 N. Suncrest Dr., Nine Mile Falls, 99026. Tel: 509-276-2219. Web: www.houseofthelordministries.com. Ramona Salvatore, Dir.

[N] NEWMAN CENTERS

CHENEY. *Catholic Newman Center at Eastern Washington University* 837 Elm St., 99004. Tel: 509-235-8402. Mailing Address: 460 N. Fifth St., 99004.

PULLMAN. *"St. Thomas More Catholic Student Center" - Washington State University* 820 N.E. B St., 99163. Tel: 509-332-6311. Email: catholiccougs@gmail.com. Web: www.catholiccougs.org. Rev. Msgr. Kevin A. Codd.

[O] MISCELLANEOUS

SPOKANE. *Cataldo Catholic School*, 425 W. 18th Ave., 99203.

Catholic Charities Foundation, P.O. Box 2253, 99210. Tel: 509-358-4255; Fax: 509-358-4259. Email: mheskett@ccspokane.org. Mary Ann Heskett, Contact Person & Planned Giving Coord.

The Catholic Foundation of the Spokane Diocese, P.O. Box 30846, 99223-3014. Tel: 509-998-0654. Email: sckphd72@msn.com. Web: www.spokanecatholicfoundation.com. Mr. Steve Kocharhook, Exec. Dir.

Diocesan Ministries Fund, P.O. Box 4000, 99210-4000. Tel: 509-358-4283. Web: www.diocesanministriesfund.org. Mr. Chris Smith, Contact Person.

Holy Names Music Center, 3910 W. Custer Dr., 99224. Tel: 509-326-9516; Fax: 509-326-7155. Email: music@hnmc.org. Web: www.hnmc.org. Craig Landron, Exec. Dir. Sponsored by Sisters of the Holy Names, Washington Province. Sisters 2; Lay Teachers 35; Students 700.

Immaculate Heart Retreat Center Foundation, S. 6910 Ben Burr Rd., 99223-1819. Tel: 509-448-1224; Fax: 509-448-1623.

Kateri Northwest Ministry Institute, P.O. Box 4693, 99220. Tel: 509-313-7024; Fax: 509-313-5892. Web: katerinmi.org. Rev. Michael Fitzpatrick, S.J., Dir.; Jenny Edgren, Office Mgr. Kateri Northwest Ministry Institute is a Jesuit-sponsored formation program dedicated to the development of all ministries needed for reservation-and urban-based Indian Catholic church communities of the Northwest. Forming church communities to be fully Indian and fully Catholic, with indigenous leadership respectful of unique cultural expression, is the goal of the Institute. The Institute also develops active leadership for those who want to take on social justice issues in their church and local communities.

**L'Arche Spokane*, 703 E. Nora, 99207-2455. Tel: 509-483-0438; Fax: 509-483-0460. Email: lura@larchespokane.org. Lura Southerland, Community Dir.

Providence Health Care (Providence Health & Services-Washington), 101 W. 8th Ave., 99220. Tel: 509-474-3335; Fax: 509-474-4925. Michael Wilson, CEO. Providence Health Care is an integrated healthcare delivery network made up of: Providence Sacred Heart Medical Center and Children's Hospital, Providence Holy Family Hospital, Providence Mount Carmel Hospital, Providence St. Joseph's Hospital, Providence Adult Day Health, Providence DominiCare, and Providence Physician Services.

Providence Medical Research Center, 101 W. 8th Ave., 99204.

Serra Club of Spokane, P.O. Box 31535, 99223. Tel: 509-466-7784. Martin Weber, Pres.

Spokane Catholic Investment Trust, P.O. Box 1453, 99210-1453. Tel: 509-358-7323. Most Rev. Blase J. Cupich, S.T.D., Pres.; Merrilin Fulton, Dir. of Fiscal Svcs. A Washington Nonprofit Corporation established to invest funds on behalf of the charitable organizations organized within the Catholic Diocese of Spokane.

POMEROY. *Holy Rosary Catholic Church Foundation of Garfield County*, 634 High St., 99347.

WAITSBURG. *St. Mark Waitsburg and St. Joseph Dayton Catholic Parish Foundation*, Mailing Address: P.O. Box 0003, Dayton, 99328.

RELIGIOUS INSTITUTES OF MEN REPRESENTED IN THE DIOCESE

For further details refer to the corresponding bracketed number in the Religious Institutes of Men or Women section.

[0520]—*Franciscan Friars* (Santa Barbara Prov.)—O.F.M.

[0690]—*Jesuit Fathers and Brothers*—S.J.

RELIGIOUS INSTITUTES OF WOMEN REPRESENTED IN THE DIOCESE

[1780]—*Congregation of the Sisters of the Third Order of St. Francis of Perpetual Adoration*—F.S.P.A.

[1070-03]—*Dominican Sisters*—O.P.

[1180]—*Franciscan Sisters of Allegany, New York*—O.S.F.

[3760]—*Order of St. Clare*—O.S.C.

[]—*Sisters for Christian Community Eastern Washington Area Communication*

[3350]—*Sisters of Providence*—S.P.

[1650]—*The Sisters of St. Francis of Philadelphia*—O.S.F.

[3840]—*Sisters of St. Joseph of Carondelet*—C.S.J.

[1990]—*Sisters of the Holy Names of Jesus and Mary*—S.N.J.M.

[2110]—*Sisters of the Humility of Mary*—H.M.

DIOCESAN CEMETERIES

SPOKANE. *Catholic Cemeteries of Spokane*, P.O. Box 18006, 99228. 7200 N. Wall St., 99208. Tel: 509-467-5496; Fax: 509-467-6649. Jim Falkner, Exec. Dir.

Holy Cross Cemetery, P.O. Box 18006, 99228. 7200 N. Wall St., 99208. Tel: 509-467-5496; Fax: 509-467-6649.

St. Joseph Cemetery, P.O. Box 18006, 99228. 17825 E. Trent, 99216. Tel: 509-467-5496; Fax: 509-467-6649.

Mary Queen of Peace Cemetery, P.O. Box 18006, 99228. 6910 S. Ben Burr Rd., 99223. Tel: 509-467-5496; Fax: 509-467-6649.

NECROLOGY

† Caffrey, Edward, (Retired)—Died March 20, 2011

† Morbeck, George H., Republic, WA Immaculate Conception; Curlew, WA St. Patrick.—Died Nov. 3, 2011

† Schoffelmeer, Arnold L., (Retired)—Died March 26, 2011

An asterisk (*) denotes an organization that has established tax-exempt status directly with the IRS and is not covered by the USCCB Group Ruling.

Diocese of Springfield-Cape Girardeau

(Dioecesis Campifontis-Capitis Girardeauensis)

Most Reverend

JOHN J. LEIBRECHT, D.D., PH.D.

Bishop Emeritus of Springfield-Cape Girardeau; ordained March 17, 1956; appointed Bishop of Springfield-Cape Girardeau October 23, 1984; consecrated December 12, 1984; retired January 24, 2008. *Res.: 1152 W. Camino Alto St., Springfield, MO 65810*. Tel: 417-987-0884. Email: jleibrecht@mchsi.com.

Most Reverend

JAMES V. JOHNSTON JR., D.D., J.C.L.

Bishop of Springfield-Cape Girardeau; ordained June 9, 1990; appointed Bishop of Springfield-Cape Girardeau January 24, 2008; ordained March 31, 2008. *Office: The Catholic Center, 601 S. Jefferson Ave., Springfield, MO 65806-3143*.

Chancery Office: The Catholic Center, 601 S. Jefferson Ave., Springfield, MO 65806-3143. Tel: 417-866-0841; Fax: 417-866-1140.

Web: www.dioscg.org

Email: treidy@dioscg.org

ESTABLISHED AUGUST 24, 1956.

Square Miles 25,719.

Comprises the following Counties in the State of Missouri: Barry, Barton, Bollinger, Butler, Cape Girardeau, Carter, Cedar, Christian, Dade, Dallas, Dent, Douglas, Dunklin, Greene, Howell, Iron, Jasper, Laclede, Lawrence, McDonald, Madison, Mississippi, New Madrid, Newton, Oregon, Ozark, Pemiscot, Polk, Reynolds, Ripley, Scott, Shannon, Stoddard, Stone, Taney, Texas, Wayne, Webster and Wright.

For legal titles of parishes and diocesan institutions, consult The Catholic Center.

STATISTICAL OVERVIEW

Personnel	
Bishop	1
Retired Bishops	1
Retired Abbots	2
Priests: Diocesan Active in Diocese	42
Priests: Diocesan Active Outside Diocese	1
Priests: Retired, Sick or Absent	19
Number of Diocesan Priests	62
Religious Priests in Diocese	56
Total Priests in Diocese	118
Extern Priests in Diocese	9
Ordinations:	
Religious Priests	2
Permanent Deacons in Diocese	16
Total Brothers	37
Total Sisters	76
Parishes	
Parishes	66
With Resident Pastor:	
Resident Diocesan Priests	38
Resident Religious Priests	6
Without Resident Pastor:	
Administered by Priests	19
Administered by Deacons	1
Administered by Religious Women	2
Missions	18
Pastoral Centers	4
Professional Ministry Personnel:	
Brothers	1
Sisters	13
Lay Ministers	16
Welfare	
Catholic Hospitals	8
Total Assisted	1,007,721
Homes for the Aged	1
Total Assisted	220
Day Care Centers	1
Total Assisted	29
Educational	
Diocesan Students in Other Seminaries	12
Total Seminarians	12
High Schools, Diocesan and Parish	3
Total Students	982
Elementary Schools, Diocesan and Parish	23
Total Students	3,572
Catechesis/Religious Education:	
High School Students	1,216
Elementary Students	3,265
Total Students under Catholic Instruction	9,047
Teachers in the Diocese:	
Brothers	1
Sisters	4
Lay Teachers	290
Vital Statistics	
Receptions into the Church:	
Infant Baptism Totals	882
Minor Baptism Totals	117
Adult Baptism Totals	108
Received into Full Communion	224
First Communions	1,193
Confirmations	788
Marriages:	
Catholic	176
Interfaith	123
Total Marriages	299
Deaths	569
Total Catholic Population	67,950
Total Population	1,353,859

Former Bishops—Most Revs. CHARLES H. HELMSING, D.D., cons. as Titular Bishop of Axomis and Auxiliary Bishop of Archdiocese of St. Louis, April 19, 1949; appt. Bishop of Springfield-Cape Girardeau, Aug. 24, 1956; transferred to Diocese of Kansas City-St. Joseph, Jan. 27, 1962; retired Aug. 17, 1977; died Dec. 20, 1993; IGNATIUS J. STRECKER, D.D., appt. April 7, 1962; cons. June 20, 1962; transferred to Archdiocese of Kansas City in Kansas, Sept. 10, 1969; retired Sept. 8, 1993; died Oct. 16, 2003; His Eminence WILLIAM CARDINAL BAUM, S.T.D. (Retired), appt. Feb. 18, 1970; cons. April 6, 1970; transferred to Archdiocese of Washington D.C., May 9, 1973; elevated to Cardinal, May 24, 1976; appt. Prefect, Congregation for Catholic Education in the Vatican, Jan. 15, 1980; Major Penitentiary, appt. April 6, 1990.; retired Nov. 22, 2001; BERNARD CARDINAL LAW, D.D., ord. May 21, 1961; appt. Bishop of Springfield-Cape Girardeau, Oct. 22, 1973; cons. Dec. 5, 1973; appt. Archbishop of Boston, Jan. 23, 1984; elevated to Cardinal, May 25, 1985; resigned Dec. 13, 2002; appt. Archpriest of St. Mary Major Basilica, Rome, Italy May 27, 2004; Most Rev. JOHN J. LEIBRECHT, D.D., Ph.D., ord. March 17, 1956; appt. Bishop of Springfield-Cape Girardeau Oct. 23, 1984; cons. Dec. 12, 1984; retired Jan. 24, 2008.

Vicar General—Rev. Msgr. THOMAS E. REIDY, V.G.

Chancery Office—The Catholic Center, 601 S. Jefferson Ave., Springfield, 65806-3143. Tel: 417-866-0841; Fax: 417-866-1140.

Chancellor—Rev. Msgr. THOMAS E. REIDY, V.G.

Vice Chancellor—Rev. THOMAS P. KIEFER, J.C.L.

Regional Priest Moderators—Region I: Rev. JUSTIN D. MONAGHAN. Region II: Rev. PAUL J. MCLOUGHLIN. Region III: Rev. J. PATRICK WISSMAN. Region IV: Rev. MICHAEL V. MCDEVITT, M.A., M.Div. Region V: Rev. DANIEL J. HIRTZ. Region VI: Rev. JAMES J. UNTERREINER. Region VII: Rev. JOHN M. HARTH. Region VIII: Rev. ALLAN L. SAUNDERS. Region IX: Rev. DAVID J. DOHOGNE.

Office of Administration

Catholic Foundation Of The Diocese Of Springfield-Cape Girardeau—Most Rev. JAMES V. JOHNSTON JR., D.D., J.C.L., Pres.; Rev. Msgr. THOMAS E. REIDY, V.G., Vice Pres.; Ms. JANET L. SMITH, Sec. Treas.

Development and Properties—EUGENE AUG, Ph.D., Dir.

Diocesan Development Fund—EUGENE AUG, Ph.D., Dir. Devel. & Properties; Revs. RICK L. JONES, M.Div., L.P.C.; NORMAND G. VARONE (Retired); Mr. TOM REINAGEL; Mrs. THERESA WITT.

Finance—Ms. JANET L. SMITH, Dir.

Financial Council—Ms. JANET L. SMITH, Dir. Finance; EUGENE AUG, Ph.D., Diocesan Dir., Devel. & Properties; Mrs. MAUREEN M. JERSAK, Diocesan Dir., Planned Giving; Mr. LARRY G. GRINSTEAD; Mrs. CATHY MEYER; Mr. TOM BARR; Mr. JAMES MOORE; Mr. CHRIS CHURCHWELL; Mr. STAN IRWIN; Mrs. ANN SAUNDERS.

Planned Giving—Mrs. MAUREEN M. JERSAK, Dir.

Office of Education

Catholic Schools—Mr. LEON WITT, Supt. of Schools.

Communications (Public Relations)—Mrs. RECY MOORE, Dir.

Ecumenism—Rev. JOHN F. GAGNEPAIN, C.M.

Newspaper, Diocese of Springfield-Cape Girardeau—"The Mirror" Mrs. LESLIE A. EIDSON, Editor; Mrs. ANGIE TOBIN, Circulation & Administrative Asst.

Office of Ministry

Campus Ministries—Revs. JOHN (J.) F. FRIEDEL, M.A., M.Div., Diocesan Dir. & Chap. Missouri Southern State Univ. Tel: 417-623-8643; THOMAS A. MCGANN, C.M.F., Missouri State Univ. Campus Min. Tel: 417-865-0802; PATRICK I. NWOKOYE, Ph.D., Southeast Missouri State Univ. Campus Min. Tel: 573-335-3899; Mrs. LYNN MELENDEZ, Part-time Campus Minister, College of the

Ozarks. Tel: 417-334-2928.

Diaconate (Permanent)—Rev. DAVID F. HULSHOF, M.A., Dir.; Deacon WALTER L. BIRI, Asst. Dir.

Diocesan Director of Continuing Formation of Clergy—Rev. JOHN F. GAGNEPAIN, C.M. Tel: 573-547-6533, Ext. 266.

Family Ministries—Mr. TROY S. CASTEEL, M.S., L.P.C., Dir.

Diocesan Council on Family Ministries—Mr. TROY S. CASTEEL, M.S., L.P.C., Dir. Family Ministries. Region I: DEANNA STREET, M.A., L.P.C.; ELIZABETH RUNKLE. Region II: VACANT. Region III: Rev. J. PATRICK WISSMAN. Region IV: Rev. MICHAEL V. MCDEVITT, M.A., M.Div.; SHARON WEIDELMAN; PATTI STRAUS; ERIC PICHLER; SHELLY PICHLER. Region V: Rev. ERNEST J. MARQUART. Region VI: Rev. JAMES J. UNTERREINER. Region VII: VACANT. Region VIII: JACK JACKOVIC; PAT JACKOVIC. Region IX: VACANT.

Natural Family Planning—Mr. TROY S. CASTEEL, M.S., L.P.C., Dir.

Rite of Christian Initiation of Adults—Co Directors: Rev. DAVID J. DOHOGNE; Mrs. KAREN PESEK.

Hispanic Ministries—Mrs. MILAGROS CALVETTI, Dir.

Social Ministry, Evangelization, and Formation—Mr. NICHOLAS C. LUND-MOLFESE, M.A., J.D., Dir.

Trinity Hills—formerly T A House and Farm for Christian Formation *689 S. Farm Rd. 253, Rogersville, 65742*. Tel: 417-753-7758; Fax: 417-753-7758. Email: nick@thills.org. Web: www.thills.org.

**Catholic Charities of Southern Missouri, Inc., 601 S. Jefferson Ave., Springfield, 65806*. Tel: 417-866-0841; Fax: 417-866-1140. Email: ccsomo@ccsomo.org. Mrs. MAURA A. TAYLOR, Exec. Dir.

Office of Child and Youth Protection—Mrs. KAREN PESEK, Dir.

Victim Assistance Coordinators—JOHN K. KREYMER, Psy.D., DAPA. Tel: 417-597-3755; JUDY A. ST. JOHN, L.P.C., N.C.C. Tel: 573-587-3139.

Tribunal—

Judicial Vicar—Rev. THOMAS P. KIEFER, J.C.L.

Adjutant Judicial Vicar—Rev. VINCENT E. BERTRAND, J.C.L.

Coordinator—Sr. ROBIN L. NORDYKE, C.D.P., J.C.L.

Auditor—Rev. Msgr. THOMAS E. REIDY, V.G.

Judges—Revs. VINCENT E. BERTRAND, J.C.L.; THOMAS P. KIEFER, J.C.L.; Rev. Msgr. THOMAS E. REIDY, V.G.

Promoter of Justice—Sr. ROBIN L. NORDYKE, C.D.P., J.C.L.

Advocates for the Petitioners— Parish Priests, deacons, and pastoral ministers

Advocates for the Respondent—Revs. MICHAEL V. MCDEVITT, M.A., M.Div.; DAVID F. HULSHOF, M.A.

Defender of the Bond—Rev. Msgr. MICHAEL F. SWALINA, S.T.D.

Notary—Mrs. LINDA MURPHY.

Vicar For The Religious—Rev. Msgr. THOMAS E. REIDY, V.G.

Vocations-Seminarians—Revs. JOHN (J.) F. FRIEDEL, M.A., M.Div., Dir. Vocations/Seminarians; PATRICK I. NWOKOYE, Ph.D., Dir. of Vocation Promotion.

Youth Ministry—Mr. TROY S. CASTEEL, M.S., L.P.C., Coord.; Revs. SCOTT M. SUNNENBERG, Youth Facilitator West; JOSEPH WEIDENBENNER, Youth Facilitator Central; Mr. TOM SCHUMER, Youth Facilitator East.

Catholic Scouting—Rev. PATRICK I. NWOKOYE, Ph.D., Diocesan Chap. Tel: 573-335-3899; Mr. BEN FRANCKA, Assoc. Diocesan Chap. Tel: 417-881-6518.

Camp Re-NEW-All—Ms. VIRGINIA SANDER, Camp Dir.; Mrs. MANDY WITT-AUBERT, Camp Dir.; Mrs. KIM SELLERS, Camp Dir.

Office of Worship

Office of Worship—Rev. DAVID J. DOHOGNE, Dir.

Liturgical Commission—Rev. DAVID J. DOHOGNE, Dir. Office of Worship.

Priests' Eucharistic League Confraternity of The Most Blessed Sacrament—Rev. MICHAEL V. MCDEVITT, M.A., M.Div., Dir.

Officials And Committees

Catholic Relief Services—Rev. Msgr. THOMAS E. REIDY, V.G.

Cemeteries—Rev. Msgr. THOMAS E. REIDY, V.G.

Health Affairs—Mr. NICHOLAS C. LUND-MOLFESE, M.A., J.D., Dir.

Holy Childhood Association—VACANT.

Missionary Apostolate - Society for the Propagation of the Faith—Rev. MARK G. BOYER, M.A., M.Div., M.R.E. Tel: 417-887-4811.

Mission of the Laity— Apostleship of Prayer, VACANT.

National Shrine Of The Immaculate Conception—Rev. Msgr. THOMAS E. REIDY, V.G., Dir.

Priests' Mutual Benefit Society—Rev. Msgr. THOMAS E. REIDY, V.G., Exec. Sec.; Rev. THOMAS P. KIEFER, J.C.L., Pres.; Rev. Msgrs. RAYMOND V. ORF (Retired); WILLIAM J. STANTON (Retired); Revs. NORMAND G. VARONE (Retired); RICK L. JONES, M.Div., L.P.C., Vice Pres.; RALPH J. DUFFNER (Retired); JOSEPH WEIDENBENNER.

Pro-Life Director—Mr. NICHOLAS C. LUND-MOLFESE, M.A., J.D.

Rural Life Movement—Rev. SYLVESTER W. BAUER (Retired).

Diocesan Consultative Groups

Diocesan Consultors—Rev. JOHN (J.) F. FRIEDEL, M.A., M.Div.; Rev. Msgr. MICHAEL F. SWALINA, S.T.D.; Rev. THOMAS P. KIEFER, J.C.L.; Rev. Msgr. THOMAS E. REIDY, V.G.; Revs. PAUL J. MCLOUGHLIN; JAMES J. UNTERREINER; DAVID F. HULSHOF, M.A.

Presbyteral Council—Revs. JOHN (J.) F. FRIEDEL, M.A., M.Div., Vice Chm.; DAVID F. HULSHOF, M.A., Chm.; JOHN F. GAGNEPAIN, C.M.; THOMAS A. MCGANN, C.M.F.; DANIEL ROBLES; ALLAN L. SAUNDERS; Rev. Msgr. MICHAEL F. SWALINA, S.T.D.; Rev. JOSEPH WEIDENBENNER, Sec. Appointed Member: Rev. Msgr. THOMAS E. REIDY, V.G.

Diocesan Pastoral Council—Rev. JOSEPH WEIDENBENNER.

Diocesan School Board—Mr. LEON WITT, Supt.; WILLIAM HENNESSEY; MIKE HIMMELBERG; Rev. WILLIAM M. HODGSON; KRYSTAL HUFFMAN; Mrs. KAREN POWERS; Mr. GENE KOESTER; Mrs. BECKI ESSNER; LEONARD RUGGIERO; Ms. GLORIA WILSON; Bro. DAVID ANTHONY MIGLIORINO, O.S.F.; Mrs. JEANNE SKAHAN.

Diocesan Lay Endowment Board—Rev. DAVID F. HULSHOF, M.A., Chm.; Sr. MARY JANE JANSEN, S.S.N.D.; Mrs. CHRISTINA DIEBOLD; Deacon JAMES E. LONG JR.; Mrs. NORMA PARKER.

Catholic Organizations And Movements

Charismatic Prayer Groups—Mr. KLAUS TAMME; Rev. WILLIAM M. HODGSON.

Cursillo Movement—

Secretariat for Cursillo—Rev. WILLIAM M. HODGSON, Diocesan Chap.

St. Francis de Sales Association—Rev. FRANK C. PALERMO, Chap. (Retired); Rev. Msgr. WILLIAM J. STANTON, Chap. (Retired).

Diocesan Council of Catholic Women (DCCW)—Revs. JAMES J. UNTERREINER, Diocesan Spiritual Moderator; DAVID F. HULSHOF, M.A., Assoc. Spiritual Moderator; BEVERLY SWIHART, Dir. At-Large. Tel: 417-326-7989.

Apostolates And Commissions

Apostolate to the Deaf—Rev. DAVID L. MILLER, Dir. Tel: 417-847-4948; 417-858-2518.

State Office

Diocesan Delegates To The Missouri Catholic Conference—

Public Policy Committee—Mr. NICHOLAS C. LUND-MOLFESE, M.A., J.D.; Mrs. SHARON WEIDELMAN.

CLERGY, PARISHES, MISSIONS AND PAROCHIAL SCHOOLS

CITY OF SPRINGFIELD

(GREENE COUNTY)

1—CATHEDRAL OF ST. AGNES (1908) [CEM] [JC] Revs. Michael V. McDevitt; James Long Hai Do, C.M.C.; Deacons William J. Keller; Mark A. Wand; Sisters Elizabeth Ann Weiler, A.S.C., Min. of Care; Bernadette Goessling, S.S.N.D., Office Mgr. In Res., Rev. Jeffery Fasching; Rev. Msgr. Mark C. Ernstmann (Retired).

Res.: 533 S. Jefferson Ave., 65806. Tel: 417-831-3565; Fax: 417-865-0367. Email: stagnesfrontdesk@gmail.com. Web: www.saintagnescathedral.org.

School—(Grades PreSchool-8), 531 S. Jefferson Ave., 65806. Tel: 417-866-5038; Fax: 417-866-2906. Email: jskahan@scspk12.org. Web: www.scspk12.org. Mrs. Jeanne Skahan, Prin. Lay Teachers 15; Aides 2; Students 227.

Catechesis/Religious Program—Ken Pesek, Liturgy & Music Dir.; Sabrina Schmidt, D.R.E. Students 97.

2—ST. ELIZABETH ANN SETON (1981) [CEM] Rev. Msgr. Thomas E. Reidy; Rev. Paul Anthony Suresh Samela (India); Sr. Bernadette Goessling, S.S.N.D., Parish Min.

Church: 2200 W. Republic Rd., 65807. Tel: 417-887-6472; Fax: 417-887-7027. Email: parishinfo@seaschurch.org. Web: www.seaschurch.org.

School—(Grades PreSchool-6) Tel: 417-887-6056; Fax: 417-887-2189. Email: chall@scspk12.org. Web: www.scspk12.org. Mrs. Cheryl Hall, Prin. Lay Teachers 9; Aides 5; Students 191.

Catechesis/Religious Program—Debbie Randell, D.R.E.; Melinda Lohkamp, Youth Min. Students 471.

3—HOLY TRINITY (1966) [JC] Rev. J. Fergus Monaghan. In Res., Rev. Frank C. Palermo (Retired).

Res.: 2818 E. Bennett, 65804. Tel: 417-883-3440; Fax: 417-883-0072. Email: frfergus@holytrinityspringfield.com. Web: www.holytrinity-catholic.com.

Catechesis/Religious Program—Sr. Jeanne Goessling, S.S.N.D., D.R.E. Students 161.

4—IMMACULATE CONCEPTION (1868) [JC] Revs. Lewis E. Hejna; Simon M. Diem Phuc Le, C.M.C. In Res., Rev. Msgr. Raymond V. Orf (Retired).

Res.: 3535 S. Fremont, 65804. Tel: 417-799-0062. Email: staff@ic-parish.org. Web: www.ic-parish.org. Church: 3555 S. Fremont, 65804. Tel: 417-887-0600; Fax: 417-887-0027.

School—(Grades PreSchool-8), 3555A S. Fremont, 65804. Tel: 417-881-7000; Fax: 417-881-7087. Mrs. Paula Baird, Prin. Lay Teachers 27; Aides 9; Students 498.

Catechesis/Religious Program—Mrs. Sharon Weidelman, D.R.E.; Dan Pfaff, Youth Min.; Mindy Pfaff, Youth Min.; Doris Trotter, PSR Dir. Students 48.

5—ST. JOSEPH'S (1892) [JC] Rev. Denis Dougherty, O.S.B.; Deacons Mathey F. Fletcher; Norm Ridder. In Res., Rev. Robert A. Landewe (Retired).

Res.: 1115 N. Campbell Ave., 65802. Tel: 417-865-1112; Fax: 417-865-7488. Email: stjosephspmo@yahoo.com. Web: www.stjosephspmo.org.

School—(Grades PreSchool-8), 515 W. Scott, 65802. Tel: 417-866-0667; Fax: 417-866-2862. Mrs. Marilyn Batson, Prin. Lay Teachers 12; Aides 1; Students 104.

Catechesis/Religious Program—Students 76.

6—SACRED HEART (1882) [JC] Rev. Daniel Robles; Deacon Edward Ellman; Bro. Manuel Benavides, C.M.F., Dir. Hispanic Ministries.

Mailing Address: 1609 N. Summit, 65803. Tel: 417-869-3646; Fax: 417-869-2218. Email: sheartch@sbcglobal.net. Web: www.sacredheartch.org.

Catechesis/Religious Program—Julia Valdes, C.R.E. Students 112.

CITY OF CAPE GIRARDEAU

(CAPE GIRARDEAU COUNTY)

1—CATHEDRAL OF ST. MARY OF THE ANNUNCIATION (1868) [CEM] [JC] Rev. Thomas P. Kiefer; Sr. Lucille Zerr, S.S.N.D., Pastoral Min.

Mailing Address: 615 William St., 63703.

Res.: 629 William St., 63703. Tel: 573-335-9347; Fax: 573-335-0649. Email: smparish@stmarycathedral.net. Web: www.stmarycathedral.net.

School—(Grades K-8), 210 S. Sprigg, 63703. Tel: 573-335-3840. Mrs. Carol Strattman, Prin. Lay Teachers 17; Aides 3; Students 269.

Catechesis/Religious Program—Brenda Kuhn, D.R.E.; Lisa Simmons, Family Life Min. Students 16.

Old St. Vincent's— (Chapel of Ease).

2—ST. VINCENT DE PAUL (1838) Revs. David F. Hulshof; Kizito Wenani. In Res., Rev. Robert F. Manso.

Office: 1913 Ritter Dr., 63701.

Res.: 741 N. Forest, 63701. Tel: 573-335-7667; Fax: 573-335-0034. Email: contactus@svparish.com. Web: www.svcape.com.

School—(Grades K-8), 1919 Ritter Dr., 63701. Tel: 573-334-9594. Mrs. Kay Glastetter, Prin. Lay Teachers 27; Aides 8; Students 446.

Catechesis/Religious Program—Kathy Hotop-Raines, D.R.E.; Sr. Theresa Davey, Christian Svc. Coord. Students 78.

OUTSIDE THE CITIES OF SPRINGFIELD AND CAPE GIRARDEAU

ADVANCE, STODDARD CO., ST. JOSEPH (1905) [CEM] Revs. Randolph G. Tochtrop; Ralph J. Duffner, Sr. Priest (Retired).

Res.: P.O. Box 640, 63730. Tel: 573-722-3504.

Catechesis/Religious Program—Students 26.

AURORA, LAWRENCE CO., HOLY TRINITY (1906) [CEM] Revs. Michael V. McDevitt, Canonical Pastor; William Paiz, C.M.F., Sacramental Priest; Sisters Francis Rose Rivers, S.S.N.D., Parish Min.; Mary Essner, S.S.N.D., Parish Life Coord.

Res.: Hwy. 60 & Carnation Rd., P.O. Box 533, 65605. Tel: 417-678-2403; Fax: 417-678-3714. Email: htcc@mo-net.com.

Catechesis/Religious Program—Mrs. Agnes Elsey, D.R.E. Students 62.

BENTON, SCOTT CO., ST. DENIS (1840) [CEM] Rev. Michael J. Casteel.
Res.: P.O. Box 127, 63736. Tel: 573-545-3864. Email: stdenischurch@gmail.com.
School—(Grades K-8), P.O. Box 189, 63736. Tel: 573-545-3017; Fax: 573-545-9185. Email: kspowers1123@yahoo.com. Mrs. Karen Powers, Prin. Lay Teachers 9; Aides 2; Students 118.
Catechesis/Religious Program—Students 18.

BILLINGS, CHRISTIAN CO., ST. JOSEPH (1879) [CEM] Revs. Lewis E. Hejna; Simon M. Diem Phuc Le, C.M.C.
Res.: P.O. Box 100, 65610. Tel: 417-744-2490; Fax: 417-744-2528. Email: stjosephbillinmo@aol.com.
Catechesis/Religious Program—Christi Brown, D.R.E.; Kelly Harter, Youth Dir. Students 70.

BOLIVAR, POLK CO., SACRED HEART (1946) [CEM] Rev. J. Patrick Wissman.
Res.: 1405 W. Fair Play St., 65613. Tel: 417-326-5596; Fax: 417-326-5596. Email: shoffice@windstream.net. Web: www.sacredheartbolivar.org.
Catechesis/Religious Program—Students 105.
Mission—St. Catherine P.O. Box 42, Humansville, Polk Co. 65674.

BRANSON, TANEY CO., OUR LADY OF THE LAKE (1951) Rev. Rick L. Jones; Sr. Francine Koehler, S.S.N.D., Pastoral Assoc.
Res.: 203 Vaughn Dr., 65616. Tel: 417-334-2928; Fax: 417-334-6883. Email: ladylakebranson@ladyofthelakeparish.org. Web: www.ladyofthelakeparish.org.
Catechesis/Religious Program—Mrs. Pat Hutcheson, D.R.E. & Youth Min. Students 178.

BUFFALO, DALLAS CO., ST. WILLIAM (1946) Revs. David L. Miller; Vincent E. Bertrand, Sacramental Priest.
Res.: P.O. Box 518, 65622. Tel: 417-345-2744. Email: sheartstwill@yahoo.com.
Catechesis/Religious Program—Brenda Paul, D.R.E. Students 14.

CARTHAGE, JASPER CO., ST. ANN (1872) Rev. William M. Hodgson.
Res.: 908 S. Clinton St., P.O. Box 803, 64836. Tel: 417-358-1841; Fax: 417-358-1841. Email: stannschurch@sbcglobal.net.
School—(Grades PreSchool-6), 1156 Grand, 64836. Tel: 417-358-2674; Fax: 417-358-8976. Bonnie Schaefer, Prin. Priests 1; Lay Teachers 8; Aides 1; Students 74.
Catechesis/Religious Program—Ryan Kiniry, D.R.E. Students 71.

CARUTHERSVILLE, PEMISCOT CO., SACRED HEART (1900) Rev. Jaroslaw Z. Skrzypek.
Res.: 605 Ward Ave., 63830. Tel: 573-333-4301. Email: sacredheart@cosmowireless.net. Web: www.rc.net/springfield-mo/sacred_heart.
Catechesis/Religious Program—Vicki Carter, C.R.E. Students 7.

CASSVILLE, BARRY CO., ST. EDWARD Revs. Paul J. McLoughlin; John S. Braun, Sacramental Priest; Sr. Juilana Soto, M.C.M., Pastoral Assoc.
Mailing Address: P.O. Box 492, 65625. Tel: 417-847-4948; Fax: 417-847-4947. Email: stedwardscc@centurytel.net.
Office: 101 W. 17th St., 65625.
Res.: 1802 Y Hwy., P.O. Box 492, 65625. Tel: 417-847-8526.
Church: 107 W. 17th St., 65625.
Catechesis/Religious Program—Students 74.

CHAFFEE, SCOTT CO., ST. AMBROSE (1907) [CEM] Revs. Randolph G. Tochtrop; Ralph J. Duffner (Retired); Diane Eftink, D.R.E.
Office: 418 S. Third St., 63740. Tel: 573-887-3953.
Res.: 314 Elliott, 63740. Tel: 573-887-4283.
School—(Grades K-8), 419 S. Third St., 63740. Tel: 573-887-6711; Fax: 573-887-6711. Mr. Clifford Lankheit, Prin. Priests 1; Lay Teachers 8; Students 68.
Catechesis/Religious Program—Students 46.

CHARLESTON, MISSISSIPPI CO., ST. HENRY (1874) Rev. Glenn A. Eftink.
Res.: 304 Court St., 63834. Tel: 573-683-2114. Email: sthenrychurch@att.net. Web: www.sthenrychurch.org.
School—(Grades PreSchool-8), 306 Court St., 63834. Tel: 573-683-6218; Fax: 573-683-7800. Mrs. Alice Harvell, Prin. Lay Teachers 11; Aides 3; Students 100.
Catechesis/Religious Program—

CONWAY, LACLEDE CO., SACRED HEART (1908) [CEM] Revs. Scott M. Sunnenberg; Vincent E. Bertrand, Sacramental Priest.
Res.: P.O. Box 8, 65632. Tel: 417-589-6782.
Church: 310 Spruce St., 65632.
Catechesis/Religious Program—Students 31.

DEXTER, STODDARD CO., SACRED HEART (1889) Rev. David J. Dohogne.
Office: 115 E. Market St., 63841.
Res.: 103 E. Market St., 63841. Tel: 573-624-8888.
Church: 102 E. Castor, 63841. Tel: 573-624-7333; Fax: 573-624-4076. Email: dexter.sacred.heart@gmail.com. Web: www.catholic-forum.com/churches/642sh.
Catechesis/Religious Program—Shearon Harris, D.R.E. Students 75.

DONIPHAN, RIPLEY CO., ST. BENEDICT (1859) [CEM] Revs. David N. Coon; Joseph Kappilumakkal Mathai, C.M.I.
Res.: 306 Kegler, 63935. Tel: 573-996-3301.
Catechesis/Religious Program—Terri Wright, C.R.E.; Sandra Kennon, C.R.E. Students 17.

EL DORADO SPRINGS, CEDAR CO., ST. ELIZABETH OF HUNGARY (1946) [CEM] Rev. Basil M. Toan Quang Doan, C.M.C.
Res.: 609 S. Main, 64744. Tel: 417-876-3216; Fax: 417-876-6448.
Catechesis/Religious Program—Students 17.
Mission—St. Peter the Apostle 222 N. Hwy. J, P.O. Box 583, Stockton, Cedar Co. 65785. Tel: 417-276-5588.

FORSYTH, TANEY CO., OUR LADY OF THE OZARKS (1980) Revs. Rick L. Jones; Philip J. Conlon (MAD), Sacramental Min. (Retired); Sr. Charlotte Flarlong, S.S.N.D., Pastoral Assoc.
Mailing Address: P.O. Box 639, 65653. Tel: 417-546-5208; Fax: 417-546-6615. Email: ourladyoftheozarks@yahoo.com. Web: www.ourladyoftheozarks.org.
Church: 951 Swan Valley Dr., 65653.
Catechesis/Religious Program—Students 11.

FREDERICKTOWN, MADISON CO., ST. MICHAEL (1827) [CEM] Rev. Mitchell S. Wilk.
Res.: 304 W. Main St., 63645. Tel: 573-783-2182; Fax: 573-783-5230. Email: stmic@charter.net. Web: stmichaelrcc.us.
Catechesis/Religious Program—Vicki Allgier, C.R.E. Students 67.

GLENNONVILLE, DUNKLIN CO., ST. TERESA (1905) [CEM] Revs. David J. Dohogne; Jose Thundathil Antoney, C.M.I.; Deacon Fred Hirtz.
Res.: 40694 State Hwy. JJ, Campbell, 63933-9148. Tel: 573-328-1226; 573-328-4544 (Office); Fax: 578-328-4544. Web: www.stteresa.catholicweb.com.
School—(Grades PreSchool-8) Mrs. Peggy Ogden, Prin. Lay Teachers 6; Students 61; Aides 1.
Catechesis/Religious Program—Students 15.

HOUSTON, TEXAS CO., ST. MARK (1975) Rev. Matthew J. Rehrauer.
Res.: 117 E. South Oak Crest, 65483. Tel: 417-967-3589. Email: stmarkchurch@centurytel.net.
Catechesis/Religious Program—Students 29.
Mission—St. Vincent de Paul Roby, Texas Co.
Mission—St. John The Baptist Licking, Texas Co.

IRONTON, IRON CO., STE. MARIE DU LAC (1878) [CEM] Revs. James J. Unterreiner; Anthony M. Gaydos, O.S.M., Senior Priest.
Res.: 350 S. Main St., 63650. Tel: 573-546-2611; Fax: 573-546-3711. Email: stmariedu@centurylink.net.
Catechesis/Religious Program—Susan Wessel, C.R.E.; Dennis Trowbridge, Youth Min. Students 20.
Mission—Our Lady of Sorrows Lesterville, Reynolds Co.
Mission—St. Philip Benizi Viburnum, Iron Co.

JACKSON, CAPE GIRARDEAU CO., IMMACULATE CONCEPTION (1874) [CEM] Rev. John M. Harth; Deacons Walter L. Biri; James E. Long Jr.
Res.: 208 S. Hope St., Ste. 101, 63755. Tel: 573-243-3182; Fax: 573-243-6833. Email: pastor@icjacksonmo.com. Web: www.icjacksonmo.com.
School—(Grades PreSchool-8), 300 S. Hope St., 63755. Tel: 573-243-5013. Ms. Michele Huffman, Prin. Lay Teachers 20; Students 240; Aides 3.
Catechesis/Religious Program—Alan Sellers, Youth Min.; Mrs. Kim Sellers, Youth Min.; Eddie Laws, Educ. Min.; Misti Laws, Educ. Min. Students 171.

JOPLIN, JASPER CO.
1—ST. MARY (1938) [JC] Rev. Justin D. Monaghan.
Mailing Address: P.O. Box 106, 64802.
Office: 430 W. 7th St., 64801.
Res.: 2415 Moffet Ave., 64804. Tel: 417-623-3333; Fax: 417-623-4015. Email: church@stmarysparishjoplin.com. Web: stmarysjoplin.myownparish.com.
School—(Grades PreSchool-5), 931 S. Byers Ave., 64801. Tel: 417-623-1465; Fax: 417-623-4749. Mr. Stephen Jones, Prin. Sisters 1; Lay Teachers 14; Students 206; Aides 2.
Catechesis/Religious Program—Patty Wheeler, C.R.E. Students 86.
2—ST. PETER THE APOSTLE (1877) [JC] Revs. John (J.) F. Friedel; Shoby Mathew Chettiyath.
Res.: 812 S. Pearl Ave., 64801-4396. Tel: 417-623-8643; Fax: 417-623-0866. Email: stpetersjoplin@yahoo.com. Web: www.saintpetertheapostlejoplin.com.
School—(Grades 6-8), 802 Byers, 64801-4396. Tel: 417-624-5605; Fax: 417-624-6254. Mr. Greg Emory, Prin. Sisters 1; Lay Teachers 8; Students 79.
Catechesis/Religious Program—Elizabeth Runkle, C.R.E.; Sr. Diane Langford, C.D.P., Dir. Faith Formation. Students 76.

KELSO, SCOTT CO., ST. AUGUSTINE (1878) Rev. M. Oliver Clavin.
Res.: 201 S. Messmer, Box 26, 63758. Tel: 573-264-4724; Fax: 573-264-4106. Email: stac@charter.net. Web: staugustinekelso.catholicweb.com.
School—(Grades K-8), 230 S. Hwy. 61, P.O. Box 97, 63758-0097. Tel: 573-264-4644; Fax: 573-264-1475. Mrs. Tracy Dumey, Prin. Lay Teachers 11; Aides 10; Students 179.
Catechesis/Religious Program—

KENNETT, DUNKLIN CO., ST. CECILIA (1923) Rev. Allan L. Saunders; Sisters Karen Thein, S.S.N.D., Pastoral Assoc. (Hispanic Ministry); Mary Elizabeth Runde, S.S.N.D., Pastoral Assoc. (Hispanic Ministry).
Res.: 1226 College St., P.O. Box 306, 63857. Tel: 573-888-2412; Fax: 573-888-0613. Email: saintcecilia@att.net.
Catechesis/Religious Program—Students 175.

KIMBERLING CITY, STONE CO., OUR LADY OF THE COVE (1979) Rev. Joseph M. Than Van Liem, C.M.C.
Res.: 20 Kimberling Blvd., P.O. Box 548, 65686. Tel: 417-739-4700; Fax: 417-739-5279. Email: ourlady@ourladyofthecove.net. Web: www.ourladyofthecove.net.
Catechesis/Religious Program—Jim Dobbs, D.R.E. Students 91.

LAMAR, BARTON CO., ST. MARY (1904) [CEM] Revs. John (J.) F. Friedel; Shoby Mathew Chettiyath.
Res.: 200 E. 17th St., P.O. Box 89, 64759. Tel: 417-682-2492.
Catechesis/Religious Program—Students 30.

LEBANON, LACLEDE CO., ST. FRANCIS DE SALES (1870) [CEM] Revs. David L. Miller; Vincent E. Bertrand, Sacramental Priest.
Res.: 345 Grand St., 65536. Tel: 417-532-4811; Fax: 417-532-8847. Email: lebanoncatholic@gmail.com. Web: www.catholicchurchlebanon.org.
Catechesis/Religious Program—Shellie Weaver, D.R.E.; Sr. Mary Frances Reis, B.V.M., Pastoral Care. Students 90.
Chapel—Bennett Springs, Sportman's Chapel

LEOPOLD, BOLLINGER CO., ST. JOHN (1856) [CEM] Rev. William Hennecke Jr.
Res.: 103 Main St., P.O. Box 83, 63760. Tel: 573-238-3300; Fax: 573-238-2450. Email: cwolpers471@clas.net. Web: www.stjohnscatholiccemetery.org.
Catechesis/Religious Program—Nick Elfrink, D.R.E.; Cindy Jansen, Youth Dir. Students 159.
Mission—St. Anthony [CEM] Glennon, Bollinger Co.

MALDEN, DUNKLIN CO., ST. ANN (1890) Revs. David J. Dohogne; Jose Thundathil Antoney, C.M.I.; Deacon Fred Hirtz.
Mailing Address: *c/o St. Teresa Parish*, 40694 State Hwy. JJ, Campbell, 63933. Tel: 573-328-4544. Web: www.stteresa.catholicweb.com.
Church: 304 N. Douglas St., 63863.
Catechesis/Religious Program—Students 2.

MANSFIELD, WRIGHT CO., IMMACULATE HEART OF MARY (1943) Revs. Paul Wightman, O.M.I.; Jeffery A. Fasching (WCH), Sacramental Min.
Res.: Rte. 6, Box 6700, Ava, 65608. Tel: 417-683-5249; 417-924-3779 (Office).
Catechesis/Religious Program—Mrs. B. J. Sterling, C.R.E. (Ava); Nancy Stepro, C.R.E. (Mansfield); Sheri Richardson, C.R.E. (Gainesville). Students 42.
Mission—St. Leo the Great R.R. 6, Box 6700, Ava, Douglas Co. 65608. Tel: 417-683-5249.
Mission—St. William P.O. Box 367, Gainesville, Ozark Co. 65655. Tel: 417-679-4804.

MARSHFIELD, WEBSTER CO., HOLY TRINITY (1892) Rev. Scott M. Sunnenberg; J. B. Kelly, C.R.E.
515 E. Washington, 65706-1865. Tel: 417-859-2228. Email: htmparish@centurytel.net. Web: home.catholicweb.com/marshfieldhtcc.
Res.: 125 N. Locust, 65706. Tel: 417-859-3489.
Catechesis/Religious Program—Students 71.

MONETT, BARRY CO., ST. LAWRENCE (1891) [CEM] Revs. Paul J. McLoughlin; John S. Braun, Sacramental Priest.
Res.: 311 8th St., 65708. Tel: 417-236-9273; 417-235-3286 (Office); Fax: 417-235-3721. Email: stlaw1@att.net. Web: home.catholicweb.com/stlawrence.
Church: 405 Seventh St., 65708.
School—(Grades PreSchool-6), 407 Seventh St., 65708. Tel: 417-235-3721. Mrs. Teresa Verhoff, Prin. Lay Teachers 8; Aides 1; Students 96.
Catechesis/Religious Program—Sr. Teresa Cruz, M.C.M., D.R.E. Students 169.

MOUNT VERNON, LAWRENCE CO., ST. SUSANNE (1939) Rev. Patrick A. Teter.
Res.: P.O. Box 126, 65712. Tel: 417-466-4190; Fax: 417-466-2561.

Catechesis/Religious Program—Students 58.
Mission—St. Patrick Greenfield, Dade Co.

MOUNTAIN GROVE, WRIGHT CO., SACRED HEART (1893) Revs. Paul Wightman, O.M.I., Canonical Pastor; Jeffery A. Fasching (WCH), Sacramental Priest; Deacon Joseph Kurtenbach, Parish Life Coord.
Res.: 302 E. State St., 65711. Tel: 417-926-3803.
Catechesis/Religious Program—Students 19.
Mission—St. Michael Cabool, Texas Co.

MOUNTAIN VIEW, HOWELL CO., ST. JOHN VIANNEY (1951) Rev. Ernest J. Marquart.
Res.: 808 State Rd. Y, P.O. Box 38, 65548. Tel: 417-934-2649.
Catechesis/Religious Program—Patricia Einweck, C.R.E. Students 16.
Mission—St. Sylvester Eminence, Shannon Co.

NEOSHO, NEWTON CO., ST. CANERA (1871) [JC] Rev. Henry Grodecki, C.M.
Res.: 504 S. Washington St., 64850. Tel: 417-451-3411; Fax: 417-451-3432. Email: stcanera@sbcglobal.net. Web: www.stcanera.catholicweb.com.
Catechesis/Religious Program—Students 212.
Mission—Nativity of Our Lord 227 Sulphur St., Noel, McDonald Co. 64854.

NEW HAMBURG, SCOTT CO., ST. LAWRENCE (1847) [CEM] Rev. Michael J. Casteel.
Mailing Address: P.O. Box 247, Benton, 63736-8159.
Church: 1001 State Hwy. A, Benton, 63736-0247. Tel: 573-545-3317; Fax: 573-545-3317.
Catechesis/Religious Program—Pat Moore, D.R.E. Students 72.

NEW MADRID, NEW MADRID CO., IMMACULATE CONCEPTION (1789) Rev. Jaroslaw Z. Skrzypek.
Res.: 605 Davis St., 63869. Tel: 573-748-5183; Fax: 573-748-7718. Email: immaculateconceptionnm@gmail.com.
School—(Grades PreSchool-8), 560 Powell, 63869. Tel: 573-748-5123; Fax: 573-748-5123. Mrs. Mary Shy, Prin. Lay Teachers 6; Students 68.
Catechesis/Religious Program—

NIXA, CHRISTIAN CO., ST. FRANCIS OF ASSISI (2004) Rev. Msgr. Thomas E. Reidy; Rev. Paul Anthony Suresh Samela (India).
844 S. Gregg Rd., P.O. Box 1920, 65714. Tel: 417-725-1975; Fax: 417-725-1975. Email: stfrancis@cebridge.net.
Catechesis/Religious Program—Leigh Sisk, C.R.E. Students 43.

ORAN, SCOTT CO., GUARDIAN ANGEL (1892) [CEM 2] Revs. Randolph G. Tochtrop; Ralph J. Duffner, Sr. Priest (Retired); Sr. Mary Jane Jansen, S.S.N.D., Pastoral Assoc.
Res.: 604 Church St., P.O. Box 158, 63771. Tel: 573-262-3210; Fax: 573-262-3210. Web: www.guardianangelchurch.net.
School—(Grades K-8), 514 Church St., 63771. Tel: 573-262-3583. Pamela Wilgus, Prin. Sisters 2; Lay Teachers 9; Aides 1; Students 88.
Catechesis/Religious Program—Students 40.

OZARK, CHRISTIAN CO., ST. JOSEPH THE WORKER (1961) Rev. Saviour Nundwe; Deacon Mike Steele.
Res.: 1796 N. State Hwy. NN, 65721. Tel: 417-581-6328; Fax: 417-581-4957. Email: sjwpriest@saintjosephozark.org. Web: www.saintjosephozark.org.
Catechesis/Religious Program—Students 170.

PIEDMONT, WAYNE CO., ST. CATHERINE OF SIENA (1873) Rev. Mark J. Binder; Sisters Cecelia Olinger, O.S.U., Pastoral Assoc.; Rita Schonhoff, Outreach Min.
Res.: 109 Piedmont Ave., 63957. Tel: 573-223-4924. Email: scsgolos@windstream.net.
Catechesis/Religious Program—Students 36.
Mission—St. George Van Buren, Carter Co. Tel: 573-323-8576.
Mission—Our Lady of Sorrows Williamsville, Wayne Co.

PIERCE CITY, LAWRENCE CO., ST. MARY (1883) [CEM 2] Rev. Peter J. Morciniec.
Res.: 200 Front St., 65723. Tel: 417-476-2827; Fax: 417-476-5827. Email: st_marys@live.com.
School—(Grades PreSchool-8), 202 Front St., 65723. Tel: 417-476-2824; Fax: 417-476-2824. Dr. Laryy Roberts, Prin. Lay Teachers 5; Aides 4; Students 81.
Catechesis/Religious Program—Students 72.

POPLAR BLUFF, BUTLER CO., SACRED HEART (1891) [CEM] Revs. David N. Coon; Joseph Kappilumakkal Mathai, C.M.I.
Res.: 123 N. Eighth St., 63901. Tel: 573-785-9635; Fax: 573-785-2069. Email: shparish@socket.net. Web: home.catholicweb.com/pbshparish.
School—(Grades PreSchool-8) Tel: 573-785-5836; Fax: 573-785-3908. Mrs. Janet Kuper, Prin. Sisters 3; Lay Teachers 8; Students 175; Aides 4.
Catechesis/Religious Program—Sharon Quaite, C.R.E. Students 71.

PORTAGEVILLE, NEW MADRID CO., ST. EUSTACHIUS (1902) Rev. Allan L. Saunders.
Res.: 200 W. Fourth St., 63873. Tel: 573-379-3401. Email: eustachius@sbcglobal.net.
School—(Grades PreSchool-8), 214 W. Fourth St., 63873. Tel: 573-379-3525; Fax: 573-379-3843. Mrs. Patricia Rone, Prin. Lay Teachers 6; Aides 1; Students 64.
Catechesis/Religious Program—Students 14.

PULASKIFIELD, BARRY CO., SS. PETER AND PAUL (1892) [CEM] Rev. Paul J. McLoughlin.
Mailing Address: P.O. Box 208, Pierce City, 65723. Tel: 417-476-2463. Email: stspp1892@gmail.com.
Catechesis/Religious Program—Students 12.

SALEM, DENT CO., SACRED HEART (1880) Rev. Daniel J. Hirtz; Deacon Richard F. Cole.
Res.: 602 W. Butler, 65560. Tel: 573-729-4291. Email: sacredh@catholicweb.com. Web: www.salemsacredheart.org.
Catechesis/Religious Program—June Cole, D.R.E. Students 65.
Mission—Christ the King P.O. Box 177, Bunker, Reynolds Co. 63629.
Chapel—Montauk, St. Jude

SARCOXIE, NEWTON CO., ST. AGNES (1870) [CEM] Rev. Peter J. Morciniec.
Res. & Mailing Address: P.O. Box 218, Pierce City, 65723-0218. Tel: 417-548-3540.
Catechesis/Religious Program—Jane Kutz, D.R.E. Students 10.

SCOTT CITY, SCOTT CO., ST. JOSEPH (1911) [CEM] Rev. M. Oliver Clavin.
Mailing Address: 201 S. Messmer, 63780. Tel: 573-264-4724; Fax: 573-264-1506. Email: stjosephsc@charter.net. Web: stjosephscottcity.catholicweb.com.
Church: 604 Sycamore, 63780.
School—(Grades K-8), 606 Sycamore, 63780. Tel: 573-264-2600; Fax: 573-264-1325. Betty Spalding, Prin. Lay Teachers 4; Students 26; Aides 1.
Catechesis/Religious Program—

SENECA, NEWTON CO., ST. MARY (1884) [CEM] Rev. Michael M. Quang Van Do, C.M.C., Admin. & Sacramental Priest.
Res.: P.O. Box 1169, 64865. Tel: 417-776-3786.
Church: 1209 Wyandotte, 64865.
Catechesis/Religious Program—Students 27.

SHELL KNOB, BARRY CO., HOLY FAMILY (1978) Rev. Mark G. Boyer, Parochial Admin.
Res.: 24036 FR 1255, P.O. Box 229, 65747. Tel: 417-858-2518; 417-858-3678; Fax: 417-858-6029. Email: catholicchur722@centurytel.net. Web: home.centurytel.net/holyfamilyshellknob.
Catechesis/Religious Program—Penny Muckle, C.R.E. Students 5.

SIKESTON, SCOTT CO., ST. FRANCIS XAVIER'S (1893) Rev. Glenn A. Eftink.
Res.: 217 W. Center St., 63801. Tel: 573-471-5018; 573-471-2447 (Office); Fax: 573-471-9820. Email: stfx1892@catholicweb.com. Web: www.sfxparish.catholicweb.com.
School—(Grades PreSchool-8), 106 N. Stoddard, 63801. Tel: 573-471-0841; Fax: 573-471-0841. Mrs. Debbie Pollock, Prin. Lay Teachers 12; Aides 3; Students 148.
Catechesis/Religious Program—Mrs. Toni Grojean, D.R.E. Students 36.

VERONA, LAWRENCE CO., SACRED HEART (1874) [CEM] Revs. Michael McDevitt, Canonical Pastor; William Paiz, C.M.F., Sacramental Priest.; Sr. Mary Essner, S.S.N.D., Parish Life Coord.
Mailing Address: P.O. Box 533, Aurora, 65605-0533.
In Res., Rev. John S. Braun.
Church: Adams & Second St., 65769. Tel: 417-678-2403; Fax: 417-678-3714. Email: htcc@mo-net.com.
Catechesis/Religious Program—Sr. Francis Rose Rivers, S.S.N.D., D.R.E. & Hispanic Min. Students 155.

WEBB CITY, JASPER CO., SACRED HEART (1908) Rev. Rahab Isidor, Parochial Admin.
Res.: 909 N. Madison, 64870. Tel: 417-673-2044. Email: sacredheartparish909@yahoo.com. Web: www.sacredheartwebbcity.com.
Catechesis/Religious Program—Students 75.

WEST PLAINS, HOWELL CO., ST. MARY (1902) Rev. Joseph Weidenbenner; Deacon Patrick J. Keefe.
Mailing Address: P.O. Box 67, 65775.
Res.: 1551 Bill Virdon Blvd., 65775. Tel: 417-257-7912; 417-256-2556 (Office); Fax: 417-256-9251. Email: stmarychurchwestplains@gmail.com. Web: home.centurytel.net/stmarychurch.
Catechesis/Religious Program—Hillary Tugwell, C.R.E. Students 82.
Mission—Sacred Heart Thayer, Oregon Co.

WILLOW SPRINGS, HOWELL CO., SACRED HEART (1897) [CEM] Rev. Sherman B. Wall, O.M.I.; Deacon G. Alan Bandy.
Church: 1050 W. Bus Hwy. 60-63, 65793. Tel: 417-469-2447.
Catechesis/Religious Program—Debbie Joerger, C.R.E. Students 23.
Mission—St. Joseph White Church, Howell Co. Karen Nichols, C.R.E.

Chaplains of Public Institutions

SPRINGFIELD. *Cape Girardeau Hospital Ministry*. Rev. Kizito Wenani. Tel: 573-335-7667.
St. John's Regional Health Center dba St. John's Hospital Tel: 417-820-2710. Rev. Augustine R. Njuu, A.J., Chap.
Springfield Hospital Ministry. Rev. Jeffrey A. Fasching. Tel: 417-831-3565.
U.S. Medical Center, 1900 W. Sunshine, 65802. Tel: 417-862-7041, Ext. 1669.

CHARLESTON. *Southeast Correctional Center*, Tel: 573-748-5183. Rev. Bobby Manso, Chap.

FORDLAND. *Ozark Correctional Center*, Tel: 417-887-6500.

JOPLIN. *Joplin Hospital Ministry*, Tel: 417-781-2727. Rev. Valery Burusu, (Diocese of Nyundo, Rwanda).

LICKING. *South Central Correctional Center*, Tel: 573-729-4291. Rev. Matthew J. Rehrauer, Chap. Tel: 417-967-3589.

POPLAR BLUFF. *Poplar Bluff Hospital Ministry*. Rev. David N. Coon. Tel: 573-785-9635.

Special Assignment:
Rev.—
Orthel, Joseph A., 704 S. Garfield Ave., Wagoner, OK 74467.

Health Leave of Absence:
Rev. Msgr.—
Swalina, Michael F., S.T.D., 389 Poplar Forest Dr. Apt. A, Saint Louis, 63125.

Leave of Absence:
Revs.—
Carr, Gary M., 5610 Village Royale Ln., Apt. B, Saint Louis, 63128.
Lamprea, Gefford C.

Retired:
Rev. Msgrs.—
Bucher, Philip A., V.G., 412 12th St. N.W., Albuquerque, NM 87102. Tel: 505-341-4514
Eftink, Edward M., Ph.D., 4009 N. Thistle Dr., Ozark, 65721. Tel: 417-551-4406
Ernstmann, Mark C., S.T.L., M.Ed., 533 S. Jefferson Ave., 65806. Tel: 417-831-3565
Orf, Raymond V., 3535 S. Fremont, 65804-4237. Tel: 417-887-0600; 417-799-0062
Rolwing, Richard C., 378 Etherton Dr., 63703. Tel: 573-335-3206
Stanton, William J., 358 Etherton Dr., 63703. Tel: 573-651-6465
Revs.—
Bauer, Sylvester W. (JC), Westphalia Hills, 1899 Hwy. 63, Westphalia, 65085. Tel: 573-455-2280
Biernacki, Jacob S., St. John's Mercy Villa, 1100 E. Montclair, 65807. Tel: 417-820-8316
Brath, John A., 3912 N. 15th St., Ozark, 65721. Tel: 417-581-1036
Duffner, Ralph J., 314 Elliott, Chaffee, 63740. Tel: 573-887-4048
Huggins, William A., Crescent Park Village, 551 Redstone Ave. W., Rm. 8, Crestview, FL 32536.
Landewe, Robert A., 1115 N. Campbell Ave., 65802. Tel: 417-350-3760
Lutz, Frederick J., 2268 E. Mirabeau St., 65804.
Palermo, Frank C., 2818 E. Bennett, 65804-1943. Tel: 417-883-3440
Seyer, James A., 150 S. Silver Springs Rd., #4, 63703-5076. Tel: 573-651-3939
Varone, Normand G., 383 Etherton Dr., 63703.

Permanent Deacons:
Bandy, G. Alan, Sacred Heart, Willow Springs
Biri, Walter L., Immaculate Conception, Jackson
Brewer, Thomas M., St. Elizabeth Ann Seton, Springfield
Cole, Richard F., Sacred Heart, Salem
Costello, Charles R.
Ellman, Edward V., Sacred Heart, Springfield
Fletcher, Mathey F., St. Joseph, Springfield
Hirtz, Fred, St. Teresa, Glennonville; St. Ann, Malden
Keefe, Patrick J., St. Mary, West Plains
Keller, William J., Cathedral of St. Agnes, Springfield
Kurtenbach, Joseph, Sacred Heart, Mountain Grove
Long, James E., Jr., Immaculate Conception, Jackson
Ridder, Norm, Sacred Heart, Springfield
Steele, Michael, St. Joseph the Worker, Ozark
Vrooman, David
Wand, Mark A., Cathedral of St. Agnes, Springfield

INSTITUTIONS LOCATED IN THE DIOCESE

[A] SEMINARIES, RELIGIOUS, OR SCHOLASTICATES

AVA. *Assumption Novitiate (Trappists)*, R.R. 5, Box 1056, 65608-9142. Tel: 417-683-5110; Fax: 417-683-5658. Email: assumptionabbey@wildblue.net. Rt. Revs. Cyprian Harrison, O.C.S.O., Supr.; Robert Matter, O.C.S.O., Abbot Emeritus; Rev. Alberic Maisog, O.C.S.O., Novice Master.

CARTHAGE. *Congregation of the Mother Co-Redemptrix*, 1900 Grand Ave., 64836. Tel: 417-358-7787; Fax: 417-359-9164. Email: cmc@dongcong.net. Web: www.dongcong.net. Very Rev. Louis M. Vu Minh Nhien, C.M.C., Prov.

[B] HIGH SCHOOLS, DIOCESAN

SPRINGFIELD. *Springfield Catholic High School*, (Grades 9-12), (Coed), 2340 S. Eastgate, 65809-2832. Tel: 417-887-8817; Fax: 417-885-1165. Email: ademelo@scspk12.org. Web: www.scspk12.org. Dr. Amy DeMelo, Prin.; Revs. Scott M. Sunnenberg, Chap.; Mark Clarke, C.M.F., Chap.; Saviour Nundwe, Chap.; Mrs. Debbie Seitzer, Librarian. Lay Teachers 26; Students 335; Counselors 2.

Springfield Catholic School System, 2340 S. Eastgate Ave., 65809-2832. Tel: 417-865-5567; Fax: 417-865-5278. Email: ademleo@sscspk12.org. Web: www.scspk12.org. Dr. Amy DeMelo, Dir.

CAPE GIRARDEAU. *Notre Dame Regional High School*, 265 Notre Dame Dr., 63701-8517. Tel: 573-335-6772; Fax: 573-335-3458. Email: principal@notredamehighschool.org. Web: www.notredamehighschool.org. Bro. David Anthony Migliorino, O.S.F., Prin.; Rev. William Hennecke Jr., Chap. Co-Instructional Regional High School Priests 1; Brothers 1; Lay Teachers 38; Counselors 2; Students 555.

JOPLIN. *St. Mary*, (Grades PreK-5), 931 S. Byers Ave., 64801. Tel: 417-623-7051; Fax: 417-626-8334. Email: sjones@jacss.org. Web: www.jacss.org. Mr. Stephen Jones, Prin. Sisters 1; Lay Teachers 14; Aides 2; Students 206.

McAuley Catholic High School, 930 Pearl Ave., 64801. Tel: 417-624-9320; Fax: 417-626-8334. Email: gkoester@jacss.org. Web: www.jacss.org. Mr. Gene Koester, Principal. Sisters 1; Lay Teachers 14; Counselors 2; Students 95.

St. Peter the Apostle Middle School, (Grades 6-8), 802 Byers, 64801. Tel: 417-624-5605; Fax: 417-624-6254. Email: gemory@jacss.org. Web: www.jacss.org. Mr. Greg Emory, Prin. Sisters 1; Lay Teachers 8; Students 79.

[C] CATHOLIC CHARITIES

SPRINGFIELD. **Catholic Charities of Southern Missouri, Inc.*, 601 S. Jefferson Ave., 65806. Tel: 417-866-0841; Fax: 417-866-1140. Email: ccsomo@ccsomo.org. Mrs. Maura A. Taylor, Exec. Dir.

[D] GENERAL HOSPITALS

SPRINGFIELD. *Mercy Hospital Springfield dba St. John's Hospital* 1235 E. Cherokee, 65804. Tel: 417-820-2710; Fax: 417-820-8730. Web: www.stjohns.com. Jon Swope, Pres. & CEO St. John's Health System; Rev. Augustine R. Njuu, A.J., Chap. Member of Mercy Health. Sisters 5; Bed Capacity 866; Inpatients 32,745; Outpatients 543,481.

CAPE GIRARDEAU. **Saint Francis Medical Center*, 211 St. Francis Dr., 63703-8399. Tel: 573-331-3000; Fax: 573-331-5009. Email: sfmc@sfmc.net. Web: www.sfmc.net. Mr. Steven C. Bjelich, FACHE-D, Pres. & CEO. Owned and operated by a lay board with Diocesan sponsorship. Sisters 2; Bed Capacity 280; Inpatients 11,929; Outpatients 144,763.

**Saint Francis Foundation*, 211 St. Francis Dr., 63703. Tel: 573-331-5133; Fax: 573-331-5009.

**Saint Francis Healthcare System (formerly known as St. Francis Hospital of Franciscan Sisters)*, 211 St. Francis Dr., 63703. Tel: 573-331-5128; Fax: 573-331-5009.

AURORA. *Mercy Hospital Aurora dba St. John's Hospital-Aurora* 500 Porter Ave., 65605. Tel: 417-678-2122; Fax: 417-678-7877. Web: www.stjohns.com. Douglas M. Stroemel, West Region Pres. Bed Capacity 25; Total Assisted Annually 28,363.

CARTHAGE. *Mercy Hospital Carthage*, 3125 Dr. Russell Smith Way, 64836. Tel: 417-358-8121; Fax: 417-237-7240. Web: mccune-brooks.org. Jacquelynn Richmond, Vice Pres. & Asst. Gen. Counsel.

CASSVILLE. *Mercy Hospital Cassville dba St. John's Hospital-Cassville* 94 S. Main St., 65625. Tel: 417-847-6000; Fax: 417-847-6083. Web: www.stjohnshospitalcassville.com. Douglas M. Stroemel, West Region Pres. Bed Capacity 25; Total Assisted Annually 21,755.

JOPLIN. *Mercy Hospital Joplin*, 2817 St. John's Blvd., 64804. Tel: 417-625-2200; Fax: 417-625-2910. Gary W. Pulsipher, Pres. & CEO; Rev. Valery Burusu, Chap.

LEBANON. **Mercy Hospital Lebanon*, 100 Hospital Dr., 65536. Tel: 417-533-6100; Fax: 417-533-6021. Email: Brenda.Parker@mercy.net. Web: stjohnslebanon.com. Mr. Mike Gillen, Pres. Sisters 1; Bed Capacity 62; Inpatients 2,901; Outpatients 83,020.

MOUNTAIN VIEW. *Mercy St. Francis Hospital*, P.O. Box 82, 65548. Tel: 417-934-7000; Fax: 417-934-7092. Jonathan Wade, Pres. Daughters of St. Francis of Assisi and Sisters of Mercy (Managed by Mercy Health Springfield Communities) Sisters 3; Bed Capacity 25; Total Assisted Annually 20,232.

The Sister Cornelia Blasko Foundation, Inc., 100 W. Hwy. 60, P.O. Box 82, 65548. Tel: 417-934-7090.

[E] SPECIAL HOSPITALS

SPRINGFIELD. *St. John's Mercy Villa*, 1100 E. Montclair, 65807. Tel: 417-820-8500; Fax: 417-820-8547. Donald Swafford, Admin., St. John's Mercy Villa, St. John's Health System. Skilled Care of Long Term Nursing Home, for the Aged and Chronically Ill. Bed Capacity 150.

[F] MONASTERIES AND RESIDENCES OF PRIESTS AND BROTHERS

SPRINGFIELD. *Claretians Missionaries' Residence-Villa Claret*, 1530 N. Summit, 65803. Tel: 417-869-0075. Revs. Mark Clark, C.M.F.; Thomas A. McGann, C.M.F.; William Paiz, C.M.F.; Bros. Agustin Carrillo, C.M.F.; Manuel Benavides, C.M.F.

AVA: *Assumption Abbey (Trappist)*, Rte. 5, Box 1056, 65608. Tel: 417-683-5110; Fax: 417-683-5658. Email: assumptionabbey@wildblue.net. Web: www.assumptionabbey.org. Rt. Revs. Robert Matter, O.C.S.O., Abbot Emeritus; Cyprian Harrison, O.C.S.O., Supr.; Revs. Leon Brockman, O.C.S.O.; Donald Joseph Hamilton, O.C.S.O.; Alberic Maisog, O.C.S.O.; Bros. Boniface Domas, O.C.S.O.; Francis Flaherty, O.C.S.O.; Thomas Imhoff, O.C.S.O. Priests 3; Brothers 3; Superior 1; Abbot Emeritus 1.

Our Lady of the Angels Friary, Rte. 5, Box 1042, 65608. Tel: 417-683-4303. Rev. Francis Wendling, O.F.M.; Bros. Josef Anderlohr, O.F.M.; Joseph F. Manning, O.F.M.

CARTHAGE. *Congregation of the Mother Coredemptrix, United States Assumption Province*, 1900 Grand Ave., 64836. Tel: 417-358-7787; Fax: 417-358-9508. Email: cmc@dongcong.net. Web: www.dongcong.net. Very Rev. Louis M. Vu Minh Nhien, C.M.C., Prov.; Revs. Paul M. Tai Tran, C.M.C., Asst. I; Raymond M. Dien Nguyen, C.M.C., Asst. II; Paul M. Van Nuyen, C.M.C., Asst. III; Lawrence M. Nguyen, C.M.C., Asst. IV; (John Damas. M.) Voung Duc Ngo, C.M.C., Treas.; (Philip M.) Thanh V. Do, C.M.C., Sec.; (Anselm M.) Can Vuong Dinh, C.M.C.; (Luke M.) Do Binh Dinh, C.M.C.; (Michael M.) Quang Van Do, C.M.C.; (Bartholomew M.) Hoa Thai Do, C.M.C.; (Mark M.) Bau Quang Doan, C.M.C.; (Francis Xavier M.) Tri Van Luong, C.M.C.; Camillus M. Tuan Nguyen, C.M.C.; (Dominic M.) Hoan Dinh Nguyen, C.M.C.; Andrew M. Nguyen Hong An, C.M.C.; Albert M. P. Kim Ban, C.M.C.; Bartholomew M. Van Minh Pham, C.M.C.; Matthias M. Man Minh Tran, C.M.C.; John M. Huy Quang Vu, C.M.C.; Isidore M. Dinh Thanh Bac, C.M.C.; Aloysius M. Tran Liem, C.M.C.; Peter M. Khuong Tran, C.M.C.; Timothy M. Vinh Loc Mai, C.M.C.; (Aloysius M.) Tran Ngoc Thoai, C.M.C.; Francis M. Hung Long Tran, C.M.C.; Gregory M. Vi Tran, C.M.C.; (Timothy M.) MyViet Tran, C.M.C.; Augustine M. Ky Truong, C.M.C.; Bros. John M. Tu Quang Bui, C.M.C.; Michael M. Trung Dan, C.M.C.; (Josaphat M.) Cuong Manh Do, C.M.C.; (Alphonsus M.) Ba Van Do, C.M.C.; (Maximilian M.) Loc the Do, C.M.C.; (Martin M.) Minh Le, C.M.C.; (Sylvester M.) Thuong Quy Lu, C.M.C.; (Stanislaus M.) An Ngoc Nguyen, C.M.C.; (John Baptist M.) Duc Hien Nguyen, C.M.C.; (Thomas M.) Hoc Nguyen, C.M.C.; Anthony M. Dan Huu Nguyen, C.M.C.; (Joachim M.) Khoa Quang Nguyen, C.M.C.; Thomas M. Nguyen L. Truong, C.M.C.; (Henry M.) Loc Van Nguyen, C.M.C.; Peter M. Thieu Nguyen, C.M.C.; (Bede M.) Tuyen Quang Nguyen, C.M.C.; (Tutus M.) Si Tien Nguyen, C.M.C.; (Ambrose M.) Thang Nguyen, C.M.C.; (Justin M.) Ky Tri Nguyen, C.M.C.; Pius M. Nguyen Trung Thu, C.M.C.; (Bonaventure M.) Tuan Van Nguyen, C.M.C.; Joseph M. Tho Pham, C.M.C.; (Matthew M.) Tan Nhat Pham, C.M.C.; (Francis M.) Thuan Duc Pham, C.M.C.; Justin M. Xuan Binh, C.M.C.; (Francis M.) Tan Tien Ta, C.M.C.; (Bernadine M.) Hien Khac Tran, C.M.C.; Stephen M. Chu Du Tran, C.M.C.; Martin M. Xuan Truong, C.M.C.; (Cyril M.) Chuong Van Vu, C.M.C.; Matthew M. Kim Vu, C.M.C.; (Alphonsus M.) Tri Vu, C.M.C.; (Bede M.) Tam Van Nguyen, C.M.C.; John M. Hien Duc Tran, C.M.C.; (Ignatius M.) Trieu Hai Hoang, C.M.C.; (Jerome M.) Tuan Duc Nguyen, C.M.C.; (Patrick M.) Mac The Tran, C.M.C.; Patrick M. Ngoc Nguyen, C.M.C.; (Thomas M.) Luu Duc Vuc, C.M.C.; (Barnabas M.) Anh Khai Tran Nguyen, C.M.C.; (Matthew M.) Frank Tuan Le, C.M.C.; (Peter M.) Tuyen Quang Dinh, C.M.C.; (Andrew M.) Viet Quoc Nguyen, C.M.C.; (John Vianney M.) Huy Duc Nguyen, C.M.C.; (Augustine M.) An Hong Pham, C.M.C.; (Benedict M.) Quy Duy Pham, C.M.C.; Mr. (Pius) Thao Van Nguyen, C.M.C., Collaborator. Priests 29; Brothers 45; Novices 2; Candidates 1. *Mater Dei Building*, 1900 Grand Ave., 64836. Tel: 417-358-7787; Fax: 417-358-9508. (Home for retired priests) In Res. Revs. Timothy M. Vinh Loc Mai, C.M.C.; Joseph Cao Phuong Ky, S.S., C.M.C.; Joseph Do Ba Ai, C.M.C.; James Do Ba Cong, C.M.C.; James Thuc Van Truong, O.S.B., C.M.C.; Joseph To Ngoc Lien, C.M.C.; Rochus Vu Dinh Hoat, C.M.C.

MARIONVILLE. *The Society of Our Mother of Peace, Sons of Our Mother of Peace*, Queen of Heaven Solitude, 12494 Hwy. T, 65705. Tel: 417-744-2011. Revs. Placid Guste, S.M.P., Supr.; Augustine Ibok, S.M.P.; John R. Hansen, S.M.P.

The Society of Our Mother of Peace, Sons of Our Mother of Peace - Queen of Heaven Solitude

[G] CONVENTS AND RESIDENCES FOR SISTERS

SPRINGFIELD. *St. Anne Monastery*, 424 E. Monastery St., 65807-6099. Tel: 417-881-2115; Fax: 417-881-5570. Email: ozarkcarmel@juno.com. Sr. Marya Williams, O.C.D., Prioress. Discalced Carmelite Nuns 2.

Congregation of Mary Queen, 625 S. Jefferson Ave., 65806. Tel: 417-869-9842; Fax: 417-832-0852. Email: srmtran@hotmail.com. Web: www.trinhvuong.org. Sr. Marguerite A. Tran, C.M.R., Regl. Supr. Sisters 6.

Sisters of Mercy of the Americas (St. Louis), 1330 E. Cherokee, 65804. Tel: 417-882-1297; Fax: 417-820-6960. Sisters 4.

AVA. *Nazareth Hermitage*, R.R. 5, Box 1122, 65608. Sisters 4.

MARIONVILLE. *The Society of Our Mother of Peace, Daughters of Our Mother of Peace*, 12494 Hwy. T, 65705-7121. Tel: 417-744-2011. Sr. Mary Fidelis Lane, S.M.P., Supr.

The Society of Our Mother of Peace, Daughters of Our Mother of Peace, Queen of Heaven Solitude Sisters 5.

PILOT KNOB. *Our Lady of the Valley Community*, 320 S. McCune St., P.O. Box 545, 63663-0545. Tel: 573-546-7229. Franciscan Sisters of Mary. Sisters 2.

REPUBLIC. *Little Portion Franciscans*, 645 Assisi Way, 65738. Tel: 417-732-6684. Email: biebel@att.net. Sisters 3.

[H] RETREAT HOUSES

AVA. *Assumption Abbey* (Trappist), RR. 5, Box 1056, 65608. Tel: 417-683-5110; Fax: 417-683-5658. Email: avaguesthouse@hughes.net. Web: www.assumptionabbey.org. Rt. Rev. Cyprian Harrison, O.C.S.O.

MARIONVILLE. *The Society of Our Mother of Peace, Daughters of Our Mother of Peace*, 12494 Hwy. T, 65705. Tel: 417-744-2011. Sr. Mary Fidelis, S.M.P., Dir.

The Society of Our Mother of Peace, Daughters of Our Mother of Peace, Queen of Heaven Solitude

REPUBLIC. *Little Portion Retreat Center*, 645 S. Assisi Way, 65738-2190. Tel: 417-732-6684. Email: little.portion@att.net. Web: www.littleportionfranciscansisters.org/mission-retreat.htmp. Sr. Cecilia Bergschneider, O.S.F., Coord.

[I] SHRINES

CARTHAGE. *Shrine of Immaculate Heart of Mary* 1900 Grand Ave., 64836. Tel: 417-358-8580; Fax: 417-358-3954. Email: heartofmaryshrine@yahoo.com. Web: www.dongcong.net/khiettam. Rev. Bartholomew M. Van Minh Pham, C.M.C., Dir.

[J] NEWMAN CENTERS

SPRINGFIELD. *Catholic Campus Ministry O'Reilly Catholic Student Center, Missouri State University, Drury University, Ozarks Technical Community College* 847 S. Holland, 65806-3513. Tel: 417-865-0802; Fax: 417-865-0895. Web: www.ccm847.org. Revs. Thomas A. McGann, C.M.F., Dir.; Mark Clarke, C.M.F.; Sr. Michelle

Nguyen, C.M.R., Pastoral Assoc.

CAPE GIRARDEAU. *Catholic Campus Ministry Southeast Missouri State University, Newman Center* 512 N. Pacific, 63701-4712. Tel: 573-335-3899; Fax: 573-334-0088. Email: catholic@ccmin.org. Web: www.ccmin.org. Rev. Patrick I. Nwokoye, Ph.D., Chap. & Dir.

BRANSON. *Catholic Christian Newman Association* , (College of the Ozarks), 203 Vaughn Dr., 65616. Tel: 417-334-2928; Fax: 417-334-6883. Email: lynnmelendez@aol.com. Web: www.ladyofthelakeparish.org. Mrs. Lynn Melendez, Campus Min.

JOPLIN. *Newman Club, Missouri Southern State University* 812 S. Pearl Ave., 64801-4336. Tel: 417-623-8643. Rev. John (J.) F. Friedel, M.A., M.Div., Dir. & Chap.

[K] MISCELLANEOUS

SPRINGFIELD. **McAuley Counseling Services, Inc.*, 2200 E. Sunshine, Ste. 201, 65804. Tel: 417-823-0498. Sisters Ann Crouse, R.S.M., M.A., Exec. Dir.; Victoria Incrivaglia, R.S.M., L.S.C.W., Asst. Dir.

**Mercy Clinic Springfield Communities*, 1965 S. Fremont St., Ste. 200, 65804. Tel: 417-820-2849; Fax: 417-820-3873. Web: www.stjohns.com.

Mercy Health Foundation Springfield, 1235 E. Cherokee St., 65804. Tel: 417-820-3250; Fax: 417-820-6996. Mike Peters, Pres.

Mercy Health Springfield Communities, 1235 E. Cherokee, 65804. Tel: 417-820-2710; Fax: 417-820-8730. Web: www.stjohns.com.

Mercy Medical Research Institute, 1235 E. Cherokee St., 65804. Tel: 417-820-3491; Fax: 417-820-3603. Email: michael.merrigan@mercy.net. Michael Merrigan, Gen. Counsel.

Queen of Angels Day Care Center, 625 S. Jefferson, 65806. Tel: 417-869-9842; Fax: 417-832-0852. Email: cmrusa@hotmail.com. Web: www.trinhvuong.org.

CARTHAGE. *Office of the Immaculate Heart of Mary Shrine*, 1749 Grand Ave., 64836. Tel: 417-358-8580; Fax: 417-358-3954. Web: www.dongcong.net/khiettam.

JOPLIN. *Mercy Health Foundation Joplin*, 2817 St. John's Blvd., 64804.

Mercy Health Southwest Missouri/Kansas Communities, 2817 St. John's Blvd., 64804. Tel: 417-781-2727; Fax: 417-625-2910.

Mercy Village Joplin, Inc., 1148 W. 28th St., 64804. Tel: 417-623-7123; Fax: 417-623-7223.

RELIGIOUS INSTITUTES OF MEN REPRESENTED IN THE DIOCESE

For further details refer to the corresponding bracketed number in the Religious Institutes of Men or Women section.

[]—*Apostles of Jesus*—A.J.

[0275]—*Carmelites of Mary Immaculate*—C.M.I.

[1330]—*Congregation of the Mission Western Province*—C.M.

[0865]—*Congregation of the Mother Coredemptrix*—C.M.C.

[0515]—*Franciscan Brothers of the Third Order Regular*—O.S.F.

[0520]—*Franciscan Friars*—O.F.M.

[0360]—*Missionary Sons of the Immaculate Heart of Mary (Claretians)*—C.M.F.

[0910]—*Oblates of Mary Immaculate (Oblates)* (United States Prov.)—O.M.I.

[0350]—*Order of Cistercians of the Strict Observance (Trappist)*—O.C.S.O.

[1240]—*Order of Friar Servants of Mary (Servites)* (United States Prov.)—O.S.M.

[0200]—*Order of St. Benedict (Benedictines)*—O.S.B.

[]—*The Society of Our Mother of Peace*—S.M.P.

[1290]—*Society of the Priests of Saint Sulpice*—S.S.

RELIGIOUS INSTITUTES OF WOMEN REPRESENTED IN THE DIOCESE

[0100]—*Adorers of the Blood of Christ*—A.S.C.

[0230]—*Benedictine Sisters of the Pontifical Jurisdiction* (Eau Claire, WI)—O.S.B.

[0397]—*Congregation of Mary, Queen*—C.M.R.

[2840]—*Congregation of the Poor Clare Missionary Sisters*—M.C.

[0460]—*Congregation of the Sisters of Charity of the Incarnate Word* (San Antonio)—C.C.V.I.

[0725]—*Cordi-Marian Missionary Sisters Congregation*—M.C.M.

[0920]—*Daughters of St. Francis of Assisi* (Lacon, Illinois)—D.S.F.

[0420]—*Discalced Carmelite Nuns*—O.C.D.

[1415]—*Franciscan Sisters of Mary* (St. Louis)—F.S.M.

[1240]—*Franciscan Sisters, Daughters of the Sacred Hearts of Jesus and Mary* (Wheaton)—O.S.F.

[2080]—*Home Mission Sisters of America (Glenmary)*—G.H.M.S.

[]—*Little Portion Franciscans*—O.S.F.

[]—*Nazareth Hermitage*

[2970]—*School Sisters of Notre Dame* (St. Louis)—S.S.N.D.

[0430]—*Sisters of Charity of the Blessed Virgin Mary* (Dubuque)—B.V.M.

[0990]—*Sisters of Divine Providence* (Marie de la Roche Prov.)—C.D.P.

[1010]—*Sisters of Divine Providence* (San Antonio, TX)—C.D.P.

[2360]—*Sisters of Loretto at the Foot of the Cross*—S.L.

[2575]—*Sisters of Mercy of the Americas* (West Midwest Community)—R.S.M.

[2575]—*Sisters of Mercy of the Americas* (South Central Community)—R.S.M.

[2575]—*Sisters of Mercy of the Americas* (Mid-Atlantic Community)—R.S.M.

[1720]—*Sisters of the Third Order Regular of St. Francis of Our Lady of Lourdes* (Rochester, MN)—O.S.F.

[]—*The Society of Our Mother of Peace*—S.M.P.

[4120]—*Ursuline Nuns of the Congregation of Paris* (Owensboro, KY)—O.S.U.

[4120]—*Ursuline Nuns of the Congregation of Paris* (Cleveland)

[4110]—*Ursuline Nuns (Roman Union)* (St. Louis, MO)—O.S.U.

NECROLOGY

† Krudwig, William C., (Retired)—Died Dec. 12, 2011

An asterisk (*) denotes an organization that has established tax-exempt status directly with the IRS and is not covered by the USCCB Group Ruling.

Diocese of Springfield in Illinois

(Dioecesis Campifontis in Illinois)

Most Reverend

THOMAS J. PAPROCKI

Bishop of Springfield in Illinois; ordained May 10, 1978; appointed Auxiliary Bishop of Chicago and Titular Bishop of Vulturara January 24, 2003; consecrated March 19, 2003; installed as ninth Bishop of Springfield in Illinois June 22, 2010. *Office: Catholic Pastoral Center, 1615 W. Washington St., P.O. Box 3187, Springfield, IL 62708-3187.*

Most Reverend

DANIEL L. RYAN

Retired Bishop of Springfield in Illinois; ordained May 3, 1956; ordained Titular Bishop of Surista in Mauritania and Auxiliary to the Bishop of Joliet in Illinois September 30, 1981; appointed Bishop of Springfield in Illinois November 22, 1983; installed January 18, 1984; retired October 19, 1999. *St. John Vianney Villa, 1464 Green Trail Dr., Naperville, IL 60540-8359.*

Catholic Pastoral Center: 1615 W. Washington St., P.O. Box 3187, Springfield, IL 62708-3187. Tel: 217-698-8500; Fax: 217-698-0802.

ERECTED JULY 29, 1853.

Square Miles 15,139.

Formerly Diocese of Quincy.

See Transferred to Alton, January 9, 1857. To Springfield, October 26, 1923.

Comprises the following Counties of Illinois: Adams, Bond, Brown, Calhoun, Cass, Christian, Clark, Coles, Crawford, Cumberland, Douglas, Edgar, Effingham, Fayette, Greene, Jasper, Jersey, Macon, Macoupin, Madison, Menard, Montgomery, Morgan, Moultrie, Pike, Sangamon, Scott and Shelby.

For legal titles of parishes and diocesan institutions, consult the Chancery Office.

STATISTICAL OVERVIEW

Personnel	
Bishop	1
Retired Bishops	1
Priests: Diocesan Active in Diocese	72
Priests: Diocesan Active Outside Diocese	4
Priests: Retired, Sick or Absent	30
Number of Diocesan Priests	106
Religious Priests in Diocese	49
Total Priests in Diocese	155
Extern Priests in Diocese	8
Ordinations:	
Diocesan Priests	1
Transitional Deacons	3
Permanent Deacons in Diocese	37
Total Brothers	27
Total Sisters	667
Parishes	
Parishes	130
With Resident Pastor:	
Resident Diocesan Priests	56
Resident Religious Priests	5
Without Resident Pastor:	
Administered by Priests	65
Administered by Deacons	2
Administered by Religious Women	2
New Parishes Created	1
Closed Parishes	1
Professional Ministry Personnel:	
Brothers	27
Sisters	667
Lay Ministers	60
Welfare	
Catholic Hospitals	6
Total Assisted	518,428
Homes for the Aged	1
Total Assisted	90
Residential Care of Children	1
Total Assisted	138
Day Care Centers	1
Total Assisted	140
Residential Care of Disabled	1
Total Assisted	98
Educational	
Diocesan Students in Other Seminaries	20
Total Seminarians	20
Colleges and Universities	2
Total Students	2,550
High Schools, Diocesan and Parish	1
Total Students	190
High Schools, Private	5
Total Students	1,937
Elementary Schools, Diocesan and Parish	42
Total Students	9,083
Elementary Schools, Private	1
Total Students	50
Catechesis/Religious Education:	
High School Students	1,485
Elementary Students	7,512
Total Students under Catholic Instruction	22,827
Teachers in the Diocese:	
Priests	2
Brothers	3
Sisters	45
Lay Teachers	983
Vital Statistics	
Receptions into the Church:	
Infant Baptism Totals	1,742
Minor Baptism Totals	129
Adult Baptism Totals	154
Received into Full Communion	319
First Communions	1,980
Confirmations	2,041
Marriages:	
Catholic	381
Interfaith	286
Total Marriages	667
Deaths	1,610
Total Catholic Population	142,847
Total Population	1,150,549

Former Bishops—Rt. Revs. HENRY DAMIAN JUNCKER, D.D., ord. 1834; cons. April 28, 1857; died Oct. 2, 1868; PETER JOSEPH BALTES, D.D., ord. 1853; cons. Jan. 23, 1870; died Feb. 15, 1886; JAMES RYAN, D.D., ord. 1871; cons. May 1, 1888; died July 2, 1923; Most Revs. JAMES A. GRIFFIN, D.D., ord. 1909; cons. Feb. 25, 1924; died Aug. 5, 1948; WILLIAM A. O'CONNOR, D.D., ord. 1927; cons. March 7, 1949; installed March 17, 1949; retired July 22, 1975; died Nov. 14, 1983; JOSEPH A. MCNICHOLAS, D.D., ord. 1949; cons. March 25, 1969; installed Sept. 3, 1975; died April 17, 1983; DANIEL L. RYAN, D.D., J.C.L. (Retired), ord. May 3, 1956; ord. Titular Bishop of Surista in Mauritania and Auxiliary to the Bishop of Joliet in Illinois, Sept. 30, 1981; appt. Bishop of Springfield in Illinois, Nov. 22, 1983; installed Jan. 18, 1984; retired Oct. 19, 1999; GEORGE J. LUCAS, ord. May 24, 1975; appt. Bishop of Springfield in Illinois Oct. 19, 1999; ord. and installed Dec. 14, 1999; appt. Archbishop of Omaha June 3, 2009.

Bishop's Cabinet—Rev. Msgr. CARL A. KEMME, V.G., Vicar General & Moderator of the Curia; Rev. JOSEPH G. RING, Vicar for Clergy; MARLENE MULFORD, Chancellor & Dir. Planning; JONATHAN SULLIVAN, Dir. for Catechetical Ministries.

Chancellor—MARLENE MULFORD.

Vicars Forane—

Alton Deanery—Very Rev. JEFFREY H. GOECKNER, V.F.

Decatur Deanery—Very Rev. DAVID ZIMMERMAN, V.F.

Effingham Deanery—Very Rev. DAVID J. HOEFLER, V.F., M.Div.

Jacksonville Deanery—Very Rev. CHRISTOPHER J. BREY, V.F.

Litchfield Deanery—Very Rev. JAMES L. NEUMAN, V.F.

Quincy Deanery—Rev. Msgr. MICHAEL KUSE, V.F.

Springfield Deanery—Very Rev. JOHN NOLAN, V.F.

Diocesan Curia—

All diocesan agencies and councils are located at the Catholic Pastoral Center, unless otherwise indicated. *Catholic Pastoral Center, 1615 W. Washington St., P.O. Box 3187, Springfield, 62708-3187.* Tel: 217-698-8500; Fax: 217-698-0802.

Office of the Bishop—Most Rev. THOMAS JOHN PAPROCKI; CHERYL KANNALL, Exec. Asst.

Office for Campus Ministry—Mr. ROY LANHAM, M.A., Dir., 500 Roosevelt Ave., Charleston, 61920. Tel: 217-348-0188; Fax: 217-348-8964. Email: rlanham@eiunewman.org.

Office for Catholic Charities— (Central Administration) *1625 W. Washington, Springfield, 62702.* Tel: 217-523-9201; Fax: 217-523-5624. Administrative Staff: STEVEN E. ROACH, Exec. Dir.; ELAINE PERINE, CPA, Dir. Finance & Admin.; MICHAEL SAKOLSKY, Dir. Oper.

Corporate Board Members—Most Rev. THOMAS JOHN PAPROCKI, Pres.; Rev. Msgr. CARL A. KEMME, V.G.; Mr. JOHN J. MAXWELL, CPA; MARLENE MULFORD.

Corporate Board Directors—REGINALD COLEMAN; LARRY CLARK; THOMAS CULLEN; THEODORE L. EILERMAN; JAMES M. GRAHAM; MICHAEL HOFFMANN, Chm.; BRIDGET HOGAN; Deacon WILLIAM KESSLER; AMY MAHER, Sec.; Rev. JOSEPH G. RING; ROBERT SCHULTZ, Treas.; Sr. JOMARY TRSTENSKY, O.S.F., M.H.A., M.S.N.; ANDY WATSON; JOHN C. WEBSTER; MICHAEL LUDVIGSEN; CLARE MCCULLA, Vice Chairperson.

Office for Catechesis—JONATHAN SULLIVAN, Dir.; CHRIS MALMEVIK, Assoc. Dir., Catechesis; BARB BURRIS, Assoc. Dir., School Planning; JEAN JOHNSON, Supt. Catholic Schools; MARILYN MISSEL, Assoc. Supt. Catholic Schools; CYNTHIA CALLAN, Exec. Sec. Fax: 217-698-8620; KYLE HOLTGRAVE, Assoc. Dir., Youth

& Young Adult Min.; ELIZABETH (BETH) SCHMIDT, Exec. Sec. School Personnel, Youth & Young Adult Min.

Board of Catholic Education—MARIAN ALTHOFF; Sr. RUTH CHAUSSE, S.S.N.D.; TOM HASSEN, 2nd Vice Pres.; TERRY KALLAL; Bro. ANTHONY JOSEPH MCCOY, F.F.S.C.; Rev. THOMAS C. MEYER; CATHERINE BECKER; Deacon TERRENCE J. ELLERMAN; MARC MITALSKI, Pres.; Rev. Msgr. CARL A. KEMME, V.G., Ex-Officio; Sr. M. ELISE MIERENDORF, F.S.G.M., 1st Vice Pres.; Rev. JEFFERY A. GRANT; Sr. GERALDINE KEMPER, O.P.

Office for Chancellor/Director of Pastoral Planning—MARLENE MULFORD.

Archives and Records Management—MICHELE MCVAY LEVANDOSKI, Dir.

Office for Communications—KATHIE SASS, Dir.; TAMMY WOLTERS, Sec. Tel: 217-698-8500; Fax: 217-698-0619.

"Catholic Times" Newspaper—KATHIE SASS, Editor; LAURIE WEAKLEY, Office Mgr.; WILLIAM CALLAN, Layout & Design Coord.; THERESA KELLY GEGEN, Spec. Projects Coord.; CATHY LOCHER, Reporter; PAULA RUOT, Advertising; DIANE SCHLINDWEIN, Reporter; TAMMY WOLTERS, Sec.

Office for the Diaconate—Rev. Msgr. DAVID S. LANTZ, Dir.; JOAN REED, Sec.

Office for Marriage and Family Life—Deacon PATRICK O'TOOLE, Dir.; CARLOS TEJEDA, Assoc. Dir.

Office for Finances—Mr. JOHN J. MAXWELL, CPA, Dir.; Mr. GREGORY FLECK, Assoc. Dir. Property, Bldgs. & Cemeteries; PATRICK KETCHUM, Assoc. Dir. Insurance, Fire, Extended Coverage, Vandalism, Multi-Peril Liability, Workers Compensation, Unemployment, Lay Employee Pension Plan, Priests' Personal Property, Seminarians' Medical Care and Coordinator for Diocesan Health Insurance Program.; MICHAEL KELLY, Insurance Assoc.; BERNADINE SMITH, Sec. Insurance; DAN GAUWITZ, Information Technology Assoc. Dir.; BOBBIE OZANIC, Asst. Information Technology Dept.; MICHAEL HOERNER, Web Master; JANET VESPA, Assoc. Dir. Office for Finances; AARON KUHN, Parish Fin. Coord. Accountants: ROBYN DOOLEY; BARBARA SCOGGINS; HEATHER MCMILLEN, Coord., Annual Catholic Svcs. Appeal and Sec.; THOMAS REISER, Spec. Projects. Staff, Annual Catholic Svcs. Appeal/Parish Financial Reporting Support: CHRISSY MAHER.

Diocesan Health Insurance Program Committee—EDNA MAE BROWN; BARB BURRIS; DAN JAMES; Rev. Msgr. CARL A. KEMME, V.G.; PATRICK KETCHUM; PATRICIA KORNFELD; LEO LENN; JOHN MAXWELL, Chairperson; THOMAS REISER; AUDRA SCHULTZ; KATHY WEAR; JULIE YOST.

Lay Employees' Pension Plan Administrative Committee—LEO LENN, Chm.; JOHN MAXWELL, Treas.; JERALD T. BARKMEIER, Consultant; EDNA MAE BROWN; BETH DALTON; THOMAS FRIER; DAN JAMES; Rev. Msgr. CARL A. KEMME, V.G.; PATRICK KETCHUM, Sec.; PATRICIA KORNFELD; THOMAS REISER; JANET VESPA, (Staff).

Commission for Buildings and Property—ANN M. CARR; GERALD L. GLAUS SR.; Rev. Msgr. CARL A. KEMME, V.G.; JOHN MAXWELL; THOMAS C. PAVLIK JR., Chm.; GREGORY FLECK. Consultant: THOMAS REISER.

Office for Human Resources—PATRICIA J. KORNFELD, Dir. & Victim Assistance Coord.; Mrs. SHERYL SPEARS, Administrative Asst.

Office for Ministry Formation—Rev. Msgr. DAVID S. LANTZ, Dir.; JOAN REED, Sec.

Advisory Board—Sr. JANE BOOS, S.S.N.D.; Rev. CHRISTOPHER A. HOUSE; ELIOT KAPITAN; CHRIS MALMEVIK.

Area Specialization Coordinators—Catechetical Leadership Ministry: CHRIS MALMEVIK. Clinical Pastoral Care Ministry: MARY HANDLEY. Adult Faith Formation in Life Issues: Deacon PATRICK O'TOOLE, Co Dir.; Sr. JANE BOOS, S.S.N.D., Co Dir. Liturgical Ministry: Christian Initiation of Adult Leadership: ELIOT KAPITAN. Liturgical Ministry: Liturgical Leadership: Rev. CHRISTOPHER A. HOUSE. Youth Ministry: KYLE HOLTGRAVE.

Office for the Missions—VICKI COMPTON, Dir.; RUTH STAAB, Office Asst., Mailing Address: 1615 W. Washington St., Springfield, 62702.

Office for Social Concerns—Sr. JANE BOOS, S.S.N.D., Dir.; NANCY MURRAY, Sec.; ELAINE VONDERHEIDE, Assoc. Dir., Spec. Needs. Associate Directors for Rural Life: JAMES SCHUMACHER; KAREN SCHUMACHER; CHRISTINE LANSAW, Coord. Catholic Religious Education at Illinois School for the DeafEmail: lansawfam@gmail.com; LEROY JORDAN, Coord., Black Catholic Ministry. Tel: 217-698-8500, Ext. 168 (TTY); Fax: 217-698-9581; Deacons DAVID G. SORRELL, Ministry of Charity and Justice; DAVID ERDMANN, Ministry of Charity and Justice.

Black Catholic Advisory Board—LEROY JORDAN, Chm.; Dr. LENORA BROWN, Alton Deanery; PAUL CORNELL, Springfield Deanery; Rev. DELIX MICHEL, S.S.L., Alton Deanery; Mrs. FREDDIE MCEWEN-RANDLE, Decatur Deanery; Mrs. RENEE SAUNCHES, Decatur Deanery; REGINALD COLEMAN, Quincy Deanery; HUGH HARRIS, Springfield Deanery; Mrs. DAPHNE SKRETVEDT, Alton Deanery; FRED ROBINSON, Springfield Deanery; SARAH GRIPPER, Springfield Deanery; Sr. JANE BOOS, S.S.N.D., Ex Officio; Dr. JIM FORSTALL, Ex Officio.

Campaign for Human Development Advisory Board—Sr. JANE BOOS, S.S.N.D., Dir. Deanery Representatives: WALT UNGER, Alton Deanery; JUDY UNGER, Alton Deanery; GIL WEYHAUPT, Alton Deanery; KEN HANDLEY, Decatur Deanery; MELISSA LYNCH, Decatur Deanery; KAREN MILLER, Effingham Deanery; Deacon RAYMOND L. ROTH JR., Litchfield Deanery; THOMAS DETERS, Quincy Deanery; JANE DETERS, Quincy Deanery; HUGH HARRIS, Springfield Deanery; Sr. MAUREEN IRVIN, O.S.F., Springfield Deanery; Mr. KEN STEINER, Member At Large. Ex Officio: MARTHA MAYFIELD, Coord.

Coordinator of Hispanic Ministry—Very Rev. CHRISTOPHER J. BREY, V.F.

Parish Hispanic Ministry—Sisters MARIA ANGELICA LOPEZ RODRIQUEZ, M.A.G.; MAGDALENA SERRANO-PAZ, M.A.G.; MARIA ESPERANZA OFELIA RIVERA GOMEZ, M.A.G.

Comite Diocesano de Ministerio Hispano - Diocesan Committee for Hispanic Ministry—Sisters MARIA ESPERANZA OFELIA RIVERA GOMEZ, M.A.G.; MARIA ANGELICA LOPEZ RODRIGUEZ, M.A.G.; MAGDALENA SERRANO-PAZ, M.A.G.; Very Rev. CHRISTOPHER J. BREY, V.F.; Mrs. JOHANNA GILLAN DE OROZCO; Very Rev. JEFFREY H. GOECKNER, V.F.; Revs. PAUL HABING; BARRY J. HARMON; Rev. Msgr. CARL A. KEMME, V.G., Ex Officio; Rev. THOMAS C. MEYER; Mrs. ANABELLA MELLADO; Mrs. ARIEL MARTIN; Mrs. CAROLINA MATA-WOODRUFF; CATHERINE BECKER; Rev. CHRISTOPHER COMERFORD; Mrs. DORIS NORDIN; Sisters ANN ELIZABETH LITTLE, O.P.; JANE BOOS, S.S.N.D., Ex Officio; Revs. THOMAS FOX, O.F.M.; ROBERT SPRIGGS (Retired); THOMAS SHAUGHNESSY, O.F.M.; RICHARD W. WELTIN; Sr. MARY JEAN TRAEGER, O.P.; Rev. DANIEL L. WILLENBORG.

Task Force For Racial Justice—Dr. JAMES FORSTALL, Chm.; Rev. JOSEPH ZIMMERMAN, O.F.M., Vice Chm. (Retired). Ex Officio: Sr. JANE BOOS, S.S.N.D.

Office for Stewardship and Development—Mr. SHAUN RIEDELL, Dir.; CATHY FURKIN, Sec.

Office for Tribunal Services—Revs. KEVIN LAUGHERY, J.C.L., Judicial Vicar; R. DEAN PROBST, J.C.L., Judge; Sr. M. MAXIMILIA UM, F.S.G.M., J.C.L., Defender of the Bond; BECKY DONALDSON, Office Mgr. & Notary; Bro. JOEL MARK ROUSSEAU, F.F.S.C., Sec. & Notary.

Office of the Vicar General—Rev. Msgr. CARL A. KEMME, V.G.

Moderator of the Curia—Rev. Msgr. CARL A. KEMME, V.G.

Staff—JOAN REED, Exec. Sec.; CAROL MULLER, Records Mgmt.; Bro. ANTHONY JOSEPH MCCOY, F.F.S.C., Assoc. Exec. Sec.; PATRICIA POLONUS, Receptionist for Catholic Pastoral Center; RUTH STAAB, Spec. Projects.

Vicar for Clergy—Revs. JOSEPH G. RING, Dir.; DAVID L. PETERS, Assoc. Vicar for Retired Priests.

Ongoing Formation of Clergy—Rev. RICHARD L. CHIOLA, Ph.D., Dir.

Commission for the Care of Infirm and Retired Priests—Revs. GERALD BUNSE; ALAN HUNTER; JEFFREY D. LONG; Rev. Msgrs. THOMAS P. HOLINGA, V.F.; MICHAEL KUSE, V.F.; JOHN R. OSSOLA. Ex Officios: Revs. DAVID L. PETERS; JOSEPH G. RING. Consultant: Deacon WILLIAM E. KESSLER.

Priests' Personnel Board—Rev. THOMAS HAGSTROM; Very Rev. DAVID J. HOEFLER, V.F., M.Div.; Revs. JEFFREY D. LONG; THOMAS C. MEYER; JOSEPH MOLLOY; Very Rev. JAMES L. NEUMAN, V.F.; Rev. Msgrs. JOHN R. OSSOLA; CARL A. KEMME, V.G., Consultant; MARLENE MULFORD, Chancellor, Dir. Pastoral Planning & Consultant; Rev. JOSEPH G. RING, Ex Officio.

Office for Vocations—Revs. CHRISTOPHER A. HOUSE, Dir.; DAREN J. ZEHNLE, Assoc. Dir.

Office for Worship and the Catechumenate—ELIOT KAPITAN, Dir.; VICKI WALKER, Sec.; NICHOL DELGIORNO, Assoc. Dir. Music Ministries.

Victim Assistance Coordinator—PATRICIA KORNFELD. Tel: 217-698-8500. Email: pkornfeld@dio.org.

Councils

Diocesan Finance Council—BARBARA BORDERS; JAMES DAVIS; Deacon WILLIAM KESSLER; LEO LENN, Chm.; LEE MARTEN; DAN MCGUIRE; Very Rev. JAMES L. NEUMAN, V.F.; JOHN STAUDT. Consultants: Rev. Msgr. CARL A. KEMME, V.G.; JOHN MAXWELL; MARLENE MULFORD; THOMAS REISER; JANET VESPA, Assoc. Dir. Finances.

Presbyteral Council—Most Rev. THOMAS JOHN PAPROCKI; Rev. ROY R. BAUER (Retired); Very Rev. CHRISTOPHER J. BREY, V.F.; Revs. GERALD BUNSE; ROBERT L. DEGRAND; BERNARD THOMAS DONOVAN; DONALD PATRICK GIBBONS; WILLIAM JEFFRY HOLTMAN, S.F.O.; WILLIAM KESSLER; Rev. Msgrs. MICHAEL KUSE, V.F.; JOHN R. OSSOLA; Revs. JOHN M. TITUS; RICHARD W. WELTIN; DANIEL L. WILLENBORG; Very Rev. DAVID ZIMMERMAN, V.F. Ex Officio: Rev. Msgr. CARL A. KEMME, V.G.; Rev. JOSEPH G. RING. Consultant: MARLENE MULFORD, Chancellor/Dir. Pastoral Planning.

Catholic Charities Institutions

Administrative Office—

Springfield. Catholic Charities—STEVEN E. ROACH, Exec. Dir., 1625 W. Washington, Springfield, 62702. Tel: 217-523-9201; Fax: 217-523-5624.

Area Offices—

Alton. Madison County Catholic Charities—MICHAEL SAKOLSKY, Acting Area Dir., 3512 McArthur Blvd., Alton, 62002. Tel: 618-462-0634; Fax: 618-462-3209.

Carlinville. Catholic Charities—TARYN MARKEZICH, Area Dir., 525 W. Second South St., P.O. Box 618, Carlinville, 62626-0618. Tel: 217-854-4511; Fax: 217-854-8049.

Decatur. Catholic Charities—MARIE RADEMACHER, Area Dir., 247 W. Prairie, Decatur, 62523. Tel: 217-428-3458; Fax: 217-428-4415.

Effingham. Catholic Charities—Sr. CAROL BECKERMANN, O.S.F., Area Dir., U.S. Rte. 40 E., P.O. Box 1017, Effingham, 62401. Tel: 217-857-1458; Fax: 217-857-1481.

Granite City. Madison County Catholic Charities—MICHAEL SAKOLSKY, Acting Area Dir., 2105 State St., Granite City, 62040. Tel: 618-877-1184; Fax: 618-798-4287.

Mattoon. Catholic Charities—DEBBIE ALBIN, Area Dir., 4217 DeWitt Ave., Mattoon, 61938. Tel: 217-235-0420; Fax: 217-235-0425.

Quincy. Catholic Charities—JACKIE RALEIGH, Area Dir., 620 Maine St., Quincy, 62301. Tel: 217-222-0958; Fax: 217-222-8737.

Springfield. Catholic Charities—MAUREEN ROBINSON, Area Dir., 120 S. 11th St., Springfield, 62703. Tel: 217-525-0500; Fax: 217-525-0554.

Institutions—

Alton, Catholic Children's Home—STEVEN E. ROACH, Exec. Dir.; CANDACE HOVEY, Admin., 1400 State St., Alton, 62002. Tel: 618-465-3594; Fax: 618-465-4023. Email: info@catholicchildrenshome.com.

Beardstown. St. Anne Residence—Mr. STEVEN E. ROACH, M.S., Exec. Dir., 309 E. Ninth St., Beardstown, 62618. Tel: 800-745-5194; Fax: 217-523-5624.

Springfield. St. John's Breadline—KEVIN KINDRED, Supvr., 430 N. Fifth St., Springfield, 62702. Tel: 217-528-6098; Fax: 217-528-3605.

Springfield. St. Clare's Health Clinic—SARAH WRIGHT, Clinic Supvr., 700 N. Seventh St., Ste. A, Springfield, 62702. Tel: 217-523-1474; Fax: 217-523-0194.

CLERGY, PARISHES, MISSIONS AND PAROCHIAL SCHOOLS

CITY OF SPRINGFIELD

(SANGAMON COUNTY)

1—CATHEDRAL OF THE IMMACULATE CONCEPTION (1928) [JC] Revs. Peter C. Harman; Stephen A. Thompson, Parochial Vicar; Deacon Irvin (Larry) Smith. In Res., Rev. Daren J. Zehnle.

Res.: 524 E. Lawrence Ave., 62703. Tel: 217-522-3342; Fax: 217-522-1151.

School—Cathedral School, (Grades PreK-8), 815 S. Sixth St., 62703. Tel: 217-523-2652; Fax: 217-523-2750. Web: www.cathedralschoolil.org. Sr. Elizabeth Wrenn, Librarian. Springfield Dominican Sisters 2; Lay Teachers 15; Students 149.

Catechesis/Religious Program—Students 89.

2—ST. AGNES (1889) Rev. Robert J. Jallas; Deacon Roy Harley.

Res.: 245 N. Amos Ave., 62702. Tel: 217-793-1330; Fax: 217-793-3212. Email: sac245@comcast.net. Web: stagnescatholicparish.org.

School—(Grades PreSchool-8) Tel: 217-793-1370; Fax: 217-793-1238. Email: sjsorge@stagnes.dio.org. Lay Teachers 26; Students 388.

Catechesis/Religious Program—Students 115.

3—ST. ALOYSIUS (1928) [JC] Rev. Bernard Thomas Donovan.
Res.: 2119 N. 20th St., 62702. Tel: 217-544-4554; Fax: 217-544-4963. Email: stals@saintaloysius.org. Web: www.saintaloysius.org.
School—(Grades PreSchool-8) Tel: 217-544-4553; Fax: 217-544-1680. Lay Teachers 17; Students 205.
Catechesis/Religious Program—Students 25.

4—BLESSED SACRAMENT (1924) Rev. Jeffery A. Grant; Deacons David R. Erdmann; Thomas G. Burns.
Res.: 1725 S. Walnut Ave., 62704. Tel: 217-528-7521; Fax: 217-528-3137. Email: bsacrament@dio.org. Web: www.bsps.org.
School—(Grades PreSchool-8), 748 West Laurel, 62704. Tel: 217-522-7534; Fax: 217-522-7542. Email: wear@bssbruins.org. Web: www.bssbruins.org. Leslie Shevlin, Librarian; Lori Criscione, Librarian. Lay Teachers 29; Students 475.
Catechesis/Religious Program—Students 63.

5—CHRIST THE KING (1963) Rev. Msgr. David S. Lantz; Deacon Allison (Al) Laabs.
Res.: 1930 Barberry Dr., 62704. Tel: 217-546-3527; Fax: 217-793-6393. Email: church@ctkparish.com.
School—1920 Barberry Dr., 62704. Tel: 217-546-2159; Fax: 217-546-0291. Web: www.ctkcougars.com. Lay Teachers 26; Students 397.
Catechesis/Religious Program—Elementary, 1920 Barberry Dr., 62704. Tel: 217-546-2159. Students 94.

6—ST. FRANCES CABRINI (1948) Rev. Richard L. Chiola.
Res.: 1020 N. Milton Ave., 62702. Tel: 217-522-8555; Fax: 217-523-1345.

7—ST. JOSEPH (1875) Rev. Msgr. Thomas P. Holinga; Deacon Larry Day.
Res.: 1300 N. 5th St., 62702. Tel: 217-528-6717.
Church & Office: 1345 N. Sixth St., 62702. Tel: 217-544-7426; Fax: 217-544-7467. Email: parish@stjoseph.dio.org. Web: stjoseph.dio.org.
School—(Grades K-8), 1344 N. 5th St., 62702. Tel: 217-523-6597; Fax: 217-523-6434. Lay Teachers 11; Students 102.
Catechesis/Religious Program—Students 42.

8—ST. KATHARINE DREXEL (2001) Revs. Peter C. Harman, Priest Moderator & Sacramental Priest; Stephen Thompson, Sacramental Priest; Sr. Mary Jean Traeger, O.P., Parish Life Coord.
Mailing Address: 722 S. 12th St., 62703. Tel: 217-523-5963. In Res., Rev. Paul Habing, Area Hispanic Min.
Sacred Heart Church: 730 S. 12th St., 62703. Fax: 217-523-5963.
St. Patrick Church: 1720 S. Grand Ave. East, 62703. Tel: 217-528-0453.
Catechesis/Religious Program—Tel: 217-744-0578. Students 28.

9—LITTLE FLOWER (1947) [JC] Rev. Msgr. John R. Ossola.
800 Stevenson Dr., 62703. Tel: 217-529-1606; Fax: 217-529-1649. Email: pax@littleflowerchurch.net. Web: littleflowerchurch.net.
School—(Grades PreK-8), 900 Stevenson Dr., 62703. Tel: 217-529-4511; Fax: 217-529-0405. Email: office@little-flower.org. Web: little-flower.org. Lay Teachers 28; Students 325.
Catechesis/Religious Program—Students 40.

10—ST. PATRICK, Merged with Sacred Heart of Jesus, Springfield to form St. Katharine Drexel, Springfield.

11—SS. PETER AND PAUL (1859), (German), Closed. For inquiries for parish records, contact the Cathedral of the Immaculate Conception, Springfield.

12—SACRED HEART OF JESUS (1884), (German), Merged with St. Patrick, Springfield to form St. Katharine Drexel, Springfield.

OUTSIDE THE CITY OF SPRINGFIELD

ALEXANDER, MORGAN CO., VISITATION B.V.M. (1909) [CEM] Rev. Kevin Laughery.
Mailing Address: P.O. Box 20, New Berlin, 62670. Tel: 217-488-3545; Fax: 217-488-3545. Email: visitation@quadpastoralunit.com. Clustered with Sacred Heart, Franklin.
Church: Old U.S. 36, 62601.
Catechesis/Religious Program—Students 5.

ALTAMONT, EFFINGHAM CO., ST. CLARE (1874), (German), [CEM] Rev. Joseph Simburger, Parochial Admin.
Res.: 216 N. Ninth St., 62411. Tel: 618-483-5346; Fax: 618-483-5345.
Catechesis/Religious Program—Students 57.
Mission—St. Mary St. Elmo, Fayette Co.

ALTON, MADISON CO.

1—ST. MARY'S (1858) [CEM] Revs. James Walther, O.M.V.; Shawn Monahan, O.M.V.; Thomas Cannon, O.M.V.
Mailing Address: 519 E. 4th St., 62002. Tel: 618-465-4284; Fax: 618-463-4637. Email: stmarylaurie@aol.com. Web: www.stmarysalton.com. In Res., Rev. David Beauregard, O.M.V.
Res.: 525 E. Fourth St., 62002. Tel: 618-465-4284.
School—(Grades PreSchool-8), 536 E. 3rd St., 62002. Tel: 618-465-8523; Fax: 618-465-4725. Web: www.smsalton.com. Sisters of St. Francis of the Martyr St. George 5; Lay Teachers 16; Students 354; Preschool 45.
School—Middle School, (Grades PreSchool-8), 1015 Milton Rd., 62002. Tel: 618-465-9719.
Catechesis/Religious Program—Students 47.

2—ST. MATTHEW (1947) Closed. For inquiries for parish records please see St. Mary (Immaculate Conception), Alton.

3—ST. PATRICK (1883) Closed. For inquiries for parish records, contact St. Mary's, Alton.

4—SS. PETER AND PAUL (1855) [JC] Rev. Delix Michel, S.S.L., Parochial Admin.; Kim Delp, Business Mgr.
Res.: 717 State St., 62002. Tel: 618-465-4221; Fax: 618-465-0346. Email: info@ssppalton.com. Web: www.ssppalton.com.
School—(Grades PreSchool-8), 801 State St., 62002. Tel: 618-465-8711; Fax: 618-465-6405. Lay Teachers 12; Students 93.
Catechesis/Religious Program—Students 12.

ARCOLA, DOUGLAS CO., ST. JOHN THE BAPTIST (1865) [JC] Rev. Barry J. Harmon, Parochial Admin.
Res.: 205 S. Locust St., Box 133, 61910. Tel: 217-268-3766; Fax: 217-268-3545. Email: johnbaptist@consolidated.net.
Catechesis/Religious Program—210 Pine St., 61910. Tel: 815-830-7105. Students 119.

ARENZVILLE, CASS CO., ST. FIDELIS (1853), (German—Irish), Very Rev. Christopher J. Brey.
Res.: *St. Augustine*, 320 N. Saratoga, Ashland, 62612. Tel: 217-323-4345.
Rectory—215 W. Fifth St., Beardstown, 62618.
Church: 601 W. North St., 62611.
Catechesis/Religious Program—Students 3.

ASHLAND, CASS CO., ST. AUGUSTINE (1875) [CEM] Very Rev. Christopher J. Brey.
Church & Res.: 320 N. Saratoga, P.O. Box 438, 62612. Tel: 217-476-8856.
Catechesis/Religious Program—Students 25.

ASSUMPTION, CHRISTIAN CO., ASSUMPTION B.V.M. (1870) [CEM] Rev. Donald L. Wolford; Deacon John O'Brien.
Res.: 301 St. Peter St., 62510. Tel: 217-226-3536; Fax: 217-226-3538.
Catechesis/Religious Program—Tel: 217-226-3205. Students 24.

ATHENS, MENARD CO., HOLY FAMILY (1903) [CEM] Rev. James Palkudy, S.A.C.
Mailing Address: 711 S. 6th St., Petersburg, 62675.
Res.: 212 Washington St., Petersburg, 62675. Tel: 217-632-2561; Fax: 217-632-7118. Email: stpeter234@sbcglobal.net.
Church: Springfield Rd., 62613. Tel: 217-632-7118. Web: hfa.dio.org.
Catechesis/Religious Program—Students 34.

AUBURN, SANGAMON CO.

1—ST. BENEDICT (1880) [JC] Merged with Sacred Heart, Divernon and St. Mary, Pawnee to form Holy Cross, Auburn.

2—HOLY CROSS (2006) Rev. Christopher A. House.
Office & Res.: 125 E. Washington St., P.O. Box 168, 62615. Tel: 217-438-6222; Fax: 217-438-6732. Web: hcp.dio.org.
St. Benedict Church, 128 E. Washington St., 62615.
Sacred Heart Church: 224 S. Lincoln, Divernon, 62530.
Catechesis/Religious Program—Students 118.

BARRY, PIKE CO., HOLY REDEEMER (1954) [JC] Closed. For inquiries for parish records contact the chancery.

BATCHTOWN, CALHOUN CO., ST. BARBARA (1910) [CEM] Merged with St. Mary, Brussels and St. Joseph, Meppen to form Blessed Trinity, Brussels.

BEARDSTOWN, CASS CO., ST. ALEXIUS (1853) [CEM] Very Rev. Christopher J. Brey.
Res.: *St. Augustine*, 320 N. Saratoga, Ashland, 62612.
Church & Rectory: 215 W. 5th St., 62618. Tel: 217-323-4345.
Catechesis/Religious Program—Tel: 217-323-1888. Students 125.

BELLEVIEW, CALHOUN CO., ST. AGNES (1900) [CEM] Merged with St. Anselm, Kampsville, St. Norbert, Hardin and St. Michael, Michael to form St. Francis of Assisi, Hardin.

BELTREES, JERSEY CO., ST. MICHAEL (1877) [CEM] Rev. Stephen J. Pohlman, Admin.
Res.: 820 W. Homer Adams Pkwy., Godfrey, 62035. Tel: 618-466-2921; Fax: 618-466-2929. Email: stambrose820@yahoo.com.
Church: Beltrees Rd., 62022.

BENLD, MACOUPIN CO., ST. JOSEPH (1915) Rev. Msgr. Lawrence Auda, Parochial Admin.
Res.: 304 N. Macoupin, Gillespie, 62033. Tel: 217-839-3456.
Church: 310 W. Central Ave., 62009. Tel: 217-835-4701.
Catechesis/Religious Program—Students 20.

BETHALTO, MADISON CO., OUR LADY QUEEN OF PEACE (1945) Rev. Thomas R. Liebler.
Res.: 132 Butcher St., P.O. Box 100, 62010. Tel: 618-377-6519; Fax: 618-377-9550. Email: olqpchurch@att.net; tliebler@aol.com.
School—(Grades K-8) Tel: 618-377-6401; Fax: 618-377-6146. Marian Connoyer, Librarian. Lay Teachers 13; Students 138.
Catechesis/Religious Program—Students 75.

BETHANY, MOULTRIE CO., ST. ISIDORE (1864) [CEM] Deacon James J. Ghiglione, Parish Life Coord.
Res.: 400 Woodland Ln., Mt. Zion, 62549. Tel: 217-864-3467; Fax: 217-864-3091.
Catechesis/Religious Program—Tel: 217-873-8667. Students 6.

BISHOP CREEK, EFFINGHAM CO., ST. ALOYSIUS (1865) [CEM] Closed. For inquiries for parish records contact the chancery.

BLACK JACK, MADISON CO., ST. JOHN THE BAPTIST, Closed. For inquiries for parish records contact the chancery.

BLUFFS, SCOTT CO., ST. PATRICK (1871) Closed. For inquiries for parish records contact the chancery.

BRIGHTON, MACOUPIN CO., ST. ALPHONSUS (1868), (German), Rev. Raphael Paul.
Res.: 918 N. Main St., 62012. Tel: 618-372-3352; Fax: 618-372-8133. Email: stalchurch@sbcglobal.net.
Catechesis/Religious Program—Students 39.

BROCTON, EDGAR CO., ST. THOMAS AQUINAS (1899) Closed. For inquiries for parish records contact the chancery.

BRUSSELS, CALHOUN CO.

1—BLESSED TRINITY (2005) Rev. Don J. Roberts; Deacon Michael B. Hagen.
Office: 111 E. Main, P.O. Box 38, 62013-0038. Tel: 618-883-2400; Fax: 618-883-2511. Email: blessedtrinityom@gmail.com.
Res.: Meppen Ln., Meppen, 62013. Tel: 618-883-2309.
School—Tel: 618-883-2124. Mrs. Brenda Paynic, Prin. Lay Teachers 3; Students 57.
Catechesis/Religious Program—Students 23.

2—ST. MARY (1851) [CEM] Merged with St. Barbara, Batchtown and St. Joseph, Meppen to form Blessed Trinity, Brussels.

BUFFALO, SANGAMON CO., ST. JOSEPH (1882) Closed. For inquiries for parish records please see Resurrection Parish, Illiopolis.

BUNKER HILL, MACOUPIN CO., ST. MARY (1854) [CEM] Closed. For inquiries for parish records contact the chancery.

CAMP POINT, ADAMS CO., ST. THOMAS (1860) Rev. J. Thomas Henseler (PEO), Parochial Admin.; Deacon Michael P. Ellerman.
Mailing Address: P.O. Box 252, Mount Sterling, 62353.
Res.: 401 W. North St., Mount Sterling, 62353-0252. Tel: 217-773-3233; Fax: 217-773-3233. Email: holy.family@frontier.com.
Church: 109 E. Spring St., 62320.
Parish Hall:—103 E. Spring St., 62320. Tel: 217-593-6685.
Catechesis/Religious Program—Students 65.

CARLINVILLE, MACOUPIN CO.

1—SS. MARY & JOSEPH (1996) [JC], SS. Mary & Joseph was formed by the merger of St. Mary's of the Immaculate Conception & St. Joseph. Rev. Angel Sierra; Deacon Thomas S. Lucia.
Office & Mailing Address: 2010 E. First S. St., P.O. Box 647, 62626-0647. Tel: 217-854-7151; Fax: 217-854-9228. Email: pastor@ssmjc.org. Web: ssmjc.org.
Catechesis/Religious Program—Email: dre@ssmjc.org.

2—ST. MARY'S OF THE IMMACULATE CONCEPTION, Closed. For inquiries for parish records contact Ss. Mary and Joseph, Carlinville.

CARROLLTON, GREENE CO., ST. JOHN THE EVANGELIST (1858) [CEM] Rev. Henry Schmidt.
Res.: 414 Third St., 62016-1319. Tel: 217-942-3551; Fax: 217-942-6767.
School—(Grades PreK-8), 426 Third St., 62016-1319. Tel: 217-942-6814; Fax: 217-942-6767. Lori Loveless, Prin. Lay Teachers 8; Students 118.
Catechesis/Religious Program—426 Third St., 62016. Students 9.

CASEY, CLARK CO., ST. CHARLES BORROMEO (1878) Rev. Michael B. Haag.
Res. & Mailing: 110 E. Lincoln Dr., Greenup, 62428. Tel: 217-923-3523; Fax: 217-923-3523.
Church: 300 E. Jefferson, 62420.
Catechesis/Religious Program—Students 17.

CHANDLERVILLE, CASS CO., ST. BASIL, Merged with St. Luke, Virginia.

CHARLESTON, COLES CO., ST. CHARLES BORROMEO (1873) Rev. John M. Titus; Deacon James Rupp.
Res.: 921 E. Madison St., 61920. Tel: 217-345-3332; Fax: 217-348-8449.
Catechesis/Religious Program—Students 159.

CHATHAM, SANGAMON CO., ST. JOSEPH THE WORKER (1920) Very Rev. John Nolan; Deacon Frank Maynerich Jr.; Sr. Judith Pfile, O.P., Pastoral Assoc.
Res.: 1505 Hoechester Rd., 62712. Tel: 217-960-4658.
Church: 700 E. Spruce St., 62629. Tel: 217-483-3772; Fax: 217-483-4581. Email:

info@stjoschatham.org. Web: www.stjoschatham.org.
Catechesis/Religious Program— 62629. Tel: 217-483-4514. Email: lafolder@comcast.net. Web: www-.stjoschatham.org. Lee Ann Folder, Coord., Faith Formation (K-6) & Business Mgr.; Amy McKenzie, Coord., Faith Formation (7-11); Kevin Collings, Youth Min.; John Kennedy, Dir., Music. Students 504.

COFFEEN, MONTGOMERY CO., ST. JOHN THE BAPTIST (1898) [CEM] [JC] Closed. For inquiries for parish records please see St. Agnes, Hillsboro.

COLLINSVILLE, MADISON CO., SS. PETER AND PAUL (1855), (Italian), [CEM] Rev. John P. Beveridge.
Res.: 200 Westview, 62234. Tel: 618-345-4343; Fax: 618-345-1145. Web: www.saintspeter-paul.org.
School—(Grades PreSchool-8) Tel: 618-344-5450; Fax: 618-344-5536. Web: www.sspeter-paulschool.org. Lay Teachers 22; Students 239.
Catechesis/Religious Program—Email: ronk@saintspeter-paul.org. Students 68.

DALTON CITY, MOULTRIE CO., SACRED HEART (1891) Closed. For inquiries for parish records contact the chancery.

DECATUR, MACON CO.

1—HOLY FAMILY (1959) [JC] Rev. Joseph Molloy; Sr. Janet Pfile, O.P., Pastoral Assoc.
Convent—Holy Family Convent, 2450 S. Franklin St., 62521. Tel: 217-423-0240; Fax: 217-423-6237. Email: holyfamilychurch1@comcast.net. Sisters 3.
School—(Grades PreSchool-8), 2400 S. Franklin St., 62521. Tel: 217-423-7049; Fax: 217-423-0137. Web: www.hfschool.org. Sr. Geraldine Kemper, O.P., Prin. Springfield Dominican Sisters 2; Lay Teachers 15; Students 212; Preschool 36.
Catechesis/Religious Program—Students 48.

2—ST. JAMES (1877) [JC] Merged with St. Patrick, Decatur to form Saints James and Patrick Parish, Decatur. For inquiries for parish records contact Saints James and Patrick Parish, Decatur.

3—SAINTS JAMES AND PATRICK PARISH (2007) Rev. John C. Burnette; Deacon Gregory Sullivan; Sr. Chaminade Kelley, O.S.F., Parish Nurse; Anita Olson, Sec.; Therese Allen, Pastoral Assoc.; Thomas Cantwell, Business Mgr.; Karen Redden, Sec.; James Rossi, Pastoral Assoc. & C.R.E.; Molly Sykes, Sec. & Office Asst.
407 E. Eldorado St., 62523. Tel: 217-429-5363 (Office); 217-428-7733 (Office); Fax: 217-429-8206. Email: office@saintsjamesandpatrick.org. Web: saintsjamesandpatrick.org.
School—St. Patrick School, (Grades K-8), 412 N. Jackson, 62523. Tel: 217-423-4351; Fax: 217-423-7288. Web: www.stpatricks.pvt.k12.il.us. Jan Sweet, Prin. Teachers 11; Students 170.
Catechesis/Religious Program—Students 40.

4—OUR LADY OF LOURDES (1958) [JC] Rev. Richard W. Weltin.
Res.: 3850 Lourdes Dr., 62526. Tel: 217-877-4404; Fax: 217-877-5257.
School—(Grades PreSchool-8), 3950 Lourdes Dr., 62526-1799. Tel: 217-877-4408; Fax: 217-872-3655. Addie Heckman, Librarian. Lay Teachers 18; Students 252.
Catechesis/Religious Program—Email: ololpsr@yahoo.com. Students 78.

5—ST. PATRICK (1853) [JC] Merged with St. James, Decatur to form Saints James and Patrick Parish, Decatur. For inquiries for parish records contact Saints James and Patrick Parish, Decatur.

6—ST. THOMAS THE APOSTLE (1925) Rev. Richard W. Weltin; Deacon Kevin Richardson.
Res.: 2160 N. Edward St., 62526. Tel: 217-877-4146; Fax: 217-877-4147.
Catechesis/Religious Program—Students 87.

DIETERICH, EFFINGHAM CO.

1—IMMACULATE CONCEPTION (1905) [CEM] Closed. For inquiries for parish records contact the chancery.

2—ST. ISIDORE THE FARMER CHURCH (2004) [CEM] Rev. Joseph P. Carlos, O.F.M.
19812 E. 1000th Ave., 62424. Tel: 217-925-5579; Fax: 217-925-5879. Email: stalbc@mmtcnet.com.
Catechesis/Religious Program—Students 321.

DIVERNON, SANGAMON CO., SACRED HEART (1905) [CEM] Merged with St. Benedict, Auburn and St. Mary, Pawnee to form Holy Cross, Auburn.

EAST ALTON, MADISON CO., ST. KEVIN (1959) Merged with St. Bernard, Wood River to form Holy Angels, Wood River.

EDGEWOOD, EFFINGHAM CO., ST. ANNE (1865), (German), [CEM] Rev. Joseph Simburger, Parochial Admin.
Res.: 216 N. Ninth, Altamont, 62411. Tel: 618-483-5346; Fax: 618-483-5345.
Catechesis/Religious Program—Tel: 614-238-4513. Students 9.

EDWARDSVILLE, MADISON CO.

1—ST. BONIFACE (1869), (German), [CEM] Very Rev. Jeffrey H. Goeckner; Deacon Daniel L. Corbett.
Res.: 326 N. Buchanan St., 62025. Tel: 618-656-6450; Fax: 618-656-7669.
Church: 110 N. Buchanan St., P.O. Box 423, 62025. Email: stbchurch@st-boniface.com. Web: www.st-boniface.com.
Preschool—Tel: 618-692-9315. Students 72.
School—(Grades K-8) Tel: 618-656-6917. Email: stbschool@st-boniface.com. Melanie Cruse, Librarian. Lay Teachers 12; Students 197; Preschool 72.
Catechesis/Religious Program—Students 256.

2—ST. MARY (1842) [CEM] [JC] Rev. William Kessler.
Res.: 1802 Madison Ave., 62025. Tel: 618-656-4857; Fax: 618-656-1715. Email: frbill@gmail.com.
School—(Grades PreK-8) Tel: 618-656-1230. Lay Teachers 15; Students (PreK-8) 241.
Catechesis/Religious Program—Students 170.

EFFINGHAM, EFFINGHAM CO.

1—ST. ANTHONY OF PADUA (1858) [CEM] Very Rev. David J. Hoefler; Revs. Brian C. Alford, Parochial Vicar; Sunder Ery, Parochial Vicar; Deacon Joseph A. Emmerich.
Res.: 417 N. Third, P.O. Box 764, 62401. Tel: 217-347-7129; Fax: 217-342-6980. Web: www.stanthony.com.
School—St. Anthony Grade School, 405 N. Second St., 62401. Tel: 217-347-0419; Fax: 217-347-2749. Sisters 1; Lay Teachers 25; Students 339.
High School—St. Anthony High School, 304 E. Roadway Ave., 62401. Tel: 217-342-6969; Fax: 217-342-6997. Priests 2; Lay Teachers 21; Students 190.
Catechesis/Religious Program—Tel: 217-347-7129; Fax: 217-347-6980. Students 67.

2—SACRED HEART (1892) [JC] Very Rev. David J. Hoefler; Revs. Brian C. Alford, Parochial Vicar; Sunder Ery, Parochial Vicar; Deacon Joseph A. Emmerich.
Res.: 405 S. Henrietta, P.O. Box 870, 62401. Tel: 217-347-7177; Fax: 217-347-0728. Email: shchurch@sheff.org. Web: www.sheff.org.
School—(Grades K-8) Tel: 217-342-4060; Fax: 217-342-9251. Email: shschool@sheff.org. Lay Teachers 14; Students 148.
Catechesis/Religious Program—Students 106.

FARMERSVILLE, MONTGOMERY CO., ST. MARY (1876) [CEM] [JC] Rev. Gerald L. Bunse, Parochial Admin.; Deacon Patrick J. O'Toole.
Res.: 310 Nobbie St., 62533. Tel: 217-227-3349; Fax: 217-227-3515.
Catechesis/Religious Program—Students 20.

FIELDON, JERSEY CO., ST. MARY, [CEM] Rev. William Hembrow, Parochial Admin.
Res.: 306 N. Washington, Jerseyville, 62052. Tel: 618-498-3416; Fax: 618-498-3414. Email: hgchurch@gtec.com.
Catechesis/Religious Program— Clustered with Holy Ghost, Jerseyville. Students 120.

FRANKLIN, MORGAN CO., SACRED HEART OF JESUS (1886) [CEM] Rev. Kevin Laughery.
Mailing Address: P.O. Box 20, New Berlin, 62670. Tel: 217-488-3545; Fax: 217-488-3545. Email: sacredheart@quadpastoralunit.com.
Office & Res.: P.O. Box 20, New Berlin, 62670.
Parish Center—Tel: 217-675-2631.
Catechesis/Religious Program—Students 28.

GILLESPIE, MACOUPIN CO., SS. SIMON AND JUDE (1879) [CEM] Rev. Msgr. Lawrence Auda, Parochial Admin.
Res.: 304 N. Macoupin St., 62033. Tel: 217-839-3456. Email: simonjude@frontiernet.net.
Catechesis/Religious Program—Students 53.

GIRARD, MACOUPIN CO., ST. PATRICK (1887) Rev. Christopher A. House; Deacon Dennis W. Baker.
Mailing Address: 722 N. Springfield St., Virden, 62690.
Church: 745 W. Center, 62640. Tel: 217-965-4545; Fax: 217-965-4586 (Call first).
Catechesis/Religious Program—Students 54.

GLEN CARBON, MADISON CO., ST. CECILIA (1926) Rev. Joseph P. Kerber; Deacon Jerry L. Cato.
Res.: 155 N. Main St., 62034. Tel: 618-288-3200; Fax: 618-288-3292. Email: cecilia@stcparish.org. Web: www.stcparish.org.
Catechesis/Religious Program—St. Cecilia Family Life Center, Tel: 618-288-5523. Email: faithformation@stcparish.org. Web: www.stcparish.org. Students 174.

GODFREY, MADISON CO., ST. AMBROSE (1947) [JC] Rev. Stephen J. Pohlman; Deacon William E. Kessler.
Church: 820 W. Homer M. Adams Pkwy., 62035. Tel: 618-466-2921; Fax: 618-466-2959.
Res.: 3307 Morkel Dr., 62035. Tel: 618-466-6408.
School—(Grades PreSchool-8) Tel: 618-466-4216; Fax: 618-466-4575. Web: saintambrosegodfrey.org. Cathy McGarrahan, Prin.; Marylee Jurvich, Librarian; Dorothy Stahl, Librarian. Lay Teachers 24; Students 251.
Catechesis/Religious Program—Students 55.

GRAFTON, JERSEY CO., ST. PATRICK (1871) Rev. Donald Patrick Gibbons.
11 N. Evans, P.O. Box 218, 62037. Tel: 618-786-3512; Fax: 618-786-2027. Email: stpatricks@gtec.com.
Res.: 506 S. State St., Jerseyville, 62052.
Catechesis/Religious Program—Students 12.

GRANITE CITY, MADISON CO.

1—ST. ELIZABETH (1871) [CEM] [JC] Rev. Christopher J. Comerford.
Office: 2300 Pontoon Rd., 62040. Tel: 618-877-3300; Fax: 618-877-9800. Email: secretary@stelizabethparish.net.
Res.: 3235 Edgewood, 62040. Tel: 618-877-0776.
School—(Grades PreK-8) Tel: 618-877-3300, Ext. 127; Fax: 618-877-3352. Email: steroyals@hotmail.com. Lay Teachers 15; Students 205.
St. Elizabeth Preschool—Tel: 618-877-3300, Ext. 124.
Catechesis/Religious Program—Students 56.

2—HOLY FAMILY (1988) [JC] Rev. Jeffry Holtman.
Res.: 2606 Washington Ave., 62040-4810. Tel: 618-877-7158; Fax: 618-877-7105.
School—(Grades K-8), 1900 St. Clair Ave., 62040. Tel: 618-877-5500; Fax: 618-877-5502. Debby Amberger, Librarian. Lay Teachers 14; Students 190.
Catechesis/Religious Program—Tel: 618-452-8244. Students 21.

GRANTFORK, MADISON CO., ST. GERTRUDE (1872) [CEM] Rev. Carlos M. Bohorquez.
Mailing Address: P.O. Box 457, Marine, 62061-0457.
Church: 202 N. Locust St., 62249. Tel: 618-887-4535; Fax: 618-887-9134. Email: vera.durbin@yahoo.com.
Catechesis/Religious Program—Tel: 618-675-3662. Maura Donnelly, C.R.E. Students 31.

GREEN CREEK, EFFINGHAM CO., ST. MARY HELP OF CHRISTIANS (1860), (German), [CEM] Rev. Robert L. DeGrand.
20057 N. 1525th St., Effingham, 62401. Tel: 217-844-2062; Fax: 217-844-2062.
Res.: 200 N. Church St., P.O. Box 68, Sigel, 62462-0068. Tel: 217-844-3371; Fax: 217-844-2309.
Catechesis/Religious Program—Students 55.

GREENFIELD, GREENE CO., ST. MICHAEL (1880) [CEM] Rev. Henry Schmidt.
Res.: 411 Sheffield, 62044. Tel: 217-368-2176.
Catechesis/Religious Program—Students 8.

GREENUP, CUMBERLAND CO., CHRIST THE KING (1937) Rev. Michael B. Haag.
Res.: 110 E. Lincoln Dr., 62428. Tel: 217-923-3523.
Catechesis/Religious Program—Students 26.

GREENVILLE, BOND CO., ST. LAWRENCE (1868) [CEM] Rev. Victor J. Kaltenbach, Parochial Admin.; Lisa Coleman, Contact Person.
Res.: 512 S. Prairie St., 62246. Tel: 618-664-9149; 618-664-9149. Email: stlawgrenvl@att.net.
Catechesis/Religious Program—Students 137.

GRIGGSVILLE, PIKE CO., HOLY FAMILY, Closed. For details for parish records see St. Mary, Pittsfield.

HAGAMAN, MACOUPIN CO., ST. CATHERINE (1905) Closed. For inquiries for parish records contact the chancery.

HARDIN, CALHOUN CO.

1—ST. FRANCIS OF ASSISI (2005) [CEM] Rev. Don J. Roberts.
Office:—304 French St, P.O. Box C, 62047. Tel: 618-576-2628; Fax: 618-576-9448. Email: stfrancisom@gmail.com. Web: www.stfrancisofassisiparish.com.
Res.: Meppen Ln., Meppen, 62013. Tel: 618-883-2309.
School—St. Norbert School, 401 Vineyard St., P.O. Box 525, 62047. Tel: 618-576-2514; Fax: 618-576-8074. Email: stnorbert@618connect.com. Lay Teachers 3; Aides 2; Students 51.
Catechesis/Religious Program—Tel: 618-576-2628; Fax: 618-576-9448. Email: sfaparishcre@gmail.com. Students 77.

2—ST. NORBERT (1872) [CEM] Merged with St. Agnes, Belleview, St. Anselm, Kampsville and St. Michael, Michael to form St. Francis of Assisi, Hardin.

HIGHLAND, MADISON CO., ST. PAUL (1844) [JC] Revs. Charles A. Edwards; Paul Kala, Parochial Vicar.
Res.: 1412 Ninth St., 62249. Tel: 618-654-2339; Fax: 618-654-9980. Web: stpaul-church.com.
School—(Grades PreK-8), 1416 Main St., 62249. Tel: 618-654-7525; Fax: 618-654-8795. Web: stpaul-highland.org. David Timmerman, Prin. Lay Teachers 24; Students 289.
Catechesis/Religious Program—1420 Ninth St., 62249. Tel: 618-654-2339, Ext. 216. Students 246.

HILLSBORO, MONTGOMERY CO., ST. AGNES (1840) [CEM] Very Rev. James L. Neuman.
Res.: 216 E. Tremont St., 62049. Tel: 217-532-5288; Fax: 217-532-2631. Email: fjnew@consolidated.net; agnesone_chris@consolidated.net. Web: www.stagneshillsboro.com.
Parish Office: 212 E. Tremont St., 62049.
Catechesis/Religious Program—Tel: 217-532-2631. Students 99.

HUME, EDGAR CO., ST. MICHAEL (1876) Rev. Paul H. Skelton.
Res.: 208 N. Pine, Box 17, Villa Grove, 61956. Tel:

217-832-8352; Fax: 217-832-8352.
Catechesis/Religious Program—Students 7.

ILLIOPOLIS, SANGAMON CO., RESURRECTION PARISH (1866) [CEM] [JC] Sr. Phyllis Schenk, O.P., Parish Life Coord.; Rev. Joseph G. Ring, Priest Moderator.
Church & Mailing Address: 410 Anne St., P.O. Box 47, 62539-0047. Tel: 217-486-3851; Fax: 217-486-3851. Email: resurrectionparish@comcast.net.
Res.: 112 N. 6th St., P.O. Box 590, Riverton, 62561-0590. Tel: 217-629-7717; Fax: 217-351-6590.
Catechesis/Religious Program—Students 30.

ISLAND GROVE, JASPER CO., ST. JOSEPH (1874) [CEM] Closed. For inquiries for parish records contact the chancery.

JACKSONVILLE, MORGAN CO., OUR SAVIOUR (1851) [CEM 2] Rev. Thomas C. Meyer.
Mailing Address: 453 E. State St., 62650. Tel: 217-245-6184; Fax: 217-245-6185. Email: osparish1@mchsi.com. Web: www.oursaviourparish.org.
School—(Grades K-8) Tel: 217-243-8621. Web: oss-shamrocks.com. Rita Carney, Prin.; Lynn Hollahan, Librarian. Lay Teachers 18; Students 250.
Catechesis/Religious Program—Tel: 217-245-7633. Students 76.

JERSEYVILLE, JERSEY CO.

1—ST. FRANCIS XAVIER (1857), (Irish—German), [CEM] [JC] Rev. Donald Patrick Gibbons.
Res.: 506 S. State St., P.O. Box 260, 62052-0260. Tel: 618-498-3518; Fax: 618-639-3519.
School—St. Francis/Holy Ghost School, (Grades K-8) Tel: 618-498-4823; Fax: 618-498-3827.
School—St. Francis, (Grades 5-8), 412 S. State St., 62052.
School—Holy Ghost, (Grades PreK-4), 309 N. Washington St., 62052. Tel: 618-498-4910; Fax: 618-498-2754. Mrs. Janet Goben, Prin. Lay Teachers 23; Students 486.
Catechesis/Religious Program—Twinned with Holy Ghost, Jerseyville, IL., Tel: 618-498-5497. Students 120.

2—HOLY GHOST (1883), (German), [JC] Rev. William Hembrow, Parochial Admin.
Res.: 306 N. Washington St., 62052. Tel: 618-498-3416; Fax: 618-498-3414. Email: hgchurch@gtec.com. See St. Francis/Holy Ghost School, Jerseyville under St. Francis Xavier, Jerseyville for details.
Catechesis/Religious Program—Twinned with St. Francis, Jerseyville, IL. Students 115.

KAMPSVILLE, CALHOUN CO., ST. ANSELM (1877) [CEM] Merged with St. Agnes, Belleview, St. Norbert, Hardin and St. Michael, Michael to form St. Francis of Assisi, Hardin.

KINCAID, CHRISTIAN CO., ST. RITA (1920) Rev. Alan M. Hunter; Deacon Raymond L. Roth Jr.
Res.: 30 St. Rita Ct., P.O. Box 439, 62540. Tel: 217-237-4339 (Rectory); 217-237-2333 (Office); Fax: 217-237-2477. Email: strita1@consolidated.net.
Catechesis/Religious Program—Students 27.

LIBERTY, ADAMS CO., ST. BRIGID (1860) [CEM] Rev. Jeffrey E. Stone; Deacon John M. Esselman.
Church: 706 N. Main St., P.O. Box 228, 62347. Tel: 217-645-3444; Fax: 217-645-3546. Email: sbtparishoffice@sbcglobal.net.
Rectory—806 N. Main St., 62347-0228.
Catechesis/Religious Program—Students 115.

LILLYVILLE, CUMBERLAND CO., SACRED HEART (1877), (German), [CEM] Rev. Robert L. DeGrand.
Res.: 200 N. Church St., P.O. Box 68, Sigel, 62462. Tel: 217-844-3371; Fax: 217-844-2309.
Church: 127 County Rd., 100 E., Sigel, 62462. Tel: 217-844-2062.
Catechesis/Religious Program—Tel: 217-844-2312. Students 51.

LITCHFIELD, MONTGOMERY CO., HOLY FAMILY (1988) [CEM], Formerly St. Mary, founded in 1857 & St. Aloysius founded in 1883. Very Rev. James L. Neuman.
Res.: 216 E. Tremont St., P.O. Box 98, Hillsboro, 62049. Tel: 217-532-5288; Fax: 217-532-2631.
Church: 410 S. State St., P.O. Box 8, 62056. Tel: 217-324-2776; Fax: 217-324-2868.
Catechesis/Religious Program—411 S. Jackson St., 62056. Tel: 217-324-5834. Students 81.

LIVINGSTON, MADISON CO., SACRED HEART (1913) [CEM] Rev. George Radosevich. Tel: 618-635-8490.
Res.: 188 Livingston Ave., P.O. Box 458, 62058. Tel: 618-637-2211.
Catechesis/Religious Program— Combined with St. Michael Parish, Staunton.

LOVINGTON, MOULTRIE CO., ST. MARY, Closed. Sacramental records are located at Our Lady of the Holy Spirit, Mt. Zion.

MACON, MACON CO., ST. STANISLAUS (1866) Closed. For inquiries for parish records contact the chancery.

MADISON, MADISON CO., ST. MARY AND ST. MARK (2002) [JC] Rev. William Jeffry Holtman, S.F.O.; Sr. Georgiana Stubner, O.P., Pastoral Assoc.
1621 10th St., 62060.
Rectory—Holy Family Catholic Church, 2606 Washington Ave., Granite City, 62040. Tel: 618-877-7158; Fax: 618-877-7105.

MARINE, MADISON CO., ST. ELIZABETH (1856) [CEM] Rev. Carlos M. Bohorquez.
Res.: 120 N. Windmill St., P.O. Box 457, 62061. Tel: 618-887-4535.
Catechesis/Religious Program—8669 Fruit Rd., Edwardsville, 62025. Tel: 618-406-7239. Jennifer Grotenfendt, C.R.E. Students 25.

MARSHALL, CLARK CO., ST. MARY (1847) [CEM] Rev. Michael B. Haag.
Res.: 414 S. 6th St., 62441. Tel: 217-826-2845; Fax: 217-826-1137.
Catechesis/Religious Program—Students 63.

MARYVILLE, MADISON CO., MOTHER OF PERPETUAL HELP (1938) Rev. Stephen T. Sotiroff.
Church & Office: 200 N. Lange, 62062.
Res.: 7502 S. Ridge, 62062. Tel: 618-344-6493. Email: secretary@mphparish.com.
School—St. John Neumann School, (Grades K-8) Tel: 618-345-7230; Fax: 618-345-4350. Lay Teachers 14; Students 219.
Catechesis/Religious Program—Students 70.

MATTOON, COLES CO., IMMACULATE CONCEPTION (1856) [CEM] Rev. Dennis D. Kollross.
Res.: 320 N. 21st St., P.O. Box 468, 61938-0468. Tel: 217-235-0539; Fax: 217-235-0593. Email: immaculate@mchsi.com.
School—(Grades K-5), 2000 Richmond Ave., 61938. Tel: 217-235-0431; Fax: 217-235-5447. Email: smschool1@consolidated.net. Web: www.stmary-schoolmattoon.org. Lay Teachers 8; Students 70.
Catechesis/Religious Program—Students 83.

MEDORA, MACOUPIN CO., ST. JOHN THE EVANGELIST (1914), (German), Rev. Raphael Paul, Admin.
Res.: c/o *St. Alphonsus Church*, 918 N. Main St., Brighton, 62012. Tel: 618-372-3352; Fax: 618-372-8133.
Catechesis/Religious Program— Clustered with St. Alphonsus, Brighton. Students 10.

MENDON, ADAMS CO., ST. EDWARD (1890) [CEM] Rev. Jeffrey E. Stone; Deacon John M. Esselman.
Mailing Address: P.O. Box 228, Liberty, 62347.
Res.: 806 N. Main St., Liberty, 62347. Tel: 217-645-3444; Fax: 217-645-3546. Email: sbtparishoffice@sbcglobal.net.
Church: 214 S. State Rd., 62351.
Catechesis/Religious Program—Students 69.

MEPPEN, CALHOUN CO., ST. JOSEPH (1864) [CEM] Merged with St. Barbara, Batchtown and St. Mary, Brussels to form Blessed Trinity, Brussels.

MICHAEL, CALHOUN CO., ST. MICHAEL (1864), (Irish), [CEM] Merged with St. Agnes, Belleview, St. Norbert, Hardin and St. Anselm, Kampsville to form St. Francis of Assisi, Hardin.

MONTROSE, EFFINGHAM CO., ST. ROSE OF LIMA (1879) [CEM] Revs. Austin Albers, O.F.M.; Kenneth Rosswog, O.F.M.; Vernon Olmer, O.F.M.
Mailing Address: 301 N. Springcreek Rd., P.O. Box 68, 62445. Tel: 217-924-4337; Fax: 217-924-4312.
Catechesis/Religious Program—Tel: 217-924-4184. Students 71.

MORRISONVILLE, CHRISTIAN CO., ST. MAURICE (1870) [CEM] Rev. Gerald L. Bunse, Parochial Admin.; Deacon Patrick O'Toole.
Mailing Address: 706 E. 4th St., 62546.
Res.: 310 Nobbe St., Farmersville, 62533. Tel: 217-227-3349; Fax: 217-227-3515.
Catechesis/Religious Program—Students 27.

MOUNT OLIVE, MACOUPIN CO.

1—ASCENSION (1886), (Croatian), [CEM] Consolidated with Holy Trinity to form Blessed Pope John Paul II, Mount Olive.

2—BLESSED POPE JOHN PAUL II (2011) Rev. Larry Anschutz.
Res.: 705 E. Main St., 62069. Tel: 217-999-4981; Fax: 217-999-4036.
Catechesis/Religious Program—Students 40.

3—HOLY TRINITY (1912), (Slovak), [CEM] Consolidated with Ascension to form Blessed Pope John Paul II, Mount Olive.

MOUNT STERLING, BROWN CO., HOLY FAMILY (1864) [CEM] Rev. J. Thomas Henseler (PEO); Deacon Michael P. Ellerman.
Res.: 401 W. North St., P.O. Box 252, 62353. Tel: 217-773-3233; Fax: 217-773-3233. Email: holy.family@frontier.com.
School—St. Mary, (Grades PreSchool-8), 408 W. Washington, 62353. Tel: 217-773-2825; Fax: 217-773-2399. Email: smseagle@adams.net. Ann Williamson, Prin. Lay Teachers 7; Students 77.
Catechesis/Religious Program—Students 33.

MOWEAQUA, SHELBY CO., ST. FRANCES DE SALES (1895) [JC] Rev. Donald L. Wolford; Deacon John O'Brien.
Res.: 301 St. Peter St., Assumption, 62510. Tel: 217-226-3536; Fax: 217-226-3538.
Church: 231 E.Warren St., 62550.
Catechesis/Religious Program—Tel: 217-226-3205. Students 19.

MT. ZION, MACON CO., OUR LADY OF THE HOLY SPIRIT (1974) Deacon James J. Ghiglione, Parish Life Coord.
Res.: 400 Woodland Ln., 62549. Tel: 217-864-3467; Fax: 217-864-3091. Email: deaconjim@hotmail.com. Web: mtzolhs.org.
Catechesis/Religious Program—Tel: 217-864-4941. Students 72.

MURRAYVILLE, MORGAN CO., ST. BARTHOLOMEW (1884) [CEM] Closed. For inquiries for parish records contact the chancery.

NEOGA, CUMBERLAND CO., ST. MARY OF THE ASSUMPTION (1897), (German), [CEM] [JC] Rev. Robert L. DeGrand.
Res.: 200 N. Church St., P.O. Box 68, Sigel, 62462-0068. Tel: 217-844-3371; Fax: 217-844-2309.
Church: 670 Walnut Ave., 62447. Tel: 217-895-2166.
Catechesis/Religious Program—Students 80.

NEW BERLIN, SANGAMON CO., SACRED HEART OF MARY (1858) [CEM] Rev. Kevin Laughery.
Res.: 308 E. Yates, P.O. Box 20, 62670. Tel: 217-488-3545. Email: stmarys@quadpastoralunit.com.
Catechesis/Religious Program—Tel: 217-488-3545; Fax: 217-488-3545. Students 29.

NEW DOUGLAS, MADISON CO., ST. UBALDUS (1872) [CEM] Closed. For inquiries for parish records contact the chancery.

NEWTON, JASPER CO., ST. THOMAS THE APOSTLE (1873) [CEM 3] Rev. Allen M. Kemme; Linda M. Hemrich, Office Mgr.
Res.: 501 W. Jourdan St., P.O. Box 225, 62448. Tel: 618-783-8741; Fax: 618-783-8742. Email: stthomaschurch@psbnewton.com.
School—(Grades K-8), 306 W. Jourdan St., 62448. Tel: 618-783-3517; Fax: 618-783-2224. Web: www-.stthomassaints.com. Verna Bergbower, Librarian. Lay Teachers 9; Students 136.
Catechesis/Religious Program—Students 75.

NIANTIC, MACON CO., ST. ANN (1889) [JC] Closed. For inquiries for parish records please see Resurrection Parish, Illiopolis.

NOKOMIS, MONTGOMERY CO., ST. LOUIS (1870) [CEM] Rev. Daniel L. Willenborg.
Res.: 311 S. Elm St., 62075-1310. Tel: 217-563-7146; 217-563-7808 (Personal); Fax: 217-563-8671. Email: parish@stlouis-nokomis.k12.il.us. Web: www.stlouis-nokomis.k12.il.us.
School—(Grades PreK-8), 509 E. Union, 62075. Tel: 217-563-7445; Fax: 217-563-7450. Email: school@stlouis-nokomis.k12.il.us. Web: www.stlouis-nokomis.k12.il.us. Lay Teachers 6; Students 74.
Catechesis/Religious Program—Students 43.

NORTH ARM, EDGAR CO., ST. ALOYSIUS (1817) [CEM] Very Rev. David Zimmerman.
18925 E. 1350th Rd., P.O. Box 577, Paris, 61944.
Res.: 117 E. Edgar St., P.O. Box 577, Paris, 61944. Tel: 217-465-7667; Fax: 217-466-5215. Email: pj154@aol.com.
Catechesis/Religious Program— Combined with St. Mary's, Paris.

OBLONG, CRAWFORD CO., OUR LADY OF LOURDES (1954) Rev. Aloysius Okey Ndeanaefo, Parochial Admin.
Res.: 207 E. Walnut St., Robinson, 62454. Tel: 618-544-7526; Fax: 618-544-9327. Web: www.crawfordcountycatholics.com.
Catechesis/Religious Program—Students 2.

OCONEE, SHELBY CO., SACRED HEART (1872) [CEM] Rev. Rodney A. Schwartz.
Res.: P.O. Box 45, 62553. Tel: 217-539-4325; Fax: 217-539-4569. Email: shparish@frontiernet.net.
Catechesis/Religious Program—Students 23.

PALMYRA, MACOUPIN CO., HOLY ROSARY (1954) Closed. For inquiries for parish records contact the chancery.

PANA, CHRISTIAN CO., ST. PATRICK (1858) [CEM] Rev. Rodney A. Schwartz.
Res.: 6 E. Fifth St., P.O. Box 440, 62557. Tel: 217-562-5396; Fax: 217-562-2308. Email: panastpats@consolidated.net.
Church: 303 S. Locust St., 62557.
School—Sacred Heart, (Grades PreK-8) Tel: 217-562-2425. Mike Guidish, Prin. Lay Teachers 10; Students 153.
Catechesis/Religious Program—Tel: 217-562-2308. Students 101.

PANAMA, BOND CO., SACRED HEART (1916) [JC] Closed. For inquiries for parish records please see St. Agnes, Hillsboro.

PARIS, EDGAR CO., ST. MARY (1849) [CEM] Very Rev. David Zimmerman.
Church: 528 N. Main St., P.O. Box 577, 61944. Tel: 217-466-3355; Fax: 217-466-5215. Web: www.stmaryschurchparis.org.
School—(Grades PreSchool-8), 507 Connelly St., 61944. Tel: 217-463-3005; Fax: 217-465-4703. Email: julie.davidson@smsk8.com. Web: www.smsk8.com. Lay Teachers 6; Students 51.
Catechesis/Religious Program—Email: pat.catanzariti@stmaryschurchparis.org. Students 71.

PAWNEE, SANGAMON CO., ST. MARY (1899) [CEM] Merged with St. Benedict, Auburn and Sacred Heart, Divernon to form Holy Cross, Auburn.

PETERSBURG, MENARD CO., ST. PETER (1868) [CEM] Rev. James Palakudy, S.A.C.
711 S. 6th St., 62675.
Res.: 212 Washington, 62675. Tel: 217-632-2561; Fax: 217-632-7118. Email: stpeter234@sbcglobal.net. Web: www.spp.dio.org.
Catechesis/Religious Program—Tel: 217-632-7118. Students 78.

PIERRON, MADISON AND BOND COS., IMMACULATE CONCEPTION (1892) [CEM] Rev. Jeffrey D. Long.
Res.: 971 Main St., P.O. Box 410, 62273. Tel: 618-669-2391. Email: icstn2011@gmail.com.
Catechesis/Religious Program—Students 57.

PITTSFIELD, PIKE CO., ST. MARY (1852) [CEM] [JC] Rev. Mark A. Schulte; Deacon Michael (Kim) Scott.
Res.: 226 E. Adams, 62363. Tel: 217-285-4321; Fax: 217-285-9400.
Catechesis/Religious Program—Students 35.

POCAHONTAS, BOND CO., ST. NICHOLAS (1871) [CEM] Rev. Jeffrey D. Long.
Res.: P.O. Box 410, Pierron, 62273. Tel: 618-669-2391. Email: icstn2011@gmail.com.
Catechesis/Religious Program—Students 19.

QUINCY, ADAMS CO.

1—ALL SAINTS (1999) [JC] Merged with St. Boniface, Quincy and St. Mary (Immaculate Conception), Quincy to form Blessed Sacrament, Quincy.

2—ST. ANTHONY OF PADUA (1859) [CEM] Rev. Thomas Hagstrom; Deacons William K. Neuser; Harold Parn, (Retired).
Res. & Church Address: 2223 St. Anthony Rd., 62305. Tel: 217-222-5996; Fax: 217-224-6477. Email: stanthonyparish@comcast.net.
School—St. Dominic Catholic Elementary School, (Grades PreK-8) Tel: 217-224-0041; Fax: 217-224-0042. Email: stdominicschool@adams.net. Lay Teachers 14; Students 170.
Catechesis/Religious Program—Bonnie Nytes, D.R.E. Students 76.

3—BLESSED SACRAMENT (2006) Rev. Msgr. Michael Kuse; Deacon Terrence J. Ellerman; Phyllis Schulte, Business Mgr.; Steve Buckman, Music Min.; Carole Glosemeyer, Sec.
1119 S. Seventh St., 62301. Tel: 217-222-2759; Fax: 217-222-6463.
School—(Grades K-8), 1115 S. 7th, 62301. Tel: 217-228-1477. Email: info@blessedscs.org. Web: www.blessedsas.org. Lay Teachers 15; Students 142.
Catechesis/Religious Program—Tel: 217-222-2758. Web: quincycatholicyouth.org. Ann Gage, Pastoral Assoc. Students 108.

4—ST. BONIFACE (1837) [JC] Merged with All Saints, Quincy and St. Mary (Immaculate Conception), Quincy to form Blessed Sacrament, Quincy.

5—ST. DOMINIC (1977) [JC] Merged with St. Anthony of Padua, Quincy.

6—ST. FRANCIS SOLANUS (1860) [JC] Revs. Donald Blaeser, O.F.M.; Thomas Shaughnessy, O.F.M., Parochial Vicar; Thomas Fox, O.F.M., Parochial Vicar; Bro. Ducanh Pham, O.F.M.; Deacon Wayne R. Zimmerman.
Res.: 1721 College Ave., 62301. Tel: 217-222-2898; Fax: 217-222-3020.
School—(Grades K-8) Tel: 217-222-4077; Fax: 217-222-5049. Lay Teachers 17; Students 232.
Catechesis/Religious Program—1721 College Ave., 62301. Students 117.

7—ST. JOHN THE BAPTIST (1880), (German), Merged with St. Rose of Lima, Quincy to form All Saints, Quincy. Records at Blessed Sacrament, Quincy.

8—ST. JOSEPH (1867) [CEM] Rev. Jeffrey E. Stone; Deacon John M. Esselman.
Mailing Address: P.O. Box 228, Liberty, 62347.
Church: 1435 E. 1500 St. Tel: 217-434-8442. Email: stjoe@adams.net.
Catechesis/Religious Program—Students 23.

9—ST. MARY (IMMACULATE CONCEPTION) (1867) [JC] Merged with All Saints, Quincy and St. Boniface, Quincy to form Blessed Sacrament, Quincy.

10—ST. PETER (1839) [JC] Rev. Msgr. Leo J. Enlow.
Res.: 2600 Maine St., 62301. Tel: 217-222-3155; Fax: 217-222-3584. Email: church@cospq.org. Web: www.cospq.org.
School—(Grades PreK-8), 2500 Maine St., 62301. Tel: 217-223-1120; Fax: 217-223-1173. Web: www.stpeterschool.com. Mary Ann Kroshinsky, Librarian. Sisters 1; Lay Teachers 23; Students 395.
Catechesis/Religious Program—Students 105.

11—ST. ROSE OF LIMA (1892), (Irish), Merged with St. John the Baptist, Quincy to form All Saints, Quincy.

RAMSEY, FAYETTE CO., ST. JOSEPH (1870), (German—Irish), [CEM] Rev. Joseph Havrilka.
Res.: 118 E. Main, P.O. Box 455, 62080. Tel: 618-423-2424. Email: st.josephschurch_ramsey@yahoo.com.
Catechesis/Religious Program—Students 28.

RAYMOND, MONTGOMERY CO., ST. RAYMOND (1874) [CEM] Rev. Gerald L. Bunse, Admin.; Deacon Patrick J. O'Toole.
Office: P.O. Box 349, 62560.
Church: 306 S. McElroy, P.O. Box 349, 62560. Tel: 217-854-7151.
Catechesis/Religious Program—Students 40.

RIVERTON, SANGAMON CO., ST. JAMES (1871) Rev. Joseph G. Ring.
Res.: 112 N. Sixth St., P.O. Box 590, 62561-0590. Tel: 217-629-7717; Fax: 217-391-6590. Email: stjamesrctry@gcctv.com. Web: www.stjamesrivertonil.org.
Catechesis/Religious Program—Tel: 217-629-7717. Deanna Broom, D.R.E. Students 66.

ROBINSON, CRAWFORD CO., ST. ELIZABETH (1907) Rev. Aloysius Okey Ndeanaefo, Parochial Admin.
Res.: 207 E. Walnut St., 62454. Tel: 618-544-7526. Web: www.crawfordcountycatholics.com.
Catechesis/Religious Program—Fax: 618-544-9327. Students 85.

ROCHESTER, SANGAMON CO., ST. JUDE (1976) Rev. R. Dean Probst; Deacon Thomas A. Walker.
Res.: 633 S. Walnut St., 62563. Tel: 217-498-7133; Fax: 217-498-7180. Web: stjude.dio.org.
Parish Center—635 S. Walnut St., 62563. Tel: 217-498-9524.
Catechesis/Religious Program—Tel: 217-498-9197. Students 248.

ST. ELMO, FAYETTE CO.

1—ST. BONAVENTURE (1843), (Irish—German), [CEM] Closed. For inquiries for parish records please see St. Mary, St. Elmo.

2—ST. MARY (1904), (German), Rev. Joseph Simburger, Admin.
Res.: 216 N. Ninth, Altamont, 62411. Tel: 618-483-5346; Fax: 618-483-5345.
Catechesis/Religious Program—Students 4.

ST. JACOB, MADISON CO., ST. JAMES (1894) Rev. Carlos M. Bohorquez.
Mailing Address: P.O. Box 457, Marine, 62061-0457. Tel: 618-887-4535.
Catechesis/Religious Program—P.O. Box 187, Saint Jacob, 62281. Tel: 618-644-9335. Patricia Galeaz, C.R.E. Students 15.

SHELBYVILLE, SHELBY CO., IMMACULATE CONCEPTION (1862) Rev. Donald L. Wolford; Deacon John M. O'Brien.
Rectory—1029 E. Northland Dr., P.O. Box 233, 62565. Tel: 217-774-3434; Fax: 217-774-3516. Email: icchurch@consolidated.net.
Catechesis/Religious Program—Students 40.

SHERMAN, SANGAMON CO., ST. JOHN VIANNEY (1931) [CEM] Rev. Msgr. Carl A. Kemme; Deacons David G. Sorrell; James Guy Bollman.
Res.: 712 Lost Tree Dr., 62684. Tel: 217-523-3816; Fax: 217-523-3954. Email: parish@sjv.dio.org. Web: sjv.dio.org.
Catechesis/Religious Program—Students 165.

SHIPMAN, MACOUPIN CO., ST. DENIS (1876) [CEM] Closed. For inquiries for parish records contact the chancery.

SHUMWAY, EFFINGHAM CO., ANNUNCIATION (1879) [CEM] Very Rev. David J. Hoefler; Revs. Brian C. Alford, Parochial Vicar; Sunder Ery, Parochial Vicar; Deacon Joseph A. Emmerich.
Res.: P.O. Box 96, 62461. Tel: 217-868-2752.
Catechesis/Religious Program—Tel: 217-821-3399. Students 48.

SIGEL, SHELBY CO., ST. MICHAEL THE ARCHANGEL (1867), (German), [CEM] Rev. Robert L. DeGrand.
Res.: 200 N. Church, Box 68, 62462-0068. Tel: 217-844-3371; Fax: 217-844-2309. Web: www.fourparishes.com.
School—Tel: 217-844-2231. Lay Teachers 11; Students 117.
Catechesis/Religious Program—Students 62.

STAUNTON, MACOUPIN CO., ST. MICHAEL THE ARCHANGEL (1875) [JC 2] Rev. George Radosevich.
Office: 428 E. North St., P.O. Box 240, 62088-0240. Tel: 618-635-3140; Fax: 618-635-2958. Email: stmikeof@madisontelco.com.
Res.: 322 E. Main, 62088-0240. Tel: 618-635-8490.
Church: 415 E. Main St., 62088-1451.
School—(Grades K-8), 419 E. Main, 62088. Tel: 618-635-3210; Fax: 618-635-3210. Lay Teachers 7; Students 62.
Catechesis/Religious Program—Students 99.

STE. MARIE, JASPER CO., ST. MARY (1837), (French—German), [CEM] [JC] Rev. Allen M. Kemme.
Res.: 112 W. Embarras St., P.O. Box 68, 62459. Tel: 618-455-3155; Fax: 618-455-3665.
Catechesis/Religious Program—112 W. Embarras St., P.O. Box 68, 62459. Students 46.

STONINGTON, CHRISTIAN CO., HOLY TRINITY (1879), (Irish—German), Rev. Alan M. Hunter; Deacon Raymond L. Roth Jr.
Res.: 108 N. Elm St., P.O. Box 257, 62567. Tel: 217-325-3697.
Church: 308 N. Pine, 62567. Tel: 217-824-8178.
Catechesis/Religious Program—Students 35.

SULLIVAN, MOULTRIE CO., ST. COLUMCILLE (1892) Rev. John E. Sohm, Parochial Admin.
Res.: 516 W. Jackson, P.O. Box 464, 61951. Tel: 217-728-4040.
Catechesis/Religious Program—Students 33.

TAYLORVILLE, CHRISTIAN CO., ST. MARY (1845) Rev. Alan M. Hunter; Deacon Raymond L. Roth Jr.
Res.: 116 W. Adams St., P.O. Box 470, 62568. Tel: 217-824-8178; Fax: 217-824-8225.
School—(Grades PreK-6), 422 S. Washington, 62568. Tel: 217-824-6501; Fax: 217-824-2803. Lay Teachers 13; Students 108.
Catechesis/Religious Program—Students 81.
Mission—Holy Trinity 108 N. Pine, Stonington, 62567. Tel: 217-325-3697; Fax: 217-325-4091.
Mission—St. Rita 30 St. Rita, Kincaid, 62540. Tel: 217-237-2333; Fax: 217-237-2477.

TEUTOPOLIS, EFFINGHAM CO., ST. FRANCIS OF ASSISI (1839) [CEM] Revs. Austin Albers, O.F.M.; Kenneth Rosswog, O.F.M.; Vernon Olmer, O.F.M.; Sylvano Pera, O.F.M.; Theodore Bracco, O.F.M.; Maria Wargolet, Liturgy Director/Music Dir. In Res., Rev. J. Michael Ewert, O.F.M.
Res.: 203 E. Main St., 62467. Tel: 217-857-6404; Fax: 217-857-1031.
Catechesis/Religious Program—Tel: 217-857-6477. Sr. Ann Siemer, S.S.N.D., D.R.E.; Lisa Siemer, C.R.E.; Sr. Ann Pierre Wilken, O.S.F., D.R.E. Students 653.

TROY, MADISON CO., ST. JEROME (1870) [CEM 2] Rev. Pat Gerald Jakel.
511 S. Main St., 62294.
Res.: 64 Westbrooke, 62294. Tel: 618-667-6571; Fax: 618-667-2697. Web: www.stjeromeparish.org.
School—St. John Neumann, (Grades K-8), 142 Wilma Dr., Maryville, 62062. Tel: 618-345-7230; Fax: 618-345-4350. Email: jholmes@sjncrusaders.org. Web: www.sjncrusaders.org. Teachers 15; Students 234.
Catechesis/Religious Program—Fax: 618-667-2697. Email: mchomko@stjeromeparish.org. Students 181.

TUSCOLA, DOUGLAS CO., FORTY MARTYRS (1865) Rev. Barry J. Harmon, Parochial Admin.
Res.: 201 E. Van Allen St., P.O. Box 440, 61953. Tel: 217-253-9012; Fax: 217-253-5010.
Catechesis/Religious Program—Students 109.

VANDALIA, FAYETTE CO., MOTHER OF DOLORS (1850) [CEM] Rev. Joseph Havrilka.
Res.: 322 N. Seventh St., P.O. Box 377, 62471. Tel: 618-283-0214; Fax: 618-283-0278. Email: motherofdolors@att.net. Web: www.motherofdolors.com.
Catechesis/Religious Program—Students 68.

VENICE, MADISON CO., ST. MARK (1871) Closed. For inquiries for parish records contact the chancery.

VILLA GROVE, DOUGLAS CO., SACRED HEART (1906) Rev. Paul H. Skelton.
Res.: 208 N. Pine, Box 17, 61956. Tel: 217-832-8352; Fax: 217-832-8352. Email: sacredheart@dio.org.
Catechesis/Religious Program—Students 34.
Mission—St. Michael's Center St., Hume, Edgar Co. 61932. Tel: 217-887-2482.

VIRDEN, MACOUPIN CO., SACRED HEART (1914), (Slovak), St. Catherine's (1866) Merged in 1978. Rev. Christopher A. House.
Res.: 125 E. Washington St., P.O. Box 168, Auburn, 62615. Tel: 217-438-6196.
Church & Mailing: 722 N. Springfield St., 62690. Tel: 217-965-4545; 217-965-5370 (Hall); Fax: 217-965-4586 (Call First). Email: secretary@sacredheart.dio.org. Web: sacredheart.dio.org.
Catechesis/Religious Program—Tel: 217-965-5370. Students 33.

VIRGINIA, CASS CO., ST. LUKE (1840) Very Rev. Christopher J. Brey.
Res. & Mailing Address: *St. Augustine*, 320 N. Saratoga, P.O. Box 438, Ashland, 62612. Tel: 217-476-8856.
Church: 240 E. Myrtle St., 62691. Tel: 217-371-4713.
Catechesis/Religious Program—Students 15.

WAVERLY, MORGAN CO., ST. SEBASTIAN (1856) [CEM] Rev. Kevin Laughery.
Office & Res.: 308 E. Yates, P.O. Box 20, New Berlin, 62670. Tel: 217-488-3545; Fax: 217-488-3545. Email: stsebastian@quadpastoralunit.com.
Church: 265 E. Elm St., 62692.
Catechesis/Religious Program— Clustered with Sacred Heart, Franklin. Students 11.

WHITE HALL, GREENE CO., ALL SAINTS (1883) Rev. Henry Schmidt, Parochial Admin.
Res.: 414 Third St., Carrollton, 62016. Tel: 217-942-3551; Fax: 217-942-6767.

Church: 167 Ross St., 62092.
Catechesis/Religious Program—Mary Beth Hawkins, D.R.E.; Gina Edwards, D.R.E. Students 32.

WILSONVILLE, MACOUPIN CO., HOLY CROSS (1926) Closed. For inquiries for parish records contact the chancery.

WINCHESTER, SCOTT CO., ST. MARK (1860) [CEM] Rev. Mark A. Schulte; Deacon Michael (Kim) Scott.
Res.: 226 E. Adams, Pittsfield, 62363. Tel: 217-285-4321; Fax: 217-742-5224.
Catechesis/Religious Program—Students 24.

WITT, MONTGOMERY CO., ST. BARBARA (1905) [CEM] Closed. For inquiries for parish records please see St. Louis, Nokomis.

WOOD RIVER, MADISON CO.
1—ST. BERNARD (1919) Merged with St. Kevin, Alton to form Holy Angels, Wood River.
2—HOLY ANGELS (2005) Rev. James A. Flach.
Church & Res.: 345 E. Acton Ave., 62095. Tel: 618-254-0679 (Office); Fax: 618-254-2690.
Catechesis/Religious Program—Students 40.

Chaplains of Public Institutions

ALTON. *Alton State Hospital.* Attended by the Catholic Churches in Alton. Vacant.

HILLSBORO. *Graham Correctional Center.* Rev. Gerald Bunse, Chap., St. Mary Church, 310 Nobbe St., Farmersville, 62533-7832. Tel: 217-227-3349.

JACKSONVILLE. *Illinois School for the Deaf,* 453 E. State St., 62650. Tel: 217-245-6184. Attended by Our Savior Parish.
Illinois School for the Visually Impaired, 453 E. State St., 62650. Tel: 217-245-6184. Attended by Our Savior Parish.
Jacksonville Correctional Center, 453 E. State St., 62650. Tel: 217-245-6184. Rev. Jeffrey D. Long, Chap.
Jacksonville Developmental Center, 453 E. State St., 62650. Tel: 217-245-6184. Attended by Our Savior Parish.

MOUNT STERLING. *Western Illinois Correctional Center,* 401 W. North St., 62353. Tel: 217-773-3233. Rev. J. Thomas Henseler (PEO), Chap. Attended by Holy Family Parish.

QUINCY. *Illinois Veterans' Home,* 1901 N. 18th, 62301. Tel: 217-224-0591. Rev. Donald Blickhan, Chap.

TAYLORVILLE. *Taylorville Correctional Center,* 116 W. Adams St., P.O. Box 248, 62658. Tel: 217-824-8178. Attended by St. Mary Parish.

VANDALIA. *Vandalia Correctional Center,* 322 N. Seventh, 62471. Tel: 618-283-0214. Rev. Delix Michel, S.S.L., Chap. Attended by Mother of Dolors Parish.

Special or Other Diocesan Assignment:
Rev. Msgr.—
Steffen, Kenneth C., J.C.L., M.A., M.Div., D.Min., St. Francis Convent, 1 Franciscan Way, P.O. Box 9020, Alton, 62002-9020. Tel: 618-463-2750
Revs.—
Janoski, Steven A., 718 S. 7th St., Unit #803, 62703-2249. Tel: 217-753-3239
Trojcak, Ronald, 34 Gablewood Ct., London ON N6G 2Z9 Canada. Tel: 519-473-5007

On Duty Outside the Diocese:
Rev. Msgr.—
Renken, John, V.G., St. Paul University, Faculty of Canon Law, 223 Main St., Ottowa ON K1S 1C4 Canada.
Rev.—
Gallenbach, Thomas, 7075 Del Ray, Las Vegas, NV 89117. Tel: 702-254-5488 (Home); 702-363-1902 (Office)

Military Services:
Rev.—
Bergbower, Daniel Air National Guard

Absent on Leave:
Revs.—
Brunette, Larry H.
Dennis, Thomas J.
Miller, Tyler
Schmidt, David

Retired:
Rev. Msgrs.—
Mank, Virgil W., V.F., 169 Shadow Point Dr., Wentzville, MO 63385. Tel: 636-856-0524
Sheridan, Paul W., St. Clare's Villa, 915 E. 5th St., Rm. 218, P.O. Box 340, Alton, 62002-0340. Tel: 618-465-5880
Revs.—
Bauer, Roy R., 1329 Catherine Ct., Quincy, 62301. Tel: 217-641-0617
Becker, Robert T., St. Joseph Home, 3306 S. Sixth St. Rd., 62703. Tel: 217-789-1201
Carberry, John, Villa Health Care West, 100 Stardust Dr., Sherman, 62684. Cell: 217-430-3998
Dahlby, Charles, St. Joseph's Home, 3306 S. 6th St. Rd., 62703. Tel: 217-679-2083
Donohoe, Peter, 714 Douglas Pl., Alton, 62002. Tel: 618-463-0521
Heintz, Robert L., Fountain Four, Rm. 209, 1000 Airport Rd., Godfrey, 62035. Tel: 618-466-3391
Kennedy, John, 411 Spring Lake Dr., Quincy, 62305-1051. Tel: 217-224-5288
Knuffman, Donald E., 1509 S. 15th St., Apt. 3, Quincy, 62301. Tel: 217-257-5717
Kraft, Philip G., P.O. Box 7492, 62791. Tel: 217-793-3218
McCarthy, Joseph F., c/o McCormick, Fitzpatrick, Kasper & Burchard, P.C., P.O. Box 638, Burlington, VT 05402.
Meyer, Bernard A., 4725 W. Quincy Ave., #207, Denver, CO 80236. Tel: 303-738-9936
Morelock, George L., 816 Chestnut Ct., Chatham, 62629. Tel: 217-697-8377
Nelson, Charles T., 26 Pearl St., Winchester, 62694. Tel: 217-742-3689
O'Reilly, Joseph, Villa Health Care West, Our Lady of Angels Friary, 100 Stardust Dr., Sherman, 62684. Tel: 217-528-4248
O'Shea, James D., 1729 Dial Ct., 62704-3501. Tel: 217-679-0501
Peters, David, 14 Kaeser Ct., Highland, 62249. Tel: 618-654-6801
Porter, Robert N., 203 Elizabeth Dr., Litchfield, 62056-1786. Tel: 217-324-2247
Savoree, John M., 15980 S. 1100th Rd., Paris, 61944.
Schlangen, Louis, 1905 N. 2800th Ave., Loraine, 62349. Tel: 217-938-4344
Schmidt, Anthony, 823 S. 36th St., Apt. 214, Quincy, 62301. Tel: 217-228-1097
Schmidt, Carl, 509 N. Main St., Effingham, 62401. Tel: 217-342-6487
Simpson, Roger, 271 E. Myrtle St., Virginia, 62691. Tel: 217-452-3168
Sperl, August J., St. Francis Convent, 4849 La-Verna Road, 62707. Tel: 217-522-3386
Spriggs, Robert, R.R. #1 Box 217-C, Shumway, 62461.
Sullivan, Kevin B., P.O. Box 44304, Phoenix, AZ 85064. Tel: 602-614-1207
Venvertloh, Kenneth J., 1029 Gerard St., Quincy, 62301. Tel: 217-473-5842

Permanent Deacons:
Deacons—
Baker, Dennis W., Sacred Heart, Virden
Bollman, James Guy, St. John Vianney, Sherman
Burns, Thomas G., Blessed Sacrament, Springfield
Cato, Jerry L., St. Cecilia, Glen Carbon
Corbett, Daniel L., St. Boniface, Edwardsville
Day, Larry, St. Joseph, Springfield
Ellerman, Michael P., Holy Family, Mt. Sterling
Ellerman, Terrence J., Blessed Sacrament, Quincy
Emmerich, Joseph A., annunciation, Shumway Sacred Heart, Effingham
Erdmann, David R., Blessed Sacrament, Springfield
Esselman, John M., St. Joseph, Quincy, St. Edward, Mendon
Hagen, Michael B., Blessed Trinity, Brussels; St. Francis of Assisi, Hardin
Harley, Roy, St. Agnes, Springfield
Hoefler, Benedict P., St. Aloysius, Springfield
Kessler, William E., St. Ambrose, Godfrey
Laabs, Allison (Al), Christ the King, Springfield
Lucia, Thomas S., Blessed Pope John Paul II Parish, Mt. Olive
Magerl, Roch, St. Luke, Virginia
Mauer, William J., St. Jerome, Troy
Maynerich, Frank, Jr., St. Joseph, Chatham
Neuser, William K., St. Anthony of Padua, Quincy
O'Brien, John, Immaculate Conception, Shelbyville; Assumption of the Blessed Virgin Mary, Assumption; St. Francis DeSales, Moweaqua
O'Toole, Patrick J., St. Mary, Farmersville; St. Maurice, Morrisonville, St. Raymond, Raymond
Richardson, Kevin, St. Thomas the Apostle, Decatur
Roth, Raymond L., Jr., St. Mary, Taylorville; St. Rita, Kincaid; Holy Trinity, Stonington
Rupp, James, St. Charles Borromeo, Charleston
Scott, Michael (Kim), St. Mark, Winchester; St. Mary, Pittsfield
Smith, Irvin (Larry), Cathedral of the Immaculate Conception, Springfield
Sorrell, David G., St. John Vianney, Sherman
Sullivan, Gregory, Saints James & Patrick Parish, Decatur
Walker, Thomas A., St. Jude, Rochester
Zimmerman, Wayne R., St. Francis Solanus, Quincy

INSTITUTIONS LOCATED IN THE DIOCESE

[A] SEMINARIES, RELIGIOUS OR SCHOLASTICATES

GODFREY. *Immaculate Heart of Mary Novitiate,* 4300 Levis Ln., 62035. Tel: 618-466-2233; Fax: 618-466-2430. Email: ominov@aol.com. Web: www.ominov.itgo.com/ominov.htm. Revs. Thomas C. Horan, O.M.I.; Rudolph Nowakowski, O.M.I. Priests 2; Brothers 1. In Res. Bro. Paul Daly, O.M.I.

[B] COLLEGES AND UNIVERSITIES

SPRINGFIELD. *Benedictine University at Springfield* (1929) 1500 N. Fifth St., 62702. Tel: 217-525-1420; Fax: 217-789-1698. Email: mjrappe@ben.edu. Web: www1.ben.edu/springfield. William J. Carroll, Pres.; Rev. Steven A. Janoski, Campus Min.; Brian Hickam, Asst. Librarian. Priests 2; Dominican Sisters 1; Lay Teachers 128; Students 950.

QUINCY. *Quincy University* (1860) 1800 College Ave., 62301. Tel: 217-222-8020; 217-228-5489. Web: www.quincy.edu. Robert Gervasi, Ph.D., Pres.; Revs. Fernand Cheri III, O.F.M., Dir. of Campus Ministry; John Doctor, O.F.M., Vice Pres. Mission & Ministry; Philibert Hoebing, O.F.M., Assoc. Prof. Emeritus (Retired); John J. Lakers, O.F.M., Assoc. Prof. Emeritus (Retired); Joseph Zimmerman, O.F.M. (Retired); Bros. Edward Marc Arambasich, O.F.M., Univ. Chap.; Terrence Santiapillai, O.F.M., Reference & Archive Asst., Brenner Library; Louis Massett, O.F.M., Campus Ministry Sec. & Coord. Weddings & Sacristy; Jesus Ramirez Tapia, O.F.M., Campus Min. Franciscan Friars, Sacred Heart Province. Priests 5; Brothers 3; Lay Administrators 73; Lay Teachers 57; Students 1,600.

[C] HIGH SCHOOLS, PRIVATE

SPRINGFIELD. *Sacred Heart-Griffin* (1895) 1200 W. Washington St., 62702. Tel: 217-787-1595; Fax: 217-787-9856. Email: smjg@shg.org. Web: www.shg.org. Sisters Margaret Joanne Grueter, O.P., Prin.; Katherine O'Connor, O.P., Pres.; Mr. Robert Brenneisen, Asst. Prin.; Mrs. Beverly Neisler, Vice Pres. for Advancement; Mr. Thomas Fiaush, Business Mgr.; Dr. William Moredock, Dir. Student & Family Svcs. Springfield Dominican Sisters. Sisters 9; Lay Teachers 54; Additional Support Staff 29; Executive Team 4; Students 773.

ALTON. *Marquette Catholic High School* (1927) 219 E. Fourth St., 62002. Tel: 618-463-0580; Fax: 618-465-4029. Email: scrafton@marquettecatholic.org. Web: alton-marquette.com. Michael Slaughter, Prin. Sisters 1; Lay Teachers 29; Students 374.

DECATUR. *St. Teresa High School* (1930) 2710 N. Water St., 62526. Tel: 217-875-2431; Fax: 217-875-2436. Email: stadmin@st-teresahs.org. Web: www.st-teresahs.org. Dr. Kenneth C. Hendriksen, Prin. & CEO; Laura Brosamr Senger, B.S., M.S., Librarian. Ursuline Sisters 1; Lay Teachers 30; Students 288.

JACKSONVILLE. *Routt Catholic High School* (1902) 500 E. College, 62650. Tel: 217-243-8563; Fax: 217-243-3138. Email: gthoroman@routtcatholic.com. Web: www.routtcatholic.com. Gale Thoroman, Prin.; Dee Arendt, Librarian. Lay Teachers 8; Part Time 10; Students 116.

QUINCY. *Quincy Notre Dame High School,* 1400 S. 11th, 62301-7299. Tel: 217-223-2479; Fax: 217-223-0023. Email: rheilmann@quincynotredame.org. Web: www.quincynotredame.org. Ray E. Heilmann, Prin.; Lori Shepard, Vice Prin.; Judy Oakley, Librarian. School Sisters of Notre Dame 1; Lay Teachers 21; Students 386.

[D] HIGH SCHOOLS, DIOCESAN AND PAROCHIAL

EFFINGHAM. *St. Anthony High School,* 304 E. Roadway Ave., P.O. Box 545, 62401. Tel: 217-342-6969; Fax: 217-342-6997. Web: www.stanthony.com. Very Rev. David J. Hoefler, V.F., M.Div., Supt.; Ron Niebrugge, Prin.; Roberta Meyer, Librarian. Priests 2; Lay Teachers 21; Students 190.

[E] ELEMENTARY SCHOOLS, PRIVATE

SPRINGFIELD. *Saint Patrick Catholic Grade School* (1910) (Grades K-5), 1800 S. Grand Ave. E., 62703. Tel: 217-523-7670; Fax: 217-523-0760. Sr. Marilyn Jean Runkel, O.P., Bd. Chairperson; Ms. Kim Marsaglia, Prin. Lay Teachers 5; Students 50.

[F] THE CATHOLIC CHARITIES OF THE DIOCESE OF SPRINGFIELD IN ILLINOIS

SPRINGFIELD. *Catholic Charities of Springfield*, 120 S. 11th St., 62703. Tel: 217-525-0500; Fax: 217-525-0554. Web: www.cc.dio.org. 1625 W. Washington, 62702. Maureen Robinson, Area Dir. Total Families Assisted 475; Total Staff 49.

Catholic Charities Administrative Office, 1625 W. Washington, 62702. Tel: 217-523-9201; Fax: 217-523-5624. Web: www.cc.dio.org. Mr. Steven E. Roach, M.S., Exec. Dir. Total Staff 20.

Crisis Assistance & Advocacy and Holy Family Food Pantry, 1023 E. Washington, 62703. Tel: 217-523-4551; Fax: 217-523-8425. Web: www.cc.dio.org. Total Assisted 52,950.

St. Clare's Health Clinic, 700 N. 7th St., Ste. A, 62702. Tel: 217-523-1474; Fax: 217-523-0194. Web: www.cc.dio.org. Total Assisted 3,160.

St. John's Breadline, 430 N. Fifth St., 62702. Tel: 217-528-6098; Fax: 217-528-3605. Web: www.cc.dio.org. Meals Served Annually 218,000.

ALTON. *Madison County Catholic Charities*, Mailing Address: 1625 W. Washington, 62702. 3512 McArthur Blvd., 62002. Tel: 618-462-0634; Fax: 618-462-3209. Web: www.cc.dio.org. Total Assisted 4,150; Total Staff 21.

BEARDSTOWN. *St. Anne Residence*, 309 E. Ninth St., 62618. Tel: 800-745-5194; Fax: 217-323-3228. Web: www.cc.dio.org. Mailing Address: 1625 W. Washington, 62702. Mr. Steven E. Roach, M.S., Exec. Dir. Residents 23.

CARLINVILLE. *Carlinville Catholic Charities* (1990) 525 W. Second S., 62626. Tel: 217-854-4511; Fax: 217-854-8049. Web: www.cc.dio.org. Mailing Address: 1625 W. Washington, 62702. Taryn Markezich, Area Dir. Total Staff 8; Total Assisted 26,600.

DECATUR. *Catholic Charities of Decatur* (1944) 247 W. Prairie Ave., 62523. Tel: 217-428-3458; Fax: 217-428-4415. Web: www.cc.dio.org. Mailing Address: 1625 W. Washington, 62702. Marie Rademacher, Area Dir. Total Assisted Annually 131,700; Total Staff 29.

Catholic Charities Resale Store & Food Pantry, 239 W. Prairie Ave., 62523. Tel: 217-428-3458; Fax: 217-428-4415. 1625 W. Washington, 62702.

EDWARDSVILLE. *Madison County Catholic Charities*, 500 N. Main St., 62025. Tel: 618-307-5420. Web: www.cc.dio.org. Mailing Address: 1625 W. Washington, 62702. Total Assisted 5,260; Total Staff 2.

EFFINGHAM. *Effingham Catholic Charities*, 1502 E. Fayette, 62401. Tel: 217-857-1458; Fax: 217-857-1481. Web: www.cc.dio.org. Mailing Address: 1625 W. Washington, 62702. Sr. Carol Beckermann, O.S.F., Area Dir. Total Assisted Annually 73,800; Total Staff 23.

GRANITE CITY. *Madison County Catholic Charities* (1942) 2266 Madison Ave., 62040. Tel: 618-877-1184; Fax: 618-798-4287. Web: www.cc.dio.org. Mailing Address: 1625 W. Washington, 62702. Total Assisted 10,700; Total Staff 9.

MATTOON. *Mattoon Catholic Charities* (1996) 4217 Dewitt Ave., 61938. Tel: 217-235-0420; Fax: 217-235-0425. Web: www.cc.dio.org. Mailing Address: 1625 W. Washington, 62702. Debbie Albin, Area Dir. Total Assisted 35,886; Total Staff 9.

QUINCY. *Quincy Catholic Charities*, 620 Maine St., 62301. Tel: 217-222-0958; Fax: 217-222-8737. Web: www.cc.dio.org. Mailing Address: 1625 W. Washington, 62702. Jackie Raleigh, Area Dir. Total Assisted 10,800; Total Staff 8.

WOOD RIVER. *Society of St. Vincent de Paul (Diocesan Central Council)*, 5 Eastmoor Ct., 62095. Tel: 618-254-9095. Email: cg9095@aol.com. Charles Goersch, Pres.

[G] CHILDREN'S HOMES

ALTON. *Catholic Children's Home*, 1400 State St., 62002. Tel: 618-465-3594; Fax: 618-465-4023. Email: info@catholicchildrenshome.com. Web: www.catholicchildrenshome.com. Mailing Address: 1625 W. Washington, 62702. Mr. Steven Roach, Exec. Dir.; Candace Hovey, Admin. Teachers 12; Lay Teachers 13; Residents 27; Total Staff 93; Special Ed. Students 138.

[H] GENERAL HOSPITALS

SPRINGFIELD. *St. John's Hospital* (1875) 800 E. Carpenter St., 62769. Tel: 217-544-6464; Fax: 217-535-3989. Email: robert.ritz@st-johns.org. Web: www.st-johns.org. Robert P. Ritz, Pres. & CEO; Mary Jo Wasser, Dir. Pastoral Care. Patients Assisted Annually 205,644; Bed Capacity 439; Staff 3,004.

St. John's College, Department of Nursing Tel: 217-544-6464, Ext. 45165; Fax: 217-757-6870. Brenda Jeffers, Ph.D., M.S.N., B.S.N., Chancellor. Students 111.

ALTON. *Saint Anthony's Health Center* (1925) 1 Saint Anthony's Way, 62002-0340. Tel: 618-465-2571; Fax: 618-465-4569. Web: www.sahc.org. Rev. Msgr. Kenneth C. Steffen, J.C.L., M.A., M.Div., D.Min., Chap.; E. J. Kuiper, Pres. & CEO. Three Campuses: Saint Anthony's Hospital, Saint Clare's Hospital and Saint Anthony's Medical Mall. Sisters of St. Francis of the Martyr St. George 9; Bed Capacity 199; Patients Assisted Annually 87,424; Staff 784.

DECATUR. *St. Mary's Hospital*, 1800 E. Lake Shore Dr., 62521. Tel: 217-464-2473; Fax: 217-464-1616. Web: www.stmarysdecatur.com. Hospital Sisters of the Third Order of St. Francis 5; Patients Assisted Annually 20,068; Bed Capacity 355; Staff 1,114.

EFFINGHAM. *St. Anthony's Memorial Hospital*, 503 N. Maple St., 62401. Tel: 217-342-2121; Fax: 217-347-1563. Email: communications@sae.hshs.org. Web: www.stanthonyshospital.org. Daniel J. Woods, Pres. & CEO; Rev. Ralph Zetzl, O.F.M., Chap. Bed Capacity 146; Patients Assisted Annually 115,435; Staff 684.

HIGHLAND. *St. Joseph's Hospital*, 1515 Main St., 62249. Tel: 618-651-2600; Fax: 618-651-2533. Email: jwatkins@sebh.org. Web: www.stjosephshighland.org. Peggy Sebastian, Pres. & CEO. Hospital Sisters of the Third Order of St. Francis 2; Patients Assisted Annually 35,657; Bed Capacity 25; Staff 250.

LITCHFIELD. *St. Francis Hospital*, 1215 Franciscan Dr., P.O. Box 1215, 62056. Tel: 217-324-2191; Fax: 217-324-3081. Web: www.stfrancis-litchfield.org. Daniel Perryman, CEO; Rev. Theodosius A. Schelich, O.F.M., Chap.; Sr. Mary Flynn, O.S.F., Religious Coord. Hospital Sisters of the Third Order of St. Francis 1; Patients Assisted Annually 54,200; Bed Capacity 25; Staff 261.

[I] SPECIAL CARE INSTITUTIONS

SPRINGFIELD. *Brother James Court* (1975) 2508 St. James Rd., 62707. Tel: 217-544-4876; Fax: 217-747-5971. Email: administrator@brotherjamescourt.com. Web: www.brotherjamescourt.com. Mr. Ron Wampler, M.A., Exec. Admin. Franciscan Brothers of the Holy Cross., Residence for Mentally Retarded Male Adults. Franciscan Brothers of the Holy Cross 2; Bed Capacity 95; Residents 95; Total Staff 104.

[J] HOMES FOR AGED

SPRINGFIELD. *St. Joseph's Home* (1903) 3306 S. Sixth St. Rd., 62703. Tel: 217-529-5596; Fax: 217-529-8590. Sr. M. Lenore Highland, C.S.F.N., Admin. & Pres. of Board. Residence for the Elderly & Nursing Home. Sisters of St. Francis of the Immaculate Conception 7; Sisters of the Holy Family of Nazareth 1; Bed Capacity 113; Residents 90; Staff 135; Total Assisted Annually 32,366; Total Staff 135.

[K] MONASTERIES AND RESIDENCES OF PRIESTS AND BROTHERS

SPRINGFIELD. *Franciscan Brothers of the Holy Cross* (1862) (America 1928) *St. James Monastery*, 2500 Saint James Rd., 62707-9736. Tel: 217-528-4757; Fax: 217-528-4824. Email: info@franciscanbrothers.net. Web: www.franciscanbrothers.net. Bros. John Francis Tyrrell, F.F.S.C., Supr.; Stephen Bissler, F.F.S.C., Treas.; Christian Guertin, F.F.S.C., Vicar. Represented in the Arch/Dioceses of: Springfield, IL; St. Louis, MO; Madison, WI Total in Residence 9.

Our Lady of Angels Friary, P.O. Box 2153, 62705. Tel: 217-522-9822; Fax: 217-522-5004. Email: seniorfriars@aol.com; drcollins2@hotmail.com. Bros. Doug Collins, O.F.M., Guardian; Earl Benz, O.F.M.; Revs. Charles Hart, O.F.M.; Andre Schludecker, O.F.M.; James Wheeler, O.F.M. (Sacred Heart Province). Priests 3; Brothers 2.

MADISON. *Dominican Missionaries for the Deaf Apostolate aka Mark Seven - DePaul House of Studies* 1011 Alton Ave., 62060. Rev. Jean De Dieu Ntibeshya, O.P. Miss.; Bros. Adam Zawadzki, O.P. Miss., Prior; Joseph Thermadom, O.P. Miss., Subprior.

QUINCY. *St. Francis Solanus Friary* (1860) 1721 College Ave., 62301. Tel: 217-222-2898; Fax: 217-222-3020. Email: church@stfrancissolanus.com. Web: www.stfrancissolanus.com. Revs. Donald Blaeser, O.F.M.; Thomas Shaughnessy, O.F.M., Senior Parochial Vicar; Thomas Fox, O.F.M., Parochial Vicar; Bro. Ducanh Pham, O.F.M. Priests 3; Brothers 1.

Holy Cross Friary, 720 & 724 N. 20th St., 62301. Tel: 217-223-9920; Fax: 217-223-9992. Web: www.qufriary.org. Revs. John Doctor, O.F.M., Guardian & Vice Pres. Mission, Quincy Univ.; Fernand Cheri III, O.F.M., Vicar, Campus Ministry; Irenaeus Kimminau, O.F.M. (Retired); Joseph Zimmerman, O.F.M. (Retired); Philibert Hoebing, O.F.M. (Retired); John Leonard Ostdiek, O.F.M. (Retired); Bros. Edward Marc Arambasich, O.F.M., Quincy Fire Chap., Campus Min., Quincy Univ.; Terence Santiapillai, O.F.M., Asst. Librarian/Archives, Quincy Univ.; Jesus Ramirez Tapia, O.F.M., Campus Min. Priests 7; Brothers 3.

SHERMAN. *Blessed Giles Friary*, 113 Stardust Dr., 62684-9763. Tel: 217-522-3575. Email: seniorfriars@aol.com; kleni70138@aol.com. Bro. Kevin Lenihan, Guardian; Revs. Robert Behnen, O.F.M.; Peter Fritz, O.F.M.; Victorian Haladus, O.F.M.; Zachary Hayes, O.F.M.; Victor Kingery, O.F.M.; Nick Meyer; Sylvester Micek; Fred Schneider, O.F.M.; Method Wilson, O.F.M.; Bros. Theo Ballmann, O.F.M.; Greg Bumm, Vicar; John Bush; Michel LeMier, O.F.M.; Joseph Weithman, O.F.M. Retirement Community of Our Lady of Friars Minor (Sacred Heart Province) Priests 11; Brothers 6.

TEUTOPOLIS. *St. Francis Assisi Friary* (1839) 203 E. Main St., P.O. Box 730, 62467-0730. Tel: 217-857-6404; Fax: 217-857-1031. Email: stfrancischurch@mchsi.com. Revs. Austin Albers, O.F.M.; J. Michael Ewert, O.F.M.; Sylvano Pera, O.F.M.; Joseph P. Carlos, O.F.M.; Ralph Zetzl, O.F.M.; Theodore Bracco, O.F.M.; Kenneth Rosswog, O.F.M.; Vernon Olmer, O.F.M. Priests 8.

[L] CONVENTS AND RESIDENCES FOR SISTERS

SPRINGFIELD. *Daughters of Divine Love Congregation* (1969) 1713 S. Lincoln Ave., 62704. Tel: 217-787-8648. Email: Chieze93@yahoo.com. Sisters 4.

Dominican Sisters of Springfield, Il, 1237 W. Monroe St., 62704. Tel: 217-787-0481; Fax: 217-787-8169. Email: srriley@spdom.org. Web: www.springfieldop.org. Sisters Rose Marie Riley, O.P., Prioress Gen.; Barbara Blesse, O.P., Vicaress Gen.; Judith Anne Haase, O.P., Prioress; Rev. Peter Witchousky, O.P., Chap.

Dominican Sisters of Springfield, Illinois. Motherhouse of the Springfield Dominican Sisters. Motherhouse and Novitiate of the Dominican Sisters of Springfield, Illinois. Sisters in the Congregation 231; In Motherhouse 105.

St. Francis Convent (1844, Congregation); (1875, Province) 4849 LaVerna Rd., P.O. Box 19431, 62794-9431. Tel: 217-522-3386; Fax: 217-522-2483. Web: www.hospitalsisters.org. Sisters Jomary Trstensky, O.S.F., M.H.A., M.S.N., Prov. Supr.; Helen Marie Plummer, O.S.F., Community Life Leader; Rev. Andre Schludecker, O.F.M., Chap. The Motherhouse of the Hospital Sisters of St. Francis. Sisters 79.

Other Locations: *St. Francis Convent*, 2101 Shabbona, 62702. Tel: 217-789-4936. Sisters 3. *St. Francis Convent*, 4145 Sunderland Dr., Decatur, 62526. Tel: 217-877-2278. Sisters 3. *St. Francis Convent*, 52 Fairview, 62711. *St. Francis Convent*, 75 Sunflower Dr., Highland, 62249. Tel: 618-654-9759. Sisters 2. *St. Francis Convent*, 2717 Arrowhead, 62702. Tel: 217-528-6492. Sisters 2.

Hospital Sisters of St. Francis-USA, Inc., St. Francis Convent, P.O. Box 19431, 62794-9431. Tel: 217-522-3386; Fax: 217-522-2483. Web: www.hospitalsisters.org.

Missionary Sisters of the Sacred Heart of Jesus "Ad Gentes", 260 N. Amos Ave., 62702. Tel: 217-726-8159. Email: hnamagda@yahoo.com. Sr. Magdalena Serrano-Paz, M.A.G., Local Supr. Sisters 3.

Ursuline Convent (1857) 4849 LaVerna Rd., P.O. Box 670, 62705. Tel: 217-492-5940; Fax: 217-492-5945. Sr. Brendan Jacoby, O.S.U., Prioress. Ursuline Nuns of the Roman Union in Community 6.

ALTON. *St. Clare's Villa*, 915 E. 5th St., 62002. Tel: 618-604-5066. Web: www.divineprovidenceweb.org. Sr. Agnes Marie Geringer, C.D.P., Contact Person.

St. Francis Convent (1923) 1 Franciscan Way, P.O. Box 9020, 62002-9020. Tel: 618-463-2750; Fax: 618-465-5064. Email: vocations@altonfranciscans.org. Web: www.altonfranciscans.org. Rev. Msgr. Kenneth C. Steffen, J.C.L., M.A., M.Div., D.Min., Chap.; Sr. M. Regina Pacis Coury, F.S.G.M., Prov. Supr. Sisters 113; Final Professed 88; Junior Professed 25; Novices 6; Postulants 1.

Ursuline Convent of the Holy Family of the Ursuline Nuns of the Roman Union, 845 Danforth St., 62002. Tel: 618-465-9112; Fax: 618-462-5262. Sr. Chabanel Mathison, O.S.U., Prioress. Sisters 17.

Queen of Peace Health Care Center, 845 Danforth St., 62002. Tel: 618-465-0791; Fax: 618-465-8414. Linda Begnel, Admin. Sisters 25; Total Staff 63.

[M] NEWMAN CENTERS

CARLINVILLE. *Blackburn College Newman Club* 2010 E. 1st South St., P.O. Box 647, 62626. Tel: 217-854-7151; Fax: 217-854-9228. Web: ssmjc.org. Chaplains 1; Students 200.

CHARLESTON. *Eastern Illinois University Newman Catholic Center* 500 Roosevelt Ave., 61920. Tel: 217-348-0188; Fax: 217-348-8964. Email: newman@eiunewman.org. Web: www.eiunewman.org. Rev. John M. Titus, Chap.; Mrs. Doris Nordin, Campus Minister; Mr. Roy Lanham, M.A., Dir.; Ms. Edrianne Ezell, M.Div., Instructor.

DECATUR. *Millikin University Newman Catholic Community* Campus: 1184 W. Main St., 62522. Tel: 217-348-0188; Fax: 217-348-8964. Email: rlanham@eiunewman.org. Mailing Address: 500 Roosevelt Ave., Charleston, 61920. Tel: 217-348-0188. Mr. Roy Lanham, M.A., Campus Min.

EDWARDSVILLE. *Southern Illinois University Catholic Campus Ministry The Center for Spirituality & Sustainability*, P.O. Box 1059, 62026. Tel: 618-650-3205; Fax: 618-650-3264. Email: ccalzet@siue.edu. Web: www.siue.edu/religion/catholic. Claudia Calzetta, S.L., Dir. Campus Min. Jesuit Priests 2; Total Staff 3.

JACKSONVILLE. *Illinois College Newman Catholic Community* 453 E. State St., 62650. Tel: 217-245-6184; Fax: 217-245-6185. Rev. Thomas C. Meyer, Chap.

MacMurray College Newman Catholic Community c/o 453 E. State St., 62650. Tel: 217-245-6184; Fax: 217-245-6185. Rev. Thomas C. Meyer, Chap.

[N] MISCELLANEOUS LISTINGS

SPRINGFIELD. *Catholic Care Center, Inc., Catholic Pastoral Center*, P.O. Box 3187, 62708. Tel: 217-698-8500, Ext. 195; Fax: 217-698-0802. Email: gfleck@dio.org. Web: www.dio.org. Mr. Leo A. Lenn, Pres.; John Maxwell, Treas. & Dir.; Rev. Msgr. Carl A. Kemme, V.G., Diocesan Admin.; Gregory K.J. Fleck, Exec. Sec. & Dir.; Hugh Graham III, Dir.; Thomas Reiser, Dir.; Marlene Mulford, Dir.

Diocesan Care Management, Inc., Catholic Pastoral Center, P.O. Box 3187, 62708-3187. Tel: 217-698-8500, Ext. 195; Fax: 217-698-0802. Email: gfleck@dio.org. Web: www.dio.org. Rev. Msgr. Carl A. Kemme, V.G., Diocesan Admin., Pres. & Dir.; Mr. John J. Maxwell, CPA, Treas. & Dir.; Gregory K.J. Fleck, Exec. Sec. & Dir.; Mr. Thomas E. Reiser, Dir.

Dominican Sisters of Springfield in Illinois Charitable Trust (1998) Sacred Heart Convent, 1237 W. Monroe, 62704-1680. Tel: 217-787-0481; Fax: 217-787-8169. Email: srriley@spdom.org. Web: www.springfieldop.org.

Foundation for the People of the Diocese of Springfield in Illinois, 1615 W. Washington, 62702. Tel: 217-698-8500, Ext. 114; Fax: 217-698-0802. Email: sriedell@dio.org.

The Foundation for the People of the Roman Catholic Diocese of Springfield in Illinois

Hospital Sisters Health System (1978) 4936 LaVerna Rd., P.O. Box 19456, 62794-9456. Tel: 217-523-4747. Mary Starmann-Harison, Pres. & CEO; Ann M. Carr, Vice Pres. & Treas.

Hospital Sisters Mission Outreach Corporation, P.O. Box 1665, 62705-1665. Tel: 217-525-8843; Fax: 217-523-4742. Web: www.mission-outreach.org. Rick Haberkorn, Exec. Dir.

Hospital Sisters of St. Francis Foundation, Inc. (1984) 4936 LaVerna Rd., P.O. Box 19456, 62794-9456. Tel: 217-523-4747. Daniel McCormack, Pres.

Hospital Sisters Services, Inc. (1983) 4936 LaVerna Rd., P.O. Box 19456, 62794-9456. Tel: 217-523-4747; Fax: 217-523-0542. Ann M. Carr, Vice Pres. & Treas.

Hospital Sisters Tanzania (2001) *Saint Francis Convent*, P.O. Box 19431, 62794-9431. Tel: 217-522-3386; Fax: 217-522-2483. Email: jschneider@hsosf-usa.org. Web: www.hospitalsisters.org. Sisters Jomary Trstensky, O.S.F., M.H.A., M.S.N., Pres.; Janice Schneider, O.S.F., Sec. & Treas.

Jubilee Farm, NFP, 6760 Old Jacksonville Rd., New Berlin, 62670-6747. Tel: 217-787-6927. Email: jubilee.farm@comcast.net. Web: www.jubileefarm.info. Sr. Sharon Zayac, O.P., Exec. Dir.

Leadership Conference of Women Religious, 1237 W. Monroe, 62704. Tel: 217-787-0481; Fax: 217-787-8169. Sisters Rebecca Ann Gemma, O.P., Chm.; Carol Bredenkemp, S.C.C., Sec.; Patricia Dulka, O.P., Vice-Chair; Nancy Roberta Schramm, O.S.F., Treas.

Sponsored Activity: Project IRENE Sr. Rose Mary Meyer, B.V.M., Project Dir.

Legion of Mary, 30 Monica Ln., 62702-4346. Tel: 217-544-9022. Elsie P. Venvertloh, Comitium Pres.

Priests' Purgatorial Society Catholic Pastoral Center, 1615 W. Washington, P.O. Box 3187, 62708-3187. Tel: 217-698-8500; Fax: 217-698-0802. Email: ckemme@dio.org.

**Springfield Developmental Center Ltd.* (1976) 4595 LaVerna Rd., 62707. Tel: 217-525-8271; Fax: 217-525-5801. Email: director@spflddevcenter.org. Kathi Clark, Dir. Franciscan Brothers of the Holy Cross., Developmental Training Program for Developmentally Disabled Adults. Lay Staff 20; Clients 90.

Theresian Foundation, Inc., 1237 W. Monroe St., 62704. Tel: 217-726-5484; Fax: 217-726-5631. Email: 5dimensions@att.net. Web: www.theresians.org. Victoria S. Schmidt, Exec. Dir.

Theresians International, Inc., 1237 W. Monroe St., 62704. Tel: 217-726-5484; Fax: 217-726-5631. Email: 5dimensions@att.net. Web: www.theresians.org. Victoria S. Schmidt, Exec. Dir. Sacred Heart Convent

Villa Maria - Catholic Life Center (Retreat and Conference Center), 1903 E. Lake Shore Dr., 62712-5514. Tel: 217-529-2213; Fax: 217-241-2485. Email: msmith@dio.org. Mary Ann Smith, Dir.

Weber House - Weber Care Corporation, 2520 St. James Rd., 62707. Tel: 217-522-8406. Email: webercare@sbcglobal.net. Bros. John Francis Tyrrell, F.F.S.C., Pres.; Gerald Voycheck, Business Mgr.; Constance Baker, Prog. Coord. & QSP. Bed Capacity 8.

ALTON. *Saint Anthony's Foundation* (1993) 1 Saint Anthony's Way, 62002-0340. Tel: 618-465-2571; Fax: 618-465-4569. Email: foundation@sahc.org. Web: www.sahc.org. Sr. M. Mikela Meidl, F.S.G.M., Pres.

Affiliates: Saint Anthony's Health System and Saint Anthony's Health Center. E. J. Kuiper, CEO.

Saint Anthony's Health System, 1 Saint Anthony's Way, 62002-0340. Tel: 618-465-2571; Fax: 618-465-4569. Web: www.sahc.org. Rev. Msgr. Kenneth C. Steffen, J.C.L., M.A., M.Div., D.Min., Chap.; E. J. Kuiper, Pres. & CEO. Affiliates: Saint Anthony's Health Center and Saint Anthony's Foundation and Saint Anthony's Physician Group. Sisters of St. Francis of the Martyr St. George 9.

Saint Clare's Hospital, 915 E. Fifth St., P.O. Box 340, 62002-0340. Tel: 618-463-5150; Fax: 618-463-5641. Web: www.sahc.org. E. J. Kuiper, Pres. & CEO. A Division of Saint Anthony's Health Center.

St. Francis Day Care Center, 710 College Ave., P.O. Box 9020, 62002-9020. Tel: 618-463-2766; Fax: 618-465-5064. Sr. M. Martha Weber, F.S.G.M., Dir. Day Care Center Sisters of St. Francis of the Martyr St. George 5; Assisted Daily 140; Total Staff 34.

QUINCY. *Priestly Fraternity of St. Peter*, 1009 N. 8th St., 62301-1845. Tel: 217-222-2511; Fax: 217-223-1579. *St. Rose of Lima Church*, 1009 N. 8th St., 62301-1845. Tel: 217-222-2511; Fax: 217-223-1579.

Quincy Ladies of Charity, 510 S. 4th St., 62301. Tel: 217-222-6359. Jan Barnard, Pres.

VANDALIA. **Our Sorrowful Mothers Ministry*, 331 N. 7th St., 62471.

RELIGIOUS INSTITUTES OF MEN REPRESENTED IN THE DIOCESE

For further details refer to the corresponding bracketed number in the Religious Institutes of Men or Women section.

[1320]—*Clerics of St. Viator* (Chicago Prov.)—C.S.V.

[]—*Dominican Missionaries for the Deaf* (Apostolate, San Antonio)—O.P. Miss.

[0510]—*Franciscan Brothers of the Holy Cross*—F.F.S.C.

[0520]—*Franciscan Friars* (Sacred Heart Province)—O.F.M.

[0800]—*Maryknoll*—M.M.

[0910]—*Oblates of Mary Immaculate* (Central Province)—O.M.I.

[0940]—*Oblates of the Virgin Mary*—O.M.V.

[0430]—*Order of Preachers (Dominicans)*—O.P.

[]—*The Priestly Fraternity of St. Peter*—F.S.S.P.

[0990]—*Society of the Catholic Apostolate*—S.A.C.

RELIGIOUS INSTITUTES OF WOMEN REPRESENTED IN THE DIOCESE

[0100]—*Adorers of the Blood of Christ* (Ruma, IL; Wichita, KS)—A.S.C.

[]—*Congregation of Daughters of Divine Love*—D.D.L.

[1710]—*Congregation of the Third Order of St. Francis of Mary Immaculate, Joliet, IL*—O.S.F.

[1070-10]—*Dominican Sisters*—O.P.

[1070-13]—*Dominican Sisters*—O.P.

[1430]—*Franciscan Sisters of Our Lady of Perpetual Help*—O.S.F.

[1770]—*Hospital Sisters of Third Order of St. Francis*—O.S.F.

[]—*Missionary Sisters of the Sacred Heart of Jesus "Ad Gentes"*—M.A.G.

[3230]—*Poor Handmaids of Jesus Christ*—P.H.J.C.

[2970]—*School Sisters of Notre Dame* (St. Louis, MO)—S.S.N.D.

[0990]—*Sisters of Divine Providence* (St. Louis Prov.)—C.D.P.

[1570]—*Sisters of St. Francis of the Holy Family*—O.S.F.

[1580]—*Sisters of St. Francis of the Immaculate Conception*—O.S.F.

[1600]—*Sisters of St. Francis of the Martyr St. George*—F.S.G.M.

[3270]—*Sisters of the Most Precious Blood (O'Fallon, MO)*—C.PP.S.

[4110]—*Ursuline Nuns (Roman Union)* (Central Prov.)—O.S.U.

[14120]—*Ursuline Sisters Mount Saint Joseph*—O.S.U.

DIOCESAN CEMETERIES

SPRINGFIELD. *Calvary Cemetery Association*

CARLINVILLE. *Calvary Cemetery Association*

DECATUR. *Calvary Cemetery Association*

EDWARDSVILLE. *Calvary Cemetery Association*

LITCHFIELD. *Holy Cross Cemetery Association*

MOUNT STERLING. *Catholic Cemetery Association*

QUINCY. *Catholic Cemetery Association*

NECROLOGY

† Jenkins, J. Michael—Died Sept. 21, 2011

† O'Hara, Martin, (Retired)—Died May 8, 2011

An asterisk (*) denotes an organization that has established tax-exempt status directly with the IRS and is not covered by the USCCB Group Ruling.

Diocese of Springfield in Massachusetts

(Dioecesis Campifontis)

Most Reverend

TIMOTHY A. MCDONNELL

Bishop of Springfield in Massachusetts; ordained June 1, 1963; appointed Titular Bishop of Semina and Auxiliary Bishop of New York October 30, 2001; consecrated December 12, 2001; appointed Bishop of Springfield in Massachusetts March 9, 2004; installed April 1, 2004. *Mailing Address: P.O. Box 1730, Springfield, MA 01102-1730.*

Most Reverend

JOSEPH F. MAGUIRE, D.D.

Retired Bishop of Springfield; ordained June 29, 1945; appointed Auxiliary Bishop of Boston and Titular Bishop of Mactaris December 1, 1971; consecrated February 2, 1972; appointed Coadjutor Bishop of Springfield with right of succession April 3, 1976; officially installed as Bishop of Springfield on November 4, 1977; retired December 27, 1991. *Res.: 76 Elliot St., P.O. Box 1730, Springfield, MA 01102-1730.*

ESTABLISHED JUNE 14, 1870.

Square Miles 2,822.

Comprises the Counties of Berkshire, Franklin, Hampden and Hampshire in the State of Massachusetts.

For legal titles of parishes and diocesan institutions, consult the Chancery Office.

Chancery Office: P.O. Box 1730, Springfield, MA 01102-1730. Tel: 413-732-3175; Fax: 413-737-2337.

Web: www.diospringfield.org

Email: mail@diospringfield.org

STATISTICAL OVERVIEW

Personnel	
Bishop	1
Retired Bishops	2
Priests: Diocesan Active in Diocese	88
Priests: Diocesan Active Outside Diocese	6
Priests: Diocesan in Foreign Missions	2
Priests: Retired, Sick or Absent	45
Number of Diocesan Priests	141
Religious Priests in Diocese	43
Total Priests in Diocese	184
Extern Priests in Diocese	9
Ordinations:	
Diocesan Priests	3
Permanent Deacons	5
Permanent Deacons in Diocese	78
Total Brothers	20
Total Sisters	353
Parishes	
Parishes	81
With Resident Pastor:	
Resident Diocesan Priests	66
Resident Religious Priests	6
Without Resident Pastor:	
Administered by Priests	9
Missions	8
Pastoral Centers	1
Closed Parishes	1
Professional Ministry Personnel:	
Brothers	2
Sisters	16
Lay Ministers	23
Welfare	
Catholic Hospitals	1
Total Assisted	172,612
Health Care Centers	1
Total Assisted	7,000
Homes for the Aged	9
Total Assisted	532
Special Centers for Social Services	8
Total Assisted	42,070
Other Institutions	2
Total Assisted	850
Educational	
Diocesan Students in Other Seminaries	20
Total Seminarians	20
Colleges and Universities	1
Total Students	1,482
High Schools, Diocesan and Parish	4
Total Students	943
Elementary Schools, Diocesan and Parish	15
Total Students	3,807
Catechesis/Religious Education:	
High School Students	5,482
Elementary Students	12,006
Total Students under Catholic Instruction	23,740
Teachers in the Diocese:	
Priests	2
Sisters	20
Lay Teachers	414
Vital Statistics	
Receptions into the Church:	
Infant Baptism Totals	2,267
Minor Baptism Totals	145
Adult Baptism Totals	83
Received into Full Communion	173
First Communions	2,348
Confirmations	2,143
Marriages:	
Catholic	486
Interfaith	179
Total Marriages	665
Deaths	3,481
Total Catholic Population	226,740
Total Population	824,161

Former Bishops—Most Revs. PATRICK THOMAS O'REILLY, D.D., cons. Sept. 25, 1870; died May 28, 1892; THOMAS DANIEL BEAVEN, D.D., cons. Oct. 18, 1892; died Oct. 5, 1920; THOMAS M. O'LEARY, D.D., cons. Sept. 8, 1921; died Oct. 10, 1949; CHRISTOPHER J. WELDON, D.D., cons. March 24, 1950; retired Oct. 15, 1977; died March 19, 1982; JOSEPH F. MAGUIRE, D.D. (Retired), cons. Auxiliary Bishop of Boston, Feb. 2, 1972; installed Bishop of Springfield, Nov. 4, 1977; retired Dec. 27, 1991; JOHN A. MARSHALL, D.D., cons. Bishop of Burlington, Jan. 25, 1972; installed Bishop of Springfield, Feb. 18, 1992; died July 3, 1994; THOMAS LUDGER DUPRE, D.D., J.C.D. (Retired), ord. May 23, 1959; appt. Auxiliary Bishop of Springfield and Titular Bishop of Hodelm April 19, 1990; cons. May 31, 1990; appt. Bishop of Springfield March 14, 1995; installed May 8, 1995; resigned Feb. 11, 2004.

Vicar General and Moderator of the Curia—Rev. Msgr. CHRISTOPHER D. CONNELLY, J.C.L., 65 Elliot St., P.O. Box 1730, Springfield, 01102-1730.

Chancery Office—76 Elliot St., P.O. Box 1730, Springfield, 01102. Tel: 413-732-3175; Fax: 413-737-2337.

Vicar for Canonical Affairs and Chancellor—Rev. Msgr. DANIEL P. LISTON, J.C.L.

Vice-Chancellor—Rev. ROBERT W. THRASHER, J.C.D. (Retired).

Judicial Vicar—Rev. Msgr. JOHN J. BONZAGNI, M.Ed., J.C.L., J.D. Attorney at Law..

Episcopal Vicars—Rev. Msgrs. MICHAEL SHERSHANOVICH, Berkshire Vicariate; RONALD G. YARGEAU, Franklin-Hampshire Vicariate; DAVID J. JOYCE, Hampden East Vicariate; HOMER P. GOSSELIN, Hampden Central and Hampden West Vicariate. Vicars for the Clergy: Rev. Msgrs. DAVID J. JOYCE; GEORGE A. FARLAND.

Vicar for Religious—Sr. JUDITH O'CONNELL, S.S.J., Vicar, 65 Elliot St., P.O. Box 1730, Springfield, 01102-1730. Tel: 413-452-0609.

Diocesan Tribunal—Sr. CLAIRE LAPOINTE, S.A.S.V., J.C.L., Dir., 65 Elliot St., P.O. Box 1730, Springfield, 01102. Tel: 413-452-0664; Fax: 413-747-8482.

Judges—Rev. Msgrs. DANIEL P. LISTON, J.C.L.; CHRISTOPHER D. CONNELLY, J.C.L.; Revs. DANIEL R. FOLEY, J.C.D.; JOHN L. SULLIVAN, J.C.L.

Promoter of Justice—Rev. DANIEL R. FOLEY, J.C.D.

Defenders of the Bond—Sr. CLAIRE LAPOINTE, S.A.S.V., J.C.L.; Rev. ROBERT W. THRASHER, J.C.D.

Procurator-Advocate—Rev. Msgr. JUAN GARCIA; Deacons WILLIAM F. KERN, J.D.; JAMES MC ELROY, J.D.

Psychological Consultants—Rev. DONALD R. LAPOINTE, S.T.L., L.I.C.S.W.; MARTIN J. MARKEY, Ph.D.; ROBERT SAISI, Ph.D., Ed.D.; DAVID ARMSTRONG, L.I.C.S.W.

Auditors—Deacons WILLIAM F. KERN, J.D.; GARY DOANE; LEO COUGHLIN; JOHN ANTAYA; GEORGE KEATOR; FRANCIS RYAN; THEODORE T. TUDRYN.

Notary—Ms. MARIE DUSSAULT.

Presbyteral Council—Most Rev. TIMOTHY A. MCDONNELL; Rev. Msgrs. CHRISTOPHER D. CONNELLY, J.C.L., Vicar Gen.; DANIEL P. LISTON, J.C.L.; JUAN F. GARCIA; HOMER P. GOSSELIN; DAVID J. JOYCE; Revs. THOMAS M. SHEA; KENNETH J. TATRO; HENRY L. DORSCH; WAYNE C. BIERNAT; DANIEL R. FOLEY, J.C.D.; WILLIAM H. LUNNEY; JOHN E. CONNORS; ROBERT A. GENTILE JR.; STANLEY J. AKSAMIT; STEFAN J. NIEMCZYK; MARK M. MENGEL, S.S.C.; CHRISTOPHER A. MALATESTA.

Deans—Revs. BRIAN F. MCGRATH, Hampden West Deanery; ROBERT J. COONAN, Hampshire Deanery;

TIMOTHY J. CAMPOLI, Franklin Deanery; CHRISTOPHER A. MALATESTA, Berkshire Deanery; ROBERT A. GENTILE JR., Greater Holyoke Deanery; Rev. Msgr. GEORGE A. FARLAND, Springfield Deanery; Revs. DAVID M. DARCY, Hampden Central Deanery; STEFAN J. NIEMCZYK, Hampden East Deanery.

Diocesan Consultors—Rev. Msgrs. CHRISTOPHER D. CONNELLY, J.C.L.; JOHN J. BONZAGNI, M.Ed., J.C.L., J.D.; JUAN GARCIA; DANIEL P. LISTON, J.C.L.; DAVID J. JOYCE; Revs. CHRISTOPHER A. MALATESTA; BRIAN F. MCGRATH; ROBERT A. GENTILE JR.; HOWARD W. MCCORMICK (Retired).

Bishop's Commission for Clergy—Most Rev. TIMOTHY A. MCDONNELL; Rev. Msgrs. CHRISTOPHER D. CONNELLY, J.C.L.; GEORGE A. FARLAND; RONALD G. YARGEAU; DAVID J. JOYCE; DANIEL P. LISTON, J.C.L.; Revs. DAVID M. DARCY; ROBERT A. GENTILE JR.; BRIAN F. MCGRATH; FRANCIS M. KENNEDY (Retired); MICHAEL F. BERNIER; THOMAS M. SHEA; WILLIAM A. TOURIGNY.

Bishop's Cabinet—Rev. Msgrs. CHRISTOPHER D. CONNELLY, J.C.L.; JOHN J. BONZAGNI, M.Ed., J.C.L., J.D. Attorney at Law.; DANIEL P. LISTON, J.C.L.; Sisters JUDITH O'CONNELL, S.S.J.; M. ANDREA CISZEWSKI, F.S.S.J.; CATHERINE HOMROCK, S.S.J.; WILLIAM F. LABROAD JR.; PATRICIA FINN MCMANAMY, L.I.C.S.W.; KATHRYN BUCKLEY-BRAWNER; PETER SCHMIDT; MARK DUPONT.

Diocesan Diaconate Council—Deacon LEO COUGHLIN, Dir.; Rev. Msgr. JOHN J. BONZAGNI, M.Ed., J.C.L., J.D., Advisor.

Diocesan Diaconate Formation Board—Deacon LEO COUGHLIN, Dir.

Diocesan Commission for Ecumenism—Rev. WILLIAM A. POMERLEAU, 76 Elliot St., P.O. Box 1730, Springfield, 01101. Tel: 413-732-3175; MARTIN PION.

Diocesan Commission for the Liturgy—65 Elliot St., P.O. Box 1730, Springfield, 01102-1730. Tel: 413-452-0839. Revs. VERNON P. DECOTEAU; GEOFFREY J. DEEKER, C.S.S.; WARREN J. SAVAGE; Deacon ROGER CARRIER.

Diocesan Pastoral Council—Most Rev. TIMOTHY A. MCDONNELL; RICHARD BUTLER; ROBERT DIGAN; CHRIS CLARK; LYNN DUBREUIL; F. WILLIAM EULIANO JR.; LISA FUSINI; ROBERT GRENIER; Deacon DONALD HIGBY; EVERETT HUME; Rev. Msgrs. DAVID J. JOYCE; CHRISTOPHER D. CONNELLY, J.C.L.; LUIS NEVAREZ; PAUL PAJAK; CAROL PIROG, Chm.; Sisters CATHERINE HOMROCK, S.S.J.; MARY QUINN, S.S.J.; RITA STANISIEWSKI.

Finance Officer—WILLIAM F. LABROAD JR., 65 Elliot St., P.O. Box 1730, Springfield, 01102. Tel: 413-732-3175.

Diocesan Offices and Directors

Apostolate to the Handicapped—Sr. JOAN MAGNANI, S.S.J., Dir., Bureau for Exceptional Children and Adults, 537 Northampton St., P.O. Box 1039, Holyoke, 01041. Tel: 413-538-7450 (Voice and TTY); Fax: 413-536-5691.

Apostolate of the Suffering—Bro. ROBERT J. LETASZ, S.O.D.C., Pres.; JEANNINE GAGNON, Sec., P.O. Box 535, Chicopee, 01021.

Building Commission—Rev. DONALD R. LAPOINTE, S.T.L., L.I.C.S.W., Chm. (Retired), 65 Elliot St., P.O. Box 1730, Springfield, 01102-1730.

Building Consultant—RICHARD WILK.

Campaign for Human Development—KATHRYN BUCKLEY-BRAWNER, Dir., 65 Elliot St., P.O. Box 1730, Springfield, 01102. Tel: 413-452-0697; Fax: 413-746-3421.

Counseling Office—PATRICIA FINN MCMANAMY, L.I.C.S.W., Dir. Tel: 413-452-0624.

Catholic Charities Agency—KATHRYN BUCKLEY-BRAWNER, Dir., 65 Elliot St., P.O. Box 1730, Springfield, 01102-1730. Tel: 413-452-0606.

Annual Catholic Appeal—65 Elliot St., Springfield, 01101. Tel: 413-452-0629; Fax: 413-732-4297. *Mailing Address: P.O. Box 1730, Springfield, 01102*.

Catholic Relief Services—KATHRYN BUCKLEY-BRAWNER, 65 Elliot St., P.O. Box 1730, Springfield, 01102. Tel: 413-732-3175.

Cemeteries—JOSEPH KOSTEK, Pres. Cemeteries, 65 Elliot St., Springfield, 01101-1730. Tel: 413-782-0349; Fax: 413-785-5449. Saint Michael's Cemetery, 1601 State St., Springfield, 01109. Tel: 413-733-0659. Gate of Heaven Cemetery, 421 Tinkham Rd., Springfield, 01129. Tel: 413-782-4731. St. Aloysius Cemetery, 1601 State St., Springfield, 01109. Tel: 413-733-0695. St. Benedict Cemetery, Liberty St., Springfield, 01104. Tel: 413-782-4731. St. Matthew Cemetery, 366 Springfield St., Springfield, 01109. Tel: 413-733-0659. St. Mary Cemetery, 203 Southampton Rd., Westfield, 01085. Tel: 413-568-7775. Notre Dame Cemetery, Lyman St., South Hadley, 01075. Tel: 413-782-4731. Calvary Cemetery, Northampton St., Holyoke, 01040. Tel: 413-782-4731. Precious Blood Cemetery, Willimansett St., South Hadley, 01075. Tel: 413-782-4731. St. Rose Cemetery, Lyman St., South Hadley, 01075. Tel: 413-420-0001.

Censor of Librorum—Rev. MARK S. STELZER, S.T.D.

Clergy Counseling Service—Rev. Msgr. GEORGE A. FARLAND, Sacred Heart Rectory, 395 Chestnut St., Springfield, 01104. Tel: 413-732-3721.

Communications and Public Relations—MARK DUPONT, Dir., 65 Elliot St., P.O. Box 1730, Springfield, 01102-1730. Tel: 413-452-0648; 413-737-4744; Fax: 413-747-0273.

Catholic Communications Corporation—MARK DUPONT, Pres., 65 Elliot St., P.O. Box 1730, Springfield, 01102-1730. Tel: 413-737-4744; Fax: 413-747-0273.

Services—

Chalice of Salvation (Televised Mass)—Bro. TERRENCE A. SCANLON, C.P., Exec. Dir., 65 Elliot St., P.O. Box 1730, Springfield, 01102-1730. Tel: 413-452-0642.

Real to Reel (Television News Magazine)—MARK DUPONT, Exec. Producer, 65 Elliot St., P.O. Box 1730, Springfield, 01102-1730. Tel: 413-452-0648.

The Catholic Mirror (Magazine)—REBECCA DRAKE, Editor, 65 Elliot St., P.O. Box 1730, Springfield, 01102-1730. Tel: 413-452-0636.

Continuing Education for Priests—Rev. JOHN T. SMEGAL, St. Brigid Rectory, 122 N. Pleasant St., Amherst, 01004. Tel: 413-256-6181.

Office of Faith Formation—Sr. PAULA ROBILLARD, S.S.J., Dir.

Cursillo Movement—Rev. Msgr. DAVID J. JOYCE, Dir. English-Speaking Cursillo Movement, 65 Elliot St., P.O. Box 1730, Springfield, 01102-1730. Tel: 413-732-3175; MARY VAZQUEZ, Spanish-Speaking Cursillo Movement. Tel: 413-535-0163.

Diocesan Office of Black Catholic Ministry—MARION M. JOHNSON, Administrative Dir., 235 Eastern Ave., Springfield, 01109. Tel: 413-788-9790. Email: marionmarie@rcn.com. Web: www.diospringfield.org/ministries/bc.html.

Diocesan Office for Communications—MARK DUPONT, 65 Elliot St., P.O. Box 1730, Springfield, 01102-1730. Tel: 413-737-4744; Fax: 413-747-0273.

Education—Sr. M. ANDREA CISZEWSKI, F.S.S.J., Supt. of Schools; Dr. GAIL FURMAN, Asst. Supt. Student Svcs., 65 Elliot St., P.O. Box 1730, Springfield, 01102-1730. Tel: 413-452-0830; Fax: 413-452-0817.

Family Life Bureau—Sr. CATHERINE HOMROCK, S.S.J., 65 Elliot St., P.O. Box 1730, Springfield, 01102-1730. Tel: 413-732-3175.

Fiscal Affairs—WILLIAM F. LABROAD JR., Finance Officer, 65 Elliot St., P.O. Box 1730, Springfield, 01102-1730. Tel: 413-452-0687; Fax: 413-785-5449.

Holy Childhood Association—Rev. DONALD R. LAPOINTE, S.T.L., L.I.C.S.W. (Retired).

Holy Family League of Charity—c/o Office of Catholic Charities, P.O. Box 1730, Springfield, 01102-1730. Tel: 413-732-3175.

Human Resources—PETER SCHMIDT, Dir., 65 Elliot St., P.O. Box 1730, Springfield, 01102-1730. Tel: 413-452-0691.

Office of Lay Ministry Formation—Rev. WILLIAM CYR, Dir.; Sr. CATHERINE HOMROCK, S.S.J., Coord.

Massachusetts Catholic Conference—Most Rev. TIMOTHY A. MCDONNELL; Rev. Msgr. CHRISTOPHER D. CONNELLY, J.C.L.; Sr. ANNETTE MCDERMOTT, S.S.J.; JOHN EGAN ESQ., 65 Elliot St., P.O. Box 1730, Springfield, 01102-1730. Tel: 413-732-3175.

Ministry to the Deaf—Sr. CAROL LAREAU, S.S.J., 34 Nye St., Springfield, 01104. Tel: 413-736-0020.

Ministry to the Divorced and Separated—Pastoral Ministry Office, 65 Elliot St., P.O. Box 1730, Springfield, 01102-1730. Tel: 413-732-3175.

Newman Apostolate and Campus Ministry—Revs. GARY M. DAILEY, Dir.; MICHAEL J. TWOHIG, Asst. Dir., Newman Center, 472 N. Pleasant St., Amherst, 01002. Tel: 413-549-0300.

Office for the Protection of Children and Youth—PATRICIA FINN MCMANAMY, L.I.C.S.W., Dir., 65 Elliot St., P.O. Box 1730, Springfield, 01102-1730. Tel: 413-452-0624.

Office of Social Concerns—PATRICIA FINN MCMANAMY, L.I.C.S.W., Dir., 65 Elliot St., P.O. Box 1730, Springfield, 01102-1730. Tel: 413-452-0615.

Pastoral Ministry—Mailing Address: 65 Elliot St., P.O. Box 1730, Springfield, 01102-1730. Tel: 413-732-3175.

Permanent Diaconate—Deacon LEO COUGHLIN, Dir., 65 Elliot St., P.O. Box 1730, Springfield, 01102-1730. Tel: 413-452-0674; Fax: 413-747-0273.

Priests' Retirement Program—Rev. FRANCIS J. MANNING, Liaison (Retired), 65 Elliot St., P.O. Box 1730, Springfield, 01102-1730.

Pro-Life Commission—TIMOTHY BIGGINS, Chm., 65 Elliot St., P.O. Box 1730, Springfield, 01102-1730. Tel: 413-732-3175.

Propagation of the Faith—Rev. DONALD R. LAPOINTE, S.T.L., L.I.C.S.W., Dir. (Retired), 65 Elliot St., P.O. Box 1730, Springfield, 01102-1730. Tel: 413-452-0675.

Refugee Resettlement Program/Immigration Services—Catholic Charities Agencies, Inc., 65 Elliot St., P.O. Box 1730, Springfield, 01102-1730. Tel: 413-452-0606.

Office of Social Concerns—65 Elliot St., P.O. Box 1730, Springfield, 01102-1730. Tel: 413-732-3175.

Retired Priests' Service—Rev. FRANCIS J. MANNING (Retired).

Southeast Asian Apostolate—Rev. QUYNH DINH TRAN, Dir., St. Paul the Apostle Church, 235 Dwight Rd., Springfield, 01108. Tel: 413-737-4422; Fax: 413-746-8378.

Catholic Latino Ministry—Mr. ANDRES LOPEZ, Dir.; LUCY RAMOS, Exec. Sec., 65 Elliot St., P.O. Box 1730, Springfield, 01102-1730. Tel: 413-452-0631. Email: hispanicmin@diospringfield.org.

The Saint Thomas More Society—Deacon WILLIAM KERN, Esq., Pres.

Bishop Marshall Center—Ms. MARGO MORAN, Dir., St. Michael's Cathedral, 260 State St., Springfield, 01105. Tel: 413-732-2301.

Springfield Diocesan Council of Catholic Women—MARY BLAIS, Pres., Mailing Address: Diocese of Springfield, P.O. Box 1730, Springfield, 01102-1730.

Victim Assistance Coordinator—PATRICIA FINN MCMANAMY, L.I.C.S.W.

Vocations—Rev. GARY M. DAILEY, 65 Elliot St., P.O. Box 1730, Springfield, 01102-1730. Tel: 413-452-0816; Fax: 413-452-0817.

Office of Youth Ministry—Sr. CATHERINE HOMROCK, S.S.J., 65 Elliot St., P.O. Box 1730, Springfield, 01101-1730. Tel: 413-732-3175.

CLERGY, PARISHES, MISSIONS AND PAROCHIAL SCHOOLS

CITY OF SPRINGFIELD

(HAMPDEN COUNTY)

1—ST. MICHAEL'S CATHEDRAL (1847) Rev. Msgr. Christopher D. Connelly, Rector; Sisters Margaret McNaughton, S.S.J., Pastoral Min.; Eileen Sullivan, S.S.J., Outreach Min.; Deacons Leo Coughlin; Angel Perez. In Res., Rev. Msgr. Daniel P. Liston; Rev. Daniel R. Foley (Retired).
Res.: 260 State St., 01103. Tel: 413-781-3656; Fax: 413-788-7752.
Catechesis/Religious Program—Students 63.
Mission—St. Francis Chapel 254 Bridge St., Hampden Co. 01102-1730. Tel: 413-452-0631.

2—ALL SOULS (1908), (Spanish), Rev. Msgr. Juan F. Garcia (Peru); Rev. Jose Siesquen Flores (Peru), Parochial Vicar. In Res., Deacon Jose Rivera.
Office & Res.: 445 Plainfield St., 01107. Tel: 413-736-8208; 413-736-2167; 413-736-0076 (Res.); Fax: 413-731-0962 (Res.).
Catechesis/Religious Program—Students 6.

3—ST. ALOYSIUS (1873), (French), Merged with St. Matthew, Springfield, to form St. Jude, Indian Orchard.

4—BLESSED SACRAMENT (1953), (Hispanic), Rev. Msgr. Juan F. Garcia (Peru); Rev. Jose Siesquen Flores (Peru), Parochial Vicar; Deacons Genaro Medina; Kevin McCarthy.
Pastoral Center & Res.: 445 Plainfield St., 01107. Tel: 413-736-8208; 413-736-2167; 413-736-0076 (Res.); Fax: 413-731-0962.
Catechesis/Religious Program—Tel: 413-736-8208. Nilda Resto, D.R.E. Students 141.

5—ST. CATHERINE OF SIENA (1961) Rev. Mark Glover, Admin.; Deacons Joseph M. Garde; John Antaya.
Res.: 1023 Parker St., 01129. Tel: 413-783-8619; Fax: 413-783-2344. Email: stcatherine1023@comcast.net. Web: www.scsparish.4Lpi.com.
Catechesis/Religious Program—Students 282.

6—HOLY CROSS (1949) Rev. Anthony F. Cullen; Deacon William Toller. In Res., Revs. Robert H. Riel (Retired); Robert W. Thrasher (Retired).
Res.: 221 Plumtree Rd., 01118. Tel: 413-783-4111; Fax: 413-783-4112. Email: hcparish@hcparish.org. Web: www.hcparish.org.
Catechesis/Religious Program—175 Eddywood St., 01118. Tel: 413-796-7675. Students 118.

7—HOLY FAMILY (1901), (African American—Hispanic), Closed. Merged into St. Michael's Cathedral with records being kept at St. Michael's Cathedral, Springfield.

8—HOLY NAME (1909) Rev. Mark M. Mengel, S.S.C., Admin.; Rev. Msgr. David J. Joyce, Parochial Vicar; Sr. Catherine Leary, S.S.J., Pastoral Min.; Mary

Reale, Finance Mgr.
Res.: 323 Dickinson St., 01108. Tel: 413-733-5823; Fax: 413-788-6481.
Center—57 Alderman St., 01108. Tel: 413-734-7113.
Catechesis/Religious Program—Tel: 413-733-5823, Ext. 123. Claudine Bouchard Collins, C.R.E. Students 82.

9—IMMACULATE CONCEPTION (1905), (Polish), Rev. Stanislaw Sokol.
Res.: 25 Parker St. (Indian Orchard), 01151. Tel: 413-543-3627; Fax: 413-543-4301. Email: iccma@verizon.net.
Catechesis/Religious Program—Alicia Jasiel, D.R.E. Students 69.

10—ST. JOSEPH'S (1873), (French), Closed. For inquiries for parish records please contact St. Michael's Cathedral, Springfield.

11—MARY MOTHER OF HOPE PARISH (2010) Rev. Michael F. Bernier. In Res., Revs. Donatus Ironuma; Adolf Busobozi.
Res.: 840 Page Blvd., 01104. Tel: 413-739-0456; Fax: 413-733-6155. Email: stmary@the-spa.com. Web: www.stmary-springfield.org.
Catechesis/Religious Program—Tel: 413-736-1622; Fax: 413-736-9299. Lee Lyon, D.R.E. Students 294.

12—ST. MARY'S (1948), Merged with Our Lady of Hope, Springfield to form Mary Mother of Hope Parish, Springfield. All records located at Mary Mother of Hope Parish, Springfield.

13—OUR LADY OF HOPE (1906) Closed. Merged with St. Mary's, Springfield to form Mary Mother of Hope Parish, Springfield. All records located at Mary Mother of Hope Parish, Springfield.

14—OUR LADY OF MT. CARMEL (1907), (Italian), Rev. Robert S. White, C.S.S.; Sr. Elizabeth A. Matuszek, S.S.J., Pastoral Assoc. In Res., Rev. Anthony M. Corigliano, C.S.S.
Res.: 123 William St., 01105. Tel: 413-734-5433; Fax: 413-731-0680. Email: olmcspfld@comcast.net. Web: www.olmcspfld.com.
Catechesis/Religious Program—Tel: 413-204-7789. Email: loisdegray@yahoo.com. Web: www.olmcspfld-.com. Students 85.

15—OUR LADY OF THE ROSARY (1917), (Polish), [JC] Rev. Stanislaw Sokol.
Res.: 28 Underwood St., 01104. Tel: 413-733-0508; Fax: 413-733-7512.
Catechesis/Religious Program—Tel: 413-739-2210. Students 87.

16—OUR LADY OF THE SACRED HEART (1929) Revs. William A. Pomerleau; Tomasz P. Parzynski, Parochial Vicar; Deacons Michael Perkins; Odell Daniel; Christina Olejarz, Business Mgr.
Office: 51 Rosewell St., 01109. Tel: 413-782-8041; Fax: 413-783-9150. Email: churchinfo@olshaa.com.
Res.: 417 Boston Rd., 01109. Tel: 413-782-8041; Fax: 413-783-9150.
Catechesis/Religious Program—Sharon Sabourin, D.R.E. Students 110.
Mission—St. Jude Indian Orchard (1998)

17—ST. PATRICK'S (1961) Rev. Francis H. Crombie; Deacon George Kozach. Tel: 413-783-2458.
Res.: 1900 Allen St., 01118-1820. Tel: 413-783-6201; Fax: 413-783-7787. Email: stpatspringfield@aol.com.
Catechesis/Religious Program—Alan E. O'Dell, D.R.E. Students 84.

18—ST. PAUL THE APOSTLE (1960) Rev. Quynh Dinh Tran, Admin.; Deacons Francis D. Rogers; Ly X. Cao; Khanh Tran.
Res.: 235 Dwight Rd., 01108. Tel: 413-737-4422 (Parish Office); Fax: 413-746-8378. Email: stpaulsapostle@aol.com.
Catechesis/Religious Program—Students 163.

19—SACRED HEART (1872) Rev. Msgr. George A. Farland. In Res., Rev. Mark S. Stelzer.
Res.: 395 Chestnut St., 01104. Tel: 413-732-3721; Fax: 413-733-5731. Email: shc395@aol.com.
Catechesis/Religious Program—Students 163.

20—ST. THOMAS AQUINAS (1908), (French—Vietnamese), Closed. For inquiries for sacramental records contact Blessed Sacrament, Springfield.

OUTSIDE THE CITY OF SPRINGFIELD

ADAMS, BERKSHIRE CO.

1—NOTRE DAME DES SEPT DOULEURS (1882), (French), Merged with St. Thomas Aquinas, Adams, to form Notre Dame des Sept Douleurs and St. Thomas Aquinas, Adams.

2—NOTRE DAME DES SEPT DOULEURS AND ST. THOMAS AQUINAS (1998) Merged see Pope John Paul the Great, Adams.

3—POPE JOHN PAUL THE GREAT PARISH, (Merged parishes of Notre Dame/St. Thomas Aquinas & St. Stanislaus Kostka) Rev. Daniel J. Boyle; Deacon Gregory Lafreniere.
P.O. Box 231, 01220-0231. Tel: 413-743-0577; Fax: 413-743-4665.
Catechesis/Religious Program—Jill Staffin, D.R.E. (K-6); Sue LaFrance, D.R.E. (7-11). Students 200.

4—ST. STANISLAUS KOSTKA (1902), (Polish), [CEM] Closed. Merged with Notre Dame des Sept Douleurs and St. Thomas Aquinas, Adams, to form Pope John Paul the Great, Adams. For inquiries for parish records please see Pope John Paul the Great, Adams.

5—ST. THOMAS AQUINAS (1875) Merged with Notre Dame des Sept Douleurs, Adams, to form Notre Dame des Sept Douleurs and St. Thomas Aquinas, Adams.

AGAWAM, HAMPDEN CO.

1—ALL SAINTS (2001) Closed. For inquiries for parish records contact Sacred Heart, Feeding Hills.

2—ST. JOHN THE EVANGELIST (1946) Rev. John J. Brennan; Deacon Paul Briere; Mary Scannell, Pastoral Min. In Res., Revs. Warren J. Savage; John S. Lis (Retired).
Res.: 833 Main St., 01001. Tel: 413-786-8105; Fax: 413-789-6266. Email: info@stjohnevangelistchurch.org. Web: www.stjohnevangelistchurch.org.
Catechesis/Religious Program—Tel: 413-789-2484. Students 463.

3—ST. THERESA OF THE CHILD JESUS (1883) Merged with Saint Anthony Mission to form All Saints, Agawam. For inquiries for parish records please see Sacred Heart, Feeding Hills.

AMHERST, HAMPSHIRE CO., ST. BRIGID'S (1872) [CEM] Rev. John T. Smegal.
Res.: 122 N. Pleasant St., P.O. Box 424, 01004-0424. Tel: 413-256-6181.
Catechesis/Religious Program—Students 90.

BELCHERTOWN, HAMPSHIRE CO., ST. FRANCIS OF ASSISI (1926) Rev. Vernon P. Decoteau.
Res. & Church: 24 Jabish St., P.O. Box 612, 01007-0612. Tel: 413-323-6272; Fax: 413-323-6272. Web: stfrancisbtown.org.
Catechesis/Religious Program—Dr. Carolyn Vogt Groves, C.R.E.; Deborah Robinson, C.R.E. Students 460.

BONDSVILLE, HAMPDEN CO.

1—ST. ADALBERT'S (1910) Closed. Sacramental Records at Saint Thomas Parish, Palmer.

2—ST. BARTHOLOMEW'S (1878) [JC] Closed. Merged with St. Thomas the Apostle, Palmer. All records will be transferred to St. Thomas the Apostle, Palmer.

BRIMFIELD, HAMPDEN CO., ST. CHRISTOPHER'S (1953) Rev. Jeddie P. Brooks.
Church: 20 Sturbridge Rd., Rte. 20, P.O. Box 387, 01010. Tel: 413-245-7274; Fax: 413-245-7372. Email: stchrisbrimfield@gmail.com. Web: stchrisbrimfield.org.
Rectory—16 Sturbridge Rd., Rte. 20, P.O. Box 387, 01010-0387.
Catechesis/Religious Program—Students 119.
Mission—St. Monica Wales, Hampden Co. (Closed)

CHESHIRE, BERKSHIRE CO., ST. MARY OF THE ASSUMPTION (1926) [JC] Rev. David R. Raymond; Deacon Robert Hitter.
Res.: 159 Church St., 01225. Tel: 413-743-2110. Email: stmarys159@verizon.net. Web: stmarycheshire.com.
Catechesis/Religious Program—Tel: 413-743-5423; Fax: 413-743-5423. Email: mtamosfarm@roadrunner.com. Students 124.

CHICOPEE, HAMPDEN CO.

1—ST. ANNE'S (1912) Revs. William C. Rousseau; Richard M. Turner, Parochial Vicar.
Res.: 30 College St., 01020. Tel: 413-532-7503; Fax: 413-532-5970. Web: stanneparishchicopee.org.
Catechesis/Religious Program—Tel: 413-533-8038. Students 164.

2—ST. ANTHONY OF PADUA (1926), (Polish), St. Mary of the Assumption and Nativity of the B.V.M., Chicopee merged into St. Anthony. Rev. Benedict Fagone, O.F.M.Conv. In Res., Bro. Frank Grimaldi, O.F.M.Conv.
Res.: 56 St. Anthony St., 01013. Tel: 413-538-9475; Fax: 413-538-9859.
Catechesis/Religious Program—Tel: 413-534-1493. Students 125.

3—ASSUMPTION (1885), (French), Closed. Merged with Holy Name of Jesus, Chicopee. All records kept at Holy Name of Jesus, Chicopee.

4—ST. GEORGE'S (1893), (French), Closed. Merged into Holy Name of Jesus, Chicopee. All records kept at Holy Name of Jesus, Chicopee.

5—HOLY NAME OF JESUS (1838) [CEM], Merged with Assumption, St. George's & St. Patrick's, Chicopee. All records for these parishes will be located at Holy Name of Jesus, Chicopee. Rev. David M. Darcy.
Office: 33 South St., 01013. Tel: 413-594-8700; Fax: 413-592-3871. Email: holynamechicopee@aol.com. Web: holynameassumption.org.
School—(Grades PreK-8), 63 South St., 01013. Tel: 413-592-6857; Fax: 413-598-0150. Email: hnprincipal@aol.com. Patricia Kern, Prin.; Ms. Carol Ann Robitaille, Librarian. Lay Teachers 11; Students 147.
Catechesis/Religious Program—Students 148.

6—ST. MARY'S (1939) Closed. Merged into St. Anthony of Padua, Chicopee. All records kept at St. Anthony of Padua, Chicopee.

7—NATIVITY OF THE BLESSED VIRGIN MARY (1897), (French), [JC] Closed. Merged with St. Anthony of Padua, Chicopee. All records kept at St. Anthony, Chicopee.

8—ST. PATRICK'S (1872), (Irish), [CEM] Closed. Merged into Holy Name of Jesus, Chicopee. All records kept at Holy Name of Jesus, Chicopee.

9—ST. ROSE DE LIMA (1909), (French), [CEM] Rev. William A. Tourigny.
Res.: 600 Grattan St., 01020. Tel: 413-536-4558; Fax: 413-534-9130. Web: www.sterose.org.
School—St. Joan of Arc, (Grades PreK-8), 587 Grattan St., 01020. Tel: 413-533-1475; Fax: 413-533-1418. Email: sjsg@stjoan-stgeorge.org. Web: sjachicopee.org. Paula Jenkins, Prin.; Rene Ruel, Librarian. Lay Teachers 21; Students 260.
Catechesis/Religious Program—Students 353.

10—ST. STANISLAUS BASILICA (1891), (Polish), [CEM] Revs. Michael Zielke, O.F.M.Conv.; Mieczyslaw Wit, O.F.M.Conv.; Pedro de Oliveira, O.F.M.Conv.; Bros. Hugh Dymski, O.F.M.Conv., Admin.; Michael Duffy, O.F.M.Conv.; Deacons Charles Wainwright; Joseph Peters. In Res., Rev. Noel Danielewicz.
Res.: 566 Front St., 01013. Tel: 413-594-6669; Fax: 413-594-5259.
School—(Grades PreK-8), 534 Front St., 01013. Tel: 413-592-5135; Fax: 413-598-0187. Sr. Cecelia Haier, F.S.S.J., Prin.; Rosemary Ankiewicz, Librarian. Franciscan Sisters of St. Joseph 2; Lay Teachers 27; Students 344.
Catechesis/Religious Program—Students 121.

DALTON, BERKSHIRE CO., ST. AGNES (1907) Rev. Christopher A. Malatesta; Deacons Pasqual Baldasaro; George Morrell; Richard Radzick.
Res.: 489 Main St., 01226. Tel: 413-684-0125; Fax: 413-684-0734. Email: stagnes@stagnescc.com. Web: www.stagnescc.com.
School—(Grades K-8), 30 Carson St., 01226. Tel: 413-684-3143; Fax: 413-684-3124. James Stankiewicz, Headmaster. Sisters of St. Joseph 1; Lay Teachers 12; Students 148.
Catechesis/Religious Program—513 Main St., 01226. Tel: 413-684-1803. Students 470.
Chapel—St. Patrick Chapel 43 Church St., Hinsdale, 01235.

EAST LONGMEADOW, HAMPDEN CO., ST. MICHAEL'S (1894) Rev. James J. Scahill; Sisters Mary McGeer, S.S.J., Pastoral Assoc.; Betty Broughan, S.S.J., Pastoral Assoc.
Mailing Address: 128 Maple St., 01028.
Res.: 108 Maple St., 01028. Tel: 413-525-4253; Fax: 413-525-2443. Email: pbaran@charter.net.
Catechesis/Religious Program—Tel: 413-525-0371. Miss Rose Stella, D.R.E. Students 997.

EASTHAMPTON, HAMPSHIRE CO.

1—IMMACULATE CONCEPTION (1871) [CEM] Merged with Sacred Heart, Easthampton and Our Lady of Good Counsel, Easthampton to form Our Lady of the Valley, Easthampton.

2—OUR LADY OF GOOD COUNSEL (1906), (French), Merged with Sacred Heart, Easthampton and Immaculate Conception, Easthampton to form Our Lady of the Valley, Easthampton.

3—OUR LADY OF THE VALLEY Revs. Douglas McGonagle; Piotr Pawlus, Parochial Vicar.
33 Adams St., 01027.
School—Our Lady's Child Care Center, (Grades PreK), 35 Pleasant St., 01027. Perri Taylor, Dir. (Child Care). Lay Teachers 15; Students 66.
Catechesis/Religious Program—Students 412.

4—SACRED HEART (1909), (Polish), [CEM] Closed. Merged with Immaculate Conception, Easthampton and Our Lady of Good Counsel, Easthampton to form Our Lady of the Valley, Easthampton.

FEEDING HILLS, HAMPDEN CO., SACRED HEART (1946) Rev. Steven Amo, Admin.
Res.: 1103 Springfield St., 01030. Tel: 413-786-8200; Fax: 413-786-7802. Email: office@sacredheartfeedinghills.org. Web: www.sacredheartfeedinghills.org.
Catechesis/Religious Program—Tel: 413-789-6705. Students 461.

FLORENCE, HAMPSHIRE CO., ANNUNCIATION (1878) Changed to a chapel under newly formed parish of Saint Elizabeth Ann Seton, Northampton. All records transferred to Saint Elizabeth All Seton, Northampton.

GRANBY, HAMPSHIRE CO., IMMACULATE HEART OF MARY (1951) Rev. Charles H. Kuzmeski.
Res.: 256 State St., 01033. Tel: 413-467-9821; Fax: 413-467-2988. Email: parish@ihmgranby.org. Web: www.ihmgranby.org.
Catechesis/Religious Program—Tel: 413-467-3566. Email: faithformation@ihmgranby.org. Students 183.

GREAT BARRINGTON, BERKSHIRE CO., ST. PETER'S (1864) [CEM] Rev. William P. Murphy.
Res.: 16 Russell St., 01230. Tel: 413-528-1157; Fax: 413-644-8916. Email: stpetersgb@verizon.net.

Catechesis/Religious Program—Students 87.

GREENFIELD, FRANKLIN CO.

1—BLESSED SACRAMENT (1960) [CEM] Rev. Timothy J. Campoli; Deacon John Leary.
Res.: 182 High St., 01301. Tel: 413-773-3311; Fax: 413-773-5785. Email: blessedsacrament@crocker.com. Web: blessedsacramentgreenfieldma.org.
Catechesis/Religious Program—Tel: 413-774-2918. Students 60.

2—HOLY TRINITY (1868) Rev. Msgr. Ronald G. Yargeau; Rev. Tomasz Gorny, Parochial Vicar; Deacons Channing L. Bete Jr.; Paul F. DeCarlo.
Res.: 133 Main St., 01301-3209. Tel: 413-774-2884; Fax: 413-774-3852. Email: churchlady@crocker.com. Web: www.holytrinitychurchgfld.org.
Catechesis/Religious Program—Students 88.

3—SACRED HEART (1912), (Polish), [CEM] Closed. Merged with St. Mary, Turner Falls & St. Ann, Turner Falls to form Our Lady of Peace, Turner Falls.

HADLEY, HAMPSHIRE CO.

1—HOLY ROSARY (1916), (Polish), Merged with St. John, Hadley, to form Most Holy Redeemer, Hadley.

2—ST. JOHN'S (1915) Merged with Holy Rosary, Hadley, to form Most Holy Redeemer, Hadley.

3—MOST HOLY REDEEMER (1998) [CEM] Rev. Shaun O'Connor.
Res.: 120 Russell St., P.O. Box 375, 01035-0375. Tel: 413-584-1326; Fax: 413-587-0224. Email: mhchurch@yahoo.com. Web: www.mhrparish.org.
Catechesis/Religious Program—Tel: 413-586-6209. Students 192.

HAMPDEN, HAMPDEN CO., ST. MARY'S (1951) [CEM] Rev. Timothy J. Murphy.
Res.: 27 Somers Rd., 01036. Tel: 413-566-8843; Fax: 413-566-5845. Email: stmarys@the-spa.com.
Catechesis/Religious Program—Students 199.

HATFIELD, HAMPSHIRE CO.

1—HOLY TRINITY (1916), (Polish), [CEM] Merged with St. Joseph, Hatfield to form Our Lady of Grace, Hatfield effective 11/28/10. For inquiries for parish records please see Our Lady of Grace, Hatfield.

2—ST. JOSEPH (1899) Merged with Holy Trinity, Hatfield to form Our Lady of Grace, Hatfield.

3—OUR LADY OF GRACE PARISH (2010) Rev. Robert J. Coonan.
Mailing Address: P.O. Box 34, 01038.
Res.: 11 School St., 01038. Tel: 413-247-9079; Fax: 413-247-9080. Email: ourladyofgracehatfield@yahoo.com.
Catechesis/Religious Program—Students 109.

HAYDENVILLE, HAMPSHIRE CO.

1—ST. MARY'S (1889) [CEM] Closed. Merged with St. Catherine's, Leeds to form Our Lady of the Hills, Haydenville.

2—OUR LADY OF THE HILLS (2007) Rev. Galadima G. Goni, Admin. (pro-tem).
173 Main St., P.O. Box 277, 01039-0277. (Merged or yoked parishes St. Catherine of Alexandria Parish, Leeds & St. Mary of the Assumption, Haydenville.) In Res., Rev. Vincent M. O'Connor (Retired).
Catechesis/Religious Program—Students 101.

HINSDALE, BERKSHIRE CO., ST. PATRICK'S (1868) Closed. Now a chapel under St. Agnes, Dalton.

HOLYOKE, HAMPDEN CO.

1—BLESSED SACRAMENT (1913) Rev. Robert A. Gentile Jr. In Res., Rev. Richard A. Riendeau (Retired).
Res.: 1945 Northampton St., 01040. Tel: 413-532-0713.
School—(Grades K-8), 21 Westfield Rd., 01040. Tel: 413-536-2236; Fax: 413-534-0795. Kathleen Labon, Prin. Sisters of St. Joseph 1; Lay Teachers 22; Students 290.
Catechesis/Religious Program—Fax: 413-532-0713. Roberta Cassidy, D.R.E. Students 160.
Mission—Holyoke Soldier's Home Chapel 110 Cherry St., Hampden Co. 01040. Tel: 413-532-9475.

2—HOLY CROSS (1905) Merged with Mater Dolorosa, Holyoke to form Our Lady of the Cross, Holyoke. Parish records are located at Our Lady of the Cross.

3—HOLY FAMILY (1949) Closed. For inquiries for parish records please see Blessed Sacrament, Holyoke.

4—IMMACULATE CONCEPTION (1905) [JC] Rev. James Aherne, M.S.; Deacon Frederick Pelletier.
Res.: 54 N. Summer St., 01040-6279. Tel: 413-532-5784; Fax: 413-532-8852.
Catechesis/Religious Program—Students 45.

5—ST. JEROME (1854) [CEM] Revs. William H. Lunney; Raymond T. Cordani, Parochial Vicar.
Res.: 169 Hampden St., 01040-4597. Tel: 413-532-6381; Fax: 413-540-9831. Email: st.jerome@comcast.net.
Catechesis/Religious Program—Students 208.

6—MATER DOLOROSA (1896), (Polish), [CEM] Merged with Holy Cross Holyoke to form Our Lady of the Cross, Holyoke. Parish records are located at Our Lady of the Cross.

7—OUR LADY OF GUADALUPE (2001) [CEM 3] [JC] Revs. William H. Lunney; Raymond T. Cordani, Parochial Vicar.
Res.: 435 Maple St., 01040. Tel: 413-532-4282; Fax: 413-532-2182.
Catechesis/Religious Program—Students 154.

8—OUR LADY OF PERPETUAL HELP (1890), (French), Merged with Sacred Heart to form Our Lady of Guadalupe, Holyoke.

9—OUR LADY OF THE CROSS 2011 Revs. Alexander B. Cymerman, O.F.M.Conv.; Stanley Sobiech, O.F.M.Conv., Parochial Vicar.
23 Sycamore St., 01040.
Offices—Fax: 413-535-1759.
Res.: *Blessed John Paul II Friary*, 71 Maple St., 01041-4698. Tel: 413-532-5661.
School—Mater Dolorosa School, (Grades K-8), 25 Maple St., 01040. Tel: 413-532-2831; Fax: 413-532-8588. Email: mrs.tierney@mater-dolorosa.com. Web: www.mater-dolorosa.com. Tracey Tierney, Prin. Lay Teachers 19; Students 256.
Catechesis/Religious Program—Tel: 413-532-8272; Fax: 413-538-6754. Students 256.

10—OUR LADY OF THE ROSARY (1886) Closed. For inquiries for parish records contact the chancery.

11—PRECIOUS BLOOD (1869) Closed. For inquiries for parish records contact Our Lady of Guadalupe, Holyoke.

12—SACRED HEART (1876) Merged with Our Lady of Perpetual Help to form Our Lady of Guadalupe, Holyoke.

HOUSATONIC, BERKSHIRE CO.

1—ALL SAINTS (1913), (Polish), Closed. For inquiries for parish records contact Blessed Teresa of Calcutta, Housatonic.

2—BLESSED TERESA OF CALCUTTA PARISH (2009), (Merged parishes of Corpus Christi & All Saints) Rev. William P. Murphy.
1085 Main St., P.O. Box 569, 01236. Tel: 413-274-3443.
Catechesis/Religious Program—Students 74.

3—CORPUS CHRISTI (1899) [CEM] Closed. Merged. See Blessed Teresa of Calcutta, Housatonic.

HUNTINGTON, HAMPSHIRE CO., ST. THOMAS (1886) [CEM] Closed. Merged with Our Lady of the Rosary, Russell & St. John Mission, Chester to form Holy Family Parish, Russell. All records located at Holy Family Parish, Russell.

LANESBORO, BERKSHIRE CO., NORTH AMERICAN MARTYRS (1969) Closed. For inquiries for parish records contact St. Mary, Cheshire.

LEE, BERKSHIRE CO., ST. MARY'S (1857) [CEM] Rev. John K. Sheaffer.
Res.: 40 Academy St., 01238. Tel: 413-243-0275; Fax: 413-243-1926. Email: lcsmchurch@gmail.com.
School—(Grades PreK-8), 115 Orchard St., 01238. Tel: 413-243-1079; Fax: 413-243-1022. Email: jfurey@stmarysschoolonline.com. Web: stmarysschoolonline.com. Jane Furey, Prin. Lay Teachers 16; Students 126.
Catechesis/Religious Program—Tel: 413-243-0275. Students 117.
Mission—St. Mary of the Lakes Otis, Berkshire Co. Tel: 413-269-4200.
Mission—Saint Joseph Stockbridge, Berkshire Co. 01263. Tel: 413-298-3748.

LEEDS, HAMPSHIRE CO., ST. CATHERINE'S (1911) [JC] Closed. Yoked with St. Mary, Haydenville to form Our Lady of the Hills, Haydenville.

LENOX DALE, BERKSHIRE CO., ST. VINCENT DE PAUL'S (1904) Rev. Christopher J. Waitekus.
Mailing Address: P.O. Box 259, 01242-0259. In Res., Rev. Msgr. John J. Bonzagni. Tel: 413-637-1085.
Church & Res.: 29 Crystal St., 01242. Tel: 413-637-3525.
Catechesis/Religious Program—Tel: 413-637-0519. Students 11.

LENOX, BERKSHIRE CO., ST. ANN (1891) [CEM] Rev. Christopher J. Waitekus; Deacons George Keator; John Zick.
Res.: 134 Main St., 01240. Tel: 413-637-0157; Fax: 413-637-2945. Email: stannlenox@verizon.net. Web: stannlenox.org.
Catechesis/Religious Program—Tel: 413-637-4027; Fax: 413-637-2945. Email: berkrex@yahoo.com. Students 111.

LONGMEADOW, HAMPDEN CO., ST. MARY'S (1936) Revs. Francis E. Reilly; James Longe, Parochial Vicar; Deacons Donald J. Higby; David Southworth.
Res.: 519 Longmeadow St., 01106. Tel: 413-567-3124; Fax: 413-567-4640. Email: parishoffice@stmarylong.org.
School—(Grades PreK-8), 56 Hopkins Pl., 01106. Tel: 413-567-0907; Fax: 413-567-7695. Email: stmarysacademy@comcast.net. Joan MacDonald, Prin. Lay Teachers 23; Students 251.
Catechesis/Religious Program—Tel: 413-567-3420; Fax: 413-567-0264. Students 968.

LUDLOW, HAMPDEN CO.

1—CHRIST THE KING (1948), (Polish), Rev. Raymond A. Soltys.
Res.: 41 Warsaw Ave., 01056. Tel: 413-583-2630; Fax: 413-583-2630. Email: ctkludlow@gmail.com.
Catechesis/Religious Program—Students 182.

2—SAINT ELIZABETH PARISH Rev. Msgr. Homer P. Gosselin; Deacons Thomas Rickson; Norman Grondin. In Res., Rev. Norman B. Bolton.
Res.: 181 Hubbard St., 01056. Tel: 413-583-3467; Fax: 413-583-2036. Email: stelizabethrectory@yahoo.com.
School—(Grades PreK-8), 217 Hubbard St., 01056. Tel: 413-583-8550; Fax: 413-589-0544. Email: sjbsoffice@gmail.com. Web: diospringfield.org/sjbschool. Mrs. Shelly Rose, Prin. Lay Teachers 17; Students 270.
Catechesis/Religious Program—Tel: 413-583-4204. Michael Witowski, D.R.E. Students 518.

3—ST. JOHN THE BAPTIST (1904), (French), Merged with St. Mary, Ludlow to form Saint Elizabeth Parish. All records kept at Saint Elizabeth Parish, Ludlow.

4—ST. MARY (1968) Closed. Merged with St. John the Baptist, Ludlow to form Saint Elizabeth Parish, Ludlow. All records kept at Saint Elizabeth Parish, Ludlow.

5—OUR LADY OF FATIMA (1948), (Portuguese), Rev. Vitor Oliveira.
Res.: 438 Winsor St., 01056. Tel: 413-583-2312; Fax: 413-547-0207.
Catechesis/Religious Program—Students 261.

MILLERS FALLS, FRANKLIN CO., ST. JOHN'S (1898) Closed. For inquiries for parish records contact Our Lady Peace, Turners Falls.

MONSON, HAMPDEN CO., ST. PATRICK'S (1878) [CEM] Rev. Jeddie P. Brooks; Deacon Bernard Pellissier; Wilfred Fredette, Pastoral Assoc.
Res.: 22 Green St., P.O. Box 473, 01057. Tel: 413-267-3622; Fax: 413-267-0272. Email: stpatmon@aol.com. Web: stpatrickmonson.org.
Catechesis/Religious Program—Students 237.

NORTH ADAMS, BERKSHIRE CO.

1—ST. ANTHONY OF PADUA (1903), (Italian), Closed. Merged. See St. Elizabeth of Hungary, North Adams.

2—SAINT ELIZABETH OF HUNGARY PARISH Rev. William Cyr.
Mailing Address: P.O. Box 868, 01247-0868. 70 Marshall St., 01247.
Catechesis/Religious Program—Kate Annichiarico, D.R.E. (Elementary); Connie Therrien, D.R.E. (H.S.). Students 159.

3—ST. FRANCIS (1863) [CEM] Closed. Merged. See St. Elizabeth of Hungary, North Adams.

4—HOLY FAMILY (1997) Merged with Our Lady of Incarnation, North Adams, to form Our Lady of Mercy, North Adams.

5—NOTRE DAME (1875) Closed. For inquiries for parish records contact the chancery.

6—OUR LADY OF MERCY (1997) Closed. See St. Elizabeth of Hungary, North Adams.

7—OUR LADY OF MERCY SHRINE (1997), Consolidation of Holy Family, North Adams, and Our Lady of the Incarnation, North Adams., 1288 Massachusetts Ave., 01247. Tel: 413-663-7131; Fax: 413-664-4940.

8—OUR LADY OF THE INCARNATION (1955) Merged with Holy Family, North Adams, to form Our Lady of Mercy, North Adams.

NORTHAMPTON, HAMPSHIRE CO.

1—BLESSED SACRAMENT (1899) Closed. Merged with Saint Elizabeth Ann Seton Parish, Northampton. All records to Saint Elizabeth Ann Seton Parish, Northampton.

2—SAINT ELIZABETH ANN SETON (2010), (French), Revs. John E. Connors; Sean O'Mannion, Parochial Vicar.
Mailing Address: 3 Elm St., 01060. Tel: 413-584-7310; Fax: 413-584-4788.
Church: 99 King St., 01060.
Catechesis/Religious Program—Students 217.
Chapel—Our Lady of the Annunciation 87 Beacon St., Florence, 01062.

3—ST. JOHN CANTIUS (1904), (Polish), Closed. Merged with Saint Elizabeth Ann Seton Parish, Northampton. All records to Saint Elizabeth Ann Seton Parish, Northampton.

4—ST. MARY OF THE ASSUMPTION (1866), (Irish), [CEM] Closed. Merged with Saint Elizabeth Ann Seton Parish, Northampton. All records to Saint Elizabeth Ann Seton Parish, Northampton.

NORTHFIELD, FRANKLIN CO., ST. PATRICK (1973) [CEM] Deacon Arthur E. Ratte.
Res.: 80 Main St., 01360-1022. Tel: 413-498-2728; Fax: 413-498-2728. Email: stpats2@msn.com.
Catechesis/Religious Program—Students 23.

ORANGE, FRANKLIN CO., ST. MARY (1903) Rev. Jose Bermudez, Admin.; Deacon Joseph S. Bucci Jr.
Res.: 19 Congress St., 01364. Tel: 978-544-2900; Fax: 978-544-8105. Email: stmorang@earthlink.net.
Catechesis/Religious Program—Students 46.

PALMER, HAMPDEN CO., ST. THOMAS THE APOSTLE (1864) [CEM], Merged with St. Bartholomew's,

Bondsville. Rev. Eugene J. Plasse.
Res.: 1076 Thorndike St., 01069. Tel: 413-283-5091; Fax: 413-289-1940.
Catechesis/Religious Program—Tel: 413-283-5651. Students 212.

PITTSFIELD, BERKSHIRE CO.

1—ST. CHARLES (1893) Rev. Peter A. Gregory; Sr. Barbara A. Faille, S.S.J., Pastoral Assoc.; Deacon William G. Moesley.
Res.: 89 Briggs Ave., 01201. Tel: 413-442-7470; Fax: 413-445-5267.
Catechesis/Religious Program—100 Briggs Ave., 01201. Tel: 413-442-0591. Students 295.

2—ST. FRANCIS (1960) Closed. For inquiries for parish records contact St. Joseph, Pittsfield.

3—HOLY FAMILY (1912), (Polish), Closed. For inquiries for parish records contact St. Joseph, Pittsfield.

4—ST. JOSEPH'S (1849) [CEM] Rev. Msgr. Michael Shershanovich; Deacon Pasqual Baldasaro. In Res., Rev. Geoffrey J. Deeker, C.S.S.
Res.: 414 North St., 01201. Tel: 413-445-5789; Fax: 413-443-5466. Email: msgrmike@berkshire.rr.com. Web: stjoemotherchurch.org.
Catechesis/Religious Program—Students 201.

5—ST. MARK'S (1913) Rev. John C. Salatino.
Office & Church: 400 West St., 01201. Tel: 413-447-7510; Fax: 413-448-2164.
Catechesis/Religious Program—400 Columbus Ave. Ext., 01201. Tel: 413-442-8444; Fax: 413-448-2164. Students 184.

6—ST. MARY THE MORNING STAR (1915) Closed. For inquiries for parish records contact St. Joseph, Pittsfield.

7—NOTRE DAME (1868) Closed. Sacramental Records at Saint Joseph, Pittsfield.

8—OUR LADY OF MT. CARMEL (1903), (Italian), Closed. For inquiries for parish records contact St. Joseph, Pittsfield.

9—SACRED HEART (1919) Rev. James K. Joyce; Deacon Robert Esposito; Sr. Kathryn Flanagan, S.S.J., Pastoral Min.; Deacon James A. Hager, Pastoral Min.; Kathleen Casella, Parish Nurse.
Res.: 191 Elm St., 01201. Tel: 413-443-6960; Fax: 413-442-9649. Email: pinkchurch@aol.com. Web: www.thepinkchurch.com.
Catechesis/Religious Program—Tel: 413-442-5564. Nicole Salvie, Admin. Asst.; Heather King, Admin. Asst. Students 415.

10—ST. TERESA (1926) Closed. For inquiries for parish records contact St. Joseph, Pittsfield.

RUSSELL, HAMPDEN CO.

1—HOLY FAMILY PARISH (2010) [JC] Rev. Ronald F. Sadlowski; Deacon David Baillargeon.
Res.: 5 Main St., P.O. Box 405, 01071-0405. Tel: 413-862-4418. Email: rfs4600@russellma.net.
Catechesis/Religious Program—Jo-Anne Auclair, D.R.E.; Christine Lindberg, D.R.E. Students 65.

2—OUR LADY OF THE ROSARY (1969) Closed. Merged with St. Thomas, Huntington & St. John Mission, Chester to form Holy Family Parish, Russell. All records located at Holy Family Parish, Russell.

SHEFFIELD, BERKSHIRE CO., OUR LADY OF THE VALLEY (1901) [CEM] Rev. Bruce Teague, Admin.; Deacons Herbert L. Cary; Richard Maginis.
Res. & Mailing Address: 99 Maple Ave., P.O. Box 515, 01257. Tel: 413-229-3028.
Catechesis/Religious Program—Students 75.
Mission—Immaculate Conception Main St., Mill River, Berkshire Co. 01244.
Mission—Our Lady of the Hills Beartown Rd., Monterey, Berkshire Co. 01245.

SHELBURNE FALLS, FRANKLIN CO., ST. JOSEPH'S (1883) Rev. Paul A. Bombardier; Deacon Thomas Rabbitt.
Res.: 34 Monroe Ave., 01370. Tel: 413-625-6405; Fax: 413-625-9951.
Catechesis/Religious Program—Students 21.
Mission—St. John the Baptist, (located in Colrain, MA), Colrain, Franklin Co. 01340.
Mission—St. Christopher Mailing Address: 01370. Charlemont, Franklin Co. 01339.

SOUTH DEERFIELD, FRANKLIN CO.

1—HOLY FAMILY PARISH (2008), (Merged parishes of St. Stanislaus & St. James) Rev. Philippe D. Roux; Deacon Theodore J. Tudryn.
27 Sugarloaf St., 01373.
Catechesis/Religious Program—Denis Roux, D.R.E. Students 159.
Mission—St. Marks Delabarre Ave., Conway, 01341.

2—ST. JAMES (1895) Closed. Merged see Holy Family, South Deerfield.

3—ST. STANISLAUS B. AND M. (1908) [CEM] Closed. Merged see Holy Family, South Deerfield.

SOUTH HADLEY, HAMPSHIRE CO.

1—ST. PATRICK'S (1878) Rev. Thomas M. Shea; Deacon John Bledsoe. In Res., Rev. Eugene D. Honan (Retired).
Res.: 30 Main St., 01075. Tel: 413-532-2850; Fax: 413-552-0241.
Catechesis/Religious Program—Tel: 413-534-7080. Students 402.

2—ST. THERESA OF LISIEUX (1946) Rev. Richard A. Bondi; Deacon Thomas Gaudrault.
Res.: 9 E. Parkview Dr., 01075-2103. Tel: 413-532-3228; Fax: 413-540-0964. Email: sainttheresachurch@comcast.net. Web: diospringfield.org/sttheresas.
Catechesis/Religious Program—Tel: 413-532-3228, Ext. 18; Fax: 413-540-0944. Anne Cormier, C.R.E. Students 98.

SOUTHWICK, HAMPDEN CO., OUR LADY OF THE LAKE (1951) Rev. Henry L. Dorsch; Deacon David Przybylowski.
Res.: 224 Sheep Pasture Rd., P.O. Box 1150, 01077. Tel: 413-569-0161; Fax: 413-569-0081. Web: ollsouthwick.org.
Catechesis/Religious Program—Lynda Daniele, D.R.E. Students 301.

STOCKBRIDGE, BERKSHIRE CO., ST. JOSEPH'S (1922) [CEM] Closed. Now a mission of St. Mary, Lee.

THORNDIKE, HAMPDEN CO., ST. MARY'S (1876) Closed. For inquiries for parish records contact the chancery.

THREE RIVERS, HAMPDEN CO.

1—ST. ANNE'S (1882), (French), [CEM] Closed. Merged with SS. Peter and Paul to form Divine Mercy Parish, Three Rivers. All records kept at Divine Mercy Parish, Three Rivers.

2—DIVINE MERCY PARISH Rev. Stefan J. Niemczyk.
Mailing Address: P.O. Box 157, 01080.
Res.: 2267 Main St., 01080. Tel: 413-283-6030.
Catechesis/Religious Program—Joan Brigham, D.R.E. Students 177.

3—SS. PETER AND PAUL (1903), (Polish), [CEM] Closed. Merged with St. Anne's to form Divine Mercy Parish, Three Rivers. All records kept at Divine Mercy Parish, Three Rivers.

TURNERS FALLS, FRANKLIN CO.

1—ST. ANNE (1884), (French), [CEM] Closed. Merged with Sacred Heart, Greenfield & St. Mary, Turner Falls to form Our Lady of Peace, Turner Falls.

2—ST. MARY'S (1872) [CEM] Closed. Merged with Sacred Heart, Greenfield & St. Anne, Turner Falls to form Our Lady of Peace, Turner Falls.

3—OUR LADY OF CZESTOCHOWA (1909), (Polish), [CEM] Rev. Charles J. DiMascola.
Res.: 84 K St., 01376. Tel: 413-863-4748; Fax: 413-863-9263. Web: ourladyofczestochowa.org.
Catechesis/Religious Program—Students 102.

4—OUR LADY OF PEACE Rev. Stanley J. Aksamit.
Rectory—90 Seventh St., 01376. Tel: 413-863-2585; Fax: 413-863-8978. Email: frstan@ourladyofpeacetf.com. Web: ourladyofpeacetf.com.
Church: 80 Seventh St., 01376.
Catechesis/Religious Program—Carol Holubecki, D.R.E. Students 160.

WARE, HAMPSHIRE CO.

1—ALL SAINTS (1860) [CEM] [JC 2] Rev. Edward T. Fitzgerald.
Res.: 17 North St., 01082. Tel: 413-967-4963.
Catechesis/Religious Program—Students 145.

2—ST. MARY'S (1905), (Polish), [CEM] Rev. Jeffrey A. Ballou.
Res.: 60 South St., 01082. Tel: 413-967-5913; Fax: 413-967-4679. Email: smcrectory@comcast.net.
School—(Grades PreK-8), 59 South St., 01082. Tel: 413-967-9936; Fax: 413-967-8217. Web: www.st-marysware.org. Mrs. Paul Moran, Prin. Sisters of Immaculate Conception 3; Lay Teachers 13; Students 125.
Catechesis/Religious Program—Tel: 413-967-5913; Fax: 413-967-4679. Students 78.

3—OUR LADY OF MT. CARMEL (1871), (French), Closed. For inquiries for sacramental records contact All Saints, Ware.

WEST SPRINGFIELD, HAMPDEN CO.

1—ST. FRANCES XAVIER CABRINI PARISH (2009), (Merged parishes of Immaculate Conception & St. Louis de France) Rev. Michael Lillpopp; Deacon Donald Philip.
495 Main St., 01089-3998.
Res. & Mailing Address: 475 Main St., 01089-3921. Tel: 413-736-4071; Fax: 413-734-5484.
Catechesis/Religious Program—Celeste Labbe, D.R.E. Students 30.

2—IMMACULATE CONCEPTION (1877) Closed. Merged see St. Frances Xavier Cabrini, West Springfield.

3—ST. LOUIS DE FRANCE (1895), (French), Closed. Merged see St. Frances Xavier Cabrini, West Springfield.

4—ST. THOMAS THE APOSTLE (1900) [CEM] Revs. Kenneth J. Tatro; Michael J. Wood Jr., Parochial Vicar; Deacon James Conroy.
Res.: 47 Pine St., 01089. Tel: 413-739-4779; Fax: 413-739-1608. Email: stthomassecretary@comcast.net.
School—(Grades PreK-8), 75 Pine St., 01089. Tel: 413-739-4131. Email: phottinssj@comcast.net. Sr. Patricia Hottin, S.S.J., Prin. Sisters of St. Joseph 5; Lay Teachers 25; Students 355.
Catechesis/Religious Program—89 Pine St., 01089. Tel: 413-737-8267; Fax: 413-731-8768. Students 546.

WEST STOCKBRIDGE, BERKSHIRE CO., ST. PATRICK'S (1871) [CEM] Rev. Christopher J. Waitekus.
Res.: 30 Albany Rd., 01266. Tel: 413-232-4427; Fax: 413-232-4427. Email: stpatricksws@verizon.nt.
Catechesis/Religious Program—Students 18.

WESTFIELD, HAMPDEN CO.

1—ST. CASIMIR'S (1915) Merged with St. Peter's, Westfield to form St. Peter and St. Casimir, Westfield.

2—HOLY TRINITY (1903), (Polish), Revs. Rene L. Parent, M.S.; Lukasz Krzanowski, M.S., Parochial Vicar.
Res.: 335 Elm St., 01085. Tel: 413-568-1506; Fax: 413-572-2533. Email: htoffice@comcast.net.
Catechesis/Religious Program—Students 124.

3—ST. MARY'S (1862) Revs. Brian F. McGrath; Ryan Rooney, Parochial Vicar; Deacons Pedro Rivera; Roger Carrier.
Res.: 30 Bartlett St., 01085. Tel: 413-562-5477; Fax: 413-562-5478.
School—St. Mary Elementary School, (Grades K-8), 35 Bartlett St., 01085. Tel: 413-568-2388; Fax: 413-568-7460. Sr. Christine Lavoie, S.S.J., Prin. Sisters 2; Lay Teachers 15; Students 204.
School—St. Mary Preschool, (Age 4 yrs.), 23 Bartlett St., 01085. Lay Teachers 2; Students 30.
High School—St. Mary High School, 27 Bartlett St., 01085. Tel: 413-568-5692; Fax: 413-562-3501. Mrs. Nichole Nietsche, Prin. Lay Teachers 16; Students 124.
Catechesis/Religious Program—Office of Rel. Educ., 86 Mechanic St., 01085. Tel: 413-568-1127; Fax: 413-562-5478. Mrs. Kay Mowatt, D.R.E. (Elementary); Mrs. Joanne Bagge, D.R.E. (High School). Students 667.
Convent—Sisters of St. Joseph 3.

4—OUR LADY OF THE BLESSED SACRAMENT (1910) Rev. Daniel S. Pacholec; Deacon Paul Federici, Dir. Faith Formation.
Mailing Address: P.O. Box 489, 01086-0489.
Rectory—85 Ridgeview Terrace, 01085.
Church & Parish Center: 127 Holyoke Rd., P.O. Box 489, 01086-0489. Fax: 413-562-9875. Email: olbsoffice@aol.com. Web: diospringfield.org/olbs.
Catechesis/Religious Program—Tel: 413-562-3450. Email: olbsccd@verizon.net. Sheila Conroy, Coord. Elementary Educ.; Lisa Laferriere, Coord. of Middle/High School Educ. Students 326.

5—ST. PETER AND ST. CASIMIR (2003) Rev. William H. Wallis.
Res.: 22 State St., 01085. Tel: 413-568-5421; Fax: 413-562-3879. Email: sspetetcas@comcast.net.
Catechesis/Religious Program—32 State St., 01085. Tel: 413-568-6261. Sr. Marcella Meluch, O.S.F., D.R.E. Students 165.

6—ST. PETER'S (1913) Merged with St. Casimir, Westfield to form St. Peter and St. Casimir, Westfield.

WILBRAHAM, HAMPDEN CO., ST. CECILIA'S (1951) Revs. Joseph M. Soranno; Dariusz P. Wudarski, Parochial Vicar; Sr. Mary McCue, S.N.D., Pastoral Min. Tel: 413-596-4232, Ext. 105.
Res.: 7 Maple St., 01095. Tel: 413-596-4232; Fax: 413-596-6272. Web: www.saintceciliawilbraham.org.
Catechesis/Religious Program—42 Main St., 01095. Tel: 413-596-4232, Ext. 104. Sr. Mary Patrice Mahoney, S.N.D., D.R.E. Students 1,052.

WILLIAMSTOWN, BERKSHIRE CO.

1—SS. PATRICK AND RAPHAEL (1997) Rev. Wayne C. Biernat; Deacon Francis Ryan.
Res. & Mailing Address: 54 Southworth St., 01267-2414. Tel: 413-458-4946; Fax: 413-458-4954. Email: saintpatrickandraphael@gmail.com. Web: www.williamstowncatholics.org.
Catechesis/Religious Program—53 Southworth St., 01267. Tel: 413-458-5443. Students 100.

2—ST. PATRICK'S (1887) Merged with St. Raphael, Williamstown, to form SS. Patrick and Raphael, Williamstown.

3—ST. RAPHAEL (1891) Merged with St. Patrick, Williamstown, to form SS. Patrick and Raphael, Williamstown.

Chaplains of Public Institutions

SPRINGFIELD. *Baystate Medical Center*, Office of Pastoral Ministry at Baystate, 01199.
Olympus Specialty Hospital, Sacred Heart Rectory, 395 Chestnut St., 01104. Tel: 413-732-3721.

HOLYOKE. *Soldiers' Home*, Tel: 413-532-0713. Served by Blessed Sacrament Parish.

MONSON. *State Hospital*. Bureau for Exceptional Children and Adults.
537 Northampton St., Box 1039, Holyoke, 01041. Tel: 413-538-7450. Deacon Gary Doane.

NORTHAMPTON. *Veterans Administration Hospital*, 421 N. Main St., 01060. Tel: 413-584-4040. Rev. Lionel E. Bonneville (Retired).

PITTSFIELD. *Berkshire Medical Center*, Tel: 413-447-2000. Rev. Leroy Smith.
One County Rte. 13, Chatham Center, NY 12184-9639. Tel: 413-392-4516.

WESTFIELD. *Western Massachusetts Hospital*, Tel: 413-562-3450. Served by Our Lady of the Blessed Sacrament Parish.

On Duty Outside the Diocese:
Revs.—
Cournoyer, Alfred C., A.P. 207, San Pedro Sula, Honduras.
Marchese, Joseph P., Boston College, Chestnut Hill, 02167. Chap.
McDonagh, John P., Catholic Student Ctr., Duke Univ., P.O. Box 90974, Durham, NC 27708.
Papineau, Daniel R., Diocese of Charleston, SC
Schmitt, Thomas F., Pope John XXII National Seminary, 558 South Ave., Weston, 02493.
Tuohey, John F., Providence St. Vincent Medical Center, 9205 S.W. Barnes Rd., Portland, OR 97225.
Twardzik, Michael W.T., Holy Family Catholic Community, 40 Elizabeth St., Dansville, NY 14437.

On Sabbatical:
Revs.—
Champigny, Thomas R.
Lessard-Thibodeau, John G.
Noiseux, Donald A.
Sipitkowski, James A.

Absent on Leave:
Revs.—
Gawienowski, John
Giroux, Regis J.
Minkler, Jeffrey R.

Retired:
Rev. Msgrs.—
Sniezyk, Richard S., 112 S.W. 15th St., Cape Coral, FL 33991.
Walsh, Francis E., The Arlington Hotel, 23-25 Bachelor Walk O'Connell Bridge, Dublin, Ireland.
Revs.—
Begley, Thomas B., P.O. Box 517, Hinsdale, 01235.
Benoit, Adrian J., 281 Chauncey Walker St., #153, Belchertown, 01007.
Bombardier, Dennis P., 12 Myers Farm Ln., Greenfield, 01301.
Bonneville, Lionel E., P.O. Box 282, Wilbraham, 01095.
Breton, Albert, Mt. Marie, 34 Lower Westfield Rd., Ste. 1, Holyoke, 01040.
Brunton, Daniel B., 80 Brush Hill Ave., Unit 42, West Springfield, 01089.
Chwalek, John, 420 Old Cheshire Rd., P.O. Box 56, Windsor, 01270.
Crean, Hugh F., Providence Pl., 5 Gamelin St., Holyoke, 01040.
Creane, Anthony, Devonshire Place, 48 Holy Family Rd., Apt. W 315, Holyoke, 01040.
Dean, John T., 7 Corser St., Holyoke, 01040.
Diemand, James E., P.O. Box 141, Turners Falls, 01376.
Duquette, Roy H., 100 Wood Ave., East Longmeadow, 01028.
Foley, Daniel R., J.C.D., St. Michael's Cathedral Rectory, 260 State St., 01105.
Galipeau, Roland J., Pinevalley Plantation, Belchertown, 01007.
Gallerini, Philip G., 867 Knightbridge Cr., Davenport, FL 33896.
Gardner, Royal J., Sacred Heart Rectory, 191 Elm St., Pittsfield, 01201.
Gilbertson, Lee C., 29 Shoreline Dr., Belfast, ME 04915.
Gonet, Charles F., St. Mary Rectory, 10 Hopkins Pl., Longmeadow, 01106.
Greenway, George G., 220 Villager Dr., Saint Simons Island, GA 31522.
Hallahan, Timothy J., P.O. Box 150112, Cape Coral, FL 33915.
Hebert, Earl, 281 Chauncey Walker St., #350, Belchertown, 01007.
Hoar, Leo James, Holy Cross Rectory, 221 Plumtree Rd., 01118.
Honan, Eugene D., St. Patrick Rectory, 30 Main St., South Hadley, 01075.
Jutt, Anthony J., 47 Bates Rd., 01085.
Kennedy, Francis M., P.O. Box 677, Southampton, 01073.
Lapointe, Donald R., S.T.L., L.I.C.S.W., 6 Old Stagecoach Rd., Easthampton, 01027.
Lavoie, Merle L., 114 College Hwy., Southampton, 01073.
Lis, John S., St. John the Evangelist Rectory, 833 Main St., Agawam, 01001.
Manning, Francis J., 29 Oakhurst St., 01104.
McCormick, Howard W., Sacred Heart Rectory, 395 Chestnut St., 01104.
O'Connor, Matthew J., 69 Beacon St., Holyoke, 01040.
O'Connor, Vincent M., P.O. Box 346, Leeds, 01053.
Pagano, Peter E., 1215 Massachusetts Ave., North Adams, 01247.
Riel, Robert H., Holy Cross Rectory, 221 Plumtree Rd., 01118.
Riendeau, Richard A., Blessed Sacrament Parish, 1945 Northampton St., Holyoke, 01040.
Sullivan, Francis X., 102 Allyn St., Holyoke, 01040.
Thrasher, Robert W., J.C.D., Holy Cross Rectory, 221 Plumtree Rd., 01118.

Permanent Deacons:
Antaya, John, St. Catherine of Sienna, Springfield
Badame, Joseph, (Retired), 9541 W. Carol Ave., Peoria, AZ 85345.
Baillargeon, David, Holy Family, Russell
Baldasaro, Pasqual, St. Joseph, Pittsfield
Bergeron, Leo, St. Rose de Lima, Chicopee
Bete, Joseph Channing, Holy Trinity, Greenfield
Bledsoe, John, V.F., St. Patrick, South Hadley
Brawner, William, St. Francis of Assisi, Belchertown
Briere, Paul, St. John the Evangelist, Agawam
Bucci, Joseph, St. Mary's, Orange
Cao, Ly X., St. Paul, Springfield
Carrier, Roger, St. Mary, Westfield
Cary, Herbert L., Our Lady of the Valley, Sheffield
Conroy, James, St. Thomas, West Springfield; Cao, Ly X., St. Paul, Springfield
Coughlin, Leo, St. Michael's Cathedral, Springfield
Cyr, Ralph R., Berkshire Medical Ctr. & Berkshire House of Correction
Daniel, Odell, Our Lady of the Sacred Heart, Springfield
DeCarlo, Paul F., Holy Trinity, Greenfield
Diaz, Celso B., (On Duty Outside the Diocese)
Digan, Robert, St. Mary, Lee
Digiacomo, Enzo
Doane, Gary, St. Thomas, Palmer
Duval, Robert L., (Retired), St. Elizabeth, Ludlow
Esposito, Robert, Sacred Heart, Pittsfield
Faber, Edward H., (Retired), Hanward Hill E., East Longmeadow, 01028.
Farrell, Robert, Our Lady of Mt. Carmel, Springfield
Federici, Paul, Our Lady of the Blessed Sacrament, Westfield
Fleury, Bernard J., (Retired), 244 Main Rd., Westhampton, 01027.
Garde, Joseph, St. Catherine, Springfield
Gaudrault, Thomas, St. Theresa, South Hadley
Gois, Antonio, Our Lady of Fatima, Ludlow
Grondin, Norman, St. Elizabeth, Ludlow
Hager, James A., Sacred Heart, Pittsfield
Herbert, Romeo, St. Anne, Chicopee
Higby, Donald, St. Mary, Longmeadow
Hitter, Robert, St. Mary, Cheshire
Hodges, Michael, Holy Name, Springfield
Kaiser, L. Joseph, (Retired)
Keator, George, St. Ann, Lenox
Kern, William, Sacred Heart, Springfield
Kolasinski, Mark, Most Holy Redeemer, Hadley
Kozach, George, St. Patrick Church, Springfield
Lafreniere, Gregory, Pope John Paul the Great, Adams
Leary, John, Blessed Sacrament, Greenfield
Lingham, Michael, St. John the Evangelist, Agawam
Magenis, Richard, Our Lady of the Valley, Sheffield
Mazzariello, Paul, Hampden Co. Correctional Facility
Mc Elroy, James, J.D., St. Mary, Lee
McCarthy, Kevin, Blessed Sacrament, Springfield
Medina, Genaro, Sr., All Souls, Latino Ministry, Springfield
Meyer, Edward, St. Elizabeth, Ludlow
Miller, Lucien M., Campus Ministry, University of Massachusetts, Amherst
Mireault, Leon, (Retired)
Moesley, William C., St. Charles, Pittsfield
Monat, Noe, 240 Skycrest Loop, Davenport, FL 33837.
Morrell, George, St. Agnes, Dalton
Mulholland, Sean, St. Marks, Pittsfield
Mutti, Al, Mary Mother of Hope, Springfield
Nolan, George, Our Lady of Peace, Turners Falls
O'Brien, John P., (On Duty Outside the Diocese)
O'Connell, Terrence, Providence Place and Providence Hospital, W. Springfield
Pelletier, Frederick J., Immaculate Conception, Holyoke
Pellissier, Bernard, St. Patrick, Monson
Pennell, Wendell, Blessed Sacrament, Holyoke
Perez, Angel, St. Michael's Cathedral, Springfield
Perkins, Michael, Our Lady of the Sacred Heart, Springfield
Peters, Joseph, St. Stanislaus, Chicopee
Phillip, Donald, St. Frances Xavier Cabrini, West Springfield
Przybylowski, David, Our Lady of the Lake, Southwick
Rabbitt, Thomas, St. Joseph, Shelburne Falls
Radzick, Richard, St. Agnes, Dalton
Rael, Lincoln C., (Retired), 47 Nonotuck St., Holyoke, 01040.
Ratte, Arthur E., St. Patrick, Northfield
Reagan, John, Our Lady of the Hills, Haydenville
Rickson, Thomas, St. Elizabeth, Ludlow
Rivera, Jose, All Souls, Springfield
Rivera-Burgos, Pedro, Our Lady of Guadalupe, Holyoke
Rivera-Moran, Pedro, St. Mary, Westfield
Rogers, Francis D., (Retired), St. Paul the Apostle, Springfield
Ryan, Francis, Sts. Patrick & Raphael, Williamstown
Shaw, Edward, Blessed Teresa of Calcutta, Housatonic
Smith, Joseph, (Retired)
Southworth, David, St. Mary, Longmeadow
Talbot, Richard, Newman Center, Amherst
Toller, William, Holy Cross, Springfield
Tran, Khanh, St. Paul, Springfield
Tudryn, Theodore, Holy Family, South Deerfield
Vernard, John, Holy Name, Springfield
Wainwright, Charles, St. Stanislaus, Chicopee
Wallen, Paul, (Retired), Springfield, MA
Zick, John, St. Patrick, W. Stockbridge
Ziemba, James, St. Cecilia, Wilbraham
Ziter, Bruce, St. Elizabeth of Hungary, North Adams

INSTITUTIONS LOCATED IN THE DIOCESE

[A] COLLEGES AND UNIVERSITIES

CHICOPEE. *College of Our Lady of the Elms* 01013. Tel: 413-265-2293; Fax: 413-265-2346. Email: breauw@elms.edu. Web: www.elms.edu. Most Rev. Timothy A. McDonnell; Sr. Mary Reap, I.H.M., Ph.D., Pres.; Dr. Walter C. Breau, Vice Pres. Academic Affairs; Patricia Bombardier, Librarian. Sisters of St. Joseph. Sisters 3; Professors 69; Lay Teachers 64; Students 1,482; Total Staff 155.

[B] HIGH SCHOOLS, DIOCESAN

SPRINGFIELD. *Cathedral High School* (1883) 260 Surrey Rd., 01118. Tel: 413-782-5285; Fax: 413-782-5065. Email: info@cathedralhigh.org. Web: www.cathedralhigh.org. Mr. John Miller, Prin.; Ms. Susan French, Librarian. Sisters 2; Lay Teachers 38; Students 345.

CHICOPEE. *Holyoke Catholic High School*, 134 Springfield St., 01013. Tel: 413-331-2480; Fax: 413-331-2708. Email: gaels@holyokecatholichigh.org. Web: www.holyokecatholichigh.org. Mrs. Theresa Kitchell, Prin.; Mrs. Jeanne O'Connell, Librarian. Sisters of St. Joseph. Sisters of St. Joseph 1; Lay Teachers 23; Students 300.

PITTSFIELD. *St. Joseph Central High School*, 22 Maplewood Ave., 01201. Tel: 413-447-9121; Fax: 413-443-7020. Web: www.stjoehigh.org. Francis F. Foley, Prin.; Sr. Jean Bostley, Librarian. Sisters of St. Joseph. Lay Teachers 19; Students 174; Total Staff 29.

[C] ELEMENTARY SCHOOLS, DIOCESAN

SPRINGFIELD. *Saint Michael's Academy*, (Grades PreSchool-8), 153 Eddywood St., 01118. Maria-Manuela deCarvalho, Head Admin. Sisters 1; Lay Teachers 38; Students 676.

Preschool Campus, 80 Arvilla St., 01118. Tel: 413-783-3532. Joanne Powers.

Elementary Campus, 153 Eddywood St., 01118. Tel: 413-782-5246; Fax: 413-782-8137. Ann Dougal, Prin.

Middle Campus, 153 Eddywood St., 01118. Tel: 413-782-5246; Fax: 413-782-8137. Carol Raffaele, Prin.; Maria-Manuela deCarvalho, Head Admin.

ADAMS. *St. Stanislaus Kostka*, (Grades PreK-8), 108 Summer St., 01220. Tel: 413-734-1091. Sr. Jacqueline M. Kazanowski, C.S.S.F., Prin. Felician Sisters 1; Lay Teachers 11; Students 140.

PITTSFIELD. *Saint Mark School*, (Grades PreSchool-8), 400 Columbus Ave., Ste. 1, 01201. Tel: 413-442-6040; Fax: 413-448-5645. Email: stmark2@verizon.net. Web: www.stmarkpittsfield.com. Ms. Margaret (Meg) Skowron, Prin. Tel: 413-442-6040; Patricia Meader, Librarian. Staff 21; Enrollment 109.

[D] GENERAL HOSPITALS

SPRINGFIELD. *CHE - The Mercy Hospital, Inc.*, 271 Carew St., Box 9012, 01102-9012. Tel: 413-748-9000; Fax: 413-781-7217. Web: www.mercycares.com. Sr. Madeline Joy, S.P., Chap.; Rev. Donatus Ironuma, Chap.; David Teague, Chap.; Katherine Mastorakis, Chap.; Yvonne M. Boudreau, M.Div., Senior Vice Pres. Mission. For both Mercy Campuses. Sisters of Providence 2; Bed Capacity 251; Patients Assisted Annually 172,612; Total Staff (Mercy Hospital) 1,443.

Providence Behavioral Health Hospital, 1233 Main St., Holyoke, 01040. Tel: 413-536-5111; Fax: 413-539-2992. Sr. Therese Dube, S.A.S.V. Spiritual Care Dept. 1; Bed Capacity 131; Total Staff 460.

Brightside, Inc. Private, Nonprofit Agency., 1233 Main St., Holyoke, 01040. Tel: 413-788-7366; Fax: 413-539-2496. Email: mariezygmont@sphs.com. Web: www.mercycares.com. *Sisters of Providence Health System*, P.O. Box 9012, 01102-9012. Tel: 413-827-4244; Fax: 413-827-4250. Mr. Richard Moen, Pres.; Mark Paglia, Dir. Outpatient Svcs.; Maria Zygmont, Dir. Brightside. Sisters of Providence. Family Stabilization Team 250; Total Staff 55.

TURNERS FALLS. *Farren Care Center, Inc.*, 340 Montague City Rd., 01376. Tel: 413-774-3111; Fax: 413-774-7049. Web: www.mercycares.com. Mailing Address: *Sisters of Providence Health Systems*, P.O. Box 9012, 01102. Email: jim.clifford@sphs.com. Sr. Madeline Joy, S.P., Chap.; James Clifford, Admin.; Christopher McLaughlin, COO Senior Care Network. Bed Capacity 122; Total Assisted Annually 121; Total Staff 175.

[E] FAMILY SERVICES

SPRINGFIELD. *Diocesan Office for Counseling, Prevention and Victim Services*, 65 Elliot St., P.O. Box 1730, 01102-1730. Tel: 413-732-3175; 413-452-0624; Fax: 413-452-0618. Web: www.diospringfield.org/MC.html. Total Assisted Annually 100; Total Staff 1.

HOLYOKE. *Providence Ministries for the Needy, Inc.*, 51 Hamilton St., P.O. Box 6269, 01041. Tel: 413-536-9109; Fax: 413-536-1137. Email: PMN3@hotmail.com. Web: www.provministries.com. Karen M. Blanchard, Admin. Sponsored by the Sisters of Providence of Holyoke, MA. Total Assisted Annually 38,950; Total Staff 18.

Broderick House, 56 Cabot St., P.O. Box 6269, 01041. Tel: 413-534-7610; Fax: 413-536-1137. SRO (single room occupancy), permanent housing for low income sober men/women. Capacity 20.

Margaret's Pantry Tel: 413-538-8026; Fax: 413-536-1137. Provides emergency food to families and individuals.

St. Jude's Center Tel: 413-538-8026; Fax: 413-536-1137. Distributes clothing and household items to the poor.

Mother Mary's Pre-owned Furniture, Clothing and Accessories, 390 Main St., 01040. Tel: 413-536-9109; Fax: 413-536-1137. Provides new and pre-owned furniture, furnishings, clothing and accessories to the community.

Loreto House, 51 Hamilton St., 01041. Tel: 413-533-5909; Fax: 413-536-1137. An around-the-clock shelter for homeless men. Capacity 24.

Kate's Kitchen, 51 Hamilton St., 01040. Tel: 413-532-0233; Fax: 413-536-1137. A community kitchen which provides one meal daily to anyone in need - no questions asked. Capacity 99.

TURNERS FALLS. *Montague Catholic Social Ministries, Inc.* (1994) 41 Third St., P.O. Box 792, 01376. Tel: 413-863-4804; Fax: 413-863-4844. Susan Mareneck, Exec. Dir. Purpose: To be a resource to children and families in the areas of parent education, family literacy, positive conflict resolution, communication skills, and community building; to assist in providing information and referral, the formation of community partnerships and neighborhood development and to facilitate parish concerns and social justice efforts. Montague Catholic Social Ministries nurtures connections, resilience and self-sufficiency in Franklin County families through preventative strength-based support, education, leadership development and empowerment. Total Assisted 3,020; Total Staff 7.

[F] HOMES FOR AGED

SPRINGFIELD. *Sisters of Providence Care Centers, Inc.*, 271 Carew St., 01104. Tel: 413-748-9000; Fax: 413-781-7217. Web: www.mercycares.com. Total Assisted Annually 327; Total Staff 251.

Beaven Kelly Home (1909) 25 Brightside Dr., Holyoke, 01040. Tel: 413-532-4892; Fax: 413-535-2355. Lori Naumowicz, Admin. Residents 55; Staff 22.

Mount St. Vincent Care Center (1972) 35 Holy Family Rd., Holyoke, 01040-2758. Tel: 413-532-3246; Fax: 413-532-0309. Persons Under Care 122; Total Staff 130. In Res. Sr. Ramona Williams, S.P., Chap.; Eriko Umana, Admin.

St. Luke's Home (1916) 85 Spring St., 01105. Tel: 413-736-5494; Fax: 413-746-5075. Barbara Tadeo, Admin. Residents 84; Staff 30.

Providence Care Center of Lenox (1999) 320 Pittsfield Rd., Lenox, 01240. Tel: 413-627-2660; Fax: 413-637-3085. David Lovelace, Admin.; Sharon Laverda, Spiritual Care Coord. Residents 67; Staff 69.

HOLYOKE. *Mary's Meadow at Providence Place, Inc.*, c/o Sisters of Providence, Inc., 12 Gamelin St., 01040. Tel: 413-536-7511, Ext. 2551; Fax: 413-536-7917. Sr. Kathleen Popko, S.P., Pres.

Mont Marie Health Care Center, Inc., 36 Lower Westfield Rd., 01040-2749. Tel: 413-538-6050; Fax: 413-533-4505. Email: tillman@ssjspringfield.com. Diane Tillman, L.S.W., Admin. Total Resident Days 30,660; Total Census 84; Total Staff 136.

Mont Marie Senior Residence, Inc., 32 Lower Westfield Rd., 01040. Tel: 413-532-9356; Fax: 413-532-9358. Sr. Denise Granger, S.S.J., Pres.

Providence Place, Inc., 5 Gamelin St., 01040. Tel: 413-534-9700; Fax: 413-534-9782. Web: provideneplace.org. Richard Pelland, Exec. Dir. Sisters of Providence. Total in Residence 139; Total Staff 51.

St. Joseph Residence at Mont Marie, Inc., 38 Lower Westfield Rd., 01040. Tel: 413-536-0853, Ext. 227. Email: lreilly@ssjspringfield.com. Web: www.ssjspringfield.org. Sr. Lillian Reilly, S.S.J., Pres.

[G] MONASTERIES AND RESIDENCES OF PRIESTS AND BROTHERS

STOCKBRIDGE. *Congregation of Marian Fathers of The Immaculate Conception of the Most Blessed Virgin Mary*, Eden Hill, 2 Prospect Hill Rd., 01262. Tel: 413-298-1101; Fax: 413-298-0207. Email: provincial@marian.org. Web: www.marian.org; www.thedivinemercy.org. *Provincial Office* Tel: 413-298-1101; Fax: 413-298-0207. Very Rev. Kazimierz Chwalek, M.I.C., Prov. Supr.; Revs. Donald Callaway, M.I.C., Vicar Prov.; Timothy Roth, M.I.C., 2nd Councilor & Prov. Sec. & Prov. Treas.; Matthew Lamoureux, M.I.C., 3rd Councilor; Bro. Brian Manian, M.I.C., 4th Councilor. *The National Shrine of The Divine Mercy* Tel: 413-298-3931; Fax: 413-298-3910. Email: dmshrine@marian.org. Web: www.thedivinemercy.org/shrine. Rev. Kenneth Dos Santos, M.I.C., Rector; Bro. Kenneth Galisa, M.I.C., Sec. to Prov. *Association of Marian Helpers, Marian Helpers Center*, Eden Hill, 01263. Tel: 413-298-3691; Fax: 413-298-3583. Email: info@marian.org. Web: www.marian.org. Revs. Anthony Gramlich, M.I.C., Dir. Office of Evangelization & Devel.; Michael Gaitley, M.I.C., Dir. Marion Helpers Center; Bros. Michael Opalacz, M.I.C., Grounds; Andrew Maczynski, M.I.C., Promoter of Marian Missions; Mr. Francis Bourdon, Exec. Dir. Marian Helpers Center. *John Paul II Institute of Divine Mercy* Tel: 413-298-1184; Fax: 413-298-4559. Email: jpii@marian.org. Web: www.thedivinemercy.org/jpii. Rev. Seraphim Michalenko, M.I.C., Dir. Emeritus; Dr. Robert Stackpole, S.T.D., Dir. Tel: 866-895-3236. Web: www.thedivinemercy.org/jpii. *Marian Fathers of the Immaculate Conception of the B.V.M., Inc. Marian Services Corporation National Shrine of the Divine Mercy Corporation Marian Helpers Corporation Marian Real Estate Trust Marian Endowment Trust Marian Education and Training Trust Marian Charitable Annuity Trust Marian Continuing Care Trust*

Lay Outreach of the Province:

Eucharistic Apostles of the Divine Mercy (EADM) Tel: 877-380-0727. Email: eadm@marian.org. Web: www.thedivinemercy.org. Dr. Bryan Thatcher, M.D., Dir.

Mother of Mercy Messengers (MOMM) Tel: 830-634-0727. Email: momm@marian.org. Web: www.thedivinemercy.org/momm. Dave Maroney, Dir.; Joan Maroney, Dir. Tel: 877-380-0727. Web: www.thedivinemercy.org/momm.

Healthcare Professionals for Divine Mercy Tel: 877-380-0727. Email: marie@nursesfordivinemercy.org. Web: www.thedivinemercy.org/healthcare. Marie Romagnano, R.N., B.S.N., Dir. In Res. Very Rev. Kazimierz Chwalek, M.I.C.; Bro. Kenneth Galisa, M.I.C., Local Supr.; Revs. Richard Drabik, M.I.C.; Andrzej Gorczyca, M.I.C.; Walter Gurgul, M.I.C.; Victor Incardona, M.I.C.; David Lord, M.I.C.; Diego Maximino, M.I.C.; Seraphim Michalenko, M.I.C.; Anthony Nockunas, M.I.C.; Martin Rzeszutek, M.I.C.; Robert Vennetti, M.I.C., Asst. Rector; Bros. John Bryda, M.I.C.; Andrew Maczynski, M.I.C.; Ronald McBride, M.I.C.; Michael Opalacz, M.I.C.; Fred Wells, M.I.C. On Duty Outside of House: Revs. Ireneusz Chodakowski, M.I.C., Portland, ME; Donald Van Alstyne, M.I.C. Arch for the Military, MO On Duty Outside of the USA: Revs. Joseph Petraitis, M.I.C., Australia; Joseph Roesch, M.I.C., Generalate in Rome, Italy.

[H] CONVENTS AND RESIDENCES FOR SISTERS

HOLYOKE. *Congregation of the Sisters of St. Joseph of Springfield* (1883) 34 Lower Westfield Rd., 01040. Tel: 413-536-0853; Fax: 413-533-3275. Email: mail@ssjspringfield.com. Web: www.ssjspringfield.org. Sisters Maxyne D. Schneider, S.S.J., Pres.; Elizabeth Sullivan, S.S.J., Vice Pres. The Congregation of the Sisters of St. Joseph of Springfield. Motherhouse of the Sisters of St. Joseph of Springfield. Sisters 265; Total Staff 49.

Daughters of the Heart of Mary Provincial Residence (1791) 1339 Northampton St., 01040-1958. Tel: 413-533-6681; Fax: 413-533-4217. Email: dhmprovadm@aol.com. Web: www.dhmna.org. Mona Balicki, Prov. Sec. Total in Residence 1; Total Staff 3.

Franciscan Missionary Sisters of Assisi Vice-Provincial House and Formation House, 1039 Northampton St., 01040-1320. Tel: 413-532-8156; Fax: 413-534-7741. Email: fmsausa@comcast.net. Web: www.sistersofassisi.org. Sr. Theresa Mwelwa, S.F.M.A., Vice Prov. Supr.

Franciscan Missionary Sisters of Assisi - Saint Francis Convent - Viceprovincial House and Formation House Sisters 14.

Marian Center, Inc., 1365 Northampton St., 01040. Tel: 413-534-4502; Fax: 413-534-7353. Sr. Miriam Najimy, D.H.M., Supr. Total in Residence 20; Total Staff 50.

Sisters of Providence (1873) 5 Gamelin St., 01040. Tel: 413-536-7511; Fax: 413-536-7917. Motherhouse of the Sisters of Providence. Sisters 48.

Providence Ministries for the Needy, Inc., P.O. Box 6269, 01041-6269. Tel: 413-536-9109; Fax: 413-536-1137.

TYRINGHAM. *Order of the Visitation of Holy Mary, Monastery of the Visitation*, 14 Beach Rd., P.O. Box 432, 01264. Tel: 413-243-3995; Fax: 413-243-3543. Email: vistyr@aol.com. Web: www.vistyr.org. Sr. Mary Ruth, V.H.M., Supr. Order of the Visitation of Holy Mary 15.

WEST SPRINGFIELD. *Monastery of the Mother of God, Dominican Nuns (Contemplative)*, 1430 Riverdale St., 01089-4698. Tel: 413-736-3639; Fax: 413-736-0850. Sr. Mary St. John, O.P., Prioress. Adoration to the Blessed Sacrament Chapel. Solemnly Professed Nuns 16.

[I] RETREAT HOUSES AND CHRISTIAN LIFE CENTERS

WESTFIELD. *Genesis Spiritual Life and Conference Center, Inc.*, 53 Mill St., 01085. Tel: 413-562-3627; Fax: 413-572-1060. Email: genesis@genesiscenter.us. Web: www.genesiscenter.us. Sr. Ann Horgan, S.P., Admin. Retreats, workshops and spiritual guidance designed to promote health of body, mind and spirit. Also, host day and overnight conferences. Total Staff 15; Total in Residence 3.

[J] SPANISH APOSTOLATES

SPRINGFIELD. *Catholic Latino Ministry*, 65 Elliot St., P.O. Box 1730, 01102-1730. Tel: 413-452-0631. Email: a.lopez@diospringfield.org. Mr. Andres Lopez, Dir.; Lucy Ramos, Exec. Sec.

[K] BUREAU FOR EXCEPTIONAL CHILDREN AND ADULTS

HOLYOKE. *Bureau for Exceptional Children and Adults Inc.* (1972) 537 Northampton St., Box 1039, 01041. Tel: 413-538-7450; Fax: 413-536-5691. Email: jerichobeca@comcast.net. Sr. Joan Magnani, S.S.J., Dir.; Nicole Beaulieu, Prog. Dir. Sisters 1; Lay Staff 5.

[L] YOUTH SERVICES

GOSHEN. *Holy Cross Camp Grounds*, 108 Cape St., 01032. Tel: 413-268-7819; 413-684-0125; Fax: 413-684-0734. Email: frcm@stagnescc.com. Web: www.campholycross.org. Mailing Address: 489 Main St., Dalton, 01226. Rev. Christopher A. Malatesta. Total Staff 2.

PITTSFIELD. *Catholic Youth Center*, 26 Melville St., 01201. Tel: 413-445-5496; Fax: 413-445-5248. Email: jadcyc@verizon.net. Jodi Astore-Davine, Exec. Dir. Total Assisted 850; Total Staff 25; Volunteer Base 150.

[M] NEWMAN APOSTOLATES AND CAMPUS MINISTRIES

SPRINGFIELD. *Newman Apostolates and Campus Ministries* 65 Elliot St., P.O. Box 1730, 01102-1730. Tel: 413-452-0819; Fax: 413-452-0555.

Email: n.bolton@diospringfield.org. Rev. Norman B. Bolton, Dir.
Campus Outreach in Higher Education 65 Elliot St., P.O. Box 1730, 01102-1730.
The Newman Catholic Center 472 N. Pleasant, Amherst, 01002-1739. Tel: 413-549-0300, Ext. 34; Fax: 413-548-9182. Email: g.dailey@diospringfield.org. Web: www.newmanumass.org. Rev. Gary Daily, Dir.
Amherst, MA:
Amherst College Cardigan Center for Religious Life, 38 Woodside Ave., Amherst, 01002-5000. Tel: 413-687-1858. Email: mcclark@amherst.edu. Chris Clark, Campus Min.
Center for Religious Life
University of Massachusetts Newman Center, 472 N. Pleasant St., Amherst, 01002-1739. Tel: 413-549-0300; Fax: 413-548-9182. Web: www.umass.edu/catholic. Revs. Gary Daily, Dir. & Chap.; Michael J. Twohig, Asst. Dir.; Deacons Lucien Miller, Campus Min.; Richard Talbot, Campus Min.; Ms. Chris Clark, Campus Min., Newman Center, 472 N. Pleasant St., Amherst, 01002. Tel: 413-687-1858 In Res. Rev. John Gawienowski.
Chicopee, MA:
College of Our Lady of the Elms College 291 Springfield St., Chicopee, 01013. Tel: 413-265-2289, Ext. 289; Fax: 413-594-6699. Web: www.elms.edu. Sr. Carol Allan, S.S.J., Dir. Campus Ministry.
American International College 202 E. Main St., Chicopee, 01020. Tel: 413-539-0835. Email: bolt1983@gmail.com. Rev. Norman B. Bolton, Chap.
Longmeadow, MA:
Bay Path College 202 E. Main St., Chicopee, 01020. Tel: 413-539-0835. Email: bolt1983@gmail.com. Rev. Norman B. Bolton. Diocese of Springfield, Campus Outreach
North Adams, MA:
Massachusetts College of Liberal Arts , Served by St. Anthony, North Adams, *St. Anthony Parish*, 375 Church St., North Adams, 01247. Tel: 413-663-3112. Rev. William Cyr, Chap., P.O. Box 868, North Adams, 01247-0868.
Northampton, MA:
Smith College Rev. John Connors, Chap. Served by St. Elizabeth Seton Parish, Northampton, MA.
Pittsfield, MA:
Berkshire Community College 400 West St., Pittsfield, 01201-3194. Tel: 413-447-7510. Rev. John C. Salatino. Served by St. Mark's.
South Hadley, MA:
Mount Holyoke College Office of the Chaplain, Eliot House, South Hadley, 01075. Tel: 413-538-2054; Fax: 413-538-2787. Email: amagovern@mtholyoke.edu. Anita Magovern, Rel. Advisor. Tel: 413-538-2787. Served by St. Theresa.
Springfield, MA:
Springfield College Campus Ministry Center Beveridge Center, 263 Alden St., 01109-3797. Tel: 413-748-3210; Fax: 413-748-3764. Deacon Bill Toller.
Western New England College 1215 Wilbraham Rd., 01119-2684. Tel: 413-782-1221; Fax: 413-585-2752. Ms. Sheila Hanifan, Campus Min.
Westfield, MA:
Westfield State College Interfaith Center, Westfield, 01085. Tel: 413-572-5567; Fax: 413-562-3613. Rev. John T. Dean, Chap. (Retired).
Williamstown, MA:
Williams College , Served by St. Patrick's.
Res.: 39 Chapel Hill Dr., Williamstown, 01267-2569. Tel: 413-597-2483; Fax: 413-597-3955. Email: gary.c.caster@williams.edu. Rev. Gary C. Caster, Campus Min.

[N] MISCELLANEOUS

SPRINGFIELD. *The Foundation of the Roman Catholic Diocese of Springfield, Massachusetts, Inc.*, 65 Elliot St., P.O. Box 1730, 01102. Tel: 413-452-0687; Fax: 413-785-5449. Email: william.labroad@diospringfield.org. Web: www.diospringfield.org.
Mercy LIFE, Inc., 271 Carew St., 01104. Tel: 413-748-7315. Web: www.mercycares.com. Daniel P. Moen, Pres. & CEO.
Sisters of Providence Health System, Inc., 271 Carew St., 01104. Tel: 413-748-9000; Fax: 413-781-7217. Web: www.mercycares.com. Yvonne M. Boudreau, M.Div., Sr. Vice Pres. Mission.

CHICOPEE. *The Friends of the Elms College, Inc.*, 291 Springfield St., 01013. Tel: 413-265-2372; Fax: 413-265-2346. Brian Doherty, Contact Person.

HOLYOKE. *Mary's Meadow at Providence Place, Inc.*, c/o Sisters of Providence, Inc., 5 Gamelin St., 01040. Tel: 413-536-7511, Ext. 2550; Fax: 413-536-7917. Sr. Kathleen Popko, S.P., Pres. Fax: 413-536-7917.

PALMER. *Apostolate of the Suffering, Inc.*, 1915 Ware St., 01069-9560. Tel: 413-283-4529. Web: www.sodcvs.org. Bro. Robert J. Letasz, S.O.D.C., Pres.; Lois Smus, Vice Pres.; Jeannine Gagnon, Sec.; Cecile Dufresne, Treas.

WESTFIELD. *Genesis Spiritual Life and Conference Center, Inc.*, 53 Mill St., 01085. Tel: 413-536-7511. Email: kpopko@sisofprov.org. Sr. Kathleen Popko, S.P., Contact Person.

RELIGIOUS INSTITUTES OF MEN REPRESENTED IN THE DIOCESE

For further details refer to the corresponding bracketed number in the Religious Institutes of Men or Women section.

[]—*The Association of Marian Helpers of Stockbridge, MA*
[0470]—*The Capuchin Fathers* (St. Mary's Prov.)—O.F.M.Cap.
[0270]—*Carmelite Fathers and Brothers* (St. Elias Prov.)—O.Carm.
[0740]—*Congregation of Marians of the Immaculate Conception*—M.I.C.
[1000]—*Congregation of the Passion* (Union City, NJ)—C.P.
[0480]—*Conventual Franciscans*—O.F.M.Conv.
[0720]—*The Missionaries of Our Lady of La Salette*—M.S.
[1280]—*Stigmatine Fathers and Brothers*—C.S.S.

RELIGIOUS INSTITUTES OF WOMEN REPRESENTED IN THE DIOCESE

[0860]—*Daughters of Mary of the Immaculate Conception*—D.M.
[0810]—*Daughters of the Heart of Mary*—D.H.M.
[0820]—*Daughters of the Holy Spirit*—D.H.S.
[1050]—*Dominican Contemplative Nuns*—O.P.
[1170]—*Felician Sisters*—C.S.S.F.
[1330]—*Franciscan Missionary Sisters of Assisi*—S.F.M.A.
[1470]—*Franciscan Sisters of St. Joseph*—F.S.S.J.
[1180]—*Franciscan Sisters of the Allegany, New York*—O.S.F.
[]—*Immaculate Heart of Mary* (Scranton)—I.H.M.
[]—*Little Sisters of St. Francis*—L.S.O.G.
[]—*Missionary Sisters of Our Lady of Africa*
[]—*Missionary Sisters of Our Lady of Perpetual Help*
[]—*Oblate Sisters of the Most Holy Eucharist*—O.S.S.E.
[]—*Schonestatt Sisters of Mary*
[1700]—*School Sisters of St. Francis*—O.S.F.
[]—*Sisters of Charity Seton Hill*—S.C.
[]—*Sisters of Mercy of the Americas*—R.S.M.
[3000]—*Sisters of Notre Dame de Namur*—S.N.D.deN.
[3340]—*Sisters of Providence*—S.P.
[3718]—*Sisters of St. Ann*—S.S.A.
[3830-16]—*Sisters of St. Joseph*—S.S.J.
[3850]—*Sisters of St. Joseph of Chambery*—C.S.J.
[0150]—*Sisters of the Assumption*—S.A.S.V.
[3310]—*Sisters of the Presentation of Mary*—P.M.
[4190]—*Visitation Nuns*—V.H.M.

DIOCESAN CEMETERIES

SPRINGFIELD. *St. Benedict Cemetery*, Mailing Address: *Springfield Diocesan Cemeteries, Inc.*, 421 Tinkham Rd., 01129. Liberty St., 01104. Tel: 413-782-0341; Fax: 413-782-5450. Web: www.diospringfield.org.
Gate of Heaven, 421 Tinkham Rd., 01129. Tel: 413-782-0341; Fax: 413-782-5450. Web: www.diospringfield.org. Joseph Kostek, Pres. Tel: 413-452-0692.
St. Matthew Cemetery, Mailing Address: *Springfield Diocesan Cemeteries, Inc.*, 421 Tinkham Rd., 01129. 366 Springfield St., 01109. Tel: 413-782-0341; Fax: 413-782-5450. Web: www.diospringfield.org.
St. Michael's Cemetery, 1601 State St., 01109. Tel: 413-782-0341; Fax: 413-782-5450. Web: www.diospringfield.org.

HOLYOKE. *Calvary Cemetery*, Mailing Address: *Springfield Diocesan Cemeteries, Inc.*, 1601 State St., 01109. Tel: 413-782-0341; Fax: 413-782-5450. Web: www.diospringfield.org. Office: Northampton St., 01040.

INDIAN ORCHARD. *St. Aloysius Cemetery*, Mailing Address: *Springfield Diocesan Cemeteries, Inc.*, 1601 State St., 01109. Tel: 413-782-0341; Fax: 413-782-5450. Web: www.diospringfield.org. Office: Berkshire Ave., 01151.

SOUTH HADLEY. *Notre Dame Cemetery, Springfield Diocesan Cemeteries, Inc.*, 63 Lyman St., 01075. Tel: 413-420-0001; Fax: 413-420-0004. Email: j.kostek@diospringfield.org. Web: www.diospringfield.org.
Precious Blood Cemetery, Springfield Diocesan Cemeteries, Inc., 63 Lyman St., 01075. Tel: 413-420-0001; Fax: 413-420-0004. Email: j.kostek@diospringfield.org. Web: www.diospringfield.org.
St. Rose Cemetery, Springfield Diocesan Cemeteries, Inc., 63 Lyman St., 01075. Tel: 413-420-0001; Fax: 413-420-0004. Email: jkostek@diospringfield.org. Web: www.diospringfield.org.

WESTFIELD. *Saint Mary Cemetery*, 203 Southampton Rd., 01085. Tel: 413-568-7775; Fax: 413-568-2727. Web: www.diospringfield.org. Joseph Kostek, Pres.

NECROLOGY

† Darling, Franklin, (Retired)—Died Nov. 7, 2011

An asterisk (*) denotes an organization that has established tax-exempt status directly with the IRS and is not covered by the USCCB Group Ruling.

Diocese of Steubenville

(Dioecesis Steubenvicensis)

Most Reverend

ALBERT H. OTTENWELLER, D.D., S.T.L.

Bishop Emeritus of Steubenville; ordained June 19, 1943; appointed Titular Bishop of Perdices and Auxiliary of Toledo April 17, 1974; consecrated May 29, 1974; appointed to Steubenville October 11, 1977; installed November 22, 1977; retired April 2, 1992. *Res.: 2544 Parkwood Ave., Toledo, OH 43610-1317.*

(VACANT SEE)

Chancery Office: 422 Washington St., P.O. Box 969, Steubenville, OH 43952-5969. Tel: 740-282-3631; Fax: 740-282-3327.

Web: www.diosteub.org

Email: lnichols@diosteub.org

Most Reverend

GILBERT I. SHELDON, D.D., D.MIN.

Bishop Emeritus of Steubenville; ordained February 28, 1953; appointed Auxiliary and Titular Bishop of Taparura April 20, 1976; consecrated June 11, 1976; appointed to Steubenville January 28, 1992; installed April 2, 1992; retired August 6, 2002.

ESTABLISHED 1944.

Square Miles 5,913.

Comprises these thirteen Counties in the State of Ohio: Athens, Belmont, Carroll, Gallia, Guernsey, Harrison, Jefferson, Lawrence, Meigs, Morgan, Monroe, Noble and Washington.

For legal titles of parishes and diocesan institutions, consult the Chancery Office.

STATISTICAL OVERVIEW

Personnel	
Retired Bishops	2
Priests: Diocesan Active in Diocese	44
Priests: Diocesan Active Outside Diocese	5
Priests: Retired, Sick or Absent	30
Number of Diocesan Priests	79
Religious Priests in Diocese	30
Total Priests in Diocese	109
Extern Priests in Diocese	5
Ordinations:	
Diocesan Priests	1
Permanent Deacons in Diocese	6
Total Brothers	7
Total Sisters	59
Parishes	
Parishes	58
With Resident Pastor:	
Resident Diocesan Priests	38
Without Resident Pastor:	
Administered by Priests	20
Missions	3
Professional Ministry Personnel:	
Brothers	1
Sisters	7
Lay Ministers	16
Welfare	
Catholic Hospitals	1
Total Assisted	231,643
Special Centers for Social Services	1
Total Assisted	28,191
Residential Care of Disabled	1
Total Assisted	257
Educational	
Diocesan Students in Other Seminaries	6
Total Seminarians	6
Colleges and Universities	1
Total Students	2,548
High Schools, Diocesan and Parish	3
Total Students	466
Elementary Schools, Diocesan and Parish	10
Total Students	1,700
Catechesis/Religious Education:	
High School Students	506
Elementary Students	1,482
Total Students under Catholic Instruction	6,708
Teachers in the Diocese:	
Priests	1
Sisters	5
Lay Teachers	167
Vital Statistics	
Receptions into the Church:	
Infant Baptism Totals	343
Minor Baptism Totals	66
Adult Baptism Totals	71
Received into Full Communion	480
First Communions	520
Confirmations	547
Marriages:	
Catholic	103
Interfaith	73
Total Marriages	176
Deaths	620
Total Catholic Population	37,011
Total Population	514,926

Former Bishops—Most Revs. JOHN KING MUSSIO, D.D., J.C.D., named First Bishop of Steubenville; ord. for Diocese of Cincinnati Aug. 15, 1935; appt. First Bishop of Steubenville March 16, 1945; cons. May 1, 1945; retired Oct. 11, 1977; died April 15, 1978; ALBERT H. OTTENWELLER, D.D., S.T.L. (Retired), named Second Bishop of Steubenville; ord. June 19, 1943; appt. Titular Bishop of Perdices and Auxiliary of Toledo April 17, 1974; cons. May 29, 1974; appt. Second Bishop of Steubenville Oct. 11, 1977; installed Nov. 22, 1977; retired April 2, 1992; GILBERT I. SHELDON, D.D., D.Min. (Retired), named Third Bishop of Steubenville.; ord. Feb. 28, 1953; appt. Auxiliary and Titular Bishop of Taparura April 20, 1976; cons. June 11, 1976; appt. Third Bishop of Steubenville Jan. 28, 1992; installed April 2, 1992; retired Aug. 6, 2002; R. DANIEL CONLON, D.D., J.C.D., Ph.D., ord. Jan. 15, 1977; appt. Bishop of Steubenville May 22, 2002; cons. and installed Aug. 6, 2002; appt. Bishop of Joliet May 17, 2011; installed July 14, 2011.

Diocesan Administrator—Rev. Msgr. KURT H. KEMO, J.C.L., M.Div.

Vicar General—VACANT, 422 Washington St., P.O. Box 969, Steubenville, 43952-5969. Tel: 740-282-3631.

Executive Assistant to the Bishop—Mr. JAMES PIAZZA, 422 Washington St., P.O. Box 969, Steubenville, 43952-5969. Tel: 740-282-3631. Email: jpiazza@diosteub.org.

Episcopal Vicar for Pastoral Planning & Personnel—VACANT, 422 Washington St., P.O. Box 969, Steubenville, 43952-5969. Tel: 740-282-3631. Email: tchillog@diosteub.org.

Chancellor—Mrs. LINDA A. NICHOLS.

Chancery Office—422 Washington St., P.O. Box 969, Steubenville, 43952-5969. Tel: 740-282-3631; Fax: 740-282-3327. Email: lnichols@diosteub.org.

Diocesan Finance Office—Mr. JAMES PIAZZA, Finance Officer (pro tem).; Mr. DAVID FRANKLIN, Comptroller, Mailing Address: P.O. Box 969, Steubenville, 43952-5969. Tel: 740-282-3631.

Diocesan/Parish Share Campaign—Mr. JAMES PIAZZA, Dir.; Mr. MARTIN B. THOMPSON, Assoc. Dir. Tel: 740-282-3631.

Diocesan Tribunal—422 Washington St., P.O. Box 969, Steubenville, 43952-5969. Tel: 740-282-3631.

Judicial Vicar—Very Rev. WILLIAM D. CROSS, J.C.L.

Auditors—Revs. THOMAS A. CHILLOG, M.Div.; DANIEL HEUSEL, M.Div.

Notaries—Rev. DANIEL HEUSEL, M.Div.; Ms. COLLEEN BAHEN.

Defenders of the Bond—Rev. Msgr. GERALD E. CALOVINI, V.F.; Revs. THOMAS A. CHILLOG, M.Div.; DANIEL HEUSEL, M.Div.

Director of the Tribunal & Notary—Ms. COLLEEN BAHEN.

Judges—Most Rev. GILBERT I. SHELDON, D.D., D.Min. (Retired); Rev. Msgr. MARK J. FROEHLICH; Rev. JAMES M. DUNFEE, V.F.; Rev. Msgr. GENE W. MULLETT; Rev. VINCENT J. HUBER, M.Ed. (Retired).

Information & Technology—Mr. MARTIN B. THOMPSON, Dir.; Mr. ANTHONY TARGOSS, Mgr., 422 Washington St., P.O. Box 969, Steubenville, 43952-5969. Tel: 740-282-3631.

Diocesan Deaneries and Deans

Deans—Rev. JAMES M. DUNFEE, V.F., Mother of Hope Deanery; Rev. Msgr. PATRICK GAUGHAN, V.F., Nativity of Mary Deanery; Rev. DALE F. TORNES, Presentation Deanery; Rev. Msgr. ROBERT J. KAWA, Visitation Deanery.

Child Protection Review Board—Rev. Msgr. KURT H. KEMO, J.C.L., M.Div., Contact Person, Mailing Address: P.O. Box 969, Steubenville, 43952-5969. Tel: 740-282-3631; Fax: 740-282-3327. Email: kkemo@diosteub.org. Members: JANE ENGOTT; Judge FRANK A. FREGIATO; Dr. JOSEPH DIPALMA; Judge JULIE SELMON; DAN FRY, Esq.; Rev. DALE F. TORNES.

Presbyteral Council—Revs. DAVID A. GAYDOSIK; DANIEL HEUSEL, M.Div.; TIMOTHY P. MCGUIRE; Rev. Msgrs. GEORGE R. COYNE (Retired); J. MICHAEL CAMPBELL; Revs. DAVID CORNETT; TIMOTHY J. HUFFMAN; Rev. Msgr. KURT H. KEMO, J.C.L., M.Div., Vice Chm.; Revs. THOMAS A. CHILLOG, M.Div., Chm.; RICHARD DAVIS, T.O.R.; PATTI PIASECKI, Recording Sec.

College of Consultors—Rev. Msgrs. GERALD E. CALOVINI, V.F.; KURT H. KEMO, J.C.L., M.Div.; Revs. DAVID CORNETT; CHARLES E. MASCOLINO (Retired); Rev. Msgr. J. MICHAEL CAMPBELL; Revs. THOMAS A. CHILLOG, M.Div.; JOHN J. MCCOY JR.; TIMOTHY P. MCGUIRE; Rev. Msgr. GEORGE R. COYNE (Retired); Rev. DANIEL HEUSEL, M.Div.

Priests Personnel Board—Rev. Msgr. PATRICK GAUGHAN, V.F., Senior Clergy; Rev. DAVID A. GAYDOSIK, Middle Age Clergy; Rev. Msgr. ROBERT J. KAWA, Southern Area; Revs. WAYNE E. MORRIS,

Younger Clergy; JOHN MUCHA, Central Area; BRADLEY GREER, Northern Area; Rev. Msgr. KURT H. KEMO, J.C.L., M.Div.; Rev. THOMAS A. CHILLOG, M.Div., Ex Officio.

Diocesan Offices and Directors

Building Commission—VACANT, Mailing Address: P.O. Box 969, Steubenville, 43952-5969. Tel: 740-282-3631; Fax: 740-282-3327.

Building & Property Director—VACANT, Mailing Address: P.O. Box 969, Steubenville, 43952-5969. Tel: 740-282-3631; Fax: 740-282-3327.

Campus Ministry—Rev. MARK MOORE, 75 Stewart St., Athens, 45701. Tel: 740-592-2711.

Censores Librorum—Mrs. LINDA A. NICHOLS, Chancellor & Coord.; Rev. JAMES M. DUNFEE, V.F.; Dr. ALAN SCHRECK.

Office of Christian Formation and Schools—Mr. PAUL WARD, Mailing Address: P.O. Box 969, Steubenville, 43952-5969. Tel: 740-282-3631; Fax: 740-282-3327.

Diocesan Communications—Mrs. PATRICIA DEFRANCIS, Mailing Address: P.O. Box 160, Steubenville, 43952. Tel: 740-282-3631; Fax: 740-282-3238.

Office of Civil Law—Mr. THOMAS S. WILSON ESQ., Mailing Address: P.O. Box 969, Steubenville, 43952-5969. Tel: 740-282-3631; Fax: 740-282-3327.

Continuing Education of Priests—Rev. THOMAS A. CHILLOG, M.Div., Dir., Mailing Address: P.O. Box 969, Steubenville, 43952-5969. Tel: 740-282-3631; Fax: 740-282-3327.

Diocesan Finance Council—Mailing Address: 422 Washington St., P.O. Box 969, Steubenville, 43952-5969. Tel: 740-282-3631; Fax: 740-282-3327. Email: kkemo@diosteub.org. Most Rev. R. DANIEL CONLON, D.D., J.C.D., Ph.D., Pres.; Rev. Msgr. KURT H. KEMO, J.C.L., M.Div., Chm. Council Members: GREGORY J. AGRESTA; RICHARD DOLAN; COLLEEN OESS; MARK BRADLEY; DAVID A. FRANKLIN; THOMAS H. HISRICH; PETER STEIGERWALD; Mrs. SUSAN TOLBERT; Rev. Msgr. JOHN C. KOLESAR, V.F.

Diocesan Director of Cemeteries—Rev. Msgr. JOHN C. KOLESAR, V.F., 221 Hanna Ave., Adena, 43901. Tel: 740-546-3463.

Diocesan Director of Ecumenism—Rev. THOMAS F. HAMM JR., St. Louis Church, 91 State St., Gallipolis, 45631. Tel: 740-446-0669.

Diocesan Office of Worship—Mr. JASON LEWIS, Dir., Mailing Address: P.O. Box 969, Steubenville, 43952-5969. Tel: 740-282-3631; Fax: 740-282-3327.

Health Panel of the Clergy—Rev. THOMAS A. CHILLOG, M.Div., Contact Person, Mailing Address: P.O. Box 969, Steubenville, 43952-5969. Tel: 740-282-3631.

Hospitals— Trinity Health System: *Trinity Medical Center, West, 4000 Johnson Rd., Steubenville, 43952.* Tel: 740-264-8000; Fax: 740-283-7104. *Trinity Medical Center, East, 380 Summit Ave., Steubenville, 43952.* Tel: 740-283-7000; Fax: 740-283-7104. FRED B. BROWER, Pres. Tel: 740-283-7390; 740-264-8303; Rev. BRADLEY GREER, Chap. Tel: 740-264-4880.

Catholic Rural Life—Rev. DAVID L. GAYDOSIK, 334 S. Main St., Woodsfield, 43793. Tel: 740-472-0187; Fax: 740-472-0182.

Office of Family and Social Concerns— Services: Campaign for Human Devel.; Respect Life; Hispanic Ministry; Marriage & Family Life. Mrs. MICHELE SANTIN, Dir., Mailing Address: P.O. Box 969, Steubenville, 43952-5969. Tel: 740-282-3631; 800-339-7890; Fax: 740-282-3327.

Priests' Retirement Board—Rev. VINCENT J. HUBER, M.Ed., Chm. (Retired).

Propagation of the Faith—Rev. TIMOTHY J. KOZAK, Asst. Dir.

Publication, "Steubenville Register"—Most Rev. R. DANIEL CONLON, D.D., J.C.D., Ph.D., Pres. & Publisher; Mrs. PAT DEFRANCIS, Editor, 422 Washington St., P.O. Box 160, Steubenville, 43952-5969. Tel: 740-282-3631; Fax: 740-282-3238.

RCIA—Rev. THOMAS F. HAMM JR., Dir., 85 State St., Gallipolis, 45631. Tel: 740-732-4576; 740-446-0669.

Schools—Mr. PAUL WARD, Supt., Mailing Address: P.O. Box 969, Steubenville, 43952-5969. Tel: 740-282-3631; Fax: 740-282-3327. Email: pward@diosteub.org.

Stewardship and Development—Mr. JAMES PIAZZA, Mailing Address: P.O. Box 969, Steubenville, 43952-5969. Tel: 740-282-3631; Fax: 740-282-3327. Email: jpiazza@diosteub.org.

Vicar for Priests—Rev. THOMAS A. CHILLOG, M.Div., Mailing Address: P.O. Box 969, Steubenville, 43952-5969. Tel: 740-282-3631.

Vicar for Religious—Rev. Msgr. J. MICHAEL CAMPBELL, Mailing Address: St. Mary Church, 506 Fourth St., Marietta, 45750. Tel: 740-373-3643.

Vicar for Retired Priests—Rev. VINCENT J. HUBER, M.Ed. (Retired), 1225 N. River Ave., Toronto, 43964. Tel: 740-537-4433.

Victim Assistance Coordinator—Rev. Msgr. KURT H. KEMO, J.C.L., M.Div., Contact, Mailing Address: P.O. Box 969, Steubenville, 43952. Tel: 740-282-3631; Fax: 740-282-3327. Email: kkemo@diosteub.org.

Vocations—422 Washington St., Steubenville, 43952. Tel: 740-282-3631. Rev. TIMOTHY J. SHANNON, Dir. Email: tshannon@diosteub.org. Assistant Directors: Revs. DANIEL HEUSEL, M.Div., Mailing Address: 411 S. 5th St., Steubenville, 43952. Tel: 740-282-3631; Fax: 740-282-3327. Email: dheusel@diosteub.org; MARK J. MOORE, Mailing Address: 38 College St., Athens, 45701. Tel: 740-593-7822; BRADLEY GREER, Mailing Address: P.O. Box 908, Steubenville, 43952. Tel: 740-264-6177; Sr. JEAN DAUGHERTY, T.O.R., 369 Little Church Rd., Toronto, 43964. Tel: 740-544-5534.

Woman's Club—Rev. TIMOTHY P. MCGUIRE; Mrs. DEDE KIDDER, Pres., Mailing Address: P.O. Box 31, Toronto, 43964. Tel: 740-544-5925.

CLERGY, PARISHES, MISSIONS AND PAROCHIAL SCHOOLS

CITY OF STEUBENVILLE

(JEFFERSON COUNTY)

1—HOLY NAME CATHEDRAL, [JC] Revs. Thomas R. Nau, Rector; Bradley Greer; Deacons Lawrence Meagher; Gerald Hickey; Randall Redington.
Office: P.O. Box 908, 43952. Tel: 740-264-6177; Fax: 740-266-2844. Email: tnau@diosteub.org. Web: www.triumphofthecross.org.
Please see Catholic Central High School, Bishop John King Mussio Central Junior High School & Bishop John King Mussio Central Elementary Schools located in the Institution section.

2—ST. ANTHONY OF PADUA, [JC] Closed. For inquiries for parish records contact Triumph of the Cross, Steubenville.

3—HOLY FAMILY, [JC] Rev. Msgr. Gerald E. Calovini.
Res.: 2608 Hollywood Blvd., 43952. Tel: 740-264-2825; Fax: 740-264-9348. Email: rectory@holyfamilyweb.org. Web: www.holyfamilyofsteubenville.4lpi.com.
Please see Catholic Central High School, Bishop John King Mussio Central Junior High School & Bishop John King Mussio Central Elementary School located in the Institution section

4—HOLY ROSARY, [JC] Closed. For inquiries for parish records contact Triumph of the Cross, Steubenville.

5—IMMACULATE HEART OF MARY CHAPEL, Closed. For inquiries for parish records contact the chancery.

6—OUR LADY OF NORTH AMERICA MARTYRS, Closed. For inquiries for parish records please see St. Peter's, Steubenville.

7—ST. PETER'S, [JC] Rev. Msgr. George W. Yontz; Bro. Patrick Geary, I.H.M., Pastoral Assoc.
Res.: 425 N. Fourth St., 43952. Tel: 740-282-7612; Fax: 740-282-9263. Email: jeanne@catholicweb.com. Web: www.stpeterschurch.catholicweb.com.
Please see Catholic Central High School, Bishop John King Mussio Central Junior High School & Bishop John King Mussio Central Elementary School located in the Institution section.

8—ST. PIUS X, [JC] Closed. For inquiries for parish records contact Triumph of the Cross, Steubenville.

9—SERVANTS OF CHRIST THE KING, Closed. For inquiries for parish records contact Triumph of the Cross, Steubenville.

10—ST. STANISLAUS, [JC] Closed. For inquiries for parish records contact Triumph of the Cross, Steubenville.

11—TRIUMPH OF THE CROSS Revs. Thomas R. Nau; Bradley Greer; Deacons Gerald Hickey; Randall Redington; Lawrence Meagher.
P.O. Box 908, 43952. Tel: 740-264-6177; Fax: 740-266-2844. Email: totcmanager@comcast.net. Web: www.triumphofthecross.org.
Please see Catholic Central High School, Bishop John King Mussio Central Junior High School & Bishop John King Mussio Central Elementary School located in the Institution section.

OUTSIDE THE CITY OF STEUBENVILLE

ADENA, JEFFERSON CO., ST. CASIMIR'S, [CEM] Rev. Msgr. John C. Kolesar.
Res.: 221 Hanna Ave., 43901. Tel: 740-546-3463; Fax: 740-546-3763. Email: stcadena@frontier.com.
Catechesis/Religious Program—Students 34.

AMSTERDAM, JEFFERSON CO., ST. JOSEPH, [CEM] Rev. John J. McCoy Jr.
Res.: 7457 State Hwy. 152, Richmond, 43944. Tel: 740-765-4142.
Church: 346 N. Main St., 43903.

ATHENS, ATHENS CO.

1—CHRIST THE KING UNIVERSITY PARISH Rev. Msgr. Patrick Gaughan; Rev. Mark Moore, Parochial Vicar.
Res.: 38 N. College St., 45701. Tel: 740-592-2711; Fax: 740-593-8908. Email: ctkinfo@ctkathens.org. Web: www.ctkathens.org.
Church: 75 Stewart St., 45701.
Catechesis/Religious Program—Email: ndenhart@ctkathens.org. Nancy Denhart, D.R.E. Students 94.

2—ST. PAUL'S, [CEM] Rev. Msgr. Patrick Gaughan; Rev. Mark Moore, Parochial Vicar.
Res.: 38 N. College St., 45701-2530. Tel: 740-593-7822.
Catechesis/Religious Program—Tel: 740-592-2711. Nancy Denhart, D.R.E. Students 62.
Chapel—Guysville, St. John

BARNESVILLE, BELMONT CO., ASSUMPTION, [CEM] Rev. Msgr. Mark J. Froehlich.
Res.: 306 W. Main St., P.O. Box 340, 43713. Tel: 740-425-2181; Fax: 740-425-3720. Email: mmjf6@comcast.net.
Catechesis/Religious Program—Students 58.

BARTON, BELMONT CO., OUR LADY OF ANGELS, Closed. For inquiries for parish records see St. Joseph, Bridgeport.

BELLAIRE, BELMONT CO.

1—ST. JOHN, [JC] Rev. Daniel Heusel.
Res.: 3745 Tallman Ave., 43906. Tel: 740-676-0051; Fax: 740-671-9776. Email: stjohns3745@comcast.net. Web: www.bncatholic.org.
School—Central Grade School, (Grades PreK-8) Tel: 740-676-2620; Fax: 740-676-8502. Email: bsje_jd@omeresa.net. Web: www.sjcgradeschool-.catholicweb.com. Joseph DeGenova, Prin. Lay Teachers 10; Students 112.

2—ST. MICHAEL'S, [CEM] [JC] Closed. For inquiries for parish records please see St. John, Bellaire.

BELLE VALLEY, NOBLE CO., CORPUS CHRISTI, [CEM] Revs. Wayne E. Morris; Chester J. Pabin.
Res.: P.O. Box 186, Caldwell, 43724. Tel: 740-732-4129; Fax: 740-732-1575. Email: wmorris@diosteub.org.
Church: Main St., 43717. Tel: 614-732-7202.

BEVERLY, WASHINGTON CO., ST. BERNARD, [CEM] Rev. Msgr. Robert J. Kawa.
Res.: 309 Seventh St., P.O. Box 331, 45715. Tel: 740-984-2555; Fax: 740-984-2555. Email: stberbev@frontier.com.
Catechesis/Religious Program—Tel: 740-984-4566. Yvonne Huck, D.R.E. Students 121.

BLAINE, BELMONT CO., ALL SAINTS, Closed. For inquiries for parish records please see St. Joseph, Bridgeport.

BRIDGEPORT, BELMONT CO.

1—ST. ANTHONY OF PADUA, [JC] Rev. John Mucha.
Res.: 68210 Neola Ave., 43912. Tel: 740-635-0408.

2—ST. JOSEPH, [JC] Rev. John Mucha.
Res.: 68210 Neola Ave., 43912. Tel: 740-635-0408; Fax: 740-635-1166. Email: jmucha@diosteub.org. Web: www.stjoschurch.com.

BRILLIANT, JEFFERSON CO., OUR LADY OF FATIMA, Closed. Sacramental records are located at St. Agnes, Mingo Junction.

BUCHTEL, ATHENS CO., ST. PATRICK, Consolidated with St. Andrew to form St. Mary of the Hills, Nelsonville.

BURKHART, MONROE CO., ST. JOSEPH'S, [CEM 2] Closed. For inquiries for parish records please contact St. Sylvester, Woodsfield.

BYESVILLE, GUERNSEY CO., HOLY TRINITY, [CEM] Closed. For inquiries for parish records please contact Christ our Light, Cambridge.

CADIZ, HARRISON CO., ST. TERESA Rev. Timothy P. McGuire.
Res.: 143 E. South St., 43907. Tel: 740-942-2211. Email: harrcntcath@frontier.com.

CALDWELL, NOBLE CO., ST. STEPHEN, [CEM] Revs. Wayne E. Morris; Chester J. Pabin.
Res.: 1036 Belford St., Box 186, 43724. Tel: 740-732-4129; Fax: 740-732-1575. Email: wmorris@diosteub.org.

CAMBRIDGE, GUERNSEY CO.

1—ST. BENEDICT, Closed. For inquiries for parish records see Christ Our Light, Cambridge.

2—CHRIST OUR LIGHT PARISH, [CEM 2] Rev. Robert D. Borer.
Office & Res.: 701 Gomber Ave., 43725. Tel: 740-432-7609; Fax: 740-439-0800. Email: stben_office@catholicweb.com.
School—St. Benedict, (Grades K-8), 220 N. 7th St., 43725. Tel: 740-432-6751; Fax: 740-432-4961. Sr. Theresa Feldcamp, O.S.F., Prin. Franciscan Sisters of Christian Charity 4; Lay Teachers 10; Students 113.
Catechesis/Religious Program—Patricia Farley, D.R.E. Students 110.

CARLISLE, NOBLE CO., ST. MICHAEL, [CEM] Revs. Wayne Morris; Chester J. Pabin.

Mailing Address: P.O. Box 286, Caldwell, 43724.
Res.: 43700 Fulda Rd., Caldwell, 43724. Tel: 740-732-4576.
Church: 43925 County Rd. 43, Caldwell, 43724. Email: wmorris@diosteub.org.

CARROLLTON, CARROLL CO., OUR LADY OF MERCY Rev. Anthony R. Batt.
Res.: 616 Roswell Rd., N.W., P.O. Box 155, 44615. Tel: 330-627-4664; Fax: 330-627-4664. Email: info@olmcarrollton.org.
Catechesis/Religious Program—Sr. Rita Murphy, D.R.E. Students 58.

CHESAPEAKE, LAWRENCE CO., ST. ANN Rev. Charles Moran.
310 Third Ave., Box 428, 45619-0428. Tel: 740-867-4434; Fax: 740-867-5829. Email: stannchurch@frontier.com.
Catechesis/Religious Program—Tel: 740-867-4434, Ext. 10. Linda McCombs, D.R.E. Students 43.

CHURCHTOWN, WASHINGTON CO., ST. JOHN THE BAPTIST, [CEM] Rev. Virgil Reischman.
Res.: 17784 State Rte. 676, Marietta, 45750. Tel: 740-896-2060; Fax: 740-896-3700.
School—Central Grade School, (Grades K-8) Tel: 740-896-2697; Fax: 740-896-2555. Jane Frances Hofbauer, Prin. Lay Teachers 12; Students 161.

COLERAIN, BELMONT CO., ST. FRANCES CABRINI Rev. Dale F. Tornes.
Res.: U.S. Rte. 250, P.O. Box 38, 43916. Tel: 740-635-9933; Fax: 740-738-0013. Email: dtornes@diosteub.org.

DILLONVALE, JEFFERSON CO., ST. ADALBERT, [CEM] Rev. Msgr. John C. Kolesar.
Res.: c/o 221 Hanna Ave., Adena, 43901. Tel: 740-546-3463; Fax: 740-546-3763. Email: stcadena@frontier.com.
Catechesis/Religious Program—Tel: 740-769-7858. Rosemary Zelek, D.R.E. Students 26.

FAIRPOINT, BELMONT CO., ST. JOSEPH Rev. Thomas J. Graven.
Mailing Address: 71793 Church St., P.O. Box 308, Maynard, 43937. Tel: 740-695-2618; Fax: 740-695-2618. Email: tgraven@diosteub.org.
Church: 46982 Columbia St., 8, 43927. Tel: 740-695-0840.
Catechesis/Religious Program—Students 7.

FLUSHING, BELMONT CO., ST. PAUL'S, [CEM] Rev. Frederick C. Kihm.
Res.: 115 Morristown Rd., Box 45, 43977. Tel: 740-968-4159.

FULDA, NOBLE CO., IMMACULATE CONCEPTION, [CEM] Revs. Wayne Morris; Chester J. Pabin.
P.O. Box 286, Caldwell, 43724.
Res.: 43700 Fulda Rd., Caldwell, 43724. Tel: 740-732-4576. Email: wmorris@diosteub.org.

GALLIPOLIS, GALLIA CO., ST. LOUIS, [CEM] Rev. Thomas F. Hamm Jr.
Res.: 85 State St., 45631. Tel: 740-446-0669; Fax: 740-446-9858.

GLOUSTER, ATHENS CO., HOLY CROSS, [CEM] Rev. David Cornett.
Mailing Address: 110 E. Washington St., Nelsonville, 45764. Tel: 740-753-1770; Fax: 740-753-4480.
Rectory—31 Republic Ave., 45732. Tel: 740-767-3068.
Church: Corner of Madison & Republic Avenues, 45732.

HARRIETTSVILLE, NOBLE CO., ST. HENRY, [CEM] Rev. Timothy J. Huffman.
Mailing Address: 5001 Lowell Hill Rd., Lowell, 45744. Tel: 740-896-2207; Fax: 740-896-2800.
Church: Rte. 1, 36575 Church St., CR 47, Lower Salem, 45745. Tel: 740-585-2383.

HOPEDALE, HARRISON CO., SACRED HEART, [JC] Rev. Timothy P. McGuire.
Res. & Mailing Address: 143 E. South St., Cadiz, 43907. Tel: 740-942-2211. Email: harrcntcath@frontier.com.
Church: 205 Cross St., 43976.

IRONTON, LAWRENCE CO.
1—ST. JOSEPH, [JC] Revs. David L. Huffman; Mark Purcell.
Res.: 905 S. Fifth St., P.O. Box 499, 45638. Tel: 740-532-0561; 740-532-0712; Fax: 740-534-0557. Email: stjoelaw@roadrunner.com. Web: www.irontoncatholicchurches.com.
Catechesis/Religious Program—Jane Rudmann, D.R.E. Students 50.
2—ST. LAWRENCE, [JC] Revs. David L. Huffman; Mark Purcell.
Res.: 905 S. Fifth St., P.O. Box 499, 45638-0499. Tel: 740-532-0561; Fax: 740-534-0557. Email: stjoelaw@roadrunner.com. Web: www.irontoncatholicchurches.com.
School—St. Lawrence Central Grade School, (Grades K-6), 315 S. 6th St., 45638. Tel: 740-532-5052; Fax: 740-532-5082. Web: irontoncatholicschools.org. James J. Mains III, Prin. Lay Teachers 12; Students 102.
High School—St. Joseph Central High School, (Grades 7-12), 912 S. 6th St., 45638. Tel: 740-532-0485; Fax: 740-532-3699. Web: irontoncatholicschools.com. James J. Mains III, Prin. Lay Teachers 10; Students 86.
Convent—615 Center St., 45638. Tel: 740-533-1206.

LAFFERTY, BELMONT CO., ST. MARY, [CEM] Rev. Frederick C. Kihm.
Res.: Box 45, Flushing, 43977. Tel: 740-968-4159.
Church: 70230 Church St., P.O. Box 188, 43951. Tel: 740-968-3200; Fax: 740-968-1881. Email: fkihm@diosteub.org.
Catechesis/Religious Program—Tel: 740-782-1487. Jill A. Clift, D.R.E. Students 24.

LITTLE HOCKING, WASHINGTON CO., ST. AMBROSE, [CEM] Rev. Robert A. Gallagher.
Res.: 5080 School House Rd., 45742. Tel: 740-423-7422.
Catechesis/Religious Program—Tel: 740-374-0848. Mrs. Cheryl Hayes, D.R.E. Students 75.

LORE CITY, GUERNSEY CO., SS. PETER AND PAUL, [CEM] Closed. For inquiries for parish records please see Christ Our Light, Cambridge.

LOWELL, WASHINGTON CO., OUR LADY OF MERCY, [CEM] Rev. Timothy J. Huffman.
Res.: 5001 Lowell Hill Rd., 45744. Tel: 740-896-2207; Fax: 740-896-2800.

MALVERN, CARROLL CO., ST. FRANCIS XAVIER (1848) [CEM] Rev. Victor Cinson.
Res.: 125 Carrollton St., P.O. Box 275, Minerva, 44657. Tel: 330-863-0305; Fax: 330-863-0760. Email: smstgabriel@frontier.com.
Catechesis/Religious Program—Tel: 330-863-3050; Fax: 330-868-2188. Denise Laubacher, D.R.E. Students 32.

MARIETTA, WASHINGTON CO., ST. MARY'S, [CEM 2] Rev. Msgr. John Michael Campbell; Rev. H. Christopher Foxhoven.
Res.: 506 Fourth St., 45750. Tel: 740-373-3643; Fax: 740-376-2956.
School—(Grades PreK-8), 320 Marion St., 45750. Tel: 740-374-8181; Fax: 740-374-8602. Rita Angel, Prin. Lay Teachers 22; Students 192.
Catechesis/Religious Program—Students 183.

MARTINS FERRY, BELMONT CO., ST. MARY, [CEM] Rev. Thomas Marut.
Res.: 20 N. Fourth St., 43935. Tel: 740-633-1416; Fax: 740-633-1490. Email: stmarymf@sbcglobal.net.
School—St. Mary Central, (Grades PreSchool-8), 24 N. Fourth St., 43935. Tel: 740-633-5424; Fax: 740-633-5462. Mary Carolyn Nichelson, Prin. Lay Teachers 9; Students 101; Aides 2.
Catechesis/Religious Program—Tel: 740-633-1416. Judy Kacsmar, D.R.E. Students 14.

MAYNARD, BELMONT CO., ST. STANISLAUS Rev. Thomas J. Graven.
Res.: 71793 Church St., P.O. Box 308, 43937. Tel: 740-695-2618; Fax: 740-695-2618. Email: tgraven@diosteub.org.

MCCONNELSVILLE, MORGAN CO., ST. JAMES Rev. Paul Walker.
Res.: 257 Bell Ave., 43756. Tel: 740-962-2856.

MILTONSBURG, MONROE CO., ST. JOHN THE BAPTIST, [CEM 2] Rev. David L. Gaydosik.
Res.: 334 S. Main St., Woodsfield, 43793.
Church: 35560 Miltonsburg-Calais Rd., Woodsfield, 43793. Tel: 740-472-0187; Fax: 740-472-0182. Email: dgaydosik@diosteub.org.

MINERVA, CARROLL CO., ST. GABRIEL THE ARCHANGEL Rev. Victor Cinson.
Res.: 400 West High, P.O. Box 275, 44657. Tel: 330-868-4498; Fax: 330-868-2188. Email: smstgabriel@frontier.com.
Catechesis/Religious Program—Students 132.

MINGO JUNCTION, JEFFERSON CO.
1—ST. AGNES, [JC] Rev. James M. Dunfee.
Mailing Address: 204 St. Clair Ave., 43938-1047. Tel: 740-535-1491.
Catechesis/Religious Program— Twinned with Triumph of the Cross, Steubenville. Students 10.
2—ANNUNCIATION, Closed. Parish records can be found at St. Agnes Church, Mingo Junction.
3—ST. BERNADETTE, Closed. Sacramental records are located at St. Agnes, Mingo Junction.

MORGES, CARROLL CO., ST. MARY, [CEM] Rev. Anthony R. Batt.
Res.: P.O. Box 690, Waynesburg, 44688. Tel: 330-866-2023.
Catechesis/Religious Program—Suzanne Tozzi, D.R.E. Students 12.

NEFFS, BELMONT CO., SACRED HEART Rev. Daniel Heusel.
Res.: 54038 St. Mary Ave., P.O. Box 425, 43940-0425. Tel: 740-676-3277; Fax: 740-676-3400.
Catechesis/Religious Program—Students 7.

NELSONVILLE, ATHENS CO., ST. MARY OF THE HILLS, Consolidated with St. Andrew, Nelsonville and St. Patrick, Buchtel to form St. Mary of the Hills. Rev. David Cornett.
Res.: 110 E. Washington St., 45764. Tel: 740-753-1770; Fax: 740-753-4480.

PINE GROVE, LAWRENCE CO., ST. MARY, [CEM] Rev. David L. Huffman.
Res.: 905 S. Fifth St., Ironton, 45638. Tel: 740-532-0712; Fax: 740-534-0557. Email: stjoelaw@roadrunner.com.

PINEY FORK, JEFFERSON CO., ST. THERESE, Closed. For inquiries for Sacramental records please see St. Casimir, Adena.

POMEROY, MEIGS CO., SACRED HEART, [CEM] Rev. Timothy J. Kozak.
Res.: 161 Mulberry Ave., 45769. Tel: 740-992-5898; Fax: 740-444-5058.
Catechesis/Religious Program—Cindy Nau, D.R.E. Students 55.

POWHATAN POINT, BELMONT CO., ST. JOHN VIANNEY Rev. Samuel Saprano.
Mailing Address: *St. Mary Church*, 350 E. 40th St., Shadyside, 43947. Tel: 740-676-3282.
Church: 295 Hwy. 7 N., 43942.

RICHMOND, JEFFERSON CO., ST. JOHN FISHER Rev. John J. McCoy Jr.
Res.: 7457 St. Hwy. 152, 43944. Tel: 740-765-4142.

ST. CLAIRSVILLE, BELMONT CO., ST. MARY'S Revs. Thomas A. Chillog; Michael Gossett.
Office: 212 W. Main St., 43950. Tel: 740-695-9993. Email: stmarysc@comcast.net.
Res.: 230 W. Main St., 43950. Tel: 740-695-2076.
School—St. Mary Central Grade School, (Grades PreSchool-8), 226 W. Main St., 43950. Tel: 740-695-3189; Fax: 740-695-3851. Lay Teachers 10; Students 165.
Catechesis/Religious Program—Fax: 740-695-6503. Michal Zabrecky, D.R.E. Students 83.

SHADYSIDE, BELMONT CO., ST. MARY'S (1946) Rev. Samuel Saprano.
350 E. 40th St., 43947. Tel: 740-676-3282; Fax: 740-676-1424.
Catechesis/Religious Program—Lyn Velkovich, D.R.E. Students 23.

SMITHFIELD, JEFFERSON CO., OUR LADY, QUEEN OF PEACE, [JC] Closed. For inquiries for Sacramental records please see St. Casimir, Adena.

TEMPERANCEVILLE, BELMONT CO., ST. MARY'S, [CEM] Rev. Msgr. Mark J. Froehlich.
Res.: P.O. Box 340, Barnesville, 43713. Tel: 740-425-2181.

TILTONSVILLE, JEFFERSON CO., ST. JOSEPH (1917) Rev. Msgr. Gene W. Mullett.
Mailing Address: P.O. Box 8, 43963-0008.
Res.: 204 Mound St., 43963-1017. Tel: 740-859-4018; Fax: 740-859-6041. Email: gmullett@diosteub.org.
Catechesis/Religious Program—(Combined with St. Lucy, Yorkville) Students 26.

TORONTO, JEFFERSON CO.
1—ST. FRANCIS OF ASSISI, [JC] Rev. Thomas A. Vennitti; Bro. Anthony Motto, I.H.M., Pastoral Assoc.
Res.: 1225 N. River Ave., 43964. Tel: 740-537-4433; Fax: 740-537-9305. Web: home.catholicweb.com/sfsjtoronto.
Church: 406 Findley St., 43964.
Catechesis/Religious Program—Judy Koehnlein, D.R.E. Students 26.
2—ST. JOSEPH'S, [JC] Rev. Thomas A. Vennitti; Bro. Anthony Motto, I.H.M., Pastoral Assoc.
Res.: 1225 N. River Ave., 43964. Tel: 740-537-4433; Fax: 740-537-9305. Web: home.catholicweb.com/sfsjtoronto.
Catechesis/Religious Program—Judy Koehnlein, D.R.E. Students 20.

VINCENT, WASHINGTON CO., ST. AMBROSE, Consolidated with St. Ambrose, Little Hocking.

WINTERSVILLE, JEFFERSON CO.
1—BLESSED SACRAMENT, [JC] Rev. Msgr. Kurt H. Kemo; Very Rev. William D. Cross; Rev. Vincent J. Huber (Retired).
Res.: 852 Main St., 43953-3870. Tel: 740-264-0868; Fax: 740-264-5449. Email: mail@wintersvilleparishes.org. Web: www.wintersvilleparishes.org.
Please see Catholic Central High School, Bishop John King Mussio Central Junior High School & Bishop John King Mussio Central Elementary School located in the Institution section
Catechesis/Religious Program—Patty D'Anniballe, D.R.E. Students 35.
2—OUR LADY OF LOURDES, [JC] Rev. Msgr. Kurt H. Kemo; Very Rev. William D. Cross.
Res.: 852 Main St., 43953-3870. Tel: 740-264-0868. Email: mail@wintersvilleparishes.org. Web: www.wintersvilleparishes.org.
Church: 1521 Bantam Ridge Rd., 43953-0612. Tel: 740-264-2798 (Church).
Please see Catholic Central High School, Bishop John King Mussio Central Junior High School & Bishop John King Mussio Central Elementary School located in the Institution section

WOODSFIELD, MONROE CO., ST. SYLVESTER, [CEM] Rev. David L. Gaydosik.
Res.: 38867 Briar Ridge Rd., 43793. Tel: 740-472-0187; Fax: 740-472-0182. Email: dgaydosik@diosteub.org.
Rectory—334 S. Main St., 43793.

School—Central Grade School, (Grades PreSchool-8) Tel: 740-472-0321; Fax: 740-472-1994. Jill Schumacher, Prin. & D.R.E. Lay Teachers 8; Students 86.

Catechesis/Religious Program—Students 38.

YORKVILLE, JEFFERSON CO., ST. LUCY'S Rev. Msgr. Gene W. Mullett.

Mailing Address: P.O. Box 8, Tiltonsville, 43963-0008. Tel: 740-859-4018; Fax: 740-859-6041.

DIOCESAN MISSIONS

BLOOMINGDALE, JEFFERSON CO., ST. THOMAS MORE MISSION, Closed. Sacramental records are located at St. John Fisher, Richmond.

CHAUNCEY, ATHENS CO., ST. JUDE MISSION, Closed. Sacramental records are located at St. Paul Church, Athens.

CRESCENT, BELMONT CO., ST. ELIZABETH MISSION, Closed. Sacramental records are located at St. Stanislaus Church, Maynard.

FREEPORT, HARRISON CO., ST. MATTHIAS MISSION Rev. Timothy P. McGuire.

Res.: 143 E. South St., Cadiz, 43907. Tel: 740-942-2211. Email: tmcguire@diosteub.org.

Church: Main St., Box 195, 43973. Tel: 740-658-3300.

HAMMONDSVILLE, JEFFERSON CO., NATIVITY OF OUR LORD MISSION, Closed. Sacramental records are located at St. Joseph Church, Toronto.

JEWETT, HARRISON CO., OUR LADY OF PERPETUAL HELP MISSION, Closed. Sacramental records located at 1435 E. South St., Cadiz, OH 43907.

SARDIS, MONROE CO., ST. JOHN BOSCO MISSION, [CEM] Rev. David L. Gaydosik.

Res.: 334 S. Main St., Woodsfield, 43793. Tel: 740-472-0187; Fax: 740-472-1994.

TAPPAN LAKE, HARRISON CO., CHRIST THE KING SUMMER MISSION, Closed. Sacramental records are located at: 143 E. South St., Cadiz 43907. Tel: 740-942-2211.

TUPPER PLAINS, MEIGS CO., OUR LADY OF LORETTO CHURCH, Closed. Sacramental records are located at Sacred Heart Church, Pomeroy.

On Duty Outside the Diocese:

Rev. Msgr.—

Wippel, John, Ph.D., 10105 Portland Pl., Silver Springs, MD 20901. Tel: 301-593-9345; 202-319-6648

Revs.—

Calabrese, Charles L., TCU, Box 297310, Fort Worth, TX 76129-0001. Tel: 817-923-2176; 817-921-7830

DiRenzo, Michael J. (LA), U.S.A.F. Chap. (Lt. Col.), 2731 Englewood Dr., Melbourne, FL 32940. Tel: 321-253-3303

Hrezo, Paul, Pontifical College Josephinum, 7625 N. High St., Columbus, 43235-1498. Tel: 614-885-5585

Massucci, Joseph D. (CIN), University of Dayton, 324 Chaminade Hall, Dayton, 45469-0534. Tel: 937-229-3737; 937-229-3730. Email: josephmassucci@notes.udayton.edu

Smith-Soucier, Martin D., 292 Durnan St., Rochester, NY 14621. Tel: 585-544-8778; 585-705-0188. Email: ms809oh@aol.com

---

Administrative Leave:

Rev.—

Zaleski, Gary A.

Retired:

Most Revs.—

Ottenweller, Albert H., D.D., S.T.L.

Sheldon, Gilbert I., D.D., D.Min.

Rev. Msgrs.—

Adams, George J., 785 Broad St., Brockway, PA 15824. Tel: 814-265-8371

Boehm, James A., 501 W. Chestnut Dr., Hendersonville, NC 28739. Tel: 828-697-8269

Cornelius, William R., 4333 Steuben Woods Dr., 43953. Tel: 740-264-0741

Coyne, George R., 67330 Ebbert Rd., S. Unit 2, Saint Clairsville, 43950. Tel: 740-296-5038

Cymbor, John A., 54345 High Ridge Rd., Bridgeport, 43912. Tel: 740-676-5545

Giannamore, Anthony J., 709 Brockton Pl. E., Sun City Center, FL 33573. Tel: 813-633-3553

Horak, Donald E., 149 Otter Rd., Hilton Head Island, SC 29928. Tel: 843-363-2933

Kakascik, Edward, Inn at Marietta, 150 Browns Rd., Ste. C, Marietta, 45750.

Metzger, Paul E., 428 Cambridge Dr., Middletown, 45042. Tel: 513-424-4576

Myers, William R., Transfiguration Center, 3505 Calurnet Rd., Apt 2B, Ludlow Falls, 45339. Tel: 937-719-3235

Nealon, Joseph A., P.O. Box 158, Carrollton, 44615-0158. Tel: 330-627-7083

Nugent, James B., 25 Noe Bixby Rd., Unit 101, Columbus, 43213. Tel: 614-367-1924

Pasquinelli, Frederick A., 4337 Steuben Woods Dr., 43953. Tel: 740-264-0970

Petronek, Thomas C., 1810 National Rd., B3-109, Wheeling, WV 26003. Email: tpetronek@diosteub.org

Uram, Kenneth J., 231 Woodridge Dr., Apt. A303, Wintersville, 43953. Tel: 740-264-9600

Revs.—

Belfield, John, Crowne Point, 5005 Sun N. Lakes Blvd., Sebring, FL 33872. Tel: 813-386-0631

Cencula, Leonard T., 1127 Euclid Ave., Apt. 1405, Cleveland, 44115. Tel: 740-632-4624

Deasio, August J., M.A., 935 Yellow Mills Rd., Shortsville, NY 14548. Tel: 716-289-3074

Heinz, Walter E., 57 Bayshore Rd., Lot 244, Palmetto, FL 34221. Tel: 701-541-5029

Holler, Martin J., 75 Stewart St., Athens, 45701. Tel: 740-592-2289

Huber, Vincent J., M.Ed., P.O. Box 2613, Wintersville, 43953. Tel: 740-317-4939

Krajcovic, Bernard, 1515 California Ave., Louisville, 44641. Tel: 330-875-4635

Lyden, Dennis P., St. Joseph Church, P.O. Box 98, Fairpoint, 43927. Tel: 740-695-0840

Magary, Thomas A., 4339 Steuben Woods Dr., 43953. Tel: 740-296-1898

Martinosky, Joseph A., 603 Franklin Ave., Apt. #1, Columbus, 43215. Tel: 614-224-4498

Mascolino, Charles E., 4338 Steuben Woods Dr., Wintersville, 43953. Tel: 740-266-9032

Ryland, Raymond (SD), 900 Granard Pkwy., 43952. Tel: 740-282-3009

Safraniec, Joseph N., St. Francis Way, Eagan, MN 55123-1167. Tel: 651-405-6705

Stromski, Adam F.X., St. Joseph Care Center, 1882 Knob St., Louisville, KY 44541. Tel: 330-875-1491

Tuttle, Richard J., 917 Glendora Rd., Kissimmee, FL 34759. Tel: 863-496-4246

Permanent Deacons:

Cerrato, Dominic, 162 Twp. Hwy. 202, Bloomingdale, 43910. Tel: 740-944-1846 (On Duty Outside the Diocese)

Hickey, Gerald, 1803 Williams Pl., 43952. Tel: 740-283-1585

Meagher, Lawrence, 4620 Lexington Dr., 43952. Tel: 740-264-3122

Miravalle, Mark, 315 High St., Hopedale, 43976. Tel: 740-283-3771

Pettie, Paul, (Outside the Diocese)

Piasecki, Stanley T., 67341 Ebbert South Rd., Saint Clairsville, 43950. Tel: 740-296-5123. Email: stpplpiasecki@aim.com

Poyo, Ralph, 1106 Jackson Pl., 43952. Tel: 740-314-5528

Redington, Randall, 401 Rosemont Ave., 43952. Tel: 740-266-7255; 740-765-5500

INSTITUTIONS LOCATED IN THE DIOCESE

[A] COLLEGES AND UNIVERSITIES

STEUBENVILLE. *Franciscan University of Steubenville*, 1235 University Blvd., 43952. Tel: 740-283-3771; Fax: 740-283-6472. Email: admissions@franciscan.edu. Web: www.franciscan.edu. Rev. Terence Henry, T.O.R., Pres.; Mr. David M. Skiviat, Vice Pres. Finance & Admin.; Dr. Daniel R. Kempton, Vice Pres., Academic Affairs; Mr. David Schmiesing, Vice Pres. Student Life; Dr. Robert Filby, Exec. Vice Pres.; Mr. Joel Recznik, Vice Pres., Enrollment Mgmt.; Mrs. Elizabeth Loizzo, Sec. to the Pres.; Revs. Bradley LePage, T.O.R., Asst. Coord. Household Life; Brian Cavanaugh, T.O.R., Assoc. in Information Technology; Richard Davis, T.O.R., Vice Pres. Community Rels. & Religious Admin.; Donald S. Frinsko, T.O.R., Theology Prog.; Dennis Gang, T.O.R., Chap., Student Life; Vincent Inghilterra, Pastoral Counseling & Campus Min.; Conrad Harkins, O.F.M., Assoc. Prof. Theology; Laurence Uhlman, T.O.R., Campus Min., Austria Campus; Daniel Pattee, T.O.R, Asst. Prof. Theology; Dominic Scotto, T.O.R., Univ. Chap. & Lecturer in Theology; Joseph Yelenc, T.O.R., Biology Prof.; David Morrier, T.O.R., Coord. Household Life; Seraphim Beshoner, T.O.R., Asst. Prof. History; Dominic Foster, T.O.R., Dir. Evangelization; Bro. John Paul McMahon, T.O.R., Instr. Economy; Revs. Gregory Plow, T.O.R., Coord. Household Life; Richard Martignetti, O.F.M., Priestly Discernment Program; Ronald J. Mohnickey, T.O.R., Campus Min. & Austrian Prog.; Andrew Draper, T.O.R, Campus Min.; Mr. Michael Hernon, Vice Pres. Advancement; Mr. Adam Scurti Esq., Vice Pres. Human Resources & Legal Counsel; Mr. William Jakub, Librarian. Priests 20; Brothers 1; Sisters 1; Lay Teachers 198; Students 2,548.

[B] HIGH SCHOOLS, CENTRAL

STEUBENVILLE. *Catholic Central High School*, 320 West View, 43952. Tel: 740-264-5538; Fax: 740-264-5443. Email: r.wilinski@steubenvillecatholiccentral.org. Web: cchs.sbd.pvt.k12.oh.us. Mr. Richard Wilinski, Prin.; Kathy Lally, Librarian. Priests 1; Chaplain 1; Lay Teachers 20; Students 263.

BELLAIRE. *St. John Central High School*, (Grades 7-12), 3625 Guernsey St., 43906. Tel: 740-676-4932; Fax: 740-676-4934. Web: www.bellairestjohn.sbd.pvt.k12.oh.us. Sheila Blackmon, Prin. Sisters 1; Lay Teachers 10; Students 104.

[C] JUNIOR-SENIOR CENTRAL HIGH SCHOOLS

IRONTON. *St. Joseph Central*, (Grades 7-12), 912 S. Sixth St., 45638. Tel: 740-532-0485; Fax: 740-532-3699. Email: jmains@stjoe.k12.oh.us. James J. Mains III, Prin. Total Staff 15; Students 99.

[D] CENTRAL JUNIOR HIGH SCHOOLS

STEUBENVILLE. *Bishop John King Mussio Central Junior High School*, (Grades 7-8), 320 W. View, Ste. 2, 43952. Tel: 740-346-0028; Fax: 740-346-0070. Email: santinone@bishopmussiojh.org. Theresa Danaher, Prin. Lay Teachers 12; Students 132.

[E] ELEMENTARY SCHOOLS, CENTRAL

STEUBENVILLE. *Bishop John King Mussio Central Elementary School*, (Grades PreK-6), 100 Etta Ave., 43952. Tel: 740-264-2550; Fax: 740-266-2843. Email: theresa.dipiero@omeresa.net. Theresa DiPiero, Prin. Lay Teachers 21; Students 393.

[F] GENERAL HOSPITALS

STEUBENVILLE. *Trinity Health System*, 380 Summit Ave., 43952. Tel: 740-283-7212; Fax: 740-283-7104. Web: www.trinityhealth.com. Sisters 5; Nurses 402; LPNs 23; Nurse Anesthetists 18; Admissions 11,964; Outpatients 180,178; Emergency Room 49,500; Births 557; Bed Capacity 500.

Trinity Medical Center, West, 4000 Johnson Rd., 43952. Tel: 740-264-8000; Fax: 740-283-7104. Web: www.trinityhealth.com. Rev. Bradley Greer, Chap.

Trinity Medical Center, East, 380 Summit Ave., 43952. Tel: 740-283-7000; Fax: 740-283-7104. Sisters Magdala Davlin, O.S.F., Pastoral Care Coord.; Mary Patrick Gillen, O.S.F., Staff Chap.

Trinity Health System Foundation, 380 Summit Ave., 43952. Tel: 740-283-7212; Fax: 740-283-7104.

[G] RESIDENTIAL CARE FACILITY

CARROLLTON. *St. John Villa*, P.O. Box 457, 44615. Tel: 330-627-9789; Fax: 330-627-4826. Web: stjohnsvilla.net. Richard A. Brown, M.P.A., Pres. Residential facility for persons with developmental disabilities. Faculty 135; Child Care Services 200; Adult Day Care 5; Residents 52.

[H] MONASTERIES AND RESIDENCES OF PRIESTS AND BROTHERS

STEUBENVILLE. *Diocesan Brotherhood of Immaculate Heart of Mary*, Villa Maria Motherhouse, 609 N. Seventh St., 43952. Tel: 740-283-2462. Email: dcarroll@diosteub.org. Bro. Dominic Carroll, I.H.M., Supr. Gen. Professed Brothers 4.

Holy Spirit Friary, 1235 University Blvd., 43952. Tel: 740-283-6403; Fax: 740-283-6348. Web: www.franciscan.edu. Revs. Bradley LePage, T.O.R.; Seraphim Beshoner, T.O.R.; Brian Cavanaugh, T.O.R.; Richard Davis, T.O.R., Local Min.; Andrew Draper, T.O.R; Dominic Foster, T.O.R.; Donald S. Frinsko, T.O.R.; Dennis Gang, T.O.R.; Terence Henry, T.O.R., Pres.; Benedict Jurchak, T.O.R.; Ronald J. Mohnickey, T.O.R.; David Morrier, T.O.R.; Daniel Pattee, T.O.R; Gregory Plow, T.O.R.; Dominic Scotto, T.O.R.; Joseph Yelenc, T.O.R.; Laurence Uhlman, T.O.R.; Bros. John Paul McMahon, T.O.R.; John Patrick Calvey, T.O.R.; Sean Mary Fitzwater, T.O.R.; Patrick Whittle, T.O.R. Priests 21; Brothers 4. In Res. Revs. Vincent Inghilterra; Conrad Harkins, O.F.M.; Richard Martignetti, O.F.M.

BLOOMINGDALE. *Holy Family Hermitage*, 1501 Fairplay Rd., 43910-7971. Tel: 740-765-4511; Fax: 740-765-4511. Web: www.camaldolese.org. Revs. Basil Corriere, E.C., Prior; Paul Vankeirsbilck, E.C.; Nicolas Luna, E.C.; Martin Flum, Novice;

Bro. Daniel Perron, Novice. Hermits 7.

[I] CONVENTS AND RESIDENCES FOR SISTERS

STEUBENVILLE. *Sacred Heart Villa*, 36 Villa Dr., 43953-7129. Tel: 740-282-3801; Fax: 740-282-3801. Sr. Rosalba Putrino, A.R., Supr. Handmaids of Reparation of the Sacred Heart of Jesus, Motherhouse of America Foundation. Engaged in Kindergarten, Pre-Kindergarten and Parish work.

CARROLLTON. *Union of Our Lady of Charity United States Province*, 620 Roswell Rd., N.W., P.O. Box 158, 44615-0158. Tel: 330-627-7647; Fax: 330-627-4415. Email: nauolc@eohio.net. Web: nauolc.org. Sr. Rosa Hernandez, Local Supr. Professed Sisters 26.

[J] ASSOCIATIONS OF THE FAITHFUL

STEUBENVILLE. *Sisters of Reparation to the Most Sacred Heart of Jesus*, 354 Rinker Rd., P.O. Box 9, 43952. Tel: 740-282-2144; Fax: 740-282-7919. Email: srmwendy@yahoo.com. Web: www.sistersofreparation.org. Sr. Wendy McMenamy, S.R., Local Supr. Sisters 8.

BLOOMINGDALE. *Mount Carmel Hermitage of Ohio, Inc*, 1619 Township Rd. 204, 43910. Tel: 740-765-5409. Sisters Immaculata St. Anthony, O.C.D.; Barbara Wright, O.C.D. Sisters 2.

HOPEDALE. *The Order of the Sacred and Immaculate Hearts of Jesus and Mary*, 48765 Annapolis Rd., 43976. Tel: 740-946-9000. Email: twohearts1@mac.com. Rev. Francis Dankoski; Sr. Teresa Condit, Vocations Dir. Priests 1; Brothers 2; Sisters 2.

TORONTO. *Franciscan Sisters Third Order Regular of Penance of the Sorrowful Mother*, 170 Little Church Rd., 43964. Tel: 740-544-5542; Fax: 740-544-5543. Email: franciscansisters@torsisters.org. Web: www.torsisters.org. Sr. Katherine Caldwell, T.O.R., Supr. Sisters 26; Novices 3; Postulants 3.

[K] SHRINES

FRANKLIN FURNACE. *Our Lady of Fatima Shrine* Old Rte. 52, 45629. P.O. Box 499, Ironton, 45638-0499. Rev. David L. Huffman. Tel: 740-532-0712; Fax: 740-534-0557.

[L] NEWMAN CENTERS

ATHENS. *Christ the King University Parish - Ohio University* 75 Stewart St., 45701. Tel: 740-592-2711; Fax: 740-593-8908. Email: pgaughan@diosteub.org; mmoore@diosteub.org. Web: www.ctkathens.org. Rev. Martin J. Holler, Dir. Campus Ministry (Retired).

MARIETTA. *Marietta College* c/o St. Mary Church, 506 Fourth St., 45750. Tel: 740-373-3643; Fax: 740-376-2956. Email: mcampbell@diosteub.org. Web: www.stmarysmarietta.org. Rev. Msgr. John Michael Campbell, Dir.

NELSONVILLE. *Hocking Technical College* Rev. David Cornett, Dir.

Res.: 110 E. Washington St., 45764. Tel: 740-753-1770.

RIO GRANDE. *Rio Grande University* 91 State St., Gallipolis, 45631. Tel: 740-446-0669. Rev. Thomas F. Hamm, Contact Person.

ST. CLAIRSVILLE. *Ohio University - Eastern* c/o St. Mary's Church, 212 W. Main St., 43950. Tel: 740-695-9993; Fax: 740-695-6503. Email: stmarysc@comcast.net. Rev. Thomas A. Chillog, M.Div., Contact Person.

[M] MISCELLANEOUS LISTINGS

STEUBENVILLE. *Boy Scouts*, 7457 State Hwy. 152, Richmond, 43944. Tel: 740-765-4142. Email: jmccoy@diosteub.org. Rev. John J. McCoy Jr., Dir.

Campaign for Human Development, Office of Family & Social Concerns, P.O. Box 969, 43952. Tel: 740-282-3631; Fax: 740-282-3327. Email: msantin@diosteub.org. Web: www.diosteub.org. Mrs. Michele Santin, Diocesan Dir.

**Catholics United for the Faith, Inc.*, 827 N. Fourth St., 43952. Tel: 740-283-2484; Fax: 740-283-4011. Email: shughes@cuf.org. Web: www.cuf.org. Michael Sullivan, Pres.; Shannon Minch-Highes, Vice Pres. Opers.

**Dietrich Von Hildebrand Legacy Project*, 417 Belleview Blvd., 43952. Tel: 740-282-0883. Email: jimhostetler@sbcglobal.net. Web: www.hildebrandlegacy.org. James M. Hostetler, Trustee & Sec.

**Fraternity of Priests, Inc.*, 100 Belleview Blvd., 43952. Tel: 740-283-4400; Fax: 740-283-3622. Email: contact@fraternityofpriests.org. Web: www.fraternityofpriests.org.

Lay Employees Pension Plan, P.O. Box 969, 43952. Tel: 740-282-3631; Fax: 740-282-1409.

Mt. Calvary Cemetery Association, 94 Mt. Calvary Ln., 43952. Tel: 740-264-1331; Fax: 740-264-9203. Email: mtcalvarycemetery@att.net.

**Pastoral Solutions Institute*, 234 St. Joseph Dr., 43952. Tel: 740-266-6461. Web: www.catholiccounselors.com. Gregory K. Popcak, Pres.

**St. Paul Center for Biblical Theology*, 2228 Sunset Blvd., Ste. 2A, 43952. Tel: 740-264-9535; Fax: 740-264-7908. Email: scotthahn@salvationhistory.com. Web: www.salvationhistory.com. Dr. Scott Hahn, Pres.

BEVERLY. *Marriage Encounter, c/o St. Bernard Church*, 307 Seventh St., P.O. Box 331, 45715. Tel: 740-984-2555. Email: stberbev@frontier.com. Rev. Msgr. Robert J. Kawa, Dir.

BLOOMINGDALE. *Apostolate for Family Consecration aka Catholic Familyland/John Paul II Holy Family Center* 3375 County Rd. 36, 43910-7903. Tel: 740-765-5500; Fax: 740-765-4941. Email: robert@familyland.org. Web: www.familycatechism.com; www.familyland.org; www.familyholiness.com; www.familylandtv.com. Mr. Robert Coniker, Pres.

CARROLLTON. *Our Lady of Charity Center Caritas House, Inc.*, 620 Roswell Rd., N.W., P.O. Box 158, 44615. Tel: 330-627-5765; Fax: 304-627-4415. Sr. Mary Annunciata Mason, O.L.C., Prog. Dir.

GALLIPOLIS. *RCIA*, 85 State St., 45631. Tel: 740-446-0669. Email: thamm@diosteub.org. Web: www.diosteub.org. Rev. Thomas F. Hamm Jr., Dir.

RELIGIOUS INSTITUTES OF MEN REPRESENTED IN THE DIOCESE

For further details refer to the corresponding bracketed number in the Religious Institutes of Men or Women section.

[0680]—*Brothers of the Immaculate Heart of Mary*—I.H.M.

[0230]—*Camaldolese Hermits of the Congregation of Monte Corona*—ER. CAM.

[0740]—*Marians of the Immaculate Conception (B.V.M. Mother of Mercy Province)*—M.I.C.

[]—*The Order of the Sacred & Immaculate Hearts of Jesus & Mary*

[0560]—*Third Order of Saint Francis. (Sacred Heart Prov.)*—T.O.R.

RELIGIOUS INSTITUTES OF WOMEN REPRESENTED IN THE DIOCESE

[0370]—*Carmelite Sisters of the Most Sacred Heart of Los Angeles*—O.C.D.

[1230]—*Franciscan Sisters of Christian Charity, Manitowac, WI*—O.S.F.

[1880]—*Handmaids of the Sacred Heart of Jesus for Reparation*—A.R.

[]—*Institute of the Sisters of Mercy of the Americas*—R.S.M.

[3070]—*North American Union Sisters of Our Lady of Charity*—O.L.C.

[2970]—*School Sisters of Notre Dame*—S.S.N.D.

[0500]—*Sisters of Charity of Nazareth*—S.C.N.

[]—*Sisters of St. Francis of Perpetual Adoration*—O.S.F.

[1530]—*Sisters of St. Francis of the Congregation of Our Lady of Lourdes* (Sylvania, OH)—O.S.F.

[1600]—*Sisters of St. Francis of the Martyr St. George*—F.S.G.M.

NECROLOGY

† Reasbeck, Rev. Msgr. David E., (Retired)—Died Oct. 6, 2011

† Rothbauer, Francis, (Retired)—Died Feb. 7, 2011

An asterisk (*) denotes an organization that has established tax-exempt status directly with the IRS and is not covered by the USCCB Group Ruling.

Diocese of Stockton

(Dioecesis Stocktoniensis)

Most Reverend

STEPHEN E. BLAIRE, D.D.

Bishop of Stockton; ordained April 29, 1967; appointed Titular Bishop of Lamzella on March 20, 1990; ordained Auxiliary Bishop of Los Angeles May 31, 1990; appointed Bishop of Stockton January 19, 1999; installed March 16, 1999. *Office: 212 N. San Joaquin St., Stockton, CA 95202.* Tel: 209-466-0636.

Chancery Office: 212 N. San Joaquin St., Stockton, CA 95202. Tel: 209-466-0636; Fax: 209-941-9722.

ESTABLISHED JANUARY 13, 1962

Square Miles 16,131.

Comprises six Counties in the State of California-viz., Alpine, Calaveras, Mono, San Joaquin, Stanislaus and Tuolumne.

Legal Title: The Roman Catholic Bishop of Stockton, a Corporation Sole.
For legal titles of parishes and diocesan institutions, consult the Chancery Office.

STATISTICAL OVERVIEW

Personnel	
Bishop	1
Priests: Diocesan Active in Diocese	43
Priests: Diocesan Active Outside Diocese	4
Priests: Diocesan in Foreign Missions	1
Priests: Retired, Sick or Absent	9
Number of Diocesan Priests	57
Religious Priests in Diocese	16
Total Priests in Diocese	73
Extern Priests in Diocese	20
Ordinations:	
Diocesan Priests	2
Permanent Deacons	3
Permanent Deacons in Diocese	45
Total Brothers	3
Total Sisters	61
Parishes	
Parishes	34
With Resident Pastor:	
Resident Diocesan Priests	31
Resident Religious Priests	3
Missions	12
Professional Ministry Personnel:	
Brothers	3
Sisters	21
Lay Ministers	31
Welfare	
Catholic Hospitals	1
Total Assisted	632,064
Health Care Centers	1
Total Assisted	9,584
Homes for the Aged	1
Total Assisted	1,046
Special Centers for Social Services	1
Total Assisted	32,662
Educational	
Diocesan Students in Other Seminaries	13
Total Seminarians	13
High Schools, Diocesan and Parish	2
Total Students	1,387
Elementary Schools, Diocesan and Parish	11
Total Students	2,898
Catechesis/Religious Education:	
High School Students	956
Elementary Students	19,017
Total Students under Catholic Instruction	24,271
Teachers in the Diocese:	
Priests	2
Brothers	1
Lay Teachers	220
Vital Statistics	
Receptions into the Church:	
Infant Baptism Totals	5,901
Minor Baptism Totals	264
Adult Baptism Totals	183
Received into Full Communion	687
First Communions	5,194
Confirmations	4,628
Marriages:	
Catholic	642
Interfaith	130
Total Marriages	772
Deaths	1,434
Total Catholic Population	227,338
Total Population	1,316,079

Former Bishops—Most Revs. HUGH A. DONOHOE, D.D., Ph.D., ord. June 14, 1930; appt. Titular Bishop of Taium and Auxiliary of San Francisco Aug. 2, 1947; cons. Oct. 7, 1947; appt. to Stockton Feb. 21, 1962; installed April 24, 1962; transferred to Fresno Aug. 27, 1969; died Oct. 26, 1987; MERLIN J. GUILFOYLE, D.D., J.C.D., ord. June 10, 1933; appt. Titular Bishop of Bulla and Auxiliary of San Francisco Aug. 15, 1950; cons. Sept. 21, 1950; translated to Bishop of Stockton Nov. 19, 1969; installed Jan. 13, 1970; retired Feb. 26, 1980; died Nov. 20, 1981; ROGER M. MAHONY, D.D., ord. May 1, 1962; appt. Titular Bishop of Tamascani and Auxiliary of Fresno, Jan. 7, 1975; cons. March 19, 1975; translated Bishop of Stockton Feb. 26, 1980; installed April 17, 1980; elevated to Archbishop of Los Angeles July 16, 1985; elevated to Cardinal, June 28, 1991; DONALD W. MONTROSE, D.D., ord. May 7, 1949; appt. Titular Bishop of Vescovio and Auxiliary of Los Angeles March 25, 1983; cons. May 12, 1983; translated Bishop of Stockton Dec. 19, 1985; installed Feb. 20, 1986; retired Jan. 19, 1999; died May 7, 2008.

Chancery Office—212 N. San Joaquin St., Stockton, 95202. Tel: 209-466-0636; Fax: 209-941-9722. Web: www.stocktondiocese.org.

Vicar General—Rev. Msgr. RICHARD J. RYAN, J.C.D., V.G.

Chancellor—Sr. BARBARA THIELLA, S.N.D.deN.

Vicar for Priests—Rev. Msgr. HARMON SKILLIN, J.C.D. (Retired).

Chief Financial Officer—Mr. DOUG ADEL.

Director of Human Resources—Mr. JOHN HALE.

Social Action Consultor—Mr. RICH FOWLER.

Diocesan Tribunal—212 N. San Joaquin St., Stockton, 95202. Tel: 209-466-0636; Fax: 209-941-9722. Web: stocktondiocese.org.

Judicial Vicar—Rev. JOVITO B. ROLDAN, J.C.L.

Vice-Officialis—Rev. Msgr. RICHARD J. RYAN, J.C.D., V.G.

Judges—Ms. CHERRY CLARK, J.C.L.; Rev. JOHN J.M. FOSTER, J.C.D.; Mrs. LYNDA ROBITAILLE, J.C.D.; Ms. LYNETTE TAIT, J.C.L.; Ms. MARY TARVER, J.C.L.

Moderator—VACANT.

Tribunal Personnel—Notaries: PAT CUMPIAN; JO ANNE GARCIA-JONES; DIANE LEWIS; DIANE TARICCO.

Defenders of the Bond—Ms. ANNE KIRBY, J.C.L.; Ms. LYNETTE TAIT, J.C.L.

Presbyteral Council—President: Most Rev. STEPHEN E. BLAIRE, D.D. Members at Large: Revs. RAMON BEJARANO; DAVID DUTRA; MICHAEL KELLY, V.F.; Rev. Msgr. IVO D. ROCHA, Chm. Members by Age Group: Rev. SALVADOR LEDESMA; Rev. Msgr. ROBERT J. SILVA. Members Appointed: Revs. MICHAEL BRADY; JOSEPH MAGHINAY; TUAN NGUYEN, S.D.B. Ex Officio: Rev. Msgr. RICHARD J. RYAN, J.C.D., V.G. Observer: Sr. BARBARA THIELLA, S.N.D.deN.

Deans—Rev. Msgr. JOHN ARMISTEAD, S.T.L., Deanery 1; Revs. DEAN MCFALLS, Deanery 2; MICHAEL KELLY, V.F., Deanery 3; J. PATRICK WALKER, V.F., Deanery 4; RICHARD MORSE, O.S.F.S., Deanery 5; MANUEL F. SOUSA, Deanery 6; JOSEPH P. ILLO, Deanery 7; JOHN E. FITZGERALD, Deanery 8.

The Roman Catholic Welfare Corporation of Stockton—212 N. San Joaquin St., Stockton, 95202. Tel: 209-466-0636; Fax: 209-941-9722.

Diocesan Building Committee—Rev. Msgr. RICHARD J. RYAN, J.C.D., V.G., Chm.; Mr. DOUG ADEL; Rev. Msgr. WILLIAM MOORE; Deacons GREG YEAGER; ALAN MOZNETT; Mr. RAYMOND TUNKEL.

Diocesan Finance Council—Mr. PAUL SCHAEFER, Chm.; Mr. JOSEPH ARIAS; Mr. DOUG ADEL, Staff; Mr. KEVIN DOUGHERTY; Mr. TOM DRISCOLL; Mr. MICHAEL DUFFY; Revs. JOHN P. FALLON, O.S.F.S.; MICHAEL BRADY; Mr. FRED LEE; Mr. DAVID ROSE, CPA, C.F.E.; Mrs. MARIA STOKMAN; Rev. Msgr. RICHARD J. RYAN, J.C.D., V.G., Staff & Consultant.

Personnel Board—Rev. Msgr. HARMON SKILLIN, J.C.D. (Retired); Rev. ARMANDO VERGARA; Rev. Msgrs. LAWRENCE MCGOVERN, S.T.L.; RICHARD J. RYAN, J.C.D., V.G.; ROBERT J. SILVA; Revs. JUAN SERNA, S.T.L.; MICHAEL KELLY, V.F.

Diocesan Offices and Directors

Apostleship of the Sea—Mr. MIKE DETORO. Tel: 209-466-0636.

Catholic Charities—Ms. ELVIRA RAMIREZ. Tel: 209-444-5900; Fax: 209-444-5933.

Catholic Youth Organization—Mr. DENNIS DEVENCENZI, Sports Dir., 212 N. San Joaquin St., Stockton, 95202. Tel: 209-466-0636.

Cemeteries—Mr. AL VIGIL, Supt. Cemeteries, Mailing Address: P.O. Box 1137, Stockton, 95201.

Censor Librorum—VACANT.

Apostolado Hispano—Mrs. DIGNA RAMIREZ-LOPEZ, Dir., 212 N. San Joaquin St., Stockton, 95202. Tel: 209-466-0636.

Development—Mrs. SHARON CAPORUSSO, Dir.

Continuing Education of Clergy—Rev. Msgr. ROBERT J. SILVA, 212 N. San Joaquin St., Stockton, 95202. Tel: 209-466-0636; Fax: 209-941-9722.

Communications Office—Sr. TERRY DAVIS, S.N.D.deN.

Cursillo Movement-English and Spanish—Mr. JESUS GONZALES, Dir.

Ecumenism— Office of the Bishop.

Office for Pastoral Leadership Development—Rev. Msgr. ROBERT J. SILVA.

Office of Religious Education—Sr. GLORIA DEJESUS SANCHEZ, E.F.M.S., Dir., 212 N. San Joaquin St., Stockton, 95202. Tel: 209-466-0636 Contact this office for various CCD Centers.

Office of Special Education—Mrs. YVONNE HARROLD, Consultant, 212 N. San Joaquin St., Stockton, 95202. Tel: 209-466-0636 Programs for physically & mentally impaired.

Office for Deacon Formation—

Office for Seminarians—Sr. WANDA BILLION, M.S.C.

Engaged Encounter—Mr. ED MANN; Mrs. LAURA MANN. Tel: 209-505-9005.

School of Ministry—Mrs. WANDA SCHEUERMANN, Dir.,

212 N. San Joaquin St., Stockton, 95202. Tel: 209-466-0636; Rev. GILBERTO ARANGO, Assoc. Dir.

Episcopal Liaison of Catholic Charismatic Renewal—English: Deacon WILLIAM BRENNAN, Ph.D., 13 Pardee Ln., Stockton, 95207. Tel: 209-474-0571. Spanish: Rev. JOSE DOMINGO RUIZ. Tel: 209-465-0416.

Liturgical Commission—Mr. DAVID SPRINGER, Chm., 505 W. Granger Ave., Modesto, 95350. Tel: 209-524-7421.

Newman Apostolate— The Newman House at University of the Pacific Mrs. DYAN HOLLENHORST, Dir.; Rev. SALVADOR LEDESMA, All Saints Newman Community at Stanislaus State University, 4040 McKenna Dr., Turlock, 95382. Tel: 209-669-0473.

Filipino Pastoral Ministry—Rev. JOSEPH MAGHINAY. Tel: 209-472-2150.

Office of Catechumenate—Mr. DAVID CORDER, Dir., 212 N. San Joaquin St., Stockton, 95202. Tel: 209-466-0636.

Permanent Diaconate Program—Deacon GREGORY YEAGER, Dir., P.O. Box 550, San Andreas, 95249. Tel: 209-754-3815.

Diaconate Formation—Sr. WANDA BILLION, M.S.C.; Mrs. WANDA SCHEUERMANN.

Pontifical Association of Holy Childhood—Mrs. MICHELLE ROMANO, 212 N. San Joaquin St., Stockton, 95202. Tel: 209-466-0636.

Propagation of the Faith—Mrs. MICHELLE ROMANO, 212 N. San Joaquin St., Stockton, 95202. Tel: 209-466-0636.

Respect Life Office--Community of Caring Program & Natural Family Planning Program—Mrs. KIM FUENTES, Dir., 212 N. San Joaquin St., Stockton, 95202. Tel: 209-466-0636.

Synod Office—Sr. TERRY DAVIS, S.N.D.deN.

Vicar for Religious Women—Sr. WANDA BILLION, M.S.C., 212 N. San Joaquin St., Stockton, 95202. Tel: 209-466-0636.

Catholic Schools Office—Mr. THOMAS BUTLER, Supt., 212 N. San Joaquin St., Stockton, 95202. Tel: 209-466-0636; Fax: 209-941-9722.

Vocations—Rev. JOSE LUIS GUTIERREZ, Dir., 212 N. San Joaquin St., Stockton, 95202. Tel: 209-466-0636.

Office for Worship—Mrs. VIRGINIA MEAGHER, Dir.; Mr. DAVID CORDER, Asst. Dir., 212 N. San Joaquin St., Stockton, 95202. Tel: 209-466-0636.

Office of Youth Ministry—Mrs. ANN MARIE AVANSINO, English Coord.; JOSE LOPEZ CEJA, Spanish Coord., 212 N. San Joaquin St., Stockton, 95202. Tel: 209-466-0636.

Catholic Committee on Scouting—LISA BALOGH. Tel: 209-815-8636.

Migrant Ministry Team—Mr. JOSE LOPEZ-CEJA, Leader; Sisters ROSA MARIA HERNANDEZ CASILLAS, M.G.Sp.S.; VERONICA SARAY TEJADA, M.G.Sp.S.; ESTER RAMIREZ, M.G.Sp.S.

Victim Assistance Coordinator—Sr. BARBARA THIELLA, S.N.D.deN. Tel: 209-466-0636. Email: bthiella@stocktondiocese.org.

CLERGY, PARISHES, MISSIONS AND PAROCHIAL SCHOOLS

CITY OF STOCKTON

(SAN JOAQUIN COUNTY)

1—CATHEDRAL OF THE ANNUNCIATION (PASTOR OF) (1944) Rev. Msgr. John M. Armistead; Rev. Benjamin Puente (Mexico), Parochial Vicar; Deacons Michael Wofford; Matthew Joseph. In Res., Rev. Gilberto Arango.
Res.: 425 W. Magnolia St., 95203-2412. Tel: 209-463-1305; Fax: 209-463-0807.
School—1110 N. Lincoln St., 95203. Tel: 209-444-4000; Fax: 209-444-4013. Mrs. Carla Donaldson, Prin. Lay Teachers 18; Students 294.
Catechesis/Religious Program—Students 716.

2—ST. BERNADETTE CHURCH (PASTOR OF) (1955) Rev. Msgr. William C. Moore.
Res.: 2544 Plymouth Rd., 95204. Tel: 209-465-3081; Fax: 209-547-1327.
Catechesis/Religious Program—Students 111.

3—ST. EDWARD CHURCH (PASTOR OF) (1967), (Hispanic), Rev. Alvaro H. Delgado.
Res.: 731 S. Cardinal Ave., 95215. Tel: 209-466-3020; Fax: 209-466-0719. Email: stedwardsoffice@aol.com.
Catechesis/Religious Program—Students 469.

4—ST. GEORGE CHURCH (PASTOR OF) (1951) Revs. David Dutra; Edwin Musico (Philippines); Deacons Jim Janukites; Don Rodgers; Jesus Aguilar; Kevin Amen.
Res.: 120 W. Fifth St., 95206-2695. Tel: 209-463-3413; Fax: 209-463-0167. Email: stgeorgechurch@att.net.
School—144 W. Fifth St., 95206. Tel: 209-463-1540; Fax: 209-463-2707. Mr. Frank Remkiewicz, Prin. Lay Teachers 5; Students 131.
St. George REALMS Foundation—
Catechesis/Religious Program—Tel: 209-463-3564. Students 533.
Mission—Good Shepherd P.O. Box 354, French Camp, San Joaquin Co. 95231. Tel: 209-982-0578; Fax: 209-858-4836.

5—ST. GERTRUDE CHURCH (PASTOR OF) (1913), (Mexican-American), [CEM] Revs. Alvaro U. Araque (Colombia); Eduardo Perez (Colombia), Parochial Vicar; Deacons Louis Juarez; Dennis Monbureau.
Res.: 1663 E. Main St., 95205. Tel: 209-466-0278; Fax: 209-466-1927. Email: gertrudeschurch@sbcglobal.net.
Catechesis/Religious Program—Tel: 209-969-5345. Students 148.

6—ST. LINUS CHURCH (PASTOR OF) (1956), (Hispanic—Asian), Rev. Gustavo V. Quintero; Deacon Joe Orzal. In Res., Rev. Jose Domingo Ruiz.
Res.: 2620 S. B St., 95206. Tel: 209-465-1430; Fax: 209-465-0299.
Catechesis/Religious Program—Students 485.

7—ST. LUKE CHURCH OF STOCKTON (PASTOR OF) (1951), (Vietnamese), Revs. Gael Sullivan; Tuan Nguyen, S.D.B. (Vietnam); Ramon Zarate; Deacons Haet Tansaeng; Glenn Sell; Ms. Victoria Kimball, Parish Admin.
Res.: 3847 N. Sutter St., 95204. Tel: 209-948-3450; Fax: 209-948-2841.
School—4005 N. Sutter St., 95204. Tel: 209-464-0801; Fax: 209-466-1150. Ms. Pat Simon, Prin. Lay Teachers 11; Students 199.
Catechesis/Religious Program—Tel: 209-462-0410. Paul C. DeValle, Dir. Youth Ministries; Sisters Odetta Bonini, Dir. Religious Ed.; Guia Jimenez, Dir. R.C.I.A. Students 620.
Convent—230 E. Atlee St., 95204. Tel: 209-463-6533.

8—ST. MARY OF THE ASSUMPTION CHURCH (PASTOR OF) (1851) Rev. Dean McFalls; Deacons Jorge Torres; Mel R. Tahod. In Res., Revs. Christian Ezeh; Louis Garcia; Alvaro M. Lopez (Colombia).
Res.: 203 E. Washington St., 95202. Tel: 209-948-0661; Fax: 209-948-0673.
Catechesis/Religious Program—Tel: 209-948-0665. Students 744.

9—ST. MICHAEL CHURCH OF STOCKTON (PASTOR OF) (1921), (Italian), Rev. Msgr. Agustin Gialogo; Deacon Allen Moznett.
Mailing Address: 5882 N. Ashley Ln., 95215-9307. In Res., Rev. Msgr. Richard J. Ryan.
Catechesis/Religious Program—Tel: 209-931-2696. Email: stmichaelcatmin@sbcglobal.net. Students 246.

10—PRESENTATION CHURCH (PASTOR OF) (1952) Rev. Msgr. Lawrence McGovern; Revs. Jose Luis Gutierrez, Parochial Vicar; Jose Maghinay; Deacons William Brennan; Scott Johnson; Mike Navarec. In Res., Rev. George Okoro.
Res.: 6715 Leesburg Pl., 95207. Tel: 209-472-2150; Fax: 209-472-0541. Email: frontdesk@presentationchurch.net. Web: presentationchurch.net.
School—1635 W. Benjamin Holt Dr., 95207. Tel: 209-472-2140; Fax: 209-320-1515. Email: office@presentationschool.org. Web: presentationschool.org. Diane Rothschild, Prin. Lay Teachers 13; Students 289.
Catechesis/Religious Program—Tel: 209-320-5714. Email: religioused@presentationchurch.net. Students 798.

OUTSIDE CITY OF STOCKTON

ANGELS CAMP, CALAVERAS CO., ST. PATRICK CHURCH OF ANGELS CAMP (PASTOR OF) (1856) [CEM] [JC] Revs. Rolando C. Petronio (Philippines); Lonachan W. Arouje (India).
Res.: 820 S. Main St., P.O. Box 576, 95222. Tel: 209-736-4575; Fax: 209-736-2217. Email: stpatricks_acamp@sbcglobal.net.
Catechesis/Religious Program—820 S. Main, 95222. Tel: 209-736-9180. Students 105.
Mission—St. Patrick 621 Sheep Ranch Rd., Murphys, Murphys Co. 95247. Tel: 209-728-2854.
Mission—Our Lady of the Sierra 1301 Linebaugh Rd., Arnold, Arnold Co. 95223. Tel: 209-795-7625.
Mission—St. Ignatius Mission

CERES, STANISLAUS CO., ST. JUDE CHURCH (PASTOR OF) (1962), (Hispanic), Revs. Ariel Munoz-Sanchez, O.R.C. (Mexico); Ascencion Rea Lagunas, O.R.C. (Mexico).
Res.: 3824 Mitchell Rd., 95307-9422. Tel: 209-537-0516; Fax: 209-537-3412. Web: www.stjudesparish.org.
Catechesis/Religious Program—Tel: 209-537-7439 (English Prog.); 209-538-8136 (Spanish Prog.). Students 1,149.
Mission—Ntra. Senora de Guadalupe 425 Broadway Ave., Modesto, Stanislaus Co. 95351. Tel: 209-606-6246.

HUGHSON, STANISLAUS CO., ST. ANTHONY CHURCH OF HUGHSON (PASTOR OF) (1921), (Hispanic), [CEM] Revs. Armando Vergara; Jeffrey Wilson.
7820 Fox Rd., 95326-9309.
Res.: 2020 Euclid Rd., 95326. Tel: 209-883-4310; Fax: 209-883-2531.
Catechesis/Religious Program—Tel: 209-883-1632. Students 680.
Mission—St. Louis [CEM] Floto St., La Grange, Stanislaus Co. 95329. Tel: 209-852-0144; Fax: 209-852-0818. Doris Quinones, Contact Person.

LATHROP, SAN JOAQUIN CO., OUR LADY OF GUADALUPE CHURCH (PASTOR OF) (2002) Rev. Francisco Naranjo, Admin.
Mailing Address: 16200 Cambridge Dr., 95330. Tel: 209-858-4466; Fax: 209-858-4978. Web: www.ourladyofguadalupelathrop.org.
Catechesis/Religious Program—Students 484.

LINDEN, SAN JOAQUIN CO., HOLY CROSS CHURCH (PASTOR OF) (1963), (Italian—Hispanic), Rev. Msgr. Robert J. Silva.
Res.: 18633 E. Front St., P.O. Box 52, 95236. Tel: 209-887-3341; Fax: 209-887-2973.
Catechesis/Religious Program—Tel: 209-887-4063. Students 153.

LOCKEFORD, SAN JOAQUIN CO., ST. JOACHIM CHURCH OF LOCKEFORD (PASTOR OF) (1882), (Hispanic), [CEM] Rev. Michael Kelly; Deacon Bill Warren, Bible Study & Prayer Group Leader.
Mailing Address: P.O. Box 232, 95237. Tel: 209-727-3912; Fax: 209-727-0403. Email: joachim@sonnet.com.
Catechesis/Religious Program—Tel: 209-727-5192. Students 197.

LODI, SAN JOAQUIN CO., ST. ANNE CHURCH (PASTOR OF) (1904) [CEM] Revs. Brandon M. Ware; William Kraft; Hung Joseph Nguyen (Vietnam), Parochial Vicar; Deacons Porfirio Cisneros; Karl Welsbacher.
Mailing Address: P.O. Box 480, 95241. Tel: 209-369-1907; Fax: 209-369-1971.
Office: 215 W. Walnut St., 95240. Tel: 209-369-1907; Fax: 209-369-1971.
Res.: 150 S. Pleasant St., 95240.
School—200 S. Pleasant St., 95240. Tel: 209-333-7580. Mr. Dennis Taricco, Prin. Lay Teachers 15; Students 246.
Catechesis/Religious Program—Sisters Isabel de la Eucaristia Abril, E.F.M.S., D.R.E.; Rosalia Cano, E.F.M.S., D.R.E. Students 632.
Mission—Mater Ecclesiae 26500 Sacramento Blvd., Thornton, San Joaquin Co. 95686.

MAMMOTH LAKES, MONO CO., ST. JOSEPH CHURCH OF MAMMOTH LAKES (1939) Rev. Paul Boudreau.
Res.: 58 Ranch Rd., P.O. Box 372, 93546. Tel: 760-934-6276; Fax: 760-934-4047. Email: info@mammothcatholicchurch.org. Web: mammothcatholicchurch.org.
Mission—Infant of Prague Mission Church 74936 Hwy. 395, Bridgeport, Mono Co. 93517. Fax: 760-934-4047.
Mission—Our Savior of the Mountains 72 Mono Lake Ave., Lee Vining, Mono Co. 93541. Tel: 760-934-6276; Fax: 760-934-4047.
Catechesis/Religious Program—Students 90.

MANTECA, SAN JOAQUIN CO., ST. ANTHONY CHURCH OF MANTECA (PASTOR OF) (1917) Revs. J. Patrick Walker; Camilo Garcia (Mexico); Dante U. Dammay (Philippines); Michael Brady; Deacons Harvey Parolari; Jeff Vierra.
505 E. North St., 95336.
Res.: 525 E. North St., 95336. Tel: 209-823-7197; Fax: 209-823-5238. Web: st-anthonys.org.
School—323 N. Fremont, 95336. Tel: 209-823-4513; Fax: 209-825-7447. Web: sasmanteca.org. Mary Lou Hoffman, Prin. Lay Teachers 12; Students 256.
Catechesis/Religious Program—Students 952.
St. Vincent de Paul Society—Tel: 209-823-8099.
St. Anthony School Educational Foundation—Tel: 209-239-4513.

MODESTO, STANISLAUS CO.

1—HOLY FAMILY CHURCH (PASTOR OF) (2006) Rev. Juan Serna; Deacon Philip Vallejo; Rev. Samuel A. Woods.
4220 Dale Rd., 95356. Tel: 209-545-3553; Fax: 209-545-3332.
Catechesis/Religious Program—Students 267.
Mission—Our Lady of San Juan de los Lagos 4643 Flint Ave., Salida, Stanislaus Co. 95368.

2—ST. JOSEPH CHURCH OF MODESTO (PASTOR OF) (1967) Revs. Joseph P. Illo; Benny Kottarathil (Italy); Deacons Kenneth Ochinero; Ernest Ciccarelli. In Res., Rev. Larry Guererro.
Res.: 1813 Oakdale Rd., 95355. Tel: 209-551-4973; Fax: 209-551-3213. Web: www.stjmod.com.
Catechesis/Religious Program—Students 1,060.

3—OUR LADY OF FATIMA CHURCH (PASTOR OF) (1951) Rev. Khoi Pham; Rev. Msgr. Bonifacio Baldonado, Parochial Vicar; Rev. Martin Garcia, Parochial Vicar; Deacon James Johnson.
Res.: 505 W. Granger Ave., 95350. Tel: 209-524-7421; Fax: 209-524-7713.
School—501 W. Granger Ave., 95350. Tel: 209-524-4170; Fax: 209-524-3960. Linda Partlow, Prin. Lay Teachers 14; Students 242; Extended Day Care 125.
Catechesis/Religious Program—Tel: 209-491-3462; Fax: 209-524-7713. Students 510.
The Monsignor William P. Kennedy Education Foundation:—
4—ST. STANISLAUS CHURCH (PASTOR OF) (1881) Revs. Ramon Bejarano; Jorge W. Arboleda, Parochial Vicar; Samuel G. West, Parochial Vicar; Deacons Jose Reyes; Jim Kottinger.
Res.: 709 J St., 95354. Tel: 209-524-4381; Fax: 209-524-1910. Email: info@ststansparish.org. Web: www.ststanscc.org.
School—1416 Maze Blvd., 95351. Tel: 209-524-9036; Fax: 209-524-4344. Web: www.ststansparish-school.com. Russel Antracoli, Prin. Lay Teachers 14; Students 201.
Catechesis/Religious Program—Tel: 209-522-6534; Fax: 209-523-9128. Students 900.

NEWMAN, STANISLAUS CO., ST. JOACHIM CHURCH OF NEWMAN (PASTOR OF) (1909), (Spanish—English), Rev. Hector Villegas; Deacon Lance Valez.
Res.: 1121 Main St., 95360. Tel: 209-862-3528; Fax: 209-862-3512. Email: hectovi@yahoo.com.
Catechesis/Religious Program—Tel: 209-862-2878. Students 230.

OAKDALE, STANISLAUS CO., ST. MARY OF THE ANNUNCIATION CHURCH (PASTOR OF) (1902) Rev. Msgr. Aloys Conrad Gruber; Rev. Antony Chacko, Parochial Vicar; Deacons Roberto Magdaleno, (Retired); Thomas Ciccarelli.
Res.: 1225 Olive St., 95361. Tel: 209-847-2715; Fax: 209-847-7348. Email: stmarysoakdale@aol.com.
Catechesis/Religious Program—Tel: 209-847-3498. Email: abcorissetto@gmail.com. Students 353.

PATTERSON, STANISLAUS CO., SACRED HEART CHURCH OF PATTERSON (PASTOR OF) (1925) Revs. Richard Rex Hays, C.M.; Jeremy Dixon, C.M., Parochial Vicar.
Res.: 529 I St., 95363. Tel: 209-892-9321; Fax: 209-892-2102. Email: sheartpatterson@juno.com. Web: www.sacredheartpatterson.org.
School—505 M St., 95363. Tel: 209-892-3544; Fax: 209-892-3214. Web: www.shcs-patterson.org. Jason Oliveira, Prin. Lay Teachers 13; Students 227.
Catechesis/Religious Program—503 M St., 95363. Tel: 209-892-6381; Fax: 209-892-6381. Students 381.
Mission—Immaculate Heart of Mary H St., Crows Landing, Stanislaus Co. 95313.

RIPON, SAN JOAQUIN CO., ST. PATRICK CHURCH OF RIPON (PASTOR OF) (1878) Rev. Peter Carota.
Res.: 19399 E St., Rte. 120 Hwy., 95366. Tel: 209-838-2133; Fax: 209-838-1077.
Catechesis/Religious Program—Tel: 209-838-3101. Students 650.

RIVERBANK, STANISLAUS CO., ST. FRANCES OF ROME CHURCH (PASTOR OF) (1953) Revs. Misael Avila, Admin.; John Peter Pragasam (Italy), Parochial Vicar; Deacons Fred Ybarra; Richard Williamsen.
Res.: 2827 Topeka St., 95367. Tel: 209-869-2996; Fax: 209-863-1004. Email: francesofrome@aol.com.
Catechesis/Religious Program—Students 499.

SAN ANDREAS, CALAVERAS CO., ST. ANDREW CHURCH OF SAN ANDREAS (PASTOR OF) (1963) [CEM] Rev. Patrick Curran; Deacon Greg Yeager.
Mailing Address: 162 Church Hill Rd., P.O. Box 550, 95249.
Res.: 261 Sunset, P.O. Box 550, 95249. Fax: 209-754-5116. Email: standrew@comcast.net.
Catechesis/Religious Program—Tel: 209-754-3815; Fax: 209-754-5116. Students 48.
Mission—St. Thomas Aquinas 8398 Lafayette St., Mokelumne Hill, Calaveras Co. 95245. Tel: 209-754-3815; Fax: 209-754-5116.
Mission—Our Lady of Fatima 22581 Hwy. 26, West Point, Calaveras Co. 95255. Tel: 209-754-3815; Fax: 209-754-5116.

SONORA, TUOLUMNE CO., ST. PATRICK CHURCH OF SONORA (PASTOR OF) (1851) [CEM 5] [JC] Revs. Ray Abella, O.S.F.S.; Editho Mascardo, Parochial Vicar; Deacon Michael Kubasek.
Res.: 116 Bradford St., 95370. Tel: 209-532-7139; Fax: 209-532-4389. Email: stpats@stpatssonora.org. Web: parishesonline.com.
Catechesis/Religious Program—Tel: 209-532-7139, Ext. 110; Fax: 209-532-4389. Students 106.
Mission—Our Lady of Mt. Carmel Cemetery Rd., Big Oak Flat, Tuolumne Co. 95305.
Mission—St. Anne 22518 Church Ln., Columbia, Tuolumne Co. 95310. Tel: 209-532-7139.

TRACY, SAN JOAQUIN CO., ST. BERNARD CHURCH (PASTOR OF) (1908) Rev. Msgr. Ivo D. Rocha (Portugal); Revs. Francis A. Joseph, O.C.D. (India), Parochial Vicar; Jorge A. Roman, Parochial Vicar; Jovito B. Roldan, Parochial Vicar; Deacons Ray Whitlock; Peter Ryza.
Res.: 163 W. Eaton Ave., 95376. Tel: 209-835-4560; Fax: 209-835-4588. Web: www.st-bernards.org.
School—165 W. Eaton Ave., 95376. Tel: 209-835-8018; Fax: 209-835-2496. Web: www.st-bernardschool.org. Gary Abate, Prin. Lay Teachers 13; Students 264.
Catechesis/Religious Program—Tel: 209-835-4560, Ext. 189 (or Ext. 121). Students 1,793.
Convent—Daughters of the Cross, 165 W. Eaton Ave., 95376. Tel: 209-835-7391; Fax: 209-830-6137.

TURLOCK, STANISLAUS CO.
1—OUR LADY OF THE ASSUMPTION OF THE PORTUGUESE CHURCH (PASTOR OF) (1973), (Portuguese), Rev. Manuel F. Sousa; Deacon Edwin Santiago.
Mailing Address: P.O. Box 2030, 95381. Fax: 209-634-2366.
Res.: 1343 W. Greenway, 95380. Tel: 209-634-2222; 209-634-3140. Email: frmanuelsousa@att.net. Web: www.olassumption.net.
Catechesis/Religious Program—Connie Madruga, C.R.E. Students 348.
2—SACRED HEART CHURCH OF TURLOCK (PASTOR OF) (1910) Revs. Mark Wagner; Luis Corderro, Parochial Vicar; Jairo H. Ramirez (Colombia), Parochial Vicar.
Mailing Address: 1301 Cooper Ave., 95380.
Res.: 650 Rose St., 95380. Tel: 209-634-8578; 209-634-8579; Fax: 209-634-7124. Email: church@shparish.net.
School—1225 Cooper Ave., 95380. Tel: 209-634-7787; Fax: 209-634-0156. Mrs. Donna Noceti, Prin. Lay Teachers 12; Students 237.
Preschool—Tel: 209-667-5512; Fax: 209-669-9647. Debra Cannella, Prin. Lay Teachers 15; Students 120.
Catechesis/Religious Program—Sacred Heart Religious Education, 1250 Cooper #1, 95380. Tel: 209-634-5111. Students 2,088.

TWAIN HARTE, TUOLUMNE CO., ALL SAINTS CHURCH (PASTOR OF) (1962) [JC] Rev. John E. Fitzgerald; Deacon Joseph Gomes.
Res.: 18674 Cherokee Dr., P.O. Box 642, 95383. Tel: 209-586-3161; Fax: 209-586-3161. Email: omnsanct@goldrush.com. Web: www.omnsanct.org.
Catechesis/Religious Program—Students 59.
Mission—St. Joseph Gardner St., Tuolumne, Tuolumne Co. 95379.
Station— Pinecrest. (Summer)

Chaplains of Public Institutions

STOCKTON. *DeWitt Nelson Training Center*, 7650 Newcastle Rd., P.O. Box 213003, 95213-9003. Tel: 209-944-6187. Rev. Randall Rainwater, Chap.
O.H. Close School, 7650 Newcastle Rd., P.O. Box 213002, 95213-9001. Tel: 209-944-6364. Deacon Louis Juarez.

FRENCH CAMP. *San Joaquin County Jail*, 999 W. Matthews Rd., 95231. Tel: 209-468-4562. Vacant.
San Joaquin General Hospital, 500 W. Hospital Rd., 95231. Tel: 209-468-6000. St. George Church.

JAMESTOWN. *Sierra Conservation Center*, P.O. Box 497, 95327-1213. Tel: 209-984-5291, Ext. 5281. Rev. Ray Abella, O.S.F.S., Chap.

TRACY. *Deuel Vocational Institution*, P.O. Box 400, 95376-3593. Tel: 209-835-4141, Ext. 5076. Deacon Edwin Santiago.

On Duty Outside the Diocese:
Revs.—
Bitterman, John L., S.S., S.T.B., M.A.
Foster, John J.M., J.C.D.
Myers, William
O'Neill, Robert
Pintacura, Michael

Absent on Leave:
Revs.—
Barrera, Fernando (Colombia)
McDonald, William
Pelaez, Oskar
Suarez, Leo

Retired:
Rev. Msgrs.—
Cain, James E., Vicar Gen. Emeritus, 1105 N. Lincoln St., 95203.
Donohoe, Edward, 5835 Cherokee Rd., #69, 95215.
Skillin, Harmon, J.C.D.
Revs.—
Ford, William A., St. Mary Star of the Sea, 888 Blvd. of the Arts, #1508, Sarasota, FL 34236.
Maguire, Enda J.
O'Dwyer, James, Pastor Emeritus, Casa Santa Fe, 24 Dillon St., Clonmel, Ireland.
Pacheco, Alexandre (India)
Pereira, Robert J., P.O. Box 78072, 95267.
Rajanayagam, Thomas M.
Ryan, William
Wang, John, 3700 N. Sutter St. #352, 95204.
White, Nathan R., 6740 Deer Valley Rd., Ste. D107-#231.

Permanent Deacons:
Aguilar, Jesus, St. George, Stockton
Amen, Kevin, St. George, Stockton
Artesi, Joseph, (Retired), St. Luke's, Stockton
Brennan, William, Ph.D., Church of the Presentation, Stockton
Broderick, Thomas, School of Ministry, Stockton
Ciccarelli, Thomas, St. Mary's of the Annunciation, Escalon
Cisneros, Porfirio, St. Anne, Lodi
Flanders, Raymond, St. Anthony, Hughson
Janukites, James, St. George, Stockton
Johnson, James, Our Lady of Fatima, Modesto
Johnson, Scott, Church of the Presentation, Stockton
Joseph, Matthew, Annunciation, Stockton
Juarez, Louis, St. Gertrude's, Stockton
Kottinger, Jim, Our Lady of Guadalupe, Lathrop
Kubasek, Michael, St. Patricks, Twain Harte
Magdaleno, Roberto, St. Mary, Oakdale
Mendez, Juan, (Retired)
Monbureau, Denis, St. Gertrude, Stockton
Moznett, Al, St. Michael, Stockton
Ochinero, Kenneth, St. Jude's, Ceres
Orzal, Joe, St. George, Stockton
Parolari, Harvey, St. Anthony, Manteca
Pietras, Adam, St. Patrick, Angel's Camp
Reyes, Jose, St. Stanislaus, Modesto
Rodgers, Donald, Good Shepherd, French Camp
Ryza, Peter, St. Bernard's, Tracy
Santiago, Edwin, Our Lady of the Assumption, Turlock
Sell, William (Glenn), St. Luke's, Stockton
Tahod, Mel R., St. Mary's Assumption, Stockton
Tansaeng, Haet, St. Luke, Stockton
Torres, Jorge, St. Mary's, Stockton
Vallejo, Felipe, St. Frances of Rome, Riverbank
Velez, Lance, St. Joachim, Newman
Vierra, Jeffrey, Our Lady of Guadalupe, Lathrop
Warren, William E., St. Joachim, Lockeford
Welsbacher, Karl, St. Anne, Lodi
Whitlock, Ray, St. Bernard, Tracy
Wofford, Michael, Cathedral of Annunciation, Stockton
Ybarra, Fred, St. Patrick, Copperopolis
Yeager, Gregory, St. Andrews, San Andreas
Ryan, John G., St. Bernard, Tracy

INSTITUTIONS LOCATED IN THE DIOCESE

[A] HIGH SCHOOLS, DIOCESAN

STOCKTON. *St. Mary's High School* (1876) 5648 N. El Dorado St., P.O. Box 7247, 95267-0247. Tel: 209-957-3340; Fax: 209-957-0861. Email: jfallon@saintmaryshighshool.org. Web: www.saintmaryshighschool.org. Rev. John P. Fallon, O.S.F.S., Pres.; Mr. Peter Morelli, Prin.; Rev. Clark T. Kelley, O.S.F.S.; Bro. James Dorazio, O.S.F.S. Non-resident students. Priests 2; Brothers 1; Sisters 1; Lay Teachers 70; Students 988.
St. Mary's High School Foundation Tel: 209-957-3340; Fax: 209-957-0861.

MODESTO. *Central Catholic High School* (1966) 200 S. Carpenter Rd., 95351. Tel: 209-524-9611; Fax: 209-524-5646. Email: jehardee@cchsca.org. Web: www.cchsca.org. Mr. Jim Pecchenino, Pres.; Melissa Bengtson, Prin.; Wendy Habeeb, Asst. Prin.; Rev. Michael Brady; Mrs. Theresa Hubert, Librarian. Non-resident students. Lay Teachers 30; Administrators 7; Students 409.
Central Catholic High School Foundation Tel: 209-524-6822; Fax: 209-524-5646.

[B] CATHOLIC CHARITIES

STOCKTON. *Catholic Charities of the Diocese of Stockton* (1980) 1106 N. El Dorado St., 95202. Tel: 209-444-5900; Fax: 209-444-5933. Email: eramirez@ccstockton.org. Ms. Elvira Ramirez, Exec. Dir.; Mark Croce, Chm. Corp. Bd.
Catholic Charities Services for Seniors & Caregivers, 1106 N. El Dorado St., 95202. Tel: 209-444-5931; Fax: 209-444-5929. Email: jhoman@ccstockton.org. Juliana Homan, Prog. Dir. Telephone Reassurance, Homemaker (Housekeeping), Personal Care, Respite Care Program, Caregiver Respite, Caregiver

Training, Caregiver Chore & Home Modification. Clients 634.

Multipurpose Senior Service Program (MSSP) Care Management, Respite In-Home, Emergency Call Device, Minor Home Repair, Home Safety Evaluations. Transportation, Massage, Physical, Occupational, Speech & Aquatic Therapies., 1106 N. El Dorado St., 95202. Tel: 209-444-5931; Fax: 209-444-5929. Email: jhoman@ccstockton.org. Clients 208.

Immigration Legal Services, 1106 N. El Dorado St., 95202. Tel: 209-444-5910; Fax: 209-460-1624. Email: rdarcy@ccstockton.org. Rosie D'Arcy, Prog. Coord. Naturalization/Citizenship, Green Card Renewal/ Replacement, Special Case Waivers, Adjustment of Status, Family Immigration, Family Petitions, TPS, Affidavit of Support. Clients 1,011.

Catholic Charities ESL/Citizenship Education Program Offers English as a Second Language (ESL)/Citizenship classes to help prepare Legal Permanent Residents (LPR's) for Citizenship and advance their integration in the United States., 1106 N. El Dorado St., 95202. Tel: 209-444-5910; Fax: 209-460-1624. Email: rdarcy@ccstockton.org.

ADVOCACY

Environmental Justice Program (EJ), 1106 N. El Dorado St., 95202. Tel: 209-444-5925; Fax: 209-444-5929. Email: betsyr@ccstockton.org. Betsy Reifsnider. Serves to educate and motivate Catholics in the Stockton Diocese to a deeper reverence and respect for God's creation and to engage local parishes in activities to resolve environmental problems, particularly as they affect the poor. Clients 99.

Stanislaus County Senior Services, 400 12th St., Ste. 4, Modesto, 95354. Tel: 209-529-3784; Fax: 209-529-6083. Email: mramos@ccstockton.org. Monica Ramos, Prog. Dir. Homemaker Program, Long-term Care, Ombudsman Program, Senior Transportation, Social Security Representative Payee Program, Stanislaus Elder Abuse Prevention Alliance. Clients 3,851.

Mother Lode Ombudsman Program Ombudsman Program, Legal Advocacy for Seniors Program, Elder Abuse Prevention Program, Social Security Representative Payee Program, Older Adult Outreach and Engagement Program., 14855 Mono Way, Ste. 101, Sonora, 95370. Tel: 209-532-7632; Fax: 209-532-8448. Email: ktoepel@ccstockton.org. Kathi Toepel, Prog. Dir. Clients 1,212.

Children's Health Initiative, 1106 N. El Dorado St., 95202. Tel: 209-444-5940; Fax: 209-460-1624. Email: jgalindo@ccstockton.org. Joanna Galindo, Prog. Dir. Services: Enroll Children to Medical, Healthy Families or Kaiser Insurance Program. Clients 2,022.

Catholic Charities Prenatal Care Outreach Educates mothers on the importance of early prenatal care. Case manages expectant mothers, referrals according to need. Coordinates Nutrition and Child Safety Classes., 1106 N. El Dorado St., 95202. Tel: 209-444-5934; Fax: 209-460-1624. Email: gguzman@ccstockton.org. Glenda Guzman, Program Coord. Clients 350.

Nutritional Assistance Services Program (Calfresh), 1106 N. El Dorado St., 95202. Tel: 209-444-5900; Fax: 209-460-1624. Email: srios@ccstockton.org. This program is an outreach and eligibility screening campaign designed to increase access by eligible individuals and families in San Joaquin and Stanislaus counties to the Supplemental Nutrition Assistance Program (SNAP). It is the name for the federal food stamp program, and Calfresh is the new name at the state level. The food stamp program is our nation's first line of defense against hunger and malnutrition and can be an effective way to increase a household's ability to purchase healthy food. Clients 3,482.

Family Counseling Services The Family Counseling Services Program provides low-cost, short-term counseling services as well as community education workshops and mental health resource and referrals in Stanislaus County., 400 12th St., Ste. 4, Modesto, 95354. Tel: 209-593-6122; Fax: 209-532-8448. Email: pmunoz@ccstockton.org.

[C] GENERAL HOSPITALS

STOCKTON. *St. Joseph's Behavioral Health Center* (1993) a dba of Catholic Healthcare West, 2510 N. California St., 95204. Tel: 209-948-2100; Fax: 209-464-2270. Web: www.stjosephscanhelp.org. Paul Rains, Pres. Sponsored by the Dominican Sisters of San Rafael, California. Bed Capacity 35; Total Assisted Annually 9,584; Total Staff 116.

St. Joseph's Medical Center of Stockton (1899) a dba of Catholic Healthcare West, 1800 N. California St., 95204-9008. Tel: 209-943-2000; Fax: 209-461-3299. Web: www.stjosephscares.org. Donald J. Wiley, Pres. Sponsored by the Dominican Sisters of San Rafael, California. Sisters 5; Bed Capacity 359; Total Assisted Annually 632,064; Total Staff 2,547.

[D] HOMES FOR AGED

STOCKTON. *Casa Manana Inn*, 3700 N. Sutter St., 95204. Tel: 209-466-4046; Fax: 209-466-3450. Delea Mercado, Admin. Total in Residence 162; Total Staff 4.

St. Joseph's Regional Housing Corp., 3400 Wagner Heights Rd., 95209. Tel: 209-956-3400; Fax: 209-952-6201. Email: info@oconnorwoods.org. Web: www.oconnorwoods.org. E. G. Schroeder, Pres.; R. Scot Sinclair, Exec. Dir. St. Joseph's Regional Housing Corp., sponsored by the Sisters of the Third Order of St. Dominic, Congregation of the Most Holy Name, provides a residential community for seniors offering a variety of living arrangements from active to assisted, skilled and rehabilitation services

O'Connor Woods Housing Corp., 3400 Wagner Heights Rd., 95209. Tel: 209-956-3400; Fax: 209-952-6201. E. G. Schroeder, Pres.; R. Scot Sinclair, Exec. Dir. O'Connor Woods Housing Corp., a nonprofit Corporation operates O'Connor Woods, Garden Oaks, Oak Creek and Meadowood Health and Rehabilitation Center. Bed Capacity 421; Total Assisted Annually 1,046; Total Staff 312.

O'Connor Woods, A Calif. Corp., 3400 Wagner Heights Rd., 95209. Tel: 209-956-3400; Fax: 209-952-6201. E. G. Schroeder, Pres. and CEO; R. Scot Sinclair, Exec. Dir.

[E] CONVENTS AND RESIDENCES FOR SISTERS

STOCKTON. *Dominican Sisters of San Rafael Convent*, 5042 Gadwell Cir., 95207. Tel: 209-956-6953.

Eucharistic Franciscan Missionary Sisters, 1205 N. San Joaquin St., 95202. Tel: 209-462-3906; Fax: 209-469-3759. Sisters 4.

Sacro Costato Missionary Sisters (1908) St. Luke's Convent, 230 E. Atlee St., 95204. Tel: 209-462-6533; Fax: 209-464-5342. Email: mscstockton@comcast.net. Sisters 4.

Sisters of Notre Dame de Namur (1804) 212 N. San Joaquin St., 95202. Tel: 209-466-0636; Fax: 209-941-9722. Sisters Barbara Thiella, S.N.D.deN., Chancellor; Terry Davis, S.N.D.deN., Dir. Communication. Sisters 2.

MODESTO. *Sisters of the Cross of the Sacred Heart of Jesus* (1897) Cloistered Convent., 1320 Maze Blvd., 95351. Tel: 209-526-3525; Fax: 209-526-3525. Email: sistersofthecross@sbcglobal.net. Web: www.sistersofthecross.org. Sisters 10.

PATTERSON. *Daughters of the Holy Spirit* (1706) Sacred Heart Convent., *Daughters of the Holy Spirit*, 624 N. 64th St., 95363. Tel: 209-892-3410. Email: lucilledhs@gvni.com. Sisters Anne Marie Berthiaume, D.H.S., Mistress, Postulants; Lucille Carreau, D.H.S., Asst. Dir., Spiritual Services. Sisters 2.

TRACY. *The Daughters of the Cross* (1833) St. Bernard Convent, 165 W. Eaton Ave., 95376. Tel: 209-835-7391; Fax: 209-830-6137. Email: fc1833@sbcglobal.net. Sisters 6.

TURLOCK. *Sisters of the Sacred Hearts of Jesus and Mary* Sacred Heart Convent, 1201 Lyons Ave., 95380-4120. Tel: 209-634-7708; Fax: 209-634-7124; 209-669-0173. Sr. Christina Doona, S.H.J.M., Pastoral Min.

[F] RETREAT CENTERS

COPPEROPOLIS. *Madonna of Peace Renewal Center* (1982) (Youth Facility), 2010 Hunt Rd., P.O. Box 71, 95228. Tel: 209-785-2157 (Office); Fax: 209-785-2157. Total in Residence 2; Total Staff 2.

[G] MISCELLANEOUS

STOCKTON. *The Bishop's Educational Foundation, Diocese of Stockton*, 212 N. San Joaquin St., 95202-2409. Tel: 209-466-0636; Fax: 209-941-9722.

Catholic Professional and Business Club, 212 N. San Joaquin St., 95202-2409. Tel: 209-466-0636; Fax: 209-941-9722.

Church for Tomorrow Fund, 212 N. San Joaquin St., 95202.

Instituto Fe y Vida (1994) 1737 W. Benjamin Holt Dr., 95207. Tel: 209-951-3483; Fax: 209-478-5357. Email: info@feyvida.org. Web: www.feyvida.org. Total Staff 6.

St. John Vianney House of Formation, 4101 N. Manchester, 95207. Tel: 209-451-3220. Rev. Jose Luis Gutierrez, Dir.

St. Joseph's Foundation of San Joaquin, 1800 N. California St., 95204. Tel: 209-467-6347; Fax: 209-461-6893. Email: abby.newton@chw.edu. Web: www.stjosephscares.org.

St. Mary's High School Foundation (1982) Box 7247, 95267-0247. Tel: 209-957-3340; Fax: 209-957-0861. Email: jfallon@saintmaryshighschool.org. Web: www.saintmaryshighschool.org.

San Lorenzo Ruiz De Manila (1988) P.O. Box 6817, 95206. Tel: 209-570-8222. Email: nbanasihan@yahoo.com. Natie R. Banasihan, Pres. & Founder.

SEEDS (Assistance for Catholic Education within the Roman Catholic Diocese of Stockton) (2004) 212 N. San Joaquin St., 95202. Tel: 209-466-0636; Fax: 209-463-5937.

LODI. *St. Anne's Endowment* (1986) 801 S. Ham Ln., Ste. H, 95242. Tel: 209-369-1907; Fax: 209-369-1971.

MODESTO. *The Catholic Social Service Guild* (1975) 2613 Illinois Ave., 95358. Tel: 209-522-6140. Els Blom, Pres.

Central Catholic High School Foundation, 200 Carpenter Rd., 95351. Tel: 209-524-6822; Fax: 209-524-5646. Email: hart@cchsca.org. Web: www.cchsca.org. Volunteer Board Members 25.

Father John C. Silva Education Foundation, P.O. Box 4304, 95352. Tel: 209-524-4381; Fax: 209-524-1910.

**Mary Mother of God Mission Society*, 1736 Milestone Cir., 95357. Tel: 209-408-0728; Fax: 209-408-0728.

The Monsignor William P. Kennedy Education Foundation, 501 W. Granger Ave., 95350. Tel: 209-524-4170; Fax: 209-524-7713.

TURLOCK. *The Father McElligott Sacred Heart School Foundation*, 1225 Cooper St., 95380-4113. Tel: 209-634-7787; 209-669-5336; Fax: 209-634-0156. Email: shs.development@yahoo.com. Jackie Cotta, Exec. Dir. Students 245; Total Staff 28.

RELIGIOUS INSTITUTES OF MEN REPRESENTED IN THE DIOCESE

For further details refer to the corresponding bracketed number in the Religious Institutes of Men or Women section.

[0220]—*Congregation of the Blessed Sacrament*—S.S.S.

[]—*Congregation of the Mission* (Vincentians)—C.M.

[0260]—*Discalced Carmelite Friars*—O.C.D.

[0920]—*Oblates of St. Francis De Sales* (Toledo-Detroit Prov.)—O.S.F.S.

[]—*Operarios del Reinode Christo*—O.R.C.

[1190]—*Salesians of St. John Bosco*—S.D.B.

[]—*Society of St. Sulpice (Sulpicians)*—S.S.

RELIGIOUS INSTITUTES OF WOMEN REPRESENTED IN THE DIOCESE

[1920]—*Congregation of the Sisters of the Holy Cross* (Notre Dame, IN)—C.S.C.

[]—*Daughters of Mary Immaculate Conception*

[0780]—*Daughters of the Cross of Liege*—F.C.

[0820]—*Daughters of the Holy Spirit* (Putnam, CT)—D.H.S.

[1070-04]—*Dominican Sisters* (San Rafael)—O.P.

[1150]—*Eucharistic Franciscan Missionary Sisters*—E.F.M.S.

[1310]—*Franciscan Sisters of Little Falls* (Minnesota)—O.S.F.

[1845]—*Guadalupan Missionaries of the Holy Spirit*—M.G.Sp.S.

[]—*Missionary Sisters of the Sacred Side of Jesus and the Sorrowful Mother* (Italy)—M.S.C.

[3465]—*Religious of the Sacred Heart of Mary*—R.S.H.M.

[]—*Sisters for Christian Community*—S.F.C.C.

[2575]—*Sisters of Mercy of the Americas*—R.S.M.

[3000]—*Sisters of Notre Dame de Namur*—S.N.D.deN.

[3340]—*Sisters of Providence*—S.P.

[1630]—*Sisters of St. Frances of Penance & Christian Charity*—O.S.F.

[1710]—*Sisters of St. Francis of Mary Immaculate*—O.S.F.

[3830-03]—*Sisters of St. Joseph of Orange*—C.S.J.O.

[]—*Sisters of the Cross of the Sacred Heart of Jesus* (Mexico City, Mexico)—R.C.S.C.J.

[1960]—*Sisters of the Holy Family* (San Francisco)—S.H.F.

[4070]—*Society of the Sacred Heart*—R.S.C.J.

DIOCESAN CEMETERIES AND MAUSOLEUMS

STOCKTON. *San Joaquin Cemetery and Mausoleum* Mr. Al Vigil, Supt.

ESCALON. *St. John Cemetery* Cynthia A. Rodriguez, Office Mgr.

MODESTO. *St. Stanislaus Cemetery and Chapel Crypts* Gretchen Storm, Office Mgr.

NECROLOGY

(No Deaths)

An asterisk (*) denotes an organization that has established tax-exempt status directly with the IRS and is not covered by the USCCB Group Ruling.

Diocese of Superior

(Dioecesis Superiorensis)

Most Reverend

PETER F. CHRISTENSEN

Bishop of Superior; ordained May 25, 1985; appointed Bishop of Superior June 28, 2007; consecrated September 14, 2007; installed September 23, 2007. *Office: 1201 Hughitt Ave., Superior, WI 54880.* Tel: 715-394-0205; Fax: 715-395-3149. *Res.: 1 Gitchinadji Dr., Superior, WI 54880. Mailing Address: Box 969, Superior, WI 54880.*

Chancery Office: 1201 Hughitt Ave., Box 969, Superior, WI 54880. Tel: 715-392-2937; Fax: 715-392-2015.

Most Reverend

RAPHAEL M. FLISS, D.D.

Retired Bishop of Superior; ordained May 26, 1956; appointed Coadjutor Bishop of Superior with right of succession November 6, 1979; ordained December 20, 1979; succeeded to See, June 27, 1985; retired June 28, 2007. *Res. & Mailing Address: 7218 Ogden Ave., P.O. Box 3067, Superior, WI 54880.* Tel: 715-392-2932; Fax: 715-392-0910.

ESTABLISHED MAY 3, 1905

Square Miles 15,715.

Comprises the Counties of Ashland, Barron, Bayfield, Burnett, Douglas, Iron, Lincoln, Oneida, Polk, Price, Rusk, Sawyer, St. Croix, Taylor, Vilas and Washburn in the State of Wisconsin.

Incorporated under the laws of the State of Wisconsin as the Diocese of Superior.

For legal titles of parishes and diocesan institutions, consult the Chancery.

STATISTICAL OVERVIEW

Personnel	
Bishop	1
Retired Bishops	1
Priests: Diocesan Active in Diocese	34
Priests: Diocesan Active Outside Diocese	2
Priests: Retired, Sick or Absent	34
Number of Diocesan Priests	70
Religious Priests in Diocese	6
Total Priests in Diocese	76
Extern Priests in Diocese	2
Ordinations:	
Diocesan Priests	2
Religious Priests	5
Transitional Deacons	1
Permanent Deacons	2
Permanent Deacons in Diocese	71
Total Sisters	73
Parishes	
Parishes	104
With Resident Pastor:	
Resident Diocesan Priests	34
Resident Religious Priests	4
Without Resident Pastor:	
Administered by Priests	52
Administered by Deacons	12
Administered by Religious Women	1
Administered by Lay People	2
Professional Ministry Personnel:	
Sisters	5
Lay Ministers	29
Welfare	
Catholic Hospitals	6
Total Assisted	253,592
Health Care Centers	1
Total Assisted	155
Homes for the Aged	12
Total Assisted	377
Day Care Centers	2
Total Assisted	233
Special Centers for Social Services	4
Total Assisted	381
Residential Care of Disabled	10
Total Assisted	149
Other Institutions	548
Total Assisted	640
Educational	
Diocesan Students in Other Seminaries	7
Total Seminarians	7
Elementary Schools, Diocesan and Parish	15
Total Students	2,508
Catechesis/Religious Education:	
High School Students	1,948
Elementary Students	4,455
Total Students under Catholic Instruction	8,918
Teachers in the Diocese:	
Sisters	5
Lay Teachers	222
Vital Statistics	
Receptions into the Church:	
Infant Baptism Totals	726
Minor Baptism Totals	149
Adult Baptism Totals	37
Received into Full Communion	134
First Communions	921
Confirmations	881
Marriages:	
Catholic	151
Interfaith	104
Total Marriages	255
Deaths	1,085
Total Catholic Population	74,697
Total Population	439,182

Former Bishops—Rt. Revs. AUGUSTIN FRANCIS SCHINNER, D.D., ord. March 7, 1886; cons. July 25, 1905; resigned Jan. 15, 1913; appt. Bishop of Spokane, WA, March 18, 1914; died Feb. 7, 1937; JOSEPH M. KOUDELKA, D.D., ord. Oct. 8, 1875; cons. Auxiliary Bishop of Cleveland and Titular Bishop of Germanicopolis, Feb. 25, 1908; transferred to Milwaukee as Auxiliary Bishop, Sept. 4, 1911; appt. to the See of Superior, Aug. 6, 1913; died June 24, 1921; JOSEPH G. PINTEN, D.D., ord. Nov. 1, 1890; elected Dec. 3, 1921; cons. May 3, 1922; transferred to the See of Grand Rapids, June 25, 1926; retired Nov. 1, 1940; died Nov. 6, 1945; Most Revs. THEODORE H. REVERMAN, D.D., ord. July 26, 1901; cons. Nov. 30, 1926; died July 18, 1941; WILLIAM PATRICK O'CONNOR, D.D., Ph.D., ord. March 10, 1912; cons. March 7, 1942; transferred to the See of Madison, Jan. 15, 1946; ALBERT GREGORY MEYER, S.S.L., D.D., ord. July 11, 1926; appt. Feb. 18, 1946; cons. April 11, 1946; promoted to Archbishop of Milwaukee, July 21, 1953; transferred to Archbishop of Chicago, Sept. 19, 1958; created Cardinal, Dec. 14, 1959; died April 9, 1965; JOSEPH JOHN ANNABRING, D.D., ord. May 3, 1927; appt. Jan. 27, 1954; cons. March 25, 1954; died Aug. 27, 1959; GEORGE A. HAMMES, D.D., Bishop Emeritus of Superior; appt. March 28, 1960; cons. May 24, 1960; retired June 27, 1985; died April 11, 1993; RAPHAEL M. FLISS, D.D., ord. May 26, 1956; appt. Coadjutor Bishop of Superior with right of succession Nov. 6, 1979; ord. Dec. 20, 1979; succeeded to See, June 27, 1985; retired June 28, 2007.

Chancery—1201 Hughitt Ave., Box 969, Superior, 54880. Tel: 715-392-2937; Fax: 715-392-2015.

Vicar General—Very Rev. JAMES P. POWERS, J.C.L., V.G., Mailing Address: Office, P.O. Box 969, Superior, 54880. Tel: 715-394-0219; Fax: 715-392-2015.

Chancellor—Mrs. DEBRA J. LIEBERG.

Secretary to Bishop—Mrs. PATRICIA WILDENBERG.

Diocesan Tribunal—

Judicial Vicar—Very Rev. JAMES F. TOBOLSKI, J.C.L.

Adjutant Judicial Vicar—Very Rev. JAMES P. POWERS, J.C.L., V.G.

Promoter of Justice— Appointed by case.

Defender of the Bond—Rev. WILLIAM G. HORATH.

Procurator and Advocate—Ms. PATTI J. HOLT.

Vicar for Canonical Affairs—Very Rev. JAMES F. TOBOLSKI, J.C.L.

Diocesan Pastoral Council—Most Rev. PETER F. CHRISTENSEN, M.A.S. South Central Deanery: CAROL EWAN; RODNEY MAHNER; ROGER RIVARD. Eastern Deanery: JANICE DONNER; YVONNE GLONCHAK. Northwest Deanery: LOUISE POPE; ERNEST SWARTZ. North Central Deanery: JOHN GREK; SHIRLEY TRAUTT; MICHAEL PUTZER. Southwest Deanery: CATHERINE SMOLINSKE; Deacon DAVID B. DISERA, Bishop's Appointee. Ex Officio Members: Very Rev. JAMES P. POWERS, J.C.L., V.G.; Sisters CELINE GOESSL, S.C.S.C.; THERESA SANDOK, O.S.M.

Deaneries and Deans—Northwest Deanery: Very Rev. JAMES F. TOBOLSKI, J.C.L. Southwest Deanery: Very Rev. JOHN A. DRUMMY. North Central Deanery: Very Rev. PAUL PARE, O.F.M. South Central Deanery: Very Rev. PHILIP J. JUZA. East Deanery: Very Rev. JOHN C. ANDERSON.

Pastoral Consultors—Very Rev. PHILIP J. JUZA; Revs. JAMES J. KINNEY; RONALD OLSON, O.F.M.Conv.; MICHAEL J. TUPA.

Presbyteral Council & Diocesan Consultors—Most Rev. PETER F. CHRISTENSEN, M.A.S., Pres.; Rev. NORBERT D'MELLO, C.S.C.; Very Revs. JAMES F. TOBOLSKI, J.C.L., Sec.; JAMES P. POWERS, J.C.L., V.G.; Rev. JOHN R. GERRITTS, Treas.; Very Rev. KEVIN M. GORDON; Revs. GERALD A. HAGEN, Chm.; GERALD P. HARRIS; EDWIN C. ANDERSON; AARON P. KALMON; MICHAEL J. TUPA, Vice Chm.; THOMAS E. THOMPSON; GERARD I. WILLGER.

Personnel Placement Board—Very Revs. JOHN C. ANDERSON; KEVIN M. GORDON; Deacon TIMOTHY J. KUEHN; Rev. THOMAS E. THOMPSON; Very Revs. JOHN A. DRUMMY; PHILIP J. JUZA; JAMES F. TOBOLSKI, J.C.L.

Diocesan Offices and Directors

Bureau of Information—JULIE KELEMAN, Dir., 1201 Hughitt Ave., P.O. Box 969, Superior, 54880. Tel: 715-394-0213.

Catholic Charities Bureau—Mr. BRIAN K. SOLAND,

M.A., Exec. Dir., Office, 1416 Cumming Ave., Superior, 54880. Tel: 715-394-6617; Fax: 715-394-5951.

Catholic Boy and Girl Scout Chaplain—Rev. EDWIN C. ANDERSON, Mailing Address: St. Francis de Sales Church, 409 Summit St., Spooner, 54801. Tel: 715-635-3105; Fax: 715-635-7341.

Catholic Mutual Group—PAUL ALTMANN, Claims/Risk Mgr., 1201 Hughitt Ave., P.O. Box 969, Superior, 54880. Tel: 715-394-0222.

Catholic Women, Council of—PAT WILLIAMS, Pres., 701 N. State Rd. 46, Lot #40, Balsam Lake, 54810. Tel: 715-405-3727.

Moderator—Rev. GERARD I. WILLGER, Mailing Address: Our Lady of the Holy Rosary Church, P.O. Box 503, Medford, 54451.

Charismatic Renewal Liaison—Deacon MICHAEL D. CULLEN, St. Joseph Church, 827 E. LaSalle Ave., Barron, 54812. Tel: 715-637-3255; Fax: 715-637-3252.

Catholic Formation, Department of—VACANT.

Diocesan Coordinator of Health Affairs—Very Rev. KEVIN M. GORDON, 1201 Hughitt Ave., P.O. Box 969, Superior, 54880. Tel: 715-394-0229.

Diocesan Sisters Council—Sr. PHYLLIS WILHELM, O.S.F., Pres., 715 Third Ave. E., Ashland, 54806. Tel: 715-209-6825.

Ecumenical Commission—Very Rev. JAMES F. TOBOLSKI, J.C.L., Mailing Address: P.O. Box 969, Superior, 54880. Tel: 715-394-0207.

Evangelization, Office of—VACANT.

Finance, Department of—RONALD C. NELSON, Dir., 1201 Hughitt Ave., P.O. Box 969, Superior, 54880. Tel: 715-394-0221.

Holy Childhood Association—Rev. GREGORY J. HOPEFL, Dir., 13891 W. Mission Rd, Stone Lake, 54876. Tel: 715-865-3669.

Insurance/Employee Benefits and Payroll, Office of—CINDY GRONSKI, Dir., 1201 Hughitt Ave., P.O. Box 969, Superior, 54880. Tel: 715-394-0230; Fax: 715-395-3758.

Newman Apostolate— Superior: Newman and Young Adult Ministry Center, University of Wisconsin Directors: JENNA HALVERSON, Dir., 823 N. 16th St., Superior, 54880. Tel: 715-394-7710. St. Thomas More Newman Center: Deacon THOMAS J. WEISS, Coord., Newman Ministry, 423 E. Cascade Ave., River Falls, 54022. Tel: 715-425-7234; Fax: 715-425-6959. Email: thomas.j.weiss@uwrf.edu.

Catholic Herald, Superior Edition—JULIE KELEMAN, Editor, 1201 Hughitt Ave., P.O. Box 969, Superior, 54880. Tel: 715-394-0213.

Parish Accounting, Office of—CINDY GRONSKI, Contact, 1201 Hughitt Ave., P.O. Box 969, Superior, 54880. Tel: 715-394-0230.

Pastoral Services, Department of—VACANT.

Planning, Office of—VACANT.

Permanent Diaconate—Deacon TIMOTHY J. KUEHN, Dir., Mailing Address: 1201 Hughitt Ave., P.O. Box 969, Superior, 54880. Tel: 715-394-0217.

Respect Life Office—Mrs. DEBRA J. LIEBERG, Mailing Address: P.O. Box 969, Superior, 54880. Tel: 715-394-0240.

Propagation of the Faith—Rev. GREGORY J. HOPEFL, 13891 W. Mission Rd., Stone Lake, 54876. Tel: 715-865-3669.

Radio and Television—JULIE KELEMAN, Dir., 1201 Hughitt Ave., P.O. Box 969, Superior, 54880. Tel: 715-394-0213.

The Bishop George A. Hammes Center—Deacon ROGER L. CADOTTE, Dir., 315 W. Fifth St., P.O. Box 280, Haugen, 54841. Tel: 715-234-5044; Fax: 715-234-5241.

St. Pius Priest Fund—Board of Directors: Most Rev. PETER F. CHRISTENSEN, M.A.S., Pres.; Rev. DENNIS M. MULLEN, Vice Pres.; Very Rev. JAMES P. POWERS, J.C.L., V.G., Sec.; Revs. ANDREW P. RICCI; JAMES J. BRINKMAN; DENNIS T. MEULEMANS (Retired); MICHAEL J. TUPA; DAVID R. LUSSON; JOHN R. GERRITTS; WILLIAM J. MURPHY (Retired); THOMAS E. THOMPSON.

Stewardship and Development, Department of—Mr. STEVEN P. TARNOWSKI, Dir., 1201 Hughitt Ave., P.O. Box 969, Superior, 54880. Tel: 715-394-0223; Fax: 715-392-2015.

Superintendent of Schools—PEGGY SCHOENFUSS, Office: Bishop George A. Hammes Center, 315 W. Fifth St., P.O. Box 280, Haugen, 54841. Tel: 715-234-5044, Ext. 4405; Fax: 715-234-5241.

Diocesan Coordinators of Assistance—Mailing Address: P.O. Box 969, Superior, 54880. CATHY KOERPEL. Tel: 715-369-2676; GARY NELSON. Tel: 715-363-2623.

Vocations, Office of—Rev. THOMAS E. THOMPSON, Mailing Address: 1201 Hughitt Ave., P.O. Box 969, Superior, 54880. Tel: 715-394-0234.

Office of Worship—PAUL J. BIRCH, 1201 Hughitt Ave., P.O. Box 969, Superior, 54880. Tel: 715-394-0233.

CLERGY, PARISHES, MISSIONS AND PAROCHIAL SCHOOLS

CITY OF SUPERIOR

(DOUGLAS COUNTY)

1—CATHEDRAL OF CHRIST THE KING (1886) [CEM] Rev. Andrew P. Ricci, Rector; Deacon Arthur Gil de Lamadrid.
Mailing Address: 1410 Baxter Ave., 54880.
Church: 1111 Belknap Ave., 54880. Tel: 715-392-8511; Fax: 715-392-3457.
School—Cathedral School, (Grades PreK-8), 1419 Baxter Ave., 54880. Tel: 715-392-2976; Fax: 715-392-2977. Mrs. Marilyn Pekol, Prin. Lay Teachers 23; Students 291.
Catechesis/Religious Program—Lynn Tracy, C.R.E.; Mary Jo Edge, C.R.E.; Pam Dawson, C.R.E.; Mary Kay Jensen, C.R.E.; Susan Collins, C.R.E. Students 84.

2—ST. ANTHONY (1870), Also serves St. Anthony, Lake Nebagamon. Rev. Donald A. Kania, Parochial Admin.; Deacon Kevin Feind.
Church & Mailing Address: 4315 E. 3rd St., 54880. Tel: 715-398-3261; Fax: 715-398-3257.
Catechesis/Religious Program—Stephanie Winter, D.R.E. Students 48.

3—SS. CYRIL AND METHODIUS, (Slovak), Closed. For inquiries for sacramental records contact Cathedral of Christ the King.

4—ST. FRANCIS XAVIER (1854) [CEM] Very Rev. James F. Tobolski; Deacon Timothy J. Kuehn.
Church and Mailing Address: 2316 E. 4th St., 54880. Tel: 715-398-7174; Fax: 715-398-3074.
Catechesis/Religious Program—Ernest Swartz, D.R.E. Students 194.

5—HOLY ASSUMPTION OF THE B.V.M. (1891), Also serves St. William, Superior. Rev. Ronald Olson, O.F.M.Conv.; Deacon Robert J. Chammings.
Church & Mailing Address: 5601 Tower Ave., 54880. Tel: 715-394-7919; Fax: 715-394-4883.
Catechesis/Religious Program—Lucinda Wnuk, C.R.E. Students 61.

6—ST. LOUIS, Closed. For inquiries for sacramental records contact Cathedral of Christ the King.

7—ST. PATRICK, Closed. For inquiries for sacramental records contact Cathedral of Christ the King.

8—ST. STANISLAUS, (Polish), Closed. For inquiries for sacramental records contact Cathedral of Christ the King.

9—ST. WILLIAM (1908) [CEM], Also serves Holy Assumption, Superior. Rev. Ronald Olson, O.F.M-.Conv.
Mailing Address: 4315 E. 3rd St., 54880.
Church: 3095 E. County Rd. B, 54880. Tel: 715-398-3261.
Catechesis/Religious Program—Lucinda Wnuk, C.R.E.

OUTSIDE THE CITY OF SUPERIOR

ALMENA, BARRON CO., SACRED HEART OF JESUS CHURCH (1890) [CEM] Rev. David R. Lusson.
Mailing Address: 900 St. Anthony St., Cumberland, 54829. Tel: 715-822-2948; Fax: 715-822-3588.
Church: 114 Soo Ave., 54805.
Catechesis/Religious Program—Mary DeNoyer, C.R.E.

AMERY, POLK CO., ST. JOSEPH (1890) [CEM] Very Rev. John A. Drummy; Deacons Larry K. Bauer; Florian Heiser; J. Patrick Derrington. Also serves Our Lady of the Lakes, Balsam Lake.
Church and Mailing Address: 1050 Keller Ave. N., 54001. Tel: 715-268-7717; Fax: 715-268-9986.
Catechesis/Religious Program—Mary Modjeski, D.R.E.; Joyce Holt, C.R.E. Students 138.

ASHLAND, ASHLAND CO.

1—HOLY FAMILY, (Polish), Closed. For inquiries for sacramental records contact Our Lady of the Lake Catholic Community, Ashland.

2—OUR LADY OF THE LAKE CATHOLIC COMMUNITY (1872) [CEM], Also serves St. Mary, Odanah. Very Rev. Paul Pare, O.F.M.; Rev. Gary Bernhardt, O.F.M.; Deacons William J. Holzhaeuser; Owen T. Gorman.
Mailing Address: 106 N. 2nd Ave. E., 54806.
Church: 201 Lake Shore Dr. E., 54806. Tel: 715-682-7620; Fax: 715-682-7626.
School—(Grades PreK-8), 215 Lake Shore Dr. E., 54806. Tel: 715-682-7622. Mr. Dan Bell, Prin. Lay Teachers 13; Students 139.
Catechesis/Religious Program—Tim Mika, C.R.E.; Sr. Phyllis Wilhelm, O.S.F., D.R.E. Students 134.

BALSAM LAKE, POLK CO., OUR LADY OF THE LAKES (1875) [CEM 2] Very Rev. John A. Drummy.
Mailing Address: P.O. Box 399, 54810.
Church: 507 W. Main, 58410. Tel: 715-405-2253; Fax: 715-405-2743.
Catechesis/Religious Program—Tel: 715-294-2243. Sally Christiansen, C.R.E. Students 70.

BARRON, BARRON CO., ST. JOSEPH (1907), Also serves St. Peter, Cameron, St. Boniface, Chetek, and Assumption of the Blessed Virgin Mary, Strickland. Deacon Michael D. Cullen, Parish Life Coord.; Rev. James P. Bartelme.
Church and Mailing Address: 827 E. LaSalle Ave., 54812. Tel: 715-637-3255; Fax: 715-637-3252.
Catechesis/Religious Program—Anne Stephens, D.R.E. Students 71.

BAYFIELD, BAYFIELD CO., HOLY FAMILY (1878) [CEM], Also serves St. Ann, Cornucopia, St. Joseph, La Pointe, St. Louis, Washburn. Rev. Aaron P. Kalmon, Parochial Admin.; Very Rev. Kevin M. Gordon, Weekend Sacramental Min.; Deacon Roger L. Cadotte.
Mailing Address: P.O. Box 1290, 54814.
Church: 232 N. 1st. St., 54814. Tel: 715-779-3316; Fax: 715-779-9804.
Catechesis/Religious Program—

BIRCHWOOD, WASHBURN CO., ST. JOHN EVANGELIST (1908) Rev. David P. Oberts.
Mailing Address: 2411 23rd St., Rice Lake, 54868.
Church: 408 S. Main, 54817. Tel: 715-234-2917; Fax: 715-236-7865.
Catechesis/Religious Program—Amie Vos, C.R.E. (6-12); Kristine Deering, C.R.E. (K-5). Students 33.

BLOOMVILLE, LINCOLN CO., ST. JOHN THE BAPTIST (1908) [CEM] Rev. Ronald Serrao, C.S.C.
Mailing Address: N10090 County Rd. B., Tomahawk, 54487.
Church: Hwy. 17 & County Rd. J, Gleason, 54435. Tel: 715-453-2561; Fax: 715-453-4813.
Catechesis/Religious Program—Vincent Geisler, C.R.E. Students 23.

BOULDER JUNCTION, VILAS CO., ST. ANNE (1938) [CEM], Also serves St. Mary, Sayner, and St. Rita, Presque Isle. Rev. Michael T. Hayden; Sr. Constance Walton, F.S.P.A., D.R.E.
Mailing Address: P.O. Box 110, 54512.
Church: 10315 Main St., 54512. Tel: 715-385-2390; Fax: 715-385-2282.
Catechesis/Religious Program—Students 18.

BRUCE, RUSK CO., ST. MARY (1893) [CEM 2] Revs. Shaji Joseph Pazhukkathara, Parochial Admin.; Christopher J. Kemp.
Mailing Address: 611 1st St. S., Ladysmith, 54848.
Church: 727 N. 2nd St., 54819. Tel: 715-353-2400; Fax: 715-353-4758.
Catechesis/Religious Program—Students 24.

BUTTERNUT, ASHLAND CO., IMMACULATE CONCEPTION (1880) [CEM] Rev. Daniel Gonzalez, Parochial Admin.; Deacon Chester E. Ball Jr.
Mailing Address: P.O. Box 6, 54514.
Church: 410 Michigan St., 54514. Tel: 715-769-3644; Fax: 715-769-3644.
Catechesis/Religious Program—Bette Hirtreiter, D.R.E. Students 39.

CABLE, BAYFIELD CO., ST. ANN (1902) Sr. Virginia Schwartz, O.S.M., Parish Dir.
Mailing Address: P.O. Box 37, 54821-0037.
Church: 13645 County Hwy. M, 54821. Tel: 715-798-3855; Fax: 715-798-3850.
Catechesis/Religious Program—Celia Peterson, C.R.E. Students 13.

CAMERON, BARRON CO., ST. PETER (1908) Deacon Michael D. Cullen, Parish Life Coord.; Rev. James P. Bartelme; Deacon Russell E. Cabak.
Mailing Address: 827 E. LaSalle Ave., Barron, 54812.
Church: Creamery Rd. & Hwy. 8, 54822. Tel: 715-637-3255.
Catechesis/Religious Program—Patty Gerber, C.R.E. Students 109.

CATAWBA, PRICE CO., ST. PAUL THE APOSTLE (1907) [CEM] Rev. Gerald A. Hagen.
Mailing Address: 125 N. Argyle Ave., Phillips, 54555.
Church: W9485 Hwy. 8, 54515. Tel: 715-339-2222; Fax: 715-339-2216.
Catechesis/Religious Program—Gloria Lyons, C.R.E. Students 42.

CENTURIA, POLK CO., ST. PATRICK (1856) Closed. For inquiries for sacramental records, please contact Our Lady of the Lakes, Balsam Lake.

CHELSEA, TAYLOR CO., ASSUMPTION OF THE BLESSED VIRGIN MARY (1887) Closed. For Inquiries for sacramental records please contact Good Shepherd, Rib Lake.

CHETEK, BARRON CO., ST. BONIFACE (1880) [CEM] Deacon Michael D. Cullen, Parish Life Coord.; Rev. James P. Bartelme; Deacon James M. Dennis.
Mailing Address: 827 E. LaSalle Ave., Barron, 54812.
Church: 425 S. 3rd St., 54728. Tel: 715-924-3514; Fax: 715-924-3514.
Catechesis/Religious Program—Dawn Langman, C.R.E. Students 46.

CLAM LAKE, ASHLAND CO., ST. GEORGE (1890), Summer Chapel for Worship Rev. William D. Brenna.
Mailing Address: P.O. Box 17, Mellen, 54546.
Church: W. Hwy. 77, 54517. Tel: 715-264-3471.

CLEAR LAKE, POLK CO., ST. JOHN (1890), Also serves St. John the Baptist, Glenwood City & St. Bridget, Wilson. Rev. Norbert D'Mello, C.S.C.
Mailing Address: P.O. Box 337, 54005.
Church: 811 Fourth St., 54005. Tel: 715-263-2032; Fax: 715-263-2032.
Catechesis/Religious Program—Paul Mara, D.R.E. Students 40.

CORNUCOPIA, BAYFIELD CO., ST. ANN (1914) [CEM] Rev. Aaron P. Kalmon, Parochial Admin.; Very Rev. Kevin M. Gordon, Weekend Sacramental Min.
Mailing Address: 8350 Superior Ave., P.O. Box 311, 54827. Tel: 715-779-3316; Fax: 715-779-9804.
Church: Superior Ave. & Ash St., 54827.
Catechesis/Religious Program—

CRESCENT LAKE, BURNETT CO., SACRED HEARTS OF JESUS AND MARY (1857) [CEM] Rev. Michael J. Tupa.
Mailing Address: P.O. Box 7, Webster, 54893.
Church: County Rd. A & H, 54830. Tel: 715-866-7321; Fax: 715-866-7305.
Catechesis/Religious Program—Colleen Monfre, D.R.E.

CUMBERLAND, BARRON CO., ST. ANTHONY ABBOT (1883) [CEM 2], Also serves Sacred Heart of Jesus, Almena and St. Ann, Turtle Lake. Rev. David R. Lusson.
Church and Mailing Address: 900 St. Anthony St., 54829. Tel: 715-822-2948; Fax: 715-822-3588.
Catechesis/Religious Program—Mary DeNoyer, C.R.E. Students 145.

DANBURY, BURNETT CO., OUR LADY OF PERPETUAL HELP (1920) Rev. Michael J. Tupa.
Mailing Address: P.O. Box 7, Webster, 54893.
Church and Mailing: 7586 Main St., 54830. Tel: 715-866-7321; Fax: 715-866-7305.
Catechesis/Religious Program—Colleen Monfre, D.R.E.

DAUBY, BAYFIELD CO., ST. PETER (1918) [CEM] Rev. Michael L. Crisp.
Mailing Address: P.O. Box 97, Iron River, 54847.
Church: Hwy. 2 & County Rd. F, 54847. Tel: 715-372-4756.
Catechesis/Religious Program—Betty Franzel, C.R.E. Students 4.

DOBIE, BARRON CO., OUR LADY OF LOURDES (1875) [CEM], (Also serves Holy Trinity, Haugen, and St. John the Evangelist, Birchwood.) Rev. David P. Oberts.
Church and Mailing Address: 2411 23rd St., Rice Lake, 54868. Tel: 715-234-2917; Fax: 715-236-7865.
Catechesis/Religious Program—Amie Vos, C.R.E. (6-12); Kristine Deering, C.R.E. (K-5). Students 123.

EAGLE RIVER, VILAS CO., ST. PETER THE FISHERMAN (1890) [CEM] Rev. Robert J. Koszarek; Sr. Jeanne Wiest, O.P., Pastoral Assoc.
Church and Mailing Address: 5001 County Rd. G, 54521. Tel: 715-479-8704; Fax: 715-477-2017.
Catechesis/Religious Program—Adele Svetnicka, C.R.E. Students 73.

ERIN, ST. CROIX CO., ST. PATRICK (1857) [CEM 2] Rev. James J. Brinkman.
Mailing Address: 151 S. Washington Ave., New Richmond, 54017.
Church: 1880 County Rd. G, 54017. Tel: 715-246-4652; Fax: 715-246-2526.
Catechesis/Religious Program—Jody Lenz, C.R.E. Students 27.

FARMINGTON, ST. CROIX CO., ASSUMPTION OF THE BLESSED VIRGIN MARY (1869) [CEM] Rev. Thomas E. Thompson.
Mailing Address: P.O. Box 399, Osceola, 54020-0399.
Church: 255 State Hwy. 35, 54025. Tel: 715-294-2243; Fax: 715-294-2495.
Catechesis/Religious Program—Gwen Nies, D.R.E.

FIFIELD, PRICE CO., ST. FRANCIS OF ASSISI (1888) Rev. Daniel Gonzalez, Parochial Admin.; Deacon Chester E. Ball Jr.
Mailing Address: 276 S. 5th Ave., Park Falls, 54552.
Church: Balsam St., 54524. Tel: 715-762-4494.
Catechesis/Religious Program—Jane Gustafson, D.R.E.; Ann Gotz, C.R.E. (1-6); Steve Eitrem, C.R.E. (7-9).

FLAMBEAU, RUSK CO., ST. FRANCIS OF ASSISI (1866) [CEM] Revs. Shaji Joseph Pazhukkathara, Parochial Admin.; Christopher J. Kemp; Deacon Craig J. Voldberg.
Mailing Address: 611 1st St. S., Ladysmith, 54848.
Church: W10193 Lehman Rd., Holcombe, 54745. Tel: 715-353-2400; Fax: 715-353-4758.
Catechesis/Religious Program—Shawna Strzok, C.R.E. Students 15.

FREDERIC, POLK CO., ST. DOMINIC (1904) [CEM], (Also serves Immaculate Conception, Grantsburg). Rev. Dennis M. Mullen; Deacon Stanley J. Marczak.
Mailing Address: P.O. Box 606, 54837.
Rectory & Parish Office: 107 W. Birch St., 54837.
Church: 103 W. Birch St., 54837. Tel: 715-327-8119; Fax: 715-327-8125.
Catechesis/Religious Program—Melody Dian, D.R.E.; Marie Onstad, C.R.E. Students 49.

GEORGETOWN, POLK CO., OUR LADY OF THE HOLY ROSARY, Closed. For inquiries for sacramental records contact Our Lady of the Lakes Balsam Lake.

GILMAN, TAYLOR CO., SS. PETER AND PAUL (1910) [CEM], (Also serves St. Michael, Jump River; St. John the Apostle, Sheldon and St. Stanislaus, Lublin). Rev. John R. Long.
Church and Mailing: 315 E. Davlin St., 54433. Tel: 715-447-8510; Fax: 715-447-5742.
Catechesis/Religious Program—Sr. Marianna Ableidinger, F.S.P.A., D.R.E. Students 63.

GLENWOOD CITY, ST. CROIX CO., ST. JOHN THE BAPTIST (1886) [CEM], Also serves St. John, Clear Lake & St. Bridget, Wilson. Rev. Norbert D'Mello, C.S.C.; Deacon Wesley G. Tuttle.
Mailing Address: 761 1st St., 54013.
Church: 757 1st St., 54013. Tel: 715-265-7133 (Phone and Fax).
Catechesis/Religious Program—Bonnie Cronk, C.R.E. (K-12). Students 178.

GLIDDEN, ASHLAND CO., MOST PRECIOUS BLOOD (1884) [CEM] Rev. William D. Brenna, Admin.
Mailing Address: P.O. Box 17, Mellen, 54546. Tel: 715-264-3471.
Church: Grant St., 54527.
Catechesis/Religious Program—Vicky Ellias, C.R.E. Students 19.

GORDON, DOUGLAS CO., ST. ANTHONY OF PADUA (1878) Rev. James J. Kinney.
Mailing Address: P.O. Box 303, Solon Springs, 54873.
Church: 9718 E. County Rd. Y, 54838. Tel: 715-378-4431.
Catechesis/Religious Program—Pat Den Hartog, C.R.E.; Barbara Schuyler, D.R.E.

GRANTSBURG, BURNETT CO., IMMACULATE CONCEPTION (1909) Rev. Dennis M. Mullen.
Mailing Address: P.O. Box 606, Frederic, 54837.
Church: 411 State Rd. 70, 54840. Tel: 715-327-8119.
Catechesis/Religious Program—Melody Dian, D.R.E.; Marie Ohnstad, C.R.E. Students 45.

HAMMOND, ST. CROIX CO., IMMACULATE CONCEPTION (1877) [CEM], Also serves St. Bridget, River Falls. Rev. Gerald P. Harris; Deacon Joseph F. Paron.
Mailing Address: P.O. Box 18, 54015-0018.
Church: 1265 Ridgeway, 54015. Tel: 715-796-2244; Fax: 715-796-2599.
Catechesis/Religious Program—Jackie Aune, C.R.E.; Diane Johnson, C.R.E. Students 239.

HARRISON, LINCOLN CO., ST. AUGUSTINE (1905) [CEM], Also serves St. John the Baptist, Bloomville. Rev. Ronald Serrao, C.S.C.; Deacon Clarence D. Towle.
Mailing Address: Tomahawk N10090 Cty. B, Tomahawk, 54487. Tel: 715-453-2561; Fax: 715-453-4813.
Church: Highways B & D, Tomahawk, 54487.
Catechesis/Religious Program—Jewel Towle, C.R.E. Students 22.

HAUGEN, BARRON CO., HOLY TRINITY (1896) [CEM] Rev. David P. Oberts; Deacon Harvey G. Drost.
Mailing Address: 2411 23rd St., Rice Lake, 54868.
Church: 317 W. 5th St., 54841. Tel: 715-234-2917; Fax: 715-236-7865.
Catechesis/Religious Program—Kris Deering, C.R.E. (K-5); Amie Vos, C.R.E. (6-12). Students 41.

HAWKINS, RUSK CO., ST. MARY OF CZESTOCHOWA (1913) [CEM] Revs. Shaji Joseph Pazhukkathara; Christopher J. Kemp.
Mailing Address: 611 1st St. S., Ladysmith, 54848.
Church: N7386 Cty. Rd. M, 54530. Tel: 715-532-3051; Fax: 715-532-7368.
Catechesis/Religious Program—

HAYWARD, SAWYER CO., ST. JOSEPH (1882), Also serves St. Ann, Cable. Very Rev. Philip J. Juza.
Mailing Address: P.O. Box 877, 54843.
Church: 10586 N. Dakota Ave., 54843. Tel: 715-634-2867; Fax: 715-634-9037.
Catechesis/Religious Program—Teri Radcliffe, C.R.E. (Grades PreK-11). Students 126.

HIGHBRIDGE, ASHLAND CO., ST. ANTHONY (1880) Rev. William D. Brenna.
Mailing Address: P.O. Box 17, Mellen, 54546.
Church: Hwy. 13, 54846. Tel: 715-274-3701; Fax: 715-274-3703.
Catechesis/Religious Program—Debbie Schutte, C.R.E. Students 9.

HUDSON, ST. CROIX CO., ST. PATRICK (1840) [CEM] Rev. Eugene A. Murphy, Temp. Parochial Admin.; Deacons Gregg Miller; Howard Cameron.
Church and Mailing Address: 1500 Vine St., 54016. Tel: 715-381-5120; Fax: 715-381-5125.
School—(Grades PreK-8), 403 St. Croix St., 54016. Tel: 715-386-3941. Mary Piasecki, Prin. Sisters 1; Lay Teachers 24; Students 313.
Catechesis/Religious Program—Tel: 715-386-9209. Larry Huiras, D.R.E.; Tim O'Brien, D.R.E.; Jeanne Darrold, C.R.E.; Becky Swanson, C.R.E.; Craig Swanson, C.R.E. Students 514.

HURLEY, IRON CO., ST. MARY OF THE SEVEN DOLORS (1885) [CEM], Also serves St. Issac Jogues and Companions, Mercer. Rev. Frank Kordek, O.F.M.
Mailing Address: 404 Iron St., 54534.
Church: Iron St. & 5th Ave., 54534. Tel: 715-561-2606; Fax: 715-561-3739.
Catechesis/Religious Program—Ann Marie Batiste, C.R.E. Students 63.

INO, BAYFIELD CO., ST. FLORIAN (1913) [CEM] Rev. Michael L. Crisp.
Mailing Address: P.O. Box 97, Iron River, 54847.
Church: 19315 Keystone Rd., Mason, 54856. Tel: 715-372-4756.
Catechesis/Religious Program—Loretta Skaj, D.R.E.

IRON RIVER, BAYFIELD CO., ST. MICHAEL (1893) [CEM], Also serves St. Peter, Dauby; St. Florian, Ino; SS. Peter & Paul, Moquah. Rev. Michael L. Crisp.
Mailing Address: P.O. Box 97, 54847.
Church: 68105 S. George St., 54847. Tel: 715-372-4756; Fax: 715-372-4753.
Catechesis/Religious Program—Cathy Berube, C.R.E. Students 34.

JUMP RIVER, TAYLOR CO., ST. MICHAEL (1915) Rev. John R. Long.
Mailing Address: 315 E. Davlin St., Gilman, 54433. Tel: 715-447-8510; Fax: 715-447-5742.
Church: WI 4764 Hwy. 73, 54434.
Catechesis/Religious Program—Sr. Marianna Ableidinger, F.S.P.A., D.R.E.

LA POINTE, BAYFIELD CO., ST. JOSEPH (1669) [CEM] Rev. Aaron P. Kalmon, Parochial Admin.; Very Rev. Kevin M. Gordon, Weekend Sacramental Min.
Mailing Address: P.O. Box 1290, Bayfield, 54814.
Church: 266 Airport Rd., 54850. Tel: 715-779-3316; Fax: 715-779-9804.
Catechesis/Religious Program—

LAC DU FLAMBEAU, VILAS CO., ST. ANTHONY OF PADUA (1862), Also serves Our Lady Queen of Peace, Manitowish Waters, and St. Isaac Jogues & Companions, Mercer. Rev. Lourdumar Reddy Mandapati; Deacon John J. Bardos.
Mailing Address: P.O. Box 38, 54538.
Church: 650 Old Abe Rd., 54538. Tel: 715-588-3148; Fax: 715-588-3889.
Catechesis/Religious Program—Tel: 715-588-7439. Debra Soulier-Ramsey, C.R.E. Students 10.

LADYSMITH, RUSK CO., OUR LADY OF SORROWS (1906), Also serves St. Mary, Hawkins, and St. Anthony de Padua, Tony; St. Mary, Bruce; St. Francis of Assisi, Flambeau; SS Peter & Paul, Weyerhaeuser. Revs. Shaji Joseph Pazhukkathara; Christopher J. Kemp; Deacons Jerome J. Drahos; Richard D. Leonhard; Douglas L. Sorenson.
Church and Mailing Address: 611 1st St. S., 54848. Tel: 715-532-3051; Fax: 715-532-7368.
School—(Grades K-8), 105 E. Washington Ave., 54848. Tel: 715-532-3232. Tami Stewart, Prin. Lay Teachers 11; Students 105.
Catechesis/Religious Program—Tel: 715-532-3703. Students 79.

LAKE NEBAGAMON, DOUGLAS CO., ST. ANTHONY (1899) [CEM] Rev. Donald A. Kania, Parochial Admin.
Mailing Address: P.O. Box 397, 54849.
Church: 11648 E. County Rd. B, 54849. Tel: 715-374-3570.
Catechesis/Religious Program—Tammy Brown, D.R.E. Students 50.

LAKE TOMAHAWK, ONEIDA CO., ST. JOHN VIANNEY (1859) Closed. For inquiries for sacramental records please contact Holy Family, Woodruff.

LAND-O'-LAKES, VILAS CO., ST. ALBERT (1894), Also serves St. Mary, Phelps. Michele Rein, Parish Dir.; Deacon Norman J. Mesun Jr.
Mailing Address: P.O. Box 237, Land O'Lakes, 54540.
Church: 4351 Hwy. B, Land O'Lakes, 54540. Tel: 715-547-3558; Fax: 715-547-3614.
Catechesis/Religious Program—Students 21.

LUBLIN, TAYLOR CO., ST. STANISLAUS (1907), (Polish), [CEM] Rev. John R. Long.
Mailing Address: 315 E. Davlin St., Gilman, 54433.
Church: W13381 South St., 54447. Tel: 715-447-8510; Fax: 715-447-5742.
Catechesis/Religious Program—Sr. Marianna Ableidinger, F.S.P.A., D.R.E.

MANITOWISH WATERS, VILAS CO., OUR LADY QUEEN OF PEACE (1958) Rev. Lourdumar Reddy Mandapati.
Mailing Address: P.O. Box 325, 54545.
Church & Office: 193 S. Hwy. 51, 54545. Tel: 715-543-8428; Fax: 715-543-8428.
Catechesis/Religious Program—Veronica McGraw, D.R.E. Students 40.

MEDFORD, TAYLOR CO., OUR LADY OF THE HOLY ROSARY (1870) [CEM], Also serves Our Lady of Perpetual Help, Whittlesey. Rev. Gerard I. Willger; Deacon Joseph Stefancin, Pastoral Assoc.

Mailing Address: P.O. Box 503, 54451.
Church: 215 S. Washington Ave., 54451. Tel: 715-748-3336; Fax: 715-748-6643.
School—(Grades PreK-6) Fax: 715-748-5110. Tim Havican, Prin.; Mary Heboda, Librarian. Lay Teachers 14; Students 154.
Catechesis/Religious Program—Renata Kingsbury, C.R.E. Students 357.

MELLEN, ASHLAND CO., MOST HOLY ROSARY (1886), Also serves St. Anthony, Highbridge; St. Anne, Sanborn; Most Precious Blood, Glidden. Rev. William D. Brenna, Parochial Admin.
Mailing Address: P.O. Box 17, 54546.
Church: 203 N. Main St., 54546. Tel: 715-274-3701; Fax: 715-274-3703.
Worship Site: St. George—Summer Chapel: *St. George*, W. Hwy 77, Clam Lake, Grant & 2nd St., Clam Lake, 54517.
Catechesis/Religious Program—Vicky Ellias, C.R.E. Students 54.

MERCER, IRON CO., ST. ISAAC JOGUES AND COMPANIONS (1912) Rev. Lourdumar Reddy Mandapati; Deacon Norbert G. Brossmer.
Mailing Address: P.O. Box 575, 54547.
Church: 2611 W. Garnet St., 54547. Tel: 715-476-2697; Fax: 715-476-2704.
Catechesis/Religious Program—Margie Richards, D.R.E.

MERRILL, LINCOLN CO.
1—ST. FRANCIS XAVIER (1875) [CEM] Rev. Michael D. McLain; Deacon John E. Ramassini.
Church and Mailing Address: 1708 E. 10th St., 54452. Tel: 715-536-2803; Fax: 715-536-7536.
School—St. Francis, (Grades PreK-8) Tel: 715-536-6083. Jaclyn Behnke, Prin. Lay Teachers 15; Students 114.
Catechesis/Religious Program—Joseph Vilie, D.R.E. Students 221.
2—ST. ROBERT BELLARMINE (1886) Closed. For inquiries for sacramental records contact St. Francis Xavier, Merrill.

MINOCQUA, ONEIDA CO., ST. PATRICK (1894) [CEM] Closed. For inquiries for sacramental records, contact Holy Family, Woodruff.

MINONG, WASHBURN CO., ST. MARY (1904) Rev. James J. Kinney.
Mailing Address: P.O. Box 303, Solon Springs, 54873.
Office & Rectory: 11651 Business 53, Solon Springs, 54873.
Church: 506 Main St., 54859. Tel: 715-378-4431; Fax: 715-378-2480.
Catechesis/Religious Program—Pat Den Hartog, C.R.E.; Barbara Schuyler, D.R.E. Students 12.

MONTREAL, IRON CO., SACRED HEART OF JESUS (1904) Closed. For inquiries for parish records please see St. Mary of the Seven Dolors, Hurley.

MOQUAH, BAYFIELD CO., SS. PETER AND PAUL (1912) [CEM 2] Rev. Michael L. Crisp; John Grek.
Mailing Address: P.O. Box 97, Iron River, 54847.
Church: 23505 County Rd. G, 54806. Tel: 715-372-4756.
Catechesis/Religious Program—Kathy Huybrecht, C.R.E. Students 23.

NEW POST, SAWYER CO., ST. IGNATIUS (1884) Rev. Gregory J. Hopefl.
Mailing Address: 13891 W. Mission Rd., Stone Lake, 54876. Tel: 715-865-3669; Fax: 715-865-3669.
Catechesis/Religious Program—Sr. Felissa Zander, S.S.S.F., D.R.E.

NEW RICHMOND, ST. CROIX CO., IMMACULATE CONCEPTION (1883) [CEM], Also serves St. Patrick, Erin. Rev. James J. Brinkman; Deacon Michael J. Germain.
Church and Office Address: 151 S. Washington Ave., 54017-1523. Tel: 715-246-4652; Fax: 715-246-2526.
School—(Grades K-8), 257 S. Washington Ave., 54017. Tel: 715-246-2469; Fax: 715-246-6195. Mari Zarcone-Patterson, Prin. Lay Teachers 14; Students 109.
Catechesis/Religious Program—Kim Palmer, D.R.E.; Patty Berger, C.R.E. Students 276.

ODANAH, ASHLAND CO., ST. MARY (1855) Very Rev. Paul Pare, O.F.M.; Rev. Gary Bernhardt, O.F.M.; Sr. Phyllis Wilhelm, O.S.F., Pastoral Assoc.
Mailing Address: 106 N. Second Ave. E., Ashland, 54806. Tel: 715-682-7620; Fax: 715-682-7626.
Church: 300 Old Hwy. 2, 54861.
Catechesis/Religious Program—Students 3.

OSCEOLA, POLK CO., ST. JOSEPH (1915), Also serves Assumption of the Blessed Virgin Mary, Farmington. Rev. Thomas E. Thompson; Deacons Fred E. Johnson; Richard T. Peterson; Thomas P. Rausch.
Mailing Address: P.O. Box 399, 54020-0399.
Church: 255 10th Ave., 54020. Tel: 715-294-2243; Fax: 715-294-2495.
Catechesis/Religious Program—Tel: 715-294-4163. Gwen Nies, D.R.E. Students 150.

PARK FALLS, PRICE CO., ST. ANTHONY OF PADUA (1904), Also serves Immaculate Conception, Butternut; St. Francis of Assisi, Fifield. Rev. Daniel Gonzalez, Parochial Admin.; Deacon Chester E. Ball Jr.
Church and Mailing Address: 276 S. 5th Ave., 54552. Tel: 715-762-4494; Fax: 715-762-0079.
School—(Grades PreK-8), 200 S. 5th Ave., 54552. Tel: 715-762-4476. Michael Plemon, Prin. Lay Teachers 15; Students 129.
Catechesis/Religious Program— Jane Gustafson, D.R.E.; Ann Gotz, C.R.E. (1-6); Steve Eitrem, C.R.E. (7-9). Students 115.

PELICAN LAKE, ONEIDA CO., ST. JOHN (1905) [CEM] Rev. John R. Gerritts.
Mailing Address: 1350 N. Stevens St., Rhinelander, 54501.
Parish Office: 105 Pelham St., Rhinelander, 54501.
Church: Appleton St. & Cty. Hwy. B, 54463. Tel: 715-362-3169.
Catechesis/Religious Program—Madonna Jensen, D.R.E. Students 12.

PENCE, IRON CO., HOLY REDEEMER (1908) Closed. For inquiries for parish records please see St. Mary of the Seven Dolors, Hurley.

PHELPS, VILAS CO., ST. MARY (1908) Michele Rein, Parish Dir.; Deacon Norman J. Mesun Jr.
Mailing Address: P.O. Box 237, Land O'Lakes, 54540.
Church: 4494 Town Hall Rd., 54554. Tel: 715-547-3558; Fax: 715-547-3614.
Catechesis/Religious Program—Students 15.

PHILLIPS, PRICE CO., ST. THERESE OF LISIEUX (1876) [CEM], Also serves St. Paul The Apostle, Catawba; St. John The Baptist, Prentice. Rev. Gerald A. Hagen; Deacon James J. Celba.
125 N. Argyle Ave., 54555.
Church and Mailing Address: 655 S. Lake Ave., 54555. Tel: 715-339-2222; Fax: 715-339-2216.
Catechesis/Religious Program—Sherrie Kandutsch, C.R.E. Students 100.

PIER-WILLOW, ONEIDA CO., ST. FRANCIS OF ASSISI (1887) [CEM] Very Rev. John C. Anderson.
Mailing Address: 320 E. Washington Ave., Tomahawk, 54487.
Church: N. Willow Rd., Tripoli, 54564. Tel: 715-453-2878.
Catechesis/Religious Program—Brad O'Leary, D.R.E.

PRENTICE, PRICE CO., ST. JOHN THE BAPTIST (1886) Rev. Gerald A. Hagen.
Mailing Address: 125 N. Argyle Ave., Phillips, 54555.
Church: 935 Town St., 54556. Tel: 715-339-2222; Fax: 715-339-2216.
Catechesis/Religious Program—Gloria Lyons, C.R.E. Students 31.

PRESQUE ISLE, VILAS CO., ST. RITA (1950) Rev. Michael T. Hayden.
Mailing Address: P.O. Box 110, Boulder Junction, 54512.
Church: Lake St., 54557. Tel: 715-385-2390.
Catechesis/Religious Program—Sr. Constance Walton, F.S.P.A., D.R.E.

RADISSON, SAWYER CO., SACRED HEART (1919) Rev. J. Patrick Hardy, Parochial Admin.; Deacon James E. Frederick.
Mailing Address: P.O. Box 216, Winter, 54896.
Church: Hwy. 27, 54867. Tel: 715-266-3441; Fax: 715-266-3440.
Catechesis/Religious Program—Jill Petit, C.R.E.

RED CLIFF, BAYFIELD CO., ST. FRANCIS (1861) [CEM] Deacon Roger L. Cadotte, Parish Life Coord.; Rev. Aaron P. Kalmon, Sacramental Min.; Very Rev. Kevin M. Gordon, Weekend Sacramental Min.
Mailing Address: P.O. Box 1290, Bayfield, 54814.
Church: Church Rd., 54814. Tel: 715-779-3316; Fax: 715-779-9804.
Catechesis/Religious Program—

RESERVE, SAWYER CO., ST. FRANCIS OF SOLANUS (1885), (Indian), [CEM], Also serves St. Ignatius, New Post; St. Philip, Stone Lake. Rev. Gregory J. Hopefl.
Church and Mailing Address: 13891 W. Mission Rd., Stone Lake, 54876. Tel: 715-865-3669; Fax: 715-865-3669.
School—St. Francis Solanus, (Grades PreK-8), 13885 W. Mission Rd., Stone Lake, 54876. Tel: 715-865-3662; Fax: 715-865-4055. Sr. Felissa Zander, S.S.S.F., Prin. Sisters of St. Francis 2; Lay Teachers 1; Students 30.
Catechesis/Religious Program—Sr. Felissa Zander, S.S.S.F., D.R.E.

RHINELANDER, ONEIDA CO.
1—IMMACULATE CONCEPTION (1883) [CEM] Closed. For inquiries for sacramental records please contact Nativity of Our Lord, Rhinelander.
2—ST. JOSEPH'S (1909) [CEM] Closed. For inquiries for sacramental records contact Nativity of Our Lord, Rhinelander.
3—NATIVITY OF OUR LORD, Also serves St. John, Pelican Lake. Rev. John R. Gerritts; Deacons Ronald J. Bosi; Michael O. Harvey; Richard J. Meier; William D. Miller; Mathew C. Porten.
Mailing Address: 105 S. Pelham St., 54501. Tel: 715-362-3169; Fax: 715-362-1811. Email: stjoe@frontiernet.net.
Worship Sites:—
St. Mary—125 E. King St., 54501.
St. Joseph—1360 N. Stevens St., 54501.
School—(Grades PreK-8), North Bldg.: 1360 N. Stevens St., 54501. Tel: 715-362-3366. South Bldg. (Main Office): 103 E. King St., 54501. Tel: 715-362-5588; Fax: 715-362-0952. Shirley Heise, Prin. Lay Teachers 24; Students 323.
Catechesis/Religious Program—Joyce Wagner, C.R.E. (Grades 9-12); Lori Novak, D.R.E. (Grades 6-7); Patti Shepard, D.R.E. (Grades K-5). Students 173.

RIB LAKE, TAYLOR CO.
1—GOOD SHEPHERD Rev. Otto N. Bucher, O.F.M.Cap.; Deacon Mark E. Priniski.
Mailing Address: P.O. Box 295, 54470. Tel: 715-427-5259; Fax: 715-427-0381. Email: goodshepherd@newnorth.net.
Church: 513 State Rd., 54470.
Catechesis/Religious Program—Mary Kauer, C.R.E. Students 64.
2—ST. JOHN THE BAPTIST (1896) Closed. For inquiries for sacramental records, contact Good Shepherd, Rib Lake.

RICE LAKE, BARRON CO., ST. JOSEPH (1878) [CEM] Very Rev. James P. Powers; Deacon Dennis C. Geisler.
Church and Mailing Address: 111 W. Marshall St., 54868. Tel: 715-234-2032; Fax: 715-234-7757.
School—St. Joseph School, (Grades PreK-8), 128 W. Humbird St., 54868. Tel: 715-234-7721; Fax: 715-234-5062. Jill Bennett, Prin. Sisters 1; Lay Teachers 13; Students 180.
Catechesis/Religious Program—Rose Schullo, D.R.E.; Laura Schissel, C.R.E. Students 148.

RIVER FALLS, ST. CROIX CO., ST. BRIDGET (1854) [CEM], Also serves Immaculate Conception, Hammond. Rev. Gerald P. Harris; Deacons Lawrence P. Hennemann; Thomas J. Weiss.
Mailing Address: P.O. Box 86, 54022. Tel: 715-425-1870; Fax: 715-425-1871.
Church: 211 E. Division St., 54022.
School—(Grades PreK-8), 135 E. Division St., 54022. Tel: 715-425-1872; Fax: 715-425-1873. Sue Steckbauer, Prin. Lay Teachers 17; Students 163.
Catechesis/Religious Program—Tel: 715-425-1874. Diane Wengelski, C.R.E.; Tessa Schuermann, C.R.E.; Amy Zimniewicz, C.R.E. Students 477.

SANBORN, ASHLAND CO., ST. ANNE (1895) Rev. William D. Brenna, Parochial Admin.
Mailing Address: P.O. Box 17, Mellen, 54546.
Church: County Hwy. E, 54806. Tel: 715-274-3701; Fax: 715-274-3703.
Catechesis/Religious Program—Tom Henke, C.R.E. Students 5.

SARONA, WASHBURN CO., ST. CATHERINE (1917) Rev. Edwin C. Anderson, Parochial Admin.
Mailing Address: 409 Summit St., Spooner, 54801.
Church: W5262 County Hwy. D, 54870. Tel: 715-635-3105; Fax: 715-635-7341.
Catechesis/Religious Program—Susan Hughes, C.R.E. (1-8).

SAXON, IRON CO., ST. ANN (1886) Unassigned. Rev. Frank Kordek, O.F.M., Parochial Admin.
Mailing Address: P.O. Box 100, 54559.
Church: 14233 N. Church St., 54559. Tel: 715-893-2236.
Catechesis/Religious Program—Monica Kolpin, D.R.E. Students 24.

SAYNER, VILAS CO., ST. MARY (1912) Rev. Michael T. Hayden.
Mailing Address: P.O. Box 110, Boulder Junction, 54512.
Church: 2820 Hwy N, 54560. Tel: 715-542-3480.
Catechesis/Religious Program—Sr. Constance Walton, F.S.P.A., D.R.E.

SHELDON, RUSK CO., ST. JOHN THE APOSTLE (1955) Rev. John R. Long.
Mailing Address: 315 E. Davlin St., Gilman, 54433.
Church: N657 County Rd. VV, 54766. Tel: 715-447-8510; Fax: 715-447-5742.
Catechesis/Religious Program—Tel: 715-452-5374. Sr. Marianna Ableidinger, F.S.P.A., D.R.E. Students 30.

SHELL LAKE, WASHBURN CO., ST. JOSEPH (1880) [CEM] Rev. Edwin C. Anderson, Parochial Admin.
Mailing Address: 409 Summit St., Spooner, 54801.
Church: 502 N. 2nd St., 54871. Tel: 715-635-3105; Fax: 715-635-7341.
Catechesis/Religious Program—Susan Hughes, C.R.E. Students 29.

SOLON SPRINGS, DOUGLAS CO., ST. PIUS X (1878) [CEM], Also serves St. Anthony of Padua, Gordon; St. Mary, Minong. Rev. James J. Kinney.
Mailing Address: P.O. Box 303, 54873.
Church: 11651 Business 53, 54873. Tel: 715-378-4431; Fax: 715-378-2480.

Catechesis/Religious Program—Barbara Schuyler, C.R.E.; Pat Den Hartog, D.R.E. Students 9.

SOMERSET, ST. CROIX CO., ST. ANNE (1851) [CEM] Deacon Richard T. Peterson, Parish Life Coord.; Rev. Barg G. Anderson, Parochial Vicar; Deacon Lawrence E. Amell.
Mailing Address: P.O. Box 9, 54025.
Church: 141 Church Hill Rd., 54025. Tel: 715-247-3310; Fax: 715-247-3174.
School—(Grades PreK-8), 140 Church Hill Rd., 54025. Tel: 715-247-3762; Fax: 715-247-4335. Randall Stanke, Prin. Lay Teachers 13; Students 117.
Catechesis/Religious Program—Sara Measner, C.R.E.; Rachel McGurran, D.R.E. Students 139.

SPOONER, WASHBURN CO., ST. FRANCIS DE SALES (1886) [CEM 2], Also serves St. Joseph, Shell Lake; St. Catherine, Sarona. Rev. Edwin C. Anderson; Deacons Robert T. Jetto; Joseph J. Wesley; Gregory V. Ricci.
Church and Mailing Address: 409 Summit St., 54801. Tel: 715-635-3105; Fax: 715-635-7341.
School—(Grades PreK-8), 300 Oak St., 54801. Tel: 715-635-2774. Lay Teachers 8; Students 62.
Catechesis/Religious Program—Abbie Schmidt, C.R.E.; Carmen Halvorson, D.R.E. Students 120.

STANTON, ST. CROIX CO., ST. BRIDGET (1875) Closed. For inquiries for parish records please see St. Joseph, Amery.

STETSONVILLE, TAYLOR CO., SACRED HEART OF JESUS (1884) [CEM] Rev. Madanu Sleeva Raju, Parochial Admin.; Deacon Joseph F. Roe.
Church and Mailing Address: 322 W. Cty. Hwy. A, 54480. Tel: 715-678-2395; Fax: 715-678-2395.
Catechesis/Religious Program—Karleen Sperl, C.R.E. Students 37.

STONE LAKE, SAWYER CO., ST. PHILIP (1905) Rev. Gregory J. Hopefl.
Mailing Address: 13891 W. Mission Rd., 54876.
Church: 5750 W. Frost Ave., 54876. Tel: 715-865-3669; Fax: 715-865-3669.
Catechesis/Religious Program—Sr. Felissa Zander, S.S.S.F., D.R.E.

STRICKLAND, RUSK CO., ASSUMPTION OF THE BLESSED VIRGIN MARY (1897) [CEM] Deacons Michael D. Cullen, Parish Life Coord.; James E. Roberge.
Mailing Address: 827 E. LaSalle Ave., Barron, 54812.
Church: Old Hwy. 14, 54895. Tel: 715-637-3255; Fax: 715-637-3252.
Catechesis/Religious Program—Patty Gerber, C.R.E.

SUGAR CAMP, ONEIDA CO., ST. KUNEGUNDA (1892) [CEM] Rev. William G. Horath; Deacon Albert A. Goodrich.
Mailing Address: P.O. Box 8, Three Lakes, 54562.
Church: 6895 Hwy. 17 N., 54501. Tel: 715-272-1191; Fax: 715-546-4046.
Catechesis/Religious Program—Patricia Sand, C.R.E. Students 56.

THREE LAKES, ONEIDA CO., ST. THERESA (1892), Also serves St. Kunegunda of Poland, Sugar Camp. Rev. William G. Horath; Deacon John McCaughn.
Church and Mailing Address: 6990 Forest St., 54562. Tel: 715-546-2159; Fax: 715-546-4046.
Catechesis/Religious Program—Deacon Al Goodrich, D.R.E. Students 59.

TOMAHAWK, LINCOLN CO., ST. MARY (1887) [CEM], Also serves St. Francis of Assisi, Pier-Willow. Very Rev. John C. Anderson; Deacons David C. Bablick; Bernard J. Lyngdal; Darrell P. Smerz; Clifford F. Eggett.
Church and Mailing Address: 320 E. Washington Ave., 54487. Tel: 715-453-2878; Fax: 715-453-6678.
School—(Grades PreK-5), 221 E. Washington Ave., 54487. Tel: 715-453-3542. Sonia Doughty, Prin. Lay Teachers 11; Students 116.
Catechesis/Religious Program—Kay Berg, C.R.E.; Brad O'Leary, D.R.E. Students 118.

TONY, RUSK CO., ST. ANTHONY DE PADUA (1901) [CEM] Revs. Shaji Joseph Pazhukkathara, Parochial Admin.; Christopher J. Kemp.
Mailing Address: 611 1st St. S., Ladysmith, 54848.
Church: N5323 Maple St., 54563. Tel: 715-532-3051; Fax: 715-532-7368.
Catechesis/Religious Program—Students 27.

TURTLE LAKE, BARRON CO., ST. ANN (1882) [CEM 4] Rev. David R. Lusson.
Mailing Address: 900 St. Anthony St., Cumberland, 54829.
Church: 300 Pine St. S., 54889. Tel: 715-822-2948; Fax: 715-822-3588.
Catechesis/Religious Program—Mary DeNoyer, C.R.E.

WASHBURN, BAYFIELD CO., ST. LOUIS (1882) [CEM], Also serves Holy Family, Bayfield; St. Anne, Cornucopia; St. Joseph, La Pointe; St. Francis, Red Cliff. Rev. Aaron P. Kalmon; Very Rev. Kevin M. Gordon, Weekend Sacramental Min.; Deacon Kenneth D. Kasinski.
Mailing Address: Box 070, 54891. Tel: 715-373-2676; Fax: 715-373-0365.
Church: 217 W. 7th St., 54891.
Catechesis/Religious Program—Wendie Libert, C.R.E. Students 27.

WEBSTER, BURNETT CO., ST. JOHN THE BAPTIST (1880) [CEM], Also serves Sacred Hearts of Jesus and Mary, Crescent Lake; Our Lady of Perpetual Help, Danbury. Rev. Michael J. Tupa.
Mailing Address: P.O. Box 7, 54893.
Church: 26455 S. Muskey Ave., 54893. Tel: 715-866-7321; Fax: 715-866-7305.
Catechesis/Religious Program—Colleen Monfre, D.R.E. Students 40.

WESTBORO, TAYLOR CO., ST. THERESA (1904) Closed. For inquiries for sacramental records please contact Good Shepherd, Rib Lake.

WEYERHAEUSER, RUSK CO., SS. PETER AND PAUL (1897) [CEM] Revs. Shaji Joseph Pazhukkathara, Parochial Admin.; Christopher J. Kemp; Deacons Craig J. Voldberg; James E. Roberge; Thomas E. Fuhrmann.
Mailing Address: 611 1st St. S., Ladysmith, 54848.
Church: 251 First St., 54895. Tel: 715-532-3051; Fax: 715-532-7368.
Catechesis/Religious Program—Norbert Poch, Co-C.R.E.; Barbra Poch, Co-C.R.E. Students 16.

WHITTLESEY, TAYLOR CO., OUR LADY OF PERPETUAL HELP (1891) [CEM] Rev. Gerard I. Willger; Deacon Joseph Stefancin.
Mailing Address: P.O. Box 503, Medford, 54451.
Church: W5409 Whittlesey Ave., 54470. Tel: 715-748-3336; Fax: 715-748-6643.
Catechesis/Religious Program—Wendy Hartl, C.R.E. Students 42.

WILSON, ST. CROIX CO., ST. BRIDGET (1886) [CEM] Rev. Norbert D'Mello, C.S.C.
Mailing Address: 761 First St., Glenwood City, 54013.
Church: 120 Depot St., 54027. Tel: 715-265-7133 (Phone and Fax).
Catechesis/Religious Program—Bonnie Cronk, C.R.E. (K-12).

WINTER, SAWYER CO., ST. PETER (1908) [CEM], Also serves Sacred Heart, Radisson. Rev. J. Patrick Hardy, Parochial Admin.; Deacon James E. Frederick.
Mailing Address: P.O. Box 216, 54896.
Church: 5106 N. Main St., 54896. Tel: 715-266-3441; Fax: 715-266-3440.
Catechesis/Religious Program—Jill Petit, C.R.E.; Madeline Smith, C.R.E. Students 16.

WOODRUFF, ONEIDA CO.
1—HOLY FAMILY (2004) Revs. Thomas Thakadipuram; Aaron Devett, O.S.B.; Joan Laut, Pastoral Assoc.
Church & Office: 8950 County Rd. J., 54568. Tel: 715-356-6284; Fax: 715-356-2940.
Catechesis/Religious Program—Diana Maki, C.R.E.; Sharon Winter, C.R.E. Students 202.
2—OUR LADY QUEEN OF THE UNIVERSE (1955) [CEM] Closed. For inquiries for sacramental records please contact Holy Family, Woodruff.

Chaplains of Public Institutions

On Special or Other Diocesan Assignment:
Very Rev.—
Gordon, Kevin M., Episcopal Vicar for Clergy, Chancery Box 969, 54880.

Retired:
Rev. Msgrs.—
Heslin, Philip J., 1408 E. 2nd St., 54880. Tel: 715-398-6183
Meulemans, Edward G., Reflections, 2601 E. McKellips Rd., Apt. 2020, Mesa, AZ 85213. Tel: 480-969-3180
Revs.—
Briody, Hugh J., Woodmount, Ballinasloe, Co. Galway Ireland. Tel: 011-090-964-4439
Bromley, Vincent M., 700 College Ave., #128, Ladysmith, 54848. Tel: 715-415-0332
Brost, Frederick, 615 E. Allman St., Medford, 54451. Tel: 715-748-2141
Buttrick, Dean T., 46050 West Tahkodah Lake Rd., Cable, 54821. Tel: 715-798-3430
Byrne, Bernard M., 18634 Marcy St., Elkhorn, NE 68022-5604. Tel: 402-917-2095
Cary, William J., 1802 Dublin Tr., Apt. 36, Neenah, 54956. Tel: 920-486-7911
Dabruzzi, James S., WinterGreen, 1312 Wisconsin St., Apt. 119, Hudson, 54016. Tel: 715-381-2815
Dahlberg, Daniel J., V.G., 3095 E. Cty. Rd. B, Foxboro, 54836. Tel: 218-391-7058
Fraher, Leonard W., 804 Woodland Ln., New Richmond, 54017. Tel: 715-246-7855
Green, William H., 1912 E. 2nd St., Apt. A, 54880. Tel: 715-392-2399
Heinen, Virgil O., 1336 A Carriage Dr., Hudson, 54016. Tel: 715-381-9778
Hoffman, James A., 1291 Donald Dr., Arbor Vitae, 54568. Tel: 715-358-2936
Horath, James R., 1226 Seville Rd., Mosinee, 54455.
Hornung, Eugene H., Wisconsin Veteran's Home, 600 Mitchell Ave., 219A, King, 54946.
Kelchak, Joseph M., 4156 Oakmont Ct., Crown Point, IN 46307. Tel: 219-663-6726
Kleinheinz, Joseph L., 408 East St., Merrill, 54452.
Kowalski, Wladyslaw J., St. John the Baptist Parish (Peplin), 3308 Hwy. 153, Mosinee, 54455. Tel: 715-693-3604
Kraker, Lames J., P.O. Box 1247, 54568. Tel: 715-358-7785
Levra, Ronald W., Charles Hill Villa, 300 10th St. S., Apt. 108, Park Falls, 54552. Tel: 715-663-0073
Meulemans, Dennis T., 718 Holden Rd., Rib Lake, 54470. Tel: 715-728-3803; Fax: 715-427-0832
Murphy, William J., P.O. Box 13381, Hayward, 54843. Tel: 715-462-4165
Pakosta, Francis J., 222 W. Hampton Ave., Apt. 309, Milwaukee, 53217. Tel: 414-967-9680
Powell, Edward F., W6771 Branch Rd., Tomahawk, 54487-9230. Tel: 715-453-1357
Spanjers, John J., Summer Address: P.O. Box 118, Turtle Lake, 54889. Winter Address: 501 Cotton Creek Dr., Unit 601, Gulf Shores, AL 36542.
Speerstra, William F., 9896 Morgan Oaks Dr., #4, Minocqua, 54548-8713. Tel: 715-358-3424
Trinka, Joseph C., 475 Golfview Ln., Apt. 101, Amery, 54001.
Urban, Robert M., 1715 Oakes Ave., #4, 54880. Tel: 715-394-3479
Zepczyk, Gabriel C., 23515 County Rd. G, Ashland, 54806. Tel: 715-746-2549

Permanent Deacons:
Amell, Lawrence E., St. Anne, Somerset
Bablick, David C., St. Mary, Tomahawk
Ball, Chester E., Jr., St. Anthony, Park Falls
Bardos, John J., St. Anthony of Padua, Lac Du Flambeau
Bauer, Larry K., St. Joseph, Amery
Bosi, Ronald J., Nativity of Our Lord, Rhinelander
Braam, Peter R., (Retired), St. Patrick, Hudson
Brossmer, Norbert G., St. Isaac Joques and Companions, Mercer
Byrnes, Timothy J., St. Ann, Turtle Neck
Cabak, Russell E., St. Peter, Cameron
Cadotte, Roger L., Holy Family, Bayfield
Cameron, Howard, St. Patrick, Hudson
Campbell, Clarence L., Our Lady of the Lake, Ashland
Celba, James J., St. Therese of Lisieux, Phillips
Chammings, Robert J., Holy Assumption, Superior
Cullen, Michael D., St. Joseph, Barron
Dennis, James M., St. Boniface Parish, Chetek
Derrington, J. Patrick, St. Joseph, Amery
DiSera, David B., St. Joseph, Hayward
Drahos, Jerome J., Our Lady of Sorrows, Ladysmith
Drost, Harvey G., (Retired), Holy Trinity, Haugen
Eggett, Clifford, St. Mary, Tomahawk
Feind, Kevin L., St. Anthony, Superior
Frederick, James E., Sacred Heart, Radisson; St. Peter, Winter
Fuhrmann, Thomas E., Ss. Peter & Paul, Weyerhaeuser
Geisler, Dennis C., St. Joseph, Rice Lake
Germain, Michael J., Immaculate Conception, New Richmond
Gil de Lamadrid, Arthur, Cathedral of Christ the King, Superior
Goodrich, Albert A., St. Kunegunda of Poland, Sugar Camp
Gorman, Owen T., Our Lady of the Lake, Ashland
Grek, John E., St. Peter & St. Paul, Moquah
Harvey, Michael O., Nativity of Our Lord, Rhinelander
Heiser, Florian H., (Retired), St. Joseph, Amery
Hennemann, Lawrence P., St. Bridget, River Falls
Holzhaeuser, William J., Our Lady of the Lake, Ashland
Huntowski, Peter R., (Retired), Spooner
Jetto, Robert T., St. Francis de Sales Parish, Spooner
Johnson, Fred E., St. Joseph, Osceola
Kasinski, Kenneth D., St. Louis, Washburn
Kuehn, Timothy J., St. Francis Xavier, Superior
Leonhard, Richard D., Our Lady of Sorrows, Ladysmith
Lyngdal, Bernard J., (Retired), St. Mary, Tomahawk
Marczak, Stanley J., St. Dominic, Frederic
Martineau, Philip L., (Retired)
McCaughn, John, St. Theresa, Three Lakes
McKenna, Jack, (Retired)
Meier, Richard J., Nativity of Our Lord, Rhinelander
Mercier, Stanley J., (Retired)
Mesun, Norman J., Jr., St. Albert, Land O'Lakes
Miller, Gregg St. Patrick, Hudson

Miller, William D. Nativity of Our Lord, Rhinelander
Paron, Joseph F., Immaculate Conception, Hammond
Peterson, Richard T., St. Joseph, Osceola
Porten, Mathew C., Nativity of Our Lord, Rhinelander
Prinski, Mark, Good Shepherd, Rib Lake
Ramassini, John E., St. Francis Xavier, Merrill
Ricci, Gregory J., St. Francis de Sales, Spooner
Roberge, James E., (Retired)
Roe, Joseph F., Sacred Heart of Jesus, Stetsonville
Schienebeck, Robert L., St. Anthony of Padua, Park Falls; St. Francis of Assisi, Fifield
Smerz, Darrell P., (Retired)
Sorenson, Douglas L., Our Lady of Sorrows, Ladysmith
Stefancin, Joseph, Our Lady of the Holy Rosary, Medford
Towle, C. Dan, St. Augustine, Harrison
Tuttle, Wesley G., St. John the Baptist, Glenwood City
Voldberg, Craig J., Our Lady of Sorrows, Ladysmith
Weiss, Thomas J., St. Bridget Parish, River Falls
Wesley, Joseph J., St. Frances de Sales, Spooner

INSTITUTIONS LOCATED IN THE DIOCESE

[A] GENERAL HOSPITALS

SUPERIOR. *St. Mary's Hospital of Superior*, 3500 Tower Ave., 54880. Tel: 715-817-7014; Fax: 715-392-8395. Email: mary.shaw@essentiahealth.org. Web: www.stmaryshospitalsuperior.org. Mary C. Shaw, Admin & COO; Sara Lund, Mgr. Spiritual Care Dept. Bed Capacity 25; Patients Assisted Annually 50,338; Total Staff 211.

EAGLE RIVER. **Eagle River Memorial Hospital, Inc.*, 201 Hospital Rd., 54521. Tel: 715-356-8000; Fax: 715-356-6097. Email: amy.thompson@ministryhealth.org. Web: www.ministryhealth.org. Sheila Clough, Pres. Corporate Sponsor: Ministry Health Care, Inc. (Milwaukee, WI). Sponsored by the Sisters of the Sorrowful Mother. Bed Capacity 25; Patients Assisted Annually 22,007; Total Staff 106.

MERRILL. *Good Samaritan Health Center of Merrill, Wisconsin, Inc.*, 601 S. Center Ave., 54452. Tel: 715-536-5511; Fax: 715-539-2170. Kristine McGarigle, Pres. Bed Capacity 25; Patients Assisted Annually 27,000; Total Staff 212.

RHINELANDER. *Sacred Heart-St. Mary's Hospital*, 2251 N. Shore Dr., 54501. Tel: 715-361-2000; Fax: 715-361-4877. Ms. Monica Hilt, Regl. CEO. Sisters of the Sorrowful Mother; Corporate Sponsor: Ministry Health Care., Inc. (Milwaukee, WI). Bed Capacity 73; Patients Assisted Annually 91,783; Shared Staff Rhinelander & Tomahawk Hospitals 700.

TOMAHAWK. *Sacred Heart-St. Mary's Hospitals, Inc.*, 401 W. Mohawk Dr., 54487. Tel: 715-453-7700; Fax: 715-453-7716. Ms. Monica Hilt, Pres. Corporate Sponsor: Ministry Health Care, Inc. (Milwaukee, WI). Bed Capacity 14; Patients Assisted Annually 9,037; Shared Staff Rhinelander & Tomahawk Hospitals 700.

WOODRUFF. **The Howard Young Medical Center, Inc.*, 240 Maple St., P.O. Box 470, 54568. Tel: 715-356-8000; Fax: 715-356-6097. Web: www.ministryhealth.org. Sheila Clough, Pres. Corporate Sponsor: Ministry Health Care, Inc. (Milwaukee, WI). Sponsored by the Sisters of the Sorrowful Mother. Bed Capacity 99; Patients Assisted Annually (Includes Inpatient Admissions) 53,427; Staff 426.

[B] HOMES FOR AGED

SUPERIOR. *St. Francis Home, Inc.*, 1416 Cumming Ave., 54880. Tel: 715-394-6617; Fax: 715-394-5951. Email: tclayton@ccbsuperior.org. Mr. Brian K. Soland, M.A., Acting CEO.

MERRILL. *Bell Tower Residence, Inc.*, 1500 O'Day St., 54452. Tel: 715-536-5575; Fax: 715-536-1765. Email: dives@belltowerresidence.org. Web: www.belltowerresidence.org. Sr. Peggy Jackelen, S.C.S.C., Admin. Assisted Living residence for the elderly. Bed Capacity 90; Total in Residence 85; Total Assisted Annually 79; Total Staff 106.

WOODRUFF. **Dr. Kate Newcomb Convalescent Center, Inc.*, P.O. Box 470, 54568-0470. Tel: 715-356-8000; Fax: 715-356-6097. Sheila Clough, Pres. Sponsored by the Sisters of the Sorrowful Mother. Corporate Sponsor: Ministry Health Care, Inc. (Milwaukee, WI). Total Staff 19.

[C] CONVENTS AND RESIDENCES FOR SISTERS

HUDSON. *Carmel of the Sacred Heart*, 430 Laurel Ave., 54016. Tel: 715-386-2156; Fax: 715-386-6946. Email: carmelit@pressenter.com. Web: www.pressenter.com/~carmelit/. Sr. Lucia LaMontagne, O.Carm., Prioress. Sisters 6.

LADYSMITH. *Servants of Mary*, 1000 College Ave. W., P.O. Box 389, 54848-2199. Tel: 920-898-1142, Ext. 320; Fax: 866-422-2802. Email: info@servitesisters.org. Web: www.servitesisters.org. Sr. Theresa Sandok, O.S.M., Pres. Sisters 50.

MERRILL. *Sisters of Mercy of the Holy Cross*, 1400 O'Day St., 54452-3417. Tel: 715-539-1456; Fax: 715-539-1458. Email: provincialoffices@holycrosssisters.org. Web: www.holycrosssisters.org. Sr. Celine Goessl, S.C.S.C., Prov. Sisters 33.

[D] CATHOLIC CHARITIES BUREAU

SUPERIOR. *Catholic Charities Bureau, Inc.*, 1416 Cummings Ave., 54880. Tel: 715-394-6617; Fax: 715-394-5951. Web: www.ccbsuperior.org. Mr. Brian K. Soland, M.A., Exec. Dir.; William Anderson, CFO; Terry Hendrick, Dir. Devel. Svcs.; Marilyn Christopherson, Coord. Diocesan Rels.; Teresa Clayton, Admin. Coord.; Gary Valley, Dir. Housing.

Catholic Community Services, Inc., 1416 Cumming Ave., 54880. Tel: 715-394-6617; Fax: 715-394-5951. Terry Hendrick, Dir. Email: thendrick@ccbsuperior.org.

Challenge Center, Inc., 39 N. 25th St. E., 54880. Tel: 715-394-2771; Fax: 715-394-2100. Eugene Chuzles, Dir.

Challenge Center A, Inc. dba Deer Haven Group Home 3105 Cumming Ave., 54880. Tel: 715-394-2771; Fax: 715-394-2100. Eugene Chuzles, Dir.

Cypress Group Home, 1415 Cypress, 54880. Tel: 715-394-2771; Fax: 715-394-2100. Eugene Chuzles, Dir.

The Dove, Inc., 1416 Cumming Ave., 54880. Tel: 715-392-3133; Fax: 715-392-3190. Web: thedovesuperior.com. Greg Leiviska, Admin.

The Dove Agency, Inc., 1416 Cumming Ave., 54880. Tel: 715-392-3133; Fax: 715-392-3190. Web: thedovesuperior.com. Greg Leiviska, Admin.

Foster Grandparent Program (NW WI, NE MN), 1416 Cumming Ave., 54880. Tel: 715-394-5384; Fax: 715-394-5951. Jennifer Jubenville, Dir.

Harborview Group Home, 910 E. 5th St., 54880. Tel: 715-394-2771; Fax: 715-394-2100. Eugene Chuzles, Dir.

Housing Counseling Program, 1416 Cumming Ave., 54880. Tel: 715-394-6617; Fax: 715-394-5951. Web: www.ccbsuperior.org. Sandy Carlson, Dir.

McKenzie Manor, 3317 N. 21st St., 54880. Tel: 715-394-2771; Fax: 715-394-2100. Eugene Chuzles, Dir.

Missouri Gardens Adult Family Home, 2347 Missouri Ave., 54880. Tel: 715-394-2771; Fax: 715-394-2100. Eugene Chuzles, Dir.

Mountain View Group Home, 3319 N. 16th St., 54880. Tel: 715-394-2771; Fax: 715-394-2100. Eugene Chuzles, Dir.

Phoenix Villa, Inc., 1100 Weeks Ave., 54880. Tel: 715-394-6617; Fax: 715-394-5951. Gary Valley, Dir.

Phoenix Villa, Inc. dba Elmwood Apartments 1020 Weeks Ave., 54880. Tel: 715-394-6617; Fax: 715-394-5951. Gary Valley, Dir.

Phoenix Villa of Superior, Inc. dba Oakwood Apartments 1112 John Ave., 54880. Tel: 715-394-6617; Fax: 715-394-5951. Gary Valley, Dir.

Retired Senior Volunteer Program, 1416 Cumming Ave., 54880. Tel: 715-394-4425; Fax: 715-394-5951. Joan Nurminen, Dir.

Superior Housing Alliance, 1416 Cumming Ave., 54880. Tel: 715-394-6617; Fax: 715-394-5951. Terry Hendrick, Dir.

Westbay, Inc., 1104 John Ave., 54880. Tel: 715-394-6617; Fax: 715-394-5951. Gary Valley, Dir.

Woodview Adult Family Home, 6001 E. Third St., 54880. Tel: 715-394-2771; Fax: 715-394-2100. Eugene Chuzles, Dir.

AMERY. *Apple River, Inc.*, 401 Minneapolis Ave. S., 54001. Tel: 715-925-2015; Fax: 715-925-2014. Mailing Address: 1416 Cumming Ave., 54880. Diane Weiss, Mgr.

CHETEK. *Phoenix Villa, Inc. dba Evergreen Apartments* 707 Tainter St., 54728. Tel: 715-925-2015; Fax: 715-925-2014. Mailing Address: 1416 Cumming Ave., 54880. Diane Weiss, Mgr.

CRANDON. *Phoenix Villa, Inc. dba Acorn Apartments* 508 W. Washington, 54520. Tel: 715-369-2550; Fax: 715-369-5857. Mailing Address: 1416 Cumming Ave., 54880. Paula Braun, Mgr.

CUMBERLAND. *Phoenix Villa, Inc. dba Phoenix Villa North* 1490 Arcade, 54829. Tel: 715-925-2015; Fax: 715-925-2014. Mailing Address: 1416 Cumming Ave., 54880. Diane Weiss, Mgr.

DULUTH. *Northfield Apartments, Inc.*, 2713 W. Superior St., MN 55806. Tel: 715-394-6617; Fax: 715-394-5951. Mailing Address: 1416 Cumming Ave., 54880. Gary Valley, Dir.

HAYWARD. *Phoenix Villa, Inc. dba Phoenix Villa of Hayward* 15869 Muriel St., 54843. Tel: 715-236-2366; Fax: 715-236-3161. Mailing Address: 1416 Cumming Ave., 54880. Cindy Lawrie, Mgr.

HUDSON. *United Day Care, Inc. dba Hudson Community Children's Center* 824 Fourth St., 54016. Tel: 715-386-5912; Fax: 715-386-1467. Mailing Address: 1416 Cumming Ave., 54880. Linda Groom, Dir.

IRON RIVER. *Phoenix Villa, Inc. dba Phoenix Villa of Iron River* 62155 Cty Rd. H, 54847. Tel: 715-394-6617; Fax: 715-394-5951. Mailing Address: 1416 Cumming Ave., 54880. Gary Valley, Dir.

LAKE NEBAGAMON. *Phoenix Villa, Inc. dba Phoenix Villa of Lake Nebagamon* 6250 S. Fitch Ave., 54849. Tel: 715-394-6617; Fax: 715-394-5951. Mailing Address: 1416 Cumming Ave., 54880. Gary Valley, Dir.

MEDFORD. *Black River Industries, Inc.*, 650 Jensen Dr., 54451. Tel: 715-748-2950; Fax: 715-748-6363. Web: www.blackriverindustries.org. Mailing Address: 1416 Cumming Ave., 54880. Paul Thornton, Dir.

Eastwood Apartments, Inc., 741-755 Del Rae Ct., 54451. Tel: 715-369-2550; Fax: 715-369-5857. Mailing Address: 1416 Cumming Ave., 54880. Paula Braun, Mgr.

Phoenix Villa, Inc. dba Maywood Apartments 521 Lemke Ave., 54451. Tel: 715-369-2550; Fax: 715-369-5857. Mailing Address: 1416 Cumming Ave., 54880. Paula Braun, Mgr.

MINONG. *Phoenix Villa, Inc. dba Acorn Apartments* 405 2nd St., 54859. Tel: 715-236-2366; Fax: 715-236-3161. Mailing Address: 1416 Cumming Ave., 54880. Cindy Lawrie, Mgr.

PLOVER. *Phoenix Villa, Inc. dba Maywood Apartments* 2601 Madison Ave., 54467. Tel: 715-341-7616; Fax: 715-712-0387. Mailing Address: 1416 Cumming Ave., 54880. Teri Obermeier, Mgr.

RHINELANDER. *Phoenix Villa, Inc. aka Evergreen Apartments/Timberlane* 880 E. Timber Dr., 54501. Tel: 715-369-2550; Fax: 715-369-5857. Mailing Address: 1416 Cumming Ave., 54880. Paula Braun, Mgr.

Headwaters. Inc., 1441 E. Timber Dr., P.O. Box 618, 54501. Tel: 715-369-1337; Fax: 715-369-1793. Web: www.headwatersinc.org. Mailing Address: 1416 Cumming Ave., 54880. Mary Hardtke, Dir.

Phoenix Villa, Inc. dba Phoenix Villa of Rhinelander 1011 Mason St., 54501. Tel: 715-369-2550; Fax: 715-369-5857. Mailing Address: 1416 Cumming Ave., 54880. Paula Braun, Mgr.

Retired Senior Volunteer Program, 1835 N. Stevens St., Ste. 22, 54501. Tel: 715-362-1919. Mailing Address: 1416 Cumming Ave., 54880. Lori Bushong, Dir.

Sumac Trail Apartments, Inc., 1313 Phillip St., 54501. Tel: 715-369-2550; Fax: 715-369-5857. Mailing Address: 1416 Cumming Ave., 54880. Paula Braun, Mgr.

RICE LAKE. *Blue Valley, Inc.*, 1310 N. Wisconsin Ave., 54868. Tel: 715-236-2366; Fax: 715-236-3161. Mailing Address: 1416 Cumming Ave., 54880. Cindy Lawrie, Mgr.

Phoenix Villa, Inc. dba Phoenix Villa North 1305 N. Wisconsin St., 54868. Tel: 715-236-2366; Fax: 715-236-3161. Mailing Address: 1416 Cumming Ave., 54880. Cindy Lawrie, Mgr.

SHELL LAKE. *Phoenix Villa, Inc. dba Evergreen Apartments* 797 N. Lake Dr., 54871. Tel: 715-236-2366; Fax: 715-236-3161. Mailing Address: 1416 Cumming Ave., 54880. Cindy Lawrie, Mgr.

SIREN. *Diversified Services Center, Inc.*, 7649 Tower Rd., P.O. Box 501, 54872. Tel: 715-349-5724; Fax: 715-349-5505. Web: www.sirentel.net/~dsi. Mailing Address: 1416 Cumming Ave., 54880. Joe Wacek, Dir.

Lilac Grove Apartments, Inc., 24145 1st Ave., 54872. Tel: 715-925-2015; Fax: 715-925-2014. Email: pkohnen@ccbsuperior.org. Mailing Address: 1416 Cumming Ave., 54880. Diane Weiss, Mgr. Apartments (Low-Income) 14.

Phoenix Villa, Inc. dba Evergreen Apartments/Lakewood 24121 Fourth St., 54872. Tel: 715-925-2015; Fax: 715-925-2014. Mailing Address: 1416 Cumming Ave., 54880. Diane Weiss, Mgr.

WINTER. *Winterhaven Apartments, Inc.*, 5038 N. Ellen St., 54896. Tel: 715-236-2366; Fax: 715-236-3161. Mailing Address: 1416 Cumming Ave., 54880. Cindy Lawrie, Mgr.

WISCONSIN RAPIDS. *Phoenix Villa, Inc. dba Acorn Apartments* 2721 Tenth St. S., 54494. Tel: 715-236-2366; Fax: 715-236-3161. Mailing Address: 1416 Cumming Ave., 54880. Cindy Lawrie, Mgr.

[E] RETREAT HOUSES

AMERY. *Mount Carmel Hermitage*, 897 U.S. Hwy. 8, 54001-2541. Tel: 715-268-9313; Fax: 715-268-9313. Email: mtcarmel@amerytel.net. Sr. Kristine Haugen, O.C.D.H., Coord.

ARBOR VITAE. *Marywood Franciscan Spirituality Center (FSPA)*, 3560 Hwy. 51 N., 54568-9538. Tel: 715-385-3750; Fax: 715-385-9118. Email: marywood.center@gmail.com. Web: www.marywoodsc.com. Sr. Elizabeth Amman, O.P., Dir.

[F] NEWMAN CENTERS

SUPERIOR. *Superior-UW* 823 N. 16th St., 54880. Tel: 715-394-7710. Email: newmancenter@centurytel.net. Newman Center Ministry to Young Adults.

RIVER FALLS. *St. Thomas More Newman Center* 423 E. Cascade, 54022. Tel: 715-425-7234; Fax: 715-425-6959. Email: thomas.j.weiss@uwrf.edu. Web: uwrfnewman.org. Deacon Thomas J. Weiss, Coord. for Newman Min.

[G] ASSOCIATION OF THE FAITHFUL

AMERY. *Hermits of Mt. Carmel*, 897 Hwy. 8, 54001-2541. Tel: 715-268-9313; Fax: 715-268-9313. Email: mtcarmel@amerytel.net. Sr. Kristine Haugen, O.C.D.H., Coord. Email: mtcarmel@amerytel.net.

[H] MISCELLANEOUS

SUPERIOR. *Society of St. Vincent de Paul Sacred Heart of Jesus Conference of Superior, WI*, 1416 Cumming Ave, 54880. Tel: 715-394-6617. Elizabeth Gaynor, Pres.

LADYSMITH. *Pooled Investment Trust of the Servants of Mary, Inc.*, 1000 College Ave. W., P.O. Box 389, 54848-0389. Tel: 920-898-1142, Ext. 320; Fax: 866-422-2802. Scott Wallenfelsz, Finance Dir.& Contact Person.

Mary Bradley Corporation, 1000 College Ave. W., P.O. Box 389, 54848-2199. Tel: 920-898-1142, Ext. 320; Fax: 866-422-2802. Sr. Theresa Sandok, O.S.M., Pres.

Servants of Mary Continuing Care Trust, 1000 College Ave. W., P.O. Box 389, 54848. Tel: 920-898-1142, Ext. 320; Fax: 866-422-2802. Email: smueller@salvatoriancenter.com. Rev. Scott Wallenfelsz, S.D.S., OSM Fin. Dir.

MERRILL. *Good Samaritan Health Center Foundation of Merrill, Wisconsin, Inc.* A not for profit corporation for the purpose of soliciting and receiving contributions for the benefit of Good Samaritan Health Center of Merrill, WI, Inc., 601 S. Center Ave., 54452. Tel: 715-536-5511; Fax: 715-539-2170. Kristine McGarigle, Pres. Corporate Sponsor: Ministry Healthcare, Inc. Sponsored by Sisters of the Sorrowful Mother.

Sisters of Mercy of the Holy Cross Community Support Charitable Trust, 1400 O'Day St., 54452-3417. Tel: 715-539-1460; Fax: 715-539-1458. Email: gsbr@juno.com. Sisters Pat Cormack, S.C.S.C., Trustee; Rose Jochmann, O.S.F., Trustee; Grace Sbrissa, C.S.J., Trustee; John Tortolani, Trustee; Craig Nienow, Trustee.

RHINELANDER. **Ministry Medical Group, Inc.*, 2251 N. Shore Dr., 54501. Tel: 715-361-4700; 800-866-8673; Fax: 715-361-4877. Email: kathy.richards@ministryhealth.org. Web: www.ministryhealth.org. Stewart Watson, Pres. & CEO; Kathy Richards-Bess, Regl. Admin. Corporate Sponsor: Ministry Health Care, Inc., Milwaukee, WI.

Ministry Weight Mgmt., St. Mary's Hospital, 2251 N. Shore Dr., 54501. Tel: 715-361-2000; Fax: 715-361-2011. Duane Stefonek, Dir.

WEBSTER. *Thomas More Center for Preaching and Prayer, Inc.*, 27781 Leef Rd., 54893. Tel: 715-866-7436. Web: www.thomasmorecenter.org. Revs. Michael A. Champlin, O.P., Pres.; Nicholas W. Punch, O.P., Treas.; Sr. Joan Bukrey, O.S.F., Vice Pres.

WINTER. *Camp WeHaKee* (Girls), 8104 N. Barker Lake Rd., 54896. Tel: 715-266-3263; 800-582-2267; Fax: 608-787-8257. Email: info@wehakeecampforgirls.com. Web: www.wehakeecampforgirls.com. Bob Braun, Co-Dir.; Maggie Braun, Co-Dir.

WOODRUFF. **Howard Young Health Care, Inc.*, 240 Maple St., P.O. Box 470, 54568. Tel: 715-356-8000; Fax: 715-356-6097. Web: www.ministryhealth.org. Sheila Clough, Pres. Corporate Sponsor: Ministry Health Care, Inc. (Milwaukee, WI). Sponsored by the Sisters of the Sorrowful Mother. Total Staff 14.

RELIGIOUS INSTITUTES OF MEN REPRESENTED IN THE DIOCESE

For further details refer to the corresponding bracketed number in the Religious Institutes of Men or Women section.

[0200]—*Benedictine Monks*—O.S.B.

[0470]—*Capuchin Franciscan Friars*—O.F.M.Cap.

[]—*Congregatio Filiorum Immaculate Conceptionis*—C.F.I.C.

[0480]—*Conventual Franciscans* (Arroyo Grande, CA)—O.F.M.Conv.

[0520]—*Franciscan Friars* (St. Louis, MO)—O.F.M.

[0430]—*Order of Preachers-Province of St. Albert the Great* Chicago—O.P.

[0610]—*Priests of the Congregation of the Holy Cross* (Indian Province, Inc.)—C.S.C.

RELIGIOUS INSTITUTES OF WOMEN REPRESENTED IN THE DIOCESE

[0320]—*Carmelite Nuns of the Ancient Observance*—O.Carm.

[1780]—*Congregation of the Sisters of the Third Order of St. Francis of Perpetual Adoration (Franciscan Sis*—F.S.P.A.

[1710]—*Congregation of the Third Order of St. Francis of Mary Immaculate* (Joilet, IL)—O.S.F.

[1070-13]—*Dominican Sisters of Adrian*—O.P.

[1070-40]—*Dominican Sisters of Grand Rapids*—O.P.

[]—*School Sisters of Notre Dame* (Central Pacific Province)—S.S.N.D.

[1680]—*School Sisters of St. Francis*—S.S.S.F.

[3590]—*Servants of Mary (Servite Sisters)*—O.S.M.

[2630]—*Sisters of Mercy of the Holy Cross*—S.C.S.C.

[1705]—*Sisters of St. Francis of Penance Charity*

[1570]—*Sisters of St. Francis of the Holy Family*—O.S.F.

[3840]—*Sisters of St. Joseph of Carondelet* (Prov. of St. Paul)—C.S.J.

[3930]—*Sisters of St. Joseph of the Third Order of St. Francis* (Prov. of Immaculate Conception; St. Joseph Prov.)—S.S.J.-T.O.S.F.

[4100]—*Sisters of the Sorrowful Mother* (Third Order of St. Francis)—S.S.M.

[1720]—*Sisters of the Third Order Regular of St. Francis of the Congregation of Our Lady of Lourdes*—O.S.F.

NECROLOGY

† Verdegan, Albert L., (Retired)—Died Feb. 22, 2011

† Votruba, George L., (Retired)—Died Jan. 22, 2011

An asterisk (*) denotes an organization that has established tax-exempt status directly with the IRS and is not covered by the USCCB Group Ruling.

Diocese of Syracuse

(Dioecesis Syracusensis)

Most Reverend

ROBERT JOSEPH CUNNINGHAM

Bishop of Syracuse; ordained May 24, 1969; appointed Bishop of Ogdensburg March 9, 2004; ordained and installed May 18, 2004; appointed Bishop of Syracuse April 21, 2009; installed as Tenth Bishop of Syracuse May 26, 2009. *Office: 240 E. Onondaga St., Syracuse, NY 13202.*

Chancery Office: 240 E. Onondaga, Syracuse, NY 13202. Tel: 315-422-7203; Fax: 315-478-4619.

Most Reverend

JAMES M. MOYNIHAN, D.D.

Retired Bishop of Syracuse; ordained December 15, 1957; appointed Bishop of Syracuse April 4, 1995; consecrated and installed in See of Syracuse May 29, 1995; retired April 21, 2009. *Mailing Address: 240 E. Onondaga St., Syracuse, NY 13202. Res.: 420 Montgomery St., Syracuse, NY 13202.*

Most Reverend

THOMAS J. COSTELLO, D.D., V.G.

Retired Auxiliary Bishop of Syracuse; ordained June 5, 1954; appointed Auxiliary Bishop of Syracuse and Titular Bishop of Perdices January 10, 1978; consecrated March 13, 1978; retired March 23, 2004. *Res.: 1515 Midland Ave., Syracuse, NY 13205.*

ESTABLISHED NOVEMBER 26, 1886

Square Miles 5,749.

Corporate Title: The Roman Catholic Diocese of Syracuse NY.

Comprises the Counties of Broome, Chenango, Cortland, Madison, Oneida, Onondaga and Oswego.

For legal titles of parishes and diocesan institutions, consult the Chancery Office.

STATISTICAL OVERVIEW

Personnel	
Bishop	1
Retired Bishops	2
Priests: Diocesan Active in Diocese	128
Priests: Diocesan Active Outside Diocese	7
Priests: Retired, Sick or Absent	85
Number of Diocesan Priests	220
Religious Priests in Diocese	37
Total Priests in Diocese	257
Extern Priests in Diocese	15
Ordinations:	
Diocesan Priests	1
Permanent Deacons in Diocese	85
Total Brothers	10
Total Sisters	301
Parishes	
Parishes	133
With Resident Pastor:	
Resident Diocesan Priests	103
Resident Religious Priests	5
Without Resident Pastor:	
Administered by Priests	25
Missions	11
Welfare	
Catholic Hospitals	3
Total Assisted	675,000
Health Care Centers	2
Total Assisted	400,000
Homes for the Aged	54
Total Assisted	2,500
Specialized Homes	3
Total Assisted	148
Special Centers for Social Services	2
Total Assisted	1,750
Residential Care of Disabled	14
Total Assisted	210
Educational	
Diocesan Students in Other Seminaries	16
Seminaries, Religious	1
Students Religious	14
Total Seminarians	30
Colleges and Universities	1
Total Students	3,502
High Schools, Diocesan and Parish	5
Total Students	1,591
High Schools, Private	1
Total Students	740
Elementary Schools, Diocesan and Parish	18
Total Students	3,012
Catechesis/Religious Education:	
High School Students	6,315
Elementary Students	20,672
Total Students under Catholic Instruction	35,862
Teachers in the Diocese:	
Priests	1
Brothers	2
Sisters	16
Lay Teachers	387
Vital Statistics	
Receptions into the Church:	
Infant Baptism Totals	2,963
Minor Baptism Totals	126
Adult Baptism Totals	130
Received into Full Communion	319
First Communions	3,285
Confirmations	3,222
Marriages:	
Catholic	701
Interfaith	277
Total Marriages	978
Deaths	4,024
Total Catholic Population	274,500
Total Population	1,170,374

Former Bishops—Rt. Revs. PATRICK ANTHONY LUDDEN, D.D., ord. June 21, 1864; cons. May 1, 1887; died Aug. 6, 1912; JOHN GRIMES, D.D., ord. Feb. 19, 1882; cons. May 16, 1909; Coadjutor Bishop, 1909-1912; succeeded to the See, Aug. 6, 1912; died July 26, 1922; Most Revs. DANIEL JOSEPH CURLEY, D.D., ord. May 19, 1894; cons. May 1, 1923; died Aug. 3, 1932; JOHN ALOYSIUS DUFFY, D.D., ord. June 13, 1908; cons. June 29, 1933; installed July 11, 1933; appt. Bishop of Buffalo, Jan. 9, 1937; installed in See of Buffalo, April 14, 1937; died Sept. 27, 1944; WALTER A. FOERY, D.D., Ph.D., ord. June 10, 1916; appt. May 26, 1937; cons. Aug. 18, 1937; appt. assistant at the Pontifical Throne, Dec. 11, 1961; retired and named Titular Bishop of Miseno-Cape, Aug. 4, 1970; died May 10, 1978; DAVID F. CUNNINGHAM, D.D., ord. June 12, 1926; appt. Titular Bishop of Lampsacus and Auxiliary Bishop of Syracuse, April 5, 1950; cons. June 8, 1950; appt. Coadjutor Bishop "Cum jure successiones," June 19, 1967; succeeded to the See, Aug. 4, 1970; died Feb. 22, 1979; FRANK J. HARRISON, D.D., ord. June 4, 1937; appt. Titular Bishop of Aquae and Auxiliary Bishop of Syracuse, March 1, 1971; cons. April 22, 1971; appt. Bishop of Syracuse, Nov. 16, 1976; retired June 16, 1987; died May 1, 2004; JOSEPH T. O'KEEFE, D.D., ord. April 17, 1948; appt. Titular Bishop of Tre Taverne and Auxiliary Bishop of New York, July 3, 1982; cons. Sept. 8, 1982; appt. Bishop of Syracuse, June 16, 1987; installed in See of Syracuse, Aug. 3, 1987; retired April 4, 1995; died Sept. 2, 1997; JAMES M. MOYNIHAN, ord. Dec. 15, 1957; appt. Bishop of Syracuse April 4, 1995; cons. and installed in See of Syracuse May 29, 1995; retired April 21, 2009.

Vicar General—Rev. Msgr. J. ROBERT YEAZEL, V.G., Res.: Holy Cross, 4112 E. Genesee St., DeWitt, 13214.

Vicars Forane—Northern Area Vicar: Rev. GAETANO T. BACCARO, St. Paul, 50 E. Mohawk St., Oswego, 13126. Southern Area Vicar: Rev. JOHN P. PUTANO, 157 Clark St., Vestal, 13850. Eastern Area Vicars: Revs. PHILIP A. HEARN, 105 E. Liberty St., Rome, 13440; JOSEPH A. SALERNO, 2 Barton Ave., Utica, 13502. Western Area Vicars: Rev. Msgr. RICHARD M. KOPP, 240 E. Onondaga St., Syracuse, 13202; Rev. JAMES T. O'BRIEN, St. John's, 8290 Soule Rd., Liverpool, 13090-1399.

Chancery Office—Mailing Address: 240 E. Onondaga St., Syracuse, 13202. Tel: 315-422-7203; Fax: 315-478-4619. Office Hours: Mon.-Fri. 8:30-4:30; Send official mail, including marriage dispensations, to Chancery.

Chancellor—Rev. TIMOTHY S. ELMER, J.C.L., 240 E. Onondaga St., Syracuse, 13202.

Assistant Chancellor—Mrs. DANIELLE CUMMINGS, 240 E. Onondaga St., Syracuse, 13202.

Board of Diocesan Consultors—Rev. PHILIP A. HEARN; Rev. Msgr. RICHARD M. KOPP; Revs. JAMES P. LANG; GAETANO T. BACCARO; JAMES T. O'BRIEN; JOSEPH A. SALERNO; JOHN P. PUTANO; Rev. Msgr. J. ROBERT YEAZEL, V.G.; Rev. TIMOTHY S. ELMER, J.C.L.

Management Team—Most Rev. ROBERT J. CUNNINGHAM, J.C.L., D.D.; Revs. JAMES P. LANG; TIMOTHY S. ELMER, J.C.L.; JOSEPH H. PHILLIPS; JOSEPH E. SCARDELLA; Mrs. CATHERINE CORNUE; Mr. JOHN BARSANTI; Mr. CHRISTOPHER PARKER; Mr. CHRISTOPHER MOMINEY; Mr. ROBERT WALTERS; Mr. JOSEPH G. SLAVIK; Sr. GRACE ANNE DILLENSCHNEIDER, O.S.F.; Mrs. DANIELLE CUMMINGS.

Pastoral Council—Most Rev. ROBERT J. CUNNINGHAM, J.C.L., D.D., Pres.; Ms. KATHLEEN M. DYER, Exec. Sec., Res.: 101 Ridge Rd., Fulton, 13069. Tel: 315-592-5566.

Presbyteral Council—Most Rev. ROBERT J. CUNNINGHAM, J.C.L., D.D., Pres.; Revs. GAETANO T. BACCARO; JOHN CANARRO; PAUL V. CAREY; CHRISTOPHER CELENTANO; JOHN D. MANNO; JAMES H. CAREY; JOHN J. KURGAN; DONALD H. KARLEN; TIMOTHY S. ELMER, J.C.L.; PHILIP A. HEARN; Rev. Msgr. RICHARD M. KOPP; Revs. JAMES P. LANG; JAMES T. O'BRIEN; DANIEL J. MULHAUSER, S.J.; ROBERT L. KELLY; JOHN P. PUTANO; BRAD MILUNSKI; JOSEPH A. SALERNO; Rev. Msgr. J.

ROBERT YEAZEL, V.G.

Diocesan Tribunal—

*Judicial Vicar—*Rev. TIMOTHY S. ELMER, J.C.L. Tel: 315-470-1480; Fax: 315-474-6893.

*Adjutant Judicial Vicar—*Rev. JOHN P. DONOVAN, J.C.L.

*Defender of the Bond—*Rev. CLIFFORD H. AUTH, J.C.L.

*Promoters of Justice—*Rev. Msgr. JAMES A. McCLOSKEY (Retired); Rev. ROBERT P. HYDE, J.C.L.

*Notary of the Tribunal—*BARBARA REITER.

*Case Coordinator/Staff—*BARBARA REITER.

*Vicar for Administration—*Rev. TIMOTHY S. ELMER, J.C.L., 240 E. Onondaga St., Syracuse, 13202. Tel: 315-470-1435.

*Director for Community Services—*Mr. JOSEPH G. SLAVIK, Dir., 240 E. Onondaga St., Syracuse, 13202. Tel: 315-470-1415.

*Vicar for Parishes—*Rev. JAMES P. LANG, 240 E. Onondaga St., Syracuse, 13202. Tel: 315-470-1437.

*Vicar for Priests—*Rev. Msgr. RICHARD M. KOPP, 240 E. Onondaga St., Syracuse, 13202. Tel: 315-470-1460.

*Vicar for Religious—*Sr. GRACE ANNE DILLENSCHNEIDER, O.S.F., 240 E. Onondaga St., Syracuse, 13202. Tel: 315-470-1005.

Diocesan Offices

*Accounting—*CAROL PIEKLIK, Mailing Address: 240 E. Onondaga St., Syracuse, 13202. Tel: 315-422-9045; Fax: 315-422-9139.

*Administration—*Rev. TIMOTHY S. ELMER, J.C.L., Vicar; Mr. JOHN BARSANTI, COO, Mailing Address: 240 E. Onondaga St., Syracuse, 13202. Tel: 315-422-7203.

*Archives—*Ms. MICKEY BRUCE, Archivist, Mailing Address: 240 E. Onondaga St., Syracuse, 13202. Tel: 315-470-1493. Email: syrarchivesed@aol.com.

*Asian Apostolate—*Rev. JOHN BOSCO PHAM TRUNG THUC, Chap.; Sr. JUDITH HOWLEY, C.S.J., 215 N. State St., Syracuse, 13203. Tel: 315-472-7043.

*Benefits—*Ms. ROSEMARY SMITH, Admin., Mailing Address: 240 E. Onondaga St., Syracuse, 13202. Tel: 315-422-9091.

*Boy Scouts/Girl Scouts—*Rev. JAMES P. LANG, Chap., 240 E. Onondaga St., Syracuse, 13202. Tel: 315-470-1437.

*Building Commission—*Most Rev. ROBERT J. CUNNINGHAM, J.C.L., D.D.; Revs. TIMOTHY S. ELMER, J.C.L.; JOSEPH E. SCARDELLA; Mr. EDWARD T. KING; Mr. JAMES W. MERRILL; Rev. Msgr. RICHARD M. KOPP; Rev. JAMES P. LANG; Mr. JOHN BARSANTI.

*Catholic Cemeteries—*Mr. MARK LAZAROSKI, Dir., 2315 South Ave., Syracuse, 13207. Tel: 315-475-4639; Fax: 315-422-0363.

*Catholic Charities—*Mr. JOSEPH G. SLAVIK, Dir., Mailing Address: 240 E. Onondaga St., Syracuse, 13202. Tel: 315-470-1416; Fax: 315-478-4619.

*Onondaga County Director—*Mr. MICHAEL F. MELARA, 1654 W. Onondaga St., Syracuse, 13204. Tel: 315-424-1800.

*Broome County Director—*LORI ACCARDI, Dir., 232 Main St., Binghamton, 13905. Tel: 607-729-9166.

*Chenango County Director—*Mrs. ROBIN BECKWITH, Dir., 3 O'Hara Dr., Norwich, 13815. Tel: 607-334-8244.

*Cortland County Director—*MARIE WALSH, 33-35 Central Ave., Cortland, 13045. Tel: 607-756-5992.

*Oneida and Madison Counties Director—*KATHLEEN EICHENLAUB, 1404 Genesee St., Utica, 13502. Tel: 315-724-2158.

*Oswego County Director—*MARY MARGARET PEKOW, 365 First St., Fulton, 13069. Tel: 315-598-3980.

*Catholic Deaf Community—*VACANT.

*Catholic Relief Services—*Mr. JOSEPH G. SLAVIK, Dir., Mailing Address: 240 E. Onondaga St., Syracuse, 13202. Tel: 315-470-1416.

Catholic Schools—Mailing Address: 240 E. Onondaga, Syracuse, 13202. Tel: 315-470-1450; Fax: 315-470-1470. Mr. CHRISTOPHER MOMINEY, Supt.; Mrs. ELIZABETH WARWICK, Asst. to Supt. Assistant Superintendents: Ms. CHERYL CANFIELD; Ms. DEBRA BRILLANTE; Mr. DOMINICK LISI, Dir. Technology.

Southern Region—Broome County Catholic School Office, 17 Adams St., P.O. Box 90, Binghamton, 13905. Tel: 607-723-1547; Fax: 607-723-5697.

Catholic School Endowment Fund of the Roman Catholic Diocese of Syracuse— (established to provide tuition assistance for students in diocesan Catholic schools) Most Rev. ROBERT J. CUNNINGHAM, J.C.L., D.D., Pres., 240 E. Onondaga St., Syracuse, 13202.

*"The Catholic Sun"—*CONNIE BERRY, Editor in Chief & Gen. Mgr.; Rev. DONALD E. BOURGEOIS, Episcopal Liaison, 240 E. Onondaga St., Syracuse, 13202. Tel: 315-422-8153; 800-333-0571; Fax: 315-422-7549. Email: catholicsun@yahoo.com. Web: www.sydio.org.

*Catholic Television—*Mr. ANDREW HAUFF, Production Coord., 240 E. Onondaga St., Syracuse, 13202. Tel: 315-472-3584; Fax: 315-472-8409.

*Christopher Community—*Mr. DOUGLAS REICHER, Exec. Dir., 990 James St., Syracuse, 13203. Tel: 315-414-1821.

*Clerical Fund Society of the Roman Catholic Diocese of Syracuse—*Most Rev. ROBERT J. CUNNINGHAM, J.C.L., D.D., Pres.; Rev. Msgr. J. ROBERT YEAZEL, V.G., Vice Pres.; Rev. TIMOTHY S. ELMER, J.C.L., Sec. & Treas.

*Office of Communications—*Mrs. DANIELLE CUMMINGS, Dir., Mailing Address: 240 E. Onondaga St., Syracuse, 13202. Tel: 315-470-1476; Fax: 315-478-4619. Email: dcummings@syracusediocese.org.

*Stewardship & Development Office—*Mr. CHRISTOPHER PARKER, 240 E. Onondaga St., Syracuse, 13202. Tel: 315-472-0203; 315-472-7902; Fax: 315-472-8409.

*Ecumenical Commission—*Rev. Msgr. RONALD C. BILL, Dir. (Retired), 400 Salt Springs St., Fayetteville, 13066. Tel: 315-637-9846.

*Family Life Education—*Rev. JOSEPH H. PHILLIPS, Exec. Dir., 815 Fay Rd., Syracuse, 13219. Tel: 315-472-6754; Fax: 315-472-8409.

*Finance Committee—*Most Rev. ROBERT J. CUNNINGHAM, J.C.L., D.D.; Rev. Msgrs. RICHARD M. KOPP; J. ROBERT YEAZEL, V.G., Chm.; Rev. TIMOTHY S. ELMER, J.C.L.; Mr. JOHN BARSANTI, COO; Ms. GRACE GHEZZI; Mr. RICHARD DEGROOT; Ms. CAROL FLETCHER; Mr. THOMAS PRINZING; Rev. JOHN D. MANNO; JOHN MIRABITO; Mr. JAMES TUOZZOLO; Mr. FRANK ARKINSON; Mr. FRANK DISCENZA.

*Formation for Ministry and Liturgy—*Rev. CHARLES S. VAVONESE, Dir., Mailing Address: 240 E. Onondaga St., Syracuse, 13202. Tel: 315-470-1420; Fax: 315-579-3564.

*Health Care—*Rev. JAMES H. CAREY, Dir., Mailing Address: P.O. Box 574, Tully, 13159. Tel: 315-696-5092.

Heritage Campaign—c/o Development Office, 240 E. Onondaga St., Syracuse, 13202. Tel: 315-472-0203.

*HOPE Appeal—*Mr. CHRISTOPHER PARKER, 240 E. Onondaga, Syracuse, 13202. Tel: 315-472-0203; Fax: 315-472-8409.

Ruth Ministry— Syracuse Diocese Response to Domestic Violence LISA HALL, Dir., Mailing Address: 240 E. Onondaga St., Syracuse, 13202. Tel: 315-470-1418; Fax: 315-478-4619.

*Parish Services—*Mr. NICK CROSBY, Mailing Address: 240 E. Onondaga St., Syracuse, 13202. Tel: 315-422-9089.

*Permanent Diaconate—*Deacon PHILLIP KEHOE, Dir., Mailing Address: 240 E. Onondaga St., Syracuse, 13202. Tel: 315-470-1466.

*Priest Personnel—*Rev. Msgr. RICHARD M. KOPP, Mailing Address: 240 E. Onondaga St., Syracuse, 13202. Tel: 315-470-1460; Fax: 315-478-4619.

*Priests' Personnel Committee—*Most Rev. ROBERT J. CUNNINGHAM, J.C.L., D.D.; Revs. JOSEPH S. ZARESKI; THOMAS J. RYAN; JAMES P. SEROWIK; JOHN J. KURGAN; JOHN A. BUEHLER; CLIFFORD H. AUTH, J.C.L.; Rev. Msgrs. RICHARD M. KOPP; MICHAEL T. MEAGHER; Revs. TIMOTHY S. ELMER, J.C.L., Ex Officio; ANDREW E. BARANSKI, Ex Officio; JAMES T. O'BRIEN; JAMES P. LANG, Ex Officio.

Project Rachel— Post Abortion Healing LISA HALL, Dir., 240 E. Onondaga St., Syracuse, 13202. Tel: 315-424-3737.

*Personal Resource Center—*Rev. Msgr. NEAL E. QUARTIER, Dir., 215 N. State St., Syracuse, 13217-6482. Tel: 315-470-1462.

*Propagation of the Faith—*Rev. JOSEPH H. PHILLIPS, Dir.; Sr. JUDITH MARKERT, C.S.J., Coord., Bishop Ludden Jr./Sr. High School, 815 Fay Rd., Syracuse, 13219. Tel: 315-472-3442; Fax: 315-472-8409.

*Public Policy—*Rev. CHARLES S. VAVONESE, Dir., 240 E. Onondaga St., Syracuse, 13202.

Religious Education— (Office of Faith Formation) Mrs. CATHERINE CORNUE, Dir., Mailing Address: 240 E. Onondaga St., Syracuse, 13202. Tel: 315-470-1431; Fax: 315-478-4619.

*Eastern Region—*ANDREA SLAVEN, Dir., One Sherman St., New Hartford, 13413. Tel: 315-797-4030; Fax: 315-797-4031; CHERYL SMITH, Resource Center.

*Northern Region and Director of Special Education for Catechetics—*CONSTANCE ARMSTRONG, Dir., 81 E. Albany St., Oswego, 13126. Tel: 315-596-4014; Fax: 315-343-5557; DEANNE HALL, Resource Center. Tel: 315-343-5557.

*Southern Region—*ANDREA SCHAFFER, Dir., 705 W. Main St., Endicott, 13760. Tel: 607-348-0746; Fax: 607-786-9650; PAULA SHANAHAN, Resource Center. Tel: 607-786-9649.

*Western Region—*THERESA MAY, Dir., 6651 Kirkville Rd., East Syracuse, 13057. Tel: 315-472-6753; Fax: 315-472-8409; MARGARET BABCOCK, Resource Ctr. Tel: 315-472-6752; BETH SCHAFER, Resource Ctr.

Religious Retirement Fund— Retirement Plan for The Roman Catholic Diocese of Syracuse, NY. Est. January 1, 1988. Contact: Rev. TIMOTHY S. ELMER, J.C.L., Mailing Address: 240 E. Onondaga St., Syracuse, 13202. Tel: 315-422-9045; Fax: 315-422-9139.

*Respect for Life—*LISA HALL, Dir., Mailing Address: 240 E. Onondaga St., Syracuse, 13202. Tel: 315-470-1418.

*Laymen & Laywomen Retreat Movements—*Rev. MICHAEL J. CARMOLA, Dir. (Retired), Christ the King Retreat House, 500 Brookford Rd., Syracuse, 13224. Tel: 315-446-2680.

*Spanish Apostolate—*Rev. ROBERT D. CHRYST, Dir., 170 Seymour St., Syracuse, 13204. Tel: 315-442-9390.

Syracuse Catholic Press Association, Inc.— "The Catholic Sun" CONNIE BERRY, Editor in Chief & Gen. Mgr.; Most Rev. ROBERT J. CUNNINGHAM, J.C.L., D.D., Pres., Mailing Address: 240 E. Onondaga St., Syracuse, 13202. Tel: 315-422-8153; 800-333-0571; Fax: 315-422-7549.

*Victim Assistance Coordinator—*NUALA COLLINS, 240 E. Onondaga St., Syracuse, 13202. Tel: 315-470-1465; Fax: 315-478-4619.

*Vocation Formation—*Rev. THOMAS R. SERVATIUS, Dir., Mailing Address: 240 E. Onondaga St., Syracuse, 13202. Tel: 315-470-1452; Fax: 315-478-4619.

*Vocation Promotion—*Rev. JOSEPH O'CONNOR, Dir., Mailing Address: 240 E. Onondaga St., Syracuse, 13202. Tel: 315-470-1468; Fax: 315-478-4619.

*Youth & Young Adult Ministry—*Mr. ROBERT WALTERS, Dir., Mailing Address: 240 E. Onondaga St., Syracuse, 13202. Tel: 315-470-1419; Fax: 315-478-4619.

CLERGY, PARISHES, MISSIONS AND PAROCHIAL SCHOOLS

CITY OF SYRACUSE

(ONONDAGA COUNTY)

SYRACUSE

1—THE CATHEDRAL OF THE IMMACULATE CONCEPTION (1841) Rev. Msgr. Neal E. Quartier, Rector; Most Rev. Robert J. Cunningham; Revs. John C. Schopfer; William R. Jones, Parochial Vicar; Sr. Maureen D'Onofrio, C.S.J., Pastoral Assoc.

Res.: 259 E. Onondaga St., 13202. Tel: 315-422-4177; Fax: 315-478-4619.

Consolidated with Our Lady of Pompei School, Syracuse

*Catechesis/Religious Program—*Students 32.

Station—Vivian Teal Howard, Tel: 315-478-1641.

Station—Clinton Plaza 13202. Tel: 315-475-2141.

Station—McCarthy Manor, Tel: 315-475-6390.

Station—Rosewood Heights, Tel: 315-474-4431.

2—ALL SAINTS Rev. Frederick D. Daley.

Res.: 112 Lancaster Pl., 13210. Tel: 315-472-9934; Fax: 315-472-9941. Email: parish@allsaintssyracuse.org.

*Catechesis/Religious Program—*Students 86.

3—ST. ANDREW THE APOSTLE (1953) Closed. For inquiries for parish records contact the chancery.

4—ST. ANN (1955) Rev. Brian E. Lang.

Res.: 4461 Onondaga Blvd., 13219. Tel: 315-468-1803; Fax: 315-487-6312. Email: stann4461@yahoo.com.

*Catechesis/Religious Program—*Tel: 315-487-6201. Students 172.

5—ST. ANTHONY OF PADUA (1901) Rev. Robert D. Chryst. In Res., Most Rev. Thomas J. Costello (Retired).

Res.: 1515 Midland Ave., 13205. Tel: 315-475-4114.

*Catechesis/Religious Program—*Students 1.

6—ASSUMPTION B.V.M. (1844), (German), [CEM] Revs. Brad Milunski; Jeffrey Keefe, O.F.M.Conv., Prov. Psychologist, Franciscan Counseling; Conrad Somerville, O.F.M.Conv.; Michael Taylor, O.F.M.Conv., Parochial Vicar; Ericson De La Pena, O.F.M.Conv.; Bros. Edward Falsey, O.F.M.Conv.; Nicholas Spano, O.F.M.Conv. In Res., Revs. Linus DeSantis, O.F.M.Conv.; Adam Keltos, O.F.M.Conv.

St. Francis Friary: 812 N. Salina St., 13208. Tel: 315-422-4833; 315-422-4118; Fax: 315-422-4363.

*Assumption Cemetery Corporation—*2401 Court St., 13208. Tel: 315-454-3841; Fax: 315-454-4931. Email: assump812@aol.com.

7—BASILICA OF THE SACRED HEART (1892), (Polish), [CEM 2] Revs. Andrew E. Baranski, Rector; Stanislaw Kardas (Poland), Parochial Vicar; Deacons James L. Morse; Joseph Daniszewski; Frank Timson; Richard Galloway.

Res.: 927 Park Ave., 13204. Tel: 315-422-2343; Fax:

315-422-2344.
Catechesis/Religious Program—Tel: 315-422-4086. Students 85.

8—BLESSED SACRAMENT (1921) Rev. E. Peter Reddick. In Res., Revs. Joseph O'Conner; Timothy S. Elmer.
Res.: 3127 James St., 13206. Tel: 315-437-3394; Fax: 315-432-9198.
School—(Grades PreK-6), 3129 James St., 13206. Tel: 315-437-1261; Fax: 315-463-1628. Mrs. Andrea Polcaro, Prin. Lay Teachers 18; Students 283.
Catechesis/Religious Program—Students 225.

9—ST. BRIGID AND ST. JOSEPH (1926 and 1869) Rev. John P. Fenlon.
Res.: 318 Herkimer St., 13204. Tel: 315-488-7122; Fax: 315-484-9723. Email: lkennedy@syrdio.org.
Catechesis/Religious Program—Students 32.

10—ST. CHARLES BORROMEO (1929) Rev. Brian E. Lang; Deacons Peter P. Vanelli; Robert Connelly; Anthony J. Paratore. In Res., Rev. Philip S. Keane, S.S., (Weekend: In Res.).
Res.: 417 S. Orchard Rd., 13219. Tel: 315-468-4122; Fax: 315-218-6296.
School—200 W. High Ter., 13219. Tel: 315-488-7631; Fax: 315-488-0617. Deacon Joseph Celentano, Prin. Sisters 2; Lay Teachers 12; Students 121.
Catechesis/Religious Program—Tel: 315-487-6201. Students 158.

11—ST. DANIEL (1932) Rev. Msgr. Eugene M. Yennock; Rev. Charles S. Vavonese, Parochial Vicar; Deacons Joseph Celentano; Thomas L. Kane.
Res.: 3004 Court St., 13208. Tel: 315-454-4946; Fax: 315-454-0978. Email: sdchurch@twcny.rr.com.
Catechesis/Religious Program—Students 143.

12—HOLY TRINITY (1891), (German), Merged with St. John the Baptist, Syracuse.

13—ST. JAMES (1925) Rev. John D. Manno. In Res., Sr. Carolyn Chmielewski, C.S.J., Pastoral Assoc.
Res.: 4845 S. Salina St., 13205. Tel: 315-469-7789; Fax: 315-492-2707. Email: stjamessyrinfo@verizon.net.
Catechesis/Religious Program—Students 80.
Station—Onondaga Valley

14—ST. JOHN THE BAPTIST (1827) Rev. Jon K. Werner, Admin.
Res.: 406 Court St., 13208. Tel: 315-478-0916; Fax: 315-423-8096. Email: johnthebaptist@twcny.rr.com.
Catechesis/Religious Program—Students 62.

15—ST. JOHN THE EVANGELIST (1851) Closed. For inquiries for parish records contact the chancery.

16—ST. LUCY (1872) Rev. James D. Mathews.
Res.: 432 Gifford St., 13204. Tel: 315-475-7273; Fax: 315-423-0128.
Catechesis/Religious Program—Tel: 315-478-6312. Students 30.

17—MOST HOLY ROSARY (1913) Rev. Frederick R. Mannara.
Res.: 111 Roberts Ave., 13207-1397. Tel: 315-478-5749; Fax: 315-478-8629.
School—(Grades PreK-6), 1031 Bellevue Ave., 13207. Tel: 315-476-6035; Fax: 315-476-0219. Web: www.mhrsyr.org. Brenda Reichert, Prin.; Sr. Joan Ottman, I.H.M., Librarian. Sisters 2; Lay Teachers 14; Students 153.
Catechesis/Religious Program—Students 186.

18—OUR LADY OF LOURDES (1947) Rev. Thomas P. Fitzpatrick; Deacons Michael B. McGrath; Leo Needham.
Res.: 300 Valley Dr., 13207. Tel: 315-476-9576.
Catechesis/Religious Program—Tel: 315-478-6383. Students 103.

19—OUR LADY OF POMPEI (1924), (Italian), Merged with St. Peter, Syracuse to form Our Lady of Pompei-St. Peter, Syracuse.

20—OUR LADY OF POMPEI/ST. PETER (1924), (Italian), Rev. Daniel J. Caruso. In Res., Rev. Frederick A. Pompei.
Res.: 301 Ash St., 13208. Tel: 315-422-7163; Fax: 315-422-7164.
School—915-917 N. McBride St., 13208. Tel: 315-422-8548; Fax: 315-472-0754. Sr. Helen Ann Charlebois, I.H.M., Prin. Lay Teachers 13; Students 119.
Catechesis/Religious Program—Tel: 315-472-2260. Students 180.
Convent—Franciscan Missionary Sisters of the Immaculate Conception, 920 N. McBride St., 13208. Tel: 315-422-7922.

21—OUR LADY OF SOLACE (1926), with St. Therese the Little Flower of Jesus, Syracuse to form All Saints, Syracuse.

22—ST. PATRICK (1870) Rev. John P. Fenlon.
Res.: 216 N. Lowell Ave., 13204. Tel: 315-475-2185; Fax: 315-476-1565.

23—ST. PETER (1890), (Italian), Merged with Our Lady of Pompeii, Syracuse to form Our Lady of Pompeii-St. Peter, Syracuse.

24—ST. STEPHEN (1915), (Slovak), Closed. For inquiries for parish records please contact Sacred Heart, Syracuse.

25—ST. THERESE THE LITTLE FLOWER OF JESUS (1926) Merged with Our Lady of Solace, Syracuse to form All Saints, Syracuse.

26—TRANSFIGURATION (1911), (Polish), Rev. Thomas P. Kobuszewski. In Res., Rev. Tadeusz Rudnik (Poland).
Res.: 740 Teall Ave., 13206. Tel: 315-479-6129; Fax: 315-426-0684. Email: ctransfi@twcny.rr.com.

27—ST. VINCENT DE PAUL (1893) Rev. Wilbur J. Votraw, Admin.
Res.: 342 Vine St., 13203. Tel: 315-479-6689; Fax: 315-479-6689.
Catechesis/Religious Program—Tel: 315-479-6301. Students 50.
Convent—Sisters of St. Joseph of Carondelet, 1101 Burnet Ave., 13203. Tel: 315-479-8012.

OUTSIDE THE CITY OF SYRACUSE

BAINBRIDGE, CHENANGO CO., ST. JOHN THE EVANGELIST (1914) Rev. Mark J. Gantley, Admin.
Res.: 34 S. Main St., 13733. Tel: 607-967-4481.
Catechesis/Religious Program—Students 28.
Mission—St. Agnes 18 Spring St., Afton, Chenango Co. 13730.

BALDWINSVILLE, ONONDAGA CO.

1—ST. AUGUSTINE (1966) Rev. Thomas R. Servatius, Admin.
Res.: 7333 O'Brien Rd., 13027. Email: staugustineparish@yahoo.comTel: 315-638-0585.
Catechesis/Religious Program—Students 203.

2—ST. ELIZABETH ANN SETON (1985) Rev. John S. Finnegan, Admin.; Deacon William A. Dotterer.
Res.: 3494 NY State Rte. 31, 13027. Tel: 315-652-4300; Fax: 315-622-1761. Email: mainoffice@stelizabethbville.org.
Catechesis/Religious Program—Tel: 315-652-3900. Students 747.

3—ST. MARY OF THE ASSUMPTION (1852) [CEM] Rev. Joseph E. Scardella; Deacon Robert J. Talomie.
Res.: 47 Syracuse St., 13027. Tel: 315-635-5762; Fax: 315-635-8137. Email: stmarysbaldwinsville@gmail.com.
School—(Grades PreK-6), 49 Syracuse St., 13027. Tel: 315-635-3977. Web: www.stmarysbaldwinsville.com. Mrs. Barbara A. Jacques, Admin.; Mrs. Mary Nicolucci, Librarian. Sisters of the Third Franciscan Order M.C. 1; Lay Teachers 10; Students 122.
Catechesis/Religious Program—Tel: 315-635-5762, Ext. 110. Students 453.

BINGHAMTON, BROOME CO.

1—ST. ANDREW (1955) Merged with St. John the Evangelist, Binghamton to form Saints John & Andrew, Binghamton.

2—ST. ANN (1925), (Slovak), Merged with St. Joseph, Binghamton and St. Stanislaus Kostka, Binghamton to form Holy Trinity, Binghamton.

3—ST. CATHERINE OF SIENA (1929), Merged with St. Christopher, Binghamton to form St. Francis of Assisi, Binghamton.

4—ST. CHRISTOPHER (1940), Merged with St. Catherine of Siena, Binghamton to form St. Francis of Assisi, Binghamton.

5—SS. CYRIL AND METHOD (1904), (Slovak), Rev. George Sandor, O.F.M.Conv. In Res., Revs. Simeon Rukstalis, O.F.M.Conv.; Robert Amrhein, O.F.M.Conv.
Res.: 148 Clinton St., 13905. Tel: 607-724-1372; Fax: 607-724-1468.
Catechesis/Religious Program—Students 50.

6—ST. FRANCIS OF ASSISI Rev. Timothy J. Taugher; Sr. Karen Gaube, C.S.J., Pastoral Assoc.; Deacon Raymond Goskowski.
Res.: 1031 Chenango St., 13901. Tel: 607-722-4388; Fax: 607-722-1336.
Catechesis/Religious Program—1031 Chenango St., 13901. Tel: 607-722-4177. Joseph Tiesi, D.R.E. Students 283.

7—HOLY TRINITY (2003) Revs. George Sandor, O.F.M-.Conv.; Robert Amrhein, O.F.M.Conv.; Simeon Rukstalis, O.F.M.Conv.
Res.: 346 Prospect St., 13905. Tel: 607-797-1856; Fax: 607-797-8452.
Catechesis/Religious Program—Students 60.

8—SAINTS JOHN & ANDREW Rev. Msgr. Michael T. Meagher. In Res., Revs. Krzysztof Boretto; Robert J. Sullivan (Retired).
Res.: 1263 Vestal Ave., 13903. Tel: 607-722-0493; Fax: 607-723-5171. Email: parishstsjohnandrew@stny.rr.com.
Catechesis/Religious Program—Students 255.

9—ST. JOHN THE EVANGELIST (1907) Merged with St. Andrew, Binghamton to form Saints John & Andrew, Binghamton.

10—ST. JOSEPH (1914), (Lithuanian), Merged with St. Ann, Binghamton and St. Stanislaus Kostka, Binghamton to form Holy Trinity, Binghamton.

11—ST. MARY OF THE ASSUMPTION (1887; 1913) Revs. Thomas I. Ward; Joseph Mary Offeh (Africa). In Res., Rev. Francis W. Kocik (CAM).
Res.: 37 Fayette St., 13901. Tel: 607-723-5383. Email: stmaryrectory@aol.com.
Catechesis/Religious Program—Students 198.

12—ST. PATRICK (1838), (Irish), Revs. John P. Putano; Paul Machira (Africa), Parochial Vicar.
Res.: 9 Leroy St., 13905. Tel: 607-722-1060.
Catechesis/Religious Program—Students 127.
Convent—Sisters of St. Joseph of Carondelet, 46 Oak St., 13905. Tel: 607-722-4745.

13—ST. PAUL (1896) Revs. Thomas I. Ward; Gabriel Adansi Fordjour (Africa); Francis W. Kocik (CAM); Sr. Mary Rose De Donato, D.C., Pastoral Assoc.
Res.: 15 Doubleday St., 13901. Tel: 607-722-6492. Email: stpauls_binghamton@yahoo.com.
Catechesis/Religious Program—Tel: 607-724-5449; Fax: 607-724-3377. Students 149.

14—ST. STANISLAUS KOSTKA (1914), (Polish), Merged with St. Ann, Binghamton and St. Joseph, Binghamton to form Holy Trinity, Binghamton.

15—ST. THOMAS AQUINAS (1927) Revs. John P. Putano; Paul Machira (Africa), Parochial Vicar.
Res.: One Aquinas St., 13905. Tel: 607-797-4015; Fax: 607-729-9727. Email: stthomasrec@stny.rr.com.
Catechesis/Religious Program—4 Aquinas St., 13905. Tel: 607-797-3304. Students 103.

BOONVILLE, ONEIDA CO., ST. JOSEPH (1875) [CEM] Rev. Sean P. O'Brien.
Res.: 110 Charles St., 13309. Tel: 315-942-4618.
Catechesis/Religious Program—Tel: 315-942-5955; Fax: 315-942-4618.

BREWERTON, ONONDAGA CO., ST. AGNES (1958) Rev. Christopher Celentano, Admin.; Deacon Donald Mula.
Res.: 5472 Miller Rd., 13029. Tel: 315-676-7050; Fax: 315-668-8149. Email: ypf70@clearwire.net.
Catechesis/Religious Program—Tel: 315-676-5662. Twinned with St. Michael, Central Square. Students 7.

BRIDGEPORT, ONONDAGA CO., ST. FRANCIS OF ASSISI (1951) Rev. Raynald Yudin, O.F.M.Conv.; Deacon Guy W. Hart. In Res., Friar James Moore, O.F.M.Conv.
Friary—Res.: 7820 Rte. 298, P.O. Box 550, 13030-0550. Tel: 315-633-9682; Fax: 315-633-0672. Email: stfrancisofc@cnymail.com. Web: www.stfrancisbridgeport.org.
Parish Center— 13030-0550. Tel: 315-633-2561; Fax: 315-633-2743.
Catechesis/Religious Program—Tel: 315-633-5661. Students 186.

CAMDEN, ONEIDA CO., ST. JOHN THE EVANGELIST (1852) [CEM] Rev. Carlo C. Stirpe.
Res.: 22 Church St., 13316. Tel: 315-245-1603. Email: stjohnscamden@twcny.rr.com.
Catechesis/Religious Program—Students 148.

CAMILLUS, ONONDAGA CO., ST. JOSEPH (1852) Rev. Msgr. George F. Sheehan, Temporary Admin.
Res.: 5600 W. Genesee St., 13031. Tel: 315-488-8490; Fax: 315-488-4214.
Catechesis/Religious Program—Students 1,084.

CANASTOTA, MADISON CO., ST. AGATHA (1883) [CEM] Rev. Kevin Maloney; Deacon Adolph J. Uryniak.
Res.: 329 N. Peterboro St., 13032. Tel: 315-697-7104; Fax: 315-697-5821.
Catechesis/Religious Program—Tel: 315-697-7827. Students 196.

CAZENOVIA, MADISON CO., ST. JAMES (1847) [CEM] Rev. Kevin J. Corcoran; Sr. Milice Bohrer, C.S.J., Pastoral Assoc.
Res.: 6 Green St., 13035. Tel: 315-655-3441; Fax: 315-655-3442. Email: stjames@twcny.rr.com.
Catechesis/Religious Program—Tel: 315-655-4871. Students 500.

CENTRAL SQUARE, OSWEGO CO., ST. MICHAEL (1928) Rev. Christopher Celentano, Admin.
Res.: 598 S. Main St., 13036. Tel: 315-676-2898; Fax: 315-676-3103. Email: stmike598@hotmail.com.
Catechesis/Religious Program—Tel: 315-676-4210. Students 195.

CHADWICKS, ONEIDA CO., ST. PATRICK-ST. ANTHONY (1907) Rev. Abraham L. Esper.
Res.: 3364 Oneida St., P.O. Box 429, 13319. Tel: 315-316-0338; Fax: 315-507-2528.
Catechesis/Religious Program—Students 227.

CHENANGO FORKS, BROOME CO., ST. RITA (1946) Closed. For inquiries for parish records contact the chancery.

CHITTENANGO, MADISON CO., ST. PATRICK (1853) [CEM] Rev. Edward J. Reimer.
Res.: 1341 Murray Dr., 13037. Tel: 315-687-6105; Fax: 315-687-0046.
Catechesis/Religious Program—Tel: 315-687-6561. Students 140.

CICERO, ONONDAGA CO., SACRED HEART (1888) Revs. James E. Gehl; James A. Schultz, Parochial Vicar.
Res.: 8229 S. Main St., 13039. Tel: 315-699-2752; Fax: 315-699-3775. Email: sheart@twcny.rr.com.
Catechesis/Religious Program—Tel: 315-699-7678. Students 1,040.

CLARK MILLS, ONEIDA CO., CHURCH OF THE ANNUNCIATION (1908) Rev. Kevin J. Bunger.
Mailing Address: 7616 E. South St., Clinton, 13323. Tel: 315-853-6138.
Catechesis/Religious Program—Tel: 315-853-6139. Students 155.

CLAYVILLE, ONEIDA CO., ST. PATRICK (1864) [CEM] Closed. For inquiries for parish records contact St. Patrick-St. Anthony, Chadwicks.

CLEVELAND, OSWEGO CO., ST. MARY OF THE ASSUMPTION (1854) [CEM] Rev. R. Paul Mathis.
Res.: 148 State Rte. 49, 13042. Tel: 315-675-3542.
Catechesis/Religious Program—Tel: 315-675-3165. Students 153.
Mission—St. Bernadette State Rte. 49, Constantia, Oswego Co. 13044. Tel: 315-623-9803.

CLINTON, ONEIDA CO., ST. MARY (1850) [CEM] Rev. John P. Croghan.
Res.: 13 Marvin St., 13323. Tel: 315-853-2935; Fax: 315-859-1097. Email: stmarysc@borg.com.
Catechesis/Religious Program—Tel: 315-853-6196; Fax: 315-853-1440. Students 346.

CORTLAND, CORTLAND CO.

1—ST. ANTHONY OF PADUA (1917), (Italian), Rev. Lucian Urbaniak.
Office: 59 N. Main St., 13045. Tel: 607-756-9967; Fax: 607-753-3444. Email: staoffice@centralny.twcbc.com. Web: www.saintanthonyofcortland.com.
Rectory—44 N. Main St., 13045.
Catechesis/Religious Program—Diane Passalugo, D.R.E. Students 60.

2—ST. MARY (1855) Rev. Lucian Urbaniak; Deacons Joseph During; Steve Smith.
Church: 59 N. Main St., 13045. Tel: 607-756-9967; Fax: 607-753-3444. Email: staoffice@centralny.twcbc.com.
School—61 N. Main St., 13045. Tel: 607-756-5614; Fax: 607-753-3444. Email: spmarycor@mail.odyssey.net. Mrs. Denise Hall, Prin. Lay Teachers 17; Students 226.
Catechesis/Religious Program—59 N. Main St., 13045. Email: dreatsmc@odyssey.net. Students 193.

DEPOSIT, BROOME CO., ST. JOSEPH (1851) [CEM] Rev. Thomas F. Catucci.
Res.: 975 NY Rt. 11, Kirkwood, 13795. Tel: 607-467-2291; Fax: 607-467-2288.
Parish Center—74 Second St., 13754. Tel: 607-467-2226.
Catechesis/Religious Program—Students 23.

DEWITT, ONONDAGA CO., HOLY CROSS (1943) Rev. Msgr. J. Robert Yeazel; Rev. John V. Ahern, Parochial Vicar. In Res., Rev. Charles S. Vavonese.
Res.: 4112 E. Genesee St., 13214. Tel: 315-446-0473; Fax: 315-446-7608. Email: info@holycrossdewitt.org.
School—4200 E. Genesee St., 13214. Tel: 315-446-4890; Fax: 315-446-4799. David Wheeler, Prin. Lay Teachers 14; Students 220.
Catechesis/Religious Program—Students 979.

DURHAMVILLE, ONEIDA CO., ST. FRANCIS (1860), (German), [CEM] Rev. Joseph F. Kehoe.
Res.: 5334 Foster St., P.O. Box 189, 13054. Tel: 315-363-1572.
Chapel—St. Mary [CEM] Irish Ridge.
Catechesis/Religious Program—Students 29.

EAST SYRACUSE, ONONDAGA CO., ST. MATTHEW (1880) Revs. Joseph J. Clemente; Severine Yagaza.
Res.: 229 W. Yates St., 13057. Tel: 315-437-8318; Fax: 315-463-6399.
Catechesis/Religious Program—Tel: 315-437-3685. Students 212.

ENDICOTT, BROOME CO.

1—ST. AMBROSE (1908) Revs. Charles A. Currie; Donald E. Bourgeois, Parochial Vicar. In Res., Rev. Benito Manding.
Res.: 203 Washington Ave., 13760. Tel: 607-754-2330; Fax: 607-785-6947.
Catechesis/Religious Program—Students 96.

2—ST. ANTHONY OF PADUA (1917), (Italian), Rev. James P. Serowik; Deacon Frank Longo.
Res.: 306 Odell Ave., 13760. Tel: 607-754-4333; Fax: 607-786-3965. Email: stanthonys@stny.rr.com.
St. Anthony's Learning Center—906 Jenkins St., 13760. Tel: 607-748-5184; Fax: 607-786-3965. Email: stanthonytlc@stny.rr.com. (Pre-School)
Convent—Little Sisters of St. Francis, 304 Oak Hill Ave., 13760. Tel: 607-786-5006.
Catechesis/Religious Program—Email: stajannine@stny.rr.com. Students 257.

3—ST. CASIMIR (1928), (Polish), Rev. Matthew S. Wieczorek.
Res.: 212 N. McKinley Ave., 13760. Tel: 607-785-3262; Fax: 607-785-4772. Email: stcasimirs@verizon.net.
Catechesis/Religious Program— Twinned with St. Joseph, Endicott. Students 5.

4—ST. JOSEPH (1923), (Slovak), Rev. Charles Opondo-Owora (Africa); Deacon Dominick Rossi (Ghana). In Res., Rev. Robert A. Ours.
Res.: 207 Hayes Ave., 13760. Tel: 607-748-0442; Fax: 607-748-7725.
Catechesis/Religious Program—Students 198.

5—OUR LADY OF GOOD COUNSEL (1941) Rev. Michael Galuppi; Deacon Thomas M. Harley.
Res.: 701 W. Main St., 13760. Tel: 607-748-7417; Fax: 607-785-6454.
Catechesis/Religious Program—Tel: 607-754-2213. Students 355.

ENDWELL, BROOME CO.

1—CHRIST THE KING (1949) Closed. For inquiries for parish records contact the chancery.

2—CHURCH OF THE HOLY FAMILY (2008) Rev. Clarence F. Rumble.
Res.: 3011 Phyllis St., 13760. Tel: 607-754-1266; Fax: 607-754-8942. Email: churchoftheholyfamily@gmail.com.
Catechesis/Religious Program—Tel: 607-785-4581. Students 330.

FAIRMOUNT, ONONDAGA CO., HOLY FAMILY (1935) Rev. Richard Prior Jr.; Rev. Msgr. Francis Osei-Nyarko; Deacon Nick Alvaro.
Parish Office—127 Chapel Dr., 13219. Tel: 315-488-3139; Fax: 315-487-1112.
Res.: 119 Chapel Dr., 13219. Tel: 315-488-3023.
School—130 Chapel Dr., 13219. Tel: 315-487-8515; Fax: 315-487-8515. Helen Chajka, Prin.
Catechesis/Religious Program—Tel: 315-488-5884. Students 901.

FAYETTEVILLE, ONONDAGA CO., IMMACULATE CONCEPTION (1869) [CEM] Rev. Thomas J. Ryan; Sr. Monica Zmolek, O.S.F., Pastoral Min. In Res., Rev. Msgrs. James A. McCloskey (Retired); Ronald C. Bill (Retired).
Res.: 400 Salt Springs St., 13066. Tel: 315-637-9846; Fax: 315-637-9846.
School—Tel: 315-637-3961; Fax: 315-637-2672. Mrs. Sally Lisi, Prin. Sisters of the Third Franciscan Order M.C. 1; Lay Teachers 28; Students 298.
Catechesis/Religious Program—Tel: 315-637-9840. Students 672.

FLORENCE, ONEIDA CO., ST. MARY (1845) [CEM] Rev. Carlo C. Stirpe.
Res.: 22 Church St., Camden, 13316. Tel: 315-245-1603.

FORESTPORT, ONEIDA CO., ST. PATRICK (1848) [CEM] Revs. Sean P. O'Brien; Donald H. Karlen.
Mailing Address: P.O. Box 1, 13338. Tel: 315-392-2341; Fax: 315-392-5651.
Catechesis/Religious Program—Students 140.
Mission—St. Mary of the Snows Otter Lake, Oneida Co.

FULTON, OSWEGO CO.

1—CHURCH OF THE HOLY TRINITY Rev. Stephen P. Wirkes; Deacon David Sweenie.
Office: 309 Buffalo St., 13069. Tel: 315-598-2118.
Res.: Tel: 315-598-9094; Fax: 315-598-3355.
Rectory—57 S. 3rd St., 13069.
Catechesis/Religious Program—Students 144.

2—HOLY FAMILY-ST. MICHAEL'S (1930), Merged with Immaculate Conception, Fulton to form Church of the Holy Trinity, Fulton.

3—IMMACULATE CONCEPTION (1854) [CEM], Merged with Holy Family-St. Michael's, Fulton to form Church of the Holy Trinity, Fulton.

4—ST. MICHAEL (1924), (Polish), Merged into Holy Trinity, Fulton.

GREENE, CHENANGO CO., IMMACULATE CONCEPTION (1889) Rev. Lukasz Kozlowski, Admin.
Res.: 1180 NY Hwy. 206, 13778. Tel: 607-656-9546; Fax: 607-656-7667. Email: padreward470@gmail.com.
Catechesis/Religious Program—Students 53.

HAMILTON, MADISON CO., ST. MARY (1869) [CEM] Rev. Richard B. Dunn.
Res.: 16 Wylie St., 13346. Tel: 315-824-2164. Email: stmaryschurch1@verizon.net.
Catechesis/Religious Program—Tel: 315-824-5024. Twinned with St. Joan, Morrisville. Students 68.
Mission—St. Joan of Arc (1931) 6 Brookside Dr., P.O. Box 1087, Morrisville, 13408.

HANNIBAL, OSWEGO CO., OUR LADY OF THE ROSARY (1954) Rev. John F. Hogan Jr.
Office: 923 Cayuga St., P.O. Box 185, 13074-3138. Tel: 315-564-5201.
Catechesis/Religious Program—Students 66.
Mission—St. Joseph Southwest Oswego, Oswego Co. (Closed)

HINCKLEY, ONEIDA CO., ST. ANN (1895) [CEM] Rev. Vincent P. Long.
Res.: 7125 Main St., 13352. Tel: 315-896-2540.
Catechesis/Religious Program—Students 114.

HOLLAND PATENT, ONEIDA CO., ST. LEO (1882) Rev. Vincent P. Long. In Res., Rev. Robert C. Weber.
Res.: 7937 Elm St., P.O. Box 185, 13354. Tel: 315-865-5371; Fax: 315-865-5868.
Catechesis/Religious Program—Students 425.

HOMER, CORTLAND CO., ST. MARGARET (1908) Rev. Paul J. Alciati, Admin.
Res.: 14 Copeland Ave., 13077. Tel: 607-749-2542; Fax: 607-749-4623. Email: stmargaret-homer@verizon.net.
Catechesis/Religious Program—Students 160.

JOHNSON CITY, BROOME CO.

1—BLESSED SACRAMENT (1945) Rev. Edward J. Zandy.
Rectory—13 Cenacle Plaza, 13790. Tel: 607-797-5151; Fax: 607-797-8603. Email: info@bsacjc.org.
Catechesis/Religious Program—Tel: 607-797-8603. Students 95.

2—ST. JAMES (1900) Revs. John P. Donovan; Christopher Ballard, Parochial Vicar; Deacons Edward Blaine; William Fitzpatrick; Mr. William P. Gallagher, Pastoral Assoc.; Carol Hall, Pastoral Assoc.
Office: 147 Main St., 13790. Tel: 607-729-6147; Fax: 607-797-5966.
Catechesis/Religious Program—Tel: 607-729-4083. Students 418.

JORDAN, ONONDAGA CO., ST. PATRICK (1858) [CEM] Rev. John R. DeLorenzo.
Res. & Office: 28 N. Main St., P.O. Box 567, 13080. Tel: 315-689-6240; Fax: 315-689-6240.
Catechesis/Religious Program—Students 83.

KIRKWOOD, BROOME CO., ST. MARY (1888) Rev. Thomas F. Catucci.
Res.: 975 NY Rte. 11, 13795. Tel: 607-775-0086. Email: stmaryskirkwood13795@verizon.net.
Catechesis/Religious Program—Tel: 607-775-2511. Marie Travis, D.R.E. Students 136.

LACONA, OSWEGO CO., ST. FRANCES XAVIER CABRINI (1946) Closed. For inquiries for parish records contact the chancery.

LAFAYETTE, ONONDAGA CO., ST. JOSEPH (1866) Revs. James H. Carey, Admin.; Robert Stephenson.
Res.: 6104 Cherry Valley Rd., Box 169, 13084. Tel: 315-677-3439.
Catechesis/Religious Program—Tel: 315-677-7735; Fax: 315-677-3858. Students 110.

LAKELAND, ONONDAGA CO., OUR LADY OF PEACE (1935) Rev. Amedeo G. Guida.
Res.: 203 Halcomb St., 13209. Tel: 315-487-6832; Fax: 315-487-9722. Email: ourladyofpeace@centralny.twcbc.com.
Catechesis/Religious Program—Students 130.

LEE CENTER, ONEIDA CO., ST. JOSEPH (1923) Rev. James D. Tormey.
Res.: 5748 Strokes Lee Center Rd., 13363. Tel: 315-336-2661.
Parish Center—Fax: 315-336-8418.
Catechesis/Religious Program—Tel: 315-339-3080. Students 135.

LIVERPOOL, ONONDAGA CO.

1—CHRIST THE KING (1964) Rev. James C. Fritzen; Deacons Thomas Hachey; Thomas Cuskey.
21 Cherry Tree Cir., 13090.
Res.: 26 Cherry Tree Cir., 13090. Tel: 315-652-3233; 315-652-9266 (Parish Office); Fax: 315-652-5680.
Catechesis/Religious Program—Tel: 315-652-5782. Students 221.

2—IMMACULATE HEART OF MARY (1950) Rev. Daniel J. O'Hara; Sr. Rose Marie Caravaglio, C.S.J., Dir. Music. In Res., Rev. James P. Lang.
Res.: 425 Beechwood Ave., 13088. Tel: 315-457-8060; Fax: 315-451-2110.
Catechesis/Religious Program—Students 321.

3—ST. JOSEPH THE WORKER (1890) Rev. Daniel J. O'Hara.
Res.: 1001 Tulip St., 13088. Tel: 315-457-6060; Fax: 315-457-4119. Email: admin@sjwchurch.org. Web: www.sjwkrchurch.org.
Catechesis/Religious Program—Tel: 315-453-7970. Students 254.

4—POPE JOHN XXIII RC CHURCH (1971) Rev. James T. O'Brien.
Res.: 8290 Soule Rd., 13090. Tel: 315-652-6591; Fax: 315-652-6631. Email: objmst@yahoo.com.
Catechesis/Religious Program—Tel: 315-652-1094. Students 476.

MAINE, BROOME CO., MOST HOLY ROSARY (1944) Rev. Clarence J. Cerwonka, Admin.
Res.: 2596 Main St., Box 248, 13802. Tel: 607-862-3216; Fax: 607-862-0096.
Catechesis/Religious Program—Tel: 607-862-4758. Students 124.

MANLIUS, ONONDAGA CO., ST. ANN (1920) Rev. Clifford H. Auth.
Res.: 104 Academy St., 13104. Tel: 315-682-5181; Fax: 315-682-5248. Email: stannschurch@twcny.rr.com.
Catechesis/Religious Program—Tel: 315-682-9443. Students 623.

MARATHON, CORTLAND CO., ST. STEPHEN (1870) Rev. Douglas D. Cunningham, Admin.
Res.: 12 Academy St., P.O. Box 475, 13803-0475. Tel: 607-849-3480; Fax: 607-849-4078. Email: presbyter@odssey.net.
Catechesis/Religious Program—Students 96.
Mission—Our Lady of Perpetual Help Cincinnatus, Cortland Co.

MARCELLUS, ONONDAGA CO., ST. FRANCIS XAVIER (1873) [CEM] Rev. Daniel C. Muscalino, Admin.
Res.: 1 W. Main St., P.O. Box 177, 13108. Tel: 315-673-2531; Fax: 315-673-9305.
Catechesis/Religious Program—53 North St., 13108. Tel: 315-673-4107. Students 453.

MATTYDALE, ONONDAGA CO., ST. MARGARET (1926) Revs. Robert P. Hyde; Cleophas Oseso Tuka (Africa); Deacon Donald R. Whiting.

Res.: 203 Roxboro Rd., 13211. Tel: 315-455-5534; Fax: 315-454-4102. Email: schurch@twcny.rr.com.
School—Tel: 315-455-5791; Fax: 315-455-1250. Ms. Susanne Donze, Prin. Lay Teachers 20; Students 249.
Catechesis/Religious Program—200 Roxboro Rd., 13211. Tel: 315-455-2203. Students 325.

MEXICO, OSWEGO CO., ST. ANNE, MOTHER OF MARY (1914) Rev. John Canorro; Deacon Daniel Caughey.
Res.: 3352 Main St., P.O. Box 487, 13114. Tel: 315-963-7182; Fax: 315-963-4032. Email: sstarofs@twcny.rr.com.
Catechesis/Religious Program—Fax: 315-963-4032. Students 118.

MINETTO, OSWEGO CO., OUR LADY OF PERPETUAL HELP (1932) Rev. Joseph M. Larkin.
Res.: West River Rd., P.O. Box 236, 13115. Tel: 315-343-7922.

MINOA, ONONDAGA CO., ST. MARY (1834) [CEM] Rev. Raynald Yudin, O.F.M.Conv.; Deacon Guy W. Hart.
Mailing Address: P.O. Box 550, Bridgeport, 13030.
Res.: 7820 Rte. 298, Bridgeport, 13030. Tel: 315-633-0712; Fax: 315-633-0672.
Office: Tel: 315-656-3441.
Catechesis/Religious Program—Tel: 315-656-4220. Email: dresmary@twcn.rr.com. Students 292.

MUNNSVILLE, MADISON CO., ST. THERESE OF THE INFANT JESUS (1926) Rev. Joseph F. Kehoe.
Res.: Main St., P.O. Box 735, 13409.
Catechesis/Religious Program—Students 5.

NEW BERLIN, CHENANGO CO., ST. THERESA OF THE INFANT JESUS (1955) Rev. Lester E. Smith, Admin.
Res. & Mailing Address: P.O. Box 780, 13411-0780. Tel: 607-847-6851.
Catechesis/Religious Program—Tel: 607-847-8732. Students 34.

NEW HARTFORD, ONEIDA CO.

1—ST. JOHN THE EVANGELIST (1883) Rev. Joseph S. Zareski. In Res., Rev. Arthur R. Hapanowicz.
Res.: 66 Oxford Rd., 13413. Tel: 315-732-8521; Fax: 315-735-1569.
Catechesis/Religious Program—One Sherman St., 13413. Tel: 315-724-4347. Sr. Martha Vincent Larkin, C.S.J., D.R.E. Students 724.

2—OUR LADY OF THE ROSARY (1949) Rev. Felix R. Colosimo.
Res.: 1736 Burrstone Rd., 13413. Tel: 315-724-0402.
Catechesis/Religious Program—Students 348.

3—ST. THOMAS (1957) Rev. G. David Sears. In Res., Rev. John M. Quinn.
Res.: 150 Clinton Rd., 13413. Tel: 315-735-8381.
Catechesis/Religious Program—Students 54.

NEW LONDON, ONEIDA CO., HOLY CROSS (1968) Closed. For inquiries for parish records please see St. Francis, Durhamville.

NEW YORK MILLS, ONEIDA CO., CHURCH OF SACRED HEART AND ST. MARY (1909) [CEM] Rev. Artur Krawczenko (Poland).
Res.: 201 Main St., 13417. Tel: 315-736-4432; Fax: 315-736-4432.
School—(Grades PreK-N), Consolidated. See separate listing under Institutions located in the Diocese.
Catechesis/Religious Program—Tel: 315-736-9132. Students 124.

NORTH BAY, ONEIDA CO., ST. JOHN (1843) [CEM] Rev. Leo J. Wimett.
Res.: 2191 Rte. 49, P.O. Box 289, 13123. Tel: 315-245-0853.
Catechesis/Religious Program—Students 77.
Mission—St. Mary Verona Beach, Oneida Co. 13162.

NORTH SYRACUSE, ONONDAGA CO., ST. ROSE OF LIMA (1926) Rev. Msgr. James M. Kennedy; Revs. Daniel Heintz (Retired); Jerome Amaechi; Corinne Mullen, Pastoral Min.
Parish Office—409 S. Main St., 13212. Tel: 315-458-0283; Fax: 315-458-1290.
Res.: 407 S. Main St., 13212. Tel: 315-458-0283.
Preschool—Tel: 315-458-6036. Students 83.
School—(Grades K-6), 411 S. Main St., 13212. Tel: 315-458-6036; Fax: 315-458-6038. Sisters Catherine Laboure, Prin.; Jogues, Librarian. Sisters of the Third Franciscan Order (Syracuse, NY) 2; Lay Teachers 22; Students 261; Preschool 83.
Catechesis/Religious Program—Tel: 315-458-6592; Fax: 315-458-1290. Patricia Decker, D.R.E.; Douglas Pyke, Music Dir. Students 896.

NORWICH, CHENANGO CO.

1—ST. BARTHOLOMEW THE APOSTLE (1919), (Italian), Rev. Ralph A. Bove; Deacons David Kirsch; Timothy McNerney; Sr. Soosai Raj Rose Mary, Pastoral Min.
73 E. Main St., 13815.
Parish Office: 30 Pleasant St., 13815. Tel: 607-336-2222; Fax: 607-337-2218; 607-334-6521.

2—ST. PAUL, [CEM] Rev. Ralph A. Bove; Deacons David Kirsch; Timothy McNerney; Sr. Soosai Raj Rose Mary, Pastoral Min.
Parish Office & Res.: 30 Pleasant St., 13815. Tel: 607-336-2222; Fax: 607-337-2218; 607-334-6521. Email: stpaulstbart@citlink.net. Web: www.stbartstpaul.com.
School—Holy Family School, 17 Prospect St., 13815. Tel: 607-337-2207; Fax: 607-337-2210. Mr. Gene Chilion, Prin. Students 97.
Catechesis/Religious Program—Tel: 607-337-2001. Sr. Sellapan Jacqueline Mary, D.R.E. Students 130.
Convent—79 E. Main St., 13815. Tel: 607-337-2219.

ONEIDA, MADISON CO.

1—ST. JOSEPH (1893) Rev. Richard J. Kapral; Rev. Msgr. Matthew C. Luczycki (Retired).
Res.: 121 St. Joseph Pl., 13421. Tel: 315-363-3280; Fax: 315-363-3280. Email: stjosephr@twcny.rr.com.
Parish Center—111 St. Joseph Pl., 13421. Tel: 315-363-5061.
Catechesis/Religious Program—Students 105.

2—ST. PATRICK (1843) [CEM] Rev. Richard J. Kapral.
Res.: 347 Main St., 13421. Tel: 315-363-7570. Email: stpatschurch@earthlink.net.
School—(Grades PreK-6), 354 Elizabeth St., 13421. Tel: 315-363-3620; Fax: 315-363-5075. Peg Brown, Prin. Lay Teachers 9; Students 146.
Catechesis/Religious Program—Lisa Spooner, D.R.E. Students 121.

ONONDAGA HILL, ONONDAGA CO., ST. MICHAEL & ST. PETER (1874) Rev. Henry J. Pedzich; Deacon Gregory Cross, Pastoral Assoc.
Res.: 4782 W. Seneca Tpke., 13215. Tel: 315-469-6995; Fax: 315-469-4388.
Catechesis/Religious Program—Tel: 315-469-6600.

ORISKANY FALLS, ONEIDA CO., ST. JOSEPH (1870) [CEM] Rev. Paul V. Carey.
Res.: 229 Main St., 13425. Tel: 315-821-6122. Email: stjoe@tds.net.
Catechesis/Religious Program—Students 48.

ORISKANY, ONEIDA CO., ST. STEPHEN, PROTOMARTYR (1929) Closed. For inquiries for Parish records contact St. Paul, Whitesboro.

OSWEGO, OSWEGO CO.

1—ST. JOHN THE EVANGELIST (1869) Closed. For inquiries for parish records please see St. Mary, Oswego.

2—ST. JOSEPH (1915), (Italian), Rev. Gregory J. Kreinheder, Admin.
Mailing Address: 178 W. Second St., 13126. Tel: 315-343-2160.
Catechesis/Religious Program—Tel: 315-342-3967. Students 94.

3—ST. LOUIS (1870), (French), Closed. For inquiries for parish records, please contact St. Peter, Oswego.

4—ST. MARY OF THE ASSUMPTION (1848) Rev. John F. Hogan Jr.
Res.: 103 W. Seventh St., 13126. Tel: 315-343-3953; Fax: 315-342-5538. Email: srectory@twcny.rr.com.
For further information please see Trinity Catholic School under Consolidated Schools located in the Institution section
Catechesis/Religious Program—Tel: 315-343-7210.

5—ST. PAUL (1840), (Irish), Rev. Gaetano T. Baccaro; Deacon George E. Maynard.
Res.: 50 E. Mohawk St., 13126. Tel: 315-343-2333; Fax: 315-343-2334. Email: stpaulparish@cnymail.com.
Church: 134 E. Fifth St., 13126.
For further information see Trinity Catholic School under Consolidated Schools in the Institution section
Catechesis/Religious Program—Students 99.

6—ST. PETER (1862), (German), Rev. George E. Wurz, Admin.
Res.: 83 E. Albany St., 13126. Tel: 315-343-1352.
Catechesis/Religious Program—Students 33.
Mission—Sacred Heart Scriba, Oswego Co. Tel: 315-342-5705.

7—ST. STEPHEN THE KING (1908), (Polish), Rev. Gregory J. Kreinheder, Admin.
Res.: 138 Niagara St., 13126. Tel: 315-343-0350; Fax: 315-343-0736.
Catechesis/Religious Program—Students 35.

OXFORD, CHENANGO CO., ST. JOSEPH (1849) [CEM] Rev. Lukasz Kozlowski, Admin.
Res.: 3 Scott St., P.O. Box 352, 13830. Tel: 607-843-7021; Fax: 607-843-7021. Email: stjoseph04@frontiernet.net.
Church: 1180 NY Hwy. 206, Greene, 13778.
Catechesis/Religious Program—Students 50.
Station—New York State Veterans' Home 13830. Tel: 607-843-3100.

PARISH, OSWEGO CO., ST. ANNE (1950) [CEM] Closed. Merged with St. Mary, Star of the Sea, Mexico to form St. Anne, Mother of Mary, Mexico.

PHOENIX, OSWEGO CO., ST. STEPHEN (1880) Rev. Philip C. Brockmyre; Deacon Frank Forish.
Res.: 469 Main St., 13135. Tel: 315-695-4531; Fax: 315-695-2176.
Catechesis/Religious Program—Tel: 315-695-4608.

POMPEY, ONONDAGA CO., IMMACULATE CONCEPTION (1850) [CEM] Rev. James H. Carey, Admin.
Res.: 7386 Academy St., 13138. Tel: 315-677-3061; Fax: 315-677-2873.
Catechesis/Religious Program—Tel: 315-677-5126. Students 90.

PULASKI, OSWEGO CO., CHRIST OUR LIGHT (2003) Rev. Jozef Mucha (Poland).
23 Niagara St., 13142-4425. Tel: 315-298-5350; 315-298-3863 (Res.). Email: colcc23@gmail.com.
Catechesis/Religious Program—Students 105.

ROME, ONEIDA CO.

1—ST. JOHN THE BAPTIST (1909), (Italian), [CEM] Rev. Paul F. Angelicchio.
Res.: 210 E. Dominick St., 13440. Tel: 315-337-0990; Fax: 315-336-3841. Email: rstjohn@twcny.rr.com.
Catechesis/Religious Program—Students 202.

2—ST. MARY OF THE ASSUMPTION (1848) [CEM], Merged with St. Peter, Rome to form St. Mary's-St. Peter's, Rome.

3—ST. MARY'S-ST. PETER'S Rev. Philip A. Hearn. In Res., Rev. Msgr. Francis J. Culkin (Retired).
Res.: 105 E. Liberty St., 13440. Tel: 315-336-5072; Fax: 315-336-0855.
Catechesis/Religious Program—Students 250.

4—ST. PAUL (1954) Rev. Robert L. Kelly; Deacon Edgar Doyle Jr.
Res.: 1807 Bedford St., 13440-2199. Tel: 315-336-3082; Fax: 315-336-3083. Email: stpaulsrome@twcny.rr.com.
Catechesis/Religious Program—Tel: 315-334-9570. Students 130.

5—ST. PETER (1837) [CEM], Merged with St. Mary of the Assumption, Rome to form St. Mary's-St. Peter's, Rome.

6—TRANSFIGURATION (1909), (Polish), Rev. Paul F. Angelicchio.
111 Ridge St., 13440.
Catechesis/Religious Program—Students 32.

SANITARIA SPRINGS, BROOME CO., ST. JOSEPH (1914) Rev. Thomas F. Catucci.
Res.: 975 NY Rte. 11, Kirkwood, 13795. Tel: 607-648-5209.
Catechesis/Religious Program—Students 17.

SHERBURNE, CHENANGO CO., ST. MALACHY (1858) [CEM] Rev. Lester E. Smith.
Mailing Address: 29 E. State St., P.O. Box 722, 13460-0722. Tel: 607-674-9625; Fax: 607-674-2792. Email: st_malachy_sherburne@yahoo.com.
Catechesis/Religious Program—Students 70.

SHERRILL, ONEIDA CO., ST. HELENA (1917) Rev. William A. Mesmer.
Res.: 210 Primo Ave., 13461. Tel: 315-363-3882. Email: shelenarectory@twcny.rr.com.
Catechesis/Religious Program—Tel: 315-361-1566. Students 150.

SKANEATELES, ONONDAGA CO., ST. MARY OF THE LAKE (1855) [CEM] Rev. Darr F. Schoenhofen.
Mailing Address: 10 W. Austin St., 13152.
Res.: 81 Jordan St., 13152. Tel: 315-685-5083; Fax: 315-685-8327. Email: stmarys13152@yahoo.com.
Catechesis/Religious Program—Tel: 315-685-6377. Students 307.

SOLVAY, ONONDAGA CO., ST. CECILIA (1903), (Italian), Rev. Amedeo G. Guida.
Res.: 1001 Woods Rd., 13209. Tel: 315-488-3221; Fax: 315-488-3222. Email: stcecilia@espeedusa.com.
Catechesis/Religious Program—Tel: 315-488-4648. Students 166.

SOUTH ONONDAGA, ONONDAGA CO., CORPUS CHRISTI (1938) Rev. Dennis J. Hayes.
Res.: P.O. Box 288, Marietta, 13110. Tel: 315-492-0814. Email: dennish@dreamscape.com.
Church: 3126 Cedarvale Rd., R.D. 1, Nedrow, 13120. Tel: 315-492-0814.
Catechesis/Religious Program—Students 85.
Mission—St. Patrick [CEM] P.O. Box 574, Marietta, Onondaga Co. 13110. Tel: 315-696-8601.

TABERG, ONEIDA CO., ST. PATRICK (1876) [CEM] Rev. Francis A. Wapen.
Res.: 9168 Main St., 13471. Tel: 315-336-4079.
Catechesis/Religious Program—Students 49.

TRUXTON, CORTLAND CO., ST. PATRICK (1854) [CEM] Rev. Joseph H. Phillips; Deacon Laurence Brickner.
Res.: 3656 Rte. 13, Box 15, 13158. Tel: 607-842-6326.
Catechesis/Religious Program—Students 65.
Mission—St. Lawrence De Ruyter, Madison Co.

TULLY, ONONDAGA CO., ST. LEO (1891) Revs. James H. Carey; Robert B. Stephenson, Parochial Vicar.
10 Onondaga St., P.O. Box 574, 13159. Tel: 315-696-5092.
Res.: 6104 US Rte. 20, P.O. Box 169, La Fayette, 13084. Tel: 315-677-3439; Fax: 315-696-8721.
Catechesis/Religious Program—Students 91.

UTICA, ONEIDA CO.

1—ST. AGNES (1887) Closed. For inquiries for parish records contact the chancery.

2—ST. ANTHONY OF PADUA (1911), (Italian), Rev. Anthony LaFache; Deacon William Dischiavo, Sec. In Res., Rev. Msgr. Francis J. Willenburg.
Res.: 422 Tilden Ave., 13501. Tel: 315-732-1177.
Catechesis/Religious Program—Tel: 315-732-1177, Ext. 3151.

3—BLESSED SACRAMENT (1924) Closed. Merged with St. Mary of Mt. Carmel, Utica to form St. Mary of Mt. Carmel/Blessed Sacrament.

4—ST. FRANCIS DE SALES (1876) Closed. Merged with St. John's, Utica. Parish records available at St. John's, Utica.

5—ST. GEORGE (1911), (Lithuanian), [CEM] Closed. For inquiries for parish records contact St. Joseph and St. Patrick, Utica.

6—HOLY TRINITY (1896), (Polish), [CEM] Revs. John E. Mikalajunas; Joseph E. Moskal.
Res.: 1206 Lincoln Ave., 13502. Tel: 315-724-7238; Fax: 315-732-5448.
Catechesis/Religious Program—Tel: 315-733-5492. Students 59.
Convent—1218 Lincoln Ave., 13502. Tel: 315-733-5492; Fax: 315-733-5492.

7—ST. JOHN (1819) Revs. John A. Buehler; Luis Olguin, Spanish Apostolate. Tel: 315-724-0389; Sisters Sharon Ann Whellahan, C.S.J., Pastoral Assoc.; Joan Corcoran, D.C., Pastoral Assoc. & Outreach; Deacon William R. Dischiavo, Pastoral Assoc. In Res., Rev. John P. Flanagan (Retired).
Res.: 240 Bleecker St., 13501. Tel: 315-724-6159. Email: historicstjohns@roadrunner.com.
Parish Center—520 John St., 13501. Tel: 315-732-2417. Nancy Manley.
Catechesis/Religious Program—Tel: 315-732-1334. Students 190.

8—ST. JOSEPH AND ST. PATRICK (1841 and 1849) [CEM] Rev. Richard E. Dellos; Deacon Gilbert Nadeau.
Res.: 702 Columbia St., 13502. Tel: 315-735-4429; Fax: 315-735-1691. Email: sjsp@verizon.net.
Catechesis/Religious Program—Students 50.

9—ST. MARK (1963) Rev. Mark A. Pasik; Deacon Richard Prusko.
Res.: 440 Keyes Rd., 13502. Tel: 315-724-1645; Fax: 315-738-1978.
Catechesis/Religious Program—Students 210.

10—ST. MARY (1870), (German), Closed. For inquiries for parish records contact St. John, Utica.

11—ST. MARY OF MT. CARMEL/BLESSED SACRAMENT (1896) Rev. James M. Cesta; Anthony Elacqua, Dir. Maintenance; Mary Beth La Neve, Business Admin.; Peter Elacqua, Dir. In Res., Rev. Luis Olguin.
Res.: 648 Jay St., 13501. Tel: 315-735-1482; Fax: 315-735-9806. Email: mtcutica@aol.com.
Catechesis/Religious Program—Tel: 315-724-3950. Constance Armstrong, Dir. Faith Formation. Students 138.

12—OUR LADY OF LOURDES (1919) Revs. Joseph A. Salerno; Paul J. Alciati; Deacon William P. Hotaling; Sisters Elizabeth Mary Paciello, C.S.J.; Lois Mary Paciello, C.S.J.
Res.: 2 Barton Ave., 13502. Tel: 315-724-3155; Fax: 315-732-3770.
See Notre Dame Elementary School under Consolidated Schools located in the Institution section.
Catechesis/Religious Program—Students 280.

13—ST. PETER (1872) [CEM] Rev. David J. Orzel.
Res.: 422 Coventry Ave., 13502. Tel: 315-724-6310; Fax: 315-724-4942.
Catechesis/Religious Program—Tel: 315-735-7077. Students 90.

14—SACRED HEART (1926) Closed. For inquiries for parish records contact St. Mary, New York Mills.

15—ST. STANISLAUS (1911), (Polish), [CEM], Merged with Holy Trinity, Utica.
Res.: P.O. Box 324, 13503. Tel: 315-732-5919.

VERNON, ONEIDA CO., HOLY FAMILY (1926; 1976) Rev. William A. Mesmer.
Res.: 4343 Peterboro St., P.O. Box 988, 13476. Tel: 315-829-3295.
Catechesis/Religious Program—Tel: 315-829-2820. Students 137.

VERONA, ONEIDA CO., OUR LADY OF GOOD COUNSEL (1913) Rev. Edmund A. Castronovo.
Res.: 5259 Beacon Light Rd., P.O. Box 135, 13478. Tel: 315-363-7696. Email: frcastronovo@gmail.com.
Church: 5652 E. Main St., P.O. Box 135, 13478.
Catechesis/Religious Program—Students 100.

VESTAL, BROOME CO.

1—OUR LADY OF SORROWS (1941) Rev. John J. Kurgan, Admin.; Deacon Dale Crotsley. In Res., Rev. Matthew F. Brown (Retired).
Res.: 157 Clark St., 13850-2494. Tel: 607-748-8287; Fax: 607-748-8016. Email: olsorrows@stny.rr.com.
Catechesis/Religious Program—Tel: 607-748-4766. Students 385.

2—ST. VINCENT DE PAUL (1965) Rev. Edward J. Zandy; Deacon James P. Crowley.
Res.: 165 Clifton Blvd., 13850. Tel: 607-722-3988; Fax: 607-722-8787. Email: stvincentdepaul@stny.rr.com.
Catechesis/Religious Program—465 Clubhouse Rd., 13850. Tel: 607-722-8372. Students 202.

WARNERS, ONONDAGA CO., OUR LADY OF GOOD COUNSEL (1913) Merged with St. Joseph, Camillus.

WATERVILLE, ONEIDA CO., ST. BERNARD (1850) [CEM] Rev. Paul V. Carey.
Res.: 199 Stafford Ave., 13480. Tel: 315-841-4481. Email: sbwat1@yahoo.com.
Catechesis/Religious Program—Students 104.

WHITESBORO, ONEIDA CO.

1—ST. ANNE (1965), Records are being maintained at St. Paul's Whitesboro. Rev. Thomas M. Durant, Admin.
Res.: 16 Park Ave., 13492.
Church: 8539 Clark Mill Rd., 13492-2754. Tel: 315-736-7672.
Catechesis/Religious Program—Students 263.

2—ST. PAUL (1883) Rev. Thomas M. Durant.
Res.: 16 Park Ave., 13492. Tel: 315-736-1124; Fax: 315-768-7915.
Catechesis/Religious Program—Tel: 315-736-4807. Students 346.

WHITNEY POINT, BROOME CO., THE CATHOLIC COMMUNITY OF ST. STEPHEN-ST. PATRICK (1869) [CEM] Rev. Douglas D. Cunningham.
Res.: Box 711, 13862. Fax: 607-692-7171; Tel: 607-692-3911.
Catechesis/Religious Program—Students 65.
Mission—Our Lady of Perpetual Help Cincinnatus, Cortland Co. 13040.

WINDSOR, BROOME CO., OUR LADY OF LOURDES (1947) Rev. Thomas F. Catucci.
Mailing Address: 975 NY Rt. 11, Kirkwood, 13795.
Catechesis/Religious Program—Tel: 607-655-8118. Students 43.

Chaplains of Public Institutions

Hospitals

SYRACUSE. *St. Camillus Health & Rehab Center*, 813 Fay Rd., 13219. Tel: 315-488-2951. Rev. Louis F. Aiello.
Crouse Irving Memorial Hospital, 736 Irving Ave., 13210. Tel: 315-470-7615. Rev. William R. Jones, Staff Chap., Deacon Robert Connelly, Catholic Chap., Rev. James H. Carey.
James Square Nursing Home, Tel: 315-474-1561. Attended from Blessed Sacrament Parish.
St. Joseph's Hospital Health Center, 301 Prospect Ave., 13203. Tel: 315-448-5116. Deborah Welch, Vice Pres., People, Sisters Linda Ann Palmisano, O.S.F., Pace Program, Baptiste Westbrook, St. Joseph's Home Care Program, Rev. Severine Yagaza, Sisters Alice Dunlop, O.S.F., Adelbert Durant, O.S.F., Laura Hackenberg, O.S.F., Bridget Dunn, M. Elizabeth Heffernan.
Loretto Geriatric Center, 700 E. Brighton Ave., 13205. Tel: 315-469-5570. Sr. Cathleen Mary Moore, S.S.J., Catholic Chap.
Rosewood Heights Nursing Home, 614 S. Crouse Ave., 13210. Tel: 315-474-4431, Ext. 125. Rev. Harold Sanderson, Chap., Sr. Frances Ann Thom, O.S.F.
Upstate University Hospital, 750 E. Adams St., 13210. Tel: 315-464-5540. Revs. Terry Ruth Culbertson, Dir., Innocent Onyenagubo (Nigeria), Chap., Sr. Anne McNally.
University Hospital at Community Campus Hospital, 4900 Broad Rd., 13215. Tel: 315-492-5740. Sisters Winifred Guinan, O.S.F., Mary Bernard Sabel, O.S.F.
Van Duyn Home & Hospital, 5060 W. Seneca Tpke., 13215. Tel: 315-435-5511. Mrs. Janice Rosbrook.
Veterans Administration Hospital, Res: 800 Irving Ave., 13210. Tel: 315-476-7461. Revs. Wilfred F. Evans (Retired), David J. James, Chap.

BINGHAMTON. *Binghamton General Hospital*, Tel: 607-762-2200. Rev. Corey S. Van Kuren, Chap. & UHS, Dir., Barbara Eggleston, Chaplain; UHS.
Our Lady of Lourdes Memorial Hospital, 179 Riverside Dr., 13905. Tel: 607-798-5111. Mary Alice Westerlund, Dir., Rev. Krzysztof Boretto, Chap., Bros. James Bagans, Daniel Balluci, Sisters Kathleen Haley, Diane Louttit, Rev. David Seaver.
The Greater Binghamton Health Center, Tel: 607-724-1391, Ext. 4254. Revs. Gerald J. Buckley, Catholic Chap. (Retired), Roy Carter, Chap., Deacon John Stella.

JOHNSON CITY. *Wilson Memorial Hospital*, 33 Harrison St., 13790. Tel: 607-763-6000. Rev. Corey S. Van Kuren, Chap.

UTICA. *St. Elizabeth Hospital*, 2209 Genesee St., 13501. Tel: 315-798-8100. Revs. John H. Comeskey (Retired), Anthony LaFache, Bros. Edward Bick, Andrew Siuta, Sisters Irene Zegarelli, O.S.F., Dir., Dolorosa, Anthony Marie Eddo.
Faxton - St. Lukes Health Care, 1656 Chaplin Ave., New Hartford, 13413. Tel: 315-624-6110 Pastoral Care Office. 1676 Sunset Ave., 13502. Sr. Maureen Denn, C.S.J., Dir. of Pastoral Care, Bonnie Waldron, Chap. Asst.

VESTAL. *Binghamton Nursing Homes*, Our Lady of Sorrows, 157 Clark St., 13850. Tel: 607-748-8287. Revs. Matthew F. Brown, Pastoral Care Chap. (Retired), John J. Kurgan, Deacon Dale Crotsley.

Psychiatric Facilities

MARCY. *Central New York Psychiatric Center*, Old River Rd., Box 330, 13403. Tel: 315-765-3101. Rev. Richard V. O'Neill (Retired).

UTICA. *Mohawk Valley Psychiatric Center*, 1400 Noyes at York, 13502. Tel: 315-738-3800. Sr. Sharon Ann Whellahan, C.S.J.

Jails

SYRACUSE. *Elmcrest Children's Center*, Salt Springs Rd., 13224. Tel: 315-446-6250. Rev. Wess Fleming.
Hillbrook Detention Center, 4949 Velasko Rd., 13215. Tel: 315-492-1721. Deacon John Woloszyn.
Jail Ministry Office, 208 Slocum Ave., 13204. Tel: 315-424-1877; 315-234-9262. Bros. David Burton, Supvr., PM, William Cawley, S.C., Dir., William Medina, Supvr. AM.
Justice Center, 259 E. Onondaga St., 13202. Rev. John C. Schopfer.

BINGHAMTON. *Broome County Jail*. Rev. Stanley J. Gerlock (Retired).

CORTLAND. *Cortland County Jail*. Vacant.

JAMESVILLE. *Jamesville Penitentiary*, P.O. Box 143, 13078. Tel: 315-469-5581. Rev. Edward J. Reimer, Sr. Maura Rhode.

MARCY. *Marcy Correctional Facility*, 900 Old River Rd., P.O. Box 5000, 13403-5000. Tel: 315-768-1400. Rev. Vincent P. Long.
Mid-State Correctional Facility, 210 W. Liberty St., 13403. Tel: 315-768-8581. Rev. Robert C. Weber.

NORWICH. *Norwich County Jail*. Vacant.

ONEIDA. *Mohawk Correctional Facility*, 578 Main St., P.O. Box 8450, 13421. Rev. Vincent P. Long, Deacon James Chappell.

ORISKANY. *Oneida County Jail*, 120 Dexter Ave., 13424. Tel: 315-736-9033. Vacant.

OSWEGO. *Oswego County Jail*, 178 W. Second St., 13126. Tel: 315-349-3300. Rev. George E. Wurz.

ROME. *Walsh Regional Medical Unit*, Tel: 315-339-5232. Rev. Luis Olguin.

Special Assignment:
Most Revs.—
Costello, Thomas J., D.D. (Retired)
Cunningham, Robert J., J.C.L., D.D.
Moynihan, James M., D.D. (Retired)
Rev. Msgrs.—
Kopp, Richard M.
Quartier, Neal E.
Sheehan, George F. (Retired)
Revs.—
Aho, Charles A.
Cahill, William C.
Carmola, Michael J. (Retired)
Elmer, Timothy S., J.C.L.
Jones, Robert S.
Lang, James P.
Muscalino, Daniel C.
Olguin, Luis
Ours, Robert A.
Phillips, Joseph H.
Pompei, Frederick A.
Sambor, David R.
Schopfer, John C.
Sullivan, Robert J. (Retired)
Vavonese, Charles S.
Weber, Robert C.

On Duty Outside the Diocese:
Rev. Msgrs.—
Fahey, Charles J., Fordham University, New York.
Rossetti, Stephen, 126 E. St., S.E., Washington, DC 20003.
Revs.—
Bassano, Michael, M.M., Mary Knoll (Incardinated)
Creed, Peter, St. Mary's Star of the Sea, Fort Monroe, VA 23651.
Keane, Philip S., S.S.
Nichols, Louis J.
Wallace, Harry C.
Woolever, James

Military Chaplains:
Rev. Msgr.—
Elkin, Frederic F. (Retired), 3942 Roebling Ln., Virginia Beach, VA 23452.
Revs.—
Dunn, Richard B., PSC 2 Box 953, APO, AP 96264.
Fukes, Gary M., 1st Lt. & Chap., 1420 Waterford Place #7, Manhattan, KS 66502.
Gryga, Theodore, U.S. Navy
Madej, Paul D., 3017 N. Institute St., Colorado Springs, CO 80907. U.S. Navy

---

Absent on Leave:
Revs.—
Broderick, John W.
McNally, Edward F.
Wolak, Edmund

Retired:
Rev. Msgrs.—
Bill, Ronald C., Immaculate Conception Rectory, 400 Salt Springs St., Fayetteville, 13060.
Brigandi, Paul A.
Culkin, Francis J.
Davern, Robert B.
Donovan, William
Eckermann, Charles H.
Kane, James D.
Kantor, Adolph A.
Kelly, William M.
Luczycki, Matthew C.
Lutz, James M.
Madden, John R.
McCloskey, James A.
McGraw, John T.
Sheehan, George F.
Revs.—
Baehr, David, 1633 Leisure Dr., M-37, Bradenton, FL 34207.
Baker, William S., Utica, NY
Bebel, Alfred J., Binghamton, NY
Bogan, Robert F.
Brown, Matthew F.
Buckley, Gerald J.
Carmola, Michael J.
Comeskey, John H.
Culver, James A.
DeLorme, R. Daniel
Donovan, J. Michael
Dudkiewicz, Stanley (Poland)
Durr, Edmund J., Bridgeport, NY
Dwyer, Robert D.
Esposito, William C., 104 David Dr., North Syracuse, 13212.
Evans, Wilfred F.
Fetcho, John E.
Flanagan, John P., St. John's Rectory, 240 Bleeker St., Utica, 13501-2216.
Florczyk, Walter
Fuchs, Moritz A.
Gerlock, Stanley J., Binghamton, NY
Gleba, William P.
Heagerty, John J.
Heintz, Daniel
Jutton, David J.
Katz, Jerome A.
Keebler, Paul J., Windsor, NY
Keeffe, Anthony J., 1124 Oak St., 13203.
Kelly, Vincent J.
Kennedy, Laurence W.
Kiernan, Thomas
Lauducci, James V.
Major, Charles M.
Mattice, George F.
McGrath, Thomas J.
Morbito, Angelo L.
Morelle, Edmund J.
Morisette, Richard P.
Nortz, Alfred E.
O'Neill, Richard V., St. George Rectory, 425 LaFayette St., Utica, 13502.
Pilat, Edmund S.
Pilla, P. Carl
Quinn, James F.
Regan, William P.
Roark, John D.
Sizing, Theodore C.
Slater, Dennis
Smegelsky, John J.
Thompson, Richard R., 1633 Leisure Dr., Apt. M37, Bradenton, FL 34207.
Tucker, Richard
Wagner, John P.
Wood, Raymond B.
Young, Frank

Permanent Deacons:
Altmeter, Robert, Norwich
Alvaro, Nick A., Syracuse
Ashe, Wayne, (Retired), Kirkville
Blaine, Edward, Endicott
Bonocore, Steven J., Skaneateles
Borchert, Robert, (On Leave)
Brickner, Lawrence, Marathon
Brody, John P., (Retired)
Caughey, Daniel, Pulaski, NY
Celentano, Joseph, Sr., Syracuse
Chappell, James C., Oneida
Cholette, Frederick, Liverpool
Collins, John H., Pennellville
Connelly, Robert, Syracuse, NY
Crosby, James P., Syracuse (On Leave)
Cross, Gregory
Crossett, Thomas F., (Retired), Johnson City (On Leave)
Crotsley, Dale, Vestal
Crowley, James, (Retired), Vestal
Daniszewski, Joseph, Syracuse
Dischiavo, William R., Utica
Distin, Leslie, Johnson City
Dotterer, William A., Liverpool
Downes, Timothy, Tully
Doyle, Edgar A., Rome, NY
During, Joseph
Dwyer, Richard J., (Retired)
Engle, Christopher
Forish, Frank M., Baldwinsville
Goskowski, Raymond, Binghamton
Gudaitis, Michael, Rome
Hachey, Thomas, North Syracuse
Harley, Thomas, Endicott
Hart, Guy W., Bridgeport
Heizman, Bernard, (Retired), La Fayette
Hotaling, William P., Utica
Joslin, Donald E., (On Leave)
Kearney, Garrett, Syracuse
Kehoe, Phillip, Fulton, NY
Kernan, Edward, New Hartford
Kirsch, David, Norwich
Kopec, John, NY Mills
Kulak, Jules F., Solvay
Lalande, John, Oswego
Longo, Frank, (On Leave)
Manzene, Stephen, Liverpool
Maynard, George E., Clay
McCabe, Donald, Syracuse
McGrath, Michael B., Syracuse
McNerney, Timothy, Norwich
Money, Kenneth N., (On Leave)
Morse, James L., Syracuse
Mullin, Paul, (Retired)
Mulvey, John, (On Leave)
Murray, John, Manlius
Nadeau, Gilbert, Utica
Needham, Leo I., (Retired), Syracuse
Niles, Elbert, Oneida
Paparella, Anthony, Whitesboro
Paratore, Anthony J.
Phillips, George, Endwell
Picciano, Thomas N.
Prusko, Richard, Utica, NY
Riggalls, Robert, Sr., (Retired), Waterville
Rosher, Nicholas, Rome, NY
Rossi, Dominick (Ghana), (Retired)
Smith, Steve, Cortland
Stella, John, Binghamton
Sweenie, David, Oswego
Talomie, Robert J., Baldwinsville
Timson, Frank
Uryniak, Adolph J.
Vanelli, Peter P., Syracuse
Warren, Frank, (Retired), Oswego, NY
Whiting, Donald R., North Syracuse
Wilber, Richard, Chesire, CT, (On Leave)
Woloszyn, John, Liverpool
Young, Stephen, Cazenovia

INSTITUTIONS LOCATED IN THE DIOCESE

[A] SEMINARIES, RELIGIOUS, OR SCHOLASTICATES

SYRACUSE. *Saint Andrew Hall*, 420 Demong Dr., 13214-1499. Tel: 315-445-3500; Fax: 315-446-9472. Revs. James P. Carr, S.J., Rector & Dir. Novices; Thomas G. Benz, S.J., Asst. Dir. Novices. Novitiate for the Maryland, New England, and New York Provinces, Society of Jesus. Priests 2; Novices 14.

[B] COLLEGES AND UNIVERSITIES

SYRACUSE. *Le Moyne College*, 1419 Salt Springs Rd., 13214-1302. Tel: 315-445-4100; Fax: 315-445-4540. Web: www.lemoyne.edu. Dr. Fred P. Pestello, Pres.; Dr. Linda M. LeMura, Interim Provost & Vice Pres. for Academic Affairs; Dr. Deborah M. Cady Melzer, Vice Pres. Student Devel.; Mr. Roger W. Stackpoole, Vice Pres. Fin. & Admin.; Mrs. Barbara M. Karper, Asst. Vice Pres. Student Devel.; Mr. Mark G. Godleski, Asst. Dean, Student Devel.; Dr. J. Barron Boyd, Interim Dean, Arts & Sciences; Mrs. Mary M. Chandler, Registrar; Dr. Dennis R. DePerro, Vice Pres., Enrollment Mgmt.; Dr. Wally J. Elmer, Dean Mgmt.; Dr. Gregory Stahl, Vice Pres. for Inst. Advancement; Mr. Shaun Black, Acting Dir., Information Technology; Mr. Robert C. Johnston, Library Dir. A private four-year comprehensive college founded in 1946 enrolling approximately 3,500 students in a program of liberal arts, sciences, business and pre-professional studies. Le Moyne offers 31 academic majors leading to BA and BS degrees and also offers graduate programs in business administration, education, nursing and physician assistant studies. Jesuits 6; Sisters 1; Lay Teachers 149; Total Enrollment 3,502.

[C] HIGH SCHOOLS, DIOCESAN

SYRACUSE. *Bishop Ludden Junior/Senior High School*, (Grades 7-12), 815 Fay Rd., 13219. Tel: 315-468-2591; Fax: 315-468-0097. Email: blhs@syrdiocese.org. Sr. Mary Ellen Shirtz, C.S.J., Pres.; Mr. Michael Sandore, Prin.; John Bruzdzinski, Asst. Prin.; Parker O'Mara, Librarian. Priests 1; Sisters 2; Lay Teachers 36; Students 323.

BINGHAMTON. *Seton Catholic Central of Broome County*, 70 Seminary Ave., 13905. Tel: 607-723-5307; Fax: 607-723-4601. Email: secathb@syrdiocese.org. Mr. Richard Bucci, Prin.; Dr. Anchen Schulz, Asst. Prin.; Ms. Kathryn Frech, Librarian. Priests 5; Sisters 2; Deacons 1; Lay Teachers 32; Students 384.

EAST SYRACUSE. *Bishop Grimes Jr./Sr. High School*, (Grades 7-12), 6653 Kirkville Rd., 13057. Tel: 315-437-0356; Fax: 315-437-0358. Email: bghs@syrdiocese.org. Mr. Marc Crouse, Prin.; Mrs. Cathleen Hendrick, Librarian. Sisters 2; Lay Teachers 37; Students 420.

UTICA. *Notre Dame Jr./Sr. High School*, (Grades 7-12), 2 Notre Dame Ln., 13502. Tel: 315-724-5118; Fax: 315-724-9460. Email: amcollins@syrdiocese.org. Sr. Anna Mae Collins, C.S.J., Prin.; Mr. Roy Kane, Assoc. Prin.; Deborah Danquer, Librarian. Sisters 4; Lay Teachers 30; Students 332.

[D] HIGH SCHOOLS, PRIVATE

SYRACUSE. *Christian Brothers Academy*, (Grades 7-12), 6245 Randall Rd., 13214. Tel: 315-446-5960; Fax: 315-446-3393. Web: www.cbasyracuse.org. Bro. Joseph Jozwiak, F.S.C., Prin.; Karen Shull, Librarian. Brothers of the Christian Schools 2; Sisters of Third Order of St. Francis 2; Lay Teachers 56; Students 740.

[E] CONSOLIDATED SCHOOLS

BINGHAMTON. *St. John the Evangelist*, (Grades PreK-6), 9 Livingston St., 13903. Tel: 607-723-0703; Fax: 607-772-6210. Email: mekelley@syrdiocese.org. Mary Ellen Kelley, Prin. Lay Teachers 18; Students 179.

ENDICOTT. *All Saints Catholic School*, (Grades PreK-6), 1112 Broad St., 13760. Tel: 607-748-7423; Fax: 607-484-9576. Email: allsaints@syrdiocese.org. Angela Tierno, Prin. Lay Teachers 15; Students 149.

JOHNSON CITY. *St. James School*, (Grades PreK-6), 143 Main St., 13790. Tel: 607-797-5444; Fax: 607-797-6794. Email: ePrincipal@aol.com. George Clancy, Prin. Sisters 1; Lay Teachers 18; Students 150.

NORWICH. *Holy Family School*, (Grades PreK-8), 17 Prospect St., 13815. Tel: 607-337-2207; Fax: 607-337-2210. Email: hfamilyn@syrdiocese.org. Mr. Steve Bradley, Prin. Lay Teachers 15; Students 97.

OSWEGO. *Trinity Catholic School*, (Grades PreK-6), 115 E. 5th St., 13126. Tel: 315-343-6700; Fax: 315-342-9471. Mr. Joseph Lazarski, Admin. Lay Teachers 13; Students 116.

ROME. *Rome Catholic School*, (Grades PreK-12), 800 Cypress St., 13440. Tel: 315-336-6190; Fax: 315-336-6194. Mr. Michael Powers, Prin.; Mrs. Dyanna Gardinier, Librarian. Lay Teachers 21; Students 266.

UTICA. *Notre Dame Elementary School*, (Grades PreK-6), 11 Barton Ave., 13502. Tel: 315-732-4374; Fax: 315-738-9720. Email: jhauck@syracuse.org. Web: notredameelem.org. Ms. Judy Hauck, Prin.; Angeline Lubey, Librarian. Lay Teachers 25; Students 358.

[F] CATHOLIC CHARITIES OF SYRACUSE

SYRACUSE. *Bishop Joseph T. O'Keefe, Inc.*, c/o 240 E. Onondaga St., 13202. Tel: 315-424-1830; Fax: 315-478-4619. Most Rev. Robert J. Cunningham, J.C.L., D.D.; Rev. Timothy S. Elmer, J.C.L., Chancellor; Rev. Msgr. J. Robert Yeazel, V.G., Vicar Gen.

Catholic Charities of the Roman Catholic Diocese of Syracuse, 240 E. Onondaga St., 13202. Tel: 315-470-1415; Fax: 315-478-4619. Email: jslavik@syracusediocese.org. Web: www.syrdio.org. Mr. Joseph G. Slavik, Diocesan Dir.

Catholic Charities Onondaga County: Mr. Michael F. Melara, County Exec.

1654 W. Onondaga St., 13204. Tel: 315-424-1800; Fax: 315-424-6045. Email: mmelara@ccoc.us.

Jail Ministry, Slocum House, 208 Slocum Ave., 13204. Tel: 315-234-9262. Bill Cuddy, Coord.

Keener Seniors, 1654 W. Onondaga St., 13204. Tel: 315-424-1804; Fax: 315-424-6033. Nutrition Program for the Elderly.

BINGHAMTON. *Associated Catholic Charities of Broome County*, 232 Main St., 13905. Tel: 607-729-9166; Fax: 607-729-2062. Web:

www.catholiccharitiesbc.org. Lori Accardi, Exec. Admin.

Catholic Social Services of Broome County, 232 Main St., 13905. Tel: 607-729-9166; Fax: 607-729-2062. Email: dyeager@ccbc.net. Web: www.catholiccharitiesbc.org. Mr. Daniel L. Yeager, M.A., Exec. Dir.; Grazia Tonelli, L.C.S.W.-R., Supvr. of Clinical Svcs.; Shelly Kaminsky, L.C.S.W.-R., Supvr. Pregnancy, Parenting & Adopting Program.

CORTLAND. *Catholic Charities of Cortland County*, 33-35 Central Ave., 13045. Tel: 607-756-5992; Fax: 607-756-5999. Email: info@ccocc.org. Marie Walsh, Exec. Dir.

Case Management Services Tel: 607-756-5992; Fax: 607-756-5999. Email: info@ccocc.org. Ann Marie Phelps, Assoc. Dir.

Residential Services Tel: 607-756-5992; Fax: 607-756-5999. Mike Pisa, Dir. Residential Svcs. Residential services for adult mental health and substance abuse recovery.

Emergency Assistance Tel: 607-756-5992; Fax: 607-756-5999. Email: info@ccocc.org. Web: www.c-cocc.org. Ann Marie Phelps, Assoc. Dir. Emergency & Basic Needs Assistance (Food Pantry, Medication, Advocacy Referral & Support).; Summer Lunch Program for Children.

Catholic Charities-STEPS-TASA, 33-35 Central Ave., 13045. Tel: 607-756-5992; Fax: 607-756-5999. Email: info@ccocc.org. (Supportive Teen Education-Parents Services), TASA; Case Management; Adolescent Group Activities.

FULTON. *Catholic Charities of Oswego County*, 365 W. 1st St., 13069. Tel: 315-598-3980; Fax: 315-593-8440. Mary Margaret Pekow, Area Dir.

NORWICH. *Chenango House*, 49 Fair St., 13815. Tel: 607-336-8939. Supervised by Community Residence Program.

Intensive Supportive Apartment Program
49 Fair St., 13815. Tel: 607-336-4359.

Supported Housing Program
49 Fair St., 13815. Tel: 607-336-4492.

Community Residence Program Provides housing for mentally ill adults.

Catholic Charities of Chenango County, 3 O'Hara Dr., 13815. Tel: 607-334-8244; Fax: 607-336-5779. Email: ccccharity@adelphia.net.

The Counseling Program Provides comprehensive counseling for children and adults, also specialized counseling for abused children.

Catholic Charities of Chenango County, 3 O'Hara Dr., 13815. Tel: 607-334-8244; Fax: 607-336-5779. Mrs. Robin Beckwith, Dir.

Crime Victims-Witness Assistance Program Tel: 607-334-3532; Fax: 607-336-5779. Provides 24-hour Hotline at 607-336-1101, Crisis Intervention, Safe Dwelling, Safe Housing; Court accompaniment; filing affidavits and claims with Crime Victims Board; advocacy with law enforcement agencies; information and referrals.

ONEIDA. *Catholic Charities of Oneida - Madison Counties*, 248 Main St., 13421. Tel: 315-363-5274. Kathleen C. Eichenlaub, Area Dir.

Madison County Catholic Charities, 248 Main St., Box 10, 13421. Tel: 315-363-5274; Fax: 315-363-4925. Kathleen C. Eichenlaub, Dir.

UTICA. *Catholic Charities Family & Community Support Services*, 1408 Genesee St., 13502. Tel: 315-724-2158; Fax: 315-724-5318. Email: bpotter@ ccharityon.org. Kathleen C. Eichenlaub, Area Dir.; Brad Potter, Dir. Family & Community Support Svs. Div.

Catholic Charities of Oneida - Madison Counties, 1408 Genesee St., 13502. Tel: 315-724-2158; Fax: 315-724-5318. Kathleen C. Eichenlaub, Area Dir.; Jan Stasaitis, Dir. Admin.; Anthony J. Conestabile, Dir. Finance; Jack Callaghan, Dir. Residential Support; Brad Potter, Dir. Family & Community Support Svcs.

[G] OFFICES OF HUMAN DEVELOPMENT

SYRACUSE. *Bishop Foery Foundation*, 100 Edmond Ave., 13205. Tel: 315-475-8316; Fax: 315-472-1408.

BINGHAMTON. *Broome County Catholic Charities Office of Social Concerns*, 232 Main St., 13905. Tel: 607-729-9166; Fax: 607-729-2062. Web: www.catholiccharitiesbc.org. Lori Accardi, Contact Person. Staff 450.

[H] ST. VINCENT DE PAUL SOCIETY

FULTON. *Catholic Charities Thrift Shop*, 365 W. First St., 13069. Tel: 315-598-3980; Fax: 315-593-8440. Email: kdavies-buchley@ccoswego.com.

[I] CATHOLIC YOUTH ORGANIZATIONS

SYRACUSE. *Catholic Charities of Onondaga County*, 1654 W. Onondaga St., 13204. Tel: 315-424-1800; Fax: 315-424-8262. Email: neron@ccoc.us. Mr. Michael F. Melara, Exec. Dir.

Children & Family Preservation Division, Catholic Charities of Onondaga County, 1654 W. Onondaga St., 13204. Tel: 315-424-1880; Fax: 315-424-6079. Email: mclary@ccoc.us. Mark Clary, Assoc. Dir.

Hawley Youth Organization, 716 Hawley Ave., 13203. Tel: 315-472-6343.

Northside CYO, 527 N. Salina St., 13208. Tel: 315-474-7428.

Salina Civic Center, 2826 Lemoyne Ave., Mattydale, 13211. Tel: 315-455-7096; Fax: 315-455-2352. Email: kcieplicki@ccoc.us.

Toomey Residential and Community Services Corp., 1654 W. Onondaga St., 13204. Tel: 315-424-1845; Fax: 315-424-7567. Email: jdamore@ccoc.us. Judith D'Amore, Exec. Dir.

Vincent House, 514 Seymour St., 13204. Tel: 315-475-9844; Fax: 315-474-3939.

BINGHAMTON. *Broome County CYO*, 86-88 Walnut St., 13905. Tel: 607-584-7800; Fax: 607-584-7801. Email: jtoner@ccbc.net. Sandra Ohlsen, Div. Dir.

FULTON. *Catholic Charities of Oswego Co.*, 365 W. First St., 13069. Tel: 315-598-3980; Fax: 315-593-8440. Email: mmpekow@ccoswego.com. Mary Margaret Pekow, Exec. Dir. Staff 40.

[J] CHILDREN'S INSTITUTIONS AND DAY CARE CENTERS

SYRACUSE. *Catholic Charities of Onondaga County*, 1654 W. Onondaga St., 13204. Tel: 315-424-1847; Fax: 315-424-8262. Email: neron@ccoc.us. Web: www.ccoc.us. Mr. Michael F. Melara. Records only.

Gingerbread House Preschool & Childcare Center, 2500 Grant Blvd., 13208. Tel: 315-471-4198; Fax: 315-471-4198. Email: d@gingerbreadsyracuse.com. David Cole, Dir.

[K] DIOCESAN SUMMER CAMPS

SYRACUSE. *Lourdes Camp*, Office: 1654 W. Onondaga St., 13204. Tel: 315-424-1812; 315-673-2888 (Summer).

Camp Address:, 10 Mile Point, Skaneateles, 13152. Michael Preston, Dir.

UTICA. *Camp Nazareth*, Office: 1408 Genesee St., 13502. Tel: 315-724-2158.
112 Long Lake Rd., Woodgate, 13494. Tel: 315-392-3791; Fax: 315-392-6545. Dianne DiMeo, Dir. Family & Community Support Svcs.

[L] FAMILY LIFE BUREAUS

SYRACUSE. *Family Life Education*, 815 Fay Rd., 13219. Tel: 315-472-6754; Fax: 315-472-8409. Email: familylifed@syracusediocese.org. Web: www.familylifeeducation.syracuse.org. Rev. Joseph H. Phillips, Exec. Dir.; Jennifer Kerns, Coord., Family & Marriage Enrichment; Karen Bandoblu, Coord., Marriage Prep. & Natural Family Planning; Dean Brainard, Coord., Separated/ Divorced, The Third Option, and Parenting; Sue & Ronald Kielar, Directors Eastern Region; Kathy & John Colligan, Directors Southern Region.

Northern Region Office of Faith Formation & Special Education for Catechetics, 74 W. 6th St., Oswego, 13126. Tel: 315-596-4014; Fax: 315-596-4020. Email: germcsj@verizon.net. Sr. Germaine Hilston, C.S.J., Dir.; Deanne Hall, Resource Center Admin.

EAST SYRACUSE. *Western Region Office of Faith Formation and Resource Center*, c/o 6651 Kirkville Rd., 13057. Tel: 315-472-6753; Fax: 315-472-8409. Email: tmay@syrdio.org. Theresa May, Dir.

ENDWELL. *Southern Region Family Life Education*, 400 Corey Ave., 13760. Tel: 607-748-4743. Email: JColligan@stny.rr.com. John Colligan, Dir.; Kathleen Colligan, Dir.

Cortland Resource Center, 44 N. Main St., Cortland, 13045. Tel: 607-756-2532; Fax: 607-756-2532. Amy White.

[M] GENERAL HOSPITALS

SYRACUSE. *St. Joseph's Hospital Health Center*, 301 Prospect Ave., 13203. Tel: 315-448-5111; Fax: 315-448-6161. Email: teresa.lavalle@sjhsyr.org. Web: www.sjhsyr.org. College for Nurses. Sisters of St. Francis of the Neumann Communities 20; Bed Capacity 431; Patients Assisted Annually 400,000; Total Staff 3,300; Students 279.

BINGHAMTON. *Our Lady of Lourdes Memorial Inc.*, 169 Riverside Dr., 13905. Tel: 607-798-5111; Fax: 607-798-7681. Web: lourdes.com. David Patak, Pres. Daughters of Charity of St. Vincent de Paul 9; Bed Capacity 267; Patients Assisted Annually 400,000; Total Staff 1,300.

UTICA. *St. Elizabeth Medical Center*, 2209 Genesee St., 13501. Tel: 315-798-8100; Fax: 315-734-3092. Email: rketcham@STEMC.org. Web: www.stemc.org. Mr. Richard Ketcham, Pres. & CEO; Rev. John H. Comeskey (Retired). College of Nursing. Sisters of the Third Franciscan Order 12; Bed Capacity 201; Patients Assisted Annually 434,277; Students 205; Total Staff 1,800.

[N] FACILITIES FOR THE AGED

SYRACUSE. *Bernardine Apartments, Inc.*, 417 Churchill Ave., 13205. Tel: 315-469-7786. Howard Jenkins, Admin.

St. Camillus Health & Rehabilitation Center, 813 Fay Rd., 13219. Tel: 315-488-2951; Fax: 315-488-3255. Email: aileen.balitz@st-camillus.org. Web: www.st-camillus.org. Mrs. Aileen M. Balitz, Pres. Bed Capacity 384; Total Assisted 2,700; Total Staff 670.

St. Camillus Foundation, 813 Fay Rd., 13219. Tel: 315-488-2951, Ext. 404. Michael Zandr, Foundation Chm.

Loretto Geriatric Community Residences, Inc., 5018 S. Salina St., 13205. Tel: 315-492-0896.
700 E. Brighton Ave., 13205. Tel: 315-469-8562.
50 Syracuse St., Baldwinsville, 13027. Tel: 315-635-1647.
8659 Carpenter Rd., Baldwinsville, 13027. Tel: 315-635-1763.

Loretto Rest Realty Corp., 700 E. Brighton Ave., 13205. Tel: 315-413-3733; Fax: 315-469-6558. Ms. Lisa Maxwell, Admin. Cunningham Bldg.; Sr. Cathleen Moore, S.S.V., Chap.

Loretto Health & Rehabilitation Center Bed Capacity 554; Total Assisted 2,000; Staff 800.

Loretto Rest, Inc., 700 E. Brighton Ave., 13205. Tel: 315-413-3185; Fax: 315-492-2446. Sr. Cathleen Moore, S.S.V., Chap.; Mr. Mitchell Marsh, Admin. Adult Home.

Loretto and Loretto Apartments Housing Development Fund Co., Inc., c/o Loretto, 700 E. Brighton Ave., 13205. Tel: 315-469-5570; Fax: 315-498-9073.

OSWEGO. *Saint Luke's Health Care Services*, 299 E. River Rd., 13126. Tel: 315-342-3166; Fax: 315-343-6531. Email: tgorman@stlukehs.com. Web: www.stlukehs.com. Mr. Terrence Gorman, Admin. Bed Capacity 200; Total Staff 370.

UTICA. *St. Joseph Nursing Home*, 2535 Genesee St., 13501. Tel: 315-797-1230; Fax: 315-797-5171. Email: fdeck@stjosephnh.org. Web: www.stjosephnh.org. Frederick Deck, Admin. Bed Capacity 120; Total Assisted Annually 120; Total Staff 180.

[O] SPECIALTY HOUSING

SYRACUSE. *Bartell Road Housing Development Co., Inc.* (Brewerton), 990 James St., 13203. Tel: 315-424-1821; Fax: 315-424-6048. Housing for well elderly.

Christopher Community, Inc. Professional management and consultants of housing programs for the elderly, families and special populations., 990 James St., 13203. Tel: 315-424-1821; Fax: 315-424-6048. Mr. Douglas Reicher, Exec. Dir.; Fred Zolna, Housing Devel. Specialist.

Churchill Manor, Inc., 750 E. Brighton Ave., 13205. Tel: 315-492-1329; Fax: 315-492-6076. Email: cahika@lorettosystem.org. Mary Koenig, Admin. A nonprofit corporation founded to provide housing for low and moderate income families and individuals. Bed Capacity 80.

Harbor View Housing Development Fund Co., Inc., c/o 990 James St., 13203. Tel: 315-424-1821; Fax: 315-424-6048.

Hawley Winton Housing Development Fund, Inc., Walter Ludovico Apts., 340 Winton St., 13203. Tel: 315-422-0475; Fax: 315-471-1554. 32 one-bedroom units occupied. Christopher Community, (Managing Agent).

Ludden Housing Development Fund Company, Inc., 990 James St., 13203. Tel: 315-424-1821; Fax: 315-424-6048. Fifty one-bedroom apartments for the elderly and handicapped. Christopher Community Inc., (Managing Agent).

Marcellus Apartments Housing Development Fund Company, Inc., 990 James St., 13203. Tel: 315-424-1821; Fax: 315-424-6048. Christopher Community, Inc., (Managing Agent).

Mother Marianne Cope Housing Development Fund Co., Inc., 1047 E. Fayette St., 13210. Tel: 315-422-5611; Fax: 315-478-6972. 23 Units for HIV positive patients.

Mount St. James Corporation, 990 James St., 13203. Tel: 315-424-1821; Fax: 315-424-6048. Engaged in the operation of a nonprofit housing facility known as Mount St. James Apartments, at 338 Jamesville Ave., for persons of low to moderate income. Christopher Community, Inc., (Managing Agents).

St. Peter's Italian Church Housing Development Fund Co., Inc. Villa Scalabrini Apts., 301 Ash St., 13208. Operation of a nonprofit housing facility for aged, well persons of low income at the 800 block of E. Willow St. in Syracuse. 120 units, one-bedroom apartments. Christopher Community, Inc., (Managing Agent).

Pompei Housing Development Fund Company, Inc. 50 one-bedroom apartments for the elderly and handicapped. Christopher Community, Inc., (Managing Agent).

c/o Christopher Community, Inc., 990 James St., 13203. Tel: 315-424-1821; Fax: 315-424-6048.

Pond St. Housing Development Fund Co., Inc., Bishop Harrison Apartments, 300 Pond St., 13208. Tel: 315-476-8630; Fax: 315-474-0806. Operation of 47 units, one bedroom apartments for the elderly and handicapped. Christopher Community Inc., (Managing Agent). Staff 2; Emergency Maintenance Services 24.

Providence House Apartments, 1700 W. Onondaga St., 13204. Tel: 315-471-8427; Fax: 315-474-1224. Email: mquirk@christopher-community.org. Senior citizen housing, 100 units. Christopher Community, (Managing Agent). Staff 3.

Stoneleigh Housing Development Fund Co., Inc., Stoneleigh Apartments, 400 Lamb Ave., Canastota, 13032. Fax: 315-697-9097; 315-697-2847. Engaged in the construction and operation of a nonprofit housing facility for elderly and handicapped persons of low income. 100 units, one bedroom apartments. Christopher Community, Inc., (Managing Agent). Staff 2.

Tyson Place Housing Development Fund Company, Inc. (40 apartments for the elderly), *St. Joseph Manor*, 990 James St., 13203. Tel: 315-424-1821; Fax: 315-424-6048. Christopher Community, Inc., (Managing Agent).

AUBURN. *Mercy Housing Development Fund Co., Inc.*, *Mercy Apartments*, 1 Thornton Ave., 13021. Tel: 315-424-1821; Fax: 315-424-6048. 990 James St., 13203. 40 one-bedroom units for the elderly and handicapped. Christopher Community, Inc., (Managing Agent).

BALDWINSVILLE. *Smokey Hollow Housing Development Fund Company, Inc.*, *St. Mary's Apartments c/o Christopher Community*, 990 James St., 13203. Tel: 315-424-1821; Fax: 315-424-6048. Christopher Community, Inc., (Managing Agent).

BREWERTON. *Bartell Road Housing Development Fund Co., Inc. dba Long Manor Apts.* 5500 Miller Rd., 13029. Tel: 315-668-9871 (Mon.-Fri. 1PM-4PM); Fax: 315-668-0048. Email: longmanor@christophercommunity.org. Justine Poplaski, Contact Person. 20 units, one bedroom apartments. Christopher Community, Inc., (Managing Agent).

CICERO. *Cicero Housing Development Fund Company Inc.*, 990 James St., 13203. Tel: 315-424-1821; Fax: 315-424-6048.

Sacred Heart Apartments, 990 James St., 13203. Christopher Community, Inc., (Managing Agent).

FAYETTEVILLE. *Redfield South Housing Development Fund Co., Inc.*, Redfield Village Apartments, 380 Salt Springs Rd., 13066. Tel: 315-637-8280; Fax: 315-637-2376. Email: lgrosso@christopher-community.org. 50 one-bedroom units. Christopher Community, Inc., (Managing Agent). Total Assisted 50; Total Staff 2; Units 1.

NORTH SYRACUSE. *Pitcher Hill-Christopher Housing Development Fund Co., Inc.*, 990 James St., 13203. Tel: 315-424-1821; Fax: 315-424-6048. Email: pitcherhill@christophercommunity.org. Engaged in the construction and operation of nonprofit housing facilities for elderly and handicapped persons of low income. 100 units, one bedroom apartments. Christopher Community, Inc., (Managing Agent). Total Assisted 98; Total Staff 4.

OSWEGO. *St. Luke's Housing Development Fund Co., Inc.*, St. Luke's Apartments, W. First St., 13126. Tel: 315-343-0821; Fax: 315-343-0619. Engaged in the construction and operation of a nonprofit housing facility for elderly and handicapped persons of low income. 100 units, one bedroom apartments. Christopher Community, Inc., (Managing Agent).

ROME. *C.N.C. Inc.*, 1003 W. Thomas St., 13440. Tel: 315-724-2185; Fax: 315-724-5318. *Catholic Charities of Oneida/Madison Counties*, 1408 Genese St., Utica, 13502. Facility for ten deinstitutionalized chronically mentally ill individuals living in a group home.

Rome Mall Housing Development Fund Company, Inc., 990 James St., 13203. Tel: 315-424-1821; Fax: 315-424-6048. 45 one-bedroom units for the elderly. Christopher Community, Inc., (Managing Agent).

Rome Mall Apts., 13440.

TOWN OF GATES. *Steger Housing Development Fund Co., Inc.*, 4100 Lyell Rd. 56 apartments for well elderly.

1654 W. Onondaga St., 13204. Tel: 315-424-1821; Fax: 315-424-6048.

UTICA. *Catherine St. Housing Development Fund Company, Inc.*, *Mt. Carmel Apartments*, 990 James St., 13203. Tel: 315-424-1821; Fax: 315-424-6048. Christopher Community, Inc., (Managing Agent).

[P] PROGRAMS FOR THE HANDICAPPED

SYRACUSE. *L'Arche of Syracuse, Inc.*, 920 Spencer St., 13204. Tel: 315-479-8088; Fax: 315-479-8118. Email: larchesyracuse@cnymail.com. Web: www.larchesyracuse.org. Peggy Harper, Community Leader. A Christian Community concerned with life sharing between persons with a developmental disability and persons who assist them; Homes at 310 Galster Ave, 4550 Cleveland Rd., 211 Croyden Rd., 140 Highland Ave., Syracuse. Staff 40.

UTICA. *St. John and St. Joseph Home, Inc.*, 1408 Genesee St., 13502. Tel: 315-724-2158; Fax: 315-724-5318. Kathleen C. Eichenlaub, Contact Person.

[Q] MONASTERIES AND RESIDENCES OF PRIESTS AND BROTHERS

SYRACUSE. *Jesuits at LeMoyne, Inc.*, 1419 Salt Springs Rd., 13214. Tel: 315-445-4604; Fax: 315-445-4722. Email: jesuitres@lemoyne.edu. Web: www.lemoyne.edu/jesuitheritage/tabid/482/default.aspx. Revs. William J. Bosch, S.J.; David J. Casey, S.J., Treas.; James H. Dahlinger, S.J.; William S. Dolan, S.J., Rector; Adelino P. Dunghe, S.J.; Vincent W. Hevern, S.J.; Donald J. Kirby, S.J.; Waldemer P. Los, S.J.; Donald C. Maldari, S.J.; Carsten P. Martensen, S.J.; David C. McCallum, S.J.; Daniel J. Mulhauser, S.J.; Paul S. Naumann, S.J.; Joseph B. Neville, S.J.; Robert E. Scully, S.J.; James F. Smith, S.J.; Louis P. Sogliuzzo, S.J.; Andrew L. Szebenyi, S.J. Priests 17; Scholastics 1.

Tommy Coyne Residence @ Dillon Hall, 714 E. Brighton Ave., 13205. Tel: 315-469-0078. Diocesan home for priests. In Res. Rev. Msgr. Robert B. Davern (Retired); Revs. Angelo L. Morbito (Retired); Alfred E. Nortz (Retired); William P. Regan (Retired); John D. Roock (Retired).

BINGHAMTON. *McDevitt Residence for Retired Priests*, 68 Seminary Ave., 13905. Tel: 607-771-6207. Rev. Thomas F. Hobbes (Retired); Rev. Msgr. James D. Kane (Retired); Revs. Gerald J. Buckley (Retired); Stanley J. Gerlock (Retired).

EAST SYRACUSE. *Vianney House*, 6651 Kirkville Rd., 13057. Tel: 315-727-4631. Rev. Msgr. George F. Sheehan (Retired).

MAINE. *Mount St. Francis Hermitage, Inc.*, 120 Edison Rd., P.O. Box 236, 13802. Tel: 607-754-0001; Fax: 607-754-0001. Web: www.mtstfrancis.com. Revs. Johannes Michael Mary Smith, F.I.; John Joseph Mary Cook, F.I.; Friars Juniper Mary Gold, F.I.; Faustino Mary Fulnecky, F.I. Professed Friars 2; Postulants 5.

[R] CONVENTS AND RESIDENCES FOR SISTERS

SYRACUSE. *Dominican Monastery of the Perpetual Rosary*, 802 Court St., 13208-1766. Tel: 315-471-6762. Email: violetbop@verizon.net. Sr. Helen Ann, O.P., Prioress. Cloistered Nuns 9; Extern Sisters 1.

Sisters of St. Francis of the Neumann Communities (1860) Congregational Offices: 2500 Grant Blvd., Ste. 3, 13208. Tel: 315-634-7000; Fax: 315-634-7023. Email: sisters@sosf.org. Web: www.sosf.org. Central New York Region: *St. Anthony and Jolenta Convents*, 1024 Court St., 13208. Tel: 315-422-8652; Fax: 315-422-9612. Sisters Patricia Burkard, O.S.F., Gen. Min.; Marion Rose Mansius, O.S.F., Gen. Councilor; Maria Salerno, O.S.F., Gen. Councilor; Barbara Woody, O.S.F., Gen Councilor; Frances Kowalski, O.S.F., Gen. Treas. & Gen. Councilor; Roberta Stark Smith, O.S.F., Sec. & Gen. Councilor. Professed Sisters in the Region 162; Professed Sisters in the House 79; Associates in the Region 114; Total in Community 505.

ENDICOTT. *Little Sisters of Saint Francis of Assisi Mission*, 304 Oak Hill Ave., 13760. Tel: 607-786-5006; Fax: 607-786-5066. Email: littlesrsusa@gmail.com. Sisters Anisia Muthoni, Dir.; Lilia Kagendo, Dir.

WINDSOR. *Transfiguration Monastery*, 701 NY Rte. 79, 13865-2700. Tel: 607-655-2366; Fax: 607-655-4024. Email: bendon@tds.net. Sr. Donald Corcoran, O.S.B.Cam., Prioress. Camaldolese Benedictine Nuns. Sisters 3.

[S] RETREAT HOUSES

SYRACUSE. *Christ the King Retreat House*, 500 Brookford Rd., 13224. Tel: 315-446-2680; Fax: 315-446-2689. Email: retreats@christthekingretreat.com. Rev. Mark P. Kaminski, Ph.D., D.Min., Dir.; Anne Richter, Asst.; Marianne Carbone, Admin. Asst. General retreat house for priests, nuns, laity and youth of upstate New York. Priests 1.

MAINE. *Mount St. Francis Hermitage, Inc.*, 120 Edson Rd., P.O. Box 236, 13802. Tel: 607-754-0001; Fax: 607-754-0001. Web: www.mtstfrancis.com. Rev. Johannes Michael Mary Smith, F.I.

SKANEATELES. *Stella Maris Retreat & Renewal Center* 13152. Tel: 315-685-6836; Fax: 315-685-7008. Email: info@setllamarisretreat.org. Web: www.stellamarisretreat.org. Rev. Thomas McGrath, Admin. (Retired); Denise Schochech, Admin. Asst.; Sisters Concetta Fabo, O.S.F., Prog. Dir.; Patricia Larkin, O.S.F., Prog. Dir. Sisters of the Third Franciscan Order, M.C., Franciscan oriented center for renewal.

UTICA. *The Good News Foundation of Central New York*, 10475 Cosby Manor Rd., 13502. Tel: 315-735-6210; Fax: 315-735-7090. Email: info@thegoodnewscenter.org. Web: www.thegoodnewscenter.org. Michael Buckley, Exec. Dir. & CEC; Michelle Holliday, Accounting & Opers. Mgr.

[T] NEWMAN CENTERS

SYRACUSE. *LeMoyne College Campus Ministry* 1499 Salt Springs Rd., 13214. Tel: 315-445-4110; Fax: 315-445-4797. Revs. Louis P. Sogliuzzo, S.J., Dir.; William S. Dolan, S.J., Rector, Campus Min.

Syracuse University, St. Thomas More Foundation, Inc. Alibrandi Catholic Center, 110 Walnut Pl., 13210. Tel: 315-478-5959; Fax: 315-443-4465. Email: ldesanti@syr.edu. Rev. Linus DeSantis, O.F.M.Conv.

CAZENOVIA. *Cazenovia College Newman Center* 10 Seminary St., 13035. Tel: 315-655-7237; Fax: 315-655-7536. Email: jabaron@cazenovia.edu. Web: www.cazcollege.edu/zinterfaith.htm. Rev. Kevin Corcoran, Chap.

CLINTON. *Hamilton College Newman Center* 198 College Hill Rd., 13323. Tel: 315-859-4129; Fax: 315-859-4041. Email: jcroghan@hamilton.edu. Web: www.hamilton.edu/college/newman. Rev. John P. Croghan, Chap.

CORTLAND. *Newman Foundation of Cortland, Inc. at the State University College of New York* 8 Calvert St., 13045. Tel: 607-753-6737. Email: marie.agen@cortland.edu. Web: www.cortland.edu/ministry/catholic.html. Marie C. Agen, Ph.D., Campus Min.

MORRISVILLE. *Newman Association at SUNY Morrisville* Mathasis Health Bldg., 13408. Tel: 315-684-6201. Email: YoungSR@morrisville.edu. Web: www.morrisville.edu/pages/newman. Deacon Steven R. Young, Chap.

St. Joan of Arc Newman Association at the State University of New York (SUNY) Morrisville Agricultural and Technical College

OSWEGO. *Newman Foundation, Inc., State University of New York Hall Newman Center*, 36 New St., P.O. Box 207, 13126. Tel: 315-312-7222; Fax: 315-216-6593. Email: newctr@oswego.edu.

UTICA. *Newman Center at SUNY Institute of Technology* P.O. Box 8087, 13505-8087. Tel: 315-792-3284; Fax: 315-792-4401. Rev. Paul J. Drobin, Chap.

State University of New York (SUNY) Institute of Technology Newman Center

Utica College Newman Center P.O. Box 8087, 13505-8087. Tel: 315-792-3284; Fax: 315-792-4401. Rev. Paul J. Drobin, Chap.

Res.: P.O. Box 8087, 13505-8087. Tel: 315-792-3284.

VESTAL. *Binghamton University Newman Center* 400 Murray Hill Rd., 13850. Tel: 607-798-7202. Email: frcorey@binghamton.edu. Rev. Corey S. Van Kuren, Chap.

[U] MISCELLANEOUS LISTINGS

SYRACUSE. **Brady Faith Center, Inc.*, 404 South Ave., P.O. Box 993, 13201. Tel: 315-472-9077; Fax: 315-472-9077. Web: www.bradyfaithcenter.org. Rev. John C. Schopfer, Pastoral Dir.

**David W. Barry Foundation*, 240 E. Onondaga St., 13202. Tel: 315-422-7203; Fax: 315-478-4619. Most Rev. Robert J. Cunningham, J.C.L., D.D., Pres.; Rev. Msgr. J. Robert Yeazel, V.G., Vice Pres.; Rev. Timothy S. Elmer, J.C.L., Sec. & Treas.

Father Champlin's Guardian Angel Society, 259 E. Onondaga St., 13202. Tel: 315-422-7218; Fax: 315-422-2471. Email: angel003@twcny.rr.com. Kathy Fedrizzi, Exec. Dir.

The Foundation of the Roman Catholic Diocese of Syracuse, 240 E. Onondaga St., 13202. Tel: 315-422-7023. Rev. Msgr. J. Robert Yeazel, V.G., Contact Person.

St. Francis Social Adult Day Care, Inc., 1108 Court St., 13208. Tel: 315-424-1003; 315-424-1004; Fax: 315-472-9899. Email: info@stfrancisadc.com. Web: www.stfrancisadc.com. Sr. Barbara Jean Donovan, O.S.F., Admin. Sponsored by the Sisters of St. Francis of the Neumann Communities., A non-residential adult day-service providing holistic care for the frail elderly.

Grimes Foundation (Incorporated by special act of the New York State Legislature, May 1, 1916),

240 E. Onondaga St., 13202. Tel: 315-422-7203; Fax: 315-478-4619. Most Rev. Robert J. Cunningham, J.C.L., D.D., Pres. Ex-Officio; Rev. Msgr. J. Robert Yeazel, V.G., Vice Pres.; Rev. Timothy S. Elmer, J.C.L., Treas. Corporation created to establish and maintain charitable, religious and educational facilities within the Roman Catholic Diocese of Syracuse, New York.

Lasalle Syracuse, Inc., 6245 Randall Rd., 13214. Tel: 315-446-5960; Fax: 315-446-3393. Web: www.cbasyracuse.org.

Loretto Apartments Housing Development Fund Co., Inc., 700 E. Brighton Ave., 13205. Tel: 315-413-3206; Fax: 315-498-9073. Email: jmurray@lorettosystem.org.

Onondaga County Catholic School Foundation (Western Region Catholic School Foundation), 240 E. Onondaga St., 13202. Tel: 315-470-1450; Fax: 315-470-1470.

Our Lady of Lourdes Hospitality - North American Volunteers, Ltd., P.O. Box 3820, 13220. Tel: 315-476-0026; Fax: 419-730-4540. A Public Association of the Christian Faithful founded in 2003 to share the Message of Lourdes, accompany the sick and handicapped on pilgrimage and serve the Sanctuaries at Lourdes, France.

Partners in Franciscan Ministries Inc., 2500 Grant Blvd., Ste. 3, 13208. Tel: 315-634-7086; Fax: 315-634-7087. Email: pfogle@sosf.org. Web: www.sosf.org. Sr. Patricia Fogle, O.S.F., Exec. Dir. Sponsored by the Sisters of St. Francis of the Neumann Communities.

Spiritual Renewal Center, 1118 Court St., Ste. B., 13208. Tel: 315-472-6546. Email: mail@spiritualrenewalcenter.com. Web: www.spiritualrenewalcenter.com.

The Robert L. McDevitt, K.S.G., K.C.H.S. and Catherine H. McDevitt, L.C.H.S. Foundation, Inc., 240 E. Onondaga St., 13202. Tel: 315-422-7023. Rev. Msgr. J. Robert Yeazel, V.G., Vicar General.

The Syracuse Diocesan Investment Fund, Inc., 240 E. Onondaga St., 13202. Tel: 315-422-7023. Rev. Msgr. J. Robert Yeazel, V.G., Dir. & Vicar Gen.

Saint Thomas Preparatory Seminary Fund, COO, 240 E. Onondaga St., 13202. Incorporated under the Laws of the State of New York, 1963, as a Membership Corporation to solicit funds for the construction of a diocesan seminary.

BINGHAMTON. *Ladies of Charity*, 100 Main St., 13905. Tel: 607-723-0194.

Samaritan House, 11 Fayette St., 13901. Tel: 607-724-3969; Fax: 607-771-0356.

The Robert L. McDevitt, K.S.G., K.C.H.S. and Catherine H. McDevitt, L.C.H.S. Fund of St. Patrick's Catholic Church of Binghamton, N.Y., 9 Leroy St., 13905. Tel: 607-722-1060.

The Robert L. McDevitt, K.S.G., K.C.H.S. and Catherine H. McDevitt, L.C.H.S. Fund of St. Thomas Aquinas Church, 1 Aquinas St., 13905. Tel: 607-797-4015.

CANASTOTA. *Catholic Diocese of Nakuru Mission Office, Inc.*, 406 Spencer St., 13032. Tel: 315-697-8795; Fax: 315-697-8959. Email: cdnmission@yahoo.com. Rev. Cleophas Oseso Tuka (Africa), Dir.

DEWITT. *Joseph & Elaine Scuderi Foundation*, 5786 Widewaters Pkwy., P.O. Box 3, 13214.

ENDICOTT. *Little Sisters of St. Francis of Assisi Mission* 304 Oak Hill Rd., Broome Co. 13760. Tel: 607-273-4200. Elena Salerno Flash, Esq., Contact Person.

Roman Catholic Diocese - Bishop Harrison Education Trust (1994) 240 E. Onodaga St., 13202.

JOHNSON CITY. *The Robert L. McDevitt, K.S.G., K.C.H.S. and Catherine H. McDevitt, L.C.H.S. Fund of St. James Church of Lestershire, N.Y.*, 147 Main St., 13790. Tel: 607-729-6147.

RICHLAND. *Rural & Migrant Ministry of Oswego Co. Inc.*, 15 Stewart St., P.O. Box 192, 13144-0192. Tel: 315-298-1154; Fax: 315-298-1154. Email: rmmoc@yahoo.com. Shawn Doyle, Exec. Dir.

SOLVAY. **Sacred Heart Apostolate, Inc.*, 105 Stanton Ave., 13209-1544. Tel: 315-492-6308; Fax: 315-492-3407. Email: sacredhc@verizon.net. Web: www.sacredheartapostolate.com. Gloria Anson, Pres.; Thomas Mueller, Chm./Contact Person. Tel: 714-775-1246.

UTICA. *Christ Child Society of Utica*, 140 Hawthorne Ave., 13502. Email: curling.kelly@verizon.net. Cindy Kelly, Treas.

RELIGIOUS INSTITUTES OF MEN REPRESENTED IN THE DIOCESE

For further details refer to the corresponding bracketed number in the Religious Institutes of Men or Women section.

[1350]—*Brothers of St. Francis Xavier* (St. Joseph Prov., Milton, MA)—C.F.X.

[0330]—*Brothers of the Christian Schools* (New York Prov.)—F.S.C.

[]—*Brothers of the Sacred Heart*

[0480]—*Conventual Franciscans*—O.F.M.Conv

[]—*Franciscan Friars of the Immaculate* (Griswold, CT)—F.I.

[0690]—*Jesuit Fathers and Brothers* (New York Prov.)—S.J.

RELIGIOUS INSTITUTES OF WOMEN REPRESENTED IN THE DIOCESE

[0230]—*Benedictine Sisters of Pontifical Jurisdiction* (Erie, PA)—O.S.B.

[]—*Camaldolese Benedictine Sisters*—O.S.B.Cam.

[0330]—*Carmelite Sisters for the Aged and Infirm*—O.Carm.

[]—*Congregation of the Sisters of the Cross of Chavanod* (India)

[0760]—*Daughters of Charity of St. Vincent de Paul*—D.C.

[]—*Daughters of St. Mary of Providence*—D.S.M.P

[1050]—*Dominican Contemplative Nuns*—O.P.

[1070-01]—*Dominican Sisters*—O.P.

[1170]—*Felician Sisters*—C.S.S.F.

[1180]—*Franciscan Sisters of Allegany, New York*—O.S.F.

[1410]—*Franciscan Sisters of St. Joseph (Mill Hill)*—F.M.S.J.

[2575]—*Institute of the Sisters of Mercy of the Americas* (New York, NY; Omaha, NE)—R.S.M.

[]—*Little Sisters of St. Francis*—L.S.O.S.F.

[1360]—*Missionary Franciscan Sisters of the Immaculate Conception*—O.S.F.

[1800]—*Sisters of St. Francis of the Neumann Communities*—O.S.F.

[3830-14]—*Sisters of St. Joseph* (Watertown, NY)—S.S.J.

[3840]—*Sisters of St. Joseph of Carondelet*—C.S.J.

[1970]—*Sisters of the Holy Family of Nazareth*—C.S.F.N.

[]—*Sisters of the Immaculate Heart of Mary, Mother of Christ* (Africa)—I.H.M.

[2160]—*Sisters, Servants of the Immaculate Heart of Mary*—I.H.M.

DIOCESAN CEMETERIES

SYRACUSE. *St. Mary-St. Agnes*, 2315 South Ave., 13207. Tel: 315-475-4639. Mr. Mark Lazaroski, Dir.; Ralph D'Agostino, Supt.; Daniel Moorhead, Asst. Supt.

BALDWINSVILLE. *Our Lady of Peace Cemetery*, 8668 Oswego Rd., 13027. Tel: 315-303-4901. Christopher Nacey, Supt.

CORTLAND. *St. Mary*, 4101 West Road, 13045. Tel: 607-756-8838; Fax: 607-756-8838. Andrew Cook, Supt.

JOHNSON CITY. *Calvary-St. Patrick*, 501 Fairview St., 13790. Tel: 607-797-2906. Email: rramey@syracusecatholiccemeteries.org. Randy Ramey, Supt.; Ann Adams, Sec.

OSWEGO. *St. Peter & St. Paul*, 379 E. River Rd., R.R. 04, 13126. Tel: 315-343-5002; Fax: 315-343-2421. Christopher Nacey, Supt.

UTICA. *Calvary Cemetery*, 2407 Oneida St., 13501. Tel: 315-735-2727. Timothy Moynihan, Supt.

Holy Trinity, Chaplain Ave., 13502. Tel: 315-724-0616. Timothy Moynihan, Supt.

St. Mary Cemetery, Webster St., 13501. Tel: 315-735-2727. Timothy Moynihan, Supt.

WHITESBORO. *Mount Olivet*, 70 Wood Rd., 13492. Tel: 315-736-4446. Timothy Moynihan, Supt.

NECROLOGY

† Gleba, Rev. Msgr. Peter W., Syracuse, NY Basilica of the Sacred Heart—Died March 9, 2011

† Cincotta, Anthony, (On Duty Outside the Diocese)—Died July 19, 2011

† Hartnett, George F., (Retired)—Died Sept. 14, 2011

† Murphy, Daniel G., (Retired)—Died Oct. 13, 2011

An asterisk (*) denotes an organization that has established tax-exempt status directly with the IRS and is not covered by the USCCB Group Ruling.

Diocese of Toledo

(Dioecesis Toletana in America)

Most Reverend

LEONARD P. BLAIR

Bishop of Toledo; ordained June 26, 1976; appointed Titular Bishop of Voncariana and Auxiliary Bishop of Detroit July 9, 1999; consecrated August 24, 1999; appointed Bishop of Toledo October 7, 2003; installed December 4, 2003.

Most Reverend

ROBERT W. DONNELLY, D.D.

Retired Auxiliary Bishop of Toledo; ordained May 25, 1957; appointed Titular Bishop of Garba and Auxiliary Bishop of Toledo March 14, 1984; ordained Bishop May 3, 1984; retired May 30, 2006.

Chancery: 1933 Spielbusch Ave., Toledo, OH 43604-5360. Tel: 419-244-6711; Fax: 419-244-4791.

Web: www.toledodiocese.org

Email: chancery@toledodiocese.org

ESTABLISHED APRIL 15, 1910.

Square Miles 8,222.

Comprises the following Counties of northwest Ohio: Williams, Fulton, Lucas, Ottawa, Defiance, Henry, Wood, Sandusky, Erie, Paulding, Putnam, Hancock, Seneca, Huron, Van Wert, Allen, Wyandot, Crawford and Richland.

For legal titles of parishes and diocesan institutions, consult the Chancery.

STATISTICAL OVERVIEW

Personnel	
Bishop	1
Retired Bishops	1
Priests: Diocesan Active in Diocese	105
Priests: Diocesan Active Outside Diocese	5
Priests: Retired, Sick or Absent	69
Number of Diocesan Priests	179
Religious Priests in Diocese	37
Total Priests in Diocese	216
Extern Priests in Diocese	7
Ordinations:	
Diocesan Priests	3
Permanent Deacons	9
Permanent Deacons in Diocese	199
Total Brothers	8
Total Sisters	500
Parishes	
Parishes	126
With Resident Pastor:	
Resident Diocesan Priests	78
Resident Religious Priests	10
Without Resident Pastor:	
Administered by Priests	32
Administered by Religious Women	6
New Parishes Created	1
Closed Parishes	2
Professional Ministry Personnel:	
Brothers	4
Sisters	10
Lay Ministers	280
Welfare	
Catholic Hospitals	7
Total Assisted	1,301,302
Health Care Centers	3
Total Assisted	481
Homes for the Aged	12
Total Assisted	1,046
Day Care Centers	2
Total Assisted	363
Special Centers for Social Services	10
Total Assisted	150,889
Other Institutions	7
Total Assisted	1,332
Educational	
Diocesan Students in Other Seminaries	26
Total Seminarians	26
Colleges and Universities	2
Total Students	3,475
High Schools, Diocesan and Parish	10
Total Students	2,881
High Schools, Private	4
Total Students	2,604
Elementary Schools, Diocesan and Parish	62
Total Students	12,261
Elementary Schools, Private	2
Total Students	326
Non-residential Schools for the Disabled	1
Total Students	49
Catechesis/Religious Education:	
High School Students	4,130
Elementary Students	21,789
Total Students under Catholic Instruction	47,541
Teachers in the Diocese:	
Priests	12
Scholastics	7
Sisters	29
Lay Teachers	1,416
Vital Statistics	
Receptions into the Church:	
Infant Baptism Totals	2,380
Minor Baptism Totals	626
Adult Baptism Totals	357
Received into Full Communion	395
First Communions	3,462
Confirmations	3,287
Marriages:	
Catholic	674
Interfaith	443
Total Marriages	1,117
Deaths	2,784
Total Catholic Population	317,685
Total Population	1,465,561

Former Bishops—Most Rev. JOSEPH SCHREMBS, D.D., appt. Auxiliary Bishop of Grand Rapids, MI Jan. 8, 1911; cons. Feb. 22, 1911; transferred to Toledo, Aug. 11, 1911; transferred to Cleveland, OH, May 11, 1921; died Nov. 2, 1945; His Eminence SAMUEL CARDINAL STRITCH, D.D., cons. Bishop of Toledo, Nov. 30, 1921; appt. Archbishop of Milwaukee, Aug. 30, 1930; appt. Archbishop of Chicago, Dec. 27, 1939; created Cardinal, Feb. 18, 1946; named Pro-Prefect of the Sacred Congregation of the Propagation of the Faith, March 1, 1958; died in Rome, May 27, 1958; Most Revs. KARL J. ALTER, D.D., LL.D., appt. Bishop of Toledo, April 17, 1931; cons. June 17, 1931; appt. Archbishop of Cincinnati, June 21, 1950; retired July 23, 1969; died Aug. 23, 1977; GEORGE REHRING, D.D., cons. Oct. 7, 1937; appt. Auxiliary Bishop of Cincinnati, Oct. 7, 1937; appt. Bishop of Toledo, July 18, 1950; retired Feb. 25, 1967; died Feb. 29, 1976; JOHN A. DONOVAN, D.D., ord. Dec. 8, 1935; Titular Bishop of Rhasus and Auxiliary of Detroit, Michigan Sept. 6, 1954; ord. Bishop of Detroit, Michigan Oct. 26, 1954; appt. to Toledo, Feb. 25, 1967; retired July 29, 1980; died Sept. 18, 1991; JAMES R. HOFFMAN, D.D., J.C.L., ord. July 28, 1957; appt. Titular Bishop of Italica and Auxiliary Bishop of Toledo April 18, 1978; ord. June 23, 1978; appt. Bishop of Toledo Feb. 17, 1981; died Feb. 8, 2003.

Chancery

Vicar General—Rev. Msgr. MARVIN G. BORGER, V.G., J.C.L., Catholic Center, 1933 Spielbusch Ave., Toledo, 43604-5360. Tel: 419-244-6711; Fax: 419-244-4791.

Chancellor and Moderator of the Curia—Rev. MONTE J. HOYLES, J.C.L., Catholic Center, 1933 Spielbusch Ave., Toledo, 43604-5360. Tel: 419-244-6711; Fax: 419-244-4791. Email: mhoyles@toledodiocese.org.

Archives—Catholic Center, 1933 Spielbusch Ave., Toledo, 43604-5360. Tel: 419-244-6711; Fax: 419-244-4791. Sr. NADINE MATHIAS, S.N.D., Archivist. Email: nmathias1@toledodiocese.org. Office Hours: daily 1pm-5pm.

Canonical Services—Catholic Center, 1933 Spielbusch Ave., Toledo, 43604-5360. Tel: 419-244-6711; Fax: 419-244-4791.

Delegate of the Bishop—Rev. MONTE J. HOYLES, J.C.L.

Promoter of Justice—Very Rev. DAVID M. ROSS, V.F., S.T.L., J.C.D.

Assessors—Rev. JOSEPH E. FOX, O.P., J.C.D.; Rev. Msgr. CHRISTOPHER P. VASKO, V.J., J.C.D.

Advocate—Rev. JAMES E. AUTH, J.C.L.

Ecclesiastical Notary—Rev. MONTE J. HOYLES, J.C.L.

Catholic Center Services—Catholic Center, 1933 Spielbusch Ave., Toledo, 43604-5360. Tel: 419-244-6711; Fax: 419-244-4791. Ms. PATRICIA STEIN, Mgr. Email: pstein@toledodiocese.org. Provides building services and centralized purchasing for offices located in the Catholic Center.

Court of Equity— The Court of Equity has been granted jurisdiction and authority by the bishop to be a legally constituted body to consider complaints against administrative decisions and to resolve controversies by conciliation or arbitration. This court has jurisdiction over the parishes, departments and institutions that are under the authority of the bishop of Toledo. Ms. JUDITH GAJDOSTIK, Clerk, 3250 Hazelton Dr.,

Oregon, 43616. Tel: 419-691-7436; Mr. FRANK LINK, Presiding Judge.

Judges—Sr. JOANNE MARY FRANIA, S.N.D.; Mr. WAYNE GRAVES; Rev. GREGORY R. HITE; Mr. FRANCIS LANDRY; Mr. COLIN MCQUADE; Ms. LORI SMITH; Sr. DOROTHY THUM, R.S.M.; MARY GRACE TRIMBOLI; Mr. BRUCE WINTERS.

Conciliators—Mr. WILLIAM BINGLE; Mr. RICHARD HANUSZ; Sr. THERESE MILNE, I.H.M.; Mr. JOHN J. SCHLAGETER JR.; Mr. JOHN F. WETLI; Mr. DENNIS WROBLEWSKI.

Intake Officers— (pending)

Diocesan Case Manager—Catholic Center, 1933 Spielbusch Ave., Toledo, 43604-5360. Tel: 419-244-6711, Ext. 632; 800-926-8277, Ext. 632 (outside Toledo, within Ohio). Mr. FRANK DILALLO. Email: fdilallo@toledodiocese.org.

Review Board— The Review Board reviews cases involving allegations of sexual abuse of minors and makes recommendations to the bishop concerning those cases. The Review Board consists of a number of qualified lay volunteers with professional expertise as well as a canon lawyer and a priest who are appointed by the bishop. Mr. FRANK LINK, Chm. Members: Rev. Msgr. CHRISTOPHER P. VASKO, V.J., J.C.D.; Mrs. MARY JO ANDERSON; Mr. FREDERICK FERRI; Ms. SHELLEY KILLEN; Dr. ROSALYN LISTON; Ms. SARAH MCHUGH; Dr. PAMELA OATIS; Ms. K. LAVERNE REDDEN.

Investigatory Team— The Investigatory Team is a designated group of individuals who are available to investigate allegations of sexual abuse. The Investigatory Team consists of a number of qualified lay volunteers with professional expertise and/or pastoral gifts to accomplish their task. They are appointed by the bishop. Members: Mr. LARRY ALBRIGHT; Mr. LAWRENCE KNANNLEIN; Mr. WILLIAM T. ROCCIA.

Pastoral Response Team— The Pastoral Response Team is a designated group of individuals who are available to respond to alleged victims of sexual abuse of minors and who are able to provide continuing pastoral care as needed. The Pastoral Response Team consists of a number of qualified lay volunteers with professional expertise. Members: Ms. DIANE DERR; Mr. JAMES HEYMAN; Ms. SHELLEY KILLEN; Mr. RICHARD KOHLER; Ms. ANDREA LOCH; Ms. ROSALIE STLUKA, L.I.S.W.; Mr. THOMAS WILLIAMS.

Human Resources—Catholic Center, 1933 Spielbusch Ave., Toledo, 43604-5360. Tel: 419-244-6711; Fax: 419-244-4791. Mr. GREGORY C. REED, Dir. Email: gcreed@toledodiocese.org; Mrs. MEGHAN REED, Specialist. Email: mreed@toledodiocese.org. Provides advice and counsel to diocesan offices, agencies and parishes in effective human resource practices; responsible for development, implementation and administration of personnel policies and programs in the areas of recruitment, employment, compensation/benefits and employee relations. HR Representatives: Mrs. JESSICA PARKER. Email: iparker@toledodiocese.org; Ms. KATHRYN SLIWINSKI. Email: ksliwinski@toledodiocese.org.

Retirement Plan for Lay Employees (RPLE)—Catholic Center, 1933 Spielbusch Ave., Toledo, 43604-5360. Tel: 419-244-6711; Fax: 419-244-4791. Mrs. LINDA MILLER, Admin. Email: lmiller@toledodiocese.org; Mrs. BECKY INGRAM, Asst. Email: bingram@toledodiocese.org. Maintains employees' contribution and benefit records and communicates with parishes, participants, trustees, investment and other professional counsel. Administers benefits including retirement, disability, death and survivor.

Employee Benefit Fund— Maintains employer's contribution records and administers certain employee benefits including life insurance, retiree health care stipend and the F. Edward Schaefer Scholarship.

Tax Deferred Savings Program for Employees— 403 (b). Savings plan to give lay employees' the opportunity to build savings for retirement through pre-tax paycheck.

Mareda, Inc.— MAREDA, Inc., is the Catholic diocesan low income housing corporation founded in 1978 by the late Bishop John A. Donovan. It is the successor corporation to the Catholic Better Community Development Corporation, which had been the diocesan housing corporation for the previous 11 years. This corporation extends the church's ministry of housing to the elderly and people with disabilities who are economically challenged. Rev. Msgr. MICHAEL R. BILLIAN, V.F., Pres. Managed by Vistula Management Co. P.O. Box 4719, Toledo, 43620. Tel: 419-242-2300; Fax: 419-246-4703; Mr. JOHN KIELY, Dir. Email: jkiely@vmc.org; Mr. ANDY KOTT, Assoc. Dir.

Madonna Homes— (171 units) *722 Huron St., Toledo, 43604-5360.* Tel: 419-244-3758. Ms. TRACEY FRANKLIN, Mgr.

Regina Manor— (180 units) *3739 N. Erie St., #1B, Toledo, 43611.* Tel: 419-726-6186. Ms. KIM WOODS, Mgr.

Delaware Acres— (68 units) *725 Buchanan St., Fremont, 43420.* Tel: 419-334-9558. Ms. MARCELLA WHITE, Mgr.

Moody Manor— (119 units) *2293 1/2 Kent St., Toledo, 43620.* Tel: 419-246-4737. Ms. ANNE FREEMAN, Mgr.

Hope Manor— (100 units) *4702 Violet Rd., Toledo, 43623.* Tel: 419-246-4733. Ms. CINDY KASPRZAK, Mgr.

Michaelmas Manor— (94 units) *3260 Schneider Rd., Toledo, 43614.* Tel: 419-389-4615. Ms. CHRIS VARGO, Mgr.

Plaza Apartments— (160 units) *2520 Monroe St., Toledo, 43620.* Tel: 419-244-1881. Ms. ANGELA SHAW, Mgr.

Diocesan Outreach Centers—

Assumption Center—219 Page St., Toledo, 43620. Tel: 419-243-9213; Fax: 419-243-5405. Ms. SUZANNE STAPLETON, Facility Admin. Email: sstapleton@bex.net; Ms. ELLEN MCCOMIS, Prog. Dir. Email: emccomis@bex.net.

DeSales Center—501 Cherry St., Toledo, 43604. Tel: 419-243-4242; Fax: 419-243-4243. Deacon THOMAS CARONE, Dir. Email: tomcarone56@aol.com.

Helping Hands of St. Louis—443 Sixth St., Toledo, 43605. Tel: 419-691-0613; Fax: 419-697-4223. Email: helpinghands@bex.net. Web: helpinghands.org. Mr. PAUL COOK, Dir.; Ms. SUE SHREWSBERRY, Administrative Asst.

Office of Communications—Catholic Center, 1933 Spielbusch Ave., Toledo, 43604-5360. Tel: 419-244-6711; Fax: 419-244-0468. Ms. SALLY A. OBERSKI, Dir. Email: soberski@toledodiocese.org; Ms. KELLY O'LOUGHLIN, Communications Coord. Email: koloughlin@toledodiocese.org. Represents the bishop and diocesan offices to the media; provides counsel for media and public relations and marketing efforts to the diocesan agencies, institutions and parishes; produces all news releases and places radio and television programming in the name of the diocese.

"Catholic Chronicle"—Catholic Center, 1933 Spielbusch Ave., Toledo, 43604-5360. Tel: 419-244-6711; Fax: 419-244-0468. Web: www.catholicchronicle.org. Email: ccnews@toledodiocese.org. Mrs. ANGELA KESSLER, Editor. Email: akessler@toledodiocese.org. The Catholic Chronicle is the official newspaper of the Diocese of Toledo. Its mission is to spread the good news of the Gospel by reporting information, providing education and including inspiring features about people and events in the diocese and the worldwide Catholic Church. It is published twice a month, except July.

Diocesan Directory—Catholic Center, 1933 Spielbusch Ave., Toledo, 43604-5360. Tel: 419-244-6711; Fax: 419-244-0468. ROSE ANNE CONRAD, Coordinating Sec. Email: rconrad@toledodiocese.org.

Information Technology—Catholic Center, 1933 Spielbusch Ave., Toledo, 43604-5360. Tel: 419-244-6711; Fax: 419-244-0468. Mr. DARREN GRUBMAER. Email: dgrubmaer@toledodiocese.org; Ms. SHARON LANDIS, Assoc. Dir. Email: slandis@toledodiocese.org. Provides direct information technology services to organizations within the Catholic Center and its satellite locations. Consulting, technical guidelines, recommendations, procurement of hardware and software and other related system services are provided to parishes and schools.

Priests' Personnel Board—Tel: 419-644-6527 (Assumption Holy Trinity Rectory). Rev. RONALD A. SCHOCK, Chm., Assumption Holy Trinity, 2649 US Hwy. 20, Swanton, 43558. Email: father_@hotmail.com. Advises the diocesan bishop regarding the appointment of priests to the positions he identifies; serves as liaison between the bishop and the priests and the parishes in matters dealing with appointments. Members: Revs. KENT R. KAUFMAN; FRANKLIN P. KEHRES; Rev. Msgr. DENNIS M. METZGER, V.F.; Revs. J. DOUGLAS GARAND; JOSEPH R. STEINBAUER.

Tribunal—Catholic Center, 1933 Spielbusch Ave., Toledo, 43604-5360. Tel: 419-244-6711; Fax: 419-244-4791. The mission of the Tribunal, under the guidance of our bishop, is to reflect and experience Christ in the ministry of justice through the compassionate and equitable application of church law, and to protect the rights and dignity of each person without discrimination, and to provide an opportunity for healing.

Judicial Vicar—Rev. Msgr. CHRISTOPHER P. VASKO, V.J., J.C.D. Email: cvasko@toledodiocese.org.

Judges—Rev. JAMES E. AUTH, J.C.L.; Rev. Msgr. MARVIN G. BORGER, V.G., J.C.L.; Rev. JOSEPH P. JAROS (Retired); Very Rev. GEORGE P. MILLER, J.C.L.; Rev. WILLIAM C. PARKER (Retired); Very Rev. DAVID M. ROSS, V.F., S.T.L., J.C.D.

Defenders of the Bond—Rev. JOSEPH L. VAMOS (Retired); Sr. MARCELLA HERMAN, O.S.F., J.C.L.; Rev. GARY D. YANUS, J.C.D.

Procurator-Advocate for Respondents—Revs. DAVID M. BRUNING; THOMAS J. EXTEJT; TIMOTHY F. FERRIS; KRZYSZTOF KARDZIS; ARTHUR J. NIEWIADOMSKI; Deacons JAMES D. CARUSO; THOMAS S. CARONE; Mrs. PATRICIA A. EINGLE.

Associate Judges—Revs. DAVID M. BRUNING; THOMAS J. EXTEJT; TIMOTHY F. FERRIS; KRZYSZTOF KARDZIS; ARTHUR J. NIEWIADOMSKI; Deacons JAMES D. CARUSO; THOMAS S. CARONE.

Ecclesiastical Notaries—Mrs. PAULA S. BUTLER; Mrs. ANGELA D. WALKER.

General Counsel— To support the Diocese of Toledo in its mission to serve the Body of Christ. This position serves as the principal legal advisor for the diocese, parishes, schools, cemeteries and other institutions that fall under the diocesan bishop's jurisdiction. Deacon JAMES CARUSO, Gen. Counsel.

Advisory Bodies

Priests' Council— Representing the presbyterate, the Priests' Council is to be like a senate of the bishop, assisting him in the governance of the diocese (canon 495). Rev. Msgr. CHRISTOPHER P. VASKO, V.J., J.C.D., Chm., 1933 Spielbusch Ave., Toledo, 43604. Email: cvasko@toledodiocese.org.

College of Consultors— The College of Consultors advises the bishop in the more important matters of diocesan administration (canon 502). Revs. MICHAEL O. BROWN; GREGORY L. PEATEE, V.F.; Very Revs. DAVID M. ROSS, V.F., S.T.L., J.C.D.; GEORGE E. WENZINGER, V.F.; Revs. EDWARD J. LITTELMANN (Retired); DENNIS G. WALSH; Very Rev. HERBERT F. WEBER, V.F.

Deans— Also known as a vicar forane in the Code of Canon Law, each dean has the responsibility of promoting and coordinating the pastoral activity of his deanery according to the norm of law. Together, the deans serve as advisors to the bishop (canon 553-555). Blessed Junipero Serra Deanery: Very Rev. DAVID M. ROSS, V.F., S.T.L., J.C.D. Blessed Kateri Tekakwitha Deanery: Very Rev. JEFFREY R. MCBETH, V.F. Blessed Teresa of Calcutta Deanery: Very Rev. DENNIS P. HARTIGAN, Ph.D., V.F. Our Lady of the Lake Deanery: Very Rev. JOHN C. MISSLER, V.F. Our Lady, Queen of Peace Deanery: Very Rev. DANIEL E. BORGELT, V.F. Precious Blood of Jesus Deanery: Very Rev. JOSEPH P. SZYBKA, V.F. St. Agnes Deanery: Rev. Msgr. MICHAEL R. BILLIAN, V.F. St. Francis of Assisi Deanery: Rev. Msgr. MICHAEL G. HOHENBRINK, V.F. St. George Deanery: Very Rev. GEORGE E. WENZINGER, V.F. St. John Neumann Deanery: Very Rev. FRANCIS J. SPEIER, V.F. St. Juan Diego Deanery: Very Rev. NELSON G. BEAVER, V.F. St. Katherine Drexel Deanery: Very Rev. HERBERT F. WEBER, V.F. St. Luke Deanery: Rev. Msgr. DENNIS M. METZGER, V.F. St. Maximilian Kolbe Deanery: Very Rev. G. ALLAN FILLMAN, V.F. St. Philomena Deanery: Very Rev. DAVID L. RITCHIE, V.F.

Diocesan Pastoral Advisory Council— The Diocesan Pastoral Advisory Council is a recommending body that will assist the bishop in setting the direction and vision for the diocese for pastoral ministry. The Diocesan Pastoral Advisory Council will engage in a planning process that includes assessment, development of strategies and evaluation. As it prays and works to carry out its mission, the council will promote and model collaboration, collegiality, cooperation and community. Members: Ms. SHARON BELISLE; Ms. IRMA CELESTINO; Mr. BRAD COLON; Mrs. ALVINA COSTILLA; Deacon JAMES E. DUNN; Mrs. PATRICIA A. EINGLE; Mrs. PATRICIA ENGLEHART; Mr. ROBERT GEIGER; Mr. RICHARD HANUSZ; Ms. LIZ MILLER; Mr. JOSHUA MOCEK; Ms. CHERYL PRYOR; Ms. LINDA SALMONS; Mr. DAVID SANTO; Mr. BRUCE WINTERS.

Finance Council— The council reviews quarterly financial statements and advises the bishop on financial matters and investments. Ex Officio Members: Most Rev. LEONARD P. BLAIR, S.T.D.; Rev. MONTE J. HOYLES, J.C.L.; Deacon RONALD D. HENDERSON. Members: Mr. RICHARD FAIST; Ms. BRENDA LEE, CPA; Ms. SUSAN MORGAN; Mr. HAL REED; Mr. SCOTT SAVAGE; Rev. Msgr. MICHAEL R. BILLIAN, V.F.; Ms. SUE VERES.

Bishop's Education Council— The Council advises the bishop and the superintendent of schools on all matters concerning Catholic schools below the collegiate level in the diocese. Ex Officio Members: Most Rev. LEONARD P. BLAIR; Mr. CHRISTOPHER KNIGHT; Mr. ANTHONY MARS; Mrs. MARY CHALMERS. Members: Mr. WADE KAPSZUKIEWICZ;

Mr. DAVID GERARDI; Mrs. JUDY HALL; Rev. FRANKLIN P. KEHRES; Mr. ROB LOEB; Dr. J.J. SREENAN; Dr. JANET ROBINSON; Mrs. TRESSA REITH; Rev. MARK J. HERZOG, V.F.; Mrs. MARY WERNER; Mr. WALTER KLIMASKI.

Project Review Board— The Project Review Board assists the bishop of Toledo by reviewing potential building, renovation and property expansion plans of the institutions of the diocese. Members: Most Rev. LEONARD P. BLAIR; Rev. KEITH A. STRIPE; Deacon RONALD D. HENDERSON; Sr. KATHLEEN PADDEN, O.S.U.; Very Rev. HERBERT F. WEBER, V.F.; Mr. JEFF MILLER.

Building Commission— The commission reviews all areas of architectural and structural design of plumbing, heating, air-conditioning and electrical systems involving the construction, repair or remodeling of church property. Dr. GEORGE MURNEN, Chm. Members: Rev. GERALD J. CHMIEL (Retired); Mr. JAMES CIHAK; Rev. FRANK K. ECKART (Retired); Dr. MARK A. PICKETT; Mr. FRANK RUGGIERO; Mr. ROBERT J. LYNN JR.

Liturgical Commission— At the invitation of the bishop, the Toledo Diocesan Liturgical Commission, in collaboration with the Office of Worship, assists the bishop in carrying out his function as promoter and guardian of the liturgical life of the diocese. Mrs. CHARLOTTE MARIASY, Chm. Members: Sr. JUDY BEAUDRY, O.S.F.S.; Deacon PHILLIP AVINA; Sr. JOY BARKER, O.S.F.; Rev. DAVID J. CIRATA; Mr. DANIEL J. DEMSKI; Mr. JACK GERDING; Deacon KEVIN WINTERSTELLER; Rev. KENT R. KAUFMAN; Deacon ANTHONY J. PISTILLI; Mr. MARK NEISE; Rev. Msgr. CHARLES E. SINGLER, D.Min.

Secretariat for Catechesis and Formation

Secretariat Leader—Sr. NANCY MATHIAS, O.S.U., Catholic Center, 1933 Spielbusch Ave., Toledo, 43604-5360. Tel: 419-244-6711; Fax: 419-244-4791. Email: nmathias@toledodiocese.org.

Office of Catechesis—Catholic Center, 1933 Spielbusch Ave., Toledo, 43604-5360. Tel: 419-244-6711; Fax: 419-244-4791. Mr. DAVID MCCUTCHEN, Dir. Email: dmccutchen@toledodiocese.org. The Office of Catechesis oversees all religious education within the diocese. The work of the office can be divided into five primary areas: evangelization; adult faith formation; parish and school catechetical ministry; catechetical certification and lay ecclesial ministry and stewardship. Education and information in these areas is provided especially through the Mysterium Christi Diocesan Institute.

Media Library—Web: www.toledocatholicmedia.org. The Media Resource Center, as part of the Catechetical Ministry Office, provides media resources to be used in the process of formation and spiritual development with parishes, schools and agencies of the diocese.

Office of Vocations: Priesthood and Consecrated Life—Catholic Center, 1933 Spielbusch Ave., Toledo, 43604-5360. Tel: 419-244-6711; Fax: 419-244-4791. Web: www.toledovocations.com. Rev. Msgr. CHARLES E. SINGLER, D.Min., Dir. Email: csingler@toledodiocese.org; Mrs. YVONNE M. DUBIELAK, Assoc. Dir. Email: ydubielak@toledodiocese.org. The primary mission of the Office of Vocations is to assist those men who are called by God to the diocesan priesthood to recognize, discern and respond to their vocational call. In conjunction with seminary personnel, we assume responsibility for the formation of diocesan seminarians. We aim to empower all members of the local church to grow in awareness of their responsibility to foster and nourish vocations to the priesthood and consecrated life and seek to provide them with the necessary education and tools to do so.

Vicar for Deacons—Catholic Center, 1933 Spielbusch Ave., Toledo, 43604-5360. Tel: 419-244-6711; Fax: 419-244-4791. Deacon JAMES D. CARUSO. Email: jcaruso@toledodiocese.org. The bishop's representative to permanent deacons of the diocese, providing pastoral care for deacons and their families and opportunities for spiritual and professional growth.

Deacon Formation—Catholic Center, 1933 Spielbusch Ave., Toledo, 43604-5360. Tel: 419-244-6711; Fax: 419-244-4791. Rev. Msgr. WILLIAM J. KUBACKI, Dir. Email: wkubacki@toledodiocese.org. Coordinates the promotion, recruitment and discernment of a vocation to the diaconate. Provides a program in the areas of human, spiritual, and intellectual pastoral formation. Assists Vicar for Deacons in ministry to the diaconal community.

Vicar for Priests—Catholic Center, 1933 Spielbusch Ave., Toledo, 43604-5360. Tel: 419-244-6711; Fax: 419-244-4791. Rev. Msgr. WILLIAM J. KUBACKI. Email: wkubacki@toledodiocese.org. Serves as a liaison for the bishop in providing pastoral care to the priests of the diocese.

Associate Vicar for Priests—Rev. THOMAS H. RADLOFF, S.J., 5901 Airport Hwy., Toledo, 43615. Tel: 419-865-5743, Ext. 242; Fax: 419-865-9675. Email: tradloff@gmail.com.

Continuing Formation for Priests— The provision for ongoing opportunities designed to enhance the human, spiritual, intellectual and pastoral growth for priests is mandated by the church. The office is at the service of the bishop and offers resources for the priests continuing formation and education. Rev. Msgr. WILLIAM J. KUBACKI, Dir., Catholic Center, 1933 Spielbusch Ave., Toledo, 43604-5360. Tel: 419-244-6711; Fax: 419-244-4791. Email: wkubacki@toledodiocese.org.

Vicar For Religious—Catholic Center, 1933 Spielbusch Ave., Toledo, 43604-5360. Tel: 419-244-6711; Fax: 419-244-4791. Sr. NANCY MATHIAS, O.S.U. Email: nmathias@toledodiocese.org. Serves as the liaison for the diocesan bishop to religious women and men of the diocese, responds to the needs of the religious in the diocese and raises consciousness about the service that religious render in the diocese.

Youth, Young Adult and Campus Ministry—Catholic Center, 1933 Spielbusch Ave., Toledo, 43604-5360. Tel: 419-244-6711; Fax: 419-244-4791. Deacon JERRY ZIEMKIEWICZ, Coord. Youth Ministry. Email: jziemkiewicz@toledodiocese.org; KATHERINE C. HANINGER, Coord. Young Adult & Campus Ministry. Email: khaninger@toledodiocese.org; Very Rev. JEFFREY R. MCBETH, V.F., Chap. Catholic Youth Ministry. Email: jmcbeth@bex.net; Revs. MICHAEL G. DANDURAND, Chap. Young Adult & Campus Ministry. Email: frmichael@sttoms.com; CHRISTOPHER G. BAZAR, Chap. Catholic Scouting. Email: cbazar872@yahoo.com; Mr. GARY HOLEWINSKI, Chm. Toledo Diocese Catholic Committee on Scouting. Email: gholewi889@aol.com. Working with and supporting parishes and campuses to empower youth, young adults and college students to live as disciples of Jesus Christ by fostering a deeper understanding of and participation in the Catholic faith community.

Teens Encounter Christ (T E C)— A weekend experience for high school juniors, seniors and college freshmen to encounter Christ in a faith-filled community. Deacon JERRY ZIEMKIEWICZ, Contact. Email: jziemkiewicz@toledodiocese.org.

Catholic Men's Ministry— Catholic Men's Ministry links men in supportive relationships, provides resources consistent with Catholic teaching and develops training and formation opportunities for men's ministry and evangelization. Mr. TADHG FARRELL, Coord. Email: daniel352@bex.net; Mr. DAVID MCCUTCHEN, Mod. Email: dmccutchen@toledodiocese.org.

Secretariat for Catholic Schools—Mr. CHRISTOPHER KNIGHT, Secretariat Leader & Supt. Catholic Schools, Catholic Center, 1933 Spielbusch Ave., Toledo, 43604-5360. Tel: 419-244-6711; Fax: 419-255-8269. Email: cknight@toledodiocese.org.

Mission— To assist the bishop in his teaching mission by serving, challenging and supporting the leaders of youth formation and education who minister in parishes and the diocese.

Services— 1. To provide formation, direction and support for parish leaders responsible for catechesis and sacramental preparation of children and youth. 2. To provide leadership, support and services to the local Catholic school community and its leadership and staff. 3. To provide youth formation through CYO athletic programs.

Catholic Schools—Email: schools@toledodiocese.org. Web: www.catholicschoolsoffice.org. Mr. TIMOTHY MAHONEY, Curriculum Consultant. Email: tmahoney@toledodiocese.org; Mr. MICHAEL BEIER, Dir. Govt. Programs. Email: mbeier@toledodiocese.org; Ms. KATHY TARASCHKE, Life Team Coord. Email: ktaraschke@toledodiocese.org; Mrs. SHARI BEIER, Technology Consultant. Email: sbeier@toledodiocese.org; Ms. JONI COCI, Technology Coord. & Govt. Programs Asst. Email: jcoci@toledodiocese.org; Mr. FRANK DILALLO, Prevention Intervention Consultant & Diocesan Case Mgr. Email: fdilallo@toledodiocese.org; Mrs. VICKI FITTS, Licensure/Certification. Email: vfitts@toledodiocese.org.

The Catholic Youth Organization (CYO)—Catholic Center, 1933 Spielbusch Ave., Toledo, 43604-5360. Tel: 419-244-6711; 419-243-4296 (Recorder); Fax: 419-244-3420. Web: www.cyss.org. Email: cyo@toledodiocese.org. Mr. JEFF MIELCAREK, Dir. Email: jmielcarek@toledodiocese.org; Ms. JULIE DUBIELAK, Asst. Dir. Email: jdubielak@toledodiocese.org.

Central City Ministry of Toledo Catholic School—Catholic Center, 1933 Spielbusch Ave., Toledo, 43604-5360. Tel: 419-244-6711; Fax: 419-255-8269. Mrs. JEAN BUGERT HAYWARD, Dir. Email: jhayward@toledodiocese.org. A consortium of two Catholic schools joined together to more effectively and efficiently minister to the central city community: Rosary Cathedral, Queen of Apostles.

Diocesan Schools— Tiffin, Calvert Catholic School; Defiance, Holy Cross Catholic School; Fremont, Bishop Hoffman Catholic School; Lima, Central Catholic High School; Norwalk Catholic School; Oregon, Kateri Catholic School System; Sandusky Central Catholic School; Toledo Central Catholic High School; Central City Ministry of Toledo Catholic School.

Secretariat for Finance and Administration

Secretariat Leader and Canonical Finance Officer—Deacon RONALD D. HENDERSON, Catholic Center, 1933 Spielbusch Ave., Toledo, 43604-5360. Tel: 419-244-6711; Fax: 419-244-4791. Email: rhenderson@toledodiocese.org.

Financial Services— Provides centralized accounting and payroll services for diocesan offices (including CCMT school), responsible for investments, accountable for funds of the diocese. Provides auditing services to parishes of the diocese to ensure proper accounting of parish funds. Consulting and training is available for pastors, administrators, finance councils and parish staff. Mrs. RENE YUHAS SCHMIDBAUER, Finance & Database Mgr. Email: rschmidbauer@toledodiocese.org; Mr. STEVEN SICKMILLER, Diocesan Comptroller. Email: ssickmiller@toledodiocese.org; Mr. MATTHEW S. STEINMETZ, Asst. Comptroller. Email: msteinmetz@toledodiocese.org; Ms. HONG XIAO, CPA/Inactive, Staff Accountant. Email: hxiao@toledodiocese.org; Ms. LISA ADAIR, Accounts Receivable. Email: ladair@toledodiocese.org; Mrs. CATHY COLLINS, Accounts Payable. Email: ccollins@toledodiocese.org; Ms. VICKI FINK, ParishSOFT Admin. Email: vfink@toledodiocese.org.

Catholic Foundation, Inc.—Catholic Center, 1933 Spielbusch Ave., Toledo, 43604-5360. Tel: 419-244-6711; Fax: 419-720-0053. Established in the fall of 1988 as an investment fund for Catholic parishes, schools, cemeteries and agencies of the diocese and the diocese itself.

Development Office—Catholic Center, 1933 Spielbusch Ave., Toledo, 43604-5360. Tel: 419-244-6711; Fax: 419-720-0053. Ms. KAREN SZYMANSKI, Diocesan Fund Officer. Email: kszymanski@toledodiocese.org; Mrs. JOELLEN CHOCHARD, Devel. Database Admin. Email: jchochard@toledodiocese.org; Mr. KEN MACKOWIAK, Regl. Devel. Officer-Toledo/Lucas & Wood Counties. Email: kmackowiak@toledodiocese.org; Mrs. PATRICE SCOTT, Regl. Devel. Officer-Mansfield Area. Tel: 410-469-0014. Email: pscott@toledodiocese.org. The Development Office is responsible for all fund development that includes the Annual Catholic Appeal, an annuity program and provides clearing house coordination for the sale of stocks and bonds for the diocese and affiliated parishes within the diocese. Provides support and direction to parishes, schools and departments within the diocese for major and planned gifts including but not limited to wills/bequests, life insurance and charitable gift annuities.

Central City Ministry of Toledo—Catholic Center, 1933 Spielbusch Ave., Toledo, 43604-5360. Tel: 419-244-6711; Fax: 419-720-0053. Ms. JEANIE BUGERT HAYWARD, Dir. Email: jhayward@toledodiocese.org; Ms. CLAIRE GUISFREDI, CCMT Devel. Officer. Email: cguisfredi@toledodiocese.org. CCMT is a Catholic school with two campuses (Rosary Cathedral and Queen of Apostles) that offers educational opportunities to those families within the central city community. Underwriting opportunities include The Urban All-American Celebration, Celebrity Wait Night and Adopt-a-School.

Northwest Ohio Scholarship Fund—Catholic Center, 1933 Spielbusch Ave., Toledo, 43604-5360. Tel: 419-244-6711; Fax: 419-720-0053. Ms. ANN RIDDLE, Coord. Programs. Email: ariddle@toledodiocese.org. A program that supports parents' choice of a private education. Acceptance is based on family income and follows the federal standards for subsidized lunch program, as well as the number of members in a family. The family is expected to pay the first $500 of tuition and must live in Fulton, Wood or Lucas County. This program is affiliated with the National Children's Scholarship Fund.

Protected Self Insurance—Mailing Address: Protected Self Insurance Program (PSI), P.O. Box 30, Swanton, 43558. Tel: 419-826-5300; Fax: 419-826-5306. Mr. JOSEPH SPENTHOFF, Dir. Email: jspenthoff@toledodiocese.org; Mrs. VICKY

SPENTHOFF, Administrative Asst. Email: vspenthoff@toledodiocese.org.

Catholic Cemeteries—5725 Hill Ave., (corner of Holland-Sylvania Rd.), Toledo, 43615-5852. Tel: 419-531-5747; Fax: 419-531-0946. Email: info@cathcemtoledo.org. Mr. DAVID CZECH, Diocesan Sexton. Assists parishes in bereavement ministry, provides appropriate products, services and burial sites, offers counsel to parish cemeteries in the diocese.

Cemeteries—Calvary Cemetery, 2224 Dorr St., Toledo, 43607. Tel: 419-536-3751. *Mount Carmel Cemetery, 15 E. Manhattan Blvd., Toledo, 43608.* Tel: 419-536-3751. *Resurrection Cemetery, 5725 Hill Ave., Toledo, 43615.* Tel: 419-531-5747.

Secretariat for Evangelization and Parish Life

Secretariat Leader—Mr. JASON SHANKS, Catholic Center, 1933 Spielbusch Ave., Toledo, 43624-1371. Tel: 419-244-6711; Fax: 419-244-4791. Email: jshanks@toledodiocese.org.

Mission Statement— The secretariat staff believes that baptism into Christ Jesus calls all to evangelize and to participate fully in the mission of the universal church. We serve the diverse peoples of the Diocese of Toledo by providing planning, resources, education and formation opportunities for the pastoral leadership of the Diocese of Toledo. Staff: Mrs. SUE FRENCH, Administrative Coord. Email: sfrench@toledodiocese.org; Ms. JOETTE ROZANSKI, Technology Coord. Email: jrozanski@toledodiocese.org; Mrs. TINA HORNYAK, Financial Coord. Email: thornyak@toledodiocese.org; Ms. JEAN MODER, Administrative Asst. Email: jmoder@toledodiocese.org.

Black Catholic Ministries—Catholic Center, 1933 Spielbusch Ave., Toledo, 43604-5360. Tel: 419-244-6711; Fax: 419-244-4791. Mr. MICHAEL YOUNGBLOOD, Dir. Email: myoungblood@toledodiocese.org. Assists parishes and deaneries in the area of African-American catechesis and Black Catholic celebrations and retreats; provides workshops on diversity and inclusion, racism and prejudice; facilitates diocesan Black Catholic events and promotes the National Black Catholic Congress.

Ecumenical and Interreligious Affairs—709 W. Catawba Rd., Port Clinton, 43452. Tel: 419-797-4801. Rev. JAMES E. PEIFFER, Chm. (Retired). Supports local initiatives that express the Catholic commitment to the ecumenical movement and interreligious dialogue; develops suggestions for ways in which parishes can become ecumenically involved.

Equal Access Ministries—Catholic Center, 1933 Spielbusch Ave., Toledo, 43604-5360. Tel: 419-244-6711; Fax: 419-244-4791; Teletype: 419-243-1475. Email: equalaccess@toledodiocese.org. Ms. MARSHA RIVAS, Dir. Email: mrivas@toledodiocese.org. Promotes ministry to people with disabilities ensuring inclusion in all aspects of the life of the church; assists parishes in assessing accessibility.

Evangelization—Mr. MICHAEL YOUNGBLOOD, Dir. Email: myoungblood@toledodiocese.org.

Hispanic Pastoral Ministries— (Hispano Ministerio) *Catholic Center, 1933 Spielbusch Ave., Toledo, 43604-5360.* Tel: 419-244-6711; Fax: 419-244-4791. Deacon JOSE GARCIA, Dir. Email: jgarcia@toledodiocese.org. Provides an active presence to, among and for the Hispanic population of northwest Ohio through support for Hispanic pastoral ministry; providing resources and collaborating with pastoral leadership in parishes and institutions to serve and advocate for the migrant and new immigrant populations at the local level.

Eastern Office—Rev. MICHAEL DIEMER, M.J. Email: mdiemer@toledodiocese.org.

Western Office—Rev. JOVEN MALANYAON. Email: jmalanyaon@toledodiocese.org.

Global Mission—Catholic Center, 1933 Spielbusch Ave., Toledo, 43604-5360. Tel: 419-244-6711; Fax: 419-244-4791. Deacon PAUL J. WHITE, Dir. Email: pwhite@toledodiocese.org. Provides resources for parishes and deaneries to deepen the mission consciousness and responsibility of the people of the diocese; informs them of needs; encourages prayer for the missions and missionaries; provides a conduit for material response to disasters within the country and around the world. Programs include the Society for the Propagation of the Faith, Catholic Relief Services, Holy Childhood Association and St. Peter the Apostle.

Mission of Accompaniment— The continued mission effort whereby the Diocese of Toledo supports financially the Diocese of Hwange in Zimbabwe in addressing the needs of the people of Binga and its outstations. *Catholic Center, 1933 Spielbusch Ave., Toledo, 43604-5360.* Tel: 419-244-6711; Fax: 419-244-4791. Rev. BERNARD J. BOFF, Dir. (Retired). Email: bboff@toledodiocese.org.

Marriage and Family Life—Catholic Center, 1933 Spielbusch Ave., Toledo, 43604-5360. Tel: 419-244-6711; Fax: 419-244-4860. Ms. MONICA MARTINEZ, Dir. Email: mmartinez@toledodiocese.org.

Office of Worship and Liturgical Music—Catholic Center, 1933 Spielbusch Ave., Toledo, 43604-5360. Tel: 419-244-6711; Fax: 419-244-4791. Rev. Msgr. CHARLES E. SINGLER, D.Min., Dir. Email: csingler@toledodiocese.org; Mr. DANIEL J. DEMSKI, Liturgy Coord. Email: ddemski@toledodiocese.org; Mr. PAUL J. MONACHINO, Dir. Liturgical Music. Email: pmonachino@toledodiocese.org. Leads the continued development of the liturgical vision of the diocese guided by the documents and spirit of the Second Vatican Council and the directives of the USCCB; provides liturgical formation for pastoral leadership; provides liturgical resources to pastoral leadership and ministers. Promotes musical excellence in the liturgical life of the diocese; provides resources for ongoing evaluation and growth of music ministry for parishes.

Diocesan Council of Catholic Women (DCCW)—Catholic Center, 1933 Spielbusch Ave., Toledo, 43604-5360. Tel: 419-244-6711; Fax: 419-244-4791. Mrs. SUZIE SWARTZMILLER, Pres. Email: tdccw@toledodiocese.org; Rev. MARK J. HERZOG, V.F., Mod. Affiliated with the National Council of Catholic Women, the Diocesan Council seeks to strengthen and broaden the network of affiliated parish women's organizations and individual Catholic women by providing programs, events and projects to respond to the spiritual and educational needs of diocesan women, their parishes, and communities.

Secretariat of Catholic Charities

Catholic Charities—Web: www.catholiccharitiesnwo.org. Email: ccharities@toledodiocese.org.

Secretariat Leader and Executive Director—Mr. RODNEY SCHUSTER, Catholic Center, 1933 Spielbusch Ave., Toledo, 43604-5360. Tel: 419-244-6711; Fax: 419-244-5171. Email: rschuster@toledodiocese.org.

Mission Statement— In the service ministry of the church Catholic Charities supports and enhances our parish communities' response to the social Gospel of Jesus Christ throughout the Diocese of Toledo.

History/Overview of Services— Catholic Charities began in 1914 to provide care and protection to orphans and single mothers. Since then the agency has grown to provide assistance to individuals, families and groups through direct social services, consultation, case management services, resources and in-service training for parish-based ministry programs, advocacy and justice education. While several programs are coordinated from a particular office, many services are available throughout the diocese.

Programs and Services—1933 Spielbusch Ave., Toledo, 43604-5360. Tel: 419-244-6711; Fax: 419-244-4860. Mr. DAVID MOEBIUS, Opers. Dir. Email: dmoebius@toledodiocese.org.

Family Connections/Healthy Beginnings—Catholic Center, 1933 Spielbusch Ave., Toledo, 43604-5360. Tel: 419-244-6711; Fax: 419-244-4860. Email: familyconnections@toledodiocese.org. Ms. KATHY MOTSINGER. Email: kmotsinger@toledodiocese.org. Provides diocesan-wide comprehensive support services for families and children including: Adoptions; Pregnancy Counseling; Domestic and International Home Studies; Post-Adoption Support; Infant Foster Care; Healthy Beginnings; Parenting Education.

Housing Services—Catholic Center, 1933 Spielbusch Ave., Toledo, 43604-5360. Tel: 419-244-6711; Fax: 419-244-4860. Provides qualified individuals and families with strategies to achieve future stability in their lives for home and financial management.

LaPosada (Family Emergency Shelter)—435 Eastern Ave., Toledo, 43609. Tel: 419-244-5931; Fax: 419-244-4993. Email: laposada@toledodiocese.org. Mrs. MICHELLE POOLE, Coord. Email: mpoole@toledodiocese.org.

Miriam House (Huron County Transitional Housing)—249 W. Main St., Norwalk, 44857. Tel: 419-668-3073; 419-663-6341; 800-668-3110. Email: themiriamhouse@toledodiocese.org. Ms. ROXANNE SANDLES, Coord. Email: rsandles@toledodiocese.org.

Permanent Supportive Housing Services Coordinator—Ms. MICHELE POOLE. Email: mpoole@toledodiocese.org.

Adult Advocacy Services— (Erie, Richland & Huron Counties) Guardianship services to adults 55 and older who are deemed incompetent by the court and who have no appropriate family support available. Payee services are focused on adults age 55 and older who voluntarily agree to assistance in maintaining their monthly budget.

Richland County - Mansfield—35 N. Park St., Mansfield, 44902. Tel: 419-524-0733. Ms. CAROL WHEELER, Contact. Email: cwheeler@toledodiocese.org.

Erie and Huron Counties - Norwalk—34 Woodlawn Ave., Norwalk, 44857. Tel: 419-668-3073; 800-668-3110. Ms. CAROL WHEELER, Coord. Email: cwheeler@toledodiocese.org.

Community Services—

Family Emergency Guidance—Catholic Center, 1933 Spielbusch Ave., Toledo, 43604-5360. Tel: 419-244-6711; Fax: 419-244-4860. Mr. BRIAN ROME, Coord. Email: brome@toledodiocese.org. Provides financial and lead paint education and limited financial assistance to people in need.

Informational, Referral and Resources—1933 Spielbusch Ave., Toledo, 43604-5360. Tel: 419-244-6711; Fax: 419-244-4860. Ms. LINDA KRAFT, Contact. Email: lkraft@toledodiocese.org.

Community Emergency Services—2 Smith Ave., Mansfield, 44905. Tel: 419-524-0733; Fax: 419-524-2055. Ms. REBECCA OWENS, Contact. Email: rowens@toledodiocese.org. Providing basic life sustaining services to people in need.

Disaster Relief—Ms. REBECCA OWENS, Contact. Email: rowens@toledodiocese.org.

Respect Life Ministry—2200 W. Elm St., Lima, 45805. Tel: 419-796-8005. Ms. JAN KAHLE, Dir. Email: jkahle@toledodiocese.org; Ms. PAT HALICEK, Contact. Tel: 419-244-6711. Email: phalicek@toledodiocese.org.

Project Rachel— Confidential help for anyone suffering from the grief and guilt of abortion. *Information: .* Tel: 419-796-8005. Email: jkahle@toledodiocese.org. *Project Rachel Help Line: .* Tel: 419-260-5811. Email: projectrachel@toledodiocese.org.

Bereavement Action Committee— Providing support and training to parishes for bereavement ministry programs. Ms. GERMAINE KIRK, Contact. Email: gkirk@toledodiocese.org.

Jail and Prison Ministry— Coordinating ministry throughout the diocese; providing assistance, resources, retreats and workshops. Ms. GERMAINE KIRK, Contact. Email: gkirk@toledodiocese.org.

Catholic Campaign for Human Development— Anti-poverty, social justice program of the United States Catholic Conference of Bishops that funds self-help projects nationally and locally, assisting poor and low-income people help themselves. Ms. GERMAINE KIRK, Contact. Email: gkirk@toledodiocese.org.

Regional Offices—Mansfield: 35 N. Park St., Mansfield, 44902. Tel: 419-524-0733; Fax: 419-524-2055. Email: rowens@toledodiocese.org. *Norwalk: 34 Woodlawn St., Norwalk, 44857.* Tel: 419-668-3073; 800-668-3110; Fax: 419-663-5070. Email: pulmer@toledodiocese.org. *Ottawa: SS. Peter and Paul Campus, 360 N. Locust St., Ottawa, 45875.* Tel: 419-796-8005. Email: jkahle@toledodiocese.org.

Affiliations and Licensures of Catholic Charities—

Ohio Catholic Conference—

Ohio Department of Human Services—

U.S. Catholic Conference of Bishops—

Catholic Club—1601 Jefferson Ave., Toledo, 43604. Tel: 419-243-7255; Fax: 419-243-6337. Email: info@catholicclub.org. Web: www.catholicclub.org. Mr. PAUL SZYMANSKI, Dir. Email: paul@catholicclub.org; Ms. BARB WITKOWSKI, Assoc. Dir. Email: barb@catholicclub.org.

Child Care— Mon.-Fri. 6:30 a.m. to 6:30 p.m. An educational child care and family center open to everyone, offering year-round state-licensed child care programs for infants through age 14. Infant care, toddler care, preschool care, before- and after-school care (transportation to and from school), calamity and snow day care, vacation day care and summer camp are available. Children participate in swimming, games, special events, field trips, crafts and more. Free of charge, all children receive breakfast, lunch and an afternoon snack. Children ages 3 and older receive free swim lessons as part of their child care enrollment.

Recreational Opportunities— Aquatic — Swim lessons for various levels of experience and age groups. School groups, scout troops and others may arrange group lessons. Transportation is available. Super Saturdays — 9 a.m.-1 p.m. (Oct.-May only) children in first through sixth grades enjoy a supervised day of activities including swimming, games and more.

Rentals— Facility — The pool and gym are available for parishes, class parties, birthday parties, team events, youth groups, etc. The facility is available for overnights and lock-ins. Vehicles — Two large school buses, one minibus and two 15-passenger vans are available for diocesan groups.

Licensed by: Ohio Department of Job and Family Services.

Accredited by: National Association for the Education of Young Children (NAEYC); National After School Association (NAA).

Other Organizations

Apostleship of the Sea— A ministry to the crews of ocean and lake ships that come to the Port of Toledo. VACANT, Port Chap., Port of Toledo Ohio, 3332 St. Lawrence Dr., Toledo, 43605. Tel: 419-693-7678.

Christ Child Society of Toledo— A nonprofit, volunteer organization embracing members of all denominations. It is dedicated to the welfare of needy children in the Toledo area. The Toledo Chapter was founded in 1990 and has more than 200 members. *P.O. Box 352254, Toledo, 43635.* Tel: 419-251-1218. Web: www.christchildsocietyoftoledo.org. Ms. MARY MURNEN, Pres.; Ms. CECILE BENNETT, Vice Pres.; Ms. TOOTIE MORETTE, Treas.; Ms. CAROL MORAVA, Sec.; Ms. LUCY ABU-ABSI, Parliamentarian.

Cursillo Movement— Movement to form apostolic leaders and link them together for an effective, apostolic Christian life in the day-to-day environments where their lives take place. Spiritual Directors: Revs. EDWARD J. LITTELMANN (Retired), 1248 Royalton Rd., Toledo, 43612. Tel: 419-345-0161. Email: ejl@littelmann.com; JAMES E. BROWN, 2255 Central Grove, Toledo, 43614. Tel: 419-382-5511; Sr. EDNA MICHEL, O.S.F., 200 St. Francis Ave., Tiffin, 44883. Tel: 419-447-0435. Email: emichel@tiffinfranciscans.org; Mr. BERNARD RUMSCHLAG, 2851 S. County Rd. 591, Tiffin, 44883. Tel: 419-595-2793.

Fraternity of Communion and Liberation— Communion and Liberation is an ecclesial movement whose purpose is the education to Christian maturity of its adherents and collaboration in the mission of the church in all the spheres of contemporary life. *3454 Oak Alley Court, Toledo, 43606.* Tel: 419-578-0057. Dr. JEFFREY G. SCHMAKEL, Local Contact.

Ministry To Catholic Charismatic Renewal (MCCR)— Provides pastoral guidance to parish charismatic prayer groups, promotes spiritual renewal through collaboration with prayer groups, parish staff and diocesan offices in integrating spirit baptism and spiritual gifts into the lives of Catholic people. *550 Clark St., Toledo, 43605-2273.* Tel: 419-691-6686; Fax: 419-691-1755. Web: www.mccrholyspirit.org. Email: mccr@toledolink.com. Mr. STEVEN TOTH, Dir.; Rev. JEROME F. NOWAKOWSKI, Spiritual Dir. (Retired).

Northwest Ohio Guild of the Catholic Medical Association—JEANNE WEISENBURGER, M.D., Contact, 1570 Elmore Rd., Pemberville, 43450. Tel: 419-287-4939. Email: rweisenb@verizon.net; VACANT, Spiritual Advisor.

Philippine-American Catholic Council (PACC)— Provides opportunities for spiritual growth among members of the Filipino-American Catholic Community of greater Toledo and southeastern Michigan through Filipino liturgies, popular Marian devotions and other spiritual means. *3030 Tremainsville Rd., Toledo, 43613.* Tel: 419-471-1123. Rev. PETER V. ZAFE, Dir. Email: pvz64@aol.com.

Retrouvaille— An international program, offering help to couples who live in the disappointment and pain of a troubled marriage. It is a weekend experience with six follow-up sessions put on by couples who have rebuilt their own marriages. Rev. FREDERICK J. DUSCHL, Spiritual Dir. (Retired), 11312 County Rd. 6, Edon, 43518. Tel: 419-272-2475. Email: frfred@bright.net. Executive Team Couple: BONNIE LANGMEYER; SCOTT LANGMEYER, Mailing Address: 323 W. River St., P.O. Box 123, Deerfield, MI 49238. Tel: 517-447-3477. Email: bud@cass.net.

St. Vincent dePaul Society— A Catholic lay organization that leads women and men to grow spiritually and witness God's love by offering person-to-person service to those who are needy and suffering. *Diocesan Central Council, P.O. Box 1075, Toledo, 43697.* Tel: 419-243-6963. Mrs. MARY HUFFMAN, Pres.; Ms. SANDRA BLOOMQUIST, Exec. Dir.; Rev. RONALD J. BRICKNER, Chap.

Secular Franciscan Order—Tel: 800-372-6247. Web: www.nafra-sfo.org.

Divine Mercy Region, Lower Michigan and Toledo—Ms. SHERI HAFELI, S.F.O., 8628 Merge St., Center Line, MI 48015. Tel: 586-758-5769. Email: shafelisfo@gmail.com.

St. Paschal Fraternity (Toledo)—Mailing Address: 6408 Glenhurst, Apt. 4, Maumee, 43537. Ms. LISA CRAIG, S.F.O., Contact. Tel: 419-868-8985. Email: lisa5347@yahoo.com. Meetings: 3rd Sun. 2:30 pm at Mercy St. Vincent Hospital Conference Room.

St. Maximilian Kolbe Fraternity (Toledo)—Mrs. MARIE CRISTE, S.F.O., Contact, 15275 S. Dixie Hwy. #419, Monroe, MI 48161. Tel: 734-240-2096. Email: mariecriste@comcast.net. Meetings: 2nd Tues. and 3rd Sun. 3 pm at St. Clement Church, 3030 Tremainsville Rd., Toledo.

St. Maximilian Kolbe Region, Northern Ohio—Mrs. JOANNE ANGELETTI, S.F.O., 2829 Cory Ave., Akron, 44314. Tel: 330-745-5766. Email: joanneangeletti@sbcglobal.net.

St. Anthony of Padua Fraternity, Carey—Mr. KEITH COSSEY, SFO, 108 Rosewood Pl., Carey, 43316. Tel: 419-396-7373. Email: deadseascroller@aol.com.

St. Anthony of Padua Fraternity, Fostoria—Mrs. ALICE DAUGHERTY, S.F.O., 328 W. North St., Fostoria, 44830. Tel: 419-435-8769. Email: adaugherty4@woh.rr.com.

St. Maximilian Mary Kolbe Fraternity, Findlay—Ms. LORRAINE HENRY, 200 Shinkle St., Findlay, 45840. Tel: 419-422-5083.

St. Joseph Fraternity, Green Springs—Mr. ANDREW GOOD, S.F.O., 528 Glenwood Dr., Fremont, 43420. Tel: 419-332-6706. Email: shadowfax25@juno.com.

Queen of the Angels Fraternity, Lima—Ms. KATHY REEVES, SFO, Contact, 105 Chickadee Pl., Elida, 45807. Tel: 419-339-1507. Email: songbird482003@yahoo.com.

St. Michael Fraternity, Hicksville—Ms. JEAN WONDERLY, S.F.O., 03773 Buckskin Rd., Hicksville, 43526. Tel: 419-542-8053.

Secular Order of Discalced Carmelites—

Our Lady of the Holy Rosary Chapter (Toledo)—Ms. DONNA O'CONNELL, OCDS, Contact, 2155 Hawthorne Rd., Toledo, 43606. Tel: 419-531-3426.

Holy Family of the Infant Jesus' Flame of Love Chapter (Sandusky)—Mrs. TERRI HANACEK, O.C.D.S., 1610 Hayes Ave., Sandusky, 44870. Tel: 419-625-6126 Meetings: 1st Tues. 6 pm at Sandusky St. Mary.

Serra International— Serra International is formally aggregated to the Pontifical Society for Priestly Vocations. Mr. GINO DIMATTIA, District Governor, 1824 University Blvd., Lima, 45805. Tel: 419-991-0289. Email: ginodimattia@juno.com; Mr. JOHN OSTERHART, Regl. Dir., 2120 Heather S.E., East Grand Rapids, MI 49506. Tel: 616-245-1893. Email: ejost1@att.net.

Mansfield Serra Club—Ms. FRAN LEITENBERGER, Pres., 1610 W. Hanley Rd., Mansfield, 44904. Tel: 419-884-0964. Email: fleitenberger@neo.rr.com. (2nd & 4th Mon. 6 pm at Franciscan Activity Center).

Lima Serra Club—Mr. ROBERT SCHMERGE, Pres., 18076 Golden Bridge Rd., Wapakoneta, 45895. Tel: 419-738-2255. Email: rschmerge@woh.rr.com. Meetings: 2nd & 4th Thurs. Sept. through May 5:45 pm at Lima CCHS Library.

St. John Neumann Serra Club—Mr. RICHARD ALGE, Pres., 144 Sycamore St., Norwalk, 44857. Tel: 419-668-7777. Email: ralge@ft.newyorklife.com. Meetings: 3rd Tues. of each month, 6:30 pm at Peru, St. Alphonsus.

Tiffin Serra Club—Mrs. PATRICIA ENGLEHART, Pres., 54 Hancock St., Tiffin, 44883. Tel: 419-447-0347 Meetings: 1st & 3rd Tues. 6 pm upper room of St. Joseph Parish Activity Center.

Toledo Serra Club—Mr. RICHARD WEISENBURGER, Pres., 4282 Deepwood Ln., Toledo, 43614. Tel: 419-345-0371. Email: rfwsales@sbcglobal.net. Meetings: 1st & 3rd Fri. 11:45 a.m. at The Toledo Club.

Fremont Area Vocation Committee—Ms. CAROL WONDERLY, Contact, 5863 County Rd. 33, Helena, 43435. Tel: 419-638-4305 Meetings: 3rd Wed., 1 pm at Fremont Sacred Heart.

St. Maximilian Kolbe Deanery Vocation Team—Mr. ROBERT BOCKRATH, Chm., 7 Shelly Dr., Defiance, 43512. Tel: 419-782-3071. Email: hlkrhb@toast.net. Meetings: 3rd Tues., after 6:30 pm mass at Defiance, St. John.

Worldwide Marriage Encounter— Weekend experience, which provides tools for better communication and an atmosphere for husband and wife to evaluate and deepen their relationship with each other and God. Tel: 800-795-5683. Executive Team: CRAIG MAAG; ANGIE MAAG, 12903 Rd. 4, Ottawa, 45875. Tel: 419-456-3116. Email: craigandangie-me@fairpoint.net. Liaison Team Priest: Rev. HAROLD C. BROWN, C.PP.S., 4106 State Rte. 269, Bellevue, 44811. Tel: 419-483-3435. Application Couple: BRIAN SCHROEDER; CHRIS SCHROEDER, 13934 Rd. K, Ottawa, 45875. Tel: 419-538-7210. Email: bcschroeder@bright.net.

CLERGY, PARISHES, MISSIONS AND PAROCHIAL SCHOOLS

CITY OF TOLEDO

(LUCAS COUNTY)

1—QUEEN OF THE MOST HOLY ROSARY CATHEDRAL (1915) [JC] Rev. Msgr. William J. Kubacki, Rector; Deacons Ronald D. Henderson; James D. Caruso. In Res., Most Rev. Leonard P. Blair; Rev. Monte J. Hoyles; Rev. Msgr. Charles E. Singler.

Office: 2535 Collingwood Blvd., 43610. Tel: 419-244-9575; Fax: 419-242-1901. Email: roscath@totalink.net. Web: www.rosarycathedral.org.

Res.: 2544 Parkwood Ave., 43610-1317. Tel: 419-255-1890.

Church: 2561 Collingwood Blvd., 43610.

See Rosary Cathedral Campus under Consolidated Elementary Schools located in the Institution Section.

Catechesis/Religious Program—Students 15.

2—ST. ADALBERT (1907), (Polish), [JC] Closed. For inquiries for parish records contact the chancery.

3—SS. ADALBERT & HEDWIG (2010) Rev. Joseph T. Poggemeyer; Deacon Gerald Ignatowski.

Office: 3233 Lagrange St., 43608-1898. Tel: 419-241-4179; Fax: 419-241-1361. Email: stadalbert2001@yahoo.com. Web: www.stadalbert-sthedwig.org.

4—ST. AGNES (1910) Closed. For inquiries for parish records contact the chancery.

5—ST. ANN, Consolidated with St. Teresa to form St. Martin de Porres. See separate listing.

6—ST. ANTHONY (1882), (Polish), Closed. For inquiries for parish records contact the chancery.

7—BLESSED SACRAMENT (1924) [JC] Rev. Msgr. Michael R. Billian; Rev. Samuel Punnour, Parochial Vicar; Deacon Harold Welch; Ms. Mary Janet L. Myers, Devel. Dir.

Res.: 4227 Bellevue Rd., 43613-3999. Tel: 419-472-2288; Fax: 419-472-0493. Email: parishsecretary@bsctoledo.com. Web: www.bsctoledo.com.

School—(Grades PreK-8), 4255 Bellevue, 43613. Tel: 419-472-1121; Fax: 419-472-1679. Elizabeth Strbik, Prin. Lay Teachers 17; Students 307.

Catechesis/Religious Program—Tel: 419-472-7526. Students 50.

8—ST. CATHERINE OF SIENA (1930) [JC] Rev. J. Douglas Garand; Deacon Michael R. Learned Sr.; Jim Riedy, Music Liturgy Dir.

Mailing Address: 4555 N. Haven Ave., 43612-2350. Tel: 419-478-9558. Email: stcatherine1@sbcglobal.net.

Res.: 4544 N. Haven Ave., 43612. Tel: 419-478-3281; Fax: 419-478-9434.

School—(Grades PreK-8), 1155 Corbin Rd., 43612-2366. Tel: 419-478-9900. Sandi Shinaberry, Prin. Lay Teachers 14; Students 171.

Catechesis/Religious Program—Theresa Paredes, D.R.E. Students 45.

9—ST. CHARLES BORROMEO (1903) [JC] Rev. Gregory L. Peatee; Deacon Michael W. Pence; Mrs. Alison L. VanRynen, Admin.; Mrs. Lynn Van Doran, Finance Mgr.

Res. & Church: 1842 Airport Hwy., 43609-2069. Tel: 419-385-7431; Fax: 419-535-1813.

Catechesis/Religious Program—Mr. Jerry Mocek, D.R.E. Students 25.

10—CHRIST THE KING (1953) [JC 3] Revs. William J. Rose; Dominic Savyo; Mrs. Suzanne Marciniak, Pastoral Assoc.; Deacon Robert Beisser; Ms. Kathryn L. Mumy, Liturgy & Music Min.

Office: 4100 Harvest Ln., 43623-4399. Tel: 419-475-4348; Fax: 419-475-4050. Email: mail@cktoledo.org. Web: www.cktoledo.org.

School—(Grades PreK-8) Tel: 419-475-0909. Mr. Jon Molter, Prin. Lay Teachers 23; Students 467.

Catechesis/Religious Program—Mrs. Sandra L. Trabbic, D.R.E. Students 204.

11—ST. CLEMENT (1947) [JC] Revs. Michael O. Brown; Alan D. Zobler, O.S.F.S.; Deacon Ronald J. Plenzler.

Res.: 3030 Tremainsville Rd., 43613-1901. Tel: 419-472-2111; Fax: 419-479-3215. Email: st.clement08@yahoo.com. Web: www.stclementparishtoledo.org.

Catechesis/Religious Program—Tel: 419-472-1259. Linda Gutierrez, D.R.E. Students 80.

12—COMMUNITY OF THE RISEN CHRIST (1972) Closed. For inquiries for parish records contact the chancery.

13—CORPUS CHRISTI (UNIVERSITY OF TOLEDO) (1970) [JC] Rev. James J. Bacik; Ms. Pamela A. Meseroll, Pastoral Admin.; Mr. Bryce Roberts, Pastoral Assoc. Res.: 2955 Dorr St., 43607-2023. Tel: 419-531-4992 (Office); Fax: 419-531-1775. Email: jbacik@ccup.org.

Web: www.ccup.org.

14—ST. FRANCIS DE SALES (1841) Closed. For inquiries for parish records contact the chancery. Chapel remains open.

15—GESU (1920) [JC] Revs. James F. Cryan, O.S.F.S.; Shaun Lowery, O.S.F.S. In Res., Rev. Martin C. Lukas, O.S.F.S.
Res.: 2049 Parkside Blvd., 43607-1597. Tel: 419-531-1421; Fax: 419-531-0270. Email: gesusecretary@bex.net. Web: www.gesutoledo.org.
School—(Grades PreK-8), 2045 Parkside Blvd., 43607-1555. Tel: 419-536-5634; Fax: 419-531-8932. Mr. Manuel Gonzales, Prin. Lay Teachers 23; Students 372.
Catechesis/Religious Program—Laurie Skowronski, D.R.E. Students 95.

16—GOOD SHEPHERD (1873) [JC] Very Rev. Jeffrey R. McBeth; Deacon Leon M. Holmer. In Res., Rev. Jerome F. Nowakowski (Retired).
Res.: 550 Clark St., 43605-2273. Tel: 419-691-5815; Fax: 419-693-6612.
Catechesis/Religious Program—

17—ST. HEDWIG (1875), (Polish), [JC] Closed. For inquiries for parish records contact the chancery.

18—HISTORIC CHURCH OF SAINT PATRICK (1863), (Irish), [JC] Very Rev. Dennis P. Hartigan; Deacons Thomas S. Carone; Trevor Fernandes. In Res., Rev. Msgr. Christopher P. Vasko.
Res.: 130 Avondale Ave., 43604. Tel: 419-243-6452; Fax: 419-243-7032. Email: parish@stpatshistoric.org. Web: www.stpatshistoric.org.

19—HOLY ROSARY (1906), (Slovak), Closed. For inquiries for parish records contact the chancery.

20—ST. HYACINTH (1927), (Polish), [JC] Rev. Gregory L. Peatee; Deacon Michael W. Pence; Chris J. Jakutowicz, Business Admin.; Mrs. Lynn Van Doran, Finance Mgr.
Res.: 719 Evesham Ave., 43607-3806. Tel: 419-535-7077; Fax: 419-535-1813. Email: hyacinth.office@buckeye-express.com.
Church: Parkside Blvd. at Victory Ave., 43607.
Catechesis/Religious Program—

21—IMMACULATE CONCEPTION (1868) [JC] Very Rev. Dennis P. Hartigan; Deacons Thomas S. Carone; Trevor Fernandes.
Church: 434 Western Ave., 43609-2886. Tel: 419-243-1829; Fax: 419-241-9642. Email: toldarbyicc@sbcglobal.net.

22—ST. JAMES (1913) Closed. For inquiries for parish records contact the chancery.

23—ST. JOAN OF ARC (1978) [JC] Revs. Adam L. Hertzfeld; Anthony L. Recker; Deacon Thomas M. Sheehan; Ms. Terri A. Pastura, Pastoral Assoc.
Res.: 5856 Heatherdowns Blvd., 43614-4570. Tel: 419-866-6181; Fax: 419-866-6142. Web: www.joanofarc.org.
School—(Grades K-8), 5950 Heatherdowns Blvd., 43614-4500. Tel: 419-866-6177; Fax: 419-866-4107. Jayne Swemba, Prin. Lay Teachers 27; Students 422.
Catechesis/Religious Program—Tel: 419-866-6177. Sr. Elaine Marie Clement, S.N.D., D.R.E. Students 168.

24—ST. JOHN THE BAPTIST (1918) [JC] Rev. Anthony A. Borgia; Deacon John Algee; Shirley Fischbach, Business Mgr.; Valerie Ademski, Music Min.
Res.: 5153 Summit St., 43611-2786. Tel: 419-726-2034; Fax: 419-726-1447. Email: stjohnptplace@buckeye-express.com. Web: www.stjohnthebaptisttoledo.parishesonline.com.
School—(Grades K-8), 2729 124th St., 43611-2240. Tel: 419-726-7761; Fax: 419-726-1031. Mary Jo Wilhelm, Prin. Lay Teachers 12; Students 159.
Catechesis/Religious Program—Tel: 419-726-9141. Sr. Frances Herkender, S.N.D., D.R.E. Students 56.

25—ST. JOSEPH (1854) [JC] Revs. Joseph T. Poggemeyer; Thomas Mulanjanani, C.Ss.R.; Mrs. Joyce Zielinski.
Mailing Address: P.O. Box 790, 43697-0790. Tel: 419-255-5556. Email: stjodowntown@sbcglobal.net.
Res.: 626 Locust St., 43604.
Church: Erie & Locust Sts., 43604.

26—ST. JUDE (1955) [JC] Closed. For inquiries for parish records contact the chancery.

27—LITTLE FLOWER OF JESUS (1928) [JC] Rev. Joseph R. Steinbauer; Deacon Douglas Bullimore; Christine Lewinski, Business Mgr.; Daniel J. Meyer, Music Dir. & Liturgist.
Res.: 5522 Dorr St., 43615-3612. Tel: 419-537-6655; Fax: 419-537-1469. Email: littleflower@bex.net. Web: www.littleflowertoledo.org.
See St. Benedict School under Consolidated Elementary Schools in the Institution Section.
Catechesis/Religious Program—Tel: 419-537-6655. Susan VanHersett, D.R.E. Students 132.

28—ST. LOUIS (1872), (French), Closed. For inquiries for parish records contact the chancery.

29—ST. MARTIN DE PORRES (1990) [JC] Sr. Virginia Welsh, O.S.F., Pastoral Leader; Rev. Msgr. Christopher P. Vasko, Presbyteral Moderator & Chap.
Res.: 1119 W. Bancroft, 43606-4613. Tel: 419-241-4544; Fax: 419-241-6214. Email: stmartin@totalink.net. Web: www.saintmartindeporres.com.
Catechesis/Religious Program—Darla Depp, D.R.E.

30—ST. MARY OF THE ASSUMPTION (1854) Closed. For inquiries for parish records contact the chancery.

31—ST. MICHAEL THE ARCHANGEL (1900) [JC] Rev. Anthony A. Borgia; Ms. Suzanne Stapleton, Parish Mgr.
Res.: 420 Sandusky St., 43611-3535. Tel: 419-726-1947; Fax: 419-726-3597. Email: stmichaels@sbcglobal.net.

32—OUR LADY OF LOURDES (1926) [JC] Rev. Joseph P. Cardone.
Res.: 6149 Hill Ave., 43615-5699. Tel: 419-865-2345; Fax: 419-865-2545. Web: www.olltoledo.com.
See St. Benedict School under Consolidated Elementary Schools in the Institution Section.
Catechesis/Religious Program—P.R.E.P., Tel: 419-754-9603. Lisa Pierson, D.R.E. Students 62.

33—OUR LADY OF PERPETUAL HELP (1918) [JC] Rev. James E. Brown; Deacons Robert J. Lesinski; Daniel R. Waters; Connie Skoski, Liturgy Dir.
Res.: 3464 Glynn Dr., 43614. Tel: 419-382-4992.
Church & Mailing Address: 2255 Central Grove, 43614-4321. Tel: 419-382-5511; Fax: 419-382-7360. Email: olph@bex.net. Web: www.olphtoledo.org.
School—(Grades PreK-8) Tel: 419-382-5696. Miss Lori Anderson, Prin. Lay Teachers 17; Students 243.
Catechesis/Religious Program—Mrs. Kathy Dusseau, D.R.E. Students 109.

34—ST. PATRICK OF HEATHERDOWNS (1956) [JC] Revs. Dennis G. Walsh; Vicente Antonio Vera (Philippines); Ms. Sharon Christy, Pastoral Assoc.; Deacons Joel F. Junga; David J. Karpanty; Joseph H. Kest.
Mailing Address: 4201 Heatherdowns Blvd., 43614-3099. Tel: 419-381-1540; Fax: 419-381-2727. Web: www.toledostpats.org.
Res.: 2424 Green Valley Dr., 43614-3936. Tel: 419-381-2533.
School—(Grades PreK-8) Tel: 419-381-1775; Fax: 419-389-1161. Ms. Debora E. O'Shea, Prin. Lay Teachers 31; Students 466.
Catechesis/Religious Program—7743 Chestnut Ridge, Maumee, 43537-2727. Tel: 419-381-0240. Ms. Sarah Holkes, D.R.E. Students 155.

35—SS. PETER AND PAUL (1866), (Hispanic), [JC] Rev. Juan Francisco Molina; Deacon Salvador Sanchez.
Office: 728 S. St. Clair St., 43609-2432. Tel: 419-241-5822; Fax: 419-241-5822. Web: hosea.freewebpage.org/tolssp.
Catechesis/Religious Program—Tel: 419-283-0884. Leticia Viveros, D.R.E. Students 110.

36—ST. PIUS X (1953) [JC] Rev. David M. Whalen, O.S.F.S.; Deacon Timothy Etue; Mr. Kevin Foos, Pastoral Assoc., Dir. Liturgy & Music; Thomas Gibney, Business Mgr.
Mailing Address: 3011 Carskaddon Ave., 43606-1662.
Res.: 2929 Ilger Ave., 43606. Tel: 419-535-7672; Fax: 419-535-7810. Web: www.saint-pius.org.
School—(Grades PreK-8), 2950 Ilger Ave., 43606-1661. Tel: 419-535-7688; Fax: 419-535-7829. Ms. Susan Richardson, Prin. Lay Teachers 16; Students 234.
Catechesis/Religious Program—3011 Carskaddon Ave., 43606. linda Baumann, D.R.E. Students 67.

37—REGINA COELI (1954) [JC] Rev. James E. Auth; Sr. Janice Ann Brown, O.S.U., Office Mgr.; Deacons James Dudley; George Mitchell; Jack Binder, Business Mgr.; Michael Soncrant, Music Min.
Mailing Address: 530 Regina Pkwy., 43612-3398. Tel: 419-476-0922; Fax: 419-478-5846. Web: www.regina-coeli.org.
Res.: 5505 Bennett, 43612. Tel: 419-476-2281 (Home); Fax: 419-478-5846 (7:30am-4pm).
School—(Grades PreK-8), 600 Regina Pkwy., 43612-3399. Tel: 419-476-0920; Fax: 419-476-6792. Barbara Lane, Prin. Lay Teachers 20; Students 283.
Catechesis/Religious Program—Sr. Janice Ann Brown, O.S.U., Catechetical Leader. Students 125.

38—SACRED HEART OF JESUS (1883), (German), [JC] Rev. James R. Sanford, O.S.F.S.; Sr. Mary Madelena Pohlman, S.N.D., Pastoral Assoc.; Deacon Jose Garcia; Mr. Royce Wicks, Liturgy & Music Min.; Lynn K. Van Doren, Business Mgr.
Res.: 509 Oswald St., 43605-2131. Tel: 419-698-1664; Fax: 419-698-9708. Email: sacredheart@bex.net. Web: www.sacredhearttoledo.catholicweb.com.
See The Kateri Catholic School System, Oregon under Consolidated Elementary Schools located in the Institution Section.
Catechesis/Religious Program—Ms. Brenda Degener, D.R.E. Students 81.

39—ST. STANISLAUS (1908), (Polish), Closed. For inquiries for parish records contact the chancery.

40—ST. STEPHEN (1898), (Hungarian), [JC] Rev. James R. Sanford, O.S.F.S.; Sr. Mary Madelena Pohlman, S.N.D., Pastoral Assoc.; Hank Rybaczewski, Music Dir. In Res., Revs. Juan Francisco Molina; Joseph L. Vamos (Retired).
Office: 1878 Genesee St., 43605-1440. Tel: 419-691-1673. Email: ststephen@bex.net. Web: ststephentoledo.catholicweb.com.
Res.: 1880 Genesee St., 43605-1440. Tel: 419-698-1031.
Catechesis/Religious Program—2565 York St., 43605. Tel: 419-693-2691. Ms. Brenda Degener, D.R.E.

41—ST. TERESA, Consolidated with St. Ann to form St. Martin de Porres. See separate listing.

42—ST. THOMAS AQUINAS (1915) [JC] Very Rev. Jeffrey R. McBeth; Mary VanderLinde, Pastoral Assoc.
Res.: 729 White St., 43605-2719. Tel: 419-698-1519; Fax: 419-698-2050. Email: stthomasaq@accesstoledo.com.
See The Kateri Catholic School System, Oregon under Consolidated Elementary Schools located in the Institution Section.
Catechesis/Religious Program—Sr. Rita Rogier, C.P.P.S., Catechetical Leader. Students 86.

43—ST. VINCENT DE PAUL (1928) Closed. For inquiries for parish records contact the chancery.

OUTSIDE THE CITY OF TOLEDO

ALVADA, SENECA CO., ST. PETER (1854) [CEM] Closed. For inquiries for parish records contact the chancery.

ANTWERP, PAULDING CO., ST. MARY (1868) [JC] Closed. For inquiries for parish records contact the chancery.

ARCHBOLD, FULTON CO., ST. PETER (1846) [CEM] Rev. Gary M. Ferguson.
Res.: 614 N. Defiance St., 43502-1105. Tel: 419-446-9288; Fax: 419-446-9288. Email: stpeter@rtecexpress.net.
Catechesis/Religious Program—Tel: 419-446-2150; Fax: 419-446-0282. Rita Kruse, D.R.E. Students 126.

ASSUMPTION, FULTON CO.

1—HOLY TRINITY (2003), (German—Irish), [CEM 4] Rev. Ronald A. Schock; Deacons Joseph Repka; Robert Gillen; Sr. Rita Marie Schroeder, S.N.D., Pastoral Assoc. In Res., Rev. Frederick J. Snyder (Retired).
Res. & Mailing Address: 2649 U.S. Hwy. 20, Swanton, 43558-9558. Tel: 419-644-4014; Fax: 419-644-2159. Email: holytriparish@roadrunner.com.
Church: U.S. Hwy. 20 at State Rte. 64, Swanton, 43558.
School—(Grades PreK-8), 2639 U.S. Hwy. 20, Swanton, 43558-9558. Tel: 419-644-3971; Fax: 419-644-5018. Web: www.holytrinityschool.com. Linda R. Justen, Prin. Lay Teachers 12; Students 123.
Catechesis/Religious Program—Jill Howard, D.R.E. Students 160.

2—ST. MARY OF ASSUMPTION (1877), (German—Irish), Merged with Immaculate Conception, Marygrove and Saint Elizabeth of Hungary, Richfield Center to form Holy Trinity Catholic Parish, Assumption.

ATTICA, SENECA CO.

1—OUR LADY OF HOPE Rev. Paul A. Fahrbach.
Mailing Address: P.O. Box 461, 44807-0461. Tel: 419-426-3043; Fax: 419-426-1844. Email: ourladyofhopeattica@frontier.com.
Res. & Church: 14204 E. County Rd. 56, 44807-0461.
Catechesis/Religious Program—Mrs. Linda Moylett, D.R.E. Students 195.

2—SS. PETER AND PAUL (1882) [CEM] Closed. For inquiries for parish records contact the chancery.

BASCOM, SENECA CO., SS. PATRICK & ANDREW (1864) [CEM] Rev. Timothy M. Kummerer; Deacon George Miller.
Mailing Address: P.O. Box 226, 44809.
Church: 6230 W. Tiffin, 44809-0226. Email: patrick2@bright.net.
Catechesis/Religious Program—Cynthia L. Brickner, D.R.E. Students 130.

BELLEVUE, HURON CO.

1—ST. GASPAR DEL BUFALO (2005) Rev. Paul A. Fahrbach; Mrs. Leann Smith, Business Mgr.; Ms. Jane A. Miller, Parish Coord.
Res.: 16209 E. County Rd. 46, 44811-4661. Tel: 419-483-3231; Fax: 419-483-4661. Email: stgaspar@thewavz.com.
Catechesis/Religious Program—Ms. Jane A. Miller, D.R.E. Students 136.

2—IMMACULATE CONCEPTION (1859) [CEM] Rev. Jonathan C. Wight.
Res.: 231 E. Center St., 44811-1404. Tel: 419-483-3417; 419-483-8254 (Res.); Fax: 419-483-2585. Email: parish@icbell.org. Web: www.icbell.org.
School—Immaculate Conception School, (Grades PreK-8), 304 E. Main St., 44811-1404. Tel: 419-483-6066; Fax: 419-483-2736. Mrs. Kathleen A. Bolen, Prin. Lay Teachers 11; Students 179.
Catechesis/Religious Program—Tel: 419-483-8374. Mr. Peter Schafer, D.R.E. Students 148.

BETHLEHEM, RICHLAND CO., SACRED HEART OF JESUS (1833), (German), [CEM] Rev. Michael A. Geiger.

Office: 5742 State Rte. 61 S., Shelby, 44875-9080. Tel: 419-342-2256; Fax: 419-342-2256. Email: frgeiger@sacredheartbethlehem.org.
Church: State Rte. 61, Shelby, 44875.
School—(Grades PreK-8), 5754 State Rte. 61 S., Shelby, 44875-9802. Tel: 419-342-2797; Fax: 419-342-2797. Lisa Myers, Prin. Lay Teachers 7; Students 84.
Catechesis/Religious Program—Students 25.

BISMARK, HURON CO., ST. SEBASTIAN (1846), (German), [CEM] Closed. For inquiries for parish records contact the chancery.

BLAKESLEE, WILLIAMS CO., ST. JOSEPH (1865), (German), [CEM] Closed. Church transferred to a chapel of Saint Mary, Edgerton

BLUFFTON, ALLEN CO., ST. MARY (1865) Sr. Carol Inkrott, O.S.F., Pastoral Leader; Rev. Timothy F. Ferris, Chap.
Mailing Address: 160 N. Spring, 45817. Tel: 419-358-8631; Fax: 419-358-0647. Email: cmschroede@embarqmail.com.
Res.: 144 N. Spring Rd., 45817. Tel: 419-358-1176.
Catechesis/Religious Program—Students 171.

BONO, LUCAS CO., OUR LADY OF MT. CARMEL (1917) Rev. Eric P. Schild.
Res.: 1105 Elliston Rd., Martin, 43445-9601. Tel: 419-836-7681; Fax: 419-836-7681. Email: olmc30@aol.com.
Catechesis/Religious Program—Julie Marshall, D.R.E. Students 58.

BOWLING GREEN, WOOD CO.
1—ST. ALOYSIUS (1862) Rev. Mark E. Davis; Deacons Ramon Llanas Jr.; Phillip Avina.
Mailing Address: P.O. Box 485, 43402-0485.
Church: S. Summit & Clough Sts., 43402-0485. Tel: 419-352-4195; Fax: 419-353-7865. Email: parishoffice@stalbg.org. Web: www.stalbg.org.
School—(Grades PreK-8), 148 S. Enterprise, 43402-4738. Tel: 419-352-8614; Fax: 419-352-4738. Andrea Puhl, Prin. Lay Teachers 13; Students 210.
Catechesis/Religious Program—Jean Bargiel, D.R.E. Students 236.
2—ST. THOMAS MORE UNIVERSITY PARISH (1967) Rev. Michael G. Dandurand.
Res.: 425 Thurstin Ave., 43402-1901. Tel: 419-352-7555; Fax: 419-352-7557. Email: info@sttoms.com. Web: www.sttoms.com.
Catechesis/Religious Program—Ms. Karen Mazzeo, Campus Min.; Mr. Peter Range, Campus Min.; Mr. Kevin Sretter, Campus Missionary. Students 101.

BRYAN, WILLIAMS CO., ST. PATRICK (1857) Rev. James E. Halleron; Deacons Dennis F. Jackson; Thomas F. Dominique; Bill Beber, Music Dir.; Patricia Cox, Sec.
Church & Mailing Address: 610 S. Portland St., 43506-2059. Web: www.stpatbryan.org.
Res.: 704 S. Portland, 43506.
School—(Grades PreK-8) Tel: 419-636-3592; Fax: 419-633-5054. Lisa Cinadr, Prin. Lay Teachers 15; Students 159.
Catechesis/Religious Program—Tel: 419-636-1044. Ms. Tami Kunesh, D.R.E.; Kasey Thormeier, Dir., Youth Ministry. Students 166.

BUCYRUS, CRAWFORD CO., HOLY TRINITY (1865), (German), [CEM] Rev. John A. Miller; Deacons Jerome A. Gubernath; Julius J. Fritz.
Res.: 760 Tiffin St., 44820-1551. Tel: 419-562-1346; Fax: 419-562-2784. Email: htc1@midohio.twcbc.com.
School—(Grades PreK-8), 740 Tiffin St., 44820-1551. Tel: 419-562-2741; Fax: 419-562-7659. Ms. Sally Dunbar, Prin. Lay Teachers 7; Students 53.
Catechesis/Religious Program—Tel: 419-562-2645. Students 98.

CAREY, WYANDOT CO., OUR LADY OF CONSOLATION, BASILICA-NATIONAL SHRINE (1867) [CEM] Revs. John Stowe, O.F.M.Conv.; Xavier Goulet, O.F.M-.Conv.; Deacon James F. Kitzler. In Res., Revs. Florian Tiell, O.F.M.Conv.; Paul Faroh, O.F.M-.Conv.; John Raphael Hadnagy, O.F.M.Conv.; Bros. Bryan Hoban, O.F.M.Conv.; Randy Kin, O.F.M-.Conv.; Mike Austin, O.F.M.Conv.; Angelo Catania, O.F.M.Conv.
Res.: 315 Clay St., 43316-1498. Tel: 419-396-1523; Fax: 419-396-3355. Email: olcparish@udata.com. Web: www.olcshrine.com.
School—401 Clay St., 43316-1496. Tel: 419-396-6166. Mrs. Judy Hall, Prin. Lay Teachers 14; Students 162.
Catechesis/Religious Program—Tel: 419-396-1523. Sr. Dionne Sartor, O.S.F., D.R.E. Students 65.

CECIL, PAULDING CO., IMMACULATE CONCEPTION (1879) Closed. For inquiries for parish records contact the chancery.

CLOVERDALE, PUTNAM CO., ST. BARBARA (1898), (German), [CEM] Rev. John F. Stites. In Res., Rev. Roger D. Bonifas (Retired).
Res.: 160 Main St., P.O. Box 8, 45827. Tel: 419-488-2391; Fax: 419-488-2390. Email: kb8bia@nwbright.net.
Catechesis/Religious Program—Students 31.

CLYDE, SANDUSKY CO., ST. MARY (1890) [CEM] Sr. Regina Fisher, S.N.D., Pastoral Leader; Rev. Edward J. Schleter, Presbyteral Moderator & Chap.
Res.: 609 Vine St., 43410-1537. Tel: 419-547-9610.
Catechesis/Religious Program—Students 97.

COLUMBUS GROVE, PUTNAM CO., ST. ANTHONY OF PADUA (1912), (German), [CEM] Rev. Thomas J. Extejt; Deacon James E. Dunn.
Res.: 518 W. Sycamore St., 45830-1020. Tel: 419-659-2263; Fax: 419-659-5202. Email: mormanj@sa.noacsc.org.
School—(Grades K-8), 520 W. Sycamore, 45830-1020. Tel: 419-659-2103. Jan Schimmoeller, Prin. Lay Teachers 12; Students 149.
Catechesis/Religious Program—Students 223.

CONTINENTAL, PUTNAM CO., ST. JOHN THE BAPTIST (1907) [JC] Rev. Mark Hoying, C.PP.S.; Deacon Joseph Heeter.
Church: 4893 St. Rte. 634, N, 45831. Tel: 419-488-2391; Fax: 419-488-2390. Web: www.stjohn-the-baptistchurch.org.
Catechesis/Religious Program—Denise J. Matthews, C.R.E.; Jean J. Tegenkamp, C.R.E. Students 97.

CRESTLINE, CRAWFORD CO., ST. JOSEPH (1861), (German), [JC] Rev. Michael A. Geiger; Deacon William E. Rall; Ms. Christine Carper, Business Mgr.
Res.: 331 N. Thoman St., 44827-1445. Tel: 419-683-2015; Fax: 419-683-3415. Web: www.stjosephcrestline.org.
School—(Grades K-8), 333 N. Thoman St., 44827-1445. Tel: 419-683-1284. Carolyn Price, Prin. Lay Teachers 5; Students 81.
Catechesis/Religious Program—Students 20.

CUBA, PUTNAM CO., ST. ISIDORE (1917) Closed. For inquiries for parish records contact the chancery. Shared with St. Michael, Kalida.

CUSTAR, WOOD CO., ST. LOUIS (1864) [CEM] [JC] Rev. David D. Tscherne.
Res.: 22792 Defiance Pike, 43511-9716. Tel: 419-669-1864; Fax: 419-669-3825. Email: stlouischurch@midohio.twcbc.com. Web: www.stlouiscustar.parishesonline.com.
School—(Grades PreK-6), 22767 Defiance Pike, 43511-9716. Tel: 419-669-1875. Richelle L. Piercefield, Prin.; Ellen Boyer, Librarian. Lay Teachers 6; Students 26.
Catechesis/Religious Program—

CYGNET, WOOD CO., SACRED HEART (1890) Closed. For inquiries for parish records contact the chancery.

DEFIANCE, DEFIANCE CO.
1—ST. JOHN THE EVANGELIST (1850) [CEM] Rev. Todd M. Dominique; Deacons Donald Meyer; Domick J. Varano; Ms. Carol Kurivial, Generations of Faith Dir.; Mr. David G. Moninger, Liturgy Dir.; Bonnie Nally, Office Mgr.
Office: 510 Jackson Ave., 43512-2189. Tel: 419-782-7121; Fax: 419-782-5813. Email: stjohn@stjohndefiance.org. Web: www.stjohndefiance.org.
See Holy Cross Catholic School of Defiance under Consolidated Elementary Schools located in the Institution section.
Catechesis/Religious Program—
2—ST. MARY (1873) Rev. Randy P. Giesige; Deacon Jeff M. Mayer.
Mailing Address: 715 Jefferson Ave., 43512. Tel: 419-782-2776; Fax: 419-782-1958. Email: stmarys@defnet.com. Web: www.stmarydefiance.org.
See Defiance Holy Cross Catholic School of Defiance under Consolidated Elementary Schools located in the Institution section.
Catechesis/Religious Program—Sr. Barbara Sloan, S.N.D., Dir. Sacramental Prep.; Ms. Carol Kurivial, Generations of Faith Dir.

DELPHOS, ALLEN CO., ST. JOHN THE EVANGELIST (1844), (German), [CEM] Revs. Melvin T. Verhoff; Jacob A. Gordon; Deacons Frederick C. Lisk; David J. Ricker; Ms. Trina Schultz, Pastoral Assoc.; Mr. Ted I. Hanf, Business Mgr.
Mailing Address: 210 N. Pierce St., 45833. In Res., Revs. Charles Obinwa (Nigeria); Timothy F. Ferris.
Res.: 331 E. Second St., 45833-1788. Tel: 419-695-4050; Fax: 419-695-4060. Web: www.delphosstjohnparish.org.
School—(Grades PreK-8), 110 N. Pierce St., 45833-1799. Tel: 419-692-8561; Fax: 419-692-4501. Mr. Nathan Stewart, Prin. Sisters of Notre Dame 1; Lay Teachers 31; Students 454.
High School—515 E Second St., 45833-1798. Tel: 419-692-5371; Fax: 419-879-6874. Mr. Donald Huysman, Prin. Lay Teachers 20; Students 272.
Catechesis/Religious Program—

DESHLER, HENRY CO., IMMACULATE CONCEPTION (1871) Rev. Tommy Rodrigues.
Mailing Address: 230 Allendale Ave., 43516-1103. Tel: 419-278-3686. Web: www.holyimmaculate.org.
Res.: 22767 Defiance Pike, Custar, 43511. Tel: 419-669-3920.
Catechesis/Religious Program—Students 32.

EDGERTON, WILLIAMS CO., ST. MARY (1865), (German), [CEM] Rev. Arthur J. Niewiadomski; Debra A. Schroeder, Business Mgr.
Mailing Address: P.O. Box 355, 43517. Tel: 419-298-2540; Fax: 419-298-3123. Email: stmarycatholic@frontier.com.
Office: 317 S. Locust St, 43517.
Res.: 133 W. Bement St., 43517. Tel: 419-298-2932.
Church: 300 S. Michigan Ave., 43517.
School—(Grades 1-6), 314 S. Locust St., P.O. Box 309, 43517. Tel: 419-298-2531. Mrs. Juliana M. Taylor, Prin. Lay Teachers 7; Students 98.
Catechesis/Religious Program—Mrs. Karrie Kimpel, C.R.E. Students 149.

FAYETTE, FULTON CO., OUR LADY OF MERCY (1943) Rev. Gary M. Ferguson.
Mailing Address: Box 429, 43521-0429. Email: ourladyofmercy@frontier.com. Web: www.ourladyofmercyfayette.parishesonline.com.
Church: 409 E. Main St., 43521. Tel: 419-237-2441; Fax: 419-237-1042.
Catechesis/Religious Program—P.O. Box 453, 43521. Tel: 419-237-3019. Ms. Mandy Eberly, D.R.E. Students 77.

FINDLAY, HANCOCK CO., ST. MICHAEL THE ARCHANGEL (1834) [CEM] Rev. Msgr. Michael G. Hohenbrink; Revs. Shaji R. Thomas; Christopher G. Bohnsak; Deacons David Sadler; Mark Kern; Michael Eier.
Mailing Address: 750 Bright Rd., 45840-2448. Tel: 419-422-2646; Fax: 419-422-2602. Email: parish@findlaystmichael.org. Web: www.findlaystmichael.org.
Res.: 2008 Greendale Ave., 45840. Tel: 419-423-8776.
Church (Downtown): 617 W. Main Cross, 45840.
Church (East): 750 Bright Rd., 45840.
School—(Grades PreK-8), 723 Sutton Pl., 45840-6965. Tel: 419-423-2738; Fax: 419-423-2720. Anne Brehm, Prin. Lay Teachers 30; Students 486.
Catechesis/Religious Program—Tel: 419-423-2123. Mrs. Geri Leibfarth, D.R.E. Students 324.

FORT JENNINGS, PUTNAM CO., ST. JOSEPH (1848), (German), [CEM] Rev. Joseph J. Przybysz; Deacon Lawrence Schimmoeller.
Mailing Address: P.O. Box 68, 45844-0068. Tel: 419-286-2132; Fax: 419-286-3132. Web: www.stjosephfortjennings.parishesonline.com.
Church: 135 N. Water St. at Second St., 45844.
Catechesis/Religious Program—Tel: 419-286-2019. Ms. Shirley Hammond, D.R.E. Students 330.

FOSTORIA, SENECA CO., ST. WENDELIN (1850) [CEM] Revs. Nicholas Weibl; Matthew R. Rader; Deacon John T. Kromer; Jonathan B. Hay, Pastoral Assoc.
Mailing Address: P.O. Box 836, 44830-0836. Tel: 419-435-6692.
Res.: 222 N. Wood St., 44830. Tel: 419-435-1875; Fax: 419-435-7826. Web: www.stwendelin.org.
Church: 303 N. Wood St., 44830.
School—(Grades K-12), 323 N. Wood St., 44830-2246. Mr. Michael Amlin, Prin. Sisters of Notre Dame 1; Lay Teachers 38; Students 341.
Catechesis/Religious Program—Tel: 419-435-6681. Mrs. Shellie Gabel, D.R.E.

FREMONT, SANDUSKY CO.
1—ST. ANN (1843) [JC] Rev. Michael J. Zacharias; Deacon James Heyman; Nancy Patterson, Business Mgr.
Res.: 1021 W. State St., 43420-2103. Tel: 419-332-7472; Fax: 419-332-3556.
Catechesis/Religious Program—Sr. Janice M. Peer, O.S.F., D.R.E. Clustered with St. Joseph.
2—ST. CASIMIR (1915), (Polish), Closed. For inquiries for parish records contact the chancery.
3—ST. JOSEPH (1857), (German), [CEM] [JC] Rev. Michael J. Zacharias; Deacon Norbert A. Wethington; Thomas Mosser, Business Mgr.; Nathan Herb, Music Dir.
Res.: 709 Croghan St., 43420-2482. Tel: 419-334-2638; Fax: 419-334-6929. Email: stjoefrem@sbcglobal.net. Web: www.stjosephfremont.parishesonline.com.
See Bishop Hoffman Catholic School under Consolidated Elementary Schools located in the Institution Section.
Catechesis/Religious Program—Clustered with St. Ann, Fremont. Sr. Janice M. Peer, O.S.F, D.R.E.
4—SACRED HEART (1956) [JC] Rev. Kenneth J. Lill; Deacon Alfredo Diaz.
Res.: 550 Smith Rd., 43420-9567. Tel: 419-332-7339; Fax: 419-332-7511. Email: scrdhrt@sacredheart-fremont.org. Web: www.sacredheart-fremont.org.
Catechesis/Religious Program—Ms. Tonya Caron, D.R.E. Students 92.

FRENCHTOWN, SENECA CO., ST. NICHOLAS (1856), (German—French), [CEM] Closed. For inquiries for parish records contact the chancery.

GALION, CRAWFORD CO., ST. JOSEPH (1853) [CEM] Rev. John A. Miller; Deacons Alfred Sisson; Gregory Kirk.
Res.: 135 N. Liberty St., 44833-2017. Tel: 419-468-2884; Fax: 419-468-9464. Email: stjoegal@midohio.twcbc.com. Web: www.galionsaintjoseph.org.

School—(Grades PreK-8), 138 N. Liberty St., 44833-2016. Tel: 419-468-5436; Fax: 419-468-3611. Ms. Sally Dunbar, Prin. Sisters 1; Lay Teachers 8; Students 66.
Catechesis/Religious Program—141 N. Liberty St., 44833. Tel: 419-468-6330. Students 90.

GENOA, OTTAWA CO., OUR LADY OF LOURDES (1856) Very Rev. David L. Ritchie; Sr. Gemma M. Fenbert, O.S.F., Pastoral Assoc.
Church: 204 Main St., 43430-1609. Tel: 419-855-8501; Fax: 419-855-8159. Email: ollgenoa@verizon.net. Web: www.ollgenoa.parishesonline.com.
Catechesis/Religious Program—Tel: 419-855-7181. Mr. Joshua Mocek, D.R.E. Students 170.

GIBSONBURG, SANDUSKY CO., ST. MICHAEL CHURCH (1892) [CEM], (Twinned with St. Mary, Millersville.) Rev. Theodore J. Miller.
Mailing: 317 E. Madison St., 43431-1498. Tel: 419-637-2255; Fax: 419-637-2255. Email: gburgstmichael@woh.rr.com.
Catechesis/Religious Program—Tel: 419-637-9929. Mrs. Patricia Hoffman, D.R.E. Students 214.

GLANDORF, PUTNAM CO., ST. JOHN THE BAPTIST (1834), (German), [CEM] [JC] Rev. Anthony Fortman, C.PP.S. In Res., Bro. Jerome Schulte, C.PP.S.
Res.: 109 N. Main St., Box 48, 45848-0048. Tel: 419-538-6928; Fax: 419-538-6147. Email: stjohns@bright.net. Web: www.stjohnglandorf.parishesonline.com.
Catechesis/Religious Program—Tel: 419-538-6335. Students 680.

HAMLER, HENRY CO., ST. PAUL (1886) Closed. For inquiries for parish records contact the chancery. Chapel remains open.

HICKSVILLE, DEFIANCE CO., ST. MICHAEL (1878) Attended by Edgerton. Rev. Arthur J. Niewiadomski; Deacon Joseph Timbrook.
Mailing Address: 100 Antwerp Dr., 43526. Tel: 419-542-8202; Fax: 419-542-9513. Email: stmikehi@bright.net. Web: www.home.catholicweb.com/stmikesweb/index.cfm.
Res.: 133 W. Bement St., P.O. Box 355, Edgerton, 43517. Tel: 419-298-2932.
Church: W. High St. at Antwerp Dr., 43526.
Catechesis/Religious Program— Ms. Melinda Amstutz, D.R.E. Students 184.

HOLGATE, HENRY CO., ST. MARY (1886) [CEM], (Twinned with Sacred Heart of Jesus, New Bavaria.) Rev. Stephen L. Stanbery; Deacon James Schortgen.
Res.: 316 Chicago Ave., 43527-0487. Tel: 419-264-3321. Email: shchurch@metalink.net.
Catechesis/Religious Program—Tel: 419-264-6596. Sue Like, D.R.E.; Karen Schwiebert, D.R.E.; Deacon James Schortgen, D.R.E.; Anthony Klear, Youth Min. Students 82.

HURON, ERIE CO., ST. PETER (1888) [JC] Rev. Jeffery P. Sikorski; Deacon John Busam.
Res.: 430 Main St., 44839-1678. Tel: 419-433-5725; Fax: 419-433-2118. Web: www.stpetershuron.com.
School—(Grades PreK-8), 429 Huron St., 44839-1753. Tel: 419-433-4640; Fax: 419-433-2118. Ms. Joy Tokarsky, Prin. Lay Teachers 13; Students 155.
Catechesis/Religious Program—Ms. Sally Clark, D.R.E.

JUNCTION, PAULDING CO., ST. MARY (1846) Closed. For inquiries for parish records contact the chancery.

KALIDA, PUTNAM CO., ST. MICHAEL (1878) [CEM] Rev. Mark Hoying, C.PP.S.; Deacon Robert Klausing; Miss Leslie A. Stechschulte, Sec.
Mailing Address: Box 387, 45853-0387.
Office: 312 N. Broad St., 45853-0387. Tel: 419-532-3474; Fax: 419-532-3470. Email: stmich@bright.net. Web: kalidastmichaels.org.
Res.: 206 N. Broad St., 45853. Tel: 419-532-3431.
Catechesis/Religious Program—Tel: 419-532-3494. Mrs. Connie Cleemput, D.R.E.; Mrs. Mary Siefker, Youth Min. Students 547.

KANSAS, SENECA CO., ST. JAMES (1890) Closed. For inquiries for parish records contact the chancery.

KELLEY'S ISLAND, ERIE CO., ST. MICHAEL (1861) Sr. Lucille Kime, S.N.D., Pastoral Leader; Rev. Christopher G. Bazar, Presbyteral Moderator & Chap.
Mailing Address: P.O. Box 490, 43438-0490. Tel: 419-285-2741. Email: mos&sm@hmcltd.net.
Catechesis/Religious Program—Ms. Caroline Jorski, D.R.E.; Ms. Patricia Seeholzer, D.R.E. Students 12.

KIRBY, WYANDOT CO., ST. MARY (1861) [CEM] Closed. For inquiries for parish records contact the chancery.

LANDECK, ALLEN CO., ST. JOHN THE BAPTIST (1866) [CEM] Rev. Melvin T. Verhoff.
Res.: 14755 Landeck Rd., Delphos, 45833-9438. Tel: 419-692-0636; Fax: 419-692-0636. Email: schurch1@woh.rr.com.

LEIPSIC, PUTNAM CO., ST. MARY (1873) [CEM] Very Rev. George E. Wenzinger; Deacons Thomas B. Niese; Benjamin R. Valdez.
Res.: 318 State St., 45856-1332. Tel: 419-943-2952. Email: stmaryleipsic@fairpoint.net.
School—(Grades K-8), 129 St. Mary St., 45856-1328. Tel: 419-943-2801; Fax: 419-943-3555. Sr. Carol Ann Mary Smith, S.N.D., Prin. Sisters of Notre Dame 2; Lay Teachers 8; Students 135.
Catechesis/Religious Program—Sr. M. Francis Theresa Dorsey, S.N.D., D.R.E. Students 222.

LEXINGTON, RICHLAND CO., RESURRECTION (1969) Very Rev. Nelson G. Beaver; Rev. Joseph Sekere; Deacon Thomas R. Dubois.
Res.: 2600 Lexington Ave., 44904-1426. Tel: 419-884-0060; Fax: 419-884-0261. Email: resparish@earthlink.net.
Catechesis/Religious Program—Barbara Ann Smith, D.R.E. Students 164.

LIBERTY, SENECA CO., ST. ANDREW (1834) [CEM], Merged with St. Patrick, Bascom to form SS. Patrick & Andrew.

LIMA, ALLEN CO.

1—ST. CHARLES BORROMEO (1953) [JC] Rev. Stephen J. Blum; Deacon James S. Bronder.
Res.: 2200 W. Elm, 45805-2697. Tel: 419-228-7635; Fax: 419-229-2835. Email: office@st-charles.org. Web: www.st-charles.org.
School—(Grades PreK-8), 2175 W. Elm St., 45805-2673. Tel: 419-222-2536; Fax: 419-222-8720. Mr. Chad Berndt, Prin. Lay Teachers 25; Students 409.
Catechesis/Religious Program—Mrs. Mary S. Shak, D.R.E. Students 527.

2—ST. GERARD (1916) Revs. James Szobonya, C.Ss.R.; Michael Houston, C.Ss.R.; Deacon Elias Pina.
Res.: 240 W. Robb Ave., 45801-2899. Tel: 419-224-3080; Fax: 419-225-2231. Web: www.stgerardchurch.org.
School—(Grades PreK-8), 1311 N. Main St., 45801-2818. Tel: 419-222-0431; Fax: 419-224-6580. Ms. Michelle Brandle, Prin. Lay Teachers 11; Students 154.
Catechesis/Religious Program—Amy Rohan, D.R.E. Students 140.

3—ST. JOHN THE EVANGELIST (1901) [JC] Very Rev. David M. Ross; Mrs. Joyce M. Stombaugh, Admin. Asst.
Mailing Address: 222 S. West St., 45801-4842. Tel: 419-222-5521; Fax: 419-228-8439. Email: strchurch@wcoil.com. Web: www.limacatholic.org; www.stjohnlimaohio.org.
Church: 777 S. Main St., 45804.
Catechesis/Religious Program—Ms. Kimberly Moritz, D.R.E. Students 45.

4—ST. ROSE OF LIMA (1856) [JC] Very Rev. David M. Ross; Deacon Theodore J. Kaser Jr.; Mrs. Joyce M. Stombaugh, Admin. Asst.
Mailing Address: 222 S. West St., 45801-4842. Tel: 419-222-5521; Fax: 419-228-8439. Email: strchurch@wcoil.com. Web: www.stroselimaohio.org.
Church: McKibben St. & N. West St., 45801-4294.
School—(Grades K-8), 523 N. West St., 45801-4237. Tel: 419-223-6361; Fax: 419-222-2032. Patricia Shanahan, Prin. Sisters 1; Lay Teachers 9; Students 109.
Catechesis/Religious Program—Tel: 419-222-2087. Ms. Kimberly Moritz, D.R.E. Students 76.

LYONS, FULTON CO., OUR LADY OF FATIMA (1946) Closed. For inquiries for parish records contact the chancery.

MANSFIELD, RICHLAND CO.

1—ST. MARY OF THE SNOWS (1949) [JC] Very Rev. Nelson G. Beaver; Rev. Joseph Sekere; Deacons Allan D. Kopp; Russell Shoemaker.
Res.: 1630 Ashland, 44905-1896. Tel: 419-589-5464; Fax: 419-589-7085. Web: www.mansfieldstmarys.org.
School—(Grades PreK-8) Tel: 419-589-2114; Fax: 419-589-7085. Roger Harraman, Prin. Lay Teachers 11; Students 98.
Catechesis/Religious Program—Ms. Sue Sanders, D.R.E.

2—ST. PETER (1844) [CEM] Revs. Gregory R. Hite; Thomas J. McQuillen; Deacon James Marshall; Bill Johnson, Dir. Liturgy & Music.
Mailing Address: 104 W. 1st St., 44902-2199. Tel: 419-524-2572; Fax: 419-522-2553. Web: www.mansfieldstpeters.org.
Church: 54 S. Mulberry St., 44902.
School—(Grades PreK-6), 63 S. Mulberry St., 44902-1909. Tel: 419-524-3351; Fax: 419-524-3366. Mr. James Smith, Prin. Sisters of St. Francis of Mary Immaculate (Joliet, IL) 1; Lay Teachers 24; Students 303.
High School—(Grades 7-12), 104 W. First St., 44902-2199. Tel: 419-524-0979. Mrs. Tressa Reith, Prin. Sisters of St. Francis of Mary Immaculate (Joliet, IL) 1; Lay Teachers 25; Students 198.
Catechesis/Religious Program—Sheila Hershiser, Youth Min. Students 106.

MARBLEHEAD, OTTAWA CO., ST. JOSEPH (1867), (Slovak), [CEM] [JC] Rev. Daniel J. Ring; Carol Robertson, Business Mgr.; Mr. Ronald Ossovicki, Dir. Music & Liturgy.
Mailing Address: 113 James St., 43440-2118. Tel: 419-798-4177; Fax: 419-798-4260. Email: stjoseph@cros.net.
Res.: 802 Barclay, 43440-2101.
Church: 822 Barclay St., 43440.
Catechesis/Religious Program—113 James St., 43440-2118. Tel: 419-798-5543. Ms. Carol Arntz, D.R.E. Students 74.

MARYGROVE, LUCAS CO., IMMACULATE CONCEPTION (1840) Merged with Saint Elizabeth of Hungary, Richfield Center, and St. Mary of Assumption, Assumption to form Holy Trinity Catholic Parish, Assumption.

MARYSDALE, DEFIANCE CO.

1—IMMACULATE CONCEPTION (1873) [CEM] Closed. For inquiries for parish records contact the chancery.

2—ST. ISIDORE (2005), (Twinned with St. Michael, St. Michael's Ridge.) Rev. Robert J. Kill.
Mailing Address: 05480 Moser Rd., Defiance, 43512-9150. Tel: 419-497-2161; Fax: 419-497-2058. Email: kb8big@defnet.com. Web: www.saintisidoreparish.org.
Church: 06324 State Rte. 15 at Glenburg Rd., Defiance, 43512.
Catechesis/Religious Program—Tel: 419-658-2512. Ms. Janet Smith, D.R.E. Students 95.

MARYWOOD, SENECA CO., ST. MICHAEL'S (1839), (German), [CEM] Closed. For inquiries for parish records contact the chancery.

MAUMEE, LUCAS CO., ST. JOSEPH (1841) [CEM] Revs. Keith A. Stripe; Kishore Kottana; Deacons Edgar E. Irelan; Joseph Malenfant.
Res.: 104 W. Broadway, 43537-2137. Tel: 419-893-4848; Fax: 419-891-6968. Email: parish.office@stjosephmaumee.org. Web: www.stjosephfamily.org.
School—(Grades K-8), 112 W. Broadway St., 43537-2137. Tel: 419-893-3304. Ms. Camille Knopps, Prin. Lay Teachers 16; Students 196.
Catechesis/Religious Program—Tel: 419-893-7025; Fax: 419-891-6969. Ms. Judy Virtue, Youth Formation. Students 420.

MILAN, ERIE CO., ST. ANTHONY (1862) [CEM] Very Rev. Francis J. Speier; Ms. Linda Salmons, Pastoral Assoc.
Mailing Address: P.O. Box 1200, 44846-9757.
Res.: 145 Center St., 44846-9757. Tel: 419-499-4274; Fax: 419-499-4584. Email: astanthonysc@neo.rr.com.
Catechesis/Religious Program—130 S. Main St., 44846. Tel: 419-499-4300. Students 170.

MILLER CITY, PUTNAM CO., ST. NICHOLAS (1888) [CEM] Rev. Stephen L. Schroeder.
Mailing Address: P.O. Box 40, 45864-0036. Tel: 419-876-3481; Fax: 501-665-8794. Email: snhf@fairpoint.net.
Church: 201 E. Main Cross, 45864-0036.
Catechesis/Religious Program—Combined with Holy Family, New Cleveland. Deborah Wehri, D.R.E.

MILLERSVILLE, SANDUSKY CO., ST. MARY (1859) [CEM], (Twinned with St. Michael, Gibsonburg.) Rev. Theodore J. Miller.
Res.: 875 State Rte. 635, Helena, 43435-9792. Tel: 419-638-3042; Fax: 419-638-3043. Email: msmparishoffice@cros.net.
Catechesis/Religious Program—Mrs. Rae L. Kistner, D.R.E. Students 59.

MONROEVILLE, HURON CO., ST. JOSEPH (1861) [CEM] Rev. William A. Pifher.
Res.: 66 Chapel St., 44847. Tel: 419-465-4142; Fax: 419-465-2170. Email: stjoseph@neo.rr.com. Web: stjosephmonroeville.parishesonline.com.
School—(Grades PreK-8), 79 Chapel St., 44847. Tel: 419-465-2625. James T. Francis, Prin. Lay Teachers 13; Students 125.
Catechesis/Religious Program—Students 50.

MONTPELIER, WILLIAMS CO., SACRED HEART (1911) Rev. James E. Halleron.
Mailing Address: 220 S. East Ave., 43543-1504. Tel: 419-485-5914; Fax: 419-272-3400.
Res.: 610 S. Portland St., Bryan, 43506. Tel: 419-636-1044.
Catechesis/Religious Program—Students 65.

NAPOLEON, HENRY CO., ST. AUGUSTINE (1856) [CEM] Very Rev. Daniel E. Borgelt; Deacon Robert Bost.
Office: 210 E. Clinton St., 43545-1602. Tel: 419-592-7656; Fax: 419-592-6316. Email: staugie@henry-net.com. Web: www.staugie.net.
School—(Grades PreK-8), 722 Monroe St., 43545-1631. Tel: 419-592-3641; Fax: 419-592-5156. Nancy Ann Schroeder, Prin. Lay Teachers 11; Students 89.

NEW BAVARIA, HENRY CO., SACRED HEART OF JESUS (1893), (German), [CEM] Rev. Stephen L. Stanbery; Deacon Kenneth Klear.
Res.: 13779 County Rd. Y, 43548-9738. Tel: 419-653-4157. Email: shchurch@metalink.net.
Catechesis/Religious Program—Tel: 419-635-4121.

Raffaela Peck, D.R.E. Students 120.

NEW CLEVELAND, PUTNAM CO., HOLY FAMILY (1862) [CEM] Rev. Stephen L. Schroeder; Deacon Doyle J. Erford; Jane Kuhlman, Pastoral Assoc.
Res. & Office: 7359 St. Rte. 109, c/o P. O. Box 40, Miller City, 45864-0036. Tel: 419-876-3481; Fax: 501-665-8794. Email: snhf@fairpoint.net.
Church: 7359 St. Rt. 109, 45864.
Catechesis/Religious Program—Tel: 419-876-3480. Deborah Wehri, D.R.E. Combined with St. Nicholas, Miller City. Students 259.

NEW LONDON, HURON CO., OUR LADY OF LOURDES (1853) [CEM] Rev. Douglas D. Taylor; Mary E. Harris, Sec.
Res.: 18 Park Ave., 44851-1163. Tel: 419-929-4401; Fax: 419-929-4430. Email: ololnlondon@hmcltd.net.
Catechesis/Religious Program—43 S. Main St., 44851. Tel: 419-929-4402. Students 73.

NEW RIEGEL, SENECA CO.
1—ALL SAINTS (2005) Rev. Timothy M. Kummerer; Ms. Lorrie J. Seiple, Business Mgr.; Mrs. Regina A. Wagner, Sec.
Mailing Address: P.O. Box 89, 44853-0089.
Church: 41 N. Perry St., 44853. Tel: 419-595-2567; Fax: 419-595-2303. Email: officeallsaintsparish@midohio.twcbc.com. Web: www.all-saints-parish.org.
Catechesis/Religious Program—Mrs. Kathy A. Reinhart, Catechetical Leader. Students 345.
2—ST. BONIFACE (1834) [CEM] Closed. For inquiries for parish records contact the chancery.

NEW WASHINGTON, CRAWFORD CO., ST. BERNARD (1844) [CEM] Rev. Eric J. Culler.
Mailing Address: P.O. Box 337, 44854-0337.
Church: 412 W. Mansfield, 44854-0337. Tel: 419-492-2295; Fax: 419-492-2135. Web: www.stbernardnwo.com.
School—(Grades K-8), 320 Mansfield St., 44854-9704. Tel: 419-492-2693. Susan Maloy, Prin. Lay Teachers 7; Students 97.
Catechesis/Religious Program—Laura Beeson, D.R.E. Students 52.

NORTH AUBURN, CRAWFORD CO., MOTHER OF SORROWS (1879) Closed. For inquiries for parish records contact the chancery. Chapel remains open.

NORTH BALTIMORE, WOOD CO.
1—HOLY FAMILY (2001) Rev. Tommy Rodrigues.
Mailing Address: 115 E. Cherry St., 45872-1134.
Res.: 410 Central Ave., 45872-1134. Tel: 419-257-2319; Fax: 419-257-2319. Web: www.holyimmaculate.org.
Catechesis/Religious Program—Margaret Bobb, D.R.E. Students 82.
2—OUR LADY OF THE MIRACULOUS MEDAL (1891) Consolidated with Sacred Heart, Cygnet to form Holy Family, North Baltimore.

NORTH CREEK, PUTNAM CO., ST. JOSEPH (1887), (German), Closed. For inquiries for parish records contact the chancery.

NORWALK, HURON CO.
1—ST. MARY, MOTHER OF THE REDEEMER (1860), (Irish), [CEM] Very Rev. Francis J. Speier; Ms. Linda Salmons, Pastoral Assoc.
Res.: 38 W. League St., 44857-1397. Tel: 419-668-2005; Fax: 419-663-6234. Email: lkleis@neo.rr.com. Web: www.stmarynorwalk.org.
Catechesis/Religious Program—P.O. Box 1200, Milan, 44846. Combined with St. Anthony, Milan Students 38.
2—ST. PAUL (1876), (German), [CEM] Revs. Franklin P. Kehres; Eric Mueller; Deacon James A. Reichert.
91 E. Main St., 44857-1798. Tel: 419-668-6044; Fax: 419-663-5770. Web: www.stpaulchurch.org.
Res.: 47 Executive Dr., 44857. Tel: 419-668-0411.
School—Norwalk Catholic Schools - St. Paul Campus, (Grades 1-12), 31 Milan Ave., 44857-1341. Tel: 419-668-6091; Fax: 419-668-8276. Dr. Wayne Babcanec, Pres.; Mr. James Tokarsky, Prin. Lay Teachers 45; Students 435.
Catechesis/Religious Program—Students 137.

OAK HARBOR, OTTAWA CO., ST. BONIFACE (1866) Very Rev. David L. Ritchie; Sr. Gemma M. Fenbert, O.S.F., Pastoral Assoc.
Res.: 215 N. Church St., 43449-1216. Tel: 419-898-1389; Fax: 419-898-2212. Email: stboniface@frontier.com. Web: www.stbonifaceoakharbor.parishesonline.com.
School—(Grades K-5), 215 Oak St., 43449-1227. Tel: 419-898-1340; Fax: 419-898-4193. Millie Greggila, Prin. Lay Teachers 6; Students 33.
Catechesis/Religious Program—Tel: 419-855-7181; Fax: 419-855-8159. Mr. Joshua Mocek, D.R.E. Students 76.

OREGON, LUCAS CO., ST. IGNATIUS (1883), (Territorial), [CEM] Rev. Mark J. Herzog.
Res.: 212 N. Stadium Rd., 43616-1536. Tel: 419-693-1150; Fax: 419-693-0063. Email: church@stiggys.org. Web: www.stiggys.org.
Catechesis/Religious Program—Tel: 419-693-7662. Ms. Amy Mottmiller, D.R.E. Students 330.

OTTAWA, PUTNAM CO., SS. PETER AND PAUL (1868) [CEM] Revs. Matthew Jozefiak, C.PP.S.; Alfons Minja, C.PP.S.; Deacon James A. Rump, Pastoral Assoc.
Res.: 307 N. Locust St., 45875-1495. Tel: 419-523-5216; Fax: 419-523-4048. Email: rectory1@spps.noacsc.org. Web: www.spppottawa.net.
School—320 N. Locust St., 45875-1496. Tel: 419-523-3697. Deacon Michael Eier, Prin. Lay Teachers 17; Students 238.
Catechesis/Religious Program—Mrs. Teresa Lanwehr, D.R.E. Students 266.

OTTOVILLE, PUTNAM CO., IMMACULATE CONCEPTION (1848) [CEM] Rev. John F. Stites; Deacon Jose Flores.
Church & Mailing Address: 189 Church St., Box 296, 45876-0296. Web: www.immaculateconceptionottoville.parishesonline.com.
Catechesis/Religious Program—Tel: 419-453-3702. Jean Byrne, D.R.E. Students 520.

PAULDING, PAULDING CO.
1—DIVINE MERCY PARISH Very Rev. G. Allan Fillman; Deacons David Jordan; David Laker; Rosalio M. Martinez; Robert Lee Nighswander; Leonard R. Roth.
Mailing Address: 417 N. Main St., 45879-1291. Tel: 419-399-2576; Fax: 419-399-2581.
Church: 315 N. Main St., 45879.
School—(Grades PreK-6), 120 Arturus St., P.O. Box 98, Payne, 45880. Mrs. Cathy R. Schoenauer, Prin. Teachers 5; Students 52.
Catechesis/Religious Program—Combined with St. John the Baptist, Payne. Theresa R. Conley, D.R.E. Students 262.
2—ST. JOSEPH (1894) Closed.

PAYNE, PAULDING CO., ST. JOHN THE BAPTIST (1892) [CEM] Closed. Church transferred to a chapel of Divine Mercy, Paulding

PERRYSBURG, WOOD CO.
1—BLESSED JOHN XXIII (2005) Very Rev. Herbert F. Weber.
Mailing Address: P.O. Box 48, 43552-0048. Web: www.blessedjohn.org.
Office: 24250 Dixie Hwy., 43551. Tel: 419-874-6502.
Catechesis/Religious Program—Marla Overholt, D.R.E.
2—ST. ROSE (1861) [CEM] Rev. Msgr. Marvin G. Borger; Rev. Jerome A. Schetter; Deacons Lawrence Tiefenbach; Kenneth Cappelletty; Victor DeFilippis.
Res.: 215 E. Front St., 43551-2193. Tel: 419-874-4559; Fax: 419-874-4375. Email: stroseoffice@stroseparish.com. Web: www.saintroseonline.org.
School—(Grades PreK-8), 217 E. Front St., 43551-2192. Tel: 419-874-5631; Fax: 419-874-1002. Barbara Jenks, Prin. Lay Teachers 26; Students 358.
Catechesis/Religious Program—Tel: 419-874-9474. Patricia Russo, D.R.E. Students 388.

PERU, HURON CO., ST. ALPHONSUS LIGUORI (1828), (German), [CEM] Rev. William A. Pifher.
Res.: 66 Chapel St., Monroeville, 44847. Tel: 419-465-4142; Fax: 419-465-2170. Email: stalphonsus@neo.rr.com. Web: www.stalphonsusperu.parishesonline.com.
Church: 1360 Settlement Rd., Norwalk, 44857.
Catechesis/Religious Program—1360 Settlement Dr., Norwalk, 44857. Tel: 419-668-5030; Fax: 419-663-6234. Catherine Raftery, D.R.E. Students 61.

PLYMOUTH, HURON CO., ST. JOSEPH (1864) Rev. Nicholas J. Cunningham.
Res.: 117 Sandusky St., 44865-1132. Tel: 419-687-4611; Fax: 419-687-4611. Email: stjoeplymouth@willard-oh.com.
Catechesis/Religious Program—Sr. Yvonne Fischer, O.S.F., D.R.E. Students 72.

PORT CLINTON, OTTAWA CO., IMMACULATE CONCEPTION (1861) Very Rev. John C. Missler; Deacon Maury A. Hall.
Mailing Address: 414 Madison St., 43452-1922. Tel: 419-734-4004; Fax: 419-734-3477. Email: icchurchpc@frontier.com. Web: www.iccpc.org.
School—(Grades PreK-6), 109 W. Fourth St., 43452-1816. Tel: 419-734-3315; Fax: 419-734-6172. Sr. Rosemary Hug, S.N.D., Prin. Sisters of Notre Dame 1; Lay Teachers 9; Students 102.
Catechesis/Religious Program—Sr. Mary Jane Fisher, R.S.M., D.R.E. Students 147.

PROVIDENCE, LUCAS CO., ST. PATRICK (1842), (Irish), [CEM] Rev. David D. Tscherne.
Mailing Address: 14010 U.S. Rte. 24 W., Grand Rapids, 43522-9678. Tel: 419-832-5215; Fax: 419-832-4075. Email: spgr@frontier.com.
Res.: 17680 Woodburn Ave., Grand Rapids, 43522-9745. Tel: 419-832-2414.
Catechesis/Religious Program—Ms. Christine Nelms, D.R.E. Students 140.

PUT-IN-BAY, OTTAWA CO., MOTHER OF SORROWS (1866) Sr. Lucille Kime, S.N.D., Pastoral Leader; Rev. Christopher G. Bazar, Presbyteral Moderator & Chap.
Mailing Address: 632 Catawba Ave., Box 179, 43456-0179. Tel: 419-285-2741; Fax: 419-285-2741 (call first). Email: mos&sm@hmcltd.net.

REED, SENECA CO., ASSUMPTION (1867), (German), [CEM] Closed. For inquiries for parish records contact the chancery.

REPUBLIC, SENECA CO., ST. ALOYSIUS (1879) [CEM] Closed. For inquiries for parish records contact the chancery.

RICHFIELD CENTER, LUCAS CO., ST. ELIZABETH OF HUNGARY (1914) Merged with Immaculate Conception, Marygrove and St. Mary of Assumption, Assumption to form Holy Trinity Catholic Parish, Assumption. Sacramental records at the Chancery.

ROSSFORD, WOOD CO., ALL SAINTS (1990) Rev. Kent R. Kaufman; Deacon Jerry Ziemkiewicz. Consolidated of SS. Cyril and Methodius and St. Mary Magdalene.
Church: 628 Lime City Rd., 43460. Tel: 419-666-1393; Fax: 419-666-5734. Email: parishoffice@allsaintsrossford.com. Web: www.allsaintsrossford.org.
School—(Grades PreK-8), 630 Lime City Rd., 43460. Tel: 419-661-2070; Fax: 419-661-2077. Sr. Mary Christine Cervi, S.N.D., Prin. Sisters 1; Lay Teachers 14; Students 188.
Catechesis/Religious Program—Cathleen Voyles-Baden, D.R.E. Students 138.

ST. MICHAEL'S RIDGE, DEFIANCE CO., ST. MICHAEL (1861) [CEM] Rev. Robert J. Kill.
Res.: 05480 Moser Rd., Defiance, 43512-9150. Tel: 419-497-2161; Fax: 419-497-2058. Email: kb8big@@defnet.com.
Church: Moser Rd. at Behrens Rd., Defiance, 43512.
Catechesis/Religious Program—05537 Moser Rd., Defiance, 43512. Tel: 419-497-3122. Mary K. Imber, D.R.E. Students 132.

ST. STEPHEN, SENECA CO., ST. STEPHEN (1844) [CEM] Closed. For inquiries for parish records contact the chancery.

SALEM TWP., WYANDOT CO., ST. JOSEPH (1849), (English), [CEM] Closed. For inquiries for parish records contact the chancery.

SANDUSKY, ERIE CO.
1—HOLY ANGELS (1839) [JC] Rev. Christopher Kardzis (Poland).
Res.: 428 Tiffin Ave., 44870. Tel: 419-625-3698; Fax: 419-625-5183. Web: www.holyangelssandusky.org.
See Sandusky Central Catholic School, Sandusky under Consolidated Elementary Schools located in the Institution section.
2—ST. MARY (1855), (German), [CEM] [JC 3] Revs. David W. Nuss; Jason J. Kahle; Deacons William G. Burch; Jeff Claar.
Res.: 429 Central Ave., 44870. Tel: 419-625-7465; Fax: 419-626-2834. Email: office@stmarysandusky.org. Web: www.stmary-sandusky.org.
See Sandusky Central Catholic School, Sandusky under Consolidated Elementary Schools located in the Institution section.
Catechesis/Religious Program—Tel: 419-621-7456. Debbie Geason, D.R.E. Students 155.
3—SS. PETER AND PAUL (1866) [CEM] [JC] Rev. Martin B. Nassr; Deacon John F. Weeks.
Res.: 510 Columbus Ave., 44870-2780. Tel: 419-625-6655; Fax: 419-625-6576. Email: office@stspeterpaul.com. Web: www.stspeterpaul-.com.
See Sandusky Central Catholic School, Sandusky under Consolidated Elementary Schools located in the Institution section.
Catechesis/Religious Program—Sr. Joyce Marie Bates, S.N.D., D.R.E. Students 178.

SHELBY, RICHLAND CO., MOST PURE HEART OF MARY (1866), (German), [CEM] Rev. Nicholas J. Cunningham.
Res.: 29 West St., 44875-1155. Tel: 419-347-2381; Fax: 419-347-3934.
School—(Grades PreK-6), 26 West St., 44875-1148. Tel: 419-342-2626; Fax: 419-347-2763. Ms. Barbara Pifher, Prin. Lay Teachers 7; Students 84.
Catechesis/Religious Program—Ms. Barbara Pifher, D.R.E.; Mark Seitz, Youth Min. Students 220.

SPENCERVILLE, ALLEN CO., ST. PATRICK (1858) [JC] Rev. Stephen J. Blum.
Mailing Address: 212 Oak Dr., 45887.
Office: 14755 Landeck Rd., Rte. 1, Delphos, 45833-9438.
Church & Res.: 500 S. Canal St., 45887. Tel: 419-692-0636; Fax: 419-692-0636. Email: ttbka@frontier.com.
Catechesis/Religious Program—Tel: 419-647-6202. Ms. Robin Lammers, D.R.E.; Ms. Terri Wolfe, D.R.E. Students 135.

STRYKER, WILLIAM CO., ST. JOHN THE EVANGELIST (1861) [JC] Closed. For inquiries for parish records contact the chancery.

SWANTON, FULTON CO., ST. RICHARD (1893) [CEM] Rev. Daniel Zak; Deacons Timothy R. Worline; Michael J. Sarra.

Res.: 333 Brookside Dr., 43558-1097. Tel: 419-826-2791; Fax: 419-826-7256. Web: www.saintrichard.org.
School—(Grades PreK-8), 333 Brookside Dr., 43558-1062. Tel: 419-826-5041. Ms. Susan Richardson, Prin. Lay Teachers 11; Students 67.
Catechesis/Religious Program—Ann R. Geise, D.R.E. Students 156.

SYCAMORE, WYANDOT CO., ST. PIUS X (1951) Revs. Gary R. Walters; Michael P. Roemmele; Deacon John Daniel.
Mailing Address: P.O. Box 282, 44882-0282. Tel: 419-447-2087; Fax: 419-927-6062.
Church: Saffel St., 44882.
Catechesis/Religious Program—Kelli Smith, D.R.E. Students 42.

SYLVANIA, LUCAS CO., ST. JOSEPH (1873) [CEM] Rev. Msgr. Dennis M. Metzger; Very Rev. Charles F. Ritter; Deacons Paul J. White; Anthony J. Pistilli.
Res.: 5373 Main St., 43560-2177. Tel: 419-885-5791; Fax: 419-882-5235. Email: parish@stjoesylvania.org. Web: www.stjoesylvania.org.
School—(Grades PreK-8), 5411 Main St., 43560-2155. Tel: 419-882-6670. Sally Koppinger, Prin. Sisters 1; Lay Teachers 37; Students 701.
Catechesis/Religious Program—Tel: 419-885-2181; Fax: 419-885-8251. Jane Ross, D.R.E. Students 434.

THE BEND, DEFIANCE CO., ST. STEPHEN (1855) [CEM] Closed. For inquiries for parish records contact the chancery.

TIFFIN, SENECA CO.

1—ST. JOSEPH (1845) [CEM] Very Rev. Joseph P. Szybka.
Res.: 36 Melmore St., 44883-3098. Tel: 419-447-5848; Fax: 419-447-7580. Email: stjoetif@bright.net. Web: www.tiffinsaintjoseph.org.
See Tiffin Calvert Schools under Consolidated Elementary Schools located in the Institution Section.
Catechesis/Religious Program—Jeannette Plisky, D.R.E. Students 136.

2—ST. MARY (1831) [CEM] Revs. Gary R. Walters; Michael P. Roemmele.
Res.: 85 S. Sandusky St., 44883-2140. Tel: 419-447-2087; Fax: 419-447-9940. Email: tfry@stmarychurch.com. Web: www.stmarychurch-.com.
See Tiffin Calvert Schools under Consolidated Elementary Schools located in the Institution Section.
Catechesis/Religious Program—Tel: 419-448-9341. Rose Ann Gaietto, D.R.E. Students 263.

UPPER SANDUSKY, WYANDOT CO.

1—ST. PETER (1857) [CEM] [JC] Closed. For inquiries for parish records contact the chancery.

2—TRANSFIGURATION OF THE LORD (2005) Rev. John Raphael Hadnagy, O.F.M.Conv.; Deacon Kevin Wintersteller.
Res.: 225 N. Eighth St., 43351-1299. Tel: 419-294-1268; Fax: 419-294-2030.
School—St. Peter Catholic School, (Grades K-6), 310 N. 8th St., 43351-1144. Tel: 419-294-1395; Fax: 419-209-0295. Ms. Kathy White, Prin. Lay Teachers 9; Students 137.
Catechesis/Religious Program—Ms. Yvonne Baldwin, D.R.E. Students 80.

VAN WERT, VAN WERT CO., ST. MARY OF THE ASSUMPTION (1876) Rev. Stanley S. Szybka; Deacon Andrew McMahon.
Res.: 601 Jennings Rd., 45891-9702. Tel: 419-238-3979; Fax: 419-238-3957. Email: info@stmarysvanwert.com. Web: www.stmarysvanwert.com.
School—(Grades K-6), 611 Jennings Rd., 45891-9701. Tel: 419-238-5186. David Mathew, Prin. Lay Teachers 10; Students 74.
Catechesis/Religious Program—Tel: 419-238-3079. Mrs. Cheryl Freewalt, D.R.E. Students 183.

VERMILION, ERIE CO., ST. MARY (1851) [JC] Rev. Ronald J. Brickner.
Mailing Address: 731 Exchange St., 44089-1330. Tel: 440-967-8711; Fax: 440-967-8712. Email: parish@stmaryvermilion.org. Web: www.stmaryvermilion.org.
Res.: 5418 Ohio St., 44089. Tel: 440-967-8711; Fax: 440-967-8712.
School—(Grades PreK-6), 5450 E. Ohio St., 44089-1340. Tel: 440-967-7911; Fax: 440-967-8287. Barbara Bialko, Prin. Lay Teachers 12; Students 99.
Catechesis/Religious Program—Sandra J. Smith, D.R.E. Students 258.

WAKEMAN, HURON CO., ST. MARY (1852) [CEM] Sr. Caroll Schemenauer, S.N.D., Pastoral Leader; Rev. Douglas D. Taylor, Chap. & Presbyteral Mod.
Mailing Address: P.O. Box 576, 44889-0576.
Church: 46 E. Main St., 44889. Tel: 440-839-2023; Fax: 440-839-2881. Email: wakemanstmary@verizon.net.
Catechesis/Religious Program—Mrs. Martha Tansey, D.R.E. Students 82.

WALBRIDGE, WOOD CO., ST. JEROME (1962) Rev. David J. Cirata.
Res.: 300 Warner St., 43465-1142. Tel: 419-666-2857; Fax: 419-661-2284. Email: stjeromeoffice@midohio.twcbc.com. Web: www.stjeromechurch.catholicweb.com.
See The Kateri Catholic School System, Oregon under Consolidated Elementary Schools located in the Institution Section.
Catechesis/Religious Program—Kathy Huffman, D.R.E. Students 85.

WAUSEON, FULTON CO., ST. CASPAR (1850) [CEM] [JC] Rev. David R. Bruning; Deacon Ivan James M. Dominique.
Res.: 1205 N. Shoop Ave., 43567-1828. Tel: 419-337-2322; Fax: 419-337-2413. Email: stck@bright.net. Web: www.stcaspar.com.
Catechesis/Religious Program—Ms. Barbara M. Bonfert, C.R.E.

WILLARD, HURON CO., ST. FRANCIS XAVIER (1875) [CEM] Rev. Eric J. Culler; Deacon Vincent Foos. In Res., Rev. Michael Diemer, M.J.
Res.: 21 W. Perry St., 44890-1694. Tel: 419-935-1149; Fax: 419-933-6000. Email: parishangelj@willard-oh.com. Web: www.willardstfrancis.com.
School—(Grades K-6), 25 W. Perry St., 44890-1602. Tel: 419-935-4744. Donna McDowell, Prin. Lay Teachers 8; Students 140.
Catechesis/Religious Program—Ms. Stacy Daniel, D.R.E. Students 151.

Special Assignment:
Rev.—
Cardone, Joseph P., Vice Pres. Mission & Values Integration, Mercy Medical Center.

On Duty Outside the Diocese:
Revs.—
Morman, Kenneth G., Mt. St. Mary Seminary, 6616 Beechmont Ave., Cincinnati, 45230-2006. Tel: 513-231-2223. Email: kmorman@athenaeum.edu
Oxley, Walter R., Pontifical College Josephinum, 7625 N. High St., Columbus, 43235.

Graduate Studies:
Rev.—
Smith, Philip A., Pontifical Institute for Studies on Marriage and Family

---

Military Chaplains:
Revs.—
Kirk, David R., Chap. U.S. Army
Reinhart, David A., Chap. U.S. Air Force

Health Leave:
Rev.—
Holmer, James J.

Retired:
Most Rev.—
Donnelly, Robert W., 4227 Bellevue Rd., 43613-3999.
Rev. Msgrs.—
Dunn, Edward C., 157 Grover St., Mansfield, 44903.
Schmenk, Cleo S., 4337 Mt. Carmel Dr., Melbourne, FL 32901.
Shenk, Bertrand J., 59 Executive Dr., Norwalk, 44857-2471.
Revs.—
Badger, Arthur A., 3607 Naples Dr., 43615-1155.
Beck, David J.
Blaser, John R., V.F.
Boff, Bernard J., 4035 Indian Rd., 43606.
Bonifas, Roger D., P.O. Box 8, Cloverdale, 45827-0008.
Caballero, Francisco, P.O. Box 985, 43697-0985.
Cairns, Stephen P., 1803 Brownstone Blvd., Apt. 201, 43614.
Ceranowski, Albert B., 26324 Edgewater Dr, Perrysburg, 43551.
Ceranowski, Gerald L., V.F., 524 Mariner Village, Huron, 44839.
Chmiel, Gerald J., 5153 Summit St., 43611.
Denny, Charles J., 2001 Consaul, 43605.
DeSloover, A. Robert, 7214 U.S. 224, Ottawa, 45875.
Donnelly, P. Martin, 2250 Eastbrook Dr., 43613.
Duschl, Frederick J., 11312 Cty Rd. 6, Edon, 43518. Tel: 419-272-2475 Mailing Address: P.O. Box 151 Blakeslee, OH 43505-0151
Eckart, Frank K., 2001 Consul, 43605.
Ensman, Raymond E., 1800 Fulton St., Port Clinton, 43452.
Feltman, Philip S., 2020 Sanford St., Sandusky, 44870.
Fisher, Raymond A., 1600 Cedar St. #36, Fremont, 43420.
Fleck, John W., 1289 State Rte. 309, Alger, 45812.
Fraser, Daniel J., 1175 Raintree Blvd., Monroe, MI 48161.
Gallagher, Anthony, 6500 Carrietown Ln., 43615.
Gorman, Thomas J., 20420 W. River Rd., Grand Rapids, 43522.
Haas, Robert L., 120 Carmel Ave., #1, Galion, 44833.
Holden, Robert A., 14900 County Rd. H., Unit 94, Wauseon, 43567.
Howe, J. Norbert, 165 N. Seriff Dr., Lima, 45807-2258.
Jaros, Joseph P., 29317 Bates Rd., Perrysburg, 43551.
Knueven, Gerald E., 29245 Hufford Rd., #8, Perrysburg, 43551.
Kwiatkowski, Paul M., 2200 Scottwood Ave., #303, 43620.
Laudick, John R., 2200 Scottwood, #107, 43620.
Lautermilch, David J., 318 Condley, 43608-1017.
LeJeune, Ronald J., Apartado Postal-314 Centro Cuernavaca, Morelos 62001 Mexico.
Lester, John E., 6832 Convent Blvd., Unit 1, Sylvania, 43560.
Leyland, Thomas J., 213 West Indiana Ave., Perrysburg, 43551.
Littelmann, Edward J., 1248 Royalton Rd., 43612.
Majoros, Stephen R., 3650 Victory Ave., 43607.
Mueller, Donald R., 321 E. Madison St., Gibsonburg, 43431.
Niedermier, Jerome G., 4035 Indian Rd., 43606.
Nieset, Frank E., 6832 Convent Blvd., Sylvania, 43560.
Nietfeld, Fred J., 3521 Environ Blvd. #301, Lauderhill, FL 33311.
Notter, Richard E., 5713 Bernath Ct., 43615.
Nowakowski, Jerome F., 550 Clark St., 43605-2273.
O'Brien, Joseph L., 930 S. Wynn #B213, Oregon, 43616.
Odey, Thomas E., 640 Ln 201 Ball Lake Rd., Hamilton, IN 46742.
Parker, William C., 3453 Woodley Rd., 43623.
Peiffer, James E., 709 N.W. Catawba Rd., Port Clinton, 43452.
Radvansky, Joseph R. (PRM), 350 N. Lighthouse Oval, Marblehead, 43440.
Reinhart, Robert J., 5146 Ford Ave., 43612.
Rethinger, Omer, 1010 N. Brush, Apt. A, Fremont, 43420-1410.
Ricker, John Michael, 212 N. Stadium Rd., Oregon, 43616-1536.
Risacher, James E., 8820 Walther Blvd. #4215, Baltimore, MD 21234.
Rohen, Patrick J., 1160 S. McCord Rd., Apt. K-3, Holland, 43528.
Say, James K., 6584 N. California Dr., Long Beach, Oak Harbor, 43449.
Schelling, Michael E., 1003 Dove Ln., Crestline, 44827.
Scherger, Herman F., Rte. 2, 21706 S.R. 114, Cloverdale, 45827-9632.
Schill, Frederick J., 586 Kaler, Bucyrus, 44820-2565.
Schroeder, Dennis A., 440 Autumnwood Dr., #B, Tiffin, 44883.
Sheperd, Raymond C., 11129 Dyke Rd., Curtice, 43412-9453.
Snyder, Frederick J., 2645 U.S. Rte. 20, Swanton, 43558.
Steinle, James, 312 Greenfield St., Tiffin, 44883-2427.
Vamos, Joseph L., 1880 Genesee St., 43605.
Wehinger, Thomas E., 2352 Cheyenne Blvd. #7, 43614.
Weigman, Joseph A., 930 S. Wynn Rd., #A212, Oregon, 43616.
Weithman, Robert J., 5055 Providence Dr., #112, Sandusky, 44870.
Wilhelm, Robert J., 4040 W. Bancroft, Apt. 3 E., 43606.
Wurzel, Richard T., S.T.D., 7445 Country Commons Ln., Sylvania, 43560.

Permanent Deacons:
Ackerman, Thomas
Algee, John R., III, St. John, Toledo
Arbogast, Urban
Avina, Phillip, St. Aloysius, Bowling Green
Badenhop, Donald F.
Beat, Walter
Beisser, Robert A., Christ the King, Toledo
Betz, Eugene N.
Billmaier, Robert C.
Bistak, Leo T., Archdiocese of Kansas City
Bleile, Jack, (Serving in Archdiocese of Seattle)
Bodette, Robert T., Sylvania St. Joseph
Bost, Robert, St. Augustine, Napoleon
Bronder, James S., St. Charles Borromeo, Lima
Buckmaster, Bruce
Bullimore, Douglas, Little Flower of Jesus, Toledo

Burch, William G., St. Mary, Sandusky
Burkett, Dennis W., (Serving in Diocese of Charleston, SC)
Burkhart, Joseph L., St. Joseph, Crestline
Busam, John, St. Peter, Huron
Calvillo, Pedro
Campbell, John E.
Cappelletty, Kenneth, St. Rose, Perrysburg
Carone, Thomas, Historic Church of St. Patrick & Immaculate Conception, Toledo
Caruso, James D., Our Lady, Queen of the Most Holy Rosary, Toledo
Caughlin, Donald J.
Cavera, James J., Immaculate Conception, Bellevue
Claar, Jeff, St. Mary, Sandusky
Daniel, John, St. Pius X, Sycamore
Dazley, Phillip
DeFilippis, Victor A., St. Rose, Perrysburg
Derr, Floyd
Diaz, Alfredo, Sacred Heart, Fremont
Dickey, Kenneth G.
Dominique, Ivan James M.
Dominique, Ralph J., Sacred Heart, Montpelier
Dominique, Thomas, St. Patrick, Bryan
Downey, John F., (Serving in Diocese of Cleveland)
Dubois, Thomas R., Resurrection, Lexington
Dudley, James M., Regina Coeli, Toledo
Dunn, James E., St. Anthony, Columbus Grove
Erford, Doyle J., Holy Family, New Cleveland
Etue, Timothy W., St. Pius, Toledo
Fedynich, Robert P., Blessed Sacrament, Toledo
Felter, Robert
Fernandez, Trevor, Historic Church of St. Patrick & Immaculate Conception, Toledo
Fisher, Clarence
Flores, Jose, Immaculate Conception, Ottoville
Foos, Vincent, St. Francis Xavier, Willard
Fox, Leonard
Fritz, Julius J., Holy Trinity, Bucyrus
Galernik, Gerald E., All Saints, Rossford
Garcia, Jose, Sacred Heart of Jesus, Toledo
Garza, Ignacio
Gillen, Robert, Holy Trinity, Assumption
Gleason, Richard, St. John, Lima
Gonalez, Armando, St. Michael the Archangel, Findlay
Gonzalez, Rene S.
Gottron, Jon A., St. Augustine, Napoleon
Gryczewski, Edward, Chaplain, Port of Toledo
Gubernath, Jerome A., Holy Trinity, Bucyrus
Hall, Maury A., Immaculate Conception, Port Clinton
Hammer, James E., St. Wendelin, Fostoria
Hartings, Leo J.
Heban, Richard D.
Heeter, Joseph M., St. John the Baptist, Continental
Henderson, Ronald D., Our Lady, Toledo; Queen of the Most Holy Rosary
Heyman, James, St. Ann, Fremont
Hohman, Floyd J., All Saints Parish, New Riegel
Holmer, Leon M., Good Sheperd, Toledo
Horning, William L.
Hostutler, James E., (Serving in Diocese of Phoenix)
Houghton, Leroy H.
Huffman, David A., Immaculate Conception, Port Clinton
Hulderman, Joseph
Ignatowski, Gerald, SS. Adalbert & Hedwig, Toledo
Inkrott, Donald W., St. John the Baptist, Glandorf
Irelan, Edgar E., St. Joseph, Maumee
Jackson, Dennis F., St. Patrick, Bryan
Jones, Paul R.
Jordan, David, Divine Mercy, Paulding
Junga, Joel F., St. Patrick of Heatherdowns, Toledo
Karpanty, David J., St. Patrick of Heatherdowns, Toledo
Kaser, Theodore J., Jr., St. Rose of Lima
Keller, Stephen, Sacred Heart of Jesus, Bethlehem
Kelley, Edward L.
Kern, Mark, St. Michael the Archangel, Findlay
Kest, Joseph, Jr., St. Patrick of Heatherdowns, Toledo
Kirk, Gregory, St. Joseph, Galion
Kitzler, James F., Our Lady of Consolation, Carey
Klausing, Robert R., St. Michael, Kalida
Klear, Kenneth, Sacred Heart of Jesus, New Bavaria
Kopp, Allan D., St. Mary, Mansfield
Kozek, Richard
Kromer, John T., St. Wendelin, Fostoria
Kujawa, Clifford
Lackney, Robert
Laker, David C., Divine Mercy, Paulding
Learned, Michael R., Sr., St. Catherine, Toledo
Lesinski, Robert J., Our Lady of Perpetual Help, Toledo
Lisk, Frederick, St. John the Evangelist, Delphos
Llanas, Ramon, St. Aloysius, Bowling Green
Lochotzki, William
Lopez, Valentin G., III
Lottier, Larry F., St. Joan of Arc, Toledo
Lyons, Raymond E., Jr.
Maher, Edward R., St. Thomas More University Parish, Bowling Green
Malenfant, Joseph, St. Joseph, Maumee
Marshall, James, St. Peter, Mansfield
Martinez, Rosalio M., Divine Mercy, Paulding
Mauer, Michael, (Serving in Diocese of Grand Rapids)
Mayer, Jeffrey L., St. Mary, Defiance
McCabe, Patrick, Blessed Sacrament, Toledo
McCauley, Terry L.
McMahon, Andrew P., St. Mary, Van Wert
Meyer, Donald, St. John, Defiance
Miller, George, St. Patrick; St. Andrew, Liberty
Mishler, Richard D.
Mitchell, George R., Regina Coeli, Toledo
Moncher, James, Corpus Christi, Toledo
Moore, Wilbur, St. Clement, Toledo
Morris, Paul J.
Newton, George E.
Niese, Thomas B., St. Mary, Leipsic
Nighswander, Robert Lee
Nye, Harold
Opper, Milton C.
Ovalle, Eduardo
Pacholski, Robert
Peeps, Ronald G.
Pence, Michael W., St. Charles and St. Hyacinth and St. Anne Mercy Medical Center, Toledo
Perez, Diego E.A.
Perez, William
Perryman, Clifton A., Blessed John XXIII, Perrysburg
Petersen, Laurence
Phillips, Eugene D., (Serving in Diocese of Phoenix)
Philpott, Terry B.
Pina, Elias, St. Gerard, Lima
Pistilli, Anthony J., St. Joseph, Sylvania
Plenzler, Ronald J., St. Clement, Toledo
Pluciniak, Edward R., St. Joseph, Maumee
Przybylek, Stanley
Quinn, Daniel P.
Rall, William E., St. Joseph, Crestline
Reef, John P., St. Peter, Mansfield
Reichert, James A., St. Paul, Norwalk
Reinhart, Lewis E.
Reinhart, Norbert
Repka, Joseph, Holy Trinity, Assumption
Ricker, David J., St. John, Delphos
Rodriguez, Guillermo
Rodriguez, Juan
Romo, Bernabe, (Serving in Archdiocese of Indianapolis)
Romo, Jose
Roth, Leonard R., St. Joseph, Paulding
Rump, James A., Saints Peter and Paul, Ottawa
Sadler, David L., St. Michael the Archangel, Findlay
Sanchez, Salvador, Saints Peter and Paul, Toledo
Sarra, Michael J., St. Richard, Swanton
Sauceda, Juan
Schaupp, Lawrence
Schimmoeller, Lawrence, St. Joseph, Fort Jennings
Schortgen, James, St. Mary, Holgate
Selmek, Zenon J.
Sheehan, Thomas K., St. Joan of Arc, Toledo
Shell, Melvin J., St. Joseph, Fremont
Shoemaker, Russell M., St. Mary, Mansfield
Sisson, Alfred N., St. Joseph, Galion
Snyder, William J.
Sortman, Jerome E., Christ the King, Toledo
Stepanic, George C., St. Alphonsus, Peru
Swartz, Robert L.
Thrun, Gary M., St. Thomas Moore University Parish, Bowling Green
Tiefenbach, Lawrence, St. Rose, Perrysburg
Timbrook, Joseph, St. Michael, Hicksville
Ulmer, William A.
Valdez, Benjamin R., St. Mary, Leipsic
Varano, Dominick J., St. John the Evangelist, Defiance
Veselka, Stephen J., Our Lady of Lourdes, Toledo
Villagomez, Jesus
Vogel, Curtis J.
Vrooman, David
Walter, John F., Saints Patrick & Andrew, Bascom
Warren, Richard
Waters, Daniel R., Our Lady of Perpetual Help, Toledo
Weber, John C.
Weeks, John F., SS. Peter and Paul, Sandusky
Welch, Harold, Blessed Sacrament, Toledo
Westrick, Eugene
Wethington, Norbert A., St. Joseph, Freemont
White, Paul J., St. Joseph, Sylvania
Wiciak, John
Wilson, Larry J., (Serving in Diocese of Columbus)
Wintersteller, Kevin, Transfiguration of the Lord, Upper Sandusky
Worline, Timothy R., St. Richard, Swanton
Wurm, Eugene L.
Yakir, Michael, serving in the Archdiocese for the Military Services
Ziemkiewicz, Jerry, All Saints, Rossford
Eier, Michael, St. Michael, Findlay

INSTITUTIONS LOCATED IN THE DIOCESE

[A] COLLEGES AND UNIVERSITIES

TOLEDO. *Mercy College of Northwest Ohio* (1994) 2221 Madison Ave., 43604. Tel: 415-251-1313; Fax: 419-251-6711. Web: www.mercycollege.edu. Mr. John F. Hayward, Esq., Pres.; Dr. Anne Loochtan, Interim Vice Pres. Academic Affairs; Mr. James Harter, Vice Pres. Admin. Svcs. Sisters of Mercy of the Americas, Mercy Sisters; Sister of Charity of Montreal, Grey Nuns. Sisters of Charity 1; Precious Blood Sisters 1; Sisters of Notre Dame 1; Students 803; Total Staff 97.

SYLVANIA. *Lourdes University*, 6832 Convent Blvd., 43560. Tel: 419-824-3969; Fax: 419-882-3987. Web: www.lourdes.edu. Dr. Robert Helmer, Pres.; Dr. Janet Robinson, Vice Pres. Academic Affairs; Michael Killian, Vice Pres. Finance & Admin.; Sr. Ann Carmen Barone, O.S.F., Vice Pres. Mission & Ministry. Sisters of St. Francis of the Congregation of Our Lady of Lourdes, (O.S.F.). Sisters 12; Faculty 71; Lay Instructors 59; Adjunct 140; Total Enrollment 2,200.

Franciscan Theatre and Conference Center of Lourdes College, 6832 Convent Blvd., 43560. Tel: 419-824-3969. Email: marquette@lourdes.edu. Web: www.franciscancenter.org. Penny Marks, Dir.; Sr. Sandra Rutkowski, Librarian. Total Staff 104.

[B] HIGH SCHOOLS, DIOCESAN

TOLEDO. *Central Catholic High School*, 2550 Cherry St., 43608-2394. Tel: 419-255-2280; Fax: 419-259-2848. Web: www.centralcatholic.org. Very Rev. Dennis P. Hartigan, Ph.D., V.F., Pres.; Rev. Paul M. Kwiatkowski (Retired); Mr. Michael Kaucher, Prin. Conducted by Diocesan Priests, Sisters and Laity. Priests 2; Teaching Sisters 2; Lay Teachers 69; Students 1,068.

FREMONT. *St. Joseph Central Catholic High School* (Bishop Hoffman Catholic School System), 702 Croghan St., 43420-2480. Tel: 419-332-9947; Fax: 419-332-4945. Web: www.streaks.net. Mr. Tim Cullen, Prin.; Rev. Christopher G. Bazar, Chap. Priests 1; Lay Teachers 17; Students 208.

LIMA. *Central Catholic High School* (1955) 720 S. Cable Rd., 45805. Tel: 419-222-4276; Fax: 419-222-6933. Web: www.lcchs.edu. Mr. Walter Klimaski, Pres.; Rev. Timothy F. Ferris, Chap. Priests 1; Lay Teachers 23; Students 332.

TIFFIN. *Calvert High School*, 152 Madison St., 44883-0836. Tel: 419-447-3844; Fax: 419-447-2922. Web: www.calvertcatholic.org. Mr. Hank Elchert, Supt.; Rev. Michael P. Roemmele, Chap. Priests 1; Sisters 1; Lay Teachers 19; Students 164.

[C] HIGH SCHOOLS, PRIVATE

TOLEDO. *St. Francis de Sales High School*, 2323 W. Bancroft St., 43607-1399. Tel: 419-531-1618; Fax: 419-531-9740. Web: www.sfstoledo.org. Revs. Ronald W. E. Olszewski, O.S.F.S., Pres.; John I. Extejt, O.S.F.S., Vice Pres.; Mr. Eric Smola, Prin. Oblates of St. Francis de Sales., School for boys. Priests 7; Sisters 1; Lay Teachers 44; Students 604.

St. John's Jesuit High School, (Grades 7-12), 5901 Airport Hwy., 43615-7344. Tel: 419-865-5743; Fax: 419-861-5002. Web: www.sjjtitans.org. Brad Bonham, Prin.; Rev. Joaquin Martinez, S.J., Pres. Jesuits of the Detroit Province., School for boys. Priests 3; Lay Teachers 52; Students 837.

Notre Dame Academy, (Grades 7-12), 3535 Sylvania Ave., 43623-4479. Tel: 419-475-9359; Fax: 419-724-2640. Web: www.nda.org. Mrs. Nichole Flores, Prin. Sisters of Notre Dame., School for girls. Sisters 4; Lay Teachers 41; Students 617.

St. Ursula Academy (1854) (school for girls), 4025 Indian Rd., 43606-2291. Tel: 419-531-1693; Fax: 419-534-5777. Web: www.toledosua.org. Sr. Mary Kay Homan, O.P., Pres.; Mrs. Kim Sofo, Prin. Sponsored by Ursuline Sisters of the Sacred Heart. Sisters 1; Lay Teachers 43; Students 514.

[D] CONSOLIDATED ELEMENTARY SCHOOLS

TOLEDO. *St. Benedict School*, 5522 Dorr St., 43615. Tel: 419-536-1194; Fax: 419-531-5140. Web: www.stbenedicttoledo.com. Carol Huss, Prin. Little Flower of Jesus & Our Lady of Lourdes schools consolidated to form St. Benedict School. Lay Teachers 16; Students 250.

Central City Ministry of Toledo Schools (CCMT), (Grades PreK-8), 1933 Spielbusch Ave., 43604-5360. Tel: 419-244-6711; Fax: 419-255-8269. Email: jhayward@toledodiocese.org.

Queen of Apostles Campus, (Grades K-8), 235 Courtland Ave., 43609-2699. Tel: 419-241-7829; Fax: 419-241-4180. Email: smbrendah@yahoo.com. Sr. Mary Brenda Haynes, S.N.D., Prin.; Miss Virginia Hasselschwert, Librarian. Sisters 2; Lay Teachers 10; Students 165.

Rosary Cathedral Campus, (Grades PreK-8), 2535 Collingwood Blvd., 43610-1400. Tel: 419-243-4396; Fax: 419-242-1901. Mrs. Sarah Cullum, Prin. Lay Teachers 17; Students 254.

DEFIANCE. *Holy Cross Catholic School of Defiance*, (Grades PreK-6), 1745 S. Clinton St., 43512. Tel: 419-784-2021; Fax: 419-784-2072. Web: www.defianceholycross.org. Sr. Linda Snyder, S.N.D., Prin. St. John Campus (PreK-2), St. Mary Campus (Grades 3-6) Lay Teachers 13; Students 104.

FREMONT. *Bishop Hoffman Catholic School*, 702 Croghan St., 43420. Mr. Tim Cullen, Supt.

Sacred Heart Campus (Grades K-3), 500 Smith Rd., 43420. Tel: 419-332-7102; Fax: 419-332-1542. Mrs. Cathy Krupp, Prin. Lay Teachers 9; Students 262.

Saint Joseph Campus (Grades 4-8), 716 Croghan St., 43420. Tel: 419-332-5161; Fax: 419-332-7299. Mrs. Cathy Krupp, Prin. Lay Teachers 9; Students 256.

OREGON. *The Kateri Catholic Academy - Kateri Catholic School System*, (Grades PreK-12), 3225 Pickle Rd., 43616. Rev. Eric P. Schild, Pres.; Deacon Michael Eier, Prin. PreK-12 528.

SANDUSKY. *Sandusky Central Catholic School*, (Grades PreSchool-8), 410 W. Jefferson St., 44870-2427. Tel: 419-627-9718; Fax: 419-621-2252. Email: jmonaghan@sanduskycentralcatholic.org. Dr. Judy Monaghan, Supt.; Rev. Jason J. Kahle, Chap.

Sandusky Central Catholic Early Childhood Center (Grades PreSchool-K), 1603 W. Jefferson St., 44870-2124. Tel: 419-626-3075; Fax: 419-625-5183. Email: sdwight@sanduskycentralcatholic.org. Web: www.sanduskycentralcatholicschool.org. Sally Dwight, Dir. (Early Childhood Center) Students 72.

Sandusky Central Catholic School Elementary, 410 W. Jefferson St., 44870. Tel: 419-626-1892. Web: www.sanduskycentralcatholicschool.com. Mr. David McDowell, Prin. Students 397.

Sandusky Central Catholic School, St. Mary Central Catholic Jr. HS/HS (Grades 7-12), SMCC Junior High-Grades 7-8., 410 W. Jefferson St., 44870-2427. Tel: 419-626-1892; Fax: 419-621-2252. Michael Savona, Prin. SMCC Junior High 104; SMCC High School 175.

TIFFIN. *Calvert Elementary School*, (Grades K-8), 357 S. Washington St., 44883-2879. Tel: 419-443-0263.

[E] ELEMENTARY SCHOOLS, PRIVATE

TOLEDO. *Mary Immaculate School* (1960) 3835 Secor Rd., 43623-4402. Tel: 419-474-1688; Fax: 419-479-3062. Web: www.maryimmaculatetoledo.org. Ms. Shelli Staudt, Prin. Day School for Children with Learning Disabilities, Attention Deficit Disorder and Other Health Impairments. Sisters of Notre Dame 15; Lay Teachers 8; Students 51.

SYLVANIA. *Franciscan Academy of Lourdes University*, (Grades PreSchool-8), 5335 Silica Dr., 43560. Tel: 419-885-3273; Fax: 419-882-5653. Email: rkohler@s-f-a.org. Web: www.s-f-a.org. Mr. Richard Kohler, Prin. Sisters 1; Lay Teachers 19; Students 203.

WHITEHOUSE. *Lial Elementary School* (1972) (Grades PreK-8), 5700 Davis Rd., 43571-9669. Tel: 419-877-5167; Fax: 419-877-9385. Web: www.lialschool.org. Sr. Patricia M. McClain, S.N.D., Prin. Sisters of Notre Dame. Sisters 3; Lay Teachers 14; Students 197.

[F] GENERAL HOSPITALS

TOLEDO. *Mercy Hospital St. Anne* (2002) 3404 W. Sylvania Ave., 43623. Tel: 419-407-2663; Fax: 419-407-3888. Web: www.mercyweb.org. Rev. Robert Obol (Uganda), Chap.; Deacon Michael W. Pence, Chap.; Mr. Brad Bestka, Interim Pres. & CEO. Patients Assisted Annually 181,157; Bed Capacity 128; Total Staff 768.

Mercy Medical Center St. Vincent, 2213 Cherry St., 43608-2691. Tel: 419-251-3232; Fax: 419-251-3810. Web: www.mercyweb.org. Dr. Imran Andrabi, Pres. & CEO; Ms. Elaine Ladd, Admin./Dir. Pastoral Care; Ms. Sharon Belisle, Chap.; Rev. Francis Ejimofor, S.S.Sp. (Kenya), Chap.; Sr. Maxine Young, S.N.D., Chap.; Mr. Ev Chavette, Chap. Grey Nuns., Affiliated with Mercy Health Partners. Sisters 1; Patients Assisted Annually 530,000; Bed Capacity 576; Total Staff 3,618.

Mercy Children's Hospital, 2222 Cherry St., 43608-2801. Tel: 419-251-3232; 800-860-6652; Fax: 419-251-3878. Web: www.mercyweb.org. Dr. John T. Schaeufele, M.D., Pres.; Ms. Elaine Ladd, Dir. Pastoral Care.

LIMA. *St. Rita's Medical Center* (1918) 730 W. Market St., 45801-4602. Tel: 419-227-3361; 800-467-0308; Fax: 419-226-9750. Web: www.stritas.org. Mr. Bob Baxter, Pres.; William W. Roe, Vice Pres. Finance; Mr. Mark Skaja, Vice Pres. Mission Svcs.; Rev. Charles Obinwa (Nigeria), Chap.; Deacon Thomas B. Niese, Chap.; Sr. Noel Frey, R.S.M., Chap. Sisters 1; Bed Capacity 437; Patients Assisted Annually 404,532; Total Staff 2,861.

OREGON. *Mercy Hospital St. Charles* (1953) 2600 Navarre Ave., 43616. Tel: 419-696-7200; Fax: 419-696-7328. Web: www.mercyweb.org. Robert Gospadavek, Pres. & CEO; Ms. Jennifer Discher, Pastoral Care; Rev. Robert Obol (Uganda), Chap. Mercy Health Partners. Sisters 1; Bed Capacity 390; Patients Assisted Annually 164,559; Total Staff 1,427.

TIFFIN. *Mercy Hospital of Tiffin*, 45 St. Lawrence Dr., 44883. Tel: 419-455-7000; Fax: 419-455-7066. Email: john_halstead@mhsnr.org. Web: www.mercyweb.org. Mr. Dale E. Thornton, Pres. & CEO; Rev. John Halstead, Dir. of Mission & Values Integration; Mrs. Paula Karr, R.N., Dir. Mission Pastoral Care. Sisters of Mercy of the Americas - Catholic Healthcare Partners. Sisters 2; Bed Capacity 62; Patients Assisted Annually 115,000; Total Staff 460.

WILLARD. *Mercy Hospital of Willard*, 110 E. Howard St., 44890. Tel: 419-964-5000; Fax: 419-964-5178 8. Email: paula_karr@mhsnr.org. Web: www.mercyweb.org. Mrs. Paula Karr, R.N., Dir. Mission Pastoral Care; Sisters Diane Hay, O.S.F., Chap.; Rita Mary Wasserman, R.S.M., Chap. Sisters of Mercy of the Americas. Sisters 2; Bed Capacity 25; Total Staff 220; Patients Assisted Annually 56,917.

[G] HOMES FOR AGED

TOLEDO. *Oblate Residences* (1980) 1225 Flaire Dr., 43615. Tel: 419-536-3862; Fax: 419-536-6372. c/o 2043 Parkside Blvd., 43607-1597. Tel: 419-724-9851; Fax: 419-724-9853. Apartments 100.

OREGON. *Sacred Heart Home*, 930 S. Wynn Rd., 43616. Tel: 419-698-4331; Fax: 419-698-1109. Email: msoregon@littlesistersofthepoor.org. Sr. Cecilia Sartorius, L.S.P., Supr./Pres.; Revs. Edward Donoher; Joseph L. O'Brien (Retired); Joseph A. Weigman, Chap. (Retired). Little Sisters of the Poor. Sisters 10; Aged Residents 73; Independent Living Apartments 20; Total Assisted Annually 101; Total Staff 101.

SANDUSKY. **The Commons of Providence*, 5000 Providence Dr., 44870. Tel: 419-624-1171; Fax: 419-624-1175. Email: jwindisch@providencecenters.org. Web: www.providencecenters.org. Jane Windisch, Mktg. Dir. Apartment assisted living facility. Bed Capacity 56; Residents 62; Total Assisted Annually 147; Total Staff 75.

Providence Care Center, 2025 Hayes Ave., 44870. Tel: 419-627-2273; Fax: 419-627-5588. Email: dday@providencecenters.org. Web: www.providencecarecenters.org. Denice Day, Admin. Sisters 2; Bed Capacity 138; Patients Assisted Annually 236; Total Staff 160.

**Providence Residential Community Corp Apartment and Villa Home Independent Living*, 5000 Providence Dr., 44870. Tel: 419-624-1171; Fax: 419-624-1175. Email: jwindisch@providencecenters.org. Web: www.providencecenters.org. Jane Windisch, Mktg. Dir. Independent Apartments 62; Independent Villas 21; Residents 74.

[H] MONASTERIES AND RESIDENCES OF PRIESTS AND BROTHERS

TOLEDO. *Oblates of St. Francis de Sales* Tel: 419-724-9851; Fax: 419-724-9853. Web: www.oblates.us.

Provincial Residence, 2043 Parkside Blvd., 43607-1597. Tel: 419-724-9851; Fax: 419-724-9853. Very Rev. Kenneth N. McKenna, O.S.F.S., Prov.; Revs. Martin C. Lukas, O.S.F.S., Vocation Dir.; James F. Cryan, O.S.F.S., Pastor, Gesu Church.

Priests serving elsewhere: Rev. William G. Auth, O.S.F.S., Mexican Missions, 554 E. Second St., Salt Lake City, UT 84103. Tel: 801-359-8201; Very Rev. Kenneth N. McKenna, O.S.F.S., Novice Dir.; Rev. Thomas A. Ribits, O.S.F.S., Formation Council, 152 Plymouth Ave., Buffalo, NY 14201. Tel: 716-886-6597.

St. Francis de Sales High School Faculty House 2323 W. Bancroft, 43607. Tel: 419-531-1619; Fax: 419-531-9740. Revs. Ronald W. E. Olszewski, O.S.F.S., Pres.; John I. Extejt, O.S.F.S., Vice Pres.; Thomas A. Landgraff, O.S.F.S., Guidance Office; John Lehner, O.S.F.S., Chap.; Alan D. Zobler, O.S.F.S., Instructor; Richard E. Morse, O.S.F.S., St. Pius X Church, Toledo; James F. Bradley, O.S.F.S. (Retired), Rosary Care Center, Sylvania, 43560; Bros. Alfred D. Durant, O.S.F.S.; James Rago, O.S.F.S., (Retired). *Annecy Hall*, P.O. Box 43, Childs, MD 21916-0043. Revs. Joseph Baraniewicz, O.S.F.S. (Retired); Edward P. Canavan, O.S.F.S. (Retired), Rosary Care Center, Sylvania, 43560. *St. Francis de Sale High School Endowment Fund, Inc.* Rev. Ronald W. E. Olszewski, O.S.F.S., Pres. Priests 13; Brothers 2.

BELLEVUE. **Mary Lay Center*, 4500 State Rte. 269, P.O. Box 319, 44811-0319. Tel: 419-483-0762; Fax: 419-483-6400. Total in Residence 4.

Residence for Staff of Sorrowful Mother Shrine. Revs. Robert Kunisch, C.PP.S.; Yuri (George) J. Kuzara, C.PP.S.; Harold C. Brown, C.PP.S.; Gene Wilson, C.PP.S.; Bro. Charles McCafferty, C.PP.S.

[I] CONVENTS AND RESIDENCES FOR SISTERS

TOLEDO. *Monastery of the Visitation* (1915) (Contemplative), 1745 Parkside Blvd., 43607-1599. Tel: 419-536-1343; Fax: 419-536-0685. Email: vhm-toledo@toast.net. Web: www.toledovisitation.org. Sr. Mary Bernard Grote, V.H.M., Supr.

The Contemplative Order of the Visitation of Toledo, Ohio, Contemplative Order of the Sisters of the Visitation of Toledo, Ohio. Sisters 22; Perpetual Vows 15; Novices 1; Temporary Profession 4; Postulants 2.

Notre Dame Academy Convent, 3535 Sylvania Ave., 43623. Tel: 419-475-4909; Fax: 419-724-2640. Email: chug@nda.org. Sr. Mary Charleen Hug, S.N.D. Sisters of Notre Dame. Sisters 27.

Notre Dame Provincial Center (1924) 3837 Secor Rd., 43623-4484. Tel: 419-474-5485; Fax: 419-474-1336. Email: awillman@sndtoledo.org. Web: www.sndtoledo.org. Sisters Mary Delores Gutliff, S.N.D., Prov. Supr.; Clarine Young, S.N.D., Local Supr. Sisters of Notre Dame. Perpetually Professed 217; Temporary Professed 1.

Ursuline Convent of the Sacred Heart (1854) *Congregational Offices*, 4045 Indian Rd., 43606. Tel: 419-536-9587; Fax: 419-536-0019. Email: ursulines@toledoursulines.org. Web: www.toledoursulines.org. Sr. Bernarda Breidenbach, O.S.U., Pres.; Rev. Richard J. Saelzler, Chap. Professed Sisters 48; Health Care Assisted 23; Associates 142.

FREMONT. *St. Bernardine Home* (1970) 1220 Tiffin St., 43420. Tel: 419-332-8208; Fax: 419-332-4423. Email: mercyfre@ezworks.net. Sr. Kathleen Marie Noonan, R.S.M., Dir.; Arlene Fleming, Health Coord.; Rev. Edward J. Schleter, V.F., Chap. Sisters of Mercy of the Americas, Cincinnati Regional Community. Sisters 35.

SYLVANIA. *Sisters of St. Francis of the Congregation of Our Lady of Lourdes*, 6832 Convent Blvd., 43560-2897. Tel: 419-882-2016; Fax: 419-885-8643. Email: cboratyn@sistersosf.org. Web: www.sistersosf.org. Sr. Diana Lynn Eckel, O.S.F., Congregational Min.

Sisters of St. Francis of the Congregation of Our Lady of Lourdes, Motherhouse and Novitiate Professed Sisters 183; Associates 72.

TIFFIN. *St. Francis Convent*, 200 St. Francis Ave., 44883-3458. Tel: 419-447-0435; Fax: 419-447-1612. Email: osftiffin@tiffinfranciscans.org. Web: www.tiffinfranciscans.org. Sr. Jacquelyn Doepker, O.S.F., Community Min.; Rev. Francis A. Murd, Chap. Motherhouse and Novitiate, Sisters of St. Francis of Tiffin. Sisters 100; Associates 80.

WHITEHOUSE. *Lial Residence, Sisters of Notre Dame*, 5908 Davis Rd., 43571. Tel: 419-877-0431. Email: jmfrania@toledosnd.org. Sr. Joanne Mary Frania, S.N.D., Community Coord. Sisters 4.

[J] RETREAT HOUSES AND CENTERS OF SPIRITUALITY

BELLEVUE. *Sorrowful Mother Shrine* (1850) 4106 State Rte. 269, P.O. Box 319, 44811-0319. Tel: 419-483-3435; Fax: 419-483-6400. Email: sorrowful@hughes.net. Web: www.sorrowfulmothershrine.com. Revs. Robert Kunisch, C.PP.S.; Yuri (George) J. Kuzara, C.PP.S., Shrine Dir.; Harold C. Brown, C.PP.S.; Gene Wilson, C.PP.S.; Bros. Charles McCafferty, C.PP.S.; Terrence Nufer, C.PP.S.

CAREY. *Our Lady of Consolation Retreat House*, 321 Clay St., 43316. Tel: 419-396-7970; Fax: 419-396-3355. Email: retreats@olcshrine.com. Web: www.olcshrine.com. Bro. Randy Kin, O.F.M.Conv., Retreat Dir. Diocese of Toledo, auspices of Shrine of Our Lady of Consolation, Carey, OH.

FREMONT. *Our Lady of the Pines Retreat Center* (1962) 1250 Tiffin St., 43420-3562. Tel: 419-332-6522; Fax: 419-333-0238. Email: olprc@ezworks.net. Web: www.pinesretreat.org. Sr. Christine Pratt, O.S.U., Dir. Sisters of Mercy. Total Staff 8.

SYLVANIA. *Sophia Center, Inc.*, 6832 Convent Blvd., 43560. Tel: 419-882-4529; Fax: 419-885-7612. Email: sophiacc@mindspring.com. 500 N. Main St., Findlay, 45840. Tel: 419-423-3292; Fax: 419-423-7662. Web: www.thesophiacenter.org. Sisters Rachel Marie Nijakowski, O.S.F.S., Psychologist (Ohio 4699); Sharon Pollnow, C.S.A., Counselor; Mary Ann Szydlowski, O.S.F.S., R.N., Massage & Polarity Therapy; Deborah Carney, C.F.O., Cert. Professional Organizer; Joan Dvorak, B.Ed., Learning Disability Specialist; Mary Goebel-Komala, Ph.D., Psychologist; Jeanne Holup, M.D., Psychiatrist; Bonnie Schrock, M.A., L.S.W., Counselor; Glennda Stelnicki, Psychologist; Norma Vorst, M.A., P.C.C., Licensed Professional Clinical Counselor; Craig Ward, L.I.S.W., Licensed Independent Social Worker & Counselor.

TIFFIN. *St. Francis Spirituality Center*, 200 St. Francis Ave., 44883-3491. Tel: 419-443-1485; Fax: 419-443-1612. Email: retreats@stfrancisspiritualitycenter.org. Web: www.stfrancisspiritualitycenter.org. Sr. Roberta Marie Doneth, O.S.F., Admin.; Martie J. Aiello, Prog. Dir. Sisters of St. Francis, Tiffin.

[K] CAMPUS MINISTRY

TOLEDO. *University of Toledo Campus Ministry* , Attended by Corpus Christi University Parish., 2955 Dorr St., 43607. Tel: 419-531-4992; Fax: 419-531-1775. Web: www.ccup.org. Rev. James J. Bacik; Pamela Meseroll, Pastoral Admin.

BLUFFTON. *Bluffton University Campus Ministry* 160 N. Spring St., 45817. Tel: 419-358-8631; Fax: 419-358-0647. Email: cinkrott@embarqmail.com. Sr. Carol Inkrott, O.S.F., Campus Min.

BOWLING GREEN. *Bowling Green State University Campus Ministry* , Attended by St. Thomas More University Parish., 425 Thurstin Ave., 43402. Tel: 419-352-7555; Fax: 419-352-7557. Email: info@sttoms.com. Web: www.sttoms.com. Rev. Michael G. Dandurand, Pastor. Total in Residence 27; Total Staff 15.

DEFIANCE. *Defiance College Newman Campus Ministry* 701 N. Clinton, 43512. Tel: 419-783-2563; Fax: 419-783-2597. Email: morzolek@defiance.edu. Mariah Orzolek, Advisor.

FINDLAY. *University of Findlay Campus Ministry* 750 Bright Rd., 45840. Tel: 419-422-2646; Fax: 419-422-2602. Email: dbrown@findlaystmichael.org. Donna Brown, Campus Min.

TIFFIN. *Heidelberg College Campus Ministry* 310 E. Market St., 44883. Tel: 419-448-2242; Fax: 419-448-2578. Email: bbishop@heidelberg.edu. Web: www.heidelberg.edu/offices/student/affairs/religion.html. Bobbi Bishop, Campus Min.

[L] MISCELLANEOUS LISTINGS

TOLEDO. **Catholic Charities - Diocese of Toledo, Inc.*, 1933 Spielbusch Ave., P.O. Box 985, 43697-0985. Tel: 419-244-6711. Email: bsanford@toledodiocese.org. Web: www.catholiccharitiesnwo.org. Mr. Rodney Schuster, Exec. Dir.

Catholic Club, The (1942) 1601 Jefferson Ave., 43604. Tel: 419-243-7255; Fax: 419-243-6337. Email: info@catholicclub.org. Web: www.catholicclub.org. Mr. Paul Szymanski, Dir.

Catholic Foundation of the Diocese of Toledo, P.O. Box 985, 43697-0985. Tel: 419-244-6711; Fax: 419-270-0053. Email: kszymanski@toledodiocese.org. Web: www.toledodiocese.org.

Christ Child Society of Toledo, P. O. Box 352254, 43635. Tel: 419-251-1218; Fax: 419-824-8040. Web: www.ccsoftoledo.org. Ms. Mary Murnen, Pres.; Ms. Kay Rasmus, Pres.-Elect.; Ms. Tootie Morette, Treas.; Ms. Carol Morava, Sec.; Ms. Lucy Abu-Absi, Parliamentarian.

Double ARC, 3837 Secor Rd., 43623-4484. Tel: 419-479-3060; Fax: 419-724-1372. Web: doublearc.org. Sr. Linda Falquette, R.S.M., Exec. Dir.

Family Health Plan, 2200 Jefferson Ave., Sixth Fl., 43624. Tel: 419-241-6501; Fax: 419-241-1482. Web: www.familyhealthplan.org. Samatha Platzke, Dir. Affiliated with Mercy Health Partners.

Farley Health Care Corporation, 2200 Jefferson Ave., 43604. Tel: 419-251-2889. Email: barry_hudgin@mhsnr.org. Barry Hudgin, Legal Counsel.

St. Francis de Sales High School Endowment Fund, Inc., 2323 W. Bancroft St., 43607. Tel: 419-531-1618; Fax: 419-531-9740. Email: rolszewski@sfstoledo.org. Web: sfstoledo.org.

Franciscan Care Center, Sylvania, 4111 Holland Sylvania Rd., 43624. Tel: 419-882-6582; Fax: 419-885-1422. Web: www.fccsylvania.org.

Hope Manor, 4702 Violet Rd., 43623. Tel: 419-246-4733; Fax: 419-246-4734. Ms. Cindy Kasprzak, Mgr. Units 100.

Saint John's Jesuit High School Foundation, 5901 Airport Hwy., 43615. Tel: 419-865-5743; Fax: 419-861-5002. Email: tpipp@sjjtitnans.org. Web: sjjtitans.org. Rev. Thomas Doyle, S.J., Pres.

LifeStar Ambulance, Inc. Ambulance & medical transport company., 2200 Jefferson, 43604. Tel: 419-693-1611; Fax: 419-693-5931. Web: www.mercyweb.org. Cathy Nelson, Admin. Lifestar & Life Flight.

Madonna Homes, Inc., P.O. Box 4719, 43620. 722 N. Huron St., 43604. Tel: 419-244-3758; Fax: 419-246-4738. Email: tfranklin@vmc.org. Tracy Franklin, Mgr. Units 171.

Mareda, Inc., P.O. Box 4719, 43620. 1931 Scottwood Ave., Ste. 700, 43620. Tel: 419-242-2300; Fax: 419-246-4703. Email: jkiely@vmc.org. Mr. John Kiely, Exec. Dir. Housing Agency of the Diocese of Toledo.

St. Marguerite D'Youville Foundation II (1996) 2213 Cherry St., 43608.

Mercy College of Northwest Ohio Foundation, Inc., 2221 Madison Ave., 43604. Tel: 419-251-1314. Email: john.hayward@mercycollege.edu. Web: www.mercycollege.edu. John F. Hayward, Pres.

Mercy Health System-Northern Region dba Mercy Health Partners 2200 Jefferson Ave., 43604. Tel: 419-251-0700; Fax: 419-251-0733. Web: www.mercyweb.org. Ms. Andrea Price, CEO. Total Staff 625.

Michaelmas Manor, Inc., P.O. Box 4719, 43620. 3250-3260 Schneider Rd., 46314. Tel: 419-389-4615; Fax: 419-389-4620. Email: jkiely@vmc.org. Ms. Chris Vargo, Mgr. A corporation organized and operated for the purpose of providing housing facilities and services to elderly persons and handicapped persons. Units for the Elderly 70; Units for the Physically Handicapped 24.

Moody Manor, P.O. Box 4719, 43620. 2293 1/2 Kent St., 43620. Tel: 419-241-6985; Fax: 419-246-4737. Email: afreeman@vmc.org. Anglona Freeman, Mgr. Family & Elderly Units 119.

Office of Global Concerns, P.O. Box 985, 43697-0985. 1933 Spielbusch Ave., 43604-5360. Tel: 419-244-6711; Fax: 419-244-4791. Email: pwhite@toledodiocese.org. Web: www.toledodiocese.org/globalconcerns/index.html. Deacon Paul J. White, Dir. Society for the Propagation of the Faith; Holy Childhood Association; Catholic Relief Services.

Plaza Apartments, 2520 Monroe St., 43620. Tel: 419-244-1881; Fax: 419-246-4710. Email: ashaw@vmc.org. Mr. John Kiely, Vice Pres.; Ms. Angela Shaw, Project Mgr.

Regina Manor, Inc., 3731 N. Erie St., 43611. Tel: 419-726-6186; Fax: 419-726-6343. Email: jector@vmc.org. P.O. Box 4719, 43620. Ms. Kim Woods, Mgr. Family & Elderly Units 180.

St. Vincent Mercy Medical Center Foundation, 2213 Cherry St., 43608. Tel: 419-251-2117. Tony Werner, Pres.

Toledo Catholic Charities Corporation, 1933 Spielbusch Ave., 43624. Tel: 419-244-6711; Fax: 419-720-0053. Email: rhenderson@toledodiocese.org. Deacon Ronald D. Henderson, Sec. Finance & Admin. The Catholic Charities Corporation is the Diocesan vehicle to collect and distribute endowment funds and bequests for charitable purposes.

U.T. Newman Foundation for Student Education and Development, 2955 Dorr St., 43607-3023. Tel: 419-531-4992; Fax: 419-531-1775. Rev. James J. Bacik.

St. Ursula Academy Foundation, Inc., 4025 Indian Rd., 43606.

Vision Time, Inc., 1618 W. Sylvania Ave., 43612. Tel: 419-476-0941; Fax: 419-476-8491. Email: nancy@servantleader.org. Sr. Nancy Westmeyer, O.S.F.

**Women Blessing Women* (1998) 223 Page St., 43620. Tel: 419-241-9789; Fax: 419-241-9791. Web: www.womenblessingwomen.org. Glenda Brown, Dir. Total Women Served 425.

CAREY. *Franciscan Mission Association*, 322 West St., 43316. Tel: 419-396-6455. Email: CarlosBH@aol.com. Bro. Bryan Hoban, O.F.M.Conv., Dir.

DELPHOS. *St. John Parish Foundation, Inc.*, Tel: 419-695-4050; Fax: 419-695-4060.

St. John the Evangelist Church: 331 E. Second St., 45833.

FINDLAY. *St. Michael Schools Educational Foundation*, 750 Bright Rd., 45840. Tel: 419-422-2646; Fax: 419-422-2602. Clifford Cook, Pres.

FREMONT. *Delaware Acres, Inc.* (1972) P.O. Box 4719, 43620. 725 S. Buchanan St., 43420. Tel: 419-334-9558; Fax: 419-334-9555. Email: jkiely@vmc.org. Ms. Marcella Miller, Mgr. Family Units 68.

LIMA. *Lima Central Catholic Educational Foundation* (1955) 720 S. Cable Rd., 45805. Tel: 419-222-4276; Fax: 419-222-6933. Email: lcary@lcchs.edu. Terrence J. Norton, Chm.

Magnificat of Lima, Ohio, 1612 Victoria Ln., 45805. Tel: 419-331-1763. Sharon Laurent, Coord.

S.R.H.C. Foundation, 730 W. Market St., 45801-4667. Tel: 419-226-9775; Fax: 419-226-9750. Mr. James P. Reber, Pres.; William W. Roe, Sec. & Treas.

OREGON. *St. Charles Mercy Hospital Foundation*, 2600 Navarre Ave., 43616. Tel: 419-696-7245; Fax: 419-696-7644. Web: www.mercyweb.org/stcharlesfoundation. Holly Meyers, Foundation Chm.

SANDUSKY. *Sandusky Central Catholic Educational Foundation, Inc.*, 410 W. Jefferson St., 44870.

SWANTON. *St. Richard's School Endowment Foundation* (1987) 333 Brookside Dr., 43558-1097. Tel: 419-826-2791; Fax: 419-826-7256. Email: busman@saintrichard.org. Web: saintrichard.org. Ed Snyder, Chmn.

SYLVANIA. **Franciscan Living Communities*, 6832 Convent Blvd., 43560. Tel: 419-882-8373; Fax: 419-882-7360. Email: rryan@fscsylvania.org. Rick Ryan, Pres.

Franciscan Properties, Inc. (1987) 6832 Convent Blvd., 43560. Tel: 419-824-3674; Fax: 419-824-3931. Email: dnolan@rosarycare.org. Sr. Jeanne Stack, O.S.F., Pres. Total in Residence 99; Total Staff 2; Apartments 98.

Franciscan Shelters-Bethany House, P.O. Box 80596, 43608. Tel: 419-727-4948. Email: bethany_exdirector@yahoo.com. Kathleen Griffin, Exec. Dir.

Rosary Care Center (1975) 6832 Convent Blvd., 43560. Tel: 419-824-3600; Fax: 419-824-3931. Cheryl King, Admin.

Sylvania Franciscan Health (1984) 6832 Convent Blvd., 43560. Tel: 419-882-8373; Fax: 419-882-7360. Web: www.fscsylvania.org. Mr. James W. Pope, Pres.

TIFFIN. *St. Francis Home Inc.*, 182 St. Francis Ave., 44883. Tel: 419-447-2723; Fax: 419-448-1337. Email: ceo@stfrancishome.org. Web: www.stfrancishome.org. Robert G. Hauzie, Pres. & CEO; Ms. Anne Lange, Chairperson Bd. of Trustees. Residents 168; Total Assisted Annually 285; Total Staff 290.

St. Francis Senior Ministries Memorial Foundation, Inc., 182 St. Francis Ave., 44883. Tel: 419-447-2723; Fax: 419-448-1337. Email: ceo@stfrancishome.org. Web: www.stfrancishome.org. Cliff Farmer, Chm. Bd. of Trustees; Robert G. Hauzie, Pres. & CEO.

Saint Francis Senior Ministries, Inc., 182 Saint Francis Ave., 44883. Tel: 419-447-2723.

St. Francis Villas, Inc., 182 St. Francis Ave., 44883. Tel: 419-447-2723; Fax: 419-448-1337. Email: ceo@stfrancishome.inc. Web: www.stfrancishome.org. Robert G. Hauzie, Pres. & CEO; Ms. Anne Lange, Chairperson Bd. of Trustees.

Friedman Village at Saint Francis, LLC, 175 Saint Francis Ave., 44883. Tel: 419-447-2723.

Mercy Tiffin Health Foundation, 45 St. Lawrence Dr., 44883. Tel: 419-455-7049; Fax: 419-455-7066. Email: bernie_steinmetz@mhsnr.org. Web: www.mercyweb.org. Lee Martin, Chm.

St. Francis Senior Ministries Day Care, Inc., 182 St. Francis Ave., 44883. Tel: 419-447-2723; Fax: 419-448-1337. Email: ceo@stfrancishome.org. Web: stfrancishome.org. Robert G. Hauzie, Pres./CEO; Ms. Anne Lange, Chm. Bd. Trustees.

Tiffin Calvert Foundation (1974) 152 Madison St., 44883-0836. Tel: 419-447-3844. Michael Klepper, Pres.

VERMILION. *St. Mary's Church Education Endowment Foundation*, 731 Exchange St., 44089-1330. Tel: 440-967-8711; Fax: 440-967-8712. Email: parish@stmaryvermilion.org. Web: www.stmaryvermilion.org.

WILLARD. *Mercy Willard Hospital Foundation*, 110 E. Howard St., 44890. Tel: 419-964-5107; Fax: 419-964-5109. Email: marsha.danhoff@mhsnr.org. Web: mercyweb.org. Marsha Danhoff, Dir. Organizational Planning & Devel.

RELIGIOUS INSTITUTES OF MEN REPRESENTED IN THE DIOCESE

For further details refer to the corresponding bracketed number in the Religious Institutes of Men or Women section.

[]—*Congregation of the Holy Ghost of the Immaculate Heart of Mary (Holy Ghost Fathers)* (Nigeria)

[]—*Congregation of Saint Basil*

[0480]—*Conventual Franciscans* (Our Lady of Consolation Prov.)—O.F.M.Conv.

[0690]—*Jesuit Fathers and Brothers*—S.J.

[0910]—*Oblates of St. Francis de Sales*—O.S.F.S.

[1070]—*Redemptorist Fathers* (Baltimore Prov.)—C.SS.R.

[1060]—*Society of the Precious Blood* (Cincinnati Prov.)—C.PP.S.

RELIGIOUS INSTITUTES OF WOMEN REPRESENTED IN THE DIOCESE

[3710]—*Congregation of the Sisters of Saint Agnes*—C.S.A.

[1710]—*Congregation of the Third Order of St. Francis of Mary Immaculate, Joliet, IL*—O.S.F.

[4190]—*The Contemplative Order of the Sisters of the Visitation of Toledo, Ohio*—V.H.M.

[1070-13]—*Dominican Sisters* (Adrian, MI)—O.P.

[1070-09]—*Dominican Sisters* (Racine, WI)—O.P.

[1430]—*Franciscan Sisters of Our Lady of Perpetual Help*—O.S.F.

[2575]—*Institute of the Sisters of Mercy of the Americas* (Cincinnati, OH)—R.S.M.

[2340]—*Little Sisters of the Poor* (Baltimore Prov.)—L.S.P.

[3130]—*Our Lady of Victory Missionary Sisters*—O.L.V.M.

[2090]—*Sisters Home Visitors of Mary*—H.V.M.

[0440]—*Sisters of Charity of Cincinnati, Ohio*—S.C.

[0490]—*Sisters of Charity of Montreal (Grey Nuns)*—S.G.M.

[2990]—*Sisters of Notre Dame*—S.N.D.

[1530]—*Sisters of St. Francis of the Congregation of Our Lady of Lourdes, Sylvania, Ohio*—O.S.F.

[3930]—*Sisters of St. Joseph of the Third Order of St. Francis*—S.S.J.-T.O.S.F.

[]—*Sisters of the Humility of Mary*

[3260]—*Sisters of the Precious Blood* (Dayton, OH)—C.PP.S.

[1760]—*Sisters of the Third Order of St. Francis of Penance and Charity*—O.S.F.

[2150]—*Sisters, Servants of the Immaculate Heart of Mary*—I.H.M.

[4120-06]—*Ursuline Nuns of the Congregation of Paris*—O.S.U.

[4120]—*Ursuline Sisters of the Congregation of Paris*—O.S.U.-B.C.

DIOCESAN CEMETERIES

TOLEDO. *Calvary*, 2224 Dorr St., 43607. Tel: 419-536-3751. Web: www.cathcemtoledo.org. Deacon Ronald D. Henderson, Sec. Fin. & Admin.

Mount Carmel, 15 E. Manhattan Blvd., 43608. Mailing Address: 5725 Hill Ave., 43615. Tel: 419-531-5747; Fax: 419-531-0946.

Resurrection, 5725 Hill Ave., 43615. Tel: 419-531-5747; Fax: 419-531-0946. Web: www.cathcemtoledo.org. Deacon Ronald D. Henderson, Sec. Fin. & Admin.

FREMONT. *St. Joseph*, Tel: 419-332-8756.

LIMA. *Gethsemane*

SANDUSKY. *Calvary*, 2020 Sanford St., 44870. Tel: 419-625-2673; Fax: 419-502-3011.

NECROLOGY

† Dentinger, Robert—Died Sept. 12, 2011

† Dorley, Paul D., (Retired)—Died Nov. 2, 2010

† McClure, John A., (Retired)—Died June 29, 2011

† Ringholz, Benedict E., (Retired)—Died April 17, 2011

An asterisk (*) denotes an organization that has established tax-exempt status directly with the IRS and is not covered by the USCCB Group Ruling.

Diocese of Trenton

(Dioecesis Trentonensis)

Most Reverend

DAVID M. O'CONNELL, C.M., J.C.D., D.D.

Bishop of Trenton; ordained May 29, 1982; appointed Coadjutor Bishop of Trenton June 4, 2010; consecrated July 30, 2010; appointed Tenth Bishop of Trenton December 1, 2010. *Office: Chancery/Pastoral Center, 701 Lawrenceville Rd., Trenton, NJ 08648.*

Most Reverend

JOHN M. SMITH, J.C.D., D.D.

Bishop Emeritus of Trenton; ordained May 27, 1961; appointed Titular Bishop of Tre Taverne and Auxiliary Bishop of Newark December 1, 1987; consecrated January 25, 1988; appointed Bishop of Pensacola-Tallahassee June 25, 1991; installed July 31, 1991; appointed Coadjutor Bishop of Trenton November 21, 1995; appointed Bishop of Trenton July 1, 1997; resigned December 1, 2010. *Res.: Villa Vianney, 2301 Lawrenceville Rd., Trenton, NJ 08648.*

Chancery/Pastoral Center: 701 Lawrenceville Rd., Trenton, NJ 08648. Tel: 609-406-7400; Fax: 609-406-7412.

ESTABLISHED AUGUST 11, 1881.

Square Miles 2,156.

Legal Corporate Title: "The Diocese of Trenton."

Comprises four Counties in the State of New Jersey: Burlington, Mercer, Monmouth and Ocean.

For legal titles of parishes and diocesan institutions, consult the Chancery Office.

STATISTICAL OVERVIEW

Personnel	
Bishop	1
Retired Bishops	1
Priests: Diocesan Active in Diocese	173
Priests: Diocesan Active Outside Diocese	9
Priests: Retired, Sick or Absent	65
Number of Diocesan Priests	247
Religious Priests in Diocese	66
Total Priests in Diocese	313
Extern Priests in Diocese	25
Ordinations:	
Diocesan Priests	6
Transitional Deacons	7
Permanent Deacons	12
Permanent Deacons in Diocese	360
Total Brothers	67
Total Sisters	359
Parishes	
Parishes	111
With Resident Pastor:	
Resident Diocesan Priests	96
Resident Religious Priests	11
Without Resident Pastor:	
Administered by Priests	4
Missions	7
Professional Ministry Personnel:	
Brothers	1
Sisters	29
Lay Ministers	110
Welfare	
Catholic Hospitals	2
Total Assisted	120,000
Health Care Centers	7
Total Assisted	4,500
Homes for the Aged	1
Total Assisted	430
Residential Care of Children	2
Total Assisted	25
Day Care Centers	5
Total Assisted	490
Specialized Homes	7
Total Assisted	250
Special Centers for Social Services	30
Total Assisted	27,900
Residential Care of Disabled	1
Total Assisted	180
Educational	
Diocesan Students in Other Seminaries	36
Total Seminarians	36
Colleges and Universities	1
Total Students	2,885
High Schools, Diocesan and Parish	8
Total Students	5,869
High Schools, Private	3
Total Students	1,163
Elementary Schools, Diocesan and Parish	36
Total Students	11,762
Elementary Schools, Private	3
Total Students	694
Non-residential Schools for the Disabled	1
Total Students	14
Catechesis/Religious Education:	
High School Students	951
Elementary Students	60,744
Total Students under Catholic Instruction	84,118
Teachers in the Diocese:	
Brothers	3
Sisters	34
Lay Teachers	3,576
Vital Statistics	
Receptions into the Church:	
Infant Baptism Totals	7,175
Minor Baptism Totals	95
Adult Baptism Totals	845
Received into Full Communion	282
First Communions	9,459
Confirmations	9,266
Marriages:	
Catholic	1,165
Interfaith	322
Total Marriages	1,487
Deaths	6,207
Total Catholic Population	856,355
Total Population	2,022,194

Former Bishops—Rt. Revs. MICHAEL J. O'FARRELL, D.D., cons. Nov. 1, 1881; died April 2, 1894; JAMES A. MCFAUL, D.D., LL.D., cons. Oct. 18, 1894; died June 16, 1917; Most Revs. THOMAS J. WALSH, S.T.D., J.C.D., cons. July 25, 1918; transferred to Newark, NJ, March 2, 1928; JOHN J. MCMAHON, D.D., cons. April 26, 1928; died Dec. 31, 1932; MOSES E. KILEY, S.T.D., cons. March 17, 1934; appt. Archbishop of Milwaukee, Jan. 1, 1940; WILLIAM A. GRIFFIN, D.D., appt. Bishop of Trenton, May 22, 1940; cons. May 1, 1938; died Jan. 1, 1950; GEORGE W. AHR, S.T.D., appt. Bishop of Trenton, Jan. 28, 1950; cons. March 20, 1950; retired June 23, 1979; died May 5, 1993; JOHN C. REISS, D.D., J.C.D. (Retired), ord. May 31, 1947; appt. Titular Bishop of Simidicca and Auxiliary of Trenton Oct. 21, 1967; cons. Dec. 12, 1967; appt. Bishop of Trenton March 4, 1980; installed April 22, 1980; resigned July 1, 1997; died March 4, 2012.; JOHN M. SMITH (Retired), ord. May 27, 1961; appt. Titular Bishop of Tre Taverne and Auxiliary Bishop of Newark Dec. 1, 1987; cons. Jan. 25, 1988; appt. Bishop of Pensacola-Tallahassee June 25, 1991; installed July 31, 1991; appt. Coadjutor Bishop of Trenton Nov. 21, 1995; appt. Bishop of Trenton July 1, 1997; retired Dec. 1, 2010.

Chancery/Pastoral Center—701 Lawrenceville Rd., Trenton, 08648. Tel: 609-406-7400; Fax: 609-406-7412.

Vicar General and Moderator of the Curia—Rev. Msgr. GREGORY D. VAUGHAN, V.G., 701 Lawrenceville Rd., Trenton, 08648.

Chancellor—Mr. ANTHONY J. MINGARINO, 701 Lawrenceville Rd., Trenton, 08648.

Episcopal Vicars—Ocean County: Rev. Msgr. CASIMIR H. LADZINSKI. Burlington County: Rev. Msgr. RICHARD L. TOFANI. Mercer County: Very Rev. JEFFREY E. LEE. Monmouth County: Rev. Msgr. EUGENE M. REBECK.

Vice Chancellors—Rev. Msgr. JAMES G. INNOCENZI; Revs. ALBERTO W. TAMAYO; MICHAEL T. MCCLANE, J.C.L.

Assistant Chancellor—Rev. Msgr. JOHN K. DERMOND, J.C.L.

Secretary to the Bishop—Rev. ALBERTO W. TAMAYO.

Records Manager and Archivist—Sr. CATHERINE THIBAULT, S.S.J.

Diocesan Tribunal—Chancery/Pastoral Center, 701 Lawrenceville Rd., Trenton, 08648. Tel: 609-406-7411; Fax: 609-406-7424.

Judicial Vicar—Rev. Msgr. JOHN K. DERMOND, J.C.L.

Associate Judicial Vicars—Rev. Msgr. JAMES G. INNOCENZI; Rev. OSCAR B. SUMANGA, J.C.D.

Defenders of the Bond—Revs. PETER J. ALINDOGAN, J.C.L.; MICHAEL T. MCCLANE, J.C.L.; Deacon JOSEPH A. HANNAWACKER.

Promoter of Justice—Rev. PETER J. ALINDOGAN, J.C.L.

Tribunal Judges—Rev. Msgr. EDWARD J. ARNISTER, J.C.L., V.F.; Revs. AWTE WELDU, O.Cist.; LOUIS W. KRALOVICH (Retired); Rev. Msgrs. WALTER E. NOLAN (Retired); EUGENE M. REBECK; Rev. JOHN J. SCULLY; Rev. Msgrs. JOSEPH C. SHENROCK, P.A. (Retired); RALPH W. STANSLEY; Rev. CHARLES B. WEISER.

Secretary of the Tribunal and Notary—Ms. EVELYN AGUIAR; Ms. JEANNETTE CAMERA.

College of Consultors—Rev. Msgr. EDWARD J. ARNISTER, J.C.L., V.F.; Revs. PETER JAMES R. ALINDOGAN; ANTHONY M. CAROTENUTO; Rev. Msgr. THOMAS N. GERVASIO; Rev. ROBERT S. GRODNICKI; Very Rev. KEVIN J. KEELEN, V.F.; Rev. JACEK W. LABINSKI, S.T.D.; Very Rev. DAMIAN J. MCELROY, V.F.; Rev. PHILLIP C. PFLEGER; Very Revs. DANIEL J. RYAN, V.F.; ROBERT J.W. SCHECKER, V.F.; Rev.

Msgr. LEONARD F. TROIANO.

Episcopal Council—Rev. Msgr. JOHN K. DERMOND, J.C.L.; Very Rev. DOUGLAS FREER; Rev. Msgrs. R. VINCENT GARTLAND; RICHARD D. LAVERGHETTA; CASIMIR H. LADZINSKI; Very Revs. JEFFREY E. LEE; THOMAS J. MULLELLY, J.D.; Rev. Msgrs. EUGENE M. REBECK; RICHARD L. TOFANI; GREGORY D. VAUGHAN, V.G.; MICHAEL J. WALSH, V.F.

Vicars Forane (Deans)—Very Revs. DENNIS A. APOLDITE, V.F.; TIMOTHY J. CAPEWELL, V.F.; KEVIN J. KEELEN, V.F.; STANLEY P. LUKASZEWSKI, V.F.; DAMIAN J. MCELROY, V.F.; DANIEL J. RYAN, V.F.; ROBERT J.W. SCHECKER, V.F.; G. SCOTT SHAFFER, V.F.; Rev. Msgr. MICHAEL J. WALSH, V.F.; Very Rev. H. BRENDAN WILLIAMS, V.F.

Council of Deacons and Vicariate Representatives—Deacon JOSE RODRIQUEZ, Pres. Burlington Co.: Deacons LEE ZITO; JAMES CASA. Mercer Co.: Deacons BARRY ZADWORNY; JOSE G. RODRIGUEZ. Monmouth Co.: Deacons VINCENT L. RINALDI; HENRY J. CUGINI. Ocean Co.: Deacons MICHAEL A. SMIGELSKI; JOHN R. PITT. At Large: Deacon LUIS RAMOS.

Diocesan Finance Council—Most Rev. DAVID M. O'CONNELL, C.M., Pres.; Mr. LAURENCE M. DOWNES, Chm.; Rev. Msgr. GREGORY D. VAUGHAN, V.G.; Mr. ANTHONY J. MINGARINO, Chancellor & CAO; Mr. HARRY R. HILL, Esq.; Mr. BERNARD M. MCGLONE; Mr. ROBERT J. DUNNE III; Mr. EMIL A. SCHROTH JR.; Mr. RON NOWAK; Mr. MICHAEL CASTELLANO; Mr. WILLIAM N. DOOLEY.

Censores Librorum—Revs. JOHN P. CZAHUR; PABLO T. GADENZ, S.T.D., S.S.L.; MICHAEL HALL; Very Rev. DAMIAN J. MCELROY, V.F.; Revs. GEORGE A. MEDINA; DAVID S. SWANTEK; JOEL R. WILSON.

Office of Temporal Administration

Chancellor/CAO/CFO—Mr. ANTHONY J. MINGARINO, Pastoral Center, 701 Lawrenceville Rd., Trenton, 08648. Tel: 609-406-7446; Fax: 609-406-7414.

Department of Administrative Services—Mr. JOSEPH BIANCHI, S.P.H.R., Dir.

Department of Human Resources—Mr. JOSEPH BIANCHI, S.P.H.R., Dir. Tel: 609-403-7208; Ms. ANGELA GITTO, HR Specialist. Tel: 609-403-7164.

Department of Computer Services—Ms. KATHLEEN MOORE, Dir., Chancery/Pastoral Center, 701 Lawrenceville Rd., Trenton, 08648. Tel: 609-403-7140; Fax: 609-406-7414.

Department of Finance—Ms. DARYL ROWE, Dir., Chancery/Pastoral Center, 701 Lawrenceville Rd., Trenton, 08648. Tel: 609-403-7120; Fax: 609-406-7414.

Department of Development—Mr. STEPHEN J. NICHOLL, Dir., Chancery/Pastoral Center, 701 Lawrenceville Rd., Trenton, 08648. Tel: 609-403-7128; Fax: 609-406-7443; Ms. BETHANY DOROS-GREGG, Assoc. Dir. Devel. & Dir. Foundation for Student Achievement.

Department of Property and Construction—Deacon WILLIAM A. WILSON, Dir., Chancery/Pastoral Center, 701 Lawrenceville Rd., Trenton, 08648. Tel: 609-403-7182; Fax: 609-406-7412. Associate Directors: Mr. KENNETH J. NOWAK; Deacon NEIL PIROZZI.

Department of Cemeteries—VACANT, Dir.

Building Commission—Rev. Msgr. RICHARD C. BRIETSKE, Chm. (Retired).

Office of Worship

Office of Worship—Rev. Msgr. SAM A. SIRIANNI, Dir. Tel: 609-403-7160; Sr. ELEANOR MCCANN, R.S.M., Assoc. Dir., Chancery/Pastoral Center, 701 Lawrenceville Rd., Trenton, 08648. Tel: 609-403-7132; Fax: 609-406-7413.

Office of Catholic Education

Vicar—Very Rev. DOUGLAS FREER. Tel: 609-403-7179; Fax: 609-406-7416.

Department of Catholic Schools—Mrs. JOANN TIER, Supt. Tel: 609-403-7145; Fax: 609-406-7416; Dr. MARGARET BOLAND, Assoc. Supt. Tel: 609-403-7147; Ms. CYNTHIA CASCIOLA-KITTS, Assoc. Dir. Elementary Schools, Chancery/Pastoral Center, 701 Lawrenceville Rd., Trenton, 08648. Tel: 609-403-7203; Fax: 609-406-7416.

Associate Director Athletics, School Boards, Marketing, and Government Programs—Ms. DONNA DAVIDSON, Chancery/Pastoral Center, 701 Lawrenceville Rd., Trenton, 08648. Tel: 609-403-7127; Fax: 609-406-7416.

Ministry of Catechesis & Evangelization—Associate Directors: Mr. MICHAEL FABIAN. Tel: 609-403-7220; Mr. JOHN BOUCHER. Tel: 609-403-7190.

Institute of Lay Ecclesial Ministry—Ms. JOLYNN KREMPECKI. Tel: 609-403-7130; Fax: 609-406-7436.

Holy Innocents Society—Mr. ANGELO ROMANELLO, Pres., 5 Shelburne Dr., Trenton, 08638. Tel: 609-882-4567.

Office of Communications

Executive Director—Ms. RAYANNE BENNETT, Chancery/Pastoral Center, 701 Lawrenceville Rd., Trenton, 08648. Tel: 609-403-7188; Fax: 609-406-7451.

Department of Media and Public Relations—Ms. RAYANNE BENNETT, Dir., Chancery/Pastoral Center, 701 Lawrenceville Rd., Trenton, 08648. Tel: 609-403-7188; Fax: 609-406-7451.

The Monitor—Web: www.trentonmonitor.com. Ms. RAYANNE BENNETT, Assoc. Publisher, Chancery/Pastoral Center, 701 Lawrenceville Rd., Trenton, 08648. Tel: 609-403-7188; Fax: 609-406-7451; Ms. MARY MORRELL, Mng. Editor. Tel: 609-403-7135; Fax: 609-406-7423; Mr. GEORGE W. STEVENSON, Business Dir. Tel: 609-403-7131; Fax: 609-406-7423.

Department of Radio and Television—Mrs. MARIANNE HARTMAN, Dir., Chancery/Pastoral Center, 701 Lawrenceville Rd., Trenton, 08648. Tel: 609-406-7402; Fax: 609-406-7423. Web: www.realfaithtv.com.

Department of Digital Media—JEANNE KYSELA, Dir. Tel: 609-403-7202. Web: www.dioceseoftrenton.org.

Office of Pastoral Life & Mission

Executive Director—Mrs. TERRY GINTHER. Tel: 609-403-7143; Fax: 609-406-7456.

Department of Pastoral Care—Mr. JOHN KALINOWSKI, Dir., 701 Lawrenceville Rd., Trenton, 08648. Tel: 609-403-7157; Fax: 609-406-7403.

Department of Youth, Marriage and Family Life—Mrs. LINDA G. RICHARDSON, Dir. Tel: 609-403-7155; Fax: 609-406-7403.

Department of Mulitcultural Ministry—Mrs. DEANNA V. SASS, M.A., Dir. Tel: 609-403-7189; Fax: 609-406-7415.

Department of Pastoral Planning—Mrs. TERRY GINTHER, Dir. Tel: 609-403-7143; Fax: 609-406-7456.

Expansion and Restructuring Commission—Very Rev. JEFFREY E. LEE, Chm., Chancery/Pastoral Center: 701 Lawrenceville Rd., Trenton, 08648. Tel: 609-406-7400; Fax: 609-406-7444.

Campus Ministries—Rev. WILLIAM J. LAGO, Diocesan Liaison, Catholic Campus Ministry: Bede House, 492 Ewingville Rd., Trenton, 08638. Tel: 609-771-0543.

Catholic Scouting—Rev. MICHAEL A. SANTANGELO, Chap., St. Mary of the Lakes Parish, 40 Jackson Rd., Medford, 08055. Tel: 609-654-8208; Fax: 609-654-1734.

Charismatic Renewal—Rev. JEFFREY KEGLEY, St. Raphael - Holy Angels Parish, 3500 S. Broad St., Hamilton, 08610. Tel: 609-585-7049.

Cursillo—Rev. EDWARD H. BLANCHETT, Jesus, The Good Shepherd Parish, 101 Middleton St., Riverside, 08075.

Legion of Mary—Rev. MICHAEL J. BURNS, Chap., St. Mary Church, 45 Crosswicks St., Bordentown, 08505. Tel: 609-298-0261; Fax: 609-298-7178.

Retreat Centers

Francis House of Prayer—Sr. MARCELLA SPRINGER, S.S.J., Dir., Mailing Address: P.O. Box 392, Rancocas, 08073. Tel: 609-877-0509; Fax: 609-877-5810. Web: www.fhop.org. Email: fhop@verizon.net.

Upper Room—Co-Directors: Sisters MAUREEN CHRISTENSEN, R.S.M.; MAUREEN CONROY, R.S.M.; TRUDY AHERN, S.S.J., 3455 W. Bangs Ave., Bldg. 2, Neptune, 07754. Tel: 732-922-0550; Fax: 732-922-3904. Web: www.theupper-room.org. Email: office@theupper-room.org.

Office of Clergy and Consecrated Life

Vicar—Very Rev. THOMAS J. MULLELLY, J.D. Tel: 609-403-7181; Fax: 609-406-7453.

Ministry of Clergy Personnel—Very Rev. THOMAS J. MULLELLY, J.D., Dir. Tel: 609-403-7181; Fax: 609-406-7453; Deacons LAWRENCE W. FINN SR., Assoc. Dir. Tel: 609-403-7134; Fax: 609-406-7453; JOSEPH M. DONADIEU, Asst. to Vicar, Chancery/Pastoral Center, 701 Lawrenceville Rd., Trenton, 08648. Tel: 609-403-7206; Fax: 609-406-7453.

Ministry of Consecrated Life—Tel: 609-406-7430; Fax: 609-406-7413.

Ministry of Vocations—Rev. Msgr. GREGORY D. VAUGHAN, V.G., Dir. Seminarians, Chancery/Pastoral Center, 701 Lawrenceville Rd., Trenton, 08648. Tel: 609-406-7448; Fax: 609-406-7412. Web: www.godiscallingyou.com.

Office of Catholic Social Services

Executive Director—Sr. JOANNE DRESS, D.C. Tel: 609-403-7188; Fax: 609-406-7412.

Migration & Refugee Services—Sr. JANET YURKANIN, I.H.M., Dir., 149 N. Warren St., Trenton, 08608. Tel: 609-394-8299; Fax: 609-394-0240. Email: jyurkanin@aol.com.

Catholic Charities—Ms. MARLENE LAO'-COLLINS, Exec. Dir., 383 W. State St., P.O. Box 1423, Trenton, 08607-1423. Tel: 609-394-5181; Fax: 609-695-6978. Web: www.catholiccharitiestrenton.org.

Catholic Campaign for Human Development—Rev. JOSEPH A. JAKUB, Dir., Emmaus House, 2116 Lawrenceville Rd., Trenton, 08648. Tel: 609-896-0394.

Catholic Relief Services—Mrs. MARY GOSS, 10 Pumpshire Rd., Toms River, 08753. Tel: 732-929-9013.

Martin House—Rev. BRIAN MCCORMICK, Dir., 802 E. State St., P.O. Box 1025, Trenton, 08606. Tel: 609-989-8143; Fax: 609-989-0933. Email: mhlcmaster@aol.com.

Mount Carmel Guild—Ms. MARIE GLADNEY, Exec. Dir., 73 N. Clinton Ave., Trenton, 08609. Tel: 609-392-5159; Fax: 609-392-5903. Email: mtcarmelguild@aol.com.

St. Vincent DePaul Society—Ms. PATRICIA BROOKS, Diocesan Council Pres. Tel: 609-234-0628. Email: pbrooks110@verizon.net.

Mercer County CYO—Mr. THOMAS G. MLADENETZ, Exec. Dir., 920 S. Broad St., Trenton, 08611. Tel: 609-396-8383. Email: tom@cyomercer.org.

CLERGY, PARISHES, MISSIONS AND PAROCHIAL SCHOOLS

CITY OF TRENTON

(MERCER COUNTY)

1—ST. MARY CATHEDRAL (1868) Revs. Joseph L. Roldan, Rector; Nilo Apura, Parochial Vicar; Deacons Emiliano Vazquez; Jose Beauchamps; Luis Ramos.
Res.: 151 N. Warren St., 08608. Tel: 609-396-8447; Fax: 609-396-5624. Email: stmaryscathedral@verizon.net.
Catechesis/Religious Program—Tel: 609-396-8447, Ext. 28. Email: stmaryscathedral@verizon.net. Sr. Luz Mery VeLez Quiroz, D.R.E.; Mrs. Marisol Rodriguez, C.R.E. Students 236.

2—ST. ANTHONY (1921) Closed. Sacramental records maintained at Our Lady of Sorrows-St. Anthony Parish, Hamilton.
High School—McCorristin High School, Closed. Records maintained at Trenton Catholic Academy, Hamilton.

3—BLESSED SACRAMENT (1912) Closed. Sacramental records maintained at Blessed Sacrament-Our Lady of the Divine Shepherd Parish, Trenton.

4—BLESSED SACRAMENT-OUR LADY OF THE DIVINE SHEPHERD PARISH (2005) Revs. Edward Tetteh, S.V.D.; Henry A. Militante; Guilherme A. Andrino, S.V.D.
Res.: 716 Bellevue Ave., 08618. Tel: 609-396-9231; Fax: 609-396-6432. Email: olds1948@juno.com. Web: www.cbs-olds.org.
Catechesis/Religious Program—Patricia Vincent, D.R.E. Students 40.
Station—Mercer Hospital 08618. Tel: 609-394-4000.

5—THE CHURCH OF THE INCARNATION-ST. JAMES (2006), (Merged July 1, 2006) Revs. Daniel Houde, O.S.S.T.; Santhosh George Kozhippadan, O.S.S.T., Parochial Vicar; Deacons Thomas H. Rivella; Joseph A. Hannawacker; Frances G. Golazeski. In Res., Rev. Kenneth G. Borgesen, O.S.S.T.
Res.: 1545 Pennington Rd., 08618. Tel: 609-882-2860; Fax: 609-637-0460. Email: isjoffice@yahoo.com. Web: www.incarnationstjames.org.
School—1555 Pennington Rd., 08618. Tel: 609-882-3228; Fax: 609-671-1629. Sr. Francis Michael Finsterbusch, I.H.M., Prin. Sisters, Servants of the Immaculate Heart of Mary (Immaculata, PA) 7; Lay Teachers 14; Students 140.
Catechesis/Religious Program—Tel: 609-882-8989. Sr. Diane Simons, I.H.M., Dir. Faith Formation. Students 226.
Convent—45 Harrop Pl., 08618.

6—DIVINE MERCY PARISH (2005) Revs. Charles L. Griffiths; Edward Kwoka; Deacon John R. Grussler; Sisters Karen Crawford, F.S.S.J., Pastoral Assoc.; Loretta Janiszewski, F.S.S.J., Pastoral Assoc.; Carmen Bojorge, Pastoral Assoc.
Res.: 201 Adeline St., 08611. Tel: 609-393-4826; Fax: 609-278-1192.
Catechesis/Religious Program—233 Adeline St., 08611. Tel: 609-393-5233, Ext. 101; Fax: 609-393-3538. Mrs. Rosemarie Micharski, C.R.E. Students 130.
Convent—Franciscan Sisters of St. Joseph, 333 Home Ave., 08611. Tel: 609-695-6424.

7—ST. FRANCIS OF ASSISIUM (1844) [CEM 2] Closed. Sacramental records maintained at Sacred Heart Church, Trenton.

8—ST. HEDWIG (1904), (Polish), [CEM 2] Rev. Jacek W. Labinski; Deacons Thomas H. Watkins Jr.; Barry Zadworny.
Res.: 872 Brunswick Ave., 08638. Tel: 609-396-9068; Fax: 609-396-3171.
Catechesis/Religious Program—Dorothy Zadworny,

D.R.E. Students 225.
9—HOLY ANGELS (1921) Closed. Sacramental records maintained at St. Raphael-Holy Angels Parish, Hamilton.
10—HOLY CROSS (1891) [CEM] Closed. Sacramental records maintained at Divine Mercy Parish, Trenton.
11—IMMACULATE CONCEPTION (1874) Closed. Sacramental records maintained at Our Lady of the Angels Parish, Trenton.
12—INCARNATION (1947) Closed. For inquiries for parish records, see Incarnation-St. James Parish, Trenton.
13—ST. JAMES (1919) Closed. For inquiries for parish records, see Incarnation-St. James Parish, Trenton.
14—ST. JOACHIM (1901) Closed. Sacramental records maintained at Our Lady of Angels Parish, Trenton.
15—ST. JOSEPH (1891), (Spanish), Revs. Javier A. Diaz-Munoz; George A. Medina.
Res.: 540 N. Olden Ave., 08638. Tel: 609-394-5757; Fax: 609-498-6018.
Catechesis/Religious Program—Tel: 609-394-5757, Ext. 3; Fax: 609-394-3418. Miss Ericka Rodriguez, Dir. Students 170.
Station—Helene Fuld Hospital, Tel: 609-394-6000.
16—ST. MICHAEL (1921) Closed. Sacramental records maintained at Church of St. Ann, Lawrenceville.
17—OUR LADY OF GOOD COUNSEL (1942) Rev. Msgr. Ralph W. Stansley; Deacons John Bonner; Steven K. Szmutko.
Res.: 137 W. Upper Ferry Rd., West Trenton, 08628. Tel: 609-882-3277; Fax: 609-882-4375.
Catechesis/Religious Program—Tel: 609-883-9005. Brenda O'Callaghan, Dir. Students 115.
18—OUR LADY OF MOUNT CARMEL, Closed. For Sacramental records please contact St. Mary Cathedral, Trenton.
19—OUR LADY OF SORROWS (1939) Closed. Sacramental records maintained at Our Lady of Sorrows-St. Anthony Parish, Hamilton.
20—OUR LADY OF THE ANGELS PARISH (2005) Very Rev. Jeffrey E. Lee; Rev. Roberto Padilla; Deacon Guido Mattozzi.
Res.: 19 Bayard St., 08611. Tel: 609-695-6089; Fax: 609-695-4375. Email: olatrenton05@aol.com.
Catechesis/Religious Program—Tel: 609-695-6089, Ext. 115. Mr. Edwin Sevilland, D.R.E. Students 53.
21—OUR LADY OF THE DIVINE SHEPHERD (1941) Closed. Sacramental records maintained at Blessed Sacrament-Our Lady of the Divine Shepherd Parish, Trenton.
22—SS. PETER AND PAUL (1899) [CEM] Closed. Sacramental records maintained at Divine Mercy Parish, Trenton.
23—ST. RAPHAEL (1943) Closed. Sacramental records maintained at St. Raphael-Holy Angels Parish, Hamilton.
24—SACRED HEART (1814) [CEM] Very Rev. Dennis A. Apoldite.
Res.: 343 S. Broad St., 08608. Tel: 609-393-2801; Fax: 609-989-8997. Web: www.trentonsacredheart.org.
Catechesis/Religious Program—Mrs. Linda Teresky, Dir. Students 144.
25—ST. STANISLAUS (1890) [CEM] Closed. Sacramental records maintained at Divine Mercy Parish, Trenton.
26—ST. STEPHEN (1903) [CEM] Closed. Sacramental records maintained at Our Lady of the Angels Parish, Trenton.
27—ST. VINCENT DE PAUL (1954) Revs. Stanley Krzyston; Rogatus Mpeka.
Res.: 555 Allentown Rd., Yardville, 08620. Tel: 609-585-6470; Fax: 609-585-0137.
Catechesis/Religious Program—Tel: 609-585-5484. Johanna Kraemer, D.R.E. Students 259.

OUTSIDE THE CITY OF TRENTON

ALLENTOWN, MONMOUTH CO., ST. JOHN (1878) [CEM] Rev. Patrick J. Castles; Deacon Joseph Hepp.
Res.: 1282 Yardville-Allentown Rd., 08501-1830. Tel: 609-259-3391; Fax: 609-259-0313. Email: stjohnallentown@optonline.net. Web: www.stjohnsallentownnj.org.
Catechesis/Religious Program—Tel: 609-259-3586; Fax: 609-259-0313. Mrs. Donna Millar, C.R.E. Students 506.

ASBURY PARK, MONMOUTH CO.
1—HOLY SPIRIT (1879) [CEM] Rev. Paul Janvier, Haitian Min.; Deacon Edner Andre.
Res.: 705 2nd Ave., P.O. Box 617, 07712. Tel: 732-775-0030; Fax: 732-775-7358.
Catechesis/Religious Program—Students 40.
Mt. Calvary Cemetery—Rte. 66 and Neptune Blvd., Box 2037, Ocean, 07712. Tel: 732-775-3320.
2—OUR LADY OF MT. CARMEL (1905), (Italian), Rev. Charles J. Flood, O.SS.T. In Res., Rev. Ireneusz Ekiert, O.SS.T.
Res.: 805 Pine St., 07712. Tel: 732-775-1056; Fax: 732-775-8767.
School—First Ave. & Pine St., 07712. Tel: 732-775-8989; Fax: 732-775-0108. Sr. Jude Catherine Boyce, S.S.J., Prin. Sisters 3; Lay Teachers 14; Students 169.
Catechesis/Religious Program—Tel: 732-988-5060. Sr. Christina Aldarelli, I.H.M., D.R.E. Students 210.
3—ST. PETER CLAVER (1943), (African American), Unassigned.
Res.: 705 2nd Ave., P.O. Box 617, 07712. Tel: 732-775-0030; Fax: 732-775-7358.
Catechesis/Religious Program—Mrs. Helen Jackson, D.R.E. Students 30.

ATLANTIC HIGHLANDS, MONMOUTH CO., ST. AGNES (1890) Rev. William Dunlap; Deacons Raymond Rainville; Robert J. Johnson.
Res.: 103 Center Ave., 07716. Tel: 732-291-0272; Fax: 732-291-4982. Email: church@stagnesnj.com.
Catechesis/Religious Program—Tel: 732-291-2035. Mrs. Barbara Hardiman, D.R.E. Students 411.
Convent—44 South Ave., 07716. Tel: 732-291-8246.

AVON, MONMOUTH CO., ST. ELIZABETH (1907) Rev. Daniel Gowen.
Res.: 424 Lincoln Ave., Avon By The Sea, 07717. Tel: 732-774-4089; Fax: 732-774-5848. Email: stelizabeth@verizon.net.
Catechesis/Religious Program—Mrs. Beatrice Murday, C.R.E. Students 195.

BARNEGAT, OCEAN CO., ST. MARY (1942) [CEM] Rev. Msgr. Kenard J. Tuzeneu; Revs. Thomas Kunath; John C. Garrett; Deacons Patrick Martin; Joseph A. Fiorillo; Philip Fiore; Ronald Haunss; Joseph A. Vivona; Frank Campione; John R. Pitt; Robert Klein.
Parish Center: 100 Bishop Ln., Manahawkin, 08050.
Res.: 747 W. Bay Ave., P.O. Box 609, 08005-0609. Tel: 609-698-5531; Fax: 609-698-6255. Web: stmary.shoresurfer.com.
Catechesis/Religious Program—Tel: 609-597-7600; Fax: 609-597-7178. Web: www.stmarysrep.com. Mrs. Joan Haldenwang, D.R.E. Students 1,515.
Mission—St. Mary of the Pines 100 Bishop Ln., Manahawkin, Ocean Co. 08050.

BAY HEAD, OCEAN CO., SACRED HEART (1913) Rev. Msgr. Casimir H. Ladzinski; Deacon James Lacey.
Res.: 751 Main Ave., 08742. Tel: 732-899-1398; Fax: 732-899-2233. Email: shrcbh@comcast.net. Web: sacredheartbayhead.com.
Catechesis/Religious Program—Students 115.

BAYVILLE, OCEAN CO., ST. BARNABAS (1966) Very Rev. Kevin J. Keelen; Revs. Michael Hall; Roberto Padilla; Deacons Guy C. Rasmussen, (Retired); Michael A. Smigelski; Robert Gay; George J. Swanson.
Res.: 33 Woodland Rd., P.O. Box I, 08721. Tel: 732-269-2208; Fax: 732-269-2557. Email: stbarnabas@sbrcc.com. Web: www.stbarnabasbayville.com.
Catechesis/Religious Program—Mary Britanak, C.R.E. Students 1,404.

BELMAR, MONMOUTH CO., ST. ROSE (1888) Rev. Msgr. Edward J. Arnister; Rev. Joel R. Wilson; Deacons Normand C. Bailey; Eugene G. Malhame Jr.; Richard J. Weber; Eugene Genovese.
Res.: 603 Seventh Ave., 07719. Tel: 732-681-0512; Fax: 732-280-3107. Email: parish@strose.k12.nj.us. Web: strosebelmar.com.
School—605 Sixth Ave., 07719. Tel: 732-681-5555; Fax: 732-681-5890. Williams Roberts, Prin. Lay Teachers 21; Students 321.
High School—Tel: 732-681-2858; Fax: 732-280-2745. Sr. Kathleen Nace, S.S.J., Prin. Sisters 5; Lay Teachers 39; Students 354.
Catechesis/Religious Program—Tel: 732-681-0512, Ext. 419. Sr. Donna D'Alia, D.R.E. Students 371.
Convent—610 Eighth Ave., 07719. Tel: 732-681-1039.

BEVERLY, BURLINGTON CO., ST. JOSEPH (1864) Merged with St. Peter's, Riverside to form The Church of Jesus, the Good Shepherd, Riverside, N.J.

BORDENTOWN, BURLINGTON CO., ST. MARY (1837) [CEM] Rev. Michael J. Burns; Deacons David M. Harris Jr.; Gary T. Richardson; Thomas F. Shea; Ronald F. Zalegowski; Lawrence W. Finn Sr. In Res., Rev. Felix F. Venza, Senior Priest.
Res.: 45 Crosswicks St., 08505. Tel: 609-298-0261; Fax: 609-298-7178. Email: office@stmarysbordentown.org. Web: www.stmarysbordentown.org.
School—30 Elizabeth St., 08505. Tel: 609-298-1448; Fax: 609-298-3803. Web: www.smsbordentown.org. Dr. Frank X. McAneny, Prin. Lay Teachers 14; Students 123.
Catechesis/Religious Program—Tel: 609-291-8281; Fax: 609-298-7178. Email: office@stmarysrc.org. Web: www.stmarysre.org. Mrs. Peg Corcoran, C.R.E. Students 513.

BRADLEY BEACH, MONMOUTH CO., ASCENSION (1907) Rev. Jerome M. Nolan; Deacon John Kopcak.
Res.: 501 Brinley Ave., 07720. Tel: 732-774-0456; Fax: 732-775-9335. Email: ascensionchurch@optonline.net.
Catechesis/Religious Program—Joan Rovere, Dir. Students 121.

BRANT BEACH, OCEAN CO., ST. FRANCIS OF ASSISI (1971) Revs. Stephen Kluge, O.F.M.; John R. Ullrich, O.F.M.; Thomas E. Conway, O.F.M., Parochial Vicar; James Scullion, O.F.M.; Deacons George Walker; Richard C. Titmas; Robert Cunningham.
Office: 4700 Long Beach Blvd., 08008-3926. Tel: 609-494-8813; Fax: 609-494-1466.
Catechesis/Religious Program—Ms. Sharon Desipio, D.R.E.
Mission—St. Thomas Aquinas 2nd & Atlantic, Beach Haven, Ocean Co. 08008. Tel: 609-492-2633.
Mission—St. Clare 56th & Long Beach Blvd., Loveladies, Ocean Co. 08008. Tel: 609-494-6662.
Mission—St. Thomas of Villanova 13th & Long Beach Blvd., Surf City, Ocean Co. 08008. Tel: 609-494-2371.

BRICK TOWN, OCEAN CO.
1—ST. DOMINIC (1962) Rev. Msgr. James J. Brady; Revs. Joseph Gnarackatt; Dean A. Gaudio; Deacons Damian Ayers; Gerald Riedinger; Edward Buecker; Ms. Brigid Hughes, Pastoral Ministry.
Res.: 250 Old Squan Rd., 08724. Tel: 732-840-1410; Fax: 732-840-0522.
School—Tel: 732-840-1412; Fax: 732-840-6457. Carol Bathmann, Prin. Lay Teachers 30; Students 610.
Catechesis/Religious Program—Mrs. Ann M. Cramer, D.R.E. Students 850.
2—EPIPHANY (1973) Rev. Bernadino Esguerra; Deacons Ron Nowak; Michael Mullarkey; Louis Commisso; Rene Perez.
615 Thiele Rd., 08724.
Res.: 641 Thiele Rd., 08724. Tel: 732-458-0220; Fax: 732-458-0855. Web: www.churchofepiphany.org.
Epiphany Parish Hall—621 Herbertsville Rd., 08724. Tel: 732-840-8411.
Catechesis/Religious Program—Tel: 732-785-0576; 732-785-0872; Fax: 732-458-0855. Students 386.
3—VISITATION (1942) Revs. Albert Ricciardelli; Velanmarukudiyil Christudasl, O.S.B.; Deacons Edward Fischer III; Salvatore Vicari; David S. Kohut; Richard Johnston.
755 Mantoloking Rd., 08723.
Res. & Rectory: 730 Lynnwood Ave., 08723-5397. Tel: 732-477-0028; Fax: 732-477-1274.
Catechesis/Religious Program—Tel: 732-477-5217. Mrs. Nancy Grodberg, D.R.E. Students 770.

BROWNS MILLS, BURLINGTON CO., ST. ANN (1906) Rev. Edwin J. Mathias; Deacons Walter Price; Frank Sherpensky; Michael J. O'Brien.
Church & Res.: 22 Trenton Rd., 08015-3236. Tel: 609-893-3246; Fax: 609-893-8056. Web: stannschurch.org.
Catechesis/Religious Program—Students 185.
Station—Burlington Co. Minimum Security Jail Pemberton Township.
Station—Burlington Co. Juvenile Detention Center Pemberton.
Station—Deborah Heart & Lung Center, Tel: 609-893-6611.
Station—Evergreen Park, Buttonwood Hall, Tel: 609-726-7000.

BURLINGTON, BURLINGTON CO.
1—ALL SAINTS (1910), (Polish), Closed. For inquiries for parish records please see St. Katharine Drexel Parish, Burlington.
2—THE CHURCH OF ST. KATHARINE DREXEL, BURLINGTON, N.J. (2008) [CEM 3] Revs. Michael G. Dunn; Cesar R. Anson, Parochial Vicar; Deacons Francis A. Jones; Alfred Pennise; Alexander A. Punchello Sr.; Walter J. Karpecik Jr.
Res.: 502 High St., 08016. Tel: 609-386-0163; Fax: 609-386-0085.
School—250 James St., 08016. Tel: 609-386-1645; Fax: 609-386-1345. Mrs. Donna Lee Healy, Prin. Lay Teachers 23; Students 240.
Catechesis/Religious Program—Miss Kathryn Besheer, D.R.E. Students 450.

CINNAMINSON, BURLINGTON CO., ST. CHARLES BORROMEO (1961) Rev. Peter J. Alindogan; Deacons William S. Sepich; William Gallagher; Carl Sondeen; Gerald Doughty; John Hvizdos.
Res.: 2226 Riverton Rd., P.O. Box 2220, 08077. Tel: 856-829-3322; Fax: 856-829-1852.
School—2500 Branch Pike, 08077. Tel: 856-829-2778; Fax: 856-829-3411. Mrs. Kathryn Chesnut, Prin. Lay Teachers 20; Students 282.
Catechesis/Religious Program—Tel: 856-829-9119. Mrs. Patricia Hafner, C.R.E. Students 519.

COLTS NECK, MONMOUTH CO., ST. MARY'S (1887) Rev. Thomas J. Triggs; Deacons Paul Daniele; Caleb Weller; Fernando A. Sorrentino; Sr. Jeanne Belli, S.S.J., Pastoral Assoc.; Joe Noble, Business Mgr.; Tom Carter, Music Min.
Res.: 1 Phalanx Rd., 07722. Tel: 732-780-2666; Fax: 732-780-0394.
Catechesis/Religious Program—Tel: 732-294-8841. Mrs. Joan Celiano, D.R.E. Students 1,217.

DEAL, MONMOUTH CO., ST. MARY OF THE ASSUMPTION

(1901) Revs. Harold Cullen; Matthew Thelly.
Res.: 46 Richmond Ave., 07723. Tel: 732-531-1409; Fax: 732-531-3931.
Catechesis/Religious Program—Tel: 732-531-1889. Sr. Elizabeth Toft, D.R.E. Students 250.

DELRAN, BURLINGTON CO.
1—CHURCH OF THE HOLY NAME (1972) Merged with St. Casimir, Riverside to form The Church of the Resurrection, Delran Township, N.J.
2—THE CHURCH OF THE RESURRECTION, DELRAN TOWNSHIP, N.J. (2008) Revs. David Stachurski, O.F.M.Conv.; Hilary Brzostowski, O.F.M.Conv.; Deacons Jim Manaloris; William E. Briggs; Daniel J. Meehan.
Office: 260 Conrow Rd., P.O. Box 1099, 08075. Tel: 856-461-6555; Fax: 856-461-1293. Email: resurrection2@comcast.net. Web: www.resurrection2.org.
Res.: 502 New Jersey Ave., Riverside, 08075. Tel: 856-461-0532; Fax: 856-461-5781.
Catechesis/Religious Program—Ms. Patricia Brooks, C.R.E. Students 320.

EATONTOWN, MONMOUTH CO.
1—ST. DOROTHEA (1905) Revs. Charles M. Schwartz; Vincent Guk; Deacons Stephen W. Andrews; John A. Notaro; Edward R. Herr; Nick Donofrio; Ilsoo P. Barng; Mary Escueta, Music Min.
Res.: 240 Broad St., 07724. Tel: 732-542-0148; Fax: 732-542-1531. Email: fathchuck@stdorothea.org. Web: www.stdorothea.com.
Catechesis/Religious Program—Tel: 732-542-0303. Email: john@stdorothea.com. Students 487.
2—IMMACULATE CONCEPTION (1984), (Korean), Rev. Cha Yong (Paul) Lee, Admin.
Res.: 64 Broad St., 07724. Tel: 732-389-3830; Fax: 732-389-2705.
Catechesis/Religious Program—Gabriel Park, Dir. Students 59.

ENGLISHTOWN, MONMOUTH CO., OUR LADY OF MERCY (1948) [CEM] Merged with St. Thomas More, Manalapan.

EVESHAM TOWNSHIP, BURLINGTON CO., ST. ISAAC JOGUES (1996) Revs. Phillip C. Pfleger; Charles Muorah; Deacons Frank E. Giglio, (Retired); Armando Acosta; George V. Lytle, (Retired); David O'Connor.
3 Lord Pl., Marlton, 08053. Tel: 856-797-0999; Fax: 856-797-0463. Email: saintisaacs@stisaacjogues.org.
Catechesis/Religious Program—Tel: 856-797-1811. Web: www.rc.net/trenton/st.isaac/. Sr. Clare Sabini, D.R.E. Students 808.

FAIR HAVEN, MONMOUTH CO., CHURCH OF THE NATIVITY (1954) Very Rev. Robert J.W. Schecker; Deacon James Kelly.
Res.: 180 Ridge Rd., 07704. Tel: 732-741-1714; Fax: 732-741-6837. Email: office@nativitychurchnj.org.
Catechesis/Religious Program—Email: dre@nativitychurchnj.org. Ms. Theresa Petrik, D.R.E. Students 800.

FARMINGDALE, MONMOUTH CO., ST. CATHERINE OF SIENA (1912) Rev. Michael S. Vona (Retired); Deacon Joseph J. Prioli.
Res.: 31 Asbury Rd., P.O. Box 667, 07727-0667. Tel: 732-938-5375; Fax: 732-938-3260. Email: frontoffice@sienachurch.org. Web: www.sienachurch.org.
Catechesis/Religious Program—Email: ccd@sienachurch.org. Deacon Vincent L. Rinaldi, C.R.E. Students 491.

FLORENCE, BURLINGTON CO., ST. CLARE (1874), (Irish—Italian), [CEM] Closed. For inquiries for parish records contact the chancery.

FORKED RIVER, OCEAN CO., ST. PIUS X (1961) Rev. Richard Basznianin; Deacons James Heller; Anthony Martucci; Michael Maione; Earl Lombardo.
Res.: 300 Lacey Rd., 08731-3598. Tel: 609-693-5107; Fax: 609-693-6829.
Catechesis/Religious Program—Tel: 609-693-0368. Mrs. Patricia Colando, C.R.E. Students 1,120.

FREEHOLD, MONMOUTH CO.
1—ST. ROBERT BELLARMINE (1971) Rev. Edward M. Jawidzik; Deacons Francis J. Weber Jr.; Rolf B. Friedmann; Henry J. Cugini; Andy Smith.
61 Georgia Rd., 07728. Tel: 732-462-7429; Fax: 732-409-3496. Web: www.strobert.com. In Res., Rev. Charles R. Valentine (Retired).
Catechesis/Religious Program—Tel: 732-431-3404. Deacon Rolf B. Friedmann, D.R.E. Students 1,389.
2—ST. ROSE OF LIMA (1871) [CEM] Revs. James Conover; Francisco J. Saenz, O.P., Parochial Vicar; Roman Modino, Hispanic Ministry. Tel: 732-303-7800; Fax: 732-303-1228; Stephen M. Piga; Deacons Andrew Luhman; R. Michael McKenna; Rodolfo A. Santos.
Res.: 16 McLean St., 07728. Tel: 732-462-0859; Fax: 732-462-8173. Email: stroseoflima@verizon.net. Web: www.stroseoflima.com.
School—51 Lincoln Pl., 07728. Tel: 732-462-2646; Fax: 732-462-0331. Email: stroseoflimaschool@comcast.net. Sr. Patricia Doyle, Prin. Sisters 2; Lay Teachers 27; Students 401.
Catechesis/Religious Program—Tel: 732-308-0215; Fax: 732-308-0257. Email: stroselimare@aol.com. Mr. Steven Olson, D.R.E. Students 1,183.
Convent—81 Randolph St., 07728. Tel: 732-462-0599.

HAINESPORT, BURLINGTON CO., OUR LADY QUEEN OF PEACE (1944) Rev. Msgr. Richard L. Tofani; Deacon John J. O'Donnell.
Res.: 1603 Marne Hwy., P.O. Box 188, 08036. Tel: 609-267-0230; Fax: 609-267-0372.
Catechesis/Religious Program—Tel: 609-267-3641. Mrs. Ginny Fama, C.R.E. Students 319.

HAMILTON, MERCER CO.
1—ST. GREGORY THE GREAT (1953) Revs. Ian W. Trammell; Thomas A. Fesen; Deacons Charles M. Moscarello; Neil Pirozzi; William A. Wilson; Andrew A. Sabados Sr.; Joseph E. Latini.
Res.: 4620 Nottingham Way, Hamilton Square, 08690. Tel: 609-587-4877; Fax: 609-588-0192. Web: stgregorythegreat.org.
School—4680 Nottingham Way, Hamilton Square, 08690. Tel: 609-587-1131; Fax: 609-587-0322. Mr. Jason Briggs, Prin. Sisters 1; Lay Teachers 51; Students 515.
Catechesis/Religious Program—Dorothy Conway, D.R.E. Students 1,565.
Convent—13 Stanley Dr., Robbinsville, 08691. Tel: 609-259-3384.
2—OUR LADY OF SORROWS-ST. ANTHONY PARISH (2005) Rev. Msgr. Thomas N. Gervasio; Revs. H. Todd Carter, Parochial Vicar; Eugene K. Savarimuthu (India); Pierre M. Alabie; Deacons James J. Challender; Timothy Moore; Kevin J. O'Boyle; Dennis E. Slavin; Joseph Jaruszewski; Luders Desire.
Res.: 3816 E. State St. Ext., 08619. Tel: 609-587-4372; Fax: 609-587-7998. Email: info@ols-sa.org. Web: ols-sa.org.
School—3800 E. State St. Ext., 08619. Tel: 609-587-4140; Fax: 609-584-8853. Web: olsschool.us. Mr. Donald Costantino, Prin. Lay Teachers 19; Students 240.
Catechesis/Religious Program—Tel: 609-587-4140, Ext. 2; Fax: 609-587-4213. Email: mfrancis@ols-sa.org. Mariyan Iqbal Francis, D.R.E. Students 710.
Convent—626 S. Olden Ave., 08629. Tel: 609-586-4355.
Station—Hamilton Grove, Tel: 609-588-5859.
3—ST. RAPHAEL-HOLY ANGELS PARISH (2005) Revs. Jeffrey Kegley; Genaro Daguplo; Leandro Delacruz; Deacons Richard Arcari; Manuel Iglesias; Thomas Lavelle; Salvatore Marcello; Robert Tharp; John A. DiLissio.
Res.: 3500 S. Broad St., 08610. Tel: 609-585-7049; Fax: 609-585-5876. Web: www.straphael-holyangels.com.
School—151 Gropp Ave., 08610. Tel: 609-585-7733; Fax: 609-581-8436. Mr. Timothy M. Lynch, Prin.
Catechesis/Religious Program—Tel: 609-585-3848; Fax: 609-585-4925. William Palmisano, D.R.E. Students 227.
Station—Robert Wood Johnson University Hospital at Hamilton, Tel: 609-585-7900.

HIGHLANDS, MONMOUTH CO., OUR LADY OF PERPETUAL HELP (1883) Revs. William Dunlap; Michael J. Lynch, Parochial Vicar; Deacon Don Ronning.
Res.: 141 Navesink Ave., 07732. Tel: 732-872-1290; Fax: 732-872-2796.
Catechesis/Religious Program—Mrs. Barbara Hardiman, D.R.E. Students 192.

HIGHTSTOWN, MERCER CO., ST. ANTHONY OF PADUA (1885) Revs. Patrick J. McDonnell; Eduard Munoz; Deacons Thomas Garvey; David L. Shapiro.
Res.: 251 Franklin St., 08520-3223. Tel: 609-448-0141; Fax: 609-448-8878.
Catechesis/Religious Program—Fax: 609-448-6193. Students 1,100.

HOLMDEL, MONMOUTH CO.
1—ST. BENEDICT (1959) Revs. Daniel F. Swift; Richard C. Vila; Deacons Raymond R. Pelkowski; Richard L. Morris; Stephen G. Scott; Catherine Warshaw, Parish Admin.; Tony Malone, Business & Finance Mgr.
Res.: 165 Bethany Rd., 07733-1699. Tel: 732-264-4712; Fax: 732-264-9080. Email: parish_office@stbenedictnj.org.
School—Tel: 732-264-5578; Fax: 732-264-8679. Mary Ellen Lilly, Prin. Lay Teachers 27; Students 512.
Catechesis/Religious Program—Tel: 732-264-4714; 732-264-4712, Ext. 24. Denise Contino, C.R.E.; Lori McCahill, Youth Min. Students 556.
2—ST. CATHARINE (1879) Rev. Msgr. Eugene M. Rebeck; Deacons John P. Flanagan; Christopher L. Hansen; Thomas J. DiCanio; Michael Lonie; Kathleen McBurnie, Pastoral Assoc.
Res.: P.O. Box 655, 07733. Tel: 732-842-3963; Fax: 732-842-9283. Email: parishoffice@stcatherine.net. Web: www.stcatherine.net.
Catechesis/Religious Program—Tel: 732-842-3963, Ext. 19. Mrs. Dominica Vullo, C.R.E. Students 1,146.

HOPEWELL, MERCER CO., ST. ALPHONSUS (1877) [CEM] Rev. Alex Enriquez; Deacons Robert Lafond; John Grant.
Res.: 54 E. Prospect St., 08525. Tel: 609-466-0332; Fax: 609-466-2023. Web: www.rc.net/trenton/stalphonnsus/.
Catechesis/Religious Program—Tel: 609-466-2694. Joan Wielenta, A.R.E. Students 180.

HOWELL TOWNSHIP, MONMOUTH CO.
1—ST. VERONICA (1962) Very Rev. H. Brendan Williams; Rev. Vicente Magdaraog (Philippines); Deacons Gene F. Moir Sr.; Theodore V. Gularek; James Littlefield; Tomasz Cechulski; Charles Daye Jr.
Res.: 4215 Hwy. 9 N., 07731. Tel: 732-363-4200; Fax: 732-370-3891.
School—4219 Hwy. 9 N., 07731. Tel: 732-364-4130; Fax: 732-363-4932. Sr. Cherree Ann Power, Prin. Sisters 3; Lay Teachers 20; Students 336.
Catechesis/Religious Program—Tel: 732-364-4137; Fax: 732-886-5064. Brenda Heffernan, D.R.E. Students 1,298.
Convent—4217 Hwy. 9 N., 07731. Tel: 732-364-2361.
2—ST. WILLIAM THE ABBOT (1985) Rev. Oscar B. Sumanga; Deacons Michael Abatemarco; Kevin Smith; George A. Prevosti Jr.
Mailing Address & Church: 2740 Lakewood-Allenwood Rd., 07731. Tel: 732-840-3535; Fax: 732-840-3663. Email: stwilliam@optonline.net. Web: www.stwilliamtheabbot.com.
Res.: 2400 Allenwood-Lakewood Rd., P.O. Box 500, Allenwood, 08720. Tel: 732-840-3628.
Catechesis/Religious Program—Mrs. Mary Cleary, C.R.E. Students 635.
Station—Geraldine Thompson Nursing Home 2350 Hospital Rd., Allenwood, 08720. Tel: 732-938-5250.

JACKSON, OCEAN CO.
1—ST. ALOYSIUS (1964) Very Rev. G. Scott Shaffer; Revs. Fernando A. Lopez; Matthew L. Riedlinger; Sr. Eileen Ivory, O.P., Pastoral Assoc.; Deacons Rene Perez; Frank Jackson; Uku Mannikus; John Wanat; Jennifer Schlameuss-Perry, Pastoral Assoc.
Res.: 935 Bennetts Mills Rd., P.O. Box 1285, 08527. Tel: 732-370-0500; Fax: 732-886-9336. Web: www.saintaloysiusonline.org.
School—Saint Aloysius Grammar School, Tel: 732-370-1515; Fax: 732-370-3555. Web: www.staloysiusschool.com. Ms. Elizabeth O'Connor, Prin. Lay Teachers 28; Students 350.
Catechesis/Religious Program—Tel: 732-370-1515. Ms. Rosemary V. Perry, D.R.E. Students 1,650.
2—CHURCH OF ST. MONICA (1953) Very Rev. G. Scott Shaffer; Rev. Thomas Petrillo; Deacon Michael Principato.
679 W. Veteran's Hwy., 08527. Tel: 732-928-0279; Fax: 732-928-1853. Email: stmonicanj@yahoo.com. Web: www.saintmonica.com.
Catechesis/Religious Program—Tel: 732-928-4038. Email: stmonicaccd@yahoo.com. Karen Badach, C.R.E. Students 415.

JOBSTOWN, BURLINGTON CO., ST. ANDREW'S CHURCH, JOBSTOWN (1880) Rev. Joseph G. Hlubik, Admin.; Deacons John F. Hoefling; Daniel Chase.
2489 Monmouth Rd., 08041. Tel: 609-723-4243.
Catechesis/Religious Program—Celeste Grant, D.R.E.

KEANSBURG, MONMOUTH CO., ST. ANN (1924) Revs. Daniel Cahill; Silvano B. Amora; Angelo Amaral.
Res.: 311 Carr Ave., 07734. Tel: 732-787-0315; Fax: 732-787-5254. Email: stannkean@aol.com. Web: stannchurch.catholicworld.info/.
St. Ann Child Care Center—121 Main St., 07734. Tel: 732-787-7220; Fax: 732-787-2136. Students 65.
Catechesis/Religious Program—Tel: 732-787-5744. Sr. Mary Cleary, R.S.M., D.R.E. Students 570.
Bayshore Senior Health, Education & Recreation Center—100 Main St., 07734. Tel: 732-495-2454; Fax: 732-495-7897. Sisters 2; Seniors Served 1,350.
Project Paul—211 Carr Ave., 07734. Tel: 732-787-4887; Fax: 732-495-7072.

KEYPORT, MONMOUTH CO.
1—JESUS THE LORD (1978) Rev. Kenneth W. Ekdahl.
Res.: 123 Broad St., 07735-1203. Tel: 732-739-0323; Fax: 732-264-8276.
Church: 120 Broad St., 07735.
Catechesis/Religious Program—Ms. Anne Biagianti, C.R.E. Students 128.
2—ST. JOSEPH (1854) [CEM] Revs. Ronald J. Cioffi; Nestor Chavenia; Cyril Johnson; Deacons Donald M. Policastro; Glen L. Mendonca.
Res.: 376 Maple Pl., 07735. Tel: 732-264-0322; Fax: 732-888-3280.
Catechesis/Religious Program—Tel: 732-264-0304. Ms. Kay Hetherington, D.R.E. Students 206.

LAKEHURST, OCEAN CO., ST. JOHN (1969) Rev. Bernard Keigher; Deacons Edward Holowienka; Ronald Kerr; Robert Gooden; Michael Pirylis; Robert Diehl; Richard T. Glogoza.
Res.: 619 Chestnut St., 08733. Tel: 732-657-6347;

Fax: 732-657-8690.
Catechesis/Religious Program—Tel: 732-657-2348; Fax: 732-657-8105. Mrs. Mary Ann Dempkowski, D.R.E. Students 415.

LAKEWOOD, OCEAN CO.

1—ST. ANTHONY CLARET (1977), (Hispanic Parish for Ocean Co.) Revs. Pedro L. Bou, S.V.D.; Pelagio Calambia Pateno, S.V.D.
Res.: 780 Ocean Ave., 08701-3644. Tel: 732-367-8486; Fax: 732-367-0460. Email: svdclaret@aol.com.
Catechesis/Religious Program—David Roman, D.R.E. Students 370.

2—ST. MARY OF THE LAKE (1889) [CEM] Revs. Michael J. O'Connor; John O. Chang; Edward H. Blanchett; Bernadino Esguerra; Deacons Vincent Riccardi; Silverius Galvan; John Cullinane; Anthony Martucci, Pastoral Min.; Sr. Geraldine Contento, M.P.F., Pastoral Min.
Res.: 43 Madison Ave., 08701. Tel: 732-363-0139; Fax: 732-905-1410.
School—Holy Family School, 1141 E. County Line Rd., 08701. Tel: 732-363-4771; Fax: 732-363-3146. Elaine Bicher, Prin. Lay Teachers 26; Students 492.
Catechesis/Religious Program—Tel: 732-363-3043; Fax: 732-961-0382. Donna Marie Clancy, D.R.E. Students 550.
Mission—Holy Family Church, Ocean Co. Fax: 732-905-1410.

LAVALLETTE, OCEAN CO., THE CHURCH OF ST. PIO OF PIETRECLINA, LAVALLETTE, N.J. (1921) Rev. Msgr. Leonard F. Troiano.
Res.: 103 Washington Ave., 08735. Tel: 732-793-7291; Fax: 732-793-8204.
Catechesis/Religious Program—Tel: 732-793-3020. Sr. Geraldine Contento, D.R.E. Students 22.

LAWRENCEVILLE, MERCER CO.

1—ST. ANN (1937) Rev. Msgr. R. Vincent Gartland; Rev. Kevin J. Kimtis; Sr. Beth Dempsey, R.S.M., Pastoral Assoc.; Deacons Thomas J. Everist; Edward A. Hoag; James Scott; Mr. Gary Maccaroni, Pastoral Assoc.; Christine Barranco, Pastoral Assoc.
School—34 Rossa Ave., 08648. Tel: 609-882-8077; Fax: 609-882-0327. Mr. John McKenna, Prin. Lay Teachers 24; Students 283.
Catechesis/Religious Program—Tel: 609-882-1212. Mrs. Kelly Wolf, D.R.E. Students 765.

2—THE CHURCH OF THE KOREAN MARTYRS (1994), (Korean), Rev. In hoo Bae, Admin. Email: baegepa@gmail.com.
Mailing Address: 1130 Brunswick Ave., 08638.
Catechesis/Religious Program—Students 45.

LINCROFT, MONMOUTH CO., ST. LEO THE GREAT (1958) Revs. John T. Folchetti; Marcin Kania, Parochial Vicar; Joseph M. Quinlan (Retired); Sr. Ann Barry, S.S.J., Pastoral Assoc.; Deacons Joseph DePaolis; Edward H. Wilson.
Res.: 50 Hurley's Ln., 07738. Tel: 732-747-5466; Fax: 732-219-5181. Email: parish@stleothegreat.com. Web: stleothegreat.com.
School—550 Newman-Springs Rd., 07738. Tel: 732-741-3133; Fax: 732-741-2241. Web: saintleothegreatschool.com. Joanne Kowit, Prin. Lay Teachers 33; Students 650.
Catechesis/Religious Program—Tel: 732-530-0717. Email: slreled@aol.com. Ms. Margaret Lang, D.R.E. Students 1,100.

LONG BRANCH, MONMOUTH CO.

1—THE CHURCH OF CHRIST THE KING, LONG BRANCH, N.J. (2009) [CEM] Revs. Daniel Peirano; Thomas M. Vala.
Business Office: 380 Division St., 07740. Tel: 732-222-3216; Fax: 732-222-4313.
Catechesis/Religious Program— Mrs. Madeline Ottino, C.R.E.; Mrs. Amelia Flego, C.R.E. Students 426.

2—HOLY TRINITY (1906) Closed. For inquiries for parish records contact the chancery. Rev. Sam A. Sirianni.

3—ST. JOHN THE BAPTIST (1984) Closed. For inquiries for parish records contact the chancery.

4—ST. MICHAEL (1885) Rev. Charles B. Weiser; Deacon Eugene A. Somma.
Res.: 800 Ocean Ave., West End, 07740. Tel: 732-222-8080; Fax: 732-870-1174. Email: stmichael@monmouth.com. Web: www.stmichaels-westend.com.
Catechesis/Religious Program—Tel: 732-483-0360; Fax: 732-483-0363. Email: outreachcenter@monmouth.com. Students 440.

MANALAPAN, MONMOUTH CO., ST. THOMAS MORE (1970) Revs. Mark W. Crane; Peter Kochery, Parochial Vicar; Asirvatham J. Selvam, Parochial Vicar; Deacons Keith J. Casey; James Davis; John J. Zebrowski; Mr. Steven Russell, Dir. Sacred Music; Mrs. Vincenza Magliano, Admin.
Res.: 186 Gordons Corner Rd., 07726. Tel: 732-446-6661; Fax: 732-446-6507.
Catechesis/Religious Program—Tel: 732-446-3232. Linda K. Andrew, D.R.E. Students 1,716.

MANASQUAN, MONMOUTH CO., ST. DENIS (1909) Very Rev. Stanley P. Lukaszewski; Rev. Msgr. Frederick A. Valentino (Retired); Rev. Joseph J. Miele (Retired); Sr. Josephine Wade, S.S.J., Pastoral Assoc.; Deacons George R. Kelder Jr.; Donald L. Perusi; Gary J. Pstrak.
Res.: 90 Union Ave., 08736. Tel: 732-223-0287; Fax: 732-528-1901. Email: st.denis@verizon.net. Web: www.churchofstdenis.org.
School—119 Virginia Ave., 08736. Tel: 732-223-4928; Fax: 732-223-1807. Web: stdenisonline.org. Trudy Bonavita, Prin. Lay Teachers 15; Students 162.
Catechesis/Religious Program—Tel: 732-223-1161. Ms. Barbara Evans, D.R.E. Students 1,000.
Chapel—Our Lady Star of the Sea Chapel 544 E. Main St., 08736.

MAPLE SHADE, BURLINGTON CO., OUR LADY OF PERPETUAL HELP (1920) Revs. Robert Holtz; Cesar Tolentino; Deacons Joseph A. Card; Michael P. Boehm, Pastoral Assoc.; Ronald S. Meyers; Fernando Linka.
Res.: 236 E. Main St., 08052. Tel: 856-667-8850; 856-667-3772 (Pastoral Care Office); Fax: 856-667-1046. Email: parishsec@olphparish.com. Web: www.olphparish.com.
School—236 E. Main St., 08052. Tel: 856-779-7526, Ext. 225; Fax: 856-667-3083. Email: olphmsprn@yahoo.com. Donna Satkowski, Prin. Sisters 1; Lay Teachers 14; Students 206.
Catechesis/Religious Program—Tel: 856-779-7529. Email: religiousedolphparish.com. Mrs. Michelle Salvino, C.R.E. Students 348.

MARLBORO, MONMOUTH CO., ST. GABRIEL (1885) [CEM] Revs. Eugene J. Roberts; Joy T. Chacko, Parochial Vicar; Deacons James C. Russo; Lester Owens; Stephen Sansevere, Pastoral Admin.; Richard Scotti.
Res.: 100 N. Main St., 07746. Tel: 732-946-4487; Fax: 732-946-7276.
Catechesis/Religious Program—Fax: 732-946-2080. Dr. James J. Bridges, D.R.E. Students 1,640.

MARLTON, BURLINGTON CO., ST. JOAN OF ARC (1961) Rev. Msgr. Richard D. LaVerghetta; Rev. Michael Wallack; Sr. Peg Boyle, S.S.J., Pastoral Assoc.; Deacons Barry Tarzy; George Johnston; Jeffrey DeFrehn; William R. Mueller.
Church & Res.: 100 Willow Bend Rd., 08053. Tel: 856-983-0077; Fax: 856-983-7716. Web: stjoans.org.
School—101 Evans Rd., 08053. Tel: 856-983-0774; Fax: 856-983-3270. Web: stjoansk-8.org. Sr. Patricia Pycik, S.S.J., Prin. Sisters of St. Joseph 2; Lay Teachers 25; Students 395.
Catechesis/Religious Program—Tel: 856-983-7575; Fax: 856-983-3479. Email: linda.mueller@stjoans.org. Mrs. Linda Mueller, D.R.E. Students 1,200.
Convent—99 Evans Rd., 08053. Tel: 856-983-7575.

MATAWAN, MONMOUTH CO., ST. CLEMENT (1965) Revs. John J. Scully; Philip Ruggiero; Deacons Mark Micali; Tom Wadolowski.
Res.: 172 Freneau Ave., 07747. Tel: 732-566-3616; Fax: 732-566-9275.
Catechesis/Religious Program—Tel: 732-591-8090. Patricia Thein, C.R.E. Students 801.

MEDFORD, BURLINGTON CO., ST. MARY OF THE LAKES (1943) Rev. Msgr. James H. Dubell; Revs. Richard C. Vila; Charles Muorah; Deacons Joseph R. Patton; W. Norman Talbot; Joseph Tedeschi.
Res.: 40 Jackson Rd., 08055. Tel: 609-654-8208; Fax: 609-654-1734.
School—196 Rte. 70, 08055. Tel: 609-654-2546; Fax: 609-654-8125. Mrs. Paula P. Angilletta, Prin. Sisters of St. Francis of Philadelphia 2; Sisters of St. Joseph 4; Lay Teachers 23; Students 482.
Catechesis/Religious Program—196 Rte. 70, 08055. Tel: 609-654-8243; Fax: 609-953-8630. Mrs. Cathleen Sheridan, D.R.E. Students 1,388.
Convent—Sisters of St. Francis, 27 Schoolhouse Dr., 08055. Tel: 609-654-5896.
Convent—Sisters of St. Joseph, 24 Summerhill Lane, 08055. Tel: 609-654-1941.
St. Vincent DePaul Society-Medford—P.O. Box 1131, 08055. Tel: 609-953-0021; Fax: 609-953-2432. Mr. Paul V. Cannon, Treas.

MIDDLETOWN, MONMOUTH CO.

1—ST. CATHERINE (1948) Rev. Daniel C. Hesko; Deacons John C. Orlando; John G. McGrath; Martin K. McMahon; L. Jacqueline Callahan, Pastoral Ministry.
Res.: 130 Bray Ave., 07748. Tel: 732-787-1318; Fax: 732-787-2851. Web: www.stcathek.org.
Catechesis/Religious Program—Tel: 732-495-7779; Fax: 732-495-7779. Mrs. L. Jackie Callahan, D.R.E. Students 548.

2—ST. MARY (1878) Rev. Msgr. Michael J. Walsh; Revs. Joselito M. Noche; Carlos A. Florez; Deacons Charles J. Smith; Robert F. Scharen; Carlo Squicciarini.
Res.: 19 Cherry Tree Farm Rd., 07748. Tel: 732-671-0071; Fax: 732-671-6125. Email: stmarynm@aol.com. Web: www.stmarychurchnj.org.
School—538 Church St., New Monmouth, 07748. Tel: 732-671-0129; Fax: 732-671-2653. Web: stmarye-s.org. Charles Kroekel, Prin.; Dennis Poracky, Asst. Prin. Lay Teachers 42; Students 703.
High School—Mater Dei Prep, Tel: 732-671-9100; Fax: 732-671-9214. Web: www.materdeihs.org. Mr. Steven Sciarappa, Prin. Lay Teachers 41; Students 286.
Catechesis/Religious Program—Tel: 732-671-8550; Fax: 732-671-6125. Sr. Sharon Santos, F.C.L.G., D.R.E. Students 1,193.

MONMOUTH BEACH, MONMOUTH CO., CHURCH OF THE PRECIOUS BLOOD (1947) Revs. Robert F. Kaeding; John J. Testa, Parochial Vicar.
Res.: 72 Riverdale Ave., 07750. Tel: 732-222-4756; Fax: 732-759-8212.
Catechesis/Religious Program—Tel: 732-963-9982. Eileen Lang, D.R.E. Students 334.

MOORESTOWN, BURLINGTON CO., OUR LADY OF GOOD COUNSEL (1879) [CEM] Very Rev. Damian J. McElroy; Rev. James O'Neill, Parochial Vicar; Deacons James J. Grogan; Joseph A. Paul, (Retired); Stephen J. Lucasi, Dir. of Sacred Music; Deacons David F. Papuga, Business Mgr.; Edward A. Heffernan; Thomas D. Begley III; Thomas F. Kolon; John F. Bertagnolli.
Res.: 42 W. Main St., 08057. Tel: 856-235-0181; Fax: 856-235-4987. Web: www.olgcnj.org.
School—23 W. Prospect St., 08057. Tel: 856-235-7885; Fax: 856-235-2570. Jerome McGowan, Prin. Dominic Sisters of Hope 1; Lay Teachers 28; Students 515.
Catechesis/Religious Program—Tel: 856-235-2354. Dr. Linda M. Dix, D.R.E. Students 1,500.

MOUNT HOLLY, BURLINGTON CO.

1—CHRIST THE REDEEMER (1976), (Hispanic), Rev. Joseph L. Roldan; Deacons Michael Adorno; Eduardo Trani; Brando Duarte.
Res.: 113 South Ave., 08060. Tel: 609-261-0181; Fax: 609-702-0017.
Catechesis/Religious Program—426 Pine St., Mt. Holly, 08060. Students 65.

2—SACRED HEART (1848) [CEM] Rev. John P. Czahur; Deacons Louis C. Restivo; James Casa; Amado F. Acosta; William Rowley; Leo Zito; Stanley Orkis; Michael Auleta.
Res.: 260 High St., 08060-1404. Tel: 609-267-0209; Fax: 609-267-9293.
School—250 High St., 08060. Tel: 609-267-1728; Fax: 609-267-4476. Mrs. Priscilla Vimislik, Prin. Lay Teachers 27; Students 331.
Catechesis/Religious Program—Tel: 609-267-6319; Fax: 609-518-9010. Mrs. Deborah Clardy, D.R.E. Students 900.
Station—County Jail, Tel: 609-267-3300.
Station—Burlington County Hospital Extended Care Center, Tel: 609-367-0700.

MOUNT LAUREL, BURLINGTON CO., ST. JOHN NEUMANN (1978) Revs. Lino S. Parente, O.Cist. (Italy); Maurizio Nicoletti, O.Cist. (Italy); Deacons James Cattanea; Joseph Barbara.
Res.: 560 Walton Ave., 08054. Tel: 856-235-1330; Fax: 856-235-9632.
Catechesis/Religious Program—Tel: 856-235-6555. Email: stjohnneumannmtlre@comcast.net. Web: www.sjncatholicchurch.org. Mrs. Helen Graziano, D.R.E. Students 626.

NEPTUNE, MONMOUTH CO.

1—HOLY INNOCENTS (1959) Revs. John T. Jakub; Evarist Kabagambe; Deacons James Walsh; John Klincewicz; Robert L. Cerefice.
Res.: 3455 W. Bangs Ave., P.O. Box 806, 07753. Tel: 732-922-4242; Fax: 732-922-2848.
School—3455 W. Bangs Ave., 07753. Tel: 732-922-3141; Fax: 732-922-6531. Cynthia Reimer, Prin. Lay Teachers 15; Students 182.
Catechesis/Religious Program—Tel: 732-922-4242, Ext. 20; Fax: 732-922-3752. Sr. Bernadette Schuler, O.S.F., D.R.E. Students 502.
Station—Convacenter Nursing Home, Tel: 732-774-3500.
Station—Imperial Nursing Home, Tel: 732-922-3400.
Station—Heritage Hall Nursing Home 07754. Tel: 732-922-9330.
Station—Medicenter Nursing Home 07754. Tel: 732-774-8300.
Station—The Lodge, Kings Manor, Tel: 732-922-1900.

2—OUR LADY OF PROVIDENCE (1981), (Spanish), Rev. Miguel Virella, S.V.D.
Res.: 1228 Fifth Ave., 07753. Tel: 732-776-7164; Fax: 732-776-7825.
Catechesis/Religious Program—Vanessa Otero, D.R.E. Students 133.

NEW EGYPT, OCEAN CO., THE CHURCH OF THE ASSUMPTION (1853) [CEM] Rev. Joseph J. Farrell; Deacons Raymond W. Staub Jr.; Vincent P. Ricciardi Sr.; Anthony Mammoliti; Mr. Mark Hoeler, Music Min.; Mary Steen, Business Mgr.
Res.: 76 Evergreen Rd., 08533. Tel: 609-758-2153; Fax: 609-758-6240. Web: www.churchoftheassumption.com.

Catechesis/Religious Program—Email: assumptionreled@aol.com. Mrs. Diane Gregorio, D.R.E. Students 630.

NORMANDY BEACH, OCEAN CO., OUR LADY OF PEACE (1979) Closed. For inquiries for parish records contact the chancery.

PENNINGTON, MERCER CO., ST. JAMES (1897) Rev. Msgr. Ronald J. Bacovin; Deacons James W. Palsir; Samuel Sciarrotta; Richard Currie; William Moore Hank.
Res.: 115 E. Delaware Ave., 08534. Tel: 609-737-0122; Fax: 609-737-6912. Email: stjames1@verizon.net. Web: www.stjames-nj.org.
Catechesis/Religious Program—Tel: 609-737-2717. Email: stjred@verizon.net. Nancy Lucash, D.R.E. Students 535.

PERRINEVILLE, MONMOUTH CO., ST. JOSEPH (1879) Rev. Michael P. Lang.
91 Stillhouse Rd., Millstone Township, 08510. Tel: 732-792-2270; Fax: 732-792-2271. Email: frmikestjoseph@optonline.net.
Catechesis/Religious Program—Jean Semanchick, C.R.E. Students 890.

POINT PLEASANT BEACH, OCEAN CO., ST. PETER'S (1882) Revs. Robert Benko, O.F.M.; Crispin Fuino, O.F.M.Conv. (Retired); Paul Varga, O.F.M.Conv., Parochial Vicar; Deacons George M. Korbelak; Thomas Loughran; Dawn Rusinko, Pastoral Assoc. In Res., Rev. Andrzej Brzezinski, O.F.M.Conv. (Poland).
Res.: 406 Forman Ave., 08742. Tel: 732-892-0049; Fax: 732-295-9782. Web: www.saintpetersonline.org.
School—415 Atlantic Ave., 08742. Tel: 732-892-1260; Fax: 732-892-3488. Email: info@stpschool.org. Web: www.stpschool.org. Kathleen Berlino, Prin. Lay Teachers 16; Students 194.
Catechesis/Religious Program—Tel: 732-899-4839; Fax: 732-899-6841. Email: religioused@saintpetersonline.org. Mrs. Merrie Brambilla, D.R.E. Students 428.
Convent—401 Atlantic Ave., 08742. Tel: 732-899-2390.

POINT PLEASANT, OCEAN CO., ST. MARTHA (1972) Rev. Michael D. Sullivan; Deacons John Haney; John Gimblett; Francis Groff; Ted Kotz; John Fiorelli, Business Admin. & Lay Ecclesial Min.; Bridget L. Homes, Youth Min. & Pastoral Counselor; Maryann Collett, Pastoral Assoc. & Lay Ecclesial Min.; Richard Andrejack, Lay Ecclesial Min.; Anne Matthews, Lay Ecclesial Min.
Res. & Mailing Address: 3800 Herbertsville Rd., 08742. Tel: 732-295-3630; Fax: 732-295-9315. Web: www.saintmartha.net.
Catechesis/Religious Program—Tel: 732-295-3630, Ext. 48; Fax: 732-295-9325. Jane Shaheen, D.R.E.; Catherine Giza, C.R.E.; Florence Egan, Jr. High Youth Min. Students 1,030.

PRINCETON, MERCER CO., ST. PAUL (1864) [CEM] Rev. Msgr. Joseph N. Rosie; Rev. Michael T. McClane; Deacons Paul LaChance; Joseph Kupin; Jim Knipper; Frank Crivello.
Res.: 214 Nassau St., 08542. Tel: 609-924-1743; Fax: 609-924-7510. Web: www.stpaulsprinceton.org.
School—218 Nassau St., 08542. Tel: 609-921-7587; Fax: 609-921-0264. Ryan Killeen, Prin. Sisters 3; Lay Teachers 30; Students 368.
Catechesis/Religious Program—Tel: 609-924-1743, Ext. 118. Mr. Martin J. Arsenault, D.R.E. Students 486.
Convent—216 Nassau St., 08540. Tel: 609-924-4414.

RED BANK, MONMOUTH CO.

1—ST. ANTHONY (1920), (Italian), Revs. Anthony M. Carotenuto; Jose Fernandez Bangueses; Deacon Arthur Fama.
Res.: 121 Bridge Ave., 07701. Tel: 732-747-0813; Fax: 732-224-0059. Email: st_anthonys@comcast.net.
Catechesis/Religious Program—Mrs. Michele McCue, D.R.E.; Roxane La Mont, Music Dir. Students 525.

2—ST. JAMES (1864) [CEM] Rev. Msgr. Philip A. Lowery; Revs. Ariel Robles; Christopher P. Picollo, Parochial Vicar; Daison Areepparampil; Deacon Bryan Davis.
Res.: 94 Broad St., 07701. Tel: 732-741-0500; Fax: 732-741-1489.
Preschool—Tel: 732-933-1041. Lay Teachers 3; Students 48.
School—*St. James Grammar School*, 30 Peters Pl., 07701. Tel: 732-741-3363; Fax: 732-933-4960. Mr. William A. Cardone, Prin. Lay Teachers 31; Students 528.
High School—*Red Bank Catholic High School*, 112 Broad St., 07701. Tel: 732-747-1774; Fax: 732-747-1936. Robert Abatemarco, Prin. Sisters 5; Lay Teachers 106; Students 1,069.
Catechesis/Religious Program—Tel: 732-747-6006. Mrs. Mary Ellen Connolly, C.R.E. Students 650.
Convent—*Sisters of Mercy*, 25 Drummond Pl., 07701. Tel: 732-741-0724.
Station—*Riverview Hospital*, Tel: 732-530-2231; Fax: 732-530-2394.

RIVERSIDE, BURLINGTON CO.

1—ST. CASIMIR (1913), (Polish), Merged with Church of the Holy Name, Delran to form The Church of the Resurrection, Delran Township, N.J.

2—THE CHURCH OF JESUS, THE GOOD SHEPHERD, RIVERSIDE, N.J. (2008) Revs. Edward H. Blanchett; Ricardo Benitez; Deacons Joseph Fuoco; Herman J. Mosteller; Matthew J. Stap, (Retired); Michael J. Hagan; Salvatore Lancieri; Debbie Cunningham, Music Min.
101 Middleton St., 08075. Tel: 856-461-0100; Fax: 856-764-6133.
Catechesis/Religious Program—Tel: 856-461-9343. Mrs. Maria B. Gimello, D.R.E. Students 368.

3—ST. PETER (1878) [CEM] Merged with St. Joseph, Beverly to form The Church of Jesus, the Good Shepherd, Riverside, N.J.

RIVERTON, BURLINGTON CO., SACRED HEART (1878) Revs. Michael J. Waites; Roberto Ignacio; Deacons Joseph M. Donadieu; Michael J. Stinsman; Kenneth W. Heilig; James E. Morton; Mark McKeever, Music Min. In Res., Rev. James T. Dever, O.S.F.S.
Res.: 103 Fourth St., 08077. Tel: 856-829-0090; Fax: 856-829-2087. Email: sacredheartriverton@comcast.net. Web: www.shcriverton.org.
Catechesis/Religious Program—Tel: 856-829-1848; Fax: 856-829-7404. Mrs. Patricia Hutchinson, D.R.E. Students 689.

ROEBLING, BURLINGTON CO., THE CHURCH OF SAINTS FRANCIS AND CLARE, FLORENCE TOWNSHIP, N.J. (1913) Rev. Adam Midor; Deacons Michael V. Scannella; James A. Manaloris.
Res.: 1290 Hornberger Ave., 08554. Tel: 609-499-0161; Fax: 866-422-4690.
Catechesis/Religious Program—Mrs. Peggy Schwoebel, C.R.E. Students 110.

RUMSON, MONMOUTH CO., HOLY CROSS (1884) Rev. Michael Manning; Eugenia Kelly, Pastoral Assoc.; Roger Trendowski, Business Admin.; Lori La Plante, Pastoral Assoc.
Res.: 30 Ward Ave., 07760. Tel: 732-842-0348; Fax: 732-842-3226. Email: webmaster@holycrossrumson.org. Web: www.holycrossrumson.org.
School—(Grades PreK-8), 40 Rumson Rd., 07760. Tel: 732-842-0348; Fax: 732-741-3134. Patricia Graham, Prin. Lay Teachers 30; Students 450.
Catechesis/Religious Program—Sally Kabash, C.R.E.; Michael Feerst, Youth Min. Students 600.

SEA GIRT, MONMOUTH CO., ST. MARK (1953) Rev. Msgr. Sean P. Flynn; Rev. Rodolfo Gonzalez-Ballesteros (Colombia); Deacons Dennis Saake, Business Admin.; Michael P. Grogan.
Res.: 215 Crescent Pkwy., 08750. Tel: 732-449-6364; Fax: 732-449-1646. Email: st.markseagirt@verizon.net. Web: stmarkseagirt.com.
Catechesis/Religious Program—Tel: 732-449-6364, Ext. 105. Mrs. Mary Ann Hirsch, D.R.E. Students 350.

SEASIDE HEIGHTS, OCEAN CO., OUR LADY OF PERPETUAL HELP (1942) Rev. Richard Rossell, O.F.M.Conv. In Res., Bro. Nicholas Lorson.
Res.: 100 Grant Ave., 08751. Tel: 732-793-6881; Fax: 732-793-7632. Email: olph2@optonline.net. Web: ourladyph.com.
Catechesis/Religious Program—Tammy Garcia, C.R.E.

SEASIDE PARK, OCEAN CO., ST. CATHARINE OF SIENA (1906) Rev. John L. Ruffo, O.F.M.Conv. In Res., Revs. Augustine Kapinus, O.F.M.Conv.; Terence Pescatore, O.F.M.Conv.; Christopher Balas, O.F.M.Conv.; Conall McHugh, O.F.M.Conv.; Eric Fenner, O.F.M.Conv.; Emmett Carroll, O.F.M.Conv.
Res.: 50 E. St., Box A, 08752. Tel: 732-793-0041; Fax: 732-793-6252. Email: stcatharines@optonline.net. Web: www.stcatharinesiena.com.
Catechesis/Religious Program—Renee Casadonte, C.R.E. Students 249.

SPRING LAKE, MONMOUTH CO., ST. CATHARINE (1901) [CEM 2] Rev. Msgr. Thomas A. Luebking; Rev. Raymond E. Hughes; Deacons Edward Jennings; John L. Little.
School—301 2nd Ave. Tel: 732-449-4424; Fax: 732-449-7876. Sr. Margo Kavanaugh, R.S.M., Prin. Sisters 2; Lay Teachers 24; Students 411.
Catechesis/Religious Program—Mrs. Tamara Sablom, C.R.E. Students 633.
Convent—211 Essex Ave., 07762. Tel: 732-449-5765; Fax: 732-449-7876.
Mission—*St. Margaret* 300 Ludlow Ave., Monmouth Co. 07762.

TABERNACLE, BURLINGTON CO., HOLY EUCHARIST (1982) Rev. Andrew Jamieson; Deacons Joseph De Luca; Kenneth S. Domzalski; Anthony Repice; Chris Murphy; Sr. Geraldine Muller, S.S.J., Pastoral Assoc.; Lynette DeTata, Pastoral Assoc.; Linda Midura, Dir. of Music.
Office: 520 Medford Lakes Rd., 08088. Tel: 609-268-8383; Fax: 609-268-3294.
Catechesis/Religious Program—Tel: 609-268-7742. Anne Marie Kelly, C.R.E. Students 612.
Station—*New Lisbon Developmental Center* New Lisbon. Tel: 609-726-1000.
Station—*Leisuretown Senior Citizen Community* Southampton.

TOMS RIVER, OCEAN CO.

1—ST. JOSEPH (Dover Township) (1883) [CEM] Revs. John P. Bambrick; Leon Salvador A. Buni; Patrick McPartland; Deacons Francis J. Babuschak; Edwin L. Voll Jr.; Frank J. McKenna; Romeo D. Aquino; Robert M. Barnes; Gerard Luongo; David L. Shapiro; Patrick J. Stesner Sr.; Michael A. Taylor; Thomas Genovese; Sr. Mary Anthony, O.P., Church Mgr.; Thomas Halpin, Music Min.; Jacqueline Mack, Business Admin.
Mailing Address: 685 Hooper Ave., 08753. Tel: 732-349-0018; Fax: 732-286-7064. Email: parish@stjosephtomsriver.org. Web: www.stjosephtomsriver.org.
School—711 Hooper Ave., 08753. Tel: 732-349-2355; Fax: 732-349-1064. Web: stjoeschooltr.org. Mrs. Michele Williams, Prin. Lay Teachers 37; Students 624.
High School—*Monsignor Donovan High School*, Tel: 732-349-8801; Fax: 732-349-8956. Web: www-.mondonhs.com. Dr. Edward G. Gere, Prin. Lay Teachers 61; Students 787.
Catechesis/Religious Program—Tel: 732-349-0018, Ext. 2224. Web: stjosephtomsriver.org. Mary Esther Wyman, C.R.E.; Catherine Werner, Youth Min. Students 1,077.
Mission—*St. Gertrude* Ocean & Central Aves., Island Heights, Ocean Co. 08732. Tel: 732-288-0036.

2—ST. JUSTIN (Dover Township) (1972) Revs. Mark Kreder; John A. Bogacz; Deacons Richard Hauenstein; Richard J. Napolitano; Frederick C. Ebenau Sr.; James Gonzalez; James L. Campbell; James Gillespie.
Res.: 975 Fischer Blvd., 08753. Tel: 732-270-3980; Fax: 732-929-9411. Web: www.stjustin.org.
Catechesis/Religious Program—Tel: 732-270-3797. Ellen Noble, C.R.E. Students 876.

3—ST. LUKE (Dover Township) (1982) Rev. Robert S. Grodnicki; Deacons Ronald R. Wicks; Stephen F. Delligatti; Joseph DeMaria; Louis Cartnick; Robert Puglisi. In Res., Rev. Louis W. Kralovich (Retired).
Res.: 1674 Old Freehold Rd., 08755. Tel: 732-286-2222; Fax: 732-914-1080.
Catechesis/Religious Program—Tel: 732-505-0108. Students 950.

4—ST. MAXIMILIAN KOLBE (Berkeley Township) (1985) Revs. Francis E. Santitoro (Retired); Sheldon Amasa; Raymond E. Hughes. In Res., Deacons Raymond Shea; Albert M. Pacitti; Leo Montini.
Res. & Mailing Address: P.O. Box 4144, 08756. Tel: 732-914-0300; 732-914-8550 (Res.); Fax: 732-240-9517.

TUCKERTON, OCEAN CO., ST. THERESA (1944) Rev. K. Michael Lambeth; Deacons James Petrauskas; William Sulzmann.
Parish Offices: 450 Radio Rd., Little Egg Harbor Twp, 08087. Tel: 609-296-2504; Fax: 609-296-4530. Email: info@sttheresa450. Web: sttheresa-tuckerton.com.
Catechesis/Religious Program—Tel: 609-296-2504, Ext. 24. Donnaann Powers, D.R.E. Students 615.

UNION BEACH, MONMOUTH CO., HOLY FAMILY (1942) Revs. Mark Devlin; Francis Cheruparambil, V.C.; Sr. Gloria Jean Bateman, R.S.M., Pastoral Min.
Res.: 727 Hwy. 36 W., P.O. Box 56, Keyport, 07735. Tel: 732-264-1484; Fax: 732-264-8369. Email: hfrccubnj@aol.com. Web: www.holyfamily.us.
Catechesis/Religious Program—Tel: 732-264-7043; Fax: 732-264-7043. Web: www.freewebs.com/hfreligiouseducation. Patricia McCarthy, C.R.E. Students 710.
Convent—*Mercy Convent*, 440 Sullivan Pl., 07735. Tel: 732-739-3065.

WASHINGTON CROSSING, MERCER CO., ST. GEORGE (1924) Rev. Msgr. James G. Innocenzi; Sr. Dorothy Jancola, R.S.M., Pastoral Assoc.; Deacons Lawrence E. Gallagher; Michael Riley.
Res.: 1370 River Rd., P.O. Box 324, Titusville, 08560. Tel: 609-737-2015; Fax: 609-737-7863. Email: churchofstgeorge@aol.com. Web: www.thechurchofstgeorge.org.
Catechesis/Religious Program—Tel: 609-730-1703. Margaret Dziminski, C.R.E. Students 149.
Station—*Mercer County Correction Center*, Tel: 609-989-6901.

WAYSIDE, MONMOUTH CO., ST. ANSELM (1972) Rev. Eugene B. Vavrick.
Res.: 1028 Wayside Rd., 07712. Tel: 732-493-4411; Fax: 732-493-4272. Email: stanselm2@aol.com. Web: www.stanselm.com.
Catechesis/Religious Program—Students 465.

WEST LONG BRANCH, MONMOUTH CO., ST. JEROME

(1956) Revs. Harold Cullen; Erin Brown, Parochial Vicar; Deacon Anthony N. DiCesare; James Palmer, Music Dir.
Res.: 254 Wall St., 07764. Tel: 732-222-1424; Fax: 732-222-2291. Email: stjeromec@aol.com. Web: saintjeromechurch.org.
School—250 Wall St., 07764. Tel: 732-222-8686; Fax: 732-263-0343. Sr. Angelina Pelliccia, Prin. Sisters 2; Lay Teachers 16; Students 252.
Catechesis/Religious Program—250 Wall St., 07764. Sr. Elizabeth Toft, D.R.E. Students 193.
Convent—250A Wall St., 07764. Tel: 732-222-2016.

WEST WINDSOR, MERCER CO., CHURCH OF ST. DAVID THE KING (1988) Very Rev. Timothy J. Capewell; Deacons Thomas Baker; Roger Dinella; Matthew V. Fung; Carol Sullivan, Dir. Music.
Res.: 517 Village Rd. W., Princeton Jct., 08550. Email: parishoffice@stdavidtheking.com. Web: www.stdavidtheking.com.
Church: One New Village Rd., Princeton Jct., 08550-2003. Tel: 609-275-7111; Fax: 609-799-1984.
Catechesis/Religious Program—Tel: 609-275-7111, Ext. 314; Fax: 609-799-1964. Email: dre@stdavidtheking.com. Bro. Robert Ziobro, S.C., D.R.E.; Nancy Riddell, Assoc. D.R.E.; Nancy Bachman, Adult Faith; Sonny Soi, Senior Youth Min.; Nicole Soi, Senior Youth Min.; Debbie Baker, Junior Youth Min.; Beth Kunkle, 6th Grade Youth Min. Students 650.

WHITING, OCEAN CO., ST. ELIZABETH ANN SETON (1976) Rev. Pasquale A. Papalia; Rev. Msgr. Joseph C. Shenrock, Pastor Emeritus (Retired); Rev. Thomas F. Maher; Deacons Kyran J. Purcell; Joseph Rider; Ralph Cordasco; Donald W. Miller; Edward J. Hoefling; James Hendrix; Alvin Miester; Christopher O'Brien; Ms. Linda Quinn, Business Mgr.
Res.: 30 Schoolhouse Rd., 08759. Tel: 732-350-5001; Fax: 732-350-0912. Email: pastor@easeton.org. Web: www.seaswhiting.org.
Catechesis/Religious Program—Tel: 732-350-7391. Email: ccd@easeton.org. Deborah Milecki, D.R.E. Students 225.

WILLINGBORO, BURLINGTON CO., CORPUS CHRISTI (1959) Very Rev. Daniel J. Ryan; Deacons James E. Ayrer; John F. Vassallo Jr.; Jose J. Jimenez.
Res.: 63 Sylvan Ln., 08046. Tel: 609-877-5322; Fax: 609-877-1695. Email: corpuschristiparishnj@comcast.net. Web: www.mycorpuschristichurch.com.
Catechesis/Religious Program—11 S. Sunset Rd., 08046. Tel: 609-871-4680; Fax: 609-871-5213. Sr. Rosemary Bucchi, O.S.F., D.R.E. Students 103.
Convent—150 Charleston Rd., 08046. Tel: 609-871-4226.

Chaplains of Public Institutions

TRENTON. *Capital Health System: Mercer Campus & Fluid Campus*. Attended from St. Michael Church, Tel: 609-393-4050 Rev. Henry A. Militante, Chap.
St. Francis Medical Center. Rev. Joel F. Szydlowski, O.F.M.
Katzenbach School for the Deaf. Vacant.
Mercer County Correction Center. Attended from St. George Church, Titusville, NJ 08560, Tel: 609-737-2015
New Jersey State Prison, CN 861, 08629. Sr. Elizabeth Gnaum.
Trenton Psychiatric Hospital. Rev. Joseph G. Hlubik, Chap.

BORDENTOWN. *Albert C. Wagner Youth Correction Facility*. Sr. Rose Huber, Chap.
Edward R. Johnstone Training and Research Center.

BURLINGTON. *Burlington County Hospital & Extended Care Center*. Attended from Sacred Heart Church.
260 High St., Mount Holly, 08060. Tel: 609-702-1848.
Burlington County Jail. Attended from Sacred Heart Church
260 High St., Mount Holly, 08060. Tel: 609-702-1848.

NEPTUNE. *Jersey Shore Medical Center*. Rev. Charles J. Flood, O.SS.T. Attended by St. Catherine Church, 215 Essex Ave. Spring Lake, NJ 07762, Tel: 732-449-5765

NEW LISBON. *New Jersey State Colony*. Attended from Holy Eucharist Church, Tabernacle, NJ 08088, Tel: 609-726-1000
Ocean County Jail. Attended by St. Joseph, Toms River, Tel: 732-349-0018

WAYSIDE. *Monmouth County Jail*, 1028 Wayside Rd., 07712. Tel: 732-493-4411. Attended from St. Rose Church, Freehold NJ, Tel: 732-462-7429

YARDVILLE. *Garden State Correctional Center*, P.O. Box 11401, 08620. Deacon James A. Manaloris. Tel: 609-298-6300, Ext. 2251.

Military Installations

COLTS NECK. *Naval Weapons Station Earle*. Served by chaplains. Assigned by the Archdiocese for the Military Service.

FORT DIX. *Fort Dix*. Served by chaplains. Assigned by the Archdiocese for the Military Service.

LAKEHURST. *U.S. Naval Air Warfare Center*. Served by chaplains. Assigned by the Archdiocese for the Military Service.

LITTLE SILVER. *Fort Monmouth*. Served by chaplains. Assigned by the Archdiocese for the Military Service.

MCGUIRE AIR FORCE BASE. *McGuire Air Force Base*. Served by chaplains. Assigned by the Archdiocese for the Military Service.

On Duty Outside the Diocese:
Rev. Msgr.—
Punderson, Joseph R., Villa Stritch, Via Della Nocetta 63, Rome 00164 Italy.
Revs.—
Gadenz, Pablo T., S.T.D., S.S.L., Seton Hall, South Orange, 07079.
Griswold, Edward J., St. Mary Seminary, Baltimore, MD 21210.
Hillier, David A., Our Lady of the Visitation, Shippensburg, PA 17257.
Kaeding, Robert F., Precious Blood Church, 72 Riverdale Ave., Monmouth Beach, 07750.
Krisak, Anthony F., S.S., 934 Kearny St., N.E., Washington, DC 20017-3516.
Kselman, John J., S.S., Weston School of Theology, Three Phillips Pl., Cambridge, MA 02138.
Lankford, Michael G., VAN-J Chaplain Service, East Orange, 07018.
Rubiano, Cesar A.
Tedesco, Joseph A., Mepkin Abbey, Moncks Corner, SC 29461.

Leave of Absence:
Revs.—
Butch, Brian T.
Dobrosky, John M.
Evans, William G.
Gallagher, Richard
Hughes, Joseph W.
Jackiewicz, Frederick W., 19 Pettit Ave., South River, 08882.
Kielb, John T.
Lang, Leonard P.
Polczyk, Stanislaus

Retired:
Most Revs.—
Reiss, John C., D.D., J.C.D., St. Lawrence Rehabilitation Center, 2381 Lawrenceville Rd., Lawrenceville, 08648.
Smith, John M., Villa Vianney, 2301 Lawrenceville Rd., 08648.
Rev. Msgrs.—
Brietske, Richard C., P.O. Box 771, Barnegat Light, 08006.
Carton, William J., Villa Vianney, 2301 Lawrenceville Rd., Lawrenceville, 08648.
Fitzgerald, William F., Villa Vianney, 2301 Lawrenceville Rd., Lawrenceville, 08648.
Flood, Peter J., Chap. Col., Headquarters AIA, 102 Halle Blvd., Ste. 263, San Antonio, TX 78243.
Gibbons, John, 610 Bedford Ln., Manchester, 08759.
Kelty, Leo A., P.O. Box 281, Allenwood, 08720-0281.
McGovern, James J., 3225 Brunswick Ln., Sarasota, FL 34239.
Nolan, Walter E., 122 James St., Burlington, 08016.
Ronan, Hugh F., Villa Vianney, 2301 Lawrenceville Rd., Lawrenceville, 08648.
Shenrock, Joseph C., P.A., Villa Vianney, 2301 Lawrenceville Rd., Lawrenceville, 08648.
Strano, Edward, 2301 Lawrenceville Rd., Lawrenceville, 08648.
Valentino, Frederick A., 509 Woodland Ave., Brielle, 08730.
Revs.—
Adackapara, Matthew, 25 Stanley Dr., Monroe, 08831.
Bausch, William J., Box 1068, Point Pleasant Beach, 08742.
Bianchi, Raymond S., Missionari Clarettiani, Via Del Banchi, Vecchi 12, Rome, Italy.
Bowden, John V., Villa Vianney, 2301 Lawrenceville Rd., Lawrenceville, 08648.
Brennan, Thomas, 1122 Skiff Way, Forked River, 08731.
Cammisa, James N., St. Lawrence Rehab, 2381 Lawrenceville Rd., Lawrenceville, 08648.
Cenefeldt, Harry E., Villa Vianney, 2301 Lawrenceville Rd., Lawrenceville, 08648.
Cervenak, Andrew, Janosikova 21, Presov 08001 Slovakia.
Coley, James E., St. Lawrence Rehab, 2381 Lawrenceville Rd., Lawrenceville, 08648.
Conlon, Arthur F., 1015 Nottinghill Ln., 08619.
Cuomo, Rocco A., 26D Holly St., Toms River, 08757.
Delzell, David G., Tower of David, P.O. Box 292, Uniondale, PA 18470.
DeSandre, John G., P.O. Box 483, Pine Beach, 08741.
Deutsch, George E., Pastor Emeritus, 1967 E. Lakeview Dr., Sebastian, FL 32958. Tel: 609-242-9456
Halpin, Joseph A., 72A Belhaven Ct., Whiting, 08759.
Inghilterra, Vincent J., 4518 Fairway Dr., Steubenville, OH 43953. (Col. Retired)
Kearns, Adam, Villa Vianney, 2301 Lawrenceville Rd., Lawrenceville, 08648.
Keenan, Eugene, Villa Vianney, 2301 Lawrenceville Rd., Lawrenceville, 08648.
Kralovich, Louis W., St. Luke Church, 1674 Old Freehold Rd., Toms River, 08755.
Kunnel, Lawrence K., St. Lawrence Rehab, 2381 Lawrenceville Rd., Lawrenceville, 08648.
Magee, Patrick F., 41 Osborne Ave., Bay Head, 08742.
Matera, Philip T., 1047 Lyndale Ave., 08629.
McCarron, Gerard J., Villa Vianney, 2301 Lawrenceville Rd., Lawrenceville, 08648.
McConnell, James J., Villa Vianney, 2301 Lawrenceville Rd., Lawrenceville, 08648.
Miele, Joseph J., 388 Cherry Quay Rd., Brick, 08723-6308.
Milewski, Casimir, U1.M. Karlowicza 22 33-100, Tarnow, Poland.
Pearson, Robert A., 73 Rolling Meadows Blvd. S., Ocean, 07712.
Poovakulam, Antony P., P.O. Box 325, Tonopah, NV 89049.
Radomski, Joseph A., St. Lawrence Rehab, 2381 Lawrenceville Rd., 08648.
Rauch, Laszlo F., St. Lawrence Rehab, 2381 Lawrenceville Rd., Lawrenceville, 08648.
Sanchez, Castor G., Pandan, Catanduanes, Philippines.
Santitoro, Francis E., 158 Rte. 539, Allentown, 08501.
Sauchelli, James J., 152A Gramercy Ct., Lakewood, 08701.
Schabowski, Henry F., 240 Shepherd Ave., Middlesex, 08846.
Schneider, William T., 209 Laurel Rd. #209, Voorhees, 08043.
Sloyan, Gerard S., 415 Silver Spring Ave. #107, Silver Spring, MD 20910.
Sweeny, Richard R., St. Lawrence Rehab, 2381 Lawrenceville Rd., Lawrenceville, 08648.
Thompson, James A., Emmaus House, 21 Main Ave., Ocean Grove, 07756.
Valentine, Charles R., 61 Woodstock Pl., Freehold, 07728-3143.
Vona, Michael S., 5 Doral Way, Neptune, 07753.
Zalewski, Francis, 97-07 63rd Rd. Apt. 15L, Rego Park, NY 11374.

Permanent Deacons:
Acosta, Amado F., St. Isaac Joques, Marlton
Adorno, Miguel, Christ the Redeemer, Mt. Holly
Alessi, James A., Incarnation - St. James, Trenton
Allen, John W., (Retired), St. George, Titusville
Andre, Edner, Holy Spirit, Asbury Park
Andrews, Stephen W., St. Dorothea, Eatontown
Aquino, Romeo D., (Retired), St. Joseph's, Toms River
Arcari, Richard A., St. Raphael-Holy Angels, Hamilton
Armstrong, Robert B., St. Elizabeth, Avon-by-the-Sea
Auleta, Michael A., Sacred Heart, Mt. Holly
Ayers, Damian, St. Dominic, Brick
Ayrer, James E., (Retired), Corpus Christi, Willingboro
Babuschak, Francis J., St. Joseph, Toms River
Baeza, Adolfo, St. Joseph, Trenton
Bailey, Normand C., (Retired), St. Rose, Belmar
Baker, Thomas, St. David the King, Princeton Junction
Barbara, Joseph F., St. John Newmann, Mt. Laurel
Barnes, Robert M., St. Joseph, Toms River
Barng, Ilsoo P., St. Dorothea, Eatontown
Beauchamps, Jose, St. Mary Cathedral, Trenton
Begley, Thomas D., III, Our Lady of Good Counsel, Moorestown
Bertagnolli, John F.
Billbrough, Joseph C., (Retired), Corpus Christi, Willingboro
Bittner, Robert W., (Outside Diocese)
Blackwell, M. Darrell, On Duty Outside the Diocese (Maine)
Boehm, Michael P., Our Lady of Perpetual Help, Maple Shade
Bonner, John J., Our Lady Good Counsel, West Trenton
Bonocore, Steven J., On Duty Outisde the Diocese (Syracuse)
Brannigan, Patrick R., St. James, Pennington
Briggs, William E., Church of the Resurrection, Delran

Buecker, Edward J., St. Dominic, Brick
Byrne, Kevin M., On Duty Outside the Diocese (Washington, D.C.)
Campbell, James L., St. Justin, Toms River
Caponigro, Alfred E., On Duty Outside the Diocese (Arizona)
Card, Joseph A., (Retired), Our Lady of Perpetual Help, Maple Shade
Carlin, George M., (Retired), St. Katherine Drexel, Burlington
Cartnick, Louis C., St. Luke, Toms River
Casa, James L., Sacred Heart, Mount Holly
Casey, Keith J., St. Thomas More, Manalapan
Cater, Thomas H., On Duty Outside the Diocese (Florida)
Cattanea, James F., St. John Neumann, Mt. Laurel
Cechulski, Thomas J., St. Veronica, Howell
Cerefice, Robert L., Holy Innocents, Neptune
Challender, James J., Our Lady of Sorrows-St. Anthony, Hamilton
Chase, Daniel A., (Retired), St. Andrew, Jobstown
Cheu, Richard A., On Duty Outside the Diocese (New York)
Clausen, Peter M., St. Barnabas, Bayville
Clymore, John L., Jesus the Lord, Keyport
Coccia, Brother Christopher A., On Duty Outside the Diocese (Florida)
Cole, John A., (Retired)
Comito, Charles, On Duty Outside the Diocese (Florida)
Commisso, Louis V., Epiphany, Brick
Cook, James P., On Duty Outside the Diocese (Florida)
Cordasco, Ralph, St. Elizabeth Ann Seton, Whiting
Cugini, Henry J., St. Robert Bellarmine, Freehold
Cullinane, John, On Duty Outside the Diocese (Cleveland)
Cummings, James H., St. Barnabas, Bayville
Cunningham, Robert, St. Francis of Assisi, Brant Beach
Currie, Richard J., St. James, Pennington
D'Angelo, V. Richard, On Duty Outside the Diocese (Charleston)
Davis, Bryan, St. James, Red Bank
Davis, James R., (Retired), St. Thomas More, Manalapan
Daye, Charles, Jr., St. Veronica, Howell
DeFrehn, Jeffrey, St. Joan of Arc, Marlton
DelGuidice, John V., On Duty Outside the Diocese (Orlando)
Dello Russo, Thomas J., On Duty Outside the Diocese (Scranton)
DeLuca, Joseph W., Holy Eucharist, Tabernacle
DeLuca, Peter J., On Duty Outside the Diocese (Florida)
DePaolis, Joseph, (Retired), St. Leo the Great, Lincroft
Desire, Luders, O.L. Sorrows - St. Anthony, Hamilton
DiCanio, Thomas J., St. Catherine, Holmdel
DiCesare, Anthony N., (Retired), St. Jerome, West Long Branch
DiLissio, John A., St. Raphael - Holy Angels, Hamilton
Dinella, Roger P., (Retired), St. David the King, Princeton Junction
Domzalski, Kenneth S., Holy Eucharist, Tabernacle
Donadieu, Joseph M., Sacred Heart, Riverton
Donofrio, Nicholas, St. Dorothea, Eatontown
Doughty, Gerald A., St. Charles Borromeo, Cinnaminson
Ebenau, Frederick C., Sr., St. Justin, Toms River
Ernst, Henry J., On Duty Outside the Diocese (Scranton)
Ervin, Martin A., On Duty Outside the Diocese (Florida)
Everist, Thomas J., St. Ann, Lawrenceville
Fanelle, John D., On Duty Outside the Diocese (San Diego)
Fatovic, Andrew J., St. Vincent de Paul, Yardville
Finn, Lawrence W., Sr., St. Mary, Bordentown
Fiorillo, Joseph A., St. Mary, Barnegat
Fischer, Edward, III, Visitation, Brick
Flanagan, John P., (Retired), St. Catharine, Holmdel
Folinus, Robert, St. Joseph, Millstone Twp.
Friedmann, Rolf B., St. Robert Bellarmine, Freehold
Fullen, Michael P., Sr.
Fullen, Peter J., On Duty Outside the Diocese (Venice, FL)
Fung, Matthew V., St. David the King, Princeton Junction
Fuoco, Joseph R., (Retired), Jesus the Good Shepherd, Riverside
Gallagher, Lawrence E., St. George, Titusville
Gallagher, Paul A., San Alfonso Retreat House, Long Branch
Gallagher, William J., St. Charles Borromeo, Cinnaminson
Galvan, Silverius F., St. Mary of the Lake, Lakewood
Garvey, Thomas J., St. Anthony of Padua, Hightstown
Gay, Robert, St. Barnabas, Bayville
Genovese, Eugene, St. Rose, Belmar
Genovese, Thomas, St. Joseph, Toms River
Gettlefinger, Robert J., On Duty Outside the Diocese (North Carolina)
Giglio, Frank E., (Retired), St. Isaac Jogues, Marlton
Gillespie, James
Glogoza, Richard T., St. John, Lakehurst
Golazeski, Frances G., Incarnation - St. James, Trenton
Gomez, Victor L., Jesus the Lord, Keyport
Gonzalez, James, St. Justin, Toms River
Gooden, Robert, (Retired), St. John, Lakehurst
Grant, John D., St. Alphonsus, Hopewell; On Duty Outside the Diocese (Massachusetts)
Gray, William G., On Duty Outside the Diocese (Florida)
Gregory, Gabriel, On Duty Outside Diocese (Minnesota)
Gregory, Thomas J., (Retired) Arizona
Groff, Francis W., St. Martha, Point Pleasant
Grogan, James J., Our Lady of Good Counsel, Moorestown
Groh, Alfred, On Duty Outside the Diocese (Florida)
Grussler, John R., Divine Mercy, Trenton
Gularek, Theodore V., St. Veronica, Howell
Gwiazda, Edward J., St. Isaac Jogues, Marlton; On Duty Outside the Diocese (Florida)
Hagan, Michael J., Jesus, the Good Shepherd, Riverside
Hambleton, Richard N., On Duty Outside the Diocese (Charleston)
Hank, William Moore, St. James, Pennington
Hanna, John H., St. Pio of Pietrelcina, Lavallette
Hannawacker, Joseph A., Incarnation-St. James, Trenton
Hansen, Christopher L., St. Catharine, Holmdel
Harbeck, Jay C., Holy Cross, Rumson
Harris, David M., (Retired), St. Mary, Bordentown
Hauenstein, Richard A., (Retired), St. Justin, Toms River
Haunss, Ronald J., St. Mary, Barnegat
Heffernan, Edward A., Our Lady of Good Counsel, Moorestown
Heilig, Kenneth W., Sacred Heart, Riverton
Heller, James T., (Retired), St. Pius X, Forked River
Hepp, Joseph L., St. John the Baptist, Allentown
Herr, Edward R., St. Dorothea, Eatontown
Hoag, Edward A., St. Ann, Lawrenceville
Hoch, Eugene, On Duty Outside the Diocese (Palm Beach, FL)
Hoefling, John F.
Hooker, George C., (Retired) South Carolina
Hughes, John P., (Retired), St. John Neumann, Mount Laurel
Hvizdos, John F., St. Charles Borromeo, Cinnaminson
Iadanza, John M., On Duty Outside the Diocese (Florida)
Iglesias, Manuel F., St. Raphael-Holy Angels, Hamilton
Jackson, Frank W., (Retired), St. Aloysius, Jackson
Jaruszewski, Joseph, Our Lady of Sorrows-St. Anthony, Hamilton
Jennings, Edward F., St. Catharine, Spring Lake
Jimenez, Jose J., Corpus Christ, Willingboro
Johnson, James G., On Duty Outside Diocese (Washington, D.C.)
Johnson, Robert J., St. Agnes, Atlantic Highlands
Johnston, George A., St. Joan of Arc, Marlton
Johnston, Richard, Visitation, Brick
Jones, Francis A., (Retired), St. Paul, Burlington
Karpecik, Walter J., Jr., St. Katherine Drexel, Burlington
Kelder, George R., Jr., St. Denis, Manasquan
Kelly, James A., Nativity, Fair Haven
Kennedy, Patrick W., (Retired)
Kerr, Ronald J., Sr., St. John, Lakehurst
Klein, Robert, (Retired), St. Mary, Barnegat
Klimaszewski, Norbert J., On Duty Outside the Diocese (Florida)
Klincewicz, John G., Holy Innocents, Neptune
Knipper, James J., St. Paul, Princeton
Kohut, David S., Visitation, Brick
Kolon, Thomas F., Our Lady of Good Counsel, Moorestown
Kopcak, John, Ascension, Bradley Beach
Korbelak, George M., St. Peter's, Pt. Pleasant Beach
Krupa, Bradford A., On Duty Outside Diocese (Atlanta, GA)
Kupin, Joseph, St. Paul, Princeton
Lacey, James A., (Retired), Sacred Heart, Bay Head
Lachance, Paul A., (Retired), St. Paul, Princeton
Lafond, Robert H., St. Alphonsus, Hopewell
LaMachia, Ralph A., On Duty Outside the Diocese (Atlanta)
Lancieri, Salvatore, Office of Jail & Prison Ministry, Trenton
Latini, Joseph E., St. Gregory the Great, Hamilton
Laurita, Daniel J., On Duty Outside the Diocese (Alabama)
Lavelle, Thomas J., Jr., St. Raphael-Holy Angels, Hamilton
Linka, Fernando, Our Lady Perpetual Help, Maple Shade
Little, John L., St. Catharine, Spring Lake
Little, Ronald J., On Duty Outside the Diocese (Phoenix)
Littlefield, James J., St. Veronica, Howell
Lombardo, Earl H., St. Pius X, Forked River
Lonie, Michael, St. Catherine, Holmdel
Lopez, Heriberto, On Duty Outside the Diocese (Florida)
Loughran, Thomas, St. Peter, Point Pleasant
Lovejoy, C. Doug, Jr., Aquinas Institute, Princeton
Luhman, Andrew G., Jr., St. Rose of Lima, Freehold
Luongo, Gerard, St. Joseph, Toms River
Lydick, Donald E., On Duty Outside the Diocese (Delaware)
Malhame, Eugene G., Jr., St. Rose, Belmar
Mammoliti, Anthony, Assumption, New Egypt
Manaloris, James A., Saints Francis & Clare, Florence Twp.
Mannikus, Uku R., St. Aloysius, Jackson
Marcello, Salvatore, St. Raphael-Holy Angels, Hamilton
Martin, Patrick J., St. Mary, Barnegat
Martucci, Anthony R., St. Pius X, Forked River
Mattozzi, Guido J., Our Lady of the Angels, Trenton
McCabe, John, (On Duty Outside the Diocese) Charleston
McGahran, Andrew R., On Duty Outside the Diocese (North Carolina)
McGrath, James G., (Retired), St. Mary of The Lakes, Lakewood
McGrath, John G., St. Catherine, Middletown
McHugh, Joseph P., On Duty Outside the Diocese (Camden)
McKenna, Francis A., St. Joseph, Toms River
McKenna, Robert M., St. Rose of Lima, Freehold
McKeon, James E., On Duty Outside Diocese (Richmond, VA)
McMahon, Martin K., St. Catherine, Middletown
McNally, Brent G., On Duty Outside Diocese (Venice, FL)
McNerny, Daniel J., On Duty Outside Diocese (Charleston, SC)
Meehan, Daniel J., Church of the Resurrection, Delran
Mendonca, Glen L., St. Joseph, Keyport
Meyer, Richard G., On Duty Outside the Diocese (Florida)
Meyers, Ronald S., Our Lady of Perpetual Help, Maple Shade
Micali, James Mark, St. Clement, Matawan
Miester, Alvin C., Jr., St. Elizabeth Ann Seton, Whiting
Miller, Daniel S., Sr., (On Duty Outside the Diocese) Orlando
Miller, Donald C., (Retired), St. Elizabeth Ann Seton, Whiting
Mintz, Robert E., On Duty Outside the Diocese (St. Petersburg)
Modelo, Romeo B., Jr., St. Charles Borromeo, Cinnaminson
Moir, Gene F., Sr., St. Veronica, Howell
Moore, Timothy E., Our Lady of Sorrows-St. Anthony, Hamilton
Morris, Richard L., St. Benedict, Holmdel
Morton, James E., Sacred Heart, Riverton
Moscarello, Charles M., St. Gregory The Great, Hamilton
Mosteller, Herman J., Jesus the Good Shepherd, Riverside
Motylinski, Kenneth E., Jr., St. Mary of The Lakes, Medford
Mroz, John J., On Duty Outside the Diocese (PA)
Mueller, William R., St. Joan of Arc, Marlton
Mullarkey, Michael F., Epiphany, Brick
Murphy, Christopher J., Holy Eucharist, Tabernacle
Murray, William J., On Duty Outside Diocese (Palm Beach, FL)
Mylod, Philip J., (Retired)
Napolitano, Richard J., St. Justin, Toms River
Nimon, Robert R., On Duty Outside the Diocese (Florida)
Nnajiofor, Christian M., Blessed Sacrament - OL Divine Shepherd, Trenton
Notaro, John A., St. Dorothea, Eatontown
Nowak, Ronald, Epiphany, Bricktown
O'Boyle, Kevin J., Our Lady of Sorrows-St. Anthony, Mercerville

O'Brien, Christopher D., St. Elizabeth Ann Seton, Whiting
O'Brien, Michael J., St. Ann, Browns Mills
O'Connor, David, St. Isaac Jogues, Marlton
O'Donnell, John J., (Retired), Our Lady Queen of Peace, Hainesport
Orkis, Stanley, Sacred Heart, Mt. Holly
Orlando, John C., St. Catherine, Middletown
Owens, Lester J., (Retired), St. Gabriel's, Marlboro
Pacitti, Albert, (Retired), St. Maximilian Kolbe, Toms River
Palan, Henry N., St. Theresa, Tuckerton
Palsir, James W., St. James, Pennington
Papuga, David F., Our Lady of Good Counsel, Moorestown
Patton, Joseph R., (Retired), St. Mary of the Lakes, Medford
Paul, Joseph A., Our Lady of Good Counsel, Moorestown
Pelkowski, Raymond R., St. Benedict, Holmdel
Pennise, Alfred, St. Katherine Drexel, Burlington
Perez, Rene P., St. Aloysius, Jackson
Perusi, Donald L., St. Denis, Manasquan
Petrauskas, James J., St. Theresa's, Tuckerton
Pierfy, Jeffrey, On Duty Outside the Diocese (Charleston, SC)
Pirozzi, Neil, St. Gregory the Great, Hamilton
Pitt, John R., St. Mary, Barnegat
Policastro, Donald M., St. Joseph, Keyport
Porter, Thomas P., On Duty Outside the Diocese (Raleigh)
Prevosti, George A., Jr., St. William the Abbot, Howell
Price, Walter L., St. Ann, Browns Mills
Prihoda, Frank J., Outside the Diocese (PA)
Principato, Michael, St. Monica, Jackson
Prioli, Joseph J., St. Catherine, Farmingdale
Provencher, Conrad J., On Duty Outside the Diocese (Pennsylvania)
Pstrak, Gary J., St. Denis, Manasquan
Punchello, Alexander A., Sr., St. Katherine Drexel, Burlington
Purcell, Kyran J., St. Elizabeth Ann Seton, Whiting
Rainville, Raymond R., St. Agnes, Atlantic Highlands
Ramos, Alfonso, St. Joseph, Trenton
Ramos, Luis A., St. Mary's Cathedral, Trenton
Rasmussen, Guy C., St. Barnabus, Bayville
Repice, Anthony, Holy Eucharist, Tabernacle
Ricciardi, Vincent P., Sr., Assumption, New Egypt
Richardson, Gary T., St. Mary, Bordentown
Richichi, Joseph, Diocesan Office of Worship
Rider, Joseph H., St. Elizabeth Ann Seton, Whiting
Riedinger, Gerald, St. Dominic, Brick
Riley, Michael, St. George, Titusville
Rinaldi, Vincent L., St. Catherine, Farmingdale
Rivella, Thomas H., Incarnation-St. James, Trenton
Rodriguez, Feliz, On Duty Outside the Diocese (Puerto Rico)
Rodriguez, Jose G., St. Paul, Princeton
Ronning, Donald J., Jr., St. Agnes, Atlantic Highlands
Rowley, William R., (Retired), Sacred Heart, Mt. Holly
Russo, James C., St. Gabriel, Marlboro
Sabados, Andrew A., Sr., St. Gregory the Great, Hamilton
Sansevere, Stephen A., St. Gabriel, Marlboro
Santos, Rodolfo A., St. Rose of Lima, Freehold
Scannella, Michael V., Saints Francis & Clare, Florence Twp.
Scharen, Robert F., St. Mary, Middletown
Sciarrotta, Samuel P., St. James Church, Pennington
Scott, James M., III, St. Ann, Lawrenceville
Scott, Stephen G., St. Benedict, Holmdel
Scotti, Richard, St. Gabriel, Marlboro
Seaman, Joseph F., On Duty Outside Diocese (Camden)
Seaton, George L., On Duty Outside the Diocese (Florida)
Sepich, William S., (Retired), St. Charles Borromeo, Cinnaminson
Shapiro, David L., St. Justin, Toms River
Shea, Thomas F., St. Mary, Bordentown
Sheehan, Kenneth R., (Retired), St. Joseph, Keyport
Sherpensky, Frank, (Retired), St. Ann, Browns Mills
Slavin, Dennis E., Office of Family Life, Trenton
Slee, Louis F., (Retired)
Smigelski, Michael A., St. Barnabas, Bayville
Smith, Andrew M., St. Robert Bellarmine, Freehold
Smith, Charles J., (Retired), St. Mary, Middletown
Smith, Kevin M., St. William The Abbot, Howell
Somma, Eugene A., St. Michael, West End
Sondeen, Carl R., St. Charles Borromeo, Cinnaminson
Sorrentino, Fernando A., St. Mary, Colts Neck
Squicciarini, Carlo, St. Mary, Middletown
Stap, Matthew J., (Retired), Jesus the Good Shepherd, Riverside
Staub, Raymond W., Jr., Assumption, New Egypt
Stesner, Patrick J., Sr., St. Joseph, Toms River
Stinsman, Michael J., Sacred Heart, Riverton
Stranieri, Nicola, Visitation, Brick
Sulzmann, William P., St. Theresa, Tuckerton
Swanson, George J., St. Barnabas, Bayville
Szmutko, Steven K., Our Lady of Good Counsel, W. Trenton
Tarzy, Barry R., St. Joan of Arc, Marlton
Taylor, Michael A., St. Joseph, Toms River
Tedeschi, Joseph R., (Retired), St. Mary of the Lakes, Medford
Tharp, Robert, St. Raphael-Holy Angels, Hamilton
Titmas, Richard C., St. Francis of Assisi, Brant Beach
Toca, Frederick M., On Duty Outside the Diocese (Atlanta)
Toolan, James W., On Duty Outside the Diocese (Allentown)
Torres, Benito, Our Lady of the Angels, Trenton
Trani, Eduardo, Christ the Redeemer, Mount Holly
Vagrin, Stephen R., St. Catherine, Seaside Park
Valentin, Juan E., On Duty Outside the Diocese (Florida)
Vassallo, John F., Jr., Corpus Christi, Willingboro
Vazquez, Emiliano, St. Mary Cathedral, Trenton
Vicari, Salvatore J., Jr., Visitation, Brick Town
Vignolini, Robert J., Christ the King, Long Branch
Vivona, Joseph A., St. Mary, Barnegat
Vlcej, Robert J., On Duty Outside the Diocese (Baltimore)
Vogel, Anthony D., Outside the Diocese (PA)
Voll, Edwin L., Jr., (Retired), St. Joseph, Toms River
Wadolowski, Thomas P., St. Clement, Matawan
Walsh, James P., Holy Innocents, Neptune
Wanat, John A., St. Rose of Lima, Freehold
Watkins, Thomas H., Jr., St. Hedwig, Trenton
Weber, Francis J., Jr., St. Robert Bellarmine, Freehold
Weber, Richard J., St. Rose, Belmar
Weller, Caleb J., St. Mary, Colts Neck
White, Edward A., On Duty Outside the Diocese (Washington)
Wilson, Edward H., St. Leo The Great, Lincroft
Wilson, William A., St. Gregory the Great, Hamilton Square
Young, Donald A., On Duty Outside the Diocese (Arlington, VA)
Zadworny, Barry J., St. Hedwig, Trenton
Zalegowski, Ronald F., St. Mary, Bordentown
Zapcic, William J., Jr., St. Anselm, Wayside
Zebrowski, John J., St. Thomas More, Manalapan
Zito, Lee, Sacred Heart, Mount Holly

INSTITUTIONS LOCATED IN THE DIOCESE

[A] COLLEGES AND UNIVERSITIES

LAKEWOOD. *Georgian Court University*, 900 Lakewood Ave., 08701-2697. Tel: 732-987-2200; Fax: 732-987-2018. Email: ksmith@georgian.edu. Web: www.georgian.edu. Sr. Rosemary E. Jeffries, R.S.M., Ph.D., Pres.; Evelyn Saul Quinn, Provost; Rev. John Zec. Priests 2; Sisters 22; Lay Teachers 288; Students 2,885.

[B] HIGH SCHOOLS, DIOCESAN AND PARISH

TRENTON. *Notre Dame High School*, 601 Lawrence Rd., Lawrenceville, 08648. Tel: 609-882-7900; Fax: 609-882-5723. Email: ivins@ndnj.org. Web: www.ndnj.org. Barry Breen, Pres.; Ms. Mary E. Ivins, Prin.; Miss Joan Pilkington, Asst. Prin.; Mrs. Joanna Barlow, Asst. Prin.; Rev. Joseph A. Jakub, Chap.; Mary Curtis, Librarian. Lay Teachers 92; Students 1,265.

BELMAR. *Saint Rose High School*, 607 Seventh Ave., 07719. Tel: 732-681-2858; Fax: 732-280-2745. Email: knace@strose.k12.nj.us. Web: www.strose.k12.nj.us. Sr. Kathleen Nace, S.S.J., Prin. Sisters 5; Lay Teachers 39; Students 501.

DELRAN. *Holy Cross High School*, 5035 Rte. 130 S., 08075. Tel: 856-461-5400; Fax: 856-764-0806. Email: dennis.guida@holycrosshighschool.org. Web: www.holycrosshighschool.org. Mr. Dennis M. Guida, Prin.; Sr. Bernadette Thomas, I.H.M., Librarian. Sisters of I.H.M., Scranton, PA. Priests 1; Sisters 3; Lay Teachers 40; Students 700.

HAMILTON. *Trenton Catholic Academy (Upper School)*, 175 Leonard Ave., 08610. Tel: 609-586-3705; Fax: 609-586-6584. Email: dpayne@trentoncatholic.org; mneves@trentoncatholic.org. Sr. Dorothy Payne, S.S.J., Pres.; Michele Neves, Prin.; Miss Kathleen Faraglia, Librarian. Sisters 1; Lay Teachers 26.

HOLMDEL. *St. John Vianney High School*, 540 A Line Rd., 07733. Tel: 732-739-0800; Fax: 732-739-0824. Email: deroba@sjvhs.com. Web: www.sjvhs.com. Mr. Joseph F. Deroba, Prin. Sisters 2; Lay Teachers 63; Students 1,011.

NEW MONMOUTH. *Mater Dei High School*, 538 Church St., 07748. Tel: 732-671-9100; Fax: 732-671-9214. Email: materdeihighschool@nac.net. Web: www.materdeihs.org. Mr. Frank Poleski Jr., Prin. Students 380; Lay Teachers 28.

RED BANK. *Red Bank Catholic High School*, 112 Broad St., 07701. Tel: 732-747-1774; Fax: 732-747-1936. Web: www.redbankcatholic.org. Robert Abatemarco, Prin. Sisters 5; Lay Teachers 100; Students 1,084.

TOMS RIVER. *Monsignor Donovan High School*, 711 Hooper Ave., 08753. Tel: 732-349-8801; Fax: 732-349-8956. Email: egere@mondonhs.com. Web: www.mondonhs.com. Dr. Edward G. Gere, Ed.D., Prin.; Karin Krenek, Librarian. Priests 1; Lay Teachers 70; Students 790.

[C] HIGH SCHOOLS, PRIVATE

TRENTON. *Villa Victoria Academy*, 376 W. Upper Ferry Rd., 08628. Tel: 609-882-1700; Fax: 609-882-8421. Email: srlillian@villavictoria.org. Web: www.villavictoria.org. Sr. Lesley Draper, M.P.F., Prin.; Jennifer Jacoppo, Librarian. Upper School, Grades 7-8 (Girls); Grades 9-12 (Girls). Sisters 3; Lay Teachers 13; Students 100.

LINCROFT. *Christian Brothers Academy*, 850 Newman Springs Rd., 07738. Tel: 732-747-1959; Fax: 732-747-1643. Email: adminoff@cbalincroftnj.org. Web: www.cbalincroftnj.org. Bros. Frank Byrne, F.S.C., Pres.; James Butler, F.S.C., Prin.; R. Ross Fales, Assoc. Prin.; Peter Santanello, Assoc. Prin.; Barbara Britton, Librarian. Priests 1; Brothers 9; Lay Teachers 72; Students 955.

[D] REGIONAL SCHOOLS

WILLINGBORO. *Pope John Paul II Regional School*, (Grades PreK-8), 11 S. Sunset Rd., 08046. Tel: 609-877-2144; Fax: 609-877-3153. Catherine Zagola, Prin.; Brenda Blizzard, Librarian.

[E] INTER-PARISH ELEMENTARY SCHOOLS

ATLANTIC HIGHLANDS. *Mother Teresa Regional School*, (Grades PreK-8), 55 South Ave., 07716. Tel: 732-291-1050; Fax: 732-872-2293. Melissa Whelan Wisk, Prin.; Katey Patrizio, Librarian. Lay Teachers 28; Religious 1.

HAMILTON. *Trenton Catholic Academy (Lower School)*, 177 Leonard Ave., 08610. Tel: 609-586-5888; Fax: 609-631-9295. Email: dpayne@trentoncatholic.org. Anne Reap, Prin.; Candace Andrako, Librarian. Lay Teachers 23; Sisters 1.

MANAHAWKIN. *All Saints Regional Catholic School*, (Grades PreK-8), 400 Doc Cramer Blvd., 08050. Tel: 609-597-3800; Fax: 609-597-2223. Email: asrc@asrcs.org. Web: asrcs.org. Sr. Jeannette Daily, Prin.; Pauline Barber, Librarian. Lay Teachers 22; Total Enrollment 410.

[F] ELEMENTARY SCHOOLS, PRIVATE

TRENTON. *Villa Victoria Academy*, (Grades PreK-6), (Girls), 376 W. Upper Ferry Rd., 08628. Tel: 609-883-5760; Fax: 609-882-8421. Email: sralice@villavictoria.org. Web: www.villavictoria.org. Sr. Alice Ivanyo, M.P.F., Prin.; Joanie Wentzel, Librarian. Lower School. Lay Teachers 8; Students 100.

PRINCETON. *Princeton Academy of the Sacred Heart*, 1128 Great Rd., 08540. Tel: 609-921-6499; Fax: 609-921-9198. Web: www.princetonacademy.org. Olen Kalkus, Headmaster; Ellen Dowling, Librarian. Private elementary and middle school for boys.

Stuart Country Day School of the Sacred Heart, (Grades PreK-8), 1200 Stuart Rd., 08540. Tel: 609-921-2330; Fax: 609-497-0784. Email: stuart@school.org. Web: stuartschool.org. Dr. Patty L. Fagin, Head of School. Sisters 1; Lay Teachers 79; Students 456.

[G] CATHOLIC CHARITIES, DIOCESE OF TRENTON

TRENTON. *Catholic Charities*, 383 W. State St., P.O. Box 1423, 08607-1423. Tel: 609-394-5181; Fax: 609-695-6978. Email: mlaocollins@cctrenton.org. Web: catholiccharitiestrenton.org. Ms. Marlene Lao'-Collins, Exec. Dir.; George Bontcue, Assoc. Exec. Dir., Fiscal Affairs; Kathryn Jean Turner, Assoc. Exec. Dir. Human Resources; Nancy B. Tompkins, Devel. Dir.; Joyce Campbell, M.S.W., L.C.S.W., Assoc. Exec. Dir. External Affairs; Mary Ellen Blackwell, Dir., Parish Social Min.

Behavioral Health Services Burlington County, 25 Ikea Dr., Westampton, 08060. Tel: 609-267-9339; Fax: 609-267-6655. Email: hpostel@cctrenton.org.

Harry Postel, M.S.W., L.C.S.W., Svc. Area Dir.

Behavioral Health Services Mercer County, 10 Southard St., 08609. Tel: 609-396-4557; Fax: 609-394-1412. Email: hpostel@cctrenton.org. Harry Postel, M.S.W., L.C.S.W., Svc. Area Dir.

Children & Family Services Monmouth/Ocean Counties, 145 Maple Ave., Red Bank, 07701. Tel: 732-747-9660; Fax: 732-747-7590. Email: rgering@cctrenton.org. Ronald C. Gering, L.P.C., C.C.M.H.C., Svc. Area Dir.

Emergency & Community Services, 801 Burlington Ave., Delanco, 08075. Tel: 856-764-6945; Fax: 856-764-6948. Jackie Edwards, M.H.S., Svc. Area Dir. Emergency & Community Svcs.

Emergency and Community Services (Mercer), 132 N. Warren St., 08608. Tel: 609-394-8847; Fax: 609-599-9271. Jackie Edwards, M.H.S., Svc. Area Dir. Emergency & Community Svcs.

Emergency and Community Services (Ocean), 200 Monmouth Ave., Lakewood, 08701. Tel: 732-363-5322; Fax: 732-363-3203. Jackie Edwards, M.H.S., Svc. Area Dir. Emergency & Community Svcs.

Children & Family Services Mercer County, 55 N. Clinton Ave., 08609. Tel: 609-394-7680; Fax: 609-278-1836. Email: rgering@cctrenton.org. Ronald C. Gering, L.P.C., C.C.M.H.C., Svc. Area Dir. Services for victims and perpetuators of family violence.

Providence House Domestic Violence Services, 950A Chester Ave., Delran, 08075. Tel: 856-824-0599; Fax: 856-824-9340. Email: jmetz@cctrenton.org. Jean Metz, L.C.S.W., Svc. Area Dir. Services to women and children in danger of physical abuse.

Providence House Domestic Violence Services (Ocean), 88 Schoolhouse Rd., Whiting, 08759. Tel: 732-350-2120; Fax: 732-350-2725.

St. Michael Children's Home, c/o Diocese of Trenton, 701 Lawrenceville Rd., 08648.

[H] DAY CARE CENTERS

TRENTON. *Mount Carmel Guild Day Care Center*, 73 N. Clinton Ave., 08609. Tel: 609-392-5159. Email: mtcarmelguild@aol.com. Web: www.mcgtrenton.org. Mr. Russell J. Hansel, Exec. Dir.; Paula Maugans, Contact Person.

BRANT BEACH. *St. Francis of Assisi Day Care Center*, 4700 Long Beach Blvd., 08008. Tel: 609-494-8861; Fax: 609-494-0489. Joan Wickert, Contact Person.

HAMILTON. *Our Lady of Sorrows Preschool*, 3710 E. State St. Ext., 08619. Tel: 609-586-1422; Fax: 609-586-1214. Email: moboyle@ols-sa.org. Web: www.ols-sa.org. Mary O'Boyle, Dir. Preschool and Day Care Center. Lay Teachers 12.

KEANSBURG. *St. Ann Day Care*, 121 Main St., 07734. Tel: 732-787-7220; Fax: 732-787-2136. Sr. Mary Faith, Contact Person.

LONG BRANCH. *St. John the Baptist Family Center*, 272 Willow Ave., 07740. Tel: 732-229-8905; 732-229-8527; 732-571-1003; Fax: 732-571-0280. Email: roma1960@comcast.net. Day Care and Child Development Center. Children 154.

[I] CARE INSTITUTIONS FOR CHILDREN

EWING. *Sister Georgine School*, 180B Ewingville Rd., 08638. Tel: 609-771-4300; Fax: 609-771-8521. Email: sgs@srgeorgineschool.org. Web: www.srgeorgineschool.org. Sr. Barbara Furst, Prin. Sisters of St. Francis. Students 16; Staff 9.

HOPEWELL. *St. Michael's Orphanage and Industrial School, c/o the Diocese of Trenton*, 701 Lawrenceville Rd., 08648.

[J] GENERAL HOSPITALS

TRENTON. *St. Francis Medical Center*, 601 Hamilton Ave., 08629. Tel: 609-599-5000; Fax: 609-695-2744. Email: rhansel@stfrancismedical.org. Web: www.stfrancismedical.com. Affiliate of Catholic Health East. Sisters of St. Francis of Philadelphia 7; Bed Capacity 238; Patients Assisted Annually 128,953; Total Staff 1,117.

Schools for Nurses Tel: 609-599-5785; Fax: 609-599-6463. Bonny Ross, Dir. School of Nursing; Russ Hansel, Vice Pres., Mission & Ministry. Student Nurses 63.

WILLINGBORO. *The Combined Auxiliaries of Lourdes Medical Center of Burlington County*, 218A Sunset Rd., 08046. Tel: 609-835-2900; Fax: 609-835-3061.

Parent Organization: Our Lady of Lourdes Health Foundation, Inc.

Lourdes Medical Center of Burlington County, Inc. (Parent Corporation: Our Lady of Lourdes Health Care Services, Inc.), 218A Sunset Rd., 08046. Tel: 609-835-2900; Fax: 609-835-3061. Web: www.lourdesnet.org.

Lourdes Medical Center of Burlington County

[K] SPECIAL HOSPITALS AND SANATORIA FOR INVALIDS

LAWRENCEVILLE. *Morris Hall/Saint Lawrence, Inc.*, 2381 Lawrenceville Rd., 08648. Tel: 609-896-9500; Fax: 609-895-0242. Email: dhanley@slrc.org. Web: www.slrc.org. Darlene Hanley, CEO; Rev. John Wake, Chap. St. Lawrence Rehabilitation Center. Bed Capacity 166; Bed Licensure 166; Total Assisted Annually 2,496; Total Staff 415.

Morris Hall/Saint Lawrence, Inc. Morris Hall - St. Joseph's Nursing Center, 1 Bishops' Dr., 08648-2050. Tel: 609-896-0006; Fax: 609-896-8037; 609-895-0466. Email: epetroski@morrishall.org. Web: www.morrishall.org. Ellen Petroski, M.S.W., L.S.W., L.N.H.A., Admin. & COO; Juvy Gonzales, R.N., Dir. of Nursing. Skilled Nursing Care Facility for the Chronically Ill. Bed Capacity 120; Total Assisted Annually 173; Staff 100.

Residences and Assisted Living for Senior Citizens Tel: 609-896-0006; Fax: 609-896-8037. Email: epetroski@morrishall.org. Web: www.morrishall.org.

Rosecliff Living-Inc., 2382 Lawrenceville Rd., 08648. Tel: 609-896-9500; Fax: 609-895-0242. Charles L. Brennan, CEO. Purpose is to provide housing, healthcare and social facilities and services to older adults.

[L] SPECIALIZED CHILD CARE AGENCIES

RED BANK. *Collier Group Home*, 180 Spring St., 07701. Tel: 732-842-8337; Fax: 732-530-7096. Email: pauldes21@verizon.net. Web: www.collieryouthservices.org. Mr. Paul DeSantis, Dir. Residential Programs. 24 Hour Program-Therapy and Educational Services. Provided Under the Supervision of the Sisters of the Good Shepherd. Capacity 10; Total Assisted Annually 20; Total Staff 8.

Collier House, 386 Maple Pl., Keyport, 07735. Tel: 732-264-3222; Fax: 732-264-3277. Email: pauldes21@verizon.net. Web: www.collieryouthservices.org. Mr. Paul DeSantis, Dir. Residential Prog. Transitional Aging-Out Program for Women 18-21 years old. Capacity 5; Total Staff 6.

WICKATUNK. *Collier Services, Collier School*, 160 Conover Rd., 07765. Tel: 732-946-4771; Fax: 732-946-3519. Email: info@collieryouthservices.org. Web: www.collieryouthservices.org. Raymond Bock, Prin.; Sr. Deborah Drago, Exec. Dir. Boys and Girls in grades 6-12. Capacity 150; Total Assisted Annually 200; Total Staff 70.

Kateri Environmental Education Center Tel: 732-946-9694; Fax: 732-946-9785. Web: www.collieryouthservices.org. Daniel N. Smith Jr., Prog. Dir. Kateri Day Camp serves children 5-12 years old.; Project Eco- six week extended school year program.; JET- Summer Job Experience & Training program for teens. Capacity 75; Total Assisted Annually 4,471.

[M] HOMES FOR AGED

TRENTON. *Cathedral Square Housing, Inc.*, 26 W. Hanover Pl., 08608. Tel: 609-392-1111; Fax: 609-683-7227. Email: cs@gershengroup.com. Most Rev. John M. Smith, Dir. (Retired). Senior Citizen Housing Project.

LAWRENCEVILLE. *Morris Hall-Saint Lawrence, Inc.*, 1 Bishops' Dr., 08648-2050. Tel: 609-896-0006; Fax: 609-896-8037; 609-895-0466. Email: epetroski@morrishall.org. Web: www.morrishall.org. Darlene Hanley, CEO; Ellen Petroski, M.S.W., L.S.W., L.N.H.A., COO; Rev. John Wake. Morris Hall - St. Mary's Residence & Assisted Living. Guests 62; Bed Capacity 98; Total Assisted Annually 86; Total Staff 45.

YARDVILLE. *Villa Maria Sanitarium*, 109 Rte. 156, 08620. Tel: 609-585-4660; Fax: 609-585-2759. Rev. Severin Dietrich, O.F.M.Conv., Chap. Administration: Franciscan Sisters. Total Staff 7; Residents 4.

[N] MONASTERIES AND RESIDENCES FOR PRIESTS AND BROTHERS

TRENTON. *St. Lawrence Rehabilitation Center* (Lawrenceville), 2381 Lawrenceville Rd., 08648. Tel: 609-896-9500; Fax: 609-895-0242. Email: clb950@aol.com. Web: www.slrc.org. Darlene Hanley, CEO. Nursing care for priests. In Res. Most Rev. John C. Reiss, D.D., J.C.D. (Retired); Revs. James N. Cammisa (Retired); James E. Coley (Retired); Stanislaus Polczyk; Laszlo F. Rauch (Retired); Ricard Sweeney.

Villa Vianney (Lawrenceville), 2301 Lawrenceville Rd., 08648. Tel: 609-219-0177; Fax: 609-896-8037. In Res. Most Rev. John M. Smith (Retired); Rev. Msgrs. William J. Carton (Retired); John K. Dermond, J.C.L.; William F. Fitzgerald (Retired); Hugh F. Ronan (Retired); Joseph C. Shenrock, P.A. (Retired); Edward Strano (Retired); Gregory D. Vaughan, V.G.; Revs. John V. Bowden (Retired); Harry E. Cenefeldt (Retired); G. William Evans; Leon J. Inverso; Adam Kearns (Retired); E.T. Keenan; John T. Kielb; Gerard J. McCarron (Retired); James J. McConnell (Retired); Richard R. Milewski; Joseph A. Radomski (Retired).

BORDENTOWN. *Society of the Divine Word*, 101 Park St., 08505. Tel: 609-298-0549; Fax: 609-298-6013. Revs. Vincent Burke, S.V.D.; Victor Butler, S.V.D.; Patrick Connor, S.V.D.; Quy Dang, S.V.D.; Joseph Detig, S.V.D.; Leo Dusheck, S.V.D.; Raymond Hannah, S.V.D.; Charles Heskamp, S.V.D.; Raymond T. Lennon, S.V.D., Vice Rector; John McSherry, S.V.D.; Martin Padovani, S.V.D.; Jefferson Pool, S.V.D.; Steven Schuler, S.V.D.; Gerhard Vogel, S.V.D.; Bros. Javier Eshman, S.V.D., Admin.; George Haegele, S.V.D.; Patrick Hogan, S.V.D., Rector; James Mullen, S.V.D.

EATONTOWN. *Christian Brothers of Frederick*, 444A Rte. 35 S., 07724-2200. Tel: 732-380-7926; Fax: 732-380-7937.

La Salle Provincialate Inc., 444A Rte. 35 S., 07724-2200. Tel: 732-380-7926; Fax: 732-380-7937. Brothers of the Christian Schools.

LINCROFT. *Christian Brothers, St. La Salle Auxiliary*, 850 Newman Springs Rd., P.O. Box 238, 07738-0238. Tel: 732-842-4359; Fax: 732-219-1619. Email: cards@dlsaux.org. Web: dlsaux.org. Bro. William Martin, F.S.C., Dir. *LaSalle Lincroft, Inc.*, 800 Newman Springs Rd., 07738-0238. Tel: 732-380-7926; Fax: 732-380-7937. Bro. Dennis Lee, F.S.C., Pres.

De La Salle Hall, 810 Newman Springs Rd., 07738. Tel: 732-530-9470; Fax: 732-530-3153. Bro. Michael Finnegan, F.S.C., Dir. Brothers Licensed Nursing Home. Brothers 3; Lay Staff 50; Patients 32.

MOUNT LAUREL. *Cistercian Monastery of Our Lady of Fatima*, 564 Walton Ave., 08054-9582. Tel: 856-235-1330; Fax: 856-235-9632. Revs. Lino S. Parente, O.Cist. (Italy), Prior (Italy); Maurizio Nicoletti, O.Cist. (Italy); Awte Weldu, O.Cist.; Musie Tesfayohanneso, O.Cist. Cistercian Fathers.

[O] CONVENTS AND RESIDENCES FOR SISTERS

TRENTON. *Morning Star House of Prayer*, 312 Upper Ferry Rd., 08628. Tel: 609-882-2766; Fax: 609-882-2766. Email: sisterjo@comcast.net. Web: www.morningstarprayerhouse.org. Religious Sisters Filippini.

Notre Dame Diocesan Convent, 681 Lawrence Rd., 08648. Tel: 609-406-7437; Fax: 609-406-7412. Web: dioceseoftrenton.org. Lawrenceville; Intercongregational Living. Sisters 10.

Sisters of St. Francis of Philadelphia, St. Clare Convent, 917 Melrose Ave., 08629. Tel: 609-695-7805. Email: clareconl@verizon.net. Web: osfphila.org.

Villa Victoria Academy Convent, 376 W. Upper Ferry Rd., 08628. Tel: 609-883-0064; Fax: 609-882-8066. Web: www.villavictoria.org. Religious Teachers Filippini.

ASBURY PARK. *Missionaries of Charity*, 144 Ridge Ave., 07712. Tel: 732-775-1101.

CHESTERFIELD. *Monastery of Saint Clare*, 150 White Pine Rd., 08515. Tel: 609-324-2638; Fax: 609-324-2938. Email: mvarleyosc@verizon.net. Web: www.poorclaresofnewjersey.com. Sr. Miriam Varley, O.S.C., Abbess.

DELRAN. *Holy Cross High School Convent*, Sisters of the Immaculate Heart of Mary, 5035 Rte. 130 S., 08075. Tel: 856-461-1792.

HARVEY CEDARS. *Maris Stella Retreat and Conference Center*, 7201 Long Beach Blvd., 08008. Tel: 609-361-8863; Fax: 609-494-1182. Sr. Mary Morley, S.C., Admin. Sisters of Charity of St. Elizabeth, Convent Station.

LAKEWOOD. *Sisters of Mercy of the Americas, Mid-Atlantic Community, Georgian Court University Convent*, 900 Lakewood Ave., 08701. Tel: 732-987-2576; Fax: 732-987-2019.

NEW MONMOUTH. *Siena New Hope Home*, P.O. Box 518, 07748. Tel: 732-671-3622; Fax: 732-671-3691. Email: sienanewhopehome@comcast.net. Religious Teachers Filippini.

OCEAN GROVE. *Emmaus House*, 21 Main Ave., 07756. Tel: 732-776-5458; Fax: 732-776-7065. Email: dwiswl18@aol.com. Sr. Patricia Mary Walsh, O.P., Admin.

Memorare, 20 Pitman Ave., 07756. Tel: 732-774-3158; Fax: 732-776-7065. Sr. Patricia Mary Walsh, O.P., Admin.

WICKATUNK. *Convent of the Sisters of Good Shepherd*, 160 Conover Rd., 07765. Tel: 732-946-7877; 732-946-7886; Fax: 732-332-1240. Web: www.goodshepherdsisters.org. Email: rosalyn.menard@nygoodshepherd.org. Rosalyn Menard, Coord. Sisters of Good Shepherd of New Jersey. Sisters 6.

YARDVILLE. *Congregation of the Servants of the Holy Child Jesus of the Third Order Regular of Sant Fra*, 109 Rte. 156, 08620. Tel: 609-585-4660; Fax: 609-585-2759. Sr. M. Antonia Cooper, Rel. Min. Properties owned and or sponsored: Villa Maria Sanitarium, Inc., Trenton, NJ. Ministry in Social Work; Health Care. Represented in the Dioceses of Trenton, Paterson, Metuchen. Total in American Region 17.

[P] CHAPELS

LAWRENCEVILLE. *Our Lady of the Rosary Chapel* 1 Bishops' Dr., 08648-2050. Tel: 609-896-0006; Fax: 609-895-0466. Email: info@morrishall.org. Web: www.morrishall.org. Located in Morris Hall.

[Q] HOUSES OF PRAYER

TRENTON. *Morning Star House of Prayer*, 312 W. Upper Ferry Rd., 08628. Tel: 609-882-2766; Fax: 609-882-2766. Email: sisterjo@morningstarprayerhouse.org. Web: morningstarprayerhouse.org. Sr. Josephine Aparo, M.P.F. Religious Teachers Filippini 2.

MOUNT HOLLY. *Francis House of Prayer*, P.O. Box 392, Rancocas, 08073. Tel: 609-877-0509. 39 Springside Rd., Westampton, 08060. Tel: 609-877-0509. Email: fhop@verizon.net. Web: www.fhop.org. Sr. Marcella Springer, S.S.J.

NEPTUNE. *The Upper Room Spiritual Center*, 3455 W. Bangs Ave. - Bldg. 2, 07753. Tel: 732-922-0550; Fax: 732-922-3904. Email: office@theupper-room.org. Web: www.theupper-room.org. Sisters Maureen Christensen, R.S.M., Co-Dir.; Maureen Conroy, R.S.M., Co-Dir.; Trudy Ahern, S.S.J., Co-Dir.

[R] RETREAT HOUSES

ELBERON. *Stella Maris Retreat Center*, 981 Ocean Ave., 07740. Tel: 732-229-0602; Fax: 732-229-8960. Email: stellamaris981@yahoo.com. Web: www.stellamarisretreatcenter.com. Sr. Lois Jablonski, S.S.J., Admin.

LONG BRANCH. *San Alfonso Retreat House*, 755 Ocean Ave., P.O. Box 3098, 07740. Tel: 732-222-2731; Fax: 732-870-8892. Email: info@sanalfonsoretreats.org. Web: www.sanalfonsoretreats.org. Revs. Thomas J. Siconolfi, C.Ss.R., Rector/Dir.; Dennis Foley, C.Ss.R.; John M. Connor, C.Ss.R.; James McDonald, C.Ss.R.; John McGowan, C.Ss.R.; Bro. Bernard Colleran, C.Ss.R.; Deacon Paul Gallagher. Priests 4; Brothers 1. In Res. Revs. John F. Murray, C.Ss.R.; John R. Cody, C.Ss.R.; William Gaffney, C.Ss.R.

SOUTH MANTOLOKING. *St. Joseph by the Sea Retreat House*, 400 Rte. 35 N., 08738. Tel: 732-892-8494; Fax: 732-892-9905. Email: sjbsea@comcast.net. Web: www.sjbsea.org. Sisters Frances Lauretti, M.P.F., Dir.; Barbara Ranere, M.P.F., Admin. Asst.; Brunilda Ramos, M.P.F., Admin. Asst. Sisters 3.

[S] PERSONAL PRELATURES

PRINCETON. *Opus Dei* Prelature of the Holy Cross and Opus Dei, 34 Mercer St., 08540. Tel: 609-497-9448; Fax: 609-497-0906. Email: mjm105@yahoo.com. Web: www.opusdei.org. Rev. Martin Joseph Miller.

[T] NEWMAN CENTERS

PRINCETON. *Campus Ministry for the Diocese of Trenton* Aquinas Institute, Princeton University, 65 Stockton St., 08540. Tel: 609-924-1820; Fax: 609-924-8322. Email: mullelly@princeton.edu. Very Rev. Thomas J. Mullelly, J.D., Dir. & Chap.

Emmaus House, Rider University 2116 Lawrenceville Rd., 08648. Tel: 609-896-0394; Fax: 609-219-9203. Email: bugliano@rider.edu. Rev. Joseph A. Jakub, Chap.

Mercer County Community College 1200 Old Trenton Rd., Hamilton Township, 08690. Tel: 609-896-0394; Fax: 609-219-9203. Rev. Joseph A. Jakub, Chap.

Bede House, College of New Jersey 492 Ewingville Rd., 08638. Tel: 609-771-9091. Rev. William J. Lago, Chap.

Georgian Court College 900 Lakewood Ave., Lakewood, 08701. Tel: 732-364-2200, Ext. 600; Fax: 732-901-7151. Sr. Mariann Mahon, R.S.M., Dir. Campus Ministry.

Catholic Center at Monmouth University 16 Beechwood Ave., West Long Branch, 07764. Tel: 732-229-9300; Fax: 732-229-1050. Web: mucatholic.com. Rev. Ireneusz Ekiert, O.SS.T, Chap.; Mary Jakub, Assoc. Dir.

[U] MISCELLANEOUS LISTINGS

TRENTON. *Diocese of Trenton Charitable Trust for Aged, Infirm and Disabled Priests*, 701 Lawrenceville Rd., 08648. Mr. Anthony J. Mingarino, CAO & Contact Person.

Diocese of Trenton Endowment Trust for Catholic Charities, 701 Lawrenceville Rd., 08648.

Diocese of Trenton Endowment Trust for Catholic Education and Religious Formation, 701 Lawrenceville Rd., 08648.

**Foundation for Student Achievement, Inc.*, 701 Lawrenceville Rd., 08648.

The Haitian Community Center, 530 S. Olden Ave, 08629. Tel: 609-588-8808; Fax: 609-588-8801. Mrs. Magda Dorleans, Dir.

Martin House, 802 E. State St., P.O. Box 1025, 08606. Tel: 609-989-0961; Fax: 609-989-0933. Rev. Brian McCormick. Priests 1; Total Assisted 2,000; Total Staff 7.

Martin House Learning Center, 794 E. State St., P.O. Box 1025, 08609. Tel: 609-989-8143; Fax: 609-989-0933. Deborah A. Robinson, CEO. Ministers 1; Total Assisted 700; Total Staff 35.

New Jersey Catholic Conference, 149 N. Warren St., 08608. Tel: 609-989-1120; Fax: 609-989-1152. Email: info@njcathconf.com. Web: www.njcathconf.com. Most Rev. John J. Myers, D.D., J.C.D., Pres.; Deacon Patrick R. Brannigan, Exec. Dir.

Trenton Diocesan Union of Holy Name Societies, 701 Lawrenceville Rd., P.O. Box 5147, 08638-0147. Tel: 732-295-2111; Fax: 732-295-2333. Email: hudsoncorp@comcast.net. Web: dioceseoftrenton.org.

Burlington County Federation of Holy Name Societies

Mercer County Federation of Holy Name Societies

Monmouth County Federation of Holy Name Societies

Ocean County Federation of Holy Name Societies

ASBURY PARK. *Mercy Center, Inc.*, 1106 Main St., 07712. Tel: 732-774-9397; Fax: 732-988-8709. Email: sistercarol@mercycenternj.org. Web: mercycenternj.org. Carol Ann Henry, R.S.M., Dir.

BRICK. *Mid-Life Directions*, 4 Palm Ave., 08723. Tel: 732-255-1239; Fax: 732-255-1239. Email: midlifedirections@comcast.net. Sr. Anne Brennan, C.S.J., Contact Person. Purpose: Ministry for personal and spiritual growth specifically for people in midlife and later years.

EATONTOWN. *Christian Brothers Retirement and Continuing Care Trust*, 444A Rte. 35 S., 07724-2200. Tel: 732-380-7926; Fax: 732-380-7937.

District of Eastern North America Ministry Corporation, 444A Rte. 35 S., 07724-2200. Tel: 732-380-7926; Fax: 732-380-7937.

FSC DENA Endowment Trust, 444A Rte. 35 S., 07724-2200. Tel: 732-380-7926; Fax: 732-380-7937.

FSC DENA Real Estate Holding Corporation, 444A Rte. 35 S., 07724-2200. Pager: 732-380-7926; Fax: 732-380-7937.

FSC DENA Real Estate Trust, 444A Rte. 35 S., 07724-2200. Tel: 732-380-7926; Fax: 732-380-7937.

LAWRENCEVILLE. *The Foundation of Morris Hall/St. Lawrence, Inc.*, 2381 Lawrenceville Rd., 08648. Tel: 609-896-9500, Ext. 2215; Fax: 609-895-1602. Email: jmillner@slrc.org. Web: www.slrc.org. Mr. Thomas E. Boyle, CFO & Contact Person.

Morris Hall/St. Lawrence, Inc., 1 Bishops' Dr., 08648-2050. Tel: 609-896-0006; Fax: 609-896-8037. Email: epetroski@morrishall.org. Web: www.morrishall.org. Bed Capacity 120; Bed Licensure 120.

Morris Hall Tel: 609-896-0006; Fax: 609-896-8037. Email: epetroski@morrishall.org. Darlene Hanley, CEO; Ellen Petroski, M.S.W., L.S.W., L.N.H.A., COO. Priests 1; Total Assisted 300; Total Staff 145.

LINCROFT. *The Bethlehem University Foundation, Inc.*, 800 Newman Springs Rd., 07738-1696. Tel: 732-380-7926; Fax: 732-380-7937. Sr. Irene O'Neill, C.S.J., Bd. Chm.; Bro. David Carroll, F.S.C., Sec.; Benjamin Monastero, Treas.

Brothers of the Christian Schools District of Eastern North America, Inc., 800 Newman Springs Rd., 07738-1696. Tel: 732-380-7926; Fax: 732-380-7937.

Christian Brothers of Lincroft, NJ, Inc., 854 Newman Springs Rd., 07738-1698. Tel: 732-842-6712; Fax: 732-758-8310. Bro. Ralph Montedoro, F.S.C., Contact Person.

MIDDLETOWN. *The Gathering Place*, 130 Bray Ave., 07748. Tel: 732-495-7615; Fax: 732-495-6422. Email: pnoonel@comcast.net. Sr. Margaret Noone, R.S.M., Contact Person. Ministry which promotes systemic change through programs of human development and spiritual growth, with special emphasis on those who are poor.

TOMS RIVER. *Holy Redeemer Visiting Nurse Agency, Inc., (Ocean County Office)*, 1228 Rte. 37 W., 08755. Tel: 732-240-2449; Fax: 732-288-2669.

RELIGIOUS INSTITUTES OF MEN REPRESENTED IN THE DIOCESE

For further details refer to the corresponding bracketed number in the Religious Institutes of Men or Women section.

[0140]—*The Augustinians*—O.S.A.

[0200]—*Benedictine Monks* (St. Mary's Abbey, Morristown, NJ)—O.S.B.

[0330]—*Brothers of the Christian Schools*—F.S.C.

[1100]—*Brothers of the Sacred Heart*—S.C.

[0270]—*Carmelite Fathers and Brothers*—O.Carm.

[0340]—*Cistercian Fathers* (Cistercian Monastery of Our Lady of Fatima)—O.Cist.

[0390]—*Consolata Missionaries* (US Prov.)—I.M.C.

[0480]—*Conventual Franciscans* (Provs. of the Immaculate Conception & St. Anthony of Padua)—O.F.M.Conv.

[0520]—*Franciscan Friars* (Prov. of the Most Holy Name of Jesus)—O.F.M.

[1310]—*Order of the Holy Trinity*—O.SS.T.

[1070]—*Redemptorist Fathers & Brothers* (Baltimore & Denver Prov.)—C.Ss.R.

[0420]—*Society of the Divine Word*—S.V.D.

[]—*Vincentian Congregation*—V.C.

RELIGIOUS INSTITUTES OF WOMEN REPRESENTED IN THE DIOCESE

[1810]—*Bernardine Sisters of Third Order of St. Francis*—O.S.F.

[1980]—*Congregation of the Servants of the Holy Child Jesus of the Third Order Regular of Sant Fra*—O.S.F.

[2980]—*Congregation of Notre Dame*—C.N.D.

[2410]—*Congregation of the Marianites of Holy Cross*—M.S.C.

[1170]—*Congregation of the Sisters of St. Felix (Felician Sisters)*—C.S.S.F.

[1830]—*Contemplative Sisters of the Good Shepherd*—R.G.S.

[0850]—*Daughters of Mary Help of Christians*—F.M.A.

[1070-05]—*Dominican Sisters* (Amityville, NY)—O.P.

[1070-11]—*Dominican Sisters* (Sparkhill, NY)—O.P.

[1070-15]—*Dominican Sisters* (Blauvelt, NY)—O.P.

[1070-18]—*Dominican Sisters* (Caldwell, NJ)—O.P.

[1105]—*Dominican Sisters of Hope* (Ossining, NY)—O.P.

[1115]—*Dominican Sisters of Peace*—O.P.

[1365]—*Franciscan Missionary Sisters of the Infant Jesus*—F.M.I.J.

[1180]—*Franciscan Sisters of Allegany, NY*—O.S.F.

[1470]—*Franciscan Sisters of St. Joseph* (Hamburg, NY)—F.S.S.J.

[1190]—*Franciscan Sisters of the Atonement (Graymoor)*—S.A.

[1840]—*Grey Nuns of the Sacred Heart*—G.N.S.H.

[]—*Hermanitas de la Anunciacion* (Columbia, South America)—H.A.

[2710]—*Missionaries of Charity*—M.C.

[2760]—*Missionary Sisters of the Immaculate Conception of the Mother of God*—S.M.I.C.

[3760]—*Order of St. Clare*—O.S.C.

[3465]—*Religious of the Sacred Heart of Mary*—R.S.H.M.

[3430]—*Religious Teachers Filippini*—M.P.F.

[2970]—*School Sisters of Notre Dame, Baltimore* (Province)—S.S.N.D.

[1700]—*School Sisters of the Third Order of St. Francis* (Bethlehem, PA)—O.S.F.

[1980]—*Servants of the Holy Infancy of Jesus*—O.S.F.

[]—*Sisters for Christian Community*—S.F.C.C.

[0590]—*Sisters of Charity of Saint Elizabeth, Convent Station*—S.C.

[2575]—*Sisters of Mercy of the Americas* (Mid-Atlantic Community)—R.S.M.

[3360]—*Sisters of Providence of Saint Mary of the Woods, IN*—S.P.

[3830]—*Sisters of Saint Joseph of Brentwood* (New York)—C.S.J.

[1630]—*Sisters of St. Francis of Penance and Christian Charity*—O.S.F.

[1650]—*The Sisters of St. Francis of Philadelphia*—O.S.F.

[]—*Sisters of St. Francis of the Neumann Communities*—O.S.F.

[3893]—*Sisters of St. Joseph of Chestnut Hill, Philadelphia*—S.S.J.

[3890]—*Sisters of St. Joseph of Peace*—C.S.J.P.

[1830]—*The Sisters of the Good Shepherd*—R.G.S.

[1970]—*Sisters of the Holy Family of Nazareth*—C.S.F.N.

[3480]—*Sisters of the Resurrection*—C.R.

[2170]—*Sisters, Servants of the Immaculate Heart of Mary* (Immaculata, PA)—I.H.M.

[2160]—*Sisters, Servants of the Immaculate Heart of Mary* (Scranton)—I.H.M.

[0810]—*Society of the Daughters of the Heart of Mary*—D.H.M.

[4060]—*Society of the Holy Child Jesus*—S.H.C.J.

[4070]—*Society of the Sacred Heart*—R.S.C.J.

NECROLOGY

✠ Reiss, Most Rev. John C.—Died March 4, 2012
† Smith, Rev. Msgr. Alfred D., (Retired)—Died Sept. 12, 2011
† Byrnes, John P., (Retired)—Died Oct. 26, 2011
† Donadio, Vincent J., (Retired)—Died July 6, 2011
† Dougherty, Edward J., (Retired)—Died April 14, 2011
† Horvath, Stephen G., (Retired)—Died Nov. 2, 2011
† McLaughlin, William J., Asbury Park, NJ Holy Spirit & St. Peter Claver.—Died Oct. 19, 2011
† Nolan, William J., (Retired)—Died Dec. 18, 2010
† Petri, John C., (Retired)—Died June 10, 2011

An asterisk (*) denotes an organization that has established tax-exempt status directly with the IRS and is not covered by the USCCB Group Ruling.

Diocese of Tucson

(Dioecesis Tucsonensis)

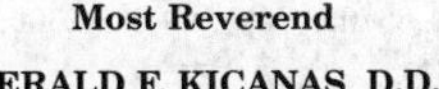

Most Reverend

GERALD F. KICANAS, D.D.

Bishop of Tucson; ordained April 27, 1967; appointed Titular Bishop of Bela and Auxiliary Bishop of Chicago January 24, 1995; consecrated March 20, 1995; appointed Coadjutor Bishop of Tucson October 30, 2001; installed January 15, 2002; succeeded to See of Tucson March 7, 2003. *Mailing Address: P.O. Box 31, Tucson, AZ 85702*. Tel: 520-838-2500; Fax: 520-838-2590.

Chancery Office: 111 S. Church Ave., P.O. Box 31, Tucson, AZ 85702. Tel: 520-838-2500.

Web: www.diocesetucson.org

Email: diocese@diocesetucson.org

ESTABLISHED A VICARIATE-APOSTOLIC 1868.

Square Miles 42,707.

Erected by His Holiness Pope Leo XIII, May 8, 1897.

Comprises the Counties of Cochise, Gila, Greenlee, Graham, La Paz, Pima, Pinal, Santa Cruz and Yuma in the State of Arizona.

For legal titles of parishes and diocesan institutions, consult the Chancery Office.

STATISTICAL OVERVIEW

Personnel	
Bishop	1
Priests: Diocesan Active in Diocese	70
Priests: Diocesan Active Outside Diocese	3
Priests: Retired, Sick or Absent	17
Number of Diocesan Priests	90
Religious Priests in Diocese	85
Total Priests in Diocese	175
Extern Priests in Diocese	47
Permanent Deacons in Diocese	139
Total Brothers	25
Total Sisters	170
Parishes	
Parishes	76
With Resident Pastor:	
Resident Diocesan Priests	53
Resident Religious Priests	17
Without Resident Pastor:	
Administered by Priests	4
Administered by Deacons	1
Administered by Religious Women	1
Missions	46
New Parishes Created	1
Professional Ministry Personnel:	
Brothers	1
Sisters	12
Lay Ministers	161
Welfare	
Catholic Hospitals	4
Total Assisted	470,000
Health Care Centers	1
Total Assisted	41,500
Special Centers for Social Services	2
Total Assisted	430,000
Educational	
Diocesan Students in Other Seminaries	13
Students Religious	1
Total Seminarians	14
High Schools, Private	6
Total Students	2,057
Elementary Schools, Diocesan and Parish	17
Total Students	4,259
Elementary Schools, Private	3
Total Students	610
Catechesis/Religious Education:	
High School Students	2,251
Elementary Students	11,278
Total Students under Catholic Instruction	20,469
Teachers in the Diocese:	
Brothers	10
Sisters	21
Lay Teachers	436
Vital Statistics	
Receptions into the Church:	
Infant Baptism Totals	4,923
Minor Baptism Totals	410
Adult Baptism Totals	243
Received into Full Communion	627
First Communions	4,503
Confirmations	2,776
Marriages:	
Catholic	636
Interfaith	97
Total Marriages	733
Deaths	2,014
Total Catholic Population	194,744
Total Population	1,820,667

Former Bishops—Most Revs. JOHN BAPTIST SALPOINTE, D.D., ord. Dec. 21, 1851; appt. Vicar Apostolic of Arizona and Titular Bishop of Doryla Sept. 25, 1868; ord. June 20, 1869; appt. Coadjutor Archbishop of Santa Fe with right of succession April 12, 1884 and Titular Archbishop of Anazarba Oct. 3, 1884; succeeded to the See of Santa Fe July 18, 1885; resigned; appt. Titular Archbishop of Tomi Jan. 27, 1894; died Tucson, July 15, 1898; PETER BOURGADE, D.D., ord. Nov. 30, 1869; appt. Vicar Apostolic of Arizona Jan. 23, 1885 and Titular Bishop of Thaumacum Feb. 7, 1885 and ord. May 1, 1885; appt. first Bishop of Tucson May 10, 1897; appt. fourth Archbishop of Santa Fe Jan. 7, 1899; died Chicago, May 17, 1908; HENRY REGIS GRANJON, D.D., ord. Dec. 17, 1887; appt. second Bishop of Tucson April 19, 1900; ord. June 17, 1900; died Brignais, France, Nov. 9, 1922; DANIEL JAMES GERCKE, D.D., ord. June 1, 1901; appt. third Bishop of Tucson June 21, 1923; ord. Nov. 6, 1923; resigned; appt. Titular Archbishop of Cotyaeum Oct. 26, 1960; died Tucson, March 19, 1964; FRANCIS JOSEPH GREEN, D.D., ord. May 15, 1932; appt. Titular Bishop of Serra in Proconsulari and Auxiliary Bishop of Tucson May 29, 1953; cons. Sept. 17, 1953; appt. Coadjutor "cum jure successionis" May 11, 1960; succeeded to See to become fourth Bishop of Tucson Oct. 26, 1960; retired July 28, 1981; died May 11, 1995; MANUEL D. MORENO, D.D. (Retired), ord. April 25, 1961; appt. Titular Bishop of Tanagra and Auxiliary of Los Angeles Dec. 20, 1976; cons. Feb. 19, 1977; appt. Bishop of Tucson Jan. 12, 1982; retired March 7, 2003; died Nov. 17, 2006.

Vicars General—Revs. RAUL P. TREVIZO, V.G.; ALBERT I. SCHIFANO, V.G., M.C.

Moderator of the Curia—Rev. ALBERT I. SCHIFANO, V.G., M.C.; Mrs. KATHY RHINEHART, Exec. Asst. Tel: 520-838-2500. Email: kathyr@diocesetucson.org.

Episcopal Vicar—Rev. Msgr. RICHARD W. O'KEEFFE, E.V., Yuma La Paz Vicariate (Retired).

Chancery Office—111 S. Church Ave., P.O. Box 31, Tucson, 85702. Tel: 520-838-2500; Fax: 520-838-2590.

Chancellor—Mr. ERNEST T. NEDDER, Office, 111 S. Church Ave., Tucson, 85701. Tel: 520-838-2500; Fax: 520-838-2581; Mrs. ANNA MARIA MAMMEN, Exec. Asst. Tel: 520-838-2511. Email: annamaria@diocesetucson.org.

Executive Assistants to the Bishop—Mrs. SONYA GUTIERREZ. Tel: 520-838-2523; Fax: 520-838-2590; Sr. CHARLOTTE ANNE SWIFT. Tel: 520-838-2500; Fax: 520-838-2590.

Fiscal Manager Office—THOMAS P. ARNOLD, CFO. Tel: 520-838-2500; DAVID KNIGHT, Senior Staff Acct., Mailing Address: P.O. Box 31, Tucson, 85702. Tel: 520-838-2500.

Matrimonial Tribunal—Office: 111 S. Church Ave., P.O. Box 31, Tucson, 85702. Tel: 520-838-2500.

Judicial Vicar—Rev. JOHN P. LYONS, J.C.L.

Adjutant Judicial Vicar—Rev. JOHN P. ARNOLD, J.C.L., V.F.

Promoter of Justice - Penal Cases—Rev. PATRICK R. LAGGES, J.C.D.

Judge—Rev. JOSEPH A. KRAUSE (Retired).

Defenders of the Bond—Revs. MICHAEL R. BUCCIARELLI, V.F.; CHARLES KNAPP (Retired); ARIEL G. LUSTAN, V.F.; RICHARD ZAMORANO.

Advocates and Auditors—Mr. KEVIN ARNOLD; Mr. CHARLES ASHLEY; Mr. RICHARD COSGROVE; Mr. LUIS KAME; Mr. MICHAEL BRESCIA; Mr. BRENDA EVEN; Mr. PEDRO NAJERA; Mr. GERALD SWEENEY; Mr. MARK WILLIMANN.

Auditors, Notaries, Case Directors—MARTHA JORDAN; HELEN EVANS, Mailing Address: P.O. Box 31, Tucson, 85702. Tel: 520-838-2500.

Professional Consultant—STEPHEN J. SCHILTZ, M.S.W.; IRENE GRAM, Ph.D.

Finance Council—Ex Officio: Most Rev. GERALD FREDERICK KICANAS, D.D., Bishop of Tucson; Rev. ALBERT I. SCHIFANO, V.G., M.C., Moderator of the Curia; THOMAS P. ARNOLD, CFO. O.F.C. Members: NANCY STEPHEN, Chm.; LUIS DABDOUB; HUMBERTO LOPEZ; LAWRENCE MCDONOUGH; Rev. PATRICK M. CRINO; RICHARD VAN EGEREN; LIRAIN URREIZTIETA; JOHN LAUER; RAYMOND BARGULL.

Diocesan Consultors—Revs. DALE A. BRANSON, V.F.; JOHN P. ARNOLD, J.C.L., V.F.; RAUL P. TREVIZO, V.G.; Rev. Msgr. THOMAS CAHALANE, V.F.; Revs. DOMENICO C. PINTI, V.F.; GONZALO J. VILLEGAS, V.F.; Most Rev. GERALD FREDERICK KICANAS, D.D.; Rev. ALBERT I. SCHIFANO, V.G., M.C.

Council of Priests—Most Rev. GERALD FREDERICK KICANAS, D.D.; Revs. RONALD A. OAKHAM, O.Carm., V.F.; JOHN P. LYONS, J.C.L.; PATRICK M. CRINO; Rev. Msgr. RICHARD W. O'KEEFFE, E.V (Retired); Revs. JAVIER H. PEREZ, V.F.; ALBERT I. SCHIFANO, V.G., M.C.; MICHAEL R. BUCCIARELLI, V.F.; EDWARD F. LUCERO, V.F.; RAUL P. TREVIZO, V.G., Vicar for Hispanic Affairs; DOMENICO C. PINTI, V.F.; ALEXANDER M. MILLS, V.F.; MARIO RICKY ORDONEZ, Dir. Vocations; STEPHEN BARNUFSKY, O.F.M., V.F.; JAY R. LUCZAK, V.F.; GONZALO J. VILLEGAS, V.F.

Vicar for Native Americans—Rev. STEPHEN

BARNUFSKY, O.F.M., V.F.
Ministry to Priests Program—Rev. JAMES M. HOBERT.
Vicar for Priests—VACANT.
Vicar for Retired Priests—Rev. Msgr. THOMAS J. MILLANE (Retired), Mailing Address: P.O. Box 31, Tucson, 85702.
Vicar for Women Religious—Sr. RINA CAPPELLAZZO, O.P., Mailing Address: P.O. Box 31, Tucson, 85702. Tel: 520-792-3410. Email: srrc@diocesetucson.org.
Vicars Forane—Revs. MICHAEL R. BUCCIARELLI, V.F., Cochise Vicariate; JAY R. LUCZAK, V.F., Gila-Pinal East; EDWARD F. LUCERO, V.F., Graham-Greenlee Vicariate; PATRICK M. CRINO, Pima-Central Vicariate; RONALD A. OAKHAM, O.Carm., V.F., Pima-East Vicariate; GONZALO J. VILLEGAS, V.F., Pima-South Vicariate; JOHN P. LYONS, J.C.L., Pima-North Vicariate; STEPHEN BARNUFSKY, O.F.M., V.F., Pima West Vicariate; DOMENICO C. PINTI, V.F., Pinal-West Vicariate; ALEXANDER M. MILLS, V.F., Santa Cruz Vicariate; JAVIER H. PEREZ, V.F., Yuma-La Paz Vicariate.

Diocesan Offices and Directors

Archives—ELIZABETH WITTENBERG, Archivist, 300 S. Tucson Blvd., Tucson, 85716. Tel: 520-886-5201. Email: bettyw@diocesetucson.org.
Board of Education—Ex Officio Members: Most Rev. GERALD FREDERICK KICANAS, D.D.; Sr. ROSA MARIA RUIZ, C.F.M.M., Supt.; Ms. SHERI DAHL, Asst. Supt. Members: THOMAS RANKIN, Pres.; DENISE MCEVOY, Vice Pres.; JOSEPH DELGADO, Sec.; DON COLEMAN; DYNSE CRUNKLETON; GERALD CURFMAN; MICHELE GRANTHAM; KAY MCLOUGHLIN; ELIZABETH MILLER; CHARLOTTE PATTERSON; NANCY WALBERT; CHRISTOPHER WINTERS.
Diocesan Building Committee—Most Rev. GERALD FREDERICK KICANAS, D.D., Honorary Chm.; Rev. ALBERT I. SCHIFANO, V.G., M.C., Moderator of the Curia; JAMES RONSTADT, Chm.; BRIAN MCCARTHY, Vice Chm.; LIZ AGUALLO, Property & Insurance Admin.; JOHN C. SHAHEEN, A.I.A., Property & Insurance Mgr.; Rev. PATRICK M. CRINO; PAT WELCHERT; HECTOR MARTINEZ; Mr. DAVID MILLER, Real Estate Specialist/Risk Mgmt.; Sr. LOIS J. PAHA, O.P.
Cemeteries—Mr. JAMES DECASTRO, Dir., Mailing Address: Holy Hope Cemetery, 3555 N. Oracle Rd., P.O. Box 5158, Tucson, 85705. Tel: 520-888-0860; Fax: 520-888-7788.
Our Lady of the Desert Cemetery—2151 S. Avenida Los Reyes, Tucson, 85748. Tel: 520-885-9173.
Desert Vista Cemetery—2151 S. Avenida Los Reyes, Tucson, 85748. Tel: 520-885-9173.
Censor Librorum—VACANT.
Office of Human Life and Dignity, Diocese of Tucson—JOANNE WELTER, Dir., P.O. Box 31, Tucson, 85702. Tel: 520-838-2500; Fax: 520-838-2583. Email: socialmission@diocesetucson.org. Includes following National Ministries: Catholic Campaign for Human Development; Catholic Relief Services
Catholic Schools—Sr. ROSA MARIA RUIZ, C.F.M.M., Supt.; Ms. SHERI DAHL, Asst. Supt., Mailing Address: P.O. Box 31, Tucson, 85702. Tel: 520-838-2546; Fax: 520-838-2589.
Communications—FRED ALLISON, Dir., Mailing Address: P.O. Box 31, Tucson, 85702. Tel: 520-838-2500.
Human Resources—RICHARD M. SERRANO, Dir.; CAROLINA CHIQUETE, Benefits Coord.; ALICIA CORTI, Employee Benefits Admin. Secretaries: ALEX NEELY; LISA NANEZ; ISELA CELAYA, 111 S. Church Ave., P.O. Box 31, Tucson, 85702. Tel: 520-838-2500; Fax: 520-838-2583.
Cursillo Movement—CINDY CHAVEZ, Lay Dir., Mailing Address: P.O. Box 31, Tucson, 85702. Tel: 928-783-3696.
Detention Ministry—MICHAEL S. GUTIERREZ, Coord., 140 W. Speedway Blvd., Ste. 230, Tucson, 85702. Tel: 520-481-9149.
Catholic Foundation for the Diocese of Tucson Stewardship and Charitable Giving—MARGIE PUERTA EDSON, Dir., 111 S. Church Ave., P.O. Box 31, Tucson, 85702. Tel: 520-838-2509.
Ecumenical Commission—Rev. Msgr. THOMAS CAHALANE, V.F., 1800 S. Kolb Rd., Tucson, 85710. Tel: 520-747-1321.
Chief Financial Officer—THOMAS P. ARNOLD, Mailing Address: P.O. Box 31, Tucson, 85702. Tel: 520-838-2500.
Holy Childhood Association—Rev. Msgr. VAN A. WAGNER, V.G., Dir. (Retired), Mailing Address: P.O. Box 31, Tucson, 85702. Tel: 520-838-2500.
Interfaith Council—LAUVER EDIE. Tel: 520-745-9443.
Legion of Decency—Chancery Office, 111 S. Church Ave., Tucson, 85701.
Diocesan Liturgical Coordinators—Rev. REMIGIO "MIGUEL" MARIANO; Sr. LOIS J. PAHA, O.P., 111 S. Church Ave., P.O. Box 31, Tucson, 85702. Tel: 520-838-2530.
Office of Catechesis for Children, Youth and Families—J. MICHAEL BERGER, Dir., 111 S. Church, P.O. Box 31, Tucson, 85702-0031. Tel: 520-838-2500; Fax: 520-838-2584. Email: mikeb@diocesetucson.org.
Office of Evangelization and Hispanic Ministry—VACANT, Dir., Mailing Address: 111 S. Church Ave., P.O. Box 31, Tucson, 85702-0031. Tel: 520-838-2500.
Office of Formation—Sr. LOIS J. PAHA, O.P., Dir., 111 S. Church, P.O. Box 31, Tucson, 85702-0031. Tel: 520-838-2500; Fax: 520-838-2584. Email: srljp@diocesetucson.org; Mr. JOE PERDREAUVILLE, Asst. Dir. Email: joep@diocesetucson.org; Mrs. ISABEL MADRID, Administrative Asst. Email: isabelm@diocesetucson.org; Mrs. OFELIA JAMES, Administrative Support. Email: ofeliaj@diocesetucson.org; VACANT, Coord. Lay Ecclesial Ministry Formation.
Office of Worship—Rev. REMIGIO "MIGUEL" MARIANO, Dir., 111 S. Church, P.O. Box 31, Tucson, 85702-0031. Tel: 520-838-2500; Fax: 520-838-2584; Mrs. GRACE LOHR, Sec. Part-time. Email: gracel@diocesetucson.org.
Pastoral Diocesana De La Renovacion Carismatica Catolica—MARGARITA R. VARELA, Mailing Address: 761 W. Tennessee St., Tucson, 85714.
Newspaper— "The New Vision/La Nueva Vision" BERNARD A. ZOVISTOSKI, Mng. Editor. Tel: 520-838-2500, Ext. 1062; Fax: 520-838-2599. Email: bernz@diocesetucson.org; OMAR RODRIGUEZ, Graphic Designer. Tel: 520-838-2500, Ext. 1063; Fax: 520-838-2599. Email: omarr@diocesetucson.org. Advertising Representatives: RUBEN C. DAVALOS; CLAUDIA BORDERS, Mailing Address: P.O. Box 31, Tucson, 85702. Tel: 520-298-1265; Fax: 520-838-2599. Email: borders.c@worldnet.att.net. Web: www.newvisiononline.org.
Office of Child, Adolescent & Adult Protection—PAUL N. DUCKRO, Ph.D., P.O. Box 31, Tucson, 85702. Tel: 520-838-2500. Email: pauld@diocesetucson.org; Ms. CATHY MOORE, Exec. Asst. Tel: 520-838-2533. Email: cathym@diocesetucson.org.
Office of Due Process—Mailing Address: Chancery Office, P.O. Box 31, Tucson, 85702. Tel: 520-838-2500.
Office of Permanent Diaconate—Deacon KENNETH MORELAND, Dir., Mailing Address: P.O. Box 31, Tucson, 85702. Tel: 520-838-2500; Fax: 520-838-2583.
Associate Vicars—Deacons JOSEPH DELGADO; DAVID SAMPSON; ERNEST TRUJILLO.
Priests' Assurance Corporation—Most Rev. GERALD FREDERICK KICANAS, D.D., Pres. Ex Officio. Directors: Rev. Msgrs. ROBERT D. FULLER, M.R.E., D.Min.; THOMAS J. MILLANE (Retired); Revs. DOMENICO C. PINTI, V.F.; JOHN F. ALLT.
Priests' Placement Advisory Board—All Vicars Forane: Revs. RONALD A. OAKHAM, O.Carm., V.F.; PATRICK M. CRINO; JAVIER H. PEREZ, V.F.; DOMENICO C. PINTI, V.F.; JAY R. LUCZAK, V.F.; GONZALO J. VILLEGAS, V.F.; MICHAEL R. BUCCIARELLI, V.F.; STEPHEN BARNUFSKY, O.F.M., V.F.; ALEXANDER M. MILLS, V.F.; EDWARD F. LUCERO, V.F.; JOHN P. LYONS, J.C.L.
Chancellor—Mr. ERNEST T. NEDDER.
Episcopal Vicar—YUMA LAPAZ, Vicariate; Rev. Msgr. RICHARD W. O'KEEFFE, E.V. (Retired).
Moderator of the Curia—Rev. ALBERT I. SCHIFANO, V.G., M.C.
Propagation of the Faith—Sr. LOIS J. PAHA, O.P., P.O. Box 31, Tucson, 85702. Tel: 520-838-2500.
Property and Insurance Manager—JOHN C. SHAHEEN, A.I.A., Office: 111 S. Church Ave., Tucson, 85701. Tel: 520-838-2500; Fax: 520-838-2581.
Rural Life Bureau—Mailing Address: P.O. Box 31, Tucson, 85702. Tel: 520-838-2500.
Council of Women Religious, Leadership Team & Office for Religious—Sr. RINA CAPPELLAZZO, O.P., 111 S. Church Ave., P.O. Box 31, Tucson, 85702. Tel: 520-838-2500; Fax: 520-838-2583. Email: srrc@diocesetucson.org.
St. Gianna Oratory—Mailing Address: P.O. Box 87350, Tucson, 85754-7350. Rev. RICHARD VON MENSHENGEN. Tel: 520-883-4360.
Korean Catholic Community—3820 N. Sabino Canyon Rd., Tucson, 85750. Mailing Address: P.O. Box 14257, Tucson, 85732-4257. Rev. AMBROSIUS YOO CHANGWOO. Tel: 520-885-0512.
Victim Assistance Coordinator—PAUL N. DUCKRO, Ph.D. Tel: 520-838-2500. Email: pauld@diocesetucson.org.
Vocations—Rev. MARIO (RICKY) V. ORDONEZ, Dir.; Mrs. MERCY ORTIZ, Sec. Email: mercyo@diocesetucson.org; Mrs. MARTY HAMMOND, Exec. Asst., 111 S. Church Ave., P.O. Box 31, Tucson, 85702. Tel: 520-838-2531; Fax: 520-838-2593. Email: vocations@diocesetucson.org.
**Catholic Commission*VACANT.

CLERGY, PARISHES, MISSIONS AND PAROCHIAL SCHOOLS

CITY OF TUCSON

(PIMA COUNTY)

1—SAINT AMBROSE ROMAN CATHOLIC PARISH - TUCSON (1946) Rev. Mark J. Long.
Res.: 300 S. Tucson Blvd., 85716. Tel: 520-622-6749; Fax: 520-882-3057. Email: stambrose@stambrosetucson.com.
School—(Grades PreK-8) Tel: 520-882-8678; Fax: 520-671-4860. Email: principal@stambrosetucson.org. Emma A. Chavez, Prin. Lay Teachers 16; Students 249.
Catechesis/Religious Program—Tel: 520-623-2925. Students 56.

2—SAINT AUGUSTINE CATHEDRAL ROMAN CATHOLIC PARISH - TUCSON (1863) Revs. Gonzalo J. Villegas, Rector; Emilio Landeros Chapa, Parochial Vicar.
Res.: 192 S. Stone Ave., 85701. Tel: 520-623-6351; Fax: 520-623-0088. Email: staugustinecathedral@staugustine.tuccoxmail.com. Web: www.staugustinecathedral.com.
Catechesis/Religious Program—Miss Barbara Valenzuela, D.R.E. Students 367.
Oratory—San Cosme 460 W. Simpson, 85701.

3—BLESSED KATERI TEKAKWITHA ROMAN CATHOLIC MISSIONS PARISH - TUCSON (1984), (Native American), Revs. Abram E. Dono, S.T.; Ermeregildo Saldana-Taneco, S.T.; Seraphim Molina, S.T.
Office: 507 W. 29th St., 85713. Tel: 520-622-5363; Fax: 520-792-0230. Email: bl_kateri_tekakwitha@yahoo.com.
Res. & Rectory: 101 W. 31st St., 85713-3336. Tel: 520-791-7774.
Catechesis/Religious Program—Tel: 520-622-5363. Students 298.
Parish Center—
Mission—Blessed Kateri Tekakwitha Parish Center 507 W. 29th St., South Tucson, Pima Co. 85713. Tel: 520-622-3681.
Mission—San Martin 418 W. 39th St., Pima Co. 85713.
Mission—Santa Rosa 2015 N. Calle Central, Pima Co. 85705. Tel: 520-622-3514.
Mission—Cristo Rey 7500 S. Camino Benem, Pima Co. 85747.
San Juan Diego Center—7465 S. Camino Benem, 85757. Tel: 520-578-0423.
Mission—El Senor de los Milagros 3410 S. 16th Ave., Pima Co. 85713.
Mission—San Ignacio de Loyola 785 W. Sahuaro, Pima Co. 85705.
Mission—San Juan Bautista Yoem Pueblo 1322 Sandario Rd., Marana, Pima Co. 85238.

4—CORPUS CHRISTI ROMAN CATHOLIC PARISH - TUCSON (1999) Rev. Richard M. Kingsley.
Res.: 300 N. Tanque Verde Loop, 85748. Tel: 520-751-4235; Fax: 520-751-1304. Email: kmontano@cccctucson.org. Web: www.cccctucson.org.
Catechesis/Religious Program—Email: pwilliams@cccctucson.org. Peggy Williams, Dir. Children's Ministry; Anita Timpani, Dir. Youth Ministry. Students 157.

5—SAINT CYRIL OF ALEXANDRIA ROMAN CATHOLIC PARISH - TUCSON (1948) Revs. Ronald A. Oakham, O.Carm.; Glenn Snow, O.Carm.; Edward S. Pietrucha, C.S.P. (Retired).
Mailing Address: 4725 E. Pima St., 85712. Tel: 520-795-1633; Fax: 520-795-1639. In Res., Rev. Ivan Marsh, O.Carm.
Res.: 1722 N. Mountain View Ave., 85712. Tel: 520-795-7640. Web: www.stcyril.com.
School—(Grades K-8) Tel: 520-881-4240; Fax: 520-795-0325. Mrs. Ann Zeches, Prin.; Erin Schudy, Librarian; Jan Ladd, Librarian. Lay Teachers 26; Students 387.
Catechesis/Religious Program—Students 202.

6—SAINT FRANCES CABRINI ROMAN CATHOLIC PARISH - TUCSON (1961) Rev. Msgr. Robert D. Fuller.
Res.: 3201 E. Presidio Rd., 85716. Tel: 520-326-7670; Fax: 520-881-8480. Email: cabrini1962@aol.com. Web: www.cabrinitucson.org.
Catechesis/Religious Program—Tel: 520-795-1110. Students 86.

7—SAINT FRANCIS DE SALES ROMAN CATHOLIC PARISH - TUCSON (1971) Revs. Robert G. Tamminga; William T.J. Shuppert; Deacons Dennis Scalpone; William Vigil; Donald Ferris; Charles "Andy" Corder; John R. Martin; Russell Kingery; Frank J. Collura, (Retired); Carlos Martinez. In Res., Rev. Robert E. Carney.

Res.: 1375 S. Camino Seco, 85710. Tel: 520-885-5908; Fax: 520-885-3109. Email: officemgr@saintfrancisdesalestucson.org. Web: www.saintfrancisdesalestucson.org.
Catechesis/Religious Program—Marian Gilbert, D.R.E.; Maureen Kingery, D.R.E. Students 448.

8—HOLY FAMILY ROMAN CATHOLIC PARISH - TUCSON (1915) Rev. Canon Richard von Menshengen, Admin. Res.: 338 W. University Blvd., 85705. Tel: 520-623-6773; Fax: 520-623-3578. Email: jackie@hfc.phxcoxmail.com. Web: www.holyfamilychurchtucson.org.
Catechesis/Religious Program—Students 81.

9—SAINT JOHN THE EVANGELIST ROMAN CATHOLIC PARISH - TUCSON (1934) Revs. Raul P. Trevizo; Franklin (Duane) Eichhurst, O.F.M.Cap., Parochial Vicar; Deacons Jose Ojeda; Don Baker; Jose Duarte. Res.: 602 W. Ajo Way, 85713. Tel: 520-624-7409; Fax: 520-740-1145.
Casa San Juan Migrant Center—Tel: 520-798-0834; Fax: 520-740-1145. Email: office@casasanjuan.org. Beth Ann Johnson, Dir. Volunteer.
School—(Grades PreSchool-8), 600 W. Ajo Way, 85713. Tel: 520-901-1975. Roseanne Villanueva, Prin. Lay Teachers 9; Students 154.
Catechesis/Religious Program—Mrs. Lydia Lopez, D.R.E. Students 456.

10—SAINT JOSEPH ROMAN CATHOLIC PARISH - TUCSON (1953) Revs. Remigio "Miguel" Mariano; Frederic F. Curry, Pastor Emeritus (Retired); Deacons George Herrick, (Retired); Leon Mazza; Richard Grijalva; Teodoro Perez. In Res., Revs. Mario (Ricky) V. Ordonez; Lawrence Lugo, A.M.
Res.: 215 S. Craycroft Rd., 85711. Tel: 520-747-3100; Fax: 520-745-4606.
School—(Grades K-8) Tel: 520-747-3060; Fax: 520-747-2024. Mrs. Donna Betterson, Prin. Lay Teachers 15; Students 252.
Catechesis/Religious Program—Dee Dee Gradillas, D.R.E. Students 287.

11—SAINT MARGARET MARY ALACOQUE ROMAN CATHOLIC PARISH - TUCSON (1951) [CEM] Revs. Robert Elias Barcelos, O.C.D.; Laurence Poncini, O.C.D., Parochial Vicar. In Res., Revs. Albert Bunsic, O.C.D.; Cyprian Killackey, O.C.D.; Deacons Miguel Lopez; Carlos Gelabert, Office Mgr.
Res.: 801 N. Grande Ave., 85745. Tel: 520-622-0168; Fax: 520-882-8022.
Catechesis/Religious Program—Tel: 520-622-5982. Students 616.

12—SAINT MARK ROMAN CATHOLIC PARISH - TUCSON (1999) Rev. Liam Leahy; Deacons Timothy Krieski; John Scott Pickett; Charles Rasmussen.
Mailing Address: P.O. Box 68650, 85742. 2727 W. Tangerine Rd., 85742. Tel: 520-469-7835; Fax: 520-219-6003. Email: stmark0799@gmail.com. Web: www.stmarktucson.org.
Catechesis/Religious Program—Students 275.

13—SAINT MONICA ROMAN CATHOLIC PARISH - TUCSON (1964) Revs. Raul Valencia Garcia; Abraham Guerrero (Ecuador); Deacons Tomas Morales, (Retired); Eugene Fernandez; Nicolas De La Torre.
Res.: 212 W. Medina, 85756. Tel: 520-294-2694; Fax: 520-295-0339. Email: stmonica5@aol.com.
Catechesis/Religious Program—Tel: 520-889-1994. Students 802.

14—MOST HOLY TRINITY ROMAN CATHOLIC PARISH - TUCSON (1975) Rev. William Remmel, S.D.S.
Res.: 1300 N. Greasewood Rd., 85745. Fax: 520-620-0977. Email: office@mhtparish.org. Web: www.mhtparish.org.
Catechesis/Religious Program—Tel: 520-884-9021. Email: maredith@mhtparish.org. Students 300.

15—SAINT ODILIA ROMAN CATHOLIC COMMUNITY - TUCSON (1965) Revs. Richard E. Troutman; Frank G. Cady, Parochial Vicar; Deacon George Scherf.
Res. & Mailing Address: 7570 N. Paseo del Norte, 85704. Tel: 520-297-7271; 520-297-7272 (Office); Fax: 520-297-8247. Email: sodilias@comcast.net. Web: www.st-odilia.org.
Catechesis/Religious Program—Teresa Bier, D.R.E.; Susanna Chapman, Youth Min. Students 219.

16—OUR LADY OF FATIMA ROMAN CATHOLIC PARISH - TUCSON (1972) Rev. Viliulfo Valderrama; Deacons Frank S. Lundgren Jr., (Retired); Robert Negrette.
Mailing Address: 1950 W. Irvington Pl., 85746. Tel: 520-883-1717.
Res.: 5576 S. Monroe St., 85746. Tel: 520-989-0345; Fax: 520-883-2450.
Catechesis/Religious Program—Tel: 520-883-1717. Students 229.
Mission—St. Mary of the Desert 1950 W. Irvington Pl., Pima Co. 85746.

17—OUR LADY OF LAVANG ROMAN CATHOLIC PARISH - TUCSON (1999), (Vietnamese), Rev. Dominic Phuc Pham, C.Ss.R.
Res.: 624 S. Tucson Blvd., 85716. Tel: 520-882-3891; Fax: 520-903-2895.
Catechesis/Religious Program—

18—OUR LADY QUEEN OF ALL SAINTS ROMAN CATHOLIC PARISH - TUCSON (1987), (Hispanic), Rev. Alonzo M. Garcia; Deacon Armando L. Valenzuela.
Res.: 2915 E. 36th St., 85713-4041. Tel: 520-622-8602; Fax: 520-622-4581.
Catechesis/Religious Program—Ms. Monica Robinson, C.R.E. (English); Mrs. Martha Cordova, C.R.E. (Spanish). Students 112.

19—OUR MOTHER OF SORROWS ROMAN CATHOLIC PARISH - TUCSON (1958) Rev. Msgr. Thomas Cahalane; Revs. Madhu George; Tersur Melchizedek Akpan, V.C.; Deacons Paul J. Welsh; George Rodriguez; Scott Thrall; Chuck Chajewski; Charles Whalen.
Res.: 1800 S. Kolb Rd., 85710. Tel: 520-747-1321; Fax: 520-790-3308. Email: omosparish@omosparish.org. Web: www.omosparish.org.
School—(Grades PreK-8) Tel: 520-747-1027; Fax: 520-747-0797. David Keller, Prin. Lay Teachers 22; Students 350.
Catechesis/Religious Program—Email: lstehle@omosparish.org. Laura Stehle, D.R.E. Students 492.

20—SAINTS PETER AND PAUL ROMAN CATHOLIC PARISH - TUCSON (1930) Revs. Patrick M. Crino; Paul Utser, Parochial Vicar; Deacon Thomas Campbell. In Res., Rev. Msgr. Van A. Wagner (Retired); Rev. Matthew Thagil, M.S.F.S.
Res.: 1946 E. Lee St., 85719-4337. Tel: 520-327-6015; Fax: 520-318-3918. Web: www.sspp-parish.org.
School—(Grades K-8), 1436 N. Campbell Ave., 85719. Tel: 520-325-2431; Fax: 520-881-4690. Web: www.sspptucson.org. Mrs. Jean McKenzie, Prin.; Debbie Nielsen, Librarian. Lay Teachers 26; Students 418.
Catechesis/Religious Program—Tel: 520-887-8346. Students 145.
Convent—1947 E. Adams St., 85719. Tel: 520-325-2234.

21—SAINT PIUS X ROMAN CATHOLIC PARISH - TUCSON (1969) Revs. Harry Ledwith; Gerry Miriani (Retired); William Dougherty (Retired); Deacon Dennis Ranke; Karen Horton, Pastoral Assoc.; Abraham Marcor, Music Min.; Linda Alexander, Fin. Mgr. In Res., Rev. Gregory Okafor.
Res.: 1800 N. Camino Pio Decimo, 85715. Tel: 520-885-3573; Fax: 520-885-0945.
Catechesis/Religious Program—Deanne Lialios, D.R.E.; Paul Flores, Youth Min. Students 452.

22—ROMAN CATHOLIC CHURCH OF SAINT ELIZABETH ANN SETON - TUCSON (1980) Revs. Joseph A. Lombardo; Clement Agamba, Parochial Vicar; Deacons Leo Longoria; Alfred Caponigro; Jose Zapata; Robert P. Carlin; Francis C. Sherlock; Rodney J. Kulpa. In Res., Rev. William (Guillo) Kohler, C.Ss.R.
Res.: 8650 N. Shannon Rd., 85742. Tel: 520-297-7357; Fax: 520-797-8886. Email: church@seastucson.org. Web: www.seastucson.org.
School—(Grades PreK-8) Tel: 520-219-7650; Fax: 520-297-1033. Email: school@seastucson.org. Web: www.school.seastucson.org. Suzanne Shadonix, Prin. Lay Teachers 41; Students 496.
Catechesis/Religious Program—Tel: 520-219-7626. Julie Espinoza, D.R.E. Tel: 520-219-7637; Sr. Gladys Echenique, O.P., Dir. Hispanic & Multicultural Ministry. Tel: 520-219-7628. Students 550.

23—SACRED HEART ROMAN CATHOLIC PARISH - TUCSON (1942) Rev. James Hobert.
Res.: 601 E. Fort Lowell Rd., 85705. Tel: 520-888-1530; Fax: 520-888-1227.
Catechesis/Religious Program—Tel: 520-888-1530, Ext. 123. Students 192.

24—SAN XAVIER MISSION ROMAN CATHOLIC PARISH - TUCSON (1692), (Native American), Revs. Stephen Barnufsky, O.F.M.; Edward Sarrazin, O.F.M.
Res.: 1950 W. San Xavier Rd., 85746. Tel: 520-294-2624; Fax: 520-294-3438. Email: sfxsteve@hughes.net. Web: www.sanxaviermission.org.
School—(Grades K-8), 1980 W. San Xavier Rd., 85746. Tel: 520-294-0628; Fax: 520-294-3465. Shirley Kalinowski, Prin. Sisters 2; Students 140.
Catechesis/Religious Program—Tel: 520-294-4639. Email: scriach@yahoo.com. Students 138.
Convent—1996 W. San Xavier Rd., 85746. Tel: 520-746-4779.

25—SANTA CATALINA ROMAN CATHOLIC PARISH - TUCSON (1981) Rev. Lawrence E. Sanders; Deacon William Krueger.
14380 N. Oracle Rd., 85739. Tel: 520-825-9611; Fax: 520-825-9866. Email: office@santacatalinaparish.org. Web: santacatalinaparish.org.
Catechesis/Religious Program—Students 101.

26—SANTA CRUZ ROMAN CATHOLIC PARISH - TUCSON (1919) Rev. Thomas R. Reeves, O.C.D., Admin.
Res.: 1220 S. 6th Ave., 85713. Tel: 520-623-3833; Fax: 520-903-2742. Web: www.santacruzparish.org.
School—(Grades PreK-8) Tel: 520-624-2093; Fax: 520-624-2833. Sr. Leonette Kochan, O.S.F., Prin. Lay Teachers 12; Students 180.
Catechesis/Religious Program—Tel: 520-882-9687. Students 275.
Mission—Our Lady of Guadalupe Capilla 401 E. 31st St., Pima Co. 85713.
Mission—St. Anthony's Catholic Instruction Center and Capilla 225 W. 34th St., Pima Co. 85713.

27—SAINT THOMAS MORE ROMAN CATHOLIC NEWMAN PARISH - TUCSON (1926) Revs. Bartholomew J. Hutcherson, O.P.; Jacek Buda, O.P.
1615 E. 2nd St., 85719. Tel: 520-327-4665; Fax: 520-327-6559. Email: newman@uacatholic.org. Web: www.uacatholic.org. In Res., Revs. Robert A. Burns, O.P.; Bede Wilks, O.P. (Retired).
Catechesis/Religious Program—Tel: 520-327-6663. Students 50.

28—SAINT THOMAS THE APOSTLE ROMAN CATHOLIC PARISH - TUCSON (1984) Rev. John P. Lyons; Rev. Msgr. Todd O'Leary, Pastor Emeritus (Retired); Rev. Alex Tigga; Deacons Edward P. Sheffer; Philip Garcia. In Res., Rev. Al Schifano.
Office: 5150 N. Valley View Rd., 85718-6121. Tel: 520-577-8780; Fax: 520-577-0441. Email: sttomapostle@yahoo.com.
Res.: 5010 N. Valley View Rd., 85718.
School—Tel: 520-577-0503. Email: sthomaspreschool@gmail.com. Lay Teachers 13; Students 76.
Catechesis/Religious Program—Tel: 520-577-8782; Fax: 520-577-0441.

OUTSIDE THE CITY OF TUCSON

AJO, PIMA CO., IMMACULATE CONCEPTION ROMAN CATHOLIC CHURCH - AJO (1916) Rev. Peter C. Nwachukwu.
Office: 101 Rocalla, P.O. Box 550, 85321. Tel: 520-387-7049; Fax: 520-413-5567. Email: iccajo@tabletoptelephone.com. Web: www.iccajo.com.
Catechesis/Religious Program—Students 35.

APACHE JUNCTION, PINAL CO., SAINT GEORGE ROMAN CATHOLIC PARISH - APACHE JUNCTION (1968) Revs. Domenico C. Pinti; Stanley J. Nadolny; Deacons Bill Jones; Elvon "Andy" Anderson.
Res.: 300 E. 16th Ave., 85119. Tel: 480-982-2929; Fax: 480-982-0036. Email: stgeorgeaz@mchsi.com. Web: stgeorgeaj.com.
Catechesis/Religious Program—Students 315.

BENSON, COCHISE CO., THE ROMAN CATHOLIC PARISH OF OUR LADY OF LOURDES - BENSON (1895) Rev. Michael R. Bucciarelli; Deacons Thomas L. Adams; Ronald J. Desmarais.
Mailing Address: 244 S. Gila, P.O. Box 2198, 85602. Tel: 520-586-3394; Fax: 520-586-3919. Email: olol@ololparish.org. Web: www.ololparish.org.
Res.: 210 E. Eighth St., 85602. Tel: 520-586-2447.
Catechesis/Religious Program—Students 75.

BISBEE, COCHISE CO., SAINT PATRICK ROMAN CATHOLIC PARISH - BISBEE (1902) Rev. Godfrey Oparaekwe; Deacons Tony Underwood, Pastoral Admin.; Guillermo Lugo; Joseph L. Delgado.
Res.: P.O. Box 164, 85603. Tel: 520-432-5753. Email: stpatricks@cableone.net.
Catechesis/Religious Program—Students 122.
Mission—St. Michael 2090 W. Martinez, Naco, Cochise Co. 85620.

CASA GRANDE, PINAL CO., SAINT ANTHONY OF PADUA ROMAN CATHOLIC PARISH - CASA GRANDE (1932) Revs. John P. Arnold; Felix Rodriquez, Parochial Vicar; Deacons Patrick L. Dugan; Francisco Solano; Florentino Tarango.
Office: P.O. Box 12335, 85130. Tel: 520-836-0601; Fax: 520-836-2985. Email: office@stanthonycg.org. Web: www.stanthonycg.org.
Res.: 309 Paseo de Paula, 85122. Tel: 520-836-0602.
School—(Grades PreK-8) Tel: 520-836-7247; Fax: 520-836-7289. Email: sas_secretary@qwest.net. Web: www.stanthonypaduaschool.org. Mr. Joe Parzych III, Prin. Lay Teachers 16; Students 230.
Catechesis/Religious Program—Students 650.
Mission—St. Mary Mission 89 N. Yaqui Way, Stanfield, Pinal Co. 85272.

CLIFTON, GREENLEE CO., SACRED HEART ROMAN CATHOLIC CHURCH AND ST. MARY'S MISSION - CLIFTON (1899) Rev. Martin Atanga Baabuge; Deacon Samuel Fullen.
Mailing Address: P.O. Box 938, 85533. Tel: 928-865-2285; Fax: 928-865-1228.
Res.: 355 Chase Creek, 85533. Tel: 928-865-2285; Fax: 928-865-1228.
Catechesis/Religious Program—North Cornado Boulevard Parish Center, Tel: 928-865-3497. Students 40.
Mission—St. Mary Third St., P.O. Box 938, Greenlee Co. 85533. Tel: 928-359-2343.

COOLIDGE, PINAL CO., SAINT JAMES ROMAN CATHOLIC PARISH - COOLIDGE (1947), (Caucasian—Hispanic), Rev. Virgilio Tabo Jr., Admin.; Deacon Viviano Leon.
Parish Center & Res: 401 W. Wilson Ave., 85228. Tel: 520-723-3063; Fax: 520-723-5137.
Catechesis/Religious Program—Tel: 520-723-3063. Students 207.

DOUGLAS, COCHISE CO.

1—IMMACULATE CONCEPTION ROMAN CATHOLIC PARISH - DOUGLAS (1905) Revs. Gilbert Malu Musumbu; Jesus Alejandro Perez-Barrera, Parochial Vicar; Robert A. Rodriguez, Parochial Vicar; Deacons Mario Castillo; Joaquin Carrasco.
Mailing Address: P.O. Box 1176, 85607. Tel: 520-364-8494; Fax: 520-364-8495.
Res.: 928 C Ave., 85607. Tel: 520-364-8494.
Lestonnac Kindergarten and Day Care Center—Tel: 520-364-3956; Fax: 520-364-3956. Rosa Delia Quintana, Dir. Sisters of the Company of Mary 4; Lay Teachers 3; Students 40.
Catechesis/Religious Program—Students 330.
Convent—Sisters of the Company of Mary, Tel: 520-364-7658; Fax: 520-364-3645.

2—SAINT LUKE ROMAN CATHOLIC CHURCH - DOUGLAS (1950) Revs. Gilbert Malu Musumbu; Jesus Alejandro Perez-Barrera, Parochial Vicar; Robert A. Rodriguez, Parochial Vicar; Deacons Armando Moulinet; Gabe Saspe; Tom Willis; Guadalupe Yanez; Ed Gomez; Raul Cantua.
Res.: 1211 15th St., 85607. Tel: 520-364-4411; Fax: 520-364-2397.
School—Loretto Central Catholic, 1200 14th St., 85607. Tel: 520-364-5754; Fax: 520-364-7707. Sr. Mary Aloysius, O.C.D., Prin. Sisters 5; Lay Teachers 14; Students 264.
Catechesis/Religious Program—Tel: 520-364-4852; Fax: 520-364-2397. Students 245.
Convent—Carmelite Sisters of the Most Sacred Heart of Los Angeles, Loretto Convent, Tel: 520-364-7571; Fax: 520-364-7844.

ELOY, PINAL CO., SAINT HELEN OF THE CROSS ROMAN CATHOLIC CHURCH - ELOY (1952) Rev. Juan Carlos Aguirre; Deacon Leonard C. Dexter.
205 W. 8th St., 85231. Tel: 520-466-7258; 520-466-3313 (Rectory); Fax: 520-466-0486. Email: office@sthelenchurch.com. Web: www.sthelenchurch.com.
Catechesis/Religious Program—Tel: 520-466-9422. Students 152.

FLORENCE, PINAL CO., ASSUMPTION OF THE BLESSED VIRGIN MARY ROMAN CATHOLIC PARISH - FLORENCE (1870) Rev. Charles W. Cloud.
Res.: 177 E. 8th St., P.O. Box 2550, 85232. Tel: 520-868-5940; Fax: 520-868-0413. Web: www.assumptionofmary.org.
Catechesis/Religious Program—Tel: 520-868-3075. Students 165.
Convent—Chapel of the Gila, (Historical Site), 255 E. 8th St., P.O. Box 2550, 85232-0550.

GLOBE, GILA CO., HOLY ANGELS ROMAN CATHOLIC CHURCH - GLOBE (1905) Deacons Frank Castillo; Richard Le Mieux; Kennard G. Brusoe Jr.
Office: 201 S. Broad St., 85501. Tel: 928-425-3137; Fax: 928-425-3136. Email: haadminasst@cableone.net.
Catechesis/Religious Program—Students 88.

GREEN VALLEY, PIMA CO., OUR LADY OF THE VALLEY ROMAN CATHOLIC PARISH - GREEN VALLEY (1970) Rev. Francisco Maldonado; Deacon Rudy Noriega.
Res.: 505 N. La Canada Dr., 85614. Tel: 520-625-4536; Fax: 520-625-1084. Email: olvbusmgr@qwestoffice.net. Web: www.olvgvpima.org.
Catechesis/Religious Program—Tel: 520-625-4536. Students 251.

HAYDEN, GILA CO., SAINT JOSEPH ROMAN CATHOLIC PARISH - HAYDEN (1913) Rev. Dale A. Branson.
Res.: 300 Mountain View Dr., P.O. Box C, 85135-1007. Tel: 520-356-7223; Fax: 520-356-7376. Email: stjoeshayden@coppernet.net.
Catechesis/Religious Program—Tel: 520-356-7223. Students 14.

KEARNY, PINAL CO., INFANT JESUS OF PRAGUE ROMAN CATHOLIC PARISH - KEARNY (1961) Rev. Thomas T. Dekaa, Admin.
Res.: 501 Victoria Cir., P.O. Box 459, 85137. Tel: 520-363-7205; Fax: 520-363-7179.
Catechesis/Religious Program—Tel: 520-363-7428. Students 45.

MAMMOTH, PINAL CO., BLESSED SACRAMENT ROMAN CATHOLIC PARISH - MAMMOTH (1970), (Hispanic), Rev. Walter Balduck, O.F.M.Cap., Admin.
Mailing Address: P.O. Box 220, 85618-0220.
Res.: 122 W. Church Dr., 85618. Tel: 520-487-2451; Fax: 520-487-0335.
Catechesis/Religious Program—Students 62.

MARANA, PIMA CO., SAINT CHRISTOPHER ROMAN CATHOLIC PARISH - MARANA (1954) Rev. Abran R. Tadeo.
Res.: 12101 W. Moore Rd., 85653. Tel: 520-682-3035; Fax: 520-395-0363. Email: stchristopher@comcast.net.
Catechesis/Religious Program—Students 117.

MARICOPA, PINAL CO., OUR LADY OF GRACE ROMAN CATHOLIC PARISH - MARICOPA (2007) Rev. Marcos Velasquez.
45295 W. Honeycutt Ave., 85139-1801. Tel: 520-568-4605; Fax: 520-568-0861. Web: www.ourladygracechurch.org.
Catechesis/Religious Program—Priscilla Santi, D.R.E.

MIAMI, GILA CO., OUR LADY OF THE BLESSED SACRAMENT ROMAN CATHOLIC CHURCH - MIAMI (1915) Rev. Jay R. Luczak.
Res.: 844 W. Sullivan St., 85539. Tel: 928-473-3568.
Catechesis/Religious Program—Students 153.
Mission—St. Joseph 5678 Pineway St., Claypool, Gila Co. 85532.
Mission—St. Theresa Roosevelt, AZ.

MORENCI, GREENLEE CO., HOLY CROSS ROMAN CATHOLIC CHURCH - MORENCI (1913) Rev. Bardo Fabian Antunez-Olea.
Res. & Mailing Address: 205 Fairbanks Rd., 85540. Tel: 928-865-3183; Fax: 928-865-1228. Email: hlycross@vtc.net.
Catechesis/Religious Program—Students 300.

NOGALES, SANTA CRUZ CO.

1—SACRED HEART OF JESUS ROMAN CATHOLIC PARISH - NOGALES (1897) Revs. Martin S. Martinez; Eduardo Lopez R., Parochial Vicar. In Res., Rev. Gerald L. Myers.
Res.: P.O. Box 968, 85628. Tel: 520-287-9221; Fax: 520-287-9224.
School—(Grades K-8), 207 W. Oak St., 85621. Tel: 520-287-2223; Fax: 520-287-3373. Marlo Lopez, Librarian.
Catechesis/Religious Program—272 N. Rodriguez St., 85621. Tel: 520-397-0963. Students 927.

2—SAN FELIPE DE JESUS ROMAN CATHOLIC PARISH - NOGALES (1987) Revs. Viliulfo Valderrama; Jesus Acuna-Delgado, Parochial Vicar.
Mailing Address: P.O. Box 6600, 85628.
Res.: 444 Camino Dona Cydney, 85621. Tel: 520-281-1961.
Church: 1901 N. Jose Gallego Dr., #1, 85628. Tel: 520-761-3100; Fax: 520-281-4380. Email: sanfelipedejesusparish@hotmail.com. Web: www.sanfelipedejesusparish.org.
Catechesis/Religious Program—Students 690.

ORACLE, PINA CO., ST. HELEN (1927) Rev. Msgr. Ambrose O. Nwohu.
Mailing Address: 66 E. Maplewood St., 85623-6148. Tel: 520-896-2708; Fax: 520-896-2631. Email: sthelensmission@msn.com.
Catechesis/Religious Program—Students 34.

PARKER, LA PAZ CO., SACRED HEART ROMAN CATHOLIC PARISH - PARKER (1950) Rev. Manuel Fragoso Carranza; Deacon Leonel Bejanaro; Cyndie Crout, Sec.
Res.: 1101 Joshua Ave., 85344. Tel: 928-669-2502; Fax: 928-669-8196.
Catechesis/Religious Program—Students 115.
Mission—Kateri Tekakwitha Indian Mission Poston.
Mission—St. John the Baptist Wenden.
Mission—Queen of Peace Quartzsite.

PATAGONIA, SANTA CRUZ CO., SAINT THERESE OF LISIEUX ROMAN CATHOLIC PARISH - PATAGONIA (1955) Rev. William P. Cosgrove, Pastoral Admin. Box 435, 85624.
Res.: 222 Third Ave., P.O. Box 435, 85624. Tel: 520-394-2954; Fax: 520-394-2831. Email: sttheresa@dakotacom.net.
Catechesis/Religious Program—Tel: 520-394-0068. Students 11.
Mission—Our Lady of Angels Renzi Residence, Sonoita, Santa Cruz Co. 85637.

PAYSON, GILA CO., SAINT PHILIP THE APOSTLE ROMAN CATHOLIC CHURCH - PAYSON (1957) Rev. William Louis Gyure; Deacons Jesus Castillo; Ed Burgin; Tom Fox.
Res.: 511 S. St. Philip St., 85541-5144. Tel: 928-474-2392; Fax: 928-474-9661. Email: fatherbill@stphilippayson.org. Web: www.stphilippayson.org.
Catechesis/Religious Program—Tel: 928-474-1269. Judy Carroll, D.R.E. Students 74.
Mission—St. Benedict Mission 98 N. Winchester Dr., Young, Gila Co. 85554. Tel: 928-462-3871.
Mission—Our Lady of the Lake Rattlesnake Ln. & Hwy. 188, Tonto Basin, 85553.

PIRTLEVILLE, COCHISE CO., SAINT BERNARD ROMAN CATHOLIC CHURCH - PIRTLEVILLE (1914) Revs. Gilbert Malu Musumbu; Jesus Alejandro Perez-Barrera, Parochial Vicar; Robert A. Rodriguez, Parochial Vicar.
Res.: 2308 N. McKinley, P.O. Box 3101, 85626. Tel: 520-364-2762; Fax: 520-364-2520.
Catechesis/Religious Program—340 Grace Ave., 85626. Tel: 520-364-5994. Students 55.
Chapel—Double Adobe, Our Lady of La Salette 3879 W. Mission Ln., Double Adobe, 85617.
Chapel—Douglas, Sacred Heart 300 17th St., Douglas, 85607.

RIO RICO, SANTA CRUZ CO., MOST HOLY NATIVITY OF OUR LORD JESUS CHRIST ROMAN CATHOLIC PARISH - RIO RICO (1987) Rev. Francisco Maldonado; Sr. Guadalupe Jurado, O.P., Pastoral Admin.
Mailing Address: P.O. Box 4024, 85648.
Res.: 395 Avenida Coatimundi, 85648. Tel: 520-281-7414; Fax: 520-281-1713. Email: mostholynativity@yahoo.com.
Catechesis/Religious Program—Students 128.

SAFFORD, GRAHAM CO., SAINT ROSE OF LIMA ROMAN CATHOLIC PARISH - SAFFORD (1937) Rev. Edward F. Lucero; Deacons Marcello Arbizo, (Retired); Carlos Vessels.
Res.: 311 Central Ave., 85546. Tel: 928-428-4920; Fax: 928-428-4922. Email: saintros@saintroselima-safford.com. Web: www.saintroselima-safford.com.
Catechesis/Religious Program—Tel: 928-348-4785. Students 464.
Mission—Pima Mission 28 S. Main, Pima, Graham Co. 85543.
Mission—Newman Center 528 4th St., Thatcher, Graham Co. 85552. Tel: 928-348-7539.

SAHUARITA, PIMA CO., ROMAN CATHOLIC PARISH OF SAN MARTIN DE PORRES - SAHUARITA (2002) Rev. Jens-Peter (Jay) Jensen Jr.
Mailing Address: P.O. Box 65, 85629. Tel: 520-625-1154; Fax: 520-399-4480. Email: smdp@hughes.net.
Catechesis/Religious Program—Students 273.

SAN CARLOS, GILA CO., SAN CARLOS APACHE ROMAN CATHOLIC COMMUNITY - SAN CARLOS (1918), (Native American), Rev. Gino L. Piccoli, O.F.M.
Res.: 460 San Carlos Ave., P.O. Box 28, 85550. Tel: 928-475-2210. Email: fathergino@theriver.com.
School—(Grades K-6), P.O. Box 339, 85550. Tel: 928-475-2449; Fax: 928-475-2050. Email: stcharlessc@theriver.com. Web: www.stcharlesindianschool.com. Anna Dillon, Librarian. Sisters of Mercy 2; Students 123.
Catechesis/Religious Program—Students 21.
Convent—St. Charles, P.O. Box 338, 85550. Tel: 928-475-2460.
Mission—Blessed Kateri Tekakwitha Bylas, 85530.

SAN LUIS, YUMA CO., SAINT JUDE THADDEUS ROMAN CATHOLIC PARISH - SAN LUIS (1982) Revs. Oscar Magallanes; Jesus Acuna, Parochial Vicar; Deacon Jose Manuel Lopez.
984 N. Main St., P.O. Box 2888, 85349. Tel: 928-627-8011; Fax: 928-627-3916. Email: sjtparish-sla@hotmail.com.
Catechesis/Religious Program—Students 563.

SAN MANUEL, PINAL CO., SAINT BARTHOLOMEW ROMAN CATHOLIC PARISH - SAN MANUEL (1954) Rev. Sebastine Bula, V.C.
Res.: 609 Park Pl., Box 607, 85631. Tel: 520-385-4156; Fax: 520-385-4742. Email: stbarth.sanmanuel@yahoo.com. Web: www.stbartsparish.net.
Catechesis/Religious Program—Students 109.

SIERRA VISTA, COCHISE CO.

1—SAINT ANDREW THE APOSTLE ROMAN CATHOLIC PARISH - SIERRA VISTA (1958) Revs. Gregory P. Adolf; Marco Basulto-Pitol, Parochial Vicar; Deacons George Gaun; Joseph Kushner III.
Res.: 800 Taylor Dr., N.W., 85635. Tel: 520-458-2925; Fax: 520-452-0235. Email: office@standrewsv.org. Web: www.standrewsv.org.
Catechesis/Religious Program—Email: christine@standrewsv.org. Students 144.
Mission—Good Shepherd Whetstone, Cochise Co.

2—OUR LADY OF THE MOUNTAINS ROMAN CATHOLIC PARISH - SIERRA VISTA (1991) Rev. Ariel G. Lustan; Deacons James Schaff; Gene Tackett; Jim Hill; Jim Burke; Reynaldo Romo.
1425 Yaqui St., 85650. Tel: 520-378-2720; Fax: 520-378-6825. Email: d.parsons@olmaz.org. Web: www.olmaz.org.
School—
Catechesis/Religious Program—Tel: 520-378-2733. Students 69.

SOLOMON, GRAHAM CO., OUR LADY OF GUADALUPE ROMAN CATHOLIC PARISH - SOLOMON (1891) [CEM] Rev. Edward F. Lucero.
Mailing Address: P.O. Box 147, 85551.
Res.: 311 Central Ave., Safford, 85546. Tel: 928-428-0149.
Catechesis/Religious Program—Students 24.
Mission—San Jose San Jose, Graham Co.

SOMERTON, YUMA CO., IMMACULATE HEART OF MARY ROMAN CATHOLIC PARISH - SOMERTON (1954) Rev. Tomas G. Munoz.
310 W. Spring St., P.O. Box 597, 85350.
Res.: 324 W. Spring St., P.O. Box 597, 85350. Tel: 928-627-2918; Fax: 928-722-5962. Email: ihmparish@live.com.
Catechesis/Religious Program—Tel: 928-627-8982. Sr. Celia DeLeon, D.R.E. Students 528.

SUNSITES, COCHISE CO., SAINT JUDE THADDEUS ROMAN CATHOLIC PARISH - PEARCE SUNSITES (1983) [JC] Rev. Jose Manuel Padilla.
Res.: P.O. Box 328, Pearce, 85625.
Church: 970 N. Hwy. 191, Mile Post 50, Cochise, 85606. Tel: 520-826-3869; Fax: 520-826-3869. Email: stjude@vtc.net.
Catechesis/Religious Program—Students 25.
Mission—St. Francis of Assisi Elfrida. *c/o St. Jude*, P.O. Box 328, Pearce, Cochise Co. 85625.

SUPERIOR, PINAL CO., SAINT FRANCIS OF ASSISI ROMAN CATHOLIC PARISH - SUPERIOR (1930) Rev. James

Aboyi, V.C. (Nigeria); Deacon Willard Kornovich.
Res.: 11 Church Ave., 85173. Tel: 520-689-2250; Fax: 520-689-5810.
Catechesis/Religious Program—St. Mary's Center, 100 Sunset Dr., 85173. Tel: 520-689-2116. Students 117.

TOMBSTONE, COCHISE CO., SACRED HEART OF JESUS ROMAN CATHOLIC PARISH - TOMBSTONE (1880) Rev. Sylvester N. Nwaogu.
Office: 592 E. Safford St., P.O. Box 547, 85638. Tel: 520-457-3364; Fax: 520-457-0017. Web: www.tombstone1880.com/sh.
Res.: 596 E. Safford St., P.O. Box 547, 85638. Tel: 520-457-3439.
Catechesis/Religious Program—Students 3.

TOPAWA, PIMA CO., SAN SOLANO MISSIONS ROMAN CATHOLIC PARISH - TOPAWA (1908), (Native American), (For office and sacramental records pertaining to Tohono O'odham Nation and mission churches on the reservation, please refer to San Solano Missions at the P.O. Box 210, Topawa, AZ, 85639 address). Friars Ponchie Vasquez, O.F.M.; David Paz, O.F.M., Guardian; Hajime Okuhara, O.F.M.; Rev. Ignatius DeGroot, O.F.M., Parochial Vicar; Deacon Alfred M. Gonzales.
Mailing Address: P.O. Box 210, 85639. Tel: 520-383-2350; Fax: 520-383-3063. Email: ssmissions@toua.net.
Catechesis/Religious Program—P.O. Box 210, 85639.

TUBAC, SANTA CRUZ CO., SAINT ANN'S ROMAN CATHOLIC PARISH AND MISSIONS - TUBAC (1987) Rev. Alexander M. Mills.
Mailing Address: 2231 E. Frontage Rd., P.O. Box 2911, 85646-2911. Tel: 520-398-2646; Fax: 520-398-3036. Email: stannschurch@qwestoffice.net.
Catechesis/Religious Program—Students 23.
Mission—Assumption Chapel Amado, Santa Cruz Co.
Mission—St. Ferdinand Arivaca, Pima Co. 85646.

VAIL, PIMA CO., SAINT RITA IN THE DESERT ROMAN CATHOLIC PARISH - VAIL (1935) Rev. John F. Allt; Deacons Kenneth Hilliard; Efren Medrano.
Res.: 13260 E. Colossal Cave Rd., 85641. Tel: 520-762-9688; Fax: 520-762-5967. Email: strita400@aol.com. Web: www.stritainthedesert.org.
Catechesis/Religious Program—Tel: 520-762-9688. Students 252.

WELLTON, YUMA CO., SAINT JOSEPH THE WORKER ROMAN CATHOLIC PARISH - WELLTON Rev. German Bartolome Vasquez Johnston.
Mailing Address: P.O. Box 157, 85356. Tel: 928-785-4275; Fax: 928-785-8706. Email: stjoseph157@hotmail.com.
Res.: 8674 S. Ave. 36 E., 85356.
Catechesis/Religious Program—Hilda Juarez, D.R.E. Students 35.

WILLCOX, COCHISE CO., SACRED HEART OF JESUS ROMAN CATHOLIC CHURCH - WILLCOX (1936) Rev. Mark J. Stein.
Res.: 215 W. Maley St., 85643. Tel: 520-384-3432; Fax: 520-384-3573.
Catechesis/Religious Program—Students 100.
Mission—Our Lady of Perpetual Help San Simon, 85605.
Mission—Our Lady of Guadalupe Bowie, 85605.

YUMA, YUMA CO.

1—SAINT FRANCIS OF ASSISI ROMAN CATHOLIC PARISH - YUMA (1948) Revs. Christopher M. Orndorff II; Gustavo Benitez; Deacons Paul Muthart; Gary Pasquinelli; Rick Hernandez; Rafael Vidal; Arnulfo Carbajal; Don Larson, (Retired); Jose Valadez; George Fischbach.
Res.: 1815 S. 8th Ave., 85364. Tel: 928-782-1875; Fax: 928-329-9479. Email: admin@stfrancisyuma.com. Web: www.stfrancisyuma.com.
School—(Grades K-8), 700 18th St., 85364. Tel: 928-782-1539; Fax: 928-782-0430. Susan Bostic, Prin.; Mary Slater, Librarian. Lay Teachers 13; Students 212.
Catechesis/Religious Program—Tel: 928-783-7461. Sr. Nancy Perez, D.R.E. Students 423.

2—IMMACULATE CONCEPTION ROMAN CATHOLIC PARISH & GUADALUPE MISSION - YUMA (1866) [JC] Revs. Javier H. Perez; Richard Kusugh; Oscar Magallanes, Parochial Vicar; Deacons Mark Nixen; David Sampson; Daniel L. Mulloy; Oscar F. Chavez; Antonio Gomez.
Res.: 509 S. Ave. B, 85364. Tel: 928-782-7516; Fax: 928-343-0172. Email: icchurchyumaaz@roadrunner.com.
School—(Grades K-8), 501 S. Ave. B, 85364. Tel: 928-783-5225. Email: icyuma@juno.com. Lydia A. Mendoza, Prin.; Denise Salgado, Librarian. Franciscan Sisters of Christian Charity 4; Lay Teachers 14; Students 226.
Catechesis/Religious Program—English and Spanish program., Tel: 928-783-1324. Mingo Coronado, D.R.E.; Armida Coronado, D.R.E. Students 740.
Mission—Our Lady of Guadalupe 417 15th Ave., Yuma Co. 85364.
Convent—500 24th Ave., 85364. Tel: 928-783-5224. Franciscan Sisters of Christian Charity 7.

3—SAINT JOHN NEUMANN ROMAN CATHOLIC CHURCH - YUMA (1986) Rev. John F. Friel; Deacons Rick Douglas; Fernando Mezquita.
Res.: 11545 E. 40th St., 85367. Tel: 928-342-3544; Fax: 928-342-7513. Email: admin@sjnyuma.com. Web: www.sjnyuma.com.
Catechesis/Religious Program—Students 200.

Chaplains of Public Institutions

TUCSON. *Arizona State Prison*, 10000 S. Wilmot Rd., 85777. Rev. Phong Bui.
Detention Ministry, P.O. Box 31, 85702. Tel: 520-792-3410, Ext. 131. Ms. Barbara Mattus, M.A., Dir.
Arizona Western College, 11750 S. Mesa Dr., 85365. Tel: 520-342-3544. Attended from St. John Neumann Parish, Yuma.
Christ the King Chapel, 355 WG/HC, Davis Monthan Air Force Base, 85707. Tel: 520-228-5411. Rev. Msgr. John J. Cusack, Revs. Timothy Butler, Michael Martinez, Chap.
St. Joseph's Hospital, 350 N. Wilmot Rd., 85732. Tel: 520-296-3211. Rev. Isaac A. Fynn.
Kino Community Hospital, 1220 S. Sixth, 85707. Tel: 520-623-3833.
2800 E. Ajo Way, 85713. Vacant.
St. Mary's Hospital, 1601 W. St. Mary's Rd., 85745. Tel: 520-622-5883. Rev. Joseph Saba.
Metropolitan Correctional Complex, 8901 S. Wilmot Rd., 85706. Tel: 520-741-3118.
Detention Ministry, P.O. Box 31, 85702. Tel: 520-792-3410, Ext. 131. Ms. Barbara Mattus, M.A., Dir.
Tucson Medical Center, 5301 E. Grant Rd., 85712. Rev. William (Guillo) Kohler, C.Ss.R., Chap. Tel: 520-324-1290; Fax: 520-324-1702.
U.S. Veterans Hospital, S. Sixth Ave., 85713. Tel: 520-792-1450. Rev. David H. Reinders.
Villa Maria Chapel, 4310 E. Grant Rd., 85712. Tel: 520-323-9351. Sr. Dorothy Ann Lesher, C.S.J., Dir. Pastoral Care.

CATALINA. *Catalina Juvenile Detention Center, Catalina Juvenile Detention Center*, 14500 N. Oracle Rd., 85713. Tel: 520-818-3484. Attended from Santa Catalina Mission.

FLORENCE. *Arizona State Prison, St. Dismas Chapel*, P.O. Box 550, 85232. Tel: 520-868-5940. Vacant.

FORT HUCHUCA. *Fort Huchuca Army Post* 85613. Rev. Krzysztof Kopec, Major.

SAFFORD. *Arizona State Prison* 85546. Tel: 928-428-4698.
Federal Correction Institute 85546. Tel: 928-428-6600. Vacant.

YUMA. *MCAS Chapel*, Marine Corps Air Station, 85369. Tel: 928-269-2371. Rev. James F. Finley, Chap.
Yuma Regional Medical Center, 1815 8th Ave., 85364. Tel: 928-782-1875. Attended from St. Francis of Assisi.

Special Assignment:
Rev. Msgr.—
O'Keeffe, Richard W., E.V., Episcopal Vicar (Retired)
Revs.—
Lyons, John P., J.C.L., Adjutant Judicial Vicar
Schifano, Albert I., V.G., M.C., Moderator Curia & Vicar Gen.
Trevizo, Raul P., V.G., Vicar Gen. & Vicar Hispanic Affairs, P.O. Box 31, 85702. Tel: 520-792-3410

On Duty Outside the Diocese:
Revs.—
Gonzales, Robert A., Ph.D.
Martinez, Michael
McCarthy, Jeremiah J., NCEA, 1005 N. Glebe Rd., Arlington, VA 22201.

Administrative Leave of Absence:
Revs.—
Cocio, Carlos
Martinez, Felipe Antonio
Taylor, Daniel

Leave of Absence:
Revs.—
Ancharski, John J.
Bradley, Michael
Cazares Haro, Salvador A.
Noriega, Arnoldo
Thuerauf, Jeffrey P.

Retired - Administrative Leave:
Rev. Msgrs.—
Coleman, James G. (HRT)
Rosensweig, Walter F.

Retired:
Rev. Msgrs.—
Brynda, Gerald J., 1724 Minnewawa, #53, Clovis, CA 93612.
Carrillo, Arsenio S., V.G., 9281 E. Summer Tr., 85749.
Carscallen, Edward C., 316 Via del Heroe, Green Valley, 85614.
O'Keeffe, Richard W., E.V.
O'Leary, Todd
Wagner, Van A., V.G., 1946 E. Lee St., 85719.
Revs.—
Brazaskas, Robert, V.F.
Bryerton, Robert R., P.O. Box 1272, Hereford, 85615.
Chavez, Luis N., San Luis Potori, Mexico.
Cote, Gerald M., 5715 W. Box R St., 85713.
Curry, Frederic F., 870 Natachee, 85710.
Emanuel, John, 1230 Encintas Point, Colorado Springs, CO 80906.
Fahey, John M., 2701-3 Star Trails Dr., 85742.
Gagnon, Ronald P., 2727 W. Star Trails Dr., #1, 85742.
Gameros, Ignacio L., 20719 Flora View Ct., Spring, TX 77379.
Hyman, Robert A., 2240 E. Monte Vista Dr., 85719.
Knapp, Charles, 4675 S. Harrison #34, 85730.
Krause, Joseph A., 4800 S. Alma Schools Rd., #1026, Chandler, 85244.
Padilla, Glibert, 1948 E. 5th St., 85716.
Pietrucha, Edward S., C.S.P., 6855 E. Dorado Blvd., 85715.
Ruiz, Antonio A., 7727 E. Black Crest Pl., 85750.

Permanent Deacons:
Ackerley, John K., St. Augustine Cathedral, Tucson
Adams, Thomas L., Our Lady of Lourdes, Benson
Aguirre-Lopez, Felix Mario
Anderson, Elvon "Andy", St. George, Apache Junction
Arbizo, Marcello A., (Retired), St. Rose of Lima, Safford
Baker, Don, St. John the Evangelist, Tucson
Bejanaro, Leonel, Sacred Heart, Parker
Bogushefsky, Joseph, St. Christopher Parish, Marana
Bracamonte, Gilbert, (Inactive)
Brusoe, Kennard G., Jr., Holy Angels Parish, Globe
Bueno, Oscar L., St. Augustine's, Tucson
Burgin, Edwin, St. Philip the Apostle, Payson
Burke, James, Our Lady of the Mountains, Sierra Vista
Burns, James, St. Elizabeth Ann Seton, Tucson
Callie, Albert, St. Joseph, Tucson
Campbell, Thomas, St. Peter & Paul Parish, Tucson
Cantua, Raul, St. Luke, Douglas
Caponigro, Alfred E., St. Elizabeth Ann Seton
Carbajal, Arnulfo, St. Francis of Assisi, Yuma
Carlin, Robert P., St. Elizabeth Ann Seton, Tucson
Carmona, Salvador, St. Augustine Cathedral, Tucson
Carrasco, Joaquin, Immaculate Conception, Douglas
Carroll, William, Most Holy Trinity, Tucson
Castillo, Frank R., Holy Angels, Globe
Castillo, Jesus, St. Philip the Apostle, Payson
Castillo, V. Mario, St. Luke, Douglas
Chajewski, Charles, Our Mother of Sorrows Parish, Tucson
Chavez, Oscar F., Immaculate Conception Parish, Yuma
Collura, Frank J., St. Francis de Sales, Tucson
Converse, Paul E., (Retired)
Corder, Charles "Andy", St. Francis de Sales Parish, Tucson
Crockette, Alvin, St. Francis de Sales, Tucson
De La Torre, Nicolas, St. Monica, Tucson
Delgado, Joseph, St. Patrick, Bisbee
Desmarais, Ronald J., Our Lady of Lourdes, Benson
Dexter, Leonard C., St. Helen of the Cross, Eloy
Douglas, Rick, St. Francis of Assisi Parish, Yuma
Duarte, Carlos V., (Retired)
Duarte, Jose, St. John the Evangelist, Tucson
Dugan, Patrick, St. Anthony of Padua, Casa Grande
Fernandez, Eugene, St. Monica, Tucson
Ferris, Donald, St. Francis de Sales, Tucson
Fischbach, George, St. Francis of Assisi, Yuma
Fisher, Donald, St. Monica, Tucson
Flam, Richard, Corpus Christi, Tucson
Fox, Tom, St. Phillip the Apostle, Payson
French, Sean, St. Francis de Sales Parish, Tucson
Fugit, James, St. Thomas the Apostle Parish, Tucson
Fullen, Samuel, Holy Cross, Morenci
Gallegos, Charles A., St. Ann's Parish, Tubac
Gamboa, Henry W., (Retired), San Xavier, Tucson
Garcia, John A., (Inactive)
Garcia, Marcario, Immaculate Heart of Mary, Somerton

Garcia, Philip, (Retired), St. Joseph, Tucson
Gaun, George, St. Andrew the Apostle, Sierra Vista
Gelabert, Carlos G., St. Margaret, Tucson
Geonnotti, Anthony, Jr., Our Lady of Fatima, Tucson
Gersitz, James M., Diocese of Phoenix
Glowdowski, Robert, Immaculate Conception, Ajo
Gomez, Antonio, Immaculate Conception, Yuma
Gomez, Edward, St. Luke Parish, Douglas
Gonzales, Alfred M., San Solano Missions, Sells
Gonzales, Jose U., (Out of Diocese)
Gonzales, Luciano, Jr., Immaculate Conception, Douglas
Gonzales, Robert J., (Retired), St. Patrick, Bisbee & St. Michael Mission, Naco
Grijalva, Richard, St. Joseph, Tucson
Grimaldo, Pedro, Our Lady of the Valley, Green Valley
Heise, George, St. George Parish, Apache Junction
Hernandez, Nieves J., Office of Catholic Chaplain, Yuma
Hernandez, Richard R., St. Francis of Assisi, Yuma
Herrick, George R., (Retired)
Hill, James, Our Lady of the Mountains, Sierra Vista
Hilliard, Kenneth, St. Rita in the Desert Parish, Vail
Hintze, Craig, (Inactive)
Hoerr, Michael "Danny", St. Joseph Parish, Hayden
Johnson, Ward, (Retired)
Kingery, Russell, St. Francis de Sales, Tucson
Kinney, William J., (Retired)
Kornovich, William, St. Francis, Superior
Krieski, Timothy, St. Mark the Evangelist, Tucson
Krikawa, Joseph, Most Holy Trinity, Tucson
Krueger, William, Santa Catalina, Tucson
Kuebler, Myron, San Martin de Porres, Sahuarita
Kulpa, Rodney J., St. Elizabeth Ann Seton Parish, Tucson
Kushner, Joseph, III, St. Andrew the Apostle, Tucson
Lambert, Frank, (Retired)
Larson, Donald L., (Retired), St. Francis of Assisi Parish, Yuma
LaSalle, James F., (Retired), St. Thomas More Newman Center, Tucson
Leinfelder, Carl, (Inactive)
LeMieux, Richard, Holy Angels, Globe
Leon, Victor, (Out of Diocese)
Leon, Viviano, St. James, Coolidge
Long, James, Holy Trinity Monastery, St. David
Longoria, Leopoldo "Leo", St. Elizabeth Ann Seton, Tucson
Lopez, Jose, St. Jude Thaddeus Mission, San Luis
Lopez, Miguel, St. Margaret Mary, Tucson
Lugo, Guillermo A. (Bill), St. Patrick's, Bisbee
Lundgren, Frank S., Jr., Our Lady of Fatima, Tucson
Martin, John R., St. Francis de Sales, Tucson
Martinez, Carlos C., St. Francis de Sales, Tucson
Mazza, Leon S., St. Joseph, Tucson
McNealy, Kenneth J., Redemptorist Renewal Center, Tucson
Medrano, Efren, St. Joseph, Tucson
Mezquita, Fernando, St. John Neumann, Yuma
Milazzo, Mike, (Retired), St. Andrew the Apostle, Sierra Vista
Miller, Anthony, St. Christopher, Marana
Miller, Rodger, Our Lady of the Mountains, Sierra Vista
Minetti, Bernard, (Inactive)
Morales, Tomas, (Retired), St. Monica, Tucson
Moreland, Kenneth, Vicar for Deacons, Most Holy Trinity, Tucson
Moreno, Florencio, Jr., (Retired)
Moulinet, Armando A., St. Luke's, Douglas
Mulloy, Daniel L., Immaculate Conception, Yuma
Munoz, Jorge, St. Christopher, Marana
Muthart, Paul, St. Francis of Assisi, Yuma
Negrette, Robert, Our Lady of Fatima, Tucson
Nehmer, David, Our Lady Queen of All Saints, Tucson
Nevins, Robert, St. Francis de Sales, Tucson
Nistler, Donald, St. John Neumann, Yuma
Nixen, Mark, Immaculate Conception, Yuma
Noriega, Rudy, Our Lady of the Valley, Green Valley
Ojeda, Jose, St. John the Evangelist, Tucson
Ornelas, Richard, Santa Cruz, Tucson
Ortega, Mario, St. Anthony of Padua, Casa Grande
Pasquinelli, Gary, St. Francis of Assisi, Yuma
Paulus, Raymond V., Sacred Heart, Tucson, (Inactive)
Pavlik, Keith F., (Out of the Diocese)
Pennington, Charles H., (Retired), St. Cyril of Alexandria, Tucson
Perez, Teodoro, St. Joseph Parish, Tucson
Pickett, John Scott, St. Mark Parish, Tucson
Prom, Mathas, Our Lady of the Valley, Green Valley
Ramirez, Frank, Santa Cruz, Tucson
Ranke, Dennis, St. Pius X, Tucson
Rasmussen, Charlie, St. Mark, Tucson
Rodriguez, George M., Our Mother of Sorrows, Tucson
Rombach, Lionel E., (Retired)
Romo, Reynaldo, Our Lady of the Mountains Parish, Sierra Vista
Roy, James, Our Lady of the Valley, Green Valley
Sadorf, Robert G., (Retired)
Saladin, Jerry, (Retired)
Sampson, David, Immaculate Conception, Yuma
Sanchez, Falvio, St. Bartholomew, San Manuel
Santiago, Nick, Santa Catalina, Tucson
Saspe, Gabriel, St. Luke, Douglas
Scalpone, Dennis R., St. Francis de Sales, Tucson
Schaff, James, Our Lady of the Mountains, Sierra Vista
Scherf, George, St. Odilia, Tucson
Sheffer, Edward P., St. Thomas the Apostle, Tucson
Sherlock, Francis C., St. Elizabeth Ann Seton, Tucson
Silva, Alfredo A., (Retired)
Solano, Francisco, St. Anthony of Padua, Casa Grande
Stotler, Jim, Our Lady of the Valley, Green Valley
Tackett, Gene, Our Lady of the Mountains, Sierra Vista
Tarango, Florentino, St. James, Coolidge
Terry, John, Most Holy Trinity, Tucson
Thrall, Scott, Our Mother of Sorrows, Tucson
Trujillo, Ernest, Assumption of the Blessed Virgin Mary, Florence
Underwood, Anthony E., St. Patrick, Bisbee
Valadez, Jose, St. Francis of Assisi, Yuma
Valenzuela, Armando L., St. Monica, Tucson
Valenzuela, Carlos, St. Augustine Cathedral, Tucson
Vessels, Carlos, St. Rose of Lima, Safford
Vidal, Rafael, St. Francis of Assisi, Yuma
Vigil, William, St. Francis de Sales, Tucson
Welsh, Paul J., Our Mother of Sorrows, Tucson
Whalen, Charles, Our Mother of Sorrows, Tucson
Willis, Thomas, St. Luke Parish, Douglas
Yanez, Guadalupe, St. Elizabeth Ann Seton Parish, Tucson
Yanez, Jesus L. "Chuy", (Retired)
Zapata, Jose S., Immaculate Conception, Douglas

INSTITUTIONS LOCATED IN THE DIOCESE

[A] HIGH SCHOOLS, PRIVATE

TUCSON. *St. Augustine Catholic High School*, 8800 E. 22nd St., 85710. Tel: 520-751-8300; Fax: 520-751-8304. Email: info@staugustinehigh.com. Web: www.staugustinehigh.com. Mrs. Lynn Cuffari, Prin. Lay Teachers 14; Students 122.

Immaculate Heart High School (1930) 625 E. Magee Rd., 85704. Tel: 520-297-2851; Fax: 520-797-7374. Email: nowanawood@ihhschool.org. Web: www.immaculateheartschool.com. Sr. Luisa Sanchez, I.H.M., Pres.; Anastasia Chao, Prin. Sisters of the Immaculate Heart of Mary 2; Lay Teachers 10; Students 92.

Salpointe Catholic High School (1950) 1545 E. Copper St., 85719. Tel: 520-327-6581; Fax: 520-327-8477. Email: president@salpointe.org. Web: www.salpointe.org. Mrs. Kay Sullivan, Pres. & Dir. of Advancement; Sr. Helen Timothy, I.B.V.M., Prin.; Sally Darcy, Librarian. Carmelite Order. Priests 3; Brothers 1; Sisters 3; Lay Teachers 70; Students 1,120.

Priory, 1540 E. Glenn St., 85719. Tel: 520-325-1537. In Res. Revs. Thomas Butler, O.Carm. (Retired); Foster Hanley, O.Carm.; Very Rev. William Harry, O.Carm.; Rev. Cyprian Hibner, O.Carm. (Retired); Very Rev. John Malley, O.Carm.; Revs. Vernon Malley, O.Carm. (Retired); Angelo Mastria, O.Carm.; Bros. Tom Conlon, O.Carm., (Retired); John Howell, O.Carm.

San Miguel of Tucson Corporation - San Miguel Catholic High School, P.O. Box 22199, 85734. 6601 S. San Fernando Rd., 85756. Tel: 520-294-6403; Fax: 520-294-6417. Email: mirandac@sanmiguelhigh.com. Web: www.sanmiguelhigh.org. Leslie Shultz-Crist, Pres.; Richard Reyes, Prin.; Christine Miranda, Registrar; Sr. Judy Franz, S.B.S., Librarian. Brothers 3; Lay Teachers 19; Students 332.

YUMA. *Yuma Catholic High School* (2000) 2100 W. 28th St., 85364. Tel: 928-317-7900; Fax: 928-317-8558. Email: jbadgley@yumacatholic.org. Web: yumacatholic.org. Judeth Badgley, Prin. Sisters 1; Lay Teachers 21; Students 265.

[B] SCHOOLS, PRIVATE

TUCSON. *Immaculate Heart Academy* (1930) (Grades PreSchool-8), 410 E. Magee Rd., 85704. Tel: 520-297-6672; Fax: 520-297-9152. Email: esoto@ihschool.org. Web: www.immaculateheartschool.com. Sisters Mary Evelyn Soto, Pres.; Veronica Loya, Prin. Sisters of the Immaculate Heart of Mary 3; Lay Teachers 25; Students 325.

NOGALES. *Lourdes Catholic School*, (Grades PreK-12), 555 Patagonia Rd., P.O. Box 1865, 85628. Tel: 520-287-5659; Fax: 520-287-2910. Email: hsprincipal@lcsnogales.org. Web: www.lcsnogales.org. Sisters Barbara Monsegur, C.F.F.M., Prin. (High School); Esther Hugues, C.F.M.M., Prin. (Elementary). Minim Daughters of Mary Immaculate (C.F.M.M.) 2; Lay Teachers 20; Students 335.

[C] CATHOLIC COMMUNITY SERVICES

TUCSON. *Catholic Community Service of Southern Arizona, Inc.* (1933) 140 W. Speedway, Ste. 230, 85705. Tel: 520-623-0344; Fax: 520-770-8514. Email: ccsinfo@ccs-soaz.org. Web: www.ccs-soaz.org. Michael Schwanenberger, Ed.D., Corp. Board Pres.; Marguerite Harmon, M.S., CEO.

Social Service Agencies: Pima County (Including City of Tucson), 140 W. Speedway, Ste. 230, 85705. Tel: 520-623-0344; Fax: 520-770-8514. Email: ccsinfo@ccs-soaz.org. Web: ccs-soaz.org.

Catholic Community Services of Southern Arizona, Inc. Marguerite Harmon, M.S., CEO of CCS; Ronald A. Dankowski, Ph.D., Exec. Dir., Catholic Social Svc.

Counseling Services, 140 W. Speedway, Ste. 130, 85705. Tel: 520-623-0344; Fax: 520-770-8578. Email: ccsinfo@ccs-soaz.org. Web: www.ccs-soaz.org. Michael Ponce, L.P.C., Clin. Dir.; Charles Fisher, M.Div., M.S.W., Exec. Dir.

Catholic Community Services in Southeastern Arizona, 155 Bartow Ave., Sierra Vista, 85635. Tel: 520-458-4203; Fax: 520-432-2009. Chuck Fisher, Exec. Dir. of CCSSEAZ.

Sierra Vista Shelter, P.O. Box 1961, Sierra Vista, 85636. Tel: 520-459-0595. Chuck Fisher, Exec. Dir.

Douglas Shelter, P.O. Box 121, Douglas, 85608. Tel: 520-364-2465. Ferdinand Lossou, Prog. Dir.

Migration and Refugee Services, 140 W. Speedway, Ste. 130, 85705. Tel: 520-623-0344; Fax: 520-770-8556. Sr. M. Teresa Apalategui, O.P., M.S.W., Prog. Dir.

Santa Cruz Project, 140 W. Speedway, Ste. 130, 85705. Tel: 520-770-8533; Fax: 520-770-8578. Ms. Linda Rumsey, M.S.R.D., Assoc. Dir.

Senior Nutrition Services, 5009 E. 29th St., 85711. Tel: 520-624-1562; Fax: 520-519-1303. Sr. Mary Ann Bogosoff, C.S.A., Prog. Dir.

Merilac Lodge and Casa de Crianza, 140 W. Speedway, Ste. 130, 85705. Tel: 520-623-0344; Fax: 520-770-8578. Rene Franco, Prog. Dir.

Immigration Counseling Service, 140 W. Speedway, Ste. 130, 85705. Tel: 520-623-0344; Fax: 520-770-8578. Ronald A. Dankowski, Ph.D., Prog. Dir.

Field Offices:

Gila County Case Management, P.O. Box 1172, Globe, 85502. Tel: 520-425-5130; Fax: 520-425-2888. Sr. Elizabeth Adams, C.S.J., M.B.A., Exec. Dir.

Catholic Community Services in Western Arizona, 690 E. 32nd St., Yuma, 85365. Tel: 520-341-9400; Fax: 520-341-8428.

Chaplaincy-Pastoral Ministry to Non-Denominational Nursing Homes, 140 W. Speedway, Ste. 230, 85705. Tel: 520-623-0344; Fax: 520-770-8514. Rev. Angelo Mastria, O.Carm., Chap.; Sr. Carolyn Nicolai, F.S.P., Prog. Coord.

Community Outreach Program for the Deaf, 268 W. Adams, 85705. Tel: 520-792-1906; Fax: 520-770-8544. Anne Levy, M.A., Exec. Dir.; Sue Henning-Mitchell, B.A., Deputy Dir.

Community Living Program, 268 W. Adams, 85705. Tel: 520-792-1906; Fax: 520-770-8544. Michael S. Gutierrez, Prog. Coord.

Detention Ministry, 140 W. Speedway, Ste. 230, 85705. Tel: 520-623-0344; Fax: 520-770-8514. Suzanne Pinon Martinez, Exec. Dir.

St. Elizabeth's Health Center, 140 W. Speedway, Ste. 100, 85705. Tel: 520-628-7871; Fax: 520-770-8528. Joyce Walker, M.A., Exec. Dir.

Pio Decimo Neighborhood Center, 848 S. 7th Ave., 85701. Tel: 520-622-2801; Fax: 520-622-4704. Anne Levy, M.A., Exec. Dir.

Valley Center for the Deaf, 5025 E. Washington St., Ste. 114, Phoenix, 85034. Tel: 602-267-1921; Fax: 602-273-1872.

[D] GENERAL HOSPITALS

TUCSON. *Carondelet Health Network*, 2202 N. Forbes Blvd., Executive Ste., 85745-2682. Tel: 520-872-7790; Fax: 520-872-7838. Web: www.carondelet.org. James Beckmann, Pres. & CEO; Odette Bolano, COO; Deb Mohesky, CFO.

Carondelet St. Joseph's Hospital, 350 N. Wilmot Rd., 85711. Tel: 520-873-3000; Fax: 520-872-3921. Mark Gregson, CEO; Mrs. Cheryl Wilson-Weiss, Dir. Spiritual Care & Mission Integration; Revs. Charles Lehman; Ronald Yabut; Isaac A. Fynn; Rev. Wendy Hackler; Mary Hill, R.N., J.D., Sr. V.P. Mission Integration. Div. of Carondelet Health Network. Sisters of St. Joseph of Carondelet 5; Bed Capacity 478; Bassinets 30; Patients Assisted Annually 223,200.

Carondelet St. Mary's Hospital, 1601 W. St. Mary's Rd., 85745-2682. Tel: 520-872-3000; Fax: 520-872-6641. Winnie Fritz, CEO; Revs. Edwin Emeli; Joseph Saba; Ukachukwu Oneyeabor. Div. of Carondelet Health Netwokk. Sisters of St. Joseph 6; Bed Capacity 425; Patients Assisted Annually 197,800.

Carondelet Foundation, 120 N. Tucson Blvd., 85716. Tel: 520-873-5000; Fax: 520-873-5030. Web: www-.carondelet.org. Richard Imwalle, CEO.

Carondelet Heart & Vascular Institute, 4888 N. Stone Ave., 85704. Tel: 520-696-2328; Fax: 520-696-0449. Web: www.carondelet.org. Deb Mohesky, CFO.

St. Elizabeth Health Center, 140 W. Speedway Blvd., Ste. 230, 85705. Tel: 520-628-7871; Fax: 520-205-8461. Email: peghccs@ccs-soaz.org. Web: www.ccs-soaz.org. Marguerite Harmon, M.S., Exec. Dir., Admin. Patients Assisted Annually 42,000; Staff 50.

NOGALES. *Holy Cross Hospital, Inc.* Div. of Carondelet Health Network, 1171 W. Target Range Rd., 85621. Tel: 520-285-3000; Fax: 520-285-8015. Email: winnie.fritz@carondelet.org. Web: carondelet.org. Sr. Isabelita Boquiren, Chap.; Ruth W. Brinkley, Pres. & CEO; Winnie Fritz, CEO, Holy Cross; Deb Mohesky, CFO. Bed Capacity 25; Total Staff 252; Patients Assisted Annually 40,000.

Holy Cross Geriatric Center, 1171 W. Target Range, 85621. Tel: 520-285-8044; Fax: 520-397-5909. Patients Assisted Annually 125; Total Geriatric Patients Days 16,890; Admissions 1,935.

[E] MONASTERIES AND RESIDENCES OF PRIESTS AND BROTHERS

TUCSON. *Carmelite Priory* (1953) 1540 E. Glenn St., 85719. Tel: 520-325-1537; Fax: 520-318-4651. Very Rev. John Malley, O.Carm., Prior; Revs. Robert C. Carroll, O.Carm., Ph.D.; Angelo Mastria, O.Carm.; Roy Conry, O.Carm. (Retired); Foster Hanley, O.Carm.; Very Rev. William Harry, O.Carm., Regl. Supr.; Revs. Vernon Malley, O.Carm. (Retired); Thomas Butler, O.Carm. (Retired); Cyprian Hibner, O.Carm. (Retired); Michael Higgins, O.Carm. (Retired); Jeffrey Smialek, O.Carm.; Bros. David Balok, O.Carm.; Thomas Conlon, O.Carm., (Retired). Fathers and Brothers at Salpointe Catholic High School. Priests 11; Brothers 2.

Discalced Carmelite Friars of St. Margaret Mary's, 801 N. Grande Ave., 85745. Tel: 520-622-0168; Fax: 520-882-8022. Revs. Cyprian Killackey, O.C.D.; Kevin McArdle, O.C.D.; Philip Sullivan, O.C.D.; Albert Bunsic, O.C.D.

Jesuit Community of the Vatican Observatory, 2017 E. Lee St., 85719. Tel: 520-795-9866; Fax: 520-326-0756. Revs. Richard P. Boyle, S.J.; Christopher Corbally, S.J.; Albert J. DiUlio, S.J.; William R. Stoeger, S.J., Vice-Supr.; Pavel Gabor, S.J.; Bros. Guy Consolmagno, S.J.; John B. Hollywood, S.J., Admin. & Treas. Jesuit Residence. **Vatican Observatory Foundation* Tel: 520-621-3225; Fax: 520-621-1532. *Offices of The Vatican Observatory*, Steward Observatory, The University of Arizona, 85721. Tel: 520-621-3225; Fax: 520-621-1532.

San Xavier Mission Friary, 1950 W. San Xavier Rd., 85746. Tel: 520-294-3015; Fax: 520-294-3438. Rev. Stephen Barnufsky, O.F.M., V.F., Vicar & Guardian; Friars Michael Bearce, O.F.M.; Ed Sarrazin, O.F.M. *Filial House, Villa Maria Care Center*, 4310 E. Grant Rd., 85712. Tel: 520-323-9351. Friars Roy Rivas, O.F.M.; Leo Sprietsma, O.F.M.

CORTARO. *Redemptorist Society of Arizona Desert House of Prayer*, 7350 W. Picture Rocks Rd., P.O. Box 570, 85652. Tel: 520-744-3825; Fax: 520-744-0774. Web: deserthouseofprayer.org.

ST. DAVID. *Holy Trinity Monastery* (1974) P.O. Box 298, 85630. Tel: 520-720-4642; 520-720-4016; Fax: 520-720-4202. Email: frhenri@theriver.com. Web: www.holytrinitymonastery.org. Rev. Henri Capdeville, O.S.B., Prior. Benedictines. Professed 6; Postulants 1; Perpetually Professed 5; Simply Professed 1; Cloister Oblate 1; Residential Oblates 20.

SONOITA. *The Benedictine Monastery of Erlac in Sonoita*, Benedict's Ln., P.O. Box 534, 85637. Tel: 520-394-2961; Fax: 520-394-0163. Email: monksonoita@hughes.net. Web: benedictinemonastery.org.

TOPAWA. *San Francisco Solano Friary*, P.O. Box 210, 85639. Fax: 520-383-3063. Friars David Paz, O.F.M., Guardian; Ponchie Vasquez, O.F.M., Vicar; Hajime Okuhara, O.F.M.; Chris Best, O.F.M.; Martin Sanabria, O.F.M. *Filial Houses* Tel: 520-361-2419. Friar Ignatius DeGroot, O.F.M. *St. Nicholas House*, 349 W. 31st St. - Front, 85713. Tel: 520-622-6393. Friars Matt Tumulty, O.F.M.; David Buer, O.F.M.

[F] CONVENTS AND RESIDENCES FOR SISTERS

TUCSON. *St. Ann Convent*, 3820 Sabino Canyon Rd., 85750-6534. Tel: 520-298-0064; Fax: 520-885-8583. Email: stanns@q.com. Sr. Luisa Sanchez, I.H.M., Supr. Sisters of the Immaculate Heart of Mary 10.

Benedictine Monastery, 800 N. Country Club Rd., 85716-4583. Tel: 520-325-6401; Fax: 520-321-4358. Email: osbtucson@benedictinesisters.org. Web: www.benedictinesisters.org. Sr. Ramona Varela, O.S.B., Prioress & Contact. Sisters 26.

Carondelet Community, 6571 E. Carondelet Dr., 85710-2156. Tel: 520-873-3832. Email: mavonderahe@csjla.org. Sisters 3.

Convento Maria Nazareth - Minim Daughters of Mary (1986) 2821 W. Calle Gardenias, 85745. Tel: 520-743-0414. Email: rmrcfmm@yahoo.com. Sr. Rosa Maria Ruiz, C.F.M.M., Rgnl. Supr. Sisters 3.

Immaculate Heart Lodge Convent, 410 E. Magee Rd., 85704. Tel: 520-742-5896. Sr. Alice M. Martinez, Prov. Supr. Sisters of the Immaculate Heart of Mary 5.

Masmitja Community, 634 E. Magee Rd., 85704. Tel: 520-575-6002. Sr. Barbara Ann Gamboa, Supr. Sisters of the Immaculate Heart of Mary 2.

Immaculate Heart Novitiate, 3820 N. Sabino Canyon Rd., 85750-6534. Tel: 520-885-4981; Fax: 520-886-4273. Email: evelyns@q.com.

Immaculate Heart of Mary Provincial House Community, 3820 N. Sabino Canyon Rd., 85750-6534. Tel: 520-886-4273; Fax: 520-886-4273. Sr. Mary Evelyn Soto, Archivist. Sisters of the Immaculate Heart of Mary 3.

St. Joseph Community, 6569 E. Carondelet Dr., 85710-2156. Tel: 520-873-3816. Email: stjoetucson@aol.com. Sisters of the St. Joseph Community 3.

Maria Community, 1835 W. St. Mary's Rd., 85745-2653. Tel: 520-872-4940. Sisters 4.

Saints Peter and Paul Convent (1933) 1947 E. Adams St., 85719. Tel: 520-325-2234. Sisters of Charity of Seton Hill. Sisters of Charity of Seton Hill 5.

San Xavier Mission (1962) 1950 W. San Xavier Rd., 85746. Tel: 520-294-2624; Fax: 520-294-3438. Email: sfxsteve@hughes.net. Web: sanxaviermission.org.

DOUGLAS. *Loretto Convent*, 1200 - 14th St., 85607. Tel: 520-364-7571; Fax: 520-364-7844. Email: lorettodepazzi@hotmail.com. Web: carmelitegeneralate.homestead.com.

GLOBE. *Holy Angels Convent* (1956) 201 S. Broad St., 85501.

NOGALES. *St. Joseph Convent*, 405 N. Carondelet Dr., 85621-2454. Tel: 520-287-7139; Fax: 520-287-2982. Email: clmrponce@yahoo.com. Sr. Celia Ma. Ponce, C.F.M.M., Supr. Minim Daughters of Mary Immaculate (C.F.M.M.) 7.

Our Lady of Lourdes Convent, P.O. Box 1865, 85628-1865. Tel: 520-287-3377; Fax: 520-287-2910. Minim Daughters of Mary Immaculate (C.F.M.M.) 7.

SAN CARLOS. *Saint Charles Convent*, Mohave Ave., P.O. Box 338, 85550. Tel: 928-475-2460; Fax: 928-475-2050. Sisters of the Holy Cross and Sisters of Mercy.

SONOITA. *Santa Rita Abbey* (1972) HC 1, Box 929, 85637-9705. Tel: 520-455-5595; Fax: 520-455-5770. Email: sracommty@gmail.com. Web: www.santaritabbey.org. Sr. Miriam Pollard, O.C.S.O., Prioress. Cistercian Nuns of the Strict Observance, O.C.S.O. Solemn Professed 9; Transfers 1.

YUMA. *Immaculate Conception Convent*, 500 - 24th Ave., 85364. Tel: 928-783-5224; Fax: 928-343-0172. Email: acharleen@hotmail.com. Sisters 7.

[G] RETREAT HOUSES

TUCSON. *Redemptorist Society of Arizona Redemptorist Renewal Center*, 7101 W. Picture Rocks Rd., 85743. Tel: 520-744-3400; Fax: 520-744-8021. Email: office@desertrenewal.org. Web: www.desertrenewal.org. P.O. Box 569, Cortaro, 85652-0569. Revs. Charles Wehrley, C.Ss.R.; Gregory Mayers, C.Ss.R.; Paul Coury, C.Ss.R., Supr. & Dir.; Patrick Hawk, C.Ss.R.; Gregory May, C.Ss.R.; Gregory Wiest, C.Ss.R.; Lawrence E. Sanders; Bro. Michael Rhodes, C.Ss.R. Priests 7; Brothers 1.

CORTARO. *Redemptorist Society of Arizona Desert House of Prayer*, P.O. Box 570, 85652. Tel: 520-744-3825; Fax: 520-744-0774. Web: deserthouseofprayer.org. In Res. Revs. Thomas D. Picton, C.Ss.R.; Hugh Ricardo Elford, C.Ss.R.; Bro. William Cloughley, C.Ss.R.

ST. DAVID. *Holy Trinity Monastery* (1974) P.O. Box 298, 85630. Tel: 520-720-4642; Fax: 520-720-4202. Email: frhenri@theriver.com. Web: www.holytrinitymonastery.org.

SIERRA VISTA. *La Purisima Retreat Center, Inc.* (2001) Mailing Address: 800 Taylor Dr., N.W., 85635. Tel: 520-458-2925; Fax: 520-452-0235. Email: lapurisima@theriver.com. Web: lpretreat.org. 10301 E. Stone Ridge Rd., Hereford, 85615. Tel: 520-378-6783. Tom Felix, Facility Mgr.; Ann S. Dickson, Contact Person.

[H] NEWMAN CENTERS

TUCSON. *University of Arizona* , St. Thomas More Newman Center, 1615 E. 2nd St., 85719. Tel: 520-327-4665; Fax: 520-327-6559. Email: uacatholic@uacatholic.org. Web: www.uacatholic.org. Revs. Bartholomew J. Hutcherson, O.P.; James J. Moore, O.P.; Sr. Diane Bridenbecker, O.P. In Res. Revs. Robert A. Burns, O.P.; Michael S. Fones, O.P. (Retired); Bede Wilks, O.P. (Retired).

CASA GRANDE. *Central Arizona College, Holy Family Newman Center* P.O. Box 12335, 85230-2335. Tel: 520-836-0601; Fax: 520-836-2985. Email: stanthony@c2i2.com. Rev. Kevin D. Clinch.

DOUGLAS. *Cochise Community College* St. Luke, 1211 15th St., 85607. Tel: 520-364-4411; Fax: 520-364-2397. Rev. Gilbert Malu Musumbu; Marsha John, Office Mgr.

SAFFORD. *Eastern Arizona Junior College* 1705 8th Ave., 85546. Rev. Ariel G. Lustan, V.F.

St. Rose of Lima 311 Central Ave., 85546. Tel: 928-348-0232; Fax: 928-348-0232. Email: deacjbt@msn.com. Betty Terry, Campus Min.

[I] MISCELLANEOUS LISTINGS

TUCSON. *Carondelet Foundation*, 120 N. Tucson Blvd., 85716-4740. Tel: 520-873-5000; Fax: 520-873-5030. Email: pdoherty@carondelet.org. Web: www.carondelet.org. Mailing Address: 2202 N. Forbes, Executive Ste., 85745. Richard Imwalle, CEO.

Casa de los Ninos Crisis Center, 1101 N. 4th Ave., 85705. Tel: 520-624-5600; Fax: 520-623-2443. Email: info@casadelosninos.org. Web: www.casadelosninos.org. Susie Huhn, Exec. Dir.

Casa Maria (1981) 401 E. 26th St., 85713. Tel: 520-624-0312. Mr. Brian Flagg, Coord.

Catholic Community Services Foundation, 140 W. Speedway Blvd., Ste. 230, 85705. Tel: 520-670-0809; Fax: 520-770-8514. Email: lizm@ccs-soaz.org. Liz McMahon, Devel. Dir.

Catholic Foundation for the Diocese of Tucson 85701. Tel: 520-838-2509; 520-838-2598; Fax: 520-838-2585. Most Rev. Gerald Frederick Kicanas, D.D.; Margie Puerta Edson, Exec. Dir.; Mary Ann Hockstad, Vice Chair; Steven Thu, Chair; Clara I. Moreno, Special Events Coord.; Lori Callas, Exec. Asst.; Robin Evans, Annual Giving Mgr.; Michele Antle, Fin. Specialist; Annette Jones, Treas.

Ex Officio Members: Rev. Albert I. Schifano, V.G., M.C.; Tom Arnold, CFO.

Members: Catherine Cosentino; Patricia (Pat) Cracchiolo; Ann Dickson; Ricardo Jaramillo; Pat Kambourian; Joe Keaney; Terisa Lopez; Richard Miranda; Mark Mistler; Deacon Kenneth Moreland; William Patient; Raul F. Pina; Cheryl J. Ponzo; Jose Rincon; James A. Romanoski; Robert Scala; Edward Steinhoff; Dan Torrington.

Catholic Relief Services, 111 S. Church Ave., P.O. Box 31, 85702. Tel: 520-838-2534; Fax: 520-838-2588. Erica Dahl-Bredine, CRS Mexico Country Mgr.; Lourdes Aguilar, Office Coord., CRS/Mexico.

Catholic Tuition Support Organization (CTSO), P.O. Box 31, 85702. Tel: 520-838-2571; Fax: 520-838-2578. Email: gracieq@diocesetucson.org. Web: www.ctso-tucson.org. Gracie Quiroz, Dir. & Contact Person; Mr. Ernest T. Nedder, Pres.

Christ Child Society of Tucson, P.O. Box 36212, 85740-6212. Tel: 520-529-5858. Email: jan@msn.com. Gail Toal, Pres.; Sylvia Blount, Vice Pres.; Merry Lewis, Treas.; Carolyn Simbari, Sec.; Norma Greenbaum, Newsletter Publisher.

Diocese of Tucson Catholic Cemeteries (Sole Corporation), 3555 N. Oracle Rd., 85705. Tel: 520-888-0860; Fax: 520-887-7360. Email: familyservice@dotcc.org. Web: www.dotcc.org.

Diocese of Tucson Catholic Committee on Scouting, P.O. Box 14256, 85732. Tel: 520-297-5245; Fax: 520-323-2026. Email: varobillard@msn.com. Web: www.diocesetucson.org/scoutindex.html.

The Diocese of Tucson Charity and Ministry Fund, Inc., P.O. Box 31, 85702-0031. Tel: 520-838-2509; 520-838-2585; Fax: 520-838-2598. Margie Puerta Edson, Exec. Dir.; Edward Steinhoff, Pres.

St. Frances Cabrini Foundation, Inc., 3201 E. Presidio Rd., 85716. Tel: 520-326-7670; Fax: 520-881-8480. Rev. Msgr. Robert D. Fuller, M.R.E., D.Min., Contact Person.

Jordan Ministry Team, Inc., 48 N. Tucson Blvd., #104, 85716. Tel: 520-623-2563; Fax: 520-623-2585. Web: www.jordanministry.org. Sr. Jane Eschweiler, S.D.S., Dir.

Knights of Columbus, 14175 W. Indian School, Ste. B4-626, Goodyear, 85395. Tel: 602-369-4814; Fax: 623-691-8119. Web: www.kofc.org.

Magnificat - Tucson Chapter, 3560 N. Via San Juanito, 85749. Tel: 520-749-0633. Email: elizabeth962@cox.net. Mrs. L.J. Elizabeth Celenza, Pres. A ministry to Catholic women.

Parish Pooled Investment Trust, P.O. Box 31, 85702. Tel: 520-792-3410. Rev. Richard M. Kingsley, Chm.

**Reachout, Inc. dba Reachout Pregnancy Center* 2648 N. Campbell Ave., 85719. Tel: 520-321-4300; Fax: 520-321-4519. Email: info@reachoutforlife.org. Web: www.reachoutforlife.org. Angela Schneider, Exec. Dir.

Retorno (Marriage Retorno), 4321 N. Ventana Dr., 85750. Tel: 520-722-2931. Email: stogskk@mindspring.com. Web: www.marriageretorno.org. Kathie & Kevin Stogsdill, Contact Person. Tel: 520-722-2931. Prayer Retreat for Couples.

The Roman Catholic Diocese of Tucson Our Faith, Our Hope, Our Future, P.O. Box 31, 85702-0031. Tel: 520-838-2509; 520-838-2598; Fax: 520-838-2585. Email: margiee@diocesetucson.org. Web: www.diocesetucson.org. Margie Puerta Edson, Exec. Dir.; Thomas P. Arnold, Dir.

**Salpointe Catholic Education Foundation*, 1545 E. Copper St., 85719. Tel: 520-547-5878; Fax: 520-327-8477.

San Miguel Corporate Internship, 6601 S. San Fernando Rd., 85706. Tel: 520-294-6403; Fax: 520-294-6427. Leslie Shultz-Crist, Pres.

Society of St. Vincent de Paul Tucson Diocesan Council, 829 S. 6th Ave., 85701. Tel: 520-628-7837; Fax: 520-624-9102. Email: inbox@svdptucson.org. Web: www.svdptucson.org.

The St. Thomas More Society of Southern Arizona, 6818 N. Oracle Rd., Ste. 414, 85704. Tel: 520-838-2507. Micah Schmit, Pres.; Mr. Mark T. Ralles, Treas.

HEREFORD. *Our Lady of the Sierras Foundation* (1993) 10310 S. Twin Oaks Rd., P.O. Box 269, 85615. Tel: 520-378-2950; Fax: 520-378-2950. Email: ourladysierrashrine@msn.com. Web: www.ourladyofthesierras.org. Mr. Gerald A. Chouinard, Pres.

NOGALES. *Kino Border Initiative* (2008) P.O. Box 159, 85628-0159. Tel: 520-287-2370; Fax: 520-287-2375. Web: www.kinoborderinitiative.org. Revs. Sean Carroll, S.J., Exec. Dir.; Peter Neeley, S.J., Assoc. Educ. & Formation; Martin McIntosh, S.J., Assoc. Socio-Pastoral Outreach; Ricardo Machuca, S.J., Dir. Mexican Programming; Sisters Maria Engracia Robles, M.E., Migrant Aid Coord.; Rosalba Avalos, M.E., Asst. Migrant Aid Coord.; Lorena Leyva, M.E., Asst. Migrant Aid Coord. Lay Employee 2.

MARANA. *Poverty 24/6 Trust*, 12101 W. Moore Rd., 85653. Tel: 520-682-3035. Email: poverty24-6@juno.com. Web: www.poverty24.6.org. Deacon Joseph Bogushefsky, Contact Person.

ST. DAVID. *San Pedro Valley Center for the Arts*, Box 298, 85630. Tel: 520-720-4642, Ext. 23. Patricia J. Don, Contact Person.

SOUTH TUCSON. *Blessed Kateri Tekakwitha Parish Center* (2003) 507 W. 29th St., 85713. Tel: 520-622-5363; Fax: 520-792-0230. Email: bl_kateri_tekakwitha@yahoo.com. Revs. Ermeregildo Saldana-Taneco, S.T.; Abram E. Dono, S.T.; Seraphim Molina, S.T.

[J] DIOCESAN CEMETERIES

TUCSON. *Holy Hope Cemetery and Mausoleum*, Office: 3555 N. Oracle Rd., 85705. Tel: 520-888-0860; Fax: 520-887-7360. Email: familyservice@dotcc.org.

Our Lady of the Desert Cemetery and Mausoleum, Office: 2151 S. Avenida Los Reyes, 85748. Tel: 520-885-9173.

[K] CLOSED INSTITUTIONS

TUCSON. *Diocese of Tucson Archives*, 300 S. Tucson Blvd., 85716. Tel: 520-886-5201; 520-792-3410. Email: bettyw@diocesetucson.org. The following parish, school or orphanage records may be found at the above address unless otherwise indicated. Notations to Sacramental Registers of closed parishes/missions on those listed below should be directed to the Archival Center and should specify the name of the parish. The location of records periodically changes. Inquiries for records of parishes, schools or institutions not on this list should be directed to the above address.

All Saints Parish (Tucson)
Blessed Martin de Porres (Tucson)
Sacred Heart Parish (Bisbee)
St. Anthony Parish (Tiger)
St. Bernard Mission Records located at: Our Lady, Queen of All Saints Parish, 2915 E. 36th St., Tucson, AZ 85713 Tel: 520-622-8602 Fax: 520-622-4581.
St. Helen Parish (Sonora)
All Saints Parochial School (Tucson)
Loretto Academy (Bisbee)
Regina Cleri Seminary (Tucson)
Sacred Heart Parochial School (Tucson)
St. Augustine Parochial School (Tucson)
St. Joseph Academy for Girls (Tucson)
St. Joseph Orphanage (Tucson)
St. Patrick Parochial School (Bisbee)

RELIGIOUS INSTITUTES OF MEN REPRESENTED IN THE DIOCESE

For further details refer to the corresponding bracketed number in the Religious Institutes of Men or Women section.

[0200]—*Benedictine Monks*—O.S.B.
[]—*Benedictine Monks of Erlac*—O.S.B.
[0330]—*Brothers of the Christian Schools*—F.S.C.
[0470]—*Capuchin Friars* (Prov. of St. Joseph)—O.F.M.Cap.
[0270]—*Carmelite Fathers and Brothers* (Prov. of Most Pure Heart of Mary)—O.Carm.
[1320]—*Clerics of St. Viator*—C.S.V.
[1330]—*Congregation of the Mission Western Province*—C.M.
[0260]—*Discalced Carmelites*—O.C.D.
[0520]—*Franciscan Friars*—O.F.M.
[]—*Friars of the Sick, Poor*—F.S.P.
[0300]—*Institute of Charity*—I.C.
[0690]—*Jesuit Fathers and Brothers*—S.J.
[0800]—*Maryknoll*—M.M.
[0720]—*Missionaries of Our Lady La Salette* (Immaculate Heart of Mary Prov.)—M.S.
[]—*Missionaries of St. Francis de Sales*
[0840]—*Missionary Servants of the Most Holy Trinity*—S.T.
[0430]—*Order of Preachers (Dominicans)*—O.P.
[1030]—*Paulist Fathers*—C.S.P.
[1070]—*Redemptorist Fathers* (Oakland Prov.)—C.SS.R.
[1200]—*Society of the Divine Savior*—S.D.S.
[]—*Via Christi Society*—V.C.

RELIGIOUS INSTITUTES OF WOMEN REPRESENTED IN THE DIOCESE

[0100]—*Adorers of the Blood of Christ*—A.S.C.
[1070-13]—*Adrian Dominican Sisters*—O.P.
[0233]—*Benedictine Nuns*—O.S.B.
[0220]—*Benedictine Sisters of Perpetual Adoration*—O.S.B.
[0370]—*Carmelite Sisters of the Most Sacred Heart of Los Angeles*—O.C.D.
[0670]—*Cistercian Nuns of the Strict Observance*—O.C.S.O.
[3710]—*Congregation of the Sisters of St. Agnes*—C.S.A.
[1920]—*Congregation of the Sisters of the Holy Cross*—C.S.C.
[1780]—*Congregation of the Sisters of the Third Order of St. Francis of Perpetual Adoration*—F.S.P.A.
[]—*Dominican Sisters of Mission San Jose*—O.P
[]—*Dominican Sisters of Oakford*—O.P.
[1115]—*Dominican Sisters of Peace*—O.P.
[1230]—*Franciscan Sisters of Christian Charity*—O.S.F.
[1310]—*Franciscan Sisters of Little Falls, Minnesota*—O.S.F.
[1415]—*Franciscan Sisters of Mary*—F.S.M.
[1425]—*Franciscan Sisters of Peace*—F.S.P.
[2575]—*Institute of the Sisters of Mercy of the Americas*—R.S.M.
[2490]—*Medical Mission Sisters*—M.M.S.
[2675]—*Minim Daughters of Mary Immaculate*—C.F.M.M.
[2720]—*Mission Helpers of the Sacred Heart*—M.H.S.H.
[]—*Oblates of St. Martha*—O.S.M.
[3130]—*Our Lady of Victory Missionary Sisters*—O.L.V.M.
[2970]—*School Sisters of Notre Dame*—S.S.N.D.
[1680]—*School Sisters of St. Francis*—S.S.S.F.
[3580]—*Servants of Mary*—O.S.M.
[3590]—*Servants of Mary (Servite Sisters)*—O.S.M.
[]—*Sisters for Christian Community*—S.F.C.C.
[0570]—*Sisters of Charity of Seton Hill, Greensburg, Pennsylvania*—S.C.
[2110]—*Sisters of Humility of Mary*—H.M.
[1705]—*The Sisters of St. Francis of Assisi*—O.S.F.
[1710]—*Sisters of St. Francis of Mary Immaculate*—O.S.F.
[1730]—*Sisters of St. Francis of Oldenberg*—O.S.F.
[1570]—*Sisters of St. Francis of the Holy Family*—O.S.F.
[3840]—*Sisters of St. Joseph of Carondelet*—C.S.J.
[0260]—*The Sisters of the Blessed Sacrament for Indians and Colored People*—S.B.S.
[1030]—*Sisters of the Divine Savior*—S.D.S.
[1990]—*Sisters of the Holy Names of Jesus and Mary*—S.N.J.M.
[2180]—*Sisters of the Immaculate Heart of Mary*—I.H.M.
[3320]—*Sisters of the Presentation of the Blessed Virgin Mary*—P.B.V.M.
[4070]—*Society of the Sacred Heart*—R.S.C.J.
[]—*Wheaton Franciscans*—O.S.F.

NECROLOGY

† Oliver, Rev. Msgr. John A. (Retired-Administrative Leave)—Died 2011
† Sherry, Bryan W., (Retired)—Died 2011

An asterisk (*) denotes an organization that has established tax-exempt status directly with the IRS and is not covered by the USCCB Group Ruling.

Diocese of Tulsa

(Dioecesis Tulsensis)

Most Reverend

EDWARD J. SLATTERY

Bishop of Tulsa; ordained April 26, 1966; appointed Bishop of Tulsa November 11, 1993; ordained January 6, 1994 in Rome; installed January 12, 1994.

Chancery Office: 12300 E. 91st St. S., Broken Arrow, OK 74012. Mailing Address: P.O. Box 690240, Tulsa, OK 74169-0240. Tel: 918-294-1904; Fax: 918-294-0920.

Web: www.dioceseoftulsa.org

Email: bishop.office@dioceseoftulsa.org

ESTABLISHED FEBRUARY 7, 1973.

Square Miles 26,417.

The Diocese of Tulsa comprises the following 31 Counties: Adair, Atoka, Bryan, Cherokee, Choctaw, Coal, Craig, Creek, Delaware, Haskell, Hughes, Latimer, LeFlore, McCurtain, McIntosh, Mayes, Muskogee, Nowata, Okfuskee, Okmulgee, Osage, Ottawa, Pawnee, Payne, Pittsburg, Pushmataha, Rogers, Sequoyah, Tulsa, Wagoner and Washington.

For legal titles of parishes and institutions, consult the Chancery Office.

STATISTICAL OVERVIEW

Personnel	
Bishop	1
Priests: Diocesan Active in Diocese	50
Priests: Diocesan Active Outside Diocese	7
Priests: Retired, Sick or Absent	19
Number of Diocesan Priests	76
Religious Priests in Diocese	24
Total Priests in Diocese	100
Extern Priests in Diocese	13
Ordinations:	
Diocesan Priests	2
Transitional Deacons	2
Permanent Deacons	13
Permanent Deacons in Diocese	67
Total Brothers	28
Total Sisters	54
Parishes	
Parishes	76
With Resident Pastor:	
Resident Diocesan Priests	43
Resident Religious Priests	5
Without Resident Pastor:	
Administered by Priests	27
Administered by Deacons	1
Missions	2
Professional Ministry Personnel:	
Sisters	4
Lay Ministers	35
Welfare	
Catholic Hospitals	6
Total Assisted	1,425,395
Health Care Centers	1
Total Assisted	5,000
Homes for the Aged	3
Total Assisted	316
Specialized Homes	3
Total Assisted	278
Special Centers for Social Services	8
Total Assisted	50,000
Educational	
Diocesan Students in Other Seminaries	16
Total Seminarians	16
High Schools, Diocesan and Parish	1
Total Students	819
High Schools, Private	1
Total Students	568
Elementary Schools, Diocesan and Parish	9
Total Students	2,093
Elementary Schools, Private	2
Total Students	945
Catechesis/Religious Education:	
High School Students	1,472
Elementary Students	5,027
Total Students under Catholic Instruction	10,940
Teachers in the Diocese:	
Priests	4
Brothers	4
Sisters	5
Lay Teachers	348
Vital Statistics	
Receptions into the Church:	
Infant Baptism Totals	1,345
Minor Baptism Totals	141
Adult Baptism Totals	120
Received into Full Communion	279
First Communions	1,250
Confirmations	919
Marriages:	
Catholic	201
Interfaith	159
Total Marriages	360
Deaths	439
Total Catholic Population	62,600
Total Population	1,650,000

Former Bishops—Most Revs. BERNARD J. GANTER, D.D., ord. May 22, 1952; appt. Bishop of Tulsa, Dec. 19, 1972; ord. Feb. 7, 1973; transferred to Beaumont, Oct. 18, 1977; EUSEBIUS J. BELTRAN, ord. May 14, 1960; appt. Bishop of Tulsa, Feb. 28, 1978; ord. April 20, 1978; transferred to Archdiocese of Oklahoma City, Nov. 24, 1992.

Vicar General—Rev. Msgr. DENNIS C. DORNEY, V.G.

Chancery Office—12300 E. 91st St. S., Broken Arrow, 74012. Mailing Address: P.O. Box 690240, Tulsa, 74169. Tel: 918-294-1904; Fax: 918-294-0920. Office Hours: Mon.-Fri. 9-5.

Chancellor—Deacon JOHN M. JOHNSON.

Finance Office—Mr. PHILIP J. CREIDER, Assets Mgr.; Mr. THOMAS SCHADLE, CFO, Mailing Address: P.O. Box 690240, Tulsa, 74169-0240. Tel: 918-294-1904, Ext. 4926.

Diocesan Senators—Most Rev. EDWARD JAMES SLATTERY; Revs. TIMOTHY L. DAVISON; JACK GLEASON; PAUL E. EICHHOFF; Rev. Msgr. DANIEL H. MUEGGENBORG; Revs. MICHAEL J. KNIPE, J.C.L.; BRIAN D. O'BRIEN; ELIAS ABI-SARKIS; LEONARD AHANOTU.

Ex Officio—Rev. Msgr. DENNIS C. DORNEY, V.G.

Diocesan Consultors—Rev. JACK GLEASON; Rev. Msgrs. PATRICK J. GAALAAS; DENNIS C. DORNEY, V.G.; DANIEL H. MUEGGENBORG; Revs. TAM N. NGUYEN; PAUL EICHHOFF; BRIAN D. O'BRIEN; TIMOTHY L. DAVISON; SAMUEL PEREZ, J.C.L.

Diocesan Marriage Tribunal—

Judicial Vicar—Rev. MICHAEL J. KNIPE, J.C.L.

Adjutant Judicial Vicar—Rev. KENNETH J. HARDER, J.C.L.

Defender of the Bond—Rev. SAMUEL PEREZ, J.C.L.

Judges—Revs. MICHAEL J. KNIPE, J.C.L.; KENNETH J. HARDER, J.C.L.; KHIET T. NGUYEN, J.C.L.

Auditors—HENRY L. HARDER, Ph.D.; Deacon KENNETH LONGBRAKE.

Notary—Mrs. MARY JONES.

Promoter of Justice—Rev. SAMUEL PEREZ, J.C.L.

Priests' Personnel Committee—Rev. Msgr. PATRICK J. GAALAAS; Revs. TAM N. NGUYEN; BRYAN V. BROOKS; Rev. Msgr. DENNIS C. DORNEY, V.G.

Seminary Board—Rev. Msgr. PATRICK J. GAALAAS; Revs. DAVID MEDINA; MATTHEW J. GERLACH; JACK GLEASON; Rev. Msgr. DENNIS C. DORNEY, V.G.; Ms. ANDREA HYATT.

Federation of Religious of the Diocese of Tulsa—Leadership Team: Sisters MARILYN NORWOOD, O.S.B.; EUGENIA BROWN, O.S.B., 2200 S. Lewis, Tulsa, 74114. Tel: 918-746-4211.

Diocesan Offices

Archivist—JOEY SPENCER, Mailing Address: P.O. Box 690240, Tulsa, 74169-0240. Tel: 918-307-4956.

Campaign for Human Development—Deacon JOHN M. JOHNSON, Mailing Address: P.O. Box 690240, Tulsa, 74169. Tel: 918-307-4914.

Campus Ministry—Rev. KERRY J. WAKULICH, Chap.; LISA HOLDEN, Dir. Devel., St. Philip Neri Newman Center at The University of Tulsa, 440 S. Florence, Tulsa, 74104. Tel: 918-599-0204; Fax: 918-587-0115. Email: tu-newman@utulsa.edu; Rev. STUART CREVCOURE, Chap., Oklahoma State University, 201 N. Knoblock St., Stillwater, 74075. Tel: 405-372-6408.

Catholic Charities of the Diocese of Tulsa—KEVIN SARTORIOUS, Exec. Dir., 2450 N. Harvard, Tulsa, 74115. Tel: 918-949-4673; Fax: 918-582-2123. Mailing Address: P.O. Box 580460, Tulsa, 74158.

Adoption Services—2450 N. Harvard, P.O. Box 580460, Tulsa, 74158. Tel: 918-949-4673.

Padre Pio Emergency Services—2450 N. Harvard, Tulsa, 74115. Mailing Address: P.O. Box 580460, Tulsa, 74158.

Madonna House—2450 N. Harvard, Tulsa, 74115. Mailing Address: P.O. Box 580460, Tulsa, 74158.

Immigration Office—2450 N. Harvard, Tulsa, 74115. Tel: 918-949-4673; Fax: 918-582-2123. *Mailing Address: P.O. Box 580460, Tulsa, 74158.*

Sallisaw Helping Center—409 N. Adam St., Sallisaw. Tel: 918-775-6111. *St. Jude Helping Center, 109 E. Washington Ave., McAlester, 74502.*

St. Elizabeth Lodge—Tulsa. Tel: 918-949-4673.

St. Joseph Residence, Inc.—Mailing Address: P.O. Box 580460, Tulsa, 74158. Tel: 918-587-6456.

Blessed Mother Teresa Health Center—2450 N. Harvard, Tulsa, 74115. Tel: 918-949-4673. *Mailing Address: P.O. Box 580460, Tulsa, 74158.*

Calvary Cemetery—9101 S. Harvard, Tulsa, 74137. Tel: 918-299-7348; Fax: 918-299-7558.

Clergy Education—Rev. Msgr. DANIEL H. MUEGGENBORG, Mailing Address: P.O. Box 690240, Tulsa, 74169. Tel: 918-294-1904, Ext. 4900.

Diocesan Catholic Committee on Scouting—Mr. DENNIS ZVACEK. Tel: 918-250-8787. Email: dzvacek@cox.net.

Diocesan Council of Catholic Women—MARY BISETT.

Tel: 918-622-4453.

Ecumenism—Rev. Msgr. PATRICK J. GAALAAS, Dir., 4001 E. 101st St., S., Tulsa, 74137.

Education—CAROL ROBINSON, Coord. Catechetical Svcs.; MARY MALCOM, Pastoral Studies Institute, Mailing Address: P.O. Box 690240, Tulsa, 74169. Tel: 918-307-4941.

Family Life Office—VACANT, Mailing Address: P.O. Box 690240, Tulsa, 74169. Tel: 918-307-4939.

Parochial Schools—TODD GOLDSMITH, Supt. Catholic Schools, 820 S. Boulder, Tulsa, 74119. Tel: 918-582-9177; Fax: 918-582-1851.

Prison and Social Ministry—VACANT, Mailing Address: P.O. Box 690240, Tulsa, 74169.

Hispanic Ministry—Mailing Address: P.O. Box 690240, Tulsa, 74169. Tel: 918-307-4950; Fax: 918-294-0920. Revs. LEONARDO MEDINA, Dir.; ROBERT M. DYE, Assoc. Dir., 1541 E. Newton Pl., Tulsa, 74106. Tel: 918-584-2424; DANIEL CAMPOS, Assoc. Dir.; OSCAR JUAN MENDOZA; SAMUEL PEREZ, J.C.L., Assoc. Dir.; JOSE MARIA BRIONES, Assoc. Dir.; Deacon CARLOS MORENO.

Pastoral Studies Institute—MARY MALCOM, Mailing Address: P.O. Box 690240, Tulsa, 74169-0240. Tel: 918-307-4941.

Office of Divine Worship—Rev. Msgr. PATRICK M. BRANKIN, Dir., Mailing Address: P.O. Box 690240, Tulsa, 74169-0240. Tel: 918-307-4955.

Magazine "Eastern Oklahoma Catholic"—DAVE CRENSHAW, Mng. Editor; MASON BEECROFT, Assoc. Editor, Mailing Address: P.O. Box 690240, Tulsa, 74169. Tel: 918-307-4946.

Office of Permanent Diaconate—Rev. Msgr. PATRICK M. BRANKIN, Vicar for Deacons, Mailing Address: P.O. Box 690240, Tulsa, 74169. Tel: 918-307-4955.

Diocesan Development Fund—Ms. MARTHA WYATT, Mailing Address: P.O. Box 690240, Tulsa, 74169. Tel: 918-307-4948.

Propagation of the Faith—Rev. MATTHEW J. GERLACH, Coord., 1727 S. 75th E. Ave., Tulsa, 74112. Tel: 918-622-4488.

Victim Assistance Coordinator—Mr. QUENTIN HENLEY. Tel: 918-508-7135.

Te Deum Institute of Sacred Liturgy—Mailing Address: P.O. Box 690240, Tulsa, 74169. JOEY SPENCER, Prog. Dir. Tel: 918-307-4956.

Vocations—Rev. MATTHEW J. GERLACH, Dir.; Mrs. THERESA WITCHER, Seminarians, Mailing Address: P.O. Box 690240, Tulsa, 74169. Tel: 918-307-4936.

Young Adult Ministry—ANTHONY KEISER, Dir.; SARAH JAMESON, Asst. Dir., Mailing Address: P.O. Box 690240, Tulsa, 74169-0240. Tel: 918-307-4940.

Youth Ministry—ANTHONY KEISER, Dir.; SARAH JAMESON, Asst. Dir., Mailing Address: P.O. Box 690240, Tulsa, 74169-0240. Tel: 918-307-4940.

CLERGY, PARISHES, MISSIONS AND PAROCHIAL SCHOOLS

CITY OF TULSA

(TULSA COUNTY)

1—HOLY FAMILY CATHEDRAL (1899) Rev. Msgr. Gregory A. Gier, Rector; Rev. James Van Nguyen; Deacons Jerry Mattox; Thomas Gorman; Nelson M. Sousa; Greg Stice; Kevin Sartorius.
Res.: 122 W. 8th St., P.O. Box 3204, 74101. Tel: 918-582-6247; Fax: 918-599-8334. Email: tulsacathedral@gmail.com. Web: holyfamilycathedralparish.com.
School—(Grades PreK-8), 820 S. Boulder St., 74119. Tel: 918-582-0422; Fax: 918-582-9705. Jay Luetkemeyer, Prin. Lay Teachers 11; Students 129.
Catechesis/Religious Program—Monica Skrzypczak, D.R.E.; Monika Davis, D.R.E. Students 85.

2—ST. AUGUSTINE'S (1955), (African American), Rev. Kenneth Iheanaho (Nigeria); Deacon Steve Litwack.
Church: 1728 E. Apache, 74110. Tel: 918-428-3280.
Catechesis/Religious Program—Students 15.

3—ST. BERNARD OF CLAIRVAUX (1978) [CEM] Rev. Msgr. Patrick J. Gaalaas; Rev. Mark Martin B. es Tillore; Deacons Richard Campbell; Alan Mikell; Robert Martin; David Johnson.
Res.: 4001 E. 101st St., 74137. Tel: 918-299-9406; Fax: 918-299-7796. Email: e-mailus@stbernardstulsa.org. Web: www.stbernardstulsa.org.
Preschool—Teachers 6; Students 30.
Catechesis/Religious Program—Sharon Lechtenberg, D.R.E. Students 480.

4—ST. CATHERINE (1925) Rev. Michael E. Cashen; Deacon Craig Victor.
Res.: 4532 S. 25th W. Ave., 74107. Tel: 918-446-8124; Fax: 918-446-4506.
School—(Grades PreSchool-8), 2515 W. 46th St., 74107. Tel: 918-446-9756. Vicky Adams, Prin. Sisters of St. Francis of the Martyr St. George 2; Lay Teachers 10; Students 110.
Catechesis/Religious Program—Students 23.
Mission—St. Joseph P.O. Box 603, Bristow, Creek Co. 74010. Deacon David C. Hamel.
Catechesis/Religious Program—Students 11.

5—CHRIST THE KING (1917) Rev. Msgr. Daniel M. Mueggenborg; Deacons Loren F. Luschen; John M. Johnson; Dean Wersal.
Res. & Office: 1520 S. Rockford Ave., 74120. Tel: 918-584-4788; 918-584-4789; 918-584-6693 (Res.); Fax: 918-584-0055. Email: ctkparish@marquetteschool.org. Web: www.christthekingtulsa.org.
School—Marquette School, (Grades K-8), 1519 S. Quincy, 74120. Tel: 918-584-4631; Fax: 918-584-0055. Pete Theban, Prin.; Annette Murray, Librarian. Lay Teachers 28; Students 401.
School—Marquette Early Childhood Development Center (ECDC), (6 mo. - 8th Grade), 1528 S. Quincy Ave., 74120. Tel: 918-583-3334. Web: www.marquetteschool.org. Lay Teachers 14; Students 100.
Catechesis/Religious Program—Students 250.

6—CHURCH OF ST. MARY (1954) Rev. Jack Gleason; Rev. Msgr. Dennis C. Dorney, Pastor Emeritus; Rev. William J. Swift; Deacon Richard Bender.
Office: 1347 E. 49th Pl., 74105. Tel: 918-749-1423; Fax: 918-747-9532. Email: church@churchofsaintmary.com. Web: www.churchofsaintmary.com.
School—(Grades PreSchool-8), 1365 E. 49th Pl., 74105. Tel: 918-749-9361; Fax: 918-712-9604. Maureen Clements, Prin. Lay Teachers 31; Students 518.
Catechesis/Religious Program—Linda Schoonover, D.R.E. Students 232.

7—CHURCH OF THE MADALENE (1946) Rev. Bryan Brooks; Sr. Marie Pierre Fleming, O.S.B., Pastoral Assoc.; Deacons Robert DeWeese; Larry E. McFadden.
Res.: 3188 E. 22nd St., 74114. Tel: 918-744-0023; Fax: 918-744-0024. Web: www.madalenetulsa.org.
Catechesis/Religious Program—Tel: 918-744-0023, Ext. 15. Becky Holder, D.R.E. Students 90.

8—ST. FRANCIS XAVIER CHURCH AND DIOCESAN MARIAN SHRINE & EXPIATORY TEMPLE OF OUR LADY OF GUADALUPE (1926), (Hispanic), Revs. David Medina; Oscar Juan Mendoza. In Res., Rev. Robert M. Dye.
Church: 2434 E. Admiral Blvd., 74110. Tel: 918-592-6770; Fax: 918-592-2208.
Res.: 2510 E. 1st St., 74104. Tel: 918-592-6828.
Instituto Bilingue Guadalupano—(Grades Pre-School) Teachers 5; Students 30.
Catechesis/Religious Program—Gloria Gerardo, D.R.E. Students 502.

9—IMMACULATE CONCEPTION (1923) Closed. For inquiries for parish records contact the chancery.

10—ST. JOSEPH CHURCH (1977), (Vietnamese), Rev. Dovan Nguyen.
Res.: 14905 E. 21st St., 74134. Tel: 918-438-1380.
Catechesis/Religious Program—Tel: 918-438-6325. Students 172.

11—ST. MONICA'S (1926), (African American), Rev. Kenneth Iheanaho (Nigeria).
Church: 633 Marshall Pl., 74106. Tel: 918-587-2965 (Office); Fax: 918-582-0699.
Catechesis/Religious Program—Students 10.

12—OUR LADY OF GUADALUPE, Closed. For inquiries for sacramental records contact St. Francis Xavier, Tulsa.

13—PARISH OF SAINT PETER (1996) Rev. Angelo Van der Putten, F.S.S.P.
Mailing Address: 1720 E. Apache, 74110. Tel: 918-747-5776.
Res.: 1728 E. Apache, 74110.
Catechesis/Religious Program—Students 44.

14—SS. PETER AND PAUL (1950) Rev. Timothy L. Davison; Deacon Robert Wilson.
Res.: 1436 N. 67th E. Ave., 74115. Tel: 918-933-4272; Fax: 918-836-2597.
Church & Mailing Address: 1419 N. 67th E. Ave., 74115. Tel: 918-836-2596.
School—(Grades PreSchool-8), 1428 N. 67th E. Ave., 74115. Tel: 918-836-2165. Patrick Martin, Prin.; Ashley Martin, Librarian. Lay Teachers 15; Students 192.
Catechesis/Religious Program—Karen Campbell, D.R.E. Students 220.

15—ST. PIUS X (1955) Rev. Matthew J. Gerlach; Deacons Ernesto Fernandez; Craig Gunter.
Church: 1727 S. 75 E. Ave., 74112. Tel: 918-622-4488; Fax: 918-622-1239.
Res.: 7628 E. 17th St., 74112. Tel: 918-664-9723.
School—(Grades PreK-8), 1717 S. 75 E. Ave., 74112. Tel: 918-627-5367; Fax: 918-627-6179. Web: spxtulsa.org. Matthew Vereecke, Prin. Lay Teachers 27; Students 364.
Catechesis/Religious Program—Arlene Hausher, D.R.E. Students 130.

16—RESURRECTION (1968) Rev. Stephen E. Austin; Deacons James Scarpitti; Peter Byrne.
Mailing Address: P.O. Box 33169, 74153. Tel: 918-663-1907; Fax: 918-663-2533.
Res.: 4338 S. Braden Pl., 74135. Tel: 918-664-8319.
Church: 4804 S. Fulton, 74135. Tel: 918-663-1907.
Catechesis/Religious Program—Amy Synar, D.R.E. Students 80.

17—ST. THOMAS MORE (1972) Revs. Samuel Perez; Jose Maria Briones (Mexico).
Church: 2720 S. 129 E. Ave., 74134-2411. Tel: 918-437-0168; 918-576-6446 (Hispanic); Fax: 918-437-0681; 918-576-6448 (Hispanic).
Catechesis/Religious Program—Alex Areualo, Hispanic D.R.E. Students 616.

OUTSIDE CITY OF TULSA

ANTLERS, PUSHMATAHA CO., ST. AGNES (1897) Rev. Joseph Vadake Chirayath (India).
Church: 503 E. Main, 74523. Tel: 580-298-5204 (Parish Ctr.).
Res.: P.O. Box 99, Hugo, 74743. Tel: 580-326-7300.
Catechesis/Religious Program—Diann Baze, D.R.E. Students 8.
Station—McLeod Correctional Center Farris. Tel: 405-889-6651; Fax: 405-889-2264.

BARTLESVILLE, WASHINGTON CO.

1—ST. JAMES (1965) Rev. Archelito Fernandez (Philippines); Deacon Gerard Rutherford.
Church: 5500 Douglas Ln., 74006. Email: office_stjms@sbcglobal.net.
Catechesis/Religious Program—Tel: 918-335-0844; Fax: 918-333-0856. Students 118.

2—ST. JOHN'S (1906) [CEM] Rev. Festus Maliwa.
Res.: 715 S. Johnstone Ave., 74003. Tel: 918-336-4353; Fax: 918-336-4354.
School—(Grades PreK-8) Tel: 918-336-0603; Fax: 918-336-0624. Jane Sears, Prin.; Lesley B. Farr, Librarian. Lay Teachers 16; Students 105.
Catechesis/Religious Program—Dorlene Martin, D.R.E. Students 196.

BIXBY, TULSA CO., ST. CLEMENT OF ROME (1957) Rev. Leonard Ahanotu (Nigeria); Deacons Jose Guzman; John L. Sommer.
Church: 15501 S. Memorial Dr., 74008. Tel: 918-366-3166; Fax: 918-365-3164. Email: stclementchurch@tulsacoxmail.com. Web: www.stclement-bixby.org.
Catechesis/Religious Program—Students 91.

BROKEN ARROW, TULSA CO.

1—ST. ANNE (1937) [JC] Rev. Michael A. Dodd; Deacon Thomas Moyes.
Res.: 301 S. 9th St., 74012. Tel: 918-251-4000; Fax: 918-251-8719.
Catechesis/Religious Program—Becky Bryant, D.R.E. Students 163.

2—ST. BENEDICT (1980) Rev. Joe C. Townsend; Deacons John Donnelly; Rick Stookey.
Res.: 3105 S. Beech Ave., 74012. Tel: 918-455-7353.
Church & Mailing Address: 2200 W. Ithica St., 74012. Tel: 918-455-4451; Fax: 918-451-2199.
Preschool—Teachers 16; Students 75.
Catechesis/Religious Program—Carol Bryan, C.R.E.; Deb Malcom, Dir. Youth Min. Students 623.

CLAREMORE, ROGER CO., ST. CECILIA (1911) Rev. Paul Eichhoff.
Res.: 1304 N. Dorothy, 74017. Tel: 918-341-2343; Fax: 918-343-2893.
Catechesis/Religious Program—Tel: 918-341-4238. Students 185.

CLEVELAND, OSAGE, ST. JOSEPH (1905), (Native American), See separate listing. Now a mission of Sacred Heart, Fairfax.

COALGATE, COAL CO., BLESSED SACRAMENT ORATORY (1889) [CEM] Closed. For inquiries for parish records contact the chancery.

COLLINSVILLE, TULSA CO., ST. THERESE CHURCH AND DIOCESAN EUCHARISTIC SHRINE OF SAINT THERESE (1908) [CEM] Rev. Richard F. Cristler.
Church: 1007 N. 19th St., 74021. Tel: 918-371-2704; Fax: 918-371-3895.
Catechesis/Religious Program—Carol Thomas, D.R.E. Students 124.

COWETA, WAGONER CO., ST. VINCENT DE PAUL (1981) Rev. Joe C. Townsend; Deacon Lamar Yarbrough.
Mailing Address: P.O. Box 597, 74429-0597. Tel: 918-486-4757.
Catechesis/Religious Program—Students 25.

CUSHING, PAYNE CO., SS. PETER AND PAUL (1894) [CEM] Rev. Matthew G. LaChance; Deacon Kenneth Longbrake.
Mailing Address: P.O. Box 828, 74023.
Res.: 214 N. Steele Ave., 74023. Tel: 918-225-0644; Fax: 918-225-0646. Email: cushingcatholicchurch@yahoo.com.
Church: 401 E. Oak St., 74023.
Catechesis/Religious Program—Alice Patterson, C.R.E. Students 60.
Mission—St. Mary 321 S. Cimarron, Drumright, Creek Co. 74030. P.O. Box 852, Drumright, 74030.

DEWEY, WASHINGTON CO., OUR LADY OF GUADALUPE

(1954) Rev. Jose K. Thottathil; Deacon James Black.
400 W. Ninth St., 74029. Tel: 918-534-3420; Fax: 918-534-3013.
Catechesis/Religious Program—Susanna Mackie, C.R.E. Students 42.
Mission—St. Catherine 217 W. Modoc, Nowata, Nowata Co. 74048. Tel: 918-273-0737. P.O. Box 804, Nowata, 74048.

DURANT, BRYAN CO., ST. WILLIAM (1914) Rev. Valerian Gonsalves.
802 University Blvd., 74701. Tel: 580-924-1989; Fax: 580-931-3044.
Catechesis/Religious Program—Students 47.
Mission—St. Patrick Church Hwy. 69 S., Atoka, Atoka Co. 74701. Tel: 580-931-3044.

FAIRFAX, OSAGE CO., SACRED HEART (1925), (Osage Indian), Rev. Bruce C. Brosnahan.
Mailing Address: 333 S. 8th St., 74637. Tel: 918-642-5053.
Catechesis/Religious Program—
Mission—(1929) 421 S. Petit, Hominy, Osage Co. 74035.
Mission—St. Joseph Osage & C Ave., Cleveland, Pawnee Co. 74020.

GROVE, DELAWARE CO., ST. ELIZABETH (1949) Rev. Alex Kennedy.
Office: 1653 113th St., N.W., 74344. Tel: 918-256-2281.
Catechesis/Religious Program—Students 53.

HARTSHORNE, PITTSBURG CO., HOLY ROSARY (1895) [CEM] Rev. Hung Viet Le.
Mailing Address: 912 Cherokee, P.O. Box 389, 74547. Tel: 918-297-2453.

HENRYETTA, OKMULGEE CO., ST. MICHAEL (1912) [JC] Rev. Chi Peter Phung.
1004 W. Gentry St., P.O. Box 148, 74437. Tel: 918-652-3445; Fax: 918-652-3445.
Catechesis/Religious Program—Students 4.

HOLDENVILLE, HUGHES CO., ST. STEPHEN'S (1905) Rev. Chi Peter Phung.
Mailing Address: P.O. Box 148, Henryetta, 74437.
Church: 515 E. Highway, 74848. Tel: 405-379-2512; Fax: 405-379-2512.
Catechesis/Religious Program—
Mission—St. Teresa (1927) 8th and Broadway, Okemah, Okfuskee Co. 74859.

HOMINY, OSAGE CO., ST. JOSEPH (1929), Now a mission under Sacred Heart, Fairfax.

HUGO, CHOCTAW CO., IMMACULATE CONCEPTION (1903) Rev. Joseph Vadake Chirayath (India).
Res.: P.O. Box 99, 74743. Tel: 580-326-7300 (Rectory); 580-326-3602 (Church); Fax: 580-326-7300.
Mission—St. Jude 511 11th St., Boswell, Choctaw Co. 74727.
Catechesis/Religious Program—Students 18.

IDABEL, MCCURTAIN CO., ST. FRANCIS DE SALES (1945) Rev. Daniel Campos.
Church: 13 S.E. Jefferson, 74745. Tel: 580-286-3275.
Catechesis/Religious Program—Students 40.

KREBS, PITTSBURG CO., ST. JOSEPH'S (1886) [CEM] Rev. James A. Caldwell Jr.; Deacon Bill Anderson.
Res.: P.O. Box 621, 74554. Tel: 918-423-6695; Fax: 918-426-4255.
Catechesis/Religious Program—Tel: 918-423-7130. Bonnie DeGiacomo, D.R.E. Students 38.
Mission—St. Paul's [CEM] 6th & Forest, Eufaula, McIntosh Co. 74554.
Catechesis/Religious Program—Students 18.

LANGLEY, MAYES CO., ST. FRANCES OF ROME (1950) Rev. Celestine Obidiegwu.
Res.: Hwy. 28, P.O. Box 267, 74350-0267. Tel: 918-782-2248.
Catechesis/Religious Program—Students 23.

MCALESTER, PITTSBURG CO., ST. JOHN (1895) [CEM] Rev. Leonard H. Higgins; Deacon Peter J. Faber.
Res.: 300 E. Washington Ave., P.O. Box 220, 74502. Tel: 918-423-0810; Fax: 918-423-0825. Email: stjohnmcalester@yahoo.com.
Catechesis/Religious Program—Students 106.
Station—Oklahoma State Penitentiary, Tel: 918-423-4700; Fax: 918-423-3862.

MIAMI, OTTAWA CO., SACRED HEART (1900) Rev. Carl Kerkemeyer.
Church: 2515 N. Main, 74354. Tel: 918-542-5281.
Catechesis/Religious Program—Tel: 918-542-5898. Karen Painter, D.R.E. Students 54.
Mission—St. Ann Welch, Craig Co. 74369.
Catechesis/Religious Program—Students 12.

MUSKOGEE, MUSKOGEE CO.
1—ASSUMPTION, Closed. For inquiries for sacramental records contact Saint Joseph Church, Muskogee.
2—SAINT JOSEPH CHURCH (1992) [CEM] Rev. Michael J. Knipe; Deacon Edwin Falleur.
Church: 321 N. Virginia, 74402.
Res. & Parish Office: 301 N. Virginia, 74403. Tel: 918-687-1351; Fax: 918-687-5541.
School—(Grades PreK-8), 323 N. Virginia, 74403. Tel: 918-683-1291; Fax: 918-682-5374. Sandra Brewer, Prin. Lay Teachers 15; Students 105.
Catechesis/Religious Program—Jimmy Perkins, D.R.E. Students 129.
3—SACRED HEART, Closed. For inquiries for sacramental records contact Saint Joseph Church, Muskogee.

OKMULGEE, OKMULGEE CO., ST. ANTHONY'S (1910) Rev. Khiet T. Nguyen.
Church: 515 S. Morton Ave., P.O. Box 698, 74447. Tel: 918-756-4385; Fax: 918-756-4385.
Catechesis/Religious Program—Freida Biddle, C.R.E. Students 28.
Mission—Uganda Martyrs 808 E. 3rd, Okmulgee Co. 74447. P.O. Box 698, 74447.

OWASSO, TULSA CO., ST. HENRY (1957) Revs. J. Richard Bradley; J. Paul Donovan, Pastor Emeritus (Retired); Deacons Vernon Foltz; Donald LeMieux; Edmundo Martinez.
Mailing Address: P.O. Box 181, 74055-0181. Tel: 918-272-3710; Fax: 918-272-1966.
Res.: 104 E. 16th St., 74055. Tel: 918-376-9141. Email: office@sthenryowasso.org. Web: www.sthenryowasso.org.
Church: 8500 Owasso Expwy., 74055.
Catechesis/Religious Program—Tel: 918-272-3740. Kelley Tucker, Dir. Faith Formation. Students 471.

PAWHUSKA, OSAGE CO., IMMACULATE CONCEPTION (1887), (Osage Indian), Rev. Christopher Daigle.
Res.: 1314 N. Lynn Ave., 74056. Tel: 918-287-1414.
Catechesis/Religious Program—Students 63.
Mission—St. Mary 3rd and Chestnut, Barnsdall, Osage Co. 74002.
Mission—St. Ann Gypsy St. & Taylor St., Shidler, Osage Co. 74652.

PAWNEE, PAWNEE CO., ST. JOHN (1907) Rev. Matthew G. LaChance; Deacon Glenn Collum.
Mailing Address: P.O. Box 828, Cushing, 74023.
Church: 1303 8th St., 74058.

PLUNKETVILLE, MCCURTAIN CO., ST. HENRY, Closed. For inquiries for parish records see St. Francis De Sales, Idabel.

POTEAU, LEFLORE CO., IMMACULATE CONCEPTION (1903) Rev. Valentine Ndebilie.
Church: 410 Bagwell St., P.O. Box 237, 74953. Tel: 918-647-3475.
Catechesis/Religious Program—Students 45.
Mission—St. Joseph 1204 N.W. 7th St., Stigler, Haskell Co. 74462.
Mission—St. Elizabeth Seton Hwy. 9, Spiro, Leflore Co. 74959.
Station—Ouachita Correctional Training Center Hodgens.

PRYOR, MAYES CO., ST. MARK'S (1942) Rev. Celestine Obidiegwu.
Res.: 1507 S. Vann, 74362. Tel: 918-824-4470; Fax: 918-825-2338. Email: stmarkspryor@sbcglobal.net.
Catechesis/Religious Program—Tel: 918-825-4186. Crystol Samford, D.R.E. Students 86.

SALLISAW, SEQUOYAH CO., ST. FRANCIS XAVIER (1952) Rev. Desmond Okpogba.
Church: 2110 N. Dogwood, 74955. Tel: 918-775-6217; Fax: 918-775-6217.
Catechesis/Religious Program—Students 32.
Mission—St. John the Evangelist P.O. Box 4, Cookson, Cherokee Co. 74427.
Mission—St. Joseph P.O. Box 53, Webbers Falls, Muskogee Co. 74470. Tel: 918-464-2422.
Mission—Blessed Kateri Tekakwitha P.O. Box 17, Roland, Sequoyah Co. 74954.

SAND SPRINGS, TULSA CO., ST. PATRICK'S (1919) Rev. Paschal Mbagwa.
Res.: 204 E. Fourth, 74063. Tel: 918-246-7253; Fax: 918-241-3100. Email: stpartrickcatholicchurch@tulsacoxmail.com. Web: www.stpatrick-sandsprings.org.
Catechesis/Religious Program—Students 40.
Mission—Our Lady of the Lake 400 Cimarron Dr., Mannford, Creek Co. 74044.

SAPULPA, CREEK CO., SACRED HEART (1907) Rev. Jovita Okonkwo (Nigeria); Deacon Mark Pittman.
Church: 1777 E. Grayson Ave., 74066. Tel: 918-224-0944; Fax: 918-512-6830. Web: www.sacredheartsapulpa.org.
Catechesis/Religious Program—Students 44.

SKIATOOK, OSAGE CO., SACRED HEART (1921), (Formerly St. William). Rev. Benjamin A. Vima (India).
Res.: 109 W. 5th St., 74070. Tel: 918-396-1179; Fax: 918-396-2112. Web: www.sacredheart-skiatook.org.
Catechesis/Religious Program—Students 64.

STILLWATER, PAYNE CO.
1—ST. FRANCIS XAVIER (1895) Rev. Kenneth J. Harder; Deacons Paul Govek; Roy Callison; Bill Moler, (Retired).
Church: 601 S. West St., 74074. Tel: 405-372-6886.
Res.: Box 909, 74076. Tel: 405-624-7243; Fax: 405-533-1728.
Catechesis/Religious Program—Students 195.
2—ST. JOHN THE EVANGELIST PARISH AND NEWMAN CENTER (1965) Revs. Stuart Crevcoure; Emmanuel Lugard Nduke; Deacons Tom Haan; Richard Berberet; Thomas Doyle.
Res.: 201 N. Knoblock, 74075. Tel: 405-372-6408; Fax: 405-372-6409. Email: saintjohnparish@yahoo.com. Web: www.stjohn-stillwater.org.
Early Childhood Center—Lay Teachers 8; Students 68.
Catechesis/Religious Program—Tel: 405-372-7987. Students 156.

TAHLEQUAH, CHEROKEE CO., ST. BRIGID (1966) Rev. Jeffrey S. Polasek; Deacons Joseph Faulds; Mark Keeley.
Res.: 807 Crafton St., 74464. Tel: 918-456-8388; Fax: 918-456-8880. Email: stbrigid2@yahoo.com.
Catechesis/Religious Program—Tel: 918-207-1737. Patsy Clifford, D.R.E. Students 84.
Mission—San Juan Mission 23 W. Division St., Stilwell, Adair Co. 74960.

VINITA, CRAIG CO., HOLY GHOST (1892) Rev. Alex Kennedy.
Res.: 120 W. Sequoyah Ave., 74301. Tel: 918-256-2281.
Catechesis/Religious Program—Tel: 918-256-3118. Debbie Lauchner, C.R.E. Students 37.
Station—Northeastern Correctional Facility

VALIANT, MCCURTAIN CO., GOOD SHEPHERD, Closed. For inquiries for parish records see St. Francis De Sales, Idabel.

WAGONER, WAGONER CO., HOLY CROSS (1895) Rev. Joseph A. Orthel, Admin.; Deacon Jim Ruyle.
Mailing Address: P.O. Box 710, 74477. Tel: 918-485-5145. Email: hcrosswag@valornet.com.
Church: S.W. 15th & Pierce, 74477.
Catechesis/Religious Program—

WILBURTON, LATIMER CO., SACRED HEART (1908) [CEM] Rev. Joshua E. Litwack; Deacon Clement Bradley.
102 Center Point Rd., Latimer Co. 74578.
Catechesis/Religious Program—Students 13.
Mission—St. Catherine of Siena 501 2nd St., Talihina, Leflore Co. 74571. Tel: 918-567-2587.
Catechesis/Religious Program—Students 10.
Mission—Holy Trinity P.O. Box 747, Clayton, Pushmataha Co. 74523. Tel: 918-569-4767.

Chaplains of Public Institutions

Special Assignment:
Rev. Msgr.—
Brankin, Patrick M., Office of the Diaconate, Chancery Office
Revs.—
Calvillo, Ernesto, (Medical Leave)
Choorackunnel, John V., C.M.I., Chap., Saint Francis Hospital, Tulsa
Coleman, Gerald J., Chap., St. John Medical Center, Tulsa
Kirby, Mark, O.S.B., Spiritual Dir. Diocesan Priests & Deacons
Kodakarakaran, Paul, Chap., St. Francis Hospital, Tulsa
Medina, Leonardo, Dir. Hispanic Ministry
Nguyen, Tam, (On Sabbatical)
O'Brien, Brian D., Pres., Bishop Kelley High School, Tulsa
Ripperger, Chad, F.S.S.P., Ministry of Deliverance
Sherman, Gary D., Chap., St. John Medical Center, Tulsa
Wakulich, Kerry J., Chap., St. Philip Neri Newman Center, Tulsa, OK
Willis, Kevin L., Chap., Franciscan Villa, 17110 E. 51st St., Broken Arrow, 74012.

On Duty Outside the Diocese:
Revs.—
Amaliri, Paul Obi, Military Chap., U.S. Air Force
Cain, Robert K.C., Military Chap., U.S. Navy
Gonzalez, Elkin, Pontificio Istituto Di Spiritualita, Rome
Kastl, Gary, Catholic Leadership Institute, 440 E. Swedesford Rd., Ste. 3040, Wayne, PA 19087.
Minh, Vu Duc, Holy Martyrs, Colorado Springs, CO
Pratt, Michael, Pontificio Istituto Di Spiritualita, Rome
Wells, Peter B., Secretary of State Office, Section of General Affairs, Vatican

Retired:
Revs.—
Casey, Denis, 2121 S. Yorktown # 503, 74114.
Courtright, Lawrence P., 1921 S. Xanthus Ave., 74104.
Donovan, J. Paul, P.O. Box 181, Owasso, 74055.
Eastman, Patrick W., 30 N. Wall, Cricklade, Wiltshire SN66DE England.
Elliott, W. Gregg, 3430 Forsythe Ter., The Villages, FL 32162.
Fulton, Kenneth S., 8437 E. 58th St., 74145.
Le, Hoang Viet, 2403 S. 141st East Ave., 74134.
Lundberg, John W., 43 California Ave., Middletown, NY 10940.
McGlinchey, James J.

Melton, Thomas K., P.O. Box 151, 74578.
Morgan, Martin J., 3105 S. Beech Ave., Broken Arrow, 74012.
Perlinski, Daniel A., 17110 E. 51st St., Apt. 4, Broken Arrow, 74012.
Richard, Edward, Franciscan Villa, 17110 E. 51st St. S., Broken Arrow, 74012.
Skeehan, William K., 3008 E. 51st St., Apt. 27, 74105.
Swett, Charles J., 2009 Xanthus, 74104.
Swift, William V., 1779 S. Wheeling, 74104.
Wade, John J., 1171 S. Wheeling, 74104.
White, James D., Santa Teresita Manor, 819 Buena Vista St., #205, Duarte, CA 91010.

Permanent Deacons:
Anderson, Bill, St. Joseph, Krebs
Barnes, Robert, (Retired)
Bender, Richard F., Church of St. Mary, Tulsa
Berberet, Richard, Stillwater Parishes
Black, James, Our Lady of Guadalupe, Dewey
Bradley, Clement W., Sacred Heart, Wilburton
Breazille, James E., Parishes of Stillwater
Byrne, Peter, Church of the Resurrection, Tulsa
Callison, Roy, St. Francis Xavier, Stillwater
Campbell, Richard, St. Bernard, Tulsa
Campbell, Sam
Cardenas, Alfonso, (Retired)
Chamberlain, Richard, (Retired)
Collum, Glenn, St. John, Pawnee
DeLeon, Felix, (Retired)
DeWeese, Robert, Church of the Madalene, Tulsa
Donnelly, John E., St. Benedict, Broken Arrow
Doyle, Thomas, Parishes of Stillwater
Faber, Peter J., St. John, McAlester
Falleur, Edwin E., St. Joseph, Muskogee
Faulds, Joseph M., St. Brigid, Tahlequah
Fernandez, Ernesto, St. Pius X, Tulsa
Foltz, Vernon, (Retired)
Garrett, James R., (Retired)
Gorman, Tom, Holy Family Cathedral, Tulsa
Govek, Paul, Stillwater Parishes
Gunter, Craig, St. Pius X, Tulsa
Guzman, Jose, St. Clement, Bixby
Haan, Tom, Stillwater Parishes
Hamel, David C., St. Joseph, Bristow
Johnson, Dave, St. Bernard, Tulsa
Johnson, John M., Christ the King, Tulsa
Keeley, Mark, St. Brigid, Tahlequah
LeMieux, Donald J., St. Henry, Owasso
Litwack, Stephen J., St. Augustine, Tulsa & St. Monica, Tulsa
Loney, Tom, (Unassigned)
Longbrake, Kenneth, Sts. Peter and Paul, Cushing
Luschen, Loren F., Christ the King, Tulsa
Martin, Robert, St. Bernard of Clairvaux, Tulsa
Martinez, Edmundo S., St. Henry, Owasso
Mattox, Jerry, Holy Family Cathedral, Tulsa
McFadden, Larry E., Church of the Madalene, Tulsa
Mikell, Alan G., St. Bernard, Tulsa
Moler, William J., (Retired)
Moreno, Carlos, Hispanic Apostolate
Morris, Marvin D., (Retired)
Moyes, Thomas, St. Anne, Broken Arrow
Mrasek, Vincent J., (Retired), St. Cecilia, Claremore
Perez, Jose, (Retired)
Pierret, James A., (Retired)
Pittman, Mark, Sacred Heart, Sapulpa
Richard, Joseph N., (Retired)
Rutherford, Gerard, St. James, Bartlesville
Ruyle, Jim, Holy Cross, Wagoner
Sartorius, Kevin, Catholic Charities, Tulsa
Scarpitti, James, Church of the Resurrection, Tulsa
Schumacher, Kenneth, St. Anne, Broken Arrow
Sommer, John L., St. Clement, Bixby
Sousa, Nelson M., Holy Family Cathedral, Tulsa
Starr, Sid
Stice, Greg, Holy Family Cathedral, Tulsa
Stookey, Rick, St. Benedict, Broken Arrow, OK
Toppins, Charles A., (Retired)
Tucker, Donel, (Retired)
Victor, Craig, St. Catherine, Tulsa
Weigant, Kasper E., (Retired)
Wersal, Dean, Christ the King, Tulsa
Willis, Daniel H., (Retired)
Wilson, Robert, Sts. Peter & Paul, Tulsa
Yarbrough, Lamar, St. Vincent de Paul, Coweta
Young, Thomas, (Retired)

INSTITUTIONS LOCATED IN THE DIOCESE

[A] HIGH SCHOOLS, DIOCESAN

TULSA. *Bishop Kelley High School* (1960) (Grades 9-12), 3905 S. Hudson, 74135-5699. Tel: 918-627-3390; Fax: 918-664-2134. Email: frobrien@bkelleyhs.org. Web: www.bkelleyhs.org. Rev. Brian D. O'Brien, Pres.; Curt Feilmeier, Prin.; Marianne Stich; Karen Govier, Librarian. Priests 2; Brothers 3; Lay Teachers 70; Students 820.

[B] HIGH SCHOOLS, PRIVATE

TULSA. *Cascia Hall Preparatory School*, (Grades 6-12), 2520 S. Yorktown Ave., 74114. Tel: 918-746-2600; Fax: 918-746-2636. Email: info@casciahall.org. Web: www.casciahall.org. 2520 S. Yorktown Ave., 74114. Tel: 918-746-2600; Fax: 918-746-2636. Mr. Roger Carter, Headmaster; Revs. Roland F. Follmann, O.S.A.; John H. Gaffney, O.S.A.; William A. Hamill, O.S.A.; William A. Perez, O.S.A.; John J. Sotak, O.S.A., Dir. Augustinian Mission; Theodore E. Tack, O.S.A.; Bro. Jack H. Hibbard, O.S.A.; Shawn Gammill, Prin.; Joan O'Brien Hubble, Librarian. Augustinians (Order of St. Augustine)., Coed College Preparatory School. Priests 7; Brothers 1; Sisters 1; Lay Teachers 46; Students 568.

[C] ELEMENTARY SCHOOLS, DIOCESAN

BROKEN ARROW. *All Saints School*, (Grades PreK-8), 299 S. 9th St., 74012. Tel: 918-251-3000; Fax: 918-258-9879. Anne Scalet, Prin.; LuAnn Cannon, Librarian. Lay Teachers 30; Students 330.

[D] ELEMENTARY SCHOOLS, PRIVATE

TULSA. *Monte Cassino School*, (Grades PreK-8), 2206 S. Lewis, 74114. Tel: 918-742-3364; Fax: 918-742-5206. Web: www.montecasino.org. Matthew Vereecke, School Dir.; Nancy Henry, Librarian; Carmen Applegate, Librarian. Sisters 4; Lay Teachers 79; Students 882.

**San Miguel School of Tulsa, Inc.* (2004) (Grades 6-8), 2444 E. Admiral Blvd., 74110. Tel: 918-728-7337; Fax: 918-660-2040. Anne Edwards, Dir., Prin. & Contact Person. Lay Teachers 10; Students 71.

[E] GENERAL HOSPITALS

TULSA. *Saint Francis Hospital*, 6161 S. Yale Ave., 74136. Tel: 918-494-2200; Fax: 918-494-8448. Web: www.saintfrancis.com. Mr. Jake Henry Jr., Pres. & CEO; Lynn Sund, Sr. Vice Pres. & Admin.; Revs. Denis Casey, Chap. (Retired); John V. Choorackunnel, C.M.I., Chap.; Elias Abi-Sarkis, Chap. (Maronite); Paul Kodakarakaran. Bed Capacity 962; Bassinets 40; Patients Assisted Annually 699,295.

**Jane Phillips Health Corp.*, Mailing Address: 1923 S. Utica Ave., 74104. 3500 E. Frank Phillips Blvd., Bartlesville, 74006. Tel: 918-331-1550. Rev. Jose K. Thottathil, Pastoral Care. Bed Capacity 144; Total Assisted 121,600.

St. John Health System, Inc. (1982) 1923 S. Utica, 74104. Tel: 918-744-2180; Fax: 918-744-2716. Web: www.stjohnhealthsystem.com. David J. Pynn, Pres.

St. John Medical Center, Inc. (1926) 1923 S. Utica Ave., 74104. Tel: 918-744-2296; Fax: 918-744-2357. Web: www.sjmc.org. Charles Anderson, Pres.; Revs. Gary D. Sherman, Chap.; Gerald J. Coleman, Chap. Sisters of the Sorrowful Mother (Third Order of St. Francis). Sisters 14; Bed Capacity 547; Patients Assisted Annually 475,000.

Marian Health System, Inc. (1989) 1923 S. Utica Ave., 74104. Tel: 918-742-9988; Fax: 918-744-2716. Web: www.marianhealthsystem.com. Sr. M. Therese Gottschalk, Pres. & CEO.

BROKEN ARROW. *St. John Broken Arrow, Inc.*, 1000 W. Boise Cir., 74012. Tel: 918-994-8000. David Phillips, CEO. Sisters 1; Bed Capacity 68; Patients Assisted Annually 46,000.

OWASSO. *Owasso Medical Facility, Inc. dba St. John Owasso* 12451 E. 100th St. N., 74055. 1923 S. Utica Ave., 74104. Tel: 918-994-8000. Bed Capacity 36; Total Assisted Annually 54,500.

[F] HOMES FOR THE AGED

TULSA. *Frances Streitel Senior Care Corporation*, 1923 S. Utica Ave., 74104. Tel: 918-355-1596.

Frances Streitel Senior Care Corp., 2300 W. Broadway, Collinsville, 74021. Tel: 918-371-2545. Bed Capacity 119; Total Assisted Annually 115; Total Staff 110; Apartments 2.

St. John Villas, Inc. (1984) 1923 S. Utica, 74104. Tel: 918-355-1596. Web: www.stjohnhealthsystem.com/departments/seniorliving. Ron Hoffman, Pres.; Revs. Gary D. Sherman, Chap.; Kevin Willis. Sisters of the Sorrowful Mother., Retirement Residence and Health Care Center for Intermediate Nursing Care. Bed Capacity 229; Apartments 97; Residents 275.

St. Teresa of Avila Villa, Inc., Mailing Address: 1923 S. Utica, 74104. 632 N. 19th St., Collinsville, 74021. Tel: 918-371-7771. Ron Hoffman, Pres. To assist in accommodating the elderly and disabled with housing facilities and services. Bed Capacity 41; Residents 41.

[G] MONASTERIES FOR MEN

TULSA. *Monastery of Our Lady of the Cenacle* (2010) 1132 E. 21st St. S., 74114. Tel: 918-749-0995. Email: cenacle@sbcglobal.net. Rev. Mark Kirby, O.S.B., Prior. Priests 1; Brothers 2.

HULBERT. *Our Lady of the Annunciation of Clear Creek Monastery* (1999) 5804 W. Monastery Rd., 74441-5698. Tel: 918-772-2454; Fax: 918-772-1044. Web: www.clearcreekmonks.org. Rt. Rev. Philip Anderson, O.S.B., Abbot; Revs. Christopher Andrews, O.S.B.; Mark Bachmann, O.S.B., Subprior; Francis Bales, O.S.B.; Francis Bethel, O.S.B., Prior; Francis Xavier Brown, O.S.B.; Lawrence Brown, O.S.B.; Philippe Le Bouteiller des Haries, O.S.B.; Vincent Hulot, O.S.B.; Joshua Morey, O.S.B.; Matthew Shapiro, O.S.B.; Ulrich Theuerer, O.S.B.; James Louis Ullmer, O.S.B. Priests 13; Brothers 24.

[H] CONVENTS AND RESIDENCES FOR SISTERS

TULSA. *St. Joseph Monastery* (1879) 2200 S. Lewis, 74114-3100. Tel: 918-742-4989; Fax: 918-744-1374. Email: sisters@stjosephmonastery.org. Web: www.stjosephmonastery.org. Sr. Christine Ereiser, O.S.B., Prioress. Motherhouse of Benedictine Sisters (Federation of St. Scholastica). Sisters in Community 21.

Sisters of Saint Joseph, 3942 S. Trenton, 74105. Tel: 918-749-8954. Sisters in Community 2.

BROKEN ARROW. *Daughters of Mary, Mother of Israel's Hope*, 466 S. 79th E. Ave., 74112. Tel: 918-576-7607.

[I] NEWMAN CENTERS

TULSA. *St. Philip Neri Newman Center at The University of Tulsa* 440 S. Florence, 74104. Tel: 918-599-0204; Fax: 918-587-0115. Email: tu-newman@utulsa.edu. Web: www.tu-newman.org. Rev. Kerry J. Wakulich, Chap.; Lisa Holden, Devel. Dir.

STILLWATER. *St. John's University Parish and Catholic Student Center* 201 N. Knoblock, 74075. Tel: 405-372-6408; Fax: 405-372-6409. Email: saintjohnparish@yahoo.com. Web: www.stjohn-stillwater.org. Rev. Stuart Crevcoure; Cathy Perry, Campus Min.

TAHLEQUAH. *Northeastern State University Catholic Student Organization* 807 Crafton St., 74464. Tel: 918-456-8388. Rev. Jeffrey S. Polasek.

[J] MISCELLANEOUS

TULSA. *Bishop Kelley High School Endowment Trust*, 3905 S. Hudson Ave., 74135. Tel: 918-627-3390; Fax: 918-664-2134. Email: frobrien@bkelleyhs.org. Web: bkelleyhs.org. Rev. Brian D. O'Brien, Pres.

Catholic Foundation of Eastern Oklahoma, Inc., P.O. Box 690240, 74169. Tel: 918-294-1904.

**Saint Francis Health System, Inc.*, 6161 S. Yale, 74136. Tel: 918-494-8452; Fax: 918-494-8435. Mr. Jake Henry Jr., Pres. & CEO.

Saint Francis of Assisi Tuition Assistance Trust, Diocese of Tulsa, P.O. Box 690240, 74169-0240.

St. John Auxiliary, Inc., 1923 S. Utica Ave., 74104. Laurie Thomas, CAVS Dir.

St. John Health System Foundation, Inc. (1981) 1923 S. Utica, 74104. Tel: 918-744-2186; Fax: 918-744-2716.

St. John Management Services Inc., 1923 S. Utica Ave., 74104. Tel: 918-744-2180. 12451 E. 100th St. N., Owasso, 74055. David Pynn, Pres. Bed Capacity 200; Total Assisted Annually 80,000.

Saint John Vianney Seminary Trust, Diocese of Tulsa, P.O. Box 690240, 74169-0240.

St. Joseph Residence, Inc., P.O. Box 580460, 74158. Tel: 918-587-6456; Fax: 918-587-3560. Total Assisted 21; Total Staff 6.

Priest Retirement Trust of the Roman Catholic Diocese of Tulsa, c/o Diocese of Tulsa, P.O. Box 690240, 74169-0240. Tel: 918-294-1904; Fax: 918-294-0920. Rev. Msgr. Dennis C. Dorney, V.G.

BROKEN ARROW. *Te Deum Institute of Sacred Liturgy*, 12300 E. 91st St. S., 74012. P.O. Box 690240, 74169. Joey Spencer, Prog. Dir.

HULBERT. *Foundation for the Annunciation Monastery of Clear Creek* (1999) 5804 W. Monastery Rd., 74441-5698. Tel: 918-772-2454; Fax: 918-772-1044. Web: www.clearcreekmonks.org.

MUSKOGEE. *St. Joseph School Endowment Trust*, P.O. Box 189, 74402. Tel: 918-687-1351.

PORTER. *Apostolate for the Most Holy Rosary and the Brown Scapular Association*, P.O. Box 1041, Coweta, 74429. Tel: 918-279-9158. Email: highlandhaven@windstream.net.

SAPULPA. *St. John Sapulpa Foundation, Inc.*, 1004 E. Bryan, 74066. Tel: 918-224-4280; Fax: 918-227-1093. Web: www.stjohnhealthsystem.com. Valerie Round, CEO.

RELIGIOUS INSTITUTES OF MEN REPRESENTED IN THE DIOCESE

For further details refer to the corresponding bracketed number in the Religious Institutes of Men or Women section.

[0140]—*The Augustinians (Province of Our Mother of Good Counsel)*—O.S.A.

[0200]—*Benedictine Monks (Solesmes Congregation)*—O.S.B.

[]—*Benedictine Monks (Diocese of Tulsa)*

[0330]—*Brothers of the Christian Schools* (Midwest Province, Burr Ridge, IL)—F.S.C.

[]—*Carmelites of Mary Immaculate*—C.M.I.

[0650]—*Holy Ghost Fathers*—C.S.Sp.

[1065]—*Priestly Order of St. Peter*—F.S.S.P.

RELIGIOUS INSTITUTES OF WOMEN REPRESENTED IN THE DIOCESE

[0230]—*Congregation of the Benedictine Sisters of the Sacred Hearts*—O.S.B.

[]—*Daughters of Mary, Mother of Israel's Hope*

[2330]—*Little Sisters of Jesus, Mexico*—L.S.J.

[]—*Medical Sisters of St. Joseph, India*

[2519]—*Religious Sisters of Mercy*—R.S.M.

[]—*Rose of Lima, Vietnam*—O.P.

[2970]—*School Sisters of Norte Dame*—S.S.N.D.

[1705]—*Sisters of St. Francis of Assisi*—O.S.F.

[1570]—*Sisters of St. Francis of the Holy Family*—O.S.F.

[1640]—*Sisters of St. Francis of the Martyr of St. George*

[3830]—*Sisters of St. Joseph*—S.S.J.

[3840]—*Sisters of St. Joseph of Carondelet*

[4100]—*Sisters of the Sorrowful Mother (Third Order of St. Francis)*—S.S.M.

CEMETERIES

TULSA. *Calvary*, 9101 S. Harvard, 74136. Tel: 918-299-7348; Fax: 918-299-7558.

NECROLOGY

† Halpine, Rev. Msgr. James F., (Retired)—Died Nov. 19, 2010

† Gomez, Jorge, (Special Assignment)—Died Aug. 21, 2011

† Pickett, Robert T., (Retired)—Died Feb. 7, 2011

An asterisk (*) denotes an organization that has established tax-exempt status directly with the IRS and is not covered by the USCCB Group Ruling.

Diocese of Tyler

(Dioecesis Tylerensis)

ESTABLISHED DECEMBER 12, 1986.

Square Miles 23,443.

Comprises the following Counties in the State of Texas: Anderson, Angelina, Bowie, Camp, Cass, Cherokee, Delta, Franklin, Freestone, Gregg, Harrison, Henderson, Hopkins, Houston, Lamar, Leon, Madison, Marion, Morris, Nacogdoches, Panola, Rains, Red River, Rusk, Sabine, San Augustine, Shelby, Smith, Titus, Trinity, Upshur, Van Zandt, and Wood.

For legal titles of parishes and diocesan institutions, consult the Chancery Office.

(VACANT SEE)

Chancery: 1015 E.S.E. Loop 323, Tyler, TX 75701-9663. Tel: 903-534-1077; Fax: 903-534-1370.

STATISTICAL OVERVIEW

Personnel

Priests: Diocesan Active in Diocese	56
Priests: Diocesan Active Outside Diocese	10
Priests: Retired, Sick or Absent	17
Number of Diocesan Priests	83
Religious Priests in Diocese	8
Total Priests in Diocese	91
Extern Priests in Diocese	10
Ordinations:	
Diocesan Priests	6
Transitional Deacons	2
Permanent Deacons in Diocese	94
Total Brothers	1
Total Sisters	50

Parishes

Parishes	45
With Resident Pastor:	
Resident Diocesan Priests	40
Resident Religious Priests	5
Missions	27
Pastoral Centers	1
New Parishes Created	2
Professional Ministry Personnel:	
Brothers	1
Sisters	13
Lay Ministers	765

Welfare

Catholic Hospitals	3
Total Assisted	1,165,343
Special Centers for Social Services	9
Total Assisted	25,000

Educational

Diocesan Students in Other Seminaries	13
Total Seminarians	13
High Schools, Diocesan and Parish	1
Total Students	256
Elementary Schools, Diocesan and Parish	5
Total Students	810
Catechesis/Religious Education:	
High School Students	796
Elementary Students	8,097
Total Students under Catholic Instruction	9,972
Teachers in the Diocese:	
Lay Teachers	29

Vital Statistics

Receptions into the Church:	
Infant Baptism Totals	2,383
Minor Baptism Totals	148
Adult Baptism Totals	75
Received into Full Communion	265
First Communions	1,664
Confirmations	2,035
Marriages:	
Catholic	255
Interfaith	35
Total Marriages	290
Deaths	288
Total Catholic Population	54,746
Total Population	1,396,736

Former Bishops—Most Revs. CHARLES E. HERZIG, D.D., First Bishop of Tyler; ord. May 31, 1955; appt. Bishop of Tyler Dec. 12, 1986; cons. Feb. 24, 1987; died Sept. 7, 1991; EDMOND CARMODY, D.D., Second Bishop of Tyler; ord. June 8, 1957; appt. Auxiliary Bishop of San Antonio, Nov. 8, 1988; cons. Dec. 15, 1988; appt. Bishop of Tyler, March 24, 1992; installed May 25, 1992; transferred to Diocese of Corpus Christi, March 17, 2000; ALVARO CORRADA DEL RIO, S.J., ord. July 6, 1974; appt. Auxiliary Bishop of Washington DC May 30, 1985; cons. Aug. 4, 1985; on assignment, as Apostolic Administrator, Diocese of Caguas; appt. Bishop of Tyler Dec. 5, 2000; installed Jan. 30, 2001; appt. Bishop of Mayaguez, Puerto Rico July 6, 2011.

Office of Bishop—VACANT, 1015 ESE Loop 323, Tyler, 75701-9663. Tel: 903-534-1077; Fax: 903-534-1370. Email: bishopoffice@dioceseoftyler.org. Secretary to the Bishop: VACANT. Tel: 903-534-1077, Ext. 132. Email: bishopoffice@dioceseoftyler.org. Bishop's Office Secretary: Ms. TERESA TISCARENO. Tel: 903-534-1077, Ext. 132. Email: mtiscareno@dioceseoftyler.org.

Apostolic Administrator—Most Rev. ALVARO CORRADA DEL RIO, S.J.

Delegate of the Apostolic Administrator—Rev. Msgr. JOSEPH E. STRICKLAND, J.C.L., 1015 ESE Loop 323, Tyler, 75701. Tel: 903-534-1077, Ext. 139. Email: vg@dioceseoftyler.org; Mrs. TERRY BOLTON, Admin. Asst. Tel: 903-534-1077, Ext. 137. Email: tbolton@dioceseoftyler.org.

Chancery—1015 E.S.E. Loop 323, Tyler, 75701-9663. Tel: 903-534-1077; Fax: 903-534-1370. Office Hours: Mon.-Fri. 8:30-5.

Chancellor—Deacon RUBEN NATERA, 1015 ESE Loop 323, Tyler, 75701-9663. Tel: 903-266-2133. Email: rnatera@dioceseoftyler.org.

Vice Chancellor—Rev. ROBERT H. (HANK) LANIK.

Moderator of the Curia—Rev. Msgr. JOSEPH E. STRICKLAND, J.C.L.

Northern Vicariate—Rev. Msgr. XAVIER PAPPU.

Southern Vicariate—Rev. Msgr. JOSEPH E. STRICKLAND, J.C.L.

Archivist—Deacon RUBEN NATERA, Chancellor. Tel: 903-534-1077, Ext. 133; 903-266-2133 (office). Email: rnatera@dioceseoftyler.org; Mrs. CINDY PLUMMER, Archivist Asst. Tel: 903-534-1077, Ext. 195.

College of Consultors—Rev. Msgrs. XAVIER PAPPU; JOSEPH E. STRICKLAND, J.C.L.; GERALD A. PRIEST, Head of Consultors (Retired); JAMES E. YOUNG; RONALD L. DIEGEL; ZACHARIAS S. KUNNAKKATTUTHARA; Revs. LUIS E. LARREA, M.F.E.; GAVIN N. VAVEREK, J.C.L.

Deans—Rev. Msgr. RON L. DIEGEL, East Central Deanery; Rev. ARIEL CORTES, Northeast Deanery; Rev. Msgrs. JAMES E. YOUNG, Southeast Deanery; ZACHARIAS S. KUNNAKKATTUTHARA, Southwest Deanery; Revs. MARK KUSMIREK, West Central Deanery; SUSAI AVULA, Northwest Deanery.

Tribunal Office—1015 E.S.E. Loop 323, Tyler, 75701-9663. Tel: 903-266-2140; Fax: 903-534-1370.

Judicial Vicar—Very Rev. ANTHONY K.W. MCLAUGHLIN, J.C.D. Tel: 903-534-1077, Ext. 139. Email: fathermclaughlin@aol.com.

Judges—Rev. Msgr. JOSEPH E. STRICKLAND, J.C.L.; Revs. ANTHONY MCLAUGHLIN, J.C.L.; CHRISTOPHER V. RUGGLES, J.C.L.

Administrator—Mrs. MARGARET OPPENHEIMER. Tel: 903-266-2140. Email: tribunal@dioceseoftyler.org; moppenheimer@dioceseoftyler.org.

Defender of the Bond—Rev. GAVIN N. VAVEREK, J.C.L.

Advocates—

Candidates Approved as Canonical Advocates for Marriage Cases—Rev. Msgr. JOHN FLYNN (Retired). Tel: 903-534-1077, Ext. 172. *Southeast Deanery*, Deacons RAY VANN, St. Patrick's, Lufkin; JOHN RAGLAND, Our Lady of Lourdes, Chireno. *Northeast Deanery*, Deacons CRAIG LASHFORD, Sacred Heart, Texarkana; TIMOTHY O'NEILL, St. Mary of the Cenacle, New Boston. *West Central Deanery*, Rev. PAUL R. KEY, S.T.L., M.Div.; Deacon JACK ROUNDS, Cathedral; VIRGINIA ROUNDS, Cathedral; Mrs. VIRGINIA S. MEDRANO, Cathedral; BEVERLY OHREN, Cathedral; Deacons DENNIS KING, Holy Family, Lindale; CLARENCE BLALOCK, St. Mary Magdalene's, Flint. *East Central Deanery*, CAROL MOLINA, St. Mary's, Longview; BILL O'ROURKE, Christ the King, Kilgore; Deacon NELSON PETZOLD, St. Matthew's, Longview; CHARLOTTE SMITH, St. Joseph's Church, Marshall; LAURA BATE, St. William of Vercelli, Carthage; Deacon LARRY BATE, St. William of Vercelli, Carthage; DEBBIE SCHOLL, St. William of Vercelli, Carthage; Deacon LEN LUSCOMB, Our Lady Queen of Angels, Overton. *Northwest Deanery*, (No candidates at the moment). *Southeast Deanery*, (No candidates at the moment).

Auditor—Rev. JOSE CORTEZ.

Ecclesiastical Notaries—Mrs. MARGARET OPPENHEIMER; Mrs. CINDY PLUMMER; Deacon RUBEN NATERA, Chancellor.

Ethics and Integrity—MARIA FLORES, Admin. Asst.

DIOCESAN ADMINISTRATION

Finance Officer—Mr. JIM SMITH, 1015 E.S.E. Loop 323, Tyler, 75701-9663. Tel: 903-534-1077, Ext. 138. Email: jsmith@dioceseoftyler.org.

Diocesan Finance Council—Rev. Msgrs. JAMES E. YOUNG, Ex Officio; JOSEPH E. STRICKLAND, J.C.L.; Mrs. LAURA REDMAN; Mr. ROBERT BREEDLOVE; Mrs. FRED ARRAMBIDEZ; Mr. LOUIS OWEN; Rev. Msgr. XAVIER PAPPU; Mr. JIM SMITH, Ex Officio; Deacon RUBEN NATERA, Chancellor; Mrs. YVETTE BRUNETTE.

Diocesan Building Board—Mr. TOM DEIBEL; Rev. GAVIN N. VAVEREK, J.C.L.; Rev. Msgr. XAVIER PAPPU; Mr. JIM SMITH.

East Texas Catholic Foundation—Mr. JIM SMITH, Dir., 1015 E.S.E. Loop 323, Tyler, 75701-9663. Email: jsmith@dioceseoftyler.org.

Priests' Pension Board—Rev. Msgrs. JAMES E. YOUNG; XAVIER PAPPU; Rev. BERNARD BOTEJU; Mr. JIM SMITH, Treas.; Rev. Msgrs. ZACHARIAS S. KUNNAKKATTUTHARA; RONALD L. DIEGEL; GERALD A. PRIEST (Retired); JOSEPH E. STRICKLAND, J.C.L.; Rev. GAVIN N. VAVEREK, J.C.L.

Catholic Campaign for Human Development—Mr. JIM SMITH. Tel: 903-534-1077, Ext. 138. Email:

jsmith@dioceseoftyler.org.

Catholic Schools Office—Dr. JAMES (JIM) KLASSEN, Supt. Catholic Schools. Tel: 903-534-1077, Ext. 142. Email: jklassen@dioceseoftyler.org; Mrs. MARY ELLIOTT, Sec., 1015 E.S.E. Loop 323, Tyler, 75701-9663. Tel: 903-534-1077, Ext. 142. Email: schooloffice@dioceseoftyler.org.

Diocesan Catholic School Advisory Council—Mrs. GRETCHEN COBB, Chair; Dr. JAMES (JIM) KLASSEN, Exec. Officer; Mrs. KRISTAN MCBRIDE; Mrs. MARY LOU TYER, Chair-Elect; Most Rev. ALVARO CORRADA, S.J.; Rev. DENZIL J. VITHANAGE; Deacon JOHN SARGENT; Ms. MICHELLE TRAMMELL, Sec.; Mrs. DIANE JAGER; Mrs. MARY ELLIOTT, Recording Sec.

Faith Formation Office—Mrs. LINDA PORTER, Dir. Email: lporter@dioceseoftyler.org; Mrs. SARAH ROBINSON, Admin. Sec. Tel: 903-534-1077, Ext. 169. Email: srobinson@dioceseoftyler.org.

Coordinator for Catechesis—Sr. ANGELICA OROZCO, E.F.M.S. Email: sistera@dioceseoftyler.org.

Diocesan Christian Initiation Team—Mrs. LINDA PORTER, Chm.; Rev. GAVIN N. VAVEREK, J.C.L., Consultant; Sr. SUSAN SEITZ, O.S.F., Tyler - Cathedral; Deacon DAVID DARBY, Nacog. - Sacred Heart; Mrs. TERESA DARBY, Nacog. - Sacred Heart; Deacon AUBREY FISK, Mineola - St. Peter the Apostle; SANDY BUNCH, Chandler - St. Boniface; Mrs. SUSAN WELLS, Longview - St. Mary's; Rev. ARIEL CORTES, Whitehouse - Prince of Peace; Sr. ANGELICA OROZCO, E.F.M.S., Diocese of Tyler; Ms. PEGGY HAMMETT, Tyler - Cathedral; Deacon TREVOR WELLS, Longview - St. Mary's.

Pastoral Ministries—Rev. ROBERT H. (HANK) LANIK.

Family Life Office—Co Directors: Deacon GERALD "JERRY" BESZE. Email: jbesze@dioceseoftyler.org; Mrs. MARY BESZE, 1015 E.S.E. Loop 323, Tyler, 75701-9663. Tel: 903-534-1077. Email: mbesze@dioceseoftyler.org.

Tyler Catholic Committee on Scouting—Mr. JOHN MCDOUGALD, Okee-Tukla District; Rev. FRANCIS O'DOWD, Chap., Mailing Address: P.O. Box 1071, Lindale, 75771-1078. Tel: 903-228-4079; Mr. BYRONE MEADS, Chm.; Mr. GARY L. HUBER, M.D.; Mr. TED KAMEL; Mr. CHARLES HEIMERDINGER; Mr. TIM RUSSELL; Mr. MIKE CONNOR, Professional Scouter, Mailing Address: 172 Luther Ln., Gun Barrel City, 75156. Tel: 903-757-7524.

Young Adult/Campus Ministries—Revs. ROBERT H. (HANK) LANIK, Catholic Campus Min. of Tyler, 1015 E.S.E. Loop 323, Tyler, 75701. Tel: 903-534-1077; Fax: 903-534-1370. Email: frlanik@dioceseoftyler.org; PAUL R. KEY, S.T.L., M.Div., St. Mary Chapel, 211 E. College, Nacogdoches, 75965. Tel: 936-564-0661; Fax: 936-559-7377. Email: frkey2007@yahoo.com; Deacon SHAUN BLACK, Chap., University of Texas at Tyler, Cathedral of the Immaculate Conception, 423 S. Broadway, Tyler, 75702. Email: deaconshaun@gmail.com.

Hispanic Ministry Advisory Council—Revs. RUBEN C. FIGUEROA, O.F.M., Chm.; LUIS E. LARREA, M.F.E.; Deacon RUBEN NATERA, Chancellor.

Priests' Personnel Board—Rev. Msgrs. JAMES E. YOUNG, Chm.; XAVIER PAPPU; Rev. ARIEL CORTES; Rev. Msgr. JOSEPH E. STRICKLAND, J.C.L., Sec.; Rev. SUSAI AVULA; Rev. Msgr. RONALD L. DIEGEL; Revs. MARK KUSMIREK; LUIS E. LARREA, M.F.E.; Rev. Msgr. ZACHARIAS S. KUNNAKKATTUTHARA.

Presbyteral Council—Rev. Msgrs. JOSEPH E. STRICKLAND, J.C.L.; JAMES E. YOUNG, Vice Chm.; RON L. DIEGEL; XAVIER PAPPU; Revs. GAVIN N. VAVEREK, J.C.L.; MARK KUSMIREK, Chm.; ARIEL CORTES; LUIS E. LARREA, M.F.E.; EFREN NANO; RAYMUNDO GARCIA; MICHAEL J. ADAMS; TIMOTHY J. KELLY.

Office of Clergy Development/Continuing Education—Rev. Msgr. JAMES E. YOUNG.

Permanent Deacon Council—Most Rev. ALVARO CORRADA, S.J., Pres.; Deacons JIM FINEGAN, Chm.; GERALD "JERRY" BESZE, Sec.; Mrs. MARY BESZE, Sec.; Deacon RICK LAWRENCE; Mrs. NELL LAWRENCE; Deacon JONATHAN BEN FADELY; Mrs. ANGIE FADELY; Deacon DAVID DARBY; Mrs. TERESA DARBY; Deacon JOHN SARGENT; Mrs. KATHY SARGENT; Mrs. PATRICIA ALFARO; Deacons REMIGIO ALFARO; RUBEN NATERA; Mrs. MARIA GUADALUPE NATERA; Deacon RAY VANN; Mrs. FE VANN; Deacon TREVOR WELLS; Mrs. SUSAN WELLS.

Vocations—Co Directors: Revs. JESUDOSS THOMAS, S.T.L., S.T.L. Tel: 903-534-1077, Ext. 184; JESUS RODRIGO ARROYAVE. Tel: 903-534-1077, Ext. 171. Email: vocations@dioceseoftyler.org.

Consecrated Life—Co Directors: Sisters CONCEPCION PONCE. Tel: 903-534-1077, Ext. 184. Email: sisterponce@dioceseoftyler.org; ANGELICA OROZCO, E.F.M.S., 1015 E.S.E. Loop 323, Tyler, 75701-9663. Tel: 903-534-1077, Ext. 145. Email: sistera@dioceseoftyler.org.

Communications Director—Mr. JIM H. D'AVIGNON, 1015 E.S.E. Loop 323, Tyler, 75701-9663. Tel: 903-534-1077, Ext. 144. Email: editorcet3@excite.com.

Discipleship and Stewardship—Deacon RICK LAWRENCE, Dir., 1015 ESE Loop 323, Tyler, 75701-9663. Tel: 903-534-1077, Ext. 161; Mrs. ADELA HERNANDEZ, Sec.

Bishop's Appeal—Deacon RICK LAWRENCE, Dir. Tel: 903-534-1077, Ext. 161. Email: rlawrence@dioceseoftyler.org. Secretaries: Mrs. ADELA HERNANDEZ, 1015 E.S.E. Loop 323, Tyler, 75701-9663. Tel: 903-534-1077, Ext. 162. Email: ahernandez@dioceseoftyler.org; Ms. BLANCA ESPINOZA. Tel: 903-534-1077, Ext. 196. Email: bespinoza@dioceseoftyler.org.

Catholic Charities—J.J. Saleh Outreach Center, 202 W. Front St., P.O. Box 2016, Tyler, 75710. Tel: 903-258-9492; Fax: 903-258-6012. Mrs. NELL LAWRENCE, Exec. Dir. Email: nlawrence@cctyler.com; Mrs. PAM MINGS, Administrative Sec. Email: pmings@cctyler.org.

Immigration Case Manager—Mrs. CLAUDIA MEAUX, VAWA (Violence Against Women Act). Email: cmeaux@cctyler.org; NYDIA MUNGIA, Asst. Email: nmungia@cctyler.org.

Society of St. Vincent de Paul—Mailing Address: Immaculate Conception Conference, 410 S. College, Tyler, 75702. Ms. SHAWN PICKETT, Dir. Tel: 903-592-0027; Cell: 903-363-5225; Fax: 903-593-7326. Email: cicsocialserv@suddenlinkmail.com; Mr. KEN WILSON, Pres.; VACANT, Vice Pres.; Mrs. KELLY JACKMAN, Treas.; Mrs. BERNIE TURES, Sec.

Newspaper "Catholic East Texas"—Mr. JIM H. D'AVIGNON, Editor; Mrs. SUSAN DEMATTEO NECESSARY, Reporter.

DIOCESAN OFFICES

Diocesan Council of Catholic Women—CATHY LAY, Pres. (2011-2013) 299 Maryland, Marshall, 75670. Tel: 903-935-4668. Email: catlay58@yahoo.com; Rev. GAVIN N. VAVEREK, J.C.L., Moderator, 2108 Ridgewood, Longview, 75605-5199. Tel: 903-757-5855, Ext. 503. Email: frgavin@stmaryslgv.org.

Pro Life Committee—JUANITA CANTU, Chm., 201 Hughes St., Marshall, 75672-7625. Tel: 888-300-5112 (Gabriel Project). Email: js_cantu@hotmail.com.

Respect Life Program—Revs. GAVIN N. VAVEREK, J.C.L., Dir., 2108 Ridgewood, Longview, 75605-5199. Tel: 903-757-5855, Ext. 503; NOLAN LOWRY, S.T.L.

Tyler Gabriel Project—THERESA MOORE, Pres. Email: theresalm58@yahoo.com; MARGIE BENGE, Assistance Chair.

Victim Assistance Coordinator—Rev. GAVIN N. VAVEREK, J.C.L. Tel: 903-266-2159. Email: promoter@dioceseoftyler.org.

Diocesan Implementation Committee On Ethics and Integrity Policy for Church Personnel—Rev. GAVIN N. VAVEREK, J.C.L., Promoter of Justice; Rev. Msgr. JOSEPH E. STRICKLAND, J.C.L., Judicial Vicar; Deacon GERALD "JERRY" BESZE; Mrs. MARY BESZE; Deacon RUBEN NATERA; Mrs. LINDA PORTER.

Diocesan Liturgical Commission—Most Rev. ALVARO CORRADA DEL RIO, S.J., Chm.; Revs. MORGAN M. WHITE; GAVIN N. VAVEREK, J.C.L.; Mr. BRIAN BRAQUET; Mrs. DIANNA BRAQUET; Ms. PEGGY HAMMETT; Mrs. LINDA PORTER; Deacon JOHN RAGLAND; MELBA RAGLAND; Sr. ANGELICA OROZCO, E.F.M.S.; Rev. JOSE LUIS VIDARTE; VINCENT MEINZER; Deacon SHAUN BLACK; Rev. VICTOR HERNANDEZ.

CLERGY, PARISHES, MISSIONS AND PAROCHIAL SCHOOLS

CITY OF TYLER

(SMITH COUNTY)

1—CATHEDRAL OF THE IMMACULATE CONCEPTION (1987) Very Rev. Anthony K.W. McLaughlin, Rector; Rev. Juan Carlos Rivera; Sisters Susan Seitz, O.S.F., Pastoral Assoc.; Sarah Kohles, O.S.F.; Deacons Bill Necessary; Jack Rounds Jr.; Steve Curry; Shaun Black; Rufino Cortez; Mark D'Eramo. In Res., Deacon Dwight (Sam) Hall.

Social Services:—Office, 423 S. Broadway, 75702. Tel: 903-592-0027; Fax: 903-593-7326.

Res.: 114 W. Front St., 75702. Tel: 903-592-5462.

School—St. Gregory Cathedral School, (Grades PreK-5), 500 S. College St., 75702. Tel: 903-595-4109; Fax: 903-592-8626. Mrs. Kathy Shieldes Harry, Prin.; Janet Simpson, Librarian. Lay Teachers 22; Students 310.

Catechesis/Religious Program—Tel: 903-592-1617. Lay Teachers 26; Students 200.

Society of St. Vincent de Paul—Tel: 903-592-0027; Fax: 903-592-0034.

Chapel—St. Paul Chapel 1015 E.S.E. Loop 323, 75701. Tel: 903-592-1617.

Mission—St. Joseph the Worker Mission 5075 FM 14, P.O. Box 4995, 75712. Tel: 903-593-5055. Rev. Scott W. Allen, F.S.S.P.

2—OUR LADY OF GUADALUPE (1999), (Hispanic), Rev. Jesus Rodrigo Arroyave.

Church & Mailing Address: 922 Old Omen Rd., 75701-3709. Tel: 903-593-2006; Fax: 903-593-6033. Email: nsgtyler@gmail.com.

Catechesis/Religious Program—Students 350.

3—ST. PETER CLAVER (1936) [CEM] [JC] Rev. Luis Eduardo Larrea, M.F.E.; Bro. Simon L. Nila.

Res.: 615 W. Cochran St., 75702. Tel: 903-595-2612; Fax: 903-596-9659. Email: st.peterclaver@att.net. Web: stpeterclavertyler.com.

Catechesis/Religious Program—Fax: 903-596-9659. Students 470.

OUTSIDE THE CITY OF TYLER

ATHENS, HENDERSON CO., ST. EDWARD CHURCH (1947) [JC] Revs. Pancras Savarimuthu; Freddy Celano, Parochial Vicar.

Res.: 800 E. Tyler, 75751-2140. Tel: 903-675-2509; Fax: 903-675-8805. Email: pancrass@yahoo.com. Web: www.stedwards-athens.com.

Catechesis/Religious Program—Email: stedwardschurch12@suddenlink.net. Zoila Hunt, D.R.E. Tel: 903-677-1922. Students 152.

Mission—St. Boniface (1997) 318 S. Broad St., P.O. Box 762, Chandler, Van Sand Co. 75758-0762. Tel: 903-849-3234; Fax: 903-849-5634. Email: stboniface3234@earthlink.net. Web: www.home.earthlink.net. Rev. Octavio Suarez; Deacon Steve Curry.

ATLANTA, CASS CO., ST. CATHERINE OF SIENA CHURCH (1965) [JC] Rev. Felix Chiraphurathel, O.Praem., Admin.

Res.: 309 N. Louise St., 75551. Tel: 903-796-4494; Fax: 903-796-9990. Email: stcathsienna@aol.com.

Catechesis/Religious Program—Tel: 903-756-5723. Irene Webster, D.R.E. Students 57.

BUFFALO, LEON CO., BLESSED KATERI TEKAKWITHA CHURCH (1979) Rev. Msgr. Theodore F. Rydelek.

Mailing Address: 208 N. Merrill, P.O. Box 878, 75831. Tel: 903-322-3705; Fax: 903-322-3155.

Catechesis/Religious Program—Email: bkateri@ezmailbox.net. Students 2.

CANTON, VAN ZANDT CO., ST. THERESE (1980) Rev. Selvaraj Sinnappan, Admin.; Deacons Richard Lawrence; Alan J. Stehsel; Jonathan Ben Fadely; Jim Burkel.

Mailing Address: 14786 FM 859, 75103-3676. Tel: 903-567-4286; Fax: 903-567-0586. Email: sttheresecanton@gmail.com.

Catechesis/Religious Program—Students 101.

Mission—St. Luke 312 W. O'Neal St., Wills Point, Van Zandt Co. 75169. Tel: 903-873-1238. Rev. Jose Ruben Lobaton, O.F.M.; Deacon Edilberto Reyes.

CARTHAGE, PANOLA CO., ST. WILLIAM OF VERCELLI (1948) Rev. Michael J. Adams.

Res.: 4088 N.W. Loop, 75633-3346. Tel: 903-693-3766 (Office); Fax: 903-693-3759. Email: stwilliamofvercelli@hotmail.com. Web: stwilliamofvercelli.com.

Catechesis/Religious Program—Students 39.

CENTER, SHELBY CO., ST. THERESE (1951) Rev. Jose Luis Vidarte, Admin.; Deacon John Ragland.

Res.: 717 FM 2974, 75935-6006. Tel: 936-598-8458.

Catechesis/Religious Program—Students 120.

Mission—Epiphany 3072 U.S. Hwy. 59 S., Timpson, Shelby Co. 75975-9350. Tel: 936-254-9662.

CLARKSVILLE, RED RIVER CO., ST. JOSEPH (1870), (Hispanic), [CEM] Rev. Guillermo Gabriel-Maisonet, Asst. Admin.; Deacon Joe Ibarra Moreno.

Res.: 406 E. Broadway, 75426-3110. Tel: 903-427-5044.

Catechesis/Religious Program—Students 8.

CROCKETT, HOUSTON CO., ST. FRANCIS OF THE TEJAS (1931) Rev. Gary Rottman.

Res.: 609 N. 4th, 75835-4001. Tel: 936-544-5338; Fax: 866-591-9583.

Catechesis/Religious Program—Students 35.

Mission—St. Leo the Great P.O. Box 356, Centerville, Leon Co. 75833-0356. Tel: 903-536-5012; Fax: 903-536-1549. Rev. Nolan Lowry, Admin.; Deacons James Finegan; Robert Dalecki.

Station—St. Thomas More Hilltop Lake Chapel Fellowship Hall, P.O. Box 1400, Hilltop Lakes. Tel: 936-855-2640; Fax: 936-855-2935. Rev. Nolan Lowry.

DAINGERFIELD, MORRIS CO., OUR LADY OF FATIMA (1951), (Hispanic), [CEM] Rev. Juan C. Sardinas-Perez.

Res.: 1305 Bert St., 75638. Tel: 903-645-5637; Fax: 903-645-3276.

Catechesis/Religious Program—Students 96.

DIBOLL, ANGELINA CO., OUR LADY OF GUADALUPE (1971), (Hispanic), [CEM] Rev. Victor Hamon (Colombia); Deacon Catarino Perez Jr.

Mailing Address: P.O. Box 310, 75941-0310. Tel: 936-829-3659; Fax: 936-829-3659.
Res.: 100 Maynard St., 75941.
Catechesis/Religious Program—Students 164.

FAIRFIELD, FREESTONE CO., ST. BERNARD OF CLAIRVAUX (1986) Rev. Devaraj Arulappa (India).
Res.: 630 W. Main, 75840-1418. Tel: 903-389-4616.
Catechesis/Religious Program—Tel: 903-389-8221. Students 10.
Mission—St. Mary 609 Cedar, Teague, Freestone Co. 75840-1617. Tel: 254-739-3692. Rev. Jose G. Marin.

FLINT, SMITH CO., ST. MARY MAGDALENE CHURCH (1998) Rev. Timothy J. Kelly (Ireland); Deacon Clarence D. Blalock Jr.
Church: 18221 FM 2493, 75762. Tel: 903-894-7647; Fax: 903-894-7739.
Catechesis/Religious Program—Lisa Ellis, D.R.E. Students 139.

GILMER, UPSHUR CO., ST. FRANCIS OF ASSISI (1994) Rev. Hector Bruno de Jesus; Deacons Guylan Blasingame; Gonzalo Rojas.
Mailing Address: 2514 FM852, P.O. Box 704, 75644-0704. Tel: 903-797-3303.
Res.: 2514 FM 852, 75644. Tel: 903-797-3090; Fax: 903-797-3090. Email: stfrancisgilmer@gmail.com.
Catechesis/Religious Program—Tel: 903-797-3303. Students 64.
Mission—Holy Spirit Church 1612 S. FM 2869, Holly Lake Ranch, Sulphur Co. 75755-9604. Tel: 903-769-3235; Fax: 903-769-1611. Rev. Msgr. Ronald L. Diegel; Deacon Sam Mullen.

GUN BARREL CITY, HENDERSON CO., ST. JUDE (1975) Revs. Daniel L. Daugherty; Freddy Celano, Parochial Vicar; Deacons Richard Sykora; Juan A. Cazares.
Res.: 172 Luther Ln., 75156. Tel: 903-887-1452 (Office); 903-887-6767 (Res.); Fax: 903-887-4906 (Office).
Catechesis/Religious Program—Tel: 903-887-9795 (Office). Mrs. Edna Beltz, D.R.E. Students 137.

HEMPHILL, SABINE CO., ST. PIUS I (1939) [CEM] Rev. Joseph M. Nasser, S.J.; Deacon Kenneth Horn.
309 Starr St., P.O. Box 1925, 75948-1925. Tel: 409-787-4189 (Res.).
Catechesis/Religious Program—Students 6.
Mission—St. Augustin Mission San Augustine, 75972. Rev. James Rowland.

HENDERSON, RUSK CO., ST. JUDE (1934) Rev. Jayaselanraj Lucas.
200 Morningside, 75652.
Res.: 110 Millville Dr., 75652. Tel: 903-657-4398; 903-657-4080; Fax: 903-657-0078. Email: judes@eastex.net. Web: www.stjudehenderson.org.
Catechesis/Religious Program—Students 85.

JACKSONVILLE, CHEROKEE CO., OUR LADY OF SORROWS (1954) Revs. Mark Kusmirek; Elpidio Lopez, Parochial Vicar; Deacon Juventino Torres.
Res.: 1023 Corinth Rd., 75766-9801. Tel: 903-586-4538; Fax: 903-586-4996. Email: pastor@oloschurch.com. Web: www.oloschurch.com.
Catechesis/Religious Program—Email: ffl@oloschurch.com. Andy Dixon, D.R.E. Students 377.
Mission—Sacred Heart P.O. Box 947, Rusk, Cherokee Co. 75785. Tel: 903-683-1862; Fax: 903-683-1853. Rev. Stephen J. Duyka; Deacon Ignacio Panuco.
Mission—Our Lady of Guadalupe Rt. 5, Box 357, Cherokee Co. 75766. Tel: 903-726-7272. In Res., Rev. Jose Cortez.
Mission—Venerable Antonio Margil 202 N. Marcus St., Alto, 75925. Tel: 903-683-1862. Rev. Elpidio Lopez, Parochial Vicar.

JEFFERSON, MARION CO., IMMACULATE CONCEPTION (1867) [CEM] [JC] Rev. Jose Kumblumkal, C.M.I.
Mailing Address: 209 W. Lafayette St., 75657.
Res. & Rectory: 201 N. Vale St., 75657-2143. Tel: 903-665-8486; Fax: 903-665-8778.
Catechesis/Religious Program—Tel: 903-665-8909; Fax: 903-665-8778. Students 21.
Mission—St. Lawrence Brindisi P.O. Box 928, Waskom, Harrison Co. 75292-0928. Tel: 903-687-2385; Fax: 903-687-4503. Rev. Joby Cheradai Thomas, M.S., Admin.
Catechesis/Religious Program—Tel: 903-687-2951. Students 40.
Mission—St. Paul of Tarsus Mission 209 W. Lafayette, 75657. Rev. Jose Kumblumkal, C.M.I.
Immaculate Conception Catholic Church, Jefferson, TX Foundation—124 W. Lafayette, 75657-2143.

KILGORE, GREGG CO., CHRIST THE KING (1936) [JC] Rev. Daniel P. Dower, S.T.L., Parish Admin.; Deacons Dennis Gilchrist; Alejandro Cisneros; Isidro Sanchez; Lino Huerta. In Res., Rev. Matias Rodriguez.
Res.: 1508 Broadway Blvd., 75662-3209. Tel: 903-984-3716.
Catechesis/Religious Program—Tel: 903-986-3573. Sr. Catherine Marie Diaz, E.F.M.S., D.R.E. Students 258.
Mission—Our Lady Queen of Angels 707 Bradford St., P.O. Box 322, Overton, Rusk Co. 75684. Tel: 903-834-6727. Deacon Len Luscomb.

LINDALE, SMITH CO., HOLY FAMILY (1994) Deacon Dennis King.
Mailing Address: P.O. Box 1071, 75771. Tel: 903-882-4079; Fax: 903-882-8382. Email: holy-family@sbcglobal.net.
Catechesis/Religious Program—Students 144.

LONGVIEW, GREGG CO.

1—ST. ANTHONY (1880), (Hispanic), Rev. Joseph B. Lincon; Deacons Joseph Pipak; Manuel Villalobos.
Res.: 908 E. Olive, 75601. Tel: 903-758-0116; 903-758-9550. Email: stanthonylgv@yahoo.comFax: 903-758-9066.
Church: 508 N. 6th St., 75601.
Catechesis/Religious Program—*Shopka Center*, 406 N. 6th St., 75601. Students 111.

2—ST. MARY (1982) Rev. Gavin N. Vaverek; Deacons John Borens; John Shaffer; Trevor Wells; Vincent James Wilson. In Res., Rev. Mark Dunne.
Res.: 2108 Ridgewood Dr., 75605-5199. Tel: 903-757-5855; Fax: 903-758-5074. Email: church@stmaryslgv.org. Web: www.stmaryslgv.org.
School—405 Hollybrook Dr., 75605-2464. Tel: 903-753-1657; Fax: 903-758-7347. Email: admin@stmaryslgv.org. Mrs. Amy Allen, Prin. Lay Teachers 18; Students 189.
Catechesis/Religious Program—Tel: 903-757-5891; Fax: 903-758-5074. Students 227.
Mission—Our Lady of Grace 415 Cypress St., Hallsville, Harrison Co. 75650. Tel: 903-668-5279; Fax: 903-668-5220. Rev. Peter McGrath, Parochial Vicar; Deacons Robert William Rhodes; Gregorio Sanchez.

3—ST. MATTHEW CATHOLIC CHURCH (1999) Rev. Jesudoss Thomas, S.T.L.; Deacons Joel Gonzalez; Francisco Lopez.
Res.: 2900 Pinetree Road, 75604. Tel: 903-295-7558.
Church: 2800 Pinetree Rd., 75604. Tel: 903-295-3890; Fax: 903-295-7559. Email: churchoffice@stmatthewlgv.org. Web: www.stmatthewlgv.org.
Catechesis/Religious Program—Email: dff@stmatthewlgv.org. Students 385.

LUFKIN, ANGELINA CO.

1—ST. ANDREW (1998) Rev. Jose J. Kannampuzha; Deacons Gary Trevino; Jesus Reyes.
Office: 1611 Feagin Dr., 75904. Tel: 936-632-9100; Fax: 936-632-0627. Email: standrewlufkin@catholicweb.com.
Catechesis/Religious Program—Students 136.

2—ST. PATRICK (1928) Revs. Francis O'Dowd; Raymundo Garcia (Mexico), Parochial Vicar; Deacons Martin Aguilar; Abelino Cordero; Juan Mijares; Manuel J. Ramos; Ray Vann.
Res.: 2118 Lowry St., 75901-1316. Tel: 936-634-6833; Fax: 936-634-6891.
School—St. Patrick School, (Grades PreK-8), 2116 Lowry St., 75901. Tel: 936-634-6719; Fax: 936-639-2776. James Menz, Prin.; Rev. Msgr. John Flynn, Advisor (Retired). Lay Teachers 13; Students 86.
Catechesis/Religious Program—Tel: 936-634-6833, Ext. 225. Oralia Aguilar, D.R.E.; Brenda Dunn, C.R.E. Students 150.

MADISONVILLE, MADISON CO., ST. ELIZABETH ANN SETON (1978) [JC] Rev. Michael J. Barone; Deacon Burke J. Landry.
Mailing Address: 100 S. Tammye Ln., 77864. Tel: 936-348-6368; Fax: 936-348-5377. Email: pastor.stelizabeth@sbcglobal.net.
Catechesis/Religious Program—Students 90.

MALAKOFF, HENDERSON CO., MARY, QUEEN OF HEAVEN CHURCH (1996) Revs. William Palmer; Freddy Celano, Parochial Vicar.
2269 CR 1730, P.O. Box 508, 75148-0508.
Catechesis/Religious Program—Neal Williams, D.R.E. Students 42.

MARSHALL, HARRISON CO., ST. JOSEPH (1874) [CEM] Revs. Denzil Vithanage, Admin.; Carlos Rangel, Parochial Vicar; Deacons Santiago Suarez; Felipe Pena; Magdaleno Aguirre; John Sargent.
Res.: 410 N. Alamo Blvd., 75670-3450. Tel: 903-935-2536; Fax: 903-938-1591. Email: saintjosephmarshall@yahoo.com. Web: stjosephmarshall.com.
School—St. Josephs School
Catechesis/Religious Program—Tel: 903-935-5502. Students 275.
Convent—2305 S. Garrett, 75670. Tel: 903-938-3998.
Mission—San Pedro the Fisherman 1835 Chaparrall, Hwy. 43, P.O. Box 430, Tatum, Panola Co. 75691-0430. Tel: 903-947-2454. Rev. Carlos Rangel; Deacon Jose Luis Mireles.

MINEOLA, WOOD CO., ST. PETER THE APOSTLE (1937) [JC] Rev. Efren Nano; Deacons Aubrey Fisk; William Faber.
203 Meadowbrook, P.O. Box 1022, 75773-7022. Email: stpeter75773@sbcglobal.net.
Rectory—
Catechesis/Religious Program—Students 133.
Mission—St. Celestine 116 W. Frank, Grand Saline, Van Zandt Co. 75140. Tel: 903-962-6350. Rev. Victor Hernandez (Colombia); Deacon William Flores.
Mission—St. John the Evangelist Church 551 E. FM 2795, Emory, Rains Co. 75140. Rev. Victor Hernandez (Colombia).

MOUNT PLEASANT, TITUS CO., ST. MICHAEL (1917) Revs. Luis Fernando Arroyave (Colombia); Steve Paradis, Parochial Vicar; Patrick Hartnett, Parochial Vicar; Deacons Joe Ibarra Moreno; Lorenzo Martinez.
Mailing Address: 1403 E. 1st St., 75455-4715. Tel: 903-572-5227; Fax: 903-572-9659.
Res.: 310 Denman Dr., 75455-4157. Tel: 903-572-5611; Fax: 903-572-9659. Email: enfo@stmichaelmp.org. Web: www.stmichaelmp.org.
Catechesis/Religious Program—Ann Decious, Dir. Faith Formation. Students 510.

MOUNT VERNON, FRANKLIN CO., SACRED HEART (1986) Rev. Ambrose Chinnappa; Deacons Carl Miller; Donald R. Brown.
Mailing Address: P.O. Box 918, 75457. Tel: 903-537-2174.
Church: 406 S. SH-37, 75457. Tel: 903-537-2174.
Catechesis/Religious Program—Tel: 903-572-3390. Students 63.

NACOGDOCHES, NACOGDOCHES CO., SACRED HEART (1716) [CEM] [JC 2] Rev. Msgr. James E. Young; Revs. Andy Puga Lorenzo; Daniel P. Dower, S.T.L.; James Rowland, Parochial Vicar; Deacons David Darby; Michael Doyle; Gary Giese; Ezequiel Tapia; Luis Alberto Hernandez; Rafael Landeros; Pedro Gonzalez; Librado Cruz Sosa; Patrick Harnett.
Res.: 2508 Appleby Sand Rd., 75965-3632. Tel: 936-564-7134 (Rectory); 936-564-7807 (Office); Fax: 936-559-5442.
Catechesis/Religious Program—Tel: 936-564-5321. Deacon Gary Giese, D.R.E. Students 360.
Mission—Our Lady of Lourdes P.O. Box 241, Chireno, Nacogdoches Co. 75937. Tel: 936-598-8458. Rev. Joseph Lourdusamy.
Mission—Immaculate Conception - Moral [CEM] [JC 3] 1422 Co. Rd. 724, Nacogdoches Co. 75964. Tel: 936-560-3200; Fax: 936-462-8825. Rev. Joseph Lourdusamy.
Mission—Our Lady of Guadalupe 4401 Old Lufkin Rd., Nacogdoches Co. 75964. Tel: 936-560-5956. Rev. Luis Alphonse Roncancio (Colombia).
Chapel—Nacogdoches, St. Mary's Chapel, Stephen F. Austin State University 211 E. College, 75961. Tel: 936-564-0661; Fax: 936-559-7377. Rev. Paul R. Key, Chap.

NEW BOSTON, BOWIE CO., ST. MARY OF THE CENACLE (1918) Rev. Michael Snider, Admin.; Deacon Timothy O'Neil.
Mailing Address: 216 W. Magnolia St., 75570-0914. Tel: 903-628-2323 Hall; Fax: 903-628-4161. Email: stmarycenacle@yahoo.com.
Res.: 216 Magnolia St., 75570. Tel: 903-628-6186.
Catechesis/Religious Program—Tel: 903-628-2323. Students 27.

PALESTINE, ANDERSON CO., SACRED HEART (1893) [CEM] Rev. Msgr. Zacharias S. Kunnakkattuthara (India); Rev. Renelmo Ramirez; Deacons Alex Kobar; Daniel Rose, Prison Chap.
Res.: 503 N. Queen St., 75801-2718. Tel: 903-729-2463; Fax: 903-723-9799. Email: shpalestine@earthlink.net.
Catechesis/Religious Program—Loiette Dixon, D.R.E.; Dr. Martin Flynn, Youth Min. Students 275.
Mission—St. Charles Borromeo 1101 Hwy. 155 N., Frankston, Anderson Co. 75763. Tel: 903-876-2089; Fax: 903-876-2089. Email: stch@gower.net. Rev. M. Jones Jayaraj.

PARIS, LAMAR CO., OUR LADY OF VICTORY (1880) [JC] Revs. Morgan M. White (Ireland); Guillermo Gabriel-Maisonet, Parochial Vicar.
Res.: 3300 Clarksville St., 75460. Tel: 903-784-1000; Fax: 903-784-3946. Email: ourladyofvictory@suddenlinkmail.com.
Catechesis/Religious Program—Nellie Denman, D.R.E. Students 240.

PITTSBURG, CAMP CO., HOLY CROSS (1987) [JC] Rev. Christians Zelaya, Admin.
501 Hill Ave., 75686-1810. Tel: 903-856-7609; 903-790-5252. Email: holycrosscc@hotmail.com.
Catechesis/Religious Program—Students 135.

SULPHUR SPRINGS, HOPKINS CO., ST. JAMES (1880) Rev. Maria Susai J. Avula; Deacons Gerald "Jerry" Besze; Loren G. Seely; Joe Ibarra Moreno; William Flores.
297 Texas St., 75482. Tel: 903-885-1222; Fax: 903-885-5855.
Res.: 303 Texas St., 75482. Tel: 903-885-2873.
Catechesis/Religious Program— Cindy Lancaster, D.R.E. Students 157.
Mission—St. Clare Mission 10 E. Side Sq., Cooper, Delta Co. 75432.

TEXARKANA, BOWIE CO., SACRED HEART (1874) [CEM 2] Rev. Msgr. Xavier Pappu; Rev. Juan Carlos

Rivera, Parochial Vicar; Deacons Keith A. Woods, (Retired); Larry Benzmiller; Craig Louis Lashford. Res.: 4505 Elizabeth St., 75503-2998. Tel: 903-794-4444; Fax: 903-792-1529.
Catechesis/Religious Program—Students 184.

TRINITY, TRINITY CO., MOST HOLY TRINITY (1972) [JC] Rev. Patrick Fenton, Admin.; Deacon John Milton.
Res.: 401 Prospect Dr., 75862-9801. Tel: 936-594-6664; Fax: 936-594-5244. Email: mhtc@valornet.com.
Catechesis/Religious Program—
Mission— Groveton, 75845.

UNION GROVE-GLADEWATER, UPSHUR CO., ST. THERESA OF THE INFANT JESUS (1945) [JC] Rev. Robert H. (Hank) Lanik, Admin.
Mailing Address: 10138 Union Grove Rd., Gladewater, 75647-0967. Tel: 903-845-2306; Fax: 903-845-7126.
Catechesis/Religious Program—Students 48.

WHITEHOUSE, SMITH CO., PRINCE OF PEACE (1995) Rev. Ariel Cortes.
Mailing Address: P.O. Box 456, 75791-0456. Tel: 903-871-3230; Fax: 903-871-3229. Web: www.opopcc.org.
Res.: 903 Langford Ln., 75791. Tel: 903-871-9771. Web: www.opopcc.org.
Catechesis/Religious Program—Tel: 903-581-9601. Email: srmmag@suddenlinkmail.com. Students 96.

Chaplains of Public Institutions

CROCKETT. *Crockett State School*, 1701 S.W. Loop 304, 75835. Tel: 936-852-5000; Fax: 936-544-2543. Email: crockett@tyc.state.tx.us. Rev. Gary Rottman, Deacon Ramiro Romo. Attended by St. Francis of the Tejas Church, Crockett.

HENDERSON. *Bradshaw State Facility, Texas Department of Criminal Justice*. Rev. Jayaselanraj Lucas. Attended by St. Jude Church, Henderson.
East Texas MTC (Management Training Corporation) Detention Center, 9000 Industrial Dr., 75652. Tel: 903-655-3300.

LOVELADY. *Eastham Unit, Texas Department of Criminal Justice*. Attended by Most Holy Trinity Catholic Parish. Tel: 936-594-6664, 2665 Prison Rd. #1, P.O. Box 16, 75851-0016. Tel: 936-636-7321, Ext. 7204.

MIDWAY. *Ferguson Prison, Texas Department of Criminal Justice*. Attended by Most Holy Trinity Catholic Parish. (Tel: 936-594-6664), 12120 Savage Dr., 75852. Tel: 936-348-3751.

NEW BOSTON. *Telford Unit, Texas Department of Criminal Justice*, 3899 State Hwy. 98, P.O. Box 9200, 75570. Tel: 903-628-3171. Rev. Michael Snider.

OVERTON. *Moore, B. (BM), TX Dept. of Criminal Justice*, 8500 N. FM 3053, 75684-1000. Rev. Daniel P. Dower, S.T.L., Chap., Deacon Lyn Luscomb.

PALESTINE. *Powledge Unit, Texas Department of Criminal Justice*, P.O. Box 2250, 75801. Rev. Msgr. Zacharias S. Kunnakkattuthara (India), Chap., Revs. Harold P. Paulsen, Renelmo Ramirez, Deacons Alex Kobar, Dan Rose, Anthony Joseph Stoeppel.

RUSK. *Hodge Unit and Skyview Unit, Texas Department of Criminal Justice*, P.O. Box 999, 75785-0999. Tel: 903-683-5781. Revs. Mark Kusmirek, Chap., Jose Cortez, Chap., Stephen J. Duyka, Deacon Ignacio Panuco.

TEAGUE. *Boyd Unit, Texas Department of Correction*, 200 Spur 113, 75860. Tel: 254-739-5555. Rev. Jose G. Marin, Chap.

TENNESSEE COLONY. *Coffield Unit, Texas Department of Hodge Unit and Skyview Unit, Texas Department of Criminal Justice*, Rte. 1, Box 150, 75861-9710. Tel: 903-928-2211. Rev. Msgr. Zacharias S. Kunnakkattuthara (India), Chap., Rev. Harold P. Paulson (Retired), Deacons Alex Kobar, Dan Rose, Anthony Joseph Stoeppel.
Gurney Unit. Rev. Msgr. Zacharias S. Kunnakkattuthara (India), Chap., Rev. Harold P. Paulson (Retired). Attended by Sacred Heart, Palestine.
Michael Unit, P.O. Box 4500, 75886-4500. Tel: 903-928-2311. Rev. Msgr. Zacharias S. Kunnakkattuthara (India), Chap., Rev. Harold P. Paulson (Retired).

TEXARKANA. *Federal Corrections Institution*, P.O. Box 9500, 75505-9500. Tel: 903-838-4587. Rev. Msgr. Xavier Pappu, Chap., Deacons Lawrence S. Benzmiller, Joe Bruick, Craig Lashford, Keith A. Woods. Attended by Sacred Heart, Texarkana.

WINNSBORO. *Clyde Johnston Unit, Texas Department of Corrections*, 703 Airport Rd., 75494-9999. Tel: 903-342-6166. Rev. Mani Mathai, C.M.I. (India).

On Duty Outside the Diocese:
Revs.—
Anthony, Alphonse
Bedoya, Dario
Dinguis, Jorge
Dobosz, Jerzy George
Doyle, Michael A.
Duran, Said
Edelen, Thomas
Gonzalez, Daniel
Martin, John Randall
Ruggles, Christopher V., J.C.L.

Graduate Studies:
Revs.—
Gomez, John Jairo, Continuing Education
Lowry, Nolan, S.T.L., Pontifical North American College 00120 Vatican City State.

Absent on Sick Leave:
Rev.—
Zakshesky, Francis (Retired), 8409 CR 31, Sinton, 78387.

Retired:
Rev. Msgrs.—
Brennan, John A.
Flynn, John
Metzger, Sam S.
Priest, Gerald A.
Revs.—
Hoan, Basil P., Lake House, Hemphill, 75948. Tel: 409-787-2310 (Residence)
Paulson, Harold P.
Walsh, Richard (Denis) L.
Zakshesky, Francis, 8409 CR 31, Sinton, 78387.

Permanent Deacons:
Aguilar, Martin, St. Patrick, Lufkin
Aguirre, Magdaleno, St. Joseph, Marshall
Alfaro, Remigio, Our Lady of Guadalupe, Tyler
Bate, Lawrence Foster, Jr., St. William of Vercelli, Carthage
Benzmiller, Lawrence S., Sacred Heart Church, Texarkana
Besze, Gerald "Jerry", St. James the Apostle Church, Sulphur Springs; Family Life Office, Tyler
Black, Shaun, Cathedral of the Immaculate Conception, Tyler; Campus Ministry, Tyler
Blalock, Clarence D., Jr., St. Mary Magdalene, Flint
Blasingame, Guylan, St. Theresa, Gladewater
Borens, John, St. Mary, Longview
Brown, Donald R., Telford Unit, New Boston; Sacred Heart, Mt. Vernon
Burkel, Jim
Cazares, Juan A., St. Jude, Gun Barrel City
Cisneros, Alejandro, Christ the King, Kilgore
Cordero, Abelino, St. Patrick, Lufkin
Cortez, Rufino, Cathedral of the Immaculate Conception, Tyler; Holy Family, Lindale; Prince of Peace, Whitehouse
Curry, Steve, Cathedral of the Immaculate Conception, Tyler
D'Eramo, Mark, Cathedral of the Immaculate Conception, Tyler
Dalecki, Robert
Daniel, Scott B. J., St. Anthony, Longview
Darby, David, Sacred Heart Church, Nacogdoches
Doyle, Micheal, Sacred Heart, Nacogdoches
Faber, William, St. Peter the Apostle Church, Mineola; St. Celestine Church, Grand Saline
Fadely, Jonathan Ben, St. Therese of Lisieux, Canton
Finegan, James, St. Thomas More Church, Hilltop Lakes; St. Leo the Great Church, Centerville; St. Elizabeth Ann Seton Church, Madisonville
Fisk, Aubrey, St. Peter the Apostle Church, Mineola
Flores, William, St. Celestine Church, Grand Saline; St. James, Sulphur Springs; St. John the Evangelist, Emory
Giese, Gary, Sacred Heart Church, Nacogdoches
Gilchrist, Dennis S., Christ the King, Kilgore
Gonzales, Pedro, Sacred Heart, Nacogdoches; Our Lady of Guadalupe, Nacogdoches
Gonzalez, Joel, St. Matthew, Longview
Hall, Dwight (Sam), Well Spring Spirituality Center; Deacon-in-Resident
Hernandez, Luis Alberto, Sacred Heart, Nacogdoches
Holda, William, Christ the King, Kilgore
Horn, Kenneth, St. Pius I, Hemphill
Huerta, Lino, Christ the King, Kilgore
King, Dennis G., Holy Family, Lindale
Kobar, Alex, Sacred Heart, Palestine
Landeros, Rafael, Our Lady of Guadalupe, Nacogdoches
Landry, Burke J., St. Elizabeth Ann Seton, Madisonville
Lashford, Craig Louis, Sacred Heart, Texarkana
Lawrence, Richard, St. Therese Church, Canton; Bishop Appeal Dir., Diocese of Tyler
Lopez, Francisco, St. Matthew, Longview
Luscomb, Len, Christ of King, Kilgore; Our Lady, Queen of Angels, Overton
Martinez, Lorenzo, St. Michael, Mount Pleasant
Martinez, Ramiro, Cathedral of the Immaculate Conception, Tyler
Martinez Blas, Lorenzo, St. Michael, Mt. Pleasant
Mijares, Juan, St. Patrick, Lufkin
Miller, Carl, Sacred Heart, Mt. Vernon
Milton, John, Most Holy Trinity, Trinity
Mireles, Jose Luis, San Pedro the Fisherman, Tatum
Mitchell, Billy, Immaculate Conception, Moral
Moreno, Joe Ibarra, St. Michael, Mt. Pleasant; St. James, Sulphur Springs
Mullen, Sam, Holy Spirit, Holly Lake Ranch
Natera, Ruben, Chancellor, Diocese of Tyler; Prince of Peace, Whitehouse TX
Necessary, William, Tyler Cathedral, with additional ministry to St. Peter Claver Church, Tyler
O'Brien, William E., St. James, Sulphur Springs; St. John the Evangelist, Emory
O'Neill, Timothy Peter, St. Mary of the Cenacle, New Boston
Panuco, Ignacio, Sacred Heart, Rusk
Pena, Felipe, St. Joseph, Marshall
Perez, Catarino, Jr., Our Lady of Guadalupe, Diboll
Petzold, Nelson R., St. Matthew, Longview
Pipak, Joseph, St. Anthony, Longview
Ragland, John Allen, Our Lady of Lourdes, Chireno; St. Mary of the Epiphany, Timpson; St. Therese of Lisieux, Center
Ramos, Manuel J., St. Patrick, Lufkin
Reyes, Jesus
Rhodes, Robert William, Our Lady of Grace, Hallsville
Rojas, Gonzalo, St. Anthony, Longview; St. Francis of Assisi, Gilmer
Romo, Ramiro, St. Francis of Tejas, Crockett
Rose, Daniel, Beto I & Powledge Unit, TDC, Palestine; Sacred Heart, Palestine
Rounds, Jack, Jr., Cathedral of the Immaculate Conception, Tyler
Sanchez, Gregorio, Our Lady of Grace, Hallsville
Sanchez, Isidro, Christ the King, Kilgore
Sargent, John, St. Joseph, Marshall
Seely, Loren G., St. James, Sulphur Springs
Shaffer, John K., St. Patrick, Lufkin
Sosa, Librado Cruz, Sacred Heart, Nacogdoches
Stehsel, Alan J., St. Therese of Lisieux, Canton
Suarez, Santiago, St. Joseph, Marshall
Sykora, Richard L., St. Jude, Gun Barrel City
Tapia, Ezequiel, Our Lady of Guadalupe, Nacogdoches
Tiscareno, Jose Angel, Our Lady of Guadalupe, Tyler
Torres, Juventino, Our Lady of Sorrows, Jacksonville
Trevino, Gerardo, St. Patrick, Lufkin; Our Lady of Guadalupe, Diboll
Vann, Raymond Kiah, Jr., St. Patrick, Lufkin
Villalobos, Manuel, St. Anthony, Longview
Wells, Trevor, St. Mary Church, Longview
Wilson, Vincent James, St. Mary, Longview
Woods, Keith A., Sacred Heart, Texarkana

INSTITUTIONS LOCATED IN THE DIOCESE

[A] REGIONAL SCHOOLS

TYLER. *Bishop T. K. Gorman Regional School*, (Grades 6-12), 1405 E.S.E. Loop 323, 75701. Tel: 903-561-2424; Fax: 903-561-2645. Mr. James P. Franz, Prin.; Rev. Msgr. Joseph E. Strickland, J.C.L., Chap.; Chi-Shim Wellmon, Librarian.

[B] GENERAL HOSPITALS

TYLER. *Trinity Mother Frances Health System* (1937) 800 E. Dawson St., 75701. Tel: 903-593-8441. Web: www.tmfhs.org. Mr. J. Lindsey Bradley Jr., Pres. & CAO; Rev. Luka U. Kalarickal, M.S.F.S., Chap. Sisters of the Holy Family of Nazareth 6; Bed Capacity 424; Staff 3,800; Total Assisted Annually 928,262.

MADISONVILLE. *Madison St. Joseph Health Center*, 100 W. Cross St., P.O. Box 698, 77864. Tel: 936-348-2631; Fax: 936-348-3404. Anthony D. Pfitzer, Pres. & CEO, St. Joseph Health System; Mr. Reed Edmundson, Admin. Bed Capacity 25; Total Assisted Annually 20,877; Total Staff 93.

TEXARKANA. *Christus Health Ark-La-Tex dba Christus St. Michael Health System* 2600 St. Michael Dr., 75503. Tel: 903-614-1000; Fax: 903-614-2030. Web: www.christusstmichael.org. Chris Karam, Pres & CEO; Revs. Felix Okey Alaribe, Chap.; Lawrence Chellaian (India), Chap. Rehabilitation Hospital., Operated by Christus Health Dallas, TX (Merged

2/1/1999). Bed Capacity 312; Total Staff 1,837; Total Assisted Annually 169,660.

Christus St. Michael Rehabilitation Hospital, 2400 St. Michael Dr., 75503. Tel: 903-614-4000; Fax: 903-614-4064. Rehabilitation Hospital., Operated by Christus Health. Bed Capacity 50; Total Staff 208; Total Assisted Annually 45,092.

St. Michael Rehabilitation Hospital, 2400 St. Michael Dr., 75503. Tel: 903-614-4000; Fax: 903-614-4064. Web: www.christusstmichael.org. Aloma R. Gender, R.N., M.S.N., Admin.; Revs. Felix Okey Alaribe, Chap.; Lawrence Chellaian (India), Chap. Operated by Christus Health, Dallas Texas. Bed Capacity 50; Total Assisted Annually 32,311; Total Staff 185.

[C] MONASTERIES AND RESIDENCES OF PRIESTS

PALESTINE. *Hermitage* (1968) 10020 An. Co. Rd. 404, 75803. Tel: 903-549-2950. Rev. Denis Walsh. Other Institutions: Houses of Religious Men 1; Total in Residence 1; Total Staff 1.

Prayer Mountain Hermitage (1985) 10089 An. Co. Rd. 404, 75803. Sr. Mary Vogel, H.S.S.R.

WHITEHOUSE. *The Missionaries of St. Francis de Sales* (1838) P.O. Box 440, 16828 FM 2964, 75791. Tel: 903-839-1280; Fax: 903-839-3486. Web: www.wellspringcommunity.net. Rev. Augustine Tharappel, M.S.F.S. (India), Regl. Supr. MSFS USA Region Wellspring. *Fransalian Center for Spirituality*, P.O Box 440, 75791. Tel: 903-839-1280; Fax: 903-839-3486. Web: www.wellspringcommunity.net. Rev. Augustine Tharappel, M.S.F.S. (India), Dir. House of Prayer - Wellspring.

Priests of the Province Not Listed Elsewhere: Revs. Nithiyaselvam Arokiaselvam, M.S.F.S., East Lansing, MI; Sebastian Conrad, M.S.F.S., Deer Park, TX; Binu Edathumparambil, M.S.F.S., Elk Grove Village, IL; Mathew Elayidathamadam, M.S.F.S., Elk Grove Village, IL; Philip Thomas Kizhakumpurath, M.S.F.S. (India), Yonkers, NY; Jose Mudavankunnel, M.S.F.S., Mobile, AL; Tom Thomas, M.S.F.S., Elk Grove Village, IL.

Priests of the Region Serving Elsewhere: Revs. John Peter Arulanandam, M.S.F.S.; John Devore, M.S.F.S.; Paul Kunnumpuram, M.S.F.S.; Joseph Mullakkara, M.S.F.S.; George Puraidam, M.S.F.S.; John Peter Ambrose, M.S.F.S.; Santhiyagu Arokiam, M.S.F.S.; Luckas Arulappa, M.S.F.S.; Anthony Bonela, M.S.F.S.; Davis Chackaleckel, M.S.F.S.; Johnbritto Chinnappa, M.S.F.S.; Benjamin Dande, M.S.F.S.; Jacob D. Dio, M.S.F.S.; Joseph Henry, M.S.F.S.; Luka U. Kalarickal, M.S.F.S.; Santy Kochupurackal, M.S.F.S.; Kurian Kollapallil, M.S.F.S.; Joseph Kuzhupil, M.S.F.S.; Ananda Prasad, M.S.F.S.; Jojaiah Mandagiri, M.S.F.S.; Augustine Mannaparambil, M.S.F.S.; Joseph Mendes, M.S.F.S.; Joseph Charles Pednekar, M.S.F.S.; Joseph Pottemmel, M.S.F.S.; Tomy Puliynampattayil, M.S.F.S.; Sunny Joseph Punnakuzhiyil, M.S.F.S.; Johnny Puthiyaparampil, M.S.F.S.; Alphonse Savarimuthu, M.S.F.S.; Mathew Thayil, M.S.F.S.; George Thayilkuzhithottu, M.S.F.S.; Mathew Thottiyil, M.S.F.S.; George Vattappara, M.S.F.S.; Joseph Xavier, M.S.F.S.

[D] CONVENTS AND RESIDENCES FOR SISTERS

TYLER. *Daughters of Divine Hope*, 1910 E.S.E. Loop 323, PMB 240, 75701. Tel: 936-554-6120.

Instituto Santa Mariana de Jesus, 2706 Shady Ln., 75702. Tel: 903-593-8933. Email: sisterponce@dioceseoftyler.org.

LUFKIN. *Monastery of the Infant Jesus*, 1501 Lotus Ln., 75904-2699. Tel: 936-634-4233; Fax: 936-634-2156. Sr. Mary John, O.P., Prioress; Rev. Paul Philibert, O.P., Chap. Cloistered Dominican Nuns. Professed Sisters 26.

[E] CAMPUS MINISTRY

TYLER. *Catholic Campus Ministry of Tyler* 1015 ESE Loop 323, 75701. Tel: 903-534-1077, Ext. 134; Fax: 903-534-1370. Rev. Hank Lanik. Diocese of Tyler

NACOGDOCHES. *St. Mary's Catholic Campus Ministry* (1959) *Stephen F. Austin, State Univ.*, P.O. Box 6125 SFASU, 75962-0001. Tel: 936-564-0661; Fax: 936-564-0661. Email: stmarysccm@gmail.com. Web: www.sfacatholic.net. Rev. Paul R. Key, S.T.L., M.Div., Chap. Other Institutions: St. Mary's Chapel Total in Residence 1; Total Staff 4.

[F] MISCELLANEOUS

TYLER. *Catholic Charities East Texas - Diocese of Tyler, J.J. Saleh Outreach Ctr.*, 202 W. Front St., P.O. Box 2016, 75710. Tel: 903-258-9492; Fax: 903-258-6012. Mrs. Nell Lawrence, Exec. Dir.; Mrs. Claudia Meaux, BIA Immigration Case Worker; Mrs. Nydia Mungia, Immigration Case Worker; Mrs. Pam Mings, Administrative Sec.

Society of St. Vincent de Paul, Immaculate Conception Conference, 410 S. College, 75702. Tel: 903-592-0027; Fax: 903-592-0034. Ms. Shawn Pickett, Dir.; Mr. Ken Wilson, Pres.; Mrs. Kelly Jackman, Treas.; Mrs. Bernie Tures, Sec.

**Tyler Catholic School Foundation*, P.O. Box 131175, 75713. Tel: 903-526-5988; Fax: 903-526-0750. Email: tcsfnd@gmail.com. Web: www.tcsf.info. D. V. Emery, Exec. Dir.

LONGVIEW. **Longview Catholic School Endowment Fund*, 405 Hollybrook, 75605. Tel: 903-753-1657; Fax: 903-758-7347. Web: www.stmaryslgv.org.

LUFKIN. **St. Patrick School Foundation* (1983) 2116 Lowry, 75901. Tel: 936-634-6719; Fax: 936-639-2776. Email: webmaster@stpatricklufkin.com. Web: www.stpatricklufkin.com.

PARIS. *St. Joseph's Community Foundation* (2004) 2800 Lamar Ave., 75460. Tel: 903-784-5136; Fax: 903-784-5481. Web: www.sjparis.org. Mailing Address: P.O. Box 6427, 75460. Stephanie Huff, Foundation Project Admin.

RELIGIOUS INSTITUTES OF MEN REPRESENTED IN THE DIOCESE

For further details refer to the corresponding bracketed number in the Religious Institutes of Men or Women section.

[]—*Carmelite of Mary Immaculate*—C.M.I.

[0220]—*Congregation of the Blessed Sacrament*—S.S.S.

[]—*Franciscan*—O.F.M.

[]—*Indian Missionary Society*—I.M.S.

[]—*Missionaries of St. Francis de Sales*—M.S.F.S.

[]—*Norbertine Fathers*—O.Praem.

[1065]—*Priestly Fraternity of St. Peter*—F.S.S.P.

RELIGIOUS INSTITUTES OF WOMEN REPRESENTED IN THE DIOCESE

[0230]—*Benedictine Sisters of Pontifical Jurisdiction*—O.S.B.

[]—*Congregation of the Mother of Carmel*—C.M.S.

[0470]—*Congregation of the Sisters of Charity of the Incarnate Word. Houston, Texas* (San Antonio, TX)—C.C.V.I.

[1070-19]—*Dominican Sisters of Houston, Texas (Congregation of the Sacred Heart)*—O.P.

[]—*Eucharistic Franciscan Sisters of Los Angeles*—E.F.M.S.

[]—*Franciscan Sisters of Dubuque*—O.S.F.

[]—*Hermit Sisters of St. Romuald*—H.S.S.R.

[]—*Instituto Santa Mariana de Jesus*—R.M.

[1570]—*Sisters of St. Francis of the Holy Family*—O.S.F.

[1970]—*Sisters of the Holy Family of Nazareth*—C.S.F.N.

NECROLOGY

(No Deaths)

An asterisk (*) denotes an organization that has established tax-exempt status directly with the IRS and is not covered by the USCCB Group Ruling.

Diocese of Venice

(Dioecesis Venetiae in Florida)

Most Reverend

FRANK J. DEWANE

Bishop of Venice; ordained July 16, 1988; appointed Coadjutor Bishop of Venice April 25, 2006; Episcopal ordination July 25, 2006; appointed Second Bishop of Venice January 19, 2007. *Res.: P.O. Box 2006, Venice, FL 34284-2006.*

Most Reverend

JOHN J. NEVINS, D.D.

Bishop Emeritus of Venice; ordained June 6, 1959; appointed Titular Bishop of Rusticiana and Auxiliary of Miami February 6, 1979; consecrated March 24, 1979; appointed First Bishop of Venice July 17, 1984; installed October 25, 1984; retired January 19, 2007. *Res.: P.O. Box 2006, Venice, FL 34284-2006.*

ESTABLISHED OCTOBER 25, 1984.

Square Miles 9,035.

Comprises the Counties of Charlotte, Collier, DeSoto, Glades, Hardee, Hendry, Highlands, Lee, Manatee and Sarasota in the State of Florida.

For legal titles of parishes and diocesan institutions, consult the Chancellor.

Catholic Center, 1000 Pinebrook Rd., Venice, FL 34285. Mailing Address: P.O. Box 2006, Venice, FL 34284-2006. Tel: 941-484-9543; Fax: 941-484-1121.

Web: dioceseofvenice.org

Email: info@dioceseofvenice.org

STATISTICAL OVERVIEW

Personnel	
Bishop	1
Retired Bishops	1
Priests: Diocesan Active in Diocese	78
Priests: Diocesan Active Outside Diocese	5
Priests: Retired, Sick or Absent	24
Number of Diocesan Priests	107
Religious Priests in Diocese	65
Total Priests in Diocese	172
Extern Priests in Diocese	91
Ordinations:	
Diocesan Priests	2
Transitional Deacons	1
Permanent Deacons	3
Permanent Deacons in Diocese	95
Total Brothers	14
Total Sisters	77
Parishes	
Parishes	59
With Resident Pastor:	
Resident Diocesan Priests	45
Resident Religious Priests	14
Missions	10
Pastoral Centers	1
New Parishes Created	1
Professional Ministry Personnel:	
Brothers	4
Sisters	12
Lay Ministers	103
Welfare	
Homes for the Aged	9
Total Assisted	588
Day Care Centers	1
Total Assisted	47
Specialized Homes	2
Total Assisted	56
Special Centers for Social Services	29
Total Assisted	40,602
Educational	
Diocesan Students in Other Seminaries	17
Total Seminarians	17
Colleges and Universities	1
Total Students	850
High Schools, Diocesan and Parish	3
Total Students	1,331
Elementary Schools, Diocesan and Parish	10
Total Students	2,770
Non-residential Schools for the Disabled	2
Total Students	123
Catechesis/Religious Education:	
High School Students	941
Elementary Students	9,598
Total Students under Catholic Instruction	15,630
Teachers in the Diocese:	
Sisters	19
Lay Teachers	372
Vital Statistics	
Receptions into the Church:	
Infant Baptism Totals	3,993
Minor Baptism Totals	505
Adult Baptism Totals	139
Received into Full Communion	264
First Communions	3,247
Confirmations	861
Marriages:	
Catholic	421
Interfaith	110
Total Marriages	531
Deaths	2,288
Total Catholic Population	226,728
Total Population	2,015,936

Former Bishop—Most Rev. JOHN J. NEVINS, D.D., ord. June 6, 1959; appt. Titular Bishop of Rusticiana and Auxiliary of Miami Feb. 6, 1979; cons. March 24, 1979; appt. First Bishop of Venice July 17, 1984; installed Oct. 25, 1984; retired Jan. 19, 2007.

Catholic Center—1000 Pinebrook Rd., Venice, 34285. Tel: 941-484-9543; Fax: 941-484-1121. *Mailing Address: P.O. Box 2006, Venice, 34284.*

Office of the Bishop—Mrs. JOHANNA MARONE, Exec. Sec.; Mrs. CAROL COMPTON, Receptionist & Sec.

Vicar General—Rev. Msgr. STEPHEN E. MCNAMARA, V.G., V.F.

Chancellor—Dr. VOLODYMYR SMERYK, M.A., M.B.A., J.C.D., J.D.

Administrative Assistant to the Chancellor—Mrs. PHYLLIS M. CURLEY.

College of Consultors—Rev. Msgrs. STEPHEN E. MCNAMARA, V.G., V.F.; GERARD FINEGAN; Very Rev. FAUSTO STAMPIGLIA, S.A.C., V.F.; Revs. JOSEPH CONNOLLY, T.O.R.; MARCIAL I. GARCIA; RAFAEL PADILLA, J.C.L.; PAUL F. MCLAUGHLIN.

Deans—Very Rev. JOSE ANTONIO GONZALEZ, V.F., Eastern Deanery; Rev. Msgr. STEPHEN E. MCNAMARA, V.G., V.F., Central Deanery; Very Revs. ROBERT KANTOR, V.F., Southern Deanery; FAUSTO STAMPIGLIA, S.A.C., V.F., Northern Deanery.

Presbyteral Council—Rev. Msgr. STEPHEN E. MCNAMARA, V.G., V.F.; Very Revs. FAUSTO STAMPIGLIA, S.A.C., V.F.; JOSE ANTONIO GONZALEZ, V.F.; ROBERT KANTOR, V.F.; Revs. PAUL F. MCLAUGHLIN; RAFAEL PADILLA, J.C.L.; STANLEY J. DOMBROWSKI, O.S.F.S.; JEAN-MARIE FRITZ LIGONDE; TEOFILO USECHE; TOMASZ ZALEWSKI; GERARD F. CRITCH; MICHAEL J. CANNON; GEORGE RATZMANN; GREGG CAGGIANELLI; HUGH J. MCGUIGAN, O.S.F.S.; Very Rev. JOHN J. LUDDEN; Rev. Msgr. GERARD FINEGAN.

Theologian to the Bishop—Very Rev. FAUSTO STAMPIGLIA, S.A.C., V.F.

Vicar for Priests—Very Rev. JOHN J. LUDDEN.

Director for Deacons—Deacon FRANCIS J. CAMACHO.

Director for Religious—Sr. MONICA PAUL FRASER, O.P.

Priest Personnel Board—Rev. Msgr. STEPHEN E. MCNAMARA, V.G., V.F., Chm.

Continuing Education of Clergy—Very Rev. JOHN J. LUDDEN.

Child Protection and Safe Environment Issues—Dr. VOLODYMYR SMERYK, M.A., M.B.A., J.C.D., J.D., Chancellor; Dr. KATHY KLEINLEIN, Dir. Awareness Training & Certification.

Victim Assistance Coordinator—Tel: 941-416-6114. Ms. BARBARA E. DICOCCO.

Official Archivist—Dr. VOLODYMYR SMERYK, M.A., M.B.A., J.C.D., J.D., Chancellor.

Historical Archivist—Ms. ROSEMARY GALLO.

Diocesan Tribunal— All Pastoral Center searches for information prior to October 25, 1984 should be directed to the Diocese of St. Petersburg for Manatee, Hardee, Sarasota, DeSoto, Glades, Charlotte and Lee Counties; to the Diocese of Orlando for Highlands Co. and to the Archdiocese of Miami for Hendry and Collier Counties

Judicial Vicar—Very Rev. ARTHUR J. ESPELAGE, O.F.M., J.C.D.; Rev. Msgr. JOHN V. DOLCIAMORE, S.T.L., J.C.L., Judicial Vicar Emeritus.

Auditors—Revs. ANTHONY HEWITT, J.C.L.; JAROSLAW SNIOSEK, J.C.L.

Defenders of the Bond—Revs. ANTHONY HEWITT, J.C.L.; PATRICK DUBOIS, J.C.L.

Promoter of Justice—Rev. RAFAEL PADILLA, J.C.L.

Judges—Rev. Msgr. JOHN V. DOLCIAMORE, S.T.L., J.C.L.; Dr. VOLODYMYR SMERYK, M.A., M.B.A., J.C.D., J.D.; Revs. DENNIS C. KLEMME, S.T.L., J.C.D.; RAFAEL PADILLA, J.C.L.; JAROSLAW SNIOSEK, J.C.L.

Ecclesiastical Notaries/Case Assessors—Mrs. ANN MANRODT; Mrs. MARIANA BARTOLILLO.

Diocesan Offices

Building Department—Mr. BOHDAN NEPIP, Dir.

Campaign for Human Development—Dr. VOLODYMYR SMERYK, M.A., M.B.A., J.C.D., J.D.

**Catholic Charities of the Diocese of Venice, Inc.*Mr. PETER ROUTSIS-ARROYO, CEO.

Catholic Relief Services/Operation Rice Bowl—VACANT.

Communications Department—Mr. WILLIAM ATWELL, Dir.

The Florida Catholic, Venice Edition—Most Rev. FRANK J. DEWANE, Publisher; Mr. ROBERT REDDY, Editor, Venice Edition. Tel: 941-486-4701; Fax: 941-486-4763.

Stewardship and Development Department—Mr. JAMES RICE, Dir. Devel. & Giving.

Diaconate—Very Rev. FAUSTO STAMPIGLIA, S.A.C., V.F.

Ecumenical and Interreligious Office—Dr. VOLODYMYR SMERYK, M.A., M.B.A., J.C.D., J.D., Dir.

Education—Dr. KATHLEEN SCHWARTZ, Dir. Educ.; Dr. KATHY KLEINLEIN, Dir., Catechetical Ministry; ANDREA LORENZO MOLINARI, Ph.D., Pres., Blessed Edmund Rice School for Pastoral Ministry; GEORGE L. SMITH, Dir. Youth Outreach.

Finance Department—Mr. PETER MCPARTLAND, Dir.; Ms. DIONNE SPOO, Risk Mgmt. Coord.

Human Resources—Mr. ARTHUR FLEISCHER, Dir.

Information Technology—RICHARD HIBBARD, Dir.; Mr. DAVID DUDLEY, Technology Admin.; Mr. SCOTT PHAYRE, Technical Asst.

Internal Financial Services—Mrs. LORRAINE VANLEDE-BROWN, Dir.

Legal— DiVito and Higham, P.A., Gen. Counsel

Hispanic, Migrant and Spanish Speaking Apostolates—Revs. CELESTINO GUTIERREZ, Dir.; VICTOR CAVIEDES; JOSE DEL OLMO; Very Rev. JOSE ANTONIO GONZALEZ, V.F.; Rev. RAFAEL PADILLA, J.C.L.

Juventud Hispana (Hispanic Youth Outreach)—Very Rev. JOSE ANTONIO GONZALEZ, V.F., Dir.

Haitian Ministry—Rev. JEAN-MARIE FRITZ LIGONDE, Dir.

Lee County—Rev. JEAN-MARIE FRITZ LIGONDE.

West Collier County—Rev. TONY CHERMEIL.

Manatee and Hardee Counties—Rev. JEAN WOADY LOUIS.

Ministry to People with HIV/AIDS—Ms. CASANDRA GALLAGHER, Sarasota and Manatee Counties.

Department of Worship—Rev. JOHN MARK KLAUS, T.O.R., Dir. Liturgy.

Department of Evangelization—ERIC SAMMONS, Dir.

Charismatic Renewal—Revs. MICHAEL A. SCHEIP, Spiritual Dir.; JUAN LORENZO.

Prison Ministry—Mr. LOUIE FAUSTINO, Coord.

Family Life Office— (includes Parenting and all Marriage Enrichment and Marriage Preparation programs) ERIC SAMMONS, Dir.; Mrs. BETTY KARSOKAS, Coord.

Divorced and Separated Ministry—ERIC SAMMONS, Dir.

Scouting—Mr. JAMES FETTERMAN, Coord.

Peace and Social Justice Department—Mr. NEIL MICHAUD, M.S.W., Dir.

Respect Life Department—Rev. DENNIS J. COONEY, Moderator; Mrs. JEANNE BERDEAUX, Dir.

Project Rachel—Tel: 877-908-1212 (Toll Free).

Real Estate Department—Dr. VOLODYMYR SMERYK, M.A., M.B.A., J.C.D., J.D., Dir.; Ms. BEVERLY KONDAS, Coord. Real Estate.

Vocations/Seminarian Formation—Rev. CORY A. MAYER, Dir.; Mrs. MARY MONTEDONICO.

Other Office

Propagation of the Faith/Mission Cooperative Program—Very Rev. JOHN J. LUDDEN, Dir.

Organizations

Catholic Volunteers in Florida—Ms. ELAINE FOWLER, Exec. Dir., Mailing Address: P.O. Box 536476, Orlando, 32853. Tel: 407-382-7071. Email: volunteer@cvif.org.

Cursillo Movement—Rev. MICHAEL A. SCHEIP, Spiritual Advisor; Mr. JOHN MEYERS, Lay Dir.

Secretariado Hispano de Cursillos—Rev. SOFONIAS ORTEZ, Spiritual Dir.; JOSE GAUTIER, Lay Dir.

Equestrian Order of the Holy Sepulchre of Jerusalem—JOHN A. ROGGE, K.C.H.S., Diocesan Representative.

International Order of Alhambra, Diego Caravan 255—Mr. MARVIN A. PESCHEL, Supreme Dir.

Knights of Columbus—EUGENE DOLECKI, Pub. Rels.; BRENT J. LABRECHE, Supreme Rep. Tel: 866-363-8022.

Legion of Mary—Rev. DAVID J. BAEHR, Manasota Curia.

St. Vincent DePaul Society—BARBARA REDMORE, Trustee.

Venice Diocesan Council of Catholic Women—Rev. JOSEPH CONNOLLY, T.O.R., Spiritual Dir.; DELORES GARVIS, Pres.

Advisory Groups to the Bishop

Audit Committee—Mr. ERNEST SKINNER, Chm.

Finance and Investment Committee—Mr. ERNEST SKINNER, Chm.

Pension Plan Board of Trustees (Archdiocese of Miami/Diocese of Venice)—Rev. JEROME A. CAROSELLA, Co Vice-Chm.

Liturgical Commission—Rev. JOHN MARK KLAUS, T.O.R., Chm.

Planning and Development Committee—Very Rev. ROBERT KANTOR, V.F., Chm.

Priest Personnel Board—Rev. Msgr. STEPHEN E. MCNAMARA, V.G., V.F., Chm.

Real Estate Advisory Board—Dr. VOLODYMYR SMERYK, M.A., M.B.A., J.C.D., J.D., Chm.

Pastor's Peer Review Committee—Rev. Msgr. STEPHEN E. MCNAMARA, V.G., V.F., Chm.

Review Board—Mr. JACK DELLORTO, Chm.

CLERGY, PARISHES, MISSIONS AND PAROCHIAL SCHOOLS

CITY OF VENICE

(SARASOTA COUNTY)

1—EPIPHANY CATHEDRAL (1955) [CEM] Revs. John F. Costello, Rector; Richard York, Parochial Vicar; John Fitch, Parochial Vicar; Cory A. Mayer, Parochial Vicar; James M. Shea (BUR) (Retired); Deacons James Hanks; Brent McNally; Epimaco Roca Jr.; Robert Tomasso. In Res., Rev. Jack Cosentino (FAR) (Retired).
Res.: 310 Sarasota St., 34285. Tel: 941-484-3505; Fax: 941-488-9333. Email: nault@epiphanycathedral.org. Web: www.epiphanycathedral.org.
School—(Grades PreK-8), 316 Sarasota St., 34285. Tel: 941-488-2215; Fax: 941-480-1565. Web: www.ec-stigers.com. Irene Lynch, Prin.; Joanne Gianopulos, Librarian. Lay Teachers 16; Students 233.
Catechesis/Religious Program—Sr. Frances Lalor, R.S.M., D.R.E. Students 287.

2—OUR LADY OF LOURDES (1986) Revs. Arnold Zebrowski, Admin.; Piotr W. Zugaj, Parochial Vicar; Deacon David Mulvaney. In Res., Very Rev. Arthur J. Espelage, O.F.M.; Revs. Patrick Dubois; Vincent J. Sheehy (Retired).
Res.: 1301 Center Rd., 34292. Tel: 941-497-2931; Fax: 941-497-5849.
Catechesis/Religious Program—Students 135.

OUTSIDE THE CITY OF VENICE

ARCADIA, DE SOTO CO., ST. PAUL (1885) Revs. Vincent L. Clemente; Sofonias Ortez, Parochial Vicar.
Res.: 1208 E. Oak St., 34266. Tel: 863-494-2611; Fax: 863-494-6385.
Catechesis/Religious Program—Tel: 863-494-2835. Students 287.
Mission—Blessed Juan Diego 5241 S.W. Hwy. 17, Nocatee, De Soto Co. 34266. Tel: 863-993-4095.

AVE MARIA, COLLIER CO., QUASI-PARISH OF AVE MARIA ORATORY Rev. Robert Tatman Jr.
5068 Annunciation Cir., Ste. 101, 34142. Tel: 239-261-5555.
Catechesis/Religious Program—

AVON PARK, HIGHLANDS CO., OUR LADY OF GRACE (1956) Rev. Nicholas McLoughlin.
Res.: 595 E. Main St., 33825. Tel: 863-453-4757; Fax: 863-453-2620. Web: ologap.org.
Catechesis/Religious Program—Tel: 863-453-7537. Students 215.

BOCA GRANDE, LEE CO., OUR LADY OF MERCY (1988) Rev. Jerome A. Carosella.
Res.: P.O. Box 181, 33921. Tel: 941-964-2254; Fax: 941-964-2173.
Catechesis/Religious Program—Students 4.

BOKEELIA, LEE CO., OUR LADY OF THE MIRACULOUS MEDAL (1965) Rev. Michael J. Hughes, O.S.A.
Church & Mailing Address: 12175 Stringfellow Rd., 33922. Tel: 239-283-0456; Fax: 239-283-1118. Email: olmmparish@embarqmail.com.
Catechesis/Religious Program—Students 38.

BONITA SPRINGS, LEE CO., ST. LEO (1962) Revs. Teofilo Useche, Admin.; Jaroslaw Sniosek, Parochial Vicar.
Res.: 28290 Beaumont Rd., 34134. Tel: 239-992-0901; Fax: 239-992-5282. Web: stleocatholicchurch.org.
Catechesis/Religious Program—Andrea Cecilli, D.R.E. Students 286.

BRADENTON, MANATEE CO.

1—ST. JOSEPH (1927) Revs. Paul F. McLaughlin; Rafal Ligenza, Parochial Vicar.
Res.: 2704 33rd Ave. W., 34205. Tel: 941-756-3732; Fax: 941-758-1244. Email: stjochurch@aol.com. Web: sjcfl.org.
School—(Grades PreK-8), 2990 26th St. W., 34205. Tel: 941-755-2611; Fax: 941-753-6339. Kellie Potter, Prin.; Ms. Dory Stovall, Librarian. Lay Teachers 24; Students 265.
Catechesis/Religious Program—Tel: 941-755-4335; Fax: 941-753-5634. Michael John, D.R.E. Students 76.

2—SS. PETER AND PAUL THE APOSTLES (1987) Revs. Mark L. Heuberger; Antonio Jean, Parochial Vicar; Russell Ruggiero, Parochial Vicar.
Office: 2850 75th St. W., 34209. Tel: 941-795-1228; Fax: 941-794-0127. Email: ss2850pp@hotmail.com. Web: www.sspeterandpaul.org. (Memorial Garden)
Catechesis/Religious Program—Tel: 941-798-9705; Fax: 941-794-3012. Students 192.

3—SACRED HEART (1969) Rev. Salvator Stefula, T.O.R.
Mailing Address: 1220 15th St. W., 34205.
Tel: 941-748-2221; Fax: 941-748-1744. Email: sacredheartchurch@tampabay.rr.com. Web: www.mysacredheart.com.
Catechesis/Religious Program—Tel: 941-748-2221, Ext. 118. Students 138.

CAPE CORAL, LEE CO.

1—ST. ANDREW (1964) Revs. Edward Gibbons, Admin.; Remigious Ssekiranda, Parochial Vicar; Andrew Malarz, Parochial Vicar.
Res.: 2628 Del Prado Blvd., 33904. Tel: 239-574-4545; Fax: 239-574-2450. Email: sacc@standrewrcc.org. Web: www.standrewcc.org.
School—(Grades PreK-8), 1509 S.E. 27th St., 33904. Tel: 239-772-3922; Fax: 239-772-7182. Sr. Elizabeth Meegan, Prin. Lay Teachers 18.
Catechesis/Religious Program—Tel: 239-574-2411. Dr. Carmine Macedonio, D.R.E. Students 430.

2—SAINT KATHARINE DREXEL (1990) Revs. John F. Deary, O.S.A.; John F. O'Rourke, O.S.A.; Deacon Richard Spiro.
Office: 1922 S.W. 20th Ave., 33991. Tel: 239-283-9501; Fax: 239-283-9502.
Catechesis/Religious Program—Theresa Idler, D.R.E. Students 551.

CLEWISTON, HENDRY CO., ST. MARGARET (1932), (Hispanic), Rev. Jiobani Batista, Admin.
208 N. Deane Duff Ave., 33440.
Res.: 312 N. Deane Duff Ave., 33440. Tel: 863-983-8585; Fax: 863-983-9673.
Catechesis/Religious Program—315 E. Pasadena Ave., 33440. Tel: 863-983-7589. Students 155.
Chapel—St. Margaret 208 N. Deane Duff Ave., 33440.
Mission—Santa Rosa de Lima 845 Mayoral St., Hendry Co. 33440. Tel: 863-983-8585; Fax: 863-983-9673.

ENGLEWOOD, SARASOTA CO., ST. RAPHAEL (1957) Revs. Mark Schaffner, O.Carm.; Niles Gillen, O.Carm.; Deacon Robert Godlewsky.
Res.: 770 Kilbourne Ave., 34223. Tel: 941-474-9595; Fax: 941-475-5697. Email: office@strapheng.org. Web: www.strapheng.org.
Catechesis/Religious Program—Tel: 941-473-2359. Anne Raczka, C.R.E. Students 29.

FORT MYERS BEACH, LEE CO., ASCENSION (1962) Revs. William Adams; Robert Murphy, Parochial Vicar.
Res.: 6025 Estero Blvd., 33931. Tel: 239-463-6754; Fax: 239-463-0690. Email: ascensionfmb@yahoo.com.
Catechesis/Religious Program—Students 2.

FORT MYERS, LEE CO.

1—ST. THERESE (2003) Rev. Mario Kono, Admin.
20115 N. Tamiami Tr., North Fort Myers, Lee Co. 33903. Tel: 239-567-2315; Fax: 239-567-2316. Email: sttheresech@aol.com. P.O. Box 3520, North Fort Myers, 33918.

2—BLESSED POPE JOHN XXIII (2002) Revs. Robert D. Tabbert; Marcin Koziola, Parochial Vicar; Bernadine Dang, C.M.C., Parochial Vicar.
13060 Palomino Ln., 33912.
Catechesis/Religious Program—Tel: 239-561-7499; Fax: 239-561-3713. Students 183.

3—ST. CECILIA (1965) [CEM] Revs. Stanley J. Dombrowski, O.S.F.S.; Francis Hanlon, O.S.F.S., Parochial Vicar.
Res.: 5632 Sunrise Dr., 33919. Tel: 239-936-3635; Fax: 239-936-2108.
Catechesis/Religious Program—Kristine Neumayer Jenkins, D.R.E. Students 80.

4—CHURCH OF THE RESURRECTION OF OUR LORD (1974) Rev. Msgr. Stephen E. McNamara; Revs. Oliver Toner, Parochial Vicar; Michal Szyszka, Parochial Vicar.
Parish Center & Mailing Address: 8121 Cypress Lake Dr., 33919. Tel: 239-481-7172; Fax: 239-481-8007. Email: parishoffice@resurrectionch.org. Web: www.resurrectionch.org.
Church: 8051 Cypress Lake Dr., 33919. Tel: 239-481-7171.
Catechesis/Religious Program—Tel: 239-482-6883. Email: resurrectionoffice@yahoo.com. Lea Pascotto, D.R.E. Students 294.

5—ST. COLUMBKILLE (1993) [CEM] Rev. Joseph G. Clifford.
Church: 12171 Iona Rd., 33908. Tel: 239-489-3973; Fax: 239-432-0066. Email: office@stcolumbkille.com.

Web: www.stcolumbkille.com.
Catechesis/Religious Program—Students 78.
6—ST. FRANCIS XAVIER (1910) Revs. Gregg Caggianelli, Admin.; James G. Simko, Parochial Vicar; Tony Chermeil, Parochial Vicar.
Res.: 2133 Heitman St., P.O. Box 912, 33902. Tel: 239-334-2161; Fax: 239-332-4178. Web: stfrancisfm.org.
School—(Grades PreK-8), 2055 Heitman St., 33901. Tel: 239-334-7707; Fax: 239-334-8605. Mrs. Janet Ortenzo, Prin. Franciscan Sisters of Allegany 2; Lay Teachers 30; Students 595.
Catechesis/Religious Program—2050 Heitman St., 33901. Tel: 239-246-2635. Students 97.
7—JESUS THE WORKER MISSION (JESUS OBRERO) (1973), (Hispanic), Revs. Patrick T. O'Connor, O.S.F.S., Admin.; Jaime Gonzalez, Parochial Vicar. Office: P.O. Box 50909, 33994. Tel: 239-693-5333; Fax: 239-693-5626.
Catechesis/Religious Program—Theresa Gomez, D.R.E. Students 227.
8—OUR LADY OF LIGHT (1990) [CEM] Revs. Hugh J. McGuigan, O.S.F.S.; Anthony Gilborges, O.S.F.S., Parochial Vicar; Deacon Francis J. Camacho.
Office: 19680 Cypress View Dr., 33967-6201. Tel: 239-267-7088; Fax: 239-267-5481. Email: info@ourladyoflight.com. Web: www.ourladyoflight.com.
Res.: 9404 Windlake Dr., 33967. Tel: 239-432-9095.
Catechesis/Religious Program—Students 255.
9—SAN JOSE MISSION (1968), (Hispanic), Revs. Patrick T. O'Connor, O.S.F.S., Admin.; Jaime Gonzalez, Parochial Vicar.
10750 Gladiolus Dr., 33908. Tel: 239-481-1143; Fax: 239-693-5626. Email: mmlcjo@earthlink.net.
Catechesis/Religious Program—Amarillys Ocasio, D.R.E. Students 56.
10—ST. VINCENT DE PAUL (1986) Rev. David Arle.
Church & Mailing Address: 13031 Palm Beach Blvd., 33905. Tel: 239-693-0818; Fax: 239-693-8459. Email: thefamilyparish@embarqmail.com.
Catechesis/Religious Program—Students 62.
GROVE CITY, CHARLOTTE CO., ST. FRANCIS OF ASSISI (1978) Revs. Adrian Wilde, O.Carm.; Marcel Dube, O.Carm.
Res. & Church: 5265 Placida Rd., 34224. Tel: 941-697-4899; Fax: 941-697-0602.
Catechesis/Religious Program—James Brantner, D.R.E. Students 80.
HOLMES BEACH, MANATEE CO., ST. BERNARD (1956) Rev. Michael Mullen.
Mailing Address: P.O. Box 1036, Bradenton Beach, 34217. In Res., Rev. Jean Woady Louis.
Res.: 246 S. Harbor Dr., Bradenton Beach, 34217. Tel: 941-778-4769; Fax: 941-778-4644. Email: stbernardcc@hotmail.com. Web: stbernard.com.
Catechesis/Religious Program— Matthew Nowicki, Dir Faith Formation. Students 40.
IMMOKALEE, COLLIER CO., OUR LADY OF GUADALUPE (1957) Revs. Carlos Reyes-Ramirez, C.S., Admin.; Onorio Benacchio, C.S., Parochial Vicar; Benjamin Casimir, C.S., Parochial Vicar.
Res.: 207 S. 9th St., 34142. Tel: 239-657-2666; Fax: 239-657-3431. Email: guadalupechurch@yahoo.com.
Catechesis/Religious Program—Mrs. Cynthia Garcia, D.R.E. Students 450.
LABELLE, HENDRY CO., OUR LADY QUEEN OF HEAVEN (1975) Revs. Chester Domaszewicz; Juan Lorenzo, Parochial Vicar.
Res.: 355 S. Bridge St., P.O. Box 357, 33935. Tel: 863-675-0030; Fax: 863-675-0756.
Catechesis/Religious Program—Students 298.
Mission—Holy Martyrs Mission 4290 Crescent Ave., S.W., Hendry Co. 33935.
LAKE PLACID, HIGHLAND CO.
1—COMMUNIDAD CATOLICA HISPANA SANTIAGO APOSTOL (SANTIAGO MISSION) (1991), (Hispanic), [JC] Rev. Luis Albarracin.
685 CR 621 E, 33852. Tel: 863-699-1561. Mailing Address: 882 Bay St., Sebring, 33870. Tel: 863-385-6762; Fax: 863-358-5169. Email: frjose@stcathe.com.
Catechesis/Religious Program—Students 130.
2—ST. JAMES (1962) [JC] Revs. Michael J. Cannon; Luis Albarracin, Parochial Vicar.
Mailing Address: 3380 Placid View Dr., 33852. Tel: 863-465-3215; Fax: 863-465-0649. 779 Hawk Ave., 33852.
Catechesis/Religious Program—Students 28.
LAKEWOOD RANCH, MANATEE CO., OUR LADY OF THE ANGELS (1999) [CEM] Rev. Daniel P. Smith, Admin.; Deacon Ronald Ochner.
12905 SR 70 E., 34202. Tel: 941-752-6770; Fax: 941-752-6821. Email: parishinfo@olangelscc.org. Web: www.olangelscc.org.
Catechesis/Religious Program—Ms. Chelle Maida, D.R.E. Students 223.
LEHIGH ACRES, LEE CO., ST. RAPHAEL (1962) Rev. Dennis J. Cooney; Deacon Joseph Allison.
Res.: 2514 Lee Blvd., 33971. Tel: 239-369-1831; Fax: 239-369-1039.
Catechesis/Religious Program—Tel: 239-369-6424. Students 293.
LONGBOAT KEY, MANATEE CO., ST. MARY STAR OF THE SEA (1973) Rev. Msgr. Gerard Finegan.
Res. & Church: 4280 Gulf of Mexico Dr., 34228. Tel: 941-383-1255; Fax: 941-383-8758. Email: stmarylbk@comcast.net. Web: stmarylbk.com.
Catechesis/Religious Program—
MARCO ISLAND, COLLIER CO., SAN MARCO (1971) Revs. Timothy M. Navin; Gordon Zanetti, Parochial Vicar; Deacons John Minicozzi; Michael Cristoforo; Norman F. McEnaney.
Res.: 851 San Marco Rd., 34145. Tel: 239-394-5181; Fax: 239-394-1385. Web: sanmarcochurch.com.
Catechesis/Religious Program—Tel: 239-394-4068. Kim Adamson, D.R.E. Students 110.
Mission—Holy Family Everglades City, Collier Co.
MOORE HAVEN, GLADES CO., ST. JOSEPH THE WORKER (1960), (Spanish), [JC] Rev. Lorenzo Gonzalez, Admin.
Res.: 24065 U.S. Hwy. 27, P.O. Box 1109, 33471. Tel: 863-946-0696; Fax: 863-946-3444.
Catechesis/Religious Program—Students 176.
Mission—St. Theresa of the Child Jesus 1027 Chobee Loop, Okeechobee, Okeechobee Co. 34974. Tel: 863-946-0696.
NAPLES, COLLIER CO.
1—ST. AGNES Very Rev. Robert Kantor; Rev. Tomasz Zalewski, Parochial Vicar.
7775 Vanderbilt Beach Rd., 34120-1641. Tel: 239-592-1949.
Catechesis/Religious Program—Ivy O'Malley, D.R.E. Students 574.
2—ST. ANN (1955) Revs. Michael Vannicola, O.S.F.S., Admin.; Thomas J. Gillespie, O.S.F.S., Parochial Vicar; Marc Gherardi, O.S.F.S., Parochial Vicar.
Res.: 475 Ninth Ave. S., 34102. Tel: 239-262-4256; Fax: 239-262-4296. Email: secretary@naplesstann.com. Web: www.naplesstann.com.
School—(Grades PreK-8), 542 Eighth Ave. S., 34102. Tel: 239-262-4110; Fax: 239-262-3991. Mr. Tommy Bridges, Prin.; Susan McKenzie, Librarian. Sisters 2; Lay Teachers 26; Students 308.
Catechesis/Religious Program—Students 130.
3—ST. ELIZABETH SETON (1975) Rev. Dennis Harten, O.S.A.
Res.: 5260 28th Ave., S.W., 34116. Tel: 239-455-3900; Fax: 239-455-6895. Email: elizabethannseton@comcast.net.
School—(Grades PreK-8) Denny Denison, Prin. Lay Teachers 16; Students 226.
Catechesis/Religious Program— Ms. Christine Roberts, D.R.E. Students 135.
4—ST. FINBARR Rev. Jean-Marie Fritz Ligonde, Admin.
13520 Tamiami Tr. E., Collier Co. 34114-8703. Tel: 239-417-2084.
5—ST. JOHN THE EVANGELIST (1988) Very Rev. John J. Ludden; Revs. Thomas N. Kelly, Parochial Vicar; Leonard Gioeli, Parochial Vicar; Deacons Harold Brenner; Al Groh; Robert Chalhoub; Frank Paniccia.
Res.: 625 111th Ave. N., 34108. Tel: 239-566-8740; Fax: 239-566-9117. Email: info@saintjohntheevangelist.com.
Catechesis/Religious Program—Tel: 239-514-2927; Fax: 239-566-9117. Mrs. Margaret Lynch, D.R.E. Students 262.
6—ST. PETER THE APOSTLE (1974) Revs. Gerard F. Critch; Russell Wright, S.T.L., Parochial Vicar; Pedro Roman, O.P., Parochial Vicar; Deacons David Nolan; Robert Tetrault; Peter Pavlyshin.
Res.: 5130 Rattlesnake Hammock Rd., 34113-7448. Tel: 239-774-3337; Fax: 239-774-3077. Email: info@stpeternaples.com. Web: stpeternapels.com.
Catechesis/Religious Program—5025 Rattlesnake Hammock Rd., 34113. Tel: 239-775-9576; Fax: 239-775-6028. Liz McGuire, D.R.E. Students 524.
7—ST. WILLIAM (1973) Revs. George Ratzmann; Paul R. D'Angelo, Parochial Vicar; Ronnie Sison, Parochial Vicar.
Res.: 750 Seagate Dr., 34103-2886. Tel: 239-261-4883; Fax: 239-261-8729. Email: cathy@saintwilliam.org. Web: www.saintwilliam.org.
Catechesis/Religious Program—Tel: 239-263-5429. Mary Jane Spirk, D.R.E. Students 249.
NORTH PORT, SARASOTA CO., SAN PEDRO (1964) Rev. Patrick C. Organ; Deacons Eugene Willis; Richard Frohmiller.
Res.: 14380 Tamiami Tr., 34287. Tel: 941-426-2500; 941-426-6810; Fax: 941-423-8710. Email: sanpedroparish@hotmail.com. Web: www.sanpedrocc.org.
Catechesis/Religious Program—Tel: 941-426-2893; Fax: 941-429-8785. Email: spreligioused@hotmail.com. Anne Raczka, D.R.E. Students 396.
OSPREY, SARASOTA CO., OUR LADY OF MOUNT CARMEL (2000) Rev. Gregory L. Klein, O.Carm.; Deacon Thomas Grant.
Parish Center: 425 S. Tamiami Tr., P.O. Box 1097, 34229. Tel: 941-966-0807; Fax: 941-966-3909. Email: ljefferson@olmc-osprey.org. Web: www.olmc-osprey.org.
Res.: 554 Pine Ranch E. Rd., 34229. Tel: 941-918-2032.
Catechesis/Religious Program—Students 31.
PALMETTO, MANATEE CO., HOLY CROSS CHURCH (1956) Revs. Marcial I. Garcia, Admin.; Pawel Kawalec, Parochial Vicar.
Church & Mailing Address: 505-26th St. W., 34221. Tel: 941-729-3891; Fax: 941-721-9402.
Catechesis/Religious Program—Tel: 941-729-4338. Students 90.
PARRISH, MANATEE CO., SAINT FRANCES XAVIER CABRINI (1992) Rev. Janusz Jay Jancarz.
Res.: 12001 69th St. E., 34219. Tel: 941-776-9097; Fax: 941-776-1307. Web: www.stfrancesxcabrini.org.
Catechesis/Religious Program—Tel: 941-776-8613. Students 195.
PORT CHARLOTTE, CHARLOTTE CO.
1—ST. CHARLES BORROMEO (1959) Revs. Thomas A. Heck; James J. Cogan, Parochial Vicar; Philip J. Scheff, Parochial Vicar; Deacon Thomas Caliguire.
Office & Church: 21505 Augusta Ave., 33952. Tel: 941-625-4754; Fax: 941-625-0256. Email: stcharlespcfl@hotmail.com. Web: stcharlespc.org.
School—(Grades PreK-8) Tel: 941-625-5533; Fax: 941-625-7359. Rita Shamrock, Prin.; Deborah Lambeth-Jones, Librarian. Lay Teachers 15; Students 176.
Catechesis/Religious Program—21505 Augusta Ave., 33952. Tel: 941-625-1292, Ext. 210. Nelson Perez, D.R.E. Students 104.
2—ST. MAXIMILIAN KOLBE (1988) Rev. Rafael Padilla.
Office: 1441 Spear St., 33948. Tel: 941-743-6877; Fax: 941-743-9176.
Res.: 1270 W. Corktree Cir., 33952.
Catechesis/Religious Program—Cindy Kuykendall, C.R.E. Students 143.
3—SAN ANTONIO (1993) Rev. Jacek Mazur, Admin.
24445 Rampart Blvd., 33980. Tel: 941-624-3799; Fax: 941-624-6184. Web: sanantoniocatholicchurch.com.
Catechesis/Religious Program—Tel: 941-624-5156; Fax: 941-624-6631. Students 79.
PUNTA GORDA, CHARLOTTE CO., SACRED HEART (1954) Revs. Jerome P. Kaywell; Leo P. Riley, Parochial Vicar.
Res.: 363 W. Charlotte Ave., 33950-5546. Tel: 941-639-3957; Fax: 941-639-2061. Web: www.sacredheartfl.org.
Catechesis/Religious Program—Tel: 941-639-9545. Sr. Josine Perez, D.R.E. Students 100.
SANIBEL, LEE CO., ST. ISABEL (1973) Rev. Christopher Senk.
Res.: 3559 Sanibel Captiva Rd., 33957. Tel: 239-472-2763; Fax: 239-472-5351. Email: saintisabel@aol.com. Web: www.saintisabel.org.
Catechesis/Religious Program—Kathy Scheer, D.R.E. Students 45.
SARASOTA, MANATEE CO., OUR LADY QUEEN OF MARTYRS (1959) Revs. Joseph F. Connolly, T.O.R.; John Mark Klaus, T.O.R., Parochial Vicar.
Res.: 833 Magellan Dr., 34243. Tel: 941-755-1826; Fax: 941-753-1654. Email: queenofmartyrs@olqm.net. Web: ourladyqueenofmartyrs.net.
Catechesis/Religious Program—Tel: 941-755-3497. Heather Felton, D.R.E. Students 129.
SARASOTA, SARASOTA CO.
1—INCARNATION (1958) Revs. Bernard P. Evanofski; Michael A. Scheip, Parochial Vicar; Leo Joseph Smith, Parochial Vicar; Deacons Joseph Cirieco; John Crescitelli.
Res.: 2929 Bee Ridge Rd., 34239. Tel: 941-921-6631; Fax: 941-927-2521. Web: www.incarnationchurch.org.
School—2911 Bee Ridge Rd., 34239. Tel: 941-924-8588; Fax: 941-925-1248. Ms. Regina Housel, Prin. Sisters 3; Lay Teachers 20; Students 153.
Catechesis/Religious Program—Tel: 941-924-9566. John Garisto, D.R.E. Students 200.
2—ST. JUDE (2006) Revs. Celestino Gutierrez; Theodoro Mata (Dominican Republic), Parochial Vicar; Anthony Hewitt, Parochial Vicar; Deacon Leonardo Pastore.
Mailing Address: 3930 17th St., 34235. Tel: 941-955-3934; Fax: 941-365-4760. Email: frcelestino@st-judeparish.org. Web: www.stjudehispamerctr.com.
Catechesis/Religious Program—Students 300.
3—ST. MARTHA (1912) Very Rev. Fausto Stampiglia, S.A.C.; Revs. Andrew Kozminski, S.A.C., Parochial Vicar; John Hoang, Parochial Vicar; C. Patrick Wilson, S.A.C., Parochial Vicar; Piotr Czerwonka, S.A.C., Parochial Vicar; Deacons C. Patrick Macaulay; William Ladroga; Kevin McKenney.
Mailing Address: 200 N. Orange Ave., 34236. Tel: 941-366-4210; Fax: 941-954-8434. Web: www.stmartha.org.
School—(Grades PreK-8), 4380 Fruitville Rd., 34232. Tel: 941-953-4181; Fax: 941-366-5580. Mrs. Siobhan Young, Prin. Religious 2; Lay Teachers 27;

Students 450.
Catechesis/Religious Program—Email: sileo@stmarth.comcastbiz.net. Mrs. Patricia Sileo, D.R.E. Students 177.
Chapel—Christ the King (2009) 1900 Meadowood St., 34231-3949. Tel: 941-924-2777; Fax: 941-924-2797. Revs. James A. Fryar, F.S.S.P., Chap.; Brian Austin, F.S.S.P.; Howard Remski, F.S.S.P.
Mission—The Vietnam Catholic Community of Our Lady of Lavang

4—ST. MICHAEL THE ARCHANGEL (1958) Rev. Msgr. Joseph E. Stearns; Deacon Kim Cohen.
Mailing Address: 5394 Midnight Pass Rd., 34242. Tel: 941-349-4174; Fax: 941-349-6388.
Res.: 1014 Glebe Ln., 34242.
Catechesis/Religious Program—Tel: 941-349-4174, Ext. 14. Students 67.

5—ST. PATRICK (1988) Rev. Robert T. Dziedziak; Deacon Raymond Lyons.
Res.: 7900 Bee Ridge Rd., 34241. Tel: 941-378-1703; Fax: 941-378-2153. Email: churchofstpatrick@churchofstpatrick.org.
Catechesis/Religious Program—Email: stpatff@churchofstpatrick.org. Students 135.

6—ST. THOMAS MORE (1979) Revs. Donald H. Henry; Jan Antonik, Parochial Vicar; Deacon John Robert Gaitens.
Mailing Address: 2506 Gulf Gate Dr., 34231. Tel: 941-923-1691; Fax: 941-923-1692. Email: stmsrq@aol.com. Web: sttmore.org.
Catechesis/Religious Program—Sr. Judy Baldino, S.S.J., D.R.E. Students 212.

SEBRING, HIGHLANDS CO., ST. CATHERINE (1929) [JC] Very Rev. Jose Antonio Gonzalez; Rev. Victor Caviedes, Parochial Vicar; Deacons James R. McGarry; Max Severe.
Mailing Address: 882 Bay St., 33870. Email: office@stcathe.com.
Res.: 862 Bay St., 33870.
Church: 820 Hickory St., 33870. Email: frjose@stcathe.com. Web: www.stcathe.com.
School—St. Catherine Catholic School (2008), (Grades PreK-5), 747 S. Franklin St., 33870. Tel: 863-385-7300. Email: school@stcathe.com. Anna V. Adam, Prin. Lay Teachers 6; Students 75.
Catechesis/Religious Program— Georgia Quick, D.R.E. Students 235.

WAUCHULA, HARDEE CO., ST. MICHAEL (1969), (Spanish—Creole), Revs. Juan Carlos Sack, I.V.E., Admin.; Esteban Soler, I.V.E., Parochial Vicar.
Res.: 408 Heard Bridge Rd., 33873. Tel: 863-773-4089; Fax: 863-773-5641.
Catechesis/Religious Program—Tel: 863-773-4215. Students 550.
Mission—Holy Child 4315 Chester Ave., Bowling Green, Hardee Co. 33834.
Mission—San Alfonso Catholic Center 3027 Schoolhouse Rd., Zolfo Springs, Hardee Co. 33890. Tel: 863-773-5641.

Military Chaplains:
Very Rev.—
Cannon, Col. Robert R., J.C.L., U.S. Air Force.
Revs.—
Kowalik, Jacek, U.S. Air Force, Germany.
Martin, Edward, U.S. Army
Sikorski, Leszek, U.S. Navy.

Absent on Leave:
Rev.—
Ochej, Tomasz

On Administrative Leave:
Revs.—
Chojnacki, Bernard
Joseph, Jean-Ronald
Strycharz, Stanislaw

Retired:
Rev. Msgrs.—
La Femina, Anthony A., S.T.L., J.C.D.
Mouch, Frank M.
Revs.—
Brubaker, Claude
Duggan, Joseph P.
Ellis, John H.R.
Feliz, Normando
Flemming, James K.
Glackin, Thomas J.
Gonzalez, Mario
Grogan, Gerald P.
Hickey, Michael
Lobato, Nicanor
Mattingly, Robert B.
McCarthy, Eugene
Mongiello, Robert
Murphy, Timothy
O'Connell, William
Pick, Edward, V.F.
Rourke, John
Ryan, Eugene
Sheehy, Vincent J.
Soy, Esteban
Sullivan, Charles K.
Walk, Donald J.

Permanent Deacons:
Allison, Joseph
Arnold, Maurice, (Retired)
Brenner, Harold
Caliguire, Thomas
Camacho, Francis, (Dir. Diaconate Personnel)
Cassidy, William
Cirieco, Joseph, (Retired)
Cole, Francis
DiMeglio, Michael, (Retired)
Esper, Michael
Fortier, W. Lorin, (Retired)
Gaitens, John Robert
Godlewsky, Robert
Grant, Thomas
Hanks, James
Healy, M. Donald
Hedge, Dennis, (Leave of Absence)
Kiesel, Charles, (Retired)
Ladroga, William, Dir. of Diaconate Formation
Lundy, Edward, (Retired)
Macaulay, Patrick C.
McKenney, Kevin
Mueller, Martin, (Unassigned)
Mulvaney, David
Nolan, David W.
Pastore, Leonardo
Roca, Epimaco, Jr.
Spiro, Richard
Willis, Eugene
Zandy, Richard, (Unassigned)

INSTITUTIONS LOCATED IN THE DIOCESE

[A] COLLEGES AND UNIVERSITIES

AVE MARIA. **Ave Maria Unversity*, 5050 Ave Maria Blvd., 34142-9505. Tel: 239-280-2500; 877-283-8648; Fax: 239-352-2392. Web: www.avemaria.edu. H. James Towey, Pres.; Terence Gallagher, Librarian. Catholic University.

[B] HIGH SCHOOLS

FORT MYERS. *Bishop Verot Catholic High School* (1962) 5598 Sunrise Dr., 33919. Tel: 239-274-6700; Fax: 239-274-6798. Email: information@bvhs.org. Web: www.bvhs.org. John A. Cavell Jr., Prin.; Lisa Dignam, Librarian. Oblates of St. Francis de Sales. Lay Teachers 46; Students 636; Total Staff 74.

NAPLES. **St. John Neumann Catholic High School, Inc.* (1985) 3000 53rd St., S.W., 34116. Tel: 239-455-3044; Fax: 239-455-2966. Email: sroche@sjnceltics.org. Web: www.sjnceltics.org. Sr. Patricia Roche, F.M.A, Prin.; Mrs. Stephanie Sweeney, Librarian. Lay Teachers 20; Students 215; Total Staff 12.

SARASOTA. *Cardinal Mooney Catholic High School, Inc.*, 4171 Fruitville Rd., 34232. Tel: 941-371-4917; Fax: 941-371-6924. Email: schristie@cmhs-sarasota.org. Web: www.cmhs-sarasota.org. Sr. Mary Lucia Haas, S.N.D., Pres.; Mr. Stephen J. Christie, Prin.; Ms. Elaine Moore, Librarian. Sisters of Notre Dame of Chardon, OH. Sisters 1; Lay Teachers 40; Total Staff 56; Students 475.

[C] SCHOOLS FOR SPECIAL NEEDS

FORT MYERS. *Father Anglim Academy at Dreams are Free*, (Grades 2-12), *Fort Myers Campus*, 2045 Heitman St., 33901. Tel: 239-337-4010; Fax: 239-337-4044. Web: www.fatheranglimacademy.org. Matthew Loge, Prin. Lay Teachers 8; Lay Speech Therapist 1; Lay Occupational Therapist 1; Lay School Counselor 1; Lay Administrators 1; Students 73.

SARASOTA. *Dreams Are Free School at Bishop Nevins Academy, Sarasota Campus*, 4380 Fruitville Rd., 34232-1623. Tel: 941-366-4010; Fax: 941-366-3819. Email: maksentis@dreamsarefree.org. Web: www.dreamsarefree.org. Mary Aksentis, Prin. Lay Teachers 5; Students 50.

[D] SCHOOLS FOR THEOLOGICAL, SPIRITUAL, PASTORAL AND PERSONAL FORMATION

ARCADIA. *Blessed Edmund Rice School for Pastoral Ministry* (1995) 10299 S.W. Peace River St., 34269-4068. Tel: 941-766-7334; Fax: 941-629-8555. Email: riceschool@daystar.net. Web: www.riceschool.org. Andrea Lorenzo Molinari, Ph.D., Pres.; Clare Miller, Librarian. Priests 3; Lay Teachers 2; Students 115; Total Staff 9.

[E] MIGRANT EDUCATION

BONITA SPRINGS. *St. Leo Parish Migrant Education Apostolate*, 28290 Beaumont Rd., 34134. Tel: 239-947-9098; Fax: 239-947-9098. Adult Education Outreach. Brothers 2.

[F] RESIDENCES FOR THE AGED

VENICE. *Blessed Pope John XXIII Housing, Inc.*, c/o 1000 Pinebrook Rd., 34285. Rev. Robert Tabbert, V.F., Pres.
St. Mark's Housing of Venice, Inc. dba Villa San Marco 1030 Albee Farm Rd., 34285. Tel: 941-483-1960; Fax: 941-483-3934. Email: villasanmarcosmgr@spm.net; villasanmarcos@comcast.net. Dr. Volodymyr Smeryk, Pres. Total Staff 4; Total in Residence 81.
St. Vincent de Paul Housing, Inc., c/o P.O. Box 2006, 34284-2006. Tel: 239-693-1333; Fax: 239-693-8459. Email: villa.vincente@earthlink.net. Dr. Volodymyr Smeryk, Pres. Total Staff 3; Total in Residence 63.

FORT MYERS. *Villa Francisco* (1984) 2140 Cottage St., 33901. Tel: 239-332-3229; Fax: 239-332-3229. Rev. Gregg Caggianelli, Pres.; Robert Beaulieu, Admin. Total in Residence 65; Total Staff 1.

PALMETTO. *Holy Cross Manor, Inc.*, 510 26th St. W., 34221. Tel: 941-729-2063; Fax: 941-729-2386. Dr. Volodymyr Smeryk, Pres. Total Staff 4; Total in Residence 70.
Holy Cross Manor II, Inc., 540 W. 26th St., 34221. 1000 Pinebrook Rd., 34285. Total Staff 3; Total in Residence 69.

PORT CHARLOTTE. *St. Charles Housing I, Inc. aka Villa San Carlos* 2550 Easy St., 33952. Tel: 941-624-2266; Fax: 941-624-2283. Email: villasancarlos@comcast.net. Rev. Thomas Heck, Pres.; Ms. Sheila Jones, Admin. Total in Residence 51; Total Staff 3.
St. Charles Housing II, Inc. dba Villa San Carlos II 22250 Vick St., 33980-2026. Tel: 941-624-4404; Fax: 941-624-5556. Email: villasancarlosii@comcast.net. Rev. Thomas Heck, Pres.; Ms. Rebecca Murray, Admin. Residents 54; Total Staff 5.

SARASOTA. *St. Martha's Housing II, Inc.* (Casa Santa Marta II), 800 N. Lemon Ave., 34236. Tel: 941-365-7913; Fax: 941-365-8887. Email: casasantamarta.csm@verizon.net. Very Rev. Fausto Stampiglia, S.A.C., V.F., Pres.; Debra Greising, Site Mgr. Total in Residence 54; Total Staff 5.
St. Martha's Housing, Inc. (Casa Santa Marta), 1576 Eighth St., 34236. Tel: 941-366-4448; Fax: 941-366-2544. Email: casasantamarta.csm@verizon.net. Very Rev. Fausto Stampiglia, S.A.C., V.F., Pres.; Debra Greising, Site Mgr. Total in Residence 81; Total Staff 6.

[G] MONASTERIES AND RESIDENCES OF PRIESTS AND BROTHERS

VENICE. *Xavieran Brothers*, 609 Cornwell on the Gulf, 34285. Tel: 941-484-9641. Web: www.xaverianbrothers.org. Brothers of St. Francis Xavier Brothers 1.

ENGLEWOOD. *Society of Saint Edmund Residence*, 603 W. Harvard St., 34223. Tel: 941-474-7683.

NOKOMIS. *Carmel at Mission Valley*, 955 Laurel Rd. E., 34275-4507. Tel: 941-412-0678; Fax: 941-485-5716. Email: ebell@carmelnet.org. Priests 6; Brothers 1.

SARASOTA. *Congregation of the Holy Spirit*, 2234 Beneva Rd., 34232. Tel: 941-921-3214. Total in Residence 1.
Holy Cross Florida Regional Center (1973) 1635 4th St., 34236-5007. Tel: 941-493-3890. Email: pnault5@comcast.net. Holy Cross Brothers Residence.

[H] CONVENTS AND RESIDENCES FOR SISTERS

FORT MYERS BEACH. *San Damiano Monastery of St. Clare.* (Solemn Vows, Papal Enclosure), 6029 Estero Blvd., 33931-4325. Tel: 239-463-5599; Fax: 239-463-4993. Email: saintclare@comcast.net. Web: www.poorclare.com/fmb. Sr. Mary Frances Fortin, O.S.C., Abbess. Poor Clares. Cloistered Sisters 8.

[I] RETREAT CENTERS

VENICE. *Our Lady of Perpetual Help Retreat and Spirituality Center* (1996) 3989 S. Moon Dr., 34292. Tel: 941-486-0233; Fax: 941-486-1524.

Email: olphsct@aol.com. Web: www.olph-retreat.org. Rev. Joseph McCarthy, O.Carm., Dir.; Sr. Carmella T. DeCosty, S.N.J.M., M.A., Admin.

LAKE PLACID. *Campo San Jose* (1996) 882 Bay St., Sebring, 33870. Tel: 863-385-6762; Fax: 863-385-5169. Email: frjose@camposanjose.com. Web: www.camposanjose.com. 170 S. Sun 'n' Lake Blvd., 33852. Very Rev. Jose Antonio Gonzalez, V.F., Dir.

[J] CATHOLIC CHARITIES

VENICE. *Catholic Charities, Diocese of Venice, Inc.*, 1000 Pinebrook Rd., 34285. Tel: 941-488-5581; Fax: 941-484-1121. Email: prarroyo@dioceseofvenice.org. Web: www.catholiccharitiesdov.org. Mr. Peter Routsis-Arroyo, CEO; Sharon Aragona, COO.

Catholic Charities, District I (Sarasota and Manatee Counties), 5055 N. Tamiami Tr., Sarasota, 34234. Tel: 941-355-4680; Fax: 941-359-8374.

Catholic Charities, District II (Lee, Henry and Glades Counties), 4235 Michigan Ave. Link, Fort Myers, 33916. Tel: 239-337-4193; Fax: 239-332-2799.

African Caribbean American Ministry (AFCAAM), 3861 Michigan Ave., Fort Myers, 33916. Tel: 239-461-0233; Fax: 239-461-0236. Email: aragona@dioceseofvenice.org.

Catholic Charities, District III (Collier County), 2210 Santa Barbara Blvd., Naples, 34116. Tel: 239-455-2655; Fax: 239-455-7235. Email: bob@catholiccharitiescc.org.

Catholic Charities, Rural Services (Charlotte, De Soto, Hardee and Highland Counties), 1210 E. Oak St., Arcadia, 34266. Tel: 863-494-1068; Fax: 863-494-1671. Email: charity2@embarqmail.com.

Casa San Jose, Inc., 3900 17th St., Sarasota, 34235. Tel: 941-952-1853; Fax: 941-952-1857. Email: prarroyo@dioceseofvenice.org.

Catholic Charities Housing, Diocese of Venice, Inc., 1000 Pinebrook Rd., 34285. Tel: 941-488-5581; Fax: 941-484-1121. Email: prarroyo@dioceseofvenice.org.

Casa San Juan Bosco, Inc., 1000 Pinebrook Rd., 34285. Tel: 941-488-5581; Fax: 941-484-1121. Email: arroyo@dioceseofvenice.org.

Marian Manor, Inc., 1000 Pinebrook Rd., 34285. Tel: 941-488-5581; Fax: 941-484-1121. Email: prarroyo@dioceseofvenice.org.

Catholic Charities Refugee Programs, 7810 S. Tamiami Tr., A-5, 34293. Tel: 941-493-8231; Fax: 941-493-8239.

Catholic Charities Immigration Programs, 1000 Pinebrook Rd., 34285.

Catholic Charities Housing Sarasota, Inc., 1000 Pinebrook Rd., 34285.

SARASOTA. *Bethesda House - HIV/AIDS Ministries*, 1670 Fourth St., 34236. Tel: 941-366-1886; Fax: 941-362-9733. Email: sgallagher@ccdis1.org. Ms. Casandra Gallagher. (AIDS Ministry)

[K] FOUNDATIONS

VENICE. *Catholic Community Foundation of Southwest Florida, Inc.*, 1000 Pinebrook Rd., P.O. Box 2006, 34284-2006. Tel: 941-441-1124; Fax: 941-484-1121. Email: citro@dioceseofvenice.org. Web: ccfswf.org. Joe Citro, Exec. Dir.

Catholic Charities Foundation of the Diocese of Venice, Inc., 1000 Pinebrook Rd., 34285. Tel: 941-488-5581; Fax: 941-484-1121. Email: prarroyo@dioceseofvenice.org. Mr. Peter Routsis-Arroyo, Contact Person.

PORT CHARLOTTE. *St. Charles Borromeo School Foundation*, 21505 Augusta Ave., 33952. Tel: 941-625-5533; Fax: 941-625-7359. Email: rita_shamrock@stcbs.org.

SARASOTA. *Cardinal Mooney High School Foundation*, c/o Cardinal Mooney High School, 4171 Fruitville Rd., 34232. Tel: 941-371-4917; Fax: 941-371-6924. Web: www.cmhs-sarasota.org.

Incarnation School Foundation, 2911 Bee Ridge Rd., 34239. Tel: 941-924-8588; Fax: 941-925-1248. Email: rhousel@incarnationschool.edu. Web: www.incarnationschool.edu.

St. Martha School Foundation, 200 N. Orange Ave., 34236. Tel: 941-366-4210; Fax: 941-954-8434. Web: www.stmarthaschool.net.

[L] MISCELLANEOUS LISTINGS

VENICE. *Diocese of Venice in Florida, Inc.*, 1000 Pinebrook Rd., P.O. Box 2006, 34284-2600. Tel: 941-484-9543. Dr. Volodymyr Smeryk, M.A., M.B.A., J.C.D., J.D., Contact Person.

Trinity Enterprise Holdings, Inc., 1000 Pinebrook Rd., P.O. Box 2006, 34284-2006. Tel: 941-484-9543. Dr. Volodymyr Smeryk, M.A., M.B.A., J.C.D., J.D., Contact Person.

Trinity Trust, 1000 Pinebrook Rd., P.O. Box 2006, 34284-2006. Tel: 941-484-9543. Dr. Volodymyr Smeryk, M.A., M.B.A., J.C.D., J.D., Contact Person.

BONITA SPRINGS. *Iona House Corporation*, 26650 Noble Ln., 34135. Tel: 239-947-9098. Bro. Robert Benedict McDonough.

FORT MYERS. *Magnificat-Ft. Myers, FL-Mother of Mercy Chapter of the Diocese of Venice*, 1828 Pine Valley Dr., Apt. 206, 33907-4705. Tel: 239-267-2684; Fax: 239-267-2684. Email: loisamader@hotmail.com. Lois Mader, Contact Person & Coord.

Societies of St. Vincent de Paul, 3010 Cleveland Ave., 33901-7001. Tel: 239-274-0660; Fax: 239-274-0659. Barbara Redmore, Pres. District Council of Charlotte, District Council of Fort Myers, District Council of Manasota, District Council of Naples.

NAPLES. *Hope for Haiti, Inc.*, 1021 Fifth Ave N., 34102. Tel: 239-434-7183. Email: info@hopeforhaiti.com. Web: www.hopeforhaiti.com. JoAnne Kuehner, Founder & Chair.

SARASOTA. *Christ Child Society of Sarasota, Inc.*, 8859 Bloomfield Blvd., 34238. Email: kmgib@aol.com. Web: www.nationalchristchildsoc.org. Kathleen Gibbons, Pres. Local affiliate of national non-profit organization whose member-volunteers serve needy children.

RELIGIOUS INSTITUTES OF MEN REPRESENTED IN THE DIOCESE

For further details refer to the corresponding bracketed number in the Religious Institutes of Men or Women section.

[0140]—*The Augustinians*—O.S.A.
[1350]—*Brothers of St. Francis Xavier*—C.F.X.
[]—*Brothers of the Catholic Apostolate*—S.A.C.
[0600]—*Brothers of the Congregation of Holy Cross*—C.S.C.
[0470]—*Capuchin Friars*—O.F.M.Cap.
[0270]—*Carmelite Fathers*—O.Carm.
[0310]—*Congregation of Christian Brothers*—C.F.C.
[0650]—*(Spiritans) Congregation of the Holy Spirit*—C.S.Sp.
[]—*Congregation of the Mother Coredemptrix*—C.M.C.
[]—*Congregation of the Resurrection*—C.R.
[0430]—*Dominican Fathers*—O.P.
[]—*Institute of the Incarnate Word*—I.V.E.
[0690]—*Jesuit Fathers*—S.J.
[]—*Legionaries of Christ*—L.C.
[]—*Marist Fathers*—S.M.
[1210]—*Missionaries of St. Charles Scalabrians*—C.S.
[0590]—*Missionaries of the Holy Apostles*—M.Ss.A.
[0920]—*Oblates of St. Francis de Sales*—O.S.F.S.
[]—*Passionist Fathers*—C.P.
[1065]—*Priestly Fraternity of St. Peter*—F.S.S.P.
[0110]—*Society of African Missions*—S.M.A.
[0440]—*Society of St. Edmund*—S.S.E.
[0990]—*Society of the Catholic Apostolate*—S.A.C.
[]—*Society of the Divine Savior*—S.D.S.
[0560]—*Third Order Regular of St. Francis*—T.O.R.

RELIGIOUS INSTITUTES OF WOMEN REPRESENTED IN THE DIOCESE

[]—*Adorers of the Blood of Christ*—A.S.C.
[]—*Congregation of Bon Secours*—C.B.S.
[1070-15]—*Congregation of St. Dominic (Sisters of St. Dominic of Blauvelt, NY)*—O.P.
[]—*Congregation of the Sisters of St. Dominic of the Immaculate Heart of Mary*—O.P.
[3832]—*Congregation of the Sisters of St. Joseph*—C.S.J.
[1105]—*Dominican Sisters of Hope*—O.P.
[1070-13]—*Dominican Sisters/Congregation of the Most Holy Rosary (Adrian Dominicans)*—O.P.
[1070-03]—*Dominican Sisters/Sinsinawa Dominican Congregation of the Most Holy Rosary*—O.P.
[1180]—*Franciscan Sisters of Allegheny, NY*—O.S.F.
[]—*Missionaries Daughters of Our Blessed Lady of the Light, Yucatan, Mexico*—M.H.M.L.
[1360]—*Missionary Franciscan Sisters of the Immaculate Conception* (Newton, MA)—M.F.I.C.
[2800]—*Missionary Sisters of the Most Sacred Heart of Jesus of Hilltrup*—M.S.C.
[]—*Order of Saint Ursula* (Cleveland)—O.S.U.
[]—*Order of St. Benedict*—O.S.B.
[3760]—*Order of St. Clare*—O.S.C.
[3465]—*Religious of the Sacred Heart of Mary* (Eastern North American Province)—R.S.H.M.
[]—*Salesian Sisters*—F.M.A.
[2970]—*School Sisters of Notre Dame* (St. Louis Prov. & Baltimore Prov.)—S.S.N.D.
[]—*Sisters of Charity of Cincinnati*—S.C.
[0590]—*Sisters of Charity of St. Elizabeth, Convent Station*—S.C.
[0430]—*Sisters of Charity of the Blessed Virgin Mary*—B.V.M.
[]—*Sisters of Christian Community*—S.C.C.
[2575]—*Sisters of Mercy of the Americas* (New Jersey Prov.)—R.S.M.
[2549]—*Sisters of Mercy, Co. Sligo, Ireland*—R.S.M.
[2990]—*Sisters of Notre Dame* (Chardon, OH)—S.N.D.
[3360]—*Sisters of Providence of St. Mary-of-the-Woods, IN*—S.P.
[1650]—*Sisters of St. Francis of Philadelphia*—O.S.F.
[3830-01]—*Sisters of St. Joseph of Boston*—C.S.J.
[3840]—*Sisters of St. Joseph of Carondelet*—C.S.J.
[]—*Sisters of St. Joseph of Chestnut Hill, Philadelphia*—S.S.J.
[1990]—*Sisters of the Holy Name of Jesus and Mary*—S.N.J.M.
[1490]—*Sisters of the Third Franciscan Order* (Syracuse, NY)—O.S.F.
[1710]—*Sisters of the Third Order of St. Francis* (Newton, MA)—O.S.F.
[]—*Sisters of the Third Order of St. Francis* (Allegeny, NY)—O.S.F.

NECROLOGY

† Brennan, George, (Retired)—Died Jan. 20, 2011

An asterisk (*) denotes an organization that has established tax-exempt status directly with the IRS and is not covered by the USCCB Group Ruling.

Diocese of Victoria in Texas

(Dioecesis Victoriensis in Texia)

Most Reverend

DAVID E. FELLHAUER, PH.D., J.C.D.

Bishop of Victoria; ordained May 29, 1965; appointed Second Bishop of Victoria in Texas April 7, 1990; consecrated and installed May 28, 1990. *Mailing Address: P.O. Box 4070, Victoria, TX 77903.*

Chancery Office: P.O. Box 4070, Victoria, TX 77903. Tel: 361-573-0828; Fax: 361-573-5725.

ESTABLISHED AND CREATED A DIOCESE, MAY 29, 1982.

Square Miles 9,609.

Comprises the Counties of Calhoun, DeWitt, Goliad, Jackson, Lavaca, Matagorda, Victoria, Wharton and Colorado; also Fayette County west of the Colorado River in the State of Texas.

Legal Title: Diocese of Victoria in Texas.
For legal titles of parishes and diocesan institutions, consult the Chancery Office.

STATISTICAL OVERVIEW

Personnel	
Bishop	1
Priests: Diocesan Active in Diocese	45
Priests: Diocesan Active Outside Diocese	1
Priests: Retired, Sick or Absent	8
Number of Diocesan Priests	54
Religious Priests in Diocese	5
Total Priests in Diocese	59
Extern Priests in Diocese	8
Ordinations:	
Transitional Deacons	1
Permanent Deacons in Diocese	35
Total Brothers	1
Total Sisters	79
Parishes	
Parishes	50
With Resident Pastor:	
Resident Diocesan Priests	37
Resident Religious Priests	2
Without Resident Pastor:	
Administered by Priests	11
Missions	17
Professional Ministry Personnel:	
Brothers	1
Sisters	15
Welfare	
Homes for the Aged	1
Total Assisted	59
Educational	
Diocesan Students in Other Seminaries	12
Total Seminarians	12
High Schools, Diocesan and Parish	2
Total Students	178
High Schools, Private	1
Total Students	316
Elementary Schools, Diocesan and Parish	12
Total Students	2,353
Elementary Schools, Private	1
Total Students	302
Catechesis/Religious Education:	
High School Students	2,059
Elementary Students	6,091
Total Students under Catholic Instruction	11,311
Teachers in the Diocese:	
Sisters	10
Lay Teachers	198
Vital Statistics	
Receptions into the Church:	
Infant Baptism Totals	1,109
Minor Baptism Totals	108
Adult Baptism Totals	70
Received into Full Communion	89
First Communions	1,126
Confirmations	882
Marriages:	
Catholic	240
Interfaith	106
Total Marriages	346
Deaths	835
Total Catholic Population	102,860
Total Population	277,995

Former Bishops—Most Rev. CHARLES V. GRAHMANN, D.D., ord. March 17, 1956; appt. Titular Bishop of Equilio and Auxiliary of San Antonio, June 30, 1981; cons. Aug. 29, 1981; appt. First Bishop of Victoria, April 14, 1982; installed May 29, 1982; appt. Coadjutor of Dallas, Dec. 18, 1989; succeeded to See, July 14, 1990; retired March 6, 2007.

Chancery Office—1505 E. Mesquite Ln., Victoria, 77901. Mailing Address: P.O. Box 4070, Victoria, 77903. Tel: 361-573-0828; Fax: 361-573-5725. Office Hours: Mon.-Fri. 8:30-4:30.

Vicar General—Rev. JOHN C. PETERS, V.F.

Chancellor—Rev. GARY W. JANAK, J.C.L., V.F., Mailing Address: P.O. Box 4070, Victoria, 77903. 1505 E. Mesquite Ln., Victoria, 77901. Tel: 361-573-0828, Ext. 14. Email: chancellor@victoriadiocese.org; St. Philip the Apostle Church, 304 W. Church St., El Campo, 77437-3317. Tel: 979-543-3770.

Diocesan Consultors—Rev. Msgr. MICHAEL HARROLD, V.F.; Revs. GARY W. JANAK, J.C.L., V.F., Chancellor; TIMOTHY KOSLER, V.F.; JOHN C. PETERS, V.F.; CHARLES O. DWOMOH, V.F.; MICHAEL LYONS, V.F.; KIRBY HLAVATY.

Vicars Forane—Victoria Deanery: Rev. Msgr. MICHAEL HARROLD, V.F., Our Lady of Victory Cathedral, 1309 E. Mesquite Ln., Victoria, 77901. Tel: 361-575-4741. Cuero Deanery: Rev. ROGER HAWES, V.F., Holy Cross Church, 1214 Zorn Rd., Yorktown, 78164. Tel: 361-564-2893; Fax: 361-564-9315. Email: holycross1214@sbcglobal.net. Edna Deanery: Rev. MICHAEL LYONS, V.F., Mailing Address: Assumption of the Blessed Virgin Mary Church, P.O. Box 369, Ganado, 77962-0369. Tel: 361-771-3425; Fax: 361-771-3526. Email: abvmchurch@ykc.com. Web: www.abvmganado.org. El Campo Deanery: Rev. GARY W. JANAK, J.C.L., V.F., Chancellor, St. Philip the Apostle Church, 304 W. Church St., El Campo, 77437. Tel: 979-543-3770; Fax: 979-578-8831. Email: apostle@stphilipapostle.org. Web: www.stphilipapostle.org; Mailing Address: P.O. Box 4070, Victoria, 77903. 1505 E. Mesquite Ln., Victoria, 77901. Tel: 361-573-0828, Ext. 14. Email: chancellor@victoriadiocese.org. Hallettsville Deanery: Rev. MATTHEW H. HUEHLEFELD, J.C.L., V.F., Mailing Address: Sacred Heart Church, P.O. Box H, Hallettsville, 77964. Tel: 361-798-5888; Fax: 361-798-4970. Email: rectory@shcatholichurch.org. Web: www.shcatholichchurch.org. Schulenburg Deanery: Rev. TIMOTHY KOSLER, V.F., St. Rose of Lima Church, 1010 Lyons Ave., Schulenburg, 78956. Tel: 979-743-3117; Fax: 979-743-4712. Email: srolc@cmaaccess.com.

Presbyteral Council—Revs. JOHN C. PETERS, V.F.; MICHAEL LYONS, V.F.; STANLEY DEBOE, O.SS.T.; Rev. Msgr. MICHAEL HARROLD, V.F.; Revs. TIMOTHY KOSLER, V.F.; CHARLES SONNIER; MICHAEL PETERING; RAPHAEL BAIDOO, O.SS.T., Immaculate Conception Church, 238 N. Commercial, Goliad, 77963. Tel: 361-645-3095; Fax: 361-645-3097. Email: catholic.church@att.net; GABRIEL D. ESPINOSA; CHARLES O. DWOMOH, V.F., St. John the Baptist Catholic Church, P.O. Box 121, Hungerford, 77448. Tel: 979-532-4747; KIRBY HLAVATY; GARY W. JANAK, J.C.L., V.F., Chancellor; ROBERT F. GUERRA; DONALD R. RUPPERT, V.F.; ROGER HAWES, V.F.; DAVID BERGER.

Diocesan Tribunal—Rev. MATTHEW H. HUEHLEFELD, J.C.L., V.F., 1505 E. Mesquite Ln., Victoria, 77901. Tel: 361-573-0760; Fax: 361-827-7176. Email: judicialvicar@victoriadiocese.org; Mailing Address: P.O. Box 4070, Victoria, 77903.

Judicial Vicar—Rev. MATTHEW H. HUEHLEFELD, J.C.L.

Judges—Rev. JOHN C. BILY; Rev. Msgr. MICHAEL HARROLD, V.F.; Revs. GARY W. JANAK, J.C.L., V.F., Chancellor; GREGORY E. KORENEK; CELESTINO SAY.

Promoter of Justice—Rev. GABRIEL MAISON, J.C.D.

Procurator Advocate—Revs. JOHNSON OWUSU-BOATENG; SAMUEL APPIASI; MICHAEL ROTHER.

Defenders of the Bond—Revs. DAN MORALES; TIMOTHY KOSLER, V.F.; MICHAEL LYONS, V.F.; CHARLES O. DWOMOH, V.F.

Notaries—Mrs. MINNIE BOCHAT; Mrs. IRENE MARTINEZ MARLER.

Priests' Personnel Board—Most Rev. DAVID EUGENE FELLHAUER; Rev. Msgr. MICHAEL HARROLD, V.F.; Revs. ROGER HAWES, V.F.; KIRBY HLAVATY; GARY W. JANAK, J.C.L., V.F., Chancellor; TIMOTHY KOSLER, V.F.; MICHAEL LYONS, V.F.; JOHN C. PETERS, V.F.

Building Board—Mr. CHARLES BLUNTZER; Mr. MICHAEL J. BROWN; Mr. JOHN GEHRKE; Mr. ED MARTINKA; Mr. JAMES MIORI; Mr. DONALD NAISER; Mr. HENRY SCHROEDER.

School Board—Mr. JOHN QUARY, Supt. Schools; Rev. GABRIEL BENTIL; Mrs. ROSANNE GALLIA; Mr. GREG HERMES; Mr. DAVID KAPAVIK; Rev. ROBERT E. KNIPPENBERG; Mrs. SHARON PARMA; Mrs. MARTHA SAWYERS; Mrs. YVONNE WAGNER.

Business Administration Office—Mr. MICHAEL J. BROWN, CFO; Mr. RENE GARCIA. Tel: 361-573-0828, Ext. 2220. Email: rgarcia@victoriadiocese.org; Mr. RYAN SPRINKLE. Tel: 361-573-0828, Ext. 2229. Email: rsprinkle@victoriadiocese.org; Mrs. JERI JOSEPH, Mailing Address: P.O. Box 4070, Victoria, 77903. Tel: 361-573-0828, Ext. 2219. Email: jjoseph@victoriadiocese.org.

Campaign For Human Development and Catholic Relief Services—Rev. DAN MORALES, Dir., St. Mary's Parish, 405 S. Main St., P.O. Box 2448, Victoria, 77902. Tel: 361-573-4328; Fax: 361-573-4308. Email: stmaryvic@suddenlinkmail.com. Web: www.stmvictoria.org.

Catholic Youth Ministry—Ms. WENDY EGGERT, Interim Dir. Youth Min., 1505 E. Mesquite Ln., P.O. Box 4070, Victoria, 77901. Tel: 361-573-0828, Ext. 2250. Email: weggert@victoriadiocese.org.

Catholic Outreach Prison Ministry—Rev. DAVID BERGER, 309 E. Church St., Cuero, 77954. Tel: 361-275-3554; Fax: 361-277-3924. Email: stmchurch@sbcglobal.net.

Council of Catholic Women (DCCW)—Rev. MICHAEL PETERING, Mod., St. Agnes Church, 506 N. Allen, Edna, 77957. Tel: 361-782-6171; Fax: 361-782-8827. Email: stagnesedna@sbcglobal.net; Mrs. JANICE OHRT, Chm., 2221 FM 237, Victoria,

77905. Tel: 361-575-2056.

Diocesan Cemeteries—GARY RANGNOW, Dir., P.O. Box 4070, Victoria, 77903. Tel: 361-573-0828; Fax: 361-573-5725.

Diocesan Finance Board—Mr. MICHAEL J. BROWN, Fin. Officer, Mailing Address: P.O. Box 4070, Victoria, 77903. Tel: 361-573-0828, Ext. 2218. Email: mbrown@victoriadiocese.org; Mrs. BEATRICE GONZALEZ; Mr. JOHN HALL; Deacon DENNIS KUTACH; Mr. HARDY MCCULLOUGH; Rev. DONALD R. RUPPERT, V.F.; Mr. ROMAN SHIMEK; Mr. JOHN STEVENSON; Mr. GLEN VILLAFRANCA; Mr. MARK WESTERMAN; Mr. JOHN ZACEK.

Diocesan Services Appeal—Mrs. JERI JOSEPH, Dir., 1505 E. Mesquite Ln., P.O. Box 4070, Victoria, 77901. Tel: 361-573-0828.

Spiritual Renewal Center—Mr. RON FRIEDEL, Admin., 718 Gussie Schmidt Rd., Victoria, 77905-4303. Tel: 361-572-0836, Ext. 3221; Fax: 361-572-0816. Email: renewalcenter@victoriadiocese.org; Ms. JULIA AMADOR, Asst. Mgr. & Exec. Cook. Tel: 361-572-0836, Ext. 3223. Email: jamador@victoriadiocese.org.

Ecumenical Commission—VACANT.

Presidio La Bahia— (located one mile South of Goliad). Mr. NEWTON WARZECHA, Dir., Mailing Address: P.O. Box 57, Goliad, 77963. Tel: 361-645-3752; Fax: 361-645-1706. Email: presidiolabahia@goliad.net. Web: www.presidiolabahia.org.

Liturgical Commission—Mrs. CYNTHIA GOERIG. Tel: 979-543-5706.

Office of Catholic Schools—Mr. JOHN QUARY, Supt. Tel: 361-573-0828, Ext. 2221. Email: jquary@victoriadiocese.org; Mrs. JANIE CARRALES, Administrative Asst., Mailing Address: P.O. Box 4070, Victoria, 77903. Tel: 361-573-0828, Ext. 2213. Email: jcarrales@victoriadiocese.org.

Permanent Diaconate Program—Rev. GABRIEL MAISON, J.C.D., Dir., P.O. Box 399, Moulton, 77975. Tel: 361-596-4674; Fax: 361-596-4826. Email: st_joe@sbcglobal.net.

Propagation of the Faith, Holy Childhood Association—Rev. GARY W. JANAK, J.C.L., V.F., Chancellor.

Mission Cooperative Plan—Rev. GARY W. JANAK, J.C.L., V.F., Chancellor, Mailing Address: Diocese of Victoria, Chancery Office, P.O. Box 4070, Victoria, 77903. 1505 E. Mesquite Ln., Victoria, 77901. Tel: 361-573-0828, Ext. 14.

Religious Education—Sr. DIGNA VELA, I.W.B.S., Dir., 1505 E. Mesquite Ln., P.O. Box 4070, Victoria, 77903. Tel: 361-573-0828, Ext. 2225. Email: dvela@victoriadiocese.org; Mrs. CHRISTELLA ALVAREZ, Assoc. Dir. Tel: 361-573-0828, Ext. 2227. Email: calvarea@victoriadiocese.org; Mrs. TANYA STARNES, Administrative Asst. Tel: 361-573-0828, Ext. 2224. Email: tstarnes@victoriadiocese.org; Mrs. MELISSA GUTIERREZ, Asst. Email: mgutierrez@victoriadiocese.org.

Respect Life-Pro Life—Rev. TOMMY CHEN, Sacred Heart Church, P.O. Box H, Hallettsville, 77964. Tel: 361-798-5888.

Scouting—Mr. DAVE KOUBA, District Chm. Eagle Court. Tel: 361-575-6693.

"The Catholic Lighthouse", Diocesan Newspaper—Mrs. CINDY BREWER. Tel: 361-573-0828, Ext. 2231. Email: cbrewer@victoriadiocese.org; Mrs. REGINA MATUS JANAK, Production & Advertising, 1505 E. Mesquite Ln., Victoria, 77903. Tel: 361-573-0828, Ext. 2230. Email: janakr@victoriadiocese.org; Mailing Address: P.O. Box 4070, Victoria, 77903.

Office of Youth and Child Protection—Mrs. MELISSA PERALES, Dir. Tel: 361-573-0828, Ext. 2249. Email: mperales@victoriadiocese.org; DORA HERNANDEZ, Administrative Asst., 1505 E. Mesquite Ln., Victoria, 77903. Tel: 361-573-0828, Ext. 2243. Email: dhernandez@victoriadiocese.org.

Vietnamese Apostolate—Rev. DOMINIC NGUYEN, C.SS.R., St. Anthony Church, P.O. Box 900, Palacios, 77465. Tel: 361-972-2446; Fax: 361-972-2606. Email: pasaop@yahoo.com.

Vocations Director—Rev. DAN MORALES; Deacon CHARLES J. GLYNN, Assoc. Dir.

Director of Seminarians—Rev. DAN MORALES, Mailing Address: St. Mary Church, P.O. Box 2448, Victoria, 77902. Tel: 361-573-4328; Fax: 361-573-4308. Email: stmaryvic@suddenlinkmail.com.

Victim Assistance Coordinators—Rev. GARY W. JANAK, J.C.L., V.F., Chancellor, St. Philip the Apostle Catholic Church, 304 W. Church St., El Campo, 77437. Tel: 979-543-3770; Fax: 979-578-8831. Email: apostle@stphilipapostle.org. Web: www.stphilipapostle.org; Mailing Address: P.O. Box 4070, Victoria, 77903. 1505 E. Mesquite Ln., Victoria, 77901. Tel: 361-573-0828, Ext. 14. Email: chancellor@victoriadiocese.org; Sr. EMILIE EILERS, I.W.B.S., Incarnate Word and Blessed Sacrament Convent, 1101 N.E. Water, Victoria, 77901. Tel: 361-575-7111.

CLERGY, PARISHES, MISSIONS AND PAROCHIAL SCHOOLS

CITY OF VICTORIA

(VICTORIA COUNTY)

1—OUR LADY OF VICTORY CATHEDRAL (1957) Rev. Msgr. Michael Harrold; Revs. Michael Rother, Parochial Vicar; Charles E. Otsiwah, Parochial Vicar; Deacon Lawrence Rossow.
Mailing Address: 1309 E. Mesquite Ln., 77901. Tel: 361-575-4741; Fax: 361-573-5555. Web: www.olvcathedral.org.
School—(Grades PreK-8) Tel: 361-575-5391; 361-578-5454 (Convent); Fax: 361-575-3473. Web: ourladyvictory.org. Email: office@ourladyvictory.org. Sr. Laura Toman, I.W.B.S., Prin.; Norma Smolik, Librarian. Sisters 2; Lay Teachers 30; Students 491.
Catechesis/Religious Program—Tel: 361-575-8132. Betty Mitchell, D.R.E. Students 696.

2—HOLY FAMILY OF JOSEPH, MARY & JESUS (1981) [JC] Revs. Robert E. Knippenberg; George Henninger; Deacon Steve Borowicz.
Office: 704 Mallette Dr., 77904. Tel: 361-573-5304; Fax: 361-573-6053. Web: www.hfccvic.org. Email: hfcc@suddenlinkmail.com.
Catechesis/Religious Program—Tel: 361-573-5398; Fax: 361-573-6053. Students 472.

3—ST. MARY'S, [JC] Revs. Dan Morales; Anthony Boateng-Mensah, Parochial Vicar; Deacon Jim Koenig.
Mailing Address: 402 S. Main, P.O. Box 2448, 77902. Tel: 361-573-4328; Fax: 361-573-4308.
Catechesis/Religious Program—Mrs. Diana Starnes, D.R.E. Students 90.

4—OUR LADY OF LOURDES (1875) Revs. P. Celestino Say; John Kollannur, Parochial Vicar.
Res.: 105 N. William, 77901. Tel: 361-575-3813.
Catechesis/Religious Program—Mrs. Laurie Bautista, D.R.E. Students 80.

5—OUR LADY OF SORROWS (1913) [JC] Revs. Stanley DeBoe, O.SS.T.; William J. Moorman, O.SS.T.; Gabriel Justus Mensah; Deacons Edward Molina; Jesus Perez.
Mailing Address: 208 W. River St., P.O. Box 2548, 77901. Tel: 361-575-2293; Fax: 361-582-0405.
Catechesis/Religious Program—Tel: 361-573-2681. Sr. Susana Islas, M.C., D.R.E. Students 830.
Convent—Missionary Catechists of the Sacred Hearts of Jesus and Mary (Violetas), 209 W. Murray St., 77901. Tel: 361-575-7654. Sisters 4.
Mission—Holy Trinity 2901 Pleasant Green Dr., Victoria Co. 77901.

OUTSIDE THE CITY OF VICTORIA

AMMANNSVILLE, FAYETTE CO., ST. JOHN THE BAPTIST, [CEM] Rev. Timothy Kosler.
Mailing Address: 7745 Mensik Rd., Schulenburg, 78956.
Mission—St. Wenceslaus [CEM] Holman, Fayette Co.

BAY CITY, MATAGORDA CO.

1—HOLY CROSS (1909) [CEM 2] [JC] Rev. Gregory E. Korenek; Deacons Guadalupe Rodriguez; Larry Koether.
Mailing Address: 2001 Katy Ave., 77414. Web: www.holycrossbaycity.org. In Res., Rev. Casimir Jarzombek (Retired).
School—(Grades K-6) Tel: 979-245-5632; Fax: 979-245-6120. Mrs. Stephanie Kucera, Prin.; Mrs. Mita Bossley, Librarian. Lay Teachers 9; Students 113; Aides 2.
Catechesis/Religious Program—Mrs. Terri Busha, D.R.E. Students 153.
Mission—Sacred Heart Wadsworth, Matagorda Co.

2—OUR LADY OF GUADALUPE Rev. Gerard Cernoch; Deacons Luan Van Tran; Joe Ramos; Billy Key.
Mailing Address: 1412 12th St., 77414. Tel: 979-245-2010; 979-245-0774 (CCD Office); Fax: 979-245-1038. Email: olg2003@sbcglobal.net.
Catechesis/Religious Program—Mrs. Esther Martinez, D.R.E. Students 488.

BLESSING, MATAGORDA CO., ST. PETER'S (1930) [CEM] [JC] Rev. Peter Yeboah-Amanfo.
Mailing Address: Box 395, 77419.
120 Live Oak, 77419. Tel: 361-588-1156; Fax: 361-588-1421. Email: stpeterblessing@tisd.net.
Catechesis/Religious Program—Mrs. Leticia Aparicio, D.R.E.; Mrs. Annette Havel, D.R.E. Students 100.
Mission—St. Robert Markham, Matagorda Co.

BLOOMINGTON, VICTORIA CO., ST. PATRICK'S (1959) Rev. Samuel Appiasi; Deacon Fred Soto.
Res. & Church: 13316 State Hwy. 185, P.O. Box 2122, 77951. Tel: 361-897-1155; Fax: 361-897-1064. Email: saintpatricks@tisd.net. Web: saintpatrickschurch.net.
Catechesis/Religious Program—Students 153.

CISTERN, FAYETTE CO., SS. CYRIL AND METHODIUS, [CEM 2] [JC 2] Rev. Joseph Hybner.
Mailing Address: P.O. Box 186, Flatonia, 78941. Tel: 361-865-3568.
Church: 113 Manchester St., Flatonia, 78941.

COLUMBUS, COLORADO CO., ST. ANTHONY'S (1930) [CEM] Rev. Augustine N. Asante; Deacons Bennie Holesovsky; Charlie Novosad.
P.O. Box 669, 78934. Tel: 979-732-2562; Fax: 979-732-8636.
School—(Grades PreK-8), 635 Bonham, 78934. Tel: 979-732-5505; Fax: 979-732-9758. Web: stanthonyschool.homestead.com. John O'Leary, Prin.; Mrs. Peggy Castillo, Librarian. Lay Teachers 13; Students 145.
Catechesis/Religious Program—Sr. Joyce Jilek, D.R.E. Students 99.

CUERO, DEWITT CO.

1—ST. MICHAEL (1875) Revs. David Berger; Daniel A. Danso, Parochial Vicar; Deacons Anthony B. Warzecha; Leo Sharron.
309 E. Church St., 77954-2906. Tel: 361-275-3554; Fax: 361-277-3924.
School—(Grades PreK-6), 208 N. McLeod, 77954. Tel: 361-277-3854; Fax: 361-275-3618. Web: www.stmichaels-cuero.org. Mrs. Judy Roeder, Prin. Lay Teachers 7; Students 72.
Catechesis/Religious Program—Tel: 361-275-0955; Fax: 361-277-3924. Students 142.

2—OUR LADY OF GUADALUPE (1923) Revs. David Berger; Daniel A. Danso, Parochial Vicar.
Catechesis/Religious Program—Tel: 361-275-0955; Fax: 361-277-3924. Students 142.

EAGLE LAKE, COLORADO CO., PARISH OF THE NATIVITY (1995) Rev. Robert F. Guerra.
Office: 545 S. Austin Rd., P.O. Box 307, 77434-0307. Tel: 979-234-2842; Fax: 979-234-5828.
Catechesis/Religious Program—Students 145.

EAST BERNARD, WHARTON CO., HOLY CROSS (1901) [CEM] Rev. Donald R. Ruppert.
Mailing Address: 839 Church St., P.O. Box 1325, 77435-1325. Tel: 979-335-7551; Fax: 979-335-7038. Email: holycross@earth-cornm.com. Web: www.eastbernardholycross.com.
Catechesis/Religious Program—Email: hcreled@elc.net. Students 269.
Religious Education & Cemetery Office—Tel: 979-335-4071. Email: hccemetery@elc.net.

EDNA, JACKSON CO., ST. AGNES (1880) Rev. Michael Petering.
Res.: 506 N. Allen, 77957. Tel: 361-782-3588; Fax: 361-782-8827. Email: stagnesedna@sbcglobal.net.
Catechesis/Religious Program—Mrs. Doris Andel, D.R.E. (Elementary); Mrs. Patricia Kromka, D.R.E. (High School). Students 248.

EL CAMPO, WHARTON CO.

1—ST. PHILIP THE APOSTLE, [CEM] Revs. Gary W. Janak; Albert Yankey, Parochial Vicar; Deacons Jarrel Nohavitza; Jerome Grahmann; Lawrence Hoelscher.
304 W. Church St., 77437. Tel: 979-543-3770; Fax: 979-578-8831. Email: apostle@stphilipapostle.org.
School—(Grades PreK-8) Tel: 979-543-2901; Fax: 979-578-8835. Mrs. Gwen Edwards, Prin. Lay Teachers 23; Students 270.
Catechesis/Religious Program—Students 249.

2—ST. ROBERT BELLARMINE (1928) Rev. Lawrence Matula; Deacon Margarito Cervantez Jr.
512 Tegner St., 77437. Tel: 979-543-4298; Fax: 979-541-5399. Email: sanroberto@sbcglobal.net.
Catechesis/Religious Program—Mrs. Janie Delgado, D.R.E. Students 450.

FLATONIA, FAYETTE CO., SACRED HEART (1912) [CEM] [JC] Rev. Joseph Hybner.
Catechesis/Religious Program—Students 115.

FRELSBURG, COLORADO CO., SS. PETER AND PAUL (1836) [CEM] Rev. Wayne N. Flagg; Deacons Charles J. Glynn; Douglas B. Tromblee.
Res.: 1031 Church Ln., New Ulm, 78950. Tel: 979-732-3430; Fax: 979-732-9204.
Catechesis/Religious Program—Mrs. Joyce Waddell, D.R.E. Students 24.

GANADO, JACKSON CO., ASSUMPTION OF THE B.V.M. (1914) [CEM] Rev. Michael Lyons.
Mailing Address: P.O. Box 369, 77962. Tel: 361-771-3425; Fax: 361-771-3526. Email: abvmchurch@ykc.com. Web: www.abvmganado.org.
Res.: 109 S. Sixth St., 77962. Tel: 361-771-3325.
Catechesis/Religious Program—Students 104.

GOLIAD, GOLIAD CO., IMMACULATE CONCEPTION, [CEM 2] Rev. Raphael Baidoo, O.SS.T.
P.O. Box 49, 77963. Tel: 361-645-3095; Fax: 361-645-3097. Email: catholic.church@att.net.
Church: 238 N. Commercial St., 77963. Tel: 361-645-3095.
Shrine—Our Lady of Loreto (Old Franciscan Mission)

HALLETTSVILLE, LAVACA CO.

1—ST. MARY (1840) [CEM 4] Rev. John C. Peters. Church: 1648 FM 340, P.O. Drawer H, 77964. Tel: 361-798-5888; Fax: 361-798-4970.
Catechesis/Religious Program—Cindy Svetlik, D.R.E. Students 63.

2—SACRED HEART (1882) [CEM] Revs. John C. Peters; Tommy Chen, Parochial Vicar; Deacons Joey Targac; W.S. (Sonny) Rogers, (Retired); Linard Harper.
Mailing Address: 400 E. Fifth St., P.O. Box H, 77964. Tel: 361-798-5888; Fax: 361-798-4970. Web: www.shcatholicchurch.org.
School—(Grades PreK-8) Tel: 361-798-4251; Fax: 361-798-4970. Mr. David Smolik, Prin. (Elementary & High School). Sisters 2; Lay Teachers 11; Students 215.
High School—313 S. Texana, 77964. Mr. David Smolik, Prin. Lay Teachers 18; Students 99.
Catechesis/Religious Program—Tel: 361-798-3124. Angela McConnell, D.R.E. Students 220.

HIGH HILL, FAYETTE CO., NATIVITY OF THE BLESSED VIRGIN MARY, [CEM] Rev. Timothy Kosler.
Mailing Address: 2833 FM 2672, Schulenburg, 78956-5603. Tel: 979-561-8455.
1010 Lyons Ave., Box 310, Schulenburg, 78956. Tel: 979-743-3117.

HILLJE, WHARTON CO., ST. ANDREW (1909) [CEM] Rev. Clement Quainoo; Deacon Edward Wendel.
Mailing Address: 270 St. Andrew St., El Campo, 77437. Tel: 979-648-2864; Fax: 979-648-2024. Email: standrew@ykc.com.
Catechesis/Religious Program—Ed Juroske, D.R.E. Students 105.
Mission—St. Procopius (1944) [CEM] Louise, Wharton Co.

HOSTYN, FAYETTE CO., HOLY ROSARY (1856) [CEM] Rev. Daniel P. Kahlich; Deacon John McCourt.
Catechesis/Religious Program—Mrs. Gina Kozelsky, C.R.E. Students 40.

HUNGERFORD, WHARTON CO., ST. JOHN THE BAPTIST (1917) [CEM] Rev. Charles O. Dwomoh.
Mailing Address: 101 Church St., P.O. Box 121, 77448. Tel: 979-532-4747; Fax: 979-532-4748.
Catechesis/Religious Program—Mrs. Janet Bubela, D.R.E. Students 70.

INEZ, VICTORIA CO., ST. JOSEPH'S (1873) [CEM] [JC 5] Rev. Gabriel Bentil, Parochial Admin.
Mailing Address: 403 Church St., P.O. Box 337, 77968.
Church: 33 Church St., P.O. Box 337, 77968. Tel: 361-782-3181; Fax: 361-781-0459. Email: stjosephchurch@tisd.net.
Catechesis/Religious Program—Ms. Kendall Pfuhl, D.R.E. Students 132.

KOERTH, LAVACA CO., ST. JOHN THE BAPTIST, [CEM] [JC] Rev. Charles Sonnier.
Mailing Address: P.O. Box 201, Sweet Home, 77987. Tel: 361-741-3206; Fax: 361-741-3206.

MENTZ, COLORADO CO., ST. ROCH (1850) [CEM] Rev. Wayne N. Flagg; Deacons Douglas B. Tromblee; Chuck Glenn.
Mailing Address: 1600 Frelsburg Rd., Alleyton, 78935. Tel: 979-732-3460; Fax: 979-733-0908.
Catechesis/Religious Program—Students 24.

MEYERSVILLE, DEWITT CO., SS. PETER & PAUL (1858) [CEM] Rev. David Berger, Parochial Admin.; Mrs. Donna Flores, Sec.
Mailing Address: 11220 FM 237, 77974. Tel: 361-275-3868; Fax: 361-277-8972. Email: stspp@gvec.net.
Catechesis/Religious Program—Mrs. Janice Ohrt, D.R.E. Students 36.
Mission—St. Aloysius Westhoff, DeWitt Co.

MOULTON, LAVACA CO., ST. JOSEPH'S (1888) [CEM] Rev. Gabriel Maison; Deacons Milburn Kram; Kenneth Fishbeck.
Mailing Address: P.O. Box 399, 77975. Tel: 361-596-4674; Fax: 361-596-4826.
601 N. Pecan St., 77975.
Catechesis/Religious Program—Tel: 361-596-7559. Students 101.

NADA, COLORADO CO., NATIVITY OF THE BLESSED VIRGIN MARY (1897) [CEM] Rev. Joseph L. Vrana.
Res. & Church: 1261 Old Nada Rd., P.O. Box 97, 77460. Tel: 979-758-3218; Fax: 979-758-3267.
Catechesis/Religious Program—Students 65.

NEW TAITON, WHARTON CO., ST. JOHN NEPOMUCENE (1912) [CEM] Rev. Gabriel Oduro Tawiah; Deacon Patrick Kubala.
Mailing Address: 1843 CR 469, El Campo, 77437. Tel: 979-543-6985; Fax: 979-543-3434. Email: stjohns@wirehand.net.
Catechesis/Religious Program—Tel: 979-543-7397. Students 62.

PALACIOS, MATAGORDA CO., ST. ANTHONY'S (1912, Mission); (1954, Parish) Revs. Bryan Heyer; Dominic Trung Nguyen, C.Ss.R., Parochial Vicar; Deacon Michael Vieira.
Mailing Address: 1004 Magnusson, Box 900, 77465. Tel: 361-972-2446; Fax: 361-972-2606. Email: pasaop@yahoo.com.
Catechesis/Religious Program—Mrs. Mary Kay Beard, D.R.E.; Mrs. Nora Aparicio, D.R.E. Students 390.
Vietnamese Apostolate—100 Vietnam, 77465. Tel: 361-972-2685. Rev. Dominic Trung Nguyen, C.Ss.R., Parochial Vicar.

PLUM, FAYETTE CO., SS. PETER AND PAUL (1897) [CEM 2] Rev. Daniel P. Kahlich; Deacon John McCourt.
Mailing Address: 936 FM 2436, La Grange, 78945. Tel: 979-247-4441; Fax: 979-247-5008. Email: hostynch@cvtv.net.
Catechesis/Religious Program—Mrs. Gina Kozelsky, C.R.E. Students 26.

PORT LAVACA, CALHOUN CO., OUR LADY OF THE GULF (1865) Revs. Ty J. Bazar; Peter Dery, Parochial Vicar; Deacon Alonzo Farias Calzada.
415 W. Austin St., P.O. Box 87, 77979. Tel: 361-552-6140; Fax: 361-552-4300. Email: olgulf@olgulf.org. Web: www.olgulf.org.
Preschool/Day Care—412 W. Austin St., P.O. Box 87, 77979. Tel: 361-552-6140, Ext. 503. Mrs. Rosie Padron, Dir. Lay Teachers 8; Students 45.
School—(Grades PreK-8) Tel: 361-552-6140, Ext. 202; Fax: 361-552-7485. Theresa Dent, Prin. Sisters 2; Lay Teachers 15; Students 90.
Catechesis/Religious Program—Tel: 361-552-6140, Ext. 100. Mrs. Linda Beard, D.R.E. Students 410.
Mission—St. Ann Point Comfort, Calhoun Co. Tel: 361-987-2855.
Mission—St. Joseph Port O'Connor, Calhoun Co. Tel: 361-983-4467.
Mission—St. Patrick Seadrift, Calhoun Co. Tel: 361-785-3405.

PRAHA, FAYETTE CO., ST. MARY'S (1855) [CEM] Rev. Gabriel Maison, Admin.
Res.: 821 FM 1295, Flatonia, 78941. Tel: 361-865-3560.
Catechesis/Religious Program—Students 2.

ST. JOHN, FAYETTE CO., ST. JOHN THE BAPTIST (1888) [CEM] Revs. John C. Peters; Tommy Chen.
Mailing Address: 7026 FM 957, P.O. Box H, Hallettsville, 77964. Tel: 361-798-5888; Fax: 361-798-4970. Email: rectory@shcatholicchurch.org.
Catechesis/Religious Program—Mrs. Dana Daughtry, D.R.E. Students 35.
Mission—Ascension of Our Lord (1913) [CEM] 11134 FM 957 (Moravia), P.O. Box H, Hallettsville, Lavaca Co. 77964.

SCHULENBURG, FAYETTE CO., ST. ROSE OF LIMA (1889) [CEM] Revs. Timothy Kosler; Edward J. Winkler, Parochial Vicar.
Mailing Address: 1010 Lyons Ave., Box 310, 78956. Tel: 979-743-3117; Fax: 979-743-4712. Email: srolc@cmaaccess.com.
School—(Grades PreK-8), 405 Black, 78956. Tel: 979-743-3080; Fax: 979-743-4228. Mrs. Rosanne Gallia, Prin. Lay Teachers 16; Students 190.
Catechesis/Religious Program—Nicole Michalke, (Grades 1-8); Mrs. Lynne Machac, (Grades 9-11). Tel: 979-561-6702. Students 210.

SHINER, LAVACA CO., SS. CYRIL AND METHODIUS, [CEM] Rev. Kirby Hlavaty; Deacons Paul Patek; Joseph Machacek.
Mailing Address: 306 S. Ave. F, 77984. Tel: 361-594-3836; Fax: 361-594-2850. Email: rectory@sscmshiner.org; frkirby@sscmshiner.org. Web: www.sscmshiner.org.
School—St. Ludmila Elementary School, (Grades PreK-8) Tel: 361-594-3843; Fax: 361-594-8599. Email: nyackel@@shinercatholicschool.org. Web: www.shinercatholicschool.org. Mrs. Neely Yackel, Prin. Sisters 1; Lay Teachers 10; Students 199.
High School—St. Paul High School, Tel: 361-594-2313; Fax: 361-594-8564. Sisters 1; Lay Teachers 7; Students 77.
Catechesis/Religious Program—Tel: 361-594-3234. Email: spatek@sscmshiner.org. Sharon Patek, Youth Min. Students 214.

SWEET HOME, LAVACA CO., QUEEN OF PEACE, [CEM] [JC] Rev. Charles Sonnier.
Mailing Address: 7372 FM 531, P.O. Box 201, 77987. Tel: 361-741-3206; Fax: 361-741-3206.
Catechesis/Religious Program—Students 127.

VANDERBILT, JACKSON CO., ST. JOHN BOSCO Rev. Johnson Owusu-Boateng.
Office: 232 Main St., P.O. Box 337, 77991-0337. Tel: 361-284-3361.
Res.: 121 Garcitas St., P.O. Box 337, 77991. Fax: 361-284-3391.
Catechesis/Religious Program—Mrs. Debbie Kuchler, D.R.E. Students 73.
Mission—St. Theresa [CEM] 4612 CR 325, La Salle, Jackson Co. 77969.

WEIMAR, COLORADO CO., ST. MICHAEL (1883) [CEM] Rev. John C. Bily.
Res. & Church: 410 N. Center, Box 36, 78962. Tel: 979-725-6714; Fax: 979-725-8146.
School—(Grades PreK-8) Tel: 979-725-8461; Fax: 979-725-8344. Ms. Kimberly Patek, Prin. Lay Teachers 13; Students 143.
Catechesis/Religious Program—Students 156.
Mission—SS. Cyril and Methodius Dubina, Fayette Co.

WHARTON, WHARTON CO.

1—HOLY FAMILY, [JC] Revs. Dominic Antwi-Boasiako, A.B.; Varghese Kunnathu, M.C.B.S., Parochial Vicar; Deacon Alvin Matthys.
Res.: 2011 Briar Ln., 77488. Tel: 979-532-3593.
Catechesis/Religious Program—Tel: 979-532-3747. Students 298.
Mission—St. Joseph Boling, Wharton Co.

2—OUR LADY OF MT. CARMEL (1948) [JC] Rev. Gabriel D. Espinosa; Deacon David Valdez.
Mailing Address: 506 S. East Ave., 77488. Tel: 979-532-3492; Fax: 979-532-2321. Email: olmc1948@sbcglobal.net.
Catechesis/Religious Program—Students 305.

YOAKUM, LAVACA CO., ST. JOSEPH (1869) [CEM] Rev. Matthew H. Huehlefeld; Deacon Dennis Kutach.
Mailing Address: 210 Schrimscher St., Box 734, 77995. Tel: 361-293-3518; 361-293-7572; Fax: 361-293-5355. Email: pastor@stjcatholicchurch.com. Web: www.stjcatholicchurch.com.
School—(Grades PreK-8) Tel: 361-293-9000; Fax: 361-293-3004. Web: www.stjcatholicschool.com. Mrs. Susan Kelley, Prin. Lay Teachers 19; Students 117.
Catechesis/Religious Program—Students 275.
Mission—St. Ann [CEM] Hochheim, DeWitt Co.

YORKTOWN, DEWITT CO., HOLY CROSS (1866) [CEM 2] Rev. Roger Hawes.
Mailing Address: 1214 Zorn Rd., 78164-1907. Tel: 361-564-2893; Fax: 361-564-9315. Email: holycross1214@sbcglobal.net; frroger@sbcglobal.net.
Catechesis/Religious Program—Students 84.
Mission—San Luis, DeWitt Co.
Mission—St. Ann's Nordheim, DeWitt Co.

On Special or Other Diocesan Assignment:
Rev.—
Moorman, William J., O.SS.T., Hospital Chap., P.O. Box 2548, 77901. Tel: 361-575-2293; Fax: 361-582-0405

On Duty Outside the Diocese:
Rev.—
Mensah, Gabriel Justus, Military Chap., U.S. Navy

Retired:
Rev. Msgrs.—
Anders, Arnold
Hermes, Eustace
McLaughlin, Thomas C.
O'Shaughnessy, Michael A.
Petru, Stanley J.
Revs.—
Higgins, Peter
Jarzombek, Casimir
Lentz, Frank
Rachunek, Henry C.

Permanent Deacons:
Borowicz, Stephen James Michael
Calzada, Alonzo Farias
Cervantez, Margarito Candelario, Jr.
Fishbeck, Kenneth
Glynn, Charles J.
Grahmann, Jerome J.
Harper, Linard
Hoelscher, Lawrence
Holesovsky, Bennie
Key, Billy
Koenig, James Nicholas
Koether, Larry
Kram, Milburn
Kubala, Patrick
Kutach, Dennis
Machacek, Joseph
Matthys, Alvin
McCourt, John
Molina, Edwardo Pina
Nohavitza, Jarrel Joseph
Novosad, Charlie
Patek, Paul, Sr.
Perez, Jesus Castillo
Ramos, Joseph
Rodriguez, Guadalupe
Rogers, Walter Smith, Jr.
Rossow, Lawrence
Ruiz, Robert
Ryan, Kenneth
Sharron, Leo
Soto, Fred
Targac, Joseph
Tran, Luan Van
Tromblee, Douglas B.
Valdez, David
Vieira, Michael
Warzecha, Anthony
Wendel, Edward

INSTITUTIONS LOCATED IN THE DIOCESE

[A] HIGH SCHOOLS, PRIVATE

VICTORIA. *St. Joseph High School*, 110 E. Red River, 77901. Tel: 361-573-2446; Fax: 361-573-4221. Email: bmcardle@stjvictoria.com. Web: www.stjvictoria.com. Mr. William H. McArdle Jr., Pres. & Prin.; Mrs. Debra Rigby Studer, Librarian. Sisters 1; Lay Teachers 26; Students 316.

[B] ELEMENTARY SCHOOLS, PRIVATE

VICTORIA. *Nazareth Academy* (1867) (Grades PreK-8), 206 W. Convent, 77901. Tel: 361-573-6651; Fax: 361-573-1829. Email: skloesel@nazarethacademy.org. Web: www.nazarethacademy.org. Mr. Scott Kloesel, Prin.; Sr. Liliane Janda, I.W.B.S., Librarian; Mrs. M. Bernarda Bludau, Asst. Prin. Attended from St. Mary's, Our Lady of Lourdes, Our Lady of Victory, Holy Family and Our Lady of Sorrows' Churches. Sisters of the Incarnate Word and Blessed Sacrament 7; Lay Teachers 20; Students 302.

[C] PERSONAL PRELATURES

SCHULENBURG. *Opus Dei, Featherock Conference Center*, 934 Holub Rd., 78956-5324. Tel: 979-743-4642. Rev. Michael Manz.

[D] CONVENTS AND RESIDENCES FOR SISTERS

VICTORIA. *Incarnate Word Convent*, 1101 N.E. Water St., 77901-9233. Tel: 361-575-2266; Fax: 361-575-2165. Web: www.iwbsvictoria.org. Sisters Evelyn Korenek, I.W.B.S., Gen. Supr.; Geraldine Pavlik, Local Supr. Sisters 55.

Missionary Catechists of the Sacred Hearts of Jesus and Mary, 203 E. Sabine St., 77901. Tel: 361-570-3332; Fax: 361-570-3377. Email: miriamp@suddenlink.net. Sr. Miriam Perez, M.C.S.H., Prov. Supr. Sisters 16.

PORT LAVACA. *Vietnamese Community, Our Lady of the Gulf Convent*, 415 W. Austin St., 77979. Tel: 361-552-6140. Sr. Francesca Bui, O.P., Supr.

[E] MISCELLANEOUS

VICTORIA. *Endowment Fund for the Catholic Diocese of Victoria in Texas*, P.O. Box 4070, 77903-4070. Tel: 361-573-0828; Fax: 361-573-5725. Email: mbrown@victoriadiocese.org. Web: www.victoriadiocese.org. Mr. Michael J. Brown, CFO.

Jeanne Chezard De Matel Fund, 1101 N.E. Water St., 77901-9233. Tel: 361-575-2266; Fax: 361-575-2165. Email: srevelynk@yahoo.com. Web: www.iwbsvictoria.org.

Sisters of the Incarnate Word and Blessed Sacrament of Victoria, Texas, Medical and Retirement Trust, 1101 N.E. Water St., 77901-9233. Tel: 361-572-9321; Fax: 361-575-2165. Email: iwbsbusofc@yahoo.com.

Sisters of the Incarnate Word and Blessed Sacrament, Victoria, Texas, Inc., 1101 N.E. Water St., 77901-9233. Tel: 361-575-2266; Fax: 361-575-2165. Email: srevelynk@yahoo.com. Web: www.iwbsvictoria.org. Sr. Evelyn Korenek, I.W.B.S., Gen Supr. & Mailing Contact. Perpetually Professed 79; Affiliate 1; Annually Professed 1; Novices 1; Postulants 1.

RELIGIOUS INSTITUTES OF WOMEN REPRESENTED IN THE DIOCESE

For further details refer to the corresponding bracketed number in the Religious Institutes of Men or Women section.

[2200]—*Congregation of the Incarnate Word and Blessed Sacrament*—I.W.B.S.

[2700]—*Missionary Catechists of the Sacred Hearts of Jesus and Mary*—M.C.SS.CC.

[0460]—*Sisters of Charity of Incarnate Word*—C.C.V.I.

[1010]—*Sisters of the Divine Providence of San Antonio, Texas*—C.D.P.

[]—*Sisters of the Incarnate Word and Blessed Sacrament of Victoria, Texas*

[]—*Vietnamese Dominican Sisters*—O.P.

NECROLOGY

(No Deaths)

An asterisk (*) denotes an organization that has established tax-exempt status directly with the IRS and is not covered by the USCCB Group Ruling.

Archdiocese of Washington

(Archidioecesis Washingtonensis)

His Eminence

THEODORE CARDINAL McCARRICK, PH.D., D.D.

Retired Archbishop of Washington; ordained May 31, 1958; appointed Auxiliary Bishop of New York and Titular Bishop of Rusibisir May 24, 1977; Episcopal ordination June 29, 1977; appointed First Bishop of Metuchen November 19, 1981; installed January 31, 1982; appointed Archbishop of Newark May 30, 1986; installed July 25, 1986; appointed Archbishop of Washington November 21, 2000; installed January 3, 2001; created Cardinal priest of Saints Nereus and Achilleus February 21, 2001; retired May 16, 2006. *Mailing Address: P.O. Box 29260, Washington, DC 20017-0260.*

Most Reverend

LEONARD J. OLIVIER, S.V.D., D.D.

Retired Auxiliary Bishop of Washington; ordained June 29, 1951; appointed Auxiliary Bishop of Washington and Titular Bishop of Legia November 10, 1988; Episcopal ordination December 20, 1988; retired May 18, 2004. *Res.: 619 Tenth St., N.W., Washington, DC 20001-4587.*

Most Reverend

FRANCISCO GONZALEZ, S.F., D.D., V.G.

Auxiliary Bishop of Washington; ordained May 1, 1964; appointed Auxiliary Bishop of Washington and Titular Bishop of Lamfua December 28, 2001; Episcopal ordination February 11, 2002. *Office: 5001 Eastern Ave., Hyattsville, MD 20782-3447. Mailing Address: P.O. Box 29260, Washington, DC 20017.*

His Eminence

DONALD CARDINAL WUERL, S.T.D.

Archbishop of Washington; ordained December 17, 1966; appointed Titular Bishop of Rosemarkie and Auxiliary Bishop of Seattle December 3, 1985; consecrated January 6, 1986; appointed and canonically installed Bishop of Pittsburgh February 12, 1988; liturgically installed March 25, 1988; appointed Archbishop of Washington May 16, 2006; installed June 22, 2006; created Cardinal priest of Saint Peter in Chains November 20, 2010. *Office: Archdiocesan Pastoral Center, 5001 Eastern Ave., Hyattsville, MD 20782-3447.* Tel: 301-853-4500; Fax: 301-853-5359. *Mailing Address: P.O. Box 29260, Washington, DC 20017-0260.*

Archdiocesan Pastoral Center: 5001 Eastern Ave., Hyattsville, MD 20782. Mailing Address: P.O. Box 29260, Washington, DC 20017. Tel: 301-853-4500; Fax: 301-853-5346.

Email: chancery@adw.org

Most Reverend

MARTIN D. HOLLEY, D.D., V.G.

Auxiliary Bishop of Washington; ordained priest May 8, 1987; appointed Auxiliary Bishop of Washington and Titular Bishop of Rusibisir May 18, 2004; Episcopal ordination July 2, 2004. *Office: 5001 Eastern Ave., Hyattsville, MD 20782-3447. Mailing Address: P.O. Box 29260, Washington, DC 20017.*

Most Reverend

BARRY C. KNESTOUT, D.D., V.G.

Auxiliary Bishop of Washington; ordained June 24, 1989; appointed Auxiliary Bishop of Washington and Titular Bishop of Leavenworth November 18, 2008; Episcopal ordination December 29, 2008. *Office: 5001 Eastern Ave., Hyattsville, MD 20782-3447. Mailing Address: P.O. Box 29260, Washington, DC 20017.*

Square Miles 2,104.

Established Archdiocese July 22, 1939; Separated from Baltimore November 15, 1947; Became a Metropolitan See October 12, 1965.

Comprises the District of Columbia and Montgomery, Prince George's, St. Mary's, Calvert and Charles Counties in Maryland.

The Province of Washington has as a Suffragan, the Diocese of St. Thomas in the Virgin Islands.

For legal titles of parishes and archdiocesan institutions, consult the Chancery Office.

STATISTICAL OVERVIEW

Personnel	
Cardinals	1
Retired Cardinals	2
Auxiliary Bishops	3
Retired Bishops	1
Abbots	1
Retired Abbots	1
Priests: Diocesan Active in Diocese	196
Priests: Diocesan Active Outside Diocese	7
Priests: Diocesan in Foreign Missions	3
Priests: Retired, Sick or Absent	84
Number of Diocesan Priests	290
Religious Priests in Diocese	373
Total Priests in Diocese	663
Extern Priests in Diocese	137
Ordinations:	
Diocesan Priests	5
Transitional Deacons	5
Permanent Deacons	4
Permanent Deacons in Diocese	205
Total Brothers	107
Total Sisters	551
Parishes	
Parishes	140
With Resident Pastor:	
Resident Diocesan Priests	121
Resident Religious Priests	16
Without Resident Pastor:	
Administered by Priests	3
Missions	9
Professional Ministry Personnel:	
Brothers	2
Sisters	34
Welfare	
Catholic Hospitals	3
Total Assisted	725,201
Health Care Centers	9
Total Assisted	43,707
Homes for the Aged	27
Total Assisted	2,545
Residential Care of Children	1
Total Assisted	260
Day Care Centers	5
Total Assisted	360
Specialized Homes	23
Total Assisted	22,234
Special Centers for Social Services	24
Total Assisted	393,000
Residential Care of Disabled	6
Total Assisted	329
Educational	
Seminaries, Diocesan	3
Students from This Diocese	51
Students from Other Diocese	84
Diocesan Students in Other Seminaries	20
Seminaries, Religious	10
Students Religious	141
Total Seminarians	212
Colleges and Universities	3
Total Students	26,277
High Schools, Diocesan and Parish	2
Total Students	771
High Schools, Private	18
Total Students	9,438
Elementary Schools, Diocesan and Parish	65
Total Students	16,039
Elementary Schools, Private	12
Total Students	1,872
Non-residential Schools for the Disabled	1
Total Students	61
Catechesis/Religious Education:	
High School Students	3,459
Elementary Students	26,688
Total Students under Catholic Instruction	84,817
Teachers in the Diocese:	
Priests	17
Brothers	9
Sisters	46
Lay Teachers	2,371
Vital Statistics	
Receptions into the Church:	
Infant Baptism Totals	3,871
Minor Baptism Totals	2,195
Adult Baptism Totals	733
Received into Full Communion	548
First Communions	5,570
Confirmations	4,501
Marriages:	
Catholic	1,026
Interfaith	481
Total Marriages	1,507
Deaths	2,780
Total Catholic Population	611,019
Total Population	2,777,359

Former Archbishops—Most Rev. MICHAEL J. CURLEY, cons. Bishop of St. Augustine, June 30, 1914; promoted to the See of Baltimore, Aug. 10, 1921; named Archbishop of Baltimore and Washington, July 22, 1939; died May 16, 1947; His Eminence PATRICK CARDINAL O'BOYLE, cons. Jan. 14, 1948; created Cardinal June 26, 1967; retired March 3, 1973; died Aug. 10, 1987; WILLIAM CARDINAL BAUM, S.T.D., installed May 8, 1973; appt. Prefect, Congregation for Catholic Education in the Vatican, Jan. 15, 1980; Major Penitentiary; appt. April 6, 1990; JAMES CARDINAL HICKEY, S.T.D., J.C.D., ord. Auxiliary Bishop of Saginaw April 14, 1967; appt. Bishop of Cleveland June 5, 1974; appt. Archbishop of Washington June 17, 1980; installed Aug. 5, 1980; created Cardinal June 28, 1988; retired Nov. 21, 2000; died Oct. 24, 2004; THEODORE CARDINAL MCCARRICK, Ph.D., D.D., ord. May 31, 1958; appt. Auxiliary Bishop of New York and Titular Bishop of Rusibisir May 24, 1977; Episcopal ord. June 29, 1977; appt. First Bishop of Metuchen Nov. 19, 1981; installed Jan. 31, 1982; appt. Archbishop of Newark May 30, 1986; installed July 25, 1986; appt. Archbishop of Washington Nov. 21, 2000; installed Jan. 3, 2001; created Cardinal priest of Saints Nereus and Achilleus Feb. 21, 2001; retired May 16, 2006.

Unless otherwise indicated, all Archdiocesan Offices, including the Chancery and the Tribunal, are located in the Archdiocesan Pastoral Center, 5001 Eastern Ave., Hyattsville, MD 20782. Mailing Address: P.O. Box 29260, Washington, 20017. Tel: 301-853-4500; Fax: 301-853-5346; Office Hours: Mon.-Fri. 8:30-5.

Vicars General—Most Revs. FRANCISCO GONZALEZ, S.F., D.D., V.G.; MARTIN D. HOLLEY, D.D., V.G.; BARRY C. KNESTOUT, D.D., V.G.

Moderator of the Curia—Most Rev. BARRY C. KNESTOUT, D.D., V.G.; Mr. WILLIAM W. GORMAN, Assoc. Mod. of the Curia.

Chancellor—JANE G. BELFORD, Esq. Tel: 301-853-4520; Fax: 301-853-5346.

Vice Chancellor—Rev. GEORGE E. STUART, J.C.D. Tel: 301-853-5327.

Office of Child Protection Services—Ms. MARCIA D. ZVARA, M.S.W., LCSW-C. Tel: 301-853-5328; Fax: 301-853-2787. Email: mzvara@adw.org.

Archivist—Rev. GEORGE E. STUART, J.C.D. Tel: 301-853-5327.

Secretary to the Archbishop—Rev. ADAM Y. PARK. Tel: 301-853-5350; Fax: 301-853-5359.

Secretariats—Mr. THOMAS W. BURNFORD, M.Div., Sec. Catholic Educ.; Rev. Msgr. MICHAEL W. FISHER, E.V., Vicar for Clergy & Sec. Ministerial Leadership; THOMAS P. DUFFY, CFO; Rev. WILLIAM D. BYRNE, Sec. Pastoral Ministry & Social Concerns, (See Separate sections for each Secretariat below); ANGELA K. FLOOD, Sec. Communications.

Office of Canonical Services—

Episcopal Vicar for Canonical Services—Rev. Msgr. CHARLES V. ANTONICELLI, J.D., J.C.L., V.F. Tel: 301-853-5325; Fax: 301-853-7674.

Canonical Consultant—Sr. ELIZABETH MCDONOUGH, O.P., J.C.D.

The Tribunal

Tribunal—Tel: 301-853-4543; Fax: 301-853-7674.

Judicial Vicars—Rev. Msgrs. JOSEPH F. SADUSKY, J.C.D. Tel: 301-853-4544; CHARLES V. ANTONICELLI, J.D., J.C.L., V.F. Tel: 301-853-4543.

Adjutant Judicial Vicar—Rev. Msgr. GODFREY T. MOSLEY, J.C.D. Tel: 301-853-4543.

Judge—Rev. MARK E. TUCKER, J.C.L. Tel: 301-853-5322.

Promoters of Justice—Revs. G. PAUL HERBERT, J.C.L. Tel: 301-853-5326; GEORGE E. STUART, J.C.D. Tel: 301-853-5327.

Defenders of the Bond—Revs. G. PAUL HERBERT, J.C.L. Tel: 301-853-5326; GEORGE E. STUART, J.C.D. Tel: 301-853-5327.

Advocates—Rev. Msgrs. GEORGE E. DOBES, J.C.L. Tel: 301-853-4543, Ext. 253; PETER J. VAGHI, J.D., V.F. Tel: 301-853-4543; KEVIN T. HART, J.C.D. Tel: 301-853-4543; Rev. AGUSTIN MATEO AYALA. Tel: 301-853-4543.

Auditors—Ms. LINDA BUDNEY, J.C.L.; Rev. JUAN ESPOSITO; Ms. PATRICIA A. PERKINSON.

Consultative Groups

Archdiocesan College of Consultors—Most Revs. FRANCISCO GONZALEZ, S.F., D.D., V.G.; MARTIN D. HOLLEY, D.D., V.G.; BARRY C. KNESTOUT, D.D., V.G.; Rev. Msgrs. MICHAEL W. FISHER, E.V.; MARK E. BRENNAN; PAUL J. LANGSFELD, S.T.D.; MICHAEL WILSON, V.F.; PETER J. VAGHI, J.D., V.F.; EDDIE E. TOLENTINO, V.F.; Revs. FREDERICK J. CLOSE, V.F.; JOHN J. DILLON, V.F., S.T.B., Ph.D.; MARIO E. DORSONVILLE.

Archdiocesan Finance Council—His Eminence DONALD CARDINAL WUERL; W. SHEPHERDSON ABELL, Esq.; RAUL FERNANDEZ; GEORGE P. CLANCY JR.; CAROL G. BATES; Sr. CAROL KEEHAN, D.C.; J. PAUL MCNAMARA; LILA O'BRIEN SULLIVAN; WILLIAM J. SHAW. Staff: Most Rev. BARRY C. KNESTOUT, D.D., V.G., Vicar Gen. & Moderator of the Curia; Rev. Msgr. JOHN J. ENZLER, E.V., Vicar for Devel.; THOMAS P. DUFFY, CFO; KATHY MCKINLESS, Sr. Advisor; SCOTT LANCASTER, Controller.

Deans—Rev. JOHN J. DILLON, V.F., S.T.B., Ph.D., Northern Prince George's County; Rev. Msgr. CHARLES J. PARRY, V.F., Middle Prince George's County; Rev. WILLIAM E. FOLEY, Southern Prince George's County; Rev. Msgrs. ROBERT G. AMEY, V.F., Upper Montgomery County; PETER J. VAGHI, J.D., V.F., Middle Montgomery County; EDDIE E. TOLENTINO, V.F., Lower Montgomery County; CHARLES E. POPE, V.F., Northeast, D.C.; JAMES D. WATKINS, V.F., Northwest East, D.C.; W. RONALD JAMESON, Northwest West, D.C.; Revs. RAYMOND H. MOORE, V.F., Southeast, D.C.; MICHAEL J. KING, J.C.D., V.F., Calvert County; Rev. Msgrs. J. WILFRID PARENT, V.F., Charles County; KARL A. CHIMIAK, V.F., St. Mary's County.

Priest Council—His Eminence DONALD CARDINAL WUERL, Pres.; Rev. Msgr. JAMES D. WATKINS, V.F.; Revs. FREDERICK J. CLOSE, V.F.; RONALD A. POTTS; Y. DAVID BRAULT; Rev. Msgr. MICHAEL WILSON, V.F.; Revs. CARLOS A. BENITEZ; DAVID H. WERNING; MARK F. HUGHES; SCOTT R. HAHN; MICHAEL T. JONES; Rev. Msgrs. PETER J. VAGHI, J.D., V.F.; EDDIE E. TOLENTINO, V.F.; PAUL M. DUDZIAK; PAUL J. LANGSFELD, S.T.D.; EDWARD J. FILARDI; Revs. RAYMOND H. MOORE, V.F.; KEITH A. WOODS; PAUL D. LEE, S.T.D.; CARTER H. GRIFFIN; JOHN J. DILLON, V.F., S.T.B., Ph.D.; Rev. Msgr. MARK E. BRENNAN; Revs. MICHAEL JOHNSON, O.F.M.; MARIO E. DORSONVILLE; Most Revs. FRANCISCO GONZALEZ, S.F., D.D., V.G.; MARTIN D. HOLLEY, D.D., V.G.; BARRY C. KNESTOUT, D.D., V.G., Vicar Gen. & Moderator of the Curia; Rev. Msgr. MICHAEL W. FISHER, E.V.

Secretariat For Education

Secretary for Catholic Education—Mr. THOMAS W. BURNFORD, M.Div. Tel: 301-853-5331; Fax: 301-853-7691. Email: tburnford@adw.org.

Superintendent of Schools—Deacon BERT L'HOMME, Ph.D. Tel: 301-853-4518, Ext. 232; Fax: 301-853-7667. Email: lhommeb@adw.org.

Associate Superintendent of Catholic Schools—Ms. KELLY BRANAMAN. Tel: 301-853-4553; Fax: 301-853-7667. Email: branamank@adw.org.

Assistant Superintendent for School Improvement and Accreditation—CATHY SPENCER. Tel: 301-853-4590; Fax: 301-853-7670. Email: spencerc@adw.org.

Assistant Superintendent for Curriculum, Instruction, and Professional Development—Mrs. WENDY ANDERSON. Tel: 301-853-4588; Fax: 301-853-7670. Email: andersonw@adw.org.

Director of Government Relations for Catholic Schools—Mrs. JENNIFER DANIELS. Tel: 301-853-5357; Fax: 301-853-7670. Email: danielsj@adw.org.

Director of Research and Planning—Mr. JEREMY MCDONALD. Tel: 301-853-4549; Fax: 301-853-7670. Email: mcdonaldj@adw.org.

Director of Special Education—Mrs. DOREEN ENGEL. Tel: 301-853-4569. Email: engeld@adw.org.

Director of Counseling—Mr. KENNETH GAUGHAN. Tel: 301-853-5353. Email: gaughank@adw.org.

Director for School Marketing and Advancement—Mrs. WENDI M. WILLIAMS. Tel: 301-853-4531. Email: williamsw@adw.org.

Assistant Director for Funding and Educational Resources—Mrs. VICKY ATIENZA. Tel: 301-853-5356; Fax: 301-853-7670. Email: atienzav@adw.org.

Assistant Director for Assessment—LESHAUN QUANDER-MOSLEY. Tel: 301-853-4598. Email: mosleylq@adw.org.

Consortium of Catholic Academies of the Archdiocese of Washington, Inc.—Ms. K. MARGUERITE CONLEY, Exec. Dir. Tel: 301-853-5358. Email: marguerite.conley@catholicacademies.org.

Director for Development (Urban Schools)—ELIZABETH ROSS. Tel: 301-853-5303. Email: elizabeth.ross@catholicacademies.org.

Board of Education—Mr. MARTIN HAHN, Bd. Pres.

Office of Catechesis—

Director of Catechesis—

Coordinator of Course Promotion and Hispanic Catechesis—

Coordinator of Children's Catechesis and Curriculum—

Coordinator for Curriculum, Assessment, and Catechist Formation—

Secretariat for Ministerial Leadership and Vicar for Clergy

Secretariat for Ministerial Leadership and Vicar for Clergy—Rev. Msgr. MICHAEL W. FISHER, E.V., Secretariat for Ministerial Leadership & Vicar for Clergy. Tel: 301-853-4550; Fax: 301-853-7668.

Pastoral Care of Priests—Rev. Msgr. JOSEPH A. RANIERI, Coord. Tel: 301-853-5361; Fax: 301-853-7668.

Vocations for Men—Revs. CARTER H. GRIFFIN, Dir. Tel: 301-853-4580; SCOTT WOODS, Asst. Dir. Tel: 301-853-5378.

Continuing Education for Clergy—Rev. Msgr. ROBERT J. PANKE, Dir. Tel: 301-853-4577.

St. John Vianney House— Kensington, MD Tel: 301-942-1191.

Executive Director, Permanent Diaconate—Rev. SCOTT HURD. Tel: 301-853-4582; Fax: 301-853-7668.

Coordinator of Pastoral Care—Deacon JOSEPH F. CURTIS JR. Tel: 301-853-4586.

Director of Formation, Permanent Diaconate—Deacon KENNETH BARRETT. Tel: 301-853-4583; Fax: 301-853-7668.

Priests Retirement Board—Rev. Msgr. KEVIN T. HART, J.C.D., Chm. Tel: 301-292-0527.

Cardinal O'Boyle Residence for Priests—Rev. Msgr. LEONARD F. HURLEY, Mailing Address: P.O. Box 29206, Washington, 20017. Tel: 202-269-7818.

Blessed John Paul II Seminary—Rev. Msgr. ROBERT J. PANKE, Rector & Dir. Priest Formation. Tel: 301-853-4580; Fax: 301-853-7668; Rev. CARTER H. GRIFFIN, Rector & Dir. Priest Vocations. Tel: 301-853-5378; Fax: 301-853-7668.

Office of Consecrated Life—Sr. MARY DOLORA KEATING, R.S.M., Delegate. Tel: 301-853-4576; Fax: 301-853-7669.

Secretariat For Pastoral Ministry and Social Concerns

Secretary for Pastoral Ministry and Social Concerns—Rev. WILLIAM D. BYRNE, Sec. Tel: 301-853-4596; Fax: 301-853-7671. Email: byrnew@adw.org.

Department for Evangelization and Family Life—Mr. RICHARD KRAMER. Tel: 301-853-4546; Fax: 301-853-7660. Email: rkramer@adw.org.

Assistant Secretary for Pastoral Ministry and Social Concerns—

Program Specialist, Pastoral Ministry and Social Concerns—SARAH YAKLIC.

Resource Coordinator (English)—

Resource Coordinator (Spanish)—

Office for Ecumenical and Interreligious Affairs—Rev. AVELINO A. GONZALEZ, Dir., St. Joseph's on Capitol Hill, 313 2nd St., N.E., Washington, 20002. Tel: 202-547-1223.

Charismatic Renewal Regional Service Committee—Rev. FREDERICK J. CLOSE, V.F., St. Anthony of Padua, 1029 Monroe St., NE, Washington, 20017. Tel: 202-526-8822.

Department of Special Needs Ministries—Ms. MARY O'MEARA, Exec. Dir., 7202 Buchanan St., Landover Hills, MD 20784. Tel: 301-459-7464 (V/TTY); Fax: 301-459-8186. Email: omearam@adw.org; Ms. MARGARET (PEG) KOLM, Coord. Office for Persons with Disabilities. Tel: 301-853-4560. Email: mkolm@adw.org.

Ministry for the Deaf—Ms. LAUREEN LYNCH-RYAN, D.R.E. Email: llynch-ryan@adw.org. Chaplains: Revs. GERARD A. TRANCONE; JOSEPH J. BRUCE, S.J., Gallaudet University, Center for Deaf Ministries, 7202 Buchanan St., Landover Hills, MD 20784. Tel: 301-459-7464 (Voice & TDD); 301-577-4184 (Video Phone).

Office of Worship

Office of Worship—Rev. MARK D. KNESTOUT, Dir. Tel: 301-853-4595; Fax: 301-853-7684. Email: knestoutm@adw.org.

Commission on Sacred Art and Architecture—Rev. Msgr. W. RONALD JAMESON, Chm. Tel: 202-347-3215; Fax: 202-347-7184.

Office of the Missions

Office of the Missions—Rev. WILLIAM M. BRAILSFORD, Dir. Tel: 301-853-4534; Fax: 301-853-7685. Email: wbrailsford@adw.org.

HCA Mission Education Coordinator—Sr. MARIA DE LA REVELACION CASTANEDA. Tel: 301-853-5388. Email: castanedar@adw.org.

Missionary Cooperative Plan Coordinator—Ms. CECILIA CORTES-PECK. Tel: 301-853-4528. Email: ccortes-peck@adw.org.

Department for Charity and Justice

Department for Charity and Justice—Mr. ANTHONY BOSNICK, Dir. Tel: 301-853-5340; Fax: 301-853-7671. Email: abosnick@adw.org.

Ministry to Persons with Disabilities— (see Margaret "Peg" Kolm under Dept. of Special Needs Ministries)

Catholic Relief Services/International Outreach and Global Solidarity/CCHD—Mr. ANTHONY BOSNICK, CRS/CCHD Diocesan Dir. Tel: 301-853-5340; Fax: 301-853-7671. Email: abosnick@adw.org.

Department for Life Issues

Department for Life Issues—Ms. CHRISTA LOPICCOLO, Exec. Dir. Tel: 301-853-5318; Fax: 301-853-7671. Email: clopiccolo@adw.org; Ms. MICHELLE CARPER, Prog. Coord. Tel: 301-853-4555; Fax: 301-853-7671. Email: mcarper@adw.org.

Project Rachel Ministry—Ms. JULIA SHELAVA, Dir. Tel: 301-853-5386; Fax: 301-853-7671. Email: projectrachel@adw.org; Ms. LUZ MENJIVAR, Prog. Coord. Pastoral Care, Project Rachel. Tel: 301-853-4562; Fax: 301-853-7671.

Office of Black Catholics

Office of Black Catholics—Deacon AL TURNER, Dir. Tel: 301-853-5371; Fax: 301-853-7671. Email: obc@adw.org.

Office of Hispanic Pastoral Affairs

Office of Hispanic Pastoral Affairs—Mr. MANUEL ALIAGA, Dir. Tel: 301-853-4567; Fax: 301-853-7671. Email: maliaga@adw.org.

Office of Youth Ministry

Office of Youth Ministry—700 Roeder Rd., Silver Spring, MD 20910. Mailing Address: P.O. Box 29260, Washington, 20017. Tel: 202-281-2460; Fax: 202-281-2470. Ms. DEBORAH MCDONALD, Exec. Dir. Tel: 202-281-2466; Fax: 202-281-2470. Email: dmcdonald@adw.org.

Associate Director, Coordinator of Athletic Ministry/CYO Sports—Mr. KEVIN DONOGHUE. Tel: 202-281-2463; Fax: 202-281-2470. Email: donoghuek@adw.org.

Associate Director, Coordinator of Youth Ministry Programs and Training—Mr. JOAQUIN TREJO. Tel: 202-281-2476; Fax: 202-281-2470. Email: jtrejo@adw.org.

African American Youth Ministry—Mr. DARREN FOSTER. Tel: 202-281-2460; Fax: 202-281-2470. Email: dfoster@adw.org.

Coordinator of Youth Ministry Resources and Programs—Ms. LAURA IRWIN. Tel: 202-281-2462; Fax: 202-281-2470. Email: lirwin@adw.org.

OYM/CYO Sports Programs Assistant—Ms. MARY

FAVA. Tel: 202-281-2465; Fax: 202-281-2470. Email: mfava@adw.org.

Our Lady of Mattaponi Youth Retreat and Conference Center—Mrs. MARY DAWN WOODS, Dir. Tel: 301-952-9074; Fax: 301-952-0609. Email: dwoods2@adw.org.

Boy Scouts/Girl Scouts/Camp Fire Boys & Girls—Mr. RICHARD STEVICK, Coord. Archdiocesan Catholic Committee on Scouting/Camp Fire. Tel: 301-490-7855. Email: dstevick@verizon.net.

Girl Scout Chair, Catholic Committee for Girl Scouts—Ms. BRENDA MURTHA. Tel: 301-349-4312. Email: breezegs@verizon.net.

Boy Scout Chair, Catholic Committee for Boy Scouts—Mrs. MARYSANTA BIGONY. Tel: 301-262-8645. Email: msbrn@aol.com.

Camp Fire Lay Coordinator—Ms. ROSEMARY PEZUTTO. Tel: 301-262-1631. Email: copier22@aol.com.

Archdiocesan Chaplain Coordinator/Catholic Committee on Boy Scouts, Girl Scouts & Camp fire—Rev. Msgr. JOHN B. BRADY (Retired). Tel: 301-769-3332.

Archdiocesan Chaplain - Catholic Committee on Boy Scouts—Rev. SCOTT WOODS. Tel: 301-862-4600.

Archdiocesan Chaplain - Catholic Committee on Girl Scouts—Rev. RONALD A. POTTS. Tel: 202-966-6575.

Lay Leadership Institute

Lay Leadership Institute—Mrs. MARY SUAREZ HAMM, Exec. Dir., Cardinal McCarrick Center, 12247 Georgia Ave., Wheaton, MD 20902. Tel: 301-946-1621; Fax: 301-946-0217. Email: mhamm@adw.org.

Secretariat for Finance and Management

Finance and Management—THOMAS P. DUFFY, CFO. Tel: 301-853-5312; SCOTT LANCASTER, Controller. Tel: 301-853-4504; KATHY MCKINLESS, Sr. Advisor. Tel: 301-853-5314.

Director of Parish and School Financial Operations—Mr. TERENCE FARRELL. Tel: 301-853-4511; Fax: 301-853-7664.

Property Risk & Liability Insurance—VACANT, Dir.

Facilities Management—Mr. RICHARD DE STWOLINSKI, Dir. Tel: 202-281-2491; Fax: 202-281-2498; Mr. SCOTT SULLIVAN, Asst. Dir. Tel: 202-281-2492; PHILIP DUCK, Asst. Dir. Pastoral Center Mgmt. Tel: 301-853-4530; Fax: 301-853-7673.

Personnel and Benefits—Deacon DANIEL F. FINN VI, Dir. Human Resources. Tel: 301-853-4513; Fax: 301-853-7680.

Secretariat for Development

Development Office— Coordinates all Archdiocesan development and fundraising efforts and oversees the Archbishop's Appeal, Parish Resource Development, planned giving, major donors, grant writing, Forward in Faith Campaign, and the Archdiocesan Tuition Assistance Fund. Tel: 301-853-4575; Fax: 301-853-7678; 301-853-7692. Email: development@adw.org.

Vicar of Development—Rev. Msgr. JOHN J. ENZLER, E.V. Tel: 202-772-4300; Fax: 301-853-7692. Email: jenzler@adw.org.

Executive Director of Development—Mr. KEVIN T. O'CONNOR. Tel: 301-853-4574; Fax: 301-853-7692. Email: oconnork@adw.org.

Cardinal's Appeal—Mr. KEVIN T. O'CONNOR, Dir. Tel: 301-853-4574; Fax: 301-853-7692. Email: oconnork@adw.org.

Planned Giving—Mr. EDWARD J. D'ANTONI, Dir. Tel: 301-853-4573; Fax: 301-853-7692. Email: dantonie@adw.org.

Forward in Faith—Mr. EDWARD J. D'ANTONI, Dir. Tel: 301-853-4573; Fax: 301-853-7692.

Archdiocesan Tuition Assistance Fund—Rev. WILLIAM L. GEORGE, S.J., Dir. Fax: 202-347-7184.

Parish Resource Development—Mr. GEORGE REED, Dir. Tel: 301-853-5374; Fax: 301-853-7692. Email: reedg@adw.org.

Archdiocesan Building Commission—Rev. Msgr. JOSEPH A. RANIERI, Chm.

Archdiocesan Sacred Arts Committee—Rev. Msgr. W. RONALD JAMESON, 1725 Rhode Island Ave. N.W., Washington, 20036. Tel: 202-347-3215; Fax: 202-347-7184.

Catholic Education Foundation of the Archdiocese of Washington, Inc.—Mr. ROBERT LANE, Chm., Mailing Address: P.O. Box 29260, Washington, 20017. Tel: 301-853-5312.

Priest Retirement Fund of the Archdiocese of Washington, Inc.—Rev. Msgr. DONALD S. ESSEX, Mailing Address: P.O. Box 29260, Washington, 20017. Tel: 301-853-5312.

Forward in Faith, Inc.—Mr. ROBERT F. COMSTOCK, Chm., Mailing Address: P.O. Box 29063, Washington, 20017-0063.

Secretariat for Communications

Secretary for Communications—ANGELA K. FLOOD. Tel: 301-853-4516; Fax: 301-853-7672.

Office of Media and Public Relations—CHIEKO NOGUCHI, Dir. Tel: 301-853-4516; Fax: 301-853-7672.

Office of Digital Media—VACANT, Dir.; Mr. CHRISTOPHER STRACKBEIN, Multi-Media Producer. Tel: 301-853-4519; Fax: 301-853-7672.

TV Mass Producer—Mr. JOHN CAPOBIANCO. Tel: 301-853-4517.

Carroll Publishing Company—His Eminence DONALD CARDINAL WUERL, Publisher.

Newspaper "The Catholic Standard"—Mr. MARK ZIMMERMANN, Editor. Tel: 202-281-2412; Fax: 202-281-2418. Email: mark@cathstan.org.

Newspaper "El Pregonero"—Mr. RAFAEL RONCAL, Editor. Tel: 202-281-2442; Fax: 202-281-2448. Email: rafael@elpreg.org.

CLERGY, PARISHES, MISSIONS AND PAROCHIAL SCHOOLS

DISTRICT OF COLUMBIA

1—ST. MATTHEW CATHEDRAL (1840) Rev. Msgr. W. Ronald Jameson; Revs. Evelio Menjivar; Kevin Regan; Deacons Ulysses Rice, (Retired); Bartholomew J. Merella, (Retired); Boyd Work; Juan Cayrampoma; Pamela Erwin, Business Mgr. In Res., Revs. Mark D. Knestout; John Hurley (Retired).
Res.: 1725 Rhode Island Ave., N.W., 20036. Tel: 202-347-3215; Fax: 202-347-7184. Email: cathstmatt@stmatthewscathedral.org. Web: www.stmatthewscathedral.org.
Catechesis/Religious Program—Students 90.

2—ST. ALOYSIUS (1859) Rev. Thomas F. Clifford, S.J.; Deacon Willis Daniels.
Res.: 19 Eye St., N.W., 20001. Tel: 202-336-7200; Fax: 202-842-3693. Email: stals@gonzaga.org. Web: www.stalschurchdc.org.
Father McKenna Center—Tel: 202-842-1112; Fax: 202-842-7401. Tom Howarth, Dir.
Catechesis/Religious Program—Students 42.

3—ST. ANN (1869) Rev. Msgr. Godfrey T. Mosley; Deacon Robert W. Whitaker.
Res.: 4001 Yuma St., N.W., 20016. Tel: 202-966-6288; Fax: 202-966-7722. Email: stann@stanndc.org. Web: www.stanndc.org.
School—(Grades PreK-8), 4404 Wisconsin Ave., N.W., 20016. Tel: 202-363-4460, Ext. 1; Fax: 202-362-6560. Email: office@stannsacademy.net. Web: www.stannsacademy.net. Mr. Thomas Wharton, Prin. Lay Teachers 17; Students 193.
Catechesis/Religious Program—Tel: 202-363-9524. Email: dre@stanndc.org. Students 75.
Mission— 4133 Yuma St., NW, 20016. Tel: 202-244-2617.

4—ANNUNCIATION (1948) Rev. Msgr. V. James Lockman; Rev. John W. Crossin, O.S.F.S. In Res., Most Rev. Barry C. Knestout.
Parish Office—Office: 3125 39th St., N.W., 20016-5409. Tel: 202-362-3323; Fax: 202-237-0652. Email: parish@annunciationdc.org. Web: www.annunciationdc.org.
Res.: 3915 Mass Ave., N.W., 20016.
School—3825 Klingle Pl., N.W., 20016-5434. Tel: 202-362-1408; Fax: 202-363-4057. Web: www.annunciationschool.net. Mr. Gary Beckley, Prin. Lay Teachers 17; Students 140.
Catechesis/Religious Program—Ms. Patrice Morace, D.R.E. Students 115.
Convent—3200 39th St., N.W., 20016. Tel: 202-362-1464.

5—ST. ANTHONY (1892) Revs. Frederick J. Close; Berard L. Marthaler, O.F.M.Conv. (Retired).
Res.: 1029 Monroe St., N.E., 20017. Tel: 202-526-8822; 202-250-8208; Fax: 202-250-6223. Email: stanthony.dc@adwparish.org. Web: www.stanthonyofpaduadc.org.
School—12th & Lawrence St., N.E., 20017. Tel: 202-526-4657; Fax: 202-832-5567. Web: www.stanthonyschooldc.org. Mr. Michael R. Thomasian, Prin. Lay Teachers 19; Students 219.
Catechesis/Religious Program—Students 47.

6—ASSUMPTION (1916) Rev. William L. Montgomery, Admin.
Res.: 3401 Martin Luther King Jr. Ave., S.E., 20032-1597. Tel: 202-561-4178; Fax: 202-561-0336.

7—ST. AUGUSTINE (1858), (African American), Revs. Patrick A. Smith; Paul John T. Camiring, Parochial Vicar.
Parish Office—1419 V St., N.W., 20009. Fax: 202-234-1787.
Res.: 1425 V St., N.W., 20009. Tel: 202-265-1470.
School—1421 V St., N.W., 20009. Tel: 202-667-2608. Donna Edwards, Prin. Lay Teachers 18; Students 173.
Catechesis/Religious Program—Students 155.

8—BASILICA OF THE NATIONAL SHRINE OF THE IMMACULATE CONCEPTION (1920) Mailing Address: 400 Michigan Ave., N.E., 20017-1566. Tel: 202-526-8300; Fax: 202-526-8313. Email: info@nationalshrine.com. Web: www.nationalshrine.com.

9—ST. BENEDICT THE MOOR (1946) Rev. Richard K. Gancayco.
Res.: 320 21st St., N.E., 20002. Tel: 202-397-3895; Fax: 202-398-3415. Email: rectory@stbenedictofdc.org. Web: www.stbenedictofdc.org.
Catechesis/Religious Program—Students 17.

10—ST. BLAISE (1984), (Croatian), (Croatian Pastoral Mission) Rev. Dubravko Turalija (Bosnia-Herzegovina).
Mailing Address: *Our Lady of Victory*, 4835 Macarthur Blvd., N.W., 20007. Tel: 202-255-0856; Fax: 202-338-4759.
Catechesis/Religious Program—Students 10.

11—BLESSED SACRAMENT, SHRINE OF THE MOST (1911) Rev. Ronald A. Potts; Rev. Msgr. Maurice V. O'Connell (Retired); Rev. Percival L. D'Silva (Retired); Deacon Daniel Thompson.
Mailing Address: 3630 Quesada St., N.W., 20015-2538. In Res., Rev. Tesfaye Fesuh (Ethiopia).
Res.: 6001 Western Ave., N.W., 20015-2423. Tel: 202-966-6575; Fax: 202-966-9255. Web: www.blessedsacramentdc.org.
School—5841 Chevy Chase Pkwy., N.W., 20015-2599. Tel: 202-966-6682; Fax: 202-966-4938. Web: www.b-sstoday.org. Mr. Christopher Kelly, Prin. Lay Teachers 45; Students 515.
Catechesis/Religious Program—Tel: 202-449-3989. Email: trecinella@blessedsacramentdc.org. Therese Recinella, D.R.E. Students 520.

12—CHURCH OF ST. LOUIS (1972), (French), (Paroisse St. Louis de France-French-speaking Parish of Washington) Rev. Jean-Marie Vincent.
Res.: 4125 Garrison St., N.W., 20016. Tel: 202-537-0709; Fax: 202-244-9649. Email: stlouisdef@aol.com. Web: www.members.aol.com/stlouisdef.
Catechesis/Religious Program—Students 240.

13—ST. DOMINIC CHURCH & PRIORY (1852) Rev. George P. Schommer, O.P.; Very Rev. R. Joseph Barranger, O.P., Prior; Revs. Norman A. Haddad, O.P., Subprior; Gerard Lessard, O.P., Parochial Vicar; J. Andrew Nicolicchia, O.P., Parochial Vicar. In Res., Revs. William Burke, O.P.; David A. Butler, O.P.; George L. Concordia, O.P.; John B. Davis, O.P.; Adrian L. Dionne, O.P.; Robert P. Fitzsimmons, O.P.; V. F. McHenry, O.P.; John T. Murphy, O.P.; Charles O'Brien, O.P.; Bede Shipps, O.P.; Robert L. Walker, O.P.; Bro. Jude Locchetto, O.P.
Res.: 630 E St., S.W., 20024. Tel: 202-554-7863; Fax: 202-554-0231.

14—EPIPHANY (1923) Rev. Paul D. Lee.
Res.: 2712 Dumbarton St., N.W., 20007. Tel: 202-965-1610; Fax: 202-337-8377.
Catechesis/Religious Program—Jane Zilles-Soberano, D.R.E. Students 22.

15—ST. FRANCIS DE SALES (1722), (African American), Rev. Carl F. Dianda; Michael Howard, Pastoral Assoc. In Res., Rev. Henry Slevin.
Res.: 2021 Rhode Island Ave., N.E., 20018. Tel: 202-529-7451; Fax: 202-529-0050. Email: dcianda@adwparish.org. Web: www.stfrancisdesaleswdc.org.
Catechesis/Religious Program—Parish Family Center, 2017 St. Frances de Sales Pl., 20018. Tel: 202-529-2147; Fax: 202-529-1630. Email: etsm@prodigy.net. Students 6.

16—ST. FRANCIS XAVIER (1924) Rev. C. Gregory Butta.
Res.: 2800 Pennsylvania Ave., S.E., 20020. Tel: 202-582-5021; Fax: 202-581-7224.
School—Tel: 202-581-2010; 202-234-4611; Fax: 202-582-5244. Harold Thomas, Prin. Lay Teachers 12; Students 250.
Catechesis/Religious Program—Tel: 202-582-2607; Fax: 202-581-1142. Mr. Robert Fuller, D.R.E. Students 40.
Convent—*Sisters of St. Joseph*, 2812 Pennsylvania Ave., S.E., 20020. Tel: 202-584-5621. Sr. Marie Brigid Monahan, S.S.J., Pastoral Min.

17—ST. GABRIEL (1919) Rev. Agustin Mateo Ayala; Deacon Robert L. Berry. In Res., Rev. Tesfamariam Baraki.
Res.: 26 Grant Cir., N.W., 20011. Tel: 202-726-9092; Fax: 202-291-0334.
Catechesis/Religious Program—Tel: 202-726-9212; Fax: 202-291-0334. Students 160.

18—HOLY COMFORTER--ST. CYPRIAN (1893), (African American), Rev. Msgr. Charles E. Pope; Deacons Charles Edelin, (Retired); Kevin Butler; Ralph Cyrus. In Res., Rev. F. Michael Bryant.
Res.: 1357 E. Capitol St., S.E., 20003. Tel: 202-546-1885; Fax: 202-544-1385.

Catechesis/Religious Program—Shirley Austin, D.R.E.

19—HOLY NAME (1891), (African American—Hispanic), Revs. Michael W. Briese; Gary T. Villanueva, Parochial Vicar; Robert Guillen; Deacon William Thomas. In Res., Rev. Francis M. Walsh.
Res.: 920 11th St., N.E., 20002. Tel: 202-397-2525; Fax: 202-397-6639.
Catechesis/Religious Program—Students 30.

20—HOLY REDEEMER (1919), (African American), Rev. David Bava.
Res.: 206 New York Ave., N.W., 20001. Tel: 202-347-7510; Fax: 202-638-4831. Email: holyredeemer.dc@adwparish.org.
School—Holy Redeemer School, (Grades PreK-8), 1135 New Jersey Ave., N.W., 20001. Tel: 202-638-5789; Fax: 301-628-0401. Ben Ketchum, Prin. Priests 1; Sisters 2; Deacons 1; Lay Teachers 15; Students 200.
Catechesis/Religious Program—Tel: 202-347-7510. Students 55.

21—HOLY ROSARY (1913), (Italian), Rev. Lydio F. Tomasi, C.S.
Res.: 595 Third St., N.W., 20001-2703. Tel: 202-638-0165; Fax: 202-638-0793. Email: casaitaldc@yahoo.com. Web: www.holyrosarychurchdc.org.
Catechesis/Religious Program—Students 12.

22—HOLY TRINITY (1787) Revs. Mark F. Horak, S.J.; Leo A. Murray, S.J.; Gregory A. Schenden, S.J.; Joseph A. Sobierajski, S.J.
Mailing Address: 36th St., N.W., between N and O Sts., 20007.
Parish Center Offices—3513 N St., N.W., 20007. Tel: 202-337-2840; Fax: 202-337-9048. Web: www.trinity.org.
Res.: 3514 O St., N.W., 20007.
School—1325 36th St. N.W., 20007-2604. Tel: 202-337-2339; Fax: 202-337-0368. Web: htsdc.org. Sisters of St. Joseph (Chestnut Hill, PA) 1; Lay Teachers 40; Students 333.
Catechesis/Religious Program—Students 700.

23—IMMACULATE CONCEPTION (1864), (African American), Rev. Msgr. James D. Watkins.
Res.: 1315 8th St., N.W., 20001. Tel: 202-332-8888; Fax: 202-332-0173. Web: www.immaculateconceptionchurchdc.org.
Catechesis/Religious Program—Students 20.

24—INCARNATION (1934), (African American), Rev. John A. Carroll, S.S.J.; Deacon Joseph E. Bell.
Res.: 880 Eastern Ave., N.E., 20019. Tel: 202-396-0942; Fax: 202-396-6064.
Catechesis/Religious Program—Students 123.

25—ST. JOSEPH ON CAPITOL HILL (1868) Revs. Avelino A. Gonzalez; Christopher T. Begg; Deacon Gary L. Bockweg. In Res., Rev. Eugene Hemrick (JOL).
Res.: 313 Second St., N.E., 20002. Tel: 202-547-1223; Fax: 202-547-4189. Web: www.st-josephs.org.
Catechesis/Religious Program—Email: parish@st-josephs.org. Students 12.

26—KIDANE-MEHRET GE'EZ RITE CATHOLIC CHURCH (1984), (Ethiopian—Eritrean), Rev. Araia Ghiday Ghebray.
Mailing Address: 1001 Lawrence St., N.E., P.O. Box 29616, 20017. Tel: 202-756-2756.
Res.: 1357 E. Capitol St., S.E., 20003. Tel: 202-546-1885.
Catechesis/Religious Program—Students 127.
Mission— 415 Michigan Ave., N.E. #65, 20017. Tel: 202-756-2756; Fax: 202-756-2755. Email: kmgeezrite@aol.com. Web: www.kidane.mehret.org.

27—ST. LUKE (1957), (African American), Revs. Joseph F. Del Vecchio, S.S.J.; Joseph N. Begay, S.S.J.; Deacon Joseph M. Conrad.
Res.: 4925 E. Capitol St., S.E., 20019-5202. Tel: 202-584-8322; Fax: 202-584-3421.
Catechesis/Religious Program—Students 39.

28—ST. MARTIN OF TOURS (1901), (African American), Rev. Michael J. Kelley.
Res.: 1908 N. Capitol St., 20002. Tel: 202-232-1144; Fax: 202-832-6772. Web: www.stmartinsdc.org.
Catechesis/Religious Program—Students 53.

29—ST. MARY, MOTHER OF GOD (1845) [CEM] Rev. Alfred J. Harris. In Res., Revs. William Cleary; Daniel D'Alliessi (NY).
Res.: 727 Fifth St., N.W., 20001. Tel: 202-289-7771; Fax: 202-408-1989. Email: stmarys20001@gmail.com.
Catechesis/Religious Program—Tel: 202-289-7770.

30—NATIVITY (1901), (African American), Revs. George Hanna, S.D.B.; Dominic DeBlase, S.D.B.; John Serio, S.D.B.; Deacon Al Douglas Turner; Revs. Paul Grauls, S.D.B.; Steve Shafran, S.D.B.; Abraham Feliciano, S.D.B.; Bro. Thomas Sweeney, S.D.B.
Res.: 6000 Georgia Ave., N.W., 20011. Tel: 202-726-6262; Fax: 202-722-7170. Email: nativityccdc2010@aol.com. Web: www.nativitychurch.net.
Catechesis/Religious Program—Students 80.

31—NIGERIAN CATHOLIC COMMUNITY (1994), (Nigerian), Closed. For inquiries for parish records contact the chancery.

32—OUR LADY OF FATIMA PARISH (1999), (Portuguese-speaking Community) Revs. Sergio Dall Agnese, C.S.; Carlos Reyes Ramirez, C.S.
Mailing Address: 5700 St. Bernard's Dr., Riverdale, MD 20737. Tel: 301-277-1000; Fax: 301-277-3464.
Catechesis/Religious Program—10830 Eastwood Ave., Silver Spring, MD 20901. Tel: 301-949-2488. Students 75.

33—OUR LADY OF PERPETUAL HELP (1920), (African American), Very Rev. Thomas R. Frank, S.S.J., Admin.; Rev. Michael K. Okechukwu, S.S.J., Parochial Vicar; Bro. Marx Tyree, S.S.J., Pastoral Assoc.; Deacon Thomas Jones.
Res.: 1600 Morris Rd., S.E., 20020-6312. Tel: 202-678-4999; Fax: 202-610-3189. Web: www.olphchurchofdc.org.
Parish Life Center—1604 Morris Rd., S.E., 20020. Tel: 202-889-1662; 202-678-0211; Fax: 202-610-1519.
Catechesis/Religious Program—Students 72.

34—OUR LADY OF VICTORY (1909) Rev. David H. Werning; Rev. Msgr. Thomas M. Duffy, Co-Chap., Sibley Hospital (Retired); Deacon Leo Flynn. In Res., Rev. Leo D. Lefebure (CHI), Matteo Ricci Chair, Georgetown University; Prof. of Theology.
Res.: 4835 MacArthur Blvd., N.W., 20007. Tel: 202-337-4835; 202-337-4836; Fax: 202-338-4759.
School—4755 Whitehaven Pkwy., N.W., 20007. Tel: 202-337-1421; Fax: 202-337-2068. Email: info@olvschooldc.org. Web: olvschooldc.org. Mrs. Sheila Martinez, Prin. Lay Teachers 25; Students 187.
Catechesis/Religious Program—Students 38.

35—OUR LADY QUEEN OF PEACE (1948), (African American), Rev. Peter M. Giovanoni; Deacon Alfred Miller.
Res.: 3800 Ely Pl., S.E., 20019. Tel: 202-582-8600; Fax: 202-575-3317.
Catechesis/Religious Program—Tel: 202-581-4986. Students 45.
Convent—3740 Ely Pl., S.E., 20019. Tel: 202-581-4963; Fax: 202-584-1922.

36—OUR LADY QUEEN OF THE AMERICAS (1986), (Hispanic), Rev. Roberto J. Cortes-Campos; Deacon Jorge W. Vargas.
Mailing Address: 2200 California St., N.W., 20008.
Catechesis/Religious Program—Tel: 202-332-8838, Ext. 200; Fax: 202-332-2967. Steward Benalcazar, D.R.E. Students 260.

37—ST. PATRICK (1794) Rev. Msgr. Salvatore A. Criscuolo. In Res., Rev. Msgr. Charles V. Antonicelli; Rev. Frederick H. MacIntyre (Retired); Most Rev. Leonard J. Olivier, S.V.D.
Res.: 619 Tenth St., N.W., 20001-4587. Tel: 202-347-2713; Fax: 202-347-1401. Email: office@saintpatrickdc.org. Web: saintpatrickdc.org.
Catechesis/Religious Program—Robert Quinlan, D.R.E. (Adult); Ronald Stolk, Music Dir.

38—ST. PETER (1821) Revs. William D. Byrne; Patrick J. Riffle, Parochial Vicar. In Res., Rev. Msgr. Joseph F. Sadusky.
Res.: 313 Second St., S.E., 20003. Tel: 202-547-1430; Fax: 202-547-5732. Email: rectory@saintpetersdc.org. Web: www.saintpetersdc.org.
School—422 Third St., S.E., 20003. Tel: 202-544-1618; Fax: 202-547-5101. Email: info@stpeterschooldc.org. Web: stpeterschooldc.org. Jennifer Ketchum, Prin. Daughters of St. Anne 2; Lay Teachers 26; Students 224.
Catechesis/Religious Program—Fax: 202-547-5732. Students 98.

39—SHRINE OF THE SACRED HEART (1899) Revs. Moises Villalta, O.F.M.Cap.; Kevin Thompson, O.F.M.Cap.; Francis X. Russo, O.F.M.Cap.; Arsene Jasmin, (Haitian Apostolate); Francis Nguyen, (Vietnamese Apostolate); Deacon Nehemias J. Molina. In Res., Revs. James P. Froehlich, O.F.M.Cap.; John Pavlik, O.F.M.Cap.
Res.: 3211 Pine St., 20010. Tel: 202-234-8000 (Day); 202-234-8002 (Night); Fax: 202-234-9159.
School—1625 Park Rd., N.W., 20010. Tel: 202-265-4828; Fax: 202-265-0595. Stephanie Margetts, Prin. Lay Teachers 16; Students 228.
Catechesis/Religious Program—Tel: 202-667-2446. Students 680.

40—ST. STEPHEN MARTYR (1867) Rev. Msgr. Paul J. Langsfeld; Rev. Klaus J. Sirianni. In Res., Rev. Gregory W. Shaffer.
Res.: 2436 Pennsylvania Ave., N.W., 20037. Tel: 202-785-0982; Fax: 202-785-1574. Email: st.stephenmartyrdc@verizon.net. Web: www.st-stephenmartyrdc.org.

41—ST. TERESA OF AVILA (1879), (African American), Rev. Msgr. Raymond G. East; Deacon William J. Hawkins.
1401 V St., S.E., 20020-5692.
Res.: 1430 Minnesota Ave., S.E., 20020-5692. Tel: 202-678-3037; Fax: 202-678-3325. Web: stachurch.org.
Church: 1244 V. St. S.E., 20020.
Catechesis/Religious Program—Students 70.
Parish Life Center: Tel: 202-678-3709; Fax: 202-678-3325.

42—ST. THOMAS APOSTLE (1913) Rev. Msgr. Michael J. Mellone; Deacon William C. Boesman.
Res.: 2665 Woodley Rd., N.W., 20008. Tel: 202-234-1488; Fax: 202-234-1480.
Catechesis/Religious Program—Students 36.

43—ST. THOMAS MORE (1952), (African American), Rev. Raymond H. Moore; Deacon Richard Walker. In Res., Rev. John P. Kinter.
Res.: 4275 4th St., S.E., 20032. Tel: 202-562-0431; Fax: 202-563-7347. Email: stmchurch@comcast.net.
School—Tel: 202-561-1189; Fax: 202-562-2336. Ms. Bridget Coates, Prin. Lay Teachers 15; Students 205.
Catechesis/Religious Program—Students 67.

44—ST. VINCENT DE PAUL (1903), (African American), Deacon Francis Kraemer. In Res., Bro. Marx Tyree, S.S.J.
Res.: 14 M St., S.E., 20003-3511. Tel: 202-488-1354; Fax: 202-488-7899.
Catechesis/Religious Program—Students 75.

CHURCHES IN MARYLAND

AVENUE, ST. MARY'S CO., HOLY ANGELS (1906) [JC] Rev. Michael E. Tietjen; Deacon Joseph W. Lloyd Jr.
Res.: 21340 Colton Point Rd., MD 20609-2422. Tel: 301-769-3332; Fax: 301-769-2541. Email: angelsinavenue@gmail.com. Web: www.parishes.org/holyangels.html.
Catechesis/Religious Program—Students 68.

BADEN, PRINCE GEORGES CO., ST. MICHAEL (1957) Rev. Louis J. Faust; Deacon Tyrone Johnson.
Mailing Address: 17510 Horsehead Rd., Brandywine, MD 20613.
Catechesis/Religious Program—Tel: 301-579-6409; Fax: 301-579-0019. Students 90.
Mission—St. Dominic's [CEM] 22300 Aquasco Rd., Aquasco, Prince Georges Co., MD 20608. Tel: 301-888-1498; Fax: 301-579-0019.

BARNESVILLE, MONTGOMERY CO., ST. MARY CHURCH AND SHRINE OF OUR LADY OF FATIMA (1807) [CEM] Rev. Kevin P. O'Reilly; Deacon David Cahoon.
Res.: 18230 Barnesville Rd., P.O. Box 67, MD 20838. Tel: 301-972-8660; Fax: 301-349-0916. Email: stmarysb@yahoo.com. Web: www.stmaryonline.com.
Catechesis/Religious Program—Students 132.

BELTSVILLE, PRINCE GEORGES CO., ST. JOSEPH (1963) Rev. J. Michael Quill; Deacons Willis R. Wolfe; Chris Schwartz. In Res., Revs. Joseph F. Wimmer, O.S.A.; John Rose.
Res.: 11007 Montgomery Rd., MD 20705. Tel: 301-937-7183; Fax: 301-937-7780. Email: stjoseph.beltsville.md@adwparish.org. Web: www.stjos.org.
School—11011 Montgomery Rd., MD 20705. Tel: 301-937-7154; Fax: 301-937-1467. Email: schooloffice@stjos.org. Lay Teachers 17; Students 210.
Catechesis/Religious Program—Email: mkeith@stjos.org. Students 227.

BENEDICT, CHARLES CO., ST. FRANCIS DE SALES (1903) Rev. Kevin M. Cusick.
Res.: 7185 Benedict Ave., P.O. Box 306, MD 20612-0306. Tel: 301-274-3416; 301-870-4991; Fax: 301-274-0689. Email: francisben@comcast.net.
Catechesis/Religious Program—7209 Benedict Ave., P.O. Box 306, MD 20612. Tel: 301-274-0904. Email: religiousedstfrancisdesalescc.org. Students 25.

BETHESDA, MONTGOMERY CO.

1—ST. BARTHOLOMEW (1960) Rev. Msgr. James T. Beattie (Retired); Rev. Joseph R. Sileo. In Res., Rev. Hugh Logan, S.M.A.
Res.: 6902 River Rd., MD 20817. Tel: 301-229-7933; Fax: 301-229-7998.
School—6900 River Rd., MD 20817. Tel: 301-229-5586; Fax: 301-229-8654. Web: www.stbartholomew.org. Mrs. Kathleen Miller, Prin. Sisters 1; Lay Teachers 25; Students 223.
Catechesis/Religious Program—Tel: 301-229-3431; Fax: 301-229-7998. Students 187.

2—ST. JANE FRANCES DE CHANTAL (1950) Rev. Msgr. Donald S. Essex; Rev. Paul Dean Nguyen; Deacons Kenneth Angell; Chester G. Chen. In Res., Rev. John F. McKay.
Res.: 9701 Old Georgetown Rd., MD 20814. Tel: 301-530-1550; Fax: 301-493-8953. Email: parish.office@stjanedechantal.org. Web: www.stjanedechantal.org.
School—9525 Old Georgetown Rd., MD 20814. Tel: 301-530-1221; Fax: 301-530-1688. Web: www.dechantal.com. Mrs. Betsy Hamilton, Prin. Lay Teachers 26; Students 500.
Catechesis/Religious Program—Tel: 301-530-1640; Fax: 301-530-5881. Email: seton.center@stjanedechantal.org. Students 381.

3—LITTLE FLOWER (1948) Rev. Msgr. Peter J. Vaghi; Revs. Anthony E. Lickteig; George E. Stuart.
Res.: 5607 Massachusetts Ave., MD 20816. Tel:

301-320-4538; Fax: 301-320-4541. Email: paw@lfchurch.org. Web: lfparish.org.
School—5601 Massachusetts Ave., MD 20816. Tel: 301-320-3273; Fax: 301-320-2867. Email: rrynn@lfschool.org. Web: lfschool.org. Sisters of the Immaculate Heart of Mary 6; Lay Teachers 18; Students 269.
Catechesis/Religious Program—Tel: 301-320-5233. Students 340.

4—OUR LADY OF LOURDES (1926), (Spanish), Rev. Msgr. Edward J. Filardi; Revs. Francisco Javier Santaballa; Marco Federico Schad; Deacon John Shewmaker. In Res., Rev. Robert Bozek.
Res.: 7500 Pearl St., MD 20814. Tel: 301-654-1287; Fax: 301-986-8716. Web: www.bethesdalourdes.org.
School—Tel: 301-654-5376; Fax: 301-654-2568. Web: www.bethesda-lourdes.org. Patricia K. McGann, Prin. Sisters 1; Lay Teachers 26; Students 220.
Catechesis/Religious Program—Tel: 301-654-5954. Students 312.

BOWIE, PRINCE GEORGES CO.

1—ASCENSION (1893) [CEM] Rev. Kyle Thomas Ingels; Deacon Nicholas J. Pitocco.
Mailing Address: 12700 Lanham-Severn Rd., MD 20720. Tel: 301-262-2227; Fax: 301-805-5053. Email: ascensionbow@aol.com. In Res., Rev. William F. Goode (Retired).
Catechesis/Religious Program—Carolyn McCart, D.R.E. Students 127.

2—ST. EDWARD (1972) Rev. John M. Barry; Deacons David Barnes; Gary Perkins.
Res.: 16304 Pond Meadow Ln., MD 20716. Tel: 301-249-9199.
Catechesis/Religious Program—Tel: 301-249-9599; Fax: 301-249-1303. Students 300.

3—ST. PIUS X (1962) Revs. Michael T. Jones; Mark Ivany; Deacon Andrew Nosacek, (Retired).
Res.: 3300 Moreland Pl., MD 20715. Tel: 301-262-2141; Fax: 301-262-2632.
Church: 14720 Annapolis Rd., MD 20715.
School—14710 Annapolis Rd., MD 20715. Tel: 301-262-0203; Fax: 301-805-8875. Lay Teachers 60; Students 700.
Catechesis/Religious Program—Tel: 301-262-3644. Maria Kaplan, D.R.E.; Cindy Ostrowski, D.R.E. Students 159.

4—SACRED HEART (1729) [CEM] Rev. Msgrs. Charles J. Parry; Patrick E. Dempsey, Parochial Vicar; Deacon Dan D. Abeyta.
Res.: 16501 Annapolis Rd., MD 20715. Tel: 301-262-0704; Fax: 301-805-4686. Email: parishoffice@sacredheartbowie.org. Web: www.sacredheartbowie.org.
Catechesis/Religious Program—Tel: 301-262-1221. Email: ccdsacredheart@gmail.com. Mrs. Mimi Shea, C.R.E. Students 237.

BRYANTOWN, CHARLES CO., ST. MARY (1793) [CEM] Rev. Rory T. Conley; Deacons Eugene Burroughs; Henry Middleton.
Res.: 13715 Notre Dame Pl., MD 20617-2224. Tel: 301-870-2220; 301-274-3187; Fax: 301-274-0253.
School—Tel: 301-932-6883; Fax: 301-274-0626. Lay Teachers 17; Students 220.
Catechesis/Religious Program—Tel: 301-274-3800. Students 101.

BURTONSVILLE, MONTGOMERY CO., RESURRECTION PARISH (1981) Revs. Robert F. Keffer; Charles E. Brown (Retired); Michael J. Blackwell (Retired).
Res.: 3315 Greencastle Rd., MD 20866. Tel: 301-236-5200; Fax: 301-236-5204. Web: www.resurrectionadw.org.
Catechesis/Religious Program—Tel: 301-236-5200, Ext. 13. Students 245.

BUSHWOOD, ST. MARY'S CO., SACRED HEART (1755) [JC] Rev. Francis J. Early.
Res.: 23080 Maddox Rd. (Rte. 238), P.O. Box 37, MD 20618. Tel: 301-769-3100; Fax: 301-769-2251.
Catechesis/Religious Program— See Holy Angels-Sacred Heart School, Avenue, MD, for details. Students 57.

CAMP SPRINGS, PRINCE GEORGES CO., ST. PHILIP THE APOSTLE (1957) Rev. Scott R. Hahn.
Res.: 5416 Henderson Way, MD 20746. Tel: 301-423-4244; Fax: 301-423-1226. Email: st.philipparish@comcast.net. Web: www.stphiliptheapostlechurch.org.
School—5414 Henderson Way, MD 20746. Tel: 301-423-4740; Fax: 301-423-4716. Lay Teachers 20; Students 283.
Catechesis/Religious Program—Students 48.

CHAPEL POINT, CHARLES CO., ST. IGNATIUS (1641) [CEM] Rev. Edward C. Dougherty, S.J.; Deacon Scott C. Stuart.
St. Thomas Manor: 8855 Chapel Point Rd., Port Tobacco, MD 20677. Tel: 301-934-8245; Fax: 301-934-0944. Web: www.chapelpoint.org.
Catechesis/Religious Program—Tel: 301-392-0962. Angela Hume, D.R.E. Students 145.

CHAPTICO, ST. MARY'S CO., OUR LADY OF THE WAYSIDE (1938) Rev. Jaroslaw Gamrot.
Tel: 301-884-3165; Fax: 301-884-3165.
Res. & Mailing Address: 37575 Chaptico Rd., P.O. Box 97, MD 20621. Tel: 301-884-2502; Fax: 301-884-0381.
School—Mother Catherine Spalding Tri Parish School, Tel: 301-884-3165. Lay Teachers 17; Students 172.
Catechesis/Religious Program—

CHEVERLY, PRINCE GEORGES CO., ST. AMBROSE (1886) Rev. Joseph B. Pierce. In Res., Rev. Alex Martinez.
Res.: 3107 63rd Ave., MD 20785. Tel: 301-773-9300; Fax: 301-773-2611. Email: stambrec@covad.net.
School—6310 Jason St., MD 20785. Tel: 301-773-0223; Fax: 301-773-9218. Mr. Carl Berger, Prin. Lay Teachers 24; Students 282.
Catechesis/Religious Program—Tel: 301-773-0627; Fax: 301-773-9647. Students 79.

CHILLUM, PRINCE GEORGES CO., ST. JOHN BAPTIST DE LA SALLE (1951) Rev. Jose Signorelli, I.V.E.
Res.: 5706 Sargent Rd., MD 20782. Tel: 301-559-3636; Fax: 301-559-3062.
Catechesis/Religious Program—Tel: 301-559-3637. Students 70.

CLINTON, PRINCE GEORGES CO., CHURCH OF ST. JOHN THE EVANGELIST (1875) [CEM] Revs. Jaime B. Hernandez; Edward Anthony Hegnauer, Parochial Vicar; Deacon Santiago T. Montalvo.
Res.: 8908 Old Branch Ave., MD 20735. Tel: 301-868-1070; Fax: 301-868-7915. Email: soc.trinidad@yahoo.com. Web: www.sjreled.org.
Church: 8910 Old Branch Ave., MD 20735.
School—8912 Old Branch Ave., MD 20735. Tel: 301-868-2010; Fax: 301-856-8941. Email: principal@saintjohnsschool.org. Web: saintjohnsschool.org. Lay Teachers 21; Students 208.
Catechesis/Religious Program—Tel: 301-868-3026. Students 165.

COLLEGE PARK, PRINCE GEORGES CO.

1—ST. ANDREW KIM (1974), (Korean), Unassigned.17615 Old Baltimore Rd., Olney, MD 20832.
Res.: 3140 Saint Florence Ter., Olney, MD 20832. Tel: 301-924-8330; Fax: 301-924-8332.
Catechesis/Religious Program—Tel: 301-275-3734. Students 210.

2—HOLY REDEEMER (1912) Rev. George A. Wilkinson Jr.
Res.: 4902 Berwyn Rd., MD 20740. Tel: 301-474-3920; Fax: 301-441-4954. Email: parish@holy-redeemer.org. Web: holy-redeemer.org.
School—Tel: 301-474-3993; Fax: 301-441-8137. Email: school@holy-redeemer.org. Maria Bovich, Prin. Lay Teachers 21; Students 256.
Catechesis/Religious Program—Tel: 301-474-4299. Email: mwinterson@holy-redeemer.org. Marie Winterson, D.R.E. & Youth Min. Students 43.

DAMASCUS, MONTGOMERY CO., ST. PAUL (1957) Rev. Peter T. Sweeney; Deacons John Finerty; David Terrar; Charles Weschler.
Res.: 9240 Damascus Rd., MD 20872. Tel: 301-253-2027; Fax: 301-391-6755.
Catechesis/Religious Program—Tel: 301-253-5941. Students 770.

DARNESTOWN, MONTGOMERY CO., OUR LADY OF THE VISITATION (1991) [CEM] Revs. Raymond L. Fecteau; Mathew Punchayil (India) (SYM); Deacon Robert Fischer.
Mailing Address: 14135 Seneca Rd., MD 20874-3337.
Res.: 14200 Darnestown Rd., MD 20874-3008. Tel: 301-948-5536; Fax: 301-948-7452.
Church: 14139 Seneca Rd., MD 20874. Tel: 301-948-5536. Email: parishoffice@olvp.org. Web: www.olvp.org.
Catechesis/Religious Program—Students 225.

DERWOOD, MONTGOMERY CO., ST. FRANCIS OF ASSISI (1972) Rev. David W. Beaubien; Deacons James J. Datovech; Daniel F. Finn VI. In Res., Rev. Msgr. Ralph J. Kuehner (Retired).
Res.: 6701 Muncaster Mill Rd., MD 20855. Tel: 301-840-1407; Fax: 301-258-5080. Email: sfaparishoffice@sfadw.org. Web: www.sfadw.org.
Catechesis/Religious Program—Tel: 301-258-9193. Email: sfareligioused@sfadw.org. Students 439.

FORESTVILLE, PRINCE GEORGE CO.

1—CHURCH OF THE HOLY SPIRIT (1966) Rev. Tam X. Tran. In Res., Rev. Jeffrey F. Samaha; Deacon Joseph Welch.
Res.: 1717 Ritchie Rd., MD 20747. Tel: 301-336-3707; Fax: 301-324-1649.
Catechesis/Religious Program— Combined with Mt. Calvary School, Forestville. Students 2.

2—MT. CALVARY (1942) [CEM] Rev. Everett Pearson; Deacon Lawrence Miles. In Res., Rev. Msgr. Richard A. Hughes (Retired).
Res.: 6700 Marlboro Pike, MD 20747. Tel: 301-735-5532; Fax: 301-735-2005. Email: mtcalvary.md@adwparish.org. Web: www.mountcalvarycatholicschool.org.
School—6704 Marlboro Pike, MD 20747. Tel: 301-735-5262; Fax: 301-736-5044. Lay Teachers 17; Students 177.
Catechesis/Religious Program—6704 Marlboro Pike, MD 20747. Tel: 301-735-5262, Ext. 17. Students 45.

FORT WASHINGTON, PRINCE GEORGES CO., ST. IGNATIUS (1849) [CEM] Rev. G. Paul Herbert.
Res.: 2315 Brinkley Rd., MD 20744. Tel: 301-567-4740; Fax: 301-567-0046. Email: office@saint-ig.org.
Catechesis/Religious Program—Tel: 301-567-4740. Students 35.

GAITHERSBURG, MONTGOMERY CO.

1—ST. JOHN NEUMANN (1978) [CEM] Revs. Thomas G. LaHood; Marcel Guarnizo, Parochial Vicar; Deacons Eugene Cummins; Carlo Caraballo; Michael W. Davy.
Mailing Address: 8900 Lochaven Dr., MD 20882-4460. Email: info@saintjohnneumann.org. Web: www.saintjohnneumann.org.
Church: 9000 Warfield Rd., MD 20882. Tel: 301-977-5492; Fax: 301-977-3559.
Catechesis/Religious Program—Tel: 301-977-7990; Fax: 301-330-3235. Students 370.

2—ST. MARTIN OF TOURS (1920) Rev. Msgr. Mark E. Brennan; Revs. Alejandro Diaz; Pawel Sass; Deacons Lawrence Bell; Ronald J. Meyer; William A. Vita Jr.; Ivan Hernandez.
Res.: 201 S. Frederick Ave., MD 20877. Tel: 301-990-3203; Fax: 301-990-7538. Email: parish@stmartinsweb.com. Web: www.stmartinsweb.com.
School—115 S. Frederick Ave., MD 20877. Tel: 301-990-2441; Fax: 301-990-2688. Web: www.smsm-d.org. Sr. Sharon Mihm, C.S.C., Prin. Lay Teachers 17; Students 236.
Catechesis/Religious Program—Tel: 301-990-2556; Fax: 301-990-2622. Email: religious-education@stmartinsweb.com. Ilsa Hernandez, D.R.E. Students 1,012.

3—ST. ROSE OF LIMA (1972) [CEM] Rev. Msgr. Paul M. Dudziak; Rev. Jose Jesus Arriaga (Mexico); Deacons John C. Liu; Mario F. Moreno; Albert L. Opdenaker; Patti Sullins, Dir Liturgy & Music.
Mailing Address: 11701 Clopper Rd., MD 20878-1024. Tel: 301-948-7545; Fax: 301-869-2170. Email: strose@strose.com. Web: www.strose.com.
Catechesis/Religious Program—Tel: 301-948-7545. Cheryl Shalgian, D.R.E. (Pre K-5, English); Sr. Gisela Rodriguez, D.R.E. (K-12, Spanish); Pat Clancy, D.R.E. (6-12, English); Kathryn Heetderks, Adult Faith Formation. Students 668.

GARRETT PARK, MONTGOMERY CO., HOLY CROSS (1960) Rev. Msgr. Robert Cary Hill; Rev. Joseph F. Perkins; Deacon Robert Hubbard.
Res.: 4900 Strathmore Ave., P.O. Box 249, MD 20896. Tel: 301-942-1020; Fax: 301-949-3543. Web: www.hcrosschurch.org.
School—Tel: 301-949-0053; Fax: 301-949-5074. Email: office@hcross.org. Web: www.hcross.org. Lisa Maio Kane, Prin. Lay Teachers 21; Students 193.
Catechesis/Religious Program—Tel: 301-942-8790. Email: keeney@hcrosschurch.org. Jeanmarie Keeney, D.R.E. Students 304.

GERMANTOWN, MONTGOMERY CO., MOTHER SETON PARISH (1974) [CEM] Revs. Mark W. Ervin; Louis J. Faust, Senior Priest; Emanuele DeNigris, Parochial Vicar; Deacons William Vita; Francis W. Bendel; Timothy Enright.
Res.: 19951 Father Hurley Blvd., MD 20874. Tel: 301-924-3838; Fax: 301-428-4951. Email: mspps@aol.com. Web: mothersetonparish.org.
Catechesis/Religious Program—Tel: 301-444-3496; 301-444-3495. Students 659.

GREAT MILLS, ST. MARY'S CO., HOLY FACE (1879) [CEM] Rev. Joseph Sileo.
Mailing Address: 20476 Point Lookout Rd., MD 20634. Tel: 301-994-0525; Fax: 301-994-1547. Email: holyface@md.metrocast.net.
School—Little Flower, 20410 Point Lookout Rd., MD 20634. Tel: 301-994-0404; Fax: 301-994-2055. Lay Teachers 15; Students 170.
Catechesis/Religious Program—Students 158.

GREENBELT, PRINCE GEORGES CO., SAINT HUGH OF GRENOBLE (1947) Rev. Walter J. Tappe.
Res.: 135 Crescent Rd., MD 20770. Tel: 301-474-4322; Fax: 301-474-9263. Web: www.sthughs.com.
Catechesis/Religious Program—Email: st.hugh.religioused@gmail.com. Students 82.

HILLCREST HEIGHTS, PRINCE GEORGES CO., HOLY FAMILY (1952), (African American), Rev. Damian Shadwell.
Res.: 2210 Callaway St., MD 20748. Tel: 301-894-2222; Fax: 301-894-2938.
School—2200 Callaway St., MD 20748. Tel: 301-894-2323.
Catechesis/Religious Program—Students 246.

HILLTOP, CHARLES CO., ST. IGNATIUS LOYOLA (1851) [CEM] Rev. Robert J. Kosty; Deacon Frank L. Hopson, (Retired).
Mailing Address: P.O. Box 278, Port Tobacco, MD 20677. Tel: 301-934-9630; Fax: 301-934-8320. Email: pappybob46@aol.com.
Catechesis/Religious Program—Tel: 301-934-9080. Students 29.

HOLLYWOOD, ST. MARY'S CO., ST. JOHN FRANCIS REGIS (1690) [CEM] Rev. Raymond F. Schmidt; Rev. Msgr. Martin P. Harris, Pastor Emeritus (Retired). In Res., Rev. Eamon Dignan (Retired).
Res. & Mailing Address: 43950 St. John's Rd., MD 20636. Tel: 301-373-2281; Fax: 301-373-8984. Email: stjohnschurch1@verizon.net. Web: stjohnsparishhollywood.org.
School—Tel: 301-373-2142; Fax: 301-373-4500. Email: office@sjshollywood.org. Web: www.sjshollywood.org. J. B. Watters, Prin. Students 196.
Catechesis/Religious Program—Email: sjcreled@verizon.net. Students 327.

HUNTINGTOWN, CALVERT CO., JESUS THE DIVINE WORD PARISH (1994) Rev. Lawrence C. Swink.
Mailing Address: 885 Cox Rd., MD 20639. Tel: 410-414-8304; Fax: 410-535-9057. Email: office@jesusdivineword.org. Web: www.jesusdivineword.org.
Catechesis/Religious Program—Email: religioused@jesusdivineword.org. Students 345.

HYATTSVILLE, PRINCE GEORGES CO.
1—ST. JEROME (1886) Rev. James M. Stack; Deacon Neal T. Conway. In Res., Revs. Isadore Dixon; Charles Edeh, Chap., Nigerian Catholic Community; Clinton Sensat.
Res.: 5205 43rd Ave., MD 20781. Tel: 301-927-6684; Fax: 301-927-9167. Email: ajstjerome@hotmail.com. Web: www.stjerome.org.
School—5207 42nd Pl., MD 20781. Tel: 301-277-4568; Fax: 301-779-2428. Mary Pat Donoghue, Prin. Lay Teachers 20; Students 270.
Convent—5300 43rd Ave., MD 20781. Tel: 301-864-2016.
Child Center—Tel: 301-699-1314.
Catechesis/Religious Program—Email: annahyatt@verizon.net. Students 30.
2—ST. MARK (1958) Revs. John J. Dillon; Paul Sullins, Parochial Vicar; Juan Esposito-Garcia, Parochial Vicar; Deacons Jose Renato Molina; Curtis Turner. In Res., Rev. Msgr. Michael W. Fisher.
Res.: 7501 Adelphi Rd., MD 20783. Tel: 301-422-8300; Fax: 301-422-2313. Email: rectory@stmarkhyattsville.org. Web: www.stmarkhyattsville.4lpi.org.
Catechesis/Religious Program—Tel: 301-422-7822. Email: mgalindo@stmarkhyattsville.org. Martha Galindo, C.R.E. Students 300.

INDIAN HEAD, CHARLES CO., ST. MARY STAR OF THE SEA (1918) [CEM] Rev. William J. Thompson (Retired); Deacon Albert S. Tompa.
Res.: 30 Mattingly Ave., MD 20640. Tel: 301-753-9177; Fax: 301-743-6670. Email: sstarofthesea@aol.com.
School—6485 Indian Head Hwy., MD 20640. Tel: 301-283-6151; Fax: 301-283-4368. Email: office@stmarystar.net. Web: www.stmarystar.net. Lay Teachers 13; Students 111.
Catechesis/Religious Program—Students 38.

ISSUE, CHARLES CO., HOLY GHOST (1880) [CEM] Rev. Gregory S. Coan; Deacon Walter G. Rourke.
Res.: 15848 Rock Point Rd., Newburg, MD 20664. Tel: 301-259-2515; Fax: 301-259-2289. Email: holyghostchurch@verizon.net. Web: parishesonline.com/holyghostissue.
Catechesis/Religious Program—Students 71.
Mission—St. Francis de Sales Newburg, MD. 13675 Furbush Rd., Rock Point, Charles Co., MD 20682.

KENSINGTON, MONTGOMERY CO., HOLY REDEEMER (1948) Revs. Mark F. Hughes; Percival L. D'Silva (Retired).
Res.: 9705 Summit Ave., MD 20895. Tel: 301-942-2333; Fax: 301-942-1041.
School—9715 Summit Ave., MD 20895. Tel: 301-942-3701; Fax: 301-942-4981. Web: hrs-ken.org. David A. Lombardi, Prin. Lay Teachers 29; Students 390.
Catechesis/Religious Program—Tel: 301-942-2333, Ext. 100. John Buchanan, D.R.E. Students 225.

LA PLATA, CHARLES CO., SACRED HEART (1901) [CEM] Revs. Robert P. Buchmeier; John F. Reutemann III; Deacons Anthony Barrasso, (Retired); Albert E. Graham Jr., (Retired); Walter G. Rourke.
Res.: 201 St. Mary's Ave., P.O. Box 1390, MD 20646. Tel: 301-934-2261; Fax: 301-934-5435. Email: shclp@verizon.net. Web: www.shclp.org.
School—Archbishop Neale School, 104 Port Tobacco Rd., MD 20646. Tel: 301-934-9595; Fax: 301-753-1717. Margaret Howard, Prin. Lay Teachers 32; Students 430.
Catechesis/Religious Program—Tel: 301-934-3386. Deacon Anthony T. Barrasso, D.R.E. Students 215.

LANDOVER HILLS, PRINCE GEORGE'S CO.
1—ST. MARY'S CATHOLIC CHURCH (1948) Revs. Samuel C. Giese; Brian Alick Coelho; Deacons Stephen M. Robinson; Dennis J. Bingham. In Res., Rev. Mathai Mannoorvadakkethil Yohannan.
Res.: 7401 Buchanan St., MD 20784-2323. Tel: 301-577-8844; Fax: 301-306-5543. Email: secretary@saintmarylandoverhills.org. Web: www.saintmarylandoverhills.org.
School—7207 Annapolis Rd., MD 20784. Tel: 301-577-0031; Fax: 301-577-5485. Email: admin.stmarys@comcast.net. Web: stmaryslh.org. Susan Junge Varrone, Prin. Lay Teachers 25; Students 227.
Catechesis/Religious Program—Tel: 301-577-2478. Students 124.
2—SYRO-MALANKARA MISSION (1985), (Indian), Rev. Jacob C. George.
Res.: 7401 Buchanan St., MD 20784-9998. Tel: 301-577-8844; Fax: 301-306-5543. Email: frjacobchi02@yahoo.com.
Catechesis/Religious Program—Students 40.

LANHAM, PRINCE GEORGES CO., ST. MATTHIAS APOSTLE (1960) Rev. Jeffrey M. Defayette.
Res.: 9475 Annapolis Rd., MD 20706-3020. Tel: 301-459-4814; Fax: 301-306-4582.
School—9473 Annapolis Rd., MD 20706-3020. Tel: 301-577-9412; Fax: 301-577-2060. Web: www.stmatthias.org. Ms. Patricia F. Wilson, Prin. Lay Teachers 15; Students 178.
Catechesis/Religious Program—Tel: 301-459-4814, Ext. 205; Fax: 301-306-4582. Students 62.
Convent—9471 Annapolis Rd., MD 20706-3020. Tel: 301-459-8078.

LARGO, PRINCE GEORGES CO., ST. JOSEPH (1922) Rev. Roy Edward Campbell; Deacon Alton Davis.
Res.: 2020 St. Joseph Dr., MD 20774. Tel: 301-773-4838; Fax: 301-773-6832.
Catechesis/Religious Program—Tel: 301-773-2480. Students 14.

LAUREL, PRINCE GEORGES CO.
1—ST. MARY (1843) [CEM] Rev. Msgr. Michael Wilson; Deacons Brandon B. Justice; Perfecto Santiago; Robert L. Gignilliat.
Res.: 114 St. Mary's Pl., MD 20707. Tel: 301-725-3080; Fax: 301-725-2409. Web: www.stmarys.laurel.md.us.
School—106 St. Mary's Pl., MD 20707. Tel: 301-498-1433; Fax: 301-498-1170. Web: www.stmaryofthemill.org. James Pavlacka, Prin. Lay Teachers 28; Students 403.
Catechesis/Religious Program—Tel: 301-490-8770. Mrs. Carol Lee, Child Protection Coord.; Jennifer Juzwiak, D.R.E. (Adult). Students 383.
2—ST. NICHOLAS (1967) Rev. James S. Betz (Retired); Deacons Francis Hannagan; Perry Iannaconi.
Res.: 8603 Contee Rd., MD 20708. Tel: 301-490-5116; 301-490-5117; Fax: 301-490-1527.
Catechesis/Religious Program—Tel: 301-776-8303. Students 77.

LEONARDTOWN, ST. MARY'S CO., ST. ALOYSIUS (1710) [CEM] Rev. John T. Dakes.
Res.: 22800 Washington St., P.O. Box 310, MD 20650. Tel: 301-475-8064; Fax: 301-475-8762. Web: www.saintaloysiuschurch.org.
School—Father Andrew White, S.J., 22850 Washington St., P.O. Box 1756, MD 20650. Tel: 301-475-9795; Fax: 301-475-3537. Email: fradwh@verizon.net. Web: www.fatherandrewwhite.org. Lay Teachers 18; Students 267.
Catechesis/Religious Program—Email: lwathen@saintaloysiuschurch.org. Students 206.

LEXINGTON PARK, ST. MARY'S CO., IMMACULATE HEART OF MARY (1947) [CEM] Revs. John H. Kennealy; David Wells, Parochial Vicar.
Mailing Address: 22375 Three Notch Rd., MD 20653-0166. Tel: 301-863-8144; Fax: 301-863-8180.
Catechesis/Religious Program—Tel: 301-863-8793. Janet Harmon, D.R.E. Students 205.

MCCONCHIE, CHARLES CO., ST. CATHERINE OF ALEXANDRIA (1911) [CEM] Rev. Robert J. Kosty; Deacon Frank L. Hopson, (Retired).
Mailing Address: P.O. Box 278, Port Tobacco, MD 20677. Tel: 301-934-9630; Fax: 301-934-8320. Email: pappybob46@aol.com.
Catechesis/Religious Program—Students 55.

MECHANICSVILLE, ST. MARY'S CO., IMMACULATE CONCEPTION (1876) Rev. John P. Caulfield; Deacons James E. Conner, (Retired); William L. Kyte.
Mailing Address: 28297 Old Village Rd., P.O. Box 166, MD 20659. Tel: 301-884-3123; Fax: 301-884-7437. Email: immaculateconception.md@adwparish.org. Web: www.icmechanicsville.com.
Catechesis/Religious Program—Tel: 301-884-3016. Email: paulamcleod26@yahoo.com. Students 285.

MEDLEY'S NECK, ST. MARY'S CO., OUR LADY'S (1767) [CEM] Rev. Thomas G. LaHood; Deacon Thomas C. Spalding Sr.
Mailing Address: 41348 Medley's Neck Rd., Leonardtown, MD 20650. Tel: 301-475-8403; Fax: 301-475-6632.
Catechesis/Religious Program—Students 71.

MITCHELLVILLE, PRINCE GEORGES CO., HOLY FAMILY (1938) [CEM] Rev. Joseph A. Jenkins.
Mailing Address: 12010 Woodmore Rd., MD 20721. Tel: 301-249-2266; Fax: 301-249-2524. Email: holyfamilyadmin@msn.com. Web: holyfamilywoodmore.com.
Catechesis/Religious Program—Tel: 301-249-1167. Students 130.

MORGANZA, ST. MARY'S CO., ST. JOSEPH (1700) [CEM 2] [JC] Rev. Keith A. Woods; Deacon James A. Somerville, (Retired).
Res.: 29119 Point Lookout Rd., P.O. Box 175, MD 20660. Tel: 301-475-3293; Fax: 301-475-0491. Email: stjosephmorganza@yahoo.com.
Catechesis/Religious Program—Students 106.

MOUNT RAINIER, PRINCE GEORGES CO., ST. JAMES (1905) Rev. Pablo Daniel Muñoz Iturrieta, I.V.E.; Deacon John H. Turner. In Res., Rev. Pablo Bonello, I.V.E.
Res.: 3628 Rhode Island Ave., MD 20712. Tel: 301-927-0567; Fax: 301-927-5289. Email: st.jamescatholicchurch@gmail.com. Web: www.stjames-mountrainier.org.
Catechesis/Religious Program—Tel: 301-927-0567. Students 650.

NEWPORT, CHARLES CO., ST. MARY (1674) [CEM] Rev. Mark W. Ervin; Deacon Jerome Butkiewicz.
Res.: 11555 St. Mary's Church Rd., Charlotte Hall, MD 20622. Tel: 301-934-8825; Fax: 301-934-0245.
Catechesis/Religious Program—Students 93.

NEWTOWNE, ST. MARY'S CO., ST. FRANCIS XAVIER (1640) [CEM] Rev. Brian P. Sanderfoot, Admin.; Deacon William J. Nickerson.
Res.: 21370 Newtowne Neck Rd., Leonardtown, MD 20650. Tel: 301-475-9885; Fax: 301-475-5662. Email: stfrancisxavier.md@adwparish.net.
Catechesis/Religious Program—Students 67.

NORBECK, MONTGOMERY CO., ST. PATRICK (1966) Rev. Msgr. Kevin T. Hart; Rev. Michael Paris; Deacons Alfred M. Barros; James T. Nalls.
Res.: 4101 Norbeck Rd., Rockville, MD 20853. Tel: 301-924-2284; 301-924-2285; Fax: 301-929-3017. Email: stpatrock@verizon.net. Web: www.stpatricksmd.org.
Catechesis/Religious Program—Tel: 301-929-9314. Students 341.

NORTH BEACH, CALVERT CO., ST. ANTHONY (1905) Rev. David P. Russell; Deacons John F. Lynch, (Retired); Francis E. Baker Jr.
Res.: 8900 Bay Ave., P.O. Box 660, MD 20714. Tel: 410-257-2368; 301-855-7756 (Washington); Fax: 240-652-8708. Email: office@stanthonycal.us. Web: www.stanthonycal.com.
Catechesis/Religious Program—Tel: 301-855-0897. Deborah Wheeler, D.R.E. & Youth Min. Students 220.

OLNEY, MONTGOMERY CO., ST. PETER (1953) Revs. Thomas M. Kalita; Ismael N. Ayala; Joseph E. Rogers; Deacons James Cadigan; Thomas Cioffi; Rory P. Crawford; Mrs. Elizabeth Harper, Business Mgr.
Res.: 2900 Olney-Sandy Spring Rd., MD 20832. Tel: 301-924-3774; Fax: 301-774-5259. Email: info@stpetersolney.org. Web: www.stpetersolney.org.
School—Tel: 301-774-9112; Fax: 301-924-6698. Email: school@stpetersolney.org. Mrs. Mary Elizabeth Whelan, Prin. Lay Teachers 44; Students 413.
Catechesis/Religious Program—Tel: 301-570-4952. Angela Busby, D.R.E. (Grades K-4); Cindy Dixon, D.R.E. (Grades 5-8). Students 645.

OWINGS, CALVERT CO., JESUS THE GOOD SHEPHERD (1985) Rev. Michael J. King; Deacons Emmett (Chad) Martin; John Verdon.
Res.: 1555 W. Mt. Harmony Rd., MD 20736. Tel: 410-257-3810, Ext. 20; Fax: 410-257-6334. Email: pastor@ccjgs.org. Web: www.ccjgs.org.
School—Cardinal Hickey Academy, 1601 W. Mt. Harmony Rd., MD 20736. Tel: 410-286-0404; Fax: 410-286-6334. Web: www.edline.net/pages/cardinal_hickey_academy. Mrs. Jennifer Griffith, Prin.
Catechesis/Religious Program—Tel: 410-257-3810, Ext. 18; Fax: 410-257-6334. Email: religoused@ccjgs.org. Students 637.

OXON HILL, PRINCE GEORGES CO., ST. COLUMBA (1960) Revs. Gary T. Villanueva; Andrew B. Gonzalo, Parochial Vicar; Deacons Richard A. Fisher, (Retired); Leandro Y. Espinosa.
Res.: 7804 Livingston Rd., MD 20745. Tel: 301-567-5506; Fax: 301-567-6546. Email: stcolumbachurch@verizon.net. Web: www.stcolumbacatholic.net.
School—7800 Livingston Rd., MD 20745. Tel: 301-567-6212; Fax: 301-567-6907. Email: schooloffice@stcolumbiafaculty.org. Web: www.stccatholic.org. Lay Teachers 20; Students 247.
Catechesis/Religious Program—Tel: 301-567-6113; Fax: 301-567-3188. Students 95.

PISCATAWAY, PRINCE GEORGES CO., ST. MARY (1640) [CEM] Rev. Timothy K. Baer; Deacons George Ames; Stephen McKimmie.
Res.: 13401 Piscataway Rd., Clinton, MD 20735-4564. Tel: 301-292-0527; Fax: 301-292-8786. Email: parish@stmaryspiscataway.org. Web: www.parishesonline.com/scripts/HostedSites/Org.asp?ID=8190.
School—13407 Piscataway Rd., Clinton, MD 20735. Tel: 301-292-2522; Fax: 301-292-2534. Email:

school@stmaryspiscataway.org. Web: www.stmaryspiscataway.org. Lay Teachers 16; Students 193.
Catechesis/Religious Program—Email: keimig@stmaryspiscataway.org. Students 58.

POMFRET, CHARLES CO., ST. JOSEPH (1763) [CEM] Rev. Mark Leo Smith; Deacon John R. Barnes.
Mailing Address: 4590 St. Joseph Way, MD 20675. Tel: 301-609-4670; Fax: 301-609-7564. Web: www.stjoepomfret.4lpi.com.
Catechesis/Religious Program—Students 156.

POOLESVILLE, MONTGOMERY CO., OUR LADY OF THE PRESENTATION (1992) Rev. Vincent J. Rigdon; Deacon William H. Stevens.
Mailing Address: P.O. Box 428, MD 20837. Tel: 301-349-2045; 301-349-2788; Fax: 301-349-5423. Email: ol-presentation.md@adwparish.org. Web: www.ol-presentation-md.org.
Catechesis/Religious Program—Students 138.

POTOMAC, MONTGOMERY CO.

1—NATIVITY OF THE BLESSED VIRGIN (GERMAN MISSION) (1992), (German), Deacon Clayton A. Nickel.
Rectory—6330 Linway Ter., McLean, VA 22101-4150. Tel: 703-356-4473.

2—OUR LADY OF MERCY (1959), (Korean), [CEM] Rev. Msgr. William J. English; Rev. Francisco Alves, S.J. (India); Deacon James Yun. In Res., Rev. Msgr. William J. Awalt (Retired); Rev. Donald P. Worch (Retired).
Res.: 9200 Kentsdale Dr., MD 20854. Tel: 301-365-1415; Fax: 301-365-3104. Web: www.olom.org.
School—9222 Kentsdale Dr., MD 20854. Tel: 301-365-4477; Fax: 301-365-3423. Mrs. Joan C. Hosmer, Prin. Lay Teachers 28; Students 276.
Catechesis/Religious Program—Tel: 301-365-1318. Students 351.

PRINCE FREDERICK, CALVERT CO., ST. JOHN VIANNEY (1965) [CEM] Rev. Peter J. Daly.
Res.: 105 Vianney Ln., MD 20678-4123. Tel: 410-535-0223; Fax: 410-535-4422. Email: sjv@chesapeake.net. Web: www.sjvc.us.
Catechesis/Religious Program—Tel: 410-535-4395. Jeanette M. Pedone, D.R.E. Students 383.

RIDGE, ST. MARY'S CO., ST. MICHAEL (1824) [CEM] Rev. Msgr. Maurice V. O'Connell (Retired).
P.O. Box 429, MD 20680.
Res.: , MD 20680. Tel: 301-872-4321.
School—P.O. Box 429, MD 20680. Tel: 301-872-5454. Mrs. Regina Housel, Prin. Lay Teachers 14; Students 170.
Catechesis/Religious Program—Students 98.

RIVERDALE PARK, PRINCE GEORGES CO., ST. BERNARD (1950) Rev. Sergio Dall Agnese, C.S.; Deacon Desmond Yorke.
Res.: 5700 St. Bernard Dr., MD 20737-2185. Tel: 301-277-1000; Fax: 301-277-3464.
Catechesis/Religious Program—Tel: 301-277-4220; Fax: 301-277-3464. Mrs. Teresa Luna, D.R.E.

ROCKVILLE, MONTGOMERY CO.

1—ST. ELIZABETH (1964) Rev. Msgr. John F. Macfarlane; Rev. Brian Alick Coelho.
Res.: 917 Montrose Rd., MD 20852. Tel: 301-881-1380; Fax: 301-881-3068.
School—Tel: 301-881-1824; Fax: 301-881-6035. Lay Teachers 39; Students 508.
Catechesis/Religious Program—Students 320.

2—ST. MARY (1813) [CEM] Rev. Msgr. Robert G. Amey; Rev. Charles M. Gallagher, Parochial Vicar; Deacons Daniel Kostka; Barry A. Levy. In Res., Rev. M. Valentine Keveny.
Res.: 520 Veirs Mill Rd., MD 20852. Tel: 301-424-5550; Fax: 301-424-5579. Email: stmaryrockville@yahoo.com. Web: www.stmarysrockville.org.
School—600 Viers Mill Rd., MD 20852. Tel: 301-762-4179. Lay Teachers 19; Students 221.
Catechesis/Religious Program—Tel: 301-762-8750. Email: smrockville@gmail.com. Students 336.

3—ST. RAPHAEL (1966) Revs. James P. Meyers; Charles Cortinovis, Parochial Vicar; Agustin Lopez, Parochial Vicar; Deacons Richard Mattocks, (Retired); Frank Salatto, (Retired); Jose R. Carbonell; Jorge Gatica. In Res., Rev. Msgr. Vincent S. Gatto (Retired).
Res. & Mailing Address: 1513 Dunster Rd., MD 20854. Tel: 301-762-2143; Fax: 301-762-0719. Web: www.straphaels.org.
Catechesis/Religious Program—Tel: 301-762-2143, Ext. 124. Students 706.

4—SHRINE OF ST. JUDE (1956) Revs. J. William Hines; John Tung Nguyen; Raphael Blake Evans-Campos; Deacons Nicholas E. Scholz; Donald Mays.
Res.: 12701 Veirs Mill Rd., MD 20853. Tel: 301-946-8200; Fax: 301-946-4527. Web: www.shrinestjude.org.
School—4820 Walbridge St., MD 20853. Tel: 301-946-7888; Fax: 301-929-8927. Email: stjudemain@yahoo.com. Web: www.stjudesschool.org. Lay Teachers 24; Students 204.
Catechesis/Religious Program—Tel: 301-949-2336. Web: shrinestjude.org/organizations. Students 394.

ROSARYVILLE, PRINCE GEORGE'S CO., CHURCH OF THE MOST HOLY ROSARY (1966) [CEM] Rev. Roger A. Soley.
Res.: 11704 Duley Station Rd., Upper Marlboro, MD 20772. Tel: 301-856-3880; 301-856-3881; Fax: 301-856-3944. Email: holyrosary.md@adwparish.org. Web: www.mostholyrosarychurch.org.
Catechesis/Religious Program— Twinned with St. Mary of the Assumption, Upper Marlboro.

ST. INIGOES, ST. MARY'S CO., ST. PETER CLAVER (1903), (African American), [CEM] Rev. Scott Woods.
Res.: 16922 St. Peter Claver Church Rd., P.O. Box 240, MD 20684-0240. Tel: 301-872-5460; Fax: 301-872-5672.
Catechesis/Religious Program—Students 50.

ST. MARY'S CITY, ST. MARY'S CO., ST. CECILIA (1974) [CEM] Rev. Scott Woods.
Res.: 47950 Mattapany Rd., P.O. Box 429, MD 20686. Tel: 301-862-4600.
Catechesis/Religious Program— Clustered with St. Michael's, Ridge.

SEAT PLEASANT, PRINCE GEORGES CO., ST. MARGARET (1908), (African American), Revs. Columban Crotty, SS.CC.; Fintan Sheeran; Deacons Sam Minor; Valentine Oguledo.
Res.: 408 Addison Rd. S., MD 20743. Tel: 301-336-3345; Fax: 301-336-5501.
Catechesis/Religious Program—Tel: 301-336-5976. Students 108.

SILVER SPRING, MONTGOMERY CO.

1—ST. ANDREW APOSTLE (1959) Revs. Daniel P. Leary; Rodolfo A. Salinas, Parochial Vicar; Deacons Michael Bond; Kenneth Barrett. In Res., Rev. Msgr. Francis G. Kazista (Retired).
Res.: 11600 Kemp Mill Rd., MD 20902. Tel: 301-649-3700; Fax: 301-681-3527. Email: standrews11600@yahoo.com. Web: standrewapostle.org.
School—Tel: 301-649-3555; Fax: 301-649-2352. Email: standrew20902@yahoo.com. Susan M. Sheehan, Interim Prin. Lay Teachers 25; Students 280.
Catechesis/Religious Program—Tel: 301-649-4200. Students 218.
McCarrick Center—12247 Georgia Ave., MD 20902. Tel: 301-946-1621; Fax: 301-789-6274. Email: andreamariat@gmail.com.

2—ST. BERNADETTE (Four Corners) (1948) Rev. Msgr. K. Bartholomew Smith; Rev. Vincent Derosa, Parochial Vicar; Deacon Thomas E. Roszkowski. In Res., Rev. Nicholas A. Zientarski (RVC).
Res.: 70 University Blvd., E., MD 20901. Tel: 301-593-0357; Fax: 301-593-3088. Email: parish@stbernadetteschurch.org.
School—80 University Blvd., E., MD 20901. Tel: 301-593-5611; Fax: 301-593-9042. Web: st_bernadetteelem.com. Lay Teachers 30; Students 430.
Catechesis/Religious Program—Tel: 301-593-5104. Email: baily@st-bernadetteelem.com. Mrs. Jane Baily, D.R.E. Students 150.

3—ST. CAMILLUS (1951) Revs. Michael Johnson, O.F.M.; Jean-Marie Kabango, O.F.M.; Jacek Orzechowski, O.F.M.; Erick Lopez, O.F.M.; Deacons Peter Barbernitz; Francisco J. Cartagena.
Res.: 1600 St. Camillus Dr., MD 20903. Tel: 301-434-8400; Fax: 301-434-8041. Web: stcamilluschurch.org.
School—1500 St. Camillus Dr., MD 20903. Tel: 301-434-2344; Fax: 301-434-7726. Email: tharkleroad@sfismd.org. Web: www.saintfrancisinternational.org. Lay Teachers 28; Students 320.
Catechesis/Religious Program—Tel: 301-434-2111. Email: officefaithformation@gmail.com. Dorothy Mensah-Aggrey, Co-Dir., Faith Formation (English and French Prog.); Gloria Canales, Co-Dir., Faith Formation (Spanish Prog.). Students 824.
Mission—Catholic Community of Langley Park 1408 Merrimac Dr., Langley Park, Prince George's Co., MD 20787. Tel: 301-328-5105; Fax: 301-328-5105 (Call first).

4—ST. CATHERINE LABOURE (Wheaton) (1951) Revs. Michael A. Salah; Thomas G. Morrow; Luis Marroquin; Bogumil Kosciesza; Deacons Raymond L. Chaput; G. Stephane Philogene.
Res.: 11801 Claridge Rd., Wheaton, MD 20902. Tel: 301-946-3636; Fax: 301-946-5064.
School—11811 Claridge Rd., Wheaton, MD 20902. Tel: 301-946-1717; Fax: 301-946-9572. Lay Teachers 19; Students 238.
Catechesis/Religious Program—Tel: 301-946-3010 (English); 301-946-1606 (Hispanic Religious Education). Email: sclreligioused@verizon.net. Students 694.

5—CHRIST THE KING (Wheaton) (1961) Rev. John F. Plans, S.F.; Deacon Stephen Mitchell.
Res.: 2300 East-West Hwy., 2301 Colston Dr., MD 20910. Tel: 301-589-8616; Fax: 301-587-1929.
Catechesis/Religious Program—Tel: 301-589-8620. Shawna Madison, D.R.E. Students 320.

6—ST. JOHN THE BAPTIST (Spring Brook) (1960) Revs. Y. David Brault; Uche Cosmas Ozoagu; Deacons John C. Cermak; James J. Gorman.
Res.: 12319 New Hampshire Ave., MD 20904. Tel: 301-622-1122; Fax: 301-625-9266. Email: stjohnbaptist.silverspring.md@adwparish.org. Web: www.sjbsilverspring.org.
School—Tel: 301-622-3076; Fax: 301-622-2453. Email: sjbsprincipal@yahoo.com. Marianne Moore, Prin. Lay Teachers 22; Students 266.
Catechesis/Religious Program—Email: dre@sjbsilverspring.org. Virginia Cohen, D.R.E. Students 229.

7—ST. JOHN THE EVANGELIST (1774) [CEM] Rev. Msgr. John R. Pennington; Rev. Mark E. Tucker; Sr. Theresa McElroy, I.H.M., Pastoral Min.
Res.: 10103 Georgia Ave., MD 20902. Tel: 301-681-7663; Fax: 301-681-8793. Web: sjeparish.org.
School—10201 Woodland Dr., MD 20902. Tel: 301-681-7656; Fax: 301-681-0754. Sr. Kathleen Lannak, I.H.M., Prin. Lay Teachers 9; (Part Time) 9; Students 259.
Catechesis/Religious Program—Tel: 301-681-7634. Sr. Roberta Harding, I.H.M., D.R.E. Students 162.

8—ST. MICHAEL (1930) Rev. Msgr. Eddie E. Tolentino; Rev. Daniel Malaver; Deacons Ronald Ealey, Life Dir.; Stephen B. Frye.
Res.: 824 Pershing Dr., MD 20910. Tel: 301-589-1155; Fax: 301-589-3470. Web: www.stmichaelsilverspring.parishesonline.com.
School—824 Wayne Ave., MD 20910. Tel: 301-585-6873; Fax: 301-587-1142. Email: sms@adwschool.org. Web: st-michaelschool.org. Mr. Larry Savoy, Prin. Lay Teachers 13; Students 157.
Catechesis/Religious Program—Tel: 301-587-2395; Fax: 301-589-3470. Email: stmichaelreled@yahoo.com. Students 406.

9—OUR LADY OF GRACE (Leisure World) (1983) Rev. Peter T. Sweeney.
Mailing Address: 3134 Adderley Ct., MD 20906. Tel: 301-924-0067; Fax: 301-924-6809. In Res., Rev. Msgr. John J. Madigan (Retired).
Res.: 15665 Norbeck Blvd., MD 20906. Tel: 301-924-4927; Fax: 301-924-6809.

10—OUR LADY OF VIETNAM (1990), (Vietnamese), Revs. Peter Nguyen-Thanh-Long; Hilary Tran-Khac Hy (Retired); Paul Tam X. Tran; Deacon John Huong Nguyen.
Res.: 11812 New Hampshire Ave., MD 20904. Tel: 301-622-4895; Fax: 301-625-9384.

11—OUR LADY QUEEN OF POLAND AND SAINT MAXIMILIAN KOLBE (Leisure World) (1983), (Polish), Rev. Jan Fiedurek, T.Chr.
Res.: 9700 Rosensteel Ave., MD 20910. Tel: 301-589-1857; Fax: 301-589-4401.
Catechesis/Religious Program—Students 80.

SOLOMONS, CALVERT CO., OUR LADY STAR OF THE SEA (1888) [CEM] Rev. Msgr. Michael Wilson; Deacons Christopher Jensen; John G. Etzel, (Retired); Robert L. Connelly, (Retired).
Mailing Address: P.O. Box 560, MD 20688. Tel: 410-326-3535; Fax: 410-326-3679.
School—Tel: 410-326-3171; Fax: 410-326-9478. Email: olssschool@comcast.net. Sr. Carolyn Marie Betsch, C.D.P., Prin. Sisters 2; Lay Teachers 12; Students 110.
Catechesis/Religious Program—Sr. Barbara Rohe, C.D.P., D.R.E. Students 216.

SUITLAND, PRINCE GEORGE'S CO., ST. BERNARDINE (1966) Unassigned. In Res., Rev. Francisco Manuel Tovar.
Res.: 2400 Brooks Dr., MD 20746-1101. Tel: 301-736-0707; Fax: 301-736-2984. Email: st.bernardine@verizon.net. Web: www.saintbernardinechurch.org.
Catechesis/Religious Program—Students 56.

TAKOMA PARK, PRINCE GEORGES CO., OUR LADY OF SORROWS (1932) Revs. Raymond J. Wadas; Jose Raul DeLeon; Deacon Trinidad Soc.
Res.: 1006 Larch Ave., MD 20912. Tel: 301-891-3500; Fax: 301-891-1523.
Catechesis/Religious Program—Tel: 301-891-2033. Students 345.

UPPER MARLBORO, PRINCE GEORGES CO., SAINT MARY OF THE ASSUMPTION (1848) [CEM] Rev. William E. Foley; Deacon Frank Klco.
Res.: 14908 Main St., MD 20772. Tel: 301-627-3255; Fax: 301-627-5533. Email: rectory@stmarysum.org. Web: www.stmarysum.org.
School—4610 Largo Rd., MD 20772. Tel: 301-627-4170; Fax: 301-627-6383. Email: tcampbell@stmarysum.org. Mr. Steven Showalter, Prin. Sisters, Servants of the Immaculate Heart of Mary 2; Students 263.
Catechesis/Religious Program—Fax: 301-627-5533. Mrs. Regina Piazza, D.R.E. Students 105.

VALLEY LEE, ST. MARY'S CO., ST. GEORGE (1851) [CEM] Rev. Msgr. Karl A. Chimiak; Deacon George H. L'Heureux, (Retired).
Mailing Address: 19199 St. George Church Rd., P.O. Box 9, MD 20692. Tel: 301-994-0607; Fax: 301-994-1793. Email: stgeorge.md@adwparish.org. Web: stgeorgercc.org.

Catechesis/Religious Program—Tel: 301-994-0737. Students 70.
Chapel—St. George's Island, St. Francis Xavier
WALDORF, CHARLES CO.
1—OUR LADY HELP OF CHRISTIANS (1980) Rev. Thomas F. Crowley; Deacon Reginald A. Thomas.
Mailing Address: 100 Village St., MD 20602-2183. Tel: 301-645-7112; Fax: 301-645-3635. Email: olhc@verizon.net. Web: www.olhoc.org.
Res.: 930 Barrington Dr., MD 20602-2183. Tel: 301-843-8823; Fax: 301-645-3635.
Catechesis/Religious Program—Mrs. Kathleen White, D.R.E. Students 308.
2—ST. PETER (1700) [CEM] Rev. Msgrs. J. Wilfrid Parent; Andrew J. Cassin, Pastor Emeritus (Retired); Oliver W. McGready (Retired); Rev. Zygmunt Kurzawinski; Deacon Robert L. Martin.
Res.: 3320 St. Peter's Dr., MD 20601. Tel: 301-843-8916; Fax: 301-843-3163. Email: parishsecretary@stpeterswaldorf.org. Web: stpeterswaldorf.org.
School—3310 St. Peter's Dr., MD 20601. Tel: 301-843-1955; Fax: 301-843-6371. J.R. West, Prin. Lay Teachers 16; Students 253.
Catechesis/Religious Program—Alice Culbreth, Dir. Christian Formation. Students 245.

Chaplains of Public Institutions

WASHINGTON. *Children's Medical Center*, 111 Michigan Ave., N.W., 20010. Tel: 202-884-5050. Rev. Tukura Michael, O.P., Chap.
St. Elizabeth's Hospital (Government Operated), 2700 Martin Luther King Jr. Ave., S.E., 20032. Tel: 202-671-1218. Rev. Maximo J. Ortiz, O.S.A., Chap.
National Rehabilitation Hospital, 102 Irving St., N.W., 20010. Tel: 202-877-1000. Rev. Lawrence Nwabueze, O.P., Chap., Fredrick Allen.
Providence Hospital (1921) 1150 Varnum St., N.E., 20017-2180. Tel: 202-269-7000. Revs. Maurus Dolcic, T.O.R., Philip Simo, O.S.B., Chap.
Washington Hospital Center, 110 Irving St. N.W., 20010. Tel: 202-877-6691. Rev. Lawrence Nwabueze, O.P., Chap.
BETHESDA, MD. *National Institutes of Health, Clinical Center*, MD. Tel: 301-496-3407. Vacant.
LANHAM, MD. *Doctor's Hospital of Prince Georges County*, MD 20706. Served by the priests of St. Matthias Parish.

Special Ministries:
Rev. Msgrs.—
Criscuolo, Salvatore A., Chap., Police and Fire Dept.
Hurley, Leonard F., Rector, Cardinal Boyle Residence
Murray, Michael J., Priest Dir., Catholic Cemeteries
Revs.—
Adams, John E., Dir., S.O.M.E.
Begg, Christopher T., Ph.D., Ph.B., S.T.D., Catholic University of America
Bryant, F. Michael, Chap., District of Columbia Jail
Conley, Rory T., Archdiocesan Historian
Hurd, R. Scott, Permanent Diaconate
Kemp, Raymond B., Fellow, Woodstock Theological Center, Georgetown University
Martin, Francis R., Chap., Mother of God Community; Instructor, John Paul II Institute (Retired)
Mudd, John, Dir. Devel., Carroll High School
O'Brien, Raymond C., J.D., Asst. Dean, Catholic University
Shaffer, Gregory W., George Washington University Newman Medical Center
Trancone, Gerard A., Chap., Center for the Deaf & Gallaudet University
Walsh, Robert E., Newman Center, University of Maryland

Pastoral Center Special Ministries:
Rev. Msgrs.—
Antonicelli, Charles V., J.D., J.C.L., V.F., V. Vicar Canonical Svcs.
Fisher, Michael W., E.V., Vicar for Clergy, Sec. Ministerial Leadership
Panke, Robert J., Rector & Dir. of Priestly Formation & Vocations
Ranieri, Joseph A., Coord. of Pastoral Care of Priests
Sadusky, Joseph F., J.C.D., Judicial Vicar Tribunal
Revs.—
Byrne, William D., Sec. for Pastoral Ministry & Social Concerns
Esposito-Garcia, Juan, J.C.L., Tribunal
Griffin, Carter H., Vice Rector, Vocations
Gurnee, William H., III, Dir. of Spiritual Formation
Herbert, G. Paul, J.C.L., Tribunal
Hurd, R. Scott, Office of Permanent Diaconate
Knestout, Mark D., Dir. Office of Worship
Park, Adam Y., Sec. to Archbishop Wuerl
Stuart, George E., J.C.D., Tribunal, Vice Chancellor, Archivist
Vidal, David, I.V.E., Sec. to Cardinal McCarrick

Hospital & Nursing Home Ministries:
Rev. Msgr.—
Hurley, Leonard F., Cardinal Boyle Residence, Carrol Manor
Revs.—
Baraki, Tesfamariam, Howard University Hospital
Kinter, John P., Greater S.E. Hospital
McKay, John F., Suburban Hosp.
Samaha, Jeffrey F., Southern Maryland Hospital
Valentine, Keveny M., Shady Grove Hospital

On Duty Outside the Archdiocese:
Rev. Msgrs.—
Albacete, Lorenzo, New York
Roensch, Roger, Vatican City State
Revs.—
Ailer, Gellert Jozsef, Szechenyi, Hungary
Culkin, Michael, Lancaster, PA
DeNigris, Emanuele, Boston, MA
DiNoia, Joseph Augustine, O.P., Ph.D., Sub-Secretary for the Congregation of the Doctrine of the Faith, Rome
Izac, Andre C., North Carolina
Kuebler, A.M. Seamus, Maine
Oberle, James P., S.S., University of Dallas, Irving, TX
Ryan, William A., Togo, West Africa
Sanz, Jose, D.L.P., California
Slevin, Henry, Vietnam
Ulshafer, Thomas, S.S., Baltimore, MD
Walsh, Francis M.
White, Mark D., Richmond, VA

Military Chaplains:
Revs.—
Fitz-Patrick, David M.
Garrett, Benton Lee
Gaskin, Grantley DaCosta
Passamonti, Paul G.
Studniewski, Gary R.

Absent On Leave:
Revs.—
Bozek, Robert
Cocca, Stephen M.
Hegedusich, William
Lee, John T. Matthew
Reeves, Harold Smith
Woods, Thomas Matthew

Retired:
Most Rev.—
Oliver, Leonard, S.V.D., 619 10th St., N.W., 20001.
Rev. Msgrs.—
Awalt, William J., Byron House, 9210 Kentsdale Dr., Potomac, MD 20854.
Bazan, Joaquin, Jeanne Jugan Residence.
Beattie, James T., Our Lady of Lourdes, Bethesda, MD
Brady, John B., 7201 Pyle Rd., Bethesda, MD 20817.
Burton, Richard W., Grand Oaks Nursing Home, 5109 MacArthur Blvd. N.W., 20016.
Cassin, Andrew J., St. Peter, Waldorf, MD.
Duffy, Thomas M., Our Lady of Victory, 20007.
Gatto, Vincent S., St. Raphael, Rockville, MD 20854.
Gillen, James G., Jeanne Jugan Residence, 4200 Harewood Rd., N.E., 20017.
Gozaloff, Paul J., P.O. Box 182, Compton, MD 20627.
Harris, Martin P., 44695 Whiteoak, #536, California, MD 20619.
Hughes, Richard A., Mt. Calvary, Forestville, MD 20747.
Kane, Thomas A., Severn House, 772A Fairview Ave., Annapolis, MD 21403-2957.
Kane, William J., Church of Little Flower, Bethesda, MD.
Kazista, Francis G., St. Andrew the Apostle, Silver Spring, MD 20902.
Kuehner, Ralph J., St. Francis of Assisi, Rockville, MD.
Laczko, T. Ansgar, 290 Devonshire Rd., Hedgesville, WV 25427.
Madigan, John J., Our Lady of Grace, 3134 Adderly Ct., Silver Spring, MD 20906.
McGready, Oliver W., St. Peter's, 3320 St. Peter's Dr., Waldorf, MD 20601.
Myslinski, John F., 196 Holmes Rd., Pittsfield, MA 01201.
O'Connell, Maurice V., Blessed Sacrament, Washington, D.C.
Otero, Henry, 613 Old Stage Rd., S.W., Glen Burnie, MD 21061.
Revs.—
Alliata, Peter R., 105 Vianney Ln., Prince Frederick, MD 20678.
Alvarez-Garcia, Julio, Carroll Manor, Miami, FL.
Barry, Paul, Carrol Manor, 1150 Varnum St., N.E., 20017.
Berry, William F., Grace House, 3214 Norbeck Rd., Silver Spring, MD 20906.
Betz, James S., 8761 Contee Rd., Apt 103, Laurel, MD 20708.
Blackwell, Michael J., Resurrection, Burtonsville, MD 20866.
Brainerd, Winthrop J., O'Boyle Residence.
Brice, Donald, O'Boyle Residence
Brown, Charles E., Riderwood, 3152 Gracefield Rd., Apt. M424, Silver Spring, MD 20904.
Conway, David, P.O. Box 173, Georgetown, DE 19947.
D'Silva, Percival L., Blessed Sacrament, 20015.
De Porter, Arnold W., 15211 Elkridge Way, Apt. 94-24, Silver Spring, MD 20906.
DeRamos, Fidel, P.O. Box 60, Lucena City 4301 Philippines.
Dignan, Eamon, St. John, Hollywood, MD.
Dixon, J. Isidore, 6335 Bumpy Oak Rd., La Plata, MD 20646.
Dolan, Michael F., 4379 Stepney Dr., Gainesville, VA 20155.
Downs, L. James, 22783 Dogwood Dr., Lewes, DE 19958.
Duggan, Robert D., 24536 Fossen Rd., Damascus, MD 20872.
Evans, Edward, Sunapee, NH.
Finamore, Robert A., P.O. Box 5146, Palm Springs, CA 92263.
Gallagher, Roger P., Carroll Manor, 1150 Varnum St., N.E., 20017.
Gardiner, Richard E., 5345 Cypress Links Blvd., Elkton, FL 32033.
Goode, William F., Ascension, Bowie, MD 20719.
Green, Charles C., Jeanne Jugan Residence.
Helwig, Alan R., 224 Dale Dr., Silver Spring, MD 20910.
Hill, W. Paul, 13901 Belle Chase Blvd., #313, Laurel, MD 20707.
Holloway, James P., 300 Ocean Blvd., #7, St. Simons Island, GA 31522.
Holt, Paul-Stephen, St. Francis Nursing Home, Hampton, VA
Hurley, John, Cathedral of St. Matthew, Washington DC
Ihrie, Bernard R., Jr., 3736 Bay Dr., Edgewater, MD 21037.
Januszkiewicz, Henry, 9910 Rookery Cir., Estero, FL 33928.
Jordan, Milton E., St. Matthias, Lanham, MD
Kennedy, Joseph P., 5 Brush Island Ct., Berlin, MD 21811.
Kleinstuber, Joseph J., 15345 Potomac River Dr., Cobb Island, MD 20625.
Liston, Paul F., O'Boyle Residence.
MacIntyre, Frederick H., St. Patrick, Washington, D.C.
Martin, Francis R., 20501 Goshen Rd., Gaithersburg, MD 20879.
McCann, Charles, Lissan, 2 Tullynore Rd., Cookstown, Northern Ireland.
McManus, Eamon, Ave Maria University, 1025 Commons Cir., Naples, FL 34119.
Metzdorf, William C., St. Vincent de Paul Village, 3350 E. St., San Diego, CA 92102.
Mudd, David A., 10519 Grove Ridge Pl., Rockville, MD 20852.
Muzzey, Charles H., Friendship Terrace, 4201 Butterworth Pl., N.W. #522, 20016-4562.
O'Sullivan, Michael J., Sacred Heart Nursing Home, 5805 Queens Chapel Rd., Hyattsville, MD 20782.
Panares, Auxentius, 8787 Country Creek Blvd., Jacksonville, FL 32221.
Pollard, Thomas W., 3312 Chiswick Ct., Apt. 62-3A, Silver Spring, MD 20906.
Reynierse, Peter, 212 Creekside Dr., Locust Grove, VA 22508.
Richardson, Robert C., Hillcrest Bldg. 27, Unit 301, 3850 Washington St., Hollywood, FL 33021.
Salcedo, Luis G., 5G Castle Hills Rd., Agawam, MA 01001.
Stack, John P., 3501 Forest Edge Dr., 14-3F, Silver Spring, MD 20906.
Thompson, Matthew E., Marian Assisted Living, 19109 Georgia Ave., Brookeville, MD 20833.
Thompson, William J., Cardinal O'Boyle Residence, 20017.
Torsiello, Ralph C., Cadbury at Lewes, 17026 Cadbury Cir., Lewes, DE 19958.
Tou, Louis A., Cardinal O'Boyle Residence, P.O. Box 29206, 20017.
Tran-Khac-Hy, Hilarius, 14201 Schaeffer Rd., Boyds, MD 20841.
Vitturino, Saverio T., 6050 California Cir., #108,

Rockville, MD 20852.
Wintermyer, John S., 15316 Pine Orchard Dr., 2K, Silver Spring, MD 20906.
Worch, Donald P., Our Lady of Mercy, Potomac, MD 20854.

Permanent Deacons:
Abeyta, Dan D., Sacred Heart, Bowie, MD
Allen, Robert F., Diocese of Richmond
Alvarez, Sergio, Diocese of Arlington
Ames, George B., Jr., St. Mary, Piscataway, MD
Angell, Kenneth, St. Jane Frances de Chantal, Bethesda, MD
Baker, Francis E., Jr., St. Anthony, North Beach, MD
Barbernitz, Peter M., St. Camillus, Silver Spring, MD
Barnes, David, St. Edwards the Confessor, Bowie
Barnes, John R., St. Joseph, Pomfret, MD
Barrasso, Anthony T., (Retired)
Barrett, Kenneth, St. Andrew the Apostle, Silver Spring, MD
Barrett, Raymond J., Diocese of Venice, FL
Barros, Alfred M., St. Patrick, Rockville, MD
Battaglia, Thomas D., Arlington
Bell, Joseph, Incarnation, Washington, DC
Bell, Lawrence G., St. Martin, Gaithersburg, MD
Beller, Edwin J., (Retired)
Bendel, Francis W., Mother Seton, Gaithersburg, MD
Berry, Robert L., Holy Family, Mitchellville, MD
Bingham, Dennis J., St. Mary, Landover, MD
Birkel, Richard, (On Leave of Absence)
Blanco-Eccleston, Julio, St. Bartholomew, Bethesda
Bobbitt, John W., (Retired)
Bockweg, Gary L., St. Joseph's on Capitol Hill, Washington, DC
Boesman, William C., St. Thomas the Apostle, Washington, DC
Bond, Stuart Michael, St. Andrew the Apostle, Silver Spring, MD
Brink, Edward J., Wilmington
Briscoe, John A., (Retired)
Brown, James E., (Retired), Holy Redeemer, Washington, DC
Brown, Sylvester, (Retired)
Burroughs, Eugene, St. Mary, Bryantown, MD
Butkiewicz, Jerome, St. Mary, Charlotte Hall
Butler, Kevin A., Sr., Holy Comforter-St. Cyprian, Washington, DC
Byrne, Kevin, St. Elizabeth, Rockville
Cadigan, James, St. Peter, Olney, MD
Cahoon, David L., Jr., St. Mary, Barnesville, MD
Cain, Leonard F., (Retired)
Caraballo, Carlo, St. John Neumann, Gaithersburg, MD
Carbonell, Jose R., St. Raphael, Rockville, MD
Carpenter, Joel P., St. George, Valley Lee, MD
Carroll, Donald T., (Wilmington)
Cartagena, Francisco J., St. Camillus, Silver Spring, MD
Cayrampoma, Juan, Cathedral of St. Matthew, Washington, DC
Cermak, John C., St. John the Baptist, Silver Spring
Chaput, Raymond L., St. Catherine Laboure, Wheaton, MD
Chase, Ira E., Basilica of the National Shrine of the Immaculate Conception, Washington, DC
Chen, Chester G., St. Jane de Chandal, Bethesda, MD
Choi, Chang Sup, St. Andrew Kim, Olney, MD
Chrzanowski, Edmund A., Jr., St. John Vianney, Prince Frederick, MD
Cioffi, Thomas, St. Peter, Olney, MD
Coates, Vincent J., Jr., (Retired), Fall River
Collins, Gerald A., Atlanta
Connelly, Robert L., (Retired)
Conner, James E., (Retired)
Connor, John E., (Retired)
Conrad, Joseph M., (Retired)
Contreras, Carlos E., (Retired), VA
Conway, Neal T., St. Jerome, Hyattsville, MD
Cooper, Philip J., Charlotte
Cordova-Ferrer, Nathaniel, (Retired)
Crawford, Rory P., St. Peter, Olney
Crowley, Ronald C., (Leave of Absence)
Cruz, George C., St. Bartholomew, Bethesda, MD
Cummins, Don E., Seattle
Cummins, Eugene, St. John Neumann, Gaithersburg, MD
Curtis, Joseph F., Jr., Basilica of the National Shrine of Immaculate Conception, Washington, DC
Cyrus, Ralph W., Holy Comforter-St. Cyprian, Washington, DC
Daniels, Willis, St. Aloysius, Washington, DC
Danko, Edward, Wilmington
Datovech, James J., St. Francis of Assisi, Derwood
Davis, Alton, Jr., St. Joseph, Largo, MD
Davis, Harry, Holy Redeemer, Kensington
Davis, William E., Las Vegas
Davy, Michael W., St. John Newmann, Gaithersburg
DeRoze, Donald G., (Retired)
Ditewig, William, St. Petersburg
Divins, David L., Jesus the Divine Word, Huntingtown, MD
Dominic, James, St. Michael, Ridge
Dubicki, Richard F., Our Lady Help of Christians, Waldorf, MD
Duggin, David, Harrisburg
Dwyer, Thomas F., Holy Redeemer, Kensington, MD
Ealey, Ronald R., DC Correctional Treatment Center & DC Jail, Washington, DC; St. Michael the Archangel, Silver Springs, MD
Edelin, Charles E., Jr., (Retired)
Elliott, Thomas B., Richmond
Emley, William P., (Retired), VA
Enright, Timothy D., Mother Seton, Germantown, MD
Espinosa, Leandro Y., St. Columba, Oxon Hill, MD
Etzel, John G., (Retired)
Feeley, John, St. Anthony of Padua, Washington, DC
Feneis, Albert G., Raleigh
Fernandez, Elmer, Archdiocese of San Antonio
Finerty, John F., St. Paul, Damascus, MD
Finn, Daniel F., VI, St. Francis of Assisi, Derwood, MD
Fischer, Robert A., Our Lady of the Visitation, Darnestown
Fisher, Richard A., (Retired)
Flores, Francisco, Diocese of Arlington
Flynn, Leo, Our Lady of Victory, Washington, DC
Frye, Stephen B., St. Michael the Archangel, Silver Spring, MD
Gallagher, Mark J., Camden; Blessed Sacrament, Washington, D.C.
Gallerizzo, William, Fall River
Garcia, David F., Santa Fe
Gatica-Delgado, Jorge, St. Raphael, Rockville
Genis, Thomas P., Immaculate Conception, Washington, DC
Gignilliat, Robert L., St. Mary of the Mills, Laurel
Glenn, Clark, (Retired), St. Ignatius, Oxon Hill, MD
Gonzalez, Fidencio, Mother Seton, Germantown, MD
Gorman, James J., St. John the Baptist, Silver Spring, MD
Gorospe, Santiago B., Honolulu
Graham, Albert E., Jr., (Retired)
Greenfield, William Mike, Incarnation, Washington, DC
Hannagan, Francis L., (Retired)
Hawkins, William J., St. Theresa of Avila, Washington DC
Haywood, Hiram H., Jr., (Retired)
Hernandez-Viera, Ivan, St. Martin of Tours, Gaithersburg, MD
Hidalgo, Alfredo, (Retired)
Hoen, David J., Fort Belvoir Army Base, VA
Hoffman, Michael R., Wilmington
Holson, Edward, Wilmington
Hong, Pascal, (Retired)
Hopson, Frank, (Retired)
Hubbard, Robert, Holy Cross, Garrett Park
Huete, Stephen, The Netherlands
Huguley, Maury, Jr., St. Paul, Damascus, MD
Hume, W. Michael, Nashville
Iannaconni, Perry F., St. Nicholas, Laurel, MD
Interlandi, Joseph S., Orlando
Jackson, Harold I., Charleston
Jensen, Christopher, Our Lady Star of the Sea, Solomons, MD
Johnson, Alfred, St. Michael, Brandywine
Jones, Thomas R., Our Lady of Perpetual Help, Washington, DC
Justice, Brandon B., St. Mary of the Mills, Laurel, MD
Keller, Grafton T., St. Augustine, FL
Keller, Norman B., (Retired)
Kelly, Richard F., St. Augustine, Washington, DC
Klco, Frank, St. Mary of the Assumption, Upper Marlboro, MD
Koeniger, Ludwig, St. John, Hollywood, MD
Kostka, Daniel S., St. Mary, Rockville, MD
Kraemer, Francis W., Sr., (Retired)
Kronschnabel, Michael C., Phoenix
Kyte, William L., Immaculate Conception, Mechanicsville, MD
L'Heureux, George G., (Retired)
L'Homme, Bert, Ph.D., St. Francis de Sales, Washington, D.C.
Lacovaro, James G., (Leave of Absence)
Lee, Kenneth, St. Anthony of Padua, Washington, DC
Lemon, John G., Wilmington
Levy, Barry A., St. Mary, Rockville, MD
Levy, Richard A., Jr., (Leave of Absence)
Liu, John C., St. Rosa of Lima, Gaithersburg, MD
Lloyd, Joseph W., Jr., Holy Angels, Avenue, MD
Locke, John W., (Retired)
Longano, Donald R., Church of the Little Flower, Bethesda, MD
Luetjen, Palmer, (Retired)
Lynch, John F., (Retired)
Lyons, Robert A., Arlington, VA
Lyons, Robert R., New York
Martin, E. Chad, Jesus the Good Shepherd, Dunkirk, MD
Martin, Robert L., St. Peter, Waldorf, MD
Maselko, Stephen M., Mother Seton, Germantown, MD
Mastrangelo, Eugene K., St. John Vianney, Prince Frederick, MD
Mattocks, Richard E., (Retired)
Mays, Donald, Shrine of St. Jude, Rockville, MD
McCann, James C., Archdiocese of Milwaukee
McCarthy, Michael, (Leave of Absence)
McGinness, John J., (Retired)
McKimmie, Stephen, St. Mary, Piscataway, MD
Merella, Bartholomew J., (Retired)
Meyer, Ronald J., St. Martin, Gaithersburg, MD
Middleton, Henry D., III, (Retired)
Migliorini, Louis, Sr., (Retired)
Miles, Lawrence A., Mount Calvary, Forestville, MD
Miller, Alfred A., Jr., Our Lady Queen of Peace, Washington, DC
Miller, Lawrence L., Military Service
Minor, Samuel L., Jr., (Retired)
Mitchell, Stephen, Christ the King, Silver Spring, MD
Molina, Jose Renato, St. Mark the Evangelist, Hyattsville, MD
Molina, Nehemias J., Shrine of the Sacred Heart, Washington, DC
Moll, Anthony W., St. John the Evangelist, Clinton, MD
Montalvo, Santiago T., St. John the Evangelist, Clinton
Montgomery, John E., Holy Rosary, Rosaryville, MD
Moreno, Mario F., St. Rose of Lima, Gaithersburg
Moskaitis, J. Vincent, (Leave of Absence)
Mukri, Kevin, Florida
Murati, George, St. Augustine
Nalls, James T., St. Patrick, Rockville, MD
Nguyen, John H., (Retired), Our Lady of Vietnam, Silver Spring, MD
Nickel, Clayton A., St. Matthew the Apostle, Washington, DC
Nickerson, William J., (Retired)
Nosacek, Andrew J., (Retired)
Oettinger, Frank F., Las Vegas
Oguledo, Valentine, St. Margaret of Scotland, Seat Pleasant, MD
Om, Michael, Epiphany, Washington, DC
Opdenaker, Albert L., St. Rose of Lima, Gaithersburg, MD
Parker, Donald A., (Retired)
Perkins, Gary, St. Edward the Confessor, Bowie, MD
Philogene, G. Stephane, St. Catherine Laboure, Wheaton, MD
Picard, Adrien D., (Retired)
Pinder, Wilbur L., Jr., Wilmington
Pineda, Roberto L., Miami
Pitocco, Nicholas J., Ascension, Bowie, MD
Price, Robert, Raleigh
Ravenscroft, F. Ian, (Retired)
Reilly, Matthew B., Charlotte
Rice, Ulysses, (Retired)
Ricker, Philip W., Wilmington
Ripple, Ammon S., St. John, Hollywood, MD
Robinson, John E., Jr., Holy Redeemer, Washington, DC
Robinson, Stephen M., St. Mary, Landover Hills, MD
Roszkowski, Thomas E., St. Bernadette, Silver Spring, MD
Rourke, Walter G., (Retired)
Ruffo, Paul, New York
Salatto, Frank J., Jr., (Retired)
Salgado, Roberto, St. Gabriel, Washington, DC
Santiago, Perfecto, St. Mary of the Mills, Laurel, MD
Schneider, Ronald W., Milwaukee
Scholz, Nicholas E., Shrine of St. Jude, Rockville, MD
Schopfer, Richard J., (Retired)
Schwartz, Patrick C., St. Joseph, Beltsville, MD
Serafini, Bartolo, (Retired)
Sferrella, Joseph J., (Retired)
Shewmaker, John B., (Retired)
Sinchak, J. Douglas, Archdiocese of Mobile
Smith, McBurnett J., Assumption, Washington, DC
Soc, Trinidad, Our Lady of Sorrows, Takoma Park, MD

Somerville, James, (Retired)
Somerville, John, (Retired)
Soto, Alfredo, Galveston-Houston
Spalding, Thomas C., Sr., (Retired)
Springer, James R., El Paso
Stackpole, Terrell U., (Retired)
Stevens, William H., Our Lady of the Presentation, Poolesville, MD
Stuart, Scott C., St. Ignatius, Chapel Point, MD
Sweeney, Anthony J., III, St. Mary's County Detention Center; St. Cecilia & St. Mary City, MD
Tan, Domingo, (Retired)
Terrar, David B., St. Paul, Damascus, MD
Testudine, Joseph, (Retired)
Thomas, Reginald A., (Retired)
Thompson, Daniel R., (Retired)
Thompson, Finis E., St. Augustine, FL
Tilghman, Timothy E., Our Lady of Perpetual Help, Washington, DC
Trichel, Allen J., (Leave of Absence)
Turner, Al Douglas, St. Joseph, Largo, MD
Turner, B. Curtis, St. Mark the Evangelist, Hyattsville, MD
Turner, John H., (Retired)
Vargas, Jorge W., Our Lady Queen of the Americas, Washington, DC
Verdon, John, Jesus the Good Shepherd, Dunkirk, MD
Vikor, Desider L., St. Hugh of Grenoble, Greenbelt, MD
Vita, William A., Jr., St. Martin of Tours, Gaithersburg, MD
Wakefield, Walter W., III, Lexington
Walker, Richard, Jr., St. Thomas More, Washington, DC
Welch, Joseph, (Retired)
Weschler, Charles A., Wilmington
Whitaker, Robert W., St. Ann, Washington, DC
White, Robert C., Sr., St. Martin of Tours, Washington, DC
Wolfe, Willis R., St. Joseph, Beltsville
Work, Boyd, Jr., Cathedral of St. Matthew, Washington, DC
Yorke, Desmond, St. Bernard, Riverdale Park, MD
Yun, James, Our Lady of Mercy, Potomac, MD

INSTITUTIONS LOCATED IN THE ARCHDIOCESE

[A] SEMINARIES, ARCHDIOCESAN

WASHINGTON. *Blessed John Paul II Seminary* (2011) 145 Taylor St., N.E., 20017. Tel: 202-636-9020; Fax: 202-636-9025. Email: jp2seminary@adw.org. Web: www.dcpriest.org. Rev. Msgr. Robert J. Panke, Rector; Revs. Carter H. Griffin, Vice-Rector; William H. Gurnee III, Spiritual Dir. Seminarians 20.

Theological College of the Catholic University of America, 401 Michigan Ave., N.E., 20017. Tel: 202-756-4900; Fax: 202-756-4909. Email: decker@theologicalcollege.org. Web: www.theologicalcollege.org.

Theological College, Inc. Sulpician Fathers. Faculty: Priests 8; Students 84.

Faculty: Revs. David D. Thayer, S.S., S.T.L., Ph.D.; Melvin C. Blanchette, S.S., M.A., Ph.D., Rector; Daniel F. Moore, S.S., M.A., S.T.L., Vice Rector; Anthony J. Pogorelc, S.S., M.Div., Ph.D.; Gerald D. McBrearity, S.S., M.A., S.T.B., D.Min., Faculty Advisor; John Slovikovski, M.Div., M.A.; James P. Froehlich, O.F.M.Cap., M.A., M.S., Ph.D.; Daniel Greenleaf, S.T.B., S.T.L.

HYATTSVILLE, MD. *Redemptoris Mater Archdiocesan Missionary Seminary* (2002) 4900 Lasalle Rd., MD 20782. Tel: 301-277-4960; Fax: 301-277-5295. Email: seminary@rmwashington.org. Web: www.rmwashington.org. Revs. José Matías Díaz, Rector; Francisco Javier Santaballa, Vice Rector; Giovanni Buontempo, Spiritual Dir. Priests 3; Students 33.

[B] SEMINARIES, RELIGIOUS OR SCHOLASTICATES

WASHINGTON. *Atonement Seminary-Franciscan Friars of the Atonement*, 5207 Colorado Ave., N.W., 20011. Tel: 202-722-0461; Fax: 202-722-1716. Revs. V. Paul Ojibway, S.A., Dir.; Dennis Polanco, S.A., Vocation Dir. Priests 2.

Deshairs Community-Oblates of St. Francis de Sales Residence, 1621 Otis St., N.E., 20018-2321. Tel: 202-529-1926. Very Rev. Donald J. Heet, O.S.F.S.; Rev. John W. Crossin, O.S.F.S.

Diocesan Laborer Priests, House of Studies (1966) 3706 15th St., N.E., 20017. Tel: 202-832-4217; Fax: 202-526-5692. Email: info@solinstitutedc.com. Web: www.solinstitutedc.com. Revs. Ovidio Pecharroman, US Delegate & Dir.; Gabriel Calvo; Victor Salomon. Priests 3; Total Enrollment 3.

Discalced Carmelite Friars (1918) 2131 Lincoln Rd., N.E., 20002-1199. Tel: 202-832-6622; Fax: 202-832-5711. Revs. Marc Foley, O.C.D., Prior; Regis Jordan, O.C.D.; Kieran Kavanaugh, O.C.D.; Francis Miller, O.C.D. (Retired); Thomas Ochieng Otanga, O.C.D.; Salvatore Sciurba, O.C.D.; Bros. Edward O'Donnell, O.C.D.; Bryan Paquette, O.C.D.; Michael Stoeghauer; Robert Sentman.

Discalced Carmelite Friars, Inc. Priests 6; Brothers 4.

Dominican House of Studies, 487 Michigan Ave., N.E., 20017. Tel: 202-495-3820; Fax: 202-495-3873. Web: www.dhs.edu. Very Rev. Steven C. Boguslawski, O.P., M.A., M.Div., S.T.M., S.T.L., Ph.D., Pres. Pontifical Faculty; Revs. J. Raymond Vandegrift, O.P.; Gabriel O'Donnell, O.P., Vice Pres. & Academic Dean, Pontifical Faculty; Joseph Alobaidi, O.P., Master of Students; Timothy Bellamah, O.P., S.T.L.; James Brent, O.P.; Brian Chrzastek, O.P., Subprior; John Dominic Corbett, O.P.; Benedict Croell, O.P., Dir. Vocations; Henry Thomas Donoghue, O.P.; Bernard Dupont, O.P., M.A.; Matthew Erickson, O.P., Procurator, Economic Admin.; Joseph Peter Fegan, O.P., S.T.L.; John Frederick Hinnebusch, O.P.; Kenneth Andrew Hofer, O.P., Asst. Master of Students; Augustine Judd, O.P.; John Chrysostom Kozlowski, O.P.; Theodore John Baptist Ku, O.P., S.T.L., Asst. Master, Students; Very Rev. Kenneth R. Letoile, O.P., Prior; Revs. Jared Austin Litke, O.P.; Nicholas E. Lombardo, O.P.; Michael J. McCormack, O.P., M.Div., M.A.; Matthew Bernard Mulcahy, O.P., Ph.D. (Cand.); Stephen Desmond Ryan, O.P.; Eugene M. Rzeczkowski, O.P., S.T.L.; John Martin Ruiz, O.P., Librarian; John Paul Walker, O.P., S.T.L.; Seth Thomas Joseph White, O.P., Ph.D.; Malcolm Sylvester Willoughby, O.P. (Pontifical Faculty) Priests 22; Brothers 2; Clerical Brothers 49; Seminarians 18. In Res. Rev. James Moore, O.P.

St. Francis Friary-Capuchin College, 4121 Harewood Rd., N.E., 20017-1593. Tel: 202-529-2188; Fax: 202-526-6664. Revs. Paul Dressler, O.F.M.Cap., Guardian - Dir. Formation; Emeh Schuler, O.F.M.Cap., Hospital Chap.; Gregory Brown, O.F.M.Cap., Treas. & Vicar; J. Daniel Mindling, O.F.M.Cap., Academic Dean, Mt. St. Mary, Emittsburgh, MD; Robert L. McCreary, O.F.M.Cap., Formation Staff & Retreat Work; Joseph Mindling, O.F.M.Cap., Prof., Washington Theological Union; Francis X. Russo, O.F.M.Cap., Hispanic Min.; Stephen Shin, O.F.M.Cap., Information; Thomas Weinandy, O.F.M.Cap., Exec. Dir. of Sec. for Doctrine & Pastoral Practices USCCB; Bros. Michael Letosak, O.F.M.Cap.; Alfred Vincent, O.F.M.Cap. Priests 9; Scholastics 17; Brothers 2; Total Enrollment 28.

Franciscan Mission Service of North America, 1323 Quincy St., N.E., 20017. Tel: 202-832-1762; Fax: 202-832-1778. Email: info@franciscanmissionservice.org. Web: franciscanmissionservice.org. P.O. Box 29034, 20017. Ms. Kim Smolik, Exec. Dir. Lay Staff 3.

St. Joseph's Seminary (1888) 1200 Varnum St., 20017. Tel: 202-526-4231; 202-526-4229 (Student); Fax: 202-526-7811. Most Rev. John Ricard, Rector; Very Rev. John L.M. Filippelli, S.S.J., Spiritual Dir.; Rev. Albert Adeleke (Nigeria), Academic Dean; Bros. Louis Tomasso, S.S.J., Assoc. Vocation Dir.; Thomas Vincent, S.S.J. St. Joseph's Society of the Sacred Heart-Josephite Fathers & Brothers. Priests 3; Brothers 2; Franciscan Sisters of St. Joseph 5; Seminarians 11. In Res. Rev. Howard Johnson (JKS) (Retired); Bro. David Andrews, C.S.C.

Josephite Pastoral Center, 1200 Varnum St., N.E., 20017. Tel: 202-526-9270; 202-526-9271; Fax: 202-526-7811. Email: ssjpastrcntr@aol.com. Rev. James E. McLinden, S.S.J., Dir.; Maria M. Lannon, Admin. Priests 1; Brothers 1; Deacons 1; Lay Women 3.

Marian Fathers Scholasticate (1673) 3885 Harewood Rd., N.E., 20017. Tel: 202-526-8884; Fax: 202-832-6551. Email: markbaron@hotmail.com. Web: www.marian.org. Revs. Mark Baron, M.I.C., Supr. & Novice Master; Lawrence Dunn, M.I.C.; Casimir Krzyzanowski, M.I.C.; Bro. Leonard Konopka, M.I.C., Treas. Priests 4; Brothers 1; Novices 3; Seminarians 7.

Marist College, Provincialate of the Marist Society in the USA (1892) 815 Varnum St., N.E., 20017-2144. Tel: 202-529-2821; Fax: 202-635-4627. Web: www.societyofmaryusa.org. Very Rev. Timothy G. Keating, S.M., Prov.; Bros. Randy T. Hoover, S.M., Admin.; John J. O'Brien III.

Maryknoll Fathers and Brothers, 4834 16th St., N.W., 20011. Tel: 202-726-4252; Fax: 202-726-0466. Email: mkldc@aol.com. Web: www.maryknoll.org. Revs. William M. Boteler, M.M.; John Sullivan, M.M., Dir. Affiliates.

Office of Justice and Peace, P.O. Box 29132, 20017. Tel: 202-832-1780; Fax: 202-832-5159. Email: mknolldc@igc.org. Marie Dennis, Dir.; Rev. James W. Kofski, M.M.; Sisters Ann Braudis, M.M., Assoc.; Meg Gallagher, M.M., Assoc.; Judy Coode, Communications Dir.; David Kane, M.L.M., Assoc.; Susan Weissert, M.L.M.; Yamileth Coreas, Admin. Asst.

Oblates of St. Francis de Sales, 721 Lawrence St., N.E., 20017. Tel: 202-269-9410; Fax: 202-526-4323. Web: www.oblates.org. Priests 3; Brothers 1; Professed 2.

DeSales Hall Residence: Bro. Edward F. Ogden, O.S.F.S., Supr. & Dir. Formation; Rev. William F. Davis, O.S.F.S.

St. Paul's College, 3015 Fourth St., N.E., 20017-1122. Tel: 202-832-6262; Fax: 202-269-2507. Email: stpaulsdc@aol.com. Revs. Paul D. Huesing, C.S.P., Ph.D., Supr. & Dir., Formation & Assoc. Dir., Novices; Richard J. Colgan, C.S.P., Dir., Novices; Kenneth G. Boyack, C.S.P., D.Min.; Francis P. DeSiano, C.S.P., D.Min.; John E. Lynch, C.S.P., Ph.D. (Retired); Louis McKernan, C.S.P.; Ronald G. Roberson, C.S.P.; Paul G. Robichaud, C.S.P., Ph.D.; Thomas Ryan, C.S.P.; Thomas F. Stransky, C.S.P. (Retired); Ms. Denise Eggers, Librarian. Paulist Fathers. Priests 9; Novices 3; Students 8.

Queen of Pious Schools House of Studies-Piarist Fathers, 1339 Monroe St., N.E., 20017-2510. Tel: 202-529-7734; Fax: 202-529-7734 (Call first). Rev. Andrew C. Buechele, Sch.P., Ph.D., Rector, Librarian, Treas. Priests 1.

Washington Theological Union (1968) 6896 Laurel St., N.W., 20012-2016. Tel: 202-726-8800; Fax: 202-726-1716. Web: www.wtu.edu. Rev. Frederick J. Tillotson, O.Carm., Pres.; Dr. C. Colt Anderson, Ph.D., Vice Pres. for Academic Affairs & Academic Dean; Mr. Alexander Moyer, Librarian.

Washington Theological Union, Inc., Established in 1968 as the Coalition of Religious Seminaries. The Union is a school of theology and ministry. Among the numerous orders and societies that make up this institution are those whose Provincials or Superiors sit on the Provincials Council of the Board of Trustees including: the Order of Carmelites, Provinces of the Most Pure Heart of Mary and St. Elias; Order of Friars Minor, Province of the Most Holy Name of Jesus; Redemptorist Fathers and Brothers, Baltimore Province; Order of Friars Minor Conventual, Province of the Immaculate Conception. Priests 12; Sisters 4; Lay Teachers 8; Students 220.

Whitefriars Hall, 1600 Webster St., N.E., 20017. Tel: 202-526-1221; Fax: 202-526-9217. Email: qconners@carmelnet.org. Revs. Quinn Conners, O.Carm., Prior & Formation Dir.; Leopold Glueckert, O.Carm.; David Blanchard, O.Carm.; Donald W. Buggert, O.Carm.; Irtikandik Darmawanto, O.Carm.; Lijoy Jacob, O.Carm (India); Patrick McMahon, O.Carm., Ph.D.; Craig Morrison, O.Carm.; Joachim Smet, O.Carm.; Francis Sulistya, O.Carm (Indonesia); Frederick J. Tillotson, O.Carm. Priests 11; Brothers 9; Friars in Solemn Profession 14; Friars in First Profession 6.

The Carmelitana Library Tel: 202-526-1221, Ext. 121; Fax: 202-526-9217. Rev. Patrick McMahon, O.Carm., Ph.D.; Patricia O'Callagan, Librarian.

BELTSVILLE, MD. *The Saint LaSalle Auxiliary* (1918) P.O. Box 1710, MD 20704-1710. Tel: 301-210-7444; Fax: 301-210-0614. Email: Lasalleauxiliary@aol.com. Bro. John Patzwall, F.S.C., Dir. The Saint La Salle Auxiliary Inc. is the Development Office for the Christian Brothers of the Baltimore Province. Brothers 3; Lay Staff 1.

SILVER SPRING, MD. *St. Bonaventure Friary*, 10400 Lorain Ave., MD 20902. Tel: 301-681-3041; Fax: 301-681-3402. Revs. Michael Lorentsen, O.F.M.Conv., M.Div., Guardian; Curt Kreml, O.F.M.Conv., Vicar; Bro. Daniel Geary, O.F.M.Conv., Vicar & Treas.; Revs. Berard L. Marthaler, O.F.M.Conv. (Retired); John Burkhard, O.F.M.Conv. Priests 2; Brothers 1; Students 8.

Holy Family Seminary, 401 Randolph Rd., P.O. Box 4138, MD 20914-4138. Tel: 301-622-1184; Fax: 301-622-1184. Email: holyfamilySeminary@gmail.com. Very Rev. Luis Picazo, S.F., Delegate Supr.; Rev. Leandro Fazolini, S.F. Priests 2.

Holy Name College (Residence), 1650 St. Camillus Dr., MD 20903. Tel: 301-434-3400; Fax: 301-434-4624. Bro. George Camacho, O.F.M.; Revs. Agoston Bagyinski, O.F.M.; Michael Blastic, O.F.M.; Thomas Conway, O.F.M., Supr. & Dir. Formation; Hoan Dinh, O.F.M.; Bro. Frank Critch, O.F.M.; Revs. Harry Monaco, O.F.M.; Binh Nguyen, O.F.M.; Vincent de Paul Cushing, O.F.M.; Bros. Juniper Capece, O.F.M.; Ross Chamberland, O.F.M.; Rev. Brian Jordan, O.F.M.; Bros. Gerald Hopeck, O.F.M.; James Hwang, O.F.M.; Jeffery Jordan, O.F.M.; Anthony LoGalbo, O.F.M.;

Stephen DeWitt, O.F.M.; Daniel Horan, O.F.M.; Geoffrey Muga, O.F.M.; Damian Park, O.F.M.; Michael Reyes, O.F.M.; David W. Schlatter, O.F.M., Vicar & Asst. Dir. Formation; Sebastian Tobin, O.F.M.; Rev. Joseph Kim, O.F.M.; Bro. Robert Lentz, O.F.M.; Rev. John Ullrich, O.F.M. House of Studies for Holy Name Province of the Order of Friars Minor. Solemnly Professed Friars 16; Simply Professed Friars 8.

Salvatorian Community (1888) 104 Bishop Dr., MD 20905. Tel: 301-236-9414; Fax: 301-384-5432. Email: glenwillis@verizon.net. Web: www.sds.org. Revs. Glen Willis, S.D.S., Area Coord.; Richard Maloney, S.D.S.; Eliot Nitz, S.D.S., First Consultor; Roman Stadtmueller, S.D.S. (Retired); Robert Nugent, S.D.S.; Julian Guzman, S.D.S.; Bogdan Palka, S.D.S.; Bros. Roger Nelson, S.D.S., M.A., Vicar Coord.; Marvin Kluesner, S.D.S.; Sean McLaughlin, S.D.S. Society of the Divine Savior/Salvatorians. Priests 8; Brothers 5; Lay Members 20.

WEST HYATTSVILLE, MD. *Pallottine Seminary at Green Hill* (1961) 2009 Van Buren St., MD 20782-1761. Tel: 301-422-3777; Fax: 301-422-4070. Rev. Frank S. Donio, S.A.C., Rector, Formation Dir. Society of the Catholic Apostolate. Priests 1.

[C] COLLEGES AND UNIVERSITIES

WASHINGTON. *Catholic University of America, The* (1887) Nugent Hall/Executive Offices, 20064. Tel: 202-319-5000; Fax: 202-319-4441. Email: webmaster@cua.edu. Web: www.cua.edu. His Eminence Donald Cardinal Wuerl, Chancellor; John H. Garvey, J.D., Pres.; James F. Brennan, Ph.D., Provost; Cathy Wood, M.F.A., Vice Pres. Finance & Treas.; Susan D. Pervi, M.A., Vice Pres. Student Life; Frank G. Persico, M.A., Vice Pres. for Univ. Rels. & Chief of Staff; Rev. Robert J. Kaslyn, S.J., Dean School of Canon Law; John C. McCarthy, Ph.D., Dean, School of Philosophy; Lawrence R. Poos, Ph.D., Dean School of Arts & Sciences; Charles C. Nguyen, Sc.D., Dean School of Engineering; Veryl V. Miles, J.D., Dean Columbus School of Law; Patricia McMullen, Ph.D., J.D., Dean School of Nursing; Grayson Wagstaff, Ph.D., Dean Benjamin T. Rome School of Music; James R. Zabora, S.C.D., Dean Natl. Catholic School of Social Svc.; Randall Ott, M.Arch., Dean School of Architecture & Planning; Sara M. Thompson, Ph.D., Dean, Metropolitan School of Professional Studies; Rev. Phillip J. Brown, S.S., J.C.D., Rector, Theological College; James J. Greene, Ph.D., Dean Graduate Studies; Ziaeddin Mafaher, M.A., M.S., CIO; Ralph Albano, M.B.A., Assoc. Provost for Sponsored Research; Rev. Jude DeAngelo, O.F.M.Conv., Univ. Chap. & Dir. Campus Ministry; Ingrid Hsieh-Yee, Ph.D., Interim Dean School of Library & Information Sciences; Adriana Farella, B.A., Registrar; Victor Nakas, M.Phil., Assoc. Vice Pres. for Public Affairs; Trevor C. Lipscombe, Ph.D., Dir., CUA Press; W. Michael Hendricks, Ed.D., Vice Pres. Enrollment Mgmt.; Lawrence J. Morris, J.D., Gen. Counsel; Christine Sportes, S.P.H.R., Assoc. Vice Pres. & Chief Human Resources Officer. Priests 31; Sisters 6; Lay Faculty 348; Students 6,894.

Priests Associated with the University Full-Time: Rev. Msgrs. Thomas J. Green, J.C.D. (BGP); Kevin W. Irwin (NY); Paul McPartlan, D. Phil.; Robert S. Sokolowski (HRT); Robert F. Trisco, Hist.Eccl.D. (CHI), Prof. Emeritus, Church History (Retired); John Wippel, Ph.D. (STU); Revs. Regis Armstrong, O.F.M.Cap., M.Div., M.Theo., M.S.Ed., Ph.D.; John P. Beal, J.C.D.; Christopher T. Begg, Ph.D., Ph.B., S.T.D.; Alexander A. Di Lella, O.F.M., S.T.L., S.S.L., Ph.D., Prof. Emeritus (Retired); John T. Ford, C.S.C., M.A., S.T.D.; John P. Galvin, D.Th. (BO); Francis T. Gignac, S.J., S.T.L., D.Phil.; Patrick Granfield, O.S.B., Ph.D., S.T.D. (Retired); Jacques Gres-Gayer, D.Theo., S.T.D. (France); Sidney H. Griffith, S.T.D., Ph.D.; John P. Heil, S.S.D.; Joseph Jensen, O.S.B., S.S.L., S.T.D., Lecturer; Brian Johnstone, C.S.S.R., S.T.D.; Joseph A. Komonchak, S.T.L., Ph.D. (NY) (Retired); Nicholas E. Lombardo, O.P.; John E. Lynch, C.S.P., Ph.D. (Retired); Berard L. Marthaler, O.F.M.Conv., Prof. Emeritus (Retired); Frank J. Matera, M.A., Ph.D. (HRT); Mark Morozowich, S.E.O.D. (SJP), Acting Dean, School of Theology & Rel. Studies; Raymond C. O'Brien, J.D.; Jon J. O'Brien, S.J. (Retired); Anthony J. Pogorelc, S.S., M.Div., Ph.D.; Dominic F. Serra, S.T.D.; Sean O. Sheridan, T.O.R.; Raymond Studzinski, O.S.B., Ph.D.; Paul Sullins; David D. Thayer, S.S., S.T.L., Ph.D.; Rt. Rev. James A. Wiseman, O.S.B., M.A., S.T.D. (Retired); Revs. Michael G. Witczak, M.Div., S.L.D. (MIL); Romuald Meogrossi, O.F.M.Conv.; John J. M. Foster; Phillip J. Brown, S.S., J.C.D.; James Brent, O.P.; Rev. Msgr. Stephen J. Rossetti, Ph.D., D.Min.

Clerical Members, Board of Trustees: His Eminence Francis Cardinal George, O.M.I., Ph.D., S.T.D.; Donald Cardinal Wuerl, Chancellor; Most Rev. Frances B. Shulte, Trustee Emeritus; His Eminence Sean Cardinal O'Malley, O.F.M.Cap., Ph.D.; Daniel N. DiNardo; Most Revs. Edward P. Cullen, D.D., Trustee Emeritus; Allen H. Vigneron, D.D., Bd. Chm.; Jose H. Gomez, S.T.D.; Wilton D. Gregory, S.L.D.; Joseph A. Pepe, D.D., J.C.D.; Rev. Msgr. Walter R. Rossi; Most Revs. Michael F. Burbidge, D.D., Ed.D., V.G.; Paul S. Loverde, D.D., S.T.L., J.C.L. (ARL); Gregory J. Mansour; Robert J. McManus; Edwin F. O'Brien; Thomas G. Wenski; Robert J. Carlson; Joseph E. Kurtz; John C. Nienstedt; Thomas J. Olmsted; Paul S. Coakley; Salvatore J. Cordileone; Nicholas A. DiMarzio; Thomas J. Tobin; Rev. Msgr. Peter J. Vaghi, V.F.

**Georgetown University* (1789) 37th and O Sts., N.W., 20057. Tel: 202-687-0100. Web: www.georgetown.edu. John J. DeGioia, Ph.D., Pres.; James J. O'Donnell, Ph.D., Provost; Stuart Bondurant, Interim Exec. Vice Pres.; T. Alexander Aleinikoff, Vice Pres. & Dean of the Law Center; Spiros Dimolitsas, Ph.D., Senior Vice Pres.; Edward M. Quinn, Univ. Sec.; Christopher Joyce, M.B.A., Senior Vice Pres., CFO & Treas.; Todd A. Olson, Ph.D., Vice Pres. Student Affairs; Jo-Ann Henry, Vice Pres. & Chief Human Resources Officer; Daniel R. Porterfield, Ph.D., Vice Pres. Public Affairs & Strategic Devel.; H. David Lambert, Vice Pres. for Information Svcs. & CIO; Jane E. Genster, Vice Pres. & Gen. Counsel; Rev. Philip L. Boroughs, S.J., Vice Pres., Mission & Ministry; Michael D. McGuire, Exec. Dir. Planning & Institute Research; Revs. Charles G. Gonzalez, S.J.; William M. King, S.J.; Paul J. McCarren, S.J.; Patrick D. Rogers, S.J.; Mr. Jaroslow Chzanowski; Mr. Francois Kabore, S.J.; Mr. Richard Ross, S.J.; Mr. Rodrique Takoudjou. Jesuits 23; Sisters 5; Lay Teachers 1,067; Total Enrollment 12,688.

The following are the Schools and Colleges which compose the University: Undergraduate Admissions.

Georgetown College (1789) Jane Dammen McAuliffe, Ph.D., Dean.

Graduate School of Arts & Sciences (1820) David W. Lightfoot, Ph.D., Dean.

School of Medicine (1851) 3900 Reservoir Rd., N.W., 20007. Ray Mitchell, M.D., Senior Assoc. Dean Academic Affairs.

Law Center (1870) 600 New Jersey Ave., N.W., 20001. T. Alexander Aleinikoff, Exec. Vice Pres. & Dean of Law Center.

School of Nursing & Health Studies (1903) 3700 Reservoir Rd., N.W., 20007. Bette Keltner, R.N., F.A.A.N., Ph.D., Dean.

Edmund A. Walsh School of Foreign Service (1919) Hon. Robert L. Gallucci, Ph.D., Dean.

Robert Emmett McDonough School of Business (1957) George Daly, Dean Mibonough School of Business.

Georgetown Public Policy Institute (1990) 3600 N. St., N.W., Ste. 200, 20007. Judith Feder, Ph.D., Dean.

School of Summer and Continuing Education (1974) Robert J. Thomas, Ph.D., Dean.

Joseph Mark Lauinger Library Artemis G. Kirk, M.A., Univ. Librarian.

Office of the University Registrar John Q. Pierce IV, M.A., Univ. Registrar.

Office of Alumni & University Relations, Box 571253, 20057. Tel: 202-687-4111.

Affirmative Action Programs, G-10 Darnall Hall, 37th St. & O St., N.W., 20057. Tel: 202-687-4798; Fax: 202-687-7778. Rosemary Kilkenny, J.D., Special Asst. to Pres. for AAP.

Trinity College, 125 Michigan Ave., N.E., 20017. Tel: 202-884-9000; Fax: 202-884-9229. Email: pauleya@Trinitydc.edu. Web: www.trinitydc.edu. Patricia A. McGuire, Pres.; Sr. Mary Johnson, S.N.D., Community Representative; Dr. Robert Preston, Vice Pres. Academic Affairs. Sisters of Notre Dame de Namur. Priests 1; Sisters 5; Lay Professors 54; Students 1,600.

[D] HIGH SCHOOLS, ARCHDIOCESAN

WASHINGTON. *Archbishop Carroll High School*, 4300 Harewood Rd., N.E., 20017. Tel: 202-529-0900; Fax: 202-529-5989. Email: carroll@archbishopcarroll.org. Web: www.archbishopcarroll.org. Dr. David S. Stofa, Ph.D., Prin. & CEO; Ms. Kimberly Burks, Vice Prin. Academic Affairs; Mr. Larry Savoy, Vice Prin. Student Affairs; Revs. George Kintiba; John Mudd; Jessica Pryde, Librarian. (Coed) Priests 2; Deacons 1; Sisters 1; Lay Teachers 41; Students 458; Staff 26.

Don Bosco Cristo Rey High School of the Archdiocese of Washington, Mailing Address: P.O. Box 56481, 20040-6481. Tel: 301-891-4750; Fax: 301-270-1459. Email: shafrans@dbcr.org. Web: www.donboscocristorey.org. Revs. Steve Shafran, S.D.B., Pres.; John Serio, S.D.B., Prin.; Mrs. Jean Cotter, Librarian. Priests 3; Brothers 1; Lay Teachers 44; Students 325.

[E] HIGH SCHOOLS, PRIVATE

WASHINGTON. *St. Anselm's Abbey School, Inc*, (Grades 6-12), 4501 South Dakota Ave., N.E., 20017. Tel: 202-269-2350; Fax: 202-269-2373. Email: mainoffice@saintanselms.org. Web: www.saintanselms.org. Rev. Dom Peter Weigand, O.S.B., Pres.; Louis Silvano, Headmaster; Bro. Marvin Kluesner, S.D.S., Librarian. Separate subsidiary corporation of The Benedictine Foundation at Washington, DC (St. Anselm's Abbey)., Seven-year college preparatory course. Priests 7; Brothers 3; Lay Faculty and Staff 43; Students 232.

Georgetown Visitation Preparatory School, 1524 35th St., N.W., 20007. Tel: 202-337-3350; Fax: 202-342-5733. Email: name@visi.org. Web: www.visi.org. Sr. Mary Berchmans Hannan, V.H.M., Pres. Emerita & Superior; Mr. Dan Kerns, Head of School; Elizabeth Burke, Librarian. Sisters 2; Lay Teachers 60; Students 480.

Gonzaga College High School, 19 Eye St., N.W., 20001. Tel: 202-336-7100; Fax: 202-336-7172. Web: www.gonzaga.org. Revs. Stephen W. Planning, S.J., Pres.; Vincent G. Conti, S.J., Headmaster; Mr. Stephen Szolosi, Dir., Campus Ministry; Rev. Thomas F. Clifford, S.J., Rector; Patricia Tobin, Librarian. Society of Jesus, Maryland Province. Priests 5; Sisters 2; Lay Teachers 76; Students 957. In Res. Revs. Kenneth E. Meehan, S.J.; Gerald V. O'Connor, S.J.; Bruce A. Steggert, S.J.

St. John's College High School (1851) (Coed Grades 9-12), 2607 Military Rd., N.W., 20015. Tel: 202-363-2316; Fax: 202-686-5162. Email: stjohnschs@stjohns-chs.org. Web: stjohns-chs.org. Bro. Michael Andrejko, F.S.C., Prin.; Mr. Jeffrey Mancabelli, Pres.

St. John's College High School Brothers of the Christian Schools., College Preparatory, Elective Army Junior ROTC. Brothers 2; Sisters 1; Lay Teachers 77; Students 1,044.

**San Miguel School*, 7705 Georgia Ave., NW, 20012. Tel: 202-232-8345; Fax: 202-232-3987. Martha W. Kendall, Exec. Dir.; Bro. Francis Eells, F.S.C., Prin.

BETHESDA, MD. *Mater Dei School, Inc.*, 9600 Seven Locks Rd., MD 20817. Tel: 301-365-2700; 301-365-2701; Fax: 301-365-2710. Mr. Edward N. Williams, Headmaster; Mr. Christopher S. Abell, Pres. Students 225.

Stone Ridge School of the Sacred Heart, 9101 Rockville Pike, MD 20814. Tel: 301-657-4322; Fax: 301-657-4393. Email: ckarrels@stoneridgeschool.org. Web: www.stoneridgeschool.org. Mrs. Catherine Ronan Karrels, Head of School; Carla Basco, Librarian. Religious of the Sacred Heart. Lay Teachers 84; Students 661.

BLADENSBURG, MD. *Elizabeth Seton High School* (1959) 5715 Emerson St., MD 20710-1844. Tel: 301-864-4532; Fax: 301-864-8946. Email: ehagar@setonhs.org. Web: www.setonhs.org. Sr. Ellen Marie Hagar, D.C., Pres.; Mrs. Sharon Pasterick, Prin.; Mrs. Kim Tremble, Librarian. Daughters of Charity of St. Vincent de Paul 7; Lay Teachers 51; Administration & Staff 34; Girls 610; Lay Staff 27.

FORESTVILLE, MD. *Bishop McNamara High School* (Coed), 6800 Marlboro Pike, MD 20747. Tel: 301-735-8401; Fax: 301-735-0934. Email: clarkm@bmhs.org. Web: www.bmhs.org. Ms. Heather Gossart, Pres.; Mr. Marco Clark, Prin. Holy Cross Brothers. Lay Teachers 75; Students 840.

HYATTSVILLE, MD. *De Matha Catholic High School*, 4313 Madison St., MD 20781. Tel: 240-764-2200; Fax: 240-764-2275. Email: dmmail@dematha.org. Web: www.dematha.org. Rev. James R. Day, O.S.S.T., Rector; Dr. Daniel J. McMahon, Ph.D., Prin.; Mrs. Zetha Ballinger, Librarian. Conducted by the Order of the Most Holy Trinity, Province of the Immaculate Heart of Mary., Boys, 9-12. Priests 2; Lay Teachers 84; Students 900.

KENSINGTON, MD. *The Academy of the Holy Cross, Inc.* (1868) 4920 Strathmore Ave., MD 20895. Tel: 301-942-2100; Fax: 301-929-6440. Email: schooloffice@academyoftheholycross.org. Web: academyoftheholycross.org. Claire M. Helm, Ph.D., Pres.; Ann Nichols, Prin.; Catharine Stoll, Librarian.

The Academy of the Holy Cross, Inc. Sisters 1; Students 550; Lay Teachers 49.

LAUREL, MD. *St. Vincent Pallotti High School* (1921) , MD 20707. Tel: 301-725-3228; Fax: 301-776-4343. Email: admissions@pallottihs.org. Web: www.pallottihs.org. Stephen J. Edmonds, Pres. & Prin.; Mrs. Amy Seigel, Librarian. Pallottine Missionary Sisters of the Catholic Apostolate. Priests 1; Sisters 1; Lay Teachers 36; Students 500.

LEONARDTOWN, MD. *St. Mary's Ryken High School* (1885) 22600 Camp Calvert Rd., MD 20650. Tel: 301-475-2814; 301-932-4422; Fax: 301-373-4195. Web: www.smrhs.org. Mrs. Mary Joy Hurlburt, Pres.; Rick Wood, Prin. Sponsored by the Xaverian Brothers. Lay Teachers 56; Students 680.

NORTH BETHESDA, MD. *Georgetown Preparatory School* , MD 20852. Tel: 301-493-5000; Fax: 301-530-9531. Web: www.gprep.org. Mr. Jeffrey Jones, Headmaster; Revs. Richard S. McCouch, S.J., Supr.; Michael J. Marco, S.J., Pres.; William J. Elliott, S.J.; Gerard P. Bell, S.J.; George S. Williams, S.J.; Leonard A. Martin, S.J.; Philip J. Rosato, S.J.; David A. Sauter, S.J.; Erica Lodish, Librarian. Jesuit Community; Society of Jesus. Priests 8; Lay Teachers 51; Students 483.

OLNEY, MD. *Our Lady of Good Counsel High School*, 17301 Old Vic Blvd., MD 20832. Tel: 240-283-3209; Fax: 240-283-3390. Email: raimo@olgchs.org. Web: olgchs.org. Mr. Arthur Raimo, Pres.; John Graham, Prin.; Rev. Barry R. Gross (LFT). Xaverian Brothers. Priests 1; Lay Teachers 89; Students 1,200.

POTOMAC, MD. *Connelly School of the Holy Child*, (Grades 6-12), 9029 Bradley Blvd., MD 20854. Tel: 301-365-0955; Fax: 301-365-0981. Web: www.holychild.org. Maureen K. Appel, Headmistress; Teri Boragno, Head of Upper School; Sarah Stonesifer, Librarian. Sisters of the Holy Child Jesus., College Preparatory for Girls. Lay Teachers 44; Students 295.

[F] ELEMENTARY SCHOOLS, ARCHDIOCESAN

DARNESTOWN, MD. *Mary of Nazareth Roman Catholic Elementary School* (1994) (Grades PreSchool-8), 14131 Seneca Rd., MD 20874. Tel: 301-869-0940; Fax: 301-869-0942. Email: marynaz@comcast.net. Web: www.maryofnazareth.org. Mr. Michael J. Friel, Prin.; Mrs. Lorraine Palmer, Librarian.

[G] ELEMENTARY SCHOOLS, PRIVATE

BETHESDA, MD. *The Woods Academy*, 6801 Greentree Rd., MD 20817. Tel: 301-365-3080; Fax: 301-469-6439. Email: jpowers@woodsacademy.org. Web: www.woodsacademy.org. Joseph E. Powers, Head of School; Susan Powers, Librarian. Students 295; Lay Teachers 39.

GAITHERSBURG, MD. *Emmanuel, Inc.* (1987) 20501 Goshen Rd., MD 20879. Tel: 301-990-2088; Fax: 301-947-0574. Email: mog@mogschool.com. Web: www.mogschool.com. Ms. Mary Reinhard, Prin.; Sheila Martin, Librarian. Total Staff 31; Students 210.

POTOMAC, MD. *The Heights School*, 10400 Seven Locks Rd., MD 20854. Tel: 301-365-4300; Fax: 301-365-4303. Email: adevicente@heights.edu. Web: www.heights.edu. Mr. Alvaro de Vicente, Headmaster; Revs. Gerald S. Kolf, Chap.; John Debicki, Chap.; Mr. Michael Moynihan, Upper School Head; Mr. Andrew Reed, Middle School Head; Colin Gleason, Lower School Head; Mr. Joseph Cardenas, Dean Advisory; Mr. Thomas Royals, Asst. Headmaster; James Nelson, Librarian. Private, Independent, Spiritual Formation and Religious Education provided by the Prelature of Opus Dei. Priests 2; Lay Teachers 59.

[H] SPECIAL SCHOOLS

WASHINGTON. *Lt. Joseph P. Kennedy, Jr., Institute*, 801 Buchanan St., N.E., 20017. Tel: 202-529-7600; Fax: 202-529-2028. Email: gadair@kennedyinstitute.org. Web: www.kennedyinstitute.org. Deacon Richard C. Birkel, Ph.D., Pres. & CEO. The Lt. Joseph P. Kennedy, Jr., Institute of the Archdiocese of Washington is a private, nonprofit organization providing education, training and employment, therapeutic and residential services to children and adults with developmental disabilities.

Nonprofit Organizations Serving Children and Adults With Developmental Disabilities:

Adult Learning & Employment Services Tel: 202-529-0500; Fax: 202-529-8211. Participants 364.

Family & Personal Support Services Tel: 301-251-2860; Fax: 301-251-8559. Staff 25; Participants 102.

Early Intervention & Preventive Services Tel: 202-529-7600; Fax: 202-529-2028. Staff 45; Participants 82.

Kennedy Education Tel: 202-529-7600; Fax: 202-529-2028. (Includes Kennedy School, Outreach Program to Catholic Schools and Inclusion 2000) Staff 52; Students 140.

Residential Division Tel: 202-529-7600; Fax: 202-529-2028. Total Staff 81; Residents 61.

Administration Division Tel: 202-529-7600; Fax: 202-529-2028. Total Staff 25.

Community Living Partnership Total Staff 3; Families 50.

[I] CATHOLIC CHARITIES OF THE ARCHDIOCESE

WASHINGTON. *Catholic Charities of the Archdiocese of Washington, Inc.*, 924 G St., N.W., 20001. Tel: 202-772-4300; Fax: 202-772-4308. Email: john.enzler@catholiccharitiesdc.org. Web: catholiccharitiesdc.org. Rev. Msgr. John Enzler, V.E., Pres.

Anchor Mental Health Association / Division of Adult and Family Services, 1001 Lawrence St., N.E., P.O. Box 29058, 20017. Tel: 202-635-5940; Fax: 202-481-1431.

CCS Housing, Inc., 924 G St., N.W., 20001.

Calvert County Family Center, 855 Main St., Prince Frederick, MD 20678. Tel: 410-535-0309; Fax: 410-257-1002.

The Catholic Charities Foundation of the Archdiocese of Washington, 924 G St., N.W., 20001. Rev. Msgr. John Enzler, V.E., Pres. Tel: 202-772-4373; Fax: 202-772-4411; Carol Shannon, Exec. Dir. Tel: 202-772-4395; Fax: 202-772-4411.

Division of Catholic Charities Enterprises Tel: 202-635-5970; Fax: 202-481-1431. Email: scott.lewis@catholiccharitiesdc.org. Scott Lewis, Dir.

Division of Housing and Support Service Tel: 202-481-1435; Fax: 202-481-1430. Email: trinette.hawkins@catholiccharitiesdc.org. Trinette Hawkins, Dir.

Lt. Joseph P. Kennedy Institute / Division of Development Disabilities Services, 801 Buchanan St., N.E., 20017. Tel: 202-281-2759; Fax: 202-529-1673. Email: daphne.pallozzi@catholiccharitiesdc.org. Daphne Pallozzi, M.S., Dir.

Montgomery County Family Center, 12247 Georgia Ave., Silver Spring, MD 20902. Tel: 301-933-3164; Fax: 301-949-1371.

N.E. Family Center / Division of Children's Services, 1438 Rhode Island Ave., N.E., 20018. Tel: 202-526-4100; Fax: 202-526-1829. Email: meha.desai@catholiccharitiesdc.org.

Prince George's County Family Center, 6706 Marlboro Pike, Forestville, MD 20747. Tel: 301-568-9529; Fax: 301-568-9567.

Rollingcrest Commons, Inc., 924 G St., N.W., 20001-4532. Tel: 202-772-4308.

SHARE Food Network, 5170 Lawrence Pl., Hyattsville, MD 20781. Tel: 301-864-3115; Fax: 301-864-5370. P.O. Box 768, Bladensburg, MD 20710. Scott Lewis.

Southeast Family Center, 220 Highview Pl., S.E., 20032. Tel: 202-574-3442; Fax: 202-574-3474. Total Assisted 102,895; Total Staff 850.

Spanish Catholic Center, Inc. / Division of Immigrant and Refuge Services, 1618 Monroe St., N.W., 20010. Tel: 202-939-2437; Fax: 202-234-7323. Email: mario.dorsonville@catholiccharitiesdc.org. Rev. Mario E. Dorsonville, Dir.

[J] ARCHDIOCESAN VOLUNTEER ORGANIZATIONS

WASHINGTON. *Archdiocesan Association of Ladies of Charity*, P.O. Box 10038, 20018. Vivian M. Chase, Pres. Purpose: Individual charity work, usually of emergency nature and supports various other agencies, foodbanks, child care centers and pregnancy aid centers.

Christ Child Society, Inc., 5101 Wisconsin Ave., N.W., Ste. 304, 20016. Tel: 202-966-9250; Fax: 202-966-2880. Email: kcurtin@christchilddc.org. Ms. Kathleen Curtin, Exec. Dir.

Serra Club of Downtown Washington, 4409 Westover Pl., N.W., 20016. Tel: 202-362-2477. Mr. Gerrald Giblin, Pres.

Society of St. Vincent de Paul, Archdiocesan Council of Washington, 1438 Rhode Island Ave., N.E., 20018-3709. Tel: 202-281-2033.

Office of Archdiocesan Council

St. Vincent de Paul Society

The Washington Cursillo Movement, 6312 2nd St. N.W., 20011. Tel: 202-330-7227. Jacquelyn DeMesme-Gray, Dir.; Rev. William E. Foley, Spiritual Dir.

BERLIN, MD. *Holy Name Society*, 141 Nottingham Ln., MD 21811-1663. Tel: 443-614-5411. Email: joelatchford@gmail.com. Mr. Joseph Latchford, Vice Pres., Region XIV.

BETHESDA, MD. *Ladies of Charity*, 5403 Linden Ct., MD 20814. Tel: 301-564-5793. Ms. Maryanne Rooney, Pres.; Rev. Carl F. Dianda, Spiritual Dir.

Serra Club of Washington, D.C., 5602 Ontario Cir., MD 20816. Tel: 301-229-2176. Mr. Joseph F. Spaniol Jr., Pres.

CHARLOTTE HALL, MD. *Serra Club of Southern Maryland*, 10548 Wicomoco Ridge Rd., MD 20622. Mrs. Walter Rourke, Pres.

HYATTSVILLE, MD. *Serra Club of Prince George's Co.*, 4014 Nicholson St., MD 20782. Tel: 301-779-3150. Miss Judith Barr, Pres.

SILVER SPRING, MD. *Archdiocesan Council of Washington*, 12247 Georgia Ave., MD 20902. Tel: 301-946-3702. Email: svdpwashdc@aol.com. Mrs. Alice Garvey, Pres.

[K] ORPHANAGES AND INFANT HOMES

HYATTSVILLE, MD. *St. Ann's Infant and Maternity Home*, 4901 Eastern Ave., MD 20782. Tel: 301-559-5500; Fax: 301-853-6985. Email: donations@stanns.org. Web: www.stanns.org. Sisters Mary Bader, D.C., CEO; Virginia Ann Brooks, D.C., Local Supr. Daughters of Charity. Sisters 6; Residential Children 57; Day Care 75; Teen Mother-Baby Program: Mothers 20; Children 20; Faith House - 8 mothers & 8 children 16.

Faith House, 4903 Eastern Ave., MD 20782. Tel: 301-559-5500; Fax: 301-853-6985. Email: peggy.gatewood@stanns.org. Mrs. Peggy Gatewood, Dir.

[L] GENERAL HOSPITALS

WASHINGTON. *De Paul Foundation, Inc.*, 1150 Varnum St., N.E., 20017. Tel: 202-269-7039; Fax: 202-269-7029. Email: jboland@provhosp.org. De Paul Foundation, Inc. was Organized to Provide Fund Development, Financial and Other Assistance to Provide Hospital and Other Subsidiaries of De Paul Foundation for the Health Care, Medical, Educational and Human Needs of the District of Columbia and Vicinity, by Functioning as a Charitable Nonprofit, Nonstock Corporation.

Providence Health Foundation, 1150 Varnum St., N.E., 20017. Tel: 202-269-7776; Fax: 202-269-7687. Providence Health Foundation, Inc. (PHF), a District of Columbia Charitable Nonprofit Corporation, was Organized to Support the Mission of Providence Hospital by Conducting Fundraising and Development Activities, by Receiving and Managing Donations, by Making Grants and by Promoting Educational Activities and Scientific Research.

Georgetown University Hospital, 3800 Reservoir Rd., N.W., 20007. Tel: 202-444-3000; Fax: 202-444-3095. Email: conleyb@gunet.georgetown.edu. Web: www.georgetownuniversityhospital.org. Richard Goldberg M.D., Interim Pres.; Revs. Brian J. Conley, S.J., Dir. Mission & Pastoral Care; Gustaaf M. Keppens, S.J., Chap.; Norman Schwartz, Chap.; Azuka Iwuchukwu, Chap. Priests 4; Bed Capacity 609; Total Assisted Annually 195,383; Total Staff 3,538.

Providence Health Services, Inc., 1150 Varnum St., N.E., 20017. Ambulatory-Outpatient Care, Promote Wellness and Carry Out Educational Activities and Scientific Research.

Providence Hospital, 1150 Varnum St., N.E., 20017. Tel: 202-269-7000; Fax: 202-269-7160. Email: amy.freeman@provhosp.org. Web: www.provhosp.org. Amy E. Freeman, Pres.; Revs. Maurus Dolcic, T.O.R., Chap.; Philip Simo, O.S.B., Chap. Daughters of Charity of St. Vincent de Paul. Sisters 10; Bed Capacity 576; Patients Assisted Annually 182,000; Total Staff 2,325.

SILVER SPRING, MD. *Holy Cross Hospital of Silver Spring, Inc.*, 1500 Forest Glen Rd., MD 20910. Tel: 301-754-7000; Fax: 301-754-7012. Web: www.holycrosshealth.org. Mr. Kevin J. Sexton, CEO; Linda Arnold, Ph.D., Dir. Pastoral Care & Mission Opers.; Rev. George Markwell, M.Afr. A member of Trinity Health which is sponsored by Catholic Health Ministries. Sisters of the Holy Cross 7; Bed Capacity 450; Patients Assisted Annually 203,527; Total Staff 3,200.

[M] HOUSING

WASHINGTON. *Cardinal O'Boyle Residence for Priests*, 1150 Varnum St., N.E., 20017. Tel: 202-269-7810 (Rector); Fax: 202-269-7820. P.O. Box 29206, 20017-0206. Suites 12; Residents 6; Total Staff 2. In Res. Rev. Msgr. Leonard F. Hurley, Chap., Carroll Manor & Rector O'Boyle Residence for Retired Priests; Revs. Winthrop J. Brainerd (Retired); Paul F. Liston (Retired); William J. Thompson (Retired); Louis A. Tou (Retired); Donald Brice (Retired).

Little Sisters of the Poor of Washington, D.C., Inc. (1871) 4200 Harewood Rd., N.E., 20017-1554. Tel: 202-269-1831; Fax: 202-269-3910. Email: mswashington@littlesistersofthepoor.org. Web: www.littlesistersofthepoor.org. Sr. Benedict Armstrong, L.S.P., Supr.; Rev. William M. Brailsford. Little Sisters of the Poor. Sisters 12; Residents 75; Apartments 22; Total Staff 100.

BETHESDA, MD. *Palmer Park Seniors Housing, Inc.* (2001) c/o Victory Housing, Inc., 5430 Grosvenor Ln., Ste. 210, MD 20814-2142. Tel: 301-493-6000; Fax: 301-493-9788. Email: info@victoryhousing.org. Web: www.victoryhousing.org. John D. Spencer, Senior Vice Pres. Apartment Units 69.

Takoma Tower, Inc. (2001) c/o Victory Housing, Inc., 5430 Grosvenor Ln., Ste. 210, MD 20814-2142. Tel: 301-493-6000; Fax: 301-493-9788. Email: info@victoryhousing.org. Web:

www.victoryhousing.org. John D. Spencer, Senior Vice Pres. Apartment Units 187.

Victory Housing, Inc., 5430 Grosvenor Ln., Ste. 210, MD 20814. Tel: 301-493-6000; Fax: 301-493-9788. Email: jbrown@victoryhousing.org. Mr. James A. Brown Jr., Pres.

Andrew Kim House, 2100 Olney Sandy-Spring Rd., Olney, MD 20832. Tel: 301-260-2500; Fax: 301-260-2720. Email: manager435@habitatamerica.com. Ms. Deysi Fuentes, Community Mgr.

Raphael House, 1515 Dunster Rd., Rockville, MD 20854. Tel: 301-217-9116; Fax: 301-217-9119. Email: raphael@victoryhousing.org. Sheila Griffith, Dir.

Byron House, 9210 Kentsdale Dr., Potomac, MD 20854. Tel: 301-469-9400; Fax: 301-765-8112. Email: sborcwiec@victoryhousing.org. Ms. Sharon Borcwiec, Dir.

Marian Assisted Living, 19109 Georgia Ave., Brookeville, MD 20833. Tel: 301-570-3190; Fax: 301-570-3638. Email: msmith@victoryhousing.org. Ms. Margaret H. Smith, Dir.

Malta House, 4916-18 LaSalle Rd., Hyattsville, MD 20782-3302. Tel: 301-699-8600; Fax: 301-699-1696. Email: eorchard@victoryhousing.org. Ms. Elizabeth Orchard, Dir.

Bartholomew House, 6904 River Rd., MD 20817. Tel: 301-320-6151; Fax: 301-320-4420. Email: jblue@victoryhousing.org. Miss Jeanne Blue, Dir.

Mary's House, 600-A Veirs Mill Rd., Rockville, MD 20852. Tel: 301-279-9520; Fax: 301-279-2080. Email: marys@victoryhousing.org. Ms. Bridget Desnoes, Dir.

Grace House, 3214 Norbeck Rd., Silver Spring, MD 20906. Tel: 301-924-4424; Fax: 301-924-4427. Email: mdeschriver@victoryhousing.org. Ms. Meg DeSchriver, Dir.

Cambridge Apartments, Inc., 676 Houston Ave., Takoma Park, MD 20912. Tel: 301-585-3750; Fax: 301-585-4072. Email: epuleo@habitatamerica.com. Ms. Eleanor Puleo, Property Mgr.

Avondale Park Apartments, 4915 Eastern Ave., Hyattsville, MD 20782. Tel: 301-853-7787; Fax: 301-853-3988. Email: manager418@habitatamerica.com. Ms. Barbara Miller, Property Mgr.

Manor Apartments, Inc., 4907 Eastern Ave., Hyattsville, MD 20782. Tel: 301-853-2900; Fax: 301-853-3418. Email: manager417@habitatamerica.com. Ms. Barbara Miller, Property Mgr.

Victory Forest, 10000 Brunswick Ave., Silver Spring, MD 20910. Tel: 301-589-4030; Fax: 301-589-7349. Email: manager406@habitatamerica.com. Ms. Valerie Richardson, Property Mgr.

Trinity Terrace, 6001 Fisher Rd., Temple Hills, MD 20748. Tel: 301-630-7717; Fax: 301-630-1798. Email: trinityterrace@habitatamerica.com. Ms. Arlita Matthews, Property Mgr.

Victory Tower, 7051 Carroll Ave., Takoma Park, MD 20912. Tel: 301-270-1858; Fax: 301-270-4715. Email: manager412@habitatamerica.com. Ms. Darcia Young, Property Mgr.

Winslow House Apartments, 666 Houston Ave., Takoma Park, MD 20912. Tel: 301-585-3750; Fax: 301-585-4072. Email: epuleo@habitatamerica.com. Ms. Eleanor Puleo, Property Mgr.

Victory Terrace Apartments, 9440 Newbridge Dr., Potomac, MD 20854. Tel: 301-983-9600; Fax: 301-983-9606. Email: manager401@habitatamerica.com. Ms. Ingrid Geissler, Property Mgr.

Victory House of Palmer Park, 7801 Barlowe Rd., Palmer Park, MD 20785. Tel: 301-341-4995; Fax: 301-341-4997. Email: manager405@habitatamerica.com. Ms. Brenda Wines, Property Mgr.

Cheval Court Apartments, 2611 Luana Dr., Forestville, MD 20747. Tel: 301-736-0685; Fax: 301-736-0705. Email: chevalcourt@habitatamerica.com. Ms. Arlita Matthews, Property Mgr.

Victory Crest, 6100 Sargent Rd., Hyattsville, MD 20782. Tel: 301-559-3891; Fax: 301-559-3868. Email: choward@hrehllc.com. Ms. Corinne Howard, Property Mgr.

Victory Heights, 1369 Irving St., N.W., 20010. Tel: 202-939-1431; Fax: 202-939-1433. Email: manager320@habitatamerica.com. Ms. Delphine Duckett, Property Mgr.

Parkfair Apartments, 1611 Park Rd., N.W., 20010. Tel: 202-986-1600; Fax: 202-986-4100. Email: manager319@habitatamerica.com. Ms. Marcia Urquiza, Property Mgr.

Winslow House, Inc. (2002) c/o Victory Housing, Inc., 5430 Grosvenor Ln., Ste. 210, MD 20814-2142. Tel: 301-493-6000; Fax: 301-493-9788. Email: info@victoryhousing.org. Web: www.victoryhousing.org. John D. Spencer, Senior Vice Pres. Apartment Units 46.

HYATTSVILLE, MD. *Sacred Heart Home Inc.*, 5805 Queens Chapel Rd., MD 20782. Tel: 301-277-6500; Fax: 301-277-3181. Email: sistervacha@sacredhearthome.org. Web: www.sacredhearthome.org. Sr. Waclawa Kludziak; Rev. Stan Ukwe. Sisters, Servants of Mary Immaculate. Sisters 6; Residents 102.

MITCHELLVILLE, MD. *Villa Rosa Nursing Home, Inc.*, 3800 Lottsford Vista Rd., MD 20721-4026. Tel: 301-459-4700; Fax: 301-429-0646. Rev. Dominic Rodighiero, C.S., Dir.; Mrs. Neva Babcock, R.N., B.S.N., L.N.H.A., Admin.; Sr. Teolide Cecagno, M.S.C.S., Supr. Comprehensive Care Nursing Facility. Sisters 4; Residents 100.

[N] MISSIONARIES OF CHARITY

WASHINGTON. *Gift of Peace House*, 2800 Otis St., N.E., 20018. Tel: 202-269-3313. Sr. Clovis, Supr.

Queen of Peace House, 3310 Wheeler Rd., S.E., 20032. Sr. Maria Bernadette, M.C., Supr.

TAKOMA PARK, MD. *Casa Nuestra Senora de Guadalupe*, 8114 Carroll Ave., MD 20912. Tel: 301-408-0091. Sr. Benedict Anne, M.C., Supr.

[O] MONASTERIES AND RESIDENCES OF PRIESTS AND BROTHERS

WASHINGTON. *St. Anselm's Abbey* (1923) 4501 S. Dakota Ave., N.E., 20017. Tel: 202-269-2300; Fax: 202-269-2312. Web: www.stanselms.org. Rt. Revs. Aidan Shea, O.S.B.; James A. Wiseman, O.S.B., M.A., S.T.D. (Retired); Revs. Patrick Granfield, O.S.B., Ph.D., S.T.D. (Retired); Michael Hall, O.S.B., M.A., Ph.D., Prior; Hilary Hayden, O.S.B., S.T.L.; Edmund Henkels, O.S.B.; Joseph Jensen, O.S.B., S.S.L., S.T.D.; Gabriel Myers, O.S.B.; Philip Simo, O.S.B.; Boniface von Nell, O.S.B.; Peter Weigand, O.S.B.; Christopher Wyvill, O.S.B.; Bros. Dunstan Robidoux, O.S.B.; Matthew Nylund, O.S.B. Benedictine Foundation at Washington, DC, Order of St. Benedict. Priests 12; Brothers 2.

Brothers of Charity, 1359 Monroe St., N.E., 20017. Tel: 202-636-4306. Web: www.brothersofcharity.org. Email: donald.joyal.fc@fracarita.org. Bro. Donald Joyal, F.C., Dir. Formation.

Center for Assisted Living (1993) Dominican Fathers and Brothers., 630 E St., S.W., 20024. Tel: 202-488-4188; Fax: 202-554-5735. Email: jmcmahon@opfriars.org. Rev. Norman A. Haddad, O.P., S.T.L., Interim Dir.

Commissariat of the Holy Land, Franciscan Monastery - Mount St. Sepulchre, 1400 Quincy St., N.E., 20017. Tel: 202-526-6800, Ext. 887; Fax: 202-529-9889. Email: commissarywdcusa@myfranciscan.com; secretariatusa@myfranciscan.com. Web: www.myfranciscan.com. Very Rev. Jeremy Harrington, O.F.M.; Rev. Garrett Edmunds, O.F.M., Vice Commissary; Friar John-Sebastian Laird-Hammond, O.F.M., Secretariat. Priests 9; Friars 19; Solemnly Professed 19. *Franciscan Monastery USA Inc.*, 1400 Quincy St. N.E., 20017. Tel: 202-526-6800; Fax: 202-529-9889. Email: secretariatusa@myfranciscan.com. Web: www.myfranciscan.com. Very Rev. Jeremy Harrington, O.F.M., Guardian; Friars Thomas Courtney, O.F.M.; John-Sebastian Laird-Hammond, O.F.M., Secretariat to Franciscan Monastery; Revs. Garrett Edmunds, O.F.M., Vice Commissary; Edward Flanagan, O.F.M.; Romuald Green, O.F.M.; Friars Simon McKay, O.F.M.; Roger Petras, O.F.M.; Revs. Stephen F. Sabbagh, O.F.M. (Retired); Francis X. Sihuay, O.F.M. (Peru) (Retired); Jacob-Matthew Smith, O.F.M., Vocation Dir.; Kevin Treston, O.F.M.; David Wathen, O.F.M., Dir. Holy Land Tours; Friars Callistus Welch, O.F.M., Treas. Holy Land Foundation; Maximilian Wojciechowski, O.F.M., Gift Shop Mgr.; Rev. Manuel Ybarra, O.F.M., Finance Office; Friar Christopher Coppock, O.F.M. Priests 11; Deacons 1; Brothers 8; Solemnly Professed 20.

Holy Redeemer College (1930) 3112 Seventh St., N.E., 20017. Tel: 202-529-4410; 202-529-4484; Fax: 202-832-1321. Very Rev. Gerard H. Chylko, C.Ss.R., Rector/Superior; Revs. Kevin O'Neil, C.Ss.R.; James Wallace, C.Ss.R., Vicar; Thomas Forrest, C.Ss.R.; Brian Johnstone, C.Ss.R., Moral Theol. CUA; John Kingsbury, C.Ss.R., North American Conference Coord.; Bro. Thomas Rochacewicz, C.Ss.R.

Holy Redeemer College, Opened in 1930. Redemptorist House of Studies 2009. Priests 10; Religious Brother 1.

The Jesuit Community at Georgetown University, 37th and O Sts., N.W., 20057-1200. Tel: 202-687-4000; Fax: 202-687-7679. Email: langanj@georgetown.edu. Revs. Joseph E. Lingan, S.J., Rector; Ronald J. Anton, S.J.; Edward W. Bodnar, S.J. (Retired); Thomas J. Buckley, S.J.; Gerard J. Campbell, S.J. (Retired); Matthew E. Carnes, S.J.; David J. Collins, S.J.; Brian J. Conley, S.J., Treas.; Richard J. Curry, S.J.; Jonathan Dela Luna, S.J., M.D.; Francisco Javier Diaz-Diaz, S.J., M.D.; James F. Duffy, S.J.; Stephen M. Fields, S.J.; Kevin T. FitzGerald, S.J.; Gerald P. Fogarty, S.J.; Mark Fusco, S.J.; Thomas P. Gaunt, S.J.; William L. George, S.J.; Francis T. Gignac, S.J., S.T.L., D.Phil.; Timothy S. Godfrey, S.J.; Charles G. Gonzalez, S.J.; Howard J. Gray, S.J.; John C. Haughey, S.J.; Patrick A. Heelan, S.J. (Ireland); Mark Henninger, S.J.; Otto H. Hentz, S.J.; J. Leon Hooper, S.J.; Salvador R. Jordan, S.J.; Mr. Francois Kabore, S.J.; Revs. Gustaaf M. Keppens, S.J.; John P. Langan, S.J.; Robert B. Lawton, S.J.; Peter L'Estrange, S.J. (Australia); Gasper F. LoBiondo, S.J.; Daniel A. Madigan, S.J. (Australia); Ryan J. Maher, S.J.; Jean Baptiste Mazarati, S.J.; William C. McFadden, S.J.; Dennis L. McNamara, S.J.; Ralph E. Metts, S.J.; G. Ronald Murphy, S.J.; Lan Ngo, S.J.; Eugene A. Nolan, S.J., Admin.; Jon J. O'Brien, S.J. (Retired); Kevin F. O'Brien, S.J., Vice Pres., Mission & Ministry; John W. O'Malley, S.J.; Ladislas Orsy, S.J.; Thomas J. Reese, S.J.; Patrick D. Rogers, S.J.; Peter Rozic, S.J.; Solomon I. Sara, S.J.; James V. Schall, S.J.; Joseph J. Schad, S.J.; Francis Schemel, S.J.; John R. Siberski, S.J.; Christopher W. Steck, S.J.; Rodrigue Takoudjou, S.J.; James P.M. Walsh, S.J. Priests 55.

The Jesuit Community of St. Aloysius Gonzaga, 19 Eye St., N.W., 20001. Tel: 202-336-7207; Fax: 202-336-7217. Email: tclifford@gonzaga.org. Revs. Thomas F. Clifford, S.J., Rector; Joseph J. Bruce, S.J.; Vincent G. Conti, S.J.; George A. Aschenbrenner, S.J.; David R. Brooks, S.J.; Henry G. Heffernan, S.J.; Robert J. Kaslyn, S.J.; Robert J. Kroll, S.J.; Joseph M. McCloskey, S.J.; Michael T. McNulty, S.J.; Kenneth E. Meehan, S.J.; Gerald V. O'Connor, S.J.; Stephen W. Planning, S.J., Pres., High School; Michael T. Siconolfi, S.J.; Bruce A. Steggert, S.J.

La Salette Formation Community (1968) 1243 Monroe St., N.E., 20017. Tel: 202-526-8070; Fax: 202-269-0775. Email: mlsadmin@aol.com. Web: www.lasalette.org. Revs. Brian Schloth, M.S., Dir., Pre-Novitiate; Donald Jeffrey, M.S., Asst. Dir.; John A. Welch, M.S., Vocation Dir.

Missionaries of La Salette Corporation

Leonard Neale House, 1726 New Hampshire Ave., N.W., 20009. Tel: 202-387-5375; 202-387-5376; Fax: 202-387-8220. Very Rev. Thomas H. Smolich, S.J., Pres., Jesuit Conference; Revs. Robert R. Ballecer, S.J., Dir. National Vocation Promotion of Jesuit Conference; Patrick J. Conroy, S.J., Chap., U.S. House of Representatives; Charles L. Currie, S.J.; Allan F. Deck, S.J., Exec. Dir. USCCB Secretariat Cultural Diversity in Church; Steven C. Dillard, S.J.; Michael A. Evans, S.J., Natl. Dir. Jesuit Refugee Svcs. USA; Edward S. Fassett, S.J., Supr. & Sec. Secondary & Pre-Secondary Educ. & Sec. Partnership Formation Jesuit Conference; David A. Godleski, S.J., Delegate, Formation & Jesuit Life, Jesuit Conference; James E. Hug, S.J., Pres., Center of Concern; Gregory N. P. Konz, S.J., Sec. Finance, Higher Educ. & Devel. Jesuit Conference; Gregory F. Lucey, S.J., Pres., Assn. of Jesuit Colleges & Universities; Gerard L. Stockhausen, S.J., Exec. Sec. Jesuit Conference; James A. Stoeger, S.J., Pres., Jesuit Secondary Educ. Assoc. Priests 14; Total Staff 14.

St. Louis Friary, 831 Varnum St., N.E., 20017-2144. Tel: 202-529-0171; Fax: 202-832-8513. Revs. David Pivonka, T.O.R., Rel. Supr.; Alberto Bueno, T.O.R.; Ambrose K. Phillips, T.O.R.; John Shanahan, T.O.R.; Sean O. Sheridan, T.O.R.; Maurus Dolcic, T.O.R. House of Post-Novitiate Formation for Franciscan Friars, T.O.R., Province of the Most Sacred Heart of Jesus. Priests 6; Friars in Post-Novitiate Formation 9; Solemn Vows Religious Brothers 1; First Vows (Students) 4; Total in Residence 15.

Marist Center (1900) 4408 8th St., N.E., 20017-2298. Tel: 202-529-4800; Fax: 202-526-2295. Revs. Joseph Fenton, S.M., Chap. Admin., The Claremont Colleges; Peter R. Blanchard, S.M., 15219 Hwy. 1078, Unit 1, Folsom, LA 70437-3410. Tel: 985-264-7073; Raymond J. Carr, S.M., Chap. (Retired), Braddock Apts. #4, 155 Edgington Ln., Wheeling, WV 26003-1546. Tel: 304-639-1236; Fax: 504-948-9123; Richard K. Colbert, S.M. (Retired), Three Palms Pointe, Unit 801-W, 400 64th Ave., St. Petersburg Beach, FL 33706-2138. Tel: 727-367-8744; Colonel Joseph M. Fleury, S.M., Army Chap., P.O. Box 11041, Fort Irwin, CA 92310-1041. Tel: 808-227-6511; Paul Frechette, S.M., The Marist House, 518 Pleasant St., Framingham, MA 01701-2896. Tel: 508-250-7592; Fortune C. Frenoy, S.M. (Retired), The Welty Home, #214, 21 Washington Ave., Wheeling, WV 26003-6261. Tel: 304-312-0781; Edward F. Fuss, S.M. (Retired); Philip S. Gage, S.M.; Andre L. Gosselin, S.M., Chap., Sisters of the Presentation of Mary, 209 Lawrence St., Methuen, MA

01844-3849. Tel: 978-686-9884; Stanley W. Hosie, S.M. (Retired), 723 Palisades Beach Rd., Unit 211, Santa Monica, CA 90402-2479. Tel: 301-451-2479; Fax: 301-939-9562; Edwin L. Keel, S.M., 8 Fifth St., Apt. #311, Wheeling, WV 26003-2582. Tel: 304-559-7732; Mark G. Kenney, S.M., Theology Prof., Catholic Inst. of Sydney, 99 Albert Rd., Strathfield NSW 2135, Australia. Tel: 011-61-2-9752-9500; Roland A. Lajoie, S.M.; Gerard E. Pelletier, S.M., Chap., Sacred Heart Manor, 261 Benham St., Hamden, CT 06514-2801. Tel: 860-305-7868; Joseph M. Pusateri, S.M. (Retired); Mariano J. Rizzuto, S.M. (Retired), Malta Park, Apt. #313, 1101 Aline St., New Orleans, LA 70115-2456. Tel: 504-894-6113; William F. Seli, S.M. (Retired), Welty Apts., Apt. #404, 1276 National Rd., Wheeling, WV 26003-5770. Tel: 304-232-4746; Howard C. Smith, S.M.; Gerard Timmerman, S.M., 1900 Purdy Ave., Apt. #1403, Miami, FL 33139-1436. Tel: 305-531-1147; H. Joseph Wilhelm, S.M. (Retired), Welty Apartments, 1276 National Rd., Apt. 409, Wheeling, WV 26003-5770. Tel: 304-242-5177. The Marist Finance Center of the Atlanta Province of the Society of Mary, Marist Fathers and Brothers.

Missionaries of Africa (1868) 1624 21st St., N.W., 20009-1003. Tel: 202-232-5154; Fax: 202-332-8640. Email: jeangorilla@aol.com. Revs. Michel J. Lavoie, M.Afr. (Retired); John Lynch, M.Afr. (Retired); George Markwell, M.Afr., Hospital Chap.; Robert C. McGovern, M.Afr. (Retired); Thomas W. Reilly, M.Afr., Guestmaster (Retired); Jean-Claude Robitaille, M.Afr., Delegate Supr.; Diego Ramon Sarrio Cucarella, M.Afr., Studies at Georgetown Univ.; Brian Denis Starkey, M.Afr., Treas. Province of North America. Priests 8; Total Staff 8.

Missionary Oblates of Mary Immaculate (1816) Tel: 202-529-4505; Fax: 202-529-4572. Email: province@omiusa.org. Web: www.omiusa.org. *Provincial Offices of the United States Province of the Missionary Oblates of Mary Immaculate* (1999) 391 Michigan Ave., N.E., 20017-1516. Tel: 202-529-4505; Fax: 202-529-4572. Revs. William Antone, O.M.I., Prov.; Louis Studer, O.M.I., Vicar Prov.; Seamus P. Finn, O.M.I., Dir. Justice & Peace; Bryan Silva, O.M.I., Dir. Special Svcs.; Thomas Ovalle, O.M.I., Councilor-at-Large; Normand Bonneau, O.M.I., Prof.; Bro. William Johnson, O.M.I., Councilor-At-Large; Revs. Warren Brown, O.M.I., Gen. Councilor; Joseph H. Hitpas, O.M.I., Treas.; Dale Schlitt, O.M.I., Prof.; Ronald Young, O.M.I., Prof.; Gregory Gallagher, O.M.I., Admin. Councilor & Dir., Mission; Raymond John Marek, O.M.I., Asst. Treas.; James Taggart, O.M.I., Councilor; James Brobst, O.M.I., Councilor; Arthur Flores, O.M.I., Councilor; Stephen Conserva, O.M.I., Councilor; Gregory Cholewa, O.M.I., Teacher; George Knab, O.M.I., Preacher; Donald Dietz, O.M.I., Chap.

Legal Titles and Holdings: *The United States Province of the Missionary Oblates of Mary Immaculate, Inc.* (1999) Tel: 202-529-4505; Fax: 202-529-4572. *Oblate Service Corporation* (1999) Tel: 202-529-4505; Fax: 202-529-4572. *Oblate Shrines and Renewal Centers, Inc.* (1999) Tel: 202-529-4505; Fax: 202-529-4572. *Oblate Title Holding Corporation* (1999) Tel: 202-529-4505; Fax: 202-529-4572. *Oblate Continuing Care Trust* (1999) Tel: 202-529-4505; Fax: 202-529-4572. *Oblate Education and Formation Trust* (1999) Tel: 202-529-4505; Fax: 202-529-4572. *Oblate Annuity Trust* (1999) Tel: 202-529-4505; Fax: 202-529-4572. *Oblate Endowment Trust* (1999) Tel: 202-529-4505; Fax: 202-529-4572. *Oblate Patrimony Trust* (1999) Tel: 202-529-4505; Fax: 202-529-4572. *Oblate Service Trust* (1999) Tel: 202-529-4505; Fax: 202-529-4572.

Oblate Real Estate Trust (1999) Tel: 202-529-4505; Fax: 202-529-4572.

Oblate Community, 391 Michigan Ave., N.E., 20017-1516. Tel: 202-529-4505; Fax: 202-529-4572. Web: www.omiusa.org. Revs. Louis Studer, O.M.I., Vicar Prov.; Seamus P. Finn, O.M.I., Dir. of Justice & Peace; Charles Hurkes, O.M.I., Newsletter Editor; Raymond A. Lebrun, O.M.I., Spiritual Dir. Natl. Shrine of the Immaculate Conception; Joseph H. Hitpas, O.M.I., Treas.; David N. Power, O.M.I., S.T.D., Prof.; Andrew Small, O.M.I., Dir., Pontifical Mission Societies in U.S.; J. William Morell, O.M.I., Dir., Fundraising; Bryan Silva, O.M.I., Dir. Special Svcs.; Daniel LeBlanc, O.M.I., Assoc. Justice & Peace Ministry; Bevil Bramwell, O.M.I., Prof.; Joseph Phiri, O.M.I., (In Res.); William Antone, O.M.I., Provincial; Gregory Gallagher, O.M.I., Admin. Councilor & Dir., Mission; George Kirwin, O.M.I., In Residence; Thabang Nkadimeng, O.M.I., Student; Raymond John Marek, O.M.I., Asst. Treas. Priests 14.

Society of the Divine Word/Divine Word House, 832 Varnum St., N.E., 20017. Tel: 202-635-7810; Fax: 202-635-7813. Email: frbob.mertes@gmail.com. Revs. John Szukalski, S.V.D.; Michio Akao, S.V.D. (Japan); Rejimon Varghese, S.V.D. (India); Marianus Pale Hera, S.V.D. (Indonesia); Georges Kintiba, S.V.D.; Thomas Krosnicki, S.V.D.; Robert Mertes, S.V.D., Rector; Binh Thanh Nguyen, S.V.D.; Khoa Quang Nguyen, S.V.D.; Attilio Rossi, S.V.D., (Italy). Presently, 10 S.V.D. Priests. Residents 10.

Woodstock Jesuit Community, 1419 35 St., N.W., 20007. Tel: 202-337-7750; Fax: 202-687-5835. Email: woodstock@georgetown.edu. Revs. Gasper F. LoBiondo, S.J.; John C. Haughey, S.J.; J. Leon Hooper, S.J.; Thomas J. Reese, S.J.; George Karuvelil, S.J. (India); Daniel A. Madigan, S.J. (Australia). Priests 6.

ADELPHI, MD. *Father Judge Missionary Cenacle*, 1733 Metzerott Rd., MD 20783. Tel: 301-439-3171; Fax: 301-434-0848. Email: fjcenacle@aol.com. Rev. Edwin Dill, S.T., M.A., Dir.; Bro. William Coombs, S.T., Asst. Dir.; Revs. Francis Conkle, S.T.; Anselm Deehr, S.T.; Stephen T. Ernst, S.T.; Gabriel Hannan, S.T.; Maurice Haiss, S.T.; Daniel McLaughlin, S.T.; John McSpiritt, S.T.; Eugene Mueller, S.T.; Louis Murphy, S.T.; Kevin Nugent, S.T.; Walter O'Donnell, S.T.; Edward Sittinger, S.T.; Bros. Jordan Baxter, S.T.; Jonathan Daneski, S.T.; Boris Farrah, S.T.; Gregory Martin, S.T.; Richard McCann, S.T.; Hilary Mettes, S.T.; Alexis Norton, S.T.; Finbarr Ray, S.T. Senior Ministry Residence.

BELTSVILLE, MD. *Ammendale Normal Institute of Prince George's County-La Salle Hall* (1880) 6001 Ammendale Rd., MD 20705. Tel: 301-210-7443; Fax: 301-210-7466. Email: ammendaleni@comcast.net. Bro. John P. McErlean, F.S.C., Dir. Brothers of the Christian Schools., Residence for Retired and Convalescent Brothers. Brothers 30.

BETHESDA. *Priestly Fraternity of the Missionaries of St. Charles Borromeo, Inc.*, 7600 Carter Ct., MD 20817. Tel: 301-983-4624. Revs. Antonio Lopez, F.S.C.B.; Roberto Amoruso, F.S.C.B.; Pietro Rossotti, F.S.C.B.; Franco Soma, F.S.C.B.; Jose Maria Cortes, F.S.C.B.; Paolo Prosperi, F.S.C.B.; Patricio Antonio Hacin, F.S.C.B.

BROOKEVILLE, MD. *Marian Monastery-Brookeville* Marian Residence & Marian Assisted Living, 19101 Georgia Ave., Box 220, MD 20833. Tel: 301-774-4478; 301-774-2242; Fax: 301-570-8645. Web: www.marian.org. Rev. Joseph Sielski, M.I.C. Priests 2.

POTOMAC, MD. *Legionaries of Christ*, 10211 Norton Rd., MD 20854. Tel: 301-299-0806; Fax: 301-299-0809. Email: washington@legionaries.org. Revs. Joseph Brickner, L.C., Supr.; Anthony Sortino, L.C., Vice-Rector; John Hopkins, L.C., Retreat Dir.; Michael Sliney, L.C., Youth Dir.; Charles Sikorsky, L.C., Pres., IPS; Daniel Wilson, L.C., Chap.; Jaime Paniagua, L.C., Student; Donal O'Keeffe, L.C., Spiritual Dir.; Bros. James Wilson, L.C., Youth Asst.; Joseph A'Hearn, L.C., Youth Asst.; Keegan McDermott, L.C., Youth Asst.

RIVERDALE, MD. *Holy Spirit Missionary Cenacle* (1996) 5809 Riverdale Rd., MD 20737. Tel: 301-277-7442; Fax: 301-277-7442 (Call first). Bro. Howard F. Piller, S.T., Local Supr. In Res. Revs. Sidney H. Griffith, S.T.D., Ph.D., Semantics & Early Christian Studies. Tel: 301-927-4919 Faculty, Catholic University of America; John S. Edmunds, S.T., Supr. General; Domingo Rodriguez, S.T., Vicar Gen.; Charles E. Piatt III, S.T.; Bros. Stephen Vesely, S.T., Sec. General; Loughlan Sofield, S.T.

SILVER SPRING, MD. *Gemelli House* Franciscan Friars-Holy Name Province, 10400 Lorain Ave., MD 20901. Tel: 301-681-9478; Fax: 301-681-7170. Revs. Vincent de Paul Cushing, O.F.M., Guardian; Paul Lininger, O.F.M.Conv., Exec. Dir. Conference of Major Superiors of Men; John Burkhard, O.F.M.Conv., Pres., Washington Theological Union; Russel T. Murray, O.F.M., Washington Theological Union Faculty; James G. Sabak, O.F.M. Priests 5.

Missionary Servants of the Most Holy Trinity, Generalate, 9001 New Hampshire Ave., Ste. 300, MD 20903-3626. Tel: 301-434-0092; Fax: 301-434-0255. Email: generalate@trinitymissions.org. Web: www.mssst.org. Rev. John S. Edmunds, S.T., Gen. Custodian; Bro. Steven Vesely, S.T., Sec. Gen.

TAKOMA PARK, MD. *Society of African Missions (S.M.A.) House of Studies*, 209 Lincoln Ave., MD 20912-5738. Tel: 301-270-2008; Fax: 301-270-0132. Email: smausa-o@smafathers.org. Web: www.smafathers.org. Rev. Austin Charles Ochu, S.M.A., Local Supr. *Lay Missionary Program*, 256 N. Manor Cir., MD 20912-4551. Tel: 301-270-2009 (Home); 301-891-2037; Fax: 301-270-6370. Email: smausa-v@smafathers.org. Rev. Daniel Lynch, S.M.A.; Theresa Hicks, Dir.; Dr. Steve Price; Rev. Frank Wright, S.M.A.

[P] MINISTRY TO PRIESTS

KENSINGTON, MD. *St. John Vianney House*, 4214 Saul Rd., MD 20895. Tel: 301-942-1191; Fax: 301-942-1191.

[Q] CONVENTS AND RESIDENCES FOR SISTERS

WASHINGTON. *Carmelite Sisters of Charity, U.S. Delegation Regional House*, 1222 Monroe St., N.E., 20017. Tel: 202-832-2114. Email: maureenfoltz@hotmail.com. Sisters Maureen Foltz, C.C.V., Regl. Supr.; Rosa M. Alvarez, C.C.V., First Councilor; Carmen Soto, C.C.V., Second Councilor; Francisca Mota, C.C.V., Sec.; Maria Pilar Chamorro, C.C.V., Treas.

Congregation of The Religious of Jesus and Mary, Provincialate (1818) 125 Michigan Ave. N.E., 4th Floor, 20017. Tel: 202-884-9795; Fax: 202-884-9794. Sr. Eileen C. Reid, R.J.M., Prov. Administrative Team 3; Total Staff 1.

Other Residences: *Religious of Jesus and Mary* (1818) 6709 41st Ave., University Park, MD 20782. Tel: 301-779-0662; Fax: 301-779-3843. Sisters 2. *Religious of Jesus and Mary*, 4602 Clemson Rd., College Park, MD 20740. Tel: 301-699-3931; Fax: 301-927-4157. Sisters 3. *Religious of Jesus and Mary*, 3521 13th St., N.W., 20010. Tel: 202-265-8812; Fax: 202-265-1842. Sisters 3.

Franciscan Sisters of Atonement, 4000 Harewood Rd., N.E., 20017. Tel: 202-529-1111. Sr. Mary Harper, S.A., Dir. Sisters 7; Total Staff 9.

Georgetown Visitation Monastery (1799) 1500 35th St., N.W., 20007. Tel: 202-337-3350, Ext. 2283; Fax: 202-558-7976. Email: berchmans@visi.org. Web: www.georgetownvisitation.org. Sr. Mary Berchmans Hannan, Supr. Professed Sisters 21.

Institute of Our Lady of Mount Carmel (1854) *Scrilli Day Care Center*, 4415 8th St., N.E., 20017. Tel: 202-526-5106; Fax: 202-526-7101. Total Assisted 45; Total Staff 7.

Missionaries of Charity, 3310 Wheeler Rd., S.E., 20032. Tel: 202-562-6890. Sr. Mary Clovis, M.C., Supr. Sisters 7; Total Assisted 16,181.

Missionaries of Charity, Gift of Peace Convent (1986) 2800 Otis St., N.E., 20018. Tel: 202-269-3313. Sr. M. Lisseria, M.C., Supr. Total Assisted 75; Total in Residence 38.

Oblates Sisters of the Most Holy Eucharist, 2907 Ellicott Ter., N.W., 20008. Tel: 202-244-7714. Email: oblatesdc@hotmail.com. Sr. Margarita Jaime, O.S.S.E., Supr. Sisters 7.

Poor Clares of Perpetual Adoration (1954) 3900 13th St., N.E., 20017-2699. Tel: 202-526-6808; Fax: 202-526-0678. Email: ourprayer4u@poorclareswdc.org. Web: www.poorclareswdc.org. Cloistered Monastery of Perpetual Adoration. Cloistered Nuns 5.

Religious of the Sacred Heart Oakview Community., 1215 Perry St., N.E., 20017. Tel: 202-832-0071. Sr. Fleisa Garcia, Contact Person.

Rosary House of Studies-Dominican Sisters of The Presentation, 1201 Monroe St., N.E., 20017. Tel: 202-529-1768; Fax: 202-529-1768. Email: rosaryhouseop@yahoo.com. Sisters 3.

Sisters of the Holy Child Jesus, 1033 Newton St., N.E., 20017. Tel: 202-526-6832. Web: www.shcj.org. Novitiate Community. Sisters 3.

Other Convents:

St. Anthony's School Sisters 1.

Sisters of St. Francis of the Neumann Communities Emmaus Convent, *B1. Marianne Cope Ste.*, 4008 8th St., N.E. #2, 20017. Tel: 202-248-3397. Email: smcosf@aol.com. Web: www.sosf.org. Sisters Margaret Christi Karwowski, O.S.F., Contact Person & Treas.; Mary Farrell, O.S.F., Historian. Sisters 1.

Society of the Sacred Heart, 1235 Otis St., N.E., 20017. Tel: 202-832-1598; Fax: 202-526-3506. Email: kcollins@rscj.org. Web: www.rscj.org. Sr. Catherine Collins, R.S.C.J., Dir. Center for Educational Design & Communication. Tel: 202-635-7987. Sisters 3.

U.S. Delegation House of the Carmelites of Charity - Vedruna, 1222 Monroe St., N.E., 20017. Tel: 301-277-2963; 202-832-2114.

ANACOSTIA, WASHINGTON. *Missionaries of Charity (Contemplatives)*, 1244 V St., S.E., 20020-7016. Tel: 202-889-6100. Sr. M. Concepcion Membreno, M.C., Supr.

CLINTON, MD. *Religious Sisters of Mercy of Alma, MI* (1973) St. Andrew Home of Mercy, 6100 Wolverton Lane, MD 20735. Tel: 301-297-5617; Fax: 301-297-5618. Email: rsmofalma@comcast.com. Web: www.rsmofalma.com. Sr. Gabrielle Mary Braccio, R.S.M., Local Supr. & Contact Person. Sisters 10.

FORT WASHINGTON, MD. *The Missionary Catechists of St. Therese of the Infant Jesus, Inc.*, 2400 Brinkley Rd., MD 20744. Tel: 301-839-7751; Fax: 301-839-7751. Email: mcstusa@yahoo.com. Sr. Helen B. Sumander, M.C.S.T., Pres. Sisters 4.

KENSINGTON, MD. *Congregation of the Sisters of the Holy Cross*, St. Angela Hall, 4910 Strathmore Ave., MD 20895. Tel: 301-946-7750; Fax: 301-946-7751.
Sisters of the Holy Cross, Inc., Independent Living House for the Sisters of the Holy Cross. Sisters 30.

LA PLATA, MD. *Carmel of Port Tobacco* (1790) 5678 Mt. Carmel Rd., MD 20646-3625. Tel: 301-934-1654; Fax: 301-934-0958. Web: www.carmelofporttobacco.com. Professed 11.

LAUREL, MD. *Pallotti Convent*, 404 Eighth St., MD 20707. Tel: 301-725-1717. Sr. M. Karen Lester, S.A.C., Sponsorship Dir. Professed Sisters 4; Total Staff 1.

NORTH BEACH, MD. *Sisters of St. Dominic of St. Cecilia of Nashville, TN, St. Anthony Convent*, 4104 First St., P.O. Box 600, MD 20714. Tel: 410-286-3393; Fax: 410-286-3275. Sr. Mary Juliana Cox, O.P., Convent Supr. Sisters 4.

RIVERDALE, MD. *Carmelite Sister of Christ - Vedruna*, 5410 56th Pl., #101, MD 20737. Tel: 301-277-2963.

SILVER SPRING, MD. *Sisters of Charity of St. Charles Borromeo, St. Elizabeth Convent*, 11320 Classical Ln., MD 20901. Tel: 301-681-9665; Fax: 301-681-0693.
Sisters of Mercy of the Americas - Institute Administrative Offices (1831) 8380 Colesville Rd., Ste. 300, MD 20910. Tel: 301-587-0423; Fax: 301-587-0533. Web: www.sistersofmercy.org. Legal Holdings: Mercy Action, Inc.; Mercy Volunteer Corps, Inc.; Sisters of Mercy of the Americas, Inc. Administrative Team 5; Total in Congregation 3,676.
Institute Leadership Team: Sisters Patricia McDermott, R.S.M., Pres.; Eileen Campbell, R.S.M., Vice Pres.; Anne Curtis, R.S.M., Councilor; Mary Patricia Garvin, R.S.M., Councilor; Deborah Troillett, R.S.M.
Sisters of the Good Shepherd, 504 Hexton Hill Rd., MD 20904-3300. Tel: 301-384-1169; Fax: 301-384-8889. Email: sg1504@aol.com. Web: www.goodshepherdsistersna.org. Sisters 4.
Sisters of the Holy Names (S.N.J.M.), 9603 Flower Ave., MD 20901. Tel: 301-587-1717. Email: kksnjml@gmail.com. Web: www.snjmusontario.org. Sisters 3.
Other Convents: *Sisters of the Holy Names (S.N.J.M.)*, 519 Varnum St., N.W., 20011. Tel: 202-829-8671. Sisters 3.
Sisters of the Holy Names (S.N.J.M.), 9212 Glenville Rd., MD 20901. Tel: 301-445-0309. Sisters 2.
Sisters of the Holy Names (S.N.J.M.), Church of the Annunciation, 3200 39th St. N.W., 20016. Sisters 2.

[R] RETREAT HOUSES

WASHINGTON. *Washington Retreat House, Inc.* (1930) 4000 Harewood Rd., N.E., 20017. Tel: 202-529-1111; Fax: 202-259-2102. Email: washretreat@juno.com. Sr. Mary Harper, S.A., Dir. Franciscan Sisters of the Atonement. Sisters 7; Total in Residence 7; Total Staff 10.

FAULKNER, MD. *Loyola Retreat House*, P.O. Box 9, MD 20632. Tel: 301-392-0801; 301-870-3515; Fax: 301-392-0808. Email: director@loyolaretreat.org. Web: www.loyolaretreat.org. Rev. Frank T. Kaminski, S.J., Assoc. Dir. Total in Residence 4; Total Staff 5.
Staff: Revs. John Thomas Kelly, S.J.; Richard C. Schmidt, S.J.; Sr. Patricia McDermott, I.H.M., Dir.; Rev. Gerald J. Fitzpatrick, S.J.

UPPER MARLBORO, MD. *Our Lady of Mattaponi Youth Retreat and Conference Center* (1987) 11000 Mattaponi Rd., MD 20772. Tel: 301-952-9074; Fax: 301-952-0609. Email: mattaponi@adw.org. Total Staff 2.

[S] NATIONAL SHRINE

WASHINGTON. *Basilica of the National Shrine of the Immaculate Conception* 400 Michigan Ave., N.E., 20017-1566. Tel: 202-526-8300; Fax: 202-526-8313. Email: info@nationalshrine.com. Web: www.nationalshrine.com. Rev. Msgr. Walter R. Rossi (SCR), Rector; Revs. Raymond A. Lebrun, O.M.I., Spiritual Dir.; Michael D. Weston (ARL), Dir. Liturgy; Vito A. Buonanno (BRK), Dir. Pilgrimages.

[T] HOUSES OF PRAYER

WASHINGTON. *Catholic Information Center*, 1501 K St., N.W., Ste. 175, 20005-1401. Tel: 202-783-2062; Fax: 202-783-6667. Email: frarnep@gmail.com. Web: www.cicdc.org. Rev. Arne A. Panula, S.T.D., Dir. Total Staff 7.
Madonna House, 220 C St., N.E., 20002. Tel: 202-547-0177; Fax: 202-547-8117. Web: www.madonnahouse.org. Cynthia Donnelly, Dir. Total in Residence 3; Total Staff 3.

[U] OFFICES OF CAMPUS MINISTRY

WASHINGTON. *Archdiocesan Campus Ministry*
American University Catholic Community Kay Spiritual Life Center, 4400 Massachusetts Ave., N.W., 20016-8010. Tel: 202-885-3327; Fax: 202-885-3317. Email: priest@american.edu. Rev. Augustine Judd, O.P., Chap.; Dr. Karin Thornton, Assoc. Campus Min. Tel: 202-885-3326.
Gallaudet University Catholic Community 800 Florida Ave., N.E., 20002. Tel: 202-651-5102. Rev. Gerard A. Trancone, Chap.
7202 Buchanan St., Landover Hills, MD 20784. Tel: 301-459-7467; 301-459-7464; Fax: 301-459-8186.
George Washington Univ. Newman Center 2210 F St., N.W., 20037. Tel: 202-676-6855; Fax: 202-676-6859. Very Rev. James J. Greenfield, O.S.F.S., Chap.
Howard Univ. Newman Center 818 Newman Center, 20059. Tel: 202-238-2687; Fax: 202-806-4641. Rev. John Raphael, S.S.J., Chap.
University of Maryland Catholic Student Center 4141 Guilford Dr., College Park, MD 20740. Tel: 301-864-6223; 301-864-6224; Fax: 301-864-8411. Rev. William D. Byrne, Chap.; Sr. Rita Ricker, R.J.M., Assoc.
St. Mary's College Campus Ministry P.O. Box 67, St. Mary's City, MD 20686. Tel: 301-862-4600. Rev. Francis W. Krastel.

[V] PERSONAL PRELATURES

WASHINGTON. *Prelature of the Holy Cross and Opus Dei*, 2301 Wyoming Ave., N.W., 20008. Tel: 202-234-1567; Fax: 202-238-0621. Web: www.opusdei.org. Revs. Arne A. Panula, S.T.D.; John Debicki; William G. Shaughnessy.
Other Centers:
Tenley Study Center, 4300 Garrison St., N.W., 20016. Tel: 202-362-2419; Fax: 202-362-0318. Revs. Gregory Coyne; Gerald S. Kolf.

[W] SECULAR INSTITUTES

WASHINGTON. *Caritas Christi* (1937) 5410 Connecticut Ave., N.W. #506, 20015-2821. Tel: 202-363-2839. Therese Druart, Gen. Councilor. A Secular Institute of Pontifical Right.
Community of Christ, 1003 Kearney St., N.E., 20017. Tel: 202-832-9710; 202-797-8806; Fax: 202-265-3849. Email: frjohn@some.org. Rev. John E. Adams, Moderator. A Private Association Community of Archdiocesan Right for Priests, Lay Men and Lay Women. The Community of Christ Purpose is Simple Lifestyle, Poverty Ministry, Spiritual Growth and Prayer of Community Members.

WEST BETHESDA, MD. *Missionaries of the Kingship of Christ*, 3025 4th St., N.E. #10, 20017. Tel: 202-525-1267; Fax: 508-386-1417. Email: angela218@aol.com. Web: www.simkc.org. Rev. Gene Pistacchio, O.F.M. Tel: 617-542-6440.
A Franciscan Secular Institute of Pontifical Right., Tel: 301-990-8630; Fax: 508-386-1417. Rev. Gene Pistacchio, O.F.M., Ecclesiastical Asst. Tel: 617-542-6440.

[X] MISCELLANEOUS

WASHINGTON. **Africa Faith & Justice Network*, 125 Michigan Ave. N.E., 20017. Tel: 202-884-9780; Fax: 202-884-9774. Email: afjn@afjn.org. Web: www.afjn.org. Rev. Aniedi Okure, O.P., Exec. Dir. Priests 1; Total Staff 3.
"The Americas" (1944) Catholic University of America, Gibbons Hall, Room B 17, 20064. Tel: 202-319-5890; Fax: 202-319-5569. Email: americas@cua.edu. Web: www.theamericasjournal.org.
St. Anselm's Abbey School Donor Trust, 4501 S. Dakota Ave., N.E., 20017. Tel: 202-281-1645; Fax: 202-281-1648.
Archbishop Carroll High School, 4300 Harewood Rd., N.E., 20017. Tel: 202-529-0900; Fax: 202-529-5989. Email: dstofa@archbishopcarroll.org. Web: www.archbishopcarroll.org. Dr. David S. Stofa, Ph.D., Prin.; Jessica Pryde, Librarian; Crystal Rucker, Dir. Devel. Tel: 202-529-0900, Ext. 160. Records Center for the Archdiocese of Washington. Priests 2; Deacons 1; Sisters 1; Lay Teachers 41; Students 458.
Alumni Office Tel: 202-529-0900, Ext. 160; Fax: 202-529-5989.
Archdiocese of Cotabato, 391 Michigan Ave., N.E., 20017. Tel: 202-529-4505; Fax: 202-529-4572. Most Rev. Orlando Quevedo, O.M.I., D.D.; Rev. Joseph H. Hitpas, O.M.I.
Association of Catholic Colleges & Universities (1899) One Dupont Cir., Ste. 650, 20036. Tel: 202-457-0650; Fax: 202-728-0977. Email: kladdbush@accunet.org. Web: www.accunet.org. Michael Galligan-Stierle, Pres. & CEO. Total Staff 6.
Association of Jesuit Colleges and Universities, One Dupont Cir., N.W., Ste. 405, 20036. Tel: 202-862-9893; Fax: 202-862-8523. Email: office@ajcunet.edu. Web: www.ajcunet.edu. Rev. Gregory F. Lucey, S.J., Pres. Established in 1970, The Association of Jesuit Colleges and Universities (AJCU) is a national voluntary organization whose mission is to serve its member institutions, the 28 Jesuit colleges and universities in the United States, and its associate members. Though each institution is separately chartered and is legally autonomous under its own board of trustees, the institutions are bonded together by a common heritage, vision and purpose. They engage in a number of collaborative projects in the United States and around the world.
Black Leadership and Christ's Kingdom Society, P.O. Box 410, Waldorf, MD 20604-0410. Tel: 301-888-2566; Fax: 301-888-2566. Rev. Robert S. Pittman, S.S.S., Pres. Total Staff 4.
CARA, Center for Applied Research in the Apostolate (1964) 2300 Wisconsin Ave., N.W., Ste. 400, 20007. Tel: 202-687-8080; Fax: 202-687-8083. Email: cara@georgetown.edu. Web: cara.georgetown.edu. Rev. Stephen J. Fichter, Interim Exec. Dir.
Carmelite Institute (1993) 1600 Webster St., N.E., 20017. Tel: 800-334-9922; Fax: 202-726-1716. Email: mail@carmeliteinstitute.org. Web: www.carmeliteinstitute.org. Dr. Keith Egan, T.O.C., Ph.D., Pres. Tel: 202-832-6622; Rev. Frederick J. Tillotson, O.Carm., Exec. Dir. (Acting).
Carroll Manor Nursing & Rehabilitation Center, 1150 Varnum St., N.E., 20017-2180. Tel: 202-269-7100; Fax: 202-269-7816. Rev. Msgr. Leonard F. Hurley, Chap.
Catholic Biblical Association (1936) *Catholic University of America*, 433 Caldwell Hall, 20064. Tel: 202-319-5519; Fax: 202-319-4799. Email: cua-cathbib@cua.edu. Web: cba.cua.edu. Rev. Joseph Jensen, O.S.B., S.S.L., S.T.D., Exec. Sec.
Catholic Daughters of the Americas Court #2344 - Our Lady of the Americas, 1510 Crittenden St., SW, 20011. Tel: 202-829-9034. Joan Tillery, Regent.
Catholic Historical Society of Washington, 619 10th St., N.W., 20001. Revs. William Richardson, S.F.O., Pres.; Paul F. Liston, Bd. Member (Retired).
Center of Concern (1971) 1225 Otis St., N.E., 20017-2516. Tel: 202-635-2757; Fax: 202-832-9494. Email: coc@coc.org. Web: www.coc.org. Rev. James E. Hug, S.J., Pres.
Centro Maria (1996) 650 Jackson St., N.E., 20017-1424. Tel: 202-635-1697; Fax: 202-526-1708. Email: centromaria@verizon.net. Web: www.religiosasmariainmaculada.org. Sr. Clara Echeverria, R.M.I., Local Supr. Residence for young students and working women (18-30). Religious 7; Bed Capacity 40; Total Assisted Annually 160.
Christ Child Society of Washington, DC , Inc. (1887) 5101 Wisconsin Ave., N.W., #304, 20016. Tel: 202-966-9250; Fax: 202-966-2880. Email: info@christchilddc.org. Web: www.charityadvantage.com/christchilddc. Ms. Kathleen Curtin, Exec. Dir. A nonprofit, volunteer organization of approximately 600 persons serving the emotional and material needs of children, through layette distribution, school counseling, camp scholarships, uniform assistance, and community outreach. Total Assisted 16,000; Total Staff 21.
Christ Our Hope Foundation, Inc., P.O. Box 29260, 20017.
Christian Brothers Conference, Hecker Center, 3025 Fourth St., N.E., #300, 20017-1102. Tel: 202-529-0047; Fax: 202-529-0775. Web: www.lasallian.info. Bros. Robert Schieler, F.S.C., Gen. Councilor; Gerard J. Frendreis, F.S.C., C.F.O.
Christian Brothers Major Superiors, Inc. Institutions owned and/or sponsored: Bethlehem University of the Holy Land; Sangre de Cristo Center, Santa Fe, NM; Christian Brothers Services, Romeoville, IL., Organizations and programs served by this office: Regional Conference of Christian Brothers; Lasallian Volunteers; Huether Lasallian Conference; Buttimer Institute of Lasallian Studies; Lasallian Leadership Institute; Lasallian Social Justice Institute and Regional Council of Lasallian Association for Mission.
Christian Life Communities, Washington Area Promoters: 5040 Nebraska Ave., N.W., 20008-2938. Tel: 202-363-4593. Ms. Margaret Fox.
201 E. Wayne Ave., Silver Spring, MD 20901-3808. Tel: 301-495-2969; Fax: 301-495-7318. Fred Leone; Betty Leone.
Communio: International Catholic Review, The Catholic University of America, McGivney Hall, 620 Michigan Ave., N.E., 20064. Tel: 202-526-0251; Fax: 202-526-1934. Email: communio@aol.com. Web: www.communio-icr.com.
Council for Research in Values and Philosophy (1983) The Catholic University of America, 20064. Tel: 202-319-6089; Fax: 202-319-6089. Email:

mclean@cua.edu. Web: www.crvp.org. Rev. George F. McLean, O.M.I., Pres.

**Culture of Life Foundation*, 1413 K St., N.W., Ste. 1000, 20005. Tel: 202-289-2500; Fax: 202-289-2502. Email: info@culture-of-life.org. Web: www.culture-of-life.org.

Diocesan Laborer Priests, 3706 15th St., N.E., 20017. Tel: 202-832-4217; Fax: 202-526-5692.

District of Columbia Detention Facility, Office of Chaplain, 1357 E. Capitol St. S.E., 20003. Tel: 202-547-1715 (Office); Fax: 202-544-1385. Email: mbryantabc@msn.com. Rev. F. Michael Bryant, Chap. Total in Residence 2,500; Total Staff 9.

Don Bosco Cristo Rey Work-Study of the Archdiocese of Washington, Mailing Address: P.O. Box 56481, 20040-6481. Tel: 301-891-4750; Fax: 301-270-1459. Email: shafrans@dbcr.org. Web: www.donboscocristorey.org. 1010 Larch Ave., Takoma Park, MD 20912. Rev. Steve Shafran, S.D.B., Pres.; Ms. Alicia Bondanella, Exec. Dir.

**Education for Parish Service Program* (1978) 125 Michigan Ave., N.E., 20017-1094. Tel: 202-884-9020; Fax: 202-483-0253. Email: WaltzB@TrinityDC.edu. Web: eps.trinitydc.edu. Margaret McCarty, D.Min., Pres. Education for Parish Service Program.

Engaged Encounter, 6514 7th Pl., N.W., 20012. Tel: 202-320-3254. Email: registration@dcengagedencounter.org. Adam Hughes, Registration Coord.; Mary Kate Hughes, Registration Coord.

Equestrian Order of the Holy Sepulchre of Jerusalem - Middle Atlantic Lieutenancy U.S.A., Mailing Address: P.O. Box 5105, Arlington, VA 22205. Tel: 571-594-7605. *Franciscan Monastery of the Holy Land*, 1400 Quincy St., N.E., 20017. Tel: 202-526-4217; Fax: 202-526-4218. H.E. Ronald G. Precup, Lieutenant.

Ethiopian and Eritrean Catholic Mission, USA, 415 Michigan Ave., N.E., P.O. Box 29616, 20017. Tel: 202-529-8420; Fax: 202-529-8523. Web: www.catholic-forum.com/churches/kidanemehret. Rev. Tesfay Woldemarian Fesuh, Dir.

Fellowship of Catholic Scholars, John Paul II Institute, 620 Michigan Ave., N.E., 20064. Tel: 718-817-3291; Fax: 718-817-3300. Email: koterski@fordham.edu. Web: www.catholicscholars.org. Rev. Joseph W. Koterski, S.J., Pres.

**Foundation for the Nativity & Miguel Schools*, 900 Varnum St., N.E., 20017. Tel: 202-832-3667; Fax: 202-832-8098. Email: jjordan@nativitymiguel.org. Web: www.nativitymiguelschools.org. Rev. Msgr. John W. Jordan, Exec. Dir.

The Franciscan Federation, Third Order Regular of the Sisters and Brothers of the United States, P.O. Box 29080, 20017. Tel: 202-529-2334; Fax: 202-529-7016. Email: franfed@aol.com. Web: www.franfed.org.

**Friends of the Pontifical Irish College, Rome, Inc.* (2000) *c/o Roha & Flaherty*, 1725 I St., N.W., Ste. 300, 20006. Tel: 202-833-0033. Email: tom@princebush.com. Thomas Prince, Pres.

**Imago Dei, Inc.*, 4393 Embassy Park Dr., NW, 20016. Tel: 202-962-0040.

Institute of Carmelite Studies and ICS Publications (1973) 2131 Lincoln Rd., N.E., 20002-1199. Tel: 800-832-8489; Fax: 202-832-8967. Email: brpaquette@aol.com. Web: www.icspublications.org. Rev. Kieran Kavanaugh, O.C.D., Publisher & Editorial Asst.; Bro. Bryan Paquette, O.C.D., Business Mgr. & Promotion Dir.

Jesuit Conference, Inc., 1016 16th St. N.W., Ste. 400, 20036. Tel: 202-462-0400; Fax: 202-328-9212. Email: usjc@jesuit.org. Web: www.jesuit.org. Very Rev. Thomas H. Smolich, S.J., Pres.; Rev. Gerard L. Stockhausen, S.J., Exec. Sec.

Jesuit Missions, Inc., 1016 16th St., N.W., Ste. 400, 20036. Tel: 202-462-0400; Fax: 202-328-9212. Email: outreach@jesuit.org. Rev. Thomas P. Greene, S.J., Exec. Dir.

Jesuit Refugee Service (1984) 1016 16th St. N.W., Ste. 500, 20036. Tel: 202-462-0400; Fax: 202-328-9212. Email: mevans@jesuit.org. Web: www.jrsusa.org. Rev. Michael A. Evans, S.J., Natl. Dir.

Jesuit Secondary Education Association, 1016 16th St. N.W., 20036. Tel: 202-667-3888; Fax: 202-387-6305. Email: jsea@jsea.org. Web: www.jsea.org. Rev. James A. Stoeger, S.J., Pres.; Bernard L. Bouillette, Ph.D., Vice Pres.; Bill Hobbs, Vice Pres.; Mari Thomas, Vice Pres.; Kathreja A. Sarfati, Communications Mgr. Total Staff 6.

Jesuit Social and International Ministries-National Office, 1016 16th St. N.W., Ste. 400, 20036. Tel: 202-462-0400; Fax: 202-328-9212. Email: outreach@jesuit.org. Web: www.jesuit.org. Rev. Thomas P. Greene, S.J., Sec.

Jesuit Volunteers, 1016 16th St., N.W., Ste. 400, 20036. Rev. Gerard L. Stockhausen, S.J., Contact Person.

Jesuit Volunteers International (1984) 1016 16th St. N.W., Ste. 400, 20036. Tel: 202-462-5200; Fax: 202-328-9212. Email: jvi@JesuitVolunteers.org. Web: www.JesuitVolunteers.org. Meghan Romey, Program Dir. Lay Volunteers 45; Foreign Missions 7; Total Staff 5.

Jesuit Volunteers, 1016 16th St., 20036.

The John Carroll Society, P.O. Box 454, Glen Echo, MD 20812. Tel: 202-537-6110. Email: jcs@johncarrollsociety.org. Web: www.johncarrollsociety.org. Gregory J. Granito, J.D., Pres.; Rev. Msgr. Peter J. Vaghi, J.D., V.F.

**John Paul II Fellowship*, P.O. Box 29482, 20017. Tel: 202-384-8182.

St. Joseph Trust, 28 15the St., S.E., 20003.

Knights of St. Jerome Bobby Gant, Pres.

McKenna House, 1501 Park Rd., N.W., 20010. Tel: 202-332-7333. Hagos Weldegiorgis, Prog. Mgr.

Morley Publishing Group, Inc., 2100 M St. N.W., #170-339, 20037. Tel: 202-861-7790; Fax: 202-403-3362. Email: mail@insidecatholic.com. Web: www.insidecatholic.com.

Mount Carmel House, 471 G Pl., N.W., 20001. Tel: 202-289-6315; Fax: 202-289-1710. Mary Bridget Klinkenbergh, Senior Program Mgr. Transitional Housing for Women with 20 beds.

National Black Sisters' Conference, 1200 Varnum St., N.E., 20017-2740. Tel: 202-529-9250; Fax: 202-529-9370. Email: nbsc68@verizon.net. Web: www.nbsc68.com. Sr. Roberta Fulton, S.S.M.N., Pres. Total Staff 3.

National Catholic Conference for Interracial Justice, 1200 Varnum St., N.E., 20017-2796. Tel: 202-529-6480; Fax: 202-526-1262. Deacon Joseph M. Conrad Jr., Exec. Dir.

National Institute for the Family (1979) 1200 Varnum St., N.E., 20017-2796. Tel: 202-302-1339; 202-557-4468 (alternate); Fax: 202-526-7811. Email: nationalinstituteforthefamily@gmail.com. Rev. Donald B. Conroy, S.T.L., Ph.D. (GBG), Pres.; Dr. Carolyn Gutowski, M.A.T., Ph.D., Assoc. Dir. Special Progs. Research Program: Parish Renewal, Intergenerational Ministry and Lay Leadership Formation in cooperation with the Christian Family Movement.

Oblate Missionary Society, Inc., 391 Michigan Ave., N.E., 20017.

Paulist Evangelization Ministries (1977) 3031 Fourth St., N.E., 20017-1102. Tel: 202-832-5022; Fax: 202-269-0209. Email: admin@pemdc.org. Web: www.pemdc.org. Revs. Francis P. DeSiano, C.S.P., D.Min., Pres.; Kenneth G. Boyack, C.S.P., D.Min., Vice Pres.; Mr. Denny Marcotte, Dir. Production, Fulfillment & Facilities; Rev. Anthony F. Krisak, Dir. Training & Online Resources.

Pax Romana / Catholic Movement for Intellectual and Cultural Affairs-USA (1927) 1025 Connecticut Ave., NW, Ste. 1000, 20036. Tel: 202-657-4613. Email: pax-romana-cmica-usa@comcast.net. Web: www.paxromanausa.org. Edward "Joe" Holland, Ph.D., Pres.

**Prison Outreach Ministry* (1982) P.O. Box 51583, 20091. Tel: 202-347-3218; Fax: 202-347-9217. Email: pomsvb@yahoo.com. Rev. F. Michael Bryant, Chap.

RJM Endowment and Continuing Care Trust, 125 Michigan Ave., NE, 4th Fl., 20017. Tel: 202-884-9795; Fax: 202-884-9794.

RJM Ministry Corporation, 125 Michigan Ave., NE, 4th Flr., 20017. Tel: 202-884-9795; Fax: 202-884-9794.

RJM Real Estate Trust, 125 Michigan Ave, NE, 4th Flr., 20017. Tel: 202-884-9795; Fax: 202-884-9794.

Rosary Shrine of St. Jude , Dominican Fathers and Brothers., St. Dominic's Church, 501 Sixth St., S.W., 20024. Tel: 202-554-7863; Fax: 202-554-3492. Very Rev. Dominic Izzo, O.P., S.T.L., Dir.

Roundtable Association of Catholic Social Action Directors, 1225 Otis St., N.E., 20017.

S.N.D.B.C. Charitable Trust, 1004 Newton St., N.E., 20017. Tel: 302-229-5736 (Day). Email: shsnd@comcast.net. Sisters Marie-Louise Rossi, S.N.D., Trustee; Seton Cunneen, S.N.D., Trustee; Helen Bellew, S.N.D., Trustee.

Sisters of Notre Dame de Namur Base Communities, Inc. (1989) 125 Michigan Ave. N.E., 20017-1004. Tel: 202-884-9750. Email: sndbcunit@aol.com. Web: www.SNDdeN.org. Sisters 12.

Sovereign Military Order of Malta-Federal Association, 1730 M St., N.W., Ste. 403, 20036. Tel: 202-331-2494; Fax: 202-331-1149. Email: info@orderofmalta-federal.org. Web: www.orderofmalta-federal.org. Joseph J. Dempsey Jr., Exec. Dir.

Spanish Catholic Center, Administrative Office, P.O. Box 11450, 20008-0650. Tel: 202-939-2437; Fax: 202-234-7323. Email: infoscc@yahoo.com. Web: www.centrocatolicohispano.org. Rev. Donald F. Lippert, O.F.M.Cap.

Mt. Pleasant Branch, 1618 Monroe St., N.W., 20010. Tel: 202-939-2437; Fax: 202-234-7323.

Medical Clinic Tel: 202-939-2400; Fax: 202-232-1970.

Dental Clinic Tel: 202-939-2423; Fax: 202-234-7349.

Social Services Tel: 202-939-2414; Fax: 202-232-1970.

Immigration Services Tel: 202-939-2420; Fax: 202-234-7349.

Maryland Locations:

Langley Park Office, 1015 University Blvd. E., Silver Spring, MD 20903. Tel: 301-431-3773; Fax: 301-431-0886.

Adult Clinic Tel: 301-434-8381; Fax: 301-434-8067.

Pediatric Clinic Tel: 301-434-3999; Fax: 301-434-5160.

Piney Branch Office, 8545 Piney Branch Rd., Silver Spring, MD 20901.

Social, Employment & Immigration Services Tel: 301-587-0582; Fax: 301-587-8209.

Medical Clinic Tel: 301-929-0207; Fax: 301-929-0594.

Gaithersburg Branch, 117 N. Frederick Ave., Gaithersburg, MD 20877. Tel: 301-417-9113; Fax: 301-417-9895.

Social, Employment & Immigration Services Tel: 301-417-9113; Fax: 301-417-9895.

Spiritual Life (1954) 2131 Lincoln Rd., N.E., 20002-1199. Tel: 888-616-1713; Fax: 202-832-5711. Email: editor@spiritual-life.org. Web: www.spiritual-life.org. Rev. Regis Jordan, O.C.D., Notices Editor; Bros. Edward O'Donnell, O.C.D., Editor; Bryan Paquette, O.C.D., Business & Promotion Mgr. A Quarterly of Contemporary Spirituality. Priests 1; Total Staff 4.

Support Our Aging Religious, Inc. (SOAR!) (1986) (Support Our Aging Religious), 3025 4th St., N.E. - Ste. 14, 20017. Tel: 202-529-7627; Fax: 202-529-7633. Email: info@soar-usa.org. Web: www.soar-usa.org. Sr. Kathleen Lunsmann, I.H.M., Pres.; Deborah H. Vornbrock, Vice Pres. Opers.

**The Foundation for the Sacred Arts*, 1413 K St., N.W., Ste. 1000, 20005.

**The Paulus Institute*, 4401-A Connecticut Ave., N.W., # 228, 20008. Tel: 202-626-6627. Web: www.thepaulusinstitute.org.

US Province of the Religious of Jesus and Mary, Inc., 125 Michigan Ave., NE, 4th Flr., 20017. Tel: 202-884-9795; Fax: 202-884-9794.

St. Vincent Pallotti Center for Apostolic Development, Inc. (1984) 415 Michigan Ave., N.E., 20017-1518. Tel: 202-529-3330; 877-865-5465 (Toll free); Fax: 202-529-0911. Email: pallotti@pallotticenter.org. Web: www.pallotticenter.org. Mr. Michael J. Goggin, M.A., Natl. Dir. Total Assisted 15,000; Total Staff 4.

**Washington Jesuit Academy*, 900 Varnum St., N.E., 20017. Tel: 202-832-7679; Fax: 202-832-8098. Email: wwhitaker@wjacademy.org. Web: www.wjacademy.org. William B. Whitaker, Pres.

**The Washington Middle School for Girls*, 1901 Mississippi Ave. SE, 20020. Tel: 202-678-1113; Fax: 202-678-1114. Email: smbourdon@washingtonmiddleschoolforgirls.org. Web: www.washingtonmiddleschoolforgirls.org. Sr. Mary Bourdon, R.J.M., Head of School.

Womens Retreat League, 4000 Harewood Rd., N.E., 20017. Tel: 202-529-1111; Fax: 202-529-2102. Mrs. Leona Mahon, Pres.

Woodstock Theological Center, Box 571137, 20057-1137. Tel: 202-687-3532; Fax: 202-687-5837. Email: woodstock@georgetown.edu. Web: www.woodstock.georgetown.edu. Revs. J. Leon Hooper, S.J., Senior Fellow; Raymond B. Kemp, Senior Fellow; Gasper F. LoBiondo, S.J., Dir.; John C. Haughey, S.J., Senior Research Fellow; Thomas J. Reese, S.J., Senior Fellow; Daniel A. Madigan, S.J. (Australia), Senior Fellow.

**Workers of St. Joseph*, 5542 Friendship Station, 20016.

ALEXANDRIA, VA. *Catholic War Veterans of the United States*, 411 N. Lee St., VA 22314. Tel: 703-549-3622; Fax: 703-684-5196. Fred Schwally, Natl. Commander; Lupita Martinez, Pres.

BETHESDA, MD. **Alliance for Communities in Action, Inc.*, 5403 Waneta Rd., MD 20816-2131. Tel: 301-229-0351. Email: richard@allact.org. Deacon Richard Schopfer, Pres.; Juan Claudio Devincenti, Vice Pres.

Alpha Omega, Inc., Our Lady of Bethesda Retreat Center, 7007 Bradley Blvd., MD 20817. Tel: 301-365-0612; Fax: 301-469-7522. Email: manager@ourladyofbethesda.org. Web: www.ourladyofbethesda.org. Rev. John Hopkins, L.C., Pres.

Avondale Park Apartments, Inc (1997) c/o Victory Housing, 5430 Grosvenor Ln., Ste. 210, MD 20814-2142. Tel: 301-493-6000; Fax: 301-493-9788. Email: info@victoryhousing.org. Web: www.victoryhousing.org.

Catholic Institute for the Psychological Science, Inc., 7007 Bradley Blvd., MD 20817. Tel: 203-281-4798. Bro. Juan Sabadell, L.C., Sec. & Treas.

Holy Family Hospital of Bethlehem Foundation, 4960 Sentinel Dr., Apt. 106, MD 20816. Tel: 301-320-1600; Fax: 301-320-1881. Email: info@hfhfoundation.org. Web: www.hfhfoundation.org.

Lay Women's Association, 3025 4th St., N.E. #10, 20017. Tel: 202-525-1267. Email: angela218@aol.com. Web: www.simkc.org. National Headquarters of the LWA.

Mission Network Young Mens Program USA, Inc., 7007 Bradley Blvd., MD 20817. Tel: 301-365-7614; Fax: 301-299-0809. Email: msliney@legionaries.org. Rev. Jose Felix Ortega, L.C., Sec. & Treas.

National Christ Child Society, Inc. (1887) 4340 E. West Hwy., Ste. 202, MD 20814. Tel: 800-814-2149; Fax: 301-718-8822. Email: office@nationalchristchildsoc.org. Web: www.nationalchristchildsoc.org. Mrs. Christine Sheehan, Exec. Dir. A national nonprofit organization with 40 affiliate chapters consisting of over 7,000 member volunteers serving needy children across the United States through educational and clothing programs.

Natural Family Planning Center of Washington, DC, Inc., 4400 East West Hwy. #911, MD 20814-4510. Tel: 301-897-9323; Fax: 301-571-5267. Email: hannaklaus@earthlink.net. Web: www.teenstarprogram.org. Sr. Hanna Klaus, M.D., M.D., Exec. Dir. Teen STAR & Holistic Sexuality Programs. Total in Residence 1; Total Staff 6.

Victory Court, Inc., 5430 Grosvenor Ln., Ste. 210, MD 20814-2100.

Victory Crest, Inc., c/o Victory Housing, Inc., 5430 Grosvenor Ln., Ste. 210, MD 20814-2142. Tel: 301-493-6000; Fax: 301-493-9788. Email: info@victoryhousing.org. Web: www.victoryhousing.org. Mr. James A. Brown Jr., Pres. & CEO; John D. Spencer, Senior Vice Pres.

Victory Oaks, Inc., 5430 Grosvenor Ln., Ste.210, MD 20814-2100.

Woodmont Educational Foundation, Inc., 7007 Bradley Blvd., MD 20817. Tel: 914-773-1368. Rev. Jose Felix Ortega, L.C., Contact Person.

BLADENSBURG, MD. *St. Luke's Ordinariate Catholic Community, Inc.*, 4002 53rd St., MD 20710.

BOWIE, MD. *Sodality Union*, 3300 Moreland Pl., MD 20715. Tel: 301-262-2141; Fax: 301-262-2632. Rev. Lawrence C. Swink, Spiritual Dir. & Moderator; Cindy Perry, Pres.

Washington Catholic Charismatic Service Committee, 16304 Pond Meadow Ln., MD 20716. Tel: 301-249-9199; Fax: 301-769-2541; 301-249-1303. Email: oremus2005@earthlink.net. Rev. John M. Barry, Dir.

COTTAGE CITY, MD. *Marriage Encounter-Worldwide*, 4011 Parkwood St., MD 20722. Tel: 301-395-5369. Email: dlf68@juno.com. Web: dc.wwme.org. Don Flanders, Contact Person; Wink Flanders, Contact Person.

FORT WASHINGTON, MD. *Birhen Ng Antipolo, USA, Inc.* (1997) 8504 Oxon Hill Road, MD 20744. Tel: 301-567-4914; Fax: 301-567-4914. Web: www.antipolo.us. Eddie D. Caparas, Pres. & Chm.

GAITHERSBURG, MD. *Knights of Columbus*, 16584 Sioux Ln., MD 20878. Tel: 301-921-4035; Fax: 301-921-4035 (Call First). Email: tryzub1@verizon.net. Lawrence Sosnowich, Immediate Past State Deputy.

GLEN ECHO, MD. *John Carroll Society*, P.O. Box 454, MD 20812. Tel: 301-654-4399. *Church of the Little Flower*, 5607 Massachusetts Ave., Bethesda, MD 20816. Rev. Msgr. Peter J. Vaghi, J.D., V.F., Chap.; Gregory Granitto, Pres.; Colleen Mudlaff, Exec. Dir.

HYATTSVILLE, MD. *Faith House, Inc.*, 4901 Eastern Ave., MD 20782. Tel: 301-559-5500; Fax: 301-853-6985. Email: maternity@stanns.org. Web: www.stanns.org. Sr. Mary Bader, D.C., CEO. Total Assisted Families 8.

KENSINGTON, MD. *Inter Mirifica*, 2812 Jutland Rd., MD 20895. Tel: 301-949-4840; Fax: 301-949-4840. Email: jdhoconnell@comcast.net. Rev. John Hardon, S.J., Founder; John O'Connell, Contact Person. Religious publications.

Victory Youth Centers, Inc., 10415 Armory Ave., MD 20895. Tel: 301-654-6200; Fax: 301-692-1990. Email: gdyer@dyercpa.com. Gregory B. Dyer, Pres.

LANDOVER HILLS, MD. *The Center for Deaf Ministries of the Archdiocese of Washington*, 7202 Buchanan, MD 20784. Tel: 301-459-7464 (TTY/Voice); Fax: 301-459-8186. Email: deafmindc@aol.com. Rev. Gerard A. Trancone, Dir. Total in Residence 1; Total Staff 3.

LAUREL, MD. *Pallotti Early Learning Center at St. Mary of the Mills*, 113 Saint Mary's Pl., MD 20707. Tel: 301-776-6471; 410-724-0097; Fax: 301-776-0019. Email: pelc.mia@verizon.net. Web: pallottiearlylearningcenter.net. Mia Laughlin, Dir.; Sr. Karen Lester, S.A.C., Rel. Teacher (part-time). Sisters 1; Lay Teachers 15; Students 129; Day Care 68; Kindergarten 14; After School 47.

MCLEAN, VA. *German Speaking Catholic Mission, Washington DC*, 6330 Linway Ter., VA 22101-4150. Tel: 703-356-4473. Email: nachcenich@adwparish.org. Web: www.kathde.org.

MOUNT RAINIER, MD. *Dominican Fathers & Brothers Inc. Province of Nigeria, Development and Mission Office*, 4504 21st St., MD 20712. Tel: 301-927-0387; Fax: 301-927-0388. Email: nigopmissions@nig.op.org. Web: www.dominicans.org.ng/. Rev. Lawrence Nwabueze, O.P., Mission Dir. Priests 96; Total Assisted 162.

IVE Real Estate Trust, 3706 Rhode Island Ave., MD 20712.

MT. VICTORIA, MD. *Sacred Military Constantinian Order of St. George, American Delegation*, P.O. Box 7, Mount Victoria, MD 20661. Tel: 301-870-1033; Fax: 301-870-0993. Email: mtvictoriafarm@gmail.com. Web: constantinianorderofstgeorge.org. Michael J. Sullivan, Delegate & Contact Person.

POTOMAC, MD. *Little Sisters of the Holy Family*, 13529 Magruder Farm Ct., MD 20854. Tel: 301-947-1955; Fax: 240-631-1786. Sr. Domina Son, L.S.H.F., Supr.

Potomac Pastoral Center Inc., 10211 Norton Rd., MD 20854. Tel: 301-299-0806; Fax: 301-299-0809.

ROCKVILLE, MD. *Archdiocesan Council of Catholic Women*, 520 Veirs Mill Rd., MD 20852. Tel: 301-424-5550; Fax: 301-424-5579. Rev. Msgr. Robert G. Amey, V.F., Moderator & Spiritual Dir.; Alice Wilson, Pres., 311 Wren Ct., Upper Marlboro, MD 20774. Tel: 301-249-4770.

SILVER SPRING, MD. *All Hallows Mission Fund, Inc.*, P.O. Box 3691, MD 20918. Tel: 301-593-4461; Fax: 301-593-4461.

Apostleship of Prayer, League of the Sacred Heart, 15107 Interlachen Dr., #722, MD 20906-5632. Tel: 301-438-3753; Fax: 301-441-4954. Web: www.apostleshipofprayer.org. Rev. Gerard P. Bell, S.J., Archdiocesan Dir.

Archdiocese of Washington Division, The Blue Army World Apostolate of Fatima, P.O. Box 4934, MD 20914. Tel: 301-589-7829. Mrs. Jane Baily, Pres.; Rev. Msgr. Charles E. Pope, V.F., Spiritual Dir.

Camp St. Charles, Inc. (1952) 104 Bishop Dr., MD 20905. Tel: 240-372-9437; 301-259-2645 (Summer); Fax: 240-523-9437. Email: glenwillis@verizon.net. Web: www.campstcharles.org. Summer Camp Address: *Camp St. Charles*, 15375 Stella Maris Dr., Rock Point, MD 20664. Rev. Glen Willis, S.D.S., Exec. Dir.; Ms. Laura Hall, Dir.; Bros. Roger Nelson, S.D.S., M.A., Asst. Dir.; Marvin Kluesner, S.D.S., Dir. Arts & Crafts. Priests 1; Brothers 2; Lay Staff 40; Children Served 600.

Catholics Committed to Support the Pope, 9402 Stateside Ct., MD 20903. Tel: 301-434-3245; 301-434-7763; Fax: 301-434-5486. Email: patmorse@comcast.net. George P. Morse, K.G.C.S.G., Pres. & Publisher; His Eminence Edward Cardinal Egan, Councilor; George Cardinal Pell, Councilor; Josef Cardinal Tomko, Councilor; Donald Cardinal Wuerl, Councilor; Timothy M. Dolan, Councilor; Most Revs. William E. Lori, Councilor; Peter J. Elliott, Councilor; Rev. Archimandrite Robert L. Stern, Councilor; Dr. William E. May, Councilor. Prepares, publishes and distributes world-wide thirteen-volume series of PRECIS OF OFFICIAL CATHOLIC TEACHING for use by rectors and faculty of seminaries, for seminarians, bishops, Catechetical Directors and DRE's, theologians and academics, for Catholic education courses and teaching, writers and teachers, Catholic Study Groups and laity and highly recommended for Anglican bishops and priests considering joining the Catholic Church. CCSP authors, publishes and distributes "THE MASS: ITS MYSTERIES REVEALED."

Conference for Mercy Higher Education (2002) 8630 Fenton St., Ste. 934, MD 20910. Tel: 301-587-8988; Fax: 301-587-0077. Web: www.mercyhighered.org. Moya K. Dittmeier, Ed.D., Exec. Dir.; Paphasi Manickam, M.A., Exec. Asst. The Conference for Mercy Higher Education is separately incorporated for the preservation and development of the Catholic identity and mission of Mercy higher education in accord with the spirit, mission, and heritage of the Sisters of Mercy of the Americas. Each of the 16 active member institutions of the Conference is separately chartered and is legally incorporated with its own board of trustees.

The Daughters of Mary Immaculate, Inc., 13004 Marlow Farm Dr., MD 20904. Tel: 301-288-7663; Fax: 866-840-3937.

Friends of John Paul II Foundation (1985) 9700 Rosensteel Ave., MD 20910. Tel: 703-790-1984. Email: virginiaegg@cox.net. Web: jp2friends.org. Rev. Jan Fiedurek, T.Chr; Cecilia Glembocki, Pres. 2009-2010, 2011-2012.

Holy Cross Health Corp., 1500 Forest Glen Rd., MD 20910-1484. Tel: 301-754-7000; Fax: 301-754-7413. Web: www.holycrosshealth.org. Mr. Kevin J. Sexton, Pres. & CEO. Includes Holy Cross Hospital, Home Health Agency, and other services.

Leadership Conference of Women Religious in the U.S.A., 8808 Cameron St., MD 20910. Tel: 301-588-4955; Fax: 301-587-4575. Email: director@lcwr.org. Web: www.lcwr.org. Sisters Patricia Farrell, O.S.F., M.S.W., Pres.; Florence Deacon, O.S.F., Ph.D., Pres.-Elect; Mary Hughes, O.P., Ed.D., Past Pres.; Barbara Blesse, O.P., M.A., M.Div., Sec.; Sheila Megley, R.S.M., C.P.A., Ph.D., Treas.; Janet Mock, C.S.J., B.A., Exec. Dir.

**St. Luke Institute Foundation*, 8901 New Hampshire Ave., MD 20903.

Saint Luke Institute, Inc., 8901 New Hampshire Ave., MD 20903. Tel: 301-445-7970; Fax: 301-422-5400. Email: getinfo@sli.org. Web: www.sli.org. Rev. Msgr. Edward J. Arsenault, S.T.L., Pres. & C.E.O. The Institute is a licensed and accredited treatment center for clergy and religious, and a center for education and research. Total Assisted Annually 535; Total Staff 60.

Lumen Catechetical Consultants, Inc. (1982) P.O. Box 1761, MD 20915. Tel: 301-593-1066; 800-473-7980; Fax: 301-593-1689. Email: lumen@lifeaftersunday.com. Web: lifeaftersunday.com. Mr. John M. Capobianco, Pres. Provides Consulting & Production Services to Catholic Organizations; Assist in Development and Production of Catechetical Materials in Various Media. Publishes "Life After Sunday."

National Association for Treasurers of Religious Institutes (1981) 8824 Cameron St., MD 20910-4152. Tel: 301-587-7776; Fax: 301-589-2897. Email: trcri@trcri.org. Web: www.trcri.org. Sr. Hertha Longo, C.S.A., Pres.; Rev. Daniel Ward, O.S.B., Exec. Dir.

North American Conference of Provincials, Corporation National Advocacy Center of the Sisters of the Good Shepherd., 504 Hexton Hill Rd., MD 20904. Tel: 301-622-6838; Fax: 301-384-1025. Email: natlcor@gsadvocacy.org. Web: www.gsadvocacy.org. Sr. Gayle Lwanga Crumbley, R.G.S., Natl. Coord.

Sisters of Mercy of the Americas CCASA Community, Inc., 8380 Colesville Rd., Ste. 300, MD 20910. Tel: 301-587-0423; Fax: 301-587-0533.

SPRINGFIELD, VA. *St. Francis de Sales Association*, 8002 Gosport Ln., VA 22151-2007. Brenda Soares, Directress of the Washington Group, 8002 Gosport Ln., VA 22151-2007. Tel: 703-321-7856. Email: bmsoares@verizon.net.

WHEATON, MD. *U.S. Foundation for the Congregation of the Holy Ghost and the Immaculate Heart of Mary, Inc.* (Sharelink - Spiritan Worldwide Aid Foundation), P.O. Box 2000, MD 20902. Tel: 877-443-1703; Fax: 301-942-5993. Email: spiritan@thespiritans.org. Web: www.thespiritans.org. Rev. George J. Spangenberg, C.S.Sp., Dir.

RELIGIOUS INSTITUTES OF MEN REPRESENTED IN THE ARCHDIOCESE

For further details refer to the corresponding bracketed number in the Religious Institutes of Men or Women section.

[0140]—*The Augustinians*—O.S.A.
[0200]—*Benedictine Monks*—O.S.B.
[]—*Brothers of Charity*—F.C.
[1350]—*Brothers of St. Francis Xavier*—C.F.X.
[0330]—*Brothers of the Christian Schools* (Baltimore Prov.)—F.S.C.
[0600]—*Brothers of the Congregation of Holy Cross*—C.S.C.
[0470]—*The Capuchin Friars* (Prov. of St. Augustine)—O.F.M.Cap.
[0270]—*Carmelite Fathers & Brothers*—O.Carm.
[]—*Congregation of the Sacred Hearts of Jesus and Mary*—SS.CC
[0480]—*Conventual Franciscans*—O.F.M.Conv.
[0260]—*Discalced Carmelite Fathers (Prov. of the Immaculate Heart of Mary)*—O.C.D.
[0520]—*Franciscan Friars (Commissariat of the Holy Land)*—O.F.M.
[0530]—*Franciscan Friars of the Atonement*—S.A.
[]—*Institute of the Incarnate Word*—IVE
[0690]—*Jesuit Fathers and Brothers (Prov. of Maryland)*—S.J.
[0730]—*Legionaries of Christ*—L.C.
[0740]—*Marian Fathers*—M.I.C.
[0780]—*Marist Fathers and Brothers*—S.M.
[0800]—*Maryknoll*—M.M.
[0850]—*Missionaries of Africa*—M.Afr.
[0720]—*The Missionaries of Our Lady of La Salette*—M.S.
[1210]—*Missionaries of St. Charles (Scalabrinians)*—C.S.

[0590]—*Missionaries of the Holy Apostle*—M.S.A.
[]—*Missionary Servants of Christ*—M.S.C.
[0840]—*Missionary Servants of the Most Holy Trinity*—S.T.
[0910]—*Oblates of Mary Immaculate (Eastern Prov.)*—O.M.I.
[0920]—*Oblates of St. Francis de Sales*—O.S.F.S.
[0430]—*Order of Preachers (Dominican) (Prov. of St. Joseph)*—O.P.
[1310]—*Order of the Holy Trinity (American Prov.)*—O.SS.T.
[1030]—*Paulist Fathers*—C.S.P.
[1040]—*Piarist Fathers*—Sch.P.
[1205]—*Priestly Fraternity of the Missionaries of St. Charles Borromeo*—F.S.C.B.
[1070]—*Redemptorist Fathers* (Baltimore Prov.)—C.SS.R.
[]—*Salesians of Don Bosco*—S.D.B.
[0110]—*Society of African Missions*—S.M.A.
[1260]—*Society of Christ*—S.Ch.
[0990]—*Society of the Catholic Apostolate (Immaculate Conception Prov.)*—S.A.C.
[1200]—*Society of the Divine Savior* (Milwaukee, WI)—S.D.S.
[0420]—*Society of the Divine Word*—S.V.D.
[1290]—*Society of the Priests of Saint Sulpice*—S.S.
[0640]—*Sons of the Holy Family*—S.F.
[0700]—*St. Joseph Society of the Sacred Heart*—S.S.J.
[0560]—*Third Order Regular of Saint Francis (Prov. of the Immaculate Conception)*—T.O.R.

RELIGIOUS INSTITUTES OF WOMEN REPRESENTED IN THE ARCHDIOCESE

[0100]—*Adorers of the Blood of Christ*—A.S.C.
[1810]—*Bernardine Franciscan Sisters*—O.S.F.
[0340]—*Carmelite Sisters of Charity*—C.C.V.
[]—*Congregation of the Daughters of Mary Immaculate*—D.M.I.
[1170]—*Congregation of the Sisters of St. Felix Cantalice (Felician Sisters)*—C.S.S.F.
[3832]—*Congregation of the Sisters of St. Joseph* (Baden, PA)—C.S.J.
[1920]—*Congregation of the Sisters of the Holy Cross*—C.S.C.
[0760]—*Daughters of Charity of St. Vincent de Paul*—D.C.
[]—*Daughters of Divine Love*—D.D.L.
[]—*Daughters of Mary Mother of Mercy*—D.M.M.M.
[]—*Daughters of St. Anne*—F.S.A.
[0420]—*Discalced Carmelite Nuns*—O.C.D.
[1070-13]—*Dominican Congregation of the Most Holy Rosary* (Adrian, MI)—O.P.
[1070-03]—*Dominican Sisters* (Sinsinawa, WI)—O.P.
[1100]—*Dominican Sisters of Charity of the Presentation of the Blessed Virgin*—O.P.
[]—*Dominican Sisters of Our Lady of the Rosary of Fatima*—O.P.
[O.S.F.]—*Franciscan Sisters of Allegany, New York*—1180
[1470]—*Franciscan Sisters of St. Joseph*—H.F.S.J.
[1190]—*Franciscan Sisters of the Atonement*—S.A.
[0793]—*Handmaids of the Holy Child Jesus*—H.H.C.J.
[0410]—*Institute of the Sisters of Our Lady of Mt. Carmel*—O.Carm.
[]—*Institute Servants of the Lord and the Virgin of Matara*—S.S.V.M.
[2340]—*Little Sisters of the Poor*—L.S.P.
[2345]—*Little Workers of the Sacred Hearts of Jesus and Mary*—P.O.S.C.
[2490]—*Medical Mission Sisters*—M.M.S.
[2720]—*Mission Helpers of the Sacred Heart*—M.H.S.H.
[2710]—*Missionaries of Charity*—M.C.
[1475]—*Missionary Catechists of St. Therese*—M.C.S.T.
[1360]—*Missionary Franciscan Sisters of the Immaculate Conception*—M.F.I.C.
[2820]—*Missionary Sisters of Our Lady of Africa*—M.S.O.L.A.
[2900]—*Missionary Sisters of St. Charles Borromeo*—M.S.C.S.
[2865]—*Missionary Sisters of the Sacred Heart of Jesus and Our Lady of Guadalupe*—M.S.C.Gpe.
[]—*Oblate Sisters of the Most Holy Eucharist*—O.S.S.E.
[3210]—*Poor Clares of Perpetual Adoration*—P.C.P.A.
[3450]—*Religious of Jesus and Mary*—R.J.M.
[3460]—*Religious of Mary Immaculate*—R.M.I.
[2519]—*Religious Sisters of Mercy* (Alma, MI)—R.S.M.
[2970]—*School Sisters of Notre Dame*—S.S.N.D.
[3620]—*Sister Servants of Mary Immaculate*—S.S.M.I.
[]—*Sisters of Charity of St. Charles Borromeo*—S.C.B.
[]—*Sisters of Charity of St. Vincent de Paul of Halifax*—S.C.
[]—*Sisters of Charity of the Blessed Virgin Mary*—B.V.M.
[0660]—*Sisters of Christian Charity*—S.C.C.
[1000]—*Sisters of Divine Providence* (Melbourne, KY)—C.D.P.
[2575]—*Sisters of Mercy of the Americas*—R.S.M.
[2630]—*Sisters of Mercy of the Holy Cross*—S.C.S.C.
[2990]—*Sisters of Notre Dame*—S.N.D.
[3000]—*Sisters of Notre Dame de Namur* (Maryland, Chesapeake & Base Communities, Prov.; Boston and Connecticut)—S.N.D.deN.
[3360]—*Sisters of Providence of St. Mary-of-the-Woods, IN*—S.P.
[3893]—*Sisters of Saint Joseph of Chestnut Hill, Philadelphia*—S.S.J.
[1070-07]—*Sisters of St. Dominic of St. Cecilia* (Nashville, TN)—O.P.
[1650]—*Sisters of St. Francis of Philadelphia*—O.S.F.
[1600]—*Sisters of St. Francis of the Martyr St. George*—F.S.G.M.
[3890]—*Sisters of St. Joseph of Peace*—C.S.J.P.
[3850]—*Sisters of St. Joseph, Canondelet*—C.S.J.
[3980]—*Sisters of St. Paul de Chartres*—S.P.C.
[3150]—*Sisters of the Catholic Apostolate (Pallotines)*—S.A.C.
[1830]—*Sisters of the Good Shepherd*—R.G.S.
[1990]—*Sisters of the Holy Names of Jesus and Mary*—S.N.J.M.
[3270]—*Sisters of the Most Precious Blood*—C.P.P.S.
[3320]—*Sisters of the Presentation of the Blessed Virgin Mary*—P.B.V.M.
[4100]—*Sisters of the Sorrowful Mother*—S.S.M.
[1490]—*Sisters of the Third Franciscan Order* (Syracuse, NY)—O.S.F.
[1720]—*Sisters of the Third Order Regular of St. Francis of the Congregation of Our Lady of Lourdes*—O.S.F.
[2160]—*Sisters, Servants of the Immaculate Heart of Mary*—I.H.M.
[4060]—*Society of the Holy Child Jesus*—S.H.C.J.
[4070]—*Society of the Sacred Heart*—R.S.C.J.
[4120-06]—*Ursuline Nuns of the Congregation of Paris* (Toledo, OH)—O.S.U.
[]—*Vietnamese Dominican Sisters*—O.P.
[4190]—*Visitation Nuns*—V.H.M.

ARCHDIOCESAN CEMETERIES

WASHINGTON. *The Catholic Cemeteries of the Archdiocese of Washington, Inc.*, 13801 Georgia Ave., Silver Spring, MD 20906. Tel: 301-871-1300 (All offices 9-4:30 P.M.). Email: lkb@ccaw.org.

Mount Olivet Cemetery & St. Mary's Cemetery, 1300 Bladensburg Rd., N.E., 20002. Tel: 202-399-3000. Email: mto@ccaw.org. Jeffrey L. McConnell, Mgr.

CLINTON, MD. *Resurrection Cemetery*, 8000 Woodyard Rd., P.O. Box 151, MD 20735. Tel: 301-868-5141. Email: res@ccaw.org. Janet L. Richardson, Mgr.

GERMANTOWN, MD. *All Souls Cemetery*, 11401 Brink Rd., MD 20876. Tel: 301-428-1995. Email: asc@ccaw.org. John A. Geiger, Mgr.

MECHANICSVILLE, MD. *St. Mary's Queen of Peace Cemetery*, 38888 Dr. Johnson Rd., P.O. Box 497, MD 20659. Tel: 301-932-1766. Email: qop@ccaw.org. John A. Spalding, Mgr.

SILVER SPRING, MD. *The Catholic Cemeteries of the Archdiocese of Washington, Inc.*, 13801 Georgia Ave., MD 20906. Tel: 301-871-1300. Ms. Lauri K. Brown, Dir.

Gate of Heaven Cemetery, 13801 Georgia Ave., MD 20906. Tel: 301-871-6500. Email: goh@ccaw.org. Samuel E. French Jr., Mgr.

NECROLOGY

† Duffy, George Ralph, (Retired)—Died July 26, 2011
† McCaffrey, Patrick J., (Retired)—Died Aug. 20, 2011
† Reid, George B., (Retired)—Died May 9, 2011

An asterisk (*) denotes an organization that has established tax-exempt status directly with the IRS and is not covered by the USCCB Group Ruling.

Diocese of Wheeling-Charleston

(Dioecesis Vhelingensis Carolopolitanus)

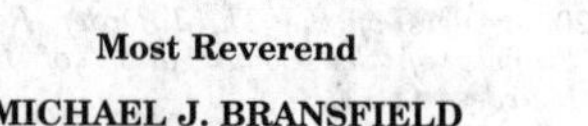

Most Reverend

MICHAEL J. BRANSFIELD

Bishop of Wheeling-Charleston; ordained May 15, 1971; appointed Bishop of Wheeling-Charleston December 9, 2004; ordained February 22, 2005.

Chancery Office: 1300 Byron St., P.O. Box 230, Wheeling, WV 26003. Tel: 304-233-0880; Fax: 304-230-2029.

Web: www.dwc.org

Email: ccarter@dwc.org

Square Miles 24,282.

Established as Diocese of Wheeling July 19, 1850; Redesignated Diocese of Wheeling-Charleston October 4, 1974.

Comprises the entire State of West Virginia.

For legal titles of parishes and diocesan institutions, consult the Chancery Office.

STATISTICAL OVERVIEW

Personnel	
Bishop	1
Priests: Diocesan Active in Diocese	67
Priests: Diocesan Active Outside Diocese	2
Priests: Retired, Sick or Absent	37
Number of Diocesan Priests	106
Religious Priests in Diocese	51
Total Priests in Diocese	157
Extern Priests in Diocese	16
Ordinations:	
Diocesan Priests	2
Transitional Deacons	1
Permanent Deacons in Diocese	45
Total Brothers	11
Total Sisters	137
Parishes	
Parishes	110
With Resident Pastor:	
Resident Diocesan Priests	84
Resident Religious Priests	26
Without Resident Pastor:	
Administered by Priests	25
Missions	18
Pastoral Centers	4
Professional Ministry Personnel:	
Brothers	4
Sisters	14
Welfare	
Catholic Hospitals	3
Total Assisted	633,117
Homes for the Aged	5
Residential Care of Children	1
Total Assisted	16
Day Care Centers	2
Total Assisted	200
Specialized Homes	1
Total Assisted	16
Special Centers for Social Services	11
Total Assisted	41,723
Educational	
Diocesan Students in Other Seminaries	9
Total Seminarians	9
Colleges and Universities	1
Total Students	1,372
High Schools, Diocesan and Parish	7
Total Students	1,430
Elementary Schools, Diocesan and Parish	22
Total Students	4,505
Catechesis/Religious Education:	
High School Students	766
Elementary Students	4,142
Total Students under Catholic Instruction	12,224
Teachers in the Diocese:	
Priests	2
Brothers	2
Sisters	1
Lay Teachers	567
Vital Statistics	
Receptions into the Church:	
Infant Baptism Totals	836
Minor Baptism Totals	140
Adult Baptism Totals	190
Received into Full Communion	164
First Communions	955
Confirmations	897
Marriages:	
Catholic	179
Interfaith	32
Total Marriages	211
Deaths	1,006
Total Catholic Population	83,129
Total Population	1,819,777

Former Bishops—Rt. Revs. RICHARD VINCENT WHELAN, D.D., cons. March 21, 1841; Bishop of Richmond; transferred to Wheeling in 1850; died July 7, 1874; JOHN JOSEPH KAIN, D.D., cons. May 23, 1875; transferred June 15, 1893, to the Titular Archiepiscopal See of Oxyrynchia; appt. July 6, 1893; Coadjutor "cum jure successionis" to the Most Rev. Archbishop of St. Louis, MO; created Archbishop of St. Louis, May 21, 1895; died Oct. 13, 1903; PATRICK JAMES DONAHUE, D.D., cons. April 8, 1894; died Oct. 4, 1922; Most Revs. JOHN J. SWINT, D.D., LL.D., appt. Auxiliary Bishop of Wheeling Feb. 22, 1922; cons. May 11, 1922; appt. Bishop of Wheeling Dec. 11, 1922; promoted to rank of Archbishop "ad personam," March 12, 1954; died Nov. 23, 1962; THOMAS J. MCDONNELL, D.D., LL.D., cons. Sept. 15, 1947; appt. Auxiliary Bishop of New York, June 21, 1947; appt. Coadjutor of Wheeling, "cum jure successionis," March 7, 1951; died Feb. 25, 1961; JOSEPH H. HODGES, D.D., ord. Dec. 8, 1935; appt. Titular Bishop of Rusadus and Auxiliary of Richmond Aug. 8, 1952; cons. Oct. 15, 1952; transferred to Wheeling See as Coadjutor, "cum jure successionis", May 24, 1961; succeeded to the See Nov. 23, 1962; died Jan. 27, 1985; FRANCIS B. SCHULTE, D.D., ord. May 10, 1952; appt. Titular Bishop of Afufenia and Auxiliary Bishop of Philadelphia June 27, 1981; cons. Bishop Aug. 12, 1981; transferred to Wheeling July 31, 1985; transferred to Archdiocese of New Orleans Feb. 14, 1989; retired Jan. 3, 2002.; BERNARD W. SCHMITT, D.D., ord. May 28, 1955; appt. Titular Bishop of Walla Walla and Auxiliary Bishop of Wheeling-Charleston May 31, 1988; ord. to the Episcopacy Aug. 1, 1988; app. Seventh Bishop of Wheeling-Charleston March 30, 1989; installed May 17, 1989; retired Dec. 9, 2004; died Aug. 16, 2011.

Vicar General and Moderator of the Curia—Rev. Msgr. FREDERICK P. ANNIE, V.G., Mailing Address: P.O. Box 230, Wheeling, 26003. Tel: 304-233-0880; Fax: 304-230-2231.

Chancery Office—Mailing Address: P.O. Box 230, Wheeling, 26003. Tel: 304-233-0880; Fax: 304-233-0890. Office Hours: Mon.-Fri. 8:30-4:30.

Chancellor—Mr. CHAD R. CARTER, M.B.A., B.A., Mailing Address: P.O. Box 230, Wheeling, 26003. Tel: 304-233-0880; Fax: 304-230-2029.

Assistant to the Bishop—Rev. Msgr. KEVIN M. QUIRK, J.C.D., J.V.

Priest-Secretary for Bishop—Rev. PAUL A. HUDOCK.

Diocesan Tribunal— All Rogatory Commissions should be addressed to the office of the Diocesan Tribunal, *Mailing Address: P.O. Box 230, Wheeling, 26003.* Tel: 304-233-0880.

Judicial Vicar—Rev. Msgr. KEVIN M. QUIRK, J.C.D., J.V.

Promotor Justitiae—Rt. Rev. JOHN M. LOGAN, O.Praem., J.C.L.

Defenders of Bond—Deacon DENNIS W. NESSER, J.C.L.; Rev. JOSEPH AUGUSTINE, H.G.N., J.C.L.

Judges—Revs. JAMES R. DEVIESE, J.C.L.; ELPIDIO M. GENETA, J.C.L.

Diocesan Consultors—Rev. Msgr. FREDERICK P. ANNIE, V.G.; Very Revs. ANTHONY CINCINNATI, S.T.D., V.E.; JOSEPH L. PETERSON, V.F.; Rev. Msgrs. SAMUEL S. SACUS, V.F.; P. EDWARD SADIE, S.T.L., V.F.

Delegate for Consecrated Life—Sr. ELLEN F. DUNN, O.P., Mailing Address: P.O. Box 230, Wheeling, 26003-0010. Tel: 304-233-0880; Fax: 304-233-8551.

Episcopal Vicar for Clergy—Very Rev. ANTHONY CINCINNATI, S.T.D., V.E., Mailing Address: P.O. Box 230, Wheeling, 26003-0010. Tel: 304-233-0880; Fax: 304-230-1583.

Vicars Forane—Rev. EUGENE S. OSTROWSKI, V.F., Wheeling Vicariate; Rev. Msgrs. SAMUEL S. SACUS, V.F., Beckley Vicariate; P. EDWARD SADIE, S.T.L., V.F., Charleston Vicariate; Very Revs. MARK WARD, C.P., V.F., Clarksburg Vicariate; WILLIAM P. LINHARES, T.O.R., U.F., B.A., M.Ed., S.T.B., Martinsburg Vicariate; JOSEPH L. PETERSON, V.F., Parkersburg Vicariate; DONALD X. HIGGS, V.F., Weston Vicariate.

Finance Council—Mailing Address: P.O. Box 230, Wheeling, 26003.

Finance Officer—Mr. WILLIAM G. FISHER, CPA, Mailing Address: P.O. Box 230, Wheeling, 26003. Tel: 304-233-0880.

Diocesan Offices and Directors

Apostleship of Prayer—Rev. Msgr. KEVIN M. QUIRK, J.C.D., J.V., Mailing Address: P.O. Box 230, Wheeling, 26003.

Archivists—Mr. RYAN RUTKOWSKI; Mr. CHAD R. CARTER, M.B.A., B.A., Chancellor, Mailing Address: 77 14th St., P.O. Box 230, Wheeling, 26003. Tel: 304-230-2079; Fax: 304-233-0890. Email: rrutkowski@dwc.org.

Behavioral Counseling and Ministry—Rev. ROBERT G. PARK, Dir., Mailing Address: P.O. Box 230, Wheeling, 26003. Tel: 304-233-0880.

Diocesan School Board—Mr. BRANN ALTMEYER, Chm.,

Mailing Address: P.O. Box 230, Wheeling, 26003. Tel: 304-233-0880.

Buildings and Properties—Mr. JOHN REARDON, Dir., Mailing Address: P.O. Box 230, Wheeling, 26003. Tel: 304-233-0880.

(CCWVa) Catholic Charities West Virginia—Mr. MARK SLITER-HAYS, Exec. Dir., Mailing Address: 2000 Main St., Wheeling, 26003. Tel: 304-905-9860; Fax: 304-233-9293. Email: msliterhays@ccwva.org; Central Regional Office, 827 Fairmont Rd., Ste. 203, Morgantown, 26505. Tel: 304-292-6597. Eastern Regional Office, 224 S. Queen St., Martinsburg, 25401. Tel: 304-267-8837. Northern Regional Office, 125 18th St., P.O. Box 6176, Wheeling, 26003. Tel: 304-232-7157. Parkersburg Regional Office, 521 Market St., #24, Parkersburg, 26101. Tel: 304-424-3457. Southern Regional Office, P.O. Box 386, Princeton, 24740-2909. Tel: 304-425-4306. Western Regional Office, 1420 Kanawha Blvd. W., Charleston, 25312. Tel: 304-345-2103. Weston Regional Office, 103 Randolph Ave., P.O. Box 2764, Elkins, 26241. Tel: 304-636-4875.

(CCWVa) Development Office—Ms. PATRICIA PHILLIPS, Dir., 2000 Main St., Wheeling, 26003. Tel: 304-905-9860.

(CCWVa) Child and Adult Care Food Program—Ms. ANNETTE "LYNN" WALLACE, State Dir., 2000 Main St., Ste. 200, Wheeling, 26003. Tel: 304-230-1280.

(CCWVa) Child Care Resource Center—Mrs. TRACI KINNEY, Dir., 2000 Main St., Ste. 100, Wheeling, 26003. Tel: 304-232-1603.

(CCWVa) Medicaid/Homemaker Services—Mrs. BARBARA HIGGINBOTHAM, Dir., 1116 Kanawha Blvd. E., Charleston, 25312. Tel: 304-345-2103.

(CCWVa) WV Birth to Three Region One—Mrs. WENDY MILLER, Dir., 2000 Main St., Ste. 121, Wheeling, 26003. Tel: 304-214-5775.

Diocesan Newspaper: "The Catholic Spirit"—Mrs. COLLEEN ROWAN, Editor, Mailing Address: P.O. Box 230, Wheeling, 26003-0030. Tel: 304-233-0880.

Diocesan Spokesperson—Mr. BRYAN MINOR, Mailing Address: P.O. Box 230, Wheeling, 26003-0030. Tel: 304-233-0880; Fax: 304-233-0890.

Catholic University, Friends of—Rev. Msgr. FREDERICK P. ANNIE, V.G., Mailing Address: P.O. Box 230, Wheeling, 26003. Tel: 304-233-0880.

Cemeteries—Mr. BRETT COCHRAN, Mailing Address: 1685 National Rd., Wheeling, 26003. Tel: 304-242-0460.

Censor Librorum—Rev. Msgr. KEVIN M. QUIRK, J.C.D., J.V.

Wheeling-Charleston Diocesan Council of Catholic Women—Sr. ELLEN F. DUNN, O.P., Diocesan Moderator, Mailing Address: P.O. Box 230, Wheeling, 26003. Tel: 304-233-0880; Very Rev. DONALD X. HIGGS, V.F., Diocesan Chap.; Mrs. BARBARA BELLDINA, Pres.

Computer Information Systems—Mr. RICHARD A. HARROLD, Dir. Technological Svcs.; Mrs. KAREN KOVACS, Coord. Technology Support Svcs.; Mr. ROBERT WICKHAM, Sr. Internet Technologies Engineer.

Stewardship and Development, Office of—Mr. BRYAN MINOR, Exec. Dir.; Mrs. KRISTEN BENSON, Dir.; Mrs. HEIDI SFORZA, Asst. Dir.

Diaconate Executive Committee—Deacon N. ROLLIN FAGERT, Chm., 202 E. Robinson St., Paden City, 26159. Email: rodgail2@verizon.net.

Finance Office—Mr. WILLIAM G. FISHER, CPA, CFO; Mr. ALEX J. NAGEM, CPA, Comptroller; Mr. FRANK BONACCI, Asst. Comptroller; Mr. JOHN L. HOFFMAN, Property Specialist; Mr. SCOTT M. MILLARD, Purchasing Agent, Mailing Address: P.O. Box 230, Wheeling, 26003-0010. Tel: 304-233-0880; Fax: 304-233-0890.

Martinsburg Vicariate—VACANT.

Holy Childhood Association—Rev. Msgr. FREDERICK P. ANNIE, V.G., Mailing Address: P.O. Box 230, Wheeling, 26003. Tel: 304-233-0880.

Diocesan and Foreign Missions, Office of—Rev. Msgr. FREDERICK P. ANNIE, V.G., Coord., Mailing Address: P.O. Box 230, Wheeling, 26003.

Diocesan (Home) Missions—Rev. Msgr. FREDERICK P. ANNIE, V.G., Dir., Mailing Address: P.O. Box 230, Wheeling, 26003.

Propagation of the Faith, Pontifical Society for—Rev. Msgr. FREDERICK P. ANNIE, V.G., Mailing Address: P.O. Box 230, Wheeling, 26003.

Human Resources, Office of—Mr. MICHAEL NAU, Dir., Mailing Address: P.O. Box 230, Wheeling, 26003. Tel: 304-233-0880.

Priests' Health and Retirement Association—Most Rev. MICHAEL J. BRANSFIELD, Pres.; Very Rev. ANTHONY CINCINNATI, S.T.D., V.E., Vice Pres. & Moderator; Mr. CHAD R. CARTER, M.B.A., B.A., Sec., Mailing Address: P.O. Box 230, Wheeling, 26003. Tel: 304-233-0880.

Justice and Life, Office of—Deacon TODD E. GARLAND, 1116 Kanawha Blvd. E., Charleston, 25301. Tel: 304-380-0155.

Migration and Refugee Services, Office of—Mrs. KIM KEENE, Dir., 1116 Kanawha Blvd. E., Charleston, 25301. Tel: 304-343-1036.

Faith Formation, Office of—Mrs. MICHELLE TOMSHACK, Dir., Mailing Address: 1322 Eoff St., 4th Fl., P.O. Box 230, Wheeling, 26003. Tel: 304-233-0880.

Youth and Young Adult Ministry—Mr. ROBERT PERRON, Dir., Mailing Address: 1322 Eoff St., 4th Fl., P.O. Box 230, Wheeling, 26003. Tel: 304-233-0880.

Marriage and Family Life—Mrs. REBECCA ROYSE, Coord., Mailing Address: 1322 Eoff St., 4th Fl., P.O. Box 230, Wheeling, 26003. Tel: 304-233-0880.

Permanent Diaconate Formation—Very Rev. ANTHONY CINCINNATI, S.T.D., V.E., Dir.; Deacon LOUIS J. BELLDINA, M.S., Prog. Assoc., Mailing Address: P.O. Box 230, Wheeling, 26003. Tel: 304-233-0880.

Presbyteral Council—Rev. R. ERIC HALL IV, Chm., St. Francis Xavier Parish, 532 Market St., Parkersburg, 26101-5144.

Prison Ministry, Office of—

Federal Facilities—Deacon JOHN W. SARRAGA, Dir., Mailing Address: c/o St. Patrick, P.O. Box 99, Coalton, 26257-0099. Tel: 304-472-1217.

State Facilities—Deacon RUE C. THOMPSON JR., Dir., Mailing Address: c/o Holy Rosary, 35 Franklin St., Buckhannon, 26201. Tel: 304-472-1217.

Religious Unity, Diocesan Commission for—Deacon DENNIS W. NESSER, J.C.L., 1116 Kanawha Blvd., E., Charleston, 25301. Tel: 304-925-2864.

Safe Environment, Office of—Deacon DOUGLAS W. BREIDING, Coord., 27 13th St., Wheeling, 26003. Tel: 304-233-0880.

Diocesan Committee on Scouting—Mr. DAVID TAMPLEN, Chm.; Rev. DENNIS R. SCHUELKENS JR., Diocesan Chap. to Boy Scouts of America.

Victim Assistance Coordinator—Dr. PATRICIA M. BAILEY, Ph.D., Professional Center III, Ste. 231, 30 Medical Park, Wheeling, 26003. Contacts to Report: Rev. Msgr. FREDERICK P. ANNIE, V.G. Email: fannie@dwc.org; Very Rev. ANTHONY CINCINNATI, S.T.D., V.E., Episcopal Vicar for Clergy. Email: acincinnati@dwc.orgTel: 304-233-0880; Sr. ELLEN F. DUNN, O.P. Email: edunn@dwc.org; Mr. BRYAN MINOR. Email: bminor@dwc.org.

Vocations, Office of—Rev. PAUL A. HUDOCK, Dir., Mailing Address: P.O. Box 230, Wheeling, 26003-0010.

Vocations Promoters—Mr. PATRICK B. MCCARTHY; Revs. CHRISTOPHER M. TURNER; DENNIS R. SCHUELKENS JR.

Catholic Conference of West Virginia—Rev. Msgr. P. EDWARD SADIE, S.T.L., V.F., Exec. Dir.; Very Rev. BRIAN P. O'DONNELL, S.J., Ph.D., Exec. Sec., Mailing Address: 1116 Kanawah Blvd. E., Charleston, 25301-2407.

Women, Office of—Sr. ELLEN F. DUNN, O.P., Dir., Mailing Address: P.O. Box 230, Wheeling, 26003-0010. Tel: 304-233-0880.

Catholic Charismatic Renewal—Deacon GARY W. LANE, Liaison, Mailing Address: Blessed John XXIII Pastoral Center, 100 Hodges Rd., Charleston, 25314. Tel: 304-342-0507; Fax: 304-342-4786.

Office of Worship and Sacraments—Ms. BERNADETTE MCMASTERS, Dir., Mailing Address: P.O. Box 230, Wheeling, 26003-0030. Tel: 304-233-0880.

Diocesan Liturgical Commission—Ms. BERNADETTE MCMASTERS, Mailing Address: P.O. Box 230, Wheeling, 26003. Tel: 304-233-0880.

Department of Catholic Schools—

Schools, Superintendent of—Mr. VINCENT DE PAUL SCHMIDT, Ed.S., M.A., Supt.

Associate Superintendent of Schools—Ms. ROBYN HAMMOND, Dir., Mailing Address: P.O. Box 230, Wheeling, 26003-0030. Tel: 304-233-0880.

Instructional Technology—Ms. JENNIFER L. HORNYAK, Dir., Mailing Address: P.O. Box 230, Wheeling, 26003. Tel: 304-233-0880.

CLERGY, PARISHES, MISSIONS AND PAROCHIAL SCHOOLS

CITY OF WHEELING

(OHIO COUNTY)

1—ST. JOSEPH'S CATHEDRAL (1828), Including former parishes: Blessed Trinity, St. Joan of Arc, and Sacred Heart. Rev. Msgr. Kevin M. Quirk, Rector; Mr. Chris Bayardi, Pastoral Assoc. In Res., Very Rev. Anthony Cincinnati; Rev. Robert G. Park.
Res.: 14 13th St., 26003-0051. Tel: 304-233-4121.

2—ST. ALPHONSUS (1856), Including former parishes St. Mary and St. Ladislaus. Rev. Francis A. O'Kruta; Deacon George Smoulder.
Church & Res. Address: 2111 Market St., 26003-3827. Tel: 304-232-4353; Fax: 304-232-1993.

3—BLESSED TRINITY (1931) Closed. Merged with St. Joseph's Cathedral.

4—CORPUS CHRISTI (1916) Rev. Eugene S. Ostrowski; Deacon Douglas W. Breiding.
Mailing Address: 1518 Warwood Ave., 26003-7197.
Res.: 1516 Warwood Ave., 26003-7197. Tel: 304-277-2911; Fax: 304-277-1287.
School—Tel: 304-277-1220; Fax: 304-277-2823. Mr. Dick Taylor, Prin. Lay Teachers 13; Students 162.
Catechesis/Religious Program—Students 50.

5—IMMACULATE CONCEPTION (ST. MARY) (1873) Closed. Merged with St. Alphonsus.

6—ST. JOAN OF ARC (1923) Closed. Merged with St. Joseph's Cathedral.

7—ST. LADISLAUS (1902) Closed. Merged with St. Alphonsus.

8—ST. MICHAEL (1897) [CEM] Revs. Jeremiah F. McSweeney; William K. Matheny Jr.
Church & Res.: 1225 National Rd., 26003-5791. Tel: 304-242-1560; Fax: 304-243-5710. Email: stmikes@stmikesparish.org. Web: www.stmikesparish.org.
School—1221 National Rd., 26003. Tel: 304-242-3966; Fax: 304-214-6578. Email: school@stmikesparish.org. Mrs. Marilyn Richardson, Prin. Lay Teachers 25; Students 347.
Catechesis/Religious Program—Students 120.

9—OUR LADY OF PEACE (Mt. Olivet) (1962) Rev. Dennis R. Schuelkens Jr., Admin.
Res.: 2 Allendale Rd., Mt. Olivet, 26003-4602. Tel: 304-242-6575.
School—Tel: 304-242-1383; Fax: 304-243-5410. Mrs. C'Ann Reilly, Prin. Lay Teachers 14; Students 192.
Catechesis/Religious Program—Students 22.

10—SACRED HEART (1903) Closed. Merged with St. Joseph's Cathedral.

11—ST. VINCENT DE PAUL (1895) [CEM] Revs. John P. Mulcahy; Gary P. Naegele; Raju Antony; Sr. Diane McCalley, C.S.J., Pastoral Assoc.
Res.: 2244 Marshall Ave., 26003-7440. Tel: 304-242-0406; Fax: 304-243-0837. Email: stvincentdepaulparish@juno.com. Web: www.saintvincentparish.org.
School—127 Key Ave., 26003. Tel: 304-242-5844; Fax: 304-243-1624. Mrs. Rebecca Beabout, Interim Prin. Religious teacher 1; Lay Teachers 25; Students 182.
Catechesis/Religious Program—Sr. Rosella Uding, C.D.P., D.R.E. Students 30.
Mission—Our Lady of Seven Dolors [CEM]Tel: 304-547-5342.

CITY OF CHARLESTON

(KANAWHA COUNTY)

1—ST. AGNES (1923) Rev. Christopher M. Turner; Deacon Gary W. Lane.
Res.: 4807 Staunton Ave., S.E., 25304. Tel: 304-925-2836. Email: stagneschurch@suddenlink.net.
School—4801 Staunton Ave., S.E., 25304. Tel: 304-925-4341; Fax: 304-925-4423. Mrs. Theresa O'Leary, Prin. Lay Teachers 15; Students 130.
Catechesis/Religious Program—Students 44.

2—ST. ANTHONY (1905) Revs. James Kurtz, O.F.M. Cap.; Benjamin F. Madden, O.F.M. Cap.; Anil Gonsalves, O.F.M. Cap.; Deacon David Wuletich. In Res., Rev. Roy Schuster, O.F.M.Cap (Retired).
Res.: 1000 Sixth St., 25302. Tel: 304-342-2716; Fax: 304-342-2716.

3—BASILICA OF THE CO-CATHEDRAL OF THE SACRED HEART (1866) [CEM] Rev. Msgr. P. Edward Sadie, Rector; Rev. Carlos L. Melocoton Jr., Assoc. Rector; Mrs. Ann Weimar, Pastoral Assoc.
Rectory—1114 Virginia St. E., 25301-2879. Tel: 304-342-8175; Fax: 304-344-3907. Email: sacredheart@shccwv.us. Web: www.shccwv.us.
Church: 1032 Virginia St. E., 25301-2879.
School—1035 Quarrier St. E., 25301. Tel: 304-346-5491. Web: shgs.us. Mrs. Terri L. Maier, Prin. Lay Teachers 28; Students 400.
Catechesis/Religious Program—Students 118.

OUTSIDE THE CITIES OF WHEELING AND CHARLESTON

ALDERSON, GREENBRIER CO., ST. MARY (1978), See St. Patrick, Hinton

ANSTED, FAYETTE CO., MISSION OF JESUS OUR SAVIOR, Mission has been suppressed. Records are at Immaculate Conception, Montgomery.

BANCROFT, PUTNAM CO., ST. PATRICK (1892) Rev. Manuel T. Gelido, Admin.
c/o Holy Trinity Parish, P.O. Box 339, Nitro, 25143.

BARRACKVILLE, MARION CO., ALL SAINTS, Merged with St. Joseph, Fairmont; St. Anthony, Grant Town, and Our Lady of the Assumption, Rivesville to form St. Peter the Fisherman, Fairmont.

BARTOW, POCAHONTAS CO., ST. MARK, See St. John Neumann, Marlinton

BECKLEY, RALEIGH CO., ST. FRANCIS DE SALES (1907) [CEM] Rev. Msgr. Samuel S. Sacus; Rev. J. Michael O. Lecias; Deacons W. Donald Wise; John F. Ziolkowski.
Res.: 614 S. Oakwood Ave., 25801. Tel: 304-253-3695 (Parish Office); 304-256-3594 (Rectory); Fax: 304-253-3594. Email: church@stfrancis-wv.org. Web: www.stfrancis-wv.org.
School—622 S. Oakwood Ave., 25801. Tel: 304-252-4087. Fax: 304-252-4087. Email: sfschool@suddenlinkmail.com. Mrs. Karen Wynne, Prin. Lay Teachers 13; Students 158.
Montessori School—Lay Teachers 1; Students 10.
Catechesis/Religious Program—626 S. Oakwood Ave., 25801. Tel: 304-255-4694. Email: osfjanice@stfrancis-wv.org. Students 102.

BEECH BOTTOM, BROOKE CO., HOLY FAMILY, Closed. See St. John, Wellsburg.

BELLE, KANAWHA CO., ST. JOHN (1951) Rev. Albert Alexandrunas, O.F.M.Cap.
Res.: 321 E. Tenth St., 25015. Tel: 304-949-3063.
Catechesis/Religious Program—Students 18.
Mission—Good Shepherd, Tel: 304-595-6002.

BENWOOD, MARSHALL CO., ST. JOHN (1875) Rev. Bekeh U. Utietiang.
Res.: 622 Main St., 26031. Tel: 304-232-6455.
School—Sts. James and John Consolidated School, Tel: 304-232-1587. Marilyn McWhorter, Prin. Lay Teachers 14; Students 115.
Catechesis/Religious Program—Mrs. Jonette Giovengo, D.R.E.

BERKELEY SPRINGS, MORGAN CO., ST. VINCENT DE PAUL (1931) [CEM] Rev. Leonard A. Smith; Deacons John W. Locke; Robert B. Lilly.
67 Liberty St., 25411.
Res.: 38 S. Mercer St., 25411. Tel: 304-258-1311; Fax: 304-258-3936.
Church: 67 Liberty St., P.O. Box 634, 25411.
Catechesis/Religious Program—Students 66.

BLUEFIELD, MERCER CO., SACRED HEART (1895) Rev. Paul J. Wharton; Deacon Donald Hammond.
Res.: 1003 Wyoming St., P.O. Box 608, 24701-0608. Tel: 304-327-5623; Fax: 304-327-7769. Email: shcc@sacredheartblfd.org. Web: www.sacredheartblfd.org.
Catechesis/Religious Program—Students 72.

BOOMER, FAYETTE CO., ST. ANTHONY'S SHRINE (1954), See Immaculate Conception, Montgomery

BRIDGEPORT, HARRISON CO., ALL SAINTS (1946) Rev. Harry N. Cramer.
Res.: 317 E. Main St., 26330-1750. Tel: 304-842-2283; Fax: 304-842-2299. Email: ascwv1@frontier.net. Web: allsaintsbridgeport.com.
School—Harrison Co. Catholic School System, Tel: 304-624-5129.
Catechesis/Religious Program—Students 193.

BRUCETON MILLS, PRESTON CO., MARY HELP OF CHRISTIANS (1983), See St. Luke, Cheat Lake

BUCKHANNON, UPSHUR CO., HOLY ROSARY (1921) Rev. Ronald J. Nikodem, S.M.; Bro. Roy Madigan, S.M.; Deacon Rue Thompson Jr.
Church: 35 Franklin St., P.O. Box 848, 26201-0848. Tel: 304-472-3414.
Rectory—9 Lincoln Heights, 26021.
Catechesis/Religious Program—Students 56.
Mission—Sacred Heart (1902) [CEM] Pickens, Randolph Co. 26230.

BURNSVILLE, BRAXTON CO., ST. MICHAEL'S CENTER, See St. Thomas, Gassaway

CAIRO, RITCHIE CO., ST. WILLIAM CHURCH, Closed. See Christ Our Hope, Harrisville

CAMDEN, LEWIS CO., ST. BONIFACE (Leading Creek) (1875) [CEM] Rev. George Manjadi.
Res.: 9140 U.S. Hwy. 33 W., 26338-8256. Tel: 304-269-1767.
Chapel—St. Clare, St. Clare [CEM]
Catechesis/Religious Program—Students 3.

CAMERON, MARSHALL CO., ST. MARTIN OF TOURS (1871) [CEM] Unassigned.Mailing Address: 64 Frohnapfel Ln., Proctor, 26055.
Church: 5 Fitzgerald Ave., 26033. Tel: 304-447-3999.
Catechesis/Religious Program—Cindy Fox, D.R.E. Students 5.

CAROLINA, MARION CO., ST. MARY, See St. Peter, Farmington, 204 Furbee Ave., Mannington, 26582-1399.

CENTURY, UPSHUR CO., OUR LADY OF SORROWS, Closed. See Holy Rosary, Buckhannon. Suppressed as a mission 12/20/96.

CHAPMANVILLE, LOGAN CO., ST. BARBARA (1979), See St. Francis, Logan
Catechesis/Religious Program—
Mission—St. Barbara Catholic Community Church HC-74, P.O. Box 3018, 25508. Tel: 304-855-7962.

CHARLES TOWN, JEFFERSON CO., ST. JAMES (1889) [CEM], Includes St. Peter, Harper's Ferry. Revs. John S. Ledford; Jose Manuel Escalante; Deacon David E. Galvin; Mrs. Jackie Moler, Pastoral Assoc.; Mr. Gary Penkala, Liturgy & Music.
Mailing Address: 49 Crosswinds Dr., 25414-3933. Fax: 304-728-9039.
Res.: 311 S. George St., 25414-1633. Tel: 304-725-6801.
Catechesis/Religious Program—Students 350.

CHEAT LAKE, MONONGALIA CO., ST. LUKE THE EVANGELIST (1980) Rev. Vincent Ezhanikatt Joseph (India).
Res.: 19 Jo Glen Dr., Morgantown, 26508-4434. Tel: 304-594-2353; Fax: 304-594-2359. Email: stlukeschurch@comcast.net.
School—St. Francis Central Catholic School, 41 Guthrie Ln., Morgantown, 26508. Tel: 304-291-5070; Fax: 304-291-5104. Mr. John Downey, Prin. Students 380.
Catechesis/Religious Program—Email: education.stlukes1980@comcast.net. Students 132.
Mission—Mary Help of Christians (1983) Bruceton Mills, Preston Co. 26525.

CHESTER, HANCOCK CO., SACRED HEART (1902) Rev. Eric B. Antwi.
Res.: 424 Fourth St., 26034-0313. Tel: 304-387-0198; Fax: 304-387-0198.
Catechesis/Religious Program—Mr. Robert Glass, D.R.E. Students 50.

CLARKSBURG, HARRISON CO.

1—HOLY ROSARY, See Immaculate Conception, Clarksburg

2—HOLY TRINITY, See Immaculate Conception, Clarksburg

3—IMMACULATE CONCEPTION (1864) [CEM] Rev. Casey B. Mahone.
Res.: 126 E. Pike St., 26301-2155. Email: immaculateconcep@ma.rr.com. Web: www.parishic.com.
Parish Office—Tel: 304-622-8243.
Catechesis/Religious Program—Students 140.

4—ST. JAMES THE APOSTLE (1924) Rev. Alfred U. Obiudu (Nigeria); Deacon Thomas Trunzo, Pastoral Assoc.
Res.: 2107 Pride Ave., 26301-1819. Tel: 304-622-1668; Fax: 304-622-4618. Email: stjameschurch@wvdsl.net.
School—Harrison County Catholic School System, Tel: 304-623-1026; 304-622-9831; Fax: 304-623-1026. See Immaculate Conception
Catechesis/Religious Program—Tel: 304-624-5811. Students 52.

5—ST. JOHN THE BAPTIST, See Immaculate Conception, Clarksburg

CLENDENIN, KANAWHA CO., ST. ANNE, See Our Lady of the Hills, Elkview

COALBURG, GOOD SHEPHERD (1866), See St. John, Belle
Catechesis/Religious Program—Students 12.

COALTON, RANDOLPH CO., ST. PATRICK CHURCH (1918) [CEM 4] Very Rev. Donald X. Higgs.
Res.: 200 Church St., P.O. Box 99, 26257-0099. Tel: 304-636-5754.
Catechesis/Religious Program—Students 15.

DAVIS, TUCKER CO., ST. VERONICA (1897) Closed. For inquiries for parish records, please see St. Thomas Aquinas Church, Thomas.

DUNBAR, KANAWHA CO., CHRIST THE KING (1942) Rev. Manuel T. Gelido.
Mailing Address: P.O. Box 339, Nitro, 25143. Tel: 304-755-0791; Fax: 304-755-3473.
Church: 1504 Grosscup Ave., 25064-2925. Students 35.
Catechesis/Religious Program—Students 17.

ELIZABETH, WIRT CO., ST. ELIZABETH OF HUNGARY (1977), See Holy Redeemer, Spencer

ELKINS, RANDOLPH CO., ST. BRENDAN (1897) [CEM] Very Rev. Donald X. Higgs; Deacons John W. Sarraga; Raymond Godwin; Lou Belldina.
Res.: Rte. 4, Box 515, 26241. Tel: 304-636-0467; 304-636-0546. Email: frdxh@aol.com. Web: www.stbrendanwv.org.
Catechesis/Religious Program—Students 105.
Chapel—St. John Bosco (1948) Rte. 1, Box 9D, Huttonsville, 26273-9737.
Station—Huttonsville Correctional Center Huttonsville. Tel: 304-338-6323.

ELKVIEW, KANAWHA CO., OUR LADY OF THE HILLS (1977) Rev. James Kurtz, O.F.M. Cap.
Res.: 100 Jackson Dr., 25071-9324. Tel: 304-965-7670.
Catechesis/Religious Program—Students 19.
Mission—St. Anne, (Suppressed as a mission)

FAIRMONT, MARION CO.

1—ST. ANTHONY (1964) Rev. Saju Puthenpurackal Joseph.
Res.: 1660 Mary Lou Retton Dr., 26554. Tel: 304-363-1328.
School—Fairmont Catholic Grade School, Tel: 304-363-5313.
Catechesis/Religious Program—Students 201.

2—IMMACULATE CONCEPTION (1960) Rev. Richard Ulam, O.S.B.; Sr. Stella Cronauer, C.S.J., Pastoral Assoc.
Mailing Address: 406 Alta Vista Ave., 26554. Tel: 304-363-5796; Fax: 304-366-4937.
School—Fairmont Catholic Grade School, 407 Jackson St., 26554. Tel: 304-363-5313.
Catechesis/Religious Program—Faculty 24; Students 190.

3—ST. JOSEPH'S (1909) Merged with St. Peter's, Fairmont to form The New St. Peter the Fisherman, Fairmont.

4—ST. PETER THE FISHERMAN CATHOLIC CHURCH (1873) [CEM 2], (Formerly St. Peter's, Fairmont.) Merged with St. Joseph, Fairmont; St. Anthony, Grant Town; Our Lady of the Assumption, Rivesville, and All Saints, Barrackville. Rev. Robert A. Perriello; Deacon David P. Lester.
Res.: 407 Jackson St., 26554-2941. Tel: 304-363-7434; Fax: 304-363-2660. Email: stpeterfisherman@wvdsl.net. Web: www.thefisherman.org.
School—Fairmont Catholic Grade School, 416A Madison St., 26554. Tel: 304-363-5313; Fax: 304-363-7701. Email: office@fairmontcatholic.com. Mr. Richard Pellegrin, Prin. Faculty 15; Students 182.
Catechesis/Religious Program—Students 189.

FARMINGTON, MARION CO., ST. PETER'S (1921) Rev. Douglas B. Sutton.
Mailing Address: 204 Furbee Ave., Mannington, 26582-1399. Tel: 304-986-2321; Fax: 304-986-1419.
Catechesis/Religious Program—Tel: 304-825-1397. Students 17.

FOLLANSBEE, BROOKE CO., ST. ANTHONY (1906) Revs. Pete A. Giannamore; James R. DeViese.
Res.: 1017 Jefferson St., 26037-1334. Tel: 304-527-2286; Fax: 304-527-2548.
Catechesis/Religious Program—Tel: 304-527-3966. Students 150.

FORT ASHBY, MINERAL CO., ANNUNCIATION OF OUR LORD (1981) Rev. Benedict E. Kapa.
Res.: 238 North Hwy. 28, P.O. Box 1560, 26719-1560. Tel: 304-298-3392; Fax: 304-298-3419. Email: annunciationchurch@atlanticbbn.net.
Catechesis/Religious Program—Students 43.

FRANKLIN, PENDLETON CO., ST. ELIZABETH ANN SETON (1975) Rev. Mario R. Claro; Deacon John E. Windett.
Church & Res.: 141 Walnut St., P.O. Box 890, 26807. Tel: 304-358-7012.
Catechesis/Religious Program—Students 22.

GARY, MCDOWELL CO., OUR LADY OF VICTORY (1904) [CEM] Rev. Thomas Paulose Manickathan, H.G.N.
Church: 38 Church St., P.O. Box 130, 24836-0130. Tel: 304-448-2749.
Catechesis/Religious Program—Students 4.

GASSAWAY, BRAXTON CO., ST. THOMAS (1973) Revs. Matheus B. Ro, S.V.D. (Indonesia); Dominikus Baok, S.V.D.
Res.: 624 Kanawha St., 26624-1208. Tel: 304-364-5895; Fax: 304-364-8099.
Catechesis/Religious Program—Students 37.

GLEN DALE, MARSHALL CO., ST. JUDE (1968) Rev. Edward G. Stafford, T.O.R.
Res.: 710 Jefferson Ave., P.O. Box 147, 26038-0147. Tel: 304-845-8165 (Rectory); 304-845-2646 (Office); Fax: 304-845-3015.
Catechesis/Religious Program—Students 50.

GLENVILLE, GILMER CO., GOOD SHEPHERD (1958) Rev. Charles E. McGinnis Jr.
Res.: 701 Mineral Rd., 26351-1310. Tel: 304-462-7130; Fax: 304-462-7130. Email: svdglenville@rtol.net.
Catechesis/Religious Program—Tel: 304-462-7130; Fax: 304-462-7130. Students 7.

GRAFTON, TAYLOR CO., ST. AUGUSTINE (1852), (Irish), [CEM 2] Rev. James E. O'Connor.
Res.: 17 W. Washington St., 26354-1398. Tel: 304-265-3861 (Office); Fax: 304-265-2810.
Catechesis/Religious Program—Students 65.

GRANT TOWN, MARION CO., ST. ANTHONY'S (1907) Merged with St. Joseph, Fairmont; Our Lady of the Assumption, Rivesville and All Saints, Barrackville to form St. Peter the Fisherman, Fairmont.

GRANTSVILLE, CALHOUN CO., JESUS CHRIST, PRINCE OF PEACE (1977) Closed. See Holy Redeemer, Spencer. Suppressed as a mission 12/1/08.

HAMLIN, LINCOLN CO., CHRIST IN THE HILLS, See St. Stephen, Ona or St. Mary, Madison

HARPERS FERRY, JEFFERSON CO., ST. PETER (1830) Closed. Merged with St. James, Charles Town.

HARRISVILLE, RITCHIE CO., CHRIST OUR HOPE (1980) [CEM] Rev. Ronald G. Prechtl; Sr. Maureen Mylott, S.C., Pastoral Assoc.
Res.: Rte. 1, Box 44A, 26362-9707. Tel: 304-643-4261. Email: mmylottsc@yahoo.com.
Church: Pullman Rd. & E. Main, 26362-9707.
Catechesis/Religious Program—Students 17.
Chapel—Pennsboro, St. Joseph (1870) [CEM] Penn Ave., Pennsboro, 26415.

HEDGESVILLE, BERKELEY CO., ST. BERNADETTE (1982), See St. Joseph, Martinsburg
Catechesis/Religious Program—Students 20.

HINTON, SUMMERS CO., ST. PATRICK (1874), (Irish),

[CEM 2] Rev. Thomas W. Dagle.
309 Second Ave., 25951-0008.
Mission—St. Mary of the Greenbrier 101 Davis St., State Rte. 12, P.O. Box 441, Alderson, Greenbrier Co. 24910.
Chapel—St. Colman (1882), (Irish Mountain, WV)
Catechesis/Religious Program—Students 12.

HOLDEN, LOGAN CO., ST. MARY'S (1961) Consolidated with Our Lady of Mount Carmel, Logan, to form St. Francis of Assisi, Logan.

HUNTINGTON, CABELL CO.

1—ST. JOSEPH'S (1872) [CEM] Rev. Msgr. Lawrence J. Luciana.
Res.: 1304 Sixth Ave., P.O. Box 369, 25708. Tel: 304-525-5202; Fax: 304-525-0903.
School—1326 Sixth Ave., 25701. Tel: 304-522-2644; Fax: 304-522-2512. Mrs. Carol Templeton, Prin. Lay Teachers 10; Students 131.

2—OUR LADY OF FATIMA (1952) Rev. James M. Sobus.
Res.: 545 Norway Ave., 25705. Tel: 304-525-0866; Fax: 304-781-3841.
School—535 Norway Ave., 25705. Tel: 304-523-2861; 304-523-2863. Mr. Jeff Jackson, Prin. Lay Teachers 18; Students 172.
Catechesis/Religious Program—Students 60.

3—ST. PETER CLAVER (1937), (African American), Rev. Livinus Uba.
Res.: 828 Fifteenth St., 25701. Tel: 304-523-7311.
Catechesis/Religious Program—Students 16.

4—SACRED HEART (1934) Rev. Livinus Uba; Deacon Michael R. Prestera Jr.; Sr. Mary Terence Wall, S.A.C., Pastoral Assoc.
Res.: 2015 Adams Ave., 25704-1419. Tel: 304-429-4318 (Office); Fax: 304-429-4319.
Catechesis/Religious Program—Students 33.

HURRICANE, PUTNAM CO., CATHOLIC CHURCH OF THE ASCENSION (1980) Rev. Neil R. Buchlein.
Res.: 905 Hickory Mill Rd., 25526. Tel: 304-562-5816. Email: ascensionwv@hotmail.com.
Catechesis/Religious Program—Students 202.

INWOOD, BERKELEY CO., ST. LEO (1982) Rev. D. Brian Shoda; Deacon Charles C. Quigley.
Res.: 2109 Sulphur Springs Rd., P.O. Box 93, 25428-0093. Tel: 304-229-8945; Fax: 304-229-9755.
Catechesis/Religious Program—Students 451.

KEYSER, MINERAL CO., ASSUMPTION (1874) [CEM] Rev. Ivan M. Lebar, T.O.R.; Bro. Richard Gates, T.O.R., Pastoral Assoc.
Res.: 34 James St., 26726-2721. Tel: 304-788-2488; Fax: 304-788-0647. Email: acckwv@frontier.com. Web: www.dwc.org.
Catechesis/Religious Program—Students 45.

KINGWOOD, PRESTON CO., ST. SEBASTIAN (1914) [CEM 3] Rev. Arthur Bufogle; Sr. Mary Priscilla Weidenschlager, C.S.J., Pastoral Assoc.
Res.: 322 E. Main St., 26537-1237. Tel: 304-329-1519; Fax: 304-329-2546. Email: ccpccath@frontier.com.
Church: 324 E. Main St., 26537.
Catechesis/Religious Program—Students 66.
Mission—St. Edward 1204 E. State Ave., Terra Alta, Preston Co. 26764.

LEWISBURG, GREENBRIER CO., ST. LOUIS, KING OF FRANCE, Closed. See St. Catherine, Ronceverte

LITTLETON, WETZEL CO., ASSUMPTION OF THE BLESSED VIRGIN MARY, See St. Patrick, Mannington

LOGAN, LOGAN CO., ST. FRANCIS OF ASSISI (1996) Rev. Yesu Golla, H.G.N.; Mrs. Connie Bazzilla, Pastoral Assoc.
Res.: 561 Main St., 25601-3899. Tel: 304-752-3017; Fax: 304-752-3017.
Church: Stratton St., 25601.
Catechesis/Religious Program—Students 12.

LOVEBERRY, ST. BERNARD, See St. Patrick, Weston

LUBECK, WOOD CO., ST. MONICA'S (1976) [CEM] Rev. Eric Hall IV.
Res.: 532 Market St., Parkersburg, 26101. Tel: 304-422-6799; Fax: 304-422-6789.
Church: State Rte. 68, Lubeck Washington.
Catechesis/Religious Program—Students 12.

MADISON, BOONE CO., ST. MARY, QUEEN OF HEAVEN (1957) Rev. Soosai Arpudam Arokiadass, H.G.N. (India), Admin.
Res.: P.O. Box 467, 25130-0467. Tel: 304-369-4538.
Church: 51 Madison Ave., 25130.
Catechesis/Religious Program—Students 8.

MAN, LOGAN CO., ST. EDMUND (1961) Rev. Yesu Golla, H.G.N., Admin.
110 Bridge St., 25635.
Res.: 561 Main St., Logan, 25601-3899. Tel: 304-752-3017.
Church & Mailing Address: 106 N. Bridge St., 25635.

MANNINGTON, MARION CO., ST. PATRICK'S (1897), (Irish), Rev. Douglas B. Sutton.
Res.: 204 Furbee Ave., 26582-1399. Tel: 304-986-2321; Fax: 304-986-1419.
Catechesis/Religious Program—Tel: 304-986-1624. Students 23.
Mission—Assumption of the Blessed Virgin Mary (1859) [CEM 2], (Suppressed Sept. 1, 2001)

MARLINTON, POCAHONTAS CO., ST. JOHN NEUMANN (1977) [CEM] Rev. Mark T. Gallipeau.
Res.: 714 10th Ave., 24954-1314. Tel: 304-799-6778.
Mission—St. Mark the Evangelist (1977) Rt. 92-250, Bartow, Pocahontas Co. 24920.
Chapel—St. Bernard
Catechesis/Religious Program—Students 23.

MARTINSBURG, BERKELEY CO., ST. JOSEPH'S (1803) [CEM 2] Rev. Msgr. Patrick L. Fryer; Sr. Patricia Endres, D.C., Pastoral Assoc.
Mailing Address: 336 S. Queen St., 25401-3213. In Res., Rev. Michael Cavanaugh, O.S.F.S.
Res.: 219 S. Queen St., 25401-3213. Tel: 304-264-8947; Fax: 304-263-7357. Email: stjoemart@frontier.com. Web: www.parishesonline.com/stjosephmartinsburg.
School—110 E. Stephen St., 25401. Tel: 304-267-6447; Fax: 304-267-6573. Email: info@stjosephparishschool.us. Web: www.stjosephparishschool.us. Daughters of Charity of St. Vincent de Paul 1; Lay Teachers 22; Students 303.
Catechesis/Religious Program—Students 89.
Mission—St. Bernadette Office: 113 W. Main St., P.O. Box 11, Hedgesville, Berkeley Co. 25427. Tel: 304-754-7830; Fax: 304-754-7830. Email: stbernadette@frontier.com. Church: 109 W. Main St., Hedgesville, 25427.

MASONTOWN, PRESTON CO., ST. ZITA (1962) Rev. Arthur Bufogle; Sr. Mary Priscilla Weidenschlager, C.S.J., Pastoral Assoc.
322 E. Main St., Kingwood, 26537-1237.
Rectory—St. Zita Rectory, 152 Roosevelt Ave., 26542.
Email: ccpccath@frontier.com.
Church: 33 Maple St., 26542.
Catechesis/Religious Program—Students 15.

MAYSEL, CLAY CO., RISEN LORD (1972) Rev. Matheus B. Ro, S.V.D. (Indonesia).
Mailing Address: 67 Wallback Rd., 25133. Tel: 304-587-4740.
Catechesis/Religious Program—Students 14.

MCMECHEN, MARSHALL CO., ST. JAMES (1900) Rev. Bekeh Ukelina Utietiang.
Mailing Address: 328 Logan St., 26040. Tel: 304-232-1227.
School—Sts. James and John Consolidated Schools, Tel: 304-232-1587. Mrs. Jennifer Marsh, Prin. Lay Teachers 7; Students 98.
Catechesis/Religious Program—Students 254.

MIDDLEBOURNE, TYLER CO., ST. LAWRENCE, See Mater Dolorosa, Paden City
Catechesis/Religious Program—Darlene Koerber, D.R.E.

MONONGAH, MARION CO., HOLY SPIRIT (1975), (Polish—Italian), [CEM] Rev. Saju Puthenpurackal Joseph.
Res.: 687 Maple Ter., 26554-1116. Tel: 304-534-3020; Fax: 304-534-5910.
Catechesis/Religious Program—Students 38.

MONTGOMERY, FAYETTE CO., IMMACULATE CONCEPTION (1888) Rev. John Rice; Deacon John Divita.
Res.: P.O. Box 65, 25136. Tel: 304-442-2101. Email: ic_sa@frontier.com.
Mission—St. Anthony Shrine (1928) P.O. Box 428, Boomer, Fayette Co. 25031. Tel: 304-779-2561.
Catechesis/Religious Program—Tel: 304-442-5224. Students 50.

MOOREFIELD, HARDY CO., EPIPHANY OF THE LORD (1980) [CEM] [JC] Rev. Giles LeVasseur.
Church: 2029 State Rd. 55, 26836. Tel: 304-434-2547.
Catechesis/Religious Program—Tel: 304-257-1057; Fax: 304-257-9442. Students 12.

MORGANTOWN, MONONGALIA CO.

1—ST. FRANCIS DE SALES CATHOLIC CHURCH (2003), (Formerly St. Theresa's, Morgantown. Merged with St. Elizabeth Ann Seton, Westover to form The St. Theresa/St. Elizabeth Ann Seton, Morgantown.); (Formerly The New St. Theresa & St. Elizabeth Ann Seton) Very Rev. Mark Ward, C.P.; Sr. Nancy White, C.S.J., Pastoral Assoc.
Res.: One Guthrie Ln., 26508. Tel: 304-296-5353; Fax: 304-296-8200. Email: desaleswv01@comcast.net. Web: www.stfrancisdesalesparish.com.
School—St. Francis Central Catholic School, 41 Guthrie Ln., 26508. Tel: 304-291-5070. Mr. John Downey, Prin.
Catechesis/Religious Program—Students 90.

2—ST. JOHN UNIVERSITY PARISH, NEWMAN HALL (1966) Revs. Frederick Byrne, O.S.B.; Rey D. Landicho; Deacons Joseph Prentiss; Stephen A. Olenchock.
Res.: 1481 University Ave., 26505-5598. Tel: 304-296-8231; Fax: 304-296-4650. Email: stjohnmorgantown@comcast.net. Web: www.stjohnmorgantown.com.
School—St. Francis Central Catholic School, 41 Guthrie Ln., 26508. Tel: 304-291-5070; Fax: 304-291-5104. Mr. John Downey, Prin.
Catechesis/Religious Program—Students 125.

MOUNDSVILLE, MARSHALL CO., ST. FRANCIS XAVIER'S (1857) Revs. Edward G. Stafford, T.O.R.; Terrance Adams, T.O.R.; Ranjan Prekash Ekka, T.O.R.
Church: 610 Jefferson Ave., 26041-2106.
Res.: 912 Seventh St., 26041-2106. Tel: 304-845-1593; Fax: 304-845-2006.
School—(Grades PreK-2), 600 Jefferson Ave., 26041. Tel: 304-845-2562; Fax: 304-845-0016. Ms. Sharon Ublen, Prin. Lay Teachers 5; Students 15; Preschool 27.
Catechesis/Religious Program—Students 30.
Station—Northern Regional Jail and Correctional Facility, Tel: 304-843-4067.

MOUNT HOPE, FAYETTE CO.
MISSION—ST. ANTHONY, Suppressed as a mission June 21, 1994.

MULLENS, WYOMING CO., ST. JOHN THE EVANGELIST (1923) Rev. John C. Reich.
Res.: 13 Terry St., 25882-1624. Tel: 304-294-8128; Fax: 304-294-8128.
Catechesis/Religious Program—Students 9.
Mission—Holy Cross 595 Appalachian Hwy., P.O. Box 375, Pineville, Wyoming Co. 24874. Tel: 304-732-6199.

NEW CUMBERLAND, HANCOCK CO., IMMACULATE CONCEPTION (1904) Rev. Eric B. Antwi.
Res.: 1016 Ridge Ave., 26047-0666. Tel: 304-564-5068; Fax: 304-564-7063. Email: iccparish@comcast.net.
Catechesis/Religious Program—Students 15.

NEW MARTINSVILLE, WETZEL CO., ST. VINCENT DE PAUL (1901) Rev. John P. McDonough.
Res.: 21 Rosary Rd., 26155-1602. Tel: 304-455-4615; Fax: 304-455-4617. Email: office@svdpnm.org. Web: www.svdpnm.org.
Catechesis/Religious Program—Students 80.

NITRO, KANAWHA CO., HOLY TRINITY (1962) Rev. Manuel T. Gelido.
Mailing Address: P.O. Box 339, 25143-0339. Tel: 304-755-0791; Fax: 304-755-3473.
Res.: 2219-22nd St., P.O. Box 339, 25143-0339. Tel: 304-755-0791; Fax: 304-755-3473.
Catechesis/Religious Program—Students 61.
Mission—St. Patrick 207 Jefferson St., P.O. Box 238, Bancroft, Putnam Co. 25011. Tel: 304-586-3485; Fax: 304-586-3485.

OAK HILL, FAYETTE CO., SS. PETER AND PAUL (1906) [CEM] Rev. Paul D. Yuenger.
Res.: 129 Elmore St., 25901-2628. Tel: 304-465-5445. Email: pastor@ssppcatholic.org. Web: www.ssppcatholic.org.
School—123 Elmore St., 25901-2628. Tel: 304-465-5045; Fax: 304-465-8726. Email: principal@ssppcatholic.org. George Scott Vargo, Prin. Lay Teachers 8; Students 120.
Catechesis/Religious Program—Students 73.

ONA, CABELL CO., ST. STEPHEN (1980) Rev. James M. Sobus.
Res.: 2491 James River Tpke., 25545-9722. Tel: 304-743-3234. Email: ststephens@suddenlinkmail.com. Web: www.ststephens1.com.
Catechesis/Religious Program—Students 20.

PADEN CITY, TYLER AND WETZEL COS., MATER DOLOROSA (1921) Rev. James B. McCafferty, S.M.; Deacon N. Rollin Fagert. In Res., Rev. James LaCrosse, S.M.
Res.: 302 E. Main St., 26159-1736. Tel: 304-337-9837.
Catechesis/Religious Program—Students 6.
Mission—St. Lawrence P.O. Box 267, Middlebourne, Tyler Co. 26149. Tel: 304-758-4649.

PARKERSBURG, WOOD CO.

1—ST. FRANCIS XAVIER'S (1853) [CEM 3] Rev. Eric Hall IV; Deacons Douglas A. Deem; James R. Kelly.
Res.: 532 Market St., 26101-5144. Tel: 304-422-6799. Email: stxoffice@stx-pburg.org. Web: www.stx-pburg.org.
Catechesis/Religious Program—Tel: 304-422-6786; Fax: 304-422-6789. Students 27.

2—ST. MARGARET MARY (1923) Very Rev. Joseph L. Peterson; Rev. Andrew M. Switzer; Deacons George B. Showalter; John Maher.
Res.: 2500 Dudley Ave., 26101-2695. Tel: 304-428-1262; Fax: 304-422-4905. Email: stmmpastor@suddenlinkmail.com. Web: stmmdwc.org.
Catechesis/Religious Program—Tel: 304-865-1470. Email: stmmpsr@suddenlinkmail.com. Students 146.

PARSONS, TUCKER CO., OUR LADY OF MERCY (1959), See St. Thomas, Thomas, P.O. Box 300, Thomas, 26292-0300.
Catechesis/Religious Program—Students 22.

PENNSBORO, RITCHIE CO., ST. JOSEPH CHAPEL, See Christ Our Hope, Harrisville

PETERSBURG, GRANT CO., ST. MARY'S (1971) [JC] Rev. Giles LeVasseur.
Rectory—5 Pierpont St., 26847-1633. Tel: 304-257-1057. Email: smcc2@frontiernet.net.
Church: 4 Grant St., 26847-1633. Fax: 304-257-9442. Email: smcc2@frontiernet.net.
Catechesis/Religious Program—Students 4.

PHILIPPI, BARBOUR CO., ST. ELIZABETH PARISH (1953) Rev. James O'Connor; Deacon A. Ray Shaw III.
Res.: Rte. 3, Box 257, 26416-9581. Tel: 304-457-2641.
Catechesis/Religious Program— Patty Bowmar, D.R.E. Students 7.

PICKENS, RANDOLPH CO., SACRED HEART (1963), See Holy Rosary, Buckhannon, 35 Franklin St., P.O. Box 848, Buckhannon, 26201-0848.
Catechesis/Religious Program—Doris Sandreth, D.R.E. Students 1.

PINEVILLE, WYOMING CO., HOLY CROSS (1963), See St. John the Evangelist, Mullens, 13 Terry St., Mullens, 25882-1624.
Catechesis/Religious Program—Students 1.

POINT PLEASANT, MASON CO., SACRED HEART (1948) Rev. David J. Schmitt (Retired).
Res.: 2222 Jackson Ave., 25550-2004. Tel: 304-675-4602.
Catechesis/Religious Program—Students 22.
Mission—St. Joseph (1856) [CEM] 3rd St. & Pomeroy St., Mason, Mason Co. 25260.
Catechesis/Religious Program—Students 6.

POWHATAN, MCDOWELL CO., SACRED HEART (1895) Rev. Thomas Paulose Manickathan, H.G.N.
Res.: HC 76, Box 402, 24877. Tel: 304-862-3494.
Catechesis/Religious Program—Students 5.

PRINCETON, MERCER CO., SACRED HEART (1915) Rev. Paul J. Wharton; Deacon Don M. Hammond, Campus Minister.
Res.: 507 Harrison St., 24740-3198. Tel: 304-425-3664; Fax: 304-425-3676. Email: church@sacredheartprinceton.org.
Catechesis/Religious Program—Students 96.
Campus Ministry, Concord College—Athens, 24712. Tel: 304-384-9502.

RAINELLE, GREENBRIER CO., SACRED HEART (1951) [CEM 2] Rev. Thomas W. Dagle.
401 13th St., 25962. Tel: 304-438-8687.
Res.: 309 2nd Ave., Hinton, 25951. Tel: 304-466-3966.
Chapel—SpringDale, Sacred Heart [CEM], (1876)
Catechesis/Religious Program—Students 6.

RAVENSWOOD, JACKSON CO., ST. MATTHEW (1957) Rev. Arok Sundar, O.F.M. (India).
Res.: 600 Crooks Ave., 26164-1312. Tel: 304-273-2175. Email: stmatthewravens@gmail.com.
Catechesis/Religious Program—Students 47.

RICHWOOD, NICHOLAS CO., HOLY FAMILY (1902) [CEM] Rev. Jerome D. Rawa, S.M.; Deacon John F. Ceslovnik; Bro. Richard McKenna, S.M., Pastoral Assoc.
Res.: 4 Maple St., 26261-1318. Tel: 304-846-2873; Fax: 304-846-2873. Email: hofam2@frontier.com.
Catechesis/Religious Program—Students 8.

RIDGELEY, MINERAL CO., ST. ANTHONY (1916) Rev. Benedict E. Kapa.
Res.: 238 N. Hwy. 28, P.O. Box 1560, Fort Ashby, 26719. Tel: 304-298-3392; Fax: 304-298-3419. Email: annunciationchurch@atlanticbbn.net.
Catechesis/Religious Program—Students 8.

RIVESVILLE, MARION CO., OUR LADY OF THE ASSUMPTION, Merged with St. Joseph, Fairmont; St. Anthony, Grant Town; Our Lady of the Assumption, Rivesville, and All Saints, Barrackville to form St. Peter the Fisherman, Fairmont.; See St. Anthony, Grant Town

ROANOKE, LEWIS CO., ST. BRIDGET, See St. Patrick, Weston

ROMNEY, HAMPSHIRE CO., OUR LADY OF GRACE (1951) Rev. Benedict E. Kapa, Temp. Admin.; Deacon Lawrence Hammel.
Res.: 299 School St., 26757-0871. Tel: 304-822-5561.
Catechesis/Religious Program—Students 41.

RONCEVERTE, GREENBRIER CO., ST. CATHERINE OF SIENA (1892) Rev. John Chapin Engler Jr.; Deacon William B. Strange Jr.
Res. & Mailing Address: 325 W. Main St., White Sulphur Springs, 24986-2413. Tel: 304-647-4514.
Catechesis/Religious Program—Tom Soper, D.R.E. Students 30.
Chapel—The Immaculate Conception of the Blessed Virgin Mary [CEM]
Chaplaincy—WV School of Osteopathic Medicine, Lewisburg, 24901.

ST. ALBANS, KANAWHA CO., ST. FRANCIS OF ASSISI (1947) [CEM] Rev. Patrick M. McDonough.
Res.: 1023 Sixth Ave., 25177. Tel: 304-727-3033; Fax: 304-727-6640.
School—(Grades PreK-5), 525 Holley St., Saint Albans, 25177. Tel: 304-727-5690; Fax: 304-727-5690. Priests 1; Lay Teachers 8; Students 163.
Catechesis/Religious Program—Students 40.

ST. CLARA, ST. CLARE, See St. Boniface, Camden

ST. JOSEPH SETTLEMENT, MARSHALL CO., ST. JOSEPH'S (1853), (German), [CEM] Unassigned.
Res. & Mailing Address: 64 Frohnapfel Ln., Proctor, 26055. Tel: 304-447-3999; Fax: 304-447-3999.
Catechesis/Religious Program—Cindy Fox, D.R.E. Students 10.

ST. MARYS, PLEASANTS CO., ST. JOHN (1913) [JC] Rev. Ronald G. Prechtl.
Mailing Address: P.O. Box 338, 26170-0338.
Res.: 310 Washington St., 26170-1313. Tel: 304-684-7669. Email: stjohnsm@suddenlinkmail.com.
Catechesis/Religious Program—Students 24.

SALEM, HARRISON CO., SACRED HEART (1915) [CEM] Rev. Alfred U. Obiudu (Nigeria).
Res.: Rte. 23 S. off Rte. 50, R.R. 5 Box 1424, 26426. Tel: 304-782-2277. Email: shp@verizon.net.
Catechesis/Religious Program—Students 18.

SHEPHERDSTOWN, JEFFERSON CO., ST. AGNES (1794) [CEM] Rev. T. Matthew Rowgh; Deacon Anthony F. Maciorowski.
Mailing Address: P.O. Box 1603, 25443-1603.
Res.: 216 S. Duke St., 25443-1603. Tel: 304-876-6436; Fax: 304-876-6436. Email: stagnescenter@frontiernet.net. Web: stagnesshepherdstown.org.
Catechesis/Religious Program—Students 126.

SHINNSTON, HARRISON CO., ST. ANN'S (1923) Rev. Karl R. Wohinc.
Res.: 610 Pike St., 26431-1451. Tel: 304-592-2733.
Mission—Holy Family (1925) Spelter, Harrison Co. 26438.

SISTERSVILLE, TYLER CO., HOLY ROSARY (1898) Rev. James B. McCafferty, S.M.; Deacon N. Rollin Fagert.
Church: 519 Main St., 26175-1405. Tel: 304-652-6381; 304-337-9837 (Rectory).
Catechesis/Religious Program—Students 6.

SOUTH CHARLESTON, KANAWHA CO., BLESSED SACRAMENT (1941) [CEM] Rev. John H. Finnell; Deacon John J. Hanna.
Res.: 305 E St., 25303-1597. Tel: 304-744-5523; Fax: 304-744-5669. Email: blessedsac@suddenlinkmail.com. Web: blessedsacramentwv.org.
Catechesis/Religious Program—Students 115.

SPELTER, HARRISON CO., HOLY FAMILY, See St. Ann's, Shinnston

SPENCER, ROANE CO., HOLY REDEEMER (1957) Rev. Tom Chacko.
Res.: 602 Parkersburg Rd., 25276-1024. Tel: 304-927-2013. Email: holy_redeemer@verizon.net. Web: mysite.verizon.net/holy_redeemer.
Catechesis/Religious Program—Students 14.
Mission—St. Elizabeth of Hungary (1977) Rt. 1, Box 118N3, Elizabeth, Wirt Co. 26143. Tel: 304-275-4226. Email: casamblanet@verizon.net. Web: mysite.verizon.net/stelizofhungary. Sr. Cheryl Samblanet, H.M., Pastoral Assoc.

STAR CITY, MONONGALIA CO., ST. MARY (1953) [CEM] Rev. John V. DiBacco Jr.
Res.: 3334B University Ave., Morgantown, 26505. Tel: 304-599-3747; Fax: 304-599-3769. Email: stmaryschurch@comcast.net. Web: www.stmarystarcity.com.
School—St. Francis Central Catholic School, 41 Guthrie Ln., Morgantown, 26508. Tel: 304-598-0133; Fax: 304-598-2690.
Catechesis/Religious Program—Tel: 304-225-1163. Email: kkerzak@comcast.net. Students 145.

STONEWOOD, HARRISON CO., OUR LADY OF PERPETUAL HELP (1955) Rev. D. Kent Durig.
Res.: 707 3rd St., 26301-4854. Tel: 304-623-2334; Fax: 304-623-2334 (Call first).
Catechesis/Religious Program—Tel: 304-623-2334, Ext. 19. Students 176.

SUMMERSVILLE, NICHOLAS CO., ST. JOHN THE EVANGELIST (1849) [CEM] Rev. Xavier Cooney, S.V.D.; Deacon John F. Ceslovnik.
Res.: 1704 Webster Rd., 26651-1096. Tel: 304-872-2554; Fax: 304-872-0580. Email: stjohnsummersville@gmail.com. Web: www.stjohnsummersville.org.
Catechesis/Religious Program—Students 52.

SWEET SPRINGS, MONROE CO., ST. JOHN, Closed. See St. Charles, White Sulphur Springs

TERRA ALTA, PRESTON CO., ST. EDWARD (1975) [CEM 2], See St. Sebastian, Kingwood
Catechesis/Religious Program—Sr. Priscilla Weidenschlager, D.R.E. Students 2.

THOMAS, TUCKER CO., ST. THOMAS AQUINAS (1897) [CEM] Rev. Timothy J. Grassi.
Res.: P.O. Box 300, 26292-0300. Tel: 304-463-4488.
Church: Brown St. & Third St., 26292.
Catechesis/Religious Program—Students 17.
Mission—Our Lady of Mercy (1960)

TRIADELPHIA, OHIO CO., OUR LADY OF SEVEN DOLORS (1869) [CEM] Closed. For inquiries for parish records, please see St. Vincent de Paul, Wheeling.

UNION, MONROE CO., ST. ANDREW, Closed. See St. Catherine of Siena, Ronceverte

VIENNA, WOOD CO., ST. MICHAEL (1956) [JC] Rev. John R. Gallagher.
Res.: 5501 Fourth Ave., 26105-2007. Tel: 304-295-6109. Email: stmoffice@frontier.com.
Catechesis/Religious Program—Students 98.

WAR, MCDOWELL CO., CHRIST THE KING (1942) Rev. That Son Ngoc Nguyen.
Church: Rt. 16 S., P.O. Box 728, 24892-0728. Tel: 304-875-3827.
Catechesis/Religious Program—Email: ctk@wv.securespeed.us. Students 5.

WAYNE, WAYNE CO., NATIVITY OF OUR LORD (1980) Rev. Julian Marneni; Deacon Michael R. Prestera Jr.
Church: Rte. 4, Box 2502, 25570-9738. Tel: 304-272-5832; 304-525-5202.
Catechesis/Religious Program—Students 12.
Station—Genoa Christian Center P.O. Box 67, Genoa, 25517. Tel: 304-385-4583; Fax: 304-385-4583.

WEBSTER SPRINGS, WEBSTER CO., ST. ANNE'S (1920) Rev. Matheus B. Ro, S.V.D. (Indonesia); Bro. James J. Zabransky, S.V.D., Pastoral Assoc.; Deacon Todd E. Garland.
Res.: 160 McGraw, 26288-1134. Tel: 304-847-5512; Fax: 304-847-5512.
Catechesis/Religious Program—Students 4.

WEIRTON, BROOKE CO., ST. PAUL'S (1910) [CEM] Rev. Larry W. Dorsch.
Res.: 140 Walnut St., 26062-4521. Tel: 304-748-6710; Fax: 304-748-3749. Email: stpaulschurch@comcast.net.
School—Tel: 304-748-5225. Email: stpaulschool3@comcast.net. James S. Lesho, Prin. Lay Teachers 15; Students 267.
Catechesis/Religious Program—Students 35.

WEIRTON, HANCOCK CO.

1—ST. JOSEPH THE WORKER (1957) Rev. Dean Borgmeyer.
Res.: 229 California Ave., 26062-3790. Tel: 304-723-2054; Fax: 304-723-3961.
School—St. Joseph the Worker Grade School, 151 Michael Ave., 26062. Tel: 304-723-1970. Mr. Alfred Boniti, Prin. Lay Teachers 13; Students 217.
Catechesis/Religious Program—Students 97.

2—SACRED HEART OF MARY (1911), (Polish), Revs. Dean Borgmeyer; Joseph Augustine, H.G.N.
Office: 200 Preston Ave., P.O. Box 2247, 26062-3994. Tel: 304-723-7175; 304-723-0707 (Rectory); Fax: 304-723-7176. Email: shmparish@frontier.com.
Catechesis/Religious Program—Students 21.

WELCH, MCDOWELL CO., ST. PETER (1923) Rev. Paulose Manickathan.
Res.: 111 Virginia Ave., 24801-2424. Tel: 304-436-2014; Fax: 304-436-2332.
Chapel—Kimball, Our Lady Queen of the Apostles, (1959)
Catechesis/Religious Program—Students 9.

WELLSBURG, BROOKE CO., ST. JOHN THE EVANGELIST (1857) [CEM] Rev. Joseph Daniel Pisano.
Res.: 1300 Charles St., 26070-1408. Tel: 304-737-0429; Fax: 304-737-0429. Email: stjohn1300@comcast.net. Web: www.stjohnwellsburgwv.org.
Catechesis/Religious Program—Students 35.
Mission—Holy Family (1980) Box 7, Beech Bottom, Brooke Co. 26030-0007. Tel: 304-394-5929; Fax: 304-394-1256.

WEST UNION, DODDRIDGE CO., ST. PATRICK CHAPEL (1856) See separate listing. See Sacred Heart, Salem

WESTON, LEWIS CO., ST. PATRICK'S (1845) Rev. J. Stephen Vallelonga.
210 Center Ave., 26452-2029. Tel: 304-269-3048. Email: office@spchurchweston.net. Web: www.spchurchweston.net.
Res.: 222 Center Ave., 26452-2029.
School—Tel: 304-269-5547. Email: st.pats@stpatswv.org. Lay Teachers 8; Students 165.
Catechesis/Religious Program—Students 40.
Chapel—Loveberry, St. Bernard [CEM]
Chapel—Roanoke, St. Bridget [CEM]
Chaplaincy—Weston State Hospital. Tel: 304-269-3048.

WESTOVER, MONOGALIA CO., ST. ELIZABETH ANN SETON (1977) Merged with St. Theresa, Morgantown, to form The New St. Theresa & St. Elizabeth Ann Seton, Morgantown.

WHITE SULPHUR SPRINGS, GREENBRIER CO., ST. CHARLES BORROMEO (1903) [CEM] [JC] Rev. John Chapin Engler Jr.; Deacon William B. Strange Jr.
Res.: 325 W. Main St., 24986. Tel: 304-536-1813.
Catechesis/Religious Program—St. Louis Catholic Center, Lewisburg, 24901. Students 32.
Chapel—Sweet Springs, St. John [CEM 2] [JC 2]Tel: 304-536-1813. (1859)

WHITESVILLE, BOONE CO., ST. JOSEPH THE WORKER (1958) Closed. See St. Mary Queen of Heaven, Madison.

WILLIAMSON, MINGO CO., SACRED HEART (1911) Rev. Elpidio M. Geneta.
Res.: 110 W. Fourth Ave., 25661-3112. Tel: 304-235-2982; Fax: 304-235-3027.
Catechesis/Religious Program—Students 12.

WINDSOR HEIGHTS, BROOKE CO., ST. THERESE, Closed. For inquiries for parish records, please see St. John, Wellsburg.

Absent on Sick Leave:
Rev.—
Petro, William

Absent on Leave:
Revs.—
Jagela, Walter M.
Kranyc, Andrew G.
Nguyen, That Son Ngoc
Owens, Brian S.
Wash, Pat J.

Retired:
Revs.—
Alexander, Leon F., 100 Hodges Rd., 25314.
Anderson, William A., The Alphonsus House, P.O. Box 108, Salem, 26426.
Bandiera, Colombo F., 1117 University Ave., Apt. 103, Morgantown, 26505.
Bauer, Carl E., 106 Johnstone St., Hampton, SC 29924.
Bell, Edward M., V.F., 149 Otter Rd., Hilton Head Island, SC 29928.
Beyer, Leroy O., 889 Wess Rd., Mineral Point, PA 15942.
Campi, Vincent L., Good Shepherd Nursing Home, 159 Edgington Ln., Rm. 207, 26003.
Cann, Hilarion V., 174 Ridgeway Dr., Bridgeport, 26330.
Chalany, Robert, 17 Cedar Lake Rd., Chester, CT 06412.
Conlon, Anthony J., 8 Beech Park, Swinford Co., Mayo, Ireland.
Cullinane, Jeremiah J., Felisian Village, # 135, 1700 S. 18th St., Manitowoc, WI 54220.
Cupp, Edwin F., Good Shepherd Nursing Home, 159 Edgington Ln., Room 209, 26003-1597.
Duhaime, John N., P.O. Box 116, Rainelle, 25962.
Ebejer, Lino P., 1304 Woodland Ct., Chester, 26034.
Fahey, John H., P.O. Box 2226, Parkersburg, 26101.
Federico, Cesidio J., 112 Boley St., Weirton, 26062.
Getsinger, Ronald A., P.O. Box 2843, Weirton, 26062.
Iaquinta, Patsy J., RR1 Box 605, Volga, 26238.
Lombard, Roy A., Welty Apartments, #405, 1276 National Rd., 26003-5743.
Lukas, Andrew F., P.O. Box 201, Fairmont, 26555-0201.
Lydon, Leo B., 236 Parkway Dr., Clarksburg, 26301.
Maguire, Seamus J., 1276 National Rd., #407, 26003.
Mascioli, Joseph M., P.O. Box 11, Morgantown, 26505.
McDonnell, John H., 4703 Kanawha Ave. S.E., 25304.
McGinnity, John C., P.O. Box B, Hot Springs, VA 24445.
Murphy, James J., 32 Elm Rd., Donnycarney, Dublin 9, Ireland.
Nash, Robert C., P.O. Box 1093, Deltaville, VA 23043.
O'Donovan, Donal, Westwood, Chapel St., Dunmanway, Co. Cork Ireland.
O'Reilly, Joseph F., P.O. Box 22303, Hilton Head Island, SC 29926.
Ralph, John, 1757 State St., Biloxi, MS 39531.
Schmitt, David J., 241 Hawthorne Ln., Point Pleasant, 25550.
Wrenn, Lawrence, Welty Apartments, 1276 National Rd., #406, 26003.

Permanent Deacons:
Belldina, Louis J., M.S., Bishop Hodges Pastoral Center & St. John Bosco, Huttonsville
Bittner, Robert W. St. Elizabeth Ann Seton, Franklin
Breiding, Douglas W. Office of Safe Environment, Diocese of Wheeling-Charleston; Corpus Christi Parish, Wheeling
Ceslovnik, John F. St. John the Evangelist, Summersville & Holy Family, Richwood
Deem, Douglas A., St. Francis Xavier, Parkersburg
Divita, John, Immaculate Conception, Montgomery
Doerr, George J., (On Leave Outside the Diocese)
Fagert, Rollin N., Mater Dolorosa, Paden City
Galvin, David E., St. James, Charles Town
Garland, Todd E., Dir. Dept. of Social Ministries & St. Anne, Webster Springs
Godwin, Raymond G. St. Brendan, Elkins; St. Patrick, Coalton
Goetemann, Gerald B., (Retired)
Grant, Russell J., (On Leave Outside the Diocese)
Hammel, Lawrence, Our Lady of Grace, Romney
Hammond, Don M., Campus Ministry, Beckley Vicariate & Sacred Heart, Bluefield
Hanna, John J., Blessed Sacrament, South Charleston
Iafrate, Albert L., (Retired)
Kelly, James R., St. Francis Xavier, Parkersburg
Lane, Gary W. Director, Blessed John XXIII Pastoral Center, Charleston
Lester, David P., Pastoral Associate, St. Peter the Fisherman, Fairmont
Lilly, Robert B., St. Vincent De Paul, Berkeley Springs
Lipscomb, Truman A., (Retired)
Locke, John W., St. Vincent de Paul, Berkeley Springs
Lynch, John J., (Retired)
Maciorowski, Anthony F. Priest Field Pastoral Center, Kearneysville & St. Agnes, Shepherdstown
Maher, John F., St. Margaret Mary Parish, Parkersburg
Mankowski, Richard W., (Retired)
Nesser, Dennis W., J.C.L. Tribunal Dir., Office of Religious Unity, Charleston
Olenchock, Stephen A. Engaged Encounter, Wheeling & Clarksburg Vicariates & St. John University, Morgantown
Prentiss, Joseph J., St. John University, Morgantown
Prestera, Michael R., Jr., Dir., Genoa Christian Center; Pastoral Assoc., Sacred Heart, Huntington
Quigley, Charles C., Ecumenical Ministry, Martinsburg Vicariate & St. Leo, Inwood
Sarraga, John W., Office of Prison Ministry (Federal Prison) & St. Brendan, Elkins
Shaw, A. Ray, III, St. Elizabeth, Phillipi
Showalter, George B., St. Margaret Mary, Parkersburg
Smith, Paul J., (Retired)
Smoulder, George St. Alphonsus, Wheeling
Strange, William B., Jr., St. Charles Borromeo, White Sulphur Springs
Thompson, Rue C., Jr. Office of Prison Ministry (State Prisons and Regional Jails) & Holy Rosary, Buckhannon
Trunzo, Thomas Notre Dame High School, Clarksburg; St. James the Apostle, Clarksburg; Sacred Heart, Salem
Windett, John E. Pastoral Svcs. (Home Health Care) & St. Elizabeth Ann Seton, Franklin
Wise, W. Donald, St. Francis De Sales, Beckley
Wojcicki, Ronald J., (Retired)
Wuletich, David E., St. Anthony, Charleston
Ziolkowski, John F., St. Francis De Sales, Beckley

INSTITUTIONS LOCATED IN THE DIOCESE

[A] COLLEGES AND UNIVERSITIES

WHEELING. *Wheeling Jesuit University*, 316 Washington Ave., 26003-6243. Tel: 304-243-2000; Fax: 304-243-2120. Web: www.wju.edu. Very Rev. Brian P. O'Donnell, S.J., Ph.D., Rector, Jesuit Community; Revs. James J. Fleming, S.J.; Harry F. Geib, S.J.; George R. Hohman, S.J.; Joseph E. Kolb, S.J.; James A. O'Brien, S.J.; Donald M. Serva, S.J.; Michael F. Steltenkamp, S.J. Jesuit Fathers. Priests 8; Lay Teachers 71; Students 1,304.

[B] HIGH SCHOOLS, CENTRAL

WHEELING. *Central Catholic High School*, 75-14th St., 26003. Tel: 304-233-1660; Fax: 304-233-3187. Web: www.cchsknights.org. Mrs. Julie Shively, Prin. Sisters of St. Joseph 1; Lay Teachers 33; Students 289.

CHARLESTON. *Charleston Catholic High School* (1923) (Grades 6-12), 1033 Virginia St. E., 25301. Tel: 304-342-8415; Fax: 304-342-1259. Email: debraksullivan@hotmail.com. Web: www.charlestoncatholic-crw.org. Mrs. Debra K. Sullivan, Prin.; Dara Krack, Librarian. Lay Teachers 33; Students 422.

CLARKSBURG. *Harrison Co. Catholic School System. Notre Dame High School* (1924) (Grades 7-12), 127 E. Pike St., 26301. Tel: 304-623-1026; Fax: 304-623-1026. Email: ndhs@iolinc.net. Dr. Carroll Kelly Morrison, Prin.; Ian McAra, Advancement Dir. Teaching one class together. 2; Faculty 18; Lay Teachers 16; Students 155.

HUNTINGTON. *St. Joseph Catholic High School*, 600 13th St., 25701. Tel: 304-525-5096; Fax: 304-525-0781. Email: barcher@stjoseph.org. Web: www.stjosephhs.org. William Archer, Prin.; Susan Popp, Librarian. Faculty 20; Students 196.

MCMECHEN. *Bishop Donahue Memorial High School* (1955) 325 Logan St., 26040. Tel: 304-233-3850; Fax: 304-233-8677. Email: twise76@hotmail.com. Web: www.bishopdonahue.org. Mr. Thomas Wise, Prin. (For Marshall Co.) Faculty 15; Students 144.

PARKERSBURG. *Parkersburg Catholic Junior-Senior High School*, (Grades 7-12), 3201 Fairview Ave., 26104. Tel: 304-485-6341; Fax: 304-485-4697. Email: pchs@pchs1.com. Web: pchs1.com. Ms. Karen Robinson, Prin.; Mrs. Yvonne Powderly, Librarian. Faculty 22; Students 195.

WEIRTON. *Madonna High School*, 150 Michael Way, 26062. Tel: 304-723-0545; Fax: 304-723-0564. Email: jmihalyo@weirtonmadonna.org. Web: www.weirtonmadonna.org. John Mihalyo, Prin. Faculty 14; Students 160.

[C] ELEMENTARY SCHOOLS, CENTRAL

BENWOOD. *SS. James and John Elementary School*, (Grades PreK-8), 52 Seventh St., 26031. Tel: 304-232-1587; Fax: 304-232-4707. Email: saints527@yahoo.com. Marilyn McWhorter, Prin. Consolidation of the following parishes: St. John, Benwood; St. James, McMechen. Lay Teachers 12; Students 130.

CLARKSBURG. *Harrison County Catholic School System. St. Mary's Central Grade School* (1914) (Grades PreSchool-6), 107 E. Pike St., 26301. Tel: 304-622-9831; Fax: 304-622-9831. Email: stmaryswv@gmail.com. Nicole A. Folio, Prin.; Christy Smith, Librarian. Consolidation of the following parishes: All Saints, Bridgeport; Immaculate Conception, Clarksburg; St. James, Clarksburg; Our Lady of Perpetual Help, Stonewood; St. Ann, Shinnston; Sacred Heart, Salem. Total Faculty 17; Lay Teachers 15; Students 167.

FAIRMONT. *Fairmont Catholic Grade School* (1928) (Grades K-8), Consolidation of the following parishes: St. Peter; Immaculate Conception; St. Anthony., 416 Madison St., 26554. Tel: 304-363-5313; Fax: 304-363-7701. Email: FCSSSchool@aol.com. Mr. Richard Pellegrin, Prin. Lay Teachers 11; Students 190.

MORGANTOWN. *St. Francis de Sales Central Catholic School*, (Grades PreK-8), 41 Guthrie La., 26508. Tel: 304-291-5070; Fax: 304-291-5104. Email: jdowney@stfrancismorgantown.com. Web: www.stfrancismorgantown.com. Mr. John M. Downey V., Prin. Lay Teachers 27; Students 391.

PARKERSBURG. *Parkersburg Catholic Elementary School*, (Grades PreK-6), 810 Juliana St., 26101. Tel: 304-422-6694; Fax: 304-422-2469. Email: pces@pchs1.com. Web: pceswv.org. Mr. Kevin Simonton, Prin. Lay Teachers 11; Staff 20; Students 167.

[D] PASTORAL CENTERS

WHEELING. *Paul VI Pastoral Center*, 667 Stone & Shannon Rd., 26003. Tel: 304-277-3300; Fax: 304-277-4320. Email: info@paulvi.org. Web: www.paulvi.org. Rev. Dismas Young, O.F.M.Cap.; Bro. Robert Herrick, O.F.M.Cap., Assoc. Dir. Capacity 72.

CHARLESTON. *Blessed John XXIII Pastoral Center* (1985) 100 Hodges Rd., 25314. Tel: 304-342-0507; Fax: 304-342-4786. Email: johnxxiii@suddenlink.net. Deacon Gary W. Lane, Dir. Capacity 166.

HUTTONSVILLE. *Bishop Hodges Pastoral Center* (1977) Rte. 1, Box 9D, 26273. Tel: 304-335-2165; Fax: 304-335-2165. Email: info@bhpc-dwc.org. Web: bhpc-dwc.org. Deacon Louis J. Belldina, M.S., Dir.; Barbara Belldina, Asst. Dir. Capacity 72.

KEARNEYSVILLE. *Priest Field Pastoral Center*, 4030 Middleway Pike, 25430. Tel: 304-725-1435; Fax: 304-725-1437. Email: priestfield@aol.org. Very Rev. William P. Linhares, T.O.R., U.F., B.A., M.Ed., S.T.B., Dir. Capacity 90.

[E] ASSOCIATED SPIRITUAL AND PASTORAL LIFE CENTERS

WHEELING. *St. Joseph Center*, 137 Mount St. Joseph Rd., 26003-1799. Tel: 304-232-8160; Fax: 304-232-0506. Email: mclark@dsjoseph.org. Web: www.csjoseph.org. Sr. Mary Clark, C.S.J., Dir. Congregation of St. Joseph Overnight Capacity 10; Daytime Capacity 25.

Maryhill Hermitage, 155 Edgington Ln. Apt. 6, 26003. Tel: 304-639-4669.

OLD FIELDS. *Holy Spirit Hermitage* (1979) Hickory Hill Rd., H.C. 66, Box 20, 26845-9201. Tel: 304-289-3997. In Res. Rev. Richard B. Hite, M.S.A.

[F] GENERAL HOSPITALS

WHEELING. *Bishop Joseph H. Hodges Continuous Care Center*, 600 Medical Park, P.O. Box 6316, 26003. Tel: 304-243-3800; Fax: 304-243-3398. Email: ctarr@wheelinghospital.com. Web: www.wheelinghospital.com. Christy Tarr, Admin. Skilled and Intermediate Care. Bed Capacity 120; Total Assisted Annually 400; Total Staff 170.

Wheeling Hospital (1850) One Medical Park, 26003. Tel: 304-243-3000; Fax: 304-243-3060. Web: www.wheelinghospital.org. Mr. Ronald L. Violi, CEO; Sr. Mary Ann Rosenbaum, C.S.J., Dir. of Pastoral Care Dept.; Rev. Anthony Thurston, Chap.; Bro. John McDonogh, F.M.S., Chap.; Sisters Mairead Scanlon, C.S.J., Chap.; Mona

Farthing, C.S.J., Chap. Sisters of St. Joseph 3; Patients Assisted Annually 451,238; Total Staff 2,090; Bed Capacity 397.

BUCKHANNON. *St. Joseph's Hospital of Buckhannon, Inc.* (1921) 1 Amalia Dr., 26201. Tel: 304-473-2000; Fax: 304-472-6620. Web: www.stj.net. Sue Johnson-Phillippe, CEO. Attended by Marist Fathers. Sisters of the Pallottine Missionary Society 4; Bed Capacity 95; Patients Assisted Annually 89,902; Home Health Care & Hospice Patients 6,063; Total Staff 368.

St. Joseph's Foundation of Buckhannon, Inc. (1993) 1 Amalia Dr., 26201. Tel: 304-473-6819.

HUNTINGTON. *St. Mary's Medical Center,* 2900 First Ave., 25702. Tel: 304-526-1234; Fax: 304-526-1538. Web: www.st-marys.org. Michael G. Sellards, Pres. & CEO. Pallottine Missionary Sisters 6; Bed Capacity 393; Patients Assisted Annually 252,921.

School of Nursing Tel: 304-526-1270; Fax: 304-526-1538. Student Nurses 176; Total Staff 2,225.

[G] NURSING HOMES

WHEELING. *Good Shepherd Nursing Home LC,* 159 Edgington Ln., 26003. Tel: 304-242-1093; Fax: 304-242-1121. Mr. Donald R. Kirsch, Admin.; Revs. John Beckley, S.M., Chap.; Raymond Carr, S.M., Chap. Sisters 2; Bed Capacity 192; Total Assisted Annually 300; Total Staff 240.

[H] HOMES FOR AGED

WHEELING. *Welty Home for the Aged, Inc.,* 159 Edgington Ln., 26003-6261. Tel: 304-242-1093.

Welty Home LC, 21 Washington Ave., 26003-6261. Tel: 304-242-5233; Fax: 304-230-1132.

Welty Trust, Inc., 83 Edgington Ln., 26003. Tel: 304-242-2300; Fax: 304-243-0890.

Trustees: Most Rev. Michael J. Bransfield, Pres.; Very Rev. Anthony Cincinnati, S.T.D., V.E.; Mr. William Yaeger, Treas.; Mr. Lawrence Bandi.

Welty Retirement Apartments LC, 1276 National Rd., 26003. Tel: 304-242-5820; Fax: 304-230-5600. 1315 National Rd., 26003. Tel: 304-230-5611.

[I] HEALTH SERVICES

HUNTINGTON. *Pallottine Health Services, Inc.* (1988) 2900 First Ave., 25702. Tel: 304-526-8915; Fax: 304-526-1538. Web: www.st-marys.org. Sr. M. Diane Bushee, S.A.C., Contact Person. Sponsored by the Pallottine Missionary Sisters.

Parent Corp. for:

St. Mary's Medical Center, Inc. (1924) 2900 First Ave., 25702. Tel: 304-526-1270; Fax: 304-526-1538. Web: www.st-marys.org.

St. Joseph's Hospital of Buckhannon, Inc. (1921) 1 Amalia Dr., Buckhannon, 26201. Tel: 304-473-2111; Fax: 304-472-6620. Web: www.stj.net. Bed Capacity 488; Total Assisted Annually 386,908; Total Staff 3,021.

PINEVILLE. *Children's Health Care, Inc.,* Box 430, 24874. Tel: 304-732-7069; Fax: 304-732-7098. Email: ecatters@marshall.edu. Sr. Eileen Catterson, D.W.M.D., Dir.; Donna Musgrave, Office Mgr. Total Assisted Annually 6,040; Total Staff 13.

RHODELL. *Rhodell Health Clinic* (1975) P.O. Box 158, 25915. Tel: 304-683-4318.

Appalachian Health Cooperative, Inc.

[J] SOCIAL SERVICE INSTITUTIONS

WHEELING. *Catholic Charities Neighborhood Center,* 125-18th St., P.O. Box 6176, 26003-0713. Tel: 304-232-7157; Fax: 304-238-7133. Email: wheelingccnc@comcast.net. Patrick J. Reindel, Dir.

HUTTONSVILLE. *Camp Tygart,* Rte. 1, Box 9D, 26273. Tel: 304-335-2130 (In Season); 304-233-0880 (Out of Season); Fax: 304-230-0508. Mrs. Michelle Tomshack, Admin. Diocesan Children's Camp.

KERMIT. *A.B.L.E. Families, Inc.* (1994) P.O. Box 1249, 25674. Tel: 304-393-4987; Fax: 304-393-4987. Web: www.ablefamilies.org. Sr. Patricia Ann Murray, O.S.F., Exec. Dir.

SALEM. *Nazareth Farm, Inc.* (1979) Rte. 2, Box 194-3, 26426. Tel: 304-782-2742; Fax: 304-782-4358. Email: nazarethfarm@gmail.com. Web: www.nazarethfarm.org.

[K] HOMES FOR DEPENDENT CHILDREN

WHEELING. *St. John's Home for Children* (1856) 141 Key Ave., 26003-7412. Tel: 304-242-5633; Fax: 304-243-4911. Email: stjterry@stratuswave.net. Web: www.stjohnshomeforchildren.org. Terence A. McCormick, Exec. Dir. Children 8; Total Assisted 16.

[L] MONASTERIES AND RESIDENCES OF PRIESTS AND BROTHERS

WHEELING. *Capuchin Hermitage of St. Joseph, St. Joseph of Leonissa Capuchin Heritage,* 665 Stone & Shannon Rd., 26003. Tel: 304-277-2971; Fax: 304-277-2972. Email: caphermitage@att.net. Revs. Scott Seethaler, O.F.M.Cap.; Dismas Young, O.F.M.Cap.; John Petrikovic, O.F.M.Cap.; Joseph Tuscan, O.F.M.Cap.; Bro. Robert Herrick, O.F.M.Cap.

CHARLESTON. *Capuchins-St. Anthony Friary,* 1000 Sixth St., 25302. Tel: 304-342-2716. Revs. Albert Alexandrunas, O.F.M.Cap.; Anil Gonsalves, O.F.M. Cap.; James Kurtz, O.F.M. Cap.; Benjamin F. Madden, O.F.M. Cap.; Roy Schuster, O.F.M.Cap (Retired).

HINTON. *Monastery of Christ on the Mountain* (1968) P.O. Box 429, 25951-0429. Tel: 304-466-4782; Fax: 304-466-3716. Rev. Bonaventure Lussier, O.C.D., Supr.; Bro. Gilbert Tovares, O.C.D. Discalced Carmelite Hermits.

[M] CONVENTS AND RESIDENCES FOR SISTERS

WHEELING. *Union of Our Lady of Charity United States Province* (1900) 141 Edgington Ln., 26003. Tel: 304-242-7070; Fax: 304-242-0042. Web: nauolc.net. Sr. Deana Kohlman, Local Supr. & Business Mgr.

North American Union Sisters of Our Lady of Charity, Inc.

Wheeling Center, Congregation of St. Joseph, 137 Mount St. Joseph Rd., 26003-1799. Tel: 304-232-8160; Fax: 304-232-0506. Email: ccrinkey@csjoseph.org. Web: www.csjoseph.org. Sr. Mary Alice Girrens, C.S.J., Admin. & Coord. Wheeling Center-Congregation of St. Joseph.

Attended by Wheeling Jesuit University.

[N] FOUNDATIONS

WHEELING. *Central Catholic High School Educational Foundation, Inc.,* 75-14th St., 26003. Tel: 304-233-1660; Fax: 304-233-3187.

**Clarence L. Christ Trust,* Office of the Chancellor: *Diocese of Wheeling-Charleston,* P.O. Box 230, 26003. Tel: 304-233-0880; Fax: 304-230-2029.

John S. Thoner Family Charitable Trust (1995) P.O. Box 230, 26003. Tel: 304-233-0880; Fax: 304-230-2029.

Medical Park Foundation (1995) One Medical Park, 26003. Tel: 304-243-2969.

**Michael Christ Trust,* Office of the Chancellor: *Diocese of Wheeling-Charleston,* P.O. Box 230, 26003. Tel: 304-233-0880; Fax: 304-230-2029.

The Sisters of St. Joseph Health & Wellness Foundation, 137 Mount St. Joseph Rd., 26003-1799. Tel: 304-233-4500; Fax: 304-232-1404. Email: ssjhwf@aol.com; helenssj@aol.com. Web: www.ssjhealthandwellnessfoundation.org. Sisters Janice Landwehr, C.S.J., Co-Exec. Dir.; Helen Skormisley, C.S.J., Co-Exec. Dir.

Sisters of St. Joseph of Wheeling Foundation, Inc. (1974) 137 Mount St. Joseph Rd., 26003-1799. Tel: 304-232-8160; Fax: 304-232-0506. Email: ccrinkey@csjoseph.org. Web: www.csjoseph.org.

West Virginia Catholic Foundation, P.O. Box 230, 26003. Tel: 304-233-0880; Fax: 304-233-0890. Email: bminor@dwc.org. Web: wvcf.dwc.org. Mr. Bryan E. Minor, Exec. Dir.

CLARKSBURG. *Harrison County Catholic Education Foundation, Inc.,* 126 E. Pike St., 26301-2720.

PARKERSBURG. *Parkersburg Catholic Schools Foundation, Inc.,* 3201 Fairview Ave., 26104-2111. Tel: 304-428-7528. Email: pcsf@pchs1.com. Web: pchs1.com.

Sisters of St. Joseph Charitable Fund, Inc. (1997) 4420 Rosemar Rd., Ste. 204, P.O. Box 4440, 26104-4440. Tel: 304-424-6080; Fax: 304-424-6081. Email: info@ssjcharitablefund.org. Web: www.ssjcharitablefund.org. Sr. Jane Harrington, C.S.J., Exec. Dir.; Renee L. Steffen, Grants Mgr.; Sr. Molly Bauer, C.S.J., Prog. Dir.

[O] NEWMAN CENTERS

CHARLESTON. *John Paul II Campus Ministry Center* 310-26th St., 25304. Tel: 304-342-9940; Fax: 304-342-9942.

ATHENS. *Concord University Newman Center* , See Sacred Heart, Princeton, P.O. Box 447, 24712. Tel: 304-327-5623. Deacon Don M. Hammond.

BETHANY. *St. John Fisher Catholic Chapel* 201 Richardson St., Box W, 26032. Tel: 304-829-4622. Revs. James R. DeViese, J.C.L., Co-Chap.; Pete A. Giannamore, Co-Chap.; Mrs. Shirley Carter, Campus Ministry.

BUCKHANNON. *West Virginia Wesleyan College Newman Center* 35 Franklin St., Box 848, 26201-0848. Tel: 304-472-3414. Email: frronsm@comcast.net. Rev. Ronald J. Nikodem, S.M.; Bro. Ray Madigan, S.M.

FAIRMONT. *Fairmont State University Newman Center* 1200 College Park, 26554. Tel: 304-363-2300. Rev. Robert Periello, Chap.

HUNTINGTON. *Marshall Newman Center* 1609 Fifth Ave., 25703. Tel: 304-525-4618; Fax: 304-522-4115. Web: www.marshallcatholic.com. Natalie Rohan, Dir. Campus Min.

PHILIPPI. *Alderson-Broaddus College Newman Center* Rte. 3, Box 257, 26416. Tel: 304-457-2641. Rev. James O'Connor.

SHEPHERDSTOWN. *Good Shepherd Catholic Campus Ministry Center* P.O. Box 1163, 25443. Tel: 304-433-2526. Rev. Jose Manuel Escalante, Chap.

WEST LIBERTY. *West Liberty State College, St. Thomas Aquinas Campus Ministry* 134 Chatham St., 26074. Tel: 304-336-7751. Rev. Pete A. Giannamore, Chap.

[P] CHILD CARE CENTERS

WHEELING. *Holy Family Child Care & Development Center, Inc.,* 161 Edgington Ln., 26003. Tel: 304-242-5222; Fax: 304-242-5379. Email: hfcccoffice@wirefire.com. Michele Forsythe, Exec. Dir. Total Assisted 86; Total Staff 22.

CLARKSBURG. *Madonna Day Care Center,* 444 E. Pike St., 26031. Tel: 304-622-4453. Ms. Sandra Mitchell, Dir. Total Staff 6.

[Q] MISCELLANEOUS

WHEELING. *St. Joseph Health Initiative, Inc.,* 137 Mount St. Joseph Rd., 26003-1799. Tel: 304-232-8160; Fax: 304-232-0506. Email: ccrinkey@csjoseph.org. Sr. Marguerite O'Brien, C.S.J., Pres.

Retirement Trust Agreement of the Priests' Health and Retirement Association (1997) P.O. Box 230, 26003. Tel: 304-233-0880; Fax: 304-230-2029.

Wheeling-Charleston Diocesan Council of Catholic Women, P.O. Box 230, 26003. Tel: 304-233-0880, Ext. 264; Fax: 304-233-8551. Sr. Ellen F. Dunn, O.P., Diocesan Moderator; Barbara Belldina, Pres.; Toni DiStefano, Sec. & Treas.

CLAYTON. *Bethlehem Farm, Inc.,* P.O. Box 415, Talcott, 24981. Tel: 304-445-7143; Fax: 304-445-2936.

MADISON. *Heralds of the Good News Missionary Society Inc.,* 51 Madison Ave., 25130-0467. Tel: 304-369-4538.

MORGANTOWN. *Morgantown Magnificat Chapter of the Diocese of Wheeling-Charleston,* 24 Millan St., 26501.

RELIGIOUS INSTITUTES OF MEN REPRESENTED IN THE DIOCESE

For further details refer to the corresponding bracketed number in the Religious Institutes of Men or Women section.

[0200]—*Benedictine Monks*—O.S.B.

[]—*Canons Regular of the New Jerusalem*—C.R.N.J.

[0470]—*The Capuchin Franciscan Friars*—O.F.M.Cap.

[1000]—*Congregation of the Passion*—C.P.

[0260]—*Discalced Carmelite Friars*—O.C.D.

[0585]—*Heralds of Good News*—H.G.N.

[0690]—*Jesuit Fathers and Brothers*—S.J.

[0770]—*Marist Brothers*—F.M.S.

[0780]—*Marist Fathers*—S.M.

[0840]—*Missionary Servants of the Most Holy Trinity*—S.T.

[0920]—*Oblates of St. Francis de Sales*—O.S.F.S.

[]—*Order of Friars Minor* (Bangalou, India)—O.F.M.

[0420]—*Society of the Divine Word*—S.V.D.

[0590]—*Society of the Missionaries of the Holy Apostles*—M.S.A.

[0570]—*The Glenmary Home Missioners*—G.H.M.

[0560]—*Third Order Regular of St. Francis*—T.O.R.

[]—*Third Order Regular of St. Francis of Assisi (St. Francis Province)* (Ranchi, India)—T.O.R.

RELIGIOUS INSTITUTES OF WOMEN REPRESENTED IN THE DIOCESE

[0130]—*Apostles of the Sacred Heart of Jesus*—A.S.C.J.

[3110]—*Congregation of Our Lady of the Retreat in the Cenacle* (North American Prov.)—R.C.

[3832]—*Congregation of the Sisters of St. Joseph* (Wheeling Center)—C.S.J.

[0760]—*Daughters of Charity of St. Vincent De Paul* (Province of St. Louis)—D.C.

[0960]—*Daughters of Wisdom*—D.W.

[1105]—*Dominican Sisters of Hope* (Ossining, NY)—O.P.

[1115]—*Dominican Sisters of Peace*—O.P.

[1450]—*Franciscan Sisters of the Sacred Heart*—O.S.F.

[2430]—*Marist Sisters*—S.M.

[3070]—*North American Union Sisters of Our Lady of Charity*—N.A.U.-O.L.C.

[3150]—*Pallottine Missionary Sisters*—S.A.C.

[2970]—*School Sisters of Notre Dame*—S.S.N.D.

[1680]—*School Sisters of St. Francis*—O.S.F.

[0570]—*Sisters of Charity of Seton Hill, Greensburg, PA*—S.C.

[0590]—*Sisters of Charity of St. Elizabeth Convent Station*—S.C.

[0990]—*Sisters of Divine Providence (Marie de la Roche Prov.)*—C.D.P.

[1930]—*Sisters of Holy Cross*—C.S.C.

[2575]—*Sisters of Mercy of the Americas*—R.S.M.

[3000]—*Sisters of Notre Dame de Namur* (Chesapeake Province)—S.N.D.DeN.

[1630]—*Sisters of St. Francis of Penance and Christian Charity*—O.S.F.

[1530]—*Sisters of St. Francis of the Congregation of Our Lady of Lourdes*—O.S.F.

[3893]—*Sisters of St. Joseph of Chestnut Hill* (Philadelphia)—S.S.J.

[3830-13]—*Sisters of St. Joseph of Pittsburgh* (Baden)—C.S.J.

[3830-05]—*Sisters of St. Joseph of Rockville Centre* (Brentwood)—C.S.J.

[]—*Sisters of the Child Jesus* Zimbabwe—S.J.I.

[2110]—*Sisters of the Humility of Mary*—H.M.

[3220]—*Sisters of the Poor Child Jesus*—P.C.J.

[1760]—*Sisters of the Third Order of St. Francis of Penance and Charity*—O.S.F.

[4120-03]—*Ursuline Nuns of the Congregation of Paris*—O.S.U.

DIOCESAN CEMETERIES

WHEELING. *Mount Calvary* (1872) 1685 National Rd., 26003-5599. Tel: 304-242-0460; Fax: 304-242-9506.

NECROLOGY

✠ Schmitt, Most Rev. Bernard W., Retired Bishop of Wheeling-Charleston.—Died Aug. 16, 2011

† Gillooly, Patrick J., (Retired)—Died June 18, 2011

† Stenger, William J., (Retired)—Died Feb. 8, 2011

† Valdes, Bert W., (Retired)—Died Feb. 18, 2011

An asterisk (*) denotes an organization that has established tax-exempt status directly with the IRS and is not covered by the USCCB Group Ruling.

Diocese of Wichita

(Dioecesis Wichitensis)

Most Reverend

MICHAEL OWEN JACKELS, S.T.D.

Bishop of Wichita; ordained May 30, 1981; appointed Bishop of Wichita January 28, 2005; ordained April 4, 2005. *The Chancery, 424 N. Broadway, Wichita, KS 67202.*

Most Reverend

EUGENE J. GERBER, D.D.

Bishop Emeritus of Wichita; ordained May 19, 1959; appointed Bishop of Dodge City October 16, 1976; ordained December 14, 1976; installed December 15, 1976; appointed Bishop of Wichita November 23, 1982; installed February 9, 1983; retired October 4, 2001. *Res.: 424 N. Broadway, Wichita, KS 67202.*

ESTABLISHED AUGUST 2, 1887.

Square Miles 20,021.

New boundaries established by Apostolic Letters dated May 19, 1951. Bounded on the west by the west lines of Rice, Reno, Kingman and Harper counties, south by Oklahoma, east by Missouri, and north by the north lines of Bourbon, Allen, Woodson, Greenwood, Morris, Marion, McPherson and Rice Counties in Kansas.

For legal titles of parishes and diocesan institutions, consult the Chancery Office.

The Chancery: 424 N. Broadway, Wichita, KS 67202. Tel: 316-269-3900; Fax: 316-269-3902.

Web: *www.CatholicDioceseOfWichita.org*

STATISTICAL OVERVIEW

Personnel	
Bishop	1
Retired Bishops	1
Priests: Diocesan Active in Diocese	80
Priests: Diocesan Active Outside Diocese	8
Priests: Retired, Sick or Absent	33
Number of Diocesan Priests	121
Religious Priests in Diocese	1
Total Priests in Diocese	122
Extern Priests in Diocese	6
Ordinations:	
Diocesan Priests	4
Transitional Deacons	1
Permanent Deacons in Diocese	4
Total Sisters	258
Parishes	
Parishes	90
With Resident Pastor:	
Resident Diocesan Priests	66
Without Resident Pastor:	
Administered by Priests	24
Pastoral Centers	22
Professional Ministry Personnel:	
Sisters	11
Lay Ministers	35
Welfare	
Catholic Hospitals	8
Total Assisted	510,175
Health Care Centers	2
Total Assisted	61,774
Homes for the Aged	7
Total Assisted	1,161
Specialized Homes	1
Total Assisted	38
Special Centers for Social Services	1
Total Assisted	24,575
Residential Care of Disabled	1
Total Assisted	437
Educational	
Diocesan Students in Other Seminaries	48
Total Seminarians	48
Colleges and Universities	1
Total Students	3,021
High Schools, Diocesan and Parish	4
Total Students	2,565
Elementary Schools, Diocesan and Parish	34
Total Students	8,106
Catechesis/Religious Education:	
High School Students	2,058
Elementary Students	5,981
Total Students under Catholic Instruction	21,779
Teachers in the Diocese:	
Priests	3
Sisters	16
Lay Teachers	740
Vital Statistics	
Receptions into the Church:	
Infant Baptism Totals	2,372
Minor Baptism Totals	200
Adult Baptism Totals	208
Received into Full Communion	302
First Communions	2,576
Confirmations	2,014
Marriages:	
Catholic	387
Interfaith	262
Total Marriages	649
Deaths	1,010
Total Catholic Population	114,595
Total Population	987,240

Former Bishops—Most Revs. JAMES O'REILLY, D.D., Bishop-Elect; died July 26, 1887; JOHN JOSEPH HENNESSY, D.D., cons. Nov. 30, 1888; died July 13, 1920; AUGUSTUS JOHN SCHWERTNER, D.D., ord. June 12, 1897; cons. June 8, 1921; installed June 22, 1921; died Oct. 2, 1939; CHRISTIAN HERMAN WINKELMANN, S.T.D., ord. June 11, 1907; cons. Auxiliary Bishop of St. Louis, Nov. 30, 1933; installed March 5, 1940; died Nov. 18, 1946; MARK K. CARROLL, S.T.D., ord. June 10, 1922; appt. Feb. 15, 1947; cons. April 23, 1947; installed May 6, 1947; resigned Sept. 27, 1967; died Jan. 12, 1985; LEO C. BYRNE, D.D., ord. June 10, 1933; appt. Titular Bishop of Sabidia and Auxiliary of St. Louis, May 21, 1954; cons. June 29, 1954; transferred to Wichita, "cum jure successionis" 1961; appt. Apostolic Administrator, Feb. 25, 1963; transferred to St. Paul and Minneapolis, Sept. 27, 1967; died Oct. 21, 1974; DAVID M. MALONEY, S.S., S.T.L., J.C.D., former Bishop of Wichita; ord. Dec. 8, 1936; appt. Titular Bishop of Ruspae Auxiliary of Denver, Nov. 9, 1960; cons. Jan. 4, 1961; transferred to Wichita, Dec. 6, 1967; resigned July 16, 1982; died Feb. 15, 1995; EUGENE J. GERBER, D.D., Bishop of Wichita; ord. May 19, 1959; appt. Bishop of Dodge City Oct. 16, 1976; ord. Dec. 14, 1976; installed Dec. 15, 1976; appt. Bishop of Wichita Nov. 23, 1982; installed Feb. 9, 1983; resigned Oct. 4, 2001; THOMAS J. OLMSTED, J.C.D., ord. July 2, 1973; appt. Coadjutor Bishop of Wichita Feb. 16, 1999; Episcopal ord. April 20, 1999; appt. Bishop of Wichita Oct. 4, 2001; appt. Bishop of Phoenix Dec. 20, 2003.

Chancery Office—424 N. Broadway, Wichita, 67202. Tel: 316-269-3900; Fax: 316-269-3902. Web: www.catholicdioceseofwichita.org.

Vicar General—Rev. Msgr. ROBERT E. HEMBERGER, J.C.L.

Moderator of the Diocesan Curia—Rev. Msgr. ROBERT E. HEMBERGER, J.C.L., 424 N. Broadway, Wichita, 67202.

Vicar for Clergy—Rev. MATTHEW C. MCGINNESS.

Director of Diocesan Planning—Rev. Msgr. ROBERT E. HEMBERGER, J.C.L.

Chancellor—Rev. JOHN P. LANZRATH, S.T.L.

Presbyteral Council/College of Consultors—Most Rev. MICHAEL O. JACKELS, S.T.D.; Revs. JAMES J. BILLINGER; DWIGHT J. BIRKET; JOHN P. LANZRATH, S.T.L.; Rev. Msgr. ROBERT E. HEMBERGER, J.C.L.; Revs. JOHN V. HOTZE, J.C.L.; JASON W. BORKENHAGEN; Rev. Msgr. JOHN P. GILSENAN, J.C.L.; Revs. BRIAN D. NELSON; DANIEL L. VACCA; ERIC M. WELDON; DANIEL J. SPEXARTH; MATTHEW C. MCGINNESS.

Tribunal—424 N. Broadway, Wichita, 67202. Tel: 316-269-3960.

Judicial Vicar—Rev. JOHN V. HOTZE, J.C.L.

Adjutant Judicial Vicar—Rev. MICHAEL E. NOLAN, J.C.L.

Promoters of Justice—Rev. Msgr. JOHN P. GILSENAN, J.C.L.; Rev. STUART M. SMELTZER, J.C.L.

Judges—Revs. STEPHEN R. BAXTER, J.C.L.; DOUGLAS L. CAMPBELL, J.C.L.; Rev. Msgr. ROBERT E. HEMBERGER, J.C.L.; Revs. JOHN V. HOTZE, J.C.L.; MICHAEL E. NOLAN, J.C.L.

Defenders of the Bond—Rev. Msgr. JOHN P. GILSENAN, J.C.L.; Revs. CHARLES F. SEIWERT, J.C.L.; STUART M. SMELTZER, J.C.L.

Notaries—Mrs. ROBERTA RAU; Mrs. CLAUDINE WALD; Mrs. JANET MILLER; Mrs. DENISE NORTHUP.

Ongoing Formation of the Clergy Committee—Most Rev. MICHAEL O. JACKELS, S.T.D.; Revs. JOSEPH M. GILE, S.T.D.; KENNETH S. VAN HAVERBEKE; JOHN P. LANZRATH, S.T.L., Prog. Dir.; MICHAEL E. NOLAN, J.C.L.; BENJAMIN N. NGUYEN; MATTHEW D. MARNEY; JOHN F. JIRAK; Rev. Msgr. ROBERT E. HEMBERGER; Rev. BENJAMIN S. SAWYER.

Diocesan Offices and Directors

Catholic Diocese of Wichita—Most Revs. MICHAEL O. JACKELS, S.T.D., Bishop of Wichita; EUGENE J. GERBER, D.D., Bishop Emeritus.

Apostleship of Prayer—Rev. MATTHEW C. MCGINNESS, 6900 E. 45th St., N., Wichita, 67226.

Catholic Charities—Ms. CYNTHIA COLBERT, Dir., 532 N. Broadway, Wichita, 67214. Tel: 316-264-8344.

Catholic Care Center—Ms. WENDY MENDEZ, Admin., 6700 E. 45th St., N., Wichita, 67226. Tel: 316-744-2020; Fax: 316-744-2182.

Cemeteries—Mr. JIM SHELDON, 1640 N. Maize Rd.,

Wichita, 67212. Tel: 316-722-1971.

Communications Office—AMY PAVLACKA, Dir., 424 N. Broadway, Wichita, 67202. Tel: 316-269-3900; Fax: 316-269-3902.

Cursillo (Spanish language)—Rev. JEROME A. BEAT, Spiritual Dir. (Retired), 6900 E. 45th St. N., Wichita, 67226. Tel: 316-518-4683.

Cursillo (English language)—Rev. STEPHEN R. BAXTER, J.C.L., Spiritual Dir., P.O. Box 149, Halstead, 67056. Tel: 316-835-2173.

Building Commission—Rev. JAMES J. BILLINGER, Chm.; Mr. BRYAN R. COULTER, CPA; Rev. KENT A. HEMBERGER; Rev. Msgr. ROBERT E. HEMBERGER, J.C.L.; Mrs. LINDA SNOOK; Rev. MICHAEL E. NOLAN, J.C.L.; Mr. MICHAEL W. WESCOTT; Mr. LARRY MCLAIN; Mr. WILLIAM WILHELM.

Stewardship Office—Rev. KENNETH S. VAN HAVERBEKE, Dir.; Mr. DANIEL L. LOUGHMAN, Coord.

Office of Faith Formation—Rev. C. JARROD LIES, Dir., 424 N. Broadway, Wichita, 67202. Tel: 316-269-3946; Ms. CHRISTINE EDMONDS, Youth & Young Adult; Ms. SHELLY BOLE, Rel. Educ.; Sr. URSULA FOTOVICH, C.S.J., Missions; VACANT, Totus Tuus & College Outreach.

Finance and Administrative Services Office—Mr. BRYAN R. COULTER, CPA, Dir. Finance, 424 N. Broadway, Wichita, 67202. Tel: 316-269-3900.

Finance Council—Most Rev. MICHAEL O. JACKELS, S.T.D., Bishop of Wichita; Mr. MICHAEL AYLWARD; Rev. JOHN P. LANZRATH, S.T.L.; Mr. BRYAN R. COULTER, CPA; Ms. JOYE HANEBERG; Rev. Msgr. ROBERT E. HEMBERGER, J.C.L.; Mr. RICHARD KERSCHEN; Mr. FRANK REMAR; Mr. DALE WIGGINS.

Health Affairs - Diocesan Liaison—Rev. Msgr. ROBERT E. HEMBERGER, J.C.L., 424 N. Broadway, Wichita, 67202. Tel: 316-269-3962.

Ministry with Persons with Disabilities Office—Mr. THOMAS K. RACUNAS, Dir., 424 N. Broadway, Wichita, 67202. Tel: 316-269-3900.

Catholic School Office—Mr. ROBERT VOBORIL, Supt., 424 N. Broadway, Wichita, 67202. Tel: 316-269-3950.

Legion of Mary—Rev. JAMES S. MAINZER, St. Mary Church, 106 E. Eighth, Newton, 67114. Tel: 316-282-0459.

Family Life and Natural Family Planning Office—Ms. JUDITH LEONARD, Dir.

Newspaper: "The Catholic Advance"—Mr. CHRISTOPHER M. RIGGS, Editor; Mr. BRYAN R. COULTER, CPA, Business Mgr., 424 N. Broadway, Wichita, 67202. Tel: 316-269-3965.

Development and Planned Giving Office—Mr. MICHAEL W. WESCOTT, Dir., 424 N. Broadway, Wichita, 67202. Tel: 316-269-3917.

Worship Office—Rev. MICHAEL E. NOLAN, J.C.L., Dir.

Respect Life and Social Justice Office—Mrs. BONNIE TOOMBS, Dir.; Rev. THOMAS M. HOISINGTON, S.T.L., Spiritual Mod., 424 N. Broadway, Wichita, 67202. Tel: 316-269-3935.

Retreats—Rev. KENNETH S. VAN HAVERBEKE, Dir., Spiritual Life Center, 7100 E. 45th St. N., Wichita, 67226. Tel: 316-744-0167.

Rural Life Ministry—Mrs. BONNIE TOOMBS, 424 N. Broadway, Wichita, 67202. Tel: 316-269-3900.

Social Service—Ms. CYNTHIA COLBERT, Catholic Charities, 532 N. Broadway, Wichita, 67214. Tel: 316-264-8344.

Victim Assistance Coordinator—Ms. VICTORIA JACKSON. Tel: 316-200-5951. Email: vjackson14@att.net; Rev. Msgr. ROBERT E. HEMBERGER, J.C.L., Review Bd. Chm.

Vocations—Rev. MICHAEL M. SIMONE, S.T.L., Dir., 424 N. Broadway, Wichita, 67202. Tel: 316-269-3900.

Hispanic Ministry Office—Mrs. JOSEFA FERNANDEZ, Dir., 1518 N. Broadway, Wichita, 67214. Tel: 316-269-3919.

St. Dismas Ministry to the Incarcerated—Mr. JIM RUNDELL, Prog. Coord., 7100 E. 45th St. N., Wichita, 67226. Tel: 316-744-0167. Email: jrundell@slcwichita.org.

Human Resource Office—Mrs. THERESE SEILER, Dir.; Mrs. KELLY MCCAGUE, Personnel/Benefits Dir., 424 N. Broadway, Wichita, 67202. Tel: 316-269-3900; Fax: 316-269-3902.

Harvest House—Sr. MARILYN STAHL, Dir.; Rev. PAUL J. OBORNY, Spiritual Mod. (Retired), 424 N. Broadway, Wichita, 67202. Tel: 316-269-3900.

CLERGY, PARISHES, MISSIONS AND PAROCHIAL SCHOOLS

CITY OF WICHITA

(SEDGWICK COUNTY)

1—CATHEDRAL OF THE IMMACULATE CONCEPTION (1887) Revs. John P. Sherlock, Rector; Patrick R. Reilley. Office: 442 N. Emporia, 67202. Tel: 316-263-6574; Fax: 316-201-1306. Email: parish@wichitacathedral.com. Web: www.wichitacathedral.com.
440 N. Topeka St., 67202.
Catechesis/Religious Program—Students 236.

2—ALL SAINTS (1946) [JC 3] Rev. H. Jay Setter.
Res.: 3205 E. Grand St., 67218. Tel: 316-682-1415; Fax: 316-682-1096.
School—(Grades K-8), 3313 E. Grand, 67218. Tel: 316-682-6021; Fax: 316-682-8734. Joyce Frederiksen, Prin. Lay Teachers 16; Students 238.
Catechesis/Religious Program—Sandra Nettleton, D.R.E. Students 64.

3—ST. ANNE (1955) Rev. David Marstall; Elhe Marx, Pastoral Assoc. In Res., Rev. Michael M. Simone.
Office: 2801 S. Seneca, 67217-2399. Tel: 316-522-2383; Fax: 316-524-2370. Email: church@stannewichita.org. Web: www.stannewichita.org.
School—(Grades PreK-8) Tel: 316-522-6131; Fax: 316-469-0096. Email: school@stannewichita.org. Mr. Winston Kenton, Prin.; Diana Bowles, Librarian. Lay Teachers 14; Students 208.
Catechesis/Religious Program—Students 174.

4—ST. ANTHONY (1887), (German), Rev. Hung Q. Pham.
Res. & Mailing Address: 325 Ohio, 67214. Tel: 316-269-4641; 316-264-9352.
Catechesis/Religious Program—Students 110.

5—BLESSED SACRAMENT (1927) [JC] Revs. John F. Jirak; Maximilian K. Biltz. In Res., Rev. Joseph M. Gile.
Rectory—401 S. Roosevelt Ave., 67218. Tel: 316-681-2204.
Church Office: 124 N. Roosevelt, 67208. Tel: 316-682-4557; Fax: 316-682-4558. Web: www.blessedsacramentwichita.com.
School—(Grades PreK-8) Tel: 316-684-3752; Fax: 316-687-1082. Mr. Dan Dester, Prin.; Pam Loyle, Vice Prin.; Kerry Seiwert, Librarian. Lay Teachers 25; Students 447.
Catechesis/Religious Program—Julie Zluticky, Dir. Faith Formation. Students 142.

6—ST. CATHERINE OF SIENA (2008) Rev. Daniel J. Spexarth.
7335 W. 33rd St. N., 67205. Tel: 316-425-0595; Fax: 316-425-0685. Email: nancy@saintcatherinewichita.com. Web: www.saintcatherinewichita.com. In Res., Rev. Msgr. John P. Gilsenan.
Catechesis/Religious Program—Polly Blum, D.R.E. Students 153.

7—CHRIST THE KING (1950) Rev. Matthew D. Marney; Deacon Len Fennewald. In Res., Rev. Benjamin S. Sawyer.
Res.: 4411 Maple Ave., 67209. Tel: 316-943-4353; Fax: 316-943-8196. Email: maplestchurch@yahoo.com.
School—(Grades PreK-8), 4501 Maple Ave., 67209. Tel: 316-943-0111; Fax: 361-943-0147. Web: ctkwichita.org. Mrs. Cindy Chrisman, Prin. (ME Admin K-9). Sisters, Adorers of the Blood of Christ 1; Lay Teachers 11; Students 134.
Catechesis/Religious Program—Students 67.
Convent—4601 W. Maple Ave., 67209.

8—CHURCH OF THE MAGDALEN (1950) Revs. Patrick G. York; John P. Fogliasso; Sr. Connie Beiriger, C.S.J., Pastoral Assoc. In Res., Rev. Aaron Spexarth.
Res.: 12626 E. 21st St. N., 67206. Tel: 316-634-2315; Fax: 316-634-3948.
School—(Grades PreK-8), 2221 N. 127th St. E, 67226. Tel: 316-634-1572; Fax: 316-634-6957. Janice Palmer, Prin.; Margo Funk, Librarian. Lay Teachers 32; Students 537.
Catechesis/Religious Program—Students 162.

9—CHURCH OF THE RESURRECTION (1965) Rev. James F. Weldon.
Res.: 4910 N. Woodlawn, 67220. Tel: 316-744-2776; Fax: 316-744-3027. Email: church@resurrectionwichita.com. Web: www.resurrectionwichita.com.
School—(Grades PreK-8) Tel: 316-744-3576; Fax: 316-744-1582. James E. Finkeldei, Prin.; Lisa Hinson, Librarian. Lay Teachers 17; Students PreK-8 240.
Catechesis/Religious Program—Dustin Gates, D.R.E. Students 71.

10—ST. ELIZABETH ANN SETON (1982) Revs. Sherman A. Orr; Marco A. de Loera.
Res.: 645 N. 119th St. W., 67235. Tel: 316-721-1686; Fax: 316-721-1723.
School—(Grades K-8) Tel: 316-721-5693. Mr. David Charles, Prin.; Mrs. Kitty Garcia, Asst. Vice Prin.; Mrs. Vicki Munsinger, Librarian. Lay Teachers 41; Students 671.
Catechesis/Religious Program—Students 242.

11—ST. FRANCIS OF ASSISI (1959) Revs. Daryl Befort; Curtis L. Robertson; Jeremy S. Huser.
Res.: 861 N. Socora, 67212. Tel: 316-722-4404; Fax: 316-722-4738.
School—(Grades PreSchool-8) Mary Carter, Prin.; Mary Bird, Vice Prin.; Margaret Raine, Librarian. Adorers of the Blood of Christ 1; Lay Teachers 39; Students 731.
Catechesis/Religious Program—Tel: 316-729-1350. Students 276.

12—HOLY SAVIOR (1948), (African American), Rev. James J. Billinger.
Res.: 1425 N. Chautauqua, 67214. Tel: 316-682-8712; Fax: 316-682-4797. Email: holysavior@holysavior.org.
School—(Grades PreK-8), 4640 E. 15th St., 67208. Tel: 316-684-2141; Fax: 316-684-4318. Delia Shropshire, Prin. Lay Teachers 17; Students 155.
Catechesis/Religious Program—Students 30.

13—ST. JOSEPH (1886) [JC] Rev. Stuart M. Smeltzer.
Res.: 132 S. Millwood Ave., 67213. Tel: 316-261-5800; Fax: 316-261-5806.
School—(Grades PreK-8), 139 S. Millwood Ave., 67213. Tel: 316-261-5801; Fax: 316-261-5804. Ms. Ellen Albert, Prin. Sisters 1; Lay Teachers 8; Students 111.
Catechesis/Religious Program—Mrs. Betty Ewing, D.R.E. Students 33.

14—ST. JUDE (1958) Rev. Daniel L. Vacca.
3030 Amidon Ave., 67204. Tel: 316-440-7098. Web: stjudewichita.net.
Res.: 3130 Amidon Ave., 67204.
School—(Grades PreK-8) Tel: 316-838-0800; Fax: 316-838-0866. Mrs. Brooker Smith, Prin.; Carolyn Rooney, Librarian. Lay Teachers 16; Students 236.
Catechesis/Religious Program—Nicole Donohue, D.R.E. Students 131.

15—ST. MARGARET MARY (1954) Rev. Eric M. Weldon.
Res.: 2701 Pattie St., 67216. Tel: 316-262-1821; Fax: 316-262-4057.
Church: 2635 Pattie St., 67216. Tel: 316-267-4911; Fax: 316-267-1707.
School—(Grades PreK-8), 2635 Pattie St., 67216. Tel: 316-267-4911; Fax: 316-267-1707. Kori Heiman, Prin.; Lisa Hinson, Librarian. Email: lhinson@smmwichita.com. Lay Teachers 15; Students 189.
Catechesis/Religious Program—Tel: 316-522-4104. Esther Caire, C.R.E.; Sr. Rosa Cruz, C.R.E. Students 240.

16—OUR LADY OF GUADALUPE, Closed. For sacramental records contact St. Margaret Mary, Wichita.

17—OUR LADY OF PERPETUAL HELP (1927) [JC] Rev. Jose Machado.
Res.: 2351 N. Market St., 67219. Tel: 316-838-8373; Fax: 316-821-9250. Email: jmachado@cox.net.
Catechesis/Religious Program—Students 172.
Convent—2354 N. Market St., 67219. Tel: 316-838-3190.
Parish Center—2409 N. Market St., 67219. Tel: 316-838-5750.

18—ST. PATRICK (1910) [JC] Rev. Jerome J. Spexarth.
Church: 2007 Arkansas Ave., 67203. Tel: 316-262-4683; Fax: 316-262-0051. Email: stpatswichita.org. Web: www.stpatswichita.org.
School—(Grades PreK-8), 2023 Arkansas Ave., 67203. Tel: 316-262-4071; Fax: 316-262-6217. Email: principal@stpatswichita.org. Mrs. Theresa Lam, Prin.; Joy Kirk, Librarian. Lay Teachers 16; Students 202.
Catechesis/Religious Program—Sr. Rosa Cruz, D.R.E., (English & Spanish). Students 364.
Convent—2045 Arkansas Ave., 67203. Tel: 316-267-0021.

19—ST. PAUL PARISH (1970) Rev. John N. Hay.
Res.: 1810 N. Roosevelt, 67208. Tel: 316-684-6896; Fax: 316-684-2679.
St. Paul Parish/Newman Center—Email: parish@wsunewmancenter.com. Web: www.wsunewmancenter.com.

20—ST. THOMAS AQUINAS (1957) Revs. Matthew C. McGinness; Daniel J. Duling; Kim Scanlan, Parish Admin.
Res.: 1321 Stratford Ln., 67206. Tel: 316-683-6569; Fax: 316-683-6672. Email: church@stthomaswichita.com. Web: www.stthomaswichita.com.
School—(Grades PreK-8) Tel: 316-684-9201; Fax: 316-684-7421. Miss Mary Sweet, Prin.; Mr. Scott Landwehr, Asst. Prin.; Barbara Evans, Librarian. Lay Teachers 42; Students 734.
Catechesis/Religious Program—Students 689.

21—ST. VINCENT DE PAUL (1955) Rev. Kent A. Hemberger; Lori Porter, Dir. Music; Sr. Kathleen Vasselli, S.S.N.D., Spiritual Enrichment Min.
Res.: 123 N. Andover Rd., Andover, 67002. Tel: 316-733-1423; Fax: 316-733-1687. Email: office@svdpks.org. Web: www.svdpks.org.
Catechesis/Religious Program—Gayle Beuke, D.R.E.; John Wagle, Youth Min. (MS); Desirae Cox, Youth Min. (HS). Students 385.

OUTSIDE THE CITY OF WICHITA

ALEPPO, SEDGWICK CO., IMMACULATE CONCEPTION (1890), (German), [CEM] Revs. Samuel J. Pinkerton; John C. Reinkemeyer.
Church: 25741 W. 13th St. N., Garden Plain, 67050. Tel: 316-531-2662.
Catechesis/Religious Program— With St. Anthony, Garden Plain. Students 9.

ANDALE, SEDGWICK CO., ST. JOSEPH (1890), (German), [CEM] Rev. Reinhard C. Eck.
Res.: 318 Rush Ave., Box 8, 67001. Tel: 316-444-2196.
Catechesis/Religious Program—Mary Jo Hieger, D.R.E. Students 299.

ANTHONY, HARPER CO., SACRED HEART (1934) Closed. For inquiries for parish records contact St. Joan of Arc, 1023 W. Main St., Box 218, Harper, KS 67058. Merged with Immaculate Conception, Danville & St. Patrick, Harper to form Joan of Arc, Harper.

ARKANSAS CITY, COWLEY CO., SACRED HEART (1886) Rev. Ruben Ortiz-Montelongo.
Res.: 302 S. B St., 67005. Tel: 620-442-0566; Fax: 620-441-0935.
School—(Grades PreK-5), 312 S. B St., 67005. Tel: 620-442-6550; Fax: 620-441-0935. Richard Sleefe, Prin. Lay Teachers 5; Students 78.
Catechesis/Religious Program—Theresa Kuffler, D.R.E. (Grades 1-12). Students 78.

ARMA, CRAWFORD CO., ST. JOSEPH (1934) Rev. Roger S. Lumbre.
Res.: 310 W. South St., P.O. Box 948, 66712. Tel: 620-347-4525. Email: stjoseph@ckt.net.

AUGUSTA, BUTLER CO., ST. JAMES (1879) [CEM] Rev. Michael Schemm.
Res.: 1012 Belmont Ave., 67010. Tel: 316-775-2155; Fax: 316-775-2131.
School—(Grades K-6) Tel: 316-775-5721; Fax: 316-775-7160. Richard Guy, Prin.; Sharon Hoffman, Librarian. Lay Teachers 9; Students 91.
Catechesis/Religious Program—Kathi Martinez, D.R.E. Students 126.

BAXTER SPRINGS, CHEROKEE CO., ST. JOSEPH (1917) [JC] Rev. Chrysostom Ah Maung.
Res.: 115 W. Walnut, Columbus, 66725. Tel: 620-429-2639.
Catechesis/Religious Program—Students 4.

BURNS, MARION CO., IMMACULATE CONCEPTION, Closed. For sacramental records contact Holy Family, Marion.

BUSHTON, RICE CO., HOLY NAME OF JESUS (1878), (German), [CEM] Rev. Robert K. Spencer.
Res. & Office: 415 St. Francis St., Lyons, 67554. Tel: 620-257-3503.
Church: 296 3rd Rd., 67427.
Catechesis/Religious Program—Tel: 620-562-3662. Roxanna Habiger, D.R.E. Students 9.

CALDWELL, SUMNER CO., ST. MARTIN OF TOURS (1888) [JC] Rev. Steven Scheier.
Res.: 428 N. Main, 67022. Tel: 620-845-6763; Fax: 620-845-6733.
Catechesis/Religious Program—Students 10.

CANEY, MONTGOMERY CO., SACRED HEART (1914) Rev. Sixtus Ye Myint (Burma).
Res.: 301 N. Hooker, 67333. Tel: 620-647-3577.
Catechesis/Religious Program—Tel: 620-879-2883. Students 22.

CAPALDO, CRAWFORD CO., ST. ALICE, Closed. For sacramental records contact Sacred Heart, Frontenac.

CASTLETON, RENO CO., ST. AGNES (1872) Closed. For inquiries for sacramental records contact St. Teresa, Hutchinson.

CEDAR VALE, CHAUTAUQUA CO., ST. JOSEPH, Closed. For inquiries for parish records contact the chancery.

CHANUTE, NEOSHO CO., ST. PATRICK (1873) [CEM 2] Rev. Bernard X. Gorges.
Res.: 424 S. Central, 66720. Tel: 620-431-3165; Fax: 620-431-6587. Email: salonzo@stpatrickchanute.org.
School—(Grades PreK-5) Tel: 620-431-4020. Fey Barles, Prin. Sisters 1; Lay Teachers 9; Students 90.
Catechesis/Religious Program—Tel: 620-431-4287. Students 90.

CHASE, RICE CO., ST. MARY (1888), (German), Closed. For inquiries for sacramental records contact St. Paul, Lyons.

CHEROKEE, CRAWFORD CO., ST. ANASTASIA, Closed. For sacramental records contact Our Lady of Lourdes, Pittsburg.

CHERRYVALE, MONTGOMERY CO., ST. FRANCIS XAVIER'S (1871), (German), [CEM] Rev. Andrew Heiman.
Res. & Office: 210 N. 4th, Independence, 67301. Tel: 620-331-1789; Fax: 620-331-6496.
Church: 202 S. Liberty St., 67335.
Catechesis/Religious Program—Tel: 620-336-2310. Students 55.

CHETOPA, LABETTE CO., SACRED HEART (1873) [CEM] Closed. For sacramental records contact Mother of God Parish, Oswego.

CHICOPEE, CRAWFORD CO., ST. BARBARA, Closed. For sacramental records contact Our Lady of Lourdes, Pittsburg.

CLONMEL, SEDGWICK CO., ST. JOHN (1878) [CEM] Rev. C. Jarrod Lies.
Church: 18630 W. 71st St., Viola, 67149. Tel: 316-545-7171; Fax: 620-545-7191.
Parish Center—Tel: 620-545-7211.
Catechesis/Religious Program—Deborah Tamburro, P.C.L.; Art Gentry, P.C.L. Students 93.

COFFEYVILLE, MONTGOMERY CO., HOLY NAME (1869), (Irish—German), [CEM 2] Rev. Benjamin N. Nguyen.
Res.: 408 Willow St., 67337. Tel: 620-251-0475; Fax: 620-251-0475. Email: holynamecoffeyville@gmail.com. Web: holynamecoffeyville.com.
School—(Grades PreK-6), 406 Willow St., 67337. Tel: 620-251-0480; Fax: 620-251-1651. Lisa Payne, Prin. Lay Teachers 10; Students 96.
Catechesis/Religious Program—Students 67.

COLUMBUS, CHEROKEE CO., ST. ROSE (1887) [JC] Rev. Chrysostom Ah Maung.
Res.: 115 W. Walnut St., 66725. Tel: 620-429-2639; Fax: 620-429-2639.
Catechesis/Religious Program—Tel: 620-429-2938. Students 32.

COLWICH, SEDGWICK CO., SACRED HEART (1901) [CEM] Rev. Kenneth J. Schuckman.
Office: 311 S. Fifth St., P.O. Box 578, 67030. Tel: 316-796-1224; Fax: 316-796-0735.
Res.: 231 S. Fifth St., 67030. Tel: 316-796-0759.
Catechesis/Religious Program—Students 250.

CONWAY SPRINGS, SUMNER CO., ST. JOSEPH (1886), (German), [CEM] Rev. Andrew J. Seiler.
Res.: 217 N. Sixth St., 67031. Tel: 316-456-2276; Fax: 316-456-3317.
School—(Grades K-6), 218 N. 5th St., 67031. Tel: 316-456-2270; Fax: 316-456-2272. Email: stjoeprinc@havilandtelco.com. Mr. Patrick Carl, Prin. Lay Teachers 7; Students 129.
Catechesis/Religious Program—Students 165.

COUNCIL GROVE, MORRIS CO., ST. ROSE (1883) [CEM] [JC 2] Rev. Theodore Khin.
Res.: 300 Spencer St., 66846. Tel: 620-767-6412; Fax: 620-767-5370. Email: rosalima@tctelco.net.
Catechesis/Religious Program—Maureen Adams, C.R.E. Tel: 620-767-6607. Students 34.

CUNNINGHAM, KINGMAN CO., SACRED HEART (1908), (German), [CEM] Rev. John P. Miller.
Res.: P.O. Box 216, 67035. Tel: 316-298-2601; Fax: 316-298-2926.
Catechesis/Religious Program—Tel: 316-246-5241; 620-243-7666. Linda Kerschen, D.R.E.; Renee D. Adelhardt, D.R.E. Students 35.

DANVILLE, HARPER CO., IMMACULATE CONCEPTION (1883) Closed. For inquiries for parish records contact St. Joan of Arc, 1023 W. Main St., Box 218, Harper, KS 67058. Merged with St. Patrick, Harper & Sacred Heart, Anthony to form Joan of Arc, Harper.

DERBY, SEDGWICK CO., ST. MARY CATHOLIC CHURCH (1954) Rev. David J. Lies; Sr. Marie Zoglman, A.S.C., Pastoral Assoc., Liturgy Dir., Music Min., & RCIA.
Parish Office: 2300 E. Meadowlark Rd., 67037. Tel: 316-788-5525; Fax: 316-788-1577. Web: www.stmarysderby.com.
School—(Grades K-8), 2306 E. Meadowlark Rd., 67037. Tel: 316-788-3151; Fax: 316-788-6895. Mr. Richard Montgomery, Prin.; Jean Schif, Librarian. Lay Teachers 24; Students 329.
Catechesis/Religious Program—Janet Clark, Youth Dir.; Catherine Wilson, P.S.R. Dir. Students 172.

EL DORADO, BUTLER CO., ST. JOHN THE EVANGELIST (1915) Rev. Brian D. Bebak.
Res.: 302 N. Denver Ave., 67042. Tel: 316-321-4796; Fax: 316-321-1831. Email: mail@stjohneldorado.com. Web: www.stjohneldorado.com.
Catechesis/Religious Program—Tel: 316-321-4933. Karen Ebersole, D.R.E. & Youth Min. Students 93.

ERIE, NEOSHO CO., ST. AMBROSE (1915) Rev. Thomas Leland.
Res: P.O. Box 216, St. Paul, 66771. Tel: 620-449-2224; Fax: 620-449-8986.
Church: 519 N. Main, 66733.
Catechesis/Religious Program—

EUREKA, GREENWOOD CO., SACRED HEART (1881), (German), [JC] Rev. Stephen F. Gronert.
Res.: 514 N. Elm St., 67045. Tel: 620-583-7100.
Catechesis/Religious Program—Students 38.
Mission—St. John Hamilton, Greenwood Co.
Mission—St. Teresa Of Avila Madison, Greenwood Co. Tel: 316-437-2504.

FLORENCE, MARION CO., ST. PATRICK, Closed. Merged with St. Mark, Marion; St. John Nepomucene, Pilsen and Holy Redeemer, Tampa to form Holy Family, Marion.

FORT SCOTT, BOURBON CO., MARY QUEEN OF ANGELS (1860) [CEM] Rev. Darrin M. May.
Res.: 705 S. Holbrook St., 66701-2506. Tel: 620-223-4340; Fax: 620-223-6060.
School—(Grades PreK-5) Tel: 620-223-6060; Fax: 620-223-6060. Krista Gorman, Prin.; Jill Gorman, Librarian. Lay Teachers 5; Students 87.
Catechesis/Religious Program—Peggy Niles, D.R.E. Students 56.

FREDONIA, WILSON CO., SACRED HEART (1906) [CEM] Rev. Stephen M. Thapwa (Burma).
Res.: 428 N. 12th St., 66736. Tel: 620-378-2694. Email: sacredheart.fkb@gmail.com.
Catechesis/Religious Program—Tel: 620-378-2114 (Work); 620-378-2328 (Home). Lewis Bambick, D.R.E. Students 41.

FRONTENAC, CRAWFORD CO., SACRED HEART (1891), (Italian), [CEM] Rev. Thomas J. Stroot, Admin.
Res.: 100 S. Cherokee St., 66763. Tel: 620-231-7747; Fax: 620-232-7006.
Catechesis/Religious Program—Mona Wachter, P.C.L. (Parish Catechetical Leader). Students 102.

FULTON, BOURBON CO., ST. PATRICK, Closed. For sacramental records contact Mary Queen of Angels, Fort Scott.

GALENA, CHEROKEE CO., ST. PATRICK (1879) [JC] Rev. Chrysostom Ah Maung.
Res.: 115 W. Walnut, Columbus, 66725. Tel: 620-429-2639; Fax: 620-429-2639.
Church: 307 Galena, 66739.
Catechesis/Religious Program—Students 13.

GARDEN PLAIN, SEDGWICK CO., ST. ANTHONY (1901), (German), [CEM] Rev. Samuel J. Pinkerton.
Res.: 615 N. Main, 67050. Tel: 316-531-2252.
Catechesis/Religious Program—Tel: 316-535-2593. Students 316.
Mission—Immaculate Conception 25741 W. 13th St. N., 67050. Tel: 316-531-2662.

GIRARD, CRAWFORD CO., ST. MICHAEL (1925), (Irish—German), Rev. Roger S. Lumbre.
Res.: 106 N. Western St., 66743. Tel: 620-724-8717.
Catechesis/Religious Program—Michelle Pucket, D.R.E. Grade School; Faith Paoni, D.R.E. (6-12th grade). Students 94.

GODDARD, SEDGWICK CO., HOLY SPIRIT (1998) Rev. Michael E. Nolan.
Church: 18218 W. Hwy. 54, 67052. Tel: 316-794-3496; Fax: 316-794-3795. Web: www.holyspiritwichita.com.
Res.: 1206 Harvest Ln., 67052.
School—(Grades PreSchool-8) Tel: 316-794-8139; Fax: 316-794-2055. Kelly Bright, Prin. Teachers 7; Students 146.
Catechesis/Religious Program—Students 146.

GREENBUSH, CRAWFORD CO., ST. ALOYSIUS, Closed. For sacramental records contact St. Michael, Girard.

HALSTEAD, HARVEY CO., SACRED HEART PARISH (1874) [JC] Rev. Stephen R. Baxter.
Res.: 419 Poplar, P.O. Box 231, 67056. Tel: 316-835-2173; Fax: 316-830-2889.
Catechesis/Religious Program—Tel: 316-830-2764. Carolyn Armendariz, D.R.E. Students 74.

HAMILTON, GREENWOOD CO., ST. JOHN (1888), (German), Rev. Stephen F. Gronert.
Res.: 514 N. Elm St., Eureka, 67045. Tel: 620-583-7100.
Catechesis/Religious Program—Students 5.

HARPER, HARPER CO.

1—ST. JOAN OF ARC (1997), (Irish—German), Consolidation of St. Patrick, Harper; Immaculate Conception, Danville & Sacred Heart, Anthony. Merged in 1997. Rev. Michael Peltzer.
Rectory Office: 1023 W. Main, P.O. Box 218, 67058. Tel: 620-896-7886; Fax: 620-896-2249.
Catechesis/Religious Program—Cheryl Kernohan, D.R.E. Tel: 620-254-7792. Students 56.

2—ST. PATRICK (1882) Closed. For inquiries for parish records contact St. Joan of Arc, 1023 W. Main St., Box 218, Harper, KS 67058. Merged with Immaculate Conception, Danville & Sacred Heart, Anthony to form Joan of Arc, Harper.

HAYSVILLE, SEDGWICK CO., ST. CECILIA (1959) Rev. Thomas Than Wai (Burma).
Res.: 1900 W. Grand, 67060. Tel: 316-524-7801; Fax: 316-524-6183. Email: mbowmaker@stceciliahaysville.org. Web: stceciliahaysville.org.
School—(Grades PreK-8), 1912 W. Grand, 67060. Tel: 316-522-0461. Mr. Winston Kenton, Prin.; Jane Betzen, Librarian. Lay Teachers 8; Students 90.
Catechesis/Religious Program—Marcia Miller, D.R.E. Students 65.

HUMBOLDT, ALLEN CO., ST. JOSEPH (1867) [CEM] Rev. Bernard X. Gorges.
Res.: 424 S. Central Ave., Chanute, 66720. Tel: 620-431-3165.
Catechesis/Religious Program—Tel: 620-431-3165; Fax: 620-431-6587. Students 10.

HUTCHINSON, RENO CO.

1—CHURCH OF THE HOLY CROSS (1957) [CEM 3] [JC] Rev. Joseph A. Eckberg.
Res.: 2631 Independence Rd., 67502. Tel: 620-665-5163; Fax: 620-662-5085. Email: hcchurch@holycross.kscoxmail.com. Web: www.holycross-hutch.com.

School—(Grades K-6), 2633 Independence Rd., 67502. Tel: 620-665-6168; Fax: 620-665-6168. Mr. Kevin Hedrick, Prin. Lay Teachers 22; Students 319.
Catechesis/Religious Program—Students 146.
2—OUR LADY OF GUADALUPE (1927), (Hispanic), Rev. Brian D. Nelson.
Res.: 612 S. Maple, South Hutchinson, 67505-2099. Tel: 620-662-6443; Fax: 620-669-0215.
Catechesis/Religious Program—Kristy Shadoin, D.R.E. Students 109.
3—ST. TERESA (1897) [CEM] Rev. Nicholas A. Voelker.
Res.: 211 E. Fifth St., 67501. Tel: 620-662-7812; Fax: 620-662-7812.
Catechesis/Religious Program—Students 40.

INDEPENDENCE, MONTGOMERY CO., ST. ANDREW (1869), (German—Mexican), [CEM 2] Rev. Andrew Heiman.
Res.: 210 N. Fourth St., 67301. Tel: 620-331-1789; Fax: 620-331-6496. Email: standrewindp@sbcglobal.net.
School—(Grades PreK-8) Tel: 620-331-2870. Email: school@standrewindependence.com. Rebecca Brown, Prin. Lay Teachers 10; Students 160.
Catechesis/Religious Program—Tel: 316-253-5989. Students 30.

IOLA, ALLEN CO., ST. JOHN (1897) [CEM] [JC] Rev. Robert B. Wachter; Deacon Theodore Stahl.
Office: 310 S. Jefferson, 66749. Tel: 620-365-2277.
Res.: 314 S. Jefferson Ave., 66749. Tel: 316-365-3454.
Catechesis/Religious Program—Tel: 316-365-8488. Mr. David Roos, D.R.E. Students 105.
Oratory—St. Martin 1368 Xylan Rd., Piqua, Woodson Co. 66761.

KINGMAN, KINGMAN CO., ST. PATRICK (1885), (Irish), [JC] Rev. Benjamin D. Shockey, Admin.
Res.: 638 Ave. D W., 67068. Tel: 316-532-5440; Fax: 316-532-5549. Web: stpatskingman.org.
School—(Grades PreK-8) Tel: 316-532-2791; Fax: 316-532-2966. Robert Lyall, Prin.; Mary Meng, Librarian. Lay Teachers 12; Students 155.
Catechesis/Religious Program—Tel: 316-532-5440. Students 50.

LIBERTY, MONTGOMERY CO., ALL SAINTS, Closed. For inquiries for parish records contact the chancery.

LINDSBORG, MCPHERSON CO., ST. BRIDGET OF SWEDEN (1985) Rev. Dwight J. Birket.
Church: 206 W. Swensson, P.O. Box 268, 67456. Tel: 785-227-3588; Fax: 620-245-9677. Email: stbridget@att.net.
Res.: 1524 Sonora Dr., McPherson, 67460. Tel: 620-241-0821; Fax: 620-241-8497.
School—(Grades PreK-K) Tel: 785-227-2910. Students 21.
Catechesis/Religious Program—Students 53.

LITTLE RIVER, RICE CO., HOLY TRINITY (1885) [JC] Rev. Robert K. Spencer.
Mailing Address: 455 Harrison St., 67457.
Office & Res.: 415 St. Francis St., Lyons, 67554. Tel: 620-662-7812.
Catechesis/Religious Program—Gary Grasser, D.R.E. Tel: 620-257-2969; Shayla Grasser, D.R.E. Students 41.

LYONS, RICE CO., ST. PAUL (1927) [JC] Rev. Robert K. Spencer.
Res.: 415 St. Francis St., 67554. Tel: 620-257-3503; Fax: 620-257-3021.
Catechesis/Religious Program—Tel: 620-257-3809. Kathi Gomez, D.R.E. Students 86.

MADISON, GREENWOOD CO., ST. TERESA OF AVILA (1954), (German), [JC] Rev. Stephen F. Gronert.
Res.: 514 N. Elm St., Eureka, 67045. Tel: 620-583-7100.
Catechesis/Religious Program—Students 5.

MARION, MARION CO., HOLY FAMILY (1992) [CEM 5] [JC 2], Parish formed from merger of St. Mark, Marion; St. John Nepomucene, Pilsen; St. Patrick, Florence; Holy Redeemer, Tampa and Immaculate Conception, Burns. Rev. Hien Paul Nguyen.
Res. & Mailing Address: 415 N. Cedar St., 66861. Tel: 620-382-3369; 620-382-3369 (Office); Fax: 620-382-3369. Email: hfpmarion@yahoo.com.
Catechesis/Religious Program— Jackie Palic, D.R.E., Marion; Sandra Oborny, D.R.E., Pilsen; Mary Jirak, D.R.E., Tampa; Jean Rziha, D.R.E., Tampa. Students 146.
Oratory—Holy Redeemer Church Tampa, 67483.

MCPHERSON, MCPHERSON CO., ST. JOSEPH (1880) Rev. Dwight J. Birket.
Church: 520 E. Northview, 67460. Tel: 620-241-0821; Fax: 620-245-9677. Web: www.stjosephmcpherson.com.
Res.: 1524 Sonora Dr., 67460. Tel: 620-504-6037.
School—(Grades PreK-6) Tel: 620-241-3913. Lay Teachers 10; Students 138.
Catechesis/Religious Program—Raschelle Jirak, D.R.E. Students 112.
Mission—St. Bridget of Sweden Box 268, Lindsborg, McPherson Co. 67456. Tel: 785-227-3588. Email: stbridget@att.net.

MOLINE, ELK CO., ST. MARY'S (1899) [CEM] Rev. Sixtus Ye Myint (Burma).
Res.: 320 N. Main, Box 276, 67353-0276. Tel: 620-647-3577.
Catechesis/Religious Program—Students 14.

MOUNT VERNON, KINGMAN CO., ST. ROSE (1911), (German—Irish), [CEM] Rev. Ivan C. Eck.
Res.: 13015 E. Maple Grove Rd., Mount Hope, 67108. Tel: 316-444-2210.
Catechesis/Religious Program—Tel: 316-542-3990. Students 136.

MULBERRY, CRAWFORD CO., ST. GABRIEL, Closed. For sacramental records contact Sacred Heart, Frontenac.

MULVANE, SUMNER CO., ST. MICHAEL THE ARCHANGEL (1948) Rev. Michael J. Maybrier.
Res.: 545 E. Main St., 67110. Tel: 316-777-4221; Fax: 316-777-9456. Email: stmichaelmulvane@sbcglobal.net. Web: www.mulvaneks.org/stmichaels/Home.html.
Catechesis/Religious Program— Karen Oblinger, D.R.E. Students 232.

NEODESHA, WILSON CO., ST. IGNATIUS (1876) [CEM] Rev. Stephen M. Thapwa (Burma).
P.O. Box 186, 66757. Tel: 620-325-5215.
Rectory—428 N. 12th, Fredonia, 66736.
Catechesis/Religious Program—Tel: 620-325-8935. Jessica Busse, D.R.E. Students 37.

NEWTON, HARVEY CO.
1—ST. MARY (1872) [CEM] Rev. James S. Mainzer.
Res.: 106 E. Eighth St., 67114. Tel: 316-282-0459. Email: sschmidt@smcsnewton.org. Web: www.stmarynewton.org.
School—(Grades PreK-8) Tel: 316-282-1974; Fax: 316-283-3642. Email: mkellogg@smcsnewton.org. Philip Stutey, Prin.; Jeanette Roberts, Librarian. Lay Teachers 16; Students 169.
Catechesis/Religious Program—Carrie Reida, D.R.E. Students 91.
2—OUR LADY OF GUADALUPE (1919), (Hispanic), [JC] Rev. Juan G. Garza.
Res.: 415 S. Ash St., 67114.
Church: 421 S. Ash St., 67114. Tel: 316-283-3499; Fax: 316-283-6813.
Catechesis/Religious Program—Students 63.

OST, RENO CO., ST. JOSEPH (1880), (German), [CEM] Rev. Ivan C. Eck.
Res.: 13015 E. Maple Grove Rd., Mount Hope, 67108. Tel: 316-444-2210.
School—St. Joseph Catholic School - Ost, (Grades K-8), 12917 E. Maple Grove Rd., Mount Hope, 67108. Tel: 316-444-2548; Fax: 316-444-2448. Lay Teachers 8; Students 100.
Catechesis/Religious Program—Tel: 316-444-2637. Students 22.

OSWEGO, LABETTE CO., MOTHER OF GOD (1878) [JC] Rev. Larry Parker.
Res.: 1105 4th St., 67356. Tel: 620-795-2262.
Catechesis/Religious Program—Students 57.

OXFORD, SUMNER CO., ST. MARY (1872) [JC] Rev. Michael A. Klag.
Res.: 412 E. Eighth St., Winfield, 67156. Tel: 620-221-3610; Fax: 620-221-3528.
Catechesis/Religious Program—Myra Jacobs, D.R.E. Students 18.

PARSONS, LABETTE CO.
1—MARY QUEEN OF PEACE (1909) Closed. For inquiries for parish records contact St. Patrick, Parsons.
2—ST. PATRICK (1872) [CEM 2] Rev. Jason W. Borkenhagen.
Res.: 1807 Stevens Ave., 67357. Tel: 620-421-6762; Fax: 620-421-1628.
School—(Grades PreK-8), 1831 Stevens Ave., 67357. Tel: 620-421-0710; Fax: 620-421-2429. Tim Born, Prin.; Jane Alexander, Librarian. Lay Teachers 13; Students 119.
Catechesis/Religious Program—Students 88.

PILSEN, MARION CO., ST. JOHN NEPOMUCENE, Closed. Merged with St. Mark, Marion; St. Patrick, Florence and Holy Redeemer, Tampa to form Holy Family, Marion.

PIQUA, WOODSON CO., ST. MARTIN (1884), (German), Closed. For inquiries for sacramental records contact St. John, Iola.

PITTSBURG, CRAWFORD CO., OUR LADY OF LOURDES (1881) [CEM] Revs. Michael E. Baldwin; Adam Keiter; Chad J. Arnold.
Res.: 916 N. Locust St., P.O. Box 214, 66762. Tel: 620-231-2135; Fax: 620-231-4804. Email: kratz@ourladypittsburg.com. Web: www.ourladypittsburg.org.
School—St. Mary's Elementary School, (Grades PreK-6), (Elementary), 301 E. Ninth, 66762. Tel: 620-231-6941; Fax: 620-235-7442. Web: www.smcschools.com. Mr. John C. Kraus, Pres. Schools, Dir. Admin.; Nancy Hicks, Prin. (Pre-K-6); Janie Burrow, Librarian. Lay Teachers 21; Students 360.
School—St. Mary's Colgan Junior High, (Grades 7-8), 212 E. 9th, 66762. Tel: 620-231-4690. Email: kraus@smcschools.org. Web: www.smcschools.com. Beverley Mitchelson, Librarian. Lay Teachers 5; Students 97.
High School—St. Mary's Colgan High School Lay Teachers 18; Students 148.
Catechesis/Religious Program—Cheryl Greer, D.R.E. Students 54.

ST. LEO, KINGMAN CO., ST. LEO THE GREAT (1906), (German), [CEM] Rev. John P. Miller.
Res.: 8035 S.W. 160 Ave., Nashville, 67112. Tel: 316-246-5370.
Catechesis/Religious Program—P.O. Box 216, Cunningham, 67035. Tel: 316-298-2601. Students 16.

ST. MARK'S, SEDGWICK CO., ST. MARK (1876), (German), [CEM] Rev. Thomas M. Hoisington.
Res.: 19230 W. 29th St. N., Colwich, 67030. Tel: 316-796-1604; Fax: 316-769-0511. Email: stmksec@pixius.net. Web: www.stmarkcolwich.org.
Catechesis/Religious Program—Tel: 316-640-8527. Vanessa Condreay, D.R.E.

ST. PAUL, NEOSHO CO., ST. FRANCIS (1847) [CEM 2] Rev. Thomas Leland.
Res.: 208 Washington St., P.O. Box 216, 66771-0216. Tel: 620-449-2224; Fax: 620-449-8986.
Catechesis/Religious Program—Tel: 620-449-2672. Suzie Diskin, D.R.E. Students 160.

SCAMMON, CHEROKEE CO., ST. BRIDGET'S (1868) [CEM] Rev. Chrysostom Ah Maung.
Res.: 115 W. Walnut, Columbus, 66725. Tel: 620-429-2639; Fax: 620-429-2639.
Catechesis/Religious Program—Tel: 620-479-2236. Students 61.

SCHULTE, SEDGWICK CO., ST. PETER THE APOSTLE (1905) [CEM] Rev. Andrew Kuykendall.
Parish Offices—11000 S.W. Blvd., 67215. Tel: 316-524-4259; Fax: 316-524-0932. Email: psecretary@stpeterschulte.com. Web: www.stpeterschulte.com.
Res.: 10980 S.W. Blvd., 67215. Tel: 316-522-4728.
School—(Grades PreK-8), 11010 S.W. Blvd., 67215. Tel: 316-524-6585; Fax: 316-524-1656. Brenda Hickok, Prin.; Mattie McCuiston, Librarian. Sisters 1; Lay Teachers 24; Students 431.
Catechesis/Religious Program—Tel: 316-529-1902. Mrs. Tama Dutton, Faith Formation Dir. Students 116.

SEDAN, CHAUTAUQUA CO., ST. ROBERT BELLARMINE (1962) Rev. Sixtus Ye Myint (Burma).
Res.: 320 N. Main, P.O. Box 276, Moline, 67353-0276. Tel: 620-647-3577.
Catechesis/Religious Program—Tel: 620-725-3812. Students 10.

STRONG CITY, CHASE CO., ST. ANTHONY OF PADUA (1880) [CEM] [JC] Rev. Theodore Khin.
Res.: 300 Spencer, Council Grove, 66846. Tel: 620-767-6412; Fax: 620-767-5370.
Catechesis/Religious Program—Tel: 620-273-8617. Jeanette Black, C.R.E. Students 30.

TAMPA, MARION CO., HOLY REDEEMER, See separate listing. Now an oratory of Holy Family, Marion.

WALNUT, CRAWFORD CO., ST. PATRICK, Closed. For sacramental records contact St. Francis Church, St. Paul.

WATERLOO, KINGMAN CO., ST. LOUIS (1881), (German—Irish), [JC] Rev. Ivan C. Eck.
Res.: 13015 E. Maple Grove Rd., Mount Hope, 67108. Tel: 316-444-2210.
Catechesis/Religious Program—Students 2.

WEIR, CHEROKEE CO., SACRED HEART, Closed. For sacramental records contact St. Rose of Lima, Columbus.

WELLINGTON, SUMNER CO.
1—ST. ANTHONY (1884) Merged with St. Rose of Lima, Wellington to form St. Anthony/St. Rose, Wellington. For inquiries for parish records contact St. Anthony/St. Rose.
2—ST. ANTHONY/ST. ROSE 1907 Rev. Lawrence D. Carney III.
217 N. C. St., 67152. Tel: 620-326-2522; Fax: 620-326-3480. Email: stanthony@sutv.com.
Catechesis/Religious Program—Tel: 620-326-3480. Carol Susong, D.R.E. Students 201.
3—ST. ROSE OF LIMA (1949), (Hispanic), Merged with St. Anthony, Wellington to form St. Anthony/St. Rose, Wellington. For inquiries for parish records, contact St. Anthony/St. Rose, Wellington.

WEST MINERAL, CHEROKEE CO., IMMACULATE CONCEPTION, Closed. For sacramental records contact St. Rose of Lima, Columbus.

WILLOWDALE, KINGMAN CO., ST. PETER'S (1884), (German), [CEM] Rev. John P. Miller.
Res.: P.O. Box 86, Zenda, 67159. Tel: 620-243-5451.
Catechesis/Religious Program—Students 3.

WINFIELD, COWLEY CO., HOLY NAME (1878) [JC] Rev. Michael A. Klag.
Res.: 412 E. Eighth St., 67156. Tel: 620-221-3610; Fax: 620-221-3528. Email: sec_holyname@yahoo.com. Web: www.holynamewinfield.org.
School—(Grades PreK-6) Tel: 620-221-0230; Fax: 620-221-4047. Email: holynamecatholicschool@yahoo.com. Kimberly Porter, Prin. Lay Teachers 4; Students 61.

Catechesis / Religious Program—Students 59.
Mission—*St. Mary's* 608 N. Sumner, Oxford, 67119. Tel: 620-455-9955.

YATES CENTER, WOODSON CO., ST. JOSEPH (1957) [JC] Rev. Robert B. Wachter.
Res.: 314 S. Jefferson, Iola, 66749.
Catechesis / Religious Program—Tel: 620-365-6082. St. Joseph students come to St. John, Iola for PSR classes. Students 5.

ZENDA, KINGMAN CO., ST. JOHN (1908), (German), [CEM] Rev. John P. Miller.
Res.: P.O. Box 86, 67159. Tel: 620-243-5451.
Catechesis / Religious Program— Renee D. Adelhardt, D.R.E. Students 7.

Chaplains of Public Institutions

WICHITA. *El Dorado Correctional Facility*. Rev. Brian D. Bebak.
Sedgwick County Adult Local Detention Facility. Rev. John P. Sherlock.
Veterans Administration Hospital. Rev. H. Patrick Malone (Retired).

HUTCHINSON. *Kansas State Industrial Reformatory*. Revs. Stephen R. Baxter, J.C.L., Juan G. Garza, Nicholas A. Voelker.

On Duty Outside the Diocese:
Revs.—
Blick, Ned J.
Fasching, Jeffery A.
Lorimer, Daniel S.
McKinney, Floyd E.
McKnight, W. Shawn, S.T.D.
Nguyen, Scott C.
Seiwert, Charles F., J.C.L.
Tatro, Joseph C.

Retired:
Rev. Msgrs.—
Carr, William, 6900 E. 45th St., 67226.
McGread, Thomas, 6900 E. 45th St. N., 67226.
Regan, Charles W., 6900 E. 45th St. N., 67226.
Revs.—
Beat, Jerome A., 6900 E. 45th St. N., 67226.
Bieberle, Victor, 6900 E. 45th St. N., 67226.
Boor, Colin J., 2823 River Park Dr., 67203.
Busch, Arthur, 6900 E. 45th St. N., 67226.
Cox, Francis, 6900 E. 45th St. N., 67226.
Garrahy, Michael, 6900 E. 45th St. N., 67226.
Grabner, Eugene W., 82 Porterfield Ln., Noel, MO 64854.
Harvey, Charles K., 6900 E. 45th St. N., 67226.
Joyce, Raymond, 115 S. Rutan #4D, 67218.
Kerschen, Leon J., 6900 E. 45th St. N, 67226.
Larkin, Patrick, 6900 E. 45th St. N., 67226.
Linnebur, Leroy, 2101 W. MacArthur, Lot 902, 67217.
Malone, H. Patrick, 7077 E. Central, 67206.
Mannion, J. Patrick, 6900 E. 45th St., 67226.
McElwee, Robert W., 4084 Mt. Carmel Rd., Frontenac, 66763.
Nolan, Joseph T., 8 Wesley St., Newton, MA 02458.
O'Hare, Donal J., 6900 E. 45th St., 67226.
O'Shea, John J., 6900 E. 45th St., 67226.
Oborny, Paul J., 6900 E. 45th St. N., 67226.
Pepe, Robert F., 6900 E. 45th St. N., 67226.
Reinkemeyer, John, St. Mary, 25741 W. 13th St. N., Garden Plain, 67050.
Roth, James J., 6900 E. 45th St. N, 67226.
Scaletty, Thomas F., 514 Central, Humboldt, 66748.
Schmid, Wayne L., 1408 S. Gasaway Dr., Derby, 67037.
Slomski, Joseph P., 6900 E. 45th St. N., 67226.
Spexarth, James, R.R. 1, P.O. Box 30, Marion, 66861.
Thissen, Donald R., 6900 E. 45th St., 67226.
Walsh, Ulich, 21 The Lawn, Dalton St., Claremorris Ireland.

INSTITUTIONS LOCATED IN THE DIOCESE

[A] COLLEGES AND UNIVERSITIES

WICHITA. *Newman University*, 3100 McCormick Ave., 67213-2097. Tel: 316-942-4291; Fax: 316-942-4483. Web: www.newmanu.edu. Revs. Michael Linnebur, Chap.; Joseph M. Gile, S.T.D., Grad. Theology Dir. & Asst. Prof. Theology; Michael Austin, Ph.D., Provost & Vice Pres. Acad. Affairs; Mark Dresselhaus, Vice Pres. Finance & Admin.; Shirley Rueb, Registrar; Joseph Forte, Librarian; Noreen M. Carrocci, Ph.D., Pres.; Rhonda Cantrell, M.S., Vice Pres. Human Resources; John Clayton, M.Ed., Dean of Admissions; Tom Borrego, J.D., Vice Pres. Inst. Advancement; Victor Trilli, M.S.Ed., Dir. Athletics. Coeducational liberal arts college, founded in 1933 by the Sisters Adorers of the Blood of Christ. (Accredited by the Higher Learning Commission of the North Central Association of Colleges and Schools). Priests 2; Sisters 4; Lay Teachers 86; Total Staff 141; Total Faculty 88; Students 3,021.

[B] HIGH SCHOOLS, DIOCESAN

WICHITA. *Bishop Carroll Catholic High School* (1964) 8101 W. Central, 67212. Tel: 316-722-2390; Fax: 316-722-6670. Email: nielsenleticia@bcchs.org. Web: www.bcchs.org. Leticia C. Nielsen, Pres.; Mrs. Vanessa Harshberger, Prin.; Rev. Benjamin S. Sawyer, Chap.; Peggy Ochs, Librarian. Priests 1; Sisters 3; Lay Teachers 69; Total Staff 73; Students 1,150.
Kapaun Mt. Carmel Catholic High School, 8506 E. Central, 67206. Tel: 316-634-0315; Fax: 316-636-2437. Email: mburrus@kapaun.org. Web: www.kapaun.org. Rev. Aaron Spexarth, Chap.; David Kehres, Prin.; Mrs. Shirley Sharma, Librarian. Priests 1; Sisters 2; Lay Teachers 62; Total Staff 82; Students 901.

HUTCHINSON. *Trinity Catholic Endowment Fund*, (Grades 7-12), 1400 E. 17th, 67501. Tel: 620-662-5800; Fax: 316-662-1233. Email: suehall@trinity-hutch.com. Web: www.trinity-hutch.com. 424 N. Broadway, 67202. Tel: 316-269-3950. Joe Hammersmith, Prin. Priests 1; Sisters 3; Lay Teachers 16; Total Staff 19; Total Enrollment 262.
Trinity Catholic High School (1966) (Grades 7-12), 1400 E. 17th, 67501. Tel: 620-662-5800; Fax: 320-662-1233. Email: jhammersmith@trinity-hutch.com. Web: www.trinity-hutch.com. Joe Hammersmith, Prin.; Rev. Brian D. Nelson, Chap.; Kelli Cramer, Librarian. Priests 1; Sisters 3; Lay Teachers 15; Total Staff 18; Students 256.

PITTSBURG. *St. Mary Colgan High School*, (Grades 7-12), 212 E. 9th St., 66762. Tel: 620-231-4690; Fax: 620-231-0690. Email: smithd@smcschools.org. Web: www.smcschools.com. Rev. Michael Baldwin (TR), Admin.; Mr. John C. Kraus, Pres. Schools; Ms. Bev Mitchelson, Librarian. Priests 3; Lay Teachers 20; Total Staff 25; Students 245.

[C] GENERAL HOSPITALS

WICHITA. *Via Christi Hospital Wichita St. Teresa, Inc.*, 14800 W. St. Teresa, 67235. Tel: 316-796-7000; Fax: 316-796-7018. Total Staff 231; Bed Capacity 68; Inpatients 1,688; Outpatients 15,938; Total Assisted Annually 17,626.
Via Christi Hospitals Wichita, Inc., 929 N. St. Francis, 67214. Tel: 316-268-5000; Fax: 316-291-7999. Web: www.Via-Christi.org. Mr. Randy Peterson, Pres. & CEO; Sisters Sherri Marie Kuhn, S.S.M., Sr. Vice Pres. Mission Integration; Anne Dolores LaPlante, C.S.J., Vice Pres. Pastoral Care & Mission. Bed Capacity 759; Licensed Beds 1,532; Inpatients 33,753; Outpatients 296,054; Total Assisted Annually 329,807; Total Staff 3,875.
Via Christi Hospital on North St. Francis, 929 N. St. Francis, 67214. Tel: 316-268-5000; Fax: 316-291-7999. Rev. Yancey O. Burgess, Chap.
Via Christi Hospital on Harry Street, 3600 E. Harry, 67218. Tel: 316-685-1111; Fax: 316-689-4786. Rev. Douglas L. Campbell, J.C.L., Chap.
Via Christi Rehabilitation Hospital, Inc. (1995) 1151 N. Rock Rd., 67206. Tel: 316-634-3400; Fax: 316-634-1141. Email: cindy.lafleur@viachristi.org. Web: www.viachristi.org. Ms. Cindi S. Unruh, Bd. Chm.; Ms. Cindy LaFleur, Pres., Post Acute Care. Bed Capacity 58; Patients Assisted Annually 10,392; Staff 220.

COLUMBUS. *Mercy Health MHMCH, Inc. dba St. John's Maude Norton Memorial Hospital* 220 N. Pennsylvania Ave., 66725. Tel: 620-429-2545; Fax: 620-429-1984. Email: cynthia.neely@mercy.net. Cynthia Neely, Pres. & Admin. Bed Capacity 25; Patients Assisted Annually 9,135; Total Staff 59.

FORT SCOTT. *Mercy Health Center*, 401 Woodland Hills Blvd., 66701. Tel: 620-223-7057; Fax: 620-223-5327. Reta Baker, Pres. & CEO. Pastoral Care Dir. 1; Lay Staff 390; Bed Capacity 61; Bassinets 6; Patients Assisted Annually 72,816; Home Health Visits 8,629.

INDEPENDENCE. *Mercy Health Systems of Kansas, Inc.-Independence*, 800 W. Myrtle St., P.O. Box 388, 67301. Tel: 620-331-2200; Fax: 620-332-3270. Email: eric.ammons@mercy.net. Web: www.mercykansas.com. Eric Ammons, CEO. Sisters of Mercy 2; Total Staff 260; Bed Capacity 40; Patients Assisted Annually 51,411.

PITTSBURG. *Via Christi Hospital Pittsburg, Inc.* (1903) 1 Mt. Carmel Way, 66762. Tel: 620-231-6100; Fax: 620-232-0493. Web: www.viachristi.org. Mr. Randy Cason, Pres. & CEO. Total Staff 632; Bed Capacity 188; Patients Assisted Annually 20,380.
Mount Carmel Foundation (1983) Tel: 620-235-3512; Fax: 620-235-7862.

[D] HOMES FOR AGED

WICHITA. *Catholic Care Center, Inc.*, 6700 E. 45th St. N., 67226. Tel: 316-744-2020; Fax: 316-744-2182. Email: tom.church@viachristi.org. Web: www.catholiccarecenter.org. Thomas Church, CEO. Operated by Catholic Diocese of Wichita & Via Christ Health. Sisters 11; Total Staff 544; Bed Capacity 298.
Shepherd's Crossing Staff 1; Independent Living Units 30; Total Assisted Annually 40.
Cornerstone Assisted Living, Inc. (2001) 1240 N. Broadmoor, 67206. Tel: 316-636-5101; Fax: 316-636-2576. Email: joanne.rogers@viachristi.org. Web: www.viachristi.org/villages. Joanne Rogers, Exec. Dir.; Mr. Monty Warren, Exec. Dir. Total Assisted 37; Total Staff 23.
3636 N. Ridge Rd., #400, 67205. Tel: 316-462-3636; Fax: 316-462-3676. Web: www.viachristi.org/villages. Mr. Jerry Carley, CEO. Total Assisted 59; Total Staff 38.
Sheridan Village, Inc., 1051 S. Bluffview, 67218. Tel: 316-681-1172; Fax: 316-681-0979. Web: www.viachristi.org/sheridanvillage. Mr. Jerry Carley, CEO. (HUD Low Income Senior Housing) Apartments 66; Total Staff 3.
Via Christi Village Georgetown, Inc. (1985) 1655 Georgetown St., 67218. Tel: 316-685-0400; Fax: 316-685-0174. Web: www.viachristi.org/villages. Margaret Carol Bettam, CEO. Staff 93; Total Assisted 68; Independent Living 130; Condominiums 17; Personnel 118.
Via Christi Village McLean, Inc., 777 N. McLean Blvd., 67203. Tel: 316-942-7000; Fax: 316-946-5727. Web: www.viachristi.org/villages. Mark Mains, CEO. Total Assisted 54; Total Staff 135; Total Nursing 36; Total Independent 42.

MULVANE. *Villa Maria, Inc.* (1950) 116 S. Central, 67110. Tel: 316-777-1129; Fax: 316-777-4406. Email: dena@villamariainc.com. Dena Johnson, CEO. Home for Disabled Men and Women. Adorers of the Blood of Christ 2; Total Staff 100; Guests 98; Total Assisted 142.
Maria Court Assisted Living, 633 E. Main, 67110. Tel: 316-777-9917. Chad Bos, Dir. Bed Capacity 35; Total Assisted Annually 52; Total Staff 18.

PITTSBURG. *Via Christi Village Pittsburg, Inc.* (2003) 1502 E. Centennial, 66762. Tel: 620-235-0020; Fax: 620-235-0520. Email: melinda.ewan@viachristi.org. Web: www.viachristi.org/villages. Melinda Ewan, CEO. Total Staff 150; Skilled Nursing Beds 96; Total Assisted 40.

[E] MONASTERIES AND RESIDENCES FOR PRIESTS AND BROTHERS

WICHITA. *Priests Retirement Center*, 6900 E. 45th St. N., 67226. Tel: 316-744-2020; Fax: 316-744-2182. Thomas M. Church, CEO. Residents 24.

[F] CONVENTS AND RESIDENCES FOR SISTERS

WICHITA. *Adorers of the Blood of Christ U.S. Region*, Wichita Center, 1165 Southwest Blvd., 67213. Tel: 316-942-2201; Fax: 877-942-0859. Web: www.adorers.org. Rev. Thomas Welk, C.PP.S., Chap. Professed Sisters 300.
Dominican Sisters of Peace (1933) 201 S. Millwood, 67213. Tel: 316-267-4551. Residents 3.
Medical Sisters of St. Joseph-United States Foundation (1985) 3435 E. Funston, 67218. Tel: 316-686-4746. Email: josmy61@yahoo.com.au. Sr. Lacy J. George, Supr. Professed Sisters 3.
Sisters of the Immaculate Heart of Mary of Wichita, Inc. (I.H.M.) (1979) 145 S. Millwood St., 67213. Tel: 316-722-9316; Fax: 316-722-4568. Email: ihmmail@sistersihmofwichita.org. Web: www.sistersihmofwichita.org. Sr. Mary Magdalene O'Halloran, I.H.M., Gen. Supr. Professed Sisters 18; Novices 2.
Wichita Center, Congregation of the Sisters of St. Joseph, 3700 E. Lincoln, 67218-2099. Tel: 316-686-7171; Fax: 316-689-4056. Email: amcdonald@csjoseph.org. Web: www.csjoseph.org. Sr. Arlys McDonald, C.S.J., Admin.; Rev. Msgr. Robert E. Hemberger, J.C.L., Chap. Professed Sisters 118.

VALLEY CENTER. *Discalced Carmelite Monastery of Divine Mercy and Our Lady of Guadalupe*, P.O. Box 278, 67147. Tel: 316-744-2652; Fax: 316-744-2652. Total Assisted 150.

[G] RETREAT HOUSES

WICHITA. *Spiritual Life Center*, 7100 E. 45th N., 67226. Tel: 316-744-0167; Fax: 314-744-8072. Email: slc@slcwichita.org. Web: www.slcwichita.org. Rev. Kenneth S. Van Haverbeke, Dir. Residents 1; Staff 15; Total Assisted Annually 13,968.

Ministry Staff: Mr. Jim Rundell, Admin.; Laura Bliss, Facility Coord.

[H] COMMUNITY CENTERS

WICHITA. **Center of Hope, Inc.*, 400 N. Emporia, 67202-2514. Tel: 316-267-3999; Fax: 316-267-7778. Email: george@centerofhopeinc.org. Web: www.centerofhopeinc.org. George Dinkel, Exec. Dir. Tel: 316-267-0222; Fax: 316-267-7778. Sponsored by Adorers of the Blood of Christ. Total Assisted Annually 8,012.

The Lord's Diner (2002) 520 N. Broadway, 67214. Tel: 316-266-4966; Fax: 316-265-6646. Email: janh@thelordsdiner.org. Web: www.thelordsdiner.org. Jan Haberly, Dir. Meals Served to Date 1,426,470.

Sisters of St. Joseph "Dear Neighbor" Ministries, Inc., 1329 S. Bluffview, 67218. Tel: 316-684-5120; Fax: 316-684-3983. Ms. Katherine J. Lambertz, L.M.S.W., Exec. Dir. Congregation of St. Joseph. Total Assisted 12,378; Total Staff 10.

**StepStone, Inc.*, 1329 S. Bluffview, 67218. Tel: 316-265-1611; Fax: 316-265-0738. Web: www.stepstoneks.org. Ms. Katherine J. Lambertz, L.M.S.W., Exec. Dir.

[I] NEWMAN CENTERS

WICHITA. *St. Paul Newman Center (Wichita State University)* (1970) 1810 N. Roosevelt, 67208. Tel: 316-684-6896; Fax: 316-684-2679. Email: parish@wsunewmancenter.com. Web: www.wsunewmancenter.com. Rev. John N. Hay, Chap.

PITTSBURG. *St. Pius X Newman Center (Pittsburg State University)* 301A E. Cleveland, 66762. Tel: 620-235-1138. Email: fradam@catholicgorillas.org. Web: catholicgorillas.org. Rev. Adam Keiter, Chap.

[J] CATHOLIC CHARITIES

WICHITA. *Catholic Charities, Inc.* (1943) 532 N. Broadway St., 67214. Tel: 316-264-8344; Fax: 316-264-4442. Email: info@catholiccharitieswichita.org. Web: catholiccharitieswichita.org. Ms. Cynthia Colbert, Exec. Dir. Total Agency Staff 120; Total Individuals Assisted 24,575.

Foster Grandparent Program (1981) 5920 W. Central Ave., 67212. Tel: 316-264-8344; Fax: 316-262-5356. Provides 119,114 hours of service. Hours of Service to Children 118,622; Total Foster Grandparents 153; Staff 2.

Food Pantry, 241 N. Indiana, 67214. Tel: 316-262-8898; Fax: 316-262-5356. Total Assisted 16,777; Total Staff 3; Total Assisted (Christmas Sharing Program) 1,491.

Immigration & Refugee Services, 532 N. Broadway St., 67214. Tel: 316-264-0282; Fax: 316-262-5356. Total Assisted 1,135; Staff 3.

Pregnancy and Adoption Services, 425 N. Topeka St., 67202. Tel: 316-263-6941; Fax: 316-263-5259. Total Assisted 201; Adoptions Completed 3; Total Staff 3.

Community Counseling Services, 425 N. Topeka St., 67202. Tel: 316-263-6941; Fax: 316-263-5259. Individuals Served 1,334; Total Staff 7.

Adult Day Services (1975) 5920 W. Central Ave., 67212. Tel: 316-942-2008; Fax: 316-942-2260. Total Assisted 96; Staff 19.

St. Anthony Family Shelter (1988) 256 N. Ohio, 67214. Tel: 316-264-7233; Fax: 316-267-3774. Individuals Assisted In Shelter 520; In Follow-Up 30; Staff 17.

Harbor House (1992) P.O. Box 3759, 67201. Tel: 316-263-6000; Fax: 316-263-8347. Women & Children Assisted and Victim's Advocate Program 1,522; Staff 35.

Interpreter Services (2001) 437 N. Topeka, 67202. Tel: 316-264-8344; Fax: 316-262-5356. Clients Served 71; Total Staff 1; Contracted Interpreters 4.

Southeast Kansas Emergency Services - Pittsburg, 411 E. 12th St., Pittsburg, 66762. Tel: 620-235-0633; Fax: 620-235-0633. Clients Served 856; Staff 1.

Marriage For Keeps (A Project of Catholic Charities), 425 N. Topeka St., 67202. Tel: 316-263-6941; Fax: 316-262-5356. Total Staff 14; Total Served 868.

[K] MISCELLANEOUS

WICHITA. *Marriage Encounter*, 6900 E. 45th St., N. #4, 67226. Tel: 316-440-3087. Rev. Paul J. Oborny, Contact Person (Retired).

St. Dismas/Ministry to the Incarcerated (1991) 7100 E. 45th St. N., 67226. Tel: 316-744-0167; Fax: 316-744-8072. Email: jrundell@slcwichita.org. Web: www.catholicdioceseofwichita.org. Total Staff 1; Inmates Served 6,100.

Father Kapaun Guild (Office for the Beatification and Canonization of Father Emil Kapaun), 424 N. Broadway, 67202. Tel: 316-269-3900. Email: hotzej@catholicdioceseofwichita.org. Web: www.frkapaun.org. Revs. John V. Hotze, J.C.L., Episcopal Delegate; Thomas M. Hoisington, S.T.L., Promoter of Justice.

Gerard House, Inc. (1989) 3144 N. Hood, 67204. Tel: 316-832-0777; Fax: 316-832-1327. Deneen Dryden, Dir. Shelter for Needy Pregnant Women. Education Program 48; Total Assisted 38.

Guadalupe Clinic, Inc. (1985) 940 S. St. Francis, 67211. Tel: 316-264-8974; Fax: 316-262-4938. Email: guadalupe@guadalupeclinic.kscoxmail.com. Web: www.guadalupeclinic.com. Karl N. Hesse, Attorney; Marlene Dreiling, M.N., R.N., Exec. Dir. Total Assisted Annually 61,774; Total Staff 15.

Guadalupe Health Foundation, 940 S. St. Francis, 67202. Tel: 316-264-8974; Fax: 316-262-4938. Purpose: to support, assist and promote the interests and welfare of the programs and activities of the Diocese of Wichita which provide health care services and health education to poor, distressed and underprivileged individuals.

Harvest House (1989) 424 N. Broadway, 67202. Tel: 316-269-3900; Fax: 316-269-3902. Staff 1; Centers 32; Members Assisted 1,820.

Holy Family Special Needs Foundation, 424 N. Broadway, 67202. Tel: 316-269-3900; Fax: 316-269-3902. Web: catholicdioceseofwichita.org/offices/disabilities. Tom Racunas, Staff to Board of Directors.

Leaven International Corporation, 1165 Southwest Blvd., 67213. Tel: 316-943-1203; Fax: 316-943-1426. Email: bergkampv@adorers.org. Web: www.adorers.org. Sisters Jan E. Renz, A.S.C., Pres.; Vicki Bergkamp, A.S.C., Treas. A charitable organization of the Adorers of the Blood of Christ.

The Mary Magdalen Foundation, 12626 E. 21st St. N., 67206. Tel: 316-634-2315; Fax: 316-634-3948. Email: fknoblauch@magdalenwichita.com. Web: www.magdalenwichita.com. Priests 2.

Ministry with Persons with Disabilities Office, 424 N. Broadway, 67202. Tel: 316-269-3900; Fax: 316-269-3902. Web: catholicdioceseofwichita.org/offices/disabilities. Priests 29; Total Assisted 437; Volunteers 222; Total Staff 2.

Priests' Retirement and Education Fund of Wichita (2001) 424 N. Broadway, 67202. Tel: 316-269-3900; Fax: 316-269-3902. Rev. Michael M. Simone, S.T.L.

Serra Club of Reno County, 424 N. Broadway, 67202. Rev. Nicholas A. Voelker, Chap.

Serra Club of Wichita - Downtown, 424 N. Broadway, 67202. Tel: 316-269-3900. Rev. Kenneth J. Schuckman, Chap.

Serra Club of Wichita - Metro, 424 N. Broadway, 67202. Tel: 316-269-3900. Rev. Michael M. Simone, S.T.L., Chap.

Sisters of St. Joseph of Wichita, Kansas, 3700 E. Lincoln, 67218. Tel: 316-686-7171; Fax: 316-689-4056.

Via Christi Foundation, Inc. (1957) 723 N. McLean, Ste. 310, 67203. Tel: 316-946-5020; Fax: 316-946-5034. Email: james.barber@viachristi.org. Mr. James N. Barber, Pres. A subsidiary of Via Christi Hospitals Wichita, Inc. Staff 15.

Via Christi Health, Inc. (1995) 8200 E. Thorn, 67226. Tel: 316-858-4900. Web: www.viachristi.org. Jeffrey O. Korsmo, Pres. & CEO. Affiliated with the Marian Health System and Ascension Health and co-sponsored by the Sisters of the Sorrowful Mother and the sponsoring congregations of Ascension Health. Owned organizations include: four acute care facilities, fifteen senior care facilities and one 50% owned, managed acute care facility, located in two states.

Via Christi Health Partners, Inc. (1982) 8200 E. Thorn, 67226. Tel: 316-858-4908. Web: www.Via-Christi.org. Total Staff 3.

Via Christi Healthcare Outreach Program for Elders, Inc. (HOPE) (2002) 2622 W. Central, Ste. 101, 67203. Tel: 316-858-1111; Fax: 316-858-1166. Email: justin.loewen@viachristi.org. Web: www.viachristi.org/villages. Justin Loewen, CEO. Long Term Care Bed Capacity 24; Total Assisted Annually 196; Total Staff 209.

Via Christi Home Health Inc. (1983) 555 S. Washington, 67211. Tel: 316-268-8588; Fax: 316-269-1556. Email: joy.scott@viachristi.org. Web: www.via-christi.org. Registered Nurses 30; Physical Therapists 8; CPTA's 6; Medical Social Workers 3; Speech Therapists 3; Occupational Therapists 5; COTA's 4; Total Staff 65; Home Health Aides 3.

Via Christi Immediate Care, 1152 S. Clifton Ave., 67218. Tel: 316-695-5121. Email: sistersherrimarie.kuhn@viachristi.org.

Via Christi Property Services, Inc. (1998) 1100 N. St. Francis, Ste. 240, 67214. Tel: 316-268-6810; Fax: 316-291-4785 1. Web: www.Via-Christi.org. Total Staff 7.

Via Christi Villages, Inc. (1985) 2622 W. Central, Ste. 100, 67203. Tel: 316-946-5200; Fax: 316-946-5299. Email: jerry.carley@viachristi.org. Web: www.viachristi.org/villages. Mr. Jerry Carley, CEO. Total Staff 90.

DERBY. *Engaged Encounter, St. Mary Catholic Church*, 2300 E. Meadowlark Rd., 67037. Tel: 316-788-5525; Fax: 316-788-1577. Rev. David J. Lies, Contact Person.

RELIGIOUS INSTITUTES OF MEN REPRESENTED IN THE DIOCESE

For further details refer to the corresponding bracketed number in the Religious Institutes of Men or Women section.

[1060]—*Society of the Precious Blood* (Kansas City Prov.)—C.PP.S.

RELIGIOUS INSTITUTES OF WOMEN REPRESENTED IN THE DIOCESE

[0100]—*Adorers of the Blood of Christ*—A.S.C.

[]—*Carmelite Sisters of St. Teresa*—C.S.S.T.

[3832]—*Congregation of the Sisters of St. Joseph*—C.S.J.

[]—*Discalced Carmelite Sisters of Divine Mercy and Our Lady of Guadalupe*—O.C.D.

[1115]—*Dominican Sisters of Peace*—O.P.

[]—*Guadalupan Missionaries of the Holy Spirit*—M.G.S.p.S.

[2500]—*Medical Sisters of St. Joseph*—M.S.J.

[]—*Missionary Catechists of the Poor*—M.C.P.

[]—*Sisters of Mercy South Central Regional Community*—R.S.M.

[]—*Sisters of St. Joseph of Concordia*—C.S.J.

[2185]—*Sisters of the Immaculate Heart of Mary of Wichita*—I.H.M.

[4100]—*Sisters of the Sorrowful Mother (Third Order of St. Francis)*—S.S.M.

NECROLOGY

(No Deaths)

An asterisk (*) denotes an organization that has established tax-exempt status directly with the IRS and is not covered by the USCCB Group Ruling.

Diocese of Wilmington

(Dioecesis Wilmingtoniensis)

Most Reverend

WILLIAM FRANCIS MALOOLY, D.D.

Bishop of Wilmington; ordained May 9, 1970; appointed Titular Bishop of Flumenzer and Auxiliary Bishop of Baltimore December 12, 2000; Episcopal ordination March 1, 2001; appointed Bishop of Wilmington July 7, 2008; installed September 8, 2008. *Chancery: 1925 Delaware Ave., P.O. Box 2030, Wilmington, DE 19899.* Tel: 302-573-3100; Fax: 302-573-6817. Email: pbossi-smedley@cdow.org.

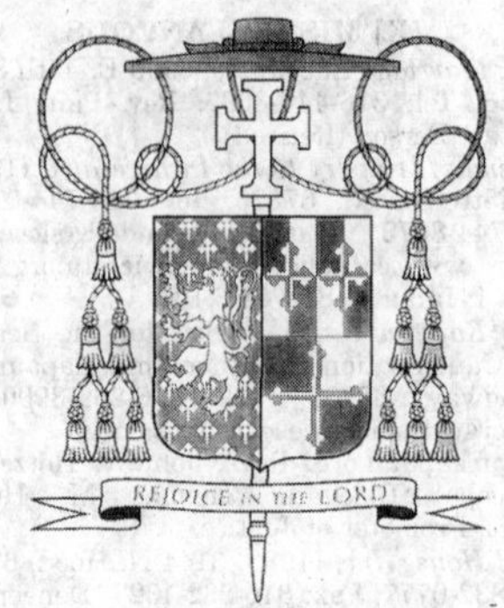

Chancery Office: P.O. Box 2030, Wilmington, DE 19899-2030. Tel: 302-573-3100; Fax: 302-573-6836.

Web: www.cdow.org

Email: chancery@cdow.org

ESTABLISHED MARCH 3, 1868.

Square Miles Delaware 1,932; Maryland 3,375; Total 5,307.

Comprises the State of Delaware and the Counties of Caroline, Cecil, Dorchester, Kent, Queen Anne's, Somerset, Talbot, Wicomico and Worcester in Maryland.

For legal titles of parishes and diocesan institutions, consult the Chancery Office.

STATISTICAL OVERVIEW

Personnel	
Bishop	1
Priests: Diocesan Active in Diocese	81
Priests: Diocesan Active Outside Diocese	4
Priests: Retired, Sick or Absent	41
Number of Diocesan Priests	126
Religious Priests in Diocese	70
Total Priests in Diocese	196
Extern Priests in Diocese	12
Ordinations:	
Diocesan Priests	3
Permanent Deacons in Diocese	107
Total Brothers	23
Total Sisters	213
Parishes	
Parishes	57
With Resident Pastor:	
Resident Diocesan Priests	47
Resident Religious Priests	6
Without Resident Pastor:	
Administered by Priests	4
Missions	19
Professional Ministry Personnel:	
Brothers	1
Sisters	10
Lay Ministers	305
Welfare	
Catholic Hospitals	1
Total Assisted	177,113
Health Care Centers	1
Total Assisted	175
Homes for the Aged	6
Total Assisted	510
Day Care Centers	3
Total Assisted	151
Specialized Homes	3
Total Assisted	75
Special Centers for Social Services	16
Total Assisted	228,778
Residential Care of Disabled	1
Total Assisted	100
Other Institutions	3
Total Assisted	10,562
Educational	
Diocesan Students in Other Seminaries	7
Total Seminarians	7
High Schools, Diocesan and Parish	5
Total Students	2,488
High Schools, Private	3
Total Students	1,654
Elementary Schools, Diocesan and Parish	18
Total Students	6,616
Elementary Schools, Private	4
Total Students	1,216
Non-residential Schools for the Disabled	1
Total Students	78
Catechesis/Religious Education:	
High School Students	529
Elementary Students	7,413
Total Students under Catholic Instruction	20,001
Teachers in the Diocese:	
Priests	15
Brothers	6
Sisters	20
Lay Teachers	973
Vital Statistics	
Receptions into the Church:	
Infant Baptism Totals	2,367
Minor Baptism Totals	215
Adult Baptism Totals	104
Received into Full Communion	269
First Communions	2,484
Confirmations	2,126
Marriages:	
Catholic	414
Interfaith	194
Total Marriages	608
Deaths	1,742
Total Catholic Population	239,017
Total Population	1,347,160

Former Bishops—Rt. Revs. THOMAS A. BECKER, D.D., ord. June 18, 1859; cons. Aug. 16, 1868; transferred to Savannah, 1886; died July 29, 1899; ALFRED A. CURTIS, D.D., ord. Dec. 19, 1874; cons. Nov. 14, 1886; resigned 1896; named Titular Bishop of Echinus; died July 11, 1908; Most Revs. JOHN J. MONAGHAN, D.D., ord. Dec. 19, 1880; cons. May 9, 1897; resigned and named Titular Bishop of Lydda, July 10, 1925; died Jan. 7, 1935; EDMOND JOHN FITZMAURICE, D.D., ord. May 1904; cons. Nov. 30, 1925; resigned March 2, 1960 and named Titular Archbishop of Tomi; died July 25, 1962; HUBERT J. CARTWRIGHT, D.D., ord. June 11, 1927; cons. Coadjutor "with right of succession," Oct. 24, 1956; Titular Bishop of Neve; died March 6, 1958; MICHAEL W. HYLE, D.D., ord. March 12, 1927; cons. Sept. 24, 1958 as Titular Bishop of Christopolis and Coadjutor with right of succession; succeeded to See, March 2, 1960; died Dec. 26, 1967; THOMAS J. MARDAGA, D.D., ord. May 14, 1940; cons. Jan. 25, 1967; named Titular Bishop of Mutugenna; appt. Bishop of Wilmington, March 13, 1968; installed April 6, 1968; died May 28, 1984; JAMES C. BURKE, O.P., ord. June 18, 1956; cons. May 25, 1967; named Titular Bishop of Lamiggiga; Vicar Apostolic of Chimbote, Peru, 1962-1978; Served in Diocese of Wilmington, 1978-1994; died May 28, 1994; ROBERT E. MULVEE, D.D., J.C.D., ord. June 30, 1957; Auxiliary Bishop of Manchester and Titular Bishop of Summa, Feb. 15, 1977; cons. April 14, 1977; appt. Bishop of Wilmington, Feb. 19, 1985; installed April 11, 1985; appt. to Diocese of Providence as Coadjutor Bishop of Providence, Feb. 7, 1995; installed March 27, 1995; succeeded to See, June 11, 1997; MICHAEL A. SALTARELLI, D.D., ord. May 28, 1960; appt. Titular Bishop of Mesarfelta and Auxiliary Bishop of Newark, June 12, 1990; Episcopal ord. July 30, 1990; appt. Eighth Bishop of Wilmington Nov. 21, 1995; installed Jan. 23, 1996 retired July 7, 2008; died Oct. 8, 2009.

Office of the Bishop—Mailing Address: P.O. Box 2030, Wilmington, 19899. PATRICIA BOSSI-SMEDLEY, Sec. to Bishop & Notary for the Curia. Tel: 302-573-3100; Fax: 302-573-6817. Email: pbossi-smedley@cdow.org.

Chancellor—Very Rev. STEVEN P. HURLEY, S.T.L., 1925 Delaware Ave., P.O. Box 2030, Wilmington, 19899. Tel: 302-573-3100; Fax: 302-573-6836.

Vicar General for Administration and Moderator of the Curia—Rev. Msgr. J. THOMAS CINI, V.G., 1925 Delaware Ave., P.O. Box 2030, Wilmington, 19899. Tel: 302-573-3118; Fax: 302-573-6947.

Vicar General for Pastoral Services—Rev. Msgr. JOSEPH F. REBMAN, V.G., S.T.L., J.C.L., C.C.C.E., 1925 Delaware Ave., P.O. Box 2030, Wilmington, 19899. Tel: 302-573-3100; Fax: 302-573-6836.

Vicar for Priests—Rev. Msgr. CLEMENT P. LEMON, 1925 Delaware Ave., P.O. Box 2030, Wilmington, 19899. Tel: 302-573-3144; Fax: 302-573-6947.

Pastoral Services Department

Secretary, Pastoral Services Department—Rev. Msgr. JOSEPH F. REBMAN, V.G., S.T.L., J.C.L., C.C.C.E.

Chancery Office—Very Rev. STEVEN P. HURLEY, S.T.L., Chancellor, Mailing Address: P.O. Box 2030, Wilmington, 19899. Office, 1925 Delaware Ave., Wilmington, 19806. Tel: 302-573-3100; Fax: 302-573-6836. Email: chancery@cdow.org. Web: www.cdow.org. Office Hours: Mon.-Fri. 8:30-4:30; Send all marriage dispensation requests to Chancery Office.

Archives—Mr. DONN DEVINE, J.D., C.G., C.G.L., Archivist, 8 Old Church Rd., Greenville, 19807. Tel: 302-655-0597. Email: donndevine@aol.com.

Censor of Books—Rev. JAMES S. LENTINI, Prin., St. Thomas More Academy, 133 Thomas More Dr., Magnolia, 19962.

Diocesan Tribunal—Mailing Address: P.O. Box 2030, Wilmington, 19899. 1925 Delaware Ave., Wilmington, 19806. Tel: 302-573-3107; Fax: 302-573-6947.

Judicial Vicar—Rev. Msgr. GEORGE J. BRUBAKER, J.C.L.

Office Supervisor—Mrs. JOANN KUBASKO.

Court of First Instance Judges—Rev. Msgr. GEORGE J. BRUBAKER, J.C.L.; Ms. JACQUELINE E. HANNEM, J.C.L.

Auditor—Deacon FRANCIS STAAB.

Defenders of the Bond—Mr. JACK D. ANDERSON, J.C.D.; Rev. CYPRIAN ROSEN, O.F.M.Cap., S.T.L.; Sr. PATRICIA SMITH, O.S.F., J.C.D.

Secretary/Notary—Mrs. GAIL ESPOSITO.

Catholic Cemeteries—Rev. Msgr. JOSEPH F. REBMAN, V.G., S.T.L., J.C.L., C.C.C.E., Dir.; Mr. MARK A. CHRISTIAN, C.C.C.E., Exec. Dir., Mailing Address: P.O. Box 2506, Wilmington, 19805. Tel: 302-656-3323; Fax: 302-656-1069.

Coordinator of Institutional Chaplains—Rev. JOHN J. MINK, Dir., 801 Dupont Blvd., New Castle, 19720. Tel: 302-328-1790.

Priest Personnel Committee—Rev. JOHN J. MINK, Dir., 801 Dupont Blvd., New Castle, 19720. Tel: 302-328-1790.

Office of Priestly and Religious Vocations and Seminarians and Newly Ordained—Rev. JOSEPH M.P.R. COCUCCI, Dir., 1626 N. Union St., P.O. Box 2030, Wilmington, 19899. Tel: 302-573-3113; Fax: 302-573-6944.

Office for Deacons—Deacon HAROLD D. JOPP JR., Dir., 1626 N. Union St., P.O. Box 2030, Wilmington, 19899. Tel: 302-573-2390; Fax: 302-573-6944.

Office of Worship—Rev. MICHAEL J. CARRIER, Dir., 1626 N. Union St., Wilmington, 19899. Tel: 302-573-3137; Fax: 302-573-6944.

Office for Marriage and Family Life—Mr. MICHAEL J. STANKEWICZ, Mailing Address: P.O. Box 2030, Wilmington, 19899. Tel: 302-295-0684.

Office for Pro Life Activities—Rev. LEONARD R. KLEIN, Dir., Mailing Address: P.O. Box 2030, Wilmington, 19899. Tel: 302-295-0626.

Delegate for Religious—Sr. MARGARET CUNNIFFE, O.S.F., 1626 N. Union St., P.O. Box 2030, Wilmington, 19899. Tel: 302-573-3124; Fax: 302-573-6944.

Mission Office— Propagation of the Faith and Holy Childhood Association, Deacon JOSEPH C. ROMANS, Dir., 1626 N. Union St., P.O. Box 2030, Wilmington, 19899. Tel: 302-573-3104; Fax: 302-573-6944.

Apostolate for Ethnic Ministries—Mailing Address: P.O. Box 2030, Wilmington, 19899. Tel: 302-573-3100.

Ministry of Black Catholics—Mr. PRESTON TAYLOR, Dir., 2810 Monroe St., Wilmington, 19802. Tel: 302-762-6848; Fax: 302-764-8244.

Hispanic Ministry—

Wilmington Office—Rev. CHRISTOPHER J. POSCH, O.F.M., Dir., 1010 W. Fourth St., Wilmington, 19805. Tel: 302-576-4123; Fax: 302-655-7684; Sr. AGNES OMAN, C.S.B., Assoc. Dir., Mailing Address: P.O. Box 45, Selbyville, 19975-0045. Tel: 443-235-7247.

Korean Catholics—Rev. JOHN (B) LEE GYE-CHUN, Pastoral Min.; Mr. PETER SANG JIN PARK, Community Pres., 2710 Duncan Rd., Wilmington, 19808. Tel: 302-994-0251.

Native American Community—Contacts: SHERYL PERSINGER, 505 Rochelle Ave., Wilmington, 19804. Tel: 302-992-0708; DEBRA GOERGER, Mailing Address: P.O. Box 2030, Wilmington, 19899. Tel: 302-573-3100.

Catholic Education Department

Secretary—VACANT.

Catholic Schools—Mrs. CATHERINE P. WEAVER, Supt. Assistant Superintendents: CAROL RIPKEN; LOUIS DEANGELO, 1626 N. Union St., Wilmington, 19806. Tel: 302-573-3133; Fax: 302-573-6945.

Religious Education—Mr. MICHAEL J. STANKEWICZ, Diocesan Dir.

Education Ministry for Persons With Special Needs—LYNN LEMON, Coord. Spec. Rel. Educ. Tel: 302-573-3130; Mrs. MARGARET WYNN, Coord. Hearing Impaired, 1626 N. Union St., Wilmington, 19806. Tel: 302-573-3130.

Catholic Youth Ministry—Mr. PATRICK DONOVAN, Dir.; JOE MCNESBY, Dir. Athletics, 1626 N. Union St., Wilmington, 19806. Tel: 302-658-3800; Fax: 302-658-7617. Web: www.cdow.org.

Catholic Scouting Program—Revs. MICHAEL J. CARRIER, Chap. for Girl Scouts, 2500 Naamans Rd., Wilmington, 19810. Tel: 302-475-6486; MICHAEL P. DARCY, Chap. Boy Scouts, 7200 Lancaster Pike, Hockessin, 19707. Tel: 302-239-7100.

Catholic Campus Ministry—Rev. AMBROSE ECKINGER, O.P.; KIM ZITZNER, Campus Min., University of Delaware, 45 Lovett Ave., Newark, 19711. Tel: 302-368-4728; Fax: 302-368-2548.

Communications Department

Secretary—Mr. ROBERT KREBS.

Office of Public Relations and Media—Mr. ROBERT KREBS, Dir., 1626 N. Union St., Wilmington, 19899. Tel: 302-573-3116; Fax: 302-573-6944.

Finance Department

Chief Financial Officer and Secretary—Mr. JOSEPH P. CORSINI, Mailing Address: P.O. Box 2030, Wilmington, 19899. 1925 Delaware Ave., Wilmington, 19806. Tel: 302-573-3105; Fax: 302-573-6869.

Development Department

Secretary and Diocesan Development Director—Mrs. DEBORAH A. FOLS, Mailing Address: P.O. Box 2030, Wilmington, 19899. Tel: 302-573-3121; Fax: 302-573-6947.

Annual Catholic Appeal—Mrs. DEBORAH A. FOLS, Dir., Mailing Address: P.O. Box 2030, Wilmington, 19899. Tel: 302-573-3100; Fax: 302-573-6947.

Catholic Charities Department

Catholic Charities—Ms. RICHELLE A. VIBLE, M.B.A., Exec. Dir., Fourth St. & Greenhill Ave., P.O. Box 2610, Wilmington, 19805. Tel: 302-655-9624; Fax: 302-655-9753 (Refer to separate listings in the Institutions for detailed information on Catholic Charities and related organizations).

Offices Reporting to Vicar General for Administration/Moderator of the Curia

Catholic Press Inc., "The Dialog"—Most Rev. W. FRANCIS MALOOLY, D.D., Publisher; Mr. JOSEPH KIRK RYAN, Editor & Gen. Mgr., Mailing Address: P.O. Box 2208, Wilmington, 19899. 1925 Delaware Ave., Wilmington, 19806. Tel: 302-573-3109 (Newsroom); 302-573-3112 (Advertising); Fax: 302-573-6948. Email: news@thedialog.org. Web: www.thedialog.org.

Human Resources Office—Sr. SUZANNE M. DONOVAN, S.C., Dir., Mailing Address: P.O. Box 2030, Wilmington, 19899. Tel: 302-573-3126; Fax: 302-573-6944.

Management Information System (MIS)—Mrs. NANCY MOORE, Dir., Mailing Address: P.O. Box 2030, Wilmington, 19899. 1925 Delaware Ave., Wilmington, 19806. Tel: 302-573-3122; Fax: 302-573-6947.

Diocesan Planning—Rev. Msgr. J. THOMAS CINI, V.G., Mailing Address: P.O. Box 2030, Wilmington, 19899. Tel: 302-573-3118; Fax: 302-573-6947.

Diocesan Real Estate Committee—Rev. Msgr. J. THOMAS CINI, V.G., Sec., Mailing Address: P.O. Box 2030, Wilmington, 19899. Tel: 302-573-3118; Fax: 302-573-6947.

Catholic Ministry to the Elderly—Rev. Msgr. J. THOMAS CINI, V.G., Sec., Mailing Address: P.O. Box 2030, Wilmington, 19806. Tel: 302-573-3118; Fax: 302-573-6947.

Other Ministries

Liaison for Non-Christian Religions—Rev. LEONARD J. KEMPSKI, Liaison (Retired), Holy Rosary, 3200 Philadelphia Pike, Claymont, 19703. Tel: 302-798-2904.

Liaison for Evangelization—Rev. WILLIAM J. LAWLER, Liaison, Mailing Address: P.O. Box 218, Cambridge, MD 21613. Tel: 410-228-4770.

Ecumenical Liaison—Rev. Msgr. JOSEPH F. REBMAN, V.G., S.T.L., J.C.L., C.C.C.E., Dir., Mailing Address: P.O. Box 2030, Wilmington, 19899. Tel: 302-573-3100.

Marian Devotions—Rev. Msgr. JOSEPH F. REBMAN, V.G., S.T.L., J.C.L., C.C.C.E., Dir. Associate Directors: Revs. TIMOTHY M. NOLAN; JOSEPH J. PIEKARSKI; JOHN S. GRIMM, Mailing Address: P.O. Box 2030, Wilmington, 19899. Tel: 302-573-3100.

Volunteer Liaison for the Physically Challenged—Mr. BOB CICHOCKI, M.H.S., 67 Lowry Dr., Wilmington, 19805. Email: quiet4343@yahoo.com.

Principal Advisory Groups to the Bishop

College of Consultors—Rev. Msgrs. JOSEPH F. REBMAN, V.G., S.T.L., J.C.L., C.C.C.E.; J. THOMAS CINI, V.G.; CLEMENT P. LEMON; GEORGE J. BRUBAKER, J.C.L.; JOHN P. HOPKINS; Very Rev. DAVID F. KELLEY.

Priests' Council—Rev. Msgr. JOHN P. HOPKINS, Exec. Officer; Very Rev. STEVEN P. HURLEY, S.T.L., Sec., Mailing Address: P.O. Box 2030, Wilmington, 19899. Tel: 302-573-3100.

Deans—Very Revs. NORMAN P. CARROLL, V.F.; PAUL F. JENNINGS JR., V.F.; Rev. Msgr. CHARLES L. BROWN III, V.F.; Very Revs. DAVID F. KELLEY; STEVEN B. GIULIANO, V.F.; MICHAEL B. ROARK; STANLEY J. RUSSELL, V.F.

Finance Council—Mr. JOSEPH P. CORSINI, Sec., Mailing Address: P.O. Box 2030, Wilmington, 19899. Tel: 302-573-3105.

Priests' Personnel Committee—Rev. JOHN J. MINK, Dir., Mailing Address: P.O. Box 2030, Wilmington, 19899. Tel: 302-328-1790; Fax: 302-328-8364.

Other Advisory Groups

Priests' Continuing Formation Committee—Rev. Msgr. JOHN P. HOPKINS, Chm., St. Margaret of Scotland, 2431 Frazer Rd., Newark, 19702. Tel: 302-834-0225; Fax: 302-834-0840.

Council of Religious—Sr. MARGARET CUNNIFFE, O.S.F., Contact, Mailing Address: P.O. Box 2030, Wilmington, 19899. Tel: 302-573-3124; Fax: 302-573-6944.

Diocesan School Board—Mrs. CATHERINE P. WEAVER, Sec., Mailing Address: P.O. Box 2030, Wilmington, 19899. Tel: 302-573-3133.

Diocesan Religious Education Board—Mr. MICHAEL J. STANKEWICZ, Sec., Mailing Address: 1626 N. Union St., Wilmington, 19806. Tel: 302-573-3130; Fax: 302-573-6944.

Diocesan Building Committee—Mr. HENRY STEENKAMER, Chm.; Rev. Msgr. J. THOMAS CINI, V.G., Episcopal Liaison, Mailing Address: P.O. Box 2030, Wilmington, 19899. Tel: 302-573-3118; Fax: 302-573-6947.

Pastoral Council—Mr. MICHAEL RUSH, Exec. Officer, Mailing Address: P.O. Box 2030, Wilmington, 19899. Tel: 302-573-3100; Fax: 302-573-6836.

Public Affairs Advisory Committee—Rev. Msgr. J. THOMAS CINI, V.G., Chm., Mailing Address: P.O. Box 2030, Wilmington, 19899. Tel: 302-573-3118; Fax: 302-573-6947.

Due Process Commission—Contact: Rev. Msgr. GEORGE J. BRUBAKER, J.C.L., Clerk, Mailing Address: P.O. Box 2030, Wilmington, 19899. Tel: 302-573-3107; Fax: 302-573-6947.

Diocesan Corporations

Catholic Cemeteries, Inc.—Rev. Msgr. JOSEPH F. REBMAN, V.G., S.T.L., J.C.L., C.C.C.E., Vice Pres.; Mr. MARK A. CHRISTIAN, C.C.C.E., Sec., Mailing Address: P.O. Box 2506, Wilmington, 19805. Tel: 302-656-3323.

Catholic Diocese of Wilmington, Inc.— A corporation sole under the laws of the State of Delaware. Rev. Msgrs. JOSEPH F. REBMAN, V.G., S.T.L., J.C.L., C.C.C.E., Vice Pres.; J. THOMAS CINI, V.G., Sec., Mailing Address: P.O. Box 2030, Wilmington, 19899. Tel: 302-573-3118. Office, 1925 Delaware Ave., Wilmington, 19899.

Catholic Diocese Foundation—Mr. JOSEPH P. CORSINI, Exec. Dir., Mailing Address: P.O. Box 2030, Wilmington, 19899. Tel: 302-573-3105.

Catholic Ministry to the Elderly, Inc.—Rev. Msgr. J. THOMAS CINI, V.G., Vice Pres., Mailing Address: P.O. Box 2030, Wilmington, 19899. Tel: 302-573-3118.

Catholic Press of Wilmington, Inc.—Rev. Msgr. J. THOMAS CINI, V.G., Vice Pres., Mailing Address: P.O. Box 2208, Wilmington, 19899. Tel: 302-573-3118.

Catholic Charities, Inc.—Rev. Msgr. J. THOMAS CINI, V.G., Contact Person, Fourth St. & Greenhill Ave., P.O. Box 2610, Wilmington, 19806. Tel: 302-655-9624.

Catholic Youth Organization, Inc.—Rev. Msgr. J. THOMAS CINI, V.G., Vice Pres., Mailing Address: P.O. Box 2030, Wilmington, 19899. Tel: 302-573-3118.

Children's Home, Inc.—Rev. Msgr. J. THOMAS CINI, V.G., Contact Person, 4th St. & Greenhill Ave., P.O. Box 2610, Wilmington, 19806. Tel: 302-655-9624.

Diocese of Wilmington Schools, Inc.—Mrs. CATHERINE P. WEAVER, Sec., 1626 N. Union St., Wilmington, 19806. Tel: 302-573-3133.

Seton Villa, Inc.—Rev. Msgr. J. THOMAS CINI, V.G., Contact Person, 4th St. & Greenhill Ave., P.O. Box 2610, Wilmington, 19806. Tel: 302-655-9624.

Siena Hall, Inc.—Rev. Msgr. J. THOMAS CINI, V.G., Contact Person, 4th St. & Greenhill Ave., P.O. Box 2610, Wilmington, 19806. Tel: 302-655-9624.

Activities

Apostleship of Prayer—Rev. JOSEPH R. MCMAHON, 7 Sharpley Rd., Wilmington, 19803. Tel: 302-652-6800.

Catholic Campaign for Human Development—4th St. & Greenhill Ave., P.O. Box 2610, Wilmington, 19806. Tel: 302-655-9624.

Catholic Charismatic Renewal—Rev. THOMAS A. FLOWERS, Chap., St. Polycarp, 135 Ransom Lane, Smyrna, 19977. Tel: 302-653-8279.

Catholic Relief Services, Inc.—Rev. Msgr. GEORGE J. BRUBAKER, J.C.L., Diocesan Dir., 506 Seabury Ave., Milford, 19963. Tel: 302-422-5123.

Black & Native American Missions—Rev. Msgr. JOSEPH F. REBMAN, V.G., S.T.L., J.C.L., C.C.C.E., Diocesan Dir., Mailing Address: P.O. Box 2030, Wilmington, 19899. Tel: 302-573-3100; Fax: 302-573-6836.

Cursillo Movement—Deacon JOSE RODRIQUEZ-TREJO, Spiritual Dir., St. Michael the Archangel Church, Georgetown, 19947; Ms. JUDITH A. LOVETT, Lay Dir., 2041 Dinah's Corner Rd., Dover, 19901. Tel: 302-741-2336.

Delmarva Catholic Network, Inc.—Mr. ROBERT KREBS, Contact Person, Mailing Address: P.O. Box 2030, Wilmington, 19899. Tel: 302-573-3116.

Diocesan Healing Ministry—JEANNE CASEY, Lay Dir., 533 Waterford Dr., Hockessin, 19707. Tel: 302-239-5982.

KAIROS Ministries, Inc.—Rev. GREGORY M. CORRIGAN, Contact Person.

Korean Catholic Community, Inc.—Rev. JOHN (B) LEE GYE-CHUN, Chap.; Mr. PETER SANG JIN PARK, Pres., Community Council, 2712 Duncan Rd., Wilmington, 19808. Tel: 302-998-7730.

St. Thomas More Society—Rev. LEONARD R. KLEIN, Chap., St. Mary of the Immaculate Conception, 1414 King St., Wilmington, 19801. Tel: 302-652-0743.

St. Vincent dePaul Society—Mr. PAUL COLLINS, 312 Hazlett Rd., New Castle, 19720. Tel: 302-328-5166.

Diocese of Wilmington - Serra Club In-formation—1626 N. Union St., Wilmington, 19806. Tel: 302-573-3116. Dr. HERBERT CASALENA, Pres.; Rev. JOSEPH M.P.R. COCUCCI, Chap.

Organizations With Which Diocese Has Liaison

**Birthright of Delaware, Inc.*NAN BERNARDO, Dir., 1311 N. Scott St., Wilmington, 19806. Tel: 302-656-7080.

**Delaware Citizens for Life*Mr. THOMAS JEWETT, Chm., 4019 Greenmount Rd., Wilmington, 19810. Tel: 302-478-3428.

Delawareans United for Education—Rev. Msgr. J. THOMAS CINI, V.G., Mailing Address: P.O. Box 2030, Wilmington, 19899. Tel: 302-573-3118.

Maryland Catholic Conference— (An agency of the Archdiocese of Baltimore, Washington and the Diocese of Wilmington) MARY ELLEN RUSSELL, Exec. Dir., 10 Francis St., Annapolis, MD 21401. Tel: 410-269-1155; Fax: 410-269-1790. Mailing Address: P.O. Box 2030, Wilmington, 19899. Tel: 302-573-3118.

National Conference for Community and Justice—Rev. CLEMENS D. MANISTA JR., St. Paul Church, 209 Washington St., Delaware City, 19706. Tel: 302-834-4321.

Regina Coeli Society—Rev. LEONARD R. KLEIN, 1414 King St., Wilmington, 19801. Tel: 302-652-0743.

Victim Assistance Coordinator—PEGGY MCLAUGHLIN. Tel: 302-655-9624. Email: mmclaughlin@ccwilm.org.

World Wide Marriage Encounter—Contact Persons: BARNEY BELLARD; KATHY BELLARD, St. John the Beloved Parish. Tel: 302-239-2571. Email: ktbellard@verizon.net.

CLERGY, PARISHES, MISSIONS AND PAROCHIAL SCHOOLS

DELAWARE, CITY OF WILMINGTON

(NEW CASTLE COUNTY)

1—CATHEDRAL OF ST. PETER (1796) Rev. Joseph M.P.R. Cocucci, Rector.
Res.: 500 N. West St., 19801. Tel: 302-654-5920; Fax: 302-654-3197. Email: rector19801@comcast.net. Web: www.cathedralofstpeter.com.
School—310 W. 6th St., 19801. Tel: 302-656-5234; Fax: 302-658-6489. Sr. Barbara Ann Curran, D.C., Prin. Daughters of Charity of St. Vincent de Paul 2; Lay Teachers 13; Students 206.

2—ST. ANN (1887) Rev. Msgr. J. Thomas Cini; Rev. Joseph F. Wisniewski.
Res.: 2013 Gilpin Ave., 19806. Tel: 302-654-5519; 302-652-0152; Fax: 302-654-5527. Email: stannschurch1@verizon.net. Web: www.st-ann.net.
School—Tel: 302-652-6567; Fax: 302-652-4156. Sr. Virginia Pfau, I.H.M., Prin. Lay Teachers 22; Students 272.
Catechesis/Religious Program—Tel: 302-654-8504. Patricia Walker, D.R.E. Students 151.

3—ST. ANTHONY OF PADUA (1924), (Italian), Revs. John F. McGinley, O.S.F.S.; Francis Rinaldi, O.S.F.S.; Gerard J. Mahoney, O.S.F.S.; Deacon Robert J. Leonzio. In Res., Rev. Roberto Balducelli, O.S.F.S.; Bro. Michael J. Rosenello, O.S.F.S.
Res.: 901 N. DuPont St., 19805. Tel: 302-421-3700; Fax: 302-421-3709. Email: parish@stanthonynet.org. Web: www.stanthonynet.org.
School—9th & Scott Sts., 19805. Tel: 302-421-3743; Fax: 302-421-3796. Mrs. Virginia Bahr, Prin. Sisters of St. Francis of Philadelphia 1; Lay Teachers 22; Students 278.
High School—Padua Academy, 905 N. Broom St., 19806. Tel: 302-421-3739; Fax: 302-421-3748. Web: www.paduaacademy.org. Cindy Hayes Mann, Prin. Lay Teachers 45; Students 601.
Catechesis/Religious Program—Fax: 302-421-3705. Students 53.
St. Anthony's Education Fund, Inc.—901 N. DuPont St., 19805. Tel: 302-421-3700; Fax: 302-421-3709.

4—CHRIST OUR KING (1926) Rev. William T. Cocco; Deacon William J. Johnston Jr.
Res.: 2810 N. Monroe St., 19802. Tel: 302-762-4140; Fax: 302-762-8414. Web: www.christourkingcatholicchurch.org.
Catechesis/Religious Program—Students 3.

5—ST. ELIZABETH (1908) Very Rev. Norman P. Carroll; Rev. John B. Gabage; Deacon Kenneth Pulliam Sr. In Res., Rev. Daniel W. Gerres (Retired).
Res.: 809 S. Broom St., 19805-4296. Tel: 302-652-3626; Fax: 302-658-5957. Email: rectory809@aol.com.
School—1500 Cedar St., 19805-4249. Tel: 302-655-8208; Fax: 302-655-5457. Ms. Alexandria Cirko, Prin. Lay Teachers 22; Aides 4; Students 320.
High School—Tel: 302-656-3369; Fax: 302-656-7513. Mrs. Shirley Bounds, Prin. Sisters 1; Lay Teachers 30; Students 361.
Catechesis/Religious Program—809 S. Broom St., 19805. Students 34.

6—ST. HEDWIG (1890), (Polish), Rev. Andrew Molewski.
Res.: 408 S. Harrison St., 19805. Tel: 302-594-1400; Fax: 302-594-1415. Email: sthedwigchurch@comcast.net. Web: www.sthedwig.org.
Catechesis/Religious Program—Tel: 302-594-1400, Ext. 3. Students 34.

7—ST. JOSEPH'S R.C. CHURCH OF WILMINGTON, INC. (1889) Rev. John Frambes, O.F.M.; Deacons Robert J. Cousar Jr.; Robert J. Levesque.
Church: 1012 French St., 19801. Tel: 302-658-4535; Fax: 302-658-2006.
Res.: 1010 W. 4th St., 19805.

8—ST. MARY OF THE IMMACULATE CONCEPTION (1858) Rev. Leonard R. Klein.
Res.: 1414 King St., 19801. Tel: 302-652-0743; Fax: 302-652-7678.
Church: 6th & Pine Sts., 19801.

9—ST. PATRICK (1880) Rev. Leonard R. Klein.
Res.: 1414 King St., 19801. Tel: 302-652-0743; Fax: 302-652-7678.
Catechesis/Religious Program—Tel: 302-622-8581. Students 5.

10—ST. PAUL'S (1869) Rev. Todd Carpenter, O.F.M. In Res., Revs. John Frambes, O.F.M.; Christopher J. Posch, O.F.M.; Ronald J. Pecci, O.F.M.; Bro. William Herbst, O.F.M.
Res.: 1010 W. 4th St., 19805. Tel: 302-655-6596; Fax: 302-655-7684.
Catechesis/Religious Program—Students 130.

11—SACRED HEART (1874), Reopened as Sacred Heart Oratory, Inc. (1998) A Center for Evangelization. Sacramental records 1874-1948 at Diocesan Archives. Sacramental records 1949-1996 at Cathedral of St. Peter. Rev. Ronald Giannone, O.F.M-.Cap.; Deacon Gianni Chicco; Sr. Mary Daniel Jackson, S.S.C.J., Dir., Outreach & Evangelization; Joseph Graney, Pastoral Team.
Res.: 917 N. Madison St., 19801. Tel: 302-428-3658; Fax: 302-428-3655.

12—ST. STANISLAUS KOSTKA (1912), (Polish), Sacramental records at Diocesan Archives.

13—ST. THOMAS THE APOSTLE (1903) Very Rev. Steven P. Hurley; Deacon Francis A. Quinlan. In Res., Rev. Xavier Bruce Rajendran.

DELAWARE

OUTSIDE THE CITY OF WILMINGTON

BEAR, NEW CASTLE CO., ST. ELIZABETH ANN SETON (1978) Revs. Roger F. DiBuo; James M. Jackson; Deacon William Kibler.
Res.: 345 Bear-Christiana Rd., 19701-1048. Tel: 302-322-6430; Fax: 302-322-6297. Email: office@setonparish.net. Web: setonparish.net.
Catechesis/Religious Program—Tel: 302-322-6430, Ext. 102; Fax: 302-322-6297. Theresa Burke, C.R.E. Students 480.

BELLEFONTE, NEW CASTLE CO., ST. HELENA (Wilmington P.O.) (1936) Very Rev. Stanley J. Russell. In Res., Rev. Edward J. Fahey.
Res.: 602 Philadelphia Pike, 19809-2520. Tel: 302-764-0325; Fax: 302-764-1068.
Catechesis/Religious Program—Tel: 302-762-4280. Hummy Pennell, D.R.E. Students 102.
Convent—610 Philadelphia Pike, 19809. Tel: 302-764-3427.

BELVEDERE, NEWPORT CO., OUR MOTHER OF MERCY (1927) Closed. 1971. Sacramental records 1927-1971 at Diocesan Archives.

BETHANY BEACH, SUSSEX CO., ST. ANN (1955) Very Rev. David F. Kelley; Rev. Christopher Hanley; Deacons Edward Danko; Dennis Hayden; John Freebery.
Res.: 691 Garfield Ave., 19930. Tel: 302-539-6449; Fax: 302-539-0657.
Catechesis/Religious Program—Tel: 302-539-5443; Fax: 302-539-5509. Students 174.
Mission—Our Lady of Guadalupe 35318 Church Rd., Frankford, Sussex Co. 19945.

BRANDYWOOD, NEW CASTLE CO., CHURCH OF THE HOLY CHILD (Wilmington P.O.) (1969) Rev. Michael J. Carrier; Deacons John C. McVoy III; Joseph Cilia Jr.; Sr. Ann Hughes, S.S.J., Pastoral Assoc.
Res.: 2500 Naamans Rd., 19810. Tel: 302-475-6486; Fax: 302-475-3458.
Catechesis/Religious Program—Students 264.

CLAYMONT, NEW CASTLE CO., HOLY ROSARY (1921) Rev. John J. Gayton; Deacons Richard J. Maichle; Allen Wolf. In Res., Rev. Leonard J. Kempski (Retired).
Res.: 3200 Philadelphia Pike, 19703. Tel: 302-798-2904.
Catechesis/Religious Program—Tel: 302-798-0123. Students 130.

DELAWARE CITY, NEW CASTLE CO., ST. PAUL (1852) Rev. Clemens D. Manista Jr., Admin.
Res.: 209 Washington St., P.O. Box 544, 19706. Tel: 302-834-4321; Fax: 302-834-7517.
Catechesis/Religious Program—409 Adams St., 19706. Sr. Lawrence Therese Hudson, O.S.F.S., D.R.E. Students 24.

DOVER, KENT CO., HOLY CROSS (1870) [CEM] Rev. Msgr. Daniel J. McGlynn; Revs. Carlos Ochoa; Joseph F. McQuaide IV; Deacons Weston "Pete" Nellius; Robert McMullen; Philip Belt; Vincent Pisano. In Res., Rev. James S. Lentini.
Res.: 631 S. State St., 19901. Tel: 302-674-5787; Fax: 302-674-5783.
School—Haydee Rosario, Prin. Lay Teachers 37; Students 584.
Catechesis/Religious Program—Tracie Reinhart, C.R.E. Students 450.

ELSMERE, NEW CASTLE CO., CORPUS CHRISTI (Wilmington P.O.) (1948) Rev. Timothy M. Nolan; Deacon David M. DeGhetto.
Res.: 905 New Rd., Elsmere, 19805. Tel: 302-994-2922; Fax: 302-892-3315.
Catechesis/Religious Program—Tel: 302-998-2864. Debbie Ciafre, C.R.E. Students 56.
Convent—912 New Rd., Elsmere, 19805. Tel: 302-998-2864.

FAIRFAX, NEW CASTLE CO., ST. MARY MAGDALEN (Wilmington P.O.) (1951) Revs. Joseph R. McMahon; James T. Kirk; Deacon Joseph C. Romans. In Res., Rev. Philip P. Sheekey (Retired).
Res.: 7 Sharpley Rd., 19803. Tel: 302-652-6800; Fax: 302-652-4771.
School—9 Sharpley Rd., 19803. Tel: 302-656-2745; Fax: 302-656-7889. Barbara Wanner, Prin. Lay Teachers 41; Students 539.
Catechesis/Religious Program—Tel: 302-652-7141. Karen Yasik, D.R.E. Students 275.

GARFIELD PARK, NEW CASTLE CO., HOLY SPIRIT (New Castle P.O.) (1954) Rev. John S. Grimm, Admin.; Deacon Patrick Johnston.
Res.: 12 Winder Rd., Garfield Park, New Castle, 19720. Tel: 302-658-1069; Fax: 302-658-6890. Email: hscathchurch@aol.com. Web: holyspiritcatholicchurchde.4lpi.com.
Catechesis/Religious Program—Students 35.

GEORGETOWN, SUSSEX CO., ST. MICHAEL THE ARCHANGEL (1956) Revs. Robert J. Burk, M.S.A.; James E. Downs, M.S.A.; Cesar Gomez (Honduras); Deacons David S. McDowell; Philip Ricker; Jose Rodriquez-Trejo; Martin J. Barrett.
Res.: 202 Edward St., 19947. Tel: 302-856-6451; Fax: 302-856-2353. Email: stmichrc@verizon.net.
Catechesis/Religious Program—Students 261.
Mission—Mary Mother of Peace 30839 Mt. Joy Rd. at Rte. 24, Millsboro, Sussex Co. 19966. Tel: 302-856-6451; Fax: 302-856-2353.

GLASGOW, NEW CASTLE CO., ST. MARGARET OF SCOTLAND (1999) Rev. Msgr. John P. Hopkins; Deacons Raymond R. Zolandz Jr.; Thomas E. Watts.
Res.: 2431 Frazer Rd., Newark, 19702. Tel: 302-834-0225; Fax: 302-834-0840.
Catechesis/Religious Program—Tel: 302-834-0225, Ext. 105. Students 521.

GREENVILLE, NEW CASTLE CO., ST. JOSEPH ON THE BRANDYWINE (1841) [CEM 2] Rev. Msgr. Joseph F. Rebman; Rev. David F. Murphy; Deacon F. Edmund Lynch.
Res.: 10 Old Church Rd., 19807. Tel: 302-658-7017; Fax: 302-428-0639. Web: www.stjosephonthebrandywine.org.
Catechesis/Religious Program—Tel: 302-656-7185; Fax: 302-658-8723. Ms. Maryanne Bemiller, D.R.E. Students 219.

HOCKESSIN, NEW CASTLE CO., ST. MARY OF THE ASSUMPTION (1772) [CEM] Revs. Charles C. Dillingham; James B. Smith; Michael P. Darcy; Deacons John Giacci; Joseph W. Jackson Sr.; Larry Morris.
Res.: 7200 Lancaster Pike, 19707. Tel: 302-239-7100; Fax: 302-239-8219. Web: www.stmaryoftheassumption.com.
Catechesis/Religious Program—Tel: 302-239-7100, Ext. 17. Sheila Meara, D.R.E. Students 650.

LEWES, SUSSEX CO., ST. JUDE THE APOSTLE (2002) Revs. James D. Hreha; Mark J. Connelly; William T. Small (Retired); Deacons Edward J. Brink, (Retired); William J. Pyrek; Kenneth J. Hall; Robert J. Sprouse; Donald E. Lydick.
Office:—152 Tulip Dr., 19958. Tel: 302-644-7300; Fax: 302-644-7415.
Catechesis/Religious Program—Tel: 302-644-7413. Students 188.

LIFTWOOD, NEW CASTLE CO., IMMACULATE HEART OF MARY (Wilmington P.O.) (1955) Rev. Msgr. Clement P. Lemon; Rev. Robert A. Wozniak; Deacons Austin M. Snow Jr.; Francis C. Conway; Theresa H. Gerlach, Pastoral Assoc.

Res.: 4701 Weldin Rd., Liftwood, 19803. Tel: 302-764-0357; Fax: 302-764-4381.
School—(Grades PreK-8), 1000 Shipley Rd., Liftwood, 19803. Tel: 302-764-0977; Fax: 302-764-0375. Jan Chapdelaine, Prin.; Joy Heck, Librarian. Lay Teachers 32; Students 528.
Catechesis/Religious Program—Tel: 302-762-5550. Claire D. Dasalla, C.R.E. Students 226.

MIDDLETOWN, NEW CASTLE CO., ST. JOSEPH (1883) [CEM 2], Sacramental records 1790-1964 at Diocesan Archives. Very Rev. Steven B. Giuliano; Rev. John Grasing; Deacons Cruz Rodriguez; Fred Wendt.
Res.: 371 E. Main St., 19709. Tel: 302-378-5800; Fax: 302-378-5808. Email: office@stjosephmiddletown.com. Web: www.stjosephmiddletown.com.
Catechesis/Religious Program—Susan Pascoe, Co-ord.; Mark Winterbottom, Coord. Students 950.
Mission—St. Rose of Lima Lock St., Chesapeake City, Cecil Co., MD 21915.
Shrine—St. Francis Xavier-Old Bohemia Warwick, MD.

MILFORD, KENT AND SUSSEX COS., ST. JOHN THE APOSTLE (1910) Rev. Msgr. George J. Brubaker; Rev. Johnny Laura Lazo; Deacons James D. Malloy; Robert C. Herzog; John Yaeger; J. Scott Landis; R. Paul Woofert.
Res.: 504 Seabury Ave., 19963-2217. Tel: 302-422-5123; Fax: 302-422-5720.
Catechesis/Religious Program—Tel: 302-422-5123, Ext. 12; Fax: 302-422-5720. Students 291.
Mission—St. Bernadette 109 Dixon, Harrington, Kent Co. 19952. Tel: 302-398-8269; Fax: 302-398-0253.

NEW CASTLE, NEW CASTLE CO., ST. PETER THE APOSTLE (1845) [CEM] Rev. John P. Klevence; Deacon Thomas G. Halko.
Church, Mailing & Res. Address: 521 Harmony St., 19720. Tel: 302-328-2335; Fax: 302-328-0519. Web: www.stpetertheapostlede.org. Email: parish@stpetertheapostlede.org.
School—515 Harmony Sts., 19720. Tel: 302-328-1191; Fax: 302-328-8049. Lay Teachers 14; Students 225.
Catechesis/Religious Program—Students 35.

NEWARK, NEW CASTLE CO.

1—ST. JOHN THE BAPTIST-HOLY ANGELS (1891) [CEM] Revs. Arthur B. Fiore; J.M. Gregory Lee; Alan Reyna; Deacon Charles Schauber Sr.
Res.: 14 N. Chapel St., 19711. Tel: 302-731-2200; Fax: 302-731-2434. Email: aahar@holyangels.net. Web: www.stjohn-holyangels.com.
School—Tel: 302-731-2210; Fax: 302-731-2211. Mrs. Barbara Snively, Prin. Lay Teachers 27; Students 422.
Catechesis/Religious Program—Tel: 302-731-2209. Students 446.

2—PARISH OF THE RESURRECTION (1969) Revs. William F. Graney; Gregory M. Corrigan; Deacons Francis J. Huhn, (Retired); John J. Falkowski; Bernardus C. Stam.
Office:—3000 Videre Dr., Skyline Ridge, 19808. Tel: 302-368-0146; Fax: 302-368-0146.
Catechesis/Religious Program—Tel: 302-368-0146, Ext. 104. Cory Zolandz, C.R.E. Students 87.

3—ST. THOMAS MORE ORATORY (1975), (Personal Parish for Students & Faculty of University of Delaware). Rev. Ambrose Eckinger, O.P.; Kim Zitzner, Pastoral Assoc. & Campus Min.
Church: 45 Lovett Ave., 19711. Tel: 302-368-4728; Fax: 302-368-2548.
Catechesis/Religious Program—Tel: 302-368-4728. Students 43.

OGLETOWN, NEW CASTLE CO., HOLY FAMILY (Newark P.O.) (1979) Revs. James Nash; Michael J. Cook; Deacon Joseph F. Certesio Sr. In Res., Rev. Antony William Rajayan.
Res.: 15 Gender Rd., Newark, 19713. Tel: 302-368-4665; Fax: 302-368-4667.
Catechesis/Religious Program—21 Gender Rd., Newark, 19713. Tel: 302-368-8976; Fax: 302-368-5184. Sr. Carol Heffner, D.R.E.; Mare Draper, Youth Min. Students 265.

PRICES CORNER, ST. CATHERINE OF SIENA (Wilmington P.O.) (1960) Rev. John M. Hynes; Deacon Francis J. Staab. In Res., Revs. Salvador Magana; Thomas J. Peterman (Retired).
Res.: 2503 Centerville Rd., 19808. Tel: 302-633-4900; Fax: 302-633-4960.
Catechesis/Religious Program—Tel: 302-633-4903; Fax: 302-633-4960. Mrs. Eva Lyons, D.R.E. Students 400.

REHOBOTH BEACH, SUSSEX CO., ST. EDMOND (1952) Revs. Raymond L. Forester; John A. Lunness; Deacons G. Jerry Shaw; James M. Walls; Dana J. Ackerson.
409 King Charles St., P.O. Box 646, 19971. Tel: 302-227-4550; Fax: 302-227-4557.
Res.: 402 King Charles St., P.O. Box 646, 19771.
Catechesis/Religious Program—Tel: 302-227-4553. Sr. Maryanne Zakreski, D.R.E. Students 225.

SEAFORD, SUSSEX CO., OUR LADY OF LOURDES (1945) [CEM] Revs. George Blasick, C.Ss.R.; Charles Hergenroeder, C.Ss.R.
Res.: 528 Stein Hwy., P.O. Box 719, 19973-0719. Tel: 302-629-3591; Fax: 302-629-6758.
Catechesis/Religious Program—Tel: 302-629-7999. Mrs. Debra Depta, D.R.E. Students 246.

SHERWOOD PARK, NEW CASTLE CO., ST. JOHN THE BELOVED (1955) Rev. Msgr. Charles L. Brown III; Revs. Ralph T. Castelow; Anthony Giamello; Deacons James Haley, (Retired); George Taylor, (Retired); Dennis Wuebbels; Thomas A. Bailey.
Res.: 907 Milltown Rd., 19808. Tel: 302-999-0211; Fax: 302-999-9184. Email: sjbchurch907@yahoo.com. Web: www.sjbde.org.
School—905 Milltown Rd., 19808. Tel: 302-998-5525; Fax: 302-998-1923. Richard D. Hart, Prin. Sisters of St. Francis of Philadelphia 1; Lay Teachers 34; Students 587; Students in Early Learning 4-yr-old program 40.
Catechesis/Religious Program—Tel: 302-994-7757; Fax: 302-996-9166. Pauline Berlingieri, D.R.E. Students 382.

SMYRNA, KENT CO., ST. POLYCARP (1883) Rev. Thomas A. Flowers; Deacons Charles Robinson; Michael Boyd.
Res.: 135 Ransom Ln., 19977. Tel: 302-653-8279; Fax: 302-653-3509.
Catechesis/Religious Program—Tel: 302-653-4101. Mrs. Carol Simpers, D.R.E. Students 286.

WILMINGTON MANOR, NEW CASTLE CO., OUR LADY OF FATIMA (New Castle P.O.) (1948) Revs. John J. Mink; Idongesit A. Etim; Deacons William Murrian; Eliezer Soto.
Res.: 801 Dupont Blvd., New Castle, 19720. Tel: 302-328-3431; 302-328-5773; Fax: 302-328-6318.
School—Tel: 302-328-2803; Fax: 302-328-5427. Lay Teachers 14; Students 270.
Catechesis/Religious Program—Tel: 302-328-0307. Mrs. Madeline Romano, D.R.E. Students 275.

WOODCREST, NEW CASTLE CO., ST. MATTHEW (1941) Revs. Joseph J. Drobinski; William J. Klapps (Retired); Deacons Harold Chalfant; Michael T. Wilber; William A. Kaper. In Res., Rev. William M. Hazzard (Retired).
Res.: 1013 E. Newport Pike, 19804. Tel: 302-633-5850; Fax: 302-633-5850.
Catechesis/Religious Program—Tel: 302-633-5860, Ext. 2. Students 120.

MARYLAND

BERLIN, WORCESTER CO., ST. JOHN NEUMANN ROMAN CATHOLIC CHURCH (2007) Very Rev. John J. Kavanaugh, Admin. (Retired); Deacons John G. Lemon; Charles A. Weschler; Wilbur Pinder.
11211 Beauchamp Rd., MD 21811. Tel: 410-208-2956; Fax: 410-208-4584.
Catechesis/Religious Program—Nancy F. Groves, D.R.E. Students 230.

CAMBRIDGE, DORCHESTER CO., ST. MARY REFUGE OF SINNERS (1885) [CEM] Rev. William J. Lawler.
Res.: 1515 Glasgow St., P.O. Box 218, MD 21613. Tel: 410-228-4770; Fax: 410-228-0969.
Catechesis/Religious Program—Rosemary Robbins, D.R.E. Students 32.
Mission—St. Mary, Star of the Sea [CEM] Church Creek, Dorchester Co., MD.

CENTREVILLE, QUEEN ANNE CO., OUR MOTHER OF SORROWS (1892) [CEM] Rev. Mark A. Kelleher.
Res.: 303 Chesterfield Ave., MD 21617. Fax: 410-758-5463. Web: www.sorrowsparish.org.
Catechesis/Religious Program—Tel: 410-758-0143. Mary Wood, D.R.E. Students 224.
Mission—St. Peter 5319 Ocean Gateway, Queenstown, Queen Anne Co., MD 21658. Tel: 410-827-8404.

CHESTER , KENT ISLAND QUEEN ANNE CO., ST. CHRISTOPHER (1954) Very Rev. Paul F. Jennings Jr.; Deacons John E. Robinson Jr.; James Massacci.
Res.: 1861 Harbor Dr., Box 660, MD 21619. Tel: 410-643-6220; Fax: 410-643-4055. Email: rectory@stchristopherki.org. Web: www.stchristopherki.org.
Catechesis/Religious Program—Tel: 410-643-8489. Students 33.

CHESTERTOWN, KENT CO., SACRED HEART (1876) [CEM] Rev. Paul J. Campbell; Deacon John Davis.
Res.: 508 High St., MD 21620. Tel: 410-778-3160; Fax: 410-810-0427.
Catechesis/Religious Program—Tel: 410-778-4650. Barbara Kelly, C.R.E. Students 94.
Mission—St. John W. Main St., Rock Hall, Kent Co., MD 21661. Tel: 410-778-3160.

EASTON, TALBOT CO., SS. PETER AND PAUL (1868) [CEM] Revs. Robert E. Coine; John E. Olson.
Res.: 7906 Ocean Gateway, MD 21601. Tel: 410-822-2344; Fax: 410-770-5080.
School—900 High St., MD 21601. Tel: 410-822-2251; Fax: 410-820-0136. Mrs. Connie Webster, Prin. Lay Teachers 30; Students 427.
High School—Tel: 410-822-2275; Fax: 410-822-1767. Mr. James Nemeth, Prin. Lay Teachers 24; Students 206.
Catechesis/Religious Program—Tel: 410-822-6581; Fax: 410-822-3207. Linda Steinmiller, D.R.E. Students 214.
Mission—St. Joseph 13209 Church Ln., Cordova, Talbot Co., MD 21625.
Mission—St. Michael 109 Lincoln Ave., St. Michaels, Talbot Co., MD 21663.

ELKTON, CECIL CO., IMMACULATE CONCEPTION (1849) [CEM 2] Revs. Joseph J. Piekarski; John T. Solomon; Deacons Joseph J. Kosman; Michael Truman.
Office: 455 Bow St., P.O. Box 345, MD 21922. Tel: 410-398-1100; Fax: 410-398-1175. Email: office@iccparish.org. Web: www.iccparish.org.
Res.: 300 Maryland Ave., MD 21922.
School—452 Bow St., MD 21921. Tel: 410-398-2636; Fax: 410-398-1190. Ms. Mary Kirkwood, Prin. Felician Sister 1; Lay Teachers 19; Students 259.
Catechesis/Religious Program—Tel: 410-392-3551. Sr. Grace Andrew, D.R.E. Students 387.
Mission—St. Jude 928 Turkey Point, North East, Cecil Co., MD 21901.

GALENA, KENT CO., ST. DENNIS (1855) [CEM] Rev. Leonard J. Blakely.
Mailing Address: P.O. Box 249, MD 21635. Tel: 410-648-5145; Fax: 410-648-5767. Email: stdennischurch@aol.com. Web: stdennischurch.org.
Catechesis/Religious Program—Tel: 410-648-5287. Students 62.

MARYDEL, CAROLINE CO., IMMACULATE CONCEPTION (1916) Very Rev. Michael B. Roark; Deacons James M. Tormey; Sherman Mitchell III.
Church: 522 Main St., P.O. Box 399, MD 21649. Tel: 410-482-7687; Fax: 410-482-7253.
Catechesis/Religious Program—Tel: 410-482-8939. Students 120.

OCEAN CITY, WORCESTER CO.

1—ST. LUKE AND ST. ANDREW (1985) Revs. Richard Smith; Anthony F. Cardone; Deacons Edward Holson; Joseph Carraro; Robert J. McNulty Jr.
Office: 14401 Sinepuxent Ave., MD 21842. Tel: 410-250-0300; Fax: 410-250-0417.
Catechesis/Religious Program—Students 59.

2—ST. MARY, STAR OF THE SEA (1877) Rev. Stanislao Esposito; Deacon Edward Gardner Sr., (Retired).
Res. & Office: 1705 Philadelphia Ave., MD 21842. Tel: 410-289-0652; Fax: 410-289-1026.
Catechesis/Religious Program—Tel: 410-289-7038. Students 139.
Mission—Holy Savior 1705 Philadelphia Ave., Worcester Co., MD 21842.

PERRYVILLE, CECIL CO., CHURCH OF THE GOOD SHEPHERD (1949) Rev. Jay R. McKee; Deacon Luke Yackley.
810 Aiken Ave., MD 21903.
Res.: 828 Aiken Ave., MD 21903. Tel: 410-642-6534; Fax: 410-642-2234.
School—800 Aiken Ave., MD 21903. Tel: 410-642-6265; Fax: 410-642-6522. Mrs. Sharon Hodges, Prin. Lay Teachers 15; Students 103.
Catechesis/Religious Program—Students 144.
Mission—St. Teresa 162 N. Main St., Port Deposit, Cecil Co., MD 21904.
Mission—St. Patrick, (Inactive), 287 Pleasant Grove Rd., Conowingo, Cecil Co., MD 21918.
Mission—St. Agnes 150 S. Queen St., Rising Sun, Cecil Co., MD 21911.

POCOMOKE CITY, WORCESTER CO., HOLY NAME OF JESUS (1943) Rev. William J. Porter; Deacons Stephen J. Kuczma; Thomas S. Cimino, (Retired).
Res.: 1913 Old Virginia Rd., P.O. Box 179, MD 21851. Tel: 410-957-1215; Fax: 410-957-1214.
Catechesis/Religious Program—Jason Pfirman, C.R.E. Students 87.
Mission—St. Elizabeth 8734 Old Westover Rd., Westover, Somerset Co., MD 21871.

RIDGELY, CAROLINE CO., ST. BENEDICT (1896) [CEM 2] Rev. Hilary R. Rodgers; Deacons Harold D. Jopp Jr.; William G. Nickum.
Res.: 408 Central Ave., P.O. Box 459, MD 21660. Tel: 410-634-2253; Fax: 410-634-1997.
Catechesis/Religious Program—Students 140.
Mission—St. Elizabeth of Hungary [CEM] First St. & Franklin St., Denton, Caroline Co., MD 21629.

SALISBURY, WICOMICO CO., ST. FRANCIS DE SALES (1910) Revs. Edward M. Aigner Jr.; Raymond F. Weisman; Christopher W. LaBarge; Deacons James E. Dean; Bruce Abresch.
Res.: 514 Camden Ave., MD 21801. Tel: 410-742-6443; Fax: 410-742-9410.
School—500 Camden Ave., MD 21801. Tel: 410-749-9907; Fax: 410-749-9507. Mr. Rob Costante, Prin. Lay Teachers 18; Students 205.
Catechesis/Religious Program—Tel: 410-546-2908. Pat Burbage, D.R.E.; Michele Harris, D.R.E.; Samantha Oscar, Coord. Youth Min. Students 247.
Mission—Holy Redeemer Bi-State Blvd. & Chestnut St., Delmar, Wicomico Co., MD 21875.

SECRETARY, DORCHESTER CO., OUR LADY OF GOOD COUNSEL (1891) [CEM] Rev. Stephen C. Lonek.
Res.: 109 Willow St., P.O. Box 279, MD 21664. Tel: 410-943-4300; Fax: 410-943-1357.
Catechesis/Religious Program—Students 35.

Chaplains of Public Institutions
National Guard

WILMINGTON. *Delaware Air National Guard.* 801 DuPont Blvd., New Castle, 19720. Tel: 302-328-3431. Revs. John J. Mink, Chap., David F. Murphy, Chap., Anthony Giamello.

Health Care

WILMINGTON. *St. Francis Hospital*, 7th St. & Clayton St., 19805. Tel: 302-421-4577. Revs. Joseph J. McKenna, O.S.F.S., Xavier Bruce Rajendran.

DELAWARE CITY. *Governor Bacon Health Center*. Rev. Clemens D. Manista Jr., Chap. Tel: 302-834-4321.

ELSMERE. *Veteran's Hospital*, 1601 Kirkwood Hwy., 19805. Tel: 302-994-2511. Revs. Sean P. Connery, O.S.F.S., Chap., Azuka Iwuchukwu.

NEW CASTLE. *Delaware Psychiatric Hospital*.

NEWARK. *Christiana Care Health Services, Inc.*, 4755 Ogletown-Stanton Rds., 19726. Tel: 302-733-1900; 302-733-1280.
Wilmington Hospital, 14th & Washington Sts., 19805. Tel: 302-733-1280. Revs. Gregory M. Corrigan, Leonard R. Klein, Clemens D. Manista Jr., Antony William Rajayan.

PERRY POINT, MD. *Veterans Admin*. Rev. Mark E. Oguamana.

SMYRNA, MD. *Delaware Home & Hospital for the Chronically Ill*. Rev. Thomas A. Flowers, Chap. Tel: 302-653-8279.

Correctional Facilities

WILMINGTON. *Ferris School*. Vacant.
Howard R. Young Correctional Institution. Deacon Gianni Chicco.

NEW CASTLE. *Delores J. Baylor Women's Correctional Institution*. Vacant, Chap.

SMYRNA, MD. *Delaware State Correctional Center*. Deacon Michael Truman, Coord. Prison Ministry.

WESTOVER, MD. *Eastern Correctional Institution*. Rev. Edward M. Aigner Jr., Chap. Tel: 410-742-6443.

Campus Ministry

CHESTERTOWN, MD. *Washington College*, Sacred Heart, 508 High St., MD 21620. Tel: 410-778-3160. Rev. Paul J. Campbell, Chap.

DOVER. *Wesley College, Holy Cross Parish*, 631 S. State St., 19901. Tel: 302-674-5787; Fax: 302-674-5783. Vacant, Chap. Tel: 410-778-3160; Fax: 410-810-0427.

NEWARK. *University of Delaware*, St. Thomas More Oratory, 45 Lovett Ave., 19711. Tel: 302-368-4728. Rev. Ambrose Eckinger, O.P., Chap., Kim Zitzner, Pastoral Assoc./Campus Min.

SALISBURY, MD. *Salisbury State College*, 211 W. College Ave., MD 21801. Tel: 410-219-3376. Mrs. Regina Yankalunas, M.P.S., Campus Min.
University of Maryland, Eastern Shore, 211 W. College Ave., MD 21801. Tel: 410-219-3376. Mrs. Regina Yankalunas, M.P.S., Campus Min.

Nursing Homes:
Rev.—
Fahey, Edward J., NCC Health Care Facilities, 602 Philadelphia Pike, 19809. Tel: 302-764-0325

Unassigned or Leave of Absence:
Revs.—
Angeloni, Michael A., P.O. Box 2030, 19899.
Breslin, Cornelius J., P.O. Box 2030, 19899.
Kauffman, William B., P.O. Box 2030, 19899.
Kopacz, Mark W., P.O. Box 2030, 19899.
McDermott, Michael J., P.O. Box 2030, 19899.
Melnick, William D., P.O. Box 2030, 19899.
Protack, Thomas J., S.T.L.

On Duty Outside the Diocese:
Rev. Msgrs.—
Koper, Francis B., SS. Cyril and Methodius Seminary, Orchard Lake, MI 48033.
McMahon, Kevin T., S.T.B., S.T.L., S.T.D., P.O. Box 2030, 19899.
Rev.—
Gallagher, Michael J., Trinity College, Theology Dept., 125 Michigan Ave., Washington, DC 20017.

Military Chaplains:
Rev.—
Kopec, Christopher A., c/o Archdiocese for the Military Service, P.O. Box 4469, Washington, DC 20017-0469.

Retired:
Rev. Msgrs.—
Martin, Ralph L., 167 Cross Ave., New Castle, 19720.
Szupper, Michael F., Ph.D., 309 Apple Rd., Newark, 19711.
Very Rev.—
Kavanaugh, John J., P.O. Box 264, Charlestown, MD 21914.
Revs.—
Byrolly, Bruce, 2 Bay View Ave., P.O. Box 43, Cambridge, MD 21613.
Casari, Michael T., P.O. Box 146, Secretary, MD 21664.
Clark, Howard T., P.O. Box 147, Essington, PA 19029.
Coppinger, Edmund, 225 28th St., Richmond, CA 94804.
Frundt, Oscar H., 417 Delaware Ave., 19803.
Gardocki, Thomas F., 4620 Sylvanus Dr., 19803.
Gerres, Daniel W., V.F., 809 Broom St., 19805.
Glapiak, Edward, ul. Krolowej Jadwig, #48, 63-400, Ostrow WLKP, Poland.
Gomolski, Joseph T., 921 Begonia Rd., Apt. 201, Celebration, FL 34747.
Greco, Anthony F., 6115 Red Haven Rd., East New Market, MD 21631.
Hanley, Thomas E., 63 Sackarackin St., Dover, 19901.
Hazzard, William M., 1013 E. Newport Pike, 19804.
Jennings, William E., Jeanne Jugan Residence, 185 Salem Church Rd., Newark, 19713-2997.
Kaczorowski, Edward J., 1012 Brandywine Dr., Bear, 19701.
Kandathiparampil, Joseph, India.
Kempski, Leonard J., 3200 Philadelphia Pike, Claymont, 19703.
Klapps, William J., Caravel Farms, 260 Benjamin Blvd., Bear, 19701.
Kochan, Frederick A., 2201-A Baltimore Ave., Lavellette, NJ 08735.
Mathesius, William P., 103 Atlantic Ave., Washington Hgts., Rehoboth Beach, 19971.
McGann, L. Philip, 316 Cedar Ln., Mount Laurel, NJ 08054.
Mullen, Owen J., 9141 Ronda Ave., San Diego, CA 92123-3553.
Narimattam, Joseph T., P.O. Box 2030, 19899.
Peterman, Thomas J., 2505 Centerville Rd., 19808.
Pollard, Roy F., P.O. Box 185, Charlestown, MD 21914-0185.
Reissmann, Richard A., P.O. Box 2030, 19899.
Richardson, James E., 2504 Blackwood Rd., 19810.
Sheekey, Philip P., 7 Sharpley Rd., 19803.
Siry, Philip L., 417 Brandywine Dr., Bear, 19701.
Storck, Edward J., 1504-2 N. Broom St., #17, 19806.
Turley, Sean F., Staffordshire, England.
Volmi, Dennis G., 10 E. Green Ln., Milford, 19963.

Permanent Deacons:
Abresch, Bruce, St. Francis de Sales, Salisbury, MD
Ackerson, Dana J., St. Edmond, Rehoboth Beach, DE
Bailey, Thomas A., St. John the Beloved Parish, Wilington, DE
Baker, Joseph G., (Retired)
Barrett, Martin J., St. Michael the Archangel, Georgetown, DE
Belt, Philip, Holy Cross, Dover, DE
Boyd, Michael, St. Polycarp, Smyrna, DE
Brink, Edward J., (Retired), St. Jude the Apostle, Lewes, DE
Campbell, Jack H., (Retired)
Carraro, Joseph, St. Luke & St. Andrew, Ocean City, MD
Carroll, Donald T., (Retired)
Certesio, Joseph F., Sr., Holy Family Parish, Newark, DE
Chalfant, Harold F., St. Matthew, Wilmington, DE
Chicco, Gianni, Sacred Heart Oratory and Howard Young Correctional Institution, Wilmington, DE
Cilia, Joseph A., Jr., Asst. Chap., Next Step Group, Church of the Holy Childhood, Wilmington, DE
Cimino, Thomas S., (Retired)
Conway, Francis C., Immaculate Heart of Mary, Wilmington, DE
Cousar, Robert J., Jr., St. Joseph Parish, Wilmington, DE
Danko, Edward, St. Ann, Bethany Beach, DE
Davis, John, Sacred Heart, Chestertown, MD
Dean, James E., St. Francis de Sales Parish, Salisbury, MD
DeGhetto, David M., Corpus Christi Parish, Wilmington, DE
Falkowski, John J., Resurrection Parish, Wilmington, DE
Freebery, John W., Jr., St. Ann, Bethany Beach, DE
Gardner, Edward, Sr., (Retired)
Giacci, John, St. Mary of the Assumption, Hockessin, DE
Haley, James J., (Retired)
Halko, Thomas G., St. Peter the Apostle Parish, New Castle, DE
Hall, Kenneth, St. Jude the Apostle, Lewes, DE
Handlir, James, (Retired)
Hayden, Dennis L., St. Ann, Bethany Beach, DE
Herzog, Robert C., St. John the Apostle, Milford, DE
Holson, Edward G., St. Luke/St. Andrew, Ocean City, MD
Huhn, Francis J., (Retired)
Jackson, Joseph W., Sr., St. Mary of the Assumption Parish, Hockessin, DE
Johnston, Patrick K., Holy Spirit Parish, New Castle, DE
Johnston, William J., Christ Our King Parish, Wilmington, DE
Jopp, Harold D., Jr., St. Benedict's, Ridgely, MD
Kaper, William A., St. Matthew Parish, Wilmington, DE
Kibler, William, III, St. Elizabeth Ann Seton, Bear, DE
Kosman, Joseph J., Immaculate Conception Parish, Elkton, MD
Kuczma, Stephen, Holy Name of Jesus, Pocomoke, MD
Lafferty, James J., Jr., (Retired)
Landis, Scott J., St. John the Apostle, Milford, PA
Lemon, John G., St. John Neumann, Berlin, MD
Leonzio, Robert J., St. Anthony of Padua Parish, Wilmington, DE
Levesque, Robert J., St. Joseph Parish, Wilmington, DE
Lydick, Donald E., St. Jude the Apostle, Lewes, DE
Lynch, Edmund F., St. Joseph on the Brandywine, Greenville, DE
Maichle, Richard J., Holy Rosary, Claymont, DE
Malloy, James D., St. John the Apostle, Milford, DE
Maloney, William, Jr., (Retired)
Masino, Thomas R., (Retired)
Massacci, James, St. Christopher Church, Kent, MD
McDowell, David S., St. Michael the Archangel, Georgetown, DE
McMullen, Robert E., Holy Cross Parish, Dover, DE
McNulty, Robert J., St. Luke, Ocean City, MD
Mitchell, Sherman, III, Immaculate Conception, Marydel, MD
Morris, Larry, St. Mary of the Assumption, Hockessin, DE
Murrian, William J., Our Lady of Fatima, New Castle, DE
Nellius, Weston E., Holy Cross Parish, Dover, DE
Nickum, William G., St. Benedict Parish, Ridgely, MD
O'Connor, Howard J., (Retired)
Ortiz, Hector, St. Joseph, Middletown, DE
Paolucci, Robert, St. Mary Refuge of Sinners, Cambridge, MD
Parisi, John G., (Retired)
Passwaters, Arcy A., (Retired)
Perez, Jose, Holy Rosary, Claymont, DE
Pinder, Wilbur, St. John Neumann, Berlin, MD
Pisano, Vincent, Holy Cross, Dover, DE
Pulliam, Kenneth, Sr., St. Elizabeth, Wilmington, DE
Pyrek, William J., St. Jude the Apostle, Lewes, DE
Quinlan, Francis A., St. Thomas the Apostle, Wilmington, DE
Recce, Richard L., (Retired)
Ricker, Philip, St. Michael the Archangel; Mary, Mother of Peace
Rivera, Angel, St. Paul, Wilmington, DE
Robinson, Charles, St. Polycarp, Smyrna, DE
Robinson, John R., Jr., St. Christopher, Chester, MD
Rodriguez, Cruz, St. Joesph, Middletown, DE
Rodriguez-Trejo, Jose N., St. Michael the Archangel, Georgetown, DE
Romans, Joseph C., Dir., Mission Office, Wilmington, DE; Mary Magdalen, Wilmington, DE
Schauber, Charles, Sr., St. John, Holy Angels, Newark, DE
Shaw, G. Jerry, St. Edmond, Rehoboth Beach, DE
Siers, Ronald, (Retired)
Smith, John A., (Retired)
Snow, Austin M., Jr., Immaculate Heart of Mary, Wilmington, DE
Soto, Eliezer, Our Lady of Fatima, New Castle, DE
Sprouse, Robert J., St. Jude the Apostle, Lewes, DE
Staab, Francis J., St. Catherine of Siena, Wilmington, DE
Stam, Bernardus C., Resurrection, Wilmington, DE
Taylor, Bradley D., SS. Peter & Paul, Easton, MD
Taylor, George M., Jr., St. John the Beloved, Wilmington, DE
Tormey, James M., Immaculate Conception, Marydel, MD
Tracy, Robert, (Retired)
Truman, Michael, Immaculate Conception, Elkton, MD
VanBourgondien, Cornelius J., (Retired)
Walls, James M., St. Edmond, Rehoboth, DE

Watts, Thomas, St. Margaret of Scotland, Newark, DE
Wendt, Fred, St. Joseph, Middletown, DE
Weschler, Charles A., St. John Neumann, Berlin, MD
Wilber, Michael T., St. Matthew Parish, Wilmington, DE
Wolf, Allen S., Claymont, DE, Holy Rosary; Christiana Div.
Woofter, R. Paul, St. John the Apostle, Milford, DE
Wuebbels, Dennis, St. John the Beloved, Wilmington, DE
Yackley, Luke, Church of the Good Shepherd, Perryville, MD
Yaeger, John A., St. John the Apostle, Milford, DE
Zolandz, Raymond R., Jr., St. Margaret of Scotland Parish, Glasgow, DE

INSTITUTIONS LOCATED IN THE DIOCESE

[A] HIGH SCHOOLS, DIOCESAN

WILMINGTON. *St. Mark's High School*, 2501 Pike Creek Rd., 19808. Tel: 302-738-3300; Fax: 302-738-5132. Email: principal@stmarkshs.net. Web: www.stmarkshs.net. Mr. Mark John Freund, Prin.; Rev. William T. Cocco, Chap.; Sr. Sandra Grieco, I.H.M., Pastoral Counselor; Voula Hadjipanayis, Librarian. Priests 1; Sisters 2; Lay Teachers 97; Students 1,083.

MAGNOLIA. *St. Thomas More Academy* (1999) 133 Thomas More Dr., 19962. Tel: 302-697-8100; Fax: 302-697-8122. Email: jlentini@saintmore.org. Web: www.saintmore.org. Rev. James S. Lentini, Prin. & Chap. Priests 1; Lay Teachers 20; Students 235.

[B] HIGH SCHOOLS, PRIVATE

WILMINGTON. *Salesianum School*, 1801 N. Broom St., 19802. Tel: 302-654-2495; Fax: 302-654-7767. Email: principal@salesianum.org. Web: www.salesianum.org. Revs. J. Christian Beretta, O.S.F.S., Prin.; Michael C. Connolly, O.S.F.S., Supr.; William F. Davis, O.S.F.S.; Patrick J. Kifolo, O.S.F.S., Dir., Campus Ministry; John M. Mokluk, O.S.F.S.; Joseph G. Morrissey, Vice Pres. Finance & Planning; Francis J. Pileggi, O.S.F.S.; Edward J. Roszko, O.S.F.S.; John P. Spellman, O.S.F.S.; Bros. Harry F. McGovern, O.S.F.S.; Harry G. Schneider, O.S.F.S.; Elizabeth E. Diemer, Librarian; Mr. Michael A. Vogt, O.S.F.S., Deacon. Priests 11; Brothers 2; Deacons 1; Lay Teachers 68; Boys 981. In Res. Rev. Sean P. Connery, O.S.F.S.

Ursuline Academy of Wilmington, DE, Inc., 1106 Pennsylvania Ave., 19806. Tel: 302-658-7158; Fax: 302-658-4297. Web: www.ursuline.org. Susan L. Long, Prin. Middle & Upper School; Judy Teoli, Prin. Lower School; Cathie Field Lloyd, Pres. (Coed Grades Early Childhood-3, All Girls Grades 4-12) Lay Faculty 90; Ursuline Nuns 1; Students 600.

CLAYMONT. *Archmere Academy* (1932) 3600 Philadelphia Pike, 19703. Tel: 302-798-6632; Fax: 302-798-7290. Email: generale-mailbox@archmereacademy.com. Web: www.archmereacademy.com. Michael Marinelli, Headmaster; Rev. Joseph P. McLaughlin, O.Praem., Chap.; Dr. William J. Doyle, Prin.; Ms. Rosemary Conway-Bauer, Librarian. High School (Private Preparatory). Priests 1; Lay Teachers 58; Students 481.

[C] INTERPAROCHIAL SCHOOLS

WILMINGTON. *All Saints Catholic School*, (Grades PreK-8), 907 New Road, 19805. Tel: 302-995-2231; Fax: 302-993-0767. Web: www.ascsde.org. Mrs. Diana R. Thompson, Prin. Sisters 2; Lay Teachers 32; Students 492; Total Staff 54.

BERLIN, MD. *Most Blessed Sacrament Catholic School*, 11242 Racetrack Rd., MD 21811. Tel: 410-208-1600; Fax: 410-208-4957. Mr. Mark J. Record, Prin.; Gwen Kangas, Librarian. Lay Teachers 22; Students 289; Total Staff 29.

NEWARK. *Christ the Teacher Catholic School*, (Grades PreK-8), 2451 Frazer Rd., 19702. Tel: 302-838-8850; Fax: 302-838-8854. Email: slking@christtheteacher.org. Web: ChristTheTeacher.org. Sr. La Verne King, R.S.M., Prin.; Mrs. Marjorie Taggart, Librarian. Sisters 3; Lay Teachers 26; Students 622; Total Staff 50.

[D] ELEMENTARY SCHOOLS, PRIVATE

WILMINGTON. *Saint Edmond's Academy*, (Grades PreK-8), 2120 Veale Rd., 19810. Tel: 302-475-5370; Fax: 302-475-2256. Web: stedmondsacademy.org. Bros. Michael A. Smith, C.S.C., Headmaster; Joseph Ash, C.S.C.; Thomas Meany, C.S.C.; Edward Quintal, C.S.C.; Tammy Hayes-Hartman, Librarian. Brothers of Holy Cross 3; Lay Teachers 30; Boys 285.

Nativity Preparatory School, 1515 Linden St., 19805. Tel: 302-777-1015; Fax: 302-777-1225. Email: ydeadwyler@nativitywilmington.org. Web: nativitywilmington.org. Michael Hassler, Prin. Priests 1; Lay Teachers 8.

CHILDS, MD. *Mount Aviat Academy*, (Grades PreK-8), 399 Childs Rd., MD 21916. Tel: 410-398-2206; Fax: 410-398-8063. Email: school@mountaviat.org. Web: www.mountaviat.org. Sr. John Elizabeth Callaghan, O.S.F.S., Prin.; Gale Casini, Librarian. Oblate Sisters of St. Francis de Sales. Sisters 4; Lay Teachers 15; Students 250.

RIDGELY, MD. *The Benedictine School*, 14299 Benedictine Ln., MD 21660. Tel: 410-634-2112; Fax: 410-634-2640. Email: admissions@benschool.org. Web: www.benschool.org. Sr. Jeannette Murray, O.S.B., Dir. Sisters of St. Benedict. Sisters 2; Lay Teachers 17; Students 73.

Benedictine School for Exceptional Children Foundation, Inc., 14299 Benedictine Ln., MD 21660. Tel: 410-634-2292; Fax: 410-634-1855. Email: foundation@benschool.org. Web: benschool.org. Sr. Jeannette Murray, O.S.B., Dir. Sisters 1; Lay Staff 5.

[E] DIOCESAN CATHOLIC CHARITIES PROGRAM

WILMINGTON. *Catholic Charities, Inc.*, 2601 W. 4th St., P.O. Box 2610, 19805-0610. Tel: 302-655-9624; Fax: 302-655-9753. Web: www.cdow.org/charities.html. Ms. Richelle A. Vible, M.B.A., Exec. Dir; Ms. Katrina Eichler, B.A., Southern Regional Dir.; Mr. Frederick Jones, M.S., Northern Regional Dir. Total Staff 94; Individuals Served 80,000; Fuel Program 20,257.

Delaware Energy Assistance Program

New Castle County Office, 2601 W. 4th St., 19805. Tel: 302-655-9624; Fax: 302-654-9757. Email: energy@ccwilm.org.

Sussex County Office, 406 S. Bedford St., Ste. 9, Georgetown, 19947. Tel: 302-856-6310; Fax: 302-856-6332.

Kent County Office, 2099 S. DuPont Hwy., Dover, 19901. Tel: 302-674-1600; Fax: 302-674-4018.

Counseling Services

Wilmington Office, 2601 W. 4th St., 19805. Tel: 302-655-9624; Fax: 302-654-6432. Email: counseling@ccwilm.org.

Dover Office, 2099 S. DuPont Hwy., Dover, 19901. Tel: 302-674-1600; Fax: 302-674-1005.

Georgetown Office, 406 S. Bedford St., Ste. 9, Georgetown, 19947. Tel: 302-856-9578; Fax: 302-856-6297.

HIV Services, 2601 W. 4th St., 19805. Tel: 302-655-9624; Fax: 302-654-6432. Email: HIVServices@ccwilm.org.

Dover Office, 2099 S. DuPont Hwy., Dover, 19901. Tel: 302-674-1600; Fax: 302-674-4018.

Georgetown Office, 406 S. Bedford St., Ste. 9, Georgetown, 19947. Tel: 302-856-9578; Fax: 302-856-6297.

Crisis Alleviation

Wilmington Office, 2601 W. 4th St., 19805. Tel: 302-655-9624; Fax: 302-654-6432. Email: basieneeds@ccwilm.org.

Dover Office, 2099 S. DuPont Hwy., Dover, 19901. Tel: 302-674-4016; Fax: 302-674-4018.

Immigration & Refugee Services

2601 W. 4th St., P.O. Box 2610, 19805-0610. Tel: 302-654-6460; Fax: 302-654-9757. Email: immigration@ccwilm.org.

Dover Office, 2099 S. DuPont Hwy., Dover, 19901. Tel: 302-674-1600.

406 S. Bedford St., Ste. 9, Georgetown, 19947. Tel: 302-856-9578; Fax: 302-856-6297.

Catholic Charities Thrift Center, 1320 E. 23rd St., 19802. Tel: 302-764-2717; Fax: 302-764-2743. Email: thriftcenter@ccwilm.org.

CACFP (Child & Adult Care Food Program), 2604 W. 4th St., 19805. Tel: 302-655-9624; Fax: 302-654-9753.

Dover Office, 2099 S. DuPont Hwy., Dover, 19901. Tel: 302-674-1600; Fax: 302-674-4018. Email: CACFP@CCWilm.org.

Georgetown Office, 406 S. Bedford St., Ste. 9, Georgetown, 19947. Tel: 302-856-9578; Fax: 302-856-6332.

Addictions and Substance Abuse Counseling, 2601 W. 4th St., 19805. Tel: 302-655-9624; Fax: 302-654-6432. Email: substanceabuse@ccwilm.org.

Dover Office, 2099 S. DuPont Hwy., Dover, 19901. Tel: 302-674-1600; Fax: 302-674-4018.

Residential Services

Bayard House, Maternity Services, Pregnancy Counseling, 300 Bayard Ave., 19805. Tel: 302-654-1184; Fax: 302-654-8570. Email: bayardhouse@ccwilm.org.

Casa San Francisco, 127 Broad St., P.O. Box 38, Milton, 19968. Tel: 302-684-8694; Fax: 302-684-2808. Email: casa@ccwilm.org.

Seton Center, 30632 Hampden Ave., P.O. Box 401, Princess Anne, MD 21853. Tel: 410-651-9608; Fax: 410-651-1437. Email: setoncenter@ccwilm.org.

[F] CHILDREN'S SERVICES

WILMINGTON. *Seton Villa, Inc.* (Catholic Charities), 4th St. & Greenhill Ave., 19805. Web: www.cdow.org.

[G] OTHER WELFARE AGENCIES
(Not under jurisdiction of Department of Social Concerns)

WILMINGTON

Family Counseling Center of St. Paul's, Inc., 1010 W. 4th St., 19805-3602. Tel: 302-576-4121; Fax: 302-655-7684. Web: www.familyrelationshiphelp.com.

Ministry of Caring, Inc. (1977) 506 N. Church St., 19801-4812. Tel: 302-652-5523; Fax: 302-652-1919. Email: mail@ministryofcaring.org. Mark L. Reardon Esq., Pres.; Rev. Ronald Giannone, O.F.M.Cap., Exec. Dir.; Debbe Philips, Chief of Staff; Annie Halverson, Exec. Asst. & Paralegal; Louisa Teoli, Personal Asst. & Community Rels. Coord.

Sacred Heart Administration, 903 N. Madison St., 19801. Tel: 302-888-1420; Fax: 302-594-9450. Anthea Piscarick, Advancement - Grant Writer.

Nazareth Long Term Housing, 207 S. Van Buren St., 19805. Tel: 302-652-5523; Fax: 302-652-1919. Mark Poletunow, Deputy Dir. Transitional residence for families.

Nazareth Long Term Housing, 109-1/2 & 111 N. Jackson St., 19805. Tel: 302-652-5523; Fax: 302-652-1919. Mark Poletunow, Deputy Dir. Transitional residence for families.

Benedictine Park, 731 W. 9th St., 19801. Tel: 302-652-5523; Fax: 302-652-1919.

Andrisani Building (1996) 1801 W. 6th St., 19805. Tel: 302-428-3702; Fax: 302-428-3705. Mark Poletunow, Chief Fin. Officer & Deputy Dir. Programs.

Sacred Heart House (1997) 917 N. Madison St., 19801. Tel: 302-428-3652; Fax: 302-428-3655. Marie Keefer, Deputy Dir. Human Resources.

Child Care Center (1992) 221 N. Jackson St., 19805-3649. Tel: 302-652-8992; Fax: 302-594-9442. Paulette Annane, Prog. Dir. Child care for homeless children, from infancy to 4 years old.

Guardian Angel Child Care (1998) 1000 Wilson St., 19801-3432. Tel: 302-428-3620; Fax: 302-428-3622. Email: jchandler@ministryofcaring.org. Janet Chandler, Site Mgr.

Il Bambino (2002) 903 N. Madison St., 19801. Tel: 302-594-9449; Fax: 302-594-9450. Paulette Annane, Prog. Dir. Infant day care program. Capacity 24.

Il Cappuccino Banquet Room 1 Culinary Job Training., 221 N. Jackson St., Lower Level, 19805. Tel: 302-652-5516. William Bradley, Chief Chef & Banquet Mgr.

St. Clare Medical Outreach (1992) 7th & Clayton Sts., 19805-3156. Tel: 302-575-8218. Dr. Oswaldo Necastro, M.D., Medical Dir.; Maryann Merrylees, R.N. Mobile medical van which provides health services for the poor.

Mary Mother of Hope House Transitional Residence, 818-820 Jefferson St., 19801-1432. Tel: 302-594-9448; Fax: 302-594-9434. Email: mmatarese@ministryofcaring.org. Mary Anne Matarese, Prog. Dir. Transitional residence for single women. Capacity 12.

House of Joseph II, 9 W. 18th St., 19802-4833. Tel: 302-594-9473; Fax: 302-594-9494. Email: srjean@ministryofcaring.org. Sr. Jean Rupertus, O.S.F., Prog. Dir. Hospice for people with AIDS. Capacity 16.

Maria Lorenza Longo House (2003) 822 Jefferson St., 19801. Mary Anne Matarese, Prog. Dir.; Tracey Brown, Mgr. Transitional Residence for Families. Capacity 5.

Pierre Toussaint Dental Office (1995) 830 Spruce St., 19801-4205. Tel: 302-652-8947; Fax: 302-652-8994. Gary Isaacs, D.M.D. Dental office for the homeless.

Angela Merici House (1993) 1105 W. 8th St., 19806-4605. Tel: 302-655-4817. Residence for Sisters of St. Francis. Religious Sisters 5.

St. Francis Transitional Residence (1995) 103-107 & 111 N. Jackson St., 19805-3648. Renee Mosley, Prog. Dir. Transitional living for women and children.

House of Joseph Transitional Residence (1998) 704 West St., 19801-1523. Tel: 302-652-7968; Fax: 302-594-9472. Email: wnewson@ministryofcaring.org. Willie Newson,

Prog. Dir. Transitional residence for employable, formerly homeless persons.

Samaritan Outreach (1995) 1410 N. Claymont St., 19802-5227. Tel: 302-594-9476; Fax: 303-594-9478. Noris Perdomo, Prog. Dir. Social outreach for the homeless.

Mary Mother of Hope House I (1977) 1103 W. 8th St., 19806. Tel: 302-652-8532; Fax: 302-594-9434. Email: mmatarese@ministryofcaring.org. Mary Anne Matarese, Prog. Dir. Emergency shelter for homeless women. Capacity 20.

Mary Mother of Hope House II (1983) 121 N. Jackson St., 19805-3670. Tel: 302-652-1935; Fax: 302-594-9475. Renee Mosley, Prog. Dir. Emergency shelter for women with children. Capacity 23.

Mary Mother of Hope House III (1988) 515 N. Broom St., 19805-3114. Tel: 302-652-0970; Fax: 302-594-9496. Renee Mosley, Prog. Dir. Emergency shelter for women with children. Capacity 21.

Job Placement Center (1985) 1100 Lancaster Ave., 19805-4009. Tel: 302-652-5522; Fax: 302-652-0917. Email: mking@ministryofcaring.org. Ms. Marva King-Poynter, Prog. Dir. Employment agency to assist the poor.

House of Joseph I (1985) 917 N. Madison St., 19801. Tel: 302-652-0904; Fax: 302-594-9472. Email: wnewson@ministryofcaring.org. Willie Newson, Prog. Dir. Shelter for homeless employable men who are seeking employment. Capacity 13.

Emmanuel Dining Room, West (1979) 121 N. Jackson St., 19805-3670. Tel: 302-652-3228; Fax: 302-652-2576. Bro. Rudolph Pieretti, O.F.M.Cap., Prog. Dir.

Emmanuel Dining Room, East, 226 N. Walnut St., 19801-3934. Tel: 302-652-2577; Fax: 302-652-2576. Mr. DeWitt Smith, Site Mgr.

Emmanuel Dining Room, South, 500 Rogers Rd., New Castle, 19720. Tel: 302-577-2951; Fax: 302-652-2576. Sr. Bernadette McGoldrick, O.S.F., Senior Site Mgr.

Ministry of Caring Distribution Center, 1410 N. Claymont St., 19802-5227. Tel: 302-652-0969; Fax: 302-594-9478. Mr. Eugene McLaughlin, Dir. Maintenance & Safety.

Ministry of Caring Guild (1990) 506 N. Church St., 19801-4812. Tel: 302-427-9447; Fax: 302-778-5286. Danielle Andrisani Nowaczyk, Pres.

Nazareth House I (1998) 106 N. Broom St., 19805-4241. Tel: 302-652-0790; Fax: 302-594-9496. Renee Mosley, Prog. Dir. Capacity (Families) 3.

Bethany House (1999) 601 N. Jackson St., 19805-3241. Tel: 302-656-8391. Email: mmatarese@ministryofcaring.org. Annie Mountain, Prog. Dir. Permanent housing for women with special needs. Capacity 8.

Nazareth House II (1998) 898 Linden St., 19805-4423. Tel: 302-428-3635; Fax: 302-428-3636. Renee Mosley, Prog. Dir. Transitional residence for families. Capacity 4.

Nazareth Long Term Housing (1998) 203 N. Jackson St., 19805-3649. Tel: 302-652-5523; Fax: 302-652-1919. Mark Poletunow, Deputy Dir. Long term housing

Nazareth Long Term Housing (1998) 807 W. 6th St., 19805. Tel: 302-652-5523; Fax: 302-652-1919. Mark Poletunow, Deputy Dir. Programs. Long term housing Capacity 1; Families 1.

Francis X. Norton Center (2002) 917 N. Madison St., 19801. Tel: 302-594-9455; Fax: 302-428-3655. Ms. Linda Richardson, Prog. Dir. Multigenerational community center.

Padre Pio House, 213 N. Jackson St., 19805. Email: wnewson@ministryofcaring.org. Willie Newson, Program Dir.; Gordon Corbitt, Resident Mgr. Permanent housing for men with special needs. Capacity 6.

Sacred Heart Convent, 700 W. 9th St., 19801. Tel: 302-692-8532. Capacity 3.

NEWARK

Our Lady of Grace Home, Inc., 487 E. Chestnut Hill Rd., 19713-2682. Tel: 302-738-4658; 302-737-6650; Fax: 302-369-1395. Email: olghch@comcast.net. Felician Sisters 2.

RIDGELY, MD

St. Martin's Ministries, Inc. (1983) 14259 Benedictine Ln., MD 21660. Tel: 410-634-2497; Fax: 410-634-1410. Email: srpatricia@stmartinsministries.org. Web: www.stmartinsministries.org. Sr. Patricia Gamgort, O.S.B., Exec. Dir.; Jean F. Austin, Opers. Dir. Sisters of St. Benedict.

St. Martin's Barn, 14376 Benedictine Ln., MD 21660. Tel: 410-634-1140; Fax: 410-634-1507. Web: stmartinsministries.org. Odette Boyce-Galvez, Dir. Volunteers 165; Total Staff 5; Total Assisted 3,300.

St. Martin's House, 14374 Benedictine Ln., MD 21660. Tel: 410-634-2537; Fax: 410-634-1293. Denise Ransome, Dir. Volunteers 12; Staff 7; Total Assisted 25.

[H] HOMES FOR AGED

WILMINGTON. *The Antonian*, 1701 W. 10th St., 19805. Tel: 302-421-3758; Fax: 302-421-3759. Tori Daniello, Mgr. Congregate Housing for the Elderly Residents 143; Apartments 136; Total Staff 6.

HOCKESSIN. *Franciscan Health System/Care at Brackenville* (1992) 100 St. Clare Dr., 19707. Tel: 302-234-5420; Fax: 302-234-5424. Email: lbranco@che-east.org. Web: www.stfrancishealthcare.org. Linda Branco, Chap. A 104-bed skilled nursing facility Total Staff 135.

NEWARK. *Jeanne Jugan Residence* (1978) 185 Salem Church Rd., 19713. Tel: 302-368-5886; Fax: 302-738-5610. Email: msnewark@littlesistersofthepoor.org. Sr. Joseph Beutler, L.S.P., Supr. Conducted by the Little Sisters of the Poor. Residents 80; Sisters 11.

Marydale Retirement Village, 135 Jeandell Dr., 19713. Tel: 302-368-2784; Fax: 302-731-0584. Ray Lloyd, Admin.; Sr. Mary Rita Smith, Pastoral Care Coord. Apartments for Elderly. Apartments 108; Residents 112; Total Assisted 98.

[I] GENERAL HOSPITALS

WILMINGTON. *St. Francis Hospital, Inc.*, 7th and Clayton Sts., P.O. Box 2500, 19805-0500. Tel: 302-575-8305; Fax: 302-575-8320. Email: jmmonahan@che-east.org. Web: www.stfrancishealthcare.org. Julie A. Hester, Pres. & CEO; Revs. Joseph J. McKenna, O.S.F.S.; Joseph Monahan, T.O.R., Vice Pres. Mission & Min.; Xavier Bruce Rajendran; Linda Branco, Dir. Spiritual Care. Bed Capacity 395; Total Staff 847; Patients Assisted Annually 186,259.

LIFE at St. Francis Healthcare, Inc., 7th & Clayton Sts., 19805. Tel: 302-421-4100; Fax: 302-575-8320.

[J] MONASTERIES AND RESIDENCES OF PRIESTS AND BROTHERS

WILMINGTON. *Brothers of Holy Cross, Saint Edmond's Academy*, 2120 Veale Rd., 19810. Tel: 302-475-5370; Fax: 302-475-2256. Email: advancement@stedmondsacademy.org. Bros. Joseph W. Ash, C.S.C., Dir. Religious; Thomas Meany, C.S.C., Trans. Coord.; Michael A. Smith, C.S.C., Headmaster. Brothers 3.

Capuchin Franciscan Friars, St. Francis Renewal Center, 1901 Prior Rd., 19809. Tel: 302-798-1454; Fax: 302-798-3360. Revs. Cyprian Rosen, O.F.M.Cap., S.T.L.; Francis Sariego, O.F.M.Cap., Vicar; William Arlia, O.F.M.Cap.

DeSales House, 1600 Brinckle Ave., 19806. Tel: 302-656-4342; Fax: 302-656-6108. Web: www.oblates.org. Revs. William R. Gore, O.S.F.S., Supr.; William E. Davis, O.S.F.S.; Gerald Dunne, O.S.F.S.; John A. Finn, O.S.F.S.; John J. Hurley, O.S.F.S.; William J. Keech, O.S.F.S.; Joseph J. McKenna, O.S.F.S. Priests 5.

St. Felix Friary, 119 N. Jackson St., 19805-3670. Tel: 302-652-7010; Fax: 302-652-8943. Email: mail@ministryofcaring.org. Rev. Ronald Giannone, O.F.M.Cap., Guardian; Bros. Robert Perez, O.F.M.Cap.; Rudolph Pieretti, O.F.M.Cap. Priests 1; Brothers 2.

Wilmington-Philadelphia Province of the Oblates of St. Francis de Sales, 2200 Kentmere Pkwy., 19806. Tel: 302-656-8529; Fax: 302-658-8052. Email: bstrong@oblates.org. Web: www.oblates.org. Very Rev. James J. Greenfield, O.S.F.S., Provincial; Revs. Barry R. Strong, O.S.F.S., Dir. Prov. Admin.; Kevin M. Nadolski, O.S.F.S., Dir. Communications & Devel.; Nicholas R. Waseline, O.S.F.S. Priests 10.

Rev. Oblates Attached to the Provincial Residence: Revs. William J. Hultberg, O.S.F.S.; Mark A. Hushen, O.S.F.S.; Thomas J. Palko, O.S.F.S.; William T. McCandless, O.S.F.S.; William E. Davis, O.S.F.S.

CHILDS, MD. *Oblates of St. Francis De Sales* (1907) , MD. Tel: 410-398-3040; Fax: 410-620-6131. Web: www.oblates.org. *Retirement and Assisted Care Facility*, 1120 Blue Ball Rd., MD 21916-0043. Tel: 410-398-3040; Fax: 410-620-6131. Web: www.oblates.org. Very Rev. Michael S. Murray, O.S.F.S., Rel. Supr. Priests 20; Brothers 7. In Res. Revs. Robert D. Ashenbrenner, O.S.F.S. (Retired); Joseph Baraniewicz, O.S.F.S. (Retired); Joseph D. Bowler, O.S.F.S. (Retired); John W. Brennan, O.S.F.S. (Retired); John J. Dennis, O.S.F.S. (Retired); Hugh E. Duffy, O.S.F.S. (Retired); Joseph J. Griffin, O.S.F.S. (Retired); Peter J. Harvey, O.S.F.S. (Retired); Mark A. Hushen, O.S.F.S.; Eugene L. Kelly, O.S.F.S. (Retired); John F. Kenny, O.S.F.S. (Retired); John A. Kowalewski, O.S.F.S.; Anthony J. Larry, O.S.F.S. (Retired); Richard D. Leone, O.S.F.S. (Retired); Eugene J. McBride, O.S.F.S. (Retired); John J. Muzdakis, O.S.F.S. (Retired); R. Douglas Smith, O.S.F.S. (Retired); Thomas J. Tucker, O.S.F.S. (Retired); Bros. Thomas P. Brophy, O.S.F.S. (Retired); John M. Carroll, O.S.F.S. (Retired); Robert M. Carter, O.S.F.S. (Retired); John J. Dochkus, O.S.F.S.; Joseph H. Hayden, O.S.F.S.; Neil McMenamin, O.S.F.S. (Retired); Gerald M. Sweeney, O.S.F.S., Ordinary (Retired).

DOVER. *Oblate Apostles of the Two Hearts*, 749 Bison Rd., 19904. Tel: 302-697-6544. Revs. Edgardo M. Arellano, Supreme Moderator; Welthy Gorecho, Local Servant; John Richard F. Santos, National Servant; Robert Tiqual; Jose Viola, Foremater; Bros. Francis Platon, Foremater; Zidney Platon, Foremater.

MIDDLETOWN. *Immaculate Conception Priory of the Canons Regular of Premontre* (1997) 1269 Bayview Rd., 19709. Tel: 302-449-1840, Ext. 31; Fax: 302-449-1217. Very Rev. James D. Bagnato, O.Praem., Admin. Dir. Vocation & Novice Master; Revs. Martin A. Frigo, O.Praem.; Brian Zielinski, O.Praem., Subprior. Priests 5.

Norbertine Fathers of Delaware, Inc. (1997) 1269 Bayview Rd., 19709. Tel: 302-449-1840; Fax: 302-449-1217. Very Rev. James D. Bagnato, O.Praem., Pres.; Rev. Brian Zielinski, O.Praem., Vice Pres.

[K] CONVENTS AND RESIDENCES FOR SISTERS

WILMINGTON. *St. Benedict*, 113 Canterbury Dr., 19803. Tel: 302-478-3754; Fax: 302-478-9305. Email: margosb@aol.com. Sisters of St. Benedict 3.

Monastery of St. Veronica Giuliani (Strict Enclosure), 816 Jefferson St., 19801. Tel: 302-654-8727; Fax: 302-652-3929. Email: stveronicagiuliani@MSN.com. Sr. Maria Magdalena Cacho, O.S.C.Cap., Abbess; Rev. Ronald Giannone, O.F.M.Cap., Chap. Capuchin Poor Clare Nuns of Delaware. Sisters 10.

Ursuline Academy Inc., The (1893) 1104 Pennsylvania Ave., 19806. Tel: 302-656-5890; Fax: 302-656-2315. Sr. Stephanie Wilson, O.S.U., Delegate Supr. Sisters 9.

CHILDS, MD. *Oblate Sisters of St. Francis de Sales, Inc.*, 399 Childs Rd., MD 21916. Tel: 410-398-3699; Fax: 877-398-8063. Email: oblatesisters@mountaviat.org. Web: www.oblatesisters.org. Sr. Anne Elizabeth, O.S.F.S., Delegate. Oblate Sisters of St. Francis de Sales. Sisters 11.

Aviat Foundation Endowment Trust, 399 Childs Rd., MD 21916.

Villa Aviat, Inc., 399 Childs Rd., MD 21916. Tel: 410-398-3699; Fax: 877-398-8063.

DOVER. *Leaven of the Immaculate Heart of Mary (LIHM)*, 207 Northdown Dr., Village of Westover, 19904. Tel: 302-734-0847; Fax: 302-734-0847. Email: lihmdover@comcast.net. Sr. Maria Cecilia Garcia, Mother General; Rev. Edgardo M. Arellano, Spiritual Dir.; Sisters Eberlene Icalla, L.I.H.M., Apostolic Head & Natl. Sec.; Marie Angelie Dorol, L.I.H.M., Natl. Servant; Marianne Morales, L.I.H.M., Vocation Head.

NEW CASTLE. *Caterina Benincasa Dominican Monastery, Inc.*, 6 Church Dr., 19720. Tel: 302-654-1206. Sisters 3.

PRINCESS ANNE, MD. *St. Joseph Novitiate*, 10572 Anderson Rd., MD 21853. Tel: 410-651-5309; Fax: 410-742-3390. Email: lsjm@comcast.net. Web: thejosephhouse.org. Sr. Constance R. Ladd, L.S.J.M., Supr. Gen. Sisters 6; Postulants 2.

Seton Center, Sisters of Charity (1983) (Convent Station), P.O. Box 401, MD 21853. Tel: 410-651-9608; Fax: 410-651-1437. Email: setoncenter@comcast.net. Sisters 4; Assisted 8,200.

RIDGELY, MD. *St. Gertrude's Monastery, Motherhouse and Novitiate of the Sisters of St. Benedict* (1857) 14259 Benedictine Ln., MD 21660-1434. Tel: 410-634-2497; Fax: 410-634-1410. Web: www.ridgelybenedictines.org. Sr. Colleen Quinlivan, O.S.B., Admin. Sisters 23.

SALISBURY, MD. *Joseph House, Little Sisters of Jesus & Mary.*, P.O. Box 1755, MD 21802. Tel: 410-543-1645; Fax: 410-742-3390. Email: lsjm@comcast.net. Web: www.thejosephhouse.org. Sr. Constance R. Ladd, L.S.J.M., Supr. Gen. Sisters 6.

[L] SECULAR INSTITUTES

WILMINGTON. *De Sales Secular Institute*, 3127 Charing Cross, 19808. Tel: 302-234-8616. Web: www.secularinstitutes.org/sfs.htm. Mary Robinson, Dir.

Secular Franciscan Order (San Damiano Fraternity), 2508 Oakfield Ln., 19810. Tel: 302-478-6593. Email: carisio@yahoo.com. Teresa Carisio, Min.; Sr. Elise Betz, O.S.F., Spiritual Asst.

Secular Franciscan Order (St. Patrick's Fraternity), 1901 Prior Rd., 19809. Tel: 302-798-1454. John Oscar, S.F.O., Local Min.; Rev. William Arlia, O.F.M.Cap., Spiritual Asst.

BEAR, MD. *Secular Order of Discalced Carmelites*, 769 Fox Chase Cir., 19701. Tel: 302-836-3843. Mary An Love, Pres.; Bro. Bryan Paquette, O.C.D., Spiritual Asst. (Annunciation Community).

DOVER. *Secular Institute of the Two Hearts*, P.O. Box 1719, 19903. Tel: 302-678-1358; Fax: 302-678-3246. Email: ahfisecretariat@aol.com. Sisters

Agnes Frias, S.I.T.H., Intl. Supr.; Deanna Crisologo, S.I.T.H., Intl. Vicar; Rev. Edgardo M. Arellano, Supr. Gen.

SALISBURY, MD. *Secular Order of Discalced Carmelites* (Community of Mary), 631 Ridge Rd., MD 21801. Tel: 410-742-1777. Mrs. Marianne Chapin; Bro. Bryan Paquette, O.C.D., Spiritual Asst.

[M] RETREAT HOUSES, GENERAL

WILMINGTON. *De Sales Spirituality Services*, 2200 Kentmere Pkwy., 19806. Tel: 302-383-3585; Fax: 302-658-8052. Email: mmurray@osfs.org. Web: www.oblates.org/dss. Very Rev. Michael S. Murray, O.S.F.S., Dir.

St. Francis Renewal Center, 1901 Prior Rd., 19809. Tel: 302-798-1454; Fax: 302-798-3360. Revs. Cyprian Rosen, O.F.M.Cap., S.T.L.; Francis Sariego, O.F.M.Cap., Vicar; William Arlia, O.F.M.Cap. Priests 3.

**Jesus House*, 2501 Milltown Rd., 19808. Tel: 302-995-6859; Fax: 302-995-6833. Mr. Christian Malmgren, Dir.

[N] RETREAT HOUSES, WOMEN

CHILDS, MD. *Oblate Sisters of St. Francis de Sales*, Villa Aviat, 399 Childs Rd., MD 21916. Tel: 410-398-3699; Fax: 877-398-8063. Email: oblatesisters@mountaviat.org. Web: www.oblatesisters.org.

RIDGELY, MD. *Berg Retreat Center*, St. Gertrude's Monastery, 14259 Benedictine Ln., MD 21660. Tel: 410-634-2497; Fax: 410-634-1410. Web: www.ridgelybenedictines.org. Benedictine Sisters.

[O] NEWMAN CENTERS

NEWARK. *Catholic Campus Ministry, Univ. of Delaware* St. Thomas More Oratory, 45 Lovett Ave., 19711. Tel: 302-368-4728; Fax: 302-368-2548. Web: www.udcatholic.org. Rev. Ambrose Eckinger, O.P.

Delmar Organization of Catholic Students - DOCS Tel: 302-368-4728; Fax: 302-368-2548. Kimberly S. Zitzner, B.A., Dir.

Salisbury University 211 W. College Ave., Salisbury, MD 21801. Tel: 410-219-3376; Fax: 410-219-3376. Mrs. Regina Yankalunas, M.P.S., Campus Min.

University of Maryland Eastern Shore 211 W. College Ave., Salisbury, MD 21801. Tel: 410-219-3376; Fax: 410-219-3376. Email: campusministry@hotmail.com. Mrs. Regina Yankalunas, M.P.S., Campus Min.

Wesley College Newman Center Tel: 302-368-4728; Fax: 302-368-2548.

Washington College 45 Lovett Ave., 19711. Tel: 302-368-4728; Fax: 302-368-2548. Rev. Paul J. Campbell.

Wesley College Catholic Campus Ministry St. Thomas More Oratory, 45 Lovett Ave., 19711. Tel: 302-368-4728; Fax: 302-368-2548.

[P] MISCELLANEOUS

WILMINGTON. *Brisson Fund* (1989) 2200 Kentmere Pkwy., 19806. Tel: 302-656-8529. Very Rev. James J. Greenfield, O.S.F.S., Pres.

Nativity Preparatory School of Wilmington Trust, 2200 Kentmere Pkwy., 19806.

OSFS Wilmington-Philadelphia Province, Inc., 2200 Kentmere Pkwy., 19806.

OSFS Childs Real Estate Corporation, 2200 Kentmere Pkwy., 19806.

OSFS Endowment Trust, 2200 Kentmere Pkwy., 19806.

OSFS Mission Corporation, 2200 Kentmere Pkwy., 19806.

OSFS Real Estate Holding Corporation, 2200 Kentmere Pkwy., 19806.

OSFS Real Estate Trust, 2200 Kentmere Pkwy., 19806.

OSFS Service Corporation, 2200 Kentmere Pkwy., 19806.

Salesianum School Endowment Trust I, 2200 Kentmere Pkwy., 19806.

Salesianum School Endowment Trust II, 2200 Kentmere Pkwy., 19806.

RELIGIOUS INSTITUTES OF MEN REPRESENTED IN THE DIOCESE

For further details refer to the corresponding bracketed number in the Religious Institutes of Men or Women section.

[0600]—*Brothers of the Congregation of Holy Cross* (Eastern Province)—C.S.C.

[0900]—*Canons Regular of Premontre*—O.Praem.

[0470]—*The Capuchin Friars* (Prov. of the Stigmata)—O.F.M.Cap.

[0520]—*Franciscan Friars* (Holy Name Province)—O.F.M.

[590]—*Missionaries of the Holy Apostles*—M.S.A.

[]—*Oblate Apostles of the Two Hearts*—O.A.T.H.

[0920]—*Oblates of St. Francis de Sales*—O.S.F.S.

[0430]—*Order of Preachers* (Prov. of St. Joseph)—O.P.

[1070]—*Redemptorist Fathers* (Baltimore, MD)—C.SS.R.

[1200]—*Society of the Divine Savior*—S.D.S.

[0560]—*Third Order Regular of Saint Francis*

RELIGIOUS INSTITUTES OF WOMEN REPRESENTED IN THE DIOCESE

[0100]—*Adorers of the Blood of Christ*—A.S.C.

[0230]—*Benedictine Sisters of Pontifical Jurisdiction*—O.S.B.

[3765]—*Capuchin Poor Clare Sisters*—O.S.C.Cap.

[]—*Carmelites of Charity of Vedruna*—C.C.V.

[3735]—*Congregation of St. Brigid*—C.S.B.

[0760]—*Daughters of the Charity of St. Vincent de Paul*—D.C.

[1050]—*Dominican Contemplative Nuns*—O.P.

[1070-11]—*Dominican Sisters*—O.P.

[1170]—*Felician Sisters*—C.S.S.F.

[]—*Leaven of the Immaculate Heart of Mary Sisters*—L.I.H.M.

[2331]—*Little Sisters of Jesus and Mary*—L.S.J.M.

[2340]—*Little Sisters of the Poor*—L.S.P.

[2790]—*Missionary Servants of the Most Blessed Trinity*—M.S.B.T.

[3060]—*Oblates Sisters of St. Francis de Sales*—O.S.F.S.

[2575]—*Religious Sisters of Mercy Mid-Atlantic Community* (Baltimore, MD; Merion, PA)—R.S.M.

[2575]—*Religious Sisters of Mercy South Central Community*—R.S.M.

[2970]—*School Sisters of Notre Dame*—S.S.N.D.

[]—*Secular Institute of the Two Hearts*—S.I.T.H.

[3630]—*Servants of the Most Sacred Heart of Jesus*—S.S.C.J.

[]—*Sisters for Christian Community*—S.F.C.C.

[0440]—*Sisters of Charity of Cincinnati*—S.C.

[0590]—*Sisters of Charity of Saint Elizabeth, Convent Station* (Southern, Western Provs.)—S.C.

[3000]—*Sisters of Notre Dame* (Base Communities Prov.; Maryland Prov.)—S.N.D.deN.

[1650]—*Sisters of St. Francis of Philadelphia*—O.S.F.

[3893]—*Sisters of St. Joseph of Chestnut Hill, Philadelphia*—S.S.J.

[2160]—*Sisters, Servants of Immaculate Heart of Mary* Scranton, PA—I.H.M.

[2150]—*Sisters, Servants of Immaculate Heart of Mary* Monroe, MI—I.H.M.

[4110]—*Ursuline Nuns (Roman Union)* (Eastern Prov.)—O.S.U.

DIOCESAN CEMETERIES

WILMINGTON. *All Saints Cemetery*, 6001 Kirkwood Hwy., 19805. Tel: 302-737-2524; Fax: 302-737-4091. Email: tkane@cathcemde.com. Web: www.cathcemde.com. Office: 6001 Kirkwood Hwy., 19808. Mr. Mark A. Christian, C.C.C.E., Exec. Dir.; Thomas J. Kane, Supt.

Cathedral Cemetery, P.O. Box 2506, 19805. Tel: 302-656-3323; Fax: 302-656-1069. Web: www.cathcemde.com. Office: 2400 Lancaster Ave., 19805. Mr. Mark A. Christian, C.C.C.E., Exec. Dir.; Scott Hudson, Supt.

DAGSBORO. *Gate of Heaven Cemetery*, 32112 Vines Creek Rd., 19939. Tel: 302-732-3690; Fax: 302-732-3692. Mr. Mark A. Christian, C.C.C.E., Exec. Dir.; Nicholas Hoopes, Supt.

NECROLOGY

† Bozzelli, Joseph V., (Retired)—Died June 1, 2011
† Connell, Stephen J., (Retired)—Died April 1, 2011
† McCloskey, Daniel J. Jr., (Retired)—Died Oct. 13, 2011
† Vazquez, Carlos R., (Retired)—Died July 16, 2011

An asterisk (*) denotes an organization that has established tax-exempt status directly with the IRS and is not covered by the USCCB Group Ruling.

Diocese of Winona

(Dioecesis Vinonaensis)

Most Reverend

JOHN M. QUINN, M.DIV.

Bishop of Winona; ordained March 17, 1972; appointed Auxiliary Bishop of the Archdiocese of Detroit and Titular See of Ressiana August 12, 2003; appointed Coadjutor Bishop of Winona October 15, 2008; Mass of Welcome December 11, 2008; Succeeded to See May 7, 2009. *Pastoral Center: 55 W. Sanborn St., P.O. Box 588, Winona, MN 55987.*

Most Reverend

BERNARD J. HARRINGTON, D.D.

Retired Bishop of Winona; ordained June 6, 1959; appointed Auxiliary Bishop of the Archdiocese of Detroit and Titular Bishop of Uzali November 23, 1993; ordained January 6, 1994; appointed Bishop of Winona November 5, 1998; installed January 6, 1999; retired May 7, 2009.

Pastoral Center: 55 W. Sanborn St., P.O. Box 588, Winona, MN 55987. Tel: 507-454-4643; Fax: 507-454-8106.

Web: www.dow.org

Email: dioceseofwinona@dow.org

ESTABLISHED NOVEMBER 26, 1889.

Square Miles 12,282.

Comprises the Counties of Winona, Wabasha, Olmsted, Dodge, Steele, Waseca, Blue Earth, Watonwan, Cottonwood, Murray, Pipestone, Rock, Nobles, Jackson, Faribault, Martin, Freeborn, Mower, Fillmore and Houston in the State of Minnesota.

For legal titles of parishes and diocesan institutions, consult the Pastoral Center.

STATISTICAL OVERVIEW

Personnel	
Bishop	1
Retired Bishops	1
Abbots	1
Priests: Diocesan Active in Diocese	59
Priests: Diocesan Active Outside Diocese	5
Priests: Retired, Sick or Absent	49
Number of Diocesan Priests	113
Religious Priests in Diocese	6
Total Priests in Diocese	119
Extern Priests in Diocese	13
Permanent Deacons in Diocese	30
Total Brothers	21
Total Sisters	377
Parishes	
Parishes	114
With Resident Pastor:	
Resident Diocesan Priests	45
Resident Religious Priests	4
Without Resident Pastor:	
Administered by Priests	64
Administered by Lay People	1
Pastoral Centers	2
Professional Ministry Personnel:	
Sisters	9
Lay Ministers	49
Welfare	
Catholic Hospitals	2
Total Assisted	149,850
Health Care Centers	1
Total Assisted	1,236
Homes for the Aged	10
Total Assisted	677
Day Care Centers	3
Total Assisted	17,398
Special Centers for Social Services	7
Total Assisted	4,392
Other Institutions	1
Total Assisted	100
Educational	
Seminaries, Diocesan	1
Students from This Diocese	8
Students from Other Diocese	47
Diocesan Students in Other Seminaries	3
Total Seminarians	11
Colleges and Universities	1
Total Students	1,372
High Schools, Diocesan and Parish	4
Total Students	977
Elementary Schools, Diocesan and Parish	26
Total Students	4,248
Catechesis/Religious Education:	
High School Students	3,385
Elementary Students	6,627
Total Students under Catholic Instruction	16,620
Teachers in the Diocese:	
Brothers	8
Sisters	4
Lay Teachers	334
Vital Statistics	
Receptions into the Church:	
Infant Baptism Totals	1,431
Minor Baptism Totals	65
Adult Baptism Totals	35
Received into Full Communion	240
First Communions	1,207
Confirmations	1,327
Marriages:	
Catholic	288
Interfaith	149
Total Marriages	437
Deaths	776
Total Catholic Population	132,545
Total Population	576,284

Former Bishops—Rt. Revs. JOSEPH B. COTTER, D.D., ord. May 3, 1871; cons. Dec. 27, 1889; died June 28, 1909; PATRICK R. HEFFRON, D.D., ord. Dec. 22, 1884; cons. May 19, 1910; died Nov. 23, 1927; Most Revs. FRANCIS M. KELLY, D.D., ord. Nov. 1, 1912; cons. June 9, 1926; transferred to Diocese of Winona, Feb. 10, 1928; transferred to Titular See of Nasal, Oct. 17, 1949; died June 24, 1950; EDWARD A. FITZGERALD, D.D., ord. July 25, 1916; cons. Sept. 12, 1946; appt. Titular Bishop of Cantanus and Auxiliary Bishop of Dubuque; transferred to Winona, Oct. 20, 1949; retired and transferred to the Titular See of Zerta, Jan. 8, 1969; died March 30, 1972; LORAS J. WATTERS, D.D. (Retired), ord. June 7, 1941; appt. Titular Bishop of Fidoloma and Auxiliary Bishop of Dubuque, June 23, 1965; cons. Aug. 26, 1965; transferred to Winona, Jan. 8, 1969; retired Oct. 14, 1986; appt. Apostolic Administrator, Oct. 14, 1986; died March 30, 2009; JOHN G. VLAZNY, D.D., ord. Dec. 20, 1961; appt. Auxiliary Bishop of Chicago and Titular Bishop of Stagno, Oct. 31, 1983; cons. Dec. 13, 1983; appt. Bishop of Winona, May 19, 1987; installed July 29, 1987; appt. Archbishop of Portland, Oct. 28, 1997; BERNARD J. HARRINGTON, D.D., ord. June 6, 1959; appt. Auxiliary Bishop of Archdiocese of Detroit and Titular Bishop of Uzali Nov. 23, 1993; ord. Jan. 6, 1994; appt. Bishop of Winona Nov. 5, 1998; installed Jan. 6, 1999; retired May 7, 2009.

Vicar General—Very Rev. RICHARD M. COLLETTI, Mailing Address: 55 W. Sanborn St., P.O. Box 588, Winona, 55987. Tel: 507-858-1267; Fax: 507-454-8106. Email: rcolletti@dow.org.

Moderator of the Curia—Very Rev. THOMAS E. COOK.

Chancellor—Very Rev. RICHARD M. COLLETTI, Mailing Address: 55 W. Sanborn St., P.O. Box 588, Winona, 55987. Tel: 507-858-1267; Fax: 507-454-8106.

Vicar for Clergy—Very Rev. THOMAS P. MELVIN, S.T.L., Mailing Address: 55 W. Sanborn St., P.O. Box 588, Winona, 55987. Tel: 507-454-4643; Fax: 507-454-8106.

Vice Chancellor—Mr. WILLIAM L. DANIEL, J.C.L., Mailing Address: 55 W. Sanborn St., P.O. Box 588, Winona, 55987. Tel: 507-858-1260; Fax: 507-454-8106.

Deans—Very Revs. THOMAS J. HARGESHEIMER, Winona; KEVIN CONNOLLY, Rochester; STEVEN J. PETERSON, Austin-Albert Lea; MARTIN T. SCHAEFER, Mankato; RUSSELL G. SCEPANIAK, Worthington.

Diocesan Consultors—Very Rev. RICHARD M. COLLETTI; Rev. Msgr. DONALD P. SCHMITZ, M.Ch.A.; Revs. MARK C. MCNEA; ROBERT G. MEYER (Retired); THOMAS J. JENNINGS; Very Revs. THOMAS J. HARGESHEIMER; KEVIN CONNOLLY.

Finance Council—Most Rev. JOHN M. QUINN, M.Div.; Very Rev. RICHARD M. COLLETTI; Rev. THOMAS A. LOOMIS; Mr. LAWRENCE J. DOSE, Dir. & Exec. Sec.; Sr. JEAN KENIRY, O.S.F.; Mr. JAMES ANDERSON, CPA; Ms. MARGARET V. MICHALETZ; Mr. ROBERT WOODEN.

Diocesan Board of Administration— (Civil Corporation): Most Rev. JOHN M. QUINN, M.Div., Pres.; Very Rev. RICHARD M. COLLETTI, Chancellor & Sec.; Mr. JAMES ANDERSON, CPA; Ms. MARGARET V. MICHALETZ.

Deposit and Loan Board—Most Rev. JOHN M. QUINN, M.Div.; Very Rev. RICHARD M. COLLETTI; Mr. LAWRENCE J. DOSE, Treas.; Rev. JOSEPH P. PETE; Ms. CAROL ORLOWSKE, Sec.; Mr. MICHAEL KIEFFER; Mr. JAMES E. BRUNNER; Mrs. MICHELLE FOLK.

Tribunal— (First and Second Instance); Please direct all inquiries concerning marriage nullity, dispensations and permissions, and pre-marriage documentation to this office: *Tribunal: 55 W. Sanborn St., P.O. Box 588, Winona, 55987-0588.* Tel: 507-454-4643; Fax: 507-454-8106.

Judicial Officers—Very Rev. R. PAUL HEITING, J.C.L., Judicial Vicar; Mr. WILLIAM L. DANIEL, J.C.L., Dir.

Censors of Books and Periodicals—Revs. WILLIAM M. BECKER, S.T.D.; JOHN M. SAUER, S.T.L.; TIMOTHY T. REKER, S.T.L.; Very Rev. ANDREW J. BEERMAN, S.T.L.; Rev. ROBERT S. HORIHAN, S.T.D. (Cand.).

Associate Judges—Revs. WILLIAM J. KULAS, J.C.L.; DAVID WECHTER, O.C.S.O., J.C.L.; Mr. WILLIAM L. DANIEL, J.C.L.

Defenders of the Bond—Sr. VICTORIA VONDENBERGER, R.S.M., J.C.L.; Mr. TIMOTHY FERGUSON, J.C.L.; Revs. JOHN GRIFFITHS, J.C.D.; THOMAS M. NIEHAUS, J.C.L. Experts: Dr. JOHN JOHNSON; Deacon DAVID PLEVAK.

Advocates—Rev. GERALD C. KOSSE; Mr. TIMOTHY FERGUSON, J.C.L.; Mr. THOMAS SZYSZIEWICZ; Sisters RITA MARIE SCHNEIDER, S.S.N.D.; MARILYN GEIGER, O.S.F.

Second Instance Court— Archdiocesan Tribunal of St. Paul/Minneapolis

Promoter of Justice—Mr. TIMOTHY FERGUSON, J.C.L.

Ecclesiastical Notaries—Mrs. KATHY BORCK; Mrs. JULIE WRIGHT.

Diocesan Offices and Directors

All Diocesan Offices and Directors are located at the Pastoral Center (unless otherwise indicated), 55 W. Sanborn St., P.O. Box 588, Winona, 55987. Tel: 507-454-4643; Fax: 507-454-8106. Web: www.dow.org.

Curia—

Vicar General—Very Rev. RICHARD M. COLLETTI. Email: rcolletti@dow.org.

Chancellor—Very Rev. RICHARD M. COLLETTI. Email: rcolletti@dow.org.

Vicar for Clergy—Very Rev. THOMAS P. MELVIN, S.T.L. Email: tmelvin@dow.org.

Vice Chancellor—Mr. WILLIAM L. DANIEL, J.C.L. Email: wldaniel@dow.org.

Finances—Mr. LAWRENCE J. DOSE, Dir. Email: ldose@dow.org.

Catholic Charities—Mr. ROBERT TEREBA, Exec. Dir., 111 Market St., P.O. Box 379, Winona, 55987. Tel: 507-454-2270; Fax: 507-457-3027. Email: rtereba@ccwinona.org.

Mission Advancement— Communications "The Courier" - Stewardship & Development. Mr. JOEL HENNESSY, Dir. Email: jhennessy@dow.org.

Divine Worship—Rev. JOHN M. SAUER, S.T.L., Dir. Email: jsauer@dow.org.

Human Resources—Mr. GARY MARTINI, Dir. Email: gmartini@dow.org.

Apostolate—Mr. TODD GRAFF, Dir. Lay Formation. Email: tgraff@dow.org; Mr. EDUARDO FORTINI, Dir. Hispanic Min. Email: efortini@dow.org.

Catholic Education— Schools. Mrs. MARSHA STENZEL. Email: mstenzel@dow.org.

Vocations—Very Rev. THOMAS P. MELVIN, S.T.L., Dir., Immaculate Heart of Mary Seminary #43, 700 Terrace Heights, Winona, 55987-1399. Tel: 507-457-7380; 507-454-4643 (DOW); Cell: 507-259-1747. Email: tmelvin@dow.org.

Life— Family; Marriage; Natural Family Planning; Safe & Sacred. Mr. PETER MARTIN, Dir. Email: pmartin@dow.org.

Youth and Young Adults—Mr. BEN FROST. Email: bfrost@dow.org.

Vicar for Clergy—Very Rev. THOMAS P. MELVIN, S.T.L., Dir. Tel: 507-454-4643; 507-457-7380 (Seminary); Cell: 507-259-1747; Fax: 507-454-8106. Email: tmelvin@dow.org.

Additional Ministries—

Annual Diocesan Appeal—Mr. JOEL HENNESSY, Dir. Email: jhennessy@dow.org.

Permanent Deacons—Very Rev. RICHARD M. COLLETTI, Interim Dir. Email: rcolletti@dow.org.

Vicar for Senior Priests—Rev. Msgr. DONALD P. SCHMITZ, M.Ch.A., Church of Nativity of the Blessed Virgin Mary, 640 First Ave., S.W., Harmony, 55939. Tel: 507-886-2393; Fax: 507-886-2394. Email: fdpsch@harmonytel.net.

Ecumenism—Mr. TODD GRAFF. Email: tgraff@dow.org.

Propagation of the Faith—Rev. CHARLIE I. COLLINS, 55 W. Sanborn St., P.O. Box 588, Winona, 55987. Tel: 507-454-4643; Fax: 507-454-8106. Email: jherdina@dow.org.

Coordinator of Diocesan Health Ministry—Rev. JAMES F. BURYSKA, Diocesan Dir. of Hospitals, Rochester Methodist Hospital Chaplain Services, 201 W. Center St., Rochester, 55902. Tel: 507-255-5551; Fax: 507-255-3125. Email: buryska.james@mayo.edu.

Advisory Bodies—

Presbyteral Council—

Ex Officio—Very Rev. RICHARD M. COLLETTI.

Elected Senior Member—Rev. CHARLES J. QUINN (Retired).

Appointed Members—Revs. MATTHEW J. FASNACHT; GLENN K. FRERICHS; MARREDDY POTHIREDDY; Very Rev. MARTIN T. SCHAEFER.

Elected At-Large Representatives—Rev. PETER L. SCHUSTER; Very Rev. KEVIN CONNOLLY.

Elected Deanery Representatives—Rev. THOMAS J. JENNINGS; Very Rev. THOMAS P. MELVIN, S.T.L.; Revs. JOHN M. SAUER, S.T.L.; DONALD J. SCHMITZ; JOSEPH P. PETE.

Priest Assignments Committee—Very Rev. RICHARD M. COLLETTI; Revs. JOSEPH B. FOGAL; PAUL W. SURPRENANT; THOMAS A. LOOMIS; Very Revs. KEVIN CONNOLLY; THOMAS P. MELVIN, S.T.L.; Rev. PETER J. KLEIN.

Priests' Pension Board—Most Rev. JOHN M. QUINN, M.Div.; Very Rev. RICHARD M. COLLETTI; Mr. LAWRENCE J. DOSE, Treas.; Rev. WILLIAM J. KULAS, J.C.L.; Very Rev. STEVEN J. PETERSON; Rev. PAUL E. NELSON; Mr THOMAS CROWLEY; Mr. DANIEL KUTZKE; Mr. ROBERT HOODECHECK.

Commission on Sacred Liturgy—Rev. TIMOTHY T. REKER, S.T.L.; Sr. LORRAINE LOECHER, O.S.F.; Ms. JACI JAMES; Ms. JOANN FAGAN; Mr. DAVID U'REN; Deacon MICHAEL ELLIS.

Diocese of Winona Incardination Board—Very Revs. THOMAS P. MELVIN, S.T.L., Chm.; RICHARD M. COLLETTI; Rev. Msgr. DONALD W. GRUBISCH (Retired); Rev. JOHN M. SAUER, S.T.L.

Winona Diocesan Organizations-Agencies-Programs

Archives—Very Rev. RICHARD M. COLLETTI. Tel: 507-858-1267; Fax: 507-454-8106.

Scouting—Mr. BEN FROST. Tel: 507-585-1258; Fax: 507-454-8106. Email: bfrost@dow.org.

Chaplain—Rev. WILLIAM THOMPSON, St. John Baptist De La Salle, 20 2nd St., N.E., Dodge Center, 55927-0310. Tel: 507-374-6830.

Catholic Charities—Mr. ROBERT TEREBA, Exec. Dir., Administrative and Winona Regional Office, 111 Market St., P.O. Box 379, Winona, 55987. Tel: 507-454-2270; Fax: 507-457-3027. Email: rtereba@ccwinona.org. Web: www.ccwinona.org.

Catholic Charities Board—Deacon CHRISTOPHER WALCHUK. Email: cwalchuk@hickorytech.net. Web: www.ccwinona.org.

Regional Offices—Mankato: 816 Hubbell Ave., Mankato, 56001. Tel: 507-387-5586; Fax: 507-387-5587. *Rochester: 903 W. Center St., Ste. 220, Rochester, 55902.* Tel: 507-287-2047; Fax: 507-287-2050. *Worthington: 1234 Oxford St., Worthington, 56187.* Tel: 507-376-9757; Fax: 507-376-9758.

Field Offices—Albert Lea: 308 E. Fountain, Albert Lea, 56007. Tel: 507-377-3664. *Austin: 405 4th St., N.W., Austin, 55912.* Tel: 507-433-3062. *Owatonna: 577 State Ave., Owatonna, 55060.* Tel: 507-455-2008.

Parish and Community Social Action Office—Mr. ROBERT TEREBA, Dir., 111 Market St., P.O. Box 379, Winona, 55987. Tel: 507-454-2270; Fax: 507-457-3027 Coordination of: Parish Social Ministry, Rural Life Ministry, Catholic Campaign for Human Development, Catholic Relief Services, HIV-AIDS Ministry, Disaster Relief Services.

Refugee Resettlement—Ms. MARY ALESSIO, Dir., 903 W. Center St., Ste. 220, Rochester, 55902. Tel: 507-287-2047; Fax: 507-287-2050. Email: malessio@ccwinona.org.

Clinical Counseling and Pregnancy, Parenting and Adoption—Mrs. VALERIE CUNNINGHAM, Dir., 903 W. Center St., Ste. 220, Rochester, 55902. Tel: 507-287-2047; Fax: 570-287-2050. Email: valerie@ccwinona.org.

Senior Services—Mrs. JENNIFER HALBERG, Dir., 111 Market St., P.O. Box 379, Winona, 55987. Tel: 507-454-2270; Fax: 507-457-3027. Email: jhalberg@ccwinona.org.

Court Appointed Services—MICHELLE ST. AMOUR-SMITH, Dir., 111 Market St., P.O. Box 379, Winona, 55987. Tel: 507-454-2270; Fax: 507-457-3027. Email: msmith@ccwinona.org.

Cemeteries—Mr. LAWRENCE J. DOSE, Pastoral Center, 55 W. Sanborn St., P.O. Box 588, Winona, 55987. Tel: 507-858-1248; Fax: 507-454-8106. Email: ldose@dow.org.

Council of Catholic Women—Ms. BEV McCARVEL, Pres., 39574 160th St., Brewster, 56119. Tel: 507-842-5460. Email: bmccarvel@roundlk.net; Very Rev. THOMAS J. HARGESHEIMER, Diocesan Moderator, St. Stanislaus Kostka Church, 625 E. 4th St., Winona, 55987. Tel: 507-452-5430.

Diocesan Self-Insurance Plan—Mr. RYAN CHRISTIANSON, Catholic Mutual Group, 111 Riverfront, Ste. 405, Winona, 55987. Tel: 507-454-6452; 800-494-6452; Fax: 800-335-8141; 507-454-8141. Email: rchristensen@catholicmutual.org.

Diocese of Winona Foundation—Mr. JOEL HENNESSY, Dir. Tel: 507-858-1249; Fax: 507-454-8106. Email: jhennessy@dow.org. Web: www.dow.org.

Hospitals—Rev. JAMES F. BURYSKA, Rochester Methodist Hospital, 201 W. Center St., Rochester, 55902. Tel: 507-255-5551; Fax: 507-255-3125.

Catholic Medical Association—Dr. JOHN I. LANE, M.D., 200 First St., S.W., Rochester, 55905. Tel: 507-266-3412; Fax: 507-266-1657. Email: lane.john@mayo.edu.

Marriage Preparation/Enrichment—Mr. PETER MARTIN, Dir., 55 W. Sanborn St., P.O. Box 588, Winona, 55987. Tel: 507-858-1264; Fax: 507-454-8106. Email: pmartin@dow.org.

Pathways TEC (Teens Encounter Christ)—Rev. TIMOTHY E. BIREN, Spiritual Dir., 1331 Warren St., Mankato, 56001. Tel: 507-387-4154; Fax: 507-385-0679. Email: timothy.biren@mnsu.edu.

Misconduct Issues—Very Revs. RICHARD M. COLLETTI, Mailing Address: 55 W. Sanborn St., P.O. Box 588, Winona, 55987. Tel: 507-858-1267; Fax: 507-454-8106. Email: rcolletti@dow.org; R. PAUL HEITING, J.C.L., Mailing Address: 55 W. Sanborn St., P.O. Box 588, Winona, 55987. Tel: 507-858-1261; Fax: 507-454-8106. Email: pheiting@dow.org; Mr. ROBERT TEREBA, Catholic Charities, 111 Market St., P.O. Box 379, Winona, 55987. Tel: 507-454-2270; Fax: 507-457-3027. Email: rtereba@ccwinona.org.

Diocesan Review Board—Very Rev. R. PAUL HEITING, J.C.L.; Ms. NELLE MORIARTY, Chair; Mr. JEFF HENRICH; Ms. JEAN O'MALLEY-LAURSEN; Ms. BETSY SINGER; Mr. KENNETH REED; Mr. BRIAN ROTTY; Mr. ROBERT TEREBA; Very Rev. RICHARD M. COLLETTI.

Retrouvaille—Rev. THEODORE J. HOTTINGER, S.J., 423 W. 7th St., Mankato, 56001. Tel: 507-317-8194.

Victim Assistance Coordinator—Very Rev. RICHARD M. COLLETTI, Interim Coord., Mailing Address: 55 W. Sanborn St., P.O. Box 588, Winona, 55987. Tel: 507-858-1267, Ext. 223. Email: rcolletti@dow.org.

CLERGY, PARISHES, MISSIONS AND PAROCHIAL SCHOOLS

CITY OF WINONA

(WINONA COUNTY)

1—CATHEDRAL OF THE SACRED HEART (1950) [JC] Very Rev. Richard M. Colletti, Rector; Rev. Michael J. Cronin; Deacon James Welch.
Res.: 360 Main St., 55987-3299. Tel: 507-452-4770; Fax: 507-454-1974. Email: info@cathedralwinona.org. Web: www.cathedralwinona.org.
School— See listings under Centralized Catholic Schools.
Catechesis/Religious Program—James Ballard, Liturgy Dir.

2—ST. CASIMIR'S (1906) [JC] Attended by Cathedral of the Sacred Heart, 360 Main St., Winona. Very Rev. Richard M. Colletti; Rev. Michael J. Cronin; Deacon James Welch.
Church: 624 W. Broadway, 55987-2721. Tel: 507-452-4770; Fax: 507-454-1974. Email: info@cathedralwinona.org.
Catechesis/Religious Program—Students 52.

3—ST. JOHN NEPOMUCENE (1888) Attended by St. Stanislaus, Winona. Very Rev. Thomas J. Hargesheimer; Deacon Justin Green.
625 E. Fourth St., 55987-4297. Tel: 507-452-5430; Fax: 507-452-3355. Email: ststans@hbci.com. Web: ststans-stjohn-winonamn.4lpi.com.
Catechesis/Religious Program—626 E. Fifth St., 55987. Students 107.

4—ST. MARY'S (1911) [JC] Rev. James C. Berning.
Res.: 1303 W. Broadway, 55987-2395. Tel: 507-452-5656; Fax: 507-452-5477. Email: stmarys@wacs1.org. Web: www.stmaryswinona.org.
See St. Mary's Primary School, Winona under Centralized Catholic Schools located in the Institution section.
Catechesis/Religious Program—Tel: 507-452-5656; Fax: 507-452-5477. Students 85.

5—ST. STANISLAUS (1871) Very Rev. Thomas J. Hargesheimer; Deacon Justin Green.
Res.: 625 E. Fourth St., 55987-4297. Tel: 507-452-5430; Fax: 507-452-3355. Email: ststans@hbci.com. Web: ststans-stjohn-winonamn.4lpi.com.
See St. Stanislaus Middle School, Winona under Centralized Catholic Schools located in the Institution section.
Catechesis/Religious Program—626 E. Fifth St., 55987. Students 107.

OUTSIDE THE CITY OF WINONA

ADAMS, MOWER CO., SACRED HEART (1886) [CEM] Rev. Thomas A. Loomis.
Res.: 412 Main St., P.O. Box 352, 55909-9998. Tel: 507-582-3321; Fax: 507-582-1033. Email: frtomloomis@yahoo.com.
School—Tel: 507-582-3120. Darlene Boe, Prin. Lay Teachers 8; Students 83.
Catechesis/Religious Program—Tel: 507-582-3321. Students 59.

ADRIAN, NOBLES CO., ST. ADRIAN (1877) [CEM] Rev. Timothy J. Hall.
Res.: 512 Maine Ave., P.O. Box 475, 56110-0475. Tel: 507-483-2317; Fax: 507-483-2460. Email: stadrian@frontiernet.net. Web: www.frontiernet.net/~stadrian.
Catechesis/Religious Program—108 E. Sixth St., 56110. Tel: 507-483-2480; Fax: 507-483-2480. Email: stafaith@frontiernet.net. Students 118.

ALBERT LEA, FREEBORN CO., ST. THEODORE (1882) [CEM] Rev. Timothy T. Reker; Deacon Michael Ellis.
Mailing Address: 308 E. Fountain St., 56007-2456. Tel: 507-373-0603; Fax: 507-373-0604. Web: www.sttheo.org.
Res.: 311 E. Clark St., 56007-2456. Tel: 507-373-9661.
Parish Center & School—323 E. Clark St., 56007. Tel: 507-373-9657; Fax: 507-373-9657. See listings under Centralized Catholic Schools.
Catechesis/Religious Program—Tel: 507-373-2987; Fax: 507-373-9657. Students 240.

ALTURA, WINONA CO., ST. ANTHONY'S (1919) [JC] Attended by St. Rose of Lima. Rev. Marreddy Pothireddy.
180 S. Fremont, Lewiston, 55952-0727. Tel: 507-796-6271; 507-523-2428 (Rectory). Email: dowstrose@embarqmail.com. Web: www.st-rose.org.
Catechesis/Religious Program—Included with St. Rose of Lima, Lewiston, MN and Immaculate Conception, Wilson, MN. Students 227.

AUSTIN, MOWER CO.
1—ST. AUGUSTINE'S (1857) [JC] Very Rev. James P. Steffes; Deacons John Kluczny; Richard Aho.
Mailing Address: 2000 Oakland Ave. W., 55912-1599. Tel: 507-433-1841; Fax: 507-433-9680.
Church: 405 Fourth St. N.W., 55912-3091. Tel: 507-437-4537; Fax: 507-437-4537.
See Austin Catholic Elementary School, under Centralized Catholic Schools located in the Institution section.
Catechesis/Religious Program—Tel: 507-437-3250. Austin Tri-Parish Students 300.
2—ST. EDWARD'S (1960) [JC] Very Rev. James P. Steffes; Deacons John Kluczny; Richard Aho; Sr. Lorraine Loecher, Pastoral Assoc. In Res., Rev. Richard P. Loomis (Retired).
Res.: 2000 Oakland Ave. W., 55912-1599. Tel: 507-433-1841; Fax: 507-433-9680.
See Austin Catholic Elementary School, under Centralized Catholic Schools located in the Institution section.
Catechesis/Religious Program—Tel: 507-437-3250. Austin Tri-Parish Students 330.
3—QUEEN OF ANGELS (1936) [JC] Very Rev. Dale E. Tupper; Rev. Gregory Parrott, Parochial Vicar; Deacon David Blake.
Res.: 1001 Oakland Ave. E., 55912-3896. Tel: 507-433-1888; Fax: 507-433-1889. Email: qofaparish@chartermi.net. Web: www.austincatholic.org.
See Austin Catholic Elementary School, under Centralized Catholic Schools located in the Institution section.
Catechesis/Religious Program—311 4th St., N.W., 55912. Tel: 507-437-3250. Austin Tri-Parish Students 71.
Catechesis/Religious Program—Spanish Catechesis, Tel: 507-433-8474. Total Enrollment 80.
Queens of Angels Hermitage—1009 E. Oakland Ave., 55912. Tel: 507-437-4015. Rev. Jon H. Moore.

BLOOMING PRAIRIE, STEELE CO., ST. COLUMBANUS (1878) [CEM] Rev. William J. Kulas.
Res.: 114 E. Main St., 55917-1427. Tel: 507-583-2529; 507-583-2784; Fax: 507-583-7738.
Catechesis/Religious Program—Tel: 507-583-2784; Fax: 507-583-7738. Students 74.

BLUE EARTH, FARIBAULT CO., SS. PETER AND PAUL'S (1866) [CEM] Rev. Leo Charles Koppala, Parochial Admin.
Res.: 214 S. Holland, 56013-1331. Tel: 507-526-5626.
Catechesis/Religious Program—Tel: 507-526-2816. Students 122.

BREWSTER, NOBLES CO., SACRED HEART (1901) [CEM] Attended by St. Francis Xaiver, 548 17th St., P.O. Box 39. Windom. Very Rev. Russell G. Scepaniak.
Catechesis/Religious Program—Tel: 507-842-5584. Loretta Smith, Dir. Faith Formation. Students 27.

BROWNSDALE, MOWER CO., OUR LADY OF LORETTO (1946) Attended by Queen of Angels, Austin. Very Rev. Dale E. Tupper; Rev. Gregory Parrott; Deacon David Blake.
1001 Oakland Ave. E., Austin, 55912-1599. Tel: 507-433-1888; Fax: 507-433-1889. Email: qopapastor@chartermi.net.
Catechesis/Religious Program—Tel: 507-567-2456. Students 11.

BROWNSVILLE, HOUSTON CO., ST. PATRICK'S (1871) [CEM] [JC 2] Attended by St. Mary, Caledonia. Rev. Gregory P. Leif.
Mailing Address: P.O. Box 406, Caledonia, 55921-0406. Tel: 507-725-3804. Email: stpatricks@acegroup.cc.
Church: 604 Adams, 55919. Tel: 507-482-6818; Fax: 507-482-6818.
Catechesis/Religious Program—P.O. Box 155, 55919. Students 17.

BYRON, OLMSTED CO., CHRIST THE KING (1965) Rev. Paul W. Surprenant.
Res.: 202 Fourth St., N.W., P.O. Box 1000, 55920-1000. Tel: 507-775-6455; Fax: 507-775-6473. Email: ckhf@churchofchristtheking.net.
Catechesis/Religious Program—Tel: 507-775-0501. Students 185.

CALEDONIA, HOUSTON CO., ST. MARY (1975) [CEM] Rev. Gregory P. Leif.
Mailing Address: P.O. Box 406, 55921-0406. Email: stmary1@acegroup.cc. Web: www.churchofstmary.net.
Office: 453 S. Pine St., 55921. Tel: 507-725-3804.
Res.: 513 S. Pine St., 55921-0406. Tel: 507-725-4408.
School—(Grades PreK-8) Tel: 507-725-3355. Mr. Thomas Reichenbacher, Prin. Priests 1; Lay Teachers 14; Students 160.

CANTON, FILLMORE CO., THE ASSUMPTION (1891) [CEM] [JC] Attended by Nativity of B.V.M. Rev. Msgr. Donald P. Schmitz.
640 First Ave., S.W., Harmony, 55939-0596. Tel: 507-886-2393; Fax: 507-886-2394.
Catechesis/Religious Program—Tri-parish Combined Rel Ed Program with Nativitiy, Harmony; & St. Olaf. Mabel Students Attend at Assumption, Canton.Email: nativity@harmonytel.net. Total Enrollment 26.

CHATFIELD, FILLMORE CO., ST. MARY'S (1866) [CEM 2] Rev. Patrick O. Arens.
405 Twiford St., S.W., 55923. Tel: 507-867-3148; Fax: 507-867-0073.
Catechesis/Religious Program—Tel: 507-867-3922. Students 122.

CLAREMONT, DODGE CO., ST. FRANCIS DE SALES (1869) [CEM] [JC] Attended by St. John Baptist de La Salle, Dodge Center. Rev. William Thompson.
20 Second St., N.E., P.O. Box 310, Dodge Center, 55927-0310. Tel: 507-374-6830. Email: tritonparishes@frontiernet.net.
Catechesis/Religious Program—P.O. Box 117, West Concord, 55985. Tel: 507-527-2384. Students 30.

CURRIE, MURRAY CO., IMMACULATE HEART OF MARY (1883) Attended by St. Gabriel, Fulda. Rev. Jeffrey L. Dobbs.
Mailing Address: 307 W. Lake Ave., Fulda, 56131. Fax: 507-763-3545.
Church: 510 Mill St., 56123.
Catechesis/Religious Program—Students 66.

DAKOTA, WINONA CO., HOLY CROSS (1890) Attended by Crucifixion Church, LaCrescent. Rev. Gregory G. Havel; Deacons Gerald Trocinski; Robert Yerhot.
Res. & Mailing Address: 423 S. 2nd St., La Crescent, 55947-1326. Tel: 507-895-4720; Fax: 507-895-6880. Email: cruxch@acegroup.cc.
Church: 820 River St., 55925.
Catechesis/Religious Program—Tel: 507-895-4120. Attend Crucifixion Faith Formation. Students 11.

DEERFIELD, STEELE CO., CORPUS CHRISTI (1869) Attended by Christ the King, Medford. Rev. Robert D. Herman (Retired); Ms. Amy Hellevik, Parish Dir.
205 N.W. Second Ave., P.O. Box 120, Medford, 55049-0120. Tel: 507-451-6353; Fax: 507-451-6353. Email: christthekingcc@q.com.
Catechesis/Religious Program—Tel: 507-451-8898. Students 20.

DELAVAN, FARIBAULT CO., MATER DOLOROSA (1889) Closed. For inquiries for parish records contact the chancery.

DODGE CENTER, DODGE CO., ST. JOHN BAPTIST DE LA SALLE (1945) Rev. William Thompson.
Res.: 20 Second St., N.E., P.O. Box 310, 55927-0310. Tel: 507-374-6830; Fax: 612-605-4315. Email: revwthompson@kmtel.com.
Catechesis/Religious Program—Tel: 507-633-6765; 507-527-2384; Fax: 612-605-4315. Students 80.

DUNDEE, NOBLES CO., ST. MARY, Closed. For inquiries for parish records contact the chancery.

EAST CHAIN, MARTIN CO., HOLY FAMILY (1897) [CEM] [JC] Attended by St. John Vianney, Fairmont. Rev. Peter L. Schuster; Deacon Edwin C. Bonnarens.
Res.: 901 S. Prairie Ave., Fairmont, 56031-3098. Tel: 507-235-5535; Fax: 507-235-5536. Email: sjv-church@midconetwork.com.
Catechesis/Religious Program—Tel: 507-773-4491. Students 21.

EASTON, FARIBAULT CO., OUR LADY OF MOUNT CARMEL (1866) [CEM] Attended by S. Casimir, Wells. Rev. Thomas M. Niehaus; Deacon Eugene Paul.
Res.: 320 2nd Ave., S.W., Wells, 56097-1399. Tel: 507-553-5391. Email: olmc@bevcomm.net.
Church: 27 Main St., 56025. Tel: 507-787-2303; Fax: 507-787-2221.
Catechesis/Religious Program—Students 41.

ELBA, WINONA CO., ST. ALOYSIUS (1877) [CEM] Attended by St. Charles Borromeo, St. Charles. Rev. Kurt P. Farrell; Deacon Placido Zavala.
1900 E. 6th St., St. Charles, 55972-1426. Tel: 507-932-3294; Fax: 507-932-3393. Email: borromeo@hbcsc.net.
Catechesis/Religious Program— Attending St. Charles Borromeo program, Tel: 507-932-3303. Students 5.

ELLENDALE, FREEBORN CO., ST. AIDAN (1857) [CEM] Attended by All Saints, New Richland. Rev. Swaminatha R. Pothireddy.
Mailing Address: 307 SW First St., P.O. Box 185, New Richland, 56072-0185. Tel: 507-465-8217. Email: newrichlandbulletin@yahoo.com.
Catechesis/Religious Program—Tel: 507-684-2245. Students 18.

ELLSWORTH, NOBLES CO., ST. MARY'S (1885) [CEM] Attended by St. Catherine, Luverne. Rev. Thomas J. Jennings.
203 E. Brown St., Luverne, 56156-1599. Tel: 507-283-8502. Email: stcatherine@iw.net. Web: www.stmaryellsworth.org.
Catechesis/Religious Program—Tel: 507-283-8071; Fax: 507-449-3638. Email: kbaustian@iw.net. Students 20.

EYOTA, OLMSTED CO., HOLY REDEEMER (1891) Attended by St. Charles Borromeo, St. Charles. Rev. Kurt P. Farrell; Deacon Placido Zavala.
Mailing Address: 1900 E. 6th St., St. Charles, 55972-1426. Tel: 507-932-3294; Fax: 507-932-3393.
Catechesis/Religious Program—Tel: 507-545-2161; Fax: 507-545-2161. Students 95.

FAIRMONT, MARTIN CO., ST. JOHN VIANNEY (1952) [CEM] Rev. Peter L. Schuster; Deacon Edwin C. Bonnarens.
Parish Office—901 S. Prairie Ave., 56031-3023. Tel: 507-235-5535; Fax: 507-235-5536. Email: sjv-church@midconetwork.com.
School—(Grades PreK-6), 911 S. Prairie Ave., 56031. Tel: 507-235-5304; Fax: 507-235-9099. Email: jschaffer@sjvschool.net. Joan Schaffer, Prin. Priests 1; Lay Teachers 10; Students 100.
Catechesis/Religious Program—Tel: 507-235-5639; Fax: 507-235-5536. Email: sjr-tamarac@midconetwork.com. Students 185.

FOUNTAIN, FILLMORE CO., ST. LAWRENCE O'TOOLE (1872) Closed. For inquiries for parish records contact the chancery.

FULDA, MURRAY CO., ST. GABRIEL'S (1882) [CEM] Rev. Jeffrey L. Dobbs.
Church: 309 W. Lake Ave., 56131-9402. Tel: 507-425-2595; 507-425-2369 (Office); Fax: 507-425-2227. Email: stgab2369@centurytel.net (Office).
Catechesis/Religious Program—Tel: 507-425-2369. Students 91.

GENEVA, FREEBORN CO., ST. MARY (1867) [CEM] Attended by All Saints, New Richland. Rev. Swaminatha R. Pothireddy.
307 1st St., S.W., P.O. Box 185, New Richland, 56072-0185. Tel: 507-465-8217; Fax: 507-465-8381.
Catechesis/Religious Program—Tel: 507-583-7530. Students 17.

GOOD THUNDER, BLUE EARTH CO., ST. JOSEPH (1879) [CEM] Attended by St. Teresa, Mapleton. Rev. Brian F. Sutton, Parochial Admin.
Mailing Address: 104 Silver St., W., Mapleton, 56065. Tel: 507-524-3127; Fax: 507-524-4423.
Catechesis/Religious Program—Tel: 507-278-3444. Students 37.

GRAND MEADOW, MOWER CO., ST. FINBARR'S (1878) [CEM] Attended by St. Ignatius, Spring Valley. Very Rev. Steven J. Peterson.
Mailing Address: 213 W. Franklin St., Spring Valley, 55975-1312. Tel: 507-346-7565.
Church: 504 1st St., S.W., P.O. Box 326, 55936. Tel: 507-754-5190.
Catechesis/Religious Program—Students 83.

GUCKEEN, FARIBAULT CO., OUR LADY OF MERCY (1902) Closed. For inquiries for parish records contact the chancery.

HAMMOND, WABASHA CO., ST. CLEMENT'S, Closed. For inquiries for parish records contact SS. Peter and Paul, Mazeppa.

HARMONY, FILLMORE CO., THE NATIVITY OF THE BLESSED VIRGIN (1906) Rev. Msgr. Donald P. Schmitz.
Res.: 640 First Ave., S.W., 55939-0596. Tel: 507-886-2393; Fax: 507-886-2394.
Catechesis/Religious Program— Tri- parish combined Rel Ed Program with Assumption, Canton and St. Olaf, Mabel. Students attend at Assumption, Canton. Students 26.

HAYFIELD, DODGE CO., SACRED HEART (1935) Attended by St. Columbanus, Blooming Prairie. Rev. William J. Kulas.
114 E. Main St., Blooming Prairie, 55917-1427. Tel: 507-583-2529; Fax: 507-583-7738. Email: stcolumbanus@frontiernet.net.
Church: 150 2nd St., N.E., 55940. Tel: 507-477-2256 Sacred Heart Office; Fax: 507-477-2938 (sacred Heart Office).
Catechesis/Religious Program—Students 86.

HERON LAKE, JACKSON CO., SACRED HEART (1884) [CEM] Attended by St. Francis Xavier, 548 17th St., P.O. Box 39, Windom. Very Rev. Russell G. Scepaniak.
321 9th St., P.O. Box 377, 56137. Tel: 507-793-2357; Fax: 507-793-2357. Email: ssacred@centurytel.net.
Catechesis/Religious Program—Tel: 507-793-2773. Students 93.

HOKAH, HOUSTON CO., ST. PETER'S (1876) [CEM] [JC 2] Attended by St. Joseph, Rushford. Rev. Joseph P. Pete.
101 Rushford Ave. W., P.O. Box 577, Rushford, 55971-0577. Tel: 507-864-2257; Fax: 507-864-3716. Email: paradm@acegroup.cc.
Church: 34 Main St., P.O. Box 355, 55941-0355. Tel: 507-894-4242; Fax: 507-894-4375.
School—(Grades PreK-8) Tel: 507-894-4375; 507-894-4944. Email: stpeter@acegroup.ccc. Mrs. Rachel Fishel, Prin. Students 60.
Catechesis/Religious Program—Students 15.

HOUSTON, HOUSTON CO., ST. MARY'S (1873) [CEM] Attended by St. Joseph, Rushford. Rev. Joseph P. Pete.
101 Rushford Ave. W., P.O. Box 577, Rushford, 55971-0557. Tel: 507-864-2257. Email: paradm@acegroup.cc. Web: www.sjsmsp.org.
Catechesis/Religious Program—Students 45.

IONA, MURRAY CO., ST. COLUMBA'S (1891) [CEM] Attended by St. Ann, Slayton. Rev. James J. Seitz.
2747 29th St., Slayton, 56172-1485. Tel: 507-836-8030; Fax: 507-836-6261.
Catechesis/Religious Program—Email: triparish@frontiernet.net. Students 18.

JACKSON, JACKSON CO., GOOD SHEPHERD (1891) [CEM] Rev. James Von Tobel, S.J.
Res.: 311 N. Sverdrup Ave., P.O. Box 65, 56143-1329. Tel: 507-847-2504; Fax: 507-847-3734. Email: goodshep@msn.com.
Catechesis/Religious Program—Tel: 507-847-2719. Susanne Foster, D.R.E. Students 120.

JANESVILLE, WASECA CO., ST. ANN'S (1876) [CEM] Rev. Peter J. Klein.
307 W. Second St., P.O. Box 218, 56048-0218. Tel: 507-234-6244; Fax: 507-234-6237. Email: stannjan@hickorytech.net.
Catechesis/Religious Program—Tel: 507-234-5753. Students 159.

JASPER, PIPESTONE CO., ST. JOSEPH'S (1890) [CEM] Attended by St. Leo's, Pipestone. Rev. Gerald C. Kosse.
415 Hiawatha Ave. S., P.O. Box 36, Pipestone, 56164. Tel: 507-825-3152; Fax: 507-825-4492. Email: om@triparishmn.org.
Rectory—121 Smith St., N., Woodstock, 56186. Tel: 507-777-4160; Fax: 507-825-4492.
Church: 415 2nd St. E., 56144.
Catechesis/Religious Program—Students 27.

JEFFERS, COTTONWOOD CO., ST. AUGUSTINE'S (1912) Closed. For inquiries for parish records contact the chancery.

JOHNSBURG, MOWER CO., ST. JOHN'S (1859) [CEM] Attended by Sacred Heart, Adams. Rev. Thomas A. Loomis.
412 Main St., P.O. Box 352, Adams, 55909. Tel: 507-582-3321; Fax: 507-582-1033.
Catechesis/Religious Program—Students 31.

KASSON, DODGE CO., HOLY FAMILY (1976) [CEM] Attended by Christ the King, Byron. Rev. Paul W. Surprenant.
202 Fourth St., N.W., P.O. Box 1000, Byron, 55920-1000. Fax: 507-634-7200. Email: ckhf@churchofchristtheking.net; holyfamilyjen@kmtel.com.
Church: 1904 N. Mantorville Ave., P.O. Box 171, 55944. Tel: 507-634-7520.
Catechesis/Religious Program—Tel: 507-634-7599. Students 207.

KELLOGG, WABASHA CO.

1—ST. AGNES (1900) Attended by St. Felix, Wabasha. Very Rev. Thomas E. Cook; Deacon John Hust.
117 3rd St. W., Wabasha, 55981-1201. Tel: 651-565-3931; Fax: 651-565-4363. Email: stfelix@hbci.com.
Catechesis/Religious Program—Tel: 651-565-3718; Fax: 651-565-0244. Email: stfelixgrowthinfaith@yahoo.com. Students 12.

2—IMMACULATE CONCEPTION (1881) Attended by St. Joachim, Plainview. Rev. William M. Becker.
900 W. Broadway, Plainview, 55964-1039. Tel: 507-534-3321; Fax: 507-534-3687. Email: stjoachimchurch@hotmail.com. Web: immconception-church.org.
Catechesis/Religious Program—Tel: 507-534-3588. Students 86.

LA CRESCENT, HOUSTON CO., THE CHURCH OF THE CRUCIFIXION (1856) [CEM 2] Rev. Gregory G. Havel; Deacons Gerald Trocinski; Robert Yerhot.
407 S. Second St., 55947-1326.
Res. & Parish Office: 423 S. Second St., 55947-1326. Tel: 507-895-4720 (Office); 507-895-6867; 507-895-2207 (Res.); Fax: 507-895-6880. Email: cruxch@acegroup.cc.
School—(Grades PreK-6), 420 S. Second St., 55947. Tel: 507-895-4402; Fax: 507-895-4403. Mrs. Gail Trocinski, Prin. Lay Teachers 10; Students 108.
Catechesis/Religious Program—1380 Lancer Blvd., 55947. Tel: 507-895-2700. Students 200.

LAKE CITY, WABASHA CO., ST. MARY'S OF THE LAKE (1877) Rev. Richard J. Dernek; Deacon David Dose.
Res.: 419 Lyon Ave., 55041-1649. Tel: 651-345-4134; Fax: 651-345-6134.
Catechesis/Religious Program—Email: stmarysff@embarqmail.com. Students 250.

LAKE CRYSTAL, BLUE EARTH CO., HOLY FAMILY (1900) [CEM] Attended by St. Joseph the Worker, Mankato. Rev. John P. Wilmot; Deacon Preston Doyle.
Church: 201 N. Hunt St., 56055. Email: sjwhf@hickorytech.net. Web: www.sjwhf.org.
Res.: 423 W. 7th St., Mankato, 56001-2197. Tel: 507-388-3766; Fax: 507-388-2101.
School—Tel: 507-388-2997; Fax: 507-388-8081. Web: www.mankatoareacatholicschool.org.
Catechesis/Religious Program—Tel: 507-388-8018; Fax: 507-388-2101. Email: esnyder@hickorytech.net. Students 150.

LAKE WILSON, MURRAY CO., ST. MARY (1916) [JC] Attended by St. Ann, Slayton. Rev. James J. Seitz.
2747 29th St., Slayton, 56172-1485. Tel: 507-836-8030; Fax: 507-836-6261. Email: stabusiness@frontiernet.net.
Catechesis/Religious Program—Students 26.

LAKEFIELD, JACKSON CO., ST. JOSEPH (1897) [CEM] Attended by Good Shepherd, Jackson. Rev. James Von Tobel, S.J.
311 N. Sverdrup Ave., P.O. Box 65, Jackson, 56143-1329. Tel: 507-847-2504; Fax: 507-847-3734. Email: sjcc@frontiernet.net; goodshep@msn.com.
Catechesis/Religious Program—410 Broadway Ave., Box 517, 56150. Tel: 507-662-5819; Fax: 507-662-5924. Students 79.

LAMOILLE, WINONA CO., PRECIOUS BLOOD (1900) Closed. For inquiries for parish records contact the chancery.

LANESBORO, FILLMORE CO., ST. PATRICK (1871) [JC] Attended by St. Mary's, Chatfield. Rev. Patrick O. Arens.
Mailing Address: 405 Twiford St., S.W., Chatfield, 55923. Tel: 507-867-3922; Fax: 507-867-0073. Email: tostmarys@gamil.com.
Church: 200 Ridgeway Ln., P.O. Box 307, 55949. Tel: 507-467-2480.
Catechesis/Religious Program—Students 25.

LE ROY, MOWER CO., ST. PATRICK'S (1878) [CEM] Attended by St. Ignatius, Spring Valley. Very Rev. Steven J. Peterson.
213 W. Franklin St., Spring Valley, 55975-1312. Tel: 507-346-7565; Fax: 507-324-5203.
Catechesis/Religious Program—Students 60.

LEWISTON, WINONA CO., ST. ROSE OF LIMA (1876) [CEM] Rev. Marreddy Pothireddy.
Res.: 180 S. Fremont, 55952-0727. Tel: 507-523-2428; Fax: 507-523-2645. Email: dowrose@embarqmail.com. Web: www.st-rose.org.
Catechesis/Religious Program—Included with St. Anthony, Altura, MN.; Immaculate Conception, Wilson, MN., Tel: 507-523-3548. Email: dowstrose@embarqmail.com. Students 227.

LISMORE, NOBLES CO., ST. ANTHONY'S (1887) [CEM] Attended by St. Adrian, Adrian. Rev. Timothy J. Hall; Roxanne Kemper, Pastoral Min.
Mailing Address: 310 Third Ave. S., P.O. Box 158, 56155-0158. Tel: 507-472-8262; Fax: 507-472-8454. Email: santhony@myclearwave.net. Web: www.frontiernet.net/~stadrian.
Catechesis/Religious Program—Tel: 507-472-8262; Fax: 507-472-8454. Students 55.

LITOMYSL, STEELE CO., HOLY TRINITY (1877) Attended by Sacred Heart, Owatonna. Revs. John M. Sauer; Andrew P. Vogel, Parochial Vicar.
810 S. Ceder Ave., Owatonna, 55060. Tel: 507-451-1588; Fax: 507-446-9979.
Church: 9946 S.E. 24th Ave., Owatonna, 55060.
School—St. Isidore, (Grades PreK-5) Tel: 507-451-5876; Fax: 507-433-9680. Mrs. Mary Hawkins, Prin. Lay Teachers 3; Students 23.
Catechesis/Religious Program—Tel: 507-583-7591. Students 36.

LUVERNE, ROCK CO., ST. CATHERINE'S (1881) [CEM] Rev. Thomas J. Jennings.
203 E. Brown, 56156-1599. Tel: 507-283-8502. Email: stcatherine@iw.net. Web: www.stcatherineluverne.org.
Catechesis/Religious Program—Tel: 507-283-8071; Fax: 507-449-3638. Email: kbaustian@iw.net. Students 226.

LYLE, MOWER CO., QUEEN OF PEACE (1946), (German), Attended by Sacred Heart, Adams. Rev. Thomas A. Loomis.
Mailing Address: 412 Main St., P.O. Box 352, Adams, 55909-0352. Tel: 507-582-3321; Fax: 507-582-1033.
Catechesis/Religious Program—Students 34.

MABEL, FILLMORE CO., ST. OLAF (1954) [JC] Attended by Nativity of B.V.M., Harmony. Rev. Msgr. Donald P. Schmitz.
640 First Ave., S.W., Harmony, 55939-0596. Tel: 507-886-2393; Fax: 507-886-2394.
Catechesis/Religious Program— Combined Rel Ed with Nativity, Harmoy & Assumption, Canton. Students attend at Assumption Canton. Students 35.

MADELIA, WATONWAN CO., ST. MARY (1872) Revs. Thien Van Nguyen; Luis Vargas, (Hispanic Ministry). Tel: 507-341-0403.
Res.: 212 First St., N.E., 56062-1702. Tel: 507-642-8305; Fax: 507-642-8310.
School—(Grades PreK-6) Tel: 507-642-3324; Fax: 507-642-3899. Email: stmarysjd@ccinternet.net. John DeZeeuw, Prin. Priests 1; Lay Teachers 5; Students 50.
Catechesis/Religious Program—Students 134.

MADISON LAKE, BLUE EARTH CO., ALL SAINTS (1894) [CEM] Rev. Robert J. Schneider.
600 3rd St., P.O. Box 217, 56063-0217.
Parish Endowment Fund, Inc. of All Saints Church—605 4th St., P.O. Box 217, 56063-0217. Tel: 507-243-3319; Fax: 507-243-4308. Email: asoffice@hickorytech.net. Web: as-ic.org.
School—(Grades PreK-4), P.O. Box 158, 56063-0158. Tel: 507-243-3819. Email: ascs@hickorytech.net. Priests 1; Lay Teachers 4; (K-5) 27; Preschool 27.
Catechesis/Religious Program—Tel: 507-327-2976. Email: colleenterrell@hotmail.com. Students 126.
Mission—Immaculate Conception 101 Church St., P.O. Box 100, Saint Clair, 56080-0100. Tel: 507-245-3447; Fax: 507-245-3448. Email: icoffice@hickorytech.net.

MANKATO, BLUE EARTH CO.

1—ST. JOHN THE BAPTIST (1884) [JC] Rev. John M. Kunz.
Church: 632 S. Broad St., 56001-3890. Tel: 507-625-3131; Fax: 507-625-3270. Email: stjohnch@hickorytech.net. Web: www.stjohnscatholicchurch.com.
Rectory—321 E. Liberty St., 56001-3890.
School—Tel: 507-388-2997; Fax: 507-388-3081. Web: www.mankatoareacatholicschools.org. See listings under Centralized Catholic Schools.
Catechesis/Religious Program—Tel: 507-387-6928. Email: mbn@hickorytech.net. Students 368.

2—ST. JOSEPH THE WORKER (1957) [JC] Rev. John P. Wilmot; Deacon Preston Doyle.
Res.: 423 W. 7th St., 56001-2197. Tel: 507-388-3766; Fax: 507-388-2101. Email: sjwhf@hickorytech.net.
School—Kirsten Davis, Admin. Asst.; Lauren Guetter, Sec.; Susan Funfsinn, Sec.; Ben Druffel, Music. See listings under Centralized Catholic Schools.
Catechesis/Religious Program—423 W. 7th St., 56001. Tel: 507-388-8018. Ed Snyder, D.R.E.; Adam Isakson, D.R.E. Students 172.
Convent—Tel: 507-388-2515.

3—SS. PETER AND PAUL'S (1854) Revs. Mariano O. Varela; Joseph LoJacono, I.V.E.; Deacon Christopher Walchuk.
Res.: 105 N. Fifth St., 56001-4442. Tel: 507-388-2995; Fax: 507-388-7661. Email: sspp@hickorytech.net.
School—Tel: 507-388-2997. See listings under Centralized Catholic Schools.
Catechesis/Religious Program—Students 95.

MAPLETON, BLUE EARTH CO., ST. TERESA'S (1876) [CEM] Rev. Brian F. Sutton, Parochial Admin.
104 Silver St., W., P.O. Box 305, 56065-0305.
Catechesis/Religious Program—Tel: 507-524-4606. Students 94.

MAZEPPA, WABASHA CO., SS. PETER AND PAUL (1860) Attended by Pax Christi, Rochester. Revs. Joseph B. Fogal; Pratap Reddy Salibindia, Parochial Vicar; Deacon Christopher Orlowski; Frank Irwin, Parish Admin.
4135 18th Ave., N.W., Rochester, 55901-0460.
Church: 222 First Ave. S., P.O. Box 224, 55956-0224. Tel: 507-843-3885; Fax: 507-843-3900. Email: secretary@sspnp.com.
Catechesis/Religious Program—Tel: 507-843-4600. Students 67.

MEDFORD, STEELE CO., CHRIST THE KING (1943) Rev. Robert D. Herman, Priest Moderator (Retired).
Res.: 205 N.W. Second Ave., P.O. Box 120, 55049-0120. Tel: 507-451-6353; Fax: 507-451-6353.

Email: christthekingcc@q.com.
Catechesis/Religious Program—Tel: 507-451-8898. Students 110.

MINNEISKA, WABASHA CO., ST. MARY'S (1867) Attended by Holy Trinity, Rollingstone. Very Rev. Thomas P. Melvin, Parish Admin. Tel: 507-457-7380.
83 Main St., Rollingstone, 55969-9759. Tel: 507-689-2351; Fax: 507-689-2251. Email: holymary@charter.net.
Catechesis/Religious Program—Total Enrollment 1.

MINNESOTA CITY, WINONA CO., ST. PAUL'S (1924) [CEM] Attended by Holy Trinity, Rollingstone Very Rev. Thomas P. Melvin, Parish Admin. Tel: 507-457-7380. Email: tmelvin@dow.org.
Res.: 83 Main St., Rollingstone, 55969-9759. Tel: 507-689-2351; Fax: 507-689-2251. Email: holymary@charter.net.
Catechesis/Religious Program—Students 4.

MINNESOTA LAKE, FARIBAULT CO., ST. JOHN THE BAPTIST (1865) [CEM] Attended by St. Casimir, Wells. Rev. Thomas M. Niehaus; Deacon Eugene Paul.
Mailing Address: 320 2nd Ave. S.W., Wells, 56097-1399. Tel: 507-553-5391. Email: scasimir@bevcomm.net.
Church: 100 Park St., P.O. Box 158, 56068. Tel: 507-462-3636; Fax: 507-462-3212. Email: stjb@bevcomm.net.
Catechesis/Religious Program—25 Higbie Ave., P.O. Box 158, 56068. Email: stjbff@bevcomm.net. Students 43.

NEW RICHLAND, WASECA CO., ALL SAINTS (1879) [CEM] Rev. Swaminatha R. Pothireddy.
Res.: 307 1st St., S.W., P.O. Box 185, 56072-0185. Tel: 507-465-8217; Fax: 507-465-8381. Email: asbulletin@earthlink.net.
Catechesis/Religious Program—Students 25.

OAK RIDGE, WINONA CO., IMMACULATE CONCEPTION (1875) Closed. For inquiries about sacramental records contact Holy Trinity, Rollingstone.

OWATONNA, STEELE CO.

1—ST. JOSEPH'S (1891) Rev. Edward F. McGrath, Parochial Admin.; Deacon Patrick Fagan.
Res.: 512 S. Elm St., 55060-3399. Tel: 507-451-4845; Fax: 507-451-4651. Email: stjosephparishowatonna@charter.net.
School— See listings under Centralized Catholic Schools.
Catechesis/Religious Program—Students 411.

2—SACRED HEART (1866) [JC] Revs. John M. Sauer; Andrew P. Vogel.
Res.: 810 S. Cedar Ave., 55060-3297. Tel: 507-451-1588; Fax: 507-446-9979. Web: www.sacredheartowatonna.org.
School—St. Mary's, Tel: 507-446-2300; Fax: 507-446-2304. See listings under Centralized Catholic Schools.
Catechesis/Religious Program—730 S. Cedar Ave., 55060. Tel: 507-446-2302. Students 350.

PIPESTONE, PIPESTONE CO., ST. LEO'S (1887) [CEM] Rev. Gerald C. Kosse.
Mailing Address: 415 Hiawatha Ave. S., P.O. Box 36, 56164-0036. Tel: 507-825-3152. Email: om@triparishmn.org.
Res.: 121 Smith St., N., Woodstock, 56186. Tel: 507-777-4160; Fax: 507-825-4492.
Catechesis/Religious Program—Students 208.

PLAINVIEW, WABASHA CO., ST. JOACHIM'S (1858) [CEM] Rev. William M. Becker.
Res.: 900 W. Broadway, 55964-1039. Tel: 507-534-3321; Fax: 507-534-3687. Email: stjoachimchurch@hotmail.com.
Catechesis/Religious Program—Tel: 507-534-2887. Students 296.

PRESTON, FILLMORE CO., ST. COLUMBAN (1869) [CEM 2] [JC] Attended by St. Mary's, Chatfield. Rev. Patrick O. Arens.
Mailing Address: *Tri-Parish*, 405 Bench St. N.W., Chatfield, 55923.
Church: 408 N.W. Preston St., 55965. Tel: 507-765-3886; Fax: 507-765-3886. Email: singwjoy@acegroup.com.
Catechesis/Religious Program—Students 53.

ROCHESTER, OLMSTED CO.

1—ST. FRANCIS OF ASSISI (1937) [JC] Revs. Mark C. McNea; Ubaldo Rogue Huerta, Parochial Vicar; Deacons Richard Mangen; David Plevak.
Res.: 1114 3rd St., S.E., 55904-7293. Tel: 507-288-7313; Fax: 507-281-5997. Email: francis@stfrancis-church.org. Web: www.stfrancis-church.org.
See St. Francis of Assisi School, Rochester under Centralized Catholic Schools located in the Institution section.
Catechesis/Religious Program—Tel: 507-289-2427. Students 576.

2—HOLY SPIRIT (1990) [JC] Rev. Donald J. Schmitz; Deacons Richard Quinn; Joseph Weigel; Mary Margaret Yaeger, Pastoral Assoc.
Office: 5455 50th Ave., N.W., 55901. Tel: 507-280-0638; 507-281-8323 (Res.); Fax: 507-292-9547. Email: hspirit@holyspiritrochester.org.
See Holy Spirit School, Rochester under Centralized Catholic Schools located in the Institution section.
Catechesis/Religious Program—Students 200.

3—ST. JOHN THE EVANGELIST (1863) [JC] Rev. Msgr. Gerald A. Mahon; Rev. John Lugala Lasuba, Parochial Vicar; Deacons Gerald Freetly; John DeStazio.
Res.: 11 4th Ave., S.W., 55902-3098. Tel: 507-288-7372; Fax: 507-288-7373. Email: stjohn@sj.org. Web: www.sj.org.
See St. John School, Rochester under Centralized Catholic Schools located in the Institution section.
Catechesis/Religious Program—Students 243.

4—PAX CHRISTI (1973) [JC] Revs. Joseph B. Fogal; Pratap Reddy Salibindia; Deacon Christopher Orlowski.
Res.: 4135 18th Ave., N.W., 55901-0460. Tel: 507-282-8542. Email: receptionist@paxchristichurch.org. Web: www.paxchristichurch.org.
School—Tel: 507-280-0349; Fax: 507-289-4008. See listings under Centralized Catholic Schools.
Catechesis/Religious Program—Students 385.

5—ST. PIUS X (1954) [JC] Revs. Charlie I. Collins; Paul E. Nelson; Deacon Thomas DeRienzo.
Res.: 4833 Salley Ln., NW, 55901.
Church: 1315 12th Ave., N.W., 55901-1744. Tel: 507-288-8238; Fax: 507-286-8769. Email: church@piusx.org. Web: www.piusx.org.
See St. Pius X School, Rochester under Centralized Catholic Schools located in the Institution section.
Catechesis/Religious Program—Tel: 507-289-6317; Fax: 507-286-8769. Students 117.

6—RESURRECTION (1967) [JC] Very Rev. Kevin Connolly; Rev. Shawn T. Haremza.
Res.: 1600-11th Ave., S.E., 55904-5499. Tel: 507-288-5528; Fax: 507-252-0763. Email: communications@resurrection-catholic.org. Web: www.resurrection-catholic.org.
School— See listings under Centralized Catholic Schools.
Catechesis/Religious Program—Students 301.

ROLLINGSTONE, WINONA CO., HOLY TRINITY (1862) [CEM] Very Rev. Thomas P. Melvin, Parish Admin. Tel: 507-454-1241.
Res.: 83 Main St., 55969-9759. Tel: 507-689-2351; Fax: 507-689-2251. Email: holymary@charter.net. Web: holytrinity-rollingstone.org.
Catechesis/Religious Program—Students 42.

ROSE CREEK, MOWER CO., ST. PETER'S (1885) [CEM] Attended by Sacred Heart, Adams. Rev. Thomas A. Loomis.
Mailing Address: 412 Main St., P.O. Box 352, Adams, 55909. Tel: 507-582-3321.
Church: 302 Maple St., S.W., 55970-9701. Tel: 507-433-1532.
Catechesis/Religious Program—Tel: 507-433-6472. Students 68.

RUSHFORD, FILLMORE CO., ST. JOSEPH'S (1868) [CEM] Rev. Joseph P. Pete.
Res.: 101 Rushford Ave. W., P.O. Box 577, 55971-0577. Tel: 507-864-2257. Email: jpete@acegroup.cc. Web: home.catholicweb.com/stspetermaryjoseph/index.cfm.
Catechesis/Religious Program—Students 75.

ST. CHARLES, WINONA CO., ST. CHARLES BORROMEO (1867) [CEM] Rev. Kurt P. Farrell; Deacon Placido Zavala.
Church: 1900 E. 6th St., 55972-1426. Tel: 507-932-3294; Fax: 507-932-3393. Email: borromeo@hdscs.net. Web: www.borromeochurch.org.
Catechesis/Religious Program—Students 275.

ST. CLAIR, BLUE EARTH CO., IMMACULATE CONCEPTION (1874) [CEM] Attended by All Saints Church, 600 3rd St., P.O. Box 217, Madison Lake 56063-0217. Rev. Robert J. Schneider.
Tel: 507-245-3447. Email: icoffice@hickorytech.net. Web: www.as-ic.org.
Catechesis/Religious Program—Students 141.

ST. JAMES, WATONWAN CO., ST. JAMES (1876) [CEM] Revs. Thien Van Nguyen; Luis Vargas, (Hispanic Ministry).
Church: 707 4th St. S., 56081-1808. Tel: 507-375-3542; Fax: 507-375-4170.
Catechesis/Religious Program—Nonnie Hanson, D.R.E. Students 178.

ST. KILIAN, NOBLES CO., ST. KILIAN (1903) [CEM] Attended by St. Adrian, Adrian. Rev. Timothy J. Hall; Roxanne Kemper, Pastoral Min.
Mailing Address: 310 Third Ave. S., P.O. Box 158, Lismore, 56155-0158. Tel: 507-472-8262; Fax: 507-472-8454. Email: santhony@myclearwave.net. Web: frontiernet.net/~stadrian.
Catechesis/Religious Program—Students 23.

SHERBURN, MARTIN CO., ST. LUKE'S (1888) [CEM] Attended by Good Shepherd, Jackson. Rev. James Von Tobel, S.J.
Res.: 311 N. Sverdrup Ave., P.O. Box 65, Jackson, 56143-1329. Tel: 507-764-7831; Fax: 507-847-3734. Email: goodshep@msn.com.
Catechesis/Religious Program—Tel: 507-764-7831; Fax: 507-764-7831. Students 58.

SIMPSON, OLMSTED CO, ST. BRIDGET'S (1857) [CEM] Attended by St. Bernard, Stewartville. Rev. Matthew J. Fasnacht.
116 4th Ave., S.E., Stewartville, 55976. Tel: 507-533-8257; Fax: 507-533-1053. Email: stbernard116@aol.com. Web: www.stbernardsparish.org.
Catechesis/Religious Program—Students 42.

SLAYTON, MURRAY CO., ST. ANN'S (1897) [CEM] Rev. James J. Seitz.
Res.: 2747 29th St., 56172-1485. Tel: 507-836-8030; Fax: 507-836-6261.
Catechesis/Religious Program—Email: triparish@frontiernet.net. Students 123.

SPRING VALLEY, FILLMORE CO., ST. IGNATIUS (1878) [CEM] Very Rev. Steven J. Peterson.
Res.: 213 W. Franklin St., 55975-1312. Tel: 507-346-7565; Fax: 507-346-7725.
Catechesis/Religious Program—Tel: 507-346-7194. Students 64.

STEWARTVILLE, OLMSTED CO., ST. BERNARD'S (1894) [CEM] Rev. Matthew J. Fasnacht.
Res.: 116 Fourth Ave., S.E., 55976. Tel: 507-533-8257; Fax: 507-533-1053. Email: stbernard116@aol.com. Web: www.stbernardsparish.org.
Catechesis/Religious Program—Tel: 507-533-8192. Students 180.

THEILMAN, WABASHA CO., ST. JOSEPH'S (1903) [CEM] Closed. For inquiries for sacramental records, contact St. Mary of the Lake, Lake City.

TRIMONT, MARTIN CO., ST. JOSEPH, Closed. For inquiries for parish records contact the chancery.

TRUMAN, MARTIN CO., ST. KATHERINE (1954) Attended by St. Mary, Madelia. Rev. Thien Van Nguyen.
212 First St., N.E., Madelia, 56062-1702. Tel: 507-642-8305; Fax: 507-642-8310.
Church: 518 E. 2nd St. S., 56088.
Catechesis/Religious Program—

TWIN LAKES, FREEBORN CO., ST. JAMES (1876) Attended by St. Theodore, Albert Lea. Rev. Timothy T. Reker; Deacon Michael Ellis.
Mailing Address: 308 E. Fountain St., Albert Lea, 56007. Tel: 507-373-0603; Fax: 507-373-0604.
Church: 106 W. Main St., 56089.
Catechesis/Religious Program—Email: dlm@sttheo.org. Students 5.

VERNON CENTER, BLUE EARTH CO., ST. MATTHEW (1911) [CEM] Attended by St. Teresa, Mapleton. Rev. Brian F. Sutton, Parochial Admin.
104 Silver St., W., P.O. Box 305, Mapleton, 56065-0305. Tel: 507-524-3127; Fax: 507-524-4423.
Catechesis/Religious Program—Students 28.

WABASHA, WABASHA CO., ST. FELIX (1858) [CEM] Very Rev. Thomas E. Cook; Deacon John Hust.
Parish Office: 117 W. Third St., 55981-1201. Tel: 651-565-3931; Fax: 651-565-4363. Email: stfelix@hbci.com. Web: www.stfelixchurch.org.
Rectory—36 Bailey Ave., 55981. Tel: 651-565-4578.
School—(Grades PreK-6), 130 Third St. E., 55981. Tel: 651-565-4446; Fax: 651-565-0244. Email: mainoffice@stfelixschool.org. Web: stfelixschool.org. Trisha Frost, Prin. Lay Teachers 10; Students 109.
Catechesis/Religious Program—Tel: 651-565-3718. Email: stfelixgrowthinfaith@yahoo.com. Students 86.

WALDORF, WASECA CO., ST. JOSEPH'S (1878) [CEM] Attended by St. Ann, Janesville, 307 W. 2nd St., P.O. Box 218, Janesville, MN 56048-0218. Rev. Peter J. Klein.
Catechesis/Religious Program—Students 28.

WASECA, WASECA CO., SACRED HEART (1869) [JC 2] Very Rev. Martin T. Schaefer.
Res.: 111 Fourth St., N.W., 56093-2413. Tel: 507-835-1222; Fax: 507-833-1498. Email: sacredheart@hickorytech.net. Web: www.sacredheartwaseca.org.
School—(Grades PreK-4), 308 W. Elm Ave., 56093. Tel: 507-835-2780. Email: shschool@hickorytech.net. LeAnn Dahle, Prin. Priests 1; Lay Teachers 9; Students 155.
Sacred Heart Children's House—400 Second Ave., N.W., 56093. Tel: 507-835-1044. Pauline Holman, Dir. Students 84.
Catechesis/Religious Program—Tel: 507-835-1500. Students 475.

WELLS, FARIBAULT CO., ST. CASIMIR'S (1880) [CEM] Rev. Thomas M. Niehaus; Deacon Eugene Paul.
Res.: 320 Second Ave., S.W., 56097-1399. Tel: 507-553-5391; Fax: 507-553-5391. Email: scasimir@bevcomm.net.

School—(Grades K-8), 330 Second Ave., S.W., 56097. Tel: 507-553-5822. Email: casimir@bevcomm.net. Joanne Tibodeau, Prin. Lay Teachers 11; Students 73.
Catechesis/Religious Program—Students 87.

WEST ALBANY, WABASHA CO., ST. PATRICK OF WEST ALBANY (1865) [CEM] Attended by St. Mary of the Lake, Lake City. Rev. Richard J. Dernek; Deacon David Dose.
419 W. Lyon Ave., P.O. Box 224, Lake City, 55041. Tel: 651-345-4134. Email: fatherdernek@embarqmail.com.
Catechesis/Religious Program—Tel: 507-753-2424; Fax: 507-843-3900. Students 47.

WEST CONCORD, DODGE CO., ST. VINCENT DE PAUL (1945) [CEM] Attended by St. John Baptist de La Salle, Dodge Center. Rev. William Thompson.
20 Second St., N.E., P.O. Box 310, Dodge Center, 55927-0310. Tel: 507-374-6830. Email: tritonparishes@frontiernet.net.
Church: 310 Clyde St., 55985. Tel: 507-527-2384.
Catechesis/Religious Program—P.O. Box 117, 55985. Tel: 507-527-2384; Fax: 612-605-4315. Students 56.

WESTBROOK, COTTONWOOD CO.
1—ST. ANTHONY'S (1909) [CEM], Attended by St. Gabriel, Fulda. Rev. Jeffrey L. Dobbs.
307 Lake Ave., Fulda, 56131. Tel: 507-274-5946. Email: anthonys@centurytel.net.
Church: 1153 1st Ave., P.O. Box 278, 56183. Tel: 507-763-3145; Fax: 507-274-5946.
Catechesis/Religious Program—Students 29.

WILMONT, NOBLES CO., OUR LADY OF GOOD COUNSEL (1903) [CEM] Attended by St. Adrian, Adrian. Rev. Timothy J. Hall.
512 Main Ave., P.O. Box 475, Adrian, 56110-0475. Tel: 507-483-2317; Fax: 507-483-2460. Email: stadrian@frontiernet.net. Web: www.frontiernet.net/~stadrian.
Catechesis/Religious Program—Tel: 507-926-5305. Email: faithform4@frontiernet.net. Students 69.

WILSON, WINONA CO., IMMACULATE CONCEPTION (1874) Attended by St. Rose of Lima, Lewiston. Rev. Marreddy Pothireddy.
180 S. Fremont St., Lewiston, 55952-0727. Tel: 507-523-2428; Fax: 507-523-2645. Email: dowstrose@embarqmail.com.
Catechesis/Religious Program— Combined with St. Rose of Lima, Lewiston, MN. and St. Anthony, Altura, MN. Students 227.

WINDOM, COTTONWOOD CO., ST. FRANCIS XAVIER'S (1898) Very Rev. Russell G. Scepaniak.
Res.: 548 17th St., P.O. Box 39, 56101-0039. Tel: 507-831-3300; Fax: 507-831-0717.
Catechesis/Religious Program—532 17th St., 56101. Tel: 507-831-1985 (Office); 507-830-1406. Email: fossing.stfrancisxavier@gmail.com. Students 114.

WINNEBAGO, FARIBAULT CO., ST. MARY'S (1893) [CEM] Attended by Ss. Peter and Paul, Blue Earth. Rev. Leo Charles Koppala, Parochial Admin.
Mailing Address: 214 S. Holland, Blue Earth, 56013.
Church: 32 1st St., N.E., P.O. Box 424, 56098-0424. Tel: 507-526-5626; Fax: 507-526-2456. Email: leokoppala@yahoo.com.
Catechesis/Religious Program—Students 20.

WOODSTOCK, PIPESTONE CO., ST. MARTIN'S (1882) [CEM] Attended by St. Leo, Pipestone. Rev. Gerald C. Kosse.
Mailing Address: 415 Hiawatha Ave. S., P.O. Box 36, Pipestone, 56164. Tel: 507-825-3152; Fax: 507-825-4492. Email: om@triparishmn.org.
Rectory—121 Smith St. N., 56186.
Church: 101 Smith St. N., 56186. Tel: 507-777-4160.
Catechesis/Religious Program—Students 25.

WORTHINGTON, NOBLES CO., ST. MARY'S (1886) [CEM] Revs. James F. Callahan; Jose L. Morales, Parochial Vicar; Deacon Vernon Behrends.
Res.: 1215 Seventh Ave., 56187-2297. Tel: 507-376-6005; Fax: 507-376-9167. Email: stmaryschurch@knology.net.
School—(Grades K-6), Twelfth St. & Eighth Ave., 56187. Tel: 507-376-5236; Fax: 507-376-6159. Brittany Larson, Prin.; Barb Stirn, Librarian. Lay Teachers 7; Students 115.
Catechesis/Religious Program—Tel: 507-372-2090. Students 275.
Convent—1221 Seventh Ave., 56187. Tel: 507-376-4035.

WYKOFF, FILLMORE CO., ST. KILIAN'S (1887) Closed. For inquiries for parish records contact the chancery.

Chaplains of Public Institutions

WINONA. *Winona County Law Enforcement Center*, 466 Chestnut St., 55987. Tel: 507-452-4723. Deacon Justin Green, Chap.

ROCHESTER. *Federal Medical Center, Bureau of Prisons*, 2110 Center St. E., 55904. Sr. Emile Bormann, P.B.V.M., Chap.

WASECA. *Federal Correctional Institution*. Deacon Eduardo Fortini, Chap.

On Special or Other Diocesan Assignment:
Revs.—
Buryska, James F., Chap., Rochester Methodist Hospital, 201 W. Center St., Rochester, 55902. Tel: 507-255-5551
Byrne, David, Chap., Church of the Resurrection, 1600 S.E. 11th Ave., Rochester, 55904. Tel: 507-255-4074 Mayo Clinic Hospitals
Chacko, Joseph P., Chap., Saint Mary's Hospital, 1216 2nd St., S.W., Rochester, 55902. Tel: 507-255-9025
Kunz, James H., Chap., Mayo Medical Center, 1216 2nd St., S.W., Rochester, 55902. Tel: 507-255-5780

On Duty Outside the Diocese:
Rev.—
Brandenhoff, Peter B., 8859 Spring Ln., Woodbury, 55125. Tel: 651-578-0957

On Special Assignment:
Rev.—
Klein, Eugene M.

Absent on Leave:
Rev.—
Brixius, Hilary R.

Additional Diocesan Assignments:
Very Revs.—
Beerman, Andrew J., S.T.L., Immaculate Heart of Mary Seminary, 700 Terrace Heights, #43., 55987. Tel: 507-457-7371
Heiting, R. Paul, J.C.L., Immaculate Heart of Mary Seminary, 700 Terrace Heights, #43, 55987. Tel: 507-457-7370
Revs.—
Dittmer, Antonio, Immaculate Heart of Mary Seminary, 700 Terrace Heights, #43, 55987. Tel: 507-457-7373
Fabian, Andrew C., O.P., Saint Mary's University of Minnesota, 700 Terrace Heights, 55987. Tel: 507-457-1539
Nienaber, Paul J., S.J., Saint Mary's University of Minnesota, 700 Terrace Heights, #32, 55987. Tel: 507-457-1532

Retired:
Rev. Msgrs.—
Egan, Eugene E., 401 N. Maple St., Ellsworth, 56129.
Evers, Paul C., 12106 Grant Blvd. W., Wabasha, 55981.
Galles, Francis A., 500 Preston St., N.W., Preston, 55965. Tel: 507-765-2756
Grubisch, Donald W., 12 Sand Prairie Circle Ct., #42, Wabasha, 55981. Tel: 651-565-4625
Habiger, James D., Univ. of St. Thomas, 2115 Summit Ave., Box 4174, St. Paul, 55105. Tel: 651-962-8065 (Res); 651-227-8777
Literski, Roy E., 1328 D. McNally Dr., 55987. Tel: 507-452-7685
Mountain, Joseph W., 4001 N.W. 19th Ave., Apt. 804, Rochester, 55901.
Revs.—
Arnoldt, David L., 118 Central Park Ln., Evans, GA 30809. Tel: 706-650-9222
Breza, Paul J., 102 Liberty St., 55987. Tel: 507-643-0441
Connelly, Donald F., 125 N.E. 2nd Ave., Apt. 105, Stewartville, 55976. Tel: 651-565-4531
Conway, Gerald W., 14208 N. Newcastle Dr., Sun City, AZ 85351. Tel: 623-505-7106
Dandelet, James D., P.O. Box 46, Easton, 56025-0046. Tel: 507-787-2520
Engels, Richard J., 205 Dugan St., Wabasha, 55981. Tel: 651-565-3432
Ernster, Milo L., 64540 140th Ave., Wabasha, 55981. Tel: 651-565-2191
Ginther, Lawrence P., 5125 W. Seventh St., Apt. 8, 55987-5616. Tel: 507-454-4789
Gits, Douglas J., 1420 4th St. S.E., Rochester, 55904-4716. Tel: 507-286-7874
Haberman, Clayton J., 5371 Elkton Tr., Faribault, 55021-8453. Tel: 507-334-0610
Halloran, Paul F., 7646 Sixth Lake Rd., N.W., Akeley, 56433-9507.
Hennessy, James W., c/o St. Elizabeth Medical Center, 1200 Grant Blvd. W., Wabasha, 55981-1098. Tel: 608-685-4095
Herman, Robert D., 205 N.W. 2nd Ave., P.O. Box 120, Medford, 55049. Tel: 507-451-6353
Jewison, Harry P., 1024 Ninth St., N.E., Rochester, 55906. Tel: 507-285-5515
Keefe, Joseph L., 5840 Summit Ln. N.E., Rochester, 55906.
Kellen, Elmer W., 12104 W. Grant Blvd., Wabasha, 55981. Tel: 651-565-5513
Kerrigan, Bernard A., St. Elizabeth Health Care Center, 626 Shields Ave., Wabasha, 55981.
Kunz, Francis P., 240 Hudson Ave. E., Mankato, 56001. Tel: 507-625-6217
LaPlante, Joseph A., 67643 154th Ave, Wabasha, 55981. Tel: 651-565-2441
Leary, Donald G., 220 S. Broadway, #1504, Rochester, 55902. Tel: 507-288-5813
Loomis, Richard P., St. Edward Church, 2000 Oakland Ave. W., Austin, 55912. Tel: 507-433-1841
Lovas, Donald J., 807 W. Mark St., 55987. Tel: 507-454-1887
Maher, Robert G., 9505 Salem Hills Court, Las Vegas, NV 89134-4600. Tel: 702-804-2718
Marek, Dean V., 1951 Tiffany Cove Ln., Rochester, 55902. Tel: 507-282-4799
McCauley, James A., P.O. Box 203, Brownsville, 55919. Tel: 507-482-6631
Meyer, Robert G., 1312 N. 7th St., Apt. 134, Lake City, 55041. Tel: 651-345-4022
Mountain, Edward C., 420 11th St., S.E., Owatonna, 55060-4008. Tel: 507-451-6752
Olsem, Andrew D., 610 Reed St., Mankato, 56001.
Quinn, Charles J., 405 S. Lake St., Sherburn, 56171. Tel: 507-764-4069
Russell, James D., 202 B Alpine Ridge, Wabasha, 55981. Tel: 651-565-3632
Schaefer, Edgar J., 9659 111th Ave. N, Sun City, AZ 85351. Tel: 623-875-9749
Schiltz, Roger J., 1532 Glenrosa Dr., North Las Vegas, NV 89031-5548.
Smith, Leland J., 468 Center St., 55987. Tel: 507-454-8464
Spinler, Ruben C., 302 Maple St. S.W., Rose Creek, 55970. Tel: 507-433-1532
Stamschror, Robert P., 2480 Goodview Rd., 55987. Tel: 507-452-4202
Stenzel, Eugene F., 60659 200th St., Wells, 56097. Tel: 507-553-5505
Traufler, John F., 200 18th St. N.W., Austin, 55912. Tel: 507-434-7702
Trocinski, LaVern F., 4513 Ruby Ln., N.W., Rochester, 55901. Tel: 507-536-0747
Verdick, Jerome F., 210 E. Paddock, P.O. Box 87, Alpha, 56111-0087. Tel: 507-847-2939
Zenk, Donald W., 602 31st St., N.W., Austin, 55912. Tel: 507-437-3579

Permanent Deacons:
Aho, Richard, St. Edward, Austin; St. Augustine Austin
Anderberg, George, (Diocese of Winona)
Behrends, Vernon, St. Mary, Worthington
Blake, David, Queen of Angels, Austin; Our Lady of Loretto, Brownsdale
Bonnarens, Edwin C., St. John Vianney, Fairmont; Holy Family, East Chain
DeRienzo, Thomas, St. Pius X, Rochester
DeStazio, John, St. John the Evangelist, Rochester
Dose, David, St. Mary, Lake City; St. Patrick, West Albany
Doyle, Preston, St. Joseph, Mankato; Holy Family, Lake Crystal
Ellis, Michael, St. Theodore, Albert Lea; St. James, Twin Lakes
Fagan, Patrick, St. Joseph, Owatonna
Fortini, Eduardo, Federal Prison Chap., Waseca
Freetly, Gerald, St. John the Evangelist, Rochester
Fuller, Leonard L., Diocese of Winona
Green, Justin, St. Stanislaus, Winona; St. John Nepomucene, Winona
Hust, John, St. Felix, Wabasha; St. Agnes, Kellogg
Kluczny, John, St. Edward, Austin; St. Augustine, Austin
Kunkel, Jerrold, St. Thomas More Newman Center, Mankato
Mangen, Richard, (Retired), St. Francis of Assisi, Rochester.
McMillan, Adam, (Diocese of Winona)
Orlowski, Christopher, Pax Christi, Rochester; Ss. Peter & Paul, Mazeppa
Paul, Eugene, St. Casimir, Wells; Our Lady of Mt. Carmel, Easton; St. John the Baptist, Minnesota Lake
Plevak, David, St. Francis of Assisi, Rochester
Quinn, Richard, Holy Spirit, Rochester
Richard, Gordon, (Diocese of Winona)
Trocinski, Gerald, Crucifixion, LaCrescent; Holy Cross, Dakota
Walchuk, Christopher, Ss. Peter & Paul, Mankato
Weigel, Joseph, Holy Spirit, Rochester
Welch, James, Cathedral of the Sacred Heart, Winona; St. Casimir, Winona
Yerhot, Robert, Crucifixion, LaCrescent; Holy Cross, Holy Cross, Dakota
Zavala, Placido, St. Charles Borromeo, St. Charles; St. Aloysius, Elba; Holy Redemer, Eyota

INSTITUTIONS LOCATED IN THE DIOCESE

[A] SEMINARIES, DIOCESAN

WINONA. *Immaculate Heart of Mary Seminary*, 700 Terrace Hts. #43, 55987-1399. Tel: 507-457-7373; Fax: 507-457-8601. Email: ihms@smumn.edu. Web: www.ihmseminary.org. Very Revs. Andrew J. Beerman, S.T.L., Rector; R. Paul Heiting, J.C.L., Vice Rector; James P. Steffes, Extern Spiritual Dir.; Revs. Jon H. Moore, Spiritual Dir.; Antonio Dittmer, Spiritual Life Dir.; Very Rev. Thomas P. Melvin, S.T.L., Spiritual Dir.; Rev. David Wechter, O.C.S.O., J.C.L., Extern Spiritual Dir.; Ellen Speltz, Dir. Devel. Affiliated with Saint Mary's University of MN. Priests 5; Lay Staff 6; Students 47.

[B] COLLEGES AND UNIVERSITIES

WINONA. *Saint Mary's University of Minnesota* (Coed), 700 Terrace Hts., 55987-1399. Tel: 507-457-1600; Fax: 507-457-1722. Email: admissions@smumn.edu. Web: www.smumn.edu. Bros. William Mann, F.S.C., D.Min., Pres.; Louis De Thomasis, F.S.C., Chancellor; Sr. Judith Schaefer, O.P., Ph.D., University Dean for Univ. Affairs; Cynthia Marek, Vice Pres. Fin. Affairs; Ann Merchlewitz, Exec, Vice Pres. & Gen. Counsel; James Bedtke, Vice Pres. of the College; Dr. Marilyn Frost, Vice Pres. Academic Affairs; Dr. Donna Aronson, Vice Pres. of Academic Affairs; Robert Conover, Vice Pres. Communications & Mktg.; Linka Holey, Assoc. Vice Pres. Graduate & Professional Programs, Academic Dean; Chris Kendall, Vice Pres. Student Devel.; Laura Oanes, Librarian; Steven Titus, Senior Vice Pres. Univ. Advancement; Dr. Marcel Dumestre, Vice Pres. Schools of Graduate & Professional Prog. DeLaSalle Christian Brothers. Priests 6; Brothers 8; Sisters 1; Lay Faculty 97; Students 1,372.

[C] CENTRALIZED CATHOLIC SCHOOLS

WINONA. *Cotter High School & Junior High School*, (Grades 7-12), 1115 W. Broadway, 55987. Tel: 507-453-5002; Fax: 507-453-5006. Email: sblank@cotterschools.org; dforney@cotterschools.org. Web: www.cotterschools.org. Jennifer Elfering, Pres.; Sandra Blank, Prin.; Dave Forney, Dir. Cotter Junior High School; Marisa Corcoran, Campus Min.; Jenny Carpenter, Activities Dir.; John Broadwater, CFO; Will Gibson, Admissions Dir.; Megan Sadowski, Devel. Dir. Tel: 507-453-5102; Mary Forney, Librarian. Lay Teachers 36; Students 380.

Winona Area Catholic Schools, 602 E. 5th St., 55987. Tel: 507-452-3766; Fax: 507-452-5497. Email: pbowlin@wacs1.org. Web: www.wacsl.org. Patrick Bowlin, School Admin. Lay Teachers 31.

St. Mary's Primary School (Grades PreK-K), 1315 W. Broadway, 55987. Tel: 507-452-2890; Fax: 507-452-2898. Patrick Bowlin; Christine Nichols, Prog. Dir. Students 175.

St. Stanislaus Elementary School (Grades 1-6), 602 E. Fifth St., 55987. Tel: 507-452-3766; Fax: 507-452-5497. Patrick Bowlin. Students 285.

Winona Area Catholic Schools Foundation (Grades PreK-12), 1115 W. Broadway, 55987. Tel: 507-453-5102; Fax: 507-453-5013. Sara Brandon, Pres.

ALBERT LEA. *St. Theodore School*, (Grades K-6), 323 E. Clark St., 56007. Tel: 507-373-9657; Fax: 507-373-9657. Email: jfc@sttheo.org. Web: www.sttheo.org. Rev. Timothy Reker, Pastor & Admin.; Deacon Michael Ellis, Admin.; Jean Calderon, Admin.; Brenda Appel, Librarian. Lay Teachers 7; Students 89.

AUSTIN. *Austin Catholic Schools Inc. dba Pacelli Catholic School* (Grades PreK-6), 511 N.W. Fourth Ave., 55912. Tel: 507-433-8859; Fax: 507-433-6630. Web: www.pacellionline.net. Mary P. Holtorf, Prin. Lay Teachers 15; Students 221.

Pacelli Catholic Middle/Senior High School (Grades 6-12), 311 Fourth St., N.W., 55912. Tel: 507-437-3278; Fax: 507-433-5693. Web: www.pacellionline.net. Rev. Gregory Parrott, Campus Min.; Joseph Steepleton, Prin. & Pres. of Schools. Lay Teachers 9; Students 124.

United Catholic Schools Foundation of Austin, MN, Inc., 511 N.W. Fourth Ave., 55912. Tel: 507-433-6630; Fax: 507-433-6630.

MANKATO. *Loyola Catholic School*, (Grades PreK-12), 145 Good Counsel Dr., 56001-3146. Tel: 507-388-2997; Fax: 507-388-3081. Email: sschultz@loyolacatholicschool.org. Web: loyolacatholicschool.org. Shelley Schultz, Interim Admin.; Sr. Mary Beth Schraml, S.S.N.D., Prin.; William Schumacher, Prin.; Ruth Corcoran, Librarian. Priests 1; Sisters 1; Lay Teachers 60; Total Enrollment 650.

OWATONNA. *St. Mary's School*, (Grades PreK-8), 730 South Cedar Ave., 55060. Tel: 507-446-2300; Fax: 507-446-2304. Web: www.stmarys-owatonna.org. Mrs. Mary Hawkins, Prin.; Sharleen Berg, Media Specialist. Lay Teachers 24; Students 385.

ROCHESTER. *Rochester Catholic Schools*, (Grades PreSchool-12), 621 W. Center St., 55901. Tel: 507-218-3028. Web: rochestercatholicschools.org. Mr. Michael Brennan, Dir. of Schools.

St. Francis of Assisi School (Grades PreSchool-8), 318 11th Ave. S.E., 55904. Tel: 507-288-4816; Fax: 507-288-4815. Email: bplenge@rochestercatholic.k12.mn.us. Mrs. Barb Plenge, Prin. Lay Teachers 53; Students 518.

St. John the Evangelist (Grades 5-8), 424 W. Center St., 55902. Tel: 507-282-5248; Fax: 507-282-1343. Email: dvalentine@rochestercatholic.k12.mn.us. Mr. Don Valentine, Prin. Lay Teachers 15; Students 188.

St. Pius X School (Grades PreSchool-4), 1205 12th Ave., 55901. Tel: 507-282-5161; Fax: 507-282-5107. Email: dvalentine@rochestercatholic.k12.mn.us. Mr. Don Valentine, Prin. Lay Teachers 11; Students 271.

Lourdes High School of Rochester, Inc., 621 W. Center St., 55902. Tel: 507-289-3991; Fax: 507-289-4008. Email: tdonlon@rochestercatholic.k12.mn.us. Mr. Thomas Donlon, Prin.; Rita Hendrickson, Campus Min.; Rev. William Thompson, Instructor. Priests 1; Lay Teachers 40; Students 460.

Holy Spirit School (Grades PreK-8), 5455 50th Ave., N.W., 55901. Tel: 507-288-8818; Fax: 507-288-5155. Email: mklebe@rochestercatholic.k12.mn.us. Lynette Lenoch, Prin. Lay Teachers 25; Students 345.

[D] GENERAL HOSPITALS

ROCHESTER. *Diocese of Winona Catholic Medical Association*, 200 First St., S.W., 55905. Tel: 507-266-3412; Fax: 507-266-1657. Email: lane.john@mayo.edu. Dr. John I. Lane, M.D.

**Saint Mary Hospital* 55902-1970. Tel: 507-255-5123; Fax: 507-255-3125. B. Lynn Frederick, Admin.; Revs. James H. Kunz. Tel: 507-255-5780; James F. Buryska. Tel: 507-255-5780; William D. Byrne. Tel: 507-255-5780; Joseph P. Chacko. Tel: 507-255-5780; John Evans. Tel: 507-255-5780. Sisters of the Third Order Regular of St. Francis of the Congregation of Our Lady of Lourdes 21; Bed Capacity 1,265; Patients Assisted Annually 60,700.

WABASHA. *Saint Elizabeth's Medical Center*, 1200 Grant Blvd., W., 55981. Tel: 651-565-4531; Fax: 651-565-2482. Email: carmen.tiffany@ministryhealth.org. Web: www.StElizabethsWabasha.org. Mr Thomas Crowley, Pres. Corporate Sponsor: Ministry Health Care, Inc. (Milwaukee, WI); Sponsored by Sisters of the Sorrowful Mother. Sisters of the Third Order of St. Francis of the Sorrowful Mother 1; Bed Capacity 25; Patients Assisted Annually 26,500; Total Staff 170.

[E] SPECIAL HOSPITALS AND REHABILITATION FACILITIES

ROCHESTER. *Guest House*, 4800 48th St., N.E., P.O. Box 954, 55903. Tel: 800-634-4155; Fax: 507-288-1240. William C. Morgan, Dir. Residential treatment center for priests, brothers, deacons and seminarians. Bed Capacity 37; Total Assisted 100.

[F] HOMES FOR AGED

WINONA. *Saint Anne of Winona*, 1347 W. Broadway, 55987. Tel: 507-454-3621; Fax: 507-452-2556. Rand Gettler, CEO & Admin. Subsidiary of Benedictine Health Systems, sponsored by the Sisters of St. Scholastica Monastery.

St. Anne of Winona Callista Court, 1455 W. Broadway, 55987. Tel: 507-457-0280; Fax: 507-494-5117. Subsidiary of Benedictine Health Systems, sponsored by the Sisters of St. Scholastica Monastery., Assisted living for seniors. Units 105; Residents 95; Total Staff 65; Resident Days 29,000.

St. Anne of Winona Benedictine Adult Day Center, 1455 W. Broadway, 55987. Email: tammy.ross@bhshealth.org. Tammy Ross, Dir. Guest Days 11,600.

St. Anne of Winona Extended Health Care, 1347 W. Broadway, 55987. Tel: 507-454-3621; Fax: 507-452-2556. Email: rand.gettler@bhshealth.org. Rand Gettler, CEO & Admin.; Jo Hassinger, Dir. of Nursing Svcs. Nursing care for the aged, chronically ill or rehab. Bed Capacity 109; Residents 107; Resident Days 39,055; Total Staff 260.

St. Anne of Winona Training Center, 1455 W. Broadway, 55987. Tel: 507-457-3811; Fax: 507-494-5117. Email: rand.gettler@bhshealth.org. Joyce Nelson, Contact Person.

AUSTIN. *Sacred Heart Care Center, Inc.*, 1200 Twelfth St., S.W., 55912. Tel: 507-433-1808; Fax: 507-434-9572. Rebecca Mathews Halverson, Admin.; Rev. Donald W. Zenk, Chap. (Retired). Bed Capacity 59; Residents 59; Assisted Living Apartments (filled) 26; Adult Day Care (Client Days) 3,041; Alzheimer's Day Program (Client Days) 2,606; Home Health Care (Clients) 84; Total Staff 145.

PLAINVIEW. *Benedictine Care Centers, St. Isidore Health Center of Greenwood Prairie*, 800 2nd Ave., N.W., 55964. Tel: 507-534-3191; Fax: 507-534-2778. Email: paula.lewis@bhshealth.org. Paula Lewis, Admin. Benedictine Health System, sponsored by Srs. of St. Scholastica Monastery Total Staff 116; Long Term Care Bed Capacity 53.

Benedictine Care Centers, Green Prairie Place, 810 2nd Ave., N.W., 55964. Tel: 507-534-4204; Fax: 507-534-0139. Email: joann.klavetter@bhshealth.org. Joann Klavetter, Resident Services Mgr.; Paula Lewis, Admin. Benedictine Health System, sponsored by Srs. of St. Scholastica Monastery Total Assisted 10; Total Staff 15; Independent Apts. 26.

ROCHESTER. *Madonna Meadows of Rochester*, 3035 Salem Meadows Dr., S.W., 55902. Tel: 507-252-5400. Email: mark.noble@bhshealth.org. Mark Noble, Admin. & Corp. Exec. Officer. Benedictine Health System and Sisters of St. Scholastica Monastery., Assisted living facility. Bed Capacity 78; Guests 70; Total Staff 72.

Madonna Towers of Rochester, Inc., 4001 19th Ave., N.W., 55901. Tel: 507-288-3911; Fax: 507-288-0393. Email: mark.noble@bhshealth.org. Mark Noble, Admin. & Corp. Exec. Officer. Independent, assisted and nursing care facility; T. Emil Gauthier Memory Care. Subsidiary of Benedictine Health System. Bed Capacity 62; Total Staff 230; Apartments 107.

Chapel of St. Benedict and Chapel of St. Scholastica Tel: 507-288-3911; Fax: 507-288-0393.

Madonna Living Community Foundation of Rochester, 4001 19th Ave., N.W., 55901. Tel: 507-288-3911; Fax: 507-288-0393.

WABASHA. *St. Elizabeth's Health Care Center*, 626 Shields Ave., 55981. Tel: 651-565-4581; Fax: 651-565-3414. Web: www.ministryhealth.org. Mr Thomas Crowley, Admin.; Rev. Bernard A. Kerrigan (Retired). (Conducted in connection with St. Elizabeth's Medical Center.) Skilled Beds 81; Admissions 56; Total Staff 130; Total Assisted Annually 115.

[G] CONVENTS AND RESIDENCES FOR SISTERS

HOUSTON. *Hermits of St. Mary of Carmel, (H.S.M.C.)* Carmelite Eremitical Community of Diocesan Right, 33005 Stinson Ridge Rd., 55943-4033. Tel: 507-896-2125; Fax: 507-896-4349. Sr. Rosemary Therese Quinn, H.S.M.C., Prioress; Rev. David Wechter, O.C.S.O., J.C.L. Tel: 507-896-2125. Sisters 5.

JACKSON. *Convent of Religious Sisters of Mercy*, 51437 800th St., 56143. Tel: 507-847-5498; Fax: 507-847-5689. Web: www.rsmofalma.org. Sr. Mary Raphael Paradis, R.S.M., Local Supr. Sisters 4.

MANKATO. *School Sisters of Notre Dame, Convent of Our Lady of Good Counsel*, 170 Good Counsel Dr., 56001-3138. Tel: 507-389-4200; Fax: 507-389-4125. Email: dhoman@ssndmankato.org. Web: www.ssndmankato.org. Religious in Province 306; Sisters in Motherhouse 135; Lay Staff 122.

School Sisters of Notre Dame at Mankato, MN, Inc. Tel: 507-389-4200; Fax: 507-389-4125.

School Sisters of Notre Dame at Mankato, MN, Inc. Charitable Trust Tel: 507-389-4200; Fax: 507-389-4125.

School Sisters of Notre Dame Cooperative Investment Fund Tel: 507-389-4200; Fax: 507-389-4125.

ROCHESTER. *Sisters of St. Francis of the Third Order Regular of the Congregation of Our Lady of Lourdes*, Assisi Heights Admin. Ctr., 1001 14th St., N.W., Ste. 100, 55901-2511. Tel: 507-282-7441; Fax: 507-282-7762. Web: www.rochesterfranciscan.org. Sr. Tierney Trueman, O.S.F., Pres. & Congregational Min. *Academy of Our Lady of Lourdes* Religious in Province 248; Sisters in Motherhouse 120; Lay Staff 98.

[H] RETREAT HOUSES AND CENTERS OF SPIRITUALITY

AUSTIN. *Annunciation Hermitage, Carmelites of St. Joseph*, 1009 Oakland Ave. E., 55912. Tel: 507-437-4015. Rev. Jon H. Moore, Prior. Brothers 3.

JANESVILLE. *Holy Spirit Retreat Center*, 3864 420th Ave., 56048. Tel: 507-234-5712; Fax: 507-234-6188. Email: retreat@frontiernet.net. Web: www.RochesterFranciscan.org. Sisters Monique Schwirtz, O.S.F., Dir.; JoAnn Haney, O.S.F.; Charlotte Hesby, O.S.F.; Carmen Sonnek, O.S.F.

[I] NEWMAN CENTERS

WINONA. *St. Thomas Aquinas Newman Center* 475 Huff St., 55987. Tel: 507-452-2781. Email: newman@hbci.com. Web: studentsclubs.winona.edu/cnc. Very Rev. Richard M. Colletti, Chap.; Mr. Thomas Parlin.

MANKATO. *St. Thomas More Newman Center, Minnesota State University* 1331 Warren St., 56001. Tel: 507-387-4154. Rev. Timothy E. Biren, Chap. & Dir.

[J] MISCELLANEOUS LISTINGS

WINONA. *Diocese of Winona Deposit & Loan*, 55 W. Sanborn St., P.O. Box 588, 55987. Tel: 507-858-1248; Fax: 507-454-8106. Email: ldose@dow.org. Web: www.dow.org.

Diocese of Winona Foundation, 55 W. Sanborn St., P.O. Box 588, 55987. Tel: 507-858-1249; Fax: 507-454-8106. Email: jhennessy@dow.org. Web: www.dowgift.org.

Saint Mary's Press, Christian Brothers Publications, 702 Terrace Hts., 55987. Tel: 800-533-8095; Fax: 800-344-9225. Email: smpress@smp.org. Web: www.smp.org. Bro. Damian Steger, F.S.C., Chm. Corp.; John M. Vitek, Pres. & CEO.

ALBERT LEA. *St. Theodore Catholic School Endowment*, 308 E. Fountain St., 56007-2456. Tel: 507-373-0603; Fax: 507-373-0603. Email: ttreker@sttheo.org. Web: www.sttheo.org. Rev. Timothy T. Reker, S.T.L., Contact.

JACKSON. *Sacred Heart Mercy Health Care Center* (Pro Life Clinic, N.F.P. Family Practice), 803 Fourth St., 56143. Tel: 507-847-3571; Fax: 507-847-5664. Email: paradism@sacredheartmercy.net. Sr. Mary Raphael Paradis, R.S.M., Admin. Patients Assisted Annually 1,236; Total Staff 7.

MANKATO. *IVE Formation Program, Inc.*, 512 E. Mulberry St., 56001. Tel: 507-387-2565; Fax: 507-388-7661. Email: mvarela@hickorytech.net. Rev. Mariano O. Varela, IVE Dir.

ROCHESTER. *Poverello Foundation*, St. Mary's Hospital, 1216 S.W. Second St., 55902. Tel: 507-255-5158; Fax: 507-255-3125. Email: hanson.sandra@mayo.edu. Sr. Generose Gervais, O.S.F., Pres.

The Roman Catholic Pontifical Lay Association Memores Domini, 6006 Woodridge Ct., N.E., 55906. Tel: 507-292-0551. Email: smodarelli@sj.org. Web: www.comunioneliberazione.org.

Seeds of Wisdom in South Sudan, 11 Fourth Ave., S.W., 55902. Tel: 507-288-7372; Fax: 507-288-7373.

RELIGIOUS INSTITUTES OF MEN REPRESENTED IN THE DIOCESE

For further details refer to the corresponding bracketed number in the Religious Institutes of Men or Women section.

[0330]—*Brothers of the Christian Schools*—F.S.C.

[0340]—*Cistercian Fathers* (Abbey of Our Lady of New Malleray)—O.S.C.O.

[]—*Institute of the Incarnate Word*—I.V.E.

[0690]—*Jesuit Fathers and Brothers* (Wisconsin Province)—S.J.

[0430]—*Order of Preachers (Dominicans)* (Chicago Province)—O.P.

RELIGIOUS INSTITUTES OF WOMEN REPRESENTED IN THE DIOCESE

[1780]—*Congregation of the Sisters of the Third Order of St. Francis of Perpetual Adoration* (Eastern, Central Regions)—F.S.P.A.

[]—*Hermits of St. Mary of Carmel (Contemplative Community)*—H.S.M.C.

[2519]—*Religious Sisters of Mercy of Alma, Michigan*—R.S.M.

[2970]—*School Sisters of Notre Dame*—S.S.N.D.

[1680]—*School Sisters of St. Francis*—O.S.F.

[]—*Sinsinawa Dominican Sisters*—O.P.

[0430]—*Sisters of Charity of the Blessed Virgin Mary*—B.V.M.

[1705]—*The Sisters of St. Francis of Assisi*—O.S.F.

[1570]—*Sisters of St. Francis of the Holy Family*—O.S.F.

[]—*Sisters of the Missionary Helpers of the Holy Savior*

[3320]—*Sisters of the Presentation of the B.V.M.*—P.B.V.M.

[4100]—*Sisters of the Sorrowful Mother (Third Order of St. Francis)*—S.S.M.

[1720]—*Sisters of the Third Order Regular of St. Francis of the Congregation of Our Lady of Lourdes*—O.S.F.

DIOCESAN CEMETERIES

WINONA. *Catholic Cemeteries of Winona*, 55 W. Sanborn St., P.O. Box 588, 55987. Tel: 507-454-4643; Fax: 507-454-8106. Mr. Lawrence J. Dose, Dir. Fin.

INTER-PAROCHIAL CATHOLIC CEMETERIES

WINONA. *Saint Mary's Cemetery*, 1190 Sugar Loaf Rd., 55987.

AUSTIN. *Calvary Cemetery, St. Augustine Church*, 405 Fourth St., N.W., 55912-3091. 1803 Fourth Ave., S.W., 55912.

MANKATO. *Calvary Cemetery*, P.O. Box 4143, 56002. 200 Goodyear Ave., 56001.

OWATONNA. *Sacred Heart Cemetery, c/o St. Joseph Church*, 512 S. Elm Ave., 55060-3399. Cedar Ave. & 22nd St., S.E.

ROCHESTER. *Calvary Cemetery*, 411 Lowry Ct., N.W, 55901.

NECROLOGY

† Eikens, Leroy F., (Retired)—Died Dec. 2, 2011

An asterisk (*) denotes an organization that has established tax-exempt status directly with the IRS and is not covered by the USCCB Group Ruling.

Diocese of Worcester

(Dioecesis Wigorniensis)

Most Reverend

ROBERT J. McMANUS

Bishop of Worcester; ordained May 27, 1978; appointed Auxiliary Bishop of Providence and Titular Bishop of Allegheny December 1, 1998; consecrated February 22, 1999; appointed Bishop of Worcester March 9, 2004; installed May 14, 2004. *Chancery Office: 49 Elm St., Worcester, MA 01609.*

Most Reverend

DANIEL P. REILLY, D.D.

Retired Bishop of Worcester; ordained May 30, 1953; appointed Bishop of Norwich June 17, 1975; consecrated August 6, 1975; appointed Bishop of Worcester October 27, 1994; installed December 8, 1994; retired March 9, 2004. *Res.: St. Paul Cathedral, 38 High St., Worcester, MA 01609.*

Chancery Office: 49 Elm St., Worcester, MA 01609. Tel: 508-791-7171; Fax: 508-754-2768.

Web: www.worcesterdiocese.org

Most Reverend

GEORGE E. RUEGER, D.D., V.G.

Retired Auxiliary Bishop of Worcester; ordained January 6, 1958; appointed Auxiliary Bishop of Worcester and Titular Bishop of Maronana January 19, 1987; consecrated February 25, 1987; retired January 25, 2005. *Res.: St. Stephen's Rectory, 16 Hamilton St., Worcester, MA 01604.*

ESTABLISHED JANUARY 14, 1950.

Square Miles 1,532.

Comprises the County of Worcester in the State of Massachusetts.

For legal titles of parishes and diocesan institutions, consult the Chancery Office.

STATISTICAL OVERVIEW

Personnel	
Bishop	1
Retired Bishops	2
Abbots	2
Priests: Diocesan Active in Diocese	132
Priests: Diocesan Active Outside Diocese	9
Priests: Retired, Sick or Absent	46
Number of Diocesan Priests	187
Religious Priests in Diocese	91
Total Priests in Diocese	278
Ordinations:	
Diocesan Priests	7
Religious Priests	2
Transitional Deacons	5
Permanent Deacons	8
Permanent Deacons in Diocese	108
Total Brothers	64
Total Sisters	265
Parishes	
Parishes	105
With Resident Pastor:	
Resident Diocesan Priests	93
Resident Religious Priests	2
Without Resident Pastor:	
Administered by Priests	10
Missions	4
Pastoral Centers	1
New Parishes Created	1
Closed Parishes	3
Professional Ministry Personnel:	
Brothers	1
Sisters	14
Lay Ministers	75
Welfare	
Catholic Hospitals	1
Total Assisted	248,569
Health Care Centers	2
Total Assisted	226
Homes for the Aged	3
Total Assisted	175
Residential Care of Children	1
Total Assisted	12
Day Care Centers	21
Total Assisted	1,860
Specialized Homes	2
Total Assisted	40
Special Centers for Social Services	6
Total Assisted	48,000
Educational	
Diocesan Students in Other Seminaries	25
Total Seminarians	25
Colleges and Universities	3
Total Students	8,863
High Schools, Diocesan and Parish	4
Total Students	1,588
High Schools, Private	5
Total Students	1,535
Elementary Schools, Diocesan and Parish	19
Total Students	3,831
Elementary Schools, Private	3
Total Students	392
Non-residential Schools for the Disabled	1
Total Students	23
Catechesis/Religious Education:	
High School Students	5,801
Elementary Students	18,551
Total Students under Catholic Instruction	40,609
Teachers in the Diocese:	
Priests	17
Sisters	28
Lay Teachers	1,173
Vital Statistics	
Receptions into the Church:	
Infant Baptism Totals	2,333
Minor Baptism Totals	159
Adult Baptism Totals	82
Received into Full Communion	171
First Communions	3,330
Confirmations	2,688
Marriages:	
Catholic	426
Interfaith	85
Total Marriages	511
Deaths	3,028
Total Catholic Population	301,000
Total Population	784,992

Former Bishops—His Eminence JOHN CARDINAL WRIGHT, D.D., S.T.D., ord. Dec. 8, 1935; appt. Titular Bishop of Aegea and Auxiliary Bishop of Boston, May 10, 1947; cons. June 30, 1947; transferred to new See of Worcester, Jan. 14, 1950; enthroned March 7, 1950; appt. Bishop of Pittsburgh, Jan. 28, 1959; created Cardinal, April 28, 1969; transferred to the Roman Curia Prefect, Sacred Congregation for the Clergy; died Aug. 10, 1979; Most Revs. BERNARD J. FLANAGAN, D.D., J.C.D., retired March 31, 1983; died Jan. 28, 1998; TIMOTHY J. HARRINGTON, D.D., retired Oct. 27, 1994; died March 23, 1997; DANIEL P. REILLY, D.D., ord. May 30, 1953; appt. Bishop of Norwich June 17, 1975; cons. Aug. 6, 1975; appt. Bishop of Worcester Oct. 27, 1994; installed Dec. 8, 1994; retired March 9, 2004.

Vicar General—Most Rev. GEORGE E. RUEGER, D.D., V.G. (Retired), St. Stephen's Rectory, 16 Hamilton St., Worcester, 01604. Tel: 508-755-3165.

Chancery Office—Rev. Msgr. THOMAS J. SULLIVAN, Chancellor. Tel: 508-929-4346; Fax: 508-754-2768; Mr. RAYMOND L. DELISLE, Vice Chancellor, 49 Elm St., Worcester, 01609. Tel: 508-929-4313.

Diocesan Co Directors of Fiscal Affairs—Mrs. CAROL A. ADAMS; Mr. JEROME JUSSAUME.

Director of Catholic Relief Services—Rev. Msgr. THOMAS J. SULLIVAN, 1052 Pleasant St., Worcester, 01602. Tel: 508-929-4346.

Diocesan Expansion Fund—Rev. Msgr. THOMAS J. SULLIVAN; Mr. PETER J. DAWSON, 49 Elm St., Worcester, 01609.

Diocesan Finance Committee—JOSEPH GIOVINO, Chm., 49 Elm St., Worcester, 01609.

Diocesan Tribunal—Address all communications to, 49 Elm St., Worcester, 01609. Tel: 508-791-7171.

Judicial Vicar and Vicar for Canonical Affairs—Rev. Msgr. F. STEPHEN PEDONE, J.C.L., 49 Elm St., Worcester, 01609.

Associate Judicial Vicar—Rev. PAUL T. O'CONNELL, J.C.D.

Judges—Rev. PAUL T. O'CONNELL, J.C.D.; Rev. Msgr. F. STEPHEN PEDONE, J.C.L.; Rev. BRICE A. LEAVINS, O.F.M.

Promoter of Justice—Sr. MARY L. WALSH, S.N.D., J.C.L.

Psychologist—Sr. MARY DANIEL MALLOY, R.S.M.

Auditor—Rev. BRICE A. LEAVINS, O.F.M.

Secretary to the Tribunal—EILEEN CHARBONNEAU.

Defenders of the Bond—Rev. Msgr. ANTHONY S. CZARNECKI, J.C.L.; Rev. RICHARD F. REIDY.

Advocates—Revs. THOMAS E. MAHONEY; JAMES P. KERRIGAN; GEORGE J. RIDICK; MICHAEL A. DIGERONIMO; WILLIAM F. SANDERS; TERENCE T. KILCOYNE, D.Min.

Notary—EILEEN CHARBONNEAU Address all requests for dispensations to: Diocesan Tribunal, 49 Elm St., Worcester, 01609.

Diocesan College of Consultors—Most Rev. GEORGE E. RUEGER, D.D., V.G. (Retired); Rev. Msgr. THOMAS J. SULLIVAN; Revs. H. EDWARD CHALMERS; JOSEPH M. NALLY; Rev. Msgr. FRANCIS T. GOGUEN; Rev. BRIAN P. O'TOOLE; Rev. Msgrs. F. STEPHEN PEDONE, J.C.L.; ROCCO M. PICCOLOMINI; FRANCIS J. SCOLLEN; Rev. JOSEPH F. SZWACH; Rev. Msgr. EDMOND T. TINSLEY, P.A. (Retired).

Deans—Rev. WALTER J. RILEY, Area I; Rev. Msgr. ROBERT K. JOHNSON, Area II; Revs. JAMES B. O'SHEA, Area III; WILLIAM F. SANDERS, Area IV;

PAUL M. LAPALME, Area V; MICHAEL F. ROSE, Area VI; Rev. Msgr. ANTHONY S. CZARNECKI, J.C.L., Area VII; Revs. STEVEN M. LABAIRE, Area VIII; DAVID B. GALONEK, Area IX; Rev. Msgr. FRANCIS T. GOGUEN, Area X; Revs. TIMOTHY M. BREWER, Area XI; JOSEPH J. JURGELONIS, Area XII; MARTIN P. DONAHUE, Area XIII (Retired).

Director of Priest Personnel—Rev. JOSE A. RODRIGUEZ.

Vicar for Religious—Sr. PAULA KELLEHER, S.S.J., 49 Elm St., Worcester, 01609. Tel: 508-791-7171.

Diocesan Offices and Directors

The Adopt-A-Student Endowment Trust—ROBERT PAPE, 49 Elm St., Worcester, 01609. Tel: 508-791-7171.

African Ministry—Rev. ANTHONY MPAGI, Chap., St. Peter, 929 Main St., Worcester, 01610. Tel: 508-752-4674.

Haitian Apostolate—Sr. JUDITH DUPUY, S.S.A., Dir. Tel: 508-929-4328.

Hmong Ministry—St. Anthony, Fitchburg, 01420. Tel: 978-342-4706. Rev. ROBERT D. BRUSO, Contact Person.

Vietnamese Ministry—Our Lady of Vilna, Worcester, 01610. Tel: 508-752-1825. Rev. TAM M. BUI.

Brazilian Ministry—Rev. ANSELMO GOMEZ, C.Ss.R., Office: 4 Caroline St., Worcester, 01604. Tel: 508-752-6364.

European Ministries—

Lithuanian Churches— St. John, Worcester. VACANT.

Polish Ministry—St. Joseph, Webster, 01570. Tel: 508-943-0467. Rev. Msgr. ANTHONY S. CZARNECKI, J.C.L., Natl. Delegate, Our Lady Czestochowa, Worcester; St. Andrew Bobola, Dudley; St. Joseph, Gardner; St. Hedwig, Southbridge; St. Stanislaus, West Warren.

Portuguese Ministry—St. Mary, Milford, 01757. Tel: 508-473-2000. Rev. RAYMOND M. GOODWIN.

Hispanic Ministry—

St. Paul—19 Chatham St., Worcester, 01609. Tel: 508-754-3195. Rev. ANGEL R. MATOS; Sr. MARIA DALLARI, X.M.M.; Deacon FRANCISCO ESCOBAR.

St. Peter—929 Main St., Worcester, 01610. Tel: 508-752-4674. Rev. MANUEL A. CLAVIJO; Sr. ANN MARSHALL, R.S.M.

St. Joan of Arc—570 Lincoln St., Worcester, 01605. Tel: 508-852-3232. Rev. JOSE A. RODRIGUEZ; Sr. YALILE RUIZ, R.O.D.A.

Our Lady of Providence—7 Auburn St., Worcester, 01605. Tel: 508-755-3820. Rev. WILLIAM E. REISER, S.J.; Sr. REBECA SANCHEZ, X.M.M.

St. John—149 Chestnut St., Clinton, 01510. Tel: 978-368-0366. Rev. MIGUEL PAGAN; Sr. PAULA CORMIER, P.B.V.M.

St. Francis—63 Sheridan St., Fitchburg, 01420. Tel: 978-342-9651. Rev. EMERITO ORTIZ.

Holy Spirit—45 Metcalf St., Gardner, 01440. Tel: 978-632-3333. Rev. JESUS E. MARTINEZ; Deacon STANLEY H. BACZEWSKI.

Sacred Heart of Jesus—166 Cross St., Gardner, 01440. Tel: 978-632-0237. Rev. EDWIN MONTANA.

Holy Trinity—69 Lincoln Terr., Leominster, 01453. Tel: 978-534-5258. Chaplain: Rev. MIGUEL PAGAN.

St. Mary—27 Pearl St., Milford, 01757. Tel: 508-473-2000. Rev. GUILLERMO J. OCHOA.

St. Mary—263 Hamilton St., Southbridge, 01550. Tel: 508-765-0394. Rev. PETER JOYCE; Sr. MARIA DE LOS ANGELES BALLESTERO, R.O.D.A.; Deacon TEODORO CAMACHO.

St. Louis—15 Lake St., Webster, 01570. Tel: 508-943-0240. Ms. NOELIA RIVERA.

St. Luke—70 W. Main St., Westborough, 01581. Tel: 508-366-5502. Rev. EDWIN A. GOMEZ; Sr. SOLEDAD CHACON, R.O.D.A.; ELENA TELLO.

Black Catholics: African American—St. Peter, 929 Main St., Worcester, 01610. Tel: 508-752-4674. Rev. Msgr. FRANCIS J. SCOLLEN, Contact Person.

Catholic Charities—10 Hammond St., Worcester, 01609. Tel: 508-798-0191.

Refugee Apostolate—Little Store, 27 Chandler St., Worcester, 01609. Tel: 508-831-7455.

Apostleship of Prayer and Eucharistic Crusade—Rev. THADDEUS X. STACHURA, Our Lady of Czestochowa, 34 Ward St., Worcester, 01610. Tel: 508-755-5959.

Apostolate for Healing—Rev. RALPH A. DIORIO, Dir., Mailing Address: P.O. Box 344, Auburn, 01501. Tel: 508-832-7892.

Archivist—Rev. Msgr. THOMAS J. SULLIVAN, Chancellor, 49 Elm St., Worcester, 01609. Tel: 508-929-4346.

The Annual Partners in Charity Appeal—Mr. MICHAEL GILLESPIE, 49 Elm St., Worcester, 01609. Tel: 508-929-4346.

Diocesan Building Commission Members—Rev. Msgrs. THOMAS J. SULLIVAN; ROBERT K. JOHNSON; Revs. JOHN FOLEY, Chm.; THADDEUS X. STACHURA; Mr. JORDAN O'CONNOR; Mr JOHN LAURING; Mr RICHARD BREAGY, Staff; Mr. ROBERT JOHNSON; Mr. KEVIN SEAMAN.

Campus Ministry—Rev. PETER J. SCANLON, S.T.L., Vicar (Retired), 35 Julio Dr., Shrewsbury, 01545.

Catholic Charities—CATHERINE LOEFFLER, Dir., 10 Hammond St., Worcester, 01610-1513. Tel: 508-798-0191 (Refer to separate listings for detailed information on Catholic Charities and related organizations).

Diocesan Cemeteries Office—260 Cambridge St., Worcester, 01603. Tel: 508-757-7415. Mr. ROBERT ACKERMAN, Dir.

Charismatic Renewal, Office of—Sr. CATHERINE MARIE WALSH, R.S.M., Liaison, 72 Birmingham Ct., Milford, 01757. Tel: 508-381-0987. Email: scmwalsh@yahoo.com.

Clergy Benefit Plan—Rev. EDWARD D. NICCOLLS, Treas., Mailing Address: P.O. Box 498, North Uxbridge, 01538; Ms. MARY LOU VERLA, Admin. Tel: 508-887-8623.

Communication Office—Mr. RAYMOND L. DELISLE, Dir., 49 Elm St., Worcester, 01609. Tel: 508-929-4313; Mr. STEPHEN KAUFMAN, TV Ministry Production Mgr. Tel: 508-791-2039.

Office of Ongoing Priestly Formation—Rev. RONALD G. FALCO, Dir., 40 Brattle St., Worcester, 01606. Tel: 508-853-0183.

Cursillo—Rev. ROBERT A. GRATTAROTI, Dir., Mailing Address: P.O. Box 338, Charlton City, 01508. Tel: 508-248-7862.

Stewardship and Development Office— The Annual Partners in Charity Appeal, Annual Catholic School Appeal. Mr. MICHAEL GILLESPIE, Dir. Tel: 508-929-4368.

Diocesan Expansion Fund—49 Elm St., Worcester, 01609. Rev. Msgr. THOMAS J. SULLIVAN. Members: Rev. Msgr. JOHN E. DORAN; Rev. RICHARD A. JAKUBAUSKAS; Mr. TERRENCE SULLIVAN; Mr. JEROME JUSSAUME, Staff; MARTIN CONNORS JR.; JOHN GRAHAM; Mr. PETER J. DAWSON, Chm.; WILLIAM JONES.

Diocesan Scouts—Boy Scout Office/Girl Scout Office, 49 Elm St., Worcester, 01609. Tel: 508-791-7171. Rev. JAMES S. MAZZONE, Chap.

Ecumenical and Interreligious Affairs, Diocesan Office for—VACANT.

Evangelization, Office of—VACANT.

Office of Marriage and Family—ALLISON LEDOUX, Dir., 49 Elm St., Worcester, 01609. Tel: 508-929-4311.

Finance Office—Mr. JEROME D. JUSSAUME, Co Dir.; Mrs. CAROL A. ADAMS, Co Dir., 49 Elm St., Worcester, 01609. Tel: 508-791-7171.

Haitian Apostolate of the Diocese of Worcester—Sr. JUDITH DUPUY, S.S.A., Dir., 49 Elm St., Worcester, 01609. Tel: 508-929-4328; Fax: 508-753-7180. Email: sjudith41@yahoo.com.

Holy Childhood Association—Most Rev. GEORGE E. RUEGER, D.D., V.G., Dir. (Retired), 16 Hamilton St., Worcester, 01604. Tel: 508-755-3165.

Meet-the-Father Ministry, Inc.—Mrs. EILEEN GEORGE, Contact Person, 363 Greenwood St., Millbury, 01527.

Newspaper— "The Catholic Free Press" Mrs. MARGARET M. RUSSELL, Exec. Editor, 51 Elm St., Worcester, 01609. Tel: 508-757-6387.

Office for Divine Worship—Rev. Msgr. ROBERT K. JOHNSON, Dir.; ELIZABETH MARCIL, 19 Chatham St., Worcester, 01609. Tel: 508-798-0417.

Permanent Diaconate—Deacon ANTHONY R. SUROZENSKI, Dir., 49 Elm St., Worcester, 01609. Tel: 508-929-4332.

Presbyteral Council—Most Rev. ROBERT JOSEPH MCMANUS, Pres.; Rev. Msgrs. F. STEPHEN PEDONE, J.C.L., Ex Officio; THOMAS J. SULLIVAN, Ex Officio; ROBERT K. JOHNSON; Revs. WALTER J. RILEY; DAVID B. GALONEK; Rev. Msgr. ANTHONY S. CZARNECKI, J.C.L.; Revs. WILLIAM F. SANDERS; JOSEPH J. JURGELONIS; STEVEN M. LABAIRE; TIMOTHY M. BREWER; JAMES B. O'SHEA; PAUL M. LAPALME, Chm.; JOHN E. KELLEY (Retired); MICHAEL F. ROSE; ROBERT D. BRUSO, Chancery Bldg.: 49 Elm St., Worcester, 01609. Tel: 508-791-7171.

Priests' Personnel Board—Rev. JOSE A. RODRIGUEZ, Dir., 570 Lincoln St., Worcester, 01605. Tel: 508-852-3232.

Ministry to Retired Priests—Sr. MARY ANN BARTELL, C.S.E., 188 Old Worcester Rd., Charlton, 01507. Tel: 508-868-9239.

Respect Life—ALLISON LEDOUX, 49 Elm St., Worcester, 01609. Tel: 508-791-7171.

Propagation of the Faith—Most Rev. GEORGE E. RUEGER, D.D., V.G., Dir. (Retired), 16 Hamilton St., Worcester, 01604. Tel: 508-755-3165.

Religious Education Office—ELIZABETH MARCIL, Dir., 49 Elm St., Worcester, 01609. Tel: 508-929-4303.

St. Paul Catholic Schools Consortium—MARCUS MORAN, Chm., 49 Elm St., Worcester, 01609. Tel: 508-929-4317; Fax: 508-929-4386.

School Department—Dr. DELMA JOSEPHSON, Supt. Associate Superintendents: Mr. WILLIAM J. MULFORD; Sr. MARGUERITE TIMOTHY YOUNG, S.N.D.

Diocesan Hispanic Apostolate—Rev. ANGEL R. MATOS, Dir., 38 High St., Worcester, 01609.

St. Vincent dePaul Society—— Central District Council Mrs. FRANCES PIKE, Pres.; Rev. WILLIAM E. CHAMPLIN, Spiritual Dir.

Northern Worcester County District Council—JOHN YOVINO, Pres.

Central Worcester County District Council—ROBERT F. PIKE, Pres.

South Worcester County District Council—MARIE BASTONE, Pres.

Tri-Conference Retirement Fund for Religious—Sr. PAULA KELLEHER, S.S.J., Diocesan Coord., 49 Elm St., Worcester, 01609. Tel: 508-791-7171.

Director of Priest Personnel—Rev. JOSE A. RODRIGUEZ, 570 Lincoln St., Worcester, 01605.

Vicar for Religious—Sr. PAULA KELLEHER, S.S.J., 49 Elm St., Worcester, 01609. Tel: 508-791-7171.

Vietnamese Apostolate—Rev. TAM M. BUI, 153 Sterling St., Worcester, 01610. Tel: 508-752-1825.

Victim Assistance Coordinator—FRANCES J. NUGENT. Tel: 508-929-4363. Email: fnugent@worcesterdiocese.org.

Vocation Office—Rev. JAMES S. MAZZONE, Dir., 51 Illinois St., Worcester, 01610. Tel: 508-799-2792.

Minister to Priests—Rev. JOSEPH M. NALLY, Mailing Address: P.O. Box 488, North Oxford, 01537.

Worcester Diocesan Commission for Women—ANNE ARCONA, Chm., 21 Searhill Rd., Boylston, 01505. Tel: 508-869-6748.

Youth Ministry—Deacon EDUARDUS MEILUS, Dir. Youth Ministry, Office, 120 Hill St., Whitinsville, 01588. Tel: 508-234-0346.

CLERGY, PARISHES, MISSIONS AND PAROCHIAL SCHOOLS

CITY OF WORCESTER

(WORCESTER COUNTY)

1—ST. PAUL CATHEDRAL (1866) Rev. Msgr. Robert K. Johnson, Rector; Rev. Angel R. Matos; Deacons Francisco Escobar; Isreal Fernandez; Franklon Lizardo; Colin Novick; Anthony J. Xatse. In Res., Most Rev. Daniel P. Reilly.
Res.: 38 High St., 01609. Tel: 508-799-4193; Fax: 508-752-6308. Email: msgrrkj@cathedralofsaintpaul.com. Web: www.cathedralofsaintpaul.com.
Catechesis/Religious Program—Tel: 508-755-1414; Fax: 508-755-1414. Students 311.

2—ST. ANDREW THE APOSTLE (1954), Now a mission of St. Peter, Worcester.

3—ASCENSION (1911) Closed. For inquiries for parish records, please see St. John's, Worcester.

4—ST. BERNARD (1916) Closed. Merged with Our Lady of Fatima, Worcester to form Our Lady of Providence, Worcester.

5—BLESSED SACRAMENT (1912) Rev. Chester J. Misiewicz.
Res.: 551 Pleasant St., 01602. Tel: 508-755-5291; Fax: 508-755-6891. Email: blessedsacrament@charter.net. Web: www.blessedsacrament.us.
Catechesis/Religious Program—Epiphany House, Tel: 508-752-4368. Students 133.

6—ST. CASIMIR (1894), (Lithuanian), Closed. For inquiries for parish records contact St. John, Worcester.

7—ST. CATHERINE OF SWEDEN (1952) Merged with Sacred Heart of Jesus, Worcester to form Sacred Heart of Jesus-St. Catherine of Sweden, Worcester.

8—ST. CHARLES BORROMEO (1954) Closed. For inquiries for parish records please see Blessed Sacrament, Worcester.

9—CHRIST THE KING (1936) Rev. Msgr. Thomas J. Sullivan; Rev. John M. Lizewski; Deacons Joseph M. Baniukiewicz; Michael Chase.
Res.: 1052 Pleasant St., 01602. Tel: 508-754-5361; Fax: 508-753-0448.
Catechesis/Religious Program—Tel: 508-752-5514. Lauren E. Bjork, C.R.E. Students 266.

10—ST. CHRISTOPHER (1956) Rev. Stanley F. Krutcik; Deacon Christopher C. Meyers.
Res.: 950 W. Boylston St., 01606. Tel: 508-853-1492; Fax: 508-853-4338. Email:

parish@stchristopherparishworcester.org.
Catechesis/Religious Program—Tel: 508-853-3302; Fax: 508-854-4338. Students 83.

11—St. George (1951) Revs. Ronald G. Falco; Michael N. Lavallee.
Res.: 40 Brattle St., 01606. Tel: 508-853-0183; Fax: 508-854-0864. Email: office@saintgeo.com. Web: www.saintgeo.com.
Catechesis/Religious Program—Tel: 508-852-1784. Peggy Moynahan, D.R.E. Students 349.

12—Holy Family Parish Rev. Richard G. Roger.
Rectory—5 Whitman Rd., 01609. Tel: 508-754-6722; Fax: 508-438-0368.
Church: *St. Joseph Church*, 35 Hamilton St., 01604.
Catechesis/Religious Program—Michelle Zellmer, C.R.E. Students 44.

13—Holy Name of Jesus (1893), (French), Closed. For inquiries for parish records, please see Holy Family, Worcester.

14—Immaculate Conception (1873) Rev. Walter J. Riley.
Res.: 353 Grove St., 01605. Tel: 508-754-8419; Fax: 508-754-8508. Web: www.icworc.com.
Catechesis/Religious Program—Father Connors Center, Tel: 508-791-5887; Fax: 508-754-8508. Web: www.icworc.com. Students 71.

15—St. Joan of Arc (1950) Rev. Jose A. Rodriguez; Sisters Yalile Ruiz, R.O.D.A., Pastoral Assoc.; Frances Barry, S.S.J., Pastoral Assoc.
Res.: 570 Lincoln St., 01605. Tel: 508-852-3232; Fax: 508-852-3223. Email: stjoan570@hotmail.com. Web: www.stjoanofarcworcester.com.
Catechesis/Religious Program—Sindy Collazo, C.R.E. Students 225.

16—St. John's (1834) Rev. John F. Madden; Rev. Msgr. Edmond T. Tinsley (Retired).
Res.: 44 Temple St., 01604. Tel: 508-756-7165; Fax: 508-754-5153. Web: stjohnsworcester.org.
Catechesis/Religious Program—Mrs. Donna Mastrovito, D.R.E. Students 113.

17—St. Margaret Mary (1922) Closed. For inquiries for parish records, please see St. Anne, Shrewsbury.

18—Notre Dame des Canadiens - St. Joseph (1869), (French), [CEM] Closed. For inquiries for parish records please see Holy Family, Worcester.

19—Our Lady of Czestochowa (1903), (Polish), Revs. Thaddeus X. Stachura; Ryszard Polek.
Res.: 34 Ward St., 01610. Tel: 508-755-5959; Fax: 508-767-1644. Email: olc.worcester@verion.net.
School—St. Mary's Elementary, (Grades PreK-6), 50 Richland St., 01610. Tel: 508-753-0484; Fax: 508-767-1384. Corey E. Maloney, Prin. Lay Teachers 8; Students 124.
High School—St. Mary's Jr. & Sr. High School, (Grades 7-12) Tel: 508-753-1170; Fax: 508-795-0560. Michael E. Dudek, Prin. Lay Teachers 16; Students 144.
Catechesis/Religious Program—Students 105.

20—Our Lady of Fatima (1952), (Spanish), Closed. Merged with St. Bernard, Worcester to form Our Lady of Providence, Worcester.

21—Our Lady of Loreto (1966) Rev. Charles R. Armey; Deacon Paul T. Audette, Pastoral Assoc.
Res.: 33 Massasoit Rd., 01604. Tel: 508-753-5001; Fax: 508-754-1537.
Catechesis/Religious Program—37 Massasoit Rd., 01604. Tel: 508-799-2445. JoAnn Bafaro, D.R.E. Students 36.

22—Our Lady of Lourdes (1949) Rev. James B. O'Shea. In Res., Revs. Francis J. Roach; Robert E. Kelley (Retired).
Res.: 1290 Grafton St., 01604. Tel: 508-757-0789; Fax: 508-757-0048. Email: lourdeslady@aol.com.
Catechesis/Religious Program—Tel: 508-753-5773. Jo-Ann Bafaro, D.R.E. Students 92.

23—Our Lady of Mt. Carmel and St. Ann (1872), (Italian—Irish), Rev. Msgr. Rocco M. Piccolomini.
Res.: 53 E. Central St., 01605. Tel: 508-797-4546; Fax: 508-755-3506. Web: www.mtcarmel.ws.
Catechesis/Religious Program—Tel: 508-791-6139. Joan D'Argenis, D.R.E. Students 158.

24—Our Lady of Providence Parish Rev. Edward M. Ryan.
Rectory—7 Auburn St., 01605. Tel: 508-755-3820; Fax: 508-755-7196.
St. Bernard Church: 228 Lincoln St., 01605.
Catechesis/Religious Program—Students 41.

25—Our Lady of the Angels (1916) Rev. Charles F. Monroe; Karen Barrows, Pastoral Asst. In Res., Rev. Terrence Dougherty, O.C.D.
Res.: 1222 Main St., 01603. Tel: 508-791-0951; Fax: 508-753-9531. Web: www.ourladyoftheangels.org.
School—(Grades PreK-8), 1220 Main St., Rear, 01603. Tel: 508-752-5609; Fax: 508-798-9634. Doreen J. Albert, Prin. Lay Teachers 26; Students 270.
Catechesis/Religious Program—Students 195.

26—Our Lady of the Rosary (1911) Rev. William F. Sanders.
Res.: 23 Fales St., 01606. Tel: 508-853-1640; Fax: 508-853-2426.
Catechesis/Religious Program—Father Riley Center, 9 Emerson Rd., 01606. Tel: 508-852-5474. Sr. Irene Moran, M.P.V., D.R.E. Students 170.

27—Our Lady of Vilna (1925), (Lithuanian—Vietnamese), Rev. Peter Tam Bui. In Res., Rev. Son Anh Nguyen.
Res.: 153 Sterling St., St. 2, 01610. Tel: 508-752-1825; Fax: 508-752-9245.
Catechesis/Religious Program—Students 185.

28—St. Peter (1884) Rev. Msgr. Francis J. Scollen; Revs. Manuel Clavijo; Donald C. Ouellette; Deacons Robert Devine; Scott R. Reisinger; George Estremera; Sr. Ann Marshall, R.S.M., Pastoral Assoc.
Res.: 929 Main St., 01610. Tel: 508-752-4674; Fax: 508-767-1511. Email: stpeters_standrewsparishes@verizon.net.
Catechesis/Religious Program—Tel: 508-752-0797. Students 155.
Mission—St. Andrew the Apostle Mission Spaulding St., 01603. Tel: 508-752-4674; Fax: 508-767-1511.

29—Sacred Heart of Jesus-St. Catherine of Sweden (1880) Rev. George J. Ridick; Deacon James Denning.
Res.: 596 Cambridge St., 01610. Tel: 508-752-1608; 508-753-2555; Fax: 508-757-2462. Web: www.home.catholicweb.com/sacredheartworcester.
Catechesis/Religious Program—Students 36.

30—St. Stephen's (1887) Rev. H. Edward Chalmers; Deacon Bruce Vidito Sr. In Res., Most Rev. George E. Rueger (Retired); Rev. Joseph P. Mahoney.
Res.: 16 Hamilton St., 01604. Tel: 508-755-3165; Fax: 508-755-0937.
School—(Grades PreK-8), 355 Grafton St., 01604. Tel: 508-755-3209; Fax: 508-770-1052. Ms. Laurie Murphy, Prin. Sisters 1; Lay Teachers 16; Students 178.
Catechesis/Religious Program—Jean Orawsky, D.R.E. Students 102.

OUTSIDE THE CITY OF WORCESTER

(In the County of Worcester)

Ashburnham, St. Denis (1951) [CEM] Rev. John E. Horgan; Deacon Richard DesJardins.
Res.: 85 Main St., P.O. Box 418, 01430. Tel: 978-827-5806; Fax: 978-827-1191. Email: stdenis@comcast.net.
Catechesis/Religious Program—Tel: 978-827-4892. Students 310.

Athol

1—St. Francis (1912), (Lithuanian), Revs. Richard A. Jakubauskas; Krzysztof Korcz; Deacon Scott Colley.
Res.: 105 Main St., 01331. Tel: 978-249-3361.
Catechesis/Religious Program—Included in Our Lady Immaculate. Students 1.

2—Our Lady Immaculate (1882) Revs. Richard A. Jakubauskas; Krzysztof Korcz; Deacon James L. Linderman.
Res.: 192 School St., 01331-2399. Tel: 978-249-2738; Fax: 978-249-0447. Email: ourladyrectory@hotmail.com. Web: www.nqcatholic.org.
Catechesis/Religious Program—Tel: 978-249-7690; Fax: 978-249-7639. Donna Findlay, D.R.E. Students 126.
Mission—Our Lady Queen of Heaven Rte. 68, South Royalston, Worcester Co. 01368. Tel: 978-249-4103.

Auburn

1—St. Joseph's (1907) Revs. Edward D. Niccolls; Patrick Ssekyole; Deacon Peter Ryan.
Res.: 194 Oxford St. N., 01501. Tel: 508-832-2074; Fax: 508-832-8894. Email: stjoesbulletin@charter.net. Web: www.stjosephauburn.org.
Catechesis/Religious Program—Tel: 508-832-0492; Fax: 508-832-6629. Lisa Wass, D.R.E. Students 580.

2—North American Martyrs (1952) Rev. John F. Gee.
Res.: 8 Wyoma Dr., 01501. Tel: 508-798-8779; Fax: 508-791-6614. Email: namoffice@verizon.net. Web: www.auburncatholiccommunity.org.
Catechesis/Religious Program—Tel: 508-798-0612; Fax: 508-798-0612. Email: namparish@aol.com. Joan Sundstrom, C.R.E. Students 254.

Baldwinville, St. Vincent De Paul (1955) Rev. Francis A. Roberge; Deacon James A. Connor.
Mailing Address: P.O. Box 14, 01436.
Res.: 18 Pleasant St., 01436. Tel: 978-939-8851; Fax: 978-939-2120. Email: stvindepaul05@aol.com. P.O. Box 14, 01436.
Church: 1 Forest St., 01436.
Catechesis/Religious Program—Tel: 978-939-8290. Mrs. Jennifer McNeaney, Coord. Students 79.

Barre, St. Joseph (1896) [CEM] Rev. Thomas H. Hultquist.
Res.: 90 Common St., P.O. Box 598, 01005. Tel: 978-355-4463; Fax: 978-355-0136.
Catechesis/Religious Program—Tel: 978-355-6402. Students 66.

Berlin, St. Joseph the Good Provider (1973) Rev. Robert M. Spellman. In Res., Deacon Joseph V. Clonan.
Res.: 52 West St., Box 284, 01503-0284. Tel: 978-838-9922; Fax: 978-838-9933.
Catechesis/Religious Program—Mary Jane Ciesluk, D.R.E. Students 121.

Blackstone

1—St. Paul (1850) [CEM] Rev. Dennis Timothy O'Mara.
Res.: 48 St. Paul St., 01504. Tel: 508-883-6726; Fax: 508-883-2079. Email: stpaulblackstone@comcast.net. Web: www.stpaulblackstone.org.
Catechesis/Religious Program—Tel: 508-883-2590. Email: religiousedstpaulblackstone.org. Students 246.

2—St. Theresa (1929), (French), Rev. Paul M. Bomba.
Res.: 630 Rathbun St., 01504. Tel: 508-883-7206; Fax: 508-883-5250. Email: theresaparish630@verizon.net.
Catechesis/Religious Program—Tel: 508-883-7527. Students 106.

Bolton, St. Francis Xavier (1954) Merged with St. Theresa's, Harvard to form Holy Trinity, Harvard.

Boylston, St. Mary of the Hills (1952) Rev. Paul J. Tougas; Marcella Wilson, Pastoral Assoc.
Res.: 620 Cross St., 01505. Tel: 508-869-6771.
Catechesis/Religious Program—Tel: 508-869-6771; Fax: 508-869-0418. Anne Dowen, D.R.E. (K-10). Students 225.

Brookfield, St. Mary's (1885) Rev. David B. Galonek.
Res.: 10 Milk St., West Brookfield, 01585. Tel: 508-867-6469; Fax: 508-867-3670.
Catechesis/Religious Program—Students 37.

Charlton City, St. Joseph's (1900) Revs. Robert A. Grattaroti; Nicholas Desimone; J. Normand Tremblay, Senior Priest; Deacons Lawrence F. Miskell; Robert F. Dio.
Res.: 10 H. Putnam Ext., Box 338, 01508. Tel: 508-248-7862; Fax: 508-248-5832. Email: stjoecharlton@aol.com. Web: stjosephcharlton.com.
Catechesis/Religious Program—Tel: 508-248-7986. Elizabeth Cotrupi, D.R.E. (High School); Oscar Rivera Jr., D.R.E. (Junior High); Sr. Agnes Patricia, D.R.E. (Grades 1-5). Students 469.

Clinton

1—St. John the Guardian of Our Lady (1849) [CEM] Revs. Thomas V. Walsh; Miguel Pagan; Deacon William Griffin; Sisters Paula Cormier, P.B.V.M., Pastoral Assoc. & Hispanic Min.; Sheila Finnigan, S.N.D., Pastoral Assoc.
Res.: 149 Chestnut St., 01510. Tel: 978-368-0366; Fax: 978-368-4359. Web: www.stjohnsclinton.org.
Catechesis/Religious Program—80 Union St., 01510. Tel: 508-368-0052; Fax: 978-368-4360. Students 554.

2—Our Lady of Jasna Gora (1913), (Polish), Closed. For inquiries for parish records please see St. John the Guardian of Our Lady, Clinton.

3—Our Lady of the Rosary (1909) Closed. For inquiries for parish records please see St. John the Guardian of Our Lady, Clinton.

Douglas, St. Denis (1870) [CEM] Rev. William N. Cormier.
Res.: 23 Manchaug St., 01516. Tel: 508-476-2002; Fax: 508-476-2022. Email: wcormier@saintdenischurch.com.
Catechesis/Religious Program—Students 523.

Dudley

1—St. Andrew Bobola (1963), (Polish), [JC] Rev. Joseph F. Szwach.
Res.: 54 W. Main St., P.O. Box 98, 01571. Tel: 508-943-5633; Fax: 508-949-6701.
Catechesis/Religious Program—Students 57.

2—St. Anthony (1905) [CEM] Rev. Paul F. Campbell; Deacon William White.
Res.: 22 Dudley Hill Rd., Box 277, 01571-0277. Tel: 508-943-0470; Fax: 508-943-5663.
Catechesis/Religious Program—Tel: 508-949-0335. Email: stanthonyreled@charter.net. Linda Brink, D.R.E. Students 211.

East Brookfield, St. John the Baptist (1952) Rev. George A. Charland.
Res.: 121 Blaine Ave., 01515. Tel: 508-867-3738; Fax: 508-867-3301. Email: stjohnseb01515@verizon.net.
Catechesis/Religious Program—Tel: 508-885-4506. Students 77.

East Templeton, Holy Cross (1952) Rev. Joseph J. Jurgelonis; Deacon Richard J. Tatro.
Res.: 25 Lake Ave., P.O. Box 418, 01438. Tel: 978-632-2121; Fax: 978-630-3890. Email: hcchurchet@comcast.net.
Catechesis/Religious Program—Tel: 978-632-2194. Students 169.
Mission—St. Martin 247 State Rd., Otter River, 01436. Tel: 978-939-5588; Fax: 978-939-2305.
Catechesis/Religious Program—Students 31.

FISKDALE, ST. ANNE'S AND ST. PATRICK'S (1883) [CEM] Revs. Peter Precourt, A.A., Shrine Dir. & Pastor; Salvatore Musuande, A.A.; Philip Bonvouloir; Deacons Richard Olson; Steve Miller.
Res.: 16 Church St., 01518. Tel: 508-347-7338; Fax: 508-347-2982. Web: stannestpat.org.
Catechesis/Religious Program—Tel: 508-347-9353; Fax: 508-347-2496. Students 299.

FITCHBURG

1—ST. ANTHONY OF PADUA (1908), (Italian), Revs. Robert D. Bruso; Edwin Montana; Deacon Salvatore Tantillo.
Res.: 2 Beekman St., 01420. Tel: 978-342-4706; Fax: 978-342-8160. Email: stanthonyfitchburg@comcast.net. Web: stanthonyfitchburg.net.
Church: 84 Salem St., 01420.
School—(Grades PreK-8), 123 Salem St., 01420. Tel: 978-345-7785; Fax: 978-342-5110. Email: principal@stanthony.net. Web: stanthonyschool-.net. John Ginnity, Prin.; Patricia Joubert, Librarian. Lay Teachers 18; Students 237.
Catechesis/Religious Program— Ellen DePatie, D.R.E. Students 79.

2—ST. BERNARD (1847) [CEM] Merged with and located at St. Camilus de Lellis, Fitchburg.

3—ST. BERNARD PARISH AT ST. CAMILLUS DE LELLIS (1953) Rev. Joseph M. Dolan; Deacon Benjamin A. Nogueira.
Res.: 333 Mechanic St., 01420. Tel: 978-342-7921; Fax: 978-345-2688. Email: st.camillus@verizon.net. Web: www.saintcamillusparish.org.
Catechesis/Religious Program—Students 145.

4—ST. CAMILLUS DE LELLIS (1953) Merged with St. Bernard, Fitchburg to form St. Bernard Parish at St. Camillus de Lellis, Fitchburg.

5—ST. FRANCIS OF ASSISI (1903) Rev. Emerito Ortiz.
Res.: 63 Sheridan, 01420. Tel: 978-342-9651; Fax: 978-342-7936. Web: www.saintfrancis-fitchburg.com.
Catechesis/Religious Program—Tel: 978-342-3521. Yesenia Quinones, D.R.E. Students 78.

6—IMMACULATE CONCEPTION (1886), (French), Closed. For inquiries for parish records please see St. Joseph Parish, Fitchburg.

7—ST. JOSEPH'S (1890) [CEM] Rev. Richard F. Trainor; Deacon James Couture. In Res., Revs. Laurie L. Leger, M.S.; John Hughes, M.S.
Res.: 49 Woodland St., 01420. Tel: 978-345-7997; Fax: 978-345-7678.
Catechesis/Religious Program—Tel: 978-345-7997. Bette Brunell, D.R.E. Students 67.

8—MADONNA OF THE HOLY ROSARY (1955) Closed. For inquiries for parish records please see St. Joseph, Fitchburg.

9—SACRED HEART OF JESUS (1878), (Irish), Closed. For inquiries for parish records please see St. Joseph, Fitchburg.

GARDNER

1—HOLY SPIRIT (1955) Rev. Thomas M. Tokarz; Deacon Stanley H. Baczewski.
Res.: 45 Metcalf St., 01440. Tel: 978-632-3333; Fax: 978-632-3630.
Catechesis/Religious Program—Holy Spirit & St. Joseph Combined Rel. Educ. Prog. Students 62.

2—ST. JOSEPH'S (1908), (Polish), [CEM] Rev. Thomas M. Tokarz.
Res.: 358 Pleasant St., 01440. Tel: 978-632-0375; Fax: 978-632-1282.
Catechesis/Religious Program—Combined with Holy Spirit, Gardner. Students 14.

3—OUR LADY OF THE HOLY ROSARY (1884) [CEM] Rev. Brian P. O'Toole.
Res.: 135 Nichols St., 01440. Tel: 978-632-0253; Fax: 978-630-1773.
School—(Grades PreK-8), 99 Nichols St., 01440. Tel: 978-632-8656; Fax: 978-630-1433. Email: d.bresnahan@holyrosaryschool.org. Web: www.holyrosaryschool.org. Lay Teachers 20; Students 267.
Catechesis/Religious Program—Students 136.

4—SACRED HEART OF JESUS (1874) [CEM] Revs. Brian P. O'Toole; Frederick D. Fraini III; Deacon Paul J. Carrier.
Res. & Parish Hall: 135 Nichols St., 01440. Tel: 978-632-0253; Fax: 978-630-2459. Email: shoffice2011@gmail.com. Web: www.sacredheartgardner.org.
Parish Center & The Caring Place—100 Central St., 01440. Tel: 978-632-0217 (Deacon's Office).
School—*Sacred Heart of Jesus School*, (Grades PreK-8), 53 Lynde St., 01440. Tel: 978-632-0950; Fax: 978-630-2448. Maureen Lapan, Prin. Lay Teachers 19; Students 159.
Catechesis/Religious Program—Tel: 978-632-0218. Students 90.
Day Care—Tel: 978-632-5745. Mrs. Jane Pineo, Dir.

GILBERTVILLE, ST. ALOYSIUS (1872) [CEM] Rev. Richard Lembo (PRT).
Res.: 58 Church St., P.O. Box 542, 01031-0542. Tel: 413-477-6493; Fax: 413-477-0140.
Catechesis/Religious Program—Students 35.
Mission—*St. Augustine* 98 Church Ln., Wheelwright, Hardwick Co. 01094.

GRAFTON, ST. PHILIP'S (1869) [CEM] Rev. Kenneth Cardinale.
12 West St., 01519. Tel: 508-839-3325; Fax: 508-839-1310.
Catechesis/Religious Program—Tel: 508-839-9130. Students 104.

HARVARD

1—HOLY TRINITY (2009) Rev. Terence T. Kilcoyne.
15 Still River Rd., P.O. Box 746, 01451. Tel: 978-456-3563; Fax: 978-456-8352. Email: htpboltonharvard@aol.com. Web: www.htpboltonharvard.org.
Catechesis/Religious Program—Tel: 978-456-8807. Students 485.

2—ST. THERESA'S (1950) Merged with St. Francis Xavier, Bolton to form Holy Trinity, Harvard.

HOPEDALE, SACRED HEART OF JESUS (1935) Rev. William C. Konicki; Deacons Joseph Manella; Roland R. Michaud; Pam Chaplin, Ministry Coord.
Res.: 187 Hopedale St., 01747. Tel: 508-473-1900; Fax: 508-473-1745. Email: parishoffice@shchopedale.org. Web: www.shchopedale.org.
Catechesis/Religious Program—Tel: 508-473-1701. Students 622.

JEFFERSON, ST. MARY (1884) [CEM] Rev. Andre N. Remillard.
Res.: 114 Princeton St., P.O. Box 2200, 01522. Tel: 508-829-4508; Fax: 508-829-0429. Email: stmaryjeff@charterinternet.com. Web: www.stmarysjeff.com.
Catechesis/Religious Program—Tel: 508-829-6758. Email: stmaryreled@charterinternet.com. Students 546.

LANCASTER, IMMACULATE CONCEPTION (1915) Rev. Edward P. Lettic; Deacon Robert Connor Jr.
Res.: 28 Packard St., P.O. Box 95, 01523. Tel: 978-365-6582; Fax: 978-365-3097.
Catechesis/Religious Program—Students 104.

LEICESTER

1—ST. ALOYSIUS-ST. JUDE (1904) Rev. Peter H. White.
Res.: 491 Pleasant St., 01524. Tel: 508-892-8296; Fax: 508-892-9054.
Catechesis/Religious Program—Mrs. Cynthia Garabedian, C.R.E. Students 89.

2—ST. JOSEPH (1851) [CEM] Rev. Robert A. Loftus.
Res.: 759 Main St., 01524. Tel: 508-892-7407; Fax: 508-892-4753. Web: www.stjoseph-stpiusx.com.
Catechesis/Religious Program—Tel: 508-892-0660. Combined with St. Pius X. Students 80.

3—ST. PIUS X (1956) Rev. Robert A. Loftus.
Mailing Address: 759 Main St., 01524. Tel: 508-892-7407; Fax: 508-892-4753.
Church: 1161 Main St., 01524.
Catechesis/Religious Program— Combined with St. Joseph's, Leicester.

LEOMINSTER

1—ST. ANNA (1937), (Italian), Rev. James B. Callahan.
Res.: 199 Lancaster St., 01453. Tel: 978-537-5293; Fax: 978-537-2950.
School—(Grades PreK-8) Tel: 978-534-4770; Fax: 978-466-1167. Web: www.stannaschool.org. Danielle Colvert, Prin. Priests 1; Lay Teachers 16; Students 185.
Catechesis/Religious Program—Students 100.

2—ST. CECILIA (1900), (French), [CEM] Rev. Msgr. Francis T. Goguen; Rev. Edward Michalski; Deacon Ronald J. Aubuchon.
Res.: 170 Mechanic St., 01453. Tel: 978-537-6541; Fax: 978-840-1965.
Catechesis/Religious Program—Tel: 978-537-4673. Patricia Secino, D.R.E. Students 211.

3—HOLY FAMILY OF NAZARETH (1963) Rev. Thomas F. Egan.
Res.: One S. Flagg St., 01602.
Church: 750 Union St., 01453. Tel: 978-537-3016; Fax: 978-534-1119. Email: churchonhill@aol.com.
Catechesis/Religious Program—Tel: 978-537-5660. Email: churchonhill@aol.com. Anne Booth, D.R.E. Students 163.

4—ST. LEO (1872) [CEM] Rev. Msgr. John E. Doran; Rev. Thien Nguyen.
Res.: 108 Main St., 01453. Tel: 978-537-7257; Fax: 978-840-6182. Email: stleoparish@verizon.net. Web: stleosparish.org.
School—(Grades PreK-8), 120 Main St., 01453. Tel: 978-537-1007; Fax: 978-537-2828. Web: www-.stleoschool.org. Mrs. Carolyn Polselli, Prin.; Sr. Mary Anne Seliga, P.B.V.M., Librarian. Sisters of the Presentation of the Blessed Virgin Mary 2; Lay Teachers 34; Students 275.
Catechesis/Religious Program—Tel: 978-537-1194; Fax: 978-840-6182. Web: www.stleosparish.org. Students 354.

5—OUR LADY OF THE LAKE (1952) Rev. Timothy M. Brewer; Deacon Fred A. Harkins.
Res.: 1400 Main St., 01453. Tel: 978-342-2978; Fax: 978-342-8738. Email: ourladylake@comcast.net. Web: www.ourladylake.org.
Catechesis/Religious Program—Tel: 978-345-7469. Lisa Sciacca, D.R.E. Students 573.

LINWOOD, GOOD SHEPHERD (1904) Rev. Lawrence J. Esposito; Deacon Marc E. Gervais.
Res.: 121 Linwood St., P.O. Box 517, 01525. Tel: 508-234-7726; Fax: 508-234-0964. Email: gshepherd7726@charter.net. Web: www.gdshphrd.com.
Catechesis/Religious Program—Tel: 508-234-5340. Carol A. Zabinski, Music Min. Students 232.

LUNENBURG, ST. BONIFACE (1950) Rev. John A. Dwyer.
Res.: 817 Massachusetts Ave., 01462. Tel: 978-582-4008; Fax: 978-582-9355. Email: stbonifaceparish@verizon.net.
Catechesis/Religious Program—Tel: 978-582-6650; Fax: 978-582-9355. Maura L. Sweeney, D.R.E. Students 186.

MANCHAUG, ST. ANNE (1900) Rev. Patrick J. Hawthorne.
Res.: 31 Main St., P.O. Box 311, 01526. Tel: 508-476-2405; Fax: 508-476-4443.
Catechesis/Religious Program—Students 47.

MENDON, ST. MICHAEL (1952) Merged with Holy Angels, Upton to form St. Gabriel the Archangel, Upton.

MILFORD

1—ST. MARY OF THE ASSUMPTION (1848), (Portuguese—Spanish), [CEM] Revs. Raymond M. Goodwin; Guillermo J. Ochoa; Sr. Theresa Lucier, S.P., Pastoral Assoc.
Catechesis/Religious Program—*St. Mary's Parish Center*, 17 Winter St., 01757. Tel: 508-478-7440; Fax: 508-473-6907. Sandra Piwko, C.R.E. (Children & Teens). Students 683.

2—SACRED HEART OF JESUS (1905) [CEM] Rev. Richard A. Scioli, C.S.S.; Deacon Pasquale G. Mussulli.
Res.: 5 E. Main St., 01757. Tel: 508-634-5435; Fax: 508-478-4993. Email: shbulletineditor@comcast.net (For Bulletin News); office@sacredheartmilford.org. Web: sacredheartmilford.org.
Catechesis/Religious Program—Tel: 508-473-1036. Amy Donahue, C.R.E.; Caren Ante, C.R.E. Students 437.

MILLBURY

1—ASSUMPTION (1884), (French), Rev. Richard A. Fortin.
Res.: 12 Waters St., 01527. Tel: 508-865-2657; Fax: 508-865-4866. Email: apsecretary@charter.net.
School—(Grades PreK-8), 17 Grove St., 01527. Tel: 508-865-5404; Fax: 508-581-8974. Dr. Rita Bernard, Prin. Lay Teachers 11; Students 212.
Catechesis/Religious Program—Students 35.

2—ST. BRIGID (1849) Revs. Paul M. LaPalme; Donald C. Ouellette; Deacon Ronald B. Buron.
Res.: 59 Main St., 01527. Tel: 508-865-6624; Fax: 508-865-3101. Email: stbrigidchurch@charter.net.
Catechesis/Religious Program—Tel: 508-865-2752; Fax: 508-865-0101. Students 273.

MILLVILLE, ST. AUGUSTINE (1884) Rev. Daniel R. Mulcahy Jr.; Deacon William Lucier.
Res.: 17 Lincoln St., P.O. Box 710, 01529. Tel: 508-883-6678; Fax: 508-883-5878. Email: st.augustinemillville@charter.net.
Catechesis/Religious Program—15 Lincoln St., 01529. Tel: 508-883-8794. Students 81.

NORTH BROOKFIELD, ST. JOSEPH (1867) [CEM] Rev. Kevin F. Hartford.
Res.: 28 Mt. Pleasant St., 01535. Tel: 508-867-6811; Fax: 508-867-7756. Email: stjosephsrectory@charter.net. Web: www.nbstjosephs.org.
Church: 296 N. Main St., 01535.
Catechesis/Religious Program—27 Mt. Pleasant St., 01535. Tel: 508-867-9302; Fax: 508-867-7756. Students 122.

NORTH GRAFTON, ST. MARY (1952) Rev. Kenneth Cardinale; Deacon Frederick Coggins; Lisa Stewart, Business Mgr.
Res.: 17 Waterville St., 01536. Tel: 508-839-3993; Fax: 508-839-1330. Web: stmarysgrafton.org.
Catechesis/Religious Program—Tel: 508-839-3993, Ext. 12. Sr. Yvonne Millman, S.S.A, D.R.E. Students 305.

NORTH OXFORD, ST. ANN (1906) Rev. Richard F. Reidy; Sr. Jeanne Rouillard, S.A.S.V., Pastoral Assoc.
Res.: 652 Main St., P.O. Box 488, 01537. Tel: 508-987-8892; Fax: 508-987-1598. Email: stannsrectory@charterinternet.com.
Catechesis/Religious Program—P.O. Box 488, 01537. Students 150.

NORTHBORO

1—ST. BERNADETTE (1959) Rev. Stephen M. Gemme; Deacon George O'Connor.
Res.: 266 Main St., 01532. Tel: 508-393-2223; Fax: 508-393-2718. Email: stbernadetteparish@stb-parish.net. Web: www.stb-parish.org.
School—(Grades PreK-8), 266 Main St., 01532. Tel: 508-351-9905; Fax: 508-351-2941. Email: principal@stb-school.org. Deborah O'Neil, Prin.; Jan Berry, Librarian; Mary Bardellini, Librarian. Sisters 1; Lay Teachers 53; Students 540.

Catechesis/Religious Program—Tel: 508-393-7445. Students 363.
2—ST. ROSE OF LIMA (1883) Rev. James A. Houston.
Res.: 244 W. Main St., P.O. Box 685, 01532. Tel: 508-393-2413; Fax: 508-393-4922. Email: saintrose1@verizon.net. Web: www.saintroseoflima.com.
Catechesis/Religious Program—P.O. Box 387. Tel: 508-393-6444. Mrs. Susan McGoldrick, D.R.E. Students 613.

NORTHBRIDGE, ST. PETER (1904) Rev. James F. Carmody; Deacon Lee Packard.
Res.: 39 Church Ave., P.O. Box 446, 01534. Tel: 508-234-2156; Fax: 508-234-5123.
Catechesis/Religious Program—Tel: 508-234-6355. Students 135.

OTTER RIVER, ST. MARTIN MISSION (1864) Rev. Joseph J. Jurgelonis.
Church & Res.: 248 State Rd., 01438. Tel: 978-939-8858. Email: info@saintmartinchurch.org. Web: saintmartinchurch.org.
Catechesis/Religious Program—Students 30.

OXFORD, ST. ROCH (1886) [CEM] Rev. Michael J. Roy; Deacon Wesley Stevens.
Res.: 334 Main St., 01540. Tel: 508-987-8987; Fax: 508-987-8938. Web: www.strochoxford.parishesonline.com.
Catechesis/Religious Program—Tel: 508-987-2382. Students 172.

PAXTON, ST. COLUMBA (1951) Rev. David E. Doiron.
Res.: 10 Richards Ave., 01612. Tel: 508-755-0408; Fax: 508-767-0759. Email: stcolumba@charter.net. Web: www.stcolumbapax.org.
Catechesis/Religious Program—Tel: 508-755-0601. Students 239.

PETERSHAM, ST. PETER (1968) Revs. Richard A. Jakubauskas; Krzysztof Korcz; Deacon Paul Mello. Mailing Address: 18 North St., 01366. Tel: 978-249-3361.
Res.: 192 School St., Athol, 01331. Tel: 978-249-2738.
Catechesis/Religious Program—Tel: 978-249-7690. High School is done with Our Lady Immaculate. Students 22.

PRINCETON, PRINCE OF PEACE (1967) Rev. James J. Caldarella; Sr. Teresa Rose Carchidi, M.P.V., Pastoral Assoc.
Res.: 5 Worcester Rd., P.O. Box 305, 01541. Tel: 508-464-2871; Fax: 508-464-0449. Email: princeofpeace@verizon.net. Web: www.princeofpeace.41pi.com.
Catechesis/Religious Program—Students 153.

RUTLAND, ST. PATRICK (1938) Rev. James P. Kerrigan; Deacon Pierre G.L. Gemme.
Res.: 290 Main St., Box 939, 01543. Tel: 508-886-4309; Fax: 508-886-2897. Email: stpatsrutland@aol.com. Web: stpatrickrutland.org.
Church: 258 Main St., 01543. Tel: 508-886-6131.
Catechesis/Religious Program—9 Pommogusset Rd., 01543. Tel: 508-886-4984; Fax: 508-886-7414. Christine Mulry, D.R.E.; Mrs. Jean Urbanowski, D.R.E. Students 394.

SHREWSBURY
1—ST. ANNE (1950) [CEM] Revs. John Foley; Paul T. O'Connell, Senior Priest; Deacon Dennis J. Klug; Eleanor Smith, Pastoral Assoc. In Res., Rev. Paul W. Lemire.
Res.: 130 Boston Tpke., 01545. Tel: 508-757-5154; Fax: 508-797-9520. Email: starec@aol.com. Web: www.stannesparish.org.
Catechesis/Religious Program—Tel: 508-752-5040. Karen Etre, D.R.E. Students 486.
2—ST. MARY'S (1922) Revs. Michael F. Rose; Leo Lancaster; Marcin Nowicki.
Mailing Address: 18 Summer St., 01545.
Res.: 11 Summer St., 01545. Tel: 508-845-0161; Fax: 508-842-9132.
School—(Grades PreK-8) Tel: 508-842-1601; Fax: 508-845-1535. Joan Barry, Prin. Sisters 1; Lay Teachers 26; Students 276.
Catechesis/Religious Program—Tel: 508-845-1154. Students 1,002.

SOUTH ASHBURNHAM, ST. ANNE (1895) Rev. John E. Horgan; Deacon Richard DesJardins.
Pastoral Office—85 Main St., P.O. Box 418, Ashburnham, 01430-0418. Tel: 978-827-5806; Fax: 978-827-1191. Email: stdenis@comcast.net.
Catechesis/Religious Program—Tel: 978-827-4892. Combined with St. Denis.

SOUTH BARRE, ST. THOMAS-A-BECKET (1918) Rev. Ernest Allega.
Res.: 398 Vernon Ave., P.O. Box 186, 01074. Tel: 978-355-2228; Fax: 978-355-0042. Email: e.allegra@yahoo.com.
Catechesis/Religious Program—Tel: 508-882-3353; Fax: 508-882-9517. Students 80.

SOUTH GRAFTON, ST. JAMES (1887) Rev. Edward J. Hanlon; Deacon Edward Richards.
Res.: 89 Main St., 01560. Tel: 508-839-5354; Fax: 508-839-5430.
Catechesis/Religious Program—Tel: 508-839-6800. Students 285.

SOUTHBOROUGH
1—ST. ANNE (1886) Rev. Conrad S. Pecevich.
Res.: 20 Boston Rd., 01772. Tel: 508-485-0141; Fax: 508-481-9374. Email: stanne403@charter.net. Web: stanne-southboro.org.
Catechesis/Religious Program—Tel: 508-481-3159. Cynthia dela Pena, D.R.E. Students 485.
2—ST. MATTHEW (1956) [JC] Rev. James B. Flynn.
Res.: 105 Southville Rd., 01772. Tel: 508-485-2285; Fax: 508-485-4437. Email: office@stmatthewsb.org. Web: stmatthewcatholic-southboro.org.
Catechesis/Religious Program—Tel: 508-229-2429. Email: reled@stmatthewsb.org. Students 511.

SOUTHBRIDGE
1—BLESSED JOHN PAUL II Revs. Peter Joyce; Nelson Rivera; Deacon Thomas A. Skonieczny.
Res.: 61 Marcy St., 01550. Tel: 508-765-0601; Fax: 508-764-4148.
Catechesis/Religious Program—Religious Education Center, 20 Marcy St., 01550. Tel: 508-764-8018. Students 198.
2—ST. HEDWIG (1916), (Polish), [CEM] Merged into Blessed John Paul II, Southbridge.
3—ST. MARY (1861) [CEM] Merged into Blessed John Paul II, Southbridge.
4—NOTRE DAME (1869) Merged with St. Hedwig, Southbridge and St. Mary Southbridge to form Blessed John Paul II, Southbridge.
5—NOTRE DAME OF THE SACRED HEART (1869) Merged with Sacred Heart of Jesus, St. Hedwig & St. Mary to form Blessed John Paul II, Southbridge.
6—SACRED HEART OF JESUS (1908), (French), Merged into Blessed John Paul II, Southbridge.

SPENCER
1—MARY, QUEEN OF THE ROSARY (1994) [CEM], Merger of St. Mary, Spencer and Our Lady of the Rosary, Spencer. Rev. James F. Hoey; Deacon Harry M. Sweet.
Office: 60 Maple St., 01562. Tel: 508-885-3111; Fax: 508-885-4905. Email: mqroffice@parishmail.com. Web: www.maryqueenoftherosary.org.
Res.: 46 Maple St., 01562. Tel: 508-885-3806.
Catechesis/Religious Program—Tel: 508-885-0211. Mrs. Judith Brennan, C.R.E. Students 331.
2—OUR LADY OF THE ROSARY (1854) Merged with St. Mary's, Spencer to form Mary, Queen of the Rosary, Spencer.

STERLING, ST. RICHARD OF CHICHESTER (1953) Rev. James M. Steuterman; Sr. Anne Marie Wildenhain, S.S.J., Pastoral Assoc.; Kathleen Majikas, Admin. Asst.
Res.: 4 Bridge St., P.O. Box 657, 01564. Tel: 978-422-8881; Fax: 978-422-0291. Email: strichardsterling@comcast.net. Web: www.strichardsterling.org.
Catechesis/Religious Program—Tel: 508-422-8921. Susan Gallivan, D.R.E. Students 375.

SUTTON, ST. MARK (1964) [CEM] Rev. Michael A. DiGeronimo; Deacon Paul Dacri.
Res.: 356 Boston Rd., 01590. Tel: 508-865-3860; Fax: 508-865-5095. Email: st.mark-office@verizon.net. Web: www.stmarksparish.org.
Catechesis/Religious Program—Tel: 508-845-3860, Ext. 16. Amanda Proulx, Youth Min. Students 149.

UPTON
1—ST. GABRIEL THE ARCHANGEL Revs. Laurence V. Brault, Co-Pastor; Thomas E. Mahoney, Co-Pastor.
Church & Res.: 151 Mendon St., 01568. Tel: 508-603-1430; Fax: 508-529-1629. Web: www.stgabrielma.org.
Catechesis/Religious Program—Tel: 508-529-3109. Simone Caron, D.R.E. Students 720.
2—HOLY ANGELS (1900) Merged with St. Michael, Mendon to form St. Gabriel the Archangel, Upton.

UXBRIDGE, ST. MARY'S (1853) [CEM] Rev. Steven M. Labaire.
Res.: 77 Mendon St., 01569. Tel: 508-278-2226; Fax: 508-278-7949.
Catechesis/Religious Program—Tel: 508-278-3777. Students 194.

WARREN, ST. PAUL (1872) [CEM] Rev. Daniel J. Becker.
Res.: 1082 Main St., P.O. Box 1027, 01083-1027. Tel: 413-436-7327.
Catechesis/Religious Program—Tel: 413-436-7492. Clustered with St. Thomas Aquinas, West Warren. Students 35.

WEBSTER
1—ST. JOSEPH BASILICA (1887), (Polish), [CEM] Rev. Msgr. Anthony S. Czarnecki; Rev. Grzegorz Chodkowski.
Res.: 53 Whitcomb St., 01570. Tel: 508-943-0467; Fax: 508-943-0808. Email: rectory@stjosephwebster.com. Web: www.saintjosephbasilica.com.
School—(Grades PreK-8) Tel: 508-943-0378; Fax: 508-949-0581. Email: principal@saintjosephwebster.com. Web: www.saintjosephschool.net. Donald Cushing, Prin. Felician Sisters 3; Lay Teachers 16; Students 128.
Catechesis/Religious Program—Students 95.
2—ST. LOUIS (1853) Rev. Joseph A. Marcotte.
Res.: 15 Lake St., 01570. Tel: 508-943-0240; Fax: 508-943-0801. Email: saintlouischurch@verizon.net. Web: www.stlouischurchwebster.org.
School—(Grades PreK-8) Tel: 508-943-0257; Fax: 508-943-0257. Mrs. Katherine Kelly, Prin. Lay Teachers 12; Students 212.
Catechesis/Religious Program—Tel: 508-943-0817; Fax: 508-943-0817. Email: stlouisreled@stlouisschool.org. Students 325.
3—SACRED HEART OF JESUS (1870) [CEM] [JC] Rev. Adam R. Reid; Deacons Anthony R. Surozenski; Paul J. Lesieur.
Res.: 18 E. Main St., 01570. Tel: 508-943-3140; Fax: 508-943-2213. Email: shp1870@verizon.net.
School—St. Anne, (Grades PreK-8), Day St., 01570. Tel: 508-943-2735; Fax: 508-943-6215. Sr. Constance Bayeur, S.S.A., Prin. Sisters of St. Anne 2; Lay Teachers 16; Students 162.
Catechesis/Religious Program—Tel: 508-943-0113. Students 77.

WEST BOYLSTON, OUR LADY OF GOOD COUNSEL (1869) [CEM] Rev. Thirburse F. Millott. In Res., Rev. Msgr. F. Stephen Pedone.
Res.: 111 Worcester St., 01583. Tel: 508-835-3606; Fax: 508-835-5456. Email: goodcounsel@charter.net.
Catechesis/Religious Program—Tel: 508-835-6336. Sr. Elaine Potvin, S.S.A., D.R.E. Students 228.

WEST BROOKFIELD, SACRED HEART OF JESUS (1950) Rev. David B. Galonek.
Res.: 10 Milk St., 01585-0563. Tel: 508-867-6469; Fax: 508-867-3670.
Parish Center—Tel: 508-867-4460.
Catechesis/Religious Program—Tel: 508-867-4460. Students 110.

WEST WARREN
1—ST. STANISLAUS (1913), (Polish), Rev. Daniel J. Becker.
Res.: 2270 Main St., P.O. Box 723, 01092-0723. Tel: 413-436-5110.
Catechesis/Religious Program—Students 3.
2—ST. THOMAS AQUINAS (1893) Closed. For inquiries for parish records contact St. Paul, Warren.

WESTBOROUGH, ST. LUKE THE EVANGELIST (1870) [CEM] Rev. Msgr. Michael G. Foley; Rev. Edwin A. Gomez.
Res.: 70 W. Main St., 01581. Tel: 508-366-5502; Fax: 508-366-6049. Email: office@stlukes-parish.org. Web: www.stlukes-parish.org.
Catechesis/Religious Program—One Ruggles St., 01581. Tel: 508-366-8509. Email: religiouseducation@stlukes-parish.org. Dianne Patrick, D.R.E.; Gloria Josephs, Youth Dir. Students 745.

WESTMINSTER, ST. EDWARD THE CONFESSOR (1951) Rev. William E. Champlin; Deacon Roderick F. Cashes.
Res.: 10 Church St., 01473. Tel: 978-874-2362; Fax: 978-874-1024. Email: edwardconf@aol.com.
Catechesis/Religious Program—Tel: 978-874-1559. Students 284.

WHITINSVILLE, ST. PATRICK (1889) [CEM] Revs. C. Michael Broderick; Juan David Echavarria; Deacon Patrick W. Stewart.
Res.: 7 East St., P.O. Box 60, 01588. Tel: 508-234-5656; Fax: 508-234-6845. Web: www.mystpatricks.com.
Catechesis/Religious Program—Tel: 508-234-3511. Mary Lou Petty, D.R.E. Students 498.

WINCHENDON, IMMACULATE HEART OF MARY (1870) [CEM] Rev. Leo-Paul J. LeBlanc; Deacon Mark J. Carrier.
Res.: 52 Spruce St., 01475. Tel: 508-297-0280; Fax: 508-297-3577. Email: ihmwinchendon@aol.com.
Catechesis/Religious Program—Tel: 508-297-2699. Mrs. Anita Bourque, D.R.E. Students 53.
Convent—110 Summer St., 01475. Tel: 508-297-0275. Sisters of the Presentation of Mary 2.

Chaplains of Public Institutions

WORCESTER. *Memorial Hospital*. Rev. Thomas J. Sheehan, S.J.
University of Mass Medical Center. Rev. Francis J. Roach.
Worcester Belmont House. Serviced by St. Anne Church, Shrewsbury.
Worcester State Hospital. Rev. Msgr. Rocco M. Piccolomini.

BOYLSTON. *Worcester County Jail and House of Correction*. Deacon Gary Miller.

GARDNER. *Massachusetts Correctional Institution*.

LEOMINSTER. *Leominster Hospital*. Cathleen Pimley, Catholic Pastoral Min.

OTTER RIVER. *Templeton Developmental Center*. Rev. Joseph J. Jurgelonis.

On Administrative Leave of Absence:
Rev.—
Doherty, Paul J.

On Special or Other Diocesan Assignment:
Rev. Msgr.—
Banach, Michael, Vatican Diplomatic Corp.
Rev.—
Diorio, Ralph A., Apostolate of Healing

On Duty Outside the Diocese:
Rev. Msgrs.—
Banach, Michael, Dir., Theresianumgasse 33/4, Vienna A-1040 Austria.
Kelly, Francis D., Rector, Superior, Casa Santa Maria, Via dell'Umitta, 30, Rome 00187 Italy.
Mongelluzzo, James A., 158 Berrington Rd., Leominster, 01453.
Moroney, James P., 127 Lake St., Brighton, 02135.
Revs.—
Boucher, Roger R., C.D.R., C.H.C., U.S.N., P.O. Box 148, Gilmanton Iron Works, NH 03837.
Damian, Ronald, Chap., V.A. Medical Center, Miami, FL
Dunkley, George, St. Mark, San Marcos, CA 92069.
Hill, George H., 1759 Castle Hill Ave., Bronx, NY 10462.

Unassigned:
Rev.—
Herrera, Juan

Military Chaplains:
Rev.—
Kazarnowicz, Anthony S., Chap., U.S. Army, 1319-A Mississippi Ave., P.O. Box 1134, Fort Campbell, KY 42223.

On Medical Leave of Absence:
Rev.—
Landry, Thomas

Retired:
Rev. Msgrs.—
Collette, Richard, Southgate, 30 Julio Dr., Shrewsbury, 01545.
Roy, F. Gilles, Southgate of Shrewsbury, 35 Julio Dr., Shrewsbury, 01545.
Sirois, Joseph V., 258 Mechanic St., Leominster, 01453.
Tinsley, Edmond T., P.A., 8 Berwick St., 01602.
Revs.—
Bafaro, Michael, Southgate, 30 Julio Dr., Shrewsbury, 01545.
Banach, Henry S., 64 Oakwood Ln., 01604.
Bielonko, Joseph, 53 Whitcomb St., Webster, 01570.
Carey, Richard T., 2 King Rd., Phillipston, 01331.
Connell, John F., P.O. Box 43, Northbridge, 01534.
Dargis, Andre E., 9031 E. Corrine Dr., Scottsdale, AZ 85260.
Debitetto, Ronald E., 66 Stetson St., Hyannis, 02601.
Donahue, Martin P., 101 Wilson Ave., Spencer, 01562.
Dumphy, Charles, 30 Julio Dr., Shrewsbury, 01545.
Dutram, Charles J., 12 Elizabeth St., Dudley, 01571.
Gallagher, William J., 35 Julio Dr., Shrewsbury, 01545.
Gariepy, Andre M., 855 John Fitch Hwy., Unit 27, Fitchburg, 01420.
Gariepy, Robert E., Southgate, 35 Julio Dr., Apt. 311, Shrewsbury, 01545.
Gionet, Urbain J., Southgate of Shrewsbury, 30 Julio Dr., Apt. 112, Shrewsbury, 01545.
Gould, Louis J., 875 John Fitch Hwy., #15, Fitchburg, 01420.
Grochowski, Bernard J., Box 9839, Las Vegas, NV 89191.
Hamernik, Peter P., Immaculate Conception Rectory, 25 Parker St., Indian Orchard, 01151.
Kelley, John E., 35 Julio Dr., Apt. 317, Shrewsbury, 01545.
Kelley, Robert E., 1290 Grafton St., 01604.
Labonte, Richard H., 41 Providence St., 01604.
Lamothe, C. Romeo, Southgate of Shewsbury, 30 Julio Dr., Shrewsbury, 01545.
Lange, George O., Southgate, 30 Julio Dr., Apt 236, Shrewsbury, 01545.
Laperle, Theodore R., St. Bernard Rectory, 240 Water St., Fitchburg, 01420.
Lewandowski, Richard P., M.A., 49 Elm St., 01609.
Liistro, Frank J., 87 Carriage Ct., Apt. 317, Leominster, 01453.
Marteka, Anthony T., Southgate, 30 Julio Dr., Shrewsbury, 01545.
McKiernan, Joseph W., 35 Julio Dr., Shrewsbury, 01545.
McNamara, Philip D., 30 Julio Dr., Shrewsbury, 01545.
Moran, Edward J., Southgate, 30 Julio Dr., Shrewsbury, 01545.
Munoz, Eusiquio-Arranz, 27 Pearl St., Milford, 01757.
O'Brien, Thomas F., 662 Windsurf Ln., Naples, FL 34108.
O'Brien, William G., P.O. Box 362, West Brookfield, 01585.
O'Donoghue, Brendan W., 30 Julio Dr., Apt. 246, Shrewsbury, 01545.
O'Leary, Cornelius F., Notre Dame Assisted Living.
Ouillette, Arthur A., 30 Julio Dr., Shrewsbury, 01545.
Scanlon, Peter J., S.T.L., 35 Julio Dr., Shrewsbury, 01545.

Permanent Deacons:
Aliskevicz, John J., St. Bernard, Fitchburg
Archibald, Norbert H., St. George, Worcester, MA
Arsenault, Roger D., (Retired), Holy Rosary, Gardner
Aubuchon, Ronald J., St. Cecilia, Leominster
Audette, Paul T., Our Lady of Loreto, Worcester, MA
Baczewski, Stanley H., Holy Spirit, Gardner
Baniukiewicz, Joseph M., Christ the King, Worcester
Barton, John, Holy Family, Worcester
Bosse, Raymond J., (Retired)
Briggs, Roy F., Blessed Sacrament, Worchester
Buron, Ronald B., St. Brigid, Millbury
Camacho, Teodoro, St. Mary, Southbridge
CaraDonna, Nicholas M., Jr.
Carrier, Mark, Immaculate Heart of Mary, Winchendon
Carrier, Paul J., Sacred Heart of Jesus, Gardner
Cashes, Roderick F., St. Edward the Confessor, Westminster
Chase, Michael, Christ The King, Worcester
Clonan, Joseph V., St. Joseph the Good Provider, Berlin
Coggins, Frederick, St. Mary, North Grafton
Colgate, Malcolm, St. Anna, Leominster
Colley, Scott, St. Francis of Assisi, Athol
Colon, William B.
Connor, James A., St. Vincent de Paul, Baldwinville
Connor, Robert, Jr., Immaculate Conception, Lancaster
Corby, Michael P., St. Joseph & St. Pius, Leicester
Cormier, Dennis J., St. Richard of Chichester, Sterling
Couture, James, St. Joseph, Fitchburg
Croteau, Andre W., (Retired)
Daluga, Richard B., Henderson, NV
Deignan, Kevin, Immaculate Conception, Worcester
Denning, James, St. Catherine of Sweden, Worcester
Desautels, Alphonse T., Our Lady of the Angels, Worcester
Desjardin, Richard C., St. Dennis/St. Ann, Ashburnham
Desmarais, Ernest E., (Retired)
Devine, Philip E., Chaplain, N. Central Correctional Institute, Gardner
Devine, Robert, St. Peter, Worcester
DeVito, Frederick A., (Retired)
Dio, Robert F., St. Joseph, Charlton City
DiPadua, James F., 86 Old East St., Petersham
Doyle, Walter F., Refugee Apostolate, Worcester
Driscoll, Patrick M., Refugee Apostolate, Our Lady of the Rosary, Worcester
Dugan, John, St. Mary, Uxbridge
Dunphy, Melvin A., New Port Richey, FL
DuVarney, Joseph T., (Retired)
Escobar, Francisco, St. Paul Cathedral, Worcester
Estremera, George, St. Peter & St. Andrew, Worcester
Faford, Peter R., Eveche Des Cayes, Haiti
Fernandez, Isreal, St. Paul, Worcester
Fiore, Anthony, St. Boniface, Lunenburg
Franchi, John A., Anna Maria College, Paxton
Gagliani, Tony, St. Paul, Blackstone
Gemme, Pierre G.L., St. Patrick, Rutland
Gendron, Steven P., St. Bernard, Fitchburg
Gervais, Mark E., Good Shepherd, Linwood
Giard, Arthur J., Jr., (Retired)
Graves, James E., St. Anna, Leominster
Green, Amos H., Sr., (Retired)
Griffin, William, St. John, Guardian of our Lady, Clinton
Harkins, Frederick A., Our Lady of the Lake, Leominster
Hayes, Myles, Our Lady of Providence, Worcester
Isabelle, David R., Souza-Baranowski Correction Center, Lancaster
King, Loren M., (Retired)
Klug, Dennis J., St. Anne, Shrewsbury
Leger, Robert, (Retired)
Lesieur, Paul J., Sacred Heart of Jesus, Webster
Linderman, James L., Our Lady Immaculate, Athol
Lizardo, Franklon, St. Paul, Worcester
Lucier, William J., St. Augustine, Millville
Manella, Joseph R., Sacred Heart, Hopedale
Martino, Richard C., St. Rose of Lima, Northboro
McCaffrey, Joseph A., (Retired)
Meilus, Eduardas, Youth Ministry & St. Mark, Sutton
Mello, Paul, St. Peter, Petersham
Meyers, Christopher C., St. Christopher, Worcester
Michaud, Roland R., (Leave of Absence)
Miller, Gary, (Retired), (Worcester County Jail and House of Correction)
Miller, William S., St. Mary, Southbridge
Miskell, Lawrence F., St. Joseph, Charlton
Montiverdi, Gerald M., University of Massachusetts Medical Center, Worcester
Motyka, Peter J., St. Louis, Webster
Mussulli, Pasquale, Sacred Heart, Milford
Myska, Frank B., Jr., St. Mary, Shrewsbury
Nogueira, Benjamin A., Campus Ministry, Fitchburg State College, Fitchburg
Novick, Colin, Cathedral of St. Paul, Worcester
O'Connor, George, St. Bernadette, Northborough
Olson, Richard V., St. Anne, St. Patrick, Sturbridge
Packard, Lee, St. Peter, Northbridge
Pizzarella, Paul, St. John, Worcester
Prince, Norman A., (Retired)
Reisinger, Scott R., St. Peter, Worcester
Richards, Edward J., St. James, South Grafton
Ryan, Peter, St. Joseph, Auburn
Shields, Court J., Holy Trinity, Harvard
Skonieczny, Thomas A., Notre Dame of the Sacred Heart, Southbridge
Stevens, Wesley, St. Roch, Oxford
Stewart, Patrick W., St. Patrick, Whitinsville
Surozenski, Anthony R., Office of the Diaconate; Sacred Heart, Webster
Sweet, Harry M., Mary Queen of the Rosary, Spencer
Tantillo, Salvatore, St. Anthony di Padua, Fitchburg
Tatro, Richard J., Holy Cross, East Templeton
Vaillancourt, David F., St. Stephen, Worcester
Vidito, Bruce R., St. Joseph, Auburn
Wagner, Thomas A., (On Duty Outside the Diocese)
Weiss, Stephen J., El Mirage, AZ
Werner, Robert, Federal Medical Ctr, Devens
White, William, St. Anthony, Dudley
Xatse, Anthony J., Cathedral of St. Paul, Worcester

INSTITUTIONS LOCATED IN THE DIOCESE

[A] COLLEGES AND UNIVERSITIES

WORCESTER. *Assumption College* (1904) 500 Salisbury St., 01609. Tel: 508-767-7000; Fax: 508-756-1780. Email: info@assumption.edu. Web: www.assumption.edu. Dr. Francesco C. Cesareo, Pres.; Christian McCarthy, Exec. Vice Pres.; Frederick F. Travis, Provost; Rev. Dennis Gallagher, A.A., Vice Pres. Mission; Thomas E. Ryan, Vice Pres. Inst. Advancement; Catherine M. Woodbrooks, Vice Pres. Student Life; Doris Ann Sweet, Dir. Library Svcs. A Catholic Liberal Arts College under the auspices of the Augustinians of the Assumption (Assumptionists). Priests 1; Sisters 1; Lay Teachers 155; Students 2,726; Total Enrollment 4,462.

College of the Holy Cross, Inc. (1843) 01610. Tel: 508-793-2011; Fax: 508-793-3030. Email: relias@holycross.edu. Web: www.holycross.edu. Rev. Michael C. McFarland, S.J., Pres.; Dr. James Hogan, Librarian. A College for Boarders and Day Scholars. Sisters 1; Lay Teachers 321; Students 2,901; Jesuit Teachers 13.

PAXTON. *Anna Maria College*, 50 Sunset Ln., 01612. Tel: 508-849-3300; Fax: 508-849-3334. Email: pgreen@annamaria.edu. Web: www.annamaria.edu. Jack P. Calareso, Ph.D., Pres.; Barbara Zawalich, Registrar; Paula Green, Vice Pres.; Ms. Ruth Pyne, Librarian. Sisters of St. Anne., A Coeducational Catholic College. Priests 2; Lay Teachers 194; Students 1,500.

[B] HIGH SCHOOLS, CENTRAL

WORCESTER. *Holy Name Central Catholic Junior/Senior High School* (1942) (Grades 7-12), 144 Granite St., 01604. Tel: 508-753-6371; Fax: 508-831-1287. Email: ereynolds@holyname.net. Web: www.holyname.net. Mrs. Mary E. Riordan, B.A., M.Ed., M.A., Dir. Inst. Advancement; Mr. Edward M. Reynolds, B.A., M.Ed., Headmaster; Mr. Ray Greenwood, B.A., Prin., Upper School; Mrs. Arlene Maurello, M.Ed., Prin., Lower School; Rev. James B. Flynn, B.A., L.S.T., Ph.D., Senior Counselor; Susan Hughes, Librarian. Priests 1; Lay Teachers 38; Students 615.

St. Peter-Marian Central Catholic Junior/Senior High School (1976) (Grades 7-12), 781 Grove St.,

01605-3196. Tel: 508-852-5555; Fax: 508-852-7238. Email: spmsroffice@spmguardians.org. Mr. Matthew R. Sturgis, B.A., M.A., M.Ed., Headmaster; Mrs. Joanne Ethier, B.A., M.Ed., C.A.E.S., Prin. Jr. High; Mrs. Denise Allain, B.A., M.A., Prin., High School; Mary Andrysick, Librarian. Lay Teachers 34; Students 579.

FITCHBURG. *St. Bernard's Central Catholic High School* (1926) 45 Harvard St., 01420. Tel: 978-342-3212; Fax: 978-345-8067. Web: stb.echalk.com. James Conry, Headmaster; Robert Blanchard, M.A., Prin. Priests 1; Lay Teachers 21; Students 285; Total Staff 6.

[C] HIGH SCHOOLS, PAROCHIAL

WORCESTER. *St. Mary's Junior/Senior High School*, (Grades 7-12), 50 Richland St., 01610. Tel: 508-753-1170; Fax: 508-795-0560. Email: mdudekstmaryshigh@gmail.com. Michael E. Dudek, Prin. Congregation of the Sisters of the Holy Family of Nazareth. Lay Teachers 16; Students 134.

[D] HIGH SCHOOLS, PRIVATE

WORCESTER. *Notre Dame Academy*, 425 Salisbury St., 01609. Tel: 508-757-6200; Fax: 508-757-7200. Email: amorrison@nda-worc.org. Web: www.nda-worc.org. Sr. Ann Morrison, S.N.D., Prin. A Private Day School for Girls. Sisters of Notre Dame de Namur 3; Lay Teachers 31; Girls 286.

FITCHBURG. *Notre Dame Preparatory School*, 171 South St., 01420. Tel: 978-343-7635; Fax: 978-343-4379. Email: ndpfa@hotmail.com. Web: www.npdschool.com. Mr. Jeff Hammond, Headmaster. Lay Teachers 7; Students 37.

LANCASTER. *Trivium School* (1979) (Grades 7-12), 471 Langen Rd., 01523. Tel: 978-365-4795; Fax: 978-365-4795. Email: triviumschool@aol.com. Web: triviumschool.com. Dr. William M. Schmitt, Headmaster. Lay Teachers 15; Students 77.

SHREWSBURY. *St. John's High School* (1898) 378 Main St., 01545. Tel: 508-842-8934; Fax: 508-842-3670. Email: jconca@stjohnshigh.org. Web: www.stjohnshigh.org. Mr. Michael W. Welch, Headmaster; Dr. Jacob A. Conca, Prin.; Elizabeth Kavanagh, Librarian. Xaverian Brothers. Lay Teachers 63; Boys 1,000.

STILL RIVER. *Immaculate Heart of Mary School* (1976) 282 Still River Rd., Box 1000, 01467. Tel: 978-456-8877; Fax: 978-456-9052. Email: brthomas@saintbenedict.com. Web: www.saintbenedict.com. Bro. Thomas Augustine, M.I.C.M., Prin.; Ann Cutress, R.N., Librarian. Sisters 11; Students 135; Total Staff 20.

[E] MIDDLE SCHOOLS, PRIVATE

WORCESTER. *The Nativity School of Worcester*, (Grades 7-9), 10 Irving St., 01606. Tel: 508-799-0100; Fax: 508-799-3951. Email: info@nativityworcester.org. Web: www.nativityworcester.org. Matthew Brunell, Exec. Dir. Tel: 508-799-0100; David Roach, Prin.; Charles Weiss, Chm. Bd. Teachers 13; Boys 55.

[F] ELEMENTARY SCHOOLS, CENTRAL

WORCESTER. *St. Peter's Central Catholic Elementary School* (1921) 865 Main St., 01610. Tel: 508-791-6496; Fax: 508-770-0818. Web: www.stpetercentralcatholic.com. Mrs. Meg Kursonis, Head of School. Lay Teachers 21; Students 319; Preschool 66; Total Enrollment 385.

MILFORD. *Milford Catholic Elementary School* (1975) (Grades PreK-6), 11 E. Main St., 01757. Tel: 508-473-7303; Fax: 508-478-4902. Email: info@milfordcatholic.org. Web: milfordcatholic.org. Mrs. Andrea Tavaska, Prin. Lay Teachers 12; Aides 3; Students 140.

UXBRIDGE. *Our Lady of Valley Regional Elementary School* (1964) 75 Mendon St., 01569. Tel: 508-278-5851; Fax: 508-278-0391. Pauline Hayward, Librarian. Lay Teachers 9; Part-Time Teachers 4; Students 186.

[G] ELEMENTARY SCHOOLS, PAROCHIAL

SOUTHBRIDGE. *Trinity Catholic Academy*, (Grades PreK-8), 11 Pine St., 01550. Tel: 508-765-5991; Fax: 508-765-0017. Email: mbrouillard@tcall.com. Web: www.trinitycatholicacademy.net. Mrs. Madeleine Brouillard, Prin. Lay Teachers 14; Students 200; Total Staff 24.

[H] ELEMENTARY SCHOOLS, PRIVATE

WORCESTER. *Venerini Academy*, (Grades PreK-8), 27 Edward St., 01605. Tel: 508-753-3210; Fax: 508-754-6050. Email: fredetted@veneriniacademy.com. Web: www.veneriniacademy.com. David E. Fredette, Ed.D., Prin.; Patricia Avis, Librarian. Sisters 5; Lay Teachers 25; Students 292.

[I] CATHOLIC CHARITIES

WORCESTER. *Catholic Charities* (1950) 10 Hammond St., 01610-1513. Tel: 508-798-0191; Fax: 508-797-5659. Web: www.ccworc.org. Catherine Loeffler, Diocesan Dir.; Cynthia Ross, Dir. Financial Mgmt.; Judith Zeh, Admin. Personnel & Training.

Northern Worcester Co. Offices, 196 Mechanic St., Leominster, 01453. Tel: 978-840-0696; Fax: 978-345-4161.

12 Riverbend St., Athol, 01331-2520. Tel: 978-249-4563; Fax: 978-249-2545. Jacqueline Hager, Area Admin.

Southern Worcester Co. Offices

Southbridge Office, 79 Elm St., Southbridge, 01550-2601. Tel: 508-765-5936; Fax: 508-764-4153. Lisa Genest, Area Admin.

Blackstone Valley/Greater Milford Area Office, 9 Spring St., Whitinsville, 01588-1409. Tel: 508-234-3800; Fax: 508-234-2321. Email: nlandry@ccworc.org.

126 Main St., Rm. 6, Milford, 01757. Tel: 508-478-9632; Fax: 508-478-9632. Noreen Landry, Area Admin.

Senior Employment Service, 10 Hammond St., 01610-1513. Tel: 508-798-0191; Fax: 508-797-5659. Susan Maedler, Prog. Admin. Senior Aid Employment.

Refugee Senior Aid Employment, 10 Hammond St., 01610-1513. Tel: 508-798-0191; Fax: 508-797-5659. Sr. Theresa Khen Doan, Prog. Admin. Refugee Resettlement & Community Educ.

Family & Community Services, 10 Hammond St., 01610-1513. Tel: 508-798-0191; Fax: 508-797-5659. Diane Lambert, Admin. Family Community Svcs.

Literacy Volunteers, 10 Hammond St., 01610-1513. Tel: 508-798-0191; Fax: 508-797-5659. Madelyn Hennessy, Prog. Admin. Literacy.

Crozier House, 10 Hammond St., 01610-1513. Tel: 508-798-0191; Fax: 508-797-5659. J. David Mulrooney, Prog. Admin. A Half-Way House for Substance Abusing Men.

Mercy Centre (Developmental Disabilities), 25 W. Chester St., 01605-1136. Tel: 508-852-7165; Fax: 508-856-9755. Heather MacDonald, Admin. Special Education Day Program and Employment Training Youngsters and Adults with Developmental Disabilities.

Youville House Shelter for Homeless Families, 133 Granite St., 01604-4500. Tel: 508-753-3084; Fax: 508-754-0139. Kenneth Michaud, Prog. Admin. Family Shelter. Total Assisted 48,000; Total Staff 230.

[J] CHILD CARE AGENCIES

WORCESTER. *Guild of St. Agnes*, 133 Granite St., 01604. Tel: 508-755-2238; Fax: 508-754-2026. Email: swoodbury@guildofstagnes.org. Web: www.guildofstagnes.org. Mr. Edward Madaus, Dir. Day Care Centers for Infants, Toddlers, Preschoolers & School-age Children. Children aged 4 weeks-12 years.; Family Day Care Program ages 6 weeks-5 years. Children 1,327; Total Staff 225.

FITCHBURG. *Guild of St. Agnes*, 62 Dover St., 01420. Tel: 978-343-3042; Fax: 978-343-2610. Total Assisted 110; Total Staff 7.

LEICESTER. *McAuley Nazareth Home for Boys* (1901) 01524. Tel: 508-892-4886; Fax: 508-892-9736. Email: naz1901@verizon.net. Web: www.nazareth-home.org. Kim E. Pare, M.Ed., C.A.G.S., Exec. Dir.; Rev. Msgr. Edmond T. Tinsley, P.A., Chap. (Retired). Diocese of Worcester. Sisters 3; Lay Teachers 2; Boys 7; Special Education School: Boys 14.

[K] SPECIAL HOSPITALS AND SANATORIA

WORCESTER. *Notre Dame Health Care Center, Inc.*, 559 Plantation St., 01605. Tel: 508-852-3011; Fax: 508-852-0397. Email: klemay@notredameltcc.org. Web: www.notredameltcc.org. Katherine Lemay, Admin. Bed Capacity 123; Total Staff 170.

WHITINSVILLE. *St. Camillus Nursing Home Inc.*, 447 Hill St., 01588. Tel: 508-234-7306. William Graves, Admin.; Bro. Thomas Farrell, O.S.Cam., Dir. Pastoral Care. Priests 1; Brothers 2; Bed Capacity 123.

[L] HEALTH SERVICES

WORCESTER. *Pernet Family Health Service*, 237 Millbury St., 01610. Tel: 508-755-1228; Fax: 508-797-3477. Email: sdooley@pernetfamilyhealth.org. Web: pernetfamilyhealth.org. Sheilah Dooley, Exec. Dir. Mission of the Little Sisters of the Assumption.; Certified Home Health and Social Service Agency. Focus of services toward the parent and young child. Parenting groups, family activities available, Early Childhood Development services also available. Total Staff 28; Little Sisters of the Assumption 2; Total Volunteers 50.

[M] HOMES FOR AGED

WORCESTER. *Notre Dame du Lac*, 555 Plantation St., 01605. Tel: 508-852-5800; Fax: 508-852-1700. Email: csessions@nddul.org. Web: www.notredamedulac.org. Margaret Coffin, Exec. Dir. Apartments 108; Total Staff 97.

LEOMINSTER. *Presentation Health Care Center* (1993) 99 Church St., 01453-3147. Tel: 978-537-7856; Fax: 978-840-1564. Email: admjuliec@juno.com. Sr. Patricia Anastasio, P.B.V.M., Pres. Purpose: To operate and maintain a rest home for aged and/or infirmed sisters at Presentation Convent. Bed Capacity 10; Total in Residence (Closed Skilled Unit) 8; Total Staff 25.

SPENCER. *St. Joseph's Abbey Resident Care Facility, Inc.* (2003) 167 N. Spencer Rd., 01562-1233. Tel: 508-885-8702; Fax: 508-885-8701. Web: www.spencerabbey.org. Bro. Amadeus Hamilton, O.C.S.O., M.S.N., N.P., Admin. Bed Capacity 12; Total Staff 7; Total Assisted 12.

[N] MONASTERIES AND RESIDENCES OF PRIESTS AND BROTHERS

WORCESTER. *Assumptionists (Augustinians of the Assumption)* (1845) 50 Old English Rd., 01609. Tel: 508-754-6276; Fax: 508-797-1789. Web: www.assumptio.org. Revs. Alexis A. Babineau, A.A.; Eugene LaPlante, A.A., Chap. (Retired); Paul Vaudreuil, A.A., A.A., Supr.; Robert Fortin, A.A.; Aidan M. Furlong, A.A.; Oliver (Robert) Blanchette, A.A.; Theodore L. Fortier, A.A.; Norman Meiklejohn, A.A.; Bros. Armand Lemaire, A.A.; John-Thomas McHugh, A.A.; Richard Gagnon, A.A., Treas. Priests 8; Brothers 3; Total Staff 2.

Assumptionists of Assumption College, Emmanuel House, 512 Salisbury St., 01609-1326. Tel: 508-767-7523; Fax: 508-793-9701. Email: dgallagh@assumption.edu. Web: www.assumptionists.com. Revs. Donat R. Lamothe, A.A., Treas.; Barry Bercier, A.A.; Dennis Gallagher, A.A., Regional Supr.; Roger R. Corriveau, A.A.; Malumba Matsongani; Richard E. Lamoureux, A.A, Prov. Dir. of Formation; Vo Tran Gia Dinh, A.A. Total in Residence 8; Total Staff 1.

Jesuits of the Holy Cross, Inc. (1843) 1 College St., 01610. Tel: 508-793-2427; Fax: 508-793-2624. Web: www.holycross.edu/index.html. Revs. John E. Brooks, S.J.; William A. Clark, S.J.; Terrence M. Curry, S.J.; John J. Donohue, S.J.; Charles J. Dunn, S.J.; John Enslin, S.J.; John E. Fagan, S.J.; John F. Gavin, S.J.; J. Thomas Hamel, S.J.; Paul F. Harman, S.J.; James M. Hayes, S.J.; Anthony J. Kuzniewski, S.J.; Vincent A. Lapomarda, S.J.; Gregory A. Lynch, S.J.; Michael C. McFarland, S.J.; Earle L. Markey, S.J.; John P. Reboli, S.J.; William E. Reiser, S.J.; Philip C. Rule, S.J.; John D. Savard, S.J.; Thomas J. Sheehan, S.J.; Simon E. Smith, S.J.; William E. Stempsey, S.J.; Edward J. Vodoklys, S.J.; Thomas W. Worcester, S.J.; Christopher Ryan, S.J., (Scholastic). Priests 16; Scholastics 1.

FITCHBURG. *Missionaries of La Salette (MA), Inc.*, St. Joseph, 46 Woodland St., 01420. Tel: 978-342-7907; Fax: 978-345-7678. Total in Residence 2.

PETERSHAM. *St. Mary's Monastery*, 271 N. Main St., P.O. Box 345, 01366. Tel: 978-724-3350; Fax: 978-724-3109. Email: monks@stmarysmonastery.org. Web: www.stmarysmonastery.org. Rev. Gregory Phillips, O.S.B., Supr. Priest-Monks 1; Monks 4.

SHREWSBURY. *Xaverian Brothers*, 378 Main St., 01545. Tel: 508-845-1878; Fax: 508-842-3670. Email: pfeeney@stjohnshigh.org. Bros. Paul Feeney, C.F.X., Dir.; James Mahoney, C.F.X.; Regis Moynihan, C.F.X.; J. Conal Owens, C.F.X. Brothers 4.

SPENCER. *St. Joseph's Abbey* 01562-1233. Tel: 508-885-8700; Fax: 508-885-8701. Email: monks@spencerabbey.org. Web: www.spencerabbey.org. Rt. Rev. Damian Carr, O.C.S.O.; Revs. Dominic Whedbee, O.C.S.O., Prior; Laurence Bourget, O.C.S.O.; Basil Byrne, O.C.S.O.; Eugene Lacasse, O.C.S.O.; Robert Kevin Anderson, O.C.S.O., (In Service Outside the Community); Edward Steriti, O.C.S.O.; Matthew Flynn, O.C.S.O.; Gabriel Bertoniere, O.C.S.O.; Patrick Brown, O.C.S.O.; Kevin Hunt, O.C.S.O.; Robert Morhous, O.C.S.O.; Henry Scarborough, O.C.S.O.; Peter Schmidt, O.C.S.O.; Gerald Sears, O.C.S.O.; Kizito Thompson, O.C.S.O.; Aquinas Keane, O.C.S.O.; Luke Truhan, O.C.S.O., Novice Dir.; Aidan (Arthur H.) Logan, O.C.S.O., (On Leave to Military Ordinariate); Francis Rodriguez, O.C.S.O.; David Lavich, O.C.S.O., (In Service Outside the Community); Paulinus O'Brien, O.C.S.O.; James Palmigiano; Isaac Keeley, O.C.S.O.; Timothy Scott, O.C.S.O.; Vincent Rogers, O.S.C.O.

Cistercian Abbey of Spencer, Inc. Cistercian Order of the Strict Observance (Trappists). Solemnly Professed 63; Novices 4; Total Priests in

Community 27; Total in Community 68.

STILL RIVER. *Benedictine Monks, St. Benedict Abbey* (Harvard), 252 Still River Rd., P.O. Box 67, 01467. Tel: 978-456-3221; Fax: 978-456-8181. Email: saintbenedict@abbey.org. Web: www.abbey.org. Rt. Rev. Xavier Connelly, O.S.B., Prior; Revs. Basil Rechenburg, O.S.B.; Peter Connelly, O.S.B.; Anthony Kloss, O.S.B.; Marc Crilly, O.S.B.; Very Rev. James Doran, O.S.B., Prior; Rev. Augustine Senz, O.S.B. Priests 7; Brothers 4; Oblates 1.

WHITINSVILLE. *St. Camillus Community*, 447 Hill St., 01588. Tel: 508-234-7306; Fax: 508-234-7597. Email: bgraves@stcamillus.com. Web: www.stcamillus.com. Rev. John Gallagher, M.I., Chap. Priests 1.

[O] CONVENTS AND RESIDENCES FOR SISTERS

WORCESTER. *Little Franciscans of Mary* (1889) 12 Jones St., Apt. 1, 01604. Tel: 508-755-0878; Fax: 508-755-6822. Email: jjapfm@aol.com. Sr. Jacquelyn Alix, P.F.M., Regl. Supr. Tel: 508-755-0878. Sisters 6.

Little Sisters of the Assumption, Pernet Family Health Service, Inc., 237 Millbury St., 01610. Tel: 508-755-1228; Fax: 508-797-3477. Email: sdooley@pernetfamilyhealth.org. Web: www.pernetfamilyhealth.org. Family Health Agency. Nursing and Family Development Services-Home Based.

Religious Venerini Sisters Provincial Office, 23 Edward St., 01605. Tel: 508-745-1020; Fax: 508-886-2017. Email: himpv3@yahoo.com. Web: www.religiousvenerinisisters.org. Sr. Hilda Ponte, M.P.V., Prov. Sisters 22.

Sisters of St. Anne, Esther House (1973) 1015 Pleasant St., 01602. Tel: 508-757-6053. Email: smdugas@hotmail.com. Web: www.sistersofsaintanne.org. Sisters 4; Total in Residence 4; Total Staff 4.

Sisters of St. Joseph, S.S.J., 783 Grove St., 01605. Tel: 508-852-1659. Sisters 3.

Sisters of the Assumption of the Blessed Virgin, 316 Lincoln St., 01605. Tel: 508-856-9383; Fax: 508-853-0881. Email: lono9595@aol.com. Sisters Lorraine Normand, S.A.S.V., Treas. Tel: 508-856-9450; Muriel Lemoine, S.A.S.V., Congregational Leader.

Xaverian Missionary Society of Mary, Inc., Headquarters: 242 Salisbury St., 01609-1639. Tel: 508-757-0514; Fax: 508-757-0514. Email: xavsistersusa@msn.com. Sr. Rosa Maria G. Serra, X.M.M., Supr. Sisters 5.

CHARLTON. *Carmelite Sisters of the Eucharist of Worcester, MA*, 188 Old Worcester Rd., 01507. Tel: 508-248-2936; Fax: 508-248-3814. Sisters 3.

LEOMINSTER. *The Sisters of the Presentation of the Blessed Virgin Mary, New Windsor, NY*, 99 Church St., 01453. Tel: 978-537-7108; Fax: 978-537-3789. Email: campjoynh@hotmail.com. Web: www.sistersofthepresentation.org. Ministries are in the areas of education in parochial elementary schools; pastoral services; health care; social services. Professed Sisters 126.

Mt. St. Joseph, 84 Presentation Way, New Windsor, NY 12553. Tel: 914-564-0513 (Admin. Office); Fax: 845-567-0219 (Admin. Office). Sisters Patricia Anastasio, P.B.V.M., Pres.; Mary Anne Seliga, P.B.V.M., House Coord.

PETERSHAM. *Assumption Residence of the Sisters of the Assumption of the Blessed Virgin*, 211 N. Main St., 01366. Tel: 978-724-3468; Fax: 978-724-0200. Email: erdube30@verizon.net. Web: www.sasv.ca. Sisters Estelle Dube, S.A.S.V., Co-Admin.; Sandra Dupre, S.A.S.V., Co-Admin. Professed Sisters 22.

St. Scholastica Priory (1980) 271 N. Main St., Box 606, 01366-0606. Tel: 978-724-3213. Email: sspriory@aol.com. Web: www.stscholasticapriory.org. Very Sr. Mary Elizabeth Kloss, O.S.B., Prioress; Sr. Mary Angela Kloss, O.S.B., Subprioress. Benedictine Nuns (Cloistered). Nuns in Solemn Vows 11; Simple Vows 3.

STILL RIVER. *Sisters of Saint Benedict Center, Slaves of the Immaculate Heart of Mary Inc.* (1949) *St. Ann House*, 254 Still River Rd., P.O. Box 22, 01467. Tel: 978-456-8017; Fax: 978-456-8508. Email: micm@verizon.net. Professed Sisters 11; Novices 1.

WEBSTER. *St. Joseph Convent*, 5 Maynard St., 01570-2433. Tel: 508-943-2228. Email: cssfwebster@yahoo.com. Sr. Jeanne Marie Akalski, C.S.S.F., Supr. Felician Sisters 2.

[P] RETREAT HOUSES AND HOUSE OF PRAYER

SPENCER. *St. Joseph Abbey*, 167 N. Spencer Rd., 01562-1233. Tel: 508-885-8710; Fax: 508-885-8701. Web: www.spencerabbey.org. Rev. Aquinas Keane, O.C.S.O., Guest Master. Guest house and Retreat house.

Mary House, Inc. (1969) 186 N. Spencer Rd. (Rte. 31), P.O. Box 20, 01562. Tel: 508-885-5450. Web: maryhousespencer.com. Ms. Joyce Thomasmeyer, Pres. House of Prayer and Contemplation.

STILL RIVER. *Benedictine Monks, St. Benedict Abbey* (Harvard); (See separate listing under Monasteries and Residences for Men.), 252 Still River Rd., P.O. Box 67, 01467. Tel: 978-456-3221; Fax: 978-456-8181. Email: saintbenedict@abbey.org. Web: www.abbey.org. Rt. Rev. Xavier Connelly, O.S.B., Abbot.

[Q] NEWMAN CHAPLAINS AND CENTERS

WORCESTER. *Campus Ministry* 35 Julio Dr., Apt. 101, Shrewsbury, 01545. Tel: 508-925-5004. Email: priest@WPI.edu. Web: www.wpi.edu/~newman. Rev. Peter J. Scanlon, S.T.L., Vicar (Retired).

Assumption College 500 Salisbury St., 01609. Tel: 508-767-7419. Email: godonline@assumption.edu. James Rizza, Dir.; Stephanie McCaffrey.

Clark University 930 Main St., 01610. Tel: 508-793-7737. Rev. Msgr. Francis J. Scollen, Chap.

Holy Cross College The Office of the College Chaplain. Tel: 508-793-2448. Ms. Katherine McElaney, Dir. Sisters 1.

Worcester State College Campus Ministry Center, 486 Chandler St., 01602. Tel: 508-793-8017. Email: rmcginn@juno.com. Ruth O. McGinn, Chap.

Worcester Polytechnic Institute Religious Center at WPI, 19 Schussler Rd., 01609. Tel: 774-262-6562. Email: lrob@wpi.edu. Rev. Tomasz Borkowski.

Fitchburg State College (Fitchburg) Newman Center, 333 Mechanic St., Fitchburg, 01420. Tel: 978-342-7921. Rev. Joseph M. Dolan, Chap.; Deacon Benjamin A. Nogueira; Lois I. Nogueira, Chap.

PAXTON. *Anna Maria College* Office of Campus Ministry, 01612-1198. Tel: 508-849-3205; Fax: 508-849-3319. Web: www.annamaria.edu. Rev. Manuel Clavijo; Deacon John Franchi. Total Staff 3.

[R] MISCELLANEOUS

WORCESTER. *The Charlton Charitable Corporation, Inc.* Diocese of Worcester., 49 Elm St., 01609. Tel: 508-791-7171; Fax: 508-754-2768.

Dismas House of Massachusetts, P.O. Box 30125, 01603. Tel: 508-799-9389; Fax: 508-767-9930. Email: cmdismashouse@aol.com. Web: www.dismashouse.org. David McMahon, Co-Dir.; Colleen Hilferty, Co-Dir. To provide transition for those who are leaving prison.

The Guild of Our Lady of Providence, Chancery Office of the Diocese of Worcester, 49 Elm St., 01609. Tel: 508-791-7171; Fax: 508-753-7180.

Mendon Charitable Corporation, Inc., 49 Elm St., 01609. Tel: 508-791-7171; Fax: 508-754-2768. Mr. Jerome D. Jussaume, Mgr. Finance.

Monsignor Thomas Griffin Foundation, 49 Elm St., 01609. Tel: 508-929-4339; Fax: 508-929-4380. Email: jjussaume@worcesterdiocese.org. Mr. Jerome Jussaume.

St. Peter-Marian Endowment Trust (1998) c/o St. Peter-Marian Central Catholic Junior/Senior High School, 781 Grove St., 01605. Tel: 508-852-5555; Fax: 508-852-7238. Email: alumni@spmguardians.org; spmsroffice@spmguardians.org. Mr. Matthew R. Sturgis, B.A., M.A., M.Ed., Headmaster; Mrs. Joanne Ethier, B.A., M.Ed., C.A.E.S., Jr. High Prin.; Mrs. Denise Allain, B.A., M.A., Prin. Staff 63; Total Assisted 850.

Religious Oblates to Divine Love, 50 Moore Ave., 01602-1820.

Visitation House, P.O. Box 60115, 01606. 119 Endicott St., 01610. Tel: 508-798-8002; Fax: 508-798-8902. Email: evelindquist@visitationhouse.org. Eve Lindquist, Exec. Dir.; Sherry Robbins, Social Svcs. Mgr. A transitional home for homeless pregnant women in crisis.

AUBURN. *Kateri Tekakwitha Development, Inc.*, 8 Wyoma Dr., 01501. Tel: 508-798-8779; Fax: 508-791-6614. Email: namoffice@verizon.net. Rev. John F. Gee, Contact Person.

Kateri Tekakwitha Housing Corp., 8 Wyoma Dr., 01501. Tel: 508-798-8779; Fax: 508-791-6614.

CHARLTON. *Ministry to Retired Priests*, 188 Old Worcester Rd., 01507. Tel: 508-868-9239; Fax: 508-248-3814. Sr. Mary Ann Bartell, C.S.E., Dir.

LANCASTER. *Community of St. John*, 471 Langen Rd., 01523. Tel: 978-368-6125; Fax: 978-365-4795. Email: wschmitt@triviumschool.com. Dr. William M. Schmitt, Contact Person. Total in Residence 1.

PETERSHAM. *St. Bede's Publications* (1977) 271 N. Main St., P.O. Box 545, 01366-0545. Tel: 978-724-3217. Web: www.fordhampress.com. Sr. Mary Clare Vincent, O.S.B.

St. Mary and St. Scholastica Church, Inc. (1996) P.O. Box 606, 01366-0606.

SOUTHBRIDGE. *The Worcester Guild of the Catholic Medical Association*, 141 Main St., 01550. Tel: 508-764-9800; Fax: 508-764-0333. Web: www.worcestercma.org. Dr. John Howland, Contact Person, Sec. & Treas.

WHITINSVILLE. *St. Camillus Institute, Inc.*, 497 Hill St., 01588. Tel: 508-266-1045. Order of the Servants of the Sick (St. Camillus).

RELIGIOUS INSTITUTES OF MEN REPRESENTED IN THE DIOCESE

For further details refer to the corresponding bracketed number in the Religious Institutes of Men or Women section.

[]—*Augustinians of the Assumption*

[1350]—*Congregation of St. Francis Xavier*—C.F.X.

[]—*Congregation of the Most Holy Redeemer*

[]—*Congregation of the Sacred Stigmata*

[0790]—*Maronite Monks of Adoration*—M.M.A.

[0720]—*Missionaries of Our Lady of LaSalette* (Seven Dolors Prov.)—M.S.

[]—*Order of Friars Minor*

[0200]—*Order of St. Benedict* (Petersham; Still River)—O.S.B.

[0240]—*Order of St. Camilus*—O.S.Cam.

[]—*Society of Jesus*—S.J.

[0370]—*Society of St. Columban*—S.S.C.

[0350]—*The Cistercians Order of the Strict Observance (Trappists)*—O.C.S.O.

RELIGIOUS INSTITUTES OF WOMEN REPRESENTED IN THE DIOCESE

[0192]—*Carmelite Sisters of the Eucharist, Inc.*—C.S.E.

[]—*Congregation of Sisters of St. Felix of Cantalice*

[3830-01]—*Congregation of St. Joseph* (Boston, Brighton)—C.S.J.

[0820]—*Daughters of the Holy Spirit*—D.H.S.

[1115]—*Dominican Sisters of Peace*—O.P.

[]—*Franciscan Sisters of the Immaculate Heart of Mary* (India)—F.I.H.M.

[]—*Fransciscan Sisters Minor*—F.S.M.

[2575]—*Institute of the Sisters of Mercy of the Americas* (New York, NY)—R.S.M.

[2280]—*Little Franciscans of Mary*—P.F.M.

[2310]—*Little Sisters of the Assumption*—L.S.A.

[]—*Order of St. Benedict* Petersham—O.S.B.

[]—*Religious Oblates of Divine Love*—R.O.D.A.

[3390]—*Religious of the Assumption*—R.A.

[4180]—*Religious Venerini Sisters*—M.P.V.

[2540]—*Sisters of Mercy* (Institute of Religious Sisters of Mercy of the Americas)—R.S.M.

[3000]—*Sisters of Notre Dame de Namur* (Boston, Ipswich, Japan and Connecticut Provs.)—S.N.D.

[3340]—*Sisters of Providence* (Holyoke)—S.P.

[3720]—*Sisters of Saint Anne*—S.S.A.

[3830-16]—*Sisters of St. Joseph* (Springfield)—S.S.J.

[0150]—*Sisters of the Assumption of the Blessed Virgin*—S.A.S.V.

[3310]—*Sisters of the Presentation of Mary*—P.M.

[3320]—*Sisters of the Presentation of the B.V.M.*—P.B.V.M.

[]—*Slaves of the Immaculate Heart of Mary*—M.I.C.M.

[4230]—*Xaverian Missionary Society of Mary, Inc.*—X.M.M.

DIOCESAN CEMETERIES

WORCESTER. *St. John's*

Sacred Heart Cemetery, Worcester Rd., Webster, 01570.

Sacred Heart Cemetery, W. Main St., West Brookfield, 01585.

Saint Brigid Cemetery, West St., Millbury, 01527.

Saint George Cemetery, Paige Hill, Southbridge, 01550.

Saint Mary Cemetery, Main St., Holden, 01520.

Saint Philip Cemetery, Millbury St., Grafton, 01519.

Calvary Cemetery, 191 Vine St., Athol, 01331.

Calvary Cemetery, Oxford Ave., Dudley, 01571.

Gethsemane Cemetery, Fielding Way, Athol, 01331.

New Notre Dame Cemetery, Woodstock Rd., Southbridge, 01550.

Old Notre Dame Cemetery, Charlton St., Southbridge, 01550.

Saint Anne Cemetery, Arnold Rd., Sturbridge, 01518.

NECROLOGY

† Piermarini, Rev. Msgr. Louis R., Oxford, MA St. Roch—Died June 26, 2011

† Burke, John F., (Retired)—Died Nov. 3, 2011

† Coonan, Joseph A., (Retired)

† Dorais, Gerald A., Gardner, MA Our Lady of the Holy Rosary—Died Sept. 23, 2011

† Falvey, Edmund F., (Retired)—Died 2011

† Garlick, Thomas B., Southborough, MA St. Anne—Died May 22, 2011

† Gelineau, Raymond H., (Retired)—Died Sept. 12, 2011
† Gilbert, Maurice L., Millville, MA St. Augustine—Died July 22, 2011
† Gilgun, Bernard E., (Retired)—Died April 25, 2011
† Hebert, Roland G., (Retired)—Died April 3, 2011
† Johnson, Stephen D., Leicester, MA St. Pius X & St. Joseph—Died Sept. 15, 2011
† McGovern, William W., (Retired)—Died April 5, 2011
† O'Brien, George L., (Retired)—Died Feb. 15, 2011

An asterisk (*) denotes an organization that has established tax-exempt status directly with the IRS and is not covered by the USCCB Group Ruling.

Diocese of Yakima

(Dioecesis Yakimensis)

Most Reverend

JOSEPH J. TYSON

Bishop of Yakima; ordained June 10, 1989; appointed Auxiliary Bishop of Seattle and Titular Bishop of Migirpa May 12, 2005; ordained June 6, 2005; appointed Bishop of Yakima April 12, 2011; installed May 31, 2011. *710 9th Ave., Seattle, WA 98104*. Tel: 206-382-4560.

Most Reverend

CARLOS A. SEVILLA, S.J., D.D.

Bishop Emeritus of Yakima; ordained June 3, 1966; appointed Auxiliary Bishop of San Francisco December 6, 1988; Episcopal ordination January 25, 1989; appointed Bishop of Yakima December 31, 1996; installed February 17, 1997; retired April 12, 2011. *Address all correspondence to: 5301-A Tieton Dr., Yakima, WA 98908.*

ESTABLISHED JUNE 23, 1951.

Square Miles 17,787.

Comprises the following Counties in the State of Washington: Benton, Chelan, Douglas, Grant, Kittitas, Klickitat and Yakima.

Legal Title: Corporation of the Catholic Bishop of Yakima.
For legal titles of parishes and diocesan institutions, consult the Pastoral Office.

Pastoral Office (Chancery): 5301-A Tieton Dr., Yakima, WA 98908. Tel: 509-965-7117; Fax: 509-966-8334.

Email: info@yakimadiocese.org

STATISTICAL OVERVIEW

Personnel	
Bishop	1
Retired Bishops	1
Priests: Diocesan Active in Diocese	47
Priests: Diocesan Active Outside Diocese	1
Priests: Retired, Sick or Absent	27
Number of Diocesan Priests	75
Religious Priests in Diocese	2
Total Priests in Diocese	77
Extern Priests in Diocese	1
Permanent Deacons in Diocese	44
Total Brothers	2
Total Sisters	30
Parishes	
Parishes	41
With Resident Pastor:	
Resident Diocesan Priests	40
Resident Religious Priests	1
Without Resident Pastor:	
Administered by Priests	8
Missions	3
Pastoral Centers	1
Professional Ministry Personnel:	
Brothers	3
Sisters	30
Lay Ministers	16
Welfare	
Health Care Centers	1
Total Assisted	65,925
Day Care Centers	1
Total Assisted	174
Special Centers for Social Services	5
Total Assisted	49,389
Educational	
Diocesan Students in Other Seminaries	11
Total Seminarians	11
High Schools, Private	1
Total Students	176
Elementary Schools, Diocesan and Parish	6
Total Students	1,644
Catechesis/Religious Education:	
High School Students	2,135
Elementary Students	5,852
Total Students under Catholic Instruction	9,818
Teachers in the Diocese:	
Brothers	2
Sisters	3
Lay Teachers	171
Vital Statistics	
Receptions into the Church:	
Infant Baptism Totals	3,412
Minor Baptism Totals	234
Adult Baptism Totals	96
Received into Full Communion	147
First Communions	2,683
Confirmations	1,027
Marriages:	
Catholic	380
Interfaith	88
Total Marriages	468
Deaths	514
Total Catholic Population	72,980
Total Population	681,556

Former Bishops—Most Revs. JOSEPH P. DOUGHERTY, D.D., First Bishop of Yakima; ord. June 14, 1930; appt. July 9, 1951; cons. Sept. 26, 1951; resigned Feb. 5, 1969; died July 10, 1970; CORNELIUS M. POWER, D.D., Second Bishop of Yakima; ord. June 3, 1939; appt. Feb. 5, 1969; cons. May 1, 1969; elevated to Metropolitan See of Portland in Oregon, Jan. 24, 1974; died May 22, 1997; NICOLAS E. WALSH, D.D., Third Bishop of Yakima; ord. June 6, 1942; appt. Sept. 5, 1974; cons. Oct. 28, 1974; installed Oct. 30, 1974; transferred to Archdiocese of Seattle as Auxiliary Bishop, Aug. 10, 1976; resigned Sept. 6, 1983; died April 22, 1997; WILLIAM S. SKYLSTAD, D.D., Fourth Bishop of Yakima; ord. May 21, 1960; appt. Feb. 22, 1977; cons. May 12, 1977; transferred to Spokane as Bishop of Spokane, April 17, 1990; FRANCIS E. GEORGE, O.M.I., Ph.D., S.T.D., Fifth Bishop of Yakima; ord. Dec. 21, 1963; appt. July 10, 1990; cons. Sept. 21, 1990; appt. Metropolitan See of Portland in Oregon, April 30, 1996; appt. Metropolitan See of Chicago, April 8, 1997; created Cardinal Priest, Feb. 21, 1998.

Pastoral Office (Chancery)—5301-A Tieton Dr., Yakima, 98908. Tel: 509-965-7117; Fax: 509-966-8334.

Vicar General—Rev. Msgr. JOHN A. ECKER, 5301-A Tieton Dr., Yakima, 98908-3493.

Vicar for Priests—Revs. MARIO A. SALAZAR; LAWRENCE T. REILLY.

Moderator of the Curia—Rev. Msgr. ROBERT M. SILER.

Chancellor—Rev. Msgr. ROBERT M. SILER.

Vice Chancellor—Mrs. ELVIA GONZALEZ.

Office of Canonical Concerns—5301-D Tieton Dr., Yakima, 98908. Tel: 509-965-7123.

Judicial Vicar—Very Rev. MICHAEL J. IBACH, J.C.L.

Adjutant Judicial Vicar—Rev. DAVID J. JIMENEZ.

Judges—Very Rev. MICHAEL J. IBACH, J.C.L.; Revs. JOHN F. HENEGHAN (Retired); DAVID J. JIMENEZ.

Defenders of the Bond—Revs. THOMAS C. CHAMPOUX; SALOMON COVARRUBIAS PINA; Ms. KAY SHEPARD.

Advocates— Clergy and pastoral ministers by appointment.

Notaries—Mrs MARIA G. FLORES; Mrs. EILEEN M. WALKER.

Diocesan Consultors—Revs. OSMAR R. AGUIRRE; JAIME H. CHACON, M.Div.; Very Rev. MICHAEL J. IBACH, J.C.L.; Rev. Msgr. JOHN A. ECKER; Revs. ARGEMIRO OROZCO; FELIPE PULIDO; LAWRENCE T. REILLY; Rev. Msgr. ROBERT M. SILER.

Diocesan Offices, Commissions, Committees

Adults with Developmental Disabilities—MICHELE WALL, 12203 Klendon Dr., Yakima, 98908. Tel: 509-965-4642.

Calvary Cemetery—Rev. DARELL J. MITCHELL, Dir., 1405 S. 24th Ave., Yakima, 98902. Tel: 509-457-8462; Fax: 509-457-6267.

CYO—DON ERICKSON, 410 S. 47th Ave., Yakima, 98908. Tel: 509-965-3382.

Campaign for Human Development—Rev. Msgr. ROBERT M. SILER, 5301-A Tieton Dr., Yakima, 98908.

Catholic Charities—Mr. JOHN L. YOUNG, Exec. Dir., Office, 5301-C Tieton Dr., Yakima, 98908. Tel: 509-965-7100.

Charismatic Renewal, English—5301-A Tieton Dr., Yakima, 98908. Tel: 509-965-7117.

Charismatic Renewal, Spanish—Rev. GUSTAVO GOMEZ, Mailing Address: St. Juan Diego Parish, 15800 Summitview Rd., Cowiche, 98923. Tel: 509-678-4164.

Cursillo, English—Rev. JOHN M. SHAW, Spiritual Dir. (English) (Retired), 213 N. Beech, Toppenish, 98948. Tel: 509-865-4725; JUDY KITCHEN, Lay Dir., 118 Fairwood Ct., Richland, 99352. Tel: 509-628-3428.

Spanish—Deacon FRANK MARTINEZ, Spiritual Dir., 3790 Rd. 10.2 S.W., Royal City, 99357. Tel: 509-346-9536; JOSE GONZALEZ, Coord., 2467 N. Ashland Ave., East Wenatchee, 98802. Tel: 509-884-6009.

Native American—Rev. JOHN M. SHAW, Spiritual Dir. (Retired), 213 N. Beech St., Toppenish, 98948. Tel: 509-865-2400; MARY GARCIA, Mailing Address: P.O. Box 191, White Swan, 98952.

Director of Planned Giving—Rev. BROOKS F. BEAULAURIER, 5301-A Tieton Dr., Yakima, 98908. Tel: 509-965-7117.

Development Office/Stewardship—Rev. BROOKS F. BEAULAURIER, Dir., 5301-A Tieton Dr., Yakima, 98908. Tel: 509-965-7117.

Diocesan Coordinator for Health Affairs—Rev. THOMAS C. CHAMPOUX, 5301-C Tieton Dr., Yakima, 98908. Tel: 509-965-7100.

Diocesan Commission for the Catechumenate—Most Rev. JOSEPH J. TYSON; Rev. JUAN M. FLORES ALFEREZ; Ms. KAY SHEPARD, Chm.; Mrs DANETTE HESTER; Mr. RICK PINNELL; Deacon ROBERT J. SCHROM; Sr. MARIA ELENA CASILLAS, M.D.P.V.M.; Deacon KERRY TURLEY.

Diocesan Commission on Public Worship—Revs. JUAN MANUEL FLORES; THOMAS S. KUYKENDALL, Chm.; Mrs. PAT MANDELAS; Deacon RAY MILLER.

Diocesan Pastoral Council—

Ecumenical Liaison—Rev. Msgr. JOHN A. ECKER, 15 S. 12th Ave., Yakima, 98902. Tel: 509-575-3713.

Engaged Encounter—FRANK BECKER; TRACY BECKER, 2080 New Haven Loop, Richland, 99352.

Diocesan Finance Council—Most Rev. CARLOS ARTHUR SEVILLA, S.J., D.D., Pastoral Center, 5301-A Tieton Dr., Yakima, 98908; Rev. Msgr. JOHN A. ECKER; Mrs. COLLEEN KELLEHER; Mrs. PAT MYERS; Rev. DANIEL G. DUFNER; JEFF PETERSON, Consultant; JAMES PERKO, CFO; Mr. PETER SPADONI; Rev. Msgr. ROBERT M. SILER, Ex Officio.

Gang Outreach Ministry—VACANT.

Home Schooling—Deacon DUANE BERGER, Chap., 1706 Lower Ahtanum, Yakima, 98903. Tel: 509-457-1926; JONELLA LEADON.

Lay Advisory Board—Mr. RUSSELL MAZZOLA, Chm. Tel: 888-276-4490; Mr. THOMAS DITTMAR; Rev. Msgr. JOHN A. ECKER; Dr. MARK MAIOCCO; Dr. JORGE TORRES-SAENZ, PsyD.; Mrs. YVONNE SMITH.

Marriage Encounter, English—VACANT.

Spanish—Rev. JOSE DE JESUS RAMIREZ, Mailing Address: P.O. Box 340, Royal City, 99357-0340. Tel: 509-346-2730.

Natural Family Planning Advisory Committee—Rev. JUAN MANUEL GODINA, Dir. Tel: 509-965-7117; SHIRA WISE; ANNE NEALEN, M.D.; THEODORE F. O'DONNELL, M.D.; Dr. JAN HEMSTAD; Mrs. JAN R. HEMSTAD, M.D.

Ministry & Education Center—Rev. THOMAS S. KUYKENDALL, Dir. Catholic Schools, 5301-B Tieton Dr., Yakima, 98908. Tel: 509-965-7117.

Hispanic Ministries/Hispanic Ministry Formation—Rev. JAIME H. CHACON, M.Div., Dir. Hispanic Ministry, 5301-B Tieton Dr., Yakima, 98908. Tel: 509-965-7117.

Evangelization, Deacon Formation, Pastoral Council, Small Church Communities—VACANT, Dir.

Family Ministries—VACANT.

Religious Education and Hispanic Catechesis—Rev. TOMAS VASQUEZ TELLEZ, 5301-B Tieton Dr., Yakima, 98908. Tel: 509-965-7117.

Youth/Young Adult Director—Rev. WILMAR ZABALA, 5301-B Tieton Dr., Yakima, 98908. Tel: 509-965-7117.

Youth/Young Adult Hispanic Ministry—Rev. MIGUEL GONZALEZ CASTILLO, 5301-B Tieton Dr., Yakima, 98908. Tel: 509-965-7117.

Deacon Council—Deacon INDALECIO "ANDY" GONZALEZ; Mrs. ELVIA GONZALEZ; Deacon BILL MICH; MARGO MICH; Deacon ROBERT J. SCHROM; TERESA SCHROM.

Permanent Diaconate Liaison—Deacon ROBERT J. SCHROM, 7240 Rd. 17 S.W., Royal City, 99357. Tel: 509-346-9464.

Clergy Personnel Board—Most Rev. JOSEPH J. TYSON; Rev. Msgr. JOHN A. ECKER; Revs. DANIEL G. DUFNER; RONALD J. PATNODE (Retired); CESAR VEGA M.; MARIO A. SALAZAR; THOMAS C. CHAMPOUX; Rev. Msgr. ROBERT M. SILER; Rev. LAWRENCE T. REILLY, Ex Officio.

Press (Central Washington Catholic)—Rev. Msgr. ROBERT M. SILER.

Presbyteral Council Executive Committee—Most Rev. JOSEPH J. TYSON; Rev. Msgr. JOHN A. ECKER; Revs. CESAR VEGA; RICARDO A. VILLARREAL; MIGUEL GONZALEZ; THOMAS S. KUYKENDALL; Rev. Msgr. PERRON J. AUVE; Rev. ARGEMIRO OROZCO; Rev. Msgr. ROBERT M. SILER; Revs. JAIME H. CHACON, M.Div.; RICHARD D. SEDLACEK; JOHN M. SHAW (Retired); BROOKS F. BEAULAURIER; WILMAR ZABALA.

Native American Ministries—Rev. JOHN M. SHAW (Retired), 213 N. Beech, Toppenish, 98948. Tel: 509-865-4725.

Natural Family Planning—Rev. JUAN MANUEL GODINA, 5301-B Tieton Dr., Yakima, 98908. Tel: 509-965-7117.

Jail Ministry—Deacon GENARO RAMOS, 373 Lombard Loop Rd., Wapato, 98951; Rev. BROOKS F. BEAULAURIER.

Respect Life Committee—Mr. GEORGE BRIGGS; Mr NORM HILBERT; Mrs CATHY HILBERT; VICKIE MONTGOMERY; FRANK SCHNEIDER; SHERYL SCOTT; Rev. JUAN MANUEL GODINA, 5301-B Tieton Dr., Yakima, 98908. Tel: 509-965-7117.

Diocesan Catholic Committee on Scouting—Deacon WILLIAM A. DRONEN, Chap., 306 Railroad Ave., Cashmere, 98815. Tel: 509-782-3976; Mr PHIL PIEPEL, Chm., 2897 Riviera Blvd., Malaga, 98828. Tel: 509-665-0892; Mr. MARC DESGROSEILLIER; Mr RICHARD MANKA; Mr SCOTT MELTON; Rev. NEILL R. MEANY, S.J.; Mr CURT NEALEN; Mr RICK URLACHER; Ms DONNA VAN DOREN.

Social Justice and Human Life Commission—Rev. JUAN MANUEL GODINA; Mr. JOHN L. YOUNG; Rev. WILLIAM VOGEL, S.J.

St. Joseph Mission at the Ahtanum—Directors: ED CAMPBELL; CARY CAMPBELL, 17740 Ahtanum Rd., Yakima, 98903. Tel: 509-966-0865; Fax: 509-966-5649. Email: casprus2@prodigy.net.

St. Vincent de Paul Society—Rev. THOMAS C. CHAMPOUX, Spiritual Dir., 1126 Long Ave., Richland, 99352. Tel: 509-946-1675.

Serra Club—BILL HAYES, 800 S. 46th St., Yakima, 98908. Tel: 509-966-7056; JOAN TOTH, 504 N. Rd. 40, Pasco, 99301.

Victim Assistance Coordinators—Mrs. JANET ERICKSON. Email: jerickson@cfcsyakima.org; BLANCA VARGAS. Email: bvargas@cfcsyakima.org.

Vocations—Revs. FELIPE PULIDO; WILMAR ZABALA.

CLERGY, PARISHES, MISSIONS AND PAROCHIAL SCHOOLS

CITY OF YAKIMA

(YAKIMA COUNTY)

1—ST. PAUL CATHEDRAL (1914) [CEM] Rev. Msgr. John A. Ecker; Rev. Eleazar Diaz; Deacon Ray Miller; Alma Jauregui, Pastoral Care for Senior Citizens.
15 S. 12th Ave., 98902.
Res.: 1208 W. Chestnut, 98902. Tel: 509-575-3713; Fax: 509-453-7497. Email: parish@stpaulyakima.org. Web: www.stpaulyakima.org.
School—(Grades PreK-8), 1214 W. Chestnut Ave., 98902. Tel: 509-575-5604; Fax: 509-577-8817. Email: merskine@stpaulsch.org. Web: www.stpaulcathedralschool.org. Lay Teachers 15; Students 216.
Catholic Student Center—810 S. 16th Ave., 98902. Tel: 509-249-6238.
Catechesis/Religious Program—Students 340.

2—HOLY FAMILY (1959) Revs. Cesar Vega M.; Gary L. Desharnais, Parochial Vicar; Deacons John Cornell; James Kramper. In Res., Revs. Thomas V. Lane (Retired); Ronald J. Patnode (Retired); Very Rev. Michael J. Ibach.
Church Office: 5315 Tieton Dr., 98908. Tel: 509-966-0830; Fax: 509-965-1742. Email: office@holyfamilyyakima.org. Web: www.holyfamilyyakima.org.
Rectory—302-304 & 306 S. 50th, 98908.
Catechesis/Religious Program—5502-04 Chestnut Ave, Rm. #11, 98908. Tel: 509-966-0788; Fax: 509-965-0288. Students 303.
Mission—St. Joseph Mission at the Ahtanum 17740 Ahtanum Rd., Yakima Co. 98908. Tel: 509-966-5649; Fax: 509-966-5649.

3—HOLY REDEEMER (1962), (Hispanic), [JC] Rev. Francisco Gutierrez; Deacon Duane Berger.
Res.: 1607 Landon Ave., 98902. Tel: 509-248-2241; Fax: 509-457-3312. Email: holyredeemer_o@questoffice.net. Web: www.holyredeemeryakima.org.
Church: 1707 S. Third Ave., 98902.
Catechesis/Religious Program—Students 184.

4—ST. JOSEPH PARISH (1847) Revs. Felipe Pulido; Jose M. Herrera; Deacons Nestor Chavez; William D. Hudson.
212 N. 4th St., 98901-2426. Tel: 509-248-1911; Fax: 509-248-2604.
School—St. Joseph/Marquette, 202 N. 4th St., 98901. Tel: 509-575-5557; Fax: 509-457-5621. Lay Teachers 24; Students 334.
Catechesis/Religious Program—Students 298.

OUTSIDE THE CITY OF YAKIMA

BENTON CITY, BENTON CO., ST. FRANCES XAVIER CABRINI (1963) Revs. Richard D. Sedlacek; John C. Vogl.
Mailing Address: P.O. Box 179, 99320-0179. Fax: 509-588-3636.
Church: 1000 Horn Rd., 99320. Tel: 509-588-3636. Email: sfxc-secretary@frontier.com.
Catechesis/Religious Program—Students 59.

BRIDGEPORT, DOUGLAS CO., ST. ANNE'S (1964) Rev. Ricardo A. Villarreal.
Mailing Address: P.O. Box 1089, Chelan, 98816-1089. Tel: 509-682-2433; Fax: 509-682-9147. Email: stfrancischurch@nwi.net.
Catechesis/Religious Program—Students 47.

CASHMERE, CHELAN CO., ST. FRANCIS XAVIER (1915) Rev. Alejandro E. Trejo; Deacon Bill Dronen.
Res.: 307 Angier, 98815. Tel: 509-782-2643; Fax: 509-782-2686.
Catechesis/Religious Program—Students 55.

CHELAN, CHELAN CO., ST. FRANCIS DE SALES (1904) [CEM] Rev. Ricardo A. Villarreal.
215 W. Allen Ave., P.O. Box 1089, 98816-1089. Tel: 509-682-2433; Fax: 509-682-9147. Email: stfrancischurch@nwi.net.
Catechesis/Religious Program—Students 79.
Mission—St. Mary (1909) Mansfield Blvd. & 2nd, Mansfield, Douglas Co. 98830. Tel: 509-682-2433; Fax: 509-682-9147. Email: stfrancischurch@nwi.net.

CLE ELUM, UPPER KITTITAS CO., ST. JOHN THE BAPTIST (1913) Rev. Lawrence T. Reilly.
Office: 303 W. 2nd St., 98922. Tel: 509-674-2531; Fax: 509-674-1894.
Catechesis/Religious Program—Students 18.

COWICHE, YAKIMA CO., ST. JUAN DIEGO (1959), (Spanish), (Formerly known as St. Peter the Apostle). Rev. Gustavo Gomez.
Res.: 15800 Summitview Rd., 98923. Tel: 509-678-4164; Fax: 509-678-4165. Email: stjuandiego@centurytel.net.
Catechesis/Religious Program—Students 133.

EAST WENATCHEE, DOUGLAS CO., HOLY APOSTLES (1962) Revs. Argemiro Orozco; Jacob Davis; Deacons Thomas Richtsmeier; Carlos Luna; Cary Parnell; Peter Fadich.
Res.: 1315 NE Eight St., 98802. Tel: 509-884-5444; Fax: 509-886-3424. Email: holyapostles@nwi.net. Web: www.holyapostlesparish.org.
Catechesis/Religious Program—1315 8th St. N.E., 98802. Tel: 509-884-5444. Students 359.

ELLENSBURG, KITTITAS CO., ST. ANDREW'S (1884) [CEM] Rev. Tomas Vazquez.
Mailing Address: 401 S. Willow St., 98926.
Res.: 403 S. Willow St., 98926. Tel: 509-962-9821. Email: standrewparish@yahoo.com.
Catechesis/Religious Program—Students 230.

EPHRATA, GRANT CO., ST. ROSE OF LIMA (1915) [CEM] Rev. Miguel Gonzalez; Deacon Armando Escamilla.
Mailing Address: 323 D St., S.W., 98823. Email: strose@nwi.net. In Res., Rev. Seamus Kerr (Retired).
Parish Office—560 Nat Washington Way, 98823. Tel: 509-754-3640; Fax: 509-754-4064. Email: strose@nwi.net.
School—(Grades PreK-6), 520 Nat Washington Way, 98823. Tel: 509-754-4901; Fax: 509-754-9274. Lay Teachers 7; Students 100.
Catechesis/Religious Program—Students 90.

GOLDENDALE, KLICKITAT CO., HOLY TRINITY (1884) [CEM] Rev. William Byron.
Res.: 210 S. Schuster St., 98620. Tel: 509-773-4516; Fax: 509-773-6983. Email: holytrinity@gorge.net.
Catechesis/Religious Program—Jackie Bugler, D.R.E. Students 40.

GRAND COULEE, GRANT CO., ST. HENRY'S (1955) [JC] Rev. Robert P. Himes.
Res.: 590 Grand Coulee Ave. W., P.O. Box P, 99133. Tel: 509-633-1180; Fax: 509-633-6859.
Catechesis/Religious Program—

GRANDVIEW, YAKIMA CO., BLESSED SACRAMENT (1954) Revs. Jaime H. Chacon; Roleto B. Amoy.
Res.: 1201 Missouri, 98930. Tel: 509-882-1657; Fax: 509-882-1107. Email: blessedsacramentchurch@embarqmail.com.
Catechesis/Religious Program—Students 540.

GRANGER, YAKIMA CO., OUR LADY OF GUADALUPE (1966), (Hispanic), [JC] Rev. Mario P. Salazar.
Res.: 608 Granger Ave., P.O. Box 308, 98932. Tel: 509-854-1558; Fax: 509-854-7326.
Catechesis/Religious Program—Tel: 509-854-2164. Students 60.

HARTLINE, GRANT CO., ST. PATRICK'S (1955) [CEM], Served from St. Henry's, P.O. Box P, Grand Coulee 99133. Rev. Robert P. Himes.
Mailing Address: P.O. Box 925, Coulee City, 99115. Tel: 509-633-1180; Fax: 509-633-6859.
Catechesis/Religious Program—
Mission—Holy Angels P.O. Box 925, Coulee City, Grant Co. 99115.

KENNEWICK, BENTON CO.

1—HOLY SPIRIT (1980) Rev. Msgr. Perron J. Auve; Deacons John E. Powers; Ronald J. Mertens. In Res., Rev. John G. O'Shea.
Office: 7409 W. Clearwater, 99336. Tel: 509-735-8558; Fax: 509-735-8559. Email: office@holyspiritkennewick.org. Web: www.holyspiritkennewick.org.
Catechesis/Religious Program—Jennifer Moore, D.R.E.; Pat Moore, D.R.E. & Youth Min. Students 194.

2—ST. JOSEPH'S (1911) Revs. Richard D. Sedlacek; Rafael Hinojosa; Deacons William Mich; Jose Cortez; Simon Jada. In Res., Rev. Msgr. Desmond P. Dillon (Retired).
Res.: 520 S. Garfield, 99336. Tel: 509-586-3820; Fax: 509-586-3558. Email: parish.office@stjoseph-kennewick.org.
School—(Grades PreSchool-8), 901 W. 4th Ave., 99336. Tel: 509-586-0481; Fax: 509-585-9781. Lay Teachers 23; Students 378.
Catechesis/Religious Program—Tel: 509-582-8460. Students 545.

LEAVENWORTH, CHELAN CO., OUR LADY OF THE SNOWS (1912) Rev. Alejandro E. Trejo.
Res.: 145 Wheeler St., 98826. Tel: 509-548-5119; Fax: 509-548-5051.
Catechesis/Religious Program—Students 40.

MABTON, YAKIMA CO., IMMACULATE CONCEPTION (1910) Revs. Jaime H. Chacon; Roleto B. Amoy.
Mailing Address: P.O. Box 275, 98935. Tel: 509-882-1657; Fax: 509-882-1107.
Res.: 1201 Missouri, Grandview, 98930. Tel: 509-882-1657; Fax: 509-882-1107.
Catechesis/Religious Program—Students 105.

MATTAWA, GRANT CO., OUR LADY OF THE DESERT (1987) [JC] Rev. Jorge Granados.
Mailing Address: 301 8th St., P.O. Box 2268, 99349. Tel: 509-932-5424; Fax: 509-932-4055.
Catechesis/Religious Program—Students 318.

MOSES LAKE, GRANT CO., OUR LADY OF FATIMA (1955), (Spanish), [CEM] Revs. Dan Dufner; Tomas Vidal; Deacons Robert J. Schrom; Agapito Gonzales Jr. In Res., Rev. Msgr. Martin O. Skehan (Retired).
Res.: 200 N. Dale Rd., 98837. Tel: 509-765-6729; Fax: 509-765-0114.
Parish Center—210 N. Dale Rd., 98837. Tel: 509-765-6729.
Catechesis/Religious Program—Doris Rosenow, Rel. Educ. & Faith Formation. Students 470.

MOXEE CITY, YAKIMA CO., HOLY ROSARY (1900) [CEM] Rev. John J. Murtagh.
Res.: 201 N. Iler., P.O. Box 279, 98936. Tel: 509-453-4061; Fax: 509-576-6290.
Catechesis/Religious Program—Tel: 509-453-6754. Students 273.

NACHES, YAKIMA CO., ST. JOHN (1959) Rev. Richard M. House; Deacon Don Griek.
Res.: 204 Moxee Ave., P.O. Box 128, 98937-0128. Tel: 509-653-2534; Fax: 509-653-2534.
Catechesis/Religious Program—Tel: 509-653-2534. Students 25.

PROSSER, BENTON CO., SACRED HEART (1899) Rev. Osmar R. Aguirre.
Res.: 1905 Highland Dr., 99350. Tel: 509-786-1783; Fax: 509-786-1747. Email: shcc@embarqmail.com.
Catechesis/Religious Program—Cynthia O'Brien, D.R.E., (English Prog.). Tel: 509-786-1783; Kathy Moore, D.R.E. (English Prog.); Maria Zepeda, D.R.E., (Spanish Program). Tel: 509-786-1783. Students 312.

QUINCY, GRANT CO., ST. PIUS X (1955), (Hispanic), Rev. Mario A. Salazar.
Res.: 805 N. Central Ave., P.O. Box 308, 98848. Tel: 509-787-2622; Fax: 509-787-6068. Email: st.piusx@verizon.net.
Catechesis/Religious Program—Rita Keene, D.R.E.; Ana Argueta, D.R.E., (Spanish). Students 210.

RICHLAND, BENTON CO., CHRIST THE KING (1946) Revs. Thomas C. Champoux; Teodulo G. Taneo, S.V.D. (Philippines); Vandennis Nguyen; Deacons Robert DaValle; LeRoi Rice; Mikhail Alnajjar; Doroteo Collado; Alfredo Jocson; Thomas Huntington; Ross Ronish.
Office: 1111 Stevens Dr., 99354. Tel: 509-946-1675; Fax: 509-946-9940. Web: www.ckparish.org.
School—1122 Long Ave., 99354. Tel: 509-946-6158; Fax: 509-943-8402. Web: www.CKschoolRichland.org. Lay Teachers 25; Students 428.
Catechesis/Religious Program—Tel: 509-946-1154; Fax: 509-946-9940. Email: erin@ckparish.org. Lori Wasner, D.R.E. Students 405.

ROSLYN, UPPER KITTITAS CO., IMMACULATE CONCEPTION (1887) Rev. Lawrence T. Reilly.
Mailing Address: 303 W. 2nd St., Cle Elum, 98922. Tel: 509-674-2531; Fax: 509-674-1894.
Res.: 211 N. B St., 98941.
Catechesis/Religious Program— Twinned with St. John the Baptist, Cle Elum. Students 14.

ROYAL CITY, GRANT CO., ST. MICHAEL THE ARCHANGEL (1966), (Hispanic), Rev. J. Jesus Ramirez; Deacon Francisco Martinez.
Res.: 145 Daisy St., N.W., P.O. Box 340, 99357. Tel: 509-346-2730; Fax: 509-346-2901. Email: fr.jesusramirez@centurytel.net.
Catechesis/Religious Program—Tel: 509-346-2236. Students 120.

SELAH, YAKIMA CO., OUR LADY OF LOURDES (1975) Rev. David J. Jimenez.
Res.: 1112 W. Fremont, 98942. Tel: 509-697-4633; Fax: 831-664-4633. Email: ollselah@hotmail.com.
Catechesis/Religious Program—1111 W. Fremont, 98942. Students 102.

SUNNYSIDE, YAKIMA CO., ST. JOSEPH'S (1936) Rev. Thomas J. Bunnell, S.J.; Deacon Kerry Turley.
Res.: 920 S. 6th St., 98944. Tel: 509-837-2243; Fax: 509-837-7063.
Catechesis/Religious Program—Tel: 509-839-4758. Students 565.

TOPPENISH, YAKIMA CO., ST. ALOYSIUS (1908) Rev. Juan M. Flores; Deacon Berny Alvarado.
Mailing Address: 213 N. Beech St., 98948. Tel: 508-865-4725; Fax: 508-865-7882. Email: st.aloysius@charter.net. In Res., Rev. John M. Shaw (Retired).
Religious Education Center—214 N. Beech St., 98948. Tel: 509-865-2565.
Catechesis/Religious Program—Fax: 509-865-3077. Manuel Castillejo, D.R.E. Students 265.

WAPATO, YAKIMA CO., ST. PETER CLAVER (1906) Rev. Juan Manuel Godina; Deacons John Kassinger; Genaro Ramos.
509 S. Satus Ave., 98951. Tel: 509-877-2813.
Catechesis/Religious Program—Tel: 509-877-2081. Students 222.

WARDEN, GRANT CO., QUEEN OF ALL SAINTS (1966), (Spanish), Revs. Dan Dufner; Tomas Vidal; Deacon Andres Escamilla.
c/o 200 N. Dale Rd., Moses Lake, 98837. Tel: 509-765-6729; Fax: 509-765-0114.
Catechesis/Religious Program—Roldan Capetillo, D.R.E. (K-12). Students 200.

WATERVILLE, DOUGLAS CO., ST. JOSEPH'S (1892) [CEM] [JC] Rev. Gary Norman.
Res.: 103 Poplar St., P.O. Box 519, 98858. Tel: 509-745-8205.
Catechesis/Religious Program—Tel: 509-745-8787. Noreen Daling, D.R.E. Students 15.

WENATCHEE, CHELAN CO., ST. JOSEPH'S (1903) Revs. Thomas S. Kuykendall; Rogelio Gutierrez; Deacons Robert Hulligan II; Bill Osborn.
Res.: 625 Elliott, 98801. Tel: 509-662-4569; Fax: 509-663-8437. Email: stjoewen@stjoewen.org.
School—(Grades PreK-5), 600 St. Joseph Pl., 98801. Tel: 509-663-2644; Fax: 509-663-8474. Religious 3; Lay Teachers 12; Students 188.
Catechesis/Religious Program—600 St. Joseph Pl., 98801. Students 375.

WHITE SALMON, KLICKITAT CO., ST. JOSEPH (1912), (Spanish), Rev. Salomon Covarrubias-Pina.
Res.: 240 N.W. Washington, P.O. Box 2049, 98672. Tel: 509-493-2828; Fax: 509-493-2175. Web: church.gorge.net/stjoes-ws/. Email: stjosephs@embarqmail.com.
Catechesis/Religious Program—Tel: 509-493-2386. Email: hshultzy5@yahoo.com. Students 125.

WHITE SWAN, YAKIMA CO., ST. MARY'S (1889), (Native American), Rev. William E. Shaw; Deacon Andy Gonzalez.
Res.: 360 Signal Peak Rd., P.O. Box 417, 98952-0417. Tel: 509-874-2436; Fax: 509-874-1197.
Catechesis/Religious Program—Students 50.

ZILLAH, YAKIMA CO., RESURRECTION (1963) Rev. Juan M. Flores.
Mailing Address: P.O. Box 567, 98953-0567. Tel: 509-829-5433; Fax: 509-829-5312.
Catechesis/Religious Program—Tel: 509-829-5433. Students 100.

Special Assignment:
Revs.—
Magaña, Alberto O., 5301-A Tieton Dr., 98908.
Mitchell, Darell J., 5301-A Tieton Dr., 98908.
Vogl, John C., 5301-A Tieton Dr., 98908.

On Duty Outside the Diocese:
Revs.—
DeLoza, Jose, Mexico
Hernandez, Francisco J. (Retired), 214 San Bernardo Ave., Laredo, TX 78040.
Higuera, Francisco, 521 Fair St., Lodi, WI 53555.
Inman, Robert D.
Kenna, Joseph J. (Retired), 9103 Wellington Pl., Lanham, MD 20706.
Keolker, Richard F., Mount Angel Seminary, 119 Anselm, St. Benedict, OR 97373.
Milich, Nicholas, 1335 Byron Dr., Salinas, CA 93901.
Rodriguez, Felix M., P.O. Box 12335, Casa Grande, AZ 85230.

Retired:
Rev. Msgrs.—
Dillon, Desmond P., St. Joseph Parish, 520 S. Garfield, Kennewick, 99336.
Skehan, Martin O., 200 N. Dale Rd., Moses Lake, 98837.
Revs.—
Cerezo, Alberto F., 11637 100th Ave., N.E., #C2, Kirkland, 98034-6518.
Greene, Daniel (ORL), 7851 54th Ave. N., St. Petersburg, FL 33709-2338.
Hannick, Anthony S., 1600 Roosmoor Pkwy., Walnut Creek, CA 94553.
Heneghan, John F., Waverly Collacoon, Mayo, Ireland.
Hernandez, Francisco J., 214 San Bernardo Ave., Laredo, TX 78040.
Kenna, Joseph J.
Kerr, Seamus
Lane, Thomas V., 304 S. 50th, 98908.
Patnode, Ronald J.
Peterson, Maurice F., 5301-A Tieton Dr., 98908.
Senvello, Robert, P.O. Box 6, Plentywood, MT 59254.
Shaw, John M.
Shields, Robert J., 4602 Tieton Dr., Apt. D 24, 98908.
Surman, Darrell, P.O. Box 12523, Thorndon Wellington, New Zealand.
Tholen, John, 5301-A Tieton Dr., 98908.

Permanent Deacons:
Alnajjar, Mikhail, 140 Canyon Rd., Richland, 99352.
Alvarado, Berney, 15 S. Date St., Toppenish, 98948.
Berger, Duane, 1706 Lower Ahtanum, 98903.
Chavez, Nestor, 710 E. Race St., 98901.
Collado, Doroteo, 108 Patton St., Richland, 99354.
Cornell, John, 2504 W. Chestnut, 98902.
Cortez, Jose, 4324 W. 15th Ave, Kennewick, 99338.
DaValle, Robert, 1837 Marshall Ave., Richland, 99352.
Dronen, Bill, 306 Railroad Ave., Cashmere, 98815.
Escamilla, Andres, 4765 Rd. V., S.E., Warden, 98857.
Escamilla, Armando, 2022 S. Division St., Moses Lake, 98837.
Fadich, Peter, 1702 8th St. N.E., East Wenatchee, 98802.
Farrell, Daniel J., 923 Straitview Dr., Port Angeles, 98362.
Gonzales, Agapito, Jr., P.O. Box 551, Warden, 98857.
Gonzalez, Indalecio, 2760 Brownstown Rd., Harrah, 98933.
Griek, Don, P.O. Box 1023, Leavenworth, 98826.
Haberman, Gregory, 290 Road B, S.W., Waterville, 98858.
Hudson, William D., 8819 S.E. 213th St., Renton, 98058.
Hulligan, Robert, II, 22 French St., East Wenatchee, 98802.
Huntington, Thomas, 1008 Fitch St., Richland, 99352.
Jada, Simon, 2115 W. Grand Ronde Ave., Kennewick, 99336.
Jocson, Alfredo, 1633 Venus Cir., Richland, 99352.
Kassinger, John, 1314 N. Ave., #4, Sunnyside, 98944.
Kramper, James, 7304 Tieton Dr., 98908.
Legg, George, P.O. Box 572, Warden, 98857.
Luna, Carlos, 1947 Easy St., Wenatchee, 98801.
Martinez, Frank, 3790 Rd. 104, S.W., Royal City, 99357.
Mertens, Ronald J., 4202 Riverhill Rd., Pasco, 99301.
Mich, William, 601 N. Reed, Kennewick, 99336.
Miller, Ray, 2412 W. Chestnut, 98902.
Munns, James, 917 S. 32nd Ave., 98902.
Oriz, Angel, 200 N.W. Simmons Rd., White Salmon, 98672.
Osborn, Bill, 1613 Fairview Ave., Wenatchee, 98801.
Parnell, Cary, 655 4th St. N.E., G203, East Wenatchee, 98802.
Powers, John, 3614 S. Green St., Kennewick, 99337.
Ramos, Genaro, 373 Lombard Loop Rd., Wapato, 98951.
Reyna, Lupe, (Retired), 1130 S. Grand, Moses Lake, 98837.
Rice, LeRoi, 1845 Mahan Ave., Richland, 99352.
Richtsmeier, Thomas, 2901 8th St., S.E., East Wenatchee, 98802.
Rizzo, Al, 135 MacArthur St., Richland, 99352.
Ronish, Ross, 621 Meadows Dr. S., Richland, 99352.
Schrom, Robert J., 7240 Rd. 17, S.W., Royal City, 99357.
Sherman, Del, 122 Chelan Falls, P.O. Box 137, Chelan Falls, 98817.
Solorzano, Miguel, 810 Juniper Dr., Moses Lake, 98837.
Turley, Kerry, 304 E. Woodin Rd., Sunnyside, 98944.

INSTITUTIONS LOCATED IN THE DIOCESE

[A] COLLEGES AND UNIVERSITIES

TOPPENISH. **Heritage University* (1982) (Interdenominational University with an Independent Board), 3240 Fort Rd., 98948. Tel: 509-865-8600; Fax: 509-865-7976. Email: ross_k@heritage.edu. Web: www.heritage.edu. John Bassett, Pres.; Sr. Kathleen Ross, S.N.J.M., Pres. Emerita & Prof.; Bill McCay, Librarian. Sisters 4; Lay Teachers 52; Students 1,500; Lay Staff 101.

[B] HIGH SCHOOLS

UNION GAP. *La Salle High School*, 3000 Lightning Way, 98903. Tel: 509-225-2900; Fax: 509-225-2950. Email: office@lasalleyakima.org. Web: www.lasalleyakima.org. Timothy McGree, Pres.; Bro. James Joost, F.S.C., Prin. Brothers 3; Sisters 1; Lay Teachers 12; Staff 8; Students 190.

[C] HOSPITALS

RICHLAND. *Lourdes Counseling Center*, 1175 Carondelet Dr., 99354. Tel: 509-943-9104; Fax: 509-943-7206. Email: bmead@lourdesonline.org. Web: www.lourdeshealth.net. Barbara Mead, Vice Pres. Behavioral Health & Physician Clinics. Bed Capacity 32; Total Assisted Annually 73,658; Total Staff 165.

[D] CATHOLIC SOCIAL SERVICE CATHOLIC CHARITIES

YAKIMA. *Carroll Children's Center*, 5301 Tieton Dr., Ste. C, 98908. Tel: 509-965-7104; Fax: 509-966-9750. Email: khelseth@cfcsyakima.org. Kathy Helseth, Prog. Mgr. Capacity 120; Total Assisted Annually 174; Total Staff 25.

Catholic Charities of the Diocese of Yakima, 5301-C Tieton Dr., 98908. Tel: 509-965-7100; Fax: 509-972-0167. Email: jyoung@ccyakima.org. Web: www.ccyakima.org. Mr. John L. Young, Pres. & CEO.

Catholic Family and Child Service, 5301 Tieton Dr., Ste. C, 98908. Tel: 509-965-7100; Fax: 509-966-9750. Email: info@cfcsyakima.org. Web: www.cfcsyakima.org. Mrs. Darlene Darnell, M.S.W., Vice Pres. Total Assisted Annually 37,489; Total Staff 125.

Child Care Nutrition, 4704 Tieton Dr., Ste. A, 98908. Tel: 509-965-7107; 800-449-9005; Fax: 509-965-8337. Email: coliphant@cfcsyakima.org.

St. Vincent Center, 2629 Main St., Union Gap, 98903. Tel: 509-457-5111; Fax: 509-457-3526. Email: stores@stvincentyakima.org. Web: www.ccyakima.org. Mr. John L. Young, Pres. Total Staff 14.

ELLENSBURG. *St. Vincent Center*, 1200 S. Canyon Rd., 98926. Tel: 509-925-2167; Fax: 509-925-9547. Email: stores@stvincentyakima.org. Web: www.ccyakima.org. Total Staff 8.

KENNEWICK. *St. Vincent Centers*, 120 N. Morain, 99336. Tel: 509-783-7020; Fax: 509-783-7039. Email: kdavis@ccyakima.org. Web: www.ccyakima.org.

MOSES LAKE. *Catholic Family and Child Service of Moses Lake-Ephrata*, 5301 Tieton Dr., Ste. C, 98901. Tel: 509-965-7100; Fax: 509-972-0167. Email: jyoung@cfcyakima.org. Web: www.ccyakima.org. Total Assisted 1,500; Total Staff 4.

RICHLAND. *Catholic Family and Child Service*, 2139 Van Giesen, 99354. Tel: 509-946-4645; Fax: 509-943-2068. Email: jyoung@ccyakima.org. Maureen C. McGrath, M.A., Agency Dir. Total Assisted 6,700; Total Staff 57.

SUNNYSIDE. *Catholic Family and Child Service of Yakima*, 320 N. 16th St., 98944. Tel: 800-793-4453. Email: jyoung@cfcsyakima.org. Web: www.ccyakima.org. Total Assisted 1,200; Total Staff 2.

WENATCHEE. *Catholic Family and Child Service*, 640 S. Mission St., 98801. Tel: 509-662-6761; Fax: 509-663-3182. Email: jyoung@cfcyakima.org. Web: www.ccyakima.org. Total Assisted 2,500; Total Staff 35.

[E] RETIREMENT HOMES

YAKIMA. **The Gamelin Association-Providence House dba dba Providence House** 312 N. 4th St. #106, 98901. Tel: 509-452-5017; Fax: 509-452-1947. Email: Dawn.Rodrigues@providence.org. Web: www.providence.org/Long_Term_Care/Housing/e20ProvHouse.htm. Dawn Rodrigues, Dir. Email: dawn.rodrigues@providence.org. Providence Ministries: Johnny Cox, Vice Pres., Barbara Savage, Past Pres., Anita Butler, SP, Treas., Barbara Schamber, SP, Sec., Low income housing for elderly.

[F] VOLUNTEER SERVICES

YAKIMA. *St. Paul's Parish Conference*, 15 S. 12th Ave., 98902. Tel: 509-575-3713; Fax: 509-453-7497. Email: stpaul@wolfenet.com. Greg Vavricka, Pres.; Jeffrey Arkills, Treas.; Patty Schumm, Sec.

Society of St. Vincent de Paul, Particular Council of Yakima, 269 D St., S.E., #209, Ephrata, 98823. Tel: 509-754-4246.

EAST WENATCHEE. *Holy Apostles Parish*, 1315 8th St., N.E., 98801. Tel: 509-884-5444; Fax: 509-886-3424. Email: holyapostles@nwi.net. Web: www.holyapostlesparish.org. Lee Gale, Pastoral Council Pres.; Rev. Argemiro Orozco.

KENNEWICK. *St. Joseph Parish Conference*, 520 S. Garfield, 99336. Tel: 509-586-3820; Fax: 509-586-3558. Email: parish.office@stjoseph-kennewick.org.

RICHLAND. *Christ the King Parish Conference* (1955) 1111 Stevens Dr., 99354. Tel: 509-946-1675; Fax: 509-946-9940. Email: bulletin@ckparish.org. Web: www.ckparish.org. Bob Morford, Pres.

WENATCHEE. *St. Joseph Parish Conference, St Vincent de Paul*, 625 S. Elliott, 98801. Tel: 509-662-4569; Fax: 509-663-8437. Pat Lynam, Pres.

[G] CAMPUS MINISTRY

ELLENSBURG. *Catholic Campus Ministry at Central Washington University* 706 N. Sprague, 98926. Tel: 509-925-3043; Fax: 509-925-3043. Email: ccmcwu@fairpoint.net. Rev. Wilmar Zabala, Dir. & Campus Min. Total in Residence 1; Total Staff 1.

[H] MISCELLANEOUS LISTINGS

YAKIMA. **Catholic Charities Housing Services, Diocese of Yakima*, 5301 Tieton Dr., Ste. G, 98908-3479. Tel: 509-853-2800; Fax: 509-853-2805. Mr. John L. Young, Pres.

**Central Washington Catholic Foundation* (2002) 5301 Tieton Dr., Ste. F, 98908-3479. Tel: 509-972-3732; Fax: 509-972-2417. Email: info@cwcatholicfoundation.org. Web: www.cwcatholicfoundation.org. Daniel C. Fortier, Exec. Dir.

Diocese of Yakima Capital Revolving Program, 5301-A Tieton Dr., 98908. Tel: 509-965-7117; Fax: 509-966-8019. James Perko, C.F.O.

Irrevocable Priest Retirement Trust for the Diocese of Yakima, 5301-A Tieton Dr., 98908. Tel: 509-965-7117; Fax: 509-966-8019. James Perko, C.F.O.

Irrevocable Seminarian Education Trust for the Diocese of Yakima, 5301-A Tieton Dr., 98908. Tel: 509-965-7117; Fax: 509-966-8019. James Perko, C.F.O.

St. Vincent Centers of the Diocese of Yakima, 5301-C Tieton Dr., 98908. Tel: 509-853-2796; Fax: 509-972-0167. Email: stores@stvincentyakima.org. Web: www.ccyakima.org. Mr. John Young, Pres.

TOPPENISH. *Association of Catholic Sisters for Educational Opportunities for the Poor*, 3240 Fort Rd., 98948. Tel: 509-865-3836. Sr. Kathleen Ross, S.N.J.M., Pres.

UNION GAP. *La Salle Foundation of Yakima*, 3000 Lightning Way, 98903. Tel: 509-225-2991; Fax: 509-225-2994. Email: foundation@lasalleyakima.org. Web: www.lasalleyakima.com. Timothy McGree, Pres.

ZILLAH. *Catholics In Action* (200) P.O. Box 673, 98953. Tel: 509-790-7696; Fax: 509-829-9503. Email: yakimacatholicradio@gmail.com. Mr. Richard Sevigny, Pres.

RELIGIOUS INSTITUTES OF MEN REPRESENTED IN THE DIOCESE

For further details refer to the corresponding bracketed number in the Religious Institutes of Men or Women section.

[0200]—*Benedictine Monks (American Cassinese Congregation)*—O.S.B.

[0330]—*Brothers of the Christian Schools* (Prov. of San Francisco)—F.S.C.

[0690]—*Jesuit Fathers and Brothers (Oregon Province)*—S.J.

RELIGIOUS INSTITUTES OF WOMEN REPRESENTED IN THE DIOCESE

[1070-20]—*Dominican Sisters*—O.P.

[1115]—*Dominican Sisters of Peace*—O.P.

[]—*Misioneras Trabajadoras Sociales de la Inglesia*—M.T.S.I.

[]—*Missionary Daughters of the Most Pure Virgin Mary*—M.D.P.V.M.

[3350]—*Sisters of Providence* (Mother Joseph Prov.)—S.P.

[]—*Sisters of St. Francis*—O.S.F.

[3840]—*Sisters of St. Joseph of Carondelet*—C.S.J.

[1990]—*Sisters of the Holy Names of Jesus and Mary*—S.N.J.M.

[2160]—*Sisters, Servants of the Immaculate Heart of Mary*—I.H.M.

NECROLOGY

(No Deaths)

An asterisk (*) denotes an organization that has established tax-exempt status directly with the IRS and is not covered by the USCCB Group Ruling.

Diocese of Youngstown

(Dioecesis Youngstoniensis)

Most Reverend

GEORGE V. MURRY, S.J.

Bishop of Youngstown; ordained June 9, 1979; appointed Auxiliary Bishop of Chicago and Titular Bishop of Fuerteventura January 24, 1995; appointed Coadjutor Bishop of Saint Thomas in the Virgin Islands May 5, 1998; succeeded June 29, 1999; appointed Bishop of Youngstown January 30, 2007; installed March 28, 2007. *Chancery Office: 144 W. Wood St., Youngstown, OH 44503.* Tel: 330-744-8451; Fax: 330-742-6448.

Chancery Office: 144 W. Wood St., Youngstown, OH 44503. Tel: 330-744-8451; Fax: 330-742-6448; 330-744-2848.

Web: www.doy.org

Email: chancery@doy.org

ESTABLISHED MAY 15, 1943.

Square Miles 3,404.

Canonically Erected July 22, 1943.

Comprises six Counties in the northeastern part of the State of Ohio, namely, Ashtabula, Columbiana, Mahoning, Portage, Stark and Trumbull Counties.

For legal titles of parishes and diocesan institutions, consult the Chancery Office.

STATISTICAL OVERVIEW

Personnel	
Bishop	1
Priests: Diocesan Active in Diocese	97
Priests: Diocesan Active Outside Diocese	2
Priests: Retired, Sick or Absent	43
Number of Diocesan Priests	142
Religious Priests in Diocese	18
Total Priests in Diocese	160
Extern Priests in Diocese	3
Ordinations:	
Diocesan Priests	4
Transitional Deacons	1
Permanent Deacons in Diocese	77
Total Brothers	11
Total Sisters	211
Parishes	
Parishes	94
With Resident Pastor:	
Resident Diocesan Priests	72
Resident Religious Priests	4
Without Resident Pastor:	
Administered by Priests	18
Missions	1
New Parishes Created	9
Closed Parishes	5
Professional Ministry Personnel:	
Sisters	26
Lay Ministers	78
Welfare	
Catholic Hospitals	4
Total Assisted	50,461
Health Care Centers	32
Total Assisted	1,217,872
Homes for the Aged	10
Total Assisted	2,172
Day Care Centers	1
Total Assisted	74
Specialized Homes	5
Total Assisted	593
Special Centers for Social Services	16
Total Assisted	45,284
Educational	
Diocesan Students in Other Seminaries	8
Total Seminarians	8
Colleges and Universities	1
Total Students	2,982
High Schools, Diocesan and Parish	6
Total Students	2,163
Elementary Schools, Diocesan and Parish	28
Total Students	5,223
Elementary Schools, Private	2
Total Students	107
Catechesis/Religious Education:	
High School Students	3,026
Elementary Students	10,089
Total Students under Catholic Instruction	23,598
Teachers in the Diocese:	
Priests	4
Sisters	5
Lay Teachers	489
Vital Statistics	
Receptions into the Church:	
Infant Baptism Totals	1,672
Minor Baptism Totals	126
Adult Baptism Totals	148
Received into Full Communion	322
First Communions	2,128
Confirmations	2,364
Marriages:	
Catholic	428
Interfaith	239
Total Marriages	667
Deaths	2,656
Total Catholic Population	198,332
Total Population	1,195,478

Former Bishops—Most Revs. JAMES A. MCFADDEN, S.T.D., LL.D., appt. Titular Bishop of Bida and Auxiliary of Cleveland, May 13, 1932; cons. Sept. 8, 1932; appt. Bishop of Youngstown, June 2, 1943; died Nov. 16, 1952; EMMET M. WALSH, D.D., ord. Jan. 15, 1916; appt. Bishop of Charleston, June 20, 1927; appt. Titular Bishop of Rhaedestus and Coadjutor, Sept. 8, 1949; succeeded to See, Nov. 16, 1952; died March 16, 1968; JAMES W. MALONE, D.D., ord. May 26, 1945; appt. Titular Bishop of Alabanda and Auxiliary, Jan. 2, 1960; appt. Apostolic Administrator, Jan. 22, 1966; succeeded to See, May 2, 1968; retired Dec. 4, 1995; died April 9, 2000; THOMAS J. TOBIN, D.D., ord. July 21, 1973; appt. Titular Bishop of Novica and Auxiliary Bishop of Pittsburgh, Nov. 3, 1992; appt. Fourth Bishop of Youngstown installed Feb. 2, 1996; appt. Bishop of Providence March 31, 2005.

All Diocesan offices and personnel can be reached at 144 W. Wood St., Youngstown, OH, 44503. Tel: 330-744-8451, Fax: 330-742-6448; 744-2848 unless otherwise indicated.

Chancery Office

Vicar General & Moderator of the Curia—Rev. Msgr. ROBERT J. SIFFRIN.

Chancellor—Mrs. NANCY YUHASZ.

"The Catholic Exponent", Diocesan Newspaper—Most Rev. GEORGE VANCE MURRY, S.J., Publisher; Mr. LOUIS JACQUET, Editor & Gen. Mgr. Tel: 330-744-5251.

College of Consultors—Rev. Msgrs. MICHAEL J. CARIGLIO JR., J.C.L.; JOHN P. ASHTON, Ph.D. (Retired); DAVID W. RHODES; ROBERT J. SIFFRIN; Rev. BERNARD R. BONNOT; Very Rev. GREGORY F. FEDOR, V.F.; Revs. JOSEPH W. WITMER (Retired); JOHN JEREK.

Presbyteral Council—Rev. Msgrs. MICHAEL J. CARIGLIO JR., J.C.L.; JOHN ZURAW, J.C.L.; WILLIAM J. CONNELL, J.C.L.; ROBERT J. SIFFRIN; Revs. RICHARD MURPHY; BERNARD R. BONNOT; PAT FERRARO; CHRISTOPHER HENYK; KEVIN PETERS; EDWARD R. BRIENZ; THOMAS MCCARTHY; PETER HALADEJ; DAVID WEIKART; WILLIAM B. KRAYNAK; DAVID M. MISBRENER; JOHN JEREK; Very Rev. GREGORY MATURI, O.P.

Finance Council—Rev. Msgrs. ROBERT J. SIFFRIN, Chm.; FRANK A. CARFAGNA; PETER M. POLANDO, J.C.L.; THERESA DELLICK; MARY BETH HOUSER; Sr. ANDRIENE IHNOT, H.M.; ROBERT MARKS; PARKER MCHENRY; Mr. PAT KELLY; Mr. ROBERT A. HOFFMAN.

Diocesan Pastoral Council— To be reestablished.

Communications—

Catholic Television Network of Youngstown (CTNY)—Rev. J. JAMES KORDA, Pastoral Dir.; BOB GAVALIER, Gen. Mgr., Mailing Address: P.O. Box 430, Canfield, 44406-0430. Tel: 330-533-2243.

Public-Media Relations—Mrs. NANCY YUHASZ.

Development / Stewardship—Mr. PAT PALOMBO, Dir.

Ecumenism—Rev. JOSEPH W. WITMER, Dir., Ecumenical Commission (Retired), 1515 California Ave., Louisville, 44641. Tel: 330-875-4635.

Office of Missions / Evangelization—Rev. EDWARD R. BRIENZ, Dir.

Office of Parish Planning Reconfiguration—Rev. NICHOLAS R. SHORI, Dir.

Scouting, Diocesan Office—Rev. TERRENCE J. HAZEL.

Department of Canonical Services

Department of Canonical Services—Rev. Msgr. MICHAEL J. CARIGLIO JR., J.C.L., Exec. Dir., 141 W. Rayen Ave., Youngstown, 44503. Tel: 330-744-8451; Fax: 330-742-6450.

Office of Conciliation—

Matrimonial Dispensations—

Tribunal—

Judicial Vicar—Rev. Msgr. MICHAEL J. CARIGLIO JR., J.C.L.

Adjutant Judicial Vicar—Rev. Msgr. PETER M. POLANDO, J.C.L.

Judges—Rev. Msgrs. FRANK A. CARFAGNA; WILLIAM J. CONNELL, J.C.L.; DAVID W. RHODES; MARTIN S. SUSKO (Retired); Revs. MARTIN CELUCH, J.C.L.; BERNARD N. GAETA; ROBERT G. GIBAS (Retired); JOHN KEEHNER, J.C.L.; DANIEL J. KULESA (Retired); THOMAS J. MCCARTHY; JOHN R. OLSAVSKY, J.C.L.; ROBERT F. PFEIFFER, J.C.L.; GARY D. YANUS, J.C.D.

Defenders of the Bond—Rev. Msgr. JOHN A. ZURAW, J.C.L.; Revs. TERRENCE J. HAZEL; RAYMOND L. PAUL.

Advocates—Rev. BERNARD N. GAETA; PHYLLIS KULICS; Mrs. BARBARA ROGICH; VICKI KIDD.

Promoter of Justice—Rev. Msgr. JOHN A. ZURAW, J.C.L.

Notary—LINDA TEDDE.

Department of Catholic Charities Services

Department of Catholic Charities Services—Mr. BRIAN CORBIN, Exec. Dir., Health & Human Svcs. Commission; Liaison to St. Vincent DePaul Society.

Office of Social Action—Mr. BRIAN CORBIN, Dir.; Mr. GEORGE GARCHAR, Assoc. Dir. Rural Life; Catholic Relief Services; Migration and Refugee Services; Catholic Campaign for Human Development; Parish Social Ministry.

Criminal Justice Ministry—Mr. JOSEPH MILES, Coord.

Office of Social Services—Mrs. MARY ELLEN ANDERSEN, Pres., Diocese of Youngstown Catholic Charities Corp.; Dir., Social Svcs. Dept.

Hispanic Ministry—Mr. BRIAN CORBIN, Dir.

Immigrant Services—EFRAIN RUANO, Coord., Pastoral Care for Migrants and Refugees, 144 W. Wood St., Youngstown, 44503. Tel: 330-744-8451; 330-755-3633.

Diocese of Youngstown Legal Immigration Services—(an affiliate of CLINIC) NAOMI HOKKY, J.D., Senior Attorney; Mr. JOSEPH MILES, Interpreter & Bureau of Immigration Affairs Accredited. Tel: 866-901-3700. Offices: 206 W. Main St., Ravenna, OH 44266; 3112 Cleveland Ave., N.W., Canton, OH 44709; 4200 Park Ave., Ashtabula, OH 44004.

Department of Clergy and Religious Services

Department of Clergy and Religious Services—Rev. JOHN JEREK, Vicar Clergy & Rel. Svcs.

Office of Vocations—Revs. JOHN JEREK; CHRISTOPHER LUONI.

Serra Club of Mahoning County—Rev. FREDERICK LUKEHART, Chap. (Retired), 50 Warner Rd., Hubbard, 44425.

Office of Clergy Services—Rev. JOHN JEREK.

Office of Continuing Education and Formation of Priests—Rev. NICHOLAS R. SHORI.

Office of Permanent Diaconate—Rev. Msgr. JOHN A. ZURAW, J.C.L., Dir.

Office of Religious—Sr. JOYCE CANDIDI, O.S.H.J., Dir.

Diocesan Conference of Religious—Sr. JOYCE CANDIDI, O.S.H.J., Dir.

Department of Financial Services

Department of Financial Services—Mr. PATRICK A. KELLY, CFO.

Office of Finance—VACANT, Dir. Finance; Mrs. CHRISTINE JICKESS, Assoc. Dir. Finance.

Office of Information Systems Services—Mr. MATTHEW PECCHIA, Dir.

Department of Pastoral and Educational Services

Pastoral and Educational Services—

Office of Catholic Schools—Dr. NICHOLAS WOLSONOVICH, Acting Supt.; MARY FIALA, Asst. Supt. Curriculum, Accreditation & Personnel; Mr. RANDAL RAIR, Asst. Supt. Govt. Progs., Athletics & Institutional Advancement; Dr. MICHAEL SKUBE, Asst. to Bishop for Regl. School Planning & High School Bd. Devel.

The Catholic Diocese of Youngstown Educational Fund, Inc.—

Office of Religious Education—BARBARA WALKO, Diocesan Dir., 225 Elm St., Youngstown, 44503. Tel: 330-744-8451; THOMAS SAULINE, Consultant; CARLA HLAVAC, Consultant.

Council for Catechesis—Rev. JOHN-MICHAEL LAVELLE, D.Min., Chm.; Sr. ROSE ANNE KRANTZ, C.D.P., Vice Chair.

Office of Youth and Young Adult Ministry—CINDEE CASE, Dir.

Office of Campus Ministry—Ms. CARMEN ROEBKE, Diocesan Dir., 1424 Horning Rd., Kent, 44240. Tel: 330-678-0240.

Hiram College—Rev. LEO J. WEHRLIN, St. Ambrose Parish, 10692 Freedom St., Garrettsville, 44231. Tel: 330-527-4105.

University Parish Newman Center (Kent State)—Rev. STEVEN J. AGOSTINO, S.J., Admin.

Walsh University—Rev. ANSELM ZUPKA, O.S.B., Chap.; MIGUEL CHAVEZ, Dir., 2020 Easton St., N.W., North Canton, 44720. Tel: 330-490-7341.

Youngstown State University—Rev. CHRISTOPHER LUONI, Chap.; Mr. THOMAS BAGOLA, Dir., 254 Madison Ave., Youngstown, 44504. Tel: 330-747-9202.

Office of Worship—FRAN AMER, Dir.

Office of Lay Ministry Formation—Mr. JOHN DAMICO, Dir.

Office of Pro-Life, Marriage & Family Ministry—MELINDA KNIGHT, Dir.; Mr. DANIEL THIMONS, Assoc. Dir.

Other Ministries

Bishop's Delegate for Retired Priests—Rev. JOSEPH W. WITMER (Retired), 1515 California Ave., Louisville, 44641. Tel: 330-875-4635.

Catholic Women, Diocesan Council of—Rev. FREDERICK LUKEHART, Moderator (Retired), 50 Warner Rd., Hubbard, 44425.

Charismatic Prayer Group—Rev. ROBERT R. EDWARDS, Dir., 935 E. State St., Salem, 44460. Tel: 330-332-0336.

Disabled Services—

Physically and Developmentally—Rev. TERRENCE J. HAZEL, Chap., 300 N. Broad St., Canfield, 44406. Tel: 330-533-6839.

Deaf and Hearing Impaired—Rev. TERRENCE J. HAZEL, Chap., 300 N. Broad St., Canfield, 44406. Tel: 330-533-6839.

Victim Assistance Coordinator—Mrs. NANCY YUHASZ. Tel: 330-744-8451. Email: nyuhasz@youngstowndiocese.org.

CLERGY, PARISHES, MISSIONS AND PAROCHIAL SCHOOLS

CITY OF YOUNGSTOWN

(MAHONING COUNTY)

1—CATHEDRAL OF ST. COLUMBA (1847) [JC] Merged with St. Casimir, Youngstown to form St. Columba Parish, Youngstown.

2—ST. ANGELA MERICI PARISH (2011) Rev. Kevin Peters.
Rectory—400 Lincoln Park Dr., 44506. Tel: 330-747-6080; Fax: 330-747-7003. Email: eastsidecatholics@yahoo.com.
Catechesis/Religious Program—Tel: 330-747-3533. Sr. Kathleen McCarragher, O.S.U., D.R.E. Students 60.
Worship Site: Immaculate Conception-Sacred Heart of Jesus Parish—400 Lincoln Park Dr., 44506.
Sacred Heart of Jesus Parish

3—ST. ANTHONY (1898), (Italian), Rev. Msgr. Michael J. Cariglio Jr., Admin.
Mailing Address: 1125 Turin Ave., 44510. Tel: 330-744-5091; Fax: 330-744-1407.
Res.: *Our Lady of Mt. Carmel Rectory*, 343 Via Mt. Carmel, 44505.
Catechesis/Religious Program— Twinned with Our Lady of Mt. Carmel, Youngstown. Students 10.

4—ST. BRENDAN (1923) Unassigned.
Res.: 2800 Oakwood Ave., 44509. Tel: 330-792-3875; Fax: 330-792-9080. Email: pastor@stbrendanyo.org. Web: www.stbrendanyo.org.
Catechesis/Religious Program—Tel: 330-792-3875, Ext. 12. Email: dff@stbrendanyo.org. Students 59.

5—ST. CASIMIR (1906) Merged with Cathedral of St. Columba, Youngstown to form St. Columba Parish, Youngstown.

6—ST. CHRISTINE (1953) Rev. Msgr. David W. Rhodes; Rev. Christopher Cicero; Deacons Robert Cuttica, Pastoral Min.; David Beil; Ronald Layko; Jim Brown.
Res.: 3165 S. Schenley Ave., 44511. Tel: 330-792-3829; Fax: 330-792-6587. Email: parishoffice@stchristine.org. Web: www.stchristine.org.
School—(Grades PreK-8), 3125 S. Schenley Ave., 44511. Tel: 330-792-4544; Fax: 330-792-6888. Marge Gatto, Librarian. Lay Teachers 21; Students 405.
Catechesis/Religious Program—Tel: 330-793-0544. Email: stchcb@aol.com. Colleen Boyle, Dir. Faith Formation. Students 378.

7—ST. COLUMBA PARISH (2010) Rev. John Keehner, Rector; Sr. Isabel Rudge, Pastoral Min.; Deacon Roy West III; Dr. Daniel Laginya, Music Min. In Res., Rev. Edward R. Brienz.
Res.: 159 W. Rayen Ave., 44503. Tel: 330-744-5233; Fax: 330-744-2282.
Catechesis/Religious Program—Students 76.

8—SS. CYRIL AND METHODIUS (1896), (Slovak), Rev. Msgr. Peter M. Polando.
Res.: 252 E. Wood St., 44503. Tel: 330-743-5291; Fax: 330-746-1207.
Catechesis/Religious Program— Twinned with St. Stephen of Hungary & Our Lady of Mt. Carmel. Students 5.

9—ST. DOMINIC (1923) Very Rev. Gregory Maturi, O.P.; Revs. C. Antoninus Niemiec, O.P.; Regis Heuschkel, O.P.; William J. Rock, O.P.
Res.: 77 E. Lucius Ave., 44507. Tel: 330-783-1900; Fax: 330-783-2396. Email: stdomsytn@yahoo.com. Web: www.saintdominic.org.
Catechesis/Religious Program—Students 56.

10—ST. EDWARD (1917) Rev. Msgr. Robert J. Siffrin, Admin.; Deacon James Smith.
Res.: 240 Tod Ln., 44504. Tel: 330-743-2308; Fax: 330-743-8321.
Catechesis/Religious Program—Email: treerichosu@yahoo.com. Web: www.saintedwardparish.org. Students 23.

11—ST. ELIZABETH (1922), (Slovak), Closed. For inquiries for parish records contact the chancery.

12—HOLY APOSTLES PARISH (2011), (Hungarian), Rev. Joseph Rudjak.
Church: 854 Wilson Ave., 44506. Tel: 330-743-1905; Fax: 330-743-1905.
Catechesis/Religious Program— Twinned with SS. Cyril and Methodius, 252 E. Wood St., Youngstown Tel: 330-743-5291. Students 4.
Worship Site: SS. Peter and Paul—421 Covington St., 44510.

13—HOLY NAME OF JESUS (1916), (Slovak), Rev. Msgr. Peter M. Polando.
Res.: 613 N. Lakeview Ave., 44509. Tel: 330-799-8873; Fax: 330-799-1721.
Catechesis/Religious Program—Students 8.

14—IMMACULATE CONCEPTION (1882) Closed. Merged with Sacred Heart of Jesus to form Immaculate Conception-Sacred Heart of Jesus Parish, Youngstown.

15—IMMACULATE HEART OF MARY (1954) Rev. Msgr. Kenneth E. Miller; Deacon Nicholas G. Moliterno.
Res.: 4490 Norquest Blvd., 44515. Tel: 330-793-9988; Fax: 330-799-9269.
School—St. Joseph and Immaculate Heart of Mary School, (Grades K-8), 4470 Norquest Blvd., 44515. Tel: 330-799-1944; Fax: 330-799-0151. Lay Teachers 12; Students 204.
Catechesis/Religious Program—Tel: 330-799-4202. Students 252.

16—ST. JOSEPH (1966) Very Rev. Gregory F. Fedor; Mrs. Terry Supancic, Pastoral Assoc.; Deacon Gerald L. Savo.
Res.: 4545 New Rd., Austintown, 44515. Tel: 330-792-1919; Fax: 330-792-5233. Email: austjoseph@zoominternet.net. Web: saintjosephaustintown.org.
Catechesis/Religious Program—Mrs. Jocelyn Welsh, C.R.E. Students 247.

17—ST. MATTHIAS (1914), (Slovak), Rev. Msgr. Peter M. Polando; Deacon Salvatore DiFrancesco.
Mailing Address: 915 Cornell St., 44502-2765.
Catechesis/Religious Program—Tel: 330-788-5082. Students 18.

18—OUR LADY OF MT. CARMEL (1908), (Italian), Rev. Msgr. Michael J. Cariglio Jr.; Deacon Joseph Nohra.
Res.: 343 Via Mt. Carmel, 44505. Tel: 330-743-4144; Fax: 330-743-1035.
Catechesis/Religious Program—Tel: 330-743-3508. Sisters Karen Marie Barile, O.S.H.J., C.R.E.; Teresina Rosa, O.S.H.J., C.R.E.; Mark Izzo, Music Min. Students 190.

19—ST. PATRICK (1911) Rev. Edward P. Noga.
Res.: 1420 Oak Hill Ave., 44507. Tel: 330-743-1109; Fax: 330-743-8810. Email: stpatricks@neo.rr.com. Web: www.stpatsyoungstown.com.
Catechesis/Religious Program—Students 140.

20—SS. PETER AND PAUL, Merged with St. Stephen of Hungary, Youngstown to form Holy Apostles Parish, Youngstown.

21—SACRED HEART OF JESUS (1888) Merged with Immaculate Conception, Youngstown to from Immaculate Conception-Sacred Heart of Jesus Parish, Youngstown.

22—ST. STANISLAUS KOSTKA (1902), (Polish), Rev. Edward J. Neroda; Deacon Michael Schlais.
Res.: 430 Williamson Ave., 44507. Tel: 330-747-8503; Fax: 330-747-6334. Email: stans430@yahoo.com. Web: www.ststansyoungstown.org.

23—ST. STEPHEN OF HUNGARY, Merged with SS. Peter and Paul, Youngstown to form Holy Apostles Parish, Youngstown.

OUTSIDE THE CITY OF YOUNGSTOWN

ALLIANCE, STARK CO.

1—ST. JOSEPH (1854) [CEM] Rev. Maciej Mankowski.
Res.: 427 E. Broadway, 44601. Tel: 330-821-5760; Fax: 330-821-5783. Web: www.stjoseph-alliance.org.
Catechesis/Religious Program—Students 52.

2—REGINA COELI (1958) [JC] Rev. Howard Ziemba.
Res.: 663 Fernwood Blvd., 44601-2796. Tel: 330-821-5880; Fax: 330-821-8837. Email: rcchurch@rcyd.net.
School—(Grades PreK-8), 733 Fernwood Blvd., 44601-2796. Tel: 330-829-9239; Fax: 330-823-1877. Monica Ketler, Librarian. Lay Teachers 11; Students 137.
Catechesis/Religious Program—Amy Benedetti, D.R.E. Students 140.

ANDOVER, ASHTABULA CO., OUR LADY OF VICTORY (1949) [CEM] Rev. Kevin McCaffrey.
Res.: 481 S. Main St., P.O. Box 669, 44003-0669. Tel: 440-293-6218; Fax: 440-293-7778.
Catechesis/Religious Program—Students 19.

ASHTABULA, ASHTABULA CO.

1—ST. JOSEPH, Merged with Our Lady of Mt. Carmel, Ashtabula & Mother of Sorrows, Ashtabula to form Our Lady of Peace Parish, Ashtabula.

2—MOTHER OF SORROWS, Merged with St. Joseph, Ashtabula & Our Lady of Mt. Carmel, Ashtabula to form Our Lady of Peace Parish, Ashtabula.

3—OUR LADY OF MT. CARMEL, Merged with St. Joseph, Ashtabula & Mother of Sorrows, Ashtabula to form Our Lady of Peace Parish, Ashtabula.

4—OUR LADY OF PEACE PARISH (2011) [CEM] Revs. Raymond J. Thomas; Ernesto Rodriguez; Deacons Richard Johnson; Donald Johnson; Peter Olsen, Business Mgr.
Res.: 3312 Lake Ave., 44004. Tel: 440-992-0330; Fax: 440-993-3579. Email: stjoeparish@hotmail.com. Web: www.stjcc.com.
Catechesis/Religious Program—Students 120.
Worship Sites—
Mother of Sorrows— (1890) 1464 W. 6th St., 44004-3310.
Our Lady of Mt. Carmel— (1897) 1200 E. 21st St., 44004.

AURORA, PORTAGE CO., OUR LADY OF PERPETUAL HELP (1955) Rev. James M. Daprile; Sr. Lu Haidnick, C.D.P., Pastoral Assoc.; Deacon Joseph Pepoy.
Res.: 342 S. Chillicothe Rd., 44202-7814. Tel: 330-502-8135; Fax: 330-562-2529. Web: www.olphaurora.org.
Catechesis/Religious Program—Margaret A. Clapp, D.R.E. Students 321.

BOARDMAN, MAHONING CO.

1—ST. CHARLES BORROMEO (1926) Revs. Philip E. Rogers; Michael Marcelli; Gerald M. DeLucia; Deacons Paul Lisko, Pastoral Assoc.; Michael A. Kocjancic, Pastoral Assoc.; Mark Heagerty, Dir. Finance; Janette Koewacic, Pastoral Assoc.; Diana Hancmarenko, Pastoral Assoc.; Natalie Wardle, Coord. Youth Min.; Jacek Sobieski, Dir. Music.
Res.: 7345 Westview Dr., 44512. Tel: 330-758-2325; Fax: 330-758-2004.
School—(Grades K-8), 7325 Westview Dr., 44512. Tel: 330-758-6689; Fax: 330-758-7404. Mary Welsh, Prin.; Mrs. Kim De Pietro, Librarian. Lay Teachers 22; Students 428.
Catechesis/Religious Program—Tel: 330-758-8063. Miss Stephanie Taracjak, D.R.E. Students 370.
Convent—7515 Oregon Tr., 44512. Tel: 330-758-2396.

2—ST. LUKE (1962) Rev. Joseph A. Fata; Deacons Richard Milanek; Robert T. Redig. In Res., Rev. James E. O'Brien (Retired).
Res.: 5235 South Ave., 44512. Tel: 330-782-9783; Fax: 330-782-1574. Email: saintlukes@zoominternet.net.
School—Early Childhood Learning Center, (Grades PreK), 5225 South Ave., 44512. Tel: 330-782-4060; Fax: 330-782-4842. Email: stlukeelementary@youngstowndiocese.org. Lay Teachers 6; Students 31.
Catechesis/Religious Program—Students 133.

BREWSTER, STARK CO., ST. THERESE (1928) [JC] Merged with St. Clement, Navarre to form Holy Family Parish, Navarre.

CAMPBELL, MAHONING CO.

1—ST. JOHN THE BAPTIST (1919), (Slovak), [CEM] Revs. Joseph Ruggieri; Shawn Conoboy; Deacon Ronald J. Bunofsky.
Office: 394 Tenney Ave., 44405.
Res.: 159 Reed Ave., 44405. Tel: 330-755-4141 (Office); Fax: 330-755-1022.
Catechesis/Religious Program—Marge O'Malley, D.R.E. Students 13.

2—ST. JOSEPH THE PROVIDER (1919), (Polish), Revs. Joseph Ruggieri, Res.: 159 Reed Ave., 44405; Shawn Conoboy, Res.: 633 Porter Ave., 44405; Deacon Anthony Falasca Jr. In Res., Rev. Paul R. Tobin (Retired).
Office: 394 Tenney Ave., 44405.
Res.: 633 Porter Ave., 44405. Tel: 330-755-0266; Fax: 330-755-1988.
See St. Joseph the Provider Catholic School under Section (F) Diocesan Schools located in the Institution section.
Catechesis/Religious Program—Students 69.

3—ST. LUCY (1937), (Italian), Revs. Joseph Ruggieri; Shawn Conoboy.
Res.: 394 Tenney Ave., 44405-1695. Tel: 330-755-4132; Fax: 330-755-1367.
Catechesis/Religious Program—Marge O'Malley, D.R.E. Students 25.

4—ST. ROSE OF LIMA (1961), (Hispanic), Revs. Joseph Ruggieri; Shawn Conoboy; Deacon John Rentas.
394 Tenney Ave., 44405. Tel: 330-755-3633; Fax: 330-755-3683.
Catechesis/Religious Program—Students 80.

CANAL FULTON, STARK CO., SS. PHILIP AND JAMES (1845) [CEM] Rev. Thomas S. Acker, S.J., Admin.
Res.: 412 High St., 44614. Tel: 330-854-2332; Fax: 330-854-2599. Email: sspj@sssnet.com.
School—(Grades PreSchool-8) Tel: 330-854-2823; Fax: 330-854-1109. Email: sspandjelem@youngstowndiocese.org. Web: www-.saintsphilipandjames.org. Marcy Watry, Prin. Lay Teachers 12; Students 133.
Catechesis/Religious Program—Tel: 330-854-3988. Jackie Prosise, D.R.E. Students 89.

CANFIELD, MAHONING CO., ST. MICHAEL (1962) Rev. Terrence J. Hazel; Sr. Brendan Sherlock, O.S.U., Pastoral Min., (Homebound); Deacon Tom Soich.
300 N. Broad St., 44406.
Res.: 281 Glenview Dr., 44406. Tel: 330-533-6839; Fax: 330-702-0432. Email: info@stmichaelcanfield.org. Web: www.stmichaelcanfield.org.
Catechesis/Religious Program—Tel: 330-533-5275. Joan Lawson, Pastoral Min. Catechesis; Maureen Hall, Pastoral Min., Youth Liturgy, RCIA. Students 450.

CANTON, STARK CO.

1—ALL SAINTS (1920), (Polish), Closed. Merged with St. Anthony, Canton to form St. Anthony/All Saints Parish, Canton.

2—ST. ANTHONY (1908), (Italian), Merged with All Saints, Canton to form St. Anthony/All Saints Parish, Canton.

3—ST. ANTHONY/ALL SAINTS PARISH (2011) Rev. Thomas G. Bishop.
Res.: 1530 11th St., S.E., 44707. Tel: 330-452-9539; 330-456-0266 (Hall); Fax: 330-452-4870.
Catechesis/Religious Program—Ann Marie Vega, D.R.E.; Sr. Karen Lindenberger, Coord. Hispanic Ministry; Roger Herstine, Dir. Youth Min. Students (English & Spanish) 205.

4—ST. BENEDICT (1923) Merged with St. Mary of the Immaculate Conception, Canton to form St. Mary/St. Benedict Parish, Canton.

5—CHRIST THE SERVANT PARISH (2010) Rev. Msgr. Lewis F. Gaetano, Admin.
Mailing Address & Res.: 833 39th St., N.W., 44709. Tel: 330-492-0757; Fax: 330-492-1214.
Worship Site: Our Lady of Peace Church— (1952) 833 39th St., N.W, 44709.
School—(Grades K-8), 1001 39th St., N.W., 44709. Tel: 330-492-0622; Fax: 330-492-0959. Lay Teachers 15; Students 224.
Catechesis/Religious Program—Students 68.

6—ST. JOAN OF ARC (1944) Rev. William B. Kraynak; Deacon David Conversino.
Res.: 4940 Tuscarawas St. W., 44708-5012. Tel: 330-477-6796; 330-477-6797; Fax: 330-477-0594. Email: rstjoanofar@neo.rr.com. Web: www.sjacanton.com.
School—(Grades PreK-8), 120 Bordner Ave., S.W., 44710. Tel: 330-477-2972; Fax: 330-478-2606. Lay Teachers 23; Students 282.
Catechesis/Religious Program—166 Bordner Ave., S.W., 44710. Students 173.

7—ST. JOHN THE BAPTIST (1823) [CEM] Rev. Ronald M. Klingler; Deacon Carl Burkhardt.
Res.: 627 McKinley Ave., N.W., 44703. Tel: 330-454-8044; Fax: 330-454-1397. Email: canton-stjohn@ameritech.net. Web: www.stjohncanton.com.
Catechesis/Religious Program—Students 55.

8—ST. JOSEPH (1902) Rev. Msgr. Frank A. Carfagna; Deacon Wilbur J. Bagley.
Res.: 2427 W. Tuscarawas St., 44708. Tel: 330-453-2526. Email: stjosephcanton@catholicweb.com. Web: stjosephcanton.catholicweb.com.
School—(Grades K-8), 126 Columbus Ave., N.W., 44708. Tel: 330-454-9787; Fax: 330-454-9866. Lay Teachers 10; Students 108.
Catechesis/Religious Program—Tel: 330-454-2144. Students 71.

9—ST. MARY OF THE IMMACULATE CONCEPTION (1899) Merged with St. Benedict, Canton to form St. Mary/St. Benedict Parish, Canton.

10—ST. MARY/ST. BENEDICT PARISH (2011) Rev. Benson Claret Okpara, Admin.
Office: 1602 Market Ave., S., 44707. Email: benedictparish@sbcglobal.net.
Res.: 2207 Third St. S.E., 44707.
Worship Sites—
St. Mary of the Immaculate Conception— 1899
St. Benedict— 1923Fax: 330-452-7299.
Catechesis/Religious Program—Students 109.

11—ST. MICHAEL THE ARCHANGEL (1952) Revs. Donald E. King; Brian James Cline; Sisters Carol McHenry, S.N.D., Pastoral Assoc.; Dorothy Fuchs, S.N.D., Pastoral Assoc.; Deacons Mark J. Fuller; Peter P. Pohl; Mrs. Faith Wackerly, Pastoral Assoc.; Mrs. Mary Germann, Parish Admin.; Mr. Jeff Fricker, Youth Min.; Patricia Berring, Liturgy Dir.
Res.: 3430 St. Michael Blvd., N.W., 44718. Tel: 330-492-3119; Fax: 330-492-0339. Web: www.stmichaelcanton.org.
School—(Grades PreK-8), 3431 St. Michael's Blvd., N.W., 44718. Tel: 330-492-2657; Fax: 330-492-9618. Mrs. Sally Roden, Prin.; Mrs. Connie Benner, Librarian. Lay Teachers 25; Students 350.
Catechesis/Religious Program—Tel: 330-492-3119, Ext. 17. Email: mike@stmichaelcanton.org. Mr. Michael Ress, D.R.E. Students 545.

12—OUR LADY OF PEACE (1952) Merged with St. Paul, Canton to form Christ the Servant Parish, Canton.

13—ST. PAUL (1907) [JC] Merged with Our Lady of Peace, Canton to form Christ the Servant Parish, Canton.

14—ST. PETER (1845) [CEM] Revs. Edward L. Beneleit; John Sheridan.
Res.: 726 Cleveland Ave., N.W., 44702. Tel: 330-453-8493; Fax: 330-453-8083. Web: www.stpeter.org.
School—(Grades PreK-8), 702 Cleveland Ave., N.W., 44702. Tel: 330-452-0125. Email: office@stpetercanton.org. Lay Teachers 12; Students 135.
Catechesis/Religious Program—Students 96.

CHAMPION, TRUMBULL CO., ST. WILLIAM (1963) Rev. Michael D. Balash.
Res.: 5411 Mahoning Ave., N.W., Warren, 44483. Tel: 330-847-8677; Fax: 330-847-6275. Web: www.stwilliamchampion.org.
Catechesis/Religious Program—Tel: 330-847-8627. Carol Timko, C.R.E. Students 148.

COLUMBIANA, COLUMBIANA CO., ST. JUDE (1966) Rev. Thomas G. Ziegler; Deacons Louis Cosentino; Terry L. Coulter.
Res.: 180 Seventh St., 44408. Tel: 330-482-2351; Fax: 330-482-0993. Email: burkeymary@comcast.net.
Catechesis/Religious Program—Tel: 330-482-2888. Dr. Thomas Brozich, D.R.E. Students 106.

CONNEAUT, ASHTABULA CO.

1—ST. FRANCES CABRINI (1955) [JC] Merged with St. Mary of the Immaculate Conception, Conneaut to form Saint Mary/Saint Frances Cabrini, Conneaut.

2—ST. MARY OF THE IMMACULATE CONCEPTION (1888) [CEM] [JC] Merged with St. Frances Cabrini, Conneaut to form Saint Mary/Saint Frances Cabrini, Conneaut.

3—SAINT MARY/SAINT FRANCES CABRINI (2008) [JC] Rev. Philip Miller.
Office: 744 Mill St., P.O. Box 619, 44030. Tel: 440-599-8570; Fax: 440-593-6772. Email: stmsfc@hotmail.com. Web: www.stmsfc.org.
Church: 744 Mill St., 44030.
Church: 480 State St., P.O. Box 619, 44030. Tel: 440-599-8570.
Catechesis/Religious Program—Students 90.

CORTLAND, TRUMBULL CO., ST. ROBERT BELLARMINE PARISH (1952) Rev. Carl Kish; Corey Fowler, Music Min.
Res.: 4659 Niles-Cortland Rd., N.E., 44410. Tel: 330-637-4886; Fax: 330-637-0608.
Catechesis/Religious Program— Sandy Bailey, D.R.E. Students 415.

DUNGANNON, COLUMBIANA CO., ST. PHILIP NERI (1817) [CEM] Rev. James Paul Lang.
Mailing Address: P.O. Box 309, Hanoverton, 44423-0309.
Office: 271 W. Chestnut St., Lisbon, 44432. Tel: 330-424-7648.
Catechesis/Religious Program— Combined with St. John, Summitville. Students 4.

EAST LIVERPOOL, COLUMBIANA CO.

1—ST. ALOYSIUS (1838), (Irish), [CEM] Merged with Immaculate Conception, Wellsville to form Holy Trinity Parish, East Liverpool.

2—ST. ANN (1915) Closed. For inquiries for parish records contact the chancery.

3—HOLY TRINITY PARISH (2011) [CEM 2] Rev. Peter Haladej.
Office & Mailing Address: 512 Monroe St., 43920. Tel: 330-385-7131; Fax: 330-385-3025. Email: immconc01@comcast.net.
School—(Grades PreK-8), 335 W. 5th St., 43920. Tel: 330-385-5963; Fax: 330-385-6455. Email: ygnaloysius@doy.org. Web: www.staloysius.k12.oh.us. Nicole Shaw, Librarian. Lay Teachers 10; Students 91.
Catechesis/Religious Program—Mr. Robert Barto, D.R.E. (H.S. Holy Trinity Parish, E. Liv. Ohio 43920) Students 67.
Worship Site: St. Aloysius Church— (1838) 235 W. 5th St., 43920.

EAST PALESTINE, COLUMBIANA CO., OUR LADY OF LOURDES (1880) [CEM] Rev. Thomas G. Ziegler, Admin.
Mailing Address: 200 E. Main St., 44413.
Office: 180 Seventh St., Columbiana, 44408. Tel: 330-482-2351; Fax: 330-482-0993.
Catechesis/Religious Program— At St. Jude Church, 180 Seventh St., Columbiana, OH 44408 Students 75.

GARRETTSVILLE, PORTAGE CO., ST. AMBROSE (1944) Rev. Leo J. Wehrlin; Deacons Robert Rapp; Gerolome P. Scopilliti.
Res.: 10692 Freedom St., 44231. Tel: 330-527-4105; Fax: 330-527-2500. Email: st_ambrose44231@yahoo.com. Web: www.stambroseonline.com.
Catechesis/Religious Program—Students 141.

GENEVA, ASHTABULA CO., ASSUMPTION B.V.M. (1915) [JC] Rev. Melvin E. Rusnak.
Res.: 594 W. Main St., 44041. Tel: 440-466-3427; Fax: 440-466-4670. Web: assumptiongeneva.org.
School—(Grades PreK-6), 30 Lockwood St., 44041. Tel: 440-466-2104; Fax: 440-466-7769. Web: www-.genevaassumption.com. Charlotte Brafford, Prin. Lay Teachers 8; Students 124.

Catechesis/Religious Program—(Grades K-8) Students 80.

GIRARD, TRUMBULL CO., ST. ROSE (1892) Rev. Msgr. John Zuraw; Rev. John S. Trimbur; Deacon Paul Milligan. In Res., Rev. Matthew Albright.
Res.: 48 E. Main St., 44420. Tel: 330-545-4351; Fax: 330-545-0119. Web: www.strosecatholic.com.
School—(Grades K-8), 61 E. Main St., 44420. Tel: 330-545-1163. Web: www.stroseschool.info. Mrs. Linda Borton, Prin. Sisters 1; Lay Teachers 15; Students 251.
Sunny Days Day Care Center—Tel: 330-545-1490; Fax: 330-545-1584. Email: sunnydayscсc@att.net. Michelle Frease, Dir. (Preschool)
Catechesis/Religious Program—Tel: 330-545-1216. Susan Lipkovich, D.R.E. Students 250.

HUBBARD, TRUMBULL CO., ST. PATRICK (1869) [CEM] Rev. Timothy H. O'Neill; Deacon Robert Friedman, Pastoral Assoc.
Res. & Mailing Address: 225 N. Main St., 44425. Tel: 330-534-1928; Fax: 330-534-0820.
School—(Grades K-8), 38 E. Water St., 44425. Tel: 330-534-2509; Fax: 330-534-0305. Lay Teachers 12; Students 120.
Catechesis/Religious Program—225 N. Main St., 44425. Tel: 330-534-8304. Email: spreled@aol.com. Web: www.stpatshub.org. Karen Bartos, C.R.E.; Teri Ray, Coord. Youth Min. Students 474.

JEFFERSON, ASHTABULA CO., ST. JOSEPH CALASANCTIUS (1858) Rev. Charles Poore.
Res.: 32 E. Jefferson St., 44047. Tel: 440-576-3651; Fax: 440-576-3651.
Catechesis/Religious Program—Tel: 440-576-3339. Students 81.

KENT, PORTAGE CO.
1—ST. PATRICK'S (1864) [JC] Rev. Richard J. Pentello; Deacons Timothy DeFrange; Michael W. Stabilla.
Res.: 313 N. Depeyster St., 44240. Tel: 330-673-5849; Fax: 330-673-5849.
School—(Grades K-8), 127 Portage St., 44240. Tel: 330-673-7232; Fax: 330-678-6612. Lay Teachers 21; Students 316.
Catechesis/Religious Program—(Grades PreK-8) Tel: 330-677-4453. Students 255.
2—UNIVERSITY PARISH NEWMAN CENTER (1953) Rev. Steven J. Agostino, S.J.
Res.: 1424 Horning Rd., 44240. Tel: 330-678-0240; Fax: 330-678-7780. Web: www.kentnewmancenterparish.org.
Catechesis/Religious Program—Students 72.

KINGSVILLE, ASHTABULA CO., ST. ANDREW BOBOLA (1936) Rev. Charles Poore.
Res.: 3700 Rte. 193, 44048. Tel: 440-224-0987 (Church).
Catechesis/Religious Program—Students 33.

KINSMAN, TRUMBULL CO., ST. PATRICK (1957) Attended by Our Lady of Victory, Andover. Rev. Kevin McCaffrey.
Res.: 481 S. Main St., P.O. Box 669, Andover, 44003-0669. Tel: 440-293-6218; Fax: 410-293-7778.
Catechesis/Religious Program—Students 21.

LAKE MILTON, MAHONING CO.
1—ST. CATHERINE (1956) Merged with St. James Parish, North Jackson to form Our Lady of the Lakes Parish, St. Catherine Church, Lake Milton.
2—OUR LADY OF THE LAKES PARISH, ST. CATHERINE CHURCH (2010) Rev. David W. Merzweiler.
Office & Mailing Address: 50 Rosemont Rd., North Jackson, 44451. Tel: 330-538-2602; Fax: 330-538-9580.
Church & Res.: 1254 Grandview Rd., 44429. Tel: 330-654-4001.

LEETONIA, COLUMBIANA CO., ST. PATRICK (1861) [CEM] Rev. Robert R. Edwards, Canonical Admin.; Deacon Lawrence Parks; Sr. Joan Franklin, O.P., Pastoral Assoc.
Mailing Address: 167 W. Main St., 44431. Tel: 330-427-6577.
Res.: 157 Ohio Ave., Salem, 44460. Tel: 330-332-0336; Fax: 330-332-7982.
Catechesis/Religious Program—Students 48.

LISBON, COLUMBIANA CO., ST. GEORGE (1820) Rev. James Paul Lang.
Res.: 271 W. Chestnut St., 44432. Tel: 330-424-7648.
Catechesis/Religious Program—Tel: 330-424-0109. Students 24.
Mission—St. Agatha, Tel: 330-424-0155 (Sunday only).

LOUISVILLE, STARK CO.
1—ST. LOUIS (1838), (French—German), [CEM] Rev. David C. Menegay (PIT).
Res.: 300 N. Chapel St., 44641. Tel: 330-875-1658; Fax: 330-875-1657. Web: stlouiscatholicchurchlouisvilleoh.4lpi.com.
School—(Grades PreSchool-8) Tel: 330-875-1467; Fax: 330-875-2511. Email: ygnlouis@doy.com. Web: stlouiscatholicschool.com. Carole von Buelow, O.S.F., Prin.; Samor Salvino, Librarian. Lay Teachers 11; Students 76.
Catechesis/Religious Program—(Grades K-8) Rachel Schmidt, C.R.E.; Daniel Kelly, Music Min.; Marsha Dalsky, Ministry Coord. Students 169.
2—SACRED HEART OF MARY (1833) [CEM] Rev. Nicholas Mancini.
Res.: 8277 Nickelplate Ave., N.E., 44641. Tel: 330-875-2827; Fax: 330-875-5511. Email: rsacred@neo.rr.com.
Catechesis/Religious Program—Students 45.

LOWELLVILLE, MAHONING CO., OUR LADY OF THE HOLY ROSARY (1867) [CEM] Rev. John Jerek, Admin.
Res.: 131 E. Wood St., 44436. Tel: 330-536-6436; Fax: 330-536-9188.
Catechesis/Religious Program—Students 185.

MANTUA, PORTAGE CO., ST. JOSEPH (1923) Rev. Michael Garvey; Deacon Gary Keefer.
Res.: 4534 Pioneer Tr., 44255. Tel: 330-274-2114.
Church & Mailing Address: 11045 St. Joseph Blvd., 44255.
Parish Office Center—Tel: 330-274-2253; Fax: 330-274-2254. Email: parishoffice@stjosephmantua.com. Web: www.stjosephmantua.com.
Catechesis/Religious Program—Tel: 330-274-2268; Fax: 330-274-2269. Students 122.

MASSILLON, STARK CO.
1—ST. BARBARA (1867), (German), [CEM] Rev. Thomas W. Cebula.
Res.: 2813 Lincoln Way, N.W., 44647. Tel: 330-833-6898; Fax: 330-833-5164. Email: stbarbmassillon@aol.com. Web: www.stbarbmassillon.com.
School—(Grades PreK-8), 2809 Lincoln Way, N.W., 44647. Tel: 330-833-9510; Fax: 330-833-3297. Email: ygnbarbara@doy.org. Lay Teachers 11; Students 151.
Catechesis/Religious Program—Mr. Henry Kappel, D.R.E. Students 109.
2—ST. JOSEPH (1863) [CEM] Rev. Raymond L. Paul; Deacons Steven A. Wyles; Donald F. Molinari.
Res., Parish Center & Office: 322 Third St., S.E., 44646. Tel: 330-833-2607; 330-833-4907; 330-833-6088; Fax: 330-833-3907. Web: www.stjoemassillon.catholicweb.com.
Catechesis/Religious Program—Students 95.
3—SAINT MARY (1839) [CEM] Rev. A. Edward Gretchko; Deacon Joseph Fries.
Parish Office—726 1st St., N.E., 44646. Tel: 330-833-8501; Fax: 330-833-3359. Email: stmarysmassilon@yahoo.com. Web: www.stmarysonline.org.
Res.: 206 Cherry Rd., N.E., 44646. Tel: 330-832-1270.
School—(Grades PreK-8), 640 First St., N.E., 44646. Tel: 330-832-9355; Fax: 330-832-9030. Lisa Channel, Librarian. Sisters 1; Lay Teachers 13; Students 218.
Catechesis/Religious Program—Students 74.

MASURY, TRUMBULL CO.
1—ST. BERNADETTE (1940) Merged with St. Vincent de Paul, Vienna to form St. Thomas the Apostle Parish, St. Vincent De Paul Church, Vienna.
2—ST. THOMAS THE APOSTLE PARISH, ST. BERNADETTE CHURCH (2010) Rev. Frank L. Zanni; Deacon Frank Marino.
Mailing Address: 7800 Locust St., 44438.
Res.: 4453 Warren-Sharon Rd., Vienna, 44473. Tel: 330-394-2461.

MAXIMO, STARK CO., ST. JOSEPH (1850) [CEM] Rev. Howard Ziemba.
Res.: P.O. Box 219, 44650. Tel: 330-823-7809.
Catechesis/Religious Program—Tel: 330-823-5233. Students 67.

MCDONALD, TRUMBULL CO., OUR LADY OF PERPETUAL HELP (1943) Rev. John P. Madden.
Res.: 618 Ohio Ave., 44437. Tel: 330-530-6929; Fax: 330-530-2488. Email: olphmcdonald@aol.com. Web: ourladymcdonald.com.
Catechesis/Religious Program—601 Indiana Ave., 44437. Tel: 330-530-1111. Email: olphmcdonaldccd@aol.com. Students 132.

MIDDLEBRANCH, STARK CO., ST. THERESE LITTLE FLOWER (1929) Revs. John E. Zuzik; Robert J. Hannon, Admin. (Retired).
Res.: 2040 Diamond St., N.E., Canton, 44721. Tel: 330-494-2759; Fax: 330-494-2536.
Catechesis/Religious Program—Email: bbuzenski@littleflowerparish.com. Web: www.littleflowerparish.com. Students 290.

MINERAL RIDGE, TRUMBULL CO., ST. MARY (1870) Revs. Thomas P. Kraszewski; Richard Murphy.
Res.: 3504 Main St., 44440. Tel: 330-652-7761; Fax: 330-652-7765. Email: saintmary@zoominternet.net.
Catechesis/Religious Program—Students 90.

NAVARRE, STARK CO.
1—ST. CLEMENT (1832) [CEM] Merged with St. Therese, Brewster to form Holy Family Parish, Navarre.
2—HOLY FAMILY PARISH (2011) Rev. Michael D. Seifert.
216 Wooster St. E., 44662. Tel: 330-879-5900; Fax: 330-879-5138. Email: stclementnavarre@sssnet.com.
Catechesis/Religious Program—Students 69.
Worship Sites—
St. Clement Church— (1832)
St. Therese Church— (1928) 456 Wabash Ave., S., Brewster, 44613.

NEW MIDDLETOWN, MAHONING CO., ST. PAUL THE APOSTLE (1952) [JC] Rev. Stephen E. Popovich.
Res.: 10143 Main St., P.O. Box 515, 44442. Tel: 330-542-3466; Fax: 330-542-2448.
Catechesis/Religious Program—Tel: 330-542-3824. Students 279.

NEWTON FALLS, TRUMBULL CO.
1—ST. JOSEPH (1923), (Slovak), [CEM] Merged with St. Mary, Newton Falls to form Saint Mary and Saint Joseph, Newton Falls.
2—ST. MARY (1928), (Polish), [JC] Merged with St. Joseph, Newton Falls to form Saint Mary and Saint Joseph, Newton Falls.
3—ST. MARY AND ST. JOSEPH PARISH (1928) [CEM] Rev. Thomas Ungashick.
Office: 120 Maple Dr., 44444. Tel: 330-872-5742.
Church & Rectory: 131 W. Quarry St., 44444-1560. Tel: 330-872-4193; Fax: 330-872-0038. Email: parishssmaryjoseph@yahoo.com. Web: www.stmaryandstjosephparish.com.
Catechesis/Religious Program—Students 49.

NILES, TRUMBULL CO.
1—OUR LADY OF MT. CARMEL (1906), (Italian), Rev. Lawrence Frient.
Res.: 381 Robbins Ave., 44446. Tel: 330-652-5825; Fax: 330-544-1872. Email: mountcarmelniles@yahoo.com. Web: www.mountcarmelniles.org.
Catechesis/Religious Program—(Grades K-8) Students 160.
2—ST. STEPHEN (1853) [CEM] Rev. Thomas P. Kraszewski.
Res.: 129 W. Park Ave., 44446. Tel: 330-652-4396; Fax: 330-652-9317. Email: churchofsaintstephen@yahoo.com.
School—(Grades PreK-8), 45 S. Chestnut, 44446. Tel: 330-652-5511; Fax: 330-652-4264. Religious 1; Lay Teachers 13; Students 78; Preschool 38.
Catechesis/Religious Program—Students 182.

NORTH CANTON, STARK CO., ST. PAUL (1845) Rev. Msgr. James A. Clarke; Revs. James E. McKarns (Retired); Donald J. Oser (Retired); Stephen Zeigler; Judy Piero, Pastoral Min.; Deacons William Lambert; Ron Reolfi, Business Admin.; Edward Laubacher; Peter D. Watry; Carl Jerzyk.
Res.: 241 S. Main St., 44720. Tel: 330-499-2201; Fax: 330-499-8106. Web: stpaulncanton.org.
School—(Grades K-8), 303 S. Main St., 44720. Tel: 330-494-0223; Fax: 330-494-3226. Jackie Zufall, Prin.; Kathy Yackshaw, Librarian. Lay Teachers 21; Students 355.
Catechesis/Religious Program—Marcy Fessler, D.R.E. Students 712.

NORTH JACKSON, MAHONING CO.
1—ST. JAMES PARISH (1943) Merged with St. Catherine, Lake Milton to form Our Lady of the Lakes Parish, St. James Church, North Jackson.
2—OUR LADY OF THE LAKES PARISH, ST. JAMES CHURCH (2010) Rev. David W. Merzweiler.
Church, Parish Offices & Social Hall: 50 Rosemont Rd., 44451. Tel: 330-538-2602; Fax: 330-538-9580.
Res.: 1254 Grandview Rd., Lake Milton, 44429.
Catechesis/Religious Program—Carol Muldowney, D.R.E. Students 108.

ORWELL, ASHTABULA CO., ST. MARY (1922) [CEM] Rev. G. David Weikart, Admin.
Res.: 103 N. Maple, Box 217, 44076-0217. Tel: 440-437-6262; Fax: 440-437-8216. Email: stmaryofc@fairpoint.net.
Catechesis/Religious Program—Tel: 440-437-8216. Students 110.

POLAND, MAHONING CO., HOLY FAMILY (1956) Rev. Msgr. William J. Connell; Rev. Martin Celuch; Deacons Ray Hatala; Ernest Formichelli.
Res.: 2729 Center Rd., 44514. Tel: 330-757-1545; Fax: 330-757-4443. Email: holy_family@sbcglobal.net. Web: www.holyfamilypoland.org.
School—(Grades K-8) Tel: 330-757-3713; Fax: 330-757-7648. Email: hfelem@youngstowndiocese.org. Web: hfspoland.org. Lay Teachers 19; Students 282.
Catechesis/Religious Program—Students 718.

RANDOLPH TOWNSHIP, PORTAGE CO., ST. JOSEPH (1831) [CEM] Rev. Edward R. Wieczorek; Deacons James White; Steven Gies, Parish Life & Family Life Chairperson.
Res.: 2643 Waterloo Rd., Mogadore, 44260. Tel: 330-628-9941; Fax: 330-628-9942. Email: stjoerandolph@yahoo.com. Web: www.stjosephrandolph.org.
School—(Grades K-8), 2617 Waterloo Rd., Mogadore, 44260. Tel: 330-628-9555. Email: stjoeelemmogadore@youngstonwdiocese.org. Web: sjsrandolph.org. Lay Teachers 10; Students 125.
Catechesis/Religious Program—Tel: 330-628-4844. Email: msgrlin@aol.com. Linda Shaw, D.R.E. Students 187.

RAVENNA, PORTAGE CO., IMMACULATE CONCEPTION (1854) [CEM] Revs. John-Michael Lavelle; Robert M. Miller; Deacon Russell J. Brode.
Res.: 409 W. Main St., 44266. Tel: 330-296-6434; Fax: 330-296-9193.
Catechesis/Religious Program—Tel: 330-296-4549. Students 120.

ROCK CREEK, ASHTABULA CO., SACRED HEART (1956) [JC] Rev. G. David Weikart, Admin.
Office: 3049 SR 45, P.O. Box 310, 44084. Tel: 440-563-3010. Email: shc305@windstream.net.
Catechesis/Religious Program—Tel: 440-563-5255. Students 47.

ROOTSTOWN, PORTAGE CO., ST. PETER OF THE FIELDS (1868), (German), [CEM] Rev. David M. Misbrener.
Mailing Address: 3487 Old Forge Rd., 44272. Tel: 330-325-7543.
Catechesis/Religious Program—Students 140.

SALEM, COLUMBIANA CO., ST. PAUL (1881) Rev. Robert R. Edwards.
Res.: 157 Ohio Ave., 44460. Tel: 330-332-0336; Fax: 330-332-7982.
Parish Administration Center—935 E. State St., 44460.
School—925 E. State St., 44460. Tel: 330-337-3451; Fax: 330-337-3452. Lay Teachers 12; Students 140.
Catechesis/Religious Program—Sr. Mary McFadden, S.N.D., Pastoral Assoc.; Donna Dermotta, C.R.E. Students 137.

SALINEVILLE, COLUMBIANA CO., ST. PATRICK (1873) [CEM] Closed. For inquiries for parish records contact the chancery.

SEBRING, MAHONING CO., ST. ANN (1908) Rev. Maciej Mankowski.
Res.: 323 S. 15th St., 44672. Tel: 330-938-2033; Fax: 330-938-6544. Email: stannsebring@sbcglobal.net.
Catechesis/Religious Program—Students 75.

STREETSBORO, PORTAGE CO., ST. JOAN OF ARC (1965) Rev. Pat Ferraro; Deacon John F. Carney.
Res.: 8894 State Rte. 14, 44241. Tel: 330-626-3424; Fax: 330-626-3422.
Catechesis/Religious Program—Students 233.

STRUTHERS, MAHONING CO.

1—CHRIST OUR SAVIOR PARISH (2011) Revs. Bernard R. Bonnot; Bernard N. Gaeta; Deacon John Terranova.
Res.: 250 N. Bridge St., 44471. Tel: 330-755-2115.
Parish Office—764 5th St., 44471-1704. Tel: 330-755-9819; Fax: 330-755-9949.
School—(Grades K-8), 762 5th St., 44471-1702. Tel: 330-755-2128. Lay Teachers 15; Students 151.
Catechesis/Religious Program—Tel: 330-755-6245. Mrs. Alvera Bell Y, D.R.E. Students 208.
Worship Sites—
St. Nicholas Church—
Holy Trinity Church—250 N. Bridge St., 44471.

2—HOLY TRINITY (1907), (Slovak), Merged with St. Nicholas, Struthers to form Christ Our Savior Parish, Struthers.

3—ST. NICHOLAS (1865) Merged with Holy Trinity, Struthers to form Christ Our Savior Parish, Struthers.

SUMMITVILLE, COLUMBIANA CO., ST. JOHN (1839) [CEM] Revs. John P. Tully; James Paul Lang.
Mailing Address: P.O. Box 309, Hanoverton, 44423-0309.
Office: 271 W. Chestnut St., Lisbon, 44432. Tel: 330-424-7648.
Res.: 16017 Smith Rd., 43962. Tel: 330-223-1871.
Catechesis/Religious Program—Students 60.

UNIONTOWN, STARK CO., HOLY SPIRIT (1979) Rev. John Zapp.
Res.: 2952 Edison St., N.W., 44685. Tel: 330-699-4500. Email: holyspiritunoh@sbcglobal.net. Web: www.holyspiritunoh.org.
Catechesis/Religious Program—Students 198.

VIENNA, TRUMBULL CO.

1—QUEEN OF THE HOLY ROSARY (1997) Rev. Denis Bouchard, F.S.S.P.
Res.: 291 Scoville Dr., 44473. Tel: 330-856-4204; Fax: 330-856-9587.
Catechesis/Religious Program—Students 47.

2—ST. THOMAS THE APOSTLE PARISH, ST. VINCENT DEPAUL CHURCH (2010) Rev. Frank L. Zanni; Deacons Kevin T. Lamar; Frank Marino.
Mailing Address: P.O. Box 148, 44473.
Church & Res.: 4453 Warren-Sharon Rd., 44473. Tel: 330-394-2461; Fax: 330-609-0320.
Catechesis/Religious Program—Tel: 330-394-2361. Students 140.

3—ST. VINCENT DE PAUL (1879) Merged with St. Bernadette, Masury to form St. Thomas the Apostle Parish, St. Vincent DePaul Church, Vienna.

WARREN, TRUMBULL CO.

1—BLESSED JOHN PAUL II PARISH (2011) Rev. Christopher Henyk.
Office: 1401 Moncrest Ave., N.W., 44485. Tel: 330-399-8881.
Res.: 1346 Vernon St., N.W., 44483. Tel: 330-393-0226; Fax: 330-393-0226.
Catechesis/Religious Program—James E. Johnston, D.R.E. Students 10.
Worship Sites—
St. Joseph Church— (1928) 420 North St., N.W., 44483.
St. Pius X Church— (1959)

2—BLESSED SACRAMENT (1959) Rev. Thomas C. Eisweirth. In Res., Rev. Thomas J. McCarthy.
Res.: 3020 Reeves Rd., N.E., 44483. Tel: 330-372-2215; Fax: 330-372-6380. Email: info@e-blessedsacramentparish.org. Web: e-blessedsacramentparish.org.
See John F. Kennedy Catholic School, Lower Campus in the Institution Section under Diocesan Schools.
Catechesis/Religious Program—Students 372.

3—SS. CYRIL AND METHODIUS (1928), (Slovak), Revs. James P. Walker; Jeffrey Stealey; Deacon Joseph P. Toth.
Res.: 185 Laird Ave., N.E., 44483. Tel: 330-393-9766; Fax: 330-393-0555. Email: warrenstcyril@aol.com. Web: www.sscmwarren.org.
Catechesis/Religious Program—Tel: 330-393-0781. Students 25.

4—ST. JAMES (1947) Revs. James P. Walker; Charles W. Crumbley; Jeffrey Stealey.
Res.: 2532 Burton St., S.E., 44484. Tel: 330-369-3518; Fax: 330-369-2761.
Catechesis/Religious Program—2106 Arbor St., S.E., 44484. Tel: 330-369-3518. Sr. Yvonne Horning, O.P., D.R.E. Students 52.

5—ST. JOSEPH, Merged with St. Pius X, Warren to form Blessed John Paul II Parish, Warren.

6—ST. MARY (1835) [CEM] Rev. Bernard R. Schmalzried.
Res.: 232 Seneca St., N.E., 44481. Tel: 330-393-8721; 330-394-3426.
Catechesis/Religious Program—Students 69.

7—ST. PIUS X, Merged with St. Joseph, Warren to form Blessed John Paul II Parish, Warren.

WAYNESBURG, STARK CO., ST. JAMES (1928) Rev. Joseph Zamary.
Res.: 400 W. Lisbon St., 44688. Tel: 330-866-9449; Fax: 330-866-1750. Email: jjzamary@aol.com.
School—(Grades PreK-6) Tel: 330-866-9556; Fax: 330-866-1750. Lay Teachers 8.
Catechesis/Religious Program—Tel: 330-866-9449. Students 91.

WELLSVILLE, COLUMBIANA CO., IMMACULATE CONCEPTION (1842) [CEM] Merged with St. Aloysius, East Liverpool to form Holy Trinity Parish, East Liverpool.

WINDHAM, PORTAGE CO., ST. MICHAEL'S (1943) Rev. Leo J. Wehrlin.
Mailing Address: 10692 Freedom St., Garrettsville, 44231.
Res.: 9736 E. Center St., 44288. Fax: 330-527-4105; 330-527-2500. Email: parish410@youngstowndiocese.org.
Catechesis/Religious Program—Students 7.

On Duty Outside the Diocese:
Revs.—
Deffenbaugh, Joseph T., Pensacola, FL
Nuzzi, Ronald, Notre Dame, IN

Military Chaplains:
Rev.—
Mikstay, Michael, U.S. Navy

Retired:
Rev. Msgrs.—
Adamko, Cyril A.
Ashton, John P., Ph.D.
Kolp, James
Reidy, Robert
Ronik, Michael
Sabatino, Robert
Susko, Martin S.
Torok, Dezso
Revs.—
Balasko, George J.
Bantz, William
Brobst, Richard A.
Cavanaugh, James K.
Cipar, Daniel
Czaja, Joseph S.
Dobosiewcz, Leon W.
Esposito, Anthony
Fasline, Anthony
Forgach, Carl J.
Franko, George M.
Gibas, Robert G.
Grabowski, Dennis
Hannon, Robert J.
Johnson, James
Karas, Stephen
Kulesa, Daniel J.
Lehnerd, Frank M.
Lody, John
Loperfido, Ernest
Lukehart, Frederick
Lyons, John F.
McKarns, James E.
Mintjal, Frank
Mulqueen, John D.
Nentwick, John
O'Brien, James E.
Oser, Donald J.
Platt, Stewart
Pleban, Leo
Reiss, John E.
Santucci, Louis
Smar, Michael J.
Summers, John
Tobin, Paul R.
Witmer, Joseph W.
Yablonsky, Gabriel

Permanent Deacons:
Arend, David H., (On Duty Outside Diocese)
Bagley, Wilbur J., St. Joseph, Canton
Beil, David C., St. Christine, Youngstown
Brode, Russell J., Immaculate Conception, Ravenna
Brown, James, St. Christine, Youngstown
Bunofsky, Ronald J., St. John, Campbell
Burkhardt, Carl R., St. John the Baptist, Canton
Carney, John F., St. Joan of Arc, Streetsboro
Chase, Ralph, St. Ann, Sebring
Conversino, David, St. Joan of Arc, Canton
Cosentino, Louis A., St. Jude, Columbiana
Coulter, Terry L., D.C., St. Jude, Columbiana
Cuttica, Robert J., St. Christine, Youngstown
Davies, Martin H., (On Duty Outside Diocese)
DeFrange, Tim, St. Patrick, Kent
DiFrancesco, Salvatore, St. Matthias, Youngstown
Falasca, Anthony, Jr., St. Joseph, Campbell
Formichelli, Ernest, Holy Family, Poland
Friedman, Robert J., St. Patrick, Hubbard
Fries, Joseph K., St. Mary, Massillon
Fuller, Mark J., St. Michael, Canton
Gies, Steven R., Immaculate Conception, Ravenna
Hatala, Ray H., (Office of Permanent Diaconate)
Hawkins, Edward, St. Patrick, Youngstown
Heinz, Edward, Sts. Peter and Paul, Youngstown
Ivan, Ellis C., Holy Spirit, Uniontown
Jerzyk, Carl, St. Paul, North Canton
Johnson, Don, St. Joseph, Ashtabula
Johnson, Richard M., St. Joseph, Ashtabula
Keefer, Gary, St. Joseph, Mantua
Kocjancic, Michael A., St. Charles, Boardman
Krause, Harold R., (Retired)
Lamar, Kevin T., St. Vincent de Paul, Vienna
Lambert, William H., St. Paul, North Canton
Laubacher, Edward, St. Paul, North Canton
Layko, Ronald J., St. Christine, Youngstown
Lisko, Paul, St. Nicholas, Struthers
Marino, Frank, St. Bernadette, Masury
Milanek, Richard, St. Luke, Boardman
Milligan, Paul, St. Rose, Girard
Mintus, Robert, St. Pius X, Warren
Molinari, Donald F., St. Joseph, Massillon
Moliterno, Nicholas G., Immaculate Heart of Mary, Youngstown
Nohra, Joseph S., St. Maron & Mt. Carmel, Youngstown
O'Neill, Russell, Holy Spirit, Uniontown
Pallo, John D., Sacred Heart, Rock Creek
Pasko, Lawrence, St. Patrick, Leetonia
Pepoy, Joseph E., Our Lady of Perpetual Help, Aurora
Pfleger, James W., (On Duty Outside the Diocese)
Pohl, Peter P., SS. Philip & James, Canal Fulton
Prasek, Alan, (Retired)
Rapp, Robert, St. Ambrose, Garrettsville
Redig, Robert T., St. Luke, Boardman
Rentas, John, St. Rose of Lima, Youngstown
Reolfi, Ron, St. Paul, North Canton
Roberts, Michael R., Jr., St. Joseph, Austintown
Santiago, Enrique, St. Rose of Lima, Youngstown
Savo, Gerald L., St. Joseph, Austintown
Schlais, Michael, St. Stanislaus, Youngstown
Scopilliti, Gerolome P., St. Ambrose, Garrettsville
Seaman, Michael T., St. Peter, Canton
Sherwood, Ronald D., (On Duty Outside the Diocese)
Simmerly, Robert, St. James, Warren
Smith, James, St. Edward, Youngstown
Soich, Thomas G., St. Michael, Canfield
Stabilla, Michael W., St. Patrick, Kent
Terranova, John, St. Nicholas, Struthers
Toth, Joseph P., Blessed Sacrament, Warren
Waldron, Michael K., Sts. Philip & James, Canal Fulton
Watry, Peter D., St. Paul, North Canton
West, Raymond F., III, St. Columba, Youngstown
White, James A., (On Duty Outside Diocese)
Wood, Gregory J., St. Peter, Canton
Wyles, Steve, St. Joseph, Massillon

INSTITUTIONS LOCATED IN THE DIOCESE

[A] SEMINARIES, RELIGIOUS, OR SCHOLASTICATES

CANFIELD. *Society of St. Paul*, 9531 Akron-Canfield Rd., P.O. Box 595, 44406. Tel: 330-533-5503; 330-533-1076; Fax: 330-533-1076. Email: paultheapostle@msn.com. Web: www.albahouse.org. Revs. Ignatius Staniszewski, S.S.P.; Anthony Chenevy, S.S.P.; Thomas Fogarty, S.S.P.; Jeffrey Mickler, S.S.P., Local Supr.; Anthony Warren, S.S.P.; Tony Bautista, S.S.P.; Bros. Dismas Beique, S.S.P.; Dominic Calabro, S.S.P.; Paschal Duesman, S.S.P.; John Naranjo, S.S.P.; Peter Scalise, S.S.P. Priests 6; Brothers 5; Total Staff 11.

[B] COLLEGES AND UNIVERSITIES

NORTH CANTON. *Walsh University* (Coed), 2020 E. Maple St., 44720-3396. Tel: 330-490-7090; Fax: 330-490-7165. Email: admissions@walsh.edu. Web: www.walsh.edu. Rev. Anselm Zupka, O.S.B., Univ. Chap.; Richard Jusseaume, Pres.; Mr. Dale Howard, Vice Pres. Student Affairs; Brett Freshour, Vice Pres. Enrollment Mgmt.; Philip Daniels, Vice Pres. Business & Finance; Bridgette Neisel, Vice Pres. Devel. & Univ. Rels.; Rev. J. Patrick Manning, Chair, Theology Dept.; Daniel Suvak, Librarian. Brothers of Christian Instruction. Priests 4; Sisters 1; Lay Teachers 114; Total Staff 286; Students 2,982.

[C] HIGH SCHOOLS, DIOCESAN

YOUNGSTOWN. *Cardinal Mooney High School* (1956) 2545 Erie St., 44507. Tel: 330-788-5007; Fax: 330-788-4511. Email: mooneyhigh@youngstowndiocese.org. Web: www.cardinalmooney.com. John Young, Prin.; Rev. Gerald DeLucia, Chap.; Debra Scarnechia, Librarian. Priests 1; Lay Teachers 52; Students 587.

Ursuline High School (1905) 750 Wick Ave., 44505. Tel: 330-744-4563; Fax: 330-744-3358. Email: ursulinehigh@youngstowndiocese.org. Web: www.ursuline.com. Rev. Richard Murphy, Pres.; Patricia Fleming, Prin. Priests 1; Sisters 1; Lay Teachers 27; Students 402.

ASHTABULA. *SS. John & Paul School* (1953) (Grades 7-12), St. John High School Building, 541 W. 34th St., 44004. Tel: 440-997-5531; Fax: 440-998-1661. Web: www.ssjp.org. Sr. Maureen Burke, S.N.D., Pres.; Mrs. Cheryl Woodward, Prin.; Janis Brown, Librarian. Lay Teachers 10; Students 99; Sisters 2.

CANTON. *Central Catholic High School* (1905) 4824 Tuscarawas St. W., 44708-5198. Tel: 330-478-2131; Fax: 330-478-6086. Email: rkaylor@cchsweb.com. Web: www.cchsweb.com. Mr. John Korecki, Asst. Prin.; Mr. Leo DeMatteis, Dean of Students; Mr. James Naegeli, Campus Ministry Dir.; Lue Schwing, Librarian. Priests 1; Lay Teachers 40; Total Staff 41; Students 410.

LOUISVILLE. *St. Thomas Aquinas High School* (1964) 2121 Reno Dr., N.E., 44641. Tel: 330-875-1631; Fax: 330-875-8469. Web: www.stahs.org. Rev. Thomas P. Dyer, Pres. & CEO; Mr. Joseph Vagedes, Prin.; Mrs. Michelle May, Campus Min. Clergy 1; Lay Teachers 26; Total Staff 50; Students 310.

[D] ELEMETARY SCHOOLS, DIOCESAN

ASHTABULA. *SS. John & Paul School* (1996) (Grades PreK-6), Our Lady of Mt. Carmel Building, 2150 Columbus Ave., 44004. Tel: 440-997-5821; Fax: 440-998-0514. Email: cheryl.woodward@neomin.org. Web: www.ssjp.org. Lay Teachers 7; Students 154.
Consolidated school for Mother of Sorrows, St. Joseph & Our Lady of Mt. Carmel. Mrs. Cheryl Woodward, Prin.; Michelle Martino, Sec.; Jaime Carr, Librarian.

[E] PRIVATE SCHOOLS

CANFIELD. *Ursuline Preschool/Kindergarten*, 4300 Shields Rd., 44406. Tel: 330-792-4150; Fax: 330-792-8177. Email: upsk43@yahoo.com. Sr. Charlotte Italiano, O.S.U., Dir. & Prin. Ursuline Sisters 1; Lay Teachers 10; Assistants 8; Students 241.

HUBBARD. *Villa Maria Teresa Daycare and Kindergarten*, 50 Warner Rd., 44425. Tel: 330-759-7383; Fax: 330-759-7290. Sr. Kristen Quicker, Prin. & Dir. Sisters 6; Lay Teachers 3; Students 110.

[F] DIOCESAN SCHOOLS

YOUNGSTOWN. *St. Joseph the Provider Catholic School*, (Grades K-8), 1145 Turin Ave., 44510. Tel: 330-259-0353. Rev. Michael Swierz, Pres.; Mrs. Cheryl Jablonski, Prin. Lay Teachers 12; Students 110.

WARREN. *John F. Kennedy Catholic School*, 2550 Central Pkwy, S.E., 44484. Tel: 330-369-1804; Fax: 330-369-1125.

Lower Campus (Grades PreK-6), 3000 Reeves Rd., N.E., 44483. Tel: 330-372-2375; Fax: 330-372-2465. Email: bsinchak@warrenjfk.com. Mr. Brian Sinchak, Pres.; Ms. Staci Raab, Prin. Lay Teachers 41; Students 578.

Upper Campus (1964) (Grades 7-12), 2550 Central Pkwy., S.E., 44484. Tel: 330-369-1804; Fax: 330-369-1125. Web: www.warrenjfk.com. Rev. Matthew Albright, Faculty; Mr. Brian Sinchak, Pres.; Ms. Staci Raab, Prin.; Mrs. Jessica McRoberts, Dir. College Counseling & Academic Svcs.; Mr. Jim Boyle, Dir. Student Affairs; Mrs. Theresa A. Dolan-Dixon, Dir., Mission & Ministry. Priests 1; Lay Teachers 29; Students 344.

[G] GENERAL HOSPITALS

YOUNGSTOWN. *Humility of Mary Health Partners, St. Elizabeth Health Center* (1911) 1044 Belmont Ave., Box 1790, 44501. Tel: 330-746-7211; Fax: 330-480-7974. Web: www.hmpartners.org. Mr. Robert W. Shroder, Pres. & CEO; Donald Koenig, Exec. Vice Pres., HMHP. Bed Capacity 560; Bassinets 60; Patients Assisted Annually (Includes Austintown Facility) 332,413; Total Staff 2,363.

BOARDMAN. *Humility of Mary Health Partners St. Elizabeth Boardman Health Center*, 8401 Market St., 44512. Tel: 330-729-2929. Mr. Robert W. Shroder, Pres. & CEO; Eugenia L. Aubel, Pres. St. Elizabeth Boardman Health Center. Bed Capacity 134; Total Assisted 91,198; Total Staff 528.

CANTON. **Mercy Medical Center* (1908) 1320 Mercy Dr., N.W., 44708. Tel: 330-489-1000; Fax: 330-489-1312. Email: mail@cantonmercy.org. Web: www.cantonmercy.org. Thomas Cecconi, Pres. & CEO. Bed Capacity 523; Bassinets 47; Total Staff 2,577; Total Assisted Annually 606,900.

WARREN. *St. Joseph Health Center* (1924) 667 Eastland Ave., S.E., 44484. Tel: 330-841-4000; Fax: 330-841-4019. Web: www.hmpartners.org. Mr. Robert W. Shroder, Pres. & CEO; John Finizio, Pres. Sisters of the Humility of Mary 3; Bed Capacity 219; Bassinets 17; Total Assisted Annually 172,026; Total Staff 821.

[H] SPECIAL CARE FACILITIES

GIRARD. *Humility of Mary Health Partners, Home Health Services*, 979 Tibbetts-Wick Rd., Ste. A, 44420. Tel: 330-480-3776; Fax: 330-480-4584. Robert Shroder, Pres. & CEO; Michael Robinson, Dir. Home Health Svcs. Patients Assisted Annually 15,335; Total Staff 120; Total Assisted Annually 16,402.

NORTH LIMA. *The Assumption Village, Marian Living Center (Assisted Living Facility)*, 9800 Market St., 44452. Tel: 330-549-0740; Fax: 330-549-0701. Jason Cicchillo, Exec. Dir.; Kristine Mariotti, Dir. Assisted Living Svcs. & Mktg.; Susan Bangor, L.P.N., Wellness Mgr. Sponsorship: Sisters of the Humility of Mary., Member: Catholic Healthcare Partners and Humility of Mary Health Partners.; Special Care Unit for residents with Alzheimer's or Dementia; Skilled Nursing Unit with Subacute Care Program; Intermediate Care. Assisted Living Rooms 48; Assisted Living Total Staff 31; Total Assisted Annually 66; Total Staff 31; Bed Capacity 60.

POLAND. *Hospice of the Valley, Hospice House*, 9803 Sharrott Rd, 44514. Tel: 330-549-5850; Fax: 330-549-5859. Richard T. Bell, Dir. Bed Capacity 16; Staff 50; Total Assisted Annually 1,260.

[I] HOMES FOR AGED

AUSTINTOWN. *Humility House*, 755 Ohltown Rd., 44515. Tel: 330-505-0144; Fax: 330-544-5694. Jason Cacchillo, Exec. Dir. LTC. Nursing Home Beds 70; Assisted Living Beds 32; Total Assisted 202; Total Staff 120.

CANTON. *House of Loreto*, 2812 Harvard Ave., N.W., 44709. Tel: 330-453-8137; Fax: 330-453-8140. Sisters Marilee Heuer, C.D.S., Admin.; Janet Harold, C.D.S., Admin.; Michele Beauseigneur, Supr. Administered by the Congregation of the Divine Spirit. Sisters of the Congregation of the Divine Spirit 18; Bed Capacity 50; Residents 50; Total Assisted Annually 65; Total Staff 50. In Res. Rev. Msgr. Homer C. DeWalt (E) (Retired); Revs. Richard E. Powers (E) (Retired); Gerald J. Sommer, M.S.C. (Retired); Adam F.X. Stromski (STU) (Retired).

HUBBARD. *Villa Maria Teresa* (1894) 50 Warner Rd., 44425. Tel: 330-759-9329 (Villa); 330-875-4635 (Emmaus House); Fax: 330-759-7290. Email: jcoblate@aol.com. Web: www.oblatesistersofshj.com. Retired Priests' Residence. Villa Residents 6; Emmaus House Residents 3; Bed Capacity 17; Total Assisted Annually 10; Total Staff 4.

LOUISVILLE. *Emmaus House* (1977) 1515 California Ave., 44641-8708. Tel: 330-875-4635. Rev. Joseph W. Witmer, Admin. Retired Priests' Residence. Bed Capacity 10; Residents 3; Total Assisted Annually 3; Total Staff 3.

St. Joseph Care Center, 2308 Reno Dr., 44641. Tel: 330-875-5562; Fax: 330-875-8947. Email: sjcc@neo.rr.com. Web: www.thealsatian.com. John T. Banks, Admin.; Sr. Andriene Ihnot, H.M., Assoc. Admin. Sisters of St. Joseph of St. Mark 11; Sisters of the Humility of Mary 1; Notre Dame Sisters 1; Nursing Home 100; Assisted Living 67; Independent Living 66; Adult Day Care 25; Bed Capacity 264; Total Assisted Annually 340; Total Staff 240.

NORTH LIMA. *The Assumption Village, Humility Health Center (Nursing Care)*, 9800 Market St., 44452. Tel: 330-549-0740; Fax: 330-549-0701. Tony Maroni, Admin.; Lisa Peretti, R.N., Dir. Nursing. Sponsorship: Sisters of the Humility of Mary., Member: Catholic Healthcare Partners and Humility of Mary Health Partners; Skilled Nursing Unit with Subacute Care Program; Special Care Unit for residents with Alzheimer's or cognitive impairment. Nursing Home Beds 150; Total Assisted 322; Total Staff 177.

[J] MONASTERIES AND RESIDENCES OF PRIESTS AND BROTHERS

YOUNGSTOWN. *Mt. Alverna Friary*, 517 S. Belle Vista Ave., 44509. Tel: 330-799-1888; Fax: 330-799-0723. Revs. Jules Wong, O.F.M.; Vit Fiala, O.F.M., Local Min. & Dir. Shrine. Franciscan Friars. Total in Residence 2; Total Staff 2.

[K] CONVENTS AND RESIDENCES FOR SISTERS

CANFIELD. *Motherhouse and Educational Center of the Ursuline Sisters* (1874) 4250 Shields Rd., 44406. Tel: 330-792-7636; Fax: 330-792-9553. Email: admainosuyo@yahoo.com. Web: www.theursulines.org. Sr. Nancy Dawson, O.S.U., Gen. Supr. Total in Community 52; Total in Residence 31; Total Staff 5.

Ursuline Center, 4280 Shields Rd., 44406. Tel: 330-799-4941; Fax: 330-799-4988.

CANTON. *Sancta Clara Monastery* (1946) 4200 N. Market Ave., 44714. Tel: 330-492-1171; Fax: 330-492-8657. Email: srmagdalenpcpa@hotmail.com. Web: www.poorclares.org. Rev. Stephen Mallya, A.J., Chap.; Sr. Magdalen Colson, P.C.P.A., Abbess. Poor Clares of Perpetual Adoration. Cloistered Professed Nuns 9.

HUBBARD. *Oblate Sisters of the Sacred Heart of Jesus Institute, Villa Maria Teresa* (1984) 50 Warner Rd., 44425. Tel: 330-759-9329; Fax: 330-759-7290. Email: oblatesisters@aol.com. Web: www.oblatesistersofshj.com. Sr. Vittoria Nisi, O.S.H.J., Regl. Supr. & Convent Supr. Novitiate and American Headquarters of Oblate Sisters of the Sacred Heart of Jesus. Sisters 16; Total Staff 8; Novices 2; Postulants 2.

[L] CATHOLIC CHARITIES SOCIAL SERVICE AGENCIES

YOUNGSTOWN. *Catholic Charities Housing Opportunities Corporation*, 225 Elm St., 44503. Tel: 330-744-8451; Fax: 330-742-6447. Email: ggarchar@youngstowndiocese.org. Web: www.catholiccharitiesyoungstown.org. Brigid Kennedy, Pres.; Mr. George Garchar, Exec. Dir. Purpose: Provides coordination, integration and leadership in the provision of housing services which promote affordable housing in the community. Total Families Assisted 25; Total Staff 1.

Catholic Charities Regional Agency (1946) 2401 Belmont Ave., 44505. Tel: 330-744-3320; Fax: 330-744-3677. Email: nvoitus@ccregional.org. Nancy Voitus, Exec. Dir. Family and child welfare work in various social services and counseling in Mahoning, Trumbull and Columbiana Counties. Total Staff 52.

Diocese of Youngstown Catholic Charities Corporation (1999) 144 W. Wood. St., 44503. Tel: 330-744-8451; Fax: 330-742-6447. Email: mandersen@youngstowndiocese.org. Web: www.catholiccharitiesyoungstown.org.

ASHTABULA. *Catholic Charities of Ashtabula County* (1944) 4200 Park Ave., 3rd Fl., 44004. Tel: 440-992-2121; Fax: 440-992-5974. Email: lynnz@doyccac.org. Web: www.doyccac.org. Lynn M. Zalewski, Exec. Dir. Total Assisted 14,000; Total Staff 15.

CANTON. *Catholic Charities of Stark County* (1999)

3112 Cleveland Ave., N.W., 44709. Tel: 330-491-0896; Fax: 330-491-1298. Email: ccstark@sbcglobal.net. James E. Armour, Exec. Dir. Total Assisted (Estimated) 7,450; Total Staff 22.

Catholic Charities Adult Day Services, 2308 Reno Dr., Louisville, 44641. Tel: 330-875-7979; Fax: 330-875-3006.

RAVENNA. *Catholic Charities of Portage County*, 206 W. Main St., 44266. Tel: 330-297-7745; Fax: 330-297-7763. Email: ccstark@global.net. James E. Armour, Exec. Dir.

[M] HOMES FOR WOMEN

YOUNGSTOWN. *Beatitude House* (1991) 238 Tod Ln., 44504. Tel: 330-744-3147; Fax: 330-744-3991. Email: info@beatitudehouse.com. Web: www.beatitudehouse.com. Sr. Patricia McNicholas, O.S.U., Exec. Dir. Permanent supportive housing, transitional housing, job preparation, job training, counseling, education and case management for economically disadvantaged women and children. Bed Capacity 150; Total Assisted 550; Total Staff 26.

[N] RETREAT HOUSES

YOUNGSTOWN. *Our Lady of the Woods Pastoral Center* (1994) 144 W. Wood St., 44503. Tel: 330-744-8451; Fax: 330-744-1702.

[O] NEWMAN CENTERS

YOUNGSTOWN. *Newman Center at Youngstown State University* 254 Madison Ave., 44504-1627. Tel: 330-747-9202; Fax: 330-747-1667. Email: ysunewmancenter@sbcglobal.net. Web: www.ysunewmancenter.org. Total Staff 1.

KENT. *Kent State University Newman Center* 1424 Horning Rd., 44240. Tel: 330-678-0240; Fax: 330-678-7780. Web: www.kentnewmancenterparish.org. Rev. Steven J. Agostino, S.J.; Ms. Carmen Roebke, Pastoral Assoc. & Christian Formation; Ms. MaryLynn Delfino, Pastoral Assoc. & Campus Min.; Dr. John Roebke, Music Dir. Total in Residence 1; Total Staff 5.

[P] MISCELLANEOUS LISTINGS

YOUNGSTOWN. *Caritas Communities*, 225 Elm St., 44503. Tel: 330-744-8451; 330-384-1555; Fax: 330-742-6447. Email: ggarchar@youngstowndiocese.org. Web: www.catholiccharitiesyoungstown.org. Mr. George Garchar, Pres.; Ken Radigan, Chm. As a member Corporation of Catholic Charities Housing Opportunities and the Humility of Mary Housing Program, Caritas Communities will serve as Property Management Corporation for low income and special needs housing. Families Assisted 165; Total Staff 1.

"The Catholic Exponent", P.O. Box 6787, 44501-6787. Tel: 330-744-5251; Fax: 330-744-5252. Email: exponent@doyweb.org. Web: www.cathexpo.org.

Conference of Slovak Clergy, 144 W. Wood St., 44503. Tel: 330-744-8451; Fax: 330-742-6448. Most Rev. Joseph Victor Adamec, D.D., S.T.L., Vice Chm.; Rev. Msgrs. Robert J. Siffrin, Chm.; Peter M. Polando, J.C.L., Sec. The Conference was founded April 22, 1985, and incorporated on June 14, 2000. It associates bishops, priests and deacons of Slovak ancestry in the United States for the purposes of mutual pastoral support and financial assistance to those preparing themselves for ordained ministry of the churches in union with Rome, particularly those of Slovak ancestry.

Declaration of Trust of Trumbull, Department of Education, 144 W. Wood St., 44503. Tel: 330-744-8451; Fax: 330-744-8451; 330-744-5099. Email: nwolsonovich@youngstowndiocese.org. County Catholic School Endowment Fund.

First Friday Club of Greater Youngstown, P.O. Box 11146, 44511. Tel: 330-533-1023; Fax: 330-533-1023.

Humility of Mary Health Partners Development Foundation (1966) 250 DeBartolo Pl., Ste. 2560, 44512. Tel: 330-729-1180; Fax: 330-729-9473. Email: james_schultis@hmis.org. Web: www.hmpartners.org. James Schultis, Pres. & CEO. Total Staff 8.

Lake to River Telecommunications Corporation, 144 W. Wood St., 44503.

Midwest Canon Law Society, 141 W. Rayen Ave., 44503. Tel: 330-744-8451.

Roman Catholic Diocese of Youngstown "Today's Sacrifice...Tomorrow's Church" Capital Campaign, 144 W. Wood St., 44503. Tel: 330-744-8451; Fax: 330-742-6447. Web: www.doy.org. Mr. Pat Palombo, Dir. Devel. & Stewardship, 144 W. Wood St., 44503. Tel: 330-744-8451; Mr. Patrick A. Kelly, CFO.

Roman Catholic Diocese of Youngstown Foundation, 144 W. Wood St., 44503. Tel: 330-744-8451; Fax: 330-744-2848. Mr. Patrick A. Kelly, CFO.

Roman Catholic Diocese of Youngstown Property Corporation, 144 W. Wood St., 44503. Tel: 330-744-8451; Fax: 330-744-2848. Mr. Patrick A. Kelly, CFO.

CANFIELD. *The Ursuline Center* (1993) 4280 Shields Rd., 44406. Tel: 330-799-4941; Fax: 330-799-4988. Email: ndawsonosu@aol.com. Web: www.theursulines.org. Resource and outreach services for the poor, including prison ministry, AIDS ministry, retreats, water therapy, adult formation, speech and hearing services, school of music, massage therapy, college courses, Walsh University Masters Programs, undergrad degree programs, preschool, and kindergarten. Total Assisted Annually 40,000; Sisters 8; Total Staff 18.

CANTON. *Catholic Migrant Farmworker Network, Inc.*, 701 Walnut Ave. N.E., 44702. Tel: 330-454-6754; Fax: 330-454-2255.

Early Childhood Resource Center, 1718 Cleveland Ave., N.W., 44703. Tel: 330-491-3272. Web: www.sistersofcharityhealth.org. Sr. Judith Ann Karam, C.S.A., Pres. & CEO.

Sisters of Charity Foundation of Canton (1996) 400 Market Ave. N., Ste. 300, 44702-1556. Tel: 330-454-5800; Fax: 330-454-5909. Email: jclose@scfcanton.org. Web: www.scfcanton.org. Joni T. Close, Pres.

LOUISVILLE. *St. Thomas Aquinas High School Endowment Fund* (1964) 2121 Reno Drive, N.E., 44641. Tel: 330-875-1631; Fax: 330-875-8469. Web: www.stahs.org. Rev. Thomas P. Dyer, Pres. & CEO; Victoria Frustaci, Business Mgr.

MASSILLON. *National Shrine of St. Dymphna* (1938) 3000 Erie St. S., P.O. Box 4, 44648-0004. Tel: 330-833-8478; Fax: 330-833-5193. Rev. A. Edward Gretchko, Chap. Located on the grounds of Heartland Behavioral Healthcare.

[Q] DIOCESAN CEMETERIES

YOUNGSTOWN. *Calvary*, 248 S. Belle Vista Ave., 44509. Tel: 330-792-4721; Fax: 330-792-1885.

Catholic Cemeteries of the Diocese of Youngstown, Inc., 144 W. Wood St., 44503. Tel: 330-744-8451; Fax: 330-742-6448. Rev. Msgr. Frank A. Carfagna, Dir.; Mr. Joseph Kun, Asst. Dir.

Resurrection, 300 N. Raccoon Rd., 44515. Tel: 330-799-1900; Fax: 330-799-5241.

CORTLAND. *All Souls*, 3823 Hoagland Blackstub Rd., 44410. Tel: 330-637-2761; Fax: 330-637-9522.

MASSILLON. *Calvary*, 3469 Lincoln Way E., 44646. Tel: 330-832-1866; Fax: 330-832-0059. Email: calvary3469@sbcglobal.net. Becky Tully, Supt.

RELIGIOUS INSTITUTES OF MEN REPRESENTED IN THE DIOCESE

For further details refer to the corresponding bracketed number in the Religious Institutes of Men or Women section.

[]—*Apostles of Jesus*—AJ
[]—*Benedictine Order of Cleveland*
[0320]—*Brothers of Christian Instruction*—F.I.C.
[0520]—*Franciscan Friars* (Immaculate Conception Prov. of New York)—O.F.M.
[]—*Missionaries of the Sacred Heart*—M.S.C.
[0430]—*Order of Preachers (Dominicans)* (Prov. of St. Joseph)—O.P.
[1065]—*Priestly Fraternity of St. Peter*—F.S.S.P.
[]—*Society of Jesus*—SJ
[1020]—*Society of St. Paul*—S.S.P.

RELIGIOUS INSTITUTES OF WOMEN REPRESENTED IN THE DIOCESE

[0100]—*Adorers of the Blood of Christ*—A.S.C.
[]—*Antonine Sisters*—A.S.
[]—*Benediction Sisters (Byzantine Sisters)*—O.S.B.
[1040]—*Congregation of the Divine Spirit*—C.D.S.
[1115]—*Dominican Sisters of Peace*
[]—*Little Sisters of Mary Immaculate*—L.S.M.I.G.
[3050]—*Oblate Sisters of the Sacred Heart of Jesus*—O.S.H.J.
[3210]—*Poor Clares of Perpetual Adoration*—P.C.P.A.
[0580]—*Sisters of Charity of St. Augustine*—C.S.A.
[0990]—*Sisters of Divine Providence*—C.D.P.
[]—*Sisters of Mercy of the Americas*
[2990]—*Sisters of Notre Dame*—S.N.D.
[]—*Sisters of Our Lady of Kilimanjaro*—C.D.N.K.
[1710]—*Sisters of St. Francis of Mary Immaculate, Joliet, IL*—O.S.F.
[]—*Sisters of St. Francis of Tiffin, OH*—OSF/T
[3910]—*Sisters of St. Joseph of St. Mark*—S.J.S.M.
[]—*Sisters of St. Joseph of the Third Order of St. Francis*—SSJ-TOSF
[2110]—*Sisters of the Humility of Mary*—H.M.
[3730]—*Sisters of the Order of St. Basil the Great*—O.S.B.M.
[]—*Ursuline Sisters of Cleveland*—O.S.U.
[4120-07]—*Ursuline Sisters of Youngstown*—O.S.U.

NECROLOGY

† DeMarinis, Rev. Msgr. John H., Youngstown, OH St. Anthony—Died June 12, 2011
† Finnigan, Rev. Msgr. John C., Canton, OH St. Peter—Died March 29, 2011
† Slaven, Rev. Msgr. Frederick, (Retired)—Died March 25, 2011
† Friedrich, Ralph J., (Retired)—Died April 18, 2011
† O'Leary, Patrick D., (Retired)—Died Dec. 26, 2010
† Witt, William, (Retired)—Died Feb. 22, 2011

Apostolate to Hungarians

Most Reverend

FERENC CSERHATI, S.T.D.

Titular Bishop of Centuria, Auxiliary to Esztergom-Budapest, especially entrusted with the coordination of the pastoral service of Hungarians abroad; ordained April 18, 1971 in Alba Julia; appointed June 15, 2007; consecrated in Esztergom August 15, 2007. *Res.: Ung.Kath.Delegatur, Landwehrstr.66, Munchen D-80336 Germany*. Tel: 49-89-532-8288; Fax: 49-89-532-8245. Email: ung.delegat@gmx.de.

ESTABLISHED MAY 20, 1983.

The Apostolate of the Bishop of Hungarians living outside of Hungary extends territorially to all the Hungarian communities existing outside of Hungary. The main purpose of the Apostolate is to give spiritual assistance to them through and in cooperation with the local ordinary and pastors.

Former Bishops—Most Revs. LADISLAUS A. IRANYI, Sch.P., ord. March 13, 1938; appt. May 20, 1983; cons. July 27, 1983; died March 6, 1987; ATTILA MIKLOSHAZY, S.J., S.T.D., Titular Bishop of Castel Minore and Bishop for the Spiritual Assistance to the Hungarian Emigrant People; ord. June 18, 1961; appt. Aug. 12, 1989; cons. Nov. 4, 1989; resigned April 5, 2006.

Delegate in North America—Rev. BARNABAS G. KISS, O.F.M., Holy Cross Hungarian R.C. Church, 8423 South St., Detroit, 48209-2709. Tel: 313-842-1133; Fax: 313-842-2773. Email: sztkereszt@comcast.net.

Hungarian Priests' Association in Canada—Rev. SZABOLCS SAJGO, S.J., St. Elizabeth of Hungary, 432 Sheppard Ave. E., Toronto ON M2N 3B7 Canada. Tel: 416-225-3300; Fax: 416-225-3814. Email: sajgosz@gmail.com.

American Hungarian Catholic Priests' Association (USA)—Rev. BARNABAS G. KISS, O.F.M., Holy Cross Hungarian R.C. Church, 8423 South St., Detroit, 48209-2709. Tel: 313-842-1133; Fax: 313-842-2773. Email: sztkereszt@comcast.net.

Hungarian Catholic League of America, Inc.—Rev. Msgr. WILLIAM I. VARSANYI, P.A., J.C.D., Chm., One Cathedral Sq., Providence, RI 02903. Tel: 401-278-4520; Fax: 401-278-4548.

Newspapers & Magazines—

"Eletunk" (Our Life)—Most Rev. FERENC CSERHATI, Editor, Landwehrstrasse 66, D-80336, Munchen 2, Germany. Tel: 49-89-532-8288; Fax: 49-89-532-8245.

"Tavlatok"— (Perspectives), Quarterly on Worldview, Spirituality and Culture, ed. by the Unio Cleri Hungarici. Rev. FERENC SZABO, S.J., Sodras u. 13., H-1026, Budapest, Hungary. Tel: 36-1-200-9476/105; Fax: 36-1-275-0249. Email: tavlatok@jezsuita.hu.

"A Sziv"— (Heart, Hungarian Journal), monthly, published by the Hungarian Jesuit Fathers. Rev. ARPAD HORVATH, S.J., Editor, Sodras u. 15., H-1026, Budapest, Hungary. Tel: 36-1-200-8054/102; Fax: 36-1-275-0269. Email: asziv@jezsuita.hu.

STATISTICS

Most personnel and institutions are under the jurisdiction of their local ordinaries.

NECROLOGY

Incorporated in diocesan and archdiocesan listings.

An asterisk (*) denotes an organization that has established tax-exempt status directly with the IRS and is not covered by the USCCB Group Ruling.

Apostolate For Lithuanian Catholics

Living Outside Lithuania

Very Reverend Monsignor

EDMOND PUTRIMAS, J.C.L.

Delegate of the Lithuanian Bishops Conference appointed August 19, 2003 to coordinate the pastoral care of Lithuanian Catholics living outside of Lithuania. *Office: 1 Resurrection Rd., Toronto ON M9A 5G1 Canada.* Tel: 416-233-7819; Fax: 416-233-5765. Email: putrimas@sielovada.org.

Most Reverend

PAUL A. BALTAKIS, O.F.M.

Former Bishop For Lithuanian Catholics; ordained August 24, 1952; appointed Titular Bishop of Egara and Bishop for Spiritual Assistance of Lithuanian Catholics June 1, 1984; cons. Sept. 14, 1984; retired July 12, 2003. *Res.: St. Anthony's Friary, 28 Beach Ave., P.O. Box 980, Kennebunkport, ME 04046.* Tel: 207-967-2011, Ext. 30.

ESTABLISHED JUNE 1, 1984.

The Apostolate for Lithuanian Catholics, extends worldwide to all Lithuanian communities existing outside Lithuania. Seventy-five percent of them in the U.S.A. The purpose of the apostolate is to give spiritual assistance to them in cooperation with the local ordinaries and pastors.

(VACANT SEE)

Email: putrimas@sielovada.org

Former Lithuanian Bishops—Most Revs. VINCENTAS BRIZGYS, Ph.D., J.C.D., cons. May 19, 1940; Titular Bishop of Bosana; Auxiliary Bishop of Kaunas, Lithuania (Impeditus); died April 23, 1992; ANTANAS DEKSNYS, Ph.D., cons. Jan. 15, 1969; Titular Bishop of Lavello; died May 5, 1999; PAUL A. BALTAKIS, O.F.M. ord. Aug. 24, 1952; appt. Titular Bishop of Egara and Bishop of Spiritual Assistance of Lithuanian Catholics in diaspora June 1, 1984; cons. Sept. 14, 1984; retired July 12, 2003.

Office of General Counsel—SAULIUS V. KUPRYS, 150 S. Wacker Dr., Ste. 1050, Chicago, IL 60606. Tel: 312-346-5275; Fax: 312-346-5640. Email: svkuprys@gmail.com.

Lithuanian R. Catholic Priests' League of Canada—Rev. VYTAUTAS STASKEVICIUS, Pres., Lithuanian Martyr's Parish, 494 Isabella Ave., Mississauga, Ontario L5B 2G2 Canada. Tel: 905-277-4320.

Lithuanian R. Catholic Priests' League of America—Rev. Msgr. ALBERT CONTONS, Pres., P.O. Box 1025, Humarock, MA 02047. Tel: 781-834-4079.

Lithuanian Franciscan Province of St. Casimir—Very Rev. PLACIDAS BARIUS, O.F.M., Delegate, Kennebunkport, ME 04046. Tel: 207-967-2031; Fax: 207-967-5721.

Lithuanian Jesuit Province—Very Rev. ANTANAS GRAZULIS, S.J., Delegate, 2345 W. 56th St., Chicago, IL 60636. Tel: 773-737-8400.

Marian Province of Mary Mother of Mercy—Very Rev. KAZIMIERZ CHWALEK, M.I.C., Prov., Stockbridge, MA 01262.

Pontifical Lithuanian College of St. Casimir—Very Rev. PETRAJ SIURYS, L.I.C., Rector, via Casalmonferrato 20, Rome 00182 Italy. Tel: 06-70-24-908; Fax: 06-70-11-659.

Sisters of the Immaculate Conception of the Blessed Virgin Mary—Sr. IGNE MARIJOSIUTE, Prov., Rte. 21, R.D. 2, Putnam, CT 06260. Tel: 860-928-7955; Fax: 860-928-1930.

Poor Sisters of Jesus Crucified and the Sorrowful Mother—Sr. MARY J. VALLERE, Supr. Gen., 261 Thatcher St., Brockton, MA 02402. Tel: 617-588-5070.

Sisters of St. Casimir—Sr. IMMACULATA WENDT, Gen. Supr., 2601 W. Marquette Rd., Chicago, IL 60609. Tel: 773-776-1324.

Sisters of St. Francis—Sr. JANET GARDNER, O.S.F., Supr. Gen., 3603 McRoberts Rd., Pittsburgh, PA 15234. Tel: 412-882-9911.

**Lithuanian R. Catholic Religious Aid, Inc.*Very Rev. Msgr. EDMOND PUTRIMAS, J.C.L., Pres.; Mrs. VIDA JANKAUSKAS, Mgr., 64-25 Perry Ave., Maspeth, 11378. Tel: 718-326-5202; Fax: 718-326-5206. Email: lcra@earthlink.net.

Lithuanian American R. Catholic Federation—Youth Camp, 15100 Austin Rd., Manchester, MI 48158.

Lithuanian Roman Catholic Charities, Inc.—4545 W. 63rd St., Chicago, IL 60629.

Publications— Draugas (Chicago, IL); The Observer (Chicago, IL); Teviskes Ziburiai (Toronto, Ontario, Canada); Teviskes Aidai (Adelaide, Australia)

INSTITUTIONS LOCATED IN THE DIOCESE

[A] SCHOOLS

CHICAGO. *Maria High School*

THOMPSON. *Marionapolis Prep School*

[B] HOSPITALS

CHICAGO. *Holy Cross Hospital*

[C] NURSING HOMES AND HOMES FOR THE AGED

BROCKTON. *St. Joseph Manor Nursing Home*

ELMHURST. *St. Mary's Villa*

HOLLAND. *St. Joseph Nursing Home*

LEMONT. *Holy Family Villa*

PUTNAM. *Matulaitis Nursing Home*

[D] MISCELLANEOUS

CHICAGO. *Catholic Action Fund*

Jesuit Lithuanian Center

**Lithuanian Catholic Press Society*, 4545 W. 63rd St., IL 60629.

Lithuanian Roman Catholic Charities, 4545 W. 63rd St., IL 60629.

Matulaitis Institute

MANCHESTER. *Lithuanian American R. Catholic Federation Youth Camp*, 15100 Austin Rd., MI 48158.

PUTNAM. *American Lithuanian Catholic Archives*

WEST BRATTLEBORO. *Camp Neringa*

[E] CEMETERIES

CHICAGO. *St. Casimir Lithuanian*

RELIGIOUS INSTITUTES OF MEN REPRESENTED IN THE DIOCESE

For further details refer to the corresponding bracketed number in the Religious Institutes of Men or Women section.

[]—*Congregation of the Marians Province of Mary Mother of Mercy* (Stockbridge, MA)

[]—*Franciscan Fathers of the Lithuanian Province of St. Casimir* (Kennebunkport, ME)

[]—*Jesuit Fathers of Della Strada* (Chicago, IL)

RELIGIOUS INSTITUTES OF WOMEN REPRESENTED IN THE DIOCESE

[3240]—*Poor Sisters of Jesus Crucified and the Sorrowful Mother* (Brockton, MA)—C.J.C.

[2140]—*Sisters of Immaculate Conception of the Blessed Virgin Mary* (Putnam, CT)

[3740]—*Sisters of St. Casimir* (Chicago, IL)—S.S.C.

[1690]—*Sisters of St. Francis* (Pittsburgh, PA)—O.S.F.

STATISTICS

Most personnel and institutions are under the jurisdiction of their local ordinaries.

NECROLOGY

(No Deaths)

An asterisk (*) denotes an organization that has established tax-exempt status directly with the IRS and is not covered by the USCCB Group Ruling.

Prelature of the Holy Cross and Opus Dei

(Praelatura Sanctae Crucis et Operis Dei)

Most Reverend

JAVIER ECHEVARRIA, J.D., J.C.D.

Prelate of the Prelature of the Holy Cross and Opus Dei ordained August 7, 1955; appointed April 20, 1994; episcopal ordination January 6, 1995. *Curia of the Prelature, Viale Bruno Buozzi 73, Rome 00197 Italy.* Tel: 011-39-06-808-961.

PRELATURE OF OPUS DEI

Erected by the Apostolic Constitution, "Ut sit," on November 28, 1982 by Pope John Paul II.

Opus Dei was founded on October 2, 1928 by Saint Josemaria Escriva, to spread in all sectors of society a profound awareness of the universal call to sanctity in ordinary life and, more specifically, in the exercise of one's work.

Curia of the Prelature—Viale Bruno Buozzi 73, Rome 00197 Italy. Tel: 011-39-06-808-961.

Vicar General—Rev. Msgr. FERNANDO OCARIZ, Ph.D., S.T.D., Viale Bruno Buozzi 73, Rome 00197 Italy.

Regional Vicar for the United States—Rev. Msgr. THOMAS G. BOHLIN, Ph.D., S.T.D., 139 E. 34th St., New York, NY 10016. Tel: 646-742-2700.

Vicar for the Midwest—Very Rev. PETER V. ARMENIO, B.S., Ph.D., 5800 N. Keating Ave., Chicago, IL 60646. Tel: 312-283-5800. Embracing the states of Illinois, Indiana, Missouri and Wisconsin.

Vicar for California—Very Rev. LUKE J. MATA, 770 S. Windsor Blvd., Los Angeles, CA 90005. Tel: 323-930-2844.

Vicar for Texas—Very Rev. PAUL D. KAIS, B.A., M.A., Ph.D., 5505 Chaucer Dr., Houston, TX 77005. Tel: 715-523-4351.

Represented in the Archdioceses of Boston, Chicago, Galveston-Houston, Los Angeles, Miami, Milwaukee, Newark, New York, St. Louis, San Antonio, San Francisco, Washington and in the Dioceses of Burlington, Dallas, Fort Wayne-South Bend, Gary, Oakland, Palm Beach, Peoria, Pittsburgh, Providence, Trenton and Victoria.

Regional Vicar for Puerto Rico—Rev. Msgr. JUSTINIANO GARCIA ARIAS, M.A., J.C.D., Villa Caparra, A35 A St., Guaynabo, PR 00966-2211. Tel: 787-781-9123.

Represented in the Archdiocese of San Juan and the Dioceses of Mayaguez and Ponce.

CHAPLAINS FOR THE UNITED STATES

State of New York

New Rochelle. Revs. Bradley K. Arturi, J.C.D. (NY), Paul G. Grant (NY), Thomas Lamb (NY), 99 Overlook Cir., New Rochelle, NY 10804.

New York. Rev. Msgrs. Thomas G. Bohlin, Ph.D., S.T.D. (NY), Reg. Vicar, Javier Garcia de Cardenas (NY), Revs. James W. Albrecht (NY), John C. Agnew (NY), Robert A. Brisson (NY), Deo G. Rosales (NY), 139 E. 34th St., New York, NY 10016. Tel: 646-742-2700, Malcolm M. Kennedy (NY), 330 Riverside Dr., New York, NY 10025. Tel: 212-222-3285.

District of Columbia

Washington. Revs. Arne A. Panula, Ph.D., S.T.D. (NY), Orestes Gonzalez (NY), John P. Debicki (CHI), 2301 Wyoming Ave., N.W., Washington, DC 20008. Tel: 202-234-1567, Gregory Coyne (WDC), Gerald S. Kolf, B.S., M.B.A., S.T.D. (GAL), 4300 Garrison St., N.W., Washington, DC 20016. Tel: 202-362-2419, Diego Daza, 4300 Garrison St., N.W., Washington, DC 20016. Tel: 202-362-2419.

State of Massachusetts

Cambridge. Revs. George A. Crafts, David J. Cavanagh (BO), 25 Follen St., Cambridge, MA 02138. Tel: 617-354-3204.

Chestnut Hill. Revs. Richard W. Rieman (BO), Jose P. Ruisanchez (BO), Salvador S. Vahi (PMB), Alvaro Silva (BO), Robert P. Bucciarelli (BO), 481 Hammond St., Chestnut Hill, MA 02467. Tel: 617-738-7348.

State of New Jersey

Princeton. Rev. Martin Joseph Miller (TR), 34 Mercer St., Princeton, NJ 08540. Tel: 609-497-9448.

South Orange. Rev. Robert A. Connor, 170 Montrose Ave., South Orange, NJ 07079. Tel: 973-763-8397.

State of Pennsylvania

Pittsburgh. Revs. Rene J. Schatteman (PIT), Martin John Miller, 5090 Warwick Ter., Pittsburgh, PA 15213. Tel: 412-683-8448.

State of Florida

Delray Beach. Rev. Victor Cortes (DAL), 4409 Frances Dr., Delray Beach, FL 33445. Tel: 305-498-1249.

Miami. Revs. Christopher Schmitt (PMB), Eduardo Castillo, 4415 S.W. 88th Ave., Miami, FL 33165. Tel: 305-551-7965.

State of Rhode Island

Providence. Rev. George A. Crafts, 224 Bowen St., Providence, RI 02906. Tel: 401-272-7834.

State of Illinois

Chicago. Very Rev. Peter V. Armenio, B.S., Ph.D. (CHI), Vicar for the Midwest, Revs. Javier del Castillo (WDC), Edward G. Maristany (CHI), Frank J. Hoffman (CHI), 5800 N. Keating Ave., Chicago, IL 60646. Tel: 312-283-5800, Hilary F. Mahaney (CHI), Charles M. Ferrer (CHI), C. John McCloskey (CHI), 1825 N. Wood St., Chicago, IL 60622. Tel: 312-278-2644, John R. Waiss (NY), Joseph P. Landauer (PIT), John Grieco, 7225 N. Greenview Ave., Chicago, IL 60646. Tel: 312-465-3486.

Oak Park. Revs. James Socias (CHI), Mark Mannion, 829 S. Euclid, Oak Park, IL 60304. Tel: 708-383-0928, G. Barry Cole, Derrick Esclanda.

Urbana. Rev. G. Barry Cole, 715 W. Michigan, Urbana, IL 61801. Tel: 217-367-6650.

State of Indiana

South Bend. Rev. Charles Trullols, 1121 N. Notre Dame Ave., South Bend, IN 46617. Tel: 219-232-0550.

State of Missouri

Kirkwood. Revs. Michael E. Giesler (STL), John J. Alvarez (STL), 100 E. Essex Ave., Kirkwood, MO 63122. Tel: 314-821-1608.

State of Wisconsin

Brookfield. Revs. Timothy J. Uhen (MIL), John C. Kubeck (MIL), 12900 W. North Ave., Brookfield, WI 53005. Tel: 414-784-1523.

State of California

Los Angeles. Very Rev. Luke J. Mata, Rev. John R. Meyer, D.D.S., S.T.D. (SFR), Rev. Msgr. William Stetson, 770 S. Windsor Blvd., Los Angeles, CA 90002. Tel: 323-930-2844, Revs. Paul A. Donlan, Matthew Bloomer, Chap., 655 Levering Ave., Los Angeles, CA 90024. Tel: 213-208-0941.

San Francisco. Revs. Torlach Delargy, Chap., Juan R. Velez, 765 14th Ave., San Francisco, CA 94118. Tel: 415-386-0431.

Menlo Park. Rev. Msgr. James A. Kelly, 1160 Santa Cruz Ave., Menlo Park, CA 94025. Tel: 415-327-1675.

Berkeley. Rev. Jerome L. Jung (SFR), 2710 College Ave., Berkeley, CA 94705. Tel: 510-548-2819.

State of Texas

Houston. Very Rev. Paul D. Kais, B.A., M.A., Ph.D. (GAL), Vicar for Texas, Revs. Francisco Vera, Michael J. Barrett, S.T.D., Michael J. Manz (GAL), 5505 Chaucer Dr., Houston, TX 77005. Tel: 713-523-4351.

Irving. Revs. John E. Solarski, Joseph Thomas, 3610 Wingren, Irving, TX 75062. Tel: 214-650-0064.

San Antonio. Rev. Michael J. Manz (GAL), 1979 Summit Ave., San Antonio, TX 78212. Tel: 210-732-3065.

State of Virginia

Reston. Revs. Ronald S. Gillis, Lawrence A. Kutz, 1810 Old Reston Ave., Reston, VA 20190. Tel: 703-689-3433, William G. Shaughnessey, 1810 Old Reston Ave., Reston, VA 20190. Tel: 703-689-3433.

Puerto Rico

Guaynabo. Rev. Msgr. Justiniano Garcia Arias, M.A., J.C.D., Reg. Vicar, Revs. Juan Aramendi (SJN), Ramon Alvarez, Villa Caparra, A35 A St., Guaynabo, PR 00966-2211. Tel: 787-781-9123, Gonzalo Diaz, Alfredo Gastalver, Villa Caparra, A48 A St., Guaynabo, PR 00966. Tel: 787-783-1987.

San Juan. Revs. Martin Llambias (SJN), 51 Margarita St., San Juan, PR 00925. Tel: 787-759-6193, Juan Ignacio Ballesteros, 51 Margarita St., San Juan, PR 00925. Tel: 787-759-6193.

Ponce. Revs. Javier Bernaola (PCE), 8 Alcazar St., La Alhambra, Ponce, PR 00731. Tel: 787-844-2661, Jaime Bermudez, 8 Alcazar St., Ponce, PR 00731. Tel: 787-844-2661.

Mayaguez. Rev. Andres Eiroa (MGZ), 69 Orquideas St., Ensanche Martinez, Mayaguez, PR 00680. Tel: 787-833-6461.

Holy Protection of Mary Byzantine Catholic Eparchy of Phoenix

Most Reverend

GERALD N. DINO

Bishop of Eparchy of Phoenix; ordained March 21, 1965; appointed Bishop of Phoenix Byzantine December 6, 2007; consecrated and enthroned March 27, 2008. *Office: 8105 N. 16th St., Phoenix, AZ 85020.*

Chancery Office: 8105 N. 16th St., Phoenix, AZ 85020. Tel: 602-861-9778; Fax: 602-861-9796.

Web: eparchyofphoenix.org

Email: evnbishop@qwestoffice.net

ESTABLISHED DECEMBER 3, 1981.

Established in 1981 as the Byzantine Catholic Eparchy of Van Nuys. The name was changed to Holy Protection of Mary Byzantine Catholic Eparchy of Phoenix on February 10, 2010 by the Holy See.

Embraces all Catholics of the Byzantine-Ruthenian Church in the States of California, Oregon, Washington, Idaho, Nevada, Arizona, Utah, Wyoming, Montana, Colorado, New Mexico, Alaska and Hawaii.

Principal Patron-Holy Protection of the Mother of God (Pokrov).

Legal Title: Byzantine Catholic Bishop of Van Nuys, A Corporation Sole.

STATISTICAL OVERVIEW

Personnel	
Bishop	1
Priests: Diocesan Active in Diocese	16
Priests: Diocesan Active Outside Diocese	1
Priests: Retired, Sick or Absent	5
Number of Diocesan Priests	22
Religious Priests in Diocese	1
Total Priests in Diocese	23
Extern Priests in Diocese	3
Ordinations:	
Diocesan Priests	1
Permanent Deacons	1
Permanent Deacons in Diocese	12
Total Brothers	2
Total Sisters	3
Parishes	
Parishes	19
With Resident Pastor:	
Resident Diocesan Priests	17
Resident Religious Priests	1
Without Resident Pastor:	
Administered by Priests	1
Missions	1
Welfare	
Other Institutions	1
Total Assisted	26
Educational	
Diocesan Students in Other Seminaries	2
Total Seminarians	2
Catechesis/Religious Education:	
High School Students	77
Elementary Students	325
Total Students under Catholic Instruction	404
Vital Statistics	
Receptions into the Church:	
Infant Baptism Totals	72
Minor Baptism Totals	1
Adult Baptism Totals	6
Received into Full Communion	15
First Communions	91
Confirmations	99
Marriages:	
Catholic	17
Interfaith	2
Total Marriages	19
Deaths	38
Total Catholic Population	2,402

Former Bishops—Most Revs. THOMAS V. DOLINAY, D.D., ord. May 16, 1948; cons. Nov. 23, 1976; appt. Titular Bishop of Thyatira and Auxiliary of Passiac, Sept. 23, 1976; appt. First Ordinary of the Byzantine Catholic Diocese of Van Nuys, CA; enthroned March 9, 1982; appt. Coadjutor Archbishop of Pittsburgh Byzantine Rite, March 13, 1990; succeeded to June 12, 1991; died April 13, 1993; GEORGE M. KUZMA, D.D. (Retired), ord. May 29, 1955; appt. Auxiliary Bishop of the Byzantine Eparchy of Passaic, Nov. 11, 1986; cons. Feb. 4, 1987; appt. Bishop of Eparchy of Van Nuys Oct. 23, 1990; enthroned as Second Bishop of Van Nuys, Jan. 15, 1991; retired Dec. 5, 2000; died Dec. 7, 2008.; WILLIAM C. SKURLA, ord. May 23, 1987; appt. Bishop of Eparchy of Van Nuys Feb. 19, 2002; cons. April 23, 2002; appt. Bishop of Passaic Dec. 6, 2007; enthroned Jan. 29, 2008.

Chancery Office—Byzantine Catholic Eparchy of Phoenix, Pastoral Center, 8105 N. 16th St., Phoenix, 85020. Tel: 602-861-9778; Fax: 602-861-9796. Email: evnsecretary@qwestoffice.net. Web: www.eparchyofphoenix.org. Office Hours: Mon.-Fri. 10-3.

Protosyncellus (Vicar General)—Rt. Rev. STEPHEN G. WASHKO. Email: sstparish@qwestoffice.net.

Chancellor—Rt. Rev. WESLEY W. IZER, S.T.M.

College of Consultors—Very Revs. KURT BURNETTE, J.C.L.; JOSEPH HUTSKO; Rt. Rev. WESLEY W. IZER, S.T.M.; Very Rev. ROBERT M. PIPTA; Rt. Revs. FRANCIS M. VIVONA, S.T.M., J.C.L.; STEPHEN G. WASHKO.

Finance Officer—Rt. Rev. WESLEY W. IZER, S.T.M. Email: evntreasurer2@aol.com.

Finance Assistant—Sr. ALPHONSA DANOVICH, O.S.B.M.

Finance Council—Rt. Revs. WESLEY W. IZER, S.T.M.; STEPHEN G. WASHKO; Very Rev. KURT BURNETTE, J.C.L.; Sr. ALPHONSA DANOVICH, O.S.B.M.; Deacon JAMES DANOVICH.

Presbyteral Council— All priests having a Pastoral Assignment within the Eparchy.

Secretary for the Presbyteral Council & The College of Consultors—Rev. JAMES M. LANE.

Eparchial Tribunal—Office of the Tribunal Eparchy of Van Nuys, P.O. Box 18316, Las Vegas, NV 89114. Tel: 702-735-1210; Fax: 702-735-5146.

Judicial Vicar—Rt. Rev. FRANCIS M. VIVONA, S.T.M., J.C.L.

Adjutant Judicial Vicar—Very Rev. KURT BURNETTE, J.C.L.

Promoter of Justice—Rev. PETER ROMEO, J.C.L.

Secretary—Mrs. PAMELA MORLEY.

Defender of the Bond—VACANT.

Judge—VACANT.

Auditors—Rev. MARK GOMORI; Deacon STEPHEN CASMUS, M.A.

Notaries—Mrs. PAMELA MORLEY; Mrs. MARGARITA HERNANDEZ.

Bishop's Appeal—Sr. CHRISTOPHER MALCOVSKY, O.S.B.M.

Building and Sacred Arts Commission—Rt. Revs. STEPHEN G. WASHKO; WESLEY W. IZER, S.T.M.; Rev. Msgr. GEORGE N. VIDA; Deacon JOHN MONTALVO III; Mr. KEVIN KOWALCHUK.

Director of Religious Education—Rev. ANTHONY HERNANDEZ; Sr. JEAN MARIE CIHOTA, O.S.B.M., Asst. Dir.

Director of Evangelization—Rt. Rev. JOSEPH STANICHAR.

Safe Environment Coordinator—Sr. JEAN MARIE CIHOTA, O.S.B.M. Email: jean.sister@cox.net.

Victim Advocate and Assistance Coordinator—ROSEMARIE LUDWIG, Ph.D. Tel: 602-997-1550. Email: rstussy@cox.net.

Vocations Office—Very Rev. ROBERT M. PIPTA, Dir.; Rev. MICHAEL O'LOUGHLIN, Asst. Dir.; Deacon JAMES DANOVICH; Sr. JEAN MARIE CIHOTA, O.S.B.M.

Ecclesiatical Notaries—Rt. Revs. STEPHEN G. WASHKO; WESLEY W. IZER, S.T.M.

Newsletter— "Light of the West" KATHLEEN SLONKA, Editor. Email: lightofthewest@cox.net.

Director of Ecumenical Affairs—Rt. Rev. STEPHEN G. WASHKO.

Censor—Rt. Rev. FRANCIS M. VIVONA, S.T.M., J.C.L.

Pro-Life Coordinator—Rev. LEE PERRY.

Communication and Eparchial Web Site—KATHLEEN SLONKA.

Pension Committee—Rt. Revs. STEPHEN G. WASHKO; WESLEY W. IZER, S.T.M.; Rev. Msgr. GEORGE N. VIDA; Very Rev. KURT BURNETTE, J.C.L.; Rev. MARK GOMORI.

Personnel Board—Rt. Revs. STEPHEN G. WASHKO; WESLEY W. IZER, S.T.M.; Very Rev. ROBERT M. PIPTA.

Youth—Very Rev. JOSEPH HUTSKO; Rev. ROBERT RANKIN.

CLERGY, PARISHES, MISSIONS AND PAROCHIAL SCHOOLS

STATE OF ARIZONA

PHOENIX, MARICOPA CO., ST. STEPHEN CATHEDRAL (1968) [CEM] Rt. Rev. Stephen G. Washko, Rector; Rev. Diodoro Mendoza, Parochial Vicar; Sr. Christopher Malcovsky, O.S.B.M., Admin. Sec.; Deacons John Montalvo III; James Danovich; Michael Hanafin.

Res.: 8141 N. 16th St. Frnt., 85020-3999. Tel: 602-943-5379; Fax: 602-997-4093. Email: sstparish@qwestoffice.net. Web: www.ststephenbyzantine.org. Sisters 2.

Catechesis/Religious Program—Sr. Jean Marie Cihota, O.S.B.M., D.R.E. Students 60.

Convent—St. Stephen Convent, 8141 N. 16th St. #27, 85020. Tel: 602-944-5121; Fax: 602-997-4093. Sisters 3.

GILBERT, MARICOPA CO., ST. THOMAS THE APOSTLE (1982) Rt. Rev. Wesley W. Izer; Deacon Michael Sullivan.
Mailing Address: P.O. Box 667, 85299-0667. Tel: 480-497-6726; Fax: 480-497-6726. Email: pastor.st.thomas@cox.net.
Rectory—Tel: 480-584-6676.
Church: 19 W. Bruce Ave., 85233.
Catechesis/Religious Program—Students 19.

TUCSON, PIMA CO., ST. MELANY (1974) Rev. Robert Rankin.
Church: 1212 N. Sahuara, 85712-5018. Tel: 520-886-4225; Fax: 520-751-4574. Web: byzantinetucson.com.
Catechesis/Religious Program—Students 22.

STATE OF ALASKA

ANCHORAGE, ANCHORAGE CO., SAINT NICHOLAS OF MYRA (1958) Rev. James R. Barrand.
Res.: 2200 Arctic Blvd., AK 99503-1909. Tel: 907-277-6731.
Catechesis/Religious Program—Students 18.
Mission—Blessed Theodore Romzha Mission Old Sacred Heart Church, 1201 Bogard Rd., Wasilla, AK 99654.

STATE OF CALIFORNIA

ANAHEIM, ORANGE CO., ANNUNCIATION (1969) Rev. Msgr. George N. Vida.
Res.: 995 N. West St., CA 92801-4305. Tel: 714-533-6292; Fax: 714-991-9738.
Rectory—999 N. West St., CA 92801-4305.
Catechesis/Religious Program—Students 30.

FONTANA, SAN BERNARDINO CO., ST. NICHOLAS (1958) Very Rev. Joseph Hutsko.
Res.: 9112 Oleander Ave., CA 92335-5599. Tel: 909-822-9917; Fax: 909-822-7663. Email: huts1009@roadrunner.com.
Catechesis/Religious Program—Pager: 909-822-7663.

FRESNO, FRESNO CO., BYZANTINE CATHOLIC COMMUNITY OF FRESNO, CA, Closed. For inquiries for parish records contact the chancery.

LOS GATOS, SANTA CLARA CO., ST. BASIL THE GREAT (1986) Rev. Anthony Hernandez.
Res.: 14263 Mulberry Dr., CA 95032-1208. Tel: 408-871-0919; Fax: 408-871-0911. Email: pastor@stbasil.org. Web: www.stbasil.org.
Catechesis/Religious Program—Students 2.
Salinas Monterey Byzantine Catholic Outreach—, Location: Blessed Edmund Rice Chapel at Palma High School, 919 Iverson St., Salinas, CA. (Div. Liturgy 4th Sat. of month at 4:30 PM), 14263 Mulberry Dr., CA 95032. Email: pastor@stbasil.org. Web: www.bcmonterey.org.

PALM SPRINGS, RIVERSIDE CO., BYZANTINE CATHOLIC COMMUNITY OF PALM SPRINGS, CA, Closed. For inquiries for parish records contact the chancery.

SACRAMENTO, SACRAMENTO CO., ST. PHILIP THE APOSTLE (1971) Rev. Frantisek Murin; Margaret Dean, Fin. Admin.
Church & Mailing Address: 3866 65th St., CA 95820. Tel: 916-452-1888 (Office); Fax: 916-452-6333. Email: stphilpastor@juno.com.

SAN DIEGO, SAN DIEGO CO., HOLY ANGELS (1958) Very Rev. Robert M. Pipta.
Mailing Address: 2235 Galahad Rd., CA 92123-3931. Tel: 858-277-2511; Fax: 858-277-5792. Web: www.holyangelssandiego.com.
Catechesis/Religious Program—Students 29.

SAN LUIS OBISPO, SAN LUIS OBISPO CO., SAINT ANNE (1986) Rev. James M. Lane; Deacon John Bradley; Mr. Paul Sawko, Fin. Admin.
Mailing Address: 222 E. Foothill Blvd., CA 93405-1540. Tel: 805-543-8883; Fax: 805-543-8832.
Catechesis/Religious Program—Students 32.

SAN MATEO, SAN MATEO CO., ST. MACRINA, Closed. All records at the Chancery Office.

SHERMAN OAKS, LOS ANGELES CO., ST. MARY PROTO-CATHEDRAL (1956) Very Rev. Melvin Rybarczyk, C.R., Rector.
Res.: 5329 Sepulveda Blvd., CA 91411-3441. Tel: 818-907-5511; Fax: 818-981-7107.
Catechesis/Religious Program—5335 Sepulveda Blvd., CA 91411. Cynthia Bosak, D.R.E. Students 10.

STOCKTON, SAN JOAQUIN CO., BYZANTINE CATHOLIC COMMUNITY OF STOCKTON, Closed. For inquiries for parish records contact the chancery.

STATE OF COLORADO

COLORADO SPRINGS, EL PASO CO., BYZANTINE CATHOLIC MISSION, Closed. For inquiries for parish records contact the chancery.

DENVER, DENVER CO., HOLY PROTECTION OF THE MOTHER OF GOD (1974) Rev. Michael O'Loughlin; Deacon Andrew Bodnar.
Mailing Address: 1074 S. Cook St., CO 80209-4923. Tel: 303-778-8283; Fax: 303-778-8283. Email: pastor@holyprotection.org. Web: www.holyprotection.org.
Church: 1201 S. Elizabeth St., CO 80210.
Catechesis/Religious Program—Students 17.

STATE OF NEVADA

LAS VEGAS, CLARK CO.
1—ST. GABRIEL THE ARCHANGEL (1977) Rev. Mark A. Gomori.
Church: 2250 E. Maule Ave., NV 89119-4607. Tel: 702-361-2431 (Office); 702-433-1935 (Rectory); Fax: 702-361-3772.
Catechesis/Religious Program—Students 13.
2—OUR LADY OF WISDOM ITALO-GREEK (1993) Rt. Rev. Francis M. Vivona; Deacon Stephen Casmus.
Church: 2120 Lindell Rd., NV 89146. Tel: 702-873-5101; Fax: 702-873-5104. Web: www.ourladyofwisdom.net.
Catechesis/Religious Program—Students 39.
Our Lady of Mt. Carmel Outreach—Outreach: 8530 Robertson Rd., NV 89146.

STATE OF NEW MEXICO

ALBUQUERQUE, BERNALILLO CO., OUR LADY OF PERPETUAL HELP (1974) Very Rev. Kurt Burnette. In Res., Rev. Christopher L. Zugger (Retired).
Church: 1837 Alvarado Dr., N.E., NM 87110. Tel: 505-256-1539 (Rectory); 505-268-2877; Fax: 505-256-1278. Web: www.olphnm.org.
Catechesis/Religious Program—Students 19.

LAS CRUCES, DONA ANA CO., BYZANTINE CATHOLIC MISSION, Closed. Records are located at Albuquerque Parish.

STATE OF OREGON

PORTLAND, MULTNOMAH CO., ST. IRENE BYZANTINE CATHOLIC CHURCH Rev. Frank Knusel.
Rectory—34799 N. Honeyman Rd., Scappoose, OR 97056. Tel: 971-322-5646.
Church & Mailing Address: 4630 N. Maryland Ave., OR 97217.

STATE OF UTAH

SALT LAKE CITY, SALT LAKE CO., BYZANTINE CATHOLIC MISSION, Closed. For inquiries for parish records contact the chancery.

STATE OF WASHINGTON

OLYMPIA, THURSTON CO., ST. GEORGE BYZANTINE CATHOLIC CHURCH (1989) Rev. Lee Perry; Deacon Joseph Wargacki.
Res.: 9730 Yelm Hwy., WA 98513. Tel: 360-413-5651; Fax: 360-413-5651.
Catechesis/Religious Program—Students 36.

SEATTLE, KING CO., ST. JOHN CHRYSOSTOM (1981) Rt. Rev. Joseph Stanichar.
Res.: 1305 S. Lander St., WA 98144-5038. Tel: 206-329-9219; Fax: 206-322-6930. Web: www.stjohnchrysostom.org.
Catechesis/Religious Program—Students 50.
Whatcom, Skagit & Island Outreach—, Location: Immaculate Conception Church, Mt. Vernon, WA. (Div. Liturgy Sunday at 5:30 PM)

SPOKANE, SPOKANE CO., SS. CYRIL & METHODIUS (1979) Rev. William O'Brien.
Mailing Address: P.O. Box 15314, Spokane Valley, WA 99216-5314.
Res.: 4317 N. Evergreen Rd., WA 99216-1298. Tel: 509-922-4527.
Catechesis/Religious Program—Students 10.

WALLA WALLA, WALLA WALLA CO., BYZANTINE CATHOLIC MISSION, Closed. For inquiries for parish records contact the Spokane parish.

On Special Assignment:
Rev.—
Michalenko, Alexei, Chap., Georgetown Law Center, 600 New Jersey Ave., N.W., Washington, DC 20001.

Retired:
Revs.—
Daigle, Robert E., 6505 O'Bannon Dr., Las Vegas, NV 89146.
Gnall, Julian, 11986 Tivoli Park Row #3, San Diego, CA 92128. Tel: 619-532-6043
Zugger, Christopher L., 1838 Palomas Dr. N.E., Albuquerque, NM 87110.
Very Rev. Archpriest—
Moran, Michael, J.C.D., 16701 Algonquin St., #307, Huntington Beach, CA 92649-3126.

Permanent Deacons:
Anderson, Craig, Los Gatos, CA
Bodnar, Andrew, Denver, CO
Bradley, John, San Luis Obispo, CA
Casmus, Stephen, M.A., Las Vegas, NV
Danovich, James, Phoenix, AZ
Escobedo, Brian, 3605 Perrysville Ave, Pittsburgh, PA 15214.
Hanafin, Michael, Phoenix, AZ
Hess, David, P.O. Box 139, Granville, OH 43023. San Diego, CA
Mandelas, Michael, 3605 Perrysville Ave., Pittsburgh, PA 15214.
Martonick, Gregory, Spokane, WA
Montalvo, John, III, Phoenix, AZ
Sullivan, Michael, Gilbert, AZ
Wargacki, Joseph, Olympia, WA

INSTITUTIONS LOCATED IN THE DIOCESE

[A] RELIGIOUS COMMUNITIES

PHOENIX. *St. Stephen Convent*, 8141 N. 16th St., #27, 85020. Tel: 602-944-5121; Fax: 602-861-9796. Sisters Jean Marie Cihota, O.S.B.M.; Christopher Malcovsky, O.S.B.M.; Alphonsa Danovich, O.S.B.M.

[B] RETIREMENT HOMES

PHOENIX. *St. Stephen Senior Citizen Apartments*, 8141 N. 16th St., 85020. Tel: 602-943-5379; Fax: 602-997-4093. Web: www.ststephenbyzantine.org. Rt. Rev. Stephen G. Washko, Contact Person. Senior Citizens Apartments 26; Residents 28.

[C] MONASTERIES AND RESIDENCES OF PRIESTS AND BROTHERS

CALIMESA. *Byzantine Brothers of St. Francis, St. Francis Monastery*, 9443 Sharondale Rd., CA 92320. Tel: 909-446-8648. Bro. John Gray, B.B.S.F., Supr.

RELIGIOUS INSTITUTES OF MEN REPRESENTED IN THE DIOCESE

For further details refer to the corresponding bracketed number in the Religious Institutes of Men or Women section.

[]—*Byzantine Brothers of St. Francis*—B.B.S.F.

[1080]—*Congregation of the Resurrection*—C.R.

RELIGIOUS INSTITUTES OF WOMEN REPRESENTED IN THE DIOCESE

[3730]—*Sisters of the Order of St. Basil the Great*—O.S.B.M.

NECROLOGY

† Idranyi, Edmund M., (Retired)—Died Aug. 3, 2011
† Ridella, Joseph, (Retired)—Died Feb. 26, 2011

An asterisk (*) denotes an organization that has established tax-exempt status directly with the IRS and is not covered by the USCCB Group Ruling.

Eparchy of Newton (Melkite-Greek Catholic)

Most Reverend

NICHOLAS JAMES SAMRA, D.D.

Bishop of Newton; ordained May 10, 1970; appointed Auxiliary Bishop of Newton June 29, 1989; appointed fifth Bishop of Newton June 15, 2011; enthroned August 23, 2011. *Mailing Address: 3 VFW Pkwy., West Roxbury, MA 02132.*

Most Reverend

JOHN A. ELYA, B.S.O., D.D.

Retired Eparch of Newton; ordained February 17, 1952; appointed Auxiliary Bishop of Newton April 2, 1986; appointed Eparch of Newton November 25, 1993; installed January 25, 1994; retired August 18, 2004. *Res.: 30 East St., Methuen, MA 01844.* Tel: 978-683-2471. Email: bpjohn3@aol.com.

The Chancery: 3 Veterans of Foreign Wars Pkwy., West Roxbury, MA 02132. Tel: 617-323-9922; Fax: 617-323-0944.

Web: melkite.org

ESTABLISHED AS AN APOSTOLIC EXARCHATE JANUARY 10, 1966.

Elevated to Eparchy, June 28, 1976; Embraces all members of the Melkite Greek Catholic Church in the United States.

For legal titles of parishes and institutions, consult the Chancery Office.

STATISTICAL OVERVIEW

Personnel	
Bishop	1
Retired Bishops	1
Priests: Diocesan Active in Diocese	28
Priests: Diocesan Active Outside Diocese	9
Priests: Retired, Sick or Absent	10
Number of Diocesan Priests	47
Religious Priests in Diocese	14
Total Priests in Diocese	61
Extern Priests in Diocese	2
Permanent Deacons in Diocese	58
Total Sisters	5
Parishes	
Parishes	36
With Resident Pastor:	
Resident Diocesan Priests	24
Resident Religious Priests	6
Without Resident Pastor:	
Administered by Priests	2
Administered by Deacons	4
Missions	7
Educational	
Diocesan Students in Other Seminaries	1
Seminaries, Religious	1
Students Religious	2
Total Seminarians	3
Catechesis/Religious Education:	
High School Students	122
Elementary Students	636
Total Students under Catholic Instruction	761
Vital Statistics	
Receptions into the Church:	
Infant Baptism Totals	317
Minor Baptism Totals	6
Adult Baptism Totals	12
Received into Full Communion	2
First Communions	180
Confirmations	203
Marriages:	
Catholic	172
Interfaith	10
Total Marriages	182
Deaths	128
Total Catholic Population	21,000

Former Eparchs—Most Revs. JUSTIN A. NAJMY, B.A.O., D.D., born April 23, 1898; ord. Dec. 25, 1926; cons. May 29, 1966; installed June 4, 1966; died June 11, 1968; JOSEPH E. TAWIL, D.D., LL.D., ord. July 20, 1936; cons. Jan. 1, 1960; appt. Apostolic Exarch, Oct. 30, 1969; appt. Eparch, June 28, 1976; became emeritus Dec. 2, 1989; died Feb. 17, 1999; IGNATIUS GHATTAS, B.S.O., D.D., born Dec. 25, 1920; ord. July 7, 1946; appt. Dec. 2, 1989; cons. Feb. 23, 1990; died Oct. 11, 1992; JOHN A. ELYA, B.S.O., D.D., ord. Feb. 17, 1952; appt. Auxiliary Bishop of Newton April 2, 1986; appt. Eparch of Newton Nov. 25, 1993; installed Jan. 25, 1994; retired Eparch of Newton Aug. 18, 2004; CYRIL SALIM BUSTROS, S.M.S.P., ord. June 29, 1962; appt. Archbishop of Baalbek (Melkite) Lebanon Oct. 25, 1988; ord. Nov. 27, 1988; appt. Eparch of Newton June 22, 2004; enthroned August 18, 2004; selected Archbishop of Beirut and Jbeil June 25, 2010; confirmed June 15, 2011.

Diocesan Administration

Chancery Office—3 VFW Pkwy., West Roxbury, 02132. Tel: 617-323-9922; Fax: 617-323-0944. Office Hours: Mon.-Fri. 9-5.

Protosyncellus—Rt. Rev. Archimandrite PHILIP RACZKA.

Chancellor—Rev. Deacon PAUL J. LEONARCZYK.

Eparchial Tribunal—6458 Tapestry Circle, Spring Hill, FL 34606. Tel: 352-683-7637.

Judicial Vicar—Rt. Rev. Archimandrite GERASIMOS MURPHY, J.C.D., 6458 Tapestry Cir., Spring Hill, FL 34606.

Judges—Rt. Rev. MICHAEL K. SKROCKI, J.C.L.; Revs. JOSEPH KOURY, J.C.D.; HERBERT MAY, J.C.L.; Rev. Msgr. MICHAEL SOUCKAR, J.C.D.

Defender of the Bond and Promoter of Justice—Rt. Rev. Exarch JOSEPH S. HAGGAR, J.C.L.

Notaries—Rev. Archdeacon GEORGE YANY; Rev. Deacon PAUL J. LEONARCZYK; LUCILLE LAROCHE; JANICE M. TERRIS.

Chief Finance Officer—Rev. Deacon ROBERT SHALHOUB. Tel: 973-785-4144; Fax: 973-890-9599.

Protopresbyters—Rt. Rev. JOSEPH FRANCAVILLA, Mid-Atlantic; Rt. Rev. Exarch JOSEPH S. HAGGAR, J.C.L., New England; Rt. Revs. FRANK J. MILIENEWICZ, Southeast; ALEXEI SMITH, M.A., M.Div., West; Very Rev. PHILARET LITTLEFIELD, Great Lakes.

Consultative Bodies

College of Eparchial Consultors—Rt. Rev. JOSEPH FRANCAVILLA; Rt. Rev. Exarch GABRIEL GHANOUM, B.S.O.; Very Rev. PHILARET LITTLEFIELD; Rt. Rev. Exarch JOSEPH S. HAGGAR, J.C.L.; Rt. Revs. FRANK J. MILIENEWICZ; ALEXEI SMITH, M.A., M.Div.; Rt. Rev. Archimandrite PHILIP RACZKA.

Presbyteral Council—Rt. Revs. CHARLES ABOODY (Retired); JOSEPH FRANCAVILLA; LAWRENCE GOSSELIN; Rt. Rev. Exarch JOSEPH S. HAGGAR, J.C.L.; Rt. Rev. FRANK J. MILIENEWICZ; Rt. Rev. Archimandrites PHILIP RACZKA; KENNETH SHERMAN; Rt. Rev. ALEXEI SMITH, M.A., M.Div.; Very Rev. PHILARET LITTLEFIELD; Rev. PETER BOUTROS; Rt. Rev. Archimandrite ROBERT RABBAT; Rt. Revs. JOHN AZAR; MICHAEL K. SKROCKI, J.C.L.; Revs. NAIM KHALIL, B.S.O.; CHRISTOPHER MANUELE; SAMIR ABU-LAIL; ANTOINE RIZK, B.S.O.

Diocese of Newton for the Melkites in the USA, Inc., a Massachusetts Corporation—Most Rev. NICHOLAS J. SAMRA; Rt. Rev. Archimandrite PHILIP RACZKA; Rev. Deacons PAUL J. LEONARCZYK; ROBERT SHALHOUB.

Finance Council—Rt. Rev. Exarch JOSEPH S. HAGGAR, J.C.L.; Dr. JOHN NAZARIAN; CHARLES JOSEPH; Rev. Deacons ROBERT SHALHOUB; THOMAS DAVIS; CAMILLE F. SARROUF JR.; BASIL ZALOOM; JOSEPH LIAN; ALBERT HADDAD.

Legal Consultants—CAMILLE F. SARROUF; CAMILLE F. SARROUF JR., 95 Commercial Wharf, Boston, 02110. Tel: 617-227-5800.

Pastoral Offices and Commissions

Continuing Education of Clergy Office—Rt. Rev. PAUL G. FRECHETTE; Rt. Rev. Exarch GABRIEL GHANOUM, B.S.O.; Rt. Rev. ALEXEI SMITH, M.A., M.Div.; Rev. IGNATIUS HARRINGTON.

National Association of Melkite Youth—Rev. THOMAS P. STEINMETZ, 140 Mitchell St., Manchester, NH 03102.

MAYA (Melkite Assoc. of Young Adults)—Rev. JUSTIN ROSE, 923 W. Congress St., San Bernardino, CA 92410. Tel: 909-889-3579.

Ambassadors—Rev. PETER BOUTROS, 3718 E. Greenway Rd., Phoenix, AZ 85032. Tel: 602-787-4787.

National Association of Melkite Women—VACANT.

Liturgical Commission—Rt. Rev. Archimandrite DAMON GEIGER.

Office of Communications—Rev. Deacon PAUL LEONARCZYK, Dir., 3 VFW Pkwy., West Roxbury, 02132.

Educational Services—Dr. FRANCES COLIE, Ph.D., Dir., 1710 Surf Ave., Belmar, NJ 07719. Tel: 732-280-1774.

Vocations Office—Rt. Rev. Archimandrite PHILIP RACZKA, Coord., 8525 Cole Ave., Warren, MI 48093. Tel: 586-751-6017; Fax: 586-751-1877.

"Sophia" (A Journal)—Rt. Rev. Archimandrite JAMES K. BABCOCK, Editor-in-Chief; Rev. Deacon PAUL LEONARCZYK, Production.

Order of St. Nicholas—Mailing Address: 3 VFW Pkwy., West Roxbury, 02132. Tel: 617-323-9922; Fax: 617-323-0692. GREGORY OUSSANY, Natl. Chm.; Rt. Rev. Exarch GABRIEL GHANOUM, B.S.O., Chap.

Associated Melkite Charities—Very Rev. PHILARET LITTLEFIELD, 1617 W. State St., Milwaukee, WI 53233. Tel: 414-342-1543.

Sophia Press—Rev. Deacon PAUL J. LEONARCZYK, Office: 3 VFW Pkwy., West Roxbury, 02132. Tel: 617-323-9922, Ext. 206; Fax: 617-323-0944; Rt. Rev. MICHAEL K. SKROCKI, J.C.L.

Victim Assistance Coordinator—Rt. Rev. Exarch GABRIEL GHANOUM, B.S.O., Mailing Address: 126 S.E. 15 Rd., Miami, FL 33129. Tel: 305-856-8666; Fax: 305-859-7982.

CLERGY, PARISHES, MISSIONS AND PAROCHIAL SCHOOLS

STATE OF MASSACHUSETTS

BOSTON, SUFFOLK CO., ANNUNCIATION CATHEDRAL Rt. Rev. Archimandrite Philip Raczka, Rector; Rev. Deacons John Moses; Ibrahim Zeinieh; Thomas Burke.
Res.: 7 V.F.W. Pkwy., 02132. Tel: 617-323-5242; Fax: 617-325-2662. Email: ourlady3@verizon.net.

LAWRENCE, ESSEX CO., ST. JOSEPH Rt. Rev. Archimandrite Mark E. Melone; Protodeacon Bryan McNeil; Rev. Deacon John MacMillan.
Res.: 241 Hampshire St., 01841. Tel: 978-682-8152; Fax: 978-682-6114.

WORCESTER, WORCESTER CO., OUR LADY OF PERPETUAL HELP Rt. Rev. Paul G. Frechette; Rev. Deacons Dennis J. McCarthy; Elias (Richard) Bailey.
Res.: 256 Hamilton St., 01604. Tel: 508-752-4174; Fax: 508-752-8351.

STATE OF ALABAMA

BIRMINGHAM, JEFFERSON CO., ST. GEORGE Rt. Rev. Frank J. Milienewicz; Rev. Deacon Seraphim Ritchey.
Res.: 425 Sixteenth Ave. S., AL 35205. Tel: 205-252-5788; Fax: 205-252-0063.

STATE OF ARIZONA

PHOENIX, MARICOPA CO., ST. JOHN OF THE DESERT Rev. Peter Boutros; Rev. Deacon Marion Rimmer.
Res.: 3718 E. Greenway Rd., AZ 85032. Tel: 602-787-4787; Fax: 602-795-4752. Email: frpeter@stjohnofthedesert.com.

STATE OF CALIFORNIA

EL SEGUNDO, LOS ANGELES CO., ST. PAUL Rt. Rev. Alexei Smith, Admin.; Rev. Deacon Irenaeus Dionne.
Res.: 538 Concord St., CA 90245. Tel: 310-322-1892; Fax: 310-322-1919.

NORTH HOLLYWOOD, LOS ANGELES CO., ST. ANNE Rev. Albert Wehby, B.A.O.; Protodeacon George Sayegh; Rev. Deacons George Karout; Tareq Nasrallah; Thom O'Malley; Estephanos Helo.
Res.: 11245 Rye St., CA 91602. Tel: 818-761-2034; Fax: 818-761-2922.
Mission—Annunciation Mission 381 Center St., Covina, CA 91723. Tel: 626-359-3976. Rt. Rev. George Said Bisharat.

PLACENTIA, ORANGE CO., HOLY CROSS Rt. Rev. Archimandrite James K. Babcock; Rev. Deacon Elias Kashou.
Church & Res.: 451 W. Madison Ave., CA 92870. Tel: 714-985-1710; Fax: 714-985-1765. Email: hcmelkite@holycrossmelkite.org.

SACRAMENTO, SACRAMENTO CO., ST. GEORGE Rev. Brendan McAnerney, O.P.
Church: 1620 Bell St., CA 95825. Tel: 916-920-2900; Fax: 916-920-2900. Email: brendanjoes@aol.com.

SAN BERNARDINO, SAN BERNARDINO CO., ST. PHILIP Rev. Justin Rose; Protodeacon Stephen Ghandour; Rev. Deacons Jacob Pesta; Joseph Kaiser; Michael Mobley.
Mailing Address: 923 W. Congress St., CA 92410. Tel: 909-889-3579. Email: comeandsee@earthlink.net.

SAN DIEGO, SAN DIEGO CO., ST. JACOB MISSION, Services at Holy Angels Church, San Diego. Rev. Saba Shofany; Protodeacon Edward Bagdasar; Rev. Deacon Antoine Kabane.
Mailing Address: 6281 Cowles Mountain Blvd., CA 92119. Tel: 619-825-9344; Fax: 619-825-9344.

SAN JOSE, SANTA CLARA CO., ST. ELIAS Rev. James K. Graham.
Church: 4411 Hyland Ave., CA 95127. Tel: 408-259-0259. Email: frjamie@earthlink.net.

WILDOMAR, RIVERSIDE CO., VIRGIN MARY MISSION, Services at St. Mark Church, San Marcos. Protodeacon Habib Khasho, Admin.
Mailing Address: 33881 Orange St., CA 92595. Tel: 909-674-3162.

STATE OF CONNECTICUT

DANBURY, FAIRFIELD CO., ST. ANN Rt. Rev. Michael K. Skrocki; Rev. Deacons Nicholas Bourjaili; Thomas Davis; Stephen McGrath.
Mailing Address: 181 Clapboard Ridge Rd., CT 06811. Tel: 203-743-5119.

WATERFORD, NEW LONDON CO., ST. ANN Rt. Rev. Edward Kakaty.
Res.: 41 Cross Rd., CT 06385. Tel: 860-442-2211; Fax: 860-442-2211. Email: edkakaty@gmail.com.

STATE OF FLORIDA

DELRAY BEACH, PALM BEACH CO., ST. NICHOLAS, Served by Miami. Rt. Rev. Exarch Gabriel Ghanoum, B.S.O.; Protodeacon Magdi Negm.
Res.: 5715 Lake Ida Rd., FL 33484. Tel: 305-856-8666.

MIAMI, DADE CO., ST. JUDE Rt. Rev. Eugene Mitchell, B.S.O.; Protodeacon Magdi Negm.
Res.: 126 S.E. 15 Rd., FL 33129. Tel: 305-856-8666; Fax: 305-859-7982.

STATE OF GEORGIA

ATLANTA, DEKALB CO., ST. JOHN CHRYSOSTOM Rt. Rev. John Azar.
Res.: 1428 Ponce de Leon Ave., N.E., GA 30307. Tel: 404-373-9522; Fax: 404-373-9755. Email: stjchrys@bellsouth.net.

AUGUSTA, RICHMOND CO., ST. IGNATIOS OF ANTIOCH Rev. Deacons Michael Willoughby, Admin.; Kent Plowman.
Mailing Address: P.O. Box 3351, GA 30914-3351.
Res.: 4220 Wood Creek Ct., Martinez, GA 30907. Tel: 706-228-4938.
Church: 1003 Merry St., GA 30904. Tel: 706-738-9388; Fax: 706-738-6559. Email: stignatios@aol.com.

STATE OF ILLINOIS

NORTHLAKE, COOK CO., ST. JOHN THE BAPTIST Rt. Rev. Fouad Sayegh; Rev. Archdeacon Elias Sahyouni; Protodeacon Antoine Shehata; Rev. Deacon Fadi Rafidi.
Res.: 318 E. Hirsch Ave., IL 60164. Tel: 708-938-5804; Fax: 708-492-0391. Email: stjohnthebaptistchicago@hotmail.com.

STATE OF INDIANA

HAMMOND, LAKE CO., ST. MICHAEL THE ARCHANGEL (1978) Rt. Rev. Fouad Sayegh.
Res.: 606 141st St., IN 46327. Tel: 219-933-1457; Fax: 219-852-0727. Email: michaelarchangel@comcast.net.

SOUTH BEND, ST. JOSEPH CO., ST. JOHN OF DAMASCUS Rev. Sean Labat, Admin.
Church: 839 Woodcliff Dr., IN 46615. Tel: 574-282-2140.

STATE OF MICHIGAN

LANSING, INGHAM CO., ST. JOSEPH Protodeacon Joseph Daratony, Admin.

PLYMOUTH, WAYNE CO., ST. MICHAEL Rev. Elie Eid, Admin.; Protodeacon Joseph Daratony.
Church: 585 N. Mill St., MI 48170. Tel: 734-414-9930; Fax: 734-414-9932.

WARREN, MACOMB CO., OUR LADY OF REDEMPTION Rev. Michel Cheble; Rev. Deacons David Herr; Rick Trabulsy.
Res.: 29293 Lorraine, MI 48093. Tel: 586-574-0140; Fax: 586-751-1877.

STATE OF NEW HAMPSHIRE

MANCHESTER, HILLSBOROUGH CO., OUR LADY OF THE CEDARS Rev. Thomas P. Steinmetz; Rt. Rev. Andre St. Germain (Retired); Rev. Deacons Robert Spencer; Paul J. Leonarczyk.
Res.: 140 Mitchell St., NH 03103. Tel: 603-623-8944; Fax: 603-645-6017. Email: oloc.church@comcast.net.

STATE OF NEW JERSEY

CLIFFSIDE PARK, BERGEN CO., ST. DEMETRIUS Rev. Joseph Nahas.
Church: 184 Cliff St., NJ 07010. Tel: 201-840-8554.

WEST PATERSON, PASSAIC CO., ST. ANN Rt. Rev. Archimandrite Kenneth Sherman; Rev. Archdeacon Edward Bsarany; Rev. Deacons Roland Basinski; Robert Shalhoub; Choukri Sabbagh.
Res.: 802 Rifle Camp Rd., Woodland Park, NJ 07424. Tel: 973-785-4144; Fax: 973-890-9599.

STATE OF NEW YORK

BROOKLYN, KINGS CO., CHURCH OF THE VIRGIN MARY Rev. Antoine Rizk, B.S.O.; Rev. Deacon Nagi Youssef.
Res.: 216 Eighth Ave., NY 11215. Tel: 718-788-5454; Fax: 718-499-7702.

ROCHESTER, MONROE CO., ST. NICHOLAS Rev. Christopher Manuele; Rev. Deacons Edmond Elhilow; Elias Sarkis.
Res.: 1492 Spencerport Rd., NY 14606. Tel: 585-426-4218.

UTICA, ONEIDA CO., ST. BASIL Rev. Jean Ghaby.
Res.: 901 Sherman Dr., NY 13501. Tel: 315-732-4662.

YONKERS, WESTCHESTER CO., CHRIST THE SAVIOR CHURCH Rev. Dany N. Touma; Protodeacon Saleem Naber.
Church: 491 Palisade Ave., NY 10703. Tel: 914-963-6680.

STATE OF OHIO

AKRON, SUMMIT CO., ST. JOSEPH Rt. Rev. Archimandrite Damon Geiger; Rev. Deacon Dennis Jebber.
Church & Res.: 600 W. Exchange St., OH 44302. Tel: 330-535-7364; Fax: 330-535-8037. Email: stjomelk@sbcglobal.net.

BROOKLYN, CUYAHOGA CO., ST. ELIAS Rev. Naim Khalil, B.S.O.
Res.: 8023 Memphis Ave., OH 44144. Tel: 216-661-1155; Fax: 216-661-3838.

COLUMBUS, FRANKLIN CO., HOLY RESURRECTION Rev. Ignatius Harrington.
Res.: 8148 Wildflower Ln., Westerville, OH 43081. Tel: 614-987-7239; Fax: 614-987-7239.
Church: 4611 Glen Mawr Ave., OH 43224.

ZANESVILLE, MUSKINGUM CO., HOLY TRINITY Rev. Ignatius Harrington.
Res.: 8148 Wildflower Ln., Westerville, OH 43081. Tel: 614-987-7239; Fax: 614-987-7239.
Church: 3745 W. Pike, OH 43701.

STATE OF PENNSYLVANIA

SCRANTON, LACKAWANNA CO., ST. JOSEPH Protodeacon Michael Jolly, Admin.
130 St. Francis Cabrini Ave., PA 18504. Tel: 570-343-6092. Email: scrantonmelkite@comcast.net.

STATE OF RHODE ISLAND

LINCOLN, PROVIDENCE CO., ST. BASIL THE GREAT Rt. Rev. Exarch Joseph S. Haggar; Rev. Archdeacon George M. Yany; Rev. Deacon Edmond Raheb.
Church: 15 Skyview Dr., RI 02865.
Res.: 111 Cross St., Central Falls, RI 02863. Tel: 401-722-1345; Fax: 401-722-2436.

WOONSOCKET, PROVIDENCE CO., ST. ELIAS Rt. Rev. Exarch Joseph S. Haggar.
Church: 80 Hamilton St., RI 02895.
Res.: 111 Cross St., Central Falls, RI 02863. Tel: 401-722-1345.

STATE OF VIRGINIA

MCLEAN, FAIRFAX CO., HOLY TRANSFIGURATION Rt. Rev. Joseph F. Francavilla; Rev. Ephrem Handal; Protodeacon David Baroody; Rev. Deacons David Black; Joseph Olt; John Fleshman; Deacon Sabatino Carnazzo.
Res.: 8501 Lewinsville Rd., VA 22102. Tel: 703-734-9198; Fax: 703-734-5148. Email: office@holytransfiguration.org.

STATE OF WASHINGTON

SEATTLE, KING CO., ST. JOSEPH MISSION Rev. Samir Abu-Lail.
Res.: 12038 31st Ave. N.E. #306, WA 98125. Tel: 206-362-2519; Fax: 206-362-2519. Email: samirabulail@gmail.com.

STATE OF WISCONSIN

MILWAUKEE, MILWAUKEE CO., ST. GEORGE Very Rev. Philaret Littlefield.
Res.: 1617 W. State St., WI 53233. Tel: 414-342-1543.

Military Chaplain:
Rev.—
Brown, Shaun S.

Leave of Absence:
Revs.—
Ferrara, Angelus
Golini, Ronald
Koury, James
Nasr, Kamil
Saato, Fred
Rev. Deacon—
Klockowski, Daniel A.

Retired:
Rt. Revs.—
Aboody, Charles
Dagher, George, B.S.O.
Samaha, Victor, B.C.O.
St. Germain, Andre
Revs.—
Alam, Alam
Azoon, Philip

Kerby, Robert
Leonard, John
Moloney, Patrick W.
Samra, Basil

Archdeacons:
Rev. Archdeacons—
Bsarany, Edward, Woodland Park, NJ
Sahyouni, Elias, Northlake, IL
Yany, George M., Lincoln, RI

Protodeacons:
Protodeacons—
Bagdasar, Edward, El Cajon, CA
Baroody, David, McLean, VA
Daratony, Joseph, Plymouth, MI
Ghandour, Stephen, San Bernardino, CA
Jolly, Michael, Scranton, PA
Khasho, Habib, Northlake, IL
McNeil, Bryan, Lawrence, MA
Naber, Saleem, (Yonkers, NY)
Negm, Magdi, Miami, FL
Sayegh, George, North Hollywood, CA
Shehata, Antoine, Northlake, IL
Soloman, James, Warren, MI

Deacons:
Rev. Deacons—
Ayala, Sergio, Northlake, IL
Bailey, Elias (Richard), Worcester, MA
Basinski, Roland, West Paterson, NJ
Black, David, McLean, VA
Bourjaili, Danbury, CT
Burke, Thomas, Boston, MA
Davis, Thomas J., Jr., Danbury, CT
Dionne, Irenaeus, El Segundo, CA
Elhilow, Edmond, Rochester, NY
Fleshman, John, McLean, VA
Herr, David, Warren, MI
Jebber, Dennis, Akron, OH
Kabbane, Antoine
Kaiser, Joseph, San Bernardino, CA
Karout, George, North Hollywood, CA
Kashou, Elias, Placentia, CA
Klockowski, Daniel A., Utica, NY
Layous, Ziad, Lawrence, MA
Leonarczyk, Paul J., Manchester, NH
MacMillan, John, Lawrence, MA
McCarthy, Dennis, Worcester, MA
McGrath, Stephen, Danbury, CT
Mobley, Michael, San Bernardino, CA
Moses, John, Boston, MA
Nasrallah, Tareq, North Hollywood, CA
O'Malley, Thom, N. Hollywood, CA
Olt, Joseph, McLean, VA
Pesta, Jacob, San Bernardino, CA
Plowman, Kent, Augusta, GA
Rafidi, Fadi, Northlake, IL
Raheb, Edmond, Lincoln, RI
Richardson, David W., Charleston, SC
Rimmer, Marion, Phoenix, AZ
Ritchey, Seraphim, Birmingham, AL
Sabbagh, Choukri, Brooklyn, NY
Sarkis, Elias, Rochester, NY
Shalhoub, Robert, West Paterson, NJ
Spencer, Robert, Manchester, NH
Trabulsy, Rick, Warren, MI
Willoughby, Michael, Augusta, GA
Youssef, Nagi, Brooklyn, NY
Zeinieh, Ibrahim, Boston, MA

Priests Serving Outside the Eparchy:
Rt. Rev.—
Russo, Romanos V.
Revs.—
Brown, Shaun S.
Gallaro, George D., J.C.O.D.
McCarthy, Emmanuel Charles
Parent, Basil R.

Deacons Serving Outside the Eparchy:
Deacon—
Haddad, Gregory
Rev. Deacons—
Hill, James A.
Nasser, Andre P. (FR)

INSTITUTIONS LOCATED IN THE DIOCESE

[A] SEMINARIES

STATE OF MASSACHUSETTS

METHUEN. *Seminary of St. Basil the Great*, 30 East St., 01844. Tel: 978-683-2471. Rev. Martin A. Hyatt, B.S.O., Dean. Priests 4.

WEST ROXBURY. *Seminary of St. Gregory the Theologian*, 3 VFW Pkwy., 02132. Rt. Rev. Archimandrite Philip Raczka, Rector. Priests 1.

[B] MONASTERIES AND RESIDENCES FOR PRIESTS AND BROTHERS

STATE OF MASSACHUSETTS

METHUEN. *Basilian Salvatorian Order*, 30 East St., 01844. Tel: 978-683-2471; Fax: 978-794-3452. Rt. Rev. George Dagher, B.S.O. (Retired); Revs. Youssef Clement, B.S.O.; Martin A. Hyatt, B.S.O., Local Supr.; Rt. Rev. Eugene Mitchell, B.S.O., Gen. Economos; Revs. Joseph Thomas, B.S.O.; Lawrence Tumminelli, B.S.O.

[C] CONVENTS AND RESIDENCES FOR SISTERS

STATE OF CONNECTICUT

DANBURY. *Community of The Mother of God of Tenderness*, 79 Golden Hill Rd., CT 06811-4631. Tel: 203-794-1486. Email: sophiamic711@sbcglobal.net. Sr. Mary Ann Socha, C.M.G.T., Pres. Sisters 3.

[D] MISCELLANEOUS

STATE OF MASSACHUSETTS

METHUEN. *St. Basil's Salvatorian Center*, 30 East St., 01844. Tel: 978-683-2959; Fax: 978-794-3379. Patricia Paduano, Dir.

STATE OF PENNSYLVANIA

WARREN CENTER. *Our Lady of Solitude Cloister & Retreat*, Physical Address: 550 Lake of Meadows Rd., Little Meadows, PA 18830. Fax: 570-395-0235.

RELIGIOUS INSTITUTES OF MEN REPRESENTED IN THE EPARCHY

For further details refer to the corresponding bracketed number in the Religious Institutes of Men or Women section.

[]—*Basilian Chouerite Order* (St. John Monastery, Khonchara, Lebanon)—B.C.O.

[0190]—*Basilian Salvatorian Order* (Holy Saviour Monastery, Sidon, Lebanon)—B.S.O.

NECROLOGY

† King, James E., (Retired)—Died Nov., 2011

An asterisk (*) denotes an organization that has established tax-exempt status directly with the IRS and is not covered by the USCCB Group Ruling.

Diocese of Our Lady of Deliverance

For Syriac Catholics in the United States and Canada

Most Reverend

MAR BARNABA YOUSIF HABASH

Second Bishop of Our Lady of Deliverance; ordained priest August 31, 1975; ordained Bishop June 11, 2010; installed Bishop of Our Lady of Deliverance Syriac Catholic Diocese in the United States and Canada July 31, 2010. *Mailing & Residential Address: 317 Avenue E, Bayonne, NJ 07002-4678.* Tel: 201-455-8151; Fax: 201-455-8152.

Chancery Office: 317 Avenue E, Bayonne, NJ 07002-4678. Tel: 201-455-8151; Fax: 201-455-8152.

Web: www.ourladyofdeliverance.org

Email: marbarnaba@yahoo.com

DIOCESE ESTABLISHED NOVEMBER 16, 1995.

Comprises the United States and Canada.

STATISTICAL OVERVIEW

Personnel	
Bishop	1
Priests: Diocesan Active in Diocese	11
Priests: Diocesan Active Outside Diocese	2
Number of Diocesan Priests	13
Total Priests in Diocese	13
Permanent Deacons in Diocese	4
Parishes	
Parishes	9
With Resident Pastor:	
Resident Diocesan Priests	8
Without Resident Pastor:	
Administered by Priests	1
Missions	7
Educational	
Diocesan Students in Other Seminaries	1
Total Seminarians	1
Catechesis/Religious Education:	
High School Students	94
Elementary Students	400
Total Students under Catholic Instruction	495
Vital Statistics	
Receptions into the Church:	
Infant Baptism Totals	76
Adult Baptism Totals	4
Received into Full Communion	40
First Communions	80
Confirmations	15
Marriages:	
Catholic	14
Interfaith	12
Total Marriages	26
Deaths	18
Total Catholic Population	22,500

Former Bishop—Most Rev. MAR EPHREM JOSEPH YOUNAN, ord. Sept. 12, 1971; ord. Bishop of Our Lady of Deliverance Diocese Jan. 7, 1996; installed Feb. 10, 1996; appt. Patriarch of the Syriac Catholic Church of Antioch, Mar Ignatius Yousif III Younan, Lebanon; confirmed Jan. 22, 2009; installed Feb. 15, 2009.

Chancery—

Chancellor—VACANT, Mailing and Residential Address: 317 Ave. E., Bayonne, 07002-4678. Tel: 201-455-8151; Fax: 201-455-8152.

Episcopal Vicar—Rt. Rev. Chorbishop TOMA B. AZIZO, 317 Ave. E, Bayonne, 07002-4678. Tel: 201-455-8151; Fax: 201-455-8152.

Officialis—SAMI DIB, 317 Ave. E., Bayonne, 07002-4678. Tel: 201-455-8151; Fax: 201-455-8152.

CLERGY, PARISHES, MISSIONS AND PAROCHIAL SCHOOLS

STATE OF NEW JERSEY

BAYONNE, HUDSON CO.

1—SAINT JOSEPH SYRIAC CATHOLIC CATHEDRAL Rev. Bassim Shoni, Rector.
Res.: 317 Avenue E, 07002-4678. Tel: 201-455-8151; Fax: 201-455-8152.

2—OUR LADY OF DELIVERANCE PARISH (1986), Served by chancery.
Res.: 317 Avenue E, 07002-4678. Tel: 201-471-2762; Fax: 201-455-8152.
Catechesis / Religious Program—Sisters Maria Magdalena, D.R.E.; Clare Marie, D.R.E. Students 20.

STATE OF ARIZONA

SCOTTSDALE, SAINTS BEHNAM AND SARAH MISSION Very Chorbishop Sadei Toma, Admin.; Mr. Sabah Gewargis, Mission Council Chair.
Mailing Address: 3630 N. 71st Ave., Phoenix, AZ 85033. Tel: 623-755-0531.
Worship Site: Saint Augustine Roman Catholic Church—
Catechesis / Religious Program—Mr. Petros Kahayat, D.R.E. Students 32.

STATE OF CALIFORNIA

LOS ANGELES, LOS ANGELES CO., JESUS SACRED HEART CHURCH Rev. Andrwos Habash, Admin.; Deacons Joseph Yaqoob; Hanna Nasi; George Ibrahim Maida, Parish Council Chair.
Res.: 10837 Collins St., North Hollywood, CA 91601-2009. Tel: 818-766-7001; Fax: 818-766-7254.
Catechesis / Religious Program—Mrs. Layla Touma, D.R.E. Students 46.

OCEANSIDE, SAN DIEGO CO., SAINT JOSEPH MISSION Rev. Msgr. Emad Hanna Al-Shaikh.
1101 S. Mollison Ave., El Cajon, CA 92020. Tel: 619-440-5555.
Worship Site: San Luis Rey R.C. Church—

SAN DIEGO, SAN DIEGO CO., OUR MOTHER OF PERPETUAL HELP CHURCH, (Worship at Santa Sophia Church) Rev. Msgr. Emad Hanna Al-Shaikh; Mr. Sami Awakeem, Parish Council Chair.
Mailing Address: 1101 S. Mollison Ave., El Cajon, CA 92020. Fax: 619-440-5555.
Catechesis / Religious Program—Mr. Diah Tozi, D.R.E. Students 25.

STATE OF FLORIDA

JACKSONVILLE, DUVAL CO., SAINT EPHREM SYRIAC CHURCH Rev. Selwan Sulaiman Taponi; Mr. Haissam Yazji, Parish Council Chair; Deacon Joseph Al-Saigh.
Res.: 4650 Kernan Blvd., S., FL 32224. Tel: 904-998-7800; Fax: 904-997-5676.
Catechesis / Religious Program—Mrs. Emtethal Yazji, D.R.E. Students 125.

STATE OF ILLINOIS

CHICAGO, COOK CO., SAINT MARY VIRGIN IMMACULATE MISSION (1999), Served by Chancery personnel.
Res.: 1243 Church St., Northbrook, IL 60062. Tel: 201-455-8151; Fax: 201-455-8152.

STATE OF MASSACHUSETTS

JAMAICA PLAINS, SUFFOLK CO., OUR LADY OF MESOPOTAMIA MISSION, (Worship at Our Lady of Cedars Lebanon Church) Rev. Bassim Shoni, Admin.; Mr. Sermed Ashkouri, Mission Council Chair.
Mailing Address: 61 Rockwood St., MA 02130. Tel: 603-880-0099; Fax: 617-830-4459.

STATE OF MICHIGAN

FARMINGTON HILLS, OAKLAND CO., SAINT TOMA CHURCH Rt. Rev. Chorbishop Toma B. Azizo; Rev. Safaa Habash, Parochial Vicar; Mr. Abdulahad Augustine, Parish Council Chair.
Res.: 25600 Drake Rd., MI 48335. Tel: 248-478-0835; Fax: 248-478-9074.
Catechesis / Religious Program—Sr. Mary Beth, D.R.E. Students 65.

STERLING HEIGHTS, MACOMB CO., CHRIST THE KING MISSION, (Worship at Saint Rene Goupil Parish) Rev. Safaa Habash, Admin.; Mr. Isho Salman, Parish Council Chair.
Mailing Address: 35955 Ryan Rd., MI 48310. Tel: 248-478-0835; Fax: 248-478-9074.
Catechesis / Religious Program—Mrs. Heather Farjo, D.R.E.; Miss Ban Mukhtar, Asst. D.R.E. Students 30.

STATE OF PENNSYLVANIA

ALLENTOWN, LEHIGH CO., OUR LADY OF MERCY PARISH, (Worship at Immaculate Conception Church) Rev. Bassim Shoni; Mr. Salim Shehadah, Parish Council Chair.
Res.: 501 Ridge Ave., PA 18102. Tel: 601-297-6101; Fax: 601-433-8401. Web: www.ladyofmercychurch.com.
Catechesis / Religious Program—Mrs. Rein Kassis, D.R.E. Students 60.

CANADA

PROVINCE OF QUEBEC

LAVAL

1—PAROISSE SAINT EPHREM Rev. Khalid Karomi.
Mailing Address: 3155 Boulevard Cartier Ouest QC H7V 2T5 Canada.
Res.: 3000 Boulvard Edouard Monpetit QC H7T 2T5 Canada. Tel: 450-682-7546; 450-688-9579; Fax: 450-682-7603.
Catechesis / Religious Program—Students 30.

2—PAROSSIE NOTRE DAME DE L'ASSOMPTION Rev. Richard Daher.
Mailing Address: 1625 Montee Masson QC H7E 2P2 Canada. Tel: 450-661-9990; Fax: 450-661-9977.
Catechesis / Religious Program—Students 25.

PROVINCE OF ONTARIO

MISSISSAUGA, SAINT JOSEPH SYRIAC CATHOLIC CHURCH
Rev. Thaer Abba, Parochial Vicar; Dr. Basil Behnam, Parish Council Chair.
999 Lakeshore Rd., E. ON L5E 1E5 Canada.
Res.: 999 Lakeshore Rd., E. ON L5E 1E5 Canada.
Tel: 905-278-0511; Fax: 905-278-9513. Web: www.stjosephsyriaccc.com.

Catechesis/Religious Program—Mr. Nael Barbary, D.R.E.; Mrs. Silvana Barbary, D.R.E. Students 50.

CAMBRIDGE, SAINTS BEHNAM AND SARAH MISSION, (Worship at Saint Clement's Roman Catholic Church) Rev. Thaer Abba, Admin.
Mailing Address: 745 Duke St. ON M3H 3T7 Canada. Tel: 905-278-0511; Fax: 905-278-9513.

OTTAWA

MISSION—SAINT PAUL MISSION 344 Cyr Ave. ON K1L 7P1 Canada. Tel: 613-869-3463. Rev. Fadi Atalla, Admin.

NECROLOGY

(No Deaths)

An asterisk (*) denotes an organization that has established tax-exempt status directly with the IRS and is not covered by the USCCB Group Ruling.

Eparchy of Our Lady of Lebanon of Los Angeles

Most Reverend

ROBERT J. SHAHEEN

Bishop of the Eparchy of Our Lady of Lebanon of Los Angeles; ordained May 2, 1964; appointed December 5, 2000; consecrated February 15, 2001.

Comprises the States of Ohio, West Virginia, Illinois, Alabama, Michigan, Minnesota, Missouri, Texas, Utah, Arizona, Nevada, Oregon, California, Alaska, Hawaii, Indiana, Kentucky, Tennessee, Mississippi, Wisconsin, Iowa, Arkansas, Louisiana, North Dakota, South Dakota, Kansas, Oklahoma, Nebraska, Montana, Wyoming, Colorado, New Mexico, Idaho and Washington.

Pastoral Center: 1021 S. 10th St., St. Louis, MO 63104. Tel: 314-231-1021; Fax: 314-231-1418.

Web: www.usamaronite.org

Email: mdenny@usamaronite.org

STATISTICAL OVERVIEW

Personnel	
Bishop	1
Abbots	1
Priests: Diocesan Active in Diocese	27
Priests: Diocesan Active Outside Diocese	4
Priests: Retired, Sick or Absent	4
Number of Diocesan Priests	35
Religious Priests in Diocese	15
Total Priests in Diocese	50
Permanent Deacons in Diocese	19
Total Sisters	6
Parishes	
Parishes	30
With Resident Pastor:	
Resident Diocesan Priests	22
Resident Religious Priests	8
Missions	9
Welfare	
Residential Care of Children	1
Total Assisted	20
Other Institutions	1
Total Assisted	65
Educational	
Diocesan Students in Other Seminaries	4
Total Seminarians	4
Elementary Schools, Private	1
Total Students	39
Catechesis/Religious Education:	
High School Students	349
Elementary Students	1,509
Total Students under Catholic Instruction	1,901
Teachers in the Diocese:	
Lay Teachers	1
Vital Statistics	
Receptions into the Church:	
Infant Baptism Totals	381
Adult Baptism Totals	28
Received into Full Communion	12
First Communions	288
Confirmations	394
Marriages:	
Catholic	84
Interfaith	22
Total Marriages	106
Deaths	171
Total Catholic Population	46,000

Former Bishop—Most Rev. JOHN GEORGE CHEDID, D.D. (Retired), ord. Dec. 21, 1951; appt. Titular Bishop of Callinicum and Auxiliary Bishop of St. Maron of Brooklyn, Oct. 28, 1980; cons. Jan. 25, 1981; appt. Bishop of Our Lady of Lebanon of Los Angeles, Feb. 19, 1994; retired Dec. 5, 2000; died March 21, 2012.

Pastoral Center—Chorbishop FAOUZI ELIA, Vicar Gen. & Chancellor; Mrs. MARY DENNY, Vice Chancellor & Chief Fiscal Officer; Deacon WISSAM G. AKIKI, Pastoral Assoc., 1021 S. 10th St., St. Louis, 63104. Tel: 314-231-1021; Fax: 314-231-1418.

College of Consultors—Chorbishops FAOUZI ELIA; RICHARD D. SAAD; MICHAEL J. KAIL; ALFRED BADAWI; Revs. PETER KARAM; ABDALLAH E. ZAIDAN, M.L.M.; Rev. Msgr. SHARBEL MAROUN; Rev. GARY GEORGE, C.Ss.R.

Commission for Lebanon—Rev. ABDALLAH E. ZAIDAN, M.L.M.

Tribunal—

Defender of the Bond—Rev. ROBERT BISHOP, S.T.L., C.F.M.

Judicial Vicar—Chorbishop WILLIAM LESER, S.T.B.

Moderator of the Tribunal—Most Rev. ROBERT JOSEPH SHAHEEN.

Procurator/Advocate—Revs. ABDALLAH E. ZAIDAN, M.L.M.; ELIAS SLEIMAN, M.L.M.

Promoter of Justice—Rev. ROBERT BISHOP, S.T.L., C.F.M.

Notary—Ms. KATARINA LEIGH.

Eparchial Newsletter— "The Maronite Voice" Rev. Msgr. GEORGE SEBAALI, St. Anthony, 4611 Sadler Rd., Glen Allen, VA 23060. Tel: 804-762-4301; Fax: 804-273-9914. Email: gmsebaali@aol.com.

Office for Immigration—Chorbishop FAOUZI ELIA.

Office for Missions—Rev. Msgrs. DONALD J. SAWYER, D.Mim.; ANTHONY SPINOSA.

Office of Communications—Chorbishop RICHARD D. SAAD.

Office of Inter-faith/Ecumenical Affairs—Rev. Msgr. ANTHONY SPINOSA.

Office of Liturgy—Chorbishop MICHAEL J. KAIL.

Office of Ministries—Deacon LOUIS PETERS.

Office of Priestly Vocations—Rev. Msgr. SHARBEL MAROUN; Rev. TONY MASSAD.

Office of Religious Education—Deacon LOUIS PETERS.

Office of Youth Ministries—Rev. GARY GEORGE, C.Ss.R.

Master of Ceremonies—VACANT.

Office of Young Adult Ministry—Rev. ELIAS SLEIMAN, M.L.M.

Presbyteral Council—Chorbishops FAOUZI ELIA, Ex Officio; RICHARD D. SAAD; Rev. ABDALLAH E. ZAIDAN, M.L.M.; Chorbishops ALFRED BADAWI; MICHAEL J. KAIL; Rev. Msgr. SHARBEL MAROUN; Revs. GARY GEORGE, C.Ss.R.; ELIAS ABI-SARKIS; GHASSAN MATTAR, M.L.M.; PIERRE BASSIL.

Pro-Life & Family Life Office—Rev. NABIL MOUANNES.

Eparchial Webmaster—Rev. ARMANDO ELKHOURY.

Properties Owned—

Father Tobia Retirement Home— North Jackson, OH.

Maronite Catholic Pastoral Center— St. Louis, MO

Protopresbyters—Rev. Msgr. SHARBEL MAROUN, Mid-America Region; Chorbishop MICHAEL J. KAIL, Midwest Region; Rev. ABDALLAH E. ZAIDAN, M.L.M., Southwest Region; Chorbishop RICHARD D. SAAD, Southern Region.

Spiritual Director for the National Apostolate of Maronites—Chorbishop RICHARD D. SAAD.

Order of St. Sharbel—Chorbishop JOSEPH KADDO, Spiritual Dir.; Mrs. ROSANNE SOLOMON, Natl. Pres.; Mrs. WANDA ELKHOURIE, Vice Pres., Eparchy of Our Lady of Lebanon of Los Angeles, 1021 S. 10th St., St. Louis, 63104.

Victim Assistance Coordinator—Rev. PETER KARAM Cleveland, OH.

Office of Protection of Minors—Rev. PETER KARAM, Dir., 1245 Carnegie Ave., Cleveland, OH 44115. Tel: 216-781-6161; Fax: 216-781-6162. Web: www.usamaronite.org.

Personnel Board—Rev. ABDALLAH E. ZAIDAN, M.L.M.; Chorbishops RICHARD D. SAAD; MICHAEL J. KAIL; Rev. Msgr. SHARBEL MAROUN; Rev. GARY GEORGE, C.Ss.R.

Board of Pastors—Chorbishop RICHARD D. SAAD; Rev. ABDALLAH E. ZAIDAN, M.L.M.; Chorbishop MICHAEL J. KAIL.

Advisor for Priests—Rev. ABDALLAH ZAIDAN, M.L.M.

CLERGY, PARISHES, MISSIONS AND PAROCHIAL SCHOOLS

STATE OF CALIFORNIA

LOS ANGELES, LOS ANGELES CO., OUR LADY OF MT. LEBANON-ST. PETER MARONITE CATHOLIC CATHEDRAL (1923) Revs. Abdallah E. Zaidan, M.L.M., Rector; Elias Sleiman, M.L.M.; Deacon Edward Corey.
Res.: 333 S. San Vicente Blvd., CA 90048. Tel: 310-275-6634; Fax: 310-858-0856.
Catechesis/Religious Program—

MILLBRAE, SAN MATEO CO., OUR LADY OF LEBANON MARONITE CATHOLIC CHURCH (1979) [JC] Rev. John Nahal.
Mailing Address: 600 El Camino Real, CA 94030. Email: ollsf@aol.com. Web: www.maronite-sf.org.
Res.: 19 Hermosa Ave., CA 94030. Tel: 650-652-6445; Fax: 650-652-6445.
Catechesis/Religious Program—Minaise Minaise, D.R.E.
Mission—St. Sharbel Maronite Catholic Mission Stockton, San Joaquin Co., CA. Tel: 209-954-0200.

ORANGE, ORANGE CO., ST. JOHN MARON MARONITE CATHOLIC CHURCH (1988) Rev. Antoine Bakh; Deacon Alfred Harb; Subdeacons John Younes; Sharbel Abi-Saber.
Mailing Address: c/o 300 S. Flower St., CA 92868. Tel: 714-940-0009; Fax: 714-594-4036. Email: email@johnmaron.org. Web: www.johnmaron.org.
Catechesis/Religious Program—
Mission—St. Joseph Maronite Catholic Mission

SAN DIEGO, SAN DIEGO CO., ST. EPHREM MARONITE CATHOLIC CHURCH (1989) [CEM] Rev. Nabil

Mouannes; Deacon Georges Ghosn.
Mailing Address: 750 Medford St., El Cajon, CA 92020. Tel: 619-337-1350.
Res.: 766 Medford St., El Cajon, CA 92020. Tel: 619-697-3040; Fax: 619-697-3042. Email: stephrem@sbcglobal.net. Web: www.stephrem.org. Students 39.
School—Saint Ephrem Maronite Catholic Academy, Tel: 619-337-1350. Rachael Farich, Prin. Students 39.
Catechesis/Religious Program—Students 100.
Mission—Maronite Catholic Community of Sacramento

THOUSAND OAKS, VENTURA CO., SAINTS PETER AND PAUL MARONITE CATHOLIC MISSION (2002) Rev. Abdallah E. Zaidan, M.L.M.
P.O. Box 4455, CA 91359-1455. Tel: 310-275-6634; Fax: 310-858-0856.
Catechesis/Religious Program—Elie ElHage, D.R.E.

WEST COVINA, LOS ANGELES CO., ST. JUDE MARONITE CATHOLIC CHURCH (1999) Rev. Samuel Madel; Subdeacon Pierre El-Khoury.
1437 W. Badillo St., CA 91790.
Res.: Email: maronitechurch@yahoo.com. Web: saintjudemaronitemission.com.
Rectory—Tel: 626-962-0222; Fax: 626-962-7222.
Catechesis/Religious Program—

STATE OF ALABAMA

BIRMINGHAM, JEFFERSON CO.
1—ST. ELIAS MARONITE CATHOLIC CHURCH (1910) Chorbishop Richard D. Saad; Deacons Joseph Stephens; Samuel J. Wehby.
Res.: 836 Eighth St. S., AL 35205-4567. Tel: 205-251-5057; 205-252-3867; Fax: 205-251-5028. Email: eliasbham@aol.com. Web: stelias.org.
Catechesis/Religious Program—Beverly Kimes, D.R.E.; Dora Bolus, D.R.E.
2—MARONITE CATHOLIC COMMUNITY OF LOUISIANA (1910) Chorbishop Richard D. Saad, Parochial Admin.
Mailing Address: St. Elias Church, 836 8th St. S., AL 35205. Tel: 205-251-5057; Fax: 205-251-5028.
Catechesis/Religious Program—

STATE OF ARIZONA

PHOENIX, MARICOPA CO., ST. JOSEPH MARONITE CATHOLIC CHURCH (1992) Rev. Ghattas Khoury.
Res.: 5406 E. Virginia Ave., AZ 85008. Tel: 602-667-3280; Fax: 602-468-0174. Email: ghattaskhoury@cox.net. Web: www.stjosephmaronitechurch.org.
Catechesis/Religious Program—Maggy Makhlouf Eid, D.R.E. Students 70.
Mission—Maronite Catholic Mission of Tuscan

STATE OF COLORADO

LAKEWOOD, JEFFERSON CO, ST. RAFKA MARONITE CATHOLIC CHURCH Rev. Bakhos Chidiac.
Res.: 2301 Wadsworth Blvd., CO 80214. Tel: 720-833-0354; Fax: 720-833-0390. Email: father@saintrafka.org. Web: www.saintrafka.org.
Catechesis/Religious Program—

STATE OF ILLINOIS

LOMBARD, DUPAGE CO., OUR LADY OF LEBANON MARONITE CATHOLIC CHURCH (1952) Chorbishop Alfred Badawi; Deacons John Sfire; William Nijm.
Res.: 950 N. Grace St., IL 60148. Tel: 630-932-9640; Fax: 630-932-9463. Email: abouna65!@sbcglobal.net.
Catechesis/Religious Program—
Mission—Maronite Catholic Community Sacred Heart Church, Eighth St., Michigan City, La Porte Co., IN 46360.

PEORIA, PEORIA CO., ST. SHARBEL MARONITE CATHOLIC CHURCH (1973) Chorbishop Faouzi Elia; Rev. Bechara Awada; Deacons James Siedlecki; George Geagea.
Res.: 2914 W. Scenic Dr., IL 61615. Tel: 309-688-5555; Fax: 309-688-0431. Email: stsharbel@sbcglobal.net.
Catechesis/Religious Program—

STATE OF KENTUCKY

LOUISVILLE, JEFFERSON CO., MARONITE CATHOLIC COMMUNITY OF LOUISVILLE (1910) Closed.

STATE OF LOUISIANA

Maronite Community of Louisiana, Closed. For inquiries for parish records contact the chancery.

BATON ROUGE, EAST BATON ROUGE PARISH, ST. SHARBEL MARONITE CATHOLIC MISSION Chorbishop Richard D. Saad, Admin.
c/o 1021 S. 10th St., Saint Louis, 63104.

LAFAYETTE, CONTRA COSTA PARISH, MARONITE CATHOLIC COMMUNITY, Closed. For inquiries for parish records contact the chancery.

LAKE CHARLES, CALCASIEU PARISH, MARONITE CATHOLIC COMMUNITY, Closed. For inquiries for parish records contact the chancery.

NEW ORLEANS, ORLEANS PARISH, MARONITE CATHOLIC COMMUNITY, Closed. For inquiries for parish records contact the chancery.

STATE OF MICHIGAN

DETROIT, WAYNE CO., ST. MARON MARONITE CATHOLIC CHURCH (1910) [CEM] Rev. Msgr. Louis Baz.
Res.: 11466 Kercheval/St. Jean, MI 48214. Tel: 313-824-0196; Fax: 313-824-6418.
Catechesis/Religious Program—

FLINT, GENESEE CO., OUR LADY OF LEBANON MARONITE CATHOLIC CHURCH (1973) Rev. Paul Tarabay, O.M.M.; Deacons Martin J. Rachid; Earl Matte.
Res.: 4133 Calkins Rd., MI 48532. Tel: 810-733-1259; Fax: 810-732-2760.
Catechesis/Religious Program—

WARREN, MACOMB CO.
1—ST. RAFKA MARONITE CATHOLIC MISSION (2003) Rev. Gaby Hoyek, Admin.; Deacon Al Morad, (Retired).
Mailing Address: 32801 Lydon Ave., Livonia, MI 48154. Tel: 734-634-9225.
Catechesis/Religious Program—
2—ST. SHARBEL MARONITE CATHOLIC CHURCH (1987) Rev. Msgr. Jibran BouMerhi; Rev. Gaby Hoyek; Subdeacons Michael Magyar; Elias Aouad; Michael Coakley; Paul Makhoul.
Res.: 31601 Schoenherr Rd., MI 48088-1977. Tel: 586-826-9688; Fax: 586-826-3521. Email: stsharbelwarren@aol.com. Web: stsharbelwarren.com.
Catechesis/Religious Program—Christina Akroush, Youth Min.

STATE OF MINNESOTA

MINNEAPOLIS, HENNEPIN CO., ST. MARON MARONITE CATHOLIC CHURCH (1903) [CEM] [JC] Rev. Msgr. Sharbel Maroun.
Res.: 600 University Ave., N.E., MN 55413. Tel: 612-379-2758; Fax: 612-379-7647. Email: abouna@stmaron.com. Web: www.stmaron.com; www.vineyardofthelord.com.
Catechesis/Religious Program—Tel: 651-714-4740. Carla Bedros, D.R.E.

MENDOTA HEIGHTS, DAKOTA CO., HOLY FAMILY MARONITE CATHOLIC CHURCH (1918) [CEM] Rev. Rodrigue Constantin.
Res.: Tel: 651-291-1116; Fax: 651-222-3033. Email: holyfamilychurch@comcast.net; rodriguec@hotmail.com. Web: www.holyfamilymaronite.org.
Rectory & Church Office: 203 E. Robie St., Saint Paul, MN 55107.
Church: 1960 Lexington Ave., MN 55118.
Catechesis/Religious Program—

STATE OF MISSOURI

SAINT LOUIS, ST. LOUIS CITY CO., ST. RAYMOND MARONITE CATHOLIC CATHEDRAL (1913) Rev. Gary George, C.Ss.R., Rector; Deacons Louis Peters; Wissam G. Akiki; Subdeacon George Simon.
Res.: 931 Lebanon Dr., 63104. Tel: 314-621-0056; Fax: 314-231-9057. Email: straymondscathedral@hotmail.com. Web: www.straymonds.net.
Catechesis/Religious Program—

STATE OF NEVADA

LAS VEGAS, CLARK CO., ST. SHARBEL MARONITE CATHOLIC MISSION (1991) Rev. Nadim Abou Zeid, M.L.M., Admin.
10325 Rancho Distino Rd., NV 89183. Tel: 702-824-1444; Fax: 702-616-4032. Email: abnadim@gmail.com; stsharbel.lv@gmail.com. Web: www.stsharbellasvegas.org.
Catechesis/Religious Program—Danelle Marek, D.R.E.

STATE OF OKLAHOMA

TULSA, TULSA CO., ST. THERESE OF THE CHILD JESUS MARONITE CATHOLIC CHURCH (1998) Rev. Elias Abi-Sarkis.
Rectory—8311 S. 107th Ave., E., OK 74133. Tel: 918-872-7400; Fax: 918-286-6619. Email: padre@sainttherese.org. Web: www.sainttherese.org.
Church & Office: 8315 S. 107th Ave., E., OK 74133.
Catechesis/Religious Program—

STATE OF OHIO

CINCINNATI, HAMILTON CO., ST. ANTHONY OF PADUA MARONITE CATHOLIC CHURCH (1910) [CEM] [JC] Rev. David Fisher; Subdeacons Joseph Mousie; Tom Simon; Donald George; Ann Kuhlman, Admin. Asst. Bookkeeper.
Res.: 2530 Victory Pkwy., OH 45206. Tel: 513-961-0120; Fax: 513-861-5075. Email: david_andrew1@mac.com.
Catechesis/Religious Program—Kimberly Simon, D.R.E.

CLEVELAND, CUYAHOGA CO., ST. MARON MARONITE CATHOLIC CHURCH (1915) [JC] Revs. Peter Karam; Tony Massad; Deacon George M. Khoury; Subdeacons James Peters; Lattouf Lattouf; Ghazi Faddoul; Georges Faddoul; Bechara Daher.
Res.: 1245 Carnegie Ave., OH 44115. Tel: 216-781-6161; Fax: 216-781-6162.
Catechesis/Religious Program—

DAYTON, MONTGOMERY CO.
1—SAINT IGNATIUS OF ANTIOCH MARONITE CATHOLIC CHURCH (1993) [JC] Rev. Pierre Bassil.
Mailing Address: 5915 Springboro Pike, OH 45449. Tel: 937-428-0372; Fax: 937-428-0371.
Catechesis/Religious Program—William Thomas, D.R.E.; Laura Thomas, D.R.E.
2—OUR LADY OF LEBANON MARONITE CATHOLIC MISSION (2003) Rev. Pierre Bassil, Admin.
5915 Springboro Pike, OH 45449. Tel: 937-428-0372; Fax: 937-428-0371. Web: www.ourladyoflebanon.info.

FAIRLAWN, SUMMIT CO., OUR LADY OF THE CEDARS OF MT. LEBANON MARONITE CATHOLIC CHURCH (1937) Rev. Toufic M. Nasr; Deacons Robert Foster; Tom Maroon.
Res.: 507 S. Cleveland-Massillon Rd., OH 44333-3019. Tel: 330-666-3598; Fax: 330-666-3598.
Catechesis/Religious Program—

TOLEDO, LUCAS CO., MARONITE CATHOLIC COMMUNITY (1999) Closed.

YOUNGSTOWN, MAHONING CO., ST. MARON MARONITE CATHOLIC CHURCH (1902) Chorbishop Michael J. Kail; Deacons Joseph Nohra; William George; Subdeacons Michel Bassil; James Essad.
Res.: 1555 S. Meridian Rd., OH 44511-1199. Tel: 330-792-2371; 330-792-7671 (Center); Fax: 330-792-3026. Email: parishoffice@stmaronyoungstown.org. Web: stmaronyoungstown.org.
Catechesis/Religious Program—Tel: 330-538-2567; Fax: 330-538-9820.

STATE OF OREGON

PORTLAND, MULTNOMAH CO., SAINT SHARBEL MARONITE CATHOLIC CHURCH (1970) [CEM 2] Rev. Jonathan Decker, M.M.J. M.J.; Subdeacon Wadih Kaldawi.
Res.: 1804 S.E. 16th Ave., OR 97214. Tel: 503-231-3853; Fax: 503-533-8524. Email: saintsharbel@saintsharbel.com. Web: www.saintsharbel.com.
Catechesis/Religious Program—Email: n.redmond@comcast.net. Nadia Redmond, D.R.E.

STATE OF TEXAS

AUSTIN, TRAVIS CO., OUR LADY'S MARONITE PARISH (1982) Rev. Msgr. Donald J. Sawyer; Deacons Joseph Crowley; Ron Lastovica.
Mailing Address: 1320 E. 51st St., TX 78723. Tel: 512-458-3693; Fax: 512-451-9554. Email: email@ourladysmaronite.org. Web: www.ourladysmaronite.org.
Catechesis/Religious Program—

EL PASO, EL PASO CO., ST. ANTHONY OF THE DESERT MARONITE CATHOLIC MISSION/HOLY FAMILY CHURCH (1997) Rev. Msgr. Donald J. Sawyer, Admin.; Subdeacon George Karam.
Mailing Address: c/o 1320 E. 51st St., Austin, TX 78723.
Res.: 3617 Breckenridge Dr., TX 79936. Tel: 512-458-3693; Fax: 512-451-9554. Web: stanthonyofthedesert.org.
Catechesis/Religious Program—

HOUSTON, HARRIS CO., OUR LADY OF THE CEDARS MARONITE CATHOLIC CHURCH (1990) [JC] Revs. Milad T. Yaghi, M.L.M.; Andre S. Estephan, M.L.M.; Pierre El Khoury.
Res.: 11935 Belfort Village Dr., TX 77031. Tel: 281-568-6800; Fax: 281-564-6961. Web: www.ourladyofthecedars.net.
Catechesis/Religious Program—Tommy L. Cordova, D.R.E.

LEWISVILLE, DENTON CO., OUR LADY OF LEBANON MARONITE CATHOLIC CHURCH (1990) Rev. Assaad El Basha, M.L.M.
Res. & Church: 719 University Pl., TX 75067. Tel: 972-436-7617; Fax: 972-221-3430. Web: ourladylebanon.com.
Catechesis/Religious Program—Tommy L. Cordova, D.R.E.

SAN ANTONIO, BEXAR CO., ST. GEORGE MARONITE CATHOLIC CHURCH (1925), (Maronite), [JC] Revs. Ghassan Mattar, M.L.M.; Charles H. Khachan, M.L.M.
Church: 6070 Babcock Rd., TX 78240. Tel: 210-690-9569; Fax: 210-690-5093.
Catechesis/Religious Program—

STATE OF UTAH

MURRAY, SALT LAKE CO., SAINT JUDE MARONITE CATHOLIC CHURCH (1975) Chorbishop William Leser, Temp. Admin.
Res.: 4893 Wasatch St., UT 84107. Tel: 801-268-2820; Fax: 801-268-4404.
Church: 4900 Wasatch St., UT 84107. Email: stjudechurch@stinger.net.
Catechesis/Religious Program—

STATE OF WEST VIRGINIA

WHEELING, OHIO CO., OUR LADY OF LEBANON MARONITE CATHOLIC CHURCH (1906) [JC] Rev. Msgr. William D. Bonczewski.
Res.: 2216 Eoff St., WV 26003. Tel: 304-233-1688; Fax: 304-233-4714.
Catechesis/Religious Program—

STATE OF WASHINGTON

SEATTLE, KING CO., ST. JOSEPH MARONITE CATHOLIC MISSION (2001) Unassigned.
Catechesis/Religious Program—

Special Assignment:
Revs.—
Kimes, John Paul, Congregation for the Doctrine of the Faith, Vatican City, Rome.
Mhanna, Andre, Studying in Rome/Ph.D. in Liturgy.
Salim, Anthony, St. Theresa Church, P.O. Box 2567, Brockton, MA 02305-2567. Tel: 508-586-1428; Fax: 508-587-8139

Retired:
Rev. Msgrs.—
Kayrouz, Victor
Michael, Kenneth
Rev.—
Grunewald, Bernard, Er.O.L.S, M.A., S.T.B.
Chorbishop—
Khachan, Bernard C.

INSTITUTIONS LOCATED IN THE DIOCESE

[A] MONASTERIES AND RESIDENCES OF PRIESTS AND BROTHERS

LOS ANGELES. *The Congregation of Maronite Lebanese Missionaries*, 333 S. San Vicente Blvd., CA 90048. Tel: 310-275-6634; Fax: 310-858-0856. Rev. Abdallah E. Zaidan, M.L.M.

ANN ARBOR. *Maronite Order of the Blessed Virgin Mary*, 4405 Earhart Rd., MI 48105. Tel: 734-662-4822; Fax: 734-662-4822. Email: paultorbey@hotmail.com. Revs. Paul Tarabay, O.M.M.; Nabil Habchi, O.M.M.; Victor Daw, O.M.M. Total in Residence 3.

HOUSTON. *The Congregation of Maronite Lebanese Missionaries* (1865) Our Lady of the Cedars, 11935 Bellfort Village, TX 77031. Tel: 281-568-6800; Fax: 281-564-6961. Email: azaidan@earthlink.net. Revs. Abdallah E. Zaidan, M.L.M., Supr.; Pierre El Khoury; Milad T. Yaghi, M.L.M.; Andre S. Estephan, M.L.M.; Assaad El Basha, M.L.M.; Ghassan Mattar, M.L.M.; Samuel Tanios Madel, M.L.M.; Elias Sleiman, M.L.M.; Charles H. Khachan, M.L.M., Asst.; Sami Chaaya, M.L.M.; Nadim Abou Zeid, M.L.M.

[B] CONVENTS AND RESIDENCES FOR SISTERS

NORTH JACKSON. *Antonine Maronite Sisters of Youngstown, Inc.*, 2691 N. Lipkey Rd., OH 44451. Tel: 330-538-2567; 330-538-9822; Fax: 330-538-9820. Email: anto9srs@aol.com. Web: www.antoninesisters.com. Sr. Marie M. Iskandar, A.S., Dir. Sisters 6. *Antonine Sisters Adult Day Care, Inc.*, 2675 N. Lipkey Rd., OH 44451. Tel: 330-538-9822; Fax: 330-538-9820. Email: anto9srs@aol.com. Web: www.antoninesistersadultdaycare.com. Total Staff 14; Total Assisted 65.

[C] NATIONAL SHRINES

NORTH JACKSON. *National Shrine of Our Lady of Lebanon* 2759 N. Lipkey Rd., OH 44451. Tel: 330-538-3351; Fax: 330-538-0455. Email: ololshrine@aol.com. Web: www.ourladyoflebanonshrine.com. Rev. Msgr. Anthony Spinosa, Rector.

[D] RELIGIOUS COMMUNITIES OF MEN

PHILIPPI. *Our Lady of Solitude Maronite Hermitage, Inc.* (1966) 334 S. Main St., WV 26416-1252. Tel: 304-457-3330; Fax: 304-457-3330. Email: monkbg7@aol.com. Rev. Bernard Grunewald, Er.O.L.S, M.A., S.T.B., Supr. (Retired). Total in Residence 1.

PORTLAND. *Oblates of Jesus, Mary & Joseph, Maronite Monks of Jesus, Mary & Joseph*, 1804 S. E. 16th Ave., OR 97214. Tel: 503-231-3853; Fax: 503-533-8524. Email: nasheesho@frontier.com. Rev. Jonathan Decker, M.M.J. M.J., Prior; Bro. Anthony J. Alles, M.M.J.M.J.

[E] RESIDENCES FOR CLERGY

NORTH JACKSON. *Father Tobia Retirement Home*, 2759 N. Lipkey Rd., OH 44451. Tel: 330-538-3351; Fax: 330-538-0455. Email: ololshrine@aol.com. Web: www.ourladyoflebanonshrine.com. Rev. Msgr. Anthony Spinosa, Rector & Contact Person.

[F] MISCELLANEOUS

SAINT LOUIS. *St. Anthony of the Desert Maronite Catholic Mission-El Paso Real Estate Trust*, 1021 S. 10th St., 63104.

Bishop's Charities, 1021 S. 10th St., 63104. Tel: 314-231-1021; Fax: 314-231-1418. Email: mdenny@usamaronite.org. Most Rev. Robert J. Shaheen, Chm.

Caritas Lebanon, 1021 S. 10th St., 63104. Tel: 314-231-1021; Fax: 314-231-1418. Email: mdenny@usamaronite.org.

Catholic School Assistance Fund, 1021 S. 10th St., 63104. Tel: 314-231-1021; Fax: 314-231-1418. Email: mdenny@usamaronite.org. Web: www.usamaronite.org. Most Rev. Robert Joseph Shaheen.

Eparchial Endowments, 1021 S. 10th St., 63104. Tel: 314-231-1021; Fax: 314-231-1418. Chorbishop Faouzi Elia.

St. George Maronite Catholic Church-San Antonio Real Estate Trust, 1021 S. 10th St., 63104.

St. John Maron Maronite Catholic Church-Orange Real Estate Trust, 1021 S. 10th St., 63104.

St. Joseph Maronite Catholic Church-Phoenix Real Estate Trust, 1021 S. 10th St., 63104.

St. Jude Maronite Catholic Church-W. Covina Real Estate Trust, 1021 S. 10th St., 63104.

LEAF USA, Inc., 1021 S. 10th St., 63104. Tel: 314-231-1021; Fax: 314-231-1418.

Maronite Heritage Institute, 1021 S. 10th St., 63104. Tel: 314-231-1416; Fax: 314-588-7399. Most Rev. Robert J. Shaheen, Contact Person.

Maronite Outreach, 1021 S. 10th St., 63104. Tel: 314-231-1021; Fax: 314-231-1418. Email: info@maroniteoutreach.org. Web: www.maroniteoutreach.org. Most Rev. Robert Joseph Shaheen, Chm.

Our Lady of Lebanon Maronite Catholic Church-Lewisville Real Estate Trust, 1021 S. 10th St., 63104.

Our Lady of Lebanon Maronite Mission-Norman Real Estate Trust, 1021 S. 10th St., 63104.

Our Lady of Mt. Lebanon-St. Peter Maronite Catholic Cathedral-LA Real Estate Trust, 1021 S. 10th St., 63104.

Our Lady of Smiles Orphanage, 1021 S. 10th St., 63104. Tel: 314-231-1021; Fax: 314-231-1418. Email: mdenny@usamaronite.org. Rev. Mansour Labaky, Pres.

Our Lady of the Cedar Maronite Catholic Church-Houston Real Estate Trust, 1021 S. 10th St., 63104.

Our Lady's Maronite Catholic Church-Austin Real Estate Trust, 1021 S. 10th St., 63104.

Priest's Retirement Fund, 1021 S. 10th St., 63104. Tel: 314-231-1021; Fax: 314-231-1418. Email: mdenny@usamaronite.org. Web: www.usamaronite.org.

St. Rafka Maronite Catholic Church-Lakewood, CO Real Estate Trust, 1021 S. 10th St., 63104.

St. Raymond Maronite Catholic Cathedral - Real Estate Trust, 931 Lebanon Dr., 63104.

St. Sharbel Maronite Catholic Church-Portland Real Estate Trust, 1021 S. 10th St., 63104.

St. Sharbel Maronite Catholic Mission-Las Vegas Real Estate Trust, 1021 S. 10th St., 63104.

RELIGIOUS INSTITUTES OF MEN REPRESENTED IN THE DIOCESE

For further details refer to the corresponding bracketed number in the Religious Institutes of Men or Women section.

[0785]—*The Congregation of Maronite Lebanese Missionaries* (Houston, TX)—M.L.M.

[]—*Maronite Monks of Jesus, Mary & Joseph*

[0782]—*Maronite Order of Blessed Virgin Mary* (Ann Arbor, MI)—O.M.M.

[]—*The Congregation of Maronite Lebanese Missionaries* (Los Angeles, CA)—M.L.M.

NECROLOGY

✠ Chedid, Most Rev. John G., Retired Bishop of Our Lady of Lebanon of Los Angeles.—Died March 21, 2012

Armenian Catholic Eparchy of Our Lady of Nareg in the United States of America and Canada

Most Reverend

MIKAEL ANTOINE MOURADIAN, I.C.P.B.

Armenian Catholic Eparch of Our Lady of Nareg ordained October 24, 1987; appointed Eparch of Our Lady of Nareg May 21, 2011; ordained July 31, 2011; installed October 2, 2011. *Chancery: 21 Nassau Ave., Brooklyn, NY 11222.*

Most Reverend

MANUEL BATAKIAN

Eparch Emeritus of Our Lady of Nareg; born November 5, 1929; ordained December 8, 1954; appointed Titular Bishop of Caesarea of Cappadocia January 8, 1995; ordained March 12, 1995; appointed third Apostolic Exarch for Armenian Catholics in United States and Canada November 30, 2000; installed January 20, 2001; nominated as the first Eparch of Our Lady of Nareg September 12, 2005; retired May 21, 2011. *Office: 21 Nassau Ave., Brooklyn, NY 11222.*

Legal Title: Armenian Catholic Eparchy of Our Lady of Nareg in the United States and Canada.

Chancery & Vicar General Office: 21 Nassau Ave., Brooklyn, NY 11222. Tel: 718-388-4218; Fax: 718-486-0615.

STATISTICAL OVERVIEW

Personnel	
Bishop	1
Retired Bishops	1
Priests: Diocesan Active in Diocese	4
Number of Diocesan Priests	4
Religious Priests in Diocese	10
Total Priests in Diocese	14
Permanent Deacons in Diocese	1
Total Sisters	10
Parishes	
Parishes	9
With Resident Pastor:	
Resident Diocesan Priests	3
Resident Religious Priests	6
Professional Ministry Personnel:	
Sisters	10
Educational	
Diocesan Students in Other Seminaries	1
Total Seminarians	1
High Schools, Diocesan and Parish	1
Total Students	389
Elementary Schools, Private	4
Total Students	542
Catechesis/Religious Education:	
High School Students	35
Elementary Students	85
Total Students under Catholic Instruction	1,052
Teachers in the Diocese:	
Priests	1
Sisters	1
Lay Teachers	146
Vital Statistics	
Receptions into the Church:	
Infant Baptism Totals	161
First Communions	132
Marriages:	
Catholic	54
Interfaith	15
Total Marriages	69
Total Catholic Population	37,500

Former Bishops—Most Revs. NERSES MIKAEL SETIAN, ord. April 13, 1941; appt. Titular Bishop of Ancera and Apostolic Exarch for the Armenian Catholics in the U.S.A. and Canada July 3, 1981; ord. Dec. 5, 1981; installed Dec. 27, 1981; retired Sept. 18, 1993; died Sept. 9, 2002; HOVHANNES TERTZAKIAN, O.M.Ven., ord. Sept. 8, 1948; appt. Titular Bishop of Trebisonda and Apostolic Exarch for Armenian Catholics in the United States and Canada Jan. 6, 1995; ord. April 29, 1995; installed May 7, 1995; retired Nov. 30, 2000; died Jan. 28, 2002; MANUEL BATAKIAN, born Nov. 5, 1929; ord. Dec. 8, 1954; appt. Titular Bishop of Caesarea of Cappadocia Jan. 8, 1995; ord. March 12, 1995; appt. third Apostolic Exarch for Armenian Catholics in United States and Canada Nov. 30, 2000; installed Jan. 20, 2001; nominated as the first Eparch of Our Lady of Nareg Sept. 12, 2005; retired May 21, 2011.

Chancery & Vicar General Office—21 Nassau Ave., Brooklyn, 11222. Tel: 718-388-4218; Fax: 718-486-0615.

Vicar General—Rev. GEORGES ZABARIAN. Tel: 718-388-4218.

Business Chancellor—Rev. RAPHAEL ANDONIAN, O.Mech. Tel: 718-388-4218; 617-489-2280.

Newspaper Diocesan Bulletin— "The Eternal Flame" *21 Nassau Ave., Brooklyn, 11222.* Tel: 718-388-4218.

Newspaper Diocesan Bulletin "VERELK"—Office: 1327 Pleasant Ave., Los Angeles, CA 90033-2328. Tel: 323-267-1740.

CLERGY, PARISHES, MISSIONS AND PAROCHIAL SCHOOLS

STATE OF NEW YORK

NEW YORK, NEW YORK CO., ST. ANN'S ARMENIAN CATHOLIC CATHEDRAL (1983) Rev. Antoine Noradounghian.
Res.: 21 Nassau Ave., 11222. Tel: 718-388-4218; Fax: 718-486-0615.

STATE OF CALIFORNIA

GLENDALE, LOS ANGELES CO., ST. GREGORY ARMENIAN CATHOLIC CHURCH (1998) Revs. Krikor Chahinian; Armenag Bedrossian.
Res.: 1510 E. Mountain St., CA 91207-1226. Tel: 818-243-8400; Fax: 818-243-0095.

LOS ANGELES, LOS ANGELES CO., OUR LADY QUEEN OF MARTYRS (1951) Rev. Antoine Panossian.
Res.: 1327 Pleasant Ave., CA 90033-2328. Tel: 323-261-9898; Fax: 323-261-0522.

STATE OF MASSACHUSETTS

BOSTON, MIDDLESEX CO., HOLY CROSS (1940) Rev. Raphael Andonian, O.Mech.; Deacon M.J. Connolly.
Res.: 200 Lexington St., Belmont, MA 02478-1241. Tel: 617-489-2280; Fax: 617-484-0218.

STATE OF MICHIGAN

DETROIT, WAYNE CO., ST. VARTAN'S (1948) Rev. Antoine Adamian.
Res.: 34080 Edmonton St., Farmington, MI 48335. Cell: 248-877-3718; Tel: 248-991-3766 (Church); Fax: 248-991-3766 (Church).

STATE OF NEW JERSEY

PATERSON, PASSAIC CO., SACRED HEART (1927) Rev. George Kalousieh.
Res.: 155 Long Hill Rd., Little Falls, NJ 07424-2374. Tel: 973-890-0447; Fax: 973-890-0292.

STATE OF PENNSYLVANIA

PHILADELPHIA, PHILADELPHIA CO., ST. MARK'S ARMENIAN CATHOLIC (1924) Rev. Michel Bassaleh.
Res.: 400 Haverford Rd., Wynnewood, PA 19096-2699. Tel: 610-896-7789; Fax: 610-896-0915.

INSTITUTIONS LOCATED IN THE DIOCESE

[A] SCHOOLS

STATE OF CALIFORNIA

MONTROSE. *Armenian Sisters of the Immaculate Conception*, 2361 Florencita Dr., CA 91020-1817. Tel: 818-249-8783; Fax: 818-249-9773. Sr. Lucia Al-Haik, Prin.

TUJUNGA. *Mekhitarist School*, 6470 Foothill Blvd., CA 91042-2729. Tel: 818-353-3003; Fax: 818-353-0815. Rev. Tavit Ghazarian, Prin.
6507 Alta Gracia Dr., CA 91042-3403. Tel: 818-352-3048; Fax: 818-352-2647.

STATE OF MASSACHUSETTS

LEXINGTON. *Armenian Sisters Academy*, 20 Pelham Rd., MA 02421-5702. Tel: 781-861-8303; Fax: 781-862-8479. Sr. Cecile Keheyan, Prin.

STATE OF PENNSYLVANIA

RADNOR. *Armenian Sisters Academy*, 440 Upper Gulph Rd., PA 19087-4699. Tel: 610-687-4100; Fax: 610-687-2430. Web: ameniansrsacademy.org. Sr. Emma Moussayan, Prin.

[B] RELIGIOUS INSTITUTES AND CONVENTS FOR WOMEN

STATE OF CALIFORNIA

MONTROSE. *Armenian Sisters of the Immaculate Conception*, 2361 Florencita Dr., CA 91020-1817. Tel: 818-249-7493 (convent). Sr. Lucia Al-Haik, Prin.

STATE OF MASSACHUSETTS

LEXINGTON. *Armenian Sisters of the Immaculate Conception*, 6 Eliot Rd., MA 02173. Tel: 781-863-5962; Fax: 781-674-0410. Sr. Cecile Keheyan, Prin.

STATE OF PENNSYLVANIA

RADNOR. *Armenian Sisters of the Immaculate Conception*, 440 Upper Gulph Rd., PA 19087-4699. Tel: 610-687-4100; 610-688-9360 (convent); Fax: 610-687-2430. Sr. Emma Moussayan, Supr.

NECROLOGY

(No Deaths)

An asterisk (*) denotes an organization that has established tax-exempt status directly with the IRS and is not covered by the USCCB Group Ruling.

Byzantine Eparchy of Parma

Most Reverend

JOHN M. KUDRICK

Bishop of Parma; ordained May 3, 1975; consecrated and installed July 10, 2002.

Chancery Office: 1900 Carlton Rd., Parma, OH 44134. Tel: 216-741-8773; Fax: 216-741-9356.

Web: www.parma.org

ESTABLISHED FEBRUARY 21, 1969.

Embraces all Byzantine Ruthenian Rite Catholics in the States of Illinois, Indiana, Iowa, Kansas, Michigan, Minnesota, Missouri, Nebraska, North Dakota, South Dakota and Wisconsin. Also the entire State of Ohio excluding the Counties of Ashtabula, Trumbull, Mahoning, Columbiana, Carroll, Harrison, Guernsey, Noble, Morgan, Athens, Meigs, Gallia and Lawrence.

For legal titles of parishes and diocesan institutions, consult the Chancery Office.

STATISTICAL OVERVIEW

Personnel	
Bishop	1
Priests: Diocesan Active in Diocese	22
Priests: Diocesan Active Outside Diocese	1
Priests: Retired, Sick or Absent	17
Number of Diocesan Priests	40
Religious Priests in Diocese	1
Total Priests in Diocese	41
Extern Priests in Diocese	4
Ordinations:	
Permanent Deacons	3
Permanent Deacons in Diocese	16
Total Sisters	8
Parishes	
Parishes	29
With Resident Pastor:	
Resident Diocesan Priests	24
Without Resident Pastor:	
Administered by Priests	5
Missions	5
Pastoral Centers	1
Closed Parishes	1
Professional Ministry Personnel:	
Sisters	6
Welfare	
Day Care Centers	1
Total Assisted	28
Special Centers for Social Services	5
Total Assisted	16,500
Educational	
Diocesan Students in Other Seminaries	3
Total Seminarians	3
Elementary Schools, Diocesan and Parish	1
Total Students	161
Catechesis/Religious Education:	
High School Students	107
Elementary Students	339
Total Students under Catholic Instruction	610
Vital Statistics	
Receptions into the Church:	
Infant Baptism Totals	55
Minor Baptism Totals	3
Adult Baptism Totals	8
Received into Full Communion	21
First Communions	48
Confirmations	60
Marriages:	
Catholic	22
Interfaith	3
Total Marriages	25
Deaths	143
Total Catholic Population	8,659

Former Bishops—Most Revs. EMIL J. MIHALIK, D.D., ord. Sept. 21, 1945; appt. first Bishop of the Ruthenian Eparchy of Parma, March 22, 1969; installed June 12, 1969; died Jan. 27, 1984; ANDREW PATAKI, D.D., appt. Titular Bishop of Tellmisus and Auxiliary of Passaic, NJ, May 30, 1983; installed Aug. 23, 1983; succeeded to See, June 19, 1984; transferred to Parma See, Aug. 16, 1984; transferred to Byzantine Eparchy of Passaic, Nov. 21, 1995; BASIL MYRON SCHOTT, O.F.M., ord. Aug. 29, 1965; cons. and installed as Bishop of Parma July 11, 1996; transferred to Archeparchy of Pittsburgh July 9, 2002; died June 10, 2010.

Chancery Office—1900 Carlton Rd., Parma, 44134. Tel: 216-741-8773; Fax: 216-741-9356.

Protosyncellus—Rt. Rev. Mitred Archpriest JOHN S. KACHUBA, M.A.

Syncellus for Clergy and Religious—Very Rev. STEVEN KOPLINKA, M.Div.

Syncellus for Parishes and Laity—Very Rev. THOMAS LOYA, S.T.B., M.A.

Syncellus for Doctrine and Worship—Very Rev. Archpriest MICHAEL HAYDUK.

Chancellor—Very Rev. Archpriest DENNIS M. HRUBIAK.

Presbyteral Council—Rt. Rev. Mitred Archpriest JOHN S. KACHUBA, M.A.; Very Rev. NICHOLAS RACHFORD, J.C.L.; Very Rev. Archpriest MICHAEL HAYDUK; Very Revs. DAVID A. HANNES, J.C.L.; STEVEN KOPLINKA, M.Div.; JAMES KUBAJAK, M.Div.; THOMAS LOYA, S.T.B., M.A.; Rev. BASIL HUTSKO; Very Rev. BRYAN R. EYMAN, D.Min.; Rev. TERRENCE FARMER; Very Rev. Archpriest DENNIS M. HRUBIAK; Rev. JAMES J. BATCHA.

Eparchial Pastoral Council—Rt. Rev. Mitred Archpriest JOHN S. KACHUBA, M.A.; Very Rev. Archpriest MICHAEL HAYDUK; Very Revs. STEVEN KOPLINKA, M.Div.; THOMAS LOYA, S.T.B., M.A.; Rev. JOSEPH REPKO, M.Div.; Deacon JOHN PETRUS, M.D.; CATHERINE BARANKO; VIRGILDEE DANIEL; NICHOLAS J. NAGRANT; LORETTA NEMETH; MICHAEL ROBUSTO; ANN SEABRIGHT; KATHRYN SZILAGYE.

Eparchial Finance Council—Rev. JAMES J. BATCHA, Finance Officer.

Eparchial Finance Officer—Rt. Rev. Mitred Archpriest JOHN S. KACHUBA, M.A.; JENIFER NEMETH, Sec.; JEROME J. LUCAS; EDWARD MAHER.

Eparchial Consultors—Rt. Rev. Mitred Archpriest JOHN S. KACHUBA, M.A.; Very Rev. Archpriest DENNIS M. HRUBIAK; Very Rev. NICHOLAS RACHFORD, J.C.L.; Rev. Msgr. FRANK KORBA, V.F.; Very Rev. Archpriests DAVID PETRAS, S.E.O.D. (Retired); MICHAEL HAYDUK.

Protopresbyters—Ohio: Very Rev. BRYAN R. EYMAN, D.Min. Midwest: Rev. Msgr. FRANK KORBA, V.F. Great Lakes: Very Rev. JAMES KUBAJAK, M.Div.

Vicar Judicialis—Very Rev. NICHOLAS RACHFORD, J.C.L.

Judges—Very Rev. DAVID A. HANNES, J.C.L.; Rev. MICHAEL J. HUSZTI.

Secretary of the Tribunal—VACANT.

Defender of the Bond—Very Rev. JAMES KUBAJAK, M.Div.

Promoter of Justice—Very Rev. JAMES KUBAJAK, M.Div.

Notaries—MARILYN MUCHA; Rev. RICHARD PLISHKA.

Eparchial Censor—Very Rev. Archpriest DAVID PETRAS, S.E.O.D. (Retired).

Priest Secretary to the Bishop—Rev. RICHARD PLISHKA.

Eparchial Commissions

Sacred Liturgy—Very Rev. Archpriest DAVID PETRAS, S.E.O.D., Chm. (Retired); Rev. ROBERT BARTER (Retired); Very Rev. Archpriest MICHAEL HAYDUK; Very Rev. STEVEN KOPLINKA, M.Div.

Building Commission—Very Rev. Archpriest DAVID PETRAS, S.E.O.D. (Retired); Very Rev. BRYAN R. EYMAN, D.Min., Chm.; Deacon WILLIAM FREDRICK; FRANK TOMBAZZI.

Cantors' Institute—NICOLETTE BOROS, Dir. Cantors' Institute Faculty: Very Rev. Archpriests DAVID PETRAS, S.E.O.D. (Retired); DENNIS M. HRUBIAK; MICHAEL HAYDUK; Revs. MICHAEL J. HUSZTI; JAMES J. BATCHA; Very Rev. NICHOLAS RACHFORD, J.C.L.

Office of Religious Education—Rt. Rev. Mitred Archpriest JOHN S. KACHUBA, M.A., Dir. Tel: 216-741-4102. Associates: Rev. Msgr. FRANK KORBA, V.F., Midwest; Deacon WILLIAM FREDRICK, Safe Environment Coord.

Catechetical Board—Rev. Msgr. FRANK KORBA, V.F.; LISA STANICH.

Office of Youth Ministry—Rev. BRUCE RIEBE, Dir.; Very Rev. THOMAS LOYA, S.T.B., M.A., Midwest.

Young Adults—Revs. TERRENCE FARMER; RICHARD PLISHKA; Sr. JULIE HRITZ.

Office of Family Life—VIRGILDEE DANIEL, Dir.

Office of Evangelization and Missionary Activity—Revs. JAMES J. BATCHA, Dir.; RICHARD PLISHKA; LORETTA NEMETH.

Office of Vocations—Very Rev. Archpriest DENNIS M. HRUBIAK, Dir.

Seminary Education Formation Board—Very Rev. Archpriests DAVID PETRAS, S.E.O.D., Chm. (Retired); MICHAEL HAYDUK; DENNIS M. HRUBIAK; Rt. Rev. Mitred Archpriest JOHN S. KACHUBA, M.A.; Very Rev. STEVEN KOPLINKA, M.Div.

Priest's Pension Board—Rt. Rev. Mitred Archpriest JOHN S. KACHUBA, M.A.; Revs. BASIL HUTSKO; JOSEPH MARQUIS; Very Rev. Archpriest DENNIS M. HRUBIAK; Revs. SIDNEY SIDOR (Retired); JAMES J. BATCHA, Chm.

Office of Ecumenical Activity—Very Rev. Archpriest DAVID PETRAS, S.E.O.D., Dir. (Retired).

Stewardship Office—Rev. JAMES J. BATCHA; FRANCINE MAKUH.

Eparchial Shrine of the Weeping Madonna of Mariapoch— (Burton, OH): President, The Most Rev. Ordinary of the Parma Eparchy. Tel: 440-834-0700. Rev. JAMES J. BATCHA, Admin.

Respect Life Office—Very Rev. THOMAS LOYA, S.T.B., M.A.

Pre-Cana Office—VIRGILDEE DANIEL; LOUISE DANIEL.

Victim Assistance Coordinator—SHARON DILAURO PETRUS, M.D. Tel: 216-741-8773, Ext. 246. Email: dilauropetrus@yahoo.com.

Office of Communications—LORETTA NEMETH, Dir. Tel: 216-741-3312. Email: viscom@parma.org.

Boy Scout Chaplain—Very Rev. NICHOLAS RACHFORD, J.C.L.

Sexual Allegation Review Board—MADELINE ZAWORSKI, Chm.; MICHAEL ROBUSTO, Sec.; Rev. JAMES J. BATCHA; RITA BASALLA; WILLIAM BOCKANIC; ROBERT KINKELA; JEAN MCNOSKY; LISA NEWBURGER; JODI STARRE. Ex Officio: Rt. Rev. Mitred Archpriest JOHN S. KACHUBA, M.A.; Very Rev. JAMES KUBAJAK, M.Div.

Byzantine Catholic Cultural Center—Most Rev. JOHN M. KUDRICK, Pres.; Rev. RICHARD PLISHKA, Co Dir; Deacon MICHAEL LEE, Co Dir; Rev. JAMES J. BATCHA, Museum Dir.

CLERGY, PARISHES, MISSIONS AND PAROCHIAL SCHOOLS

STATE OF OHIO

PARMA, CUYAHOGA CO.

1—SAINT JOHN THE BAPTIST, CATHEDRAL (1898), (Ruthenian), Very Rev. Archpriest Michael Hayduk; Deacons Andrew Nagrant; Gregory Loya.
Church: 1900 Carlton Rd., 44134-3129. Tel: 216-661-8658; Fax: 216-661-8221.
Res.: 1703 Carlton Rd., 44134.
Catechesis/Religious Program—Students 28.

2—HOLY SPIRIT (1969) [CEM 2] Rev. James J. Batcha.
Res.: 5500 W. 54th St., 44129-2274. Tel: 440-884-8452; Fax: 440-884-8453. Email: contactus@holyspiritbyzantine.org. Web: holyspiritbyzantine.org.
Catechesis/Religious Program—

AKRON, SUMMIT CO., ST. MICHAEL THE ARCHANGEL (1916) [CEM] Rev. Robert Stash.
Res.: 847 Crouse St., 44306-1125. Tel: 330-376-6633; Fax: 330-376-7007.
Catechesis/Religious Program—

BARBERTON, SUMMIT CO., ST. NICHOLAS (1918) [CEM] Rev. Miron Kerul'-Kmec, Admin.
Church: 1051 E. Robinson St., 44203-3852. Tel: 330-753-2031; Fax: 330-745-5500. Email: stnickbyz@gmail.com. Web: www.stnickbyz.com.
Catechesis/Religious Program—Students 14.

BEDFORD, CUYAHOGA CO., ST. EUGENE (1963) Rev. Joseph Repko.
Res.: 264 Warrensville-Center Rd., 44146-2741. Tel: 440-232-7302; Fax: 440-439-9537. Email: frrepko@ameritech.net.
Catechesis/Religious Program—Students 3.

BRECKSVILLE, CUYAHOGA CO., ST. JOSEPH (1913) Rev. Bruce Riebe; Deacon William Fredrick.
Res.: 8111 Brecksville, 44141-1204. Tel: 440-526-1818; Fax: 440-526-6464. Email: stjoebyz@sbcglobal.net. Web: www.stjoebyz.com.
Catechesis/Religious Program—Students 57.

BRUNSWICK, MEDINA CO., ST. EMILIAN (1975) Rev. Marek Visnovsky; Deacon Robert Cripps.
Res.: 4705 Hickory Ridge Ave., 44212. Tel: 330-225-7799.
Church: 1231 Substation Rd., 44212-0843. Tel: 330-225-9857; Fax: 330-220-5963.
Catechesis/Religious Program—Students 21.

BURTON, GEAUGA CO., CHURCH OF MARIAPOCH (1956) Rev. James J. Batcha, Admin.
Church: 17486 Mumford Rd., P.O. Box 388, 44021-9640. Tel: 440-834-8807.
Shrine—Shrine of Mariapoch, Tel: 440-834-0700.

CLEVELAND, CUYAHOGA CO.

1—HOLY GHOST (1909) Closed. For inquiries for parish records contact the chancery.

2—ST. MARY (1938) Very Rev. Steven Koplinka; Deacon Joseph Hnat.
Res.: 3518 Stickney Ave., 44109. Tel: 216-741-7979; Fax: 216-741-6622.
School—(Grades K-8) Tel: 216-749-7980; Fax: 216-749-7775. Rita Basalla, Prin.; Mary Somrak, Librarian. Sisters of St. Basil the Great 2; Lay Teachers 12; Students 163.
Catechesis/Religious Program—Students 4.
Convent—Sisters of St. Basil the Great., 3600 Biddulph Ave., Apt 1, 44109. Tel: 216-398-5939.

3—ST. NICHOLAS (1902), (Croatian), Rev. Richard Plishka.
Church: 3431 Superior Ave., 44114-4160. Tel: 216-361-5069; Fax: 216-361-2455.
Catechesis/Religious Program—

COLUMBUS, FRANKLIN CO., ST. JOHN CHRYSOSTOM (1961) Rev. Terrence Farmer; Deacon Jeffrey Martin.
Res.: 5858 Cleveland Ave., 43231-2862. Tel: 614-882-7578; Fax: 614-890-6048.
Catechesis/Religious Program—Students 25.

DAYTON, MONTGOMERY CO., ST. BARBARA, Closed. For inquiries for parish records contact the chancery.

EUCLID, CUYAHOGA CO., ST. STEPHEN (1955) Rt. Rev. Mitred Archpriest John S. Kachuba; Deacon Robert Kirschner.
Res.: 532 Lloyd Rd., 44132-1721. Tel: 216-732-7292; Fax: 216-732-9434.
Catechesis/Religious Program—Students 36.

FAIRPORT HARBOR, LAKE CO., ST. MICHAEL (1926) Rev. Robert D. Kelly.
Mailing Address: *St. Andrew*, c/o 5768 Andrews Rd., Mentor-on-the-Lake, 44060-2608.
Res.: 630 Plum St., 44077-5660. Tel: 440-257-3620; Fax: 440-257-6524.
Catechesis/Religious Program—

FAIRVIEW PARK, CUYAHOGA CO., ST. MARY MAGDALENE (1966) Very Rev. Archpriest Dennis M. Hrubiak; Deacon Daniel Surniak.
Res.: 5390 W. 220th St., 44126-2968. Tel: 440-734-4644; Fax: 440-734-4645. Email: fdhrubiak@yahoo.com. Web: ebni.com/stmarymagdalene.
Catechesis/Religious Program—Students 19.

LAKEWOOD, CUYAHOGA CO., ST. GREGORY THE THEOLOGIAN (1905) Rev. Robert D. Kelly.
Res.: 2035 Quail Ave., 44107-5217. Tel: 216-521-1081; Fax: 216-521-1020.
Catechesis/Religious Program—

LORAIN, LORAIN CO.

1—ST. MICHAEL, Closed. For inquiries for parish records contact the chancery.

2—ST. NICHOLAS (1914) Very Rev. Nicholas Rachford.
Res.: 2711 W. 40th St., 44053-2252. Tel: 440-282-7525; Fax: 440-282-9185. Email: pastor@stnicks.org. Web: www.stnicks.org.
Catechesis/Religious Program—Students 13.

MARBLEHEAD, OTTAWA CO., ST. MARY (1897) [CEM] Very Rev. Bryan R. Eyman.
Res.: 506 E. Main St., 43440-2232. Tel: 419-798-4283; Fax: 419-798-4095.
Catechesis/Religious Program—Students 6.

MENTOR-ON-THE-LAKE, LAKE CO., ST. ANDREW THE APOSTLE (1974) Rev. Robert D. Kelly.
Res.: 630 Plum St., Fairport Harbor, 44077.
Church: 5768 Andrews Rd., 44060-2608. Tel: 440-257-3620; Fax: 440-257-6524.
Catechesis/Religious Program—

NORTHWOOD, LUCAS CO., ST. MICHAEL THE ARCHANGEL (1915) Very Rev. James Kubajak; Deacon James Sofalvi.
Res.: 2526 Skagway Dr., 43619. Tel: 419-691-5656; Fax: 419-691-7669.
Church: 4001 Navarre Ave., Oregon, 43616.
Catechesis/Religious Program—Students 1.

SOLON, CUYAHOGA CO., ST. JOHN THE BAPTIST (1892) Rev. Joseph Repko.
Res.: 264 Warrensville Center Rd., Bedford, 44146. Tel: 440-232-7302.
Church: 36125 Aurora Rd., 44139-3841. Tel: 440-248-0417; Fax: 440-248-8044.
Catechesis/Religious Program—Students 3.

STATE OF ILLINOIS

CHICAGO, COOK CO., ST. MARY, Closed. For inquiries for parish records contact the chancery.

HOMER GLEN, WILL CO., ANNUNCIATION BYZANTINE CATHOLIC CHURCH (1999) [CEM] Very Rev. Thomas Loya; Deacons J. Timothy Tkach; John Evancho.
Res.: 14610 S. Will-Cook Rd., IL 60491-9212. Tel: 708-645-0241; Fax: 708-645-0243. Email: annuncbyzchurch@aol.com. Web: www.byzantinecatholic.com.
Catechesis/Religious Program—Students 50.

JOLIET, WILL CO., ST. MARY ASSUMPTION, Closed. For inquiries for parish records contact the chancery.

STATE OF INDIANA

EAST CHICAGO, LAKE CO., ST. BASIL'S, Closed. For inquiries for parish records contact the chancery.

INDIANA, HARBOR CO., HOLY GHOST, Closed. For inquiries for parish records contact the chancery.

INDIANAPOLIS, MARION CO., ST. ATHANASIUS CHURCH (1980) Rev. Sidney Sidor (Retired).
Res.: 1117 S. Blaine Ave., IN 46221-1110. Tel: 317-632-4157; Fax: 317-632-2988. Email: stathanasius@pngusa.net. Web: http://r-fol.com./st.athanasius.
Catechesis/Religious Program—

MERRILLVILLE, LAKE CO., ST. MICHAEL (1911) Rev. Basil Hutsko.
Res.: 557 W. 57th Ave., IN 46410-2540. Tel: 219-980-0600; Fax: 219-980-0127.
Catechesis/Religious Program—Students 17.

MUNSTER, LAKE CO., SAINT NICHOLAS (1922) [CEM] Rev. Msgr. Frank Korba.
Res.: 8103 Columbia Ave., IN 46321-1802. Tel: 219-838-9380; Fax: 219-838-1265.
Catechesis/Religious Program—

WHITING, LAKE CO., ASSUMPTION OF THE BLESSED VIRGIN (1899) [CEM] Rev. Stephen Muth; Deacon J. Timothy Tkach.
Res.: 2011 Clark St., IN 46394-2023. Tel: 219-659-0277; Fax: 219-659-1687.
Catechesis/Religious Program—Students 11.

STATE OF MICHIGAN

ALLEN PARK, WAYNE CO., ST. STEPHEN (1941) Rev. Cyril Attak (Retired).
Res.: 4141 Laurence Ave., MI 48101-3049. Tel: 313-382-5901; Fax: 313-382-5902.
Catechesis/Religious Program—Students 22.

BAY CITY, BAY CO., SAINT GEORGE (1967) Rev. Innocenti Rossi, Admin.
Res.: 204 N. Van Buren St., MI 48706-6519. Tel: 616-322-6462; Fax: 989-892-0763.
Catechesis/Religious Program—Students 5.

CLINTON TOWNSHIP, ST. NICHOLAS (1921) Rev. Robert Barter (Retired).
Church & Res.: 23300 King Dr., MI 48035. Tel: 586-791-1052; Fax: 586-791-1059.
Catechesis/Religious Program—Students 19.

DETROIT, WAYNE CO., ST. JOHN THE BAPTIST, Closed. For inquiries for parish records contact the chancery.

FLUSHING, GENESEE CO., ST. MICHAEL (1917) Very Rev. David A. Hannes.
Res.: 2333 N. Elms Rd., MI 48433-9426. Tel: 810-659-4887; Fax: 810-659-8363. Email: stmichaelbyz@aol.com. Web: www.stmichaelbyz.com.
Catechesis/Religious Program—Students 36.

LIVONIA, WAYNE CO., SACRED HEART (1957) Rev. Joseph Marquis; Deacon Lawrence Hendricks.
Res.: 16881 Savoie St., MI 48154.
Church: 29125 W. Six-Mile Rd., MI 48152-3661. Tel: 734-522-3166; Fax: 734-261-8562. Email: shbyzantine@sbcglobal.net.
Catechesis/Religious Program—Students 12.

OMER, ARENAC CO., ST. JOHN (1981) Rev. Innocenti Rossi.
Res.: 204 N. Van Buren St., Bay City, MI 48706-6519. Tel: 616-322-6462; Fax: 989-892-0763.
Church: 125 High St., P.O. Box 236, MI 48749-0236.

STERLING HEIGHTS, MACOMB CO., ST. BASIL (1962) Rev. Mychail Rozmarynowycz, Admin.; Deacon Paul Latcha.
Res.: 4700 Metropolitan Pkwy., MI 48310-3905. Tel: 586-268-1082; Fax: 586-268-2548.
Catechesis/Religious Program—Students 17.

TAYLOR, WAYNE CO., CHRIST THE KING, Closed. For inquiries for parish records contact the chancery.

STATE OF MINNESOTA

MINNEAPOLIS, HENNEPIN CO., ST. JOHN THE BAPTIST (1907) Rev. Ihar Labacevich.
Res.: 2215 Third St., N.E., MN 55418-3422. Tel: 612-789-6252; Fax: 612-789-2607. Email: stjohnminneapolis@comcast.net.
Catechesis/Religious Program—Students 5.

STATE OF MISSOURI

ST. LOUIS, ST. LOUIS CO., ST. LOUIS MISSION (1981) Revs. Eugene P. Selzer; Paul Niemann; Joseph A. Weber.
Mailing Address: 796 Buckley Rd., MO 63125. Tel: 314-892-5109; Fax: 314-892-0629.
Blessed John XXIII Center: 8300 Morganford Rd., MO 62123.

SUGAR CREEK, JACKSON CO., ST. LUKE, BYZANTINE CATHOLIC PARISH (1980) Deacon Nicholas Szilagye, Admin.
Mailing Address: P.O. Box 8673, MO 64054.
Church: 11411 Chicago, MO 64054. Tel: 816-231-7100.

STATE OF WISCONSIN

BRISTOL, KENOSHA CO., ST. IRENE, Closed. For information regarding the Byzantine Catholic Community contact the Chancery.

On Duty Outside the Diocese:
Revs.—
Atkins, James (Retired), Archeparchy of Pittsburgh
Huszti, Michael J., Sisters of St. Basil the Great, 500 W. Main St., Uniontown, PA 15401. Tel: 724-439-4475
Very Rev. Archpriest—
Petras, David, S.E.O.D. (Retired), Byzantine Catholic Seminary, 3605 Perrysville Ave., Pittsburgh, PA 05214. Tel: 412-321-5133; Fax: 412-321-9936

Absent on Leave:
Revs.—
Chelena, Thomas
St. Germain, Brian

Retired:
Very Revs.—
Evanick, Michael, 2371 Deerpath Dr., Unit 111, Schererville, IN 46375.
Zavell, Edward, 11644 Katherine, Taylor, MI 48180. Tel: 734-250-8594
Revs.—
Atkins, James

Attak, Cyril, 4141 Laurence Ave., Allen Park, MI 48101.
Barter, Robert, 34475 Jefferson, Harrison Township, MI 48045.
Ivan, Nicholas, Mt. Macrina Manor, 520 W. Main St., Uniontown, PA 15401.
Jadwisiak, Edmund, 5000 Providence Dr. #321, Sandusky, 44870-1414. Tel: 419-625-1354
Kovach, John, P.O. Box 20510, Los Angeles, CA 90006.
Linowski, Eugene R., 2221 Glenmere Rd., Columbus, 43220. Tel: 614-488-0427
Pohorlak, Joseph, 1511 Warwick Ave., Apt 1S, Whiting, IN 46394. Tel: 219-473-0197
Radvansky, Joseph R., 350 N. Lighthouse Oval, Marblehead, 43440. Tel: 419-503-0507
Sidor, Sidney, 1117 S. Blaine Ave., Indianapolis, IN 46221.
Wojciechowski, Edward C., Albertine Home, 1501 Hoffman St., Hammond, IN 46327. Tel: 219-937-0575

Very Rev. Archpriest—
Petras, David, S.E.O.D.

Permanent Deacons:
Cripps, Robert, St. Emilian Church, Brunswick, OH
Evancho, John, Annunciation Byzantine Church, Homer Glen, IL
Fredrick, William, St. Joseph, Brecksville, OH
Hendricks, Lawrence, Sacred Heart, Livonia, MI
Hnat, Joseph, St. Mary, Cleveland, OH
Kirschner, Robert, St. Stephen Byzantine Church, Euclid, OH
Latcha, Paul, St. Basil, Sterling Heights, MI
Loya, Gregory, Cathedral of St. John the Baptist, Parma, OH
Martin, Jeffrey, St. John Chrysostom, Columbus, OH
Petrus, John, M.D., St. John Cathedral, Parma, OH
Sofalvi, James, St. Michael, Northwood, OH
Surniak, Daniel, St. Mary Magdalene, Fairview Park, OH
Szilagye, Nicholas, M.D., St. Luke, Sugar Creek, MO
Tkach, J. Timothy, Annunciation Byzantine Church, Homer Glen, IL; St. Mary, Whiting, IN

INSTITUTIONS LOCATED IN THE DIOCESE

[A] CONVENTS AND RESIDENCES FOR SISTERS

NORTH ROYALTON. *Motherhouse and Novitiate*, 6688 Cady Rd., 44133. Tel: 440-237-6800. Sr. Mary Lucille Tepper, B.P.C.N., Supr.

[B] RELIGIOUS SHRINES

BURTON. *Shrine of Mariapoch* 17486 Mumford Rd., 44021. Tel: 440-834-0700.

[C] MISCELLANEOUS

CLEVELAND. *St. Mary Hospitality House*, 5500 W. 54th St., 44129. Tel: 440-884-8452; Fax: 440-884-8453. Dorothy Papke, Dir.

DAYTON. *St. Barbara Prayer Community* Prayer Center., 5915 Springboro Pike, 45449. Tel: 513-434-9205. Rev. John Kapitan Jr., O.F.M.

RELIGIOUS INSTITUTES OF WOMEN REPRESENTED IN THE DIOCESE

For further details refer to the corresponding bracketed number in the Religious Institutes of Men or Women section.

[]—*Byzantine Nuns of St. Clare* (Parma Eparchy)—B.P.C.N.

[3730]—*Sisters of the Order of St. Basil the Great*—O.S.B.M.

NECROLOGY

† Smochko, Rev. Msgr. Basil, (Retired)—Died May 9, 2011

An asterisk (*) denotes an organization that has established tax-exempt status directly with the IRS and is not covered by the USCCB Group Ruling.

Byzantine Catholic Eparchy of Passaic

ESTABLISHED JULY 31, 1963.

Embraces all Catholics of the Byzantine-Ruthenian Rite in the States of New Jersey, Connecticut, Delaware, District of Columbia, Florida, Georgia, Maine, Maryland, Massachusetts, New Hampshire, New York, North Carolina, Rhode Island, South Carolina, Vermont, Virginia and all Eastern Pennsylvania within the western boundaries of the Counties of Franklin, Juniata, Lycoming, Mifflin, Union and Tioga.

For legal titles of parishes and diocesan institutions, consult the Chancery Office.

(VACANT SEE)

Chancery Office: 445 Lackawanna Ave., Woodland Park, NJ 07424. Tel: 973-890-7777; Fax: 973-890-7175.

Web: www.eparchyofpassaic.com

Email: bishop@dioceseofpassaic.org

STATISTICAL OVERVIEW

Personnel	
Priests: Diocesan Active in Diocese	43
Priests: Diocesan Active Outside Diocese	3
Priests: Retired, Sick or Absent	21
Number of Diocesan Priests	67
Religious Priests in Diocese	10
Total Priests in Diocese	77
Extern Priests in Diocese	6
Permanent Deacons in Diocese	26
Total Brothers	1
Total Sisters	16
Parishes	
Parishes	84
With Resident Pastor:	
Resident Diocesan Priests	43
Resident Religious Priests	5
Without Resident Pastor:	
Administered by Priests	36
Missions	4
Educational	
Diocesan Students in Other Seminaries	2
Total Seminarians	2
Catechesis/Religious Education:	
High School Students	164
Elementary Students	509
Total Students under Catholic Instruction	675
Vital Statistics	
Receptions into the Church:	
Infant Baptism Totals	144
Minor Baptism Totals	2
Adult Baptism Totals	3
Received into Full Communion	16
First Communions	149
Confirmations	133
Marriages:	
Catholic	45
Interfaith	7
Total Marriages	52
Deaths	457
Total Catholic Population	14,729

Former Bishops—Most Revs. STEPHEN J. KOCISKO, D.D., ord. March 30, 1941; appt. Titular Bishop of Theveste and Auxiliary of Exarchate of Pittsburgh, July 20, 1956; appt. First Eparch of Passaic, July 31, 1963; appt. Eparch of Pittsburgh, Dec. 21, 1967; installed March 5, 1968; elevated to Metropolitan Archbishop of Pittsburgh, Feb. 21, 1969; retired June 12, 1991; died March 7, 1995; MICHAEL J. DUDICK, D.D. (Retired), ord. Nov. 13, 1945; appt. Bishop of Passaic, Aug. 21, 1968; installed Oct. 24, 1968; retired Nov. 21, 1995; died May 30, 2007.; ANDREW PATAKI, J.C.L., D.D., ord. Feb. 24, 1952; appt. Titular Bishop of Tellmisus and Auxiliary Bishop of Passaic, May 30, 1983; cons. Aug. 23, 1983; appt. Bishop of Parma June 19, 1984; enthroned Aug. 16, 1984; transferred to Passaic Nov. 6, 1995; enthroned Feb. 8, 1996; retired & appt. Apostolic Administrator Dec. 6, 2007; appt. Protosyncellus and Moderator of Eparchial Curia March 1, 2008; died Dec. 8, 2011.; WILLIAM C. SKURLA, ord. May 23, 1987; appt. Bishop of the Eparchy of Van Nuys Feb. 19, 2002; cons. and enthroned April 23, 2002; transferred to the Eparchy of Passaic Dec. 6, 2007; enthroned Jan. 29, 2008; appt. Metropolitan Archbishop of Pittsburgh Jan. 19, 2012.

Protosyncellus-Vicar General and Moderator of the Curia—Very Rev. EDWARD G. CIMBALA, D.Min.

Syncellates and Protopresbyterates—

Susquehanna Valley Syncellate—

Syncellus—Very Rev. JAMES HAYER, St. Mary's Church, 695 N. Main St., Wilkes Barre, PA 18705. Tel: 570-822-6028.

Northern Pennsylvania/Northern New York Protopresbyterate—Rev. Msgr. JOHN T. SEKELLICK, J.C.L., Protopresbyter, Holy Ghost Church, 313 First St., Jessup, PA 18434. Tel: 570-489-2353.

Wyoming Valley Protopresbyterate—Very Rev. MICHAEL SALNICKY, Protopresbyter, Carpathian Village, 802 Snow Hill Rd., Cresco, PA 18326. Tel: 570-595-3265.

Central Pennsylvania Syncellate—

Syncellus—Very Rev. PETER J. HOSAK, M.S., SS. Peter & Paul Church, 1140 Johnston Dr., Bethlehem, PA 18017. Tel: 610-867-2322.

Mid-Pennsylvania Protopresbyterate—Very Rev. FRANCIS M. TWARDZIK, S.D.B., SS. Peter & Paul Church, 107 S. Fourth St., Minersville, PA 17954. Tel: 570-544-2074.

South Pennsylvania Protopresbyterate—Very Rev. EDWARD J. HIGGINS, Protopresbyter, Holy Ghost Church, 2310 S. 24th St., Philadelphia, PA 19145. Tel: 215-334-5129.

New Jersey Syncellate—

Syncellus—Very Rev. MICHAEL MONDIK, St. Thomas the Apostle Church, 1410 Church St., Rahway, 07065. Tel: 732-382-5300.

Northern New Jersey Protopresbyterate—Very Rev. MARCEL SZABO, Protopresbyter, St. Michael Cathedral, 96 First St., Passaic, 07055. Tel: 973-777-2553.

Central New Jersey Protopresbyterate—Very Rev. GREGORY J. NOGA, M.A., Protopresbyter, St. Mary Church, 411 Adeline St., Trenton, 08611. Tel: 609-394-5004.

New York-New England Syncellate—

Syncellus—Very Rev. ROBERT J. HOSPODAR, J.C.L., St. Mary Church, 246 E. 15th St., New York, NY 10003. Tel: 212-677-0516.

New York/New England Protopresbyterate—VACANT.

Middle States Syncellate—

Syncellus—Very Revs. JOHN G. BASARAB, M.A., Epiphany of Our Lord Church, 3410 Woodburn Rd., Annandale, VA 22003. Tel: 703-573-3986; CONAN H. TIMONEY, Ph.D., Protopresbyter, Patronage of Mother of God Church, 1260 Stevens Ave., Baltimore, MD 21227. Tel: 410-247-4936.

Southern States Syncellate—

Syncellus—Very Revs. PETER LICKMAN, St. Basil Church, 1475 N.E. 199th St., Miami, FL 33179. Tel: 305-651-0991; ROBERT EVANCHO, Protopresbyter, St. Therese Church, 4265 13th Ave. N., St. Petersburg, FL 33713. Tel: 727-323-4022.

Chancery Office—Eparchial Center, 445 Lackawanna Ave., Woodland Park, 07424. Tel: 973-890-7777; Fax: 973-890-7175. Office Hours: Mon.-Fri. 9-12 & 1-4.

Chancellor—Very Rev. ROBERT J. HOSPODAR, J.C.L.

Eparchial Finance Officer—Mr. BERT REIMANN.

Eparchial Financial Controller—Ms. LINDA FISHER.

Eparchial Finance Council—Mr. BERT REIMANN; Mr. THOMAS P. DEVITA, Attorney at Law; Mr. JERRY LUCAS, CPA; Ms. LINDA FISHER.

Eparchial College of Consultors—Very Revs. FRANCIS M. TWARDZIK, S.D.B.; MICHAEL MONDIK; JOHN G. BASARAB, M.A.; PETER LICKMAN; Rev. JAMES CARROLL, O.F.M.; Very Revs. RONALD BARUSEFSKI; ROBERT J. HOSPODAR, J.C.L., Sec.

Presbyteral Council—Very Revs. RONALD BARUSEFSKI; JOHN G. BASARAB, M.A.; ROBERT J. HOSPODAR, J.C.L.; PETER LICKMAN; MICHAEL MONDIK; Rev. JAMES CARROLL, O.F.M.; Very Revs. CONAN H. TIMONEY, Ph.D.; FRANCIS M. TWARDZIK, S.D.B.; Rev. Msgr. JOHN T. SEKELLICK, J.C.L.; Rev. PETER M. DONISH; Very Rev. EDWARD J. HIGGINS; Revs. GARY J. MENSINGER; MICHAEL SOPOLIGA; CARMEN SCUDERI, O.F.M.; CHARLES YASTISHOCK; MICHAEL J. YURISTA.

Eparchial Tribunal—445 Lackawanna Ave., Woodland Park, 07424. Tel: 973-890-7777.

Judicial Vicar—Rev. Msgr. JOHN T. SEKELLICK, J.C.L.

Defender of the Bond—Very Rev. MICHAEL M. WALTERS, J.C.L.

Advocate—VACANT.

Promoter of Justice—Very Rev. ROBERT J. HOSPODAR, J.C.L.

Notaries—Rev. GARY J. MENSINGER; Very Rev. GREGORY J. NOGA, M.A.; Rev. EDWARD SEMKO; Mrs. MAUREEN FRENCH; Mrs. DIANE RABIEJ.

Commissions, Departments and Institutions

Building and Properties Commission—Very Revs. MICHAEL MONDIK, Chm.; JAMES HAYER.

Cemeteries Commission—Rev. Msgr. JOHN T. SEKELLICK, J.C.L., Chm.

Clergy Continued Education—VACANT.

Commission for Ecumenism—Very Rev. EDWARD J. HIGGINS, Chm.

Communications and Telecommunications—Very Rev. JAMES HAYER.

Evangelization—Revs. JOSEPH BERTHA, Ph.D., Chm.;

JOHN S. CUSTER, S.T.D.; Very Revs. MICHAEL MONDIK; JOHN G. BASARAB, M.A.; CONAN H. TIMONEY, Ph.D.

Respect Life—Very Rev. ROBERT J. HOSPODAR, J.C.L., Dir.; Rev. G. SCOTT BOGHOSSIAN, Asst. Dir.

Family Life—Rev. Msgr. JOHN T. SEKELLICK, J.C.L., Dir.

Eparchial Historian—Very Rev. ROBERT J. HOSPODAR, J.C.L.

Eparchial Liturgy and Art Commission—Very Rev. MICHAEL MONDIK, Chm.

Eparchial Music Commission—Mr. ELIAS ZAREVA, Member & Representative.

Eparchial Newspaper— "The Eastern Catholic Life" Very Rev. JAMES HAYER, Editor; Mrs. DIANE RABIEJ, Assoc. Editor. Tel: 973-890-7794.

Office for Eastern Christian Formation (formerly: Office of Religious Education)—Very Rev. GREGORY J. NOGA, M.A., Dir.

Secretariat for Youth—Mrs. ANDREA BABILYA, Moderator.

Retirement Plan Board—Very Rev. ROBERT J. HOSPODAR, J.C.L., Chm.; Mr. BERT REIMANN, Treas.; Revs. MICHAEL J. YURISTA; HARRY P. UNTEREINER, Sec.; JOSEPH BERTHA, Ph.D.; GARY J. MENSINGER; PETER M. DONISH; MICHAEL KERESTES, Vice Chm.; SALVATORE A. PIGNATO; JOHN J. CIGAN, J.C.B.

Saint Nicholas Shrine - Carpathian Village—Very Rev. MICHAEL SALNICKY, Dir., Mailing Address: P.O. Box 616, Canadensis, PA 18325. Tel: 570-595-3265; Fax: 570-595-6177.

Vocations—Rev. SALVATORE A. PIGNATO.

Priesthood & Diaconate Formation Programs—Very Rev. EDWARD G. CIMBALA, D.Min., Dir.

Eastern Catholic Associates— Publication: "God With Us" *445 Lackawanna Ave., Woodland Park, 07424.*

Safe Environment Program—Rev. DAVID J. BARATELLI, Coord. Email: fr.dave.ewr@juno.com.

Victims Advocate—Mrs. MAUREEN DADDONA, Ph.D. Tel: 516-623-6446. National Child Abuse Hotline: Tel: 800-442-4453.

CLERGY, PARISHES, MISSIONS AND PAROCHIAL SCHOOLS

STATE OF NEW JERSEY

PASSAIC, PASSAIC CO., ST. MICHAEL CATHEDRAL, [CEM] Very Rev. Marcel Szabo; Rev. Jody Baran.
Res.: 96 First St., 07055. Tel: 973-777-2553; Fax: 973-777-9474.
Chapel— 415 Lackawanna Ave., 07424. Tel: 973-256-0134; Fax: 973-777-9474.

BAYONNE, HUDSON CO., ST. JOHN THE BAPTIST Rev. Michael J. Yurista.
Res.: 15 E. 26th St., 07002. Tel: 201-339-1840; Fax: 201-339-6255.

CARTERET, MIDDLESEX CO., ST. ELIAS Rev. Edward Semko.
Res.: 42 Cooke Ave., 07008. Tel: 732-541-5213; Fax: 732-541-9637.

DUNELLEN, MIDDLESEX CO., ST. NICHOLAS, Administered from Nativity, East Brunswick, NJ.
Res.: 121 Madison Ave., 08812. Tel: 732-968-3337.

EAST BRUNSWICK, MIDDLESEX CO., NATIVITY OF OUR LORD, Closed. For inquiries for parish records contact the chancery. Rev. Gregory Hosler, Admin.
Res.: 700 Old Bridge Tpke., 08816. Tel: 732-238-0865; Fax: 732-238-2950.

EDISON, MIDDLESEX CO., ST. NICHOLAS, Closed. For inquiries for parish records, please contact the chancery.

ELIZABETH, UNION CO., SS. PETER AND PAUL, Administered from St. George's, Linden, NJ.
Res.: 316 First Ave., 07206. Tel: 908-486-6500; Fax: 908-486-6523.

FLANDERS, MORRIS CO., HOLY WISDOM, Administered from St. Michael Cathedral, Passaic, NJ.
Res.: 197 Emmans Rd., 07836. Tel: 973-584-0414.

HILLSBOROUGH TOWNSHIP, SOMERSET CO., ST. MARY'S Very Rev. Edward G. Cimbala.
Res.: 1900 Brooks Blvd., 08844. Tel: 908-725-0615; Fax: 908-725-9615.

JERSEY CITY, HUDSON CO., ST. MARY'S, Administered from St. John the Baptist, Bayonne, NJ.
Res.: 231 Pacific Ave., 07304. Tel: 201-333-2975.

LINDEN, UNION CO., ST. GEORGE'S Rev. G. Scott Boghosian.
Res.: 417 McCandless St., 07036. Tel: 908-486-6500; Fax: 908-486-6523.

MAHWAH, BERGEN CO., HOLY SPIRIT, Administered from St. Michael Cathedral, Passaic, NJ. , Mailing Address: c/o 96 First St., Passaic, 07055.
Church: Island Rd. at Church St., 07430.

NEW BRUNSWICK, MIDDLESEX CO., ST. JOSEPH Rev. Harry P. Untereiner.
Res.: 30 High St., 08901. Tel: 732-545-1686.

NEWARK, ESSEX CO., ST. GEORGE, Administered from St. John the Baptist, Bayonne, NJ.
Res.: 214 Warwick St., 07105. Tel: 973-589-7202; Fax: 973-589-7202.

PERTH AMBOY, MIDDLESEX CO.
1—ST. MICHAEL, [CEM] Rev. Martin Vavrak (Ukraine), Eparchy of Mukacevo, Ukraine.
Res.: 401 Hall Ave., 08861. Tel: 732-826-0792; Fax: 732-826-7993.
2—ST. NICHOLAS, [CEM] Rev. Martin Vavrak (Ukraine), Admin.
Church: 320 Washington St., 08861. Tel: 732-442-0418.

PHILLIPSBURG, WARREN CO., SS. PETER AND PAUL Very Rev. Peter J. Hosak, Admin.
Res.: 723 S. Main St., 08865. Tel: 908-454-5482; Fax: 908-859-6174.

RAHWAY, UNION CO., ST. THOMAS THE APOSTLE Very Rev. Michael Mondik.
Res.: 1410 Church St., 07065. Tel: 732-382-5300; Fax: 732-382-3265.

ROEBLING, BURLINGTON CO., ST. NICHOLAS, [CEM], Administered from St. Mary's, Trenton, NJ.
Res.: 191 Norman Ave., 08554. Tel: 609-499-0058; Fax: 609-394-5045.

SOMERSET, SOMERSET CO., SS. PETER AND PAUL Rev. Robert Kemeter.
Res.: 285 Hamilton St., 08873. Tel: 732-545-5500; Fax: 732-545-2525.

TOMS RIVER, OCEAN CO., OUR LADY OF PERPETUAL HELP Rev. Charles Yastishock.
Res.: 1937 Church Rd., 08753. Tel: 732-255-6272; Fax: 732-255-6272.

TRENTON, MERCER CO.
1—ST. MARY, [CEM] Very Rev. Gregory J. Noga.
Res.: 411 Adeline St., 08611. Tel: 609-394-5004; Fax: 609-394-5045.
2—ST. NICHOLAS, Closed. For parish records contact St. Mary of the Assumption, Trenton, NJ.

STATE OF CONNECTICUT

BRIDGEPORT, FAIRFIELD CO., HOLY TRINITY, Closed. For inquiries for parish records contact the chancery.

DANBURY, FAIRFIELD CO., ST. NICHOLAS Rev. John J. Cigan.
Res.: 13 Pembroke Rd., CT 06811. Tel: 203-743-1106; Fax: 203-743-5326.

MERIDEN, NEW HAVEN CO., ST. NICHOLAS OF MYRA, Administered from St. Nicholas, Danbury, CT., Mailing Address: c/o 13 Pembroke Rd., Danbury, CT 06810.
Church: 89 Summer St., CT 06450. Tel: 203-743-1106.

NEW BRITAIN, HARTFORD CO., HOLY TRINITY, [CEM] Rev. Frank A. Hanincik, Admin.
Res.: 121 Beaver St., CT 06051. Tel: 860-229-2531; Fax: 860-827-0564.

TRUMBULL, FAIRFIELD CO., ST. JOHN THE BAPTIST Rev. Frank A. Hanincik.
Res.: 100 St. John's Dr., CT 06611. Tel: 203-377-5967; Fax: 203-377-5968.

STATE OF FLORIDA

COCONUT CREEK, BROWARD CO., OUR LADY OF THE SIGN Rev. Michael Kane.
Res.: 7311 Lyons Rd., FL 33073. Tel: 954-429-0056.

FORT PIERCE, PORT ST. LUCIE CO., SS. CYRIL AND METHODIUS Rev. Michael Sopoliga, Admin.
Res.: Tel: 772-595-8862.
Church: 1002 Bahama Ave., FL 34982. Tel: 772-595-1021.

JACKSONVILLE, DUVAL CO., PROTECTION OF THE MOTHER OF GOD, Closed. For parish records, contact Holy Dormition, Ormond Beach, FL.

LAKE WORTH, DUVAL CO., HOLY APOSTLES, Closed. For parish records contact St. Basil, Miami, FL.

MIAMI, DADE CO., ST. BASIL (1966) Very Rev. Peter Lickman.
Res.: 1475 N.E. 199 St., FL 33179-5162. Tel: 305-651-0991; Fax: 786-320-5126.

NEW PORT RICHEY, PASCO CO., ST. ANNE'S Rev. Michael Krulak.
Church: 7120 Massachusetts Ave., FL 34653. Tel: 727-849-1190.

NORTH FORT MYERS, LEE CO., ALL SAINTS BYZANTINE CATHOLIC, Administered from St. Basil's, Miami, FL., Mailing Address: c/o 1475 N.E. 199 St., Miami, FL 33179. Tel: 305-651-0991.
Res.: 10291 Bayshore Rd., FL 33917. Fax: 786-320-5126.

ORLANDO, ORANGE CO., ST. NICHOLAS OF MYRA Rev. Salvatore A. Pignato.
Res.: 5135 Sand Lake Rd., FL 32819. Tel: 407-351-0133; Fax: 407-351-8886.

ORMOND BEACH, VOLUSIA CO., HOLY DORMITION, Administered from St. Nicholas of Myra, Orlando, FL. Rev. Vincent M. Brady.
Mailing Address: 5135 Sand Lake Rd., Orlando, FL 32819.
Church: 17 Buckskin Ln., FL 32174. Tel: 386-677-8704; Fax: 386-677-8704.

ST. PETERSBURG, PINELLAS CO., ST. THERESE Very Rev. Robert Evancho.
Res.: 4236 13th Ave. N., Saint Petersburg, FL 33713. Tel: 727-323-4022; Fax: 727-323-8351.
Convent—Sisters of Saint Basil the Great, 1200 37th St. N., FL 33713. Tel: 727-322-0003.

STATE OF GEORGIA

ROSWELL, FULTON CO., EPIPHANY BYZANTINE CHURCH Rev. Philip P. Scott.
Res.: 2030 Old Alabama Rd., GA 30076. Tel: 770-993-0973; Fax: 770-993-2419.

STATE OF MARYLAND

BALTIMORE, BALTIMORE CO., PATRONAGE OF THE MOTHER OF GOD Very Rev. Conan H. Timoney.
Church: 1260 Stevens Ave., MD 21227. Tel: 410-247-4936; Fax: 410-247-1542.
Mission—St. Francis Abingdon, Harford Co., MD.
Mission—St. Ann's Hagerstown, Washington Co., MD.

BELTSVILLE, PRINCE GEORGE'S CO., ST. GREGORY OF NYSSA Rev. Michael Kerestes.
Res.: 12420 Old Gunpowder Rd. Spur, MD 20705. Tel: 301-953-9323; Fax: 301-953-1529.

STATE OF MASSACHUSETTS

SOUTH HADLEY, HAMPSHIRE CO., ST. MICHAEL'S, Closed. For inquiries for parish records contact the chancery.

STATE OF NEW YORK

AMHERST, ERIE CO., ST. STEPHEN'S, Closed. For inquiries for parish records contact the chancery.

BINGHAMTON, BROOME CO., HOLY SPIRIT, [CEM] Rev. Peter Tomas.
Res.: 360 Clinton St., NY 13905. Tel: 607-797-2122; Fax: 607-797-2167.

BROOKLYN, KINGS CO., ST. ELIAS, Closed. For inquiries for parish records please contact St. Mary's, New York., Mailing Address: c/o 246 E. 15th St., New York, NY 10003.

ENDICOTT, BROOME CO., SS. PETER AND PAUL'S, [CEM], Administered from Holy Spirit, Binghamton, NY., Mailing Address: c/o 360 Clinton St., Binghamton, NY 13905.
Church: 106 N. Rogers Ave., NY 13763. Tel: 607-797-2122.

GRANVILLE, WASHINGTON CO., SS. PETER AND PAUL, [CEM], Administered from St. Mary's, New York, NY., Mailing Address: c/o 246 E. 15th St., New York, NY 10003. Tel: 212-677-0516. In Res., Rev. Harold R. Stockert (Retired).
Church: 2 Park Ave., NY 12832.

NEW YORK, NEW YORK CO.
1—EXALTATION OF HOLY CROSS, Administered from St. Mary's, New York, NY., Mailing Address: 246 E. 15th St., NY 10003.
Church: 323 E. 82nd St., NY 10028. Tel: 914-681-0659.
2—ST. MARY'S Very Rev. Robert J. Hospodar.
Res.: 246 E. 15th St., NY 10003. Tel: 212-677-0516; Fax: 212-260-6071.

OLEAN, CATTARAGUS CO., ST. MARY'S Rev. Leonard A. Martin, S.J., Admin.
Church: 718 Fountain St., NY 14760. Tel: 716-688-9290.

PEEKSKILL, WESTCHESTER CO., SS. PETER AND PAUL Rev. John J. Cigan, Admin.; Rev. Msgr. Robert Senetsky, Pastor Emeritus (Retired).
Res.: 705 Shenandoah Ave., NY 10566. Tel: 914-737-8249; Fax: 914-737-8438.

SMITHTOWN, SUFFOLK CO., RESURRECTION, [CEM] Rev. John S. Custer.
Res.: 225 Ellison Ave., Westbury, NY 11590. Tel: 631-759-6083.
Edgewater at Mayflower, NY 11787.

WESTBURY, NASSAU CO., ST. ANDREW THE APOSTLE Rev. John S. Custer, Admin.
Church: 225 Ellison Ave., NY 11590. Tel: 631-759-6083.

WHITE PLAINS, WESTCHESTER CO., ST. NICHOLAS OF MYRA Very Rev. Robert J. Hospodar, Admin. In Res., Rev. Vasyl Chepelskyy (Ukraine), (Eparchy of Buchach, Ukraine).
Res. & Church: 768 North St., NY 10605. Tel: 914-681-0659.

YONKERS, WESTCHESTER CO., ST. NICHOLAS OF MYRA, Closed. For inquiries for parish records please contact St. Nicholas of Myra, White Plains, New York., Mailing Address: 768 North St., White Plains, NY 10605.

STATE OF NORTH CAROLINA

CARY, WAKE CO., SS. CYRIL & METHODIUS BYZANTINE CATHOLIC Rev. Richard Rohrer.
Res.: 2510 Piney Plains Rd., NC 27518. Tel:

919-851-9266; Fax: 919-233-3997.

STATE OF PENNSYLVANIA

ALLENTOWN, LEHIGH CO.

1—ST. ANDREW THE APOSTLE, Closed. For parish records, contact St. Michael, Allentown.

2—ST. MICHAEL Rev. J. Michael Venditti (MET).
Res.: 156 Green St., PA 18102. Tel: 610-432-6773; Fax: 610-423-6702.

BEAVER MEADOWS, CARBON CO., SS. PETER AND PAUL, [CEM] Rev. James J. Demko.
Res.: P.O. Box 206, PA 18216. Tel: 570-455-1442; Fax: 570-455-7144.

BETHLEHEM, NORTHAMPTON CO., SS. PETER AND PAUL Very Rev. Peter J. Hosak.
Res.: 1140 Johnston Dr., PA 18017. Tel: 610-867-2322; Fax: 610-867-7274.

BROCKTON, SCHUYLKILL CO., ST. MARY'S, [CEM], Administered from St. Mary's, Mahanoy City, PA., Mailing Address: c/o 621 Mahanoy Ave., Mahanoy City, PA 17948.
Church: Green St., PA 17925.

CLARKS SUMMIT, LACKAWANNA CO., TRANSFIGURATION, Closed. For parish records contact St. Mary, Scranton, PA.

COATESVILLE, CHESTER CO., ST. MARY'S, Administered from St. Michael, Mont Clare, PA.
Church: 88 Gap Rd., PA 19320.

DUNMORE, LACKAWANNA CO., ST. MICHAEL, [CEM] Rev. Robert W. Lozinski, C.S.C.
Res.: 511 E. Drinker St., PA 18512. Tel: 570-344-2521; Fax: 570-344-4535.

FOREST CITY, SUSQUEHANNA CO., ST. JOHN THE BAPTIST, [CEM], Administered from Holy Ghost, Jessup, PA., Mailing Address: c/o 313 First Ave., Jessup, PA 18434. Tel: 570-489-2353; Fax: 570-489-7049.
Church: 306 Susquehanna St., PA 18421.

FREELAND, LUZERNE CO., ST. MARY'S, [CEM] Rev. Peter M. Donish, Admin.; Rev. Msgr. Nicholas I. Puhak, Pastor Emeritus (Retired).
Res.: 643 Fern St., PA 18224. Tel: 570-636-0700; Fax: 570-636-1955.

GLEN LYON, LUZERNE CO., ST. MICHAEL, Closed. For parish records contact St. Mary's, Kingston, PA.

HARRISBURG, DAUPHIN CO., ST. ANN Rev. Michael G. Popson.
Res.: 5408 Locust Ln., PA 17109. Tel: 717-652-1415; Fax: 888-356-3080.

HAZLETON, LUZERNE CO.

1—ST. JOHN THE BAPTIST CHURCH, [CEM] Rev. Carmen Scuderi, O.F.M.
Res.: 5 E. 20th St., PA 18201. Tel: 570-454-1142; Fax: 570-454-6120.

2—ST. MARY'S Rev. Peter M. Donish.
Res. & Church: 227 E. Beech St., PA 18201. Tel: 570-455-3232; Fax: 570-455-5654.

HILLTOWN, BUCKS CO., BYZANTINE CATHOLIC MISSION OF BUCKS COUNTY, PA, Closed. For mission records contact Holy Ghost, Philadelphia, PA.

JESSUP, LACKAWANNA CO., HOLY GHOST, [CEM] Rev. Msgr. John T. Sekellick.
Res.: 313 First Ave., PA 18434. Tel: 570-489-2353; Fax: 570-489-7049.

KINGSTON, LUZERNE CO., ST. MARY'S, [CEM] Rev. Mykhaylo Prodanets, Eparchy of Mukachevo, Ukraine.
Res.: 321 Chestnut Ave., PA 18704. Tel: 570-287-0282; Fax: 570-283-0464.

LANSFORD, CARBON CO., ST. JOHN THE BAPTIST, [CEM] Very Rev. Peter J. Hosak, Admin. In Res., Rev. Ronald J. Hatton.
Church: 116 E. Bertsch St., PA 18232. Tel: 570-645-2640; Fax: 570-645-8718.

LEVITTOWN, BUCKS CO., OUR LADY OF PERPETUAL HELP Very Rev. Edward J. Higgins, Admin.; Rev. Myron M. Badnerosky, Pastor Emeritus.
Res.: 1787 Woodburne Rd., PA 19056. Tel: 215-945-5122.

LOPEZ, SULLIVAN CO., SS. PETER AND PAUL, [CEM] Closed. For inquiries for parish records please contact St. Mary's, Scranton, PA.

MAHANOY CITY, SCHUYLKILL CO., ST. MARY'S, [CEM] Rev. James Carroll, O.F.M., Admin.
Res.: 621 W. Mahanoy Ave., PA 17948. Tel: 570-773-2631; Fax: 570-773-0548.

MCADOO, SCHUYLKILL CO., ST. MICHAEL, [CEM] Revs. Peter M. Donish, Admin.; George A. Bujnak, Pastor Emeritus (Retired).
Res.: 17 E. Blaine St., PA 18237. Tel: 570-929-1062; Fax: 570-929-3239.

MINERSVILLE, SCHUYLKILL CO., SS. PETER AND PAUL, [CEM] Very Rev. Francis M. Twardzik, S.D.B.
Res.: 107 S. Fourth St., PA 17954. Tel: 570-544-2074; Fax: 570-544-9441.

MONT CLARE, MONTGOMERY CO., ST. MICHAEL, [CEM] Rev. James Badeaux.
Church: 203 Jacob St., PA 19453. Tel: 610-933-2819; Fax: 610-935-9460.

NANTICOKE, LUZERNE CO., ST. MARY'S, Closed. (Hanover) For inquiries for parish records contact St. John's, Wilkes-Barre, PA.

NESQUEHONING, CARBON CO., ST. MARY'S, [CEM], Administered from St. John the Baptist, Lansford, PA.
Church: 141 W. High St., PA 18240.

OLD FORGE, LACKAWANNA CO., ST. NICHOLAS, [CEM] Rev. Gary J. Mensinger.
Res.: 140 Church St., PA 18518. Tel: 570-457-3042; Fax: 570-457-1906.

PALMERTON, CARBON CO., SS. PETER AND PAUL, Administered from St. Michael's, Allentown, PA., Mailing Address: c/o 156 Green St., Allentown, PA 18102.
Church: 142 Lafayette Ave., PA 18071.

PHILADELPHIA, PHILADELPHIA CO.

1—HOLY GHOST Very Rev. Edward J. Higgins.
Res.: 2310 S. 24th St., PA 19145. Tel: 215-334-5129; Fax: 215-334-1797.

2—HOLY TRINITY, Administered from Holy Ghost, Philadelphia, PA., Mailing Address: c/o 2310 S. 24th St., PA 19145.
Church: 6801 N. 10th St., PA 19126. Tel: 215-548-2837.

PITTSTON, LUZERNE CO., ST. MICHAEL, [CEM] Rev. Joseph Bertha.
Res.: 205 N. Main St., PA 18640. Tel: 570-654-4564; Fax: 570-654-5349.

POCONO SUMMIT, MONROE CO., ST. NICHOLAS Very Rev. Michael Salnicky, Admin.
Rte. 940 & Commerce St., P.O. Box 515, PA 18346. Tel: 570-839-8090; Fax: 570-595-6177.

POTTSTOWN, MONTGOMERY CO., ST. JOHN THE BAPTIST, [CEM] Rev. Nicholas DeProspero.
Res.: 301 Cherry St., PA 19464. Tel: 610-326-1877; Fax: 610-326-1890.

ST. CLAIR, SCHUYLKILL CO., ST. MARY'S, [CEM], Administered from SS. Peter and Paul, Minersville, PA., Mailing Address: c/o 107 S. 4th St., Minersville, PA 17954.
Church: 131 S. Morris St., PA 17970.

SCRANTON, LACKAWANNA CO.

1—ST. JOHN THE BAPTIST, [CEM], Administered from St. Mary's, Scranton, PA., Mailing Address: c/o 310 Mifflin Ave., PA 18503. Tel: 570-342-8429; Fax: 570-342-6773.
Church: 310 Broadway, PA 18505.

2—ST. MARY'S, [CEM] Rev. Leonard A. Martin, S.J.
Res.: 310 Mifflin Ave., PA 18503. Tel: 570-342-8429; Fax: 570-342-6773.

SHEPPTON, SCHUYLKILL CO., ST. MARY'S, [CEM], Administered from SS. Peter and Paul, Beaver Meadows., Mailing Address: c/o P.O. Box 206, Beaver Meadows, PA 18216.

SWOYERSVILLE, LUZERNE CO., ST. NICHOLAS, [CEM], Administered from St. Michael, Pittston, PA., Mailing Address: c/o 205 N. Main St., Pittston, PA 18640. Tel: 570-654-4564; Fax: 570-654-5349.
Church: 271 Tripp St., PA 18704.

TAYLOR, LACKAWANNA CO., ST. MARY'S, [CEM], Administered from St. Nicholas, Old Forge., Mailing Address: c/o 140 Church St., Old Forge, PA 18518.
Church: 700 Oak St., PA 18517. Tel: 570-457-3042.

WILKES-BARRE, LUZERNE CO.

1—ST. JOHN'S, Administered from St. Mary's, Kingston, PA.
Res.: 526 Church St., PA 18702. Tel: 570-825-4338; Fax: 570-825-0786.

2—ST. MARY'S, [CEM] Very Rev. James Hayer.
Res.: 695 N. Main St., PA 18705. Tel: 570-822-6028; Fax: 570-822-5423.

WILLIAMSTOWN, DAUPHIN CO., HOLY SPIRIT, [CEM] Closed. For inquiries for parish records contact SS. Peter and Paul, Minersville, PA.

STATE OF VIRGINIA

ANNANDALE, FAIRFAX CO., EPIPHANY OF OUR LORD Very Rev. John G. Basarab.
3410 Woodburn Rd., VA 22003. Tel: 703-573-3986; Fax: 703-573-0344.
Mission—Mother of God Community School 20501 Goshen Rd., Gaithersburg, MD 20879.

WILLIAMSBURG, YORK CO., ASCENSION OF OUR LORD Rev. Alex Shuter, Archeparchy of Lviv, Ukraine.
Mailing Address: P.O. Box 5096, VA 23188. Tel: 757-253-5641; Fax: 757-253-9423.
Church: 114 Palace Ln., VA 23185. Tel: 757-220-8098.
Mission—Our Lady of Perpetual Help 216 S. Parliament Dr., Virginia Beach, Virginia Beach Co., VA 23462. Tel: 757-456-0809.

Special or Other Diocesan Assignment:
Rev.—
DeFronzo, Anthony P.

On Duty Outside Diocese:
Revs.—
Fulton, Eugene J., Larchmont Trinity Retreat, One Pryer Manor Rd., Larchmont, NY 10538. Tel: 914-632-3743
Hamperzonian, Jerry, Chap., VA Medical Center, 3350 Lajolla Village Dr., San Diego, CA 92161. Tel: 619-582-5722
Siroki, David

Leave of Absence:
Revs.—
Davidowich, Glenn M.
Drucker, James N. (Retired)
Kapron, Alan
Malitz, George M.
Mitchko, James
Slesinski, Robert F., Ph.D.
Woytek, Robert

Retired:
Rev. Msgrs.—
Puhak, Nicholas I., 643 Fern St., Freeland, PA 18224. Tel: 570-636-0700
Senetsky, Robert, J.C.D., 705 Shenandoah Ave., Peekskill, NY 10566.
Revs.—
Badnerosky, Myron, 1787 Woodburne Rd., Levittown, PA 19056.
Bitsko, Daniel J.
Brown, Charles, M.D., Santa Teresita del Nino Jesus, 2 Poniente #2714, Puebla CP 72140 Mexico. Tel: 011-22-48-38-78
Bujnak, George A., 17 E. Blaine St., McAdoo, PA 18237.
Eles, Joseph, 150 Horizons E., Apt. 305, Boynton Beach, FL 33435. Tel: 407-731-2682
Gera, Francis
Kraynak, Nicholas, 328 S. Belle Vista Ave., Youngstown, OH 44509.
Petruska, Christopher, 15544 Bellflower Blvd., Apt. C, Bellflower, CA 90706.
Skurla, Robert J., c/o Little Sisters of the Poor, 110-30 221 St., Queen of Peace Rm. 215, Queens Village, NY 11429.
Stockert, Harold R., 2 Park Ave., Granville, NY 12832.
Tigyer, Paul, P.O. Box 658, Hamlin, PA 18427. Tel: 717-689-2153
Zeyack, John, S.T.L., 53 Blue Ridge Dr., Brick, 08724.

Permanent Deacons:
Behrens, Robert
Daddona, Nicholas
Dunlop, Richard
Foran, Lawrence
Frey, Edward
Guze, John G.
Hook, Thomas
Koscinski, Mark
Kotlar, Anthony, (Leave of Absence)
Kubik, Alexander
Laskowski, Charles J.
McDonnell, Gerald E.
Opalka, Michael
Pataki, Michael
Pekarik, Elmer
Russo, Stephen
Senoyuit, Michael, III
Soroka, Basil
Sotack, Nicholas
Szewczyk, William
Thomas, David
Tizio, William, (Retired)
Tokarcsik, George M.
Vanisko, Thomas L.
Wolfe, Daniel
Worlinsky, Lawrence

INSTITUTIONS LOCATED IN THE DIOCESE

[A] MONASTERIES

MATAWAN. *Basilian Fathers of Mariapoch,* 360 Monastery Ln., 07747-9703. Tel: 732-566-8445; Fax: 732-566-8762. Very Rev. Joseph J. Erdei, O.S.B.M., Supr.; Rev. Lawrence Robert Wolf, O.S.B.M.

SYBERTSVILLE, PA. *Holy Dormition Friary,* P.O. Box 270, PA 18251. Tel: 570-788-1212; Fax: 570-788-2431. Revs. Carmen Scuderi, O.F.M.; Anthony Skurla, O.F.M.; James Carroll, O.F.M.; Laurian Janicki, O.F.M., Guardian; Jerome Wolbert, O.F.M.; Bro. Augustine Paulik, O.F.M.

[B] CONVENTS AND RESIDENCES FOR SISTERS

SUGARLOAF, PA. *Holy Annunciation Monastery*, 403 W. County Rd., PA 18249. Tel: 570-788-1205; Fax: 570-788-3329. Discalced Carmelite Nuns of the Byzantine Rite Nuns with Solemn Vows 12.

WILKES-BARRE, PA. *Sisters of Saint Basil The Great Saint Mary of the Assumption Convent*, 522 Madison St., Wilkes Barre, PA 18705. Tel: 570-824-3973.

[C] SHRINES AND SPIRITUAL RENEWAL CENTERS

CANADENSIS, PA. *Carpathian Village* 802 Snow Hill Rd., Cresco, PA 18326. Tel: 570-595-3265; Fax: 570-595-6177. Very Rev. Michael Salnicky, Dir.

[D] MISCELLANEOUS

WEST PATERSON. *Eastern Catholic Associates*, 445 Lackawanna Ave., 07424. Tel: 973-890-7777; Fax: 973-890-7175.

God with Us Publications Most Revs. John M. Kudrick, Pres.; Richard S. Seminack, Sec.

RELIGIOUS INSTITUTES OF MEN REPRESENTED IN THE DIOCESE

For further details refer to the corresponding bracketed number in the Religious Institutes of Men or Women section.

[0520]—*Franciscan Friars*—O.F.M.

[0180]—*Order of St. Basil the Great*—O.S.B.M.

RELIGIOUS INSTITUTES OF WOMEN REPRESENTED IN THE DIOCESE

[0420]—*Discalced Carmelite Nuns (Byzantine Rite)*—O.C.D.

[3730]—*Sisters of the Order of St. Basil the Great*—O.S.B.M.

NECROLOGY

✠ Pataki, Most Rev. Andrew, Perth Amboy, NJ St. Nicholas—Died Dec. 8, 2011

† Paulshock, Emil, (Retired)—Died Feb. 15, 2011

† Safko, Steven, Phillipsburg, NJ SS. Peter and Paul—Died Dec. 30, 2011

An asterisk (*) denotes an organization that has established tax-exempt status directly with the IRS and is not covered by the USCCB Group Ruling.

Metropolitan Archeparchy of Philadelphia Ukrainian

Most Reverend

STEFAN SOROKA

Archbishop of Philadelphia Ukrainian; ordained June 13, 1982; appointed Auxiliary Bishop of Winnipeg (Ukrainian) March 29, 1996; ordained Auxiliary Bishop of Winnipeg (Ukrainian) June 13, 1996; appointed Archbishop of Philadelphia Ukrainian November 29, 2000; installed Archbishop of Philadelphia Ukrainian February 27, 2001.

Most Reverend

JOHN BURA

Auxiliary Bishop of Philadelphia Ukrainian; ordained February 14, 1971; appointed Auxiliary Bishop of Philadelphia Ukrainian and Titular Bishop of Limisa January 3, 2006; ordained February 21, 2006; appointed Apostolic Administrator of the Eparchy of St. Josaphat in Parma July 29, 2009.

Most Reverend

STEPHEN SULYK

Archbishop Emeritus of Philadelphia Ukrainian; ordained June 14, 1952; appointed Archbishop of Philadelphia Ukrainian December 29, 1980; ordained March 1, 1981; retired November 29, 2000.

Chancery Office: 827 N. Franklin St., Philadelphia, PA 19123-2097. Tel: 215-627-0143; Fax: 215-627-0377.

Email: ukrmet@catholic.org

ESTABLISHED MAY 28, 1913.

The jurisdiction of the Metropolitan Archdiocese of Philadelphia includes the District of Columbia, the States of Virginia, Maryland, Delaware, New Jersey and eastern Pennsylvania to the eastern boundaries of the following Counties: Potter, Clinton, Center, Mifflin, Huntington and Fulton. With regard to persons, his subjects are all Catholics of the Byzantine Rite: 1. Who immigrated to this country from Galicia, Bucovina and other Ukrainian provinces; 2. Who descend from such persons (can. 755); 3. Women married to men referable to 1. and 2. if they comply with can. 98, n. 4; 4. Who in accordance with can. 98, n. 3 changed their Rite; 5. Converts to the Catholic Church of the Byzantine Rite; 6. And in fact all other Catholics of the Byzantine Rite who are attached to parishes subject to the jurisdiction of the Archbishop.

For legal titles of parishes and archdiocesan institutions, consult the Chancery Office.

STATISTICAL OVERVIEW

Personnel	
Archbishops	1
Retired Archbishops	1
Priests: Diocesan Active in Diocese	39
Priests: Retired, Sick or Absent	9
Number of Diocesan Priests	48
Religious Priests in Diocese	5
Total Priests in Diocese	53
Extern Priests in Diocese	6
Permanent Deacons in Diocese	7
Total Sisters	49
Parishes	
Parishes	66
With Resident Pastor:	
Resident Diocesan Priests	41
Resident Religious Priests	2
Without Resident Pastor:	
Administered by Priests	23
Professional Ministry Personnel:	
Sisters	33
Lay Ministers	2
Welfare	
Homes for the Aged	2
Total Assisted	279
Educational	
Seminaries, Diocesan	1
Students from This Diocese	1
Students from Other Diocese	2
Diocesan Students in Other Seminaries	1
Total Seminarians	2
Colleges and Universities	1
Total Students	969
High Schools, Private	1
Total Students	324
Elementary Schools, Diocesan and Parish	4
Total Students	567
Catechesis/Religious Education:	
High School Students	96
Elementary Students	409
Total Students under Catholic Instruction	2,367
Teachers in the Diocese:	
Priests	2
Sisters	12
Lay Teachers	78
Vital Statistics	
Receptions into the Church:	
Infant Baptism Totals	232
Minor Baptism Totals	7
Adult Baptism Totals	3
Received into Full Communion	9
First Communions	191
Confirmations	233
Marriages:	
Catholic	46
Interfaith	26
Total Marriages	72
Deaths	519
Total Catholic Population	15,779

Former Bishops—Most Revs. STEPHEN SOTER ORTYNSKY, O.S.B.M., D.D., First Ukrainian Catholic Bishop of the United States; ord. July 18, 1891; cons. May 12, 1907; died March 24, 1916; CONSTANTINE BOHACHEVSKY, D.D., S.T.D., appt. Bishop in the United States, May 20, 1924; appt. Metropolitan Archbishop of the Philadelphia Archeparchy, Byzantine Rite, Aug. 6, 1958; cons. June 15, 1924; died Jan. 6, 1961; AMBROSE SENYSHYN, O.S.B.M., D.D., appt. Auxiliary Bishop to the Philadelphia Bishop, July 6, 1942; appt. Exarch of Stamford, July 20, 1956; appt. Eparch of Stamford, Nov. 1, 1958; appt. Metropolitan Archbishop of Philadelphia, Aug. 14, 1961; died Sept. 11, 1976; JOSEPH M. SCHMONDIUK, D.D., appt. Titular Bishop of Zeugma and Auxiliary of the Archeparchy of Philadelphia, July 20, 1956; cons. Nov. 8, 1956; transferred to the Diocese of Stamford See, Nov. 9, 1961; appt. Metropolitan Archbishop of Philadelphia, Oct. 1, 1977; died Dec. 25, 1978; His Eminence MYROSLAV CARDINAL LUBACHIVSKY, D.D., appt. Metropolitan Archbishop of Philadelphia, Sept. 21, 1979; appt. Apostolic Administrator of Philadelphia, Oct. 3, 1979; cons. in Rome, Nov. 12, 1979; named Coadjutor Major Archbishop of Lviw, March 24, 1980; transferred to Rome; Assumed position of Major Archbishop of Lviw, Sept. 7, 1984. Created Cardinal, May 25, 1985; died Dec. 14, 2000; Most Rev. STEPHEN SULYK, D.D. (Retired), appt. Archbishop of Philadelphia for Ukrainians and Metropolitan of the Ukrainian Catholic Church in the USA, Dec. 29, 1980; ord. March 1, 1981; retired Nov. 29, 2000.

Protosyncellus—Rev. Msgr. PETER D. WASLO, J.C.L.

Chancellor—Rev. Msgr. PETER D. WASLO, J.C.L. Tel: 215-627-0143. Email: chancellor@catholic.org.

Vice Chancellor—Very Rev. ANDRIY RABIY, J.C.L.

Secretary to the Archbishop—Sr. LYDIA ANN SAWKA, O.S.B.M.

Chancery Office—827 N. Franklin St., Philadelphia, 19123-2097. Tel: 215-627-0143; Fax: 215-627-0377.

College of Archeparchial Consultors—Rev. Msgr. PETER D. WASLO, J.C.L.; Very Rev. ANDRIY RABIY, J.C.L.; Very Rev. Archpriest JOHN M. FIELDS; Very Revs. IVAN DEMKIV; ROBERT HITCHENS; JOSEPH SZUPA.

Presbyteral Council—Rev. Msgr. PETER D. WASLO, J.C.L.; Very Revs. ANDRIY RABIY, J.C.L.; IVAN DEMKIV; ROBERT HITCHENS; Very Rev. Archpriest DANIEL TROYAN; Very Rev. VOLODYMYR POPYK; Very Rev. Archpriest DANIEL GUROVICH; Very Revs. NESTOR IWASIW; ROMAN PITULA; MARK FESNIAK; WASYL KHARUK; JOHN CIURPITA; JOSEPH SZUPA; Very Rev. Archpriest JOHN M. FIELDS.

Archeparchial Corporation—Most Rev. STEFAN SOROKA, D.D., Ph.D., Pres.; JOHN DROZD, Treas.; Rev. Msgr. PETER D. WASLO, J.C.L., Sec.

Archdiocesan Tribunal—827 N. Franklin St., Philadelphia, 19123. Tel: 215-627-0143. Email: metropolitantribunal@catholic.org.

Judicial Vicar—Rev. Msgr. PETER D. WASLO, J.C.L.

Adjunct Judicial Vicars—Very Rev. Archpriest DANIEL GUROVICH; Revs. PAUL LUNIW, Eparchy of Stamford; RICHARD WHETSTONE, Diocese of Youngstown.

Procurator/Advocate—Very Revs. JOSEPH SZUPA; NESTOR IWASIW.

Auditor—Very Rev. ANDRIY RABIY, J.C.L.

Defender of the Bond—Rev. MYKOLA IVANOV, Ukraine.

Notary—GLORIA LEINART.

Director of Evangelization—Very Rev. Archpriest DANIEL TROYAN.

Archeparchial Council for Economic Affairs—Most Rev. STEFAN SOROKA, D.D., Ph.D.; Rev. Msgr. PETER D. WASLO, J.C.L.; JOHN DROZD; HELEN CHELOC; LEONARD MAZUR; ANDREW FYLYPOWYCH; KEN HUTCHINS; ADRIAN HAWRYLIW; ANNA KERDA; Sr. LYDIA ANN SAWKA, O.S.B.M., Sec.

Financial Officer—JOHN DROZD.

Protopresbyters (Deans)—Rev. Msgr. RONALD P. POPIVCHAK, Ph.D., Lehigh-Schuylkill Valley; Very Revs. IVAN DEMKIV, Philadelphia; JOHN SENIW, North Anthracite; JOSEPH SZUPA, New Jersey; Very Rev. Archpriest JOHN M. FIELDS, South Anthracite; Very Rev. ROBERT HITCHENS, Washington.

Diocesan Offices and Directors

Youth Ministry—VACANT, Dir.

Pro-Life and Family Ministry—Very Rev. TARAS LONCHYNA.

Apostolate—Most Rev. STEFAN SOROKA, D.D., Ph.D.;

JOHN DROZD.

Cemeteries—TARAS HANKEWYCH.

Censor—Rev. Msgr. RONALD P. POPIVCHAK, Ph.D.

Ecumenical Relations—Rev. Msgr. PETER D. WASLO, J.C.L.

Insurance Commission—JOHN DROZD.

Director of Communication—Rev. Msgr. PETER D. WASLO, J.C.L. Email: ukrcomm@yahoo.com.

The Way - Online Newspaper—Web: www.ukrarcheparchy.us. Email: theway@ukrarcheparchy.us. TERESA SIWAK, Editor; Rev. IHOR ROYIK, Asst. Editor; Rev. Msgr. PETER D. WASLO, J.C.L.

Archdiocesan Bulletin—Office: 827 N. Franklin St., Philadelphia, 19123. Rev. Msgr. PETER D. WASLO, J.C.L.; Very Rev. ANDRIY RABIY, J.C.L.

Priests Beneficial Fund—Most Rev. STEFAN SOROKA, D.D., Ph.D., Pres.; Very Rev. Archpriest DANIEL GUROVICH, Sec. & Treas. Board Members: Rev. Archpriest MICHAEL HUTSKO; Very Rev. Archpriest JOHN M. FIELDS; Very Rev. JOHN SENIW; Rev. Msgr. JAMES T. MELNIC; Very Rev. WASYL KHARUK, Alternate Member.

Office of Vocations—Rev. PAUL J. MAKAR, Dir. Tel: 202-529-1177, Ext. 115. Email: ukrvocations@catholic.org.

Archeparchial Seminary Advisory and Admissions Board—Most Rev. STEFAN SOROKA, D.D., Ph.D.; Very Revs. ROBERT HITCHENS; NESTOR IWASIW; ANDRIY RABIY, J.C.L.

Sheptytsky Educational Center—Most Rev. STEFAN SOROKA, D.D., Ph.D.; Very Rev. Archpriest DANIEL TROYAN.

Evangelization Center—Very Rev. Archpriest DANIEL TROYAN.

Department of Religious Education—Very Rev. VOLODYMYR POPYK, Dir. Email: ukrcatecheticaloffice@catholic.org.

Byzantine Church Supplies—Mrs. MYROSLAVA DEMKIV. Tel: 215-627-0660. Email: supplies@ukrarcheparchy.us.

Archeparchial Museum— Treasury of Faith. Tel: 215-627-3389. Email: tofmuseum@catholic.org. Sisters NADIA BARANICK, M.S.M.G.; EVHENIA PRUSNAY, M.S.M.G.; TIMOTHEA KONYU, M.S.M.G.; Very Rev. Archpriest DANIEL TROYAN.

Victim Assistance Coordinator—Very Rev. ANDRIY RABIY, J.C.L. Tel: 215-873-6162. Email: ukrchildprotection@catholic.org.

Deacon Formation—Very Rev. Archpriest JOHN M. FIELDS, Dir.

CLERGY, PARISHES, MISSIONS AND PAROCHIAL SCHOOLS

CITY OF PHILADELPHIA

(PHILADELPHIA COUNTY)

1—IMMACULATE CONCEPTION OF BLESSED VIRGIN MARY, CATHEDRAL, [CEM] Very Rev. Ivan Demkiv; Rev. Myron Myronyuk (Ukraine); Deacon Charles Schultz III.
Res.: 833 N. Franklin St., 19123. Tel: 215-922-2845; Fax: 215-922-4635. Email: cathedralonfranklin@comcast.net. Web: www.ukrcathedral.com.
Mission—St. Nicholas 871 N. 24th St., Philadelphia Co. 19130. Tel: 215-769-3863; Fax: 215-769-2018.
Mission—Our Lady of Fatima Church 2913 Street Rd., Bensalem, 19020.
Chapel—Missionary Sisters of Mother God Convent

2—ST. ANDREW, Closed. For inquiries for parish records contact the Cathedral of the Immaculate Conception, Philadelphia.

3—ANNUNCIATION OF THE B.V.M. (1962) Rev. Ihor Royik.
Res.: 1206 Valley Rd., Melrose Park, 19027-3035. Tel: 215-635-1627; Fax: 215-635-9203. Email: a.b.v.m@comcast.net.
Church: 1204 Valley Rd., Melrose Park, 19027-3035.

4—CHRIST THE KING (1949) Rev. Yaroslav Kurpel.
Res.: 1629 W. Cayuga St., 19140. Tel: 215-455-2416; Fax: 215-455-6614. Email: ctkucc@aol.com.
Catechesis/Religious Program—Maria Kasian, D.R.E.

5—ST. JOSAPHAT'S Rev. Ihor Bloshchynskyy (Ukraine), Admin.
Res.: 6932 Ditman St., 19135. Tel: 215-332-8488; Fax: 215-332-0315. Email: bloshchynskyy@yahoo.com.
School—(Grades K-8), 4521 Longshore Ave., 19135. Tel: 215-332-8008; Fax: 215-332-1876. Christine McIntyre, Prin. Sisters 1; Lay Teachers 12; Students 148.

6—ST. NICHOLAS (1943) Attended by the Cathedral of the Immaculate Conception, Philadelphia.
Res.: 871 North 24th St., 19130. Tel: 215-769-3863; Fax: 215-769-2018.
Church: 24th & Poplar Sts., 19130-1988.

7—PROTECTION OF BLESSED VIRGIN MARY, Closed. For inquiries for parish records please see SS. Peter and Paul, Clifton Heights.

8—SACRED HEART, Closed. For inquiries for parish records contact the chancery.

STATE OF DELAWARE

WILMINGTON, NEW CASTLE CO., ST. NICHOLAS Rev. Volodymyr Klanichka.
Res.: 801 Lea Blvd., DE 19802. Tel: 302-762-5511; Fax: 302-762-5849. Email: stnicholas2@verizon.net. Web: st-nicholas-church.org.

STATE OF MARYLAND

BALTIMORE, BALTIMORE CO., ST. MICHAEL'S, [CEM] Rev. Vasyl Sivinskyi, Admin.
Res.: 2401 Eastern Ave., MD 21224. Tel: 410-675-7557; Fax: 410-732-0839. Email: tserkva@yahoo.com.

CHESAPEAKE CITY, CECIL CO., ST. BASIL THE GREAT, Attended by St. Nicholas, Wilmington., Mailing Address: 801 Lea Blvd., Wilmington, DE 19802.

CURTIS BAY, BALTIMORE CO., SS. PETER AND PAUL, Attended by St. Michael's, Baltimore., Mailing Address: 2401 Eastern Ave., Baltimore, MD 21224.
Church: 1506 Church St., MD 21226-1440.

SILVER SPRING, MONTGOMERY CO., HOLY TRINITY (1980) Very Rev. Taras Lonchyna.
Res.: 16631 New Hampshire Ave., MD 20905-3919. Tel: 301-421-1739; Fax: 301-421-1869.

STATE OF NEW JERSEY

BAYONNE, HUDSON CO., ASSUMPTION B.V.M. (1916) Attended by SS. Peter and Paul, Jersey City., Mailing Address: *c/o SS. Peter and Paul*, 30 Bentley Ave., Jersey City, NJ 07304. Tel: 201-432-3122; Fax: 201-432-0111.
Church: 30 E. 25th St., Box 260, NJ 07002.

CARTERET, MIDDLESEX CO., ST. MARY'S (1949) Rev. Vasyl Vladyka.
719 Roosevelt Ave., NJ 07008. Tel: 732-366-2156.

CHERRY HILL, CAMDEN CO., ST. MICHAEL'S Rev. Ruslan Romanyuk.
Res.: 675 Cooper Landing Rd., NJ 08002. Tel: 856-482-0938; Fax: 609-482-9092. Email: stmichaelucc@comcast.net.

ELIZABETH, UNION CO., ST. VLADIMIR'S (1903) Very Rev. Joseph Szupa.
Res.: 312 Grier Ave., NJ 07202-3310. Tel: 908-352-8823; Fax: 908-352-7648.
Catechesis/Religious Program—Students 12.

GREAT MEADOWS, WARREN CO., ST. NICHOLAS (1923) Attended by Holy Ghost, West Easton, PA. Rev. Petro Zvarych, Admin.
Mailing Address: c/o 315 Fourth St., West Easton, 18042. Tel: 610-252-4266; Fax: 610-252-8533.
Church: Rte. 46, P.O. Box 162, NJ 07838.
Catechesis/Religious Program—Susan McMaster, D.R.E. Students 12.

HILLSIDE, UNION CO., IMMACULATE CONCEPTION (1957) Attended by St. Vladimir, Elizabeth.
Church: Bloy St. and Liberty Ave., NJ 07205.
Catechesis/Religious Program—Joseph Shatynski, D.R.E. Students 13.

JERSEY CITY, HUDSON CO., SS. PETER AND PAUL (1886) Rev. Vasyl Putera.
Res.: 30 Bentley Ave., NJ 07304. Tel: 201-432-3122; Fax: 201-432-0111.
Catechesis/Religious Program—Orest Polishchuk, D.R.E. Students 17.

HILLSBOROUGH, SOMERSET CO., ST. MICHAEL'S (1950) Very Rev. Roman Pitula.
Res.: 63 N. 18th Ave., Manville, NJ 08835. Tel: 908-526-9195; Fax: 908-725-5089.
Church: 1700 Brooks Blvd., NJ 08844.

MARLBORO, MONMOUTH CO., ST. VOLODYMYR'S, Closed. For inquiries for parish records contact the chancery.

MILLVILLE, CUMBERLAND CO., ST. NICHOLAS, [CEM], Attended from St. Stephen, Toms River, NJ. Rev. Oleksandr Dumenko (Ukraine).
Church: 801 Carmel Rd., NJ 08332. Tel: 856-825-4826; Fax: 856-825-4826.

NEW BRUNSWICK, MIDDLESEX CO., NATIVITY OF B.V.M. (1951) Attended by St. Michael, Hillsborough, NJ. Very Rev. Roman Pitula.
Mailing Address: 80 Livingston Ave., NJ 08901.

NEWARK, ESSEX CO., ST. JOHN THE BAPTIST Revs. Leonid Malkov, C.Ss.R.; Andriy Manko, C.Ss.R.; Taras Svirchuk, C.Ss.R.
Res.: 719 Sandford Ave., NJ 07106. Tel: 973-371-1356; Fax: 973-416-0085.
Catechesis/Religious Program—Students 35.

PASSAIC, PASSAIC CO., ST. NICHOLAS Rev. Andriy Dudkevych (Ukraine).
Res.: 60 Holdsworth Ct., NJ 07055. Tel: 973-471-9727; Fax: 973-471-4714.
School—(Grades K-8) Tel: 973-779-0249; Fax: 973-779-6309. Sisters 2; Lay Teachers 10; Students 98.
Catechesis/Religious Program—Sr. Eliana Ignitski, S.S.M.I., D.R.E. Students 11.

PERTH AMBOY, MIDDLESEX CO., ASSUMPTION OF B.V.M. (1908) Rev. Ivan Turyk; Deacon Paul Makar.
Res.: 684 Alta Vista Pl., NJ 08861. Tel: 732-826-0767; Fax: 732-826-6744. Email: assumptionchurch@verizon.net. Web: www.assumptioncatholicchurch.net.
School—(Grades K-8) Tel: 732-826-8721; Fax: 732-826-5013. Michael Szpyhulsky, Prin. Missionary Sisters of Mother of God 2; Lay Teachers 11; Students 170.
Catechesis/Religious Program—Sr. Yosaphata Litvenczuk, M.S.M.G., D.R.E. Students 8.

RAMSEY, BERGEN CO., ST. PAUL, Attended by St. John the Baptist, Whippany. Rev. Archpriest Mitrat Roman Mirchuk.
Mailing Address: 60 N. Jefferson Rd., Whippany, NJ 07981. Tel: 845-356-1634.
Church: 79 Cherry Ln., NJ 07446.

RUTHERFORD, BERGEN CO., ANNUNCIATION B.V.M., Closed. For inquiries for parish records please see St. Vladimir, Elizabeth.

TOMS RIVER, OCEAN CO., ST. STEPHEN'S Rev. Oleksandr Dumenko (Ukraine).
1344 White Oak Bottom Rd., NJ 08755. Tel: 732-505-6053; Fax: 732-505-6295. Web: www.st-stephenchurch.us.

TRENTON, MERCER CO., ST. JOSAPHAT'S (1949) Very Rev. Volodymyr Popyk.
Res.: 1195 Deutz Ave., NJ 08611. Tel: 609-695-3771; Fax: 609-815-0232.

WHIPPANY, MORRIS CO., ST. JOHN THE BAPTIST Rev. Archpriest Mitrat Roman Mirchuk.
Res.: 60 N. Jefferson Rd., NJ 07981. Tel: 973-887-3616; Fax: 973-585-7188.
Catechesis/Religious Program—Students 129.

WILLIAMSTOWN, GLOUCESTER CO., SS. PETER AND PAUL (1920) [CEM] Rev. Ruslan Romanyuk, Admin.
Mailing Address: 675 Cooper Landing Rd., Cherry Hill, NJ 08002. Tel: 856-482-0938; Fax: 856-482-9092.
Church: Black Horse Pike & Cecil Rd., NJ 08094.

WOODBINE, CAPE MAY CO., ST. NICHOLAS, Closed. For inquiries for parish records contact St. Nicholas, Millville, NJ

STATE OF PENNSYLVANIA

ALDEN STATION, LUZERNE CO., ST. VLADIMIR, Closed. For inquiries for parish records contact St. Nicholas, Glen Lyon, PA.

ALLENTOWN, LEHIGH CO., IMMACULATE CONCEPTION OF B.V.M., Closed. For inquiries for parish records contact St. Josaphat, Bethlehem, PA.

BERWICK, COLUMBIA CO., SS. CYRIL AND METHODIUS (1909) [CEM] Very Rev. John Seniw.
Res.: 706 Warren St., 18603. Tel: 717-752-3172; Fax: 570-752-0378. Email: sscm1@verizon.net.
Catechesis/Religious Program—Students 4.

BETHLEHEM, LEHIGH CO., ST. JOSAPHAT'S (1918) [CEM] Very Rev. Archpriest Daniel Gurovich.
Res.: 1826 Kenmore Ave., 18018-3305. Tel: 610-865-2521; Fax: 610-865-4490. Email: yaroway@aol.com.
Catechesis/Religious Program—Students 30.

BRIDGEPORT, MONTGOMERY CO., SS. PETER AND PAUL (1924) [CEM] Rev. Msgr. Ronald P. Popivchak.
Res.: 519 Union Ave., P.O. Box 126, 19405. Tel: 610-272-7035; Fax: 610-272-5620.
Catechesis/Religious Program—George Maxim, D.R.E. Students 85.

BRISTOL, BUCKS CO., ST. MARY'S (1954) Rev. Gregory Maslak.
Res.: 2026 Bath Rd., 19007. Tel: 215-788-7117; Fax: 215-788-7175.
Catechesis/Religious Program—Students 10.

CENTRALIA, COLUMBIA CO., ASSUMPTION OF B.V.M. (1911) [CEM] Attended by Mt. Carmel. Rev. Archpriest Michael Hutsko, Admin.
Mailing Address: 131 N. Beech St., Mount Carmel, 17851.
Church: 538 S. Center St., Aristes, 17920.

CHESTER, DELAWARE CO., HOLY GHOST Very Rev. John Ciurpita.
Res.: 3015 W. Third St., 19013. Tel: 610-494-7899; Fax: 610-494-2350.
Catechesis/Religious Program—Students 14.

CLIFTON HEIGHTS, DELAWARE CO., SS. PETER AND PAUL Very Rev. John Ciurpita, Admin.
Res. & Church: 100 S. Penn St., 19108. Tel: 610-626-9495; Fax: 610-626-0326.

EDWARDSVILLE, LUZERNE CO., ST. VLADIMIR'S (1910) [CEM] Rev. Orest Kunderevych.
Mailing Address: 70 Zerby Ave., 18704. Tel: 570-287-9718.
Catechesis/Religious Program—Tel: 717-822-1589. Christine Mash, D.R.E. Tel: 570-735-1784. Students 3.

FRACKVILLE, SCHUYLKILL CO., ST. MICHAEL'S (1921) [CEM] Very Rev. Archpriest John M. Fields; Deacon Paul Mark Spotts.

Res.: 45 S. Second St., 17931. Tel: 570-874-1101; Fax: 570-874-0448. Email: IBAH@aol.com.
Catechesis/Religious Program—Tel: 717-874-1101. Students 25.

GLEN LYON, LUZERNE CO., ST. NICHOLAS, Attended by Ss Cyril and Methodius, Berwick., Mailing Address: 706 Warren St., Berwick, 18603. Tel: 570-752-3172. Church: 153 Main St., 18617.
Catechesis/Religious Program—Students 2.

HAZLETON, LUZERNE CO., ST. MICHAEL'S (1910) [CEM] Attended by St. Mary's, McAdoo. Rev. Msgr. James T. Melnic.
Mailing Address: 210 W. Blaine St., McAdoo, 18237. Tel: 570-455-0643. Email: stmarysmcadoo@aol.com.
Church: 74 N. Laurel St., 18201.
Catechesis/Religious Program—Students 3.

JENKINTOWN, MONTGOMERY CO., ST. MICHAEL THE ARCHANGEL (1976) Rev. Volodymyr Kostyuk (Ukraine).
Res.: 1013 Fox Chase Rd., 19046. Tel: 215-576-5827; Fax: 215-576-8500.

LANSDALE, MONTGOMERY CO., PRESENTATION OF OUR LORD (1969) Attended by St. Anne's, Warrington. Rev. Wasyl Bunik, Admin.
Mailing Address: 1545 Easton Rd., Warrington, 18976.
Church: 1564 Allentown Rd., 19446. Tel: 215-368-3993; Fax: 215-343-8060. Web: www.presentationukrainiancc.com.
Catechesis/Religious Program—Students 9.

MAHANOY CITY, SCHUYLKILL CO., ST. NICHOLAS, [CEM] Closed. For inquiries for parish records contact the chancery.

MAIZEVILLE, SCHUYLKILL CO., ST. JOHN THE BAPTIST (1908) [CEM] Attended by St. Michael, Frackville. Very Rev. Archpriest John M. Fields.
Mailing Address: 45 S. Second St., Frackville, 17931. Tel: 570-874-1101.
Church: Main St., 17934. Tel: 570-874-1101; Fax: 570-874-0448.

MARION HEIGHTS, NORTHUMBERLAND CO., PATRONAGE OF THE MOTHER OF GOD (1911) Attended by Transfiguration, Shamokin. Rev. Stepan Bilyk, Admin.
Mailing Address: 303 N. Shamokin St., Shamokin, 17872.

MCADOO, SCHUYLKILL CO., ST. MARY'S (1891) [CEM] Rev. Msgr. James T. Melnic.
Church: 210 W. Blaine St., 18237. Tel: 570-929-2804.

MIDDLEPORT, SCHUYLKILL CO., NATIVITY OF B.V.M. (1910) [CEM] Rev. Mark Fesniak, Admin.
Mailing Address: 415 N. Front St., Minersville, 17954. Tel: 570-544-4581; Fax: 570-544-9653.
Church: Kaska St., 17953.

MINERSVILLE, SCHUYLKILL CO., ST. NICHOLAS (1896) [CEM] Rev. Mark Fesniak, Admin.
Res.: 415 Front St., 17954. Tel: 570-544-4581; Fax: 570-544-9653.
School—(Grades K-8) Tel: 570-544-2800; Fax: 570-544-6471. Email: altssn@ptd.net. Sr. Thomas Hyrnewich, S.S.M.I., Prin.; Sofie Smith-Frantz, Librarian. Sisters 3; Lay Teachers 13; Students 151.
Catechesis/Religious Program—Students 16.

MOSCOW, LACKAWANNA CO., HOLY GHOST, Closed. For inquiries for parish records contact St. Vladimir, Scranton, PA.

MOUNT CARMEL, NORTHUMBERLAND CO., SS. PETER AND PAUL (1891) [CEM] Rev. Archpriest Michael Hutsko.
Res.: 131 N. Beech St., 17851. Tel: 570-339-0650; Fax: 570-339-2715.
Catechesis/Religious Program—Christine Bogner, D.R.E. Students 16.

NANTICOKE, LUZERNE CO.
1—ST. NICHOLAS, Closed. For inquiries for parish records contact Transfiguration of Our Lord, 240 Center St., Nanticoke.
2—TRANSFIGURATION OF OUR LORD (1912) [CEM] Rev. Roman Petryshak (Ukraine), Admin.
Res.: 240 Center St., 18634. Tel: 570-735-2262; Fax: 570-735-6020. Email: holytransfiguration@verizon.net. Web: transfigurationofourlord.org.

NORTHAMPTON, NORTHAMPTON CO., ST. JOHN THE BAPTIST, [CEM] Rev. Archpriest David Clooney.
Res.: 1343 Newport Ave., 18067. Tel: 610-262-4104; Fax: 610-262-7393. Email: stjohn1900@verizon.net.
Catechesis/Religious Program—Students 23.

OLYPHANT, LACKAWANNA CO., SS. CYRIL AND METHODIUS (1888) [CEM] Very Rev. Nestor Iwasiw.
Res.: 135 River St., 18447. Tel: 570-489-2271; Fax: 570-489-6918. Email: sscyrilmethodius@comcast.net.
Catechesis/Religious Program—Sandra Berta, D.R.E. Students 33.

PALMERTON, CARBON CO., ST. VLADIMIR'S Rev. Evhan Moniuk.
Res.: 101 Lehigh Ave., 18071. Tel: 610-826-2359.

PHOENIXVILLE, CHESTER CO., SS. PETER AND PAUL, [CEM] Attended by St. Michael, Pottstown. Rev. Mykola Ivanov, Admin.
Mailing Address: 425 W. Walnut St., Pottstown, 19464-6654. Tel: 610-933-5453; Fax: 610-933-9826.
Church: 472 Emmett St., 19460.

PLYMOUTH, LUZERNE CO., SS. PETER AND PAUL (1898) Rev. Roman Petryshak (Ukraine), Admin.
Res.: 240 Center St., Nanticoke, 18634. Tel: 570-735-2262; Fax: 570-735-6020.
Church & Mailing Address: 20 Nottingham St., P.O. Box 60, 18651.

POTTSTOWN, MONTGOMERY CO., ST. MICHAEL'S (1936) [CEM] Rev. Mykola Ivanov, Admin.
Res.: 425 W. Walnut St., 19464. Tel: 610-326-2150; Fax: 610-326-2150. Email: mykolaivan1977@yahoo.com.
Catechesis/Religious Program—Students 1.

READING, BERKS CO., NATIVITY OF BLESSED VIRGIN MARY (1906) [CEM] Very Rev. Andriy Rabiy, Admin.
Res.: 1814 Philadelphia Ave., 19607. Tel: 610-376-0586; Fax: 610-376-0586. Email: nativitybvmucc@catholic.org.

ST. CLAIR, SCHUYLKILL CO.
1—HOLY TRINITY, [CEM] Closed. For inquiries for parish records, contact St. Nicholas, St. Clair, PA.
2—ST. NICHOLAS, [CEM] Attended by St. Michael, Shenandoah. Rev. Msgr. Myron Grabowsky, Admin.
Mailing Address: 114 S. Chestnut St., Shenandoah, 17976. Tel: 570-462-0809; Fax: 570-462-0517.
Church: N. Morris St., 17970.

SAYRE, BRADFORD CO., ASCENSION OF OUR LORD (1912) [CEM] Attended by Sacred Heart, Johnson City, NY Rev. Teodor Czabala Jr. Tel: 607-797-6293.
Church: 108 N. Higgins Ave., 18840. Tel: 607-857-0703.

SCRANTON, LACKAWANNA CO., ST. VLADIMIR'S, [CEM] Rev. Paul Wolensky, Admin.
Res.: 430 N. Seventh Ave., 18503. Tel: 570-342-7023; Fax: 570-342-7130. Email: stvladimirscr430@verizon.net.
Catechesis/Religious Program—Shirley Nidoh, D.R.E. Students 16.
Mission—*SS. Peter & Paul* 47 Rittenhouse St., Simpson, 18407.

SHAMOKIN, NORTHUMBERLAND CO., TRANSFIGURATION OF OUR LORD, [CEM] Rev. Stepan Bilyk; Deacon Theodore Spotts.
Res.: 303 N. Shamokin St., 17872-5460. Tel: 570-648-5932; Fax: 570-648-3871.
Catechesis/Religious Program—

SHENANDOAH, SCHUYLKILL CO., ST. MICHAEL'S (1884) [CEM] Rev. Msgr. Myron Grabowsky.
Res.: 114 S. Chestnut St., 17976. Tel: 570-462-0809; Fax: 570-462-0517. Email: stmichaelsukrainian@verizon.net. Web: www.firstukrainian.com.
Catechesis/Religious Program—Alice Brcznik, D.R.E. Students 14.

SIMPSON, LACKAWANNA CO., SS. PETER AND PAUL (1904) [CEM] Attended by St. Vladimir Church, Scranton. Rev. Paul Wolensky, Admin.
430 N. Seventh Ave., Scranton, 18503. Tel: 570-342-7023.
Church: 47 Rittenhouse St., 18407.

WARRINGTON, BUCKS CO., ST. ANNE'S (1963) Rev. Wasyl Bunik, Admin.
Res.: 1545 Easton Rd., 18976. Tel: 215-343-0779; Fax: 215-343-8060. Web: www.stanneukrainiancc.com.
Catechesis/Religious Program—Students 19.

WEST EASTON, NORTHAMPTON CO., HOLY GHOST (1921) [CEM] Rev. Petro Zvarych, Admin.
Res.: 315 Fourth St., 18042. Tel: 610-252-4266; Fax: 610-252-8533.
Catechesis/Religious Program—Christine Mattes, D.R.E. Students 7.

WILKES-BARRE, LUZERNE CO., SS. PETER AND PAUL, [CEM] Rev. Orest Kunderevych.
Church: 635 N. River St., 18701. Tel: 570-823-1821; Fax: 570-822-7391. Email: sspeterandpaulwb@gmail.com.
Catechesis/Religious Program—Students 5.

STATE OF VIRGINIA

MANASSAS, PRINCE WILLIAM CO., ANNUNCIATION OF THE BLESSED VIRGIN MARY (1925) [CEM] Rev. Volodymyr Baran, C.Ss.R., Admin.
Mailing Address: P.O. Box 2735, VA 20108.
Church: 6719 Token Valley Rd., VA 20108-0878. Tel: 703-791-6635.
Catechesis/Religious Program—Helen Troy, D.R.E. Students 15.

RICHMOND, HENRICO CO., ST. JOHN THE BAPTIST (1966) Attended by Annunciation of the Blessed Virgin Mary, Manassas. Rev. Volodymyr Baran, C.Ss.R., Admin.
Mailing Address: P.O. Box 2735, Manassas, VA 20108. Tel: 703-791-6635.
Chapel—*Comboni Sisters Chapel* 1307 Lakeside Ave., VA 23228. Tel: 804-272-3844.

DISTRICT OF COLUMBIA

WASHINGTON, DISTRICT OF COLUMBIA, UKRAINIAN CATHOLIC NATIONAL SHRINE OF THE HOLY FAMILY Very Revs. Robert Hitchens; Wasyl Kharuk, Parochial Vicar; Deacon Theophil Staruch.
Res.: 4250 Harewood Rd., N.E., DC 20017. Tel: 202-526-3737; Fax: 202-526-1327. Web: www.ucns-holyfamily.org.
Catechesis/Religious Program—Students 6.

Absent on Leave:
Rev.—
Worschak, D. George

Special Assignment:
Rev.—
Makar, Paul J., Vocations Dir.

Retired:
Most Rev.—
Sulyk, Stephen, D.D., 1113 Cobble Creek Cir., Cherry Hill, NJ 08003.
Very Rev. Msgr.—
Hrynuck, Stephen
Revs.—
Dubitsky, Roman
Labinsky, Paul, 1101 Heartwood Dr., Cherry Hill, NJ 08003.
Levandusky, Edward
Patrylak, Frank, St. Mary's Catholic Home, 210 St. Mary's Dr., Cherry Hill, NJ 08003.
Sinatra, Leonard, 1114 Chestnut St. Alden, Nanticoke, 18634.
Wysochansky, John, 118 Second St., Blakely, 18447.
Very Rev. Archpriest—
Markewych, Uriy, 990 Summerhill Rd., Auburn, 17922.

Permanent Deacons:
Latrick, Donald, (On Leave)
Makar, Paul, Assumption B.V.M., Perth Amboy
Schultz, Charles, III, Cathedral of Immaculate Conception, Philadelphia
Spotts, Paul Mark, St. Michael, Frackville, PA
Spotts, Theodore, Transfiguration, Shamokin, PA; Assumption B.V.M., Centralia, PA
Staruch, Theophil, Holy Family Ukrainian Catholic National Shrine, Washington, DC
Waak, Michael P., Cathedral of the Immaculate Conception, Philadelphia

INSTITUTIONS LOCATED IN THE ARCHDIOCESE

[A] SEMINARIES, ARCHEPARCHY

WASHINGTON. *St. Josaphat Seminary*, 201 Taylor St., N.E., DC 20017. Tel: 202-529-1177; Fax: 202-529-9366. Email: stjosaphatseminary@catholic.org. Web: www.sjucs.org. Very Revs. Robert Hitchens, Rector; Wasyl Kharuk, Spiritual Dir.

[B] COLLEGES AND UNIVERSITIES

JENKINTOWN. *Manor College*, 700 Fox Chase Rd., 19046. Tel: 215-885-2360; Fax: 215-576-6564. Email: scecilia@manor.edu. Web: www.manor.edu. Sr. M. Cecilia Jurasinski, O.S.B.M., Pres.; Sally Mydlowec, Exec. Vice Pres. & Dean Academic Affairs; Barbara Ozer, Contact Person; Beth Lander, Librarian. Sisters of St. Basil the Great., Approved by the Commonwealth of Pennsylvania and accredited by the Middle States Association of Colleges and Secondary Schools. Sisters 1; Professors 25; Students 969.

[C] HIGH SCHOOLS, PRIVATE

JENKINTOWN. *St. Basil Academy*, 711 Fox Chase Rd., 19046. Tel: 215-885-3771; Fax: 215-885-4025. Email: admissions@stbasilacademy.org. Web: www.stbasilacademy.org. Sr. Carla Hernandez, O.S.B.M., Prin.; Connie D'Angelo, Dean Students & Vice Prin.; Melissa Norman, Librarian. High School Sisters 5; Lay Teachers 32; Students 324.

[D] HOMES FOR SENIOR CITIZENS

PHILADELPHIA. *Ascension Manor, Inc.*, 911 N. Franklin St., 19123. Tel: 215-922-1116. Most Revs. Stefan Soroka, D.D., Ph.D.; John Bura; Rev. Msgrs. James T. Melnic; Peter D. Waslo, J.C.L., Sec. Treas.; Very Rev. Archpriest John M. Fields, Exec. Vice Pres.; Andrew Fylypowych, Dir.; Jeanne Karbiwnyk, Dir.; Ihor Shust, Dir.; John Siwak, Gen. Mgr. Units 279; Staff 9; Total Assisted 229.
Ascension Manor I, 911 N. Franklin St., 19123. Tel:

215-922-1116; Fax: 215-922-3735. Bill Malinowski, Asst. Mgr.

Ascension Manor II, 970 N. Seventh St., 19123. Tel: 215-923-3907; Fax: 215-922-3735. Tonja Starkey, Asst. Mgr.

[E] MONASTERIES AND RESIDENCES OF PRIESTS AND BROTHERS

WASHINGTON. *Monastery of the Holy Cross*, 1302 Quincy St., N.E., DC 20017-2614. Tel: 202-832-8519; Fax: 202-526-3316. Email: holycrossdc@aol.com. Rev. Archimandrite Joseph (Richard) Lee.

[F] CONVENTS AND RESIDENCES FOR SISTERS

PHILADELPHIA. *Motherhouse of the Missionary Sisters of Mother of God*, 711 N. Franklin St., 19123. Tel: 215-627-7808; Fax: 215-627-4225. Sr. Evhenia Prusnay, M.S.M.G., Supr. Gen.

Sacred Heart Convent, 160 W. Carpenter Ln., 19119. Tel: 215-843-2266. Sr. Maria Rita Donnelly, P.O.S.C., Supr.

FOX CHASE MANOR. *Provincial Motherhouse of the Sisters of St. Basil the Great*, 710 Fox Chase Rd., 19046. Tel: 215-379-3998; Fax: 215-728-6129. Email: province@stbasils.com. Web: www.stbasils.com. Sisters Dorothy Ann Busowski, O.S.B.M., Prov. Supr.; Joan Sosler, O.S.B.M., Asst. Prov.; Maria Rozmarynowycz, Councilor; Lydia Ann Sawka, O.S.B.M., Councilor; Ann Laszok, O.S.B.M., Councilor; Very Rev. Archpriest Daniel Troyan, Chap. Professed Sisters 40.

[G] MISCELLANEOUS

PHILADELPHIA. *Archieparchial Museum and Educational Center*, 814 N. Franklin St., 19123. Tel: 215-627-3389; Fax: 215-627-0377. Sr. Evhenia Prusnay, M.S.M.G., Admin.

FOX CHASE MANOR. *Basilian Spirituality Center*, 710 Fox Chase Rd., 19046. Tel: 215-780-1227; Fax: 215-780-1743. Email: basilcenter@stbasils.com. Sr. Marina Bochnewich, O.S.B.M., Dir.

JENKINTOWN. *The Basileiad Library/Manor College*, 700 Fox Chase Rd., 19046. Tel: 215-885-2360, Ext. 238; Fax: 215-576-6564. Email: basileiad@manor.edu. Web: www.youseemove.com/manorcollege/. Beth Lander, Library Dir. Sisters of St. Basil the Great.

RELIGIOUS INSTITUTES OF MEN REPRESENTED IN THE ARCHEPARCHY

For further details refer to the corresponding bracketed number in the Religious Institutes of Men or Women section.

[1070]—*Redemptorist Fathers*—C.Ss.R.

RELIGIOUS INSTITUTES OF WOMEN REPRESENTED IN THE ARCHEPARCHY

[2345]—*Little Workers of the Sacred Heart of Jesus and Mary*—P.O.S.C.

[2810]—*Missionary Sisters of Mother of God*—M.S.M.G.

[3730]—*Sisters of the Order of St. Basil the Great*—O.S.B.M.

[3610]—*Sisters Servants of Mary Immaculate*—S.S.M.I.

ARCHDIOCESAN CEMETERIES

LANGHORNE. *Mother of Sorrows*, Langhorne & Yardley Rd., 19047. Tel: 215-627-0143; Fax: 215-627-0377. 827 N. Franklin St., 19123.

NECROLOGY

† Fedorowich, Rev. Msgr. Michael, (Retired)—Died April 25, 2011

† Molodowitz, Augustine, (Retired)—Died June 15, 2011

An asterisk (*) denotes an organization that has established tax-exempt status directly with the IRS and is not covered by the USCCB Group Ruling.

Metropolitan Archeparchy of Pittsburgh, Byzantine

Most Reverend

WILLIAM C. SKURLA

Metropolitan Archbishop of Pittsburgh; ordained November 1, 1993; appointed Bishop of Van Nuys February 19, 2002; ordained April 23, 2002; appointed Bishop of Passaic December 6, 2007; installed January 29, 2008; appointed Metropolitan Archbishop of Pittsburgh January 19, 2012; installed April 18, 2012. *66 Riverview Ave., Pittsburgh, PA 15214.*

Chancery: 66 Riverview Ave., Pittsburgh, PA 15214. Tel: 412-231-4000; Fax: 412-231-1697.

ESTABLISHED FEBRUARY 25, 1924.

Raised to Archeparchy February 21, 1969.

Embraces all Byzantine Ruthenian Rite Catholics in that part of the State of Pennsylvania west of the western boundaries of the Counties of Tioga, Lycoming, Union, Mifflin, Juniata and Franklin. In the State of Ohio, the Counties of Ashtabula, Athens, Belmont, Carroll, Columbiana, Gallia, Guernsey, Harrison, Jefferson, Lawrence, Mahoning, Meigs, Morrow, Morgan, Noble, Trumbull and Washington and also the States of Alabama, Arkansas, Kentucky, Louisiana, Mississippi, Oklahoma, Tennessee, Texas and West Virginia.

For legal titles of parishes and diocesan institutions, consult the Chancery.

STATISTICAL OVERVIEW

Personnel	
Abbots	1
Priests: Diocesan Active in Diocese	43
Priests: Diocesan Active Outside Diocese	1
Priests: Retired, Sick or Absent	11
Number of Diocesan Priests	55
Religious Priests in Diocese	9
Total Priests in Diocese	64
Extern Priests in Diocese	9
Ordinations:	
Permanent Deacons	6
Permanent Deacons in Diocese	21
Total Brothers	2
Total Sisters	69
Parishes	
Parishes	76
With Resident Pastor:	
Resident Diocesan Priests	40
Resident Religious Priests	5
Without Resident Pastor:	
Administered by Priests	29
Administered by Deacons	2
Missions	2
Pastoral Centers	2
Closed Parishes	3
Professional Ministry Personnel:	
Sisters	3
Welfare	
Homes for the Aged	2
Total Assisted	548
Educational	
Seminaries, Diocesan	1
Students from This Diocese	1
Students from Other Diocese	9
Total Seminarians	1
Catechesis/Religious Education:	
High School Students	271
Elementary Students	652
Total Students under Catholic Instruction	924
Vital Statistics	
Receptions into the Church:	
Infant Baptism Totals	133
Adult Baptism Totals	6
Received into Full Communion	33
First Communions	157
Confirmations	143
Marriages:	
Catholic	43
Interfaith	17
Total Marriages	60
Total Catholic Population	58,200

Former Bishops—Most Revs. BASIL TAKACH, ord. Dec. 12, 1902; appt. May 20, 1924; cons. June 15, 1924; died May 13, 1948; DANIEL IVANCHO, D.D., Titular Bishop of Europus; ord. Sept. 30, 1934; appt. Coadjutor Bishop, Aug. 29, 1946; cons. Nov. 5, 1946; succeeded to May 13, 1948; retired Dec. 2, 1954; died Aug. 2, 1972; NICHOLAS T. ELKO, D.D., ord. Sept. 30, 1934; cons. March 6, 1955; transferred to Rome, Dec. 22, 1967; died May 18, 1991; STEPHEN J. KOCISCKO, D.D., ord. March 30, 1941; appt. Titular Bishop of Theveste and Auxiliary Bishop of Pittsburgh July 20, 1956; cons. Oct. 23, 1956; appt. First Eparch of Passaic July 31, 1963; appt. Eparch of Pittsburgh Dec. 21, 1967; enthroned March 5, 1968; elevated to Metropolitan Archbishop of Pittsburgh Feb. 21, 1969; retired June 12, 1991; died March 7, 1995; THOMAS V. DOLINAY, ord. May 16, 1948; appt. Titular Bishop of Thyatira and Auxiliary of Passaic, Sept. 23, 1976; cons. Nov. 23, 1976; appt. First Ordinary of the Byzantine Catholic Eparchy of Van Nuys; installed March 1982; appt. Coadjutor Archbishop of Pittsburgh, March 13, 1990; installed May 29, 1990; succeeded to June 12, 1991; died April 13, 1993; JOHN M. BILOCK, ord. Feb. 3, 1946; appt. Titular Bishop of Pergamo and Auxiliary Bishop to the Metropolitan Archbishop of Pittsburgh; installed March 1, 1973; cons. May 15, 1973; appt. Archieparchial Administrator, April 20, 1993; died Sept. 8, 1994; JUDSON M. PROCYK, ord. May 19, 1957; appt. Metropolitan Archbishop of Pittsburgh Nov. 15, 1994; installed Feb. 7, 1995; died April 24, 2001; BASIL M. SCHOTT, O.F.M., ord. Aug. 29, 1965; appt. Eparch of Parma May 3, 1996; enthroned July 11, 1996; appt. Metropolitan Archbishop of Pittsburgh May 3, 2002; enthroned July 9, 2002; died June 10, 2010.

Chancery—66 Riverview Ave., Pittsburgh, 15214. Tel: 412-231-4000; Fax: 412-231-1697. Email: archpitt@aol.com. Office Hours: Mon.-Fri. 9:30-12 and 12:30-4.

Administrator—Very Rev. EUGENE P. YACKANICH.

Protosyncellus—Rev. Msgr. RUSSELL A. DUKER, S.E.O.D.

Vicar for Canonical Services—Rev. GEORGE D. GALLARO, J.C.O.L., J.C.O.D., S.T.L.

Finance Officer—GREGORY S. POPIVCHAK.

Consultors—Very Rev. Archpriest DENNIS M. BOGDA; Rev. Msgr. RUSSELL A. DUKER, S.E.O.D.; Very Rev. RICHARD I. LAMBERT; Revs. SIMEON B. SIBENIK; JAMES A. SPONTAK.

Protopresbyters—Very Rev. JOSEPH BORODACH, Clairton; Rev. Msgr. RAYMOND A. BALTA, Johnstown; Very Revs. JOHN H. SALKO, Mon-Valley; JOHN J. MIHALCO, S.E.O.L., North-Central; EUGENE P. YACKANICH, Pittsburgh; ELIAS L. RAFAJ, Southwest; JOSEPH J. JUGAN, Tri-State; RICHARD I. LAMBERT, Youngstown.

Finance Advisory Council—GREGORY S. POPIVCHAK; Very Rev. EUGENE P. YACKANICH; MICHAEL I. ROMAN; BERNARD J. KOSAR SR.; CATHY A. CHROMULAK, Attorney.

Tribunal—

Judicial Vicar—Rev. GEORGE D. GALLARO, J.C.O.L., J.C.O.D., S.T.L.

Pro-Synodal Judges—Revs. MICHAEL HUSZTI, J.C.O.L.; MICHAEL K. SKROCKI, J.C.O.L.

Defender of the Bond—Very Rev. JOHN J. MIHALCO, S.E.O.L.

Promoter of Justice—Very Rev. JOHN J. MIHALCO, S.E.O.L.

Secretary—Sr. ELAINE KISINKO, O.S.B.M.

Notaries—Rev. GREGORY J. MICHALISIN; Sr. VALERIA EVANYO, O.S.B.M.; DONNA OBSINCS.

Archieparchial Choir—DARLENE FEJKA, Dir.

Archives—Revs. JOHN L. MINA, Ph.D., Archivist; ROBERT F. ORAVETZ, Asst.; Sr. ELAINE KISINKO, O.S.B.M., Asst.

Communications—DARLENE FEJKA; Rev. ANDREW J. DESKEVICH, Asst. Dir. Media.

Diaconate Program—Very Rev. Archpriest JOHN G. PETRO, Dir.

Evangelization, Mission Activity and Ecumenism—Rev. ROBERT F. ORAVETZ, Dir.

Vocations—Very Rev. Archpriest DENNIS M. BOGDA, Dir.; Rev. KEVIN E. MARKS, Assoc. Dir.; DARLENE FEJKA, Admin. Coord.

Priests' Pension Board— Ex Officio Members: GREGORY S. POPIVCHAK, Finance Officer; Rev. Msgr. RUSSELL A. DUKER, S.E.O.D., Protosyncellus & Chancellor.

Elected Deanery Representatives—Revs. R. JOSEPH RAPTOSH, Sec., Clairton; DAVID A. BOSNICH, Greater Pittsburgh; GREGORY J. MICHALISIN, Johnstown; JEROME G. BOTSKO, Mon Valley; Very Rev. JOHN J. MIHALCO, S.E.O.L., North Central; Revs. KEVIN E. MARKS, Tri State; JOHN J. CUCCARO, Youngstown.

Office of Religious Education—Sr. MARION DOBOS, O.S.B., Dir.; Very Rev. ELIAS L. RAFAJ, Asst. Dir., Archeparchial Catechetical Center, 3605 Perrysville Ave., Pittsburgh, 15214. Tel: 412-322-8773; Fax: 412-322-8737.

Revitalization and Renewal Commission—Very Rev. Archpriest DENNIS M. BOGDA; Revs. JOSEPH KAPUSNAK; ROBERT J. KARL; ANDREW J. DESKEVICH; HELEN KENNEDY; Deacons DENNIS M. PRESTASH; RAYMOND J. ZADZILKO.

Archieparchial Newspaper— "Byzantine Catholic World" DARLENE FEJKA, Layout & Graphics; CHRISTINA CALISE; STEVEN HORGER, Business Mgr.; DONNA OBSINCS, Circulation Mgr.; Sr. ELAINE KISINKO, O.S.B.M., Copy Editor, 66 Riverview Ave., Pittsburgh, 15214. Tel: 412-231-4000; Fax: 412-231-1697.

Byzantine Catholic Seminary Press—CATHY SILVESTRI, Dir., 3643 Perrysville Ave., Pittsburgh, 15214. Tel: 412-322-8307; Fax: 412-322-9530.

Victim Assistance Coordinator—Sr. BARBARA JEAN MIHALCHICK, O.S.B.M., 500 W. Main St., P.O. Box 878, Uniontown, 15401-0878. Tel: 724-438-7149.

Safe Environment Coordinator—Sr. AGNES KNAPIK, O.S.B., Queen of Heaven Monastery, 169 Kenmore Ave., N.E., Warren, OH 44483. Tel: 330-856-1813.

CLERGY, PARISHES, MISSIONS AND PAROCHIAL SCHOOLS

STATE OF PENNSYLVANIA

ALIQUIPPA, BEAVER CO., ST. GEORGE THE GREAT MARTYR (1915) Rev. Kevin E. Marks; Deacon Michael E. George.
Res.: 1001 Clinton St., 15001-3903. Tel: 724-375-2742; Fax: 724-375-8776.

AMBRIDGE, BEAVER CO., ST. MARY'S (1940) Rev. Kevin E. Marks; Deacon Thomas J. Klacik.
Res.: 624 Park Rd., 15003. Tel: 724-266-2030; Fax: 724-266-1834.

ARCADIA, INDIANA CO., ASCENSION, [CEM] Closed. For inquiries for parish records contact the chancery.

AVELLA, WASHINGTON CO., ST. JOHN THE BAPTIST (1916) [CEM] Attended by St. Mary's, Weirton, WV.
Res.: 176 Cross Creek Rd., P.O. Box 565, 15312. Tel: 304-748-2087; Fax: 304-748-7550.

BEAVER, BEAVER CO., SAINT NICHOLAS CHAPEL (1995) Very Rev. Archpriest John G. Petro, Admin.
5400 Tuscarawas Rd., 15009-9513. Tel: 412-321-7550. Web: www.gcuusa.com. Mailing Address: 3605 Perrysville Ave., 15214.

BEAVERDALE, CAMBRIA CO., ST. MARY'S (1906) [CEM] Attended by Sts. Peter and Paul, Portage. Deacon Daniel F. Perich.
Church: 513 Cameron Ave., P.O. Box 610, 15921. Tel: 814-736-9780.

BRADDOCK, ALLEGHENY CO., SS. PETER AND PAUL (1896) Attended by Sts. Peter and Paul, Duquesne.
Church: 431 George St., P.O. Box 441, 15104. Tel: 412-466-3578.

BRADENVILLE, WESTMORELAND CO., ST. MARY'S (1902) [CEM] Very Rev. Joseph Borodach.
Res.: 112 St. Mary's Way, 15620-1017. Tel: 724-537-5839; Fax: 724-532-1499.

BROWNSVILLE, FAYETTE CO., ST. NICHOLAS (1911) [CEM] Rev. Jerome G. Botsko.
Res.: 302 Third Ave., 15417. Tel: 724-785-7573; Fax: 724-785-4649.

CANONSBURG, WASHINGTON CO., ST. MICHAEL (1912) [CEM] Very Rev. Joseph J. Jugan; Deacon Lance D. Weakland.
Res.: 166 E. College St., 15317. Tel: 724-745-7117; Fax: 724-745-3097.

CHARLEROI, WASHINGTON CO., HOLY GHOST (1899) Rev. James A. Ragan.
Res.: 828 Meadow Ave., 15022. Tel: 724-483-8622; Fax: 724-483-0696. Email: golden15739@gmail.com.

CLAIRTON, ALLEGHENY CO., ASCENSION OF OUR LORD (1907) [CEM] Rev. John L. Mina.
Res.: 318 Park Ave., 15025. Tel: 412-233-7422. Email: ivanmina@verizon.net.

CLARENCE, CENTRE CO., DORMITION OF THE MOTHER OF GOD (1906) [CEM] Attended by St. John the Baptist Church, Hawk Run. Rev. William Rupp, Admin.
Mailing Address: *c/o St. John the Baptist Church*, P.O. Box 2, Hawk Run, 16840. Tel: 814-342-4315. Web: www.byzcath.org/centralpa.

CLYMER, INDIANA CO., ST. ANNE (1907) Rev. William A. Lascelles.
48 Franklin St., 15728. Tel: 814-938-4244.

COAL RUN, INDIANA CO., HOLY CROSS, Closed. For inquiries for parish records contact the chancery.

CONEMAUGH, CAMBRIA CO., HOLY TRINITY (1908) [CEM] Rev. Robert K. Yetsko, T.O.R.
Church: 217 Fourth St., 15909. Tel: 814-535-5231.

DONORA, WASHINGTON CO., ST. MICHAEL (1904) [CEM] Rev. Stephen J. Wahal.
Church: 511 Murray Ave., 15033. Tel: 724-379-9751; Fax: 724-379-9752.

DU BOIS, CLEARFIELD CO., NATIVITY OF THE MOTHER OF GOD (1910) Attended by Holy Trinity, Sykesville. Very Rev. John J. Mihalco; Deacons Paul M. Boboige; George M. Fatula.
Res.: 200 McCullough St., 15801. Tel: 814-894-5440; Fax: 814-894-2412.

DUNLO, CAMBRIA CO., SS. PETER AND PAUL (1909) [CEM] Attended by Sts. Peter and Paul, Portage., Mailing Address: 143 Church Rd., Portage, 15946. Tel: 814-736-9780.

DUQUESNE, ALLEGHENY CO.

1—ST. MARY'S (1915) Closed. For inquiries for parish records contact the chancery.

2—SS. PETER AND PAUL (1904) [CEM] Rev. David A. Bosnich; Deacon Sean Petrisko.
Res.: 701 Foster Ave., 15110. Tel: 412-466-3578; Fax: 412-466-3578.

EAST PITTSBURGH, ALLEGHENY CO., ST. MARY'S (1930) Rev. Daniel J. Loya.
Res.: 317 Howard St., 15112. Tel: 412-824-1622.

ERIE, ERIE CO., SS. PETER AND PAUL (1912) Rev. Robert J. Karl.
Res.: 3415 Wallace St., 16504. Tel: 814-825-8140; Fax: 814-825-7582.

ERNEST, INDIANA CO., ST. JUDE THADDEUS (1949) Rev. William A. Lascelles.
Res.: 320 Main St., Box 130, 15739. Tel: 814-938-4244.

GIBSONIA, ALLEGHENY CO., ST. ANDREW THE APOSTLE (1975) Rt. Rev. Leo R. Schlosser.
Res.: 235 Logan Rd., 15044-6093. Tel: 724-625-1160; Fax: 724-625-1160.

GIRARD, ERIE CO., SS. CYRIL AND METHODIUS (1952) Attended by Sts. Peter and Paul, Erie Rev. Robert J. Karl.
Res.: 1022 Tilden Ave., 16417. Tel: 814-774-3281; Fax: 814-774-5405.

GREENSBURG, WESTMORELAND CO., ST. NICHOLAS OF MYRA (1955) Rev. Regis J. Dusecina.
Res.: 624 E. Pittsburgh St., 15601. Tel: 724-837-0295; Fax: 724-837-9042.

HANNASTOWN, WESTMORELAND CO., ST. MARY'S (1906) Attended by St. Nicholas of Myra, Greensburg., 624 E. Pittsburgh St., Greensburg, 15601. Tel: 724-837-0295.

HAWK RUN, CLEARFIELD CO.

1—ST. JOHN THE BAPTIST (1904) [CEM] Rev. William Rupp, Admin.; Deacons John A. Custaney; Dennis M. Prestash.
Mailing Address: 24 Fulton St., P.O. Box 2, 16840. Tel: 814-342-4315; Fax: 814-342-3254. Web: www.byzcath.org/centralpa.

2—STATE COLLEGE PA BYZANTINE CATHOLIC COMMUNITY (2005) Rev. William Rupp, Admin.
P.O. Box 431, State College, 16804-0431. Tel: 814-861-2005; Fax: 814-342-3254. Web: www.byzcath.org/centralpa.

HERMINIE, WESTMORELAND CO., ST. MARY'S (1923) Attended by St. Stephen's, North Huntington., 5 Second St., 15637. Tel: 724-446-5570.

HERMITAGE, MERCER CO., ST. MICHAEL (1905) [CEM] Rev. John J. Cuccaro.
Res.: 2230 Highland Rd., 16148. Tel: 724-981-6680; Fax: 724-981-7422.

HOMER CITY, INDIANA CO., ST. MARY'S HOLY PROTECTION formerly Holy Protection of Mary, The Mother of God (1919) Rev. Cuthbert A. Jack, O.S.B.; Deacon Richard A. Ciganko.
Res.: 279 Yellow Creek St., 15748. Tel: 724-479-2206; Fax: 724-479-9506.

JEROME, SOMERSET CO., SS. PETER AND PAUL (1913) [CEM] Attended by St. Mary, Windber. Rev. Gregory J. Michalisin; Deacon Paul J. Pipta.
803 Somerset Ave., Windber, 15963. Tel: 814-467-8044; Fax: 814-467-8044.

JOHNSTOWN, CAMBRIA CO., ST. MARY'S (1895) [CEM] Rev. Msgr. Raymond A. Balta.
Res.: 411 Power St., 15906. Tel: 814-535-4132; Fax: 814-536-9017.

LATROBE, WESTMORELAND CO., ST. MARY (1894) [CEM] Rev. Paul-Alexander Shutt, O.S.B.
Res.: 4480 Rte. #981, 15650. Tel: 724-423-3673; Fax: 724-423-1808.

LEISENRING, FAYETTE CO., ST. STEPHEN (1892) [CEM] Rev. Joseph Kapusnak.
Res.: P.O. Box 128, 15455. Tel: 724-628-6611; Fax: 724-628-5009.

LYNDORA, BUTLER CO., ST. JOHN THE BAPTIST (1910) [CEM] Rev. Robert F. Oravetz; Deacon Paul Simko.
Res.: 105 Kohler Ave., 16045. Tel: 724-287-5000; Fax: 724-287-6769. Email: byzbob@aol.com.

MCKEES ROCKS, ALLEGHENY CO., HOLY GHOST (1907) Rev. Frank A. Firko.
Res.: 225 Olivia St., 15136. Tel: 412-771-3324; Fax: 412-331-1870.

MCKEESPORT, ALLEGHENY CO.

1—ST. NICHOLAS (1901) [CEM] Rev. Donald J. Voss.
Res.: 410 Sixth Ave., 15132. Tel: 412-664-9131; Fax: 412-664-0854.

2—TRANSFIGURATION OF OUR LORD (1913) Closed. Parish Supressed - Sept. 18, 2011. For inquiries for parish records, contact St. Nicholas, McKeesport

MONESSEN, WESTMORELAND CO., ASSUMPTION OF THE BLESSED VIRGIN (1902) [CEM] Rev. Stephen J. Wahal; Deacon John M. Hanchin.
Res.: 125 McKee Ave., 15062. Tel: 724-684-5662; Fax: 724-684-3301.

MONONGAHELA, WASHINGTON CO., ST. MACRINA, Closed. For inquiries for parish records contact the chancery.

MONROEVILLE, ALLEGHENY CO., CHURCH OF THE RESURRECTION (1969) Rev. R. Joseph Raptosh, Admin.
Res.: 455 Center Rd., 15146. Tel: 412-372-8650; Fax: 412-372-1442.

MUNHALL, ALLEGHENY CO.

1—ST. JOHN THE BAPTIST CATHEDRAL (1897) [CEM] Very Rev. Archpriest Dennis M. Bogda, Rector; Deacon Timothy J. Corbett.
Res.: 210 Greentree Rd., 15120. Tel: 412-461-0944; Fax: 412-462-3495.

2—ST. ELIAS (1907) [CEM] Very Rev. Eugene P. Yackanich.
Res.: 4200 Homestead-Duquesne Rd., 15120. Tel: 412-461-1712; Fax: 412-461-1712.

NANTY-GLO, CAMBRIA CO., ST. NICHOLAS (1919) Attended by Holy Trinity, Conemaugh.
Church: 1191 Second St., 15943. Tel: 814-535-5231.

NEW SALEM, FAYETTE CO., ST. MARY'S (1903) [CEM] Attended by St. Nicholas, Brownsville., Mailing Address: P.O. Box 487, 15468. Tel: 724-245-7188.

NORTH HUNTINGDON, WESTMORELAND CO., ST. STEPHEN'S (1972) Rev. James D. Hess, O.Carm.
Res.: 90 Bethel Rd., 15642. Tel: 724-863-6776; Fax: 724-864-9685. Email: jimocarm@mac.com.

NORTHERN CAMBRIA, CAMBRIA CO., ST. JOHN THE BAPTIST (1897) [CEM] Rev. Oliver J. Hebert, T.O.R.
Res.: 719 Chestnut Ave., 15714-1459. Tel: 814-948-8242; Fax: 814-948-8252. Email: stjohn@pennswoods.net. Web: ssppandjbyzcatholic-.com.

PATTON, CAMBRIA CO., SS. PETER AND PAUL (1900) [CEM] Attended by St. John, Northern Cambria. Rev. Oliver J. Hebert, T.O.R.; Deacon Raymond J. Zadzilko.
Church: 516 Palmer Ave., 16668. Tel: 814-674-5552; Fax: 814-948-8252. Email: stjohn@pennswoods.net. Web: ssppandjbyzcatholic.com.

PERRYOPOLIS, FAYETTE CO., ST. NICHOLAS (1911) [CEM] Rev. Robert E. Halus.
Res.: 102 Railroad St., 15473. Tel: 724-736-4344; Fax: 724-736-4642.

PITTSBURGH, ALLEGHENY CO.

1—HOLY GHOST (1902) Attended by Holy Ghost, McKees Rocks.
Church: 1437 Superior Ave., 15212. Tel: 412-321-5072; Fax: 412-321-0260.

2—HOLY SPIRIT (1907) Rev. Msgr. Russell A. Duker, S.E.O.D.
Res.: 4815 Fifth Ave., 15213. Tel: 412-687-1220; Fax: 412-687-1520.

3—ST. JOHN CHRYSOSTOM (1910) Rev. Thomas Schaefer.
Res.: 506 Saline St., 15207. Tel: 412-421-0243; Fax: 412-422-3624.

4—ST. JOHN THE BAPTIST (1900) [CEM] Rev. Thomas Schaefer.
Res.: 1720 Jane St., 15203. Tel: 412-431-1090; Fax: 412-431-2059.

5—NATIVITY OF B.V.M. (1932) Closed. For inquiries for parish records, contact the Cathedral of St. John the Baptist, Munhall.

6—ST. PIUS X (1954) Rev. Msgr. Russell A. Duker, S.E.O.D.
Res.: 2336 Brownsville Rd., 15210. Tel: 412-881-8344.

PORTAGE, CAMBRIA CO., SS. PETER AND PAUL (1917) [CEM] Rev. James A. Spontak.
Res.: 143 Church Rd., 15946. Tel: 814-736-9780; Fax: 814-736-8701.

PUNXSUTAWNEY, JEFFERSON CO., SS. PETER AND PAUL (1893) [CEM 2] Rev. Simeon B. Sibenik; Deacon Steven F. White.
Res.: 714 Sutton St., 15767. Tel: 814-938-6564; Fax: 814-938-6551.

RANKIN, ALLEGHENY CO., ST. JOHN'S, Closed. For inquiries for parish records contact the chancery.

SAGAMORE, ARMSTRONG CO., ST. MARY'S, [CEM] Closed. For inquiries for parish records contact the chancery.

SCOTTDALE, WESTMORELAND CO., ST. JOHN THE BAPTIST (1912) [CEM] Very Rev. John H. Salko.
Res.: 525 Porter Ave., 15683. Tel: 724-887-5072; Fax: 724-887-3365.

SHEFFIELD, WARREN CO., ST. MICHAEL (1905) [CEM] Rev. Roy R. Schubert.
Res.: 407 School St., P.O. Box 801, 16347. Tel: 814-968-5478; Fax: 814-968-4445.

SOUTH FORK, CAMBRIA CO., ST. MICHAEL'S, [CEM] Closed. Nov. 13, 2011. For inquiries for parish records, contact Sts. Peter and Paul, Portage.

SYKESVILLE, JEFFERSON CO., HOLY TRINITY (1907) [CEM] Very Rev. John J. Mihalco; Deacon Lucas M. Crawford.
Res.: 104 Shaffer St., 15865. Tel: 814-894-5440; Fax: 814-894-2412.

TARENTUM, ALLEGHENY CO., STS. PETER AND PAUL (1918) Rev. Wesley M. Mash.
Res.: 339 E. 10th Ave., 15084-1003. Tel: 724-224-3026; Fax: 724-224-5242. Web: www.stspeterpaul-byz.org.

UNIONTOWN, FAYETTE CO., ST. JOHN THE BAPTIST (1911) [CEM] Rev. Ronald P. Larko.
Res.: 185 E. Main St., 15401. Tel: 724-438-6027; Fax: 724-438-1382.

UPPER ST. CLAIR, ALLEGHENY CO., ST. GREGORY NAZIANZUS (1971) Rev. Thomas J. Wesdock.
Res.: 2005 Mohawk Rd., 15241. Tel: 412-835-7800; Fax: 412-835-7898.

WALL, ALLEGHENY CO., HOLY TRINITY (1928) Attended by St. Mary, East Pittsburgh.
Res.: 470 Wall Ave., 15148. Tel: 412-823-9857.

WINDBER, SOMERSET CO., ST. MARY (DORMITION) CHURCH (1900) [CEM] Rev. Gregory J. Michalisin.
Res.: 803 Somerset St., 15963. Tel: 814-467-8044; Fax: 814-467-8044.

STATE OF LOUISIANA

NEW ORLEANS, ST. NICHOLAS OF MYRA MISSION (1976) Deacon Gregory A. Haddad, Admin.; Rev. Phillip J. Linden Jr., S.S.J.

2435 S. Carrollton Ave., LA 70118. Tel: 504-861-0806; Fax: 985-872-9123. Email: stnicholasnola@yahoo.com. Mailing Address: P.O. Box 1359, Gray, LA 70359-1359.

STATE OF OHIO

ASHTABULA, ASHTABULA CO., ST. NICHOLAS (1906) Rev. A. Edward Gretchko.
Res.: 206 Cherry Rd., N.E., Massillon, OH 44646.
Church: 1104 E. Fifteenth St., OH 44004. Tel: 330-833-8501; Fax: 330-833-3359.

BOARDMAN, MAHONING CO., INFANT JESUS OF PRAGUE (1907) Rev. Christopher R. Burke.
Res.: 7754 S. Ave., OH 44512. Tel: 330-758-6019; Fax: 330-758-0768.

CAMPBELL, MAHONING CO., ST. MICHAEL (1922) [CEM] Rev. Msgr. Victor G. Romza.
Res.: 463 Robinson Rd., Box 426, OH 44405. Tel: 330-755-4831; Fax: 330-755-1818.

MINGO JUNCTION, JEFFERSON CO., ST. JOHN THE BAPTIST (1923) Attended by St. Joseph, Toronto.
Church: 207 Standard St., OH 43938. Tel: 740-535-0271; Fax: 740-537-9802.

NEWTON FALLS, TRUMBULL CO., ST. MICHAEL (1924) Rev. Andrew Kolitsos.
Church: 737 Ridge Rd., P.O. Box 485, OH 44444. Tel: 330-652-5199.

PLEASANT CITY, GUERNSEY CO., ST. MICHAEL THE ARCHANGEL (1898) [CEM] Rev. John J. Kapitan Jr., O.F.M.
Res.: 408 Walnut St., OH 43772. Tel: 740-685-3292; Fax: 740-685-3292.

TORONTO, JEFFERSON CO., ST. JOSEPH (1901) Deacon Paul Simko, Admin.; Rev. James Atkins, Admin. Emeritus.
Res.: 814 N. Fifth St., OH 43964. Tel: 740-537-1026; Fax: 740-537-9802. Email: fr.james@sbcglobal.net.

WARREN, TRUMBULL CO., SS. PETER AND PAUL'S (1925) [CEM] Rev. Andrew J. Deskevich.
Res.: 180 Belvedere Ave., N.E., OH 44483. Tel: 330-372-1875; Fax: 330-372-1896.

YOUNGSTOWN, MAHONING CO.
1—ASSUMPTION OF THE BLESSED VIRGIN (1899) [CEM] Very Rev. Richard I. Lambert.
Res.: 356 S. Belle Vista, OH 44509. Tel: 330-799-8163; Fax: 330-793-5360.
2—ST. GEORGE (1914) Attended by St. Nicholas, Youngstown., 1726 Canfield Rd., OH 44511. Tel: 330-782-2865.
3—ST. JOHN THE BAPTIST, Closed. For inquiries for parish records contact St. Nicholas, 1898 Wilson Ave., Youngstown, OH 44506. Tel: 330-743-0419.
4—ST. NICHOLAS (1912) [CEM] Rev. David J. Shortt.
Res.: 1898 Wilson Ave., OH 44506. Tel: 330-743-0419; Fax: 330-743-6888. Email: stnick9000@aol.com.

STATE OF TEXAS

HOUSTON, HARRIS CO., ST. JOHN CHRYSOSTOM (1982) Very Rev. Elias L. Rafaj; Deacon Andrew F. Veres.
Res.: 5402 Acorn St., TX 77092-4255. Tel: 713-681-3580; Fax: 713-681-3466. Email: houstonelias@gmail.com. Web: www.st-john-chrysostom-houston.org.

IRVING, DALLAS CO., ST. BASIL THE GREAT (1988) Rev. Daniel A. Forsythe.
Res.: 1118 E. Union Bower Rd., TX 75061. Tel: 972-438-5644; Fax: 972-767-2246. Web: stbasilsinirving.org.

STATE OF TENNESSEE

KNOXVILLE, KNOX CO., HOLY RESURRECTION MISSION (1999) Rev. Thomas P. O'Connell, Admin.; Deacon Ronald J. Volek.
Res.: 806 Villa View Way, TN 37920. Tel: 865-256-4880.
Church: 1031 N. Central St., TN 37917.

STATE OF WEST VIRGINIA

MORGANTOWN, MONONGALIA CO., ST. MARY HOLY PROTECTION (1918) Attended by Chaplain, Mt. St. Macrina, Uniontown, PA, Mailing Address: 2115 Listravia Ave., WV 26505.
Church: Tel: 304-296-2455; 724-439-4475 (Res.). Web: www.saintmarybyz.org.

WEIRTON, HANCOCK CO., ST. MARY'S (1924) Rev. Edward M. Lucas.
Res.: 3116 Elm St., WV 26062. Tel: 304-748-2087; Fax: 304-748-7550.

Retired:

Rev. Msgrs.—
Mihalik, Alexis E., 4300 Westford Pl., #6-C, Canfield, OH 44406-7010.
Tay, Peter P., 1200 San Pedro St., 15212.

Revs.—
Borsuk, Ronald W., 180 Van Buren St., Johnstown, 15909.
Chewning, Seraphim John, 821 Clark St., Cambridge, OH 43725.
Evancho, George, P.O. Box 568, Avella, 15312-0568.
Kolcun, Stephen J., 4469 Country Club Dr., 15236.
Petruska, Gregory, 15544 Bellflower Blvd., #C, Bellflower, CA 90706.
Pyo, Edward J., 200 Butler St., Kingston, 18704.
Whetstone, Richard, 7626 Pegotty Dr. N.E., Warren, OH 44484.

INSTITUTIONS LOCATED IN THE ARCHDIOCESE

[A] SEMINARIES, ARCHIEPARCHIAL

PITTSBURGH. *Byzantine Catholic Seminary of SS. Cyril and Methodius*, 3605 Perrysville Ave., 15214-2229. Tel: 412-321-8383; Fax: 412-321-9936. Email: office@bcs.edu. Web: www.bcs.edu. Very Rev. Archpriest John G. Petro, Rector. Tel: 412-321-7550; Revs. David M. Petras, Spiritual Dir. Tel: 412-321-8383, Ext. 12; R. Joseph Raptosh, Academic Dean; Sandra A. Collins, Ph.D., Librarian. Tel: 412-321-8383, Ext. 23; Rev. George D. Gallaro, J.C.O.L., J.C.O.D., S.T.L., Coord. Student Life. Tel: 412-321-8383, Ext. 15. Priests 3; Sisters 1; Students for Priesthood 10.

[B] HOMES FOR AGED

UNIONTOWN. *Mt. Macrina Manor*, 520 W. Main St., 15401-2602. Tel: 724-437-1400; Fax: 724-430-1172. Email: pbenford@mtmacrinamanor.com. Web: www.mtmacrinamanor.com. Patricia A. Benford, Admin. Sisters of St. Basil the Great 1; Bed Capacity 139.

WARREN. *Infant of Prague Manor*, 169 Kenmore, N.E., OH 44483. Tel: 330-372-4700. Rev. Andrew J. Deskevich. Housing for the elderly. Apartments 46; Total Staff 3; Total in Residence 31.

[C] MONASTERIES AND RESIDENCES OF PRIESTS AND BROTHERS

BUTLER. *Holy Trinity Monastery*, 134 Trinity Ln., P.O. Box 990, 16003. Tel: 724-287-4461; Fax: 724-287-6160. Rt. Rev. Leo R. Schlosser, Abbot/Hegumen; Rev. Anselm Orlosky, Prior; Bros. Michael Zetzer, Procurator; James Merva. Priests 2; Brothers 2.

[D] CONVENTS AND RESIDENCES FOR SISTERS

ALIQUIPPA. *St. George Convent*, 1000 Clinton St., 15001. Tel: 724-378-0238.

UNIONTOWN. *Monastery and Novitiate of the Sisters of St. Basil the Great*, 500 W. Main St., P.O. Box 878, 15401. Tel: 724-438-8644; Fax: 724-438-8660. Email: osbmolph@verizon.net. Web: www.sistersofstbasil.org. Sr. Seraphim Olsafsky, O.S.B.M., Prov. Supr.; Rev. Michael Huszti, J.C.O.L. Professed Sisters 61.

WARREN. *Queen of Heaven Monastery*, 169 Kenmore Ave. N.E., OH 44483. Tel: 330-856-1813; Fax: 330-856-9528. Email: qohm@netdotcom.com. Web: www.benedictinebyzantine.org. Sr. Margaret Mary Schima, O.S.B., Admin. Benedictine Sisters of the Byzantine Rite 7.

YOUNGSTOWN. *Byzantine Convent*, 3295 Cricket Dr., OH 44511. Tel: 330-757-9186. Sisters of St. Basil the Great 2.

[E] MISCELLANEOUS

UNIONTOWN. *Mt. St. Macrina House of Prayer*, 510 W. Main St., P.O. Box 878, 15401-0878. Tel: 724-438-7149; Fax: 724-438-3048. Email: hpmsm@verizon.net. Web: www.sistersofstbasil.org. Sr. Carol Petrasovich, O.S.B.M., Dir.

RELIGIOUS INSTITUTES OF WOMEN REPRESENTED IN THE ARCHDIOCESE

For further details refer to the corresponding bracketed number in the Religious Institutes of Women section.

[0230]—*Benedictine Sisters of the Byzantine Church*—O.S.B.

[3730]—*Sisters of the Order of St. Basil the Great*—O.S.B.M.

NECROLOGY

(No Deaths)

Romanian Catholic Diocese of Saint George in Canton

Most Reverend

JOHN MICHAEL BOTEAN, D.D.

Bishop for the Romanian Catholic Diocese of Canton; ordained May 18, 1986; appointed Bishop for the Romanian Catholic Diocese of Canton July 15, 1996; Episcopal Ordination August 24, 1996. *Res.: 1325 Skyway St., N.E., Canton, OH 44721.* Tel: 330-493-9355; Fax: 330-493-9963.

Chancery: 1121 44th St., N.E., Canton, OH 44714-1297. Tel: 330-493-9355; Fax: 330-493-9963.

Web: www.romaniancatholic.org

Email: ovim@rcdcanton.org

Elevated from Apostolic Exarchate for Romanian Byzantine to the Rank of an Eparchy (Diocese) March 26, 1987

The Jurisdiction of the Romanian Catholic Diocese of Canton extends territorially to all of the United States

Legal Title: The Romanian Catholic Diocese of Canton.

STATISTICAL OVERVIEW

Personnel	
Bishop	1
Abbots	1
Priests: Diocesan Active in Diocese	12
Priests: Retired, Sick or Absent	7
Number of Diocesan Priests	19
Religious Priests in Diocese	2
Total Priests in Diocese	21
Extern Priests in Diocese	4
Ordinations:	
Diocesan Priests	1
Transitional Deacons	1
Permanent Deacons in Diocese	7
Total Brothers	5
Total Sisters	4
Parishes	
Parishes	15
With Resident Pastor:	
Resident Diocesan Priests	10
Resident Religious Priests	1
Without Resident Pastor:	
Administered by Priests	4
Missions	4
Professional Ministry Personnel:	
Lay Ministers	4
Educational	
Diocesan Students in Other Seminaries	2
Total Seminarians	2
Catechesis/Religious Education:	
High School Students	45
Elementary Students	78
Total Students under Catholic Instruction	125
Vital Statistics	
Receptions into the Church:	
Infant Baptism Totals	37
Minor Baptism Totals	3
Adult Baptism Totals	1
Received into Full Communion	7
First Communions	37
Confirmations	38
Marriages:	
Catholic	15
Interfaith	7
Total Marriages	22
Deaths	15
Total Catholic Population	5,675

Former Bishop—Most Rev. LOUIS PUSCAS, D.D., ord. May 14, 1942; appt. Exarch, Dec. 4, 1982; Episcopal ordination, June 26, 1983; installed Aug. 28, 1983; promoted to first Eparch, April 16, 1987; retired July 15, 1993; died Oct. 3, 2009.

Protosyncellus—Very Rev. GEORGE DAVID, V.G.

Chancery—1121 44th St., N.E., Canton, 44714.

Chancellor and Moderator of the Curia—Very Rev. OVIDIU IOAN MARGINEAN.

Economos—JAMES P. DERSHAW, CPA, Reader.

College of Consultors—Very Revs. GEORGE DAVID, V.G.; AUREL PATER; ANDRE MATTHEWS, Vicar for Clergy; Rev. MICHAEL MOISIN; Rev. Msgr. GREGORY DUMA (Retired); Rev. GEORGE GAGE.

Protopresbyters: Deans—

Canton Deanery—Rev. Msgr. GREGORY DUMA (Retired).

Aurora Deanery—Very Rev. AUREL PATER.

Trenton Deanery—Very Rev. GEORGE DAVID, V.G.

Vicar for Theological Affairs—Sr. THERESA KOERNKE, I.H.M., Ph.D.

Vicar for Clergy—Very Rev. ANDRE MATTHEWS.

Director of Religious Education—VACANT.

Pro-Life Commission—Dr. DAN FARCASIU.

Director of Vocations—Very Rev. GEORGE DAVID, V.G.

Office to Aid the Church in Romania—Rev. MICHAEL MOISIN, Coord.

Diocesan Collections Coordinator—JAMES P. DERSHAW, CPA, Economos.

Evangelization—Rev. PAUL VOIDA.

Finance Council—Most Rev. JOHN MICHAEL BOTEAN, D.D.; Very Revs. GEORGE DAVID, V.G.; AUREL PATER, Protopresbyter; OVIDIU IOAN MARGINEAN; Rev. MICHAEL MOISIN.

Victim Assistance Coordinator—ANN FOSNAUGHT, 1121 44th St., N.E., Canton, 44714. Tel: 330-493-9355. Email: annf@rcdcanton.org.

Communications Director—Rev. ALIN NADIR DOGARU.

Tribunal of the Eparchy— The Romanian Catholic Eparchy of St. George in Canton has as its Tribunal the Tribunal of the Eparchy of St. Maron of Brooklyn.

Judicial Vicar—Very Rev. FRANCIS J. MARINI, J.D., J.C.D.

CLERGY, PARISHES, MISSIONS AND PAROCHIAL SCHOOLS

STATE OF OHIO

ALLIANCE, STARK CO., ST. THEODORE (1909) Attended by St. George Cathedral., Mailing Address: 1121 44th St. N.E., 44714-1297. Tel: 330-493-9355; Fax: 330-493-9963.
Church: 820 S. Linden St., 44601.

CANTON, STARK CO., ST. GEORGE CATHEDRAL (1912) Very Rev. Ovidiu Ioan Marginean, Rector; Deacon George Wendt.
Church & Res.: 1121 44th St., N.E., 44714-1297. Tel: 330-492-8413; Fax: 330-493-9963.
Bishop's Residence:—1325 Skyway St., N.E., 44721. Tel: 330-493-9355; Fax: 330-493-9963.
Catechesis/Religious Program—Carol Popa, D.R.E.; Jaime Moran, D.R.E. Students 15.

CHESTERLAND, GEAUGA CO., MOST HOLY TRINITY (1912) Attended by St. Helena, Cleveland. Rev. Gabriel Didita, Admin.
Church: 8549 Mayfield Rd., 44026-2625. Tel: 216-729-7636.
Catechesis/Religious Program—Students 6.

CLEVELAND, CUYAHOGA CO., ST. HELENA (1904) Rev. Gabriel Didita, Admin.; Adrian V Rosca, Lector; Florentin O. Popa, Cantor.
Church & Res.: 1367 W. 65th St., 44102-2109. Tel: 216-651-0965.
Catechesis/Religious Program—Students 10.

YOUNGSTOWN, MAHONING CO., ST. MARY (1906) Rev. George Gage.
Church & Res.: 7782 Glenwood Ave., Boardman, 44512-5823. Tel: 330-726-8573; Fax: 330-726-8573.

STATE OF CALIFORNIA

LOS ANGELES, LOS ANGELES CO., ST. MARY ROMANIAN CATHOLIC MISSION Rev. Calin Tamiian.
5329 Sepulveda Blvd., Sherman Oaks, CA 91411.
Res. & Mailing Address: 1447 Iguana Cir., Ventura, CA 93003-6337. Tel: 805-671-9936. Email: ctamiian@hotmail.com.

LAGUNA HILLS, ORANGE CO., ST. JOHN THE BAPTIST ROMANIAN CATHOLIC MISSION (2009) Rev. Chris Terhes, Admin.
St. Jeanne de Lestonnac School Chapel, 16791 E. Main St., Tustin, CA 92780.
Res. & Mailing Address: 24891 Hon Ave., CA 92653. Tel: 949-340-6703. Email: cterhes@gmail.com. Web: www.sfioan.org.

OXNARD, VENTURA CO., ST. JOHN THE EVANGELIST ROMANIAN CATHOLIC MISSION (2009) Rev. Calin Tamiian.
150 N. I St., CA 93030.
Res. & Mailing Address: 1447 Iguana Cir., Ventura, CA 93003-6337. Tel: 805-671-9936.

STATE OF ILLINOIS

AURORA, KANE CO.

1—ST. GEORGE (1935) Revs. Frederick Peterson, O.S.B.; Ronald H. Hilt; Deacons George Dzwricsko; Paul Crawford.
Res.: 850 Butterfield Rd., IL 60502-8609. Tel: 630-897-7215, Ext. 326; Fax: 630-897-0393.
Church: 720 Rural St., IL 60505-2551. Tel: 630-851-4002.
Catechesis/Religious Program—Carol Glover, D.R.E. Students 27.

2—ST. MICHAEL (1906) Very Rev. Aurel Pater.
Res. & Church: 609 N. Lincoln Ave., IL 60505-2112. Tel: 630-897-8115; Fax: 630-897-5923.

CHICAGO, COOK CO., SS. PETER AND PAUL CHURCH (1994) Rev. Sergiu Cornea.
Res.: 1472 Burr Oak Cir., Aurora, IL 60506-1396. Tel: 630-205-4806; Fax: 630-896-4807. Email: slcornea@aol.com.
Church: 3107 Fullerton Ave., IL 60647-2809. Tel:

773-342-7373; Fax: 773-342-7373.

STATE OF INDIANA

EAST CHICAGO, LAKE CO., ST. NICHOLAS (1913) Rev. Alin Nadir Dogaru, Admin.
Church & Res.: 4309 Olcott Ave., IN 46312-2649. Tel: 219-398-3760; Fax: 219-398-3760. Email: adogaru@romaniancatholic.org.

STATE OF MASSACHUSETTS

BOSTON, MIDDLESEX CO., ROMANIAN CATHOLIC MISSION OF BOSTON (2000) Rev. Michael Moisin, Admin.
Res. & Mailing Address: 8 Druce St., Brookline, MA 02445-4213. Tel: 617-216-4980; Fax: 617-566-3073.

STATE OF MICHIGAN

DEARBORN, WAYNE CO., ST. MARY Rev. Gheorghe Opris, Admin.
Church & Res.: 823 S. Military, MI 48124-2109. Tel: 313-274-2347.

DETROIT, WAYNE CO., ST. JOHN THE BAPTIST Very Rev. Emmanuel G. Samayoa.
Res.: 2371 Woodstock Dr., MI 48203-1060. Tel: 313-731-8548.
Catechesis / Religious Program—Annamaria Silveri, D.R.E.

STATE OF NEW JERSEY

ROEBLING, BURLINGTON CO., ST. MARY, Attended by St. Basil, Trenton. Very Rev. George David.
Church: 180 Alden Ave., NJ 08554-1125. Tel: 609-695-6093.

TRENTON, MERCER CO., ST. BASIL (1909) Very Rev. George David.
Church & Res.: 238 Adeline St., NJ 08611-2420. Tel: 609-695-6093; Fax: 609-695-6093.

STATE OF NEW YORK

ASTORIA, QUEENS CO., ST. MARY ROMANIAN CATHOLIC MISSION
Holy Cross Church: 31-12 30th St., Long Island City, NY 11106-2802. Tel: 718-845-5366. Rev. Radu N. Titonea.
Res.: 11814 83rd Ave., Apt. 2E, Kew Gardens, NY 11415-1309. Tel: 347-935-5378.

STATE OF PENNSYLVANIA

MCKEESPORT, ALLEGHENY CO., ST. MARY Rev. Paul Voida.
Church & Res.: 318 26th St., PA 15132-7014. Tel: 412-673-5552.

Unassigned:
Very Rev.—
Matthews, Andre
Revs.—
Kovacevich, Steve
Yossa, Kenneth F.

On Loan to Other Diocese (Eparches):
Rev.—
Kolitsos, Andrew
Deacons—
Puscas, Michael
Puscas, Steven
Puscas, Victor

Retired:
Rev. Msgr.—
Duma, Gregory
Revs.—
Buga, John
Kirila, Michael
Streza, Charles V.

INSTITUTIONS LOCATED IN THE DIOCESE

[A] MONASTERIES

NEWBERRY SPRINGS, CA. *Holy Resurrection Monastery*, Mailing Address: 300 S. 2nd Ave., Saint Nazianz, WI 54232. Tel: 760-644-6127. Rt. Rev. Archimandrite Nicholas Zachariadis, Abbot; Revs. Maximos Davies, Hieromonk; Moses Wright, Hierodeacon.

OLYMPIA, WA. *Holy Theophany Monastery*, 10220 66th Ave., S.E., WA 98513-9207. Tel: 360-491-8233. Email: htheophany@earthlink.net. Web: www.holytheophanymonastery.org. Sr. Anastasia, Abbess.

NECROLOGY

† Brown, Konstantin K.—Died Dec. 30, 2010

An asterisk (*) denotes an organization that has established tax-exempt status directly with the IRS and is not covered by the USCCB Group Ruling.

Ukrainian Catholic Diocese of St. Josaphat in Parma

(Editor's Note: 2012 information was not received)

Most Reverend

ROBERT M. MOSKAL, D.D.

Retired Bishop of St. Josaphat in Parma; ordained March 25, 1963; appointed Titular Bishop of Agathopolis and Auxiliary Bishop of the Archeparchy of Philadelphia August 3, 1981; consecrated October 13, 1981; appointed First Bishop of St. Josaphat in Parma December 5, 1983; retired July 29, 2009. *Res.: 5720 State Rd., P.O. Box 347180, Cleveland, OH 44134.*

Most Reverend

JOHN BURA

Auxiliary Bishop of Philadelphia Ukrainian and Apostolic Administrator of St. Josaphat in Parma; ordained February 14, 1971; appointed Auxiliary Bishop of Philadelphia Ukrainian and Titular Bishop of Limisa January 3, 2006; ordained February 21, 2006; appointed Apostolic Administrator of St. Josaphat in Parma July 29, 2009.

(VACANT SEE)

Chancery: 5720 State Rd., P.O. Box 347180, Parma, OH 44134-7180. Tel: 440-888-1522; Fax: 440-888-3477.

Email: josaphateparchy@cs.com

ESTABLISHED DECEMBER 3, 1983.

The jurisdiction of the Bishop of St. Josaphat in Parma extends territorially through all the States of Ohio, Mississippi, West Virginia, Kentucky, Tennessee, Alabama, Georgia, North Carolina, South Carolina, Florida and western Pennsylvania. With regards to persons, his subjects are Catholics of the Byzantine Ukrainian Rite: 1. Who immigrated to this country from Galicia, Bucovina and other Ukrainian provinces; 2. Who descend from such persons (Can. 755); 3. Women married to men referable to 1 and 2, if they comply with (Can. 98, n.4); 4. Who in accordance with (Can. 98, n.3) changed their Rite; 5. Converts to the Catholic Church of the Byzantine Ukrainian Rite; 6. And in fact, all other Catholics of the Byzantine Ukrainian Rite who are attached to parishes subject to the jurisdiction of the Bishop of St. Josaphat in Parma.

For legal titles of parishes and diocesan institutions, consult the Chancery.

STATISTICAL OVERVIEW

Personnel
- Auxiliary Bishops . . . 1
- Retired Bishops . . . 1
- Priests: Diocesan Active in Diocese . . . 32
- Priests: Diocesan Active Outside Diocese . . . 4
- Priests: Retired, Sick or Absent . . . 12
- Number of Diocesan Priests . . . 48
- Religious Priests in Diocese . . . 1
- Total Priests in Diocese . . . 49
- Extern Priests in Diocese . . . 4

Ordinations:
- Diocesan Priests . . . 1
- Transitional Deacons . . . 2
- Permanent Deacons in Diocese . . . 8
- Total Brothers . . . 3
- Total Sisters . . . 2

Parishes
- Parishes . . . 38

With Resident Pastor:
- Resident Diocesan Priests . . . 30
- Resident Religious Priests . . . 1

Without Resident Pastor:
- Administered by Priests . . . 7
- Missions . . . 4

Professional Ministry Personnel:
- Brothers . . . 3
- Sisters . . . 2

Welfare
- Other Institutions . . . 3

Educational
- Diocesan Students in Other Seminaries . . . 2
- Total Seminarians . . . 2

Catechesis/Religious Education:
- High School Students . . . 32
- Elementary Students . . . 101
- Total Students under Catholic Instruction . . . 135

Vital Statistics

Receptions into the Church:
- Infant Baptism Totals . . . 48
- Minor Baptism Totals . . . 1
- Adult Baptism Totals . . . 1
- Received into Full Communion . . . 110

First Communions . . . 50

Confirmations . . . 54

Marriages:
- Catholic . . . 6
- Interfaith . . . 1

Total Marriages . . . 7

Deaths . . . 109

Total Catholic Population . . . 8,500

Former Bishop—Most Rev. ROBERT M. MOSKAL, ord. March 25, 1963; appt. Titular Bishop of Agathopolis and Auxiliary Bishop of the Archeparchy of Philadelphia Aug. 3, 1981; cons. Oct. 13, 1981; appt. First Bishop of St. Josaphat in Parma Dec. 5, 1983; retired July 29, 2009.

Chancery—5720 State Rd., P.O. Box 347180, Parma, 44134-7180. Tel: 440-888-1522; Fax: 440-888-3477. Web: stjosaphateparchy.org. Office Hours: Mon.-Thurs. 10-12 & 2-4, Fri. 10-12

Chancellor—Very Rev. Canon STEVEN PALIWODA.

Vice Chancellor—Rev. VALERIAN MICHLIK.

Vicar General—Rev. Msgr. GEORGE APPLEYARD.

Judicial Vicar—VACANT.

Consultors—Rev. Msgr. GEORGE APPLEYARD; Very Rev. Canon STEVEN PALIWODA; Very Rev. MICHAEL POLOSKY; Very Rev. Canon ANDREW HANOWSKY; Rev. MICHAEL KRUPKA; Very Rev. IGNATIUS KURY.

Eparchial Corporation—Most Rev. JOHN BURA, Pres.; Rev. Msgr. GEORGE APPLEYARD, Vice Pres.; Very Rev. Canon STEVEN PALIWODA, Sec. & Treas.

Administrative Council—Most Rev. JOHN BURA; Very Rev. Canon ANDREW HANOWSKY; Revs. MARK MOROZOWICH, S.E.O.D.; IHOR KASIYAN; Deacons DONALD BILLY; MARK PROKOPOWICH.

Vicar for Clergy—Very Rev. ANTHONY BALISTRERI.

Vicar for Religious—Rev. Msgr. GEORGE APPLEYARD.

Tribunal—

Judicial Vicar—VACANT.

Judge—VACANT.

Defender of the Bond—VACANT.

Notary—VACANT.

Liturgical Commission—Most Rev. JOHN BURA; Revs. VALERIAN MICHLIK; IVAN CHIROVSKY; Rev. Msgr. GEORGE APPLEYARD; Rev. MARK MOROZOWICH, S.E.O.D.

Examiners of Clergy—Rev. Msgr. GEORGE APPLEYARD; Rev. JOSEPH TAMBURRO.

Personnel Board—Very Rev. ANTHONY BALISTRERI, Chm.; Very Rev. Canon STEVEN PALIWODA, Sec.; Very Rev. MICHAEL POLOSKY; Revs. VALERIAN MICHLIK; MICHAEL KRUPKA.

St. Josaphat Sacerdotal Society— (next election in May 2011) Most Rev. JOHN BURA, Ex Officio; Very Rev. Canons STEVEN PALIWODA, Ex Officio; ANDREW HANOWSKY, Sec.; Rev. IVAN CHIROVSKY; Very Rev. IGNATIUS KURY; Rev. PETER TOMAS, S.J.P. Alternates: Revs. VALERIAN MICHLIK; IHOR KASIYAN; GREGORY MAYDYA; IHOR HOHOSHA.

Religious Education—Sr. ANN LASZOK, O.S.B.M., Dir.

League of Ukrainian Catholics—Rev. VALERIAN MICHLIK, Western PA Spiritual Dir.

Obnova Societies—Rev. Mitred Archpriest WOLODYMYR WOLOSZCZUK (Retired).

Vocations—Rev. MARK MOROZOWICH, S.E.O.D.

Acolyte Confraternity—Deacon DONALD BILLY; Mr. JOSEPH LEVY.

Permanent Deacon Program—Rev. Msgr. GEORGE APPLEYARD.

Priests' Continuing Education—Rev. JOSEPH TAMBURRO.

Eparchial Convention—Rev. Msgr. GEORGE APPLEYARD.

Youth Ministries—Very Rev. MICHAEL POLOSKY.

Lay Ministries—Sisters ANN LASZOK, O.S.B.M.; OLGA MARIE FARYNA, O.S.B.M.

Presbyteral Council—Most Rev. JOHN BURA; Rev. Msgr. GEORGE APPLEYARD; Rev. Msgr. Mitred JOHN P. STEVENSKY; Rev. IHOR HOHOSHO; Very Rev. ANTHONY BALISTRERI; Very Rev. Canon STEVEN PALIWODA; Very Rev. MICHAEL POLOSKY; Revs. JOSEPH TAMBURRO; VALERIAN MICHLIK.

Arbitration Board—Rev. Msgr. GEORGE APPLEYARD; Rev. Archpriest PHILIP BUMBAR; Rev. IVAN CHIROVSKY; Rev. Msgr. Mitred JOHN P. STEVENSKY; Rev. XAVIER ELAMBASSERY.

Protopresbyteries—

Western Protopresbytery—Very Rev. Canon STEVEN PALIWODA, 3038 Charleston Ave., Lorain, 44055-2464. Tel: 440-277-7114 Akron, OH; Austintown, OH; Brunswick, OH; Canton, OH; Cleveland, OH; Lorain, OH; Parma, OH (Cathedral); Parma, OH (St. Andrew); Parma, OH (Pokrova); Rossford, OH; Solon, OH; Youngstown, OH.

Central Protopresbytery—Rev. Msgr. GEORGE APPLEYARD, 726 Washington Ave., Carnegie, PA 15106. Tel: 412-279-4652 Aliquippa, PA; Ambridge, PA; Arnold, PA (New Kensington); Carnegie, PA; Jeannette, PA; Lyndora, PA; McKees Rocks, PA; McKeesport, PA; Pittsburgh, PA (St. George); Pittsburgh, PA (St. John); Wheeling, WV; Wilmerding, PA.

Eastern Protopresbytery—Very Rev. ANTHONY BALISTRERI, 22 Bentz St., Ramey, PA 16671. Tel: 814-378-7688 Altoona, PA; Ford City, PA; Johnstown, PA; Latrobe, PA; New Alexandria, PA; Northern Cambria, PA (Barnesboro); Ramey, PA; Revloc, PA; West Leechburg, PA.

Southern Protopresbytery—Rev. Msgr. Mitred JOHN P. STEVENSKY, 434 90th Ave., N., St. Petersburg, FL 33702. Tel: 727-576-1001 Apopka, FL; Conyers, GA; Spring Hill (Brooksville), FL; Miami, FL; North Port, FL; St. Petersburg, FL.

Mid-Atlantic Protopresbytery—Very Rev. MARK SHUEY, 4801 Topstone Rd., Raleigh, NC 27603. Tel: 919-779-7246 Garner, NC (Ss. Volodymyr and Olha); Raleigh, NC (St. Nicholas); Charlotte,

NC (St. Basil); Knoxville, TN (St. Thomas the Apostle).

Presbyters—Rev. Msgr. GEORGE APPLEYARD, Holy Trinity, 726 Washington Ave., Carnegie, PA 15106-4109. Tel: 412-279-4652; Fax: 412-279-5109; Cell: 724-290-6561; Tel: 814-385-6775 (Cabin). Email: apple@cboss.com; Rev. RICHARD ARMSTRONG, St. Thomas the Apostle, 2044 Farmstead Ln., Powell, TN 37849; Very Rev. ANTHONY BALISTRERI, Annunciation BVM, 22 Bentz St., Ramey, PA 16671. Tel: 814-378-7688; Rev. MICHAEL BLISZCZ (on loan to St. Nicholas Eparchy) St. Michael, 4390 Woodside Oaks Dr., S.E., Grand Rapids, MI 49546-6216. Tel: 616-949-1151; Rev. Archpriest PHILIP BUMBAR, 726 Washington Ave., Carnegie, PA 15106-4109. Tel: 412-279-4652; Fax: 412-279-5109; Rev. Msgr. Mitred MARTIN A. CANAVAN, S.T.L., J.C.L., 2850 N. Palm Aire Dr. #604, Pompano Beach, FL 33069. Tel: 305-450-8003. Email: pmsgr@en.com; Revs. JASON CHARRON, Ss. Volodymyr and Olha, 8312 White Oak Rd., Garner, NC 27529. Tel: 919-376-8099; IVAN CHIROVSKY, St. John the Baptist, 109 S. 7th St., Pittsburgh, PA 15203-1028. Tel: 412-431-2531; Fax: 412-431-0727; Cell: 786-251-9522. Email: ugveg@aol.com; CRAIG DE PAULO (on leave); MICHAEL DERBISH, O.F.M. (Retired), 2001 Main St., Aliquippa, PA 15001-2724. Tel: 724-375-7016; IHOR HOHOSHO, St. John the Baptist, 204 Olivia St., Mc Kees Rocks, PA 15136. Tel: 412-331-5605; MICHAEL DROZDOVSKY, Pokrova, 6790 Broadview Rd., Parma, 44134. Tel: 216-524-0918 (Residence & Office); Fax: 216-524-0919; Tel: 216-524-6872 (Hall Office); 216-524-6871 (Hall); BORIS DUKELEY (Retired), 415 Montpellier Court, Spring Hill, FL 34608. Tel: 352-684-4876; XAVIER ELAMBASSERY, Assumption BVM/Nativity BVM, 4827 Rte. 982, Latrobe, PA 15650. Tel: 724-537-6450; JOHN GRIBIK, St. Demetrius/Ss. Peter and Paul, 1013 Gaskill Ave., Jeannette, PA 15644. Tel: 724-523-9389; VOLODYMYR GRYTSYUK, Protection BVM, 27275 Aurora Rd., Solon, 44139-1804. Tel: 440-248-4549; Cell: 440-539-2621; Very Rev. Canons ANDREW HANOWSKY, Ss. Peter & Paul, 2280 W. 7th St., Cleveland, 44113. Tel: 216-861-2176; Cell: 216-401-0004; ROBERT HNATYSHYN (Retired), 452 E. McMurray Rd., Mc Murray, PA 15317. Tel: 724-969-5003; Revs. JERRY IKALOWYCH, Mother of God, 2880 Hwy. 138, N.E., Conyers, GA 30013. Tel: 770-760-1111; Fax: 770-922-2992. 143 McBride, Canonsburg, PA 15317; JOHN IZRAL, St. Vladimir, 1601 Kenneth Ave., Arnold, PA 15068-4219. Tel: 724-339-9622; OLEH KACHUR (on loan to Toronto Eparchy) 251 Bolton St., Apt. 20, Ottawa, Canada ON K1N 5B5; IHOR KASIYAN, St. Andrew, 7700 Hoertz Rd., Parma, 44134-6404. Tel: 440-843-9149; 440-845-2270 (Residence); Cell: 440-391-8500. Email: pastor@standrewucc.org. Web: www.standrewucc.org; MICHAEL KOUTS, St. Andrew, 8064 Weeping Willow St., Brooksville, FL 34613. Tel: 352-596-2433; SEVERYN KOVALYSHIN (Entrance BVM into Temple) 1078 N. Biscayne Dr., North Port, FL 34291. Tel: 941-426-7931. Email: severinokov@yahoo.it. Web: www.ukrainiancatholicflorida.com; ANDREW KRASULSKI, St. John/Protection BVM, 606 Maple Ave., Johnstown, PA 15901. Tel: 814-535-2634. Email: stjohnbaptist@yahoo.com; MICHAEL KRUPKA, Our Lady of Perpetual Help, 4136 Jacob St., Wheeling, WV 26003. Tel: 304-232-2168; 304-232-1774 (Hall). Email: krupka@juno.com; IVAN KUBISHYN, St. Mary's Protection, 305 Lake McCoy Dr., Apopka, FL 32712. Tel: 407-880-1640; MICHAEL KULICK, 8455 Sunnydale Dr., Brecksville, 44141. Tel: 440-526-4517; 440-888-8811 (Office); Fax: 440-888-5818; Cell: 440-537-0175; Pager: 440-948-2976. Email: dddfriend@sbcglobal.net; Very Rev. IGNATIUS KURY, Holy Ghost/St. Nicholas, 1859 Carter Ave., Akron, 44301-3198. Tel: 330-724-8277; Cell: 202-270-6153; Revs. SEAN J. LABAT, St. Basil Mission, Charlotte, NC. 1315 Pickens St., Apt. 1, Columbia, SC 29201. Tel: 803-381-7073. Email: sjlabat@yahoo.com; DOUGLAS LORANCE, 610 Hansen Ave., Lyndora, PA 16045-1325. Tel: 724-283-6230; Fax: 724-283-0363; GREGORY MADEYA, B.H.S., St. John the Baptist, 1907 Eden Park Blvd., Mc Keesport, PA 15132. Tel: 412-672-0923. 111 Third St., Dravosburg, PA 15034. Tel: 412-896-1668; Cell: 412-805-3451. Email: greggorio2@aol.com; ANDREW MARKO (Retired), 33225 Electric Blvd., Avon Lake, 44012. Tel: 440-933-6954; VALERIAN MICHLIK, St. George, 3455 California Ave., Pittsburgh, PA 15212-2180. Tel: 412-766-8801; Fax: 412-766-3379; Tel: 412-766-8800 (Hall); 412-766-8802 (Sheptytsky Hall). Email: frvalmichlik@yahoo.com; saintgeorgepghs@aol.com. Web: saintgeorgepittsburgh.org; MARK MOROZOWICH, S.E.O.D., 3900 B Watson Pl., N.W., Apt. G3A, Washington, DC 20016. Tel: 202-965-1572 (House); Cell: 202-468-5166; Tel: 202-319-6515 (Voice Mail); Fax: 202-319-4967. Email: morozowich@cua.edu; GEORGE MULLONKAL, St. Michael, 133 Walnut St., Rossford, 43460-1248. Tel: 419-666-5627; Rev. Msgr. MICHAEL NESTOR (Retired), 867 N. Concord St., Gilbert, AZ 85234. Tel: 480-507-5015. Email: imike@worldnet.att.net; Very Rev. Canon STEVEN PALIWODA, Protopresbyter, Western, St. John the Baptist, 3038 Charleston Ave., Lorain, 44055-2464. Tel: 440-277-7114. Email: steve@eriennet.net; Rev. VASYL PETRIV, St. Josaphat Cathedral, 5720 State Rd., Parma, 44134. Tel: 440-886-2108; Very Rev. MICHAEL POLOSKY, Ss. Peter & Paul, 404 Sixth St., Ambridge, PA 15003. Tel: 724-266-2262 (Office); Fax: 724-266-2262. Email: sspandp@aol.com; Rev. Msgrs. Mitred MICHAEL POLOWAY (Retired), Shevchenko Manor, 5620 W. 24th St., #211, Parma, 44134. Tel: 216-741-8106; Cell: 216-235-7001; MICHAEL REWTIUK (Retired) (on leave) 3112 Marioncliff Dr., Parma, 44134. Email: 2stm@buckeye-express.com; markmorozowich@comcast.net; THOMAS A. SAYUK (on leave); Revs. MATTHEW SCHROEDER, Assumption BVM, 11000 S.W. 128th St., Miami, FL 33176. 39 N.W. 57th Court, Miami, FL 33126. Tel: 305-262-4192; Fax: 305-261-9759; Tel: 786-242-8146 (Home). Email: father@uccm.us. Web: www.uccm.us; JAROSLAV SHUDRAK; Very Rev. MARK SHUEY, St. Nicholas Mission; St. Basil the Great, Charlotte. Email: george.gulyas@lpl.com. Web: www.saintbasilcharlotte.org; 4801 Topstone Rd., Raleigh, NC 27603. Tel: 919-779-7246. Email: rfmark@nc.rr.com; Revs. JOHN SMEREKA (visiting priest) 410 7th Ave., Carnegie, PA 15106; MICHAEL SOPP (on leave of absence) P.O. Box 49, Kittanning, PA 16201; ANIBAL SOUTUS, 2941 Lookout, Atlanta, GA 30035. Tel: 404-723-7396; Rev. Msgr. Mitred JOHN P. STEVENSKY, Protopresbyter, Southern, Epiphany of Our Lord, 434 90th Ave., N., St. Petersburg, FL 33702-3022. Tel: 727-576-1001. Email: msgrjps@mindspring.com; Revs. JOSEPH TAMBURRO, Immaculate Conception/Imm. Con., 3711 Campbell Ave., P.O. Box 1335, Northern Cambria, PA 15714-1335. Tel: 814-948-9193 (Res.). Email: rublievht@sbcglobal.net; PETER TOMAS, S.J.P., St. Anne, Holy Trinity, 3055 S. Raccoon Rd., Austintown, 44515-5351. Tel: 330-793-5436 (Res.); Fax: 330-793-5436. Office: 4310 Kirk Rd., Austintown, 44511-1899. Tel: 330-792-8555. Email: stannechurch@yahoo.com; frpetertomas@yahoo.com; Rev. Mitred Archpriest WOLODYMYR WOLOSZCZUK (Retired), 4240 Timberline Blvd., Venice, FL 34293. Tel: 941-493-7299; Rev. Canon WALTER WYSOCHANSKY (Retired), 404 Sixth St., Ambridge, PA 15003. Tel: 724-266-2262; Rev. STEVEN ZARICHNY, Holy Trinity, 526 W. Rayen Ave., Youngstown, 44502-1124. Tel: 330-744-5820.

CLERGY, PARISHES, MISSIONS AND PAROCHIAL SCHOOLS

STATE OF OHIO

PARMA

1—ST. ANDREW (1965) Rev. Ihor Kasiyan; Deacon Roman Turchyn.
Res.: 7700 Hoertz Rd., 44134-6404. Tel: 440-843-9149; Fax: 440-845-2986.
Catechesis/Religious Program—Mary Sulhan, D.R.E. Students 19.

2—ST. JOSAPHAT CATHEDRAL (1959) Revs. Michael Kulick; Vasyl Petriv; Claudio Melnicki; Archdeacon Jeffrey Smolilo.
Res.: 5720 State Rd., 44134-2536. Tel: 440-886-2108.

3—POKROVA UKRAINIAN CATHOLIC PARISH (1973) [CEM] Rev. Michael Drozdovsky.
Mailing Address: 6790 Broadview Rd., 44134.
Res.: 6810 Broadview Rd., 44134-4804. Tel: 216-524-0918; Fax: 216-524-0919.

AKRON, SUMMIT CO., HOLY GHOST Very Rev. Ignatius Kury.
Res.: 1859 Carter Ave., 44301. Tel: 330-724-8277.

AUSTINTOWN, MAHONING CO., ST. ANNE (1967) [JC] Unassigned.
Res.: 3055 S. Raccoon Rd., 44515-5351. Tel: 330-792-8555; Fax: 330-793-5436. Email: stannechurch@yahoo.com.
Catechesis/Religious Program—Mrs. Michelle Tomas, D.R.E. Students 7.

CANTON, STARK CO., ST. NICHOLAS, Attended by Akron. Very Rev. Ignatius Kury.
Res.: 1859 Carter Ave., Akron, 44301. Tel: 330-724-8277.

CLEVELAND, CUYAHOGA CO., SS. PETER AND PAUL, [CEM] Very Rev. Canon Andrew Hanowsky.
Res.: 2280 W. 7th St., 44113. Tel: 216-861-2176.

LORAIN, LORAIN CO., ST. JOHN THE BAPTIST (1913) Very Rev. Canon Steven Paliwoda.
Res.: 3038 Charleston Ave., 44055-2164. Tel: 440-277-7114.
Church: 2445 E. 31st St., 44055.

ROSSFORD, WOOD CO., ST. MICHAEL Rev. George Mullonkal.
Res.: 133 Walnut St., 43460-1248. Tel: 419-666-5627; Fax: 419-666-3077.

SOLON, CUYAHOGA CO., PROTECTION B.V.M. Rev. Volodymyr Grytsyuk.
Res.: 27275 Aurora Rd., 44139-1804. Tel: 440-248-4549.
Catechesis/Religious Program—Students 7.

YOUNGSTOWN, MAHONING CO., HOLY TRINITY Rev. Steven Zarichny.
Res.: 526 W. Rayen Ave., 44502-1124. Tel: 330-744-5820.

STATE OF FLORIDA

APOPKA, ORANGE CO., ST. MARY'S Rev. Ivan Kubishyn; Deacon Richard Wilhelm.
Res.: 245 Lake McCoy Dr., FL 32712. Tel: 407-880-1640.
Catechesis/Religious Program—

BROOKSVILLE, HERNANDO CO., ST. ANDREW Rev. Michael Kouts.
Mailing Address: 8064 Weeping Willow St., FL 34613. Tel: 352-597-4366.

MIAMI, DADE CO., ASSUMPTION OF B.V.M. Rev. Matthew Schroeder.
Res.: 11000 S.W. 128th St., FL 33176. Tel: 305-262-4192; Fax: 305-261-9759.
Church: 39 N.W. 57th Ct., FL 33126.
Catechesis/Religious Program—Students 10.
Mission— Lantana, Palm Beach Co., FL.

NORTH PORT, SARASOTA CO., ENTRANCE OF B.V.M. INTO THE TEMPLE (ST. MARY'S) Rev. Severyn Kovalyshin.
Res.: 1078 N. Biscayne Dr., FL 34286. Tel: 941-426-7931; Fax: 941-426-7931.

ST. PETERSBURG, PINELLAS CO., EPIPHANY OF OUR LORD Rev. Msgr. Mitred John P. Stevensky.
Res.: 434 90th Ave. N., FL 33702. Tel: 727-576-1001 (Res.); Fax: 727-576-6821.

STATE OF GEORGIA

CONYERS, ROCKDALE CO., MOTHER OF GOD Revs. Jerry Ikalowych; Anibal Soutus.
Res.: 2880 Hwy. 138, N.E., GA 30013. Tel: 770-760-1111.

STATE OF NORTH CAROLINA

CHARLOTTE, MECKLENBURG CO., ST. BASIL THE GREAT MISSION Very Rev. Mark Shuey; Rev. Sean J. LaBat.
c/o Rev. Mark Shuey, 4801 Topstone Rd., Raleigh, NC 27603. Tel: 919-779-7246.
Res.: 729 Aiken St., Columbia, SC 29201. Tel: 803-381-7073.

GARNER, WAKE CO., SS. VOLODYMYR AND OLHA MISSION (2006) Rev. Msgr. Mitred Martin A. Canavan.
8312 White Oak Rd., NC 27529. Tel: 919-376-8099.
Catechesis/Religious Program—Students 5.

RALEIGH, WAKE CO., ST. NICHOLAS MISSION Very Rev. Mark Shuey.
4801 Topstone Rd., NC 27603. Tel: 919-779-7246.

STATE OF PENNSYLVANIA

ALIQUIPPA, BEAVER CO., SS. PETER AND PAUL (1916) Rev. Ihor Hohosha. Served from St. John the Baptist, McKees Rocks.
Res.: 2001 Main St., PA 15001. Tel: 724-375-7016.

ALTOONA, BLAIR CO., IMMACULATE CONCEPTION, [CEM], Served by Northern Cambria , Mailing Address: 2024 20th St., PA 16601.

AMBRIDGE, BEAVER CO., SS. PETER AND PAUL (1907) [CEM] Very Rev. Michael Polosky. In Res., Rev. Canon Walter Wysochansky (Retired).
Res.: 404 6th St., PA 15003. Tel: 412-266-2262; Fax: 412-266-2262.
Catechesis/Religious Program—Michael Cross, D.R.E. Students 55.
Convent—542 Melrose Ave., PA 15003. Tel: 724-266-5578. Sisters of St. Basil the Great.

CARNEGIE, ALLEGHENY CO., HOLY TRINITY (1951) [CEM] Rev. Msgr. George Appleyard; Rev. John Smereka; Rev. Canon Philip Bumbar.
Res.: 730 Washington Ave., PA 15106. Tel: 412-279-4652; Fax: 412-279-5109.
Catechesis/Religious Program—Donna Sradomski, D.R.E. (Elementary); Mark Medwig, D.R.E. (High School). Students 17.

FORD CITY, ARMSTRONG CO., ST. MARY, [CEM] Rev. John Gribik.
Res.: 514 Ninth St., PA 16226. Tel: 724-763-1203.

JEANNETTE, WESTMORELAND CO., ST. DEMETRIUS Rev. John Gribik.
Res.: 1013 Gaskill Ave., PA 15644-3307. Tel: 724-523-9389.

JOHNSTOWN, CAMBRIA CO., ST. JOHN THE BAPTIST, [CEM] Rev. Andrew Krasulski.

Res.: 606 Maple Ave., PA 15901. Tel: 814-535-2634; Fax: 814-535-2634.
Catechesis/Religious Program—Miss Mary Anne Varholak, D.R.E. Students 4.

LATROBE, WESTMORELAND CO., ASSUMPTION OF B.V.M. Rev. Xavier Elambassery.
Res.: 4827 Rt. 982, PA 15650. Tel: 412-537-6450.

LYNDORA, BUTLER CO., ST. MICHAEL Rev. Douglas Lorance.
Res.: 610 Hansen Ave., PA 16045-1325. Tel: 724-283-6230; Fax: 724-283-0363. Email: stmikeschurch@zoominternet.net.
Catechesis/Religious Program—Students 7.

MCKEES ROCKS, ALLEGHENY CO., ST. JOHN THE BAPTIST (1941) Rev. Ihor Hohosha.
Res.: 204 Olivia St., PA 15136. Tel: 412-331-5605; Fax: 412-331-8809.

MCKEESPORT, ALLEGHENY CO., ST. JOHN THE BAPTIST Rev. Gregory Madeya, B.H.S.
Res.: 1907 Eden Park Blvd., PA 15132. Tel: 412-672-0923.

NEW ALEXANDRIA, WESTMORELAND CO., NATIVITY B.V.M., [CEM] Attended by Assumption of B.V.M., Latrobe., Mailing Address: 4827 Rte. 982, Latrobe, PA 15650. Tel: 412-537-6450.
Church: Shersburg Rd., PA 15670.

NEW KENSINGTON (ARNOLD), WESTMORELAND CO., ST. VLADIMIR (1912) Rev. John Izral.
Res.: 1601 Kenneth Ave., Arnold, PA 15068. Tel: 724-339-9622.

NORTHERN CAMBRIA, CAMBRIA CO., IMMACULATE CONCEPTION, Unassigned.
Res.: 300 Campbell Ave., P.O. Box 1335, PA 15714. Tel: 814-948-9193.

PITTSBURGH, ALLEGHENY CO.
1—ST. GEORGE Rev. Valerian Michlik.
Res.: 3455 California Ave., PA 15212. Tel: 412-766-8801; Fax: 412-766-3379.
2—ST. JOHN THE BAPTIST, [CEM] Rev. Ivan Chirovsky.
Res.: 109 S. Seventh St., PA 15203. Tel: 412-431-2531; Fax: 412-431-6404.

RAMEY, CLEARFIELD CO., ANNUNCIATION B.V.M., [CEM] Very Rev. Anthony Balistreri.
Mailing Address: P.O. Box 205, PA 16671.
Res.: 22 Bentz St., PA 16671-0205. Tel: 814-378-7688.

REVLOC, CAMBRIA CO., PROTECTION BLESSED VIRGIN MARY (1926) Attended by Johnstown., 606 Maple Ave., Johnstown, PA 15901. Tel: 814-535-2634.
Church: 560 Cambria Ave., P.O. Box 194, PA 15948-0914.
Catechesis/Religious Program—Mrs. Robin Wagner, D.R.E. Students 9.

WEST LEECHBURG, ARMSTRONG CO., ST. MICHAEL, Attended by Ford City, PA., Mailing Address: 514 Ninth St., Ford City, PA 16226. Tel: 724-763-1203.
Church: Main St., PA 15656.

WILMERDING, ALLEGHENY CO., SS. PETER AND PAUL, Attended by Jeannette, PA., Mailing Address: 1013 Gaskill Ave., Jeannette, PA 15644-3307. Tel: 724-523-9389.
Church: 163 State St., PA 15148-1323. Tel: 724-829-1833.

STATE OF WEST VIRGINIA

WHEELING, OHIO CO., OUR LADY OF PERPETUAL HELP Rev. Michael Krupka.
Res.: 4136 Jacob St., WV 26003. Tel: 304-232-2168; Fax: 304-232-8719.

On Assignment Outside the Diocese:
Revs.—
Bliszcz, Michael, St. Michael, 4390 Woodside Oaks Dr., S.E., Grand Rapids, MI 49506.
Kachur, Oleh, 251 Bolton St., Apt. 20, Ottawa ON K1N5B5 Canada.
Morozowich, Mark, S.E.O.D., 3900 B Watson Pl., N.W., Apt. G3A, Washington, DC 20016.
Shudrak, Jaroslav, 1555 Bloor St. W., Toronto ON M6P 1A4 Canada.

On Leave:
Revs.—
de Paulo, Craig
Sopp, Michael, P.O. Box 49, Kittanning, PA 16201.
Tamburro, Joseph
Rev. Msgrs. Mitred—
Rewtiuk, Michael (Retired), 3112 Marioncliff Dr., 44134.
Sayuk, Thomas A.

Retired:
Rev. Msgr.—
Nestor, Michael, 867 N. Concord St., Gilbert, AZ 85234. Tel: 602-507-5015
Revs.—
Derbish, Michael, O.F.M., 2001 Main St., Aliquippa, PA 15001.
Dukeley, Boris, 415 Montpellier Ct., Spring Hill, FL 34608.
Marko, Andrew, 33225 Electric Blvd., Avon Lake, 44012.
Very Rev. Canon—
Hnatyshyn, Robert, 452 E. McMurray Rd., Mcmurray, PA 15317.
Rev. Msgr. Mitred—
Poloway, Michael, 5620 W. 24th St., #211, 44134.
Rev. Mitred Archpriest—
Woloszczuk, Wolodymyr, 4240 Timberline Blvd., Venice, FL 34293.
Rev. Canon—
Wysochansky, Walter, 404 6th St., Ambridge, PA 15003.

Permanent Deacons:
Aftanas, Stephen, 3009 Wachter Ave., Lower Burrell, PA 15068.
Billy, Donald, 2515 McCollum Rd., Youngstown, 44509. Tel: 330-792-3166
Dozier, Daniel, P.O. Box 2264, Southern Pines, NC 28388. Tel: 860-938-2582
Dozier, Gordon, 15 Village By the Lake, Southern Pines, NC 28387.
Gregory, John, 7629 Normandy Blvd., Apt. B28, Middleburg Heights, 44130-6560.
Prokopovich, Mark, 38 Anthony Wayne Ter., Baden, PA 15005.
Smolilo, Jeffery, 4546 Shelly Dr., Seven Hills, 44131. Tel: 216-328-0743 (Home); 216-344-8315 (Office)
Suchan, Stephen, 133 Willow Village Dr., Pittsburgh, PA 15239.
Wirag, Joseph, 807 Pine St., Ambridge, PA 15003-1734. Cell: 724-709-9640
Wroblicky, Alexander, 818 Hershire Dr., Bethel Park, PA 15102. Tel: 412-527-8456

INSTITUTIONS LOCATED IN THE DIOCESE

[A] MONASTERIES AND RESIDENCES FOR PRIESTS AND BROTHERS

BROOKLYN. *Holy Spirit Monastery*, 4150 Rabbit Run, 44144. Tel: 216-741-3653. Email: brotherdale@catholicweb.com. Bros. Dale Sefcik, B.H.S.; David Robert, B.H.S.

[B] CONVENTS

PARMA. *St. Josaphat Cathedral Convent*, 5710 State Rd., 44134-2536. Tel: 440-885-1245. Email: janinajp3@yahoo.com. Sisters of St. Basil the Great.

AMBRIDGE. *Ss. Peter & Paul Convent*, 542 Melrose Ave., PA 15003. Tel: 724-266-5578. Sisters of St. Basil the Great.

[C] HOMES FOR THE AGED

PARMA. *Shevchenko Manor*, 5620 W. 24th St., 44134-2751. Tel: 216-459-1440; Fax: 216-459-1442. Jean Waschtschenko, Mgr.

PITTSBURGH. *St. George's Close*, 3505 Mexico St. at Chidel St., PA 15212. Amy Rumsky, Mgr.
Sheptytsky Arms, 3503 Mexico St., PA 15212. Tel: 412-766-8802. Amy Rumsky, Mgr.

[D] MISCELLANEOUS

PITTSBURGH. *Pastoral Ministry Office*, 727 E. Carson St., PA 15203. Tel: 412-481-9778; Fax: 412-481-4914.

RELIGIOUS INSTITUTES OF MEN REPRESENTED IN THE DIOCESE

For further details refer to the corresponding bracketed number in the Religious Institutes of Men or Women section.

[]—*Brothers of the Holy Spirit*—B.H.S.

NECROLOGY

(No Deaths)

An asterisk (*) denotes an organization that has established tax-exempt status directly with the IRS and is not covered by the USCCB Group Ruling.

Eparchy of St. Maron of Brooklyn

Most Reverend

GREGORY J. MANSOUR

Bishop of Saint Maron of Brooklyn; ordained September 18, 1982; appointed Bishop of Saint Maron of Brooklyn January 10, 2004; consecrated March 2, 2004; installed April 27, 2004. *109 Remsen St., Brooklyn, NY 11201.*

Most Reverend

STEPHEN HECTOR DOUEIHI, S.T.D.

Retired Bishop of Saint Maron of Brooklyn; born June 25, 1927; ordained August 14, 1955; appointed Second Eparchial Bishop of the Eparchy of Saint Maron of Brooklyn November 23, 1996; consecrated January 11, 1997; enthroned February 5, 1997; retired January 10, 2004. *Res.: 113 Remsen St., Brooklyn, NY 11201.*

Chancery Office, 109 Remsen St., Brooklyn, NY 11201. Tel: 718-237-9913; Fax: 718-243-0444.

Email: chancerystmaron@verizon.net

Web: www.stmaron.org

Established as an Apostolic Exarchate January 10, 1966; Elevated to a Diocese November 11, 1971.

The jurisdiction of the Diocese extends to all the Maronite Catholics in New York, New Jersey, Pennsylvania, Florida, Georgia, North Carolina, South Carolina, Delaware, Virginia, District of Columbia, Maine, New Hampshire, Vermont, Massachusetts, Rhode Island, Connecticut and Maryland.

For legal titles of parishes and diocesan institutions, consult the Chancery Office.

STATISTICAL OVERVIEW

Personnel	
Bishop	1
Retired Bishops	1
Abbots	1
Priests: Diocesan Active in Diocese	33
Priests: Diocesan Active Outside Diocese	3
Priests: Retired, Sick or Absent	12
Number of Diocesan Priests	48
Religious Priests in Diocese	13
Total Priests in Diocese	61
Extern Priests in Diocese	7
Permanent Deacons in Diocese	16
Total Brothers	7
Total Sisters	2
Parishes	
Parishes	34
With Resident Pastor:	
Resident Diocesan Priests	30
Resident Religious Priests	3
Missions	8
Welfare	
Other Institutions	1
Total Assisted	70
Educational	
Seminaries, Diocesan	1
Students from This Diocese	2
Students from Other Diocese	3
Diocesan Students in Other Seminaries	1
Total Seminarians	3
Catechesis/Religious Education:	
High School Students	329
Elementary Students	1,441
Total Students under Catholic Instruction	1,773
Vital Statistics	
Receptions into the Church:	
Infant Baptism Totals	350
Minor Baptism Totals	9
Adult Baptism Totals	8
Received into Full Communion	14
First Communions	330
Confirmations	404
Marriages:	
Catholic	74
Interfaith	20
Total Marriages	94
Deaths	240
Total Catholic Population	31,800

Former Bishops—Most Revs. FRANCIS M. ZAYEK, D.D., S.T.D., J.C.D., born Oct. 18, 1920; ord. March 17, 1946; appt. Titular Bishop of Callinicum May 30, 1962; cons. Aug. 5, 1962; appt. Bishop of the Diocese of Saint Maron Nov. 11, 1971; installed June 4, 1972; elevated to Archbishop Dec. 22, 1982; retired Nov. 11, 1996; died Sept. 14, 2010.; STEPHEN HECTOR DOUEIHI, S.T.D., born June 25, 1927; ord. Aug. 14, 1955; appt. Second Eparchial Bishop of the Eparchy of Saint Maron of Brooklyn Nov. 23, 1996; cons. Jan. 11, 1997; enthroned Feb. 5, 1997; retired Jan. 10, 2004.

Protosyncellus (Vicar General)—Chorbishop MICHAEL G. THOMAS, J.C.D.

Chancellor—Chorbishop MICHAEL G. THOMAS, J.C.D.

The Chancery—109 Remsen St., Brooklyn, 11201. Tel: 718-237-9913; Fax: 718-243-0444. Email: chancerystmaron@verizon.net. Office Hours: Mon.-Fri. 9-4. Closed on holy days of obligation and national holidays.

Tribunal of the Eparchy of Saint Maron of Brooklyn—300 Wyoming Ave., Scranton, PA 18503-1279. Tel: 570-207-2246; Fax: 570-207-2274. Email: maronitetribunal@aol.com.

Tribunal—

Judicial Vicar—Very Rev. FRANCIS J. MARINI, J.D., J.C.D.

Judges—Chorbishop MICHAEL G. THOMAS, J.C.D.; Rev. Msgr. ANDREW L. ANDERSON, J.C.D.; Rev. JOHN PAUL KIMES, J.C.D.; Rev. Msgr. PATRICK J. PRATICO, J.C.D.

Promoter of Justice—Very Rev. WILLIAM J. KING, J.C.D.

Defender of the Bond—Rev. Msgr. JOSEPH G. QUINN, J.D., J.C.L.

Advocates—Rev. TANIOS KOZHAYA AKOURY, J.C.L.; Rev. Msgr. NEVIN J. KLINGER, J.C.L.

Notaries—Mrs. JOAN MATELIS; Ms. CAMILLE P. MANNING; Ms. PAT VANCOSKY; Ms. CARYN BUTLER.

Presbyteral Council—Rev. Msgr. PETER F. AZAR, Ex Officio; Chorbishop SEELY BEGGIANI, S.T.D., Ex Officio; Revs. PETER BOULOS, Ex Officio; GEORGES Y. EL-KHALLI, Ph.D., Ex Officio; Chorbishop JOSEPH F. KADDO; Very Rev. FRANCIS J. MARINI, J.D., J.C.D.; Rev. SAMUEL A. NAJJAR, Ex Officio; Rev. Msgr. JAMES A. ROOT, Ex Officio; Rev. BASSAM SAADE; Rev. Msgr. GEORGE M. SEBAALI; Chorbishop MICHAEL G. THOMAS, J.C.D., Ex Officio; Rev. JEAN YOUNES.

Protopresbyters (Deans)—Rev. Msgr. PETER F. AZAR, New England Region; Revs. PETER BOULOS, Far South Region; GEORGES Y. EL-KHALLI, Ph.D., Mid-Atlantic West Region; Rev. Msgr. JAMES A. ROOT, Mid-Atlantic East Region; Rev. SAMUEL A. NAJJAR, South Region.

Lebanon Commission—Chorbishop SEELY BEGGIANI, S.T.D., Chm., 7164 Alaska Ave., N.W., Washington, DC 20012. Tel: 202-723-8831. Email: ololsem@maroniteseminary.org.

National Apostolate of Maronites National Office—MIKE J. NABOR, Exec. Dir., Mailing Address: P.O. Box 717, Yonkers, 10702. Tel: 914-964-3070; Fax: 914-964-3071. Email: nam@namnews.org.

Diocesan Offices and Directors

Communications—Rev. Msgr. GEORGE M. SEBAALI, 4611 Sadler Rd., Glen Allen, VA 23060. Tel: 804-270-7234; Fax: 804-273-9914. Email: gmsebaali@aol.com.

(Diocesan Newspaper) "The Maronite Voice"—Rev. Msgr. GEORGE M. SEBAALI, Editor, 4611 Sadler Rd., Glen Allen, VA 23060. Tel: 804-762-4301; Fax: 804-273-9914. Email: gmsebaali@aol.com.

Finance Council—Chorbishops MICHAEL G. THOMAS, J.C.D.; SEELY BEGGIANI, S.T.D.; Mr. ANTHONY BUDWAY, Finance Officer; Ms. CLAIRE HABIB; Mr. RODNEY THOMAS; Mr. ALBERT ASHKOUTI; Dr. PETER GABRIEL; Mr. PETER HABIB.

Ministries (Permanent Deacons and Subdeacons)—Rev. JACK MORRISON, 11 Franklin St., New Bedford, MA 02740. Tel: 508-996-8934; Fax: 508-996-2744. Email: aboonajack@aol.com.

Order of Saint Sharbel—Mrs. BEVERLY MIKE-NARD, Pres., 3330 Partridge Park Dr., Poland, OH 44514; BERNADETTE SHALHOUB, Vice Pres., 8429 W. Lake Dr., Lake Clarke Shores, FL 33406.

Office of Ecumenism and Interreligious Dialogue—Rev. SAMUEL A. NAJJAR, St. Michael the Archangel Church, 806 Arsenal Ave., Fayetteville, NC 28305. Tel: 910-484-1531; Fax: 910-484-5387. Email: stmikemcc@embarqmail.com.

Family and Sanctity of Life—Deacon NICHOLAS MAMMI, 669 Dulany Rd., Floyd, VA 24091. Tel: 540-763-3333; Fax: 540-763-3000. Email: nmammi@swva.net.

Religious Education—Rev. GEORGES Y. EL-KHALLI, Ph.D., 61 Rockwood St., Jamaica Plain, MA 02130. Tel: 617-522-0225; Fax: 617-522-0194.

Email: rockcedars@yahoo.com.

Victim Assistance Coordinator—ROSANNE SOLOMON, 15 Raven Rd., Canton, MA 02021. Tel: 781-828-5183. Email: rosannesolomon@hotmail.com.

Vocations—Rev. DOMINIQUE HANNA, St. Joseph Church, 502 Seminole Ave., N.E., Atlanta, GA 30307. Tel: 404-525-2504; Fax: 404-589-1744. Email: sjmcc@sjmcc.org.

Youth Ministry Office—Rev. GARY GEORGE, Saint Maron Church, 1555 S. Meridian Rd., Youngstown, OH 44511. Tel: 330-792-2371; Fax: 330-792-3026. Email: abounag1@hotmail.com.

Young Adult Ministry—Rev. ELIE HARES MIKHAEL, Our Lady of Lebanon, 2055 Coral Way, Miami, FL 33145. Tel: 305-856-7449; Fax: 305-856-5740. Email: ololmiami@bellsouth.net.

Board of Pastors—Rev. Msgr. PETER F. AZAR; Very Rev. FRANCIS J. MARINI, J.D., J.C.D.; Rev. Msgr. GEORGE M. SEBAALI.

College of Consultors—Rev. Msgr. PETER F. AZAR; Revs. PETER BOULOS; GEORGES Y. EL-KHALLI, Ph.D.; Very Rev. FRANCIS J. MARINI, J.D., J.C.D.; Rev. Msgr. GEORGE M. SEBAALI.

Immigration Office—MICHAEL J. KOURY JR., Attorney. Tel: 610-905-3781; Fax: 610-253-0673. Email: kourylaw@msn.com.

CLERGY, PARISHES, MISSIONS AND PAROCHIAL SCHOOLS

STATE OF NEW YORK

BROOKLYN, KINGS CO., CATHEDRAL OF OUR LADY OF LEBANON (1902) [JC] Rev. Msgr. James A. Root, Rector. In Res., Rev. Geoffrey Abdallah.
Res.: 113 Remsen St., 11201. Tel: 718-624-7228; Fax: 718-624-8034.
Catechesis/Religious Program—Students 90.
Mission— Rev. Naji Kiwan, Admin.

OLEAN, CATTARAUGUS CO., ST. JOSEPH (1919) [JC] Rev. Anthony J. Salim.
Res.: 225 N. 4th St., 14760. Tel: 716-372-4311. Email: stjosepholean@roadrunner.com.
Catechesis/Religious Program—Students 11.

TROY, RENSSELAER CO., ST. ANN (1905) Rev. Georges Bouchaaya, M.L.M.
Church: 184 Fourth St., 12180. Tel: 518-272-6073; Fax: 518-272-6073. Email: stann1905@gmail.com. Web: www.sainteann.com.
Rectory—1919 Third Ave., Watervliet, 12189.
Catechesis/Religious Program—Students 16.

UTICA, ONEIDA CO., ST. LOUIS GONZAGA (1910) Chorbishop John D. Faris; Deacon Paul A. Salamy.
Res.: 520 Rutger St., 13501. Tel: 315-732-6019; Fax: 315-732-6018. Email: stlouisgonzaga@gmail.com.
Catechesis/Religious Program—Students 55.

WHITE PLAINS, BLESSED JOHN PAUL II CATHOLIC CHURCH, 52 N. Broadway, 10603.

WILLIAMSVILLE, ERIE CO., ST. JOHN MARON (1903) Rev. Elie G. Kairouz.
Res.: 2040 Wehrle Dr., 14221-7041. Tel: 716-634-0669; Fax: 716-634-0674. Email: stjmaron@gmail.com. Web: www.stjohnmaron.com.
Catechesis/Religious Program—Students 105.

STATE OF CONNECTICUT

DANBURY, FAIRFIELD CO., ST. ANTHONY (1932) Rev. Jean Younes.
Res.: 17 Granville Ave., CT 06810. Tel: 203-744-3372; Fax: 203-794-0949. Email: stanthonyoffice@yahoo.com.
Catechesis/Religious Program—Students 54.

TORRINGTON, LITCHFIELD CO., ST. MARON (1912) Rev. Lawrence P. Michael; Subdeacons Paul Comeau; David Leand; Deacon Steve P. Marcus.
Mailing Address: 605 Main St., CT 06790.
Res.: 613 Main St., CT 06790. Tel: 860-489-9015; Fax: 860-482-1614. Email: stmaronchurch@aol.com.
Catechesis/Religious Program—Students 97.

WATERBURY, NEW HAVEN CO., OUR LADY OF LEBANON (1975) Rev. Dany Abi-Akar, Admin.
Mailing Address: 8 E. Mountain Rd., CT 06706. Email: our_lady_lebanon@sbcglobal.net.
Res.: 1544 Hamilton Ave., CT 06706. Tel: 203-753-9428; Fax: 203-573-8384.
Catechesis/Religious Program—Students 25.

STATE OF FLORIDA

FORT LAUDERDALE, BROWARD CO., HEART OF JESUS CATHOLIC CHURCH Chorbishop Michael G. Thomas, Admin.
1800 N.E. 6th Ct., FL 33304. Tel: 954-522-3939; Fax: 954-522-3949. Email: heartofjesusfll@gmail.com.

JACKSONVILLE, DUVAL CO., ST. MARON MARONITE (1995) [JC] Rev. Elie Abi-chedid; Deacon Elias Shami.
Res.: 7032 Bowden Rd., FL 32216. Tel: 904-448-0203; Fax: 904-448-8277. Email: frchedid@hotmail.com. Web: stmaronjax.com.
Catechesis/Religious Program—Students 47.

MIAMI, DADE CO., OUR LADY OF LEBANON (1973) Rev. Elie Hares Mikhael.
Mailing Address: 2055 Coral Way, FL 33145. Tel: 305-856-7449; Fax: 305-856-5740. Email: ololmiami@bellsouth.net. Web: www.ololmiami.org.
Res.: 420 Como Ave., Coral Gables, FL 33146. Tel: 305-663-8601.
Catechesis/Religious Program—Students 33.

ORLANDO, ORANGE CO., ST. JUDE (2003) Rev. Bassam Saade.
Mailing Address: 5555 Dr. Phillips Blvd., FL 32819.
Res.: 7832 Pine Haven Ct., FL 32819-7110. Tel: 407-363-7405; Fax: 407-363-7793. Email: saintjudemaronitecatholicchurch@gmail.com. Web: www.saintjudechurch.org.
Catechesis/Religious Program—Students 35.

TAMPA, PASCO CO., MISSION OF STS. PETER & PAUL (2000) [JC] Rev. Peter Boulos.
6201 Sheldon Rd., FL 33615. Tel: 813-886-7413 (Church & Rectory); Fax: 813-885-6346. Email: peterandpaulmcc@gmail.com. Web: www.peterpaultampa.com.
Catechesis/Religious Program—Students 7.

WEST PALM BEACH, PALM BEACH CO., MARY MOTHER OF THE LIGHT MARONITE MISSION Rev. Jorge Perales, Admin.; Subdeacon Dennis Somerville.
Mailing Address & Church: 4891 Lake Worth Rd., Greenacres, FL 33463. Tel: 561-433-8831; Fax: 561-841-1153. Email: rbfish1404@gmail.com.
Catechesis/Religious Program—Students 18.

STATE OF GEORGIA

ATLANTA, FULTON CO., ST. JOSEPH'S MARONITE CHURCH (1911) [JC] Rev. Dominique Hanna; Deacon Robert Calabrese.
Res.: 502 Seminole Ave., N.E., GA 30307. Tel: 404-525-2504; Fax: 404-524-8572. Email: sjmcc@sjmcc.org. Web: www.sjmcc.org.
Catechesis/Religious Program—Students 52.

STATE OF MAINE

WATERVILLE, KENNEBEC CO., ST. JOSEPH (1927) Rev. Larry Jensen; Deacon Peter P. Joseph.
Res.: 3 Appleton St., ME 04901. Tel: 207-872-8515; Fax: 207-872-8089. Email: stjoesinmaine@yahoo.com.
Catechesis/Religious Program—Students 12.

STATE OF MASSACHUSETTS

BROCKTON, PLYMOUTH CO., ST. THERESA (1932) Rev. Tanios Mouannes, Admin.
Res.: P.O Box 2567, MA 02305-2567. Tel: 508-586-1428; Fax: 508-587-8139. Email: saintheresa@comcast.net.
Catechesis/Religious Program—Students 49.

FALL RIVER, BRISTOL CO., ST. ANTHONY OF THE DESERT (1911) Chorbishop Joseph F. Kaddo; Deacons Donald P. Massoud; Andre Nasser.
Res.: 300 N. Eastern Ave., MA 02723. Tel: 508-672-7653; Fax: 508-678-1474. Email: saotd@saotd.com. Web: www.saotd.com.
Catechesis/Religious Program—Students 73.

JAMAICA PLAIN, SUFFOLK CO., OUR LADY OF THE CEDARS OF LEBANON (1893) Rev. Georges Y. El-Khalli.
Res.: 61 Rockwood St., MA 02130. Tel: 617-522-0225; Fax: 617-522-0194. Email: rockcedars@yahoo.com. Web: www.ourladyofthecedars.org.
Catechesis/Religious Program—Students 68.

LAWRENCE, ESSEX CO., ST. ANTHONY (1903) [CEM] Rev. Msgr. Peter F. Azar; Deacons Allan Ramey; Simon Abi Nader; Subdeacon James Demers.
Res.: 145 Amesbury St., MA 01841. Tel: 978-685-7233; Fax: 978-688-4475. Email: rectory@stanthonylawrence.org. Web: stanthonylawrence.org.
Catechesis/Religious Program—Students 150.

NEW BEDFORD, BRISTOL CO., OUR LADY OF PURGATORY (1917) Rev. John A. Morrison; Deacon Jean E. Mattar; Subdeacon Joseph Abraham.
Res.: 11 Franklin St., MA 02740. Tel: 508-996-8934; Fax: 508-996-2744.
Catechesis/Religious Program—Students 4.

SPRINGFIELD, HAMPDEN CO., ST. ANTHONY (1905) Rev. George Zina; Deacon Enzo DiGiacomo; Subdeacon Norman Hannoush.
Mailing Address: 375 Island Pond Rd., MA 01118-1002.
Res.: 419 Island Pond Rd., MA 01118-1002. Tel: 413-732-0589; Fax: 413-732-6320. Email: stanthony419@comcast.net.
Catechesis/Religious Program—Students 25.

WORCESTER, WORCESTER CO., OUR LADY OF MERCY (1923) Rev. Paul Mooradd.
Mailing Address: 74 Mulberry St., MA 01605.
Res.: 341 June St., MA 01602-2845. Tel: 508-752-4287. Web: www.ourladyofmercy.parishesonline.com.
Catechesis/Religious Program—Students 16.

STATE OF NEW HAMPSHIRE

DOVER, STRAFFORD CO., ST. GEORGE (1949) Rev. Joseph Khoueiry.
Mailing Address: 15 Chapel St., P.O. Box 2210, NH 03821-2210.
Res.: 46 Hough St., NH 03820. Tel: 603-742-1149; Fax: 603-740-9624. Email: joekhoveiry@aol.com.
Church: 15 Chapel St., NH 03821. Tel: 603-740-4287.
Catechesis/Religious Program—Fred Ouellette, D.R.E. Students 5.

STATE OF NEW JERSEY

PLEASANTVILLE, ATLANTIC CO., OUR LADY STAR OF THE EAST (2002) Unassigned.*c/o St. Peters Maronite Catholic Church*, 25 W. Black Horse Pike, NJ 08232. Tel: 609-363-1042 (Res.); Fax: 609-407-0901 (Bus.).

SOMERSET, SOMERSET CO., ST. SHARBEL Rev. Tony Akoury; Subdeacon Joseph Chebli.
Res.: 7 Reeve St., NJ 08873. Tel: 732-828-2055; Fax: 732-828-5488.
Catechesis/Religious Program—Email: secretary@saintsharbelnj.us. Students 70.

STATE OF NORTH CAROLINA

CARY, WAKE CO., SAINT SHARBEL MISSION (2000) Rev. Kamil Alchouefati.
Mailing Address: P.O. Box 4093, NC 27513. Tel: 610-905-2859; 610-739-8586; 919-931-5781; Fax: 866-748-8522. Email: st.charbel.rql.nc@gmail.com. Web: www.marsharbel.org.
Rectory—8908 Taymouth Court, Raleigh, NC 27613.
Catechesis/Religious Program—Students 27.

FAYETTEVILLE, CUMBERLAND CO., ST. MICHAEL THE ARCHANGEL (1973) Rev. Samuel A. Najjar.
Mailing Address: 806 Arsenal Ave., NC 28305. Tel: 910-484-1531; Fax: 910-484-5387.
Res.: 212 Bradford Ave., NC 28301. Tel: 910-429-0808. Email: stmikemcc@embarqmail.com. Web: www.stmichaelsmaronite.org.
Catechesis/Religious Program—Students 14.

STATE OF PENNSYLVANIA

CARNEGIE, ALLEGHENY CO., OUR LADY OF VICTORY (1902) Revs. Rodolph Wakim; Simon Elhajj, Parochial Vicar.
Res.: 1000 Lindsay Rd., PA 15106. Tel: 412-278-0841; Fax: 412-278-0846. Email: abounarodolph@gmail.com. Web: www.olov.info.
Catechesis/Religious Program—Students 30.
Mission—Maronite Mission of Aliquippa 2001 Main St., Aliquippa, Beaver Co., PA 15001. Tel: 724-252-7112.

EASTON, NORTHAMPTON CO., OUR LADY OF LEBANON (1931) Rev. Paul Damien; Deacon Anthony P. Koury.
Res.: 54 S. Fourth St., PA 18042. Tel: 610-252-5275; Fax: 610-252-1737. Email: oLoLchurch@yahoo.com. Web: www.mountlebanon.org.
Catechesis/Religious Program—Students 40.

NEW CASTLE, LAWRENCE CO., ST. JOHN THE BAPTIST (1926) Rev. Claude W. Franklin Jr.; Subdeacon Andrew Demko; Deacon Richard E. Stone.
Res.: 2 W. Reynolds St., PA 16101. Tel: 724-658-0787; Fax: 724-658-2711. Email: stjohnmaronite@hotmail.com.
Catechesis/Religious Program—Students 40.

NEWTOWN SQUARE, DELAWARE CO., ST. SHARBEL (1983) Rev. Paul Mouawad; Deacon Martin LoMonaco.
Res.: 3679 Providence Rd., PA 19073. Tel: 610-353-5952; Fax: 610-353-0343.
Catechesis/Religious Program—Students 18.

PHILADELPHIA, PHILADELPHIA CO., ST. MARON (1862) Rev. Vincent Farhat, Admin.; Deacon Joseph Regan.
Res. & Office: 1013 Ellsworth St., PA 19147. Tel: 215-389-2000; Fax: 215-334-5080. Email: parishstmaronphiladelphia@hotmail.com.
Catechesis/Religious Program—Students 30.

SCRANTON, LACKAWANNA CO., ST. ANN (1903) [JC] Very Rev. Francis J. Marini; Subdeacon Robert Rade.
Res.: 1320 Price St., PA 18504-3336. Tel: 570-344-2129; Fax: 570-344-3920. Email: stannscranton@aol.com.
Catechesis/Religious Program—Students 12.

UNIONTOWN, FAYETTE CO., ST. GEORGE (1927) Rev. Nadim Helou, M.L.M.; Subdeacon Thomas George. Students 35.
Res.: 6 Lebanon Ter., PA 15401-3011. Tel: 724-437-5589; Fax: 724-437-3819. Email: sixleb@atlanticbb.net. Web: www.stgeorgemaronite.com.
Catechesis/Religious Program—Students 32.

WILKES-BARRE, LUZERNE CO., ST. ANTHONY + ST. GEORGE (1911) Rev. Hanna Karam; Subdeacon Oliver Crosby Sparks.
Res.: 79 Loomis St., PA 18702-4610. Tel: 570-824-3599; Fax: 570-824-1747.
Catechesis/Religious Program—Students 40.

STATE OF RHODE ISLAND

LINCOLN, PROVIDENCE CO., ST. GEORGE (1911) Rev. Edward T. Nedder.
Church & Res.: 171 Twin Rivers Rd., RI 02865. Tel: 401-723-8444 (Rectory); Fax: 401-728-2032. Email: stgeorgemaronitechurch@earthlink.net.
Catechesis/Religious Program—Students 44.

STATE OF SOUTH CAROLINA

GREENVILLE, GREENVILLE CO., ST. RAFKA MARONITE MISSION (2002) Rev. Bartholomew Leon, O.S.B., Admin.
1215 S. Hwy. 14, Greer, SC 29650.
Res.: 111 Hampton Ave., SC 29601. Tel: 864-271-8422; Fax: 864-370-9880. Email: saintrafkagreenville@gmail.com. Web: www.saintrafka.net.
Catechesis/Religious Program—Mr. Elie Alam, D.R.E. Students 3.

STATE OF VIRGINIA

GLEN ALLEN, HENRICO CO., ST. ANTHONY (1912) [JC] Rev. Msgr. George M. Sebaali.
Res.: 4611 Sadler Rd., VA 23060. Tel: 804-270-7234; Fax: 804-273-9914. Email: stanthonymaronitechurch@verizon.net. Web: www.stanthonymaronitechurch.org.
Catechesis/Religious Program—Students 200.

ROANOKE, ROANOKE CITY CO., ST. ELIAS (1917) Rev. Kevin J. Beaton, S.F.O.
Res.: 4730 Cove Rd., N.W., VA 24017. Tel: 540-562-0012 (Church); 540-562-2525 (Rectory); Fax: 540-562-1300. Email: fr@steliaschurch.org. Web: www.steliaschurch.org.
Catechesis/Religious Program—Students 35.

DISTRICT OF COLUMBIA

WASHINGTON, DISTRICT OF COLUMBIA, OUR LADY OF LEBANON CHURCH (1967) Chorbishop Dominic F. Ashkar.
Res.: 7237 15th Pl. N.W., DC 20012. Tel: 202-829-5554; Fax: 202-291-5153. Web: ourladyoflebanon-dc.org.
Church: 7142 Alaska Ave., N.W., DC 20012.
Catechesis/Religious Program—Students 112.

On Duty Outside the Diocese:
Revs.—
Amar, Joseph P.
Bartoul, William
Michael, David F.

On Sabbatical:
Rev. Msgr.—
George, David M.

Retired:
Most Rev.—
Doueihi, Stephen Hector, S.T.D.
Rev. Msgrs.—
Asmar, Maroun
Hayek, Sami
Khoury, James T.
Lahoud, Joseph F.
Sadek, Ignace
Revs.—
Andary, John S.
Basinow, Leonard
Boackle, Paul H.
Henderson, Christopher
Shaheen, Joseph

Permanent Deacons:
Abi Nader, Simon, Bow, NH
Calabrese, Robert, Cummings, GA
DiGiacomo, Enzo, Springfield, MA
Gebron, Charles, (Retired), Springfield, MA
Jarius, John, Ft. Lauderdale, FL
Joseph, Peter P., Waterville, ME
Koury, Anthony P., Easton, PA
Lomomaco, Martin, Newtown Square, PA
Marcus, Steven
Massoud, Donald P., Fall River, MA
Mattar, Jean E., New Bedford, MA
Nasser, Andre, Fall River, MA
Ramey, Allan, Lawrence, MA
Regan, Joseph W., Sewell, NJ
Salamy, Paul A., Utica, NY
Shami, Elias, Jacksonville, FL
Stone, Richard E., New Castle, PA

INSTITUTIONS LOCATED IN THE DIOCESE

[A] SEMINARIES, DIOCESAN

WASHINGTON. *Our Lady of Lebanon Maronite Seminary*, 7164 Alaska Ave., N.W., DC 20012. Tel: 202-723-8831; Fax: 202-829-6053. Email: ololsem@maroniteseminary.org. Web: www.maroniteseminary.org. Chorbishop Seely Beggiani, S.T.D., Rector. Priests 1. In Res. Rev. Msgr. Ignace Sadek (Retired).

[B] RELIGIOUS COMMUNITIES OF MEN

PETERSHAM. *Maronite Monks of Adoration Most Holy Trinity Monastery*, 67 Dugway Rd., MA 01366-9725. Tel: 978-724-3347. Rt. Rev. William J. Driscoll, M.M.A., Abbot; Very Rev. Louis Marie Dauphinais, M.M.A., Prior; Revs. Michael Gilmary Cermak, M.M.A.; John Marie Choiniere, M.M.A.; Ignatius (Allen) Dec, M.M.A.; Martin Ferland, M.M.A.; Giles R. Goyette, M.M.A.; Elias Havel, M.M.A.; Robert Nortz, M.M.A.; Bros. Benedict Henricks, M.M.A.; Patrick Kokorian, M.M.A.; John Baptist Livingston, M.M.A.; Augustine Martin, M.M.A.; Ephrem Martin, M.M.A.; Jerome Sauber, M.M.A.; Bernard Choupin, M.M.A. Priests 9; Brothers 8; Novices 1.

[C] RELIGIOUS COMMUNITIES OF WOMEN

DARTMOUTH. *Servants of Christ the Light*, 856 Tucker Rd., MA 02747. Tel: 508-996-1753. Email: sister@maroniteservants.org. Web: www.maroniteservants.org.

[D] RESIDENCES FOR CLERGY

BROOKLYN. *Bishop's Residence*, 8070 Harbor View Ter., 11209.

[E] ASSISTED LIVING

NEW BEDFORD. *Cedar Holdings, Inc.*, c/o 11 Franklin St., MA 02740. Tel: 508-996-8934; Fax: 508-996-2744. Web: www.thecedarsassistedliving.com. Rev. Jack Morrison.

[F] MISCELLANEOUS

BROOKLYN. *Bishops Retirement Trust Fund*, 109 Remsen St., 11201.
Order of St. Sharbel Trust Fund, 109 Remsen St., 11201.
Priest Retirement Trust Fund, 109 Remsen St., 11201.
Tele Lumiere / Noursat, 109 Remsen St., 11201.

SHELBURNE. *Saint Rafka Retreat Center*, 6420 Rte. 116, VT 05482-7191. Tel: 802-660-2528; Fax: 802-660-2528.

NECROLOGY

† Beshara, Rev. Msgr. Ronald, (Sabbatical)—Died Sept. 7, 2011
† Lischaa, Rev. Msgr. Sharbel, (Retired)—Died Aug. 2, 2011
† El-Hayek, Nehmatallah, (Retired)—Died May 10, 2011

An asterisk (*) denotes an organization that has established tax-exempt status directly with the IRS and is not covered by the USCCB Group Ruling.

Diocese of St. Nicholas in Chicago for Ukrainians

Most Reverend

RICHARD S. SEMINACK

Bishop of St. Nicholas in Chicago; ordained May 25, 1967; appointed Bishop of St. Nicholas in Chicago March 25, 2003; ordained June 4, 2003. *Office: 2245 W. Rice St., Chicago, IL 60622.* Tel: 773-276-5080.

Most Reverend

INNOCENT LOTOCKY, O.S.B.M.

Retired Bishop of St. Nicholas in Chicago; ordained November 24, 1940; appointed Second Bishop of Chicago January 29, 1981; consecrated March 1, 1981; installed April 2, 1981; retired September 28, 1993. *Mailing Address: 2245 W. Rice St., Chicago, IL 60622.* Tel: 773-276-8981.

Comprises all of the United States west of the western borders of Ohio, Kentucky, Tennessee and Mississippi.

For legal titles of parishes and diocesan institutions, consult the Chancery Office.

Chancery Office: 2245 W. Rice St., Chicago, IL 60622. Tel: 773-276-5080; Fax: 773-276-6799; 773-276-0314.

Email: sneparchy@iols.com

STATISTICAL OVERVIEW

(Editor's Note: 2012 statistical information was not received)

Personnel	
Bishop	1
Retired Bishops	1
Abbots	2
Retired Abbots	1
Priests: Diocesan Active in Diocese	36
Priests: Diocesan Active Outside Diocese	1
Priests: Retired, Sick or Absent	6
Number of Diocesan Priests	43
Religious Priests in Diocese	12
Total Priests in Diocese	55
Extern Priests in Diocese	5
Ordinations:	
Diocesan Priests	2
Religious Priests	1
Permanent Deacons in Diocese	11
Parishes	
Parishes	38
With Resident Pastor:	
Resident Diocesan Priests	22
Resident Religious Priests	3
Without Resident Pastor:	
Administered by Priests	12
Administered by Deacons	1
Missions	4
Closed Parishes	2
Educational	
Diocesan Students in Other Seminaries	1
Total Seminarians	1
Elementary Schools, Diocesan and Parish	2
Total Students	245
Catechesis/Religious Education:	
High School Students	40
Elementary Students	105
Total Students under Catholic Instruction	391
Teachers in the Diocese:	
Priests	1
Sisters	2
Lay Teachers	20
Vital Statistics	
Receptions into the Church:	
Infant Baptism Totals	250
Adult Baptism Totals	5
Received into Full Communion	5
First Communions	120
Confirmations	256
Marriages:	
Catholic	50
Interfaith	35
Total Marriages	85
Deaths	200
Total Catholic Population	10,500

Former Bishops—Most Revs. JAROSLAV GABRO, D.D., appt. First Bishop of Chicago, July 12, 1961; cons. Oct. 26, 1961; died March 28, 1980; INNOCENT LOTOCKY, O.S.B.M., D.D., Ph.D., ord. Nov. 24, 1940; appt. Second Bishop of Chicago, Jan. 29, 1981; cons. March 1, 1981; installed April 2, 1981; retired Sept. 28, 1993; MICHAEL WIWCHAR, C.Ss.R., D.D., ord. June 28, 1959; appt. Third Bishop of St. Nicholas July 2, 1993; ord. Sept. 28, 1993; appt. Bishop of Saskatoon (Ukrainian), Nov. 29, 2000; secondary appt. Apostolic Administrator of St. Nicholas in Chicago, Dec. 9, 2000.

Protosyncellus—Very Rev. Canon WAYNE J. RUCHGY.

Chancellor—VACANT.

Vice Chancellor—Subdeacon PETRO RUDKA.

Bishop's Personal Secretary—Mr. NAZAR SLOBODA.

Chief Financial Officer and Eparchial Finance Director—JAROSLAW HANKEWYCH. Tel: 773-772-6131. Email: hankewych@msn.com.

Chancery Office—2245 W. Rice St., Chicago, 60622. Tel: 773-276-5080; Fax: 773-276-6799; 773-276-0314. Email: sneparchy@iols.com. Office Hours: Mon.-Fri. 9-4. Closed all major holy days and legal holidays.

Diocesan Consultors—Very Rev. Canon WAYNE J. RUCHGY; Very Rev. VARCILIO BASIL SALKOVSKI, O.S.B.M.; Rev. RICHARD JANOWICZ; Very Rev. Canon MICHAEL STELMACH; Very Rev. Archpriest MYKHAILO KUZMA.

Presbyteral Council—Most Rev. RICHARD S. SEMINACK, D.D., Ex Officio; Very Rev. Canon WAYNE J. RUCHGY; Very Rev. Archpriest MYKHAILO KUZMA; Rev. HUGO SOUTUS, Chm.; Very Rev. YAROSLAV MENDYUK, Sec.; Rev. MYRON MYKYTA; Very Revs. VARCILIO BASIL SALKOVSKI, O.S.B.M.; VOLODYMYR PETRIV.

Personnel Board—Most Rev. RICHARD S. SEMINACK, D.D.; Very Rev. Canon WAYNE J. RUCHGY, Chm.; Very Rev. Archpriest MYKHAILO KUZMA; Very Rev. JAMES M. KAREPIN, O.P.; Rev. RICHARD JANOWICZ.

Tribunal— Through Special Permission of the Holy See, Local Latin Rite Tribunals Handle the Cases Within the Diocese.

Protopresbyteries (Deans)—Detroit: Very Rev. VOLODYMYR PETRIV, Protopresbyter. Chicago: Very Rev. VARCILIO BASIL SALKOVSKI, O.S.B.M., Protopresbyter; Very Rev. Archpriest MYKHAILO KUZMA, Vice Protopresbyter. Minneapolis: Very Rev. Canon MICHAEL STELMACH, Protopresbyter. South-West: Rev. RICHARD JANOWICZ, Protopresbyter.

Eparchial Censor—Rev. DEMETRIUS WYSOCHANSKY, O.S.B.M.

Eparchial Office of Religious Education & Catechesis—Rev. LEONARD KORCHINSKY, Vicar Catechesis & Faith Formation.

Eparchial Ecumenical Officer—Very Rev. JAMES M. KAREPIN, O.P.

Stewardship and Development Office—Mr. SERGE MICHALUK, Dir., 2245 W. Rice St., Chicago, 60622. Tel: 773-276-9500; Fax: 773-276-9502.

Office for Protection of Children and Youth—Mr. SERGE MICHALUK, Dir.

Task Force for a Safe Environment—Dr. LINDA HRYHORCZUK, Chm.

"New Star" - Eparchial Newspaper—Rev. JOHN P. LUCAS, English Editor. Tel: 773-291-0168; Subdeacon PETRO RUDKA, Ukrainian Editor. Tel: 773-276-5080.

CLERGY, PARISHES, MISSIONS AND PAROCHIAL SCHOOLS

STATE OF ILLINOIS

CHICAGO, COOK CO.

1—ST. NICHOLAS UKRAINIAN CATHOLIC CATHEDRAL (1906), (Ukrainian), [CEM] Revs. Bohdan Nalysnyk, Rector; Volodymyr Hudzan, Vice Rector; Deacons Mychajlo Horodysky; Michael Huskey.

Res.: 2238 W. Rice St., 60622. Tel: 773-276-4537 (parish phone); Fax: 773-276-5558. Email: office@stnicholaschicago.org. Web: www.stnicholaschicago.org.

School—(Grades PreK-8), 2200 W. Rice St., 60622-4811. Tel: 773-384-7243; Fax: 773-384-7283. Sr. Irenea Hankewych, O.S.B.M., Supr.; Maria Klysh-Finiak, Prin.; Renata Kwit, Librarian. Sisters 2; Lay Teachers 12; Students 127.

Convent—Sisters of St. Basil the Great, 2230 W. Rice St., 60622-4811. Tel: 773-486-6820.

2—ST. JOSEPH (N.W. Chicago) (1956), (Ukrainian), Rev. Mykola Buryadnyk. Tel: 312-421-5230; Very Rev. Canon Thomas Glynn; Rev. Volodymyr Kushnir. Tel: 773-979-4737.

Res.: 5000 N. Cumberland Ave., 60656. Tel: 773-625-4833; 773-625-4805 (Office); Fax: 773-625-4148.
Catechesis / Religious Program—Students 35.
3—ST. MICHAEL'S (1917), (Ukrainian), [JC] In Res., Rev. John Lucas.
Church & Mailing Address: 12211 S. Parnell, 60628. Tel: 773-291-0168.
4—SS. VOLODYMYR AND OLHA (1968), (Ukrainian), [JC] Rev. Oleh Kryvokulsky. Tel: 312-829-6805; Rt. Rev. Mitred Archpriest Ivan Krotec, Pastor Emeritus. Tel: 312-455-0178; Revs. Ihor Koshyk. Tel: 773-276-1493; Stepan Kostiuk.
Parish Office—2245 W. Superior St., 60612. Tel: 312-829-5209; Fax: 312-829-4113.
MADISON, MADISON CO., ST. MARY'S, [JC] Rev. Robert Piorkowski, Admin.
Res.: 1312 Iowa St., 62060. Tel: 616-452-9118.
PALATINE, COOK CO., IMMACULATE CONCEPTION (1963), (Ukrainian), Very Rev. Archpriest Mykhailo Kuzma; Rev. Andrew Plishka.
Res.: 745 S. Benton, 60067. Tel: 847-991-0820; Fax: 847-991-7873. Email: frmykhailo@att.net.
Catechesis / Religious Program—Tel: 847-639-9188. Students 31.
PALOS PARK, COOK CO., NATIVITY OF B.V.M. (1911), (Ukrainian), Very Rev. Varcilio Basil Salkovski, O.S.B.M.; Rev. Demetrius Wysochansky, O.S.B.M.; Deacon Michael Cook.
Res.: 8530 W. 131 St., 60464. Tel: 708-361-8876; Fax: 708-361-8820. Email: nativityukrainian@sbcglobal.net.
Catechesis / Religious Program—Patricia Kuzmak, D.R.E. Students 7.

STATE OF ARIZONA

PHOENIX, MARICOPA CO., ASSUMPTION OF B.V.M. (1959) Rev. Hugo Soutus.
Res.: 3730 W. Maryland Ave., AZ 85019. Tel: 602-973-3667; Fax: 602-973-3667.
Church: 3720 W. Maryland Ave., AZ 85019.
Mission—Flagstaff Mission 16 W. Cherry Ave., Flagstaff, AZ 86001. Served by Phoenix.
TUCSON, PIMA CO., ST. MICHAEL (1978), (Ukrainian), [JC] Rt. Rev. Andriy Chirovsky.
Mailing Address: 715 W. Vanover Rd., AZ 85705-4137.
Res.: 1616 W. Gleaming Moon Trail, AZ 85704-1454. Tel: 480-217-8505.
Catechesis / Religious Program—Mrs. Halyna Chirovsky, D.R.E. Students 4.

STATE OF CALIFORNIA

LOS ANGELES, LOS ANGELES CO., NATIVITY OF B.V.M. (1947), (Ukrainian), Rev. Myron Mykyta.
Res.: 5154 De Longpre Ave., Hollywood, CA 90027. Tel: 323-663-6307; Fax: 323-663-0369.
CITRUS HEIGHTS, SACRAMENTO CO., HOLY WISDOM (2001) Rev. Theodore P. Wroblicky.
Mailing Address: 1324 La Serra Dr., Sacramento, CA 95864.
Chapel— Christ the King Retreat Center, 6520 Van Maren Ln., CA 95621. Tel: 916-482-8423.
DESERT HOT SPRINGS, RIVERSIDE CO., ST. SOPHIA, Closed. For inquiries for parish records contact the chancery.
LA MESA, SAN DIEGO CO., ST. JOHN THE BAPTIZER (1960), (Ukrainian), Rev. James Bankston.
Church: 4400 Palm Ave., CA 91941. Tel: 619-697-5085; Fax: 619-697-7374.
Catechesis / Religious Program—Students 10.
SACRAMENTO, SACRAMENTO CO., ST. ANDREW THE APOSTLE Rev. Petro Kozar.
Res.: 7001 Florin Rd., CA 95828. Tel: 916-383-8614; 916-381-1179.
Catechesis / Religious Program—Tel: 916-381-2529; Fax: 916-381-2529.
SAN FRANCISCO, SAN FRANCISCO CO., IMMACULATE CONCEPTION CATHOLIC CHURCH (1957), (Ukrainian), Rev. Petro Dyachok, Admin.
Res.: 215 Silliman, CA 94134. Tel: 415-468-2601; Fax: 415-468-2601.
Catechesis / Religious Program—Tel: 415-468-2601.
SANTA CLARA, SANTA CLARA CO., ST. VOLODYMYR UKRAINIAN CATHOLIC MISSION (1963) Attended by Immaculate Conception, San Francisco. Rev. Petro Dyachok, Admin.
445 Washington Ave., CA 95050. Email: st_volodymyr_ucc@att.net. Web: https//stvolodymyrucc.org/index.html.
UKIAH, UKIAH CO., ST. PETER EASTERN CATHOLIC MISSION (1999), (Ukrainian), Rev. David Anderson, Admin.
Res.: 190 Orr St., CA 95482. Tel: 707-468-4348; Fax: 707-467-0505.

STATE OF COLORADO

DENVER, DENVER CO., TRANSFIGURATION OF OUR LORD (1954), (Ukrainian), [JC] Rev. Vasyl Hnatkivskyy, Admin.; Deacon Michael Bozio.
Res.: 4118 Shoshone St., CO 80211. Tel: 303-433-2347. Email: denverukrainian@comcast.net.

STATE OF HAWAII

HONOLULU, ST. SOPHIA BYZANTINE MISSIONS, Unassigned.
Res.: 5919 Kalanianaole Hwy., HI 96821. Tel: 808-396-0551.

STATE OF INDIANA

MISHAWAKA, ST. JOSEPH CO., ST. MICHAEL (1962) Rev. Leonard Korchinsky.
Res.: 712 E. Lawrence St., IN 46544. Tel: 574-259-7173. Email: archangelmishawaka@comcast.net.
MUNSTER, LAKE CO., ST. JOSAPHAT (1958), (Ukrainian), Very Rev. Yaroslav Mendyuk.
Res.: 8624 White Oak Ave., IN 46321. Tel: 219-923-0984; Fax: 219-923-0984.
Catechesis / Religious Program—Students 6.

STATE OF KANSAS

WICHITA, SEDGWICK
MISSION—HOLY APOSTLES 7100 E. 45th St. N., KS 67226. Tel: 316-734-1295; 316-744-0167, Ext. 118. Deacon Randall Brown, Temporary Admin.

STATE OF MICHIGAN

DEARBORN, WAYNE CO., ST. MICHAEL'S (1962) Very Rev. Canon Wayne J. Ruchgy.
Res.: 6340 Chase Rd., MI 48126. Tel: 313-582-1424; Fax: 313-582-8157.
Mission—Holy Ascension Salem, MI 48175.
DEARBORN HEIGHTS, WAYNE CO., OUR LADY OF PERPETUAL HELP (1963), (Ukrainian), Very Rev. Volodymyr Petriv; Rev. Andriy Burda.
Res.: 26606 Ann Arbor Trail, MI 48127. Tel: 313-278-0470. Email: olphukr@gmail.com.
Catechesis / Religious Program—Students 7.
DETROIT, WAYNE CO., ST. JOHN THE BAPTIST (1918), (Ukrainian), Rev. Valeriy Kandyuk, Admin.
Res.: 3877 Clippert Ave., MI 48210. Tel: 313-897-7300; Fax: 313-897-7304.
FLINT, GENESEE CO., ST. VLADIMIR'S (1950) Rev. Bogdan Rybchuk.
Res.: c/o 24932 Marigold Ave., Warren, MI 48089. Tel: 586-757-3834.
GRAND RAPIDS, KENT CO., ST. MICHAEL'S (1949), (Ukrainian), [JC] Rev. Michael Bliszcz (SJP), Admin.
Mailing Address: 154 Gold Ave., N.E., MI 49504. Tel: 616-742-0874.
HAMTRAMCK, WAYNE CO., IMMACULATE CONCEPTION OF B.V.M. (1914), (Ukrainian), Revs. Daniel Schaicoski, O.S.B.M., Supr. & Pastor; Roman Hykavy, O.S.B.M.; Joseph Ihor Kralka, O.S.B.M.
Res. & Church: 11700 McDougall St., MI 48212. Tel: 313-893-1710; Fax: 313-893-0770.
School—Immaculate Conception Ukrainian Catholic Schools Association, (Grades K-8), 29500 Westbrook, Warren, MI 48093. Tel: 586-574-2480; Fax: 586-574-2723. Christine Juzych, Librarian. Priests 1; Lay Teachers 20; Students 169.
Catechesis / Religious Program—Students 145.
Immaculate Conception Endowment Fund Inc.—
WARREN, MACOMB CO., ST. JOSAPHAT (1961), (Ukrainian), [CEM] Revs. Mario Dacechen, O.S.B.M.; Walter Rybicky, O.S.B.M.
Res.: 26401 St. Josaphat Dr., MI 48091. Tel: 586-755-1740; Fax: 586-755-1399.
Catechesis / Religious Program—Marie Heshchuk, D.R.E. Students 16.

STATE OF MINNESOTA

MINNEAPOLIS, HENNEPIN CO., ST. CONSTANTINE (1913), (Ukrainian), [CEM] Very Rev. Canon Michael Stelmach.
Res.: 515 University Ave., N.E., MN 55413-1944. Tel: 612-379-2394; Fax: 612-379-2470.
Catechesis / Religious Program—Students 21.

STATE OF MISSOURI

ST. JOSEPH, BUCHANAN CO., ST. JOSEPH'S (1918), (Ukrainian), Attended by Omaha, NE. Rev. Bohdan Kudleychuk, Temporary Admin.
Church: 526 Virginia, MO 64504. Tel: 816-238-1187; Fax: 402-345-1552.
ST. LOUIS, ST. LOUIS CO., ASSUMPTION B.V.M. (1894), (Ukrainian), Rev. Andrew Plishka, Admin. Served by Chicago.
Church: 11363 Oak Branch Dr., MO 63129. Tel: 314-487-1786.

STATE OF NEBRASKA

LINCOLN, LANCASTER CO., ST. GEORGE'S (1950), (Ukrainian), Rev. Bohdan Kudleychuk, Temporary Admin.
Res.: 1513 Martha St., Omaha, NE 68108.
Church: 3330 N. 13th St., NE 68521. Tel: 402-435-5882; 402-345-1552.
OMAHA, DOUGLAS CO., ASSUMPTION OF B.V.M. (1950), (Ukrainian), Rev. Bohdan Kudleychuk, Temporary Admin.
Res.: 1513 Martha St., NE 68108. Tel: 402-345-1552.

STATE OF NORTH DAKOTA

BELFIELD, STARK CO.
1—ST. DEMETRIUS (1905), (Ukrainian), [CEM 2] Rev. Michael Taras Miles; Deacon Leonard Kordonowy.
Res.: P.O. Box 428, ND 58622-0428. Tel: 701-575-4281.
Catechesis / Religious Program—Students 8.
2—ST. JOHN THE BAPTIST (1946), (Ukrainian), [CEM 2] Rev. Michael Taras Miles; Deacon Leonard Kordonowy.
Mailing Address: P.O. Box 428, ND 58622-0428.
Res.: 307 6th St., N.E., P.O. Box 428, ND 58622-0428. Tel: 701-575-4281.
Catechesis / Religious Program—Students 3.
WILTON, MCLEAN CO., SS. PETER AND PAUL (1906), (Ukrainian), [CEM] Rev. George L. Pruys, Admin.
Res.: 106 N. 7th St., P.O. Box 275, ND 58579. Tel: 701-734-6464.
Catechesis / Religious Program—
Mission—St. Michael 812 N. Main St., Minot, Ward Co., ND 58703. Tel: 701-839-4756.

STATE OF OREGON

SPRINGFIELD, LANE CO., NATIVITY OF THE MOTHER OF GOD (1981), (Ukrainian), Rev. Richard Janowicz.
Res.: 704 Aspen St., OR 97477. Tel: 541-726-7309; Fax: 541-726-7309.
Catechesis / Religious Program—Students 18.

STATE OF TEXAS

HOUSTON, HARRIS CO., PROTECTION OF THE MOTHER OF GOD (1957), (Ukrainian), [JC] Rev. Mykola Dovzhuk, Admin.
Res.: 9102 Meadowshire St., TX 77037. Tel: 713-447-2749; Fax: 713-447-2749.
Catechesis / Religious Program—Students 27.
THE COLONY, ST. SOPHIA UKRAINIAN CATHOLIC CHURCH (1999), (Ukrainian), Rev. Pavlo Popov, Admin.; Deacon John Novocilsky.
Church & Res.: 5600 N. Colony Blvd., TX 75056-1927. Tel: 469-384-2855 (Res.); 972-370-4700 (Office); Fax: 972-370-4700. Web: www.stsophiaukrainian.cc.

STATE OF WASHINGTON

SEATTLE, KING CO., OUR LADY OF ZARVANYTSYA (1959) Rev. Abraham Miller.
5321 17th Ave., S., WA 98108. Tel: 206-762-1055.
Catechesis / Religious Program—Ulana Petersen, D.R.E. Students 10.

STATE OF WISCONSIN

MILWAUKEE, MILWAUKEE CO., ST. MICHAELS (1950), (Ukrainian), [JC] Rev. Volodymyr Savchyn; Deacon Michael Chabin.
Res.: 1025 S. 11th St., P.O. Box 64012, WI 53204. Tel: 414-672-5616; Fax: 414-672-5616.

Chaplains of Public Institutions

Hospitals Rev. Mykola Buryadnyk, Resurrection Health Care Center, Very Rev. Archpriest Mykhailo Kuzma, Resurrection Health Care Center, Alexian Brothers, Rev. Jaroslav Mendyuk, Illinois Masonic Hospital.

On Leave:
Rev.—
Panchuk, Myron

Retired:
Revs.—
Bucsek, Basil, 17648 W. Voltaire St., Surprise, AZ 85388-5057. Tel: 623-243-5207
Dohman, William
Marick, Thomas D., 1801 Dallas Ave., Royal Oak, MI 48067. Tel: 248-398-9196
Zaiats, Volodymyr
Very Rev. Archpriest—
Dobrowolski, Thomas. Tel: 313-768-5474
Rev. Msgr. Canon—
Bilinsky, William M., 84031 Pine Dr., Folsom, LA 70437.

Permanent Deacons:
Bozio, Michael, Transfiguration of Our Lord, Denver, CO
Brown, Randall, Holy Apostles Mission, Wichita, KS
Chabin, Nicholas, St. Michael, Milwaukee, WI
Cook, Michael, Nativity of the Blessed Virgin Mary
Horodysky, Mychajlo, St. Nicholas Cathedral, Chicago, IL
Huskey, Michael, St. Nicholas Cathedral, Chicago, IL
Kordonowy, Leonard, St. John the Baptist, Belfield, ND; St. Demetrius, Belfield, ND
Logusch, Eugene, St Mary's Assumption, St. Louis, MO

INSTITUTIONS LOCATED IN THE DIOCESE

[A] MONASTERIES

EAGLE HARBOR. *Holy Transfiguration Skete* (1983) Society of St. John, 6559 State Hwy. M26, MI 49950. Tel: 906-289-4484; Fax: 906-289-4388. Email: htskete@gmail.com. Web: societystjohn.com. Very Rev. Nicholas Glenn, Hegumen; Deacon Ambrose Nemeth; Rev. Basil Paris. Priests 2; Deacons 1; Professed Monks 5.

REDWOOD VALLEY. *Holy Transfiguration Monastery*, 17001 Tomki Rd., CA 95470. Tel: 707-485-8959; Fax: 707-485-1122. Email: monksmttabor@gmail.com. Web: www.byzcath.org/monastery. P.O. Box 217, CA 95470. Rev. Theodore Zientek, Admin. Monks of Mount Tabor. Priests 2; Deacons 1; Professed Monks 5.

[B] MISCELLANEOUS

CHICAGO. **Ukrainian Catholic Education Foundation*, 2247 W. Chicago Ave., 60622. Tel: 773-235-8462; Fax: 773-235-8464. Email: ucef@ucef.org. Web: www.ucef.org. Alexander B. Kuzma, Exec. Dir.

TEMPE. *Metropolitan Andrey Sheptytsky Institute of Eastern Christian Studies*, 1616 W. Gleaming Moon Trail, Tucson, AZ 85704-1454. Tel: 480-217-8505. Web: www.sheptytskyinstitute.ca.

RELIGIOUS INSTITUTES OF MEN REPRESENTED IN THE DIOCESE

For further details refer to the corresponding bracketed number in the Religious Institutes of Men or Women section.

[]—*Monks of Mt. Tabor*

[0180]—*Order of St. Basil the Great*—O.S.B.M.

[]—*Skete of Mt. Tabor*

RELIGIOUS INSTITUTES OF WOMEN REPRESENTED IN THE DIOCESE

[3730]—*Sisters of the Order of St. Basil the Great*—O.S.B.M.

NECROLOGY

(No Deaths)

An asterisk (*) denotes an organization that has established tax-exempt status directly with the IRS and is not covered by the USCCB Group Ruling.

Eparchy of St. Peter the Apostle (Chaldean)

(Editor's Note: 2012 information was not received)

Most Reverend

SARHAD Y. JAMMO

First Bishop-Eparch of the Eparchy of Saint Peter the Apostle-Chaldean; ordained December 19, 1964; appointed Chaldean Bishop May 4, 2002; consecrated Bishop July 18, 2002 in Detroit, Michigan; installed July 25, 2002 in San Diego, California; appointed First Bishop Eparch to the Eparchy of Saint Peter the Apostle-Chaldean Catholic Diocese of America July 25, 2002. *Res.: St. Peter Chaldean Diocese, 1627 Jamacha Way, El Cajon, CA 92019.*

Chancery Office: 1627 Jamacha Way, El Cajon, CA 92019. Tel: 619-579-7997; Fax: 619-588-8281.

Email: sjammo@gmail.com

ESTABLISHED JULY 25, 2002.

The Jurisdiction of the Eparchy extends territorially to all Western States in the United States of America inclusive. With regards to persons, its subjects are all Catholics of the Chaldean or Assyrian Ancestry: (1) Who immigrated to this country from the Middle East, especially from Iraq and Iran; (2) Who descends from such persons (can. 755); (3) Women married to men referable to (1) & (2) if they comply with can. 98, n.4; (4) Who in accordance with can. 98, n. 3, changed their Rite; (5) converts to the Catholic Church of the Chaldean Rite; (6) And in fact, all other Catholics of the Chaldean Rite who are attached to the parishes subject to the jurisdiction of the Eparch. For legal titles of parishes and diocesan institutions, consult the Chancery Office.

Legal Title: The Chaldean Catholic Diocese of St. Peter the Apostle.

STATISTICAL OVERVIEW

Personnel	
Bishop	1
Priests: Diocesan Active in Diocese	13
Priests: Diocesan Active Outside Diocese	2
Number of Diocesan Priests	15
Religious Priests in Diocese	5
Total Priests in Diocese	20
Permanent Deacons in Diocese	10
Total Sisters	10
Parishes	
Parishes	9
With Resident Pastor:	
Resident Diocesan Priests	6
Resident Religious Priests	5
Welfare	
Homes for the Aged	2
Total Assisted	92
Vital Statistics	
Receptions into the Church:	
Infant Baptism Totals	447
Adult Baptism Totals	9
First Communions	437
Confirmations	447
Marriages:	
Catholic	154
Total Marriages	154
Deaths	109
Total Catholic Population	60,000

Chancery Office—1627 Jamacha Way, El Cajon, 92019. Tel: 619-579-7997; Fax: 619-588-8281.

Vicar General—Rev. Msgr. Archdeacon SABRI A. KEJBO, 799 E. Washington Ave., El Cajon, 92020. Tel: 619-444-9911; Fax: 619-444-7989.

Chancellor—Rev. Msgr. Chorbishop SAEED D. SAEED (Felix Shabi).

Judicial Officer—Rev. Msgr. Chorbishop SAEED D. SAEED (Felix Shabi).

Director of Finance—Rev. Msgr. Chorbishop SAEED D. SAEED (Felix Shabi).

Diocesan Advisory Council—Mr. AZIZ RAZOKY.

Director of Religious Education—Ms. KHELOUD ALLOS.

Media Center—WASAN JARBO, Mgr. Tel: 619-590-9028; Fax: 619-590-8273.

Child Protection Review Board—NADIA NAJOR; KUSAY ARABO.

Victim Assistance Coordinator—Rev. Msgr. Archdeacon SABRI A. KEJBO. Tel: 619-444-9911; Fax: 619-444-7989. Email: st.michaels@cox.net.

CLERGY, PARISHES, MISSIONS AND PAROCHIAL SCHOOLS

STATE OF CALIFORNIA

CERES, STANISLAUS CO., ST. MATTHEW'S ASSYRIAN-CHALDEAN CATHOLIC CHURCH Rev. Michael Barota. 3005 6th St., 95307. Tel: 209-541-1660; Fax: 209-541-3952.

EL CAJON, SAN DIEGO CO.

1—**ST. PETER CHALDEAN CATHEDRAL* (1973), (Chaldean), Rev. Michael J. Bazzi; Rev. Msgr. Polis Karkees; Rev. Andrew Younan.
Res.: 1627 Jamacha Way, 92019. Tel: 619-579-7913; 619-588-9921; Fax: 619-588-8281.
Catechesis/Religious Program—Tel: 619-447-8876; Fax: 615-588-8281. Ms. Kheloud Allos, D.R.E. Students 810.
Convent—Chaldean Sisters, 1591 Jamacha Way, 92019. Tel: 619-447-4842; Fax: 619-590-0052.
Convent—Worker of the Vineyard, 552 E. Camden Ave., 92020. Tel: 619-663-9683. Web: www.workersofthevineyard.org.

2—ST. MICHAEL CHALDEAN CATHOLIC CHURCH (1999), (Chaldean), Rev. Msgr. Archdeacon Sabri A. Kejbo; Revs. Peter Lawrence; Michael Mansoor.
Church: 799 E. Washington Ave., 92020. Tel: 619-444-9911; Fax: 619-444-7989.
Catechesis/Religious Program—Sr. Miskenta Mariam (Reem) Salman, D.R.E. Students 304.

EL DORADO HILLS, EL DORADO CO., OUR LADY OF PERPETUAL HELP CHALDEAN/ASSYRIAN CATHOLIC CHURCH, (Sacramento, CA) Rev. Kamal Warda Bidawid, Admin.; Tom Simon, Parochial Board Pres.
P.O. Box 4154, 95762. Tel: 916-709-3784; Fax: 916-772-9394.

NORTH HOLLYWOOD, LOS ANGELES CO., ST. PAUL ASSYRIAN-CHALDEAN CATHOLIC PARISH (1980), (Chaldean—Assyrian), [JC] Revs. Samuel Dinkha; Tomy Tomikeh.
Res.: 13050 Vanowen St., 91605. Tel: 818-765-3665; Fax: 818-765-0493.
Catechesis/Religious Program—Students 30.

PERRIS, RIVERSIDE CO., ST. HORMIZDAH MISSION Revs. Awraha Mansoor, Admin.; Pieter Georgis.
13985 Descanso Dr., 92570. Tel: 951-780-1593.

POWAY, SAN DIEGO CO., MAR ADDAI MISSION Rev. Peter Lawrence.
17252 Bernardo Center Dr., San Diego, 92128.

SAN JOSE, SANTA CLARA CO., ST. MARY ASSYRIAN-CHALDEAN PARISH (1987) Rev. Zuhair G. Toma.
Assyrian Chaldean Catholic Church California Corporation—
Church & Rectory: 109 N. First St., Campbell, 95008. Tel: 408-378-6212; Fax: 408-379-0496.
Catechesis/Religious Program—Students 70.

SANTA ANA, ORANGE CO., ST. GEORGE CHALDEAN CATHOLIC CHURCH (2001), (Chaldean), [JC] Rev. Awraha Mansoor, Admin.
Church: 4807 W. McFadden, 92704. Tel: 714-531-7760; Fax: 714-775-1442.
Catechesis/Religious Program—Students 24.

TURLOCK, STANISLAUS CO., ST. THOMAS ASSYRIAN-CHALDEAN PARISH (1964), (Chaldean), [CEM] [JC] Rev. Kamal Warda Bidawid.
Res.: 2901 N. Berkeley Ave., 95380. Tel: 209-668-4500; Fax: 209-668-2762.
Catechesis/Religious Program—Students 45.
Convent—Chaldean Sisters, 2937 N. Berkeley Ave., 95380. Tel: 209-634-2043; Fax: 209-634-6384.
St. Thomas Retirement Center—Tel: 209-634-7252.

STATE OF ARIZONA

GLENDALE, MARICOPA CO., HOLY FAMILY MISSION Rev. Msgr. Chorbishop Saeed D. Saeed, (Felix Shabi).
3847 W. Bluefield Ave., AZ 85305.

SCOTTSDALE, MARICOPA CO., MAR AURAHA CHALDEAN CATHOLIC PARISH (1992), (Chaldean), [JC] Rev. Msgr. Chorbishop Saeed D. Saeed, (Felix Shabi); Rev. Reemon Sarkees.
The Chaldean Catholic Church of Arizona Corporation—
Res.: 6816 E. Cactus Rd., AZ 85254. Tel: 480-596-6798; Fax: 480-596-9067.
Catechesis/Religious Program—Students 210.
Convent—Chaldean Sisters, 6308 E. Shea Blvd., AZ 85254. Tel: 480-596-1012; Fax: 480-596-1012. Sisters 2.

STATE OF NEVADA

LAS VEGAS, CLARK CO., ST. BARBARA ASSYRIAN-CHALDEAN CATHOLIC CHURCH Rev. Poulos Ghozairan.
4514 Meadows Ln., NV 89107. Tel: 702-870-0045; Fax: 702-430-8566.

INSTITUTIONS LOCATED IN THE DIOCESE

[A] SEMINARIES

EL CAJON. *Seminary of Mar Abba the Great*, 1245 Jamacha Rd., 92019. Tel: 619-334-8427. Web: www.marabba.org. Rev. Andrew Younan, Rector.

[B] RETIREMENT CENTERS

EL CAJON. *Good Samaritan Retirement Center*, 1515 Jamacha Way, 92019. Tel: 619-590-1515; Fax: 619-590-0052. Web: www.goodsamretirement.org. Sr. Alexandra Matti, Exec. Dir.

[C] MONASTERIES AND RESIDENCES FOR PRIESTS AND BROTHERS

PERRIS. *St. George Monastery/Retreat Center*, 13985 Descanso Dr., 92570. Rev. Awraha Mansoor, Admin.

[D] MISCELLANEOUS

EL CAJON. *Chaldean Media Center*, 1627 Jamacha Way, 92019. Tel: 619-590-9028; Fax: 619-590-8273. Email: infokaldu@yahoo.com. Web:

www.kaldu.org; kaldaya.net. Wasan Jarbo, Dir.

NECROLOGY

(No Deaths)

An asterisk (*) denotes an organization that has established tax-exempt status directly with the IRS and is not covered by the USCCB Group Ruling.

Eparchy of Saint Thomas the Apostle (Chaldean)

(Editor's Note: 2012 information was not received)

Most Reverend

IBRAHIM N. IBRAHIM, D.D.

First Bishop-Eparch of the Eparchy of Saint Thomas the Apostle-Chaldean Catholic Diocese of America; ordained December 30, 1962; appointed Chaldean Apostolic Exarch and Titular Bishop of Anbar January 26, 1982; consecrated Bishop March 7, 1982 in Baghdad, Iraq; installed April 18, 1982 in Detroit; appointed First Bishop Eparch to the Eparchy of Saint Thomas the Apostle-Chaldean Catholic Diocese of America September 14, 1985. *Res.: St. Thomas the Apostle, Chaldean Catholic Diocese of U.S.A., 25603 Berg Rd., Southfield, MI 48033.*

Exarchate Erected January 26, 1982. Elevated to the Rank of Eparchy September 14, 1985.

The Jurisdiction of the Eparchy extends territorially to all Eastern States in the United States of America inclusive. With regard to persons, its subjects are all Catholics of the Chaldean or Assyrian Ancestry: (1) Who immigrated to this country from the Middle East, especially from Iraq and Iran; (2) Who descends from such persons (can. 755); (3) Women married to men referable to (1) & (2) if they comply with can. 98, n. 4; (4) Who in accordance with can. 98, n. 3., changed their Rite; (5) Converts to the Catholic Church of the Chaldean Rite; (6) And in fact, all other Catholics of the Chaldean Rite who are attached to the parishes subject to the jurisdiction of the Eparch.

For legal titles of parishes and diocesan institutions, consult the Chancery Office.

STATISTICAL OVERVIEW

Personnel	
Bishop	1
Priests: Diocesan Active in Diocese	15
Priests: Diocesan Active Outside Diocese	1
Priests: Diocesan in Foreign Missions	1
Priests: Retired, Sick or Absent	4
Number of Diocesan Priests	21
Total Priests in Diocese	21
Ordinations:	
Diocesan Priests	1
Permanent Deacons in Diocese	120
Total Sisters	10
Parishes	
Parishes	9
With Resident Pastor:	
Resident Diocesan Priests	9
Missions	1
New Parishes Created	1
Welfare	
Homes for the Aged	1
Total Assisted	60
Special Centers for Social Services	1
Total Assisted	150
Educational	
Diocesan Students in Other Seminaries	7
Total Seminarians	7
Total Students under Catholic Instruction	7
Vital Statistics	
Receptions into the Church:	
Infant Baptism Totals	978
Adult Baptism Totals	7
First Communions	680
Confirmations	985
Marriages:	
Catholic	323
Interfaith	5
Total Marriages	328
Deaths	269
Total Catholic Population	125,000

Chancery Office—25603 Berg Rd., Southfield, 48033. Tel: 248-351-0440; Fax: 248-351-0443. Email: chaldeandiocese-detroit@comcast.net. Web: www.chaldeandiocese.org. Most Rev. IBRAHIM N. IBRAHIM, D.D.; Rev. SAMEEM BALINS.

Vicar General—Rev. MANUEL Y. BOJI, 43700 Merrill Rd., Sterling Heights, 48314. Tel: 586-803-3114; Fax: 586-803-3140.

Eparchial College of Consultors—Revs. MANUEL Y. BOJI; STEPHEN H. KALLABAT; JACOB O. YASSO; SULEIMAN DENHA (Retired); JIRJIS ABRAHIM; WISAM MATTI; EMANUEL HANA SHALETA; FRANK KALABAT; RUDY ZOMA; ANTHONY KATHAWA.

Diocesan Corporation-The Chaldean Catholic Church of U.S.A.—Most Rev. IBRAHIM N. IBRAHIM, D.D., S.T.D., Pres.; Revs. MANUEL Y. BOJI, Treas.; FRANK KALABAT, Sec.

Eparchial Tribunal—Rev. STEPHEN H. KALLABAT, Court of the First Instance, Chancery Office, 25603 Berg Rd., Southfield, 48033. Tel: 248-351-0440.

CLERGY, PARISHES, MISSIONS AND PAROCHIAL SCHOOLS

STATE OF MICHIGAN

DETROIT, WAYNE CO., SACRED HEART CHALDEAN PARISH (1973), (Chaldean), Rev. Jacob O. Yasso.
Res.: 310 W. Seven Mile Rd., 48203. Tel: 313-368-6214 (Church); Fax: 313-891-0132. Email: fryasso@hotmail.com.
Catechesis/Religious Program—Tel: 248-548-0066. Students 30.

OAK PARK, OAKLAND CO., MAR ADDAI CHALDEAN PARISH (1979), (Chaldean), Rev. Stephen H. Kallabat.
Res.: 24010 Coolidge Hwy., 48237. Tel: 248-547-4648; Fax: 248-399-9089.
Catechesis/Religious Program—Students 220.

SHELBY TWP., OAKLAND CO., ST. GEORGE CHALDEAN CATHOLIC CHURCH (2005) Revs. Emanuel Hana Shaleta; Basel Yaldo.
Mailing Address: 45700 Dequinder Rd., 48317. Tel: 586-254-7221; Fax: 586-254-2874.
Catechesis/Religious Program—Students 350.

SOUTHFIELD, OAKLAND CO., OUR LADY OF CHALDEANS CATHEDRAL, MOTHER OF GOD CHALDEAN PARISH (1948), (Chaldean), Most Rev. Ibrahim N. Ibrahim; Revs. Wisam Matti; Anthony Kathawa.
Mailing Address: 25585 Berg Rd., 48033. Tel: 248-356-0565; 248-356-0569; 248-356-9809 (Hall); Fax: 248-356-5235.
Catechesis/Religious Program—Tel: 248-356-2448. Students 180.
Convent—Chaldean Sisters, Daughters of Mary Immaculate Conception, 24900 Middlebelt Rd., Farmington, 48336. Tel: 248-615-2951; Fax: 248-615-3482.
Chaldean Manor Housing for Elders—25775 Berg Rd., 48033. Tel: 248-355-9491. (Middle age & up).

STERLING HEIGHTS, HOLY MARTYRS CHALDEAN CATHOLIC CHURCH (2010) Rev. Manuel Y. Boji.
43700 Merrill Rd., 48314. Tel: 586-803-3114; Fax: 586-803-3140.

TROY, OAKLAND CO., ST. JOSEPH CHALDEAN PARISH (1981), (Chaldean), Rev. Msgr. Zouhair Toma; Rev. Rudy Zoma.
Res.: 2442 E. Big Beaver Rd., 48083. Tel: 248-528-3676; 248-524-1144 (Church); Fax: 248-524-1957.

WARREN
MISSION—OUR LADY OF PERPETUAL HELP 11200 Twelve Mile Rd., 48093. Tel: 586-804-2114; Fax: 586-933-2590. Rev. Fadi Habib.

WEST BLOOMFIELD, OAKLAND CO., ST. THOMAS CHALDEAN CATHOLIC PARISH (1992), (Chaldean), Revs. Frank Kalabat; Jirjis Abrahim.
Res. & Mailing Address: 6900 Maple Rd., 48322. Tel: 248-788-2460; Fax: 248-788-2153.
St. Ephrem Re-Evangelization Center—4875 Maple Rd., Bloomfield Township, 48301. Tel: 248-538-9903; Fax: 248-538-0969.
Catechesis/Religious Program—Tel: 248-306-6004. Students 370.

STATE OF ILLINOIS

CHICAGO, COOK CO.

1—ST. EPHREM'S CHURCH (1904), (Chaldean-Assyrian), [JC] Rev. Zaya Marano.
Res.: 2537 W. Bryn Mawr Ave., IL 60659-4996. Tel: 773-271-8899; Fax: 773-271-8866.
Catechesis/Religious Program—Tel: 773-506-9957. Students 50.
Convent—Chaldean Sisters, Daughters of Mary Immaculate Conception, 2908 Morse, IL 60645. Tel: 773-338-8832.

2—MART MARIAM PARISH (1986), (Chaldean-Assyrian), [JC] Rev. Sanharib Youkhanna.
Church: 2849 W. Chase Ave., IL 60645. Tel: 773-761-9401; Fax: 773-761-9045. Web: www.martmariamchurch.org.

Retired:
Rev. Msgr.—
Bikoma, Edward J.
Revs.—
Denha, Suleiman
Rayes, Emanuel, 6900 Maple Rd., West Bloomfield, 48322. Tel: 248-788-2460

INSTITUTIONS LOCATED IN THE DIOCESE

RELIGIOUS INSTITUTES OF WOMEN IN THE EPARCHY

For further details refer to the corresponding bracketed number in the Religious Institutes of Men or Women section.

[]—*Daughters of Mary Immaculate* (Baghdad, Iraq); (Farmington Hills, MI; Chicago, IL)—D.M.I.

NECROLOGY

(No Deaths)

An asterisk (*) denotes an organization that has established tax-exempt status directly with the IRS and is not covered by the USCCB Group Ruling.

St. Thomas Syro-Malabar Catholic Diocese of Chicago

Most Reverend

JACOB ANGADIATH

Bishop of St. Thomas Syro-Malabar; ordained January 5, 1972; appointed Bishop of St. Thomas Syro-Malabar Catholic Diocese of Chicago March 13, 2001; Episcopal Ordination July 1, 2001. *Office: 372 S. Prairie Ave., Elmhurst, IL 60126-4020.* Tel: 630-279-1386; 630-279-1383; Fax: 630-279-1479.

ESTABLISHED MARCH 13, 2001.

Comprises all of the United States and Canada.

Diocesan Office: 372 S. Prairie Ave., Elmhurst, IL 60126-4020. Tel: 630-279-1386; 630-279-1383; Fax: 630-279-1479.

STATISTICAL OVERVIEW

Personnel	
Bishop	1
Priests: Diocesan Active in Diocese	38
Number of Diocesan Priests	38
Religious Priests in Diocese	15
Total Priests in Diocese	53
Total Sisters	18
Parishes	
Parishes	27
With Resident Pastor:	
Resident Diocesan Priests	26
Resident Religious Priests	3
Missions	37
New Parishes Created	5
Educational	
Diocesan Students in Other Seminaries	2
Total Seminarians	2
Catechesis/Religious Education:	
High School Students	962
Elementary Students	3,181
Total Students under Catholic Instruction	4,145
Vital Statistics	
Receptions into the Church:	
Infant Baptism Totals	303
Minor Baptism Totals	81
Adult Baptism Totals	69
Received into Full Communion	97
First Communions	669
Confirmations	766
Marriages:	
Catholic	77
Interfaith	9
Total Marriages	86
Deaths	57
Total Catholic Population	87,000

Diocesan Office—372 S. Prairie Ave., Elmhurst, 60126-4020. Tel: 630-279-1386; 630-279-1383; Fax: 630-279-1479.

Administration

Vicar General (Protosyncellus)—Rev. ANTONY C. THUNDATHIL, M.S.T., 372 S. Prairie Ave., Elmhurst, 60126-4020. Tel: 630-279-1386; 630-279-1453; Fax: 630-279-1479. Email: vicargeneral@syromail.com.

Vicar General (Syncellus)—Rev. ABRAHAM MUTHOLATHU JACOB, Our Lady of Victory Church, 5212 W. Agatite Ave., Chicago, 60630. Cell: 773-412-6254.

Procurator, Chancellor & Secretary to Bishop—Rev. VINOD MADATHIPARAMBIL, 372 S. Prairie Ave., Elmhurst, 60126-4020. Tel: 630-279-1386; 630-279-1383; Fax: 630-279-1479.

Eparchial Consultors—Revs. ANTONY C. THUNDATHIL, M.S.T.; ABRAHAM MUTHOLATHU, V.G.; VINOD MADATHIPARAMBIL, Procurator; VARGHESE NAICKAMPARAMBIL; JOY ALAPPATT; THOMAS MULAVANAL.

Cathedral—Mar Thoma Sleeha Cathedral, 5000 St. Charles Rd., Bellwood, 60104. Tel: 708-544-6419; Fax: 708-544-5890.

Victim Assistance Coordinator—Dr. PAUL CHERIAN. Tel: 630-769-9603 (USA).

CLERGY, PARISHES, MISSIONS AND PAROCHIAL SCHOOLS

STATE OF ILLINOIS

BELLWOOD, COOK CO.

1—MAR THOMA SLEEHA CATHEDRAL (CHICAGO) (1985), (Indian), [JC 2] Revs. Joy Alappat; Emmanuel Madukkakuzhy.
5000 St. Charles Rd., 60104. Tel: 708-544-7250; Fax: 708-544-5890.
Catechesis/Religious Program—Sr. Jeslin Thalachira, C.M.C., D.R.E. Students 710.

2—SYRO-MALABAR CATHOLIC MISSION OF THE DIOCESE OF CHICAGO (1985), (Indian), Closed. For inquiries for parish records contact the chancery.

MAYWOOD, COOK CO.

1—ST. MARY'S SYRO-MALABAR KNANAYA CATHOLIC CHURCH (MORTON GROVE) (2010) Rev. Abraham Mutholathu, Pastor/Vicar.
Church: 7800 W. Lyons St., Morton Grove, 60053. Tel: 773-412-6254; Fax: 773-286-8579. Email: mutholath2000@yahoo.com. Web: www.knanayaregion.us/chicago. 5212 W. Agatite Ave., Chicago, 60630.
Catechesis/Religious Program—Maneesh Kaimoolayil, D.R.E. Students 208.

2—SACRED HEART SYRO-MALABAR KNANAYA CATHOLIC CHURCH (MAYWOOD) (2006), (Indian), [JC] Rev. Saji Kurian Pinarkayil.
611 Maple St., 60153. Tel: 773-412-6254; Cell: 224-659-6586; Fax: 773-286-8579. Email: sajipinarkayil@gmail.com. Web: www.knanayaregion.us/chicago.
Catechesis/Religious Program—Saji Poothrukayil, D.R.E. Students 445.

MORTON GROVE, COOK CO., VISITATION CONGREGATION, Mailing Address: 7801 W. Maple St., 60053. Tel: 847-603-8881; Fax: 847-603-8881. Email: svminchicago@yahoo.com.

STATE OF ARIZONA

PHOENIX, MARICOPA CO., HOLY FAMILY SYRO-MALABAR CATHOLIC MISSION (PHOENIX) (2007) Rev. Mathews Kurian Munjanath, Dir.
Mailing Address: 2936 N. 81st Ave., AZ 85033. Tel: 623-328-5784; Cell: 602-410-8843; Fax: 623-328-5784. Email: info@holyfamilychurchphx.org. Web: www.syromalabaraz.org.
Catechesis/Religious Program—Sajan Mathew, D.R.E. Students 100.

STATE OF CALIFORNIA

LOS ANGELES, LOS ANGELES CO.

1—ST. ALPHONSA SYRO-MALABAR CATHOLIC CHURCH OF LOS ANGELES (2008), (Asian—Indian), Rev. Kuriakose Chacko Vadana, M.S.T.
Mailing Address: 11320 Laurel Cyn. Blvd., San Fernando, CA 91340.
Church: 607 Fourth St., San Fernando, CA 91340. Tel: 818-365-5522; 818-361-1706; Cell: 617-717-4018; Fax: 818-365-6646. Email: alphonsa.angeles@gmail.com. Web: www.syromalabarla.org.
Catechesis/Religious Program—Students 80.

2—BL. CHAVARA SYRO-MALABAR CATHOLIC MISSION (BAKERSFIELD) (2011) [JC] Rev. Kuriakose Chacko Vadana, M.S.T.
11320 Laurel Canyon, San Fernando, CA 91340. Tel: 818-365-5522; 617-717-4018; Fax: 818-365-6646. Email: alphonsa.angeles@gmail.com. Web: www.syromalabar.org.

3—ST. PIUS X SYRO-MALABAR KNANAYA CATHOLIC MISSION OF LOS ANGELES (2010), (Indian), Rev. Thomas Mulavanal.
Mailing Address: 8912 S. Gate Ave., South Gate, CA 90280. Tel: 310-709-5111; Fax: 323-563-0161. Email: mulavan@hotmail.com. Web: www.knanyaregion.us/losangeles.
Church: 124 N. 5th St., Montebello, CA 90640. Tel: 310-709-5111.
Catechesis/Religious Program—Students 32.

SACRAMENTO, SACRAMENTO CO., INFANT JESUS SYRO-MALABAR CATHOLIC MISSION OF SACRAMENTO, CA (2009) Rev. John Kutty George.
6210 McMahon Dr., CA 95820. Cell: 916-803-5307. Email: frjohnyg@gmail.com. Web: infantjesussyromalabarsacramento.org. Services held at: 6210 McMahon Dr., Sacramento, CA 95820.
Res. & Mailing Address: 1017 11th St., CA 95814. Tel: 916-444-3071; Fax: 916-443-2749.
Catechesis/Religious Program—Students 39.

SAN FRANCISCO, SAN FRANCISCO CO., ST. THOMAS SYRO-MALABAR CATHOLIC CHURCH OF SAN FRANCISCO (2009), (Indian), [JC] Rev. Kurian Neduvelichalumkal.
Church: 200 N. Abbott Ave., Milpitas, CA 95035. Tel: 510-688-7805; 408-385-1123; Fax: 408-941-9580. Email: frneduveli@gmail.com. Web: syromalabarsf.org.
Catechesis/Religious Program—Paul C. Akkarakalam, D.R.E. Tel: 510-386-7015. Students 157.

SAN JOSE, SANTA CLARA CO., ST. MARY SYRO-MALABAR KNANAYA CATHOLIC MISSION OF SAN JOSE (2000), (Indian), Rev. Thomas Adathiparampil, Dir.
47385 Warm Springs Blvd., Fremont, CA 94539. Mailing Address: 37588 Fremont Blvd., Fremont, CA 94536. Cell: 650-293-1968; Fax: 408-736-4968. Services held at: 47385 Warm Springs Blvd., Fremont, CA 94539
Catechesis/Religious Program—Tel: 510-745-9244. Jessy Villian, D.R.E. Students 36.

SANTA ANA, ORANGE CO., ST. THOMAS APOSTLE SYRO-MALABAR CATHOLIC CHURCH (SANTA ANA) (2001), (Indian), Rev. Augustine Palackaparampil.
Mailing Address: 5021 W. 16th St., CA 92703. Tel: 714-530-2900; Cell: 714-800-3648. Web:

www.stthomassyromalabar.com.
Catechesis/Religious Program—Mini Raju, D.R.E. Students 116.

STATE OF CONNECTICUT

HARTFORD, HARTFORD CO., ST. THOMAS SYRO-MALABAR CATHOLIC MISSION OF HARTFORD (1998), (Indian), Rev. Joseph J. Naduvilekoot, Dir.
Mailing Address: 15 Maplewood Ave., East Hartford, CT 06108. Tel: 860-289-7916, Ext. 12; Cell: 860-287-2859. Email: frjosen@gmail.com. Web: syromalabarct.com. Services held at: St. Helena Catholic Church, 30 Echo Ln., West Hartford, CT 06107
Catechesis/Religious Program—Students 14.

WEST HARTFORD, HARTFORD CO., SYRO-MALABAR KNANAYA CATHOLIC MISSION CONNECTICUT (2009) Rev. James Mathew (India), Dir.
1969 Crompond Rd., Cortlandt Manor, NY 10567. Tel: 914-309-5822; Fax: 914-737-6882.

STATE OF FLORIDA

BRANDON, HILLSBOROUGH CO., SACRED HEART SYRO-MALABAR KNANAYA CATHOLIC CHURCH (TAMPA) (2010) Rev. Pathros Champakara.
Mailing Address: 3920 S. Kings Ave., FL 33511. Tel: 813-315-9838 (Office); Cell: 813-458-0518. Email: tampaknanayamission@gmail.com.
Catechesis/Religious Program—Students 150.

CORAL SPRINGS, BROWARD CO., OUR LADY OF HEALTH SYRO-MALABAR CATHOLIC CHURCH (CORAL SPRINGS) (2002), (Indian), Rev. Zacharias Thottuvelil.
Mailing Address: 159 N.W. 95th Ln., FL 33071. Tel: 954-227-6985; Cell: 469-688-9511; Fax: 954-227-6985. Email: fr_zacharias@yahoo.com. Web: syromalabarflorida.org.
Church: 201 N. University Dr., FL 33071.
Catechesis/Religious Program—Tel: 786-382-7903. Jimmy Emanuel, D.R.E. Students 207.
Mission—St. Joseph Syro-Malabar Catholic Mission West Palm Beach, FL. Tel: 561-585-5970.
Mission—St. George Syro-Malabar Catholic Mission Miami, FL. Tel: 305-274-6333.

LONGWOOD, SEMINOLE, CO., ST. MARY SYRO-MALABAR CATHOLIC MISSION (ORLANDO) (2008) Rev. John Kudiyiruppil. Services held at: Nativity Catholic Church, 3255 N. Ronald Reagan Blvd., Longwood, FL 32750.
Church & Res.: 3255 Ronald Reagan Blvd., FL 32750. Tel: 407-324-9394; Cell: 407-489-2390; Fax: 407-322-8981. Email: johnk@nativity.org.
Catechesis/Religious Program—Students 12.

MIAMI, MIAMI-DADE CO., ST. GEORGE SYRO-MALABAR CATHOLIC MISSION, MIAMI FL Rev. Zacharias Thottuvelil, Dir.
Mailing Address: 159 N.W. 95th Ln., Coral Springs, FL 33071. Tel: 754-366-6765; Cell: 469-688-9511; Fax: 954-227-6985.

MIAMI BEACH, MIAMI-DADE CO., ST. JUDE SYRO-MALABAR KNANAYA CATHOLIC MISSION OF SOUTH FLORIDA (2007) Rev. Stephen J. Vettuvelil, Dir.
Mailing Address: 2512 Barbara Dr., Fort Lauderdale, FL 33316. Tel: 954-525-4133; Cell: 786-370-8649; Fax: 954-524-9347. Email: vettuvelilstephen@gmail.com. Web: miamikna.com.
Catechesis/Religious Program—Students 58.

TAMPA, HILLSBOROUGH CO., ST. JOSEPH SYRO-MALABAR CATHOLIC CHURCH (TAMPA) (2008) Rev. George Maliekal Paulos.
Church: 5501 Williams Rd., Seffner, FL 33584. Tel: 813-621-0570 (Office); Cell: 813-420-3436. Email: vicar@stjosephsmcc.com. Web: www.stjosephsmcc.corn/org.
Catechesis/Religious Program—Email: skarijirakattu@yahoo.com. Sr. Christy Kanjirakkattu, D.R.E. Students 91.

WEST PALM BEACH, PALM BEACH CO., ST. JOSEPH SYRO-MALABAR CATHOLIC MISSION Rev. Zacharias Thottuvelil.
Mailing Address: 159 N.W. 95th Ln., Coral Springs, FL 33071. Tel: 754-366-6765; Cell: 469-688-9511; Fax: 954-227-6985.

STATE OF GEORGIA

ATLANTA, HOLY FAMILY SYRO-MALABAR KNANAYA CATHOLIC CHURCH (ATLANTA) (2009) Rev. Dominic Joseph.
Mailing Address: 2140 Beaver Ruin Rd., Norcross, GA 30071.
Church: 3885 Rosebud Rd., Loganville, GA 30052. Tel: 813-446-9868; Cell: 210-284-8585; Fax: 770-448-7046. Email: hfchurchatlanta@gmail.com. Web: www.knanayacommunity.net/holyfamily-church.
Catechesis/Religious Program—Students 92.

LOGANVILLE, GWINNETT CO., ST. ALPHONSA SYRO-MALABAR CATHOLIC CHURCH, ATLANTA (2001), (Indian), Rev. Abraham P. Schariah.
Mailing Address: 4561 Rosebud Rd., GA 30052. Tel: 404-921-1267 (Office); 678-512-0295 (Rectory); Cell: 404-935-8658; Fax: 678-512-0295. Email: frjohnyp@gmail.com. Web: www.stalphonsacatholicchurch.org.
Catechesis/Religious Program—Students 154.

STATE OF KENTUCKY

LOUISVILLE, JEFFERSON CO.
1—BLESSED CHAVARA SYRO-MALABAR CATHOLIC CHURCH CINCINNATI, OH (2005) Rev. Joseph Anson Kattuthara, Dir. Cell: 859-308-8394.
Mailing Address: *St. Francis Xavier*, 401 Berry St., Dayton, KY 41074. Email: director.blchavara@gmail.com (Office). Web: www-.blessedchavara.cincinnati.org. Services held at: Our Lady of the Rosary Catholic Church, 17 Farragut Rd., Cincinnati, OH 45218.
Catechesis/Religious Program—Students 10.
2—SYRO-MALABAR CATHOLIC MISSION LOUISVILLE, KENTUCKY (2006) Rev. Anthony Thundathil.
Mailing Address: 372 S. Prairie Ave., 60126. *Assumption Cathedral*, 433 S. Fifth St., KY 40202. Tel: 630-279-1453; Fax: 630-279-1479. Email: shajitgl@gmail.com.

STATE OF MARYLAND

BALTIMORE, BALTIMORE CO., SYRO-MALABAR CATHOLIC MISSION OF BALTIMORE (2004), (Asian—Indian), Rev. James Nirappel, Dir. Services held at: St. Gabriel Catholic Church, 6950 Dogwood Rd., Baltimore, MD 21244.
St. Mary Catholic Church—Church & Mailing Address: 224 W. Washington St., Hagerstown, MD 21740. Tel: 301-739-0390; Cell: 443-414-2250; Fax: 301-739-7082. Email: nirappeljames@yahoo.com. Web: www.syromalabarbaltimore.com.
Catechesis/Religious Program—Students 43.

STATE OF MASSACHUSETTS

BOSTON, SUFFOLK CO., ST. THOMAS THE APOSTLE SYRO-MALABAR CATHOLIC CHURCH (BOSTON) (2004) Rev. Varghese Naickamparampil.
41 Brook St., Framingham, MA 01701. Tel: 508-532-8620; Cell: 586-365-9062; Fax: 508-969-2849. Email: syromalabarchurchboston@gmail.com. Web: www.malayamchurchboston.com.
Catechesis/Religious Program—Students 81.

STATE OF MICHIGAN

BERKLEY, OAKLAND CO., ST. MARY'S SYRO-MALABAR KNANAYA CATHOLIC CHURCH OF DETROIT (2010) Rev. Mathew Meladath.
Mailing Address: 3238 Royal Ave., MI 48072. Tel: 248-820-2086; Fax: 248-677-3686.
Catechesis/Religious Program—Biju Thekkilakattil, D.R.E. Tel: 248-497-1966. Students 30.

SOUTHFIELD, OAKLAND CO., ST. THOMAS SYRO-MALABAR CATHOLIC CHURCH, DETROIT (1995), (Indian), [JC] Rev. George Elambasseril.
Church & Mailing Address: 17235 Mt. Vernon St., MI 48075. Tel: 248-552-6620; Cell: 248-794-4343; Fax: 248-552-6620. Email: secretary.stmcc@gmail.com. Web: www.syromalabardetroit.com.
Catechesis/Religious Program—Students 108.

STATE OF MINNESOTA

ST. PAUL, RAMSEY CO.
1—ST. ALPHONSA SYRO-MALABAR CATHOLIC CHURCH MINNESOTA (1999), (Indian), Rev. Joseph J. Arackal, V.C., Dir.
Mailing Address: *Syro-Malabar Catholics of MN*, 210 5th Ave., S.E., St. Cloud, MN 56304. Tel: 651-437-7103; 320-229-7759; Cell: 320-339-1923. Services held at: St. Richard Church, 7540 Penn Ave. S., Richfield, MN 55423
Catechesis/Religious Program—
2—SYRO-MALABAR KNANAYA CATHOLIC MISSION OF MINNESOTA (2009) Rev. Abraham Mutholathu Jacob.
261 8th St. E., MN 55101. Tel: 773-412-0254; Fax: 773-286-8579. Email: muthalath2000@yahoo.com. Web: www.knanayaregion.us/minnesota_mission.htm. *Our Lady of Victory*, 5212 W. Agatite Ave., Chicago, 60630.

STATE OF NEVADA

LAS VEGAS, CLARK CO.
1—BL. MOTHER THERESA SYRO-MALABAR CATHOLIC CHURCH (2006) Rev. Kuriakose Chacko Vadana, M.S.T.
Mailing Address: 11320 Laurel Canyon, San Fernando, CA 91340. Cell: 617-717-4018. Email: frkvadana@gmail.com. Web: www.syromalabar-.la.org.
2—ST. STEPHEN'S SYRO-MALABAR KNANAYA CATHOLIC MISSION, LAS VEGAS (2009) Rev. Thomas Mulavanal.
2461 E. Flamingo Rd., NV 89121. Tel: 702-376-6717.

STATE OF NEW JERSEY

EAST MILLSTONE, SOMERSET CO., ST. THOMAS SYRO-MALABAR CATHOLIC CHURCH (EAST MILLSTONE) (2006), (Indian), Rev. Thomas Kadukappillil.
Mailing Address: 44 Livingston Ave., Somerset, NJ 08873. Tel: 908-837-9484; Cell: 908-235-8449. Email: trustee@stthomassyronj.org. Web: www.stthomassyronj.org.
Catechesis/Religious Program—Thomas Vengathadam, D.R.E. Students 161.

GARFIELD, BERGEN CO., SYRO-MALABAR CATHOLIC MISSION OF GARFIELD (2004), (Indian), Rev. Paul Kottackal, Dir. Tel: 973-772-7889; Fax: 973-772-7806.
Mailing Address: 69 Market St., NJ 07026. Email: olosc@optonline.net (Office). Web: www.syromalabarmissiongarfield.com.
Catechesis/Religious Program—Students 170.

NEWARK, ESSEX CO., SYRO-MALABAR KNANAYA CATHOLIC MISSION OF NEWARK NEW JERSEY (1993), (Indian), [JC] Rev. Joseph Tharackal, Dir. Services held at: 411 Rutgers Ave., Hillside, NJ 07205.
Res.: 188-16 91st Ave., Hollis, NY 11423. Cell: 847-322-9503; Fax: 718-468-3136. Email: josetharackal@yahoo.com.

STATE OF NEW YORK

BRONX, WESTCHESTER CO., ST. THOMAS SYRO-MALABAR CATHOLIC CHURCH (BRONX) (2002), (Asian—Indian), [CEM] [JC] Rev. Jos Kandathikudy.
Mailing Address: 810 E. 221 St., NY 10467. Tel: 718-944-4747; Cell: 201-681-6021; Fax: 347-920-4296. Email: stsmcc@optonline.net. Web: www.stsmcc.org.
Catechesis/Religious Program—Tel: 718-944-4747. Sabu Ooluthua, D.R.E. Tel: 845-942-5320. Students 131.

FLORAL PARK, NASSAU CO., SYRO-MALABAR KNANAYA CATHOLIC MISSION OF BROOKLYN, NY (1993), (Asian—Indian), [JC] Rev. Joseph Tharackal, Dir. Services held at: 80-45 Winchester Blvd., Queens Village, NY 11427.
Res.: 188-16 91st Ave., Hollis, NY 11423. Cell: 847-322-9503; Fax: 718-468-3136. Email: josetharackal@yahoo.com.
Catechesis/Religious Program—Lissy Joseph, D.R.E. Students 62.

HAVERSTRAW, ROCKLAND CO., SYRO-MALABAR KNANAYA CATHOLIC MISSION OF ROCKLAND, NY (1994), (Indian), [JC] Rev. James Mathew (India), Dir.
Res.: 1969 Compond Rd., Cortlandt Manor, NY 10567. Tel: 914-309-5822; Fax: 914-737-6882. Email: jponganayil@yahoo.com.
Catechesis/Religious Program—Students 51.

ROCKLAND, SULLIVAN CO., SYRO-MALABAR CATHOLIC MISSION, ROCKLAND (2001), (Indian), Rev. Thadeus J. Aravindathu, Dir.
Mailing Address: 128 Parrott Rd., West Nyack, NY 10994-1097. Tel: 845-490-9307; Cell: 845-490-9307. Email: thadeusa@gmail.com. Web: syromalabarrockland.org. Services held at: Our Lady Queen of Peace Chapel, Orangburg.
Catechesis/Religious Program—James Kanachery, D.R.E. Tel: 845-267-0353. Students 69.

STATEN ISLAND, RICHMOND CO., BLESSED KUNJACHAN SYRO-MALABAR CATHOLIC MISSION, STATEN ISLAND, NY (2002), (Indian), Rev. Thadeus J. Aravindathu, Dir.
Mailing Address: 128 Parrot Rd., Rosebank, West Nyack, NY 10994. Tel: 973-772-7889; Cell: 201-951-1701; Fax: 973-772-7806.
Catechesis/Religious Program—

WEST HEMPSTEAD, NASSAU CO., ST. MARY SYRO-MALABAR CATHOLIC CHURCH (WEST HEMPSTEAD) (2004) Rev. Ligory Johnson Philips.
Mailing Address: 24 Westminster Rd., NY 11552. Tel: 516-505-7940; Cell: 281-935-7275. Email: kattiakaran@yahoo.com. Web: www.stmaryssyromalabar.org. Services held at: St. Thomas the Apostle Catholic Church, 875 Hempstead Ave., West Hempstead, NY 11552.
Catechesis/Religious Program—Sherry George Nampiaparambil, D.R.E. Students 202.

WESTCHESTER, WESTCHESTER CO., SYRO-MALABAR KNANAYA CATHOLIC MISSION OF WESTCHESTER, NY (1994), (Indian), [JC] Rev. James Mathew (India), Dir.
Mailing Address: 1969 Crompond Rd., Cortlandt Manor, NY 10567. Tel: 914-309-5822; Fax: 914-737-6882. Email: jponganayil@yahoo.com.
Catechesis/Religious Program—

STATE OF NORTH CAROLINA

RALEIGH-DURHAM, WAKE CO., LOURDES MATHA SYRO-MALABAR CATHOLIC CHURCH (NORTH CAROLINA) (2006) Rev. Augustine Kizhakkedam, O.C.D.
Church: 1400 Vision Dr., Apex, NC 27523. Tel: 919-439-0305; 919-749-4455. Email: akizhakkedam@yahoo.com. Web: www.lourdesmatha.org. Mailing Address: 503 Fantail Ln., Apex, NC 27523.
Catechesis/Religious Program—Joseph Francis, D.R.E. Students 60.

STATE OF OHIO

CLEVELAND, CUYAHOGA CO., ST. RAPHEL SYRO-MALABAR MISSION CLEVELAND, OH (2009) Rev. John Thomas.
Mailing Address: 893 Hamlet St., Columbus, OH 43201. Tel: 614-299-4191; Cell: 630-202-2989. Email: syromalabarcleveland@gmail.com (Office). Web: syromalabarccc.org. Services held at: Our Lady of Peace, 126th St., Shaker Blvd.-12503 Buckingham Ave., Cleveland, OH 44120.
Catechesis/Religious Program—Brijesh George, D.R.E. Students 10.

COLUMBUS, DELAWARE CO., ST. MARY SYRO-MALABAR CATHOLIC MISSION COLUMBUS, OH (2009) Rev. John Thomas.
c/o Sacred Heart Church, 893 Hamlet St., OH 43201. Tel: 614-372-5249; Cell: 630-202-2989. Email: jthachara@gmail.com; columbus-nazrani@googlegroups.com (Office). Web: www.columbusnazrani.googlepages.com.
Catechesis/Religious Program—Medona Jose, D.R.E. Students 12.

STATE OF OKLAHOMA

OKLAHOMA CITY, OKLAHOMA CO., HOLY FAMILY SYRO-MALABAR CATHOLIC CHURCH OKLAHOMA (2005) Rev. Davis Cherayath, Dir.
Mailing Address: P.O. Box 267, OK 73101. Tel: 405-677-7976 (Office); Cell: 630-901-6416. Email: oksyromalabarchurch@yahoo.com (Office). Web: holyfamilyok.org.
Church: 3916 S. Highland Park Dr., OK 73129.
Catechesis/Religious Program—Cell: 630-901-6416. Email: frdavischerayath@gmail.com. Students 43.

STATE OF PENNSYLVANIA

AMBLER, MONTGOMERY CO., SYRO-MALABAR KNANAYA CATHOLIC MISSION OF GREATER PHILADELPHIA (1999), (Indian), Rev. Mathew Manakatt, Dir.
Mailing Address: 212 Welsh Rd., Huntingdon Valley, PA 19006. Tel: 215-947-3500 (Rectory); Cell: 914-954-7081; Fax: 215-938-9071.
Catechesis/Religious Program—Students 21.

PHILADELPHIA, PHILADELPHIA CO., ST. THOMAS SYRO-MALABAR CATHOLIC CHURCH (PHILADELPHIA) (2005), (Asian—Indian), Rev. John Melepuram.
Church: 608 Welsh Rd., PA 19115. Tel: 215-464-4008; Cell: 215-808-4052; Fax: 215-464-4055. Email: johnmelepuram@gmail.com. Web: www.syromalabarphila.org.
Catechesis/Religious Program—Dr. James Kurichy, D.R.E. Students 325.

PITTSBURGH, ALLEGHENY CO., ST. MARY SYRO-MALABAR CATHOLIC MISSION PITTSBURGH, PA (2006) Rev. Vincent Ezhanikkatt, Dir. Cell: 304-723-8007.
Mailing Address: 19 Jo-Glen Dr., Morgantown, WV 26508. Email: syromalabarpittsburgh@gmail.com (Office). Web: www.syromalabarpittsburgh.org. Services held at: 1607 Greentree Rd., Scott Township, Pittsburgh, PA 15220.

STATE OF TENNESSEE

NASHVILLE, DAVIDSON CO., BLESSED MOTHER THERESA SYRO-MALABAR MISSION NASHVILLE, TN (2008) Rev. Tomy Joseph Puliyanampattayil, M.S.F.S.
Mailing Address: 1225 Gallatin Pike S., Madison, TN 37115. Tel: 615-865-1071 (office); 615-844-4154 (Res.); Cell: 615-943-8706; Fax: 615-868-4900. Email: tjpuly@gmail.com. Web: www.syromalabarnashville.com.
Catechesis/Religious Program—Students 13.

STATE OF TEXAS

AUSTIN, HAYS CO., ST. ALPHONSA SYRO-MALABAR CATHOLIC MISSION AUSTIN, TX (2008) Rev. Prince Kuruvilla.
Mailing Address: *St. John of the Cross Church*, 200 S. Metz St., P.O. Box 329, Orange Grove, TX 78372. Tel: 361-756-9028; Fax: 361-756-9028. Email: mcaustin@googlegroups.com (Office). Web: stalphonsa.org. Services held at: 111 Montropolis Dr., Austin, TX 78741.
Dolores Catholic Church—1111 Montopolis Dr., TX 78741.

COPPELL, DALLAS CO., ST. ALPHONS SYRO MALABAR CATHOLIC CHURCH (COPPELL) (2010) Rev. Mathew Varghese, M.S.T.
Mailing Address: P.O. Box 1862, TX 75019.
Church: 200 S. Heartz Rd., TX 75019. Tel: 972-782-4197; Cell: 630-201-8875; Fax: 972-782-4197. Email: stalphonsa1@gmail.com. Web: www.saintalphonsachurch.org.
Catechesis/Religious Program—Students 226.

EDINBURG, HIDALGO CO., DIVINE MERCY SYRO-MALABAR CATHOLIC CHURCH (EDINBURG) (2011) Rev. Cyriac John Valachanath.
Mailing Address: 300 W. Cano St., TX 78539. Tel: 956-380-1363; Cell: 361-660-8786; Fax: 956-380-1363. Email: divinemercymalabar@gmail.com. Web: www.divinemercymalabarparish.com.
Catechesis/Religious Program—Students 36.

FARMERS BRANCH, DALLAS CO., CHRIST THE KING SYRO-MALABAR KNANAYA CATHOLIC CHURCH DFW (2010) Rev. Joseph Sauriamakkel.
Mailing Address: 13406 Onyx Ln., TX 75234. Tel: 972-241-1171; 214-432-0155 (Rectory); Cell: 972-302-5652; Fax: 972-241-1323. Email: pastorchristthekingknanaya.org. Web: christthekingknanaya.org.
Church: 13565 Webb Chapel Rd., TX 75234.
Catechesis/Religious Program—Joseph Elakodikal, D.R.E. Students 180.

GARLAND, DALLAS CO., ST. THOMAS THE APOSTLE CATHOLIC CHURCH/DALLAS (SYRO-MALABAR) (1992), (Indian), Rev. Sebastian Kaniampadickal.
4922 Rosehill Rd., TX 75043. Tel: 972-240-1100; Cell: 708-268-3819; Fax: 972-240-1489. Email: jojiachan@gmail.com. Web: www.syromalabarchurchdallas.org. Mailing Address: 1118 Dandelion Dr., TX 75043. Tel: 972-303-7063.
Catechesis/Religious Program—Josey Angiliuelil, D.R.E. Students 220.

HOUSTON, HARRIS CO., ST. MARY'S SYRO-MALABAR KNANAYA CATHOLIC CHURCH OF HOUSTON (2011), (Indian), [JC] Rev. Jose Mathew, Dir.
Mailing Address: 2430 Bradford Dr., Missouri City, TX 77489. Tel: 847-912-5673. Email: frillijose@gmail.com.
Church: 2210 Staffordshire, Missouri City, TX 77489.
Catechesis/Religious Program—Students 255.

MISSOURI CITY, FORT BEND, CO., ST. JOSEPH SYRO-MALABAR CATHOLIC CHURCH (2001) Rev. Jacob Christy Parampakattil.
Mailing Address: 231 Boardwalk Pkwy., Stafford, TX 77477. Tel: 281-904-6622. Email: jacobchristy@gmail.com. Web: www.sjsmcc.org.
Catechesis/Religious Program—Benny Chacko, D.R.E. Students 441.

SAN ANTONIO, BEXAR CO.
1—ST. ANTHONY SYRO-MALABAR KNANAYA CATHOLIC CHURCH (SAN ANTONIO) (2010) Rev. Dominic Joseph.
Mailing Address: 2140 Beaver Ruins Rd., Norcross, GA 30071. Tel: 210-284-8585; Cell: 210-284-8585. Web: www.sakcpwebs.com.
Catechesis/Religious Program—Students 7.
2—ST. THOMAS SYRO-MALABAR CATHOLIC MISSION OF SAN ANTONIO (2006) Rev. George C. George, Dir.
Mailing Address: 15519 Luna Ridge, Helotes, TX 78023. Cell: 210-385-3961. Email: george.george3@va.gov.
Catechesis/Religious Program—Sr. Licy George, M.S.M.I., D.R.E. Students 32.

SUGAR LAND, FORT BEND CO., ST. JOSEPH SYRO-MALABAR CATHOLIC CHURCH (HOUSTON) (2001), (Indian), Rev. Jacob Christy Parampakattil.
Res. & Mailing Address: 231 Boardwalk Pkwy., Stafford, TX 77477. Tel: 281-904-6622; Fax: 281-969-7088. Email: jacobchristy@gmail.com.
Catechesis/Religious Program—Students 461.

STATE OF VIRGINIA

CENTREVILLE, FAIRFAX CO., ST. JUDE SYRO-MALABAR CATHOLIC MISSION OF NORTHERN VIRGINIA (2010) Revs. Mathew Punchayil (India); Joseph Elamparayil.
14135 Seneca Rd., Darnestown, MD 20874. Tel: 301-948-5536; Cell: 301-873-7006; Fax: 301-948-7452. Email: matpunchayil@yahoo.com. Web: syromalabargw.org.
Catechesis/Religious Program—Students 38.

RICHMOND, HENRICO CO., ST. ALPHONSA SYRO-MALABAR MISSION OF RICHMOND (2010) Rev. Joseph Elamparayil.
Mailing Address: 905 Park Ave., Falls Church, VA 22046. Tel: 703-999-4179. Services held at: St. Epiphany, 11000 Smoketree Dr., Richmond, VA 23236.
Catechesis/Religious Program—Students 4.

STATE OF WISCONSIN

WEST ALLIS, MILWAUKEE CO., ST. ANTONY SYRO-MALABAR CATHOLIC MISSION (WISCONSIN) Rev. Sojan Vathappallil, M.C.B.S., Dir.
Mailing Address: 2322 S. 106th St., WI 53227. Tel: 262-945-8071. Web: www.malayalammass.com. Services held at: St. Aloysius Catholic Church, 1414 S. 93rd St., West Allis, WI 53227.

DISTRICT OF COLUMBIA

DISTRICT OF COLUMBIA, SYRO-MALABAR CATHOLIC MISSION OF GREATER WASHINGTON (1980) Rev. Mathew Punchayil (India), Dir.
Mailing Address: 14135 Seneca Rd., Darnestown, MD 20874. Tel: 301-948-5536, Ext. 101; Cell: 301-873-7006; Fax: 301-948-7452. Email: matpunchayil@yahoo.com. Web: syromalabargw.org.
St. Rose of Lima—11701 Clopper Rd., Gaithersburg, MD 20878.
Catechesis/Religious Program—Roy Mathew, D.R.E. Students 31.

INSTITUTIONS LOCATED IN THE DIOCESE

[A] CONVENTS AND RESIDENCES FOR SISTERS

CHICAGO. *Congregation of Mother of Carmel*, 8120 S. California Ave., 60652. Tel: 773-737-9440. Sr. Geena Chittinappilly, C.M.C., Regl. Supr.

MARGATE. *Sisters of Adoration of the Blessed Sacrament, St. Thomas Adoration Convent*, 6981 N.W. 18th Ct., FL 33063. Tel: 954-323-8373. Sr. Maria Thengumthottathil, S.A.B.S., Mother Supr.

SAN ANTONIO. *Missionary Sisters of Mary Immaculate*, 19 Kenrock Ridge, TX 78254. Tel: 210-647-2947. Sr. Licy George, M.S.M.I., Mother Supr.

STAFFORD. *Missionary Sisters of Mary Immaculate*, 630 Easy Jet Dr., TX 77477. Tel: 281-499-0030; Fax: 281-499-0030. Sr. Agnes Marie, M.S.M.I., Mother Supr.

[B] MISCELLANEOUS

WASHINGTON. *Divine Mercy Healing Center, Inc.*, 426 Rte. 57 W., NJ 07882. Tel: 908-835-9989. Rev. Antony Thekkanath, V.C., Dir.

GLENVIEW. *Missionary Society of St. Thomas the Apostle, M.S.T.*, 2909 Central Ave., 60025-4047. Tel: 847-730-5765. Rev. Skariya Azhikannikkal Poulose, Dir.

RELIGIOUS INSTITUTES OF MEN REPRESENTED IN THE ARCHDIOCESE

For further details refer to the corresponding bracketed number in the Religious Institutes of Men or Women section.

[]—*Missionary Society of St. Thomas the Apostle*—M.S.T.

[]—*Vincentian Congregation - Marymatha Province*

RELIGIOUS INSTITUTES OF WOMEN REPRESENTED IN THE ARCHDIOCESE

[]—*Congregation of Mother of Carmel* (Chicago, IL)

[]—*Missionary Sisters of Mary Immaculate* (Stafford, TX)

[]—*Missionary Sisters of Mary Immaculate* (San Antonio, TX)

[]—*Sisters of Adoration of Blessed Sacrament* (Margate, FL)

NECROLOGY

(No Deaths)

Ukrainian Catholic Diocese of Stamford

Most Reverend

PAUL PATRICK CHOMNYCKY, O.S.B.M.

Bishop of Stamford; ordained October 1, 1988; appointed Apostolic Exarch of Great Britain, Faithful of Eastern Rite & Titular Bishop of Buffada April 5, 2002; ordained June 11, 2002; appointed Bishop of Stamford for Ukrainians January 3, 2006; installed February 20, 2006. *Office: 14 Peveril Rd., Stamford, CT 06902-3019.*

Most Reverend

BASIL H. LOSTEN, D.D., S.T.L., LL.D. (HON.)

Retired Bishop of Stamford; ordained June 10, 1957; appointed Titular Bishop of Arcadiopolis and Auxiliary of Ukrainian Catholic Archeparchy of Philadelphia March 15, 1971; consecrated May 25, 1971; appointed Apostolic Administrator of Archeparchy of Philadelphia June 8, 1976; Transferred to the Stamford See September 20, 1977; retired January 3, 2006. *Res.: 122 Clovelly Rd., Stamford, CT 06902.*

ESTABLISHED AUGUST 8, 1956.

The jurisdiction of the Bishop of Stamford extends territorially throughout all of New York State and the New England States. With regard to persons, his subjects are all members of the Ukrainian Catholic Church (Byzantine Rite), irrespective of where they received Baptism.

For legal titles of parishes and diocesan institutions, consult the Chancery Office.

Chancery Office: 14 Peveril Rd., Stamford, CT 06902-3019. Tel: 203-324-7698; Fax: 203-967-9948.

Email: stamfordeparchy@optonline.net

STATISTICAL OVERVIEW

Personnel	
Bishop	1
Retired Bishops	1
Priests: Diocesan Active in Diocese	33
Priests: Retired, Sick or Absent	6
Number of Diocesan Priests	39
Religious Priests in Diocese	10
Total Priests in Diocese	49
Extern Priests in Diocese	12
Ordinations:	
Diocesan Priests	1
Transitional Deacons	1
Permanent Deacons in Diocese	10
Total Brothers	1
Total Sisters	42
Parishes	
Parishes	51
With Resident Pastor:	
Resident Diocesan Priests	48
Resident Religious Priests	3
Missions	3
Welfare	
Homes for the Aged	1
Total Assisted	26
Day Care Centers	1
Total Assisted	48
Educational	
Seminaries, Diocesan	1
Students from This Diocese	2
Diocesan Students in Other Seminaries	5
Total Seminarians	7
High Schools, Diocesan and Parish	1
Total Students	210
Elementary Schools, Diocesan and Parish	2
Total Students	198
Catechesis/Religious Education:	
High School Students	218
Elementary Students	642
Total Students under Catholic Instruction	1,275
Vital Statistics	
Receptions into the Church:	
Infant Baptism Totals	171
Adult Baptism Totals	7
Received into Full Communion	9
First Communions	151
Confirmations	178
Marriages:	
Catholic	31
Interfaith	13
Total Marriages	44
Deaths	213
Total Catholic Population	13,783

Former Bishops—Most Revs. AMBROSE SENYSHYN, O.S.B.M., D.D., installed as first Bishop of Stamford, Dec. 15, 1956; transferred to the Archeparchy of Philadelphia, Oct. 26, 1961; died Sept. 11, 1976; JOSEPH M. SCHMONDIUK, D.D., Bishop of Stamford, Nov. 9, 1961; transferred to the Archeparchy of Philadelphia, Sept. 20, 1977; died Dec. 25, 1978; BASIL H. LOSTEN, D.D., S.T.L., LL.D. (Hon.), ord. June 10, 1957; appt. Titular Bishop of Arcadiopolis and Auxiliary of Ukrainian Catholic Archeparchy of Philadelphia March 15, 1971; cons. May 25, 1971; appt. Apostolic Administrator of Archeparchy of Philadelphia June 8, 1976; transferred to the Stamford See Sept. 20, 1977; retired Jan. 3, 2006.

Chancery Office—14 Peveril Rd., Stamford, 06902-3019. Tel: 203-324-7698; Fax: 203-967-9948. Email: chancellor@optonline.net. Web: www.stamforddio.org. Office Hours: Mon.-Fri. 9-12 & 1-5.

Vicar General—Rt. Rev. Mitred Archpriest IHOR MIDZAK.

Econome—Rt. Rev. Mitred Msgr. JOHN TERLECKY, B.A., M.A., M.L.S.

Vice Econome—Rt. Rev. Mitred Archpriest MIHAI DUBOVICI, B.A., S.T.B.

Chancellor & Archivist—Very Rev. Archpriest KIRIL ANGELOV.

Chancery Secretary—OKSANA DRAGAN.

Notary Publics—Rt. Rev. Mitred Archpriest MIHAI DUBOVICI, B.A., S.T.B.; OKSANA DRAGAN.

Diocesan Consultors—Rt. Rev. Mitred Archpriest IHOR MIDZAK; Rt. Rev. Mitred Msgr. JOHN TERLECKY, B.A., M.A., M.L.S.; Very Rev. PAUL LUNIW; Very Rev. Archpriests EDWARD CANON YOUNG; KIRIL ANGELOV; Very Rev. MAXIM KOBASUK, O.S.B.M.

Diocesan Tribunal—14 Peveril Rd., Stamford, 06902-3019. Tel: 203-324-7698.

Judicial Vicar—Very Rev. PAUL LUNIW.

Judge—Rev. THEODOSIUS ILNICKI, O.S.B.M., J.C.L.

Defender of the Bond— "Ad Hoc" Appointment

Notary—Rev. MARK HIRNIAK.

Diocesan Protopresbyters (Deans)—Albany: Rev. VLADIMIR MARUSCEAC. Boston: Rev. JAROSLAW NALYSNYK. Brooklyn: Very Rev. VASILE TIVADAR. Buffalo: Very Rev. MARIJAN PROCYK. Hartford: Very Rev. PAUL LUNIW. New York: Very Rev. Archpriest KIRIL ANGELOV. Syracuse: Very Rev. Mitred Archpriest PHILIP WEINER.

Presbyteral Council—Most Rev. PAUL P. CHOMNYCKY, O.S.B.M.; Rt. Rev. Mitred Archpriest IHOR MIDZAK; Very Rev. Archpriests KIRIL ANGELOV; EDWARD CANON YOUNG; Rt. Rev. Mitred Archpriest MIHAI DUBOVICI, B.A., S.T.B.; Very Rev. Archpriest IVAN KASZCZAK, Ph.D., M.A., B.A.; Rev. THEODOR CZABALA; Very Rev. MAXIM KOBASUK, O.S.B.M.; Rt. Rev. Mitred Msgr. JOHN TERLECKY, B.A., M.A., M.L.S.; Rev. VASILE COLOPELNIC; Very Rev. PAUL LUNIW; Very Rev. Archpriest BOHDAN DANYLO, B.A., S.T.B.

Diocesan Offices and Directors

All offices are located at the following address unless otherwise noted *14 Peveril Rd., Stamford, 06902-3019.* Tel: 203-325-2116; Fax: 203-967-9948. Email: chancellor@optonline.net.

Administrative Council—Most Rev. PAUL P. CHOMNYCKY, O.S.B.M.; Rt. Rev. Mitred Msgr. JOHN TERLECKY, B.A., M.A., M.L.S.; Very Rev. YAROSLAW KOSTYK; Very Rev. Archpriest KIRIL ANGELOV; Rt. Rev. Mitred Archpriests MIHAI DUBOVICI, B.A., S.T.B.; IHOR MIDZAK.

Personnel Board—Most Rev. PAUL P. CHOMNYCKY, O.S.B.M.; Rt. Rev. Mitred Archpriest IHOR MIDZAK; Very Rev. MICHAEL BUNDZ; Rev. MARIAN KOSTYK; Rt. Rev. Mitred Msgr. JOHN SQUILLER, B.A., S.T.L. (Retired); Sr. MICHELLE YAKYMOVITCH, S.S.M.I.

Apostleship of Prayer—Rev. OLVIAN POPOVICI.

Catechetics—Revs. ALBERT FORLANO; VASILE COLOPELNIC.

Cemeteries—Holy Spirit Ukrainian Catholic Cemetery, 141 Sarah Wells Trail, Campbell Hall, NY 10916. Tel: 845-496-5506. Directors: Most Rev. PAUL P. CHOMNYCKY, O.S.B.M., Pres. & Chm.; Rev. JAROSLAW KOSTYK, Exec. Dir.; Very Rev. Archpriest KIRIL ANGELOV; Rt. Rev. Mitred Archpriest IHOR MIDZAK; Rt. Rev. Mitred Msgr. JOHN TERLECKY, B.A., M.A., M.L.S.; Mr. LOUIS NIGRO; Mr. JOHN SENKO; ANDRIJ SZUL, Esq.

Censor—Very Rev. Archpriests EDWARD CANON YOUNG; IVAN KASZCZAK, Ph.D., M.A., B.A.

Communications—Rev. VASYL BEHAY.

Development Office—Mrs. NATALIYA PISTUN, B.A., S.T.B., J.C.L.

Diaconate, Permanent—Very Rev. MAXIM KOBASUK, O.S.B.M.

Diocesan Charities and Missions—Most Rev. PAUL P. CHOMNYCKY, O.S.B.M.; Rt. Rev. Mitred Msgr. JOHN TERLECKY, B.A., M.A., M.L.S.; Ms. MARIAN KOZANSKI.

Ecumenical Commission—Most Revs. PAUL P.

CHOMNYCKY, O.S.B.M.; BASIL H. LOSTEN, D.D., S.T.L., LL.D. (Hon.); Very Rev. Archpriest KIRIL ANGELOV.

Educational Institutions—Most Rev. PAUL P. CHOMNYCKY, O.S.B.M.; Rev. JAMES MORRIS; Deacon PETER SHYSHKA, Supt. Schools.

Family Life—Sr. NATALYA STOCZANYN, S.S.M.I.

Holy Name Societies—Rev. BOHDAN HEDZ.

League of Ukrainian Catholics—Very Rev. MARIJAN PROCYK, Spiritual Dir. (New York).

Liturgical Commission—Very Rev. MAXIM KOBASUK, O.S.B.M.; Very Rev. Archpriest BOHDAN DANYLO, B.A., S.T.B.; Rev. VOLODYMYR SYBIRNYY.

Missionaries, Diocesan—Rev. BERNARD J. PANCZUK, O.S.B.M.

Ukrainian Museum and Library of Stamford, Inc.—161 Glenbrook Rd., Stamford, 06902. Museum Library Research Center, 39 Clovelly Rd., Stamford, 06902. Tel: 203-327-7899. Ms. LUBOW WOLYNETZ, B.A., M.L.S., Curator, Librarian & Archivist; Mrs. NATALIYA PISTUN, B.A., S.T.B., J.C.L.; Mrs. ANNA BOYCHUK; Rt. Rev. Mitred Msgr. JOHN TERLECKY, B.A., M.A., M.L.S., Librarian.

Press, Diocesan: "The Sower"—Sr. NATALYA STOCZANYN, S.S.M.I., Editor-in-Chief. Email: thesower@optonline.net; Rev. VASYL BEHAY, Ukrainian Editor.

Priests' Benevolent Association—Rt. Rev. Mitred Archpriest MIHAI DUBOVICI, B.A., S.T.B.

Religious Communities, Vicar—Very Rev. PHILIP SANDRICK, O.S.B.M.

Religious Education—Rev. VASILE COLOPELNIC.

Sodalities, B.V.M.—Very Rev. CYRIL ISZEZUCK, O.S.B.M.

Vocations—Very Rev. Archpriest BOHDAN DANYLO, B.A., S.T.B.

Youth Apostolate—Deacon TARAS CHAPARYN.

Youth-For-Christ Association—Deacon TARAS CHAPARYN.

Office of Safe Environment—ANDRIJ SZUL, Esq.; Sr. NATALYA STOCZANYN, S.S.M.I.

Director of Religious Education for Ukrainian Heritage Schools—Rev. ROMAN SYDOROVYCH.

Chaplain to the Ukrainian American Youth Association—Rt. Rev. Mitred Archpriest IHOR MIDZAK.

Chaplain to the Ukrainian Scouts Plast Organization—Very Rev. Archpriest IVAN KASZCZAK, Ph.D., M.A., B.A.

CLERGY, PARISHES, MISSIONS AND PAROCHIAL SCHOOLS

STATE OF CONNECTICUT

ANSONIA, NEW HAVEN CO., SS. PETER AND PAUL (1897), (Ukrainian), [CEM] Rt. Rev. Mitred Msgr. John Terlecky; Rev. Stepan Yanovsky, Parochial Vicar.
Res.: 105 Clifton Ave., 06401. Tel: 203-734-3895; Fax: 203-732-3191. Email: st_peter_st_paul@sbcglobal.net. Web: st-peter-st-paul.com.

BRIDGEPORT, FAIRFIELD CO., PROTECTION OF B.V.M. (1950), (Ukrainian), Rt. Rev. Mitred Archpriest Mihai Dubovici.
Holy Protection of B.V.M. Ukrainian Catholic Church: 457 Noble Ave., 06608. Tel: 203-367-5054; Fax: 203-367-5054.
Res.: 255 Barnum Ave., 06608. Tel: 203-367-5054.

COLCHESTER, NEW LONDON CO., ST. MARY DORMITION (1948), (Ukrainian), [CEM] Rev. Kiril Manolev.
Res.: 178 Linwood Ave., 06415. Tel: 860-537-2069; Fax: 860-537-2069. Email: frcyril@sbcglobal.net.

GLASTONBURY, HARTFORD CO., ST. JOHN THE BAPTIST (1925), (Ukrainian), Attended by St. Mary Dormition, Colchester. Rev. Kiril Manolev.
Church: 26 New London Tpke., 06033.
Res.: 178 Linwood Ave., Colchester, 06415. Tel: 860-537-2069.

HARTFORD, HARTFORD CO., ST. MICHAEL (1910), (Ukrainian), [CEM] Very Rev. Pawlo Martyniuk.
Church: 125 Wethersfield Ave., 06114.
Res.: 135 Wethersfield Ave., 06114. Tel: 860-525-7823; Fax: 860-548-1049. Email: st-michael@att.net.
School—Saturday Ukrainian School, (Grades K-8) Tel: 860-728-8792. Ivanna Omeliach, Prin. Priests 1; Lay Teachers 14; Students 86.

NEW BRITAIN, HARTFORD CO., ST. JOSAPHAT (1951), (Ukrainian), Rev. Stepan Bereza.
Res.: 303 Eddy Glover Blvd., 06053. Tel: 860-225-7340; Fax: 860-229-5490.
Catechesis/Religious Program—Priests 1; Lay Teachers 2; Students 18.

NEW HAVEN, NEW HAVEN CO., ST. MICHAEL (1909), (Ukrainian), Rev. Iura Godenciuc.
Res.: 569 George St., 06511. Tel: 203-865-0388; Fax: 203-752-0327. Email: stmichaels@snet.net.
School—St. Michaels Ukrainian Heritage School Myron Melnyk, Prin. (Saturdays) Priests 1; Lay Teachers 5; Students 37.

STAMFORD, FAIRFIELD CO., ST. VLADIMIR CATHEDRAL (1916), (Ukrainian), Rt. Rev. Mitred Archpriest Ihor Midzak.
Res.: 24 Wenzel Ter., 06902. Tel: 203-324-0242; Fax: 203-316-8284.
Catechesis/Religious Program—Priests 1; Sisters 1; Lay Teachers 1; Students 35.

TERRYVILLE, LITCHFIELD CO., ST. MICHAEL (1910), (Ukrainian), [CEM] Very Rev. Paul Luniw.
Res.: 35 Allen St., 06786. Tel: 860-583-7588; Fax: 860-582-8064. Email: stmichael@adelphia.net. Web: www.stmichaelterryville.org.
Catechesis/Religious Program—Tel: 860-582-1850. Kristine Meinert, D.R.E.; Ann Kerry, D.R.E.; Dan Czuchta, D.R.E.; John Stefanczyk, D.R.E. Priests 1; Students 11; Lay Teachers 4.

WILLIMANTIC, WINDHAM CO., PROTECTION OF B.V.M. (1950), (Ukrainian), Rev. Ivan Bilyk.
Res.: 69 Oak St., 06226. Tel: 860-423-5031; Fax: 860-423-5031.

STATE OF MASSACHUSETTS

BOSTON, SUFFOLK CO., CHRIST THE KING (1968) [CEM] Rev. Jaroslaw Nalysnyk.
Res.: 146 Forest Hills St., Jamaica Plain, MA 02130. Tel: 617-522-9720; Fax: 617-983-0309. Email: yaroslavnalysnyk@aol.com.
School—Saturday Ukrainian School Priests 1; Lay Teachers 2; Students 15.
Catechesis/Religious Program—Priests 1; Lay Teachers 2; Students 9.

FALL RIVER, BRISTOL CO., ST. JOHN-THE-BAPTIST (1914) [JC] Attended by Woonsocket, RI. Rev. Msgr. Roman Golemba.
Church: 339 Center St., MA 02724. Tel: 508-673-2353.

LUDLOW, HAMPDEN CO., SS. PETER AND PAUL (1912)(1924), (Ukrainian), Very Rev. Archpriest Edward P. Young.
Res.: 45 Newbury St., MA 01056. Tel: 413-583-2140; Fax: 413-583-2140. Email: eyoung8073@aol.com.
Catechesis/Religious Program—Priests 1; Students 4.

PITTSFIELD, BERKSHIRE CO., ST. JOHN THE BAPTIST (1921), (Ukrainian), Attended by Hudson, New York Rev. Janusz Jedrychowski.
Mailing Address: 206 Union St., Hudson, NY 12534.
Res.: Tel: 518-828-5226; Fax: 518-828-6749.

SALEM, ESSEX CO., ST. JOHN THE BAPTIST (1918), (Ukrainian), Rev. James Morris, Admin.
Mailing Address: P.O. Box 206, MA 01970-0206. Tel: 978-745-3151.
Church: 124 Bridge St., MA 01970. Email: saintjohnsukr@comcast.net.
Catechesis/Religious Program—Tel: 617-599-8138. Students 1.

SOUTH DEERFIELD, FRANKLIN CO., HOLY GHOST (1920), (Ukrainian), Very Rev. Archpriest Edward P. Young.
Res.: 44 Sugarloaf St., MA 01373. Tel: 413-665-3880.
Catechesis/Religious Program—Priests 1; Students 8.

STATE OF NEW HAMPSHIRE

MANCHESTER, HILLSBORO CO., PROTECTION OF B.V.M. (1908), (Ukrainian), Rev. Robert Smolley.
Church: 54 Walnut St., NH 03104. Tel: 603-622-0034; Fax: 603-642-8961.
Catechesis/Religious Program—Priests 1; Lay Teachers 2; Students 14.

STATE OF NEW YORK

AMSTERDAM, MONTGOMERY CO., ST. NICHOLAS (1909), (Ukrainian), [CEM] Rev. Marian Kostyk.
Res.: 24 Pulaski St., NY 12010. Tel: 518-842-8731; Fax: 518-842-1384.

AUBURN, CAYUGA CO., SS. PETER AND PAUL (1901), (Ukrainian), Rev. Ivan Mazuryk.
Res.: 136 Washington St., NY 13021. Tel: 315-252-5573; Fax: 315-252-5567.
School—(Grades K-8) Tel: 315-252-5567. Sr. Kathleen Hutsko, S.S.M.I., Prin.; Mrs. Geri Pelc, Librarian. Lay Teachers 8; Students 91.
Catechesis/Religious Program—Lay Teachers 3; Students 15.

BEDFORD HILLS, WESTCHESTER CO., HOLY PROTECTION OF THE MOTHER OF GOD (2000) Very Rev. Archpriest Ivan Kaszczak.
Res.: 195 Glenbrook Rd., 06902. Tel: 203-324-4578.
Catechesis/Religious Program—Elizabeth Gardasz, D.R.E. Students 5.

BRONX, BRONX CO., ST. MARY PROTECTRESS (1943), (Ukrainian), [JC] Rev. Lawrence Lawryniuk, O.S.B.M.
Church: 1745 Washington Ave., NY 10457. Tel: 718-731-9392.
Res.: E. Beach Dr., Glen Cove, NY 11542. Tel: 516-671-0545; Fax: 516-676-7465.

BROOKLYN, KINGS CO.

1—HOLY GHOST (1913), (Ukrainian), Rev. Ivan Tykhovytch.
Mailing Address: 161 N. Fifth St., NY 11211.
Church: 160 N. 5th St., NY 11211. Tel: 718-782-9592; Fax: 718-599-2905.

2—ST. NICHOLAS (1916), (Ukrainian), Very Rev. Vasile Tivadar, Admin.; Rev. Vasyl Kadylo, Visiting Priest. 256 19th St., NY 11215. Tel: 718-389-8744.
Mission—Blessed Nicholas Chernetsky, Manhattan Beach, NY

BUFFALO, ERIE CO., ST. NICHOLAS (1894), (Ukrainian), Very Rev. Marijan Procyk; Rev. Raymond Palko.
Res.: 308 Fillmore Ave., NY 14206. Tel: 716-852-7566; Fax: 716-855-1319.
Catechesis/Religious Program—Elaine P. Nowadly, D.R.E. Priests 2; Students 32.

COHOES, ALBANY CO., SS. PETER AND PAUL (1907), (Ukrainian), Rev. Vladimir Marusceac.
Res.: 198 Ontario St., NY 12047. Tel: 518-237-0535; Fax: 518-237-2397.
Catechesis/Religious Program—Priests 1; Lay Teachers 1; Students 7.

ELMIRA HEIGHTS, CHEMUNG CO., ST. NICHOLAS (1895), (Ukrainian), Rev. Robert Batcho.
Res.: 410 E. McCanns Blvd., NY 14903. Tel: 607-734-1221.
Catechesis/Religious Program—Irene Moffe, D.R.E. Priests 1; Lay Teachers 3; Students 10.

FRESH MEADOWS, QUEENS CO., ANNUNCIATION OF THE B.V.M. (1957), (Ukrainian), Very Rev. Zbigniew Canon Brzezicki.
Res.: 48-26 171st St., NY 11365. Tel: 718-939-4116; Fax: 718-939-3696.

GLEN SPEY, SULLIVAN CO., ST. VOLODYMYR (1961), (Ukrainian), [JC] Attended by Campbell Hall, New York Very Rev. Yaroslaw Kostyk.
Res.: 141 Sarah Wells Tr., Campbell Hall, NY 10916. Tel: 845-496-5506.

HAMPTONBURGH (CAMPBELL HALL), ORANGE CO., ST. ANDREW'S (1983), (Ukrainian), Very Rev. Yaroslaw Kostyk.
Res.: 141 Sarah Wells Tr., Campbell Hall, NY 10916. Tel: 845-496-5506; Fax: 845-496-5564.
Catechesis/Religious Program—Priests 1; Lay Teachers 1; Students 4.

HEMPSTEAD , NASSAU CO., ST. VLADIMIR (1944), (Ukrainian), Rev. Wasyl Hrynkiw.
Res.: 709 Front St., NY 11550. Tel: 516-481-7717; Fax: 516-481-3435.
Parish Center—226 Uniondale Ave., Uniondale, NY 11553. Tel: 516-485-0775.
School—Saturday Ukrainian School, (Grades 1-12) Priests 1; Lay Teachers 8; Students 60.
Catechesis/Religious Program—Priests 1; Lay Teachers 9; Students 38.

HUDSON, COLUMBIA CO., ST. NICHOLAS (1923), (Ukrainian), Rev. Janusz Jedrychowski (Attends St. John the Baptist, Pittsfield, MA).
Res.: 206 Union St., NY 12534. Tel: 518-828-5226; Fax: 518-828-6749.

HUNTER, GREENE CO., ST. JOHN THE BAPTIST (1962), (Ukrainian),Rte. 23A, P.O. Box 284, NY 12442. Tel: 518-263-3862.

JOHNSON CITY, BROOME CO., SACRED HEART UKRAINIAN CATHOLIC CHURCH (1944), (Ukrainian), [CEM] Rev. Theodor Czabala.
Res.: 230 Ukrainian Hill Rd., NY 13790. Tel: 607-797-6293; Fax: 607-797-6295. Web: www.sacredheartucc.org.
School—Saturday Ukrainian School, Tel: 607-797-6294. Students 11.
Catechesis/Religious Program—Tel: 607-797-6294. Luba Woytew, D.R.E. Lay Teachers 1; Students 20.

KENMORE, ERIE CO., ST. JOHN THE BAPTIST (1902), (Ukrainian), Rev. Mykola Drofych.
Res.: 3275 Elmwood Ave., NY 14217. Tel: 716-873-5011; Fax: 718-462-5243.

KERHONKSON , ULSTER CO., HOLY TRINITY (1965), (Ukrainian), Rev. Volodymyr Piso.
Church & Mailing Address: 211 Foordmore Rd., NY 12446. Tel: 845-626-2864; Fax: 845-626-3548.
School—Saturday Ukrainian School Bohdan Uhryn, Prin. Priests 1; Lay Teachers 3; Students 17.

LACKAWANNA, ERIE CO., OUR LADY OF PERPETUAL HELP (1925), (Ukrainian), Rev. Andriv Kasiyan.
Res.: 1182 Ridge Rd., NY 14218. Tel: 716-823-6182; Fax: 716-823-6550. Web: www.olphukrchurch.org.
Catechesis/Religious Program—Maria Slabyk, D.R.E.; Oksana Kasiyan, D.R.E. Priests 1; Lay Teachers 2.

LANCASTER, ERIE CO., ST. BASIL (1921), (Ukrainian), Rev. Robert Moreno.
Res.: 12 Embry Pl., NY 14086. Tel: 716-683-0313. Students 20.
Church: 3657 Walden Ave., NY 14086.
Catechesis/Religious Program—Michele Forkl, D.R.E. Students 20.

LINDENHURST, SUFFOLK CO., HOLY FAMILY (1924), (Ukrainian), Rev. Olvian Popovici.
Res.: 225 N. 4th St., NY 11757. Tel: 631-225-1168; Fax: 631-225-1177.
Catechesis/Religious Program—Priests 1; Lay Teachers 2; Students 67.

LITTLE FALLS, HERKIMER CO., ST. NICHOLAS (1912) Attended by Amsterdam. Rev. Marian Kostyk.
Res.: 24 Pulaski St., Amsterdam, NY 12010. Tel: 518-842-8731; Fax: 518-842-1384.

LONG ISLAND CITY, QUEENS CO., HOLY CROSS (1944), (Ukrainian), Revs. Christopher Woytyna, O.S.B.M.; Januario Lucavei, O.S.B.M.; Melecio Kraizyi.
Res.: 31-12 30th St., NY 11106. Tel: 718-932-4060; Fax: 718-932-6370. Web: www.geosites.com/church11106.
Catechesis/Religious Program—Priests 1; Lay Teachers 1; Students 4.

NEW YORK, NEW YORK CO., ST. GEORGE (1905), (Ukrainian), Rev. Bernard J. Panczuk, O.S.B.M.; Very Rev. Cyril Iszezuck, O.S.B.M.
Res.: 30 E. Seventh St., NY 10003. Tel: 212-674-1615; Fax: 212-475-7017.
School—215 E. Sixth St., NY 10003. Tel: 212-473-3130; Fax: 917-534-0819. Sr. Theodosia, O.S.B.M., Prin. Sisters of St. Basil the Great 2; Lay Teachers 8; Students 100.
High School—Tel: 212-473-3323; Fax: 917-534-0819. Deacon Peter Shyshka, Prin. Lay Teachers 13; Students 100.

NIAGARA FALLS, NIAGARA CO., PROTECTION OF B.V.M. (1920), (Ukrainian), Rev. Raymond Palko.
Res.: 2713 Ferry Ave., NY 14301. Tel: 716-284-7066; Fax: 716-282-6902.

OZONE PARK, QUEENS CO., ST. MARY PROTECTRESS (1954), (Ukrainian), Very Rev. Vasile Tivadar.
Res.: 97-06 87th St., NY 11416. Tel: 718-845-5366; Fax: 718-529-1477.

RIVERHEAD, SUFFOLK CO., ST. JOHN THE BAPTIST (1924), (Ukrainian), [CEM] Rev. Roman Malyarchuk.
Res.: 820 Pond View Rd., NY 11901. Tel: 631-727-2766; Fax: 631-727-4141.
Church: Franklin St., NY 11901.

ROCHESTER, MONROE CO.
1—EPIPHANY OF OUR LORD (1958), (Ukrainian), [JC] Rev. Roman Sydorovych.
Res.: 202 Carter St., NY 14621. Tel: 585-266-4036; Fax: 585-323-9691. Email: vasylcolopelnic@yahoo.com.
Catechesis/Religious Program—Teachers 8; Students 41.
2—ST. JOSAPHAT (1909), (Ukrainian), Very Rev. Mitred Archpriest Philip Weiner; Rev. Bohdan Hedz.
Res.: 940 Ridge Rd. E., NY 14621. Tel: 585-467-6457; Fax: 585-467-7296.
Catechesis/Religious Program—Lay Teachers 9; Students 42.

ROME, ONEIDA CO., ST. MICHAEL (1914), (Ukrainian), [CEM] Attended by St. Vladimir, Utica. Very Rev. Michael Bundz.
Res.: 296 Genessee St., Utica, NY 13502. Tel: 315-735-5138; Fax: 315-735-0443.
Church: 133 River St., NY 13440.

SPRING VALLEY, ROCKLAND CO., SS. PETER AND PAUL (1913), (Ukrainian), Rev. Vasile Colopelnic.
Res.: 41 Collins Ave., NY 10977. Tel: 845-356-1634.
Catechesis/Religious Program—Maria-Liusea Colopelnic, D.R.E. Lay Teachers 2; Students 12.

STATEN ISLAND, RICHMOND CO., HOLY TRINITY (1949), (Ukrainian), Rev. Vasile Godenciuc.
Res.: 288 Vanderbilt Ave., NY 10304. Tel: 718-442-2555.
Catechesis/Religious Program—L. Niewiadomski, D.R.E. Students 5.

SYRACUSE, ONONDAGA CO., ST. JOHN THE BAPTIST (1900) Rev. Mykhaylo Dosyak.
Res.: 207 Tompkins St., NY 13204. Tel: 315-478-5109; Fax: 315-471-9867.
Catechesis/Religious Program—Priests 1; Lay Teachers 8; Students 65.

TROY, RENSSELAER CO., PROTECTION OF B.V.M. (1952), (Ukrainian), [JC] Attended by St. Nicholas Watervilet. Revs. Mikhail Myshchuk; Volodymyr Sibirnij.
Church: 459 Second St., NY 12180. Tel: 518-274-5318.

UTICA, ONEIDA CO., ST. VOLODYMYR THE GREAT (1950), (Ukrainian), [CEM] Very Rev. Michael Bundz (Attends St. Michael's, Rome, NY).
Res.: 296 Genesee St., NY 13502. Tel: 315-735-5138.

WATERVLIET, ALBANY CO., ST. NICHOLAS (1905), (Ukrainian), [CEM] [JC] Revs. Mikhail Myshchuk; Volodymyr Sibirnij.
Res.: 2410-4th Ave., NY 12189. Tel: 518-273-6752; Fax: 866-751-4103. Email: office@cerkva.com. Web: www.cerkva.com.
School—*Saturday Ukrainian School* Lay Teachers 8; Students 29.
Catechesis/Religious Program—Students 29.

YONKERS, WESTCHESTER CO., ST. MICHAEL (1899), (Ukrainian), Very Rev. Archpriest Kiril Angelov.
Res.: 21 Shonnard Pl., NY 10703. Tel: 914-963-0209; Fax: 914-969-6269. Email: stmich@optonline.net.
Catechesis/Religious Program—*School of Ukrainian Studies* Elizabeth Gardasz, Catechist; Svetlana Khromokoska, Dir. Priests 2; Lay Teachers 9; Students 123.

STATE OF RHODE ISLAND

WOONSOCKET, PROVIDENCE CO., ST. MICHAEL (1908) [CEM] [JC] Rev. Msgr. Roman Golemba.
Res.: 394 Blackstone St., RI 02895. Tel: 401-762-2733; Fax: 401-762-2733.
Church: 396 Blackstone St., RI 02895.

Retired:
Rev.—
Mudry, Lubomyr, St. Joseph's, P.O. Box 8, Sloatsburg, NY 10974.
Rt. Rev. Mitred Msgrs.—
Mosko, Leon, 195 Glenbrook Rd., 06902.
Squiller, John, B.A., S.T.L.

Permanent Deacons:
Coleman, Paul, SS. Peter & Paul, Auburn, NY
Evans, Michael, SS. Peter & Paul, Auburn, NY
Galvin, Edward, St. John the Baptist, Syracuse, NY
Gutch, Thomas, St. Nicholas, Waterlivet, NY
Hobczuk, John, St. Nicholas, Elmira Heights, NY
Homick, Willis, SS. Peter & Paul, Auburn, NY
Malachowsky, Yourij, Holy Cross, Long Island City, NY
Stadnick, Thomas, Holy Ghost, Brooklyn, NY
Wanat, John, Protection of the BVM, Bridgeport, CT
Wisnowski, Stephen A., St. Josaphat, Rochester, NY

INSTITUTIONS LOCATED IN THE DIOCESE

[A] SEMINARIES, DIOCESAN

STAMFORD. *Ukrainian Catholic Seminary Inc. St. Basil College*, 195 Glenbrook Rd., 06902-3099. Tel: 203-324-4578; Fax: 203-357-7681. Most Rev. Paul P. Chomnycky, O.S.B.M., Chm., Bd. Trustees; Very Rev. Maxim Kobasuk, O.S.B.M.; Very Rev. Archpriests Bohdan Danylo, B.A., S.T.B., Pres. & Rector; Ivan Kaszczak, Ph.D., M.A., B.A., Acting Academic Dean; Rt. Rev. Mitred Archpriest Mihai Dubovici, B.A., S.T.B., Bursar; Ms. Lubow Wolynetz, B.A., M.L.S., Librarian; Mr. Vasile Popovici, Procurator.

[B] SEMINARIES, RELIGIOUS

GLEN COVE. *Basilian Fathers Novitiate of the Order of St. Basil the Great*, E. Beach Dr., NY 11542. Tel: 516-671-0545; Fax: 516-676-7465. Revs. Leo Goldade, O.S.B.M., Vicar, Provincial Treas.; Eugene Khomyn, O.S.B.M.; Theodosius Ilnicki, O.S.B.M., J.C.L., Provincial Sec. Priests 3; Brothers 1.

[C] NURSERY SCHOOLS

STAMFORD. *St. Ann's Nursery School*, 111 W. North St., 06902. Tel: 203-323-1237; 203-348-5675; Fax: 203-323-0262. Missionary Sisters of Mother of God 6; Nursery 44; Staff 3.

[D] ADULT FACILITIES

SLOATSBURG. *St. Joseph's Adult Care Home, Inc.*, 125 Sisters Servants Ln., NY 10974-0008. Tel: 845-753-2555; Fax: 845-753-6910. Sisters Michele Yakymovitch, S.S.M.I., Admin.; Barbara Stefaniak, S.S.M.I., Asst. Admin. Sisters Servants of Mary Immaculate 6; Residents 28; Total Staff 12.

[E] MONASTERIES AND RESIDENCES OF PRIESTS AND BROTHERS

NEW YORK. *Provincialate of Basilian Fathers*, Res.: 29 Peacock Ln., Locust Valley, NY 11560. Tel: 516-609-3262; Fax: 516-609-3264. Email: USAOSBM@aol.com. Very Rev. Philip Sandrick, O.S.B.M., Protohegumen. Priests 23; Brothers 1.

[F] MONASTERIES OF NUNS

STAMFORD. *Missionary Sisters of Mother of God*, 111 W. North St., 06902. Tel: 203-323-1237; Fax: 203-323-0262. Sr. Euhenia Prusnay, M.S.M.G., Supr.; Rev. Peter Gronski, Chap.

MIDDLETOWN. *Nuns of St. Basil the Great*, Sacred Heart Monastery, 209 Keasel Rd., NY 10940-6287. Tel: 845-343-1308; Fax: 845-343-1308. Sr. Georgianna Snihur, O.S.B.M., Supr. Sisters 4; Novices 1.

SLOATSBURG. *Sister Servants of Mary Immaculate, Inc.*, 150 Sisters Servants Ln., 9 Emmanuel Dr., P.O. Box 9, NY 10974-0009. Tel: 845-753-2840; Fax: 845-753-1956. Email: ssminy@aol.com. Sr. Kathleen Hutsko, S.S.M.I., Prov. Supr. Sisters Servants of Mary Immaculate Conception Province. Sisters 32.

[G] MISCELLANEOUS

STAMFORD. *Institute of Catechists of the Heart of Jesus*, 161 Glenbrook Rd., 06902. Tel: 203-327-6374.

SLOATSBURG. *St. Mary's Villa Spiritual, Cultural & Educational Center*, 150 Sisters Servants Ln., P.O. Box 9, NY 10974-0009. Tel: 845-753-5100; Fax: 845-753-1956. Sr. Albina Gregory, S.S.M.I., Coord.

RELIGIOUS INSTITUTES OF MEN REPRESENTED IN THE DIOCESE

For further details refer to the corresponding bracketed number in the Religious Institutes of Men or Women section.

[0180]—*Order of St. Basil the Great*—O.S.B.M.

[1070]—*Redemptorists*—C.Ss.R.

RELIGIOUS INSTITUTES OF WOMEN REPRESENTED IN THE DIOCESE

[]—*Institute of Catechists of the Heart of Jesus*

[2810]—*Missionary Sisters of Mother of God*—M.S.M.G.

[3730]—*Sisters of the Order of St. Basil the Great*—O.S.B.M.

[3610]—*Sisters Servants of Mary Immaculate*—S.S.M.I.

NECROLOGY

† Scrincosky, Rev. Msgr. Peter, (Retired)—Died Jan. 11, 2011

An asterisk (*) denotes an organization that has established tax-exempt status directly with the IRS and is not covered by the USCCB Group Ruling.

The Syro-Malankara Catholic Church Apostolic Exarchate in USA

Most Reverend

THOMAS EUSEBIUS NAICKAMPARAMBIL

Bishop of the Syro-Malankara Catholic Exarchate in USA and Apostolic Visitator of Syro-Malankara Catholics in Europe & Canada; ordained priest December 29, 1986; appointed Bishop of the Syro-Malankara Catholic Exarchate in USA July 14, 2010; consecrated September 21, 2010; installed Bishop of the Exarchate October 3, 2010. *Chancery Office & Res.: 950 Hillside Ave., New Hyde Park, NY 11040.* Tel: 516-266-1653; Fax: 516-616-0727.

Chancery Office: 950 Hillside Ave., New Hyde Park, NY 11040. Tel: 516-266-1653; Fax: 516-616-0727.

ESTABLISHED JULY 14, 2010

The jurisdiction of the Exarchate is all Syro-Malankara Catholics in the United States of America.

STATISTICAL OVERVIEW

Personnel	
Bishop	1
Priests: Diocesan Active in Diocese	12
Number of Diocesan Priests	12
Religious Priests in Diocese	1
Total Priests in Diocese	13
Total Sisters	33
Parishes	
Parishes	12
Missions	4
Educational	
Students Religious	4
Total Seminarians	4

Vicar General—Rev. Msgr. PETER KOCHERY.
Chancellor—Very Rev. AUGUSTINE A. MANGALATH.
Diocesan Curia—
Vicar General—Rev. Msgr. PETER KOCHERY.
Chancellor—Very Rev. AUGUSTINE A. MANGALATH.
Vice Chancellor—Rev. SUNNY MATHEW.
Finance Officer—Very Rev. AUGUSTINE A. MANGALATH.
Secretary—Rev. ABRAHAM LUKOSE.
Tribunal—
Office—3 Stephen Ave., New Hyde Park, 11040.
Judicial Vicar—Rev. SUNNY MATHEW.
Defender of the Bond—Rev. SATHYAN NADUVILEDATH ANTONY, O.I.C.
Promoter of Justice—Rev. MATHAI MANNOORVADAKKETHIL.
Notary—Rev. ABRAHAM LUKOSE.
Diocesan Apostolates and Directors—
Vocation Promotion Director—Rev. SAJI G. MUKKOOT.
Youth Apostolate Director—Rev. JOB KALLUVILAYIL.
Family Apostolate Director—Rev. MATHAI MANNOORVADAKKETHIL.
Faith Formation (Catechism) Director—Rev. MATHEW PERUMBILLIKUNNEL.
Seminary Formation Director—Rev. Msgr. PETER KOCHERY.
Bible Apostolate Director—Rev. SATHYAN NADUVILEDATH ANTONY, O.I.C.
Ecumenism and MCA Director—Rev. JOSEPH NEDUMANKUZHIYIL.
Liturgy Director—Rev. ABRAHAM LUKOSE.
Fathers' Forum Director—Rev. JOHN KURIAKOSE.
Mothers' Forum Director—Rev. THOMAS MALAYIL.
Malankara Catholic Children's League—Rev. ANTONY VAYALIKAROTTU.
Councils—
Presbyteral Council—Most Rev. THOMAS EUSEBIUS NAICKAMPARAMBIL, Pres.; Rev. JOSEPH NEDUMANKUZHIYIL, Sec.
Ex Officio Members—Rev. Msgr. PETER KOCHERY, (Vicar Gen.); Very Rev. AUGUSTINE A. MANGALATH, (Chancellor & Finance Officer); Rev. SUNNY MATHEW, (Vice Chancellor).
Elected Members—Revs. SAJI G. MUKKOOT; MATHAI MANNOORVADAKKETHIL; JOB KALLUVILAYIL; SATHYAN NADUVILEDATH ANTONY, O.I.C.; MATHEW PERUMBILLIKUNNEL; ANTONY VAYALIKAROTTU; THOMAS MALAYIL; ABRAHAM LUKOSE.
Pastoral Council—Most Rev. THOMAS EUSEBIUS NAICKAMPARAMBIL, Pres. Secretaries: Very Rev. AUGUSTINE A. MANGALATH; Mr. PHILIP JOHN.
Ex Officio Members—Rev. Msgr. PETER KOCHERY, (Vicar Gen.); Rev. SUNNY MATHEW, (Vice Chancellor); Mr. MOHAN VARGHESE, PRO.
Priests - Heads of Apostolates—Revs. SAJI G. MUKKOOT; JOB KALLUVILAYIL; MATHAI MANNOORVADAKKETHIL; MATHEW PERUMBILLIKUNNEL; JOSEPH NEDUMANKUZHIYIL; SATHYAN NADUVILEDATH ANTONY, O.I.C.; ANTONY VAYALIKAROTTU; THOMAS MALAYIL; ABRAHAM LUKOSE; JOHN KURIAKOSE.
Elected Members—Mr. CIBY DANIEL; Mr. MINOY VARGHESE; Mr. ROY VARGHESE; Mr. JACOB JOHN; Mr. SAJI GEORGE; Mr. CHERIAN ALEX EDICHERIA; Mr. THOMAS A. GEORGE; Mr. JOHNSON S. KANJIRAVILA; Mr. GEORGE THOMAS; Mr. GIJO GEORGE; Mr. GEORGE JAMES; Mr. SAJI VARUGHESE KEEKKADAN; Mr. ALEXANDER MAMMEN; Mr. BIJU KURUVILA; Mr. JOHN EDATHIL; Mr. VARGHESE ZACHARIAH; Mr. ABRAHAM PONMELIL; Mr. ROY SAM; Mr. MATHEW JOHN; Mr. JOHN THOMAS; Mr. MATHEW THOMAS.
Representatives of Religious Orders—Rev. FRANCIS ASSISI, O.I.C.; Sisters ARPITHA, S.I.C.; LINUS MARIA, D.M.; JOVINA, D.M.
Nominated Members—Rev. JACOB JOHN; Mr. ALEX JOHN; Mr. BABUKUTTY THUDIYATHU; Mr. PHILIP MATHAI; Mr. WILSON JOSEPH; Mrs. ANNAMMA THOMAS; Mrs. DAISAMMA MATHEW; Mr. ALOYSIUS JOHN; Mr. FRANCIS THAZHAMON.
Finance Council—Most Rev. THOMAS EUSEBIUS NAICKAMPARAMBIL, Pres.
Members—Very Rev. AUGUSTINE A. MANGALATH, (Finance Officer); Mr. ABRAHAM PONMELIL; Mr. ABRAHAM PHILIP; Mr. VARGHESE ZACHARIAH; Mr. SHAJI SIMON; Mr. REJI JOSE; Mr. SIMON PLAMTHOTTAM; Mr. PRAMOD ZACHARIAH.
Council for Planning and Development—Most Rev. THOMAS EUSEBIUS NAICKAMPARAMBIL, Pres.
Members—Rev. Msgr. PETER KOCHERY, (Vicar Gen.); Very Rev. AUGUSTINE A. MANGALATH, (Finance Officer); Mr. GEORGE JAMES; Mr. ALEX JOHN THANGALATHIL; Mr. BABU STEPHEN; Mr. BENJAMIN THOMAS; Mr. ROY VARGHESE; Mr. GEEVARGHESE THANKACHAN; Mr. GEORGE SAMUEL; Mr. JOHNSON DANIEL; Mrs. CHINNAMMA RAJAN; Dr. JOCELYN EDATHIL; Mr. SEBIN ALEX; Mr. JAMES S. THOMAS.
Council for the Promotion of Culture and Heritage—Rev. SAJI G. MUKKOOT, Pres.
Members—Mr. PHILIP JOHN; Mr. THOMAS ABRAHAM; Mr. RAJAN KAKKANATTU; Mr. WILSON JOSEPH; Mr. SAJI KEEKKADAN; Mr. PHILIP VANDAKATHIL; Miss NINA DANIEL.
Exarchate Webteam—Most Rev. THOMAS EUSEBIUS NAICKAMPARAMBIL, Pres.; Very Rev. AUGUSTINE A. MANGALATH, Vice Pres. Members: Mr. BINU ABRAHAM, Chicago; Mr. GIJO GEORGE, Long Island; Mr. JOHN THOMAS, New Jersey; Mr. SUNIL CHACKO, Queens; Mr. VARGHESE SAMUEL, Philadelphia.
Public Relations Office—Rev. Msgr. PETER KOCHERY, Dir.; Mr. MOHAN VARUGHESE, PRO.

CLERGY, PARISHES, MISSIONS AND PAROCHIAL SCHOOLS

STATE OF NEW YORK

DOUGLASTON, QUEENS CO., ST. BASIL MALANKARA CATHOLIC CHURCH Rev. Sathyan Naduviledath Antony, O.I.C.
7200 Douglaston Pkwy., 11362.
Res.: 201 N. Central Ave., Valley Stream, 11580. Tel: 516-352-2127; Fax: 516-616-0727.

ELMONT, NASSAU CO., ST. CHRYSOSTOM MALANKARA CATHOLIC CHURCH Rev. Abraham Lukose.
1500 DePaul St., 11003.
Res.: 950 Hillside Ave., 11040. Tel: 516-233-1656; Fax: 516-616-0727.

NEW ROCHELLE, WESTCHESTER CO., ST. MARY'S MALANKARA CATHOLIC CHURCH Rev. Sunny Mathew.
148 Main St., 10801. Tel: 516-642-4356; Fax: 516-616-0727.

SPRING VALLEY, ROCKLAND CO. , ST. PETER'S MALANKARA CATHOLIC CHURCH Very Rev. Augustine A. Mangalath.
333 Sneeden Pl. W., 10977.
Res.: 41 Alling St., West Haven, CT 06516. Tel: 203-934-1871; Fax: 203-931-9416.

STATE OF FLORIDA

MARGATE, BROWARD CO., ST. MARY'S MALANKARA CATHOLIC CHURCH Rev. Antony Vayalikarottu.
6350 N.W. 18th St., FL 33063. Tel: 516-428-6909.

STATE OF ILLINOIS

EVANSTON, COOK CO., ST. MARY'S MALANKARA CATHOLIC CHURCH Rev. Mathew Perumbillikunnel.
Res.: 1534 Wilder Ave., IL 60202. Tel: 847-332-1794; Fax: 847-424-0889. Email: fathermathew@gmail.com.

STATE OF MARYLAND

LANDOVER HILLS, PRINCE GEORGE CO., ST. MARY'S MALANKARA CATHOLIC CHURCH Rev. Mathai Mannoorvadakkethil.
Res.: 7401 Buchanan St., MD 20784. Tel: 301-875-9273; Fax: 301-306-5543.

STATE OF MICHIGAN

CENTER LINE, MACOMB CO., ST. JOSEPH'S MALANKARA CATHOLIC CHURCH Rev. Saji G. Mukkoot.
8075 Ritter Ave., MI 48015.
Res.: 50931 Maria St., New Baltimore, MI 48047. Tel: 917-673-5318; Fax: 586-725-3647. Email: mukkudan@yahoo.com.

STATE OF NEW JERSEY

RAHWAY, UNION CO., ST. THOMAS MALANKARA CATHOLIC CHURCH Rev. Msgr. Peter Kochery.

287 Hamilton St., NJ 07065.
Res.: 186 Gordons Corner Rd., Manalapan, NJ 07726. Tel: 732-446-6311. Email: kochery@optonline.net.

STATE OF PENNSYLVANIA

PHILADELPHIA, PHILADELPHIA CO., ST. JUDE MALANKARA CATHOLIC CHURCH Rev. Thomas Malayil.
244 W. Cheltenham Ave., PA 19126.
Res.: 2319 S. 3rd St., PA 19148. Tel: 267-297-9952.

STATE OF TEXAS

GARLAND, DALLAS CO., ST. MARY'S MALANKARA CATHOLIC CHURCH Rev. Joseph Nedumankuzhiyil.
116 E. Ave. D, TX 75040.
Res.: 1224 Main St., TX 75040. Tel: 972-272-4641; Fax: 972-494-3653. Email: frsaju@msn.com.

HOUSTON, HARRIS CO., ST. PETER'S MALANKARA CATHOLIC CHURCH Rev. Job Kalluvilayil.
1323 Phyllis Rosharon, Rosharon, TX 77583.
Res.: 10330 Hillcroft St., TX 77096. Tel: 713-333-3511; Fax: 713-729-3294. Email: jobkalluvilayil@gmail.com.

MISSIONS **Los Angeles, Atlanta, Phoenix, Boston.**

INSTITUTIONS LOCATED IN THE DIOCESE

[A] CONVENTS AND RESIDENCES FOR SISTERS

BRONX. *Daughters of Mary Convent*, 176 Kilroe St., 10464. Tel: 718-885-1842. Email: dmcityisland@optimum.net.

LIVONIA. *Daughters of Mary Convent*, 33315 Broadmoor Ct., MI 48154. Tel: 248-543-4127. Email: dmdetroit@hotmail.com.

MORTON GROVE. *Bethany Convent*, 7910 Arcadia St., IL 60053. Tel: 516-225-2709. Email: bethanysisters@chicagomalankara.org.

NEW HYDE PARK. *Bethany Convent*, 1653 Highland Ave., 11040. Tel: 516-358-4597. Email: usbethany@gmail.com.

YONKERS. *Daughters of Mary Convent*, 45 Verona Ave., 10710. Tel: 914-202-9255. Email: srjovinadm@yahoo.com.

NECROLOGY

(No Deaths)

An asterisk (*) denotes an organization that has established tax-exempt status directly with the IRS and is not covered by the USCCB Group Ruling.

Archdiocese of Agana

(Editor's Note: 2012 information was not received)

Most Reverend
ANTHONY SABLAN APURON, O.F.M.CAP., D.D.

Archbishop of Agana; ordained August 26, 1972; appointed Auxiliary Bishop December 8, 1983; ordained Titular Bishop of Muzuca February 19, 1984; appointed Apostolic Administrator to the Archdiocese October 27, 1985; succeeded to Metropolitan See May 11, 1986. *Res.: Archbishop's Residence, 196-B Cuesta San Ramon, Agana, GU 96910.* Tel: 671-472-6116; Fax: 671-477-3519.

Erected by Pope Pius X, March 1, 1911 and Committed to the Order of Friars Minor Capuchin. Extended to all the Marianas Islands, July 4, 1946, Wake Island, June 14, 1948. Elevated to a Diocese, October 14, 1965, as a Suffragan of San Francisco. Elevated to Metropolitan Archdiocese, May 20, 1984 with a Suffragan See, Diocese of Caroline-Marshalls and Diocese of Chalan Kanoa (subsequently added January 13, 1985). Member of CEPAC Conference. Member of Federation of Catholic Bishops Conference of Oceania. Observer to NCCB-USCC Conference.

Guam is a Territory of the U.S.A. by Act of the U.S. Congress July 21, 1949.

Legal Title: Archbishop of Agana, a Corporation Sole.

STATISTICAL OVERVIEW

Personnel	
Archbishops	1
Priests: Diocesan Active in Diocese	37
Priests: Diocesan Active Outside Diocese	6
Number of Diocesan Priests	43
Religious Priests in Diocese	10
Total Priests in Diocese	53
Permanent Deacons in Diocese	19
Total Brothers	3
Total Sisters	85
Parishes	
Parishes	24
With Resident Pastor:	
Resident Diocesan Priests	19
Resident Religious Priests	5
Welfare	
Homes for the Aged	1
Total Assisted	60
Day Care Centers	4
Total Assisted	617
Special Centers for Social Services	2
Total Assisted	5,570
Educational	
Seminaries, Diocesan	1
Students from This Diocese	36
Diocesan Students in Other Seminaries	1
Total Seminarians	37
High Schools, Diocesan and Parish	3
Total Students	922
High Schools, Private	1
Total Students	291
Elementary Schools, Diocesan and Parish	7
Total Students	3,165
Catechesis/Religious Education:	
High School Students	1,686
Elementary Students	2,815
Total Students under Catholic Instruction	8,916
Teachers in the Diocese:	
Priests	8
Brothers	1
Sisters	35
Lay Teachers	363
Vital Statistics	
Receptions into the Church:	
Infant Baptism Totals	1,699
Minor Baptism Totals	64
Adult Baptism Totals	39
Received into Full Communion	248
First Communions	1,131
Confirmations	1,058
Marriages:	
Catholic	168
Interfaith	4
Total Marriages	172
Deaths	591
Total Catholic Population	143,650
Total Population	169,000

Former Vicars-Apostolic—Most Revs. FRANCIS X. VILLA Y MATEU, O.F.M.Cap., D.D., cons. Titular Bishop of Adraha, Oct. 1, 1911; died at Agana, Jan. 1, 1913; AUGUSTIN BERNAUS Y SERRA, O.F.M.Cap., D.D., cons. Titular Bishop of Milopotamo, May 9, 1913; transferred to Vicariate-Apostolic of Bluefields, Nicaragua, 1914; JOAQUIN FELIPE OLAIZ Y ZABALZA, O.F.M.Cap., D.D., cons. Titular Bishop of Docimeo, Nov. 30, 1914; died at Pamplona, Spain, Dec. 8, 1945; MIGUEL ANGEL OLANO Y URTEAGA, O.F.M.Cap., D.D., cons. Titular Bishop of Lagina, May 5, 1935; resigned and made Asst. at Pontifical Throne Aug. 20, 1945; died at Agana, Guam May 21, 1970; APOLLINARIS W. BAUMGARTNER, O.F.M.Cap., D.D., cons. Sept. 18, 1945; appt. First Bishop of Agana, Oct. 14, 1965; died at Agana, Guam Dec. 18, 1970; FELIXBERTO CAMACHO FLORES, ord. April 30, 1949; appt. Apostolic Admin., Diocese of Agana, May 2, 1969; appt. Titular Bishop of Stonj, March 19, 1970; cons. May 17, 1970; succeeded to See, May 15, 1971; died Oct. 25, 1985.

Chancery Office—196 B Cuesta San Ramon, Hagatna, 96910. Tel: 671-472-6116; 671-472-6573; Fax: 671-477-3519. Office Hours: Mon.-Fri. 8-12 & 1-4.

Moderator of the Curia and Vicar General—Rev. Msgr. DAVID C. QUITUGUA, J.C.D.

Chancellor—Sr. ANA LEE, O.P., J.C.L.

Finance Officer and Business Mgr.—Deacon STEPHEN W.M. MARTINEZ.

Archdiocesan College of Consultors—Rev. Msgr. DAVID C. QUITUGUA, J.C.D.; Revs. ERIC FORBES, O.F.M.Cap.; KENNETH J. HEZEL, S.J.; JOSE ALBERTO RODRIGUEZ; Rev. Msgr. JAMES L.G. BENAVENTE.

Archdiocesan Finance Council—Rev. Msgr. JAMES L.G. BENAVENTE; RICHARD UNTALAN, Pres.; Mr. JOSEPH RIVERA; Sr. MARY STEPHEN TORRES, R.S.M.

Archdiocesan Presbyteral Council—Rev. Msgr. DAVID C. QUITUGUA, J.C.D.; Revs. ERIC FORBES, O.F.M.Cap.; KENNETH J. HEZEL, S.J.; Rev. Msgr. JAMES L.G. BENAVENTE; Very Rev. Msgr. DAVID I.A. QUITUGUA; Revs. JOSEPH ENGLISH, O.F.M.Cap.; AGUSTIN GUMATAOTAO, O.F.M.Cap.; JOSE ALBERTO RODRIGUEZ; JOSE ANTONIO P. ABAD; JEFFREY C. SAN NICOLAS; MICHAEL CRISOSTOMO; PATRICK CASTRO, O.F.M.Cap.; Rev. Msgr. BRIGIDO ARROYO.

Metropolitan Tribunal—

Judicial Vicar—Rev. Msgr. DAVID C. QUITUGUA, J.C.D.

Promoter of Justice—VACANT.

Defender of the Bond—Rev. JONATHAN ALVAREZ.

Associate Judges—Rev. CARLOS S. VILA, J.C.L.; Sr. ANA LEE, O.P., J.C.L.

Notary—Rev. FELIX LEON GUERRERO, O.F.M.Cap.

Chancery Records Department—Mrs. JUNE UNGACTA.

Catholic Schools Office—Mrs. CYNTHIA AGBULOS, Supt.

Division of Pastoral Ministries—Sr. MARIAN ARROYO, R.S.M., Exec. Dir. Tel: 671-472-6116; Fax: 671-472-4406; Ms. CATHERINE LEON GUERRERO, Exec. Asst.

Office of Faith Formation—Deacon LARRY CLAROS, Dir.

Office of Family Ministry—Deacon LARRY CLAROS, Dir.

Office of Pastoral Planning—Sr. MARIAN ARROYO, R.S.M., Dir.

Office of Worship—Sr. MARIAN ARROYO, R.S.M., Dir.

Office of Communications—Mr. TONY DIAZ, Dir., 196 B Cuesta San Ramon, Hagatna, 96910. Tel: 671-472-6427; Fax: 671-477-5656.

Catholic Educational Radio, KOLG—196 B Cuesta San Ramon, Hagatna, 96910. Tel: 671-477-5654; Fax: 671-477-5656.

Pacific Voice—Mr. TONY DIAZ, Editor, 193 B Cuesta San Ramon, Hagatna, 96910. Tel: 671-472-6427; Fax: 671-477-5224. Email: pacvoice@ite.net; Ms. MARIQUITA CRUZ, Production Supvr.; Ms. LUZ OBERIANO, Office Asst.

Procurement Clerk—Ms. ANN GOGUE.

Information Resource Officer—HELEN FLORES.

Family Ministry Coordinator—CARMELITA MONDIA.

Other Archdiocesan Pastoral Offices and Directors

Catholic Campus Ministry, Newman Center, University of Guam—Rev. MICHAEL CRISOSTOMO, Dir., 196 B Cuesta San Ramon, Hagatna, 96910. Tel: 671-734-3507; Fax: 671-734-2943.

Catholic Cemetery Office—FRANK SANTOS, Exec. Dir.; Rev. Msgr. JAMES L.G. BENAVENTE, Dir., 196 B Cuesta San Ramon, Hagatna, 96910. Tel: 671-472-6201; Fax: 671-472-1729.

Office of Vocations—

Formation Program for the Permanent Diaconate—Rev. JEFFREY C. SAN NICOLAS, Dir.

Associations and Charitable Organizations in the Archdiocese

Alee Shelter Program for Spousal Abuse—Sr. BRIGID PEREZ, R.S.M., Dir., c/o Catholic Social Service, 234-A US Army Juan C. Fejeran St., Barrigada, 96913. Tel: 671-635-1409; Fax: 671-635-1444.

Catholic Charities Appeal—Deacon LARRY CLAROS, 196 B Cuesta San Ramon, Hagatna, 96910. Tel: 671-472-6116; Fax: 671-477-3519.

Catholic Pro-Life Committee—

Gentle Refuge Crisis Pregnancy Center—

Project Rachel (Abortion Aftermath Counseling)—Deacon FRANCISCO TENORIO, Exec. Dir., Mailing Address: P.O. Box 23006, GMF, 96921. Tel: 671-477-1724.

Catholic Social Service—Mrs. DIANA BALETO CALVO, Exec. Dir., 234-A US Army Juan C. Fejeran St., Barrigada, 96913. Tel: 671-635-1410; Fax: 671-635-1444. Email: css@guam.net. Web: www.catholicsocialservice.net.

Pontifical Holy Childhood Association & Pontifical Society for the Propagation of the Faith—Rev. Msgr. DAVID C. QUITUGUA, J.C.D., Contact Person, 196 B Cuesta San Ramon, Hagatna, 96910. Tel: 671-472-6116; 671-472-6573; Fax: 671-477-3519.

Groups, Ecclesial Movements and other Organizations in the Archdiocese

Catholic Daughters of the Americas—Rev. Msgr. BRIGIDO ARROYO, Chap., P.O. Box 7707, Tamuning, 96931. Tel: 671-646-7181.

Court 2047, Our Lady of Camarin—Ms. PRISCILLA MUNA, Regent.

Court 2450, Maria Rainan Y Familia—Mrs. DORA SALAZAR, Regent.
Confraternity of Christian Mothers—Rev. FELIX LEON GUERRERO, O.F.M.Cap., Spiritual Dir.
United Catholic Charismatic Community—
Catholic Covenant Community—CARLOS SAN AGUSTIN. Tel: 671-477-9118.
Cell Prayer Community—ROQUE MENDIOLA.
El Shaddai (PPFI), Prayer Partner International, Guam Chapter—ALBINA SANTOS, Coord.; Rev. PAUL M. GOFIGAN, Spiritual Dir.
Our Lady of Lourdes Catholic Charismatic Group—LINDA ESTRELLA. Tel: 671-653-2584.
Worship and Praise—FLO SANCHEZ. Tel: 671-646-8044.
Cursillo in Christianity—Rev. JOEL DE LOS REYES, Spiritual Dir., Santa Barbara Church, Dededo, 96929. Tel: 671-632-5659; Fax: 671-632-1713; Mr. SIMON PEREZ, Pres.
Evenings for the Engaged—229 San Roke St., Barrigada, 96913. Tel: 671-734-4573; Fax: 671-734-5858.
Knights of Columbus—FRANK FLORIG, State Deputy; Rev. JOSE VILLAGOMEZ, O.F.M.Cap., State Chap.
Knights of St. Sylvester—PEDRO M. CAMACHO; RICHARD UNTALAN; FRANK SANTOS; THOMAS J. CALVO; EDWARD S. TERLAJE; GONZALO REYES.
Legion of Mary—Rev. Msgr. DAVID C. QUITUGUA, J.C.D., Spiritual Dir.; Mrs. REMEDIOS SILVERIO, Pres., Mailing Address: P.O. Box 2890, Hagatna, 96932. Tel: 671-632-2281; 671-734-2829; Fax: 671-477-3519.
Marriage Encounter—Coordinators: CHARLES KEONE; ESTHER KEONE, 196 B Cuesta San Ramon, Hagatna, 96910. Tel: 671-632-7654; Fax: 671-477-3519.
Neo Catechumenal Way— Dulce Nombre de Maria Cathedral-Basilica Most Rev. ANTHONY SABLAN APURON, O.F.M.Cap., D.D., 207 Archbishop Flores St., Agana, 96910. Tel: 671-472-6201; Fax: 671-472-1729. San Vicente Ferrer Parish: Rev. JOSE ALBERTO RODRIGUEZ, Presbyter, 229 San Roke St., Barrigada, 96913. Tel: 671-734-4573; Fax: 671-734-5858. Saint Anthony Parish: Rev. Msgr. BRIGIDO ARROYO, Presbyter, P.O. Box 7707, Tamuning, 96931. Tel: 671-646-8044; Fax: 671-649-1039. Our Lady of Lourdes Parish: Rev. JEFFREY C. SAN NICOLAS, Presbyter, P.O. Box 11001, Yigo, 96929. Tel: 671-653-2584; Fax: 671-653-4746. Nino Perdido Parish (Asan): Rev. ANTONINO CAMINITI, Presbyter, P.O. Box 45, Agana, 96910. Tel: 671-477-2211.
Secular Franciscans (Third Order)—Mrs. CARMEN MANIBUSAN, Pres., 135 Chalan Kapuchino, Agana Heights, 96910.
Sponsor Couple Program—Deacon LARRY CLAROS.
Natural Family Planning Program—Deacon LARRY CLAROS, 196 B Cuesta San Ramon, Hagatna, 96910. Tel: 671-472-6116; 671-472-6573; Fax: 671-477-3519.
Youth and Young Adults Ministry—Rev. MICHAEL CRISOSTOMO.

CLERGY, PARISHES, MISSIONS AND PAROCHIAL SCHOOLS

CITY OF AGANA

ISLAND OF GUAM

1—DULCE NOMBRE DE MARIA CATHEDRAL - BASILICA (1669) Most Rev. Anthony Sablan Apuron, O.F.M.Cap., Pastor; Rev. Msgr. James L.G. Benavente, Rector; Rev. Thomas B. McGrath, S.J.; Deacons John Dierking; Augusto F. Cepeda; Stephen W.M. Martinez.
Res.: 207 Archbishop Felixberto C. Flores St., 96910. Tel: 671-472-6201; 671-477-1842; Fax: 671-472-1729. Email: info@aganacathedral.org. Web: www.aganacathedral.org.
Catechesis/Religious Program—Students 49.

2—ST. ANDREW KIM (1998), (Korean), Under the Jurisdiction of Santa Barbara Parish, Dededo., Mailing Address: P.O. Box 1555, 96910. Tel: 671-637-4148; 671-637-1116; Fax: 671-637-4149. Email: sungjoox@hanmail.net. Web: www.guam.catb.kr.
Catechesis/Religious Program—Email: bin200p@hanmail.net. Students 60.

OUTSIDE THE CITY OF AGANA

AGANA HEIGHTS, OUR LADY OF THE BLESSED SACRAMENT (1948) Rev. Joseph English, O.F.M.Cap.
Res.: 135 Chalan Kapuchino, 96919. Tel: 671-472-6246.
Catechesis/Religious Program—Cynthia Agbulos, D.R.E. Students 211.

AGAT, OUR LADY OF MOUNT CARMEL (1957) [CEM] Rev. Jason Granado.
Mailing Address: P.O. Box 8353, 96928.
Res.: 157S Eugenio St., 96928. Tel: 671-565-2136; Fax: 671-565-9678.
Catechesis/Religious Program—Students 167.
Chapel—Santa Ana Chapel Lot No. 306-4-2, 96928.

ASAN, NINO PERDIDO Y SAGRADA FAMILIA (1947) Rev. Antonino Caminiti; Deacon R. Larry Claros.
Res.: Nino Perdido St., 96910. Tel: 671-477-2211; Fax: 671-477-2211.
Catechesis/Religious Program—Students 71.

BARRIGADA, SAN VICENTE FERRER (1947) Rev. Jose Alberto Rodriguez.
Res.: 229 San Roke St., 96913. Tel: 671-734-4573; Fax: 671-734-5858.
Catechesis/Religious Program—Geraldine Dela Rosa, D.R.E. Students 290.

CHALAN PAGO, NUESTRA SENORA DE LA PAZ Y BUEN VIAJE (1959) Rev. Santiago Flor Caravia.
Res.: 520 S. Chalan Kanton Tasi, 96910. Tel: 671-734-3723; Fax: 671-734-3722. Email: olopsj@gmail.com. Web: www.olopsj.org.
Catechesis/Religious Program—Tel: 671-734-4223. Students 202.

DEDEDO, SANTA BARBARA (1947) Revs. Paul M. Gofigan; Vito San Andres, Parochial Vicar; Joel de los Reyes (Philippines), Parochial Vicar; Dan Bien, Parochial Vicar; Deacons Herbert Cruz; Peter L. Kaai.
Office: 330 Iglesias Cir., 96929. Tel: 671-632-5659; 671-632-9534; Fax: 671-632-1713. Email: welcome@sbparish.org.
Res.: 372 Gloria Cir., 96929. Tel: 671-633-7253.
Catechesis/Religious Program—Virginia Avaricio, C.R.E.; Cristeta Deliquina, C.R.E. Students 711.

INARAJAN, ST. JOSEPH (1680), (Chamorro), [CEM] Rev. Lonilo R. Torres, Admin.
Res.: P.O. Box 170022, 96917. Tel: 671-828-8102; Fax: 671-828-7062.
Catechesis/Religious Program—Students 92.

MAINA, OUR LADY OF THE PURIFICATION (1949) Rev. Simeon Balmeo.
Res.: P.O. Box 4477, 96910. Tel: 671-477-7256; Fax: 671-635-1444.
Catechesis/Religious Program—Students 39.

MALOJLO, SAN ISIDRO (1950) [JC] Rev. Hector U. Canon.
Res.: 131 San Isidro St., HC 1 Box 17083, Inarajan, 96915. Tel: 671-828-8454; Fax: 671-828-8454.
Catechesis/Religious Program—Students 96.

MANGILAO, SANTA TERESITA (1951) Rev. Felixberto C. Leon Guerrero, O.F.M.Cap.; Deacon Itoy Ruda.
Res.: 192 Vietnam Veterans Hwy., 96913. Tel: 671-734-2100; 671-734-2171; Fax: 671-734-2172. Email: santateresitaguam@gmail.com.
Catechesis/Religious Program—Email: youthandfaith@mail2kevin.com. Students 364.

MERIZO, SAN DIMAS AND OUR LADY OF THE ROSARY (1680), (Chamorro), [CEM] Rev. Wojciech B. Jaskowiak; Deacon Jeff Barcinas.
Res.: P.O. Box 6099, 96916. Tel: 671-828-8056; Fax: 671-828-3100.
Catechesis/Religious Program—Students 274.

MONGMONG, NUESTRA SENORA DE LAS AGUAS (1969) Rev. Manuel Trenchera Jr.; Deacons Stephen W.M. Martinez; Louis J. Rama.
139-A Roy T. Damian St., 96927. In Res., Rev. Manuel C. Trocio.
Res.: P.O. Box 163, 96932. Tel: 671-477-6754; Fax: 671-472-6569. Email: nsdlaguas@guam.net.
Catechesis/Religious Program— Rosa C. Santos, D.R.E. Students 62.

ORDOT, SAN JUAN BAUTISTA (1947), (Chamorro), Very Rev. Msgr. David I.A. Quitugua; Rev. Manny Ombao.
Res.: P.O. Box 49, 96910. Tel: 671-472-8341; Fax: 671-472-2324.
Catechesis/Religious Program—Students 88.

PITI, ASSUMPTION OF OUR LADY (1930), (Chamorro), Rev. Willy O. Lorilla.
Res. & Mailing Address: 314 Assumption Dr., 96915. Tel: 671-472-2272; Fax: 671-477-1955. Email: pitichurch@guam.net.
Catechesis/Religious Program—Students 84.

SANTA RITA, OUR LADY OF GUADALUPE (1944) Rev. Fabio Faiola.
Res.: P.O. Box 4632, 96932. Tel: 671-565-2160; Fax: 671-565-7078.
Catechesis/Religious Program—Students 209.

SINAJANA, SAINT JUDE THADDEUS (1962) Rev. Agustin Gumataotao, O.F.M.Cap.; Deacon Joseph Barcinas.
Church: 122 Bien Avenida Ct., 96910. Tel: 671-475-6530; Fax: 671-477-5353. Email: stjudeguam@gmail.com.
Catechesis/Religious Program—Cynthia Eclavea, D.R.E. Students 254.

TALOFOFO, SAN MIGUEL (1945), (Chamorro), Unassigned.
Res.: 138 San Miguel St., 96915-3606. Tel: 671-789-1069; Fax: 671-789-7665.
Catechesis/Religious Program—Tel: 671-789-0130. Bernie Duenas, D.R.E.; Goring Duenas, D.R.E. Students 157.

TAMUNING, ST. ANTHONY AND ST. VICTOR (1946) Rev. Msgr. Brigido Arroyo; Revs. James Ch'e; Carlos S. Vila (Philippines); Mario S. Palanca; Rodolfo G. Arejola; Val Gabriel Rodriguez.
Res.: P.O. Box 7707, 96931. Tel: 671-646-7181; 671-646-8044; Fax: 671-646-1039.
Catechesis/Religious Program—Students 244.

TOTO, IMMACULATE HEART OF MARY (1948) Rev. Michael Crisostomo; Deacon Jose E. Santos.
Res.: P.O. Box 2552, Hagatna, 96932. Tel: 671-477-9118; Fax: 671-472-2514.
Catechesis/Religious Program—Tel: 671-472-6754. Students 85.

TUMON BAY, BLESSED DIEGO LUIS DE SAN VITORES CHURCH (1970) Rev. Jose Antonio P. Abad, Pastor; Deacon William Hagen.
Res.: 884 Pale' San Vitores Rd., 96913-4013. Tel: 671-646-5649; Fax: 671-648-6887.
Catechesis/Religious Program—Students 97.

UMATAC, SAN DIONISIO (1680), (Chamorro), [CEM] Rev. Wojciech B. Jaskowiak; Deacon Jeff Barcinas.
Res.: P.O. Box 6099, Merizo, 96915. Tel: 671-828-8056; Fax: 671-828-3100.
Catechesis/Religious Program—Students 71.

YIGO, OUR LADY OF LOURDES (1947) Revs. Jeffrey C. San Nicolas; Patrick Kenny Q. Garcia, Parochial Vicar; Jonathan Alvarez, Parochial Vicar; Deacons Fred Otte; Len Stohr; David Richards.
Res.: 153 Chalan Pale Ramon Lagu, 96929. Tel: 671-653-2584; Fax: 671-653-4746. Email: ourlady@ite.net. Web: www.lourdesguam.com.
Catechesis/Religious Program—Tel: 671-653-1102. Femelyne Wesolowski, D.R.E.; Veronica Lizama, Coord. (Children's Div.); Glenda Luke, Registrar. Students 543.
Mission—Santa Bernadita Mission Chapel
Catechesis/Religious Program—Students 27.

YONA, SAN FRANCISCO D'ASSISI (1954) [CEM] Rev. Jose Villagomez, O.F.M.Cap.
San Fidelis Friary: 135 Chalan Kapuchino, Agana Heights, 96910. Tel: 671-789-1491; 671-789-1492; Fax: 671-789-1400. Email: stfrancis@teleguam.net.
Catechesis/Religious Program— Sharon O'Mallan, D.R.E. Students 246.

On Duty Outside the Archdiocese:
Rev.—
Adversario, Efren, Military Chap., U.S.A.F.

Retired:
Rev.—
Brouillard, Louis A., 525 9th St., Pine City, MN 55063.

Permanent Deacons:
Agbulos, Louis T., Jr.
Barcinas, Jeff
Barcinas, Joseph
Cepeda, Augusto F.
Claros, Larry
Cruz, Herbert
Diaz, Ramon
Dierking, John
Hagen, William
Kaai, Peter L.
Leon Guerrero, Anthony
Martinez, Steve
Otte, Fred
Rama, Louis J.
Richards, David
Ruda, Itoi
Santos, Jose E.
Stohr, Leonard
Tenorio, Francisco

INSTITUTIONS LOCATED IN THE ARCHDIOCESE

[A] SEMINARIES

YONA. *Redemptoris Mater Archdiocesan Missionary Seminary* (1999) 130 Chalan Seminariu, 96915. Tel: 671-789-2400; Fax: 671-789-2800. Email: rmsguam@ite.net. Web: www.seminaryguam.com. Revs. Pablo Ponce Rodriguez (Italy), Rector; Wojciech B. Jaskowiak, Prefect of Studies; Julio Cesar Sanchez Malagon, Vice-Rector. Seminarians 36.

[B] HIGH SCHOOLS

AGANA. *Academy of Our Lady of Guam*, 233 W. Archbishop Felixberto C. Flores St., 96910. Tel: 671-477-8203; Fax: 671-477-8555. Email: acad@aolg.edu.gu. Web: www.aolg.edu.gu. Sr. Francis Jerome Cruz, R.S.M., Pres.; Ms. Lourdes Babauta, Dean Student Affairs; Mrs. Mary Meeks, Prin.; Mrs. Daphne Castillo, Vice Prin.; Ms. Eileen Gofigan, Admission Dir.; Sr. Orlean Pereda, R.S.M., Librarian. Sisters of Mercy. Sisters 5; Lay Teachers 28; Staff 18; Students 425.

HAGATNA. *The Father Duenas Memorial School* (1949) P.O. Box FD, 96932. Tel: 671-734-2261; 671-734-2263; Fax: 671-734-5738. Email: fdms@guam.net. Web: www.fatherduenas.com. Rev. Vitaliano Dimaranan, S.D.B., Prin.; Dante Perez, Librarian. Priests 4; Lay Teachers 28; Students 428.

ORDOT. *St. Thomas Aquinas Catholic High School*, P.O. Box AC, Hagatna, 96932. Tel: 671-473-7821; Fax: 671-473-7824. Dr. Hauhouot Diambra-Odi, Ph.D., Prin.; Pilar Perez Williams, Pres.; Norman Babia, Librarian & MRC Coord. Priests 1; Lay Teachers 9; Students 69.

TALOFOFO. *Notre Dame High School*, 480 S. San Miguel St., 96915-3540. Tel: 671-789-1676; 671-789-1745; Fax: 671-789-4847. Email: info@ndhsguam.com. Web: ndhsguam.com. Sr. Jean Ann Crisostomo, S.S.N.D., Pres.; Mariesha Cruz-San Nicolas, Prin.; Sr. Barbara Lambor-Hagel, S.S.N.D., Librarian. Sisters 3; Lay Teachers 26; Students 291.

[C] ELEMENTARY AND JUNIOR HIGH SCHOOLS

AGAT. *Our Lady of Mt. Carmel School* (1957) P.O. Box 7830, 96928. Tel: 671-565-3822; 671-565-5128; Fax: 671-565-3539. Email: mcsourlady@gmail.com. Norma C. Tabayoyoug, Vice Prin. Priests 3; Lay Teachers 26; Students 410.

BARRIGADA. *San Vicente Catholic School*, 196 Bejong St., 96913. Tel: 671-735-4240; Fax: 671-734-8718; 671-735-4243. Email: sjaquinene@svcsguam.com. Web: www.geocities.com/sanvicentebraves2000/index.htm. Sr. Joseph Ann Quinene, S.S.N.D., Prin.; Maria Camacho, Library Tech; Anisia S.D. Lujan, Librarian. Sisters 2; Lay Teachers 24; Students 297.

DEDEDO. *Santa Barbara Catholic School* (1950) 274-A W. Santa Barbara Ave., 96929-5378. Tel: 671-632-5578; Fax: 671-632-1414. Email: info@santabarbaraschool.org. Web: www.santabarbaraschool.org. Sr. Jeanette Marie Pangelinan, R.S.M., Prin.; Margaret Catabay, Librarian. Sisters 2; Lay Teachers 39; Students 467.

GMF. *St. Francis School*, P.O. Box 22199, 96921. Tel: 671-789-1270; 671-789-1350; Fax: 671-789-3900. Email: info@sfcsguam.com. Web: www.sfcsguam.com. Sr. Marsha Nededog, S.S.N.D., Prin. Sisters 2; Lay Teachers 20; Students 330.

SINAJANA. *Bishop Baumgartner Memorial Catholic School*, 281 Calle Angel Flores St., 96910. Tel: 671-472-6670; 671-477-2677; Fax: 671-477-4028. Email: smartero1938@hotmail.com. Web: www.bbmcs.org. Sr. Mary Emiline Artero, R.S.M., Pres.; Mrs. Rita D. Duenas, Prin.; Merly Lacaden, Librarian. Cathedral Grade School merged with Bishop Baumgartner Middle School to form Bishop Baumgartner Memorial Catholic School. Brothers 1; Sisters 3; Lay Teachers 43; Students 690.

TAMUNING. *Saint Anthony School*, 529 Chalan San Antonio, 96913. Tel: 671-647-1140; Fax: 671-649-7130. Email: sasadm@ite.net. Web: www.stanthonyschoolguam.org. Sr. Doris San Agustin, R.S.M., Prin.; Mrs. Arlene Rodriguez, Librarian. Sisters 3; Lay Teachers 48; Students 742.

YIGO. *Dominican Catholic School* (1995) 114 Chalan Pale Ramon-Lagu Rte. 1, 96929. Tel: 671-653-3021; Fax: 671-653-3090. Email: cormosd@ite.net; admin@dcsguam.com. Web: www.dcsguam.com. Sr. Zenaida T. Ancheta, O.P., Prin.; Ms. Bernadette Alicante, Librarian. Sisters 6; Lay Teachers 21; Students 229.

[D] KINDERGARTEN AND NURSERY SCHOOLS

AGANA HEIGHTS. *Maria Artero Catholic Preschool & Kindergarten*, 161 A Sunset Dr., 96910-6451. Tel: 671-472-8777; Fax: 671-472-2326. Email: macpk@teleguam.net. Sr. Katherine E. Bromwell, M.M.B., Prin. Sisters 3; Lay Teachers 3; Students 64.

ORDOT. *Dominican Child Development Center*, P.O. Box 5668, 96932. Tel: 671-477-7228; 671-472-1524; Fax: 671-472-4282. Email: dcdcj1980@yahoo.com. Sisters Ma. Ana Lee, O.P., Local Prioress & Contact Person; Jessica Quipit, O.P., Prin. Sisters 3; Lay Teachers 13; Aides 5; Students 156.

PEREZVILLE-TAMUNING. *Mercy Heights Nursery and Kindergarten, Inc.*, 211 Fr. San Vitores St., Tamuning, 96913. Tel: 671-646-1185; Fax: 671-649-1822. Ms. Cecilia Crisostomo, Admin. Lay Teachers 16; Students 197.

TAI. *Infant of Prague Nursery and Kindergarten, Inc.*, 164 Sabanan Magas Rd., Mangilao, 96913. Tel: 671-734-2785; Fax: 671-734-1055. Email: sbu@ite.net. Sr. Barbara Ungacta, R.S.M., Admin. Institute of the Sisters of the Mercy of the Americas, South Central Community on Guam. Sisters 4; Lay Teachers 20; Students 200.

[E] CATHOLIC CHARITIES

BARRIGADA. *Catholic Social Services of Guam*, 234A U.S. Army Juan C. Fejeran St., 96913. Tel: 671-635-1409; 671-635-1406; Fax: 671-635-1444. Email: css@guam.net. Web: www.catholicsocialservices.net. Mrs. Diana Baleto Calvo, Exec. Dir.; Leo G. Casil, Deputy Dir. Total Elderly Assisted 2,218; Total Adults Assisted 2,485; Total Children Assisted 414; Total Families Assisted 453; Total Staff 230.

Elderly Programs:

Case Management Lisa Kenworthy, Prog. Mgr.

Adult Day Care Maria Timoteo, Prog. Mgr.

Dementia Care Julie Perez, Prog. Mgr.

Emergency Receiving Home Juliet Baroga, Acting Prog. Mgr.

Shelter Programs:

Alee I Shelter for Abused Spouses & Children Sr. Brigid Perez, R.S.M., Project Dir.

Alee II Shelter for Abused Children Sr. Brigid Perez, R.S.M., Project Dir.

Caridad I Shelter for Children with Disabilities Marie Espinosa, Acting Project Dir.

Caridad II Shelter for Adults Marie Espinosa, Acting Project Dir.

Guma San Jose Josephine Rosario, Project Dir.

Transitional Homeless (Liheng) Jesse Catahay, Project Dir.

Programs for Persons with Disabilities:

Respite Care Norbert Ungacta, Project Dir.

Community Habilitation Program Lourdes Bitanga, Project Dir.

Support Services Division:

Support Services Juan C. Chargualaf, Support Svc. Dir. & Facilities Maintenance Coord.

Federal Grant

FEMA (Food & Shelter Grant)

Emergency Food Bank

Msgr. David I.A. Quitugua Foundation

Finger Printing

Food Catering

Monthly Rummage Sale

Hidden Treasure

[F] MONASTERIES AND RESIDENCES OF PRIESTS

AGANA HEIGHTS. *St. Fidelis Friary*, 135 Chalan Kapuchino, 96910. Tel: 671-472-6339; Fax: 671-472-3335. Web: www.thepacificaps.org. Revs. Joseph English, O.F.M.Cap., Vice Prov., Guardian; Felix Leon Guerrero, O.F.M.Cap., Councilor; George Maddock, O.F.M.Cap.; Jose Villagomez, O.F.M.Cap., Councilor; Agustin Gumataotao, O.F.M.Cap.; Randolph Nowak, O.F.M.Cap.; Patrick Castro, O.F.M.Cap.; Eric Forbes, O.F.M.Cap.; Michael Tenorio, O.F.M.Cap.; Andre Eduvala, O.F.M.Cap.; Bros. Brian Champoux, O.F.M.Cap.; Joseph R. Meno Jr., O.F.M.Cap.; Nathaniel Santos, O.F.M.Cap. Headquarters of Capuchin Friars (Vice Province, Star of the Sea).

BARRIGADA. *Society of Jesus Micronesia*, P.O. Box 315244, Tamuning, 96931. Tel: 671-649-0073. Email: kenhezel@gmail.com. Revs. Kenneth J. Hezel, S.J., Supr.; Thomas B. McGrath, S.J., Chap.

[G] CONVENTS AND RESIDENCES FOR SISTERS

AGANA HEIGHTS. *Mercedarian Missionaries of Berriz*, 161 A Sunset Dr., 96910-6451. Tel: 671-477-8303; Fax: 671-472-2326. Email: mmbmicro@teleguam.net. Web: www.mmberriz.com. Sisters Isabel T. Seman, M.M.B., Regl. Coord.; Anotia Addy, M.M.B., Regl. Vicar; Fudalina Umwech, M.M.B., Admin.; Katherine E. Bromwell, M.M.B., Prin.; Marlihsa Suzumu, M.M.B., Teacher Aide MACPK & Student UOG; Ancherin Koto, M.M.B., Teacher Aide MACPK & Student UOG; Brenda Mwarike, M.M.B., Teacher Aide MACPK & Student UOG; Rosemary Laigeluw, M.M.B., Teacher Aide MACPK & Student UOG; Regina Doone, M.M.B., Student UOG. Sisters 9.

BARRIGADA. *San Vicente Community*, 201 Bejong St., 96913. Tel: 671-734-3010; Fax: 671-734-8718. Sr. Joseph Ann Quinene, S.S.N.D., Prin. Sisters teach at San Vicente Elementary, St. Francis School. Sisters 4.

DEDEDO. *Santa Barbara Convent*, 274 B. W. Santa Barbara Ave., 96929. Tel: 671-632-2384; Fax: 671-632-1414. Institute of the Sisters of Mercy of the Americas, South Central Community on Guam. Sisters 5.

HAGATNA. *Cathedral Mercy Convent*, 221 Archbishop F. C. Flores St., 96910-5102. Tel: 671-477-9291; Fax: 671-477-9293. Email: mcamacho@mercysc.org. Sisters 3.

ORDOT. *Religious Missionaries of St. Dominic*, P.O. Box 5668, 96932. Tel: 671-472-1524. Email: tribunal@ite.net. Religious 3; Total in Residence 4.

PEREZVILLE-TAMUNING. *MERCY ACTION MARIANAS, Ltd. (MAML)*, 211 Fr. San Vitores St., Tamuning, 96913. Tel: 671-649-7561; Fax: 671-649-1822. Email: mcamacho@mercysc.org. Sr. Mary Cabrini Taitano, R.S.M., Pres. Institute of the Sisters of Mercy of the Americas, South Central Community on Guam.

Mercy Heights Convent, 211 Fr. San Vitores St., Tamuning, 96913. Tel: 671-646-7246; Fax: 671-649-1822. Email: mcamacho@mercysc.org. Sr. Mary Cecilia Camacho, R.S.M., Local Admin. Sisters in residence teaching and working in Tamuning, Agana, Sinajana and infirmed; Residence, retirement residence & administrative offices of the Institute of the Sisters of Mercy of the Americas, South Central Community on Guam. Sisters 22.

SINAJANA. *St. Jude Thaddeus Convent*, P.O. Box 394, Hagatna, 96932. Tel: 671-477-7852. Email: sgamakaka@teleguam.net. Franciscan Sisters of Perpetual Adoration.

TAI. *Tai Mercy Convent and Formation House*, P.O. Box 22865 GMF, Barrigada, 96921-2865. Tel: 671-734-3312; Fax: 671-734-2260. Institute of the Sisters of Mercy of the Americas, South Central Community on Guam.; Professed Sisters in various Apostolates and Sisters in basic formation as well as retired sisters. Sisters 9.

TALOFOFO. *S.S.N.D. Notre Dame Center*, 480 San Miguel St., 96915-3540. Tel: 671-789-7763; 671-789-0501; Fax: 671-789-3810. Email: maryjuancamacho@yahoo.com. Sr. Mary Juan Camacho, S.S.N.D., Coord. Sisters 22.

Mother Theresa Tel: 671-789-0501; Fax: 671-789-3810.

Notre Dame Community Tel: 671-789-1629; Fax: 671-789-3810.

TAMUNING. *Discalced Order Of Carmelites Monastery*, P.O. Box 315225, 96931. Tel: 671-646-8972; 671-727-7737 (Work); Fax: 671-922-7737. Email: guam@carmelite-nuns.org. Sr. Dawn Marie, O.C.D., Prioress. Order of Discalced Carmelites. Sisters 9.

[H] MISCELLANEOUS LISTINGS

AGANA. *Our Lady of the Waters House of Prayer* (Retreat Center), P.O. Box 163, 96932. Tel: 671-477-6754; 671-472-1842; Fax: 671-472-6569; 671-472-1729.

Secular Franciscans, 135 Chalan Kapuchino, 96910. Tel: 671-472-6023; 671-472-6339; Fax: 671-789-7665. Rev. Daniel Cristobal, O.F.M.Cap., Spiritual Dir.; Mrs. Carmen Manibusan, Pres.

BARRIGADA. *Saint Dominic's Senior Care Home*, 350 N. Sabana Dr., Barrigada Heights, 96913-1262. Tel: 671-632-9370; 671-632-9378; Fax: 671-637-1679. Email: stdom@ite.net. Sr. Emelita Cinco, O.P., Admin. Bed Capacity 60; Total Assisted Annually 60; Total Staff 75.

MANGILAO. *Office of Youth, Young Adult & Campus Ministry* 196-B Cuesta San Ramon, Hagatna, 96910. Tel: 671-472-6116; Fax: 671-472-3514. Email: palemike@yahoo.com. Rev. Michael Crisostomo, Dir. Total Assisted Annually 15; Total Staff 1.

RELIGIOUS INSTITUTES OF MEN REPRESENTED IN THE ARCHDIOCESE

For further details refer to the corresponding bracketed number in the Religious Institutes of Men or Women section.

[0470]—*The Capuchin Friars* (Vice Prov. of Mary, Star of the Sea)—O.F.M.Cap.

[0690]—*The Society of Jesus- Jesuit Fathers and Brothers* (N.Y. Prov.)—S.J.

RELIGIOUS INSTITUTES OF WOMEN REPRESENTED IN THE ARCHDIOCESE

[1780]—*Congregation of the Sisters of the Third Order of St. Francis of Perpetual Adoration* (La Crosse, WI)—F.S.P.A.

[0420]—*Discalced Carmelite Nuns*—O.C.D.

[2510]—*Mercedarian Missionaries of Berriz*—M.M.B.

[]—*Religious Missionaries of St. Dominic*—O.P.

[2970]—*School Sisters of Notre Dame* (Mequon, WI)—S.S.N.D.

[2575]—*Sisters of Mercy of the Americas* (Belmont, NC)—R.S.M.

NECROLOGY

(No Deaths)

An asterisk (*) denotes an organization that has established tax-exempt status directly with the IRS and is not covered by the USCCB Group Ruling.

Diocese of Arecibo, Puerto Rico

(Dioecesis Arecibensis)

Most Reverend

DANIEL FERNANDEZ TORRES

Bishop of Arecibo; ordained January 7, 1995; appointed Titular Bishop of Sufes and Auxiliary Bishop of San Juan, PR February 14, 2007; ordained April 21, 2007; appointed Bishop of Arecibo September 24, 2010; installed October 3, 2010.

Most Reverend

INAKI MALLONA TXERTUDI, C.P.

Bishop Emeritus of Arecibo; ordained March 17, 1956; appointed December 14, 1991; consecrated January 6, 1992; installed January 25, 1992; retired September 24, 2010. *Res.: Hogar Irma Fe Pol, #52 Calle Comercio, Lares, PR 00669.*

ESTABLISHED APRIL 30, 1960.

Square Miles 833.

Comprises the mid-northern part of the Island.

The Chancery: 206 Dr. Salas St., P.O. Box 616, Arecibo, PR 00613. Tel: 787-878-3180; 787-878-3110; Fax: 787-880-2661.

Email: arecibo@diocesisdearecibo.org

STATISTICAL OVERVIEW

Personnel	
Bishop	1
Retired Bishops	1
Priests: Diocesan Active in Diocese	52
Priests: Diocesan Active Outside Diocese	10
Priests: Retired, Sick or Absent	10
Number of Diocesan Priests	72
Religious Priests in Diocese	49
Total Priests in Diocese	121
Extern Priests in Diocese	7
Ordinations:	
Diocesan Priests	1
Permanent Deacons in Diocese	1
Total Brothers	7
Total Sisters	139
Parishes	
Parishes	59
With Resident Pastor:	
Resident Diocesan Priests	42
Resident Religious Priests	17
Missions	241
Welfare	
Homes for the Aged	4
Total Assisted	260
Residential Care of Children	3
Total Assisted	57
Specialized Homes	1
Total Assisted	9
Special Centers for Social Services	2
Total Assisted	1,952
Educational	
Seminaries, Diocesan	1
Diocesan Students in Other Seminaries	15
Total Seminarians	15
Colleges and Universities	1
Total Students	690
High Schools, Diocesan and Parish	7
Total Students	1,306
High Schools, Private	6
Total Students	1,809
Elementary Schools, Diocesan and Parish	7
Total Students	1,583
Elementary Schools, Private	5
Total Students	5,388
Catechesis/Religious Education:	
High School Students	3,454
Elementary Students	12,089
Total Students under Catholic Instruction	26,334
Teachers in the Diocese:	
Priests	9
Brothers	4
Sisters	23
Lay Teachers	390
Vital Statistics	
Receptions into the Church:	
Infant Baptism Totals	3,860
Minor Baptism Totals	463
Adult Baptism Totals	305
Received into Full Communion	4,515
First Communions	4,481
Confirmations	3,903
Marriages:	
Catholic	292
Interfaith	31
Total Marriages	323
Deaths	3,045
Total Catholic Population	370,000
Total Population	603,469

Former Bishops—Most Revs. ALFRED F. MENDEZ, C.S.C., ord. 1935; cons. Oct. 28, 1960; retired Jan., 1974; died Jan. 28, 1995; MIGUEL RODRIQUEZ, C.S.S.R., D.D., ord. June 22, 1958; appt. Jan. 21, 1974; cons. March 23, 1974; retired March, 1990; died Aug. 13, 2001; INAKI MALLONA TXERTUDI, C.P., ord. March 17, 1956; appt. Dec. 14, 1991; cons. Jan. 6, 1992; installed Jan. 25, 1992; retired Sept. 24, 2010.

Secretary to the Bishop—Mrs. VIVIAN MALDONADO.

Chancery Office—206 Dr. Salas St., P.O. Box 616, Arecibo, 00613-0616. Tel: 787-878-3180; 787-878-3110; Fax: 787-880-2661.

Vicar General—Rev. LUIS A. COLON, S.E.M.V., Mailing Address: P.O. Box 616, Arecibo, 00613. Tel: 787-878-3180; 787-878-3110.

Secretary and Receptionist—Mrs. WALESKA CORDERO.

Administrator—Mr. MIGUEL GONZALEZ.

Accountant—VACANT.

Chancellor—Rev. JORGE L. VIRELLA VAZQUEZ, Mailing Address: P.O. Box 616, Arecibo, 00613. Tel: 787-878-3180.

Secretary—Miss SYLVIA VARGAS.

Diocesan Tribunal of Arecibo—VACANT, Judicial Vicar & Presiding Judge.

Adjutant Judges—Revs. JUAN R. MORA DELGADO, J.C.L., Mailing Address: P.O. Box 775, Vega Alta, 00692; JORGE L. VIRELLA VAZQUEZ, Official, Mailing Address: P.O. Box 9018, Sabana Branch, Vega Baja, 00694.

Promoter of Justice—Rev. GABRIEL MADURO LOPEZ.

Defenders of the Bond—Revs. ALBERTO DIAZ COLON; P. GABRIEL MADURO.

Advocate—VACANT, Mailing Address: P.O. Box 142142, Arecibo, 00614. Fax: 787-815-0022.

Notary—Mrs. WANDA RIVERA.

Secretary—Mrs. LIVIA E. SERRANO.

Vicar of Diocesan Pastoral Affairs—Rev. ADRIAN N. JIMENEZ ORTIZ; Mrs. MIRIAM NEGRON, Sec.

Diocesan Consultors—Revs. P. JESUS MONREAL PUJANTE, O.Carm.; LUIS A. COLON, S.E.M.V.; VICTOR ROJAS; ANGEL M. SANTOS; MELQUIADES ROJAS; VICTOR SANCHEZ; CARMELO URARTE.

Priest's Senate (Consejo Presbiteral)—Revs. VICTOR SANCHEZ VELEZ; LUIS A. COLON, S.E.M.V.; ANGEL M. SANTOS; FERNANDO MORELL; JESUS MONREAL, O.Carm.; TOMAS SANTOS RODRIGUEZ; ANGEL R. DÍAZ; VICTOR ROJAS; DAVID RIVAS; LUIS J. RIVERA; OVIDIO PEREZ; EDWARD MALDONADO, O.F.M.Cap.; ANGEL DIAZ CACERES; ADRIAN N. JIMENEZ ORTIZ; ROBERTO VEGA; ALBERTO DIAZ COLON.

Diocesan Offices and Directors

Ayuda Social Movimiento Juan XXIII—BRENDA RIVERA, Coord., Mailing Address: P.O. Box 241, Sabana Hoyos, 00688-0241. Tel: 787-881-7141; 787-881-2342; Fax: 787-881-7141. Email: ayudasoc@coqui.net.

Confraternity of Christian Doctrine—VACANT, Mailing Address: 5 Calle Mariano Abril, Box 1151, Arecibo, 00613. Tel: 787-878-8401. Email: catequesis_arecibo@hotmail.com.

Cursillos de Cristiandad—VACANT.

Diocesan Council of Catholic Women—Mrs. BLANCA RUIZ.

Propagation of Faith—Rev. ORLANDO CAMACHO, C.S.Sp.

Holy Childhood—Rev. ORLANDO CAMACHO, C.S.Sp.

Director of Youth—Rev. IVAN MARTINEZ.

Legion of Mary—VACANT.

Movimiento Familiar Cristiano (CFM)—Rev. VICTOR ROJAS RODRIGUEZ.

Prison Services—Rev. ELVIN A. IRIZARRY ROMAN, Mailing Address: P.O. Box 2525 CMB - 75, Utuado, 00641-2525. Tel: 787-894-7144; Fax: 787-894-7144.

Seminario Jesus Maestro College Seminary—Rev. VICTOR SANCHEZ, Mailing Address: Box 2164, Arecibo, 00613. Tel: 787-878-1528.

Seminary Board and Vocation Program—Rev. Msgr. DANIEL FERNANDEZ; Revs. VICTOR ROJAS; VICTOR SANCHEZ; RAMON OLIVENCIA.

Pastoral Vocational Program—Rev. VICTOR ROJAS.

Superintendent of Schools—JUAN A. VALDES; LUZ RIVERA VELAZQUEZ, Sec., Mailing Address: P.O. Box 1683, Arecibo, 00613. Tel: 787-878-1095; Fax: 787-878-1095.

Oficina para la Promocion y el Desarrollo Humano, Inc.—

Catholic Charities—Mrs. ANGELICA FLORES, Dir.; VACANT, In Charge of the Mission; Sr. VERONICA ORAVEC, C.D.P., Admin.; Dr. ZULMA CUEVAS, Psychology Asst., Mailing Address: P.O. Box 353, Arecibo, 00613. Tel: 787-817-6951; Fax: 787-817-7597.

Programs—

Women Head of Household—Mrs. LAURA LLERANDI.

Domestic Violence Unit—Mrs. LAURA LLERANDI.

Parenting with Love—VACANT.

Community Development—CARMEN NORIS ARBELO.

Improving Your Self Esteem—LUZ I. SOTO.

Retreat House, Centro Diocesano Mons. Mendez—Rev. VICTOR SANCHEZ, Apdo. 2164, Arecibo, 00613. Tel: 787-878-4796.

Boy Scouts—VACANT.

Hospital Chaplains—

Arecibo Hospital—JAVIER RODRIGUEZ FIGUEROA, Coord. Capellania; Dr. COLL Y TOSTE; Rev. JULIO A. ANGLADA; Miss ESTHER COSTA. Cathedral of San Felipe Apostol: Rev. ADRIAN N. JIMENEZ.

Susoni Hospital—JAVIER RODRIGUEZ FIGUEROA, Coord. Capellania; Rev. P. GABRIEL MADURO.

Vocations—Rev. VICTOR SANCHEZ, Apdo. 2164, Arecibo, 00613. Tel: 787-878-1528.

Police Chaplain—Rev. LUIS A. VAZQUEZ.

Sociedad San Vincente de Paul (Vincentinos)—Mr. ANGEL GINES, Pres. Consejo Diocesano. Tel: 787-884-5087; 787-854-2562.

CLERGY, PARISHES, MISSIONS AND PAROCHIAL SCHOOLS

CITY OF ARECIBO

1—CATHEDRAL OF SAN FELIPE APOSTOL (1616) [JC] Revs. Adrian N. Jimenez, Rector; P. Gabriel Maduro; Reinaldo I. Davila.
De Diego St.—Box 577, 00613. Tel: 809-878-1149; Fax: 787-816-5719. Email: catedralarecibo@hotmail.com.
Catechesis/Religious Program—Students 272.
Chapel—Islote II, Sagrada Familia
Chapel—Islote III (Sector Vibora), San Juan Evangelista
Chapel—Sector Boan, Maria Reina
Chapel—Islote I (Vigia), N.S. del Carmen

2—CHURCH OF CHRIST THE KING (1967) Rev. Eugenio Gayarre.
Res.: Box 1932, 00613. Tel: 787-815-4114.
Catechesis/Religious Program—
Chapel—Bo. Hato Arriba, Maria Auxiliadora

3—CHURCH OF SAGRADO CORAZON DE JESUS (1961) [JC] Revs. Alberto Diaz; Ernesto Perez Torres.
Res.: Box 140637, 00614. Tel: 787-878-4910; Fax: 787-815-0498. Email: sagradocorazon-arecibo@yahoo.com.
School—*Colegio San Felipe*, (Grades PreK-12), Box 673, 00613. Tel: 809-878-3532; Fax: 787-879-2124. Web: www.colegiosanfelipe.org. Lucy Cruz, Prin.; Felicita Beauchamp, Librarian. Lay Teachers 38; Students 500.
Catechesis/Religious Program—Students 141.
Chapel—Bo. Obrero, Inmaculada Concepcion

4—CHURCH OF SAN MARTIN DE PORRES (1973) Revs. Julio A. Anglada, Admin.; Rafael A. Ramos; Deacon Hipolito Crespo.
Res.: Calle 6 F-12, Box 14-2142, Urb. Univ. Gardens, 00614. Tel: 787-878-1822.
Catechesis/Religious Program—Students 210.
Chapel—Victor Rojas II, San Jose Obrero

5—CHURCH OF SANTA CECILIA (1981) [JC] Rev. Roy F. Martinez, O.F.M.Cap., Admin.
Res.: HC-04, Box 13674, 00612. Tel: 787-879-3364. Email: peregrino59@aol.com.
Catechesis/Religious Program—Students 117.
Chapel—Calichosa, San Jose
Chapel—Los Canos, San Martin de Porres
Chapel—La Guinea, La Milagrosa

6—CHURCH OF SANTA TERESITA (1980) [JC] Rev. Jorge L. Virella, Admin.
Res.: Road 492, KM 1.9, P.O. Box 9242, Cotto Station, 00613. Tel: 787-878-7015.
Catechesis/Religious Program—Students 143.
Chapel—Hato Arriba, N.S. La Providencia
Chapel—Barranca La Milagrosa

7—INMACULADO CORAZON DE MARIA (1987) [JC] Rev. Lisimaco Hincapie, Admin.
Res.: Box 1282, Sabana Hoyos, 00688.
Catechesis/Religious Program—Students 150.
Chapel—Bo. Asomante, San Isidro
Chapel—Bo. Carolina, Sagrado Corazon de Jesus
Chapel—Bo. Arrozal, San Jose
Chapel—Los Muertos, San Francisco

8—LA MILAGROSA (1973) [JC] Rev. Angel Diaz.
Res.: Box 204, Bajadero, 00616. Tel: 787-650-3420. Email: lamilagrosaare@hotmail.com.
Catechesis/Religious Program—Students 272.
Chapel—Bajadero, Immaculada Concepcion
Chapel—Domingo Ruiz, N.S. La Providencia
Chapel—Carreras, San Judas
Chapel—Biafara, N.S. La Virgen del Carmen

9—NUESTRA SENORA DE FATIMA (1967) [JC] Revs. Roberto Atzeni; Gianni Soro Belloni; Johnny C. Iturrizaga, C.M.V.; Michele Querin, C.M.V.
Res.: Box 667, Sabana Hoyos, 00688. Tel: 787-881-8274.
Catechesis/Religious Program—Students 193.
Chapel—Garrochales, S. Fco. de Asis
Chapel—Ballaja, N.S. del Carmen
Chapel—Garrochales, La Milagrosa, San Luis
Chapel—Espino, Immaculada Concepcion

10—NUESTRA SENORA DEL CARMEN (1961) [JC] Rev. Miguel Mercado.
Res.: Bo. Cotto No. 985, P.O. Box 9949, Cotto Sta., 00613. Fax: 787-817-5062.
School—*Hogar-Colegio La Milagrosa*, (Grades K-12), Ave. Francisco Jimenez Gonzalez, 00612-4912. Tel: 787-878-0341; 787-879-4912; Fax: 787-817-7822. Email: hogarcolegiolamilagrosa@yahoo.com. Sr. Maria D. Vicens, Prin. Sisters of Charity 2; Lay Teachers 33; Students 411.
Catechesis/Religious Program—Students 172.
Chapel—Abra S. Francisco, San Antonio
Chapel—Rodriguez Olmo, San Francisco

11—OUR LADY OF HOPE (1986) [JC] Rev. Ivan Martinez Adorno.
Res.: Box 489, 00613. Tel: 787-880-1943.
Catechesis/Religious Program—Students 221.
Chapel—Cantagallo, Sgdo. Corazon de Jesus
Chapel—Plan Bonito, San Rafael

12—SAN JUAN BOSCO (1971) Rev. Efraín Montesino, Dir.
Res.: Urb. Jardines de Arecibo, Calle R-Y-26, 00612. Tel: 787-879-1070; Fax: 787-817-4107. Email: col.sanjuanboscoare@yahoo.com.
School—(Grades PreK-9) Tel: 787-879-2069. Nilda Gonzalez, Prin. Lay Teachers 34; Students 472.
Catechesis/Religious Program—Students 262.
Chapel—Las Canelas, N.S. La Dolorosa, San Daniel Sisters of Nazaret 3.

13—SANTA ANA (1961) [JC] Revs. Edwin A. Mercado; Victor Sanchez.
Res.: Bo. Santana, Box 318, 00613. Tel: 787-881-6005.
Catechesis/Religious Program—Tel: 787-881-6882. Students 195.
Chapel—Factor II, N.S. del Carmen
Chapel—Santuario Cristo de los Milagros

14—SANTISIMO SACRAMENTO (1990) [JC] Rev. Roy F. Martinez, O.F.M.Cap.
Res.: Ste. 109, P.O. Box 474, 00613. Tel: 787-878-4310.
Catechesis/Religious Program—Students 105.
Chapel—Del Valle, La Milagrosa
Chapel—Jobos, San Pascual

OUTSIDE OF ARECIBO

BARCELONETA

1—CHURCH OF OUR LADY OF MT. CARMEL (1882) [JC] Rev. Victor Rojas.
Res.: P.O. Box 2062, 00617. Tel: 809-846-5625; Fax: 787-846-5625. Email: sradelcarmen@gmail.com.
Catechesis/Religious Program—
Chapel—Garrochales I, N.S. de Fatima
Chapel—Palmas Altas, San Antonio
Chapel—Punta Palma, N.S. del Mar

2—OUR LADY OF VICTORY (1963) [JC] Rev. Juan R. Mora, Admin.
Res.: Ste. 125, Call Box 2020, 00617. Tel: 809-846-6120.
Catechesis/Religious Program—Students 166.
Chapel—Parcelas Imberry, San Jose Obrero
Chapel—Quebrada, Immaculate Heart of Mary
Chapel—Tiburones, N.S. de Fatima
Chapel—Palenque, San Juan Bautista

CAMUY

1—ST. JOSEPH (1827) [JC] Revs. Pedro N. Montoya; Orlando Lugo Perez.
Res.: P.O. Box 414, 00627. Tel: 787-898-3620; Fax: 787-898-3620.
Catechesis/Religious Program—Students 455.
Convent—San Jose Hermanas Terciarias Capuchinas 4.
Chapel—Membrillo, N.S. La Monserrate
Chapel—Puente (Zarzas), Sagrado Corazon
Chapel—Puente (Zarza Parcelas), N.S. La Milagrosa
Chapel—Puente (Sector Pica), N.S. del Rosario
Chapel—Abra Honda, Espiritu Santo
Chapel—Zanjas, Immaculada Concepcion

2—OUR LADY OF ASUMPTION (1984) [JC] Rev. Marcos A. Cepeda Contreras, M.N.M.
Res.: HC-02, Box 8047, 00627. Tel: 787-898-8038.
Catechesis/Religious Program—Students 231.
Chapel—Cibao Ocasio, N.S. del Perpetuo Socorro
Chapel—Callejones, Sagrado Corazon
Chapel—Callejones II, San Pablo de la Cruz
Chapel—Cibao Lugo, Maria Auxiliadora

3—OUR LADY OF MONSERRATE (1961) [JC] Rev. Joaquín J. Rojas, M.N.M.
Res.: HC-03, Box 16512, Quebradillas, 00678-9820. Tel: 787-898-6784.
Catechesis/Religious Program—Students 330.
Chapel—Piletas (Lares), N.S. del Carmen
Chapel—Guajataca (Queb.), N.S. de Fatima
Chapel—Aibonito Beltran, San Antonio
Chapel—Cibao (S. Sebastian), Santa Ana
Chapel—Planas I (Isabela), Santa Cruz
Chapel—Planas II, N.S. del Rosario

4—OUR LADY OF THE MIRACULOUS MEDAL (1962) [JC], (El Calvario) Revs. Jose B. Zapien, M.N.M.; Israel Medina, M.N.M.
Res.: HC-01 Buzon 5240, 00627. Tel: 787-898-5825.
Catechesis/Religious Program—Tel: 787-898-4841. Students 519.
Chapel—Planas II, Santiago Apostol
Chapel—Puertos, Sagrado Corazon
Chapel—Cienaga, Cristo Rey
Chapel—Camuy Arriba, N.S. del Carmen
Chapel—Sector Riego, Santa Clara
Chapel—Sector Mani, Sagrado Corazon

CIALES

1—HOLY ROSARY (1820) [JC] Revs. Jorge L. Rivera, O.Carm.; Jorge R. Betancourt, O.Carm.
Res.: P.O. Box 26, 00638. Tel: 787-871-2205; 787-871-3485. Email: zelozeletussum@hotmail.com.
School—P.O. Box 1334, 00638. Tel: 787-871-2222; Fax: 787-871-5797. Email: cnsrciales@hotmail.com. Blanca Marrero, Prin. Lay Teachers 20; Students 224.
Catechesis/Religious Program—Students 300.
Chapel—Pozas, San Elias
Chapel—Cialitos, Buen Pastor
Chapel—Hato Viejo, Corazon de Jesus
Chapel—Hato Viejo, San Antonio
Chapel—Jaguas, Santa Clara
Chapel—Pesa, San Ignacio
Chapel—Cialitos-Cruces, Corazon de Maria
Chapel—Toro Negro, N.S.
Chapel—Bo. Marias, Maternidad de la Virgen

2—N.S. MADRE DEL REDENTOR (1988) [JC] Rev. Wiktor Tarnawski.
Res.: P.O. Box 1181, 00638. Tel: 787-871-2404.
Catechesis/Religious Program—
Chapel—Yunes, San Jose
Chapel—Fronton (Sabana), Perpetuo Socorro
Chapel—Cordillera 5, N.S. La Providencia
Chapel—Cordillera 7, Sagrada Familia

COROZAL, HOLY FAMILY (1804) [JC] Revs. Ovidio Perez; Delfin Rodriguez.
Res.: P.O. Box 474, 00783. Tel: 787-859-2595; Fax: 787-859-5018.
School—(Grades PreK-12) Tel: 787-859-2420; Fax: 787-859-4115. Email: csfcorbiblio@yahoo.com. Sr. Maria Salvador, Prin. Sisters of St. Joseph 9; Lay Teachers 53; Students 1,187.
Catechesis/Religious Program—Students 764.
Chapel—Guarico Palmarejo I, San Judas Tadeo
Chapel—Palmarejo II, San Vicente
Chapel—Palmarejo II, San Francisco de Asis
Chapel—Dos Bocas II, Santa Teresita
Chapel—Cibuco, N.S. del Carmen
Chapel—Abras, San Jose
Chapel—Urb. Sylvia, Perpetuo Socorro

COROZAL-PADILLA, OUR LADY OF THE SEVEN SORROWS (1984) Rev. Miguel Rivera.
Res.: P.O. Box 740, 00783-0740. Tel: 787-859-1900. Email: 7dolores@catholicnet.zzn.co.
Catechesis/Religious Program—Students 480.
Chapel—Padilla Hermita, San Rafael
Chapel—Padilla Hormiga, San Martin
Chapel—Cieneguita (V.A.), N.S. del Perpetuo Socorro

COROZAL-PALMARITO, LA MILAGROSA Revs. Rafael J. Gonzalez, C.R.L.; Felix A. Reyes, C.R.L., Vicar.
Res.: HC-03, Box 13976, 00783-9803. Tel: 787-859-5306. Email: crl-milagrosa@hotmail.com.
Catechesis/Religious Program—Students 570.
Convent—P.O. Box 80267, Bo. Palmarito, Corozal, 00783-8267. Tel: 787-859-5181. San Francisco (Secular Institute) 1.
Chapel—Maguelles, Cristo Rey
Chapel—Mana, N.S. de Fatima
Chapel—Radio Oro, Nuestra Senora del Carmen

COROZAL-PALOS BLANCOS, CHRIST THE KING (1968) [JC] Rev. Edison Navarro, C.R.L.
Res.: P.O. Box 1091, 00783-1091. Tel: 787-859-7313.
Catechesis/Religious Program—Students 391.
Chapel—Cuchillas, N.S. del Perpetuo Socorro
Chapel—Negros, N.S. del Rosario
Chapel—Palos Blancos, Santa Teresita
Chapel—Palos Blancos, San Antonio

FLORIDA, OUR LADY OF MERCY (1887) [JC] Rev. Cesar E. Santos.
Res.: P.O. Box 1184, 00650. Tel: 787-822-2670; Fax: 787-822-2670.

Catechesis/Religious Program—Tel: 787-822-2045.
Chapel—Monte Bello, N.S. del Carmen
Chapel—Pajonal - Santa Rosa de Lima
Chapel—La Fuente - San Pablo

HATILLO

1—OUR LADY OF GUADALUPE (1961) [JC] Revs. Rene A. Colon; Marcos A. Conelly, Vicar; Luis R. Banchs, S.E.M.V., Vicar; Victor R. Borrero, S.E.M.V., Vicar; Luis A. Colon, S.E.M.V.; Luis A. Mendez, S.E.M.V.; Sr. Teresa Maria V. de la Eucaristia.
Res.: Carr. Ins. 129, Arecibo to Lares, P.O. Box 1131, 00613. Tel: 787-898-8035. Email: guadalupehatillo@hotmail.com.
Catechesis/Religious Program—Students 225.
Chapel—Pajuil, Santa Rosa de Lima
Chapel—Buena Vista, Inmaculada Concepcion
Chapel—Sector Naranjito, San Jose

2—OUR LADY OF MT. CARMEL (1830) [JC] Revs. Fernando Morell, Pastor; Nicolas De la Cruz, C.R.L.
Res.: P.O. Box 2, 00659. Tel: 809-898-5300.
School—(Grades PreK-12) Tel: 787-898-2800; 787-898-5235; Fax: 787-820-5258. Email: mmielescnsc@yahoo.com. Rev. Fernando Morell, Dir.; Mr. Frederico Lopez, Prin. (High School). Sisters 3; Lay Teachers 54; Students 743.
Catechesis/Religious Program—Tel: 787-898-3302. Students 294.
Chapel—Carrizales, Sagrado Corazon
Chapel—Corcovados, Immaculada Concepcion
Chapel—Capaez, N.S. Perpetuo Socorro
Chapel—Carrizales, San Jose
Chapel—Santa Rosa, Santa Rosa de Lima
Chapel—Lechuga: San Pio X
Chapel—Palma Gordo: Sagrada Familia

3—PERPETUAL HELP (1961) [JC] Rev. Antonio Portalatin.
Res.: Ste. 393, P.O. Box 69001, 00659. Tel: 787-898-7771.
Catechesis/Religious Program—Tel: 787-820-2819. Students 294.
Chapel—Aibonito, Cristo Rey
Chapel—Berrocal, Sagrado Corazon de Jesus
Chapel—Sonadora, La Milagrosa
Chapel—Mariposa, N.S. del Carmen
Chapel—Cantera, Ntra. Sra. de la Providencia

ISABELA

1—ST. ANTHONY (1835) [JC] Revs. Manuel E. Salgado, O.SS.T., Admin.; Wilfredo Echevarria, O.SS.T., Vicar.
Res.: #81 Corchado St., Box 525, 00662. Tel: 787-872-0126; Fax: 787-872-4393.
School—(Grades K-12)Email: csaisabela@yahoo.com. Sr. Ida Negrón, O.P., Prin. Sisters of St. Dominic 3; Lay Teachers 36; Students 526.
Catechesis/Religious Program—Students 716.
Chapel—Medina, Sma. Trinidad
Chapel—Curva, Santa Rosa de Lima
Chapel—Cotto, San Martin de Porres
Chapel—Arenales Bajo, N.S. La Monserrate
Chapel—Vendrel, N.S. La Providencia
Chapel—Jobos, Buen Pastor
Chapel—Guayabos, Espiritu Santo
Chapel—Arenales A., El Salvador
Chapel—Arenales Alto, Sagrado Corazon, Tel: 787-872-0015. Sisters of Trinity (Valencia) 4.
Chapel—Hogar Infantil/Jesus Nazareno, Isabella Sisters of Trinity (Valencia) 2.

2—OUR LADY OF MOUNT CARMEL (1983) [JC] Rev. German LLona, O.SS.T.
Res.: Box 1555, 00662. Tel: 787-872-5550.
Catechesis/Religious Program—Students 200.
Chapel—Poncito, Santos Inocentes
Chapel—Planas, San Juan Bautista
Chapel—La Tuna, San Juan de Mata
Chapel—Galateo Bajo, La Milagrosa

LARES

1—ST. JOSEPH (1827) [JC] Revs. Carlos L. Rodriguez, C.P.; Luis A. Lopez, C.P.; Jesus Etxeandia, C.P.
Res.: P.O. Box 103, 00669-0103. Tel: 787-897-2067.
School—(Grades PreK-9) Tel: 787-897-2640; Fax: 787-897-2640. Maritza Lopez Pol, Prin. Hermanas Pasionistas 3; Lay Teachers 17; Students 136.
Catechesis/Religious Program—Tel: 787-897-2717. Students 421.
Chapel—Piletas II, San Carlos
Chapel—Sebruguillo, La Resurreccion
Chapel—Piletas Arece, La Milagrosa
Chapel—Piletas, Saint Maria Goretti
Chapel—Tabonuco, La Providencia Hermanas Josefinas de Mexico 4.

2—ST. JUDAS TADEOS (1986) [JC] Rev. David Rivas.
Res.: P.O. Box 1109, 00669. Tel: 809-897-3540. Email: pdavidrivasrivera@parroquia.org.
Catechesis/Religious Program—Students 210.
Chapel—Palmar Llano, Perpetuo Socorro
Chapel—Vega de los Acevedo, La Dolorosa
Chapel—Buenos Aires, Sgda. Familia de Nazaret
Chapel—Matilde, San Antonio

MANATI

1—LA CANDELARIA (1738) [JC] Revs. Emilio Tovar, C.M.; Ignacio Alonso.
Res.: Calle Padial #2, 00674. Tel: 787-854-2013. Email: manaticm@atenas.com.
School—(Grades PreK-12) Tel: 787-854-2079; Fax: 787-854-2202. Email: cinmacul@yahoo.com. Sr. Rosalina Santiago, Prin. Sisters of Charity 3; Lay Teachers 50; Students 945.
Catechesis/Religious Program—Tel: 787-854-4021. Students 270.
Convent—Monastery Mother of God Sisters 33.
Chapel—Pugnado, N.S. del Perpetuo Socorro
Chapel—Villa Amalia, La Milagrosa
Chapel—Cortes, Sagrado Corazon
Chapel—Polvorin, La Monserrate
Chapel—Ceiba, Espiritu Santo

2—NUESTRA SENORA DEL MAR (1978) [JC] Rev. Elmon Hernandez Fana.
Res.: Apdo. 1183, 00674. Tel: 787-854-5388.
Catechesis/Religious Program—Tel: 787-854-9252.
Chapel—Tierras Nuevas, Santa Rosa de Lima
Chapel—Sector Cantito, La Milagrosa
Chapel—Sector Laguna, Nuestra Senora de Lourdes

3—OUR SAVIOR Rev. Melquiades Rojas.
Res.: P.O. Box 465, 00674. Tel: 787-884-3664. Email: parroquia.elsalvador@yahoo.com.
School—Colegio Marista, (Grades K-12), P.O. Box 462, 00764. Tel: 787-854-1075; 787-854-2485; Fax: 787-854-6733. Email: maristamanote@yahoo.com. Bro. Carlos Velez, Dir.; Margarita Santiago, Prin. Marist Brothers 3; Lay Teachers 35; Students 520.
Catechesis/Religious Program—
Chapel—San Jose, San Jose
Chapel—Urb. Atenas - Ntra. Sra. de la Salud
Chapel—Guayaney, San Martin de Porres

4—SAGRADA FAMILIA (1972) [JC] Revs. Ricardo Fernandez, C.M.; Bernardo Hernandez, C.M.
Res.: P.O. Box 704, 00674. Tel: 787-854-2858.
Catechesis/Religious Program—Students 182.
Chapel—Parcelas Marquez, San Judas Tadeo
Chapel—Palo Alto, N.S. La Monserrate
Chapel—Polvorin, La Milagrosa

MOROVIS

1—NUESTRA SENORA DEL CARMEN (1820) [JC] Revs. Jesus Monreal, O.Carm.; Enrique Oria, O.Carm.; Jose Oliveras; Tomas Ciscar, O.Carm.
Res.: Box 428, 00687. Tel: 787-862-2620.
Catechesis/Religious Program—Students 1,623.
Chapel—San Lorenzo, N.S. del Rosario
Chapel—Perchas, N.S. del Carmen
Chapel—Pastos, N.S. del Carmen
Chapel—Rio Grande, La Milagrosa
Chapel—Morovis Sur, San Jose
Chapel—Unibon, San Miguel
Chapel—Vaga III, La Milagrosa
Chapel—MPatron I, Sagrada Familia
Chapel—Cuchillas, Segrado Corazon
Chapel—Morovis Sur, Inmaculada Concepcion

2—ST. PAUL APOSTLE (1985) [JC] Rev. Tomas Santos, Admin.
Res.: P.O. Box 537, 00687. Tel: 787-862-3445.
Catechesis/Religious Program—
Chapel—Franquez, Nino de Praga
Chapel—Franquez Carretera, La Providencia
Chapel—Torrecillas, Senor de los Milagros

OROCOVIS

1—OUR LADY OF FATIMA (1975) [JC] Revs. Osualdo Perez, C.S.Sp.; Tosello Giangiacomo, C.S.Sp.; Bro. Irving Oquendo Romero, C.S.Sp.
Res.: Box 2118, 00720. Tel: 787-867-3277. Email: fatimaorocovis@hotmail.com.
Catechesis/Religious Program—Students 272.
Chapel—Bermejales, Cristo de la Salud
Chapel—Bauta, N.S. de los Dolores
Chapel—Damian Arriba, N.S. del Perpetuo Socorro
Chapel—Pellejas I, Espiritu Santo
Chapel—Miraflores, San Martin

2—SAN JUAN BAUTISTA (1838) [JC] Revs. Adan Marrero; Demetrio Coello, S.D.B.; Julian San Nicasio, S.D.B.; Juan Martinez, S.D.B.; P. Jorge R. Burgos, S.D.B.
Res.: P.O. Box 2114, 00720. Tel: 787-867-2210; Fax: 787-867-5675. Email: sdboro@coqui.net.
School—(Grades PreK-9) Tel: 787-867-2295; Fax: 787-867-6269. Email: margfont28@yahoo.com. Sor Margarita Fontan, Prin. Salesian Sisters 3; Lay Teachers 19; Students 278.
Catechesis/Religious Program—
Chapel—Sabana, Angeles Custodios
Chapel—Botijas I, Cristo Resucitado
Chapel—Botijas II, Santa Clara
Chapel—El Puente, San Pablo
Chapel—Mata de Cana, Sagrado Corazon
Chapel—Damian Arriba, Espiritu Santo
Chapel—Montebello, N.S. del Carmen
Chapel—Guadalupe, N.S. La Guadalupe
Chapel—Gato Bajura, N.S. La Providencia
Chapel—Gato, San Judas Tadeo

QUEBRADILLAS

1—SACRED HEART (1977) [JC] Rev. Carmelo Urarte.
Res.: Box 1569, 00678. Tel: 787-895-3033; Fax: 787-895-3033.
Catechesis/Religious Program—Students 549.
Chapel—San Antonio, San Miguel
Chapel—Yeguada, N.S. del Perpetuo Socorro
Chapel—El Verde, Madre Dolorosa

2—SAN RAPHAEL (1828) [JC] Rev. Jose A. Acaba.
Res.: Box 57, 00678. Tel: 787-895-3463.
School—(Grades K-9) Tel: 809-895-2280; Fax: 787-895-2280. Email: csrque@q.mail.com. Mrs. Carmen Diaz, Prin. Lay Teachers 22; Students 282.
Catechesis/Religious Program—Students 669.
Chapel—San Jose, San Jose
Chapel—Quebrada, N.S. del Carmen
Chapel—Chivos, Santa Cruz
Chapel—Cacao, La Milagrosa
Chapel—Parcelas San Antonio, N.S. La Monserrate
Chapel—San Antonio, San Antonio
Chapel—Charcas, N.S. del Perpetuo Socorro
Chapel—Las Talas, La Guadalupe

UTUADO

1—NUESTRA SENORA DEL MONTE CARMELO (1981) [JC] Rev. Rafael Rodriguez, Admin.
Res.: P.O. Box 299, Caonillas-Utuado, 00641. Tel: 787-894-7340. Email: parrmontecarmelo@yahoo.com.
Catechesis/Religious Program—Students 123.
Chapel—Mameyes, San Antonio
Chapel—Tetuan III, Sagrado Corazon
Chapel—Tetuan I, Cristo Salvador
Chapel—Don Alonso, La Milagrosa

2—OUR LADY OF ANGELS (1967) [JC] Rev. Miguel S. Bido.
Res.: Box 98, Angeles, 00611. Tel: 809-894-3964.
Catechesis/Religious Program—Students 94.
Chapel—Corcho, San Jose
Chapel—Santa Isabela, N.S. La Monserrate
Chapel—Las Vegas, Sagrada Familia

3—OUR LADY OF SORROWS (1983) [JC] Rev. Elvin A. Irizarry.
Res.: CMB-73, P.O. Box 2525, 00641-2525. Tel: 787-894-7144.
Catechesis/Religious Program—Students 177.
Chapel—Roncador, San Martin de Porres
Chapel—Cayuco, Cristo Rey
Chapel—Jacanas, N.S. la Monserrate

4—SAN MIQUEL (1746) [JC] Revs. Edward Maldonado, O.F.M.Cap.; Carlos Reyes, O.F.M.Cap.; Bro. Jose F. Irizarry, O.F.M.Cap.
Res.: 8 Barcelo St., P.O. Box 10, 00641-0010. Tel: 787-894-2696; 787-894-3108; Fax: 787-894-3812. Email: parroquiasanmiguel@utuadoweb.com.
Catechesis/Religious Program—Students 315.
Chapel—Puente Blanco, San Fidel
Chapel—Arenas, San Martin
Chapel—Sabana Grande, N.S. del Perpetuo Socorro
Chapel—Rio Abajo - San Jose

5—SAN PEDRO Y SAN PABLO (1988) [JC] Rev. Rafael Nuno.
Res.: Box 679, 00641. Tel: 787-894-0696.
Catechesis/Religious Program—Students 139.
Chapel—Las Palmas, San Francisco
Chapel—Vivi Arriba, Inmaculada Concepcion
Chapel—La Pica, La Milagrosa
Chapel—Consejo, San Jose
Chapel—Vivi Abajo, Nuestra Senora de la Divina Providencia

VEGA-ALTA

1—IMMACULATE CONCEPTION OF BLESSED VIRGIN MARY (1805) Revs. Roberto Vega; Bertulfo Acevedo (Retired).
Res.: P.O. Box 775, 00692. Tel: 787-883-4875.
Catechetical Center—Calle Colon 17, 00692. Students 388.
Chapel—Maricao IV, Sagrado Corazon
Chapel—Bajura II, San Vicente
Chapel—Bajura I, Santa Ana
Chapel—Candelaria, Inmaculado Corazon de Maria
Chapel—Maricao II, N.S. La Guadalupe

2—PERPETUO SOCORRO (1975) [JC] Rev. Luis A. Vazquez.
Res.: Sabana Branch, Box 9018, Vega-Baja, 00694-9018. Tel: 787-883-5776; Fax: 787-270-3103.
Catechesis/Religious Program—Students 197.
Chapel—Sabana (V.B.), San Vicente
Chapel—Cerro Gordo, N.S. del Carmen

3—SANTA ANA (1967) Rev. Angel Diaz Caceres.
Res.: Urb. Santa Ana, Apartado 2105, Calle 3H9, 00692. Tel: 787-883-2502. Email: diazcaceres@prw.net.
Catechesis/Religious Program—Students 200.
Chapel—Espinosa, N.S. del Carmen

VEGA-BAJA

1—THE BLESSED TRINITY (1971) Rev. Angel M. Santos.
Res.: P.O. Box 58, Almirante Sur Station, 00694-0058. Tel: 809-858-8743.
Catechesis/Religious Program—
Chapel—Almirante Norte, Sagrada Familia
Chapel—Patron II, N.S. La Providencia

2—HOLY ROSARY (1794) [JC] Revs. Jorge Paredes; Marc A. Santiago.
Res.: P.O. Box 1388, 00694. Tel: 787-858-2969.
School—(Grades K-12) Tel: 787-858-2538; 787-858-4111; Fax: 787-858-6648. Email: melendez@colros.org. Lay Teachers 39; Students 542. Principals:, Nilda Fontan, Elementary; Miguelina Melendez, High School.
Catechesis/Religious Program—Students 236.
Chapel—Arenales, San Jose
Chapel—Almirante, N.S. de Fatima

3—N.S. DE LA PROVIDENCIA (1970) [JC] Rev. Carlos E. Granados, Admin.
Res.: Box 4056, Vega Baja, 00694-4056. Tel: 809-858-2171; Fax: 809-858-2171.
Catechesis/Religious Program—Students 372.
Chapel—Brisas de Tortuguero, San Jose
Chapel—Vega Baja Lakes, San Pedro

4—OUR LADY OF CARMEN-PLAYA (1976) [JC] Rev. Jesus A. Rodriguez, Admin.
Res.: Apdo. 4095, 00694-4095. Tel: 787-855-5226; Fax: 787-855-5115.
Catechesis/Religious Program—
Chapel—Naranjos, San Judas Tadeo
Chapel—San Demetrio, Divino Nino Jesus

5—OUR LADY OF LOURDES (1984) [JC] Rev. Luis J. Rivera.
Res.: P.O. Box 4414, 00694-4414. Tel: 787-855-4942; Fax: 787-807-9249.
Catechesis/Religious Program—Students 270.
Convent—Tel: 787-855-0341. Hermanas Terciarias Capuchinas 3.
Chapel—Rio Abajo, Santa Rosa de Lima
Chapel—Quebrada Arenas, San Juan Bautista
Chapel—Las Granjas, S. Francisco de Asis

6—OUR LADY OF MT. CARMEL (1968) [JC] Rev. Pedro Hernandez.
Camelia St. #48-A, Bo. Carmelita, Vega Alta, 00692.
Res.: P.O. Box 1417, 00694-1417. Tel: 787-855-0159; Fax: 787-855-0159.
Catechesis/Religious Program—Students 275.
Chapel—Pueblo Nuevo, La Milagrosa
Chapel—Sabana Hoyos, San Judas
Chapel—Santa Rosa, La Guadalupe

7—PARROQUIA DE SAN MARTIN DE PORRES (1967) [JC] Revs. Jose Colon, Admin.; Martin Sadaba.
Res.: P.O. Box 254, Vega Baja, 00694. Tel: 787-858-1485; Fax: 787-858-1485.
Catechesis/Religious Program—Tel: 787-858-8651. Students 139.
Chapel—Panaini, Sagrado Corazon
Chapel—Pugnado Adentro, San Jose
Chapel—Villa Colombo, St. Anthony

On Duty Outside the Diocese:
Revs.—
Davila, Andres, Arecibo, P.R.
Guerrero, Jose Ma., Spain
Irizarry, Alan M., Favetteville, NC
Lopez, Carlos A., Boston, MA
Lopez, Jose M., Quebradillas, P.R.
Lopez, Juan J., Sunrise, FL
Munoz, Jesus M., Military Service
Santana, Edward, J.C.L., Homestead, FL

Retired:
Revs.—
Acevedo, Bertulfo, Vega Alta, P.R.
Caraballo, Antonio, Spain
Estensoro, Jose, Hogar Sta. Teresa Jornet, San Juan, PR
Fernandez Minguez, Serapio, Spain
Garcia, Jose L., Sevilla, Spain
Hernandez, Jimmy, Quebradillas, Puerto Rico
Jimenez, Francisco, Hogar Sta. Teresade Jesus Jornet, San Juan
Jimenez, Victorino, Spain
Morales, Salomon J.
Perez, Leon, Zaragoza, Spain
Soberal, Jose D., V.G., Lares, P.R.

INSTITUTIONS LOCATED IN THE DIOCESE

[A] EDUCATIONAL

ARECIBO. *Pontificia Universidad Catholica de Puerto Rico, Recinto de Arecibo*, P.O. Box 144045, 00614-4045. Tel: 787-881-1212; Fax: 787-881-0777. Web: www.pucpr.edu. Rev. Ivan Martinez Adorno, Chap.; Mrs. Nora Garcia de Lopez, Dir. Priests 3; Lay Teachers 71; Students 708.

Seminario de Jesus Maestro, P.O. Box 2164, 00613. Tel: 787-878-1528; Fax: 787-880-2661. Email: arecibo@diocesisdearecibo.org. Rev. Victor Sanchez Velez, Dir. Total Enrollment 15.

[B] HOMES FOR AGED AND ORPHANS

ARECIBO. *Hogar de Ancianos San Vicente de Paul*, P.O. Box 4196, Vega Baja, 00694. Bo. Almirante Sur-Carr 645 Km. 6.6, Vega Baja, 00693. Tel: 787-855-0487; Fax: 787-858-3103. Email: svpaulpr@gmail.com. Nelson De Leon, Dir. Tel: 787-862-5257; Cell: 787-318-6695. Guests 50.

Hogar Sta. Maria Eufrasia, P.O. Box 1909, 00613. Fax: 787-880-2632. Carr. Est. 651-10, Sector Junco, 00612. Tel: 787-878-5166. Email: eufrasia86@gmail.com. Web: www.hogareufrasia.org. House for pregnant teens. Good Shepherd Sisters 4; Unwed Mothers 9; Babies 5.

La Milagrosa Home for Abused Girls, Ave. Francisco Jimenez Gonzalez #987, 00612-3877. Tel: 787-878-6231; 787-878-0341; Fax: 787-817-7822. Email: hogarcolegiolamilagrosa@yahoo.com. Sisters of Charity 5; Girls 16.

San Rafael Geriatric Center, #49 Calle Cervantes, 00612. Tel: 787-878-3813; Fax: 787-879-4592. Sisters of Charity 6; Guests 30.

Centro Geriatrico San Rafael, Calle Cervantes #49, 00612. Tel: 787-878-3813; Fax: 787-879-4592. Email: nydia.montijo@hotmail.com. Mrs. Nydia G. Montijo Soto, Exec. Dir.

ISABELA. *Hogar Infantil Jesus Nazareno, Inc.*, P.O. Box 1671, 00662. Tel: 787-872-0015; Fax: 787-872-0015. Email: hogarinfantiljesusnazareno@gmail.com. Residential Care of Children 23.

LARES. *Hogar Envejecientes Irma Fe Pol Mendez, Inc.*, P.O. Box 1185, 00669. Tel: 787-897-6090; Fax: 787-897-0612. Charity Sisters of St. Joseph (Mexico) 4; Guests 25.

VEGA-ALTA. *Centro Actividades Multiples/Conferencia San Vicente de Paul*, P.O. Box 1613, 00692. Tel: 787-270-4517; Fax: 787-883-2370. Email: centrojan@coqui.net. Orlando Garcia, Dir. Tel: 787-270-4517. Guests 155.

Centro Geriatrico Juan de los Olivos, P.O. Box 1613, 00692. Tel: 787-883-2370; Fax: 787-883-2370.

[C] MISCELLANEOUS

ARECIBO. *Hogar Infantil Santa Teresita del Nino Jesus, Inc.*, P.O. Box 140057, 00614-0057. Tel: 787-817-6651; 787-650-7731; Fax: 787-817-6651. Email: hogarsantateresita@hotmail.com. Mrs. Melva Arbelo Mangual, Dir.; Mrs. Maria del Carmen Alonso, Admin. Hermanas Dominicas de la Presentacion 3; Children 15.

Oficina para la Promocion y el Desarrollo Humano, Inc., P.O. Box 353, 00613. Tel: 787-817-6951; 787-817-6954; 787-817-6955; Fax: 787-817-7597. Email: opdhinc@gmail.com.

UTUADO. *Fondita Santa Marta*, #1 Calle Betances, P.O. Box 10, 00641. Tel: 787-814-0735; Fax: 787-814-0735. Bro. Jose F. Irizarry, O.F.M.Cap., Pres. Guests 52.

RELIGIOUS INSTITUTES OF MEN REPRESENTED IN THE DIOCESE

For further details refer to the corresponding bracketed number in the Religious Institutes of Men or Women section.

[]—*Canonigos Regulares Lateranenses de San Agustin* (Bronx, NY)—C.R.L.
[0470]—*Capuchin Friars* (Province of Pittsburgh)—O.F.M.Cap.
[0270]—*Carmelite Fathers and Brothers* (Province de Aragon, Valencia, Espana)—O.Carm.
[]—*Comunidad Misionera de Villaregia*—C.M.V.
[1330]—*Congregation of the Mission* (Vice-Province of Puerto Rico)—C.M.
[1000]—*Congregation of the Passion* (Bilbao, Spain)—C.P.
[]—*Esclavos de la Eucaristia y Maria Virgen*—E.E.M.V.
[0650]—*Holy Ghost Fathers* (Eastern Province)—C.S.Sp.
[0770]—*Marist Brothers*—F.M.S.
[]—*Misioneros Natividad de Maria* (Mexico)—M.N.M.
[1310]—*Order of the Holy Trinity* (Viscaya, Spain Province)—O.SS.T.
[1190]—*Salesians of Don Bosco* (Province of Madrid)—S.D.B.

RELIGIOUS INSTITUTES OF WOMEN REPRESENTED IN THE DIOCESE

[]—*Comunidad Misionera de Villaregia*—C.M.V.
[]—*Congregation of Sisters of Passion* (Mexico)
[]—*Convento Madre de Dios, Inc.*
[0760]—*Daughters of Charity of St. Vincent de Paul*—H.C.
[]—*Dominican Sisters of Amityville, N.Y.*
[1100]—*Dominican Sisters of Charity of the Presentation of the Blessed Virgin*—O.P.
[]—*Dominican Sisters of Fatima* (Yauco PR)
[]—*Dominicas Divina Misericordia* (Lares, Puerto Rico)
[]—*Hermanas de San Jose de Corozal* (Corozal)
[]—*Hermanas del Buen Pastor*
[]—*Hermanas Esclaves del Santisimo y la Inmaculada*
[]—*Hermanas Josefinas* (Mexico)
[]—*Hnas. Apostolado Corzon de Jesus* (Madrid)—R.A.
[]—*Hnas. de Nazaret* (El Salvador)
[]—*Instituto Sma. Trinidad* (Valencia, Spain)
[]—*Misioneras de la Sagrada Familia* (Instituto Secular)
[]—*Salesian Sisters* (Roma)
[]—*San Francisco* (Instituto Secular)
[]—*Siervas de Maria* (Roma)
[0990]—*Sisters of Divine Providence* (Pittsburgh)—C.D.P.
[]—*Terciarias Capuchina Sgda. Familia* (Roma)

NECROLOGY

(No Deaths)

An asterisk (*) denotes an organization that has established tax-exempt status directly with the IRS and is not covered by the USCCB Group Ruling.

Diocese of Caguas, Puerto Rico

(Dioecesis Caguana)

Most Reverend

RUBEN ANTONIO GONZALEZ MEDINA, C.M.F.

Bishop of Caguas; ordained February 9, 1975; appointed Bishop of Caguas December 12, 2000; consecrated February 4, 2001.

Most Reverend

ENRIQUE HERNANDEZ RIVERA, D.D.

Bishop Emeritus of Caguas; ordained June 8, 1968; appointed Titular Bishop of Vanalla, North Africa and Auxiliary Bishop of San Juan June 11, 1979; consecrated August 17, 1979; appointed Bishop of Caguas February 13, 1981; officially installed March 8, 1981; retired July 28, 1998. *Res.: Bishop's House, HC 04 Box 44015, Caguas, PR 00727.* Tel: 787-747-5885; 787-747-5787; Fax: 787-747-5616; 787-747-5767.

ESTABLISHED NOVEMBER 1964.

Square Miles 737.

Comprises east and southeast portion of Puerto Rico.

Patroness of the Diocese: Maria, Madre de la Iglesia - November 12, 1988.

Web: www.home.coqui.net/obicag

Email: obicag@coqui.net

STATISTICAL OVERVIEW

Personnel	
Bishop	1
Retired Bishops	1
Priests: Diocesan Active in Diocese	44
Priests: Diocesan Active Outside Diocese	3
Priests: Diocesan in Foreign Missions	1
Number of Diocesan Priests	48
Religious Priests in Diocese	34
Total Priests in Diocese	82
Ordinations:	
Transitional Deacons	1
Permanent Deacons in Diocese	102
Total Sisters	95
Parishes	
Parishes	34
With Resident Pastor:	
Resident Diocesan Priests	27
Resident Religious Priests	7
Welfare	
Specialized Homes	2
Total Assisted	362
Educational	
Seminaries, Diocesan	2
High Schools, Diocesan and Parish	2
High Schools, Private	7
Elementary Schools, Diocesan and Parish	2
Elementary Schools, Private	7
Vital Statistics	
Receptions into the Church:	
Infant Baptism Totals	3,326
Minor Baptism Totals	107
Adult Baptism Totals	359
First Communions	3,398
Confirmations	4,215
Marriages:	
Catholic	422
Interfaith	16
Total Marriages	438
Deaths	2,219
Total Catholic Population	350,000
Total Population	503,000

Former Bishops—Most Revs. RAFAEL GROVAS, D.D., S.T.D., Ph.D., J.C.L., ord. April 7, 1928; appt. Jan. 19, 1965; cons. March 28, 1965; retired Feb. 13, 1981; died Sept. 9, 1991; ENRIQUE HERNANDEZ RIVERA, D.D. (Retired), ord. June 8, 1968; cons. Aug. 17, 1979; appt. Feb. 13, 1981; retired July 28, 1998.

Vicar General—Rev. ANTONIO CARTAGENA.

Sec. Chancellor—Rev. ANGEL MOLINA.

Sec. Vice Chancellor—VACANT.

Diocesan Consultors—Revs. HIPÓLITO TORRES; AURELIO ADAN; ANTONIO CARTAGENA; OSCAR RIVERA; CAMPO E. ARIZA; ISRAEL BERRIOS.

Diocesan Tribunal of Caguas—Rev. FELIX NUNEZ, Judicial Vicar; Sr. CARMEN GONZALEZ, C.D.P., J.C.L., Dir.; Revs. MIGUEL A. MERCED; ORLANDO DE JESUS, Mailing Address: P.O. Box 9779, Caguas, 00726. Tel: 787-286-8595; Fax: 787-286-8620.

Board of Diocesan Government—Rev. FELIX OLIVERAS VILLANUEVA.

Priests Senate—Revs. ANTONIO CARTAGENA; FRANCISCO HERNANDEZ; FELICIANO RODRIQUEZ; ANGEL MOLINA; OSCAR RIVERA; MELVIN MONTANEZ; FELIX NUNEZ; ISRAEL BERRIOS; MIGUEL CLAUDIO; JORGE D. CARDONA; YAMIL A. VELAZQUEZ; RAUL MORALES; JUAN LUIS NEGRON; ANGEL COLON; GIOVANNI RUIZ; LUIS RIVERA.

Diocesan Offices and Directors

Economic Administrator—Rev. FELIX OLIVERAS VILLANUEVA; Mr. ABDEL ALVAREZ GONZALEZ; Deacon JOSE RODRIGUEZ, Mailing Address: HC 04, P.O. Box 44015, Caguas, 00727. Tel: 787-747-5885; 787-747-5787, Ext. 227.

Planning Vicar—VACANT, Mailing Address: Diocesis de Caguas, HC 04, P.O. Box 44015, Caguas, 00727. Tel: 787-747-5885; 787-747-5787.

Movimientos y Organizaciones Diocesanas—

Cursillos de Cristiandad—FELIPE SANCHEZ RAMOS. Tel: 787-734-7068.

Legion de Maria—ANTONIO RODRIGUEZ.

Renovacion Carismatica—ADELAIDA CRUZ.

Juan XXIII—FLORENCIO MARTINEZ. Tel: 787-747-3748.

Apostolado de la Cruz—ELVIN PENA. Tel: 787-715-1768.

Caballeros de Colon—JOSE SOTO CARMONA. Tel: 787-746-4747.

Equipos Ntra. Sra.—GUILLERMO TORRES; MILAGROS ORTIZ.

Equipo Ntra. Sra.—LUIS Y AMPARO URBINA. Tel: 787-739-8581.

Hijas Catolicas—IRMA RUIZ DE MERCED.

Hnos. Cheos—ESTEBAN RIVERA. Tel: 787-850-5224.

Misioneros Padre Ntro.—RAMON L. RAMOS.

Schoenstatt—JOSE N. BRACERO. Tel: 787-722-3941.

Vicentinos—CARMENCITA COLON. Tel: 787-747-6546.

Talleres de Oracion y Vida—PETRONILA RUIZ. Tel: 787-745-4123.

Sociedad del Santo Nombre—VICTOR COTTO.

La Piedra que Cristo edifico en mi—JAVIER LEBRON.

Camino Neo Catecumenal—DOMINGO VEGA.

CASSE—Sr. CARMEN D. ROSADO. Tel: 787-286-3333.

Comisiones Diocesanas—

Pastoral de Multitudes—MARINY VAZQUEZ. Tel: 787-738-1941.

Pastoral Familiar—Deacon VICTOR M. CRUZ. Tel: 787-733-3592.

Pastoral Preadolescentes—*Hnas. Salesianas.* Tel: 787-744-0858.

Pastoral Social—Rev. FELICIANO RODRIQUEZ. Tel: 787-745-8183.

Espiritualidad Comunitaria—HERMINIA FONSECA. Tel: 787-746-2669.

Misiones—Deacon JOSE BERRIOS. Tel: 787-869-3042.

Pastoral Penitenciaria—D. ANIBAL GONZALEZ. Tel: 787-263-0976.

Pastoral Nec. Especiales—VACANT.

Formacion Diac. Permanentes—Rev. FRANCISCO HERNANDEZ.

Catholic Youth—Rev. MIGUEL CLAUDIO, Mailing Address: Diocesis de Caguas, HC 04, P.O. Box 44015, Caguas, 00727. Tel: 787-744-6738, Ext. 229.

Catholic Social Action—VACANT, Mailing Address: Diocesis de Caguas, HC 04, P.O. Box 44015, Caguas, 00727. Tel: 787-747-5885; 787-747-5787.

Catholic School Consultors—MARIA MERCEDES AGOSTO, Mailing Address: P.O. Box 8699, Caguas, 00726. Tel: 787-743-1171.

Catechetical Vicar—Sr. CLETA M. LOPEZ.

Building Commission—VACANT, Mailing Address: Diocesis de Caguas, HC 04, P.O. Box 44015, Caguas, 00727. Tel: 787-747-5885; 787-747-5787.

Liturgical Consultor—Rev. MELVIN MONTANEZ, Mailing Address: Diocesis de Caguas, HC 04, P.O. Box 44015, Caguas, 00727. Tel: 787-747-5885, Ext. 222.

Communication Office—MARINY VAZQUEZ, Mailing Address: Diocesis de Caguas, HC 04, P.O. Box 44015, Caguas, 00727. Tel: 787-747-5885.

Red de Esperanzay Solidaridad (REDES)—MAGALY MILLAN; Sr. MARIA JESUS MOMPO, Mailing Address: Diocesis de Caguas, HC 04, P.O. Box 44015, Caguas, 00727. Tel: 787-747-5767.

Vincentian Society—CARMENCITA COLON, Mailing Address: Diocesis de Caguas, HC 04, P.O. Box 44015, Caguas, 00727.

Hospitals—Rev. ENCARNACIÓN NIEVES, Mailing Address: Diocesis de Caguas, HC 04, P.O. Box 44015, Caguas, 00727.

Legion of Mary—Mr. ISABELO HUERTAS, Mailing

Address: Diocesis de Caguas, HC 04, P.O. Box 44015, Caguas, 00727.

Master of Ceremonies—Rev. MELVIN MONTANEZ, Mailing Address: Diocesis de Caguas, HC 04, P.O. Box 44015, Caguas, 00727. Tel: 809-747-5885.

Pastoral Vicar—Rev. FELICIANO RODRIGUEZ, Mailing Address: Diocesis de Caguas, HC 04, P.O. Box 44015, Caguas, 00727. Tel: 787-286-0075, Ext. 245.

Schools—Mailing Address: P.O. Box 8699, Caguas, 00726. Tel: 787-743-1171.

School Superintendent—MARIA MERCEDES AGOSTO.

Vocations—Revs. JOSE A. DE LEON, Rector; ISRAEL BERRIOS, Mailing Address: Diocesis de Caguas, HC 04, P.O. Box 44015, Caguas, 00727. Tel: 787-747-5885, Ext. 243; Fax: 787-857-3585.

Catholic Charities—VACANT, Mailing Address: Diocesis de Caguas, HC 04, P.O. Box 44015, Caguas, 00727. Tel: 787-703-0775; Fax: 787-747-5616.

Commission of Permanent Deacons—Deacon CARLOS LUGO.

CLERGY, PARISHES, MISSIONS AND PAROCHIAL SCHOOLS

CITY OF CAGUAS

1—CATHEDRAL DULCE NOMBRE DE JESUS (1771) Revs. Campo E. Ariza, Rector; Aurelio Adan; Kevin Cintron Gonzalez.
Res.: 44 Betances St., Box 665, 00726-0665. Tel: 787-743-4311; 787-743-2927; Fax: 787-746-5399.
Chapel—Nuestra S. Perpetuo Socorro (1929) 24 Aguayo St., 00726.
Chapel—San Gerardo (1940) 221 B St., B-14, Jardines de Caguas, 00726.
Chapel—San Vicente de Paul 221 B St., Brooklyn, NY 11209.
Chapel—La Sagrada Familia (1978) 1004 P St., Bda. Morales.

2—DIVINO NINO (1995) Rev. Hermenegildo Alayón; Deacons Moise's Vargas; Rolando Rocafort.
Mailing Address: P.O. Box 9416, 00726. Tel: 787-746-1450; Fax: 787-744-3497.
Catechesis/Religious Program—Fax: 787-744-3497. Students 120.
Chapel—San Francisco Javier, Tel: 787-286-0440.

3—EL SALVADOR (1970) Rev. Victor G. Ortiz; Deacon Pablo Gonzalez.
Parcelas Bo. Boringuen—HC 08, Buzon 38888, 00725-9723. Tel: 787-747-0091; Fax: 787-747-0091 (call first). Email: elsalvador@caribe.net.
Catechesis/Religious Program—Students 300.
Chapel—Bo. San Salvador, Cristo Rey (1922)
Chapel—Sector Anon, San Alfonso (1929)
Chapel—Sector Hato, Nuestra S. del Carmen (1911)

4—INMACULADO CORAZON DE MARIA (1971) [JC] Revs. Vincent Penalba (Spain); Tomas Cabello, C.M.F. (Spain); Deacon Jose A. Velez Velazquez.
Mailing Address: HC 05, P.O. Box 57564, 00725-9233. Tel: 787-747-6336; Fax: 787-258-4910.
Catechesis/Religious Program—Students 435.
Chapel—Bo. La Barra, Cristo Rey (1971)
Chapel—San Antonio (1950)
Chapel—Bo. La Mesa, N.S. Providencia (1982)
Chapel—Bo. Quebrada Arenas, San Felipe
Chapel—Guasabara, Sta. Teresa del Nino Jesus (1995)

5—MARIA MADRE DE LA IGLESIA (1972) Rev. Encarnación Nieves; Deacons Francisco Gonzalez; Hipolito Montanez; Felix Cotto Velez.
Calle Juan M. Morales D-23 Urb Valle Tolima, 00725. Tel: 787-258-4481; Fax: 787-747-5616.
Chapel—Bo. Canabon, Maria Reina
Chapel—Las Carolinas, Ntra. Sra. del Carmen

6—NUESTRA SENORA DE LA PROVIDENCIA (1966) Rev. Angel Colon; Deacon Ruben Villodas.
Res.: Urb. Villa del Carmen, Box 6318, 00726. Tel: 787-743-8200; Fax: 787-743-8200.
Station—Urb. Mariolga
Station—Caserio Publico
Station—Los Flamboyanes
Station—Rio Verde
Station—Villa Carmen
Station—Villa del Rey I
Station—Residencial San Carlos 00726.
Station—Residencial San Alfonso

7—NUESTRA SENORA DEL PERPETUO SOCORRO (1966) Revs. Raul Morales; Carlos J. Vazquez; Deacons Francisco Santiago; Miguel Laguerre; Mario Cardona; Jose M. Garcia.
Res.: Calle 2, A-13, Villa Nueva, 00725. Tel: 787-744-1420; Fax: 787-258-4341. Email: vpsocorro@hotmail.com.
Station—San Patricio (1926) Bo. Canaboncito.
Station—San Judas Tadeo (1960) Villa Esperanza.
Station—Sagrado Corazon Bo. Canaboncito (Las Parcelas).
Station—Nuestra S. del Carmen (1988) Urb. Turabo Gardens.

8—SAGRADO CORAZON DE JESUS (1963) Rev. Hipólito Torres.
Res.: HC 04, Box 45078, Bo. Beatriz, 00726. Tel: 787-747-5170.
Chapel—Bo. Beatriz, Cristo Rey (1960)
Chapel—San Martin (1994)

9—SAN JOSE (1960), (Discalced Carmelites from Spain) Revs. Fernando Sanchez, O.C.D.; Alejandro Moral, O.C.D.; Samuel Fernandez, O.C.D.; Deacons Rafael Torres; Bruno Dueno.
Res.: Coral St., Villa Blanca, P.O. Box 1749, 00726. Tel: 787-743-5889; Fax: 787-258-0683. Email: sanjose_caguas@yahoo.com. Web: www.parroquiasanjose.net.
School—P.O. Box 1101, 00726. Tel: 787-743-2032; Fax: 787-258-0683. Email: csje-sec@csje-sec.org. Web: www.csje-sec.org. Sr. Nelly O. Rodriguez, C.M., Prin. (Spanish Carmelite Missionaries Sisters) Priests 2; Sisters 5; Lay Teachers 29; Students 596.
High School—Tel: 787-744-8993; Fax: 787-744-4111. Email: webmaster_csjs@yahoo.com. Mrs. Brenda Figueroa de Soler, Prin. Priests 1; Lay Teachers 21; Students 450.
Chapel—Nuestra Senora del Rosario (1981) Boi Bairoa La 25, Puerto Rico. Tel: 787-743-5889.
Catechesis/Religious Program—Norma Otie, D.R.E.; Helen Nolasco, D.R.E. Students 120.

10—SAN JUAN APOSTOL Y EVANGELISTA (1982) Rev. Angel Molina; Deacons Kenny Figueroa; Francisco Gonzalez; Ruben Huertas.
Res.: Apartado 459, Avenida Bairoa, 00726. Tel: 787-744-6359; Fax: 787-743-8266.
Catechesis/Religious Program—Tel: 787-743-8266. Students 200.

11—SAN PABLO APOSTOL (1980), (Hispanic), Rev. Juan B. Medina.
Res.: Kennedy U-32-B Urb. Jose Mercado, 00725. Tel: 787-743-3546; Fax: 787-743-3546.
Chapel—Bo. Tomas de Castro I, Nuestra S. de Guadalupe (1928)
Chapel—Bo. Tomas de Castro II, Santa Rose de Lima
Chapel—Sector Ramal, San Martin de Porres (1969)
Chapel—Sector Buenos Aires, San Juan Bautista y Santa Ines
Chapel—Sector RM5, Ntra. Sra. de la Monserrate
Catechesis/Religious Program—Students 134.

12—SAN PEDRO APOSTOL (1982) Rev. Roberto Solivan.
Res.: Urb. Bonneville, P.O. Box 8878, 00726. Tel: 787-744-2036; Fax: 787-743-4695.

13—SANTISIMA TRINIDAD (1986) Rev. Efrain Zabala; Deacon Esteban Dominguez.
Res.: P.O. Box 9630, 00726-9630. Tel: 787-747-6967; Fax: 787-747-6967. Email: pstcaguaspr@yahoo.com.

14—SANTISIMO SACRAMENTO (1967), Blessed Sacrament Fathers. Revs. Jose Martin Eguiguren, S.S.S.; Jesus Maria Maiza, S.S.S.; Antonio Odriozola, S.S.S.
Res.: Calle Caney A-11, Caguax, 00725. Tel: 787-743-8444; Fax: 787-745-5165.
Chapel—Urb. Caguas Norte, San Antonio de Padua
Chapel—Nuestra S. de Guadalupe 5th St., 00725.

OUTSIDE THE CITY OF CAGUAS FROM LAS AMERICAS EXPRESSWAY TOWARD THE WEST

AGUAS BUENAS, AGUAS BUENAS CO.

1—CHURCH OF TRES SANTOS REYES (1838), Redemptorist Fathers. Revs. Gerardo Hernandez, C.Ss.R.; Luis Adorno, C.Ss.R.; Antonio Hernandez, C.Ss.R.; Jose Checchia, C.Ss.R.
Res.: 4 Munoz Rivera St., P.O. Box 1, 00703. Tel: 787-732-2741; Fax: 787-732-2185.
School—Academia San Alfonso, Tel: 787-732-8288; Fax: 787-732-4115. Email: sanalfonso@prtc.net. Ms. Luz Rodriguez, Prin. Religious 1; Lay Teachers 16; Students 172.
Chapel—Bo. Sumidero, Nuestra S. del Perpetuo Socorro (1933)
Chapel—Sector Las Corujas del Barrio Sumidero, Buen Pastor (1984)
Chapel—Bo. Sonadora, Sagrado Corazon (1937)
Chapel—Bo. Jagueyes Abajo, San Jose (1939)
Chapel—Bo. Jagueyes Quintas, Santisimo Redentor (1947)
Chapel—Bo. Caguitas, Madre del Perpetuo Socorro (1941)
Chapel—Bo. Caguitas, Sector La Brusca, Ntra. del Rosario (1996)
Chapel—Parcelas Santa Clara, Santa Clara (1974)

2—ESPIRITU SANTO (1991) Rev. Felix Nunez; Deacons Juan Lopez; Jose Rivera; Domingo Falcon; Nelson Garcia.
Res.: P.O. Box 1250, 00703. Tel: 787-732-1270.
Chapel—Carr. 156, Santa Teresita (1929)
Chapel—Bo. Mulitas Alvelo, De Todos los Santos (1974)
Chapel—Bo. Mulitas Tiza, San Gerardo Mayela (1974)
Chapel—Bo. Juan Ascencio, San Alfonso

AIBONITO, AIBONITO CO., CHURCH OF ST. JOSEPH (1897) Revs. Yamil A. Velazquez; Israel Ramos Cintron; Deacons Modesto Reyes; Ezequiel Collazo; Cristobal Rolon; Carlos Lugo; Humberto Martinez.
Res.: P.O. Box 2038, 00705. Tel: 787-735-3741; 787-735-7235; Fax: 787-735-4436.
Catechesis/Religious Program—Tel: 787-735-4856. Students 1,900.
Mission—Barrio Algarrobo Barrio La Plata, Amoldadero. Tel: 787-735-5032.
Chapel—Bo. Asomante (Cuadritos), Nuestra S. del Carmen (1959)Tel: 787-735-1811.
Chapel—Bo. Asomante (Abejas), Inmaculada Concepcion (1965), Tel: 787-735-6455.
Chapel—Bo. Pasto, Nuestra S. de Guadalupe (1970)Tel: 787-735-6977.
Chapel—Nuestra S. de la Providencia (1982) Palestina St. Tel: 787-735-3072.
Chapel—Bo. Rabanal (Parcelas), Nuestra S. de Fatima (1972)Tel: 787-735-0395.
Chapel—Ext. San Luis, Nuestra S. del Carmen (1986)Tel: 787-735-7189.
Chapel—La Plata, La Milagrosa (1986)Tel: 787-735-4038.
Chapel—Llanos, Sector El Juicio, Tel: 787-735-1973.
Chapel—La Sierra, San Judas Tadeo, Tel: 787-735-2835.

BARRANQUITAS, BARRANQUITAS CO.

1—CHURCH OF ST. ANTHONY OF PADUA (1808; 1988) Revs. Baltazar Nunez; Jose A. de Leon; Deacon Carlos Colon Bernardi.
Res.: P.O. Box 1099, 00794. Tel: 787-857-3585; Fax: 787-857-3585.
Catechesis/Religious Program—Students 1,800.
Chapel—San Francisco de Asis (1960)
Chapel—Bo. Mana, Virgen del Carmen (1963)
Chapel—Bo. Canabon, Virgen de la Providencia (1968)
Chapel—Bo. Helechal, San Jose Obrero (1968)
Chapel—Bo. Quebrada Grande, Nuestra Sra. de la Monserrate (1968)
Chapel—Bo. Palo Hincado, Virgen del Perpetuo Socorro (1975)
Chapel—Bo. Lajitas, Nuestra S. del Pilar (1970)
Chapel—Sector La Torre, Santa Cruz (1975)
Chapel—Bo. Helechal, San Martin de Porres (1950)

2—SAN ANDRES APOSTOL (1986) Rev. Israel Berrios; Deacons Optaciano Rivera Ortiz; Angel Mercado.
In Res., Rev. Raúl Santos.
Res.: Bo. Quebradillas, Box 490, 00794. Tel: 787-875-5424; Fax: 787-875-5424.
Catechesis/Religious Program—Students 241.
Chapel—Bo. Palomas, Comerio, San Jose (1925)
Chapel—Bo. Quebradillas, Barranquitas, Corazon de Jesus (1940; 1987)
Chapel—Bo. Cedro Arriba, Naranjito, San Antonio de Padua (1864)
Chapel—Bo. Quebradillas, Barranquitas, Inmaculada Concepcion y Santa Cruz (1957)
Chapel—Bo. Cedro Arriba, Naranjito, Santuario Maria Auxiliadora (1992)

CAYEY, CAYEY CO.

1—NUESTRA SENORA DE LA ASUNCION (1787), Mercedarian Fathers. Revs. Elias Lorenzana, O.M.; Antonio Garcia, O.M.
Casa Parroquial: P.O. Box 372887, 00737-2887. Tel: 787-738-2763; Fax: 787-738-2763. Email: asuncion.cayey@hotmail.com.
Catechesis/Religious Program—Students 1,069.
Chapel—Bo. Jajome, Sagrado Corazon de Jesus (1935)
Chapel—Bo. Pasto Viejo, Nuestra S. del Carmen (1937; 1988)
Chapel—Bo. Toita, Nuestra S. de la Merced (1946)
Chapel—Res. Brisas de Cayey, San Ramon Nonato (1978)
Chapel—Bo. Maton Arriba, Santa Teresita del Nino Jesus (1987)

2—NUESTRA SENORA DE LA MERCED (1968) Revs. Benigno Lopez; Wilfredo Riveros; Gregorio Dafonte Vaz.
Reparto Montellano—P.O. Box 372798, 00737. Tel: 787-738-3872; Fax: 787-263-1810.
Chapel—Bo. Vegas, San Ramon Nonato (1961)
Chapel—Bo. Culebras, Nuestra S. del Carmen (1973)
Chapel—Bo. Farallon, San Pedro Nolasco (1980)
Chapel—San Pedro Armengol (La Plata) (1994)

3—SAN ESTEBAN PROTOMARTIR (1985) Rev. Edwin R. Hernandez; Deacons Anibal Gonzalez Vazquez; Felix Montanez Perez; Silvestre Rodriguez Flores.
Res.: Bo. Guavate, 22601 Sector Nieves, 00736-9522. Tel: 787-747-4555.
Chapel—Bo. Borinquen Pradera, Nuestr Senora del Carmen (1910)
Chapel—Bo. Guavate, San Jose de la Montana (1951; 1990)

CIDRA, CIDRA CO.
1—NUESTRA SENORA DE FATIMA (1963) Rev. Luis Rivera; Deacons Reyes Santos; Israel Santiago.
Bo. Rabanal—Box 214, 00739. Tel: 787-739-0633.
Catechesis/Religious Program—Students 596.
Chapel—Bo. Toita, Sagrado Corazon de Jesus (1960)
Chapel—Bo. Salto, San Vicente (1965)
Chapel—Bo. Honduras, Perpetuo Socorro (1970)
Chapel—Bo. Rabanal, Jesus Salvador (1970)
Chapel—Bo. Parcelas, La Milagrosa (1978)
Chapel—Bo. Salto, Nuestra Senora de la Providencia
Chapel—Bo. Salto, Santa Teresita (1982)
Chapel—Santo Cristo de Los Milagros (1987)
2—NUESTRA SENORA DEL CARMEN (1818) Rev. Orlando de Jesus Gomez; Deacons Diego Reyes Vasquez; Hector Orlando Santos Reyes; Jose Antonio Flores Colon; Ramon Hernandez Zayas; Angel Alberto Perez Arroyo; Rafael Santos Cruz.
Centro Plaza Municipal—P.O. Box 359, 00739. Tel: 787-739-2406; Fax: 787-739-4991.
Chapel—Bo. Rio Abajo, Madre del Salvador
Chapel—Urb. Treasure Valley, La Milagrosa
Chapel—Bo. Bayamon-Centenejas I, La Inmaculada
Chapel—Bo. Montellano, Santa Teresa del Nino Jesus
Chapel—Bo. Bayamon-Certenejas II, Perpetuo Socorro
Chapel—Bo. Bayamon-Juan del Valle, Nuestra Senora del Rosario
Chapel—Bo. Arena-Santa Clara, San Joaquin
Chapel—Bo. Ceiba-Hevia, Nuestra Senora del Rosario
Chapel—Bo. Arenas, Nuestra Senora de la Providencia
Chapel—Bo. Ceiba, Cristo Rey
Chapel—Bo. Bayamon-San Jose, San Jose
Chapel—Bo. Rincon, San Francisco de Asis
Chapel—Bo. Sud, La Milagrosa
Chapel—Bo. Sud, San Pablo
COMERIO, COMERIO CO., SANTO CRISTO DE LA SALUD (1832) Revs. Oscar Rivera; David Diaz; Deacon Manuel Rivera Gonzalez.
Mailing Address: P.O. Box 1139, 00782. Tel: 787-875-4525; Fax: 787-875-3481.
Res.: Calle Santiago R Palmer #12, 00782.
Chapel—Bo. Sabana, Nuestra Senora del Santisimo Rosario (1966)
Chapel—Bo. Rio Hondo, Nuestra Senora de Fatima (1953)
Chapel—Bo. Palomas, Santa Ceceilia (1954)
Chapel—Bo. Cedrito, Virgen de la Providencia (1958)
Chapel—Bo. Rio Hondo-Sector Las Parcelas, San Pablo (1965)
Chapel—Bo. Pinas Arriba, Nuestra Senora del Carmen (1973)
Chapel—Bo. Naranjo-Sector Las Parcelas, San Antonio de Padua (1977)
Chapel—Bo. Vega Redonda, San Francisco de Asis (1977)
Chapel—Bo. Cejas, Santa Rose de Lima (1980)
Chapel—Bo. Dona Elena, San Martin de Porres (1950)
Chapel—Rio Hondo II, Maria Madre de la Iglesia
NARANJITO, NARANJITO CO., SAN MIGUEL ARCANGEL (1831) Revs. Felix Oliveras Villanueva; Juan J. Colon; Deacons Abigail Matos; Jose Berrios.
Res.: Centro Parroquial, P.O. Box 68, 00719. Tel: 787-869-2840; 787-869-4080; 787-869-4690; Fax: 787-869-3050.
Chapel—Bo. Nuevo, Santa Rosa de Lima (1953)
Chapel—Bo. Lomas Centro, Virgen del Carmen (1954)
Chapel—Bo. Anones, La Milagrosa (1962)
Chapel—Bo. Lomas Valles, San Judas Tadeo (1963)
Chapel—Bo. Guadiana, La Monserrate (1967)
Chapel—Bo. Achiote, Sagrado Corazon (1978)
Chapel—Bo. Nuevo Parcelas, San Vicente de Paul (1981)
Chapel—Bo. Cedro Abajo, San Jose (1981)

OUTSIDE THE CITY OF CAGUAS FROM LAS AMERICAS EXPRESSWAY TOWARD THE EAST COAST

GURABO, GURABO CO., SAN JOSE (1822) Rev. Antonio Cartagena.
Res.: 7 Santiago Iglesias St., P.O. Box 733, 00778. Tel: 787-737-2656; Fax: 787-737-2656.
Catechesis/Religious Program—Students 240.
Chapel—Bo. Jagual, Sagrado Corazon de Jesus (1951)
Chapel—Bo. Jaguas Llano, Virgen del Carmen (1967)
Chapel—Bo. Santa Rita, Santa Rita (1968)
Chapel—La Milagrosa (1973) Bo. Hato Nuevo, 00778.
Chapel—Bo. Celada, Santa Francisca Javier Cabrini (1967)
Chapel—Bo. Hato Nuevo, La Milagrosa (1982)
Chapel—Bo. Jaguas Loma, San Miguel (1989)
Chapel—Bo. Mamey II, Ntra. Sra. del Carmen
JUNCOS, JUNCOS CO., INMACULADA CONCEPCION (1797) Revs. Feliciano Rodriquez; Angel L. Cintron; Deacons Luis Almodovar; Avelino Perez; Carlos Sola.
Res.: Munoz Rivera St. #25 B, 00777.
Office: Algarin St., #6, P.O. Box 1728, 00777. Tel: 787-734-2431; Fax: 787-734-0350. Email: immaculada_juncos@hotmail.com.
Catechesis/Religious Program—Students 200.
Chapel—Bo. Canta Gallo, Cristo Redentor (1975)
Chapel—Bo. Ceiba Sur, Sagrado Corazon (1976)
Chapel—Bo. Valenciano Sector Amigo, Espiritu Santo (1976)
Chapel—Bo. Ceiba Norte, Cristo Rey (1978)
Chapel—Bo. Valenciano Arriba, San Juan Bautista (1979)
Chapel—Bo. Ceiba Norte Sector Chinos, Buen Pastor (1979)
Chapel—Bo. Pinas, Santa Cruz (1981)
Chapel—Bo. Lirios, San Jose (1978)
Chapel—Bo. Canta Gallo Secto Reparto Valenciano, Maria Madre de la Iglesia (1993)
Chapel—Santisima Trinidad Bo. Placita.
LAS PIEDRAS, LAS PIEDRAS CO.
1—INMACULADA CONCEPCION (1801) Revs. Melvin Montanez; Enrique Gómez.
Res.: Box 324, 00771. Tel: 787-733-2381; Fax: 787-733-1180.
Catechesis/Religious Program—Tel: 787-733-8325. Hnas Fatima, D.R.E.; Sr. M. Ines Zayas, O.P., C.R.E. Students 450.
Chapel—Bo. Montones I, Perpetuo Socorro (1935)
Chapel—Bo. Tejas Asomante, Nuestra Senora de la Providencia (1955)
Chapel—Bo. La Fermina, Jesus de Nazaret (1979)
Chapel—Bo. Montones IV, Santa Teresa del Nino Jesus (1980)
Chapel—Bo. Montones II, San Juan Bautista (1982)
Mission— Salon Usos Multiples-Urb. April Gardens, Las Piedras.
2—SAN JUAN BAUTISTA (Bo. Pueblito del Rio) (1971) Rev. Pastor A. Arroyave; Deacons Angel Luis Santiago; Efrain Gomez.
Bo. Pueblito del Rio—HC 02, Buzon 4467, 00771. Tel: 787-733-6444; Fax: 787-733-1479. Email: psjb@prtc.net.
Chapel—Finca Roig, San Juan Bautista (1911; 1940)
Chapel—Bo. Boqueron, La Sagrada Familia (1957)
Chapel—Bo. Pena Pobre, Sagrado Corazon (1964)
Chapel—Bo. Rio Blanco, La Milagrosa (1972)
Chapel—Bo. Mango, San Francisco Javier
Chapel—Bo. Pasto Seco, El Buen Pastor 00771.
MAUNABO, MAUNABO CO., SAN ISIDRO LABRADOR (1799) Rev. Jorge D. Cardona.
Res.: P.O. Box 248, 00707. Tel: 787-861-2595; Fax: 787-861-2595.
Chapel—Nuestra Senora del Carmen (1962)
Chapel—Bo. Calzada, Nuestra Senora de la Providencia (1971)
Chapel—Bo. Matuyas, Nuestra Senora de la Candelaria (1974)
Chapel—Bo. Palo Seco, San Judas Tadeo (1975)
Chapel—Bo. Emajaguas, San Antonio de Padua (1977)
Mission— Bo. Quebrada Arenas.
Mission— Bo. Lizas.
Chapel—N.S. del Rosario de Fatima Bo. Talante.
Mission— Bo. Paloseco.
Mission— Bo. Talante (La Pica).
Mission— Bo. Calzada.
SAN LORENZO, SAN LORENZO CO.
1—NUESTRA SENORA DE LA MERCEDES (1810), (Hispanic), Revs. Angel Lopez, C.Ss.R.; Juan Ramon Hernandez, C.Ss.R.; Andres Spacht, C.Ss.R.; Santiago Mallen, C.Ss.R.; Rafael Torres, C.SS.R.
Res.: Munoz Rivera 55, Apartado 1280, 00754-1280. Tel: 787-736-2571; Fax: 787-736-1213.
Chapel—Bo. Jagual, Nuestra Senora del Carmen (1952)
Chapel—Bo. Quemados, Nuestra Senora del Perpetuo Socorro (1957)
Chapel—Bo. Cerro Gordo Abajo, Cristo Redentor (1965)
Chapel—Bo. Quebrada, Jesus Maestro
Chapel—Bo. Florida, Santa Monica
Chapel—Bda. Roosevelt, Nuestra Senora del Carmen (1968)
Chapel—Bo. Hato Km. 6, Nuestra Senora del Perpetuo Socorro (1968)
Chapel—Bo. Cerro Gordo Arriba, Inmaculada Concepcion (1977)
Chapel—Bo. Lorenzo del Valle, Inmaculado Corazon de Maria (1978)
Chapel—Bo. Santa Clara, San Gerardo (1986)
Chapel—Urb. Los Flamboyanes, Bo. Florida, Nuestra Senora de Lourdes (1988)
Catechesis/Religious Program—Students 1,115.
2—SAGRADO CORAZON DE JESUS Y 12 APOSTOLES (Bo. Espino) (1986) Revs. Boris Espinosa; Franklin Rodriguez; Giovanni Ruiz.
Bo. Espino—HC 30, Box 32716, 00754-9726. Tel: 787-715-6947; Fax: 787-715-6947.
Chapel—San Francisco de Asis (1988) Carr. 181, 00754.
Chapel—Santa Rosa de Lima (1989) Carr. 181, 00754.
Chapel—San Jose (1959) Carr. 181, 00754.
Chapel—Nstra. Sra. del Rosario (1994) Carr. 181, Ramal 745, 00754.
Chapel—Maria Madre de la Iglesia (1990) Carr. 181, 00754.
Chapel—San Pedro (1998) 00754.
Chapel—Santa Teresita del Nino Jesus (1950) 00754.
YABUCOA, YABUCOA CO., SANTOS ANGELES CUTODIOS (1793) Revs. Miguel A. de Angel; Ricardo Santin; Deacon Carlos M. Ramos.
Res.: Degetau St. #2, P.O. Box 7, 00767. Tel: 787-893-2250 (Res.); 787-893-3347 (Office); Fax: 787-266-0841.
Catechesis/Religious Program—Students 930.
Chapel—Bo. Rosa Sanchez, Santa Rosa de Lima
Chapel—Bo. Jacanas Granjas, San Juan Evangelista
Chapel—Bo. Jac. Piedra Blanca, Sagrado Corazon (1976)
Chapel—Bo. Tejas Piedra Azul, Sta. Maria Reina Paz
Chapel—Bo. Martorell, Santa Teresita del Nino Jesus
Chapel—Bo. Tejas, Ntra. Sra. de la Divina Providencia
Chapel—Bo. Playita Cuesta, San Bernardo
Chapel—Bo. Playita Arriba, S. Antonio de Padua (1947)
Chapel—Bo. Playita Parcelas, Virgen Milagrosa
Chapel—Bo. Quebradillas, Ntra. Sra. del Carmen
Chapel—Bo. Guayabota, La Sagrada Familia (1948)
Chapel—Bo. Calabazas Arriba, San Jose (1942)
Chapel—Bo. Quebrada Grande, San Benito
Chapel—Bo. Playa Guayanes, Ntra. Sra. del Carmen
Chapel—Bo. Aguacate, Ntra. Sra. del Perpetuo Socorro (1937)
Chapel—Bo. Jagueyes, Inmaculada Concepcion (1910)
Chapel—Bo. Ingenio, Santisima Trinidad
Chapel—Bo. Camino Nuevo, San Jeronimo
Chapel—Bo. Jacanas Sur, Divino de Jesus y Beato Diego (1999)
Chapel—Bo. Tejas Valerio, Corpus Christi.
Chapel—Camino Nuevo, El Guano, San Esteban
Chapel—Jacanas, Piedra Blanca, Sagrado Corazon de Jesus
Chapel—Limones, Campo Alegre, San Francisco de Asis

Chaplains of Public Institutions

CAGUAS. *Hospital Interamericano de Medicina Avanzada (HIMA)*Rev. Encarnación Nieves.
*San Juan Bautista Hospital*Rev. Encarnación Nieves.

Retired:
Revs.—
Chocarro, Antonio
Martinez, Alfredo

INSTITUTIONS LOCATED IN THE DIOCESE

[A] PAROCHIAL SCHOOLS

CAGUAS. *Academia Cristo de los Milagros* (1982) Box 7618, 00726-7618. Tel: 787-743-3131; 787-743-4242; 787-743-4855; Fax: 787-746-1428. Email: cristo@acmpr.org. Mrs. Leonides Parrilla de Carrión, Gen. Dir.; Mrs. Nilda Aponte, Librarian. Priests 1; Deacons 1; Lay Teachers 63; Students 1,304.

Colegio Catolico Notre Dame Elemental (1916) P.O. Box 967, 00726. Tel: 787-743-2385; 787-743-2524; Fax: 787-743-7567; 787-744-6464. Email: prsbm@yahoo.com.du. Web: www.ccnde.org. Ms. Luz Rodriguez, Prin. Priests 1; Lay Teachers 46; Aides 7; Students 866.

Colegio Catolico Notre Dame Superior, Box 937, 00726. Tel: 787-743-3693; 787-743-5501; Fax: 787-258-9648. Web: www.ccnd.org. Mr. Jose G. Grillo, Prin.; Aurora Vazquez, Librarian. Priests 2; Lay Teachers 86; Students 1,174.

Colegio San Jose Elemental (1963) P.O. Box 2005, 00726. Tel: 787-743-2032; 787-743-3205; Fax: 787-258-0683. Email: csje-sec@csje-sec.org. Web: www.csje-sec.org. Margarita Rosales, Prin.; Rev. P. Samuel Fernandez Paulino, O.C.D., Dir.; Mrs.

Judith Perez, Librarian. Priests 1; Sisters 4; Lay Teachers 26; Students 409.

Colegio San Jose Superior (1977) Y/O 1749, P.O. Box 1101, 00726. Tel: 787-744-8993; Fax: 787-744-4111. Email: colegiosanjosesuperior@hotmail.com. Rev. Alejandro Moral, O.C.D., Dir.; Mrs. Brenda Figueroa de Soler, Prin.; Mrs. Sonia Fernandez, Librarian. Priests 1; Lay Teachers 21; Students 293.

Colegio San Juan Apostol y Evangelista (1992) P.O. Box 459, 00726-0459. Tel: 787-743-8266; 787-747-4302; 787-744-6359; Fax: 787-747-4301. Marie Lozano, Prin.; Wilma Roman, Admin.; Carmen Martinez, Librarian. Lay Teachers 43; Students 816.

AGUAS BUENAS. *Academia San Alfonso*, (Grades PreK-7), Pio Rechani St., P.O. Box 97, 00703. Tel: 787-732-8288; Fax: 787-732-4115. Email: bmfontanez@yahoo.com. Luz E. Rodriguez-Marrero, Prin. Lay Teachers 16; Students 172.

BARRANQUITAS. *Colegio San Francisco de Asis Elemental y Superior*, P.O. Box 789, 00794. Tel: 787-857-2123; Fax: 787-857-2123. Email: matriculateya@csfa-sec.org. Mr. Celestino Mercado Cartagena, Dir. Students 137.

CAYEY. *Colegio Nuestra Senora de la Merced*, P.O. Box 372678, 00736. Tel: 787-738-3438; Fax: 787-263-5837. Email: www.lamercedcayey@yahoo.com. Mrs. Nancy Diaz Morales, Prin.; Maricarmen Lopez, Librarian. (Nuestra Senora de la Asuncion Parish) Priests 1; Lay Teachers 47; Students 826.

GURABO. *Colegio Ntra. Sra. De Pilar*, P.O. Box 1332, 00778. Tel: 787-737-1400; 787-737-1401; Fax: 787-737-1400. Mrs. Adelaida Cruz Zayas. Priests 1; Lay Teachers 16; Total Staff 26; Students 191.

NARANJITO. *Academia Santa Teresita*, P.O. Box 244, 00719. Tel: 787-869-7968; 787-869-6731; 787-869-8357; Fax: 787-869-8357. Email: astnar@prtc.net. Mrs. Josefina Lopez Caldero, Prin. Lay Teachers 21; Students 360.

[B] RETREAT HOUSES

AGUAS BUENAS. *Casa Cristo Redentor* (1967) P.O. Box 8, 00703-0008. Tel: 787-732-5161; Fax: 787-732-1115. Email: pdamian@coqui.net. Revs. Terence Damian Wall, C.Ss.R., S.T.D., Supr.; Miguel A. Torres, C.Ss.R., Dir.; Hector Garcia, C.Ss.R.

AIBONITO. *Casa Manresa*, P.O. Box 1319, 00705. Tel: 787-735-8016; 787-735-8017; Fax: 787-735-2421. Email: manresa@caribe.net. Web: www.casamanresaaibonito.org. Rev. Francisco Hernandez, Dir.

JUNCOS. *Casa Cursillos de Cristiandad of Caguas* (Lay Corp. of Cursillistas), Salida de Juncos Carretera 919, P.O. Box 1762, 00777. Tel: 787-734-7068; Fax: 787-713-9725.

SAN LORENZO. *Casa Charlie Rodriguez*, P.O. Box 1190, 00754. Tel: 787-736-5750; Fax: 787-715-8946. Email: santuariopr@gmail.com. Web: www.santuariopr.org. Rev. Giovanni Ruiz Esquivel.

[C] MONASTERIES AND RESIDENCES OF PRIESTS

CAGUAS. *Misioneros Hijos del Inmaculado Corazon de Maria (Claretianos)*, Bo. Rio Canas HC-05, Box 57564, 00725-9233. Tel: 787-747-6336; Fax: 787-258-4910. Email: jvicente@coqui.net; jvmsg@hotmail.com.

AIBONITO. *Casa Salesiana de Retiros*, P.O. Box 2019, 00705. Tel: 787-735-2486; Fax: 787-735-5501. Email: sdbaibon@coqui.net. Revs. Homero Betancourt, S.D.B.; Orlando Cejas, S.D.B.; Luis Dalbon; Francisco Juan, S.D.B.; Antonio Robles, S.D.B.

[D] CLOISTER SISTERS

CAGUAS. *Hnas. Hijas de Santa Maria de la Ternura*, Calle Naranjito 220 - Barrio Boringuen Parcelas Viejas, P.O. Box 5097, 00726. Tel: 787-653-5813; Fax: 787-653-5813. Sr. Sonia Maria La Luz, H.S.M.T., Prior.

AGUAS BUENAS. *Santa Clara Monastery* Hermanas Clarisas, P.O. Box 884, 00703. Tel: 787-732-5771.

[E] SHRINES

SAN LORENZO. *Diocesan Shrine Our Lady of Mount Carmel* P.O. Box 1190, 00754. Tel: 787-736-5750; Fax: 787-715-8946. Email: santuariopr@gmail.com. Web: www.santuariopr.org. Rev. Giovanni Ruiz Esquivel, Rector.

[F] MISCELLANEOUS

CAGUAS. *Centro de Acompanamiento Sico Social Espiritual (CASSE)*, P.O. Box 656, 00726. Tel: 747-286-3333; Fax: 787-286-3612.

Diocesan Tribunal of Caguas, P.O. Box 9779, 00726. Tel: 787-286-8595; Fax: 787-286-8620. Rev. Felix Nunez, Judicial Vicar.

Instituto Secular de Ntra. Sra. de la Altagracia, Calle 13, L23. Urb. Delgado, 00725. Tel: 787-744-3628; Fax: 787-744-3628. Isabel Vazquez Rivera; Maria Melendez Sanchez; Ramonita Lopez Diaz; Zoraida Santos Santos; Judith Colon Cruz; Olga Rodriguez Berrios; Maria Isabel Colon; Prixda Santos Agosto; Doris Roque Julia; Natividad Ramos Ramos; Evelyn Rosado Rivera; Brenda Y. Abreu Garcia.

Movimiento Juan XXIII, P.O. Box 7229, 00726. Tel: 787-747-3748. Revs. Hipólito Torres; Karlos Lopez.

NARANJITO. *Seminario Pablo VI - Theological*, P.O. Box 302, 00719. Tel: 787-869-0861; Fax: 787-869-0861. Email: jcardona@prtc.net.

Casa del Apostol San Andres Rev. Israel Berrios.

RELIGIOUS INSTITUTES OF MEN REPRESENTED IN THE DIOCESE

For further details refer to the corresponding bracketed number in the Religious Institutes of Men or Women section.

[]—*Claretian Fathers*—C.M.F.

[0220]—*Congregation of the Blessed Sacrament* (N. Spain Prov.)—S.S.S.

[]—*Mercedarian Fathers* (Spain)

[]—*Order of Carmelites*—O.Carm.

[1070]—*Redemptorist Fathers* (San Juan Prov.)—C.SS.R.

[1190]—*Salesians of Don Bosco* (Antillas)—S.D.B.

RELIGIOUS INSTITUTES OF WOMEN REPRESENTED IN THE DIOCESE

[0420]—*Discalced Carmelite Nuns* (Spain)—O.C.C.

[]—*Doninicas de la Santisima Virgen*

[]—*Dominicas del Rosario de Fatima*

[]—*Hermanas Carmelitas Misioneras*

[]—*Hermanas Clarisas*

[]—*Hermanas de Notre Dame*

[]—*Hermanas Dominicas del Rosario de Fatima*

[]—*Hermanas Hijas de Santa Maria de la Ternura*

[]—*Hermanas Mercedarias*

[]—*Hermanas Misioneras de los Sagrados Corazones*

[]—*Hermanas Misioneras del Buen Pastor*

[]—*Hermanas Misioneras Dominicas del Santo Rosario*

[]—*Hijas de Maria Auxiliadora*

[]—*Misioneras de Maria Corredentora*

[]—*Misioneras del Sagrado Corazon*

[2790]—*Missionary Servants of the Most Holy Trinity* (Spain)—M.S.B.T.

[3760]—*Order of St. Clare*—P.C.C.

[]—*Religiosas del Sagrado Corazon*

[]—*Sacred Heart Sisters*

[]—*Salesian Sisters*

[2970]—*School Sisters of Notre Dame* (Wilton, CT)—S.S.N.D.

[]—*Siervas de Maria* (Spain)

[]—*Siervas de Maria*

[0640]—*Sisters of Charity of St. Vincent de Paul* (Puerto Rico Prov.)—S.C.

[]—*Sisters of Fatima* (P.R.)

[2150]—*Sisters Servants of the Immaculate Heart of Mary*—I.H.M.

NECROLOGY

(No Deaths)

An asterisk (*) denotes an organization that has established tax-exempt status directly with the IRS and is not covered by the USCCB Group Ruling.

Diocese of the Caroline Islands

(Editor's Note: 2012 information was not received)

Most Reverend

AMANDO SAMO, D.D.

Bishop of the Caroline Islands; ordained Priest December 10, 1977; appointed Titular Bishop of Libertina and Auxiliary Bishop of the Caroline and Marshalls May 10, 1987; ordained Bishop August 15, 1987; named Coadjutor February 3, 1994; named Bishop of the Diocese March 25, 1995; installed June 6, 1995. *Res.: P.O. Box 939, Chuuk, FM 96942.* Tel: 691-330-2399; Fax: 691-330-4585.

Chancery Office: P.O. Box 939, Chuuk, FM 96942. Tel: 691-330-2399; Fax: 691-330-4585.

Web: www.diocesecarolines.org

Email: diocese@mail.fm

Square Miles Ocean 1,725,000.

Total Population of 135,831.

Vicariate of the Caroline Islands erected December 10, 1905 and committed to the Order of Friars Minor Capuchin, extended to the Mariana Islands March 1, 1911.

Vicariate of the Marianas and Caroline and Marshall Islands erected May 4, 1923 and committed to the Society of Jesus. Marianas Islands separated July 4, 1946. Diocese of the Caroline-Marshalls created February 3, 1980. The Marshalls made a separate Prefecture Apostolic August 15, 1993, and the Diocese renamed "Diocese of the Caroline Islands."

Civilly it includes the four Federated States of Micronesia (Chuuk, Kosrae, Pohnpei and Yap) and the Republic of Palau.

STATISTICAL OVERVIEW

Personnel	
Bishop	1
Priests: Diocesan Active in Diocese	10
Priests: Diocesan Active Outside Diocese	2
Priests: Retired, Sick or Absent	1
Number of Diocesan Priests	13
Religious Priests in Diocese	15
Total Priests in Diocese	28
Ordinations:	
Diocesan Priests	1
Transitional Deacons	3
Permanent Deacons	23
Permanent Deacons in Diocese	65
Total Brothers	2
Total Sisters	34
Parishes	
Parishes	29
With Resident Pastor:	
Resident Diocesan Priests	10
Resident Religious Priests	7
Without Resident Pastor:	
Administered by Priests	2
Administered by Deacons	12
Missions	2
Professional Ministry Personnel:	
Brothers	2
Sisters	34
Educational	
Diocesan Students in Other Seminaries	12
Total Seminarians	12
High Schools, Diocesan and Parish	3
Total Students	620
High Schools, Private	1
Total Students	175
Elementary Schools, Diocesan and Parish	4
Total Students	1,221
Catechesis/Religious Education:	
High School Students	798
Elementary Students	1,309
Total Students under Catholic Instruction	4,135
Teachers in the Diocese:	
Scholastics	2
Brothers	2
Sisters	24
Lay Teachers	134
Vital Statistics	
Receptions into the Church:	
Infant Baptism Totals	1,424
Minor Baptism Totals	345
Adult Baptism Totals	113
First Communions	1,171
Confirmations	886
Marriages:	
Catholic	245
Interfaith	31
Total Marriages	276
Total Catholic Population	77,733
Total Population	140,368

Former Bishops—Most Revs. SALVADOR WALLAESER, O.F.M.Cap., cons. Vicar Apostolic and Titular Bishop of Tanagra, Aug. 21, 1912; resigned June 23, 1919; died Jan. 1, 1946; SANTIAGO LOPEZ DE REGO, S.J., cons. Vicar Apostolic and Titular Bishop of Dionisiopolis, Aug. 26, 1923; resigned June 2, 1939; died Aug. 5, 1940; THOMAS J. FEENEY, S.J., cons. Vicar Apostolic and Titular Bishop of Agno, Sept. 8, 1951; died Sept. 9, 1955; VINCENT I. KENNALLY, S.J., cons. Vicar Apostolic and Titular Bishop of Sassura, March 25, 1957; resigned Sept. 20, 1971; died April 12, 1977; MARTIN J. NEYLON, S.J., D.D., ord. Bishop, Feb. 2, 1970; succeeded to as Vicar Apostolic, Sept. 20, 1970; named to be Bishop of the new diocese, May 3, 1979; installed as first Bishop of the Diocese of the Carolines-Marshalls, Feb. 3, 1980; retired June 6, 1995; died April 13, 2004.

Chancery Office—Mailing Address: P.O. Box 939, Chuuk, 96942. Tel: 691-330-2399; Fax: 691-330-4585.

Vicar General—Rev. JOHN F. CURRAN, S.J., J.C.L.

Chancellor—Rev. ROSENDO RUDOLF.

Diocesan Consultors—Revs. DAVID ANDRUS, S.J.; RUSK SABURO; JOHN S. HAGILEIRAM, S.J.; NICHOLAS P. RAHOY.

Finance Committee—Rev. JOHN F. CURRAN, S.J., J.C.L.; Mr. SANTI ASANUMA; Mr. IGNACIO STEPHEN; Mr. TONY GANNGIYAN; Mr. ALBINO KERMAN; Rev. ROSENDO RUDOLF.

Episcopal Vicars—

Chuuk—Rev. NICHOLAS P. RAHOY, Mailing Address: P.O. Box 337, Chuuk, 96942. Tel: 691-330-2672; Fax: 691-330-4394.

Palau—Rev. RUSK SABURO, Mailing Address: P.O. Box 128, Palau, PW 96940. Tel: 680-488-6539; 680-488-2226; Fax: 680-488-1819.

Pohnpei-Kosrae—Rev. DAVID ANDRUS, S.J., Mailing Address: P.O. Box 160, Pohnpei, 96941. Tel: 691-320-4661; Fax: 691-320-5876.

Yap—Rev. JOHN S. HAGILEIRAM, S.J., Mailing Address: P.O. Box "A", Yap, 96943. Tel: 691-350-2265; Fax: 691-350-2784.

Diocesan Tribunal—

Judical Vicar—Rev. WILLIAM J. RAKOWICZ, S.J., Mailing Address: P.O. Box 128, Palau, PW 96940. Tel: 680-488-2226; Fax: 680-488-1819.

Defenders of the Bond—Revs. NICHOLAS P. RAHOY; RUSK SABURO.

Notaries—Rev. JOHN F. CURRAN, S.J., J.C.L.; Mrs. MIRIAM CHIN; Ms. FILIPANA PHILLIP.

Vocations—Rev. JULIO ANGKEL.

CLERGY, PARISHES, MISSIONS AND PAROCHIAL SCHOOLS

CHUUK (TRUK) STATE, CAROLINE ISLANDS

Mailing Address for the Vicariate of Chuuk: Rev. Nicholas Rahoy, P.O. Box 250, Chuuk, Caroline Islands, FM 96942. Tel: 691-330-2672; Fax: 691-330-4394 (unless otherwise noted).

FEFAN, SACRED HEART Deacon Iowanes Reim, Admin.
Mission— Parem.

MORTLOCK ISLANDS, MORTLOCK Revs. John Ikataere, M.S.C.; Tatieru Ewenteang, M.S.C.; Deacons Soichy Buliche; Petrus Soumwei.
Mission— Satowan.
Mission— Kuttu.
Mission— Moch.
Mission— Ettal.
Mission— Namoluk.
Mission— Lukunor.
Mission— Oneop.
Mission— Ta.
Mission— Nama.
Mission— Piis.
Mission— Losap.

NEEPWUKOS, HOLY FAMILY CHURCH Rev. Basilio Dilipy; Deacons Eliot Cholymay; Bername Itiraw; Rikarto Fabian; Julio Akapito.

TOL, ASSUMPTION OF THE BLESSED VIRGIN MARY Rev. Fernando Titus; Deacons Angken Rapun; Roke Rokop; Kintin Rawit; Itoi Ruta; Oiken Victus; Missa Sewell; Francisco Ykuta; Lukas Paulus; Gabriel Ykuda; Krispino Raphael; Siano Pius; Enato Rapun.

TOLOWAS, ST. ANTHONY'S Rev. Julio Angken; Deacons Tobias Soram; Rinder Fidel.

TUNNUK, IMMACULATE HEART OF MARY CATHEDRAL Rev. Nicholas P. Rahoy; Deacons Chitaro William; Yostaro Noporu; Edwin Shuru, (Retired); Angken Xymoon.
School—St. Cecilia's, Tel: 691-330-4525; Fax: 691-330-4394. Mr. Kaspar Berry, Prin. Mercedarian Missionaries of Berriz 4; Peace Corps Volunteer 1; Lay Teachers 25; Students 634.

UDOT, ST. FRANCIS ASSISI Rev. Fernando Titus; Deacons John Fritz; Eichy Karsom; Julian Ranu; Kerno Sam.
Mission—St. Joseph Romanum.

UMAN, HOLY CROSS Revs. Edmond Ludwick; Lomano Kauvaetupu, M.S.C.; Deacons Audreas Nimas; Carlos Sam; Salvador Mailos; Akiuo Meisa; Joseph Albert; Nori Oneitam; Atitor Edmond; Istor Aien.

POHNPEI STATE, CAROLINE ISLANDS

Mailing Address for the Vicariate of Pohnpei: Rev. Dave Andrus, S.J., P.O. Box 160, Pohnpei, Caroline Islands, FM 96941. Tel: 691-320-4661; Fax: 691-320-5876 (unless otherwise noted).

AWAK, ST. JOSEPH Deacons Adelino Lorens, Admin.; Manuel Amor, (Retired).
Tel: 691-320-6025.

IPWUTEK, ST. AUGUSTINE Deacon Tarsisio Amon, Admin.
Tel: 691-320-8930.

KOLONIA, OUR LADY OF MERCY Revs. Cuthbert Yiftheg; Kasiano Paul (Special Studies Philippines).; Deacons Edgar Martin; Martiniano Rodriguez.
Tel: 691-320-2557; Fax: 691-320-5876.
School—Pohnpei Catholic School, Tel: 691-320-2556. Sisters 3; Lay Teachers 11; Students 213.

PALIKIR, STS. PAUL AND BARNABAS Deacon Thomas Santos, Admin.
Tel: 691-320-5822.

PORRASSAPW, CHRIST THE KING Deacons Saulus Olbet, Admin.; Koropin Kermen.
Tel: 691-320-3744.

SEINWAR, MOST PURE HEART OF MARY Deacon Luciano Iowanis.
Tel: 691-320-3573.

SOKEHS, ST. PETER'S Deacon Albert Linny, Admin.
Tel: 691-320-4667; 691-320-6923.

TAMOROI, SACRED HEART Rev. Gregory F. Muckenhaupt, S.J.
Mission— Pohnpei, 96941.

YAP STATE, CAROLINE ISLANDS

Mailing Address for the Vicariate of Yap: Rev. Paul L. Horgan, S.J., Vicar, P.O. Box A, Yap, FM 96943. Tel: 691-350-2265; Fax: 350-2784.

GAGIL-TOMIL, ST. JOSEPH Rev. Eddy Anthony, S.J.
Tel: 691-350-2598.

NEMAR, ST. MARY
School—St. Mary's Sr. Vincent Marie Balajadia, S.S.N.D., Prin. Priests 1; Sisters 1; Lay Teachers 13; Students 310.

ULITHI AND NEIGHBORING ISLANDS, QUEEN OF HEAVEN Deacon John Rulmal.
Mission— Ngulu.

WOLEAI AND NEIGHBORING ISLANDS, ST. IGNATIUS Rev. John S. Hagileiram, S.J.

REPUBLIC OF PALAU, CAROLINE ISLANDS

Mailing Address for the Vicariate of Palau: Rev. Rusk R. Sabaro, Vicar, P.O. Box 128, Koror, Palau PW 96940. Tel: 680-488-1758; Fax: 680-488-1819.

BABELDAOB, ST. THOMAS APOSTLE Rev. Wayne Tkel, S.J., Admin.

IOUELDOAB, ST. JOHN BAPTIST Rev. John Paul Ililau.

KOROR, SACRED HEART Rev. Rusk R. Saburo.
School—Maris Stella Mr. Felix Okabe, Prin. Mercedarian Missionaries of Berriz 6; Lay Teachers 23; Students 330.
Mission— Ngcheangl.
Mission— Sonsorol.
Convent—Our Lady of Lourdes Mercedarian Missionaries of Berriz 7.
Manresa Jesuit Novitiate—

Permanent Deacons:
Afeiluk, Christino, Weno, Chunk
Aien, Istor, Uman, Chuuk
Akapito, Camirino, Fefan, Chuuk
Akapito, Julio, Fefan, Chuuk
Albert, Joseph, Uman, Chuuk
Amor, Manuel, Awak, Pohnpei
Amor, Tarsisio, Ipwutek, Pohnpei
Buliche, Soichy, Satawan, Chuuk
Cholymay, Eliot, Neepwokos, Moen, Chuuk
Easu, Mariano, Polowot, Chuuk
Edgar, Martin, Kolonia, Pohnpei
Edmond, Atitor, Uman, Chuuk
Else, Pelsiano, Sapwuahfik, Pohnpei
Elukan, Augustine, (Retired), Maap, Yap
Fabian, Rikarto, Weno, Chuuk
Felichoo, Francisco, Gagil-Tomil, Yap
Fichiman, Donald, Gagil-Tomil, Yap
Fidel, Rinder, Tolas, Chuuk
Fritz, John, Udot, Chuuk
Iowanis, Tuciano, Seinwar, Pohnpei
Itiraw, Bername, Neepwukos, Chuuk
James, Kawaichy, Murilo, Chuuk
Kanas, Patrick, Fefan, Chuuk
Karsom, Eichy, Udot, Chuuk
Kermen, Koropin, Kiti, Pohnpei
Kerno, Sam, Udot, Chuuk
Linny, Albert, Sokehs, Pohnpei
Lorens, Adelino, Uh, Pohnpei
Mailos, Salvador, Uman, Chuuk
Meisa, Akiuo, Uman, Chuuk
Naich, Julio, Pollap, Chuuk
Nimas, Andreas, Uman, Chuuk
Noporu, Yostaro, Fono, Chuuk
Olbet, Saulus, Porrassapw, Pohnpei
Oneitam, Nory, Uman, Chuuk
Paulus, Lucas, Fanapanges, Chuuk
Pius, Siano, Wonei, Chuuk
Rano, Julian, Romanum, Chuuk
Raphael, Krispino, Polle, Chuuk
Rapun, Angken, Tol, Chuuk
Rapun, Enato, Tol, Chuuk
Rawit, Kintin, Wonei, Chuuk
Reim, Iowanes, Fefan, Chuuk
Robert, Pisek, Mekur (Weito), Chuuk
Rodriguez, Martiniano, Kolonia, Pohupei
Rokop, Roke, Tol, Chuuk
Rulmal, John B., Ulithi, Yap
Ruta, Itoi, Tol, Chuuk
Sadlin, Anasio, Fefan, Chuuk
Sam, Karlos, Uman, Chuuk
Santos, Thomas, Palikir, Pohnpei
Sewell, Meisa, Tol, Chuuk
Shuru, Edwin, (Retired), Moen, Chuuk
Silbanuz, Peter, Tamworoi, Pohnpei
Soram, Tobias, Tolowas, Chuuk
Sos, Iakim, Uman, Chuuk
Soumwei, Petrus, Kuttu, Chuuk
Victus, Oiken, Pwene, Chuuk
William, Chitaro, Tunnuk, Moen, Chuuk
Xymon, Angken, Fefan, Chuuk
Ykuda, Gabriel, Polle, Chuuk
Ykuta, Francisco, Pwene, Chuuk

INSTITUTIONS LOCATED IN THE DIOCESE

[A] PASTORAL RESEARCH INSTITUTE

POHNPEI. *Micronesian Seminar*, P.O. Box 160, 96941. Tel: 691-320-4067; Fax: 691-320-5876. Rev. Francis X. Hezel, S.J., Dir. Lay Assistants 2.

[B] HIGH SCHOOLS

CHUUK. *Saramen Chuuk Academy*, P.O. Box 662, 96942. Tel: 691-330-4442; Fax: 691-330-4452. Mr. Wayne Olap, Prin. Sisters 4; Lay Teachers 18; Students 249.
Xavier High School, P.O. Box 220, 96942. Tel: 691-330-4266; Fax: 691-330-4753. Rev. Richard McAuliff, S.J., Dir.; Ms. Anne Traynor, Prin. Lay Teachers 13; Scholastics 2; Students 153.

PALAU. *Mindszenty High School*, P.O. Box 69. Tel: 680-488-2437. Ms. Justa Polloi, Prin. Priests 1; Mercedarian Sisters 1; Lay Teachers 17; Students 197.

POHNPEI. *Our Lady of Mercy Vocational Training School*, P.O. Box 73, 96941. Tel: 691-320-3168. Sr. Maria Perez-Caballero, M.M.B., Prin. Mercedarian Sisters 3; Lay Teachers 6; Students 61.

[C] RESIDENCES OF PRIESTS AND BROTHERS

KOLONIA, POHNPEI. *Jesuit House*, P.O. Box 160, 96941. Tel: 691-320-2317; Fax: 691-320-5876. In Res. Revs. Joseph A. Cavanagh, S.J.; John F. Curran, S.J., J.C.L., Vicar Gen. & E. Vicar; Francis X. Hezel, S.J., Supr.; Dave Andrews, S.J.; Gregory F. Muckenhaupt, S.J.

KOROR, PALAU. *Manresa Jesuit House*, P.O. Box 128. Tel: 680-488-2226; Fax: 680-488-1819; 680-488-1725. Revs. Kenneth J. Hezel, S.J., Regl. Supr.; Rusk R. Saburo; John Paul Ililau; Wayne Tkel, S.J.

TUNNUK, CHUUK. *Vicariate Residence*, P.O. Box 250, 96942. Tel: 691-330-2313; Fax: 691-330-4394. In Res. Revs. Julio Angkel; Basilio Dilipy, Admin.; David Lewis; Edmond Ludwick; Nicholas P. Rahoy; Rosendo Rudolf; Fernando Titus.

[D] RESIDENCES OF SISTERS

AWAK, POHNPEI. *Sisters of Marie Auxiliatrice*, P.O. Box 1375, 96942. Tel: 691-320-2626. Sisters 6.

COLONIA, YAP. *Maryknoll Sisters*, P.O. Box 26, 96943. Tel: 691-350-2148 (Colonia). Sr. Joanne McMahon, M.M., Contact Person. Sisters 3.
School Sisters of Notre Dame, P.O. Box 111, 96943. Tel: 691-350-2345. Sr. Vincent Marie Balajadia, S.S.N.D., Contact Person. Sisters 2.

KOLONIA, POHNPEI. *Mercedarian Missionaries of Berriz*, P.O. Box 73, 96941. Tel: 691-320-2558. Sr. Gloria Billimont, M.M.B., Coord. Sisters 4.

KOROR, PALAU. *Mercedarian Missionaries of Berriz*, P.O. Box 56. Tel: 680-488-2272. Sr. Micaela Udui, M.M.B., Coord. Sisters 7.

NEEPWUKOS, CHUUK. *Religious Sisters of Mercy* 96942. Tel: 691-330-3363. Sr. Grace Joseph, R.S.M., Coord. Sisters 1.

WENO, CHUUK. *Mercedarian Missionaries of Berriz*, P.O. Box 67, 96942. Tel: 691-330-4587. Sr. Faustina Nedelec, M.M.B., Coord. Sisters 5.

RELIGIOUS INSTITUTES OF MEN REPRESENTED IN THE DIOCESE

For further details refer to the corresponding bracketed number in the Religious Institutes of Men or Women section.

[0690]—*Jesuit Fathers and Brothers* (New York Prov.)—S.J.
[1110]—*Missionaries of the Sacred Heart*—M.S.C.

RELIGIOUS INSTITUTES OF WOMEN REPRESENTED IN THE DIOCESE

[2470]—*Maryknoll Sisters of St. Dominic*—M.M.
[2510]—*Mercedarian Missionaries of Berriz*—M.M.B.
[2970]—*School Sisters of Notre Dame*—S.S.N.D.
[]—*Sisters of Marie Auxiliatrice*—M.A.
[2575]—*Sisters of Mercy of the Americas*—R.S.M.
[]—*Sisters of the Immaculate Heart of Mary*—S.I.H.M.

NECROLOGY

(No Deaths)

An asterisk (*) denotes an organization that has established tax-exempt status directly with the IRS and is not covered by the USCCB Group Ruling.

Diocese of Chalan Kanoa

(Dioecesis Vialenbensis)

Reverend

RYAN P. JIMENEZ

Apostolic Administrator; ordained priest June 8, 2003 by Most Rev. Tomas A. Camacho; appointed Apostolic Administrator December 28, 2010 by his Holiness Pope Benedict XVI.

(VACANT SEE)

Web: www.cnmicatholic.org

Email: diocese@pticom.com

Most Reverend

TOMAS A. CAMACHO, D.D.

Bishop Emeritus of Chalan Kanoa; ordained June 14, 1961; appointed Prelate of Honor by Pope Paul VI in 1974; appointed Bishop of Chalan Kanoa November 8, 1984; consecrated and installed January 13, 1985; retired April 6, 2010. *Res.: Bishop's Residence, P.O. Box 500745 CK, Saipan, MP 96950.* Tel: 670-235-1114.

ESTABLISHED NOVEMBER 8, 1984.

Square Miles 184.

Corporate Title: "Bishop of Chalan Kanoa, a Corporation Sole."

Comprises the Mariana Island chain except for Guam, known legally as the Commonwealth of the Northern Mariana Islands.

For legal titles of parishes and diocesan institutions, consult the Diocesan Curia.

STATISTICAL OVERVIEW

Personnel	
Retired Bishops	1
Priests: Diocesan Active in Diocese	12
Number of Diocesan Priests	12
Religious Priests in Diocese	1
Total Priests in Diocese	13
Parishes	
Parishes	12
With Resident Pastor:	
Resident Diocesan Priests	11
Resident Religious Priests	1
Missions	1
Pastoral Centers	1
Professional Ministry Personnel:	
Lay Ministers	70
Welfare	
Specialized Homes	1
Total Assisted	138
Special Centers for Social Services	2
Total Assisted	3,258
Educational	
Diocesan Students in Other Seminaries	1
Total Seminarians	1
High Schools, Private	1
Total Students	156
Elementary Schools, Diocesan and Parish	3
Total Students	169
Catechesis/Religious Education:	
High School Students	697
Elementary Students	663
Total Students under Catholic Instruction	1,686
Teachers in the Diocese:	
Priests	2
Sisters	2
Lay Teachers	20
Vital Statistics	
Receptions into the Church:	
Infant Baptism Totals	459
Minor Baptism Totals	21
Adult Baptism Totals	20
Received into Full Communion	25
First Communions	610
Confirmations	632
Marriages:	
Catholic	53
Interfaith	2
Total Marriages	55
Deaths	127
Total Catholic Population	43,000
Total Population	71,850

Former Bishop—Most Rev. TOMAS A. CAMACHO, ord. June 14, 1961; appt. Prelate of Honor by Pope Paul VI in 1974; appt. Bishop of Chalan Kanoa Nov. 8, 1984; cons. and installed Jan. 13, 1985; retired April 6, 2010.

Diocesan Curia—Mailing Address: P.O. Box 500745, Saipan, 96950. Tel: 670-234-3000; Fax: 670-235-3002.

Vicar General—VACANT.

Chancellor—Rev. RYAN JIMENEZ.

Finance Officer—Mrs. BETTINA LYNETTE G. TERLAJE.

Personnel Officer—VACANT.

Director of Vocations—Rev. JESSE T. REYES, Dir.

Director of Religious Education—Sr. ESTELA V. ALTEA, S.G.B.P., Dir.

Superintendent of Catholic Schools—Rev. RYAN JIMENEZ.

Director of Worship—Rev. ISAAC M. AYUYU.

Director of Youth Ministry—VACANT.

Diocesan Curia Staff—Mrs. LOLITA M. BABAUTA, Office Mgr.; Mrs. MARITES L. VILLANUEVA, Accountant; Sr. ESTELA ALTEA, S.G.B.P., Archivist Librarian.

Consultative Bodies

Presbyteral Council—Rev. RYAN JIMENEZ; Rev. Msgr. LOUIS ANTONELLI; Revs. ISAAC M. AYUYU; KENNETH J. HEZEL, S.J.; CHARLITO A. BORJA; JAE (LUKE) HYEONG LEE; REY ROSAL; ISIDRO T. OGUMORO; AURELIUS E. STOIA; JESSE T. REYES; RAUL SALGADO; FLORENTINO E. RECAIDO JR.; FRANCISCO M. SANTOS; CELSO MAGBANUA JR.

College of Consultor—VACANT.

Diocesan Finance Council—Mr. EDWARD MANIBUSAN, Ex Officio; ROSE SOLEDAD; Mr. KARL REYES; EDWARD C. SABLAN; Mr. CHARLES V. CEPEDA; CRISPIN M. SABLAN.

Diocesan Pastoral Council— Representatives from every Parish, Clergy and Religious. Sr. MARYANN HARTMANN, M.M.B.; CHRISTOPHER TENORIO; VIRGINIA C. VILLAGOMEZ; HERBERT S. DELROSARIO; JAMES LG. SABLAN; ROSIKY F. CAMACHO; JOSEFA C. TAITANO; MARIE T. MUNA; Sr. VERONICA A. BENAVENTE; FRANCES T. JOHNSON; TRICIA T. TENORIO; NIEVES L. BABAUTA; NOMINANDA L. KOSAKA; PRESCILLA SN. MUNA; MARGARET C. DELACRUZ; MARCELINA P. CEPEDA; MARIA MALUA T. PETER; FRANCISCO M. DIAZ; BAE IN HWA; HAN GI YANG; RITA A. MANGLONA; ROSA P. ACQUININGOC; ANICETO MUNDO; FRANCISCO S. CALVO; VINCENT M. CALVO.

Diocesan Tribunal

Judicial Vicar—Rev. Msgr. DAVID C. QUITUGUA, J.C.D.

Marriage Tribunal Judge—VACANT.

Defender of the Bond—VACANT.

Tribunal Auditor—VACANT.

Diocesan Commissions

Commission on Worship—Rev. ISAAC M. AYUYU.

Commission on Justice and Development—Mr. JOHN GONZALES, Coord.

Commission on Evangelization—VACANT.

Commission on Family Life—ROSIKY CAMACHO, Chm.

Commission on Ministerial Development—VACANT.

Commission on Vocation Team—Rev. JESSE T. REYES.

Commission on Heritage Cultural of the Church—Rev. RYAN JIMENEZ, Chm.

Apostolic Works of the Diocese

Diocesan Publications Office—Revs. RYAN JIMENEZ, Dir.; CELSO MAGBANUA JR., Editor of "North Star" (Diocesan Newspaper); Ms. JOCELYN GUERRERO, Advertising Mgr.

Electronic Media—Rev. RYAN JIMENEZ.

Hospital Chaplaincy (Saipan)—Rev. RAUL SALGADO.

Mt. Carmel Catholic Cemetery—Mr. EDWARD S. TENORIO, Chm.

Prison Chaplaincy—Rev. JESSE T. REYES.

Police and Fire Departments Chaplaincy—Rev. JESSE T. REYES.

St. Joseph Catholic School (Tinian)—Rev. ISIDRO T. OGUMORO, Acting Prin.

Civilly Incorporated Activities of the Diocese

Mount Carmel School, Inc. (Saipan)—Mrs. ELIZABETH S. BALAJADIA, Chm.; Mrs. MARGARET C. DELA CRUZ, Pres.; Mr. BOBBY NELSON BALDAZO; Rev. CELSO MAGBANUA JR., Chap.

Eskuelan San Francisco de Borja School, Inc. (Rota)—Mr. FRANK CALVO, Chm.; Sisters ZOSIMA CAPUA, R.V.M., Admin.; JOSIELINDA S. TANUDTANUD, R.V.M.

Karidat, Inc.—Ms. JUDY DLG. TORRES, Pres. Bd. Directors; Ms. ANGIE V. GUERRERO, Exec. Dir.

Associations of the Faithful

A.G.A.P.E. (Almighty God and People Encounter)—(Inactive) Adult Leaders: CRIS SABLAN; LUCINDA SABLAN; Rev. FLORENTINO E. RECAIDO JR., Spiritual Dir.

Catholic Daughters of America— (Inactive) Mrs. FELICIDAD OGUMORO, Regent.

Children of God the Father, Inc.—Mr. CARLOS VALERO, Pres.; Ms. ROXANN D. ARANDA, Vice Pres.; Rev. REY ROSAL, Spiritual Dir.

Confraternity of Christian Mothers—Mrs. ANGELICA MANGARERO, Diocesan Bd. Pres.; Rev. JESSE T. REYES, Spiritual Dir.

Couples for Christ—Household Leader: Mr. NEL MATANGUIHAN.

Cursillo Movement—STANLEY BENAVENTE, Pres.; Rev. RYAN JIMENEZ, Spiritual Dir.

El Shaddai Movement—Sr. CORA SAN GABRIEL, Leader.

Eucharistic Adoration Society—Most Rev. TOMAS AGUON CAMACHO, Bishop Emeritus; ELIZABETH CHO; FRANCISCO PALACIOS.

Knights of Columbus—Sir Knight ROBERT ALDAN, District Deputy; Rev. CHARLITO A. BORJA, Spiritual Dir. for Rev. Msgr. Vicente T. Martinez Council & Pale Luis Medina Council.

Legion of Mary—Rev. AURELIUS E. STOIA, Diocesan Spiritual Dir.

San Roque Parish - Mother of Divine Love Praesidium—Mrs. RIZALINA CANO, Pres.; VACANT, Spiritual Dir.

Legion of Mary at San Antonio Parish/Mother of Perpetual Help Praesidium—VACANT, Spiritual Dir.

Legion of Mary at Kristo Rai Parish/Mother Refuge of Sinners, Praesidium—Ms. OLIVE ONEDERA, Pres.; Rev. CELSO MAGBANUA JR., Spiritual Dir.

Legion of Mary at San Jose Parish/Rainan i Gef Santos Na Lisayo—Mrs. ANGELICA MANGARERO, Pres.; Rev. JESSE T. REYES, Spiritual Dir.

Light & Salt Catholic Charismatic Community—CELY ZAMORA, Head Servant; VACANT, Spiritual Dir.

Divine Mercy—Rev. JESSE T. REYES, Spiritual Dir.

Marriage Encounter—Main Contact: Mr. CHARLES V. CEPEDA, Ecclesial Team; Mrs. CATHY S. CEPEDA; Rev. ISAAC M. AYUYU, Spiritual Dir.

CLERGY, PARISHES, MISSIONS AND PAROCHIAL SCHOOLS

ISLAND OF SAIPAN

CHALAN KANOA VILLAGE, CATHEDRAL OF OUR LADY OF MT. CARMEL Most Rev. Tomas Aguon Camacho, Bishop Emeritus; Revs. Ryan Jimenez; Isaac M. Ayuyu; Florentino E. Recaido Jr.
Rectory—Mt. Carmel, P.O. Box 500745, 96950. Tel: 670-234-3000.
Mission—Korean Catholic Community P.O. Box 693, 96950. Tel: 670-235-1449; 670-235-1450. Rev. Jae Hyeong (Luke) Lee.
Oratory—Mercedarian Missionary Sisters of Berriz, Formation House.

GARAPAN VILLAGE, DISTRICT 11, KRISTO RAI PARISH Rev. Celso Magbanua Jr.
Oratory—Maturana House of Prayer
Oratory—Navy Hill, Commonwealth Health Center Chapel

KAGMAN VILLAGE, SANTA SOLEDAD MISSION PARISH Rev. Raul Salgado.
Mailing Address: P.O. Box 500745, 96950. Tel: 670-256-4568; 670-234-3000.

SAIPAN, SAN JUDE PARISH Rev. Kenneth J. Hezel, S.J.
Rectory—P.O. Box 500745, 96950. Tel: 670-288-0007; Fax: 670-235-3002.

SAN ANTONIO VILLAGE, DISTRICT 6, SAN ANTONIO PARISH, Unassigned.
Rectory—San Antonio, P.O. Box 500745, 96950. Tel: 670-235-4515.

SAN JOSE VILLAGE, DISTRICT 7, SAN JOSE PARISH Rev. Jesse T. Reyes.
Rectory—P.O. Box 500745, 96950. Tel: 670-234-6991.

SAN ROQUE VILLAGE, DISTRICT 9, SAN ROQUE PARISH, Unassigned.
Rectory—P.O. Box 500745, 96950. Tel: 670-322-2404.

SAN VICENTE VILLAGE, DISTRICT 10, SAN VICENTE PARISH Rev. Rey Rosal.
Rectory—San Vicente, P.O. Box 500745, 96950. Tel: 670-235-8208.
Oratory—Our Lady of the Most Holy Rosary Dandan.

TANAPAG VILLAGE, DISTRICT 8, SANTA REMEDIOS PARISH Rev. Aurelius E. Stoia.
Rectory—P.O. Box 500745, 96950. Tel: 670-322-7254.

ISLAND OF ROTA

SONGSONG VILLAGE
1—SAN FRANCISCO DE BORJA PARISH Rev. Charlito A. Borja.
Rectory—San Francisco de Borja, Songsong Village, P.O. Box 542, Rota, 96951. Tel: 670-532-3522.
2—SAN ISIDRO PARISH (Sinapalo) Rev. Msgr. Louis Antonelli.
Rectory—Sinapalo Village, P.O. Box 590, Rota, 96951. Tel: 670-532-0720.

ISLAND OF TINIAN

SAN JOSE VILLAGE, SAN JOSE Rev. Isidro T. Ogumoro.
Catholic Rectory, San Jose Village—Tinian, 96952. Tel: 670-433-3000.
School—St. Joseph Catholic School, (Grades K-6), P.O. Box 282, Tinian, 96952. Tel: 670-433-7527; Fax: 670-433-7527.

DIOCESAN MISSIONS

San Ignacio Chapel (Island of Pagan)San Jose Chapel (Island of Anatahan)Santa Cruz Chapel (Island of Alamagan)Santa Cruz Chapel (Island of Agrihan)

INSTITUTIONS LOCATED IN THE DIOCESE

[A] ELEMENTARY AND HIGH SCHOOLS

TINIAN. *St. Joseph Catholic School*, (Grades K-6), P.O. Box 282, 96952. Tel: 670-433-7527; Fax: 670-433-7527. Rev. Isidro T. Ogumoro, Acting Prin.

[B] RESIDENCES OF SISTERS

SAIPAN. *Chalan Kanoa Formation House*, P.O. Box 500136, 96950. Tel: 670-234-6214. Sr. Martha Ramarui, M.M.B., Local Coord. Sisters 3.

MMB Maturana Community, P.O. Box 501178-CK, 96950. Tel: 670-322-9713. Email: mmbmaturana@pticom.com. Web: www.mmberriz.com. Sr. MaryAnn Hartmann, M.M.B., Local Coord. Sisters 12.

Pastorelle Sisters Convent (San Antonio Parish), P.O. Box 745, 96950. Tel: 670-234-1213. Sisters Estela Altea, S.G.B.P., Local Coord.; Teresa Han, S.G.B.P., Local Coord.

RELIGIOUS INSTITUTES OF MEN REPRESENTED IN THE DIOCESE

For further details refer to the corresponding bracketed number in the Religious Institutes of Men or Women section.

[0690]—*The Society of Jesus*—S.J.

RELIGIOUS INSTITUTES OF WOMEN REPRESENTED IN THE DIOCESE

[2510]—*Mercedarian Missionaries of Berriz*—M.M.B.
[]—*Pastorelle Sisters*
[]—*Religious of the Virgin Mary*—R.V.M.
[1830]—*Sisters of the Good Shepherd*—R.G.S.

NECROLOGY

† Corcuera, Manuel R., Apostolic Administrator of Chalan Kanoa.—Died Dec. 19, 2010

An asterisk (*) denotes an organization that has established tax-exempt status directly with the IRS and is not covered by the USCCB Group Ruling.

Diocese of Fajardo-Humacao, Puerto Rico

(Dioecesis Faiardensis-Humacaensi)

(Editor's Note: 2012 information was not received)

Most Reverend

EUSEBIO RAMOS MORALES

Bishop of Fajardo-Humacao; ordained December 15, 1983; appointed Bishop of Fajardo-Humacao March 11, 2008; consecrated May 31, 2008.

Bishop House: *Carr #987 Km. 0.2 Santa Isidra I #206, Fajardo, PR 00738. Mailing Address: Apartado 888, Fajardo, PR 00738.* Tel: 787-801-5700; 787-801-5800; Fax: 787-801-2600.

Email: diocesisfajardohumacao@gmail.com

ESTABLISHED JUNE 1, 2008

Comprises southeast municipalies of Puerto Rico: Humacao, Naguabo; east municipalies of Puerto Rico: Ceiba, Fajardo, Luquillo, northeast municipalies of Puerto Rico Rio Grande, Loiza, Canovanas and the Islands Municipalies of Culebra and Vieques.

Patroness of the Diocese: Nuestra Senora del Carmen and Santiago Apostol (extra-official).

STATISTICAL OVERVIEW

Personnel	
Bishop	1
Priests: Diocesan Active in Diocese	19
Number of Diocesan Priests	19
Religious Priests in Diocese	11
Total Priests in Diocese	30
Extern Priests in Diocese	3
Ordinations:	
Transitional Deacons	1
Permanent Deacons in Diocese	26
Total Brothers	6
Total Sisters	27
Parishes	
Parishes	21
With Resident Pastor:	
Resident Diocesan Priests	16
Resident Religious Priests	5
Welfare	
Day Care Centers	1
Total Assisted	26
Special Centers for Social Services	1
Total Assisted	27
Educational	
Diocesan Students in Other Seminaries	1
Total Seminarians	1
High Schools, Diocesan and Parish	6
Total Students	1,676
Elementary Schools, Diocesan and Parish	5
Total Students	1,243
Catechesis/Religious Education:	
Elementary Students	215
Total Students under Catholic Instruction	3,135
Vital Statistics	
Receptions into the Church:	
Infant Baptism Totals	588
Adult Baptism Totals	85
First Communions	529
Confirmations	392
Marriages:	
Catholic	85
Interfaith	12
Total Marriages	97
Deaths	381
Total Catholic Population	97,869
Total Population	293,000

Vicar General—Rev. VICENTE PARQUALETTO, S.T.

Sec. Chancellor—Rev. MIGUEL A. MERCED REYES.

Diocesan Offices and Directors

Economic Administrator—Mr. HECTOR N. GONZALEZ, CPA, Mailing Address: P.O. Box 888, Fajardo, 00738. Tel: 787-801-5700; 787-801-5800; Fax: 787-801-2600.

Movimientos y Organizaciones Diocesanas—

Cursillos de Cristiandad—Mr. JOHNNY MORALES; Mr. JOSE MARRERO.

Legion de Maria—Mrs. AIDA JIMENEZ.

Renovacion Carismatica—Mrs. LUCY FIGUEROA; NILDA VELAZQUEZ.

Juan XXIII—Mr. MIGUEL ESCALERA.

Caballeros de Colon—Mr. JUSTINO CRUZ.

Vicentinos—VACANT.

Talleres de Oracion y Vida—VACANT.

Catechetical Vicar—Rev. ANGEL LUIS CINTRON.

Master of Ceremonies—Rev. JOSE A. AROCHO, Mailing Address: P.O. Box 888, Fajardo, 00738.

Pastoral Vicar—Rev. OSCAR SANCHEZ, Mailing Address: P.O. Box 888, Fajardo, 00738.

Vocations—Rev. ANGEL LUIS CINTRON.

CLERGY, PARISHES, MISSIONS AND PAROCHIAL SCHOOLS

CITY OF FAJARDO

1—CATHEDRAL SANTIAGO APOSTOL (1766) Rev. Angel L. Cintron Ortiz, Rector.
Res.: 16 Garrido Morales St., P.O. Box 806, 00738. Tel: 787-863-2365; Fax: 787-860-1837.
Catechesis/Religious Program—Students 55.
Chapel—Bo. Florencio, Santa Elena (1962)
Chapel—Bo. Quebrada Vueltas, Perpetuo Socorro (1965)
Chapel—La Milagrosa (1978)
Chapel—Santa Isidra, Santiago Apostol

2—SANTISIMO REDENTOR (1993) Rev. Jose A. Arocho.
Res.: Urb. Monte Brisas, Calle C-V-19, 00738. Tel: 787-863-5227; Fax: 787-860-0560.
Catechesis/Religious Program—Students 140.
Chapel—Puerto Real, Ntra. Sra. de Carmen
Chapel—Sardinera, San Juan Bautista
Chapel—Las Croabas, Maria, Madre del Senor
Chapel—Fajardo Gardens, Maria, Madre de la Providencia

CITY OF HUMACAO

3—CONCATHEDRAL DULCE NOMBRE DE JESUS (Pueblo) (1763) [CEM 3] [JC] Revs. Floyd Mercado, Rector; Raguiel Rodriguez Leon; Deacons Angel Cruz Cruz; Eduardo Del Rivero; Rafael Medinc; Angel M. Rodriguez.
Res.: 3 Font Martelo St., Box 9087, Humacao, 00791. Tel: 787-852-0868; Fax: 787-850-6448.
Catechesis/Religious Program—Students 380.
Chapel—San Agustin (1955) Parcela No. 44, Bo. Anton Ruiz, Humacao, 00792.
Chapel—Nuestra Senora de la Candelaria (1956) Parcela No. 30, Candelero Arriba, Humacao, 00791.
Chapel—San Jose (1957) Carr. 922 Cotto Mabu, Humacao, 00791.
Chapel—Nuestra Senora de Fatima (1962) Bo. Juniquito, Humacao, 00791.
Chapel—Santa Teresita (1965) Bo. Candelero Abajo, Humacao, 00791.
Chapel—Nuestra Senora de la Providencia (2000) Bo. Catano, Humacao, 00791.
Chapel—Perpetuo Socorro (1944) Bo. Buena Vista, Humacao, 00791.
Chapel—Inmaculada Concepcion (1996) Urbanizacion Villa, Humacao, 00791.
Chapel—Maria Auxiliadora (1999) Bo. Candelero Abajo, Parcelas Martinez.

4—MARIA REINA DE LA PAZ (Pueblo) (1989) Revs. Kharlosg Lopez; Jose A. Marrero; Deacons Rafael Ulfret; Jose L. Ortiz; Juan Cintron.
Res.: Urb. Villa Universitaria, Calle 4 A-20, Humacao, 00791. Tel: 787-850-3081; 787-285-0351; Fax: 787-850-3080. Email: mariapaz@libertypr.net.
Catechesis/Religious Program—Students 210.
Chapel—Sagrado Corazon de Jesus (1940)
Chapel—San Martin de Porres (1962)
Chapel—Buen Pastor (1970)
Chapel—Bo. Tejas, Cristo Rey (1976)
Chapel—Bo. Mariana II, Santa Rosa de Lima (1978)
Chapel—Comunidad Vista Hermosa

OUTSIDE THE CITIES OF FAJARDO AND HUMACAO

CANOVANAS

1—NUESTRA SENORA DEL PILAR (1960) Rev. Fabio Moncada (Colombia); Deacon Jose R. Rivera.
P.O. Box 1615, 00729-1615.
Res.: Luis Hernaiz St., #3, 00729. Tel: 787-876-2655; 787-876-3002; Fax: 787-256-5767.
School—3 Luis Hernaiz St., 00729. Iris Del Valle, Dir. Lay Teachers 50; Students 900.
Catechesis/Religious Program—Raquel Ortiz, D.R.E. Students 11.
Mission—San Francisco Javier Bo. Camabalache, 00729.

2—RESURRECCION DEL SEÑOR (1978) Rev. Jesus Palomanes-Vega, S.T. (Mexico); Deacons Pedro Flores; Miguel Roman.
Mailing Address: P.O. Box 896, 00729-0896.
Res.: Las Parcelas de San Isidro, Carret. 188 Km. 2.0, 00729. Tel: 787-876-3917; Fax: 787-256-4836.
Mission—Ntra. Sra. de la Providencia Villas De Loiza.

3—SAGRADO CORAZON DE JESUS (1991) Rev. Fabian Rodriguez, S.J.; Deacon Anthony Calderon.
PMB 20147, P.O. Box 35000, 00729-0014.
Res.: Bo. Cubuy, Carretera 186 Km. 77, 00729. Tel: 787-876-1355; Fax: 787-886-3668.
Mission—La Milagrosa Bo. Cuatrocientas, 00729.
Mission—San Pedro Apostol Bo. Lomas, PR.

4—SAN JOSE (1971) Rev. Oscar Alberto Sanchez-Lopez; Deacon Felipe Rivera.

P.O. Box 807, 00729-0807.
Res.: Bo. Campo Rico, Carretera 185, 00729. Tel: 787-876-7167.
Mission—Ntra. Sra. de la Asuncion Carrt. 957 Km. 6.8, Palma Sola.
Mission—Ntra. Sra. del Carmen Carrt. 185 Km. 5.3, Alturas de Campo Rico.

5—SANTA MARIA MADRE DE DIOS (1971) Rev. Jose A. Rivera Maldonado; Deacon Jose L. Casaigne.
Res.: Urb. Loiza Valley, Calle Girasol E189, 00729. Tel: 787-876-0827; Fax: 787-876-0827.
Catechesis/Religious Program—Sr. Gloria Mercedes Gonzalez, M.S.B.T., D.R.E. Students 58.
Mission—Capilla Cristo Salvador Sector Pueblo Indio.
Mission—Iglesia Santa Maria Madre De Dios Carr. 8874-Bo. La Central. Tel: 787-876-1490; Fax: 787-876-1490.

CEIBA, CEIBA CO., SAN ANTONIO DE PADUA (1840) Rev. Adrian Alicea Rivera, Admin.
Res.: 561 Escolastico Lopez St., P.O. Box 77, 00735. Tel: 787-885-2530; Fax: 787-885-2218.
Mission—Sagrado Corazon de Jesus Parcelas Aguas Claras, 00735.
Mission—N.S. del Perpetuo Socorro Bo. Rio Abajo, Ceiba Co. 00735.
Chapel—Nuestra Senora de Fatima (1968) Bo. Daguao, 00735.
Catechesis/Religious Program—Students 112.

HUMACAO PLAYA, HUMACAO CO., NUESTRA SENORA DEL CARMEN (Punta Santiago) (1970) Rev. Miguel A. Merced; Deacon Jose A. Nevarez.
Res.: P.O. Box 91, Punta Santiago, 00741. Tel: 787-850-2125; Fax: 787-850-2125.
Catechesis/Religious Program—Calle 5, #103 Verde Mar, P.O. Box 91, Punta Santiago, 00741. Tel: 787-852-3882. Students 125.
Chapel—Bo. Pasto Viejo, Sector El Batey, Nuestra Senora del Perpetuo Socorro (1937; 1986)Tel: 787-852-4421.

LOIZA
1—SAN PATRICIO (1719) Rev. Felix Rivera Rivera; Deacons Santiago Acosta; Marcos Penaloza; Pastor Perez.
Box 504, 00772-0504.
Res.: Calle Espiritu Santo #10, 00772. Tel: 787-886-1539; Fax: 787-876-7828.
Catechesis/Religious Program—Glorivee Davila, D.R.E. Students 79.
Mission—Santa Rosa Bo. Pinones.
Mission—Ntra. Sra. del Perpetuo Socorro Bo. La Torre.
Mission—Santisima Trinidad Bo. Mediana Baja.
Mission—San Antonio Bo. Las Cuevas, 00772.
Mission—Ntra. Sra. de Fatima Villa Canona, 00772.
Mission—San Rafael Villa Alvarez, 00772.

2—SANTIAGO APOSTOL, EL MAYOR (1971) Revs. Marco Sanchez, S.T.; Harold Stone, S.T.
P.O. Box 118, 00772-0118.
Res.: Carretera 187 Km. 6.1 Bo. Mediania Alta, 00772-0118. Tel: 787-876-1879.
Catechesis/Religious Program—Students 70.
Mission—Ntra. Sra. Perpetuo Socorro Parcelas Suarez.
Mission—La Milagrosa Bo. El Jobos.
Mission—La Providencia Bo. Mini Mine.
Mission—N. Sra. De Fatima Parcelas Vieques.

LUQUILLO
1—MADRE DEL REDENTOR (1997) Rev. Luis A. Alicea Rivera; Deacon Frank Rivera.
P.O. Box 591, 00773-0591.
Res.: Barrio Pitaya, Sector Casablanca, Carr. 173, Km. 1.5, 00773. Tel: 787-889-0733; Fax: 787-889-0733.
Catechesis/Religious Program—Students 35.
Mission—N. Sra. del Carmen Carr. 983 K.2 H.0, Bo. Pitahaya.
Mission—N. Sra. Milagrosa Carr. 983 K.6 H.3, Bo. Sabana.
Mission—S. Vicente de Paul Carr. 3H 43 H.9.
Mission—N. Sra. del Perpetuo Socorro Carr. 984 K.2 H.2, San Martin.

2—SAN JOSE (1797) Revs. Vicente Pasqualetto, S.T.; Mariano Fernandez-Diaz, S.T. (Colombia); Deacon Jesus Ramos.
P.O. Box 493, 00773-0493.
Res.: Calle Soledad No. 15, fronte a Plaza de Recreo, 00773. Tel: 787-889-2590; Fax: 787-889-2590.
Mission—San Judas Bo. Mata de Platano.
Mission—Ntra. Sra. del Cobre Parcelas Fortuna.

NAGUABO, NAGUABO CO., NUESTRA SENORA DEL ROSARIO (1794), (Hispanic), [CEM 2] [JC] Rev. Leonardo Rodriguez Ochoa.
Res.: Box 655, 00718. Tel: 787-874-2235; Fax: 787-874-0150. Email: pvrosario@hotmail.com.
Chapel—Nuestra Senora del Perpetuo Socorro (1946)
Chapel—Bo. Maizales, Nuestra Senora de la Altagracia (1963)
Chapel—Bo. Duque, Nuestra Senora de Fatima (1965)
Chapel—Bo. Florida, Nuestra Senora del Perpetuo Socorro (1942)
Chapel—Nuestra Senora del Carmen Playa Hucares (1920)
Chapel—Bo. Mariana, Nuestra Senora de la Providencia (1965)
Chapel—Bo. Santiago y Lima (Botija), Santa Rosa de Lima (1975)
Mission— Barrio Rio, Sector Brazo Seco.
Mission— Barrio Cecilia, Sector La Fe.

RIO GRANDE
1—SAN FRANCISCO DE ASIS (1986) Deacon Manuel Llanos.
Bo. Malpica, P.O. Box 1449, 00745-1449.
Res.: Barrio Malpica, 00745. Tel: 787-888-5302; Fax: 787-888-5302.

2—CRISTO REY (1970) Rev. Emerito Gomez Ortiz, O.F.M.; Deacon Pedro J. Rivera Viera.
P.O. Box 382, Palmer, 00721-0382.
Res.: Calle Principal, #50, Palmer, 00721. Tel: 787-887-3552. Email: pcristorey@libertypr.net.
Mission—La Milagrosa Palmer. Parcela 69 Hato Rio Grande, Bo. Carola, 00721.
Mission—Ntra. Sra. de la Providencia Bloque S-1 #7, Palmer, 00721.

3—NUESTRA SENORA DEL CARMEN (1840) Rev. Manuel R. Villamor; Deacons Jose Carrasquillo; Vidal Diaz; Juan Rodriguez.
P.O. Box 845, 00745. Tel: 787-887-2365; Fax: 787-887-2365.
Res.: No. 9 del Carmen St., Apartado 845, 00745. Tel: 787-888-3991. Email: delcarmen_9@yahoo.com.
School—Calle 14 Urb. Alturas de Rio Grande, Apartado 1389, P.O. Box 818, 00745. Tel: 787-887-4099; Fax: 787-887-0872. Email: cnscrg@yahoo.com. Raquel Ortiz, Prin.
Catechesis/Religious Program—Students 95.
Mission—Nuestra Senora de Fatima Bo. El Verde.
Mission—Ntra. Sra. de Guadalupe Jardines de Rio Grande, 00745.
Mission—San Pedro Bo. Bartolo.
Mission—La Milagrosa Calle 14, Alturas de Rio Grande, 00745.
Mission—Sagrado Corazon de Jesus Coco Beach, 00745.

OUTSIDE THE MAIN ISLAND OF PUERTO RICO, THE SMALL ISLANDS

CULEBRA, CULEBRA CO., NUESTRA SENORA DEL CARMEN (1889; 1990) Rev. Luis M. Ruiz.
Mailing Address: P.O. Box 236, 00775. Tel: 787-742-0133.

VIEQUES, VIEQUES CO., INMACULADA CONCEPCION (1844), (Hispanic), Rev. Nelson Lopez Aponte; Deacon Justino Lopez Ortiz.
Res.: 442 Lebrum St., 00765. Tel: 787-741-2241; Fax: 787-741-2241.
Chapel—Bo. Puerto Real, Sagrado Corazon de Jesus (1949)
Chapel—Bo. Esperanza, San Gerardo (1952)
Chapel—Bo. Monte Santo, Nuestra Senora del Perpetuo Socorro (1945)
Chapel—Bo. Santa Maria, Virgen del Carmen (1942)
Chapel—Bo. Destino, Nuestra Senora de Fatima (1950)

Chaplains of Public Institutions

Otero Lugo, Jose
Rivera Viera, Pedro J.

INSTITUTIONS LOCATED IN THE DIOCESE

[A] PAROCHIAL SCHOOLS

FAJARDO. *Colegio Santiago Apostol*, (Grades K-12), Call Box 70007, 00738. Tel: 787-863-0445; Fax: 787-860-6655. Email: santiagoapostolprl@yahoo.com. Web: www.csa-sec.org. Rev. Luis A. Alicea Rivera, Educ. Vicar; Mr. Daniel Ruben Ortiz, Prin.

HUMACAO. *Colegio Nuestra Senora del Perpetuo Socorro de Humacao, Inc.* (1984) P.O. Box 9107, 00792. Tel: 787-852-0845; Fax: 787-852-8706. Email: nuestrasocorro@gmail.com. Mrs. Mercedes M. De Arroyo, Prin.; Miss Diana Ortiz Salcedo, Librarian. Lay Teachers 26; Students 470.

Colegio San Antonio Abad (Benedictines), P.O. Box 729, 00792. Tel: 787-852-1616; Fax: 787-852-1920. Email: santabad@east-net.net. Glenda Bermudez, Prin. Brothers 3; Priests 3; Lay Teachers 29; Students 441.

Colegio San Benito (1963) P.O. Box 728, 00792. Tel: 787-850-7075; Fax: 787-285-8137. Sisters Mary Ruth Santana, Prin. (K-6); Myriam Pacheco, Dir.; Mrs. Isabel Sandel, Librarian. Sisters 6; Lay Teachers 43; Students 740.

[B] MONASTERIES AND RESIDENCES OF PRIESTS

HUMACAO. *San Antonio Abad Abbey of the Order of St. Benedict*, P.O. Box 729, 00792. Tel: 787-852-1616; Fax: 787-852-1920. Email: santabad@east-net.com. Rt. Rev. Oscar Rivera, O.S.B., Abbot; Revs. Rafael Perez, O.S.B.; Jaime Reyes, O.S.B.; Eric Buermann, O.S.B.; Mauro Simpson, O.S.B.; Ignacio Aguirre, O.S.B.; Bros. Aristedes Pacheco, Subprior; Felix Neussendorfer; Tarcisio Medina; Gregorio Valentin; Randolph Perkins; Antonio Hernandez. Brothers 8; Novices 2.

[C] HOMES AND RESIDENCES

CANOVANAS. *Hogar Teresa Toda* (1993) (For Girls), P.O. Box 868, 00729. Tel: 787-886-2060; Fax: 787-886-2075. Email: hteresatoda@aol.com; teresatoda@prtc.net. Web: www.teresatodapr.org. Calle 5-A, R-14, Villa De Loiza, Loiza, 00729. Tel: 787-886-2060; Fax: 787-886-2075. Sr. Ines Pena, Dir. Bed Capacity 28; Total Assisted Annually 60; Total Staff 15.

[D] MISCELLANEOUS

LOIZA. *Centro Esperanza, Inc.*, Calle 1, Esquina 4, Paracelas Vieques, 00772. Tel: 787-876-1545; Fax: 787-876-3389. Email: cesperanza@coqui.net. P.O. Box 482, 00772-0482. Sr. Carmen Gloria Alayon, H.C., Dir. & Contact Person. Sponsored by: Sisters of Charity, Saint Vincent de Paul.

Centro Providencia, 2 #175 Parcelas Suarez, 00772. Tel: 787-256-2320; Fax: 787-256-2320. Mailing Address: P.O. Box 482, 00772. Jose Alayon Martinez, Admin. Asst.

RELIGIOUS INSTITUTES OF WOMEN REPRESENTED IN THE DIOCESE

For further details refer to the corresponding bracketed number in the Religious Institutes of Men or Women section.

[]—*Carmelitas Teresas de San Jose*
[]—*Cenaculo Misionero Rafael Cordero*
[]—*Hermanas de Nazareth*
[]—*Hermanas Dominicas de la Santa Cruz*
[]—*Hijas de la Caridad de San Vicente de Paul*
[]—*Hijas del Corazon de Maria*
[]—*Monasterio Santa Escolastica*

NECROLOGY

(No Deaths)

Prefecture Apostolic of the Marshall Islands

Reverend Monsignor

RAYMUNDO T. SABIO, M.S.C.

Second Prefect Apostolic of the Marshall Islands; ordained December 20, 1971; appointed December 21, 2007; installed January 6, 2008. *Res.: Cathedral of the Assumption, Uliga, P.O. Box 8, Majuro, MH 96960.* Tel: 962-625-6675; Fax: 962-625-5520.

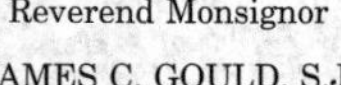

Reverend Monsignor

JAMES C. GOULD, S.J.

First Prefect Apostolic of the Marshall Islands; ordained May 4, 1974; appointed First Prefect Apostolic of the Marshall Islands April 23, 1993; installed August 15, 1993; retired January 5, 2008.

Mailing Address: Assumption, Uliga, Majuro, P.O. Box 8, Majuro, MH 96960. Tel: 962-625-6675; Fax: 962-625-5520.

Email: prefecture.marshalls@gmail.com

Square Miles 500,000.

Total Population (est.) 59,200.

Prefecture Apostolic of the Marshall Islands divided from the Diocese of the Carolines-Marshall Islands and erected on August 15, 1993 and committed to the Society of Jesus, New York Province; and on January 6, 2008 committed to the Missionaries of the Sacred Heart. Area is that of the Republic of the Marshall Islands which is related by Compact of Free Association to the United States.

STATISTICAL OVERVIEW

Personnel	
Priests: Diocesan Active in Diocese	1
Number of Diocesan Priests	1
Religious Priests in Diocese	5
Total Priests in Diocese	6
Total Sisters	10
Parishes	
Parishes	5
With Resident Pastor:	
Resident Diocesan Priests	1
Resident Religious Priests	4
Missions	8
Professional Ministry Personnel:	
Sisters	10
Lay Ministers	36
Welfare	
Special Centers for Social Services	1
Total Assisted	270
Educational	
Seminaries, Religious	1
Students Religious	2
High Schools, Diocesan and Parish	2
Total Students	180
Elementary Schools, Diocesan and Parish	3
Total Students	626
Catechesis/Religious Education:	
High School Students	82
Elementary Students	382
Total Students under Catholic Instruction	1,272
Teachers in the Diocese:	
Sisters	8
Lay Teachers	55
Vital Statistics	
Receptions into the Church:	
Infant Baptism Totals	96
Minor Baptism Totals	14
Received into Full Communion	23
First Communions	81
Confirmations	26
Marriages:	
Catholic	4
Interfaith	7
Total Marriages	11
Deaths	22
Total Catholic Population	4,925
Total Population	52,558

Former Prelate—Rev. Msgr. JAMES C. GOULD, S.J., ord. May 4, 1974; appt. First Prefect Apostolic of the Marshall Islands April 23, 1993; installed Aug. 15, 1993; resigned Jan. 5, 2008.

Prefecture Consultors—Revs. YOHANES SUJONO, M.S.C.; ARIEL GALIDO, M.S.C.; AMANDUS REYAAN, M.S.C.; SAIMON KOKORIA, M.S.C.; Deacon ALFRED CAPELLE.

Secretary—Mrs. VERONICA KILUWE, Assumption, P.O. Box 8, Majuro, 96960.

Religious Formation Ministry Coordinator—Deacon ALFRED CAPELLE.

Catholic Education Ministry Coordinator—Sr. DOROTHY NOOK, M.M.B.

Pastoral and Social Ministry Coordinator—Sr. KANTARAWA YEE-ON, F.D.N.S.C.

Finance Committee—Mr. ALAN FOWLER; Mr. DENNIS MOMOTARO; Mr. VINCENT MULLER.

Catechists Coordinators—Mrs. ROSITA CAPELLE; Mrs. NEWIN CAPELLE.

Vocations—Rev. Msgr. RAYMUNDO T. SABIO, M.S.C.

CLERGY, PARISHES, MISSIONS AND PAROCHIAL SCHOOLS

MARSHALL ISLANDS

Mailing Address for the Marshalls: P.O. Box 8, Majuro, MH 96960. Tel: (011) 962-625-6675; Fax: (011) 962-625-5520, unless otherwise noted.

MAJURO, CATHEDRAL OF THE ASSUMPTION Rev. Ariel Galido, M.S.C.; Rev. Msgr. Raymundo T. Sabio, M.S.C.
Tel: 692-625-8307; Fax: 692-625-6507.
School—Assumption Elementary School, (Grades K-8) Ms. Biram Stege, Prin.; Mr. Luke Roverove, Asst. Prin.; Ms. Cathy Kiluwe, Librarian. Lay Teachers 19; Students 307.
High School—Assumption High School Ms. Biram Stege, Prin.; Mr. Richard David, Asst. Prin. Sisters 1; Lay Teachers 10; Students 95.
Mission—Laura, (St. Francis Xavier), Majuro Atoll.

EBEYE, QUEEN OF PEACE Rev. Yohanes Sujono, M.S.C. Mailing Address: P.O. Box 5065, 96970. Tel: 692-329-3828.
School—Queen of Peace Elementary School, (Grades K-8) Mr. Gary Elaisha, Dir.; Nolan deBrum, Prin.; Mrs. Mary Peter, Librarian. Sisters 2; Lay Teachers 12; Students 224.
High School—Fr. Hacker High School Mr. Raphael Capelle, Prin.; Mrs. Brenda Loeak, Librarian. Sisters 1; Lay Teachers 6; Students 84.
Mission—Santo, (St. Leonard), Gugeegue, MH.

JALUIT, SACRED HEART OF JESUS Rev. Amandus Reyaan, M.S.C. Cell: 692-455-1223; Sr. Lumine Beckmann, M.S.C., Pastoral Coord.
Jabor, Jaluit, MI. Mailing Address: P.O. Box 8, 96960.
School—St. Joseph Elementary School, (Grades K-8) Ms. Moten Naisher, Prin. Sisters 2; Lay Teachers 7; Students 95.
Mission—Namdrik, (Our Lady of the Sacred Heart)

KWAJALEIN

1—BLESSED SACRAMENT Rev. Victor Langhans.

2—OUTER ISLAND PARISH Rev. Msgr. Raymundo T. Sabio, M.S.C.
Mission—Arno, (St. Paul)
Mission—Ailinglaplap: Buoj, (Immaculate Heart of Mary)
Mission—Ailinglaplap: Woja, (St. James)

LIKIEP, HOLY ROSARY Rev. Saimon Kokoria, M.S.C.; Sr. Anita Selidio, M.S.M., Pastoral Coord.
Mailing Address: P.O. Box 8, 96960.
Catechesis / Religious Program—Sr. Marivic Cabote, M.S.M., C.R.E.
Mission—Wotje, (St. Thomas)

INSTITUTIONS LOCATED IN THE DIOCESE

[A] MISCELLANEOUS

MAJURO. *Catholic Pastoral Center: Ajeltake*, P.O. Box 8, 96960. Tel: (011) 692-247-7762; (011) 692-247-7797. Penny Hone, Contact Person.

NECROLOGY

(No Deaths)

An asterisk (*) denotes an organization that has established tax-exempt status directly with the IRS and is not covered by the USCCB Group Ruling.

Diocese of Mayaguez, Puerto Rico

(Dioecesis Maiaguezensis)

Most Reverend

ALVARO CORRADA DEL RIO, S.J.

Bishop of Mayaguez; ordained July 6, 1974; appointed Auxiliary Bishop of Washington DC May 30, 1985; consecrated August 4, 1985; on assignment, as Apostolic Administrator, Diocese of Caguas; appointed Bishop of Tyler December 5, 2000; installed January 30, 2001; appointed Bishop of Mayaguez, Puerto Rico July 6, 2011. *Mailing Address: P.O. Box 2272, Mayaguez, PR 00681.*

Most Reverend

ULISES AURELIO CASIANO VARGAS, D.D.

Bishop Emeritus of Mayaguez; ordained May 30, 1967; appointed Bishop March 4, 1976; ordained April 30, 1976; retired July 6, 2011. *Res.: P.O. Box 2272, Mayaguez, PR 00681.* Tel: 787-831-2942; 787-833-5411 (Office).

Erected by the Bull "Qui arcano Dei" on March 1, 1976, by Pope Paul VI.

Comprises a portion of the southwest of the Island.

STATISTICAL OVERVIEW

Personnel	
Bishop	1
Retired Bishops	1
Priests: Diocesan Active in Diocese	41
Priests: Diocesan Active Outside Diocese	3
Priests: Retired, Sick or Absent	3
Number of Diocesan Priests	47
Religious Priests in Diocese	26
Total Priests in Diocese	73
Extern Priests in Diocese	3
Ordinations:	
Transitional Deacons	2
Permanent Deacons	15
Permanent Deacons in Diocese	24
Total Brothers	2
Total Sisters	112
Parishes	
Parishes	30
With Resident Pastor:	
Resident Diocesan Priests	21
Resident Religious Priests	9
New Parishes Created	1
Professional Ministry Personnel:	
Brothers	2
Sisters	7
Lay Ministers	743
Welfare	
Catholic Hospitals	1
Total Assisted	38,911
Homes for the Aged	3
Total Assisted	287
Day Care Centers	5
Total Assisted	267
Specialized Homes	1
Total Assisted	110
Special Centers for Social Services	1
Total Assisted	14,938
Educational	
Diocesan Students in Other Seminaries	5
Total Seminarians	5
Colleges and Universities	1
Total Students	1,810
High Schools, Diocesan and Parish	4
Total Students	408
High Schools, Private	6
Total Students	900
Elementary Schools, Diocesan and Parish	5
Total Students	1,035
Elementary Schools, Private	6
Total Students	1,685
Catechesis/Religious Education:	
High School Students	310
Elementary Students	2,989
Total Students under Catholic Instruction	9,142
Teachers in the Diocese:	
Brothers	1
Sisters	5
Lay Teachers	287
Vital Statistics	
Receptions into the Church:	
Infant Baptism Totals	3,674
Minor Baptism Totals	193
Adult Baptism Totals	129
Received into Full Communion	81
First Communions	3,253
Confirmations	3,729
Marriages:	
Catholic	282
Interfaith	25
Total Marriages	307
Deaths	708
Total Catholic Population	342,899
Total Population	489,857

Former Bishop—Most Rev. ULISES AURELIO CASIANO VARGAS, ord. May 30, 1967; appt. Bishop March 4, 1976; ord. April 30, 1976; retired July 6, 2011.

Vicar General—Rev. Msgr. GONZALO DIAZ.

Episcopal Vicars—

For Pastoral—Rev. Msgr. ROGELIO MUR, O.Carm.

For Diocesan Administration—Rev. Msgr. HECTOR E. RIVERA.

Chancery Office—Mailing Address: P.O. Box 2272, Mayaguez, 00681. Tel: 787-833-5411.

Chancellor—Rev. Msgr. GONZALO DIAZ HERNANDEZ.

Diocesan Consultors—Rev. Msgrs. GONZALO DIAZ; ROGELIO MUR, O.Carm.; Rev. JOSE L. DIEZ, O.S.A.

Diocesan Board of Administration—Rev. Msgrs. GONZALO DIAZ HERNANDEZ; ROGELIO MUR, O.Carm.; Rev. ALBERTO CASTRO, P.D.

Administrator—Mr. ALBERTO RODRIGUEZ.

Censor Librorum—Revs. JULIO FERNANDEZ; ISAIAS REVILLA, O.S.A.

Parish Priests Consultors—Rev. Msgrs. GONZALO DIAZ HERNANDEZ; ROGELIO MUR, O.Carm.; Rev. JOSE L. DIEZ, O.S.A.

Diocesan Offices and Directors

Youth Apostolate—Deacon CARLOS VALENTIN.

Communications Media—Rev. EDGARDO ACOSTA OCASIO.

Cursillos de Cristiandad—Rev. EDGARDO ACOSTA OCASIO.

Holy Childhood—Most Rev. HERMIN NEGRON.

Legion of Mary—VACANT.

Superintendent of Schools—YOLANDA PAGAN.

Religious Consultor—Rev. JULIO FERNANDEZ.

Catechetics—VACANT.

Christian Family Movement—Rev. DELROY THOMAS SCOTT.

Religious Coordinator—Rev. JULIO FERNANDEZ.

Development and Planification—Rev. Msgr. ROGELIO MUR, O.Carm.

Vocations—Revs. ORLANDO ROSAS; DANIEL ENRIQUE HERNANDEZ VELEZ; WILSON MONTES RODRÍGUEZ.

Catholic Social Services—Rev. ORLANDO ROSAS, Dir., Carr. 108 Km. 2.8 Int., Calle Obispado Final, Bo. Miradero, Mayaguez, 00681. Tel: 787-833-3627; 787-833-3638; Fax: 787-833-3627. Email: sscdmaya@gmail.com.

Seasonal Head Start Program—Calle Dr. Veve #44, San German, 00683. Tel: 787-892-3800; Fax: 787-892-3866. Ms. MYRNA CARRERO, Dir.

CLERGY, PARISHES, MISSIONS AND PAROCHIAL SCHOOLS

CITY OF MAYAGUEZ

1—CATHEDRAL OF OUR LADY OF PURIFICATION (1763) Rev. Msgr. Humberto Lopez Bonilla, Rector; Rev. P. Paulino Mazuelos; Deacon Israel Valentin.

Res.: P.O. Box 220, 00681-0220. Tel: 787-831-2444; 787-805-5952; Fax: 787-831-2444.

School—Academy of the Immaculate Conception, Tel: 787-834-5400; 787-834-7824 (High School); Fax: 787-834-5400. Rebeca Perez, Elementary Prin.; Mr. Rene Torres, High School Prin. Lay Teachers 42; Elementary Students 300; High School Students 381.

School—Colegio La Milagrosa, Tel: 787-834-0350; Fax: 787-834-0350. Sr. Delma Morales, Prin. Sisters of Charity 1; Lay Teachers 24; Elementary Students 133; High School Students 120.

Mission—Maria Socorro de los Cristianos Barrio Leguisamo.

Mission—Santa Ana Quebrada Grande.

Catechesis/Religious Program—Students 143.

2—ASCENSION (1968) Rev. Msgr. Santiago Rivera Allende; Deacon Gilberto Martinez.

Res.: Salud Sta., Box 4361, 00681-4361. Tel: 787-832-0766; Fax: 787-832-0766. Email: p.santiagoriverallende@hotmail.com.

Mission—St. Teresita Bo. Limon.

Mission—Our Lady of Perpetual Help Bo. Las

Vegas.
Mission—Ntra. Sra. de la Providencia (Rep. Masias) Bo. El Porvenir.
Catechesis/Religious Program—Students 60.
3—CHURCH DE EL BUEN PASTOR (1986) Revs. Jose Aponte, S.J.; Jorge Ferrer, S.J.
Res.: Urb. Mayaguez Ter., 5000 Calle San Gerardo, 00682-6627. Tel: 787-833-8800; Fax: 787-805-3660. Email: elpastor_bueno@yahoo.com.
Catechesis/Religious Program—Students 74.
Mission—El Cristo de Los Milagros 1116 Calle Perpetuo Socorro, Bo. Algarrobo, 00682. Tel: 787-265-5936.
Mission—Sta. Teresita Parcelas Soledad, 00682.
4—CHURCH OF THE RESURRECTION (1988) Rev. Daniel Enrique Hernandez Velez, Admin.; Deacon Jose Luis Rodriguez.
Res.: Balboa 285, 00680. Tel: 787-831-6180.
Catechesis/Religious Program—Students 46.
Chapel—Consumo, Jesus Redentor
Chapel—Rio Canas, Nuestra Senora del Perpetuo Socorro
Chapel—Barrio Quemado, Nuestra Senor del Carmen
5—NUESTRA SENORA DE FATIMA (1986) [JC] Rev. Gerardo E. Caraballo Galindo, Admin.
Res.: Parcelas Castillo C-2, 00680. Tel: 787-833-0794.
Catechesis/Religious Program—Students 101.
Mission—Cristo Rey Andalucia St., Sultana, 00680.
Mission—Espiritu Santo Sagitario St., Villa del Oeste, Sabalos, 00680.
Mission—Corpus Christi Urb. Vista Verde, 00680.
6—OUR LADY OF MT. CARMEL (1957) Revs. Carlos González, S.F.M., Admin.; William Saltar.
Res.: Box 3166, 00681. Tel: 787-652-4999 (Office); 787-832-2203; Fax: 787-834-2777.
Mission—Infant of Prague Mani.
Mission—Perpetuo Socorro Jardines del Caribe.
Catechesis/Religious Program—Students 207.
7—SACRED HEART (1959) Revs. P. Angel Luis Rios Matos; Juan Chavajay.
Res.: *Marina Station*, P.O. Box 3626, 00681-3626. Tel: 781-831-3940.
School—St. Benedict, Tel: 787-832-9626. Lay Teachers 31; Elementary Students 342; High School Students 225.
Catechesis/Religious Program—Students 320.
Mission—San Jose Rosario.
Mission—San Carlos y San Antonio Rio Hondo.
Mission—La Milagrosa Bo. Malezas.
8—SAN VICENTE (1965) [JC] Revs. Manuel Aznar Bello, C.M.; Prudencio Sanchez, C.M.; Tomàs de la Puebla, C.M. (Retired).
Res.: Ave. Guanajibo, No. 401, 00680. Tel: 787-832-8874. Email: maznarbe1@yahoo.es.
Catechesis/Religious Program—Students 65.
9—SANTA TERESITA (1970) Rev. Orlando Rosas Muniz, Admin.
Res.: Principe St., 203 Bo. Colombia, 00680. Tel: 787-806-0881; Fax: 787-806-0881.
Catechesis/Religious Program—Students 88.

OUTSIDE THE CITY OF MAYAGUEZ

AGUADA
1—ST. FRANCIS OF ASSISI (1692) Revs. Jose Luis Diez Gabela, O.S.A. (Spain); Isaias Revilla, O.S.A. (Spain); Ildefonso Blanco, O.S.A. (Spain); Aridio Taveras, O.S.A.; Deacons Hector Vargas; Benjamin Echevarria; Jorge Lopez; Wilfredo Valle.
Mailing Address: P.O. Box 608, 00602.
Res.: Calle Paz #225, 00602. Tel: 787-868-2630; Fax: 787-868-8561. Email: psfcoaguada@hotmail.com. Web: www.psfcoaguada.tripod.com.
Catechesis/Religious Program—Students 1,300.
Convent—Hermanas de la Caridad del Cardenal Sancha, Calle Jose Hernandez, Box 1136, 00602. Tel: 787-868-8257; Fax: 787-868-8257.
Mission—San Jose Sabana.
Mission—Santa Rita Laguna.
Mission—Santa Monica Cruces.
Mission—Santo Tomas de Villanueva Galicia-Columbani.
Mission—San Augustin Jaguey Chiquito.
Mission—Perpetuo Socorro Rio Grande.
Mission—Ntra. Madre de la Consolacion Naranjo Militar.
Mission—Ntra. Sra. de Altagracia Atalaya.
Mission—San Pablo Naranjo-Guanabanas.
Mission—Asuncion de Maria Marias.
Mission—Buen Consejo Cerro Gordo.
Mission—Perpetuo Socorro Mamey.
Mission—Ntra. Sra. del Carmen Guaniquilla.
Mission—Centro de Espintualidad, Madre de la Consolacion Piedras Blancas, Puerto Rico.
Mission—Ntra. Sra. de las Mercedes Carrizales.
Mission—Inmaculada Concepcion Malpaso-Cesar Ruiz.
Mission—Sagrada Familia Bajio.
Mission—Sgdo. Corazon de Jesus Quebrada Larga.
Mission—Ntra. Sra. del Carmen Rio Grande-Playa.
Mission—El Buen Pastor Guayabo.
Mission—Ntra. Sra. Reina de la Paz Piedras Blancas.
2—SANTUARIO PROTOMARTIRES DE LA CONCEPCION (1524) Revs. Luis Oscar Padilla Cruz, O.F.M.Cap; Juan Rolando Gonzalez, O.F.M.Cap., Vicar; Bro. Jaime Perez, O.F.M.Cap.; Deacon Nicolas Mejias.
Res.: Bo. Espinar, Buzon 1162, 00602. Tel: 787-891-2889.
Chapel—Bo. Palmar, El Buen Pastor
Chapel—Bo. Tablonar, El Nino Jesus
Catechesis/Religious Program—Students 88.
AGUADILLA
1—ST. CHARLES BORROMEO (1780) [CEM] Revs. Angel Valle Nieves, Admin.; P. Harry Lopez; Deacon Victor M. Morales; Rev. P. Carlos F. Mendez.
Res.: P.O. Box 238, 00605-0238. Tel: 787-891-0575; Fax: 787-882-2579.
School—Tel: 787-891-1445; Fax: 787-882-3270. Mr. Raymond Pérez, Prin. Lay Teachers 27; Elementary Students 114; High School Students 274.
Catechesis/Religious Program—Students 377.
Convent—Tel: 787-882-3629. Sr. Julia del Carmen Perez Rodriguez, Supr. Salesian Sisters 4.
Convent—Tel: 787-891-7496. Sr. Violetta Meduvely, M.C. Missionaries of Charity 4.
Chapel—Bo. Corrales, Our Lady of Perpetual Help
Chapel—Caimital Alto, St. John Baptist
Chapel—Victoria-Our Lady of Mt. Carmel
Chapel—Esteves, Our Lady of Rosary
Chapel—Bda. Caban, Holy Family
2—LA MILAGROSA (1974) Rev. Msgr. Ramon E. Albino; Rev. Perfecto Pérez; Deacons Jorge Casanova; Herminio Blas.
Res.: Urb. Marbella, Calle 1 Num. 379, 00603. Tel: 787-891-7014; Fax: 787-891-7014. Email: p_lamilagrosa@yahoo.com.
School—Educational Service Corpus Christi School, Tel: 787-882-8433. Esmeralda Perez, Prin. Students 239.
Catechesis/Religious Program—Students 205.
Mission—Our Lady of Victory Borinquen.
Mission—Our Lady of Fatima Camaseyes.
Mission—San Judas Tadeo Playuela, Puerto Rico.
3—SAN JOSE OBRERO (1975) Revs. Wilfredo Calderon, S.D.B.; Franklin Santana, S.D.B.
Res.: P.O. Box 787, San Antonio, 00690-0787. Tel: 787-890-2449; Fax: 787-890-0436.
Catechesis/Religious Program—Students 200.
Mission—La Providencia Bo. Guerrero.
Mission—Los Santos Reyes Ramey-Maleza.
ANASCO, ST. ANTHONY ABBOT (1730) Revs. Tomas Ciscar, O.Carm.; Rogelio Mur Aguilar, O.Carm.; Hector Garcia, O.Carm.; Deacon Victor M. Rosado Cortes.
Res.: Box 392, 00610. Tel: 787-826-2215. Email: antabad@coqui.net.
School—LaSalle, Tel: 787-826-6071. Bro. Angel Suarez, F.S.C., Prin. Students 264.
Catechesis/Religious Program—Students 450.
Mission—Chapel of Our Lady of Perpetual Help Miraflores.
Mission—Our Lady of Carmel La Playa.
Mission—St. Lawrence Martyr Bo. Espino.
Mission—La Immaculade Bo. Pinales.
Mission—La Providencia Bo. Carreras.
Mission—Our Lady of Monserrat Bo. Cerro Gordo.
Mission—St. Rita Bo. Marias.
Mission—Cristo Redentor Bo. Oveja.
Mission—Santa Rosa de Lima Bo. Pozo Hondo.
Jesus Maestro Casa de Formacion—
CABO ROJO, ST. MICHAEL (1783) Revs. Angel Ortiz, Admin.; Jose R. Linares.
Res.: Box 625, 00623. Tel: 787-851-1283; Fax: 787-851-1970.
*School—San Agustin*Email: colegiosanagustin @hotmail.com. Miss Madeline Ortiz, Dir. Sisters 2; Lay Teachers 38; Students: High School 302; Elementary 304.
Catechesis/Religious Program—Students 621.
Mission—Our Lady of Mt. Carmel Puerto Real.
Mission—St. John the Baptist Joyuda.
Mission—Our Lady of Good Counsel Llanos Tunas.
Mission—St. Jude Thaddeus Monte Grande.
Mission—St. Martin de Porres Conde Avila.
Mission—Ntro. Sra. de la Providencia Bo. Miradero.
HORMIGUEROS
1—EL SALVADOR (1969) Rev. Edgar Carlo; Deacon Angel Rivera.
Res.: Box 567, 00660. Tel: 787-834-1993.
Catechesis/Religious Program—Students 80.
Chapel—Valle Hermoso Arriba, San Judas Tadeo
Chapel—Parcelas S. Romualdo, Sta. Teresita
2—SHRINE OF OUR LADY OF MONSERRATE (1874) Rev. Msgr. Gonzalo Diaz Hernandez; Rev. Floyd McCoy Jordain; Deacon Gilberto H. Rodriguez.
Res.: Box 24, 00660. Tel: 787-849-2260. Web: www.santuariolamonserrate.org.
Convent—Box 185, 00660. Tel: 787-849-2055; Fax: 787-849-2035. Sr. Maria Concepcion, O.P. Sisters of Fatima for Social Work 3.
Mission—Sagrado Corazon de Jesus Bo. Lavadero.
Mission—Ntra. Sra. de la Paz Bo. Jaquitas.
Mission—La Asuncion Bo. Carretera Nueva.
Mission—San Martin de Porres Bo. Guanajibo.
Mission—Santa Rosa de Lima Bo. El Hoyo.
LAJAS
1—DE LA MERCED PARISH (1971) Rev. Rafael Sastre, Admin.; Deacon Ramon Cardona, P.D.
Res.: Calle Violeta #113, P.O. Box 1023, 00667-1023. Tel: 787-899-1910.
Catechesis/Religious Program—Students 110.
Mission—Ntra. Sra. de la Monserrate Carr. 101 Ramal 303 K.2.4, Bo. Maguayo, 00667.
Mission—San Pedro Carr. 304 Calle Principal, Bo. Parguera, 00667.
Mission—Ntra. Sra. de Monserrate Carr. 116 Parcellas Cuesta Blanca #264, Bo. Cuesta Blanca, 00667.
Mission—Ntra. Sra. del Carmen Carr. 324 K. 5.6, Bo. Salinas, 00667.
Mission—Ntra Sra. del Perpetuo Socorro Carr. 306, Bo. Paris, 00667.
2—OUR LADY OF THE PURIFICATION (1883) Revs. Edwin Lugo Silva, Admin.; Nomar Jose Calero Gómez.
Res.: Box 425, 00667. Tel: 787-899-1911; Fax: 787-899-2455.
School—St. Louis Academy Sisters of St. Joseph, Tel: 787-899-4080; Fax: 787-899-4080. Sr. Teresita Alicea, C.S.J., Prin. (Brooklyn) Sisters 2; Lay Teachers 21; Elementary Students 76; High School Students 44.
Catechesis/Religious Program—Students 24.
Convent—La Providencia, Tel: 787-899-5180.
Mission—Sagrado Corazon de Jesus Parcelas #201, Bo. La Plata, 00667.
Mission—Ntra. Sra. del Perpetuo Socorro Carretera 118 Km 0, Bo. Lajas Arriba (La Tea), 00667.
Mission—San Pablo Parcelas #48, Bo. Lajas Arriba (Parcelas), 00667.
Mission—Santa Rosa de Lima Comunidad Sta. Rosa #35, Bo. Parcelas Santa Rosa, 00667.
Mission—San Judas Tadeo Parcelas #172, Bo. Parcelas Palmarejo, 00667.
Mission—San Juan Bautista Parcela #80, Bo. Palmarejo II, 00667.
Mission—Santa Rosa de Lima Bo. La Haya.
LAS MARIAS, IMMACULATE HEART OF MARY (1863) Rev. Edward Acevedo, Admin.
Res.: Box 126, 00670. Tel: 787-827-3300.
Catechesis/Religious Program—Students 177.
Mission—San Jose Carr. 406, Km. 3.9, Anones, 00607.
Mission—La Milagrosa Carr. 124, R. 370, Km. 6.8 Int Buena Vista, Buena Vista, 00670.
Mission—N.S. de Fatima Palma Escrita.
MARICAO, ST. JOHN THE BAPTIST (1864) Rev. David Perez Mendez, Admin.
Res.: Box 453, 00606. Tel: 787-838-2014.
Catechesis/Religious Program—Students 142.
Mission—Sagrado Corazon Bucarabones.
Mission—Santa Rosa Indiera Fria.
Chapel—Montoso, Immaculado Corazon de Maria, Tel: 787-838-2272. Sr. Angeles Marie Pacheco, O.P., Supr. Dominican Sisters of Our Lady of Fatima 6.
MOCA, OUR LADY OF MONSERRATE (1772) Revs. Wilson Mintes; P. Luis Jusino; Angel Mendez Mendez; Rev. Msgr. Angel Latre; Revs. Enrique Ascencio; Julio A. Vera Gonzalez; Deacons Domingo Lerenzo; Norberto Perez; German Colon.
Res.: P.O. Box 435, 00676. Tel: 787-877-2765; Fax: 787-877-7795. Email: parroquialamonserrate@gmail.com.
*School—Colegio Ntra. Sra. de La Monserrate*Email: colegiolamonserratemoca@yahoo.com. Damaris Gonzalez, Prin.; Hebe Mabel Saavedra, Librarian. Students 163.
Catechesis/Religious Program—Carmen A. Lorenzo, D.R.E. Students 1,200.
Mission—San Judas Tadeo Bo. Plata.
Mission—Espiritu Santo Bo. Voladoras Lomas.
Mission—Sagrada Familia Bo. Voladoras Parcelas.
Mission—Sagrado Corazon de Jesus Bo. Naranjo.
Mission—Santos Guillermo Abad y San Mateo, Bo. Cuchillas Lassalle, PR
Mission—Inmaculado Corazon de Maria, Bo. Cuchillas Sabana, PR
Mission—Virgen del Perpetuo Socorro, Bo. Cuchillas Limon, PR
Mission—Cristo Rey Bo. Cuchillas Loperena.
Mission—Virgen de la Monserrate Bo. Cuchillas Cordero.
Mission—Virgen de La Providencia Bo. Rocha Magueyes.
Mission—San Pedro Apostol Bo. Rocha Sec. Lassalle.
Mission—Virgen del Rosario Bo. Capa Barreto.
Mission—Corpus Christi Bo. Capa Bosque.
Mission—El Buen Pastor Bo. Cerro Gordo.
Mission—San Martin de Porres Bo. Aceituna.
RINCON, ST. ROSE OF LIMA (1789) Revs. Delroy Thomas Scott, Admin.; Angel Roman Ramos;

Deacons Heriberto Santana; Gilberto Medina Agron.
Res.: Box 128, 00677. Tel: 787-823-2650; Fax: 787-823-4400.
Catechesis/Religious Program—Students 600.
Mission—Santa Rosa Bo. Calvache.
Mission—El Cristo de la Reconciliacion Bo. Atalaya.
Mission—La Milagrosa Bo. Corcega.
Mission—La Virgin de Guadalupe Bo. Rio Grande.
Mission—Sagrado Corazon de Jesus Bo. Cruces.
Mission—Nuestra Senora del Carmen Bo. Puntas.
Mission—San Jose Bo. Jaguey.

ROSARIO, OUR LADY OF ROSARY (1831) Rev. Javier Aquino Florenciani.
Res.: 348 St., 7.5 Kilometer, Box 692, 00636. Tel: 787-831-7232.
Mission—Nuestra Senora del Rosario
Mission—La Milagrosa Bo. Rosario Alto.
Mission—La Monseirate Bo. Rosario Penon, 00680.
Catechesis/Religious Program—Students 628.

SABANA GRANDE, CHURCH OF SAN ISIDRO (1813) Revs. Jorge L. Caro Morales; Edgardo Acosta Ocasio; Edgardo Lopez Hernandez; Deacon Roberto De Jesus.
Res.: Box 817, 00637. Tel: 787-873-4475; Fax: 787-804-0327.
Catechesis/Religious Program—Students 406.
Convent—Tel: 787-873-2750. Sr. Maximina, O.P., Supr. Sisters 3.
Mission—Cristo Rey Carr.368 R.367 KM.2.0, El Papayo, 00637.
Mission—La Resurreccion Carr.121 Calle Azucena, Susua, 00637.
Mission—Sagrado Corazon de Jesus Calle Rable #44-Carr.121 K. 5.0, Bo. Maginas, 00637.
Mission—San Jose Carr.121 Km. 4.1, Bo. La Pica, 00637.
Mission—San Francisco de Asis Carr.369 Km.1.4, Bo. Cerro Gordo, 00637.
Mission—Ntra. Sra. de Monserrate Carr.2 R.365 Km.2.8 Int., Bo. Molinas, 00637.
Mission—Ntra. Sra. de Fatima Carr.328 Km.3.6, Bo. Guaras, 00637.
Mission—Santa Catalina de Siena Carr.388 Km.5.9 Int., Bo. La Torre, 00637.
Mission—Santa Ana Carr.114 R.363 Km.2.4, Bo. La Maquina, 00637.
Mission—Ntra. Sra. del Rosario Carr.120 Km.6, Bo. Santana Pichel, 00637.
Mission—La Virgen Milagrosa Carr.364 Km.7 Interior, Bo. El Hoyo, 00637.
Mission—San Judas Tadeo Carr.117 Km.10.7, Bo. Rayo Plata, 00637.
Mission—Divino Nino Jesus Carr. 102 Km 38.1, Int. Bo. Rayo, Sector David Mendez, Sab. Gde, P.R.
Mission—Sta Lucia Carr.120 Km.3.1, Bo. Sta. Ana Moreno, 00637.

SAN GERMAN

1—ST. ROSE OF LIMA (1967) Revs. Eliseo Garcia, O.S.A.; Francisco Larran, O.S.A.; Abdon Atienza, O.S.A.
Res.: Box 364, 00683. Tel: 787-892-1276; Fax: 787-892-1276. Email: rosalima@prtc.net. Web: www.mysantarosa.org.
Catechesis/Religious Program—Students 542.
Mission—N. Sra. de la Consolacion Bo. Guama.
Mission—Perpetuo Socorro Bo. Minillas Carretera.
Mission—Santa Rita Bo. Retiro Tea.
Mission—Santa Monica Bo. Minillas Valle.
Mission—St. Martin de Porres Bo. Cain.

2—SAN GERMAN DE AUXERRE Revs. Rafael Mendez; Angel L. Soto Barreto; Tomas Galarza Figueroa.
Mailing Address: Box 305, 00683.
Res.: 2 Jose J. Acosta St., 00683. Tel: 787-892-1027. Web: www.sangermanauxerre.com.
School—Colegio San Jose, Tel: 787-892-1009; Fax: 787-892-2275. Lay Teachers 27; Elementary Students 217; High School Students 111.
Catechesis/Religious Program—Students 425.
Mission—Chapel of St. Augustin Duey.
Mission—Chapel of St. Joseph Hoconuco.
Mission—Gruta de Lourdes Maresua.
Mission—Our Lady of Fatima Cotuy.
Mission—San Judas Tadeo Sabana Eneas.

SAN SEBASTIAN, SAN SEBASTIAN MARTIR (1752) Revs. Angel Antonio Perez, C.P.; Jose Lizarralde, C.P.; Gregorio Paredes; Deacons Miguel Angel San Martin; Nestor Gonzalez; Bernardino Medina.
Res.: P.O. Box 801, 00685. Tel: 787-896-1028. Email: parroquiass@gmail.com.
School—San Sebastian Martir, Administrated by the Passionist Sisters "Hijas de la Pasion", Tel: 787-896-5728; Fax: 787-280-6521. Nia K. Méndez, Prin. Lay Teachers 30; Elementary Students 361; High School Students 68.
Catechesis/Religious Program—Students 675.
Mission—Cristo Rey Bo. Perchas I.
Mission—La Pasion del Señor Bo. Perchas II.
Mission—San Gabriel de la Dolorosa Bo. Calabazas.
Mission—La Immaculada Concepcion Bo. La Lechuza.
Mission—Santa Teresita del Nino Jesus Bo. Juncal.
Mission—Ntra. Sra. del Carmen Bo. Aibonito Guerrero.
Mission—San Judas Tadeo Bo. Saltos.
Mission—San Patricio Bo. Hato Arriba.
Mission—San Pablo de la Cruz Bo. Hato Arriba (Parcelas).
Mission—Ntra. Sra. de Fatima Bo. Altozano.
Mission—Sagrado Corazon de Jesus Bo. Robles.
Mission—San Jose Obrero Bo. Hoyamala.
Mission—Santa Cruz Bo. Parcelas Guacio (Parcelas).
Mission—Espiritu Santo Bo. Culebrinas.
Mission—Cristo Resucitado Bo. Sonador.
Mission—Ntra. Sra. de La Providencia Bo. Eneas.
Mission—Sagrada Familia Bo. Pozas.

On Special Assignment:
Rev.—
Diaz, Gonzalo, Vicar Gen., Box 24, Hormigueros, PR.

INSTITUTIONS LOCATED IN THE DIOCESE

[A] COLLEGES AND UNIVERSITIES

ANASCO. *De La Salle Catholic College*, Apartado 61, 00610. Tel: 787-826-6071; Fax: 787-826-5185. Rene Hernandez Perez, Contact Person.

AQUADILLA. *Corpus Christi College*, Apartado 4021, 00605-4021. Tel: 787-882-8433; Fax: 787-891-4555. Email: colegiocorpuschristi@yahoo.com. Rev. Msgr. Ramon E. Albino.

MOCA. *Nuestra Senora de la Monserrate College*, Apartado 435, 00676. Tel: 787-877-2765; Fax: 787-877-7795. Damaris Gonzalez, Prin.

[B] HOSPITALS

SAN GERMAN. *Hospital of the Immaculate Conception*, Box 285, 00683. Tel: 787-892-1860; Fax: 787-264-7908. Web: www.hospconcepcion.org. Sr. Juanita Flores, H.C.; Rev. Angel Leonides Soto, Chap. Sisters of Charity. Sisters 7; Bed Capacity 167; Total Staff 735; Patients Assisted Annually (Admissions) 8,968; Emergency Visits 41,832.

[C] INSTITUTIONS

MAYAGUEZ. *Asylum for the Poor and Aged*, Calle Ramon E. Betances 162 Sur., 00680. Sisters of Charity (Spanish). Sisters 4; Bed Capacity 68; Residents 68.
Comunidad Belen, c/o P.O. Box 2272, 00681. Rev. P. Carlos Gonzalez, Contact Person.
Convent of the Servants of Mary, Hostos Ave., 401, 00680. Tel: 787-832-0391; Fax: 787-805-6160. Sr. Rosaura Morales Rivera, Supr. Sisters care for the sick in their homes and hospital. Sisters 14.

HORMIGUEROS. *Residence for the Aged, San Jose*, Valle Hermoso, 00660. Tel: 787-832-4243; Fax: 787-833-4529. Sr. Maria Guadalupe Rivera, Supr. Sisters 9; Residents 120.

[D] PERSONAL PRELATURES

MAYAGUEZ. *Opus Dei (Prelature of the Holy Cross and Opus Dei)*, 69 Orquideas St., Ensanche Martinez, 00680. Tel: 787-833-6461. Rev. Andres Eiroa.

RELIGIOUS INSTITUTES OF MEN REPRESENTED IN THE DIOCESE

For further details refer to the corresponding bracketed number in the Religious Institutes of Men or Women section.

[]—*Acies Christi* (Spain)
[0140]—*Augustinians*—O.S.A.
[0200]—*Benedictine Monks* Spain—O.S.B.
[0270]—*Carmelite Fathers and Brothers* (Spain)—O.Carm.
[1330]—*Congregation of the Mission* (Vice Province of Puerto Rico)—C.M.
[1000]—*Congregation of the Passion*—C.P.
[]—*Salesian Fathers*

RELIGIOUS INSTITUTES OF WOMEN REPRESENTED IN THE DIOCESE

[]—*Acies Christi* (Spain)
[]—*Carmelitas de Clausura* (Spain)
[]—*Hermanas de la Caridad*
[]—*Hermanas Salesianas* (Spain)
[]—*Hermanas Teatinas* (Spain)
[2340]—*Little Sisters of the Poor*—L.S.P.
[2790]—*Missionary Servants of the Most Blessed Trinity*—M.S.B.T.
[]—*Monasterio Santa Maria del Monte Carmelo*
[3580]—*Servants of Mary* (Spain)—O.S.M.
[0650]—*Sisters of Charity of St. Vincent de Paul* (Spanish)—S.C.
[]—*Sisters of Fatima* (Puerto Rico)
[]—*Sisters of Schoenstatt* (Germany)
[]—*Sisters of St. Joseph* (Brooklyn)

NECROLOGY

† Morales Santana, Juan Bautista, Moca, PR Our Lady of Monserrate—Died 2011

An asterisk (*) denotes an organization that has established tax-exempt status directly with the IRS and is not covered by the USCCB Group Ruling.

Diocese of Ponce, Puerto Rico

(Dioecesis Poncensis)

Most Reverend

FELIX LAZARO, SCH.P.

Bishop of Ponce; ordained April 9, 1961; appointed Coadjutor Bishop of Ponce March 20, 2002; consecrated April 25, 2002; appointed Bishop of Ponce June 11, 2003. *Res.: Bishop's House, P.O. Box 32205, Ponce, PR 00732-2205.* Tel: 787-848-5265; Fax: 787-841-1778.

ESTABLISHED NOVEMBER 21, 1924.

Square Miles 830.

Comprises the south portion of the Island of Puerto Rico and is in the Ecclesiastical Province of Puerto Rico.

Email: obispadoponce@direcway.com

flazaro@direcway.com

STATISTICAL OVERVIEW

Personnel	
Bishop	1
Priests: Diocesan Active in Diocese	57
Priests: Diocesan Active Outside Diocese	10
Priests: Retired, Sick or Absent	14
Number of Diocesan Priests	81
Religious Priests in Diocese	36
Total Priests in Diocese	117
Extern Priests in Diocese	2
Permanent Deacons in Diocese	106
Total Brothers	3
Total Sisters	185
Parishes	
Parishes	43
With Resident Pastor:	
Resident Diocesan Priests	29
Resident Religious Priests	14
Pastoral Centers	248
Professional Ministry Personnel:	
Brothers	3
Sisters	185
Lay Ministers	1,936
Welfare	
Health Care Centers	7
Total Assisted	336,690
Homes for the Aged	2
Total Assisted	225
Residential Care of Children	1
Total Assisted	26
Day Care Centers	2
Total Assisted	10,052
Specialized Homes	10
Total Assisted	325,117
Special Centers for Social Services	4
Total Assisted	52,823
Educational	
Seminaries, Diocesan	1
Students from This Diocese	12
Students from Other Diocese	12
Seminaries, Religious	2
Students Religious	9
Total Seminarians	21
Colleges and Universities	1
Total Students	9,908
High Schools, Diocesan and Parish	11
Total Students	1,683
High Schools, Private	4
Total Students	680
Elementary Schools, Diocesan and Parish	17
Total Students	5,028
Elementary Schools, Private	4
Total Students	1,183
Catechesis/Religious Education:	
High School Students	2,469
Elementary Students	7,606
Total Students under Catholic Instruction	28,578
Teachers in the Diocese:	
Priests	12
Sisters	6
Lay Teachers	227
Vital Statistics	
Receptions into the Church:	
Infant Baptism Totals	2,980
Minor Baptism Totals	1,574
Adult Baptism Totals	414
First Communions	3,511
Confirmations	3,423
Marriages:	
Catholic	527
Interfaith	22
Total Marriages	549
Total Catholic Population	424,263
Total Population	565,683

Former Bishops—Most Revs. EDWIN V. BYRNE, D.D., cons. in Philadelphia, Nov. 30, 1925; transferred to San Juan, PR; promoted to Archbishop of Santa Fe, NM, June 15, 1943; died July 25, 1963; ALOYSIUS J. WILLINGER, C.Ss.R., D.D., ord. July 2, 1911; appt. Bishop of Ponce March 8, 1929; cons. Oct. 28, 1929; appt. Titular Bishop of Bida and Coadjutor of Monterey-Fresno (cum jure successionis), Dec. 12, 1946; installed Bishop of Monterey-Fresno, Jan. 3, 1953; resigned Oct. 25, 1967; died July 25, 1973; JAMES E. MCMANUS, C.Ss.R., D.D., J.C.D., transferred to the Archdiocese of New York, Nov. 18, 1963; died July 1, 1976; His Eminence LUIS CARDINAL APONTE MARTINEZ, D.D., ord. April 10, 1950; appt. Titular Bishop of Lares and Auxiliary of Ponce, July 23, 1960; cons. Oct. 12, 1960; appt. Coadjutor Bishop of Ponce, April 16, 1963; appt. Bishop of Ponce, Nov. 18, 1963; installed Feb. 20, 1964; promoted to Archbishop of San Juan, Nov. 4, 1964; installed Jan. 15, 1965; created Cardinal, March 5, 1973; resigned May 8, 1999; Most Revs. FREMIOT TORRES OLIVER, D.D., ord. April 10, 1950; appt. Bishop Nov. 4, 1964; cons. Dec. 21, 1964; retired Nov. 10, 2000; died Jan. 26, 2012.; RICARDO SURINACH CARRERAS, D.D., ord. April 13, 1957; appt. Auxiliary Bishop of Ponce May 26, 1975; cons. July 25, 1975; appt. Bishop of Ponce Nov. 10, 2000; installed Nov. 30, 2000; retired June 11, 2003; died Jan. 19, 2005.

Vicar General—Rev. Msgr. ROBERTO GARCIA BLAY.

Pro-Vicar General—VACANT.

Chancellor—Rev. Msgr. HERMINIO DE JESUS.

Episcopal Vicar for Diocesan Administration—Rev. Msgr. ROBERTO GARCIA BLAY.

Episcopal Vicar for Pastoral Coordination—Rev. Msgr. JUAN RODRIGUEZ ORENGO.

Episcopal Vicar for Religious—Rev. MARIO MASTRANGELO, O.F.M.Cap.

Episcopal Vicar for Education—VACANT.

Episcopal Vicar for Sick—Rev. DAIRO H. ARBOLEDA, O.SS.T.

Tribunal Interdiocesano de Puerto Rico—Calle Isabel No. 31, P.O. Box 32229, Ponce, 00732-2229. Tel: 787-843-4630; Fax: 787-841-7483. First instance for the Dioceses of Mayaguez and Ponce. Second Instance for the Archdiocese of San Juan.

Judicial Vicar—Rev. Msgr. ELIAS S. MORALES.

Associate Judicial Vicars—Rev. MANUEL SANTIAGO.

Moderator—Most Rev. FELIX LAZARO, Sch.P.

Judge—Mayaguez: Rev. Msgr. GONZALO DIAZ.

Diocesan Consultors—Rev. Msgrs. ROBERTO GARCIA BLAY; HERMINIO DE JESUS; MARCOS A. PANCORBO; ELIAS S. MORALES; JOSE LOZANO; JUAN RODRIGUEZ ORENGO.

Diocesan Board of Administration—Rev. Msgrs. ROBERTO GARCIA BLAY; MARCOS A. PANCORBO; Deacon ALBERTO CASTRO; Mr. SANTIAGO RAMOS; Mr. JAIME SANTIAGO CANET; FELIX NEGRON MARTINEZ.

Parish Priests Consultors—Rev. Msgr. MARCOS A. PANCORBO; Rev. JOSE DIEGO RODRIGUEZ; Rev. Msgrs. JUAN RODRIGUEZ ORENGO; JOSE LOZANO.

Notaries—Mrs. LUZ DELIA MEDINA; GLADYSBETH ORTIZ GONZALEZ.

Censores Librorum—Rev. ADALIN RIVERA.

Administrator—Rev. Msgr. ROBERTO GARCIA BLAY.

Diocesan Offices and Directors

Propagation of the Faith—Rev. Msgr. JUAN RODRIGUEZ ORENGO, Diocesan Dir., Mailing Address: Diocese of Ponce, P.O. Box 32205, Ponce, 00732-2205. Tel: 787-848-5265.

Police Chaplains—Rev. Msgr. MARCOS PANCORBO. Tel: 787-842-0134; Revs. SAMUEL SANTIAGO. Tel: 787-848-3313; SEGISMUNDO CINTRON. Tel: 787-856-3617; JUAN SALIVA. Tel: 787-839-3465.

Catholic Charismatic Renewal—Rev. JUAN ALBERTO TORRES, O.C.D.; HERMAN ORTIZ PADILLA, Diocesan Dir., Mailing Address: P.O. Box 728, Mercedita, 00715. Tel: 787-662-3961.

Master of Ceremonies to the Bishop—Rev. Msgr. JUAN RODRIGUEZ ORENGO, Mailing Address: Diocese of Ponce, P.O. Box 32205, Ponce, 00732-2205. Tel: 787-848-5265.

Holy Name Society—Sr. GILBERTO GONZALEZ, Bo. Clausells, 107 Colon St., Ponce, 00731. Tel: 787-844-1384.

Equipo de Ntra. Senora Parroquia La Monserrate—13 Figueras St., Jayuya, 00664. Tel: 787-828-6350.

Catholic Daughters of America—ADA MELENDEZ, Mailing Address: P.O. Box 6530, Ponce, 00730. Tel: 787-840-4330.

Knights of Columbus—Mr. JOSE MARTINEZ CHAMORRO, Mailing Address: Consejo 1719, P.O. Box 7921, Ponce, 00732.

Nocturnal Adoration—

Talleres de Oracion y Vida - P. Larranaga—Mrs. MARTA ALVAREZ.

Hogar Catholico Divino Nino Jesus—Mailing Address: P.O. Box 2106, Guayama, 00785. Tel: 787-866-1486.

Pro-Life Center—Deacon FRANCISCO LUGO, Mailing Address: P.O. Box 32214, Ponce, 00732-2214. Tel: 787-848-6018.

Franciscan Third Order (Secular Franciscans Order)—JORGE F. IRIZARRY SANTANA, Dir., Mailing

Address: P.O. Box 7244, Ponce, 00732.

Cofradia Sagrado Corazon—Rev. Msgr. Herminio de Jesus Viera, Chap.; Mrs. Daisy Guzman, Urb. Tomas Carrion Maduro, St. 2 #58, Juana Diaz, 00795. Tel: 787-837-3562.

Movimiento Juan XXIII—Rev. Msgr. Herminio de Jesus Viera, Chap.; Mr. Rafael Lopez, Mailing Address: P.O. Box 560296, Guayanilla, 00656-0296. Tel: 787-267-3309.

Movimiento Schoensttat—

Juventud Mariana Vicentina—Mr. Heriberto Velazquez, Dir., Parraquia San Vicente de Paul, 67 Paseo Cantera, Ponce, 00730-3026.

Neocatacumenal Way—Lic. Felix Negron. Tel: 787-364-9209.

Movimiento Sacerdotal Mariano—Rev. Msgr. Herminio de Jesus Viera, Mailing Address: P.O. Box 32205, Ponce, 00732-2205. Tel: 787-848-5265.

Siervas de Cristo Vivo—Yolanda Amadeo, Mailing Address: P.O. Box 2206, Coamo, 00769. Tel: 787-803-6074.

Orden Ecuestre del Santo Sepulcro—Mr. Santiago Ramos, Lugarteniencia de P.R., Mailing Address: P.O. Box 331110, Ponce, 00733-1110. Tel: 787-841-0384.

Estudios Biblicos Peregrinos en la Fe—Mrs. Nancy Bonilla, Mailing Address: Centro Catequistico Diocesano, P.O. Box 33164, Ponce, 00733-1064. Tel: 787-842-9178.

Comunidad de Oracion y Reflexion Biblica—Mrs. Gilda Cruz Batiz, Urb. Los Caobos, 2353 calle Pendula, Ponce, 00716. Tel: 787-843-8207.

Comunion y Liberacion—Mr. Wadi Adames Roman, Urb. Villa Grillasca, 2040 Calle Eduardo Cuevas, Ponce, 00717-0897. Tel: 787-473-0897.

Cofradia Ntra. Sra. de la Dolorosa—Parroquia Cristo Rey, Urb. La Rambla, 2933 Valladolid St., Ponce, 00730-4011. Rev. Msgr. Juan Rodriguez Orengo, Chap.; Mrs. Juanita Pena.

Ministerio de Evangelizacion Catolico Jesus Misericordioso—Mailing Address: P.O. Box 334151, Ponce, 00733-4151. Mr. Juan Perez. Tel: 787-602-8287.

Boy Scouts of America—Mr. Anibal Diaz Colon, Urb. Villa El Encanto, Calle 7 #50, Juana Diaz, 00795. Tel: 787-837-2806.

Radio Station WEUC - FM Catholic Radio—Mr. Jose Leon Almodovar, Dir., 2250 Ave. Las Americas, Ste. 529, Ponce, 00717-9997. Tel: 787-844-8809.

Television Station - Catholic TV - Channel 14—Mr. Ivan Falto, Dir., 2250 Ave. Las Americas, Ste. 529, Ponce, 00717-9997. Tel: 787-841-2000, Ext. 2536.

Pastoral Carcelaria—Rev. Gerardo Ramirez, Chap., Parroquia Ntra. Srs. de la Providencia, HC-01 Box 3471, Villalba, 00766. Tel: 787-867-2052.

Pastoral de la Salud - Hospitales—Rev. Dairo H. Arboleda, O.SS.T., Dir., Hospital Dr. Pila, Ave. Las Americas, Ponce, 00717. Tel: 787-848-5600, Ext. 3202; 787-631-5522.

Catechesis—Sr. Amarilis Rosario, O.P.

Catholic Youth Organization—Rev. Manuel Santiago Hernandez.

Children of Mary—Rev. Msgr. Juan Rodriguez Orengo.

Committee for Community Planning—Rev. Msgr. Roberto Garcia Blay.

Communications—Sr. Socorro Bonilla, O.P., Mailing Address: P.O. Box 330986, Ponce, 00733-0986. Tel: 787-843-1548.

Cursillos de Cristiandad—Revs. Gerardo Ramirez Torres, 4072 Ave. Tito Castro, Ste. 201, Ponce, 00716-4702; Samuel Santiago, Parroquia Santa Maria Reina, P.O. Box 32101, Ponce, 00732-2101.

Ecumenism—Rev. Msgr. Juan Rodriguez Orengo, Mailing Address: P.O. Box 32205, Ponce, 00732-2205.

Legion of Mary—Rev. Msgr. Juan Rodriguez Orengo, Mailing Address: P.O. Box 32205, Ponce, 00732-2205.

Liturgical Commission—Most Rev. Felix Lazaro Martinez, Sch.P., Mailing Address: P.O. Box 32205, Ponce, 00732-2205.

Sacred Music Commission—Rev. Msgr. Abel A. DiMarco.

St. Vincent de Paul Conferences—Mr. Ibrahim Maldonado, Cristo Rey Parish, Urb La Rambla, 2933 Calle Valladolid, Ponce, 00730-4011.

Superintendent of Schools—Mrs. Nancy Ghigliotti, Mailing Address: P.O. Box 32552, Ponce, 00732-2552. Tel: 787-848-4020; Fax: 787-844-5987.

Vigilance for the Faith—Most Rev. Felix Lazaro Martinez, Sch.P.

Vocations—Rev. Msgr. Elias S. Morales, Mailing Address: P.O. Box 32110, Ponce, 00732-2110. Tel: 787-848-4380; Fax: 787-848-4380.

Institute of Family Orientation—Deacon Francisco Lugo, Mailing Address: P.O. Box 32214, Ponce, 00732-2214. Tel: 787-840-6018; Fax: 787-848-4523.

CLERGY, PARISHES, MISSIONS AND PAROCHIAL SCHOOLS

CITY OF PONCE

1—Cathedral of Our Lady of Guadalupe (1692) Rev. Msgr. Marcos A. Pancorbo; Rev. Jayson Orsini Baez; Deacons Jose Ramon Mercado; Carlos J. Rodriguez.
Res.: 32 Cristina St., Box 32210, 00732-2210. Tel: 787-842-0134; Fax: 787-848-9104.
Chapel—Church of Our Lady of Miraculous Medal P.O. Box 32210, 00732-2210.

2—Christ the King (1964) Rev. Msgr. Juan Rodriguez Orengo; Rev. Arnaldo Ortiz Dominichi; Deacons Anibal Rosario; Eduardo A. Dosal; Jose Plaud Medina; Manuel Roman Perez.
Res.: Urb La Rambla, 2933 Calle Valladolid, 00730-4011. Tel: 787-843-3028; Fax: 787-848-1861.
Catechesis/Religious Program—Zaida Diaz Medina, D.R.E. Students 617.
Mission—Santa Teresita Santa Luisa, Ponce Co. 00730.
Mission—Nino Jesus de Praga Bo. Los Claves, Rio Chiquito, Ponce Co.
Mission—La Dolorosa Villa Ponce - Rambla, Calle Castellana Final, Ponce Co. 00730-4011. Tel: 787-840-8380.

3—Church of the Resurrection (1967) Rev. Msgr. Roberto Garcia Blay; Revs. Esteban Santaella; Victor Rene Sanchez Muniz; Deacon Rafael Castro.
Glenview Gardens—PMB-98, P.O. Box 2000, Mercedita, 00715. Tel: 787-842-7167; Fax: 787-841-8718.
Mission—Immaculate Heart of Mary Bo. La Yuca, Ponce Co.
Mission—Our Lady of Monserrate Bo. Collado, Ponce Co.
Mission—San Lucas Bo. Las Vallas, Ponce Co.
Mission—Saint Joseph Bo. La Yuca, Ponce Co.
Mission—Our Lady of Carmel Bo. Carmelita, Ponce Co.

4—Church of the Sacred Heart (1969) Rev. Jose M. Galan; Deacon Reinaldo Rivera.
Res.: P.O. Box 577, Mercedita, 00715-0577. Tel: 787-843-4891; Fax: 787-848-9212.
Catechesis/Religious Program—Students 100.

5—Church Santisimo Sacramento (1984) Rev. Eliud Aponte Rivera.
Res.: Urb. Vistas del Mar, 2238 Calle Marlin, 00716-0834. Tel: 787-843-0245.

6—Good Shepherd Parish (1968) Rev. Winston R. Mendez; Deacons Rafael D. Ruiz; Luis A. Gonzalez Gonzalez.
Res.: Calle 40-NN25, Jardines del Caribe, 00728-2675. Tel: 787-843-6202; Fax: 787-843-4422. Email: pastorbonus@prw.net. Web: www.elbuenpastorponce.parroquia.org.
Catechesis/Religious Program—Students 89.
Mission—La Milagrosa Calle 5 #69, Bo. Quebrado del Agua, Ponce, Ponce Co. 00731. Tel: 787-843-6202.

7—La Merced (1928) Rev. Jesus Saez Castrillo, O.de.M., Vicar; Deacons Carlos M. Rodriguez-Guilbe; José D. Ruiz; Victor Fabre.
Res.: 4632 Luna St., 00717-2000. Tel: 787-842-0069; Fax: 787-842-0603.

8—La Milagrosa (1928) Revs. Juan Lamela, C.M.; Basilio Roldan Ricarte; Deacons Ramon L. Vazquez; Carlos Juan Ramos Torres.
Res.: Guadalupe No. 2, 00730-3110. Tel: 787-842-3188; Fax: 787-284-1100. Email: parmilagrosa@rsisp.net.
School—Tel: 787-842-6349; Fax: 787-284-1100. Liz Marie Santiago, Prin.
Catechesis/Religious Program—Students 200.

9—La Santisima Trinidad (1971) Revs. Dairo H. Arboleda, O.SS.T.; Johnny Cruz, O.SS.T., Vicar; Deacons Francisco Lugo; Nestor Rentas; Jose Rodriguez.
Las Delicias—Box 8226, 00732. Tel: 787-842-6073; Fax: 787-842-6073.
Catechesis/Religious Program—Students 171.
Mission—San Juan de Mata Box 8226, Bo. Magueyes, Ponce Co. 00732.
Mission—San Andres Bo. Guaraguao, Ponce Co. 00732.
Mission—Santa Ana Bo. Guaraguao Arriba, Ponce Co. 00732.
Mission—N.S. Fatima Sector Jaguas, Bo. Marueno, Arriba, Ponce Co. 00732.
Mission—San Antonio de Padua Parcelas de Marueno, Ponce Co. 00732.
Mission—N.S. del Rosario Bo. Madrigal, Ponce Co. 00730.
Mission—Inmaculada Bo. Pastillo, Ponce Co. 00732.
Mission—Cristo Rey Bo. Corral Viejo, Ponce Co. 00732.
Mission—San Miguel de los Santos Las Delicias 11, Ponce Co. 00732.
Mission—Resurreccion Bo. Santas Pascuas, Ponce Co. 00732.

10—Our Lady of Mt. Carmel (1883) Revs. Felix Ganuza, Sch.P.; Miguel Alvarez, Sch.P., Vicar; Cecilio Lacruz, Sch.P. (Spain); Deacons Arnaldo Figueroa Rivera; Jose Rivera Saez.
Res.: P.O. Box 7760, 00732-7760. Tel: 787-842-1333; Fax: 787-841-6861.
School—Tel: 787-842-5018; Fax: 787-842-5018. Mrs. Paquita Alvarado, Prin.
Mission—San Martin de Porres Constancia Ave., Villa del Carmen, Ponce Co. 00734. Tel: 787-848-4355.
Mission—Santa Marta c/o Santa Marta #8, Bo. Salistral, Ponce Co. 00732.

11—Our Lady of Mt. Carmel (1973) Rev. Jose Antonio Lopez Vega; Deacon Juan Altori Vargas.
Res.: P.O. Box 800187, Coto Laurel, 00780. Tel: 787-848-2030.
Mission—Santa Maria Virgen Bo. Hoyos, Ponce Co. 00780.
Mission—Sagrado Corazon de Jesus Carr. 511 K. 15, Bo. Las Raices, Ponce Co. 00780.
Mission—San Mateo Bo. Real Anon Abajo, Ponce Co. 00780.
Mission—San Martin de Porres Bo. Real Anon Arriba, Ponce Co. 00780.

12—San Conrado (1948) Rev. Jose R. Alvarado de Jesus; Deacons Emerito Lopez Cosme; Joseph Burgos.
Res.: Box 7362, 00732. Tel: 787-843-0560; Fax: 787-843-0600. Email: psconrado@prw.net. Web: psconrado.web.prw.net.
School—P.O. Box 7111, 00732. Tel: 787-843-1405; 787-842-2293; Fax: 787-841-7303. Email: sanconrado@coqui.net. Sr. Nildred Rodriguez, C.S.J., Prin.
Catechesis/Religious Program—Students 712.

13—San Jose (1965) Revs. Orlando Ramos, O.C.D.; Jacinto Rosario, O.C.D.; Mariano Fraile, O.C.D.; Alexio Jose de Armas, O.C.D.; Deacons Benjamin Pagan Diaz; Edgardo Muniz; Arnaldo Gierbolini.
Res.: Urb. San Jose, 416 Calle Beato Francisco Palau, Box 8414, 00728-1905. Tel: 787-843-3910; Fax: 787-843-1994. Email: carmelitasponce@yahoo.com.

14—San Jose Obrero (1979) Revs. Manuel Santiago; P. Omar Martinez Medina, Vicar; Deacon Vicente Aponte Arroyo.
Res.: *Parcelas El Tuque*, Calle Ramos Antonini #632, P.O. Box 8027, 00732-8027. Tel: 787-843-9072; Fax: 787-290-5339. Email: psjoseobrero@yahoo.com.
Mission—Ntra. Sra. del Pilar 616 M #7, Punto Oro, Ponce Co. 00728.
Mission—Cristo de la Misericordia Nueva Vida Calle J D-9.
Mission—Inmaculado Corazon de Maria Calle Lorencita Ferre, Brisas del Caribe.
Mission—Natra. Sra. de la Medalla Milagrosa Punta Diamante. Tel: 787-259-3992. (Encargada - Hermanas Dominicas de Fatima)

15—San Vicente-Cantera (1964) Revs. Osner Domond, C.M., Admin.; Francisco Javier Ramirez, C.M., Vicar; Deacons Jorge Almodovar Capielo; Hector Luis Santiago.
Res.: Paseo La Cantera No. 67, 00730-3026. Tel: 787-843-1976; Fax: 787-812-0212. Email: poncecm@hotmail.com.
Catechesis/Religious Program—Students 100.
Mission—San Vicente Rio Chiquito, Ponce Co.
Mission—Santos Reyes Bo. La Mocha, Ponce Co.
Mission—Santa Luisa Bo. Nuevo Mameyes, Ponce Co.
Mission—La Inmaculada Sector San Patricio, Ponce Co.

16—Santa Maria Reina (1952) Rev. Samuel Santiago; Deacon David Ramos.
Res.: P.O. Box 32101, 00732-2101. Tel: 787-848-5370; 787-848-3313; Fax: 787-290-4189.
School—Tel: 787-842-1164; Fax: 787-843-6755 (Elem.); 787-290-3711 (H.S.). Lydia Otero, Prin., Elem.; Carmen Ojeda, Prin., H.S.

17—Santa Teresita (1930) Revs. P. Ramon Lopez, O.F.M.Cap.; Mario Mastrangelo, O.F.M.Cap., Vicar; P. Jose Antonio Villaran, O.F.M.Cap., Guardian Formation Dir.; P. Juis Gonzalez, O.F.M.Cap., Parish Vicar Formation Team; Deacons Casildo Rodriguez; Ildefonso Gonzalez Plaza; Arnaldo Lopez Quirindongo.
Res.: 342 Victoria St., Box 7244, 00732. Tel: 787-842-3137; 787-842-5055 (Friary); Fax: 787-844-7267.
Catechesis/Religious Program—Lorena Ayala, D.R.E. Students 100.

18—Santuario San Judas Tadeo (1964) Revs. Angel

Cuadrado, O.de.M.; P. Javier Erralcalde, O.de.M.; P. Ramón Conde Ocampo, O.de.M.; Vicente Salas Avello, O.de.M.
Res.: Constancia 2518, Urb Constancia P.O. Box 7046, 00732-7046. Tel: 787-843-0572; Fax: 787-842-0148. Email: psjudasponce@hotmail.com.
School—San Judas Tadeo, Tel: 787-844-2610; Fax: 787-843-3802. Nancy Torres Garcia, Prin.; Rev. Ramon Conde, Dir. Congregacion Religiosa de la Merced
Catechesis/Religious Program—Urb. Constancia Calle Coloso 2929. Students 668.
PARISHES IN FORMATION, CHURCH SAN PATRICIO, Closed. Now a Mission of Our Lady of Monserrate.

OUTSIDE THE CITY OF PONCE

ADJUNTAS, ADJUNTAS CO., ST. JOACHIM (1815) Revs. Carlos Reynoso Valdez, O.R.C.; Rosalino Aguirre, O.R.C.; Deacons Samuel Sepulveda; Radames Marcucci; Efrain Bernard Sierra; Jose M. Maldonado Plaza; Edwin Portalatin Padua; Edgardo Rivera Garcia.
Res.: 14 Rius Rivera St., 00601. Tel: 787-829-3145.
School—San Joaquin Elementary and Intermediate, 12 Primo Delgado St., 00601. Tel: 787-829-3040; Fax: 787-829-3040. Mrs. Carmen Zelideth Ortiz Reyes, Prin.
Catechesis/Religious Program—Students 164.
Mission—San Francisco Garzas, Adjuntas Co.
Mission—Sta. Ana Vegas Arriba, Adjuntas Co.
Mission—Santa Teresita Tres de Jayuya, Adjuntas Co.
Mission—Santa Rosa Pellejas, Adjuntas Co.
Mission—Virgen del Carmen Yahuecas, Adjuntas Co.
Mission—Sagrado Corazon Tanama, Adjuntas Co.
Mission—San Antonio Guilarte, Adjuntas Co.
Mission—La Milagrosa Vegas Abajo, Adjuntas Co.
Mission—Ntra Sra Fátima Juan González formerly Inm. Corazon de Maria Limani, Adjuntas Co.
AGUIRRE, SALINAS CO., SACRED HEART (1946) Rev. Pedro Faustino Echeverria; Deacons Benjamin Lopez; Wenceslao Cruz Rivera.
Res.: Box 260, 00704-0260. Tel: 787-853-3620; Fax: 787-853-2131.
School—Perpetuo Socorro, Street 3 Km 151, 00704-2499. Tel: 787-853-2270. Sr. Aurea E. Fuentes, R.A., Prin. Students 426.
Mission—St. Judas Las Mareas, Salinas Co.
Mission—Our Lady of Perpetual Help Coqui, Salinas Co.
Mission—St. Martin de Porres San Felipe, Salinas Co.
Mission—La Milagrosa, Salinas Co.
ARROYO, ARROYO CO., OUR LADY OF MT. CARMEL (1855) Revs. Juan Jose Saliva Gonzalez; Alonso Escobar Giraldo; Deacons Jacinto Rodriguez; Esteban Rivera.
Res.: General Brooke No. 18, Box 388, 00714. Tel: 787-839-3465; Fax: 787-839-1552. Email: parroquia_carmen@hotmail.com. Web: www.yaucoweb.com/parroquiadelcarmen.
Mission—Ntra Sra. del Carmen Bo. Pitahaya Carr. 3 K.43.
Mission—La Milagrosa Carr. 3 Bda. Marin, Arroyo Co.
Mission—San Jose Sector Palmarejo - Carr 3 K 6 H 3.
Mission—Ntra Sra. de Fatima Bo. Palmas Parcela 526, Arroyo Co.
Mission—San Martin Sector Santa Clara Carr. 3, Arroyo Co.
CASTAÑER, LARES CO., OUR LADY OF THE MIRACULOUS MEDAL (1969) Rev. Rosalino Aguirre Bahena, O.R.C.; Deacons Wilfredo Torres Maldonado; William Ramos.
Res.: Box 1006, Castaner, 00631. Tel: 787-829-6389.
Catechesis/Religious Program—Tel: 787-829-6389.
Chapel—La Milagrosa Chapel Bartolo, Rio Grande Co. 00669.
Chapel—La Milagrosa Chapel Bo. Mirasol, Lares Co. 00669.
Chapel—La Milagrosa Chapel Bo. Rio Prieto, Lares Co. 00669.
COAMO, COAMO CO.
1—ST. BLASE (1616) Revs. Jose Diego Rodriguez; Vicente Perez Roig; Cristobal Reilly, S.T.; Juan Carlos Rivera Medina; Deacons Angel A. Negron; Orlando Martinez Rodriguez; Jaime Ortiz; Alfredo Rivera Cardona.
Res.: Box 196, 00769. Tel: 787-825-1122; Fax: 787-825-7006. Email: psblas@hotmail.com.
School—Ntra. Sra. de Valvanera, Box 1903, 00769. Tel: 787-825-1145; Fax: 787-825-8082. Ada Pedrogo, Prin.
Catechesis/Religious Program—Thelma Sanchez, D.R.E. Students 900.
Mission—Immaculate Heart of Mary Palmarejo, Coamo Co. 00769.
Mission—Christ the King Pulguillas, Coamo Co. 00769.
Mission—Our Lady of Mt. Carmel Hayales, Coamo Co. 00769.
Mission—Miraculous Virgin Descalabrado, Coamo Co. 00769.
Mission—Santa Catalina Santa Catalina, Coama Co. 00769.
Mission—Saint James Cilantro, Coamo Co. 00769. Fax: 787-825-1122.
Mission—Miraculous Virgin Pedro Garcia, Coamo Co. 00769.
Mission—Santa Ana Santa Ana, Coamo Co. 00769.
Mission—San Diego San Diego, Coamo Co. 00769.
Mission—Holy Family Emanueli, Coamo Co. 00769.
Mission—Our Lady of Providence Melendez, Coamo Co. 00769. Fax: 787-825-1122.
Mission—Our Lady of Fatima Bo. Cuyon.
Mission—Sacred Heart of Jesus Coamo Arriba.
2—SAN ANTONIO DE PADUA (2002) Rev. Emiliano Alamo; Deacon Pedro Garcia.
Res.: 545. Carr. 14 Hec 2, KM 26 Barrio Los Llanos, P.O. Box 2227, 00769. Tel: 787-803-4801.
Catechesis/Religious Program—Students 93.
Mission—San Martin Las Flores, Coamo, Coamo Co. 00769.
Mission—Our Lady of Lourdes Rio Jueyes, Coamo, Coamo Co. 00769.
ENSENADA, GUANICA CO., SACRED HEART (1963) Rev. Jery Rivera Martinez; Deacon Wallis S. Sanchez.
Res.: Box 179, 00647. Tel: 787-821-2857.
Mission—Divina Providencia Salinas-Providencia, Guanica Co.
Mission—Monserrate Bo. Fuig., Guanica Co.
Mission—Virgen del Rosario Bo. Guaypao, Guanica Co.
GUANICA, GUANICA CO., ST. ANTHONY ABBOT (1888) Rev. Jose Carlos Vargas; Deacon Reinaldo Galarza.
Res.: Box 804, 00653. Tel: 787-821-2147.
School—Blessed Imelda, Dr. Veve Str. 26, 00653. Tel: 787-821-2714; Fax: 787-821-2714. Students 117.
Mission—Cristo Rey Bo. Belgica, Guanica Co.
Mission—N. Sra. Rosario Bo. Santa Juanita, Guanica Co.
Mission—San Judas Bo. La Laguna, Guanica Co.
Mission—N. Sra Fatima Bo. La Luna, Guanica Co.
Mission—La Providencia Bda. Esperanza, Guanica Co.
GUAYAMA, GUAYAMA CO., ST. ANTHONY OF PADUA (1736) Revs. José J. Rached, C.Ss.R.; Manuel Rodrgiez, C.Ss.R.; Terry Tull, C.Ss.R.; Henry Beauchamp, C.Ss.R.; Felipe Santiago, C.Ss.R.; Deacons Genaro Rivera Alicea; Francisco Carrasquillo; Juan B. Garcia.
Res.: Box 2820, 00785. Tel: 787-864-4100; Fax: 787-864-5494.
School—St. Anthony, Box 777, 00785. Tel: 787-864-2062; Fax: 787-864-1450. Wanda Pomales, Prin.
Catechesis/Religious Program—Adelina Baerga, D.R.E. Students 287.
Mission—Our Lady of Perpetual Help Caimital, Guayama Co.
Mission—San José Obrero Branderi - Guayama, Puerto Rico.
Mission—St. Gerard Palmas, Guayama Co.
Mission—Our Lady of Mt. Carmel Pueblito del Carmen, PR.
Mission—Cristo Rey Bo. Olimpo, Guayama Co.
Mission—La Candelaria Bo. Corazon, Guayama Co.
Mission—Sgdo. Corazon Bo. Guamani, Guayama Co.
Mission—San Martin Bo. Carite, Guayama Co.
GUAYANILLA, GUAYANILLA CO., IMMACULATE CONCEPTION (1841) Revs. Raymond L. Rivera; Carlos Manuel Grullon; Deacon Miguel Sepuelveda.
Res.: P.O. Box 560573, 00656-0573. Tel: 787-835-3035; Fax: 787-835-3082. Email: inmaculada@caribe.net.
School—Immaculate Conception, P.O. Box 560573, 00656-0573. Tel: 787-835-2230. Email: info@inmaculadapr.org. Web: inmaculadapr.org. Rafael Ortiz Rodriguez, Prin.
Catechesis/Religious Program—Tel: 787-835-2230. Students 168.
Mission—Our Lady of Mt. Carmel Barrio Sierra Baja, Guayanilla Co.
Mission—Perpetuo Socorro Magas Arriba, Guayanilla Co.
Mission—San Francisco de Asis Quebradas, Guayanilla Co.
Mission—San Juan Bosco Barrio Indios, Guayanilla Co.
Mission—La Monserrate Consejo Alto, Guayanilla Co.
Mission—Virgen de Fatima Macana Rio, Guayanilla Co.
Mission—Nuestra Senora La Milagrosa Quebrada Honda, Guayanilla Co.
Mission—San Martin de Porres Macana Parcelas, Guayanilla Co.
JAYUYA, JAYUYA CO., OUR LADY OF MONSERRATE (1883) Revs. Oran de Jesus Ramirez; P. Ramon Arellano Dedia; P. Nicolas Perez Lopez; Deacons Luis Rosario; Carlos Orama; Darvin Orama de Jesus; Jose A. Perez Santos.
Res.: Calle Figueras 13, 00664. Tel: 787-828-6350; Fax: 787-828-5062. Web: www.monserratejayuya.com.
Mission—Ntra Sra del Carmen Bo. Santa Clara - Jayuya, Puerto Rico.
Mission—Bo. Veguita Fama Puerto Rico.
Mission—Divino Niño Jesús Bo. Salientito - Jayuya, Puerto Rico.
Mission—Cristo Rey Bo. Collores - Jayuya.
Mission—San Jorge Bo. Coabey - Jayuya, Jayuya Co. 00664.
Mission—La Milagrosa Bo. Canalizo - Jayuya, Jayuya Co. 00664.
Mission—Buen Pastor Bo. Gripinas - Jayuya, Jayuya Co. 00664.
Mission—Santa Cecila Bo. Zama - Jayuya, Jayuya Co. 00664.
Mission—Ntra Sra de la Divina Providencia Bo. Hoyo Planes - Jayuya, Jayuya Co. 00664.
Mission—S. Antonio Bo. Mameyes - Jayuya, Jayuya Co. 00664.
Mission—Santos Reyes Bo. El Salto - Jayuya.
Mission—San Francisco Bo. Saliente - Jayuya, Jayuya Co. 00664.
Mission—San Juan Evangelista Bo. Puerto Plata - Jayuya.
Mission—San Patricio Bo. La Pica - Jayuya, San Patricio Co. 00664.
Mission—San Jose de la Montaña Bo. Hogares Seguros - Jayuya, San Antonio Co. 00664.
Mission—San Patricio La Pica Cr. Buzon 234-B, Ponce Co. 00730.
JUANA DIAZ, JUANA DIAZ CO.
1—NUESTRA SENORA DE LOURDES (Aguilita) (1984) Rev. Edwin Vazquez-Vega; Deacons Cirilo Carmona; Jaime Velez; Fernando Perez De La Cruz; Marcelino Lebron Romero.
Res.: P.O. Box 1824, 00795. Tel: 787-837-1097.
Mission—Virgen del Carmen Bo. Tiburones, Juana Diaz Co. 00795.
Mission—Sagrado Corazon Bo. Buyones, Juana Diaz Co. 00795.
Mission—San Pedro Nolasco Bo. La Cuarta, 00795.
2—ST. RAYMOND NONATO (1798) Rev. Msgr. Jose Lozano; Revs. Mario Genaro Isla Chavez; Pedro J. Guzman Quintana; Deacons Narciso Ortiz Negron; Orlando Pagan Figueroa; Norberto Santiago; William Santiago Figueroa.
Res.: Munoz Rivera 48, Box 1426, 00795. Tel: 787-837-2390; Fax: 787-837-2390. Email: parroco@juanadiaz.org. Web: www.juanadiaz.org/parroquia.
Catechesis/Religious Program—Maria Isabel Martinez, D.R.E.
Mission—San Judas Rio Canas Abajo, Juana Diaz Co.
Mission—N.S. de Fatima Bo. Jacaquas, Juana Diaz Co. Tel: 787-260-7021.
Mission—La Milagrosa Collores Parcelas, Juana Diaz Co.
Mission—Santiago, Ap. Las Margaritas, Bo. Collores, Bo. Collores Arriba.
Mission—Our Lady of the Rosary Bo. Guayaba, Juana Diaz Co.
Mission—San Ramon Callabo, Bo. Callabo.
Mission—La Merced Bo. Rio Cana Arriba, Juana Diaz Co.
Mission—La Merced Sector Cuatro Calles, 00795.
3—SANTA TERESITA DEL NINO JESUS (Arus) (1984) Rev. Orlando Rivera-Soto; Deacon David Rodriguez.
Barrio Arus carr., 1 Km 190 Hm. 7, 00795-1620.
Res.: P.O. Box 1620, 00795-1620. Tel: 787-214-8083.
Mission—San Martin de Porres, (Singapur)
Mission—Ntra Sra de la Monserrate, Juana Diaz Co. (Galicia)
Chapel—Chapel Divine Mercy (Piedra Aguza), Juana Diaz Co.
PATILLAS, PATILLAS CO., INMACULADO CORAZON DE MARIA (1811) Revs. Patricio Gallego Cifuentes; Martin Garcia Cano; Jaime Rojas Hidalgo; Deacons Luis Melendez Ortiz; Ruben Pabon; Hector Pagan Morales; Juan F. Rodriguez Rivera.
Res.: Cristo #1, Box 635, 00723. Tel: 787-839-5333; Fax: 787-839-5525.
Mission—Perpetuo Socorro Bo. Marin Alto, Patillas, Patillas Co.
Mission—Madre Cabrini Bo. Guarderraya, Patillas, Patillas Co.
Mission—Sto. Cristo de Los Milagros Bo. Recio, Patillas, Patillas Co.
Mission—Nuestra Senora del Carmen Bo. Jacaboa, Patillas, Patillas Co.
Mission—Cristo Rey Bo. El Bajo, Patillas, Patillas Co.
Mission—Ntra Sra de la Providencia Bo. Providencia, Patillas, Patillas Co.
Mission—Santa Rosa de Lima Bo. Los Pollos, Patillas, Patillas Co.

Mission—S. Juan Evangelista Bo. Los Barros, Patillas, Patillas Co.
Mission—San Guillermo Bo. El Real, Patillas, Patillas Co.
Mission—Nuestra Senora del Carmen Bo. Jagual, Patillas, Patillas Co.

PENUELAS, PENUELAS CO.

1—ST. JOSEPH (1793) Revs. Octavio Gonzalez, Admin.; Francesco Donnarumma, Vicar; Deacons Jose E. Gelpi Ortiz; Joaquin Massoller; Glidden R. Perez; Jose A. Rosario Colon; Jose Torres Santiago; Carmelo Vazquez.
Res.: Dr Loyola #603, P.O. Box 25, 00624. Tel: 787-836-1038; Fax: 787-836-0167.
Catechesis/Religious Program—Students 347.
Mission—La Milagrosa Carr. #132 R 391 K. 5 Sec Pueblito, El Rucio, Penuelas Co. 00624.
Mission—San Antonio de Padua Carr. #132 K-16 H 9, Bo. Pastillo - Penuelas, Penuelas Co. 00624.
Mission—Ntra. Sra. de Fatima Carr. #131 Km 5 Sect, La Vega, Bo. Macana, Penuelas Co. 00624.
Mission—Santa Ana Carr. #132 K 14. 7, Bo. Tallaboa Alta, Penuelas Co. 00624.
Mission—Santa Cruz Carr. #132 Rte. 386 Km 6. H-7, Sector Felipe Quinones Barreal, Penuelas Co. 00624.
Mission—La Milagrosa Carr. #387, Sector la Gelpa - Quebrada Ceiba, Penuelas Co. 00624.
Mission—Ntra Sra del Carmen Carr. #132 K. 7 H. 9, Bo. Santo Domingo, Penuelas Co. 00624.
Mission—San Judas Tadeo Carr. #132, Bo. Coto el Mato, Penuelas Co. 00624.
Mission—San Martin de Porres 996 Com. Caracoles III, Penuelas Co. 00624.
Mission—Divino Nino 363 Bo Tallaboa Alta III, Penuelas Co. 00624.

2—SACRED HEART (Tallaboa) (1928) Rev. Christopher De Herrera, O.S., Penuelas, PR Sacred Heart of Jesus Parish.
Res.: HC 03, P.O. Box 13063, 00624. Tel: 787-836-1164.
Catechesis/Religious Program—Students 55.
Mission—Corazon de Maria Bo. Juncos, PR.

PUENTE JOBOS, GUAYAMA CO., SS. PETER AND PAUL (2003) Rev. Manuel I. Sala; Deacon Rene Antonetty Giraud.
Mailing Address: P.O. Box 837, Guayama, 00785-0837. Tel: 787-864-2912. Email: parroquiapedroypablo@yahoo.es. St 6B #33 Puente de Jobos, Guayama, 00784.

SALINAS, SALINAS CO., OUR LADY OF MONSERRAT (1854) Revs. Alberto Muniz; Wilson Saldana; Deacon Jose Luis Rodriguez Collazo.
Res.: Box 1172, 00751. Tel: 787-824-2215.
Mission—San Jose Plena, Salinas Co.
Mission—Santa Ana Coco, Salinas Co.
Mission—Esp. Santo Parcelas Vazquez, Salinas Co.
Mission—Virg. del Carmen Bo. Las Palmas, Salinas Co.
Mission—Santa Marta Naranjo, Salinas Co.
Mission—Inmaculada Concepcion Las Ochenta, Salinas Co.
Mission—Virgen Milagrosa Bo. Playita, Salinas Co.
Mission—Carmen Bo. Playa, Salinas Co.
Mission—Perpetuo Socorro Sabana Llana, Salinas Co.

SANTA ISABEL, SANTA ISABEL CO., ST. JAMES (1854) Revs. Juan Alberto Torres Reyes; Angel Berrios, Vicar; Deacons Jaime Martinez; Jose Manuel Rivera Colon.
Res.: Hostos - #2, Box 137, 00757. Tel: 787-845-2450; Fax: 787-845-2485.
Catechesis/Religious Program—Students 160.
Mission—San Patricio Bo. Playita Cortada - Santa Isabel, PR.
Mission—Virgen del Rosario Bo. Penuelas Santa Isabel.
Mission—Virgen del Perpetuo Socorro
Mission—Ntra. Sra. del Carmen Bo. Playa.
Mission—Virgen de Monserrate Bo. Ollas - Santa Isabel, Santa Isabel Co.
Mission—San Ignacio de Loyola Bo. Jauca - Santa Isabel, Santa Isabel Co.

VILLALBA, VILLALBA CO.

1—OUR LADY MOTHER OF DIVINE PROVIDENCE (Mission Noell) (1962) Rev. Gerardo Ramirez Torres.
Res.: Bo Cacao Carr. 157 Km. 2.2, Orocovis, 00720. Tel: 787-867-2052.
Catechesis/Religious Program—
Mission—Our Lady of Mt. Carmel Bo. Alturita Carr 157, Orocovis, Cacao Co.
Mission—Imm. Concepcion Bo. Cacao Carr 157, Orocovis, Cacao Co.
Mission—Nino de Praga Bo. El Frio carra 143, Orocovis, Ala de La Piedra Co.
Mission—N.S. del Rosario Bo. Bauta Carr 590, Orocovis, Bauta Abajo Co.
Mission—N.S. del Pilar Bo. Damian Abajo Carr 157, Orocovis, Damian Abajo Co.
Mission—N.S. Monserrate Bo. Pozas Carr 615, Orocovis, Damian Abajo Co.
Mission—O.L. of Perp. Help Bo. La Piedra Carr 149, Orocovis, Ala de La Piedra Co.
Mission—Sacred Heart of Jesus Bo. Matrullas Carr 564, Orocovis.
Mission—San Mateo Bo. Ortiga Carr 143, Orocovis, Bauta Abajo Co.

2—OUR LADY OF MT. CARMEL (1917) Revs. Angel Sanchez; Cruz Cruz Ferdinand; Deacons Javier Gonzalez; Cruz M. La Torre Ramos; Jose A. Pagan; Ramon A. Resto; Jaime Luis Rivera Rivera.
Res.: Box 432, 00766. Tel: 787-847-0695; Fax: 787-847-8137.
School—Box 1033, 00766. Tel: 787-847-2875.
Mission—Sagrado Corazon HC01 Box 5081, Romero, Villalba Co. 00766. Tel: 787-847-1591.
Mission—Jesus Crucificado Bo. Vista Alegre, Villalba Co. 00766.
Mission—Santisima Trinidad Bo. Mogote, Villalba Co. 00766.
Mission—Espiritu Santo Bo. Cerro Gordo, Villalba Co. 00766.
Mission—La Milagrosa, Villalba Co. 00766.
Mission—San Pedro Bo. Corillo, Villalba Co. 00766.
Mission—San Jose Bo. Palmarejo, Villalba Co. 00766.
Mission—Santisimo Sacramento Bo. Higuero, Villalba Co. 00766.
Mission—Jesus Crucificado Bo. Camarones, Villalba Co. 00766.
Mission—Maria Madre de la Iglesia Bo. Canonilla Abajo, Villalba Co. 00766.
Mission—Cristo de la Salud Bo. Sierrita Caonillas, Villalba Co. 00766.
Mission—Madre Cabrini Barrio Jaguey, Villalba Co. 00766.
Mission—Santa Cecilia Barrio Semil, Villalba Co. 00766.
Mission—San Alfonso Barrio Apeadero, Villalba Co. 00766.
Mission—Sagrada Familia Barrio Hatillo, Villalba Co. 00766.
Mission—San Antonio Bo. Camarones-Los Robles, Villalba Co. 00766.
Mission—La Milagrosa Bo. Hatillo Viejo, Villalba Co. 00766.
Mission—La Asuncion Bo. Cuchilla del Limon, Villalba Co. 00766.
Mission—Virgen de la Amargura Bo. Limon, Villalba Co. 00766.
Mission—N.S. del Carmen Bo. Dajas, Villalba Co. 00766.
Mission—San Francisco de Asis Bo. La Sierrita de Vacas, Villalba 00766.
Mission—La Milagrosa Bo. El Pino, Villalba 00766.
Mission—San Juan Evangelista Bo. Chichon, Villalba 00766.

YAUCO, YAUCO CO.

1—HOLY ROSARY (1756) Revs. P. Jose Fernando Osorio Osorio, O.P.; Victor Perez Aviles, O.P.; P. Angel Diaz; Deacons Jesus Vazquez Orengo; Luis M. Jusino Cintron; David Fuentes Rivera; Ramon Santiago Ortiz; Rafael Vargas Roman; Jose Ramon Feliciano Baez.
Res.: Box 46, 00698. Tel: 787-856-1222; Fax: 787-856-6845.
School—Box 26, 00698. Tel: 787-856-1001; Fax: 787-267-1238. Mrs. Judith Negron, Prin.
Catechesis/Religious Program—Tel: 787-856-1573. Students 545.
Mission—Virgin of Mt. Carmel Duey, Yauco Co.
Mission—St. James Barinas, Yauco Co.
Mission—Our Lady of Perpetual Help Cambalaches, Yauco Co.
Mission—Our Lady of Montserrat Carrizales, Hatillo Co.
Mission—St. Lucy Sierra Alta, Yauco Co.
Mission—St. Anthony Naranjo, Yauco Co.
Mission—St. Anthony Diego Hdez, Yauco Co.
Mission—Sacred Heart Quebradas, Yauco Co.
Mission—La Milagrosa formerly St. Martin Mogotes, Puerto Rico.

2—ST. MARTIN DE PORRES (1969) Rev. Segismundo Cintron.
Res.: Las Palomas, Box 2005, 00698. Tel: 787-856-3617.
Convent—Sisters of Fatima-Motherhouse, P.O. Box 62, Santa Rita, 00698. Tel: 787-856-1476; Fax: 787-821-2439. Sr. Celeste Ortiz, O.P., Mother Gen. Sisters 126; Novices 3; Postulants 3.
Mission—Ntra. Sra. de Lourdes Bo. Susua, PR, Guanica Co.
Mission—N.S. de La Providencia Bo. Susa, Guanica Co.
Mission—S. Martin de Porres Bo. Arenas de Guancia, Guanica Co.
Mission—S. Francisco de Asis Bo. Susa, Yauco Co.
Mission—N.S. de La Monserrate Bo. Susa, Yauco Co.

3—SANTO DOMINGO DE GUZMAN (2001) Revs. Melvin Diaz Aponte; Francisco Santiago Torres, Vicar.
Mailing Address: P.O. Box 3036, 00698-3036. Tel: 787-856-8212; Fax: 787-856-8212.
Mission—Sacred Heart Bo. Collores - Yauco, Yauco.
Mission—Sta. Teresita Bo. Las Vegas - Yauco, Yauco.
Mission—St. Joseph Bo. Lluberas Yauco, Yauco.
Mission—Our Lady of Fatima Bo. Algarrobos - Yauco, Yauco.
Mission—St. Martin de Porres Bo. Almacigo Bajo - Yauco, Yauco.
Mission—St. Juan Macias Bo. Almacigo Alto - Yauco, Yauco.
Mission—Our Lady of Montserrat Bo. Rio Loco - Yauco, Yauco.
Mission—St. Rosa de Lima Bo. El Cafetal - Yauco, Yauco.

On Duty Outside the Diocese:
Revs.—
Alvarez, Pablo D., F.S.S.P., 13780 S.W. 17 Ter., Miami, FL 33175.
Barrett, Kevin S., Chap., Apostolate of Family Consecration, P.O. Box 151, Bloomingdale, OH 43910-0151.
Espona Jimenez, Juan, Madrid, Spain.
Fletcher, Patrick, 62 AW/Chapel, 746 Main St., McChord AFB, WA 98438.
Gusiora, Alphonsus, P.O. Box 61, Enugwu-Ukwu (Anambra State), Nigeria.
Harrison, Brian W., O.S., P.O. Box 13230, Saint Louis, MO 63157.
Kelty, Edward J., O.S., Associazione SACRI, Via Antonio Zanoni, 44, Roma (Castel di Leva) 00134 Italy.
MacIssac, Charles S., O.S. (Retired), St. Joseph's Home, 140 Shepherd Ln., Totowa, NJ 07512.
Malachowski, Christopher, O.S., Bethlehem-Domus Panis Vital, Nadliwe 05-281 Urle Poland.
Medina, George, P.O. Box 286, East Boston, MA 02128.
Mezquida, Ramon, San Jose 4, Alqueria Condesa 46715, Valencia, Spain.
Munoz, Rafael, P.O. Box 187, Barceloneta, 00657.
Nieves, Carlos, HC763, Buzon 4240, Patillas, 00723.
Nischan, James R., 1625 Mayo Ave., Owensboro, KY 42301.
Quinones, Leoncio, Urb. Apolo, Guaynabo, 00657.
Roman, Carlos, (la Crosse Diocese, WI)
Sancho Piquer, Enrique, Calvario 49, 2, 4, Pafelbunoli, Valencia, Spain.
Serrano, Dionisio, Maestro Ripoll 14, 28006 Madrid, Spain.
Sirvent, Francisco, Capitan Cortes 8-2, Valencia, Spain.
Zayas, Antonio, Naranjito, 00719.

Retired:
Revs.—
Garcia Echevarria, Roberto, Bo. Real Anon, Coto Laurel, 00780.
MacIssac, Charles S., O.S., St. Joseph's Home, 140 Shepherd Ln., Totowa, NJ 07512.
Weslin, Norman U., O.S., Cherry Hill Haven, 4825 N. Long Lake Rd., Traverse City, MI 49684.

Permanent Deacons:
Almodovar Capielo, Jorge
Altori Vargas, Juan
Antonetty Giraud, Rene
Aponte Arroyo, Vicente
Bernard Sierra, Efrain
Burgos Roca, Joseph
Carmona Cruz, Cirilo
Carrasquillo, Francisco
Castro Belen, Rafael
Castro Toro, Alberto
Cruz Rivera, Wenceslao
Dosal Lines, Eduardo
Fabre Torres, Antonio Victor
Feliciano Baez, Jose Ramon
Figueroa Rivera, Arnaldo
Figueroa Santana, Edwin
Fuentes Rivera, David
Galarza, Reinaldo
Garcia Malavet, Pedro
Garcia Rivera, Juan B.
Gelpi Ortiz, Jose E.
Gierbolini Rodriguez, Arnaldo
Gonzalez, Javier
Gonzalez Gonzalez, Luis A.
Gonzalez Plaza, Ildefonso
Jusino Cintron, Luis M.
La Torre Ramos, Cruz M.
Lebron Romero, Marcelino
Lopez Cosme, Emerito
Lopez Quirindongo, Arnaldo
Lopez Sanchez, Benjamin
Lugo, Francisco
Maldonado Plaza, Jose M.
Marcucci, Radames

Martinez, Jaime
Martinez Rodriguez, Orlando
Masollet, Joaquin
Melendez Ortiz, Luis
Mendez Molina, Angel
Mendez Purcell, Jose M.
Mercado, Jose Ramon
Miranti, Pablo
Montanez, Alberto
Morales Colon, Angel R.
Muniz Rivera, Edgardo
Negron Ortiz, Angel
Niewiadonski, Arthur
Orama de Jesus, Darvin
Oramas, Carlos
Orsini, Pablo
Ortiz, Jaime
Ortiz Negron, Narciso
Pabon Gonzalez, Ruben
Pagan Diaz, Benjamin
Pagan Figueroa, Orlando
Pagan Morales, Hector
Pagan Rivera, Jose E.
Perez De La Cruz, Fernando
Perez Diaz, Glidden
Perez Santos, Jose A.
Plaud Medina, Jose
Portalatin Padua, Edwin
Ramos Rivera, William
Ramos Torres, Carlos Juan
Ramos Torres, David
Rentas, Nestor
Resto, Ramon
Reyes, Ruperto
Rivera, Esteban
Rivera, Juan Esteban
Rivera, Reinaldo
Rivera Alicea, Genaro
Rivera Cardona, Alfredo
Rivera Colon, Jose Manuel
Rivera Garcia, Edgardo
Rivera Rivera, Jaime Luis
Rivera Saez, Jose
Rivera Velazquez, Esteban
Rodriguez, Casildo
Rodriguez, David
Rodriguez, Feliz
Rodriguez, Jacinto
Rodriguez, Jose
Rodriguez Collazo, Jose Luis
Rodriguez Guilbe, Carlos
Rodriguez Rivera, Juan F.
Rodriguez Sanchez, Carlos
Roman Perez, Manuel
Rosario, Anibal
Rosario, Luis
Rosario Colon, Jose A.
Ruiz, Jose D.
Ruiz, Rafael
Sanchez, Wallis
Santiago, Hector Luis
Santiago, William
Santiago Negron, Norberto
Santiago Ortiz, Ramon
Sepulveda, Miguel
Sepulveda, Samuel
Torres Maldonado, Wilfredo
Torres Santiago, Jose
Vargas Roman, Rafael
Vazquez, Carmelo
Vazquez, Ramon
Vazquez Orengo, Jesus
Velazquez, Jose A. Velez
Velez, Jaime

INSTITUTIONS LOCATED IN THE DIOCESE

[A] SEMINARIES

PONCE. *Diocesan Seminary Regina Cleri* (Major), P.O. Box 32110, 00732-2110. Tel: 787-812-3024. Email: meliasalvador@hotmail.com. Rev. Msgr. Elias S. Morales, Rector; Rev. Julio A. Rolon Torres, Admin. Priests 2; Lay Staff 5; Seminarians 24.

[B] COLLEGES & UNIVERSITIES

PONCE. *The Pontifical Catholic University of Puerto Rico*, 2250 Avenida de las Americas, 00717-9997. Tel: 787-841-2000; Fax: 787-651-2034. Web: www.pucpr.edu. The University is composed of the following: College of Arts and Humanities and Graduate Studies in Hispanic Studies; College of Business Administration and Graduate Studies; College of Education and Graduate Studies; College of Science and Graduate Studies; School of Law; College of Graduate Studies in Behavioral Science and Community Affairs; Institute of Social Doctrine of the Church; Student Support Services; Post-Baccalaureate Achievement Program; Upward Bound Program. Priests 21; Sisters 5; School of Law 57; Lay Teachers 611; Students 9,908.

Administration: Most Rev. Felix Lazaro, Sch.P., Grand Chancellor; Dr. Jorge Velez Arocho, Pres.; Dr. Leandro Colon-Alicea, Vice Pres. Academic Affairs; Mrs. Irma Rodriguez, Vice Pres. Fin. Affairs; Mr. Freddie Martinez Sotomayor, Vice Pres. Student Affairs; Ms. Karen Morales Rodriguez, Interim Dir. Continuing Education; Dr. Felix M. Cortes Morales, Vice Pres. Office Devel., Research & Planning; Mr. Alfonso Santiago-Cruz, Dean College of Arts and Humanities; Dr. Jaime Santiago Canet, Dean College of Business Admin.; Ms. Carmen L. Velazquez-Almodovar, Dean College of Science; Angel Gonzalez Roman, Dean School of Law; Mr. Ivan E. Davila-Ostolaza, Registrar; Dr. Ana Bonilla de Sanchez, Dir. Admissions; Ms. Carmen Gonzalez-Martinez, Dir. Guidance Center; Mrs. Magda I. Vargas Rodriguez, Dir. Libraries; Mrs. Noelia Padua, Esq., Dir. Law Library; Dr. Herman A. Vera-Rodriguez, Dean of College Graduate Studies; Ms. Gilda Rivera-Aponte, Exec. Dir. Information Technology & Telecommunications.

Faculty: Rev. Msgrs. Herminio De Jesus; Abel A. DiMarco, Lecturer in History; Juan Rodriguez Orengo, Lectures in Theology; Revs. José D. Rodriguez Martino, Lecturer in Theology; Perfecto Alvarez, O.S.A., Lecturer in Theology; Adalin Rivera; Mario Mastrangelo, O.F.M.Cap.; Segismundo Cintron, Lecturer in Theology; Alvaro Huerga Teruelo; P. Julio A. Vera Gonzalez; Juan Javier Inigo Monreal, C.M., Delegado para la Mision Inst.; Friar P. Omar A. Martinez Medina, O.P.; Hna Nancy Arroyo Gonzalez; Nydia E. Rivera Aponte.

Mayaguez: Edgardo Acosta Ocasio, Lecturer in Theology; Revs. Jose R. Linares Pagan, Lecturer in Theology; Luis A. Rodriguez Vientos, Chap. Precinct Mayaguez, Dept. Teologia y Filosofia.

Ponce: Revs. Julio A. Rolon Torres, Lecturer in Theology; Antonio Portalatin Rodriguez, Lecturer in Theology; Francisco Medina Santos-Lecturer, Lecturer in Theology; P. Angel L. Rios Matos, J.C.D.

Recinto De Arecibo: Rev. Omar Bedoya Gaviria, Lectures in Theology; Victor Rojas Rodriguez, Lecture in Graduate Studies; Rev. P. Ivan Martinez Adorno.

Extension De Coamo: Emiliano Alamo Hernando, Lecturer in Theology.

[C] SCHOOLS - INSTITUTES OF EDUCATION

PONCE. *Academia Cristo Rey Inc.*, Urb. La Rambla, c/o San Judas 3011, 00730-4091. Miss Gicela Bonilla, Prin. Students 617.

Centro San Francisco, Box 10479, 00732. Tel: 787-842-2776; 787-290-0271; Fax: 787-842-2776. Email: csfinc@aol.com. Web: www.csfinc.aol.com. Sonial Pagan Figueroa, Dir.; Mrs. Lizabeth Quinones Vargas, Prin.; Ms. Vivian Arroyo Torres, Teacher; Mrs. Mariselly Santiago O'Conner, Librarian. Sisters of St. Joseph. Lay Teachers 28; Librarians 2; Social Workers 1; Counselors 1.

Colegio Del Sagrado Corazon De Jesus (1916) 2511 Calle Obispado, 00716-3836. Tel: 787-842-0339; Fax: 787-843-0250. Email: sagrado@coqui.net. Web: www.home.coqui.net/sagrado. Mrs. Maria Serrano, Prin.; Miss Lydia Mendez, Librarian. Religious of the Sacred Heart. Priests 1; Lay Teachers 55; Total Staff 82.

Colegio El Ave Maria, 4506 Dr. Bartolomei, Reparto Valle Alegre, 00728-3151. Tel: 787-284-2453; Fax: 787-284-2453. Email: avemaria@pucpr.edu. Sr. Milagros Pizarro, O.D.M., Dir. & Prin. Operarias del Divino Maestro (Avemarianas). Sisters 4; Lay Teachers 13; Total Staff 17; Total Enrollment 13.

Holy Family School (1913) 1270 Ave. Hostos, 00717-0928. Tel: 787-842-3208; Fax: 787-844-6773. Email: sagradafamilia1270@yahoo.com. Sisters Cecilia Serrano Guzman, H.C., Prin.; Elena Cintron, H.C., Librarian. Sisters of Charity - Saint Vincent de Paul. Sisters 2; Lay Teachers 24; Total Staff 26; Students 223.

COTO LAUREL. *Colegio Ponceno* (Day School), 1900 Carr. 14, 00780-2147. Tel: 787-848-2525; Fax: 787-259-4282. Email: colegio@copin.net. Web: www.copin.net. Revs. Hector Cruz, Sch.P., Chap. & Teacher; P. Jesus Romero, Sch.P., Teacher; Very Rev. Fernando Torres, Sch.P., Dir.; Luis de Leon, Supr.; Carmen Rizzo, Prin. (Elementary); Milagros Carmona, Librarian. Piarist Fathers. Priests 3; Deacons 2; Lay Teachers 67; Total Enrollment 965; Total Staff 75.

PLAYA PONCE. *Centros Sor Isolina Ferre, Inc.* (1969) Vocational School, P.O. Box 7282, 00732-7282. Tel: 787-843-1910 (Tabaiba - Playa Ponce); 787-842-0000 (Admin.); Fax: 787-844-7665; 787-540-5020. Email: mperez@csifpr.org. Web: www.csifpr.org. Sr. Rosita M. Bauza, M.S.B.T., Historian. Missionary Servants of the Most Blessed Trinity., Non-profit organization dedicated to community revitalization through education and vocational, technological training programs. We help natural leaders from these communities become its advocates and counselors. Our efforts are aimed at: juvenile delinquency prevention - decreasing school dropout rates - special education, vocational & technological training - preparing youngsters & adults for employment - community self-development. We provide the necessary tools to become fully alive & rediscover their abilities. Our emphasis is to promote dignity & self-respect as a preventive measure for high risk groups. Sisters 5; Total Staff 450.

[D] HOMES FOR THE AGED

PONCE. *Residencia Santa Marta* Home for Aged and Infirm, Barrio Sabanetas, P.O. Box 242, Mercedita, 00715-0242. Tel: 787-840-7575; Fax: 787-651-1080. Email: rsmarta@hotmail.com. Sr. Hilda M. Rodriguez Rodriguez, Supr.; Rev. P. Miguel Alvarez Hernando, Chap. Bed Capacity 215; Total Assisted Annually 175; Total Staff (Religious) 15; Residents 196.

[E] MONASTERIES AND RESIDENCES OF PRIESTS AND BROTHERS

PONCE. *Fraternidad Santa Teresita, Frailes Capuchinos* (Postulantado), 342 Victoria St., Box 7244, 00732. Tel: 787-842-5055; Fax: 787-844-7267. Email: frfernandoirizarrysantana@yahoo.com. Friar Jose Fernando Irizarry Santana, O.F.M.Cap., Guardian & Dir. Postulantado; Rev. Mario Mastrangelo, O.F.M.Cap., Prof. at P.U.C.P.R.; Friars Ramon Luis Lopez; Henry Felix Silva Maldonado. Postulants 2.

[F] CONVENTS & RESIDENCES OF SISTERS

PONCE. *Blessed Trinity Missionary Cenacle* (1950) P.O. Box 7282, 00732-7282. Tel: 787-844-1627; Fax: 787-842-6745. Email: msbtponce@coqui.net. Web: www.msbt.org. Sr. Rosita M. Bauza, M.S.B.T., Historian (Centros Sor Isolina Ferre, Inc.). Sisters 5.

Convent of Servants of Mary (1891) Urb. La Rambla, 1703 Calle Siervas de Maria, 00730-4027. Tel: 787-842-2336; Fax: 787-844-5449. Sr. Elena Rolon Rosado, S. de M., Supr. Religious 21; Novices 6; Administered in the home 2,300; Aspirants 3.

Religiosas del Apostolado del Sagrado Corazon de Jesus (1891) P.O. Box 8300, 00732-8300. Tel: 787-842-4340; Fax: 787-813-2066. Sisters Apostolate of the Sacred Heart of Jesus 23.

Colegio Perpetuo Socorro, Bo. Coqui, Aguirre - Salinas, PR 00704. Tel: 787-853-2270; Fax: 787-853-2531. Sr. Aurea E. Fuentes, R.A., Supr., Delegada Regl. Representante de la Superiora Gen.

YAUCO. *Hermanas Dominicas de Fatima, Hermanas Dominicas de Nuestra Senora del Rosario de Fatima*, P.O. Box 62, 00698-0062. Tel: 787-856-4256; 787-856-4330; Fax: 787-821-2439.

[G] PERSONAL PRELATURES

PONCE. *Prelature of the Holy Cross and Opus Dei*, Urb. Alhambra, 1814 calle Alcazar, 00716-3829. Tel: 787-844-2661; Fax: 787-844-2661. Email: pricoinf@coqui.net. Web: opusdei.org.pr. Revs. Javier Bernaola; Jaime Bermudez Onopa.

[H] MISCELLANEOUS

PONCE. *Albergue La Providencia para El Bienestar Social, Inc.*, P.O. Box 10142, 00732. Tel: 787-841-2119; Fax: 787-840-6642. Email: albergueprovi@gmail.com. Web: www.laprovidencia.org. Rev. Francisco Garcia, O.F.M.Cap., Dir. Refuge Center for AIDS patients. Total Assisted 7; Total Staff 8.

Casa de Formacion Residencia Asis, c/o Chancery, P.O. Box 32205, 00732-2205.

Centro Calasanz

Centro Madre Dominga, Casa Belen (2000) Urb. San Jorge, 3504 Calle Andino Apt. 2, 00717-0777. Tel: 787-290-3627; Fax: 787-844-3240. Email: centromadredominga@hotmail.com. Sr. Elena Santana, O.P., Dir.

Fundacion Surinach, P.O. Box 32205, 00732-2205. Most Rev. Felix Lazaro, Sch.P., Pres.; Rev. Msgr. Juan Rodriguez Orengo, Treas.; Mr. Fernando Luis Rosado, Sec.

Institucion Magdalena Aulina - Operarias Parroquiales (Secular Institute), Simon de la Torre 43, 00730. Tel: 787-842-7209. Email: jiaulina@hotmail.com.

Jardin Infantil Aulina I and II, (I) Calle Simon de la Torre #43; (II) Calle Torre #48, Esq. Juan Seix, 00730. Grades: (I) 0-18 months; (II) 19 months-4 years

Instituto Santa Ana, P.O. Box 554, Adjuntas, 00601. Tel: 787-829-2504; Fax: 787-829-2504.

Jardin Infantil Amor De Dios, Urb. Constancia, 2456 Calle Eureka, 00717-2218. Tel: 787-842-5079; Fax: 787-984-5254. Sr. Martina Barreira, R.A.D., Dir.

Memores Domini, P.O. Box 32197, 00732-2197. Tel: 787-515-6464. Email: zaffagiu@yahoo.com.

Missionaries of Charity (1989) Mailing Address: P.O. Box 32177, 00732-2177. Tel: 787-841-5443. *Hna. Selma M.C. (D) Home for the Aged*, 683 Ramos Antonini, El Tuque, 00728. Tel: 787-841-5443. Sr. M. Selma Thomas, M.C., Supr. Missionaries of Charity (Mother Theresa of Calcutta). Sisters 6; Residents 44; Bed Capacity 46; Total Assisted Annually 42; Total Staff 22.

Pastoral Care of the Sick (1982) Parroquia Santisima Trinidad, Ave Ponce de Leon 985, Urb Las Delicias, P.O. Box 8226, 00732-8226. Tel: 787-848-5600, Ext. 3202 (Operator - Dr. Pila Metropolitan Hospital); 787-842-6073 (Parish Private); 787-651-5522 (Office - Dr. Pila Metropolitan Hospital); Fax: 787-290-0693. Rev. Dairo Hernando Arboleda Ibarra, O.SS.T., Dir.

COTO LAUREL. *Diocesan Fathers of Schoenstatt-Santuary of Schoenstatt*, P.O. Box 800371, 00780-0371. Tel: 787-526-6362. Rev. Ramon Fco. Garcia Lantigua, Rector.

GUAYAMA. **Hogar Catolico Divino Nino Jesus, Inc.*, P.O. Box 2106, 00785.

OROCOVIS. *Nuestra Senora del Encuentro con Dios*, HC-01, Box 6267, OR 00720. Tel: 787-867-1801; Fax: 787-867-5262. Email: hprfem@gmail.com.

Santuario Nuestra Senora del Encuentro con Dios - Hilasterio Masculino, HC-01, Box 6267, 00720. Tel: 787-867-0773; Fax: 787-867-5262. Email: poncesac1@gmail.com. Rev. Roberto Maldonado, L.D.

PENUELAS. *Congregacion San Juan Evangelista*, P.O. Box 118, 00624. Tel: 787-836-1512; Fax: 787-836-1512. Email: aberrios75@yahoo.com. Rev. Angel Berrios, Dir.; Bro. Arturo Ramos Ruiz, Pres. Brothers 138.

Oblates of Wisdom (1979) *Sagrado Corazon Parish*, HC-03 Box 13063, 00624-9717. Tel: 787-836-1164; 787-605-1195. Web: www.rtforum.org. Rev. Christopher De Herrera, O.S.

YAUCO. *Instituto Especial para el Desarrollo Integral del Individuo, la Familia y la Communidad, Inc.*, P.O. Box 1241, 00968-1241. Tel: 787-856-3798; Fax: 787-856-4192. Email: instyco@coqui.net. Calle Madre Dominga #66, 00968-1241. Tel: 787-856-3798; 787-856-1573; Fax: 787-856-4192. Sr. Lizandra Rosa Pagan, Dir. Sisters 2; Total Assisted 1,900; Staff 29.

RELIGIOUS INSTITUTES OF MEN REPRESENTED IN THE DIOCESE

For further details refer to the corresponding bracketed number in the Religious Institutes of Men or Women section.

[0470]—*The Capuchin Friars (Vice Province of Puerto Rico)*—O.F.M.Cap.
[0270]—*Carmelite Fathers & Brothers*—O.Carm.
[1330]—*Congregation of the Mission*—C.M.
[0650]—*Holy Ghost Fathers* (Eastern Prov.)—C.S.Sp.
[]—*Lumen Dei*—L.D.
[]—*Mercedarian Fathers*—O.deM.
[]—*Oblates of Wisdom*
[]—*Operarios Del Reino De Cristo*—O.R.C.
[0430]—*Order of Preachers-Dominicans* (Holland Prov.)—O.P.
[1310]—*Order of the Holy Trinity* (Spain)—O.SS.T.
[1040]—*Piarist Fathers* (Spain)—Sch.P.
[1070]—*Redemptorist Fathers* (San Juan Prov.)—C.SS.R.
[]—*Santuario Nuestra Senora Del Encuentro Con Dios Hislaterio Masculino Lumen Dei*

RELIGIOUS INSTITUTES OF WOMEN REPRESENTED IN THE DIOCESE

[0130]—*Apostles of the Sacred Heart of Jesus*—A.S.C.J.
[0340]—*Carmelite Sisters of Charity*—C.a.Ch.
[1070-05]—*Dominican Sisters*—O.P.
[]—*Hermanas de los Ancianos Desamparados*
[]—*Hermanas del Servicio Social*
[]—*Hermanas Del-Amor De Dios*
[]—*Hermanas Dominicas de Fatima*—O.P.
[]—*Hermanas Ntra. Sra. del Perpetuo Socorro* Juana Diaz, Ponce—N.S.P.S.
[]—*Hnas. Clarisas*—O.S.C.
[2340]—*Little Sisters of the Poor*—L.S.P.
[2710]—*Missionaries of Charity*—M.C.
[2790]—*Missionary Servants of the Most Blessed Trinity*—M.S.B.T.
[]—*Operarias del Divino Maestro (Avemarianas)*
[]—*Operarias Parroquiales*
[]—*Religious de los Santos Angeles Custodios (Adjuntas, Ponce)*—R.A.C.
[]—*Santuario Nuestra Senora Del Encuentro Con Dios Hislaterio Femenino Lumen Dei*
[]—*School Sisters of Notre Dame*—S.S.N.D.
[3580]—*Servants of Mary*—O.S.M.
[]—*Sisters of Charity of St. Vincent de Paul*—H.C.
[]—*Sisters of Perpetual Socorro*—N.S.P.S.
[]—*Sisters of St. Joseph*—S.S.J.
[2150]—*Sisters, Servants of the Immaculate Heart of Mary*—I.H.M.

NECROLOGY

✠ Oliver, Most Rev. Fremiot Torres, Bishop emeritus of Ponce.—Died Jan. 26, 2012
† Ferrer, Rev. Msgr. Jose Colon, (Retired)—Died Feb. 4, 2011
† Guerrero Fernandez, Rev. Msgr. Andres, Juana Diaz, PR San Ramon Nonato.—Died March 14, 2011
† Colon Hernandez, Jose E., (Retired)—Died June 24, 2011
† Solla, P. Santiago, (Retired)—Died May 23, 2011

An asterisk (*) denotes an organization that has established tax-exempt status directly with the IRS and is not covered by the USCCB Group Ruling.

Diocese of St. Thomas in the Virgin Islands

Most Reverend

HERBERT A. BEVARD

Bishop of St. Thomas in the Virgin Islands; ordained May 20, 1972; appointed Bishop of St. Thomas in the Virgin Islands July 7, 2008; ordained and installed September 3, 2008.

Chancery Office: P.O. Box 301825, Charlotte Amalie, VI 00803. Tel: 340-774-3166; Fax: 340-774-5816.

Web: www.catholicvi.com

Email: vichancery@vipowernet.net

ESTABLISHED AS PRELATURE OF VI, JULY 23, 1960.

Established as Diocese of St. Thomas in the Virgin Islands April 20, 1977.

Comprises the Islands of St. Thomas, St. Croix, St. John and Water Island.

STATISTICAL OVERVIEW

Personnel	
Bishop	1
Retired Bishops	1
Priests: Diocesan Active in Diocese	8
Priests: Diocesan Active Outside Diocese	4
Priests: Retired, Sick or Absent	2
Number of Diocesan Priests	14
Religious Priests in Diocese	4
Total Priests in Diocese	18
Extern Priests in Diocese	2
Ordinations:	
Diocesan Priests	1
Permanent Deacons in Diocese	27
Total Brothers	1
Total Sisters	16
Parishes	
Parishes	8
With Resident Pastor:	
Resident Diocesan Priests	5
Resident Religious Priests	2
Without Resident Pastor:	
Administered by Priests	1
Missions	1
Welfare	
Special Centers for Social Services	4
Total Assisted	787
Educational	
Diocesan Students in Other Seminaries	2
Total Seminarians	2
High Schools, Diocesan and Parish	2
Total Students	136
Elementary Schools, Diocesan and Parish	3
Total Students	453
Catechesis/Religious Education:	
High School Students	103
Elementary Students	438
Total Students under Catholic Instruction	1,132
Teachers in the Diocese:	
Brothers	1
Sisters	2
Lay Teachers	68
Vital Statistics	
Receptions into the Church:	
Infant Baptism Totals	196
Minor Baptism Totals	18
Adult Baptism Totals	11
Received into Full Communion	12
First Communions	144
Confirmations	108
Marriages:	
Catholic	42
Interfaith	10
Total Marriages	52
Deaths	192
Total Catholic Population	30,000
Total Population	120,917

Former Bishops—Most Revs. EDWARD J. HARPER, C.Ss.R., D.D., ord. June 18, 1939; appt. July 23, 1960; cons. Oct. 6, 1960; named first residential bishop of Diocese of St. Thomas in the Virgin Islands, April 20, 1977; retired Oct. 15, 1985; died Dec. 2, 1990; SEAN P. O'MALLEY, O.F.M.Cap., ord. Aug. 29, 1970; named coadjutor, May 30, 1984; ord. Bishop, Aug. 2, 1984; installed Oct. 16, 1985; transferred to Fall River Aug. 11, 1992; ELLIOTT G. THOMAS, D.D. (Retired), ord. June 6, 1986; cons. and installed as Bishop Dec. 12, 1993; retired June 30, 1999; GEORGE V. MURRY, S.J., ord. June 9, 1979; appt. May 5, 1998; installed June 30, 1999; appt. Bishop of Youngstown Jan. 30, 2007.

Chancery Office—Mailing Address: P.O. Box 301825, Charlotte Amalie, 00803. Tel: 340-774-3166; Fax: 340-774-5816.

Chancellor—Rev. NEIL SCANTLEBURY. Tel: 340-774-3166; Fax: 340-774-5816.

Fiscal Officer—VACANT.

Diocesan Consultors—Rev. E. PATRICK LYNCH, C.Ss.R.; Rev. Msgrs. JEROME FEUDJIO; MICHAEL F. KOSAK, P.A.; Revs. NEIL SCANTLEBURY; JOHN K. MARK.

Hispanic Ministry—Revs. CHARLES CRESPO, Mailing Address: P.O. Box 301767, St. Thomas, 00803. Tel: 340-774-0201; Fax: 340-776-9586; JOHN K. MARK, Mailing Address: P.O. Box 2150, St. Croix, 00851. Tel: 340-692-2005; Fax: 340-692-2748.

Catholic Charities of the Virgin Islands, Inc.—Mr. MICHAEL AKIN, Exec. Dir., Mailing Address: P.O. Box 10736, Charlotte Amalie, 00801. Tel: 340-777-8518; Fax: 340-777-4875.

Catholic Schools Office—Rev. E. PATRICK LYNCH, C.Ss.R., Supt., 416 Custom House St., Frederiksted, 00840. Tel: 340-772-0138; Fax: 340-772-0142.

Vocations—Rev. Msgr. JEROME FEUDJIO, Mailing Address: P.O. Box 301767, St. Thomas, 00803. Tel: 340-774-0201; Fax: 340-776-9586.

Charismatic Movement—Sr. PATRICIA ALEXANDER, W.I.F., St. Croix, VI; Rev. ANTHONY ABRAHAM, Dir., Mailing Address: P.O. Box 502218, St. Thomas, 00805. Tel: 340-775-1650; Fax: 340-775-1750.

Caribbean Catholic Network (CCN)— Channel 7, Rev. Msgr. MICHAEL F. KOSAK, P.A., Gen. Mgr., P.O. Box 1160, Kingshill, 00851. Tel: 340-779-3000; Fax: 340-779-3151.

Catholic Television Network (CTN)— Channel 16, Rev. Msgr. JEROME FEUDJIO, Mailing Address: P.O. Box 301825, Charlotte Amalie, 00803. Tel: 340-774-3166; Fax: 340-774-5816.

Diocesan Newspaper— "The Catholic Islander" Rev. CHARLES CRESPO, Editor, Mailing Address: P.O. Box 301825, St. Thomas, 00803. Tel: 340-774-3166; Fax: 340-774-5816.

Communications Coordinator—Rev. Msgr. MICHAEL F. KOSAK, P.A., Mailing Address: P.O. Box 1160, Kingshill, 00851. Tel: 340-778-0484; Fax: 340-779-3151.

Prison Ministry—Rev. Msgr. JEROME FEUDJIO, St. Thomas. Tel: 340-774-3166; Fax: 340-774-5816.

Shelters for the Homeless—Mr. MICHAEL AKIN, Exec. Dir., Mailing Address: Bethlehem House, P.O. Box 10736, Charlotte Amalie, 00801. Tel: 340-774-4663. St. Croix. Tel: 340-778-1227. Administration. Tel: 340-777-8518; Fax: 340-777-4475.

Vicar for Clergy and Religious—Rev. Msgr. JEROME FEUDJIO, Mailing Address: P.O. Box 301825, St. Thomas, 00803-1825. Tel: 340-774-3166; Fax: 340-774-5816.

CLERGY, PARISHES, MISSIONS AND PAROCHIAL SCHOOLS

ISLAND OF ST. THOMAS

(CATHOLIC POPULATION, 12,500)

1—CATHEDRAL OF STS. PETER AND PAUL (1773), (West Indian), Rev. Msgrs. Jerome Feudjio, Rector; Antonio Verzosa; Deacons Jose Vasquez; Wilfredo Acosta; Clement Danet.

Mailing Address: P.O. Box 301767, 00803. Tel: 340-774-0201; 340-776-7384; Fax: 340-776-9586. Web: www.catholicvi.com.

Res.: 22A Kronprindsens Gade (Main St.), 00803. Tel: 340-774-0201; Fax: 340-776-9586.

School—Sts. Peter and Paul School, (Grades PreK-12), P.O. Box 301706, St. Thomas, 00803. Tel: 340-774-5662; 340-774-2199; Fax: 340-777-5355. Mrs. Marie Jules-Daniel, Librarian. Lay Teachers 30; Students 240.

School—Mr. Samuel Belmar, Prin.; Austin Walters, Vice Prin.

Catechesis/Religious Program—Students 65.

Mission—Chapel of St. Anne P.O. Box 306810, Carenage, 00803. Tel: 340-714-1101; Fax: 340-714-5231. Rev. Charles Crespo, Admin. In Res., Rev. Louis Kemayou.

2—HOLY FAMILY PARISH (1969), (West Indian), [JC] Rev. Neil Scantlebury; Deacons Roy Bruney; Austin Medina. In Res., Rev. Anthony Abraham.

Res.: *213 Anna's Retreat*, P.O. Box 502218, St. Thomas, 00805. Tel: 340-775-1650; Fax: 340-775-1750. Email: holyfamilyvi@msn.com. Web: www.holyfamilyvi.com.

Catechesis/Religious Program—Students 84.

3—OUR LADY OF PERPETUAL HELP (1926), (West Indian), [CEM] Rev. Eduardo Ortiz-Santiago, Admin.; Deacon Bernard Gibs.
Mailing Address: P.O. Box 304983, 00803. Tel: 340-774-0885; Fax: 340-774-5896. Email: olphmafolie@yahoo.com.
Catechesis/Religious Program—Students 40.

ISLAND OF ST. JOHN

(CATHOLIC POPULATION 300), OUR LADY OF MT. CARMEL PARISH (1962) Rev. Anthony Abraham, Admin.
Res.: P.O. Box 241, St. John, 00831. Tel: 340-776-6339 (Res. & Office); Fax: 340-693-7685. Email: olmc@hotmail.com.
Catechesis/Religious Program—Mrs. Rita Peltier, D.R.E. Students 27.

ISLAND OF ST. CROIX

(CATHOLIC POPULATION, APPROX. 17,200)

1—CHURCH OF ST. JOSEPH (1947) [JC] Rev. John K. Mark; Deacons Conrad Williams; Neville Charles; James Verhoff; Guillermo Huertas.
Mailing Address: P.O. Box 2150, Kingshill, 00851-2150. Tel: 340-692-2005; Fax: 340-692-2748.
In Res., Bro. James Petrait.
Res.: Mt. Pleasant #1, Frederiksted, Frederiksted, 00840.
Catechesis/Religious Program—Students 77.
Sacred Heart Society—Tel: 340-692-2005; Fax: 340-692-2748. Mrs. Agneta Bailey.

2—CHURCH OF ST. PATRICK (1846), (African-Caribbean), Rev. E. Patrick Lynch, C.Ss.R.; Deacons Ed Cave; Emith Fludd; Lambert Heyliger; Louis Soto Jr.
Mailing Address: 416 Custom House St., Frederiksted, 00840. Tel: 340-772-0138; Fax: 340-772-0142. Email: stpatrick@catholicvi.org. Web: stpatrickstc.com. In Res., Rev. Kevin MacDonald.
School—P.O. Box 988, Frederiksted, St. Croix, 00841. Tel: 340-772-5052; Fax: 340-772-4488. Elizabeth John Baptiste, Prin. Lay Teachers 10; Students 93.
Catechesis/Religious Program—Sr. Florine Bailey, I.C.M., D.R.E. Students 26.
Convent—Missionary Sisters of the Immaculate Heart of MaryCaribbean Center, P.O. Box 95, Frederiksted, St. Croix, 00841. Tel: 340-772-0341; Fax: 340-772-4908.
DeMeester Residence—P.O. Box 52, St. Croix, 00841. Tel: 340-772-0132.
Light of Christ Retreat Center—310 New St., P.O. Box 52, Kingshill, 00851. Tel: 340-772-4782; Fax: 340-772-4385.

3—CHURCH OF THE HOLY CROSS (1755), (West Indian), [CEM 3] [JC] Revs. John Juszczak, C.Ss.R.; Andrzej Szorc, C.Ss.R.; Deacons Ulric Benjamin; David Capriola; Vincent Colianni; Hector Rivera.
Res.: 2182 Queen St., Christiansted, 00820. Tel: 340-773-7564; Fax: 340-713-9149.
School—St. Mary's, P.O. Box 224620, Christiansted, 00822. Tel: 340-773-0117; Fax: 340-773-1166. Email: stmaryschool@hcccstx.org. Lay Teachers 15; Students 192.
Catechesis/Religious Program—Tel: 340-773-7564; Fax: 340-713-9149. Rev. David Capriola, Coord. Students 75.
Mission—Sacred Heart Chapel Christiansted, U.S.V.I. 00820. Tel: 340-773-7564; Fax: 340-713-9149.
Convent—Missionaries of Charity, P.O. Box 3058, Christiansted, 00821. Tel: 340-773-1950; Fax: 340-713-9149.
Convent—Sisters of the Good Shepherd, P.O. Box 222984, Christiansted, 00822. Tel: 340-713-8724.
Convent—Dominican Sisters of the Immaculate Mother, O.P., Christiansted, 00820. Tel: 340-719-7299.

4—CHURCH ST. ANN (1823), (Caribbean), Rev. Msgr. Michael F. Kosak; Rev. Simon Peter Opira; Deacons Arnold Helenese; Joseph Mark; Norbert Xavier; Denis Griffith; Eugene Thompson; Hyacinthe George.
Mailing Address: 42 Barrenspot Hill, P.O. Box 1160, Kingshill, 00851-1160. Tel: 340-778-0484; Fax: 340-779-3151. Email: stannbarrenspot@yahoo.com. Web: www.catholicvi.com.
Catechesis/Religious Program—Students 147.
Chaplaincy—Herbert Grigg Home for the Aged, Kingshill, 00851. Tel: 340-778-0708.
Shrine—Our Lady of Barrenspot Hill

Chaplaincies

These chaplaincies only pertain to the Island of St. Thomas.

ST. THOMAS. *Lucinda Millin Home for the Aged.*
Queen Louise Home for the Aged.
Seaview Nursing and Rehabilitation Center.
St. Thomas Hospital and Community Health Center.

On Duty Outside the Diocese:
Revs.—
Corneille, Cecil
Herrera, Jose
Obeng, Simon
Sanchez, Alejandro

Permanent Deacons:
Acosta, Wilfredo
Benjamin, Ulric
Bruney, Roy
Capriola, David
Cave, Edward
Charles, Neville
Colianni, Vincent
Danet, Clement
Fludd, Emith
George, Hyacinthe
Gibs, Bernard
Griffith, Denis
Helenese, Arnold
Heyliger, Lambert
Huertas, Guillermo
Kenny, William, (Retired)
Mark, Joseph T.
Matthew, James
Medina, Austin
Monsanto, Leonard, (Retired)
Rivera, Hector
Soto, Louis, Jr.
Summer, William, (On Leave)
Thompson, Eugene
Vazquez, Jose
Verhoff, James, (On Leave)
Williams, Conrad
Xavier, Norbert

INSTITUTIONS LOCATED IN THE DIOCESE

[A] INTERPAROCHIAL HIGH SCHOOLS

ST. CROIX. *St. Joseph High School* (1964) 3 Mt. Pleasant, Rte. 2, Frederiksted, 00840. Tel: 340-692-2455; Fax: 340-692-2458. Email: sjhs@islands.vi. Web: www.islands.vi/~sjhs. Rev. John F. Mark, Prin.; Bro. James Petrait. Brothers 1; Lay Teachers 9; Students 64.

[B] ORGANIZATIONS IN THE DIOCESE

ST. THOMAS. *Miscellaneous Organizations* (For further information contact the Chancery Office), Box 301825, 00803-1825. Tel: 340-774-3166; Fax: 340-774-5816. Email: vichancery@vipowernet.net.
Catholic Charismatic Renewal Tel: 340-775-1650; Fax: 340-775-1750. Rev. Anthony Abraham, Dir.; Sr. Patricia Alexander, W.I.F., Asst. Dir.
Catholic Daughters of the Americas Tel: 340-775-7846; Fax: 340-775-1750. Ms. Alicia Doute, Regent.
Children of Mary Tel: 340-775-2890; Fax: 340-775-1750. Wende Rouse, Pres. Tel: 340-775-1351; Fax: 340-775-1750.
Good Shepherd Center Tel: 340-713-2984; Fax: 340-713-9149. Sr. Digna Maria Rivas, R.G.S., Dir.
Hispanic Ministry, St. Croix. Tel: 340-692-2005; Fax: 340-692-2748. Rev. John K. Mark.
Knights of Columbus Council 6482, St. Croix. Tel: 340-513-8172. Louis Soto Jr., Grand Knight.
Knights of Columbus Council 6187 Tel: 340-775-3537; Fax: 340-776-9586. Anthony Francis, Grand Knight.
Legion of Mary, St. Croix. Tel: 340-773-7564; Fax: 340-713-9149. Betty Schnieder, Pres. Tel: 340-778-1670.
Legion of Mary (St. John), St. John, 00831. Tel: 340-776-6054; Fax: 340-693-7685. Maggie Metor.
Legion of Mary, St. Thomas Tel: 340-775-3503; Fax: 340-775-1750. Eubald Rene, Pres. Tel: 340-775-3503.
Lumen 2000/Caribbean Region Tel: 340-778-0484; Fax: 340-779-3151. Rev. Msgr. Michael F. Kosak, P.A. Tel: 340-778-0484; Fax: 340-779-3151.
Magnificat Ministry Tel: 340-774-0201; Fax: 340-776-9586. Carmen Grant, Coord. Tel: 340-775-5369.
Secular Franciscans Sr. Patricia Alexander, W.I.F., Spiritual Asst. Tel: 340-778-5773; Fax: 340-719-3037.
Fraternity Our Lady of the Angels Ms. Fredericka Leonce, S.F.O. Tel: 340-772-9131; Mrs. Cleo Hobson, Min. Tel: 340-775-0666.
St. Vincent de Paul Society, St.Thomas. Tel: 340-774-3320; Fax: 340-775-1750. Ms. Nellie Gumbs, Pres. Tel: 340-775-0839.
Catholic Charities of the Virgin Islands Tel: 340-777-8518; Fax: 340-777-4475. Mr. Michael Akin, Exec. Dir.
St. Joseph Workers Tel: 340-775-2890; 340-775-1351; Fax: 340-775-1750. Web: www.holyfamilyvi-.com. Orville Rouse, Pres. Tel: 340-775-1351.
Secular Order Discalced Carmelites, St. Croix. Tel: 340-778-8386. Rita M. Schuster, Dir. Tel: 340-778-8386.
Cursillo Movement, St. Croix. Tel: 340-692-2005; Fax: 340-692-2748. Petra Arroyo.
Hispanic Ministry, P.O. Box 301767, 00803. Tel: 340-774-0201; Fax: 340-776-9586. Rev. Charles Crespo, Contact Person.
New Catechumenal Way, St. Croix. Tel: 340-692-2005; Fax: 340-692-2748. Deacons Conrad Williams, Contact Person; Neville Charles, Contact Person.
Sacred Heart Society, St. Patrick Church, 416 Custom House St., Frederiksted, 00840. Tel: 340-772-3042. Julia Pankey, Pres.
Shepherds of Christ Associates Tel: 340-692-2005; Fax: 340-692-2748. St. Croix, VI.
Sacred Heart Society, St. Joseph Church. Tel: 340-692-2005; Fax: 340-692-2748.

ST. CROIX. *Miscellaneous Organizations*
St. Ann's Youth Group, P.O. Box 1160, Kingshill, 00851-1160. Tel: 340-778-0484; Fax: 340-779-3151. Patricia Browne, Youth Coord.
Magnificat Organization, P.O. Box 1847, Kingshill, 00851-1847. Tel: 340-778-5773; Fax: 340-719-3037. Jeanne Garcia, Coord.; Sr. Patricia Alexander, W.I.F., Spiritual Advisor.
Shepherds of Christ Associates, 00824. Tel: 340-692-2005; Fax: 340-692-2748. Mrs. Merle Seepersad, Contact Person.

RELIGIOUS INSTITUTES OF MEN REPRESENTED IN THE DIOCESE

For further details refer to the corresponding bracketed number in the Religious Institutes of Men or Women section.

[0920]—*Oblates of St. Francis De Sales*—O.S.F.S.
[1070]—*Redemptorist Fathers*—C.SS.R.

RELIGIOUS INSTITUTES OF WOMEN REPRESENTED IN THE DIOCESE

[]—*Association of West Indian Franciscans*—W.I.F.
[]—*Dominican Sisters of the Immaculate Mother* (Philippines)—O.P.
[2710]—*Missionaries of Charity*—M.C.
[2750]—*Missionary Sisters of the Immaculate Heart of Mary*—I.C.M.
[1830]—*Sisters of the Good Shepherd*—R.G.S.

NECROLOGY

(No Deaths)

An asterisk (*) denotes an organization that has established tax-exempt status directly with the IRS and is not covered by the USCCB Group Ruling.

Diocese of Samoa-Pago Pago

Most Reverend

JOHN QUINN WEITZEL, M.M.

Bishop of Samoa-Pago Pago; ordained June 11, 1955; appointed First Bishop of Samoa-Pago Pago June 9, 1986; ordained October 29, 1986. *Fatuoaiga: P.O. Box 596, Pago Pago, AS 96799*. Tel: 684-699-1402; Fax: 684-699-1459. Email: quinn@samoatelco.com.

CREATED A DIOCESE NOVEMBER, 1982.

The Diocese of Samoa-Pago Pago includes the islands of Tutuila; Swains; Manu'a Is., Ofu, Olosega & Ta'u; Aunu'u and Rose Island.

STATISTICAL OVERVIEW

Personnel	
Bishop	1
Priests: Diocesan Active in Diocese	15
Priests: Retired, Sick or Absent	1
Number of Diocesan Priests	16
Religious Priests in Diocese	2
Total Priests in Diocese	18
Ordinations:	
Diocesan Priests	1
Permanent Deacons in Diocese	23
Total Sisters	9
Parishes	
Parishes	17
With Resident Pastor:	
Resident Diocesan Priests	11
Resident Religious Priests	1
Without Resident Pastor:	
Administered by Priests	5
New Parishes Created	1
Welfare	
Homes for the Aged	1
Total Assisted	20
Day Care Centers	1
Total Assisted	70
Special Centers for Social Services	1
Total Assisted	170
Educational	
Students from This Diocese	4
Diocesan Students in Other Seminaries	4
Total Seminarians	4
High Schools, Diocesan and Parish	1
Total Students	273
Elementary Schools, Diocesan and Parish	2
Total Students	317
Catechesis/Religious Education:	
High School Students	435
Elementary Students	3,085
Total Students under Catholic Instruction	4,114
Teachers in the Diocese:	
Priests	4
Sisters	6
Lay Teachers	61
Vital Statistics	
Receptions into the Church:	
Infant Baptism Totals	180
Minor Baptism Totals	40
Adult Baptism Totals	90
Received into Full Communion	40
First Communions	210
Confirmations	240
Marriages:	
Catholic	15
Interfaith	20
Total Marriages	35
Deaths	40
Total Catholic Population	14,250
Total Population	65,000

Vicar General of Diocese—Rev. VIANE ETUALE, V.G., M.A., M.Ed.

Chancellor—Mrs. IVONA T. MAUGA.

Diocesan Consultors—Most Rev. J. QUINN WEITZEL, M.M., D.D.; Revs. VIANE ETUALE, V.G., M.A., M.Ed.; KELEMETE PUA'AULI; ANDREW ATONIO, M.F.; KOLIO ETUALE, M.Div.; Rev. Msgr. ETUALE LEALOFI, J.C.D.

Diocesan Pastoral Council—Rev. VIANE ETUALE, V.G., M.A., M.Ed., Chm.

Fatuoaiga Multipurpose Cultural and Pastoral Center—Rev. Msgr. ETUALE LEALOFI, J.C.D. Faculty Members: Revs. VIANE ETUALE, V.G., M.A., M.Ed.; KELEMETE PUA'AULI; FALANIKO ATONIO; KOLIO ETUALE, M.Div.

St. Anne Society—Mrs. KALALA KAIO, Pres.; Mrs. PELESIA PETELO, Vice Pres.; Mrs. LAGI SAGOTE, Treas.; Mrs. ONETI AOELUA, Sec.

Sacred Heart Society—Mrs. RUFO TUITELELEAPAGA, Pres.; Mrs. SUNI FELISE, Vice Pres.; Mrs. JOANNE KIMOTO, Treas.; Mrs. PALU VITALE, Sec.

Legion of Mary—Mrs. AGNES VARGO, Pres.

Children of Mary—LUPE MAUGAOTEGA; Miss KAREN FA'ASAVALU, Vice Pres.; Miss MARY AULAUMEA, Treas.; Miss ROSE LAFAELE, Sec.

Divine Mercy—Mrs. THERESA BURGOS, Pres.

Youth—Deacon MALAKI TIMU, F.K., Pres.

Women's Organization—Mrs. PALEPA LEMANA, Pres.; Mrs. VALELIA TALO, Vice Pres.; Mrs. PALU VITALE, Treas.; Mrs. TELESIA LEOTA.

Rosary Society—Mrs. KALALA TUITELE, Pres.

Matrimonial Tribunal—

Judicial Vicar—Most Rev. J. QUINN WEITZEL, M.M., D.D.

Adjunct Judicial Vicar—Rev. Msgr. ETUALE LEALOFI, J.C.D.

Judges—Rev. Msgr. SCOTT L. MARCZUK, J.C.L.; Rev. VIANE ETUALE, V.G., M.A., M.Ed.

Defender of the Bond—VACANT.

Auditors—Revs. SETEFANO T. LUAMANU; KELEMETE PUA'AULI; KOLIO ETUALE, M.Div.; HILDRITHO RANOLA, M.A., M.Ed., M.Div.; Mrs. IVONA T. MAUGA.

Tribunal Administrator—Mrs. IVONA T. MAUGA.

Ecclesiastical Notaries—Mrs. IVONA T. MAUGA; Mrs. THERESA H. SILAO.

Vicar for Diocesan Youth—Deacon MALAKI TIMU, F.K., Dir.

Director of Vocations—Rev. KOLIO ETUALE, M.Div.

Port Chaplain—Deacon TAVITA PEREIRA.

Prison Chaplain—Deacon AUGUST GABRIEL.

Director of Propagation of the Faith—Rev. ANDREW ATONIO, M.F.

Hospital Chaplain—JOHN PEREIRA, F.K., Catechist.

CLERGY, PARISHES, MISSIONS AND PAROCHIAL SCHOOLS

SAMOA-PAGO PAGO

1—CATHEDRAL OF THE HOLY FAMILY (1986) Most Rev. John Quinn Weitzel, M.M.; Rev. Faitau Lemautu, Rector; Deacons Iosefo Vitaliano; August Gabriel; Avaletalia Hunkin; Isidore Taaga.
Mailing Address: *Fatuoaiga*, P.O. Box 3594, AS 96799-3594. Tel: 684-699-1446; Fax: 684-699-1459.
Catechesis/Religious Program—Tel: 684-699-2209. Mrs. Patricia Letuli, D.R.E.; Tualesolo Talo, D.R.E.; Iosefo Vitaliano, D.R.E. Students 510.
Mission—Mary, Star of the Sea Manu'a Island, AS. Tel: 684-677-3103. Deacon Alefosio Uelese.

2—CHRIST THE KING (Amanave) Rev. Vaiula Iulio.
Mailing Address: P.O. Box 5408, AS 96799. Tel: 684-688-1542.
Catechesis/Religious Program—Aukusitino Paaniani, D.R.E. Students 50.

3—CHRIST THE KING (Malaeloa) (1997) Rev. Teofilo Schmidt.
Mailing Address: P.O. Box 596, AS 96799. Tel: 684-688-2438; Fax: 684-699-1459.
Catechesis/Religious Program—Meaalofa Lotomau, Catechetical Leader. Students 75.

4—CHRIST THE KING (Nu'uuli) (1983) Rev. Viane Etuale, Admin.; Deacons Niuatoa Andy Puletasi; Sauileone Aigofie.
Mailing Address: P.O. Box 596, AS 96799. Fax: 684-699-1459.
Catechesis/Religious Program—Students 85.

5—CHURCH OF SACRED HEART (Alao) (1989) Rev. Eneliko Auva'a.
Mailing Address: *Alao*, P.O. Box 4175, AS 96799. Tel: 684-622-7029; Fax: 684-699-1459.
Catechesis/Religious Program—Nu'u Ituau, Catechist. Students 220.
Mission— Aoa, AS. Tel: 684-622-7416. Esitio Savelio, F.K., Catechist.
Mission— Amouli, AS. Tel: 684-622-7613. Esitio Savelio, F.K., Catechetical Leader.

6—CHURCH OF ST. PETER AND PAUL (Lauli'i) (1969) Rev. Asalemo Asalemo Jr.; Deacons Setefano Lesa; Moli Toilolo.
Mailing Address: P.O. Box 985, AS 96799. Tel: 684-644-5581.
Catechesis/Religious Program—Tel: 684-644-4697. Students 130.

7—CHURCH OF THE HOLY CROSS (Leone) (1861) Rev. Kolio Etuale; Deacon Toetofi Tavale.
Mailing Address: *Leone*, P.O. Box 1206, AS 96799. Tel: 684-688-7663; Fax: 684-699-1459.
Catechesis/Religious Program—Students 280.

8—CHURCH OF THE IMMACULATE CONCEPTION (Lepua) (1867) Rev. Andrew Atonio, M.F., Admin.; Deacon Iosefo Tarangi, (Mission Afono).
Mailing Address: *Lepua*, P.O. Box 398, AS 96799. Tel: 684-644-5512.
Catechesis/Religious Program—Tel: 684-644-2411. Tumaai Solimalo, F.K., Catechist, Mission Lepua. Students 120.
Mission— Afono, AS. Tel: 684-644-4797.
Mission— Lepua, AS.

9—CO-CATHEDRAL OF ST. JOSEPH THE WORKER (Fagatogo) (1974) Rev. Kelemete Pua'auli.
Mailing Address: *Fagatogo*, P.O. Box AA, AS 96799. Tel: 684-633-1548.
Catechesis/Religious Program—Students 275.
Mission— Utulei, AS. Lui Polu, F.K., Catechist.
Mission— Faga'alu, AS. Tel: 684-633-2560. Deacon Samuelu Aoelua, F.K., Catechist.

10—ST. JOSEPH THE WORKER FUTIGA (2006) Rev. Msgr. Etuale Lealofi.
Mailing Address: P.O. Box 596, AS 96799. Tel: 684-688-7765.
Catechesis/Religious Program—Paunga Lolesio, D.R.E. Students 95.

11—OUR LADY OF FATIMA (2002) Rev. Fila Filipo Petelo, M.F.; Deacon Tavete Maugaotega.
Mailing Address: *Aua Parish*, P.O. Box 4052, AS 96799. Tel: 684-644-5826; Fax: 684-699-1459.
Catechesis/Religious Program—Students 160.

12—ST. PAUL (Ili'ili) (1974) Rev. Iosefo Vaitele Tupuola; Deacons Iosefo Toilolo; Sanele Paselio, F.K.
Mailing Address: *Ili'ili*, P.O. Box 2004, AS 96799. Tel: 684-699-7572; Fax: 684-699-1459.
Office: Fatuoaiga, P.O. Box 596, AS 96799. Tel: 684-699-7575.
Catechesis/Religious Program—Lutovi'o Uti, F.K., Catechist; Ameto Lemana, F.K., Catechist. Students 420.
Mission— Faleniu, AS. Deacon Sanele Paselio, F.K., Catechist.
Mission— Pava'ia'i, AS. Tel: 684-699-7613. Deacon Malaki Timu, F.K., Catechist.
Mission— Aasu/Aoloau, AS. Tel: 684-699-9766. Lutovi'o Uti, F.K., Catechist.

13—STS. PETER & PAUL, (Asili) Rev. Vaiula Iulio, Admin.
Mailing Address: P.O. Box 7286, AS 96799. Tel: 684-688-7236.
Catechesis/Religious Program—Leafa Gasio, F.K., Catechist. Students 110.
Mission—Amaluia

14—ST. PETER CHANEL PARISH FAGASA, P.O. Box 596, AS 96799.

15—ST. PETER CHANEL-SA'ILELE Rev. Asalemo Asalemo Jr.
Mailing Address: P.O. Box 596, AS 96799. Tel: 684-622-7512.
Catechesis/Religious Program—Moe Sagote, Catechetical Leader; Faleagafulu Filipo, F.K., Catechist. Students 40.
Mission— Masefau, AS. Tel: 684-622-7131. Ierenimo Vaina, F.K., Catechist.
Mission— Faga'itua, AS. Tel: 684-622-7130. Faleagafulu Filipo, F.K., Catechist.

16—SACRED HEART OF JESUS PARISH, VAILOA (2003) Rev. Teofilo Schmidt; Deacon Felise Toilolo.
Mailing Address: P.O. Box 596, AS 96799. Tel: 684-688-1243.
Catechesis/Religious Program—Students 65.

17—SACRED HEART PARISH-PAGO PAGO (2001) Rev. Falaniko Atonio.
Res.: P.O. Box 596, AS 96799. Tel: 684-633-4035.
Catechesis/Religious Program—Ioane Afoa, Catechist. Total Enrollment 120.

Permanent Deacons:
Aigofie, Sauileone, F.K.
Aoelua, Samuelu, F.K.
Auva'a, Lino
Gabriel, August, Chap. Pago-Pago Intl. Airport
Hunkin, Avaletalia
Lafaele, Setefano
Lemana, Penitito
Maugaotega, Tavete
Paselio, Sanele, F.K.
Pepe, Anitele'a Tolu
Pereira, Tavita
Puletasi, Andy Niuatoa
Sipiliano, Nua
Taaga, Isidore
Tarangi, Iosefo
Tavale, Toetofi
Tia, Vaipuna
Timu, Malaki, F.K.
Toilolo, Felise
Toilolo, Filipo
Toilolo, Iosefo
Toilolo, Moli
Uelese, Alefosio

INSTITUTIONS LOCATED IN THE DIOCESE

[A] PRESCHOOLS

PAGO PAGO. *Mary The Mother Montessori Early Education Center, c/o Diocese of Samoa-Pago Pago*, Fatuoaiga, P.O. Box 596, AS 96799. Tel: 684-644-1311; Fax: 684-699-1459. Sr. Marilyn Evans, M.M., Prin. & Supr. Sisters 1; Lay Teachers 5; Students 36.

[B] ELEMENTARY SCHOOLS, PAROCHIAL

LEONE. *St. Theresa*, (Grades 1-8), P.O. Box 883, AS 96799-0596. Tel: 684-688-1105; Fax: 684-688-1114. Mrs. Maria Pepe Talatau, Prin. Lay Teachers 15; Students 183.

LEPUA. *Marist St. Francis*, (Grades 1-8), Fatuoaiga, P.O. Box 429, AS 96799-0429. Fax: 684-699-1459. Sr. Carol Tevaga, F.M.A., Prin.; Mr. Sililo Asalemo, Librarian. Priests 2; Sisters 3; Lay Teachers 13; Students 134.

[C] HIGH SCHOOLS, PAROCHIAL

LEPUAPUA. *Faasao Marist College Preparatory School*, P.O. Box 729, AS 96799. Tel: 684-688-7731; Fax: 684-688-2055. Email: courgars@faasao.com. Mr. Victor Langkilde, Prin. Priests 2; Deacons 3; Lay Teachers 18; Students 273.

[D] HOMES FOR AGED & SPECIAL CARE FOR CHILDREN

PAGO PAGO. *Hope House*, P.O. Box 596, AS 96799. Tel: 684-699-2101; Fax: 684-699-6051. Sr. Elsa O. Sintilias, O.P., Admin. Aged Residents 11; Special Care Children 9; Montessori Early Education 69; Day Care Center 70; Total Staff 48; Teachers 10.

[E] MISCELLANEOUS

PAGO PAGO. *Catholic Social Services, Inc.*, P.O. Box 596, AS 96799. Tel: 684-699-5683; Fax: 684-699-1340. Email: ccs1@samoatelco.com. Total Staff 3.
Diocesan Eucharistic League, P.O. Box 596, AS 96799. Tel: 684-699-1402; Fax: 684-699-1459. Email: ivonamauga@yahoo.com. Mrs. Ivona T. Mauga, Pres.

RELIGIOUS INSTITUTES OF MEN REPRESENTED IN THE DIOCESE

For further details refer to the corresponding bracketed number in the Religious Institutes of Men or Women section.

[0800]—*Maryknoll*—M.M.

[]—*Missionaries of the Faith*—M.F.

RELIGIOUS INSTITUTES OF WOMEN REPRESENTED IN THE DIOCESE

[]—*Dominican Sisters of the Holy Trinity*—O.P.

[2470]—*Maryknoll Sisters of St. Dominic*—M.M.

[]—*Salesian Sisters (Daughters of Mary Help of Christians)*—F.M.A.

NECROLOGY

(No Deaths)

An asterisk (*) denotes an organization that has established tax-exempt status directly with the IRS and is not covered by the USCCB Group Ruling.

Archdiocese of San Juan, Puerto Rico

(Sancti Joannis Portoricensis)

Most Reverend

ROBERTO O. GONZALEZ NIEVES, O.F.M.

Archbishop of San Juan; ordained May 8, 1977; appointed Titular Bishop of Ursona and Auxiliary Bishop of Boston July 19, 1988; consecrated October 3, 1988; appointed Coadjutor Bishop of Corpus Christi May 16, 1995; transferred to Corpus Christi June 26, 1995; succeeded to See April 1, 1997; appointed Archbishop of San Juan March 26, 1999; installed May 8, 1999.

Most Reverend

HECTOR M. RIVERA, D.D.

Retired Auxiliary Bishop of San Juan PR; ordained June 12, 1966; appointed Titular Bishop of Tubune in Numidia and Auxiliary Bishop of San Juan PR June 11, 1979; consecrated August 17, 1979; retired October 31, 2009. *Res.: Valle Arriba Heights, Calle Alamo, BF #20, Carolina, PR 00983.* Tel: 787-276-1413. *Mailing Address: P.O. Box 31155, San Juan, PR 00929-2155.*

ERECTED AUGUST 8, 1511.

Square Miles 353.

Erected an Archdiocese April 30, 1960.

Comprises the northeast portion of the Island of Puerto Rico, with a Total Population of 1,451,146

Chancery Office: P.O. Box 9021967, San Juan, PR 00902-1967. Tel: 787-727-7373; Fax: 787-726-8280.

STATISTICAL OVERVIEW

Personnel	
Archbishops	1
Retired Bishops	1
Priests: Diocesan Active in Diocese	84
Priests: Diocesan Active Outside Diocese	12
Priests: Retired, Sick or Absent	25
Number of Diocesan Priests	121
Religious Priests in Diocese	106
Total Priests in Diocese	227
Extern Priests in Diocese	48
Ordinations:	
Diocesan Priests	1
Religious Priests	3
Transitional Deacons	1
Permanent Deacons in Diocese	161
Total Brothers	18
Total Sisters	331
Parishes	
Parishes	143
With Resident Pastor:	
Resident Diocesan Priests	96
Resident Religious Priests	106
Missions	143
Professional Ministry Personnel:	
Brothers	23
Sisters	331
Lay Ministers	1,961
Welfare	
Catholic Hospitals	5
Total Assisted	17,699
Health Care Centers	3
Total Assisted	76,944
Homes for the Aged	7
Total Assisted	16,513
Residential Care of Children	8
Total Assisted	936
Day Care Centers	1
Total Assisted	85
Specialized Homes	17
Total Assisted	65,543
Special Centers for Social Services	8
Total Assisted	46,467
Other Institutions	2
Total Assisted	2,500
Educational	
Seminaries, Diocesan	1
Students from This Diocese	14
Students from Other Diocese	5
Diocesan Students in Other Seminaries	3
Seminaries, Religious	6
Students Religious	11
Total Seminarians	28
Colleges and Universities	2
Total Students	8,995
High Schools, Diocesan and Parish	15
Total Students	3,234
High Schools, Private	28
Total Students	6,323
Elementary Schools, Diocesan and Parish	21
Total Students	6,391
Elementary Schools, Private	37
Total Students	13,247
Non-residential Schools for the Disabled	1
Total Students	120
Catechesis/Religious Education:	
High School Students	9,557
Elementary Students	19,638
Total Students under Catholic Instruction	67,533
Teachers in the Diocese:	
Priests	12
Scholastics	52
Brothers	23
Sisters	331
Lay Teachers	1,961
Vital Statistics	
Receptions into the Church:	
Infant Baptism Totals	3,161
Minor Baptism Totals	2,103
Adult Baptism Totals	766
Received into Full Communion	12
First Communions	4,609
Confirmations	3,520
Marriages:	
Catholic	876
Interfaith	77
Total Marriages	953
Total Catholic Population	897,325
Total Population	1,281,893

Former Bishops—Most Revs. ALONSO MANSO, D.D., appt. May 1511; JAMES H. BLENK, S.M.D.D., appt. Bishop of Puerto Rico, June 12, 1899; died April 20, 1917; WILLIAM A. JONES, O.S.A., cons. Feb. 24, 1907; died Jan. 1921; GEORGE J. CARUANA, D.D., appt. Bishop 1921; promoted to the Apostolic Delegation of Mexico, 1925; promoted to Nunciature Apostolic of Cuba, 1927; EDWIN VINCENT BYRNE, D.D., former Bishop of Ponce, Puerto Rico; cons. Nov. 30, 1925; appt. March 1929; promoted to Archdiocese of Santa Fe, June 15, 1943; died July 25, 1963; JAMES PETER DAVIS (Retired), appt. 1943; cons. Oct. 9, 1943; transferred to Archdiocese of Santa Fe, June, 1963; installed Feb. 25, 1964; retired Oct. 1974; His Eminence LUIS CARDINAL APONTE MARTINEZ, D.D. (Retired), appt. Auxiliary Bishop of Ponce July 23, 1960; cons. Oct. 12, 1960; appt. Coadjutor Bishop of Ponce April 16, 1963; succeeded to Nov. 18, 1963; installed Feb. 22, 1964; appt. Archbishop of San Juan Nov. 4, 1964; installed Jan. 15, 1965; created Cardinal March 5, 1973; retired March 26, 1999; died April 10, 2012.

Vicar General—Rev. Msgr. LEONARDO J. RODRIGUEZ-JIMENES.

Episcopal Moderator—

for Administration of Temporalities—Rev. Msgr. LEONARDO J. RODRIGUEZ-JIMENES, Moderator.

for Education—Rev. JUAN SANTA GUZMANWeb: www.escueloscatolicos-sj.org.

for Pastoral Affairs—Rev. Msgr. ALBERTO LOPEZ FIGUEROA.

for Geographic-Pastoral Zones—San Juan-Santurce: Rev. TARSICIO GOTAY FIGAREDO, O.Carm. Bayamon: Rev. CARLOS ALGARIN LOPEZ, O.S.A. Del Toa y La Plata: Rev. ANGEL PAGAN TORRES. Carolina: Rev. NESTOR YULFO-HOFFMAN. Rio Piedras: Rev. JOAQUIN MAYORGA-FONSECA. Guaynabo-Puerto Nuevo: Rev. WALTER S. GOMEZ-BACA.

Chancery Office—Mailing Address: P.O. Box 9021967, San Juan, 00902-1967. Web: www.arqsj.org.

Chancery Affairs—Miss LUCIA GUZMAN ORTA, Chancellor. Email: luciagu@arqsj.org.

Vice Chancellor—VACANT.

Metropolitan Curia—

Moderator—Rev. Msgr. LEONARDO J. RODRIGUEZ-JIMENES.

Secretary to the Archbishop—Rev. ALFONSO GUZMAN ALFARO, O.F.M. Tel: 787-725-4975; 787-977-0672.

Executive Assistant to the Archbishop—Mr. SAMUEL SOTO-ALONSO. Tel: 787-725-4975; 787-977-0672.

Assistant to the Archbishop and Secretary to the Cardinal—Miss MIRIAM RAMOS. Tel: 787-725-4975; 787-977-0672.

Judicial Vicar—Rev. RICARDO AUGUSTO ROIG LORENZO.

Adjunct Vicars—Revs. LUIS NORBERTO CORREA-GARCIA; PEDRO LUIS REYES LEBRÓN.

Judges—Miss MARIA LUCIA SANCHEZ; Rev. LUIS NORBERTO CORREA-GARCIA; Mr. ABRAHAM MORALES BERRIOS.

Defender of the Bond—MARIA DEL ROSARIO RINCON-BECERRA.

Instructors—Mr. RIGOBERTO HIRALDO RIOS; Mr. JOSE GARCIA FERNANDEZ; Revs. JOSE A. LANDRAU-ROMAN; CARMELO SOTO TANON; ALBITA DARILA; Mrs. CARMEN J. ACOSTA; Mrs. ANGELA GARCIA. Email: tribunal@arqsj.org.

Lawyers—ORLANDO DURAN; MILAGROS GONZALEZ-RODRIQUEZ; XAVIER HIRALDO-SANCHEZ; MARJORIE STEWART.

Diocesan Consultors—Rev. Msgrs. LEONARDO J. RODRIGUEZ-JIMENES; ALBERTO LOPEZ FIGUEROA; JOSE E. CUMMINGS-ESPADA; Revs. ANGEL L. CIAPPI-AZCORRA; MILTON AGUSTIN RIVERA-VIGO; MARCO ANTONIO RIVERA PEREZ; RICARDO AUGUSTO ROIG LORENZO; PEDRO LUIS REYES LEBRÓN; Rev. Msgr. EFRAIN RODRIGUEZ-OTERO; Revs. ANGEL PAGAN TORRES; JOSE FRANCISCO QUINTERO ANGUEIRA.

Censor Librorum—Rev. Msgr. FERNANDO B. FELICES-SANCHEZ.

Vicar of Social Communication—VACANT.

Auxiliary Vicar of Social Communication—VACANT.

Vicar of Cultural Affairs—Rev. Msgr. EFRAIN RODRIGUEZ-OTERO.

Vicar of Development—Rev. ANGEL L. CIAPPI-AZCORRA.

Vicar of Economic Affairs—VACANT.

Director of Economic Affairs—Mr. SANTIAGO MORALES-ROSARIO; Mrs. SANDRA RODRIGUEZ, Asst. to Dir.

Vicar of Ecumenism—Rev. WILLIAM TORRES-PAGAN.

Vicar of Family Affairs—Rev. PHILLIP NUNEZ-CARRION.

Vicar for Pastoral Affairs—Rev. Msgr. ALBERTO LOPEZ FIGUEROA.

Vicar for Education—Rev. JUAN SANTA GUZMAN.

Vicar of Religious—Rev. ALFONSO GUZMAN ALFARO, O.F.M.

Examinatores Cleri—VACANT.

Vicar for Vocations—Rev. Msgr. IVAN LUIS HUERTAS-COLON.

Pro-Synodal Examiner—VACANT.

Vicar for Priests—Rev. JOSE FRANCISCO QUINTERO-ANGUEIRA.

Vicar for Youth—Rev. RAMON HIRAM NEGRON, O.F.M.Cap.

Archdiocesan Offices and Directors

Boy Scouts—VACANT.

Catechetics—Rev. RAMON J. CASELLAS RIVERA, O.F.M.Cap.

Catechetics Center—Sr. MERCEDES CADENAS, Mailing Address: San Juan-Santurce, P.O. Box 9021967, San Juan, 00902-1967. Tel: 787-727-7373. Carolina: Deacon JORGE RIVERA, Valle Arriba Heights, BF-20 Calle Alamo, Carolina, 00983. Bayamon: Sr. LISSIE AVILES, O.P., Mailing Address: P.O. Box 4152, Bayamon, 00958. Tel: 787-780-1173. Rio Piedras: Sr. ISABEL SOTO, M.SS.S., Mailing Address: P.O. Box 20884, San Juan, 00920. Tel: 787-761-4280. Guaynabo-PtoNuevo: Sr. ROSE MORALES, M.S.B.T., Mailing Address: P.O. Box 9021967, San Juan, 00902-1967. Tel: 787-731-6100.

Catholic Charities—Rev. ENRIQUE MANUEL CAMACHO-MONSERRATE, Mailing Address: P.O. Box 8812, San Juan, 00910-0812. Tel: 787-727-7373; Fax: 787-728-4100. Email: ssc@arqsj.org.

"El Visitante"— Weekly Catholic Paper for All Dioceses (Interdiocesan). Published By The P.R., Episcopal Conference. Revs. RUBEN GONZALEZ-MEDINA, C.M.F., Pres.; EFRAIN ZABALA, Editor; JAIME TORRES TORRES, Dir., Mailing Address: P.O. Box 41305, Minillas Sta., San Juan, 00940-1305. Tel: 787-728-3710; Fax: 787-268-1748. Offices, Pumarada St. 1704, Santurce, 00914.

Radio Stations— WORO-FM and WKVM-AM 81, Mr. ALAN CORALES, Dir., Urb. Baldrich, 415 Calle Ingeniero Carbonell, San Juan, 00918. Mailing Address: P.O. Box 9021967, San Juan, 00902-1967. Tel: 787-731-1380; 787-751-1018; Fax: 787-758-9967. Email: radiooro@arqsj.org.

Television Station— WPRV-TV CHANNEL 13, Tele Oro, Mr. JUAN M. MUNIZ, Gen. Mgr., Ave Iturregui Esq. Marginal, Baldorioty De Castro Ave., Carolina, 00982. Tel: 787-276-1300; Fax: 787-276-1307. Mailing Address: P.O. Box 9021967, San Juan, 00902-1967.

Commission for Sacred Liturgy and Popular Piety—Rev. Msgr. LEONARDO J. RODRIGUEZ-JIMENES.

Subcommission for Sacred Art—Rev. Msgr. LEONARDO J. RODRIGUEZ-JIMENES; Rev. RODOLFO LAMAS; Dr. ARTURO DAVILA, Urb. Baldrich, Calle Rossy #202, San Juan, 00918. Tel: 787-763-9154; Dr. TERESA TIO; FRANCISCO JAVIER BLANCO; HECTOR BALVANERA; Rev. Msgr. JOSE E. CUMMINGS-ESPADA.

Subcommission for Sacred Music—Rev. MIGUEL TRINIDAD.

Subcommission for Popular Piety—Rev. TARSICIO GOTAY FIGAREDO, O.Carm.

Subcommission for Ministries—Rev. Msgr. LEONARDO J. RODRIGUEZ-JIMENES.

Clergy Social Security (Prevision Social del Clero)—VACANT, Pres.; Revs. RICARDO HERNANDEZ, Treas.; ALBERTO DIAZ; ANGEL MENDEZ; Rev. Msgr. MANUEL GARCIA PEREZ; VACANT, Sec., Mailing Address: CEP, P.O. Box 4682, San Juan, 00940-0682. Tel: 787-728-1650; Fax: 787-728-1654.

Istepa—Rev. Msgr. FRANCISCO MEDINA, Urb. Caparra Heights, 1564 Calle Encarnacion, San Juan, 00920. Tel: 787-200-6891; Fax: 787-200-6305.

San Juan Bautista Regional Seminary—Rev. JUAN LUIS NEGRON, Rector; Rev. Msgr. IVAN L. HUERTAS-COLON, Vice Rector. Spiritual Directors: Revs. JOSE VICENTE MARTINEZ, C.M.F.; EDWIN ALBEIRO LONDONO ZULUAGA, Mailing Address: P.O. Box 11714, San Juan, 00922-1714. Tel: 787-783-0645; 787-273-8090; Fax: 787-783-0645. Ave. De Diego 930, Urb. La Riviera, Rio Piedras, 00921. Email: seminary@coqui.net.

Serra Club—VACANT.

Vocations Promoter—Rev. EDWIN ALBEIRO LONDONO ZULUAGA, Mailing Address: P.O. Box 11714, San Juan, 00922-1714. Tel: 787-706-9455; 787-273-8090.

Superintendent of Schools—Mrs. ANA CORTES, Supt.; VACANT, Rel. Prog. Dir., Mailing Address: Urb. Los Maestros, 789 Calle Jaime Drew, San Juan, 00923. Tel: 787-731-6100; Fax: 787-731-0000. Web: www.esculelascatolicas-sj.org.

Archdiocesan Historical Archive—Mrs. ELSE ZAYAS LEON, Calle San Sebastian 5-N, San Juan, 00902. Mailing Address: P.O. Box 9021967, San Juan, 00902-1967. Tel: 787-977-1447.

Youth Ministries—Rev. RAMON HIRAM NEGRON, O.F.M.Cap., Calle Auzuaga 218, Rio Piedras, 00925. Mailing Address: P.O. Box 25177, San Juan, 00928-5177. Tel: 787-765-0606.

Police Chaplains—Rev. Msgrs. BAUDILIO MERINO. Tel: 787-767-6552; VALERIANO MIGUÉLEZ. Tel: 787-754-0570; Rev. ANTONIO GARCIA CASTEJON. Tel: 787-757-4454; Deacon JOSE PENA GONZALEZ. Tel: 787-786-5309.

Society for the Protection of Children—Most Rev. ROBERTO OCTAVIO GONZÁLEZ NIEVES, O.F.M., Mailing Address: P.O. Box 9021967, San Juan, 00902-1967. Tel: 787-727-7373.

United Against Hunger (Unidos Contra El Hambre)—Deacon HECTOR CRUZ DECHOUDENS, San Jorge St., No. 201, Santurce, 00914. Mailing Address: P.O. Box 11547, San Juan, 00910-2647. Tel: 787-727-7373, Ext. 240; Fax: 787-727-7938. Email: uch@arqsj.org.

Propagation of the Faith—Rev. JOSE ORLANDO CAMACHO-TORRES, C.S.Sp., 106 Ruiz Belvis St., P.O. Box 191882, Floral Park, San Juan, 00919.

Pius Union of the Clergy—VACANT, Mailing Address: P.O. Box 9021967, San Juan, 00902-1967. Tel: 787-727-7373.

Catholic Charismatic Renewal—Rev. Msgr. BAUDILIO MERINO MERINO, Dir., Arzobispado de San Juan. Tel: 787-765-6240; 787-727-7373.

Master of Ceremonies to the Archbishop—Mr. LUIS DACOSTA-DEJESUS.

Pre Cana Conferences—VACANT, Dir., Parroquia Santa Rosa Lima, 1765 Calle Lesbos, San Juan, 00926. Tel: 787-761-6586; Mr. MANUEL SANCHEZ, Urb. Country Club, 1031 Calle Genoveva De Lugo, San Juan, 00924. Tel: 787-769-3565.

Caritas of Puerto Rico—Rev. ENRIQUE MANUEL CAMACHO-MONSERRATE, Exec. Dir., Mailing Address: P.O. Box 8812, San Juan, 00910-0812. Tel: 787-727-7373; Fax: 787-728-4100.

Centro Apostolado De La Cruz—MARICARMEN RIVERA, Coord., Urb. Sans Souci, Z 10 Calle 19, Bayamon, 00956. Tel: 787-797-1481; Fax: 787-269-3190.

Cursillos De Cristiandad—Rev. TOMAS GONZALEZ-GONZALEZ.

Immigrant Aid—Mrs. CANDIDA ROSA MATOS, Mailing Address: Catholic Social Services, P.O. Box 9021967, San Juan, 00902-1967. Tel: 787-727-7373.

Holy Childhood Association—Rev. JOSE ORLANDO CAMACHO-TORRES, C.S.Sp.

Holy Name Society—Mr. MIGUEL A. RODRIGUEZ, Archdiocesan Dir., Mailing Address: P.O. Box 31164, San Juan, 00929. Tel: 787-276-2212; 787-605-9292; Mr. FRANCISCO FIGUEROA, Sec. Tel: 787-768-4787.

Renovacion Conyugal (Fundacion Fernando Martinez Calle, Inc.)—Rev. JORGE AMBERT, S.J., Dir., Urb. Ext. Roosevelt, 576 Calle Eddie Gracia, San Juan, 00918. Tel: 787-751-6001; 787-766-1363. Email: ambertsj@aol.com. Web: www.renovacion.net.

Courage Puerto Rico—Rev. OVIDIO ORTEGA Encourage: Padres, Familia y AmigosTel: 787-941-7311. Email: poncepr@courage-latino.org; sanjuanpr@courage-latino.org.

Equipo De Impacto Matrimonial—Deacon MIGUEL A. MARRERO, Dir., Urb Sabana Gardens, #15 Calle 9 Blq 4, Carolina, 00983. Tel: 787-750-0609; Fax: 787-750-0609.

Grupo Misioneros De Amor Y Fe—JOSE A. MENDEZ, Coord. y Fundador, Urb. Paseo Las Vistas, B31 Calle 1, San Juan, 00926. Tel: 787-397-1612. Email: joseamendez@misionerosdeamoryfe.org. Web: www.misionerosdeamoryfe.org.

La Mujer Por La Familia Catolica En Puerto Rico—TERUCA RULLAN, Pres., Mailing Address: Fernandez Juncos Station, P.O. Box 19241, San Juan, 00910. Tel: 787-723-1620; Fax: 787-725-9455.

Proyecto Reencuentro Familiar—MAXIMINO DIAZ GUZMAN, Dir., 500 Ave Los Filtros, Boulevard del Rio II Apt. 119, Guaynabo, 00971. Tel: 787-797-4500 (Office); 787-797-4288 (Casa de Retiro).

Legion of Mary—Miss DORIS MARTINEZ, Pres., Mailing Address: PMB 822, Box 7891, Guaynabo, 00970-7891; Rev. ANGEL L. CIAPPI-AZCORRA, Spiritual Dir., Urb. Munoz Rivera, C. Betania #34, Guaynabo, 00969. Tel: 787-360-0508.

Marriage Encounter—Mr. GERARDO SALAZAR; Mrs. MILLY SALAZAR, Jardines del Parque, 59 Boulevard Media Luna, Apt. 1803, Carolina, 00987-4935. Tel: 787-757-3432.

Spiritual Director—VACANT.

Catholic Daughters of America—Mrs. IRMA BONILLA, c/o Julio Bonilla #50, Isabela, 00662. Tel: 787-872-6831.

Spiritual Director—VACANT.

Knights of Columbus—Mr. MIGUEL A. TORRES ORTEZ, RR4, Box 3451, Bayamon, 00956. Tel: 787-782-8250, Ext. 6280; Fax: 787-792-7553.

Nocturnal Adoration—Mr. ANGEL PAGAN, Pres., Mailing Address: P.O. Box 190199, San Juan, 00919-0199. Tel: 787-749-0502; Mr. ISMAEL SUAREZ, Sec. Guaynabo. Tel: 787-728-0670; Mr. RAMON MENDEZ, Santa Maria de Cana. Cell: 787-312-2224.

Spiritual Director—Rev. RICARDO HERNANDEZ MORALES.

Talleres De Oracion y Vida P. Larranaga—Mrs. EMILIA DIAZ, Dir., Urb. Montehiedra, 33 Calle Garza, San Juan, 00926-9537. Tel: 787-728-2894; 787-731-1358.

Tourism and Apostleship of the Sea—

Casamar—VACANT.

UPR Catholic Student Center—Rev. RAFAEL RODRÍGUEZ, S.J., Mariana Bracetti 10, Rio Piedras, 00925-2201. Tel: 787-767-3348; Fax: 787-758-4145.

San Juan International Airport Chapel— Ntra. Sra de la Providencia Deacon EDUARDO GONZALEZ. Tel: 789-487-3731.

Carmelite Third Order—Rev. LUIS MIRANDA, O.Carm. Tel: 787-726-2631.

Casa San Clemente—

Psychological and Pastoral Counseling—257 Ponce De Leon, San Juan, 00906. Tel: 787-723-6915.

Pro-Life Center (Human Life International)—VACANT.

Pro-Life Pharmacists International—Miss SANDRA FABREGAS, Dir.

Consejo De Accion Social Arquidiocesano—Most Rev. HECTOR RIVERA, Dir., Mailing Address: P.O. Box 31155, San Juan, 00929-2155. Tel: 787-276-1413; Mrs. IDIS OTERO, Coord.

Servicios Pastorales Paules—Rev. SANTIAGO ARRIBAS, C.M., Dir., 1650, Ave. Fernandez Juncos, San Juan, 00910-0118. Tel: 787-728-0670; Fax: 787-728-0670. Mailing Address: P.O. Box 19118, San Juan, 00910-9118.

Franciscan Third Order (Secular Franciscan Order)—VACANT, Spiritual Dir.; Mrs. AWILDA VASQUEZ, Natl. Min., Mailing Address: P.O. Box 3915, Carolina, 00984. Tel: 787-752-7363.

Focolares—Deacon JOSE HERNANDEZ, Dir., Urb Fairview, 1937 Calle Melchor Maldonado, San Juan, 00926. Tel: 787-761-4993. Womens: Miss DIANA RIVERA, Urb. Fairview, 1911 Francisco Zuniga, San Juan, 00926. Tel: 787-543-3160.

Secretariado Sagrado Corazon—Mrs. ANA M. BONET, Pres., Urb. Prado Alto, C6 Calle 4, Guaynabo, 00966. Tel: 787-781-6295.

Grupo Reina De La Paz—Miss IVETTE PACHECO, Pres., PMB 258, Ste. 2, Ave. Esmeralda 405, Guaynabo, 00969. Tel: 787-644-8256; Fax: 787-731-8256; Mrs. IVONNE MELENDEZ, Sec. Tel: 787-754-8383; VACANT, Spiritual Dir.

Union Eucaristica Reparadora (UNER)—Rev. VICTORIANO RAMOS, Spiritual Dir. (Retired); Mrs. MARIA MERCEDES MAIZ, Dir., Cond. El Paraiso, 7-D Calle Parania 1560, San Juan, 00926. Tel: 787-751-1821; Mrs. ESTHER VARGAS, Urb. Ponce de Leon, Calle 23 #250, Guaynabo, 00969. Tel: 787-789-6660; DOLLIE MORALES; MARIZA BELARANA; LUIGUI BENITEZ; SONIA RENIOS.

Consejo Arquidioceseano De Accion Social (CASA)—Mr. MIGUEL A. RODRIGUEZ, Coord., Apartado 31164, San Juan, 00929. Tel: 787-605-9292.

Sociedad San Vicente De Paul—Mrs. CARMEN E. ARROYO, Calle Rafallar 566, Urb. La Merced, San Juan, 00918.

Maranatha House of Prayer—SILVIA SAAVEDRA DE BADIA, Dir., Urb. La Arboleda, Calle Alameda B #13, Guaynabo, 00966. Tel: 787-759-7734. Email: cmaranatha@prw.net. Web: www.casamaranathapr.org; Rev. BANDILIO GUZMAN, S.J., Dir. Esp.

Cofradia De Los Santos Angeles De La Guarda—MARIA T. PAGAN, Pres., Urb. Colinas Verdes, A-43 Calle 1, San Juan, 00924.

Cofradia Peregrinos De Tierra Santa—Deacon ANGEL ANTONIO NIEVES, Urb. Levittown, #1214 Paseo Doncella, Toa Baja, 00949. Tel: 787-948-1512.

Grupo Devocion Divina Misericordia—Deacon JULIO SANCHEZ, Oficina Diaconal, Caparra Heights, Calle Encarnacion 1564, San Juan, 00920-4739. Tel: 787-720-5714.

Grupos Para La Juventud—

Consejo Arquidiocesano De Pastoral Juvenil—Rev. RAMON HIRAM NEGRON, O.F.M.Cap., Vicario Pastoral Juvenil, Calle Arzuaga 218, Rio Piedras, 00925. Tel: 787-765-0606.

Grupo Juvenil Damasco—GEORGIE FERNANDEZ, Dir., Mailing Address: P.O. Box 360764, San Juan, 00936. Tel: 787-281-0707 (Office); 787-706-8906 (Res.); Fax: 787-281-0708.

Grupos De Retiros—

Grupo de Retiros Paz y Bien—Sr. OSVALDO ROMAN, Dir., Urb. Levittown, 1418 Paseo Delfin, Toa Baja, 00949. Tel: 787-784-5579.

Juventud Mariana Vicenciana (JMV)—Miss DAMARIS RIVERA, Dir. Seminario San Vicente De Paul Ave Ponce de Leon, 1711 Pda. 26, Santurce, San Juan, 00909. Tel: 787-727-3963; Sr. MILAGROS OLIVENCIA, H.C., Archdiocesan Representative, Hospital Auxilio Mutuo.

Asociacion De Profesionales Catolicos—Mr. JOSE VARELA, Committee Coord. Tel: 787-738-5189; LELIS RODRIGUEZ. Tel: 787-565-4884. Email: lelis@onelinkpr.net.

Hermandad N. Sra. De La Caridad—Mailing Address: P.O. Box 32, Guaynabo, 00970-0032. CALLE S. PEDRO MARTIR. Tel: 787-720-2361; Rev. Msgr. MARIO GUIJARRO, Dir. Espiritual; VACANT, Dir., Mailing Address: P.O. Box 10151, San Juan, 00922-0151. Tel: 787-783-3522.

Movimiento Juan XXIII—Mr. ANGEL L. RIOS, Pres., Villa Contessa, F35 Calle Aragon, Bayamon, 00976. Tel: 787-787-5984; Fax: 787-785-1024.

Movimiento De Schoenstatt—Mr. MARIO SANCHEZ; Mrs. MARIO SANCHEZ, Urb. Pinero, 12 Calle Alanebra, San Juan, 00917-3128.

World Apostolate of Fatima—Prof. AMERICO LOPEZ-ORTIZ, Intl. Pres.; Rev. Msgr. FERNANDO B. FELICES, Spiritual Dir., Mailing Address: P.O. Box 1968, Fernandez Juncos Sta., Mayaguez, 00681-1968. Tel: 787-833-0509; 787-487-5383. Web: www.apostoladomundialdefatima.org. Email: alfatima@coqui.net.

Neocatecumenal Way—Deacon JULIO ALVAREZ, Dir., Urb. El Conquistador, F-7 Calle 8, Trujillo Alto, 00976. Tel: 787-761-1667.

Our Lady of Providence Association—VACANT.

Perpetual Adoration—Mrs. VIRGINIA ALVAREZ, Asst., Mailing Address: Box S-763, San Juan, 00902. Tel: 787-725-7734.

Padre Nuestro—Mr. SAMUEL VALENTIN, Pres., Urb. Las Colinas, Calle 6, F. 35, Toa Baja, 00949. Tel: 787-368-3810.

Movimiento De Seglares Claretianos—Mrs. CARMEN SANCHEZ, Dir., San Antonio Maria Claret Parish. Tel: 787-797-3337.

Apostolado Del Cenaculo Misionero—Rev. VICENTE PASQUALETTO, S.T., Spiritual Dir.; Mrs. ALMA ROBLES, Urb. Los Colobos, Calle Robles #516, Carolina, 00987. Tel: 787-752-9327; 787-876-0827.

Conferencia Mariana De Puerto Rico—Mr. RICARDO HERNANDEZ; Mrs. RICARDO HERNANDEZ. Spiritual Directors: Rev. Msgr. FERNANDO B. FELICES-SANCHEZ; Rev. RICARDO HERNANDEZ MORALES.

CLERGY, PARISHES, MISSIONS AND PAROCHIAL SCHOOLS

CITY OF SAN JUAN

1—CATEDRAL DE SAN JUAN BAUTISTA (1522), (Nuestra Sra. de los Remedios). Rev. Jose Emilio Cummings, Rector; Deacons Louis Marin; Rafael Morales; Luis Echegaray Martinez.
Res.: 151 Cristo St., Box 9022145, 00902-2145. Tel: 787-722-0861; Fax: 787-722-0861.
Chapel—Santo Cristo
Chapel—San Jose, Tel: 787-725-7501.
Chapel—Santa Ana

2—ASUNCION DE LA VIRGEN (1972) Unassigned.
Res.: Calle Calve No. 1484, Urb. Antonsanti, Rio Piedras, 00927. Tel: 787-250-6771; Fax: 787-463-0894.

3—CORPUS CHRISTI (1972) Rev. Pablo Valenzuela (Spain); Deacons Francisco Gierbolini; Miguel Mendez; Juan Figueroa; Reinaldo Del Valle; Jose Perez; Casiano Lugo; Luis Fernando Amador; Luis A. Aparicio Amengual.
Res. & Mailing Address: Calle Jose Abad, 1224 Urb. Club Manor, 00924. Tel: 787-757-5821; Fax: 787-257-2741.
Mission—Santo Domingo de Guzman Carretera 849 Km. 8.7, Sector Santo Domingo, Penuelas CoEmail: pvalenzuelaz@onelinkpr.net.

4—CRISTO REDENTOR (1971) Rev. Angel L. Ciappi-Azcorra.
Res. & Mailing Address: Calle Ganges 140, Urb. El Paraiso, 00926. Tel: 787-946-1999.

5—CRISTO REY (1956) Rev. Carlos D. Cruz-Davila; Deacons Victor Reyes; Miguel Roman Del Valle.
Mailing Address: 65 Inf. Sta., P.O. Box 29695, 00929-0695.
Res.: Calle Jaime Drew, No. 789, Urb. Los Maestros, Rio Piedras, 00923. Tel: 787-767-3289.

6—ESPIRITU SANTO (1941) Rev. Msgr. Valeriano Miguélez (Spain); Deacon David Henriquez.
Mailing Address: P.O. Box 190259, 00919-0259. Calle Pachin Marin, Esq. Suiza, Hato Rey, 00919.
Res.: 75 Ruiz Belvis St., Floral Park, Hato Rey, 00919. Tel: 787-754-0570.
School—P.O. Box 191715, 00917. Tel: 787-754-0490; 787-754-0555; Fax: 787-754-7154. Olga Iris Torres, Assoc. Prin. Priests 1; Lay Teachers 46; Students 756.

7—FRANCISCA JAVIERA CABRINI (1968), (Mother Cabrini) Rev. Prisciliano Cardenas.
Res.: 1564 Encarnacion St., 00920. Tel: 787-783-7447; Fax: 787-706-2073.
Catechesis/Religious Program—Students 90.

8—INMACULADO CORAZON DE MARIA (1961) Rev. Jose Maria Solano-Uribe (Colombia); Deacons Benjamin Antonio Ramos Rivera; Israel Suarez; Benjamin Totti Lugo.
Urb. Santiago Iglesias, #1740 Calle Rodriguez Vera, Rio Piedras, 00921. Tel: 787-782-0245; Fax: 787-782-4176. Email: corazondemaria1704@hotmail.com. Web: inmaculadocorazon.tripod.com.
Res.: Rodriguez Vera y Ferrer St., Urb. Santiago Iglesias, 00922.
Catechesis/Religious Program—Students 121.
Mission—Monacillos San Fernando, San Juan Co.
Chapel—N. Sra. del Camino, Metropolitan Hospital [JC]

9—JESUS MAESTRO (1969) Revs. Anulfo Del Rosario, C.M. (Dominican Republic); Santiago Arribas, C.M.; Manuel Araujo, C.P.; Deacon Rafael Velazquez.
Res.: Segre 1725 Urb. Rio Piedras Heights, 00926. Tel: 787-763-8291; Fax: 787-763-8291.
Mission—Jesus Nazareno Calle Guadiana #1666, Urb. El Cerezal, 00926.

10—JESUS MEDIADOR (1988) Rev. Luis A. Cruz-Gonzalez; Deacons Candido Martinez; Edwin Rivera.
Res. & Mailing Address: Calle Demetrio O'Daly 1000, Urb. Country Club, 00924. Tel: 787-752-2410; Fax: 787-752-2410.

11—MARIA AUXILIADORA (1962) Revs. Nicolas Navarro, S.D.B.; Andres Rivera, S.D.B.; Antonio Polo, S.D.B.; Bro. Jose Cabo.
Mailing Address: P.O. Box 14367, 00916.
Res.: C. Constitucion Esq. Sta. Elena, Cantera, 00916. Tel: 787-727-5346; 787-726-1995, Ext. 267.
Catechesis/Religious Program—Students 300.
Mission—Sagrado Corazon, Sector Buenavista.
Mission—Nra. Sra. del Altagracia, Sector Buenavista.
Mission—Ntra. Sra. de Fatima, Sector Ultimo Chance-Cerro.
Mission—Santisima Trinidad Ave. Borinquen Final.

12—MARIA MADRE DE LA IGLESIA (1967) Rev. Edgardo Sanabria Santaliz; Deacons George Gonzalez; Eugenio Torres Diaz.
Res.: 1120 Calle 5, Urb. Villa Nevarez, 00927. Tel: 787-765-0600.

13—MARIA REINA DEL MUNDO (1971) Rev. Mariano Martínez Galvez, O.M.I.
Mailing Address: G.P.O. Box 3828, 00936-3828. Tel: 787-781-0303; Fax: 787-781-0303.
Res.: Caserio Nemesio Canales, Roosevelt Ave., 00936.
Catechesis/Religious Program—Students 20.

14—NTR. SRA. DE LA CARIDAD DEL COBRE (1969) Rev. Luis R. Brioso Texidor.
Res.: Urb. Buena Vista, Calle 5, No. 124, 00917. Tel: 787-689-4804.
Mission—Sma. Trinidad Calle Buenos Aires, No. 25, Parada 27, Hato Rey, San Juan Co. 00919.

15—NTRA. SRA. DE FATIMA (1967) Revs. Jose Reyes-Garcia, O.de.M.; Martin Garamendi, O.M. (Spain); Jose M. Gallego, O.M. (Spain); Jose B. Osorio Mourino.
Mailing Address: P.O. Box 190396, 00919-0396. Tel: 787-753-6334; Fax: 787-764-3571.
Res.: 608 Munoz Rivera Ave., Stop 34, Urb. Baldrich, Hato Rey, 00919.
School—La Merced (1949) P.O. Box 364048, 00936-4048. Tel: 787-765-7342; 787-754-1162; Fax: 787-765-3970. Mrs. Rosa M. Figueroa, Prin. Lay Teachers 36; Students 485.
Mission—Egida del Maestro

16—NTRA. SRA. DE LA MEDALLA MILAGROSA (1957) Rev. Carlos Verdia Nay; Deacon De Jesús Robles Filiberty.
Mailing Address: Urb. Perez Moris, Calle Mayaguez 209, 00917-5147.
Res.: 209 Mayaguez St., 00917. Tel: 787-751-2335; Fax: 787-274-0939.

17—NTRA. SRA. DE LA MONSERRATE (1919) Rev. Oscar Jimenez Portes, O.S.A.
Mailing Address: P.O. Box 13726, 00908-3726.
Res.: 1058 Fernandez Juncos Ave., 00907. Tel: 787-722-3134; Fax: 787-723-7838. Email: oscarjp@msn.com.
School—Santa Monica, Tel: 787-723-2573 (Elem.); 787-723-3845 (H.S.); Fax: 787-723-3992. Rev. Carlos R. Morales, O.S.A., Dir. Lay Teachers 34; Students 376.
Catechesis/Religious Program—Students 37.
Mission—Trastalleres Santa Ana, San Juan Co.

18—NTRA. SRA. DEL PERPETUO SOCORRO (1941) Rev. Msgr. Carlos Quintana-Puente.
Res.: Calle Marti 704, Miramar, Santurce, 00907-3227. Tel: 787-721-1015; 787-721-1016.
School—Jose Marti St. 704, 00907. Tel: 787-724-1447; 787-721-4540; Fax: 787-725-8104 (Elem.); 787-723-4550 (H.S.). Marie Ellen Gemel, Prin. Priests 1; Lay Teachers 102; Students 1,312.

19—NUESTRA SENORA DE BELEN (1960) Rev. Reinaldo Sagardia.
Mailing Address: P.O. Box 10845, 00922-0845. Tel: 787-793-2485; Fax: 787-792-8541.
Res.: Calle Jacinto Galib Final, Ave. San Patricio, Guaynabo.

20—NUESTRA SENORA DE LA ALTAGRACIA (1958) Rev. Gabriel Maria Torres-Rivera; Deacons Ildefonso Lugo; Rafael Colon; Euripides Lugo Lugo.
Mailing Address: Apartado 29493, 00929-0493. Tel: 787-765-0281.
Res.: Calle Felipe Gutierrez 672, Urb. Villa Prades, Rio Piedras, 00924. Tel: 787-765-0281.
Catechesis/Religious Program—Tel: 787-764-0614. Students 376.

21—NUESTRA SENORA DE LA CARIDAD DEL COBRE Rev. Pedro Luis Zaballa.
Res.: Urb. La Riviera, Calle 3 S.O. 1027, 00921-2517. Tel: 787-268-1325.

22—NUESTRA SENORA DE LA ESPERANZA (1962) Rev. Victor Aurelio Vargas Galan.
Mailing Address: P.O. Box 8532, 00910-8532.
Res.: Calle Republica No. 864, Urb. Hipodromo, Parada 20, Santurce, 00910. Tel: 787-999-7620.
Mission—Ntra. Sra. de la Providencia Barriada Figueroa.
Chapel—Doctors Hospital, Tel: 787-723-2950; Fax: 787-721-3155.

23—NUESTRA SENORA DE LA MERCED (1940) Revs. Jose Fernandez Martinez, O.de.M.; Jose Benito Osorio Mourino, O.de.M. (Spain); Javier Errecalde, O.de.M. (Spain).
Mailing Address: P.O. Box 364133, 00936-4133.
Res.: C/Pedro Espada 430, Urb. Roosevelt, Hato Rey, 00919. Tel: 787-763-3657.
Catechesis/Religious Program—Students 50.

24—NUESTRA SENORA DE LA PIEDAD (1956) Revs. Juan Bautista Benguria, C.P.; Manuel Elejalde, C.P.; Jesús Etxeandia Ormaetzea, C.P., Supr.; Florencio Landa, C.P. (Spain).
Mailing Address: P.O. Box 79520, Carolina, 00984. Email: lapiedad_cp@yahoo.com.
Res.: 1001 Marginal, Villamar, Carolina, 00979. Tel: 787-726-2880; 787-726-2794; Fax: 787-982-2155.
School—Tel: 787-727-7585 (H.S.); 787-727-2460 (Elem.); Fax: 787-268-0664 (H.S.); 787-728-0125 (Elem.). Mrs. Lizette Matos, Prin.; Rev. Florencio Landa, C.P. (Spain), Dir. Priests 1.

25—NUESTRA SENORA DE LA PROVIDENCIA (1959) Rev. Msgr. Baudilio Merino (Spain); Deacons Luis Vazquez; Ricardo Martinez.
Res. & Mailing Address: Santa Agueda St., No. 1730, Urb. San Gerardo, Rio Piedras, 00926. Tel: 787-765-6240; 787-765-8613; Fax: 787-765-4821.
School—Carretera #176, Km. 2.7, Calle Santa Agueda 1733, Urb. San Gerardo, Rio Piedras, 00926. Tel: 787-767-6552; 787-767-6755; Fax: 787-765-4821. Yolanda I. Martínez, Prin. Lay Teachers 30; Students 337.
Catechesis/Religious Program—Students 337.

26—NUESTRA SENORA DE LA PROVIDENCIA (1973) Rev. Hermenegildo Vicedo (Spain).
Res. & Mailing Address: 219 Aponte St., 00912. Tel: 787-727-1878.

27—NUESTRA SENORA DE LOURDES (1969) Rev. Angel L. Morales Figueroa.
Mailing Address: Bo. Obrero Sta., P.O. Box 14452, 00916.
Res.: Gilberto Monroig Ave., Cor. of Colton St., 288, 00916. Tel: 787-726-4643; Fax: 787-268-5255.

28—NUESTRA SENORA DEL CARMEN (1923) Rev. Giovanni Perez Berrios.
Mailing Address: P.O. Box 7275, 00916-7275. Tel: 787-727-0737; Fax: 787-728-4860.
Res.: Ave., Borinquen, Esq., Calle Tapia, Barrio Obrero, Santurce, 00916-7275.
School—Colegio Padre Berrios, (Grades K-9), P.O. Box 7717, 00916. Tel: 787-726-4851; Fax: 787-728-4860. Sr. Nilsa Cruz, H.C.C.S., Prin. Sisters 4; Lay Teachers 11; Students 160.
Catechesis/Religious Program—Sr. Tercida Y. De Leon, H.C.C.S., D.R.E. Students 56.
Mission—San Martin de Porres Calle: Tito Rodriguez #719 Barrio Obrero, Barrio Obrero, 00916.

29—NUESTRA SENORA DEL PILAR (1714) Revs. Jose Ramon Jimenez Lopez, C.O.R.C.; Jorge Alberto Ramirez Jonelez; Deacon Jose L. Velazquez; Bro. Jose Antonio Varcarcel.
Mailing Address: Box 21134, 00928-1134.
Res.: Plaza de Recreo, Rio Piedras, 00928. Tel: 787-764-5088; 787-763-3161.
Mission—Santa Teresita de Nino Jesus Calle, Tanque #37, Barriada Venezuela, Rio Piedras, San Juan Co. 00925.
Chapel—Colegio La Milagrosa De Diego St. 107, Rio Piedras, 00936. Tel: 787-765-6114.
Chapel—Hogar Crea Barriada Venezuela. Tel: 787-751-5640.

30—NUESTRA SRA. DE GUADALUPE (1951) Rev. Neil Macaulay, O.M.I. (Canada).
Mailing Address: G.P.O. Box 364125, 00936-4125. Tel: 787-782-0016; Fax: 787-782-0016. In Res., Rev. Mariano Martínez Galvez, O.M.I.
Res.: Calle 19 N.E. No. 1, Puerto Nuevo, 00920.
School—Tel: 787-782-0330; Fax: 787-782-0454. Mrs. Genevieve Zayas, Prin. Lay Teachers 37; Students 676.
Catechesis/Religious Program—Students 85.

31—RESURRECCION DEL SENOR (1968) Revs. Esteban Meliams-Figueredo; Mariano Errasti, O.F.M.
Res. & Mailing Address: Calle 31, S.O. #797, Urb. Las Lomas, 00921-1205. Tel: 787-792-1416; 787-792-5939; Fax: 787-792-1416.

32—SAGRADA FAMILIA (1971) Rev. Joaquin Mayorga-Fonseca.
Mailing Address: P.O. Box 29311, 00929.
Res.: Ave 65 de Inf., Esquina Calle 7, No. 112, Hills Brothers, Sabana Llana, 00924. Tel: 787-767-1723.
Catechesis/Religious Program—Students 2.

33—SAGRADO CORAZON DE JESUS (1971) Rev. Faustino Burgos Brisman, C.M. (Dominican Republic).
Res. & Mailing Address: Calle Oxford 251, Esq. Howard Urb. University Gardens, 00927. Tel: 787-765-4798; Fax: 787-765-5456.
School—Esq. Iteramericana y Palma Real: Urb. University Gardens, Rio Piedras, 00927-4826. Tel: 787-765-9430; Fax: 787-765-5267. Mary Andreen, O.S.F., Prin.
Catechesis/Religious Program—Students 37.

34—SAGRADO CORAZON DE JESUS (1909) Rev. Ovidio Ortega Lemus (Cuba); Deacon Pedro Nel Are.
Mailing Address: F. Juncos Sta., Box 8312, 00910-8312.
Res.: Ponce de Leon Ave., #1308, Stop 19, Santurce, 00910. Tel: 787-722-0235; Fax: 787-722-4845.

35—SAN AGUSTIN (1889) Rev. Miguel A. Garcia, C.Ss.R.
Mailing Address: 265 Ave. Constitucion, P.O. Box 9066557, 00906-6557. In Res., Revs. Felipe Santiago Burgos, C.Ss.R.; Jorge Colon, C.Ss.R.
Res.: 265 Ave. Constitución, Pta. de Tierra, 00906. Tel: 787-722-4289; Fax: 787-725-7737.
School—Colegio San Agustin, 255 Constitution Ave., Box 9066547, 00906. Tel: 787-722-4544; Fax: 787-977-1700. Marie Benitez Alonso, Prin. Lay Teachers 17; Students 269.
Catechesis/Religious Program—Students 10.

36—SAN ANTONIO (1908) [JC] Revs. Ramon Hiram Negron, O.F.M.Cap.; Ramon J. Casellas Rivera, O.F.M.Cap.; Roberto Martinez, O.F.M.Cap.
Res.: Calle Arzuaga #218, Esq. Frailes Capuchinos, Apartado 25177, 00928. Tel: 787-765-0606; Fax: 787-765-1180.
School—Tel: 787-764-0090; Fax: 787-763-7592. Minerva Feliciano, Elementary Prin.; Rev. Fray Jorge Macias, O.F.M.Cap., School Dir.; Miguel Rosa, Prin. (Intermediate & High School). Sisters 3; Lay Teachers 102; Students 1,411.
Catechesis/Religious Program—Students 51.
Mission—Nuestra Senora del Buen Consejo Calle Alto, 00926.

37—SAN FRANCISCO DE ASIS (1858) Revs. Jose A. Cruz Collazo, O.F.M. Cap.; Stephen Carter, O.F.M. Cap.
Res.: 301 San Francisco St., Box 9024231, 00902-4231. Tel: 787-724-1131; Fax: 787-721-4616.
Catechesis/Religious Program—Students 12.
Mission—Capilla San Conrado Bo. La Perla, 00902.

38—SAN FRANCISCO DE MONTE ALVERNIA (1985) Rev. Jose Antonio Landrau Roman; Deacon Juan Bautista Perez.
Res.: Calle 10, #15 Ext. San Agustin, 00926. Tel: 787-765-8824.

39—SAN FRANCISCO JAVIER (1967) Rev. Marco Antonio Rivera Perez; Deacons Abel De Varona; Jose Hernandez.
Res.: Calle 19, G46. Urb. Fair View, 00926. Tel: 787-761-2115; Fax: 787-761-2115. Email: santj@onelinkpr.net.
Catechesis/Religious Program—Students 48.

40—SAN IGNACIO DE LOYOLA (1956) Revs. Baudilio Guzmán, S.J.; Donald M. Vega, S.J.; Deacon Carmelo Rivera.
Res. & Mailing Address: Calle Narciso 1904, 00927-6706. Tel: 787-293-7960; 787-751-7512; Fax: 787-751-7000. Email: psi@coqui.net; parroquiasanignaciopr@hotmail.com.
School—Academia San Ignacio de Loyola, 1908 Calle Narcisco, Rio Piedras, 00936. Tel: 787-765-8190; Fax: 787-765-3635. Glorimar Soegaard, Prin.; Rev. Bandilio Guzman, S.J., Dir. Students 631.
Chapel—Cond. Jardines de San Francisco

41—SAN JORGE (1965) Rev. Jesus A. Garcia (Venezuela).
Mailing Address: Loiza Sta., P.O. Box 6427, 00914-6427.
Res.: Calle San Jorge 157, Santurce, 00914. Tel: 787-724-7780.

42—SAN JOSE (Villa Caparra) (1948) Rev. Ricardo Hernandez Morales; Deacon Luis Cordero.
Res.: Urb. Villa Caparra, Bloque ZM 215, Guaynabo, 00966. Tel: 787-781-1155; Fax: 787-774-8985. Email: acadparrsj@prtc.net. Web: www.parroquiasanjosevcpr.org.
School—Calle Josemaria Escriva 32, Guaynabo (Villa Caparra), 00966-2209. Tel: 787-783-1995 (H.S.); 787-792-7489 (Elem.); Fax: 787-792-7440 (Elem.); 787-781-3029 (H.S.). Sisters Catherine Ortiz, O.P., Prin. (Elementary); John Christian, Prin. (High School). Priests 1; Sisters 3; Lay Teachers 90; Students 800.

43—SAN JOSE OBRERO (1956) Rev. Rogelio Salazar-Valero (Mexico); Deacon Jose Lionel Cruz Trinidad.
Mailing Address: Calle Belmonte 470, 00923. Tel: 787-767-1448; Fax: 787-753-5392.
Res.: Urb. San Jose, Calle Belmonte 470, Rio Piedras, 00923.
Catechesis/Religious Program—Students 65.
Mission—San Antonio Ma. Claret, Embalse Sector.

44—SAN JUAN BOSCO (1945) Revs. Narciso De La Iglesia; Miguel Rivera, S.D.B.; Lorenzo Ruiz.
Mailing Address: Barrio Obrero Sta., P.O. Box 14125, 00915.
Res.: 370 Lutz St., Villa Palmeras, 00915. Tel: 787-726-7317; Fax: 787-726-1420.
Mission—La Milagrosa Villa Palmeras, C. Lutz 300 Final, Santurce, Mayaguez Co. 00915. Tel: 787-728-2175; Fax: 787-726-7313.
Mission—Ntra. Sra. del Rosario Fajardo St., 00915.
Mission—San Martin de Porres Union St. #58, Playita, Yabucoa Co. 00915.

45—SAN JUAN DE LA CRUZ (1990) Rev. Jose-Juan Cardona Diaz; Deacons Jorge Colon Velez; Luis Francisco Hernandez; Omar Santamarina.
Mailing Address: MSC 216, Urb. La Cumbre, Emiliano Pol Sta., 00926.
Res.: Urb. La Cumbre, Calle Julio Ruedas #1925, Borinquen Gardens, Rio Piedras, 00926. Tel: 787-731-2016; Fax: 787-708-0812.

46—SAN JUAN M. VIANNEY (1972), (Santo Cura de Ars) Rev. James Gil de la Madrid, M.SS.CC.; Deacon Manuel Caban.
Res. & Mailing Address: Calle 2, F-14, Urb. Hillside, 00926. Tel: 787-790-2014.
Mission—La Milagrosa, San Juan Co.
Mission—Cristo del Perdon Parcelas Canejas, Bo. Caimito Bajo.
Mission—Dulce Nombre de Maria Bo. Dulce, Caimito Bajo.
Mission—Ntra. Sra. del Carmen Calle Fidalgo, Sector Corea, Bo. Caimito Bajo.

47—SAN LUCAS (1972) Rev. Ramon Orlando Tirado; Deacons Jose Rodriguez; Hector Cruz DeChoudens.
Mailing Address: Urb. El Senorial, Calle Pio Baroja 380, 00926. Web: psanlucas.org; www.parroquiasanlucas.org.
Res.: Pio Baroja St., No. 380, Urb. El Senorial, 00926. Tel: 787-761-5476; Fax: 787-761-5476.
Catechesis/Religious Program—Students 72.

48—SAN LUIS GONZAGA (1965) Rev. Eddie Rivera Marzan.
Res. & Mailing Address: Calle Ronda A-17, Urb. Villa Andalucia, 00926. Tel: 787-761-9438; Fax: 787-761-9438.

49—SAN LUIS REY (1968) Rev. Msgr. Manuel Garcia Perez.
Mailing Address: Ste. #65, P.O. Box 71325, 00936-8425.
Res.: Calle 43 S.E. Final, Urb. Reparto Metropolitano, Rio Piedras, 00921. Tel: 787-767-6235.

50—SAN MATEO (1773) Rev. Olin Pierre Louis.
Mailing Address: P.O. Box 6081, 00914-6081.
Res.: Calle San Mateo, Esq. San Jorge, Stop 25, Santurce, 00912. Tel: 787-722-4158; Fax: 787-722-4158.

51—SAN PABLO (1965) Rev. Jose Miguel Cardona Matta.
Res.: Duero St., No. 370, Urb. Villa Borinquen, Puerto Nuevo, 00920. Tel: 787-706-0412; Fax: 787-706-0412.
Mission—Ntra. Sra. de la Caridad Del Cobre Borinquen Towers, Puerto Nuevo, San Juan Co. 00920.

52—SAN VICENTE DE PAUL (1940) [CEM] Revs. Luciano Frias, C.M.; Evaristo Oliveras, C.M.; Bro. Wilfredo Acevedo, C.M.
Mailing Address: P.O. Box 19118, 00910-0118.
Res.: 1650 Ave Fernandez Juncos, Stop 24, Santurce, 00910. Fax: 787-728-0670.
School—709 Bolivar St., Box 8699, 00910. Tel: 787-727-4273; Fax: 787-728-2263. Isabel Casanas, Prin. Lay Teachers 31; Students 539.
Catechesis/Religious Program—Students 80.

53—SANTA BERNARDITA SOUBIROUS (1982) Rev. Msgr. Wilfredo Pena-Moredo; Deacon Ismael Colon.
Mailing Address: 65 Infanteria Sta., P.O. Box 29826, 00929-0826. Tel: 787-762-0375; 787-257-7643; Fax: 787-757-6642. Email: santabernarditapr@yahoo.com. Web: www.parroquiasantabernardita.org.
Res.: Calle Espioncela, Esquina Calle Torcaza, Country Club, Rio Piedras, 00924.

54—SANTA CATALINA LABOURE (1977) Rev. Eusebio C. Fernandez Salazar (Colombia); Deacon Jacinto Ortiz.
Mailing Address: 267 Calle Sierra Morena, PMB 507, 00926-5583. Tel: 787-720-0303; Fax: 787-731-7166.
Res.: Carretera 842 Km. 3.6 Barrio Caimito, Rio Piedras, 00936.
Mission—Medalla Milagrosa Barrio Los Romeros, Bo. Caimito 00926-5636. Tel: 787-720-2215.
Mission—San Pablo Carretera 842, Bo. Caimito 00926.

55—SANTA CECILIA (1969) Rev. Danilo Martinez; Deacon Victor Merced de la Paz.
Mailing Address: El Senorial Sta., P.O. Box 415, 00926-0415.
Res.: Avenida Ceciliana #1, Urb. Rivieras de Cupey, Rio Piedras, 00936. Tel: 787-755-8670; 787-761-5461 (Parish House).
Catechesis/Religious Program—Students 33.
Chapel—Hogar Santa Teresa Jornet, Tel: 787-761-5805; Fax: 787-755-5575.
Chapel—Capilla San Agustin Carretera 844, Cupey Bajo.

56—SANTA LUISA DE MARILLAC (1962) Rev. Alberto Figueroa; Deacon Francisco Colon.
Mailing Address: Urb. La Cumbre Ave., Emiliano Pol Sta. 497, Ste. #17, 00926-5636.
Res.: Ave. Emiliano Pol, Urb. La Cumbre, Rio Piedras, 00926. Tel: 787-720-3150; Fax: 787-720-8779.

57—SANTA MARIA DE LOS ANGELES (1954) Rev. Luis Norberto Correa-Garcia; Deacons Rafael Reyes Crespo; Ramon Luis Rivera.
Mailing Address: Box 10716, 00922-0716. Tel: 787-792-2640; Fax: 787-792-2640.
Res.: De Diego Ave., No. 930, Urb. La Rivera, Rio Piedras, 00936.

58—SANTA ROSA DE LIMA (1971) Rev. Carlos Perez Toro; Deacons Pedro Costa; Jose R. Amezaga.
Res. & Mailing Address: Calle Lesbos No. 1765, Urb. Venus Gardens, 00926-4843. Tel: 787-761-6586; Fax: 787-761-6586. Email: santarosadelimapr@yahoo.com. Web: santarosadelimapr.blogspot.com.

59—SANTA TERESA DE JESUS JORNET (1985) Rev. Ivan Serrano Rivera; Deacons Vicente Lasanta; Martin Cuevas.
Mailing Address: El Senorial Mail Sta., P.O. Box 415, 00926-0415.
Res.: Carr. 176 Camino el Mudo, Km. 10.0 Cupey Alto, 00926. Tel: 787-748-2978.
Mission—San Martin de Porres Camino El Mudo. Cupey, Alto, 00926.
Mission—Ntra Sra de la Salud Camino Guayabos Carr. 176, Km. 9.5, Cupey, Alto, 00926.
Mission—Parroquia Santa Teresa de Jesus Jornet [CEM] Camino Los Gonzalez, Km. 5.3.

60—SANTA TERESITA DEL NINO JESUS (1930) Revs. Tarsicio Gotay Figaredo, O.Carm.; Luis M. Miranda Rivera, O.Carm.; Antonio M. Soto Torres, O.Carm.
Res.: 2059 Loiza St., 00911-1799. Tel: 787-727-0181; 787-727-0030; Fax: 787-728-0056. Email: tmgf@prmail.net. Web: www.parroquiasantateresita.com.

School—Tel: 787-727-4260; 787-727-4317; 787-727-4358. Ana R. Castro, Prin. Priests 1; Sisters 1; Lay Teachers 47; Students 360.
Mission—Sagrada Familia Residencial, Luis Llorens Torres, San Juan Co. 00913. Tel: 809-726-0570.

61—SANTISIMO SALVADOR (1966) Revs. Jesus Marques, Sch.P. (Spain); Javier Lopez, Sch.P. (Spain); Agustin Lopez, Sch.P. (Spain); Juan L. Cabrerizo, Sch.P. (Spain); Deacons Luis A. Medina; Luis O. del Rio.
Res.: Niza St., 575, Urb. Villa Capri, 00924. Tel: 787-761-3314; Fax: 787-755-1595.
School—Calasanz (1968) Ave. Montecarlo, Esq. Z, Urb. Montecarlo, P.O. Box 29067, 00929-0067. Tel: 787-750-2500; Fax: 787-257-0450. Ana Celia Santos, Prin. (High School); Glenda Laureano, Prin. (Elementary). Priests 3; Lay Teachers 25; Students 430.
Catechesis/Religious Program—Students 65.
Mission—N. Sra. Reina de la Paz Calle #1 Esq. C-8 Urb. Berwind States, Rio Piedras, San Juan Co. 00924.
Mission—San Jose de Calasanz Calle #23 408, Parc. Hills Brothers, Rio Piedras, San Juan Co. 00924.

62—SANTISMO SACRAMENTO (1967) Rev. Rogelio Salazar-Valero (Mexico).
Res.: 500 Jerusalem St., Urb. Matienzo Cintron, Rio Piedras, 00923. Tel: 787-764-3448.
Catechesis/Religious Program—Students 40.

63—SANTOS PEDRO Y PABLO LOS APOSTOLES (1980) Rev. Joaquin Mayorqa Fonscea.
Mailing Address: Las Teresas II Apt. 7F, Calle Azabache 905, 00924-3244.
Res.: Urb. Jardines De Berwind, Calle Las Casitas, Lote K, 65 Infanteria, Rio Piedras, 00929. Tel: 787-768-1424.

64—STELLA MARIS (1965) Rev. Msgr. Antonio Jose Vazquez Colon.
Res.: 69 Cervantes St., Condado, San Juan, 00907-1947. Tel: 787-723-2240; 787-723-2359; Fax: 787-722-3200.

OUTSIDE THE CITY OF SAN JUAN

BAYAMON

1—ASCENSION DEL SENOR (1984) Revs. Javier Elorriaga, O.SS.T.; Pedro Gorena, O.SS.T. (Spain); Deacon Juan Perez del Valle.
Mailing Address: P.O. Box 3367, 00958-3367. Tel: 787-799-6120; Fax: 787-730-7389.
Res.: Calle 31, Final, Urb. Rexville, 00957.

2—CATALINA DE SIENA (1963) Rev. Oscar Morales Cruz, O.P.; Deacons Francisco Cruz; Antonio Santiago; Jose Rios.
Mailing Address: *Hnas. Davila*, Q-3 Calle 1, 00959.
Res.: Urb. Hermanas Davila, Calle 10, Q-3, 00959. Tel: 787-785-2381; Fax: 787-269-5065.
Catechesis/Religious Program—Students 94.

3—CRISTO SALVADOR (1998) Rev. Luis Felipe Rodriguez Garnica.
Mailing Address: PMB 464, P.O. Box 7891, Guaynabo, 00970-7891.
Church: Parroquia Cristo Salvador, Guaynabo, 00970. Tel: 787-720-6596; 787-309-2448; Fax: 787-720-6596. Email: cristosalvador08@hotmail.com.

4—ESPIRITU SANTO (2002) Rev. José A. Santiago, O.SS.T.
Res. & Mailing Address: P.O. Box 3367, Bayamon Gardens Station, 00958-3367. Tel: 787-222-0935.

5—INVENCION DE LA SANTA CRUZ (1772) Rev. Ismael Fernandez Torres, O.P.
Res.: 12 Degetau St., 00961. Tel: 787-785-2134.

6—LA RESURRECCION DEL SENOR (1987) Rev. Edwin A. Cruz Garcia; Deacon Nicanor Mercado.
Res. & Mailing Address: *Urb. Royal Town*, F-1 Calle 12, 00956-4563. Tel: 787-730-4310; Fax: 787-730-4310.
Catechesis/Religious Program—Students 60.

7—NTRA. SRA. DE LA MONSERRATE (1985) Revs. Mario Gonzalez, O.S.A. (Spain); Perfecto Alvarez, O.S.A.; Carlos Cordero, O.S.A.
Mailing Address: P.O. Box 3948, 00958-3948.
Res.: Carr. 829, Km. 6.2, Bo. Santa Olaya, Bayamon Gardens, 00958. Tel: 787-797-0708; 787-799-7340; Fax: 787-797-9953.
Mission—Cristo Rey Bo. Guaraguao, Sector La Morenita.
Mission—Santa Monica Bo. Guaraguao, Sector Pena, Bayamon Co. 00619.

8—NUESTRA SENORA DE LA MILAGROSA (1968) Rev. Edgaro Pinto (Peru).
Mailing Address: P.O. Box 2104, 00960-2104.
Res.: Carr. 864, No. 82, Bo. Hato Tejas, 00960. Tel: 787-785-6620.

9—NUESTRA SENORA DEL PERPETUO SOCORRO (1976) Rev. Silvestre Gomez, O.P.; Deacons Ramon L. Ramon; Miguel Velez; Rafael Ortiz.
Res. & Mailing Address: Comerio St. No. 190, 00956. Tel: 787-785-2381; 787-780-4367; Fax: 787-785-2134.

10—NUESTRA SENORA DEL ROSARIO (1971) Rev. Jose Francisco Quiceno; Deacon Luis A. Navedo.
Res.: Calle Zaragoza, Bloque, B No. 34, Esq. Calle Vizcaya, Urb. Villa Espana, 00961. Tel: 787-787-0418; Fax: 787-787-0418.
Mission—Minillas San Jose.
Mission—N. Sra. del Carmen Bella Vista.
Mission—Sagrado Corazon de Jesus

11—NUESTRA SRA. DE LOS DOLORES (1976) Rev. Jose Francisco Quintero Angueira; Deacon Francisco Hernandez.
Res. & Mailing Address: 18th St., Urb. Alturas de Flamboyan, Bloque DD-25, 00957. Tel: 787-786-7494.
Catechesis/Religious Program—Students 12.

12—NUESTRA SRA. DEL ROSARIO (1993) Rev. Abelardo Mojica Paez; Deacon Hector Rivera.
Mailing Address: Box 3917, 00958.
Res.: Carr. 816 Km. 5.6, Barrio Nuevo, 00961. Tel: 787-730-6000; Fax: 787-730-6000.
Mission—San Juan Bautista, Montellano Co.
Mission—Jesus Maestro, Dajaos Co.
Mission—La Providencia, Dajaos Co.

13—SAGRADA FAMILIA (1976) Rev. Pedro Luis Reyes Lebrón; Deacons Americo Arroyo; Angel L. Oyola-Figueroa; Ramon L. Ortiz.
Mailing Address: P.O. Box 8478, 00959-8478. Email: sagfamilia@coqui.net.
Res.: #A-468 Cuba St., Urb. Ext. Forest Hills, 00960. Tel: 787-798-2010; Fax: 787-798-2010. Email: sagradafamilia@coqui.net.

14—SAN AGUSTIN (1964) Revs. Felipe Fernandez, O.S.A. (Spain); Gonzalo Gonzalez, O.S.A. (Spain); Carlos Algarin Lopez, O.S.A.; Deacons Ignacio Perez; Cristobal Rivera.
Mailing Address: Bayamon Gardens Sta., P.O. Box 4263, 00958-4283. Email: bayamonsanagustin@hotmail.com.
Res.: Urb. Lomas Verdes, Calle Duende, Bloque 2, E #21, 00956. Tel: 787-785-8611; Fax: 787-786-7631.
School—(1964) Box 4263, Bayamon Gardens Sta., 00958. Tel: 787-786-8055. Mrs. S. Morales, Prin. Lay Teachers 28; Students 406.
Mission—San Martin de Porres c/1 Barrio Juan Sanchez, Bayamon Co. 00959.
Mission—N. Sra. del Buen Consejo Villas de San Agustin, Bayamon Co. 00959.

15—SAN ANTONIO MARIA CLARET (1966) Revs. Norberto Padilla, C.M.F.; Romualdo Fernandez, C.M.F. (Spain); Deacon Jose Dolores Rivera.
Mailing Address: P.O. Box 3292, 00958-3292.
Res.: D-24 Castiglioni Ave., Urb. Bayamon Gardens, 00957. Tel: 787-797-3337.
Catechesis/Religious Program—Students 250.

16—SAN JOSE (1964) [CEM] Revs. Salvador Salgado, C.M.F.; Hector F. Cuadrado, C.M.F.; Jose Armengol, C.M.F. (Spain); Camilo Riano, C.M.F. (Spain); Severiano Garcia, C.M.F. (Spain).
Res. & Mailing Address: Dakar, F-169, Forest View, 00956. Tel: 787-785-6675; Fax: 787-785-0670.
School—Academia Claret, Tel: 787-787-6685; 787-786-7976. Israel Irizarry, Prin. Priests 3; Lay Teachers 30; Students 444.

17—SAN JUAN BAUTISTA DE LA SALLE (1979) Revs. Antonio Vallcaneras, SS.CC.; Jose M. Garcia Bastan, O.S.A. (Spain); Deacons Francisco Ortiz; Jose Vega; Jorge Rivera.
Res. & Mailing Address: A-19 Rio Cialitos St., 1ra. Secc. Estancias de Rio Hondo, 00961. Tel: 787-787-9567; Fax: 787-798-5071.

18—SAN MIGUEL ARCANGEL (1962) Rev. Ysidro Valero Castillo.
Mailing Address: P.O. Box 361714, 00936-1714. Tel: 787-787-4459; Fax: 787-787-4459.
Res.: Urb. Jardines de Caparra, Calle 12A Bloque AB., No. 32, 00959.
Mission—San Miguel Barriada San Miguel, Guaynabo, Guaynabo Co. 00657.

19—SANTA ELENA (1978) Rev. Jesus Gonzalez.
Mailing Address: P.O. Box 366, 00960-0366.
Res.: Calle 6, H-14, Urb. Sta. Elena, 00957. Tel: 787-785-6604; Fax: 787-785-6604.

20—SANTA MARIA (1984) Revs. Hector F. Cuadrado, C.M.F.; Pedro Lopez Moran, C.M.F. (Spain); Rafael Beltran, C.M.F.; Jose Daniel DeJesus Colon SJN, C.M.F.; Deacons Jose Ramon Cruz; Rafael Araya.
Mailing Address: Urb. Cana, Calle 24 #II-1, 00957.
Res.: Calle 24, Esq. 23, Urb. Cana, 00957. Tel: 787-797-7248; 787-797-8230; Fax: 787-797-7228.
Mission—San Gerardo Mayela Bo. Buena Vista, Bayamon Co. 00957.
Mission—Sagrado Corazon Bo. Cerro Gordo, Bayamon Co. 00956.

21—SANTA RITA DE CASIA (1967) Revs. Domingo Aller, O.S.A. (Spain); Benigno Palomo, O.S.A. (Spain); Deacons Ramon Luis Rivera; Noel Vasquez.
Res. & Mailing Address: Urb. Santa Juanita NS-8 Ave., Hostos, 00956-5102. Tel: 787-786-3971; Fax: 787-778-3806.
Mission—San Jose Carretera 831, Bo. Minillas, Bayamon Co. 00619.
Mission—N. Sra. Del Carmen Calle Reno P-54, Urb. Vista Bella, Bayamon Co. 00619.
Mission—Sagrado Corazon de Jesus

22—SANTA ROSA DE LIMA (1976) Rev. Virgilio Martinez (Spain); Deacon Ricardo Longueira.
Mailing Address: *Urb. Santa Rosa*, 28-9, Calle 12, 00956-6561. Tel: 787-798-2300; 787-787-1676; Fax: 787-780-3680. Email: santarosab@prtc.net. Web: www.ase-bay.org.
Res.: Urb. Sta. Rosa, Av. Main, Calles 11, 12, 13, 00959. Tel: 787-798-2300; Fax: 787-780-3680.
School—Ave. Main, Urb. Santa Rosa. Tel: 787-798-2829; 787-798-2539; Fax: 787-780-3680; 787-288-4996. Lorrie M. Cuevas Torres, Prin. Lay Teachers 33; Students 577.
Catechesis/Religious Program—Students 600.

23—SANTA TERESA DE JESUS (1983) Rev. Edwin Londono Zuluaga; Deacon Eugenio Torres Diaz.
Mailing Address: P.O. Box 9204, 00960-9204. Email: parsteresa@gmail.com.
Res.: Calle 12 F #10, Urb. Teresita, 00960. Tel: 787-269-6749; Fax: 787-269-6749.
Mission—San Martin de Porres Rio Plantation Urb., 00961. Tel: 787-269-6749; Fax: 787-269-6749.
Mission—Convento Missioneras de La Caridad Sector Punta Brava. Tel: 787-269-0207.

24—SANTIAGO APOSTOL (1966) [CEM] Revs. Julio Cesar Taveras Reymoso, M.SS.CC.; Jesus M. Ciriza, M.SS.CC. (Spain); Deacon Angel Pabon.
Res.: Urb. Sierra Bayamon, Calle 23, Bloque 23, Num. 17, 00961. Tel: 787-786-9679; 787-288-1966; Fax: 787-269-3965.
School—Tel: 787-786-9179; Fax: 787-269-3965. Mrs. Zoraida N. de Alonso, Prin. Priests 2; Lay Teachers 21; Students 359.
Catechesis/Religious Program—Students 359.

25—SANTO DOMINGO DE GUZMAN (1976) Rev. Silvestre Gomez, O.P.; Deacons Hèctor Negrón; Rubén González.
Mailing Address: Ext: La Milagrosa Calle 2, 00959.
Res.: Ext. La Milagrosa Calle 2, 00959. Tel: 787-786-8592.
Catechesis/Religious Program—

26—SANTO DOMINGO DE GUZMAN (1984) Rev. Francisco J. Quinones Diaz; Deacons Virgilio Andino; Ramon Ramos; Pedro Gonzalez Ramos.
Mailing Address: P.O. Box 3342, 00958-3342.
Res.: Parcelas Van Scoy, Calle Principal Esquina Calle, #3, 00957. Tel: 787-797-5510; 787-799-2377.
Catechesis/Religious Program—Students 173.
Mission—Santisima Trinidad Carretera 167 Km. 10, Bo. Ortiz, Corozal Co.
Mission—N. Sra. de la Providencia Urb. Los Dominicos, 00958.
Mission—Carlos Manuel Rodriguez Urb. Los Palacios, Toa Alta, 00954.

CAROLINA

1—CRISTO REY (1971) Rev. Jan Krolh.
Mailing Address: P.O. Box 1215, 00986-1215.
Res.: Urb. Parque Ecuestre, Calle Dulce Sueno U-8, 00987. Tel: 787-752-9939; Fax: 787-752-9939.
Mission—S. Francisco de Asis Entre las calles Tinajero y Dulce Sueno, Parque Encuestre.
Mission—Maria Auxiliadora Carrt. 857 Km. 3.6, Bo. Canovanillas.
Mission—Divino Nino Jesus Ubanizaciones: Ciudad Jardin y Colobos Park, Bo. Cambute, Carolina Co.
Mission—Cristo Rey Bo. Carruzos.

2—EPIFANIA DEL SENOR (1982) Rev. Francisco Moralez Feliu.
Mailing Address & Res.: Calle Calais 425, Ext. El Comandante, 00982-3601. Tel: 787-752-1149.
Catechesis/Religious Program—Students 19.

3—INMACULADA CONCEPCION (1966) Rev. Benjamin Antonio Perez Cruz.
Mailing Address: Apartado 3562, 00984-3562. Email: pinmaccon@gmail.com.
Res.: Urb. Valle Arriba Hts., Calle Almendro A-15, 00984. Tel: 787-276-1527; Fax: 787-769-4307.
Catechesis/Religious Program—Students 58.

4—NTRA. SRA. DE FATIMA (1998) Rev. Gregorz O. Karma; Deacon Orlando Rodriguez.
Mailing Address: HC 03 Box 12076, Bo. Cedros, 00987-2076.
Res.: Bo. Cedros, Carr 853, Km. 13.6, 00988. Tel: 787-750-2168; Fax: 787-750-2168.
Mission—N. Sra. del Carmen Carr 853, Km. 8.0, Barrazas 00987.
Mission—Santa Teresa de Jesus Bo. Carr 853, Km. 5.0, Cacao 00987.

5—NTRA. SRA. DEL CARMEN (1984) Rev. Antonio Garcia (Spain); Deacons Ernie Diaz; Cesar Avila.
Mailing Address: P.O. Box 299, 00986-0299.
Res.: Urb. Lomas de Carolina, Monte Membrillo Km. 8, 00987. Tel: 787-752-8708; 787-752-4454; Fax: 787-762-6656.
School—Academia del CarmenMonte Britton:, Esq. Monte Membrillo, Lomas de Carolina, 00987. Tel: 787-757-4489; 787-757-4454. Email: academiadelcarmen@gmail.com. Mrs. Aitza Vázquez-Padilla, Sub-Dir. Priests 1; Lay Teachers 20; Students 232.
Catechesis/Religious Program—Students 232.

6—NTRA. SRA. REINA DE LA PAZ (1969) Rev. Angel Cuevas Rosario; Deacons Euripides Lugo; Miguel

A. Marrero; Manuel Reyes; Efigenio Rivera.
Mailing Address: P.O. Box 3688, 00984-6388.
Res.: Calle 6, Final, Urb. Sabana Gardens, 00983. Tel: 787-750-4538; Fax: 787-750-4538.
Mission—Divino Nino Jesus

7—NTRA. SRA. REINA DE LOS ANGELES (1960) Rev. Benjamin Antonio Perez Cruz; Deacon Ildefonso Berrios.
Res. & Mailing Address: Urb. Los Angeles, 29 Calle Lira, 00979-1659. Tel: 787-791-2594; Fax: 787-791-8878. Email: reinadelosangeles@catholic.org.

8—NUESTRA SENORA DE LOURDES (1956) Rev. David Arrieta (Spain).
Mailing Address: Urb. El Comandante, 1173 Calle Alejo Cruzado, 00924.
Res.: 1173 Alejo Cruzado, Ext. El Comandante, 00988. Tel: 787-752-3716.

9—SAN ANDRES (1982) Rev. Carmelo Soto Tanon; Deacons Marino Hernandez; Gilberto Mejias.
Res. & Mailing Address: MF-15 Calle 482, Urb. Country Club (4 Ta. Extension), 00982. Tel: 787-769-7076; Fax: 787-769-7076.

10—SAN FELIPE APOSTOL (1971) Rev. Rodney Algarin-Rosado; Deacon Manuel Cruz.
Mailing Address: P.O. Box 1494, 00984-1494.
Res.: Calle 419, Bloque 165, No. 3, 4 Ta. Ext. Villa Carolina, 00964. Tel: 787-762-6520; Fax: 787-257-8995. Email: sanfelipepr@hotmail.com.

11—SAN FERNANDO (1851) Rev. Msgr. Efrain Rodriguez-Otero; Deacons Jose Birriel; Santiago Diaz Rosa; Prebistero Rivera.
Mailing Address: P.O. Box 128, 00986-0128.
Res.: Calle Ignacio Arzuaga #157, 00986. Tel: 787-769-0170; Fax: 787-769-5223.

12—SAN FRANCISCO DE ASIS (1988) Rev. Frank de la Rosa Peguero (Dominican Republic).
Res. & Mailing Address: Calle 22 #0-31 A, Urb. Metropolis, 00987. Tel: 787-998-8331. Email: parsonta@onelinkpr.net.

13—SAN JUAN DE DIOS (1971) Rev. Julio Ortiz-Mangual; Deacons Luis R. O'Neill; Jorge Fonseca; Jose Otero Lugo.
Mailing Address: P.O. Box 3179, 00984-3179.
Res.: R-19 Canaria St., Jardines de Borinquen, 00985. Tel: 787-757-5060; Fax: 787-757-5060.
Mission—La Sagrada Familia C. Progreso A-79A, Villa Esperanza, Carolina Co. 00985.

14—SAN VALENTIN (1971) Rev. Natividad Acevedo Viscaya; Deacon Jose A. Pappaterra.
Mailing Address: P.O. Box 9382, 00988-9382.
Res.: Calle San Luis 128, Urb. Rolling Hills, 00988. Tel: 787-750-5277; Fax: 787-750-5277.
Catechesis/Religious Program—Students 66.
Mission—Jardines de Carolina Calle E, esq. Calle F, Santa Rosa, 00987. Tel: 787-750-5272.
Mission—San Antonio Urb. San Anton, Calle Tomas Ortiz, esq. Kercado, Carolina Co. 00987.

15—SANTA CLARA DE ASIS (1966) Revs. Francisco Labaka, O.F.M. (Spain); Leandro Abarrategui, O.F.M. (Spain); Luis S. Olmo, O.F.M. (Spain); Deacons Luis Del Rio Pitre; Jose A. Morales, (Retired); Luis Montes.
Mailing Address: Urb. Villa Fontana, JL-456 Via 14, 00983.
Res.: Via 14 JL No. 456 Urb. Villa Fontana, 00983. Tel: 787-768-1708; Fax: 787-750-2898.
School—(1968)Tel: 787-768-7110; Fax: 787-757-5044. Mrs. Lillivette Torres, Prin.; Rev. Leanadro Abarratelegui, O.F.M., Dir. Lay Teachers 23; Students 355.
Mission—San Francisco de Asis
Mission—Parque Boliviano 5-JL Villa Fontana Park, Carolina Co. 00983.

16—SANTA GEMA GALGANI (1971) Revs. Jose R. Montanez Lopez, C.P.; Felix Barruetabena, C.P. (Spain).
Mailing Address: P.O. Box 2789, 00984-2789.
Res.: Av. Galicia Final, Urb. Vistamar, 00984. Tel: 787-769-5663; Fax: 787-750-3090.
School—Tel: 787-768-3082; 787-757-2505; Fax: 787-750-3090. Mrs. Lilia Luna de Anaya, Prin. Lay Teachers 32; Students 631.

17—SANTISIMA TRINIDAD (1982) Rev. Francisco Arana (Spain); Deacons Ibrahim Suarez; Esteban Valle; Bienvenido Domenech; Gaspar Orozco.
Mailing Address: Urb. Country Club, 3 ra Ext., Ave. Campo Rico PA-16, 00982. Tel: 787-769-5665.
Res.: Avenida Campo Rico PA-16, Urb. Country Club, 00988.
Catechesis/Religious Program—Students 175.

18—SANTO CRISTO DE LA AGONIA (1971) Rev. Juan Santa Guzman; Deacons Ernesto Rivera; Miguel A. Marrero-Nieves.
Mailing Address: P.O. Box 5108, 00984-5108.
Res.: Calle Robles 29, Urb. Eduardo J. Saldana (Ceramica), 00984. Tel: 787-768-0374.
Catechesis/Religious Program—Students 60.
Mission—N. Sra. de la Esperanza Sabana Abajo, Carolina Co.

19—SANTO CRISTO DE LOS MILAGROS (1971) Rev. Nestor Yulfo-Hoffman; Deacon Jorge Rivera.
Mailing Address: P.O. Box 834, 00986-0834.
Res.: Ave. Sanchez Castano, Urb. Villa Carolina, 00985. Tel: 787-636-0317; Fax: 787-636-0317.

CATANO

1—NUESTRA SENORA DEL CARMEN (1893) Revs. Roberto Arzola, O.P.; Ceferino Gómez Urias (Spain); Rafael Díaz Delgado; Deacon Angel Oquendo.
Mailing Address: P.O. Box 427, 00963-0427.
Res.: Calle Tren Num. 42, 00963. Tel: 787-275-1309.
Mission—San Martin de Porres Urb. Bayview.
Mission—San Jose Obrero

2—SAN FRANCISCO DE SALES (1969) Revs. Luis Rodriguez, S.D.B.; Jorge L. Gonzalez, S.D.B., Supr.
Mailing Address: P.O. Box 567, 00963-8163.
Res.: Ave. Flor del Valle Bloque BB-No. 108, Urb. Las Vegas, 00963. Tel: 787-788-5036; Fax: 787-788-8163.
Mission—Santo Domingo De Guzman Puente Blanco, Catano Co.
Mission—Maria Auxiliadora Urb. Vistas Del Morro.
Mission—San Judas Tadeo (Santuario) Parcelas Bo. Palmas.
Mission—Immaculada Concepcion Sector La Cucharilla.

DORADO

1—NTRA. SRA. DE LA SALUD (1982) Rev. Angel Pagan Torres; Deacons Hilario De Leon; Cresencio Rosario.
Mailing Address: Bo. Higuillar, P.O. Box 470, 00646-0470.
Res.: Parcela 202, Calle Principal 210, Sector San Antonio, 00646. Tel: 787-796-3418; Fax: 787-796-3418.

2—SAN ANTONIO DE PADUA (1848) Rev. Jose Angel Rodriguez Reyes; Deacons Boanerges Herrera; Benito Lugo Soto; José E. Colon; José C. Diaz.
P.O. Box 602, 00646-0602. Tel: 787-278-1416; Fax: 787-278-1154. Email: saintantny@coqui.net.
Res.: 184 Calle Norte, P.O. Box 602, 00646. Tel: 787-278-1416.
Mission—San Martin de Porres Calle Principal Bo Mameyal, 00646.
Shrine—Christ of Reconciliation (2001) Paseo Del Cristo Lot #8, Urb. Martorell, 00646.

GUAYNABO

1—BUEN PASTOR (1965) Rev. Msgr. Francisco Medina Santos.
Res. & Mailing Address: Urb. Apolo QQIA Calle Acropolis, 00969-5014. Tel: 787-200-5308; Fax: 787-789-2653.

2—CORAZON DE JESUS (1992) Rev. Victor Hugo Mira Alvarez, SS.CC.
Mailing Address: P.O. Box 225, 00970-0225. Tel: 787-731-0585.
Res.: Carr. 834 Km. 4.0, Bo. Sonadora, 00970.
Mission—San Juan Bosco Bo. Mamey 1.
Mission—Sagrada Familia Bo. Sonadora, Villa Jalena, Bo. Sonadora.

3—DIVINO NINO JESUS (1992) Rev. Rodolfo Lamas; Deacons Andres Figueroa; Milton Valladares.
Mailing Address: PBM 143, HC-01, Box 29030, Caguas, 00725. Tel: 787-720-0203; Fax: 787-720-0203.
Res.: Urb. Lomas Del Sol, Calle Principal, 00971.
Mission—San Rafael Arcangel Barrio Camarones, Carr. #20, Guaynabo Co. 00970.
Mission—Jesus Nazareno Bo. Mamey, Guaynabo Co. 00970.
Mission—El Buen Pastor Carr. #1, Guaynabo Co. 00970. Tel: 787-798-9596.
Mission—N. Sra. de la Paz Bo. Quebrada Arenas, Guaynabo Co. 00971.

4—MARIA MADRE DE LA MISERICORDIA (1995) Rev. Msgr. Leonardo J. Rodriguez-Jimenes; Revs. Rafael Mendez-Hernandez; Ricardo Augusto Roig Lorenzo; Deacon Francisco Martinez.
Mailing Address: Ave. Santa Ana. #150, 00969.
Res.: Carretera 833 Km. 13.2, Bo. Santa Rosa 3, 00969. Tel: 787-789-0090; Fax: 787-790-7596.

5—MARIA MADRE DE MI SENOR (1988) Rev. Phillip Nunez-Carrion.
Mailing Address: P.O. Box 2150, 00970-2150. Tel: 787-789-1837; 787-720-1709.
Res.: Bo. Tortugos, Carretera 873, #1904, 00970.
Mission—Ntra. Sra. del Carmen Bo. Frailes Llanos, Sector Los Baez, Guaynabo Co. 00657.

6—NUESTRA SENORA DE LA PAZ (1992) Rev. Jose Humberto Lopez Marino; Deacons Porfirio Franco; Jose M. Castillo; Pablo Manzano.
Mailing Address: PMB 774, P.O. Box 7891, 00970-7891. Tel: 787-287-5714.
Res.: 833 Rd. LM 3.5, Bo. Guaraguao, 00970.
Mission—N. Sra. de la Divina Providencia Cantagallo, Juncos Co. 00971.
Mission—Espiritu Santo Bo. Sta. Rosa I, 00971. Tel: 787-287-2335.
Mission—Inmaculada Concepcion Bo. Camarones Centro, Ciales Co. 00971.
Mission—San Jose Obrero Bo. Sta. Rosa II, 00971.

7—SAGRADOS CORAZONES (1968) Revs. Victor Hugo Mira Alvarez, SS.CC.; Mateo Mateo, SS.CC.; Luis Alfonso Padilla; Deacons Ivan E. Dominguez; Ulpiano H. Rivera; Olimpio R. Zambrana Ortega.
Mailing Address: P.O. Box 3902, 00970-3902.
Res.: Urb. Ponce de Leon, 208 Ave. Esmeralda, 00969. Tel: 787-720-6151; Fax: 787-720-6151.
School—Avenue A, 00969. Tel: 787-720-2585; 787-720-6316; Fax: 787-720-6035. Email: ssccgnb@gmail.com. Edith N. Casiano, Dir. (High School & Elementary). Lay Teachers 44; Students 731.
Catechesis/Religious Program—Sr. Bibino Acevedo, D.R.E.
Mission—Virgen de la Paz Bda. Cruz Melendez, 00969.

8—SAN JUAN EVANGELISTA (1962) Rev. Walter S. Gomez-Baca; Deacon Miguel De La Sota.
Mailing Address: P.O. Box 10151, 00922-0151. Email: psje@caribe.net; info@psje.us.
Res.: Calle Church Hill, J-5, Urb. Torrimar, 00966. Tel: 787-783-3522; Fax: 787-781-0236.
School—Tel: 787-781-5325; Fax: 787-793-8076. Priests 1; Lay Teachers 37; Students 260.
Catechesis/Religious Program—Tafty Beuicos, D.R.E.
Mission—San Francisco de Asis [CEM] Carretera 19, La Marina, Guaynabo Co. 00966.

9—SAN PEDRO MARTIR DE VERONA (1769) Rev. Msgr. Mario A. Guijarro de Corzo (Cuba); Deacons Carlos Rivera Martinez; Humberto Reyes Anciano; Angel Loyola Zayas; Gregory A. Guijarro.
Mailing Address: P.O. Box 32, 00970-0032.
Res.: Calle Tapia No. 5, 00970. Tel: 787-720-2361; 787-272-6739; 787-287-1791; Fax: 787-287-2833.
School—Alpierre St. Final, Urb. Colimar, P.O. Box 2560, 00970-2560. Tel: 787-720-2219; Fax: 787-272-8770. Mrs. Ivonne D. Carlo, Prin.; Deacon Gregory A. Guijarro, Prof. & Vice Dir. Priests 2; Sisters 9; Lay Teachers 45; Students 610.
Catechesis/Religious Program—Students 267.

10—SANTA ROSA DE LIMA (1973) Rev. Jose Gregorio Guaipo; Deacon Filiberty De Jesus.
Res. & Mailing Address: 16 Parque St., Barrio Amelia, 00965. Tel: 787-781-5855; 787-783-9731; Fax: 787-781-5855; 787-783-9731.
Mission—La Milagrosa Barriada Vietnam.

TOA ALTA

1—N. SRA. DE LA PROVIDENCIA (1968) Rev. William Torres-Pagan; Deacon Gregorio Cuevas.
Mailing Address: Bayamon Gardens Sta., P.O. Box 3836, Bayamon, 00958-3836. Tel: 787-797-1618.
Res.: Bo. Pinas, Carretera 861 Km. 5.6, 00954.
Mission—N. Sra. de Fatima Sector Rincon, Bo. Pinas, Comerio Co.
Mission—La Resurreccion Villa del Rio, Bo. Pinas, Comerio Co.
Mission—N. Sra. del Carmen Sector del 7.
Mission—Sagrada Familia Villa Juventud, Bo. Pinas, Comerio Co.

2—NUESTRA SENORA DE LA MEDALLA MILAGROSA Rev. Jose A. Ortiz Gonzalez; Deacons German Hernandez; Santos Nieves.
Mailing Address: P.O. Box 335, 00954-0335.
Res.: Bo. Quebrada Cruz, Carretera 824, Km. 3.8, 00954. Tel: 787-870-4090; Fax: 787-870-8125.
Mission—Nuestra Senora del Carmen Sector El Cuco, Bo. Quebrada Cruz, Toa Alta Co. 00758.
Mission—Sagrado Corazon de Jesus Carretera 165 Km. 3.1, Quebrada Cruz, Toa Alta Co. 00758.

3—SAN ESTEBAN, PROTOMARTIR (1997) Rev. Hernan Berdugo (Colombia); Deacons Jose Ramon Perez-Bracero; Rafael Morales Figueroa.
Res. & Mailing Address: Urb. Monte Sol, Ave. Hato Tejas, Esq. Carretera 861, 00953. Tel: 787-799-2925; Fax: 787-279-8439. Email: parroquiasanesteban@prtc.net.
Catechesis/Religious Program—Students 155.
Mission—Capilla Cristo Rey Sector La Cuerda, Barrio Bucarabones, Toa Alta Co. 00953.
Mission—N. Sra. del Rosario Bo. Pajaros, RR-5, Box 4103, Bayamon, Toa Alta Co. 00956. Tel: 787-799-7950.

4—SAN FERNANDO REY (1751) [JC] Rev. Miguel Angel Trinidad-Fonseca; Deacons Jose Narvaez; Felipe Collazo; Pablo Irene.
Mailing Address: P.O. Box 63, 00954-0063. Email: sfdo2585@coqui.net.
Res.: Calle Jose de Diego #10, 00953. Tel: 787-870-2585.
Mission—San Antonio Rio Lajas, Dorado, Dorado Co. 00646.

5—SAN JOSE (1998) Rev. Jorge Saenz-Ramos; Deacons Francisco Villamil; Enrique Laureano; Rafael Morales.
Mailing Address: P.O. Box 777, 00954-0777.
Res.: Sector Jazmin, Carretera 823, Rio Lajas, 00954. Tel: 787-870-6415.
Mission—Ntra. Sra. del Camino Bo. Espinosa, Carretera #2, Dorado, Dorado Co. 00646.
Mission—S. Francisco De Asis Bo. Maguayo, Dorado, Dorado Co. 00646.
Mission—Cristo de los Milagros

Mission—Santa Teresita Bo. Rio Lajas, Toa Alta Co. 00758.
Mission—Sagrada Familia Sector Marzan, Bo. Rio Lajas, Toa Alta Co. 00758.
Mission—Sagrado Corazon Sector Los Mudos, Bo. Quebrada Arenas, Toa Alta Co. 00758.

6—San Judas Tadeo (2002) Rev. Victor Torres, O.M.I. (Panama); Deacons Luis Rivera-Albino; Luis Alvira Colon.
Mailing Address: RP-03, Box 9169, 00954.
Res.: Carretera 804 Km. 1.2, Bo. Galateo Centro, 00954. Tel: 787-870-6643; Fax: 787-870-8018.
Mission—S. Martin de Porres Bo. Galateo.
Mission—Santa Teresa De Jesus Bo. Quebrada Cruz, Toa Alta Co. 00758.

Toa Baja

1—Espiritu Santo (1965) Revs. Milton Agustin Rivera-Vigo; Jose Ramon Zubizarreta Mugica, C.P. (Spain); Deacons Martin Estrada; Miguel A. Torres; Guillermo M. Vaello Perez.
Mailing Address: Levittown Sta., P.O. Box 50272, 00950. Email: pes@coqui.net.
Res.: Paseo Damisela No. 1453, Urb. Levittown, 00949. Tel: 787-794-4805; Fax: 787-795-1248.
School—Paseo Damisela 1454, 00949. Tel: 787-784-0905; Fax: 787-795-5418. Lay Teachers 46; Students 381.
Catechesis/Religious Program—Students 232.
Mission—N. Sra. del Carmen Calle Carmen, Bo. Palo Seco, Toa Baja Co. 00759.

2—Ntra. Sra. de la Candelaria (1960) Rev. Jose Dario Martinez Tobon (Colombia); Deacons Anselmo Miranda; Roberto Rosado Ortiz.
Mailing Address: P.O. Box 892, 00951-0892.
Res.: Carretera No. 863, Km. 0.6, Bo. Pajaros, 00951. Tel: 787-251-0503.
Mission—Cristo Rey Calle 10, Bo. Bucarabones, Toa Alta, Toa Alta Co. 00758.
Mission—Santa Maria La Mayor Carretera #2 R.063, Bo. Macun, Bo. Macun, Toa Baja Co. 00759.
Mission—Santisima Trinidad Urb. Las Colinas, Toa Baja Co. 00759.
Mission—Buen Pastor Urb. Sta. Maria, Toa Baja Co. 00759.

3—Nuestra Senora de Covadonga (1984) Rev. Jairo Salazar Castano; Deacon Efrain Narvaez.
Mailing Address: P.O. Box 9076, Bayamon, 00960-9076. Tel: 787-251-6466; Fax: 787-251-6466.
Res.: Calle 13, 2-C-4, Esq. Calle 14, Urb. Covadonga, 00949.
Mission—Ntra. Sra. de Lourdes Bo. Candelaria Arenas, Toa Baja Co. 00759.
Mission—San Martin de Porres Bo. Kennedy, Toa Baja Co. 00759.
Mission—Divino Nino Jesus Urb. El Plantio, Toa Baja Co. 00759.

4—San Jose Obrero (1965) Revs. Gerardo A. Vargas Cruz, O.F.M.; Angel Dario Carrero, O.F.M., Supr.; Alfonso Guzman, O.F.M.; Deacon Ramon L. Colon.
Mailing Address: Box 173, Sabana Seca, 00952-0173. Tel: 787-784-1400; Fax: 787-795-3141.
Res.: Carretera 2-R 866, Km. 3 #6, 00952. Tel: 787-784-1400; 787-795-3141; Fax: 787-784-1400.
Mission—Ntra. Sra. del Carmen
Mission—San Martin de Porres Carr. 816 PAR 1034, Villa Marisol, Sabana Seca.

5—San Pedro Apostol (1745) Rev. Calixto Soto Silvera (Colombia); Deacon Jose M. Sanchez.
Mailing Address: P.O. Box 513, 00951-0513.
Res.: 47 Las Flores St., 00949. Tel: 787-794-1327; Fax: 787-794-5967.
Catechesis/Religious Program—Students 295.
Mission—St. Teresita Calle Quintero.
Mission—Ntra. Sra. de Guadalupe Calle Crisantemo, Parcela 137-A.
Mission—San Jose Calle San Jose #303.
Mission—San Pablo Calle Universo, Parcela #9, Toaville.
Mission—La Virgen de la Providencia Bo. Villa Calma.

6—Santisima Trinidad (1978) Rev. Juan M. Beristain (Spain); Deacons Eusebio Jaca; Justo Ortiz; Edwin Negron.
Mailing Address: Apartado 50378, Levittown, 00950-0378. Tel: 787-784-2889; Fax: 787-261-2911.
Res.: Ave. Los Dominicos, Esquina Dr. Sanchez Cardona, Levittown, 00950.

Trujillo Alto

1—Exaltacion de la Santa Cruz (1801) Rev. Carlos Alberto Contreras Tribaldo; Deacons Domingo Vargas; Cesar Guiven.
Mailing Address: Box 1808, 00977-1808.
Res.: J. Diaz St., #515, frente a la Plaza de Recreo, 00977. Tel: 787-761-0507; Fax: 787-761-0507.
Catechesis/Religious Program—Students 51.

2—Gruta de Lourdes (1975) Rev. Msgr. Fernando Benicio Felices Sánchez; Deacon Pablo Torres.
Mailing Address: P.O. Box 1081, 00977-1081. Email: grutadelourdes1925@yahoo.com. Web: lagrutadelourdes.org.
Res.: Santuario, Gruta de Lourdes, Carretera 876 Km. 1.7, Barrio Cuevas, 00977. Tel: 787-761-0571; Fax: 787-761-0571.

3—Maria Llena de Gracia (1997) Rev. Franco Gutierrez (Spain).
Mailing Address: P.O. Box 1618, 00977-1618. Tel: 787-283-0364.
Res.: Urb. Rincon Espanol, Calle 1, Esq. Calle 4, 00977.

4—San Bartolome (1985) Rev. Rafael Delgado-Diaz, O.P.; Deacon Alberto Gomez.
Mailing Address & Res.: Urb. Ciudad Universitaria, X-1 Calle 16, 00976. Tel: 787-755-0120.

5—San Francisco de Asis (1992) Rev. David Vargas Grajales; Deacons Hector Rivera; Alfredo Aponte; William Rios.
Mailing Address: P.O. Box 1316, 00977-1316.
Res.: Carr. #181 R-852, Bo.Quelseada Negrito, Quebrada Negrito, 00977. Tel: 787-305-0660.
Mission—Espiritu Santo Bo. Kennedy Hills, Carretera 181 Km. 10.
Mission—San Jose de la Montana Carretera #181 R-851, Bo. Sabana.
Mission—La Inmaculada Concepcion Bo. Talanco, Carretera #181 R-852.

6—San Judas Tadeo (1980) Rev. Miguel Pons; Deacons Jose Baez; Jose Ramon Oliveras.
Mailing Address: Apartado 1535, 00977-1535.
Res.: Calle 7, Esq. 8, Urbanizacion El Conquistador, 00977-1535. Tel: 787-755-5993.
Catechesis/Religious Program—Students 75.
Mission—El Divino Pastor Carretera 844 Km. 0.2, Parcelas Carraizo, Trujillo Alto Co. 00760.
Mission—Ntra. Sra. del Carmen Carretera 175, Bo. Carraizo Alto, Trujillo Alto Co. 00760.

7—San Pio X (1971) Rev. Alberto Lopez; Deacons Julio Sanchez; Jose I. Bustillo; Jorge Montanez.
Mailing Address: St. Just, P.O. Box 631, 00978.
Res.: Carretera 848, K-1.4, Bo. Sain Just, 00978. Tel: 787-761-5040. Email: alfpiox2002@yahoo.com; sanpiox2010@yahoo.com.
Mission—N. Sra. del Rosario Calle Lirio, Esq. Orquidea, Urb. Round Hill, Rio Piedras, San Juan Co. 00923.

Chaplains of Public Institutions

Santurce. *Ashford Presbyterian Community Hospital*, 1451 Ave. Ashford, Condado, 00940. Tel: 787-725-8820; 787-724-8320; 787-722-5765. Rev. Msgr. Antonio Jose Vazquez Colon.
Doctors Community Hospital, 1395 Calle San Rafael, 00940. Tel: 787-723-2950. Rev. Victor Aurelio Vargas Galan. Tel: 787-723-5998.
Hospital Del Nino San Jorge, 255 Calle San Jorge, 00940. Tel: 787-727-1000. Rev. Olin Pierre Louis. Tel: 787-722-4158.
Hospital Pavia-Santurce, 1462 Calle Asia, 00940. Tel: 787-727-6060. Rev. Evaristo Oliveras, C.M. Tel: 787-727-3963.

Resident Chaplains:
Rev.—
Martinez, Danilo

On Duty Outside the Archdiocese:
Revs.—
Alecio-Rodriguez, Freddy (Sabbatical)
Del Valle, Tomas
McCoy, Floyd, Lajas, P.R.
Pierino, Vicente, U.S. Dept. of Justice, Coleman, FL.
Roldan, Juan, Caguas, P.R.
Sutil, Florencio
Torres Graciani, Ivan, Rochester, NY.

Graduate Studies:
Rev.—
Hernandez Ralat, Edwin, Rome, Italy.

Military Services:
Revs.—
Gomez-Baca, Walter S., (Air Force)
Perez Vazquez, Juan De La Cruz, (Army)
Sanchez, Alejandro, National Guard
Tirado, Orlando, C.M., (Air Force)

Awaiting Assignment:
Rev.—
Betancourt Ramirez, Jorge

Retired:
Rev. Msgrs.—
Cruz, Remberto
Maisonet-Ortiz, Tomas
Revs.—
Candela, Rafael
Coroztieta, Jose Madoz
Cruz, Gilbert J. (Spain)
Cruz Gonzalez, Gil
De Carlo Mena, Francisco
Diaz, Alvaro
Fuentes Rodriguez, Jose
Gonzalez Chao, Luis
Quinones-Rivera, Leoncio
Ramos, Victoriano
Sanz, Florentino (Spain)

Permanent Deacons:
Aguilera-Casiano, Jose Rafael
Alicea Rivera, Angel L.
Amador Melendez, Luis F.
Andino Cintron, Virgilio
Andino Santos, Manuel
Aponte Diaz, Alfredo
Araya Brenes, Rafael F.
Arroyo Acevedo, Americo
Avila Rodriguez, Cesar
Baez Cotto, Pedro J.
Baez Navarro, Jose
Berrios Berrios, Ildefonso
Birriel Rodriguez, Jose
Caban, Vicente
Carmona, Eduardo Figueroa
Castillo Lopez, Jose M.
Collazo Montalvo, Felipe
Colon Colon, Rafael
Colon Febres, Ismael
Colon Hernandez, Ramon L.
Colon Rivera, Francisco
Comulada Pabon, Gerardo
Cordero Mercado, Luis
Cosme Varela, Nicomedes
Costa, Pedro Tomas
Cruz De Choudens, Hector M.
Cruz Ortiz, Francisco
Cruz Trinidad, Jose Lionel
Cruz Vasquez, Ramon Jose
Cuevas Nieves, Gregorio
D'Auria, Ricardo
De Jesus Robles, Filiberty
De La Sota Pumarejo, Miguel
De Leon Sanchez, Hilario
De Varona Juarez, Abel
Del Rio Ortiz, Luis Orlando
Del Rio Pitre, Luis
Del Valle Gonzalez, Reinaldo
Diaz Miranda, Ernie P.
Diaz Rivera, Jose
Diaz Rosa, Santiago
Diaz Sifonte, Agapito
Domenech, Bienvenido
Dominguez, Ivan
Echegaray Martinez, Luis
Encarnacion Torres, Jorge
Estrada Galarza, Martin
Figueroa Acevedo, Andres
Figueroa Carrasquillo, Raul
Figueroa Sanchez, Juan
Franco Torres, Porfirio
Gierbolini Santiago, Francisco
Gomez Maldonado, Alberto
Gonzalez Reyes, Ruben
Gonzalez Rosario, Pablo
Gonzalez Rosario, Pedro
Gonzalez Segarra, George
Guijarro del Corzo, Gregory A.
Guiven Flores, Cesar H.
Henriquez Rodriguez, David A.
Hernandez, German
Hernandez Adorno, Francisco
Hernandez Hernandez, Marino
Hernandez Jorge, Jose A.
Hernandez Velez, Luis F.
Irene Vargas, Pablo
Jaca Hernandez, Eusebio
LaSanta Arroyo, Vicente
Laureano Molina, Enrique
Laureano Rivera, Juan
Longueira, Ricardo
Lopez Collazo, Jesus
Loyola Zayas, Angel A.
Lugo Lugo, Euripides
Lugo Soto, Benito
Marin Mingaro, Louis
Marrero Nieves, Miguel A.
Martinez Duran, Ricardo L.
Martinez Pacini, Francisco
Martinez Santiago, Candido
Medina Rivera, Luis A.
Mejias Nunez, Gilberto
Melendez Lozano, Juan R.
Mendez Santiago, Miguel
Mendia Colon, Roberto
Mercado Vila, Nicanor
Merced De La Paz, Victor
Merino Raposo, Latino
Miranda Mercado, Anselmo
Montes Quevedo, Luis J.
Morales Gonzalez, Jose A.
Morales Rodriguez, Carlos R.
Narvaez Hernandez, Jose E.

Narvaez Santiago, Efrain
Navedo Rodriguez, Luis A.
Negron Santana, Hector
Nieves Vazquez, Santos
Nunez, Quinones Pedro Arcadio
O'Neill Rosario, Luis R.
Oquendo Serrano, Angel
Orozco Carrasquillo, Gaspar
Ortiz Alvarado, Justo
Ortiz Collazo, Francisco
Ortiz Core, Ramon L.
Ortiz Rodriguez, Jacinto
Oyola Figueroa, Angel L.
Pabon Hernandez, Angel R.
Pabon Molina, Angel A.
Pacheco Diaz, Jose C.
Pappeterra Arthur, Jose A.
Pedro, Claudio Flores
Pena Gonzalez, Jose
Perez Bracero, Jose R.
Perez Del Valle, Juan B.
Perez Fuentes, Raul
Perez Gonzalez, Ignacio
Perez Guadalupe, Jose
Ramirez Abreu, Tomas
Ramos Rodriguez, Ramon L.
Reyes Anciano, Humberto
Reyes Crespo, Rafael
Reyes Matos, Manuel
Reyes Torres, Victor M.
Rios Aponte, William
Rios Arroyo, Jose M.
Rivera Albino, Luis
Rivera Alequin, Ulpiano H.
Rivera Baez, Eugenio
Rivera Collazo, Angel
Rivera De Jesus, Efigenio
Rivera Diaz, Hector R.
Rivera Fuentes, Jorge L.
Rivera Garcia, Edwin
Rivera Martinez, Carlos
Rivera Mojica, Jose D.
Rivera Negron, Ernesto
Rivera Rios, Cristobal
Rivera Rivera, Ramon L.
Rivera Rodriguez, Presbitero
Rodriguez Acevedo, Ramon
Rodriguez Melendez, Orlando
Rodriguez Rodriguez, Wilfredo
Rodriguez Serrano, William
Roman Del Valle, Miguel A.
Roman Maldonado, Jose M.
Roman Maldonado, Miguel A.
Rosado Yambo, Martin
Sanabria Lopez, Rafael
Sanchez Acosta, Oscar
Sanchez Ortiz, Julio
Santamarina Dorta, Omar
Santiago, Ramon C.
Santiago Rivera, LaTorre
Santos Negron, Marcos A.
Soto Miranda, Nelson
Suarez, Ibrahim
Suarez Molina, Israel
Toro Toro, Obed E.
Torres Acevedo, Pablo L.
Torres Burgos, Miguel A.
Torres Diaz, Eugenio
Torres Irizarry, Jose
Torres Rodriguez, Dionilo
Torres Torres, Jose A.
Totti Lugo, Benjamin
Trujillo Cardona, Gerardo
Ubarri Mestres, Juan
Valladares Almodovar, Milton
Vargas Ramos, Domingo
Vazquez Garcia, Luis A.
Vazquez Rosario, Noel A.
Vega Vega, Jose P.
Veguilla Colon, Victor
Velazquez Gonzalez, Jose L.
Velazquez Reyes, Rafael
Velez Roman, Miguel
Villamil Marrero, Fco. E.

INSTITUTIONS LOCATED IN THE ARCHDIOCESE

[A] COLLEGES & UNIVERSITIES

SAN JUAN. *Sacred Heart University*, Calle Rosales esq. San Antonio, Parada 26 1/2, Santurce, 00940. P.O. Box 12383, 00914-0383. Tel: 787-728-1515. Email: jjrivera@sagrado.edu. Web: www.sagrado.edu.
The University has the following Departments and Programs: Departments of Communications, Humanities, Business Administration, Education, Natural Sciences and Social Sciences. The Graduate Programs include: Masters of Business Administration in Management of Systems Information, Masters of Arts & Communications, Masters of Art & Education, Masters of Occupational Nursing, Medical Technology Certificate. Faculty 136; Total Enrollment 5,330.
Governing Board: Mr. Alberto Paraccini, Pres. Bd. of Trustees; Dr. Jose Jaime Rivera, Pres.; Dr. Lydia Espinet, Dean Academic Affairs; Mr. Jose L. Ricci Jr., Dean Admissions; Sr. Sororro Julia, Dean Devel.; Pedro Fraile, Dean Student Affairs; Dr. Isabel Yamin, Dir. Humanities; Carmen Garcia, Dir. Communications; Adalexis Rios, Dir. Educ.; Arturo Figueroa, Dir. Business Admin.; Dr. Francisco Fereer, Dir. Natural Sciences; Fernando Medina, Dir. Social Sciences; Hylsa Silva Janer, License & Legal Counsel; Ms. Mildred Pineiro, Registrar; Mr. Luis A. Quiles, Dir. Student Financial Aid; Rev. Rafael Rodríguez, S.J., Dir. Campus Ministry.

BAYAMON. *Bayamon Central University*, Avenida Zaya Verde, Bo. Hato Tejas, P.O. Box 1725, 00960-1725. Tel: 787-786-3030; Fax: 787-785-4365. Email: pbreyes@ucb.pr. Web: ucb.edu.pr. The University has the following Departments and Programs: Humanities; Business Administration; Natural Sciences; Education; Graduate Studies; Adult Education Program; Student Support Services; Upward Bound. Lay Teachers 60; Total Enrollment 3,028.
Governing Board: Rev. Mario Rodriguez-Leon, Pres. Council of Founders; C.P.A. Ismael Sanchez-Rivera, Pres. Bd. of Trustees.
Administration: Dr. Blanca Berio, Dean Academic Affairs; Mr. Mario Medina, Dean Admin. & Finances; Mr. Yanius Alvarado, Dean Student Affairs; Dr. Modesto Fernandez, Dir. Humanities; Dr. Nydia Cohen, Dir. Education; Dr. William A. Soler, Prof. & Dir. Natural Sciences; Mr. Pedro Bermudez, Dir. Institutional Devel.; Mr. Enrique Arias, Esq., Legal Counsel; Angela Ramos, Dir. Human Resources; Mr. Victor Colon, Registrar; Mrs. Christine Hernandez, Dir. Admissions; Ms. Vivian Cintron, Dir. Student Financial Aid; Ms. Ana Medina, Dir. Academic Resource Ctr.
Faculty: Revs. Felix A.P. Struik, O.P. (Holland); Luis Espinel, O.P.; Angel Diaz Caceres; Angel Dario Carrero, O.F.M.; Manuel Soler Pala, M.SS.CC.; Victor Ortiz; Antonio Gonzalez Pola.

GUAYNABO. *ISTEPA (Instituto Superior de Teologia y Pastoral)*, Urb. Caparra Heights, 1563 Calle Encarnacion, 00920. Tel: 787-200-6891; Fax: 787-731-6305. Rev. Msgr. Francisco Medina Santos, Rector. (Theology, Biblical and Pastoral courses for lay ministers and Deacons) Priests 3; Deacons 6; Lay Teachers 4; Students 745.

[B] ELEMENTARY & HIGH SCHOOLS

SAN JUAN. *Academia Perpetuo Socorro*, (Grades K-12), 704 Calle Jose Martí, 00907-3227. Tel: 787-721-4540 (H.S.); 787-724-8104 (Elem.); Fax: 787-723-4550 (H.S.); 787-725-8104 (Elem.). Email: perpetuo@perpetuo.org. Carlos Quintana Puente, Dir.; Mr. E. Morales, Prin. (High School); Vanessa Monserrate, Prin. (Elem.); Sr. Mary Ellen Gemmell, C.S.F.N., Prin. Priests 1; Lay Teachers 102; Total Enrollment 1,312.

Academia San Ignacio de Loyola, 1908 Calle Narciso, Urb. Santa Maria, 00927-6716. Tel: 787-765-8190; Fax: 787-765-3635. Email: academia@asiloyola.org. Web: www.asiloyola.org. Rev. Bandilio Guzman, S.J., Dir.; Blanca I. Esteves, Ed.D., Asst. Dir.; Glorimar Soegaard, Prin.; Adela Sabater, Librarian. Lay Teachers 53; Total Enrollment 651.

Academia Santa Monica (1996) (Grades PreK-12), Ave. Fernandez Juncos, 00908. Tel: 787-723-2573; 787-723-3992; Fax: 787-723-3992. Email: director@smonica.org; raulrivera-nieves-principal.asm@gmail.com. Web: www.smonica.org. P.O. Box 13726, 00908-3726. Email: santamonicapr@gmail.com. J. Oscar Jimenez, Dir.; Carmen Rodriguez, Prin.; Raul Rivere Nieves, Prin.; Shaila E. Alvira, Librarian. Lay Teachers 33; Students 379.

Colegio Angeles Custodios, Urb San Jose #13 Calle Sicilia, 00923. Tel: 787-763-3829; Fax: 787-764-9496. Email: angelescustodios1954@gmail.com. Maria Aranzazu Labak, Dir.; Sr. Luis Roberto Rivera Cepeda, Prin.; Rev. Rogelio Salazar-Valero (Mexico); Soamy Velez Perez, Librarian. Students (K-8) 81; Students (9-12) 101.

Colegio Calasanz, Montecarlo Ave., 00929-0067. Tel: 787-750-2500; Fax: 787-257-0450. Email: calasanzpr@cc-rpi.org. P.O. Box 29067, 00929-0067. Revs. Juan L. Cabrerizo, Sch.P. (Spain); Jesus Marques, Sch.P. (Spain), Campus Min.; Agustin Lopez, Sch.P. (Spain), Campus Univ.; Maritere del Rio, Counselor; Ana Celia Santos, Prin. (High School); Glenda Laureano, Prin. (Elementary); Ruben Tirado, Librarian. Priests 3; Lay Teachers 28; Total Enrollment 431.

Colegio Corazon De Maria (Archdiocesan School), Calle Ferrer y Ferrer, Urb. Santiago Igesias, 00922. Tel: 787-783-3275; Fax: 787-774-5682. Mailing Address: P.O. Box 70359, 00936-0359. Priests 1; Lay Teachers 18; Students 348.

Colegio Espiritu Santo, Pachín Marín Esq. Suiza St., 00917. Tel: 787-754-0490; Fax: 787-754-7154. P.O. Box 191715, 00917-1715. Rev. Msgr. Valeriano Miguélez (Spain), Dir.; Mrs. Milagros Zurkowsky, Prin.; Mrs. Elena Rivera, Academic Prin.; Mrs. Olga D. Torres, Librarian; Mrs. Maria I. Orta. Lay Teachers 37; Students 504.

Colegio Maria Auxiliadora, 2273 Eduardo Conde, 00915. Tel: 787-726-8288; Fax: 787-727-6497. Email: smmmfma@hotmail.com. Sr. Magna M. Martinez, F.M.A., Prin.; Elba Varela, Librarian. Sisters 8; Lay Teachers 25; Students 348.

Colegio Nuestra Senora de Guadalupe, 19 N.E. St. #1, Puerto Nuevo, 00920. Tel: 787-782-0330; Fax: 787-782-0454. P.O. Box 364125, 00936-4125. P. Neil Macaulay, Dir.; Mrs. Genevieve Zayas, Prin.; Teresita Hernández, Vice Prin.; Jackeline Wys, Librarian. Lay Teachers 35; Students 599.

Colegio Nuestra Senora de Lourdes, (Grades PreK-12), 1050 Demetrio O'Daly, Country Club, 00924. Tel: 787-769-6284; 787-769-6275; Fax: 787-750-7805; 787-757-1245. P.O. Box 29193, 65 INF Station, 00929-0193. Roxanna Vázquez, Dir. & Prin.; Melissa Carrera, Vice Prin. High School; Marisol Quinones, Librarian; Nilsa Menéndes, Librarian. Lay Teachers 45; Students 688.

Colegio Nuestra Senora Del Carmen, R.R. 2, Box 15, 00926-9701. Tel: 787-761-8010; Fax: 787-748-2505. Email: melisea@coquí.net. Sisters Arlyn Medina Vazquez, Dir.; Elizabeth Andino, Prin.; Lissette Torres, Prin.; Liliana Santiago, Prin. Sisters 8; Lay Teachers 38; Students 510.

Colegio Reina De Los Angeles, Urb. Villa Andalucia, M19 Calle Frontera, 00926-2304. Tel: 787-761-7455; Fax: 787-761-7440. Email: colegio1972reina@gmail.com. Juana F. Gomez Moya, Dir.; Ana Román, Registrar. Sisters 3; Lay Teachers 12; Students 208.

Colegio San Ignacio de Loyola, Urb. Santa Maria, 1940 Calle Sauco, 00927-6718. Tel: 787-765-3814; Fax: 787-758-4145. Rev. Mario Alberto Torres, S.J., Dir.; Mr. Rafael Fernandez, Prin. Priests 3; Students 715.

Colegio San Vicente de Paul, 709 Bolivar St., 00910. Tel: 787-727-4271; Fax: 787-728-2263. P.O. Box 8699, Fernández Juncos Sta., 00910-8699. Rev. Evaristo Oliveras, C.M., Dir.; Isabel Casanas, Prin.; Marina Perez, Librarian; Emilio Roldan, Dean Discipline; Maria del C. Cordova, Counselor. Operated by: Congregacion de la Misión de San Vincente de Paúl, Inc. (Padres Paúles) Lay Teachers 27; Students 504.

Colegio Santo Domingo Savio, Ave. Gilberto Monroig 2278, 00916. Tel: 787-728-2175; Fax: 787-982-2903. P.O. Box 14125, Bo. Obrero Sta., 00916-4125. P. Miguel A. Rivera Borges, Dir.; P. Lorenzo Ruiz Victoria, Admin. Lay Teachers 1.

Nuestra Senora De Belen (Archdiocesan School), P.O. Box 10845, 00922-0845. Tel: 787-792-3115; Fax: 787-781-4920. Email: colegiobelen11@yahoo.com. Eleonor Marrero, Prin. (Elementary); Eduardo Rodríguez, Prin. (High School); Mayra Mendez Barreto, Dir. Lay Teachers 49; Students 752.

Nuestra Senora de la Altagracia (Archdiocesan School), P.O. Box 29493, 00929-0493. Tel: 787-763-7755; Fax: 787-756-5195. Rev. Gabriel M. Torres; Mr. Angel Castillo, Dir. Students 375.

San Jorge (Archdiocesan School), 1701 Colon St., 00911-2041. Tel: 787-722-3182; Fax: 787-725-4580. Email: sanjorge@iname.com. Mrs. Maritza Rosario, Prin.; Mrs. Vanesa Valdes, Dir. Lay Teachers 70; Students 681.

BAYAMON. *Academia Maria Reina*, Urb. College Park, Glasgow #1879, 00921-4899. Tel: 787-764-0690; Fax: 787-282-7556. Sr. Judith Burchyns, C.S.J., Pres.; Rita Hernández, Prin.; Lucila Aponte, Librarian. Catholic Girls School. Sisters 1; Lay Teachers 80; Students 626.

Academia Santa Maria del Camino, (Grades PreSchool-8), P.O. Box 4228, Bayamón Gardens Station, 00958-1218. Tel: 787-780-5770; Fax: 787-785-7373. Sr. Lucy del Blanco, O.S.R., Dir.; Margarita Montesinos Ortiz, Prin.; Myrna Lee Román Miró, Librarian. Sisters 1; Lay Teachers 16; Students 231.

Colegio Beato Carlos Manuel Rodriguez, 3000 Jazmin, Urb.Lomas Verdes, 00956. Tel: 787-798-5260; 787-798-2329; 787-798-2747; Fax: 787-787-2620. Email: pjmartinez@cbcbay.org. Web: colegiobeatocmr.wordpress.com. P.O. Box 4225, 00956. P. Luis Brioso, Dir. & Prin.; Mrs. Maria Luisa M. Medina, Prin.; Jaime Solivan, Librarian. Students 400.

Colegio Ntra. Sra. del Rosario, Calle 5, AA-7, Rep.

Valencia, 00659. Tel: 787-798-5100; Fax: 787-269-7551. Sr. Ma. Ana Jimenez Maldonado, O.P., Dir.; Elba I. Soto, Prin. Students 300.

Colegio Santa Rosa, P.O. Box 6032, 00960. Tel: 787-785-1195 (H.S.); 787-785-0381 (Elem.); Fax: 787-740-0115 (H.S.); 787-785-3791 (Elem.). Neymi A. Aponte, Prin. (High School); Mrs. Nilsa Gonzales, Prin. (Elementary). Priests 1; Lay Teachers 30; Total Enrollment 976.

Santo Tomas de Aquino, P.O. Box 1557, 00960-1557. Tel: 787-785-2530 (High School); 787-785-3066 (Elementary); Fax: 787-785-5550 (H.S.); 787-780-8600 (Elem.). Lay Teachers 48; Students 1,311.

P.O. Box 4098, 00958-1098. Ricardo Oquendo, Elementary Prin.; Jannette Cintron, High School Prin.

CAROLINA. *Academia Del Carmen*, Monte Membrillo esq., Monte Britton, Lomas de Carolina, 00987. Tel: 787-757-4454; Fax: 787-762-6656. Email: academiadelcarmen@gmail.com. Web: academiadelcarmen.com; hlt:billacademiasagradocorazon. P.O. Box 299, 00986-0299. Mrs. Aitza Vázquez-Padilla, Subdirector (Elem. & High School); Mrs. Gladymir Montanez, Librarian. Priests 1; Lay Teachers 19; Total Enrollment 20.

Colegio Maria Auxiliadora, Box 7770, 00986-7770. Tel: 787-762-0350; 787-768-6924; Fax: 787-257-3760. Web: cma-car.org. Rosa Perez, Dir. Priests 1; Lay Teachers 75; Students 962.

Colegio Santa Gema, Galicia Ave., Vistamar, 00983. Tel: 787-768-3082; Fax: 787-750-3090. P.O. Box 2789, 00984-2789. Mrs. Lilia Luna de Anaya, Prin.; Wanda Sánchez, Librarian. Lay Teachers 50; Students 895.

GUAYNABO. *Colegio Marista*, Alturas de Torrimar #6 Calle Marcelino Champagnat, 00969-3251. Tel: 787-720-2186; 787-720-2187; Fax: 787-720-7020. Email: marista1@prtc.net. Bro. Ricardo Herrero, Dir.; Luz D. Romero, Prin.; Awilda Díaz, Librarian. Priests 1; Brothers 7; Lay Teachers 70; Students 1,215.

Colegio Sagrados Corazones, P.O. Box 3902, 00970-3902. Tel: 787-720-2585; Fax: 787-720-6035. Edith N. Casiano, Dir. Lay Teachers 43; Students 673.

Colegio San Pedro Martir, Alpierre (Final), 00969. Tel: 787-720-2219; Fax: 787-272-8770. P.O. Box 2560, 00970-2560. Rev. Msgr. Mario Guijarro, Dir.; Mrs. Ivonne D. Carlo, Prin. Sisters 1; Lay Teachers 28; Students 357.

Preescolar San Juan Evangelista, (Grades PreSchool), Urb. Torrimar, JA-5 Calle Church Hill, 00966-3109. Tel: 787-781-5325; Fax: 787-793-8076. Lourdes Rodríguez, Administrative Dir.; Flor María Lugo, Prin. Lay Teachers 33; Students 270.

HATO REY. *Colegio Lourdes*, 87 Mayaguez St., 00917. Tel: 787-767-6106; 787-756-5436; Fax: 787-767-5282. Email: clourdes@coqui.net. Web: colegiolourdes.net. P.O. Box 190847, 00919-0847. Sr. Maria Paz Asiain, O.P., Dir.; Thalia Lopez, Prin.; Josefina Arce, Librarian. Sisters 5; Lay Teachers 45; Students 850.

Colegio Nuestra Senora de La Merced, Calle Sargento Luis Medina #374, 00936. Tel: 787-765-7342; 787-754-1162; Fax: 787-765-3970. P.O. Box 364048, 00936-4048. William Súarez, Dir.; Mrs. Coville Auoyo, Prin.; Marina Azofra, Librarian. Lay Teachers 35; Students 376.

RIO PIEDRAS. *Colegio Mater Salvatoris*, Carretera 838 Km 4.8 de Rio Piedras Caguas, 00926-9690. Tel: 787-765-0130; Fax: 787-765-8161. R.R. 3 Box 3080, 00926-9601. Sisters 6; Lay Teachers 52; Students 905.

Colegio Nuestra Senora De La Providencia (Girls), Ave. San Ignacio #1358, Urb. Altamesa, 00921. Tel: 787-781-7506; 787-782-6344; Fax: 787-792-7888. Email: zegri@coqui.net. Mailing Address: P.O. Box 11610, 00922-1610. Sr. Lourdes Martínez, Prin. Mercedarian Sisters. Priests 1; Sisters 4; Lay Teachers 48; Students 950.

Colegio Sagrado Corazon de Jesus, (Grades PreK-8), University Gardesn, Rio Piedras, 215 Calle Palma Real, 00927-4826. Tel: 787-765-9430; Fax: 787-765-5267. Sr. Mary Andreen Rusin, O.S.F., Prin. Students 790.

Colegio San Jose, (Grades 7-12), Box 21300, 00928-1300. Tel: 787-751-8177; Fax: 866-955-7644. Email: sanjose@csj-rpi.org. Web: www.csj-rpi.org. Calle Paz Esq. Los Marianistas, 00925. Bro. Francisco T. Gonzalez, S.M., M.D., Dir. & Prin.; Alma Flores, Librarian. Priests 7; Brothers 5; Lay Teachers 38; Students 557.

SANTURCE. *Academia Sagrado Corazon, Fernandez Juncos Sta.*, Box 11368, 00910. Tel: 787-721-3300; Fax: 787-725-1865. Email: nowita@prtc.net. Rev. Francisco Javier Quinones, Spiritual Dir.; Mrs. Gladys Vélez, Prin.; Paulina Quintero, Librarian. Priests 1; Lay Teachers 25; Students 294.

Colegio de La Inmaculada, 1711 Ponce de Leon Ave. Stop 26, 00909-1997. Tel: 787-727-6673; Fax: 787-728-7768. Mrs. María Rivera de Modesto, Dir.; Mary A. Acosta Perez, Prin.; Maria Tosta Perez, Librarian. Sisters 5; Lay Teachers 30; Students 410.

Colegio Sagrada Familia (Archdiocesan School), Urb. Llorens Torres #2059, Calle Loiza, 00913. Tel: 787-726-1742; Fax: 787-726-0718. Ines Y. Elias, Prin.; Vanessa Valdes, Dir. Lay Teachers 6; Students 164.

Colegio San Juan Bosco, Carpenter Rd., Constitucion Santos Elena, 00915. Tel: 787-726-1995; Fax: 787-268-1869. Mailing Address: P.O. Box 14367, 00916-4367. Rev. Nicolas Navarro, S.D.B., Dir.; Mrs. Lissette M. Ruiz. Priests 2; Religious 15; Lay Teachers 12; Students 288.

TRUJILLO ALTO. *Santa Cruz* (Archdiocesan School), Dr. Fernandez St., #203, 00977. Tel: 787-761-1100; Fax: 787-755-3065. Mailing Address: P.O. Box 1809, 00977-1809. Rev. Carlos Alberto Contreras Tribaldo, Dir.; Mrs. Ana L. Monzon de Matos, Prin. Sisters 1; Lay Teachers 25; Students 371.

[C] SPECIAL SCHOOLS AND SEMINARIES

SAN JUAN. *Instituto Psicopedagogico De P.R.*, P.O. Box 363744, 00936-3744. Tel: 787-783-3678; 787-783-5431; Fax: 787-792-3610. Email: ippr@coqui.net. Mr. Roberto Vazquez, Prin. Bed Capacity 134; Patients Assisted Annually 134.

BAYAMON. *Casa Mision Claret* (Claretians), R.R. 12, Box 10131, Bo. Buena Vista, 00956. Tel: 787-797-8230.

Convento Ntra-Sra del Rosario (Dominicans), P.O. Box 1968, 00960. Tel: 787-785-6542; 787-786-4508; Fax: 787-798-2712. Web: dominicospr.com.

Seminario Agustiniano Sto. Tomas De Villanueva, Carretera 830 km 5.1, Camino Los Muleros, Barrio Santaolaya, 00961. P.O. Box 3948, 00958. Tel: 787-797-0708; Fax: 787-797-9953. Email: tomasdevillanuevapr@yahoo.es. Revs. Mario Gonzalez, O.S.A. (Spain), Prior; Carlos Cordero, O.S.A. (Augustinians) Priests 3; Brothers 1.

Seminario Misionero del Espiritu Santo (Holy Spirit Fathers), Calle Zaya Verde #44-A, Hato Tejas, 00959. Tel: 787-786-8231; Fax: 787-787-2398. Email: opgcssp@caribe.net. Rev. Osvaldo Perez Gonzalez, C.S.Sp., M.Div., Prin. Supr.

CATANO. *Prenoviciado Salesiano* (Don Bosco Salesians), Ave. Flor Del Valle, Bloque BB #108, Urb. Las Vegas, 00962. Tel: 787-275-1921; Fax: 787-788-8163. Email: sanfasal@coqui.net. P.O. Box 567, 00963-8163. Rev. Adan Marrero, S.D.B.

DORADO. *Estudiantado Pasionista* (Passionists), Carretera 695 km. 3.3, Sector Los Puertos, Barrio Higuillar, 00646. Tel: 787-278-0517. P.O. Box 593, 00646-0593. Rev. Ramon Gurtubay, C.P. (Spain), Supr. Priests 2; Students 6.

RIO PIEDRAS. *Colegio San Antonio*, P.O. Box 21350, 00928-1350. Tel: 787-764-0090; Fax: 787-763-7592. Email: helenperezdiaz@hotmail.com. Bro. Jorge M. Macias, O.F.M.Cap., Dir.; Minerva Feliciano, Prin. (Elementary School); Nayda Jimenez, Librarian (Intermediate & High School); Annie Rivera, Librarian (Elementary School); Mrs. Marlee Feliu; Katherine Gibbs. Priests 2; Brothers 1; Sisters 3; Lay Teachers 94.

Fraternidad San Antonio (Capuchin Postnovitiate) , P.O. Box 25177, 00928. Rev. Roberto Martinez, O.F.M.Cap., Guardian; Bros. Cecilio Figueroa; German Quinones; Orlando Reyes; Elmig M. Soto, O.F.M.Cap. Priests 4; Brothers 4. In Res. Rev. Malachy Clune, O.P. (Ireland).

Fraternidad Santa Maria de Los Angeles (Centro Capuchins), Care.877 Km.1 Hm 6, 00936. Tel: 787-761-8060; 787-761-8410; Fax: 787-293-1682. Aptdo. 29882, 00929-0882. Rev. Jose Fernando Irizzary, O.F.M.Cap., Dir.; Bro. Jaime Perez Munoz, O.F.M.Cap.

Seminario Mayor Regional San Juan Bautista (Diocesan), Ave. De Diego No. 930, Urb. La Riviera, 00922-1714. Tel: 787-273-8090; 787-783-0645; Fax: 787-783-0645. Email: seminary@coqui.net. P.O. Box 11714, 00922-1714. Rev. Juan Luis Negron, Rector; Rev. Msgr. Ivan L. Huertas-Colon, Vice Rector; Rev. Tomas Gonzalez. Priests 9; Brothers 1; Lay Teachers 7; Total Staff 17.

SANTUCE. *Seminario San Vicente De Paul* (Vincentians) , C. Victoria 1658, Pda. 24, Santurce, 00940. Tel: 787-727-4110. P.O. Box 19119, 00910. Priests 3; Brothers 4.

TOA BAJA. *Post-Noviciado San Jose Obrero* (Franciscans), Carretera 866 Km. 3.4, Sabana Seca, Sabana Seca, 00952. Tel: 787-795-3141. P.O. Box 173, Sabana Seca, 00952. Rev. Eddie Caro, O.F.M., Rector.

[D] SPECIAL CENTERS

SAN JUAN. *Renovacion Conyugal dba Fundacion Fernando Martinez* 573 Calle Alverio, 00918. Tel: 787-751-6001; Fax: 787-766-1363. Email: renovacionpr@yahoo.com. Web: geocities.com/renovacionpr. Rev. Jorge Ambert, S.J., Dir.

Santa Ana Chapel Perpetual Adoration, Calle Tetuan 203, P.O. Box 9022145, 00902. Tel: 787-722-0861; Fax: 787-722-0861. Rev. Jose Emilio Cummings, Rector.

PUERTO NUEVO. *San Gabriel School For The Deaf*, Prolongacion Calle 19 NE, 00920. Tel: 787-783-3455; Fax: 787-781-3770. P.O. 360347, 00936-0347. Sr. Amparo Blasco, Dir.

RIO PIEDRAS. *Centro De Espiritualidad Ignaciana Pedro Arrupe (CEIPA)*, R.R. 10, Buzon 5348, 00926. Tel: 787-790-3557; Fax: 787-790-3162. Email: ceipapr@gmail.com; ceipa@ceipapr.org. Rev. Lawrence P. Searles, S.J., Dir.

Centro Universitario Catolico, 10 Mariana Bracetti St., 00925-2201. Tel: 787-763-5432; 787-767-3348; Fax: 787-296-3068. Email: elcuc2003@hotmail.com. Web: www.centrouniversitariocatolicocuc.org. Revs. Rafael Rodríguez, S.J., Dir.; Juan José Santiago, S.J., Coop.

[E] CLINICS, HEALTH CENTERS

SAN JUAN. *Casa La Providencia, Inc.* Drug Rehabilitation Center, P.O. Box 9020614, 00902-0614. Tel: 787-725-5358; Fax: 787-725-0058. Email: casalaprovidencia@hotmail.com. Web: casalaprovidenciapr.org. Sr. Maria Socorro Sandoval, Dir. Sisters Oblates of the Most Holy Redeemer 4; Bed Capacity 32; Total Assisted Annually 100; Total Staff 20.

Centro Medico de P.R., Calle 10 #1030, Puerto Nuevo, 00920. Apdo. 347, 00936. Tel: 787-763-7272. Revs. Antonio Jose Vazquez Colon (ARE), Vicario. Tel: 787-777-3535; 787-723-2240; Cell: 787-562-2065; Francisco Arana (Spain), Chap., Hospital Oncologico. Tel: 787-251-6466; Pedro Luis Zaballa, Chap., Hospital Universitario; Manuel Garcia (Spain), Chap. Hospital Municipal. Tel: 787-796-3418; Bartolome Vanrell, Chap., Hospital Cardiovascular. Tel: 787-740-3425; Paules, C.M., Hosp. Pavia, Santurce. Tel: 787-727-6060; Carlos D. Cruz-Davila, Doctor's Hosp. Tel: 787-723-5998; Francisco J. Marrodan, C.M. (Spain), Hosp. Auxilio Mutuo. Tel: 787-758-2000, Ext. 3070; Rev. Msgr. Valeriano Miguélez (Spain), Hosp. Pavia, Hato Rey. Tel: 787-754-0570; Revs. Hector Diaz, Hosp. Veteranos. Tel: 787-641-7582, Ext. 3350; Eddie Rivera Marzan; Jose Maria Solano Uribe, Hosp. Metropolitano. Tel: 787-782-4176; Rev. Agustinos, O.S.A. (Spain), Hosp. Regional, Bayamon. Tel: 787-786-8611; Deacons Jose R. Rivera, Hosp. Pediatrico. Tel: 787-475-7849; Andres Figueroa, Hosp. Pediatrico. Tel: 787-505-9973; Rev. Jesus Gonzalez, Hosp. San Pablo. Tel: 787-785-6874.

VA Medical Center, 10 Calle Casia, 00921-3200. Tel: 787-641-7582; 787-641-7575. Email: hrd198254@yahoo.com. Revs. Hector Diaz Estrada, Chap.; Eddie Rivera-Marzan, Chap. Bed Capacity 535.

BAYAMON. *Hospital Hermanos Melendez, Oficina de Administracion*, P.O. Box 306, 00960-0306. Tel: 787-785-6542. Email: normanchd@gmail.com.

Hospital Hima San Pablo 00960. Tel: 787-620-4747; 787-620-4762; Fax: 787-620-9273. *Oficina de Administracion*, P.O. Box 236, 00959-0236. Rev. Jesus Gonzalez, Chap. Tel: 787-785-6874.

Hospital Matilde Brenes, Oficina de Administracion, P.O. Box 2957, 00960-2957. Tel: 787-785-2381.

Hospital Universitario, Oficina de Administracion, Ave. Laurell, 00956. Tel: 787-785-8611. Dr. Ramon Ruiz Arnau, Dir.; Rev. Agustinos, O.S.A. (Spain), Chap.

CAROLINA. *Hospital Universitario de Puerto Rico, Oficina de Administracion*, P.O. Box 6021, 00984. Tel: 787-757-1800; Fax: 787-276-2205. Email: jatorres@hospital.org. Web: hospitalupr.org. Rev. Frank de la Rosa, Chap.

HATO REY. *Hospital Auxilio Mutuo* Tel: 787-758-2000, Ext. 3070; Fax: 787-771-7960. Web: www.auxiliomutuo.com. P.O. Box 1277, 00919. Rev. Francisco J. Marrodan, C.M. (Spain), Chap. Bed Capacity 591; Total Staff 1,230.

Hospital Pavia, Ave. Pone De Leon, 00917. Tel: 787-754-0570. *Oficina de Administracion*, P.O. Box 190828, 00919-0828. Rev. Msgr. Valeriano Miguélez (Spain).

RIO PIEDRAS. *Hospital del Maestro*, Calle Flamboyanes #218, Hyde Park, 00929. Tel: 787-763-8383. Rev. Antonio Jose Vazquez. Tel: 787-723-2240.

Hospital San Francisco 00926. Tel: 787-765-0606. *Oficina de Administracion*, P.O. Box 29025, 00929-0025. Rev. Capuchinos.

SANTURCE. *Doctor's Community Hospital* 00909. Tel: 787-999-7620; Fax: 787-725-2124. Email:

echevarria@dchpr.com. *Oficina de Administracion*, P.O. Box 11338, 00910. Rev. Carlos D. Cruz-Davila, Chap.

Hospital Pavia 00912. Tel: 787-727-3963. *Oficina de Administracion*, P.O. Box 11137, 00910-1137. Vincentian Fathers (Chaplains).

Hospital San Juan Capestrano, Rio Piedras, 00926. Tel: 787-625-2900; Fax: 787-760-6875. Email: laura.vargas@uhsinc.com. Web: sjcapestrano.com. *Oficina de Administracion*, RR2 Box 11, 00926. Total Staff 230; Total Assisted Annually 5,000; Bed Capacity 108.

San Jorge's Children Hospital 00912. Tel: 787-727-1000; Fax: 787-268-3610. Email: cruz.vivaldi@sanjorgechildrenshospital.com. Web: www.sanjorgechildrenshospital.com. *Oficina de Administracion*, P.O. Box 6308, 00914-6308. Rev. Olin Pierre Louis. Bed Capacity 125.

[F] HOMES AND RESIDENCES

SAN JUAN. *Casa La Providencia* (Drug Addicted Women), Calle Norzagaray #200, 00901. Tel: 787-725-5358; Fax: 787-725-0058. Email: casalaprovidencia@hotmail.com. P.O. Box 9020614, 00902-0614. Sr. Adela Dominguez, Dir. Total Staff 18; Patients Assisted Annually 71; Bed Capacity 32.

Centro De Orientacion Vocacional Nuestra Senora del Consuelo, Floral Park, 20 C. Matienzo Citron, 00919. Tel: 787-250-6323; Fax: 787-250-6323. Email: oblahchr@prte.net. Total Assisted Annually 60; Total Staff 8.

BAYAMON. *Hogar Del Nino "El Ave Maria Corp."* (For Abused Children), Carretera 861, km 2.0, Bo. Pajaros Americanos, 00957. Tel: 787-797-2382; 787-279-3003; Fax: 787-797-2382. Mailing Address: PMS 239, P.O. Box 607061, 00960-7061. Sr. Florencia Santos, Dir.

Hogar Escuela Sor Maria Rafaela (Girls with Problems), Carretera 871, km 1.0, Bo. El Volcan, Hato Tejas, 00961. Tel: 787-785-9517; 787-785-1125; Fax: 787-787-5324; 787-779-0449. Email: hogar.sormaria@gmail.com. P.O. Box 3024, PR 00960. Sr. Nelida Gonzalez, Dir.

Hogar Fatima (Girls), Ave. Santa Juanita Final, Camino Esteban Cruz, 00961. Fax: 787-780-9763. Email: fatima001@prttc.net. Web: www.osrhogarfatimainc.com. P.O. Box 4228, Bayamon Garden Sta., Bayamon, 00958-4228. Tel: 787-787-2580; Fax: 787-780-9763. Sr. Maria Saez, Dir. Patients Assisted Annually 39; Staff 18.

DORADO. *Santuario del Espiritu Santo*, Box 187, 00646-0187. Tel: 787-796-2798; Fax: 787-796-1359. Email: espiritanospr@gmail.com. Web: www.espiritanos.com. Revs. Cornelius T. McQuillan, C.S.Sp., Rector; Eduardo Caron, C.S.Sp.; Jose Orlando Camacho-Torres, C.S.Sp.

PUERTA DE TIERRA. *Asylum For The Aged and Infirm* (Hogar de Ntra. Sra. de la Providencia), Stop 5, Edif. 205, 00906-6571. Tel: 787-722-1331; 787-723-2419; 787-724-3574; Fax: 787-725-4308. Mailing Address: P.O. Box 9066571, 00906-6571. Sr. Gladys Rosario, Supr.; Rev. Efrain Lopez, Chap. Sisters of the Poor. Sisters 12; Patients Assisted Annually 207.

RIO PIEDRAS. *Centro N. Sra. de la Providencia* Sisters of Notre Dame., R.F.D. #2, Box 16T, 00928. Tel: 787-761-0273.

Centro Santa Luisa (1972) (Services for the Elderly), Carretera 842, Camino Los Romeros km 1.5, Bo. Caimito, 00926. Tel: 787-720-2764; Fax: 787-731-7795. Email: centrosantaluisa@yahoo.com. Web: www.geocities.com/centrosantaluisa. Mailing Address: R.R. 6 Box 9492, 00926-9492. Sr. Glenda Y. Rios, H.C., Dir. Patients Assisted Annually 100; Total Staff 9.

Hermanitas de los Ancianos Desamparados Hogar Santa Teresa Jornet de Caspey Inc., Cupey Alto, Ave. Las cumbres, Km. 14. 3, 00926. Tel: 787-761-5805; Fax: 787-755-5575. 181 Calle Teresa Jornet, 00926-7542. Sr. Angeles Garrido, Mother Supr.; Rev. Cecilio de la Cruz. Sisters of the Poor. Sisters 14; Bed Capacity 200; Residents 200; Total Staff 80.

Hogar Carmelitano Julian Bengochea Final (Elderly Retirement Hospice), Calle Julian Bengoechea Final, 00924. Tel: 787-769-6510; 787-769-3110; Fax: 787-768-1240. Sr. Maribelle Mejias Muniz, Admin. Carmelite Sisters (Spain). Bed Capacity 224; Patients Assisted Annually 167; Total Staff 91.

Hogares Rafaela Ibarra (Orphan or Abused Girls), Urb.San Jose 432 Calle Torrelaguna, 00923. Tel: 787-763-1204; Fax: 787-763-6266. Web: www.hogaresrafaelaybarra.com. 432 Calle Torrelaguna, 00923-1773. Sr. Julia Jose, Dir. Patients Assisted Annually 40; Staff 14.

SANTURCE. *Casa de Ninos Manuel Fernandez Juncos* (Orphans and Abused Boys) , Calle Villa Verde Esq. Refugio, Pda 11, Miramar, 00940. Tel: 787-724-2904; 787-725-6328; Fax: 787-724-0980. P.O. Box 9020163, 00902-0163. Revs. Candido Lizarraga, RR.T.C.; Francisco J. Arizcuren Rey; Deacon Pablo Osorio Carmona; Bros. Eliecer Balladares; Juan Manual González Fzgvieedo; Abner Irom Picon. Total Staff 22.

Politecnico Amigo (For School Dropout Boys), Calle Refugio #960, Pda II, 00940. Tel: 787-725-2059; Fax: 787-722-3436. Email: polam@prtc.net. P.O. Box 13204, 00908.

TOA ALTA. *Hogar Santisima Trinidad* (Drug Addiction Rehabilitation Home), Lote A y Lote B, km 7.0, Bo Mucarabones, Carr. 861, 00954. Tel: 787-799-6208; Fax: 787-799-1977. Email: trinita@prtc.net. PMB 326, P.O. Box 607061, Bayamon, 00960-7061. Rev. Pedro Gorena, O.SS.T. (Spain). Patients Assisted Annually 87; Total Staff 15.

TOA BAJA. *Hogar Divino Nino Jesus*, Carretera 854, Km. 3.5, 00949. Tel: 787-794-0020; Fax: 787-794-3124. Email: divinoninojesus@yahoo.es. P.O. Box 2464, 00951-2662. Julio Pacheco, Dir. (Detox and Tx Residencial)

[G] PERSONAL PRELATURES

GUAYNABO. *Opus Dei* (Prelature of the Holy Cross and Opus Dei), Region of Puerto Rico of the Prelature, Urb. Villa Caparra, #35 Calle A, 00966-2211. Tel: 787-783-6206; Fax: 787-783-1201. Email: pricoinf@coqui.net. Web: www.opusdei.org.pr. Rev. Msgr. Vicente Ariza, Ph.D., J.C.D., Regl. Vicar; Revs. Alfredo Gastalver; Gonzalo Diaz; Martin Llambias; Juan Aramendi; Ramon Encarnacion; Javier Bernaola; Justiniano Garcia.

[H] MONASTERIES AND RESIDENCES FOR PRIESTS AND BROTHERS

SAN JUAN. *The Capuchin Formation Trust of Puerto Rico*, c/o P.O. Box 25177, 00928-5177. Tel: 787-764-3090; Fax: 787-764-4070. Rev. Roberto Martinez, O.F.M.Cap. *Capuchin Health and Retirement Trust of Puerto Rico*
Asociacion Frailes Capuchinos, Inc.

Comunidad Jesuita, Colegio San Ignacio, Urb. Santa Maria, 1940 Calle Sauco, 00927-6718. Tel: 787-758-1717, Ext. 1721; Fax: 787-750-8640. Revs. Baudilio Guzmán, S.J., Supr.; Jose A. Borges, S.J.; Mario Alberto Torres, S.J.; Donald M. Vega, S.J.

The Viceprovince of Saint John the Baptist, Puerto Rico, of the Order Friars Minor Capuchin (1905) 216 Arzuaga St., P.O. Box 21350, 00928-1350. Tel: 787-764-3090; Fax: 787-764-4070. Web: www.capuchinospr.org. Bros. Francisco Garcia Cervero, O.F.M.Cap., Vice Prov. Min.; Roberto Martinez, O.F.M.Cap., First Councillor & Vice Provincial Treas.; Rev. Jaime Perez, O.F.M.Cap., Second Councillor; Bro. Luis O. Padilla, O.F.M.Cap., Sec.; Rev. Ramon J. Casellas Rivera, O.F.M.Cap., Dir. Capuchin Mass Assoc.
Asociacion De Frailes Capuchinos, Inc.; Asociacion Misionera Capuchina; Capuchin Formation Trust of Puerto Rico; Capuchin Health and Retirement Trust of Puerto Rico Friars 22; Postulants 1.

HATO REY. *Jesuit Community - Casa Claver*, 398 Francisco Sein, 00917. Tel: 787-759-7654; Fax: 787-790-3162. Apto. 22634 U.P.R. Sta., 00931-2634. Rev. Fernando Pico, S.J. *Casa Spinola De Angelis* Urb. Baldrich, 580 Hostos Ave., 00902. Tel: 787-282-8522; Fax: 787-282-6087. Revs. Juan José Santiago, S.J.; Rafael Rodríguez, S.J.

TRUJILLO ALTO. *Carmelite Monastery of St. Joseph* (1651) (Monasterio Carmelita De San Jose), 00977-0568. Tel: 787-761-9548; Fax: 787-283-7235. Email: mcsjose@prtc.net. Mailing Address: P.O. Box 568, 00977-0568. Sr. Madre Ines Maria Carmona Ortiz, O.Carm, Prioress.

[I] MISCELLANEOUS

SAN JUAN. *Caritas de Puerto Rico, Inc.*, 201 San Jorge St., 00910-0812. Tel: 787-300-4953, Ext. 1156; 787-727-7373, Ext. 1106; Fax: 787-728-4100; Tel: 787-300-4953, Ext. 1156; 787-300-4953, Ext. 1110; 787-728-3207. Email: ssc@rqsj.org. Web: www.sscpr.org. Mailing Address: P.O. Box 8812, 00910-8812. Rev. Enrique Manuel Camacho-Monserrate.

Casa San Clemente (Spiritual, Personal, Pastoral, and Psychological Counseling), Ave. Ponce De Leon 257, Puerta De Tierra, 00901. Tel: 787-723-6915; Fax: 787-977-8156. P.O. Box 9066315, 00906-6315. Rev. Terence Damian Wall, C.Ss.R., S.T.D., Exec. Dir.; Bro. Mateo Perez, C.Ss.R., Ph.D.; Ms. Ela Iglesias, Exec. Dir.

Centro Sor Isolina Ferre, Box 9511, 00926. Tel: 787-731-5700; Fax: 787-272-3390. Email: lurema@coqui.net; lortiz@csifpr.org. Mrs. Lourdes M. Ortiz, M.T.S. (Social Improvement of the Poor).

El Hogar del Niño, Inc., Carr. 176 Km. 4.2 Bo. Cupey Alto, 00926. Tel: 787-761-2805; Fax: 787-283-1345. Email: elhogardelnino@prtc.net. Web: www.elhogardelninopr.org. Mailing Address: P.O. Box 20667, 00928-0667. Employees 15.

Hogar Del Buen Pastor formerly Hogar Buen Pastor (Homeless Shelter), Mailing Address: P.O. Box 9066547, 00906-6547. Constitucion #250, Puerta de Tierra, 00901. Tel: 787-721-8579; Fax: 787-921-8709. Sr. Rosemarie Gonzalez, S.S.N.D.

Hogar Padre Venard, Inc., Calle San Francisco 305, 00901. Tel: 787-724-1131; Fax: 787-727-4616. Mailing Address: Apartado Postal 9020274, 00902-0274.

R. R. Siervas de Maria Ministras de los Enfermos, 1 Calle Fortaleza, 00901-1599. Tel: 787-723-4558; 787-724-2228; Fax: 787-721-0140. Sr. Aurea Fernandez Fontan, Supr. Sisters 24.

RIO PIEDRAS. *Paulinas Multimedia* (Books, Cassettes and Catholic Publications), Calle Arzuaga #164, 00925-3322. Tel: 787-764-4885; 787-765-4390; Fax: 787-767-6214. Email: paulinas@yunque.net. Web: www.paulinas.org.

SANTURCE. *Beth Yash'ah* (Spiritual and Psychological Counseling), 1708 Calle Pumarada, 00912. Tel: 787-763-6708; 787-268-2661; Fax: 787-268-2661. Dr. Lucy Lopez-Roig, Dir.; Dr. Cecilia Arias.

Fondita De Jesus (Supportive, spiritual and psychosocial services and transitional/permanent housing), Calle Monserrate 704, PDA 16 1/2, 00909. Tel: 787-724-4051; Fax: 787-722-0992. Email: cartas@lafonditadejesus.org. P.O. Box 19384, 00910-1384. Tel: 787-725-0660; Fax: 787-722-0992. Socorro Rivera Rosa, Exec. Dir. Personnel 48; Total Assisted 3,100.

Servicios Pastorales Paules (Books, Leaflets and Catholic Publications), P.O. Box 19118, 00910. Tel: 787-728-0670. Email: centrosp@onelinkpr.net. Rev. Santiago Arribas, C.M., Dir.
Res.: 1650 Fernández Juncos, Santurce, 00910-9118. Email: centrosp@onelinkpr.net.

RELIGIOUS INSTITUTES OF MEN REPRESENTED IN THE ARCHDIOCESE

For further details refer to the corresponding bracketed number in the Religious Institutes of Men or Women section.

[0140]—*Augustinian Friars* (Spain)—O.S.A.
[0470]—*The Capuchin Friars* (Vice Prov. of Puerto Rico)—O.F.M.Cap.
[0270]—*Carmelite Fathers & Brothers* (Prov. of Aragon, Valentina, Spain)—O.Carm.
[0360]—*Claretian Missionaries* (Spain)—C.M.F.
[]—*Confraternidad de Operarios del Reino de Cristo*—C.O.R.C.
[0310]—*Congregation of Christian Brothers* (Antilles Prov.)—C.F.C.
[]—*Congregation of St. Michael Arcangel*—C.S.M.A.
[0820]—*Congregation of the Fathers of Mercy* (Madrid, Spain)—C.P.M.
[1330]—*Congregation of the Mission* (Prov. of Puerto Rico)—C.M.
[1000]—*Congregation of the Passion* (Bilbao)—C.P.
[]—*Congregation of the Sacred Heart* (Spain)—C.SS.CC.
[]—*Congregation of the Terciarios Capuchinos Ntra. Sra. de los Dolores* (Spain)—T.C.
[0520]—*Franciscan Friars* (Spain)—O.F.M.
[0650]—*Holy Ghost Fathers* (American Prov.)—C.S.Sp.
[0690]—*Jesuit Fathers and Brothers* (Prov. of Puerto Rico)—S.J.
[0740]—*Marian Fathers*—M.I.C.
[0770]—*The Marist Brothers*—F.M.S.
[]—*Misioneros Contemplativos Ad-Gentes*
[1120]—*Missionaries of the Sacred Hearts of Jesus and Mary* (Spain)—M.SS.CC.
[0840]—*Missionary Servants of the Most Holy Trinity*—S.T.
[0910]—*Oblates of Mary Immaculate* (Peru Prov.)—O.M.I.
[0430]—*Order of Preachers-Dominicans* (Gen. Vicariate of P.R.)—O.P.
[1310]—*Order of the Holy Trinity* (Spain)—O.SS.T.
[1040]—*Piarist Fathers* (Spain)—Sch.P.
[1070]—*Redemptorist Fathers* (San Juan Prov.)—C.SS.R.
[1190]—*Salesians of Don Bosco* (Antilles Prov.)—S.D.B.
[0760]—*Society of Mary* (New York Prov.)—S.M.

RELIGIOUS INSTITUTES OF WOMEN REPRESENTED IN THE ARCHDIOCESE

[]—*Custodia Franciscana del Caribe "Santa Maria de la Esperanza"* (Frailes Franciscanos)
[1070-05]—*Dominican Sisters*—O.P.
[1070-06]—*Dominican Sisters*—O.P.
[1070-13]—*Dominican Sisters*—O.P.
[]—*Dominicanas Terciarias del Santisimo Sacramento* (Cadiz, Spain)
[]—*Hermanas Carmelitas de la Caridad* (Rome, Italy)—C.ach.
[]—*Hermanas Carmelitas de Madre Candelaria (Venezuela)*

[]—*Hermanas Carmelitas Teresas de San Jose (Barcelona, Spain)*
[]—*Hermanas de la Amistad Misionera en Cristo Obrero* (Amico and Madrid, Spain)
[]—*Hermanas de la B.V. Maria del Monte Carmelo* (Madrid, Spain)—H.Carm.
[]—*Hermanas de la Caridad del Cardenal Sancha* (San Domingo)—H.C.C.S.
[]—*Hermanas de la Caridad Del Sagrado Corazon De Jesus* (Madrid, Spain)
[]—*Hermanas de la Compania del Salvador* (Spain)
[]—*Hermanas De La Divina Providencia* (Rome, Italy)—CDP
[]—*Hermanas de Santos Angeles Custodios* (Bilbao, Spain)
[]—*Hermanas Dominicas de la Presentacion* (Tours, France; Colombia)
[]—*Hermanas Dominicas de Nuestra Senora del Rosario de Fatima* (Yauco)
[]—*Hermanas Franciscanas de Los Sagrados*—HH.FF.SSCC.
[]—*Hermanas Hospitalarias de Jesus Nazareno* (Cordoba, Spain)
[]—*Hermanas Mercedarias de la Caridad* (Madrid, Spain)
[]—*Hermanas Misioneras de la Madre Dolorosa y San Francisco de Asis* (Buga, Colombia)
[]—*Hermanitas de los Ancianos Desamparados* (Valencia, Spain)
[]—*Hijas de Maria Auxiliadora* (Torino, Italy)
[]—*Hijas Del Corazon Misericordioso De Maria* (Bogota, Colombia)
[]—*Hijas de la Pasion de Jesucristo y de Maria Delorosa*—C.P.
[0950]—*Instituto Misionero Hijas de San Pablo* (Rome, Italy)
[]—*Instituto Santa Mariana de Jesus (Hermanas Marianitas)* (Ecuador)—R.M.
[]—*Lumen Dei* (Madrid, Spain)—U.L.D.
[]—*Madres de Desamparados y San Jose de la Montana* (Valencia, Spain)
[]—*Madres Escolapias* (Rome)
[]—*Misioneras de Cristo Salvador*
[2710]—*Misioneras De La Caridad* (Calcutta, India)—M.C.
[]—*Misioneras del Buen Pastor* (San Juan)
[]—*Misioneras del Santisimo Sacramento y Maria Inmaculada* (Spain)
[]—*Misioneras Dominicas del Santisimo Rosario* (Madrid, Spain)
[]—*Misioneros Contemplativos Ad-Gentes*
[2720]—*Mission Helpers of the Sacred Heart*—M.H.S.H.
[2790]—*Missionary Servants of the Most Blessed Trinity* (Philadelphia, PA)—M.S.B.T.
[]—*Monjas de la Orden de la Bienventurada Virgen Maria de Monte Carmelo*—O.Carm.
[]—*Oblatas De La Santisima Trinidad* (Spain)
[]—*Oblatas del Santisimo Redentor* (Madrid, Spain)
[]—*Operarias Del Divino Maestro* (Valenzia, Spain)
[]—*Hermanas Pasionistas de San Pablo de la Cruz*—C.P.
[]—*Religiosas del Sagrado Corazon* (Rome, Italy)
[]—*Religiosas Oblatas del Divino Amor*
[]—*Religiosas Teatinas de la Inmaculada Concepcion* (Rome)—R.T.
[]—*Religiosas Terciarias de San Francisco de Asis y de la Inmaculada Concepcion* (Valencia, Spain)
[2970]—*School Sisters of Notre Dame* (Wilton, CT)—S.S.N.D.
[]—*Siervas De La Verdad* (Bayamon, Puerto Rico)
[3600]—*Siervas de Maria y Ministras de los Enfermos* (Rome, Italy)—S.M.
[2570]—*Sisters of Mercy* (Pittsburgh, PA)—R.S.M.
[]—*Sisters of Nazareth*
[1620]—*Sisters of Saint Francis of Millvale, Pennsylvania*—O.S.F.
[1650]—*Sisters of St. Francis of Philadelphia*—O.S.F.
[1800]—*Sisters of St. Francis of the Third Order Regular* (Williamsville, New York)—O.S.F.
[3830]—*Sisters of St. Joseph* (Brentwood)—C.S.J.
[3930]—*Sisters of St. Joseph of the Third Order of St. Francis*—S.S.J.-T.O.S.F.
[1970]—*Sisters of the Holy Family of Nazareth*—C.S.F.N.
[1490]—*Sisters of the Third Franciscan Order*—O.S.F.
[2150]—*Sisters, Servants of the Immaculate Heart of Mary*—I.H.M.
[]—*Terciarias Franciscanas de la Purisima* (Murcia, Spain)

NECROLOGY

✠ Aponte Martinez, His Eminence Luis Cardinal, Retired Archbishop of San Juan.—Died April 10, 2012
✠ Negron Santana, Most Rev. Hermin, Auxiliary Bishop of San Juan, PR.—Died March 10, 2012
† Barragam, Feliciano Ganda—Died Oct. 20, 2011
† Capiello, Luis Beltran Rios, Dorado, PR San Antonio de Padua—Died June 25, 2011
† Marino, Vincente Fernandez—Died Aug. 13, 2011
† Sanchez, Angel Luis Figueroa—Died Jan. 11, 2011

An asterisk (*) denotes an organization that has established tax-exempt status directly with the IRS and is not covered by the USCCB Group Ruling.

American Foreign Missions

AUGUSTINIAN MISSIONS (O.S.A.)

Foreign Missions of the Midwestern Province of the Order of St. Augustine

Foreign Missions Provincial Headquarters

Province of Our Mother of Good Counsel (Midwestern): *Tolentine Center* 20300 Governors Hwy., Olympia Fields, IL 60461-1081. Phone: 708-748-5435; Fax: 708-481-2090. Very Rev. Bernard C. Scianna, O.S.A. Ord: '93, Prov.; Rev. Christopher C. Steinle, O.S.A. Ord: '98, Mission Procurator.

Midwestern Augustinian Religious serving in Foreign Missions: Most Rev. Daniel T. Turley, O.S.A. Ord: '68, Peru; Rev. Alfred M. Burke, O.S.A. Ord: '57, Japan; Rev. Charles J. Bodden, O.S.A. Ord: '78, Peru; Rev. John J. Dowling, O.S.A. Ord: '68, Peru; Rev. Richard Palmer, O.S.A. Ord: '87, Peru; Rev. John P. Tasto, O.S.A. Ord: '67, Mexico; Rev. John A. Tyma, O.S.A. Ord: '59, Peru.

Province of St. Thomas of Villanova (Eastern): P.O. Box 340, Villanova, PA 19085-0340. Phone: 610-527-3330; Fax: 610-520-0618. Very Rev. Anthony M. Genovese, O.S.A. Ord: '73, Prior Prov.; Rev. Anthony P. Burrascano, O.S.A. Ord: '79, Dir. Missions.

U.S. Religious Serving in Foreign Missions: Rev. Arthur P. Purcaro, O.S.A. Ord: '75, Peru; Rev. Francis J. Doyle, O.S.A. Ord: '70, South Africa; Rev. William R. Faix, O.S.A. Ord: '63, Czech Republic; Rev. Maurice J. Mahoney, O.S.A. Ord: '60, Japan; Rev. Aquilino D. Gonzalez, O.S.A. Ord: '72, Peru; Rev. Michael J. Hilden, O.S.A. Ord: '73, Japan; Rev. John F. McAtee, O.S.A. Ord: '66, South Africa; Rev. John J. Lydon, O.S.A. Ord: '84, Peru; Rev. Michael F. Di Gregorio, O.S.A. Ord: '73, Vicar General, Rome, Italy; Rev. Brian S. Lowery, O.S.A. Ord: '67, San Gimignano, Italy; Rev. George P. Lawless, O.S.A. Ord: '56, Rome, Italy; Rev. Robert J. Guessetto, O.S.A. Ord: '79, Rome, Italy.

AMERICAN BENEDICTINE FOREIGN MISSIONS (O.S.B.)

American Cassinese Congregation Foreign Missions

St. Vincent Archabbey: 300 Fraser Purchase Rd., Latrobe, PA 15650-2690. Phone: 724-532-6600. Arch Abbot (US) Douglas R. Nowicki, O.S.B. Ord: '72, Archabbot; Rev. Noel H. Rothrauff, O.S.B. Ord: '54, Mission Dir.

U.S. Religious serving in Taiwan: Bro. Nicholas Koss, O.S.B., Prior.

St. John's Abbey: Box 2015, Collegeville, MN 56321-2015. Fax: 320-363-3082. Rt. Rev. John Klassen, O.S.B. Ord: '77.

U.S. Religious serving Abroad: Rev. Kieran Nolan, O.S.B. Ord: '59, Japan; Rev. Neal Henry Lawrence, O.S.B. Ord: '60, Japan; Rev. Fintan Bromenshenkel, O.S.B. Ord: '45, Nassau; Rev. George Wolf, O.S.B. Ord: '44, Nassau; Very Rev. Thomas Wahl, O.S.B. Ord: '58, Japan; Rev. Cyprian Weaver, O.S.B. Ord: '72, Taiwan.

St. Benedict's Abbey: Atchison, KS 66002. Phone: 913-367-7853; Fax: 913-367-6230. Rt. Rev. Barnabas Senecal, O.S.B. Ord: '64, Abbot.

U.S. Religious serving in Brazil: Most Rev. Herbert Hermes; Rev. Kieran McInerney, O.S.B. Ord: '52; Rev. Denis Meade, O.S.B. Ord: '55; Rev. Duane Roy, O.S.B. Ord: '67.

St. Procopius Abbey: 5601 College Rd., Lisle, IL 60532. Phone: 630-969-6410; Fax: 630-969-6426. Rt. Rev. Dismas B. Kalcic, O.S.B. Ord: '61, Prior.

Assumption Abbey: P.O. Box A, Richardton, ND 58652. Phone: 701-974-3315; Fax: 701-974-3317. Rt. Rev. Brian Wangler, O.S.B. Ord: '69.

U.S. Religious serving in South America: Very Rev. Philip Vanderlin, O.S.B. Ord: '80, Prior; Rev. Gonzalo Blanco, O.S.B. Ord: '92, Subprior; Rev. Efraim Villegas, O.S.B. Ord: '88; Rev. Carlos Suarez, O.S.B. Ord: '86; Rev. Francis Wehri, O.S.B. Ord: '61; Rev. Nicolas Cano, O.S.B. Ord: '97; Bro. Fabio Mejia; Bro. Manuel Cely; Bro. Roberto Duarte.

St. Paul's Abbey: Newton, NJ 07860-0007. Phone: 973-383-2470; Fax: 973-383-5782. Very Rev. John Bosco Kim, O.S.B.

U.S. Religious serving Abroad: Rev. Damian Milliken, O.S.B. Ord: '58, Tanzania; Rev. Peter W. Blue, O.S.B. Ord: '70, Namibia.

Swiss-American Foreign Missions

Blue Cloud Abbey: Marvin, SD 57251. Phone: 605-398-9200; Fax: 605-398-9201. Rt. Rev. Thomas Hillenbrand Ord: '65, Mission Dir.

U.S. Religious serving in Guatemala: Rev. Basil Dilger, O.S.B. Ord: '61; Rev. Cletus Miller, O.S.B. Ord: '44; Rev. Bernardine Ness, O.S.B. Ord: '64.

Mount Angel Abbey: 1 Abbey Dr, Saint Benedict, OR 97373. Saint Benedict, OR 97373. Phone: 503-845-3030; Fax: 503-845-3594. Rt. Rev. Nathan Zodrow, O.S.B. Ord: '88.

U.S. Religious serving in Mexico: Very Rev. Konrad Shaefer, O.S.B. Ord: '80; Bro. James Bartos, O.S.B.

Marmion Abbey: 850 Butterfield Rd., Aurora, IL 60502. Phone: 630-897-7215; Fax: 630-897-0393. Rt. Rev. John Brahill, O.S.B. Ord: '82.

AMERICAN CAPUCHIN MISSIONS (O.F.M.CAP.)

Missions of the American Provinces of the Order of Friars Capuchin (The Capuchin Friars) in the United States and other countries.

General Headquarters Via Piemonte, 70, Rome, Italy, 00187, Web: www.ofmcap.org. Very Rev. Mauro Johri, O.F.M.Cap., Gen. Min.; Rev. Helmut Rakowski, O.F.M.Cap., Sec. Gen. for the Missions.

American Capuchin Missions

Provincial Headquarters

Capuchin Foreign Missions

Province of St. Joseph: Office of Overseas Missions, 1820 Mt. Elliott St., Detroit, MI 48207. Fax: 313-579-2275. Very Rev. John Celichowski, O.F.M.Cap. Ord: '93, Prov. Min.; Bro. Larry LaCross, O.F.M.Cap., Mission Sec.

U.S Religious serving Abroad: Rev. Kevin Heagerty, O.F.M.Cap. Ord: '61, Panama; Rev. Glenn Gessner, O.F.M.Cap. Ord: '60, Nicaragua; Rev. Benjamin Markwell, O.F.M.Cap. Ord: '66, Middle East; Rev. Paul Craig, O.F.M.Cap. Ord: '66, Middle East; Rev. Paul Koenig, O.F.M.Cap. Ord: '93, Middle East; Rev. Carmel Flora, O.F.M.Cap. Ord: '53, Australia; Rev. Walter Kasuboski, O.F.M-.Cap. Ord: '74, Panama; Rev. Jozef Timmers, O.F.M.Cap. Ord: '00, Panama; Rev. Andre Weller, O.F.M.Cap. Ord: '63, Panama.

Province of Mid-America: 3613 Wyandot St., Denver, CO 80211-2950. Phone: 303-477-5436; Fax: 303-477-6925. Rev. Charles Polifka, O.F.M-.Cap. Ord: '71, Prov. Min.; Stephanie Pedersen, Mission Sec.

U.S. Religious serving in Papua, New Guinea: (St. Michael the Archangel Vice Province of Papua, New Guinea and the Solomon Islands): Most Rev. Stephen Reichert, O.F.M.Cap. Ord: '69, Archbishop of Madang; Rev. Peter Meis, O.F.M-.Cap. Ord: '67; Rev. Donald Debes, O.F.M.Cap. Ord: '70.

U.S. Religious serving in Mexico: Rev. William Kraus, O.F.M.Cap. Ord: '73.

Province of St. Augustine: 220 37th St., Pittsburgh, PA 15201. Phone: 412-682-6011; Fax: 412-682-0506. Very Rev. W. David Nestler, O.F.M-.Cap. Ord: '89, Prov. Min.; Rev. John Pfannenstiel, O.F.M.Cap. Ord: '82, Coord. of Missions.

U.S. Religious serving in Papua New Guinea (St. Michael the Archangel Vice Province of Papua, New Guinea and the Solomon Islands): Most Rev. William Fey, O.F.M.Cap. Ord: '68, Bishop of Diocese of Kimbe; Rev. Donald Lippert, O.F.M-.Cap. Ord: '85; Rev. Brian Newman, O.F.M.Cap. Ord: '61; Rev. Cyril Repko, O.F.M.Cap. Ord: '62; Rev. Colman Studeny, O.F.M.Cap. Ord: '61; Rev. Allan Wasiecko, O.F.M.Cap. Ord: '68; Rev. Jonathan Williams, O.F.M.Cap. Ord: '71; Bro. Raymond Ronan, O.F.M.Cap.; Bro. James Mungovan, O.F.M.Cap.

U.S. Religious serving in Puerto Rico (St. John the Baptist Vice Province): Rev. Mario Mastrangelo, O.F.M.Cap. Ord: '58; Rev. Carlos A. Reyes, O.F.M.Cap. Ord: '06; Rev. Stephen Carter, O.F.M-.Cap. Ord: '82.

The Province of St. Mary of the Capuchin Order: 30 Gedney Park Dr., White Plains, NY 10605. Phone: 914-761-3008.

The Capuchin Foreign Missions described here are a ministry of: The Province of St. Mary of the Capuchin Order

Rev. Francis Gasparik, O.F.M.Cap. Ord: '86, Prov.; Bro. Celestino Arlas, O.F.M.Cap., Mission Sec.

U.S. Religious serving in Guam: Rev. George Maddock, O.F.M.Cap. Ord: '64; Rev. Randolph Nowak, O.F.M.Cap. Ord: '52; Bro. Brian Champoux, O.F.M.Cap.

U.S. Religious serving in Japan: Rev. Wayne Berndt, O.F.M.Cap. Ord: '83; Rev. Louis Chiusano, O.F.M.Cap. Ord: '57; Rev. Roland Daigle, O.F.M.Cap. Ord: '84; Rev. Peter Von Essen, O.F.M.Cap. Ord: '56; Rev. LaSalle Parsons, O.F.M-.Cap. Ord: '57; Rev. Patrick Sullivan, O.F.M.Cap. Ord: '71; Bro. Martin de Porres Schmitt, O.F.M.Cap.

U.S. Religious serving in Central America: Rev. John Clermont, O.F.M.Cap. Ord: '53, Honduras; Rev. Raymond Richard, O.F.M.Cap. Ord: '72, Honduras; Bro. James Donegan, O.F.M.Cap., Honduras.

The Seraphic Mass Association-Capuchin Mission Association: *St. Mary's Province* 210 W. 31st St., New York, NY 10001-2876.

This Association supports the Capuchin Foreign Mission.

AMERICAN CARMELITE MISSIONS (O.CARM.)

Carmelite Foreign Missions

Foreign Missions of the American Province of the Most Pure Heart of Mary

Provincial Headquarters, Carmelite Provincial Office: 1317 Frontage Rd., Darien, IL 60561. Fax: 630-971-0195. Very Rev. Carl Markelz, O.Carm. Ord: '91, Prov.

Mission Office, Carmelite Missions: 8501 Bailey Rd., Darien, IL 60561-8418. Phone: 630-969-5220; Fax: 630-969-5266. Very Rev. John Malley, O.Carm. Ord: '56, Mission Dir.

U.S. Religious serving in Peru: Rev. Edward Adelmann, O.Carm. Ord: '75; Most Rev. Michael LaFay, O.Carm. Ord: '60; Rev. Gerald Payea, O.Carm. Ord: '70; Rev. Michael Sgarioto, O.Carm. Ord: '85.

U.S. Religious serving in Mexico: Rev. Peter Hinde, O.Carm. Ord: '52; Rev. Thomas Jordan, O.Carm. Ord: '70.

COMBONI MISSIONARIES (VERONA FATHERS) (M.C.C.J.)

Comboni Foreign Missions

Legal Title: *Comboni Missionaries of the Heart of Jesus, Inc.*

U.S. Headquarters, Comboni Mission Center: 1318 Nagel Rd., Cincinnati, OH 45255-3120. Phone: 513-474-4997; Fax: 513-474-0382; Email: info@combonimissionaries.org. Rev. Manuel Baeza, M.C.C.J. Ord: '96, Prov. Supr.; Rev. Brian Quigley, M.C.C.J. Ord: '77, Mission Dir.

U.S. Religious serving Abroad: Rev. Albert Anichini, M.C.C.J. Ord: '62, Uganda; Rev. David Baltz, M.C.C.J. Ord: '67, Uganda; Rev. Michael Barton, M.C.C.J. Ord: '75, Sudan; Rev. James Francez, M.C.C.J. Ord: '57, Mexico.

AMERICAN CONVENTUAL FRANCISCAN MISSIONS (O.F.M.CONV.)

Conventual Franciscan Foreign Missions

General Headquarters Convento SS. XII Apostoli Piazza, SS Apostoli 51, Rome, Italy, 00187, Rev. Jaroslaw Wysoczanski, O.F.M.Conv., Sec. Gen. for the Missions; Very Rev. Justin A. Biase, O.F.M.Conv. Ord: '70, Prov. & Mission Dir.

Provincial Headquarters

Province of the Immaculate Conception: 77 St. Francis Pl., P.O. Box 629, Rensselaer, NY 12144. Phone: 518-472-1000.

U.S. Religious serving Abroad: Rev. Maury Marhafer, O.F.M.Conv. Ord: '54; Most Rev. Elias Manning, O.F.M.Conv., Bishop of Valenca, Brazil.

Province of Saint Anthony of Padua: Provincial House & Office of Mission Procurator, 12300 Folly Quarter Rd., Ellicott City, MD 21042-1419. Phone: 410-531-9200; Fax: 410-531-4881. Very Rev. James McCurry, O.F.M.Conv. Ord: '77, Minister Prov.

Franciscan Mission Association: 12300 Folly Quarter Rd., Ellicott City, MD 21042. Rev. Martin Breski, O.F.M.Conv. Ord: '69.

U.S. Religious serving Abroad: Bro. Michael Duffy,

O.F.M.Conv., Jamaica; Rev. Vincent Lachendro, O.F.M.Conv. Ord: '63, Japan.

Province of Our Lady of Consolation: Provincial Office, 101 St. Anthony Dr., Mount Saint Francis, IN 47146. Rev. James Kent, O.F.M-.Conv. Ord: '91, Minister Prov.

Religious serving Abroad: Rev. Ivan Rohloff, Russia; Rev. Terence Tobin, O.F.M.Conv. Ord: '55, Zambia; Bro. Joseph Weissling, O.F.M.Conv., Guardian; Bro. Anthony Droll, O.F.M.Conv., Zambia.

Province of Saint Bonaventure: Provincial Office, 6107 N. Kenmore Ave., Chicago, IL 60660-2797. Phone: 773-274-7681; Fax: 773-274-9751. Rev. Patrick Greenough, O.F.M.Conv. Ord: '87, Minister Prov.

U.S. Religious serving Abroad: Rev. John Calgaro, O.F.M.Conv. Ord: '74, Mexico; Rev. Abraham Crisostomo, O.F.M.Conv. Ord: '96; Bro. Paschal Metzger, O.F.M.Conv., Mexico; Bro. Joseph Schenk, O.F.M.Conv.; Bro. Stanislaus Zabkiewicz, O.F.M.Conv.

CROSIER FATHERS MISSIONS (O.S.C.)

Crosier Foreign Missions

Crosier Fathers and Brothers: (Canons Regular of the Order of the Holy Cross)

U.S. Address: Crosier Province Headquarters:, 4423 N. 24th St., Ste. 400, Phoenix, AZ 85016-5584. Phone: 602-443-7100; Fax: 602-443-7101; Email: cpowell@crosier.org. Rev. Thomas A. Enneking, O.S.C. Ord: '84, Prior Prov.; Bro. Albert Becker, O.S.C., Mission Dir.

AMERICAN DIVINE WORD MISSIONARIES (S.V.D.)

Society of the Divine Word Foreign Missions

Missions of the American Provinces of the Society of the Divine Word (S.V.D.), commonly known as Divine Word Missionaries

Latin: Societas Verbi Divini

Provincial Headquarters in the U.S.A.

Chicago Province: Society of the Divine Word - Province of Saint Joseph Freinademetz, S.V.D., 1985 Waukegan Rd., P.O. Box 6038, Techny, IL 60082-6038. Phone: 847-272-2700; Fax: 847-272-2517.

Publications: Divine Word Missionaries.
Rev. Thomas J. Ascheman, S.V.D. Ord: '82, Prov. Supr.; Bro. Dennis Newton, S.V.D., Mission Dir. for all three Provinces.

Southern Province: Society of the Divine Word Southern Province of St. Augustine, 199 Seminary Dr., Bay Saint Louis, MS 39520-4638. Phone: 228-467-4322. Very Rev. James Pawlicki, S.V.D. Ord: '73, Prov. Supr. *Divine Word Missionaries Office* 1835 Waukegan Rd., Techny, IL 60082.

American Divine Word Missionaries in Overseas Missions: Rev. Daniel Bauer, S.V.D. Ord: '74, Taiwan; Rev. Joseph Bisson, S.V.D. Ord: '63, Papua, New Guinea; Archbishop Michael Blume, S.V.D. Ord: '72, Apostolic Nuncio to Togo & Benin; Rev. Francis Budenholzer, S.V.D. Ord: '72, Taiwan; Rev. Vincent Burke, S.V.D. Ord: '61, Ghana; Rev. Dennis Callan, S.V.D. Ord: '87, Korea; Rev. Ba Thai Dai, S.V.D. Ord: '05, Vietnam; Rev. Richard Daschbach, S.V.D. Ord: '64, East Timor; Rev. Anthony Dugay, S.V.D. Ord: '62, Ghana; Rev. Loyd Fiedler, S.V.D. Ord: '70, Philippines; Bro. Ronald Fratzke, S.V.D., Thailand; Rev. Paul Gootee, S.V.D. Ord: '55, Indonesia; Rev. Lawrence Hambach, S.V.D. Ord: '61, Indonesia; Rev. James Heisig, S.V.D. Ord: '69, Japan; Rev. Xuan Ho, S.V.D. Ord: '03, St. Kitts, West Indies (Caribbean); Rev. Robert Johnson, S.V.D. Ord: '92, St. Maarten, Netherand Antilles (Caribbean); Bro. Lawrence Kieffer, S.V.D., Papua New Guinea; Rev. Robert Kisala, S.V.D. Ord: '85, Italy; Rev. Ronald Lange, S.V.D. Ord: '71, Ghana; Rev. Anthony Duc Le, S.V.D. Ord: '06, Thailand; Rev. John Hung Le, S.V.D. Ord: '04, Papua New Guinea; Rev. James Liebner, S.V.D. Ord: '85, China; Rev. Michael Lindstrom, S.V.D. Ord: '82, Japan; Bro. Damien Lunders, S.V.D., Thailand; Rev. David Mayer, S.V.D. Ord: '66, Japan; Rev. Walter Mendonca, S.V.D. Ord: '76, British Virgin Islands (Caribbean); Rev. Peter Michael, S.V.D. Ord: '40, Philippines; Rev. Theodore Murnane, S.V.D. Ord: '59, Philippines; Rev. Paul Nadolny, S.V.D. Ord: '89, Mozambique; Rev. Lawrence Nemer, S.V.D. Ord: '60, Australia; Rev. Long Phi Nguyen, S.V.D. Ord: '07, Chile; Rev. Michael Quang Nguyen, S.V.D. Ord: '02, Australia; Rev. Peter Sam Cao Nguyen, S.V.D. Ord: '86, Korea; Rev. Phong Cao Nguyen, S.V.D. Ord: '06, Brazil; Rev. Vinh Daniel Nguyen, S.V.D. Ord: '07, Mexico; Rev. Joseph Minh Vu Nguyen, S.V.D. Ord: '96, Australia; Rev. Thi Pham, S.V.D. Ord: '02, Italy; Rev. Frank Power, S.V.D. Ord: '73, Jamaica; Rev. Robert Riemer, S.V.D. Ord: '60, Japan; Rev. Bartley Schmitz, S.V.D. Ord: '44, Taiwan; Rev. John Seland, S.V.D. Ord: '68, Japan; Bro. Bernard Spitzley, S.V.D., Jamaica; Rev. Arnold Steffen, S.V.D. Ord: '57, Papua New Guinea; Rev. Victor Stevko, S.V.D. Ord: '57, Australia; Rev. Nicholas Strawn, S.V.D. Ord: '62, Indonesia; Rev. David Streit, S.V.D. Ord: '69, Rome; Rev. Richard Szippl, S.V.D. Ord: '81, Japan; Rev. Gerald Theis, S.V.D. Ord: '80, Papua New Guinea; Rev. Richard Thibeau, S.V.D. Ord: '57, Mexico; Rev. Frederick Timp, S.V.D. Ord: '71, Ghana; Rev. Joseph Huynh Tran, S.V.D. Ord: '03, Vietnam; Rev. Peter Tam Tran, S.V.D. Ord: '98, Australia; Rev. Vinh The Trinh, S.V.D. Ord: '07, Colombia; Rev. Andy Dinh Vu, S.V.D. Ord: '07, Ecuador; Rev. Joseph Tri Van Vu, S.V.D. Ord: '85, Vietnam; Rev. Toan Quoc Vu, S.V.D. Ord: '06, Ecuador; Rev. James Vorwek, S.V.D. Ord: '69, Argentina.

AMERICAN DOMINICAN MISSIONS (O.P.)

Dominican-Order of Preachers Foreign Missions

Foreign Missions of the American Provinces of the Order of Preachers

Provincial Headquarters

Province of St. Joseph (Eastern): 141 E. 65th St., New York, NY 10065. Phone: 212-861-3776. Very Rev. D. Dominic Izzo, O.P. Ord: '94, Dir., Dominican Foundation & Mission Sec.

U.S. Religious serving Elsewhere: Rev. D. G. Doherty, O.P. Ord: '57, Philippines; Most Rev. Christopher Cardone, O.P. Ord: '86, Auxiliary Bishop -Solomon Islands.

U.S. Religious serving in Kenya: Rev. Leon Martin A. Martiny, O.P. Ord: '98, Vicar Prov.; Rev. M. B. Schepers, O.P. Ord: '56; Rev. Vincent Wiseman, O.P. Ord: '71; Very Rev. David Adiletta, O.P. Ord: '98; Rev. Christopher Saliga, O.P. Ord: '05; Rev. Thomas Kraft, O.P. Ord: '84.

Province of St. Albert the Great (Central): 1909 S. Ashland Ave., Chicago, IL 60608-2994. Fax: 312-829-8471. Very Rev. Charles E. Bouchard, O.P. Ord: '79, Prov.; Rev. Gerard B. Cleator, O.P. Ord: '65, Dir., St. Dominic Mission Society.

U.S. Religious serving in Nigeria: Rev. Peter Otillio, O.P. Ord: '57; Rev. Joseph H. Kenny, O.P. Ord: '50; Rev. Justus Pokrzewinski, O.P. Ord: '60; Rev. Edward H. Riley, O.P. Ord: '60; Rev. Gilbert Thesing, O.P. Ord: '75; Bro. Stephen D. Lucas, O.P.

U.S. Religious serving in Bolivia: Rev. Daniel Roach, O.P. Ord: '56.

Province of the Holy Name (Western Dominican Province): 5877 Birch Ct., Oakland, CA 94618. Very Rev. Mark C. Padrez, O.P. Ord: '95, Prov.

U.S. Religious serving in Latin America: Rev. Timothy Conlan, O.P. Ord: '67, Guatemala; Rev. Bartholomew de la Torre, O.P. Ord: '67, Mexico; Rev. Martin de Porres Walsh, O.P. Ord: '69, Mexico; Rev. Michael Rolland, O.P. Ord: '93, Mexico; Rev. Mark Francis Manzano, O.P. Ord: '11, Mexico.

U.S. Religious Serving in Kenya: Bro. Daniel Thomas, O.P.

St. Martin de Porres Province (Southern Dominican Province): 1421 N. Causeway Blvd., Ste. 200, Metairie, LA 70001-4144. Phone: 504-837-2129; Fax: 504-837-6604. Rev. Christopher T. Eggleton Ord: '88, Prov.

U.S. Religious serving Abroad: Rev. Jose D. Padilla, O.P. Ord: '04, France; Rev. Leobardo Almazan Estevez, O.P. Ord: '05, Italy; Rev. James L. Dolan, O.P. Ord: '60, Peru; Rev. Brian J. Pierce, O.P. Ord: '83, Rome; Rev. Marcos Ramos, O.P. Ord: '01, Canada; Rev. Philip Powell, O.P. Ord: '05, Italy; Rev. Jesus Guerra deVinney, O.P. Ord: '69, Venezuela; Rev. Jaime Diaz Serna, O.P. Ord: '00, Colombia; Bro. Angel Mendez, O.P., Mexico.

AMERICAN FRANCISCAN MISSIONS (O.F.M.)

Franciscan Foreign Missions

Missions of the American Provinces of the Order of Friars Minor (Franciscan)in the United States and other countries

Holy Name Province: 135 W. 31st St., New York, NY 10001-3439. Phone: 973-778-1915; Phone: 888-372-6478; Fax: 973-777-5687; Web: www.hnp.org. Rev. Russell C. Becker, O.F.M. Ord: '72, Sec. Missionary Evangelization; Bro. Thomas J. Cole, O.F.M., Dir. & Mission Promoter.

U.S. Religious serving in Africa: Rev. Joseph B. Ehrhardt, O.F.M. Ord: '67.

U.S. Religious serving in Bolivia: Rev. Ignatius Harding, O.F.M. Ord: '72; Rev. William R. Keenan, O.F.M. Ord: '56; Rev. Thomas J. Kornacki, O.F.M. Ord: '77; Rev. Clement Comesky, O.F.M. Ord: '55.

U.S. Religious serving in Brazil: Rev. David J. Babcock, O.F.M. Ord: '53; Rev. Donald J. Chin, O.F.M. Ord: '67; Rev. Berard J. Hanlon, O.F.M. Ord: '63; Rev. Juvenal F. Leahy, O.F.M. Ord: '58; Rev. Paul J. Osborne, O.F.M. Ord: '64.

U.S. Religious serving in Japan: Rev. Russell C. Becker, O.F.M. Ord: '72; Rev. Bede Fitzpatrick, O.F.M. Ord: '55; Rev. Bartholomew McMahon, O.F.M. Ord: '62; Rev. Donnon P. Murray, O.F.M. Ord: '56; Rev. Callistus Sweeney, O.F.M. Ord: '53.

U.S. Religious serving in Peru: Rev. Mariano Gagnon, O.F.M. Ord: '57; Rev. Christopher J. Dunn, O.F.M. Ord: '82; Rev. Anthony Wilson, O.F.M. Ord: '87; Rev. Paul Breslin, O.F.M. Ord: '88; Rev. Carlos Sarmiento-Diaz, O.F.M. Ord: '99.

U.S. Religious serving in Puerto Rico: Archbishop Roberto O. Gonzalez, O.F.M. Ord: '77; Rev. Alfonso Guzman Alfaro, O.F.M. Ord: '71.

U.S. Religious serving in Taiwan: Rev. Pius Liu, O.F.M. Ord: '53.

Franciscan Province of the Immaculate Conception: 125 Thompson St., New York, NY 10012. Rev. James Goode, O.F.M. Ord: '72, Sec./Missionary Evangelization & Franciscan Missionary Union.

Province-affiliated Religious serving in Honduras: Most Rev. Maurus Muldoon, O.F.M. Ord: '66; Most Rev Roberto Camilleri, O.F.M. Ord: '75; Most Rev. Joseph Bonello, O.F.M. Ord: '85; Rev. Albert Gauci, O.F.M. Ord: '71; Rev. Angelo Falzon, O.F.M. Ord: '84; Rev. Donald Salazar, O.F.M. Ord: '67; Rev. Octavio Salinas, O.F.M. Ord: '83.

Province-affiliated Religious serving in El Salvador: Rev. Flavian Mucci, O.F.M. Ord: '63; Rev. Guy Vellardita, O.F.M. Ord: '58, San Pedro; Rev. Rafael Fernandez, O.F.M. Ord: '87.

Province-affiliated Religious serving in Guatemala: Rev. Ottaviano Battolini, O.F.M. Ord: '43; Rev. Roberto Siguere, O.F.M. Ord: '65; Rev. Michael Della Penna, O.F.M. Ord: '99; Rev. Nery Aguirre, O.F.M. Ord: '74.

Sacred Heart Province: 3140 Meramec St., Saint Louis, MO 63118. Phone: 314-353-3421; Phone: 314-353-7470. *Franciscan Missionary Union* Phone: 314-353-7729. Rev. William Spencer, O.F.M. Ord: '74, Prov.; Rev. Michael Jennrich, O.F.M. Ord: '87, Prov. Vicar; Bro. Joseph Rogenski, O.F.M., Promoter of the Missions, Holy Land Commissariat, Secretariat for Missionary Evangelization. Rev. Jesus Aguirre-Garza, O.F.M. Ord: '96, Democratic Republic of Congo; Rev. Joseph Tan Doan Nguyen, O.F.M. Ord: '86, Vietnam; Bro. Jeffery Haller, O.F.M., Democratic Republic of the Congo.

U.S. Religious serving in Alaska: Rev. Joseph Hemmer, O.F.M. Ord: '54; Bro. Robert J. Ruzicka, O.F.M.; Bro. R Justin Huber, O.F.M.

U.S. Religious serving in Brazil: Rev. Nestor Windolph, O.F.M. Ord: '55; Rev. Richard Duffy, O.F.M. Ord: '58.

St. Barbara Province: 1500 34th Ave., Oakland, CA 94601. Phone: 510-536-3722; Fax: 510-536-3970; Web: www.sbfranciscans.org.

U.S. Religious serving Overseas: Rev. Garret Edmunds, O.F.M. Ord: '82, Israel; Rev. Elias Galvez, O.F.M. Ord: '56, Mexico; Rev. John Gibbons, O.F.M. Ord: '01, Russia; Bro. Leo Gonzalez, O.F.M., Israel; Bro. Gerard Saunders, O.F.M., Peru; Bro. Ivo Toneck, O.F.M., Mexico; Bro. William Minkel, O.F.M., Mexico.

COMMISSARIAT OF THE HOLY LAND

Franciscan Monastery, 1400 Quincy St., N.E., Washington, DC 20017. Phone: 202-526-6800; Fax: 202-529-9889; Email: secretariatusa@myfranciscan.com; Web: www.myfranciscan.com. Very Rev. Jeremy Harrington, O.F.M. Ord: '59, Guardian; Rev. David Wathen, O.F.M. Ord: '99, Vocation Dir.; Rev. Garrett Edmunds, O.F.M. Ord: '82, Vice Commissary; Friar Thomas Courtney, O.F.M.; Friar-Deacon John-Sebastian Laird-Hammond, O.F.M. Ord: '91, Secretariat to the Franciscan Monastery.

Commissary Custody of the Holy Land: Jordan, Israel, Lebanon, Syria, Cyprus, Egypt, and Rhodes.

U.S. Religious serving Abroad: Rev. Fergus Clarke, O.F.M. Ord: '73, Jerusalem, Israel; Rev. David Jaeger, O.F.M. Ord: '86, Jerusalem, Israel; Rev.

George Lewett, O.F.M. Ord: '88, Bethlehem, Israel; Rev. Athanasius Macora, O.F.M. Ord: '92, Jerusalem, Israel; Rev. Matthias Rendon, O.F.M. Ord: '92, Jerusalem, Israel; Rev. Danielmose Shroeder, O.F.M. Ord: '91, Jerusalem, Israel; Rev. Peter Vasko, O.F.M. Ord: '87, Jerusalem, Israel; Bro. Leo Gonzales, O.F.M., Mt. Tabor, Israel; Bro. Angel Beda Ison, O.F.M., Jerusalem, Israel; Bro. Michael Raum, O.F.M., Jerusalem, Israel; Bro. Lawrence Bode, O.F.M., Jerusalem, Israel; Bro. Gregory Giannoni, O.F.M., Jerusalem, Israel; Bro. John Savage, O.F.M., Jerusalem, Israel.

FRANCISCAN FRIARS OF THE ATONEMENT (S.A.)

General Headquarters: Graymoor:, P.O. Box 300, Garrison, NY 10524-0300. Phone: 845-424-3671; Fax: 845-424-2166.

For detailed information on the U.S. Religious working in foreign missions, please refer to the listings under the Archdiocese of New York section entitled "Monasteries and Residences of Priests and Brothers," Graymoor, Garrison, NY.

HOLY CROSS MISSION CENTER (C.S.C.)

U.S. Headquarters and Procure: Holy Cross Mission Center:, P.O. Box 543, Notre Dame, IN 46556. Phone: 574-631-5477; Fax: 574-631-6813. Rev. Leonard Olobo, C.S.C. Ord: '04, Dir.

Legal Title: *Holy Cross Foreign Mission Society, Inc.*

Holy Cross Mission Center

Holy Cross Foreign Missions

Indiana Province: Congregation of the Holy Cross, P.O. Box 1064, Notre Dame, IN 46556-1064.

Midwest Province of Brothers: Congregation of the Holy Cross, P.O. Box 460, Notre Dame, IN 46556-0460.

Eastern Province of Priests: Congregation of the Holy Cross, 835 Clinton Ave., Bridgeport, CT 06604-2393.

South-West Province of Brothers: Congregation of the Holy Cross, 1101 St. Edward's Dr., Austin, TX 78704-6512.

Eastern Brothers Province: Congregation of the Holy Cross, 85 Overlook Cir., New Rochelle, NY 10804-4501.

U.S. Religious serving in Foreign Missions: Rev. Robert R. Baker, C.S.C. Ord: '70, Peru; Rev. James T. Banas, C.S.C. Ord: '57, Bangladesh; Rev. Gerald R. Barmasse, C.S.C. Ord: '76, Chile; Rev. David B. Burrell, C.S.C. Ord: '59, Kenya; Rev. Charles A. Delaney, C.S.C. Ord: '49, Chile; Rev. Michael M. DeLaney, C.S.C. Ord: '87, Chile; Rev. Philip T. Devlin, C.S.C. Ord: '56, Peru; Rev. Joseph A. Dorsey, C.S.C. Ord: '57, Chile; Rev. David E. Farrell, C.S.C. Ord: '68, Peru; Rev. Donald G. Fetters, C.S.C. Ord: '76, Peru; Rev. Robert Gilbo, C.S.C. Ord: '67, Chile; Rev. Robert G. Gilmour, C.S.C. Ord: '68, Ghana; Rev. Eugene Homrich, C.S.C. Ord: '55, Bangladesh; Rev. L. Peter Logsdon, C.S.C. Ord: '68, Mexico; Rev. H. Thomas McDermott, C.S.C. Ord: '79, Bangladesh; Rev. Russell K. McDougall, C.S.C. Ord: '91, Rome; Rev. Daniel A. Panchot, C.S.C. Ord: '65, Mexico; Rev. Gerald T. Papen, C.S.C. Ord: '63, Chile; Rev. Joseph Peixotto, C.S.C. Ord: '61, Bangladesh; Rev. George F. Pope, C.S.C. Ord: '58, Bangladesh; Rev. Richard L. Potthast, C.S.C. Ord: '67, Uganda; Rev. Frank J. Quinlivan, C.S.C. Ord: '70, Bangladesh; Rev. Robert G. Simon, C.S.C. Ord: '61, Chile; Rev. Thomas W. Smith, C.S.C. Ord: '72, Tanzania; Rev. Richard E. Stout, C.S.C. Ord: '71, Uganda; Rev. Richard W. Timm, C.S.C. Ord: '49, Bangladesh; Rev. Thomas Zurcher, C.S.C. Ord: '72, Mexico; Bro. Donald Becker, C.S.C., Bangladesh; Bro. John Benesh, C.S.C., Peru; Bro. Thomas Dillman, C.S.C., Ghana; Bro. Ronald Drahozal, C.S.C., Bangladesh; Bro. John Flood, C.S.C., Kenya; Bro. Vincent Gross, C.S.C., Ghana; Bro. Thomas Giumenta, C.S.C., Peru; Bro. Alan Harrod, C.S.C., Uganda; Bro. Ronald Hein, C.S.C., Brazil; Bro. Bernard Klim, C.S.C., Uganda; Bro. Donald E. Kuchenmeister, C.S.C., Chile; Bro. Alfred Ledet, C.S.C., Brazil; Bro. Dismas Lenzi, C.S.C., Brazil; Bro. Norbert Lengerich, C.S.C., Brazil; Bro. Matthew Lyons, C.S.C., Chile; Bro. Matthew McKenna, C.S.C., Chile; Bro. Harold Naudet, C.S.C., Brazil; Bro. James Nichols, C.S.C., Uganda; Bro. Leonard Reeson, C.S.C., Brazil; Bro. Frank Robinson, C.S.C., Brazil; Bro. Paul Schaefer, C.S.C., Brazil; Bro. Sergio Stolf, C.S.C., Brazil; Bro. Rodney Struble, C.S.C., Bangladesh; Bro. Nicholas Thielman, C.S.C., Bangladesh; Bro. Ernest Turk, C.S.C., Brazil; Bro. Robert Weinmann, C.S.C., Brazil.

JESUIT MISSIONS (S.J.)

Jesuit Foreign Missions

Jesuit Mission Inc. An official missionary organization of the Provinces of the United States Assistancy of the Society of Jesus.

National Headquarters: Jesuit Missions, 1016 16th St., N.W., #400, Washington, DC 20036. Phone: 202-462-0400; Fax: 202-328-9212. Rev. Thomas H. Smolich, S.J. Ord: '86, Pres.; Rev. Thomas P. Greene, S.J. Ord: '07, Vice Pres.; Rev. James M. Shea, S.J. Ord: '75, Treas.; Very Rev. Myles Sheehan, S.J. Ord: '94, Sec.

Provinces

Society of Jesus: California Province, 300 College Ave., Los Gatos, CA 95030. Rev. Michael F. Weiler, S.J. Ord: '88, Prov.; Rev. Theodore E. Gabrielli, S.J. Ord: '96, Mission Dir.

Legal Title: *California Jesuit Missionaries*

U.S. Religious serving in Foreign Missions: Rev. Louis G. Aldrich, S.J. Ord: '86, Republic of China; Rev. Walter G. Brennan, S.J. Ord: '60, Japan; Rev. Robert E. Chiesa, S.J. Ord: '68, Japan; Rev. Robert W. Cunningham, S.J. Ord: '55, Philippines; Rev. John A. Donahue, S.J. Ord: '79, Honduras; Rev. John R. Donald, S.J. Ord: '72, Honduras; Rev. Gustavo D. Fernandez, S.J. Ord: '67, Guatemala; Rev. Robert Glynn, S.J. Ord: '91, Zambia; Rev. Fred J. Green, S.J. Ord: '58, Peru; Rev. Robert B. Grimaldi, S.J. Ord: '68, Honduras; Rev. Keith Barry Martinson, S.J. Ord: '75, Republic of China; Rev. George G. Martinson, S.J. Ord: '73, Republic of China; Rev. Paul E. Pollock, S.J. Ord: '73, Thailand; Rev. Daniel J. Ross, S.J. Ord: '66, Republic of China; Rev. Richard J. Schneck, S.J. Ord: '72, Ecuador; Rev. Augustine H. Tsang, S.J. Ord: '94, Republic of China; Rev. Edward J. Thylstrup, S.J. Ord: '67, Republic of China; Rev. Charles A. Welsh, S.J. Ord: '72, Republic of China; Rev. Thomas J.E. Schwarz, S.J. Ord: '01, Uruguay; Bro. Richard J. Devine, S.J., Japan.

Residing in other provinces: Phone: 39 06 68977 703; Cell: 39 3314350589. Phone: 39 06 69526 6112; Fax: 39 06 69526 6151. Rev. Ernest R. Martinez, S.J. Ord: '62, Supr. & Prof. Emeritus New Testament Spirituality; Phone: 39 06 68977 703; Cell: 39 3314350589.Rev. Stephen Pisano, S.J. Ord: '75, Old Testament Exegesis and Criticism;Phone: 39 06 69526 6112; Fax: 39 06 69526 6151. .

Priests: 22; Brothers: 1

Society of Jesus: Chicago Province, 2050 N. Clark St., Chicago, IL 60614. Phone: 773-975-6363. Very Rev. Timothy P. Kesicki, S.J. Ord: '94, Prov.; Rev. Walter C. Deye, S.J. Ord: '75, Socius.

Legal Title: *Jesuit International Missions, (Formerly, Jesuits in Peru, Chicago Province, and Patna Jesuit Mission Society).*

U.S. Religious serving in Foreign Missions: Rev. Richard J. Baumann, S.J. Ord: '75, Ghana & Nairobi; Rev. Theodore B. Bowling, S.J. Ord: '53, India; Rev. Francis P. Chamberlain, S.J. Ord: '68, Peru; Rev. Terrence P. Charlton, S.J. Ord: '76, Kenya; Rev. Martin P. Coyne, S.J. Ord: '66, Nepal; Rev. Edwin J. Daly, S.J. Ord: '59, India; Rev. Robert M. Deiters, S.J. Ord: '58, Japan; Rev. Robert L. Dolan, S.J. Ord: '73, Peru; Rev. Jerome F. Durack, S.J. Ord: '60, India; Rev. Keith J. Esenther, S.J. Ord: '71, Zimbabwe; Rev. Kevin H. Flaherty, S.J. Ord: '83, Peru; Rev. John J. Kenealy, S.J. Ord: '58, India; Rev. Roman B. Lewicki, S.J. Ord: '65, India; Rev. Jeffrey L. Klaiber, S.J. Ord: '74; Rev. Lewis Charles Murtaugh, S.J., Peru; Rev. John L. O'Malley, S.J. Ord: '63, Japan; Rev. Edward P. Schmidt, S.J. Ord: '71, Peru; Rev. John R. Sima, S.J. Ord: '71, Peru; Rev. George Wuest, S.J. Ord: '58, Ecuador; Rev. T. Mattingly Garr, S.J. Ord: '75, Peru.

Priests: 20

Society of Jesus: *Detroit Province* 2500 N. Clark St., Chicago, IL 60614. Phone: 313-861-7500. Very Rev. Timothy P. Kesicki, S.J. Ord: '94, Prov.; Rev. Walter C. Deye, S.J. Ord: '75, Socius.

Legal Title: *Jesuit International Missions, (Formerly, Patna Jesuit Mission Society)*

U.S. Religious serving in Foreign Missions: Rev. Richard W. Cherry, S.J. Ord: '69, Sudan; Rev. Gerald A. Drinane, S.J. Ord: '62, India; Rev. Eugene F. Hattie, S.J. Ord: '53, Uganda; Rev. Casper J. Miller, S.J. Ord: '64, Nepal; Rev. Joseph E. Mulligan, S.J. Ord: '73, Nicaragua; Rev. James J. Regan, S.J. Ord: '67, Peru; Rev. Robert H. Schmidt, S.J. Ord: '69, India; Rev. Theodore W. Walters, S.J. Ord: '56, Tanzania; Rev. Martin T. Connell, S.J. Ord: '94, Tanzania; Bro. Richard L. Cure, S.J., Japan.

Priests: 9; Brothers: 1

Society of Jesus: Maryland Province, 8600 LaSalle Rd., Ste. 620, Towson, MD 21286-2014. Phone: 443-921-1310; Fax: 443-921-1313. Very Rev. James M. Shea, S.J. Ord: '75, Prov.

Legal Title: *Jesuit Mission Inc., an official missionary organization of the Provinces of the United States Assistancy of the Society of Jesus.*

U.S. Religious serving in Foreign Missions: Rev. Eugene J. Barber, S.J. Ord: '63, Chile; Rev. Edgar J. Debany, S.J. Ord: '84, Nigeria; Rev. James M. Desjardins, S.J. Ord: '77, Russia; Rev. Eugene M. Geinzer, S.J. Ord: '74, China; Rev. Michael J. Lynch, S.J. Ord: '93, China.

Priests: 8

Society of Jesus: Missouri Province, 4511 W. Pine Blvd., St. Louis, MO 63108. Phone: 314-361-7765; Fax: 314-758-7164. Rev. Douglas W. Marcouiller, S.J. Ord: '86, Prov.

Legal Title: *The Jesuits of the Missouri Province*

U.S. Religious serving in Foreign Missions: Rev. Brian J. Christopher, S.J. Ord: '09, Belize; Rev. Joseph Damhorst, S.J. Ord: '68, Belize; Rev. Mauricio Gaborit, S.J. Ord: '78, El Salvador; Rev. Jeffrey D. Harrison, S.J. Ord: '87, Belize; Rev. Steven B. Hawkes-Teeples, S.J. Ord: '93, Italy, Prof. Pontifical Oriental Institute; Rev. D. Scott Hendrickson, S.J. Ord: '08, United Kingdom; Rev. Mark A. Kramer, S.J. Ord: '05, Italy; Rev. John L. Maher, S.J. Ord: '74, Belize; Rev. Maurice M. Murray, S.J. Ord: '66, Belize; Rev. Lammert B. Otten, S.J. Ord: '65, Zambia; Rev. Raymond A. Pease, S.J. Ord: '68, Honduras; Rev. Richard D. Perl, S.J. Ord: '78, Belize; Rev. Hung Pham, S.J. Ord: '06, Spain; Rev. Jesus R. Riveroll, S.J. Ord: '88, Belize; Rev. Frank J. Schmitt, S.J. Ord: '83, Belize; Rev. William J. Snyders, S.J. Ord: '66, Belize; Rev. Ricardo Steinmetz, S.J. Ord: '55, Mexico; Rev. John J. Stochl, S.J. Ord: '54, Belize; Rev. J. Timothy Thompson, S.J. Ord: '70, Belize; Rev. Jose Antonio Vega, S.J. Ord: '00, Belize; Rev. Robert D. Voss, S.J. Ord: '72, Honduras; Rev. Jarrell D. Wade, S.J. Ord: '65, Honduras; Rev. John B. Warner, S.J. Ord: '74, Honduras; Rev. Robert A. White, S.J. Ord: '62, Tanzania; Rev. John H. Willmering, S.J. Ord: '68, Honduras; Bro. Karl D. Swift, S.J., Belize; Bro. Harold A. Teel, S.J., Belize; Bro. N. Aloysius Vogt, S.J., Belize; Bro. E. Glenn Kerfoot, S.J., Belize.

Priests: 24; Brothers: 4

Society of Jesus: New England Province, 85 School St., Watertown, MA 02472-4251. Phone: 617-607-2800; Fax: 617-607-2888. Very Rev. Myles N. Sheehan, S.J. Ord: '94, Prov.; Rev. Michael J. Linden, S.J. Ord: '80, Prov. Asst. International Ministries.

Legal Title: *The Society of Jesus of New England*

U.S. Religious serving in Foreign Missions: Rev. John A. Carty, S.J. Ord: '59, Egypt; Mr. Daniel R. Corrou, Lebanon; Rev. James A. Gillon, S.J. Ord: '74, Uganda; Rev. Julio Giulietti, S.J. Ord: '72, Vietnam; Rev. Louis L. Grenier, S.J. Ord: '49, Jamaica; Rev. Richard P. Guerrera, S.J. Ord: '73, Mozambique; Rev. Alfred J. Hicks, S.J. Ord: '66, Jordan; Rev. Michael D. Linden, S.J. Ord: '80, Jordan; Rev. Joseph A. MacWade, S.J. Ord: '61, Jamaica; Rev. Martin F. McDermott, S.J. Ord: '64, Lebanon; Rev. Joseph F. McHugh, S.J., Jamaica; Rev. Gerald L. McLaughlin, S.J. Ord: '59, Jamaica; Rev. Perard C. Monestime, S.J. Ord: '85, Haiti; Rev. Oliver E. Nickerson, S.J. Ord: '54, Jamaica; Rev. Kevin G. O'Connell, S.J. Ord: '69, Jordan; Rev. Francis J. Ryan, S.J. Ord: '56, Jamaica; Rev. Paul A. Schweitzer, S.J. Ord: '70, Brazil; Rev. David A. Skelskey, S.J. Ord: '80, Philippines; Rev. Kevin R. White, S.J. Ord: '99, Sudan.

Priests: 17; Seminarians: 1

Society of Jesus: New York Province, 39 E. 83rd St., New York, NY 10028. Phone: 212-774-5500. Very Rev. David S. Ciancimino, S.J. Ord: '88, Prov.; Rev. Thomas R. Slon, S.J. Ord: '90, Exec. Asst. to the Prov./Socius; Rev. Ramon A. Salomone, S.J. Ord: '65, Asst. Prov. International Apostolates.

U.S. Religious serving in Foreign Missions: Rev. John S. Hagileiram, S.J. Ord: '85, Supr., Micronesia; Rev. William M. Abbott, S.J. Ord: '72, Philippines; Rev. Gerald W. Aman, S.J. Ord: '73, Nigeria; Rev. John J. Carroll, S.J. Ord: '55, Philippines; Rev. Matthew J. Cassidy, S.J. Ord: '99, Ghana; Rev. Pasquale T. Giordano, S.J. Ord: '72, Philippines; Rev. Francis N. Glover, S.J. Ord: '58, Philippines; Rev. James C. Gould, S.J. Ord: '74, Micronesia; Rev. John J. Halligan, S.J. Ord: '61, Ecuador; Rev. Donald J. Hinfey, S.J. Ord: '63, North-West Africa; Rev. Victor J. Helly, S.J. Ord: '54, Philippines; Rev. Kenneth J. Hezel, S.J. Ord: '66; Rev. Robert C. Hogan, S.J. Ord: '64, Philippines; Rev. Raymond T. Holscher, S.J. Ord: '72, Philippines; Rev. William P. Klintworth, S.J.

Ord: '61, Philippines; Rev. William H. Kreutz, S.J. Ord: '69, Philippines; Rev. Dennis M. Leder, S.J. Ord: '76, Guatemala; Rev. William J. Malley, S.J. Ord: '64, Philippines; Rev. R. Richard McAuliff, S.J. Ord: '92, Micronesia; Rev. William J. McGarry, S.J. Ord: '58, Philippines; Rev. Thomas B. McGrath, S.J. Ord: '64, Guam; Rev. Daniel J. McNamara, S.J. Ord: '80, Philippines; Rev. James T. Meehan, S.J. Ord: '63, Philippines; Rev. Michael D. Moga, S.J. Ord: '64, Philippines; Rev. Gregory F. Muckenhaupt, S.J. Ord: '88, Micronesia; Rev. James A. O'Donnell, S.J. Ord: '61, Philippines; Rev. Thomas H. O'Gorman, S.J. Ord: '63, Philippines; Rev. Calvin H. Poulin, S.J. Ord: '62, Philippines; Rev. James B. Reuter, S.J. Ord: '46, Philippines; Rev. Robert A. Rice, S.J. Ord: '53, Philippines; Rev. Joseph L. Roche, S.J. Ord: '58, Philippines; Rev. Marc J. Roselli, S.J. Ord: '85, Micronesia; Rev. Herbert Schneider, S.J. Ord: '70, Philippines; Rev. John N. Schumacher, S.J. Ord: '57, Philippines; Rev. John J. Shea, S.J. Ord: '75, Japan; Rev. Joseph J. Smith, S.J. Ord: '57, Philippines; Rev. Thomas B. Steinbugler, S.J. Ord: '61, Philippines; Rev. Robert J. Suchan, S.J. Ord: '56, Philippines; Rev. Juan C. Villegas, S.J. Ord: '75, Colombia.

Society of Jesus: Oregon Province, 3215 S.E. 45th Ave., P.O. Box 86010, Portland, OR 97286-0010. Phone: 503-226-6977. Rev. Patrick J. Lee, S.J. Ord: '78, Prov.

Legal Title: *American Jesuits in Africa*

U.S Religious serving in Foreign Missions: Rev. Joseph B. Danel, S.J. Ord: '52, Zambia; Rev. Peter J. Henriot, S.J. Ord: '70, Zambia; Rev. Ronald E. Hidaka, S.J. Ord: '74, Zambia; Rev. James P. McGloin, S.J. Ord: '74, Zambia; Rev. Roy W. Thaden, S.J. Ord: '73, Zambia; Rev. Peter R. Titland, S.J. Ord: '70, Zambia; Rev. Bartholomew J. Murphy, S.J. Ord: '72, Kenya; Rev. Michael J. Schultheis, S.J. Ord: '65, South Sudan; Rev. Gary N. Smith, S.J. Ord: '71, Kenya.

Priests: 9

Society of Jesus: Wisconsin Province, 3400 W. Wisconsin Ave., P.O. Box 080288, Milwaukee, WI 53208-8004. Phone: 414-937-6949; Fax: 414-937-6950. Very Rev. Thomas A. Lawler, S.J. Ord: '99, Prov.; Rev. Patrick J. Burns, S.J. Ord: '63, Asst. Prov., Dir. Planning & Implementation for Province Reconfiguration.

U.S. Religious serving in Foreign Missions: Rev. Francis X. Buchmeier, S.J. Ord: '73, Korea; Rev. John V. Daly, S.J. Ord: '66, Korea; Rev. Emil J. Denemark, S.J. Ord: '81, East Timor; Rev. Robert W. Dundon, S.J. Ord: '69, Nigeria; Rev. John D. Mace, S.J. Ord: '68, Cambodia; Rev. H. Francis Mathy, S.J. Ord: '58, Japan; Rev. Robert K. McIntosh, S.J. Ord: '72, Korea; Rev. John R. Schak, S.J. Ord: '61, Argentina; Rev. Nicholas E. Schiel, S.J. Ord: '55, Honduras; Rev. Christopher A. Spalatin, S.J. Ord: '71, Korea; Rev. James J. Strzok, S.J. Ord: '70, Kenya; Rev. Anthony J. Wach, S.J. Ord: '72, Uganda.

Priests: 14

CONGREGATION OF THE HOLY SPIRIT (C.S.Sp.)

Holy Spirit Foreign Missions

Province of the United States, 6230 Brush Run Rd., Bethel Park, PA 15102. Fax: 412-831-0970. Very Rev. John Fogarty, C.S.Sp. Ord: '81, Prov.

U.S. Religious serving Abroad: Rev. William H. Christy, C.S.Sp. Ord: '92, Beagle Bay, Australia; Rev. Paul M. Flamm, C.S.Sp. Ord: '99, Kasulu-Kigoma; Rev. Adrien T. Hebert, C.S.Sp. Ord: '58, Pomeroy, RSA; Rev. Joseph M. Herzstein, C.S.Sp. Ord: '63, Arusha; Rev. Trinh Le, C.S.Sp. Ord: '07, Quan Tan Binh, Vietnam; Rev. Quoc Le, C.S.Sp. Ord: '10, Quan Tan Binh, Vietnam; Rev. Duc Luong, C.S.Sp. Ord: '04, Hsinchu, Taiwan; Rev. Edward T. Marchessault, C.S.Sp. Ord: '64, Arusha, Tanzania; Rev. Donald J. McEachin, C.S.Sp. Ord: '81, The Dominican Republic; Rev. Josaphat Msongore, C.S.Sp. Ord: '63, Arusha, Tanzania; Rev. Joseph Q. Nguyen, C.S.Sp. Ord: '10, Tanlajas, Mexico; Rev. Simon T. Nguyen, C.S.Sp. Ord: '10, Hsinchu, Taiwan; Rev. Patrick A. Patten, C.S.Sp. Ord: '78, Arusha, Tanzania; Rev. Binh T. Quach, C.S.Sp. Ord: '91, Hsinchu, Taiwan; Rev. Daniel Sormani, C.S.Sp. Ord: '86, Quezon City, Philippines.

JESUIT VOLUNTEERS (S.J.)

U.S. Headquarters: Jesuit Volunteers International:, 1016 16th St. N.W., Ste. 400, Washington, DC 20036. Phone: 202-462-5200; Fax: 202-328-9212. Kevin O'Brien, Pres.

Selected college graduates improve education and promote human welfare, faith communities and social justice through a two-year commitment to impoverished local communities in seven developing nations.

MARYKNOLL (M.M.)

A community of American secular priests and brothers. Established in 1911 by action of the United States Hierarchy. Authorized by Pope Pius X, with later approvals by Pope Benedict XV and Pope Pius XI.

U.S Foundation Maryknoll Society Center & Administrative Offices Catholic Foreign Mission Society of America:, P.O. Box 303, Maryknoll, NY 10545-0303. Phone: 914-941-7590; Fax: 914-944-3600. Rev. Edward M. Dougherty, M.M. Ord: '79, Supr. Gen. & Pres.; Rev. Jose A. Aramburu, M.M. Ord: '84, Vicar Gen. & Vice Pres.; Rev. Edward J. McGovern, M.M. Ord: '04, Asst. Gen.; Rev. Paul R. Masson, M.M. Ord: '72, Asst. Gen.

The Society is incorporated in New York, under the Legal Title: Catholic Foreign Mission Society of America, Incorporated. It is also incorporated in California, Hawaii, Illinois, Massachusetts, Minnesota, and Missouri.

For detailed information regarding statistics, activities in the Archdioceses and Dioceses in the United States, Properties owned or sponsored and Houses in the United States, and the placement of the Maryknollers in the various Archdioceses and Dioceses, please refer to the sections for Religious Institutes of Men and the designated Archdioceses and Dioceses.

Maryknoll Foreign Missions

Maryknollers serving Overseas: Province Office:

Religious serving in Bangladesh: Rev. Robert T. McCahill, M.M. Ord: '64; Rev. William J. McIntire, M.M. Ord: '67.

Priests 2.

Religious serving in Bolivia: Rev. Denis P. Browne, M.M. Ord: '47; Rev. Joseph M. Everson, M.M. Ord: '99; Rev. Raymond J. Finch, M.M. Ord: '76; Rev. John F. Gorski, M.M. Ord: '63; Rev. Thomas P. Henehan, M.M. Ord: '65; Rev. Francis B. Higdon, M.M. Ord: '67; Rev. Sigmund S. Jamroz, M.M. Ord: '66; Rev. Stephen P. Judd, M.M. Ord: '78; Rev. Kenneth J. Moody, M.M. Ord: '70; Rev. John J. Ogurchock, M.M. Ord: '54; Rev. Paul M. Sykora, M.M. Ord: '76; Rev. Stephen J. Taluja, M.M. Ord: '09; Rev. Eugene W. Toland, M.M. Ord: '64; Rev. Juan M. Zuniga, M.M. Ord: '88.

Priests 14; Brothers 3; Seminarians 1.

Religious serving in Brazil: Rev. Daniel F. McLaughlin, M.M. Ord: '61; Rev. Dennis Moorman, M.M. Ord: '98.

Priests 2.

Religious serving in Cambodia: Rev. Charles R. Dittmeier Ord: '70; Rev. Kevin M. Conroy Ord: '68; Rev. Robert F. Wynne, M.M. Ord: '74.

Priests 1; Priest Associates 2.

Religious serving in Chile: Rev. Dale F. Barron, M.M. Ord: '65; Rev. Frederick J. Hegarty, M.M. Ord: '53; Rev. J. Lawrence Schanberger, M.M. Ord: '49.

Priests 3; Brothers 1.

Religious serving in El Salvador: Rev. John B. Northrop, M.M. Ord: '98; Rev. John H. Spain, M.M. Ord: '70.

Priests 2.

Religious serving in Ethiopia: Rev. Richard M. Baker, M.M. Ord: '71.

Priests 1.

Religious serving in Guatemala: Rev. Edward O. Custer, M.M. Ord: '72; Rev. William F. Mullan, M.M. Ord: '62; Rev. Joseph W. Halpin, M.M. Ord: '52; Rev. James M. Lynch, M.M. Ord: '74; Rev. John C. Moynihan, M.M. Ord: '67; Rev. William L. Senger, M.M. Ord: '73.

Priests 6; Brothers 1.

Religious serving in Honduras: Rev. Robert F. Coyne, M.M. Ord: '83; Rev. Richard C. Frank, M.M. Ord: '53.

Priests 2.

Religious serving in Hong Kong: Rev. John F. Ahearn, M.M. Ord: '73; Rev. Robert F. Astorino, M.M. Ord: '70; Rev. Brian Barrons, M.M. Ord: '84; Rev. Peter J. Barry, M.M. Ord: '65; Rev. Anthony V. Brennan, M.M. Ord: '61; Rev. John A. Cioppa, M.M. Ord: '59; Rev. Dennis W. Cleary, M.M. Ord: '77; Rev. Vincent F. Corbelli, M.M. Ord: '60; Rev. John P. Cuff, M.M. Ord: '69; Rev. William J. Galvin, M.M. Ord: '56; Rev. John E. Geitner, M.M. Ord: '53; Rev. Adam B. Gudalefsky, M.M. Ord: '59; Rev. Timothy Kilkelly, M.M. Ord: '90; Rev. Denis J. Hanly, M.M. Ord: '59; Rev. James D. McAuley, M.M. Ord: '80; Rev. Thomas A. Peyton, M.M. Ord: '58; Rev. Edward J. Phillips, M.M. Ord: '74; Rev. Ronald R. Saucci, M.M. Ord: '65; Rev. Michael J. Sloboda, M.M. Ord: '85; Rev. John E. Vesey, M.M. Ord: '68; Rev. Elmer P. Wurth, M.M. Ord: '56.

Priests 20; Brothers 3; Associates 1.

Religious serving in Indonesia: Rev. Vincent P. Cole, M.M. Ord: '71.

Priests 1.

Religious serving in Italy: Rev. Clyde Phillips, M.M. Ord: '78, Procurator Gen.

Priests 1.

Religious serving in Japan: Rev. John T. Brinkman, M.M. Ord: '71; Rev. Richard S. Czajkowski, M.M. Ord: '61; Rev. LoXuan Dam, M.M. Ord: '00; Rev. Regis B. Ging, M.M. Ord: '66; Rev. William J. Grimm, M.M. Ord: '77; Rev. Joseph L. Hamel, M.M. Ord: '85; Rev. Joseph H. Hermes, M.M. Ord: '62; Rev. James R. Jackson, M.M. Ord: '58; Rev. James J. Mylet, M.M. Ord: '75; Rev. Robert V. Nehrig, M.M. Ord: '54; Rev. Bryce T. Nishimura, M.M. Ord: '56; Rev. Francis A. Riha, M.M. Ord: '68; Rev. Roberto Rodriguez, M.M. Ord: '95; Rev. Kenneth C. Sleyman, M.M. Ord: '90.

Priests 14.

Religious serving in Kenya: Rev. John E. Conway, M.M. Ord: '73; Rev. William Fryda, M.M. Ord: '88; Rev. Joseph G. Healey, M.M. Ord: '66; Rev. Makarios F. Isaac, M.M. Ord: '88; Rev. Michael C. Kirwen, M.M. Ord: '63; Rev. John J. Lange, M.M. Ord: '58; Rev. Douglas E. May, M.M. Ord: '86; Rev. Lance P. Nadeau, M.M. Ord: '90; Rev. Richard J. Quinn, M.M. Ord: '54; Rev. Kenneth F. Thesing, M.M. Ord: '69.

Priests 9; Brothers 1; Priest Associates 1.

Religious serving in Korea: Rev. Edward J. Whelan, M.M. Ord: '61; Rev. Richard Agustin, M.M. Ord: '85; Rev. Francis H. Beninati, M.M. Ord: '55; Rev. Carl A. Costa, M.M. Ord: '71; Rev. Gerald J. Farrell, M.M. Ord: '57; Rev. Russell J. Feldmeier, M.M. Ord: '80; Rev. Gerard E. Hammond, M.M. Ord: '60; Rev. Robert M. Lilly, M.M. Ord: '60; Rev. Philip W. Mares, M.M. Ord: '86; Rev. James T. Najmowski, M.M. Ord: '76; Rev. Gerald P. O'Connor, M.M. Ord: '69; Rev. Robert R. Pellini, M.M. Ord: '59; Rev. Richard S. Rolewicz, M.M. Ord: '65; Rev. Joseph A. Slaby, M.M. Ord: '66; Rev. James P. Sinnott, M.M. Ord: '60.

Priests 15.

Religious serving in Mexico: Rev. Richard L. Clifford, M.M. Ord: '53; Rev. John P. Martin, M.M. Ord: '66; Rev. Eugene A. Theisen, M.M. Ord: '53; Rev. Robert V. Tobin, M.M. Ord: '57.

Priests 4.

Religious serving in Namibia: Rev. Richard P. Albertine, M.M. Ord: '66; Rev. Richard W. Bauer, M.M. Ord: '85; Rev. Edward D. Shellito, M.M. Ord: '90.

Priests 3; Brothers 1.

Religious serving in Nepal: Rev. Joseph L. Thaler, M.M. Ord: '77; Rev. Rodrigo Ulloa-Chavarry, M.M. Ord: '11.

Priests 2.

Religious serving in the Philippine Islands: Rev. James H. Kroeger, M.M. Ord: '75; Rev. Jeremiah R. Burr, M.M. Ord: '67; Rev. Francis J. Felter, M.M. Ord: '69; Rev. James T. Ferry, M.M. Ord: '56; Rev. William J. LaRousse, M.M. Ord: '80.

Priests 5.

Religious serving in Peoples Republic of China: Rev. Thomas R. Egan, M.M. Ord: '64; Rev. Richard R. Fries, M.M. Ord: '76; Rev. John J. McAuley, M.M. Ord: '81; Rev. Lawrence D. Radice, M.M. Ord: '85.

Priests 4.

Religious serving in Peru: Rev. Thomas J. Burns, M.M. Ord: '69; Rev. Michael J. Briggs, M.M. Ord: '76; Rev. Edmund L. Cookson, M.M. Ord: '65; Rev. Joseph Fedora, M.M. Ord: '84; Rev. Robert E. Hoffman, M.M. Ord: '60; Rev. Kyungsu Son, M.M. Ord: '79.

Priests 6.

Religious serving in Samoa: Most Rev. J. Quinn Weitzel, M.M. Ord: '55.

Bishops 1.

Religious serving in South Sudan: Rev. John C. Barth, M.M. Ord: '91; Rev. Thomas A. Tiscornia, M.M. Ord: '73.

Priests 2.

Religious serving in Taiwan: Rev. Kurt J. Anderson, M.M. Ord: '72; Rev. Paul J. Brien, M.M. Ord: '60; Rev. Peter C. Brien, M.M. Ord: '60; Rev. Robert F. Crawford, M.M. Ord: '61; Rev. Alan T. Doyle, M.M. Ord: '64; Rev. Paul J. Duffy, M.M. Ord: '79; Rev. Clarence A. Engler, M.M. Ord: '59; Rev. Delos A. Humphrey, M.M. Ord: '54; Rev. Alfonso Kim, M.M. Ord: '97; Rev. J. Donald McGinnis, M.M. Ord: '53; Rev. Leonard J. Marron, M.M. Ord: '57; Rev. Eugene M. Murray, M.M. Ord: '58; Rev. Cuong H. Nguyen, M.M. Ord: '98; Rev.

Nhuan D. Nguyen, M.M. Ord: '93; Rev. Brendan M. O'Connell, M.M. Ord: '63; Rev. Norbert A. Pacheco, M.M. Ord: '79; Rev. Anthony V. Polyak, M.M. Ord: '62; Rev. Louis B. Rost, M.M. Ord: '55; Rev. Francis F. Schexnayder, M.M. Ord: '64; Rev. R. Joyalito F. Tajonera, M.M. Ord: '02.

Priests 20; Brothers 1.

Religious serving in Tanzania: Rev. Michael Bassano, M.M. Ord: '75; Rev. James A. Conard, M.M. Ord: '56; Rev. Edward V. Davis, M.M. Ord: '61; Rev. Hung M. Dinh, M.M. Ord: '08; Rev. James E. Eble, M.M. Ord: '88; Rev. Edward A. Hayes, M.M. Ord: '59; Rev. Ramon J. McCabe, M.M. Ord: '56; Rev. Daniel F. Ohmann, M.M. Ord: '55; Rev. Edward R. Schoellmann, M.M. Ord: '65; Rev. Michael J. Snyder, M.M. Ord: '79; Rev. Donald F. Sybertz, M.M. Ord: '55; Rev. John W. Waldrep, M.M. Ord: '90.

Priests 12; Brothers 2; Seminarians 2.

Religious serving in Thailand: Rev. Thomas J. Dunleavy, M.M. Ord: '75; Rev. James W. Kofski, M.M. Ord: '91.

Priests 2; Brothers 1.

Religious serving in Vietnam: Rev. Thomas J. O'Brien, M.M. Ord: '74.

MISSIONARIES OF AFRICA (M.AFR.)

Missionaries of Africa Foreign Missions

U.S. Headquarters: Province of the Americas: 1624 21st St., N.W., Washington, DC 20009-1003. Phone: 202-232-5154; Fax: 202-332-8640. Rev. Richard Archambault, M.Afr. Ord: '73, Supr.; Rev. John Lynch, M.Afr. Ord: '62; Rev. George Markwell, M.Afr. Ord: '65, Hospital Chap.; Rev. Thomas Reilly, M.Afr. Ord: '78, Guestmaster; Rev. Jean-Claude Robitaille, M.Afr. Ord: '73, Delegate Supr.; Rev. Richard Roy, M.Afr. Ord: '71; Rev. Diego Ramon Sarrio Cucarella, M.Afr. Ord: '01, Studies at G.U.; Rev. Brian Denis Starkey, M.Afr. Ord: '77, Treas.; Rev. Robert C. McGovern, M.Afr. Ord: '63; Rev. Michel J. Lavoie, M.Afr. Ord: '70; Rev. Roger Bisson, M.Afr. Ord: '55; Rev. John Joseph Braun, M.Afr. Ord: '57; Rev. Joseph Elmo Hebert, M.Afr. Ord: '63; Rev. Joseph Kay, M.Afr. Ord: '48; Rev. Youville Labonte, M.Afr. Ord: '52; Rev. Richard Roy, M.Afr. Ord: '71; Bro. Martin Chapper, M.Afr.; Bro. James Heintz, M.Afr., Bursar.

U.S. Religious serving in Africa: Rev. William Curran, M.Afr. Ord: '66, Ghana-West Africa; Rev. Roger A. LaBonte, M.Afr. Ord: '62, Uganda-East Africa; Rev. William Moroney, M.Afr. Ord: '61, Kenya-East Africa.

U.S. Religious serving in Great Britain: Rev. David Goergen, M.Afr. Ord: '69.

U.S. Religious serving in Spain: Rev. Rene Dionne, M.Afr. Ord: '61, Spain.

MISSIONARIES OF THE SACRED HEART (M.S.C.)

Missionaries of the Sacred Heart Foreign Missions

Missionaries of the Sacred Heart, 305 S. Lake St., P.O. Box 270, Aurora, IL 60507. Phone: 630-892-2371; Phone: 630-892-8400; Fax: 630-892-1678; Web: www.misacor-usa.org. Very Rev. Raymond Diesbourg, M.S.C. Ord: '74, Prov. Supr.; Bro. James Miller, M.S.C., Treas.

Publication(s): A New Heart for a New World

Religious serving in Colombia, South America: Very Rev. Luis Alfonso Segura, M.S.C. Ord: '99, Section Supr.; Very Rev. German Barona Monsalve, M.S.C. Ord: '86; Rev. Tito Abdenago Medina Mora, M.S.C. Ord: '92; Rev. Hector Eduardo Mejia Arciniegas, M.S.C. Ord: '06; Rev. Eduard Riascos, M.S.C. Ord: '10; Bro. Favio Castro Andino, M.S.C.; Bro. Juan Pablo Romero Contreras; Bro. Faiber Antonio Vargas; Bro. Ernesto Odilio Caicedo, M.S.C.; Bro. William Andres Tovar, M.S.C.; Bro. Jesus Felipe Trejo, M.S.C.; Bro. Jorge Mario Vallejo, M.S.C.; Bro. Miguel Henrry Piamba, M.S.C.

Religious serving in Italy: Very Rev. Mark McDonald, M.S.C. Ord: '68, Supr. Gen.

OBLATES OF ST. FRANCIS DE SALES MISSIONS (O.S.F.S.)

Oblates of St. Francis de Sales Foreign Missions

U.S. Mission Headquarters Office of the Mission Procurato Oblates of St. Francis de Sales:, 1600 Brinckle Ave., Wilmington, DE 19806-1123. Rev. John J. Hurley, O.S.F.S. Ord: '68, Mission Procurator.

U.S. Religious serving in Africa, Asia, Europe & South America: Rev. Leon V. Bonikowski, O.S.F.S. Ord: '65; Rev. Walter DeSa, O.S.F.S. Ord: '65; Rev. William R. Gore, O.S.F.S. Ord: '69; Rev. Thomas Hagan, O.S.F.S. Ord: '69; Rev. Robert J. Hindley, O.S.F.S. Ord: '58; Rev. John A. Kowalewski, O.S.F.S. Ord: '77; Rev. Michael Moore, O.S.F.S. Ord: '68; Rev. Harry J. Schlight, O.S.F.S. Ord: '44; Rev. Alfred J. Smuda, O.S.F.S. Ord: '66; Bro. James Petrait; Rev. Thomas Moore, O.S.F.S. Ord: '66.

AMERICAN PASSIONIST MISSIONS (C.P.)

Passionist Foreign Missions

Home and Foreign Missions of the American Provinces of the Congregation of the Passion.

General Motherhouse: St. Giovanni e Paolo 13, Rome, Italy, 00184, Most Rev. Ottaviano D'Egidio, C.P., Supr. Gen.

The Passionists Provincial Headquarters U.S.A.

St. Paul of the Cross Province: Province Pastoral Center, 20 Cedar St., Ste. 101, New Rochelle, NY 10801. *Residence St. Vincent Strambi Residence:,* 190 Mt. Tom Rd., Pelham, NY 10803. Very Rev. Robert Joerger, C.P. Ord: '77, Prov. Supr.; Very Rev. James O'Shea, C.P. Ord: '89, 3rd Consultor & Mission Procurator; Very Rev. Robin Ryan, C.P. Ord: '84, 1st Consultor; Rev. Richard Burke, C.P. Ord: '76, 2nd Consultor; Rev. Paul Zilonka, C.P. Ord: '71, 4th Consultor.

U.S. Religious serving Abroad: Rev. Richard Award, C.P. Ord: '81, West Indies; Rev. Thomas Brislin, C.P. Ord: '68, Nassau, The Bahamas; Rev. Richard Frechette, C.P. Ord: '79, Haiti; Rev. Lawrence Rywalt, C.P. Ord: '92, Rome; Rev. Francis Finnigan, C.P., France; Rev. Hilarion Walters, C.P. Ord: '47, Philippines; Rev. Paul Ruttle, C.P., Jamaica, West Indies; Bro. Robert McKenna, C.P., Philippines; Bro. Michael Stomber, C.P., West Indies; Rev. Melvin Shorter, C.P. Ord: '86, France.

Mission Procurators

Eastern: Very Rev. James O'Shea, C.P. Ord: '89; Anne Marie Gardiner, Dir., Devel.

Overseas Missions: 526 Monastery Pl., Pittsburgh, PA 15211-3398.

Canada: 2102 Kipling Ave., Rexdale, Canada, M9W 4K5.

Holy Cross Province (Western): 5700 N. Harlem Ave., Chicago, IL 60631. Phone: 773-631-6336; Fax: 773-631-8059. Very Rev. Donald Webber, C.P. Ord: '73, Prov.; Rev. Arthur Carrillo, C.P. Ord: '70.

Mission Appeals

U.S. Religious serving Abroad: Rev. Robert Coward, C.P. Ord: '68, Rome; Rev. Denis McGowan, C.P. Ord: '55, Japan; Rev. Joseph Van Leeuwen, C.P. Ord: '64, India; Rev. John B. Ormechea, C.P. Ord: '65, Rome.

Priests: 5

AMERICAN REDEMPTORIST FATHERS (C.SS.R.)

Mission of the Provinces and Vice-Provinces in the United States and other countries and lands

Redemptorist Foreign Missions

Baltimore Province: Redemptorist Fathers of New York:, 7509 Shore Rd., Brooklyn, NY 11209. Phone: 718-833-1900; Fax: 718-630-5666. Very Rev. Patrick F. Woods, C.Ss.R. Ord: '75, Prov. Supr.

U.S. Religious serving in Dominica, WI: Rev. Michael Houston, C.Ss.R. Ord: '98; Rev. Rodney J. Olive, C.Ss.R. Ord: '86.

U.S. Religious serving in Trinidad & Tobago: Archbishop Edward Joseph Gilbert, C.Ss.R. Ord: '64.

Redemptorist Office of Mission Advancement: 107 Duke of Gloucester St., Annapolis, MD 21401-2526. Phone: 410-288-8755; Phone: 877-876-7662.

Baltimore Province:

U.S. Religious serving in Brazil: Rev. Richard Blissert, C.Ss.R. Ord: '56; Rev. Karl Esker, C.Ss.R. Ord: '76; Rev. Giles Gardner, C.Ss.R. Ord: '39; Rev. Lawrence Kearns, C.Ss.R. Ord: '65; Rev. Clement Krug, C.Ss.R. Ord: '65; Rev. Patrick McGillicuddy, C.Ss.R. Ord: '79; Rev. Edward Moriarty, C.Ss.R. Ord: '42; Rev. Donald Roth, C.Ss.R. Ord: '75; Rev. John Roche, C.Ss.R. Ord: '63; Rev. William Tracey, C.Ss.R. Ord: '55; Rev. Stephen Vanyo, C.Ss.R. Ord: '62.

U.S. Religious serving in Lebanon: Rev. Charles Coury, C.Ss.R. Ord: '76.

U.S. Religious serving in St. Lucia, V.I.: Rev. Michael Houston, C.Ss.R. Ord: '98.

U.S. Religious serving in St. Croix, V.I.: Rev. Kenneth F. Gaddy, C.Ss.R. Ord: '88; Rev. E. Patrick Lynch, C.Ss.R Ord: '69; Rev. Kevin M. MacDonald, C.Ss.R. Ord: '91.

Denver Province: 1230 Parker Rd., Denver, CO 80231. Phone: 303-370-0035; Fax: 303-370-0036. Rev. Harry Grile, C.Ss.R. Ord: '68, Provincial Supr.

U.S. Religious serving in Brazil: Most Rev. Gutemberg Regis, C.Ss.R., Bishop of Coari; Most Rev. Alfred Novak, C.Ss.R. Ord: '49, Bishop of Paranagua, Brazil; Rev. John McCarthy, C.Ss.R. Ord: '62; Rev. Thomas McIntosh, C.Ss.R. Ord: '66; Rev. William H. (Carlos) Steiner, C.Ss.R. Ord: '54.

U.S. Religious serving in Nigeria: Rev. Richard Thiele, C.Ss.R. Ord: '54.

U.S. Religious serving in Thailand: Most Rev. George Yod Phimphisan, C.Ss.R. Ord: '58, Bishop of Udon Thani; Rev. Charles Cotant, C.Ss.R. Ord: '41; Rev. Francis Gautreaux, C.Ss.R. Ord: '50; Rev. Joseph Maier, C.Ss.R. Ord: '65; Rev. Robert Martin, C.Ss.R. Ord: '50; Rev. Lawrence Patin, C.Ss.R. Ord: '63; Rev. Michael Shea, C.Ss.R. Ord: '64; Rev. Leo Travis, C.Ss.R. Ord: '54; Rev. William Wright, C.Ss.R. Ord: '60.

ST. COLUMBAN'S FOREIGN MISSION SOCIETY (S.S.C.)

(The Columban Fathers)

Founded in 1918 with the approval of Pope Benedict XV. Placed under the patronage of St. Columban and made a Pontifical Society by Pope Pius XI.

PO Box 10, St Columbans, NE 68056. *Generalate Missionary Society of St. Columban:,* 504 Tower 1, Silvercord, 30 Canton Rd. TST, Kowloon, Hong Kong, Very Rev. Tommy Murphy, S.S.C., Supr. Gen.

U.S. Foundation & Administration: Columban Fathers, St Columbans, NE 68056. Phone: 402-291-1920.

The Society is incorporated in California, Florida, Illinois, Massachusetts, Nebraska, New York, Rhode Island, and Texas and registered in Pennsylvania.

Publication: Columban Mission

Very Rev. John Burger, S.S.C. Ord: '73, Dir.; Rev. Thomas P. Reynolds, S.S.C. Ord: '61, Vice Dir.

Legal Title: *Missionary Society of St. Columban a/k/a St. Columban's Foreign Mission Society*

Publication(s): Columban Mission

St. Columban's Foreign Mission

House of Post-Graduate Studies: PO Box 10, St Columbans, NE 68056. **Collegio San Colombano,** Corso Trieste, 57, Rome, Italy, 00198, Rev. Padhraic O'Loughlin, S.S.C. Ord: '57, Procurator Gen.

U.S. Religious serving Overseas: Very Rev. Brendan O'Sullivan, S.S.C. Ord: '70, Ireland; Rev. Vincent J. Busch, S.S.C. Ord: '74, Philippines; Rev. Francis P. Carroll, S.S.C. Ord: '62, Japan; Rev. David J. Clay, S.S.C., Philippines; Rev. John Comisky, C.S.C. Ord: '68, Philippines; Rev. Neil Boyle, S.S.C. Ord: '43, Ireland; Rev. Otto Imholte, S.S.C. Ord: '63, Ireland; Rev. Michael Hoban, S.S.C. Ord: '70, Chile; Rev. David Padrnos, S.S.C. Ord: '71, Japan; Rev. Ronald Kelso, S.S.C. Ord: '73; Rev. Donald Kill, S.S.C. Ord: '72, Philippines; Rev. Joseph McSweeny, S.S.C. Ord: '90, Taiwan; Rev. John P. Moran, S.S.C. Ord: '50, Philippines; Rev. William Morton, S.S.C. Ord: '60, Mexico; Rev. Robert Mosher, S.S.C. Ord: '82, Chile; Rev. Richard L. Pankratz, S.S.C. Ord: '74; Rev. Desmond Quinn, S.S.C. Ord: '54, Ireland; Rev. Edward Quinn, S.S.C. Ord: '55, Fiji; Rev. Paul Richardson, S.S.C. Ord: '54, Philippines; Rev. Christopher Saenz, S.S.C. Ord: '00, Chile; Rev. John Wanaurny, S.S.C. Ord: '59, Mexico; Rev. Vincent J. Youngkamp, S.S.C. Ord: '59, Japan.

Priests: 29

BROTHERS OF THE SACRED HEART (S.C.)

Brothers of the Sacred Heart Foreign Missions

Provincial House, 685 Steere Farm Rd., Pascoag, RI 02859-4601. Phone: 401-568-3361; Fax: 401-568-1450. Bro. Robert Croteau, S.C., Prov. Supr.; Bro. Paul J. Hebert, S.C., Mission Procurator.

Brothers: 65; Brothers in Africa: 59

The Brothers of the Sacred Heart have mission schools and other establishments in Kenya, Lesotho, Uganda, Zambia, and Zimbabwe.

SALESIANS OF DON BOSCO (S.D.B.)

Salesians of Don Bosco Foreign Missions

Salesian Provincial House, 148 Main St., Box 639, New Rochelle, NY 10802-0639. Phone: 914-636-4225. Very Rev. Thomas Dunne, S.D.B. Ord: '72, Prov.; Rev. Mark Hyde, S.D.B. Ord: '81, Procurator.

U.S. Religious serving Abroad: Rev. Henry Bonetti, S.D.B. Ord: '73, Philippines; Rev. Robert Falk, S.D.B. Ord: '63, Korea; Rev. Lawrence Gilmore, S.D.B. Ord: '84, Liberia; Rev. Harry Peterson, S.D.B. Ord: '61, Chile; Rev. John Thompson, S.D.B. Ord: '79, Swaziland; Bro. Sean McEwen, S.D.B., Ivory Coast; Rev. Jean-Paul Lebel, S.D.B. Ord: '66, Rwanda; Bro. Joseph Reza, S.D.B., Ethiopia.

SALVATORIAN MISSIONS (S.D.S.)

Salvatorian Foreign Missions

U.S.A. Provincial Headquarters: Salvatorian Provincial Offices:, 1735 N. Hi-Mount Blvd., Milwaukee, WI 53208-1720. Phone: 414-258-1735. Very Rev. David Bergner, S.D.S. Ord: '76, Prov.

Publication(s): The Salvatorian Newsletter

U.S.A. Procurator: 4033 Bacopa Pl., Lexington, KY 40509. Phone: 859-264-8058. Rev. Thomas Tureman, S.D.S. Ord: '88, Mission Dir.

U.S. Religious serving in Philippines: Rev. Gregory Coulthard, S.D.S. Ord: '67.

SOCIETY OF AFRICAN MISSIONS (S.M.A.)

Society of African Missions

U.S. Provincial Headquarters: 23 Bliss Ave., Tenafly, NJ 07670. Phone: 201-567-0450; Phone: 201-567-9085; Fax: 800-670-8328; Fax: 201-541-1280. Very Rev. Michael P. Moran, S.M.A. Ord: '81, Prov. Supr.

U.S. Religious serving Abroad: Rev. Ted Hayden, S.M.A. Ord: '58, Liberia.

SOCIETY OF ST. EDMUND (S.S.E.)

Edmundite Foreign Missions

U.S. Foundation: 270 Winooski Park, Colchester, VT 05439. Phone: 802-654-3400; Fax: 802-654-3409. Very Rev. Michael P. Cronogue, S.S.E. Ord: '77, Supr. Gen.

U.S. Religious serving Abroad: Rev. Edward J. Dubriske, S.S.E. Ord: '64, Venezuela; Rev. Philippe Simonnet, S.S.E. Ord: '52, France.

SOCIETY OF ST. JAMES THE APOSTLE

St. James the Apostle, Inc: 24 Clark St., Boston, MA 02109. Phone: 617-742-4715; Fax: 617-723-7389.

Founded by His Eminence Richard Cardinal Cushing, in 1958 to recruit Diocesan priest volunteers for South America.

Rev. David Costello Ord: '95, Dir.; Rev. Patrick Universal Ord: '75.

Serving in Ecuador: Rev. P.J. Hughes; Rev. Martin Kelly Ord: '65; Rev. Cornelius Kiely Ord: '67; Rev. Colin MacInnes Ord: '70; Rev. Patrick McIntyre Ord: '60; Rev. John Molloy; Rev. Dennis J. O'Brien Ord: '81; Rev. Thomas Oates Ord: '63; Rev. Liam Reilly Ord: '00; Rev. Robert Thomas Ord: '61.

Serving in Peru: Rev. Geoffrey Adolfo Ord: '00; Rev. Simon Cadwallader Ord: '97; Rev. George Flynn Ord: '56; Rev. Jonathan Hart Ord: '96; Rev. Kevin Hays Ord: '77; Rev. Derek Leonard Ord: '96; Rev. J. Joseph McCarthy Ord: '66; Rev. John O'Leary Ord: '67; Rev. Gerard O'Meara Ord: '56; Rev. Daniel O'Sullivan Ord: '70; Rev. Raymond S. O'Sullivan Ord: '68; Rev. Denis Parry Ord: '94; Rev. Msgr. Jules Roos Ord: '56; Rev. Desmond A. Tynan Ord: '67.

THE SOCIETY OF MARY (S.M.)

MARIST FATHERS

Marist Foreign Missions

General Motherhouse: Via Alesandro Poerio, 63, Rome, Italy, 00152, Very Rev. John Hannan, S.M. Ord: '68, Supr. Gen.; Very Rev. Lawrence Duffy, S.M. Ord: '75, Vicar Gen.

U.S. Mission Promoter: Marist Missions, 27 Isabella St., Boston, MA 02116-5216. Phone: 617-482-0832; Fax: 617-426-1884.

Missions in Brazil, Fiji, Japan, New Caledonia, Norway, Papua New Guinea, Jamaica, Peru, Philippine Islands, Samoa, Senegal, Solomon Islands, Thailand, Tonga, Vanuatu, Wallis & Futuna, Republic of Cameroon.

Rev. Joseph J. McLaughlin, S.M. Ord: '72, Mission Promoter.

U.S. Religious serving Abroad: Rev. John Bolduc, S.M. Ord: '70, Jamaica; Rev. John Galvin, S.M. Ord: '63, Solomon Islands; Rev. Louis Morosini, S.M. Ord: '56, Solomon Islands; Rev. Alfred Puccinelli, S.M. Ord: '66, Brazil; Rev. Neil Soucy, S.M. Ord: '62, New Caldonia.

THIRD ORDER REGULAR MISSIONS (T.O.R.)

THIRD ORDER REGULAR OF ST. FRANCIS

T.O.R. Foreign Missions

Provincial Residence: Province of the Most Sacred Heart of Jesus:, P.O. Box 137, Loretto, PA 15940. Phone: 814-693-2890. Rev. Christian R. Oravec, T.O.R. Ord: '64, Minister Prov.

U.S. Religious serving Abroad: Rev. Gerald J. King, T.O.R. Ord: '71, Brazil; Rev. Paul R. Pavlik, T.O.R. Ord: '59, Brazil.

MISSIONARY SERVANTS OF THE MOST HOLY TRINITY (S.T.)

Trinity Missions

International Headquarters

Generalate, 9001 New Hampshire Ave., Ste. 300, Silver Spring, MD 20903-3626. Phone: 301-434-0092; Fax: 301-434-0255. Rev. John S. Edmunds, S.T. Ord: '76, Gen. Custodian; Bro. Steven Vesely, S.T., Sec. Gen.

U.S. Religious serving Abroad: Rev. Charles Gordon, S.T. Ord: '67, Colombia; Rev. Raymond Riding, S.T. Ord: '75, Mexico.

AMERICAN VINCENTIAN MISSIONS (C.M.)

Provincial Headquarters

Vincentian Foreign Missions

Eastern Province: St. Vincent's Seminary, 500 E. Chelten Ave., Philadelphia, PA 19144. Phone: 215-713-2400; Fax: 215-844-2085; Email: cmphila88@aol.com. Very Rev. Michael J. Carroll, C.M. Ord: '77, Prov.; Rev. Gregory P. Cozzubbo, C.M. Ord: '84, Asst. Prov.

U.S. Religious serving Abroad: Rev. Osvaldo Ayala, C.M. Ord: '01, Colon, Panama; Rev. John J. Carney, C.M. Ord: '82, Balboa, Panama; Rev. Jose Manuel Delgado, C.M. Ord: '04, Panama City, Panama; Rev. Edison Famania, C.M. Ord: '94, Concepcion, Panama; Rev. Joseph Fitzgerald, C.M. Ord: '05, Soloy, Panama; Very Rev. G. Gregory Gay, C.M. Ord: '80, Rome, Italy; Rev. John W. Gouldrick, C.M. Ord: '69, Rome, Italy; Rev. Alcibiades Guerra, C.M. Ord: '90, Colon, Panama; Rev. Jose Pio Jimenez, C.M. Ord: '68, Panama City, Panama; Rev. Teodoro Justavino, C.M. Ord: '90, Puerto Armuelles, Panama; Rev. John J. MacGillivray, C.M. Ord: '76, Colon, Panama; Rev. Rolando Molina, C.M. Ord: '07, Concepcion, Panama; Rev. Geovany Morales, C.M. Ord: '01, Volcan, Panama; Rev. John P. Prager, C.M. Ord: '82, Republic of Ecuador; Rev. Teodoro A. Rios, C.M. Ord: '76, Puerto Armuelles, Panama; Rev. Secundino Rios, C.M. Ord: '01, Puerto Armuelles, Panama; Rev. Aidan R. Rooney, C.M. Ord: '84, LaPaz, Bolivia; Rev. Charles G. Schuster, C.M. Ord: '55, Soloy, Panama; Rev. Thomas Sendlein, C.M. Ord: '72, Taipei, Taiwan, Republic of China; Rev. Eliseo Troetsch, C.M., Concepcion, Panama; Bro. Crecensio Tenorio A., C.M., Concepcion, Panama; Bro. G. Edgardo Lopez, C.M., Balboa, Panama.

Western Province: Vincentian Fathers and Brothers, 13663 Rider Tr. N., Earth City, MO 63045-1512. Phone: 314-344-1184; Fax: 314-344-2989. Very Rev. Perry Henry, C.M. Ord: '83, Prov.

U.S Religious serving in Foreign Missions: Bro. James E. Donlevy, C.M., Supr.; Rev. Thomas E. Esselman, C.M. Ord: '80, Kenya; Rev. Bernard J. Quinn, C.M., Kenya; Rev. Richard B. Benson, C.M. Ord: '78, Kenya; Rev. Robert W. Chap, C.M. Ord: '66, Taiwan (Province of China); Rev. Richard Preuss, C.M. Ord: '73, Taiwan (Province of China); Rev. Richard Wehrmeyer, C.M. Ord: '91; Rev. Gilbert R. Walker, C.M. Ord: '87, Havana, Cuba.

XAVERIAN MISSIONARY FATHERS (S.X.)

Xaverian Foreign Missions

U.S. Foundation: Xaverian Missionary Fathers:, 12 Helene Ct., Wayne, NJ 07470. Phone: 201-942-2975; Fax: 201-942-5012. Rev. Carl S. Chudy, S.X. Ord: '86, Prov. Supr.; Rev. Frank B. Grappoli, S.X. Ord: '63, Local Superior & Treas. and Prov. Treas. & Mission Procurator.

Legal Title: *St. Francis Xavier Foreign Mission Society, Inc.*

Religious serving in Brazil: Rev. Danilo Lago, S.X. Ord: '77; Rev. Gino Nasini, S.X. Ord: '65.

Religious serving in Cameroon: Rev. Rene Lovat, S.X. Ord: '57; Rev. Pierino Zoni, S.X. Ord: '61; Rev. Fernandes de Araujo Herondi, S.X. Ord: '76.

U.S. Religious serving in Colombia: Rev. Mauro Loda, S.X. Ord: '99.

U.S. Religious serving in Indonesia: Rev. Franco Qualizza, S.X. Ord: '71.

Religious serving in Italy: Rev. Francis Gugliotta, S.X. Ord: '52.

U.S. Religious serving in Japan: Rev. Renato Filippini, S.X. Ord: '97; Rev. Frank Sottocornola, S.X. Ord: '69.

U.S. Religious serving in Mexico: Rev. Dan Boschetto, S.X. Ord: '70; Rev. Ramon Cerratos, S.X. Ord: '99; Rev. Pablo Nieves, S.X. Ord: '99.

U.S. Religious serving in Mozambique: Rev. Dario Maso, S.X. Ord: '82; Rev. Horacio Perez, S.X. Ord: '03.

U.S. Religious serving in Sierra Leone: Most Rev. George Biguzzi, S.X.; Rev. Luigi Brioni, S.X. Ord: '61; Rev. Eugene Montesi, S.X. Ord: '62.

U.S Religious serving in Taiwan: Rev. Joe Vignato, S.X. Ord: '93; Rev. Martino Roia, S.X. Ord: '82; Rev. Edi Foschiatto, S.X. Ord: '81.

MISSIONHURST (C.I.C.M.)

Missionhurst Foreign Missions

American Headquarters (1946): Congregation of the Immaculate Heart of Mary:, 4651 N. 25th St., Arlington, VA 22207. Phone: 703-528-3800; Fax: 703-528-5355; Email: provincial@missionhurst.org. Very Rev. Anselme Malonda Nkuanga, C.I.C.M. Ord: '92, Prov. Supr.

Publication(s): Missionhurst Magazine

U.S Religious serving Abroad: Rev. Timothy Atkin, C.I.C.M. Ord: '74, General Councillor, Rome; Rev. Paul Delaere, C.I.C.M. Ord: '43, Belgium; Rev. William Missinne, C.I.C.M. Ord: '54, Belgium; Rev. Luke Moortgat, C.I.C.M. Ord: '65, Philippines; Rev. Gerard Rogmans, C.I.C.M. Ord: '55, Belgium; Rev. Roy Shea, C.I.C.M. Ord: '86, Brazil; Rev. Stanley Szarwark, C.I.C.M. Ord: '64, Dominican Republic; Bro. Leon Delanoy, C.I.C.M., Dominican Republic; Bro. Robert Dixon, C.I.C.M., Brazil.

AMERICAN OBLATE MISSIONS (O.M.I.)

Home and Foreign Missions of the United States Province of the Missionary Oblates of Mary Immaculate.

United States Province, 391 Michigan Ave., N.E., Washington, DC 20017. Phone: 202-529-4505; Fax: 202-529-4572. Rev. William Antone, O.M.I. Ord: '80, Prov.

Religious in Scandinavian Missions: Rev. Michael Bradley, O.M.I. Ord: '66; Rev. Allen Courteau, O.M.I. Ord: '76; Rev. Leo Kertz, O.M.I. Ord: '63; Rev. Paul Marx, O.M.I. Ord: '65; Rev. Carroll Parker, O.M.I. Ord: '61.

U.S. Religious serving in Brazil: Rev. James Gibbons, O.M.I. Ord: '69; Rev. Thomas Brown, O.M.I. Ord: '55; Rev. Peter Curran, O.M.I. Ord: '71; Rev. Thomas Delaney, O.M.I. Ord: '60; Rev. John Drexel, O.M.I. Ord: '62; Rev. Edward Figueroa, O.M.I. Ord: '60; Rev. Robert Fitzpatrick, O.M.I. Ord: '71; Rev. Edmund Leising, O.M.I. Ord: '46; Rev. Paul Medeiros, O.M.I. Ord: '64; Rev. Robert Mayer, O.M.I. Ord: '67; Rev. David O'Brien, O.M.I. Ord: '59; Rev. Thomas O'Brien, O.M.I. Ord: '55; Rev. William Reinhard, O.M.I. Ord: '61; Rev. Charles Tierney, O.M.I. Ord: '73.

U.S. Religious serving in Canada: Rev. Normand Bonneau, O.M.I. Ord: '76; Rev. John Lau, O.M.I. Ord: '91, Canada; Rev. Ronald W. Young, O.M.I. Ord: '88.

U.S. Religious serving in Haiti: Rev. Alfred Charpentier, O.M.I. Ord: '71; Rev. Real Corriveau, O.M.I. Ord: '61; Rev. John Henault, O.M.I. Ord: '63; Rev. Joseph Vaillancourt, O.M.I. Ord: '46; Rev. Marc Boisvert, O.M.I. Ord: '84; Rev. John St. Cyr, O.M.I. Ord: '61.

U.S. Religious serving in Japan: Rev. Raymond Bourgoin, O.M.I. Ord: '66; Rev. John Deely, O.M.I. Ord: '70; Rev. Francis Hahn, O.M.I. Ord: '72; Rev. Thomas Maher, O.M.I. Ord: '57; Rev. William Maher, O.M.I. Ord: '66; Rev. Jerome Novotny, O.M.I. Ord: '68; Rev. Bertram Silver, O.M.I. Ord: '54; Rev. Edward Williams, O.M.I. Ord: '57.

U.S. Religious serving in Mexico: Rev. John M. Curran, O.M.I. Ord: '78; Rev. Daniel Gagnon, O.M.I. Ord: '87; Rev. Francisco Gomez, O.M.I.

Ord: '07; Rev. Robert Hickl, O.M.I. Ord: '79; Rev. Richard Junius, O.M.I. Ord: '56; Rev. James Lyons, O.M.I. Ord: '61; Rev. Augustine Petru, O.M.I. Ord: '53; Rev. Thomas Rush, O.M.I. Ord: '73; Rev. Gerald Kapustka, O.M.I. Ord: '65, Guatemala.

U.S. Religious serving in other countries: Rev. James G. Dukowski, O.M.I. Ord: '67, Peru; Rev. Robert Durette, O.M.I. Ord: '60, Bolivia; Rev. Ruben Elizondo, O.M.I. Ord: '62, Guatemala; Rev. Roger Hallee, O.M.I. Ord: '63, Colombia; Rev. Leo Guilmette, O.M.I. Ord: '63, Paraguay; Rev. Clyde Rausch, O.M.I. Ord: '68, Rome; Rev. David Ullrich, O.M.I. Ord: '71, Hong Kong.

U.S. Religious serving in the Philippine Islands: Rev. Armand Carignan, O.M.I. Ord: '53; Rev. Maurice Hemann, O.M.I. Ord: '50; Rev. Richard Pommier, O.M.I. Ord: '66; Rev. Richard Weixelman, O.M.I. Ord: '65.

U.S. Religious serving in Zambia: Rev. Patrick Gitzen, O.M.I. Ord: '75; Rev. Ronald Walker, O.M.I. Ord: '61;.

Missionary Activities

RELIGIOUS SOCIETIES ENGAGED IN MISSIONARY WORK

Augustinian Recollect Fathers: *Province of St. Nicholas Tolentine U.S. Delegation*, 3021 Frutas Ave., El Paso, TX 79905. Rev. Antonio Lasheras, O.A.R., Prov. Delegate.

Engaged in missionary work among Spanish-speaking people. Sustains mission personnel in the Archdioceses of New York and Newark, and in the Dioceses of Las Cruces and El Paso.

Caritas for Children, Inc.: 5250 Grand Ave., P.M.B. 105, Gurnee, IL 60031-1877. Phone: 888-227-4827; Fax: 414-771-3528; Web: www.caritasforchildren.org. Christopher T. Hoar, Contact Person.

Congregation of the Blessed Sacrament: *Province of St. Ann*, 5384 Wilson Mills Rd., Cleveland, OH 44143.

Brothers of the Christian Schools: *Christian Brothers Conference*, 3025 Fourth St., N.E., Hecker Center, Ste. 300, Washington, DC 20017-1102. Phone: 202-529-0047; Web: www.lasallian.info.

The De La Salle Christian Brothers serve in 82 countries. The U.S.A./Toronto region has historic responsibilities in the Holy Land, English-speaking Africa, Central America and the Philippines.

***Christian Foundation for Children and Aging:** 1 Elmwood Ave., Kansas City, KS 66103. Phone: 913-384-6500; Phone: 800-875-6564; Fax: 913-384-2211; Email: mail@cfcausa.org; Web: www.hopeforafamily.org. Robert K. Hentzen, Pres.; Paco Wertin, CEO; Larry Livingston, Contact Person.

Christian Foundation for Children and Aging is an international movement serving those living in poverty in 22 developing countries. CFCA's Hope for a Family sponsorship program connects individual sponsors with a child, youth or elderly person in need of encouragement and support. Hope for a Family sponsorship helps provide food, education, health care and livelihood programs, but it does more. It gives families hope that they can create a path out of poverty for their children. Founded by lay Catholics acting on the Gospel call to serve those living in poverty, the CFCA movement includes people of all faiths.

Claretian Missionaries: *Headquarters of Western Province*, 10203 Lower Azusa Rd., Temple City, CA 91780. Phone: 626-443-2009; Fax: 626-443-2005. Very Rev. Rosendo Urrabazo, C.F.M., Prov.

Headquarters of Eastern Province , 400 N. Euclid Ave., Oak Park, IL 60302. Phone: 708-848-2076. Very Rev. Eddie DeLeon, C.M.F., Prov.

Please refer to the Religious Institutes of Men section for activities and representation in the United States.

Claret Center , 5536 S. Everett Ave., Chicago, IL 60637.

Resources for Counseling and Spiritual Directions. Chicago, IL.

Missions outside the United States entrusted to the Claretians: Guatemala, Cameroons, Mexico.

Publications: monthly magazine, U.S. Catholic; extensive line of Pamphlets and Paperback Books; bi-monthly Newsletter; Fides-Claretian.

Comboni Missionaries of the Heart of Jesus, Inc. (Verona Fathers): *Provincial Headquarters: Comboni Mission Center*, 1318 Nagel Rd., Cincinnati, OH 45255-3120. Phone: 513-474-4997; Email: info@combonimissionaries.org; Web: www.combonimissionaries.org. Rev. Manuel Baeza Gama, M.C.C.J., Prov. Supr.; Rev. Brian Quigley, M.C.C.J., Mission Dir.; Mary Bertolini, Communications Dir.

Foreign mission society, both priests and brothers, founded by Saint Daniel Comboni, Vicar Apostolic of Central Africa.

Active in the Archdioceses of Chicago, Cincinnati, Los Angeles and Newark.

Comboni Missionaries work with local churches in: Africa - Benin, Central African Republic, Egypt, Eritrea, Ethiopia, Ghana, Kenya, Malawi, Mozambique, South Africa, Sudan, Chad, Togo, Uganda, Zambia and Democratic Republic of Congo; Asia - Philippines, China; Latin America - Brazil, Chile, Colombia, Costa Rica, Ecuador, El Salvador, Guatemala, Mexico, Nicaragua, and Peru; North America - Canada and the United States.

Training Centers: Africa - Eritrea, Ethopia, Kenya, Malawi, Mozambique, South Africa, Togo, Egypt, Sudan, Uganda, Democratic Republic of the Congo; Asia - Philippines; Europe - Austria, England, France, Germany, Italy, Poland, Portugal, and Spain; Latin America - Brazil, Colombia, Costa Rica, Ecuador, Mexico and Peru; North America - United States.

Publications: Comboni Press Network Newsletter; Comboni Press Feature Service; Comboni Mission Magazine.

Comboni Missionary Sisters: *American Headquarters*, 1307 Lakeside Ave., Richmond, VA 23228-4710. Phone: 804-262-8827; Fax: 804-264-2906; Email: cmusaprov@verizon.net; Web: www.combonisrs.com. Sr. Maria de la Luz Aguilera, C.M.S., Supr.; Sr. Mary Bernadette Hilmer, C.M.S., Delegate Supr.

An international congregation of 1,450 sisters founded by Bishop St. Daniel Comboni in 1872 in Verona, Italy. Engaged in pastoral and catechetical work; education; social services; health services; building Christian communities; committed to justice and peace making and care for creation; training local church leaders in Africa, America, Europe, and the Middle East.

The American Delegation recruits and trains sisters for the foreign mission, mission education, fundraising for missions, and pastoral ministry among the poor.

Congregation of Alexian Brothers: *Immaculate Conception Province, U.S. Provincial Headquarters*, 3040 Salt Creek Ln., Arlington Heights, IL 60005. Bro. James Classon, C.F.A., Prov.

Missionary healthcare work in Davao City, Philippines & Győr, Hungary directed by Alexian Brothers. Please refer to the Religious Institutes of Men section for activities and representation in the United States.

Congregation of Christian Brothers: *Business Office:* 21 Pryer Ter., New Rochelle, NY 10804-4418. Bro. Hugh B. O'Neill, C.F.C., Prov. Leader; Bro. Kevin M. Griffith, C.F.C., Deputy Prov. Leader.

Missionary and educational work in Central and South America and in Africa.

Congregation of the Holy Spirit (1872): 6230 Brush Run Rd., Bethel Park, PA 15102. Phone: 412-831-0302; Fax: 412-831-0970. Holy Spirit Fathers and Brothers (C.S.Sp.) Province of the United States:, Very Rev. John Fogarty, C.S.Sp., Prov.

Missionary work among the abandoned, including first evangelization, teaching, care of homeless children, and pastoral ministry.

Missionaries serve in 17 (Arch)Dioceses in the United States: the Archdiocese of San Juan and the Diocese of Arecibo in Puerto Rico; the Dioceses of Ciudad Valles, Tampico, and the Archdiocese of San Luis Potosi in Mexico; Archdiocese of Arusha, and Dioceses of Mbulu and Zanzibar in Tanzania; and Bethlehem in South Africa. Other establishments in North and South America, Europe, Africa, Australia and the Dominican Republic; also the Philippines, Taiwan and Vietnam.

Missionaries of Our Lady of La Salette: *Province of Mary, Mother of the Americas*, 915 Maple Ave., Hartford, CT 06114-2330. Phone: 860-956-8870; Fax: 860-956-8849. Very Rev. Joseph G. Bachand, M.S., Prov. Supr.; Rev. Thomas Vellappallil, M.S., Procurator.
4650 S. Broadway, Saint Louis, MO 63111-1398. Phone: 314-352-0064; Fax: 314-352-3737.

Active in Archdioceses of Buenos Aires, Argentina; Cochabamba, Bolivia; Cordoba, Argentina; and Diocese of Santiago del Estero, Argentina.

Please refer to the Religious Institutes of Men section for activities and representation in the United States.

Congregation of the Priests of the Sacred Heart, The: *U.S. Provincialate Offices*, P.O. Box 289, Hales Corners, WI 53130-0289. Phone: 414-425-6910. Very Rev. Thomas P. Cassidy, S.C.J., Prov. Supr.

Please refer to the Religious Institutes of Men section for other activities and representation in the United States.

Missionary work in the home and foreign missions; educational activities; welfare work, especially in industrial centers. Home Missions: Lower Brule and Crow Creek Indian Reservation, South Dakota; Black Missions, Diocese of Jackson, Mississippi; Spanish-speaking Apostolate, Archdiocese of Galveston-Houston and Diocese of Brownsville.

Foreign Missions: Zaire, Cameroon, Mozambique, South Africa, Brazil, Argentina, Uruguay, Chile, Venezuela, India, Indonesia, Finland, Vietnam and Philippines

Congregation of the Resurrection: *Resurrection Catholic Missions of the South, Inc.*, 2815 Forbes Dr., Montgomery, AL 36110. Phone: 334-263-4221; Fax: 334-263-4999.

The Resurrection Catholic Missions ministries includes an early childhood development facility for preschoolers, a church and elementary school, as well as an outreach program to homebound elders.

Please refer to the Religious Institutes of Men section for activities and representation in the United States. Active also in Australia, Brazil, Bolivia, Bulgaria, Canada, Germany, Jamaica, Mexico, Poland and Tanzania.

Consolata Missionaries (1901): *Provincial Headquarters (1964)*, 2301 Hwy. 27, P.O. Box 5550, Somerset, NJ 08875-5550. Phone: 732-297-9191; Fax: 732-940-3121. Rev. Robert Rezac, I.M.C., Reg. Supr.

Legal Title: *Consolata Society for Foreign Missions.*

Serving in 26 countries around the world including the United States.

Publication: Consolata Missionaries.

Consolata Missionary Sisters (1910): 6801 Belmont Ave., N.E., P.O. Box 371, Belmont, MI 49306. Phone: 616-361-2072; Fax: 616-361-2049. Sr. Zelita M. Bragagnolo, M.C., Supr.

The congregation is committed to all types of missionary apostolate, primarily in African, Asian and South American countries.

Crosier Fathers and Brothers: *Crosier Missions*, 4423 N. 24th St., Ste. 400, Phoenix, AZ 85016-5584. Phone: 602-443-7100; Fax: 602-443-7101. Bro. Albert Becker, O.S.C., Mission Coord. & Dir. Devel.

Legal Title: *Canons Regular of the Order of the Holy Cross.*

Publication: quarterly, Crossview.

Daughters of Mary Help of Christians: *St. Philip Apostle Province*, 655 Belmont Ave., Haledon, NJ 07508. Sr. Karen Dunn, F.M.A., Prov.

Legal Title: *Missionary Society of the Salesian Sisters, Inc.*

Missionary work in home and foreign countries; catechetical, educational and training centers; social services; hostels, hospitals, clinics and dispensaries; mission centers, and youth centers.

Active in U.S. within the Archdioceses of Miami, Newark, New Orleans, and New York, and the Dioceses of Paterson, Rockford, and St. Petersburg.

Franciscan Friars of the Atonement - Generalate: *Graymoor*, P.O. Box 300, Garrison, NY 10524-0300. Phone: 845-424-2113; Fax: 845-424-2166. General Council:, Very Rev. James F. Puglisi, S.A., Min. Gen.; Rev. Timothy I. MacDonald, S.A., 1st Councilor & Vicar Gen.; Rev. Elias D. Mallon, S.A., 2nd Councilor; Rev. Charles Sharon, S.A., 3rd Councilor & Sec. Gen.; Rev. V. Paul Ojibway, S.A., 4th Councilor.

Mission activities outside of the US: Japan. Also staff parishes in Canada, England, Italy and the United States. The Friars mission of reconciliation is promoted through preaching of the Gospel, ecumenism and inter-religious activity and missionary activity.

Please refer to the Religious Institutes of Men section for activities and representation in the United States.

Franciscan Missionaries of Mary, The: *U.S. Provincial House*, 3305 Wallace Ave., Bronx, NY 10467. Phone: 718-547-4693; Fax: 718-325-5102. Sr. Lois Ann Pereira, F.M.M., Prov.

The Franciscan Missionaries of Mary, founded in India in 1877 by Bl. Mary of the Passion, for Eucharistic contemplation and the work of Evangelization, is dedicated to Universal Mission. It is an international Religious Institute of Pontifical Right.

This international congregation serves 831 missions in 50 provinces and 2 delegations.

Missionary work of evangelization and development, catechetics; social work; nursing; community development programs; educational and public health programs; pastoral activity and various forms of ministry and service; immigration and prison ministries.

Franciscan Missionary Sisters for Africa: *American Headquarters Center for Promotion and Formation*, 172 Foster St., Brighton, MA 02135. Phone: 617-254-4343; Fax: 617-787-8007; Email: brightonsisters172@yahoo.com. Sr. Miriam Duggan, F.M.S.A., Supr. Gen. - Ireland; Sr. Camilla Roach, F.M.S.A., Contact Person U.S.A.

Missions in Kenya, Uganda, South Africa, Sudan, Zambia and Zimbabwe.

Publication: The Daystar.

Franciscan Mission Association: *Franciscan Mission House*, 517 Washington Ave., Rensselaer, NY 12144. Phone: 518-465-0062; Fax: 518-465-3673; Web: www.thefma.org; Web: www.franciscaneast.org. Rev. Raynald Yudin, O.F.M-.Conv., Dir.

The American branch of the Franciscan Mission Crusade founded in 1924, approved by Pope Pius XI to further the work of the Conventual Franciscan Missionary Apostolate. The purpose is to aid the Mission of the Order in every possible way. The revenues of the Association accrue from the annual and perpetual enrollments in the Association, bequests, other free-will offerings and donations, membership in monthly mission club appeal.

Franciscan Mission Association (1953): *Franciscan Missions*, 322 West St., Carey, OH 43316. Phone: 419-396-6455. Bro. Bryan Hoban, O.F.M.Conv., Dir.

The purpose of the association, which is part of the Province of Our Lady of Consolation, is to give financial and other material aid to the missionaries of Africa: the Dioceses of Ndola and Solwezi, Zambia; missionaries in the Dioceses of Olancho, Tegucigalpa and Comayagua in Honduras and San Jose in Costa Rica; and missionaries of the Southwestern United States. Both living and deceased may be enrolled as members. Members of the laity have an active part in promoting the growth of the association as outlined in Vatican II.

Franciscan Mission Association, Inc.: *Province of St. Anthony of Padua*, 12300 Folly Quarter Rd., Ellicott City, MD 21042. Phone: 410-531-3695; Fax: 410-531-4881; Email: info@companionsofstanthony.org. Rev. Martin Breski, O.F.M.Conv., Dir.

Founded to support the domestic and foreign missions of the Conventual Franciscans of St. Anthony Province.

Franciscan Sisters of Allegany: *St. Elizabeth Motherhouse*, 115 E. Main St., Allegany, NY 14706. Sr. Maureen Avril Chin Fatt, O.S.F., Congregational Min.; Sr. Chris Doherty, O.S.F., Mission Society Dir.

Sisters serve in areas of education; health-care; pastoral ministry; social ministries; and other missionary work in the Archdiocese of Kingston; the Archdioceses of Goiania and Palmas, Brazil; Prelacy of Cristalandia, Brazil; Dioceses of Anapolis, Ipameri, Goias, Rui Barbosa, Miracema do Tocantins and Jatai, Brazil. Archdiocese of La Paz and Dioceses of Cochabamba, Bolivia.

Congregation 289; Foreign Missions 75.

Publication: Zeal.

Franciscan Sisters, Daughters of the Sacred Hearts of Jesus and Mary: *Province of St. Clara*, P.O. Box 667, Wheaton, IL 60187-0667. Phone: 630-462-7422; Fax: 630-462-7148. Sr. Beatrice Hernandez, O.S.F., Prov. Dir.

Active in the United States ministering in sponsorship of Catholic hospitals; counseling, housing; education; pastoral ministry; care of elderly; wellness; long-term care; social services; spiritual direction and retreats in Archdioceses of Milwaukee; in Dioceses of Joliet, Green Bay, La Crosse and Springfield-Cape Girardeau; outside the US: Brazil and Italy.

Franciscan Sisters of Little Falls, MN: *Motherhouse*, 116 8th Ave. S.E., Little Falls, MN 56345. Phone: 320-632-2981. Sr. Beatrice Eichten, O.S.F., Pres.

Home health care; Hospice Care; Catholic elementary schools; Spirituality Farm, Native Americans; religious education; parish ministry; liturgical music ministry; music center; health and recreation center; retreat ministry; counseling; spiritual direction; social service; ministry to the poor; ministry to the migrants; art therapist; Hispanic Ministry; pastoral ministry; in the U.S. and in education, health, social services in Quito, Ecuador, S.A., San Rafael, Linares, Mexico, Monterrey, Nuevo Leon, Mexico

Franciscan Sisters of the Poor: *Congregational Office*, 133 Remsen St., Brooklyn, NY 11201. Phone: 718-643-1919; Fax: 718-643-9710. Sr. Tiziana Merletti, S.F.P., Pres.

Sisters serve in healing ministry; health care; social welfare; pastoral ministry in the U.S.; pastoral ministry and health care in the Dioceses of Assisi, Frascati, Pistoia, Rome, Padua and Messina in Italy. Mission ministry is represented in the Archdiocese of Goiania and in the Dioceses of Jatai, Ipameri & Pires Do Rio in Brazil, in the Dioceses of Dakar, Kaolack, Kolda in Senegal, West Africa, and also in the Diocese of Dumaguete in the Philippines.

Number in Congregation 138; Mission Ministry 27.

Glenmary Home Missioners (1939): *National Headquarters*, P.O. Box 465618, Cincinnati, OH 45246. Phone: 513-874-8900; Web: www.glenmary.org. Rev. Chet Artysiewicz, G.H.M., Pres.

Glenmary is an apostolic society of priests and brothers who, along with lay coworkers, establish the Catholic Church in small-town and rural America. Glenmary is the only religious community dedicated exclusively to serving the spiritually and materially poor in Appalachia, the rural South and Southwest. Glenmary missioners serve in areas where less than three percent of the population is Catholic, a significant percent have no church affiliation, and the poverty rate is almost twice the national average. Their missionary activities include nurturing Catholic communities, fostering ecumenism, evangelizing the unchurched, working for justice and social outreach. Glenmary staffs over 40 missions and ministries, including a group volunteer program at the Glenmary Farm and commissions on evangelization and justice.

Please refer to the Religious Institutes of Men section for activities and representation in the United States.

Publication: Glenmary Challenge

Glenmary Home Mission Sisters of America (1941): *Glenmary Sisters*, P.O. Box 22264, Owensboro, KY 42304-2264. Fax: 270-686-8759. Sr. Sharon Miller, Pres.

Glenmary is a community of women religious of diocesan right - a home mission community dedicated to bringing mission presence and activity to the rural, small town areas of the United States. The sisters live and work among the poor, the sick, the oppressed and unchurched in Appalachia and the South in areas where less than 2% of the total population is Catholic. When possible the sisters work in collaboration with the Glenmary Priests and Brothers. The Glenmary Sisters believe in a holistic approach to mission - the caring of the whole person - through their ministries of evangelization, pastoral outreach, religious education, home visitation and a wide variety of social services for the poor.

Please refer to the Religious Institutes of Women section for activities in the United States.

Publications: Kinship; Kinship for Kids; Kinship for Teens.

Institute of Charity (Rosminian Fathers): *Rosmini House*, 2327 W. Heading Ave., Peoria, IL 61604.

Active in the Dioceses of Peoria and St. Petersburg.

Missions and missionary work in Tanga, Tanzania; New Zealand; Venezuela; and Kerala, India.

Jesuit Volunteers International: P.O. Box 3756, Washington, DC 20027-0256. Phone: 202-687-1132; Fax: 202-687-5082. Meghan Romey, Exec. Dir.

Selected college graduates improve education and promote human welfare, faith communities and social justice through a two-year commitment to impoverished local communities in seven developing nations.

Mariannhill, Congregation of Missionaries of (1882): 23715 Ann Arbor Tr., Dearborn Heights, MI 48127-1449. Rev. Alain Rodrigue, C.M.M., Prov. Supr.

The American-Canadian province recruits and trains young men as priests and lay brothers for foreign missions, secures funds for the foreign missions, and does a limited amount of pastoral work at home.

Active in the Archdiocese of Detroit.

Outside the U.S: Austria, Botswana, Canada, Columbia, Germany, Italy, Kenya, Mozambique, Netherlands, Papua New Guinea, Poland, South Africa, Spain, Switzerland, Zambia and Zimbabwe.

Worldwide membership: Bishops 4; Priests 211; Brothers 88; Seminarians Professed 73; Total Members 376.

Publication: Leaves Magazine.

Marist Missionary Sisters: *North American Provincial Office:* 349 Grove St., Waltham, MA 02453. Phone: 781-893-0149; Fax: 781-894-7610; Web: www.maristmissionarysmsm.org. Sr. Judith Sheridan, S.M.S.M., Prov.; Sr. Pauline St. Pierre, Mission Promotor; Sr. Claire Rheaume, S.M.S.M., Vocation Directress Email: rheaumesmsm@yahoo.com.

Legal Title: *Missionary Sisters of the Society of Mary, Inc.*

Founded in France in 1845 for mission in the South Pacific, today, the International Missionary Congregation consist of 465 sisters (in seven provinces), serving the people of God in 29 countries around the world. The American Province has 98 sisters working in Massachusetts, Tennessee, Florida, California, and Jamaica, W.I. The mission is to bring the good news of God's love through spiritual and corporal works of mercy; catechetical, medical, educational and social services; pastoral ministry; formation of laity for leadership and a great concern for the poorest and most neglected. Working by preference among people of different cultures and languages, to bring about greater understanding, dignity and mutual respect.

Formation is international with a French-speaking novitiate in Senegal, an English-speaking novitiate in New Zealand and a Spanish-speaking novitiate in Peru.

Province headquarters are in the United States, Australia, France, Italy, New Caledonia, New Zealand, and Peru.

Please refer to the Religious Institutes of Women section for activities and representation in the United States.

Maryknoll Sisters of St. Dominic, Inc.: P.O. Box 311, Maryknoll, NY 10545-3011. Sr. Janice McLaughlin, M.M., Community Pres.; Sr. Rebecca Macugay, M.M., Vice Pres.; Sr. Ann Hayden, M.M., Gen. Sec.; Sr. Bitrina Kirway, M.M., Team Member.

A Pontifical Institute under the jurisdiction of the Congregation for the Institutes of Consecrated Life. The purpose of the Maryknoll Sisters Congregation is to participate in the mission presence and activity of the universal Church so that God's reign of peace, justice and love may be proclaimed and witnessed to throughout the world. The Maryknoll Sisters embrace a plurality of ministries while giving a clear sign of Christian community; faith-sharing; self-gift in service through pastoral and catechetical work; basic ecclesial communities; education; social services; medical and health promotion work; services through hostels; services to refugees; and ministries that promote human rights, social justice and the dignity and equality of women.

Please refer to the Religious Institutes of Women section for activities in the United States.

Active in Bangladesh, Bolivia, Brazil, Cambodia, Central Pacific, Chile, China, East Timor, Ecuador, El Salvador, Guatemala, Japan, Kenya, Korea, Namibia, Panama, Peru, Philippines, Taiwan, Tanzania, Thailand, USA and Zimbabwe.

Medical Missionaries of Mary: 563 Minneford

Ave., Bronx, NY 10464-1118. Phone: 718-885-0945; Fax: 718-885-0010; Email: minniefordmmm@verizon.net; Web: www.mmmusa.org. Sr. Siobhan Corkery, M.M.M., Congregational Leader; Sr. Jean Clare Eason, M.M.M., Area Leader USA.

Missionary work in hospitals, clinics and leprosy treatment; public health and pastoral ministry centers in Africa, South America and Clinchco, VA.

Please refer to the Religious Institutes of Women section for activities and representation in the United States.

Active also in Angola, Benin, Rwanda, Nigeria, Uganda, Tanzania, Honduras, Kenya, Malawi, Ethiopia, England, Ireland and Brazil.

Publication: quarterly, The Mini MMM.

Medical Mission Sisters: *North American Headquarters*, 8400 Pine Rd., Philadelphia, PA 19111. Fax: 215-342-3948. Sr. Agnes Lanfermann, M.M.S., Society Coord.; Sr. Suzanne Maschek, M.M.S., North American Sector Coord.; Monica M. McGinley, Pub. Rels. Dir.

Legal Title: *Society of Catholic Medical Missionaries, Inc.; Society of Catholic Medical Missionaries Generalate, Inc., (effective 1991).*

Medical Mission Sisters have the special call in the Church of "being a healing presence at the heart of a wounded world." Members commit themselves "to promote healing and wholeness in all aspects of life" in the spirit of Jesus. They share life with those who are sick and have been made poor, trying to help them to live fully as human beings. Medical Mission Sisters' healing presence today involves a full range of preventative, curative and promotive health services; health training programs; and development and social justice activities in Ghana, Uganda, Kenya, Ethiopia, Pakistan, India, Belgium, Venezuela, Peru, Indonesia, Philippines, Italy, Holland, Germany, England, Mexico and the United States.

Medical Mission Houses in the United States are listed under the Religious Institutes of Women Section.

Publication: Medical Mission Sisters News.

Mill Hill Missionaries: *St. Joseph's Missionary Society:* 222 W. Hartsdale Ave., Hartsdale, NY 10530. Phone: 914-682-0645; Fax: 914-682-0862; Email: mhmnyoffice@aol.com. Rev. Bartholomew Daly, M.H.M., Regl. Representative; Rev. Terence J. Lee, M.H.M., Counselor; Rev. Robert O'Neil, M.H.M., Counselor.

An international society of priests, brothers and associates, founded in 1866 by Herbert Vaughan, devoted entirely to the missionary needs of the Church.

Active in the U.S. in the Archdiocese of New York and in the Diocese of Phoenix.

Active outside the United States. Cameroon: the Archdiocese of Bamenda and the Dioceses of Buea, Kumbo, Mamfe and Ngaoundere. Congo: Diocese of Basankusu. Kenya: Archdioceses of Kisumu, Nairobi, and the Dioceses of Bungoma, Kakamega, Kisii, Malindi, Nakuru, Ngong and Homa Bay. Uganda: Archdioceses of Kampala, Tororo and the Dioceses of Jinja, Soroti, Kotido and Lugazi. South Africa: Diocese of Kroonstad, Rustenburg. Sudan: Archdiocese of Khartoum, and the Diocese of Malakal. China: Diocese of Hong Kong. India: Archdioceses of Hyderabad, and the Dioceses of Jammu-Srinagar, Varanasi and Warangal. Pakistan: Dioceses of Islamabad-Rawalpindi and Hyderabad. Malaysia: Archdiocese of Kuching, and the Dioceses of Kota Kinabalu and Sibu. Brunei: Prefecture Apostolic of Brunei. Philippines: Archdioceses of Manila, Jaro, and the Diocese of San Jose. New Zealand: Dioceses of Aukland and Hamilton. Brazil: Dioceses of Governador Valadares and Itaquai. Also Ecuador: Archdiocese of Guayaquil. Bolivia: Archdiocese of Cochabamba.

Mission Helpers of the Sacred Heart: 1001 W. Joppa Rd., Baltimore, MD 21204. Phone: 410-823-8585; Fax: 410-825-6355. Sr. Loretta Cornell, M.H.S.H., Pres.

A Pontifical, missionary congregation with principal work of evangelization and catechesis; adult religious education; instruction of youth and children; D.R.E. programs; pastoral ministers; pastoral associates; pastoral social ministers; special ministers of the Eucharist; ministry in homes and institutions; ministry to the elderly and infirm; catechesis of blind, deaf, retarded; campus ministry; Hispanic pastoral ministry to adults and youth; spiritual direction and retreat work.

Please refer to the Religious Institutes of Women for activities and representation in the United States.

Activities also in the Archdioceses of Barquisimeto, Venezuela, and San Juan.

Publication: 2 times yearly, The Mission Helper.

Missionaries of Africa (M.Afr.): *U.S. Province of the Americas Headquarters:* 1624 21st St., N.W., Washington, DC 20009-1003. Fax: 202-332-8640.

International and interracial missionary society of priests and brothers working in teams almost exclusively in Africa.

Active in the Archdiocese of Washington, D.C. and the Diocese of St. Petersburg.

Training centers in Burkina Faso, Ivory Coast, Kenya, D.R. Congo, Zambia, Jerusalem, South Africa, Ethiopia, Uganda, Malawi, Ghana, Tanzania, India, Mexico, Philippines and Poland.

Missionary work in Algeria, Burundi, Ethiopia, Ghana, Kenya, Malawi, Mali, Mozambique, Nigeria, Rwanda, Sudan, Tanzania, Tunisia, Uganda, Burkina Faso, Democratic Republic of Congo, Zambia, South Africa, Ivory Coast, Niger and Mauritania.

Publication: newsletter, Missionaries of Africa Report.

Missionaries of the Holy Apostles, Society of the: 22 Prospect Hill Rd., Cromwell, CT 06416. Phone: 860-632-3039. Very Rev. Addison Hallock, M.S.A., Prov. Animator.

Apostolic works consist of the promotion and formation of adult candidates for the diocesan and religious priesthood and preparation of the laity for Christian leadership.

Please refer to the Religious Institutes of Men section for activities and representation in the United States.

Activities also in Brazil, Venezuela, Cameroon, Colombia, Canada, Peru, Italy, and France.

Missionary Benedictine Sisters (1923): *Priory House and Novitiate: Immaculata Monastery*, 300 N. 18th St., Norfolk, NE 68701-3687. Phone: 402-371-3438; Fax: 402-379-7667. Sr. Pia Portmann, O.S.B., Prioress.

Sisters serve in elementary schools; catechetical programs; pastoral ministry; hospitals; Native American reservation; outreach programs with Hispanic & elderly; spirituality programs.

Outside the U.S: Angola, Argentina, Brazil, Bulgaria, Germany, India, Italy, Kenya, Korea, Namibia, Tanzania, Philippines, Portugal, Spain, Switzerland & Uganda.

Missionary Servants of the Most Blessed Trinity: *Motherhouse, Novitiate and Generalate:* 3501 Solly Ave., Philadelphia, PA 19136. Fax: 215-332-7559. Sr. Joan Marie Keller, M.S.B.T., Gen. Custodian.

The congregation's mission is the preservation of the faith. This involves nourishing the faith-life of those of the Roman Catholic tradition, cooperating in ecumenical endeavors, strengthening life-giving faith among all people, evangelization, actively promoting human development and social justice. The special apostolic intent is to advance and support the ministry of the laity in the mission of the Church, accomplished through the ministries of education, social work and health care on parish and diocesan levels.

Please refer to the Religious Institutes of Women section for activities and representation in the United States.

Active also in the Archdioceses of Kingston, San Juan and Mexico City and the Dioceses of Ponce and Mayaguez in Puerto Rico as well as the Diocese of Texcoco in Mexico.

Missionary Servants of the Most Holy Trinity (Trinity Missions): *The Generalate*, 9001 New Hampshire Ave., Ste. 300, Silver Spring, MD 20903-3626. Phone: 301-434-0092; Fax: 301-434-0255; Email: generalate@trinitymissions.org. Rev. John S. Edmunds, S.T., Gen. Custodian; Bro. Steven Vesely, S.T., Sec. Gen.; Bro. Jordan Baxter, S.T., Treas. Gen.; Rev. Domingo Rodriguez, S.T., Mission Procurator.

A clerical congregation of Pontifical Right founded for the preservation of the faith and missionary work wherever the Church directs. The major fields are the missionary areas of the southern United States and the Spanish-speaking people in the United States, Puerto Rico, Colombia, Costa Rica and Mexico. The principal work is the development of Catholic lay leaders. There is also training for the missionary priesthood and brotherhood of the congregation.

Please refer to the Religious Institutes of Men section for activities and representation in the United States.

Publication: Trinity Missions.

Missionary Sisters of St. Columban (1922): 73 Mapleton St., Brighton, MA 02135. Phone: 617-782-5683; Fax: 617-789-3569. Sr. Margaret Holleran, S.C.C., U.S. Area Coord.

The Missionary Sisters of Saint Columban are also known as the Columban Sisters. The Columban Sisters are religious women called to bring the good and the oppressed and those who have not yet had the Gospel proclaimed to them. The congregation strives to respond to the needs of the people by dedication to the work of evangelization through pastoral, educational, medical and social ministries, and supporting the efforts of the local church where its members are sent. The congregation also endeavors, through programs of mission education and animation, to deepen an awareness of global vision and world justice.

Active in the U.S. in the Archdioceses of Boston, and Los Angeles and in the Diocese of Buffalo.

Active outside the U.S. in Ireland, Myanmar, China, England, Scotland, Hong Kong, Korea, Philippines, Peru, Chile and Pakistan.

Missionary Sisters of Our Lady of Africa: *American Headquarters:* 47 W. Spring St., Winooski, VT 05404. Sr. Marie Heintz, Contact Person.

Missionary activities in Africa: catechetical, pastoral ministry, social work, education and health programs, and working with African Religious Congregations.

Missionary Sisters of the Immaculate Conception of the Mother of God: *Generalate:* 47 Garden Ave., West Paterson, NJ 07424-3337. Phone: 973-279-1484; Fax: 973-279-3480. Sr. Maria do Livramento Oliveira, S.M.I.C., Coord. Gen.

Missionary work in catechetical and social service centers, schools, dispensaries and hospitals.

Active in the U.S. in the Dioceses of Austin, Paterson, Portland, San Bernardino and Santa Fe.

Active outside the U.S. in Angola, Brazil, Germany, Namibia, Philippines, Taiwan and Vietnam.

Missionary Sisters of St. Peter Claver (1894): *American Headquarters:* 265 Century Ave., S., Saint Paul, MN 55125-1155. Phone: 651-738-9704. Sr. Genevieve Kudlik.

Legal Title: *The Sodality of St. Peter Claver for the African Missions.*

The congregation is of Pontifical Jurisdiction, fostering interest in and obtaining funds and requisites for the missions. Apostolate of the press in Africa

Publications: monthly magazine, Echo from Africa, annual, Claver Almanac.

Missionary Sisters of Our Lady of the Holy Rosary: 741 Polo Rd., Bryn Mawr, PA 19010. Phone: 610-520-1974. Sr. Maureen O'Malley, Congregational Leader; Sr. Helena McNeill, Regl. Leader.

Founded for the evangelization of people in Africa and Latin America through educational, medical, social, pastoral and catechetical work.

Active in the U.S. in the Archdiocese of Philadelphia.

Active outside the U.S. in England, Ireland, Nigeria, Sierra Leone, Cameroon, Ethiopia, Kenya, Liberia, South Africa, Zambia, Ghana, Mexico and Brazil.

Missionary Sisters of the Immaculate Heart of Mary (1919): 238 E. 15th St.,# 5, New York, NY 10003. Phone: 212-677-2959. Sr. Kathryn Vercelline, I.C.M., District Leader.

Please refer to the Religious Institutes of Women section for further details.

Missionary Sisters Servants of the Holy Spirit (1901): Techny, IL 60082-6026. Fax: 847-441-5587. Sr. Carol Welp, S.Sp.S., Prov. Supr.; Sr. Margaret Hansen, S.Sp.S., Supr.

Home and foreign missions including teaching, nursing and social work.

Please refer to the Religious Institutes of Women section for activities and representation in the United States.

Also active in Africa, Antigua, Australia, China, Cuba, Europe, India, Indonesia, Japan, Korea, Mexico, New Guinea, Philippine Islands, Romania, Russia, South America, Taiwan, Ukraine and Vietnam.

Publication: SSpS Mission.

Our Lady of Victory Missionary Sisters: *Victory-Noll*, P.O. Box 109, Huntington, IN 46750-0109. Phone: 260-356-0628. Sr. Beatrice Haines, O.L.V.M., Pres.; Sr. Elizabeth Anderson, O.L.V.M., Gen. Sec.

Legal Title: *Our Lady of Victory Missionary Sisters, Inc.*

A Marian congregation proclaiming the Gospel in a personal, non-institutional way through pastoral ministry, religious education, social service and health-care programs in favor of the poor and oppressed.

Please refer to the Religious Institutes of Women section for activities and representation in the United States.

Order of Augustinian Recollects (1943): *Province of St. Augustine*, 29 Ridgeway Ave., West Orange, NJ 07052. Rev. Joseph J. Gallardo, O.A.R., Prior Prov.

Missionary work among Spanish-speaking people in the U.S.

Parish Visitors of Mary Immaculate: *Motherhouse Generalate and Novitiate-Marycrest:* P.O. Box 658, Monroe, NY 10949-0658. Phone: 845-783-2251. Sr. Carole Marie Troskowski, Gen. Supr.; Sr. Maria Catherine, Novice Dir.

Founded for the missionary visitation of families and individuals in the parish and for religious instruction of children and adults; assists parish priests in their ministry of evangelization, catechetical programs, spiritual surveys, census, follow-up religious counseling, religious social services, training laity.

Please refer to the Religious Institutes of Women section for activities and representation in the United States and overseas.

Publication: The Parish Visitor.

Passionist Sisters (1924): *Sisters of the Cross and Passion American Provincialate: Holy Family Convent*, One Wright Lane, North Kingstown, RI 02852. Sr. Theresina Scully, C.P., Province Leader.

Diversified apostolic works according to the needs of the Church; catechetical, pastoral and social work; educational functions; retreats; missionary work in the United States and Africa, Argentina, Australia, Bosnia, Botswana, Chile, England, Europe, Ireland, Jamaica, Papua New Guinea, Peru, Scotland, and Wales.

Please refer to the Religious Institutes of Women section for activities and representation in the United States.

Pontifical Institute for Foreign Missions, P.I.M.E., Inc.: *North American Region:* 17330 Quincy Ave., Detroit, MI 48221. Phone: 313-342-4066; Fax: 313-342-6816. Very Rev. Kenneth Mazur, P.I.M.E., North American Reg. Supr.

Legal Title: *Pontifical Institute for Foreign Missions (P.I.M.E.), Inc.*

The U.S. Region focuses its efforts by being at the service of the Church, both locally and globally. Its members minister in local parishes sharing their missionary vocation. It strives to raise mission awareness, foster vocations and provide financial assistance to PIME's missions and missionaries in developing countries.

Active in the Archdioceses of Detroit and New York and the Dioceses of Columbus, Lansing, Palm Beach, and Paterson.

Outside the US: Bangladesh, Brazil, Cambodia, Cameroon, Guinea-Bissau, Hong Kong/China, India, Ivory Coast, Japan, Mexico, Mayanmar (Burma), Papua New Guinea, Philippines, and Thailand.

Publication: national magazine, PIME World.

St. Joseph's Society of the Sacred Heart (Josephites): *Headquarters:* 1130 North Calvert St., Baltimore, MD 21202. Phone: 410-727-3386; Fax: 410-727-1006; Web: www.josephite-.com. Rev. William L. Norvel, S.S.J., Supr. Gen.

An organization of priests and brothers doing missionary work in the African American community of the United States.

Publication: The Josephite Harvest.

St. Patrick's Missionary Society: 70 Edgewater Rd, P.O Box 3080, Cliffside Park, NJ 07010-4080. Phone: 201-943-6575; Fax: 201-943-2946. Rev. Michael E. Morris, S.P.S., Supr.; Rev. Karl Langsdorf, U.S. Supr.; Rev. Michael Moore, Supr.

A society of secular priests devoted entirely to the missionary needs of the Church.

Activities in the Archdioceses of Newark, and Chicago and the Dioceses of Paterson, and San Jose.

Outside the U.S. in Nigeria-Archdiocese of Lagos, Dioceses of Abakaliki, Calabar, Abuja, Minna, Ogoja, Warri, Port Harcourt and Missio Sui Juris Bomadi. Kenya-Archdiocese of Nairobi, Dioceses of Eldoret, Kitui, Lodwar and Nakuru. Sudan-Diocese of Torit. Malawi-Dioceses of Lilongwe, Chikwawa, Zomba and Mzuzu. Zambia-Archdiocese of Lusaka, Diocese of Chipata. Brazil-Archdiocese of Sao Paulo, Dioceses of Campo Limpo, Osasco, Santo Amaro, Sao Miguel Paulista and Campina Grande. Grenada-Diocese of St. George's. South Africa-Dioceses of Tzaneen and Witbank. Zimbabwe-Archdiocese of Harare and Diocese of Mutare. Cameroon-Archdiocese of Bamenda.

Publication: Africa, St. Patrick's Mission.

Salesian Missions: 2 Lefevre Ln., New Rochelle, NY 10801. Phone: 914-633-8344.

The Salesians were founded to help bring the Faith to all people, and contribute to their social and economic development through education, especially in trade and agricultural schools. The purpose of the society is the recruitment and preparation of vocations for the missions and the education of the American public on the needs of other people through lectures, mass media, direct mail and the magazine, Salesian. It is also the purpose of the society to educate the American public on the unique system of education developed by the society's founder, St. John Bosco, as well as to spread knowledge of his life and accomplishments. Funds are raised to implement the religious, educational and technical assistance projects of the society.

Please refer to the Religious Institutes of Men section for activities and representation in the United States. Represented in over 130 countries throughout the world.

Publication: Salesian.

School Sisters of Notre Dame: *Milwaukee Province:* 13105 Watertown Plank Rd., Elm Grove, WI 53122-2291. Phone: 262-782-9850; Fax: 262-782-5725. Sr. Debra Marie Sciano, S.S.N.D., Prov. Leader.

Please refer to the Religious Institutes of Women section I.D.# [2970] for provinces, activities and representations in the United States and overseas.

Sisters of the Blessed Sacrament for Indians and Colored People (1891): *Sisters of the Blessed Sacrament:* Bensalem, PA 19020-5796. Phone: 215-244-9900; Fax: 215-244-8174. Sr. Patricia Suchalski, Pres.

Missionary work in the educational, catechetical and social services among Black and Native Americans in the U.S. and Haiti.

Please refer to the Religious Institutes of Women section for activities and representation in the United States.

Publication: Mission.

Society of African Missions: *SMA Fathers American Province*, 23 Bliss Ave., Tenafly, NJ 07670. Phone: 201-567-9085; Phone: 201-567-0450; Fax: 800-670-8328; Fax: 201-541-1280. Very Rev. Michael P. Moran, S.M.A., Prov.

Please refer to the Religious Institutes of Men section for activities and representation in the United States.

Active also in: Liberia-Diocese of Cape Palmas, Archdiocese of Monrovia, Diocese of Gbarnga; Ivory Coast-Archdiocese of Abidjan; Dioceses of Abengourou, Bondoukou, Bouake, Daloa, Gagnoa, Katiola, Grand-Bassam, Korhogo, Odienne, Man, San Pedro, Yamoussoukro, and Yopougon; Ghana-Archdiocese of Cape Coast; Dioceses of Accra, Konongo-Mampong, Keta-Akatsi, Kumasi, Sekondi-Takoradi, Obuasi; Togo-Archdiocese of Lome; Dioceses of Kara, and Sokode; Benin-Archdiocese of Cotonou & Parakou; Dioceses of Abomey, Kandi, Djougou, Natitingou, Dassa-Zoume and Porto-Novo; Nigeria-Archdioceses of Kaduna, Abuja (Benin City) Jos, Lagos, Ibadan; Dioceses of Abeokuha, Bauchi, Ilorin, Issele-Uku, Kafanchan, Kano, Kontagor, Makurdi, Ondo and Warri; Niger-Diocese of Niamey; Central African Republic-Archdiocese of Bangui; Dioceses of Berberati. Zambia-Archdiocese of Lusaka, Dioceses of Ndola, Solwezi. Egypt-Vicarate Apostolic of Alexandria Morocco-Rabat; Congo-Kinshasa, Kikwit. Tanzania-Dioceses of Mwanza and Shinyanga. Kenya-Archdiocese of Nairobi; Diocese of Ngong & Lodwar. Argentina-Archdiocese of Cordoba. Australia-Archdiocese of Perth. South Africa-Diocese of Rustenburg, Archdiocese of Pretoria. Philippines-Archdiocese of Manila. South India: Tamilnadu. Poland-Warsaw.

Society of Mary: *Marianist Province of the United States (Society of Mary):* 4425 W. Pine Blvd., Saint Louis, MO 63108. Phone: 314-533-1207; Fax: 314-533-0778. Rev. Martin A. Solma, S.M., Prov.

Educational, parish, and development work in the following territories: (Puerto Rico) Archdiocese of San Juan, Puerto Rico; (Placements in India) Ranchi, India; Bangalore, India; Patna, India; Orissa, India; (Nepal) East Nepal, Nepal; (Placements in Mexico) Coatzacoalcos, Mexico; Queretaro, Mexico; Puebla, Mexico; (Central America) Guatemala; (South America); Davao City (The Philippines); Japan; Dublin, Ireland.

Society of St. Edmund: *Edmundite Generalate:* 270 Winooski Park, Colchester, VT 05439. Phone: 802-654-3400; Fax: 802-654-3409. Very Rev. Michael P. Cronogue, S.S.E., Supr. Gen.

Legal Title: *Society of St. Edmund, Inc.*

Major missionary endeavors in the United States are in Selma, Alabama and surrounding areas, and in the inner city of New Orleans (LA).

See the Foreign Mission section for the list of priests serving abroad.

Publications: Edmundite Missions.

Society of the Precious Blood: *Cincinnati Province:* 431 E. Second St., Dayton, OH 45402. Fax: 937-228-6878. Very Rev. Larry Hemmelgarn, C.PP.S, Prov. Dir. & Mission Coord.; Rev. Jeffrey Kirch, C.PP.S., Prov. Sec.; Bro. Joseph J. Fisher, C.PP.S., Mission Procurator.

Priests, brothers and deacons in foreign missions: 35.

Mission activities outside the U.S. in Chile, Peru, Bogota, Colombia, South America, Guatemala, Central America; Missions in La Tinta, Tucuru, Santiago, Purranque, Valdivia, LaOroya, Lima, Guatemala City, La Labor.

Publication: C.PP.S. Today.

Sons of Mary Missionary Society (1952): 567 Salem End Rd., Framingham, MA 01702-5599. Phone: 508-879-6711; Email: sonsboston@gmail.com; Web: www.sonsofmary-.com. Rev. John Murphy, F.M.S.I., Coord.; Rev. John Coss, F.M.S.I., Councilor; Bro. Francisco Tanega, F.M.S.I., Councilor.

Legal Title: *Sons of Mary, Health of the Sick, Inc.*

Dedicated to the ministry of healing: medical, catechetical and social apostolates in the home and foreign missions.

Third Order Regular of St. Francis: *Province of the Most Sacred Heart of Jesus: Franciscan T.O.R. Missions*, P.O. Box 188, Loretto, PA 15940. Phone: 814-693-2841. Bro. Mark McBride, T.O.R., Prov. Dir. of Foreign Missions; Very Rev. Christian R. Oravec, T.O.R., Min. Prov.Phone: 814-693-2890.

Secures missionaries and material aid to missions.

Active in the Archdioceses of Manaus and Sao Paulo; the Prelacy of Borba, Brazil; the Diocese of Bhagalpur, Bihar, India; and Diocese of Vice Province of Saint Joseph, Republic of South Africa.

Xaverian Missionary Fathers: *Provincial Headquarters:* 12 Helene Ct., Wayne, NJ 07470-2813. Phone: 973-942-2975; Fax: 973-942-5012. Very Rev. Carl S. Chudy, S.X.

A religious society of priests and brothers dedicated exclusively to foreign mission work and the training of candidates for missionary life.

Active in Brazil, Democratic Republic of Congo, Burundi, Chad, Cameroon, Bangladesh, Indonesia, Japan, Mexico, Sierra Leone, Colombia, Philippines, Mozambique, Taiwan, Italy, Spain, Great Britain and the United States of America.

Please refer to the Religious Institutes of Men section for activities and representation in the United States.

Publication: Xaverian Mission Newsletter.

Pontifical Mission Societies

A. The Pontifical Society for the Propagation of the Faith (1822): *National Office:* 70 W. 36th St., 8th Fl., New York, NY 10018. Phone: 212-563-8700; Fax: 212-563-8725; Email: pmsusa@propfaith.org; Web: www.onefamilyinmission.org. Rev. Andrew Small, O.M.I., Natl. Dir. & Pres.; Rev. Msgr. Robert J. Fuhrman, Vice. Pres.; Rev. Msgr. Richard L. Tofani, Acting Treas.; Rev. Msgr. Francis X. Blood, Sec.; Mr. Raymond Schroeck, Asst. Sec.

International Officers: His Eminence Ivan Dias, Prefect of the Congregation for Evangelization of Peoples; Rev. Timothy Lehane, S.V.D., Sec. Gen., Vatican City.

The Propagation of the Faith, under the direction of the Congregation for the Evangelization of Peoples, is established in every country where the Church is free to operate; it has a two-fold goal of promoting a universal missionary spirit and encouraging prayer and financial support for the local churches of the missions.

Each diocese in the United States has a director appointed by the Ordinary to promote the work of the Society through programs such as World Mission Sunday (the next-to-last Sunday in October) and Membership, presentations in seminaries, lesson plans and materials for mission animation in schools (grades 9-12) and parishes, news media and personal contact with parishes and diocesan organizations.

Offerings received by the Propagation of the Faith in the United States are joined with offerings from all other countries and distributed annually to more than 1,150 mission Dioceses and Vicariates.

Publication: Mission, Rev. Andrew Small, O.M.I., Publisher.

B. The Society of St. Peter Apostle (1889): *National Office:* 70 W. 26th St., 8th Fl., New York, NY 10018. Phone: 212-563-8700. Rev. Msgr. John E. Kozar, Natl. Dir. & Pres.; Rev. Msgr. Jan Dumon, Sec. Gen.

International Officers: His Eminence Ivan Dias, Prefect of the Congregation for Evangelization of Peoples; Rev. Msgr. Jan Dumon, Sec. Gen., Vatican City.

The Society of St. Peter Apostle, under the direction of the Congregation for the Evangelization of Peoples, is established for the support of seminarians and novices in the missions. During 2008, there were 26,792 major seminarians 50,315 minor seminarians and 9,099 novices receiving assistance from the Society of St. Peter Apostle. The Society also helps support local religious communities and retired native clergy. Each diocese in the United States has a local director who is also the Director of the Propagation of the Faith.

C. The Pontifical Missionary Union (1916): *National Office:* 70 W. 26th St., 8th Fl., New York, NY 10018. Phone: 212-563-8700. Rev. Msgr. John E. Kozar, Natl. Dir. & Pres.

International Officers: His Eminence Ivan Dias, Prefect of the Congregation for Evangelization of Peoples; Rev. Vito Del Prete, P.I.M.E., Sec. Gen., Vatican City.

The Missionary Union, under the direction of the Congregation for the Evangelization of Peoples, is established to inspire, deepen and sustain a mission spirit among priests, deacons, religious, seminarians, candidates for the religious life and others in the pastoral ministry of the Church. The director in each diocese is also the Director of the Propagation of the Faith.

D. Holy Childhood Association: *National Office:* 70 W. 36th St., 8th Fl., New York, NY 10018. Phone: 212-563-8700; Fax: 212-994-8569. Rev. Andrew Small, O.M.I., Natl. Dir. & Pres.

International Officers: His Eminence Ivan Dias, Prefect of the Congregation for Evangelization of Peoples.

The Holy Childhood Association (HCA) is one of four Pontifical Mission Societies active in some 110 countries throughout the world. Founded in France in 1843 by Bishop Charles de Forbin-Janson, HCA helps to animate the young faithful to a universal missionary spirit and to gather support from these children for the service of the local churches of Africa, Asia, remote regions of Latin America and the Pacific Islands among the poorest of the world's children.

Annually, more than two million young people, kindergarten through eighth grade, participate in HCA-sponsored programs in the United States through Catholic schools and parish religious education programs.

HCA is unique to other organizations that assist children in the Developing World in that its primary aim is to encourage children to share their faith with children in the Developing World through their prayers, personal sacrifices and financial offerings.

Contributions to HCA are allocated to mission dioceses throughout the world according to need. This system of allocating funds helps ensure that aid is distributed fairly and that those who are most desperately in need receive enough support. HCA funds are distributed to help children in 110 countries throughout the world.

More than 80% of HCA's annual funding in the United States is used for the Church's service among children in the Developing World and to provide mission education materials to children in the United States.

Parents, guardians, parish priests, religious brothers and sisters and lay people, especially teachers and catechists, play a vital role in HCA's mission. With support from these people, children can learn about children in other countries through HCA programs and learn too the message of HCA-that children are and can be missionaries today, called to share their faith and their love, in prayer and sacrifice, with the poorest of the world's children. In addition, financial contributions from adults help to underwrite the cost of education materials for children in the United States and also help support the Church's service to children in the Developing World.

Subcommittee on the Home Missions: *U.S. Conference of Catholic Bishops,* 3211 Fourth St. N.E., Washington, DC 20017. Phone: 202-541-3011; Phone: 202-541-5400; Fax: 202-722-8752; Fax: 202-541-3473. Most Rev. Michael William Warfel, Chm.; Dr. David J. Suley, Dir.; Mr. Ken Q. Ong, Grants Specialist.

A Subcommittee of the U.S. Conference of Catholic Bishops dedicated to support of the home missions. Catholic Home Missions (CHM) makes grants to extend the Church's presence as a means of salvation and to strengthen the Church's presence in rural, remote, and poor areas within the United States. Grantees include dioceses, religious institutes, and national, regional, and interdiocesan Catholic organizations in the United States and its island territories. The CHM funds a wide range of mission and evangelization activities; examples include parish support, seminary formation, lay ministry training, religious education, and ministry with culturally diverse groups. Application materials are available January 1 of each year; the deadline for submission of completed applications is April 1. The CHM makes grant decisions once a year in September, and grants are disbursed in quarterly payments January through October. The CHM's funds come from the annual Catholic Home Missions Appeal.

Publication: quarterly newsletter, Neighbors

Refer to the American Foreign Mission section of the Directory and the Religious Institutes of Men section I.D. #[0480] for detailed information on provinces and activities.

Bureau of Catholic Indian Missions (1874): 2021 H St., N.W., Washington, DC 20006-4207. Phone: 202-331-8542; Fax: 202-331-8544. Board of Directors:, His Eminence Justin Cardinal Rigali, Pres.; His Eminence Edwin F. O'Brien; His Eminence Timothy M. Dolan; Rev. Wayne C. Paysse, Exec. Dir.

Collecting and distribution of funds for the support of American Indian missions. The Bureau represents U.S. Catholic missions in government relations, specifically in Washington, DC.

Active throughout the United States, where American Indian, Eskimo and Aleute missions are present.

Office of Vice Postulator for the Cause of Blessed Kateri Tekakwitha Rev. Msgr. Paul A. Lenz, P.A., Vice Postulator. Promotes cause for canonization of Blessed Kateri Tekakwitha.

Publications: quarterly newsletter; monthly Kateri Circle Agenda.

Catholic Church Extension Society of the United States of America, The (1905): 150 S. Wacker Dr., Ste. 2000, Chicago, IL 60606-4200. Phone: 800-842-7804; Fax: 312-236-5276; Web: www.catholicextension.org. His Eminence Francis E. George, O.M.I., Chancellor; Rev. John J. Wall, Pres.; Mr. Thomas E. Gordon, COO; Ms. Julie Turley, Vice Pres. Devel.; Mr. Kevin P. McGowan, CFO.

Catholic Extension is a Papal society with a mission to strengthen the Church's presence and mission in under-resourced and isolated communities across the United States. Catholic Extension raises money through charitable contributions, gift annuities, trusts, and will bequests to support mission dioceses across America.

Requests for funds are submitted by bishops in designated American mission dioceses. Funding is for religious purposes: construction of churches and other facilities; salary subsidies for priests, religious, and lay people; seminarian education; campus ministry; pastoral and social ministry; emergency and disaster relief; evangelization, and religious education, including sponsorship of parish calendars.

Publications: EXTENSION Magazine; Catholic Extension Parish Calendars.

Catholic Near East Welfare Association (1926): 1011 First Ave., New York, NY 10022. His Eminence Timothy M. Dolan, Chm. & Treas.; Rev. Msgr. John E. Kozar, Pres.

A papal agency for humanitarian and pastoral support established by Pope Pius XI in 1926. It promotes awareness of the needs of the churches, institutions and persons under the jurisdiction of the Congregation for the Eastern Churches and the Permanent Interdiacasterial Commission for the Church on Eastern Europe. It raises and distributes funds to help meet the material and spiritual needs of the people it serves.

CNEWA works in those lands in which from ancient times the majority of Christians have been members of the Eastern churches. Its mandate extends to the churches and peoples of the Middle East, Northeast Africa, India and Eastern Europe. It encourages and provides assistance to projects and programs of pastoral support, humanitarian assistance, interfaith communication and public awareness.

Publication: ONE magazine

Catholic Negro American Mission Board: 2021 H St., N.W., Washington, DC 20006-4207. Phone: 202-331-8542; Fax: 202-331-8544. Board of Directors:, His Eminence Justin Cardinal Rigali, Pres.; His Eminence Edwin F. O'Brien, Pres.; His Eminence Timothy M. Dolan; Rev. Wayne C. Paysse, Exec. Dir.

Engaged in the support of priests and sisters throughout the states below Mason-Dixon Line, especially support in black schools.

Active in the United States, particularly all states in the South.

Commissariat of the Holy Land: 3140 Meramec St., Saint Louis, MO 63118-4339. Phone: 314-353-7729; Fax: 314-655-0563. Bro. Joseph Rogenski, O.F.M., Commissary.

Established for collecting and distributing funds for the support of the sacred places in the Holy Land. Regional Commissariat for the Ecclesiastical Provinces of Chicago, Cincinnati, Detroit, Dubuque, Indianapolis, Kansas City, Louisville, Milwaukee, Mobile, New Orleans, Oklahoma City, Omaha, St. Louis, St. Paul-Minneapolis and San Antonio.

Commissariat of the Holy Land: P.O. Box 127, Malibu, CA 90265. Rev. Warren J. Rouse, O.F.M., Commissary Email: frwarren@serraretreat.com.

Established to collect and distribute funds for support of the Sacred Shrines and educational and charitable institutions in the Holy Land. Assigned Territory: Ecclesiastical Provinces of Denver, Los Angeles, Portland (OR), San Francisco, Santa Fe and Seattle.

Commission for Catholic Missions Among the Colored People and the Indians (Black and Indian Mission Office) (1884): 2021 H St., N.W., Washington, DC 20006-4207. Phone: 202-331-8542; Fax: 202-331-8544. Board of Directors:, His Eminence Justin Cardinal Rigali, Pres.; His Eminence Edwin F. O'Brien; His Eminence Timothy M. Dolan; Rev. Wayne C. Paysse, Exec. Dir.

Organized by the Third Plenary Council as trustee of the funds collected in the churches for support of Black, Indian, Eskimo and Aleute evangelization programs in the United States. Grant applications are sent to Ordinaries each year and grant disbursements made in January and June.

Publication: annual, Annual Report.

Commissariat of the Holy Land: *Franciscan Monastery:* 1400 Quincy St., N.E., Washington, DC 20017. Phone: 202-526-6800 ext 887; Fax: 202-529-9850; Email: commissarywdcusa@myfranciscan.com; Email: secretariatusa@myfranciscan.com; Web: www-.myfranciscan.com. Rev. Jeremy Harrington, O.F.M., Commissary; Rev. Garrett Edmunds, O.F.M., Vice Commissary; Friar John-Sebastian Laird-Hammond, O.F.M., Secretariat to the Commissariat.

Administering the "Pontifical Good Friday Collection" in the United States; to promote vocations for the Holy Land Missions; to bring to light the needs of the people, especially the Christian Community in the Holy Land, and to address those needs.

Dominican Mission Secretariate: 141 E. 65th St., New York, NY 10065. Phone: 212-861-3776; Fax: 212-639-9823. Very Rev. Dominic Izzo, O.P., Dir.

Legal Title: *St. Jude Dominican Foreign Missions, Inc. (formerly Rosary Foreign Mission Society, Inc.).*

Founded by the Order of Preachers (Dominican Friars), Province of St. Joseph for the purpose of promoting American Dominican activity in the foreign missions throughout the world. Presently the Mission Office aids and supports work in the Archdioceses of Karachi and Lahore, the Dioceses of Multan, Faisalabad and Islamabad-Rawalpindi in Pakistan. The Archdioceses of Nairobi and Kisumu in Kenya; Calayan Island, Philippines, and the Solomon Islands.

Assumption B.V.M. Province: *Holy Dormition Friary,* P.O. Box 270, Sybertsville, PA 18251. Fax: 570-788-2431. Rev. Jerome J. Wolbert, O.F.M.; Rev. Anthony Skurla, O.F.M.; Rev. Laurian Janicki, O.F.M., Guardian; Bro. Augustine Paulik, O.F.M.; Rev. Michael Lenz, O.F.M.

Preparing missionaries to work among the people in the Byzantine Church.

General Secretariat of the Franciscan Missions, Inc.: P.O. Box 130, Waterford, WI 53185. Phone: 262-534-5470; Fax: 262-534-4342; Email: framis@wi.net; Web: www.franciscanmissions.org. Rev. Sereno Baiardi, O.F.M., Dir.; Rev. Sante De Angelis, O.F.M., Assoc. Dir.; Rev. Ponciano Macabalo, O.F.M.

General American office for assistance to Franciscan Missions under the auspices of the General Minister of the Order of Friars Minor.

Catholic Service Network: 6930 Carroll Ave., Ste. 820, Takoma Park, MD 20912-4423. Phone: 301-270-0900; Fax: 301-270-0901. Most Rev. Oscar A. Solis, Episcopal Advisor; James G. Lindsay, Exec. Dir.

Catholic Volunteer Network promotes, recruits and refers volunteers to missions in the United States and overseas. We represent nearly 200 faith-based volunteer programs worldwide and work with the U.S. Dioceses, religious communities and the private sector to determine their needs for help. Catholic Volunteer Network (CVN) is committed to the goal that every Catholic man and woman be invited to consider a period of service in the missions, as a vital and important manifestation of the baptismal call of all Catholic people. Currently, over 14,000 men and women are serving in CVN member mission programs offering their gifts and abilities in full-time service to people in need and living their Catholic faith more fully. These volunteers are serving domestically for a summer, six months, a year or more, and they are serving internationally for two or more years at a time. They are single and married, recent college graduates and early retirees, doctors and teachers, parish ministers and social workers, community organizers, computer programmers, legal aides and more.

Gatherings: Annual Conference; Formation Workshops, Training Seminars.

Awards: The Father George Mader Award, given annually to honor organizations and individuals who promote the value of lay mission service. The Bishop Joseph A. Francis Award to honor organizations and individuals who promote community service.

Publications: annual, Response: Directory of Volunteer Opportunities; quarterly, FaithWorks; monthly, How Can I Help?

Missionary Association of Catholic Women (1916): *National Office:* 1501 S. Layton Blvd., Box 3087, Milwaukee, WI 53203-3087. Phone: 414-758-2281; Email: wmo@archmil.org. Sr. Frances P. Cunningham, O.S.F., Contact Person.

Association providing material and financial aid to home and foreign missions.

MIVA-America Missionary Vehicle Association Inc.: *National Office:* 1400 Michigan Ave., N.E., Washington, DC 20017. Phone: 202-635-3444; Fax: 202-526-0830; Web: www.miva.org. Rev. Philip DeRea, M.S.C., Natl. Dir.; Larry Nigh, Office Admin.; Michele Marth, M.S.C., Appeal Coord.

The Missionary Vehicle Association (MIVA America) is a nonprofit organization whose sole purpose is to raise money to fund the purchase of reliable transportation for American missionaries working around the world. Without dependable transportation, missionaries are often unable to reach the people that most need their help. MIVA America's funds allow American Missionaries to purchase cars, trucks, jeeps, bicycles, motorcycles, boats, buses and ambulances.

Oblates of St. Francis de Sales (O.S.F.S.) (1906): *Wilmington-Philadelphia Province:* 2200 Kentmere Pkwy., Wilmington, DE 19806. Phone: 302-656-8529; Fax: 302-658-8052. Very Rev. James J. Greenfield, O.S.F.S., W-P Prov.; Very Rev. Kenneth N. McKenna, O.S.F.S., T-D Prov.; Rev. John J. Hurley, O.S.F.S., American Mission Procurator.

Missionary work in Republic of South Africa, Diocese of Keimeos-Upington; Nambia, Diocese of Keetmamshoop; South America—Uruguay, Archdiocese of Montevideo; Brazil, Archdiocese Porto Alegre (Rio Grande de Sol), Dioceses of Bage (RGS), Cruz Alta (RGS), Frederico Westphalen (RGS), and Senhor do Bofim (Bahia); India, Archdiocese of Bangalore (province of Karnataka); Haiti—Diocese of Les Gonaives; Mexico—Archdiocese of Merida.

Please refer to the Religious Institutes of Men section for activities and representation in the United States.

Provinces outside the United States: France, German-speaking, Italy, Netherlands, South African Region (South Africa, Namibia), De Sales Oblate Asia (India) Region, South America (Brazil).

Pontifical Mission for Palestine (1949): 1011 First Ave., New York, NY 10022. Phone: 212-826-1480. Rev. Msgr. Robert L. Stern, Pres.; Mr. Issam Bishara, Vice Pres.

A papal agency for humanitarian and charitable assistance established by Pope Pius XII in 1949. Its mission is to assist, without regard to nationality or religion, all who suffer as a result of the repeated conflicts that have devastated Palestine and neighboring regions of the Middle East.

It encourages and supports projects and programs of relief, rehabilitation, development; collaboration with other agencies; and education.

St. Paul's Guild, Inc.: 1011 First Ave., Rm. 1940, New York, NY 10022.

Formerly National Catholic Converts' League, now interested in assisting former Protestant clergymen and former Protestant religious.

Tekakwitha Conference (1939): *National Center,* P.O. Box 6768, Great Falls, MT 59406-6768. Phone: 406-727-0147; Phone: 800-842-9635; Fax: 406-452-9845; Email: tekconf@gmail.com; Web: www.tekconf.org.

Nonprofit organization established for evangelization within the Catholic Church with American Indians, Eskimos and missionaries working together at a national level to develop a Native American identity voice and presence in the Catholic Church. Catechesis, liturgy, youth ministry, inculturation and related areas within the Catholic Church are goals of the Conference.

Publication: 4 issues annually, Cross & Feathers.

Catholic Medical Mission Board, Inc. (1928): 10 W. 17th St., New York, NY 10011-5765. Members of the Board:, Rev. Msgr. Ferdinando D. Berardi; Rev. William J. Scanlan, S.J.; John A. Donnelly; Sr. Marilyn Fischer, S.F.P.; Rev. Msgr. Robert J. Fuhrman; Dr. Thomas G. Flynn; Dr. Patricia Smith; Mr. Thomas P. Melady; Most Rev. William Skylstad; Sr. Peggy Egan, O.S.F.; James A. Cunningham; Terry Kirch; Mr. Charles J. Casamento.

The Catholic Medical Mission Board (CMMB), founded in 1928, provides pharmaceuticals and health care supplies for organizations and clinical facilities that make health care available to the world's needy. In addition to its schedule of shipments, CMMB responds to health care emergencies. In 1999, over $43 million in medicines and related supplies were shipped to clinical facilities in 52 countries. Financial aid is also granted to students in accredited health care training programs. CMMB's Medical Volunteer Program places health providers interested in volunteering for short-term and long-term tours of service at selected clinical sites around the world. Catholic Medical Mission Board publishes "Medical Mission News," a quarterly journal magazine which provides in-depth information on its programs.

United States Conference of Secular Institutes

U.S.C.S.I. Attn: Sue Ann Rice, Pres. P.O. Box 2742, Ponca City, OK 74602. Tel: (580) 718-0752; Email: sueannrice1952@cableone.net. Members of the U.S.C.S.I. are Secular Institutes of Diocesan or Pontifical Right, canonically erected since 1947, following the promulgation of the Apostolic Constitution, "Provida Mater Ecclesia," by Pope Pius XII. The Institutes are listed on this page by the Congregation for the Institutes of Consecrated Life and for Societies of Apostolic Life. The purpose of the U.S.C.S.I., canonically erected by the Congregation as of its 1976 statutes, is to offer the Institutes an opportunity to exchange experiences, conduct research, and promote ways to make the vocation and Institutes known.

Company of St. Paul (Lay People and Priests): 52 Davis Ave., White Plains, NY 10605. Rev. Stuart Sandberg, Contact Person.
Founded in Milan, Italy November 17, 1920, under the auspices of Cardinal Andrew Ferrari; approved as a Secular Institute of Pontifical Right on June 30, 1950.
Aim: The practices of evangelical counsels is the expression of consecration to God. Professional work becomes the main means of the apostolate.

Diocesan Laborer Priests: 3706 15th St., N.E., Washington, DC 20017. Phone: 202-832-4217 Fax: 202-526-5692 Rev. Ovidio Pecharroman, Delegate.
A Secular Institute of Pontifical Right founded in Spain in 1883.
The aim of the Institute is the promotion, sustenance and cultivation of apostolic, religious and priestly vocations.

Don Bosco Volunteers: P.O. Box 588, Hawthorne, NJ 07507-0588. Cathy Sylvester, Contact Person.
Founded as a Secular Institute for Women by Blessed Philip Rinaldi, S.D.B., in Turin, Italy in 1917.
Approved as an Institute of Pontifical Right in 1978. Existing in 35 countries, with over 1,200 members.
Aim: to live in the spirit of St. John Bosco, in a wide variety of apostolates in one's own environment, and in the service of the local church, particularly on behalf of youth. An Institute for Men was founded in Rome in November, 1994. For information, see address above.

Missionaries of the Kingship of Christ: P.O. Box 34513, West Bethesda, MD 20827. Phone: 301-990-8630
Under this title are included two distinct and juridically separate institutes following the spirituality of St. Francis of Assisi.

Women Missionaries of the Kingship of Christ:
Founded in Italy in 1919 and approved as an Institute of Pontifical Right in 1948. Existing in thirty-two countries, the American branch began in 1950 and has spread to 25 states. Through a consecrated life in the world they give witness to Gospel values in work, family, church, civic and social environments by living the spirit of St. Francis and the beatitudes.
Rev. Gene B. Pistacchio, O.F.M., Ecclesiastical Asst.

Men Missionaries of the Kingship of Christ:
Founded in Italy in 1928 and approved as an institute of Pontifical Right in 1998. It was established in the United States in 1962. Their purpose is spreading the social reign of Christ through individual professions and occupations.

Oblate Missionaries of Mary Immaculate: 56 Brookfield St., Lawrence, MA 01843. Women: P.O. Box 764, Lowell, MA 01853.
Founded in Canada on July 2, 1952. Approved of Pontifical Right March 24, 1984.
International Membership: The members profess the evangelical counsels. Unique spirituality based on five attitudes of life: presence of God, absence of criticism and complaints, service and Charism.
Aim: A constant availability to the will of the Father to live everywhere the charity of Christ, through service, with the help of Mary.

Opus Spiritus Sancti: 301 E. 4th St., Auburn, IA 51433. Phone: 712-790-1749 Rev. James D. McCormick, Regional Coord. Phone: 712-688-2253
Founded in Mammolshain-Koenigstein, Germany in 1950.
A federation of communities having a common dedication to the Holy Spirit and life according to the evangelical counsels. Secular Institute of Priest; Secular Institute of Single Women; Apostolic Life Community of Sisters (Holy Spirit Sisters); Apostolic Life Community of Priests (Holy Spirit Father); Community of Apostolic Christians.

Secular Institute of Schoenstatt Fathers: W284 N746 Cherry Ln., Waukesha, WI 53188. Rev. Christian Christensen, Supr.
Founded by Father Joseph Kentenich in 1965, approved as a Secular Institute of Pontifical Right, June 24, 1988.
Aim: To aid the moral and religious renewal of society and the realization of the post-Vatican II mission of the Church, especially through priestly service to the International Schoenstatt Movement. In 2010, 318 ordained members in 25 nations worldwide.

Secular Institute of Schoenstatt Sisters of Mary (Women): W284 N404 Cherry Ln., Waukesha, WI 53188-9416. Phone: 262-522-4200 Fax: 262-522-4201 Email: schoenstattsisters@schsrsmary.org
Founded in Germany in 1926 by Father Joseph Kentenich; approved as a Secular Institute of Pontifical Right in 1948.
Aim: The moral and religious renewal of society. The members practice a Marian lay asceticism as a means of growing in love for God, and consecrating the world to Him. They are active within the Schoenstatt Movement and in a wide variety of professional spheres.

Servitum Christi (Women): Mailing Address: 1209 Greenwood Ave., Pueblo, CO 81003. 184 E. 76th St., New York, NY 10021. Elaine Kozlowski, Contact Person.
Founded Origin inspired by St. Peter Julian Eymard (1868), founder of the Congregation of the Blessed Sacrament. Founded in Holland, 1952; approved as a Secular Institute of Diocesan Right May 8, 1963.
Aim: To live the mystery of the Eucharist fully as consecrated lay persons and to make known its meaning so that the reign of Christ may come and the glory of God be revealed to the world.

Society of Our Lady of the Way: 2339 N. Catalina St., Los Angeles, CA 90027.
Additional members in Cleveland, OH; Daly City & Simi Valley, CA; Bridgeport, CT; Green Bay, WI; Jersey City, NJ; New Orleans, LA; Vancouver, B.C., Canada; Tokyo, Japan.
Founded in Vienna, Austria in 1936; approved as a Secular Institute of Pontifical Right in 1953. To Christianize the secular order members are consecrated to God through the vows of chastity, obdience and poverty. They pursue individual apostolates, seeking to manifest Christ in all the circumstances of their life and work. Spirituality is Marian and Ignatian.

Voluntas Dei Institute (1958): 2104 Eagle Pointe, Bloomfield Hills, MI 48304. Email: Director@voluntasdeiusa.org Rev. George F. Hazler, Contact Person.
Approved as a Secular Institute of Pontifical Right in 1987.
The Institute assembles together within a common apostolic project both clerics and celibate laymen. The Institute directs its members to discover the will of God, adhere to it and cherish it through the profession of the vows of poverty, chastity and obedience. The Institute also includes married couples as Associate Members. These commit themselves to live according to their state in life the same ideal and apostolic project as the clerics and celibate laymen, through committment to living poverty, chastity and apostolic obedience. Members of the Institute regularly gather as a team which is the place for listening to the Word and discerning the Will of God.

Alphabetical Listing of Mission Churches in the United States

A

Aasu/Aoloau, AS, c/o Pago Pago, AS, St. Paul. (SPP)
Abbeville, LA, St. James, c/o Erath, LA, St. John. (LAF)
Abeytas, NM, Socorro Co., San Antonio, c/o La Joya, NM, Our Lady of Sorrows. (SFE)
Abie, NE, Butler Co., SS. Peter and Paul, c/o Bruno, NE, St. Anthony. (LIN)
Abilene, TX, Sacred Heart Perpetual Adoration Chapel, c/o Abilene, TX, Sacred Heart. (SAN)
Abingdon, MD, Harford Co., St. Francis, c/o Baltimore, MD, Patronage of the Mother of God. (PSC)
Abo, NM, Torrance Co., c/o Mountainair, NM, St. Alice. (SFE)
Abram, TX, Hidalgo Co., St. Mary Magdalene, c/o La Joya, TX, Our Lady, Queen of Angels. (BWN)
Absarokee, MT, Stillwater Co., St. Michael, c/o Columbus, MT, St. Mary. (GF)
Absecon, NJ, St. Andrew Kim Korean Catholic Mission, Inc., c/o Absecon, NJ, Church of Saint Elizabeth Ann Seton, Absecon, N.J. (CAM)
Absarokee, MT, Stillwater Co., St. Michael, c/o Columbus, MT, St. Mary. (GF)
Acomita, NM, Cibola Co., St. Anne, c/o Pueblo of Acoma, NM, San Esteban, Acoma Catholic Indian Mission. (GLP)
Adel, GA, Cook Co., St. Margaret Mary, c/o Adel, GA, Queen of Peace. (SAV)
Adel, OR, Lake Co., St. Richard, c/o Lakeview, OR, St. Patrick. (BAK)
Adona, AR, Conway Co., St. Elizabeth, c/o Bigelow, AR, St. Boniface. (LR)
Afono, AS, c/o Pago Pago, AS, Church of the Immaculate Conception. (SPP)
Afton, NY, Chenango Co., St. Agnes, c/o Bainbridge, NY, St. John the Evangelist. (SY)
Afton, WY, Lincoln Co., Holy Family, c/o Jackson, WY, Our Lady of the Mountains. (CHY)
Agua Ramon, CO, Rio Grande Co., San Jose, c/o Del Norte, CO, Holy Name of Mary. (PBL)
Aguila, AZ, Maricopa Co., Our Lady of Guadalupe, c/o Wickenburg, AZ, St. Anthony of Padua Roman Catholic Parish. (PHX)
Aguirre, PR, Salinas Co., La Milagrosa, c/o Aguirre, PR, Sacred Heart. (PCE)
Alamillo, NM, Socorro Co., c/o Socorro, NM, San Miguel. (SFE)
Alapaha, GA, Berrien Co., St. Ann, c/o Tifton, GA, Our Divine Saviour. (SAV)
Alberton, MT, Mineral Co., St. Albert the Great, c/o Frenchtown, MT, St. John the Baptist. (HEL)
Albertville, AL, Marshall Co., Chapel of the Holy Cross, c/o Guntersville, AL, St. William. (BIR)
Albin, WY, Laramie Co., St. Joseph, c/o Pine Bluffs, WY, St. Paul's. (CHY)
Albuquerque, NM, Bernalillo Co., Morada de San Jose, c/o Albuquerque, NM, St. Anne. (SFE)
Albuquerque, NM, Bernalillo Co., Our Lady of Mount Carmel, c/o Albuquerque, NM, Nativity of the Blessed Virgin Mary. (SFE)
Albuquerque, NM, Bernalillo Co., San Jose de los Duranes, c/o Albuquerque, NM, San Felipe de Neri. (SFE)
Alcalde, NM, Rio Arriba Co., c/o Ohkay Owingeh, NM, San Juan Bautista. (SFE)
Alderson, WV, Greenbrier Co., St. Mary of the Greenbrier, c/o Hinton, WV, St. Patrick. (WH)
Alexandria, NE, Thayer Co., St. Mary's, c/o Fairbury, NE, St. Michael's. (LIN)
Alger, MI, Arenac Co., St. Joseph, c/o Standish, MI, Resurrection of the Lord. (SAG)
Algodones, NM, Sandoval Co., c/o Bernalillo, NM, Our Lady of Sorrows. (SFE)
Aliquippa, PA, Beaver Co., Maronite Mission of Aliquippa, c/o Carnegie, PA, Our Lady of Victory. (SAM)
Allegan, MI, Sacred Heart, c/o Dorr, MI, St. Stanislaus. (KAL)
Allen, SD, Bennett Co., St. John of the Cross, c/o Pine Ridge, SD, Our Lady of Sorrows. (RC)
Allendale, SC, Barnwell Co., St. Mary, c/o Orangeburg, SC, Holy Trinity. (CHR)
Alpaugh, CA, Tulare Co., Sacred Heart, c/o Corcoran, CA, Our Lady of Lourdes. (FRS)
Alpine, CA, San Diego Co., Nativity of BVM, c/o Lakeside, CA, Blessed Kateri Tekakwitha. (SD)
Alto, TN, Franklin Co., St. Margaret Mary, c/o Decherd, TN, Good Shepherd. (NSH)
Alto, TX, Venerable Antonio Margil, c/o Jacksonville, TX, Our Lady of Sorrows. (TYL)
Altoona, PA, Blair Co., Our Lady of the Assumption, c/o Altoona, PA, Our Lady of Mt. Carmel. (ALT)
Alturas de Campo Rico, PR, Ntra. Sra. del Carmen, c/o Canovanas, PR, San Jose. (FAJ)
Amado, AZ, Santa Cruz Co., Assumption Chapel, c/o Tubac, AZ, Saint Ann's Roman Catholic Parish and Missions – Tubac. (TUC)
Amagansett, NY, Suffolk Co., St. Peter the Apostle, c/o East Hampton, NY, Most Holy Trinity. (RVC)
Amalia, NM, Taos Co., c/o Questa, NM, St. Anthony. (SFE)
Ambia, IN, St. Mary's Church, c/o Fowler, IN, Sacred Heart of Jesus. (LFT)
Amelia, NE, Holt Co., St. Joseph, c/o O'Neill, NE, St. Patrick. (OM)
Amherst, NE, Buffalo Co., St. John Capistran, c/o Elm Creek, NE, Immaculate Conception. (GI)
Amouli, AS, c/o Pago Pago, AS, Church of Sacred Heart. (SPP)
Anaheim, CA, Orange Co., Sacred Heart, c/o Anaheim, CA, St. Justin Martyr. (ORG)
Andes, NY, Delaware Co., St. Ann, c/o Margaretville, NY, Sacred Heart. (ALB)
Andover, NH, Immaculate Conception, c/o New London, NH, Our Lady of Fatima. (MAN)
Angel Fire, NM, Holy Angels, c/o Cimarron, NM, Immaculate Conception Church. (SFE)
Anguilla, MS, Sharkey Co., Our Mother of Mercy, c/o Leland, MS, St. James. (JKS)
Anita, PA, Jefferson Co., St. Joseph, c/o Punxsutawney, PA, SS. Cosmas and Damian. (E)
Annapolis, MD, Anne Arundel Co., St. John Neuman, c/o Annapolis, MD, St. Mary. (BAL)
Anones, PR, San Jose, c/o Las Marias, PR, Immaculate Heart of Mary. (MGZ)
Anselmo, NE, Custer Co., St. Anselm's, c/o Broken Bow, NE, St. Joseph's. (GI)
Anthony, NM, Dona Ana Co., Immaculate Conception, c/o Anthony, NM, St. Anthony's. (LSC)
Anton, TX, Hockley, Co., St. Anthony of Padua, c/o Shallowater, TX, St. Philip Benizi. (LUB)
Antonito, CO, St. Augustine, c/o Antonito, CO, Our Lady of Guadalupe. (PBL)
Antwerp, NY, Jefferson Co., St. Michael, c/o Evans Mills, NY, St. Mary. (OG)
Aoa, AS, c/o Pago Pago, AS, Church of Sacred Heart. (SPP)
Apache, OK, Caddo Co., Mother of Sorrows, c/o Elgin, OK, St. Ann. (OKL)
Aquasco, MD, Prince Georges Co., St. Dominic's, c/o Brandywine, MD, St. Michael. (WDC)
Aquin, OH, Haiti Parish Twinning Program (Saint Thomas d' Aquin), c/o Marysville, OH, Our Lady of Lourdes. (COL)
Arago, NE, Richardson Co., St. Mary's, c/o Rulo, NE, Immaculate Conception. (LIN)
Arapahoe, NE, Furnas Co., St. Germanus, c/o Cambridge, NE, St. John's. (LIN)
Arboles, CO, Archuleta Co., SS. Peter & Rose, c/o Ignacio, CO, St. Ignatius Parish. (PBL)
Arbuckle, CA, Colusa Co., Holy Cross, c/o Williams, CA, Sacred Heart. (SAC)
Argyle, MN, Marshall Co., St. Rose of Lima, c/o Stephen, MN, St. Stephen's. (CR)
Arivaca, AZ, Pima Co., St. Ferdinand, c/o Tubac, AZ, Saint Ann's Roman Catholic Parish and Missions – Tubac. (TUC)
Arlee, MT, Lake Co., Sacred Heart, c/o St. Ignatius, MT, St. Ignatius Mission. (HEL)
Armagh, MO, Franklin Co., St. Patrick, c/o Catawissa, MO, St. James. (STL)
Arnold, CA, Arnold Co., Our Lady of the Sierra, c/o Angels Camp, CA, St. Patrick Church of Angels Camp (Pastor of). (STO)
Arnold, NE, Custer Co., St. Agnes, c/o Stapleton, NE, St. John the Evangelist. (GI)
Arock, OR, Malheur Co., Holy Family, c/o Jordan Valley, OR, St. Bernard. (BAK)
Arrey, NM, Sierra Co., San Jose, c/o Garfield, NM, San Isidro. (LSC)
Arroyo, PR, Arroyo Co., La Milagrosa, c/o Arroyo, PR, Our Lady of Mt. Carmel. (PCE)
Arroyo, PR, Arroyo Co., Ntra Sra. de Fatima, c/o Arroyo, PR, Our Lady of Mt. Carmel. (PCE)
Arroyo, PR, San Jose, c/o Arroyo, PR, Our Lady of Mt. Carmel. (PCE)
Arroyo, PR, Arroyo Co., San Martin, c/o Arroyo, PR, Our Lady of Mt. Carmel. (PCE)
Arroyo Hondo, NM, Taos Co., Nuestra Senora de Dolores, c/o Arroyo Seco, NM, La Santisima Trinidad. (SFE)
Ashdown, AR, Little River Co., St. Elizabeth Ann Seton, c/o Texarkana, AR, St. Edward. (LR)
Ashland, AL, Clay Co., St. Mark, c/o Alexander City, AL, St. John the Apostle. (BIR)
Ashland, NY, Greene Co., St. Joseph's Chapel, c/o Windham, NY, St. Theresa of Child Jesus. (ALB)
Aspermont, TX, Stonewall Co., St. Mary, c/o Rotan, TX, St. Joseph. (LUB)
Asti, CA, Our Lady of Mt. Carmel, c/o Cloverdale, CA, St. Peter's. (SR)
Astor, FL, Lake Co., St. Hubert of the Forest, c/o Ocala, FL, Our Lady of the Springs. (ORL)
Atalaya, PR, Ntra. Sra. de Altagracia, c/o Aguada, PR, St. Francis of Assisi. (MGZ)
Athena, OR, Umatilla Co., Sacred Heart, c/o Pendleton, OR, St. Andrew's Indian Mission. (BAK)
Atlanta, GA, Fulton Co., Centro Catolico del Espiritu Santo, c/o Atlanta, GA, Holy Spirit. (ATL)
Atlanta, IL, Logan Co., St. Mary's, c/o Lincoln, IL, Holy Family. (PEO)
Atlantic Mine, MI, Houghton Co., St. Mary, c/o Houghton, MI, St. Ignatius Loyola. (MAR)
Atoka, OK, Atoka Co., St. Patrick Church, c/o Durant, OK, St. William. (TLS)
Atwater, CA, Immaculate Conception, c/o Atwater, CA, St. Anthony. (FRS)
Atwood, CA, Orange Co., Santa Teresita, c/o Placentia, CA, St. Joseph. (ORG)
Augusta, MT, Lewis and Clark Co., St. Matthias, c/o Fairfield, MT, St. John the Evangelist. (HEL)
Aurora, NM, San Miguel Co., c/o Villanueva, NM, Our Lady of Guadalupe. (SFE)
Austin, PA, Potter Co., St. Augustine, c/o Galeton, PA, St. Bibiana. (E)
Austwell, TX, Refugio Co., St. Anthony of Padua, c/o Tivoli, TX, Our Lady of Guadalupe. (CC)
Autrain, MI, Alger Co., St. Therese, c/o Munising, MI, Sacred Heart of Jesus. (MAR)
Ava, MO, Douglas Co., St. Leo the Great, c/o Ava, MO, Immaculate Heart of Mary. (SPC)
Avoca, NE, Cass Co., Holy Trinity, c/o Syracuse, NE, St. Paulinus. (LIN)
Avon, MT, Powell Co., St. Theodore, c/o Helena, MT, Cathedral of St. Helena. (HEL)
Avondale, LA, Jefferson Civil Parish, Assumption of Mary, c/o Marrero, LA, St. Agnes Le Thi Thanh. (NO)
Avondale, PA, Santa Maria, Madre de Dios, c/o Avondale, PA, St. Rocco. (PH)
Azle, TX, Tarrant Co., Holy Trinity, c/o Fort Worth, TX, St. Thomas. (FWT)

B

Babb, MT, Glacier Co., St. Mary, Queen of the World, c/o Browning, MT, Church of the Little Flower. (HEL)
Badger, MN, Roseau Co., St. Mary's, c/o Roseau, MN, Sacred Heart. (CR)
Baggs, WY, Carbon Co., Our Lady of the Sage, c/o Rawlins, WY, St. Joseph's. (CHY)
Bahner, MO, Pettis Co., St. John, c/o Sedalia, MO, Sacred Heart. (JC)
Bainville, MT, Roosevelt Co., Sacred Heart, c/o Poplar, MT, Our Lady of Lourdes. (GF)
Bajio, PR, Sagrada Familia, c/o Aguada, PR, St. Francis of Assisi. (MGZ)
Baker, CA, San Bernardino Co., Our Lady of the Desert, c/o Barstow, CA, St. Joseph. (SB)
Bakersfield, CA, Kern Co., Holy Spirit, c/o Bakersfield, CA, Our Lady of Guadalupe. (FRS)
Bakersfield, CA, Kern Co., St. Jude, c/o Bakersfield, CA, Our Lady of Guadalupe. (FRS)
Bald Knob, AR, White Co., St. Richard, c/o Searcy, AR, St. James. (LR)
Billings, MT, Yellowstone Co., Sts. Cyril & Methodius, c/o Billings, MT, St. Bernard. (GF)
Ballardville, MA, St. Joseph's, c/o Andover, MA, St. Augustine. (BO)

Baltimore, MD, St. Patrick, c/o Baltimore, MD, Sacred Heart of Jesus. (BAL)
Bancroft, WV, Putnam Co., St. Patrick, c/o Nitro, WV, Holy Trinity. (WH)
Barberville, FL, Volusia Co., San Jose Mission, c/o DeLand, FL, St. Peter's Church. (ORL)
Barinas, PR, Yauco Co., St. James, c/o Yauco, PR, Holy Rosary. (PCE)
Barneston, NE, Gage Co., St. Joseph's, c/o Wymore, NE, St. Mary's. (LIN)
Barnsdall, OK, Osage Co., St. Mary, c/o Pawhuska, OK, Immaculate Conception. (TLS)
Barriada Vietnam, PR, La Milagrosa, c/o Guaynabo, PR, Santa Rosa de Lima. (SJN)
Barrington, NH, Strafford Co., Chapel of the Nativity, c/o Dover, NH, Parish of the Assumption. (MAN)
Barrio Apeadero, PR, Villalba Co., San Alfonso, c/o Villalba, PR, Our Lady of Mt. Carmel. (PCE)
Barrio Hatillo, PR, Villalba Co., Sagrada Familia, c/o Villalba, PR, Our Lady of Mt. Carmel. (PCE)
Barrio Indios, PR, Guayanilla Co., San Juan Bosco, c/o Guayanilla, PR, Immaculate Conception. (PCE)
Barrio Jaguey, PR, Villalba Co., Madre Cabrini, c/o Villalba, PR, Our Lady of Mt. Carmel. (PCE)
Barrio La Plata, Amoldadero, PR, Barrio Algarrobo, c/o Aibonito, PR, Church of St. Joseph. (CGS)
Barrio Obrero, PR, San Martin de Porres, c/o San Juan, PR, Nuestra Senora del Carmen. (SJN)
Barrio Semil, PR, Villalba Co., Santa Cecilia, c/o Villalba, PR, Our Lady of Mt. Carmel. (PCE)
Barrio Sierra Baja, PR, Guayanilla Co., Our Lady of Mt. Carmel, c/o Guayanilla, PR, Immaculate Conception. (PCE)
Barstow, TX, Ward Co., Our Lady of Refuge, c/o Pecos, TX, Santa Rosa de Lima. (ELP)
Barton, MD, St. Gabriel, c/o Westernport, MD, St. Peter. (BAL)
Bartow, WV, Pocahontas Co., St. Mark the Evangelist, c/o Marlinton, WV, St. John Neumann. (WH)
Basile, LA, Evangeline Parish, Assumption, c/o Basile, LA, St. Augustine. (LAF)
Basin, WY, Big Horn Co., St. Philip, c/o Greybull, WY, Sacred Heart. (CHY)
Basin City, WA, San Juan Diego, c/o Eltopia, WA, St. Paul. (SPK)
Bass Lake, CA, Madera Co., St. Dominic Savio, c/o Oakhurst, CA, Our Lady of the Sierra. (FRS)
Bassett, NE, Rock Co., Holy Cross, c/o Ainsworth, NE, St. Pius X. (GI)
Basye, VA, Shenandoah Co., Our Lady of the Shenandoah, c/o Woodstock, VA, St. John Bosco. (ARL)
Batesville, TX, Zavala Co., St. Patrick, c/o La Pryor, TX, St. Joseph. (LAR)
Baxley, GA, Appling Co., St. Raymond, c/o Baxley, GA, Good Shepherd. (SAV)
Baxley, GA, Appling Co., St. Rose of Lima, c/o Baxley, GA, Good Shepherd. (SAV)
Bay Mills, MI, Chippewa Co., Blessed Kateri Tekakwitha, c/o Brimley, MI, St. Francis Xavier. (MAR)
Bayamon, PR, Bayamon Co., N. Sra. Del Carmen, c/o Bayamon, PR, Santa Rita de Casia. (SJN)
Bayamon, PR, N. Sra. de la Providencia, c/o Bayamon, PR, Santo Domingo De Guzman. (SJN)
Bayamon, PR, Bayamon Co., N. Sra. del Buen Consejo, c/o Bayamon, PR, San Agustin. (SJN)
Bayamon, PR, Toa Alta Co., N. Sra. del Rosario, c/o Toa Alta, PR, San Esteban, Protomartir. (SJN)
Bayamon, PR, Bayamon Co., Sagrado Corazon, c/o Bayamon, PR, Santa Maria. (SJN)
Bayamon, PR, Bayamon Co., San Gerardo Mayela, c/o Bayamon, PR, Santa Maria. (SJN)
Bayamon, PR, Bayamon Co., San Jose, c/o Bayamon, PR, Santa Rita de Casia. (SJN)
Bayamon, PR, Bayamon Co., San Martin de Porres, c/o Bayamon, PR, San Agustin. (SJN)
Bayamon, PR, San Martin de Porres, c/o Bayamon, PR, Santa Teresa de Jesus. (SJN)
Bayamon, PR, Bayamon Co., Santa Monica, c/o Bayamon, PR, Ntra. Sra. de la Monserrate. (SJN)
Bayard, NE, Morrill Co., Sacred Heart, c/o Bridgeport, NE, All Souls. (GI)
Bayside, TX, Refugio Co., St. Mary, c/o Woodsboro, TX, St. Therese, The Little Flower. (CC)
Bda. Esperanza, PR, Guanica Co., La Providencia, c/o Guanica, PR, St. Anthony Abbot. (PCE)
Beach Haven, NJ, Ocean Co., St. Thomas Aquinas, c/o Brant Beach, NJ, St. Francis of Assisi. (TR)
Beaulieu, MN, Mahnomen Co., St. Joseph, c/o Mahnomen, MN, St. Michael's Parish. (CR)
Beaver, OK, Beaver Co., St. Frances Cabrini, c/o Guymon, OK, St. Peter's. (OKL)
Beaverton, OR, Washington Co., Mission of the Atonement, c/o Tigard, OR, St. Anthony. (P)
Beaverton, OR, Washington Co., St. Andrew Dung Lac, c/o Portland, OR, Southeast Asian Vicariate. (P)
Beaverton, OR, Washington Co., St. Andrew Dung–Lac, c/o Portland, OR, Our Lady of Lavang. (P)
Bedford Hills, NY, Westchester Co., St. Matthias, c/o Katonah, NY, St. Mary of the Assumption. (NY)
Bee, NE, Seward Co., St. Wenceslaus, c/o Dwight, NE, Assumption. (LIN)
Beech Bottom, WV, Brooke Co., Holy Family, c/o Wellsburg, WV, St. John The Evangelist. (WH)
Bel Air, MD, Harford Co., St. Mary Magdalen, c/o Bel Air, MD, St. Margaret. (BAL)
Belfair, WA, Mason Co., Prince of Peace, c/o Port Orchard, WA, St. Gabriel. (SEA)
Belgrade, MT, Gallatin Co., Valley of Flowers, c/o Three Forks, MT, Holy Family. (HEL)
Bellflower, IL, McLean Co., St. John, c/o Farmer City, IL, Sacred Heart. (PEO)
Bellingham, WA, Whatcom Co., St. Joachim (Indian Reservation), c/o Ferndale, WA, St. Joseph. (SEA)
Bellwood, NE, Butler Co., St. Joseph's, c/o Bellwood, NE, St. Peter's. (LIN)
Bemidji, MN, Beltrami Co., Holy Spirit Newman Center, c/o Bemidji, MN, St. Philip's. (CR)
Benicia, CA, St. Dominic, c/o Sacramento, CA, Vietnamese Martyrs Parish. (SAC)
Bennettsville, SC, Marlboro Co., St. Denis, c/o Cheraw, SC, St. Peter. (CHR)
Bensalem, PA, Our Lady of Fatima Church, c/o Philadelphia, PA, Immaculate Conception of Blessed Virgin Mary, Cathedral. (PHU)
Bent, NM, Otero Co., Our Lady of Guadalupe, c/o Mescalero, NM, St. Joseph. (LSC)
Benton, LA, Bossier Parish, Mary, Queen of Heaven, c/o Bossier City, LA, St. Jude. (SHP)
Benton, PA, Columbia Co., Christ the King, c/o Bloomsburg, PA, St. Columba. (HBG)
Bergland, MI, Ontonagon Co., St. Ann, c/o Ewen, MI, Sacred Heart. (MAR)
Berlin, PA, Somerset Co., St. Gregory, c/o Meyersdale, PA, SS. Philip and James. (ALT)
Bermuda, LA, Natchitoches Parish, St. Charles, c/o Natchez, LA, St. Augustine's. (ALX)
Berrien Springs, MI, Berrien Co., St. Gabriel Mission Church, c/o Bridgman, MI, Our Lady Queen of Peace. (KAL)
Berryville, AR, St. Anne, c/o Eureka Springs, AR, St. Elizabeth of Hungary. (LR)
Berryville, VA, Clarke Co., St. Bridget of Ireland, c/o Winchester, VA, Sacred Heart of Jesus. (ARL)
Berthold, ND, St. Ann, c/o Stanley, ND, Queen of the Most Holy Rosary. (BIS)
Bertram, TX, Burnet Co., Holy Cross, c/o Burnet, TX, Our Mother of Sorrows. (AUS)
Beryl, UT, Iron Co., San Pablo, c/o St. George, UT, St. George LLC 223. (SLC)
Beulah, CO, Pueblo Co., Our Lady of Lourdes, c/o Pueblo, CO, St. Francis Xavier. (PBL)
Beulaville, NC, Duplin Co., St. Teresa del Nino Jesus, c/o Kenansville, NC, Maria, Reina De Las Americas. (R)
Bevier, MO, Macon Co., Sacred Heart, c/o Macon, MO, Immaculate Conception. (JC)
Bibo, NM, Cibola Co., Our Lady of Loretto, c/o Seboyeta, NM, Our Lady of Sorrows. (GLP)
Bieber, CA, Lassen Co., St. Stephen, c/o Burney, CA, St. Francis of Assisi. (SAC)
Big Bay, MI, Marquette Co., St. Mary, c/o Marquette, MI, St. Peter Cathedral. (MAR)
Big Elbow Lake, MN, Becker Co., St. Frances Cabrini, c/o Waubun, MN, St. Ann. (CR)
Big Oak Flat, CA, Tuolumne Co., Our Lady of Mt. Carmel, c/o Sonora, CA, St. Patrick Church of Sonora (Pastor of). (STO)
Big Pine, CA, Inyo Co., St. Stephen, c/o Bishop, CA, Our Lady of Perpetual Help. (FRS)
Big Piney, WY, Sublette Co., St. Anne, c/o Pinedale, WY, Our Lady of Peace. (CHY)
Big Sky, MT, Gallatin Co., St. Joseph of Big Sky, c/o West Yellowstone, MT, Our Lady of the Pines. (HEL)
Big Sur, CA, Monterey Co., St. Francis of the Redwoods, c/o Carmel, CA, San Carlos Borromeo Basilica. (MRY)
Big Wells, TX, Dimmit Co., St. Michael, c/o Asherton, TX, Immaculate Conception. (LAR)
Bigfoot, TX, Frio Co., Our Lady of Mt. Carmel, c/o Devine, TX, St. Joseph's. (SAT)
Billings, MT, Yellowstone Co., Sts. Cyril & Methodius, c/o Billings, MT, St. Bernard. (GF)
Billings, OK, Noble Co., Sacred Heart, c/o Perry, OK, St. Rose of Lima. (OKL)
Binger, OK, Caddo Co., Our Lady of the Most Holy Rosary, c/o Anadarko, OK, St. Patrick's. (OKL)
Bird City, KS, Cheyenne Co., St. Joseph's, c/o St. Francis, KS, St. Francis of Assisi Parish. (SAL)
Birmingham, AL, Jefferson Co., St. Stephen the Martyr and Campus Center, c/o Birmingham, AL, St. Paul's Cathedral. (BIR)
Bismarck, MO, St. Francois Co., St. John, c/o Park Hills, MO, Immaculate Conception. (STL)
Bison, OK, Garfield Co., St. Joseph, c/o Hennessey, OK, St. Joseph's. (OKL)
Bison, SD, Perkins Co., Blessed Sacrament, c/o Lemmon, SD, St. Mary's. (RC)
Black Lake, LA, Natchitoches Parish, Our Lady of the Holy Rosary, c/o Campti, LA, Nativity of The Blessed Virgin Mary. (ALX)
Black Lake, NM, Colfax Co., St. Anthony, c/o Cimarron, NM, Immaculate Conception Church. (SFE)
Blackduck, MN, Beltrami Co., St. Ann, c/o Kelliher, MN, St. Patrick. (CR)
Blackville, SC, Barnwell Co., Sacred Heart, c/o Orangeburg, SC, St. Andrew. (CHR)
Blackwater, AZ, Pinal Co., Holy Family, c/o Sacaton, AZ, St. Peter. (PHX)
Blackwell's Corner, CA, Kern Co., Nuestra Senora de la Paz, c/o Wasco, CA, St. John the Evangelist. (FRS)
Blaine, WA, Whatcom Co., St. Anne, c/o Ferndale, WA, St. Joseph. (SEA)
Blanca, CO, Costilla Co., St. James, c/o San Luis, CO, Sangre de Cristo. (PBL)
Blencoe, IA, Monona Co., St. Bernard, c/o Onawa, IA, St. John. (SC)
Blooming Grove, PA, Good Shepherd, c/o Lords Valley, PA, St. John Neumann. (SCR)
Bloomingburg, NY, Sullivan Co., Our Lady of the Assumption, c/o Middletown, NY, Our Lady of Mt. Carmel. (NY)
Blowing Rock, NC, Epiphany, c/o Boone, NC, St. Elizabeth. (CHL)
Blue Hill, NE, Webster Co., Holy Trinity, c/o Campbell, NE, St. Anne. (LIN)
Blue Lake, CA, St. Joseph, c/o Arcata, CA, St. Mary's. (SR)
Blue Mountain Lake, NY, Hamilton Co., St. Paul, c/o Indian Lake, NY, St. Mary's. (OG)
Bluetown, TX, Cameron Co., Cristo Rey, c/o Progreso, TX, Holy Spirit. (BWN)
Bly, OR, Klamath Co., St. James the Apostle, c/o Chiloquin, OR, Our Lady of Mt. Carmel. (BAK)
Bo. Aceituna, PR, San Martin de Porres, c/o Moca, PR, Our Lady of Monserrate. (MGZ)
Bo. Aibonito Guerrero, PR, Ntra. Sra. del Carmen, c/o San Sebastian, PR, San Sebastian Martir. (MGZ)
Bo. Algarrobos – Yauco, PR, Yauco, Our Lady of Fatima, c/o Yauco, PR, Santo Domingo de Guzman. (PCE)
Bo. Almacigo Alto – Yauco, PR, Yauco, St. Juan Macias, c/o Yauco, PR, Santo Domingo de Guzman. (PCE)
Bo. Almacigo Bajo – Yauco, PR, Yauco, St. Martin de Porres, c/o Yauco, PR, Santo Domingo de Guzman. (PCE)
Bo. Altozano, PR, Ntra. Sra. de Fatima, c/o San Sebastian, PR, San Sebastian Martir. (MGZ)
Bo. Arenas de Guancia, PR, Guanica Co., S. Martin de Porres, c/o Yauco, PR, St. Martin de Porres. (PCE)
Bo. Atalaya, PR, El Cristo de la Reconciliacion, c/o Rincon, PR, St. Rose of Lima. (MGZ)
Bo. Bartolo, PR, San Pedro, c/o Rio Grande, PR, Nuestra Senora del Carmen. (FAJ)
Bo. Belgica, PR, Guanica Co., Cristo Rey, c/o Guanica, PR, St. Anthony Abbot. (PCE)
Bo. Cain, PR, St. Martin de Porres, c/o San German, PR, St. Rose of Lima. (MGZ)
Bo. Calabazas, PR, San Gabriel de la Dolorosa, c/o San Sebastian, PR, San Sebastian Martir. (MGZ)
Bo. Calvache, PR, Santa Rosa, c/o Rincon, PR, St. Rose of Lima. (MGZ)
Bo. Calzada, PR, c/o Maunabo, PR, San Isidro Labrador. (CGS)
Bo. Camarones, PR, Villalba Co., Jesus Crucificado, c/o Villalba, PR, Our Lady of Mt. Carmel. (PCE)
Bo. Camarones–Los Robles, PR, Villalba Co., San Antonio, c/o Villalba, PR, Our Lady of Mt. Carmel. (PCE)
Bo. Cambute, PR, Carolina Co., Divino Nino Jesus, c/o Carolina, PR, Cristo Rey. (SJN)
Bo. Canalizo – Jayuya, PR, Jayuya Co., La Milagrosa, c/o Jayuya, PR, Our Lady of Monserrate. (PCE)
Bo. Canonilla Abajo, PR, Villalba Co., Maria Madre de la Iglesia, c/o Villalba, PR, Our Lady of Mt. Carmel. (PCE)
Bo. Canovanillas, PR, Maria Auxiliadora, c/o Carolina, PR, Cristo Rey. (SJN)
Bo. Capa Barreto, PR, Virgen del Rosario, c/o Moca, PR, Our Lady of Monserrate. (MGZ)
Bo. Capa Bosque, PR, Corpus Christi, c/o Moca, PR, Our Lady of Monserrate. (MGZ)
Bo. Carite, PR, Guayama Co., San Martin, c/o Guayama, PR, St. Anthony of Padua. (PCE)
Bo. Carola, PR, La Milagrosa, c/o Palmer, PR, Cristo Rey. (FAJ)
Bo. Carreras, PR, La Providencia, c/o Anasco, PR, St. Anthony Abbot. (MGZ)
Bo. Carretera Nueva, PR, La Asuncion, c/o Hormigueros, PR, Shrine of Our Lady of Monserrate. (MGZ)
Bo. Cerro Gordo, PR, El Buen Pastor, c/o Moca, PR, Our Lady of Monserrate. (MGZ)
Bo. Cerro Gordo, PR, Villalba Co., Espiritu Santo, c/o Villalba, PR, Our Lady of Mt. Carmel. (PCE)
Bo. Cerro Gordo, PR, Our Lady of Monserrat, c/o Anasco, PR, St. Anthony Abbot. (MGZ)
Bo. Cerro Gordo, PR, San Francisco de Asis, c/o Sabana Grande, PR, Church of San Isidro. (MGZ)
Bo. Coabey – Jayuya, PR, Jayuya Co., San Jorge, c/o Jayuya, PR, Our Lady of Monserrate. (PCE)
Bo. Collado, PR, Ponce Co., Our Lady of Monserrate, c/o Mercedita, PR, Church of the Resurrection. (PCE)
Bo. Collores – Jayuya, PR, Cristo Rey, c/o Jayuya, PR,

Our Lady of Monserrate. (PCE)
Bo. Collores – Yauco, PR, Yauco, Sacred Heart, c/o Yauco, PR, Santo Domingo de Guzman. (PCE)
Bo. Corazon, PR, Guayama Co., La Candelaria, c/o Guayama, PR, St. Anthony of Padua. (PCE)
Bo. Corcega, PR, La Milagrosa, c/o Rincon, PR, St. Rose of Lima. (MGZ)
Bo. Corillo, PR, Villalba Co., San Pedro, c/o Villalba, PR, Our Lady of Mt. Carmel. (PCE)
Bo. Corral Viejo, PR, Ponce Co., Cristo Rey, c/o Ponce, PR, La Santisima Trinidad. (PCE)
Bo. Coto el Mato, PR, Penuelas Co., San Judas Tadeo, c/o Penuelas, PR, St. Joseph. (PCE)
Bo. Cruces, PR, Sagrado Corazon de Jesus, c/o Rincon, PR, St. Rose of Lima. (MGZ)
Bo. Cuchilla del Limon, PR, Villalba Co., La Asuncion, c/o Villalba, PR, Our Lady of Mt. Carmel. (PCE)
Bo. Cuchillas Cordero, PR, Virgen de la Monserrate, c/o Moca, PR, Our Lady of Monserrate. (MGZ)
Bo. Cuchillas Loperena, PR, Cristo Rey, c/o Moca, PR, Our Lady of Monserrate. (MGZ)
Bo. Cuesta Blanca, PR, Ntra. Sra. de Monserrate, c/o Lajas, PR, De la Merced Parish. (MGZ)
Bo. Culebrinas, PR, Espiritu Santo, c/o San Sebastian, PR, San Sebastian Martir. (MGZ)
Bo. Cuyon, Our Lady of Fatima, c/o Coamo, PR, St. Blase. (PCE)
Bo. Dajas, PR, Villalba Co., N.S. del Carmen, c/o Villalba, PR, Our Lady of Mt. Carmel. (PCE)
Bo. El Bajo, Patillas, PR, Patillas Co., Cristo Rey, c/o Patillas, PR, Inmaculado Corazon de Maria. (PCE)
Bo. El Cafetal – Yauco, PR, Yauco, St. Rosa de Lima, c/o Yauco, PR, Santo Domingo de Guzman. (PCE)
Bo. El Hoyo, PR, La Virgen Milagrosa, c/o Sabana Grande, PR, Church of San Isidro. (MGZ)
Bo. El Hoyo, PR, Santa Rosa de Lima, c/o Hormigueros, PR, Shrine of Our Lady of Monserrate. (MGZ)
Bo. El Jobos, PR, La Milagrosa, c/o Loiza, PR, Santiago Apostol, El Mayor. (FAJ)
Bo. El Porvenir, PR, Ntra. Sra. de la Providencia (Rep. Masias), c/o Mayaguez, PR, Ascension. (MGZ)
Bo. El Real, Patillas, PR, Patillas Co., San Guillermo, c/o Patillas, PR, Inmaculado Corazon de Maria. (PCE)
Bo. El Salto – Jayuya, PR, Santos Reyes, c/o Jayuya, PR, Our Lady of Monserrate. (PCE)
Bo. El Verde, PR, Nuestra Senora de Fatima, c/o Rio Grande, PR, Nuestra Senora del Carmen. (FAJ)
Bo. Eneas, PR, Ntra. Sra. de La Providencia, c/o San Sebastian, PR, San Sebastian Martir. (MGZ)
Bo. Espino, PR, St. Lawrence Martyr, c/o Anasco, PR, St. Anthony Abbot. (MGZ)
Bo. Fuig., PR, Guanica Co., Monserrate, c/o Ensenada, PR, Sacred Heart. (PCE)
Bo. Gripinas – Jayuya, PR, Jayuya Co., Buen Pastor, c/o Jayuya, PR, Our Lady of Monserrate. (PCE)
Bo. Guama, PR, N. Sra. de la Consolacion, c/o San German, PR, St. Rose of Lima. (MGZ)
Bo. Guamani, PR, Guayama Co., Sgdo. Corazon, c/o Guayama, PR, St. Anthony of Padua. (PCE)
Bo. Guanajibo, PR, San Martin de Porres, c/o Hormigueros, PR, Shrine of Our Lady of Monserrate. (MGZ)
Bo. Guaraguao, PR, Ponce Co., San Andres, c/o Ponce, PR, La Santisima Trinidad. (PCE)
Bo. Guaraguao Arriba, PR, Ponce Co., Santa Ana, c/o Ponce, PR, La Santisima Trinidad. (PCE)
Bo. Guaras, PR, Ntra. Sra. de Fatima, c/o Sabana Grande, PR, Church of San Isidro. (MGZ)
Bo. Guarderraya, Patillas, PR, Patillas Co., Madre Cabrini, c/o Patillas, PR, Inmaculado Corazon de Maria. (PCE)
Bo. Guayaba, PR, Juana Diaz Co., Our Lady of the Rosary, c/o Juana Diaz, PR, St. Raymond Nonato. (PCE)
Bo. Guaypao, PR, Guanica Co., Virgen del Rosario, c/o Ensenada, PR, Sacred Heart. (PCE)
Bo. Guerrero, PR, La Providencia, c/o San Antonio, PR, San Jose Obrero. (MGZ)
Bo. Hatillo Viejo, PR, Villalba Co., La Milagrosa, c/o Villalba, PR, Our Lady of Mt. Carmel. (PCE)
Bo. Hato Arriba, PR, San Patricio, c/o San Sebastian, PR, San Sebastian Martir. (MGZ)
Bo. Hato Arriba (Parcelas), PR, San Pablo de la Cruz, c/o San Sebastian, PR, San Sebastian Martir. (MGZ)
Bo. Higuero, PR, Villalba Co., Santisimo Sacramento, c/o Villalba, PR, Our Lady of Mt. Carmel. (PCE)
Bo. Hogares Seguros – Jayuya, PR, San Antonio Co., San Jose de la Montaña, c/o Jayuya, PR, Our Lady of Monserrate. (PCE)
Bo. Hoyamala, PR, San Jose Obrero, c/o San Sebastian, PR, San Sebastian Martir. (MGZ)
Bo. Hoyo Planes – Jayuya, PR, Jayuya Co., Ntra Sra de la Divina Providencia, c/o Jayuya, PR, Our Lady of Monserrate. (PCE)
Bo. Hoyos, PR, Ponce Co., Santa Maria Virgen, c/o Coto Laurel, PR, Our Lady of Mt. Carmel. (PCE)
Bo. Jacaboa, Patillas, PR, Patillas Co., Nuestra Senora del Carmen, c/o Patillas, PR, Inmaculado Corazon de Maria. (PCE)
Bo. Jacaquas, PR, Juana Diaz Co., N.S. de Fatima, c/o Juana Diaz, PR, St. Raymond Nonato. (PCE)
Bo. Jagual, Patillas, PR, Patillas Co., Nuestra Senora del Carmen, c/o Patillas, PR, Inmaculado Corazon de Maria. (PCE)
Bo. Jaguey, PR, San Jose, c/o Rincon, PR, St. Rose of Lima. (MGZ)
Bo. Jaquitas, PR, Ntra. Sra. de la Paz, c/o Hormigueros, PR, Shrine of Our Lady of Monserrate. (MGZ)
Bo. Jauca – Santa Isabel, PR, Santa Isabel Co., San Ignacio de Loyola, c/o Santa Isabel, PR, St. James. (PCE)
Bo. Juncal, PR, Santa Teresita del Nino Jesus, c/o San Sebastian, PR, San Sebastian Martir. (MGZ)
Bo. Juncos, PR, Corazon de Maria, c/o Penuelas, PR, Sacred Heart. (PCE)
Bo. La Haya, PR, Santa Rosa de Lima, c/o Lajas, PR, Our Lady of the Purification. (MGZ)
Bo. La Laguna, PR, Guanica Co., San Judas, c/o Guanica, PR, St. Anthony Abbot. (PCE)
Bo. La Lechuza, PR, La Immaculada Concepcion, c/o San Sebastian, PR, San Sebastian Martir. (MGZ)
Bo. La Luna, PR, Guanica Co., N. Sra Fatima, c/o Guanica, PR, St. Anthony Abbot. (PCE)
Bo. La Maquina, PR, Santa Ana, c/o Sabana Grande, PR, Church of San Isidro. (MGZ)
Bo. La Mocha, PR, Ponce Co., Santos Reyes, c/o Ponce, PR, San Vicente–Cantera. (PCE)
Bo. La Pica, PR, San Jose, c/o Sabana Grande, PR, Church of San Isidro. (MGZ)
Bo. La Pica – Jayuya, PR, San Patricio Co., San Patricio, c/o Jayuya, PR, Our Lady of Monserrate. (PCE)
Bo. La Plata, PR, Sagrado Corazon de Jesus, c/o Lajas, PR, Our Lady of the Purification. (MGZ)
Bo. La Torre, PR, Ntra. Sra. del Perpetuo Socorro, c/o Loiza, PR, San Patricio. (FAJ)
Bo. La Torre, PR, Santa Catalina de Siena, c/o Sabana Grande, PR, Church of San Isidro. (MGZ)
Bo. La Yuca, PR, Ponce Co., Immaculate Heart of Mary, c/o Mercedita, PR, Church of the Resurrection. (PCE)
Bo. Lajas Arriba (La Tea), PR, Ntra. Sra. del Perpetuo Socorro, c/o Lajas, PR, Our Lady of the Purification. (MGZ)
Bo. Lajas Arriba (Parcelas), PR, San Pablo, c/o Lajas, PR, Our Lady of the Purification. (MGZ)
Bo. Las Palmas, PR, Salinas Co., Virg. del Carmen, c/o Salinas, PR, Our Lady of Monserrat. (PCE)
Bo. Las Raices, PR, Ponce Co., Sagrado Corazon de Jesus, c/o Coto Laurel, PR, Our Lady of Mt. Carmel. (PCE)
Bo. Las Vallas, PR, Ponce Co., San Lucas, c/o Mercedita, PR, Church of the Resurrection. (PCE)
Bo. Las Vegas, PR, Our Lady of Perpetual Help, c/o Mayaguez, PR, Ascension. (MGZ)
Bo. Las Vegas – Yauco, PR, Yauco, Sta. Teresita, c/o Yauco, PR, Santo Domingo de Guzman. (PCE)
Bo. Lavadero, PR, Sagrado Corazon de Jesus, c/o Hormigueros, PR, Shrine of Our Lady of Monserrate. (MGZ)
Bo. Limon, PR, St. Teresita, c/o Mayaguez, PR, Ascension. (MGZ)
Bo. Limon, PR, Villalba Co., Virgen de la Amargura, c/o Villalba, PR, Our Lady of Mt. Carmel. (PCE)
Bo. Lizas, PR, c/o Maunabo, PR, San Isidro Labrador. (CGS)
Bo. Lluberas Yauco, PR, Yauco, St. Joseph, c/o Yauco, PR, Santo Domingo de Guzman. (PCE)
Bo. Lomas, PR, San Pedro Apostol, c/o Canovanas, PR, Sagrado Corazon de Jesus. (FAJ)
Bo. Los Barros, Patillas, PR, Patillas Co., S. Juan Evangelista, c/o Patillas, PR, Inmaculado Corazon de Maria. (PCE)
Bo. Los Pollos, Patillas, PR, Patillas Co., Santa Rosa de Lima, c/o Patillas, PR, Inmaculado Corazon de Maria. (PCE)
Bo. Macana, PR, Penuelas Co., Ntra. Sra. de Fatima, c/o Penuelas, PR, St. Joseph. (PCE)
Bo. Macun, PR, Toa Baja Co., Santa Maria La Mayor, c/o Toa Baja, PR, Ntra. Sra. de la Candelaria. (SJN)
Bo. Madrigal, PR, Ponce Co., N.S. del Rosario, c/o Ponce, PR, La Santisima Trinidad. (PCE)
Bo. Maginas, PR, Sagrado Corazon de Jesus, c/o Sabana Grande, PR, Church of San Isidro. (MGZ)
Bo. Maguayo, PR, Ntra. Sra. de la Monserrate, c/o Lajas, PR, De la Merced Parish. (MGZ)
Bo. Magueyes, PR, Ponce Co., San Juan de Mata, c/o Ponce, PR, La Santisima Trinidad. (PCE)
Bo. Malezas, PR, La Milagrosa, c/o Mayaguez, PR, Sacred Heart. (MGZ)
Bo. Mameyes – Jayuya, PR, Jayuya Co., S. Antonio, c/o Jayuya, PR, Our Lady of Monserrate. (PCE)
Bo. Marias, PR, St. Rita, c/o Anasco, PR, St. Anthony Abbot. (MGZ)
Bo. Marin Alto, Patillas, PR, Patillas Co., Perpetuo Socorro, c/o Patillas, PR, Inmaculado Corazon de Maria. (PCE)
Bo. Marueno, Arriba, PR, Ponce Co., N.S. Fatima, c/o Ponce, PR, La Santisima Trinidad. (PCE)
Bo. Mediana Baja, PR, Santisima Trinidad, c/o Loiza, PR, San Patricio. (FAJ)
Bo. Mini Mine, PR, La Providencia, c/o Loiza, PR, Santiago Apostol, El Mayor. (FAJ)
Bo. Minillas Carretera, PR, Perpetuo Socorro, c/o San German, PR, St. Rose of Lima. (MGZ)
Bo. Minillas Valle, PR, Santa Monica, c/o San German, PR, St. Rose of Lima. (MGZ)
Bo. Miradero, PR, Ntro. Sra. de la Providencia, c/o Cabo Rojo, PR, St. Michael. (MGZ)
Bo. Mogote, PR, Villalba Co., Santisima Trinidad, c/o Villalba, PR, Our Lady of Mt. Carmel. (PCE)
Bo. Molinas, PR, Ntra. Sra. de Monserrate, c/o Sabana Grande, PR, Church of San Isidro. (MGZ)
Bo. Naranjo, PR, Sagrado Corazon de Jesus, c/o Moca, PR, Our Lady of Monserrate. (MGZ)
Bo. Nuevo Mameyes, PR, Ponce Co., Santa Luisa, c/o Ponce, PR, San Vicente–Cantera. (PCE)
Bo. Olimpo, PR, Guayama Co., Cristo Rey, c/o Guayama, PR, St. Anthony of Padua. (PCE)
Bo. Ollas – Santa Isabel, PR, Santa Isabel Co., Virgen de Monserrate, c/o Santa Isabel, PR, St. James. (PCE)
Bo. Ortiz, PR, Corozal Co., Santisima Trinidad, c/o Bayamon, PR, Santo Domingo De Guzman. (SJN)
Bo. Oveja, PR, Cristo Redentor, c/o Anasco, PR, St. Anthony Abbot. (MGZ)
Bo. Palmarejo, PR, Villalba Co., San Jose, c/o Villalba, PR, Our Lady of Mt. Carmel. (PCE)
Bo. Palmarejo II, PR, San Juan Bautista, c/o Lajas, PR, Our Lady of the Purification. (MGZ)
Bo. Paloseco, PR, c/o Maunabo, PR, San Isidro Labrador. (CGS)
Bo. Parcelas Guacio (Parcelas), PR, Santa Cruz, c/o San Sebastian, PR, San Sebastian Martir. (MGZ)
Bo. Parcelas Palmarejo, PR, San Judas Tadeo, c/o Lajas, PR, Our Lady of the Purification. (MGZ)
Bo. Parcelas Santa Rosa, PR, Santa Rosa de Lima, c/o Lajas, PR, Our Lady of the Purification. (MGZ)
Bo. Parguera, PR, San Pedro, c/o Lajas, PR, De la Merced Parish. (MGZ)
Bo. Paris, PR, Ntra Sra. del Perpetuo Socorro, c/o Lajas, PR, De la Merced Parish. (MGZ)
Bo. Pastillo, PR, Ponce Co., Inmaculada, c/o Ponce, PR, La Santisima Trinidad. (PCE)
Bo. Pastillo – Penuelas, PR, Penuelas Co., San Antonio de Padua, c/o Penuelas, PR, St. Joseph. (PCE)
Bo. Penuelas Santa Isabel, PR, Virgen del Rosario, c/o Santa Isabel, PR, St. James. (PCE)
Bo. Perchas I, PR, Cristo Rey, c/o San Sebastian, PR, San Sebastian Martir. (MGZ)
Bo. Perchas II, PR, La Pasion del Señor, c/o San Sebastian, PR, San Sebastian Martir. (MGZ)
Bo. Pinales, PR, La Immaculade, c/o Anasco, PR, St. Anthony Abbot. (MGZ)
Bo. Pinas, PR, Comerio Co., La Resurreccion, c/o Bayamon, PR, N. Sra. de la Providencia. (SJN)
Bo. Pinas, PR, Comerio Co., N. Sra. de Fatima, c/o Bayamon, PR, N. Sra. de la Providencia. (SJN)
Bo. Pinas, PR, Comerio Co., Sagrada Familia, c/o Bayamon, PR, N. Sra. de la Providencia. (SJN)
Bo. Pinones, PR, Santa Rosa, c/o Loiza, PR, San Patricio. (FAJ)
Bo. Pitahaya, PR, N. Sra. del Carmen, c/o Luquillo, PR, Madre del Redentor. (FAJ)
Bo. Pitahaya Carr. 3 K.43, PR, Ntra Sra. del Carmen, c/o Arroyo, PR, Our Lady of Mt. Carmel. (PCE)
Bo. Plata, PR, San Judas Tadeo, c/o Moca, PR, Our Lady of Monserrate. (MGZ)
Bo. Playa, PR, Salinas Co., Carmen, c/o Salinas, PR, Our Lady of Monserrat. (PCE)
Bo. Playita, PR, Salinas Co., Virgen Milagrosa, c/o Salinas, PR, Our Lady of Monserrat. (PCE)
Bo. Playita Cortada – Santa Isabel, PR, San Patricio, c/o Santa Isabel, PR, St. James. (PCE)
Bo. Pozas, PR, Sagrada Familia, c/o San Sebastian, PR, San Sebastian Martir. (MGZ)
Bo. Pozo Hondo, PR, Santa Rosa de Lima, c/o Anasco, PR, St. Anthony Abbot. (MGZ)
Bo. Providencia, Patillas, PR, Patillas Co., Ntra Sra de la Providencia, c/o Patillas, PR, Inmaculado Corazon de Maria. (PCE)
Bo. Puerto Plata – Jayuya, PR, San Juan Evangelista, c/o Jayuya, PR, Our Lady of Monserrate. (PCE)
Bo. Puntas, PR, Nuestra Senora del Carmen, c/o Rincon, PR, St. Rose of Lima. (MGZ)
Bo. Quebrada Arenas, PR, c/o Maunabo, PR, San Isidro Labrador. (CGS)
Bo. Quebrado del Agua, Ponce, PR, Ponce Co., La Milagrosa, c/o Ponce, PR, Good Shepherd Parish. (PCE)
Bo. Rayo Plata, PR, San Judas Tadeo, c/o Sabana Grande, PR, Church of San Isidro. (MGZ)
Bo. Real Anon Abajo, PR, Ponce Co., San Mateo, c/o Coto Laurel, PR, Our Lady of Mt. Carmel. (PCE)
Bo. Real Anon Arriba, PR, Ponce Co., San Martin de Porres, c/o Coto Laurel, PR, Our Lady of Mt. Carmel. (PCE)
Bo. Recio, Patillas, PR, Patillas Co., Sto. Cristo de Los Milagros, c/o Patillas, PR, Inmaculado Corazon de Maria. (PCE)
Bo. Retiro Tea, PR, Santa Rita, c/o San German, PR, St. Rose of Lima. (MGZ)

Bo. Rio Cana Arriba, PR, Juana Diaz Co., La Merced, c/o Juana Diaz, PR, St. Raymond Nonato. (PCE)
Bo. Rio Grande, PR, La Virgin de Guadalupe, c/o Rincon, PR, St. Rose of Lima. (MGZ)
Bo. Rio Loco – Yauco, PR, Yauco, Our Lady of Montserrat, c/o Yauco, PR, Santo Domingo de Guzman. (PCE)
Bo. Robles, PR, Sagrado Corazon de Jesus, c/o San Sebastian, PR, San Sebastian Martir. (MGZ)
Bo. Rocha Magueyes, PR, Virgen de La Providencia, c/o Moca, PR, Our Lady of Monserrate. (MGZ)
Bo. Rocha Sec. Lassalle, PR, San Pedro Apostol, c/o Moca, PR, Our Lady of Monserrate. (MGZ)
Bo. Rosario Alto, PR, La Milagrosa, c/o Rosario, PR, Our Lady of Rosary. (MGZ)
Bo. Rosario Penon, PR, La Monseirate, c/o Rosario, PR, Our Lady of Rosary. (MGZ)
Bo. Sabana, PR, N. Sra. Milagrosa, c/o Luquillo, PR, Madre del Redentor. (FAJ)
Bo. Sabana, PR, San Jose de la Montana, c/o Trujillo Alto, PR, San Francisco de Asis. (SJN)
Bo. Saliente – Jayuya, PR, Jayuya Co., San Francisco, c/o Jayuya, PR, Our Lady of Monserrate. (PCE)
Bo. Salientito – Jayuya, Divino Niño Jesús, c/o Jayuya, PR, Our Lady of Monserrate. (PCE)
Bo. Salinas, PR, Ntra. Sra. del Carmen, c/o Lajas, PR, De la Merced Parish. (MGZ)
Bo. Salistral, PR, Ponce Co., Santa Marta, c/o Ponce, PR, Our Lady of Mt. Carmel. (PCE)
Bo. Saltos, PR, San Judas Tadeo, c/o San Sebastian, PR, San Sebastian Martir. (MGZ)
Bo. Santa Clara – Jayuya, Ntra Sra del Carmen, c/o Jayuya, PR, Our Lady of Monserrate. (PCE)
Bo. Santa Juanita, PR, Guanica Co., N. Sra. Rosario, c/o Guanica, PR, St. Anthony Abbot. (PCE)
Bo. Santana Pichel, PR, Ntra. Sra. del Rosario, c/o Sabana Grande, PR, Church of San Isidro. (MGZ)
Bo. Santas Pascuas, PR, Ponce Co., Resurreccion, c/o Ponce, PR, La Santisima Trinidad. (PCE)
Bo. Santo Domingo, PR, Penuelas Co., Ntra Sra del Carmen, c/o Penuelas, PR, St. Joseph. (PCE)
Bo. Sierrita Caonillas, PR, Villalba Co., Cristo de la Salud, c/o Villalba, PR, Our Lady of Mt. Carmel. (PCE)
Bo. Sonador, PR, Cristo Resucitado, c/o San Sebastian, PR, San Sebastian Martir. (MGZ)
Bo. Sonadora, PR, Sagrada Familia, c/o Guaynabo, PR, Corazon de Jesus. (SJN)
Bo. Sta. Ana Moreno, PR, Sta Lucia, c/o Sabana Grande, PR, Church of San Isidro. (MGZ)
Bo. Susa, PR, Yauco Co., N.S. de La Monserrate, c/o Yauco, PR, St. Martin de Porres. (PCE)
Bo. Susa, PR, Guanica Co., N.S. de La Providencia, c/o Yauco, PR, St. Martin de Porres. (PCE)
Bo. Susa, PR, Yauco Co., S. Francisco de Asis, c/o Yauco, PR, St. Martin de Porres. (PCE)
Bo. Susua, PR, Guanica Co., Ntra. Sra. de Lourdes, c/o Yauco, PR, St. Martin de Porres. (PCE)
Bo. Talante (La Pica), PR, c/o Maunabo, PR, San Isidro Labrador. (CGS)
Bo. Tallaboa Alta, PR, Penuelas Co., Santa Ana, c/o Penuelas, PR, St. Joseph. (PCE)
Bo. Vista Alegre, PR, Villalba Co., Jesus Crucificado, c/o Villalba, PR, Our Lady of Mt. Carmel. (PCE)
Bo. Voladoras Lomas, PR, Espiritu Santo, c/o Moca, PR, Our Lady of Monserrate. (MGZ)
Bo. Voladoras Parcelas, PR, Sagrada Familia, c/o Moca, PR, Our Lady of Monserrate. (MGZ)
Bo. Zama – Jayuya, PR, Jayuya Co., Santa Cecila, c/o Jayuya, PR, Our Lady of Monserrate. (PCE)
Bodega, CA, St. Teresa, c/o Occidental, CA, St. Philip. (SR)
Boise City, OK, Cimarron Co., Good Shepherd, c/o Guymon, OK, St. Peter's. (OKL)
Boles Acres, NM, Otero Co., Our Lady of the Desert, c/o Alamogordo, NM, Immaculate Conception. (LSC)
Bolinas, CA, Marin Co., St. Mary Magdalene, c/o Olema, CA, Sacred Heart. (SFR)
Boling, TX, Wharton Co., St. Joseph, c/o Wharton, TX, Holy Family. (VIC)
Bon Secour, AL, Baldwin Co., Our Lady of Bon Secour, c/o Magnolia Springs, AL, St. John the Baptist. (MOB)
Bonanza, OR, Klamath Co., St. Frances Cabrini, c/o Merrill, OR, St. Augustine. (BAK)
Bongard, IL, Champaign Co., Immaculate Conception, c/o Philo, IL, St. Thomas. (PEO)
Bonneau, SC, Berkeley Co., Our Lady of Peace, c/o Moncks Corner, SC, St. Philip Benizi. (CHR)
Booker, TX, Lipscomb Co., St. Peter, c/o Perryton, TX, Immaculate Conception. (AMA)
Boomer, WV, Fayette Co., St. Anthony Shrine, c/o Montgomery, WV, Immaculate Conception. (WH)
Booneville, KY, Owsley Co., Booneville Catholic Church of the Holy Family, c/o Beattyville, KY, Queen of All Saints. (LEX)
Borica, NM, Guadalupe Co., c/o Santa Rosa, NM, St. Rose of Lima. (SFE)
Borinquen, PR, Our Lady of Victory, c/o Aguadilla, PR, La Milagrosa. (MGZ)
Bosque, NM, Valencia Co., c/o Belen, NM, Our Lady of Belen. (SFE)
Boswell, OK, Choctaw Co., St. Jude, c/o Hugo, OK, Immaculate Conception. (TLS)
Boulder Valley, MT, Jefferson Co., St. John the Evangelist, c/o Boulder, MT, St. Catherine. (HEL)
Bowie, AZ, Our Lady of Guadalupe, c/o Willcox, AZ, Sacred Heart of Jesus Roman Catholic Church – Willcox. (TUC)
Bowling Green, FL, Hardee Co., Holy Child, c/o Wauchula, FL, St. Michael. (VEN)
Box Elder, MT, Hill Co., St. Anthony, c/o Box Elder, MT, St. Margaret Mary. (GF)
Box Elder, MT, St. Mary, c/o Box Elder, MT, St. Margaret Mary. (GF)
Bozrah, CT, New London Co., St. John, c/o Norwichtown, CT, Sacred Heart. (NOR)
Bradley, CA, Monterey Co., Our Lady of Guadalupe, c/o San Miguel, CA, San Miguel. (MRY)
Braithwaite, LA, Plaquemines Parish, Assumption of Our Lady, c/o Braithwaite, LA, St. Thomas. (NO)
Branch, LA, Acadia Parish, St. Edmund Chapel, c/o Rayne, LA, St. Leo IV. (LAF)
Branderi – Guayama, San José Obrero, c/o Guayama, PR, St. Anthony of Padua. (PCE)
Branford, FL, Suwannee Co., San Juan, c/o High Springs, FL, St. Madeleine Sophie Parish. (STA)
Brewster, MA, Barnstable Co., Immaculate Conception, c/o Brewster, MA, Our Lady of the Cape. (FR)
Bridge City, LA, Jefferson Parish, Holy Guardian Angels Mission, c/o Westwego, LA, Our Lady of Prompt Succor. (NO)
Bridgeport, CA, Mono Co., Infant of Prague Mission Church, c/o Mammoth Lakes, CA, St. Joseph Church of Mammoth Lakes. (STO)
Bridger, SD, Ziebach Co., Immaculate Conception, c/o Eagle Butte, SD, All Saints. (RC)
Brisas del Caribe, PR, Inmaculado Corazon de Maria, c/o Ponce, PR, San Jose Obrero. (PCE)
Brisbane, CA, San Mateo Co., Our Lady of Guadalupe, c/o San Francisco, CA, Visitacion, Church of the. (SFR)
Bristol, CO, Prowers Co., St. Mary, c/o Holly, CO, St. Frances of Rome. (PBL)
Bristol, NH, Our Lady of Grace, c/o Plymouth, NH, Holy Trinity Parish. (MAN)
Bristow, OK, Creek Co., St. Joseph, c/o Tulsa, OK, St. Catherine. (TLS)
Broadview, MT, Yellowstone Co., St. Theresa the Little Flower, c/o Roundup, MT, St. Benedict. (GF)
Brockton, MT, Roosevelt Co., St. Thomas, c/o Poplar, MT, Our Lady of Lourdes. (GF)
Bronte, TX, Coke Co., St. James, c/o Ballinger, TX, St. Mary Star of the Sea. (SAN)
Bronx, NY, St. Anthony, c/o Bronx, NY, St. Frances of Rome. (NY)
Bronx, NY, St. Francis of Assisi, c/o Bronx, NY, St. Frances of Rome. (NY)
Bronx, NY, St. Francis of Assisi, c/o Bronx, NY, Sacred Heart. (NY)
Brooklyn, NY, Kings Co., Regina Pacis Votive Shrine, c/o Brooklyn, NY, St. Rosalia–Regina Pacis. (BRK)
Brooks, MN, Red Lake Co., St. Joseph, c/o Red Lake Falls, MN, St. Joseph's. (CR)
Brown City, MI, Sanilac Co., c/o Yale, MI, Sacred Heart. (DET)
Brownstown, IN, Jackson Co., Our Lady of Providence, c/o Seymour, IN, St. Ambrose Catholic Church, Seymour, Inc. (IND)
Brownsville, OR, Linn Co., Holy Trinity, c/o Sweet Home, OR, St. Helen Catholic Church. (P)
Brownsville, TN, Haywood Co., St. John Church, c/o Jackson, TN, St. Mary Church. (MEM)
Brownsville, TX, Cameron Co., Sacred Heart, c/o Brownsville, TX, Immaculate Conception Cathedral. (BWN)
Brownsville, TX, Cameron Co., St. Thomas, c/o Brownsville, TX, Immaculate Conception Cathedral. (BWN)
Bruceton Mills, WV, Preston Co., Mary Help of Christians, c/o Morgantown, WV, St. Luke the Evangelist. (WH)
Bruni, TX, Jim Hogg Co., Sacred Heart, c/o Hebbronville, TX, Our Lady of Guadalupe. (LAR)
Brunswick, NE, Antelope Co., St. Ignatius, c/o Creighton, NE, St. Ludger. (OM)
Bryan, TX, Brazos Co., San Salvador, c/o Bryan, TX, St. Anthony. (AUS)
Bucarabones, PR, Sagrado Corazon, c/o Maricao, PR, St. John the Baptist. (MGZ)
Buckhorn, CA, Amador Co., Our Lady of the Pines, c/o Jackson, CA, St. Patrick's. (SAC)
Buena Vista, GA, Marion Co., St. Mary Magdalen, c/o Columbus, GA, Our Lady of Lourdes. (SAV)
Buena Vista, PR, La Milagrosa, c/o Las Marias, PR, Immaculate Heart of Mary. (MGZ)
Buenavista, NM, Mora Co., c/o Mora, NM, St. Gertrude. (SFE)
Bueyeros, NM, Harding Co., c/o Roy, NM, Holy Family–St. Joseph. (SFE)
Buffalo, NY, St. Adalbert, c/o Buffalo, NY, St. John Kanty. (BUF)
Buffalo, OK, Harper Co., St. Joseph, c/o Woodward, OK, St. Peter's. (OKL)
Buffalo Creek, CO, Jefferson Co., St. Elizabeth, c/o Conifer, CO, Our Lady of The Pines. (DEN)
Buffalo Twp., WI, WI, St. Andrew, c/o Pardeeville, WI, St. Mary of the Most Holy Rosary. (MAD)
Bullhead, SD, Corson Co., St. Aloysius, c/o McLaughlin, SD, St. Bernard. (RC)
Bullhead, SD, Corson Co., St. Aloysius, c/o McLaughlin, SD, Standing Rock Reservation. (RC)
Bullville, NY, Orange Co., St. Paul, c/o Middletown, NY, Our Lady of Mt. Carmel. (NY)
Bumpass, VA, Immaculate Conception, c/o Mineral, VA, St. Jude. (RIC)
Bunker, MO, Reynolds Co., Christ the King, c/o Salem, MO, Sacred Heart. (SPC)
Burchard, NE, Pawnee Co., Sacred Heart, c/o Steinauer, NE, St. Anthony. (LIN)
Burkesville, KY, Cumberland Co., Holy Cross Catholic, c/o Albany, KY, Emmanuel Catholic. (L)
Burlington, TX, St. Michael, c/o Burlington, TX, St. Ann. (AUS)
Burlington Junction, MO, Nodaway Co., St. Benedict Catholic Church, c/o Tarkio, MO, St. Paul the Apostle. (KC)
Burnsville, NC, Yancey Co., Sacred Heart, c/o Mars Hill, NC, St. Andrew the Apostle. (CHL)
Burwell, NE, Garfield Co., Sacred Heart, c/o Ord, NE, Our Lady of Perpetual Help. (GI)
Busby, MT, Big Horn Co., Christ the King, c/o Lame Deer, MT, Blessed Sacrament. (GF)
Bush, LA, St. Tammany Parish, St. Michael the Archangel, c/o Abita Springs, LA, St. Jane de Chantal. (NO)
Butler, AL, Washington Co., St. Paul, c/o Butler, AL, St. John The Evangelist. (MOB)
Butte La Rose, LA, St. Martin Parish, Sacred Heart, c/o Breaux Bridge, LA, Our Lady of Mercy. (LAF)
Bylas, AZ, Blessed Kateri Tekakwitha, c/o San Carlos, AZ, San Carlos Apache Roman Catholic Community – San Carlos. (TUC)

C

Cabezon, NM, Sandoval Co., San Jose, c/o Cuba, NM, Immaculate Conception. (GLP)
Cabool, MO, Texas Co., St. Michael, c/o Mountain Grove, MO, Sacred Heart. (SPC)
Cactus, TX, Sherman Co., Our Lady of Guadalupe, c/o Stratford, TX, St. Joseph's. (AMA)
Cade, LA, St. Martin Parish, St. Anthony, c/o Broussard, LA, St. Joseph. (LAF)
Caimital, PR, Guayama Co., Our Lady of Perpetual Help, c/o Guayama, PR, St. Anthony of Padua. (PCE)
Cairo, GA, Grady Co., St. Elizabeth Ann Seton, c/o Thomasville, GA, St. Augustine. (SAV)
Caldwell, TX, Burleson Co., Holy Rosary, c/o Caldwell, TX, St. Mary. (AUS)
California City, CA, Kern Co., St. Joseph, c/o California City, CA, Our Lady of Lourdes. (FRS)
Callabo, PR, Bo. Callabo, San Ramon, c/o Juana Diaz, PR, St. Raymond Nonato. (PCE)
Callaway, MN, Becker Co., Assumption, c/o Frazee, MN, Sacred Heart. (CR)
Callaway, NE, Logan Co., St. Boniface, c/o Stapleton, NE, St. John the Evangelist. (GI)
Calumet, OK, Canadian Co., Immaculate Heart of Mary, c/o Okarche, OK, Holy Trinity. (OKL)
Camaseyes, PR, Our Lady of Fatima, c/o Aguadilla, PR, La Milagrosa. (MGZ)
Cambalaches, PR, Yauco Co., Our Lady of Perpetual Help, c/o Yauco, PR, Holy Rosary. (PCE)
Cambridge, IL, Henry Co., St. John Vianney, c/o Woodhull, IL, St. John's. (PEO)
Camden, AL, Wilcox Co., St. Joseph, c/o Monroeville, AL, Annunciation. (MOB)
Camilla, GA, Mitchell Co., St. John Vianney, c/o Moultrie, GA, Immaculate Conception. (SAV)
Camp Sacramento, CA, El Dorado Co., Our Lady of the Sierra, c/o South Lake Tahoe, CA, St. Theresa. (SAC)
Camp Wood, TX, Real Co., St. Mary Magdalen, c/o Rocksprings, TX, Sacred Heart of Mary. (SAT)
Campbellton, TX, Atascosa Co., Sacred Heart, c/o Pleasanton, TX, St. Andrew. (SAT)
Campton, KY, Wolfe Co., Catholic Church of the Good Shepherd, c/o Jackson, KY, Holy Cross. (LEX)
Campus, IL, Sacred Heart, c/o Odell, IL, St. Paul's. (PEO)
Canaan, NH, Grafton Co., St. Mary, c/o Enfield, NH, St. Helena. (MAN)
Canadohta Lake, PA, Crawford Co., Our Lady of Fatima, c/o Union City, PA, St. Teresa of Avila. (E)
Candelaria, TX, Presidio Co., Our Lady of Peace, c/o Presidio, TX, Santa Teresa de Jesus. (ELP)
Canjilon, NM, Rio Arriba Co., San Juan Nepomuceno, c/o Chama, NM, St. Patrick. (SFE)
Canon, NM, Sandoval Co., c/o Jemez Pueblo, NM, San Diego Indian Missions. (SFE)
Canon de Vallecitos, NM, Rio Arriba Co., c/o El Rito, NM, San Juan Nepomuceno. (SFE)

Canoncito, NM, Mora Co., c/o Mora, NM, St. Gertrude. (SFE)
Canoncito, NM, Santa Fe Co., c/o Pecos, NM, St. Anthony of Padua. (SFE)
Canoncito, NM, Bernalillo Co., c/o Tijeras, NM, Holy Child. (SFE)
Canones, NM, Rio Arriba Co., c/o Abiquiu, NM, St. Thomas Apostle. (SFE)
Canovanas, PR, La Milagrosa, c/o Canovanas, PR, Sagrado Corazon de Jesus. (FAJ)
Canovanas, PR, San Francisco Javier, c/o Canovanas, PR, Nuestra Senora del Pilar. (FAJ)
Canton, NC, Haywood Co., Immaculate Conception, c/o Waynesville, NC, St. John the Evangelist. (CHL)
Cantonment, FL, Escambia Co., St. Elizabeth of Hungary, c/o Cantonment, FL, St. Jude Thaddeus. (PT)
Canyon Ferry, MT, Lewis and Clark Co., Our Lady of the Lake, c/o East Helena, MT, SS. Cyril and Methodius. (HEL)
Capitan, NM, Lincoln Co., Sacred Heart, c/o Carrizozo, NM, St. Rita. (LSC)
Capulin, NM, Rio Arriba Co., c/o Abiquiu, NM, St. Thomas Apostle. (SFE)
Carenage, VI, Chapel of St. Anne, c/o Charlotte Amalie, VI, Cathedral of Sts. Peter and Paul. (STV)
Carnation, WA, King Co., St. Anthony, c/o Snoqualmie, WA, Our Lady of Sorrows. (SEA)
Carnegie, OK, Caddo Co., St. Richard, c/o Anadarko, OK, St. Patrick's. (OKL)
Carnuel, NM, Bernalillo Co., Holy Child, c/o Tijeras, NM, Holy Child. (SFE)
Carolina, PR, Barrazas, N. Sra. del Carmen, c/o Carolina, PR, Ntra. Sra. de Fatima. (SJN)
Carolina, PR, Carolina Co., Parque Boliviano 5–JL, c/o Carolina, PR, Santa Clara de Asis. (SJN)
Carolina, PR, Carolina Co., San Antonio, c/o Carolina, PR, San Valentin. (SJN)
Carolina, PR, Cacao, Santa Teresa de Jesus, c/o Carolina, PR, Ntra. Sra. de Fatima. (SJN)
Carpenter, WY, Laramie Co., St. Peter, c/o Pine Bluffs, WY, St. Paul's. (CHY)
Carrissa Plains, CA, San Luis Obispo Co., St. James Mission, c/o Santa Margarita, CA, Santa Margarita de Cortona. (MRY)
Carrizales, PR, Ntra. Sra. de las Mercedes, c/o Aguada, PR, St. Francis of Assisi. (MGZ)
Carrizales, PR, Hatillo Co., Our Lady of Montserrat, c/o Yauco, PR, Holy Rosary. (PCE)
Carroll, NH, Coos Co., St. Patrick, c/o Lancaster, NH, Gate of Heaven. (MAN)
Caruthers, CA, Fresno Co., Our Lady of the Assumption, c/o Easton, CA, The Catholic Community of St. Jude and Our Lady of the Assumption. (FRS)
Casa Colorada, NM, Valencia Co., c/o Tome, NM, Immaculate Conception. (SFE)
Cascade, CO, El Paso Co., Holy Rosary, c/o Colorado Springs, CO, Sacred Heart. (COS)
Cascade, MT, Cascade Co., Sacred Heart, c/o Fort Shaw, MT, St. Ann. (GF)
Cascade, PA, Lycoming Co., Assumption of the B.V.M., c/o Williamsport, PA, St. Ann. (SCR)
Cascade, WI, Sheboygan Co., St. Michael Chapel, c/o Eden, WI, Shepherd of the Hills (Good Shepherd). (MIL)
Catarina, TX, Dimmit Co., St. Henry, c/o Asherton, TX, Immaculate Conception. (LAR)
Cathlamet, WA, Wahkiakum Co., St. Catherine, c/o Longview, WA, St. Rose de Viterbo. (SEA)
Cave Junction, OR, Josephine Co., St. Patrick of the Forest, c/o Grants Pass, OR, St. Anne. (P)
Cawker City, KS, Mitchell Co., SS. Peter & Paul, c/o Tipton, KS, St. Boniface Parish. (SAL)
Cazadero, CA, St. Colman, c/o Guerneville, CA, St. Elizabeth. (SR)
Cebolla, NM, Rio Arriba Co., Santo Nino, c/o Chama, NM, St. Patrick. (SFE)
Cedar Bluffs, NE, Saunders Co., St. Mary, c/o Colon, NE, St. Joseph's. (LIN)
Cedar Creek, AZ, Gila Co., St. Anthony, c/o Cibecue, AZ, St. Catherine. (GLP)
Cedar Hill, NE, Saunders Co., Sacred Heart, c/o Morse Bluff, NE, St. George. (LIN)
Cedar Hill, TN, Robertson Co., St. Michael, c/o Springfield, TN, Our Lady of Lourdes. (NSH)
Cedaredge, CO, Delta Co., St. Philip Benizi, c/o Delta, CO, St. Michael. (PBL)
Cedarville, CA, Modoc Co., St. James, c/o Alturas, CA, Sacred Heart. (SAC)
Ceiba, PR, Ceiba Co., N.S. del Perpetuo Socorro, c/o Ceiba, PR, San Antonio de Padua. (FAJ)
Ceiba, PR, Sagrado Corazon de Jesus, c/o Ceiba, PR, San Antonio de Padua. (FAJ)
Celina, TN, Clay Co., Divine Savior, c/o Cookeville, TN, St. Thomas Aquinas. (NSH)
Center, MO, Ralls Co., St. Paul (Historic Church), c/o Perry, MO, St. William. (JC)
Centermoreland, PA, Luzerne Co., Blessed Sacrament, c/o Wyoming, PA, St. Frances Cabrini. (SCR)
Centerville, MT, Cascade Co., Holy Trinity, c/o Belt, MT, St. Mark the Evangelist. (GF)
Centerville, TX, Leon Co., St. Leo the Great, c/o Crockett, TX, St. Francis of the Tejas. (TYL)
Centreville, MI, St. Joseph Co., St. Clare, c/o Three Rivers, MI, Immaculate Conception. (KAL)
Cerrito, NM, San Miguel Co., c/o Villanueva, NM, Our Lady of Guadalupe. (SFE)
Cerro, NM, Taos Co., c/o Questa, NM, St. Anthony. (SFE)
Cerro Gordo, PR, Buen Consejo, c/o Aguada, PR, St. Francis of Assisi. (MGZ)
Chacon, NM, Mora Co., c/o Mora, NM, St. Gertrude. (SFE)
Chalmette, LA, St. Bernard Parish, Chapel of St. Lawrence, c/o Chalmette, LA, Our Lady of Prompt Succor. (NO)
Chama, CO, Costilla Co., Immaculate Conception, c/o San Luis, CO, Sangre de Cristo. (PBL)
Chamisal, NM, Taos Co., Santa Cruz Mission, c/o Penasco, NM, San Antonio de Padua. (SFE)
Chamita, NM, Rio Arriba Co., c/o Ohkay Owingeh, NM, San Juan Bautista. (SFE)
Chandler, TX, Van Sand Co., St. Boniface, c/o Athens, TX, St. Edward Church. (TYL)
Chantilly, VA, Corpus Christi Mission, c/o Middleburg, VA, St. Stephen the Martyr. (ARL)
Chapmanville, WV, St. Barbara Catholic Community Church, c/o Logan, WV, St. Barbara. (WH)
Charlemont, MA, Franklin Co., St. Christopher, c/o Shelburne Falls, MA, St. Joseph's. (SPR)
Charlestown, RI, Washington Co., St. James, c/o Carolina, RI, St. Mary. (PRO)
Charley Creek, MT, Richland Co., St. Bernard, c/o Sidney, MT, St. Matthew. (GF)
Charlo, MT, Lake Co., St. Joseph's, c/o Ronan, MT, Sacred Heart. (HEL)
Chatham, MA, Our Lady of Grace, c/o Chatham, MA, Holy Redeemer. (FR)
Cherokee, NC, Swain Co., Our Lady of Guadalupe, c/o Bryson City, NC, St. Joseph. (CHL)
Cherokee, OK, Alfalfa Co., St. Cornelius, c/o Alva, OK, Sacred Heart. (OKL)
Cherry Creek, SD, Ziebach Co., St. Joseph, c/o Eagle Butte, SD, All Saints. (RC)
Chesapeake City, MD, Cecil Co., St. Rose of Lima, c/o Middletown, DE, St. Joseph. (WIL)
Chester, PA, Delaware Co., St. Hedwig Chapel, c/o Clifton Heights, PA, Sacred Heart. (PH)
Chicago, IL, Angel Guardian Croatian Catholic Mission, c/o Chicago, IL, Archdiocese of Chicago's Joseph Cardinal Bernardin Archives and Records Center. (CHI)
Chicago, IL, Our Lady of Fatima Mission, c/o Chicago, IL, Archdiocese of Chicago's Joseph Cardinal Bernardin Archives and Records Center. (CHI)
Chicago, IL, Our Lady of the Cross Mission Chapel, c/o Chicago, IL, Archdiocese of Chicago's Joseph Cardinal Bernardin Archives and Records Center. (CHI)
Chicago, IL, Cook Co., Sacred Heart, c/o Chicago, IL, Holy Name of Mary. (CHI)
Chicago, IL, San Marcello Mission, c/o Chicago, IL, Archdiocese of Chicago's Joseph Cardinal Bernardin Archives and Records Center. (CHI)
Chicago, IL, Santa Lucia Mission, c/o Chicago, IL, Archdiocese of Chicago's Joseph Cardinal Bernardin Archives and Records Center. (CHI)
Chicago, IL, St. Florian Mission, c/o Chicago, IL, Archdiocese of Chicago's Joseph Cardinal Bernardin Archives and Records Center. (CHI)
Chicago, IL, St. Hedwig Mission, c/o Chicago, IL, Archdiocese of Chicago's Joseph Cardinal Bernardin Archives and Records Center. (CHI)
Chicago, IL, St. Hyacinth Mission, c/o Chicago, IL, Archdiocese of Chicago's Joseph Cardinal Bernardin Archives and Records Center. (CHI)
Childersburg, AL, Talladega Co., Holy Name of Jesus, c/o Sylacauga, AL, St. Jude. (BIR)
Chilili, NM, Bernalillo Co., San Juan de Nepumoceno, c/o Tijeras, NM, Holy Child. (SFE)
China Spring, TX, McLennan Co., St. Philip, c/o McGregor, TX, St. Eugene Catholic Church – McGregor, Texas. (AUS)
Chireno, TX, Nacogdoches Co., Our Lady of Lourdes, c/o Nacogdoches, TX, Sacred Heart. (TYL)
Choctaw, LA, Lafourche Parish, St. James, c/o Thibodaux, LA, St. Lawrence the Martyr. (HT)
Christiansted, VI, U.S.V.I., Sacred Heart Chapel, c/o Christiansted, VI, Church of the Holy Cross. (STV)
Christine, TX, Atascosa Co., St. Ignatius, c/o Jourdanton, TX, St. Matthew's. (SAT)
Christmas Valley, OR, Lake Co., Holy Family, c/o La Pine, OR, Holy Redeemer. (BAK)
Chualar, CA, Monterey Co., Chualar Mission, c/o Gonzales, CA, St. Theodore. (MRY)
Chugwater, WY, Platte Co., Mary Queen of Heaven, c/o Wheatland, WY, St. Patrick's. (CHY)
Church Creek, MD, Dorchester Co., St. Mary, Star of the Sea, c/o Cambridge, MD, St. Mary Refuge of Sinners. (WIL)
Churubusco, NY, Immaculate Heart of Mary, c/o Ellenburg, NY, St. Edmund. (OG)
Cilantro, PR, Coamo Co., Saint James, c/o Coamo, PR, St. Blase. (PCE)
Cincinnatus, NY, Cortland Co., Our Lady of Perpetual Help, c/o Marathon, NY, St. Stephen. (SY)
Cincinnatus, NY, Cortland Co., Our Lady of Perpetual Help, c/o Whitney Point, NY, The Catholic Community of St. Stephen–St. Patrick. (SY)
Citra, FL, Christ the King, c/o Ocala, FL, Blessed Trinity. (ORL)
Clallam Bay, WA, Clallam Co., St. Thomas the Apostle, c/o Forks, WA, St. Anne Parish. (SEA)
Clancy, MT, Jefferson Co., St. John's, c/o East Helena, MT, SS. Cyril and Methodius. (HEL)
Clark, WY, Park Co., Our Lady of the Valley, c/o Cody, WY, St. Anthony. (CHY)
Clarkdale, AZ, Yavapai Co., St. Cecilia, c/o Cottonwood, AZ, Immaculate Conception Roman Catholic Parish. (PHX)
Clarkson, NE, Holy Trinity – Heun, c/o Howells, NE, SS. Peter and Paul. (OM)
Clarksville, MO, Pike Co., Mary Queen of Peace, c/o Louisiana, MO, St. Joseph. (JC)
Clatskanie, OR, Columbia Co., St. John the Baptist, c/o Rainier, OR, Nativity B.V.M. (P)
Claypool, AZ, Gila Co., St. Joseph, c/o Miami, AZ, Our Lady of the Blessed Sacrament Roman Catholic Church – Miami. (TUC)
Clayton, AL, Barbour Co., Ventress Correctional Facility, c/o Eufaula, AL, Holy Redeemer. (MOB)
Clayton, GA, Rabun Co., St. Helena, c/o Clarkesville, GA, St. Mark. (ATL)
Clayton, OK, Pushmataha Co., Holy Trinity, c/o Wilburton, OK, Sacred Heart. (TLS)
Denali National Park, AK, c/o Healy, AK, Holy Mary of Guadalupe Catholic Church Healy. (FBK)
Clear Spring, MD, Washington Co., St. Michael, c/o Hagerstown, MD, St. Mary. (BAL)
Clearmont, WY, Johnson Co., St. Mary, c/o Buffalo, WY, St. John the Baptist. (CHY)
Clearwater, NE, Mission of St. Theresa of Avila, Clearwater, NE, c/o Ewing, NE, St. Peter de Alcantara. (OM)
Cleveland, NM, Mora Co., c/o Mora, NM, St. Gertrude. (SFE)
Cleveland, OK, Pawnee Co., St. Joseph, c/o Fairfax, OK, Sacred Heart. (TLS)
Clewiston, FL, Hendry Co., Santa Rosa de Lima, c/o Clewiston, FL, St. Margaret. (VEN)
Clifton, AZ, Greenlee Co., St. Mary, c/o Clifton, AZ, Sacred Heart Roman Catholic Church and St. Mary's Mission – Clifton. (TUC)
Clinton, AR, Van Buren Co., St. Jude, c/o Fairfield Bay, AR, St. Francis Assisi. (LR)
Clinton Corners, NY, Dutchess Co., c/o Millbrook, NY, St. Joseph. (NY)
Cloudcroft, NM, Otero Co., Sacred Heart, c/o Alamogordo, NM, Immaculate Conception. (LSC)
Cloverdale, OR, Tillamook Co., St. Joseph, c/o Tillamook, OR, Sacred Heart. (P)
Clyde, TX, Callahan Co., Sts. Joachim and Ann, c/o Abilene, TX, Sacred Heart. (SAN)
Clyde Park, MT, Park Co., St. Margaret, c/o Livingston, MT, St. Mary. (GF)
Coal Mine, TX, Atascosa Co., Immaculate Conception, c/o Lytle, TX, St. Andrew. (SAT)
Coamo Arriba, Sacred Heart of Jesus, c/o Coamo, PR, St. Blase. (PCE)
Cochiti, NM, Sandoval Co., St. Bonaventure, c/o Pena Blanca, NM, Nuestra Senora De Guadalupe. (SFE)
Cochranton, PA, Crawford Co., Our Lady of Lourdes, c/o Guys Mills, PA, St. Hippolyte. (E)
Cochranville, PA, Chester Co., St. Malachy, c/o Parkesburg, PA, Our Lady of Consolation. (PH)
Coco, PR, Salinas Co., Santa Ana, c/o Salinas, PR, Our Lady of Monserrat. (PCE)
Coffman Cove, AK, c/o Craig, AK, St. John by the Sea. (JUN)
Cole Camp, MO, Benton Co., SS. Peter & Paul, c/o Warsaw, MO, St. Ann. (JC)
Collegeville, AL, Jefferson Co., Sacred Heart, c/o Birmingham, AL, Our Lady Queen of the Universe. (BIR)
Collores Parcelas, PR, Juana Diaz Co., La Milagrosa, c/o Juana Diaz, PR, St. Raymond Nonato. (PCE)
Colon, MI, St. Joseph Co., St. Barbara, c/o Bronson, MI, St. Mary's. (KAL)
Colonia Nueva, TX, Hidalgo Co., Christ the King, c/o Donna, TX, St. Joseph. (BWN)
Colonial Beach, VA, Westmoreland Co., St. Anthony's, c/o Colonial Beach, VA, St. Elizabeth of Hungary. (ARL)
Colonias, NM, Guadalupe Co., c/o Santa Rosa, NM, St. Rose of Lima. (SFE)
Colrain, MA, Franklin Co., St. John the Baptist, c/o Shelburne Falls, MA, St. Joseph's. (SPR)
Columbia, CA, Tuolumne Co., St. Anne, c/o Sonora, CA, St. Patrick Church of Sonora (Pastor of). (STO)
Columbia, KY, Adair Co., Good Shepherd, c/o Jamestown, KY, Holy Spirit. (L)
Columbia, LA, Caldwell Parish, St. John, c/o Winnsboro, LA, St. Mary. (ALX)
Columbia, NC, Tyrrell Co., All Souls, c/o Edenton, NC, St. Anne. (R)

Columbus, NM, Luna Co., c/o Deming, NM, Holy Family. (LSC)
Comal, TX, Comal Co., St. Joseph, c/o New Braunfels, TX, SS. Peter and Paul. (SAT)
Comstock, TX, Valverde Co., Mary, Queen of the Universe, c/o Del Rio, TX, Sacred Heart. (SAT)
Concepcion, TX, Duval Co., Immaculate Conception, c/o Premont, TX, St. Theresa of the Infant Jesus. (CC)
Concrete, WA, Skagit Co., St. Catherine, c/o Sedro Woolley, WA, Immaculate Heart of Mary. (SEA)
Conde Avila, PR, St. Martin de Porres, c/o Cabo Rojo, PR, St. Michael. (MGZ)
Conehatta, MS, Newton Co., St. Catherine, c/o Philadelphia, MS, Holy Rosary. (JKS)
Conowingo, MD, Cecil Co., St. Patrick, c/o Perryville, MD, Church of the Good Shepherd. (WIL)
Consejo Alto, PR, Guayanilla Co., La Monserrate, c/o Guayanilla, PR, Immaculate Conception. (PCE)
Constantia, NY, Oswego Co., St. Bernadette, c/o Cleveland, NY, St. Mary of the Assumption. (SY)
Contreras, NM, Socorro Co., San Jose, c/o La Joya, NM, Our Lady of Sorrows. (SFE)
Conway, MA, St. Marks, c/o South Deerfield, MA, Holy Family Parish. (SPR)
Cookson, OK, Cherokee Co., St. John the Evangelist, c/o Sallisaw, OK, St. Francis Xavier. (TLS)
Cooper, TX, Delta Co., St. Clare Mission, c/o Sulphur Springs, TX, St. James. (TYL)
Cooper Landing, AK, St. John Neumann Church, c/o Seward, AK, Sacred Heart. (ANC)
Copper Harbor, MI, Keweenaw Co., Our Lady of the Pines, c/o Calumet, MI, Our Lady of Peace. (MAR)
Coqui, PR, Salinas Co., Our Lady of Perpetual Help, c/o Aguirre, PR, Sacred Heart. (PCE)
Coral, MI, Montcalm Co., St. Clara, c/o Sand Lake, MI, Mary Queen of Apostles. (GR)
Cordell, OK, Washita Co., St. Anne, c/o Clinton, OK, St. Mary's. (OKL)
Cordova, MD, Talbot Co., St. Joseph, c/o Easton, MD, SS. Peter and Paul. (WIL)
Cordova, NM, Rio Arriba Co., San Antonio, c/o Chimayo, NM, Holy Family. (SFE)
Corona, NM, Lincoln Co., St. Therese of the Little Flower, c/o Carrizozo, NM, St. Rita. (LSC)
Corona, NY, Queens Co., Our Lady of Mount Carmel, c/o Corona, NY, St. Leo. (BRK)
Corpus Christi, TX, Nueces Co., St. Mary, c/o Corpus Christi, TX, St. Peter Prince of Apostles. (CC)
Costilla, NM, Taos Co., c/o Questa, NM, St. Anthony. (SFE)
Cotton City, NM, Hidalgo Co., St. Jude, c/o Lordsburg, NM, St. Joseph. (LSC)
Cottonwood, CA, Shasta Co., St. Anne, c/o Anderson, CA, Sacred Heart. (SAC)
Cotuy, PR, Our Lady of Fatima, c/o San German, PR, San German de Auxerre. (MGZ)
Coupeville, WA, Island Co., St. Mary, c/o Oak Harbor, WA, St. Augustine. (SEA)
Coushatta, LA, Red River Parish, St. George, c/o Bossier City, LA, Mary, Queen of Peace. (SHP)
Covelo, CA, Mendocino Co., Our Lady, Queen of Peace, c/o Willits, CA, St. Anthony of Padua. (SR)
Covina, CA, Annunciation Mission, c/o North Hollywood, CA, St. Anne. (NTN)
Covington, KY, Kenton Co., St. Ann, c/o Covington, KY, St. John. (COV)
Cox, SD, Harding Co., St. Agnes, c/o Buffalo, SD, St. Anthony. (RC)
Coyanosa, TX, Pecos Co., St. Isidore, c/o Crane, TX, Good Shepherd. (SAN)
Coyanosa, TX, Pecos Co., St. Isidore, c/o McCamey, TX, Sacred Heart. (SAN)
Coyote, NM, Rio Arriba Co., c/o Abiquiu, NM, St. Thomas Apostle. (SFE)
Crandall, GA, Capella Santo Toribio Romo, c/o Dalton, GA, St. Joseph. (ATL)
Crane, OR, Harney Co., St. Thomas, c/o Burns, OR, Holy Family. (BAK)
Cranfield, MS, Adams Co., St. John the Baptist, c/o Natchez, MS, Holy Family. (JKS)
Crates, PA, Clarion Co., St. Nicholas, c/o New Bethlehem, PA, St. Charles Church. (E)
Crawfordsville, AR, Crittenden Co., Sacred Heart, c/o West Memphis, AR, St. Michael. (LR)
Creede, CO, Mineral Co., Immaculate Conception, c/o Del Norte, CO, Holy Name of Mary. (PBL)
Crescent, OK, Logan Co., St. Margaret Mary, c/o Guthrie, OK, St. Mary's. (OKL)
Crescent City, IL, Iroquois Co., St. Joseph, c/o Watseka, IL, St. Edmund. (JOL)
Creswell, OR, Lane Co., St. Philip Benizi, c/o Cottage Grove, OR, Our Lady of Perpetual Help. (P)
Cripple Creek, CO, Teller Co., St. Peter's, c/o Woodland Park, CO, Teller County Catholic Community. (COS)
Cristo Rey, TX, Starr Co., Cristo Rey, c/o La Grulla, TX, Holy Family. (BWN)
Cross City, FL, Holy Cross, c/o Chiefland, FL, St. John the Evangelist. (STA)
Crosstown, MO, Perry Co., St. James, c/o Perryville, MO, St. Vincent De Paul. (STL)
Crown Point, LA, St. Pius X, c/o Lafitte, LA, St. Anthony. (NO)
Crows Landing, CA, Stanislaus Co., Immaculate Heart of Mary, c/o Patterson, CA, Sacred Heart Church of Patterson (Pastor of). (STO)
Cruces, PR, Santa Monica, c/o Aguada, PR, St. Francis of Assisi. (MGZ)
Crucible, PA, Greene Co., St. Mary, c/o Carmichaels, PA, Our Lady of Consolation. (PIT)
Cuadrilla, TX, El Paso Co., San Jose, c/o Fabens, TX, Our Lady of Guadalupe. (ELP)
Cubero, NM, Cibola Co., Our Lady of Light, c/o Seboyeta, NM, Our Lady of Sorrows. (GLP)
Cuchillo, NM, Sierra Co., St. Jose, c/o Truth or Consequences, NM, Our Lady of Perpetual Help. (LSC)
Cuervo, NM, Guadalupe Co., c/o Santa Rosa, NM, St. Rose of Lima. (SFE)
Culbertson, MT, Roosevelt Co., St. Anthony, c/o Poplar, MT, Our Lady of Lourdes. (GF)
Cullman, AL, Cullman Co., St. Boniface, c/o Cullman, AL, Sacred Heart. (BIR)
Cundiyo, NM, Rio Arriba Co., Santo Domingo, c/o Chimayo, NM, Holy Family. (SFE)
Cuny Table, SD, Shannon Co., St. Joseph, c/o Pine Ridge, SD, Holy Rosary/Red Cloud Indian School Inc. (RC)
Curtis, MI, Mackinac Co., St. Timothy, c/o Grand Marais, MI, Holy Rosary Church. (MAR)
Custer, MT, Yellowstone Co., St. Mary, c/o Hardin, MT, St. Joseph. (GF)
Cuthbert, GA, Randolph Co., St. Luke, c/o Blakely, GA, Holy Family. (SAV)

D

Dahlia, NM, Guadalupe Co., c/o Anton Chico, NM, San Jose. (SFE)
Dallas City, IL, Hancock Co., Sacred Heart, c/o Nauvoo, IL, SS. Peter and Paul. (PEO)
Dalton, NE, Cheyenne Co., St. Mary, c/o Bridgeport, NE, All Souls. (GI)
Dandan, Our Lady of the Most Holy Rosary, c/o Saipan, MP, San Vicente Parish. (CHK)
Danforth, ME, Washington Co., St. Ann, c/o Lincoln, ME, St. Mary. (PRT)
Danville, AR, Yell Co., St. Andrew, c/o Waldron, AR, St. Jude Thaddeus Church. (LR)
Darby, MT, Ravalli Co., St. Philip Benizi, c/o Hamilton, MT, St. Francis. (HEL)
Darien, GA, McIntosh Co., Nativity of Our Lady, c/o Brunswick, GA, St. Francis Xavier. (SAV)
Darlington, SC, Darlington Co., St. Joseph the Worker, c/o Hartsville, SC, St. Mary the Virgin Mother. (CHR)
Darrington, WA, Snohomish Co., St. John Mary Vianney, c/o Arlington, WA, Immaculate Conception. (SEA)
Datil, NM, Catron Co., Nativity of the Blessed Virgin Mary, c/o Reserve, NM, Santo Nino. (GLP)
David City, NE, Butler Co., Assumption, c/o David City, NE, St. Mary's. (LIN)
Dayton, OR, Yamhill Co., St. Martin de Porres, c/o McMinnville, OR, St. James. (P)
De Bruce, NY, Sullivan Co., Sacred Heart, c/o Livingston Manor, NY, St. Aloysius. (NY)
De Lancey, PA, St. Adrian, c/o Punxsutawney, PA, SS. Cosmas and Damian. (E)
De Mossville, KY, St. John's, c/o Williamstown, KY, St. William. (COV)
De Ruyter, NY, Madison Co., St. Lawrence, c/o Truxton, NY, St. Patrick. (SY)
Decatur, NE, Burt Co., Holy Family, c/o Tekamah, NE, St. Patrick. (OM)
Deep Creek Lake, MD, Garrett Co., St. Peter at the Lake, c/o Oakland, MD, St. Peter the Apostle. (BAL)
Del Rio, TX, Valverde Co., San Juan Diego Chapel, c/o Del Rio, TX, Our Lady of Guadalupe. (SAT)
Del Valle, TX, Travis Co., San Juan Diego, c/o Austin, TX, San Francisco. (AUS)
Delancey, PA, St. Adrian, c/o Punxsutawney, PA, St. Anthony of Padua. (E)
Delhi, CA, Merced Co., Blessed Teresa of Calcutta, c/o Livingston, CA, St. Jude Thaddeus. (FRS)
Delhi, LA, Richland Parish, St. Theresa, c/o Rayville, LA, Sacred Heart. (SHP)
Dell City, TX, Hudspeth Co., San Isidro, c/o Van Horn, TX, Our Lady of Fatima. (ELP)
Delmar, MD, Wicomico Co., Holy Redeemer, c/o Salisbury, MD, St. Francis De Sales. (WIL)
Delmas Dedeaux, MS, Harrison Co., Our Lady of Chartres, c/o Gulfport, MS, St. Ann. (BLX)
Delta, UT, Millard Co., St. John Bosco, c/o Milford, UT, Saint Bridget LLC 217. (SLC)
Deming, WA, Whatcom Co., St. Peter, c/o Lynden, WA, St. Joseph. (SEA)
Denali National Park, AK, c/o Healy, AK, Holy Mary of Guadalupe Catholic Church Healy. (FBK)
Dennis Port, MA, Our Lady of the Annunciation, c/o West Harwich, MA, Holy Trinity. (FR)
Denton, MD, Caroline Co., St. Elizabeth of Hungary, c/o Ridgely, MD, St. Benedict. (WIL)
Denton, MT, Fergus Co., St. Anthony, c/o Stanford, MT, St. Rose of Lima. (GF)
Denver, CO, Our Lady of Visitation, c/o Westminster, CO, Holy Trinity. (DEN)
Des Moines, NM, Union Co., Our Lady of Guadalupe, c/o Clayton, NM, St. Francis Xavier. (SFE)
Descalabrado, PR, Coamo Co., Miraculous Virgin, c/o Coamo, PR, St. Blase. (PCE)
Deweese, NE, Clay Co., Assumption, c/o Lawrence, NE, Sacred Heart. (LIN)
Dexter, OR, Lane Co., St. Henry, c/o Springfield, OR, St. Michael Catholic Church. (P)
Diego Hdez, PR, Yauco Co., St. Anthony, c/o Yauco, PR, Holy Rosary. (PCE)
Diener Ranch At Five Points, CA, Fresno Co., Holy Family Chapel, c/o Riverdale, CA, St. Ann. (FRS)
Dilia, NM, Guadalupe Co., c/o Anton Chico, NM, San Jose. (SFE)
Dilley, TX, Frio Co., St. Mary, c/o Dilley, TX, St. Joseph's. (SAT)
Dillon, CO, Summit Co., Our Lady of Peace, c/o Frisco, CO, St. Mary. (DEN)
Dixon, NE, Dixon Co., St. Anne, c/o Laurel, NE, St. Mary. (OM)
Dobbins, CA, Yuba Co., Sacred Heart Church, c/o Marysville, CA, St. Joseph. (SAC)
Dodson, MT, Phillips Co., Sacred Heart, c/o Malta, MT, St. Mary. (GF)
Dollar Bay, MI, Houghton Co., St. Francis of Assisi, c/o Hancock, MI, Resurrection. (MAR)
Dolores, CO, Our Lady of Victory Church, c/o Cortez, CO, St. Rita. (PBL)
Donaldson, IN, Maria Center, c/o Donaldson, IN, Convent Ancilla Domini. (FTW)
Donalsonville, GA, Seminole Co., Church of the Incarnation, c/o Bainbridge, GA, St. Joseph's. (SAV)
Doniphan, KS, Doniphan Co., St. John the Baptist, c/o Atchison, KS, St. Benedict's. (KCK)
Donken, MI, Houghton Co., Immaculate Heart of Mary, c/o Chassell, MI, St. Anne. (MAR)
Dorado, PR, Dorado Co., Ntra. Sra. del Camino, c/o Toa Alta, PR, San Jose. (SJN)
Dorado, PR, Dorado Co., S. Francisco De Asis, c/o Toa Alta, PR, San Jose. (SJN)
Dorado, PR, Dorado Co., San Antonio, c/o Toa Alta, PR, San Fernando Rey. (SJN)
Dorado, PR, San Martin de Porres, c/o Dorado, PR, San Antonio de Padua. (SJN)
Dorrance, KS, Russell Co., St. Joseph, c/o Wilson, KS, St. Wenceslaus Parish. (SAL)
Dorris, CA, Siskiyou Co., Our Lady of Good Counsel, c/o Tulelake, CA, Holy Cross. (SAC)
Douglas, NE, Otoe Co., St. Martin's, c/o Palmyra, NE, St. Leo's. (LIN)
Dove Creek, CO, Dolores Co., St. Jude, c/o Cortez, CO, St. Margaret Mary. (PBL)
Downey, CA, Los Angeles Co., Los Padrinos Juvenile Hall, c/o Downey, CA, St. Raymond. (LA)
Downey, CA, Los Angeles Co., Rancho Los Amigos Hospital, c/o Downey, CA, St. Raymond. (LA)
Downs, KS, Osborne Co., St. Mary's, c/o Osborne, KS, St. Aloysius Gonzaga Parish. (SAL)
Downsville, NY, Delaware Co., Holy Family, c/o Walton, NY, St. John the Baptist. (ALB)
Doylesburg, PA, Franklin Co., Our Lady of Refuge, c/o Chambersburg, PA, Corpus Christi. (HBG)
Draper, SD, Jones Co., St. Anthony of Padua, c/o Presho, SD, Christ the King. (RC)
Drewsey, OR, Harney Co., Our Lady of Loretto, c/o Burns, OR, Holy Family. (BAK)
Drifting, PA, Clearfield Co., St. Severin, c/o Frenchville, PA, St. Mary of the Assumption. (E)
Driftwood, PA, Cameron Co., St. James, c/o Emporium, PA, St. Mark. (E)
Driscoll, TX, Nueces Co., St. James, c/o Bishop, TX, St. James. (CC)
Drummond Island, MI, Chippewa Co., St. Florence, c/o Goetzville, MI, Sacred Heart. (MAR)
Drumright, OK, Creek Co., St. Mary, c/o Cushing, OK, SS. Peter and Paul. (TLS)
Dubina, TX, Fayette Co., SS. Cyril and Methodius, c/o Weimar, TX, St. Michael. (VIC)
Dubois, WY, Fremont Co., Our Lady of the Woods, c/o Riverton, WY, St. Margaret's. (CHY)
Duchesne, UT, Duchesne Co., Holy Spirit, c/o Roosevelt, UT, Saint Helen LLC 224. (SLC)
Duey, PR, Chapel of St. Augustin, c/o San German, PR, San German de Auxerre. (MGZ)
Duey, PR, Yauco Co., Virgin of Mt. Carmel, c/o Yauco, PR, Holy Rosary. (PCE)
Dulce, NM, Rio Arriba Co., St. Anthony, c/o Dulce, NM, St. Francis of Assisi. (GLP)
Duluth, GA, Gwinnett Co., Mision del Divino Nino Jesus, c/o Johns Creek, GA, St. Benedict. (ATL)
Dumas, AR, Desha Co., Holy Child, c/o Monticello, AR, St. Mark. (LR)
Duncannon, PA, Perry Co., St. Bernadette, c/o Marysville, PA, Our Lady of Good Counsel. (HBG)
Dupree, SD, Ziebach Co., Sacred Heart, c/o Eagle Butte, SD, All Saints. (RC)

Dupuyer, MT, Pondera Co., Holy Cross, c/o Valier, MT, St. Francis. (HEL)
Duran, NM, Torrance Co., c/o Vaughn, NM, St. Mary. (SFE)
Durham, CA, Butte Co., St. James, c/o Chico, CA, St. John the Baptist. (SAC)
Dyer, NV, Esmeralda Co., Our Lady of Guadalupe, c/o Tonopah, NV, St. Patrick. (LAV)

E

Eagle, AK, c/o Delta Junction, AK, Our Lady of Sorrows Catholic Church Delta Junction. (FBK)
Eagle, CO, Eagle Co., St. Mary, c/o Edwards, CO, St. Clare of Assisi. (DEN)
Eagle Harbor, MI, Keweenaw Co., Holy Redeemer, c/o Calumet, MI, Our Lady of Peace. (MAR)
Eagle Nest, NM, Colfax Co., St. Mel, c/o Cimarron, NM, Immaculate Conception Church. (SFE)
Eagles Mere, PA, Sullivan Co., St. Francis of Assisi, c/o Dushore, PA, Immaculate Heart of Mary Parish. (SCR)
Eagleville, CT, Tolland Co., St. Joseph, c/o Coventry, CT, St. Mary. (NOR)
Easley, SC, Anderson Co., St. Luke, c/o Pickens, SC, Holy Cross. (CHR)
East Barre, VT, Washington Co., St. Cecilia & St. Frances Cabrini, c/o Graniteville, VT, St. Sylvester. (BUR)
East Berkshire, VT, Franklin Co., Our Lady of Lourdes, c/o Richford, VT, All Saints. (BUR)
East Durham, NY, Greene Co., St. Mary, c/o Cairo, NY, Sacred Heart. (ALB)
East Eden, NY, Erie Co., St. Mary, c/o Boston, NY, St. John the Baptist. (BUF)
East Fairfield, VT, Franklin Co., St. Anthony–St. George, c/o Fairfield, VT, St. Patrick. (BUR)
East Glacier, MT, Glacier Co., Chapel of the Ascension, c/o Browning, MT, Church of the Little Flower. (HEL)
East Highlands, CA, San Bernardino Co., St. John Bosco, c/o Highland, CA, St. Adelaide. (SB)
East Quogue, NY, Suffolk Co., c/o Hampton Bays, NY, St. Rosalie's. (RVC)
East Sebago, ME, Cumberland Co., Our Lady of Sebago, c/o Gorham, ME, St. Anne. (PRT)
Eatonville, WA, Pierce Co., Our Lady of Good Counsel, c/o Puyallup, WA, Holy Disciples. (SEA)
Edcouch, TX, Hidalgo Co., Our Lady of Guadalupe, La Villa, c/o Edcouch, TX, St. Theresa of the Infant Jesus. (BWN)
Eden, WY, Sweetwater Co., St. Christopher, c/o Rock Springs, WY, Holy Spirit Catholic Community. (CHY)
Edenville, MI, Gladwin Co., St. Anne, c/o Coleman, MI, St. Philip Neri. (SAG)
Edgemont, SD, Fall River Co., St. James the Apostle, c/o Hot Springs, SD, St. Anthony of Padua. (RC)
Edgewater, FL, Volusia Co., St. Gerard, c/o New Smyrna Beach, FL, Sacred Heart. (ORL)
Edgewood, NM, St. Elizabeth Ann Seton, c/o Moriarty, NM, Estancia Valley Catholic Parish. (SFE)
Edinburg, TX, Hidalgo Co., Capilla de San Jose, c/o Edinburg, TX, Sacred Heart. (BWN)
Edison, NJ, St. Theresa of the Infant Jesus, c/o New Brunswick, NJ, St. Mary of Mount Virgin. (MET)
Edisto Island, SC, Charleston Co., Sts. Frederick & Stephen, c/o Yonges Island, SC, St. Mary. (CHR)
Effie, LA, Avoyelles Parish, St. Winifred, c/o Deville, LA, St. John the Baptist. (ALX)
Egan, LA, Acadia Parish, St. Michael, c/o Iota, LA, St. Joseph. (LAF)
Ekalaka, MT, Carter Co., St. Joan of Arc, c/o Baker, MT, St. John the Evangelist. (GF)
El Cajon, CA, San Diego Co., Immaculate Conception of BVM, c/o Lakeside, CA, Blessed Kateri Tekakwitha. (SD)
El Carmen, NM, Mora Co., c/o Mora, NM, St. Gertrude. (SFE)
El Duende, NM, Rio Arriba Co., c/o Espanola, NM, Sacred Heart. (SFE)
El Flaco, Hidalgo Co., TX, Centro Catolico San Juan Diego, c/o Alton, TX, San Martin de Porres. (BWN)
El Guache, NM, Rio Arriba Co., c/o Espanola, NM, Sacred Heart. (SFE)
El Guique, NM, Rio Arriba Co., c/o Ohkay Owingeh, NM, San Juan Bautista. (SFE)
El Indio, TX, Maverick Co., Our Lady of San Juan, c/o Eagle Pass, TX, Sacred Heart. (LAR)
El Macho, NM, San Miguel Co., c/o Pecos, NM, St. Anthony of Padua. (SFE)
El Nido, CA, St. George, c/o Chowchilla, CA, St. Columba. (FRS)
El Papayo, PR, Cristo Rey, c/o Sabana Grande, PR, Church of San Isidro. (MGZ)
El Paso, TX, El Paso Co., La Resurreccion Mission, c/o El Paso, TX, El Buen Pastor Mission. (ELP)
El Paso, TX, El Paso Co., Santa Teresita, c/o El Paso, TX, San Judas Tadeo. (ELP)
El Pueblo, NM, San Miguel Co., San Antonio de Padua, c/o Ribera, NM, San Miguel Del Vado. (SFE)
El Rancho, NM, Santa Fe Co., c/o Santa Fe, NM, N.S. de Guadalupe del Valle de Pojoaque. (SFE)
El Rucio, PR, Penuelas Co., La Milagrosa, c/o Penuelas, PR, St. Joseph. (PCE)
El Sauz, TX, Starr Co., Our Lady of Guadalupe, c/o Roma, TX, Sacred Heart. (BWN)
El Valle, NM, Taos Co., San Miguel Archangel, c/o Chimayo, NM, Holy Family. (SFE)
Elba, NE, Howard Co., St. Joseph, c/o St. Paul, NE, SS. Peter and Paul. (GI)
Elberta, UT, Utah Co., Mission San Isidro, c/o Orem, UT, St. Francis of Assisi LLC 221. (SLC)
Elbridge, MI, Oceana Co., Kateri Tekawitha Native American Center & St. Joseph Center, c/o Hart, MI, St. Gregory's. (GR)
Eleele, HI, Kauai Co., Sacred Heart, c/o Kalaheo, HI, Holy Cross. (HON)
Elfin Cove, AK, c/o Yakutat, AK, St. Ann. (JUN)
Elgin, OR, Union Co., St. Mary, c/o La Grande, OR, Our Lady of the Valley. (BAK)
Elizabeth, IN, Harrison Co., St. Peter, c/o Corydon, IN, St. Joseph Catholic Church, Corydon, Inc. (IND)
Elizabeth, LA, Allen Parish, St. Frances, c/o Oakdale, LA, Sacred Heart. (LKC)
Elizabeth, WV, Wirt Co., St. Elizabeth of Hungary, c/o Spencer, WV, Holy Redeemer. (WH)
Elizabethtown, NC, Bladen Co., Our Lady of the Snows, c/o Whiteville, NC, Sacred Heart. (R)
Elk, CA, Blessed Sacrament, c/o Mendocino, CA, St. Anthony. (SR)
Elk, TX, McLennon Co., St. Joseph, c/o West, TX, St. Martin. (AUS)
Elkhorn City, KY, Pike Co., St. Joseph the Worker, c/o Pikeville, KY, St. Francis of Assisi. (LEX)
Elkin, NC, Surry Co., St. Stephen, c/o North Wilkesboro, NC, St. John Baptist de LaSalle. (CHL)
Ellinger/Hostyn Hill, TX, Fayette Co., St. Mary, c/o Fayetteville, TX, St. John the Baptist. (AUS)
Elmer, LA, Rapides Parish, St. Peter, c/o Glenmora, LA, St. Louis. (ALX)
Elmwood, NE, Cass Co., St. Mary's, c/o Manley, NE, St. Patrick's. (LIN)
Elsie, NE, Perkins Co., Resurrection of Our Lord, c/o Wallace, NE, St. Mary's. (LIN)
Emanueli, PR, Coamo Co., Holy Family, c/o Coamo, PR, St. Blase. (PCE)
Eminence, KY, Henry Co., St. John Chrysostom, c/o Shelbyville, KY, Annunciation of the Blessed Virgin Mary. (L)
Eminence, MO, Shannon Co., St. Sylvester, c/o Mountain View, MO, St. John Vianney. (SPC)
Emmanuel, LA, Natchitoches Parish, Holy Rosary, c/o Cloutierville, LA, St. John the Baptist. (ALX)
Emory, TX, Rains Co., St. John the Evangelist Church, c/o Mineola, TX, St. Peter the Apostle. (TYL)
Empire, NV, Washoe Co., St. Joseph the Worker, c/o Fernley, NV, St. Robert Bellarmine. (RNO)
Encinal, NM, Valencia Co., Nativity of the Blessed Virgin Mary, c/o Laguna, NM, St. Joseph. (GLP)
Encino, NM, Torrance Co., c/o Vaughn, NM, St. Mary. (SFE)
Encino, TX, Brooks Co., St. Ann, c/o Falfurrias, TX, Sacred Heart. (CC)
England, AR, Lonoke Co., Holy Trinity, c/o Carlisle, AR, St. Rose of Lima Church. (LR)
Enid, OK, Garfield Co., St. Gregory the Great, c/o Enid, OK, St. Francis Xavier. (OKL)
Ephraim, UT, Sanpete Co., St. Jude, c/o Central Valley, UT, Saint Elizabeth LLC 220. (SLC)
Ericson, NE, St. Theresa of the Child Jesus, c/o Spalding, NE, St. Michael's. (GI)
Erie, IL, Whiteside Co., St. Ambrose, c/o Prophetstown, IL, St. Catherine. (RCK)
Errol, NH, St. Pius the Tenth, c/o Colebrook, NH, North American Martyrs Parish. (MAN)
Escalante, UT, Garfield Co., St. Sylvester, c/o Cedar City, UT, Christ the King LLC 203. (SLC)
Escobosa, NM, Bernalillo Co., San Isidro, c/o Tijeras, NM, Holy Child. (SFE)
Esopus, NY, Ulster Co., Sacred Heart, c/o Port Ewen, NY, Presentation of the Blessed Virgin Mary. (NY)
Esparto, CA, Yolo Co., St. Martin, c/o Winters, CA, St. Anthony. (SAC)
Essex, IL, Kankakee Co., St. Lawrence O'Toole, c/o Braidwood, IL, Immaculate Conception. (JOL)
Estaca, NM, Rio Arriba Co., c/o Ohkay Owingeh, NM, San Juan Bautista. (SFE)
Estancia, NM, Torrance Co., Sts. Peter & Paul, c/o Moriarty, NM, Estancia Valley Catholic Parish. (SFE)
Estherwood, LA, Acadia Parish, St. Margaret, c/o Mermentau, LA, St. John the Evangelist. (LAF)
Ethete, WY, Fremont Co., St. Joseph, c/o Saint Stephens, WY, St. Stephen's. (CHY)
Etna, CA, Siskiyou Co., St. Mary's, c/o Fort Jones, CA, Sacred Heart. (SAC)
Ettal, FM, c/o Chuuk, FM, Mortlock. (CI)
Euclid, MN, Polk Co., St. Mary, c/o Warren, MN, SS. Peter and Paul. (CR)
Eufaula, OK, McIntosh Co., St. Paul's, c/o Krebs, OK, St. Joseph's. (TLS)
Eunice, NM, St. Clare, c/o Jal, NM, St. Cecilia. (LSC)
Eureka, CA, St. Joseph, c/o Eureka, CA, St. Bernard. (SR)
Eutaw, AL, Greene Co., St. Mary, c/o Demopolis, AL, St. Leo. (BIR)
Everglades City, FL, Collier Co., Holy Family, c/o Marco Island, FL, San Marco. (VEN)
Excursion Inlet, AK, c/o Yakutat, AK, St. Ann. (JUN)
Expressway Heights, TX, Hidalgo Co., Nuestra Senora de Guadalupe, c/o Weslaco, TX, San Martin de Porres. (BWN)

F

Faga'alu, AS, c/o Pago Pago, AS, Co–Cathedral of St. Joseph the Worker. (SPP)
Faga'itua, AS, c/o Pago Pago, AS, St. Peter Chanel–Sa'ilele. (SPP)
Fairacres, NM, Dona Ana Co., San Jose Mission, c/o Mesilla, NM, Basilica of San Albino. (LSC)
Fairfield, AL, Jefferson Co., St. Mary's, c/o Birmingham, AL, Holy Family. (BIR)
Fairford, AL, Washington Co., Our Lady of Sorrows, c/o Mount Vernon, AL, St. Peter the Apostle. (MOB)
Fairplay, CO, Park Co., St. Joseph, c/o Buena Vista, CO, St. Rose of Lima. (COS)
Fairview, MT, Richland Co., St. Catherine, c/o Sidney, MT, St. Matthew. (GF)
Fairview, OK, Major Co., St. Ann, c/o Okeene, OK, St. Anthony's. (OKL)
Falcon, TX, Zapata Co., Santa Ana, c/o Zapata, TX, Our Lady of Lourdes. (LAR)
Falcon Heights, TX, Starr Co., Holy Trinity, c/o Roma, TX, Our Lady of Refuge. (BWN)
Faleniu, AS, c/o Pago Pago, AS, St. Paul. (SPP)
Fall River Mills, CA, Shasta Co., Our Lady of the Valley, c/o Burney, CA, St. Francis of Assisi. (SAC)
Falun, MN, Roseau Co., St. Philip, c/o Roseau, MN, Sacred Heart. (CR)
Farmersville, CA, Tulare Co., St. Anthony of Egypt, c/o Exeter, CA, Sacred Heart. (FRS)
Farmerville, LA, Union Parish, Our Lady of Perpetual Help, c/o West Monroe, LA, St. Paschal. (SHP)
Farnam, NE, Dawson Co., St. Joseph's, c/o Curtis, NE, St. James. (LIN)
Farwell, NE, Howard Co., St. Anthony of Padua, c/o St. Paul, NE, SS. Peter and Paul. (GI)
Fashing, TX, Atascosa Co., St. Elizabeth, c/o Karnes City, TX, St. Cornelius. (SAT)
Fayette, AL, Fayette Co., Holy Family, c/o Winfield, AL, Holy Spirit. (BIR)
Faysville, TX, Hidalgo Co., St. Theresa Faysville, c/o Edinburg, TX, St. Joseph the Worker. (BWN)
Faywood, NM, Luna Co., San Jose, c/o Hurley, NM, Infant Jesus. (LSC)
Fellsmere, FL, Indian River Co., c/o Fellsmere, FL, Our Lady of Guadalupe Mission. (PMB)
Fence Lake, NM, Valencia Co., El Morro, c/o Ramah, NM, San Lorenzo. (GLP)
Fillmore, UT, Millard Co., Holy Family, c/o Milford, UT, Saint Bridget LLC 217. (SLC)
Fine, NY, St. Lawrence Co., St. Michael, c/o Star Lake, NY, St. Hubert. (OG)
Fisher, MN, Polk Co., St. Francis, c/o East Grand Forks, MN, Sacred Heart. (CR)
Fishville, LA, Grant Parish, St. Edward, c/o Jena, LA, St. Mary. (ALX)
Fitzgerald, GA, Ben Hill Co., St. William, c/o Douglas, GA, St. Paul's. (SAV)
Flagler, CO, Kit Carson Co., St. Mary, c/o Limon, CO, Our Lady of Victory. (COS)
Flagstaff, AZ, Flagstaff Mission, c/o Phoenix, AZ, Assumption of B.V.M. (STN)
Flanagan, IL, Livingston Co., St. Joseph, c/o Pontiac, IL, St. Mary's. (PEO)
Flatwoods, LA, Rapides Parish, St. Cyril, c/o Boyce, LA, St. Margaret. (ALX)
Fleming, CO, Logan Co., St. Peter the Apostle, c/o Holyoke, CO, St. Patrick. (DEN)
Florence, MT, Ravalli Co., St. Joseph, c/o Stevensville, MT, St. Mary. (HEL)
Florian, MN, Marshall Co., Assumption Church of Florian, c/o Stephen, MN, St. Stephen's. (CR)
Floyd, VA, Floyd Co., Church of All Saints, c/o Woodlawn, VA, St. Joseph's. (RIC)
Folkston, GA, Charlton Co., St. Francis of Assisi, c/o St. Marys, GA, Our Lady Star of the Sea. (SAV)
Folsom, NM, Union Co., St. Joseph, c/o Clayton, NM, St. Francis Xavier. (SFE)
Fordyce, AR, Good Shepherd, c/o Pine Bluff, AR, St. Joseph. (LR)
Foreman, AR, Little River Co., Sacred Heart, c/o Texarkana, AR, St. Edward. (LR)
Forest City, MO, Holt Co., St. Patrick, c/o Savannah, MO, St. Rose of Lima. (KC)
Forest Park, GA, Clayton Co., San Felipe de Jesus, c/o Atlanta, GA, The Basilica of the Sacred Heart of Jesus. (ATL)
Foresthill, CA, Placer Co., St. Joseph of Foresthill, c/o Auburn, CA, St. Joseph. (SAC)
Forestville, MI, Sanilac Co., St. John Chrysostom, c/o

Port Sanilac, MI, St. Mary. (SAG)
Forestville, PA, Butler Co., St. Anthony Church, c/o Slippery Rock, PA, St. Peter. (PIT)
Forrest, IL, Livingston Co., St. James, c/o Chatsworth, IL, SS. Peter and Paul. (PEO)
Forrest City, St. Francis of Assisi, c/o Brinkley, AR, St. John the Baptist. (LR)
Fort Adams, MS, Wilkinson Co., St. Patrick, c/o Woodville, MS, St. Joseph. (JKS)
Fort Bridger, WY, Uinta Co., St. Helen, c/o Evanston, WY, St. Mary Magdalen. (CHY)
Fort Duchesne, UT, Uintah Co., Blessed Kateri Tekakwitha, c/o Roosevelt, UT, Saint Helen LLC 224. (SLC)
Fort Garland, CO, Costilla Co., Holy Family, c/o San Luis, CO, Sangre de Cristo. (PBL)
Fort Montgomery, NY, Orange Co., Blessed Sacrament, c/o Highland Falls, NY, Sacred Heart of Jesus. (NY)
Fort Stanton, NM, Lincoln Co., Sacred Heart, c/o Ruidoso, NM, St. Eleanor. (LSC)
Fort Valley, GA, Peach Co., St. Juliana, c/o Kathleen, GA, St. Patrick. (SAV)
Fossil, OR, Wheeler Co., St. Catherine, c/o Condon, OR, St. John. (BAK)
Foster City, MI, Dickinson Co., St. Joseph, c/o Bark River, MI, St. Elizabeth Ann Seton. (MAR)
Fountain, FL, Bay Co., Our Lady Queen of Peace, c/o Panama City, FL, Our Lady of the Rosary. (PT)
Fowler, CO, Otero Co., Mary Queen of Heaven, c/o Rocky Ford, CO, St. Peter. (PBL)
Frances, CO, Archuleta Co., St. Francis, c/o Pagosa Springs, CO, Immaculate Heart of Mary. (PBL)
Frances, WA, Pacific Co., Holy Family, c/o Pe Ell, WA, St. Joseph. (SEA)
Franconia, NH, Grafton Co., Our Lady of the Snows, c/o Littleton, NH, St. Rose of Lima. (MAN)
Frankford, DE, Sussex Co., Our Lady of Guadalupe, c/o Bethany Beach, DE, St. Ann. (WIL)
Franklin, NE, Franklin Co., St. Kathrine Drexel, c/o Red Cloud, NE, Sacred Heart. (LIN)
Franklin, NY, Delaware Co., St. Paul, c/o Sidney, NY, Sacred Heart. (ALB)
Franklin, VT, Franklin Co., St. Mary, c/o Sheldon Springs, VT, St. Anthony. (BUR)
Frankston, TX, Anderson Co., St. Charles Borromeo, c/o Palestine, TX, Sacred Heart. (TYL)
Frazer, MT, Valley Co., St. Joseph, c/o Wolf Point, MT, Immaculate Conception. (GF)
Frederick, OK, St. Helen Church, c/o Altus, OK, Prince of Peace. (OKL)
Fredericksburg, TX, Gillespie Co., Our Lady of Guadalupe, c/o Fredericksburg, TX, St. Mary's. (SAT)
Freeport, FL, Walton Co., Christ the King Catholic Mission, c/o Santa Rosa Beach, FL, St. Rita. (PT)
French Camp, CA, San Joaquin Co., Good Shepherd, c/o Stockton, CA, St. George Church (Pastor of). (STO)
French Village, MO, St. Francois Co., St. Anne, c/o Bonne Terre, MO, St. Joseph's. (STL)
Frewsburg, NY, Our Lady of Victory, c/o Jamestown, NY, St. James. (BUF)
Frieburg, MI, Sanilac Co., St. Ignatius, c/o Argyle, MI, St. Joseph. (SAG)
Frilot Cove, LA, Evangeline Parish, St. Ann, c/o Opelousas, LA, St. Joseph. (LAF)
Fromberg, MT, Carbon Co., St. Joseph, c/o Bridger, MT, Sacred Heart. (GF)
Fronton, TX, Starr Co., Lamb of God, c/o Roma, TX, Our Lady of Refuge. (BWN)
Fryeburg, ME, Oxford Co., St. Elizabeth Ann Seton, c/o Bridgton, ME, St. Joseph. (PRT)
Fulton, MS, Itawamba Co., Christ the King, c/o Tupelo, MS, St. James. (JKS)

G

Gabriels, NY, Franklin Co., Assumption of the B.V.M., c/o Saranac Lake, NY, St. Paul. (OG)
Gainesville, MO, Ozark Co., St. William, c/o Ava, MO, Immaculate Heart of Mary. (SPC)
Gainesville, VA, Prince William Co., St. Katharine Drexel Mission, c/o Middleburg, VA, St. Stephen the Martyr. (ARL)
Gaithersburg, MD, Mother of God Community School, c/o Annandale, VA, Epiphany of Our Lord. (PSC)
Galicia–Columbani, PR, Santo Tomas de Villanueva, c/o Aguada, PR, St. Francis of Assisi. (MGZ)
Galisteo, NM, Santa Fe Co., c/o Cerrillos, NM, St. Joseph. (SFE)
Gallegos, NM, Harding Co., c/o Roy, NM, Holy Family–St. Joseph. (SFE)
Gallina, NM, Rio Arriba Co., c/o Abiquiu, NM, St. Thomas Apostle. (SFE)
Gallinas, NM, San Miguel Co., Santo Nino, c/o Las Vegas, NM, Our Lady of Sorrows Church. (SFE)
Galway, NY, Saratoga Co., St. Mary's, c/o Hagaman, NY, St. Stephen. (ALB)
Ganado, AZ, Apache Co., St. Anne, c/o Ganado, AZ, All Saints. (GLP)
Garcia, CO, Costilla Co., Sacred Heart of Jesus, c/o San Luis, CO, Sangre de Cristo. (PBL)
Garden Plain, KS, Immaculate Conception, c/o Garden Plain, KS, St. Anthony. (WCH)
Gardena, CA, Los Angeles Co., St. Francis Korean Catholic Center, c/o Gardena, CA, St. Anthony of Padua. (LA)
Gardiner, MT, Park Co., St. William, c/o Livingston, MT, St. Mary. (GF)
Gardner, CO, Huerfano Co., Sacred Heart, c/o Walsenburg, CO, St. Mary. (PBL)
Garrison, NY, Putnam Co., St. Joseph's Chapel, c/o Cold Spring, NY, Our Lady of Loretto. (NY)
Garzas, PR, Adjuntas Co., San Francisco, c/o Adjuntas, PR, St. Joachim. (PCE)
Genesee, PA, Potter Co., Sacred Heart, c/o Galeton, PA, St. Bibiana. (E)
Geneva, AL, Geneva Co., St. Mary, c/o Enterprise, AL, St. John. (MOB)
Gentilly, MN, Polk Co., St. Peter, c/o Crookston, MN, Cathedral of the Immaculate Conception. (CR)
George West, TX, Live Oak Co., c/o George West, TX, St. George. (CC)
Georgetown, CA, El Dorado Co., St. James, c/o Placerville, CA, St. Patrick's. (SAC)
Georgetown, CO, Clear Creek Co., Our Lady of Lourdes, c/o Idaho Springs, CO, St. Paul. (DEN)
Georgetown, MN, Clay Co., St. John, c/o Moorhead, MN, St. Francis de Sales. (CR)
Georgia, VT, Franklin Co., Ascension, c/o St. Albans, VT, Holy Angels. (BUR)
Geraldine, MT, Chouteau Co., St. Margaret, c/o Fort Benton, MT, Immaculate Conception. (GF)
Germfask, MI, Schoolcraft Co., St. Therese, c/o Grand Marais, MI, Holy Rosary Church. (MAR)
Geyser, MT, Judith Basin Co., St. Cyril, c/o Stanford, MT, St. Rose of Lima. (GF)
Gila, NM, Grant Co., St. Isidore, c/o Silver City, NM, St. Vincent de Paul. (LSC)
Gila Bend, AZ, Pinal Co., San Lucy, c/o Laveen, AZ, St. John The Baptist. (PHX)
Gilchrist, OR, Klamath Co., Our Lady of the Snows, c/o La Pine, OR, Holy Redeemer. (BAK)
Giltner, NE, Hamilton Co., St. Joseph's, c/o Aurora, NE, St. Mary's. (LIN)
Girdwood, AK, Our Lady of the Snows, c/o Anchorage, AK, St. Elizabeth Ann Seton. (ANC)
Glasgo, CT, New London Co., St. Anne, c/o Voluntown, CT, St. Thomas the Apostle. (NOR)
Glencoe, LA, St. Mary Parish, St. Joan of Arc, c/o Franklin, LA, St. Peter the Apostle. (LAF)
Glencoe, NM, Lincoln Co., San Ysidro, c/o Ruidoso, NM, St. Eleanor. (LSC)
Glendale, OR, Douglas Co., Holy Family, c/o Myrtle Creek, OR, All Souls. (P)
Glendale, RI, Providence Co., St. Louis Chapel, c/o Harrisville, RI, St. Patrick. (PRO)
Glennon, MO, Bollinger Co., St. Anthony, c/o Leopold, MO, St. John. (SPC)
Glennville, GA, Tattnall Co., St. Jude, c/o Hinesville, GA, St. Stephen, First Martyr. (SAV)
Glentana, MT, Valley Co., Holy Family, c/o Glasgow, MT, St. Raphael. (GF)
Glenwood, AR, Pike Co., Our Lady of Guadalupe, c/o Mena, AR, St. Agnes. (LR)
Glidden, IA, St. Elizabeth Seton, c/o Coon Rapids, IA, Annunciation. (SC)
Glidden, IA, Carroll Co., St. Elizabeth Seton Church, c/o Lidderdale, IA, Holy Family. (SC)
Glorieta, NM, Santa Fe Co., c/o Pecos, NM, St. Anthony of Padua. (SFE)
Gloster, MS, Amite Co., Holy Family, c/o Woodville, MS, St. Joseph. (JKS)
Gobles, MI, Van Buren Co., St. Jude's Church, c/o Paw Paw, MI, St. Mary. (KAL)
Gold Beach, OR, Curry Co., St. Charles Borromeo, c/o Brookings, OR, Star of the Sea. (P)
Gold Hill, OR, Jackson Co., Our Lady of the River Mission, c/o Grants Pass, OR, St. Anne. (P)
Goldcreek, MT, Powell Co., St. Mary, c/o Drummond, MT, St. Michael. (HEL)
Golden, NM, Santa Fe Co., c/o Cerrillos, NM, St. Joseph. (SFE)
Goldens Bridge, NY, Westchester Co., St. Michael, c/o Croton Falls, NY, St. Joseph. (NY)
Golondrinas, NM, Mora Co., c/o Mora, NM, St. Gertrude. (SFE)
Goltry, OK, Alfalfa Co., St. Michael, c/o Enid, OK, St. Francis Xavier. (OKL)
Gonzales, TX, Gonzales Co., Sacred Heart, c/o Gonzales, TX, St. James. (SAT)
Gonzales Ranch, NM, San Miguel Co., c/o Villanueva, NM, Our Lady of Guadalupe. (SFE)
Goodridge, MN, Pennington Co., St. Anne, c/o Thief River Falls, MN, St. Bernards. (CR)
Gorum, LA, Natchitoches Parish, St. Margaret Mary, c/o Boyce, LA, St. Margaret. (ALX)
Gothenburg, NE, Dawson Co., Our Lady of Good Counsel, c/o Cozad, NE, Christ the King. (GI)
Goudeau, LA, Avoyelles Parish, St. Charles, c/o Evergreen, LA, Little Flower. (ALX)
Grady, AR, Lincoln Co., Blessed Sacrament, c/o Star City, AR, St. Justin. (LR)
Grafton, NE, Fillmore Co., St. Helena's, c/o Sutton, NE, St. Mary's. (LIN)
Granby, CO, Grand Co., Our Lady of the Snow, c/o Granby, CO, St. Anne. (DEN)
Grand Isle, VT, Grand Isle Co., St. Joseph, c/o South Hero, VT, St. Rose of Lima. (BUR)
Grand Junction, IA, Greene Co., St. Brigid, c/o Jefferson, IA, St. Joseph's. (SC)
Grand Ridge, IL, La Salle Co., St. Mary's, c/o Ottawa, IL, St. Columba. (PEO)
Grand Saline, TX, Van Zandt Co., St. Celestine, c/o Mineola, TX, St. Peter the Apostle. (TYL)
Grandfalls, TX, Ward Co., St. Gertrude, c/o Monahans, TX, St. John the Apostle and Evangelist. (ELP)
Grass Valley, OR, Sherman Co., St. John the Baptist, c/o Wasco, OR, St. Mary. (BAK)
Grassflat, PA, Clearfield Co., SS. Peter & Paul, c/o Frenchville, PA, St. Mary of the Assumption. (E)
Greasewood, AZ, Navajo Co., Our Lady of the Rosary, c/o Ganado, AZ, All Saints. (GLP)
Great Falls, SC, Chester Co., St. Michael, c/o Lancaster, SC, St. Catherine. (CHR)
Greeley, PA, Pike Co., Sacred Heart of Jesus, c/o Shohola, PA, St. Ann's. (SCR)
Green Lake, ME, Hancock Co., Our Lady of the Lake, c/o Ellsworth, ME, St. Joseph. (PRT)
Green River, UT, Emery Co., St. Michael, c/o East Carbon, UT, Good Shepherd LLC 204. (SLC)
Greene, ME, Androscoggin Co., St. Francis, c/o Sabattus, ME, Our Lady of the Rosary. (PRT)
Greenfield, MO, Dade Co., St. Patrick, c/o Mount Vernon, MO, St. Susanne. (SPC)
Greensboro, AL, Hale Co., Our Lady of Lourdes, c/o Demopolis, AL, St. Leo. (BIR)
Greenup, KY, St. Lawrence, c/o Ashland, KY, Holy Family. (LEX)
Greenville, CA, Plumas Co., St. Anthony, c/o Quincy, CA, St. John. (SAC)
Greenwich, CT, Fairfield Co., St. Timothy's, c/o Greenwich, CT, St. Michael the Archangel. (BGP)
Greenwood, NE, Cass Co., St. Joseph's, c/o Ashland, NE, St. Mary's. (LIN)
Greig, NY, Lewis Co., St. Thomas, c/o Lowville, NY, St. Mary. (OG)
Gretna, LA, Jefferson Parish, St. Anthony Mission, c/o Gretna, LA, St. Joseph. (NO)
Groveton, TX, c/o Trinity, TX, Most Holy Trinity. (TYL)
Gruver, TX, Hansford Co., Cristo Redentor, c/o Spearman, TX, Sacred Heart. (AMA)
Grygla, MN, Marshall Co., St. Clement, c/o Thief River Falls, MN, St. Bernards. (CR)
Guachupanque, NM, Rio Arriba Co., c/o Espanola, NM, Sacred Heart. (SFE)
Guadalupita, NM, Mora Co., c/o Mora, NM, St. Gertrude. (SFE)
Gualala, CA, Mary, Star of the Sea, c/o Point Arena, CA, St. Aloysius. (SR)
Guaniquilla, PR, Ntra. Sra. del Carmen, c/o Aguada, PR, St. Francis of Assisi. (MGZ)
Guayabo, PR, El Buen Pastor, c/o Aguada, PR, St. Francis of Assisi. (MGZ)
Guaynabo, PR, Guaynabo Co., El Buen Pastor, c/o Caguas, PR, Divino Nino Jesus. (SJN)
Guaynabo, PR, Espiritu Santo, c/o Guaynabo, PR, Nuestra Senora de la Paz. (SJN)
Guaynabo, PR, Ciales Co., Inmaculada Concepcion, c/o Guaynabo, PR, Nuestra Senora de la Paz. (SJN)
Guaynabo, PR, Guaynabo Co., Jesus Nazareno, c/o Caguas, PR, Divino Nino Jesus. (SJN)
Guaynabo, PR, Juncos Co., N. Sra. de la Divina Providencia, c/o Guaynabo, PR, Nuestra Senora de la Paz. (SJN)
Guaynabo, PR, Guaynabo Co., N. Sra. de la Paz, c/o Caguas, PR, Divino Nino Jesus. (SJN)
Guaynabo, PR, Guaynabo Co., Ntra. Sra. del Carmen, c/o Guaynabo, PR, Maria Madre de Mi Senor. (SJN)
Guaynabo, PR, San Jose Obrero, c/o Guaynabo, PR, Nuestra Senora de la Paz. (SJN)
Guaynabo, PR, Guaynabo Co., San Miguel, c/o San Juan, PR, San Miguel Arcangel. (SJN)
Guaynabo, PR, Guaynabo Co., San Rafael Arcangel, c/o Caguas, PR, Divino Nino Jesus. (SJN)
Guaynabo, PR, Virgen de la Paz, c/o Guaynabo, PR, Sagrados Corazones. (SJN)
Gugeegue, MH, MH, Santo, c/o Ebeye, MH, Queen of Peace. (MI)
Guilarte, PR, Adjuntas Co., San Antonio, c/o Adjuntas, PR, St. Joachim. (PCE)
Gulf Breeze, FL, Santa Rosa Co., Our Lady of the Assumption, c/o Gulf Breeze, FL, St. Ann. (PT)
Gulliver, MI, Schoolcraft Co., Divine Infant of Prague, c/o Manistique, MI, St. Francis de Sales. (MAR)
Gunnison, UT, Sanpete Co., San Juan Diego Mission, c/o Central Valley, UT, Saint Elizabeth LLC 220. (SLC)
Gussetville, TX, Live Oak Co., St. Joseph, c/o George West, TX, St. George. (CC)
Gustavus, AK, c/o Yakutat, AK, St. Ann. (JUN)

Gypsum, KS, Saline Co., St. Patricks, c/o Solomon, KS, Immaculate Conception of the Blessed Virgin Mary Parish. (SAL)

H

Hagerman, NM, Chavez Co., St. Catherine, c/o Dexter, NM, Immaculate Conception. (LSC)
Hagerstown, MD, Washington Co., St. Ann's, c/o Baltimore, MD, Patronage of the Mother of God. (PSC)
Hale Center, TX, St. Theresa, c/o Olton, TX, St. Peter the Apostle. (LUB)
Haleyville, AL, Winston Co., Our Lady of Guadalupe, c/o Winfield, AL, Holy Spirit. (BIR)
Halfway, OR, Baker Co., St. Therese, c/o Baker, OR, Cathedral of St. Francis De Sales. (BAK)
Hallettsville, TX, Lavaca Co., Ascension of Our Lord, c/o Hallettsville, TX, St. John the Baptist. (VIC)
Hallsville, TX, Harrison Co., Our Lady of Grace, c/o Longview, TX, St. Mary. (TYL)
Halstad, MN, Norman Co., Holy Family, c/o Ada, MN, St. Joseph's. (CR)
Hamburg, AR, Ashley Co., Holy Spirit, c/o Lake Village, AR, Our Lady of the Lake. (LR)
Hamilton, IL, Hancock Co., St. Mary, c/o Warsaw, IL, Sacred Heart. (PEO)
Hamilton, KS, Greenwood Co., St. John, c/o Eureka, KS, Sacred Heart. (WCH)
Hamilton City, CA, Glenn Co., St. Mary, c/o Orland, CA, St. Dominic. (SAC)
Hamlin, TX, Jones Co., Holy Trinity, c/o Anson, TX, St. Michael. (LUB)
Hammond, OR, Clatsop Co., St. Francis de Sales, c/o Astoria, OR, St. Mary, Star of the Sea. (P)
Hampton, CT, Windham Co., Our Lady of Lourdes, c/o Brooklyn, CT, Our Lady of La Salette. (NOR)
Hampton, IL, Rock Island Co., St. Mary, c/o Rapids City, IL, St. John the Baptist. (PEO)
Hampton, SC, Hampton Co., St. Mary, c/o Ridgeland, SC, St. Anthony. (CHR)
Hanalei, HI, Kauai Co., St. William, c/o Kapaa, HI, St. Catherine. (HON)
Hanna, WY, Carbon Co., St. Joseph, c/o Saratoga, WY, St. Ann's. (CHY)
Hanover, NM, Grant Co., Holy Family, c/o Bayard, NM, Our Lady of Fatima. (LSC)
Happy Camp, CA, Siskiyou Co., All Saints, c/o Fort Jones, CA, Sacred Heart. (SAC)
Hardeeville, SC, Jasper Co., St. Anthony, c/o Ridgeland, SC, St. Anthony. (CHR)
Hargill, TX, Hidalgo Co., St. Frances Xavier Cabrini, c/o Raymondville, TX, Our Lady of Guadalupe. (BWN)
Harlem, MT, Blaine Co., Sacred Heart, Fort Belknap, c/o Hays, MT, St. Paul's Indian Mission. (GF)
Harlem, MT, Blaine Co., St. Thomas the Apostle, c/o Chinook, MT, St. Gabriel. (GF)
Harlingen, TX, Cameron Co., San Felipe, c/o Harlingen, TX, Our Lady of the Assumption. (BWN)
Harmon, NY, Westchester Co., Church of the Good Shepherd, c/o Croton–on–Hudson, NY, Holy Name of Mary. (NY)
Harmony, WA, Lewis Co., St. Yves, c/o Morton, WA, Sacred Heart. (SEA)
Harrington, DE, Kent Co., St. Bernadette, c/o Milford, DE, St. John the Apostle. (WIL)
Harrison, NE, Sioux Co., Church of the Nativity of the Blessed Virgin Mary, c/o Crawford, NE, St. John the Baptist. (GI)
Hart, TX, Castro Co., St. John's, c/o Dimmitt, TX, Immaculate Conception. (AMA)
Hartford, AR, Sebastian Co., St. Leo's, c/o Fort Smith, AR, Immaculate Conception. (LR)
Harvard, MI, Kent Co., St. Margaret, c/o Greenville, MI, St. Charles Borromeo. (GR)
Harvey, LA, Jefferson Parish, Infant Jesus of Prague, c/o Harvey, LA, St. Martha. (NO)
Haskell, TX, Haskell Co., St. George, c/o Stamford, TX, St. Ann. (LUB)
Hato Rey, PR, San Juan Co., Sma. Trinidad, c/o San Juan, PR, Ntr. Sra. de la Caridad del Cobre. (SJN)
Hawk Run, PA, Clearfield Co., SS. Peter & Paul, c/o Morrisdale, PA, St. Agnes. (E)
Hawkinsville, CA, Siskiyou Co., Immaculate Conception, c/o Yreka, CA, St. Joseph. (SAC)
Hawley, MN, Clay Co., St. Andrew, c/o Dilworth, MN, St. Elizabeth. (CR)
Hawthorne, FL, Alachua Co., St. Philip Neri, c/o Gainesville, FL, St. Patrick Church. (STA)
Haxtun, CO, Phillips Co., Christ the King, c/o Holyoke, CO, St. Patrick. (DEN)
Hay Springs, NE, Sheridan Co., St. Columbkille, c/o Gordon, NE, St. Leo's. (GI)
Hayales, PR, Coamo Co., Our Lady of Mt. Carmel, c/o Coamo, PR, St. Blase. (PCE)
Hayden, NM, Quay Co., Holy Trinity, c/o Clayton, NM, St. Francis Xavier. (SFE)
Hayesville, NC, Clay Co., Immaculate Heart of Mary, c/o Murphy, NC, St. William. (CHL)
Hayfork, CA, Trinity Co., Holy Trinity, c/o Weaverville, CA, St. Patrick. (SAC)
Hazard, NE, Sherman Co., St. Gabriel, c/o Loup City, NE, St. Josaphat's. (GI)
Hazlehurst, MS, Copiah Co., St. Martin, c/o Crystal Springs, MS, St. John the Evangelist. (JKS)
Heart Butte, MT, Glacier Co., Holy Family Mission, c/o Heart Butte, MT, St. Anne (Blackfeet Reservation). (HEL)
Heartwell, NE, Kearney Co., Holy Family, c/o Minden, NE, St. John the Baptist. (LIN)
Hebbronville, TX, Jim Hogg Co., Inmaculada, c/o Hebbronville, TX, Our Lady of Guadalupe. (LAR)
Heber, CA, Imperial Co., Sacred Heart, c/o El Centro, CA, Our Lady of Guadalupe Catholic Parish El Centro. (SD)
Heber City, UT, Wasatch Co., St. Lawrence, c/o Park City, UT, Saint Mary of the Assumption LLC 238. (SLC)
Heber Springs, AR, Cleburne Co., St. Albert, c/o Searcy, AR, St. James. (LR)
Hedgesville, WV, Berkeley Co., St. Bernadette, c/o Martinsburg, WV, St. Joseph's. (WH)
Heidelberg, KY, Lee Co., St. Therese, c/o Beattyville, KY, Queen of All Saints. (LEX)
Helena, TX, Karnes Co., St. Helena, c/o Panna Maria, TX, Immaculate Conception of the Blessed Virgin Mary. (SAT)
Hemingford, NE, Box Butte Co., St. Bridget, c/o Alliance, NE, Holy Rosary. (GI)
Henderson, NY, Jefferson Co., Queen of Heaven, c/o Adams, NY, St. Cecilia. (OG)
Hermosa, SD, Custer Co., St. Michael's, c/o Rapid City, SD, Cathedral of Our Lady of Perpetual Help. (RC)
Hernandez, NM, Rio Arriba Co., c/o Espanola, NM, Sacred Heart. (SFE)
Hesperia, MI, Oceana Co., Christ the King, c/o Fremont, MI, St. Michael. (GR)
Hessel, MI, Mackinac Co., Our Lady of the Snows, c/o Goetzville, MI, St. Stanislaus Kostka. (MAR)
High Falls, NY, Ulster Co., Our Lady Help of Christians, c/o Rosendale, NY, St. Peter. (NY)
Highland, MO, Perry Co., St. Joseph, c/o Perryville, MO, St. Vincent De Paul. (STL)
Highlands, NC, Our Lady of the Mountains, c/o Franklin, NC, St. Francis of Assisi. (CHL)
Hill City, SD, Pennington Co., St. Rose of Lima, c/o Rapid City, SD, Blessed Sacrament. (RC)
Hillsboro, NM, Sierra Co., Our Lady of Guadalupe, c/o Garfield, NM, San Isidro. (LSC)
Hinsdale, MT, Valley Co., St. Albert, c/o Glasgow, MT, St. Raphael. (GF)
Hinton, OK, Caddo Co., Sacred Heart, c/o Weatherford, OK, St. Eugene's. (OKL)
Hobart, OK, Kiewa Co., Sts. Peter and Paul, c/o Mangum, OK, Sacred Heart. (OKL)
Hobson, MT, Judith Basin Co., Sacred Heart, c/o Stanford, MT, St. Rose of Lima. (GF)
Hochheim, TX, DeWitt Co., St. Ann, c/o Yoakum, TX, St. Joseph. (VIC)
Hoconuco, PR, Chapel of St. Joseph, c/o San German, PR, San German de Auxerre. (MGZ)
Hode, KY, Martin Co., St. John Neumann, c/o Louisa, KY, St. Jude. (LEX)
Hogeland, MT, Blaine Co., St. Thomas Aquinas, c/o Chinook, MT, St. Gabriel. (GF)
Hollandale, MS, Washington Co., Immaculate Conception, c/o Leland, MS, St. James. (JKS)
Hollis, AK, c/o Craig, AK, St. John by the Sea. (JUN)
Hollis, OK, Harmon Co., Our Lady of Guadalupe, c/o Mangum, OK, Sacred Heart. (OKL)
Holly Lake Ranch, TX, Sulphur Co., Holy Spirit Church, c/o Gilmer, TX, St. Francis of Assisi. (TYL)
Holman, NM, Mora Co., c/o Mora, NM, St. Gertrude. (SFE)
Holman, TX, Fayette Co., St. Wenceslaus, c/o Schulenburg, TX, St. John The Baptist. (VIC)
Holton, IN, Ripley Co., St. Mary Magdalen, c/o Osgood, IN, St. John the Baptist Catholic Church, Osgood, Inc. (IND)
Holualoa, HI, Hawaii Co., Immaculate Conception, c/o Kailua–Kona, HI, St. Michael The Archangel. (HON)
Holyoke, MA, Hampden Co., Holyoke Soldier's Home Chapel, c/o Holyoke, MA, Blessed Sacrament. (SPR)
Holyrood, KS, Ellsworth Co., St. Mary Parish, c/o Wilson, KS, St. Wenceslaus Parish. (SAL)
Homer, IL, Champaign Co., St. Charles Borromeo, c/o Penfield, IL, St. Lawrence's. (PEO)
Homer, LA, Claiborne Parish, St. Margaret, c/o Minden, LA, St. Paul. (SHP)
Homer, NE, Dakota Co., St. Cornelius, c/o Winnebago, NE, St. Augustine's. (OM)
Hominy, OK, Osage Co., c/o Fairfax, OK, Sacred Heart. (TLS)
Honalo, HI, Hawaii Co., St. Paul, c/o Kailua–Kona, HI, St. Michael The Archangel. (HON)
Honokahua (Kapalua), HI, Maui Co., Sacred Hearts of Jesus and Mary, c/o Lahaina, HI, Maria Lanakila. (HON)
Honomu, HI, Hawaii Co., Good Shepherd, c/o Papaikou, HI, Immaculate Heart of Mary. (HON)
Hooker, OK, Texas Co., Sacred Heart, c/o Guymon, OK, St. Peter's. (OKL)
Hoonah, AK, c/o Yakutat, AK, St. Ann. (JUN)
Hooper, NE, Dodge Co., St. Lawrence, c/o Hooper, NE, St. Rose of Lima. (OM)
Hooppole, IL, Henry Co., St. Mary's, c/o Annawan, IL, Sacred Heart. (PEO)
Hopedale, IL, Tazewell Co., St. Joseph's, c/o Delavan, IL, St. Mary's. (PEO)
Hopkins Park, IL, Kankakee Co., Sacred Heart, c/o Momence, IL, St. Patrick. (JOL)
Hopland, CA, St. Francis Mission, c/o Ukiah, CA, St. Mary of the Angels. (SR)
Hornitos, CA, Mariposa Co., St. Catherine of Siena, c/o Mariposa, CA, St. Joseph. (FRS)
Horse Cave, KY, Hart Co., Our Lady of the Caves Church, c/o Glasgow, KY, St. Helen. (L)
Horse Springs, NM, Catron Co., St. Anne, c/o Reserve, NM, Santo Nino. (GLP)
Horseshoe Bay, TX, Burnet Co., Our Lady of the Lake (Sunrise Beach), c/o Kingsland, TX, St. Charles Borromeo Catholic Church – Kingsland, Texas. (AUS)
Horseshoe Bend, AR, Izard Co., St. Mary of the Mount Church, c/o Cherokee Village, AR, St. Michael. (LR)
Horseshoe Lake, AR, Crittenden Co., St. Mary of the Lake, c/o Brinkley, AR, St. John the Baptist. (LR)
Hot Springs, MT, Sanders Co., Sacred Heart, c/o Plains, MT, St. James. (HEL)
Hotchkiss, CO, Delta Co., St. Margaret Mary, c/o Paonia, CO, Sacred Heart. (PBL)
Houma, LA, St. Holy Rosary, c/o Morgan City, LA, Thanh Gia. (HT)
Houston, MS, Chickasaw Co., Immaculate Heart of Mary, c/o Aberdeen, MS, St. Francis of Assisi. (JKS)
Hubbard, NE, Dakota Co., St. Mary, c/o Jackson, NE, St. Patrick. (OM)
Hubbard, OR, Marion Co., St. Agnes, c/o Woodburn, OR, St. Luke. (P)
Hudson, IN, Steuben Co., St. Mary of the Angels, c/o Waterloo, IN, St. Michael the Archangel. (FTW)
Hugo, CO, Lincoln Co., St. Anthony of Padua, c/o Limon, CO, Our Lady of Victory. (COS)
Hulett, WY, Crook Co., St. Matthew's, c/o Newcastle, WY, Corpus Christi. (CHY)
Humansville, MO, Polk Co., St. Catherine, c/o Bolivar, MO, Sacred Heart. (SPC)
Hume, IL, Edgar Co., St. Michael's, c/o Villa Grove, IL, Sacred Heart. (SFD)
Humphrey, NY, Cattaraugus Co., St. Pacificus, c/o Ellicottville, NY, Holy Name of Mary. (BUF)
Hunter, NY, St. Mary's Church, c/o Haines Falls, NY, Sacred Heart–Immaculate Conception Church. (ALB)
Huntingdon, TN, Carroll Co., Holy Family Church, c/o Camden, TN, St. Mary Church. (MEM)
Huntington, UT, Emery Co., San Rafael, c/o Price, UT, Notre Dame de Lourdes LLC 207. (SLC)
Huntsville, OH, Logan Co., St. George Chapel Marianists of Ohio, c/o Russells Point, OH, St. Mary of the Woods. (CIN)
Huntsville, UT, Weber Co., St. Florence, c/o Ogden, UT, Saint Joseph LLC 230. (SLC)
Hurley, MS, Jackson Co., St. Ann, c/o Moss Point, MS, St. Joseph. (BLX)
Hurley, NY, Msgr. O'Reilly Chapel, c/o Kingston, NY, St. Joseph. (NY)
Hurtsboro, AL, Russell Co., John XXIII Center, c/o Fort Mitchell, AL, St. Joseph. (MOB)
Hyannis, NE, Grant Co., All Saint's, c/o Mullen, NE, St. Mary's. (GI)
Hydaburg, AK, c/o Craig, AK, St. John by the Sea. (JUN)
Hysham, MT, Treasure Co., St. Joseph, c/o Forsyth, MT, Immaculate Conception. (GF)

I

Imperial, TX, Pecos Co., Our Lady of Lourdes, c/o Crane, TX, Good Shepherd. (SAN)
Imperial, TX, Pecos Co., Our Lady of Lourdes, c/o McCamey, TX, Sacred Heart. (SAN)
Independence, CA, Inyo Co., St. Vivian, c/o Lone Pine, CA, Santa Rosa. (FRS)
Indian Land, SC, Our Lady of Grace, c/o Fort Mill, SC, St. Philip Neri. (CHR)
Indiera Fria, PR, Santa Rosa, c/o Maricao, PR, St. John the Baptist. (MGZ)
Industry, TX, Austin Co., Immaculate Conception, c/o Bellville, TX, Sts. Peter & Paul. (GAL)
Inglis, FL, Levy Co., St. Anthony the Abbot, c/o Williston, FL, Holy Family. (STA)
Ingold, NC, Sampson Co., San Juan, c/o Clinton, NC, Immaculate Conception. (R)
Interior, SD, Jackson Co., Holy Rosary, c/o Wall, SD, St. Patrick's. (RC)
Inverness, MT, Hill Co., Sacred Heart, c/o Chester, MT, Our Lady of Ransom. (GF)
Ione, OR, St. William, c/o Heppner, OR, St. Patrick's. (BAK)
Iowa, LA, Calcasieu Parish, St. Peter Claver, c/o Welsh, LA, St. Joseph. (LKC)

Iraan, TX, Pecos Co., St. Francis, c/o Big Lake, TX, St. Margaret of Cortona. (SAN)
Irish Grove Rd., IL, Stephenson Co., St. Patrick, c/o Durand, IL, St. Mary. (RCK)
Irishtown, MI, Gratiot Co., St. Patrick, c/o Shepherd, MI, St. Vincent De Paul. (SAG)
Irvine, CA, Queen of Life Chapel, c/o Irvine, CA, St. Elizabeth Ann Seton. (ORG)
Isabel, SD, Dewey Co., St. Mary, c/o Timber Lake, SD, Holy Cross. (RC)
Island Heights, NJ, Ocean Co., St. Gertrude, c/o Toms River, NJ, St. Joseph. (TR)
Isle La Motte, VT, Grand Isle Co., St. Joseph, c/o Alburgh, VT, St. Amadeus. (BUR)
Isle of Hope, GA, Chatham Co., Our Lady of Good Hope, c/o Savannah, GA, St. James. (SAV)
Iuka, MS, Tishomingo Co., St. Mary, c/o Booneville, MS, St. Francis of Assisi. (JKS)
Ivanhoe, CA, Tulare Co., San Felipe de Jesus, c/o Woodlake, CA, St. Frances Cabrini. (FRS)

J

Jackpot, NV, Elko Co., Our Lady of Guadalupe, c/o Elko, NV, St. Joseph's. (RNO)
Jackson, AL, Clarke Co., Visitation, c/o Grove Hill, AL, Sacred Heart. (MOB)
Jackson, MI, St. Joseph the Worker Oratory, c/o Jackson, MI, St. John the Evangelist. (LAN)
Jackson, MI, St. Stanislaus Kosta, c/o Jackson, MI, St. Mary Star of the Sea. (LAN)
Jacksonville, FL, Duval Co., St. Peter, c/o Jacksonville Beach, FL, St. Paul's. (STA)
Jacksonville, OR, Jackson Co., St. Joseph, c/o Medford, OR, Sacred Heart of Jesus. (P)
Jacksonville, TX, Cherokee Co., Our Lady of Guadalupe, c/o Jacksonville, TX, Our Lady of Sorrows. (TYL)
Jacumba, CA, San Diego Co., St. Mary Magdalene, c/o Campo, CA, Saint Adelaide of Burgundy Catholic Parish. (SD)
Jaguey Chiquito, PR, San Augustin, c/o Aguada, PR, St. Francis of Assisi. (MGZ)
Jamestown, PA, Mercer Co., St. Margaret, c/o Greenville, PA, St. Michael. (E)
Jarales, NM, Valencia Co., c/o Belen, NM, Our Lady of Belen. (SFE)
Jardines del Caribe, PR, Perpetuo Socorro, c/o Mayaguez, PR, Our Lady of Mt. Carmel. (MGZ)
Jasper, FL, Hamilton Co., St. Therese of the Child Jesus, c/o Live Oak, FL, St. Francis Xavier. (STA)
Java Center, NY, St. Patrick, c/o Strykersville, NY, St. John Neumann. (BUF)
Jayton, TX, Kent Co., Epiphany, c/o Spur, TX, St. Mary. (LUB)
Jayuya, Bo. Veguita Fama, c/o Jayuya, PR, Our Lady of Monserrate. (PCE)
Jefferson, NH, Coos Co., St. Agnes, c/o Lancaster, NH, Gate of Heaven. (MAN)
Jefferson, OR, Marion Co., St. Thomas, c/o Scio, OR, St. Bernard. (P)
Jefferson, TX, St. Paul of Tarsus Mission, c/o Jefferson, TX, Immaculate Conception. (TYL)
Jeffrey City, WY, Freemont Co., St. Brendan, c/o Lander, WY, Holy Rosary. (CHY)
Jenny Lind, AR, SS. Sabina & Mary Church, c/o Barling, AR, Sacred Heart of Mary. (LR)
Jerome, AZ, Yavapai Co., Holy Family, c/o Cottonwood, AZ, Immaculate Conception Roman Catholic Parish. (PHX)
Jersey City, NJ, Hudson Co., c/o Jersey City, NJ, St. Ann's. (NEW)
Jocko, MT, Lake Co., St. John Berchman's, c/o St. Ignatius, MT, St. Ignatius Mission. (HEL)
Johnson City, TX, Blanco Co., Good Shepherd, c/o Blanco, TX, St. Ferdinand. (AUS)
Johnsonville, SC, Florence Co., St. Patrick the Apostle, c/o Lake City, SC, St. Philip the Apostle. (CHR)
Joliet, MT, Carbon Co., St. John, c/o Bridger, MT, Sacred Heart. (GF)
Jones, OK, St. Robert Bellarmine, c/o Oklahoma City, OK, Corpus Christi. (OKL)
Jonestown, PA, Lebanon Co., Our Lady of Fatima, c/o Lebanon, PA, Assumption of the Blessed Virgin Mary. (HBG)
Jonesville, LA, Catahoula Parish, St. Gerard, c/o Ferriday, LA, St. Patrick. (ALX)
Jordan, MT, Garfield Co., St. John the Baptist, c/o Miles City, MT, Sacred Heart. (GF)
Joyuda, PR, St. John the Baptist, c/o Cabo Rojo, PR, St. Michael. (MGZ)
Juana Diaz, PR, La Merced, c/o Juana Diaz, PR, St. Raymond Nonato. (PCE)
Juana Diaz, PR, Juana Diaz Co., Ntra Sra de la Monserrate, c/o Juana Diaz, PR, Santa Teresita del Nino Jesus. (PCE)
Juana Diaz, PR, Juana Diaz Co., Sagrado Corazon, c/o Juana Diaz, PR, Nuestra Senora de Lourdes. (PCE)
Juana Diaz, PR, San Pedro Nolasco, c/o Juana Diaz, PR, Nuestra Senora de Lourdes. (PCE)
Juana Diaz, PR, Juana Diaz Co., Virgen del Carmen, c/o Juana Diaz, PR, Nuestra Senora de Lourdes. (PCE)
Judith Gap, MT, Wheatland Co., Immaculate Conception, c/o Harlowton, MT, St. Joseph. (HEL)
Julian, NE, Nemaha Co., St. Bernard's, c/o Nebraska City, NE, St. Joseph's. (LIN)
Juniata, NE, Adams Co., Assumption, c/o Roseland, NE, Sacred Heart. (LIN)
Juntura, OR, Malheur Co., St. Charles, c/o Burns, OR, Holy Family. (BAK)

K

Kahakuloa, HI, Maui Co., St. Francis Xavier, c/o Waihee, HI, St. Ann. (HON)
Kahaluu, HI, Hawaii Co., St. Peter by the Sea, c/o Kailua–Kona, HI, St. Michael The Archangel. (HON)
Kahuku, HI, Honolulu Co., St. Joachim, c/o Kahuku, HI, St. Roch. (HON)
Kake, AK, c/o Yakutat, AK, St. Ann. (JUN)
Kake, AK, c/o Sitka, AK, St. Gregory of Nazianzen. (JUN)
Kalama, WA, Cowlitz Co., St. Joseph, c/o Woodland, WA, St. Philip. (SEA)
Kalaoa, HI, Hawaii Co., Holy Rosary, c/o Kailua–Kona, HI, St. Michael The Archangel. (HON)
Kaplan, LA, Vermilion Parish, St. Frances Xavier Cabrini, c/o Kaplan, LA, Our Lady of the Holy Rosary. (LAF)
Karlstad, MN, Marshall Co., St. Edward, c/o Greenbush, MN, Blessed Sacrament. (CR)
Kaupo, HI, Maui Co., St. Joseph, c/o Hana, HI, St. Mary. (HON)
Kaycee, WY, Johnson Co., St. Hubert, c/o Buffalo, WY, St. John the Baptist. (CHY)
Keaau, HI, Hawaii Co., Holy Rosary, c/o Mountain View, HI, St. Theresa. (HON)
Kealakekua, HI, Hawaii Co., St. John the Baptist, c/o Captain Cook, HI, St. Benedict. (HON)
Keenesburg, CO, Weld Co., Holy Family, c/o Roggen, CO, Sacred Heart. (DEN)
Kelly, NM, Socorro Co., c/o Socorro, NM, San Miguel. (SFE)
Kelseyville, CA, St. Peter, c/o Lakeport, CA, St. Mary Immaculate. (SR)
Kenel, SD, Corson Co., Assumption of the Blessed Virgin Mary Church, c/o McLaughlin, SD, Standing Rock Reservation. (RC)
Kenel, SD, Corson Co., Our Lady of the Assumption Parish, c/o McLaughlin, SD, St. Bernard. (RC)
Kerhonkson, NY, Ulster Co., Our Lady of Lourdes, c/o Ellenville, NY, St. Mary and St. Andrew. (NY)
Kettleman City, CA, Kings Co., St. Cecilia, c/o Avenal, CA, St. Joseph. (FRS)
Kewanna, IN, Fulton Co., St. Ann, c/o Rochester, IN, St. Joseph. (LFT)
Key West, FL, Monroe Co., St. Mary, Star of the Sea Outreach Mission, c/o Key West, FL, St. Mary Star of the Sea. (MIA)
Keyapaha, SD, Tripp Co., St. Ann, c/o Winner, SD, Immaculate Conception. (RC)
Keystone, SD, Pennington Co., Our Lady of Mt. Carmel, c/o Rapid City, SD, Blessed Sacrament. (RC)
Kilauea, HI, Kauai Co., St. Sylvester, c/o Kapaa, HI, St. Catherine. (HON)
Killington, VT, Rutland Co., Our Lady of the Mountains, c/o Woodstock, VT, Our Lady of the Snows. (BUR)
Kincaid, IL, St. Rita, c/o Taylorville, IL, St. Mary. (SFD)
King, NC, Stokes Co., Good Shepherd, c/o Winston–Salem, NC, St. Benedict the Moor. (CHL)
King Ranch, TX, Kleberg Co., Christ the King, c/o Kingsville, TX, St. Martin. (CC)
Kingman, ME, Penobscot Co., St. James, c/o Lincoln, ME, St. Mary. (PRT)
Kings Beach, CA, Placer Co., Our Lady of the Lake, c/o Truckee, CA, Assumption of the Blessed Virgin Mary. (SAC)
Kings Mountain, NC, Cleveland Co., Christ the King, c/o Shelby, NC, St. Mary's. (CHL)
Kinnear, WY, Fremont Co., St. Edward, c/o Riverton, WY, St. Margaret's. (CHY)
Kipahulu, HI, Maui Co., St. Paul, c/o Hana, HI, St. Mary. (HON)
Kirtland, NM, San Juan Co., San Juan Catholic Center, c/o Waterflow, NM, Sacred Heart. (GLP)
Kit Carson, CO, Cheyenne Co., St. Augustine, c/o Cheyenne Wells, CO, Sacred Heart. (COS)
Klamath, CA, St. Robert and Ann, c/o Crescent City, CA, St. Joseph. (SR)
Kluckwan, AK, c/o Haines, AK, Sacred Heart. (JUN)
Knickerbocker, TX, Tom Green Co., Immaculate Conception, c/o Eldorado, TX, Our Lady of Guadalupe. (SAN)
Knippa, TX, Uvalde Co., St. Joseph, c/o Sabinal, TX, St. Patrick's. (SAT)
Kovar, TX, Bastrop Co., Sts. Peter and Paul, c/o Smithville, TX, St. Paul Catholic Church. (AUS)
Kress, TX, Swisher Co., St. Paul the Apostle, c/o Tulia, TX, Church of the Holy Spirit. (AMA)
Kuttu, FM, c/o Chuuk, FM, Mortlock. (CI)

L

L'Erable, IL, Iroquois Co., St. John the Baptist, c/o Ashkum, IL, Assumption of the Blessed Virgin Mary. (JOL)
La Bajada, NM, Sandoval Co., San Miguel, c/o Pena Blanca, NM, Nuestra Senora De Guadalupe. (SFE)
La Casita, TX, Starr Co., Our Lady of the Peace, c/o La Grulla, TX, Holy Family. (BWN)
La Cienega, NM, Santa Fe Co., San Jose, c/o Santa Fe, NM, San Isidro. (SFE)
La Cueva, NM, Mora Co., c/o Mora, NM, St. Gertrude. (SFE)
La Garita, CO, Saguache Co., St. John the Baptist, c/o Del Norte, CO, Holy Name of Mary. (PBL)
La Grange, CA, Stanislaus Co., St. Louis, c/o Hughson, CA, St. Anthony Church of Hughson (Pastor of). (STO)
La Grange, MO, Lewis Co., Notre Dame, c/o Canton, MO, St. Joseph. (JC)
La Honda, CA, San Mateo Co., Our Lady of Refuge, c/o Half Moon Bay, CA, Our Lady of the Pillar. (SFR)
La Isla, TX, El Paso Co., San Luis, c/o Fabens, TX, Our Lady of Guadalupe. (ELP)
La Jara, CO, Conejos Co., Our Lady of the Valley, c/o Capulin, CO, St. Joseph. (PBL)
La Jara, NM, Sandoval Co., Santo Nino, c/o Cuba, NM, Immaculate Conception. (GLP)
La Lagunita, NM, San Miguel Co., c/o Ribera, NM, San Miguel Del Vado. (SFE)
La Madera, NM, Rio Arriba Co., c/o El Rito, NM, San Juan Nepomuceno. (SFE)
La Marina, PR, Guaynabo Co., San Francisco de Asis, c/o San Juan, PR, San Juan Evangelista. (SJN)
La Mesa, NM, Dona Ana Co., San Pedro (Del Cerro), c/o La Mesa, NM, San Jose. (LSC)
La Paloma, TX, Cameron Co., Our Lady of Lourdes, c/o San Benito, TX, St. Ignatius. (BWN)
La Playa, PR, Our Lady of Carmel, c/o Anasco, PR, St. Anthony Abbot. (MGZ)
La Rosita, TX, Starr Co., Santa Rosa de Lima, c/o Roma, TX, Sacred Heart. (BWN)
La Salle, TX, Jackson Co., St. Theresa, c/o Vanderbilt, TX, St. John Bosco. (VIC)
La Union, NM, Dona Ana Co., Our Lady of Refuge, c/o Anthony, NM, St. Anthony's. (LSC)
La Valle, WI, Holy Family, c/o Lime Ridge, WI, St. Boniface. (MAD)
La Veta, CO, Huerfano Co., Christ the King, c/o Walsenburg, CO, St. Mary. (PBL)
La Villa, TX, Hidalgo Co., Our Lady of Guadalupe, c/o Edcouch, TX, St. Theresa of the Infant Jesus. (BWN)
LaCrosse, IN, LaPorte Co., St. Martin, c/o Wanatah, IN, Sacred Heart. (GRY)
LaSal, UT, San Juan Co., Sacred Heart, c/o Moab, UT, Saint Pius X LLC 244. (SLC)
Labelle, FL, Hendry Co., Holy Martyrs Mission, c/o LaBelle, FL, Our Lady Queen of Heaven. (VEN)
Lacassine, LA, Jefferson Davis Parish, St. John the Evangelist, c/o Fenton, LA, St. Charles Borromeo. (LKC)
Lacey, MI, Barry Co., Our Lady of Great Oak, c/o Delton, MI, St. Ambrose. (KAL)
Lackawaxen, PA, Pike Co., St. Mary of the Assumption, c/o Shohola, PA, St. Ann's. (SCR)
Laddonia, MO, Audrain Co., St. John, c/o Vandalia, MO, Sacred Heart. (JC)
Lafayette, LA, Lafayette Parish, Our Lady of Good Hope, c/o Lafayette, LA, St. Paul The Apostle. (LAF)
Lagarto, TX, St. Francis of Assisi Mission, c/o Orange Grove, TX, St. John of the Cross. (CC)
Laguna, PR, Santa Rita, c/o Aguada, PR, St. Francis of Assisi. (MGZ)
Laguna Heights, TX, Cameron Co., Laguna Heights Chapel, c/o Port Isabel, TX, Our Lady Star of the Sea. (BWN)
Lajitas, TX, Brewster Co., Lajitas Mission, c/o Presidio, TX, Santa Teresa de Jesus. (ELP)
Lake Arthur, NM, Chavez Co., Our Lady of Guadalupe, c/o Dexter, NM, Immaculate Conception. (LSC)
Lake Carmel, NY, Putnam Co., Our Lady of the Lake/Mt. Carmel, c/o Carmel, NY, St. James the Apostle. (NY)
Lake Charles, LA, Calcasieu Parish, Our Lady of Fatima Chapel, c/o Lake Charles, LA, Immaculate Heart of Mary. (LKC)
Lake Hughes, CA, Los Angeles Co., St. Elizabeth, c/o Lancaster, CA, Blessed Junipero Serra. (LA)
Lake Huntington, NY, Sullivan Co., Our Lady of the Lake, c/o Narrowsburg, NY, St. Francis Xavier. (NY)
Lake Park, MN, Becker Co., St. Francis Xavier, c/o Detroit Lakes, MN, St. Mary of the Lakes. (CR)
Lake Titus, NY, Franklin Co., St. Mary, c/o Malone, NY, St. Helen. (OG)
Lake Wallenpaupack, PA, Pike Co., St. Veronica, c/o

Hawley, PA, Blessed Virgin Mary, Queen of Peace. (SCR)
Lake Wylie, SC, York Co., All Saints, c/o York, SC, Divine Saviour. (CHR)
Lakehills, TX, Bandera Co., St. Victor's Chapel, c/o Bandera, TX, St. Stanislaus. (SAT)
Lakeside, SD, Meade Co., St. Margaret, c/o Wall, SD, St. Patrick's. (RC)
Lakewood, NJ, Ocean Co., Holy Family Church, c/o Lakewood, NJ, St. Mary of the Lake. (TR)
Lambert, MT, Richland Co., St. Theresa, c/o Sidney, MT, St. Matthew. (GF)
Lamesa, TX, Dawson Co., Our Lady of Guadalupe, c/o Lamesa, TX, St. Margaret Mary. (LUB)
Lancaster, MN, Kittson Co., Holy Rosary, c/o Hallock, MN, St. Patrick's. (CR)
Langley Park, MD, Prince George's Co., Catholic Community of Langley Park, c/o Silver Spring, MD, St. Camillus. (WDC)
Lantana, FL, Palm Beach Co., c/o Miami, FL, Assumption of B.V.M. (SJP)
Laporte, MN, Hubbard Co., St. Theodore, c/o Nevis, MN, Our Lady of the Pines. (CR)
Laredo, TX, Webb Co., Santa Cruz, c/o Laredo, TX, Holy Redeemer. (LAR)
Largo, FL, Pinellas Co., Holy Martyrs of Vietnam, c/o Largo, FL, St. Matthew. (SP)
Larose, LA, St. Peter, c/o Morgan City, LA, Thanh Gia. (HT)
Las Colonias, NM, Taos Co., Santo Nino de Atocha, c/o Arroyo Seco, NM, La Santisima Trinidad. (SFE)
Las Colonias, NM, San Miguel Co., c/o Pecos, NM, St. Anthony of Padua. (SFE)
Las Flores, Coamo, PR, Coamo Co., San Martin, c/o Coamo, PR, San Antonio de Padua. (PCE)
Las Mareas, PR, Salinas Co., St. Judas, c/o Aguirre, PR, Sacred Heart. (PCE)
Las Margaritas, Bo. Collores, PR, Bo. Collores Arriba, Santiago, Ap., c/o Juana Diaz, PR, St. Raymond Nonato. (PCE)
Las Mesitas, CO, Conejos Co., San Isidro Brador, c/o Antonito, CO, Our Lady of Guadalupe. (PBL)
Las Nutrias, NM, Socorro Co., San Isidro, c/o La Joya, NM, Our Lady of Sorrows. (SFE)
Las Ochenta, PR, Salinas Co., Inmaculada Concepcion, c/o Salinas, PR, Our Lady of Monserrat. (PCE)
Las Palomas, NM, Sierra Co., San Ysidro, c/o Truth or Consequences, NM, Our Lady of Perpetual Help. (LSC)
Las Rucias, TX, Cameron Co., Sacred Heart, c/o San Benito, TX, St. Ignatius. (BWN)
Las Tablas, NM, Taos Co., c/o El Rito, NM, San Juan Nepomuceno. (SFE)
Las Vegas, NM, San Miguel Co., Los Vigiles (Our Lady of Refuge), c/o Las Vegas, NM, Immaculate Conception. (SFE)
Las Vegas, NM, San Antonio (Uppertown), c/o La Joya, NM, Our Lady of Sorrows. (SFE)
Lasara, TX, Willacy Co., St. Patrick, c/o Raymondville, TX, Our Lady of Guadalupe. (BWN)
Latimer, MS, Jackson Co., Christ the King, c/o Vancleave, MS, Holy Spirit Catholic Church. (BLX)
Laurens, SC, Laurens Co., Holy Spirit, c/o Joanna, SC, St. Boniface. (CHR)
Laveen, AZ, St. Catherine, c/o Laveen, AZ, St. John The Baptist. (PHX)
Lawrence, NE, Nuckolls Co., St. Stephen's, c/o Lawrence, NE, Sacred Heart. (LIN)
Le Bleu Settlement, LA, Calcasieu Parish, St. Joseph, c/o Iowa, LA, St. Raphael. (LKC)
Le Doux, NM, Mora Co., c/o Mora, NM, St. Gertrude. (SFE)
Le Roy, NY, St. Joseph, c/o Le Roy, NY, Our Lady of Mercy. (BUF)
LeGrand, CA, Merced Co., Our Lady of Lourdes, c/o Planada, CA, Sacred Heart. (FRS)
Leakesville, MS, Perry Co., Holy Trinity, c/o Waynesboro, MS, St. Bernadette. (BLX)
Leakey, TX, Real Co., St. Raymond of Pennafort, c/o Rocksprings, TX, Sacred Heart of Mary. (SAT)
Leavenworth, KS, Kickapoo Twp., Sacred Heart, c/o Leavenworth, KS, Immaculate Conception–St. Joseph. (KCK)
Lebanon, OH, c/o Lebanon, OH, St. Francis de Sales. (CIN)
Ledgedale, PA, Wayne Co., St. Mary, c/o Lake Ariel, PA, St. Thomas More. (SCR)
Lee Vining, CA, Mono Co., Our Savior of the Mountains, c/o Mammoth Lakes, CA, St. Joseph Church of Mammoth Lakes. (STO)
Leicester, VT, Addison Co., St. Agnes, c/o Brandon, VT, St. Mary's. (BUR)
Leming, TX, Loire Co., Our Lady of Guadalupe, c/o Pleasanton, TX, St. Luke–Loire. (SAT)
Lemitar, NM, Socorro Co., c/o Socorro, NM, San Miguel. (SFE)
Lenorah, TX, Martin Co., St. Isidore, c/o Stanton, TX, St. Joseph's. (SAN)
Lepua, AS, c/o Pago Pago, AS, Church of the Immaculate Conception. (SPP)
Lesterville, MO, Reynolds Co., Our Lady of Sorrows, c/o Ironton, MO, Ste. Marie Du Lac. (SPC)
Lewiston, CA, Trinity Co., St. Gilbert, c/o Weaverville, CA, St. Patrick. (SAC)
Lexington, IL, McLean Co., St. Mary, c/o Chenoa, IL, St. Joseph's. (PEO)
Lexington, TX, Lee Co., Holy Family, c/o Dime Box, TX, St. Joseph. (AUS)
Leyba, NM, San Miguel Co., c/o Villanueva, NM, Our Lady of Guadalupe. (SFE)
Liberty, KY, Casey Co., Sacred Heart, c/o Liberty, KY, St. Bernard. (L)
Licking, MO, Texas Co., St. John The Baptist, c/o Houston, MO, St. Mark. (SPC)
Lilburn, GA, Gwinnet Co., Our Lady of the Americas, c/o Norcross, GA, Saint Patrick. (ATL)
Limani, PR, Adjuntas Co., Ntra Sra Fátima Juan González, c/o Adjuntas, PR, St. Joachim. (PCE)
Lincoln, MA, Middlesex Co., St. Joseph, c/o Weston, MA, St. Julia. (BO)
Lincoln, MT, Lewis and Clark Co., St. Jude's, c/o Helmville, MT, St. Thomas. (HEL)
Lincoln, NM, Lincoln Co., San Juan, c/o Ruidoso, NM, St. Eleanor. (LSC)
Lindsay, OK, Garvin Co., St. Peter Church, c/o Purcell, OK, Our Lady of Victory. (OKL)
Lindsborg, KS, McPherson Co., St. Bridget of Sweden, c/o McPherson, KS, St. Joseph. (WCH)
Linlithgo, NY, Columbia Co., Nativity, c/o Hudson, NY, Parish of the Holy Trinity. (ALB)
Linville, NC, Avery Co., St. Bernadette, c/o Spruce Pine, NC, St. Lucien. (CHL)
Lisco, NE, Garden Co., St. Gall, c/o Chappell, NE, St. Joseph's. (GI)
Little Diomede, AK, Nome Census Area, St. Jude Catholic Church Little Diomede, c/o Nome, AK, St. Joseph Catholic Church Nome. (FBK)
Little Italy, AR, Pulaski Co., St. Francis of Assisi, c/o Bigelow, AR, St. Boniface. (LR)
Little Orleans, MD, Allegany Co., St. Patrick's, c/o Hancock, MD, St. Peter's. (BAL)
Littlerock, CA, Los Angeles Co., Our Lady of the Desert, c/o Palmdale, CA, St. Mary. (LA)
Live Oak, CA, Sutter Co., Our Lady of Guadalupe, c/o Gridley, CA, Sacred Heart. (SAC)
Llano Quemado, NM, Taos Co., N.S. del Carmel, c/o Ranchos De Taos, NM, San Francisco de Asis. (SFE)
Llano San Juan, NM, Taos Co., San Juan Nepomuceno Mission, c/o Penasco, NM, San Antonio de Padua. (SFE)
Llanos Tunas, PR, Our Lady of Good Counsel, c/o Cabo Rojo, PR, St. Michael. (MGZ)
Lobatos, CO, Conejos Co., Sagrada Familia, c/o Antonito, CO, Our Lady of Guadalupe. (PBL)
Loch Lomond, CA, Our Lady of the Lake, c/o Middletown, CA, St. Joseph. (SR)
Lockney, TX, Floyd Co., San Jose, c/o Plainview, TX, St. Alice. (LUB)
Lockport, NY, St. Joseph, c/o Lockport, NY, All Saints. (BUF)
Lodgepole, MT, Blaine Co., St. Thomas, c/o Hays, MT, St. Paul's Indian Mission. (GF)
Logan, KS, Phillips Co., St. John the Evangelist, c/o Phillipsburg, KS, Saints Philip and James Parish. (SAL)
Logan, NM, Quay Co., San Antonio, c/o Tucumcari, NM, St. Anne. (SFE)
Logan, UT, Cache Co., Utah State University, c/o Hyde Park, UT, Saint Thomas Aquinas LLC 247. (SLC)
Loiza, PR, Ntra. Sra. de Fatima, c/o Loiza, PR, San Patricio. (FAJ)
Loiza, PR, San Antonio, c/o Loiza, PR, San Patricio. (FAJ)
Loiza, PR, San Rafael, c/o Loiza, PR, San Patricio. (FAJ)
Loleta, CA, St. Patrick, c/o Fortuna, CA, St. Joseph. (SR)
Lolo, MT, Missoula Co., Spirit of Christ, c/o Missoula, MT, Blessed Trinity Parish. (HEL)
Lometa, TX, Lampasas Co., Good Shepherd Catholic Church, c/o Lampasas, TX, St. Mary of the Immaculate Conception. (AUS)
London, CA, Tulare Co., Santa Cruz, c/o Kingsburg, CA, Holy Family. (FRS)
Long Beach, CA, Los Angeles Co., Our Lady of Mt. Carmel Cambodian Catholic Center, c/o Long Beach, CA, St. Anthony. (LA)
Long Creek, OR, Grant Co., St. Katherine, c/o John Day, OR, St. Elizabeth. (BAK)
Long Eddy, NY, St. Patrick, c/o Callicoon, NY, Holy Cross. (NY)
Long Island, ME, Cumberland Co., c/o Portland, ME, St. Christopher's. (PRT)
Lopeno, TX, Zapata Co., San Pedro, c/o Zapata, TX, Our Lady of Lourdes. (LAR)
Loraine, TX, Mitchell Co., St. Joseph, c/o Colorado City, TX, St. Ann's. (SAN)
Lorenzo, TX, Crosby Co., San Lorenzo, c/o Idalou, TX, St. Philip Benizi. (LUB)
Loris, SC, Horry Co., Catholic Church of the Resurrection, c/o North Myrtle Beach, SC, Our Lady Star of the Sea. (CHR)
Los Alamos, CA, St. Anthony's Church, c/o Santa Maria, CA, St. Louis de Montfort. (LA)
Los Angeles, CA, Old Co., Assumption, c/o Los Angeles, CA, Assumption. (LA)
Los Angeles, CA, Hermanas Misioneras Servidoras de la Palabra, c/o Los Angeles, CA, Santa Isabel. (LA)
Los Angeles, CA, Los Angeles Co., La Purisima Chapel, c/o Los Angeles, CA, Our Lady of the Rosary of Talpa. (LA)
Los Angeles, CA, Los Angeles Co., San Conrado, c/o Los Angeles, CA, St. Peter. (LA)
Los Angeles, CA, Los Angeles Co., San Felipe, c/o Los Angeles, CA, Our Lady of Guadalupe. (LA)
Los Angeles, CA, Los Angeles Co., Santo Nino, c/o Los Angeles, CA, St. Vincent De Paul. (LA)
Los Angeles, CA, Los Angeles Co., St. John Bosco, c/o Los Angeles, CA, St. Odilia. (LA)
Los Angeles, CA, Los Angeles Co., St. Turibius, c/o Los Angeles, CA, St. Joseph. (LA)
Los Chavez, NM, Valencia Co., c/o Belen, NM, Our Lady of Belen. (SFE)
Los Cordovas, NM, Taos Co., San Isidro, c/o Ranchos De Taos, NM, San Francisco de Asis. (SFE)
Los Ebanos, TX, Hidalgo Co., St. Michael, c/o La Joya, TX, Our Lady, Queen of Angels. (BWN)
Los Garcias Ranch, TX, Starr Co., Sacred Heart, c/o Rio Grande City, TX, Immaculate Conception. (BWN)
Los Hueros, NM, Mora Co., c/o Wagon Mound, NM, Santa Clara. (SFE)
Los Le Febres, NM, Mora Co., c/o Wagon Mound, NM, Santa Clara. (SFE)
Los Lentes, NM, Valencia Co., San Antonio, c/o Los Lunas, NM, San Clemente. (SFE)
Los Lunas, NM, San Juan Diego, c/o Los Lunas, NM, San Clemente. (SFE)
Los Martinez, NM, San Juan Co., Our Lady of Guadalupe, c/o Bloomfield, NM, St. Rose of Lima. (GLP)
Los Saenz, TX, Starr Co., Holy Family, c/o Roma, TX, Our Lady of Refuge. (BWN)
Los Sauces, CO, Conejos Co., St. Anthony, c/o Capulin, CO, St. Joseph. (PBL)
Los Valdeses, CO, Rio Grande Co., St. Francis of Assisi, c/o Del Norte, CO, Holy Name of Mary. (PBL)
Losap, FM, c/o Chuuk, FM, Mortlock. (CI)
Lott, TX, Falls Co., Sacred Heart, c/o Marlin, TX, St. Joseph. (AUS)
Louisburg, NC, Our Lady of the Rosary, c/o Wendell, NC, St. Eugene. (R)
Louise, TX, Wharton Co., St. Procopius, c/o El Campo, TX, St. Andrew. (VIC)
Louisville, GA, Jefferson Co., St. Joan of Arc, c/o Waynesboro, GA, Sacred Heart. (SAV)
Loveladies, NJ, Ocean Co., St. Clare, c/o Brant Beach, NJ, St. Francis of Assisi. (TR)
Lovell, WY, St. Joseph's, c/o Powell, WY, St. Barbara. (CHY)
Lowell, VT, Orleans Co., St. Ignatius Loyola, c/o Troy, VT, Sacred Heart of Jesus. (BUR)
Lower San Francisco, NM, Catron Co., San Isidro, c/o Reserve, NM, Santo Nino. (GLP)
Loyalton, CA, Sierra Co., Holy Rosary, c/o Portola, CA, Holy Family. (SAC)
Lozano, TX, Cameron Co., St. Vincent de Paul, c/o Rio Hondo, TX, St. Helen. (BWN)
Lucedale, MS, George Co., St. Lucy, c/o Wiggins, MS, St. Francis Xavier. (BLX)
Lucerne, CA, Queen of the Rosary, c/o Clearlake, CA, Our Lady, Queen of Peace. (SR)
Lucero, NM, Mora Co., c/o Mora, NM, St. Gertrude. (SFE)
Luis Llorens Torres, PR, San Juan Co., Sagrada Familia, c/o San Juan, PR, Santa Teresita Del Nino Jesus. (SJN)
Luis Lopez, NM, Socorro Co., c/o Socorro, NM, San Miguel. (SFE)
Lukunor, FM, c/o Chuuk, FM, Mortlock. (CI)
Lyden, NM, Rio Arriba Co., San Jose, c/o Dixon, NM, St. Anthony. (SFE)
Lyman, NE, Scotts Bluff Co., Sacred Heart, c/o Mitchell, NE, St. Theresa's. (GI)
Lyons, OR, Linn Co., St. Patrick, c/o Scio, OR, Our Lady of Lourdes. (P)
Lyons Falls, NY, Lewis Co., St. John, c/o Port Leyden, NY, St. Martin. (OG)

M

Macana Parcelas, PR, Guayanilla Co., San Martin de Porres, c/o Guayanilla, PR, Immaculate Conception. (PCE)
Macana Rio, PR, Guayanilla Co., Virgen de Fatima, c/o Guayanilla, PR, Immaculate Conception. (PCE)
Macon, MS, Noxubee Co., Corpus Christi, c/o Starkville, MS, St. Joseph. (JKS)
Madawaska, ME, Aroostook Co., St. Michael's Chapel, c/o St. Agatha, ME, Our Lady of the Valley. (PRT)
Madera, CA, Madera Co., St. Agnes, c/o Madera, CA, St. Joachim. (FRS)
Madera, PA, Clearfield Co., Immaculate Conception, c/o Houtzdale, PA, Christ the King. (E)

Madison, GA, Morgan Co., St. James, c/o Covington, GA, St. Augustine of Hippo. (ATL)
Madison, KS, Greenwood Co., St. Teresa Of Avila, c/o Eureka, KS, Sacred Heart. (WCH)
Magas Arriba, PR, Guayanilla Co., Perpetuo Socorro, c/o Guayanilla, PR, Immaculate Conception. (PCE)
Magdalena, NM, Socorro Co., c/o Socorro, NM, San Miguel. (SFE)
Mageetown, PA, Crawford Co., Immaculate Conception, c/o Titusville, PA, St. Titus. (E)
Magnolia, AR, Columbia Co., Immaculate Heart of Mary, c/o Camden, AR, St. Louis. (LR)
Magnolia, MS, Pike Co., St. James, c/o Chatawa, MS, St. Teresa. (JKS)
Majuro Atoll, MH, Laura, c/o Majuro, MH, Cathedral of the Assumption. (MI)
Malaga, CA, Fresno Co., Christ the King, c/o Fresno, CA, St. Anthony Claret. (FRS)
Malaga, NM, Eddy Co., Cristo Rey, c/o Loving, NM, Our Lady of Grace. (LSC)
Malpaso–Cesar Ruiz, PR, Inmaculada Concepcion, c/o Aguada, PR, St. Francis of Assisi. (MGZ)
Mamey, PR, Perpetuo Socorro, c/o Aguada, PR, St. Francis of Assisi. (MGZ)
Manahawkin, NJ, Ocean Co., St. Mary of the Pines, c/o Barnegat, NJ, St. Mary. (TR)
Manassa, CO, Conejos Co., St. Therese of the Child Jesus, c/o Capulin, CO, St. Joseph. (PBL)
Manchester, KY, Clay Co., St. Ann, c/o London, KY, St. William. (LEX)
Manderson, SD, Shannon Co., Sacred Heart, (Wounded Knee), c/o Manderson, SD, St. Agnes. (RC)
Mani, PR, Infant of Prague, c/o Mayaguez, PR, Our Lady of Mt. Carmel. (MGZ)
Manito, IL, Mason Co., Immaculate Conception, c/o Havana, IL, St. Patrick's. (PEO)
Manitou Springs, CO, El Paso Co., Our Lady of Perpetual Help, c/o Colorado Springs, CO, Sacred Heart. (COS)
Mannford, OK, Creek Co., Our Lady of the Lake, c/o Sand Springs, OK, St. Patrick's. (TLS)
Manning, SC, Clarendon Co., Our Lady of Hope Mission, c/o Summerton, SC, St. Mary. (CHR)
Mansfield, WA, Douglas Co., St. Mary, c/o Chelan, WA, St. Francis de Sales. (YAK)
Manu'a Island, AS, Mary, Star of the Sea, c/o Pago Pago, AS, Cathedral of the Holy Family. (SPP)
Many, LA, Sabine Parish, St. Terence, c/o Many, LA, St. John the Baptist. (SHP)
Many Farms, AZ, Apache Co., St. Anthony, c/o Chinle, AZ, Our Lady of Fatima. (GLP)
Manzano, NM, Torrance Co., c/o Mountainair, NM, St. Alice. (SFE)
Maple, NC, Currituck Co., St. Katharine Drexel, c/o Elizabeth City, NC, Holy Family. (R)
Marak, TX, Milam Co., Ss. Cyril & Methodius, c/o Burlington, TX, St. Joseph. (AUS)
Marana, AZ, Pima Co., San Juan Bautista, c/o Tucson, AZ, Blessed Kateri Tekakwitha Roman Catholic Missions Parish – Tucson. (TUC)
Marathon, TX, Brewster Co., St. Mary, c/o Alpine, TX, Our Lady of Peace. (ELP)
Marcellus, MI, Cass Co., St. Margaret Mary, c/o Mattawan, MI, St. John Bosco. (KAL)
Marengo, IN, Crawford Co., St. Joseph, c/o Depauw, IN, St. Bernard Catholic Church, Frenchtown, Inc. (IND)
Marenisco, MI, Gogebic Co., St. Catherine, c/o Wakefield, MI, Immaculate Conception of the Blessed Virgin Mary. (MAR)
Maresua, PR, Gruta de Lourdes, c/o San German, PR, San German de Auxerre. (MGZ)
Marianna, AR, Lee Co., St. Andrew, c/o Helena, AR, St. Mary. (LR)
Marias, PR, Asuncion de Maria, c/o Aguada, PR, St. Francis of Assisi. (MGZ)
Maricopa, AZ, Pinal Co., St. Francis, c/o Sacaton, AZ, St. Peter. (PHX)
Marienville, PA, Forest Co., St. Ann, c/o Crown, PA, St. Mary. (E)
Marietta, OK, Good Shepherd, c/o Madill, OK, Holy Cross Church. (OKL)
Marion, NC, McDowell Co., Our Lady of the Angels, c/o Morganton, NC, St. Charles Borromeo. (CHL)
Marion, SC, Marion Co., Infant Jesus, c/o Dillon, SC, St. Louis. (CHR)
Marion, TX, Guadalupe Co., Immaculate Conception, c/o Schertz, TX, Church of the Good Shepherd. (SAT)
Marked Tree, AR, St. Norbert, c/o Blytheville, AR, Immaculate Conception. (LR)
Markham, TX, Matagorda Co., St. Robert, c/o Blessing, TX, St. Peter's. (VIC)
Marksville, LA, Avoyelles Parish, St. Richard, c/o Marksville, LA, Holy Ghost. (ALX)
Marlow, OK, Stephens Co., Immaculate Conception, c/o Duncan, OK, Assumption. (OKL)
Marshfield, MA, Plymouth Co., St. Theresa's, c/o Marshfield, MA, St. Christine. (BO)
Marshfield, VT, Washington Co., North American Martyrs, c/o Montpelier, VT, St. Augustine. (BUR)
Mascotte, FL, Mission Outreach – Santo Toribio Romo, c/o Clermont, FL, Blessed Sacrament. (ORL)
Masefau, AS, c/o Pago Pago, AS, St. Peter Chanel–Sa'ilele. (SPP)
Mason, TX, Mason Co., St. Joseph, c/o Llano, TX, Holy Trinity Catholic Church – Llano, Texas. (AUS)
Mason, WV, Mason Co., St. Joseph, c/o Point Pleasant, WV, Sacred Heart. (WH)
Matador, TX, Motley Co., Our Lady of Guadalupe, c/o Floydada, TX, St. Mary Magdalen. (LUB)
Mattituck, NY, Suffolk Co., Our Lady of Good Counsel, c/o Cutchogue, NY, Sacred Heart. (RVC)
Maupin, OR, Wasco Co., St. Mary, c/o Dufur, OR, St. Alphonsus. (BAK)
Mayaguez, PR, Corpus Christi, c/o Mayaguez, PR, Nuestra Senora De Fatima. (MGZ)
Mayaguez, PR, Cristo Rey, c/o Mayaguez, PR, Nuestra Senora De Fatima. (MGZ)
Mayaguez, PR, El Cristo de Los Milagros, c/o Mayaguez, PR, Church De El Buen Pastor. (MGZ)
Mayaguez, PR, Espiritu Santo, c/o Mayaguez, PR, Nuestra Senora De Fatima. (MGZ)
Mayaguez, PR, Maria Socorro de los Cristianos, c/o Mayaguez, PR, Cathedral of Our Lady of Purification. (MGZ)
Mayaguez, PR, Santa Ana, c/o Mayaguez, PR, Cathedral of Our Lady of Purification. (MGZ)
Mayaguez, PR, Sta. Teresita, c/o Mayaguez, PR, Church De El Buen Pastor. (MGZ)
Mayetta, KS, Jackson Co., Our Lady of the Snows Oratory, c/o Holton, KS, St. Dominic. (KCK)
Mayo, FL, Lafayette Co., Our Lady of Guadalupe, c/o Live Oak, FL, St. Francis Xavier. (STA)
Maysville, MO, DeKalb Co., St. Aloysius, c/o Cameron, MO, St. Munchin. (KC)
Mc Cool Junction, NE, York Co., St. Patrick's, c/o Exeter, NE, St. Stephen's. (LIN)
McCartys, NM, Cibola Co., Santa Maria de Acoma, c/o Pueblo of Acoma, NM, San Esteban, Acoma Catholic Indian Mission. (GLP)
McCook, NE, Red Willow Co., Sacred Heart, c/o McCook, NE, St. Patrick. (LIN)
McCook, NE, Red Willow Co., St. Ann's, c/o McCook, NE, St. Patrick. (LIN)
McCrory, AR, Woodruff Co., St. Mary, c/o Wynne, AR, St. Peter. (LR)
McDermitt, NV, Humboldt Co., Sacred Heart, c/o Winnemucca, NV, St. Paul. (RNO)
McKee, KY, Jackson Co., St. Paul, c/o Berea, KY, St. Clare. (LEX)
McLoud, OK, Saint Vincent de Paul Church, c/o Harrah, OK, St. Teresa of Avila. (OKL)
McRoberts, KY, Letcher Co., Holy Angels, c/o Jenkins, KY, St. George. (LEX)
Meadville, MS, Franklin Co., St. Ann, c/o Brookhaven, MS, St. Francis. (JKS)
Medanales, NM, Rio Arriba Co., c/o Abiquiu, NM, St. Thomas Apostle. (SFE)
Medicine Lake, MT, Sheridan Co., St. Patrick, c/o Plentywood, MT, St. Joseph. (GF)
Medicine Root, SD, Shannon Co., St. Stephens, c/o Pine Ridge, SD, Our Lady of Sorrows. (RC)
Meeker, OK, Lincoln Co., St. Michael, c/o Prague, OK, St. Wenceslaus, National Shrine of the Infant Jesus of Prague. (OKL)
Meeteetse, WY, Park Co., St. Therese, c/o Cody, WY, St. Anthony. (CHY)
Melendez, PR, Coamo Co., Our Lady of Providence, c/o Coamo, PR, St. Blase. (PCE)
Melrose, MT, Silver Bow Co., St. John The Apostle, c/o Dillon, MT, St. Rose of Lima. (HEL)
Melrose, NM, Curry Co., c/o Clovis, NM, Sacred Heart. (SFE)
Melstone, MT, Musselshell Co., Our Lady of Mercy, c/o Roundup, MT, St. Benedict. (GF)
Melvin, TX, McCullogh Co., St. Francis Xavier, c/o Brady, TX, St. Patrick's. (SAN)
Mercersburg, PA, Franklin Co., St. Luke the Evangelist, c/o Greencastle, PA, St. Mark the Evangelist. (HBG)
Mereta, TX, Tom Green Co., Holy Family, c/o Wall, TX, St. Ambrose. (SAN)
Merkel, TX, Taylor Co., Our Mother of Mercy, c/o Abilene, TX, St. Vincent Pallotti. (SAN)
Merrill, IA, Plymouth Co., St. Joseph at Ellendale, c/o Merrill, IA, Assumption Church. (SC)
Mertzon, TX, Irion Co., St. Peter's, c/o Eldorado, TX, Our Lady of Guadalupe. (SAN)
Mesa de Poleo, NM, Rio Arriba Co., c/o Abiquiu, NM, St. Thomas Apostle. (SFE)
Mesita, NM, Valencia Co., Sacred Heart, c/o Laguna, NM, St. Joseph. (GLP)
Mesquite, NM, Dona Ana Co., Our Lady of Perpetual Help, c/o San Miguel, NM, San Miguel. (LSC)
Metter, GA, Candler Co., Holy Family, c/o Swainsboro, GA, Holy Trinity. (SAV)
Meyers Chuck, AK, c/o Craig, AK, St. John by the Sea. (JUN)
Meyersdale, PA, Somerset Co., St. Mary's, c/o Salisbury, PA, St. Michael's. (ALT)
Miami, FL, La Milagrosa, c/o Miami, FL, Corpus Christi. (MIA)
Miami, FL, Nuestra Senora de Altagracia, c/o Miami, FL, Corpus Christi. (MIA)
Miami, FL, San Francisco y Santa Clara, c/o Miami, FL, Corpus Christi. (MIA)
Miami, FL, San Juan Bautista, c/o Miami, FL, Corpus Christi. (MIA)
Miami, FL, St. Robert Bellarmine, c/o Miami, FL, Corpus Christi. (MIA)
Michigan City, IN, La Porte Co., Maronite Catholic Community, c/o Lombard, IL, Our Lady of Lebanon Maronite Catholic Church. (OLL)
Michigan City, IN, Sacred Heart, c/o Michigan City, IN, St. Mary of the Immaculate Conception. (GRY)
Mico, TX, Medina Co., St. Francis of Assisi (Medina Lake Chapel), c/o Castroville, TX, St. Louis. (SAT)
Middle River, MN, Marshall Co., St. Joseph, c/o Greenbush, MN, Blessed Sacrament. (CR)
Middlebourne, WV, Tyler Co., St. Lawrence, c/o Paden City, WV, Mater Dolorosa. (WH)
Middlesboro, KY, St. Anthony, c/o Middlesboro, KY, St. Julian. (LEX)
Middletown, PA, Susquehanna Co., St. Patrick, c/o Friendsville, PA, St. Francis Xavier. (SCR)
Midkiff, TX, Upton Co., St. Thomas, c/o Garden City, TX, St. Lawrence. (SAN)
Midland, LA, St. Aloysius, c/o Morse, LA, Immaculate Conception. (LAF)
Mifflinburg, PA, Union Co., Saint George Church, c/o Lewisburg, PA, Sacred Heart of Jesus. (HBG)
Mifflintown, PA, St. Jude Thaddeus, c/o Mifflintown, PA, St. Jude. (HBG)
Milagro, NM, Guadalupe Co., c/o Santa Rosa, NM, St. Rose of Lima. (SFE)
Milan, TN, Northern Gibson Co., c/o Humboldt, TN, Sacred Heart. (MEM)
Mildred, PA, Sullivan Co., St. Francis of Assisi, c/o Dushore, PA, Immaculate Heart of Mary Parish. (SCR)
Milesville, SD, Haakon Co., St. Mary, c/o Philip, SD, Sacred Heart. (RC)
Milford Center, OH, Union Co., Sacred Heart, c/o Plain City, OH, St. Joseph. (COL)
Mill City, OR, St. Catherine of Siena, c/o Stayton, OR, Immaculate Conception. (P)
Mill Rift, PA, Pike Co., Holy Family, c/o Matamoras, PA, St. Joseph. (SCR)
Mill River, MA, Berkshire Co., Immaculate Conception, c/o Sheffield, MA, Our Lady of the Valley. (SPR)
Millen, GA, Jenkins Co., St. Bernadette, c/o Sylvania, GA, Our Lady of the Assumption. (SAV)
Millersview, TX, Concho Co., Our Lady of Guadalupe, c/o Eden, TX, St. Charles. (SAN)
Millerton, NY, Dutchess Co., St. Patrick, c/o Amenia, NY, Immaculate Conception. (NY)
Milligan, NE, Fillmore Co., St. Wenceslaus, c/o Friend, NE, St. Joseph's. (LIN)
Millington, MI, Tuscola Co., St. Bernard, c/o Vassar, MI, St. Frances Xavier Cabrini. (SAG)
Millsboro, DE, Sussex Co., Mary Mother of Peace, c/o Georgetown, DE, St. Michael the Archangel. (WIL)
Millwood, NY, Westchester Co., Our Lady of the Wayside, c/o Briarcliff Manor, NY, St. Theresa. (NY)
Milolii, HI, Honaunau Co., St. Peter, c/o Captain Cook, HI, St. Benedict. (HON)
Milwaukee, WI, Milwaukee Co., St. John's Chapel, c/o Milwaukee, WI, All Saints. (MIL)
Minerva, KY, Mason Co., St. James, c/o Maysville, KY, St. Patrick. (COV)
Minot, ND, Ward Co., St. Michael, c/o Wilton, ND, SS. Peter and Paul. (STN)
Miraflores, PR, Chapel of Our Lady of Perpetual Help, c/o Anasco, PR, St. Anthony Abbot. (MGZ)
Mirando City, TX, Jim Hogg Co., St. Agnes, c/o Hebbronville, TX, Our Lady of Guadalupe. (LAR)
Mission, SD, Todd Co., St. Thomas, c/o St. Francis, SD, St. Francis Mission/Rosebud Educational Society. (RC)
Mission, TX, Hidalgo Co., Our Lady of Fatima, c/o Mission, TX, San Cristobal Magallanes & Companions. (BWN)
Mission, TX, Hidalgo Co., Our Lady of Lourdes, c/o Mission, TX, San Cristobal Magallanes & Companions. (BWN)
Moch, FM, c/o Chuuk, FM, Mortlock. (CI)
Modesto, CA, Stanislaus Co., Ntra. Senora de Guadalupe, c/o Ceres, CA, St. Jude Church (Pastor of). (STO)
Mogotes, La Milagrosa, c/o Yauco, PR, Holy Rosary. (PCE)
Mokelumne Hill, CA, Calaveras Co., St. Thomas Aquinas, c/o San Andreas, CA, St. Andrew Church of San Andreas (Pastor of). (STO)
Monarch, MT, Cascade Co., St. Clement, c/o Belt, MT, St. Mark the Evangelist. (GF)
Moncla, LA, Avoyelles Parish, St. John the Baptist, c/o Deville, LA, St. John the Baptist. (ALX)
Monet Ferry, LA, Natchitoches Parish, Holy Family, c/o Cloutierville, LA, St. John the Baptist. (ALX)
Mongaup Valley, NY, Sullivan Co., St. Joseph, c/o Monticello, NY, St. Peter. (NY)

Monroe, NY, Sacred Heart Chapel, c/o Monroe, NY, Sacred Heart Church. (NY)
Monroeville, AL, Wilcox Co., Mission of Annunciation Parish, c/o Monroeville, AL, St. Joseph. (MOB)
Monte Alto, TX, Hidalgo Co., Christ the King, c/o Elsa, TX, Sacred Heart. (BWN)
Monte Aplanado, NM, Mora Co., c/o Mora, NM, St. Gertrude. (SFE)
Monte Cristo, Hidalgo Co., TX, Capilla Santa Cecilia, c/o Alton, TX, San Martin de Porres. (BWN)
Monte Grande, PR, St. Jude Thaddeus, c/o Cabo Rojo, PR, St. Michael. (MGZ)
Monte Rio, CA, St. Catherine, c/o Guerneville, CA, St. Elizabeth. (SR)
Montecello, NM, Sierra Co., St. Ignatius, c/o Truth or Consequences, NM, Our Lady of Perpetual Help. (LSC)
Monterey, MA, Berkshire Co., Our Lady of the Hills, c/o Sheffield, MA, Our Lady of the Valley. (SPR)
Montesano, WA, Grays Harbor Co., St. John, c/o Elma, WA, St. Joseph. (SEA)
Montezuma, GA, Macon Co., St. Michael, c/o Cordele, GA, St. Theresa. (SAV)
Montgomery, AL, Montgomery Co., Resurrection Catholic Mission, c/o Montgomery, AL, Resurrection Catholic Church. (MOB)
Montgomery, LA, Grant Parish, St. Patrick, c/o Colfax, LA, St. Joseph. (ALX)
Montgomery Center, VT, Franklin Co., St. Isidore, c/o Richford, VT, All Saints. (BUR)
Monticello, MS, Lawrence Co., St. Lawrence, c/o Bassfield, MS, St. Peter. (BLX)
Monument, OR, Grant Co., St. Anne, c/o John Day, OR, St. Elizabeth. (BAK)
Moody, TX, McLennan Co., Our Lady of San Juan, c/o McGregor, TX, St. Eugene Catholic Church – McGregor, Texas. (AUS)
Moorcroft, WY, Crook Co., St. Patrick, c/o Gillette, WY, St. Matthew's. (CHY)
Moore, MT, Fergus Co., St. Mathias, c/o Stanford, MT, St. Rose of Lima. (GF)
Moore, TX, Frio Co., St. Augustine, c/o Devine, TX, St. Joseph's. (SAT)
Mooreland, OK, Woodward Co., Sacred Heart, c/o Woodward, OK, St. Peter's. (OKL)
Moquino, NM, Valencia Co., Santa Rosalia, c/o Seboyeta, NM, Our Lady of Sorrows. (GLP)
Moretown, VT, Washington Co., St. Patrick, c/o Waterbury, VT, St. Andrew. (BUR)
Morgan City, LA, St. Mary Parish, St. Rosalie, c/o Morgan City, LA, Holy Cross. (HT)
Morning View, KY, Kenton Co., Assumption of the Blessed Virgin, c/o Morning View, KY, St. Matthew. (COV)
Morrill, NE, Scotts Bluff Co., St. Ann, c/o Mitchell, NE, St. Theresa's. (GI)
Morrison Bluff, AR, Logan Co., SS. Peter & Paul Church, c/o Scranton, AR, St. Ignatius. (LR)
Morristown, SD, Corson Co., Sacred Heart, c/o Lemmon, SD, St. Mary's. (RC)
Moses, NM, Union Co., Sacred Heart, c/o Clayton, NM, St. Francis Xavier. (SFE)
Mount Ida, AR, Montgomery Co., All Saints, c/o Mena, AR, St. Agnes. (LR)
Mount Pulaski, IL, Logan Co., St. Thomas Aquinas, c/o Lincoln, IL, St. Patrick. (PEO)
Mount Vernon, AL, Mobile Co., St. Theresa, c/o Citronelle, AL, St. Thomas. (MOB)
Mountain View, AR, Stone Co., St. Mary Church, c/o Mountain Home, AR, St. Peter the Fisherman. (LR)
Moxham, PA, Cambria Co., St. Anne's, c/o Johnstown, PA, St. Therese of the Child Jesus. (ALT)
Mt. Palatine, IL, La Salle Co., Immaculate Conception, c/o Wenona, IL, St. Mary's. (PEO)
Mt. Vernon, KY, Rockcastle Co., Our Lady of Mt. Vernon, c/o Berea, KY, St. Clare. (LEX)
Mud Butte, SD, Meade Co., St. Joseph, c/o Faith, SD, St. Joseph. (RC)
Mukilteo, WA, Snohomish Co., St. John, c/o Everett, WA, St. Mary Magdalen. (SEA)
Mulvey, LA, Vermilion Parish, St. David, c/o Gueydan, LA, St. Peter the Apostle. (LAF)
Murphys, CA, Murphys Co., St. Patrick, c/o Angels Camp, CA, St. Patrick Church of Angels Camp (Pastor of). (STO)
Myrtle Point, OR, Coos Co., Sts. Ann and Michael, c/o Coquille, OR, Holy Name. (P)

N

Naco, AZ, Cochise Co., St. Michael, c/o Bisbee, AZ, Saint Patrick Roman Catholic Parish – Bisbee. (TUC)
Nacogdoches, TX, Nacogdoches Co., Immaculate Conception – Moral, c/o Nacogdoches, TX, Sacred Heart. (TYL)
Nacogdoches, TX, Nacogdoches Co., Our Lady of Guadalupe, c/o Nacogdoches, TX, Sacred Heart. (TYL)
Nags Head, NC, Dare Co., Holy Trinity by the Sea Catholic, c/o Kitty Hawk, NC, Holy Redeemer by the Sea. (R)
Naknek, AK, Bristol Bay Borough, St. Theresa, c/o Dillingham, AK, Holy Rosary. (ANC)
Nalcrest, FL, Polk Co., St. Leo the Great, c/o Lake Wales, FL, Holy Spirit. (ORL)
Nama, FM, c/o Chuuk, FM, Mortlock. (CI)
Nambe, NM, Santa Fe Co., c/o Santa Fe, NM, N.S. de Guadalupe del Valle de Pojoaque. (SFE)
Nambe Indian Pueblo, NM, Santa Fe Co., c/o Santa Fe, NM, N.S. de Guadalupe del Valle de Pojoaque. (SFE)
Namoluk, FM, c/o Chuuk, FM, Mortlock. (CI)
Nanuet, NY, Rockland Co., St. Anthony Shrine Church, c/o Nanuet, NY, St. Anthony. (NY)
Nara Visa, NM, Quay Co., Sacred Heart, c/o Tucumcari, NM, St. Anne. (SFE)
Naranjo, PR, Salinas Co., Santa Marta, c/o Salinas, PR, Our Lady of Monserrat. (PCE)
Naranjo, PR, Yauco Co., St. Anthony, c/o Yauco, PR, Holy Rosary. (PCE)
Naranjo Militar, PR, Ntra. Madre de la Consolacion, c/o Aguada, PR, St. Francis of Assisi. (MGZ)
Naranjo–Guanabanas, PR, San Pablo, c/o Aguada, PR, St. Francis of Assisi. (MGZ)
Naschitti, NM, San Juan Co., St. Anthony, c/o Tohatchi, NM, St. Mary Church. (GLP)
Nashport, OH, Muskingum Co., St. Mary, c/o Dresden, OH, St. Ann's. (COL)
Nashua, MT, Valley Co., Queen of the Angels, c/o Glasgow, MT, St. Raphael. (GF)
Nashville, GA, Berrien Co., St. Mary, c/o Adel, GA, Queen of Peace. (SAV)
Nashville, MI, Barry Co., St. Cyril, c/o Hastings, MI, St. Rose of Lima. (KAL)
Natalia, TX, Medina Co., St. John Bosco, c/o Lytle, TX, St. Andrew. (SAT)
Natural Bridge, NY, Jefferson Co., St. Henry, c/o Harrisville, NY, St. Francis Solanus. (OG)
Naubinway, MI, Mackinac Co., St. Stephen, c/o Newberry, MI, St. Gregory. (MAR)
Naukati, AK, c/o Craig, AK, St. John by the Sea. (JUN)
Naytahwaush, MN, Mahnomen Co., St. Anne, c/o Waubun, MN, St. Ann. (CR)
Nebish, MN, Beltrami Co., St. John, c/o Kelliher, MN, St. Patrick. (CR)
Nelson, NE, Nuckolls Co., Sacred Heart, c/o Superior, NE, St. Joseph's. (LIN)
Nenzel, NE, Cherry Co., St. Mary, c/o Valentine, NE, St. Nicholas. (GI)
New Almelo, KS, Norton Co., St. Joseph's Church, c/o Norton, KS, St. Francis of Assisi Parish. (SAL)
New Braunfels, TX, Comal Co., St. John, c/o New Braunfels, TX, Our Lady of Perpetual Help. (SAT)
New Castle, VA, Craig Co., St. John the Evangelist, c/o Fincastle, VA, Church of the Transfiguration. (RIC)
New Deal, TX, Lubbock Co., Our Lady Queen of Apostles, c/o Lubbock, TX, St. Patrick. (LUB)
New Dorp Beach, NY, Richmond Co., Our Lady of Lourdes, c/o Staten Island, NY, Our Lady, Queen of Peace. (NY)
New Germany, PA, Cambria Co., Immaculate Conception, c/o Summerhill, PA, St. John. (ALT)
New Haven, MO, Franklin Co., St. Gerald, c/o New Haven, MO, Holy Family. (STL)
New Hope, TN, Marion Co., Virgin of the Poor Shrine, c/o South Pittsburg, TN, Our Lady of Lourdes. (KNX)
New Iberia, LA, Iberia Parish, St. Jude, c/o New Iberia, LA, St. Edward. (LAF)
New Middletown, IN, Harrison Co., Most Precious Blood, c/o Corydon, IN, St. Joseph Catholic Church, Corydon, Inc. (IND)
New Milford, PA, Susquehanna Co., St. John the Apostle, c/o Great Bend, PA, St. Lawrence. (SCR)
New Orleans, LA, Orleans Civil Parish, Our Lady of Guadalupe, c/o New Orleans, LA, Cathedral – Basilica of St. Louis King of France. (NO)
New Orleans, LA, Orleans Civil Parish, Our Lady of La Vang, c/o New Orleans, LA, Mary, Queen of Vietnam. (NO)
New Orleans, LA, Orleans Civil Parish, St. Joseph, c/o Marrero, LA, St. Agnes Le Thi Thanh. (NO)
New Orleans, LA, St. Mary Assumption, c/o Sheboygan, WI, Immaculate Conception. (MIL)
New York, NY, Chapel of the Resurrection, c/o New York, NY, Church of the Resurrection. (NY)
New York, NY, New York Co., Chapel of the Sacred Hearts of Jesus and Mary, c/o New York, NY, St. Stephen and Our Lady of the Scapular. (NY)
New York, NY, Richmond Co., Christ the King, c/o Staten Island, NY, St. Mary of the Assumption. (NY)
New York, NY, Church of the Nativity, c/o New York, NY, St. Teresa. (NY)
New York, NY, New York Co., Resurrection, c/o New York, NY, St. Charles Borromeo. (NY)
New York, NY, New York Co., St. Veronica, c/o New York, NY, Our Lady of Guadalupe at St. Bernard's. (NY)
Newburgh/Roseton, NY, Orange Co., Our Lady of Mercy, c/o Marlboro, NY, St. Mary. (NY)
Newfoundland, PA, Wayne Co., St. Anthony of Padua, c/o Gouldsboro, PA, St. Rita. (SCR)
Newkirk, OK, St. Francis of Assisi, c/o Ponca City, OK, Church of St. Mary. (OKL)
Newport, AR, Jackson Co., St. Cecilia, c/o Batesville, AR, St. Mary. (LR)
Newton, MS, Newton Co., St. Anne, c/o Forest, MS, St. Michael. (JKS)
Newton, PA, Lackawanna Co., St. Benedict, c/o Clarks Summit, PA, Our Lady of the Snows. (SCR)
Newton Falls, NY, St. Lawrence Co., St. Anthony of Padua, c/o Star Lake, NY, St. Hubert. (OG)
Ngcheangl, FM, c/o Palau, PW, Sacred Heart. (CI)
Ngulu, FM, c/o Yap, FM, Queen of Heaven. (CI)
Nicasio, CA, Marin Co., St. Mary, c/o Lagunitas, CA, St. Cecilia. (SFR)
Nicolaus, CA, Sutter Co., St. Boniface, c/o Lincoln, CA, St. Joseph. (SAC)
Niland, CA, Immaculate Heart of Mary, c/o Calipatria, CA, Saint Patrick Catholic Parish Calipatria. (SD)
Ninilchik, AK, St. Peter the Apostle, c/o Homer, AK, St. John the Baptist. (ANC)
No Water, SD, Shannon Co., Our Lady of Good Counsel, c/o Pine Ridge, SD, Holy Rosary/Red Cloud Indian School Inc. (RC)
Noble, LA, Sabine Parish, St. Ann, c/o Zwolle, LA, St. Joseph. (SHP)
Nocatee, FL, De Soto Co., Blessed Juan Diego, c/o Arcadia, FL, St. Paul. (VEN)
Noel, MO, McDonald Co., Nativity of Our Lord, c/o Neosho, MO, St. Canera. (SPC)
Norborne, MO, Carroll Co., Sacred Heart, c/o Carrollton, MO, St. Mary's. (KC)
Nordheim, TX, DeWitt Co., St. Ann's, c/o Yorktown, TX, Holy Cross. (VIC)
Norias Ranch, TX, Kenedy Co., Santa Elena, c/o Sarita, TX, Our Lady of Guadalupe. (CC)
North East, MD, Cecil Co., St. Jude, c/o Elkton, MD, Immaculate Conception. (WIL)
North Eastham, MA, Barnstable Co., Visitation Church, c/o Wellfleet, MA, Our Lady of Lourdes. (FR)
North Fork, CA, Madera Co., St. Joseph the Worker, c/o Oakhurst, CA, Our Lady of the Sierra. (FRS)
North Greenbush, NY, Rensselaer Co., Van Rensselaer Manor, County Nursing Home, c/o Troy, NY, St. Michael the Archangel. (ALB)
North Hollywood, CA, Los Angeles Co., Our Lady of Zapopan, c/o Sun Valley, CA, Our Lady of the Holy Rosary. (LA)
North Powder, OR, Union Co., St. Anthony, c/o La Grande, OR, Our Lady of the Valley. (BAK)
North Salem, NY, Westchester Co., St. John, c/o Croton Falls, NY, St. Joseph. (NY)
Northbrook, IL, Mission of the Holy Ghost, c/o Chicago, IL, Archdiocese of Chicago's Joseph Cardinal Bernardin Archives and Records Center. (CHI)
Northland, MI, Marquette Co., St. Joseph, c/o Gwinn, MI, St. Anthony. (MAR)
Northwood, NH, Rockingham Co., St. Joseph, c/o Pittsfield, NH, Our Lady of Lourdes. (MAN)
Norton, VT, Essex Co., St. Bernard, c/o Island Pond, VT, St. James the Greater. (BUR)
Norwich, VT, Windsor Co., St. Francis of Assisi, c/o Bradford, VT, Our Lady of Perpetual Help. (BUR)
Novinger, MO, Adair Co., St. Rose of Lima, c/o Kirksville, MO, Mary Immaculate. (JC)
Nowata, OK, Nowata Co., St. Catherine, c/o Dewey, OK, Our Lady of Guadalupe. (TLS)
Noxon, MT, c/o Thompson Falls, MT, St. William. (HEL)
Nucla, CO, Our Lady of Sorrows, c/o Telluride, CO, St. Patrick. (PBL)
Nunam Iqua, AK, St. Peter Catholic Church Nunam Iqua, c/o Alakanuk, AK, St. Ignatius Catholic Church Alakanuk. (FBK)

O

O'Connor Ranch, TX, Refugio Co., St. Dennis, c/o Tivoli, TX, Our Lady of Guadalupe. (CC)
Oak Beach, NY, Suffolk Co., c/o Babylon, NY, St. Joseph. (RVC)
Oak Creek, CO, Routt Co., St. Martin of Tours, c/o Steamboat Springs, CO, Holy Name. (DEN)
Oak Grove, MO, Jackson Co., St. Jude the Apostle, c/o Odessa, MO, St. George. (KC)
Ocala, FL, Guadalupe Catholic Mission, c/o Ocala, FL, Blessed Trinity. (ORL)
Ocala National Forest, FL, Marion Co., St. Joseph of the Forest, c/o Ocala, FL, Our Lady of the Springs. (ORL)
Ocate, NM, Mora Co., c/o Wagon Mound, NM, Santa Clara. (SFE)
Ocean City, MD, Worcester Co., Holy Savior, c/o Ocean City, MD, St. Mary, Star of the Sea. (WIL)
Oceano, CA, San Luis Obispo Co., St. Francis of Assisi, c/o Arroyo Grande, CA, St. Patrick. (MRY)
Oceanside, CA, San Diego Co., Mission San Luis Rey De Francia, c/o Oceanside, CA, Mission San Luis Rey Catholic Parish. (SD)

Odell, NE, Gage Co., St. Mary's, c/o Wymore, NE, St. Mary's. (LIN)
Odessa, TX, Ector Co., Our Lady of San Juan, c/o Odessa, TX, St. Elizabeth Ann Seton. (SAN)
Odessa, TX, Ector Co., St. Martin de Porres, c/o Odessa, TX, St. Joseph. (SAN)
Oglala, SD, Shannon Co., Our Lady of Sioux, c/o Pine Ridge, SD, Holy Rosary/Red Cloud Indian School Inc. (RC)
Oilton, TX, Jim Hogg Co., St. Bridget, c/o Hebbronville, TX, Our Lady of Guadalupe. (LAR)
Ojo Armarillo, NM, San Juan Co., Sacred Heart Missionary Cenacle, c/o Waterflow, NM, Sacred Heart. (GLP)
Ojo Caliente, NM, Rio Arriba Co., c/o El Rito, NM, San Juan Nepomuceno. (SFE)
Ojo Feliz, NM, Mora Co., c/o Mora, NM, St. Gertrude. (SFE)
Ojo Sarco, NM, Rio Arriba Co., Santo Tomas, c/o Chimayo, NM, Holy Family. (SFE)
Okeechobee, FL, Okeechobee Co., St. Theresa of the Child Jesus, c/o Moore Haven, FL, St. Joseph the Worker. (VEN)
Okemah, OK, Okfuskee Co., St. Teresa, c/o Henryetta, OK, St. Stephen's. (TLS)
Oklee, MN, Red Lake Co., St. Francis Xavier, c/o Red Lake Falls, MN, St. Joseph's. (CR)
Okmulgee, OK, Okmulgee Co., Uganda Martyrs, c/o Okmulgee, OK, St. Anthony's. (TLS)
Okreek, SD, Todd Co., St. Peter, c/o St. Francis, SD, St. Francis Mission/Rosebud Educational Society. (RC)
Okreek, SD, Todd Co., St. Peter's, c/o Mission, SD, St. Thomas the Apostle. (RC)
Olcott, NY, St. Charles Borromeo, c/o Newfane, NY, St. Brendan on the Lake. (BUF)
Old River, LA, Natchitoches Parish, St. Anne, c/o Natchez, LA, St. Augustine's. (ALX)
Old Washington, TX, Washington Co., Blessed Virgin Mary Chapel, c/o Somerville, TX, St. Ann. (AUS)
Olean, NE, Colfax Co., Sacred Heart, c/o Dodge, NE, St. Wenceslaus. (OM)
Olean, NY, Cattaraugus Co., Transfiguration, c/o Olean, NY, St. John. (BUF)
Olla, LA, La Salle Parish, St. William, c/o Winnfield, LA, Our Lady of Lourdes. (ALX)
Olmito, TX, Cameron Co., Our Heavenly Father, c/o Brownsville, TX, The Parish of the Lord of Divine Mercy. (BWN)
Olympic Valley, CA, Placer Co., Queen of the Snows, c/o Tahoe City, CA, Corpus Christi. (SAC)
Oneida, PA, Schuykill Co., St. John the Baptist, c/o Sheppton, PA, St. Joseph. (ALN)
Oneop, FM, c/o Chuuk, FM, Mortlock. (CI)
Onset, MA, Plymouth Co., St. Mary Star of the Sea, c/o Buzzards Bay, MA, St. Margaret. (FR)
Opelousas, LA, St. Landry Parish, Christ the King, c/o Grand Coteau, LA, St. Charles Borromeo. (LAF)
Orange Lake, NY, Orange Co., Our Lady of the Lake, c/o Newburgh, NY, St. Patrick. (NY)
Orange Park, FL, Clay Co., Moosehaven Chapel, c/o Orange Park, FL, St. Catherine's. (STA)
Ordway, CO, Crowley Co., St. Peter Chapel, c/o Rocky Ford, CO, St. Peter. (PBL)
Orlando, FL, Orange Co., St. Ignatius Kim Korean Mission, c/o Orlando, FL, St. James Cathedral. (ORL)
Orocovis, PR, Cacao Co., Imm. Concepcion, c/o Orocovis, PR, Our Lady Mother of Divine Providence. (PCE)
Orocovis, PR, Damian Abajo Co., N.S. Monserrate, c/o Orocovis, PR, Our Lady Mother of Divine Providence. (PCE)
Orocovis, PR, Damian Abajo Co., N.S. del Pilar, c/o Orocovis, PR, Our Lady Mother of Divine Providence. (PCE)
Orocovis, PR, Bauta Abajo Co., N.S. del Rosario, c/o Orocovis, PR, Our Lady Mother of Divine Providence. (PCE)
Orocovis, PR, Ala de La Piedra Co., Nino de Praga, c/o Orocovis, PR, Our Lady Mother of Divine Providence. (PCE)
Orocovis, PR, Ala de La Piedra Co., O.L. of Perp. Help, c/o Orocovis, PR, Our Lady Mother of Divine Providence. (PCE)
Orocovis, PR, Cacao Co., Our Lady of Mt. Carmel, c/o Orocovis, PR, Our Lady Mother of Divine Providence. (PCE)
Orocovis, PR, Sacred Heart of Jesus, c/o Orocovis, PR, Our Lady Mother of Divine Providence. (PCE)
Orocovis, PR, Bauta Abajo Co., San Mateo, c/o Orocovis, PR, Our Lady Mother of Divine Providence. (PCE)
Orting, WA, Pierce Co., SS. Cosmas and Damian, c/o Sumner, WA, St. Andrew. (SEA)
Ortiz, CO, Conejos Co., San Juan Nepomuceno y San Cayetano, c/o Antonito, CO, Our Lady of Guadalupe. (PBL)
Osceola, AR, St. Matthew, c/o Blytheville, AR, Immaculate Conception. (LR)
Osceola, MO, St. Clair Co., St. Catherine's, c/o Clinton, MO, Holy Rosary. (KC)
Osceola, NE, Polk Co., St. Mary's, c/o Osceola, NE, St. Vincent Ferrer. (LIN)
Oshkosh, NE, Garden Co., St. Elizabeth, c/o Chappell, NE, St. Joseph's. (GI)
Oslo, MN, Marshall Co., St. Joseph, c/o Warren, MN, SS. Peter and Paul. (CR)
Otis, MA, Berkshire Co., St. Mary of the Lakes, c/o Lee, MA, St. Mary's. (SPR)
Otter Lake, NY, Oneida Co., St. Mary of the Snows, c/o Forestport, NY, St. Patrick. (SY)
Otter River, MA, St. Martin, c/o East Templeton, MA, Holy Cross. (WOR)
Overton, NE, Dawson Co., Holy Rosary, c/o Elm Creek, NE, Immaculate Conception. (GI)
Overton, TX, Rusk Co., Our Lady Queen of Angels, c/o Kilgore, TX, Christ the King. (TYL)
Owasco, NY, Cayuga Co., St. Ann, c/o Auburn, NY, Sacred Heart. (ROC)
Owensboro, KY, Daviess Co., Good Samaritan Refugee Home, c/o Owensboro, KY, SS. Joseph and Paul. (OWN)
Owenton, KY, Owen Co., St. Edward, c/o Warsaw, KY, St. Joseph. (COV)
Owingsville, KY, St. Julie Catholic Church, c/o Morehead, KY, Church of Jesus Our Savior. (LEX)
Owl's Head, NY, Franklin Co., St. Joseph, c/o Malone, NY, St. Helen. (OG)
Oxford, KS, St. Mary's, c/o Winfield, KS, Holy Name. (WCH)
Oxford, NE, Furnas Co., St. Michael's, c/o Orleans, NE, St. Mary's. (LIN)
Oxnard, CA, Ventura Co., Christ the King, c/o Oxnard, CA, Our Lady of Guadalupe Parish. (LA)
Oxnard, CA, Ventura Co., Santa Clara Chapel, c/o Oxnard, CA, Santa Clara. (LA)

P

Paducah, TX, Cottle Co., St. Elizabeth, c/o Floydada, TX, St. Mary Magdalen. (LUB)
Pageland, SC, Chesterfield Co., St. Ernest, c/o Cheraw, SC, St. Peter. (CHR)
Pagosa Junction, CO, Archuleta Co., St. John Baptist, c/o Pagosa Springs, CO, Immaculate Heart of Mary. (PBL)
Paguate, NM, Valencia Co., St. Elizabeth of Hungary, c/o Laguna, NM, St. Joseph. (GLP)
Painesdale, MI, Houghton Co., Sacred Heart, c/o Chassell, MI, St. Anne. (MAR)
Paisley, OR, Lake Co., St. John the Apostle, c/o Lakeview, OR, St. Patrick. (BAK)
Palisade, CO, Mesa Co., St. Ann, c/o Grand Junction, CO, Immaculate Heart of Mary. (PBL)
Palisade, NE, Hitchcock Co., Holy Family, c/o Trenton, NE, St. James. (LIN)
Palito Blanco, TX, Jim Wells Co., St. Joseph, c/o San Diego, TX, St. Francis de Paula. (CC)
Palma Escrita, PR, N.S. de Fatima, c/o Las Marias, PR, Immaculate Heart of Mary. (MGZ)
Palma Sola, PR, Ntra. Sra. de la Asuncion, c/o Canovanas, PR, San Jose. (FAJ)
Palmarejo, PR, Coamo Co., Immaculate Heart of Mary, c/o Coamo, PR, St. Blase. (PCE)
Palmas, PR, Guayama Co., St. Gerard, c/o Guayama, PR, St. Anthony of Padua. (PCE)
Palmer, MI, Marquette Co., Our Lady Perpetual Help, c/o Negaunee, MI, St. Paul. (MAR)
Palmer, PR, Ntra. Sra. de la Providencia, c/o Palmer, PR, Cristo Rey. (FAJ)
Palmetto, LA, St. Landry Parish, St. Thomas, the Apostle, c/o Melville, LA, St. John the Evangelist. (LAF)
Palo Blanco, NM, Colfax Co., c/o Springer, NM, St. Joseph. (SFE)
Panguitch, UT, St. Gertrude, c/o Cedar City, UT, Christ the King LLC 203. (SLC)
Paoli, IN, Orange Co., Our Lord Jesus Christ the King, c/o French Lick, IN, Our Lady of the Springs Catholic Church, French Lick, Inc. (IND)
Parachute, CO, Garfield Co., St. Brendan, c/o Rifle, CO, St. Mary. (DEN)
Paradise, MI, Chippewa Co., Our Lady of Victory, c/o Newberry, MI, St. Gregory. (MAR)
Paradise Valley, NV, Humboldt Co., St. Alphonsus, c/o Winnemucca, NV, St. Paul. (RNO)
Paraje, NM, Valencia Co., St. Margaret Mary, c/o Laguna, NM, St. Joseph. (GLP)
Parcelas Fortuna, PR, Ntra. Sra. del Cobre, c/o Luquillo, PR, San Jose. (FAJ)
Parcelas Suarez, PR, Ntra. Sra. Perpetuo Socorro, c/o Loiza, PR, Santiago Apostol, El Mayor. (FAJ)
Parcelas Vazquez, PR, Salinas Co., Esp. Santo, c/o Salinas, PR, Our Lady of Monserrat. (PCE)
Parcelas Vieques, PR, N. Sra. De Fatima, c/o Loiza, PR, Santiago Apostol, El Mayor. (FAJ)
Parcelas de Marueno, PR, Ponce Co., San Antonio de Padua, c/o Ponce, PR, La Santisima Trinidad. (PCE)
Parem, FM, c/o Chuuk, FM, Sacred Heart. (CI)
Paris, MI, Mecosta Co., St. Anne, c/o Reed City, MI, St. Philip Neri. (GR)
Paris, MO, Monroe Co., St. Frances Cabrini, c/o Perry, MO, St. William. (JC)
Parishville, NY, St. Lawrence Co., St. Michael, c/o Colton, NY, St. Patrick. (OG)
Parks, LA, St. Louis, c/o Parks, LA, St. Joseph. (LAF)
Parmelee, SD, Todd Co., St. Agnes, c/o St. Francis, SD, St. Charles Borromeo. (RC)
Parmelee, SD, Todd Co., St. Agnes, c/o St. Francis, SD, St. Francis Mission/Rosebud Educational Society. (RC)
Parque Encuestre, PR, S. Francisco de Asis, c/o Carolina, PR, Cristo Rey. (SJN)
Parsons, TN, Decatur Co., St. Regina, c/o Lexington, TN, St. Andrew the Apostle. (MEM)
Pastura, NM, Guadalupe Co., c/o Vaughn, NM, St. Mary. (SFE)
Patch Grove, WI, Grant Co., St. John Parish, c/o Bloomington, WI, St. Mary. (MAD)
Patten, ME, Penobscot Co., St. Paul, c/o Houlton, ME, St. Agnes. (PRT)
Paul Smiths, NY, Franklin Co., St. Gabriel, c/o Lake Clear, NY, St. John in the Wilderness. (OG)
Pauls Valley, OK, St. Catherine of Siena, c/o Purcell, OK, Our Lady of Victory. (OKL)
Pava'ia'i, AS, c/o Pago Pago, AS, St. Paul. (SPP)
Pawnee, TX, Bee Co., Our Lady of Guadalupe, c/o Three Rivers, TX, Sacred Heart. (CC)
Paxton, NE, Keith Co., St. Patrick's Church, c/o Ogallala, NE, St. Luke's. (GI)
Pearce, AZ, Cochise Co., St. Francis of Assisi, c/o Pearce, AZ, Saint Jude Thaddeus Roman Catholic Parish – Pearce Sunsites. (TUC)
Pearl, MI, San Felipe de Jesus, c/o Hartford, MI, Immaculate Conception. (KAL)
Pecan Island, LA, Vermilion Parish, Sacred Heart, c/o Abbeville, LA, St. Anne. (LAF)
Peck, MI, Sanilac Co., St. John, c/o Sandusky, MI, St. Joseph. (SAG)
Pedro Garcia, PR, Coamo Co., Miraculous Virgin, c/o Coamo, PR, St. Blase. (PCE)
Pelican, AK, c/o Yakutat, AK, St. Ann. (JUN)
Pellejas, PR, Adjuntas Co., Santa Rosa, c/o Adjuntas, PR, St. Joachim. (PCE)
Pembroke, GA, Bryan Co., Holy Cross, c/o Claxton, GA, St. Christopher. (SAV)
Penitas, TX, Hidalgo Co., St. Anthony, c/o La Joya, TX, Our Lady, Queen of Angels. (BWN)
Pennington, MN, Beltrami Co., St. Charles, c/o Bemidji, MN, St. Philip's. (CR)
Pentwater, MI, Oceana Co., St. Vincent, c/o Hart, MI, St. Joseph's. (GR)
Penuelas, PR, Penuelas Co., Divino Nino, c/o Penuelas, PR, St. Joseph. (PCE)
Penuelas, PR, Penuelas Co., San Martin de Porres, c/o Penuelas, PR, St. Joseph. (PCE)
Pep, TX, Hockley Co., St. Philip Neri, c/o Morton, TX, St. Ann. (LUB)
Perrinton, MI, Gratiot Co., St. Martin De Porres, c/o Ithaca, MI, St. Paul the Apostle. (SAG)
Perry Park, KY, Owen Co., Transfiguration, c/o Carrollton, KY, St. John the Evangelist. (COV)
Perryville, KY, Boyle Co., St. Mary, c/o Harrodsburg, KY, St. Andrew. (LEX)
Peru, NE, Nemaha Co., St. Clara, c/o Auburn, NE, St. Joseph's. (LIN)
Petaca, NM, Taos Co., c/o El Rito, NM, San Juan Nepomuceno. (SFE)
Petersburg, TX, Sacred Heart, c/o Petersburg, TX, St. Isidore. (LUB)
Petersville, MD, Frederick Co., St. Mary's, c/o Brunswick, MD, St. Francis of Assisi. (BAL)
Petrolia, CA, St. Patrick, c/o Ferndale, CA, Church of the Assumption. (SR)
Phelps, KY, Pike Co., Jesus of the Mountains Catholic Church, c/o Pikeville, KY, St. Francis of Assisi. (LEX)
Philadelphia, MS, Neshoba Co., St. Theresa, c/o Philadelphia, MS, Holy Rosary. (JKS)
Philadelphia, NY, Jefferson Co., St. Joseph, c/o Evans Mills, NY, St. Mary. (OG)
Philadelphia, PA, Holy Redeemer Chinese Church, c/o Philadelphia, PA, St. John the Evangelist. (PH)
Philadelphia, PA, Philadelphia Co., St. Nicholas, c/o Philadelphia, PA, Immaculate Conception of Blessed Virgin Mary, Cathedral. (PHU)
Philadelphia, PA, c/o Philadelphia, PA, St. Francis Xavier. (PH)
Phillipsburg, KY, Marion Co., Our Lady of Fatima, c/o Campbellsville, KY, Our Lady of Perpetual Help. (L)
Philo, CA, St. Elizabeth Seton, c/o Fort Bragg, CA, Our Lady of Good Counsel. (SR)
Picacho, NM, Lincoln Co., St. Joseph, c/o Ruidoso, NM, St. Eleanor. (LSC)
Pickens, WV, Randolph Co., Sacred Heart, c/o Buckhannon, WV, Holy Rosary. (WH)
Pickwick Dam, TN, Hardin Co., Our Lady of the Lake, c/o Savannah, TN, St. Mary Church. (MEM)
Picuris Indian Pueblo, NM, Taos Co., San Lorenzo Mission, c/o Penasco, NM, San Antonio de Padua. (SFE)
Piedmont, AL, Calhoun Co., St. Joachim, c/o Jacksonville, AL, St. Charles Borromeo. (BIR)

Piedras Blancas, PR, Ntra. Sra. Reina de la Paz, c/o Aguada, PR, St. Francis of Assisi. (MGZ)
Piedras Blancas, Centro de Espintualidad, Madre de la Consolacion, c/o Aguada, PR, St. Francis of Assisi. (MGZ)
Piis, FM, c/o Chuuk, FM, Mortlock. (CI)
Pilar, NM, Taos Co., Nuestra Senora de los Dolores, c/o Dixon, NM, St. Anthony. (SFE)
Pima, AZ, Graham Co., Pima Mission, c/o Safford, AZ, Saint Rose of Lima Roman Catholic Parish – Safford. (TUC)
Pin Oak, TX, Bastrop Co., St. Mary's in Pin Oak, c/o Giddings, TX, St. Margaret. (AUS)
Pine Bluff, AR, Jefferson Co., St. Mary Plum Bayou, c/o Pine Bluff, AR, St. Joseph. (LR)
Pine Bluff, AR, Jefferson Co., St. Raphael, c/o Pine Bluff, AR, St. Peter. (LR)
Pine Island, NY, Orange Co., St. Stanislaus, c/o Florida, NY, St. Joseph. (NY)
Pine Springs, AZ, Apache Co., St. Rose, c/o Houck, AZ, St. John the Evangelist. (GLP)
Pinedale, CA, Fresno Co., St. Agnes, c/o Fresno, CA, St. Anthony of Padua. (FRS)
Pineville, WV, Wyoming Co., Holy Cross, c/o Mullens, WV, St. John the Evangelist. (WH)
Pinon, AZ, Navajo Co., St. Mary of the Rosary, c/o Chinle, AZ, Our Lady of Fatima. (GLP)
Pinos Altos, NM, Grant Co., Holy Cross, c/o Silver City, NM, St. Vincent de Paul. (LSC)
Pinos Wells, NM, Torrance Co., c/o Vaughn, NM, St. Mary. (SFE)
Pintada, NM, Guadalupe Co., c/o Santa Rosa, NM, St. Rose of Lima. (SFE)
Piqua, KS, Woodson Co., St. Martin, c/o Iola, KS, St. John. (WCH)
Piru, CA, Ventura Co., San Salvador, c/o Fillmore, CA, St. Francis of Assisi. (LA)
Placita, NM, Taos Co., Nuestra Senora de la Asuncion Mission, c/o Penasco, NM, San Antonio de Padua. (SFE)
Placitas, NM, Sierra Co., San Lorenzo, c/o Truth or Consequences, NM, Our Lady of Perpetual Help. (LSC)
Placitas, NM, Sandoval Co., c/o Bernalillo, NM, Our Lady of Sorrows. (SFE)
Placitas, NM, Rio Arriba Co., c/o El Rito, NM, San Juan Nepomuceno. (SFE)
Plain, WI, St. Patrick–Loreto, c/o Lime Ridge, WI, St. Boniface. (MAD)
Plains, TX, Yoakum Co., Sacred Heart, c/o Denver City, TX, St. William. (LUB)
Plainview, NE, St. Paul the Apostle, c/o Pierce, NE, St. Joseph. (OM)
Plainview, SD, Meade Co., Our Lady of Victory, c/o Faith, SD, St. Joseph. (RC)
Plasi, NE, Saunders Co., SS. Cyril and Methodius, c/o Prague, NE, St. John's. (LIN)
Playita, PR, Yabucoa Co., San Martin de Porres, c/o San Juan, PR, San Juan Bosco. (SJN)
Playuela, San Judas Tadeo, c/o Aguadilla, PR, La Milagrosa. (MGZ)
Pleasanton, NE, Buffalo Co., St. Mary's, c/o Ravenna, NE, Our Lady of Lourdes. (GI)
Pleasantville Park, NY, Westchester Co., Our Lady of Pompeii, c/o Pleasantville, NY, Holy Innocents. (NY)
Plena, PR, Salinas Co., San Jose, c/o Salinas, PR, Our Lady of Monserrat. (PCE)
Plevna, MT, Fallon Co., St. Anthony, c/o Baker, MT, St. John the Evangelist. (GF)
Plum Island, MA, St. James, c/o Newburyport, MA, Immaculate Conception. (BO)
Plush, OR, Lake Co., St. Thomas, c/o Lakeview, OR, St. Patrick. (BAK)
Plymouth, CA, Amador Co., St. Mary of the Mountains, c/o Jackson, CA, Immaculate Conception. (SAC)
Plymouth Meeting, PA, Montgomery Co., Our Lady of Mount Carmel, c/o Norristown, PA, Holy Saviour. (PH)
Pohnpei, FM, c/o Pohnpei, FM, Sacred Heart. (CI)
Point Comfort, TX, Calhoun Co., St. Ann, c/o Port Lavaca, TX, Our Lady of the Gulf. (VIC)
Pointblank, TX, San Jacinto Co., St. Stephen the Martyr, c/o New Waverly, TX, St. Joseph. (GAL)
Polvadera, NM, Socorro Co., c/o Socorro, NM, San Miguel. (SFE)
Ponce, PR, Cristo de la Misericordia, c/o Ponce, PR, San Jose Obrero. (PCE)
Ponce, PR, Ponce Co., La Dolorosa, c/o Ponce, PR, Christ the King. (PCE)
Ponce, PR, Natra. Sra. de la Medalla Milagrosa, c/o Ponce, PR, San Jose Obrero. (PCE)
Ponce, PR, Ponce Co., Our Lady of Carmel, c/o Mercedita, PR, Church of the Resurrection. (PCE)
Ponce, PR, Ponce Co., Saint Joseph, c/o Mercedita, PR, Church of the Resurrection. (PCE)
Ponce, PR, Ponce Co., San Miguel de los Santos, c/o Ponce, PR, La Santisima Trinidad. (PCE)
Ponce, PR, Ponce Co., San Patricio, c/o Jayuya, PR, Our Lady of Monserrate. (PCE)
Ponce, PR, Ponce Co., Santa Teresita, c/o Ponce, PR, Christ the King. (PCE)
Pond Creek, OH, Scioto Co., Holy Trinity, c/o West Portsmouth, OH, Our Lady of Sorrows. (COL)
Pond Creek, OK, Grant Co., St. Joseph's, c/o Medford, OK, St. Mary's. (OKL)
Pond Eddy, NY, Sullivan Co., Sacred Heart, c/o Yulan, NY, St. Anthony of Padua. (NY)
Ponderosa, NM, Sandoval Co., c/o Jemez Pueblo, NM, San Diego Indian Missions. (SFE)
Ponsford, MN, Becker Co., St. Theodore, c/o Ogema, MN, Most Holy Redeemer. (CR)
Pontotoc, MS, Pontotoc Co., St. Christopher, c/o New Albany, MS, St. Francis of Assisi. (JKS)
Poplarville, MS, Pearl River Co., St. Joseph, c/o Lumberton, MS, Our Lady of Perpetual Help. (BLX)
Porcupine, SD, Shannon Co., St. Paul, Sharpes Corner, c/o Porcupine, SD, Church of Christ the King. (RC)
Port Costa, CA, Contra Costa Co., St. Patrick, c/o Crockett, CA, St. Rose of Lima. (OAK)
Port Deposit, MD, Cecil Co., St. Teresa, c/o Perryville, MD, Church of the Good Shepherd. (WIL)
Port Huron, MI, St. Clair Co., Our Lady of Guadalupe Mission, c/o Port Huron, MI, Holy Trinity. (DET)
Port O'Connor, TX, Calhoun Co., St. Joseph, c/o Port Lavaca, TX, Our Lady of the Gulf. (VIC)
Port Orford, OR, Curry Co., St. John the Baptist, c/o Bandon, OR, Holy Trinity. (P)
Port St. Joe, FL, Gulf Co., San Blas Catholic Mission, c/o Port St. Joe, FL, St. Joseph. (PT)
Portales, NM, Roosevelt Co., Thomas More Center, c/o Portales, NM, St. Helen. (SFE)
Portland, PA, Northampton Co., St. Vincent de Paul, c/o Bangor, PA, Our Lady of Good Counsel. (ALN)
Portola Valley, CA, San Mateo Co., Our Lady of the Wayside, c/o Menlo Park, CA, St. Denis. (SFR)
Portville, NY, Oratory of the Sacred Heart, c/o Olean, NY, St. Mary of the Angels. (BUF)
Poston, AZ, Kateri Tekakwitha Indian Mission, c/o Parker, AZ, Sacred Heart Roman Catholic Parish – Parker. (TUC)
Potato Creek, SD, Jackson Co., St. Henry, c/o Pine Ridge, SD, Saint Ignatius Loyola. (RC)
Poughkeepsie, NY, Our Lady of the Rosary Chapel, c/o Poughkeepsie, NY, St. Peter. (NY)
Power, MT, Teton Co., Guardian Angel, c/o Dutton, MT, St. William. (HEL)
Prairie Laurent, LA, St. Landry Parish, St. Jules, c/o Leonville, LA, St. Catherine. (LAF)
Prairie Ronde, LA, St. Landry Parish, Sacred Heart, c/o Lawtell, LA, St. Bridget. (LAF)
Prairie View, AR, Logan Co., St. Meinrad, c/o Scranton, AR, St. Ignatius. (LR)
Prentiss, MS, Jefferson Davis Co., St. Mary's, c/o Bassfield, MS, St. Peter. (BLX)
Princeton, CA, Colusa Co., St. Joseph, c/o Colusa, CA, Our Lady of Lourdes. (SAC)
Proctorsville, VT, Windsor Co., Holy Name of Mary, c/o Ludlow, VT, Annunciation of the Blessed Virgin Mary. (BUR)
Promise, SD, Dewey Co., St. Catherine, c/o Eagle Butte, SD, All Saints. (RC)
Promised Land, PA, Monroe Co., Our Lady of Fatima, c/o Mount Pocono, PA, St. Bernadette. (SCR)
Prudence Island, RI, Newport Co., Our Lady of Prudence, c/o Bristol, RI, St. Mary. (PRO)
Puako, HI, Hawaii Co., Church of the Ascension, Puako, c/o Kamuela, HI, Church of the Annunciation. (HON)
Pueblito del Carmen, PR, Our Lady of Mt. Carmel, c/o Guayama, PR, St. Anthony of Padua. (PCE)
Pueblitos, NM, Valencia Co., c/o Belen, NM, Our Lady of Belen. (SFE)
Puente Blanco, PR, Catano Co., Santo Domingo De Guzman, c/o Catano, PR, San Francisco de Sales. (SJN)
Puerto Nuevo, PR, San Juan Co., Ntra. Sra. de la Caridad, c/o Puerto Nuevo, PR, San Pablo. (SJN)
Puerto Real, PR, Our Lady of Mt. Carmel, c/o Cabo Rojo, PR, St. Michael. (MGZ)
Puerto de Luna, NM, Guadalupe Co., c/o Santa Rosa, NM, St. Rose of Lima. (SFE)
Pulaski, VA, Davis Co., St. Edward, c/o Wytheville, VA, St. Mary the Mother of God. (RIC)
Pulguillas, PR, Coamo Co., Christ the King, c/o Coamo, PR, St. Blase. (PCE)
Punta de Agua, NM, Torrance Co., c/o Mountainair, NM, St. Alice. (SFE)
Punto Oro, PR, Ponce Co., Ntra. Sra. del Pilar, c/o Ponce, PR, San Jose Obrero. (PCE)
Putnam Valley, NY, Putnam Co., North American Martyrs, c/o Cortlandt Manor, NY, St. Columbanus. (NY)
Puuiki, HI, Maui Co., St. Peter, c/o Hana, HI, St. Mary. (HON)

Q

Quartzsite, AZ, Queen of Peace, c/o Parker, AZ, Sacred Heart Roman Catholic Parish – Parker. (TUC)
Quebrada Honda, PR, Guayanilla Co., Nuestra Senora La Milagrosa, c/o Guayanilla, PR, Immaculate Conception. (PCE)
Quebrada Larga, PR, Sgdo. Corazon de Jesus, c/o Aguada, PR, St. Francis of Assisi. (MGZ)
Quebradas, PR, Yauco Co., Sacred Heart, c/o Yauco, PR, Holy Rosary. (PCE)
Quebradas, PR, Guayanilla Co., San Francisco de Asis, c/o Guayanilla, PR, Immaculate Conception. (PCE)
Queenstown, MD, Queen Anne Co., St. Peter, c/o Centreville, MD, Our Mother of Sorrows. (WIL)
Quemado, TX, Maverick Co., Our Lady of Guadalupe, c/o Eagle Pass, TX, Our Lady of Refuge. (LAR)

R

Ragley, LA, St. Pius X Mission, c/o Lake Charles, LA, St. Theodore. (LKC)
Rainsville, NM, Mora Co., c/o Mora, NM, St. Gertrude. (SFE)
Ralls, TX, Crosby Co., St. Joseph, c/o Ralls, TX, St. Michael. (LUB)
Ralph, SD, Harding Co., St. Isidore, c/o Buffalo, SD, St. Anthony. (RC)
Ralston, PA, Lycoming Co., St. Aloysius, c/o Canton, PA, St. Michael. (SCR)
Ramey–Maleza, PR, Los Santos Reyes, c/o San Antonio, PR, San Jose Obrero. (MGZ)
Ramirez, TX, Duval Co., Our Lady of Guadalupe, c/o Premont, TX, St. Theresa of the Infant Jesus. (CC)
Ranchester, WY, Sheridan Co., St. Edmund, c/o Sheridan, WY, Holy Name. (CHY)
Ranchito, TX, Fisher Co., Sacred Heart, c/o Rotan, TX, St. Joseph. (LUB)
Ranchitos, NM, Rio Arriba Co., c/o Ohkay Owingeh, NM, San Juan Bautista. (SFE)
Rancho Murieta, CA, Sacramento Co., St. Vincent de Paul Mission Church, c/o Elk Grove, CA, St. Joseph. (SAC)
Randsburg, CA, Kern Co., Santa Barbara, c/o Ridgecrest, CA, St. Ann. (FRS)
Rangeley, ME, Franklin Co., St. Luke, c/o Oquossoc, ME, Our Lady of the Lakes. (PRT)
Rankin, TX, St. Thomas, c/o Big Lake, TX, St. Margaret of Cortona. (SAN)
Rapid City, SD, Pennington Co., Indian Health Service, Sioux San Hospital and Pennington County Jail, c/o Rapid City, SD, St. Isaac Jogues. (RC)
Raymond, CA, Madera Co., St. Anne, c/o Madera, CA, St. Joachim. (FRS)
Raymond, ME, Cumberland Co., St. Raymond Chapel, c/o Windham, ME, Our Lady of Perpetual Help. (PRT)
Raymond, MS, Hinds Co., Immaculate Conception, c/o Clinton, MS, Holy Savior. (JKS)
Raynesford, MT, Judith Basin Co., St. Mary, c/o Belt, MT, St. Mark the Evangelist. (GF)
Reading, PA, Berks Co., Holy Rosary Chapel, c/o Reading, PA, Holy Rosary. (ALN)
Realitos, TX, Duval Co., Sacred Heart, c/o Benavides, TX, Santa Rosa de Lima. (CC)
Red Cliff, CO, Eagle Co., Our Lady of Mt. Carmel, c/o Minturn, CO, St. Patrick. (DEN)
Red Owl, SD, Meade Co., St. Anthony, c/o Faith, SD, St. Joseph. (RC)
Red River, NM, Taos Co., c/o Questa, NM, St. Anthony. (SFE)
Red Scaffold, SD, Ziebach Co., Sacred Heart, c/o Eagle Butte, SD, All Saints. (RC)
Red Shirt Table, SD, Shannon Co., St. Bernard, c/o Pine Ridge, SD, Holy Rosary/Red Cloud Indian School Inc. (RC)
Reddick, IL, Kankakee Co., St. Mary, c/o Cabery, IL, St. Joseph. (JOL)
Redford, TX, Presidio Co., San Jose, c/o Presidio, TX, Santa Teresa de Jesus. (ELP)
Redwood, TX, Guadalupe Co., St. Joseph, c/o Seguin, TX, Our Lady of Guadalupe. (SAT)
Redwood City, CA, San Mateo Co., San Jose Obrero, c/o Menlo Park, CA, St. Anthony. (SFR)
Reform, AL, Pickens Co., St. Robert, c/o Tuscaloosa, AL, St. Francis of Assisi University Parish. (BIR)
Reidsville, GA, St. Andrew the Apostle, c/o Vidalia, GA, Sacred Heart. (SAV)
Reserve, NM, Catron Co., St. Francis, c/o Reserve, NM, Santo Nino. (GLP)
Reva, SD, Harding Co., Our Lady of the Prairie, c/o Buffalo, SD, St. Anthony. (RC)
Rhinecliff, NY, Dutchess Co., St. Joseph, c/o Rhinebeck, NY, The Good Shepherd. (NY)
Ricardo, TX, Kleberg Co., Sacred Heart, c/o Riviera, TX, Our Lady of Consolation. (CC)
Rices Landing, PA, Greene Co., Sacred Heart, c/o Carmichaels, PA, Our Lady of Consolation. (PIT)
Rich Hill, MO, Bates Co., St. Bridget's, c/o Nevada, MO, St. Mary. (KC)
Richey, MT, Dawson Co., St. Francis de Sales, c/o Circle, MT, St. Francis Xavier. (GF)
Richgrove, CA, Tulare Co., St. Vincent, c/o Delano, CA, St. Mary of the Miraculous Medal. (FRS)
Rico, CO, Immaculate Heart of Mary Chapel, c/o Cortez, CO, St. Rita. (PBL)
Ridgefield, WA, Clark Co., St. Mary of Guadalupe, c/o Battle Ground, WA, Sacred Heart. (SEA)

Ridgeview, SD, Dewey Co., St. Joseph, c/o Eagle Butte, SD, All Saints. (RC)
Riegelwood, NC, Columbus Co., Christ the King, c/o Wilmington, NC, St. Mark. (R)
Riley, NM, Socorro Co., c/o Socorro, NM, San Miguel. (SFE)
Rileyville, PA, Wayne Co., St. Joseph, c/o Honesdale, PA, St. John the Evangelist. (SCR)
Rimersburg, PA, Clarion Co., St. Richard, c/o East Brady, PA, St. Eusebius. (E)
Rincon, NM, Dona Ana Co., Our Lady of All Nations, c/o Hatch, NM, Our Lord of Mercy. (LSC)
Ringgold, LA, Bienville Parish, Blessed Sacrament, c/o Minden, LA, St. Paul. (SHP)
Rio Bravo, TX, Webb Co., Santa Monica Mission, c/o Rio Bravo, TX, Santa Rita de Casia. (LAR)
Rio Canas Abajo, PR, Juana Diaz Co., San Judas, c/o Juana Diaz, PR, St. Raymond Nonato. (PCE)
Rio Chiquito, NM, Rio Arriba Co., Sagrado Corazon, c/o Chimayo, NM, Holy Family. (SFE)
Rio Chiquito, PR, Ponce Co., Nino Jesus de Praga, c/o Ponce, PR, Christ the King. (PCE)
Rio Chiquito, PR, Ponce Co., San Vicente, c/o Ponce, PR, San Vicente–Cantera. (PCE)
Rio Grande, PR, La Milagrosa, c/o Rio Grande, PR, Nuestra Senora del Carmen. (FAJ)
Rio Grande, PR, Ntra. Sra. de Guadalupe, c/o Rio Grande, PR, Nuestra Senora del Carmen. (FAJ)
Rio Grande, PR, Perpetuo Socorro, c/o Aguada, PR, St. Francis of Assisi. (MGZ)
Rio Grande, PR, Sagrado Corazon de Jesus, c/o Rio Grande, PR, Nuestra Senora del Carmen. (FAJ)
Rio Grande–Playa, PR, Ntra. Sra. del Carmen, c/o Aguada, PR, St. Francis of Assisi. (MGZ)
Rio Hondo, PR, San Carlos y San Antonio, c/o Mayaguez, PR, Sacred Heart. (MGZ)
Rio Jueyes, Coamo, PR, Coamo Co., Our Lady of Lourdes, c/o Coamo, PR, San Antonio de Padua. (PCE)
Rio Lucio, NM, Taos Co., Sagrado Corazon Mission, c/o Penasco, NM, San Antonio de Padua. (SFE)
Rio Piedras, PR, San Juan Co., N. Sra. Reina de la Paz, c/o San Juan, PR, Santisimo Salvador. (SJN)
Rio Piedras, PR, San Juan Co., N. Sra. del Rosario, c/o Trujillo Alto, PR, San Pio X. (SJN)
Rio Piedras, PR, San Juan Co., San Jose de Calasanz, c/o San Juan, PR, Santisimo Salvador. (SJN)
Rio Piedras, PR, San Juan Co., Santa Teresita de Nino Jesus, c/o San Juan, PR, Nuestra Senora del Pilar. (SJN)
Rio Rancho, NM, Sandoval Co., St. John Vianney, c/o Rio Rancho, NM, St. Thomas Aquinas. (SFE)
Rio Verde, AZ, Maricopa Co., St. Dominic, c/o Fountain Hills, AZ, Ascension Roman Catholic Parish. (PHX)
Rio en Medio, NM, Santa Fe Co., Our Lady of Sorrows, c/o Santa Fe, NM, Our Lady of Guadalupe. (SFE)
Rios, TX, Duval Co., St. Francis of Assisi, c/o Premont, TX, St. Theresa of the Infant Jesus. (CC)
Ripley, TN, Lauderdale Co., Ave Maria, c/o Covington, TN, St. Alphonsus Church. (MEM)
Rising Sun, MD, Cecil Co., St. Agnes, c/o Perryville, MD, Church of the Good Shepherd. (WIL)
River Forest, IL, St. Thomas Mission, c/o Chicago, IL, Archdiocese of Chicago's Joseph Cardinal Bernardin Archives and Records Center. (CHI)
Riverside, CA, Riverside Co., Our Lady of Guadalupe, c/o Riverside, CA, St. John the Evangelist. (SB)
Riviera, TX, Kleberg Co., Our Lady of Guadalupe, c/o Riviera, TX, Our Lady of Consolation. (CC)
Roanoke, AL, Randolph Co., Immaculate Conception, c/o Lanett, AL, Holy Family. (BIR)
Robbins, IL, Cook Co., St. Peter Claver, c/o Blue Island, IL, St. Benedict. (CHI)
Robbins, NC, Moore Co., Saint Juan Diego, c/o Pinehurst, NC, Sacred Heart. (R)
Robbinsville, NC, Graham Co., Prince of Peace, c/o Andrews, NC, Holy Redeemer. (CHL)
Robert Lee, TX, Coke Co., Our Lady of Guadalupe, c/o Ballinger, TX, St. Mary Star of the Sea. (SAN)
Roberts, IL, Immaculate Conception, c/o Gibson City, IL, Our Lady of Lourdes. (JOL)
Robstown, TX, Nueces Co., St. Mary, c/o Robstown, TX, St. Anthony. (CC)
Robstown, TX, St. Vivian, c/o Corpus Christi, TX, Our Lady of Mount Carmel. (CC)
Roby, MO, Texas Co., St. Vincent de Paul, c/o Houston, MO, St. Mark. (SPC)
Rociada Abajo, NM, San Miguel Co., Santo Nino, c/o Las Vegas, NM, Our Lady of Sorrows Church. (SFE)
Rock City Falls, NY, Saratoga Co., St. Paul, c/o Greenfield Center, NY, St. Joseph. (ALB)
Rock Hall, MD, Kent Co., St. John, c/o Chestertown, MD, Sacred Heart. (WIL)
Rock Point, MD, Charles Co., St. Francis de Sales, c/o Newburg, MD, Holy Ghost. (WDC)
Rockville, NE, Sherman Co., St. Mary's, c/o Ravenna, NE, Our Lady of Lourdes. (GI)
Rockwood, ME, Somerset Co., St. Joseph's, c/o Greenville, ME, Holy Family. (PRT)
Rocky Mount, NC, Nash & Edgecombe Cos., Immaculate Conception, c/o Rocky Mount, NC, Our Lady of Perpetual Help. (R)
Rodarte, NM, Taos Co., Santa Barbara Mission, c/o Penasco, NM, San Antonio de Padua. (SFE)
Rodeo, NM, Hidalgo Co., San Felipe de Neri, c/o Lordsburg, NM, St. Joseph. (LSC)
Roland, OK, Sequoyah Co., Blessed Kateri Tekakwitha, c/o Sallisaw, OK, St. Francis Xavier. (TLS)
Romanum, FM, St. Joseph, c/o Chuuk, FM, St. Francis Assisi. (CI)
Romeo, CO, Conejos Co., Our Lady of the Immaculate Conception, c/o Capulin, CO, St. Joseph. (PBL)
Romero, PR, Villalba Co., Sagrado Corazon, c/o Villalba, PR, Our Lady of Mt. Carmel. (PCE)
Roosevelt, AZ, Gila Co., St. Theresa, c/o Miami, AZ, Our Lady of the Blessed Sacrament Roman Catholic Church – Miami. (TUC)
Ropesville, TX, Hockley Co., San Francisco de Asis, c/o Brownfield, TX, St. Anthony's. (LUB)
Rosario, PR, Nuestra Senora del Rosario, c/o Rosario, PR, Our Lady of Rosary. (MGZ)
Rosario, PR, San Jose, c/o Mayaguez, PR, Sacred Heart. (MGZ)
Roscoe, IL, Winnebago Co., Church of the Holy Spirit, c/o South Beloit, IL, St. Peter. (RCK)
Roscoe, NY, Sullivan Co., Gate of Heaven, c/o Livingston Manor, NY, St. Aloysius. (NY)
Roscoe, TX, Nolan Co., St. Albert the Great, c/o Sweetwater, TX, Immaculate Heart of Mary. (SAN)
Rosebud, SD, Todd Co., St. Bridget, c/o St. Francis, SD, St. Francis Mission/Rosebud Educational Society. (RC)
Round Mountain, NV, St. Barbara, c/o Tonopah, NV, St. Patrick. (LAV)
Round Rock, AZ, Apache Co., Our Lady of Guadalupe, c/o Lukachukai, AZ, St. Isabel. (GLP)
Rowe, NM, San Miguel Co., c/o Pecos, NM, St. Anthony of Padua. (SFE)
Roxbury, CT, Litchfield Co., St. Patrick's, c/o Washington Depot, CT, Our Lady of Perpetual Help. (HRT)
Rushville, NE, Sheridan Co., Immaculate Conception, c/o Gordon, NE, St. Leo's. (GI)
Rushville, NY, Ontario Co., St. Mary, c/o Penn Yan, NY, Our Lady of the Lakes Catholic Community. (ROC)
Rusk, TX, Cherokee Co., Sacred Heart, c/o Jacksonville, TX, Our Lady of Sorrows. (TYL)
Russell, NY, St. Lawrence Co., St. Paul–Pyrites, c/o Canton, NY, St. Mary. (OG)
Russian Mission, AK, Wade Hampton Co., Our Lady of Guadalupe Catholic Church Russian Mission, c/o Marshall, AK, Immaculate Heart of Mary Catholic Church Marshall. (FBK)
Rutherford, CA, Holy Family, c/o Yountville, CA, St. Joan of Arc. (SR)
Rutland, IL, La Salle Co., Sacred Heart, c/o Toluca, IL, St. Ann's. (PEO)
Ryan, OK, Jefferson Co., San Jose, c/o Duncan, OK, Assumption. (OKL)
Rye, CO, Pueblo Co., St. Aloysius, c/o Pueblo, CO, Holy Family. (PBL)
Ryegate, MT, Golden Valley Co., St Mathias, c/o Roundup, MT, St. Benedict. (GF)

S

Sab. Gde, P.R., Divino Nino Jesus, c/o Sabana Grande, PR, Church of San Isidro. (MGZ)
Sabana, PR, San Jose, c/o Aguada, PR, St. Francis of Assisi. (MGZ)
Sabana Eneas, PR, San Judas Tadeo, c/o San German, PR, San German de Auxerre. (MGZ)
Sabana Llana, PR, Salinas Co., Perpetuo Socorro, c/o Salinas, PR, Our Lady of Monserrat. (PCE)
Sabana Seca, PR, San Martin de Porres, c/o Sabana Seca, PR, San Jose Obrero. (SJN)
Sabin, MN, Clay Co., St. Cecilia, c/o Barnesville, MN, Assumption. (CR)
Sabinal, NM, Socorro Co., San Antonio, c/o La Joya, NM, Our Lady of Sorrows. (SFE)
Sabinoso, NM, San Miguel Co., c/o Roy, NM, Holy Family–St. Joseph. (SFE)
Sacaton, AZ, Pinal Co., St. Anthony, c/o Sacaton, AZ, St. Peter. (PHX)
Sacaton Flats, AZ, Pinal Co., Our Lady of Victory, c/o Sacaton, AZ, St. Peter. (PHX)
Saco, MT, Phillips Co., St. Francis of Assisi, c/o Malta, MT, St. Mary. (GF)
Saegertown, PA, Crawford Co., St. Bernadette, c/o Meadville, PA, St. Agatha. (E)
Sagamore, MA, Barnstable Co., St. Theresa, c/o East Sandwich, MA, Corpus Christi. (FR)
Saint Clair, MN, Immaculate Conception, c/o Madison Lake, MN, All Saints. (WIN)
Saipan, MP, Korean Catholic Community, c/o Saipan, MP, Cathedral of Our Lady of Mt. Carmel. (CHK)
Salem, IN, Washington Co., St. Patrick, c/o Scottsburg, IN, Church of the American Martyrs, Scottsburg, Inc. (IND)
Salem, MI, Holy Ascension, c/o Dearborn, MI, St. Michael's. (STN)
Salida, CA, Stanislaus Co., Our Lady of San Juan de los Lagos, c/o Modesto, CA, Holy Family Church (Pastor of). (STO)
Salinas–Providencia, PR, Guanica Co., Divina Providencia, c/o Ensenada, PR, Sacred Heart. (PCE)
Salineno, TX, Starr Co., St. Joseph, c/o Roma, TX, Our Lady of Refuge. (BWN)
Salon Usos Multiples–Urb. April Gardens, PR, Las Piedras, c/o Las Piedras, PR, Inmaculada Concepcion. (CGS)
Saltillo, MS, Lee Co., St. Thomas Aquinas, c/o Tupelo, MS, St. James. (JKS)
Salton Sea Beach, CA, Riverside Co., c/o Borrego Springs, CA, Saint Richard Catholic Parish. (SD)
San Acacio, CO, Costilla Co., San Acacio, c/o San Luis, CO, Sangre de Cristo. (PBL)
San Antonio, CO, Conejos Co., San Antonio de Padua, c/o Antonito, CO, Our Lady of Guadalupe. (PBL)
San Antonio, NM, Socorro Co., c/o Socorro, NM, San Miguel. (SFE)
San Antonio, NM, Bernalillo Co., c/o Tijeras, NM, Holy Child. (SFE)
San Antonio, TX, Bexar Co., Purisima Concepcion, c/o San Antonio, TX, St. Cecilia. (SAT)
San Antonio, TX, Bexar Co., San Francesco di Paola (Italian), c/o San Antonio, TX, Cathedral of San Fernando. (SAT)
San Antonio, TX, Bexar Co., Santa Maria Goretti, c/o San Antonio, TX, St. Jude. (SAT)
San Antonio, TX, Bexar Co., St. Catherine, c/o San Antonio, TX, St. Margaret Mary. (SAT)
San Antonio, TX, Bexar Co., St. Frances Cabrini, c/o San Antonio, TX, San Francisco de la Espada. (SAT)
San Antonio, TX, Bexar Co., St. John Vianney, c/o LaCoste, TX, Our Lady of Grace. (SAT)
San Antonito, NM, Senor de Mapimi, c/o Tijeras, NM, Holy Child. (SFE)
San Ardo, CA, Monterey Co., Our Lady of Ransom, c/o San Miguel, CA, San Miguel. (MRY)
San Augustine, TX, St. Augustin Mission, c/o Hemphill, TX, St. Pius I. (TYL)
San Benito, TX, Cameron Co., St. Joseph, c/o San Benito, TX, Our Lady, Queen of the Universe. (BWN)
San Cristobal, NM, Taos Co., San Cristobal, c/o Arroyo Seco, NM, La Santisima Trinidad. (SFE)
San Diego, CA, San Diego Co., SDSU Newman Center, c/o San Diego, CA, Blessed Sacrament Catholic Parish. (SD)
San Diego, PR, Coamo Co., San Diego, c/o Coamo, PR, St. Blase. (PCE)
San Felipe, NM, Sandoval Co., San Felipe, c/o Pena Blanca, NM, Nuestra Senora De Guadalupe. (SFE)
San Felipe, PR, Salinas Co., St. Martin de Porres, c/o Aguirre, PR, Sacred Heart. (PCE)
San Fernando, PR, San Juan Co., Monacillos, c/o Rio Piedras, PR, Inmaculado Corazon de Maria. (SJN)
San Francisco, CA, San Francisco Co., All Hallows Chapel, c/o San Francisco, CA, Our Lady of Lourdes. (SFR)
San Francisco, CA, San Francisco Co., Dominican Sisters of Mission San Jose, c/o San Francisco, CA, St. James. (SFR)
San Francisco, CO, Costilla Co., St. Francis of Assisi, c/o San Luis, CO, Sangre de Cristo. (PBL)
San Ignacio, NM, Guadalupe Co., c/o Santa Rosa, NM, St. Rose of Lima. (SFE)
San Ignacio, TX, Zapata Co., Our Lady of Refuge, c/o Zapata, TX, Our Lady of Lourdes. (LAR)
San Isidro, CO, Costilla Co., St. Isidro, c/o San Luis, CO, Sangre de Cristo. (PBL)
San Isidro, NM, Dona Ana Co., San Isidro, c/o Dona Ana, NM, Our Lady of the Purification. (LSC)
San Isidro Norte, NM, San Miguel Co., c/o Ribera, NM, San Miguel Del Vado. (SFE)
San Isidro Sur, NM, San Miguel Co., c/o Ribera, NM, San Miguel Del Vado. (SFE)
San Joaquin, CA, Fresno Co., St. Vincent de Paul, c/o Tranquillity, CA, St. Paul. (FRS)
San Jon, NM, Quay Co., Our Lady of Guadalupe, c/o Tucumcari, NM, St. Anne. (SFE)
San Jose, AZ, Graham Co., San Jose, c/o Solomon, AZ, Our Lady of Guadalupe Roman Catholic Parish – Solomon. (TUC)
San Jose, CA, Santa Clara Co., Santee Mission, c/o San Jose, CA, St. Maria Goretti. (SJ)
San Jose, NM, San Miguel Co., c/o Ribera, NM, San Miguel Del Vado. (SFE)
San Jose, PR, Minillas, c/o Bayamon, PR, Nuestra Senora del Rosario. (SJN)
San Jose Ranch, TX, Duval Co., St. Joseph, c/o Benavides, TX, Santa Rosa de Lima. (CC)
San Juan, NM, Grant Co., San Juan, c/o Hurley, NM, Infant Jesus. (LSC)
San Juan, NM, San Miguel Co., c/o Ribera, NM, San Miguel Del Vado. (SFE)
San Juan, PR, Capilla San Conrado, c/o San Juan, PR, San Francisco de Asis. (SJN)
San Juan, PR, Jesus Nazareno, c/o San Juan, PR, Jesus Maestro. (SJN)
San Juan, PR, San Juan Co., La Milagrosa, c/o San Juan, PR, San Juan M. Vianney. (SJN)
San Juan, PR, Bo. Caimito, Medalla Milagrosa, c/o San

Juan, PR, Santa Catalina Laboure. (SJN)
San Juan, PR, Ntra Sra de la Salud, c/o San Juan, PR, Santa Teresa de Jesus Jornet. (SJN)
San Juan, PR, Ntra. Sra. del Rosario, c/o San Juan, PR, San Juan Bosco. (SJN)
San Juan, PR, Nuestra Senora del Buen Consejo, c/o San Juan, PR, San Antonio. (SJN)
San Juan, PR, San Martin de Porres, c/o San Juan, PR, Santa Teresa de Jesus Jornet. (SJN)
San Juan, PR, Bo. Caimito, San Pablo, c/o San Juan, PR, Santa Catalina Laboure. (SJN)
San Juan, TX, Immaculate Conception, c/o San Juan, TX, St. John the Baptist. (BWN)
San Lorenzo, NM, Grant Co., San Lorenzo–Black Range Station, c/o Bayard, NM, Our Lady of Fatima. (LSC)
San Lucas, CA, Monterey Co., St. Luke, c/o King City, CA, St. John the Baptist. (MRY)
San Luis, NM, Sandoval Co., Saint Aloysius Gonzaga, c/o Cuba, NM, Immaculate Conception. (GLP)
San Manuel, TX, Hidalgo Co., St. Anne San Manuel, c/o Edinburg, TX, St. Joseph the Worker. (BWN)
San Marcos, CA, San Diego Co., c/o San Marcos, CA, Saint Mark Catholic Parish. (SD)
San Marcos, TX, Hays Co., Guadalupe Chapel, c/o San Marcos, TX, St. John the Evangelist. (AUS)
San Martin, PR, N. Sra. del Perpetuo Socorro, c/o Luquillo, PR, Madre del Redentor. (FAJ)
San Patricio, NM, Lincoln Co., St. Jude Thaddeus, c/o Ruidoso, NM, St. Eleanor. (LSC)
San Pedro, CO, Costilla Co., SS. Peter and Paul, c/o San Luis, CO, Sangre de Cristo. (PBL)
San Pedro, TX, Cameron Co., San Pedro, c/o Brownsville, TX, The Parish of the Lord of Divine Mercy. (BWN)
San Perlita, TX, Hidalgo Co., St. Anne, Mother of Mary, c/o Raymondville, TX, Our Lady of Guadalupe. (BWN)
San Rafael, CA, Marin Co., St. Sylvester, c/o San Rafael, CA, St. Raphael. (SFR)
San Rafael, CO, Conejos Co., San Pedro y San Rafael, c/o Antonito, CO, Our Lady of Guadalupe. (PBL)
San Simon, AZ, Our Lady of Perpetual Help, c/o Willcox, AZ, Sacred Heart of Jesus Roman Catholic Church – Willcox. (TUC)
San Ysidro, NM, Sandoval Co., c/o Jemez Pueblo, NM, San Diego Indian Missions. (SFE)
Sand Hill, GA, Our Lady of Guadalupe, c/o Claxton, GA, St. Christopher. (SAV)
Sanderson, TX, St. James, c/o Fort Stockton, TX, St. Joseph's. (SAN)
Sandersville, GA, Washington Co., St. William, c/o Dublin, GA, Immaculate Conception. (SAV)
Sandia Indian Pueblo, NM, Sandoval Co., c/o Bernalillo, NM, Our Lady of Sorrows. (SFE)
Sandy Valley, NV, Clark Co., St. Catherine of Siena, c/o Las Vegas, NV, Christ the King. (LAV)
Santa Ana, NM, Sandoval Co., c/o Jemez Pueblo, NM, San Diego Indian Missions. (SFE)
Santa Ana, PR, Coamo Co., Santa Ana, c/o Coamo, PR, St. Blase. (PCE)
Santa Ana, PR, San Juan Co., Trastalleres, c/o San Juan, PR, Ntra. Sra. de la Monserrate. (SJN)
Santa Catalina, PR, Coama Co., Santa Catalina, c/o Coamo, PR, St. Blase. (PCE)
Santa Clara, NY, St. Peter, c/o St. Regis Falls, NY, St. Ann. (OG)
Santa Cruz, CA, Santa Cruz Co., Mision Galeria, c/o Santa Cruz, CA, Holy Cross. (MRY)
Santa Fe, NM, Santa Fe Co., Our Lady of Guadalupe, c/o Santa Fe, NM, Cristo Rey. (SFE)
Santa Isabel, PR, Ntra. Sra. del Carmen, c/o Santa Isabel, PR, St. James. (PCE)
Santa Maria, TX, Cameron Co., St. Margaret Ann, c/o Progreso, TX, Holy Spirit. (BWN)
Santa Monica, TX, Willacy Co., Santa Monica, c/o Lyford, TX, Prince of Peace. (BWN)
Santa Rita, NM, San Miguel Co., c/o Ribera, NM, San Miguel Del Vado. (SFE)
Santa Rosa, PR, Jardines de Carolina, c/o Carolina, PR, San Valentin. (SJN)
Santa Teresa, NM, Dona Ana Co, Santa Teresa de Avila, c/o Sunland Park, NM, St. Martin de Porres. (LSC)
Santan, AZ, Pinal Co., St. Anne, c/o Sacaton, AZ, St. Peter. (PHX)
Santiago–Talco, NM, Mora Co., c/o Mora, NM, St. Gertrude. (SFE)
Santo Domingo, NM, Sandoval Co., Santo Domingo, c/o Pena Blanca, NM, Nuestra Senora De Guadalupe. (SFE)
Santurce, PR, Mayaguez Co., La Milagrosa, c/o San Juan, PR, San Juan Bosco. (SJN)
Sapello, NM, San Miguel Co., Our Lady of Guadalupe, c/o Las Vegas, NM, Our Lady of Sorrows Church. (SFE)
Sapphire, NC, St. Jude, c/o Brevard, NC, Sacred Heart. (CHL)
Saragosa, TX, Reeves Co., Our Lady of Guadalupe, c/o Balmorhea, TX, Christ the King. (ELP)
Saratoga Lake, NY, Saratoga Co., St. Isaac Jogues, c/o Stillwater, NY, Roman Catholic Community of All Saints on the Hudson. (ALB)
Sardis, MS, Panola Co., St. John the Baptist, c/o Batesville, MS, St. Mary. (JKS)
Sargent, NE, Cluster Co., Assumption of the Blessed Virgin Mary, c/o Broken Bow, NE, St. Joseph's. (GI)
Sartwell, PA, McKean Co., St. Mary, c/o Eldred, PA, St. Raphael. (E)
Saspamco, TX, Bexar Co., Our Lady of Perpetual Help, c/o Elmendorf, TX, St. Anthony. (SAT)
Satowan, FM, c/o Chuuk, FM, Mortlock. (CI)
Savage, MT, Richland Co., St. Michael, c/o Sidney, MT, St. Matthew. (GF)
Savannah, NY, Wayne Co., St. Patrick, c/o Clyde, NY, St. John the Evangelist. (ROC)
Savoy, LA, St. Landry Parish, St. Thomas, c/o Church Point, LA, St. Edward. (LAF)
Sawmill, AZ, Apache Co., St. Francis Mission, c/o Navajo, NM, St. Berard. (GLP)
Sawyer, MI, Berrien Co., St. Agnes, c/o Three Oaks, MI, St. Mary of the Assumption. (KAL)
Sawyer's Bar, CA, Siskiyou Co., St. Joseph, c/o Fort Jones, CA, Sacred Heart. (SAC)
Saxtons River, VT, Windham Co., St. Edmund of Canterbury, c/o Putney, VT, Our Lady of Mercy. (BUR)
Sayre, OK, Beckham Co., Queen of All Saints, c/o Elk City, OK, St. Matthew's. (OKL)
Schenevus, NY, Otsego Co., St. Mary, c/o Worcester, NY, St. Joseph. (ALB)
Schoolcraft, NE, Madison Co., St. Francis de Sales, c/o Battle Creek, NE, St. Patrick's. (OM)
Schriever, LA, Vietnam's Martyrs, c/o Morgan City, LA, Thanh Gia. (HT)
Scio, NY, Allegany Co., St. Joseph, c/o Belmont, NY, Holy Family of Jesus, Mary & Joseph. (BUF)
Scotland, CT, Windham Co., St. Margaret, c/o Willimantic, CT, St. Joseph. (NOR)
Scotland Neck, NC, Halifax Co., St. Anne, c/o Ahoskie, NC, St. Charles Borromeo. (R)
Scotts Mills, OR, Marion Co., Holy Rosary, c/o Mount Angel, OR, St. Mary. (P)
Scottsdale, AZ, St. Francis of Assisi, c/o Laveen, AZ, St. John The Baptist. (PHX)
Scottsville, VA, Albemarle Co., St. George's, c/o Charlottesville, VA, Church of the Holy Comforter. (RIC)
Scriba, NY, Oswego Co., Sacred Heart, c/o Oswego, NY, St. Peter. (SY)
Seabrook, NH, St. Elizabeth of Hungary, c/o Hampton, NH, Our Lady of the Miraculous Medal. (MAN)
Seadrift, TX, Calhoun Co., St. Patrick, c/o Port Lavaca, TX, Our Lady of the Gulf. (VIC)
Seagraves, TX, Gaines Co., St. Paul's, c/o Seminole, TX, St. James. (LUB)
Seama, NM, Valencia Co., St. Anne, c/o Laguna, NM, St. Joseph. (GLP)
Seaside, CA, Seaside, Monterey Co., c/o Seaside, CA, St. Francis Xavier. (MRY)
Seattle, WA, Plymouth Congregational Church Chapel, c/o Seattle, WA, Christ Our Hope Personal Parish. (SEA)
Sebastian, TX, Willacy Co., St. Martin, c/o Lyford, TX, Prince of Peace. (BWN)
Seco Mines, TX, Maverick Co., Our Lady of Lourdes, c/o Eagle Pass, TX, Our Lady of Refuge. (LAR)
Sector Brazo Seco, PR, c/o Naguabo, PR, Nuestra Senora del Rosario. (FAJ)
Sector Felipe Quinones Barreal, PR, Penuelas Co., Santa Cruz, c/o Penuelas, PR, St. Joseph. (PCE)
Sector La Cucharilla, PR, Immaculada Concepcion, c/o Catano, PR, San Francisco de Sales. (SJN)
Sector La Fe, PR, c/o Naguabo, PR, Nuestra Senora del Rosario. (FAJ)
Sector Punta Brava, PR, Convento Missioneras de La Caridad, c/o Bayamon, PR, Santa Teresa de Jesus. (SJN)
Sector San Patricio, PR, Ponce Co., La Inmaculada, c/o Ponce, PR, San Vicente–Cantera. (PCE)
Sector Santo Domingo, PR, Penuelas Co., Santo Domingo de Guzman, c/o San Juan, PR, Corpus Christi. (SJN)
Sector la Gelpa – Quebrada Ceiba, PR, Penuelas Co., La Milagrosa, c/o Penuelas, PR, St. Joseph. (PCE)
Sedillo, NM, Bernalillo Co., San Isidro, c/o Tijeras, NM, Holy Child. (SFE)
Seeley Lake, MT, Missoula Co., Living Water, c/o Bonner, MT, St. Ann. (HEL)
Segundo, CO, Las Animas Co., St. Ignatius, c/o Trinidad, CO, Most Holy Trinity. (PBL)
Seiling, OK, Dewey Co., St. Thomas, c/o Okeene, OK, St. Anthony's. (OKL)
Seldovia, AK, St. James the Apostle, c/o Homer, AK, St. John the Baptist. (ANC)
Selinsgrove, PA, Snyder Co., Selinsgrove Center, c/o Selinsgrove, PA, St. Pius X. (HBG)
Selinsgrove, PA, Snyder Co., Snyder County Prison, c/o Selinsgrove, PA, St. Pius X. (HBG)
Selinsgrove, PA, Snyder Co., Susquehanna University, c/o Selinsgrove, PA, St. Pius X. (HBG)
Sena, NM, San Miguel Co., c/o Villanueva, NM, Our Lady of Guadalupe. (SFE)
Seneca, OR, Grant Co., St. Charles, c/o John Day, OR, St. Elizabeth. (BAK)
Seneca, SC, Oconee Co., St. Paul the Apostle, c/o Clemson, SC, St. Andrew. (CHR)
Servilleta, NM, Taos Co., c/o El Rito, NM, San Juan Nepomuceno. (SFE)
Shafter, TX, Presidio Co., Sgdo. Corazon de Jesus, c/o Presidio, TX, Santa Teresa de Jesus. (ELP)
Shamrock, TX, Wheeler Co., St. Patrick, c/o Shamrock, TX, Our Mother of Mercy. (AMA)
Shasta Lake City, CA, Shasta Co., St. Michael, c/o Redding, CA, St. Joseph. (SAC)
Shattuck, OK, Ellis Co., Holy Name, c/o Woodward, OK, St. Peter's. (OKL)
Shawmut, MT, Wheatland Co., Blessed Sacrament, c/o Harlowton, MT, St. Joseph. (HEL)
Sheffield, TX, Pecos Co., Good Shepherd, c/o Ozona, TX, Our Lady of Perpetual Help. (SAN)
Shelton, NE, Buffalo Co., Sacred Heart, c/o Wood River, NE, St. Mary's. (GI)
Shickley, NE, Fillmore Co., St. Mary, c/o Geneva, NE, St. Joseph's. (LIN)
Shidler, OK, Osage Co., St. Ann, c/o Pawhuska, OK, Immaculate Conception. (TLS)
Shingletown, CA, Shasta Co., Mary Queen of Peace, c/o Redding, CA, Our Lady of Mercy. (SAC)
Shoreham, VT, Addison Co., St. Bernadette/St. Genevieve, c/o Middlebury, VT, Assumption of the Blessed Virgin Mary. (BUR)
Shoshone–Tecopa, CA, St. John the Baptist, c/o Lone Pine, CA, Santa Rosa. (FRS)
Shoshoni, WY, Fremont Co., St. Joseph, c/o Riverton, WY, St. Margaret's. (CHY)
Shubert, NE, Richardson Co., St. Anne's, c/o Dawson, NE, St. Mary's. (LIN)
Sieper, LA, Rapides Parish, St. Jude, c/o Glenmora, LA, St. Louis. (ALX)
Sierra Alta, PR, Yauco Co., St. Lucy, c/o Yauco, PR, Holy Rosary. (PCE)
Sierra Blanca, TX, Hudspeth Co., Our Lady of Miracles, c/o Van Horn, TX, Our Lady of Fatima. (ELP)
Sierra City, CA, St. Thomas, c/o Downieville, CA, Immaculate Conception. (SAC)
Sigel, PA, Jefferson Co., St. Dominic, c/o Brookville, PA, Immaculate Conception. (E)
Sile, NM, Sandoval Co., Santa Barbara, c/o Pena Blanca, NM, Nuestra Senora De Guadalupe. (SFE)
Siletz, OR, Lincoln Co., St. Mary, c/o Newport, OR, Sacred Heart Parish. (P)
Silt, CO, Garfield Co., Sacred Heart, c/o Rifle, CO, St. Mary. (DEN)
Silver Lake, PA, Susquehanna Co., St. Augustine, c/o Friendsville, PA, Saint Brigid Parish. (SCR)
Silverton, CO, San Juan Co., St. Patrick, c/o Ouray, CO, St. Daniel the Prophet. (PBL)
Simpson, PA, SS. Peter & Paul, c/o Scranton, PA, St. Vladimir's. (PHU)
Skagway, AK, St. Therese of the Child Jesus, c/o Haines, AK, Sacred Heart. (JUN)
Slidell, LA, Edolia Barros, c/o Slidell, LA, St. Genevieve. (NO)
Smith, NV, Lyon Co., St. John the Baptist, c/o Yerington, NV, Holy Family. (RNO)
Smithfield, NE, Gosper Co., St. John's, c/o Holdrege, NE, All Saints. (LIN)
Smiths Corners, MI, Huron Co., Most Holy Trinity, c/o Rapson, MI, St. Joseph. (SAG)
Snow Shoe, PA, Centre Co., c/o Clarence, PA, Queen of Archangels. (ALT)
Solana Beach, CA, San Diego Co., St. Leo, c/o Solana Beach, CA, Saint James Catholic Parish. (SD)
Soledad, CA, Monterey Co., Nuestra Senora de la Soledad, c/o Soledad, CA, Our Lady of Solitude. (MRY)
Sonoita, AZ, Santa Cruz Co., Our Lady of Angels, c/o Patagonia, AZ, Saint Therese of Lisieux Roman Catholic Parish – Patagonia. (TUC)
Sonsorol, FM, c/o Palau, PW, Sacred Heart. (CI)
South Colton, NY, St. Lawrence Co., St. Paul, c/o Colton, NY, St. Patrick. (OG)
South Fork, CO, Rio Grande Co., Holy Family, c/o Del Norte, CO, Holy Name of Mary. (PBL)
South Royalston, MA, Worcester Co., Our Lady Queen of Heaven, c/o Athol, MA, Our Lady Immaculate. (WOR)
South Strafford, VT, Orange Co., Our Lady of Light, c/o Bradford, VT, Our Lady of Perpetual Help. (BUR)
South Tucson, AZ, Pima Co., Blessed Kateri Tekakwitha Parish Center, c/o Tucson, AZ, Blessed Kateri Tekakwitha Roman Catholic Missions Parish – Tucson. (TUC)
Southton, TX, Bexar Co., St. Ann, c/o San Antonio, TX, San Juan Capistrano. (SAT)
Southwest Oswego, NY, Oswego Co., St. Joseph, c/o Hannibal, NY, Our Lady of the Rosary. (SY)
Spanish Lake, LA, Natchitoches Parish, St. Anne, c/o Powhatan, LA, St. Francis of Assisi. (ALX)
Sparta, NC, St. Frances of Rome, c/o Jefferson, NC, St. Francis of Assisi. (CHL)
Spelter, WV, Harrison Co., Holy Family, c/o Shinnston, WV, St. Ann's. (WH)

Spencer Mountain, NC, Gaston Co., St. Helen, c/o Charlotte, NC, Our Lady of Consolation. (CHL)
Spiro, OK, Leflore Co., St. Elizabeth Seton, c/o Poteau, OK, Immaculate Conception. (TLS)
Spofford Junction, TX, Kinney Co., St. Blaise, c/o Brackettville, TX, St. Mary Magdalen. (SAT)
Spring Creek, SD, Todd Co., St. Patrick, c/o St. Francis, SD, St. Charles Borromeo. (RC)
Spring Creek, SD, Todd Co., St. Patrick, c/o St. Francis, SD, St. Francis Mission/Rosebud Educational Society. (RC)
Spring Lake, MN, Itasca Co., St. Catherine of Spring Lake Township, c/o Jordan, MN, St. Patrick of Cedar Lake Township. (STP)
Spring Lake, NJ, Monmouth Co., St. Margaret, c/o Spring Lake, NJ, St. Catharine. (TR)
Springfield, KY, Washington Co., Holy Rosary–Manton, c/o Springfield, KY, Holy Trinity. (L)
Springfield, MA, Hampden Co., St. Francis Chapel, c/o Springfield, MA, St. Michael's Cathedral. (SPR)
Springfield, SC, Orangeburg Co., St. Theresa, c/o Orangeburg, SC, St. Andrew. (CHR)
Springhill, LA, Webster Parish, Sacred Heart, c/o Minden, LA, St. Paul. (SHP)
Squaw Valley, CA, Fresno Co., St. Rita, c/o Orange Cove, CA, St. Isidore the Farmer. (FRS)
St. Augustine, FL, St. Johns Co., St. Benedict the Moor, c/o St. Augustine, FL, Cathedral – Basilica of St. Augustine. (STA)
St. Boniface, PA, Cambria Co., St. Boniface Chapel, c/o Hastings, PA, St. Bernard. (ALT)
St. David, IL, Fulton Co., St. Michael, c/o Lewistown, IL, St. Mary's. (PEO)
St. Denis, IN, Jennings Co., St. Denis, c/o Greensburg, IN, Immaculate Conception Catholic Church, Millhousen, Inc. (IND)
St. Elmo, IL, Fayette Co., St. Mary, c/o Altamont, IL, St. Clare. (SFD)
St. Francis, SD, Todd Co., St. Charles, c/o St. Francis, SD, St. Francis Mission/Rosebud Educational Society. (RC)
St. Helena Island, SC, Beaufort Co., Holy Cross, c/o Beaufort, SC, St. Peter. (CHR)
St. Mary, NE, Johnson Co., St. Mary's, c/o Tecumseh, NE, St. Andrew's. (LIN)
St. Michaels, AZ, Apache Co., St. Michael's Mission for Navajo Indians, c/o St. Michaels, AZ, St. Michael. (GLP)
St. Michaels, MD, Talbot Co., St. Michael, c/o Easton, MD, SS. Peter and Paul. (WIL)
St. Paul, TX, San Patricio Co., St. Paul, c/o Sinton, TX, Sacred Heart. (CC)
St. Pete Beach, FL, Pinellas Co., St. Casimir Lithuanian Mission, c/o Gulfport, FL, Most Holy Name of Jesus. (SP)
St. Petersburg, FL, Pinellas Co., The Mercy of God Polish Mission, c/o St. Petersburg, FL, St. Paul. (SP)
St. Xavier, MT, Big Horn Co., St. Francis Xavier, c/o Crow Agency, MT, St. Dennis. (GF)
Staatsburg, NY, Dutchess Co., St. Paul, c/o Hyde Park, NY, Regina Coeli. (NY)
Stamford, VT, Bennington Co., St. John Bosco, c/o Readsboro, VT, St. Joachim. (BUR)
Standish, NY, Clinton Co., St. Michael, c/o Lyon Mountain, NY, St. Bernard. (OG)
Stanfield, AZ, Pinal Co., St. Mary Mission, c/o Casa Grande, AZ, Saint Anthony of Padua Roman Catholic Parish – Casa Grande. (TUC)
Starr School, MT, Sacred Heart, c/o Browning, MT, Church of the Little Flower. (HEL)
Starrucca, PA, Wayne Co., St. Paul, c/o Susquehanna, PA, St. Martin of Tours. (SCR)
Staten Island, NY, Holy Rosary, c/o Staten Island, NY, Holy Rosary. (NY)
Staten Island, NY, Staten Island Co., St. Nicholas, c/o Staten Island, NY, St. Teresa. (NY)
Stedman, NC, Cumberland Co., St. Isidore, c/o Hope Mills, NC, Good Shepherd. (R)
Steilacoom, WA, Pierce Co., Immaculate Conception, c/o Lakewood, WA, St. John Bosco. (SEA)
Stephentown, NY, Rensselaer Co., St. Joseph's, c/o New Lebanon, NY, Immaculate Conception. (ALB)
Stepstone, KY, Pendleton Co., Immaculate Conception, c/o California, KY, Sts. Peter and Paul. (COV)
Sterling, OK, Comanche Co., Our Lady of Perpetual Help, c/o Elgin, OK, St. Ann. (OKL)
Stevenson, WA, Skamania Co., Our Lady Star of the Sea, c/o Camas, WA, St. Thomas Aquinas. (SEA)
Stevinson, CA, Merced Co., St. Mary, c/o Hilmar, CA, Holy Rosary. (FRS)
Stigler, OK, Haskell Co., St. Joseph, c/o Poteau, OK, Immaculate Conception. (TLS)
Stilwell, OK, Adair Co., San Juan Mission, c/o Tahlequah, OK, St. Brigid. (TLS)
Stinnett, TX, Hutchinson Co., St. Ann's, c/o Borger, TX, St. John the Evangelist. (AMA)
Stockbridge, MA, Berkshire Co., Saint Joseph, c/o Lee, MA, St. Mary's. (SPR)
Stockton, CA, San Joaquin Co., St. Sharbel Maronite Catholic Mission, c/o Millbrae, CA, Our Lady of Lebanon Maronite Catholic Church. (OLL)
Stockton, MO, Cedar Co., St. Peter the Apostle, c/o El Dorado Springs, MO, St. Elizabeth of Hungary. (SPC)
Stoneham, CO, Weld Co., St. John, c/o Brush, CO, St. Mary. (DEN)
Stoneham, TX, Grimes Co., St. Joseph, c/o Plantersville, TX, St. Mary. (GAL)
Stonewall, LA, DeSoto Parish, St. Ann's Chapel, c/o Mansfield, LA, St. Joseph. (SHP)
Stonington, IL, Holy Trinity, c/o Taylorville, IL, St. Mary. (SFD)
Stonyford, CA, Colusa Co., St. Mary of the Mountain, c/o Williams, CA, Sacred Heart. (SAC)
Story, WY, Sheridan Co., Our Lady of the Pines, c/o Sheridan, WY, Holy Name. (CHY)
Stratford, CA, St. Joseph, c/o Lemoore, CA, St. Peter Prince of Apostles. (FRS)
Strathmore, CA, Tulare Co., St. James Catholic Church, c/o Lindsay, CA, Sacred Heart. (FRS)
Stratton, ME, Franklin Co., St. John, c/o Oquossoc, ME, Our Lady of the Lakes. (PRT)
Stratton, NE, Hitchcock Co., St. Joseph's, c/o Benkelman, NE, St. Joseph's. (LIN)
Stratton Mountain, VT, Windham Co., Chapel of the Snows, c/o Putney, VT, Our Lady of Mercy. (BUR)
Strawn, IL, Livingston Co., St. Rose, c/o Fairbury, IL, St. John the Baptist. (PEO)
String Prairie, TX, Bastrop Co., Assumption of the Blessed Virgin Mary, c/o Bastrop, TX, Sacred Heart. (AUS)
Stroud, OK, Lincoln Co., St. Louis, c/o Chandler, OK, Our Lady of Sorrows. (OKL)
Stuart, VA, Patrick, Church of the Risen Lord, c/o Woodlawn, VA, St. Joseph's. (RIC)
Sturgeon Bay, WI, c/o Sturgeon Bay, WI, Corpus Christi. (GB)
Sugar Island, MI, Chippewa Co., Sacred Heart, c/o Sault Sainte Marie, MI, Holy Name of Mary. (MAR)
Sugarloaf Shores, FL, Sugarloaf Firehouse, c/o Big Pine Key, FL, St. Peter. (MIA)
Sugarloaf U.S.A., ME, Franklin Co., Richard H. Bell Memorial Chapel, c/o Oquossoc, ME, Our Lady of the Lakes. (PRT)
Sullivan City, TX, Hidalgo Co., St. William, c/o La Joya, TX, Our Lady, Queen of Angels. (BWN)
Sulphur, OK, Murray Co., St. Francis Xavier, c/o Ada, OK, St. Joseph. (OKL)
Sunapee, NH, Sullivan Co., St. Joachim, c/o Newport, NH, St. Patrick. (MAN)
Sunburst, MT, St. Thomas Aquinas, c/o Shelby, MT, St. William. (HEL)
Sundance, WY, Crook Co., St. Paul, c/o Newcastle, WY, Corpus Christi. (CHY)
Sundown, TX, Hockley Co., San Isidro, c/o Levelland, TX, St. Michael's. (LUB)
Sunray, TX, Moore Co., Christ the King, c/o Dumas, TX, SS. Peter and Paul. (AMA)
Sunriver, OR, Deschutes Co., Holy Trinity, c/o La Pine, OR, Holy Redeemer. (BAK)
Superior, MT, Mineral Co., St. Mary Queen of Heaven, c/o Frenchtown, MT, St. John the Baptist. (HEL)
Superior, WY, Sweetwater Co., St. Vivian, c/o Rock Springs, WY, Holy Spirit Catholic Community. (CHY)
Suquamish, WA, Kitsap Co., St. Peter, c/o Poulsbo, WA, St. Olaf. (SEA)
Surf City, NC, Pender Co., St. Mary, Gate of Heaven, c/o Hampstead, NC, St. Jude the Apostle. (R)
Surf City, NJ, Ocean Co., St. Thomas of Villanova, c/o Brant Beach, NJ, St. Francis of Assisi. (TR)
Susua, PR, La Resurreccion, c/o Sabana Grande, PR, Church of San Isidro. (MGZ)
Swartz, LA, Ouachita Parish, St. Lawrence, c/o Monroe, LA, Our Lady of Fatima. (SHP)
Sweet Lake, LA, Cameron Parish, St. Patrick's, c/o Lake Charles, LA, St. Mary of the Lake. (LKC)
Sweet Springs, MO, Saline Co., Holy Family, c/o Marshall, MO, St. Peter. (JC)

T

Ta, FM, c/o Chuuk, FM, Mortlock. (CI)
Tabor, MN, Polk Co., Holy Trinity, c/o East Grand Forks, MN, Sacred Heart. (CR)
Tache Indian Reservation, CA, Kings Co., Santa Rosa, c/o Lemoore, CA, St. Peter Prince of Apostles. (FRS)
Tajique, NM, San Antonio, c/o Moriarty, NM, Estancia Valley Catholic Parish. (SFE)
Talihina, OK, Leflore Co., St. Catherine of Siena, c/o Wilburton, OK, Sacred Heart. (TLS)
Talpa, NM, Taos Co., N.S. de San Juan de Los Lagos, c/o Ranchos De Taos, NM, San Francisco de Asis. (SFE)
Tampa, FL, Hillsborough Co., Immaculate Conception Haitian Catholic Mission, c/o Tampa, FL, Epiphany of Our Lord. (SP)
Tampa, FL, Santa Maria, c/o Tampa, FL, St. Mary. (SP)
Tampa, FL, Hillsborough Co., St. Joseph Vietnamese Mission, c/o Tampa, FL, Epiphany of Our Lord. (SP)
Tampa, KS, Holy Redeemer Church, c/o Marion, KS, Holy Family. (WCH)
Tanama, PR, Adjuntas Co., Sagrado Corazon, c/o Adjuntas, PR, St. Joachim. (PCE)
Taos, NM, Taos Co., St. Jerome, c/o Taos, NM, Nuestra Senora De Guadalupe. (SFE)
Tatum, NM, Lea Co., Our Lady of the Holy Rosary, c/o Lovington, NM, St. Thomas Aquinas. (LSC)
Tatum, TX, Panola Co., San Pedro the Fisherman, c/o Marshall, TX, St. Joseph. (TYL)
Taylorsville, KY, Spencer Co., All Saints Church, c/o Mount Washington, KY, St. Francis Xavier. (L)
Taylorsville, NC, Alexander Co., Holy Trinity, c/o Statesville, NC, St. Philip the Apostle. (CHL)
Teague, TX, Freestone Co., St. Mary, c/o Fairfield, TX, St. Bernard of Clairvaux. (TYL)
Tecolotito, NM, San Miguel Co., c/o Anton Chico, NM, San Jose. (SFE)
Tehama, CA, Tehama Co., St. Stanislaus, c/o Corning, CA, Immaculate Conception. (SAC)
Tenakee Springs, AK, c/o Yakutat, AK, St. Ann. (JUN)
Tenino, WA, Thurston Co., St. Peter, c/o Yelm, WA, St. Columban. (SEA)
Tennessee, IL, McDonough Co., Sacred Heart, c/o Macomb, IL, St. Paul's. (PEO)
Terra Alta, WV, Preston Co., St. Edward, c/o Kingwood, WV, St. Sebastian. (WH)
Terra Bella, CA, Tulare Co., Blessed Miguel Agustin Pro, c/o Porterville, CA, St. Anne. (FRS)
Terry, MT, Prairie Co., Sacred Heart, c/o Miles City, MT, Sacred Heart. (GF)
Tesuque, NM, Santa Fe Co., San Ysidro, c/o Santa Fe, NM, Our Lady of Guadalupe. (SFE)
Texico, NM, Curry Co., c/o Clovis, NM, Our Lady of Guadalupe. (SFE)
Texline, TX, Dallum Co., St. Mary's, c/o Dalhart, TX, St. Anthony of Padua. (AMA)
Thatcher, AZ, Graham Co., Newman Center, c/o Safford, AZ, Saint Rose of Lima Roman Catholic Parish – Safford. (TUC)
Thayer, MO, Oregon Co., Sacred Heart, c/o West Plains, MO, St. Mary. (SPC)
Thedford, NE, Thomas Co., St. Thomas of Canterbury, c/o Mullen, NE, St. Mary's. (GI)
Theresa, NY, Jefferson Co., St. Theresa of Avila, c/o Evans Mills, NY, St. Mary. (OG)
Thermal, CA, Riverside Co., Sacred Heart of Mary & Jesus, c/o Coachella, CA, Our Lady of Soledad. (SB)
Thermal, CA, Riverside Co., San Felipe de Jesus, c/o Coachella, CA, Our Lady of Soledad. (SB)
Thomas, OK, Custer Co., Blessed Sacrament, c/o Weatherford, OK, St. Eugene's. (OKL)
Thomasville, AL, Clarke Co., St. Joseph, c/o Grove Hill, AL, Sacred Heart. (MOB)
Thoreau, NM, Risen Savior, c/o Crownpoint, NM, St. Paul. (GLP)
Thorne Bay, AK, c/o Craig, AK, St. John by the Sea. (JUN)
Thornhurst, PA, Luzerne Co., St. Mark, c/o Bear Creek, PA, St. Elizabeth. (SCR)
Thornton, CA, San Joaquin Co., Mater Ecclesiae, c/o Lodi, CA, St. Anne Church (Pastor of). (STO)
Three Rivers, CA, Tulare Co., St. Clair, c/o Woodlake, CA, St. Frances Cabrini. (FRS)
Three Rivers, NM, Otero Co., St. Patrick, c/o Mescalero, NM, St. Joseph. (LSC)
Three Rocks, CA, Fresno Co., Our Lady of Lourdes, c/o Mendota, CA, Our Lady of Guadalupe. (FRS)
Thunder Butte, SD, Ziebach Co., St. Luke, c/o Eagle Butte, SD, All Saints. (RC)
Tijeras, NM, Bernalillo Co., c/o Tijeras, NM, Holy Child. (SFE)
Tilden, TX, McMullen Co., St. Joseph, c/o Charlotte, TX, St. Rose of Lima. (SAT)
Timpson, TX, Shelby Co., Epiphany, c/o Center, TX, St. Therese. (TYL)
Tinaja, NM, Colfax Co., c/o Springer, NM, St. Joseph. (SFE)
Tioga, PA, Tioga Co., St. Mary, c/o Mansfield, PA, Holy Child. (SCR)
Tionesta, PA, Forest Co., St. Anthony, c/o Tidioute, PA, St. John. (E)
Tiskilwa, IL, Bureau Co., St. Mary, c/o DePue, IL, St. Mary's. (PEO)
Toa Alta, PR, Toa Alta Co., Capilla Cristo Rey, c/o Toa Alta, PR, San Esteban, Protomartir. (SJN)
Toa Alta, PR, Carlos Manuel Rodriguez, c/o Bayamon, PR, Santo Domingo De Guzman. (SJN)
Toa Alta, PR, Toa Alta Co., Cristo Rey, c/o Toa Baja, PR, Ntra. Sra. de la Candelaria. (SJN)
Toa Alta, PR, Toa Alta Co., Nuestra Senora del Carmen, c/o Toa Alta, PR, Nuestra Senora de la Medalla Milagrosa. (SJN)
Toa Alta, PR, Toa Alta Co., Sagrada Familia, c/o Toa Alta, PR, San Jose. (SJN)
Toa Alta, PR, Toa Alta Co., Sagrado Corazon, c/o Toa Alta, PR, San Jose. (SJN)
Toa Alta, PR, Toa Alta Co., Sagrado Corazon de Jesus, c/o Toa Alta, PR, Nuestra Senora de la Medalla Milagrosa. (SJN)
Toa Alta, PR, Toa Alta Co., Santa Teresa De Jesus, c/o

Toa Alta, PR, San Judas Tadeo. (SJN)
Toa Alta, PR, Toa Alta Co., Santa Teresita, c/o Toa Alta, PR, San Jose. (SJN)
Toa Baja, PR, Toa Baja Co., Buen Pastor, c/o Toa Baja, PR, Ntra. Sra. de la Candelaria. (SJN)
Toa Baja, PR, Toa Baja Co., Divino Nino Jesus, c/o Bayamon, PR, Nuestra Senora de Covadonga. (SJN)
Toa Baja, PR, Toa Baja Co., N. Sra. del Carmen, c/o Toa Baja, PR, Espiritu Santo. (SJN)
Toa Baja, PR, Toa Baja Co., Ntra. Sra. de Lourdes, c/o Bayamon, PR, Nuestra Senora de Covadonga. (SJN)
Toa Baja, PR, Toa Baja Co., San Martin de Porres, c/o Bayamon, PR, Nuestra Senora de Covadonga. (SJN)
Toa Baja, PR, Toa Baja Co., Santisima Trinidad, c/o Toa Baja, PR, Ntra. Sra. de la Candelaria. (SJN)
Tobias, NE, Saline Co., St. Joseph's, c/o Wilber, NE, St. Wenceslaus. (LIN)
Tollhouse, CA, Fresno Co., Infant Jesus of Prague, c/o Clovis, CA, Our Lady of Perpetual Help. (FRS)
Tomales, CA, Marin Co., St. Helen, c/o Tomales, CA, Church of the Assumption. (SFR)
Tomkins Cove, NY, Rockland Co., Immaculate Conception, c/o Stony Point, NY, Immaculate Conception. (NY)
Tompkinsville, KY, Monroe Co., Christ the King, c/o Edmonton, KY, Christ the Healer. (L)
Tonawanda, NY, Erie Co., St. Andrew Kim, c/o Kenmore, NY, St. Andrew. (BUF)
Tonto Basin, AZ, Our Lady of the Lake, c/o Payson, AZ, Saint Philip the Apostle Roman Catholic Church – Payson. (TUC)
Tonyville, CA, Tulare Co., St. Anthony Church, c/o Lindsay, CA, Sacred Heart. (FRS)
Tornillo, TX, El Paso Co., Santa Rita, c/o Fabens, TX, Our Lady of Guadalupe. (ELP)
Torreon, NM, Torrance Co., c/o Mountainair, NM, St. Alice. (SFE)
Torrey, UT, Wayne Co., St. Anthony of the Desert, c/o Central Valley, UT, Saint Elizabeth LLC 220. (SLC)
Touhy, NE, Saunders Co., St. Vitus, c/o Weston, NE, St. John Nepomucene. (LIN)
Townshend, VT, Windham Co., Our Lady of the Valley, c/o Putney, VT, Our Lady of Mercy. (BUR)
Toyah, TX, Reeves Co., St. Emily, c/o Pecos, TX, St. Catherine. (ELP)
Trail City, SD, Corson Co., Holy Rosary, c/o Timber Lake, SD, Holy Cross. (RC)
Trampas, NM, Taos Co., San Jose de Gracia, c/o Chimayo, NM, Holy Family. (SFE)
Trapper Creek, AK, St. Philip Benizi, c/o Talkeetna, AK, St. Bernard. (ANC)
Traver, CA, Tulare Co., St. John the Baptist Educational Center, c/o Kingsburg, CA, Holy Family. (FRS)
Tremonton, UT, Box Elder Co., Santa Ana, c/o Brigham City, UT, Saint Henry LLC 225. (SLC)
Trenton, GA, Dade Co., St. Katharine Drexel, c/o Lookout Mountain, GA, Our Lady of the Mount. (ATL)
Trenton, MO, Mercer Co., Immaculate Heart of Mary Church, c/o Chillicothe, MO, St. Joseph's. (KC)
Tres Piedras, NM, Taos Co., c/o El Rito, NM, San Juan Nepomuceno. (SFE)
Tres de Jayuya, PR, Adjuntas Co., Santa Teresita, c/o Adjuntas, PR, St. Joachim. (PCE)
Trichel, LA, Natchitoches Parish, St. Joseph, c/o Campti, LA, Nativity of The Blessed Virgin Mary. (ALX)
Trinidad, CA, Holy Trinity, c/o McKinleyville, CA, Christ the King. (SR)
Trout Lake, MI, Chippewa Co., St. Mary, c/o Rudyard, MI, St. Joseph. (MAR)
Troy, MT, Lincoln Co., Immaculate Conception, c/o Libby, MT, St. Joseph. (HEL)
Troy, NY, Rensselaer Co., The Springs Nursing Home, c/o Troy, NY, St. Michael the Archangel. (ALB)
Troy, PA, Bradford Co., St. John Nepomucene, c/o Canton, PA, St. Michael. (SCR)
Truchas, NM, Rio Arriba Co., Holy Rosary, c/o Chimayo, NM, Holy Family. (SFE)
Trujillo, CO, Archuleta Co., St. James, c/o Pagosa Springs, CO, Immaculate Heart of Mary. (PBL)
Trujillo, NM, San Miguel Co., San Isidro, c/o Las Vegas, NM, Our Lady of Sorrows Church. (SFE)
Trujillo Alto, PR, Trujillo Alto Co., El Divino Pastor, c/o Trujillo Alto, PR, San Judas Tadeo. (SJN)
Trujillo Alto, PR, Trujillo Alto Co., Ntra. Sra. del Carmen, c/o Trujillo Alto, PR, San Judas Tadeo. (SJN)
Tsaile, AZ, Apache Co., St. Ann, c/o Lukachukai, AZ, St. Isabel. (GLP)
Tucson, AZ, Pima Co., Cristo Rey, c/o Tucson, AZ, Blessed Kateri Tekakwitha Roman Catholic Missions Parish – Tucson. (TUC)
Tucson, AZ, Pima Co., El Senor de los Milagros, c/o Tucson, AZ, Blessed Kateri Tekakwitha Roman Catholic Missions Parish – Tucson. (TUC)
Tucson, AZ, Pima Co., Our Lady of Guadalupe Capilla, c/o Tucson, AZ, Santa Cruz Roman Catholic Parish – Tucson. (TUC)
Tucson, AZ, San Cosme, c/o Tucson, AZ, Saint Augustine Cathedral Roman Catholic Parish – Tucson. (TUC)
Tucson, AZ, Pima Co., San Ignacio de Loyola, c/o Tucson, AZ, Blessed Kateri Tekakwitha Roman Catholic Missions Parish – Tucson. (TUC)
Tucson, AZ, Pima Co., San Martin, c/o Tucson, AZ, Blessed Kateri Tekakwitha Roman Catholic Missions Parish – Tucson. (TUC)
Tucson, AZ, Pima Co., Santa Rosa, c/o Tucson, AZ, Blessed Kateri Tekakwitha Roman Catholic Missions Parish – Tucson. (TUC)
Tucson, AZ, Pima Co., St. Anthony's Catholic Instruction Center and Capilla, c/o Tucson, AZ, Santa Cruz Roman Catholic Parish – Tucson. (TUC)
Tucson, AZ, Pima Co., St. Mary of the Desert, c/o Tucson, AZ, Our Lady of Fatima Roman Catholic Parish – Tucson. (TUC)
Tulalip, WA, Snohomish Co., Tulalip Indian Reservation, St. Anne, c/o Marysville, WA, St. Mary. (SEA)
Tule Indian Reservation, CA, Tulare Co., Mater Dolorosa, c/o Porterville, CA, St. Anne. (FRS)
Tullytown, PA, Bucks Co., Sacred Heart of Jesus, c/o Bristol, PA, St. Ann. (PH)
Tuolumne, CA, Tuolumne Co., St. Joseph, c/o Twain Harte, CA, All Saints Church (Pastor of). (STO)
Turquillo, NM, Mora Co., c/o Mora, NM, St. Gertrude. (SFE)
Tuscaloosa, AL, Tuscaloosa Co., St. John, c/o Tuscaloosa, AL, Holy Spirit. (BIR)
Twin Bridges, MT, Jefferson Co., Notre Dame, c/o Whitehall, MT, St. Teresa of Avila. (HEL)
Twin Lakes, GA, Lowndes Co., St. Jose, c/o Valdosta, GA, St. John the Evangelist. (SAV)
Twin Sisters, TX, Blanco Co., St. Mary's Help of Christians, c/o Blanco, TX, St. Ferdinand. (AUS)
Twin Valley, MN, Norman Co., St. William, c/o Ada, MN, St. Joseph's. (CR)
Tyler, TX, St. Joseph the Worker Mission, c/o Tyler, TX, Cathedral of the Immaculate Conception. (TYL)
Tylertown, MS, Walthall Co., St. Paul the Apostle, c/o Columbia, MS, Holy Trinity. (BLX)
Tynan, TX, Bee Co., St. Francis Xavier, c/o Skidmore, TX, Immaculate Conception. (CC)

U

Ulupalakua, HI, Maui Co., St. James the Less, c/o Kula, HI, Our Lady Queen of the Angels. (HON)
Unadilla, NY, Otsego Co., St. Ambrose, c/o Sidney, NY, Sacred Heart. (ALB)
Union City, MI, Branch Co., Our Lady of Fatima, c/o Coldwater, MI, St. Charles Borromeo. (KAL)
Union Springs, AL, Bullock Co., Bullock County Correctional Facility, c/o Eufaula, AL, Holy Redeemer. (MOB)
Union Springs, AL, Bullock Co., St. Pius X, c/o Eufaula, AL, Holy Redeemer. (MOB)
Unionville, MO, Putnam Co., St. Mary, c/o Milan, MO, St. Mary. (JC)
Unionville, NY, Orange Co., Our Lady of the Scapular, c/o Middletown, NY, Holy Cross. (NY)
Unity, OR, Baker Co., St. Joseph, c/o Vale, OR, St. Patrick. (BAK)
Universal, IN, Vermillion Co., St. Joseph, c/o Clinton, IN, Sacred Heart Church, Clinton, Inc. (IND)
Upton, WY, Weston Co., St. Anthony, c/o Newcastle, WY, Corpus Christi. (CHY)
Urich, MO, Henry Co., Holy Trinity, c/o Holden, MO, St. Patrick's. (KC)
Ute, IA, Monona Co., St. Mary's, c/o Denison, IA, St. Boniface. (SC)
Utica, NE, Seward Co., St. Patrick's, c/o Beaver Crossing, NE, Sacred Heart. (LIN)
Utulei, AS, c/o Pago Pago, AS, Co–Cathedral of St. Joseph the Worker. (SPP)

V

Vadito, NM, Taos Co., Nuestra Senora de los Dolores Mission, c/o Penasco, NM, San Antonio de Padua. (SFE)
Valdez, NM, Taos Co., San Antonio de Padua, c/o Arroyo Seco, NM, La Santisima Trinidad. (SFE)
Valencia, NM, Valencia Co., Sangre de Cristo, c/o Peralta, NM, Our Lady of Guadalupe. (SFE)
Valentine, TX, Jeff Davis Co., Sacred Heart, c/o Van Horn, TX, Our Lady of Fatima. (ELP)
Vallecitos, NM, Rio Arriba Co., c/o El Rito, NM, San Juan Nepomuceno. (SFE)
Van Buren, MO, Carter Co., St. George, c/o Piedmont, MO, St. Catherine of Siena. (SPC)
Vanceboro, ME, Washington Co., Guardian Angel, c/o Lincoln, ME, St. Mary. (PRT)
Vanderpool, TX, Bandera Co., St. Mary, c/o Sabinal, TX, St. Patrick's. (SAT)
Variadero, NM, San Miguel Co., Holy Family, c/o Las Vegas, NM, Our Lady of Sorrows Church. (SFE)
Vegas Abajo, PR, Adjuntas Co., La Milagrosa, c/o Adjuntas, PR, St. Joachim. (PCE)
Vegas Arriba, PR, Adjuntas Co., Sta. Ana, c/o Adjuntas, PR, St. Joachim. (PCE)
Veguíta, NM, Socorro Co., San Juan, c/o La Joya, NM, Our Lady of Sorrows. (SFE)
Velarde, NM, Rio Arriba Co., Nuestra Senora de Guadalupe, c/o Dixon, NM, St. Anthony. (SFE)
Verdigre, NE, Knox Co., St. William, c/o Verdigre, NE, St. Wenceslaus. (OM)
Verdunville, LA, St. Mary Parish, Immaculate Conception, c/o Franklin, LA, St. Jules. (LAF)
Verona Beach, NY, Oneida Co., St. Mary, c/o North Bay, NY, St. John. (SY)
Versailles, MO, Morgan Co., St. Philip Benizi, c/o Laurie, MO, Shrine of St. Patrick. (JC)
Viburnum, MO, Iron Co., St. Philip Benizi, c/o Ironton, MO, Ste. Marie Du Lac. (SPC)
Victor, CO, Teller Co., St. Victor's, c/o Woodland Park, CO, Teller County Catholic Community. (COS)
Victoria, TX, Victoria Co., Holy Trinity, c/o Victoria, TX, Our Lady of Sorrows. (VIC)
Vida, MT, McCone Co., St. Ann, c/o Wolf Point, MT, Immaculate Conception. (GF)
Vienna, MO, St. Boniface, c/o Argyle, MO, St. Aloysius. (JC)
Vigil, CO, Las Animas Co., St. Isidore, c/o Trinidad, CO, Most Holy Trinity. (PBL)
Villa Esperanza, PR, Carolina Co., La Sagrada Familia, c/o Carolina, PR, San Juan de Dios. (SJN)
Villa del Carmen, PR, Ponce Co., San Martin de Porres, c/o Ponce, PR, Our Lady of Mt. Carmel. (PCE)
Villalba, PR, Villalba Co., La Milagrosa, c/o Villalba, PR, Our Lady of Mt. Carmel. (PCE)
Villalba, PR, Villalba, La Milagrosa, c/o Villalba, PR, Our Lady of Mt. Carmel. (PCE)
Villalba, PR, Villalba, San Francisco de Asis, c/o Villalba, PR, Our Lady of Mt. Carmel. (PCE)
Villalba, PR, Villalba, San Juan Evangelista, c/o Villalba, PR, Our Lady of Mt. Carmel. (PCE)
Villas De Loiza, PR, Ntra. Sra. de la Providencia, c/o Canovanas, PR, Resurreccion del Señor. (FAJ)
Viola, IL, Mercer Co., St. John, c/o Aledo, IL, St. Anthony's Church. (PEO)
Virginia Beach, VA, Virginia Beach Co., Our Lady of Perpetual Help, c/o Williamsburg, VA, Ascension of Our Lord. (PSC)
Volcano, CA, Amador Co., St. Bernard, c/o Jackson, CA, St. Patrick's. (SAC)

W

Wa Keeney, KS, Trego Co., St. Michael, c/o WaKeeney, KS, Christ the King Parish. (SAL)
Wadesboro, NC, Anson Co., Sacred Heart, c/o Hamlet, NC, St. James. (CHL)
Wadsworth, TX, Matagorda Co., Sacred Heart, c/o Bay City, TX, Holy Cross. (VIC)
Waelder, TX, Gonzales Co., St. Patrick, c/o Gonzales, TX, St. James. (SAT)
Wahneta, FL, Polk Co., Our Lady of Guadalupe, c/o Bartow, FL, St. Thomas Aquinas. (ORL)
Waiakoa, HI, Maui Co., Holy Ghost, c/o Kula, HI, Our Lady Queen of the Angels. (HON)
Waialua, HI, Honolulu Co., SS. Peter and Paul, c/o Waialua, HI, St. Michael. (HON)
Waimea, HI, Kauai Co., Sacred Hearts of Jesus & Mary, c/o Kekaha, HI, St. Theresa. (HON)
Waitsfield, VT, Washington Co., Our Lady of the Snows, c/o Waterbury, VT, St. Andrew. (BUR)
Wakefield, VA, Southampton Co., Infant of Prague, c/o Franklin, VA, St. Jude. (RIC)
Wakita, OK, Grant Co., St. Mary's Assumption, c/o Medford, OK, St. Mary's. (OKL)
Wakpala, SD, Corson Co., St. Bede, c/o McLaughlin, SD, St. Bernard. (RC)
Wakpala, SD, Corson Co., St. Bede, c/o McLaughlin, SD, Standing Rock Reservation. (RC)
Walden, CO, Jackson Co., St. Ignatius, c/o Kremmling, CO, St. Peter. (DEN)
Wales, MA, Hampden Co., St. Monica, c/o Brimfield, MA, St. Christopher's. (SPR)
Walhalla, SC, Oconee Co., St. Francis of Assisi, c/o Clemson, SC, St. Andrew. (CHR)
Walker Valley, NY, Ulster Co., Our Lady of the Valley, c/o Pine Bush, NY, The Infant Saviour. (NY)
Wallace, NC, Duplin Co., Transfiguration, c/o Burgaw, NC, St. Joseph. (R)
Wallkill, NY, Ulster Co., St. Benedict, c/o Walden, NY, Most Precious Blood. (NY)
Wallowa, OR, Wallowa Co., St. Pius X, c/o Enterprise, OR, St. Katherine's. (BAK)
Walls, MS, DeSoto Co., Sacred Heart, c/o Robinsonville, MS, Good Shepherd Catholic Church. (JKS)
Walpole, NH, St. Joseph, c/o Charlestown, NH, All Saints Parish. (MAN)
Walston, PA, Jefferson Co., St. Anthony of Padua, c/o Punxsutawney, PA, SS. Cosmas and Damian. (E)
Walterboro, SC, Colleton Co., St. James the Greater, c/o Walterboro, SC, St. Anthony. (CHR)
Walters, OK, Cotton Co., St. Patrick Church, c/o Duncan, OK, Assumption. (OKL)
Wamsutter, WY, Sweetwater Co., St. Anthony, c/o Rock Springs, WY, Holy Spirit Catholic Community. (CHY)

Wanette, OK, Pottawatomie Co., St. Mary, c/o Konawa, OK, Sacred Heart. (OKL)
Wareham, MA, Plymouth Co., St. Anthony, c/o Wareham, MA, St. Patrick's. (FR)
Warm Springs, GA, Meriwether Co., St. Elizabeth Seton, c/o LaGrange, GA, St. Peter. (ATL)
Warm Springs, OR, Jefferson Co., Blessed Kateri Tekakwitha, c/o Madras, OR, St. Patrick. (BAK)
Warner Springs, CA, San Diego Co., St. Francis of Assisi, c/o Santa Ysabel, CA, Santa Ysabel Indian Mission Catholic Parish. (SD)
Warrenton, NC, Warren Co., St. Joseph, c/o Henderson, NC, St. James. (R)
Warrenton, TX, Fayette Co., St. Martin, c/o Fayetteville, TX, St. John the Baptist. (AUS)
Warrior, AL, Jefferson Co., St. Henry, c/o Gardendale, AL, St. Elizabeth Ann Seton. (BIR)
Washburn, IL, Woodford Co., St. Elizabeth, c/o Metamora, IL, St. Mary's. (PEO)
Washington, DC, c/o Washington, DC, St. Ann. (WDC)
Washington, DC, c/o Washington, DC, Kidane–Mehret Ge'ez Rite Catholic Church. (WDC)
Washington, GA, Elbert Co., St. Mary, c/o Washington, GA, St. Joseph. (ATL)
Washoe Valley, NV, Washoe Co., Holy Spirit, c/o Reno, NV, St. Rose of Lima. (RNO)
Waskom, TX, Harrison Co., St. Lawrence Brindisi, c/o Jefferson, TX, Immaculate Conception. (TYL)
Watauga, SD, Corson Co., St. Michael, c/o McLaughlin, SD, Standing Rock Reservation. (RC)
Waterproof, LA, Tensas Parish, St. Francis of Assisi, c/o St. Joseph, LA, St. Joseph. (ALX)
Watonga, OK, Blaine Co., St. Rose of Lima, c/o Kingfisher, OK, SS. Peter and Paul. (OKL)
Watrous, NM, Mora Co., c/o Wagon Mound, NM, Santa Clara. (SFE)
Wattenburg, CO, Weld Co., Our Lady of Grace, c/o Fort Lupton, CO, St. William. (DEN)
Wauneta, NE, Chase Co., St. John's, c/o Trenton, NE, St. James. (LIN)
Waurika, OK, Jefferson Co., St. Thomas Aquinas Chapel, c/o Duncan, OK, Assumption. (OKL)
Wayland, MO, Clark Co., St. Martha, c/o Kahoka, MO, St. Michael the Archangel. (JC)
Waynoka, OK, Woods Co., Our Mother of Mercy, c/o Alva, OK, Sacred Heart. (OKL)
Webbers Falls, OK, Muskogee Co., St. Joseph, c/o Sallisaw, OK, St. Francis Xavier. (TLS)
Welch, OK, Craig Co., St. Ann, c/o Miami, OK, Sacred Heart. (TLS)
Weldona, CO, Morgan Co., St. Francis of Assisi, c/o Fort Morgan, CO, St. Helena. (DEN)
Wellfleet, NE, Lincoln Co., St. William's, c/o Curtis, NE, St. James. (LIN)
Wells River, VT, Orange Co., St. Eugene, c/o Bradford, VT, Our Lady of Perpetual Help. (BUR)
Wenden, AZ, St. John the Baptist, c/o Parker, AZ, Sacred Heart Roman Catholic Parish – Parker. (TUC)
Weslaco, TX, Hidalgo Co., St. Jude Chapel, c/o Weslaco, TX, San Martin de Porres. (BWN)
West Alton, MO, Immaculate Conception, c/o Portage Des Sioux, MO, St. Francis of Assisi. (STL)
West Barnstable, MA, Barnstable Co., Our Lady of Hope, c/o Centerville, MA, Our Lady of Victory. (FR)
West Castleton, VT, Rutland Co., St. Matthew of Avalon, c/o Fair Haven, VT, Our Lady of Seven Dolors. (BUR)
West Charleston, VT, Orleans Co., St. Benedict Labre, c/o Derby Line, VT, St. Edward. (BUR)
West Columbia, TX, Brazoria Co., St. John the Apostle, c/o Sweeny, TX, Our Lady of Perpetual Help. (GAL)
West Dundee, IL, Kane Co., St. Mary, c/o Dundee, IL, St. Catherine of Siena. (RCK)
West Gilgo Beach, NY, Suffolk Co., c/o Babylon, NY, St. Joseph. (RVC)
West Glacier, MT, Flathead Co., c/o Columbia Falls, MT, St. Richard. (HEL)
West Hempstead, NY, Nassau Co., Chapel, c/o West Hempstead, NY, St. Thomas, the Apostle. (RVC)
West Pawlet, VT, Rutland Co., St. Frances Cabrini, c/o Fair Haven, VT, Our Lady of Seven Dolors. (BUR)
West Peru, NY, Clinton Co., St. Patrick, c/o Peru, NY, St. Augustine. (OG)
West Point, CA, Calaveras Co., Our Lady of Fatima, c/o San Andreas, CA, St. Andrew Church of San Andreas (Pastor of). (STO)
West Shokan, NY, Ulster Co., St. Augustine, c/o Woodstock, NY, St. John. (NY)
Westfield, PA, Tioga Co., St. Catherine, c/o Elkland, PA, St. Thomas the Apostle. (SCR)
Westfield, WI, Marquette Co., Good Shepherd, c/o Montello, WI, St. John the Baptist. (MAD)
Westhoff, TX, DeWitt Co., St. Aloysius, c/o Meyersville, TX, SS. Peter & Paul. (VIC)
Westover, MD, Somerset Co., St. Elizabeth, c/o Pocomoke City, MD, Holy Name of Jesus. (WIL)
Westport, WA, Grays Harbor Co., St. Paul, c/o Aberdeen, WA, St. Mary. (SEA)
Westville, NY, Franklin Co., c/o Constable, NY, The Catholic Community of Constable, Westville and Trout River. (OG)
Westville Grove, NJ, St. Yi Yun Il John Korean Catholic Mission, c/o Woodbury, NJ, Holy Angels Parish, Woodbury, N.J. (CAM)
Westway, TX, El Paso Co., Immaculate Heart of Mary, c/o Canutillo, TX, St. Patrick. (ELP)
Wewahitchka, FL, Gulf Co., St. Lawrence Mission, c/o Port St. Joe, FL, St. Joseph. (PT)
Wheatfields, AZ, Apache Co., Our Lady of the Lake, c/o Lukachukai, AZ, St. Isabel. (GLP)
Wheatland, CA, Yuba Co., St. Daniel, c/o Lincoln, CA, St. Joseph. (SAC)
Wheatville, NY, Genesee Co., St. Patrick, c/o Oakfield, NY, St. Padre Pio. (BUF)
Wheelwright, MA, Hardwick Co., St. Augustine, c/o Gilbertville, MA, St. Aloysius. (WOR)
Whetstone, AZ, Cochise Co., Good Shepherd, c/o Sierra Vista, AZ, Saint Andrew the Apostle Roman Catholic Parish – Sierra Vista. (TUC)
White Church, MO, Howell Co., St. Joseph, c/o Willow Springs, MO, Sacred Heart. (SPC)
White Earth, MN, Becker Co., St. Benedict, c/o Ogema, MN, Most Holy Redeemer. (CR)
White Horse, SD, Dewey Co., St. Therese, c/o Eagle Butte, SD, All Saints. (RC)
White Horse Beach, MA, St. Catherine's Chapel, c/o Manomet, MA, St. Bonaventure. (BO)
White Lake, NY, Sullivan Co., St. Anne, c/o Monticello, NY, St. Peter. (NY)
White Pigeon, MI, St. Joseph Co., St. Joseph, c/o Sturgis, MI, Holy Angels. (KAL)
White River, SD, Mellette Co., Sacred Heart, c/o St. Francis, SD, St. Francis Mission/Rosebud Educational Society. (RC)
White River, SD, Mellette Co., St. Ignatius, c/o St. Francis, SD, St. Francis Mission/Rosebud Educational Society. (RC)
White Rock, NM, Los Alamos Co., St. Joseph, c/o Los Alamos, NM, Immaculate Heart of Mary. (SFE)
Whiteville, LA, Resurrection, c/o Morrow, LA, St. Peter. (LAF)
Whitley City, KY, Good Shepherd Chapel, c/o Somerset, KY, St. Mildred. (LEX)
Wibaux, MT, Wibaux Co., St. Peter, c/o Glendive, MT, Sacred Heart. (GF)
Wibaux, MT, Wibaux Co., St. Philip, c/o Glendive, MT, Sacred Heart. (GF)
Wiggins, CO, Morgan Co., Our Lady of Lourdes, c/o Roggen, CO, Sacred Heart. (DEN)
Wilkeson, WA, Pierce Co., Our Lady of Lourdes, c/o Buckley, WA, St. Aloysius. (SEA)
Willacoochee, GA, Atkinson Co., Holy Family, c/o Douglas, GA, St. Paul's. (SAV)
Willard, NM, Torrance Co., c/o Mountainair, NM, St. Alice. (SFE)
Williams, CA, Colusa Co., Church of the Annunciation, c/o Williams, CA, Sacred Heart. (SAC)
Williams, MN, Lake of the Woods Co., St. Joseph, c/o Baudette, MN, Sacred Heart. (CR)
Williamsfield, IL, Knox Co., St. James, c/o Brimfield, IL, St. Joseph's. (PEO)
Williamstown, PA, Dauphin Co., Sacred Heart of Jesus, c/o Lykens, PA, Our Lady Help of Christians. (HBG)
Williamstown, VT, Orange Co., St. Edward, c/o Northfield, VT, St. John the Evangelist. (BUR)
Williamsville, MO, Wayne Co., Our Lady of Sorrows, c/o Piedmont, MO, St. Catherine of Siena. (SPC)
Willow, AK, St. Christopher, c/o Big Lake, AK, Corp. of Our Lady of the Lake Church. (ANC)
Wills Point, TX, Van Zandt Co., St. Luke, c/o Canton, TX, St. Therese. (TYL)
Wilson, TX, Lynn Co., Blessed Sacrament, c/o Post, TX, Holy Cross. (LUB)
Wilton, MN, Beltrami Co., Sacred Heart, c/o Red Lake, MN, St. Mary's Mission Church. (CR)
Wimauma, FL, Hillsborough, Our Lady of Guadalupe Mission, c/o Sun City Center, FL, Prince of Peace. (SP)
Windsor, MO, Henry Co., St. Bartholomew, c/o Clinton, MO, Holy Rosary. (KC)
Wingdale, NY, Dutchess Co., Our Lady of Solace Mission, c/o Dover Plains, NY, St. Charles Borromeo. (NY)
Winifred, MT, Fergus Co., Holy Family, c/o Lewistown, MT, St. Leo. (GF)
Winn, ME, Penobscot Co., Sacred Heart, c/o Lincoln, ME, St. Mary. (PRT)
Winn, MI, Isabella Co., St. Leo, c/o Shepherd, MI, St. Vincent De Paul. (SAG)
Winnett, MT, Petroleum Co., St. Aloysius, c/o Roundup, MT, St. Benedict. (GF)
Winona, MS, Montgomery Co., Sacred Heart, c/o Lexington, MS, St. Thomas. (JKS)
Winston–Salem, NC, Forsyth Co., Our Lady of Fatima, c/o Winston–Salem, NC, Our Lady of Mercy. (CHL)
Winter Harbor, ME, Hancock Co., St. Margaret, c/o Ellsworth, ME, St. Joseph. (PRT)
Winter Park, CO, Grand Co., St. Bernard of Montjoux, c/o Granby, CO, St. Anne. (DEN)
Wisdom, MT, Beaverhead Co., Our Lady of Wisdom, c/o Dillon, MT, St. Rose of Lima. (HEL)
Wolf Creek, MT, Lewis and Clark Co., Sacred Heart, c/o Helena, MT, Our Lady of the Valley. (HEL)
Wolfforth, TX, Lubbock Co., St. Francis of Assisi, c/o Lubbock, TX, San Ramon. (LUB)
Wood, SD, Melette Co., Our Lady of Good Counsel, c/o White River, SD, St. Ignatius. (RC)
Wood, SD, Mellette Co., Our Lady of Good Counsel, c/o St. Francis, SD, St. Francis Mission/Rosebud Educational Society. (RC)
Woodland, WI, Dodge Co., St. Mary, c/o Neosho, WI, St. Matthew. (MIL)
Woodville, CA, Tulare Co., St. Francis of Assisi, c/o Tipton, CA, St. John The Evangelist. (FRS)
Worcester, MA, St. Andrew the Apostle Mission, c/o Worcester, MA, St. Peter. (WOR)
Wright, WY, Campbell Co., Blessed Sacrament, c/o Gillette, WY, St. Matthew's. (CHY)
Wrightsville, PA, Mother of Holy Purity Chapel, c/o Columbia, PA, St. Peter. (HBG)
Wyola, MT, Big Horn Co., Blessed Kateri Tekakwitha, c/o Lodge Grass, MT, Our Lady of Loretto. (GF)

Y

Yacolt, WA, Clark Co., St. Joseph the Worker, c/o Battle Ground, WA, Sacred Heart. (SEA)
Yahuecas, PR, Adjuntas Co., Virgen del Carmen, c/o Adjuntas, PR, St. Joachim. (PCE)
Yakima, WA, Yakima Co., St. Joseph Mission at the Ahtanum, c/o Yakima, WA, Holy Family. (YAK)
Yancey, TX, Medina Co., Immaculate Heart of Mary, c/o D'Hanis, TX, Holy Cross. (SAT)
Yarmouth Port, MA, Barnstable Co., Sacred Heart Chapel, c/o Hyannis, MA, St. Francis Xavier's. (FR)
Yellville, AR, Marion Co., St Andrews Catholic Church, c/o Harrison, AR, Mary, Mother of God. (LR)
Yolo, CA, Yolo Co., Our Lady of Guadalupe, c/o Woodland, CA, Holy Rosary. (SAC)
Yorktown, TX, DeWitt Co., San Luis, c/o Yorktown, TX, Holy Cross. (VIC)
Young, AZ, Gila Co., St. Benedict Mission, c/o Payson, AZ, Saint Philip the Apostle Roman Catholic Church – Payson. (TUC)
Youngsville, NM, Rio Arriba Co., c/o Abiquiu, NM, St. Thomas Apostle. (SFE)
Youngsville, NY, Sullivan Co., St. Francis of Assisi, c/o Jeffersonville, NY, St. George–St. Francis. (NY)
Yuma, AZ, Yuma Co., Our Lady of Guadalupe, c/o Yuma, AZ, Immaculate Conception Roman Catholic Parish & Guadalupe Mission – Yuma. (TUC)

Z

Zamora, CA, Yolo Co., St. Agnes, c/o Knights Landing, CA, St. Paul. (SAC)
Zia, NM, Sandoval Co., c/o Jemez Pueblo, NM, San Diego Indian Missions. (SFE)
Zolfo Springs, FL, Hardee Co., San Alfonso Catholic Center, c/o Wauchula, FL, St. Michael. (VEN)
Zortman, MT, Phillips Co., St. Joseph, c/o Hays, MT, St. Paul's Indian Mission. (GF)

Index for Religious Institutes of Men

Religious Order Initials for Men

A. Assumptionists [0130]
G.S. Little Brothers of the Good Shepherd [0580]
H.S. Brothers of the Holy Spirit [0645]
.S.O. Basilian Salvatorian Fathers [0190]
F.A. Alexian Brothers [0120]
F.C. Congregation of Christian Brothers [0310]
F.M.M. Brothers of Our Lady, Mother of Mercy [0980]
.F.P. Brothers of the Poor of St. Francis [0460]
F.R. Franciscan Friars of the Renewal [0535]
.F.X. Brothers of St. Francis Xavier [1350]
.I.C.M. Missionhurst Congregation of the Immaculate Heart of Mary [0860]
.J. Josephite Fathers [0710]
.M. Congregation of the Mission [1330]
.M.C. Congregation of Mother Coredemptrix [0865]
.M.F. Claretian Missionaries [0360]
.M.I. Carmelites of Mary Immaculate [0275]
.M.L.M. The Congregation of Maronite Lebanese Missionaries [0785]
.M.M. Congregation of Mariannhill Missionaries, Marianhill Fathers & Brothers [0750]
.O. Oratorians [0950]
.P. Congregation of the Passion [1000]
.P.M. Congregation of the Fathers of Mercy [0820]
.PP.S. Society of the Precious Blood [1060]
.R. Congregation of the Resurrection [1080]
.R. Theatine Fathers [1300]
:.R.L. Canons Regular of the Lateran [0250]
:.R.M. Adorno Fathers [0100]
'.R.S. Somascan Fathers [1250]
:.R.S.P. Clerics Regular of St. Paul [0160]
.S. Missionaries of St. Charles-Scalabrinians [1210]
.S.B. Basilian Fathers [0170]
:.S.C. Brothers of the Congregation of Holy Cross [0600]
:.S.C. Priests of the Congregation of Holy Cross [0610]
:.S.J. Congregation of St. Joseph [1150]
:.S.P. Paulist Fathers [1030]
:.S.P.X. Brothers of Saint Pius X [1180]
:.S.S. Stigmatine Fathers and Brothers. [1280]
:.S.Sp. Congregation of the Holy Spirit [0650]
:.Ss.R. Redemptorist Fathers [1070]
:.S.V. Clerics of St. Viator [1320]
:r.Cam. Camaldolese Hermits of the Congregation of Monte Corona [0230]
'.C. Brothers of Charity [0290]
'.D.P. Sons of Divine Providence [0410]
'.F.I. Franciscan Friars of the Immaculate [0533]
'.F.S.C. Franciscan Brothers of the Holy Cross [0510]
'.I.C. Brothers of Christian Instruction [0320]
'.M.M. Brothers of Mercy [0810]
'.M.M. Missionary Fraternity of Mary [0855]
'.M.S. The Marist Brothers [0770]
'.M.S.I. Sons of Mary Missionary Society [1270]
'.S.C. Brothers of the Christian Schools [0330]
'.S.C.B. Priestly Fraternity of the Missionaries of St. Charles Borromeo [1205]
'.S.E. Brothers of the Holy Eucharist [0620]

F.S.P. Brothers of St. Patrick [1160]
F.S.R. Brothers of the Congregation of Our Lady of the Holy Rosary [0960]
F.S.S.P. Priestly Fraternity of St. Peter [1065]
G.H.M. The Glenmary Home Missioners [0570]
H.G.N. Heralds of Good News [0585]
I.C. Institute of Charity [0300]
I.C. Institute of Christ the King - Sovereign Priest [0305]
I.H.M. Brothers of the Immaculate Heart of Mary [0680]
I.M.C. Consolata Missionaries [0390]
I.V.E. Institute of the Incarnate Word [0685]
L.B.S.F. Little Brothers of Saint Francis [1144]
L.C. Legionaries of Christ [0730]
M.Afr. Missionaries of Africa [0850]
M.C.C.J. Comboni Missionaries of the Heart of Jesus (Verona) [0380]
M.E.P. Paris Foreign Mission Society [0897]
M.H.M. Mill Hill Missionaries [0830]
M.I. Camillian Fathers and Brothers [0240]
M.I.C. Congregation of Marians of the Immaculate Conception [0740]
M.M. Maryknoll [0800]
M.M.A. Maronite Monks of Adoration [0790]
M.S. The Missionaries of Our Lady of La Salette [0720]
M.S.A. Society of the Missionaries of the Holy Apostles [0590]
M.S.C. Missionaries of the Sacred Heart [1110]
M.S.F. Congregation of the Missionaries of the Holy Family [0630]
M.S.F.S. Missionaries of St. Francis de Sales [0485]
M.S.P. Missionary Society of St. Paul of Nigeria [0854]
M.Sp.S. Missionaries of the Holy Spirit [0660]
M.S.S. Missionaries of the Blessed Sacrament [0825]
M.SS.CC. Missionaries of the Sacred Hearts of Jesus and Mary [1120]
O.A.R. Order of Augustinian Recollects [0150]
O.Carm. Carmelite Fathers and Brothers [0270]
O.Cart. Order of Carthusians [0280]
O.C.D. Discalced Carmelite Friars [0260]
O.Cist. Cistercian Fathers [0340]
O.C.S.O. The Cistercian Order of the Strict Observance (Trappists) [0350]
O.de.M. Order of Our Lady of Mercy [0970]
O.F.M. Franciscan Friars [0520]
O.F.M.Cap. The Capuchin Franciscan Friars [0470]
O.F.M.Conv. Conventual Franciscans [0480]
O.H. Hospitaller Brothers of St. John of God [0670]
O.M. Minim Fathers [0835]
O.M.I. Oblates of Mary Immaculate [0910]
O.M.M. Maronite Order of the Blessed Virgin Mary [0782]
O.M.V. Oblates of the Virgin Mary [0940]
O.P. Order of Preachers (Dominicans) [0430]

O.Praem. Canons Regular of Premontre [0900]
O.S.A. The Augustinians [0140]
O.S.B. Benedictine Monks [0200]
O S.B.M. Order of St. Basil the Great [0180]
O.S.C. Canons Regular of the Order of the Holy Cross [0400]
O.S.F. Congregation of the Religious Brothers of the Third Order Regular of St. Francis [0490]
O.S.F. Franciscan Brothers of the Third Order Regular [0515]
O.S.F. Franciscan Missionary Brothers of the Sacred Heart of Jesus [0540]
O.S.F.S. Oblates of St. Francis de Sales [0920]
O.S.J. Oblates of St. Joseph [0930]
O.S.M. Servites [1240]
O.S.P.P.E. Pauline Fathers [1010]
O.Ss.S. Brigittine Monks [0895]
O.SS.T. Order of the Most Holy Trinity [1310]
P.I.M.E. Pontifical Institute for Foreign Missions [1050]
R.C.J. Rogationist Fathers [1090]
S.A. Franciscan Friars of the Atonement [0530]
S.A.C. Society of the Catholic Apostolate [0990]
S.C. Brothers of the Sacred Heart [1100]
S.C. Servants of Charity [1220]
S.Ch. Society of Christ [1260]
Sch.P. Piarist Fathers. [1040]
S.C.J. Congregation of the Priests of the Sacred Heart [1130]
S.D.B. Salesians of Don Bosco [1190]
S.D.S. Society of the Divine Savior [1200]
S.D.V. Vocationist Fathers [1340]
S.F. Sons of the Holy Family [0640]
S.J. Jesuit Fathers and Brothers [0690]
S.M. Society of Mary (Marianists) [0760]
S.M. Marist Fathers [0780]
S.M.A. Society of African Missions [0110]
S.M.M. Montfort Missionaries [0870]
S.O.L.T. Society of Our Lady of the Most Holy Trinity [0975]
s.P. Servants of the Paraclete [1230]
S.P.S. St. Patrick's Missionary Society [1170]
S.S. Society of the Priests of Saint Sulpice [1290]
S.S.C. Society of St. Columban [0370]
SS.CC. Congregation of the Sacred Hearts of Jesus and Mary [1140]
S.S.E. Society of Saint Edmund [0440]
S.S.J. St. Joseph's Society of the Sacred Heart [0700]
S.S.P. Pauline Fathers and Brothers [1020]
S.S.S. Congregation of the Blessed Sacrament [0220]
S.T. Missionary Servants of the Most Holy Trinity [0840]
S.X. Xaverian Missionary Fathers [1360]
S.V.D. Society of the Divine Word [0420]
V.C. Vincentian Congregation (India) [0420]
T.O.R. Third Order Regular of Saint Francis [0560]

Religious Institutes of Men

The Conference of Major Religious Superiors of Men, U.S.A., 8808 Cameron St., Silver Spring, MD 20910. Tel: 301-588-4030; Fax: 301-587-4575; Website: cmsm.org. A canonical conference of the major superiors of religious communities and institutes of men for the purpose of promoting the spiritual and apostolic welfare of Priests and Brothers. Rev. Paul Lininger, O.F.M.Conv., Exec. Dir.; Abbot Giles Hayes, O.S.B., Pres.; Very Rev. Thomas Smolich, S.J., Vice Pres.; Bro. Ronald Talbot, S.C., Sec. & Treas.

[0100] (C.R.M.)—ADORNO FATHERS
(Clerics Regular Minor)

General Motherhouse: *Via Alpi Apuane 1*, 00141, Rome, Italy, Very Rev. Raffaele Mandolesi, C.R.M., Supr. Gen.

U.S. Foundation (1936): *St. Michael's Seminary*, 575 Darlington Ave., Ramsey, NJ 07446. Tel: 201-327-7375; Fax: 201-327-8131. Rev. Hector DiNardo, C.R.M., U.S. Delegate, Supr. & Rector.

Priests: 10; Brothers: 5

Represented in the Archdiocese of Newark and in the Diocese of Charleston.

[0110] (S.M.A.)—SOCIETY OF AFRICAN MISSIONS
(Societas Missionum ad Afros)

Founded Dec. 8, 1856 with the approval of Pope Pius IX. A clerical society of apostolic life.

Generalate: Via della Nocetta 111, 00164, Rome, Italy, Very Rev. Jean-Marie Guillaume, S.M.A., Supr. Gen; Rev. Thomas M. Wright, S.M.A., Gen. Councilor; Rev. Paul Ennin, S.M.A., Gen. Councilor.

American Province (1941): 23 Bliss Ave., Tenafly, NJ 07670. Tel: 201-567-9085; Fax: 800-670-8328. Very Rev. Michael P. Moran, S.M.A., Prov. Supr; Rev. Brendan Darcy, S.M.A., Vice Prov; Rev. Frank Wright, S.M.A., Councilor.

Legal Title: Society of African Missions, Inc. NJ.

Priests: 24; Lay Missionary in temporary commitment: 4; Lay Missionary in permanent commitment: 1; Priest Associates: 1

Represented in the Archdioceses of Boston, Newark and Washington.

[0120] (C.F.A.)—ALEXIAN BROTHERS
(Congregatio Fratrum Cellitarum seu Alexianorum)

Generalate: Signal Mountain, TN 37377. Tel: 423-886-0212. Bro. Edward Walsh, Supr. Gen; Bro. Warren Longo, Asst. Supr. Gen; Bro. Dominkus Seeberg, C.F.A., Gen. Councilor 52001, Germany,Bro. John of God Oblina, C.F.A., Gen. Councilor Davao City, Philippines,

General Motherhouse: *Congregation of Alexian Brothers*, No. 198 James Blvd., Signal Mountain, TN 37377. Tel: 423-886-0212; Fax: 423-886-0208.

United States Province: 3040 W. Salt Creek Ln., Arlington Heights, IL 60005. Tel: 847-385-7147; Fax: 847-483-7036. Councilors: Bro. James Classon, C.F.A., Prov; Bro. Theodore Loucks, C.F.A; Bro. John Howard, C.F.A; Bro. Richard Lowe, C.F.A; Bro. Lawrence Krueger, C.F.A., Vicar Prov.

Professed Brothers: 28; Novice Brothers: 5

Properties owned or sponsored: General Hospitals 4; Continuing Care Retirement Communities 2; Alzheimers Assisted Living Facility 1; Novitiates 2; Nursing Homes 2; Residential AIDS Facility 2; HUD Housing 2; Pace 2; Mobile Clinic & Wellness Center (Davo City, Philipppines) 1; Independent Living facility 1; Senior Center 1.

Represented in the Archdioceses of Chicago, Milwaukee and St. Louis and in the Diocese of Knoxville. Also in Davao City, Philippines and Györ, Hungary.

[0130] (A.A.)—ASSUMPTIONISTS
(Augustinians of the Assumption)

General House: via San Pio V, 55, 00165, Rome, Italy, Very Rev. Richard Lamoureux, A.A., Supr. Gen.

Province of North America (1946): 330 Market St., Brighton, MA 02135. Tel: 617-783-0400. Rev. Marcel Poirier, A.A., Prov. Supr. Councilors: Rev. Miguel Diaz Ayllon, A.A; Rev. Dennis Gallagher, A.A; Rev. Donald Espinosa, A.A., Prov. Treas.

Priests: 45; Brothers: 10; Parishes: 1; Shrines: 1; Colleges: 1; Formation Centers: 1; Novitiates: 1; Residences: 8

Represented in the Archdioceses of Boston and New York and in the Dioceses of Nashville and Worcester. Also in Korea, Philippines, Kenya, Mexico, Tanzania, Italy and Canada.

[0140] (O.S.A.)—THE AUGUSTINIANS
(Ordo Sancti Augustini)

Founded in 1244, first American foundation 1796.

Generalate: *Via Paolo VI - 25*, 00193, Rome, Italy, Very Rev. Robert F. Prevost, O.S.A., Prior Gen; Very Rev. Michael F. Di Gregorio, O.S.A., Vicar Gen; Very Rev. Anthony M. Genovese, O.S.A., Prior Provincial; Rev. Michael H. Bielecki, O.S.A., Province Sec; Rev. Martin L. Smith, O.S.A., Province Treas. & Counselor.

Province of St. Thomas of Villanova (1796): *Saint Augustine Friary*, 214 Ashwood Rd., P.O. Box 340, Villanova, PA 19085-0340. Tel: 610-527-3330. Counselors: Rev. Gary N. McCloskey, O.S.A; Rev. James M. Paradis, O.S.A; Rev. Raymond F. Dlugos, O.S.A; Rev. Joseph L. Farrell, O.S.A; Rev. Carlos E. Urbina, O.S.A; Paul Ashton, Abuse Prevention & Educ Coord.; Rev. Kevin DePrinzio, O.S.A., Dir. Vocations; Rev. Joseph S. Mostardi, O.S.A., Dir. Augustinian Volunteers; Rev. Anthony P. Burrascano, O.S.A., Dir. Mission Office; Rev. John J. Sheridan, O.S.A., Province Archivist; Rev. John E. Deegan, O.S.A., Dir. Justice & Peace; Rev. Gordon E. Marcellus, O.S.A., Dir. Devel.

Legal Title: The Brothers of the Order of Hermits of Saint Augustine (The Brothers of the Order of Hermits of St. Augustine, a corporation in the state of Pennsylvania 1804).

Priests: 179; Students of Theology: 4; Brothers: 5; Permanent Deacons: 1; Parishes (USA 15, Japan 4; South Africa 1): 20; Major Seminaries: 1; Colleges: 1; Universities: 1; Preparatory Schools and High Schools & Foreign Missions: 5

Represented in the Archdioceses of Boston, Miami, New York and Philadelphia and in the Dioceses of Albany, Camden and Venice.

Province of Our Mother of Good Counsel (Order of St. Augustine) (1941): *Tolentine College & Center*, 20300 Governors Hwy., Olympia Fields, IL 60461-1081. Tel: 708-748-9500; Fax: 708-481-2090; Web: www.MidwestAugustinians.org. Very Rev. Bernard C. Scianna, O.S.A., Prior Prov; Rev. Michael J. Slattery, O.S.A., Vicar Prov. & Treas; Rev. Thomas R. McCarthy, O.S.A., Vocation Dir; Bro. Thomas P. Taylor, O.S.A., Prov. Sec; Bro. Gary L. Hresil, O.S.A., Personnel Dir.

Fathers: 71; Bishops: 2; Professed Brothers: 14; Parishes: 7; High Schools: 3; Retreat Centers: 1; Residences: 3

Represented in the Archdioceses of Chicago, Detroit and Milwaukee and in the Dioceses of Joliet, Kalamazoo, Lansing and Tulsa. Also in Peru, South America.

Province of St. Augustine: 1605 28th St., San Diego, CA 92102. Tel: 619-235-0247. Rev. Gary E. Sanders, O.S.A., Prov. Counselors: Rev. James P. Retzner, O.S.A., Sec; Rev. Robert W. Gavotto, O.S.A; Rev. John D. Keller, O.S.A; Rev. Gregory D. Heidenblut, O.S.A; Rev. Kevin C. Mullins, O.S.A.

Priests: 25; Deacons: 2; Brothers: 3; Parishes: 5; High Schools: 2; Orphanages: 1

Legal Holdings or Titles: St. Augustine High School, San Diego, CA; Monica House, San Diego, CA; Tierra del Sol, Boulevard, CA; St. Rita House, San Francisco, CA; Villanova Preparatory School, Ojai, CA; Austin House, San Diego, CA.

Represented in the Archdioceses of Chicago, Los Angeles, Milwaukee and Portland in Oregon and in the Dioceses of Honolulu, Oakland and San Diego.

St. Augustine Monastery: 611 Cedar Ave., P.O. Box 279, Richland, NJ 08350. Tel: 856-697-2600; Fax: 856-697-8389. Rev. Francis X. Devlin, O.S.A., Prior; Rev. Donald F. Reilly, O.S.A., Pres; Rev. Francis J. Horn, O.S.A., Headmaster & Subprior; Rev. Ronald A. Hamaday, O.S.A., Treas; Rev. Patrick B. McStravoy, O.S.A., Asst. to Pres. for Mission & Ministry; Rev. Stephen M. Curry, O.S.A.

Represented in the Archdiocese of Philadelphia and in the Diocese of Camden.

Region U.S.A. (1993): *Cristo Rey Church*, 767 Ave. A, Beaumont, TX 77701. Tel: 409-835-7788. Rev. Luis Urriza, O.S.A.

Fathers: 4

Represented in the Archdiocese of San Antonio and in the Diocese of Beaumont.

[0150] (O.A.R.)—ORDER OF AUGUSTINIAN RECOLLECTS
(Ordo Augustinianorum Recollectorum)

General Motherhouse: Viale dell' Astronomia, 27, Casella Postale 10760, 00144, Rome, Italy, Very Rev. Miguel Miro, O.A.R., Prior Gen.

Province of St. Augustine (1943): *Augustinian Recollects*, 29 Ridgeway Ave., West Orange, NJ 07052-3297. Tel: 973-731-0616; Fax: 973-731-1033. Rev. Joseph J. Gallardo, O.A.R., Prior Prov; Rev. Domingos A. Machado, O.A.R., 1st Councilor, Vicar of Prov; Rev. Fidel Hernandez, 2nd Councilor; Rev. J. Michael Rafferty, O.A.R., 3rd Councilor; Rev. Eliseo Gonzalez, O.A.R., 4th Councilor.

Bishops: 1; Priests: 35; Brothers: 3; Professed Clerics: 4; Permanent Deacons: 3

Represented in the Archdioceses of Los Angeles, Newark and New York and in the Diocese of Orange. Also in Mexico.

Province of St. Nicholas of Tolentine (U.S.A. Delegation): 3021 Frutas Ave., El Paso, TX 79905. Rev. Antonio Lasheras, O.A.R., Prov. Delegate.

Priests: 21

Represented in the Archdioceses of Newark and New York and in the Dioceses of El Paso and Las Cruces.

[0160] (C.R.S.P.)—CLERICS REGULAR OF ST. PAUL
(Barnabite Fathers)
(Ordo Clericorum Regularium Sancti Pauli)

Founded in Milan, Italy in 1533. First foundation in the United States in 1952 in Buffalo, NY.

General Motherhouse: Historical Motherhouse: Church of St. Barnabas, Milan, since 1545. Via Giacomo Medici, 15, Rome, Italy, Most Rev. Giovanni M. Villa, C.R.S.P., Supr. Gen.

North American Province: 981 Swann Rd., P.O. Box 167, Youngstown, NY 14174-0167. Tel: 716-754-7489. Very Rev. Robert B.M. Kosek, C.R.S.P., Prov. Superior.

Legal Title: Barnabite Fathers, Inc.

Priests: 13; Novices: 1

Fathers staff and serve: Parishes; Marian Shrine; Colleges; Spiritual Centers.

Properties Owned or Sponsored: Our Lady of Fatima Shrine and Barnabite Fathers Seminary, Youngstown, NY; Barnabite Spiritual Center, Bethlehem, PA; St. Anthony M. Zaccaria Seminary.

Represented in the Dioceses of Allentown, Buffalo, and San Diego. Also in Hamilton, Ontario, Canada.

[0170] (C.S.B.)—BASILIAN FATHERS
(Congregatio Presbyterorum a St. Basilio)

General Curia: *Cardinal Flahiff Basilian Centre*, 95 St. Joseph St., M5S 3C2, Toronto, Tel: 416-921-6674; Fax: 416-920-3413.

U.S. Headquarters: *Christ the King Church*, 445 Kings Hwy. S., Rochester, NY 14614. Tel: 585-266-1288. Very Rev. George T. Smith, C.S.B., Supr. Gen; Rev. Paul F. English, C.S.B., Gen. Councilor.

[0180] (O.S.B.M.)—ORDER OF ST. BASIL THE GREAT
(Ordo Sancti Basilii Magni)

General Superior "Protoarchimandrita": Via San Giosafat 8, (Aventino), 00153, Rome, Italy, Rev. Basilio Koubetch, O.S.B.M.

American Province (1948): 29 Peacock Ln., Locust Valley, NY 11560. Tel: 516-609-3262; Fax: 516-609-3264. Very Rev. Philip Patrick J. Sandrick, O.S.B.M., Prov.

Fathers: 21; Brothers: 2; Deacons: 1; Parishes: 6; Community Houses: 6; Novitiates: 1; Monasteries: 3; Retreat Houses: 1; Libraries: 1

Represented in the Byzantine Rite Archdiocese of Philadelphia and in the Byzantine Rite Dioceses of Chicago, Parma, Passaic and Stamford.

[0190] (B.S.O.)—BASILIAN SALVATORIAN FATHERS

General Motherhouse: *Holy Savior Monastery*, Saida, Lebanon, Archimandrite Sleyman Abouzeid, B.S.O., Supr. Gen.

American Headquarters: *Basilian Salvatorian Fathers*, 30 East St., Methuen, MA 01844. Rt. Rev. John Faraj, B.S.O., Prov. Supr; Rt. Rev. Simon Hage, B.S.O; Rev. Lawrence Tumminelli, B.S.O; Rt. Rev. Archimandrite John Jadaa, B.S.O; Rev. Youssef Aziz, B.S.O; Rt. Rev. George Dagher, B.S.O; Rt. Rev. Eugene Mitchell, B.S.O., General Economos; Rev. Martin A. Hyatt, B.S.O., Local Supr; Rev. Antoine Rizk, B.S.O.

Fathers in American Region: 22

Novitiate and House of Studies: St. Basils Seminary; Methuen, MA.

Parishes: Canada 4; U.S.A. 7.

Represented in the Archdioceses of Boston and Miami, the Dioceses of Cleveland, Manchester and Norwich and the Eparchy of Newton.

[0200] (O.S.B.)—BENEDICTINE MONKS
(Ordo Sancti Benedicti)

American Cassinese Congregation of the Order of Saint Benedict (Established by Pope Pius IX, August 24, 1855.)

Headquarters: *St. Procopius Abbey*, 5601 College Rd., Lisle, IL 60532. Tel: 320-363-3935; Fax: 320-363-3082. Rt. Rev. Hugh R. Anderson, O.S.B., Abbot & Pres. President's Council: Rt. Rev. Douglas R. Nowicki, O.S.B., 1st Councilor Saint Vincent Archabbey: Rt. Rev. Matthew K. Leavy, O.S.B., 2nd Councilor; Rev. Valerian Odermann, O.S.B., 3rd Councilor; Ven. Bro. Valerian Odermann, O.S.B., 4th Councilor; Ven. Bro. David Kelly, O.S.B., Sec. The Abbeys and Priories belonging to this Congregation are as follows:

Saint Vincent Archabbey: 300 Fraser Purchase Rd., Latrobe, PA 15650-2690. Tel: 724-532-6600. Rt. Rev. Douglas R. Nowicki, O.S.B., Archabbot; Rt. Rev. Paul R. Maher, O.S.B., Archabbot (Resigned); Most Rev. Rembert G. Weakland, O.S.B., Resigned Archbishop of Milwaukee.

Legal Title: The Benedictine Society of Westmoreland County; Saint Vincent College Corporation; The Wimmer Corporation; The Saint Vincent Cemetery Corporation.
Priests: 106; Deacons: 4; Junior Professed Monks: 12; Brothers: 32
Represented in the Archdiocese of Baltimore and in the Dioceses of Altoona-Johnstown, Erie, Greensburg, Harrisburg, Pittsburgh, Richmond, Savannah and Wheeling-Charleston.

American Cassinese Congregations

St. John's Abbey: 31802 County Rd 159, P.O. Box 2015, Collegeville, MN 56321-2015. Tel: 320-363-2011; Fax: 320-363-3082. Rt. Rev. John Klassen, O.S.B., Abbot; Very Rev. Thomas Andert, O.S.B., Prior; Very Rev. Jonathan Licari, O.S.B., Subprior.
Fathers: 92; Professed Brothers: 57; Novices: 3; Abbeys: 1; Dependent Priories: 1; Parishes: 12; Chaplaincies: 7; Japanese Residences: 1; Schools of Theology: 1; Universities: 1; High Schools: 1; Novitiates: 1
Monastery founded in 1856 and raised to an Abbey in 1866.
Legal Holdings: Saint John's Seminary; Saint John's University; Saint John's Preparatory School; Saint John's Abbey.
Represented in the Archdiocese of St. Paul-Minneapolis and in the Dioceses of New Ulm, St. Cloud and San Bernardino. Also in Japan and The Bahamas.

St. Benedict's Abbey: 1020 North Second St., Atchison, KS 66002-1499. Tel: 913-367-7853; Fax: 913-367-6230. Rt. Rev. Barnabas Senecal, O.S.B.; Rt. Rev. Owen Purcell, O.S.B., Retired Abbot; Rt. Rev. Ralph Koehler, O.S.B., Retired Abbot; Very Rev. James R. Albers, O.S.B., Prior; Rev. Meinrad Miller, O.S.B., Subprior.
Bishops: 1; Fathers: 36; Brothers Professed: 13; Abbeys: 1; Parishes: 11; Missions: 1; Chaplaincies: 5; Colleges: 1; High Schools: 1
Founded in 1857 and raised to an Abbey in 1876.
Represented in the Archdiocese of Kansas City in Kansas. Also in Brazil.

St. Mary's Abbey: *Delbarton*, 230 Mendham Rd., Morristown, NJ 07960. Tel: 973-538-3231; Fax: 973-538-7109; Web: www.osbmonks.org. Rt. Rev. Giles P. Hayes, O.S.B., Abbot; Very Rev. Bruno A. Ugliano, O.S.B., Prior; Rev. Jerome Borski, O.S.B., Subprior.
Priests: 34; Brothers: 6; Deacons: 2; Juniors: 5; Novices: 1; Parishes: 2; Preparatory Schools: 1; Retreat Centers: 1
Monastery founded in 1857 and raised to an Abbey in 1884.
Represented in the Archdiocese of Newark and in the Dioceses of Metuchen, Paterson and Trenton.

Newark Abbey: 528 Dr. Martin Luther King, Jr. Blvd., Newark, NJ 07102. Tel: 973-643-4800; Fax: 973-643-6922. Rt. Rev. Melvin J. Valvano, O.S.B., Abbot; Very Rev. Augustine J. Curley, O.S.B., Prior; Very Rev. Matthew S. Wotelko, O.S.B., Subprior.
Priests: 12; Brothers: 2; Abbeys: 1; Parishes: 1; Preparatory (High) Schools: 1
Priory founded 1857; Abbey in 1884; title transferred from Newark to Morristown, N.J. in 1956; became Abbey again in 1968 and known as Newark Abbey under the patronage of the Immaculate Conception.
Legal Holding: St. Benedict Preparatory School, Newark, NJ.
Represented in the Archdioceses of Indianapolis and Newark.

Belmont Abbey: 100 Belmont-Mount Holly Rd., Belmont, NC 28012-1802. Tel: 704-825-6675; Fax: 704-825-6242. Rt. Rev. Placid D. Solari, O.S.B., Abbot; Rt. Rev. Oscar C. Burnett, O.S.B., Retired Abbot & Prior.
Legal Title: Southern Benedictine Society of North Carolina, Incorporated.
Priests: 11; Brothers: 7
Monastery founded in 1876, raised to an Abbey in 1884 and erected into an Abbey Nullius in 1910; Abbey Nullius suppressed January 1, 1977 and incorporated into Diocese of Charlotte.
Properties owned or sponsored: Belmont Abbey College, Belmont, NC.

St. Bernard Abbey (1891): Cullman, AL 35055. Tel: 256-734-8291; Fax: 256-734-3885. Rt. Rev. Cletus D. Meagher, O.S.B., Abbot; Very Rev. Kevin D. McGrath, O.S.B., Prior & Novice Master; Ven. Bro. Leo Borelli, O.S.B., Subprior.
Legal Title: St. Benedictine Society of Alabama, Inc.
Priests: 13; Brothers: 17
Represented in the Archdiocese of Mobile and in the Diocese of Birmingham.

St. Procopius Abbey: 5601 College Rd., Lisle, IL 60532. Tel: 630-969-6410; Fax: 630-969-6426; Web: www.procopius.org. Rt. Rev. Austin G. Murphy, O.S.B., Abbot; Rt. Rev. Hugh R. Anderson, O.S.B., Abbot Pres; Rev. Anthony J. Jacob, O.S.B; Very Ven. Columban Trojan, O.S.B., Prior; Very Ven. Gregory Perron, O.S.B., Subprior; Rev. James Flint, O.S.B., Treas; Rev. Becket Franks, O.S.B; Rev. David Turner, O.S.B; Rev. Edward J. Kucera, O.S.B; Rev. Joseph Chang, O.S.B; Rev. Jude D. Randall, O.S.B; Rev. Julian von Duerbeck, O.S.B; Rev. Odilo Crkva, O.S.B; Rev. Philip S. Timko, O.S.B; Rev. Theodore D. Suchy, O.S.B; Rev. Thomas Chisholm, O.S.B.
Archbishops: 1; Priests: 18; Brothers: 10
Monastery founded in 1885 and raised to an Abbey in 1894.
Legal Holdings or Titles: Benedictine University, Lisle, IL; Benet Academy, Lisle, IL; Benedictine Chinese Mission, Lisle, IL; Slav Mission, Lisle, IL; St. Procopius Abbey Endowment, Lisle, IL; St. Scholastica Mission House, Lisle, IL.
Represented in the Diocese of Joliet. Also in Taiwan.

St. Gregory's Abbey: 1900 W. MacArthur St., Shawnee, OK 74804. Tel: 405-878-5491; Fax: 405-878-5189. Rt. Rev. Lawrence Stasyszen, O.S.B., Abbot; Rt. Rev. Adrian Vorderlandwehr, O.S.B., Resigned; Rt. Rev. Charles Massoth, O.S.B., Resigned; Rt. Rev. Martin Lugo, O.S.B., Resigned, Prior; Rev. Joachim Spexarth, O.S.B., Subprior.
Legal Titles: Benedictine Fathers of Sacred Heart Mission, Inc.; St. Gregory's University, Endowment Foundation, Inc., Shawnee, OK; Saint Gregory's Abbey Benefit Trust.
Priests: 17; Brothers: 8
Monastery founded in 1875 and raised to an Abbey in 1896.
Ministries in 3 Parishes and 2 military installations.
Represented in the Archdiocese of Oklahoma City and in the Diocese of Tulsa.
Properties owned or sponsored: Mabee-Gerrer Museum of Art, Shawnee, OK; St. Gregory's University, Shawnee, OK.

Saint Leo Abbey: 33601 SR 52, P.O. Box 2350, Saint Leo, FL 33574. Tel: 352-588-8624; Fax: 352-588-5217; Email: abbey@saintleo.edu; Web: www.saintleoabbey.org. Rt. Rev. Isaac Camacho, O.S.B., Abbot.
Legal Title: Order of St. Benedict of Florida, Inc.
Fathers: 9; Brothers: 12; Internal Oblates: 1
Founded in 1889 and raised to an Abbey in 1902.
Represented in the Diocese of St. Petersburg.

Assumption Abbey: P.O. Box A, Richardton, ND 58652. Tel: 701-974-3315. Rt. Rev. Brian Wangler, O.S.B., Abbot; Rev. Patrick Moore, O.S.B., Resigned Abbot; Bro. Basil Kirsch, O.S.B., Prior; Rev. Sebastian Schmidt, O.S.B., Subprior.
Priests: 31; Brothers: 22
Founded in 1893 and raised to an Abbey in 1903.
Represented in the Dioceses of Bismarck, Cheyenne, Fargo and Indianapolis. Also in Colombia.
Properties owned or sponsored: Abbey; Dependent Priory; Parishes 4; Chaplaincies 5; Indian Mission.

St. Bede Abbey: 24 W. U.S. Hwy. 6, Peru, IL 61354. Tel: 815-223-3140. Rt. Rev. Philip D. Darcy, O.S.B., Abbot; Rt. Rev. Marion E. Balsavich, O.S.B., Resigned Abbot; Rt. Rev. Roger F. Corpus, O.S.B., Resigned Abbot; Rt. Rev. Claude J. Peifer, O.S.B., Resigned Abbot; Very Rev. Michael Calhoun, O.S.B., Prior; Very Rev. Dominic M. Garramone, O.S.B., Subprior.
Legal Title: The Benedictine Society of Saint Bede.
Priests: 19; Brothers: 6
Monastery founded in 1891 and raised to an Abbey in 1910.
Represented in the Diocese of Peoria.
Properties owned or sponsored: Parishes 1 & St. Bede Academy.

St. Martin's Abbey: 5000 Abbey Way S.E., Lacey, WA 98503-7500. Rt. Rev. Neal G. Roth, O.S.B; Rt. Rev. Adrian Parcher, O.S.B., Resigned Abbot; Very Rev. Alfred J. Hulscher, O.S.B., Prior; Very Rev. Clement Pangratz, O.S.B., Subprior.
Priests: 17; Brothers: 10
Monastery founded in 1895 and raised to an Abbey in 1914.
Legal Holdings or Titles: St. Martin's Abbey; St. Martin's University.
Represented in the Archdiocese of Seattle and in the Diocese of Spokane.

Holy Cross Abbey: 2951 E. Hwy. 50, Canon City, CO 81212. Tel: 719-275-8631. Very Rev. Maurice C. Haefling, O.S.B., Vicar Admin; Rt. Rev. Warren J. Heidgen, O.S.B., Retired Abbot; Rt. Rev. Kenneth C. Hein, O.S.B., Retired Abbot.
Fathers: 3; Oblates: 1
Founded in 1886 and raised to an Abbey in 1925.
Represented in the Archdiocese of Denver and in the Diocese of Pueblo.

St. Anselm Abbey: 100 St. Anselm Dr., Manchester, NH 03102-1310. Tel: 603-641-7000; Fax: 603-641-7267. Rt. Rev. Matthew K. Leavy, O.S.B., Abbot; Most Rev. Joseph John Gerry, O.S.B., 3rd Abbot, Tenth Bishop of Portland, ME; Bro. Isaac Murphy, O.S.B., Prior; Very Rev. Peter J. Guerin, O.S.B., Subprior.
Legal Title: Order of Saint Benedict of New Hampshire.
Bishops: 1; Abbots: 1; Fathers: 21; Brothers: 5
Monastery founded in 1889 and raised to an Abbey in 1927.
Represented in the Archdiocese of San Francisco and in the Diocese of Manchester.

St. Andrew Abbey: 10510 Buckeye Rd., Cleveland, OH 44104. Tel: 216-721-5300. Rt. Rev. Christopher Schwartz, O.S.B., Abbot; Very Rev. Gary Hoover, O.S.B., Prior; Very Rev. Albert Marflak, O.S.B., Subprior.
Bishops: 1; Abbots: 1; Brothers: 12; Abbeys: 1; Parishes: 2; High Schools: 1; Chaplaincies: 2; Novices: 1
Founded in 1922 and raised to an Abbey in 1934.
Legal Holdings or Titles: Benedictine Order of Cleveland; Benedictine High School.
Represented in the Dioceses of Cleveland and Great Falls-Billings.

Benedictine Priory: 6502 Seawright Dr., Savannah, GA 31406. Tel: 912-356-3520; Fax: 912-356-3527. Very Rev. Frank E. Ziemkiewicz, O.S.B., Prior.
Priests: 3; Brothers: 1; High Schools: 1
Founded 1877, dependent priory of St. Vincent Archabbey, Latrobe, PA.
Represented in the Diocese of Savannah.

Woodside Priory: 302 Portola Rd., Portola Valley, CA 94028. Tel: 650-851-8220. Very Rev. Martin J. Mager, O.S.B., Supr.
Legal Title: Benedictine Fathers of the Priory, Inc.
Priests: 3; Brothers: 1; High Schools: 1; Middle Schools: 1
Founded in 1956, erected as Conventual Priory 1958, became a dependent Priory upon St. Anselm's Abbey, Manchester, NH, 1976.
Represented in the Archdiocese of San Francisco.

Abadia Benedictine-de San Antonio Abad: P.O. Box 729, Humacao, PR 00792. Tel: 787-852-1616; Tel: 787-852-1766; Fax: 787-852-1920. Rt. Rev. Oscar Rivera, O.S.B., Abbot; Rev. Eduardo Torrellas, O.S.B., Prior; Bro. Aristedes Pacheco, Subprior.
Priests: 7; Brothers: 7
Monastery founded in 1947 and became an Abbey in 1984.

Mary Mother of the Church Abbey: 12829 River Rd., Richmond, VA 23238-7206. Tel: 804-784-3508; Fax: 804-708-5064. Very Rev. Luke Travers, O.S.B., Admin; Very Rev. Adrian Harmening, O.S.B., Prior.
Priests: 7; Brothers: 5; Abbeys: 1; Chaplaincies: 3; High Schools: 1
Community founded in 1911 and became an Abbey in 1989.
Legal Holdings: Benedictine High School of Richmond; Mary Mother of the Church Abbey.
Represented in the Diocese of Richmond.

Mount Saviour Monastery: 231 Monastery Rd., Pine City, NY 14871-9787. Tel: 607-734-1688; Fax: 607-734-1689; Email: info@msaviour.org. Very Rev. Martin Boler, O.S.B; Rev. James Cronen, O.S.B., Prior.
Professed Monks: 10
Monastery founded in 1950, raised to Independent Priory 1957.
Represented in the Diocese of Rochester.

Swiss-American Congregation

Marmion Abbey: 850 Butterfield Rd., Aurora, IL 60502. Tel: 630-966-7750; Fax: 630-897-0393. Rt. Rev. Vincent Bataille, O.S.B., Abbot & Pres. President's Council: Rt. Rev. Justin DuVall, O.S.B, St. Meinrad Archabbey; Rt. Rev. Gregory Polan, O.S.B, Conception Abbey; Rev. Patrick Caveglia, O.S.B, Conception Abbey; Rev. Paul Thomas, O.S.B, Mt. Angel Abbey
Established by Pope Leo XIII, April 5, 1881.
The Abbeys and Priories belonging to this Federation are as follows:

St. Meinrad Archabbey: No. 100 Hill Dr., Saint Meinrad, IN 47577. Tel: 812-357-6611; Fax: 812-357-6551. Rt. Rev. Justin DuVall, O.S.B., Archabbot; Rt. Rev. Lambert Reilly, O.S.B., Resigned Archabbot; Rt. Rev. Bonaventure Knaebel, O.S.B., Retired Archabbot; Rev. Kurt Stasiak, Prior.
Archbishops: 1; Priests: 64; Brothers: 24; Parishes: 19; Schools of Theology: 1; Chaplaincies: 7
Founded 1854; raised to an Abbey in 1870.
Represented in the Archdioceses of Chicago, Hartford, Indianapolis and Washington and in the Dioceses of Charleston, Evansville, Gary, Owensboro and Sioux Falls.

Conception Abbey: 37174 State Hwy. VV, Conception, MO 64433. Tel: 660-944-3100; Fax: 660-944-2800. Rt. Rev. Gregory Polan, O.S.B., Abbot; Rev. Daniel Petsche, O.S.B., Prior; Bro. Bernard Montgomery, O.S.B., Subprior.
Legal Title: Conception Abbey, Inc.
Archbishops: 1; Fathers: 35; Brothers: 22; Parishes: 8; Seminary College: 1; Chaplaincies: 5
Founded December 8, 1873; Abbey April 5, 1881.
Represented in the Archdioceses of Kansas City in Kansas and Omaha and in the Dioceses of Dodge City, Jefferson City, Kansas City-St. Joseph, Manchester and Springfield-Cape Girardeau.

Mount Michael Abbey: 22520 Mount Michael Rd., Elkhorn, NE 68022-3400. Tel: 402-289-2541; Fax: 402-289-4539. Rt. Rev. Michael Liebl, O.S.B., Abbot; Rev. Richard Thell, O.S.B., Prior; Rev. Louis L. Sojka, O.S.B., Subprior.
Fathers: 12; Brothers: 12
Legal Holdings & Titles: Mount Michael Benedictine Abbey; Mount Michael Benedictine School; Mount Michael Foundation.
Monks serve and staff: Parishes 2.
Represented in the Archdiocese of Omaha and in the Diocese of Pueblo.

Subiaco Abbey: Subiaco, AR 72865. Tel: 479-934-1000; Fax: 479-934-4328. Very Rt. Rev. Jerome Kodell, O.S.B., Abbot; Rev. David Bellinghausen, O.S.B., Prior; Bro. Ephrem O'Bryan, O.S.B., Subprior.
Fathers: 19; Perpetually Professed Brothers: 20; Temporarily Professed Brothers: 1; Temporarily Professed Fathers: 1; Oblates: 1
Properties staffed or sponsored: Parishes 5; High School 1.
Represented in the Diocese of Little Rock.

St. Joseph Abbey: Saint Benedict, LA 70457. Tel: 985-892-1800; Fax: 985-867-2270; Web: www.sjasc.edu. Rt. Rev. Patrick Regan, O.S.B., Retired Abbot; Rt. Rev. Justin Brown, O.S.B., Abbot; Bro. Brian Harrington, O.S.B., Prior.
Fathers: 23; Brothers: 12; Parishes: 3; Novitiates: 1; Seminary College: 1
Legal Holdings: St. Joseph Seminary College, St. Benedict, LA.
Represented in the Archdiocese of New Orleans.

Mt. Angel Abbey: *St. Benedict*, Mt. Angel Abbey &

Seminary, One Abbey Dr., Saint Benedict, OR 97373. Tel: 503-845-3030; Fax: 503-845-3594. Rt. Rev. Gregory Duerr, O.S.B., Abbot; Rev. Vincent Trujillo, O.S.B., Prior; Rev. Odo Recker, O.S.B., Subprior.
Finally Professed Monks (Priests): 32; Finally Professed Monks (Brothers): 16; Temporarily Professed Monks (Brothers): 5
Founded on Oct. 30, 1882, from Engelberg in Switzerland and raised to an Abbey on March 24, 1904.
Legal Holdings or Titles: Monastery of Our Lady of the Angels, Cuernavaca, Morelos, Mexico.

Marmion Abbey: 850 Butterfield Rd., Aurora, IL 60502. Tel: 630-897-7215. Rt. Rev. John Brahill, O.S.B., Abbot; Rt. Rev. Gerald Benkert, O.S.B., Abbot Emeritus; Rt. Rev. David J. Cyr, O.S.B., Abbot Emeritus; Rt. Rev. Vincent Bataille, O.S.B., Abbot Emeritus; Very Rev. Basil Yender, O.S.B., Prior; Rev. Kenneth Theisen, O.S.B., Subprior.
Priests: 22; Brothers: 8
Founded as Dependent Priory of St. Meinrad's Abbey, June 20, 1943; Abbey since March 21, 1947.
Represented in the Diocese of Rockford. Also in Quetzaltenango, Guatemala.
Properties staffed or sponsored: Parishes 1; High Schools 2.

St. Benedict's Abbey: 12605 224th Ave., Benet Lake, WI 53102-1000. Tel: 262-396-4311; Fax: 262-396-4365; Email: benedictines@msn.com. Rt. Rev. Edmund J. Boyce, O.S.B., Abbot; Rt. Rev. Andrew V. Garber, O.S.B., Abbot Resigned; Rt. Rev. Robert C. Schoofs, O.S.B., Abbot Resigned; Rt. Rev. Leo M. Ryska, O.S.B., Abbot Resigned; Very Rev. Henry V. Nurre, O.S.B., Subprior; Rev. Stephen E. Lattner, O.S.B., Prior.
Legal Titles: Benedictine Monks, Inc.; St Benedict's Home Missionary Society.
Priests: 9; Brothers: 10
Monastery founded in 1945 and raised to an Abbey in 1952.
Represented in the Archdiocese of Milwaukee.

Glastonbury Abbey: 16 Hull St., Hingham, MA 02043. Tel: 781-749-2155; Fax: 781-749-7236. Rev. Thomas O'Connor, Prior Admin.
Monks in Solemn Vows: 9
Represented in the Archdiocese of Boston.

Blue Cloud Abbey: P.O. Box 98, Marvin, SD 57251-0098. Tel: 605-398-9200; Fax: 605-398-9201. Rt. Rev. Denis Quinkert, O.S.B., Abbot; Bro. Benet Tvedten, O.S.B., Prior. Retired Abbots: Rt. Rev. Alan Berndt, O.S.B; Rev. Thomas Hillenbrand, O.S.B.
Legal Title: Blue Cloud Abbey, Inc.; Asociacion Benedictina de Coban.
Priests: 15; Brothers: 14
Monastery founded June 24, 1950; raised to a Priory August 5, 1952; raised to an Abbey March 21, 1954.
Represented in the Diocese of Sioux Falls. Also in Guatemala.

Prince of Peace Abbey: 650 Benet Hill Rd., Oceanside, CA 92054. Tel: 760-967-4200; Email: princeabby@aol.com; Web: www.princeofpeaceabbey.org. Rt. Rev. Charles Wright, O.S.B., Abbot; Very Rev. Sharbel Ewen, O.S.B., Prior.
Fathers: 8; Brothers: 17

St. Benedict Abbey: 252 Still River Rd., P.O. Box 67, Still River, MA 01467. Tel: 978-456-3221; Fax: 978-456-8181; Email: saintbenedict@abbey.org. Rt. Rev. Xavier Connelly, O.S.B., Abbot; Very Rev. James Doran, O.S.B., Prior.
Priests: 7; Brothers: 4; Oblates: 1
Represented in the Diocese of Worcester.

Congregation of St. Ottilien for Foreign Missions

St. Paul's Abbey: 289 U.S. Hwy. 206 South, P.O. Box 7, Newton, NJ 07860-0007. Tel: 973-383-2470; Fax: 973-383-5782. Rt. Rev. Joel P. Macul, O.S.B., Abbot; Rt. Rev. Justin E. Dzikowicz, O.S.B., Resigned Abbot; Rt. Rev. Augustine J. Hinches, O.S.B., Resigned Abbot; Very Rev. Samuel Kim, O.S.B., Prior.
Solemnly Professed Monks (Priests 10): 18
(Benedictine Missionaries)
Monastery established March 15, 1924; elevated to an Abbey June 9, 1947.
Represented in the Diocese of Paterson.

Christ the King Priory (1985) - Benedictine Mission House (1935): Benedictine Mission House was founded in 1935 and raised to the rank of Priory in 1985. P.O. Box 528, Schuyler, NE 68661. Tel: 402-352-2177; Fax: 402-352-2176. Rev. Mauritius Wilde, O.S.B., Prior; Rev. Volker Futter, O.S.B; Rev. Thomas Leitner, O.S.B; Rev. Paul L. Kasun, O.S.B.
Fathers: 4; Brothers: 3
Represented in the Archdiocese of Omaha.

Congregation of the Annunciation

St. Andrew's Abbey: P.O. Box 40, Valyermo, CA 93563. Tel: 661-944-2178. Rev. Damien Toilolo, O.S.B., Abbot; Rev. Joseph Brennan, O.S.B., Prior.
Monks in Solemn Vows: 19; Simple Vows: 2
Represented in the Archdiocese of Los Angeles.

Weston Priory (1953): 58 Priory Hill Rd., Weston, VT 05161. Tel: 802-824-5409; Fax: 802-824-3573. Very Rev. Richard Iaquinto, O.S.B., Prior.
Monks: 15
Represented in the Diocese of Burlington.

Camaldolese Benedictine Congregation (Congregatio Camaldulensis Ordinis Sancti Benedicti)

U.S. Foundation (1958): *New Camaldoli Hermitage*, 62475 Hwy. 1, Big Sur, CA 93920. Tel: 831-667-2456. Very Rev. Raniero Hoffman, O.S.B.Cam., Prior.
Fathers: 8; Professed Brothers: 7
Represented in the Dioceses of Monterey and Oakland.

English Benedictine Congregation

St. Anselm's Abbey: 4501 S. Dakota Ave. N.E., Washington, DC 20017. Tel: 202-269-2300; Fax: 202-269-2312. Rt. Rev. James Wiseman, O.S.B., Abbot.
Legal Title: Benedictine Foundation at Washington DC.
Solemnly Professed Monks: 14

Abbey of St. Gregory the Great: 285 Cory's Ln., Portsmouth, RI 02871. Tel: 401-683-2000; Fax: 401-683-5888. Rt. Rev. Caedmon Holmes, O.S.B., Abbot.
Choir Religious: 15

Abbey of St. Mary and St. Louis: 500 S. Mason Rd., Saint Louis, MO 63141-8500. Tel: 314-434-3690; Fax: 314-434-0795. Rt. Rev. Thomas Frerking, O.S.B., Abbot.
Solemnly Professed Monks (Priests 16): 26; Simply Professed Monks: 2; Oblates: 1; Novices: 1
Founded as a dependent Priory 1955, granted independence 1973, raised to status of Abbey 1989.

Sylvestrine Benedictine Congregation (Monachorum Silvestrinorum, O.S.B.)

Foundations in the U.S. (1910): *Saint Benedict Priory*, 2711 E. Drahner Rd., Oxford, MI 48370. Tel: 248-628-2249. Rev. Michael R. Green, O.S.B., Conventual Prior.
Brothers: 2; Priests: 5; Regular Oblates: 3
Represented in the Archdiocese of Detroit and in the Diocese of Paterson.

Olivetan Benedictines (Congregatio Sanctae Mariae Montis Oliveti Ordinis Sancti Benedicti)

General Motherhouse: *St. Sylvester Monastery*, Fabriano, Italy, Very Rev. Michael Kelly, O.S.B., Abbot Gen.

U.S. Foundations: *Holy Trinity Monastery*, P.O. Box 298, Saint David, AZ 85630. Tel: 520-720-4642; Fax: 520-720-4202. Rev. Henri Capdeville, O.S.B., Prior; Rev. Benedict Lemekt, O.S.B.
Solemnly Professed: 6; Postulants: 1
Represented in the Diocese of Tucson.

Our Lady of Guadalupe Abbey: P.O. Box 1080, Pecos, NM 87552-1080. Tel: 505-757-6415. Rev. Christopher Zielenski, O.S.B., Abbot; Bro. James Marron, Claustral Prior.
Priests: 6; Brothers: 6
Represented in the Archdiocese of Santa Fe.

Benedictine Monastery of Hawaii: 67-290 Farrington Hwy., P.O. Box 490, Waialua, HI 96791. Tel: 808-637-7887; Fax: 808-637-8601; Email: monastery@hawaiibenedictines.org; Web: www.hawaiibenedictines.org. Rev. David Barfknecht, O.S.B., Supr.
Priests: 3; Brothers: 2

Subiaco Benedictine Congregation

Monastery of Christ in the Desert (1964): Abiquiu, NM 87510. Tel: 801-545-8567. Rt. Rev. Philip Lawrence, O.S.B., Abbot.
Monks: 75
Independent 1983; Abbey 1996.
Represented in the Archdioceses of Chicago, Santa Fe, Dallas and Rochester. Also in Mexico and South Africa.

Saint Mary's Monastery: P.O. Box 345, Petersham, MA 01366. Tel: 978-724-3350. Rev. Dom Gregory Phillips, O.S.B., Supr.
Monks: 5
Dependent Monastery 1987.
Represented in the Diocese of Worcester.

Solesmes Congregation

Benedictine Monks, Solesmes Congregation: *Our Lady of Clear Creek Abbey*, 5804 W. Monastery Rd., Hulbert, OK 74441. Tel: 918-772-2454; Fax: 918-772-1044; Email: clearcreekmonks@gmail.com; Web: www.clearcreekmonks.org. Rt. Rev. Philip Anderson, O.S.B., Abbot.
Legal Title: Foundation for the Annunciation Monastery of Clear Creek.

[0220] (S.S.S.)—CONGREGATION OF THE BLESSED SACRAMENT

(Congregatio Sanctissimi Sacramenti)

Generalate: 46 Via Giovanni Battista de Rossi, 00161, Rome, Italy, Very Rev. Eugenio Barbosa Martins, S.S.S., Supr.

Province of St. Ann (1931): 5384 Wilson Mills Rd., Cleveland, OH 44143. Tel: 440-442-6311. Very Rev. Norman B. Pelletier, S.S.S., Prov; Rev. Anthony Schueller, S.S.S., Vicar Prov; Rev. Dana Pelotte, S.S.S., Consultor & Prov. Treas.
Priests: 37; Permanent Deacons: 1; Brothers: 13
Properties staffed or owned: Parishes 7; Seminary 1; Community Houses 9; Novitiate 1.
Represented in the Archdioceses of Galveston-Houston, New York and San Antonio and in the Dioceses of Cleveland, Chicago, and St. Petersburg.

[0230] (ER. CAM.)—CAMALDOLESE HERMITS OF THE CONGREGATION OF MONTECORONA

(Eremitae Camaldulenses Congregationis Montis Coronae)

General Motherhouse: *Sacro Eremo*, Via del Tuscolo 45, 00040 Monte Porzio Catone, Rome, Italy, Rt. Rev. Lanfranco Longhi, Er.Cam., Father Major.

U.S. Foundation (1959): *Holy Family Hermitage*, 1501 Fairplay Rd., Bloomingdale, OH 43910-7971. Tel: 740-765-4511. Very Rev. Basil Corriere, Er.Cam., Prior.
Hermit Priests: 4; Professed: 3
Represented in the Diocese of Steubenville.

[0240] (M.I.)—CAMILLIAN FATHERS AND BROTHERS OR ORDER OF ST. CAMILLUS

(Ministers of the Infirm or Sick)
(Ministri degli Infermi)

General Motherhouse: *Casa Generalizia*, Ministri degli Infermi, Piazza della Maddalena 53, 00186, Rome, Italy, Very Rev. Renato Salvatore, M.I., Supr. Gen; Rev. Jesus Ruiz, M.I., Vicar Gen; Bro. Luca Perletti, M.I., Sec. Gen. & Sec. of Formation; Rev. Paulo Guarise, M.I., Sec. of Ministry; Rev. Babychan Pazhanilath, M.I., Sec. of Missions.

U.S.A. Camillian (1923): *Delegation of Brazilian Prov.*, 3345 S. 10th St., Milwaukee, WI 53215. Tel: 414-481-3696; Fax: 414-481-8044. Very Rev. Richard O'Donnell, M.I., Prov; Rev. Louis Lussier, M.I., Vicar Prov; Rev. Joseph L. Bisoffi, M.I; Rev. Albert Schempp, M.I; Bro. Mario Crivello, M.I.
Fathers: 11; Professed Brothers: 2
Legal Titles: St. Camillus Health Center Inc., Wauwatosa, WI; St. Camillus Health System, Wauwatosa, WI; San Camillo, Inc., Wauwatosa, WI; St. Camillus Ministries Inc., Wauwatosa, WI; St. Camillus Communities Inc., Wauwatosa, WI; Order of St. Camillus Foundation, Wauwatosa, WI.
Represented in the Archdiocese of Milwaukee and in the Dioceses of Savannah and Worcester.

[0250] (C.R.L.)—CANONS REGULAR OF THE LATERAN

(Ordo Canonicorum Regularium S. Augustini Congregations Ss. Salvatoris Lateranensis)

General House: *Curia Generalizia dei Canonicio Regolari Lateranensi*, Piazza S. Pietro in Vincoli, 4A, 00184, Roma, Italy,

United States: *Canons Regular of the Lateran*, 2317 Washington Ave., Bronx, NY 10458. Tel: 212-295-9600. Rev. Jose L. Biain, C.R.L., Supr.
Priests: 6; Brothers: 4
Represented in the Archdiocese of New York and in the Diocese of Arecibo (PR).

[0260] (O.C.D.)—DISCALCED CARMELITE FRIARS

(Ordo Carmelitarum Discalceatorum)
Founded Mt. Carmel, Palestine in the 13th Century.

Generalate: *Carmelitani Scalzi*, Corso d'Italia, 38, 00198, Rome, Italy, Very Rev. Saverio Cannistra, O.C.D., Supr. Gen.

California-Arizona Province (1983): 926 E. Highland Ave., P.O. Box 2178, Redlands, CA 92373. Tel: 909-793-0424; Fax: 909-335-1304. Very Rev. Gerald Werner, O.C.D., Prov.
Legal Title: Discalced Carmelite Province of California.
Fathers: 32; Brothers: 2; Students: 13; Postulants: 2; Novices: 2
Represented in the Archdioceses of Los Angeles, Portland and Seattle and in the Dioceses of San Jose, San Bernardino, Santa Rosa and Tucson. Also in Uganda.
Properties owned, staffed or sponsored: Parishes 4; Retreat House; Novitiate; House of Studies; House of Prayer; Institute of Spirituality.

Province of St. Therese of Oklahoma (1935): *Provincial House*, 906 Kentucky Ave., San Antonio, TX 78201. Tel: 201-735-9127. Rev. Luis J. Castaneda, O.C.D., Prov.
Fathers: 20; Brothers: 2; Students of Philosophy: 3
Represented in the Archdioceses of Oklahoma City and San Antonio and in the Dioceses of Dallas and Little Rock.
Properties staffed or sponsored: Parishes 3; Community Houses 1; Novitiate 1.

Washington Province of the Immaculate Heart of Mary (1947): *Discalced Carmelites-Prov. Office*, 1233 S. 45th St., Milwaukee, WI 53214-3693. Tel: 414-672-7212; Fax: 414-672-3138. Very Rev. John Sullivan, O.C.D., Prov.
Fathers: 56; Brothers: 11; Deacons: 3; Temporary Professed Brothers: 5; Bishops: 1; Novices: 2; Postulants: 5
Represented in the Archdioceses of Boston, Milwaukee and Washington and in the Diocese of Wheeling-Charleston. Also in Kenya.
Properties owned or sponsored: Community Houses 6.

Polish Province of the Holy Spirit, Poland (1949):

Monastery of Our Lady of Mt. Carmel, 1628 Ridge Rd., Munster, IN 46321. Tel: 219-838-7111; Fax: 219-838-7214; Email: carmelmunster@yahoo.com. Rev. Franciszek Czaicki, O.C.D., Prior.
Priests: 11; Brothers: 2
Represented in the Diocese of Gary.

[0270] (O.CARM.)—CARMELITE FATHERS & BROTHERS

(Ordo Fratrum Beatissimae Virginis Mariae de Monte Carmelo)

General Curia: Via Giovanni Lanza, 138, 00184, Rome, Italy, Most Rev. Fernando Millan Romeral, O.Carm., Prior Gen.

Province of the Most Pure Heart of Mary (1864): *Carmelite Provincial Office*, 1317 Frontage Rd., Darien, IL 60561. Tel: 630-971-0050; Fax: 630-971-0195. Very Rev. John F. Welch, O.Carm., Prior Prov; Rev. Bernhard Bauerle, O.Carm., Officer & Treas. Commissary Provincials: Rev. Leonard Gilman, O.Carm., Prov. Eastern Commissary; Rev. Joseph Atcher, O.Carm., Prov. Midwest Commissary; Rev. William Harry, O.Carm., Prov. Western Commissary; Rev. Enrique Laguna Yargas, O.Carm., Prov. Peru Commissary. Councilors: Rev. Myron Judy, O.Carm; Rev. Gregory Houck, O.Carm; Rev. Sam Citero, O.Carm; Rev. Quinn Conners, O.Carm; Rev. Robert E. Colaresi, O.Carm., Dir. Little Flower Society; Rev. John Malley, O.Carm., Dir.-Carmelite Mission Office; Rev. Brian Henden, O.Carm., Delegate to Lay Carmelites.
Priests: 154; Clerics: 6; Pre-Novitiates: 7; Novices: 4; Brothers: 21
Ministries in 35 Parishes.
Properties owned: Spiritual Centers 3; Shopping-center Chapels 2; Carefree Village, residence for senior citizens, Darien, IL; High Schools 6; Community Houses 48; House of Study 7; Cemetery 1; Shrine 2.
Represented in the Archdioceses of Boston, Chicago, Galveston-Houston, Kansas City in Kansas, Los Angeles, Newark, New York, Philadelphia and Washington and in the Dioceses of Fall River, Fort Wayne-South Bend, Joliet, Oakland, Phoenix, Sacramento, Sioux Falls, Tucson and Venice. Also in Australia, Canada, El Salvador, France, Italy, Peru and Mexico.

Province of the Most Pure Heart of Mary: *St. Therese Priory*, 75 E. Mariposa St., Phoenix, AZ 85012-1631. Rev. Charles Kurgan, O.Carm; Rev. Valentine Boyle, O.Carm.

Province of St. Elias (1931): P.O. Box 3079, Middletown, NY 10940-0890. Tel: 845-344-2223. Rev. Mario Esposito, O.Carm., Prov.
Fathers: 52; Brothers: 5; Novices: 5; Pre-Novices: 5; Professed Students: 12
Legal Holdings or Titles: The Missionary Society of Our Lady of Mt. Carmel of the State of New York; The Carmelite Fathers, Inc. of New York; Carmelite Fathers, Inc. of the Commonwealth of Massachusetts; Mt. Carmel Hermitage; Order of Carmelites of Palm Beach, Inc.; National Shrine of Our Lady of Mount Carmel, Inc.
Represented in the Archdioceses of New York, Miami, Newark and Washington and in the Dioceses of Albany, Dodge City, Greensburg, Palm Beach, Rochester and Sioux Falls. Also in Trinidad & Vietnam.
Properties staffed, owned or sponsored: Parishes 7; Priories 17; Houses of Study 1; Novitiate 1; Hermitages 1; Shrines 1.

Mt. Carmel Hermitage: 244 Baileys Rd., Bolivar, PA 15923. Tel: 724-238-0423; Fax: 724-238-0423. Rev. Bede J.K. Mulligan, O.Carm; Rev. Simeon D. Marro, O.Carm.
Fathers: 2; Brothers: 1
Founded in 1970, became dependent upon St. Elias Province in 1995.
Represented in the Diocese of Greensburg.

Carmelite Hermitage of the Blessed Virgin Mary (O.Carm): 8249 de Montreville Tr. N., Lake Elmo, MN 55042-9545. Tel: 651-779-7351; Email: carmelus@earthlink.net; Web: www.decorcarmeli.com. Rev. John M. Burns, O.Carm., Prior; Rev. Joseph V. Vaccaro, O.Carm; Rev. Patrick Peter Peach, O.Carm.
Fathers: 3; Brothers: 5

[0275] (C.M.I.)—CARMELITES OF MARY IMMACULATE

(Congregatio Fratrum Carmelitarum B.V. Mariae Immaculatae)

Founded by Blessed Kuriakose Elias Chavara and Companions at Mannanam, Kerala, India in 1831.

Generalate: *CMI Generalate Chavara Hills*, P.B. No. 3105, Kakkanad P.O., 682030, Kochi, India, Tel: 484-378-137; Fax: 484-378-363. Rev. Jose Panthaplamthottiyil, C.M.I., Prior Gen.

North American Headquarters: 862 Manhattan Ave., Brooklyn, NY 11222. Tel: 718-383-3339. Rev. Walter Thelapilly, C.M.I., Coord. Gen.
Legal Title: Carmelites of Mary Immaculate, Inc.
Priests in the United States and in Canada: 106
Ministries in Parishes; Hospitals; Universities; Prisons; Mission to the Syro-Malabar Catholics.
Represented in the Archdioceses of Boston, Hartford, Los Angeles, New York and Philadelphia and in the Dioceses of Alexandria, Amarillo, Beaumont, Brooklyn, Camden, Charleston, Covington, Joliet, Lafayette, Lake Charles, Metuchen, Nashville, New Ulm, Rockville Centre, St. Augustine, St. Paul & Minneapolis, Salina, San Angelo, Shreveport, Sioux Falls, Syracuse, Toledo, Tulsa, Tyler and Victoria. Also in Canada.

[0280] (O.CART.)—ORDER OF CARTHUSIANS

(Ordo Cartusianorum)

Motherhouse: *Grande Chartreuse*, St. Pierre de Chartreuse (Isere), France, Rev. Marcellin Theeuwes, Supr. Gen.

U.S. Charterhouse of the Transfiguration (1951): *Carthusian Monastery*, 1084 Ave Maria Way, Arlington, VT 05250. Tel: 802-362-2550; Fax: 802-362-3584; Email: carthusians_in_america@chartreuse.info; Web: www.chartreux.org; Web: transfiguration.chartreux.org. Rev. Lorenzo Maria T. De La Rosa Jr., O.Cart., Prior.
Total in Community: 15
Legal Titles: Carthusian Foundation in America, Inc.; Carthusian Foundation, Association Fraternelle Romande.
Represented in the Diocese of Burlington.

[0290] (F.C.)—BROTHERS OF CHARITY

(Congregatio Fratrum Caritate)

General Motherhouse (1807): Via G.B. Pagano 35, 00167, Rome, Italy, Bro. Rene Stockman, F.C., Supr. Gen.

American Region (1963) (1963): *Region of Our Lady of Charity*, 7720 Doe Ln., Glenside, PA 19038. Bro. John Fitzgerald, F.C., Regional Supr. for U.S.
Represented in the Archdioceses of Philadelphia and Washington.

[0300] (I.C.)—INSTITUTE OF CHARITY

(Rosminians Institutum Charitatis)

General Motherhouse: *Collegio Rosmini Via Porta*, Latina 17, Rome, Italy, Very Rev. James Flynn, I.C., Supr. Gen.

U.S. Foundation (1877): 2327 W. Heading Ave., Peoria, IL 61604. Tel: 309-676-6341. Rev. William T. Miller, I.C., Vicar.
Fathers in the U.S: 11; Parishes: 8
Represented in the Dioceses of Peoria and St. Petersburg.

[0305] (I.C.)—INSTITUTE OF CHRIST THE KING-SOVEREIGN PRIEST

(Institutum Christi Regis Summi Sacerdotis)

General Motherhouse and House of Formation: *Villa Martelli*, Via di Gricigliano 52, 50065, Sieci, Italy, Rev. Msgr. Gilles Wach, Prior Gen.

U.S. Mailing Address: *Institute of Christ the King-Sovereign Priest*, 6415 S. Woodlawn Ave., Chicago, IL 60637.

American Headquarters: *Shrine of Christ the King Sovereign Priest*, 6415 S. Woodlawn Ave., Chicago, IL 60637. Tel: 773-363-7409; Fax: 773-363-7824; Email: info@institute-christ-king.org. Rev. Msgr. R. Michael Schmitz, Prov. Supr. & Vicar Gen; Rev. Matthew L. Talarico, Vice Rector & Vice Prov; Rev. Raphael Katsuyuki Ueda, Vicar.

[0310] (C.F.C.)—EDMUND RICE CHRISTIAN BROTHERS NORTH AMERICA CONGREGATION OF CHRISTIAN BROTHERS

Founded in Ireland in 1802. First foundation in the United States in 1906.

Edmund Rice Christian Brothers North America, a provice of the Congregation of Christian Brothers (1916): 21 Pryer Ter., New Rochelle, NY 10804-4418. Tel: 914-636-6194. Bro. Hugh B. O'Neill, C.F.C., Prov. Leader; Bro. Kevin M. Griffith, C.F.C., Dept. Prov. Leader. Councilors: Bro. Daniel J. Casey, C.F.C; Bro. J. Barry Lynch, C.F.C; Bro. Anthony M. Murphy, C.F.C; Bro. Raymond Vercruysse, C.F.C.
Legal Title: The Christian Brothers Institute, Inc.; Christian Brothers of Ireland, Inc.; Mount Sion Community, Inc.
Brothers: 250
Represented in the Archdioceses of Boston, Chicago, Detroit, Miami, New Orleans, New York, Newark, and Seattle and in the Dioceses of Brooklyn, Brownsville, Charleston, Honolulu, Jackson, Joliet, Monterey, Orlando, Providence, Rochester, St. Petersburg and Venice. Also in Canada and West Indies.
4; Ministries: Colleges 1; High Schools 17; Grade Schools 2; Houses of Formation 1; Migrant Education Centers 2; Care Center; Parishes 2.

Development Office: Christian Brothers Association: P.O. Box 42903, Evergreen Park, IL 60805-0903. Tel: 773-233-2949. Bro. Donald F. McGovern, C.F.C., Dir.

[0320] (F.I.C.)—BROTHERS OF CHRISTIAN INSTRUCTION

(La Mennais Brothers)
(Institutum Fratrum Instructionis Christianae)

General Motherhouse: *Casa Generalizia*, Via della Divina Provvidenza, 44, 00166, Rome, Italy, Tel: (39) 06-66-41-56-18; Fax: (39) 06-45-44-35-92. Bro. Yannick Houssay, Supr. Gen.

American Province (1946): *Notre Dame Province*, P.O. Box 159, Alfred, ME 04002. Tel: 207-324-0067. Bro. Jerome Lessard, Prov.
Brothers: 21; Colleges: 1; High Schools: 1; Retreat Centers: 1
Represented in the Dioceses of Fall River, Ogdensburg, Portland (In Maine) and Youngstown.

[0330] (F.S.C.)—BROTHERS OF THE CHRISTIAN SCHOOLS

(Fratres Scholarum Christianarum)

General Motherhouse: *Casa Generalizia*, Via Aurelia 476, CP 9099 00100, Rome, Italy, Bro. Alvaro Rodriquez Echeverria, F.S.C., Supr. Gen; Bro. Thomas Johnson, F.S.C., Vicar Gen.

Christian Brothers Conference: *USA/Toronto Region*, Hecker Center, 3025 Fourth St. N.E., Ste. 300, Washington, DC 20017-1102. Tel: 202-529-0047; Web: www.lasallian.info. Bro. Robert Schieler, F.S.C., Gen. Councilor; Bro. Gerard J. Frendreis, F.S.C., Dir. Admin. & Finance.
Legal Title: Christian Brothers Major Superiors, Inc.
Organizations and programs served by this office: Regional Conference of Christian Brothers; Lasallian Volunteers; Huether Lasallian Conference; Buttimer Institute of Lasallian Studies; Lasallian Leadership Institute; Lasallian Social Justice Institute; Regional Council of Lasallian Association for Mission.
Organizations associated with this office: Christian Brothers Major Superiors.
Institutions owned and/or sponsored: Bethlehem University of the Holy Land; Sangre de Cristo Center, Santa Fe, NM; Christian Brothers Services, Romeoville, IL.

Brothers of the Christian Schools (Midwest Province): 7650 S. Country Line Rd., Burr Ridge, IL 60527-7959. Tel: 630-323-3725; Fax: 630-323-3779; Email: info@cbmidwest.org. Bro. Larry Schatz, F.S.C., Visitor; Bro. Mark Snodgrass, F.S.C., Aux. Visitor; Bro. Joseph Saurbier, F.S.C., Dir. Admin. & Operations; Bro. Joseph Martin, F.S.C., Dir. Senior Brothers; Bro. Stephen W. Markham, F.S.C., Dir. Vocation Ministry; Mr. Robert Cummings, Chief Devel. Officer.
Brothers: 160
Legal Titles: The Christian Brothers of the Midwest, Inc.; The Christian Brothers of Illinois; Brothers of the Christian Schools of the St. Louis District; The Christian Brothers of Minnesota.
Represented in the Archdioceses of Chicago, Cincinnati, Milwaukee, St. Louis and St. Paul-Minneapolis and the Dioceses of Green Bay, Helena, Jefferson City, Joliet, Kansas City-St. Joseph, Memphis, Omaha, Tulsa and Winona.
Properties owned, staffed or sponsored: Communities 28; Universities 3; High Schools 15; Middle Schools 5; Elementary Schools 1; Retreat Houses 3; Publishing House 1.

Province of San Francisco (1868): *Brothers of the Christian Schools Provincial Office*, P.O. Box 3720, Napa, CA 94558-0372. Tel: 707-252-0222. Bro. Donald Johanson, F.S.C., Prov.
Brothers: 91
Represented in the Archdioceses of Los Angeles, Portland in Oregon and San Francisco and the Dioceses of Oakland, Orange, Sacramento, Santa Rosa, Tucson and Yakima. Also in Israel, Mexico, England, Ethiopia, Singapore, and Vietnam.
Properties owned, staffed and/or sponsored: Colleges 1; High Schools 11; Middle and Elementary Schools 1; Community Houses 14; Retreat & Conference Center 1.

Province of New Orleans-Santa Fe (1921): *De La Salle-Christian Brothers Provincialate*, 1522 Carmel Dr., Lafayette, LA 70501. Tel: 337-234-1973. Bro. Timothy Coldwell, F.S.C., Prov; Bro. Peter Tripp, F.S.C., Finance Dir; Bro. David Sinitiere, Auxiliary Prov.
Brothers: 60
Legal Holdings or Titles: NOSF, Inc.; St. La Salle Auxiliary; Brothers of the Christian Schools of Lafayette Retirement Trust; The Christian Brothers Foundation; Christian Brothers Charitable Trust; De La Salle Christian Brothers, Lafayette, LA; St. La Salle Auxiliary, Lafayette, LA; Magnolia Lafayette, Inc.
Properties owned, staffed or sponsored: College; High Schools 7; Elementary Schools 2.
Represented in the Archdioceses of Denver, New Orleans and Santa Fe and in the Dioceses of El Paso and Lafayette (LA).

District of Eastern North America: 444A Rte. 35 S., Eatontown, NJ 07724-2200. Tel: 732-380-7926; Fax: 732-380-7937; Web: www.fscdena.org. Bro. Dennis M. Malloy, F.S.C., Visitor/Prov. & Pres; Bro. Dennis Lee, F.S.C., Auxiliary; Bro. Jerome Sullivan, F.S.C., Auxiliary; Bro. Thomas Scanlan, F.S.C., Auxiliary; Bro. Timothy J. Froehlich, F.S.C., Dir. Finance & Treas; Bro. James Martino, F.S.C., Dir. Admin. & Sec; Mr. Alan Weyland, Exec. Dir. Mission & Ministry; Ms. Carroll Bennett, Admin. Asst; Mr. Philip De Rita, Dir. Communications & Public Rels; Bro. James Dries, F.S.C., Dir. Vocations; Bro. Charles Mrozinski, F.S.C., Asst. to the Visitor; Bro. William Martin, F.S.C., Dir. Devel; Bro. Kevin Stanton, F.S.C., Dir. Devel.
Legal Titles: Brothers of the Christian Schools, District of Eastern North America, Inc. (d/b/a: FSC DENA); Brothers of the Christian Schools, Long Island-New England Province; Christian Brothers of Frederick, Inc.; La Salle Provincialate, Inc.; Ammendale Normal Institute of Prince George's County, Inc.
Brothers: 357
Represented in the Archdioceses of Baltimore, Detroit,

New York, Newark, Philadelphia and Washington and in the Dioceses of Albany, Brooklyn, Buffalo, Camden, Pittsburgh, Providence, Rockville Centre, Syracuse and Trenton.

[0340] (O.CIST.)—CISTERCIAN ABBEY

(Ordo Cisterciensis)

Headquarters: *Piazza del Tempio di Diana*, 14 I-00153, Rome, Italy, Rt. Rev. Maurus-Giuseppe Lepori, O.Cist., Abbot Gen.

Cistercian Abbey: *Our Lady of Spring Bank*, 17304 Havenwood Rd., Sparta, WI 54656. Tel: 608-269-8138; Fax: 608-269-1992; Email: porter@MonksOnline.org; Web: www.MonksOnline.org. Very Rev. Bernard McCoy, O.Cist., Prior; Rev. Robert Keffer, Subprior.
Solemnly Professed: 6

Cistercian Monastery: *Our Lady of Dallas*, 3550 Cistercian Rd., Irving, TX 75039. Tel: 972-438-2044. Rt. Rev. Denis M. Farkasfalvy, O.Cist., Abbot; Rev. Peter Verhalen, O.Cist., Prior; Rev. Bernard Marton, O.Cist., Subprior.
Priests: 21; Junior Monks: 8
Staff: Universities 1; Preparatory School 1; Novitiate 1; Chaplaincies 1.
Properties owned: Abbey and Preparatory School.
Represented in the Dioceses of Dallas and Fort Worth.

Cistercian Monastery of Our Lady of Fatima: 564 Walton Ave., Mount Laurel, NJ 08054. Tel: 856-235-1330. Rev. Lino S. Parente, O.Cist., Prior; Rev. Maurizio Nicoletti, O.Cist; Rev. Awte Weldu, O.Cist; Rev. Musie Tesfayohannes.
Established in 1961 as a dependent Monastery of the Congregation of Casamari (Italy).
Property owned: Fatima House and the Monastery.

Cistercian Conventual Priory: *St. Mary's Priory*, 70 Schuylkill Rd., New Ringgold, PA 17960. Tel: 570-943-2645; Fax: 570-943-3035. Very Rev. Luke Anderson, S.O.Cist., Ph.D, Prior.
Legal Title: The Cistercian Monastery of Pennsylvania.
Monks: 2

[0350] (O.C.S.O.)—THE CISTERCIAN ORDER OF THE STRICT OBSERVANCE

(TRAPPISTS)
(Ordo Cisterciensium Strictioris Observantiae)

Generalate: *Casa Generalizia*, O.C.S.O., 33 Viale Africa, 00144, Rome, Italy, Rt. Rev. Dom Eamon Fitzgerald, O.C.S.O., Abbot Gen.

Abbey of Gethsemani (1848): No. 3642 Monks Rd., Trappist, KY 40051. Tel: 502-549-3117. Rt. Rev. Elias Dietz, O.C.S.O., Abbot.
Priests: 15; Brothers: 54

Abbey of Our Lady of New Melleray (1849): 6632 Melleray Cir., Peosta, IA 52068. Tel: 563-588-2319. Rt. Rev. Brendan J. Freeman, O.C.S.O., Abbot; Rev. Neil Paquette, O.C.S.O., Prior; Rev. Stephen Verbest, O.C.S.O., Novice Dir. & Vocation Dir; Rev. Jonah Wharff, O.C.S.O., Sub-Prior.
Priests: 14; Professed Monks: 29
Professed Monks 34 (Priests 19)

St. Joseph's Abbey (1825): 167 N. Spencer Rd., Spencer, MA 01562-1233. Tel: 508-885-8700; Fax: 508-885-8701. Rt. Rev. Damian Carr, O.C.S.O., Abbot.
Legal Title: Cistercian Abbey of Spencer, Inc.
Total in Community: 71; Priests: 28; Solemnly Professed: 64; Novices: 7

Monastery of the Holy Spirit, Inc. (1944): 2625 Hwy. 212 S.W., Conyers, GA 30094. Tel: 770-483-8705; Fax: 770-760-0989. Rev. Francis Michael Stiteler, O.C.S.O., Abbot.
Priests: 14; Professed Monks: 33
Represented in the Archdiocese of Atlanta.

Abbey of Our Lady of Guadalupe (1948): P.O. Box 97, Lafayette, OR 97127. Tel: 503-852-7174; Fax: 503-852-7748. Rt. Rev. Peter McCarthy, O.C.S.O., Abbot; Very Rev. Dismas Gannon, O.C.S.O., Prior; Bro. Phillip Wertman, O.C.S.O., Subprior.
Solemnly Professed: 30; Priests: 12

Abbey of Our Lady of the Holy Trinity (1947): 1250 S. 9500 E., Huntsville, UT 84317. Tel: 801-745-3784. Rev. David Altman, O.C.S.O., Abbot.
Priests: 7; Brothers: 7; Oblates: 1

Abbey of the Genesee (1951): 3258 River Rd., P.O. Box 900, Piffard, NY 14533. Tel: 585-243-0660. Rt. Rev. John Denburger, O.C.S.O., Abbot; Rt. Rev. John Eudes Bamberger, O.C.S.O., Abbot Emeritus; Rev. Jerome J. Machar, O.C.S.O., Prior & Guest Master; Rev. Gerard D'Souza, O.C.S.O., Novice Master Retreat House,
Solemnly Professed: 29; Professed Priests: 11

Mepkin Abbey (1949): 1098 Mepkin Abbey Rd., Moncks Corner, SC 29461. Tel: 843-761-8509; Fax: 843-761-6719. Rev. Kevin V. Walsh, O.C.S.O., Novice Master & Prior; Rt. Rev. Stan Gumula, O.S.C.O., Abbot; Bro. John Corrigan, Business Mgr; Rt. Rev. Christian Aidan Carr, O.C.S.O.
Priests: 9; Monks in Community: 20

Abbey of Our Lady of the Holy Cross (1950): 901 Cool Spring Ln., Berryville, VA 22611-2700. Tel: 540-955-1425; Fax: 540-955-1356. Rt. Rev. Robert T. Barnes, O.C.S.O., Abbot.
Legal Title: Community of Cistercians of the Strict Observance, Inc.
Solemnly Professed: 20; Priests: 10

Assumption Abbey: Rte. 5, Box 1056, Ava, MO 65608. Tel: 417-683-5110; Fax: 417-683-5658. Rt. Rev. Robert Matter, O.C.S.O., Abbot (Retired); Rt. Rev. Cyprian Harrison, O.C.S.O., Abbot (Retired), Supr.
Priests: 5; Professed: 9

Abbey of New Clairvaux (1955): *Trappist-Cistercian Abbey*, Vina, CA 96092. Tel: 530-839-2161. Rt. Rev. Paul Mark Schwan, O.C.S.O., Abbot.
Legal Title: Abbey of New Clairvaux, Inc.
Solemn Vows: 18; Simple Vows: 4; Novices: 1

St. Benedict's Monastery (1956): 1012 Monastery Rd., Snowmass, CO 81654. Tel: 970-920-5990. Rt. Rev. Joseph Boyle, O.C.S.O., Abbot; Bro. Raymond Roberts, O.C.S.O., Prior; Rev. Charles Albanese, O.C.S.O., Subprior.
Professed Monks: 12

[0360] (C.M.F.)—CLARETIAN MISSIONARIES

(Missionary Sons of the Immaculate Heart of Mary)
(Congregatio Missionariorum Filiorum Immaculati Cordis Beatae Mariae Virginis.)

General Headquarters: Via Sacro Cuore di Maria 5, Rome, Italy, Very Rev. Joseph Abella, C.M.F., Supr. Gen.

Western Province: *Provincial Headquarters*, 10203 Lower Azusa Rd., Temple City, CA 91780. Tel: 626-443-2009; Fax: 626-443-2005. Very Rev. Richard H. DeTore, C.M.F; Rev. Daryl Olds, C.M.F; Rev. Jose L. Sanchez, C.M.F; Rev. Paul J. Keller, C.M.F; Bro. Rene LePage, C.M.F.
Legal Title: Claretian Missionaries-Western Province, Inc. A not-for-profit corporation under the laws of the State of California having as its purpose the support of any Roman Catholic benevolent, charitable, educational or missionary undertakings of the Claretian Missionaries - Western Province, Inc. Other Corporations: Dominguez Seminary, Inc., Compton, CA; Claretian Educational and Renewal Center, Inc., Los Angeles, CA.
Fathers: 59; Brothers: 6; Students: 2
Ministries in the following areas: Parishes; Novitiate; House of Study; Centers for Spanish Speaking; Renewal Centers; Education; Spiritual Direction.
Represented in the Archdioceses of Los Angeles and San Antonio and in the Dioceses of Fresno and Phoenix.

Eastern Province: *Claretian Missionary Headquarters*, 400 N. Euclid Ave., Oak Park, IL 60302. Tel: 708-848-2076; Fax: 708-848-2069. Very Rev. Eddie DeLeon, C.M.F., Prov. Supr; Rev. Mark J. Brummel, C.M.F., Treas. & Consultor; Rev. Carl J. Quebedeaux, C.M.F., Sec. & Consultor; Rev. Ronald Stua, C.M.F., Vicar & Consultor; Rev. Bruce L. Wellems, C.M.F., Consultor.
Fathers: 36; Brothers: 6; Scholastics: 10; House of Study: 1
Legal Holdings or Titles: The Congregation of Sons of the Immaculate Heart of Mary of the Eastern Province, Inc.; Claret Center, Chicago, IL; Claretian Volunteer Program, Chicago, IL; Claretian Associates, Chicago, IL; Claretians, Inc.; St. Jude League, Inc.; St. Jude Seminary, Inc.
Represented in the Archdioceses of Atlanta and Chicago and in the Dioceses of Metuchen and Springfield-Cape Girardeau.

[0370] (S.S.C.)—SOCIETY OF ST. COLUMBAN

(Societas Sancti Columbani pro missionibus ad Exteros)

Central Administration (1918): *Missionary Society of St. Columban*, 504 Tower 1, Silvercord, 30 Canton Rd. TST, Kowloon, Hong Kong, Very Rev. Tommy Murphy, S.S.C., Supr.
Members: 575

Region in the United States: *Society of St. Columban*, P.O. Box 10, St Columbans, NE 68056. Tel: 402-291-1920. Very Rev. Arturo Aguilar, S.S.C., Regl. Dir; Rev. William Morton, S.S.C., Vice Dir. Council: Rev. Thomas Shaughnessy, S.S.C; Rev. Kevin Mullins, S.S.C; Rev. Charles Duster, S.S.C; Rev. Peter Kenny, S.S.C.
Fathers: 82
Legal Titles: St. Columban's Foreign Mission Society; The Columban Fathers; Missionary Society of St. Columban.
Represented in the Archdioceses of Chicago, Los Angeles, Omaha and Washington and in the Dioceses of Buffalo, El Paso, Orange, Providence and San Bernardino.

[0380] (M.C.C.J.)—COMBONI MISSIONARIES OF THE HEART OF JESUS

(Verona Fathers) Missionarii Comboniani Cordis Jesu
(A Pontifical World Missionary Congregation Of Priests And Brothers)

Founded by Saint Daniel Comboni in 1867, First foundation in the United States in 1939.

General Motherhouse: *Missionari Comboniani*, Via Luigi Lilio 80, 00142, Rome, Italy, Very Rev. Enrique Sanchez Gonzalez, M.C.C.J., Supr. Gen.

North American Province (1950): *Comboni Mission Center*, 1318 Nagel Rd., Cincinnati, OH 45255-3120. Tel: 513-474-4997; Fax: 513-474-0382; Email: info@ComboniMissionaries.org; Web: www.ComboniMissionaries.org. Rev. Manuel Baeza Gama, M.C.C.J., Prov; Rev. Brian Quigley, M.C.C.J., Mission Office Dir.
Legal Title: Comboni Missionaries of the Heart of Jesus, Inc.
Priests: 31; Brothers: 1; Home Mission Parishes: 5; Mission Centers: 3
Represented in the Archdioceses of Chicago, Cincinnati, Los Angeles and Newark.

[0390] (I.M.C.)—CONSOLATA MISSIONARIES

(Institutum Missionum a Consolata)

General Motherhouse: Viale delle Mura Aurelie 11, Rome, Italy, Very Rev. Aquileo Fiorentini, Supr. Gen.

Headquarters in the U.S: 2301 Rte. 27, P.O. Box 5550, Somerset, NJ 08875-5550. Tel: 732-297-9191; Fax: 732-940-3121. Rev. Robert Rezac, I.M.C., Regl. Supr.
Legal Title: Consolata Society for Foreign Missions.
Priests: 10
Properties owned: Mission Community House 2.
Represented in the Dioceses of Buffalo, Metuchen and San Bernardino.

[0400] (O.S.C.)—CANONS REGULAR OF THE ORDER OF THE HOLY CROSS

(Crosier Fathers and Brothers)
Canonici Regulares Ordinis Sanctae Crucis (Cruciferi)

Generalate: *Generalatus Ordinis S. Crucis*, Via del Velabro 19, 00186, Rome, Italy, Very Rev. Glen Lewandowski, O.S.C., Master Gen.

United States Province: *Province of St. Odilia, Crosier National Headquarters*, 4423 N. 24th St., Ste. 400, Phoenix, AZ 85016-5584. Tel: 602-443-7100; Fax: 602-443-7101. Rev. Thomas A. Enneking, O.S.C., Prior Prov. Provincial Councilors: Rev. Stephan Bauer, O.S.C; Rev. Richard McGuire, O.S.C; Very Rev. Kermit Holl, O.S.C; Very Rev. David Donnay, O.S.C.
Bishops: 1; Fathers: 36; Brothers: 16
Legal Titles: Crosier Fathers and Brothers Province, Inc.; Canons Regular of the Order of the Holy Cross.
Represented in the Archdiocese of Detroit and in the Dioceses of Phoenix and St. Cloud.
Properties owned, sponsored or staffed: Houses 2; Novitiates 1; Parishes 7.

[0410] (F.D.P.)—SONS OF DIVINE PROVIDENCE

(Filiorum Divinae Providentiae)

General Motherhouse: Via Etruria 6, 00183, Rome, Italy, Very Rev. Flavio Peloso, F.D.P., Supr. Gen.
Founded in 1893 by St. Don Louis Orione.

Missionary Delegation-Our Lady Mother of the Church-U.S. Foundation: 150 Orient Ave., East Boston, MA 02128. Tel: 617-569-2100; Fax: 617-569-8701. Rev. Malcolm George, Delegation Supr.
Priests: 5
Properties staffed or owned: Parishes 1; Nursing Home 2; Shrine 1.
Represented in the Archdioceses of Boston and New York and in the Diocese of Evansville.

[0420] (S.V.D.)—SOCIETY OF THE DIVINE WORD

(Societas Verbi Divini)

General Motherhouse: *Collegio del Verbo Divino*, Via dei Verbiti 1, 00154, Rome, Italy, Very Rev. Antonio Pernia, S.V.D., Supr. Gen.
Founded 1875, in Steyl, Netherlands; First U.S.A. province erected in 1897 with Headquarters at St. Mary's Mission House (Divine Word Seminary) Techny, Illinois; later separating into four provinces. In 1985 the Eastern and Northern Provinces combined.

Chicago Province (1985): *Province of Saint Joseph Freinademetz, S.V.D. Province Center*, 1985 Waukegan Rd., P.O. Box 6038, Techny, IL 60082-6038. Tel: 847-272-2700; Fax: 847-412-9505. Rev. Thomas J. Ascheman, S.V.D., Prov; Rev. Adam Oleszczuk, S.V.D., Prov; Rev. Dariusz Garbaciak, S.V.D., Treas.
Legal Titles: Society of the Divine Word; Divine Word Funds, Inc.; Divine Word International; Techny Towers Conference and Retreat Center; Blessed Arnold Charitable Trust; DWTCRE Charitable Trust; S.V.D. Funds, Inc.
Priests 177; Brothers 32; Theologians 18; Brothers in Temporary Vows 3.
Minor Seminarians: Colleges 52; Novices 7; Associates 3.
Properties owned: Theologate; College; 3 Retreat Houses; House of Studies; Conference Center; 3 Retirement Houses.
Represented in the Archdioceses of Boston, Chicago, Dubuque, Indianapolis, Milwaukee, St. Louis and Washington and in the Dioceses of Memphis, Pittsburgh, Trenton and Wheeling-Charleston. Also in Canada, Jamaica, Netherland Antilles, British Virgin Islands, and the West Indies.

Divine Word Missionaries: 1835 Waukegan Rd., P.O. Box 6099, Techny, IL 60082-6099. Bro. Dennis Newton, S.V.D., Pres.
Divine Word Missionaries is within the territory of the Chicago Province but assists members of all three United States S.V.D. Provinces serving overseas and reports directly to Rome regarding its international fundraising activities.
Legal Titles: Divine Word Missionaries, Inc.; S.V.D. Catholic Universities.

Eastern Province: Amalgamated with Northern Province. See Chicago Province.: Amalgamated with Northern Province. See Chicago Province.

Southern Province: *Southern Province of St. Augustine*, 199 Seminary Dr., Bay Saint Louis, MS 39520.

Tel: 228-467-4322; Tel: 228-467-3815; Email: svdsouthusa@yahoo.com. Very Rev. James Pawlicki, S.V.D., Prov; Rev. Paul Kahan, S.V.D., Vice Prov; Rev. George Gormley, S.V.D., Treas.

Fathers: 60; Brothers: 4; Parishes: 33; Mission Stations: 3; Elementary Schools: 4

Address applications for Retreats and Missions to: Rev. William J. Kelley, S.V.D., Retreat Center.

Represented in the Archdioceses of Galveston-Houston and New Orleans and in the Dioceses of Baton Rouge, Beaumont, Biloxi, Fort Worth, Jackson, Lafayette (LA), Little Rock, and Lake Charles.

Western Province (1964): *Province of St. Therese of the Child Jesus*, 11316 Cypress Ave, Riverside, CA 92505. Tel: 951-687-7600; Fax: 951-687-3158. Very Rev. Briccio Tamoro, S.V.D., Prov; Rev. Soney Sebastian, S.V.D., Vice Prov; Rev. Ponciano Ramos, S.V.D., Prov. Treas.

Fathers: 60; Brothers: 5

Represented in the Archdiocese of Los Angeles and in the Dioceses of Oakland, Orange, San Bernardino and San Diego.

Properties staffed, sponsored or owned: High Schools 1; Parishes 15; Hospitals 3; Prisons 1; Retreat Centers 1.

[0430] (O.P.)—ORDER OF PREACHERS

(Dominicans Fratres Sacri Ordinis Praedicatorum)

Generalitia: *Convento Santa Sabina*, Piazza Pietro d'Illiria, Aventino 00153, Rome, Italy, Most Rev. Bruno Cadore, O.P., 87th Master of the Order; Very Rev. Edward Ruane, O.P., Vicar for the Master of the Order & Socius for the United States Provs; Very Rev. Robert Ombres, O.P., Procurator Gen.

Province of St. Joseph-Eastern Dominican Province (1805): *Dominican Provincial Offices*, 141 E. 65th St., New York, NY 10065-6618. Tel: 212-737-5757; Fax: 212-861-4216. Rev. Brian Mulcahy, O.P., Prior Prov; Rev. John Albert Langlois, O.P., Socius to the Prov; Rev. William Paul Marquis, O.P., Econ. Admin; Rev. John C. Vidmar, O.P., Archivist; Rev. Joseph Torchia, O.P., Regent of Studies; Rev. Paul Keller, O.P., Dir. Continuing Formation; Rev. John B. Croell, O.P., Dir., Vocations; Very Rev. Darren Michael Pierre, O.P., Vicar, Admin. & Promoter, Dominican Lay & Priestly Fraternities; Very Rev. William Alexander Holt, O.P., Dir., Mission Office; Rev. Christopher Francis Belanger, O.P., Promoter, Social Justice; Rev. Bruno M. Shah, O.P., Promoter, Holy Name Society; Rev. John Gregory Schnakenberg, O.P., Promoter, Holy Rosary; Very Rev. David Dominic Izzo, O.P., Vicar for Advancement; Very Rev. Steven C. Boguslawski, O.P., Acting Pres., Pontifical Faculty of the Immaculate Conception (Washington, D.C.); Rev. James Dominic Brent, O.P., Promoter, Angelic Warfare Confraternity; Rev. Kevin Gabriel Gillen, O.P., Asst. Dir., Dominican Foundation.

Corporate Title: Dominican Fathers Province of St. Joseph.

Legal Titles: Retirement Plan and Pension Plan; Dominican Fathers, Province of St. Joseph; Dominican Friars' Guilds, Inc.; Deserving Poor Boys Priesthood Association, Inc.; St. Jude Dominican Missions, Inc.; St. Martin de Porres Guild, Inc.; Dominican Foreign Missions; Handicapped Children's Fund, Peru; Rosary Shrine of St. Jude, (Washington, DC); Rosary Apostolate; Dominican Foundation of Dominican Friars, Province of St. Joseph, Inc.

Represented in the following U.S. dioceses: Arlington, Baltimore, Boston, Buffalo, Camden, Cincinnati, Columbus, Fort Wayne-South Bend, Grand Rapids, Harrisburg, Hartford, Lansing, Louisville, Manchester, Nashville, New York, Newark, Oakland, Providence, Richmond, Rochester, Rockville Centre, Saint Paul and Minneapolis, Springfield, Washington, Wilmington and Youngstown.

Properties owned, staffed or sponsored: Priories 9; Houses 9; Parishes 16; Campus Ministries 7; Colleges 1; Houses of Study 1; Novitiates 1; Mission Abroad 1; Health Care Ministry 1; Health Care Facility 1.

Province of the Most Holy Name of Jesus-Western Dominican Province (1912): 5877 Birch Ct., Oakland, CA 94618-1626. Tel: 510-658-8722; Fax: 510-658-1061; Email: WDP@opwest.org. Rev. Mark Padrez, O.P., Prior Prov; Rev. Joseph Sergott, O.P., Vicar Prov. & Socius; Rev. Martin Walsh, O.P., Dir. Mission Foundation; Rev. Bryan Kromholtz, O.P., Regent of Studies; Rev. Dominic DeDomenico, O.P., Treas; Rev. Daniel Syverstad, O.P., Dir. Devel; Rev. Steven Maekawa, O.P., Dir. Vocations; Rev. Jude Eli, O.P., Dir.-Preaching; Bro. Raymond Bertheaux, O.P., Archivist.

Legal Title: Province of the Holy Name, Inc.

Fathers: 122; Brothers: 6; Professed Clerics: 19; Novices: 6; Donatus: 1; Parishes: 8; Newman Centers/Personal Parishes: 9; Retreat Houses: 1; Houses of Study: 1; Novitiates: 1

Represented in the Archdioceses of Anchorage, Los Angeles, Portland in Oregon, San Francisco, Seattle and Washington and in the Dioceses of Fall River, Las Vegas, Oakland, Providence, Sacramento, Salt Lake City, San Bernardino, San Diego, San Jose and Tucson. Also in Australia, Germany, Guatemala, Italy Kenya, Lithuania, Mexico, Switzerland and Jerusalem.

Province of St. Albert the Great-Central Dominican Province (1939): 1909 S. Ashland Ave., Chicago, IL 60608. Tel: 312-666-3244; Fax: 312-829-8471. Very Rev. Charles E. Bouchard, O.P., Prov; Rev. Louis S. Morrone, O.P., Socius, Vicar Prov. & Economic Admin; Rev. David F. Wright, O.P., Archivist; Rev. Andrew-Carl Wisdom, O.P., Promoter of Vocations & Dir.-Society Vocational Support; Rev. Patrick F. Norris, O.P., Promoter of Social Justice; Rev. Thomas K. McDermott, O.P., Regent; Rev. Robert J. Botthof, O.P., Dir., Shrine of St. Jude; Rev. Gerard B. Cleator, O.P., Dir. St. Dominic Mission Society.

Fathers: 149; Professed Clerics: 21; Novices: 6; Brothers: 16

Legal Titles: Dominicans, Province of St. Albert the Great, U.S.A.; Shrine of St. Jude Thaddeus, Inc.; Society for Vocational Support, Inc.; St. Dominic Mission Society; Dominican Social Action Fund; Dominican Laity; Dominican Central Productions; The Bolivian Trust of the Dominicans, Office for Mission Advancement.

Represented in the Archdioceses of Chicago, Denver, Detroit, Indianapolis, St. Louis, St. Paul-Minneapolis and Santa Fe and in the Dioceses of Jefferson City, Joliet, Lafayette in Indiana, Madison, Springfield in Illinois, Superior and Winona.

Properties owned, staffed or sponsored: Parishes 9; Convents 8; Houses 11; Houses of Studies 2; Novitiate; High Schools 1.

Southern Dominican Province of St. Martin de Porres (1979): 1421 N. Causeway Blvd., Ste. 200, Metairie, LA 70001-4144. Tel: 504-837-2129; Fax: 504-837-6604. Very Rev. Christopher T. Eggleton, O.P., Prov; Very Rev. David G. Caron, O.P., Socius; Rev. Justin Kauchak, O.P., Syndic; Very Rev. Paul J. Philibert, O.P., Promoter for Permanent Formation; Very Rev. Mark Wedig, O.P., Regent of Studies; Rev. John M. Pitzer, O.P., Promoter of Vocations & Devel.

Fathers: 105; Professed Clerics: 11; Brothers: 7; Novices: 2; Deacons: 1

Legal Holdings or Titles: Southern Dominican Foundation; Retirement and Community Support Plan, Southern Dominican Province, U.S.A.; Shrine of St. Martin de Porres; DePorres Property.

Represented in the Archdioceses of Atlanta, Galveston-Houston, Miami, New Orleans, San Antonio and St. Louis and in the Dioceses of Austin, Baton Rouge, Columbus, Dallas, Fort Worth, Lubbock, Memphis, Raleigh, Tucson and Venice.

Properties owned, staffed or sponsored: Parishes 10; Priories 7; Houses 8; Shrines 1; Provincial Offices 1.

U.S. Foundation (1926): *Province of Spain*, P.O. Box 279, San Diego, TX 78384. Tel: 361-279-3596. Rev. Benito Retortillo, O.P; Rev. Epifanio Rodriguez, O.P.

Priests: 2

Represented in the Diocese of Corpus Christi.

[0440] (S.S.E.)—SOCIETY OF SAINT EDMUND

(Societas Sancti Edmundi)

General Motherhouse: *Edmundite Generalate*, 270 Winooski Park, Colchester, VT 05439. Tel: 802-654-3400; Fax: 802-654-3409. Very Rev. Michael P. Cronogue, S.S.E., Supr. Gen. Councilors: Rev. Stephen W. Hornat, S.S.E; Rev. Brian J. Cummings, S.S.E; Rev. David Theroux, S.S.E; Rev. Michael P. Jacques, S.S.E.

Legal Title: Society of St. Edmund, Inc.

Bishops: 1; Fathers: 28; Brothers: 6

Represented in the Archdioceses of Detroit, Mobile and New Orleans and in the Dioceses of Burlington, Norwich and Venice. Also Venezuela and France.

Properties owned, staffed or sponsored: Parishes 13; College 1; Shrine; Novitiate.

[0460] (C.F.P.)—BROTHERS OF THE POOR OF ST. FRANCIS

(Congregatio Fratrum Pauperum)

Motherhouse: Aachen, Germany, Bro. Mark Gastel, C.F.P., Min. Gen.

USA Community of St. Joseph: P.O. Box 30359, Cincinnati, OH 45230-0359. Tel: 513-924-0111; Fax: 513-321-3777. Bro. Edward Kelser, C.F.P., U.S.A Community Min.

Professed Brothers: 15

Brothers serve and staff: Development Office; High School; Elementary Schools.

Brothers' Special Mission: Care and education of youth; elementary & secondary education; pastoral ministry.

Represented in the Archdioceses of Cincinnati and Newark and in the Dioceses of Covington, Davenport, El Paso and Little Rock.

[0470] (O.F.M.CAP.)—THE CAPUCHIN FRANCISCAN FRIARS

(Ordo Fratrum Minorum Capuccinorum)

Generalate: *Curia Generale dei Cappuccini*, Via Piemonte 70, 00187, Rome, Italy, Web: www.ofmcap.org. Bro. Mauro Johri, O.F.M.Cap., Gen. Min.

Province of St. Joseph (1857) (1857): *Calvary Province*, 1820 Mt. Elliott St., Detroit, MI 48207-3496. Tel: 313-579-2100; Fax: 313-579-2275. Very Rev. John Celichowski, O.F.M.Cap., Prov. Min; Rev. Mark Joseph Costello, O.F.M.Cap., Prov. Vicar; Bro. Randolph Graczyk, O.F.M.Cap., Sec.-Religious Affairs; Bro. T.L. Michael Auman, O.F.M.Cap., Dir.-Communications; Rev. Edward Foley, O.F.M.Cap., Dir.-Continuing Education; Rev. William Cieslak, O.F.M.Cap., Dir.-Office of Preaching & Evangelization; Bro. Larry LaCross, O.F.M.Cap., Overseas Missions; Rev. Lester Bach, O.F.M.Cap., Prov. Asst.-Secular Franciscan Order; Bro. Richard Merling, O.F.M.Cap., Dir.-Solanus Guild; Bro. Leo Wollenweber, O.F.M.Cap., Vice Postulator-Cause of Ven. Solanus Casey; Rev. Patrick McSherry, O.F.M.Cap., Archivist; Rev. Michael Crosby, O.F.M-.Cap., Corp. Responsibility Agent; Mr. Harlan Swift, Corp. Sec./Treas; Ms. Judy Gilleran, Admin. Asst; Bro. Larry LaCross, O.F.M.Cap., Prov. Devel; Mr. Jeff Parrish, Dir., Human Resources; Ms. Amy Peterson, Office of Pastoral Care & Conciliation; Ms. Colleen Crane, Dir. Public Rels; Ms. Debra Van Ermen, Dir. Wellness; Shelly Roder, Co-Dir. Cap Corps; Ms. Marcia Lee, Co-Dir. Cap Corps. Councilors: Rev. Gary Wegner, O.F.M.Cap; Rev. Francis Voris, O.F.M.Cap; Rev. Michael Sullivan, O.F.M.Cap.

Legal Title: Province of St. Joseph of the Capuchin Order, Inc.

Priests: 127; Perpetually Professed Lay Friars: 38

Parishes, Hospitals, Nursing Homes, Hospices, Prisons, Retreat Centers, Soup Kitchens; Direct Services to the Poor; Educational Institutions; Home and Foreign Missions.

Represented in the Archdioceses of Chicago, Detroit, Los Angeles, Milwaukee, New York and St. Paul-Minneapolis, and in the Dioceses of Fort Wayne-South Bend, Great Falls-Billings, Green Bay, LaCrosse, Madison, Marquette, Saginaw, San Diego, Santa Barbara, Superior and Tucson. Also the vicariate of Bluefields, Nicaragua and in Dioceses of Managua, Panama and Australia.

Province of St. Augustine (1873): *Provincial Office*, 220 37th St., Pittsburgh, PA 15201. Tel: 412-682-6011; Fax: 412-682-0506. Very Rev. W. David Nestler, O.F.M.Cap., Prov. Min; Rev. Michael Joyce, O.F.M-.Cap., Vicar Prov; Rev. John Pfannenstiel, O.F.M.Cap., Vicar Prov; Bro. Robert Toomey, O.F.M.Cap. Definitors: Rev. Thomas Betz, O.F.M.Cap; Bro. Robert Toomey, O.F.M.Cap., Exec. Sec; Mr. R. Joseph Kusnir, CFO. Vocations Director: Rev. Thomas Betz, O.F.M-.Cap., Vocation Min.

Cardinals: 1; Priests: 115; Brothers: 39; Professed in Formation: 25; Novices: 9; Postulants: 11

Legal Titles: Province of St. Augustine of the Capuchin Order; Headquarters of Capuchin Franciscan Volunteer Corps., Inc.; Augustine Province of the Capuchin Order; National Headquarters of Archconfraternity of Christian Mothers; Mission Office of Seraphic Mass Association; Secular Franciscan Order of St. Augustine, Province; Capuchin Friars Sick and Elderly Trust Fund; St. Fidelis, Inc.; Capuchin Friars Formation and Education Trust Fund.

Represented in the Archdioceses of Baltimore, Philadelphia and Washington and in the Dioceses of Altoona-Johnstown, Cleveland, Harrisburg, Pittsburgh and Wheeling-Charleston. Also in Papua New Guinea and Puerto Rico.

Properties owned, staffed or sponsored: Parishes 21; Formation Houses 2; Friaries 17; Postulancy Houses 1; Hospital Chaplain 8; Missions 2.

Province of St. Mary: *St. Conrad Friary*, 30 Gedney Park Dr., White Plains, NY 10605. Tel: 914-761-3008; Fax: 914-948-6429. Rev. Francis Gasparik, O.F.M-.Cap., Minister Prov. Definitors: Rev. Michael Marigliano, O.F.M.Cap., Vicar Prov; Bro. Joseph Yakimovich, O.F.M.Cap; Rev. Michael Connolly, O.F.M.Cap; Bro. James Peterson, O.F.M.Cap.

Legal Title: The Province of St. Mary of the Capuchin Order; Capuchin Friars International, Inc.; St. Francis of Assisi Foundation; Capuchin Friars of North America.

Bishops: 2; Priests: 100; Professed Clerical Brothers: 5; Professed Lay Brothers: 36; Novices: 5; Postulants: 9

Represented in the Archdioceses of Agana, Boston and New York and in the Dioceses of Brooklyn, Burlington, Honolulu, Manchester, Norwich, Portland (In Maine), Rochester, Rockville Centre and St. Petersburg. Also in Japan.

Properties staffed or sponsored: Parishes 12; Chaplaincies 13; Novitiate 1; Foreign Missions 3.

Development Office: *St. John's Friary*, 210 W. 31st St., New York, NY 10001.

Province of the Sacred Stigmata of St. Francis: *Our Lady Guadalupe Friary*, 319 - 36th St., P.O. Box 809, Union City, NJ 07087. Tel: 201-865-0611; Fax: 201-866-7035. Rev. Nicholas A. Mormando, O.F.M.Cap., Prov. Min; Rev. Ronald Giannone, O.F.M.Cap., Prov. Vicar. Definitors: Bro. John Paul Russo, O.F.M.Cap; Bro. Rudolph Pieretti, O.F.M.Cap; Rev. Remo DiSalvatore, O.F.M.Cap.

Priests: 30; Brothers: 12; Parishes: 8; Friaries: 4; Retreat Houses: 1; Hospital Chaplaincies: 1

Represented in the Archdioceses of Newark and New York and in the Dioceses of Charlotte, Paterson, St. Petersburg and Wilmington.

Our Lady of Angels, Western America Province: 1345 Cortez Ave., Burlingame, CA 94010. Rev. Matthew Elshoff, O.F.M.Cap., Prov. Definitors: Rev. Camillus MacRory, O.F.M.Cap., Spiritual Asst.-Secular Franciscans; Rev. Donal Burke, O.F.M.Cap., Dir.-Devel./Finances; Rev. Miguel Angel Ortiz, O.F.M.Cap., Dir.-Foreign Missions, Sec; Rev. Jesus Vela, O.F.M.Cap., Vicar; Rev. Antonio Marti, O.F.M.Cap; Rev. Harold Snider, O.F.M.Cap; Rev. Robert A. Barbato, O.F.M.Cap.

Priests: 39; Brothers: 15; Brothers in Formation: 13; Novices: 6; Postulants: 13

Ministries in Parishes, High Schools, Novitiates, Chaplaincies, House of Study, Retreats, Foreign Missions, Campus Ministry, Prison Chaplaincy and Hospital Chaplaincy.

Represented in the Archdioceses of Los Angeles and San Francisco and in the Dioceses of Oakland and San Bernardino. Also in Mexico.

Province of SS. Stanislaus and Adalbert (1948): *St. Stanislaus Friary*, 2 Manor Dr., Oak Ridge, NJ 07438.

Tel: 973-697-7757. Rev. Marek Przeczewski, O.F.M-.Cap., Prov. Minister; Rev. Krzysztof Lewandowski, O.F.M.Cap., Provincial Vicar; Deacon Jerzy Krzyskow, Admin.
Fathers: 4
Represented in the Dioceses of Metuchen and Paterson.

Vice Province of Our Lady of Guadalupe: *Capuchin Franciscan Friars of Texas*, 5605 Bernal Dr., Dallas, TX 75212. Tel: 214-500-8595; Tel: 214-637-6673; Fax: 214-637-2454. Rev. Mario Garcia, O.F.M.Cap., Vice Prov.
Fathers: 9
Members serve and staff: Parishes 2; Cursillo Centers 2.
Represented in the Dioceses of Dallas and Fort Worth.

Province of Mid-America (1977): 3613 Wyandot St., Denver, CO 80211-2950. Tel: 303-477-5436; Fax: 303-477-6925; Web: www.midamcaps.org. Rev. Charles Polifka, O.F.M.Cap., Prov. Min; Rev. Christopher Popravak, O.F.M.Cap., Prov. Vicar; Rev. David Songy, O.F.M.Cap., Initial Formation Dir; Rev. Blaine Burkey, O.F.M.Cap., Communications Dir. & Archivist; Rev. John Lager, O.F.M.Cap., Vocation Dir; Stephanie Pedersen, Dir. Devel. & Missionary Activities; Rev. James Moster, O.F.M.Cap., Councilor; Rev. John Cousins, O.F.M.Cap., Councilor; Rev. Jeff Ernst, O.F.M-.Cap., Councilor.
Bishops: 2; Priests: 38; Students: 5; Lay Brothers: 5; Temporary Professed Brothers: 2; Novices: 2; Postulants: 6
Legal Titles: Capuchin Province of Mid-America, Inc.; St. Francis Seminary Endowment Foundation, Inc.
Represented in the Archdioceses of Denver and Kansas City in Kansas and in the Dioceses of Colorado Springs, Pueblo, and Salina.

Vice Province of St. John the Baptist (1905): *Vice Provincial Offices*, 216 Arzuaga St., P.O. Box 21350, Rio Piedras, PR 00928-1350. Tel: 787-764-3090; Fax: 787-764-4070; Email: curia@capuchinospr.org; Web: www.capuchinospr.org. Bro. Francisco Garcia, O.F.M-.Cap., Vice Prov. Min; Bro. Roberto Martinez, O.F.M-.Cap., First Councilor; Bro. Fernando Irizarry, O.F.M-.Cap., Second Councilor; Bro. Elmig M. Soto Negrou, O.F.M.Cap., Dir. Capuchin Mass Assoc; Rev. Luis O. Padilla, O.F.M.Cap., Vice Provincial Sec. Capuchin Mass Assoc; Rev. Roberto Martinez, O.F.M.Cap., Vice Provincial Treas.
Friars: 25; Postulants: 3
Legal Titles: Asociacion de Frailes Capuchinos, Inc.; Asociacion Misionera Capuchina; Capuchin Formation Trust of Puerto Rico; Capuchin Health and Retirement Trust of Puerto Rico.
Represented in the Archdiocese of San Juan and in the Dioceses of Arecibo, Caguas and Ponce.
Properties owned, staffed and sponsored: Formation Fraternites 3; Parishes 4; Retreat Center 1; Friaries 6; Mission Office 1.

[0480] (O.F.M.CONV.)—CONVENTUAL FRANCISCANS

(Friars Minor Conventual)
(Ordo Fratrum Minorum S. Francisci Conventualium)

General Curia: Piazza SS. Apostoli, 51, 00187, Rome, Italy, Most Rev. Marco Tasca, O.F.M.Conv., Min. Gen.

Province of the Immaculate Conception B.V.M. (1852): *Provincial Office*, 77 St. Francis Pl., P.O. Box 629, Rensselaer, NY 12144. Tel: 518-472-1000; Fax: 518-472-1013; Web: www.franciscanseast.org. Very Rev. Justin A. Biase, O.F.M.Conv., Min. Prov; Rev. Brad A. Milunski, O.F.M.Conv., Vicar Prov; Rev. Michael Lorentsen, O.F.M.Conv., Province Sec; Bro. Raymond Sobocinski, O.F.M.Conv., Province Treas; Rev. Jobe Abbass, O.F.M.Conv., Province Definitor; Rev. Jorge Dobles, O.F.M.Conv., Province Definitor.
Fathers: 76; Professed Brothers: 19; Parishes: 18; Friaries: 17; Chaplaincies: 4; Filial Houses: 1
Legal Titles: Order of Friars Minor Conventual Immaculate Conception; Province Charitable Trust; Franciscorps, Inc., Rensselaer, NY; The Franciscan Center for Spirituality, Inc., Albany, NY; Franciscans in Collaborative Ministry, Inc., Rensselaer, NY.
Represented in the Archdioceses of New York and Washington and in the Dioceses of Albany, Charlotte, Raleigh, Syracuse and Trenton. Also in Canada and Costa Rica.

Province of St. Anthony of Padua (1906): *Provincial House*, 12300 Folly Quarter Rd., Ellicott City, MD 21042-1419. Tel: 410-531-1400; Fax: 410-531-4881. Very Rev. James McCurry, O.F.M.Conv., Minister Prov; Rev. Jude Surowiec, O.F.M.Conv., Vicar Prov; Rev. Mitchell Sawicki, O.F.M.Conv., Treas; Rev. Richard-Jacob Forcier, O.F.M.Conv., Sec. Definitors: Rev. Michael Sajda, O.F.M.Conv; Rev. Michael Zielke, O.F.M.Conv; Rev. Jude Michael Krill, O.F.M.Conv; Rev. Russell Governale, O.F.M.Conv.
Priests: 111; Brothers in Solemn Vows: 14; Clerics in Temporary Vows: 3; Novices: 2; Candidates: 3; Friaries: 25; Filial Houses: 8
Legal Titles: St. Francis High School of Athol Springs, NY, Inc.; The Father Justin Rosary Hour, Inc.; Franciscan Fathers Minor Conventuals of Buffalo, NY, Inc.; The Franciscan Center, Inc.; St. Anthony of Padua Province, Franciscan Fathers Minor Conventual, U.S.A., Inc.; Order of Friars Minor Conventual, Inc.; Conventual Franciscan Friars, St. Anthony of Padua Province, Franciscan Mission Association, Inc.; Franciscan Fathers Minor Conventual, St. Anthony of Padua Province U.S.A., MA. Inc.; Franciscan Friars, St. Anthony of Padua Province, Education Fund, Inc.; Franciscan Friars, St. Anthony of Padua Province, Fund for the Aged and Infirm, Inc.; Franciscan Minor Conventuals of Maryland, of Ellicott City, MD, Inc.; The Franciscan Fathers, Minor Conventuals of St. Stanislaus Church of Baltimore City, MD, Inc.; St. Francis of Assisi Community, Inc.; Order of Friars Minor Conventual, St. Anthony of Padua Province, U.S.A., Inc.; St. Stanislaus Cemetery, Inc.; Anthony-Corps, Inc.; Fr. Justin Ministry Fund, Inc.
Represented in the Archdioceses of Atlanta, Baltimore, Boston and Hartford and in the Dioceses of Altoona-Johnstown, Bridgeport, Brooklyn, Buffalo, Fall River, Harrisburg, Norwich, Palm Beach, Paterson, Springfield in Massachusetts and Trenton.
Apostolates owned, staffed or sponsored: Novitiates 1; House of Study 1; Parishes 28; Campus Ministries 4; High Schools 2; Youth-Crisis Shelter 1; Sisters' Chaplaincies 1; Hospital-Nursing Home Chaplaincies 3; Apostolates Radio Apostolate; Healing Ministry; Preaching Apostolate; Foreign Missions 3; Candidate House; Youth Ministry.

St. Bonaventure Province (1939): 6107 N. Kenmore Ave., Chicago, IL 60660-2797. Tel: 773-274-7681; Fax: 773-274-9751. Rev. Patrick Greenough, O.F.M.Conv., Min. Prov. Definitors: Rev. Michael J. Glastetter, O.F.M.Conv., Vicar Prov; Bro. Juniper Kriss, O.F.M-.Conv.; Rev. Patrick Stoffer, O.F.M.Conv.; Rev. John Grigus, O.F.M.Conv.; Bro. Joseph Wood, O.F.M.Conv., Sec.
Fathers: 22; Professed Clerics: 2; Brothers: 19
Legal Titles: Conventual Franciscans of St. Bonaventure Province; Franciscan Friars Educational Corp.; Conventual Franciscan Friars of Marytown; Shrine of St. Maximillian Kolbe; St. Hedwig Cemetery and Mausoleum; The Conventual Franciscans of Saint Bonaventure Province Charitable Continuing Care Trust Fund.
Represented in the Archdioceses of Chicago, Detroit and Milwaukee and in the Dioceses of Peoria and Rockford. Also in Mexico.
Properties owned or sponsored: Parishes 5; Chaplaincies; Marian Center; Shrine.

Province of Our Lady of Consolation (1926): 101 Anthony Dr., Mount Saint Francis, IN 47146. Tel: 812-923-8444. Very Rev. James Kent, Min. Prov; Bro. Robert Baxter, O.F.M.Conv., Sec.
Fathers: 74; Brothers: 26; Professed Clerics: 2; Candidates: 3; Novices: 1; Friaries: 15; Parishes: 17; Houses of Formation: 3; Retreat-Renewal Centers: 3; Missions: 15; Chaplaincies: 3

Development Office: 103 St. Francis Blvd., Mount Saint Francis, IN 47146. Tel: 812-923-5250.

Province of St. Joseph of Cupertino (1981): *St. Joseph of Cupertino Friary*, P.O. Box 820, Arroyo Grande, CA 93421-0820. Tel: 805-489-1012; Tel: 805-473-2256; Fax: 805-489-8303. Very Rev. Christopher Deitz, O.F.M.Conv., Min. Prov; Very Rev. Gary Klauer, O.F.M.Conv., Vicar; Rev. Viktor Perez, O.F.M.Conv., Definitor; Rev. Luke Vu, O.F.M.Conv., Definitor; Bro. George Cherrie, O.F.M.Conv., Definitor & Sec.
Legal Title: Conventual Franciscans of California, Inc.
Priests: 35; Brothers: 13
Represented in the Archdioceses of Los Angeles and San Francisco and in the Dioceses of Fresno, Monterey, Oakland and Reno.
Properties owned, staffed or sponsored: Parishes 6; Chaplaincies 3; High Schools 1; Houses of Formation 1.

[0485] (M.S.F.S.)—MISSIONARIES OF ST. FRANCIS DE SALES

(Missionariorum Sancti Francisci Salesi)

Founded in Annecy, France 1838. Established in the United States of America as a region on July 3, 2007.

Motherhouse: *Domus Missionariorum Sancti Francisci Salesi*, Via delle Testuggini, 21, I-00143, Roma, Italy,

American Mission: *Villa Luyet*, 3474 Pate Dr., Snellville, GA 30078-5000. Rev. Augustine Tharappel, M.S.F.S., Regional Supr; Rev. John C. DeVore, M.S.F.S; Rev. Joseph Pottemmel, M.S.F.S; Rev. George Puraidam, M.S.F.S; Rev. Joseph Mullakkara, M.S.F.S; Rev. Joseph Mendes, M.S.F.S; Rev. Sunny Punakuzhiyil, M.S.F.S; Rev. Johnny Puthiyaparampil, M.S.F.S.
Legal Title: Missionaries of St. Francis de Sales, Inc.
Fathers: 44; Fathers from provinces outside U.S: 15
Properties Staffed: Religious Houses 2; Parishes 33; Convents 1.
Properties Owned: Villa Luyet , Snellville, GA; "Wellspring", Fransalian Center for Spirituality, Whitehouse, TX.
Represented in the Archdioceses of Atlanta, Chicago, Detroit, Galveston-Houston, Kansas City in Kansas, Mobile, New York and St. Louis and in the Dioceses of Alexandria, Cleveland, Dodge City, Knoxville, Lansing, La Crosse, Nashville, St. Augustine, Tucson and St. Thomas Syro-Malabar diocese of Chicago.

[0490] (O.S.F.)—CONGREGATION OF THE RELIGIOUS BROTHERS OF THE THIRD ORDER REGULAR OF ST. FRANCIS

(Franciscan Brothers of Brooklyn)

Generalate (1858): *St. Francis Monastery*, 135 Remsen St., Brooklyn, NY 11201-4212. Tel: 718-858-8217; Fax: 718-858-8306. Bro. William Boslet, O.S.F., Supr. Gen. Councilors: Bro. Kevin Smith, O.S.F; Bro. Richard Contino, O.S.F; Bro. Joshua DiMauro, O.S.F; Bro. Jeremy Sztabnik, O.S.F.
Brothers: 77
Legal Titles and Holdings: St. Francis Monastery; Franciscan Brothers' Generalate; Franciscan Brothers, Inc., Brooklyn, NY; Mount Alvernia, Inc.; St. Francis Center, Inc., Rockville Centre, NY.
Ministries in the field of Education at all levels; Pastoral Ministries, Social Services; Spirituality Centers.
Represented in the Dioceses of Brooklyn, Rockville Centre and Springfield-Cape Girardeau.

[0510] (F.F.S.C.)—FRANCISCAN BROTHERS OF THE HOLY CROSS

Generalate: *St. Josefshaus*, 53547 Hausen/Wied, Linz Rhein, Germany, Bro. Ulrich Schmitz, F.F.S.C., Supr. Gen.

American Region (1924): 2500 St. James Rd., Springfield, IL 62707. Tel: 217-528-4757; Fax: 217-528-4824. Bro. John Francis Tyrrell, F.F.S.C., Pres./Supr; Bro. Stephen Bissler, F.F.S.C., Treas; Bro. Christian Guertin, F.F.S.C., Vice Pres./Vicar; Bro. Ulrich Schmitz, F.F.S.C; Bro. Joel Mark Rousseau, F.F.S.C., Sec.
Brothers: 12
Represented in the Archdiocese of St. Louis and in the Dioceses of Madison and Springfield in Illinois.
Properties owned, staffed or sponsored: Home for Mentally Handicapped; Adult Training Center for Mentally Handicapped; Secretarial; Chaplaincy; Novitiate; Community Living Facility; Pastoral leadership.

[0515] (O.S.F.)—FRANCISCAN BROTHERS OF THE THIRD ORDER REGULAR

Generalate: *Franciscan Brothers' Generalate*, Mountbellow, Ireland,

United States Region: 4522 Gainsborough Ave., Los Angeles, CA 90027. Tel: 323-644-2740. Bro. Paulinus Horkan, O.S.F., Reg. Supr.
Brothers: 6
Ministries in the field of secondary education.
Represented in the Archdiocese of Los Angeles.

[0520] (O.F.M.)—FRANCISCAN FRIARS

(Ordinis Fratrum Minorum)

General Headquarters: *Curia Generalizia dei Frati Minori*, Via S. Maria Mediatrice, 25, 00165, Rome, Italy, Rev. Jose R. Carballo, O.F.M., Min. Gen; Rev. Francis Walter, O.F.M., English-Speaking General Definitor.

Order of Friars Minor: *English-Speaking Conference*, 14 N. Bennet St., Boston, MA 02113. Tel: 617-248-8821; Fax: 617-248-8868. Rev. Thomas Washburn, O.F.M., Exec. Sec; Very Rev. Caoimhin O'Laoide, O.F.M., Pres; Very Rev. Uohn Hardin, O.F.M., Vice Pres; Rev. Francis Walter, O.F.M., Gen. Definitor.
Includes: Order of Friars Minor Provinces 12; Custodies 1; of the United States, Canada, England, Ireland, Lithuania and Malta.

Province of St. John the Baptist (1844): 1615 Vine St., Cincinnati, OH 45202-6400. Tel: 513-721-4700; Fax: 513-421-9672. Rev. Jeffrey Scheeler, O.F.M., Prov. Min; Rev. Donald Miller, O.F.M., Vocation Dir; Rev. Arthur Espelage, O.F.M., Prov. Canonist. Councillors: Bro. Vincent Delorenzo, O.F.M; Rev. Mark Soehner, O.F.M; Bro. Michael Dubec, O.F.M; Rev. William Farris, O.F.M; Bro. Gene Mayer, O.F.M., Prov. Sec; Rev. Kenan Freson, O.F.M., Prov. Liaison to Sponsored Ministries; Rev. Maynard Tetreault, O.F.M., Bldg. Coord; Rev. Patrick McCloskey, O.F.M., Dir. Continuing Educ./Formation; Rev. Page Polk, O.F.M., Co-Dir.-Continuing Educ./Formation; Sr. Donna Graham, O.S.F., Dir.-Office of Peace, Justice & Integrity of Creation; Bro. Vincent Delorenzo, O.F.M., Dir. Franciscan Mission Office; Bro. David Crank, O.F.M., Dir.-Office of Senior Friars; Rev. Daniel J. Anderson, O.F.M., Admin. Asst. to Prov. Min; Bro. Juniper Crouch, O.F.M., Prov. Spiritual Asst. for Secular Order; Bro. Timothy Lamb, O.F.M., Personnel Advr. & Assoc. Vocation Dir; Rev. Frank J. Jasper, O.F.M., Prov. Vicar & Treas; Mr. David O'Brien, CFO; Rev. John Bok, O.F.M., Co-Dir.-Friar Works/Franciscan Mission & Ministry; Ms. Colleen Cushard, Co-Dir. Friar Works/Franciscan Mission & Ministry; Ms. Toni Cashnelli, Dir.-Office of Communications; Bro. Allan Schmitz, O.F.M., Prov. Archivist; Rev. James Van Vurst, O.F.M, Spec. Delegate for Child Protection.
Priests: 107; Temporary Professed: 5; Novices: 5; Brothers: 55
Represented in the Archdioceses of Chicago, Cincinnati, Detroit, Galveston-Houston, Indianapolis, Milwaukee, New Orleans, Santa Fe and Washington and in the Dioceses of Allentown, El Paso, Gallup, Greensburg, Lafayette, Las Cruces, Lexington, Peoria, Phoenix, Pittsburgh, Shreveport, Springfield-Cape Girardeau, St. Petersburg, and Venice. Also in Military Services.

Province of The Sacred Heart (1858): 3140 Meramec St., Saint Louis, MO 63118. Tel: 314-353-3421. Rev. William Spencer, O.F.M., Prov. Min; Rev. Michael Jennrich, O.F.M., Prov. Vicar; Bro. Christopher Lambert, O.F.M., Prov. Sec; Rev. Michael Hill, O.F.M., Prov. Treas; Bro. Joseph Rogenski, Prov. Promoter of the Missions, Commissary of the Holy Land, Secretariat Missionary Evangelization. Councilors: Rev. James Lause, O.F.M; Rev. John Dombrowski, O.F.M; Rev. Gerald Bleem, O.F.M; Rev. John Eaton, O.F.M; Bro. Moises Gutierrez, O.F.M; Bro. Ducanh Pham, O.F.M.
Legal Titles: Franciscan Fathers of the State of Missouri; Franciscan Fathers of the State of Illinois; Franciscan Press; Franciscan Tertiary Province of the

Sacred Heart, Incorporated; Mayslake Village; Franciscan Mayslake Village; Cloister Courts; Employees of the Franciscan Orders.
Solemnly Professed: Priests 163; Brothers 57; Simply Professed: Brothers 10; Permanent Deacons 1.
Represented in the Archdioceses of Chicago, Indianapolis, Military Services, St. Louis, St. Paul-Minneapolis and San Antonio and the Dioceses of Belleville, Cleveland, Evansville, Fairbanks, Fort Worth, Gaylord, Joliet, Nashville, Shreveport, Springfield in Illinois, Springfield-Cape Girardeau and Superior.
Properties owned, sponsored or staffed: Friaries 32; Parishes 27; Missions 13; Institutional Chaplaincies 14; Chaplaincies for Religious 6; Formation Houses 2; Novitiates 1; Colleges 1; High Schools 2.

Province of the Assumption of the Blessed Virgin Mary, Inc. (1887): *Provincial Office*, 9230 W. Highland Park Ave., Franklin, WI 53132. Tel: 414-525-9253; Fax: 414-525-9289; Email: province@ofm-abvm.org; Web: ofm-abvm.org. Very Rev. John Puodziunas, O.F.M., Prov. MIn; Rev. James Gannon, O.F.M., Vicar Prov. Provincial Councilors: Rev. Edward G. Tlucek, O.F.M; Rev. Bernard Kennedy, O.F.M; Bro. Andrew Brophy, O.F.M; Rev. Gregory Plata, O.F.M; Rev. Michael Surufka, O.F.M., Prov. Dir. of Vocations; Rev. John Cella, O.F.M., Dir. of Evangelization Center; Rev. Jerome J. Wolbert, O.F.M., Prov. Spiritual Asst. of Secular Franciscan Order; Bro. Jude Lustyk, O.F.M., Prov. Archivist; Bro. Jerry Tokarz, O.F.M., Prov. Historian & Chronicler; Rev. Anthony F. Janik, O.F.M., Dir., Ongoing Formation.
Priests: 81; Professed Brothers: 38; Deacons: 1
Legal Holdings or Titles: St. Mary of the Angels Friary, Green Bay, WI; Queen of Peace Friary, Burlington, WI; St. Francis Friary, Burlington, WI; Our Lady of Lourdes Friary, Cedar Lake, IN; St. Francis of Assisi School, Greenwood, MS; Francis and Clare Friary, Franklin, WI; Franciscan Pilgrimage Programs, Inc., Franklin, WI; Holy Dormition Friary, Sybertsville, PA; Holy Name Friary, Chicago, IL; St. Francis of Assisi Friary, Greenwood, MS; Assumption BVM Friary, Pulaski, WI; Sacred Heart Friary, McAllen, TX.
Properties owned or staffed: Parishes 16; Friaries 11.
Represented in the Archdioceses of Chicago, Detroit, Milwaukee, New York, Philadelphia, Philadelphia Ukrainian and Pittsburgh Byzantine and in the Dioceses of Brownsville, Cleveland, Gary, Green Bay, Jackson and Parma.

Province of Our Lady of Guadalupe (1985): *Curia Juan Diego*, 1204 Stinson St., SW, Albuquerque, NM 87121-3440. Tel: 505-831-9199; Fax: 505-831-9577. Rev. Gino Correa, O.F.M., Min. Prov; Rev. Ron Walters, O.F.M., Vicar Prov. & Sec. Formation. Councilors: Rev. Gonzalo Moreno, O.F.M., Vocation Dir; Rev. Sean Murnan, O.F.M; Bro. Duane Torisky, O.F.M., Sec., Province Notary Council Member; Rev. Ron Walters, O.F.M., Treas; Bro. Jose Rodriguez, O.F.M.
Priests: 40; Brothers: 16; Postulants: 4
Legal Titles: The Province of Our Lady of Guadalupe of the Order of Friars Minor, Inc.
Represented in the Archdioceses of Chicago, San Antonio and Santa Fe and in the Dioceses of Gallup and Las Cruces.

Province of the Most Holy Name (1901): 129 W. 31st. St., 2nd Fl., New York, NY 10001-3403. Tel: 646-473-0265; Fax: 800-420-1078; Email: hnp@hnp.org. Very Rev. John F. O'Connor, O.F.M., Prov. Minister; Very Rev. Dominic Monti, O.F.M., Prov. Vicar. Provincial Councilors: Bro. Thomas J. Cole, O.F.M., Dir., Franciscan Missionary Union; Rev. Thomas Conway, O.F.M., Prov. Councilor; Bro. Francis Edward Coughlin, O.F.M., Prov. Councilor; Bro. Michael Harlan, O.F.M., Prov. Sec; Rev. Vincent B. Grogan, O.F.M., Canonical Counsel; Ms. Jocelyn Thomas, Dir. Communications; Rev. Dennis Wilson, O.F.M., Treas; Rev. Russell C. Becker, O.F.M., Sec.-Missionary Evangelization; Rev. Brian E. Smail, O.F.M., Dir. Vocations; Rev. Richard Trezza, O.F.M., Prov. Spiritual Asst; Rev. David Convertino, O.F.M., Dir., St. Anthony Guild & Devel; Rev. William L. Beaudin, O.F.M; Bro. Brian C. Belanger, O.F.M; Rev. Lawrence Hayes, O.F.M; Rev. Joseph J. Nangle, O.F.M.
Priests: 260; Brothers: 60; Temporary Profession: Brothers 5, Clerics 4, Novices 3: 12
Solemn Profession: Archbishop 1; Priests 272; Brothers 68; Permanent Deacons 3; Temporary Profession: Brothers 2; Clerics 8; Novices 2.
Represented in the Archdioceses of Atlanta, Baltimore, Boston, Hartford, Miami, Newark, New York, Philadelphia, San Juan and Washington and in the Dioceses of Albany, Arlington, Buffalo, Camden, Charleston, Charlotte, Columbus, Fall River, Ft. Wayne-South Bend, Paterson, Providence, Raleigh, St. Petersburg, Steubenville, Trenton and Wilmington. Also in Lima, Peru.
Properties owned or sponsored: Province Parishes 27; Missions 2; School of Theology 1; Retreat Centers 2; University 1; Colleges 1; Community Houses-Residences 42; Houses of Formation 2; Shrine Churches 3; Campus Ministry 2.

Province of St. Barbara (1915): *The Franciscan Friars of California (1900)*, 1500 34th Ave., Oakland, CA 94601. Tel: 510-536-3722; Fax: 510-536-3970. Rev. John S. Hardin, O.F.M., Prov. Minister; Rev. Kenneth J. Laverone, O.F.M., Vicar Prov. Definitors: Rev. Charles Talley, O.F.M; Rev. Oscar Mendez Guzman, O.F.M; Rev. Franklin Fong, O.F.M; Rev. Michael Doherty, O.F.M; Rev. Joe Schwab, O.F.M; Bro. Robert Rodrigues, O.F.M; Bro. Peter Boegel, O.F.M., Prov. Sec.
Priests: 114; Solemnly Professed Lay Brothers: 54; Simply Professed Brothers: 10; Novices: 3; Pre-Novitiates: 4
Legal Titles: Franciscan Friars of California; Franciscan Friars of Arizona; Franciscan Friars of Oregon.
Represented in the Archdioceses of Los Angeles, Milwaukee, Portland in Oregon and San Francisco and in the Dioceses of Fresno, Las Cruces, Monterey, Oakland, Orange, Phoenix, Sacramento, San Diego, San Jose, Spokane and Tucson.

Province of the Immaculate Conception (Friars Minor of the Order of St. Francis): 125 Thompson St., New York, NY 10012. Tel: 212-674-4388. Rev. Primo P. Piscitello, O.F.M., Minister Prov; Rev. Robert M. Campagna, O.F.M., Vicar Prov. Definitors: Rev. Patrick Boyle, O.F.M; Bro. Vincent Ciaravino, O.F.M; Rev. Dennis Wheatley, O.F.M; Rev. John R. Scarangello, O.F.M; Rev. Michael Della Penna, O.F.M; Bro. Ronald Bolfeta, O.F.M., Prov. Sec. & Treas; Rev. Vit Fiala, O.F.M., SFO Prov. Spiritual Asst; Rev. James Goode, O.F.M., Promoter of the Franciscan Missions; Ms. Madeline Bonnici, Exec. Dir. Franciscan Mission Associates 274-280 W. Lincoln Ave., Mount Vernon, NY 10550.Rev. Robert M. Campagna, O.F.M., Pius League of St. Anthony.
Fathers: 116; Bishops: 4; Brothers: 21; Permanent Deacons: 2
Properties owned or staffed: Parishes 28; Residences 16.
Represented in the Archdioceses of Boston, Hartford and New York and in the Dioceses of Albany, Brooklyn, Fall River, Manchester, Pittsburgh, St. Petersburg, Wheeling-Charleston and Youngstown. Also in Central America, Toronto and Italy.

Commissariat of The Holy Cross (1912): 14246 Main St., P.O. Box 608, Lemont, IL 60439. Tel: 630-257-2494; Fax: 630-257-6432. Rev. Blase Chemazar, O.F.M., Pres. Councilors: Rev. Athanasius Lovrencic, O.F.M; Rev. Bernard Karmanocky, O.F.M; Rev. Krizolog Cimerman, O.F.M.
Fathers: 7; Monasteries: 1; Retreat Houses: 1; Mission Centers: 1
Legal Titles: The Slovene Franciscan Fathers, Order of Friars Minor, Commissariat of the Holy Cross, Lemont, IL; St. Mary's Retreat House, Lemont, IL.
Represented in the Archdioceses of Chicago and New York and in the Diocese of Altoona-Johnstown.

Holy Family Friary: 232 S. Home Ave., Pittsburgh, PA 15202-2899. Tel: 412-761-2550. Rev. David Moczulski, O.F.M., Evangelization/Sacramental Ministry & Chap. Sisters of the Holy Family of Nazareth, Secular FranciscansRev. Michael Lenz, O.F.M., Vicar/ Sacramental Ministry/Byzantine Rite Ministry, Guardian; Bro. Paschal Dierks, O.F.M., (Retired).

Franciscan Friars: *Mt. Alverna Friary*, 517 S. Belle Vista Ave., Youngstown, OH 44509. Tel: 330-799-1888. Rev. Jules Wong, O.F.M; Rev. Vit Fiala, O.F.M., Guardian.
Represented in the Diocese of Youngstown.

Croatian Franciscan Custody of the Holy Family of U.S. & Canada (1926): 4851 S. Drexel Blvd., Chicago, IL 60615-1703. Tel: 773-536-0552; Fax: 773-536-2094; Email: custos@croatianfranciscans.org. Rev. Paul Maslach, O.F.M., Custos. Councilors: Rev. Ljubo Branimir Lebo, O.F.M; Rev. Ivica Majstorovic, O.F.M; Rev. Stjepan Pandzic, O.F.M; Rev. Nikola Pasalic, O.F.M.
Fathers: 25; Friaries: 1; Parishes: 7; Missions in Canada: 6
Represented in the Archdioceses of Chicago, Milwaukee, New York and St. Louis. Also in Canada.

Lithuanian Franciscan Province of St. Casimir: 28 Beach Ave., P.O. Box 980, Kennebunkport, ME 04046-0980. Tel: 207-967-2011; Fax: 207-967-0423; Email: jonasbac@gmail.com; Web: www.framon.net. Rev. Aurelijus Gricius, O.F.M., Guardian; Rev. John J. Bacevicius, O.F.M., Vicar of Friary; Rev. Raimudas Bukauskas, O.F.M., Treas. of Friary; Rev. Placid Barius, O.F.M., Province Delegate; Rev. Gabriel Baltrusaitis, O.F.M; Rev. Andrew R. Bisson, O.F.M; Rev. Francis Giedgaudas, O.F.M; Most Rev. Paul A. Baltakis, O.F.M., Retired Bishop.
Legal Title: Society of the Franciscan Fathers of Green, Maine.
Bishops: 1; Fathers: 8
Properties owned or sponsored: Friaries 2; Parishes 1; Summer Camps 1; Guest House 1.
Represented in the Dioceses of Portland (In Maine) and St. Petersburg. Also in Toronto, Canada.

U.S. Foundation (1940): *Province of the Holy Gospel Roger Bacon College*, 2400 Marr St., El Paso, TX 79903. Rev. J. Arturo Bustamante, O.F.M.
Priests: 3; Brothers: 1
Represented in the Diocese of El Paso.

Franciscan Monastery: 1400 Quincy St., N.E., Washington, DC 20017. Tel: 202-526-6800; Fax: 202-529-9889; Email: secretariatusa@myfrancsican.com; Web: www.myfranciscan.com. Rev. Jeremy Harrington, O.F.M., Commissary; Rev. Garrett Edmunds, O.F.M., Vice Commissary; Friar Christopher Coppock, O.F.M; Friar Thomas Courtney, O.F.M; Rev. Romuald Green, O.F.M; Friar-Deacon John-Sebastian Laird-Hammond, O.F.M., Sec. to the Commissary/Guardian; Friar Simon McKay, O.F.M; Friar Roger Petras, O.F.M; Rev. Stephen F. Sabbagh, O.F.M; Rev. Francisco Sihuay, O.F.M; Rev. Jacob-Matthew Smith, O.F.M; Rev. Kevin Treston, O.F.M; Rev. David Wathen, O.F.M., Dir. Holy Land Pilgrimage; Friar Maximilian Wojciechowski, O.F.M; Rev. Manuel Ybarra, O.F.M., Treas; Friar Callistus Welch, O.F.M; Rev. Edward Flanagan, O.F.M.
Priests: 11; Brothers: 7; Permanent Deacons: 1; Solemnly Professed: 20
Represented in the Archdiocese of Washington.

Academy of American Franciscan History: 1712 Euclid Ave., Berkeley, CA 94709. Dr. Jeffrey M. Burns, Dir.
Legal Title: Academy of American Franciscan History.

National Fraternity of the Secular Franciscan Order, U.S.A: (formerly North American Federation, Third Order of St. Francis), 1710 Chesterbrook Vale Ct., Mc Lean, VA 22101-3244. Tel: 1-800-FRANCIS; Web: www.nafra-sfo.org. Deacon Tom Bello, S.F.O., Nat'l Min.
Founded by St. Francis of Assisi in 1209, to give laity and diocesan clergy an opportunity to live the Gospel intently. There are approximately 15,000 members in nearly 741 fraternities located in 30 geographic regions.

[0530] (S.A.)—FRANCISCAN FRIARS OF THE ATONEMENT

(Societas Adunationis T.O.R.)

Motherhouse: *St. Paul's Friary*, New York Office of the Minister General P.O. Box 300, Garrison, NY 10524-0300. Tel: 845-424-2113; Fax: 845-424-2166.
Priests: 64; Professed Seminarians: 1; Professed Brothers: 33; Friaries: 13; Parishes (U.S. and Canada): 6; Overseas Ministries: England, Italy, and Japan: 1; Ecumenical Institute: 1; Pastoral Center: 1; Campus Ministries: 1; Retreat and Conference Center: 1; Rehabilitation Center for Alcoholics: 1; Shelter for Homeless Men: 1
Legal Titles: St. Christopher's Inn; St. James Friary; St. Paul's Friary; St. Francis of Assisi Novitiate.
Represented in the Archdioceses of Boston, Hartford, Los Angeles, New York and Washington and in the Dioceses of Albany, Arlington, Brooklyn, Buffalo, Charlotte, Ogdensburg, Raleigh and Steubenville.

[0533] (F.F.I.)—FRANCISCAN FRIARS OF THE IMMACULATE

General Motherhouse: Founded 1990. Benevento, Italy,

American Motherhouse: *Marian Friary of Our Lady of Guadalupe*, 199 Colonel Brown Rd., Griswold, CT 06351. Tel: 860-376-6840. Rev. Angelo Mary Geiger, F.I., American Supr.
Legal Title: Marian Friary of Our Lady of Guadalupe.
Represented in the Archdiocese of Indianapolis and in the Dioceses of Fall River, La Crosse, Norwich and Syracuse.

[0535] (C.F.R.)—FRANCISCAN FRIARS OF THE RENEWAL

Central House: *Saint Crispin Friary*, 420 E. 156th St., Bronx, NY 10455. Tel: 718-665-2441. Rev. Mariusz Casimir Koch, C.F.R., Community Servant; Rev. Richard Roemer, C.F.R., Vicar; Rev. Anthony Marie Baetzold, C.F.R. Counselors: Rev. Luke Fletcher, C.F.R; Rev. Fidelis Moscinshi, C.F.R; Bro. John Joseph Brice, C.F.R., Community Treas.
Represented in the Archdioceses of Newark, New York and Santa Fe and in the Diocese of Fort Worth.

[0540] (O.S.F.)—FRANCISCAN MISSIONARY BROTHERS OF THE SACRED HEART OF JESUS

(Fratres Missionarii sti Francisci de Sso. Corde Jesu)

Motherhouse (1927): *Our Lady of Angels Monastery*, 265 Saint Joseph Hills Rd., Pacific, MO 63069. Tel: 636-587-3661.

Mailing Address: Box 181, Eureka, MO 63025. Bro. John A. Spila, O.S.F., Dir. Gen.
Brothers: 8
Legal Holdings or Titles: The Black Madonna Shrine and Grottos (Our Lady of Czestochowa); St. Joseph Hill Infirmary, Inc.; Price Memorial, Eureka, MO; Merkle-Knipprath Nursing Home and Apartment Community, Clifton, MO.
Represented in the Archdiocese of St. Louis and in the Diocese of Joliet.

[0560] (T.O.R.)—THIRD ORDER REGULAR OF SAINT FRANCIS

(Tertius Ordo Regularis de Poenitentia)

General Motherhouse: *SS. Cosmas and Damian*, Via dei Fori Imperiali, 1, Rome, Italy, Very Rev. Michael J. Higgins, T.O.R; Rev. John Kochuchira, T.O.R. Counselors: Rev. Bernat Nebot Llinás, T.O.R; Rev. Amando Trujillo Cano, T.O.R; Rev. Francesco Masseria, T.O.R.

Province of the Most Sacred Heart of Jesus (1910): *Provincial Office*, P.O. Box 137, Loretto, PA 15940. Tel: 814-693-2890; Fax: 814-472-8992. Very Rev. Christian R. Oravec, T.O.R., Minister Prov; Rev. Nicholas Polichnowski, T.O.R., Vicar Prov. Councilors: Rev. Peter A. Lyons, T.O.R; Rev. Gabriel Zeis, T.O.R; Rev. Richard L. Davis, T.O.R; Bro. John Paul McMahon, T.O.R., Prov. Sec; Bro. Richard Gates, T.O.R., Assoc. Dir. Vocations; Rev. Jonathan St. Andre, T.O.R., Dir. Vocations; Rev. David Morrier, T.O.R., Secular Franciscans Prov. Spiritual Asst; Rev. Bernard Tickerhoof, T.O.R.
Legal Title: Province of the Most Sacred Heart of Jesus, Third Order Regular of Saint Francis (USA), Loretto, PA.
Fathers: 103; Professed Clerics: 9; Brothers: 24; Novices: 1; Postulants: 6
Ministries in Parishes; Universities and Colleges; High Schools; Chaplaincies; House of Study 1; Novitiates 1;

Laymen's Retreat League.

Represented in the Archdioceses of Baltimore, Philadelphia and Washington and in the Dioceses of Altoona-Johnstown, Arlington, Charlotte, Dallas, Fort Worth, La Crosse, Pittsburgh, Rockville Centre, St. Petersburg, Sioux Falls, Steubenville, Venice, Wilmington and Wheeling-Charleston.

Province of the Immaculate Conception: *Office of Minister Provincial*, P.O. Box 659, Hollidaysburg, PA 16648-0659. Tel: 814-696-3321; Fax: 814-695-1611. Very Rev. J. Patrick Quinn, T.O.R., Min. Prov. Councilors: Very Rev. Frank A. Scornaienchi, T.O.R., Vicar Prov; Very Rev. William P. Linhares, T.O.R., U.F; Rev. Ambrose K. Phillips, T.O.R; Very Rev. Giles A. Schinelli, T.O.R; Rev. Raphael Eagle, T.O.R.

Legal Title: Third Order Regular of St. Francis, Province of the Immaculate Conception (USA).

Priests: 34; Brothers: 8

Represented in the Archdioceses of St. Paul-Minneapolis and Washington and in the Dioceses of Altoona-Johnstown, Arlington, Fort Worth, Orlando and Wheeling-Charleston.

U.S.A. Franciscan Vice Province of Our Lady of Guadalupe - T.O.R: 301 Jefferson Ave., Waco, TX 76701. Very Rev. David Gutierrez, T.O.R., Prov. Delegate; Very Rev. Esteban Jasso, T.O.R; Very Rev. Angel Infante, T.O.R; Very Rev. Juan Carlos Bello, T.O.R; Very Rev. Florencio Rodriguez, T.O.R; Very Rev. Roman Burgos, T.O.R; Very Rev. Lorenzo Soler, T.O.R.

Fathers: 8

Represented in the Archdiocese of San Antonio and in the Dioceses of Austin and Fort Worth.

[0570] (G.H.M.)—THE GLENMARY HOME MISSIONERS

(Societas Missionariorum Domesticorum Americas)
(The Home Missioners of America)

General Headquarters: P.O. Box 465618, Cincinnati, OH 45246. Tel: 513-874-8900; Web: www.glenmary.org. Rev. Chet Artysiewicz, G.H.M., Pres; Rev. Neil Pezzulo, G.H.M., 1st Vice Pres; Bro. Jack Henn, G.H.M., 2nd Vice Pres; Sandra M. Wissel, Treas; Bro. Dennis Craig, G.H.M., House Dir; Bro. David Henley, G.H.M., Dir.-Vocation Office; Rev. Dominic R. Duggins, G.H.M., Devel. Dir.

House of Formation: *Glenmary House of Studies*, 12484 E. State Rd 62, St. Meinrad, IN 47577. Tel: 812-357-2090. Rev. Victor Subb, G.H.M., Dir. Formation; Rev. Tom Kirkendoll, G.H.M., Co-Dir. Novices; Jose Grosek, Dir. Volunteer Programs P.O. Box 7, Vanceburg, KY 41179.Lorraine Vancamp, Dir. Dept. of Pastoral Ministers & Pastoral Svcs.

Fathers: 38; Professed Brothers: 14; Seminarians: 5; Brothers in Training: 1; Novices: 1; Aspirants: 5

Represented in the Archdiocese of Cincinnati and in the Dioceses of Covington, KY, Indianapolis, Jackson, Knoxville, Lexington, Little Rock, Nashville, Owensboro, Raleigh, Richmond, Savannah, Tulsa and Wheeling-Charleston.

Properties owned, sponsored or staffed: Missions & Ministries 40; Houses of Study 1; Pastoral Center; Volunteer Center.

[0580] (B.G.S.)—LITTLE BROTHERS OF THE GOOD SHEPHERD

Villa Mathias: 901 Bro. Mathias Pl., N.W., P.O. Box 389, Albuquerque, NM 87102. Tel: 505-243-4238; Fax: 505-764-9721.

General Headquarters: 82 Stinson St., P.O. Box 1003, L8N 3R1, Hamilton, Canada, Tel: 416-869-3619. Bro. Justin Howson, B.G.S., Supr. Gen; Bro. David Lynch, B.G.S., Vicar Gen; Bro. Raphael Mieszala, B.G.S., Sec. Gen; Bro. Richard MacPhee, B.G.S., Treas. Gen; Bro. Gerard Sullivan, B.G.S., Councillor; Bro. Charles Searson, B.G.S., Dir., Novices.

Professed Brothers: 29

Legal Holdings and Titles: Caritas Deus, Inc. of New Mexico; Camillus House Inc. of Florida; Camillus Health Concern Inc. of Florida; Charity Unlimited, Inc. of New Mexico; BGS Charitable of Illinois; Brother Mathias Barrett Inc. of Illinois; Brother Mathias Barrett Inc. of New Mexico; Brothers of Good Shepherd Inc. of Florida; Brothers of The Good Shepherd Inc. of New Mexico; Brother Mathias Barrett Inc. of New Mexico; Good Shepherd Center Inc. of New Mexico; Good Shepherd Manor, Inc., Momence, IL; Little Brothers of Good Shepherd Inc. of Illinois; Villa Mathia, Inc. of New Mexico; Brothers of the Good Shepherd Inc. of California, Los Angeles, CA; Charity Unlimited Inc. of Florida.

Represented in the Archdioceses of Miami and Santa Fe and in the Diocese of Joliet.

Properties owned and /or sponsored: temporary shelters for marginalized men and women 14; shelter for battered women & children 3; residences for persons with AIDS 1.

[0585] (H.G.N.)—HERALDS OF GOOD NEWS

Founded on Oct. 14, 1984 at Eluru, Andhra Pradesh, India. Missionary Society of Apostolic Life of Pontifical Right.

Generalate: Heralds of Good News: R.S. Post, W.G. Dt., 534005, Eluru, India, Tel: 91-88-12-235973; Fax: 91-88-12-230256.

U.S. Address: Heralds of Good News: 118 E. Chester Ave., Middlesboro, KY 40965. Tel: 606-248-2068; Fax: 606-248-2207. Rev. C. Amalanathn, Mission Representative.

Legal Title: Heralds of Good News Missionary Society, Inc.

Priests in the U.S: 25

Represented in the Dioceses of Biloxi, Fort Worth, Gallup, Lexington, Owensboro, Portland, and Wheeling-Charleston. Also represented in India.

[0590] (M.S.A.)—SOCIETY OF THE MISSIONARIES OF THE HOLY APOSTLES

General Administration: *Society of the Missionaries of the Holy Apostles*, 8594 rue Berri, H2P 2G4, Montreal, Canada, Tel: 514-387-2222; Fax: 514-387-0863. Very Rev. Isaac M. Chuquizana, M.S.A., Supr. Gen. Animator.

Society of Missionaries of Holy Apostles: *Provincial Administration Headquarters*, 22 Prospect Hill Rd., Cromwell, CT 06416. Tel: 860-632-3039. Very Rev. Addison Hallock, M.S.A., Prov. Animator.

Priests: 36; Brothers: 3

Represented in the Archdioceses of Hartford, Los Angeles, New York and Washington and in the Dioceses of Norwich, Pennsacola-Tallahassee, Richmond (with US Navy), Wheeling-Charleston, Wilmington and Venice.

Properties owned, staffed or sponsored: Holy Apostles College and Seminary; 8 Parishes; Hermitage; Hospital Chaplaincies; Retreat House.

[0600] (C.S.C.)—BROTHERS OF THE CONGREGATION OF HOLY CROSS

(Congregatio A Sancta Cruce)

Generalate: *Congregazione di Santa Croce*, Via Framura 85, 00168, Rome, Italy, Tel: 011-39-06-612-962-10; Fax: 011-39-06-614-7547. Rev. Richard Warner, C.S.C., Supr. Gen; Bro. Thomas A. Dziekan, C.S.C., Vicar & 1st Asst; Rev. Roy Thalackan, C.S.C., 2nd Asst; Bro. Subal Rozario, C.S.C., 3rd Asst; Rev. Jorge Isaguirre Rafel, C.S.C., 4th Asst; Bro. George Schmitz, C.S.C., 5th Asst; Rev. Robert Epping, C.S.C., 6th Asst.

Midwest Province of the Brothers of Holy Cross (1841): 54515 State Rd. 933 N., P.O. Box 460, Notre Dame, IN 46556. Tel: 574-631-4000; Fax: 574-631-2999; Web: www.brothersofholycross.com. Bro. Chester Freel, C.S.C., Prov. Supr; Bro. Raymond Papenfuss, C.S.C., Asst. Prov. & Vicar; Bro. Thomas Minta, C.S.C., Sec; Bro. Kenneth Haders, C.S.C., Steward & Treas; Bro. Lewis T. Brazil, C.S.C., Councilor; Bro. Robert Lavelle, C.S.C., Councilor; Bro. Richard Gilman, C.S.C., Councilor.

Legal Title: Notre Dame, Ind. Brothers of Holy Cross, Inc.

Professed Brothers: 170

Properties owned, staffed or sponsored: Community Houses 4; Colleges 1; High Schools 6; Scholasticates 2; Foreign Mission Schools 3.

Represented in the Archdioceses of Chicago, Detroit, Los Angeles, Portland in Oregon and San Antonio and in the Dioceses of Austin, Cleveland, Fort Wayne-South Bend, Lansing, Oakland, Peoria, Phoenix, St. Petersburg and Venice. Also in West Africa, Chile, Peru, and Vancouver.

Congregation of Holy Cross, Moreau Province: *Brother John Baptist Province Center, St. Edward University*, 1101 St. Edwards Dr., Austin, TX 78704. Tel: 512-442-7856. Bro. William Zaydak, C.S.C., Prov. Supr; Bro. Donald Blauvelt, C.S.C., Asst. Prov; Bro. James J. Branigan, C.S.C., Sec; Bro. William Nick, C.S.C., Steward. Councilors: Bro. Richard Daly, C.S.C; Bro. Michael Winslow, C.S.C; Bro. Jonathan Beebe, C.S.C; Bro. Mark Knightly, C.S.C; Bro. Stephen J. LaMendola, C.S.C.

Legal Title: Brothers of Holy Cross Moreau Province, Inc.

Professed Brothers: 152; Temporarily Professed: 6

Represented in the Archdioceses of Hartford, Los Angeles, Miami, New Orleans, New York, San Antonio and Washington and in the Dioceses of Albany, Austin, Fort Wayne-South Bend, Oakland, San Jose and Wilmington.

Colleges 1; High Schools 8; Middle Schools 1; Schools Foreign Mission Schools 2.

Eastern Province of the Brothers of Holy Cross: 85 Overlook Cir., New Rochelle, NY 10804. Tel: 914-632-4468; Tel: 914-632-4469; Fax: 914-632-2490. Bro. William Zaydak, C.S.C., Provincial; Bro. Mark Knightly, C.S.C., Vicar; Bro. George C. Schmitz, C.S.C., Steward; Bro. Jerome Donnelly, C.S.C., Sec. Councilors: Bro. Jonathan Beebe, C.S.C; Bro. Edward Boyer, C.S.C; Bro. James J. Branigan, C.S.C; Bro. Roger Croteau, C.S.C; Bro. Stephen J. LaMendola, C.S.C. In Res. Bro. James Rio, C.S.C.

Legal Title: Brothers of Holy Cross of the Eastern Province of the United States of America, Inc.

Professed Brothers: 90; Temporarily Professed: 6

Properties owned, staffed or sponsored: High Schools 4; Foreign Mission Houses 6; Middle School; Spiritual Life Center; Provincial Residence.

Represented in the Archdioceses of Hartford, New York and Washington and in the Dioceses of Albany, Brooklyn and Wilmington.

[0610] (C.S.C.)—PRIESTS OF THE CONGREGATION OF HOLY CROSS

(Congregatio a Sancta Cruce)

Generalate: *Curia Generalizia di Santa Croce*, Via Framura 85, 00168, Rome, Italy, Rev. Richard Warner, C.S.C., Supr. Gen; Bro. Tom Dzickan, C.S.C., First Asst. & Vicar; Rev. Roy Thalackan, C.S.C., Second Asst; Bro. Subal Rozario, C.S.C., Third Asst; Rev. Jorge Izaguerre Rafael, C.S.C., Fourth Asst; Rev. Robert Epping, C.S.C., Sixth Asst; Bro. George Schmitz, C.S.C., Fifth Asst; Rev. Carl F. Ebey, C.S.C., Gen. Steward; Rev. Paul LeBlanc, C.S.C., Procurator; Bro. Edward Dailey, C.S.C., Gen. Sec; Rev. Gaspar Selvaraj, C.S.C., Asst. Steward; Bro. Patrick Sopher, C.S.C., Exec. Dir., Congregational Planning.

Congregation of Holy Cross, United States Province: *Provincial Admin. Office*, 54515 State Rd. 933 N., P.O. Box 1064, Notre Dame, IN 46556-1064. Tel: 574-631-6196.

Res: *Provincial House*, 1304 E. Jefferson Blvd., South Bend, IN 46617. Rev. David T. Tyson, C.S.C., Prov. Supr; Rev. Kenneth M. Molinaro, C.S.C., First Asst. Prov. & Vicar; Rev. Anthony V. Szakaly, C.S.C., Second Asst. Prov; Rev. Edwin H. Obermiller, C.S.C., Third Asst. Prov; Rev. Thomas P. Looney, C.S.C., Fourth Asst. Provincial Councilors: Rev. William Beauchamp, C.S.C; Rev. Thomas C. Bertone, C.S.C; Rev. Thomas E. Blantz, C.S.C; Rev. Peter A. Jarret, C.S.C; Rev. Charles W. Kohlerman, C.S.C; Rev. James R. Lackenmier, C.S.C; Rev. William M. Lies, C.S.C; Rev. Michael C. Mathews, C.S.C; Rev. James E. McDonald, C.S.C; Rev. Francis J. Murphy, C.S.C; Rev. John J. Ryan, C.S.C; Rev. Neil F. Wack, C.S.C.

Legal Title: Congregation of the Holy Cross, United States Province, Inc.

Fathers: 378; Professed Clerics: 8; Temporary Professed Clerics: 39; Novices: 23; Candidates: 48; Professed Brothers: 20

Represented in the Archdioceses of Anchorage, Baltimore, Chicago, Detroit, Los Angeles, Military Service, USA, New Orleans, New York, Portland in Oregon, San Antonio, San Francisco and Washington and in the Dioceses of Bridgeport, Cleveland, Colorado Springs, Erie, Fall River, Fort Wayne-South Bend, Gary, Kalamazoo, Monterey, Oakland, Phoenix, San Bernardino and San Jose.

Properties owned, sponsored or staffed: College Seminary; Theological Seminary; Novitiate; Mission Center; Provincial House; Postulate; Universities 2; High Schools 1; Parishes 12; Chaplaincies 17; Publishing House; Retreat House.

Holy Cross Oversea Lay Missionary Program: P.O. Box 668, Notre Dame, IN 46556. Rick Addis, Assoc. Dir.

Holy Cross Association: Box 771, Notre Dame, IN 46556. James G. Kramer, Assoc. Dir.

Represented in the Archdioceses of Anchorage, Baltimore, Chicago, Detroit, Los Angeles, Military Services, USA, New Orleans, New York, Portland in Oregon, San Antonio, San Francisco and Washington and in the Dioceses of Bridgeport, Cleveland, Colorado Springs, Erie, Fall River, Fort Wayne-South Bend, Gary, Kalamazoo, Monterey, Oakland, Phoenix, San Bernardino and San Jose.

Congregation of Holy Cross-Eastern Province, Inc: *Provincial Headquarters*, 835 Clinton Ave., Bridgeport, CT 06604. Tel: 203-367-7252; Tel: 203-367-1152; Fax: 203-366-7886. Rev. Thomas P. Looney, C.S.C., Prov. Supr; Rev. Thomas C. Bertone, C.S.C., Asst. Prov. & Vicar; Rev. James Lackenmier, C.S.C., Treas. & Steward. Prov. Councilors: Rev. Mark T. Cregan, C.S.C; Rev. John F. Denning, C.S.C; Bro. Patrick Lynch, C.S.C; Rev. Thomas J. O'Hara, C.S.C; Rev. John P. Phalen, C.S.C; Rev. John J. Ryan, C.S.C.

Fathers: 101; Temporarily Professed Clerics: 4; Candidates: 1; Brothers Professed: 8

Represented in the Archdioceses of Boston, Hartford, Los Angeles, New Orleans and New York and in the Dioceses of Albany, Austin, Bridgeport, Burlington, Fall River, Fort Wayne-South Bend, Orlando, Palm Beach, Rochester, Scranton and St. Petersburg.

Properties owned, sponsored or staffed: Colleges 2; Parishes 8; Retreat House; Chaplaincies 4; Campus Ministry 5; Family Rosary Crusade; Family Theater.

Holy Cross Southern Province (1968): *Provincial House*, 2111 Brackenridge St., Austin, TX 78704. Tel: 512-351-9780. Rev. David T. Tyson, C.S.C., Prov. Supr; Rev. Kenneth M. Molinaro, C.S.C., Asst. Prov. & Vicar; Rev. Anthony V. Szakaly, C.S.C., Asst. Prov. & Steward. Members Rev. E. William Beauchamps, C.S.C; Rev. Thomas E. Chambers, C.S.C; Rev. Robert A. Dowd, C.S.C; Rev. Peter A. Jarret, C.S.C; Rev. Patrick M. Neary, C.S.C.

Legal Title: Congregation of Holy Cross, Southern Province, Inc.

Fathers: 22; Professed Brothers: 2; Temporary Professed: 7

Ministries in Parishes; Foreign Missions; Chaplaincies; Social Service; Schools.

Represented in the Archdioceses of New Orleans and San Antonio and in the Dioceses of Austin, Fort Wayne-South Bend, Lafayette (LA) and Las Cruces.

[0620] (F.S.E.)—BROTHERS OF THE HOLY EUCHARIST

Founded in the United States 1957.

General Motherhouse and Novitiate: P.O. Box 25, Plaucheville, LA 71362. Tel: 318-922-3630; Tel: 318-922-3401. Bro. Andre M. Lucia, F.S.E., Supr. Gen.

Represented in the Archdiocese of New Orleans and in the dioceses of Alexandria and Baton Rouge.

[0630] (M.S.F.)—CONGREGATION OF THE MISSIONARIES OF THE HOLY FAMILY
(Congregatio Missionariorum a Sacra Familia)

General Motherhouse: Via Odoado Beccari, 41, 00154, Rome, Italy, Tel: 011-39-0657-250639; Fax: 011-39-0657-55192. Very Rev. Edmund Michalski, M.S.F., Supr. Gen.

MSF Center: *Provincialate USA of the Missionaries of the Holy Family, Office*, 3014 Oregon Ave., Saint Louis, MO 63118. Tel: 314-577-6300; Fax: 314-577-6301. Rev. Philip Sosa, M.S.F., Prov. Supr.

Fathers: 24; Theology Students: 1; Brothers: 2

Ministries in House of Study 2; Parishes 8; Chaplaincies 2.

Represented in the Archdioceses of St. Louis and San Antonio and in the Dioceses of Brownsville, Corpus Christi, Duluth, and Richmond. Also in Canada.

General Mission Office - M.S.F., Inc: 260 W. Euclid Blvd., P.O. Box 918, West Point, VA 23181. Tel: 804-843-2622; Fax: 804-843-3182. Rev. John Brieffies, M.S.F., Exec. Dir.

MSF Provincial Residence: 3582 Pearson Pointe Ct., Saint Louis, MO 63139. Tel: 314-416-0299.

[0640] (S.F.)—SONS OF THE HOLY FAMILY
(Congregatio Filiorum Sacrae Familiae)

General Motherhouse: Entenza 301, 08029, Barcelona, Spain, Very Rev. Jesus Diaz, S.F., Gen. Supr.

U.S. Foundation (1920): 401 Randolph Rd., P.O. Box 4138, Silver Spring, MD 20914-4138. Tel: 301-622-1184. Very Rev. Luis Picazo, S.F., Vice Prov.

Fathers: 12

Represented in the Archdioceses of Santa Fe and Washington.

[0645] (B.H.S.)—BROTHERS OF THE HOLY SPIRIT - CLEVELAND

General Motherhouse: *Holy Spirit Monastery*, 4150 Rabbit Run Dr., Brooklyn, OH 44144. Tel: 216-741-3653; Email: brotherdale@catholicweb.com. Bro. Dale Sefcik, B.H.S., Supr; Bro. David Robert, B.H.S., Community Councilor.

Legal Title: Brothers of the Holy Spirit Cleveland.

Represented in the Ukrainian Catholic Diocese of St. Josaphat in Parma.

[0650] (C.S.SP.)—CONGREGATION OF THE HOLY SPIRIT
(Congregation of the Holy Spirit under the protection of the Immaculate Heart of Mary, Spiritans.)
(Congregatio Sancti Spiritus sub tutela Immaculati Cordis Beatissimae Virginis Mariae)

Generalate: Clivo di Cinna 195, 00136, Rome, Italy, Very Rev. Jean-Paul Hoch, C.S.Sp.

Province of the United States (1872): 6230 Brush Run Rd., Bethel Park, PA 15102. Tel: 412-831-0302; Fax: 412-831-0970. Very Rev. John Fogarty, C.S.Sp., Prov. Supr. Councilors: Rev. John A. Sawicki, C.S.Sp., Prov. Treas. & Councilor; Rev. Jeffrey T. Duaime, C.S.Sp; Rev. Michael T. White, C.S.Sp; Rev. Benoit Mukamba, C.S.Sp; Rev. Brandon Nguyen, C.S.Sp.

Fathers in the U.S: 81; Professed Brothers: 2; Scholastics: 1; Candidates: 1; Lay Spiritans: 5

Legal Holdings: Archconfraternity of the Holy Ghost; Provincial Residence; Duquesne University, Laval House; Holy Ghost Preparatory School; The Spiritan Center.

Represented in the Archdioceses of Baltimore, Chicago, Cincinnati, Detroit, Galveston-Houston, Miami, New York, Philadelphia and Washington and in the Dioceses of Arlington, Baton Rouge, Little Rock, Phoenix, Pittsburgh, Providence, San Bernardino, San Diego and Venice. Also in Puerto Rico and the Dominican Republic.

Properties owned, sponsored or staffed: Parishes 19; Retirement Residences 2; Training Center 1; Spiritan Residence, Houston; Properties in Mexico.

Holy Ghost Fathers of Ireland (1971): 4849 37th St., Long Island City, NY 11101. Tel: 718-729-5273; Fax: 718-729-6949. Very Rev. Thomas Basquel, C.S.Sp., Prov. Delegate U.S.A. East; Rev. Joseph Glynn, C.S.Sp., Prov. Delegate U.S.A. West. Councilors: Very Rev. Thomas Basquel, C.S.Sp; Rev. Edmond B. Duggan, C.S.Sp; Rev. Noel P. O'Meara, C.S.Sp; Rev. Jerry Kirwin, C.S.Sp.

Fathers: 20

Represented in the Archdioceses of Boston, Miami, and San Francisco and in the Dioceses of Brooklyn, Fargo, Palm Beach, Peoria and St. Augustine.

[0660] (M.SP.S.)—MISSIONARIES OF THE HOLY SPIRIT

General Motherhouse: Av. Universidad 1702 04010, Mexico, D.F., Mexico, Tel: 5-658-74-33; Tel: 5-658-7851. Very Rev. Fernando Torre Medina-Mora, Supr. Gen.

Provincial House (Christ the Priest Province): 39085 N.W. Harrington Rd., P.O. Box 130, Banks, OR 97106. Tel: 503-324-2492; Fax: 503-324-2493. Rev. Domenico Di Raimondo, Prov. Supr. Council Members: Rev. Jose Ortega, M.Sp.S., Vicar; Rev. Juan Jose Gonzalez, M.Sp.S.

Priests: 23; Professed: 19; Novices: 3; Parishes: 4; Houses of Study: 1; Novitiates: 1; Theologates: 1

Represented in the Archdioceses of Los Angeles, Portland in Oregon and Seattle and in the Diocese of Orange.

642 S.E. 20th Ct., Hillsboro, OR 97123.

[0670] (O.H.)—HOSPITALLER BROTHERS OF ST. JOHN OF GOD

General Motherhouse: *Hospitaller Brothers of St. John of God*, Order Founded by St. John of God at Granada, Spain, in 1537. via della Nocetta 263, 00164, Rome, Italy, Rev. Donatus Forkan, O.H., Prior Gen.

American Province of Our Lady Queen of Angels (1970): *Villa Maria-Provincial Curia*, 2425 S. Western Ave., Los Angeles, CA 90018. Tel: 323-734-0233; Fax: 323-731-5987; Email: usaprov-office@sbcglobal.net. Bro. Pablo Lopez, O.H., Prov.

Brothers: 24; Solemnly Professed: 24; Priests: 3

Legal Holdings: St. John of God Retirement and Care Center, Los Angeles, CA; St. Joseph Health and Retirement Center, Ojai, CA; St. John of God Health Care Services, Victorville, CA.

Represented in the Archdiocese of Los Angeles and in the Diocese of San Bernardino.

[0680] I.H.M.—BROTHERS OF THE IMMACULATE HEART OF MARY

General Motherhouse (1948): 609 N. 7th St., Steubenville, OH 43952. Tel: 740-283-2462. Bro. Dominic Carroll, I.H.M., Supr. Gen; Bro. Anthony Motto, I.H.M., Novice Master; Bro. Patrick Geary, I.H.M., Vocation Dir.

Professed Brothers: 4

Ministries in: Novitiate; Bishop's Residence; CCD Center; Pastoral Associates 3.

Represented in the Diocese of Steubenville.

[0685] I.V.E.—INSTITUTE OF THE INCARNATE WORD

General Motherhouse: *Province of the Immaculate Conception of the Institute of the Incarnate Word*, 113 E. 117th St., New York, NY 10035. Rev. Gustavo Javier Nieto, I.V.E., Provincial Supr.

Represented in the Archdiocese of New York.

[0690] S.J.—JESUIT FATHERS AND BROTHERS
(Societas Jesu)

Generalate: Borgo S. Spirito 4, 00193, Rome, Italy, Rev. Adolfo Nicolas, S.J., Gen; Rev. Ignacio Echarte, S.J., Sec; Rev. James E. Grummer, S.J., U.S. Asst.

Jesuit Conference: *The Society of Jesus in the United States National Offices*, 1016 16th St., N.W., Ste. 400, Washington, DC 20036. Tel: 202-462-0400; Fax: 202-328-9212. Rev. Thomas H. Smolich, S.J., Pres; Rev. Gerard L. Stockhausen, S.J., Exec. Sec; Rev. David A. Godleski, S.J., Delegate, Formation & Jesuit Life; Rev. Thomas P. Greene, S.J., Sec.-Social Intl. Ministries; Rev. Gregory N.P. Konz, S.J., Sec. Finance & Higher Educ. & Devel; Rev. Edward S. Fassett, S.J., Sec. Secondary & Pre-Secondary Educ & Partnership; Rev. Robert R. Ballecer, S.J., Dir. Natl. Vocation.

Maryland Province of the Society of Jesus (1833) (1833): 8600 LaSalle Rd., Ste. 620, Towson, MD 21286-2014. Tel: 443-921-1310; Fax: 443-921-1313. Very Rev. James M. Shea, S.J., Prov; Rev. James A. Casciotti, S.J., Socius; Ms. Rose Ann D'Alesandro, Asst. Treas; Rev. Ronald J. Amiot, S.J., Asst. Healthcare Planning; Mrs. Deirdre Elmore Banscher, Asst. for Healthcare; Rev. Charles A. Frederico, S.J., Vocations Dir; Rev. Thomas H. Feely, S.J., Asst. for Formation; Rev. Gerald P. Fogarty, S.J., Archivist; Rev. Liborio J. LaMartina, S.J., Resident Archivist; Rev. James P. Carr, S.J., Novice Dir; Ms. Maureen Locher, Special Case Coord; Rev. Brian O. McDermott, S.J., Tertian Instructor; Rev. James A. O'Brien, S.J., Promoter, Christian Life Communities; Rev. William C. Rickle, S.J., Asst. for Latino Ministries; Rev. Timothy J. Stephens, S.J., Treas; Rev. James Conroy, S.J., Exec. Dir., Jesuit Collaborative; Rev. William J. Walters, S.J., Asst., Pastoral Ministries; Rev. Robert M. Hussey, S.J., Revisor, Province Finances; Rev. Richard S. McCouch, S.J., Asst. Secondary Education; Mr. Nicholas Napolitano, Asst. Social Ministries; Rev. James D. Redington, S.J., Interreligious Dialogue.

Legal Title: Corporation of the Roman Catholic Clergymen, Maryland.

Fathers: 287; Scholastics: 24; Brothers: 14

Represented in the Archdioceses of Baltimore, Philadelphia and Washington and in the Dioceses of Allentown, Charlotte, Raleigh, Richmond, Scranton and Wheeling-Charleston.

Properties owned, sponsored or staffed: Parishes 10; Universities 5; High Schools 5; Middle and Grammar Schools 4; Houses of Retreats 3; Residences 23.

Province of New York (1943): 39 E. 83rd St., New York, NY 10028. Tel: 212-774-5500; Fax: 212-794-1036. Very Rev. David S. Ciancimino, S.J., Prov; Rev. Thomas R. Slon, S.J., Socius & Exec. Asst. to the Prov; Rev. Walter F. Modrys, S.J., Prov. Treas; Rev. Thomas H. Feely, S.J., Asst. for Formation-Maryland & New York Provs; Rev. Ramon A. Salomone, S.J., Asst. for Int'l Apostolate; Rev. Charles A. Frederico, S.J., Dir. of Vocations, Maryland, New England & New York Provs; Rev. James F. Keenan, S.J., Dir. of Province Devel. Office; Rev. Vincent L. Biagi, S.J., Asst. for Sec. & Pre-Sec. Education & Lay Formation; Rev. Edward J. Quinnan, S.J., Asst. for Pastoral Ministry & Province Representative to the Jesuit Collaborative.

Legal Title: The New York Province of the Society of Jesus, New York, NY.

Fathers: 318; Scholastics: 13; Brothers: 13

Represented in the Archdioceses of Newark and New York and in the Dioceses of Albany, Brooklyn, Buffalo, Paterson, Rochester, Rockville Centre and Syracuse. Also in Guam, the Caroline Islands, Chalan Kanoa and the Prefecture Apostolic of Marshall Islands, Philippines, West Africa - Nigeria & Ghana.

Properties owned, sponsored or staffed: Parishes 8; Universities 1; Colleges 3; High Schools 8; Houses for Laymen's Retreats 3; House of Study 1; Novitiates 1; Community Houses 4.

The Jesuits of the Missouri Province (Missouri Province of the Society of Jesus): *Province Offices*, 4511 W. Pine Blvd., Saint Louis, MO 63108-2191. Tel: 314-361-7765; Fax: 314-758-7164. Rev. Douglas W. Marcouiller, S.J., Prov; Rev. J. Daniel Daly, S.J., Socius; Rev. Kevin L. Cullens, S.J., Treas; Rev. John F. Armstrong, S.J., Asst. for Formation; Rev. Louis J. McCabe, S.J., Asst. for Vocations; Mr. Sean Agniel, Asst. for Secondary & Pre-Secondary Education; Rev. Robert F. Weiss, S.J., Assoc. Dir. Jesuit Advancement Office; Rev. Michael G. Harter, S.J., Editor of Jesuit Bulletin; Dr. David P. Miros, Archivist; Rev. Daniel P. White, S.J., Asst. for Pastoral & Spiritual Ministries; Rev. Thomas M. Rochford, S.J., Asst. for Communications; Rev. Brian J. Christopher, S.J., Delegate for Social and Int'l. Ministries; Mr. Thom Digman, Asst. for Advancement; Barbara Middleton, Asst. for Healthcare.

Fathers: 188; Students in Major Seminary: 17; Novices: 8; Brothers: 15

Legal Titles: Regis Jesuit High School Corporation, Aurora, CO; Regis University, Denver, CO; Rockhurst University; Rockhurst High School, Kansas City, MO; The Province-The Jesuits of the Missouri Province; Bellarmine House of Studies - The Jesuits of the Missouri Province; Fusz Pavilion - The Jesuits of the Missouri Province; Institute of Jesuit Sources - The Jesuits of the Missouri Province; Jesuit Mission Bureau - The Jesuits of the Missouri Province; Review for Religious - The Jesuits of the Missouri Province; DeSmet Jesuit High School; Jesuit Community Corporation at Saint Louis University; Saint Louis University; St. Louis University High School; White House Retreat, Inc.; Loyola Academy, St. Louis, MO; Arrupe Jesuit High School, Denver, CO; Society of Jesus in Belize, Inc., Belize; Jesuit Retreat House, Sedalia,CO.

Ministries in Parishes; Universities; High Schools; Middle Schools; Novitiate; First Studies House; Curia; Retreat Houses.

Represented in the Archdioceses of Denver, Kansas City in Kansas and St. Louis and in the Diocese of Kansas City-St. Joseph. Also in Belize.

New Orleans Province (1907) (1907): 710 Baronne St., Ste. B, New Orleans, LA 70113-1064. Tel: 504-571-1055; Fax: 504-571-1744; Email: noprovsj@norprov.org; Web: www.norprov.org. Very Rev. Mark Lewis, S.J., Provincial; Rev. John F. Armstrong, S.J., Asst. for Formation; Mary Baudouin, Asst. for Social Ministries; Rev. Anthony F. McGinn, S.J., Asst. for Secondary Education; Rev. Warren J. Broussard, S.J., Asst. for Pastoral Ministry & Retreat Ministry; Bro. Lawrence J. Lundin, S.J., Treas; Rev. Michael A. Bouzigard, S.J., Asst. for International Ministries; Rev. Michael D. Dooley, S.J., Socius; Mike Bourg, Dir. Devel.

Legal Title: Catholic Society of Religious and Literary Education, A Louisiana Corporation.

Fathers: 160; Students in Major Seminary: 32; Novices: 10; Brothers: 15

Represented in the Archdioceses of Atlanta, Galveston-Houston, Miami, New Orleans, San Antonio and Santa Fe and in the Dioceses of Austin, Baton Rouge, Birmingham, Dallas, El Paso, Fort Worth, Lafayette (LA), Las Cruces, Mobile, St. Augustine, St. Petersburg, Tyler and Venice.

Properties owned, sponsored or staffed: Parishes 8; Universities 1; Colleges 1; High Schools 5; Elementary Schools 1; Novitiate 1; Houses of Retreat 5.

California Province (1909): 300 College Ave., P.O. Box 519, Los Gatos, CA 95031-0519. Tel: 408-884-1600. Very Rev. Michael F. Weiler, S.J., Prov; Rev. Alfred E. Naucke, S.J., Exec. Asst; Rev. Edwin B. Harris, S.J., Asst. for Secondary Education; Rev. Chi Ngo, S.J., Asst. Formation; Bro. James Siwicki, S.J., Dir. Vocations; Rev. Gerdenio M. Manuel, S.J., Asst. for Higher Educ. & Dir. Studies; Rev. Theodore E. Gabrielli, S.J., Asst. for Intl. Min. & Dir., California Jesuit Missionaries; Rev. Dennis R. Parnell, S.J., Prov. Treas; Mr. Joseph B. Naylor, Prov. Dir. Advancement; Bro. Daniel J. Peterson, S.J., Prov. Archivist; Rev. John D. Murphy, S.J., Tertian Instructor; Rev. Doan T. Hoang, S.J., Apostleship of Prayer; Rev. William J. Kelley, S.J., Asst. for Pastoral Ministries; Rev. Charles J. Tilley, S.J., Special Projects Mgr.

Legal Title: The California Province of the Society of Jesus.

Fathers: 290; Brothers: 20; Scholastics: 38; Scholastic Novices: 9

Represented in the Archdioceses of Los Angeles and San Francisco and in the Dioceses of Fresno, Oakland, Orange, Phoenix, Sacramento, San Diego, San Jose and Tucson.

Properties owned, sponsored or staffed: Parishes 10; Universities 3; High Schools 7; Novitiates 1; Retreat Center 2.

New England Province (1926): 85 School St., Watertown, MA 02472-4251. Tel: 617-607-2800; Fax: 617-607-2888. Very Rev. Myles N. Sheehan, S.J., Prov; Rev. Joseph A. Appleyard, S.J., Exec. Asst; Rev. Dennis J. Yesalonia, S.J., Prov. Treas; Rev. Thomas H. Feely, S.J., Prov. Asst. Formation; Rev. Charles A. Frederico, S.J., Dir. Vocations; Rev. Michael J. Linden, S.J., Prov. Asst. for Pastoral Social & Int'l Ministries; Rev. Robert J. Daly, S.J., Prov. Asst. Higher Educ; Rev. James M. Shaughnessy, S.J., Liaison Hospital Chaplaincy Ministry; Rev. Edward J. Quinnan, S.J., Prov. Asst. for Pastoral Ministries; Mr. Nicholas Napolitano, Prov. Asst. for Social Ministries.

Legal Title: The Society of Jesus of New England.

Fathers: 255; Scholastics: 22; Brothers: 11; Parishes: 1; Universities: 2; Colleges: 1; High Schools: 3; Houses of Retreat: 2; Seminaries: 1

Represented in the Archdioceses of Baltimore, Boston, Chicago, Newark, Milwaukee, New Orleans, New York, St. Louis, Seattle and Washington and in the Dioceses of Baton Rouge, Bridgeport, Brooklyn, Buffalo, Fall River, Fort Wayne-South Bend, Honolulu, Manchester, Nashville, Norwich, Oakland, Portland (In Maine), Raleigh, Rapid City, St. Augustine, San Diego, San Jose, Scranton, Spokane, Syracuse, Tucson, and Worcester.

Chicago Province - Society of Jesus (S.J.) (1928): 2050 N. Clark St., Chicago, IL 60614. Tel: 773-975-6363; Fax: 773-975-0230. Very Rev. Timothy P. Kesicki, S.J., Prov; Rev. Walter C. Deye, S.J., Socius; Rev. Raymond P. Guaio, S.J., Asst. for Formation; Rev. Theodore G. Munz, S.J., Prov. Treas. and Asst. for Business and Fin; Rev. James S. Prehn, S.J., Asst. for Secondary Educ; Rev. Patrick A. Fairbanks, S.J., Asst. for Vocations; Mr. John Sealey, Social & Intl. Ministries; Mr. David K. McNulty, Vice Pres., Advancement; Ms. Jenene M. Francis, Asst., Pastoral Ministries.

Legal Title: Chicago Province of the Society of Jesus.

Fathers: 167; Scholastics: 21; Brothers: 11

Represented in the Archdioceses of Chicago, Cincinnati, Indianapolis and Louisville and in the Dioceses of Covington, Fort Wayne-South Bend, Gary, Joliet, Lafayette in Indiana and Lexington.

Properties Sponsored: Parishes 3; Universities 2; High Schools 6; Retreat Houses 2; Diocesan Major Seminary 1; Residences 20; House of Writers 1.

Oregon Province - Society of Jesus (1932): 3215 S.E. 45th Ave, P.O. Box 86010, Portland, OR 97286-0010. Tel: 503-226-6977. Rev. Patrick J. Lee, S.J., Prov; Rev. Michael A. Tyrrell, S.J., Prov. Treas. & Socius; Rev. Gerald T. Cobb, S.J., Asst. for Formation; Rev. Peter D. Byrne, S.J., Asst. for Parishes & Spiritual Ministries.

Fathers: 181; Scholastics: 32; Brothers: 8

Legal Titles: Society of Jesus, Oregon Province, Portland, OR; The Pioneer Educational Society, Spokane, WA; Montana Catholic Missions, SJ; The Society of Jesus, Alaska.

Represented in the Archdioceses of Portland in Oregon and Seattle and in the Dioceses of Baker, Boise, Fairbanks, Great Falls-Billings, Helena, Spokane and Yakima.

Properties owned, sponsored or staffed: Parishes 8; Universities 2; High Schools 4; Middle Schools 1; Novitiates 1.

Detroit Province - Society of Jesus (S.J.) (1955): 7303 W. Seven Mile Rd., Detroit, MI 48221. Tel: 313-861-7500; Fax: 313-861-4230. Very Rev. Timothy P. Kesicki, S.J., Prov. Supr; Rev. Walter C. Deye, S.J., Exec. Asst; Rev. Theodore G. Munz, S.J., Treas; Mr. John Sealey, Asst. for Social & International Ministries; Rev. Raymond P. Guiao, S.J., Asst. Formation; Ms. Jenene M. Francis, Asst. Pastoral Ministries; Rev. Patrick A. Fairbanks, S.J., Asst. Vocation Promotion; Rev. James S. Prehn, S.J., Asst. Secondary Educ; Mr. David K. McNulty, Vice Pres. Advancement; Mr. Jeremy W. Langford, Asst. Communications.

Fathers: 110; Scholastics: 18; Brothers: 14

Legal Titles: Detroit Province of the Society of Jesus; Colombiere Center, Clarkston, MI; Jesuit Retreat House of Cleveland, Ohio; Jesuit Seminary Association; Jesuit International Missions; John Carroll University of Cleveland, Ohio; John Carroll Jesuit Community Corporation; Loyola High School, Detroit, MI; Manresa Jesuit Retreat House; Patna Jesuit Mission Society, Inc.; St. Ignatius High School of Cleveland, Ohio; St. John's Jesuit High School of Toledo, Ohio; University of Detroit Mercy; The Jesuit Community Corporation at the University of Detroit; University of Detroit Jesuit High School and Academy; Walsh Jesuit High School.

Represented in the Archdioceses of Baltimore, Boston, Chicago, Detroit, Los Angeles, Military Services, Mobile, New York and Washington and in the Dioceses of Charlotte, Cleveland, Columbus, Gaylord, Lansing, Lexington, Marquette, Oakland, Saginaw, Toledo, Wheeling-Charleston, Winona, and Worcester.

Properties owned, sponsored or staffed: Parishes 4; Universities 2; High Schools 5; Retreat Houses 2.

Wisconsin Province - Society of Jesus (S.J.) (1955): 3400 W. Wisconsin Ave., P.O. Box 080288, Milwaukee, WI 53208-8004. Tel: 414-937-6949; Fax: 414-937-6950. Very Rev. Thomas A. Lawler, S.J., Prov; Rev. Patrick J. Burns, S.J., Asst. Prov., Dir. Planning & Implementation for Prov. Reconfiguration; Rev. John M. Paul, S.J., Dir. Formation; Rev. Paul Coelho, S.J., Vocation Dir; Rev. Eugene M. Dutkiewicz, S.J., Prov. Asst. Pastoral & Retreat Ministries; Rev. John L. Treloar, S.J., Prov. Asst. Higher Educ; Rev. James S. Prehn, S.J., Prov. Asst. for Secondary Education; Rev. James J. Gladstone, S.J., Prov. Asst., Personnel.

Legal Title: Wisconsin Province of the Society of Jesus.

Fathers: 217; Novices: 4; Brothers: 11; Scholastics: 26

Represented in the Archdioceses of Milwaukee, Omaha and St. Paul-Minneapolis and in the Dioceses of Des Moines, Green Bay, Rapid City, Winona and Cheyenne.

Properties owned, sponsored or staffed: Parishes 5; Universities 2; High Schools 4; Middle Schools 2; Elementary Schools 2; Community Houses 15; Novitiate; Native American Missions 2; Retreat Houses 4.

U.S. Address: 12725 S.W. 6th St., Miami, FL 33184. Tel: 786-621-4595; Fax: 305-559-3160. Rev. Felix F. Polanco, S.J., Prov; Rev. Francisco Perez Lerena, S.J., Miami Reg. Supr.

Fathers: 99; Scholastics: 34; Brothers: 11

Represented in the Archdiocese of Miami. Also in Santo Domingo.

Properties owned, staffed or sponsored: High Schools: Loyola in Dominican Republic, Belen Jesuit Prep in Miami; Novitiate 1; House of Retreat 3 in Santo Domingo; Juan Pablo II in Miami; Residences 2.

Puerto Rico Province - Society of Jesus (1987): *Urb. Santa Maria*, 1940 Calle Sauco, San Juan, PR 00927-6718. Tel: 787-765-3814; Fax: 787-758-4145. Rev. Mario A. Torres, S.J., Reg. Supr; Rev. John F. Talbot, S.J., Exec. Asst. to Reg. Supr; Rev. Baudillo Guzman, S.J., Exec. Treas; Rev. Alvaro Velez, S.J., Auditor.

Fathers: 17; Scholastics: 7

Represented in the Archdiocese of San Juan and in the Dioceses of Fajardo-Humacao, Mayaguez, and Palm Beach.

Properties owned, sponsored or staffed: Parishes 3; High Schools 1; Residences 2; Campus Ministry Centers 1.

[0700] (S.S.J.)—ST. JOSEPH'S SOCIETY OF THE SACRED HEART

(The Josephites)

(Societas Sancti Joseph SSmi Cordis)

Central House Administration: 1130 N. Calvert St., Baltimore, MD 21202. Tel: 410-727-3386; Fax: 410-727-1006; Email: josephite1@aol.com; Web: www.josephite.com. Rev. William L. Norvel, S.S.J., Supr. Gen.

Fathers: 79; Brothers: 5; Seminarians: 11

Legal Titles: St. Joseph's Society of the Sacred Heart, Inc.; St. Joseph Manor Foundation, Inc.; The Josephite Retirement and Disability Benefits Trust; The Josephite Seminarian Education Trust.

Represented in the Archdioceses of Baltimore, Galveston-Houston, Los Angeles, Mobile, New Orleans and Washington and in the Dioceses of Arlington, Baton Rouge, Beaumont, Biloxi, Birmingham, Jackson and Lafayette (LA). Also in Nigeria.

Properties owned, staffed or sponsored: Parishes 40; Elementary Schools 9; High School; House of Study; Major Seminary; Novitiate; Nigerian Formation House.

[0710] (C.J.)—JOSEPHITE FATHERS

(Institutum Josephitarum Gerardimontensium)

General Motherhouse: Geraardsbergen (Ghent), Belgium, Rev. Robert Hamilton, C.J., Supr. Gen.

U.S. Foundation: *St. Joseph Seminary, Provincialate and Novitiate*, 180 Patterson Rd., Santa Maria, CA 93455. Tel: 805-937-5378; Fax: 805-937-5759. Rev. Ludo DeClippel, C.J., Prov. Supr.

Fathers: 10

Ministry to: Parishes; Academic Education.

Represented in the Archdiocese of Los Angeles.

[0720] (M.S.)—THE MISSIONARIES OF OUR LADY OF LA SALETTE

(Congregatio Missionariorum Vulgo "De la Salette")

General House: Piazza Madonna Della Salette 3, 00152, Rome, Italy, Very Rev. Dennis J. Loomis, M.S., Supr. Gen.

American Region was established in 1892; Canonically erected 1934; Divided into other Provinces in 1945, 1958, 1967 and restructured into one Province in 2000.

Province of Mary, Mother of the Americas (2000): 915 Maple Ave., Hartford, CT 06114-2330. Tel: 860-956-8870. Very Rev. Joseph G. Bachand, M.S., Prov. Supr; Rev. James H. Kuczynski, M.S., Vicar; Rev. William Kaliyadan, M.S., Asst; Rev. Brian Schloth, M.S., Prov. Treas.

Legal Title: Missionaries of LaSalette Corp.; MLS Religious Trust.

Priests: 114; Brothers: 29; Oblates: 3

Represented in the Archdioceses of Atlanta, Boston, Galveston-Houston Hartford, Milwaukee, Brooklyn, St. Louis and Washington and in the Dioceses of Albany, Beaumont, Fall River, Lake Charles, Manchester, Norwich, Orlando, Peoria, Providence, Raleigh, Rockville Centre, Springfield in Massachusetts, Tucson and Worcester. Also in Canada.

[0730] (L.C.)—LEGIONARIES OF CHRIST

Founded in Mexico in 1941, first foundation in United States 1965.

General Headquarters: Via Aurelia 677, Rome, Italy, Tel: 011-39-06-664991; Fax: 011-39-06-66499372. Very Rev. Alvaro Corcuera, L.C., Gen. Dir.

New York Territory Headquarters: 590 Columbus Ave., P.O. Box 205, Thornwood, NY 10594. Tel: 914-495-9000; Fax: 914-495-9050. Very Rev. Julio Marti, L.C., Territorial Dir; Rev. Anthony Bannon, L.C., Nat'l. Dir. Novitiate and Juniorate 475 Oak Ave., Cheshire, CT 06410.Rev. Christopher Brackett, L.C., Rector.

Priests: 60; Religious: 234; Novices: 79

Represented in the Archdioceses of Hartford, New York, Philadelphia and Washington and in the Dioceses of Manchester and Providence.

Atlanta Territory Headquarters: 55 Club Ct., Alpharetta, GA 30005. Tel: 770-671-8778; Fax: 770-676-5891. Very Rev. John Connor, L.C., Territorial Dir.

Priests: 70; Religious: 43

Represented in the Archdioceses of Atlanta, Chicago, Denver, Detroit, Galveston-Houston, Los Angeles and St. Louis and in the Dioceses of Dallas, Gary, Madison, Phoenix, Sacramento and San Jose.

[0740] (M.I.C.)—CONGREGATION OF MARIANS OF THE IMMACULATE CONCEPTION

(Congregatio Clericorum Marianorum ab Immaculatae Conceptionis Beatae Mariae Virginis)

General Motherhouse: Via Corsica 1, 00198, Rome, Italy, Tel: 011-39-06-853-7031; Fax: 011-39-06-853-7032. Rev. Andrzej Pakula, M.I.C; Very Rev. Joseph Roesch, M.I.C; Rev. Jair B. De Souza, M.I.C; Rev. Zbigniew Pilat, M.I.C; Rev. Wojciech Jasinski, M.I.C.

Blessed Virgin Mary, Mother of Mercy Province: 2 Prospect Hill Rd., Stockbridge, MA 01262-0951. Tel: 413-298-3931; Fax: 413-298-0207; Email: provincial@marian.org; Web: www.marian.org; Web: www.thedivinemercy.org. Very Rev. Kazimierz Chwalek, M.I.C., Prov. Supr. Provincial Councilors: Very Rev. Donald Calloway, M.I.C; Rev. Timothy Roth, M.I.C; Rev. Matthew Lamoureux, M.I.C; Bro. Brian Manian, M.I.C.

Fathers: 49; Brothers: 10; Seminarians: 12; Novices: 11; Postulants: 2

Legal Holdings: Marian Fathers of the Immaculate Conception of the B.V.M., Inc., 2 Prospect Hill Rd., Stockbridge, MA 01262; Congregation of Marians of the Immaculate Conception; Congregation of Marian Fathers of the Immaculate Conception of the Most Blessed Virgin Mary; Association of Marian Helpers; Marian Service Corporation; Marian Helpers Corporation; Eucharistic Apostles of the Divine Mercy (EADM); Healthcare Professionals-Nurses and Doctors-for Divine Mercy; John Paul II Institute of Divine Mercy; Marian Helpers Center; Marian House of Studies; Marian Scholasticate; Marianapolis Preparatory School; Mother of Mercy Messengers (MOMM); National Shrine of the Divine Mercy; National Shrine of the Divine Mercy Gift Shop.

Represented in the Archdioceses of Chicago, Milwaukee and Washington and in the Dioceses of Joliet, Norwich, Springfield in Massachusetts and Steubenville. Also in Argentina.

Properties owned, staffed or sponsored: 7 Religious Houses; 3 Residences; 7 Parishes; 2 High School. In Argentine Vicariate: 2 Religious Houses; 2 Parishes; 2 Grade Schools.

[0750] (C.M.M.)—CONGREGATION OF MARIANNHILL MISSIONARIES, MARIANNHILL FATHERS AND BROTHERS

(Congregatio Missionariorum de Mariannhill)

Generalate: Via S. Giovanni Eudes 91, 00163, Rome, Italy, Very Rev. Damian Weber, C.M.M., Supr. Gen.

American-Canadian Province (1938): *Our Lady of Grace Monastery*, 23715 Ann Arbor Trail, Dearborn Heights, MI 48127-1449. Tel: 313-561-7140; Fax: 313-561-9486. Rev. Thomas Heier, C.M.M., American District Supr; Rev. Thomas Szura, C.M.M., Procurator.

Fathers: 7; Brothers: 3

Legal Holdings: Mariannhill Retreat Center, Dearborn Heights, MI.

Represented in the Archdiocese of Detroit.

[0760] (S.M.)—SOCIETY OF MARY

(Marianists)

(Societas Mariae--Marianistae)

General Motherhouse: Via Latina 22, 00179, Rome, Italy, Very Rev. Manuel Cortes, S.M., Supr. Gen.

The Province of Cincinnati (1849); Province of the Pacific (1948); Province of St. Louis (1908) and the Province of New York (1961) have merged June 30th, 2002 to form the Marianist Province of the United States.

Marianist Province of the United States (Society of Mary) (2002): 4425 W. Pine, Saint Louis, MO 63108-2301. Tel: 314-533-1207; Fax: 314-533-0778. Rev. Martin A. Solma, S.M., Prov; Bro. Joseph Kamis, S.M., Asst. Prov. Councilors: Rev. William J. Meyer, S.M; Rev. Paul Marshall, S.M; Bro. Francisco T. Gonzalez, S.M; Bro. Charles J. Johnson, S.M; Bro. Edward Brink, S.M; Bro. Dennis Schmitz, S.M.

Fathers: 129; Brothers: 314; Perpetual Professed: 365; Novices: 33; Aspirants: 15

Legal Titles and Holdings - Properties owned: Marianist Provincial Office, St. Louis, MO; St. Mary's University, San Antonio, TX; Central Catholic Marianist High School, San Antonio, TX; Tecaboca: Marianist Center for Spiritual Renewal, Ingram, TX; Chaminade Preparatory, St. Louis, MO; St. John Vianney High School, St. Louis, MO; Marianist Galleries, St. Louis, MO; Marianist Retreat & Conference Center, Eureka, MO; Marianist Community, St. Louis; Mount St. John;

Bergamo Center; University of Dayton; Chaminade-Julienne High School; Marianist Mission, Dayton OH; Governor's Island, Huntsville, OH; Marianist Communities in: Cleveland, OH; Cincinnati, OH; Dayton, OH; Marianist Community, Baltimore, MD; Marianist Family Center, Cape May Point, NJ; Marianist Community Residences, Hollywood, FL; Chaminade/Madonna High School, Hollywood, FL; Colegio San Jose, Rio Piedras, PR; Chaminade University, Honolulu, HI; St. Louis School, Honolulu, HI; Marianist Center, Honolulu, HI; Marianist Communities, Honolulu, HI; Marianist Residence, Maui, HI.

Members serve and staff: Parishes; Universities, High Schools, Middle Schools and Elementary Schools; Retreat Houses; Apostolic Centers; Missions in East Nepal, India, Mexico, Nepal & Philippines.

Represented in the Archdioceses of Baltimore, Cincinnati, Hartford, Los Angeles, Miami, Philadelphia, St. Louis, San Antonio, San Francisco and San Juan and in the Dioceses of Belleville, Brooklyn, Camden, Cleveland, Columbus, Fort Wayne-South Bend, Fort Worth, Honolulu, Norwich, Orange, Oakland, Rockville Centre and San Jose. Also in Ireland.

Province of Meribah (1976): *Marianist Provincial Residence*, 240 Emory Rd., Mineola, NY 11501. Tel: 516-742-5555. Bro. Thomas J. Cleary, S.M., Prov. & Asst. for Education; Rev. Garrett J. Long, S.M., Asst. Prov. & Asst. for Religious Life; Bro. James W. Conway, S.M., Asst. for Temporalities. Councilors: Bro. Timothy S. Driscoll, S.M; Rev. Thomas A. Cardone, S.M.

Legal Holdings: Chaminade High School, Mineola, NY; Kellenberg Memorial High School, Uniondale, NY; Marianist Residence, Accord, NY.

[0770] (F.M.S.)—THE MARIST BROTHERS

(Fratres Maristae a Scholis)

Generalate: Rome, Italy, Rev. Bro. Emili Turu, F.M.S., Supr. Gen; Rev. Bro. Joseph McKee, F.M.S., Vicar Gen.

Province of the United States of America (2003): *Provincial Office*, 1241 Kennedy Blvd., Bayonne, NJ 07002. Tel: 201-823-1115; Fax: 201-823-2232. Bro. James McKnight, F.M.S., Dir. Marist Foreign Missions & Senior Brothers Liaison; Bro. Hugh Turley, F.M.S., Co-Dir. Devel; Mrs. Paulette Karas, Co-Dir. Devel; Mr. Frank Pellegrino, C.F.O. Councilors: Bro. Ben Consigli, F.M.S., Prov; Bro. Roy George, F.M.S., Asst. Prov; Bro. Stephen Schlitte, F.M.S; Bro. Hank Hammer, F.M.S., Academic Dean; Bro. Kevin Handibode, F.M.S; Bro. Ken Hogan, F.M.S; Bro. James Kearney, F.M.S; Rev. Bro. Sean D. Sammon, F.M.S.

Brothers: 172

Legal Titles: Marist Brothers of the Schools, Inc.; The Marist Brothers.

Represented in the Archdioceses of Boston, Chicago, Miami, Newark, New Orleans and New York and in the Dioceses of Albany, Brooklyn, Brownsville, Laredo, Rockville Centre and Wheeling-Charleston.

Properties owned, staffed or sponsored; High Schools 15; community houses 30; junior high school 2; community school in Japan 1.

[0780] (S.M.)—MARIST FATHERS

(Societas Mariae)

General Motherhouse: *via Alessandro Poerio 63*, 00152, Rome, Italy, Very Rev. John Hannan, S.M., Supr. Gen; Rev. Kevin Mowbray, S.M., Treas. Gen.

The first Marist foundation in the United States was in 1863, St. Michael's in Convent, Louisiana. The first Marist Province in the United States was established in 1889 under the name of American Province. This Province was subdivided in 1924 into the Washington Province and the Boston Province; On January 1, 1962, the San Francisco Province was established. On January 1, 2000 the San Francisco and Washington Provinces merged. On September 8, 2000 the merged entity became officially known as the Atlanta Province. The Boston Province continues as a separate province.

Atlanta Province (2000): P.O. Box 81144, Atlanta, GA 30366-1144. Tel: 770-458-1435. Very Rev. Timothy G. Keating, S.M., Prov; Rev. Joseph Hindelang, S.M., Vicar Prov. & Councilor; Rev. John Harhager, S.M., Prov. Treas; Rev. Joseph J. McLaughlin, S.M., Mission Promoter; Mr. Jack Ridout, Dir. Vocations; Rev. Charles Girard, S.M., Archivist; Rev. Edwin L. Keel, S.M., Promoter of Marist Laity; Rev. Peter R. Blanchard, S.M., Promoter of Marist Laity; Rev. John P. Bolduc, S.M., Prov. Council; Rev. Rene J. Iturbe, S.M., Prov. Council; Bro. Randy T. Hoover, S.M., Prov. Council; Rev. Leon M. Olszamowski, S.M., Prov. Council.

Fathers: 56; Brothers: 11

Legal Holdings & Titles: Marist Society, Inc.; Marist College and Marist Center, Washington, DC; Marist Society of GA; Marist School, Atlanta, GA; Marist Society of OH; Marist Society of LA; Marist Community, New Orleans, LA; Marist Society of PA

Properties owned, sponsored or staffed: Community Houses 7; Parishes 8; Seminaries/Houses of Study 2; High School 1.

Represented in the Archdioceses of Atlanta, Los Angeles, Miami, Military Services, USA, New Orleans, San Francisco, St. Paul-Minneapolis, Seattle and Washington and in the Dioceses of Brownsville, Monterey, Oakland, Orange, Savannah, St. Petersburg and Wheeling-Charleston

Boston Province (Marist Fathers) (1924): *Marist Fathers of Boston*, 27 Isabella St., Boston, MA 02116-5216. Tel: 617-426-4448; Fax: 617-426-1884. Rev. Timothy G. Keating, S.M., Prov; Rev. Albert DiIanni, S.M., Prov. Dir. of Third Order of Mary & Vocation Dir; Rev. Joseph Hindelang, S.M., Vicar & Council Prov; Rev. John Bolduc, S.M., Prov. Council; Rev. Rene Iturbe, S.M., Prov. Council; Rev. Leon M. Olszamowski, S.M., Prov. Council; Bro. Randy T. Hoover, S.M., Prov. Council; Rev. John Harhager, S.M., Prov. Treas; Rev. Andrew Albert, S.M., Dir. Lourdes Center.

Legal Titles: Marist Fathers of Boston; Marist Fathers of Detroit, Inc.; Marist Fathers of New York.

Fathers: 50; Brothers: 5

Properties owned, sponsored or staffed: Community Houses 5; Parishes 5; High Schools 1.

Represented in the Archdioceses of Boston, Hartford and Detroit, and in the Dioceses of Brooklyn, Burlington and Portland (In Maine).

[0782] (O.M.M.)—MARONITE ORDER OF THE BLESSED VIRGIN MARY

Maronite Order of the Blessed Virgin Mary: 4405 Earhart Rd., Ann Arbor, MI 48105. Tel: 734-662-4822; Fax: 734-662-4822. Rev. Victor Daw, O.M.M; Rev. Hanna Tayar, O.M.M; Rev. Paul Tarabay, O.M.M; Rev. Nabil Habchi, O.M.M.

[0785] (C.M.L.M.)—THE CONGREGATION OF MARONITE LEBANESE MISSIONARIES

Founded at the Monastery of Kreim-Ghosta (Mountain of Lebanon), in the year 1865. Established in the United States March of 1991: Agreement between Archbishop Zayek of the Diocese of St. Maron and the Congregation to serve the parishes of San Antonio, Dallas and Houston.

U.S. Headquarters: *Our Lady of the Cedars Maronite Church*, 11935 Bellfort Village, Houston, TX 77031. Tel: 281-568-6800; Fax: 281-564-6961. Rev. Abdallah Zaidan, C.M.L.M., Supr.

Bishops: 2; Priests: 95; Seminarians: 15; Postulants: 2; Novices: 8

Represented in the Dioceses of Our Lady of Lebanon and the Eparchy of St. Maron.

Our Lady of Mt. Lebanon: *St. Peter Cathedral*, 333 S. San Vicente Blvd., Los Angeles, CA 90048. Tel: 310-275-6634; Fax: 310-858-0856.

[0790] (M.M.A.)—MARONITE MONKS OF ADORATION

Monastery of the Most Holy Trinity: 67 Dugway Rd., Petersham, MA 01366-9725. Tel: 978-724-3347. Rt. Rev. William J. Driscoll, M.M.A., Abbot; Very Rev. Louis Marie Dauphinais, M.M.A., Prior.

Priests: 9; Brothers: 9; Monks in Community: 18

[0800] (M.M.)—MARYKNOLL

(Catholic Foreign Mission Society of America, Inc.)

U.S. Foundation (1911): *Maryknoll Society Center & Admin. Offices*, Maryknoll, NY 10545-0305. Tel: 914-941-7590; Fax: 914-944-3605. Rev. Edward M. Dougherty, M.M., Supr. Gen. & Pres; Rev. Jose A. Aramburu, M.M., Vicar Gen. & Vice Pres; Rev. Edward J. McGovern, M.M., Asst. Gen; Rev. Paul R. Masson, M.M., Asst. Gen. & Sec.

Legal Title: Catholic Foreign Mission Society of America Incorporated, Training Center; Maryknoll Society Center, Maryknoll, NY 10545.

Houses in Archdioceses and Dioceses:

Buffalo: *Maryknoll Fathers and Brothers*, 73 Adam St., Tonawanda, NY 14150. Tel: 716-213-0000; Fax: 716-213-0000.

Chicago: *Maryknoll Fathers and Brothers*, 5128 S. Hyde Park Blvd., Chicago, IL 60615-4217. Tel: 773-493-3367; Fax: 773-493-3427; Email: chicago@maryknoll.org; Web: www.maryknoll.org/society. Rev. John W. Eybel, M.M., Rector; Rev. William J. Donnelly, M.M; Rev. John P. Cuff, M.M; Bro. Joseph Bruener, M.M; Bro. Adrian R. Mazuchowski, M.M; Gregory Darr, Regl. Dir; Mr. Jay Weingarten, Major Gift Officer.

Cincinnati: *Maryknoll Fathers and Brothers*, 6930 Greenfield Dr., Cincinnati, OH 45224. Tel: 513-681-7888.

Cleveland: *Maryknoll Fathers and Brothers*, 10309 Edgewater Dr., Cleveland, OH 44102. Tel: 216-651-2121; Fax: 216-651-8242. Rev. James H. Huvane, M.M.

Denver: *Maryknoll Fathers and Brothers*, 3554 Marion St., Denver, CO 80205. Tel: 303-296-1196; Fax: 303-296-1196.

Galveston-Houston: *Maryknoll Fathers and Brothers*, 2360 Rice Blvd., Houston, TX 77005. Tel: 713-529-1912; Fax: 713-529-0372; Email: mklhouston@maryknoll.org.

Los Angeles: *Maryknoll Fathers and Brothers*, 745 W. Adams Blvd., Los Angeles, CA 90007. Tel: 213-747-9676; Fax: 213-747-8923.

St. Paul: *Maryknoll Fathers and Brothers*, P.O. Box 20626, Minneapolis, MN 55420. Tel: 952-884-1024; Fax: 952-884-1371; Email: minneapolis@maryknoll.org; Web: www.maryknoll.org.

San Jose: *Maryknoll Residence*, 23000 Cristo Rey Dr., Los Altos, CA 94024-7499. Tel: 650-967-3822; Fax: 650-965-3473.

Seattle: *Maryknoll Fathers and Brothers*, 958 16th Ave., E., Seattle, WA 98112. Tel: 206-322-8831; Fax: 206-324-6909.

Washington: *Maryknoll Fathers and Brothers*, 4834 16th St., N.W., Washington, DC 20011. Tel: 202-726-4252; Tel: 202-726-4281; Fax: 202-726-0466.

Priests: 449; Students of Theology: 13; Brothers: 62; Priest Associates: 4

Properties owned or sponsored: Major Society Center; House of Formation; U.S. Community Houses 22.

Represented in the Archdioceses of Boston, Chicago, Cincinnati, Denver, Detroit, Galveston-Houston, Los Angeles, New York, St. Louis, St. Paul-Minneapolis, San Francisco, Seattle and Washington and in the Dioceses of Buffalo, Cleveland, and San Jose.

[0810] (F.M.M.)—BROTHERS OF MERCY

General Motherhouse: D-56412, Montabaur, Germany, Bro. Stephan Geissler, F.M.M., Supr. Gen.

American Region: 4520 Ransom Rd., Clarence, NY 14031. Tel: 716-759-8341; Fax: 716-759-7243. Bro. Jude Holzfoerster, F.M.M., Regional Supr. Assistants Bro. Kenneth Thomas, F.M.M; Bro. Fidelis Verrall, F.M.M.

Brothers: 11

Legal Holdings or Titles: Brothers of Mercy Nursing Home Co., Inc.; Brothers of Mercy Housing Co., Inc.; Brothers of Mercy Sacred Heart Home, Inc.

Represented in the Diocese of Buffalo.

[0820] (C.P.M.)—CONGREGATION OF THE FATHERS OF MERCY

(Congregatio Presbyterorum a Misericordia)

Generalate and Novitiate (1808): 806 Shaker Museum Rd., Auburn, KY 42206. Tel: 270-542-4146; Fax: 270-542-4147; Web: www.fathersofmercy.com. Rev. David Wilton, C.P.M., Supr. Gen; Rev. Ben Cameron, C.P.M., Asst. Gen; Rev. William Casey, C.P.M., Consultor; Rev. Anthony M. Stephens, C.P.M., Consultor; Rev. Thomas Sullivan, C.P.M., Consultor; Rev. Louis Caporiccio, C.P.M., Sec. Gen; Rev. Charles Zmudzinski, C.P.M., Treas.Gen; Rev. Joseph R. Aytona, C.P.M., Treas. Gen.

Priests: 25; Novices: 1; Students: 8

Represented in the Archdiocese of Louisville and in the Dioceses of Altoona-Johnstown, Charlotte, Cheyenne, Covington, Green Bay, Kansas City-St. Joseph and Owensboro.

[0825] (M.S.S.)—MISSIONARIES OF THE BLESSED SACRAMENT

(Missionaries of the Blessed Sacrament)

Regional Headquarters: 2933 Street Rd., Bensalem, PA 19020. Tel: 215-244-9211; Fax: 215-244-9211. Rev. Victor P. Warkulwiz, M.S.S., Supr.

Fathers: 2

Ministries in Special Apostolate: Promotion of perpetual Eucharistic adoration.

Represented in the Archdiocese of Philadelphia and in the Diocese of Lafayette.

[0830] (M.H.M.)—MILL HILL MISSIONARIES

(St. Joseph's Missionary Society of Mill Hill)

International Headquarters: *St. Joseph's Missionary Society*, P.O. Box 3608, SL6 7UX, Maidenhead, England, Web: millhillmissionaries.com. Very Rev. Anthony Chantry, M.H.M., Gen. Supr.

American Headquarters: *Mill Hill Missionaries*, 222 W. Hartsdale Ave., Hartsdale, NY 10530-1667. Tel: 914-682-0645; Fax: 914-682-0862; Email: mhmnyoffice@aol.com. Rev. Bartholomew Daly, M.H.M., Reg. Rep.

Legal Title: Mill Hill Fathers, Inc.

Fathers: 9

Represented in the Archdiocese of New York and Diocese of Phoenix.

[0835] (O.M.)—MINIM FATHERS

General Motherhouse: Piazza San Francesco di Paola, 10 00184, Rome, Italy, Tel: 011-39-6-4882613; Fax: 011-39-6-4882613. Very Rev. Francesco Marinelli, O.M., Supr. Gen.

North American Delegation (1970): 3431 Portola Ave., Los Angeles, CA 90032. Tel: 323-223-1101. Rev. Mario Pisano, O.M., Delegate Gen.

Legal Title: Minim Fathers.

Priests: 3

Vocation Center, 6043 N. Barranca Ave., Azusa, CA 91702.

Represented in the Archdiocese of Los Angeles.

[0840] (S.T.)—MISSIONARY SERVANTS OF THE MOST HOLY TRINITY

(Missionarii Servi Sanctissimae Trinitatis)

(Trinity Missions)

Generalate-Missionary Servants of the Most Holy Trinity: 9001 New Hampshire Ave., Ste. 300, Silver Spring, MD 20903-3626. Tel: 301-434-0092; Fax: 301-434-0255. Rev. John S. Edmunds, S.T., Gen. Custodian; Rev. Domingo Rodriguez, S.T., Vicar Gen; Rev. Dennis M. Berry, S.T., Gen. Councilor; Rev. Rafael Pisso, S.T., Gen. Councilor; Bro. John A. Skrodinsky, S.T., Gen. Councilor; Bro. Steven Vesely, S.T., Sec.

Gen; Bro. Jordan Baxter, S.T., Treas. Gen.

Legal Title: Missionary Servants of the Most Holy Trinity (aka) Trinity Missions; Missionary Servants Charitable Trust; Father Judge Charitable Trust.

Priests: 87; Brothers: 25; Student Brothers: 12; Candidates: 19; Deacons: 3; Novices: 6

Ministry in the following areas: Missionary Cenacles; Parishes; Missions; Stations and Specialized Apostolates; Lay Apostolate Secretariat; Counseling Centers; Hospitals and Rest Home Chaplains; AA Programs; Protective Institutions; Prison Chaplains; Community Centers

Properties owned and or sponsored: Generalate, Silver Spring, MD; Parish, rectory and school, Holy Trinity, AL; School Buildings, Camden, MS; St. Joseph Shrine, Stirling, NJ; Former minor seminary building, Monroe, VA; Residences: Harpers Ferry, WV and Senior Ministry Residence, Adelphi, MD.

Represented in the Archdioceses of Baltimore, Los Angeles, Mobile, Newark, Philadelphia and Washington and in the Dioceses of Biloxi, Boise, Jackson, Knoxville, Paterson, Pensacola-Tallahassee, San Bernardino, San Diego, Savannah and Tucson. Also in Mexico, Puerto Rico, Colombia and Costa Rica.

[0850] (M.AFR.)—MISSIONARIES OF AFRICA

(Societas Missionariorum Africae)

Generalate: 269 via Aurelia, C.P. 9078 I-00165, Rome, Italy, Rev. Richard Baawobr, M.Afr., Supr. Gen.

USA Sector of the Province of the Americas: 1624 21st. St. N.W., Washington, DC 20009-1003. Tel: 202-232-5154; Fax: 202-332-8640. Rev. Richard Archambault, M.Afr., Supr; Rev. George Markwell, M.Afr., Hospital Chap; Rev. John Lynch, M.Afr; Bro. James Heintz, M.Afr., Bursar; Rev. Thomas Reilly, M.Afr., Guestmaster; Rev. Jean-Claude Robitaille, M.Afr., Delegate Supr; Rev. Richard Roy, M.Afr; Rev. Diego Ramon Sarrio Cucarella, M.Afr., Studies at G.U; Rev. Brian Denis Starkey, M.Afr., Treas; Rev. Joseph Elmo Hebert, M.Afr., Co-ordinator; Rev. Robert C. McGovern, M.Afr; Rev. Roger Bisson, M.Afr; Rev. John Joseph Braun, M.Afr; Bro. Martin Chapper, M.Afr; Rev. Joseph Kay, M.Afr; Rev. Youville Labonte, M.Afr; Rev. Michel J. Lavoie, M.Afr.

Priests: 22; Brothers: 2

Represented in the Archdiocese of Washington and in the Diocese of St. Petersburg.

[0854] (M.S.P.)—MISSIONARY SOCIETY OF ST. PAUL OF NIGERIA

Generalate: *Gwagwalada*, P.O. Box 23, Abuja, Nigeria, Very Rev. Anselm Umoren, M.S.P., Supr. Gen.

U.S. Region: *Missionary Society of St. Paul, Inc.*, 3607 Meriburr Ln., P.O. Box 300145, Houston, TX 77230-0145. Tel: 713-842-6090; Fax: 713-747-4263; Web: www.mspfathers.org. Very Rev. Desmond Ohankwere, M.S.P., Local Supr.

Legal Title: Missionary Society of St. Paul, Inc., Houston, TX.

Universal number of Priests: 217; Priests in U.S: 36

Represented in the Archdiocese of Galveston-Houston.

[0855] (F.M.M.)—MISSIONARY FRATERNITY OF MARY

General Headquarters: 6A Calle 48-98, Zona 7-Apartado Postal 623-I, Zona 7, Guatemala, Rev. Msgr. Eduardo Aguirre-Oestmann, Gen. Moderator.

U.S. Foundation (1991): 340 Pine St., Seaford, DE 19973. Tel: 302-629-5115. Rev. Ruben A. Soto, F.M.M., Regional Vicar; Rev. Juan Vicente Hidalgo.

Represented in the Diocese of Wilmington.

[0860] (C.I.C.M.)—MISSIONHURST CONGREGATION OF THE IMMACULATE HEART OF MARY

(Congregatio Immaculati Cordis Mariae)

Foreign and Home missions.

Generalate: *Casa Generalizia C.I.C.M.*, Via S. Giovanni Eudes, 95, 00163, Rome, Italy, Very Rev. Edouard Tsimba, C.I.C.M., Supr. Gen.

U.S. Province (1946): *Missionhurst*, 4651 N. 25th St., Arlington, VA 22207. Tel: 703-528-3800; Fax: 703-528-5355. Very Rev. Anselme Malonda Nkuanga, C.I.C.M.

Legal Title: American I.H.M. Province, Inc.; Immaculate Heart Missions, Inc.; Missionhurst, Inc.

Fathers: 39; Students: 1

Ministries in Parishes; Prison Ministry; Campus Ministry; Hospital Pastoral Work.

Represented in the Archdioceses of Boston, New York, Philadelphia and San Antonio and in the Dioceses of Arlington, Brownsville and Raleigh.

[0865] (C.M.C.)—CONGREGATION OF THE MOTHER COREDEMPTRIX

Founded in the United States 1975.

U.S. Assumption Province: *Congregation of the Mother Coredemptrix*, 1900 Grand Ave., Carthage, MO 64836-3500. Tel: 417-358-7787; Fax: 417-358-9508; Email: cmc@dongcong.net. Rev. Louis Minh Nhien, C.M.C., Prov. Supr.

Priests: 67; Brothers: 46; Novices: 2

Represented in the Diocese of Springfield-Cape Girardeau.

[0870] (S.M.M.)—MONTFORT MISSIONARIES

(Missionaries of the Company of Mary)
(Societas Mariae Montfortana)

Generalate: Viale Dei Monfortani 65, 00135, Rome, Italy, Very Rev. Santino Brembilla, S.M.M.

United States Province (1948): *Montfort Missionaries*, 101-18 104th St., Ozone Park, NY 11416. Tel: 718-849-5885; Fax: 718-849-7518. Very Rev. Matthew J. Considine, S.M.M. Counselors: Rev. Thomas Poth, S.M.M; Rev. George J. Werner, S.M.M; Rev. William Considine, S.M.M; Rev. Gerald Fitzsimmons, S.M.M.

Legal Title: Missionaries of the Company of Mary.

Fathers: 24; Brothers: 2; Parishes: 2; Community Houses: 6; Scholastics: 1

Represented in the Archdiocese of Hartford and in the Dioceses of Brooklyn and Rockville Centre.

[0895] (O.SS.S.)—BRIGITTINE MONKS

(The Order of the Most Holy Savior)

Priory of Our Lady of Consolation: 23300 Walker Ln., Amity, OR 97101. Tel: 503-835-8080; Fax: 503-835-9662; Email: monks@brigittine.org; Web: www.brigittine.org. Bro. Bernard Ner Suguitan, O.Ss.S., Prior.

Professed Monks: 6; Novices: 2

Represented in the Archdiocese of Portland in Oregon.

[0897] (M.E.P.)—PARIS FOREIGN MISSION SOCIETY

(Societas Parisiensis Missionum Ad Exteros)

Society of secular priests, without vows, of Pontifical Right.

Headquarters: 128 Rue du Bac, Paris, France, Very Rev. Georges Colomb, M.E.P., Supr. Gen.

U.S. Establishment: *Paris Foreign Mission Society*, 930 Ashbury St., San Francisco, CA 94117. Tel: 415-664-6747. Rev. Jacques R. Didier, M.E.P., Dir.

Legal Title: American Auxiliary of Paris Foreign Missions, Inc.

Priests: 2

Represented in the Archdiocese of San Francisco.

[0900] (O.PRAEM.)—CANONS REGULAR OF PREMONTRE

(Norbertines, Order of St. Norbert, Premonstratensians)
(Ordo Canonicorum Regularium Praemonstratensium)

Founded in France in the 12th century. First foundation in the United States in 1893.

Most Rev. Thomas A. Handgratinger, O.Praem., Abbot Gen.

Norbertine Generalate: 27 Viale Giotto, 00153, Rome, Italy, Tel: 011-39-06-571-766-1; Tel: 571-766-212; Fax: 011-39-06-57-80906.

United States: *St. Norbert Abbey*, 1016 N. Broadway, De Pere, WI 54115-2697. Tel: 920-337-4300; Fax: 920-337-4328. Rt. Rev. Gary J. Neville, O.Praem., Abbot; Rt. Rev. E. Thomas De Wane, O.Praem., Abbot Emeritus; Rt. Rev. Jerome G. Tremel, O.Praem., Abbot Emeritus; Very Rev. James B. Herring, O.Praem., Prior; Rev. John M. Tourangeau, O.Praem., Vocation Coord; Rev. John P. Kastenholz, O.Praem., Sec. Treas; Rev. Conrad J. Kratz, O.Praem., Dir. Norbertine Center for Spirituality; Very Rev. David M. Komatz, O.Praem., Dir. of Formation/St. Norbert Abbey.

Legal Title: The Premonstratensian Fathers; NORBERT & CO., a nominee of The Premonstratensian Fathers; Norbertine Fathers; St. Norbert Abbey, Inc.; The Walnut Markets, Inc.; Los Amigos del Peru, Inc.; Norbertine Generalate, Inc.

Fathers: 60; Brothers: 2; Novices: 3

Properties owned, staffed or sponsored: Dependent Priories 4; House of Studies 1; Colleges 1; Chaplaincies 5; Parishes 12.

Represented in the Archdioceses of Chicago, Military Services, USA and Santa Fe and in the Dioceses of Green Bay, Jackson, Madison. Also in Peru.

Daylesford Abbey: *Norbertine Fathers and Brothers*, 220 S. Valley Rd., Paoli, PA 19301-1900. Tel: 610-647-2530; Fax: 610-651-0219. Rt. Rev. Richard J. Antonucci, O.Praem., Abbot; Rt. Rev. Ronald J. Rossi, O.Praem., Abbot Emeritus; Rev. John Joseph Novielli, O.Praem., Vocation Dir; Very Rev. Steven J. Albero, O.Praem., Prior; Rev. Joseph A. Serano, O.Praem., Treas.

Legal Title: Nobertine Fathers, Inc.

Fathers: 26; Brothers: 5; Properties Owned, Staffed or Sponsored: Chaplaincies: 1; Seminaries: 1; Parishes: 3

Represented in the Archdiocese of Philadelphia.

St. Michael's Abbey: 19292 El Toro Rd., Silverado, CA 92676. Tel: 949-858-0222; Fax: 949-858-4583. Rt. Rev. Eugene J. Hayes, O.Praem., Abbot; Very Rev. Hugh C. Barbour, O.Praem., Prior P.O. Box 819, El Toro, CA 92630

Legal Title: The Norbertine Fathers of Orange, Inc.

Priests: 46; Juniors: 12; Postulants: 5; Novices: 5; Deacons: 2

Properties owned: St. Michael's College Preparatory High School, Orange, CA: Summer Camp, Orange, CA.

Represented in the Archdiocese of Los Angeles and in the Diocese of Orange.

[0910] (O.M.I.)—OBLATES OF MARY IMMACULATE

General House: *Oblati di Maria Immacolata*, C.P. 9061, 00100, Roma-Aurelio, Italy, Very Rev. Louis Lougen, O.M.I., Supr. Gen; Very Rev. Paolo Archiati, O.M.I., Vicar Gen.

United States Province (1999): *Missionary Oblates of Mary Immaculate, Provincial Admin. Office*, 391 Michigan Ave., N.E., Washington, DC 20017-1516. Tel: 202-529-4505; Fax: 202-529-4572. Rev. William Antone, O.M.I., Prov. Councilors: Rev. Louis B. Studer, O.M.I., Personnel Dir; Rev. James Taggart, O.M.I., Area Councilor-Northeast/Southeast Areas 60 Wyman St., Lowell, MA 01852-2841.Rev. James Brobst, O.M.I., Area Councilor-North Central/South Central Areas 9480 N. Demazenod Dr., Belleville, IL 62223.Rev. Raymond John Marek, O.M.I., Treas; Rev. Arthur Flores, O.M.I., Area Councilor-Southwest Area 327 Oblate Dr., San Antonio, TX 78216-6602.Rev. Stephen Conserva, O.M.I., Area Councilor-Pacific Area 1329 Griffith St., San Fernando, CA 91340-3905.Bro. William Johnson, O.M.I., Councilor-At-Large; Rev. Thomas Ovalle, O.M.I., Councilor-At-Large.

Fathers: 280; Brothers: 23; Scholastics: 12

Ministries in Retreat Centers, Shrines, Parishes, Chaplaincies, Religious Residences and Houses, Retirement Centers and the Media.

Represented in the Archdioceses of Anchorage, Boston, Chicago, Galveston-Houston, Los Angeles, Miami, New Orleans, New York, St. Louis, St. Paul-Minneapolis, San Antonio and Washington and in the Dioceses of Belleville, Brownsville, Buffalo, Columbus, Corpus Christi, Crookston, Duluth, Juneau, Laredo, Manchester, Norwich, Oakland, Palm Beach, Pensacola-Tallahassee, Portland (In Maine), San Angelo, San Diego, Sioux Falls, Springfield in Illinois, and Springfield-Cape Girardeau. Also in Brazil, Canada, Hong Kong, Mexico, and Zambia.

Missionary Oblates of Mary Immaculate: 391 Michigan Ave., N.E., Washington, DC 20017-1516. Tel: 978-458-9912; Fax: 978-458-7274. Rev. James Taggart, O.M.I., Area Councilor.

North/South Central Area Office: 9480 DeMazenod Dr., Belleville, IL 62223-1160. Tel: 618-398-7640 ext 3251; Fax: 618-398-8788. Rev. James Brobst, O.M.I., Area Councilor.

[0920] (O.S.F.S.)—OBLATES OF ST. FRANCIS DE SALES

(Congregatio Oblatorum Sancti Francisci Salesii)

General Motherhouse: Via Dandolo 49, Rome, Italy, In July 1966, the American Province was renamed the Wilmington/Philadelphia Province, and the Toledo/Detroit Province was canonically established.

Wilmington-Philadelphia Province (1906): 2200 Kentmere Pkwy., Wilmington, DE 19806. Very Rev. James J. Greenfield, O.S.F.S., Prov. Provincial Councilors: Very Rev. James Dalton, O.S.F.S; Very Rev. Robert L. Bazzoli, O.S.F.S; Very Rev. Donald J. Heet, O.S.F.S; Very Rev. Mark S. Mealey, O.S.F.S. Provincial Staff: Rev. Michael C. Connolly, O.S.F.S., Prov. Canonist; Very Rev. Donald J. Heet, O.S.F.S., Dir. Vocations; Rev. Michael S. Murray, O.S.F.S., DeSales Spirituality Svcs; Rev. Kevin M. Nadolski, O.S.F.S., Dir. Devel. & Communs; Bro. Edward F. Ogden, O.S.F.S., Dir. Formation & Pres. Prov. Conference; Rev. Barry R. Strong, O.S.F.S., Dir. Prov. Admin; Rev. Mark F. Plaushin, O.S.F.S., Dir. Planning; Rev. Michael J. McCue, O.S.F.S., Dir. De Sales Service Works; Rev. John E. McGee, O.S.F.S., Convocation Planning.

Fathers: 145; Brothers: 15; Deacons: 1; Post-Novitate: 4; Novices: 1

Properties owned, staffed or sponsored: Parishes 23; Universities 1; Houses of Study 1; Novitiates 1; High Schools 2; Chaplaincies 12; Foreign Missions 4; Middle School 1.

Represented in the Archdioceses of Baltimore, Boston, Military Services, Philadelphia and Washington and in the Dioceses of Allentown, Arlington, Camden, Charlotte, Kansas City-St. Joseph, Raleigh, Venice, Wheeling-Charleston and Wilmington.

Toledo-Detroit Province (1966): 2043 Parkside Blvd., Toledo, OH 43607-1597. Tel: 419-724-9851; Fax: 419-724-9853. Very Rev. Kenneth N. McKenna, O.S.F.S., Prov; Rev. Geoff Rose, O.S.F.S; Rev. Ronald W. E. Olszewski, O.S.F.S., Councilor & Asst. Prov; Rev. Michael E. Newman, O.S.F.S., Councilor; Rev. John J. Loughran, O.S.F.S., Councilor.

Legal Title: Oblates of St. Francis de Sales, Inc.

Priests: 54; Brothers: 11; Scholastics: 4

Ministries in Parishes; High schools; Chaplaincies; Missionaries; Armed Forces; Senior Citizens Residence.

Properties owned, staffed or sponsored: Provincialate, Toledo, OH; St. Francis de Sales High School, Toledo, OH; Oblate Residence, Jackson, MI; Oblate Residence, Toronto, Canada.

Represented in the Archdioceses of Detroit, Miami, Military Services, USA and Philadelphia and in the Dioceses of Buffalo, Erie, Kalamazoo, Lansing, Oakland, Palm Beach, Saginaw, Stockton and Toledo. Also in Canada, Mexico, and Virgin Islands.

[0930] (O.S.J.)—OBLATES OF ST. JOSEPH

(Congregatio Oblatorum S. Joseph)

Founded in Italy in 1878. Founder: Saint Joseph Marello (1844-1895). Cause of Beatification introduced May 28, 1948; Beatified 1993; Canonized 2001. First foundation in U.S. in 1929.

Motherhouse: Corso Alfieri 384, Asti, Italy,

General House: Via Boccea 364, Rome, Italy, Rev. Michael Piscopo, O.S.J., Supr. Gen; Very Rev. Sebastian Jacobi, O.S.J., Vicar Gen; Very Rev. Giocondo Bronzini, O.S.J., Procurator Gen.

Oblates of St. Joseph Eastern Province: 1880 Hwy. 315, Pittston, PA 18640. Tel: 570-654-7542; Fax: 570-654-8621. Very Rev. Philip V. Massetti, O.S.J., Prov. Councilors: Rev. Paul A. McDonnell, O.S.J; Rev. Joseph D. Sibilano, O.S.J.
Priests: 10
Parishes 4; Community Houses 1; Houses of Studies 1.
Properties owned: St. Joseph's Oblate Seminary, Pittston, PA; St. Joseph Marello Retreat House, Harveys Lake, PA.
Represented in the Diocese of Scranton.

California Province: 544 W. Cliff Dr., Santa Cruz, CA 95060. Tel: 831-457-1868; Fax: 831-457-1317. Rev. John Warburton, O.S.J., Prov. Councilors: Rev. Arnold Ortiz, O.S.J; Rev. Mariusz Beczek, O.S.J.
Legal Title: Oblates of St. Joseph.
Priests: 16; Brothers: 5; Students: 2
Parishes 4; Community Houses 5; Houses of Study 1; Shrines 1.
Properties owned: St. Joseph House of Studies, Berkeley, CA; Mount St. Joseph Seminary, Loomis, CA; Shrine of St. Joseph, Guardian of the Redeemer, Santa Cruz, CA; St. Joseph Marello House of Studies, Oxnard CA; St. Joseph's Villa, Soda Springs. CA.
Represented in the Archdiocese of Los Angeles and in the Dioceses of Fresno, Monterey and Sacramento.

[0940] (O.M.V.)—OBLATES OF THE VIRGIN MARY

(Congregation of the Oblates of the Virgin Mary)
(Congregatio Oblatorum Beatae Mariae Virginis)

Generalate: Viale XXX Aprile, 00153, Rome, Italy, Very Rev. Sergio Zirattu, O.M.V., Rector Major.

St. Ignatius Province: 2 Ipswich St., Boston, MA 02215-3607. Tel: 617-536-4141; Web: www.omvusa.org. Rev. David Nicgorski, O.M.V., Prov.
Priests in U.S: 31; Brothers: 5
Ministries in Parishes; Hospital and Prison Chaplaincies; Retreats & Parish Missions; Novitiate; Community Houses; College Seminary Shrine Chaplaincies.
Legal Holdings: St. Clement's Eucharistic Shrine, Boston, MA; St. Joseph House, Milton, MA; St. Ignatius Province of the Oblates of the Virgin Mary, Inc., Boston, Ma.
Represented in the Archdioceses of Boston, Denver, and Los Angeles and in the Diocese Springfield in Illinois. Also in the Philippines.

[0950] (C.O.)—ORATORIANS

(Confederatio Oratorii S. Philippi Nerii)

A Confederation of Autonomous Houses first founded in Rome, 1575.

General Confederation: Via Di Parione, 33, 1-00186, Rome, Italy, Tel: (39) 06-689-25-37. Rev. Edoardo Cerrato, C.O., Procurator Gen; Rev. Felix Selden, C.O., Delegate of the Holy See Landstrasser Hauptstr, 56, Wien, Austria, A-1030,

The Oratory of Rock Hill: P.O. Box 11586, Rock Hill, SC 29731. Tel: 803-327-2097. Very Rev. Fabio Refosco, C.O., Provost.
Fathers: 9; Brothers: 7
Represented in the Diocese of Charleston.

The Oratorian Community of Monterey: Monterey, CA 93942. Tel: 831-373-0476. Very Rev. Peter C. Sanders, Provost. & Major Supr; Rev. Thomas A. Kieffer, Vicar & Sec.
Total in Community: 2
Oratorian Foundation Inc., Arizona, Yarnell, AZ 85362. An outreach of the Oratorian Community in Monterey.
Represented in the Diocese of Monterey.

The Pittsburgh Oratory: *Congregation of the Oratory of St. Philip Neri,* 4450 Bayard St., Pittsburgh, PA 15213-1506. Tel: 412-681-3181. Very Rev. Drew P. Morgan, C.O., Provost; Rev. David S. Abernethy, C.O., Vicar; Rev. Michael Darcy, C.O; Bro. Paul Werley, C.O; Rev. Joshua Kibler, C.O; Rev. Stephen Lowery, C.O; Bro. Dennis Di Benedetto, C.O.
Fathers: 5; Novices: 2
Represented in the Diocese of Pittsburgh.

The Oratory of Pharr: P.O. Box 1698, Pharr, TX 78577-1630. Tel: 956-843-8217; Fax: 956-843-2946. Very Rev. Leo Francis Daniels, C.O., Provost; Rev. Mario Alberto Aviles, C.O., Treas. Deputy for Latin America & Sec; Rev. Jose Encarnacion Losoya, C.O., Vicar; Rev. Jose Juan Ortiz, C.O; Bro. Nilton Cueto, C.O.
Ministries in Parish work; Services to the poor; promotion of Mexican-American cultural services; Education at all levels; Spanish language communities.
Properties owned: Casa Maria of the Oratory, Pharr, TX; Oratory Academy-Academia Oratoriana, Pharr; TX; Oratory Athenaeum For University Preparation; Pharr Oratory of St. Philip Neri of Pontifical Right.
Represented in the Diocese of Brownsville. Also in Mexico.
Secular Oratory, Lay institute Founded by St. Philip Neri. Principal Work; Federacion Mexicana del Oratorio de San Felipe Neri, American Office, The Oratory, Rte. 4 Box 118, Pharr, TX 78577. The Pharr Oratory is a member of the Mexican Federation of Oratories and at present serves as the American office of all eleven houses.

The Oratory of St. Philip Neri: 109 Willoughby St., Brooklyn, NY 11201. Tel: 718-875-2096; Fax: 718-875-4678. Very Rev. Dennis M. Corrado, C.O., Provost.
Fathers: 5; Brothers: 1

The New Brunswick Congregation of the Oratory of St. Philip Neri: 94 Somerset St., New Brunswick, NJ 08901. Tel: 732-545-6820; Fax: 732-545-4069; Email: oratorians@nboratory.org; Web: www.nboratory.org. Very Rev. Peter R. Cebulka, C.O., Provost; Rev. Thomas A. Odorizzi, C.O., Vicar & Treas; Rev. Kevin Patrick Kelly, C.O; Rev. Jeffrey Calia, C.O., Sec.
Priests: 4

[0960] (F.S.R.)—BROTHERS OF THE CONGREGATION OF OUR LADY OF THE HOLY ROSARY

Founded in the United States in 1957.

General Motherhouse and Novitiate: 232 Sunnyside Dr., Reno, NV 89503-3510. Tel: 775-747-4441. Bro. Matthew Cunningham, F.S.R., Supr; Bro. Philip Napolitano, F.S.R., Asst. Supr.
Brothers: 3
Ministries in the field of Education and Pastoral Ministry.
Represented in the Diocese of Reno.

[0970] (O.DE.M)—ORDER OF OUR LADY OF MERCY

(Mercedarians Friars)
(Ordo de Beatae Mariae Virginis de Mercede)

Founded in Barcelona, Spain on August 10, 1218.

Generalate: *Curia Generalizia dei PP Mercedari,* Via Monte Carmelo 3 00166, Rome, Italy, Most Rev. Pablo Bernardo, O.de.M., Master Gen.

U.S.A. Provincial Headquarters: *Vicariate of Mary, Co-Redemptress,* 7758 E. Main Rd., Le Roy, NY 14482-9701. Tel: 585-768-7110. Rev. Richard S. Rasch, O.de.M., Prov. Supr.
Priests: 16; Brothers: 8
Ministries in Parishes, education, hospital and prison chaplaincies, retreats; newman campus chaplaincies; mission word.
Properties owned: St. Raymond Nonnatus Novitiate, Le Roy, NY; Monastery of Our Lady of Mercy, Philadelphia, PA; Saint Peter Nolasco Residence, St. Petersburg, FL.
Represented in the Archdiocese of Philadelphia and in the Dioceses of Buffalo, Cleveland and St. Petersburg. Also in South India.

[0975] (S.O.L.T.)—SOCIETY OF OUR LADY OF THE MOST HOLY TRINITY

International House: *Casa San Jose,* 109 W. Ave. F, P.O. Box 152, Robstown, TX 78380. Tel: 361-387-2754. Rev. Rogelio Rosalinas, S.O.L.T., Gen. Priest Servant.
Priests: 102; Deacons: 2; Novices: 5; Seminarians: 16
Pastoral Ministries: Community House; House of Study-Novitiate, Migrant Ministry, Native Americans, Marian Shrine, Parish Work, Hospital Chaplaincy, Military Chaplaincy.
Represented in the Archdioceses of Atlanta, Detroit, Galveston-Houston, Military Services, Milwaukee, Santa Fe and Seattle and in the Dioceses of Albany, Arlington, Cheyenne, Corpus Christi, Fargo, Helena, Kansas City-St. Joseph, Lafayette, Laredo, Paterson, Pensacola-Tallahassee, Phoenix, Pittsburgh, Portland (In Maine), Providence, Pueblo and Wheeling-Charleston.

[0980] (C.F.M.M.)—BROTHERS OF OUR LADY, MOTHER OF MERCY

(Congregatio Fratrum Beatae Mariae Virginis, Matris Misericordiae)

Generalate: Gasthuisring 54 5041 DT, Tilburg, The Netherlands,

U.S. Region: 7140 Ramsgate Ave., Los Angeles, CA 90045. Bro. John Grever, C.F.M.M., Contact Person.
Brothers: 3
Represented in the Archdiocese of Los Angeles.

[0990] (S.A.C.)—SOCIETY OF THE CATHOLIC APOSTOLATE

(Pallottines)

Generalate: *Pallottines,* Piazza S.V. Pallotti 204 00186, Rome, Italy,

Province of the Immaculate Conception (Eastern) (1953): 204 Raymond Ave., P.O. Box 979, South Orange, NJ 07079. Tel: 201-762-2926. Very Rev. Peter T. Sticco, S.A.C., Prov; Rev. Frank S. Donio, S.A.C., 1st Consultor; Rev. Frank Gaetano, S.A.C., Bursar. Consultors: Rev. Bernard P. Carman, S.A.C; Rev. Frank Amato, S.A.C; Bro. James Beamesderfer, S.A.C.
Fathers: 14; Professed Brothers: 2
Properties owned, sponsored or staffed: Parishes 3; Seminary; High school; Novitiate; Shrine of St. Jude, Pallottine Center for Apostolic Causes.
Represented in the Archdioceses of Baltimore, Newark and Washington and in the Dioceses of Brooklyn and Camden.

Mother of God Province (1946): *Pallottine Fathers and Brothers, Inc.,* 5424 W. Blue Mound Rd., Milwaukee, WI 53208. Tel: 414-259-0688; Fax: 414-258-9314. Very Rev. Leon J. Martin, S.A.C., Prov; Rev. Joseph Koyickal, S.A.C., 1st Consultor; Bro. James Scarpace, S.A.C., Consultor.
Fathers: 9; Brothers: 1
Ministries in Parishes; Retreat House; Hospital Chaplaincies; High School.
Represented in the Archdiocese of Milwaukee.

U.S. Foundation: 3352 4th St., P.O. Box 249, Wyandotte, MI 48192. Rev. Gerard Frawley, S.A.C., Prov. Delegate.
Fathers: 12; Brothers: 1
Parishes 4; Missions 3.
Represented in the Archdioceses of Detroit, New York and San Francisco and in the Diocese of Fort Worth.

Irish Province (1909): Homestead, Sandyford Rd., Dundrum, Dublin 16, Ireland, Rev. Eamonn Monson, S.C.A., Prov.

Queen of the Apostles Province (1909): Via Giuseppe Ferrari, 1-Rome, Italy, Very Rev. Gaetano Ianni, S.A.C., Prov.

U.S. Foundation: *Our Lady of Mt. Carmel Shrine and Church,* 448 E. 116th, New York, NY 10029. Tel: 212-534-0681.
Fathers: 7
Parishes 3.
Represented in the Archdiocese of New York and in the Dioceses of Albany and Pensacola-Tallahassee.

Infant Jesus Delegature of Christ The King Province: *Mission House and Infant Jesus Shrine,* 3452 Niagara Falls Blvd., North Tonawanda, NY 14120-0563. Rev. John Posiewala, S.A.C., Supr. & Prov. Delegate.
Priests: 11
Represented in the Dioceses of Brooklyn and Buffalo.

[1000] (C.P.)—CONGREGATION OF THE PASSION

(Congregatio Passionis Jesu Christi)

Founded in Italy in 1720 by St. Paul of the Cross. First foundation in United States in 1852.

General Motherhouse: *SS. Giovanni e Paolo Monastery,* Rome 00184, Italy, Most Rev. Ottaviano D'Egidio, C.P., Supr. Gen.
Very Rev. Robert Joerger, C.P., Prov; Very Rev. Robin Ryan, C.P., 1st Consultor; Rev. Richard Burke, C.P., 2nd Consultor; Very Rev. James O'Shea, C.P., 3rd Consultor; Rev. Paul Zilonka, C.P., 4th Consultor.
Legal Title: St. Paul's Benevolent, Educational and Missionary Institute of West Hoboken, New Jersey; Passionist Missions, Inc.; Passionist Missionaries, Inc.
Fathers: 119; Brothers: 22
Properties owned, sponsored or staffed: Parishes 5; Community Houses 19; House of Study 1.
Represented in the Archdioceses of Atlanta, Baltimore, Hartford, Newark and New York and in the Dioceses of Altoona-Johnstown, Brooklyn, Metuchen, Palm Beach, Pittsburgh, Raleigh, Scranton and Springfield in Massachusetts. Also in Canada.

Western Province, Holy Cross Province: *Passionist Provincial Office,* 5700 N. Harlem Ave., Chicago, IL 60631. Tel: 773-631-6336. Very Rev. Donald Webber, C.P., Prov. Consultors: Rev. Joseph Moons, C.P., Asst. Prov. Consultor; Rev. John Schork, C.P., Prov. Consultor; Rev. John Conley, C.P., Consultor; Rev. Richard Burke, C.P., Consultor.
Legal Title: Congregation of the Passion, Holy Cross Province.
Fathers: 55; Brothers: 7; Deacons: 1
Properties owned or sponsored: Passionist Provincial Office; Stauros, U.S.A.; Immaculate Conception Community; St. Vincent Strambi Passionist Community, Chicago, IL; Immaculate Conception Parish; Chicago, IL.
Represented in the Archdioceses of Chicago, Detroit, Galveston-Houston, Los Angeles, Louisville and San Antonio and in the Dioceses of Birmingham and Sacramento.

[1010] (O.S.P.P.E.)—PAULINE FATHERS

(Ordo Sancti Pauli Primi Eremitae)

Founded in Hungary in the 13th Century. First foundation in the United States in 1953.

General Motherhouse: *Ojcowie Paulini - Jasna Gora,* ul. Kordeckiego 2 42-225, Czestochowa, Poland, Rev. Izdydor Matuszewski, O.S.P.P.E., Gen. Supr.

American Provincial Motherhouse (1984): *Shrine of Our Lady of Czestochowa, Pauline Fathers Monastery,* Beacon Hill, P.O. Box 2049, 654 Ferry Rd., Doylestown, PA 18901. Tel: 215-345-0600; Fax: 215-348-2148; Email: info@czestochowa.us; Web: www.czestochowa.us. Rev. Mikolaj Socha, O.S.P.P.E., Prov; Rev. Jerzy Maj, O.S.P.P.E., Prior; Rev. Jan Kolmaga, O.S.P.P.E., Shrine Dir.
Priests in U.S: 27; Brothers: 5
Represented in the Archdioceses of Chicago, New York and Philadelphia and in the Dioceses of Buffalo, Greensburg, Orlando and Norwich.

[1020] (S.S.P.)—PAULINE FATHERS AND BROTHERS

(Society of St. Paul for the Apostolate of Communications)

Corporate Name: Pious Society of St. Paul

General Motherhouse: Via Alessandro Severo, 58 00145, Rome, Italy, Very Rev. Silvio Sassi, S.S.P., Supr.

Gen; Very Rev. Celso Godilano, S.S.P., Vicar Gen.

United States Province (1932): *Pious Society of St. Paul*, 2187 Victory Blvd., Staten Island, NY 10314. Tel: 718-761-0047. Rev. Ernesto Tigreros, S.S.P., Prov. Supr; Rev. Edmund C. Lane, S.S.P., Vicar Prov; Rev. Joseph Javillo, S.S.P., Prov. Bursar; Bro. Richard Brunner, S.S.P., Vocation Dir; Bro. Dismas Beique, S.S.P., Prov. Councillor; Bro. Dominic Calabro, S.S.P., Prov. Councillor; Bro. Edward Donaher, S.S.P., Prov. Councillor.
Legal Title: Pious Society of St. Paul, Inc.
Priests: 13; Brothers: 20
Represented in the Archdioceses of Detroit and New York and in the Diocese of Youngstown.

Los Angeles Province: 112 S. Herbert Ave., Los Angeles, CA 90063. Tel: 323-269-5010; Fax: 323-268-4583. Rev. Marco Antonio Vences, S.S.P., Supr; Rev. Francisco M. Rosas Zevada, S.S.P; Rev. Valeriano Giachino, S.S.P; Rev. Tomas Martinez, S.S.P.
Priests: 5

Miami Province: *Society of St. Paul*, 8455 SW 2nd St., Miami, FL 33144. Tel: 305-480-5377; Web: www.sanpablomia.com. Rev. Jose Refugio Lopez, S.S.P., Supr; Rev. Arnulfo Gomez, S.S.P., Mgr; Rev. Antonio F. Paredes, S.S.P., Admin.
Priests: 3

[1030] (C.S.P.)—PAULIST FATHERS
(Societas Missionaria a S. Paulo Apostolo)

Paulist Fathers Generalate (1858): 86-11 Midland Pkwy., Jamaica, NY 11432. Tel: 718-291-5995. Very Rev. Michael B. McGarry, C.S.P., Pres.
Legal Title: Missionary Society of St. Paul the Apostle in the State of New York.
Fathers: 131; Students in Major Seminary: 8; Novices: 6
Properties owned or sponsored: Newman Campus Chaplaincies; Information Centers; Paulist Press; Paulist Radio-TV-Film Communications Svcs.; House of Study; Novitiate; Paulist Evangelization Ministries.
Represented in the Archdioceses of Boston, Chicago, Los Angeles, Newark, New York, Portland in Oregon, St. Paul-Minneapolis, San Francisco and Washington and in the Dioceses of Austin, Brooklyn, Columbus, Grand Rapids, Knoxville, Memphis and Oakland

[1040] (SCH.P.)—PIARIST FATHERS
(Ordo Clericorum Regularum Pauperum Matris Dei Scholarum Piarum)

General Motherhouse: *San Pantaleo*, Piazza De Massimi, 00186, 4, Rome, Italy, Very Rev. Pedro Aguado, Sch.P., Supr. Gen.

USA Province (1975): *Piarist Fathers-USA Province*, 1339 Monroe St., N.E., Washington, DC 20017-2510. Tel: 305-279-2333; Fax: 305-279-0925; Email: provinceusa@yahoo.com. Very Rev. Fernando Negro, Sch.P., Prov. Supr.
Priests: 18; Professed Seminarians: 6; Novices: 3; Pre-Novices: 7
Legal Titles and Holdings: Piarist Fathers-USA Province, Inc.; Piarist Fathers, Inc.; Order of the Pious Schools, Inc.; Piarist Fathers House of Studies, Washington, DC; Piarist Fathers, Queen of Pious Schools, Inc., Washington, D.C.; The Piarist School, Martin, KY; Piarist Fathers Residence, Martin, KY; Devon Preparatory School, Devon, PA.
Represented in the Archdioceses of Miami, Philadelphia and Washington and in the Diocese of Lexington.

New York-Puerto Rico Vice Province: 1900 Road 14, Coto Laurel, PR 00780-2147. Tel: 787-848-1592; Fax: 787-841-5173. Very Rev. Fernando Negro, Sch.P., Prov. Supr.
Bishops: 1; Priests: 16; Juniors: 8; Pre-Novices: 2
Houses 4; House of Formation 2; Parishes 3; High Schools 2; Schools 4.
Represented in the Archdioceses of New York and San Juan and in the Diocese of Ponce. Also Calasanzian Fathers and Padres Escolapios de P.R.

California's Vice Province Piarist Fathers: *Piarist Fathers*, 3940 Perry St., Los Angeles, CA 90063-1174. Tel: 323-708-5864; Fax: 323-266-4907. Rev. Miguel Mascorro, Sch.P., Vice Prov.
Priests: 19; Pre-Novices: 6; Seminarians: 4
Properties owned, staffed or sponsored: Parishes 6; Grammar Schools 2; House of Formation 2.
Represented in the Archdiocese of Los Angeles.

[1050] (P.I.M.E.)—PONTIFICAL INSTITUTE FOR FOREIGN MISSIONS, INC.

General Motherhouse: Via F. D. Guerrazzi 11, 00152, Rome, Italy, Very Rev. Gian Battista Zanchi, P.I.M.E., Supr. Gen.

North American Region: 17330 Quincy Ave., Detroit, MI 48221. Tel: 313-342-4066; Fax: 313-342-6816. Very Rev. Ken Mazur, P.I.M.E., Reg. Supr.
Fathers: 21
Legal Titles and Holdings: PIME Missionaries - PIME Mission Center; PIME College Community, Detroit, MI; PIME Missionaries, Wayne, NJ & Tequesta, FL.
Formation Communities 1; Mission Houses 4.
Represented in the Archdioceses of Detroit and New York and in the Dioceses of Lansing, Paterson, Columbus and Palm Beach.

[1060] (C.PP.S.)—SOCIETY OF THE PRECIOUS BLOOD
(Congregatio Missionariorum Pretiosissimi Sanguinis Domini Nostri Jesu Christi)

General Motherhouse: Viale di Porta Ardeatina 66, 1-00154 Rome, Italy, Very Rev. Francesco Bartoloni, C.PP.S., Moderator.

Cincinnati Province: 431 E. Second St., Dayton, OH 45402. Tel: 937-228-9263. Very Rev. Larry Hemmelgarn, C.PP.S, Prov. Dir. Provincial Council: Rev. Benjamin Berinti, C.PP.S; Rev. Thomas Hemm, C.PP.S; Bro. Robert Reuter, C.PP.S; Rev. Anthony T. Fortman, C.PP.S; Rev. Kenneth Schnipke, C.PP.S; Rev. Jeffrey Kirch, C.PP.S., Prov. Sec.
Fathers: 138; Brothers: 28; Students in Major Seminaries: 6; Students in Preparatory Seminary: 14
Ministries in Parishes; Missions; Chaplaincies; Shrine; Education; Retreat Preaching; Community Houses; Houses of Study; Military Chaplains; Precious Blood Ministry of Reconciliation.
Represented in the Archdioceses of Chicago, Cincinnati, Los Angeles and Military Services, USA and in the Dioceses of Cleveland, Columbus, Fort Wayne-South Bend, Gary, Harrisburg, Lafayette in Indiana, Oakland, Orange, Orlando and Toledo.

Kansas City Province: *Precious Blood Society Provincial Office*, P.O. Box 339, Liberty, MO 64069-0339. Tel: 816-781-4344; Fax: 816-781-3639. Rev. Joseph Nassal, C.PP.S., Prov. Dir; Rev. Richard Bayuk, C.PP.S., Vice Prov. & Prov. Treas; Rev. Ronald Will, C.PP.S., 2nd Consultor & Prov. Sec; Rev. James G. Betzen, C.PP.S., 3rd Consultor; Rev. Thomas Welk, C.PP.S., 4th Consultor.
Bishops: 1; Fathers: 48; Brothers: 3
Ministries in Parishes; Missions; Houses of Study; Community House; Chaplaincies.
Represented in the Archdioceses of Chicago, Cincinnati, Denver, Dubuque, Kansas City in Kansas and Los Angeles and in the Dioceses of Davenport, Jefferson City, Joliet in Illinois, Kansas City-St. Joseph, Oakland, San Angelo and Wichita.

Atlantic Province: *Society of the Precious Blood, Atlantic Province*, 1261 Highland Ave., Rochester, NY 14620. Tel: 585-461-0318.

Provincial House: 13313 Niagara Pkwy., L2E 6S6, Niagara Falls, Canada, Tel: 905-382-1118. Very Rev. Jeffrey Finley, C.PP.S., Provincial Dir; Rev. James Reposkey, C.PP.S., Vice Provincial; Rev. Peter Nobili, C.PP.S., Treas; Rev. Ronald Wiecek, C.PP.S., Sec; Rev. John A. Colacino, C.PP.S., Council Member; Rev. Brendan Doherty, C.PP.S., Council Member.
Priests in the U.S: 4
Represented in the Archdioceses of Boston and Miami and in the Dioceses of Albany and Rochester. Also in Canada.

[1065] (F.S.S.P.)—PRIESTLY FRATERNITY OF ST. PETER

Founded in Switzerland in 1988. First foundation in United States in 1991.

General Motherhouse: *Fraternitas Sacerdotalis Sancti Petri*, Maison St. Pierre Canisius, Chemin du Schoenberg 8, CH-1700 Fribourg, Switzerland, Tel: 41-26-488-0037; Fax: 41-26-488-0038. Rev. John Berg, F.S.S.P., Supr. Gen.

International Seminary: *Priesterseminar Sankt Petrus*, Kirchstrasse 16, D-88145, Opfenbach-Wigratzbad, Germany, Tel: 49-8385 9221 0; Fax: 49-8385 9221 33. Rev. Franz Karl Banauch, F.S.S.P., Rector.

U.S. Headquarters: *Priestly Fraternity of St. Peter-North American District Headquarters*, 119 Griffin Rd., Elmhurst Twp., PA 18444. Tel: 570-842-4000; Fax: 570-842-4001. Rev. Eric Flood, F.S.S.P., Dist. Supr; Rev. Gregory Pendergraft, F.S.S.P., Dir.-Devel; Rev. Carl N. Gismondi, F.S.S.P., Dist. Bursar.

House of Formation: *Our Lady of Guadalupe Seminary*, 7880 W. Denton Rd., P.O. Box 147, Denton, NE 68339. Tel: 402-797-7700; Fax: 402-797-7705. Very Rev. Josef Bisig, F.S.S.P., Rector; Rev. James B. Buckley, F.S.S.P; Rev. Robert Ferguson, F.S.S.P; Rev. Robert Fromageot, F.S.S.P; Rev. Calvin R. Goodwin, F.S.S.P; Rev. Charles Ryan, F.S.S.P; Rev. Charles Van Vliet, F.S.S.P; Rev. Joseph Lee, F.S.S.P.
Priests: 6; Seminarians: 77
Properties owned or sponsored: Houses 34; High Schools 1.
Represented in the Archdioceses of Atlanta, Cincinnati, Denver, Indianapolis, Kansas City, Oklahoma City, Omaha and Seattle and in the Dioceses of Boise, Charleston, Colorado Springs, Corpus Christi, Dallas, Fort Worth, Fresno, Harrisburg, Joliet, Lafayette in Indiana, Lexington, Lincoln, Little Rock, Orlando, Paterson, Phoenix, Rapid City, Richmond, Sacramento, San Diego, Scranton, Springfield (IL), Tulsa, Tyler, Venice and Youngstown. Also Canada.

[1070] (C.SS.R.)—REDEMPTORIST FATHERS
(Congregatio Sanctissimi Redemptoris-Redemptorist)

Generalate: *Sant' Alfonso*, Via Merulana 31. C.P. 2458 I-00100, Rome, Italy, Rev. Michael Brehl, C.Ss.R., Supr. Gen; Rev. Enrique Lopez, C.Ss.R., Vicar Gen; Rev. John C. Vargas, C.Ss.R., Proc. Gen.

Province of Baltimore (1850): *Provincial Residence*, 7509 Shore Rd., Brooklyn, NY 11209-2807. Tel: 718-833-1900; Fax: 718-630-5666. Very Rev. Kevin J. Moley, C.Ss.R., Prov. Supr; Rev. Joseph F. Jones, C.Ss.R., Prov. Vicar; Rev. Thomas J. Travers, C.Ss.R; Rev. Carl W. Hoegerl, C.Ss.R., Prov. Archivist; Rev. Robert Pagliari, C.Ss.R., Sec; Rev. Lawrence E. Lover, C.Ss.R., Canonical Consultor; Rev. Francis Gargani, C.Ss.R., Rector.
Bishops: 3; Priests: 186; Brothers: 19; Novices: 2; Postulants: 2; Students in Vows: 4
Properties owned, staffed or sponsored: Parishes 18; Residences 3; Retreat Houses 3; Community Houses 24.
Represented in the Archdioceses of Baltimore, Boston, New York, Philadelphia and Washington and in the Dioceses of Albany, Brooklyn, Harrisburg, Rochester, Rockville Centre, Springfield, Toledo, Trenton and Wilmington. Also in the West Indies.

Redemptorist Office Mission Advancement: 107 Duke of Gloucester St., Annapolis, MD 21401-2526. Tel: 410-288-8755; Tel: 877-876-7662.

Richmond Vice Province (1942): *Vice Provincial Hqtrs.*, 313 Hillman St., P.O. Box 1529, New Smyrna Beach, FL 32170. Tel: 386-427-3094. Very Rev. Jerome L. Chavarria, C.Ss.R., Vice Prov; Rev. Peter E. Sousa, C.Ss.R., Vicar. Consultors: Deacon Darrell Cevasco, C.Ss.R., Vocation Dir; Rev. Glenn D. Parker, C.Ss.R., Cons.
Legal Title: Congregation of the Most Holy Redeemer; Redemptorist Fathers of Florida, Inc; Redemptorists Fathers of South Carolina; Redemptorists Fathers of North Carolina, Inc; Redemptorists Fathers of Virginia, Incorporated; Redemptorists Fathers of Georgia, Incorporated.
Priests: 26; Brothers: 3; Deacons: 1
Properties owned, staffed or sponsored: Parishes 6; Retreat Houses 1; Retirement Home 1; Residences 1; Missions 3.
Represented in the Dioceses of Charleston, Charlotte, Orlando and Richmond.

The Redemptorists Denver Province (1996): *The Redemptorist Provincial Offices*, 1230 S. Parker Rd., Denver, CO 80231-7556. Tel: 303-370-0035; Tel: 303-565-5450; Tel: 303-565-5409; Fax: 303-370-0036; Web: www.redemptoristsdenver.org. Rev. Harry Grile, C.Ss.R., Prov. Supr; Rev. Robert Halter, C.Ss.R., Vicar; Rev. John K. Schmidt, C.Ss.R., Prov. Consultor; Rev. Allan Weinert, C.Ss.R., Treas.
Legal Titles: The Redemptorists/Denver Province; The Redemptorists of Denver, Colorado; The Redemptorists of Greeley, Colorado, Inc., Denver, CO; Redemptorist Fathers (Boise, ID), Denver, CO; Redemptorists Society of Oregon (Portland, OR), Denver, CO; The Society of the Redemptorists of the City Grand Rapids, Michigan, Denver, CO; The Redemptorists of Nebraska (Omaha, NE), Denver, CO; Redemptorists of Hamtramck, Denver, CO; The Redemptorist Fathers of Hennepin County (St.Paul-Minneapolis, MN), Denver, CO; Redemptorist Fathers (St. Louis, MO), Denver, CO; The Redemptorist Fathers of Kansas City, Missouri, The Redemptorists of Blessed Sacrament - The Redemptorist Fathers of Chicago (Chicago, IL), Denver, CO; Redemptorist Society of Alaska (Anchorage, AK), Denver, CO; The Redemptorist Society of Arizona (Tucson, AZ), Denver, CO; The Redemptorists Society of Washington, Palisades Retreat Association, A School of Christian Living (Seattle, WA), Denver, CO; The Redemptorist Community of Wichita, Kansas, Inc., Society of the Redemptorist Fathers of Wichita, Kansas, Denver, CO.; Redemptorist Fathers of St. Alphonsus Parish (Chicago, IL), Denver, CO.; Redemptorist Fathers of Iowa; Redemptorists of Berkeley; Redemptorists of Oakland; Redemptorists of Whittier; The Redemptorists (Glenview, IL) Denver, CO.; Redemptorist Fathers, d/b/a Liguori Publications; Holy Redeemer Center; Redemptorist Society of California; Redemptorist Theology Residence; Redemptorist Hispanic Ministry, Inc.; Liguori Mission House/Redemptorists: St. Clement Health Care Center; St. John Neumann House; Our Mother of Perpetual Help Retreat House of Oconomowoc, Wisc. Inc., d/b/a/ Redemptorist Retreat Center; Redemptorist Social Services Center, Inc.; Redemptorists of Mattese; Redemptorist Fathers of Bellaire, Texas; The Redemptorists/San Antonio; The Society of Redemptorists; Redemptorist Vice-Provincialate of New Orleans; Redemptorist Fathers of Baton Rouge, Inc.; The Redemptorists of the South Endowment Fund, Inc.; The Redemptorist Education and Formation Foundation, Inc.; Redemptorists of Tennessee; Redemptorist Vietnamese Ministry; Redemptorists of Mississippi
Properties owned, sponsored or staffed: Parishes 14; Retreat Houses 3; Residences 7; Community Houses 15.
Represented in the Archdioceses of Chicago, Denver, Detroit, Los Angeles, Milwaukee, New Orleans, New York, San Antonio, St. Louis, St. Paul-Minneapolis and Seattle and in the Dioceses of Baton Rouge, Biloxi, Grand Rapids, Kansas City-St. Joseph Oakland, Tucson and Wichita. Also in Foreign Missions.

Bangkok Vice-Province: *Redemptorist*, St. John Neumann, 6 Ramkamkaeng 184, Minburi, Bangkok, 10510, Thailand, Very Rev. Joseph Apisit Kritsaralam, C.Ss.R., Vice Prov.

Manaus Vice-Province: *Redentoristas*, Caixa Postal 217, 69011-970 Manaus-AM, Amazonas South America, Brazil, Very Rev. Zenildo Luiz Pereira DaSilva, C.Ss.R., Vice Prov.

Vice Province of Nigeria: *Sts. Michael, Raphael & Gabriel Church*, P.O. Box 541, Satellite Town, Nigeria, Very Rev. Callistus Nwachukwu, Vice Prov.

[1080] (C.R.)—CONGREGATION OF THE RESURRECTION

(Congregatio a Resurrectione Domini Nostri Jesu Christi)

Generalate: Via San Sebastianello 11 00187, Rome, Italy,

U.S. of America Province: 3601 N. California Ave., Chicago, IL 60618-4602. Tel: 773-463-7506. Very Rev. Eugene Szarek, C.R., Prov. Supr; Rev. Timothy F. Keppel, C.R., Asst. Prov. Supr. Councilors: Rev. Gary Hogan, C.R; Rev. Paul Sims, C.R; Rev. Tadeusz Sosnowski, C.R.

Fathers: 54; Brothers: 3

Ministries in Parishes; Missions; High School; Chaplaincies.

Represented in the Archdioceses of Chicago, Mobile and St. Louis and in the Dioceses of Joliet, Kalamazoo, Pensacola-Tallahassee, Rockford and San Bernardino. Also in Bermuda.

Ontario Kentucky Province U.S. Address: *St. Cecila - Villa Pacis House*, 515 D S. Shelby St., Louisville, KY 40202. Tel: 502-589-6113; Fax: 502-589-6116. Rev. Raymond Hofmann, C.R; Rev. John Lesousky, C.R; Rev. John Miles, C.R; Rev. Charles Schoenbaechler, C.R; Deacon Brian Karley, C.R., Supr.

Members of Province in U.S.A: 12

Properties owned, sponsored or staffed: Community Houses 3; University 1.

Represented in the Archdiocese of Louisville.

4252 W. Pine Blvd., Saint Louis, MO 63108. Tel: 314-652-8814. Rev. Gary Hogan, C.R., Rector.

[1090] (R.C.J.)—ROGATIONIST FATHERS

(Congregatio Rogationis-a-Corde-Jesu)

Generalate: via Tuscolana 167 00182, Rome, Italy, Very Rev. Angelo Mezzari, R.C.J., Supr. Gen.

U.S.A. Delegation: 2688 S. Newmark Ave., P.O. Box 37, Sanger, CA 93657. Tel: 559-875-5808; Tel: 559-875-2025; Fax: 559-875-1281. Rev. Vito Di Marzio, R.C.J., Delegation Supr.

U.S. Foundations: *St. Mary's Church*, 828 O St., P.O. Box 335, Sanger, CA 93657. Tel: 559-875-2025. Rev. Salvatore Ciranni, R.C.J; Rev. Philip Puntrello, R.C.J; Rev. Jupiter Quinto, R.C.J; Rev. Rene Panlasigui, R.C.J.

Legal Title: Congregation of Rogationists, Inc.

Priests: 7

Ministries in Parishes; Vocation Center; Formation House; Social Service Center.

Represented in the Archdiocese of Los Angeles and in the Diocese of Fresno.

U.S. Foundations: *St. Elisabeth Church*, 6638 Tobias Ave., Van Nuys, CA 91405. Tel: 818-779-1756. Rev. Vito Di Marzio, R.C.J; Rev. John Bruno, R.C.J; Rev. Rodolfo D'Agostino, R.C.J.

[1100] (S.C.)—BROTHERS OF THE SACRED HEART

(Societas Fratrum Sacris Cordis)

Founded in Lyons, France in 1821. First foundation in the United States in Mobile in 1847.

Generalate: Piazza Sacro Cuore, No. 3, 00151, Rome, Italy, Bro. Jose Ignacio Carmonia, S.C., Supr. Gen.

New Orleans Province (1847): *Provincial Office*, 4600 Elysian Fields Ave., New Orleans, LA 70122. Tel: 504-301-4758; Fax: 504-301-4843. Bro. Ronald Talbot, S.C., Prov. Provincial Councilors: Bro. Ronald Hingle, S.C; Bro. Francis David, S.C; Bro. Ivy LeBlanc, S.C., Treas; Bro. Bernard Couvillion, S.C.

Legal Title: Brothers of the Sacred Heart, (a Louisiana Corporation); Brothers of the Sacred Heart Foundation of the New Orleans Province, Inc.

Perpetual Professed: 48; Ordained Brothers: 4; Temporary Professed: 1

Incorporated Schools: Brother Martin High School, New Orleans, LA; Catholic High School, Baton Rouge, LA; Saint Stanislaus College, Bay St. Louis, MS.

Represented in the Archdioceses of Mobile and New Orleans and in the Dioceses of Baton Rouge, Biloxi, Gallup and Houma-Thibodaux.

New England Province (1945): *Provincial House - Brothers of the Sacred Heart*, 685 Steere Farm Rd., Pascoag, RI 02859-4601. Tel: 401-568-3361; Fax: 401-568-1450. Bro. Robert Croteau, S.C., Prov. Supr. Councilors: Bro. Mark E. Hilton, S.C; Bro. Raymond Hetu, S.C; Bro. Clifford King, S.C; Bro. Willie A. Morin, S.C., Prov. Sec; Bro. Robert T. Gagne, S.C., Accts. Mgr; Bro. Daniel St. Jacques, S.C.

Brothers: 61

Properties owned: Brothers of the Sacred Heart Provincial House, Pascoag, RI; Mt. St. Charles Academy, Woonsocket, RI; Bishop Guertin High School, Nashua, NH; St. John Residence, Woonsocket, RI; Brothers of the Sacred Heart Residence Nashua, NH

Represented in the Archdiocese of Hartford and in the Dioceses of Manchester and Providence. Also in England.

Province of New York (1960): *Brothers of the Sacred Heart Provincial House*, 141-11 123 Ave., South Ozone Park, NY 11436-1426. Tel: 718-322-3309; Fax: 718-529-6004. Bro. Joseph Rocco, S.C., Prov.

Final Professed Brothers: 46

Ministries in the field of Education; Spiritual Centers; Kenya Missions; Philippines Delegation.

Properties owned: Msgr. McClancy High School, East Elmhurst, NY; St. Joseph High School, Metuchen, NJ.

Represented in the Dioceses of Brooklyn, Metuchen, Syracuse and Trenton. Also in Kenya and the Philippines.

[1110] (M.S.C.)—MISSIONARIES OF THE SACRED HEART

(Societas Missionarii Sacratissimi Cordis Jesu)

General Motherhouse: Via Asmara 11 00199, Rome, Italy, Very Rev. Mark McDonald, M.S.C., Supr. Gen.

United States Province (1939): 305 S. Lake St., P.O. Box 270, Aurora, IL 60507. Tel: 630-892-8400; Tel: 630-892-2371; Fax: 630-892-3071. Very Rev. Raymond Diesbourg, M.S.C., Prov. Supr. Consultors: Rev. David Foxen, M.S.C., Vice Prov; Bro. James Miller, M.S.C; Rev. Pierre Aubin, M.S.C; Rev. Earl Henley, M.S.C; Rev. Michael Camilli, M.S.C; Very Rev. Luis Alfonso Segura, M.S.C.

Legal Title: Society of the Missionaries of the Sacred Heart.

Fathers: 47; Brothers: 15; Professed Students: 8

Properties owned, staffed or sponsored: Residential Houses 3; Parishes 14; Chaplaincies 1.

Represented in the Archdioceses of Chicago and Philadelphia and in the Dioceses of Allentown, Ogdensburg, Orange in California, Pensacola-Tallahassee, Rockford and San Bernardino. Also in Colombia, Dominican Republic and Italy.

U.S. Section of the Irish Province for California and Southern States: *Sectional Hqtrs*, 123 W. Laurel, San Antonio, TX 78212-4667. Tel: 210-226-5514; Fax: 210-226-5725. Sectional Leadership Team Rev. William Collins, M.S.C., Supr; Rev. Kevin Shanahan, M.S.C; Rev. Michael Fitzgibbon, M.S.C.

Priests: 15

Represented in the Archdiocese of San Antonio and in the Dioceses of Austin and Charleston.

[1120] (M.SS.CC.)—MISSIONARIES OF THE SACRED HEARTS OF JESUS AND MARY

(Missionarii a Sacris Cordibus Jesus et Mariae)

Founded in Italy in 1833.

General Motherhouse: Via dei Falegnami 23, Rome, Italy, Very Rev. Salvatore Izzo, M.SS.CC., Supr. Gen.

American Headquarters: 2249 Shore Rd., Linwood, NJ 08221. Tel: 609-927-5600; Fax: 609-927-5262. Rev. Peter DiTomasso, M.SS.CC., Mission Procurator; Rev. Malcolm MacLeod, M.SS.CC; Rev. John Perdue, M.SS.CC., Vice-Rector; Rev. Robert McDade, M.SS.CC; Rev. Augustine Peter Arul, M.SS.CC; Rev. Frederick Clement, M.SS.CC; Bro. David Graber, M.SS.CC.

Legal Title: Missionaries of the Sacred Heart of Jesus and Mary.

Priests: 9; Brothers: 2

Represented in the Dioceses of Camden and Harrisburg.

[1130] (S.C.J.)—CONGREGATION OF THE PRIESTS OF THE SACRED HEART

(Priests of the Sacred Heart)

(Congregatio Sacerdotum a Corde Jesu)

General Motherhouse: *Curia Generalizia, S.C.J.*, Via Casale S. Pio v, no. 20 00165, Rome, Italy, Very Rev. Jose Ornelas Carvalho, S.C.J., Supr. Gen.

United States Province (1933): *Provincialate Offices*, P.O. Box 289, Hales Corners, WI 53130-0289. Tel: 414-425-6910. Very Rev. Thomas P. Cassidy, S.C.J., Prov. Supr.

Bishops: 1; Priests: 73; Clerics: 2; Brothers: 16; Deacons: 1

Represented in the Archdioceses of Chicago, Galveston-Houston, Milwaukee and San Antonio and in the Dioceses of Brownsville, Green Bay, Jackson, Rapid City, St. Petersburg and Sioux Falls.

[1140] (SS.CC.)—CONGREGATION OF THE SACRED HEARTS OF JESUS AND MARY

(Congregatio Sacrorum Cordium)

General Motherhouse: *Casa Generalizia-Padri Dei Sacri Cuori-Via*, Rivarone 85 00166, Rome, Italy, Very Rev. Javier Alvarez-Ossorio, SS.CC., Supr. Gen.

Legal Title: Congregation of the Sacred Hearts of Jesus and Mary.

Eastern Province (1946): *Provincial House*, 77 Adams St., Box 111, Fairhaven, MA 02719-0111. Tel: 508-993-2442; Fax: 508-996-5499. Rev. William F. Petrie, SS.CC., Prov; Rev. Thomas McElroy, SS.CC., Vicar Prov. Councilors: Bro. Paul R. Alves, SS.CC; Rev. Fintan Sheeran, SS.CC; Rev. Robert Charlton, SS.CC.

Priests: 42; Brothers: 13; Novices: 5

Properties owned or staffed: Parishes 11; Community Houses 5; House of Studies 1; Houses of Formation 2.

Represented in the Archdiocese of Washington and in the Dioceses of Brownsville, Fall River and Las Cruces. Also in Bahamas, India, and Mexico.

Western United States Province (1970): *Congregation of the Sacred Hearts of Jesus and Mary*, 2150 Damien Ave., La Verne, CA 91750. Tel: 909-593-5441; Fax: 909-593-3971. Very Rev. Paedar Cronin, SS.CC., Prov. Supr.

Priests: 22

Ministries in the field of Religious and Academic Education; Parishes; Chaplaincies.

Represented in the Archdiocese of Los Angeles and in the Dioceses of Orange and San Bernardino.

Hawaii Province: *Sacred Hearts Center*, Box 1365, Kaneohe, Oahu, HI 96744. Tel: 808-247-5035; Fax: 808-235-8849. Very Rev. Christopher Keahi, SS.CC., Prov.

Fathers: 18; Brothers: 6

Properties owned, staffed or sponsored: Churches 6; Mission 1; Chaplaincies 1.

[1144] (L.B.S.F.)—LITTLE BROTHERS OF SAINT FRANCIS

Founded in the United States in 1970 by Bro. James Curran, L.B.S.F.

Regional Fraternity and Novitiate (1970): 785-789 Parker St., Roxbury, MA 02120. Tel: 617-442-2556; Web: www.littlebrothersofstfrancis.org.

Legal Title: Little Brothers of Saint Francis - Franciscan Fraternity of Peace and Love, Inc.

Professed Brothers: 5

Represented in the Archdiocese of Boston.

[1150] (C.S.J.)—CONGREGATION OF ST. JOSEPH

(Congregatio Sancti Joseph)

Founded in Turin, Italy in 1873. First foundation in United States in 1951.

General Motherhouse: Via Belvedere Montello 77 00166, Rome, Italy, Rev. Mario Aldegani, C.S.J., Supr. Gen.

U.S. and Mexico Vice Province: *St. Leonard House*, 4076 Case Rd., Avon, OH 44011. Tel: 440-934-6270. Rev. Giuseppe Rainone, C.S.J., Prov. Supr.

Priests: 23; Brothers: 1; Scholastics: 6; Novices: 4

Properties owned, staffed or sponsored: Parishes 5; High Schools 1; Youth Retreat Center.

Properties owned: St. Leonard House, Avon, OH.

Represented in the Archdiocese of Los Angeles and in the Diocese of Cleveland. Also in Mexico.

[1160] (F.S.P.)—BROTHERS OF ST. PATRICK

(Patrician Brothers)

Founded in Ireland 1808 by Bishop Daniel Delaney.

U.S. Foundation (1948): *St. Patrick's Novitiate*, 7820 Bolsa Ave., Midway City, CA 92655. Tel: 714-897-8181; Fax: 714-898-9020. Bro. Philip Shepler, F.S.P., Pres.

Brothers: 5

Represented in the Archdiocese of Los Angeles and Diocese of Orange.

[1170] (S.P.S.)—ST. PATRICK'S MISSIONARY SOCIETY

(St. Patrick Fathers)

Founded March 17, 1932 with the approval of Pope Pius XI. A Pontifical Society of secular priests devoted entirely to the missionary needs of the Church.

International Headquarters: St. Patrick's, Kiltegan, Wicklow, Ireland, Very Rev. Seamus O'Neill, S.P.S., Supr. Gen; Rev. David Walsh, S.P.S., Vicar Gen; Rev. Brendan Cooney, S.P.S., Proc. Gen.-Rome; Rev. Karl Langsdorf, S.P.S., Supr. for North America.

Total number of Priests: 308; Priests in the U.S: 10

U.S. Foundations (1965): *St. Patrick's (1967)*, 19536 Eric Dr., Saratoga, CA 95070. Tel: 408-253-3135; Fax: 408-253-5433. Rev. Michael Moore, S.P.S., Supr; Rev. Michael E. Morris, S.P.S., Supr St. Patrick's (1965): 70 Edgewater Rd., Box 3080, Cliffside Park, NJ 07010.Rev. Karl Langsdorf, S.P.S., Supr., North America St. Patrick's (1968): 1347 W. Granville Ave., Chicago, IL 60660

Legal Title: St. Patrick's Missionary Society, Camden, NJ.

Represented in the Archdioceses of Chicago and Newark and in the Dioceses of Paterson, San Bernardino and San Jose.

[1180] (C.S.P.X.)—BROTHERS OF SAINT PIUS X

Founded in the United States in 1952.

Motherhouse: P.O. Box 284, Spring Valley, WI 54767. Tel: 715-778-4999. Bro. Charles Bisenius, Dir.

Ministries in the field of Religious and Academic Education; Health Care; Community services and Administration.

Represented in the Diocese of La Crosse.

[1190] (S.D.B.)—SALESIANS OF DON BOSCO

(Societas Sancti Francisci Salesii)

Generalate: *Salesian Don Bosco*, via Della Pisana, 1111, C.P.18333, 00163 Roma-Bravetta, Italy, Very Rev. Pascual Chavez, S.D.B., Rector Major.

Province of St. Philip the Apostle (1902): 148 Main St., New Rochelle, NY 10801. Tel: 914-636-4225. Very Rev. Thomas Dunne, S.D.B., Prov; Rev. Steven Dumais, S.D.B., Vice Prov; Bro. Thomas Dion, S.D.B., Prov. Economer & Councilor; Rev. Stephen Leake, S.D.B., Dir. Formation & Councilor; Bro. Bernard Dube, S.D.B., Councilor; Rev. Stephen Ryan, S.D.B., Dir. of Youth Ministry & Councilor.

Legal Title: Salesian Society, Province of St. Philip the Apostle, Inc.

Fathers: 138; Professed Clerics: 13; Students in Major Seminaries: 5; Coadjutor-Brothers: 35

Ministries in: Parishes; High Schools; Boys and Girls Clubs; Camps; Shrine; Retreat Center.

Represented in the Archdioceses of Boston, Chicago,

Newark, New Orleans, New York and Washington and in the Dioceses of Birmingham, Passaic and St. Petersburg.

San Francisco Province (1926): *Salesian Society - San Francisco*, 1100 Franklin St., San Francisco, CA 94109. Tel: 415-441-7144; Fax: 415-441-7155. Very Rev. Timothy Ploch, S.D.B., Prov; Rev. Thomas Prendiville, S.D.B., Vice. Prov. Councilors: Rev. Joseph Farias, S.D.B., Treas; Bro. Alphonse Vu, S.D.B; Bro. John Tom Mass, S.D.B; Rev. Gael E. Sullivan, S.D.B.
Priests: 73; Professed Brothers: 22; Seminarians: 8
Ministries in Parishes; High Schools; Retreat House; Youth Centers.
Represented in the Archdioceses of Los Angeles and San Francisco and in the Dioceses of Laredo, Monterey, Oakland, Santa Rosa and Stockton.

[1200] (S.D.S.)—SOCIETY OF THE DIVINE SAVIOR

(Salvatorian Fathers and Brothers)
(Salvatorians - Societas Divini Salvatoris)

General Motherhouse: *Curia Generalizia dei Salvatoriani*, Via Conciliazione 51, I-00193, Rome, Italy, Very Rev. Andrew Urbanski, S.D.S., Supr. Gen.

U.S.A. Province (1892): *Salvatorian Provincial Offices*, 1735 N. Hi-Mount Blvd., Milwaukee, WI 53208-1720. Tel: 414-258-1735; Fax: 414-258-1934. Very Rev. David Bergner, S.D.S., Prov; Rev. Jeffrey Wocken, S.D.S., Vicar; Rev. Scott Wallenfelsz, S.D.S., Treas. Consultors: Rev. Scott Jones, S.D.S; Bro. Sean McLaughlin, S.D.S; Rev. Robert Marsicek, S.D.S; Rev. Dennis Thiessen, S.D.S.
Fathers: 66; Brothers: 28; Clerics: 2; Total: 96
Legal Titles: Society of the Divine Savior; Society of the Divine Savior Ongoing Community Support Trust; Camp St. Charles, Inc.; Lay Salvatorians Inc.; Salvatorian Institute of Philosophy and Theology Inc.; Fund Raising and Public Relations Center; Salvatorian Center, New Holstein, WI 53061.
Properties owned, staffed or sponsored: Parishes 16; Houses of Study and Formation 2.
Represented in the Archdioceses of Milwaukee, New York, Portland in Oregon and Washington and in the Dioceses of Birmingham, Bismarck, Brooklyn, Green Bay, Harrisburg, LaCrosse, Lexington, Madison, Nashville, Oakland, Orlando, Phoenix, Sacramento, Santa Rosa, Savannah, Seattle, St. Cloud, Tucson, Venice, Wheeling-Charleston and Wilmington.

[1205] F.S.C.B.—PRIESTLY FRATERNITY OF THE MISSIONARIES OF ST. CHARLES BORROMEO

(Sacerdotalis Fraternitas Missionarium a Sancti Carolo Borromeo)

General Motherhouse: Via Boccea 761, 00166, Rome, Italy, Rev. Massimo Camisasca, F.S.C.B., Supr. Gen; Rev. Paolo Sottopietra, F.S.C.B., Gen. Vicar; Rev. Gianluca Attanasio, F.S.C.B., Gen. Sec.

North American Regional Delegation: *Priestly Fraternity of the Missionaries of St. Charles Borromeo, Inc.*, 21 Follen Rd., Lexington, MA 02421-5921. Tel: 781-864-3427; Web: www.fraternityofsaintcharles.org. Rev. Antonio Lopez, F.S.C.B., Regional Delegate; Rev. Stefano Colombo, F.S.C.B., Contact Person; Rev. Jose Medina, F.S.C.B; Rev. Luca Brancolini, F.S.C.B; Rev. Michael Carvill, F.S.C.B; Rev. Accursio Ciaccio, F.S.C.B; Rev. Gabriele Azzalin, F.S.C.B; Rev. Antonio Lopez, F.S.C.B; Rev. Roberto Amoruso, F.S.C.B; Rev. Franco Soma, F.S.C.B; Rev. Pietro Rossotti, F.S.C.B; Rev. Jose Maria Cortes, F.S.C.B; Rev. Paolo Prosperi, F.S.C.B.
Legal Title: Priestly Fraternity of the Missionaries of St. Charles Borromeo, Inc.
Priests: 12
Properties owned: House of Formation 1; Parishes staffed: 2
Represented in the Archdioceses of Boston, Denver and Washington.

[1210] (C.S.)—MISSIONARIES OF ST. CHARLES-SCALABRINIANS

(Congregatio Missionariorum A Sancto Carolo)

General Motherhouse: Via Calandrelli 42, 00153, Rome, Italy, Very Rev. Sergio Geremia, C.S., Supr. Gen.

Province of St. Charles Borromeo (188): *Scalabrinians Provincial Curia*, 209 Flagg Pl., Staten Island, NY 10304. Tel: 718-351-8808; Fax: 718-667-4598. Rev. Matthew Didone, C.S., Prov. Supr; Rev. Sergio Dall'Agnese, C.S., Treas.
Legal Title: The Pious Society of the Missionaries of St. Charles Borromeo, Inc.
Fathers: 99; Brothers: 2
Properties staffed or owned: Parishes 30; Missions 7; Homes for Aged 2; Seminaries 4; Center for Migration Studies.
Represented in the Archdioceses of Atlanta, Boston, Miami, New York and Washington and in the Dioceses of Brooklyn, Buffalo, Orlando, Palm Beach, Providence and Venice. Also in Eastern Canada, Venezuela, Colombia, the Dominican Republic and Haiti.

Province of St. John Baptist (1903): *Missionaries of St. Charles - Fathers of St. Charles*, 546 N. East Ave., Oak Park, IL 60302. Tel: 708-386-4430; Fax: 708-386-4457. Rev. Adilso Balen, C.S., Prov. Supr.
Fathers: 65; Brothers: 2
Legal Titles: The Fathers of Saint Charles; Scalabrinian Community Support Corp.; Scalabrinian Community Formation Corp.
Ministries in 20 Parishes; 1 Homes for the Aged; 3 Missions; 6 Seminaries; 6 Centers for Migrants and Refugees; 2 Diocesan office for Hispanic Ministry.
Represented in the Archdioceses of Chicago, Cincinnati, Galveston-Houston, Kansas City in Kansas and Los Angeles and in the Dioceses of Dallas, Kansas City-St. Joseph and San Jose. Also in Canada, Guatemala and Mexico.

[1220] (S.C.)—SERVANTS OF CHARITY

(Guanellians)
(Congregatio Servorum a Charitate)

General Motherhouse: Vicolo Clementi 41, Rome, Italy, Very Rev. Alfonso Crippa, S.C., Supr. Gen.

U.S. Headquarters: *Servants of Charity*, 1795 S. Sproul Rd., Springfield, PA 19064. Tel: 610-328-3406; Fax: 610-328-1019. Rev. Luigi De Giambattista, S.C., Prov., Divine Providence Province.
Legal Title: Pious Union of St. Joseph.
Priests: 10
Publication: The Voice of Providence.
Ministry for the suffering and dying: Schools for mentally handicapped boys 2; Residences for mentally handicapped adults 2; Parishes 1; House of Formation 1; Chaplaincies 1.
Represented in the Archdiocese of Philadelphia and in the Dioceses of Lansing and Providence.

[1230] (S.P.)—SERVANTS OF THE PARACLETE

Generalate: P.O. Box 539, Cedar Hill, MO 63016-0539. Tel: 636-274-1979; Fax: 636-274-1430; Web: www.theservants.org. Very Rev. David T. Fitzgerald, s.P., Servant Gen; Rev. Philip Taylor, s.P., Vicar Gen; Rev. Benedict Livingstone, Treas. Gen; Very Rev. Liam Hoare, s.P., Sec. Gen; Rev. Peter Lechner, s.P., Asst. for Apostolate.
Legal Titles: Servants of the Paraclete Generalate: A New Mexico Corporation.; Servants of the Paraclete: A New Mexico Corporation.; Servants of the Paraclete, A Missouri Corporation.; Sevants of the Paraclete Foundatiion.
Represented in the Archdioceses of St. Louis and Santa Fe.

U.S. Motherhouse (1952): *Servants of the Paraclete*, P.O. Box 10, Jemez Springs, NM 87025-0010. Tel: 505-829-3586; Fax: 505-829-3706; Email: paulsp1000@yahoo.com. Rev. Paul Valley, s.P.

[1240] (O.S.M.)—SERVITES

(Order of Friar Servants of Mary)
(Ordo Fratrum Servorum Beatae Virginis Mariae)

Generalate: *Curia Generalizia dei Servi di Maria*, Convento San Marcello Piazza San Marcello al Corso, 5, 00187, Rome, Italy,

Servite Friars (1999): *United States of America Province Servite Provincial Center*, 3121 W. Jackson Blvd., Chicago, IL 60612-2729. Tel: 773-533-0360; Fax: 773-533-8307. Very Rev. John M. Fontana, O.S.M., Prior Prov; Rev. Luke M. Stano, O.S.M., Asst. Prov; Rev. Frank M. Falco, O.S.M., Prov. Councilor; Rev. Gerald M. Horan, O.S.M., Prov. Councilor; Rev. Michael M. Pontarelli, O.S.M., Prov. Councilor & Prov. Vocation Team Coord 31520 Camino Capistrano, San Juan Capistrano, CA 92675.Rev. Lawrence M. Choate, O.S.M., Prov. Treas; Bro. Michael M. Callary, O.S.M., Prov./Corp. Sec. & Province Mission Procurator; Rev. Conrad M. Borntrager, O.S.M., Archivist & Historian; Rev. Christopher M. Krymski, O.S.M., Dir. National Shrine of St. Peregrine; Rev. Lawrence M. Choate, O.S.M., Dir. Prov. Devel; Rev. Vidal M. Martinez, O.S.M., Natl. Asst. Servite Secular Order; Rev. John M. Topper, O.S.M., Dir. Sanctuary of Our Sorrowful Mother; Rev. Robert J. Warsey, O.S.M., Dir. Marian Center & Dir. National Shrine of Our Lady of Sorrows; Rev. Paul M. Gins, O.S.M., Province Vocation Dir St. Juliana Falcomieri Priory: 1316 N. Acacia Ave., Fullerton, CA 92838
Priests: 71; Professed Brothers: 11; Temporary Professed Friars: 5
Legal Titles: The Order of Friar Servants of Mary-United States of America Province, Inc., 3121 W. Jackson Blvd., Chicago, IL, Tel: 773-533-0360; Fax: 773-533-8307; Retirement Plan of the Order of Friar Servants of Mary-United States of America Province, Inc., 3121 W. Jackson Blvd., Chicago, IL 60612-2729, Tel: 773-533-0360; Fax: 773-533-8307; Charitable Trust of the Order of Friar Servants of Mary-United States of America Province, Inc., 3121 W. Jackson Blvd., Chicago, IL 60612-2729, Tel: 773-533-0360; Fax: 773-533-8307; Servite High School, Anaheim, CA, A California Corporation, 1952 W. La Palma Ave., Anaheim, CA 92801, Tel: 714-774-7575; Fax: 714-774-1404; Sanctuary of Our Sorrowful Mother, Inc., P.O. Box 20008, Portland, OR 97294-0008, Tel: 503-254-7371; Fax: 503-254-9682.
Properties Owned, Staffed and Sponsored: Parishes 2 owned, 7 staffed; High Schools 1; Shrines 3; Residences 6; Hospital Chaplaincies 1; Nursing Home Chaplaincies 1.
Represented in the Archdioceses of Chicago, Denver, Hartford, Portland in Oregon and St. Louis and in the Dioceses of Oakland, Orange and Springfield-Cape Girardeau. Also in Australia, Ireland and South Africa.

[1250] (C.R.S.)—SOMASCAN FATHERS

(Clericorum Regularium Somaschensium)
(Order of St. Jerome Aemilian)

General Motherhouse: Via Casal Morena, 8 00040, Morena - Rome, Italy, Rev. Franco Moscone, C.R.S., Father Gen.

U.S. Foundation: *Pine Haven Boys Center*, 133 River Rd., P.O. Box 162, Suncook, NH 03275. Tel: 603-485-7141. Rev. John B. Vitali, C.R.S., Supr.
Priests: 9
Represented in the Archdiocese of Galveston-Houston and Diocese of Manchester.

[1260] (S.CH.)—SOCIETY OF CHRIST

(Societas Christi Pro Emigrantibus Polonis)

General Motherhouse: 60-962 Poznan Ulica Panny Marii 4, Poland, Very Rev. Tomasz Sielicki, S.Ch., Supr. Gen; Rev. Andrzej Duczkowski, S.Ch., Procurator Gen Via Pietro Cavallini 38, Rome, Italy, 00193,

American-Canadian Province: *Provincial House*, 786 W. Sunset Ave., Lombard, IL 60148. Tel: 630-424-0401; Fax: 630-424-0409. Rev. Pawel Bandurski, S.Ch., Prov; Rev. Jacek Walkiewicz, S.Ch., Vice Prov; Rev. Zygmunt Ostrwoski, S.Ch., Treas.
Priests: 57; Seminarians: 4
Represented in the Archdioceses of Atlanta; Baltimore, Chicago, Detroit, Galveston- Houston, Los Angeles, Milwaukee, New York, Portland in Oregon, St. Paul-Minneapolis, San Francisco, Seattle and Washington and in the Dioceses of Dallas, Joliet, Phoenix, San Diego, San Jose and Toledo. Also in Canada.

[1270] (F.M.S.I.)—SONS OF MARY MISSIONARY SOCIETY

(Sons of Mary, Health of the Sick)
(Filii Mariae Salutis Infirmorum)

General Headquarters: 567 Salem End Rd., Framingham, MA 01702-5599. Tel: 508-879-6711; Fax: 508-879-7667; Email: sonsboston@gmail.com; Web: www.sonsofmary.com. Rev. John Murphy, F.M.S.I., Coord; Bro. Francisco Tanega, F.M.S.I., Councilor; Rev. John Coss, F.M.S.I., Councilor.
Professed: 12
Represented in the Archdiocese of Boston. Also in the Philippines.

[1280] (C.S.S.)—STIGMATINE FATHERS AND BROTHERS

(Congregation of the Sacred Stigmata)

General Motherhouse: Via Mazzarino No. 16, Rome, Italy, Very Rev. Andrea Meschi, C.S.S., Supr. Gen.

North American Province (1940): 554 Lexington St., Waltham, MA 02452. Tel: 781-209-3100; Fax: 781-894-9785. Rev. Robert S. White, C.S.S., Prov. Supr.
Legal Title: Stigmatine Fathers & Brother, Inc.
Priests: 17
Properties owned, staffed or sponsored: Parishes 3; Retreat & Conference Center.
Represented in the Archdioceses of Boston and New York and in the Dioceses of Springfield in Massachusetts and Worcester.

[1290] (S.S.)—SOCIETY OF THE PRIESTS OF SAINT SULPICE

(Societas Presbyterorum a S. Sulpitio)

General Motherhouse: 6 rue du Regard, Paris 75006, France, Very Rev. Ronald D. Witherup, S.S., Supr. Gen.

U.S. Provincial House: 5408 Roland Ave., Baltimore, MD 21210. Tel: 410-323-5070; Fax: 410-433-6524. Very Rev. Thomas R. Ulshafer, S.S., Prov; Judith A. Mohan, Exec. Asst. to Prov; Rev. Gerald D. McBrearity, S.S., Dir., Formation; Rev. Michael L. Barre, S.S., Prov. Treas; Rev. Richard M. Gula, S.S., Dir. Personnel.
Legal Title: The Associated Sulpicians of the United States, Inc.
Fathers: 73
Represented in the Archdioceses of Baltimore, Hartford, Los Angeles, San Antonio, San Francisco and Washington and in the Dioceses of Bridgeport, Dallas, Lansing, Monterey, Oakland, San Jose, Scranton and Springfield-Cape Girardeau. Missions: Kabwe & Lusaka, Zambia Central Africa.

[1300] (C.R.)—THEATINE FATHERS

(Congregatio Clericorum Regularium)

General Motherhouse: *Sant' Andrea della Valle*, Piazza Vidoni, 6 00186, Rome, Italy, Very Rev. Valentin Arteaga, C.R.

U.S. Headquarters: 1050 S. Birch St., Denver, CO 80246. Tel: 303-757-4280. Very Rev. Antonio Flores, C.R.
Fathers: 17; Clerics: 5
Parishes 9; House of Formation 1; Provincial House 1.
Represented in the Archdioceses of Denver and New York and in the Diocese of Pueblo.

[1310] (O.SS.T.)—ORDER OF THE MOST HOLY TRINITY

(Holy Trinity Fathers, Inc.)
(Ordo Sanctissimae Trinitatis; The Trinitarians)

Founded in France in 1198 by St. John De Matha for the ransom of Christian slaves. First settlement in the

United States in 1911.

General Curia: Via Massimi, 114/C, 00136, Rome, Italy, Most Rev. Jose T. Narlaly, O.SS.T., Min. Gen; Very Rev. Albert M. Anuszewski, O.SS.T., Gen Councilor, Economer Gen.

U.S.A. Province (1950): *Province of the Immaculate Heart of Mary*, P.O. Box 5719, Baltimore, MD 21282-5719. Tel: 410-486-5171. Very Rev. J. Edward Owens, O.SS.T., Min. Prov. Councilors: Very Rev. William J. Axe, O.SS.T., Vicar Provincial; Very Rev. James R. Day, O.SS.T; Very Rev. Stanley W. DeBoe, O.SS.T; Very Rev. Juan J. Molina, O.SS.T; Rev. Kurt J. Klismet, O.SS.T., Treas. Prov; Rev. Damian Anuszewsi, O.SS.T., Sec. Provincial.

Trinitarian Communities in the U.S: 11; Fathers: 36; Brothers: 2

Ministries in 13 parishes; Seminary Facility Positions; High Schools; Prison Chaplaincies; Hospital Chaplaincies; India Foundation; Mission for Persecuted Christians.

Properties owned: DeMatha Catholic High School, Hyattsville, MD; Holy Trinity Monastery, Pikesville, MD; Trinitarian Residence, Ellicott, MD; Trinitarian Residence, Adelphi, MD; Domus Trinitatis, San Antonio, TX.

Represented in the Archdioceses of Baltimore, Los Angeles, Miami, Philadelphia and San Antonio and in the Dioceses of Las Vegas, Trenton and Victoria.

[1320] (C.S.V.)—CLERICS OF ST. VIATOR

(Congregatio Clericorum Sancti Viatoris)

General Motherhouse: *Chierici di San Viatore*, Via Padre Angelo Paoli, 41, Casella Postale 10793 00144, Rome, Italy, Very Rev. Mark R. Francis, C.S.V., Supr. Gen.

Province of Chicago (1882): 1212 E. Euclid Ave., Arlington Heights, IL 60004. Tel: 847-398-1354. Rev. Thomas R. von Behren, C.S.V., Prov; Bro. Michael T. Gosch, C.S.V., Asst. Prov; Rev. Corey D. Brost, C.S.V., Councilor; Rev. Daniel R. Hall, C.S.V., Councilor; Rev. Lawrence D. Lentz, C.S.V., Councilor.

Fathers: 55; Brothers: 20

Properties owned, staffed or sponsored: Parishes 11; High Schools 4; Formation Houses 3.

Represented in the Archdiocese of Chicago and in the Dioceses of Fort Wayne-South Bend, Joliet, Las Vegas, Peoria, Rockford, San Bernadino, and Tucson. Also in Belize, Colombia and Italy.

[1330] (C.M.)—CONGREGATION OF THE MISSION

(Vincentians)

(Congregatio Missionis Sti. Vincentii a Paulo)

Founded in France in 1625. First foundation in the United States in 1818.

General Motherhouse: *Curia Generalizia*, Via dei Capasso, 30 00164, Roma, Italy, Very Rev. G. Gregory Gay, C.M., Supr. Gen; Rev. Joseph Geders, C.M., Econome Gen.

Eastern Province of the U.S.A. (1888): *St. Vincent's Seminary*, 500 E. Chelten Ave., Philadelphia, PA 19144. Tel: 215-713-2400; Fax: 215-844-2085. Very Rev. Michael J. Carroll, C.M., Prov; Rev. Gregory P. Cozzubbo, C.M., Asst. Prov; Rev. Elmer Bauer III, C.M., Prov. Treas; Mr. Allen Andrews, Exec. Dir. Finance. Consultors: Rev. James J. Maher, C.M; Rev. Michael Manh Nguyen, C.M; Rev. Emmet J. Nolan, C.M.

Legal Title: Congregation of the Mission of St. Vincent de Paul in Germantown, Inc.

Priests: 125; Brothers: 9; College Seminarians: 15

Properties owned, sponsored or staffed: Parishes 11; Missions in Republic of Panama 6; Universities 2; Major Seminary Residences 1; Novitiates 1; Retreat Houses 1.

Represented in the Archdioceses of Baltimore, New York and Philadelphia and in the Dioceses of Albany, Allentown, Birmingham, Brooklyn, Buffalo, Charlotte, Grand Rapids, Metuchen and Rockville Centre.

Western Province of the U.S.A. (1888): 13663 Rider Trail N., Earth City, MO 63045-1512. Tel: 314-344-1184; Fax: 314-344-2989. Very Rev. Perry Henry, C.M., Prov; Rev. Mark S. Pranaitis, C.M., Asst. Prov.

Legal Title: Congregation of the Mission Western Province; Congregation of the Mission Western Province, Texas; Congregation of the Mission Western Province, Louisiana; Congregation of the Mission Western Province, California.

Priests: 136; Brothers: 17; Permanent Deacons: 1

Serving in 19 U.S. (arch)dioceses; Universities; Foreign Mission Stations; Houses of Apostolic Activity; Parishes; Home Mission Parishes; Seminaries; Retreat/Evangelization Centers.

Represented in the Archdioceses of Chicago, Denver, Los Angeles, Milwaukee, New Orleans, Saint Louis, and San Antonio and in the Dioceses of Dallas, Evansville, Gallup, Jefferson City, Kansas City-St. Joseph, Joliet, Little Rock, Memphis, Phoenix, Springfield-Cape Girardeau, and Stockton. Also in France, Italy and Kenya.

The New England Province of the Vincentian Fathers (1975): *DePaul Vincentian Provincial Residence*, 234 Keeney St., Manchester, CT 06040-7048. Tel: 860-643-2828; Fax: 860-533-9462. Very Rev. Andrzej Rafal Kopystynski, C.M., Prov.

Fathers: 25; Brothers: 1

Legal Title: New England Province of the Congregation of the Mission, Inc.; Charitable Trust of the New England Province of the Congregation of the Mission.

Represented in the Archdiocese of Hartford and in the Dioceses of Bridgeport, Brooklyn and Manchester.

American Italian Branch (Naples, Italy) (1922): *Our Lady of Pompei Church*, 3600 Claremont St., Baltimore, MD 21224. Tel: 410-675-7790. Rev. Luigi Esposito, Supr.

Legal Title: Vincentian Fathers of the Neapolitan Province of Maryland Charities, Inc.

Represented in the Archdiocese of Baltimore.

American Spanish Branch (Zaragoza, Spain) (1926): *Holy Agony Church*, 1834 3rd Ave., New York, NY 10029. Tel: 212-289-5589; Fax: 212-289-8321. Rev. Victor Elia, C.M; Rev. Candido Arrizurieta, C.M; Rev. Jesus Arellano, C.M.

Legal Title: Padres Paules Community - Vincentians Inc.

Fathers: 4

Represented in the Archdioceses of Los Angeles and New York.

[1335] (V.C.)—VINCENTIAN CONGREGATION

(Vincentians)

Founded by Rev. Fr. Varkey Kattarath at Thottakom, Kerala, India in 1904.

Generalate: *Vincentian Generalate*, P.O. Box No. 2250 - Edappally Kochi 682 024, Kerala, India, Very Rev. Varghese Parapuram, V.C., Supr. Gen.

St. Joseph Province: *Vincentian Provincial House*, S.H. Mount P.O. Kottayam 686 006, Kerala, India, Tel: 481-256-3559. Very Rev. George Arackal, V.C., Prov. Supr.

North American Headquarters: *Vincentian House*, 210 5th Ave., S.E., Saint Cloud, MN 56304. Tel: 320-229-7759. Rev. Joseph Thalananay, V.C., Reg. Coord; Rev. Joseph J. Arackal, V.C., Mission Procurator.

Fathers: 7

Represented in the Archdiocese of St. Paul and Minneapolis and in the Dioceses of St. Cloud and Trenton.

[1340] (S.D.V.)—VOCATIONIST FATHERS

(The Society of Divine Vocations)

Generali: Via Cortina D'Ampezzo, 140 00135, Rome, Italy, Tel: 011 39 06 33 12725; Fax: 011 39 06 33 12758. Very Rev. Louis Caputo, S.D.V., Supr. Gen.

American Headquarters: 90 Brooklake Rd., Florham Park, NJ 07932. Tel: 973-966-6262; Fax: 973-593-8381. Rev. Ignatius Okoroji, S.D.V., Rel. Supr. & Master of Novices; Rev. Vernon Kohlmann, S.D.V., Vice Supr. & Vocation Dir; Rev. Mario Muccitelli, S.D.V., Delegate Emeritus.

U.S. Foundations: *Our Lady of Perpetual Help Center*, 90 Brooklake Rd., Florham Park, NJ 07932. Tel: 973-966-6262; Fax: 973-593-8381. Rev. Ignatius Okorgi, S.D.V; Rev. Vernon Kohlmann, S.D.V.

Represented in the Archdiocese of Newark and in the Diocese of Paterson.

[1350] (C.F.X.)—BROTHERS OF ST. FRANCIS XAVIER

(Congregatio Fratrum Xaverianorum)

Generalate - Xaverian Brothers: 4409 Frederick Ave., Baltimore, MD 21229. Tel: 410-644-0034; Fax: 410-644-2762. Bro. Lawrence Harvey, C.F.X., Gen. Supr; Bro. Daniel Skala, C.F.X., Vicar; Bro. Cornelius Hubbuch, C.F.X., Pastoral Care; Bro. Paul Murray, C.F.X., Gen. Councilor for the U.S; Bro. James Connolly, C.F.X., Dir. Volunteers & Vocation; Bro. Jerimiah O'Leary, C.F.X., Coord. Peace & Justice; Ms. Alice Hession, Dir. Xaverian Sponsored Schools; Bro. Peter Campbell, C.F.X., Congregational Treas; Mr. Richard Costello, Dir. Devel.

Brothers: 241

Legal Titles: Xaverian Brothers USA Inc.; Isidore Charitable Trust; Paul van Gerwen Religious & Charitable Trust.

Ministries in the field of: Religious and Academic Education at all levels; Diocesan Offices; Pastoral Ministry; Mission Schools; Communities; Houses and House of Formation.

Represented in the Archdioceses of Baltimore, Boston, Chicago, Louisville, Milwaukee, New Orleans and Washington and in the Dioceses of Biloxi, Brooklyn, Charleston, Houma-Thibodaux, Norwich, Richmond, Syracuse, Venice and Worcester. Also in Bolivia, Belgium, Congo, England, Haiti, Kenya, Lithuania, Mexico and South Sudan.

[1360] (S.X.)—XAVERIAN MISSIONARY FATHERS

(Saint Francis Xavier Foreign Mission Society)

(Pia Societas Sancti Francisci Xaverii pro Exteris Missionibus)

General Motherhouse: *Istituto Saveriano Missioni Estere*, Viale Vaticano 40 00165, Rome, Italy, Very Rev. Rino Benzoni, S.X., Supr. Gen.

U.S. Province: *Xaverian Missionary Fathers*, 12 Helene Ct., Wayne, NJ 07470. Tel: 973-942-2975; Fax: 973-942-5012. Very Rev. Carl S. Chudy, S.X., Prov.

Fathers: 15

Mission Houses 2; Houses of Formation 2.

Represented in the Archdioceses of Boston, Chicago and Milwaukee and in the Diocese of Paterson.

Index for Religious Institutes of Women

(The initial D or P indicates Diocesan or Pontifical Jurisdiction.)

Religious Order Initials for Women

Initials	Order	Code
B.S.	Auxiliaries of the Blessed Sacrament	[]
C.J.	Handmaids of the Sacred Heart of Jesus	[1870]
D.	Sisters of the Lamb of God	[2260]
I.M.	Association of Mary Immaculate	[]
N.G.	A New Genesis	[]
P.	Nuns of Perpetual Adoration of Blessed Sacrament	[3190]
P.B.	Adorers of the Precious Blood	[0110]
P.G.	Sisters of Perpetual Adoration	[3195]
R.	Handmaids of the Sacred Heart of Jesus for Reparation	[1880]
R.	Augustinian Recollects	[]
S.C.	Adorers of the Blood of Christ	[0100]
S.C.J.	Apostles of the Sacred Heart of Jesus	[0130]
C.	Notre Dame du Bon Conseil (Quebec)	[]
ethl.	Bethlemita Daughters of the Sacred Heart of Jesus	[0910]
V.M.	Sisters of Charity of Blessed Virgin Mary	[0430]
V.M.C.	Blessed Virgin Missionaries of Carmel	[]
a.Ch.	Carmeilte Sisters of Charity	[0340]
armel.D.C.J.	Carmelite Sisters of the Divine Heart of Jesus	[0360]
B.S.	Congregation of Bon Secours	[0270]
C.	Carmel Community	[0310]
C.V.I.	Sisters of Charity of Incarnate Word	[0460]
CVI	Sisters of Charity of Incarnate Word (Houston, TX)	[0470]
C.W.	Carmeiite Community of the Word	[0315]
D.P.	Sisters of Divine Providence	[0990]
D.P.	Sisters of Divine Providence of Melbourne, Kentucky	[1000]
D.P.	Sisters of Divine Providence of San Antonio, TX	[1010]
D.P.	Capuchin Sisters (Spain)	[]
D.S.	Congregation of Divine Spirit	[1040]
F.M.M.	Minim Daughters of Mary Immaculate	[2675]
F.P.	Feminine Congregation of the Passion	[]
F.P.	Mexican Passionist Sisters	[]
G.S.	Contemplatives of Good Shepherd	[1830]
H.F.	Sisters of Holy Faith	[1940]
H.M.	Congregation of Humility of Mary	[2100]
H.S.	Community of the Holy Spirit	[2020]
I.C.	Sisters of Immaculate Conception	[2120]
I.J.	Congregation of Infant Jesus	[2230]
J.C.	Poor Sisters of Jesus Crucified and Sorrowful Mother	[3240]
K.	School Sisters of Christ the King	[]
L.H.C.	Congregation of Our Lady Help of the Clergy	[3090]
M.C.	Congregation of Mother of Carmel	[]
M.R.	Congregation of Mary Queen	[0397]
M.S.	Comboni Missionary Sisters	[0690]
M.S.	Cashel Mercy Sisters	[2515]
M.S.T.	Missionary Carmelites of St. Teresa	[0390]
N.D.	Congregation of Notre Dame	[2980]
O.C.	Companions of Christ	[]
P.	Religious of the Passion of Jesus Christ	[3170]
P.	Sisters of the Cross and Passion	[3180]
P.C.	Capuchin Poor Clares	[]
P.C.	St. Clare Capuchin Sisters	[]
P.P.S.	Sisters of the Precious Blood Dayton, Ohio	[3260]
P.P.S.	Sisters of the Most Precious Blood, (O'Fallon, MO)	[3270]
P.S.	Missionary Sisters of the Precious Blood	[2850]
C.R.	Sisters of the Resurrection	[3480]
C.S.	Company of the Savior	[0710]
C.S.	The Christian Sisters (Pious Union)	[]
C.S.A.	Sisters of Charity of St. Augustine	[0580]
C.S.A.	Sisters of St. Agnes	[3710]
C.S.A.	Albertine Sisters (Krakow, Poland)	[]
C.S.A.C.	Sisters of the Catholic Apostolate (Pallottine)	[3140]
C.S.B.	Congregation of St. Brigid	[3735]
C.S.C.	Congregation of Sisters of Holy Cross	[1920]
C.S.C.	Sisters of Holy Cross	[1930]
C.S.C.	Sisters of Holy Cross and Seven Dolors	[]
C.S.E.	Carmelite Sisters of the Eucharist	[]
C.S.F.N.	Sisters of Holy Family of Nazareth	[1970]
C.S.J.	Hermanas Carmelitas de San Jose	[1895]
C.S.J.	Sisters of St. Joseph (Boston, Brighton)	[3830-01]
C.S.J.	Sisters of St. Joseph (Orange)	[3830-03]
C.S.J.	Sisters of St. Joseph (Rockville Centre, Brentwood)	[3830-05]
C.S.J.	Sisters of St. Joseph (Pittsburgh, Baden)	[3830-13]
C.S.J.	Sisters of St. Joseph (Salina, Concordia)	[3830-15]
C.S.J.	Sisters of St. Joseph (Wichita)	[3830-18]
C.S.J.	Congregation of the Sisters of St. Joseph	[3832]
C.S.J.	Sisters of St. Joseph of Carondelet	[3840]
C.S.J.	Sisters of St. Joseph of Chambery	[3850]
C.S.J.	Sisters of St. Joseph (Lyons, France)	[3870]
C.S.J.	Sisters of St. Joseph of Medaille	[3880]
C.S.JB.	Sisters of St. John the Baptist	[3820]
C.S.J.P.	Sisters of St. Joseph of Peace	[3890]
C.S.M.	Sisters of St. Martha of Antigonish N.S	[3937]
C.S.N.	Congregation of Sisters of Nazareth	[3242]
C.S.R.	Sisters of Holy Redeemer	[2000]
C.S.S.F.	Felician Sisters	[1170]
C.S.Sp.	Sisters of Holy Spirit	[2030]
C.S.S.T.	Carmelite Sisters of St. Teresa	[]
C.S.T.	Carmelite Sisters of St. Therese of Infant Jesus	[0380]
C.V.D.	Sisters of Bethany	[0250]
C.V.I.	Congregation of Incarnate Word and Blessed Sacrament	[2190]
C.V.I.	Religious of the Incarnate Word	[3449]
D.C.	Daughters of Charity of St. Vincent de Paul	[0760]
D.C.	Daughters of the Cross	[0770]
D.C.M.	Diocesan Carmelites of Maine	[]
D.C.P.B.	Daughters of Charity of Most Precious Blood	[0740]
D.D.L.	Daughters of Divine Love	[0793]
D.H.M.	Daughters of Heart of Mary	[0810]
D.H.S.	Daughters of the Holy Spirit	[0820]
D.L.F.	Daughters of Our Lady of Fatima	[]
D.L.J.C.	Disciples of the Lord Jesus Christ	[0965]
D.M.	Daughters of Mary of the Immaculate Conception	[0860]
D.M.	Daughters of Our Lady of Mercy	[0890]
D.M.I.	Daughters of Mary Immaculate (Chaldean)	[]
D.M.J.	Daughters of Mary and Joseph	[0880]
D.O.M.	Daughters of Mercy (Croatian)	[]
D.S.F.	Daughters of St. Francis of Assisi	[0920]
D.S.M.P.	Daughters of St. Mary of Providence	[0940]
D.W.	Daughters of Wisdom	[0960]
E.F.M.S.	Eucharistic Franciscan Missionary Sisters	[1150]
E.I.N.	Servants of the Immaculate Child Mary	[3615]
E.M.S.	Eucharistic Missionary Society	[]
F.A.S.	Franciscan Apostolic Sisters	[]
F.C.	Daughters of the Cross of Liege	[0780]
F.C.J.	Society of Sisters Faithful Companions of Jesus	[4048]
F.C.S.C.J.	Daughters of Charity of the Sacred Heart of Jesus	[0750]
F.D.C.	Daughters of Divine Charity	[0790]
Fd.CC.	Canossian Daughters of Charity	[0730]
F.D.L.P.	Daughters of Providence	[]
F.D.N.S.C.	Daughters of Our Lady of the Sacred Heart	[0900]
F.D.P.	Daughters of Divine Providence	[0800]
F.D.Z.	Daughters of Divine Zeal	[0795]
F.H.I.C.	Franciscan Hospitaller Sisters of the Immaculate Conception	[1270]
F.H.M.	Franciscan Handmaids of the Most Pure Heart of Mary	[1260]
F.H.M.	Franciscan Sisters Daughters of Mercy	[1235]
F.J.	Congregation of the Daughters of Jesus	[0830]
F.L.G.	Franciscan Sisters of Our Lady of Grace	[]
F.M.A.	Daughters of Mary Help of Christians	[0850]
F.M.I.	Congregation of the Daughters of Mary Immaculate (Marianist Sisters)	[0870]
F.M.I.	Franciscan Sisters of Mary Immaculate of the Third Order of St. Francis of Assisi	[1500]
F.M.I.J.	Franciscan Missionaries of the Infant Jesus	[1365]
F.M.M.	The Franciscan Missionaries of Mary	[1370]
F.M.S.A.	Franciscan Missionary Sisters for Africa	[1320]
F.M.S.C.	Franciscan Missionary Sisters of the Sacred Heart	[1400]
F.M.S.J.	Mill Hill Sisters	[1410]
F.M.S.R.	Daughters of Our Lady of Holy Rosary	[0895]
F.N.S.S.C.	Franciscan Sisters of Our Lady of the Sacred Heart	[]
F.S.E.	The Institute of the Franciscan Sisters of the Eucharist	[1250]
F.S.G.M.	Sisters of St. Francis of the Martyr St. George	[1600]
F.S.J.	Religious Daughters of St. Joseph	[0930]
F.S.M.	Franciscan Sisters of Mary	[1415]
F.S.O.L.	Franciscan Sisters of Our Lady	[]
F.S.P.	Pious Society Daughters of St. Paul	[0950]
F.S.P.	Franciscan Sisters of Peace	[1425]
F.S.P.A.	Congregation of the Sisters of the Third Order of St. Francis of Perpetual Adoration	[1780]
F.S.R.	Franciscan Sisters of Ringwood	[1420]
F.S.S.C.	Franciscan Sisters of St. Clare (Pious Union)	[]
F.S.S.E.	Franciscan Sisters of St. Elizabeth	[1460]
F.S.S.J.	Franciscan Sisters of St. Joseph	[1470]
F S.S.M.	Franciscan Sisters of the Sorrowful Mother	[]
F.S.Sp.J.	Franciscan Sisters of the Spirit of Jesus	[]
G.H.M.S.	Home Mission Sisters of America (Glenmary)	[2080]
G.N.S.H.	Grey Nuns of the Sacred Heart	[1840]

Initials	Order	Code
H.B.S.	Hermanas Contemplativas del Buen Pastor	[]
H.C.G.	Hermanas Catequistas Guadalupanas	[1900]
H.F.deS.J.	Franciscan Sisters of St. Joseph (Mexico City)	[]
H.F.S.J.	Franciscan Sisters of St. Joseph	[1480]
H.G.S.	Congregation de Hermanas Guadalupanas de la Salle	[]
H.H.C.J.	Congregation of the Handmaids of the Holy Child Jesus	[1855]
H.H.S.	Society of Helpers	[1890]
H.J.	Hermanas Josefinas	[1910]
H.J.D.	Las Hermanas de Juan Diego	[]
H.M.	Sisters of the Humility of Mary	[2110]
H.M.C.	Hermits of Mount Carmel	[]
H.M.S.S.	Mercedarian Sisters of the Blessed Sacrament	[2590]
H.M.S.S.	Religious Sisters of the Apostolate of the Blessed Sacrament	[3370]
H.O.Carm.	Hermits of Our Lady of Mt. Carmel	[]
H.P.B.	Congregation of the Handmaids of the Precious Blood	[1860]
H.R.F.	Sisters of the Holy Rosary of Fatima (Mexico)	[]
H.S.H.	Handmaids of the Sacred Heart of Pohang	[]
H.S.M.	Hermit Sisters of Mary	[]
H.Sp.S.	Daughters of the Holy Spirit Nazareth of the Good Shepherd	[]
H.S.S.	Hermanas del Servicio Social	[]
H.S.S.R.	Hermit Sisters of Romuald	[]
H.T.	Handmaids of the Most Holy Trinity	[]
H.V.M.	Sisters, Home Visitors of Mary	[2090]
I.B.V.M.	Institute of the Blessed Virgin Mary (Loretto Sisters)	[2370]
I.B.V.M.	Institute of the Blessed Virgin Mary (Loretto Sisters)	[2380]
I.C.	Vietnamese Sisters Incarnational Consecration	[]
I.C.M.	Incarnatio-Consecratio-Missio	[2187]
I.C.M.	Missionary Sisters of the Immaculate Heart of Mary	[2750]
I.H.M.	Sisters of the Immaculate Heart of Mary at Mirinae	[2182]
I.H.M.	Sisters of the Immaculate Heart of Mary Mother of Christ	[2183]
I.H.M.	Sisters Servants of the Immaculate Heart of Mary	[2150]
I.H.M.	Sisters Servants of the Immaculate Heart of Mary	[2160]
I.H.M.	Sisters Servants of the Immaculate Heart of Mary	[2170]
I.H.M.	Sisters Servants of the Immaculate Heart of Mary	[2180]
I.H.M.	The California Institute of the Sisters of the Most Holy and Immaculate Heart of the Blessed Virgin Mary	[2930]
I.H.M.	Sisters of the Immaculate Heart of Mary of Wichita	[2185]
I.J.	Sisters of the Infant Jesus	[2240]
I.M.	Sisters of Charity of the Infant Mary	[]
I.S.S.M.	Secular Institute of Schoenstatt Sisters of Mary	[]
I.W.B.S.	Congregation of the Incarnate Word and Blessed Sacrament	[2200]
I.W.B.S.	Congregation of the Incarnate Word and Blessed Sacrament	[2205]
J.S.O.P.	Dominican Oblates of Jesus (Spain)	[]
L.B.	Ladies of Bethany	[]
L.C.M.	Sisters of the Little Company of Mary	[2270]
L.H.C.N.T.	Lovers of the Holy Cross Nha Trang	[2385]
L.H.C.	Lovers of the Holy Cross Sisters	[2390]
L.H.C.	Lovers of the Holy Cross Sisters	[2392]
L.M.S.C.	Little Missionary Sisters of Charity	[2290]
L.S.	Lasallian Sisters (Vietnam)	[]
L.S.A.	Little Sisters of the Assumption	[2310]
L.S.G.	Little Sisters of the Gospel (France)	[2315]
L.S.I.C.	Little Servant Sisters of the Immaculate Conception	[2300]
L.S.J.	Little Sisters of Jesus	[2330]
L.S.J.M.	Little Sisters of Jesus and Mary	[2331]
L.S.P.	Little Sisters of the Poor	[2340]
M.C.	Consolata Missionary Sisters	[0720]
M.C.	Missionaries of Charity	[2710]
M.C.	Poor Clare Missionary Sisters	[2840]
M.C.D.P.	Missionary Catechists of Divine Providence, San Antonio, TX	[2690]
M.Ch.R.	Missionary Sisters of Christ the King for Polonia	[2715]
M.C.M.	Cordi Marian Sisters	[0725]
M.C.P.	Missioneras Catequestas de los Pobres	[]
M.C.S.	Missionary Sisters of the Sacred Side	[]
M.C.S.J.M.	Congregation of Missionary Catechists of the Sacred Heart of Jesus and Mary	[]
M.D.	Mothers of the Helpless	[2920]
M.D.P.V.M.	Missionary Daughters of the Most Pure Virgin Mary	[2717]
M.E.	Missionary Ecumenical (Rome)	[]
M.C.SS.CC.J.M.	Missionary Catechists of the Sacred Hearts of Jesus and Mary	[2700]
M.E.S.S.T.	Eucharistic Missionaries of the Most Holy Trinity	[]
M.E.S.T.	Eucharistic Missionaries of St. Theresa (Mexico)	[]
M.F.P.	Franciscan Missionaries Our Lady of Peace	[]
M.G.Sp.S.	Guadalupan Missionaries of the Holy Spirit	[1845]
M.H.S.	Sisters of the Most Holy Sacrament	[2940]
M.H.S.H.	Mission Helpers of the Sacred Heart	[2720]
M.I.C.	Missionary Sisters of the Immaculate Conception (Canada)	[]
M.J.	Missionary Sisters of Jesus	[]
M.J.M.J.	Missionaries of Jesus, Mary and Joseph	[2770]
M.M.	Maryknoll Sisters of St. Dominic	[2470]
M.M.B.	Mercedarian Missionaries of Berriz	[2510]
M.M.D.	Servite Missionary Sisters of the Sorrowful Mother	[]
M.M.M.	Medical Missionaries of Mary	[2480]
M.M.S.	Medical Mission Sisters	[2490]
M.O.M.	Missionary Sisters of Our Lady of Mercy	[2830]
M.P.F.	Religious Teachers Filippini	[3430]
M.P.H.	Missionary Sisters of Our Lady of Perpetual Help	[]
M.P.S.	Misioneras del Perpetual Socorro	[]
M.P.S.	Missionary Sisters of Our Lady of Perpetual Help	[]
M.P.V.	Religious Venerini Sisters	[4180]
M.R.	Marianist Sisters	[]
M.S.	Marian Sisters of the Diocese of Lincoln	[2400]
M.S.B.T.	Missionary Servants of the Most Blessed Trinity	[2790]
M.S.C.	Congregation of the Marianites of the Holy Cross	[2410]
M.S.C.	Missionary Sisters of the Most Sacred Heart of Jesus of Hiltrup	[2800]
M.S.C.	Missionary Sisters of the Sacred Heart	[2860]
M.S.C.Gpe.	Missionaries of the Sacred Heart of Jesus and of Our Lady of Guadalupe	[2865]
M.S.C.K.	Missionary Sisters of Christ the King	[2715]
M.S.E.	Missionary Sisters of the Eucharist	[2725]
M.S.F.	Missionary Sisters of the Holy Family	[]
M.S.H.F.	Missionary Sisters of the Holy Family (Poland)	[]
M.S.H.R.	Missionary Sisters of the Holy Rosary	[2730]
M.S.J.	Medical Sisters of St. Joseph	[2500]
M.S.K.C.P.	Missionary Sisters of Christ the King of Polonia	[]
M.S.M.G.	Missionary Sisters of Mother of God	[2810]
M.S.O.L.A.	Missionary Sisters of Our Lady of Africa	[2820]
M.S.S.A.	Missionary Servants of St. Anthony	[2890]
M.S.S.C.B.	Missionary Sisters of St. Charles Borromeo	[2900]
M.S.S.J.	Missionary Servants of St. Joseph (Spain)	[]
M.S.Sp.	Mission Sisters of the Holy Spirit	[2740]
M.SS.S.	Missionary Sisters of the Most Blessed Sacrament	[2780]
M.T.G.	Adorers of the Holy Cross	[4155]
M.X.Y.	The Yarumal Foreign Mission Institute (Colombia)	[]
N.A.U.-O.L.C.	North American Unions of Sisters of Our Lady of Charity	[3070]
N.D.	Notre Dame Sisters	[2960]
N.D.S.	Congregation of Notre Dame de Sion	[2950]
O.A.R.	Augustinian Recollect Sisters	[]
O.B.T.	Sisters Oblates to the Blessed Trinity	[3020]
O.C.A.	Carmelite Vietnamese of Our Lady of Mt. Carmel	[]
O.Carm.	Calced Carmelites	[0300]
O.Carm.	Carmelite Nuns of the Ancient Observance	[0320]
O.Carm.	Carmelite Sisters for Aged and Infirm	[0330]
O.Carm.	Carmelite Sisters (Corpus Christi)	[0350]
O.Carm.	Congregation of Our Lady of Mt. Carmel	[0400]
O.Carm.	Institute of the Sisters of Our Lady of Mt. Carmel	[0410]
O.C.D.	Carmelite Sisters of the Most Sacred Heart of Los Angeles	[0370]
O.C.D.	Discalced Carmelite Nuns	[0420]
O.C.D.	Carmelitas del Sagrado Corazon	[]
O.Cist.	Cistercian Nuns	[0680]
O.C.S.O.	Cistercian Nuns of the Strict Observance	[0670]
O.D.N.	Company of Mary	[0700]
O.L.C.	Sisters of Our Lady of Charity	[3071]
O.L.C.	Sisters of Our Lady of Charity	[3073]
O.L.G.	Sisters of Our Lady of the Garden	[]
O.L.L.	Sisters of Our Lady of Lourdes	[]
O.L.M.	Sisters of Charity of Our Lady of Mercy	[0510]
O.L.S.	Sisters of Our Lady of Sorrows	[3120]
O.L.V.M.	Our Lady of Victory Missionary Sisters	[3130]
O.M.M.I.	Oblate Missionaries of Mary Immaculate	[]
O.M.O.	Oblates of the Mother of Orphans	[3035]
O.P.	The Congregation of the Dominican Sisters of Our Lady of the Springs of Bridgeport CT	[1045]
O.P.	Dominican Contemplative Nuns (Cloistered)	[1050]
O.P.	Dominican Contemplative Sisters (Cloistered)	[1060]
O.P.	Dominican Sisters (St. Catharine, KY)	[1070-01]
O.P.	Dominican Sisters (Columbus, OH)	[1070-02]
O.P.	Dominican Sisters (Sinsinawa, WI)	[1070-03]
O.P.	Dominican Sisters (San Rafael, CA)	[1070-04]

Initials	Order	Code
O.P.	Dominican Sisters (Amityville, NY)	[1070-05]
O.P.	Dominican Sisters (Newburgh, NY)	[1070-06]
O.P.	Dominican Sisters (Nashville, TN)	[1070-07]
O.P.	Dominican Sisters (New Orleans, LA)	[1070-08]
O.P.	Dominican Sisters (Racine, WI)	[1070-09]
O.P.	Dominican Sisters (Springfield, IL)	[1070-10]
O.P.	Dominican Sisters (Sparkill, NY)	[1070-11]
O.P.	Dominican Sisters (San Jose, CA)	[1070-12]
O.P.	Dominican Sisters (Adrian, MI)	[1070-13]
O.P.	Dominican Sisters (Grand Rapids, MI)	[1070-14]
O.P.	Dominican Sisters (Blauvelt, NY)	[1070-15]
O.P.	Dominican Sisters (Ossining, NY)	[1070-16]
O.P.	Dominican Sisters (Elkins Park, PA)	[1070-17]
O.P.	Dominican Sisters (Caldwell, PA)	[1070-18]
O.P.	Dominican Sisters (Houston, TX)	[1070-19]
O.P.	Dominican Sisters (Tacoma, WA)	[1070-20]
O.P.	Dominican Sisters (Edmonds, WA)	[1070-21]
O.P.	Dominican Sisters (Fall River, MA)	[1070-22]
O.P.	Dominican Sisters (Hawthorne, NY)	[1070-23]
O.P.	Dominican Sisters (Great Bend, KS)	[1070-24]
O P.	Dominican Sisters (Kenosha, WI)	[1070-25]
O.P.	Dominican Sisters (Oxford, MI)	[1070-26]
O.P.	Dominican Sisters (Justice, IL)	[1070-27]
O.P.	Dominican Sisters (Akron, OH)	[1070-28]
O.P.	Dominican Sisters (Spokane, WA)	[1070-29]
O.P.	Dominican Sisters (Oxford, South Africa)	[1070-30]
O.P.	Marian Society of Dominican Catechists	[1090]
O.P.	Dominican Sisters of Charity of the Presentation of the Blessed Virgin	[1100]
O.P.	Dominican Sisters of Hope	[1105]
O.P.	Dominican Sisters of Our Lady of the Rosary and of Saint Catherine of Siena, Cabra	[1110]
O.P.	Dominican Sisters of Peace	[1115]
O.P.	Dominican Sisters of the Roman Congregation	[1120]
O.P.	Dominican Rural Missionaries	[1130]
O.P.	Eucharistic Missionaries of St. Dominic	[1140]
O.P.	Dominican Sisters of Carondelet	[]
O.P.	Religious Missionaries of St. Dominic (Spanish Prov.)	[1145]
O.P.	Dominican Sisters of Mt. Thabor	[]
O.P.	Dominican Sisters of Our Lady of the Most Holy Rosary	[]
O.P.	Dominican Sisters (Vietnam)	[]
O.P.	Dominican Contemplative Sisters	[]
O.P.	Dominican Sisters (Colombia)	[]
O.P.	Dominican Sisters (Ecuador)	[]
O.P.	Hermanas Dominicanas de la Doctrine Cristiana	[]
O.S.A.	Augustinian Nuns of Contemplative Life	[0160]
O.S.A.	Congregation of Augustinian Sisters Servants of Jesus and Mary	[2145]
O.S.A.	Sisters of St. Rita	[4010]
O.S.A.	Sisters of St. Augustine	[]
O.S.A.	Augustinian Sisters of Our Lady of Consolation	[]
O.S.B.	Benedictine Nuns of the Congregation of Solesmes	[0170]
O.S.B.	Benedictine Nuns of the Primitive Observance	[0180]
O.S.B.	Benedictine Nuns	[0190]
O.S.B.	Benedictine Sisters	[0200]
O.S.B.	Missionary Benedictine Sisters	[0210]
O.S.B.	Congregation of the Benedictine Sisters of Perpetual Adoration of Pontifical Jurisdiction	[0220]
O.S.B.	Benedictine Sisters of Pontifical Jurisdiction	[0230]
O.S.B.	Benedictine Nuns	[0233]
O.S.B.	Olivetan Benedictine Sisters	[0240]
O.S.B.	Congregation of Jesus Crucified	[2250]
O.S.B.	Benedictine Congregation of Our Lady of Monte	[]
O.S.B.	Benedictine Sisters of Sacred Heart	[]
O.S.B.	Contemplative Sisters of St. Benedict	[]
O.S.B.	Benedictine Sisters of Liberty	[]
O.S.B.	Congregation of the Benedictine Sisters of the Sacred Heart	[]
O.S.B.Cam.	Camaldolese Benedictine Sisters	[0235]
O.S.B.M.	Sisters of the Order of St. Basil the Great	[3730]
O.S.B.S.	Oblate Sisters of the Blessed Sacrament	[3010]
O.S.C.	Order of St. Clare	[3760]
O.S.C.	Sisters of St. Clare	[3770]
O.S.C.Cap.	Capuchin Poor Clares	[3765]
O.S.F.	Franciscan Sisters of Allegany New York	[1180]
O.S.F.	The Franciscan Sisters of Baltimore	[1200]
O.S.F.	Franciscan Sisters of Chicago	[1210]
O.S.F.	Franciscan Sisters of Christian Charity	[1230]
O.S.F.	Franciscan Sister, Daughters of the Sacred Hearts of Jesus and Mary	[1240]
O.S.F.	Franciscan Sisters of the Immaculate Conception	[1280]
O.S.F.	Franciscan Sisters of the Immaculate Conception and St. Joseph for the Dying	[1300]
O S.F.	Franciscan Sisters of Little Falls, Minnesota	[1310]
O.S.F.	Franciscan Missionary Sisters of the Immaculate Conception	[1350]
O.S.F.	Missionary Franciscan Sisters of the Immaculate Conception	[1360]
O.S.F.	Franciscan Missionaries of Our Lady	[1380]
O.S.F.	Franciscan Missionary Sisters of Our Lady of Sorrows	[1390]
O.S.F.	Franciscan Sisters of Our Lady of Perpetual Help	[1430]
O.S.F.	Franciscan Sisters of the Sacred Heart	[1450]
O.S.F.	Franciscan Sisters of St. Paul	[1485]
O.S.F.	Sisters of the Third Franciscan Order	[1490]
O.S.F.	St. Francis Mission Community	[1505]
O.S.F.	Sisters of St. Francis	[1510]
O.S.F.	Sisters of St. Francis of Christ the King	[1520]
O.S.F.	Sisters of St. Francis of the Congregation of Our Lady of Lourdes, Sylvania, Ohio	[1530]
O.S.F.	Sisters of Saint Francis, Clinton, Iowa	[1540]
O.S.F.	Sisters of St. Francis of the Holy Cross	[1550]
O.S.F.	Sisters of St. Francis of the Holy Eucharist	[1560]
O.S.F.	Sisters of St. Francis of the Holy Family	[1570]
O.S.F.	Sisters of St. Francis of the Immaculate Conception	[1580]
O.S.F.	Sisters of St. Francis of the Immaculate Heart of Mary (Hankinson, North Dakota)	[1590]
O.S.F.	Sisters of Saint Francis of Millvale, Pennsylvania	[1620]
O.S.F.	Sisters of St. Francis of Penance and Christian Charity	[1630]
O.S.F.	Sisters of St. Francis of Perpetual Adoration	[1640]
O.S.F.	Sisters of St. Francis of the Neumann Communities	[1805]
O.S.F.	The Sisters of St. Francis of Philadelphia	[1650]
O.S.F.	Sisters of Saint Francis of the Providence of God	[1660]
O.S.F.	Sisters of St. Francis of Savannah, MO	[1670]
O.S.F.	School Sisters of St. Francis	[1680]
O.S.F.	School Sisters of the Third Order of St. Francis (Pittsburgh, PA)	[1690]
O.S.F.	School Sisters of the Third Order of St. Francis (Panhandle, TX)	[1695]
O.S.F.	School Sisters of the Third Order of St. Francis (Bethlehem, PA)	[1700]
O.S F.	The Sisters of St. Francis of Assisi	[1705]
O.S.F.	Congregation of the Third Order of St. Francis of Mary Immaculate (Joliet, IL)	[1710]
O.S.F.	Sisters of the Third Order Regular of St. Francis of the Congregation of Our Lady of Lourdes	[1720]
O.S.F.	Congregation of the Sisters of the Third Order of St. Francis (Oldenburg, IN)	[1730]
O.S.F.	Sisters of the Third Order of St. Francis of Penance and Charity	[1760]
O.S.F.	Sisters of the Third Order of St. Francis (Peoria, IL)	[1770]
O.S.F.	Sisters of St. Francis of the Third Order Regular (Williamsville, New York)	[1800]
O.S.F.	Bernardine Sisters of the Third Order of St. Francis	[1810]
O.S.F.	Hospital Sisters of the Third Order of St. Francis	[1820]
O.S.F.	Servants of the Holy Infancy of Jesus	[1980]
O.S.F.	Consolation Sisters (Highland, CA)	[]
O.S.F.	Franciscan Sisters of Christ the Divine Teacher	[]
O.S.F.	St. Francis Mission Community	[]
O.S.F.S.	Oblate Sisters of St. Francis de Sales	[3060]
O.S.H.J.	Oblate Sisters of the Sacred Heart of Jesus	[3050]
O.S.M.	Mantellate Sisters, Servants of Mary of Blue Island	[3570]
O.S.M.	Mantellate Sisters, Servants of Mary of Plainfield	[3572]
O.S.M.	Servants of Mary	[3580]
O.S.M.	Servants of Mary (Servite Sisters)	[3590]
O.S.M.	Oblates of St. Martha	[]
O.S.P.	Oblate Sisters of Providence	[3040]
O.S.S.	Sacramentine Nuns	[3490]
O.SS.R.	Order of the Most Holy Redeemer	[2010]
O.SS.R.	Oblates of the Most Holy Redeemer	[3030]
O.SS.S.	The Brigittine Sisters	[0280]
O.SS.T.	Sisters of the Most Holy Trinity	[0260]
O.S.U.	Ursuline Nuns (Roman Union)	[4110]
O.S.U.	Ursuline Nuns of the Congregation of Paris (St. Martin, OH)	[4120]
O.S.U.	Ursuline Nuns of the Congregation of Paris (Cincinnati, OH)	[4120-01]
O.S.U.	Ursuline Nuns of the Congregation of Paris (Kansas City, KS)	[4120-02]
O.S.U.	Ursuline Nuns of the Congregation of Paris (Louisville, KY)	[4120-03]
O.S.U.	Ursuline Nuns of the Congregation of Paris (Cleveland, OH)	[4120-04]
O.S.U.	Ursuline Nuns of the Congregation of Paris (Owensboro, KY)	[4120-05]
O.S.U.	Ursuline Nuns of the Congregation of Paris (Toledo, OH)	[4120-06]
O.S.U.	Ursuline Nuns of the Congregation of Paris (Youngstown, OH)	[4120-07]
O.S.U.	Ursuline Sisters of the Congregation of Tildonk, Belgium	[4130]
O.S.U.	Irish Ursuline Union	[4150]
P.B.V.M.	Presentation of the Blessed Virgin Mary Sisters	[3280]
P.B.V.M.	Sisters of the Presentation of the B.V.M	[3320]
P B.V.M.	Union of the Sisters of the Presentation of the Blessed Virgin Mary	[3330]
P.C.C.	Order of St. Clare	[3760]
P.C.I.	Pax Christi Institute	[]
P.C.J.	Sisters of the Poor Child Jesus	[3220]
P.C.P.A.	Poor Clares of Perpetual Adoration	[3210]
P.D.D.M.	Pious Disciples of the Divine Master	[0980]
P.F.M.	Franciscans of Mary	[2280]
P.H.J.C.	Poor Handmaids of Jesus Christ	[3230]
P.M.	Sisters of the Presentation of Mary	[3310]
P.O.S.C.	Little Workers of the Sacred Heart	[2345]
P.S.N.	Poor Sisters of Nazareth	[3242]
P.S.S.F.	The Little Sisters of the Holy Family	[2320]
P.S.S.J.	Poor Sisters of St. Joseph	[3250]
P.V.M.I.	The Parish Visitors of Mary Immaculate	[3160]

Q.M.H.C.	Quinhon Missionary Sisters of the Holy Cross	[]
R.A.	Religious of the Apostolate of the Sacred Heart	[3380]
R.A.	Religious of the Assumption	[3390]
R.A.	Antonine Sisters	[]
R.A.D.	Sisters of the Love of God	[]
R.C.	Congregation of Our Lady of Retreat in the Cenacle	[3110]
R.C.D.	Sisters of Our Lady of Christian Doctrine	[3080]
R.C.E.	Religious of Christian Education	[3410]
R.C.M.	Sisters of the Immaculate Conception	[2120]
R.C.S.C.J.	Sisters of the Cross of the Sacred Heart of Jesus (Mexico)	[]
R.D.C.	Sisters of the Divine Compassion	[0970]
R.F.	Sisters of St. Philip Neri Missionary Teachers	[]
R.F.R.	Sisters of Our Lady of Refuge	[]
R.G.S.	The Sisters of the Good Shepherd	[1830]
R.H.S.J.	Religious Hospitallers of Saint Joseph	[3440]
R.J.M.	Religious of Jesus and Mary	[3450]
R.M.	Marianitas	[]
R.M.I.	Claretian Missionary Sisters	[0685]
R.M.I.	Religious of Mary Immaculate	[3460]
R.M.M.	Mercedarian Sisters	[]
R.O.D.A.	Sisters Oblates to Divine Love	[]
R.O.L.C.	Our Lady of Charity of Refuge	[3072]
R.S.C.	Religious Sisters of Charity	[3400]
R.S.C.J.	Society of the Sacred Heart	[4070]
R.S.H.M.	Religious of the Sacred Heart of Mary	[3465]
R.S.J.	Religious of St. Joseph of Australia	[]
R.S.M.	Religious Sisters of Mercy of Alma, Michigan	[2519]
R.S.M.	Sisters of Mercy	[2520]
R.S.M.	Sisters of Mercy of Ardagh & Clonmacnois	[2523]
R.S.M.	Sisters of Mercy (Galway)	[2535]
R.S.M.	Sisters of Mercy	[2540]
R.S.M.	Sisters of Mercy (Sligo)	[2549]
R.S.M.	Sisters of Mercy	[2550]
R.S.M.	Sisters of Mercy of the Americas	[2575]
R.S.M.	Sisters of Mercy	[2600]
R.S.M.	Sisters of Mercy (Ballyshannon, Ireland)	[]
R.S.M.	Sisters of Mercy (Mayo, Ireland)	[]
R.S.M.	Sisters of Mercy of Mississippi, Inc.	[]
R.S.M.	Sisters of Mercy of Portland	[2655]
R.S.M.	Diocesan Sisters of Mercy	[]
R.S.R.	Congregation of Our Lady of the Holy Rosary	[3100]
R.T.	Theatine Sisters of the Immaculate Conception	[]
R.V.M.	Religious of the Blessed Virgin Mary	[]
S.A.	Franciscan Sisters of the Atonement	[1190]
S.A.A.	Sisters Auxillaries of the Apostolate	[0140]
S.A.B.	Sisters of St. Anne Bangalone	[]
S.A.C.	Sisters of the Guardian Angel	[1850]
S.A.C.	Pallottine Missionary Sisters Queen of Apostles Prov	[3150]
S.A.S.V.	Sisters of the Assumption	[0150]
S.B.S.	The Sisters of the Blessed Sacrament for Indians and Colored People	[0260]
S.C.	Sisters of Charity of Cincinnati, Ohio	[0440]
S.C.	Sisters of Charity of Seton Hill, Greensburg, PA	[0570]
S.C.	Sisters of St. Elizabeth, Convent Station	[0590]
S.C.	Sisters of Charity of St. Vincent de Paul, Halifax	[0640]
S.C.	Sisters of Charity of St. Vincent de Paul, New York	[0650]
S.C.C.	Sisters of Christian Charity	[0660]
Sch.P.	Sisters of the Pious Schools	[3200]
S.C.I.C.	Sisters of Charity of the Immaculate Conception of Ivrea	[0450]
S.C.I.M.	Servants of the Immaculate Heart of Mary	[3550]
S.C.K.	Sisters of Christ the King	[]
S.C.L.	Sisters of Charity of Leavenworth, Kansas	[0480]
S.C.M.C.	Sisters of Charity of Our Lady, Mother of the Church	[0530]
S.C.M.M.	Sisters of Charity of Our Lady Mother of Mercy	[0520]
S.C.M.M.	Medical Mission Sisters	[2490]
S.C.N.	Sisters of Charity of Nazareth	[0500]
S.C.O.	Sisters of Charity of Ottawa (Grey Nuns of the Cross)	[0540]
S.C.O.	Sisters of Charity of Quebec (Grey Nuns)	[0560]
S.C.R.H.	Sisters of Charity of Rolling Hills	[0565]
S.C.S.C.	Sisters of Mercy of the Holy Cross	[2630]
S.C.S.J.A.	Sisters of Charity of St. Joan Antida	[0600]
S.C.S.L.	Sisters of Charity of St. Louis	[0620]
S.C.S.H.	Sisters of Charity of St. Hyacinthe (Grey Nuns)	[0610]
S.C.V.	Sisters of Charity of St. Vincent de Paul of Suwon	[0655]
S.deM.	Sisters Servants of Mary	[3600]
S.deP.	Sister Servants of the Poor	[]
S.D.R.	Sisters of the Divine Redeemer	[1020]
S.D.S.	Sisters of the Divine Saviour	[1030]
S.D.S.H.	Sisters of the Society Devoted to the Sacred Heart	[4050]
S.D.V.	Vocationist Sisters	[4210]
S.E.	Sisters of Emanuel	[]
S.E.C.	Sisters of the Eucharistic Covenant	[]
S.F.C.C.	Sisters for Christian Community	[]
S.F.M.A.	Franciscan Missionary Sisters of Assisi	[1330]
S.F.p.	Franciscan Sisters of the Poor	[1440]
S.G.M.	Sisters of Charity of Montreal (Grey Nuns)	[0490]
S.G.S.	Hermanas del Buen Pastor	[]
S.H.C.J.	Society of the Holy Child Jesus	[4060]
S.H.F.	Sisters of the Holy Family	[1960]
S.H.J.M.	Sisters of the Sacred Hearts of Jesus and Mary	[3680]
S.H.S.	Sisters of the Holy Spirit	[2040]
S.H.Sp.	Sisters of the Holy Spirit and Mary Immaculate	[2050]
S.I.M.	Missionaries of the Kingship of Chnst	[]
S.I.W.	Sisters of the Incarnate Word and the Blessed Sacrament	[2210]
S.J.	Servants of Jesus	[3560]
S.J.A.	Sisters of Ste. Jeanne D'Arc	[3815]
S.J.B.	Sisters of St. John Bosco (Taylor, TX)	[]
S.J.C.	Sisters of St. Joseph of Cluny	[3860]
S.J.S.	Servants of the Blessed Sacrament	[3499]
S.J.S.	Sisters of Jesus the Savior	[2245]
S.J.S M.	Sisters of St. Joseph of St. Mark	[3910]
S.J.W.	Sisters of St. Joseph the Worker	[3920]
S.L.	Sisters of Loretto at the Foot of the Cross	[2360]
S.L.T.	Pious Society of Our Lady of the Most Holy Trinity	[]
S.L.W.	Sisters of the Living Word	[2350]
S.M.	Marist Sisters Congregation of Mary	[2430]
S.M.	Sisters of Mercy	[2516]
S.M.	Sisters of Mercy	[2518]
S.M.	Sisters of Mercy	[2570]
S.M.	Sisters of Mercy (Cork and Ross)	[2600]
S.M.	Misericordia Sisters	[2680]
S.M.	Sisters Servants of Mary	[3600]
S.M.	Sisters of Mercy (Loughrea, Ireland)	[]
S.M.	Sisters of Mercy of Tralee	[]
S.M.G.	Poor Servants of the Mother of God	[3640]
S.M.I.	Sisters of Mary Immaculate	[2440]
S.M.I.C.	Missionary Sisters of the Immaculate Conception of the Mother of God	[2760]
S.M.M.G.	Sisters of Mary, Mother of God	[]
S.M.M.I.	Sisters Minor of the Mary Immaculate	[2674]
S.M.M.S.	Society of Mary Missionary Sisters	[]
S.M.P.	Sisters of Mary of the Presentation	[2450]
S.M.P.	Daughters of Our Mother of Peace	[]
S.M.P.	Society of Our Mother of Peace	[]
S.M.R.	Society of Mary Reparatrix	[2560]
S.M.S.H.	Sisters of Saint Marthe (of St. Hyacinthe)	[3940]
S.M.S.M.	Marist Missionary Sisters	[2420]
S.N.D.	Sisters of Notre Dame	[2990]
S.N.D.deN.	Sisters of Notre Dame de Namur	[3000]
S.N.J.M.	Sisters of the Holy Names of Jesus and Mary	[1990]
S.O.L.M.	Sisters of Our Lady of Mercy	[2670]
S.O.L.P.H.	Sisters of Our Lady of Perpetual Help	[]
S.O.L.T.	Sisters of the Society of Our Lady of the Most Holy Trinity	[3105]
S.P.	Sisters of Providence	[3340]
S.P.	Sisters of Providence	[3350]
S.P.	Sisters of Providence of Saint Mary-of-the-Woods, IN	[3360]
S.P.C.	Sisters of St. Paul of Chartres	[3980]
S.R.	Sisters of Reparation of the Sacred Wounds of Jesus	[3475]
S.R.C.	Servants of Our Lady Queen of Clergy	[3520]
S.R.C.M.	Servants of Reparation of the Congregation of Mary	[3470]
S.S.A.	Sisters of St. Ann	[3718]
S.S.A.	Sisters of St. Anne	[3720]
S.S.C.	Missionary Sisters of St. Columban	[2880]
S.S.C.	Sisters of St. Casimir	[3740]
S.S.C.	Society of the Sisters of the Church	[]
SS.CC.	Congregation of the Sacred Hearts and of Perpetual Adoration	[3690]
S.S.Ch.	Sisters of St. Chretienne	[3750]
S.S.C.J.	Servants of the Most Sacred Heart of Jesus	[3630]
S.S.C.J.	Sisters of the Sacred Heart of Jesus of Saint Jacut	[3670]
S.S.C.K.	Congregation of Sister Servants of Christ the King	[3510]
S.S.C.M.	Servants of the Holy Heart of Mary	[3520]
SS.C.M.	Sisters of Saints Cyril and Methodius	[3780]
S.S.D.	Institute of the Sisters of St. Dorothy	[3790]
S.S.E.	Sisters of St. Elizabeth	[3800]
S.S.F.	Congregation of the Sisters of the Holy Family	[1950]
S.S.H.	Sisters Servants of the Most Sacred Heart	[]
S.S.H.J.	Sisters of the Sacred Heart of Jesus	[3658]
S.S.H.J.P.	Servants of the Sacred Heart of Jesus and of the Poor	[3660]
S.S.J.	Servants of St. Joseph	[3595]
S.S.J.	Sisters of St. Joseph (Buffalo)	[3830-06]
S.S.J.	Sisters of St. Joseph (Burlington)	[3830-07]
S.S.J.	Sisters of St. Joseph (Erie)	[3830-09]
S.S.J.	Sisters of St. Joseph (Kalamazoo, Nazareth)	[3830-11]
S.S.J.	Sisters of St. Joseph (Ogdensburg)	[3830-12]
S.S.J.	Sisters of St. Joseph (Rochester)	[3830-14]
S.S.J.	Sisters of St. Joseph, (Springfield, MA)	[3830-16]
S.S.J.	Sisters of St. Joseph (Wheeling, Eng)	[3830-17]
S.S.J.	Sisters of Saint Joseph of Chestnut Hill, Philadelphia	[3893]
S.S.J.	Sisters of St. Joseph of St. Augustine, Florida	[3900]
S.S.J.C.	Sisters of St. Joseph Benedict Cottolengo	[]
S.S.J.-T.O.S.F.	Sisters of St. Joseph of the Third Order of St. Francis	[3930]
S.S.L.	Congregation of the Sisters of St. Louis, Juilly-Monaghan	[3935]
S.S.LOG.	Seton Sisters of Our Lady of Guadalupe, Tucson	[]
S.S.M.	Sisters of the Sorrowful Mother (Third Order of St. Francis)	[4100]
S.S.M.I.	Sisters Servants of Mary Immaculate	[3510]
S.S.M.I.	Sisters Servants of Mary Immaculate	[3610]
S.S.M.I.	Sisters Servants of Mary Immaculate	[3620]

.S.M.N. Sisters of Saint Mary of Namur .... [3950]
.S.M.O. Sisters of St. Mary of Oregon .... [3960]
.S.N.D. School Sisters of Notre Dame .... [2970]
.S.P.C. Missionary Sisters of St. Peter Claver [3990]
.Sp.S. Missionary Sisters Servants of the Holy Spirit .... [3530]
.Sp.S.deA.P. Sister Servants of the Holy Spirit of Perpetual Adoration .... [3540]
.S.S. Servants of the Blessed Sacrament ...... [3500]
.S.S. Sisters of Social Service of Los Angeles, Inc. .... [4080]
S.S.S. Sisters of Social Service .... [4090]
S.S.S.F. School Sisters of St. Francis .... [1680]
S.S.T.V. Congregation of Sisters of St. Thomas of Villanova .... [4030]
S.T.J. Society of St. Teresa of Jesus .... [4020]
S.U. Society of St. Ursula .... [4040]
S.U.S.C. Sisters of the Holy Union .... [2070]
S.V. Sisters of Life .... [2265]
S.V.M. Sisters of the Visitation of the Congregation of the Immaculate Heart of Mary .... [4200]
V.D.C. Verbum Dei Community .... []
V.H.M. Visitation Nuns .... [4190]
V.S. Vestiarski Sisters .... []
V.S.C. Vincentian Sisters of Charity .... [4160]
V.S.C. Vincentian Sisters of Charity .... [4170]
V.Z. Sisters of Charity of St. Vincent de Paul .... [0630]
X.M.M. Xaverian Missionary Society of Mary, Inc. .... [4230]
X.S. Catholic Mission Sisters of St. Francis Xavier .... [3810]

Religious Institutes of Women

Women Leadership Conference of Women Religious of the United States of America—National Office: 8808 Cameron St., Silver Spring, MD 20910. Tel: 301-588-4955; Fax: 301-587-4575; Website: www.lcwr.org. Sr. Pat Farrell, O.S.F., Pres.; Sr. Florence Deacon, O.S.F., Pres. Elect; Sr. Mary Hughes, O.P., Past Pres.; Sr. Barbara Blesse, O.P., Sec.; Sr. Sheila Megley, R.S.M., Treas.; Sr. Janet Mock, C.S.J., Exec. Dir. Council of Major Superiors of Women Religious in the United States of America—1211 Lawrence St., N.E., P.O. Box 4467, Washington, DC 20017-0467. Tel: 202-832-2575; Fax: 202-832-6325; Website: www.cmswr.org. Mother Regina Marie Gorma, O.C.D., Chm.; Mother Ann Marie Karlovic, O.P., Asst. Chm.; Mother M. Regina Pacis Coury, F.S.G.M., Sec.; Sr. Jacquelyn Darner, M.S., Treas.

(The initial (D) or (P) indicates Diocesan or Pontifical Jurisdiction.)

[0100] (A.S.C.)—ADORERS OF THE BLOOD OF CHRIST (P)

Founded in Acuto, Italy, in 1834. First foundation in the United States in 1870.

General Motherhouse: Via Beata Maria De Mattias 10, Rome, Italy, 00183. Sr. Bernarda Kristic, A.S.C., Supr. Gen.

Regional Offices - United States Region: *Adorers of the Blood of Christ*, 4233 Sulphur Ave., Saint Louis, MO 63109. Tel: 314-351-6294; Fax: 314-351-6789. Sr. Jan E. Renz, A.S.C., Regional Leader.
Professed Sisters: 300.
Properties owned and/or sponsored: Villa Maria, Mulvane, KS; Newman University, Wichita, KS; St. Joseph Villa, David City, NE; St. Joseph Convent-Provincial House; St. Anne's Retirement Community, Inc.; De Matias Residence; St. Anne's Independent Living Retirement Village, Columbia PA.
Legal Title: *Adorers of the Blood of Christ.*
Sisters serve and staff: Colleges; Secondary & Elementary Schools; Special & Religious Education; Hospitals; Pastoral Care; Nursing Homes; Domestic Service in Communities & Institutions; Administration in Religious Orders & Parishes; Prayer Ministry; Retreat Ministry; Social Service; Pastoral & Chaplaincy Ministry; Prison & Minority Ministries; Ministry to the Homeless; Diocesan Offices; Homes for the Aged & Home Nursing; Foreign Missions.
Represented in the Archdioceses of Chicago, Kansas City in Kansas, Oklahoma City, St. Louis, San Antonio, San Francisco and Washington and in the Dioceses of Alexandria, Belleville, Dodge City, El Paso, Fort Worth, Gallup, Harrisburg, Jefferson City, Kansas City, Lexington, Lincoln, Oakland, Salina, San Diego, Springfield-Cape Girardeau, Springfield in Illinois, Tucson, Wilmington, Wichita and Youngstown. Also in Bolivia, Guatemala, Korea and Rome.

Ruma Center(1876): 2 Pioneer Ln., Red Bud, IL 62278. Tel: 618-282-3848.

Wichita Center(1929): 1165 Southwest Blvd., Wichita, KS 67213-1394. Tel: 316-942-2201.

Columbia Center(1925): 3950 Columbia Ave., Columbia, PA 17512-9714. Tel: 717-285-4536.

[0110] (A.P.B.)—THE SISTERS ADORERS OF THE PRECIOUS BLOOD (P)
(Cloistered Contemplative Order)

American Federation: Consisting of Five Autonomous Monasteries: 400 Pratt St., Watertown, NY 13601-4238. Tel: 315-788-1669. Sr. Mary Jo Divney, A.P.B., Pres. American Federation.
Professed Sisters: 75; Novices: 8; Postulants: 2.
Represented in the Dioceses of Brooklyn, Manchester, Ogdensburg and Portland (In Maine).

New York: 5400 Ft. Hamilton Pkwy., Brooklyn, NY 11219. Tel: 718-438-6371.

New Hampshire: 700 Bridge St., Manchester, NH 03104. Tel: 603-623-4264.

New York: 400 Pratt St., Watertown, NY 13601. Tel: 315-788-1669.

Maine: 166 State St., Portland, ME 04101. Tel: 207-774-0861.

Canada: 9415 165th St., Edmonton, Canada, T5R 2S5. Tel: 403-484-6691.

[0130] (A.S.C.J.)—APOSTLES OF THE SACRED HEART OF JESUS (P)

Founded in Italy in 1894. First Foundation in United States 1902.

General Motherhouse: *Apostole del Sacro Cuore di Gesu*, Via Germano Sommeiller 38, Rome, Italy, 00185. Mother Clare Millea, A.S.C.J., Supr. Gen.; Sr. Chiara Cervato, Sec.

U.S. Provincial Motherhouse: *Mt. Sacred Heart*, 295 Benham St., Hamden, CT 06514. Tel: 203-248-4225; Fax: 203-230-8341.
Professed Sisters: 127.
Properties owned and/or sponsored: Clelian House Convent, St. Louis, MO; Our Lady of Hope Convent, St. Louis, MO; Mary, Mother of the Church Convent, Hamden, CT; Mount Sacred Heart College for Sisters; Sacred Heart Academy; Sacred Heart Manor; Sacred Heart Manor Nursery and Kindergarten; Clelian Adult Day Center, Hamden, CT; Sacred Heart on the Lake, Higganum, CT; Cor Jesu Academy, St. Louis, MO; Sacred Heart Villa Nursery, St. Louis, MO; Our Lady Queen of Apostles (Convent & Retreat and Spirituality Center), Imperial, MO; Clelian Heights School for Exceptional Children, Greensburg, PA; Sacred Heart Private School, Bronx, NY.
Ministry in the fields of Education, Health Care, Parishes, Adult Day Care and Immigrant Services.
Represented in the Archdioceses of Hartford, New York and St. Louis and in the Dioceses of Bridgeport, Greensburg, Norwich and Pensacola-Tallahassee. Also in Rome and Taiwan.

[0150] (S.A.S.V.)—SISTERS OF THE ASSUMPTION (P)

Founded in Saint-Gregoire, P.Q., Canada in 1853. First foundation in the United States in 1891.

General Motherhouse: Nicolet, Canada Sr. Muriel Lemoine, S.A.S.V., Congregational Leader.

United States Region: *Regional Office*, 316 Lincoln St., Worcester, MA 01605. Tel: 508-856-9383. Sr. Lorraine Normand, S.A.S.V., Reg. Treas.
Total in Region and Professed: 69.
Legal Holdings: Assumption Residence of the Sisters of the Assumption of the Blessed Virgin, Petersham, MA; Harper Residence, Worcester, MA.
Ministry in all levels of education.
Missions in Japan, Brazil and Ecuador.
Represented in the Archdiocese of Boston and in the Dioceses of Albany, Fall River, Portland (In Maine), Providence, Springfield in Massachusetts and Worcester.

[0160] (O.S.A.)—AUGUSTINIAN NUNS OF CONTEMPLATIVE LIFE (P)

Augustinian Contemplative Nuns: *Mother of Good Counsel Convent*, 440 N. Marley Rd., New Lenox, IL 60451. Sr. Mary Grace Kuppe, O.S.A., Prioress.
Total in Community: 5.
Legal Title: *Augustinian Cloistered Nuns, Inc.*
Represented in the Diocese of Joliet.

[0170] (O.S.B.)—BENEDICTINE NUNS OF THE CONGREGATION OF SOLESMES (P)

Order originated in Italy, c.529. Congregation of Solesmes formed in France in 1837.

U.S. Establishment (1981): *Monastery of the Immaculate Heart of Mary*, 4103 VT Rte. 100, Westfield, VT 05874. Tel: 802-744-6525; Fax: 802-744-6236. Rev. Mother Laurence Couture, O.S.B., Prioress.
Total in Congregation: 882; Total in Community: 14.
Represented in the Diocese of Burlington.

[0180] (O.S.B.)—BENEDICTINE NUNS OF THE PRIMITIVE OBSERVANCE (P)

First founded in Italy in about c.529. First United States establishment in 1948.

Abbey of Regina Laudis: 273 Flanders Rd., Bethlehem, CT 06751. Tel: 203-266-7727; Fax: 203-266-5915. Rt. Rev. Mother David Serna, O.S.B., Abbess.
Professed Nuns: 29; Sisters in First Vows: 4; Postulants: 2; Novices: 3.

[0190] (O.S.B.)—BENEDICTINE NUNS (P)

First founded in Italy in c.529. Founded in the United States in 1931 from St. Walburg Abbey, Eichstatt, Bavaria, Germany.

The Sisters of St. Benedict of Westmoreland County: *St. Emma Monastery*, 1001 Harvey Ave., Greensburg, PA 15601-1491. Tel: 724-834-3060; Fax: 724-834-5772; Email: benedictinenuns@stemma.org. Mother Mary Anne Noll, O.S.B., Prioress.
Professed Nuns: 11.
Ministry in Monastic Life; Benedictine hospitality extended through adjacent St. Emma Retreat House; Monastic Guest House.
Represented in the Diocese of Greensburg.

Benedictine Nuns: *Abbey of St. Walburga*, 1029 Benedictine Way, Virginia Dale, CO 80536. Tel: 970-472-0612; Fax: 970-484-4342; Email: abbey@walburga.org. Mother Maria Michael Newe, O.S.B., Abbess; Mother Maria-Thomas Beil, O.S.B., Retired Abbess.
Sisters: 19; Novices: 3; Claustral Oblate: 1.
Represented in the Archdiocese of Denver.

[0210] (O.S.B.)—MISSIONARY BENEDICTINE SISTERS (P)

The Congregation of Missionary Benedictine Sisters is of Pontifical Jurisdiction. Its Constitutions were approved by Rome on June 25, 1934; Revised approval June 29, 1983.

Generalate: Rome, Italy

Priory House and Novitiate: *Immaculata Monastery (1923)*, 300 N. 18th St., Norfolk, NE 68701-3687. Tel: 402-371-3438; Fax: 402-379-7667. Sr. Pia Portmann, O.S.B., Prioress.
Professed Sisters: 38; Junior Sisters: 3.
Legal Holdings or Titles: Missionary Benedictine Sisters, Inc., Norfolk, NE; Providence Convent, Wayne, NE; Hildegard House, Creighton, NE.
Ministry in the fields of Retreat; Education; Health; Outreach Services with Hispanics and Elderly.
Represented in the Archdiocese of Omaha and in the Diocese of New Ulm.

[0220] (O.S.B.)—CONGREGATION OF THE BENEDICTINE SISTERS OF PERPETUAL ADORATION OF PONTIFICAL JURISDICTION (P)

Founded from Maria Rickenbach, Switzerland in 1874 with first monastery at Clyde, MO. Congregation erected by decree of the Holy See on June 16, 1936.

General Motherhouse: *Benedictine Convent of Perpetual Adoration*, 31970 State Hwy. P, Clyde, MO 64432. Tel: 660-944-2221; Fax: 660-944-2152. Sr. Patricia Nyquist, Prioress Gen.
Total in Community: 52; Total in Congregation: 80; Postulants: 1.

San Benito Monastery: Box 510, Dayton, WY 82836.

Interdependent Monasteries: 800 N. Country Club Rd., Tucson, AZ 85716.
Ministry in Monastic/Contemplative/Eucharistic Apostolate of Prayer; Liturgy of the Hours four times daily in Choir; Contemplative Prayer and Monastic Atmosphere Shared with Others; Prayer Days and Retreats for Sisters; Editing and Publishing Bimonthly Magazine: Spirit & Life; Production and Distribution of Altar Breads; Liturgical Vestments; Correspondence.
Represented in the Dioceses of Cheyenne, Kansas City-St. Joseph and Tucson.

[0230] (O.S.B.)—BENEDICTINE SISTERS OF PONTIFICAL JURISDICTION (P)

(I) The Federation of St. Scholastica

Erected by Decree of the Holy See, February 25, 1922, with final approbation by Decree of June 10, 1930. Nineteen Monasteries in the United States and two in Mexico. Total number in the Federation 760. Sr. Glenna Smith, O.S.B., Federation Pres., residing at: St. Benedict Monastery, 9535 Linton Hall Rd., Bristow, VA 20136. Phone: 703-361-7028.

Benedictine Sisters of Baltimore, Inc: *Emmanuel Monastery*, 2229 W. Joppa Rd., Lutherville Timonium, MD 21093. Tel: 410-821-5792; Fax: 410-296-9560; Email: bensrs@emmanuelosb.org; Web: www.emmanuelosb.org. Sr. Kathleen White, O.S.B., Prioress.
Total in Community: 16.
Ministry in the field of Education; Pastoral Ministry; Retreats and Spiritual Direction; Justice Ministry; Social Services; Administrative Services; Hospital Service Ministry.
Represented in the Archdioceses of Baltimore and Newark and in the Diocese of Allentown.

Benedictine Sisters of the Byzantine Rite (1969): *Queen of Heaven Monastery*, 169 Kenmore Ave., N.E., #305, Warren, OH 44483. Tel: 330-856-1813. Sr. Margaret Mary Schima, O.S.B., Admin.
Professed Sisters: 7.
Ministry in Religious and Academic Education; Pastoral Ministry; Administration.
Represented in the Archdiocese of Pittsburgh Byzantine Rite.

Mount St. Scholastica Inc. (1863): *Motherhouse of the Sisters of St. Benedict*, 801 S. Eighth St., Atchison, KS 66002-2778. Tel: 913-360-6200; Fax: 913-360-6190; Web: www.mountosb.org. Sr. Anne Shepard, O.S.B., Prioress.
Professed Sisters: 151; Novices: 1.
Legal Holdings: Dooley Center, Inc.; Mount St. Scholastica, Inc., Atchison, KS.
Ministry in the field of Academic Education at all levels; Counseling; Retreats; Spirituality Center; Spiritual Direction; Social Services; Hospitality; Music Conservatory; Pastoral Ministry; Ministry to women of all ages; Missionary Work in Brazil.
Represented in the Archdioceses of Kansas City in Kansas, Oklahoma City, and St. Louis and in the Dioceses of Des Moines, Lincoln and Kansas City-St. Joseph. Also in Brazil.

Benedictine Sisters of Elk Co. (1852): *St. Joseph Monastery*, St. Marys, PA 15857. Tel: 814-834-2267; Fax: 814-834-3270. Sr. Anne Stedman, O.S.B., Admin.
Professed Sisters: 17.
Ministry in the fields of Academic and Religious Education; Pastoral Ministry; Retreats.

Benedictine Sisters (1998): *Transfiguration Priory*, 526 Fairview St., Emmaus, PA 18049-3837. Tel: 610-965-6818. Sr. Martina Revak, O.S.B., Supr.
Professed Sisters: 3.
Legal Title: *Benedictine Sisters of Baltimore.*
Ministry in the fields of Education; Pastoral Ministry;

Hospitality and Spirituality.
A mission house of the Benedictine Sisters of Baltimore, Emmanuel Monastery, 2229 W. Joppa Rd., Lutherville, MD 21093-4601.
Represented in the Diocese of Allentown.

Benedictine Sisters of Erie (1856): *Mount St. Benedict Monastery*, 6101 East Lake Rd., Erie, PA 16511. Tel: 814-899-0614; Fax: 814-898-4004. Sr. Anne Wambach, O.S.B., Prioress.
Total in Congregation: 100; Professed Sisters: 100.
Properties owned and/or sponsored: Mount Saint Benedict Monastery; Glinodo Center; St. Benedict Education Center; Benet Center; 8 Community Houses; St. Benedict Community Center.
Sisters serve and staff: High Schools; Elementary Schools; Colleges; Day Care Centers; Residence for Elderly and Handicapped; Hospitals; Social Services; Diocesan Offices; Pastoral Ministry; Religious Education.
Represented in the Dioceses of Cleveland, Erie, and Wilmington.

Benedictine Sisters of Chicago O.S.B. (1861): *St. Scholastica Monastery*, 7430 N. Ridge Blvd., Chicago, IL 60645. Tel: 773-764-2413. Sr. Patricia Crowley, O.S.B., Prioress; Sr. Vivian Ivantic, Community Archivist.
Professed Sisters: 44.
Properties owned and/or sponsored: St. Scholastica Monastery, Chicago, IL; St. Scholastica Academy, Chicago, IL.
Ministry in High Schools; Parish Ministry; Education Administration; Religious Education; Management Consultant; Spiritual Direction; Shelter Ministry; Community Center Work; Social Service Counseling; Music; Massage Therapy; Group Facilitation; Preschool; Psychiatric Social Work; Pastoral Psychotherapy.
Represented in the Archdiocese of Chicago and in the Diocese of Pueblo.

Benedictine Sisters of the Sacred Heart O.S.B. (1895): *Sacred Heart Monastery*, 1910 Maple Ave., Lisle, IL 60532-2164. Tel: 630-725-6000. Sr. Judith Ann Heble, O.S.B., Prioress.
Professed Sisters: 28.
Legal Title: *Benedictine Sisters of the Sacred Heart Charitable Trust.*
Sisters serve and staff: High Schools; Elementary Schools; Colleges; Villa St. Benedict; Religious Education; Pastoral Ministry; Nurses Administration; Independent Positions involving Secretarial, Counseling, Liturgical Works, Occupational Therapy.
Represented in the Diocese of Joliet.

Sisters of Benedict of Colorado, Inc: 4264 W. Ponds View Dr., Littleton, CO 80123. Tel: 303-795-2378. Sr. Judith Elms, O.S.B., Supr.

Benedictine Sisters of Elizabeth, NJ O.S.B. (1868): *St. Walburga Monastery and Novitiate*, 851 N. Broad St., Elizabeth, NJ 07208. Tel: 908-352-4278. Sr. Sharon McHugh, O.S.B., Prioress; Sr. Cynthia Cunningham, O.S.B., Sub Prioress.
Professed Sisters: 43.
Legal Holdings and Titles: Benedictine Hospital, Kingston, NY; Benedictine Academy, Elizabeth, NJ.
Represented in the Archdioceses of New York and Newark.

Benedictine Sisters of Pittsburgh, PA O.S.B. (1870): *St. Benedict Monastery*, 4530 Perrysville Ave., Pittsburgh, PA 15229-2296. Tel: 412-931-2844. Sr. Benita DeMatteis, O.S.B., Prioress.
Professed Sisters: 52.
Ministry in the field of Education in all levels; Religious and Special Education; Pastoral Ministry; Childcare; Social Service; Campus Ministry; Hospital Chaplaincy; Art Education; Ministry Resource; Outreach with Poor.
Represented in the Dioceses of Greensburg, Pittsburgh and Lexington.

Sisters of Benedict O.S.B. (1968): *Red Plains Spirituality Center*, 728 Richland Rd., S.W., Piedmont, OK 73078-9324. Tel: 405-373-4565; Fax: 405-373-3392. Sr. Anne Shepard, O.S.B., Prioress.
Professed Sisters: 6.
Properties owned and/or sponsored: Red Plains Spirituality Center, Piedmont, OK.
Ministry in the fields of Spiritual Formation; Spiritual Direction; Retreats.
Represented in the Archdiocese of Oklahoma City.

Benedictine Sisters O.S.B. (1879): *St. Joseph Monastery*, 2200 S. Lewis, Tulsa, OK 74114-3100. Tel: 918-742-4989; Fax: 918-744-1374. Sr. Christine Ereiser, O.S.B., Prioress.
Professed Sisters: 22.
Legal Holdings and Titles: Congregation of the Benedictine Sisters of the Sacred Hearts; Monte Cassino School.
Ministry in the field of Academic Education; Catechetics; Evangelization; Social Work; Pastoral Ministry; Counseling & Spiritual Direction; Religious Education & Religious Formation.
Represented in the Dioceses of Lincoln and Tulsa.

Benedictine Sisters of Pontifical Jurisdiction O.S.B. (1857): *St. Gertrude Monastery*, 14259 Benedictine Ln., Ridgely, MD 21660-1434. Tel: 410-634-2497. Sr. Colleen Quinlivan, O.S.B., Admin.
Professed Sisters: 24.
Legal Holdings and Titles: The Benedictine School for Exceptional Children; Berg Retreat Facility; St. Martin's Barn; St. Martin House, Ridgely, MD; St. Benedict, Wilmington, DE.
Ministry in Special Schools and Secondary Education; Ministry to the poor and homeless; Ministry to Hospice.
Represented in the Diocese of Wilmington.

St. Walburg Monastery of Benedictine Sisters of Covington, KY O.S.B. (1859): *St. Walburg Monastery*, 2500 Amsterdam Rd., Villa Hills, KY 41017-5316. Tel: 859-331-6324; Fax: 859-331-2136. Sr. Mary Catherine Wenstrup, O.S.B., Prioress; Sr. Betty Cahill, O.S.B., Community Archivist.
Professed Sisters: 65.
Legal Titles and Holdings: Villa Madonna Montessori School; Villa Madonna Academy.
Sisters serve and staff: Diocesan Offices; Pastoral and Social Ministry; Public Health Care; all levels of academic education (elementary and high school).
Represented in the Archdiocese of Cincinnati and in the Dioceses of Covington, Lexington and Pueblo.

Benedictine Sisters (1902): *Sacred Heart Monastery*, 916 Convent Rd., Cullman, AL 35055. Tel: 256-734-2199; Fax: 256-255-0048. Sr. Janet Marie Flemming, O.S.B., Prioress; Sr. Mary Ruth Coffman, O.S.B., Community Archivist.
Professed Sisters: 47.
Properties owned and/or sponsored: Benedictine Spirituality and Conference Center; Benedictine Manor Retirement Home; Sacred Heart Monastery of Cullman, AL Foundation.
Sisters serve and staff: all levels of Academic Education; Pastoral Ministry; Diocesan Offices; Retirement Homes; Conference Centers; Rural Health Center (Doctor); Nurses; Lawyer.
Represented in the Diocese of Birmingham.

Benedictine Sisters of Virginia O.S.B. (1868): *St. Benedict Monastery*, 9535 Linton Hall Rd., Bristow, VA 20136-1217. Tel: 703-361-0106. Sr. Cecilia Dwyer, O.S.B., Prioress.
Total Professed Sisters: 31.
Legal Holdings and Titles: Benedictine Sisters of Virginia, Inc.; St. Gertrude High School, Richmond, VA; Linton Hall School; Benedictine Pastoral Center; Benedictine Counseling Services, Bristow, VA; B.E.A-.C.O.N., Bristow, VA.
Represented in the Dioceses of Arlington and Richmond.

Benedictine Sisters (1911): *St. Scholastica's Monastery and Novitiate*, 416 W. Highland Dr., Boerne, TX 78006. Tel: 830-249-2645; Fax: 830-249-1365. Sr. Bernadine Reyes, O.S.B., Prioress.
Total in Community: 17.
Properties owned and/or sponsored: St. Scholastica Monastery; Benedictine Sisters Charitable Trust I; Benedictine Sisters Charitable Trust II.
Represented in the Archdiocese of San Antonio and in the Diocese of Laredo.

Benedictine Sisters of St. Lucy's Priory Inc. O.S.B. (1956): *St. Lucy's Priory*, 19045 E. Sierra Madre Ave., Glendora, CA 91741. Tel: 626-335-1682. Sr. Elizabeth Brown, O.S.B., Prioress.
Professed Sisters: 12.
Legal Holdings: St. Lucy's Priory High School; St. Lucy's Benedictine Child Development Center.
Sisters serve and staff: all levels of Academic Education; Pastoral Ministry.
Represented in the Archdiocese of Los Angeles and in the Diocese of San Diego.

Benedictine Sisters of Florida (1889): *Holy Name Monastery*, P.O. Box 2450, St. Leo, FL 33574-2450. Tel: 352-588-8320; Fax: 352-588-8319. Sr. Roberta Bailey, O.S.B., Prioress; Sr. M. Dorothy Neuhofer, O.S.B., Community Archivist.
Professed Sisters: 15.
Represented in the Diocese of St. Petersburg.

Sisters of St. Benedict (1963): *Benet Hill Monastery-Motherhouse*, 3190 Benet Ln., Colorado Springs, CO 80921-1509. Tel: 719-633-0655; Fax: 719-471-0403. Sr. Anne Stedman, O.S.B., Prioress; Sr. Diane Liston, O.S.B., Community Archivist.
Total in Community: 38.
Properties owned and/or sponsored: Benet Hill Monastery and Ministry Center.
Represented in the Archdioceses of Denver and Santa Fe and in the Diocese of Colorado Springs. Also in Jamaica.

Benedictine Sisters O.S.B. (1989): *Queen of Angels Monastery*, 23615 N.E. 100th St., Liberty, MO 64068. Tel: 816-750-4618; Fax: 816-750-4620; Web: www.libertybenedictinesisters.org. Sr. Agnes Helgenberger, O.S.B., Prioress.
Professed Sisters: 6.
Ministry in Companioning; food for the hungry; prison ministry; thrift stores; Religious education and retreats; Nursing.
Represented in the Diocese of Kansas City-St. Joseph.
Erected by Decree of the Apostolic See on April 14, 1937, with final approbation by Decree of April 4, 1950.

(II) The Federation of St. Gertrude: 802 E. 10th St., Ferdinand, IN 47532.

Federation Office: *Monastery Immaculate Conception (1867)*, 802 E. 10th St., Ferdinand, IN 47532-9239. Tel: 812-367-1411; Fax: 812-367-2313. Sr. Joella Kidwell, O.S.B., Federation Pres.
Total in Federation: 700.

Fifteen members monasteries from this Federation as follows:

Benedictine Sisters of Belcourt O.S.B: *Queen of Peace Monastery (1956)*, 802 E. 10th St., Ferdinand, IN 47532-9239. Tel: 812-367-1411 Ext. 2917; Fax: 812-367-2313. Sr. Joella Kidwell, O.S.B., Pres. & Admin.
Community Ministry.
Represented in the Diocese of Fargo.

Mailing Address: Benedictine Sisters O.S.B: *Our Lady of Peace Monastery*, 802 E. 10th, Ferdinand, IN 47532. Tel: 812-367-1411 Ext. 2835; Fax: 812-367-2313; Email: joellak@thedome.org. Sr. Joella Kidwell, O.S.B., Admin.
Professed Sisters: 2.
Ministry in Religious Education; Home Health Care; Pastoral Care; Parish, Social and Nursing Ministries; Counseling.
Represented in the Dioceses of Jefferson City and Springfield Cape-Girardeau.

Monastery of St. Gertrude (1882): 465 Keuterville Rd., Cottonwood, ID 83522-5183. Tel: 208-962-3224; Fax: 208-962-7212. Sr. Clarissa Goeckner, O.S.B., Prioress; Rev. Meinrad Schallberger, O.S.B., Chap.
Professed Sisters: 55.
Legal Title: *Idaho Corporation of Benedictine Sisters.*
Sisters serve in Education; Parish Ministry; Health Care; Retreat Ministry; Social Work; Counseling; St. Gertrude's Museum, Spirit Center Retreat House.
Represented in the Archdioceses of Los Angeles and Seattle and in the Dioceses of Boise, St. Cloud and Spokane.

Sisters of St. Benedict of Crookston O.S.B: *Mount St. Benedict Monastery (1919)*, 620 E. Summit Ave., Crookston, MN 56716-2799. Tel: 218-281-3441; Fax: 218-281-6966. Sr. Jennifer Kehrwald, O.S.B., Admin.
Professed Sisters: 74.
Legal Titles or Holdings: Villa St. Vincent, Crookston, MN.
Sisters serve and staff: Elementary; Colleges; Nursing Homes; Assisted Living Facilities; Religious Education Center; Adult Education; Parish Ministry; Pastoral Care; Retreat Centers; Child Care; Nursery School.
Represented in the Dioceses of Brownsville, Crookston and New Ulm.

Benedictine Sisters O.S.B. (1867): *Monastery Immaculate Conception*, 802 E. 10th St., Ferdinand, IN 47532-9239. Tel: 812-367-1411; Fax: 812-367-2313. Sr. Kristine Anne Harpenau, O.S.B., Prioress.
Professed Sisters: 156; Perpetually Professed: 153; Temporary Commitment: 3.
Legal Title: *Sisters of St. Benedict of Ferdinand, Indiana, Inc.*
Sisters sponsor: Kordes Retreat Center, Ferdinand, IN.
Sisters serve and staff: on all levels of Academic Education; Religious Education; Parish Ministry; Hospitals; Public Health-Social Service Agencies; Diocesan Offices; Foreign Missions; Hispanic Ministries; Retreat House; Community Ministry; Psychology and Counseling Agencies.
Represented in the Archdioceses of Indianapolis, and Louisville and in the Dioceses of Evansville and Owensboro. Also in Rome and Peru.

Benedictine Sisters, O.S.B. of St. Scholastica Monastery (1879): *St. Scholastica Monastery*, P.O. Box 3849, Fort Smith, AR 72913-3489. Tel: 479-783-4147; Fax: 479-782-4352. Sr. Maria Goretti DeAngeli, O.S.B., Prioress.
Professed Sisters: 61.
Ministry in the fields of Retreat Center; Parish Ministry; Hospital Chaplaincy; House of Prayer; Retreat Ministry; Counseling; Spiritual Direction.

Sisters of St. Benedict of Riverside, California, Inc., (1972): *Holy Spirit Monastery*, 22791 Pico St., Grand Terrace, CA 92313-5725. Tel: 909-783-4446; Fax: 909-783-3525. Sr. Mary Ann Schepers, O.S.B., Prioress.
Professed Sisters: 5.
Ministry in Religious Education; Parish Ministry; Spritual Guidance; Retreat Ministry; Educating Mentally Challenged Children.
Represented in the Diocese of San Bernardino.

Benedictine Sisters of Mt. Angel, Oregon (1882): *Queen of Angels Monastery*, 840 S. Main St., Mount Angel, OR 97362-9527. Tel: 503-845-6141; Fax: 503-845-6585; Email: qamosb@yahoo.com; Web: www.benedictine-srs.org. Sr. Donna Marie Chartraw, O.S.B., Prioress.
Professed Sisters: 39.
Corporate Ministries: Shalom Prayer Center; St. Joseph's Shelter, Mt. Angel, OR.
Sisters serve: High School; Seminary; Parish Ministry; Retreat and Prayer Ministry; Spiritual Direction; Ministry to Poor and Hispanics.
Represented in the Archdiocese of Portland in Oregon.

Benedictine Convent of St. Martin (1889): *St. Martin Monastery*, 1851 City Spring Rd., Rapid City, SD 57702-9602. Tel: 605-343-8011; Fax: 605-399-2723. Sr. Yvette Mallow, O.S.B., Prioress.
Professed Sisters: 25.
Ministry in the fields of Religious Education; Parish and Jail Ministry; Retreat and Spiritual Direction.
Represented in the Diocese of Rapid City.

Sisters of St. Benedict of Beech Grove, Ind., Inc. (1956): *Our Lady of Grace Monastery*, 1402 Southern Ave., Beech Grove, IN 46107-1197. Tel: 317-787-3287; Fax: 317-780-2368. Sr. Juliann Babcock, O.S.B., Prioress.
Professed Sisters: 66.
Legal Titles: Sisters of St. Benedict of Beech Grove, IN,

Inc.; Charitable Trust of the Monastery of Our Lady of Grace, Sisters of the Order of St. Benedict.
Ministry in Education; Parish Ministries; Retirement Home; Educational Center; Religious Education; Hospitals.
Represented in the Archdioceses of Cincinnati, Indianapolis and Louisville.
Properties owned and sponsored: Our Lady of Grace Monastery; Benedict Inn Retreat and Conference Center; St. Paul Hermitage; Regina Retreat.

Benedictine Sisters of Richardton, O.S.B. (1916): *Sacred Heart Monastery (1916)*, P.O. Box 364, Richardton, ND 58652-0364. Tel: 701-974-2121; Fax: 701-974-2124. Sr. Paula Larson, O.S.B., Prioress.
Professed Sisters: 24.
Legal Titles or Holdings: Benedictine Sponsorship Board, Inc.; Marillac Manor, Inc.; Subiaco Manor Inc.; Sacred Heart Benedictine Foundation; Pia Tegler Foundation.
Ministry in the fields of Academic Education; Hospital Chaplaincy; Native American Ministry; Parish Ministry; Health Care.
Represented in the Diocese of Bismarck.

The Benedictine Sisters of Mother of God Monastery O.S.B: *Mother of God Monastery (1961)*, 110 28th Ave., S.E., Watertown, SD 57201-8418. Tel: 605-882-6600; Fax: 605-882-6658. Sr. Marlene Minnaert, O.S.B., Prioress.
Perpetual Vows: 53; Temporary Professed: 3; Novices: 1.
Legal Titles: The Benedictine Sisters of Mother of God Monastery, Watertown, SD; St. Ann's Corporation (includes Benet Place & Evergreen Assisted Living), Watertown, SD; Retirement Trust, Watertown, SD; Benedictine Sisters Foundation of Watertown, SD.
Sisters serve and staff: in Elementary Education; Religious Education Centers; Parish Ministry; Social Services; Hospitals and Hospices; Retreat Center; Juvenile Services; Prison Ministry; Native American Ministries; Hispanic Ministries; Libraries & Archives; and Congregate Housing for Elderly.
Represented in the Archdiocese of St. Paul-Minneapolis and in the Dioceses of Fargo, New Ulm and Sioux Falls.

St. Benedict's Monastery (1912): 225 Masters Ave., Winnipeg, Canada, R4A 2A1. Tel: 204-338-4601; Fax: 304-339-1705. Sr. Virginia Evard, O.S.B., Prioress.
Professed Sisters: 22.
Ministry in Retreat & Conference Center; Education; Health Care; Pastoral Care; St. Benedict's Place, Seniors' Residence.
Represented in the Dioceses of Calgary and Winnipeg, Canada.

Benedictine Convent of the Sacred Heart: *Sacred Heart Monastery (1880)*, 1005 W. 8th St., Yankton, SD 57078-3389. Tel: 605-668-6000; Fax: 605-668-6153. Sr. Penny Bingham, O.S.B., Prioress.
Professed Sisters: 108.
Sisters serve and staff: in Health Care Institutions; all levels of Academic Education; Social Services; Parish Ministry; Pastoral Care; Diocesan Offices; Counseling & Religious Education.
Represented in the Archdiocese of Omaha and St. Louis and in the Dioceses of Grand Island, Lincoln, Rapid City and Sioux Falls.

Benedictine Sisters of Nanaimo: *House of Bread Monastery (1993)*, 2329 Arbot Rd., Nanaimo, Canada, V9R 6S8. Tel: 250-753-1763; Fax: 250-754-3744. Sr. Barbara Rinehart, O.S.B., Prioress.
Professed Sisters: 7.
Corporate Ministries: Bethlehem Retreat Centre; Bethlehem Counseling Centre.
Sisters serve: Counseling; Retreat and Prayer Ministry; Nursing; Artist.
Represented in the Diocese of Victoria, Canada.

(III): The Federation of St. Benedict: 2200 88th Ave., W., Rock Island, IL 61201-7649. Tel: 309-283-2124; Fax: 309-283-2130. Sr. Susan Hutchens, O.S.B., Pres.
Total number of Sisters in Federation: 584.
Legal Title: *Federation of St. Benedict.*
Erected by decree of the Holy See March 24, 1947.
Ten monasteries form this Federation; in addition to the seven American monasteries listed, three autonomous monasteries exist: Japan, St. Benedict's Monastery (1985); Muroran, Hokkaido; Taiwan, St. Benedict Monastery (1988) Tanshui, Taipei; Bahamas, Saint Martin Monastery (1994) Nassau.

Sisters of the Order of Saint Benedict (1857): *Mount Benedict Monastery*, 6000 S. 1075 E., Ogden, UT 84405-4945. Tel: 801-479-6030; Fax: 801-479-4997; Email: mbmutah@mbmutah.org; Web: www.mbmutah.org. Sr. Danile Knight, O.S.B., Contact Person.
Professed Sisters: 6.
Sisters serve and staff: Health Care; Parish Ministry; Spiritual Ministry.
Represented in the Diocese of Salt Lake City.

Sisters of the Order of Saint Benedict-O.S.B. (1857): *Monasterio Santa Escolastica*, Apartado 8526, Humacao, Puerto Rico Tel: 787-852-4222; Fax: 787-850-5279. Sr. Angela Berrios, O.S.B.
Sisters: 10; Novices: 1.
Legal Title: *Sisters of the Order of Saint Benedict, Inc.*
Ministry in the field of Education at all levels; Parish Ministry.
Represented in the Diocese of Caguas.

Sisters of the Order of Saint Benedict-O.S.B. (1857): *St. Benedict's Monastery-Motherhouse and Novitiate*, 104 Chapel Ln., St. Joseph, MN 56374-0220. Tel: 320-363-7100. Sr. Michaela Hedican, O.S.B., Prioress; Sr. Renee Rau, O.S.B., Archivist.
Total Sisters in Congregation: 280.
Legal Title: *Sisters of the Order of Saint Benedict, St. Joseph, MN.*
Ministry in the field of Education at all levels; Hospitals; Nursing Homes; Individual Apostolates; Diocesan Marriage Tribunal; Parish Ministry; Social Work; Spirituality and Retreat Counseling.
Represented in the Archdioceses of Portland in Oregon and St. Paul-Minneapolis and in the Dioceses of New Ulm, St. Cloud and Santa Rosa.

Sisters of St. Benedict - St. Scholastica Monastery O.S.B. (1892): 1001 Kenwood Ave., Duluth, MN 55811. Tel: 218-723-6555. Sr. Lois Eckes, O.S.B., Prioress; Sr. Margaret Clarke, O.S.B., Archivist.
Total in Community: 90.
Ministry in the field of Academic Education at all levels; Religious Education; Indian Ministry; Residence for Elderly; Nursing Homes; Hospitals; Pastoral Care and Parish Ministries; Peace and Justice; Retreat Center.
Properties owned and/or sponsored: Benedictine Sisters Benevolent Association, McCabe Renewal Center, Duluth, MN; College of St. Scholastica; Benedictine Health System; St. Mary's Medical Center, Duluth, MN; Benedictine Living Communities, Inc., Duluth, MN: Benedictine Living Center of Garrison, Garrison, ND; Benedictine Health System Foundation, Duluth, MN; Benedictine Living Communities, Bismarck Inc., dba St. Gabriel's Community, Bismarck, ND; Prince of Peace Care Center & Evergreen Place, Ellendale, ND; St. Benedict's Health Center & Benedict's Court, Dickinson, ND; St. Catherine's Living Center, Wahpeton, ND; St. Rose Care Center & Rosewood Court, LaMoure, ND; Benedictine Living Communities Foundation, Bismarck, ND; Benedictine Health Center; Polinsky Rehabilitation Center, Duluth, MN; St. Joseph's Medical Center, Brainerd, MN; St. Mary's Regional Health Center, Detroit Lakes, MN; St. Francis Regional Medical Center, Shakopee, MN; St. Mary's Hospital & Clinics, Cottonwood, ID; Clearwater Valley Hospital & Clinics, Orifino, ID; Tekakwitha Living Center, Inc., Sisseton, SD; Madonna Towers of Rochester, Inc., Rochester, MN; St. Gertrude's Health Rehabilitation Center, Shakopee, MN; Benedictine Health Dimensions, Cambridge, MN; St. Mary's Hospital, Superior, WI; St. Anne of Winona, Winona, MN; Villa St. Benedict, Lisle, IL; Villa St. Vincent, Crookston, MN, Benedictine Care Centers: St. Brigid's at Hi-Park, Red Wing, MN; St. Isidore Health Center of Greenwood Prairie, Plainview, MN; Benedictine Health Center at Innsbruck, New Brighton, MN; St. Eligius Health Center, Duluth, MN; Green Prairie Place, Plainview, MN; The Villa at Hi-Park, Red Wing, MN; Benedictine Living Community of St. Peter, St. Peter, MN; Madonna Meadows of Rochester, Rochester, MN; Living Community of St. Joseph, St. Joseph, MO; Benedictine Senior Living at Steeple Pointe, Osseo, MN; Benedictine Health Center of Minneapolis, MN; Arrowhead Senior Living Community dba St. Michael's Health and Rehabilitation Center, Virginia, MN; Arrowhead Senior Living Community dba St. Raphael's Health and Rehabilitation Center, Eveleth, MN; Bridges Care Community, Ada, MN; Benedictine Living Community of Spooner, Spooner, WI; Benedictine Senior Living Community of New London dba Glen Oaks Senior Living Campus, New London, MN; Benedictine Senior Living Community of Mora dba Villa Health Care Center, Mora, MN; Benedictine Senior Living Community of Winsted dba St. Mary's Care Center, Winsted, MN; Holy Trinity Hospital, Graceville, MN; Graceville Health Center Clinic, Graceville, MN; Grace Home, Graceville, MN; Grace Village, Graceville, MN
Represented in the Archdioceses of Chicago, Milwaukee and St. Paul-Minneapolis, and in the Dioceses of Bismarck, Boise, Crookston, Duluth, Fargo, Joliet, Kansas City-St. Joseph; New Ulm, Peoria, Phoenix, St. Cloud, Superior, Sioux Falls and Winona.

St. Bede Monastery (1948): 1190 Priory Rd., P.O. Box 66, Eau Claire, WI 54702. Tel: 715-834-3176. Sr. Michaela Hedican, O.S.B., Prioress.
Total in Community: 29.
Properties owned and sponsored: St. Bede Monastery; St. Bede Retreat and Conference Center.
Represented in the Archdioceses of Louisville and San Antonio and in the Dioceses of La Crosse and Springfield-Cape Girardeau.

Sisters of St. Benedict O.S.B. (1874): *St. Mary Monastery*, 2200 88th Ave., W., Rock Island, IL 61201-7649. Tel: 309-283-2100; Fax: 309-283-2200. Sr. Phyllis McMurray, O.S.B., Prioress; Sr. Marilyn Roman, Archivist.
Total in Community: 53.
Ministry in the field of Religious and Academic Education; Pastoral Care; Parish Ministry.
Represented in the Diocese of Peoria.

Benedictine Sisters of the Annunciation, B.M.V. (1947): *Annunciation Monastery*, 7520 University Dr., Bismarck, ND 58504-9653. Tel: 701-255-1520. Sr. Nancy Miller, O.S.B., Prioress.
Professed Sisters: 53.
Ministry in Hospitals; Parish Ministry and Catechetical Work; Education, Health Care and Spiritual Direction.
Represented in the Diocese of Bismarck.

Sisters of St. Benedict (1948): *St. Paul's Monastery*, 2675 Benet Rd., St. Paul, MN 55109. Tel: 651-777-8181; Fax: 651-773-5124. Sr. Lucia Schwickerath, O.S.B., Prioress.
Professed Sisters: 44.
Sisters serve and staff: Schools; Long term care facilities; Administration; Child care; Retreat Center; Parish Ministry; Social Service and various other apostolic work.
Represented in the Archdiocese of St. Paul-Minneapolis and in the Diocese of Great Falls.

Sisters of St. Benedict O.S.B. (1952): *St. Placid Priory*, 500 College St., NE, Lacey, WA 98516. Tel: 360-438-1771. Sr. Maureen O'Larey, O.S.B., Prioress.
Professed Sisters: 15.
Sisters serve in the field of Education; Spirituality and Pastoral Care.
Represented in the Archdioceses of Portland in Oregon and Seattle.

[0233] (O.S.B.)—BENEDICTINE NUNS (P)
Subiaco Congregation

St. Scholastica Priory, Benedictine Nuns (Cloistered): 271 N. Main St., Box 606, Petersham, MA 01366-0606. Tel: 978-724-3213; Fax: 978-724-3216. Very Rev. Mother Mary Elizabeth Kloss, O.S.B., Prioress; Sr. Mary Angela Kloss, O.S.B., Sub-Prioress.
Nuns in Solemn Vows: 10; Junior Professed: 1; Novices: 2.

[0235] (O.S.B.CAM.)—CAMALDOLESE BENEDICTINE SISTERS (P)
Camaldolese Congregation

First founded in Italy in the 11th century, affiliated with monastery in Rome founded in 1722; United States foundation in 1988.

Transfiguration Monastery: *Camaldolese Benedictine Sisters*, 701 NY Rte. 79, Windsor, NY 13865. Tel: 607-655-2366. Sr. Donald Corcoran, O.S.B.Cam., Prioress.
Professed Nuns: 3.
Ministry in Monastic life and Benedictine hospitality.
Represented in the Diocese of Syracuse.

[0240] (O.S.B.)—OLIVETAN BENEDICTINE SISTERS (D)

Established in the Diocese of Little Rock in 1887.

Motherhouse and Novitiate (1887): *Holy Angels Convent*, P.O. Drawer 1209, Jonesboro, AR 72403-1209. Tel: 870-935-5810; Fax: 870-935-4210. Sr. Lillian Marie Reiter, O.S.B., Prioress.
Professed Sisters: 38; Postulants: 1.
Properties owned and/or sponsored: St. Bernards Healthcare, Inc., Jonesboro, AR; St. Bernards Development Foundation, Inc., Jonesboro, AR.
Sisters serve and staff: Healthcare Ministries; Grammar Schools; Diocesan Ministries; CCD Centers & Parish Services.
Represented in the Dioceses of Fort Worth and Little Rock.

[0250] (C.V.D.)—SISTERS OF BETHANY (P)

Founded in El Salvador in 1928.

General Motherhouse: *Instituto Bethania*, Santa Tecla, El Salvador Madre Luz Elena Ordonez, Supr. Gen.; Mother Foundrees Dolores de Maria Zea.

U.S. Address (1949): *Bethany House*, 850 N. Hobart Blvd., Los Angeles, CA 90029. Tel: 323-665-6937. Sr. Leticia Gomez, C.V.D., Supr.
Professed Sisters: 10.
Ministry in Parish Work, Residence.
Represented in the Archdiocese of Los Angeles.

[0260] (S.B.S.)—THE SISTERS OF THE BLESSED SACRAMENT FOR INDIANS AND COLORED PEOPLE (P)

Founded in the United States in 1891.

General Motherhouse: 1663 Bristol Pike, Bensalem, PA 19020-5796. Tel: 215-244-9900. Sr. Patricia Suchalski, Pres.
Professed Sisters: 135.
Sisters serve and staff in the field of Education on all levels; Catechetical Schools; Adult Education and Social Service; House of Prayer; Evangelization Center.
Represented in the Archdioceses of Boston, New Orleans, New York, Philadelphia, Portland in Oregon and Santa Fe and in the Dioceses of Birmingham, Biloxi, Evansville, Gallup, Memphis, Palm Beach, Phoenix, Richmond and Tucson. Also in Haiti.

[0270] (C.B.S.)—CONGREGATION OF BON SECOURS (P)

Founded in France in 1824. First foundation in the United States in 1881.

United States: *Provincial House and Novitiate*, 1525 Marriottsville Rd., Marriottsville, MD 21104. Tel: 410-442-1333; Fax: 410-442-1394. Sr. Rose Marie Jasinski, C.B.S., Leader. Sr. Patricia Eck, C.B.S., Congregation Leader.
Total Sisters in U.S: 28.
Sisters own and operate: Bon Secours Spiritual Center.
Represented in the Archdioceses of Baltimore, Newark and New York and in the Dioceses of Charleston and Richmond.

[0280] (O.SS.S.)—THE BRIGITTINE SISTERS (P)

Founded in Sweden in the 14th century.

Motherhouse: Rome, Italy

Convent in U.S.A. (1957): *Convent of St. Birgitta*, 4 Runkenhage Rd., Darien, CT 06820. Tel: 203-655-1068; Fax: 203-655-3496; Email: conventsb@optonline.net. Sr. M. Eunice Kulangarathottiyil, O.SS.S., Supr.
Professed Sisters: 8.
Legal Title: *Order of the Most Holy Savior of St. Bridget.*
Monastic tradition, Semi cloister.
Represented in the Diocese of Bridgeport.

[0300] (O.CARM.)—CALCED CARMELITES (P)

Carmelite Nuns of the Ancient Observance, Strictly Cloistered, belonging in the Second Order of Carmel.
Founded in Naples, Italy in 1536. First foundation in the United States in 1931.

Carmelite Monastery of St. Therese: *Little Flower of Jesus and St. M. Magdalen De Pazzi, St. Therese's Valley*, 3551 Lanark Rd., Coopersburg, PA 18036-9324. Web: www.carmelite-nuns.com. Mother Mary Gertrude, O.Carm., Prioress.
Professed Sisters: 7.
Legal Title: *The Carmelite Sisters of St. Therese's Valley, Inc.*
Represented in the Dioceses of Allentown, Fargo, San Angelo and Superior.

[0315] (C.C.W.)—CARMELITE COMMUNITY OF THE WORD (D)

Motherhouse & Novitiate: *Incarnation Center (1971)*, 3904 Bem Rd., Gallitzin, PA 16641. Fax: 814-886-4098. Sr. Marilyn Welch, C.C.W., Admin. Gen.
Total in Community: 15.
Ministries in Diocesan Administration; the field of Religious and Academic Education at all levels; Pastoral Care to the Imprisoned, Institutionalized, Elderly, Mentally Handicapped, Family Life Support Groups and the Poor; Parish Ministry; Mission activity in Appalachia.
Represented in the Diocese of Altoona-Johnstown.

[0320] (O.CARM.)—CARMELITE NUNS OF THE ANCIENT OBSERVANCE (P)

Carmelite Nuns of the Ancient Observance

Strictly Cloistered, belonging to the Second Order of Carmel. Founded in Guelder, Holland, in 1453. First foundation in the United States in 1930.

Carmel of Mary (1954): 17765 78th St., S.E., Wahpeton, ND 58075. Tel: 701-642-2360. Mother Joseph Marie of the Child Jesus, O.Carm., Prioress.
Total in Community: 9.
Represented in the Diocese of Fargo.

Monastery of Our Lady of Grace (1989): 6202 CR 339 Via Maria, Christoval, TX 76935-3023. Tel: 325-853-1722; Web: carmelnet.org/christoval/christoval.htm. Sr. Mary Grace, O.Carm., Vicar Prioress.
Professed Sisters: 4; Junior Professed: 1; Postulants: 1.
Represented in the Diocese of San Angelo.

Carmel of the Sacred Heart (1963): 430 Laurel Ave., Hudson, WI 54016. Tel: 715-386-2156. Sr. Lucia LaMontagne, O.Carm., Prioress & Archivist.
Professed Sisters: 6.
Legal Title: *Carmelite Nuns of the Diocese of Superior, Inc.*
Represented in the Diocese of Superior.

[0330] (O.CARM.)—CARMELITE SISTERS FOR THE AGED AND INFIRM (P)

Founded in 1929 in New York, Foundress: Mother M. Angeline Teresa, O.Carm.

Motherhouse and Novitiate: *St. Teresa's Motherhouse and Novitiate*, 600 Woods Rd., Avila on the Hudson, Germantown, NY 12526. Mother M. Mark Louis, O.Carm., Supr. Gen.
Professed Sisters: 184.
Sponsored Works: Carmelite System Inc., Germantown, NY; Carmel Terrace, Framingham, MA; St. Patrick Home, Bronx, NY; St. Margaret Hall, Cincinnati, OH; Carmel Manor, Fort Thomas, KY; Kahl Home for the Aged, Davenport, IA; St. Patrick's Manor, Framingham, MA; Marian Manor, South Boston, MA; St. Patrick's Residence, Naperville, IL; Lourdes - Noreen McKeen Residence, West Palm Beach, FL; Mother Angeline McCrory Manor, Columbus, OH; Avila Institute of Gerontology; Our Lady's Manor, Dublin, Ireland.
Represented in the Archdioceses of Boston, Cincinnati and New York and in the Dioceses of Albany, Altoona-Johnstown, Brooklyn, Columbus, Covington, Davenport, Joliet, Palm Beach, Scranton and Syracuse.

[0340] (C.A.CH.)—CARMELITE SISTERS OF CHARITY (P)

Founded in 1826.

Motherhouse: Vic, Spain

Generalate: *Carlo Zucchi*, 12, Rome, Italy, 00165. Tel: 06-662-03-52.

Provincial/Formation House: *Carmelite Sisters of Charity*, 701 Beacon Rd., Silver Spring, MD 20903. Tel: 301-434-6344. Sr. Maria Pilar Chamorro, C.C.V., Prov.
Ministry in Health Clinics; Parishes; Higher Education; Immigrants, Hispanics and Homeless, Educational Centers.
Properties owned or sponsored: Mount Carmel House; Formation House.
Represented in the Archdiocese of Washington and in the Diocese of Brooklyn.

[0350] (O.CARM.)—CARMELITE SISTERS (CORPUS CHRISTI) (P)

First foundation in the United States in 1920.

General Motherhouse: Tunapuna, Trinidad, West Indies Sr. Petronilla Joseph, O.Carm., Prioress Gen.

U.S. Address: *Mount Carmel Home-Keen's Memorial*, 412 W. 18th, Kearney, NE 68847. Tel: 308-237-2287; Tel: 308-338-1263. Sr. Dorothy Cavaness, O.Carm., Supr.
Professed Sisters: 9.
Ministry in Home and foreign missions; Academic and Religious Education; Social Work.
Represented in the Dioceses of Grand Island and Providence.

[0360] (CARMEL D.C.J.)—CARMELITE SISTERS OF THE DIVINE HEART OF JESUS (P)

Founded in Germany in 1891. First Convent in the United States in 1912.

General Motherhouse: Sittard, Netherlands Antilles Mother M. Angleina, Supr. Gen.

Northern Province: 1230 Kavanaugh Pl., Milwaukee, WI 53213. Tel: 414-453-4040; Fax: 414-453-6503. Sr. Maria Giuseppe, Prov.

Central Province: 10341 Manchester Rd., St. Louis, MO 63122. Tel: 314-965-7616. Sr. Mary Joseph, Prov. Supr.

South Western Province: 4130 S. Alameda, Corpus Christi, TX 78411. Sr. M. Lydia Ann Braun, Provincial Supr.
Professed Sisters Worldwide: 457; Total Sisters in U.S: 66; Novices: 72; Postulants: 36.
Sisters minister to Homes for Children 2; Homes for the Aged 9; Day Nurseries 4; Mission work in Africa, Iceland, Nicaragua, Venezuela and Brazil.
Represented in the Archdioceses of Milwaukee, St. Louis and San Antonio and in the Dioceses of Corpus Christi, Gary, Grand Rapids, Owensboro and San Diego.

[0370] (O.C.D.)—CARMELITE SISTERS OF THE MOST SACRED HEART OF LOS ANGELES (P)

General Motherhouse & Novitiate: *Carmelite Sisters of the Most Sacred Heart of Los Angeles*, 920 E. Alhambra Rd., Alhambra, CA 91801. Tel: 626-289-1353; Fax: 626-308-1913. Mother Regina Marie Gorman, O.C.D., Supr. Gen.
Total in Community: 145.
Legal Titles: Carmelite Sisters of the Most Sacred Heart of Los Angeles; Carmelite Educational Centers, Inc.; dba Sacred Heart Retreat House, Alhambra, CA; dba Mount Carmel in the Desert Retreat House and Day Care Center, Palmdale, CA; dba St. Joseph Center, Alhambra, CA; Little Flower Center, Inc.; dba Little Flower Missionary House, Los Angeles, CA; Avila Gardens Residence for Seniors, Duarte, CA; Santa Teresita Medical Center, Duarte, CA; Maycrest Manor, Inc. Culver City, CA; Mount Carmel Health Ministries, Inc.; Flos Carmeli Formation Centers, Inc.; Carmelite Sisters Foundation, Inc.
The sisters serve and staff: Religious and academic education; healthcare centers; skilled nursing facilities for the care of the aged; nursery schools with day care and kindergarten; retreat houses; ministry to the elderly, sick and convalescents; evangelization centers and ministry to the youth.
Represented in the Archdioceses of Denver, Los Angeles and Miami and in the Dioceses of Tucson and Steubenville.

[0380] (C.S.T.)—CARMELITE SISTERS OF ST. THERESE OF THE INFANT JESUS (D)

Founded in the United States in 1917 at Bentley, OK.

General Motherhouse: *Villa Teresa*, 1300 Classen Dr., Oklahoma City, OK 73103-2447. Tel: 405-232-7926. Sr. Patricia Ann Miller, Gen. Supr.
Total in Community: 18.
Legal Title: *Carmelite Sisters of St. Therese of the Infant Jesus.*
Ministry in the field of Academic Education; Religious Education and Parish Ministry.
Properties owned and sponsored: Villa Teresa School, Oklahoma City, OK; Villa Teresa Moore, Oklahoma City, OK.
Represented in the Archdiocese of Oklahoma City.

[0390] (C.M.S.T.)—MISSIONARY CARMELITES OF ST. TERESA (P)

Founded in Mexico City in 1903.

General Motherhouse: Fresno No. 150, Col. Santa Maria la Ribera, 06400, Mexico, D.F., Mexico Sr. Fidelina Herrera, Supr. Gen.

U.S. Holy Family Province (1983): 9548 Deer Trail Dr., Houston, TX 77038. Tel: 281-445-5520; Fax: 281-445-5748. Sr. Maria Isabel Torres, C.M.S.T, Prov. Supr.
Professed Sisters: 60.
Ministry in Pastoral; Hospital Chaplaincy and Retreats.
Represented in the Archdioceses of Galveston-Houston and Oklahoma City and in the Dioceses of Beaumont and Little Rock.

[0397] (C.M.R.)—CONGREGATION OF MARY, QUEEN (P)

Founded in Vietnam in 1670 by Bishop Pierre Lambert de la Motte. First foundation in the United States in 1979 in Springfield, MO.

U.S. Regional: 625 S. Jefferson Ave., Springfield, MO 65806. Tel: 417-869-9842; Fax: 417-832-0852. Sr. Marguerite A. Tran, C.M.R., Reg. Leader.
Professed Sisters: 20.
Legal Title: *Congregation of Mary Queen, American Region.*
Represented in the Archdiocese of St. Louis and in the Dioceses of Dallas, Kansas City-St. Joseph and Springfield-Cape Girardeau.

[0400] (O.CARM.)—CONGREGATION OF OUR LADY OF MOUNT CARMEL (P)

Founded in France in 1824. First foundation in the United States in 1833.

Generalate: P.O. Box 476, Lacombe, LA 70445. Tel: 504-524-2398; Tel: 985-882-7577; Fax: 504-524-5011. Sr. Elizabeth Fitzpatrick, O.Carm., Pres.; Sr. Andree Bindewald, Vice Pres./Sec. & Devel. Dir.; Sr. Therese Gregoire, O.Carm., Treas./Archivist.
Professed Sisters: 74.
Ministry in the field of Education on all levels; Hospitals; Social Service; Religious Education; Pastoral Ministry and Retreat Work; Prison Education Ministry; Child Care.
Represented in the Archdiocese of New Orleans and in the Dioceses of Houma-Thibodaux, Joliet in Illinois and Lafayette (LA). Also in the Philippines.

[0410] (O.CARM.)—INSTITUTE OF THE SISTERS OF OUR LADY OF MOUNT CARMEL (P)

Istituto delle Suore di Nostra Signora del Carmelo

Founded in Italy in 1854. First foundation in the United States, 1947.

General Motherhouse: *Istituto di Nostra Signora del Carmelo*, Via dei Baglioni 10, Rome, Italy

U.S. Headquarters: *Carmelite Sisters*, 5 Wheatland St., Peabody, MA 01960. Tel: 978-531-4733. Sr. Kathleen A. Bettencourt, O.Carm., Supr.
Professed Sisters: 16.
Ministry in Holy Childhood Nursery; Kindergarten; Preschools; Daycare Centers
Represented in the Archdioceses of Boston and Washington and in the Diocese of St. Augustine.

[0420] (O.C.D.)—DISCALCED CARMELITE NUNS (P)

Founded in Spain in 1562. First foundation in the United States in 1790 in Charles County, Maryland; later this monastery was moved to Baltimore.
The Monasteries listed here are strictly contemplative and belong to the Order of Discalced Carmelites.

Carmelite Monastery (1790): 1318 Dulaney Valley Rd., Baltimore, MD 21286. Tel: 410-823-7415; Email: info@baltimorecarmel.org; Web: www.baltimorecarmel.org. Sr. Colette Ackerman, O.C.D., Prioress.
Professed Sisters: 17.
Legal Title: *Carmelite Sisters of Baltimore.*

Carmel of St. Joseph (1863): 9150 Clayton Rd., St. Louis, MO 63124. Tel: 314-993-6899; Fax: 314-993-5093; Email: stlouiscarmel@sbcglobal.net; Web: www.stormpages.com/mtcarmel. Mother Mary Joseph, O.C.D., Prioress.
Professed Cloistered Nuns: 10; Professed Extern Sisters: 1; Postulants: 2; Novices: 2.

Monastery of St. Joseph and St. Teresa (1877): *Discalced Carmelite Nuns*, 73530 River Rd., Covington, LA 70435-2206. Tel: 985-898-0923; Fax: 985-871-9333; Email: covingtoncarmel@yahoo.com; Web: www-.covingtoncarmel.org. Sr. Edith Turpin, O.C.D., Prioress.
Solemnly Professed: 7.

Discalced Carmelite Monastery (1890): 61 Mt. Pleasant Ave., Boston, MA 02119. Tel: 617-442-1411; Fax: 617-442-0203; Email: bostoncarmel@juno.com; Web: www.carmelitesofboston.org. Sr. Bernadette Therese Huang, O.C.D., Prioress.
Total in Community: 10.

Monastery of the Most Holy Trinity: *Discalced Carmelite Nuns*, 4525 W. 2nd Ave., Hialeah, FL 33012. Tel: 305-558-7122; Fax: 305-558-1190. Mother Blanca Flor de Jesus Sacramentado, O.C.D., Prioress.
Total in Community: 12.
Legal Title: *Discalced Carmelite Nuns, Inc.*

Carmelite Monastery (1902): 66th Ave. and Old York Rd., Oak Ln., Philadelphia, PA 19126. Tel: 215-424-6143; Fax: 215-424-6143; Fax: 215-424-6145. Mother

Barbara of the Holy Ghost, O.C.D., Prioress.
Professed Nuns: 7.

Monastery of Our Lady of Mt. Carmel (1907): *Office of Episcopal Delegate for Religious Diocese of Brooklyn*, 310 Prospect Park W., Brooklyn, NY 11215-6214. Tel: 718-399-5900; Fax: 718-235-0542. Sr. Maryann Seton LoPiccolo, S.C., Episcopal Delegate (Diocese of Brooklyn).

Monastery of Our Lady of Mt. Carmel and St. Joseph: 361 Highland Blvd., Brooklyn, NY 11207. Tel: 718-235-0422. Mother Ana Maria, O.C.D., Prioress.
Total in Community: 8.

Carmelite Monastery of the Infant Jesus (1908): 1000 Lincoln St., Santa Clara, CA 95050. Tel: 408-296-8412. Sr. Emmanuel of Bethlehem, O.C.D., Prioress.
Sisters Solemn Vows: 19; Novices: 1.

St. Joseph's Carmelite Monastery (1908): 2215 N.E. 147th, Shoreline, WA 98155. Tel: 206-363-7150; Fax: 206-365-7335. Sr. Maria Valla, O.C.D., Prioress.
Professed Sisters: 5; Novices: 2.
Legal Title: *Carmelite Monastery of Seattle.*

Carmel of the Queen of Heaven (Formerly known as Regina Coeli Monastery) (1911): 17937 250th St., Eldridge, IA 52748-9425. Tel: 563-285-8387; Fax: 563-285-7467. Sr. Lynne Elwinger, O.C.D., Prioress.
Professed Sisters: 9.

Discalced Carmelite Nuns (1930): *Monastery of Mary Immaculate and St. Joseph*, 1740 Newburg Rd., Louisville, KY 40205. Tel: 502-451-6796; Fax: 502-458-8272. Mother Katherine, Prioress; Sr. Clare, Archivist.
Solemnly Professed Sisters: 9; In Formation: 2.
Legal Title: *Carmelite Monastery of Louisville, Inc.*

Order of Discalced Carmelites O.C.D. (1913): *Carmel of St. Teresa of Los Angeles, Inc.*, 215 E. Alhambra Rd., Alhambra, CA 91801. Tel: 626-282-2387; Fax: 626-282-2053; Email: teresacarm@aol.com. Sr. Brenda Marie, O.C.D., Prioress.
Total in Community: 17.

Carmelite Monastery (1916): 4300 Mount Carmel Dr. N.E., Ada (Parnell), MI 49301. Web: www.carmelitenuns.com. Mother Elizabeth Ann, O.C.D., Prioress.
Professed: 10; Externs: 2.

Discalced Carmelite Nuns (2000): *Carmelite Monastery*, 89 Hiddenbrooke Dr., Beacon, NY 12508-2230. Tel: 845-831-5572; Fax: 845-831-5579; Email: beaconcarmel@optonline.net; Web: www.carmelitesbeacon.org. Sr. Michaelene Devine, O.C.D., Prioress.
Total in Community: 18.

Discalced Carmelite Monastery of St. Therese of the Child Jesus (1920): 75 Carmel Rd., Buffalo, NY 14214. Tel: 716-837-6499. Mother Miriam of Jesus, O.C.D., Prioress.
Cloistered Professed Sisters: 11; Extern Professed Sisters: 2; Novices: 1; Postulants: 1.

Monastery of Discalced Carmelites (1922): 22143 Main St., P.O. Box 260, Oldenburg, IN 47036-0260. Tel: 812-932-2075. Sr. Jean Alice McGoff, O.C.D., Prioress.
Contemplative Professed Nuns: 8.
Legal Title: *Monastery of the Resurrection, Discalced Carmelites, Sisters of Our Lady of Mount Carmel Carmelite Monastery, Carmelites of Indianapolis.*

Carmel of the Holy Family (1923): 3176 Fairmount Blvd., Cleveland, OH 44118-4199. Tel: 216-321-6568; Fax: 216-321-1904; Web: clevelandcarmel.org. Sr. Barbara Losh, O.C.D., Prioress.
Contemplative Professed Nuns: 12.

Discalced Carmelites of the Order of Our Lady of Mount Carmel O.C.D. (1925): *Monastery of Our Lady and St. Therese*, 27601 Hwy. 1, Carmel, CA 93923. Tel: 831-624-3043; Fax: 831-624-5495; Email: carmelitesofcarmel2010@catholic.org; Web: carmelitesistersbythesea.net. Mother Mercedes of Mary Immaculate, O.C.D., Prioress.
Professed Sisters: 9.
Legal Title: *Carmelite Monastery of Carmel, California, Inc.*

Discalced Carmelites O.C.D. (1926): *Monastery of the Most Blessed Virgin Mary of Mount Carmel*, 189 Madison Ave., Morristown, NJ 07960. Mother Therese, O.C.D., Prioress.
Professed Sisters: 10; Novices: 2.

Order of Discalced Carmelites O.C.D. (1926): *Carmelite Monastery of the Trinity*, 5158 Hawley Blvd., San Diego, CA 92116. Tel: 619-280-5424. Sr. Yvonne Hanke, O.C.D., Prioress.
Professed Nuns: 14.

Monastery of St. Therese of the Child Jesus (1926): 35750 Moravian Dr., Clinton Township, MI 48035-2138. Tel: 586-790-7255. Mother Mary Elizabeth, O.C.D., Prioress.
Professed Nuns: 6; Professed Extern Sisters: 1.

Carmel of St. Therese of Lisieux, Inc. (1927): *Discalced Carmelite Nuns*, P.O. Box 57, Loretto, PA 15940-0057. Tel: 814-472-8620; Web: www.lorettocarmel.com. Mother John of the Cross, O.C.D., Prioress.
Solemn Professed Nuns: 10.

Discalced Carmelite Nuns O.C.D. (1928): *Carmelite Monastery of Cristo Rey*, 721 Parker Ave., San Francisco, CA 94118-4227. Tel: 415-387-2640.
Total in Community: 18.

Carmelite Nuns of Dallas: *Monastery of Discalced Carmelites (1928)*, 600 Flowers Ave., Dallas, TX 75211. Rev. Mother Juantia Marie, O.C.D., Prioress.
Professed Nuns: 12.

Discalced Carmelite Nuns (1930): *Monastery of Our Lady and St. Joseph*, 1931 W. Jefferson Rd., Pittsford, NY 14534. Tel: 585-427-7094. Mother Therese Marie of Jesus Crucified, O.C.D., Prioress.
Professed Nuns with Solemn Vows: 13.
Legal Title: *Carmelite Monastery of Rochester.*

Monastery of Discalced Carmelites O.C.D. (1930): *Monastery of Our Lady of Mount Carmel and St. Therese of the Child Jesus*, 25 Watson Ave., Barrington, RI 02806. Tel: 401-245-3421. Sr. Susan Lumb, O.C.D., Prioress.
Total in Community: 16.

Discalced Carmelite Nuns O.C.D. (1934): *Monastery of the Infant Jesus of Prague and Our Lady of Guadalupe*, 6301 Culebra Rd., San Antonio, TX 78238-4909. Tel: 210-680-1834. Mother Therese Leonard, Prioress.
Total in Community: 9.

Carmel of the Holy Family and St. Therese (1935): 6981 Teresian Way, P.O. Box 4210, Georgetown, CA 95634. Tel: 530-333-1617. Mother Christine, Prioress.
Total in Community: 16.

Discalced Carmelite Nuns O.C.D. (1936): *Monastery of Mary, Mother of Grace*, 1250 Carmel Dr., Lafayette, LA 70501. Tel: 337-232-4651. Mother Regina Mullins, O.C.D., Prioress.
12 Professed; 2 Novices; 1 Postulant; 2 Extern: 17.

Discalced Carmelite Nuns O.C.D. (1939): *Carmel of St. Joseph*, 20,000 N. County Line Rd., Piedmont, OK 73078. Sr. Donna Ross, O.C.D., Prioress.
Total in Community: 10.

Discalced Carmelite Nuns of Milwaukee O.C.D. (1940): *Carmel of the Mother of God*, W267 N2517 Carmelite Rd., Pewaukee, WI 53072. Tel: 262-691-0336; Fax: 262-695-0143; Email: pewaukeecarmel@aol.com. Sr. Mary Agnes Kramer, O.C.D., Prioress.
Total in Community: 8.

Discalced Carmelite Nuns of Alexandria, South Dakota, Inc. O.C.D: *Monastery of Our Mother of Mercy and St. Joseph*, 221 5th St. W., P.O. Box 67, Alexandria, SD 57311-0067. Tel: 605-239-4382. Mother Marie Therese of the Child Jesus, Prioress.
Total in Community: 17.

Carmelite Monastery (1943): 716 Dauphin Island Pkwy., Mobile, AL 36606. Tel: 251-471-3991; Fax: 251-471-3991; Web: www.carmelitemonasterymobileal.com. Mother Marie Therese, Prioress; Sr. M. Josepha, Supr.
Solemnly Professed Nuns: 6; Temporary Professed: 5.

Discalced Carmelite Monastery (1945): 49 Mount Carmel Rd., Santa Fe, NM 87505-0352. Tel: 505-983-7232. Mother Rose Teresa, O.C.D., Prioress.
Total in Community: 9.

Discalced Carmelite Monastery (1946): 275 Pleasant St., Concord, NH 03301-2590. Tel: 603-225-5791. Sr. Claudette Blais, O.C.D., Prioress.
Solemnly Professed Nuns: 6; Temporary Professed: 2.

Sisters of Our Lady of Mount Carmel of Terre Haute: *Carmelite Monastery*, 59 Allendale, Terre Haute, IN 47802-4751. Tel: 812-299-1410; Fax: 812-299-5820; Email: carmelth@heartsawake.org. Mother Mary Clare Trolley, O.C.D., Prioress.
Professed Nuns: 12.

Discalced Carmelite Nuns of Colorado, Inc. (1948): *Carmel of Holy Spirit*, 6138 S. Gallup St., Littleton, CO 80120-2702. Tel: 303-798-4176. Mother Gemma Marie of the Passion of Jesus, D.C., Prioress.
Professed Nuns: 9; Professed Novice: 1; Novices: 1.

Order of Discalced Carmelites O.C.D. (1949): *Carmel of Mary Immaculate and St. Mary Magdalen*, 26 Harmony School Rd., Flemington, NJ 08822. Mother Anne of Christ, O.C.D., Prioress.
Novices: 2; Professed: 15; Total in Community: 17.

Discalced Carmelite Nuns O.C.D. (1950): *Monastery of the Infant Jesus of Prague*, 3501 Silver Lake Rd., Traverse City, MI 49684-8949. Tel: 231-946-4960. Mother Mary of Jesus Markey, O.C.D., Prioress.
Solemnly Professed: 4; Sisters in Formation: 2.

Discalced Carmelite Nuns O.C.D. (1951): *Monastery of the Holy Cross*, N4028 N. Hwy. U.S. 2, P.O. Box 397, Iron Mountain, MI 49801. Tel: 906-774-0561; Fax: 906-774-0561. Mother Maria of Jesus, O.C.D., Prioress.
Total in Community: 21.

Discalced Carmelite Nuns O.C.D: *Monastery of the Holy Name of Jesus*, 6100 Pepper Rd., Denmark, WI 54208. Tel: 920-863-5055; Email: holynamecarmel@catholic.org. Mother Mary Elizabeth, O.C.D., Prioress.

Discalced Carmelite Nuns O.C.D. (1950): *Monastery of the Immaculate Heart of Mary*, 94 Main St., P.O. Box F, Montpelier, VT 05601-1455. Tel: 914-831-5572. Sr. Jeanne Gonyon, O.C.D., Prioress.
Total in Community: 10.

Discalced Carmelite Nuns O.C.D. (1950): *Discalced Carmelite Nuns of Little Rock*, 7201 W. 32nd St., Little Rock, AR 72204-4716. Tel: 501-565-5121. Sr. Cecilia Chun, O.C.D., Prioress.
Professed Sisters: 13.
Legal Title: *Discalced Carmelite Nuns of Little Rock.*

Discalced Carmelite Nuns O.C.D. (1951): *Monastery of Our Lady of Mount Carmel and The Little Flower*, 2155 Terry Rd., Jackson, MS 39204. Tel: 601-373-1460. Sr. Margaret Mary Flynn, O.C.D., Prioress.
Professed Nuns: 6.

Carmel of the Immaculate Heart of Mary (1952): 5714 Holladay Blvd., Salt Lake City, UT 84121-1599. Tel: 801-277-6075. Mother Maureen Goodwin, O.C.D., Prioress; Sr. Mary Ann Krajiceb, O.C.D., Archivist.
Solemn Vows: 8; Finally Professed Externs: 1.

Discalced Carmelite Nuns of St. Paul (1952): *Carmel of Our Lady of Divine Providence*, 8251 De Montreville Trail N., Lake Elmo, MN 55042-9547. Tel: 651-777-3882. Mother Rose of the Sacred Heart, O.C.D., Prioress.
Professed Sisters: 12.

Discalced Carmelite Nuns O.C.D. (1953): 1 Maria Hall Dr., Danville, PA 17821. Tel: 570-275-4682; Fax: 570-275-4684. Sr. Angela Pikus, O.C.D., Prioress.
Professed Sisters: 10.

Sisters of Our Lady of Mount Carmel: 1950 La Fond Dr., Reno, NV 89509-3099. Tel: 775-323-3236; Fax: 775-322-1532; Email: renocarmel@carmelofreno.net; Web: www.carmelofreno.com. Sr. Susan Weber, O.C.D., Prioress.
Professed Nuns: 15.

Carmel of Maria Regina O.C.D. (1957): 87609 Green Hill Rd., Eugene, OR 97402. Tel: 541-345-8649; Fax: 541-345-4857. Mother Elizabeth Mary, O.C.D., Prioress & Community Archivist.
Total in Community: 10.

Monastery of the Holy Family (1957): 510 E. Gore Rd., Erie, PA 16509. Web: www.eriercd.org/carmelites.asp. Mother Emmanuel of the Mother of God, O.C.D., Prioress.
Professed Sisters: 5.

Discalced Carmelite Nuns (1958): 11 W. Back St., Savannah, GA 31419-3219. Tel: 912-925-8505. Sr. Joann Gartner, O.C.D., Prioress.
Total in Community: 6; Professed Nuns: 3.

Monastery of the Most Holy Trinity (1958): 5801 Mt. Carmel Dr., Arlington, TX 76017. Tel: 817-468-1781. Mother Anne Teresa Kulinski, O.C.D., Prioress.
Total in Community: 12.

Discalced Carmelite Nuns O.C.D. (1958): *Discalced Carmelite Nuns of New Caney, Texas*, 1100 Parthenon Pl., New Caney, TX 77357-3276. Sr. Angel Teresa Sweeney, O.C.D., Prioress; Sr. Mary Ann Harrison, O.C.D., 1st Council Sister.
Total in Community: 8.
Legal Title: *Discalced Carmelite Nuns of New Caney, TX.*

Monastery of Discalced Carmelites (1959): 949 N. River Rd., Des Plaines, IL 60016. Tel: 847-298-4241. Mother Anne of Jesus, Prioress.
Total in Community: 16.

Order of Discalced Carmelites O.C.D. (1958): *Carmel of St. Therese*, 15 Mt. Carmel Rd., Danvers, MA 01923-3796. Tel: 978-774-3008. Sr. Teresa Benedicta of the Cross, O.C.D., Prioress.
Legal Title: *Discalced Carmelite Nuns of Danvers.*

Discalced Carmelite Nuns O.C.D. (1960): *Monastery of The Sacred Heart and St. Joseph*, 2201 W. Main St., Jefferson City, MO 65109. Tel: 573-636-3364. Mother Marie Therese, O.C.D., Prioress.
Solemnly Professed Nuns: 6; Novices: 1.

Carmel of the Assumption (1961): 5206 Center Dr., Latrobe, PA 15650-5204. Tel: 724-539-1056. Sr. Mary Wild, O.C.D., Prioress.
Professed Sisters: 13.

Discalced Carmelite Nuns, Inc. (1962): *Monastery of the Discalced Carmelite Nuns*, 2901 S. Cecelia St., Sioux City, IA 51106-3299. Tel: 712-276-1680. Mother Kateri Marie of the Eucharist, O.C.D., Prioress.
Total in Community: 7.

Carmelite Monastery of the Mother of God (1965): 530 Blackstone Dr., San Rafael, CA 94903. Tel: 415-479-6872; Fax: 415-491-4964; Email: srdol@motherofgodcarmel.org. Mother Dolores Sullivan, O.C.D., Prioress.
Total in Community: 5.

Discalced Carmelite Nuns O.C.D: *Carmel of St. Anne*, 424 E. Monastery St., Springfield, MO 65807. Tel: 573-881-2115.

Mailing Address: 2201 W. Main St., Jefferson City, MO 65109. Mother Marya, O.C.D., Prioress.
Total in Community: 3.

Carmel of the Holy Trinity: 6301 Pali Hwy., Kaneohe, HI 96744. Tel: 808-261-6542. Mother Agnes Marie Wong, O.C.D., Prioress.
Total in Community: 6.

Discalced Carmelite Nuns of the Byzantine Rite (1980): *Holy Annunciation Monastery*, 403 W. County Rd., Sugarloaf, PA 18249. Tel: 570-788-1205; Fax: 570-788-3329. Mother Marija of the Holy Spirit, O.C.D., Prioress.
Professed Nuns: 12.
Represented in the Diocese of Passaic.

Carmel of Port Tobacco (1976): 5678 Mt. Carmel Rd., La Plata, MD 20646. Mother Virginia Marie, O.C.D., Prioress.
Solemn Professed: 5; Simple Professed: 1; Postulants: 1; Aspirant: 1.

[0430] (B.V.M.)—SISTERS OF CHARITY OF THE BLESSED VIRGIN MARY (P)

Founded in America in 1833.

BVM Center: *Mount Carmel*, 1100 Carmel Dr., Dubuque, IA 52003-7991. Tel: 563-588-2351; Fax: 563-588-4832; Web: www.bvmcong.org. Sr. Mary Ann Zollmann, B.V.M., Pres.

Total in Congregation: 475.

Sisters serve and staff: in the field of Academic Education on all levels; Health Care Services; Religious Education; Chaplaincies; Pastoral Care and Parish Ministry; Campus Ministry; Diocesan School Offices; Diocesan Services-Administration; Social Work; Homeless Shelters; Social Justice/Advocacies.

Represented in the Archdioceses of Chicago, Denver, Dubuque, Los Angeles, Omaha, Milwaukee, Portland in Oregon, San Antonio, St. Louis, St. Paul-Minneapolis, San Francisco, Seattle and Washington and in the Dioceses of Arlington, Biloxi, Davenport, Des Moines, Fort Wayne-South Bend, Fresno, Helena, Honolulu, Jackson, Joliet, Kansas City-St. Joseph, Lafayette, Lexington, Memphis, Oakland, Orange, Orlando, Peoria, Phoenix, Rockford, Rockville Centre, San Jose, Santa Rosa, Sioux City, Springfield-Cape Girardeau and Venice. Also in Ecuador, Ghana and Guatemala.

[0440] (S.C.)—SISTERS OF CHARITY OF CINCINNATI, OHIO (P)

Founded by Saint Elizabeth Ann Seton, Emmitsburg, MD, 1809. The Cincinnati Community became independent in 1852, Papal approval in 1939.

General Motherhouse (1852): *Mount St. Joseph*, 5900 Delhi Rd., Mount Saint Joseph, OH 45051. Tel: 513-347-5300; Fax: 513-347-5228; Web: www.srcharitycinti.org. Sr. Joan Elizabeth Cook, S.C., Pres.

Professed Sisters: 387.

Legal Title: *Sisters of Charity, Cincinnati, OH.*

Sisters serve and staff: Colleges; Secondary and Elementary Schools; Parishes; Healthcare; Foreign Missions; Home for Profoundly Challenged; Senior Care Services; Social Services; Congregational Services; Marian Shrine.

Represented in the Archdioceses of Cincinnati, Denver, Detroit, Dubuque, Indianapolis, Louisville, Miami, Newark, New York, New Orleans, San Francisco and Santa Fe and in the Dioceses of Brownsville, Cleveland, Colorado Springs, Columbus, Covington, El Paso, Fort Wayne-South Bend, Helena, Juneau, Kalamazoo, Lansing, Oakland, Paterson, Pueblo, Saginaw, St. Petersburg, San Diego, Toledo, Venice and Wilmington. Also in Guatemala, Anapra, Mexico and Commonwealth of Dominica, West Indies.

[0450] (S.C.I.C.)—SISTERS OF CHARITY OF THE IMMACULATE CONCEPTION OF IVREA (P)

Founded in Italy in the 18th Century. First foundation in the United States in 1961.

General Motherhouse: Via della Renella 85, Rome, Italy Tel: 396-5818145. Sr. Palma Giuliana Porro, Supr. Gen.

Total in Congregation: 898.

U.S. Foundation (1961): *Immaculate Virgin of Miracles Convent*, 628 Prittstow Rd., Mount Pleasant, PA 15666. Tel: 412-887-0220. Sr. M. Letizia Tribuzio, S.C.I.C., Reg. Supr. Tel: 412-887-6753.

Professed Sisters in the U.S: 10.

Properties owned and/or sponsored: Verna Montessori Children's House, Middle School & Elementary School; Immaculate Virgin of Miracles Convent, Mt. Pleasant, PA.

Sisters serve and staff: Kindergarten and Elementary Schools and Middle School; Parish Services; Religious Education; Pastoral Ministry.

Represented in the Diocese of Greensburg.

[0460] (C.C.V.I.)—CONGREGATION OF THE SISTERS OF CHARITY OF THE INCARNATE WORD (P)

Founded in 1869 at San Antonio, Texas.

Generalate: 4503 Broadway, San Antonio, TX 78209-6209. Tel: 210-828-2244; Fax: 210-828-9741. Sr. Yolanda Tarango, C.C.V.I., Congregational Coord.

Incarnate Word Provincialate - U.S. Province: P.O. Box 15378, San Antonio, TX 78212-8578. Tel: 210-734-8310; Fax: 210-734-8369. Sr. Bette Anne Bluhm, C.C.V.I., Prov. Coord.

Incarnate Word Retirement Community: 4707 Broadway, San Antonio, TX 78209-6215. Tel: 210-829-7561; Fax: 210-828-0020. Mr. Steven Fuller, Exec. Dir.

Universal total in Congregation: 377; U.S. Province: 202.

Properties owned and/or sponsored: Universities 1; High Schools 3; Hospitals (co-sponsored) 27; Temporary shelter for homeless women & children 2; Retirement Center 1.

Ministry in the field of Education at all levels; Hospitals and Health Service Agencies; Nursing Homes; Pastoral Ministries; Diocesan Offices; Social Service Agencies.

Represented in the Archdioceses of Chicago, New Orleans, St. Louis, and San Antonio and in the Dioceses of Amarillo, Corpus Christi, Dallas, El Paso, Fort Worth, Jefferson City, LaCrosse, WI, Spokane, and Victoria, TX. Also in Ireland, Mexico, Peru, and Zambia.

[0470] (CCVI)—CONGREGATION OF THE SISTERS OF CHARITY OF THE INCARNATE WORD, HOUSTON, TEXAS (P)

Founded in the United States in 1866, St. Mary's Infirmary Galveston, TX.

Motherhouse: *Villa de Matel*, 6510 Lawndale St., P.O. Box 230969, Houston, TX 77223-0969. Tel: 713-928-6053; Fax: 713-928-8148. Sr. Lillian Anne Healy, Congregational Leader.

Total in Congregation: 160.

Legal Titles: Incarnate Word Charitable Trust; The Congregation of the Sisters of Charity of the Incarnate Word, Houston, Texas.

Sisters serve and staff: Hospitals; Homes for Aged; Elementary Schools; Social Services; Retreat Centers.

Represented in the Archdioceses of Galveston-Houston and Los Angeles and in the Dioceses of Alexandria, Lake Charles, San Bernardino, Shreveport, St. Louis and Tyler. Also in Ireland, Guatemala, San Salvador and Kenya.

[0480] (S.C.L.)—SISTERS OF CHARITY OF LEAVENWORTH, KANSAS (P)

Founded in the United States in 1858.

Community Offices and Motherhouse: 4200 S. 4th St., Leavenworth, KS 66048-5054. Tel: 913-758-6501; Fax: 912-682-2128. Sr. Maureen Hall, S.C.L., Community Dir.; Sr. Barbara Sellers, S.C.L., Archivist.

Total in Community: 276.

Ministries to AIDS Victims; Cross-culture; Elderly; Immigrants; Prisoners, Handicapped Adults and Youth; Health Service Agencies; Mental Health; Native Americans; and Social Service Agencies.

Properties owned and sponsored: University of Saint Mary, Leavenworth, KS; Cristo Rey Kansas City High School, KCMO. The Sisters' Health Care ministry is currently carried out and sponsored by Leaven Ministries (Public Juridic Person) for the following - Sisters of Charity of Leavenworth Health System (SCLHS), Lenexa, KS: Residential and Day Treatment Centers for Children, Mount St. Vincent Home, Denver, CO; Saint John's Health Center, Santa Monica, CA. Health Facilities: Saint John's Health Center, Santa Monica, CA; Saint Joseph Hospital, Denver, CO; St. Mary's Hospital & Medical Center, Grand Junction, CO; Saint John Hospital, Leavenworth, KS; St. Francis Health Center, Topeka, KS; Providence Medical Center, Kansas City, KS; Saint Vincent Healthcare, Billings, MT; St. James Healthcare, Butte, MT; Holy Rosary Healthcare, Miles City, MT; Marian Clinic, Topeka, KS; Marillac Clinic, Grand Junction, CO; Caritas Clinic, Inc., Kansas City, KS; Saint Vincent Clinic, Leavenworth, KS (Div. of Caritas Clinics); Duchesne Clinic, Kansas City, KS (Div. of Caritas Clinics).

Sisters serving in Elementary; Secondary and Higher Education; Nursing Education; Special Education; Religious Education; Ministry Training; Hospitals; Latin American Missions; Diocesan Offices; Parish Administration and Pastoral Ministry; Liturgy-Music Ministry; Campus Ministry; Spiritual Direction; Communications; Social Justice; Housing.

Represented in the Archdioceses of Denver, Kansas City in Kansas, Los Angeles, Milwaukee, Santa Fe and St. Louis and in the Dioceses of Charlotte, Cheyenne, Gallup, Great Falls-Billings, Helena, Kansas City-St. Joseph and Pueblo. Also in Peru and Southern Sudan.

[0490] (S.G.M.)—SISTERS OF CHARITY OF MONTREAL (P)

(Grey Nuns)

Founded in 1737 by Saint Marguerite d'Youville at Montreal, Canada. First foundation in the United States in 1855.

Generalate: *General Administration*, 138 Rue Saint-Pierre, Montreal, Canada, H2Y 2L7. Tel: 514-842-9411. Sr. Jacqueline St. Yves, S.G.M., Congregational Leader.

St. Joseph Area U.S.A: *Area Administration-SGM*, 10 Pelham Rd., Ste. 1000, Lexington, MA 02421-8499. Tel: 781-674-7407. Sr. Helene Georges, S.G.M., Dir.-Formation; Sr. June Ketterer, S.G.M., Area Coord.

Total in Community: 25.

Legal Title: *The Grey Nuns Charities, Inc.*

Ministry in religious education, retreat ministry, social justice, congregational governance & administration, housing for the elderly, hospitals, nursing homes, parish ministry, pastoral care and prayer ministry.

Represented in the Archdiocese of Boston and in the Dioceses of Manchester and Toledo.

[0500] (S.C.N.)—SISTERS OF CHARITY OF NAZARETH (P)

Founded in the United States in 1812.

SCN Center: P.O. Box 172, Nazareth, KY 40048. Tel: 502-348-1555; Fax: 502-348-1502. Sr. Mary Elizabeth Miller, S.C.N., Pres.

Total in Congregation: 648.

Legal Title: *Nazareth Literary & Benevolent Institution.*

Properties owned or sponsored: Camp Maria, Leonardtown, MD; Nazareth Villages Inc., Nazareth Villages II, Inc., Nazareth, KY; Nazareth Home, Inc., Louisville, KY; Vincentian Academy; Vincentian Collaborative System; Vincentian Home, Inc.; Vincentian Regency; Vincentian DeMarillac; Marian Manor Corp.; Vincentian Collaborative System Rehabilitation Services; Vincentian Child Development Center; Vincentian Collaborative System Charitable Foundation.

Nazareth Office: P.O. Box 187, Nazareth, KY 40048. Tel: 502-331-4072; Fax: 502-331-4076. Sr. Judy Raley, S.C.N., Prov.; Sr. Brenda Gonzales, S.C.N., Vice Prov.

Sisters serve and staff: in the field of Academic Education on all levels; Special Education Services; Social Services; Libraries; Parish Ministry; Archdiocesan Offices; Health Care Institutions; Retreat Centers; Literacy & Retirement Centers.

Represented in the Archdioceses of Boston, Indianapolis, Louisville, Mobile and Philadelphia and in the Dioceses of Charleston, Cleveland, Columbus, Covington, Greensburg, Jackson, Knoxville, Little Rock, Lexington, Madison, Memphis, Owensboro, Pittsburgh, Scranton, Steubenville and Venice. Also in Belize and Botswana.

Louisville Office: 676 Atwood, P.O. Box 17545, Louisville, KY 40217. Tel: 502-636-0411; Fax: 502-636-0412. Sr. Adeline Fehribach, S.C.N., Vice Prov.

Eastern Province: *SCN Provincial House*, E. Boring Canal Rd., KSV Raman Ln., GPO Box 219, Patna, Bihar, India, 800 001. Tel: 011-91-612-2520192. Sr. Sangeeta Ayithamattam, S.C.N., Prov.; Sr. Reena Theruvankunnel, S.C.N., Vice Prov.; Sr. Basanti Lakra, S.C.N., Vice Prov.

[0510] (O.L.M.)—SISTERS OF CHARITY OF OUR LADY OF MERCY (D)

Founded in Charleston, South Carolina in 1829.

Generalate and Motherhouse: *Sisters of Charity of Our Lady of Mercy*, 424 Fort Johnson Rd., P.O. Box 12410, Charleston, SC 29422. Tel: 843-795-2866; Fax: 843-795-6083. Sr. Bridget Sullivan, O.L.M., Gen. Supr.

Total in Community: 19.

Properties owned and/or sponsored: Motherhouse, May Forest, Charleston, SC; Our Lady of Mercy Convent, Johns Island, SC; Our Lady of Mercy Community Outreach Services, Inc. Johns Island, SC.

Legal Title: *Barry Charitable Trust.*

Sisters serve and staff: Parishes; Social Services.

Represented in the Diocese of Charleston.

[0520] (S.C.M.M.)—SISTERS OF CHARITY OF OUR LADY, MOTHER OF MERCY (P)

Founded in Holland 1832. First foundation in the United States in 1874.

General Motherhouse: Den Bosch, The Netherlands

Universal total in Congregation: 610.

SCMM Provincial Center: 32 Tuttle Pl., East Haven, CT 06512. Tel: 203-469-7872. Sr. Barbara Ann Valentine, S.C.M.M., Prov.

Total in Community: 11.

Represented in the Archdioceses of Chicago, Hartford and St. Paul-Minneapolis and in the Diocese of San Diego.

[0530] (S.C.M.C.)—SISTERS OF CHARITY OF OUR LADY, MOTHER OF THE CHURCH (P)

First foundation in the United States in 1970.

General Motherhouse: Baltic, CT 06330. Tel: 860-822-8241; Fax: 860-822-9842. Mother M. Anthony Lemire, Supr. Gen.

Professed Sisters: 59; Junior Professed: 2; Novices: 1.

Properties owned, staffed or sponsored: High Schools 1; Nursing Home 1; Elementary Schools 8; Catechetical Schools 5; Shelter for the Homeless 1; Hispanic Ministry 1; Educational Tutoring Center 1; Assisted Living, CBRF 1.

Represented in the Archdioceses of Hartford and St. Paul-Minneapolis and in the Dioceses of Madison and Norwich.

[0540] (S.C.O.)—SISTERS OF CHARITY OF OTTAWA (P)

(Grey Nuns of the Cross)

Founded in Ottawa, Canada, in 1845. First foundation in the United States in 1857.

General Motherhouse: 9 Bruyere St., Ottawa, Canada, K1N 5C9. Sr. Lorraine Desjardins, S.C.O., Gen. Supr.

Total number of Sisters in Congregation based in Ottawa: 591.

American Province (1950): *St. Joseph*, 559 Fletcher St., Lowell, MA 01854-3434. Tel: 978-458-4472; Fax: 978-441-1452. Sr. Pauline Leblanc, S.C.O., Archivist & Provincial Superior.

Professed U.S. Sisters: 20.

Properties owned and/or sponsored: D'Youville Senior Care, Inc, Lowell, MA; Bachand Hall, Lowell, MA; St. Joseph Residence, Lowell, MA; Provincial House, Lowell, MA.

Legal Title: *Sisters of Charity of Ottawa.*

Sisters staff: Grammar Schools; Health Care and Pastoral Ministries; Apostolate of Aging.

Sisters sponsor: Saints Medical Center, Lowell, MA and D'Youville Life and Wellness Community, Lowell, MA.

Represented in the Archdiocese of Boston.

[0560] (S.C.Q.)—SISTERS OF CHARITY OF QUEBEC (P)

(Grey Nuns)

Founded in Quebec in 1849. First United States foundation in 1890.

General Motherhouse: 2655 Le Pelletier St., Beauport, Canada, GIC 3X7. Tel: 418-628-8860. Sr. Morin Huguette, S.C.Q., Supr.

U.S. House (1908): *Franco-American School*, 357 Pawtucket St., Lowell, MA 01854. Tel: 508-458-1251. Sr. Lorraine Richard, S.C.Q.

U.S. House (1917): *Sacred Heart Home, Inc.*, 359 Summer St., New Bedford, MA 02740. Tel: 508-996-6751. Sr. Lorraine Richard, S.C.Q., Supr.

Professed U.S. Sisters: 4.

Sisters serve and staff: The field of education and care of the elderly; Franco American School, Lowell, MA; Sacred Heart Home, New Bedford, MA.

Represented in the Archdiocese of Boston and in the Diocese of Fall River.

[0565] (S.C.R.H.)—SISTERS OF CHARITY OF ROLLING HILLS (D)

Founded in Los Angeles, CA in 1964.

General Motherhouse & U.S. House: 28600 Palos Verdes Dr. E., Rancho Palos Verdes, CA 90275. Tel: 310-831-4104. Sr. Virginia Buchholz, S.C.R.H., Supr.

Sisters: 6.

Legal Title: *Sisters of Charity of Rolling Hills.*

Ministries: Service to those in need, supported through ministry in Catholic institutions according to the talents of each sister.

Represented in the Archdiocese of Los Angeles.

[0570] (S.C.)—SISTERS OF CHARITY OF SETON HILL, GREENSBURG, PENNSYLVANIA (P)

Founded in the United States in 1870.

Motherhouse: *Caritas Christi*, 129 DePaul Center Rd, Greensburg, PA 15601. Tel: 724-853-7948; Fax: 724-838-1512; Web: www.scsh.org. Sr. Jane Mary Kelly, S.C., Sister Servant.

Sisters: 87.

Generalate: *Sisters of Charity of Seton Hill*, 4933 W. Patterson Ave., Chicago, IL 60641-3512. Tel: 773-205-1822; Tel: 773-205-1853; Fax: 773-205-1855; Email: marlenemondalek@hotmail.com. Sr. Marlene Mondalek, S.C., Gen. Supr.

Total in Community: 423.

Properties owned and/or sponsored: Elizabeth Seton Center, Pittsburgh, PA; Korea Province in Kwangju, Korea.

Ministry in the field of Religious and Academic Education at all levels; Special Education and Rehabilitation Services for Children and Adults with physical and mental handicaps; Social and Legal Services; Health Care; Retreat Centers; Day Care Centers for Children and Adults; Pastoral and Campus Ministry; Community Service Center, Shelters for the Homeless; Spiritual Direction; Diocesan Offices; and Art Ministry.

U.S. Province - Provincialate: *DePaul Center*, 144 DePaul Center Rd, Greensburg, PA 15601. Tel: 724-836-0406; Fax: 724-836-8280; Web: sss.scsh.org. Sr. Vivien Linkhauer, S.C., Prov. Supr.; Sr. Louise Grundish, S.C., Archivist.

Represented in the Archdioceses of Chicago and Cincinnati, and in the Dioceses of Altoona-Johnstown, Erie, Cleveland, Greensburg, Orlando, Phoenix, Pittsburgh, Tucson, Wheeling-Charleston and Youngstown. Also in Israel.

[0580] (C.S.A.)—SISTERS OF CHARITY OF ST. AUGUSTINE (D)

Founded in Cleveland, Ohio in 1851.

Motherhouse: *Mount Augustine*, 5232 Broadview Rd., Richfield, OH 44286. Sr. Miriam Erb, C.S.A., Congregational Leader; Sr. Mary Denis Maher, C.S.A., Archivist.

Total in Congregation: 51.

Properties owned and sponsored: CSA Health Network, Cleveland, OH; Providence Hospitals, Columbia, SC; Sisters of Charity of St. Augustine Health System Inc., Cleveland OH; Mercy Medical Center, Inc., Canton OH; Regina Health Center, Richfield, OH; Sisters of Charity Foundation of Cleveland; Sisters of Charity Foundation of Canton; Sisters of Charity Foundation of South Carolina; St. John Medical Center; St. Vincent Charity Medical Center.

Represented in the Dioceses of Charleston, Cleveland, Lexington and Youngstown.

[0590] (S.C.)—SISTERS OF CHARITY OF SAINT ELIZABETH, CONVENT STATION (P)

Founded in Newark, New Jersey in 1859.

General Motherhouse: *Convent of St. Elizabeth - Administration Building*, P.O. Box 476, Convent Station, NJ 07961-0476. Tel: 973-290-5000; Tel: 973-290-5450; Fax: 973-290-5335. Sr. Rosemary Moynihan, Gen. Supr.; Sr. Miriam Teresa, League of Prayer.

Total in Congregation: 374.

Properties and Legal Titles: Sisters of Charity of Saint Elizabeth Academy of Saint Elizabeth, Convent Station, NJ; Saint Vincent Academy, Newark, NJ; Josephine's Place, Elizabeth, NJ.

Sisters serve and staff: Academies; High Schools; Elementary Schools; Hospitals; C.C.D.; Parish Work; Social Work; Health Services; College Teaching.

Represented in the Archdioceses of Boston, Hartford, Newark and New York and in the Dioceses of Charlotte, El Paso, Fairbanks, Fall River, Gallup, Jackson, Metuchen, Paterson, Palm Beach, Pensacola-Tallahassee, Raleigh, St. Petersburg, Trenton, Tucson, Wheeling-Charleston and Wilmington. Also in San Salvador, Central America.

[0600] (S.C.S.J.A.)—SISTERS OF CHARITY OF ST. JOAN ANTIDA (P)

Founded in France in 1799 by Saint Joan Antida Thouret. First foundation in the U.S. 1932.

General Motherhouse: *Suore della Carita di Santa Giovanna Antida*, Via S. Maria in Cosmedin 5, Rome, Italy, 00153. Sr. Nunzia De Gori, Supr. Gen.

North American Province (1976): *Regina Mundi Provincial House*, 8560 N. 76th Pl., Milwaukee, WI 53223. Tel: 414-354-9233; Fax: 414-355-6463. Sr. Anne Marie Baemmert, S.C.S.J.A., Prov.

Total in Congregation: 35.

Ministry in schools; neighborhood services and parishes.

Properties owned and sponsored: St. Joan Antida High School, Inc; Guardian Angel Learning Center, Inc.; St. Joan Antida High School Foundation, Ltd.

Represented in the Archdiocese of Milwaukee and in the Diocese of Gallup.

[0610] (S.C.S.H.)—SISTERS OF CHARITY OF ST. HYACINTHE (P)

(Grey Nuns)

Founded in 1840 in St. Hyacinthe, P.Q., Canada. First United States foundation in 1878.

General House: 16470 Avenue Bourdages, SUD, St. Hyacinthe, Canada, J2T 4J8. Sr. Diane Beaudoin, S.C.S.H., Supr. Gen.; Sr. Claudette Jacques, S.C.S.H., Gen. Sec.

Universal total in Congregation: 146.

Legal Title: *The Society of the Sisters of Charity, Portland, ME.*

U.S. Regional Administration: *Sisters of Charity of St. Hyacinthe*, Portland, ME 04103-4257. Tel: 207-773-8607. Sr. Diane Beaudoin, Pres.; Sr. Claudette Jacques, S.C.S.H., Sec.

Total number in U.S: 8.

Represented in the Dioceses of Manchester and Portland (In Maine). Also in Canada and Haiti.

[0620] (S.C.S.L.)—SISTERS OF CHARITY OF ST. LOUIS (P)

Founded in France in 1803. First foundation in the United States in 1910.

Generalate: 5169 Avenue MacDonald, Montreal, Canada, H3X 2V9. Sr. Nicole Jégo, Supr. Gen.

Universal total in Congregation: 590.

American Sector: 60 Club Rd., Unit 204, Plattsburgh, NY 12903-4926. Tel: 518-563-7410; Email: srber.du@charter.net. Sr. Bernadette Ducharme, Local Supr.

Total in Community: 5.

Represented in the Diocese of Ogdensburg.

[0630] (M.V.Z.)—SISTERS OF CHARITY OF ST. VINCENT DE PAUL OF ZAGREB (P)

Founded in Croatia (Austria-Hungary) in 1845. First U.S. foundation in 1955.

General Motherhouse: Zagreb, Croatia Mother Miroslava Bradica, Supr. Gen.

U.S. Foundation: *Sisters of Charity Convent*, 171 Knox Ave., West Seneca, NY 14224. Tel: 716-825-5859. Sr. Bogumila Kutlesa, M.V.Z., Supr.

Professed Sisters: 6.

Sisters staff: CCD Centers and Parish Services; Hospital & Health Services.

Represented in the Diocese of Buffalo.

[0640] (S.C.)—SISTERS OF CHARITY OF ST. VINCENT DE PAUL, HALIFAX (P)

Founded by Saint Elizabeth Ann Seton, Emmitsburg, Maryland in 1809. Congregation at Halifax became independent in 1856, Papal approved in 1908.

Sisters of Charity Centre: 215 Seton Rd., Halifax, Canada, B3M 0C9. Tel: 902-406-8077; Fax: 902-457-3506. Sr. Donna Geernaert, Congregational Leader; Mrs. Patti Bannister, Archivist.

Total in Congregation: 476.

Legal Title: *Sisters of Charity (Halifax).*

Commonwealth of Massachusetts: *Boston Office*, 125 Oakland St., Wellesley Hills, MA 02481-5338. Tel: 781-997-1100; Fax: 781-997-1358. Sr. Sally McLaughlin, S.C., Congregational Councillor Tel: 781-997-1355; Fax: 781-997-1358; Sr. Ann Regan, S.C., Congregational Councillor Tel: 781-997-1356; Fax: 781-997-1358.

Legal Titles: Sisters of Charity (Halifax) Supporting Corporation, 125 Oakland St. Wellesley Hills, MA 02481-5338. Phone: 781-997-1110; Fax: 781-237-8152. Sr. Donna Geernaert, Congregational Leader; Sisters of Charity (Halifax) Corporate Mission, Inc., 125 Oakland St. Wellesley Hills, MA 02481-5338. Tel: 781-997-1100; Fax: 781-997-1358. Sr. Donna Geernaert, Congregational Leader.

Mount St. Vincent Retirement Community: 125 Oakland St., Wellesley Hills, MA 02481-5338. Tel: 781-997-1110; Fax: 781-237-8152. Sr. Kathleen Crowley, S.C., Community Leadership Team Tel: 781-997-1165; Fax: 781-237-8152; Sr. Maureen Murphy, S.C., Community Leadership Team Tel: 781-997-1165; Fax: 781-237-8152.

Legal Titles and Holdings: Marillac Residence, Inc., Wellesley Hills, MA; Elizabeth Seton Residence, Inc., Wellesley Hills, MA.

State of NY: *Sisters of Charity (Halifax), New York Office*, 85-10 61st Rd., Rego Park, NY 11374. Tel: 718-651-1685; Fax: 718-651-5645; Email: scnyoffice@aol.com. Sr. Maryanne Fitzgerald, Congregational Councillor Tel: 516-622-9655; Sr. Roberta Kerins, Congregational Councillor Tel: 301-773-0208.

Ministering in education at all levels; parish ministry; spiritual direction/retreats; social services; pastoral ministry; administration.

Represented in the Archdioceses of Boston and New York and in the Dioceses of Brooklyn and Rockville Centre. Also in Canada, Bermuda, Dominican Republic and Peru.

[0650] (S.C.)—SISTERS OF CHARITY OF ST. VINCENT DE PAUL OF NEW YORK (D)

Founded in Emmitsburg, Maryland in 1809 by Saint Elizabeth Ann Seton.

General Motherhouse: *Sisters of Charity Center*, 6301 Riverdale Ave., Bronx, NY 10471-1093. Tel: 718-549-9200; Fax: 718-884-3013. Sr. Jane Iannucelli, Pres.

Total in Congregation: 333.

Sisters serve and staff: Colleges; High Schools; Elementary Schools; General Hospitals; New York Foundling Hospital; House of Prayer; Supportive Housing for low income Elderly; Residence for Senior and Invalid Sisters; Mental Health Divisions, Rest House for Community use; Housing for Homeless; Parish Pastoral Ministry; Advocacy Programs; Outreach Pastoral Ministry; Spirituality Programs.

Represented in the Archdioceses of Miami and New York and in the Dioceses of Rockville Centre. Also in Guatemala.

[0655] (S.C.V.)—SISTERS OF CHARITY OF ST. VINCENT DE PAUL OF SUWON

Motherhouse is located in Suwon, Korea.

Represented in the Archdiocese of Denver.

The sisters provide service to the poor, caring for the sick poor, elderly, mentally disabled, single mothers, dying people, prisoners, and refugees from North Korea.

Total Members: 230.

Sr. Regina Park, Pres.

Motherhouse & Generalate: 93-3 Chi-Dong Paddal-Gu, Suwon City, KyoungGi Province, Korea, North Tel: 031-241-2151.

U.S. Address(1996): *St. Anna's Home*, 3147 S. Pagosa St., Aurora, CO 80013. Tel: 303-627-2986; Fax: 720-379-6308; Email: stannashome@hotmail.com.

Total Sisters in U.S: 4.

[0660] (S.C.C.)—SISTERS OF CHRISTIAN CHARITY (P)

Daughters of the Blessed Virgin Mary of the Immaculate Conception

Founded in Germany in 1849. First foundation in the United States in 1873.

Generalate: *Suore della Carita Cristiana, Casa Generalizia*, Largo XXI Aprile, 10, Rome, Italy, 00162. Tel: 011-3906-86071-35. Sr. Adalberta Mette, Supr. Gen.

Universal total in Congregation: 543.

North American Eastern Province (1927): *Mallinckrodt Convent Div. of North American Province*, 350 Bernardsville Rd., Mendham, NJ 07945. Tel: 973-543-6528. Sr. Joan Daniel Healy, S.C.C., Prov. Supr.; Sr. Mary Pierre Koesters, S.C.C., Archivist.

Professed Sisters: 206.

Ministry in Academic Education; Retreat House; Catechetical Centers; Religion Coordinators; Health care and Parish Ministry.

Properties owned and/or sponsored: Villa Pauline, Retreat House, Mendham, NJ; Divine Providence Hospital, Williamsport, PA; Holy Spirit Hospital, Camp Hill, PA; Mallinckrodt Convent Motherhouse, Mendham, NJ; Holy Family Convent, Home for Aged and Retired Sisters, Danville, PA; Muncy Valley Hospital, Muncy, PA.

Represented in the Archdioceses of Newark, New York, Philadelphia, and Washington and in the Dioceses of Allentown, Camden, Harrisburg, Metuchen, Paterson and Scranton.

North American Western Province: *Sisters of Christian Charity - Daughters of the Blessed Virgin Mary of the Immaculate Conception*, 2041 Elmwood Ave., Wilmette, IL 60091-1431. Tel: 847-920-9341; Fax: 847-920-9346. Sr. Janice Boyer, S.C.C., Prov. Supr.; Sr. Anastasia Sanford, Archivist.

Professed Sisters: 56.

Ministry in Academic & Religious Education; Pastoral Ministry; Parish Ministry; Ministry to Aged; Prayer Ministry; Ministry to the Poor and Multi-Cultural.

Properties owned and sponsored: Maria Immaculata Convent; Sacred Heart Convent, Wilmette, IL; the Josephinum Convent and Academy, Chicago, IL.

Represented in the Archdioceses of Chicago, New Orleans and St. Louis and in the Diocese of Rapid City.

[0670] (O.C.S.O.)—CISTERCIAN NUNS OF THE STRICT OBSERVANCE (P)

Founded at Citeaux, France, in 1098. First foundation in the United States in 1949.

Generalate: Viale Africa 33, Rome, Italy, 00144.

Total universal number of Nuns in Order: 1782.

Contemplative and Monastic

U.S. Establishments:

Mount St. Mary's Abbey: 300 Arnold St., Wrentham, MA 02093-1799. Tel: 508-528-1282; Fax: 508-528-5360. Mother Maureen McCabe, O.C.S.O., Abbess.
Total in Community: 45.
Represented in the Archdiocese of Boston.

Our Lady of the Mississippi Abbey: 8400 Abbey Hill Rd., Dubuque, IA 52003. Tel: 563-582-2595; Fax: 563-582-5511. Rev. Mother Nettie Gamble, O.C.S.O., Abbess.
Total in Community: 22.
Legal Title: *Trappistine Nuns, Inc.; Iowa Cistercians of the Strict Observance.*
Represented in the Archdiocese of Dubuque.

Santa Rita Abbey: H.C. 1 Box 929, Sonoita, AZ 85637-9705. Tel: 520-455-5595. Mother Miriam Pollard, O.C.S.O., Prioress.
Total in Community: 10.
Legal Title: *Cistercian Nuns of the Strict Observance.*
Represented in the Diocese of Tucson.

Our Lady of the Redwoods Abbey: 18104 Briceland Thorn Rd., Whitethorn, CA 95589. Tel: 707-986-7419; Web: www.redwoodsabbey.org. Sr. Kathy DeVico, O.C.S.O., Abbess.
Total in Community: 10.
Represented in the Diocese of Santa Rosa.

Our Lady of the Angels Monastery: 3365 Monastery Dr., Crozet, VA 22932. Tel: 434-823-1452; Fax: 434-823-6379. Mother Marion Rissetto, O.C.S.O., Prioress.
Legal Title: *Cistercian Nuns of the Strict Observance in Virginia, Inc.*
Represented in the Diocese of Richmond.

[0680] (O.CIST.)—CISTERCIAN NUNS (P)

Founded in 1098 at Citeaux, France. It is composed of monks and nuns in independent houses.

Generalate: *Piazza del Tempio di Diana*, 14, Rome, Italy, 00153. Rt. Rev. Maurus-Giuseppe Lepori, O.Cist., Abbot Gen.

U.S. Headquarters: *Valley of Our Lady Monastery*, E11096 Yanke Dr., Prairie Du Sac, WI 53578-9737. Tel: 608-643-3520. Rev. Mother Bernarda Seferovich, O. Cist., Prioress.
Total in Community: 21.

[0685] (R.M.I.)—CLARETIAN MISSIONARY SISTERS (P)

Religious of Mary Immaculate Claretian Missionary Sisters

Founded in Santiago de Cuba, August 25, 1855. Established in the United States in 1956.

Generalate: Via Calandelli 16, Rome, Italy, 00153. Eusebia Pizarro, Supr. Gen.

U.S. Delegation: 9600 W. Atlantic Ave., Delray Beach, FL 33446. Sr. Regina Tutzo, R.M.I., Local Supr.
Sisters in the World: 600; Sisters in Florida: 11.
Legal Title: *Claretian Missionary Sisters of Florida, Inc.*
Ministry in Religious Education; Theological Formation in Pastoral Institutes and Seminaries; Social Ministries; Parish and Diocesan Ministries.
Represented in the Archdiocese of Miami and in the Diocese of Palm Beach.

[0690] (C.M.S.)—COMBONI MISSIONARY SISTERS (P)

Founded in Italy in 1872. An international congregation of 1,450 sisters serving in the mission fields of Africa, America, Europe, and the Middle East. First United States foundation in 1950.

Generalate: Rome, Italy Sr. Luzia Premoli, C.M.S., Supr. Gen.

American Headquarters: 1307 Lakeside Ave., Richmond, VA 23228-4710. Tel: 804-262-8827; Fax: 804-264-2906; Email: cmsusaprov@verizon.net; Web: www.combonisrs.com. Sr. Maria de la Luz Aguilera, C.M.S., Prov. Supr.; Sr. Mary Bernadette Hilmer, C.M.S., Delegate Supr.
Legal Titles & Holdings: Provincial House, Comboni Missionary Sisters, Inc., Richmond, VA.
Represented in the Archdiocese of Baltimore and Chicago and in the Diocese of Richmond.

[0700] (O.D.N.)—COMPANY OF MARY (P)

Founded in Bordeaux, France, April 7, 1607, by St. Jeanne de Lestonnac. First foundation in the United States in 1926, in Douglas, Arizona.

General Motherhouse: Rome, Italy Sr. Beatriz Acosta, O.D.N., Supr. Gen.
Universal total in Congregation: 1798.

U.S. Motherhouse (1926): *Company of Mary Provincial Offices*, 16791 E. Main St., Tustin, CA 92780. Tel: 714-541-3125. Sr. Leticia Salazar, O.D.N., Prov. Supr.; Sr. Kathy Schneider, O.D.N., Community Archivist.
Professed: 45.
Properties owned and/or sponsored: Divine Providence Kindergarten & Day Nursery, Los Angeles, CA; Lestonnac Kindergarten & Day Nursery, Douglas, AZ; St. Jeanne De Lestonnac School, Tustin, CA; St. Jeanne de Lestonnac Kindergarten & Day Nursery, Los Angeles, CA; St. Jeanne de Lestonnac School, Temecula, CA; St. Joseph Residence for Women, Los Angeles, CA; Vina de Lestonnac Ministry Center-Retreat, Temecula, CA; Lestonnac Residence for Women, Tustin, CA; Lestonnac Retreat Center, Tustin, CA.
Sisters serve and staff: Pre-Schools - Kindergartens; Grammar Schools; Religious Instruction Centers; Residences; Parishes & Retreat Centers.
Represented in the Archdiocese of Los Angeles and in the Dioceses of Orange, San Bernardino and Tucson.

[0710] (C.S.)—THE COMPANY OF THE SAVIOR (D)

Founded in Spain in 1952. First United States foundation in 1962.

General Motherhouse: Tajsia de Cusariego 19, Madrid, Spain, 28023. Mother Amelia Lora-Tamayo, Supr. Gen.

U.S. Foundation: 820 Clinton Ave., Bridgeport, CT 06604. Tel: 203-368-1875.
Professed Sisters: 81; Novices: 4.
Represented in the Diocese of Bridgeport.

[0720] (M.C.)—CONSOLATA MISSIONARY SISTERS (P)

Founded in Italy in 1910. First foundation in the United States in 1954.

Motherhouse: *Istituto Suore Missionarie della Consolata*, Via Cassia Km.37-BivioUmilta, Nepi, VT, Italy, 01036. Mother Simona Brambilla, M.C., Supr. Gen.
Universal total in Congregation: 710.
Represented in the Dioceses of Birmingham, Grand Rapids and Saginaw.

U.S. Headquarters: *Consolata Missionary Sisters*, 6801 Belmont Rd., P.O. Box 371, Belmont, MI 49306. Tel: 616-361-2072; Fax: 616-361-2072. Sr. Zelita M. Bragagnolo, M.C., Supr.
Total in Community: 24.
Sisters serve and staff: Catechetical and Pastoral Work; Apostolate among Minorities; Elementary Schools and Pastoral Ministries.

[0725] (M.C-M.)—CORDI-MARIAN MISSIONARY SISTERS CONGREGATION (P)

Founded in Mexico City in 1921. First United States foundation in 1926.

General Motherhouse: Apdo. Postal #1109, Toluca, Mexico, 50091. Sr. Maria Cibrian, M.C.M., Supr. Gen.

U.S. Provincial House: 11624 FM 471, Apt. 501, San Antonio, TX 78253. Tel: 210-798-8220; Fax: 210-798-8225. Sr. Matilda Jaime, M.C.M., Prov. Supr.
Total in Congregation: 108; Total number in U.S. community: 33.
Properties owned and/or sponsored: Cordi-Marian Villa-Retreat Center and Provincial House, San Antonio, TX; East St. Louis Catholic Day Care Center and Convent, East St. Louis, IL; Formation House, San Antonio, TX.
Ministry in Catechetical Centers; Pastoral Ministry Programs; Elementary Education; Kindergarten and Day Care Centers; Retreat Center; Social Service; Rel. Articles & Book Stores; Ministry to Hispanics.
Represented in the Archdiocese of San Antonio and in the Dioceses of Belleville and Springfield-Cape Girardeau.

[0730] (FD.CC.)—CANOSSIAN DAUGHTERS OF CHARITY (P)

Canossian Sisters

Founded in Verona, Italy in 1808.

General Motherhouse: via della Stazione di Ottavia 70, Rome, Italy, 00135.

U.S. Provincial House: *Cristo Rey-Canossian Sisters*, 5625 Isleta Blvd., S.W., Albuquerque, NM 87105. Tel: 505-873-2854. Sr. Anne Bosio, Prov. Supr.
Sisters in U.S: 41.
Ministry in Evangelization; Spirituality Center, Integral Promotion of the Person; Parish Pastoral Ministry; Pastoral Care of the Sick; Intermediate Care Facility for Developmentally Disabled Children; Lay Volunteer Program.
Represented in the Archdioceses of San Francisco and Santa Fe and in the Diocese of Sacramento. Also in Canada and Mexico.

[0740] (D.C.P.B.)—DAUGHTERS OF CHARITY OF THE MOST PRECIOUS BLOOD

Founded in Pagani, Italy in 1872. First foundation in United States in 1908.

Generalate: Via Vigna Fabbri 45, Rome, Italy Sr. Alfonsa Bove, Mother Gen.

U.S. Address: *Daughters of Charity of the Most Precious Blood*, 1482 North Ave., Bridgeport, CT 06604. Tel: 203-334-7000. Sr. Alfonsa Kunnel, D.C.P.B., Supr.
Total in Community: 18.
Represented in the Dioceses of Albany, Bridgeport and Paterson.

[0750] (F.C.S.C.J.)—DAUGHTERS OF THE CHARITY OF THE SACRED HEART OF JESUS (P)

First founded in France at La Salle de Vihiers in 1823. First founded in the United States at Newport, Vermont in October 1905.

Generalate: Montgeron, France

General Motherhouse: La Salle de Vihiers, France Sr. Genevieve Penisson, Supr. Gen.

Mount Sacred Heart Provincial House: *Daughters of the Charity of the Sacred Heart of Jesus (1949)*, 226 Grove St., Littleton, NH 03561. Tel: 603-444-5346; Fax: 603-444-5348. Sr. Elaine Voyer, F.C.S.C.J., Prov.
Total number in Province: 38.
Sisters serve and staff: Elementary Schools; High Schools; Catechetical Centers; Spiritual Directors; Pastoral Ministry; Preschools; Foreign Missions.
Represented in the Archdiocese of Boston and in the Dioceses of Burlington, Fall River, Manchester and Ogdensburg.

[0760] (D.C.)—DAUGHTERS OF CHARITY OF ST. VINCENT DE PAUL (P)

Founded in France in 1633. First foundation in the United States in 1809 by Saint Elizabeth Ann Seton, Emmitsburg, MD.

General Motherhouse: Paris, France Sr. Evelyne Franc, Supr. Gen.

St. Louis Province: 4330 Olive St., St. Louis, MO 63108-2622. Tel: 314-533-4770; Fax: 314-561-3226; Web: www.daughtersofcharity.org. Sr. Maureen Schmalzried, D.C., Prov.

Province of the West (Los Altos Hills) (1969): *Seton Provincialate*, 26000 Altamont Rd., Los Altos, CA 94022-4317. Tel: 650-941-4490; Fax: 650-949-8883. Sr. Marjory Ann Baez, D.C., Prov.
Total in Community: 121.
Properties owned and sponsored: Seton Medical Center, Daly City, CA; Seton Provincialate, Los Altos Hills, CA; St. Vincent Medical Center, Los Angeles, CA; St. Vincent's Senior Citizen Nutrition Program, Los Angeles, CA; St. Francis Medical Center, Lynwood, CA; Maryvale, Rosemead, CA; Mount St. Joseph-St. Elizabeth, San Francisco, CA; O'Connor Hospital, San Jose, CA; Villa Siena, Mountain View, CA; St. Louise Regional Hospital, Gilroy, CA; St. Vincent's, Santa Barbara, CA; Our Lady of the Rosary of Talpa School, Los Angeles, CA; Our Lady of the Miraculous Medal School, Montebello, CA; Our Lady of the Visitacion School, San Francisco, CA; St. Patrick School, San Jose, CA; St. Elizabeth Seton School, Palo Alto, CA; Sacred Heart Cathedral Preparatory, San Francisco, CA.
Represented in the Archdioceses of Anchorage, Los Angeles and San Francisco and in the Dioceses of Gallup, Phoenix, Salt Lake City and San Jose.

[0770] (D.C.)—DAUGHTERS OF THE CROSS (D)

Founded in France in 1640. First foundation in the United States in 1855.

Motherhouse: *Daughters of the Cross Motherhouse*, 411 E. Flournoy-Lucas Rd., Shreveport, LA 71115-3901. Tel: 318-797-0887. Sr. Maria Smith, Pres.
Total in Community: 3.
Represented in the Diocese of Shreveport.

[0780] (F.C.)—DAUGHTERS OF THE CROSS OF LIEGE (P)

Founded in Liege, Belgium in 1833. First foundation in the United States in 1958.

Principal House: *St. Bernard Convent*, 165 W. Eaton Ave., Tracy, CA 95376. Sr. Maureen O'Brien, F.C., Supr.
Total in Community: 6.
Represented in the Diocese of Stockton.

[0790] (F.D.C.)—DAUGHTERS OF DIVINE CHARITY (P)

Founded in Austria on November 21, 1868 by Mother Franziska Lechner. First founded in the United States on October 8, 1913, in New York City.

General Motherhouse: Vienna, Austria

Generalate: *Grottaferrata*, Rome, Italy

Holy Family Province (2012): *Provincialate:*, 850 Hylan Blvd., Staten Island, NY 10305-2021. Tel: 718-981-4402; Fax: 718-556-3550; Email: sisterwilliam@gmail.com; Web: www.god'slovefdc.org. Sr. M. William McGovern, F.D.C., Prov. Supr.
Professed Sisters: 46.
Properties owned and/or sponsored: St. Mary's Residence, NY; St. Joseph Hill Academy, Staten Island, NY; St. Elizabeth Briarbank Home for the Aged, Bloomfield Hills, MI; St. Mary's Residence, Detroit, MI; Leonora Hall, Akron, OH.
Ministry in Education; Nursing; Residence for Young Women; CCD; Youth Ministry; Care of the Elderly.
Represented in the Archdiocese of New York, Detroit, Milwaukee and in the Diocese of Cleveland, Fort Wayne-South Bend and San Diego.

[0793] (D.D.L.)—DAUGHTERS OF DIVINE LOVE (P)

Founded in Ukpor, Nigeria in 1969. First United States Foundation in 1990.

General House: Fifth Avenue, P.O. Box 546, Enugu, Nigeria Tel: 042-559071; Tel: 042-551742. Rev. Mother Chilota Elochukwu, D.D.L., Mother Gen.
Professed Sisters in Congregation: 800.

U.S. Regional House: 2601 N. Sayer Ave., Chicago, IL 60707. Tel: 773-622-2434; Fax: 773-622-2499; Email:

ddloveus@aol.com. Sr. M. Magdalene Ogah, D.D.L., Reg. Supr.
Professed Sisters in U.S: 49.
Ministry in the field of Administration; Religious and Academic Education at all levels; Special Education; Health Services; Parish and Diocesan Services; Retreat Work; Social Work.
Represented in the Archdioceses of Chicago, Galveston-Houston, Newark, and Washington and in the Dioceses of Brooklyn, Brownsville and Springfield in Illinois.

[0795] (F.D.Z.)—DAUGHTERS OF DIVINE ZEAL (P)

Founded in Messina, Italy in 1887 by Saint Hannibal Maria DiFrancia. First foundation in the United States in 1951.

Generalate: *Figlie Del Divino Zelo*, Circonvallazione Appia 144, Rome, Italy, 00179. Mother M. Teolinola Salemi, F.D.Z., Supr. Gen.
Universal total in Congregation: 1000.

U.S. Headquarters: *Hannibal House Spiritual Center*, 1526 Hill Rd., Reading, PA 19602. Tel: 610-375-1738; Tel: 610-375-9072; Fax: 610-374-0369; Email: srdivinezeal@hotmail.com. Sr. Gesulmina Micali, F.D.Z., Supr.
Total in Community: 3.
Ministry in the field of Religious and Academic Education; Parish and Youth Ministry; Retreat, Vocation, Prayer and Apostolate.
Represented in the Diocese of Allentown.

[0810] (D.H.M.)—DAUGHTERS OF THE HEART OF MARY (P)

Founded in France in 1790. First United States foundation in 1851.

Generalate: 39 rue Notre Dame des Champs, Paris, France, 75006.

Provincialate: 1339 Northampton St., Holyoke, MA 01040-1958. Tel: 413-532-7406; Fax: 413-533-4217. Sr. Anita Price Baird, D.H.M., Prov.
Professed Sisters U.S.A: 47.
Represented in the Archdioceses of Chicago, New York, St. Louis and St. Paul-Minneapolis and in the Dioceses of Buffalo and Springfield in Massachusetts.
Properties owned or sponsored: Marian Center, Holyoke, MA; Maryhill, St. Paul, MN; Ephpheta Center, Chicago, IL; Nardin Academy, Buffalo, NY; Heart of Mary Center, St. Louis, MO; St. Joseph's School for the Deaf, Bronx, NY.

[0820] (D.H.S.)—DAUGHTERS OF THE HOLY SPIRIT

Founded in France in 1706. First foundation in the U.S. in 1902.

Generalate: *Congregation des Filles du Saint Esprit*, 15 Boulevard Sebastopol, B.P. 50148, Rennes Cedex 3, France, 35101. Sr. Agnes Stephan, F.S.E., Supr. Gen.

General Motherhouse: *Maison-mere des Filles du Saint Esprit*, 20 rue des Capucins - BP 4538, Saint-Brieuc Cedex 2, France, 22045.

Provincial House: *Daughters of the Holy Spirit, Inc.*, 72 Church St., Putnam, CT 06260. Tel: 860-928-0891. Sr. Norma Bourdon, D.H.S., Prov.
Total in Community: 97.
Ministry in the field of Academic Education at all levels; Home/District Nursing; Health Care Center for Daughters of the Holy Spirit; and Various Social and Pastoral Ministries of Service.
Represented in the Archdioceses of Hartford and Mobile and in the Dioceses of Bridgeport, Burlington, Norwich, Providence, Richmond, Sacramento, Springfield in Massachusetts, Stockton and Worcester.

[0850] (F.M.A.)—DAUGHTERS OF MARY HELP OF CHRISTIANS (P)

Salesian Sisters of St. John Bosco

Founded in Mornese, Italy, in 1872. First foundation in the U.S. in 1908 at Paterson, NJ.

General Motherhouse: Via Ateneo Salesiano, 81, 00139, Rome, Italy Very Rev. Mother Yvonne Reungoat, F.M.A., Mother Gen.
Universal total in Congregation: 14115.

Province of St. Philip, Apostle: *Provincial House*, 655 Belmont Ave., Haledon, NJ 07508-2398. Tel: 973-790-7963. Mother Phyllis Neves, F.M.A., Prov.
Total in Community: 100.
Properties owned and/or sponsored: Provincial House, Haledon, NJ; Mary Help of Christians Academy, North Haledon, NJ; Sacred Heart Center, Newton, NJ; Villa Madonna School-Salesian Sisters of Tampa, Inc., Tampa, FL; Camp Auxilium Learning Center, Newton, NJ.
Legal Title: *Missionary Society of the Salesian Sisters, Inc.; Salesian Sisters of Tampa, Inc.*
Ministry in the field of academic and religious education at all levels; Youth Ministry.
Represented in the Archdioceses of Miami, Newark, New Orleans and New York and in the Dioceses of Paterson and St. Petersburg.

Province of Mary Immaculate: *FMA Provincial House*, 6019 Buena Vista, San Antonio, TX 78237. Tel: 210-432-0090; Fax: 210-432-4016. Sr. Sandra Neaves, F.M.A., Prov.
Total in Community: 103.
Properties owned and/or sponsored: FMA Provincial House & St. John Bosco School, San Antonio, TX; Mary Help of Christians School, Laredo, TX; Salesian Sisters School - Salesian Sisters: MHC Youth Center, Inc., Corralitos, CA; Salesian Sisters Convent, Colorado Springs, Co; Formation House, Bellflower, CA.
Legal Title: *Institute of the Daughters of Mary Help of Christians - Salesian Sisters of St. John Bosco, San Antonio, TX.*
Ministry in Education; Youth Ministry; Religious Education and Outreach to the Poor.
Represented in the Archdioceses of Los Angeles, New Orleans, San Antonio and San Francisco and in the Dioceses of Austin, Colorado Springs, Laredo, Monterey, and Phoenix.

[0860] (D.M.)—DAUGHTERS OF MARY OF THE IMMACULATE CONCEPTION (P)

Founded in New Britain in 1904.

Motherhouse - Main Headquarters: *Admin. Offices*, 314 Osgood Ave., New Britain, CT 06053.

General Motherhouse: 314 Osgood Ave., New Britain, CT 06053. Tel: 860-225-9406. Mother Mary Jennifer, Supr. Gen.
Total in Community: 41.
Properties owned and/or sponsored: St. Lucian's Home, New Britain, CT; Monsignor Bojnowski Manor, New Britain, CT; Motherhouse and Novitiate Comples, New Britain, CT; St. Joseph's Home, NY; St. Agnes Residence, NY; Our Lady's Guild House, Boston, MA; Santa Maria Nursing Facility, Cambridge MA; Marian Heights; Prudence Crandall; Mary Immaculate; Miriam House.
Legal Title: *Congregation of the Daughters of Mary of the Immaculate Conception, Inc.*
Ministry in the field of Education; Home for the Aged; Homes for Working Girls and Students; Skilled Care.
Represented in the Archdioceses of Boston, Hartford and New York and in the Diocese of Springfield in Massachusetts.

[0870] (F.M.I.)—CONGREGATION OF THE DAUGHTERS OF MARY IMMACULATE (P)

Marianist Sisters

Founded in France in 1816.

Motherhouse: Rome, Italy Mother C. Joelle Bec, Supr. Gen.

U.S. Foundation (1949): *Marianist Sisters Residence*, 235 W. Ligustrum Dr., San Antonio, TX 78228. Tel: 210-433-5501; Fax: 210-433-0300. Sr. Gretchen Trautman, F.M.I., Prov. Supr.
Total in Community: 16.
Properties owned and/or sponsored: Marianist Sisters Residence, San Antonio, TX.
Represented in the Archdioceses of Cincinnati and San Antonio.

[0880] (D.M.J.)—DAUGHTERS OF MARY AND JOSEPH (P)

Founded in Belgium in 1817. First U.S. Foundation in 1926.

Generalate: Via dei Lucchesi, 3, Roma, Italy, 00187. Sr. Kate Creedon, Supr. Gen.

Novitiate: 5300 Crest Rd., Rancho Palos Verdes, CA 90275-5004. Tel: 310-377-9968; Fax: 310-541-5967. Sr. Sheila Collins, Vocation Dir.; Sr. Christina O'Connor, Formation Contact.

Regionalate: 5300 Crest Rd., Rancho Palos Verdes, CA 90275-5004. Tel: 310-377-9968. Sr. Kitty Moloney, D.M.J., Regional Admin.
Professed Sisters: 45.
Legal Title: *Daughters of Mary and Joseph, California.*
Sisters staff: Grammar & High Schools, Parish Ministry; Health Ministry; Retreat Work.
Represented in the Archdioceses of Los Angeles and San Francisco and in the Dioceses of Monterey and San Bernardino.

[0890] (D.M.)—DAUGHTERS OF OUR LADY OF MERCY (P)

Founded in Italy in 1837 by Saint Mary Joseph Rossello. First foundation in the United States in 1919.

Generalate: Via Monte Grappa, No. 7, Savona, Italy Rev. Mother M. Beatriz Lassalle, Supr. Gen.

Provincialate and Novitiate: *Villa Rossello*, 1009 Main Rd., Newfield, NJ 08344. Tel: 856-697-2983. Sr. Daniel Marie Catherine, Prov. Supr.; Sr. Loretta Marie Stevens, D.M., Community Archivist.
Total in Community: 45.
Legal Holdings: Our Lady of Mercy Academy, Newfield, NJ.
Ministry in the field of Education; Health Services; Skilled Nursing Center; Pastoral Counseling, C.C.D. and Parish Work.
Represented in the Dioceses of Camden, Harrisburg and Scranton. Also in the West Indies.

[0895] (F.M.S.R.)—DAUGHTERS OF OUR LADY OF THE HOLY ROSARY (P)

Founded in 1946 in Trung Linh, Bui Chu, North Vietnam by Bishop Dominic Maria Ho Ngoc Can. First foundation in the United States in 1967.
Sr. Maria Nen Thi Tran, F.M.S.R.

U.S. Provincial Office: *Annunciation Convent*, 1492 Moss St., New Orleans, LA 70119-2904. Sr. Mary James Hang-Nga Thi Tran, F.M.S.R., Prov. Supr.
Total in Community: 55.
Properties owned and/or sponsored: Five residences.
Ministry in the field of Education; Health Services; Pastoral Ministry.
Represented in the Archdioceses of New Orleans and Oklahoma City and in the Dioceses of Biloxi and Houma-Thibodaux.

[0900] (F.D.N.S.C.)—DAUGHTERS OF OUR LADY OF THE SACRED HEART (P)

Founded in France in 1882.

Motherhouse: Via Casale S. Pio V, 37, Rome, Italy Sr. Mary Fyfe, Supr. Gen.

U.S. Foundation (1955): *St. Francis de Sales Convent*, 424 E. Browning Rd., Bellmawr, NJ 08031. Tel: 856-931-8973; Fax: 856-931-7018.
Professed Sisters in the U.S: 11.
Represented in the Diocese of Camden.

[0910] (BETHL.)—BETHLEMITA, DAUGHTER OF THE SACRED HEART OF JESUS (P)

Founded in Guatemala in 1861. First foundation in the United States in Dallas, TX.

Motherhouse: Bogota, Colombia

U.S. Foundation: *St. Joseph Residence, Inc.*, 330 W. Pembroke St., Dallas, TX 75208. Tel: 214-948-3597. Sr. Carolina Sanchez Botero, Admin.
Professed Sisters: 9.
Represented in the Diocese of Dallas.

[0920] (D.S.F.)—CONGREGATION OF THE DAUGHTERS OF ST. FRANCIS OF ASSISI

Founded in Hungary, 1894. First foundation in the United States in 1946.

Motherhouse: *American Province: St. Joseph's Convent*, 507 N. Prairie St., Lacon, IL 61540. Tel: 309-246-2175. Sr. Adriana Zdila, D.S.F., Pres.
Professed Sisters: 13.
Legal Title: *Congregation of the Daughters of St. Francis of Assisi, American Province.*
Represented in the Dioceses of Peoria and Springfield-Cape Girardeau.

[0930] (F.S.J.)—RELIGIOUS DAUGHTERS OF ST. JOSEPH (P)

Founded in Gerona, Spain in 1875.

General Motherhouse: *General Asensio Cabanillas*, 18, Madrid, Spain, 28003. Mother Ma. Benita de la Cuerda, Supr. Gen.
Universal total in Congregation: 680.

Regional House: *Calzada Ermita Istapalapa*, Mexico Sr. Maria Mendia Ajona, Prov.

U.S. Foundation: 6677 Del Rosa Ave., San Bernardino, CA 92404. Tel: 909-888-4877. Sr. Maria Belen Manso, Supr.
Total in Community: 5.
Legal Title: *Daughters of St. Joseph of California, Inc.*
Represented in the Archdiocese of Los Angeles.

[0940] (D.S.M.P.)—DAUGHTERS OF ST. MARY OF PROVIDENCE (P)

Founded in Italy in 1881. First foundation in the United States in 1913.

Generalate: Rome, Italy Mother Serena Ciserani, D.S.M.P., Supr. Gen.

Provincialate: *Daughters of St. Mary of Providence Immaculate Conception Province*, 4200 N. Austin Ave., Chicago, IL 60634. Tel: 773-205-1313; Tel: 773-545-8300. Sr. Patricia McCafferty, Prov.
Professed Sisters: 68.
Represented in the Archdioceses of Boston, Chicago and Philadelphia and in the Dioceses of Camden, Gary, Lansing, Milwaukee, New Ulm, Providence, Sioux Falls and Syracuse.

[0950] (F.S.P.)—PIOUS SOCIETY DAUGHTERS OF ST. PAUL (P)

Missionary Sisters of the Media of Communications

Founded in Alba, Piedmont, Italy, on June 15, 1915. First founded in the United States on June 28, 1932, in New York.

General Motherhouse: Rome, Italy Sr. Maria Antonieta Bruscato, Supr. Gen.
Universal total in Congregation: 2247.

Provincial House, Novitiate, Publishing House: 50 St. Paul's Ave., Jamaica Plain, MA 02130. Tel: 617-522-8911. Sr. Joan Paula Arruda, F.S.P., Local Supr.; Sr. Mary Leonora Wilson, F.S.P., Prov. Supr.
Total in Community: 135.
Properties owned and/or sponsored: Pauline Book and Media Centers, found in 12 locations throughout the U.S.; Provincialate, Boston, MA; St. Thecla Retreat House, Billerica, MA.
Legal Title: *Daughters of St. Paul, Inc.*
Represented in the Archdioceses of Boston, Chicago, Los Angeles, Miami, New Orleans, New York, Philadelphia, St. Louis and San Francisco and in the Dioceses of Arlington, Charleston, Honolulu, and San

Diego. Also in Canada.

[0960] (D.W.)—DAUGHTERS OF WISDOM (P)
Founded in France in 1703. First foundation in the United States in 1904.

General Motherhouse: *St. Laurent-sur-Sevre*, Vendee, France
Superior General Headquarters located in Rome, Italy.

U.S. Province (1949): *Provincial House*, 385 Ocean Ave., Islip, NY 11751-4600. Tel: 631-277-2660; Fax: 631-277-3274. Sr. Ann Gray, D.W., Prov.
Professed Sisters: 97.
Properties owned and/or sponsored: Wisdom House Center for Spirituality, Litchfield, CT; Our Lady of Perpetual Help Convent (Rest Home for Sisters), Sound Beach, NY; Provincial House, Islip, NY.
Ministry in all levels of Education; Retreat House; Hospital & Health Services; Orphanage; Social Work; Pediatrics Clinic.
Represented in the Archdioceses of Hartford and Washington and in the Dioceses of Brooklyn, Charleston, Portland (In Maine), Raleigh, Richmond, Rockville Centre, St. Petersburg and Wheeling-Charleston.

[0965] (D.L.J.C.)—DISCIPLES OF THE LORD JESUS CHRIST (P)
Founded in the United States in 1972.

Motherhouse: P.O. Box 64, Prayer Town, TX 79010. Tel: 806-534-2312; Fax: 806-534-2223; Email: sisters@dljc.org; Web: www.dljc.org. Mother Lucy Lukasiewicz, Supr. Gen.
Total in Community: 37.
Legal Holdings and Titles: Prayertown Emmanuel Retreat House, Prayer Town, TX.
Ministry in Retreat Work and Evangelization.
Represented in the Archdiocese of Santa Fe, NM and Diocese of Amarillo. Also in Mexico.

[0970] (R.D.C.)—SISTERS OF THE DIVINE COMPASSION (D)
Founded in the United States in 1886.

General Motherhouse: *Good Counsel Convent*, 52 N. Broadway, White Plains, NY 10603. Tel: 914-798-1300; Fax: 914-949-5169. Sr. Susan Merritt, R.D.C., Pres.
Total in Community: 90.
Legal Holdings and Titles: Academy of Our Lady of Good Counsel High School and Elementary School, White Plains, NY; Preston High School, New York, NY; Divine Compassion Center for Spiritual Renewal, NY; Migrant Ministry, Goshen, NY; Residence, Hampton Bays, NY; RDC Center for Counseling and Human Development.
Ministry in Preschool, Elementary, Secondary, College and University Education; Religious Education; Educational Consultation; Adult Education; Special Education; Pastoral Ministry; Retreat Work and Spiritual Direction; Counseling; Social Services; Migrant Ministry; Health Services; Administration and Business Services.
Represented in the Archdiocese of New York.

[0980] (P.D.D.M.)—PIOUS DISCIPLES OF THE DIVINE MASTER (P)
Founded in 1924. First foundation in the United States in 1948.

General Motherhouse: Rome, Italy Sr. M. Regina Cesarato, Supr. Gen.
Universal total in Congregation: 1426.

U.S. Headquarters: 60 Sunset Ave., Staten Island, NY 10314. Tel: 718-494-8597; Fax: 718-494-2123. Sr. M. Nieves Salinas, P.D.D.M., Reg. Supr.
Total number in Region: 48.
Ministry is a Three Dimensional Mission: Eucharistic, Priestly, Liturgical.
Represented in the Archdioceses of Boston, Los Angeles and New York and in the Dioceses of Fresno and San Jose.

[0990] (C.D.P.)—SISTERS OF DIVINE PROVIDENCE (P)
Founded in Germany in 1851. First foundation in the United States in 1876; incorporation granted September 17, 1881.
Amended and restated articles of incorporation on December 28, 2001.

General Motherhouse: *Mother of Providence Convent*, 12 Christopher St., Wakefield, RI 02879. Tel: 401-782-1785; Fax: 401-782-6967. Sr. Janet Folkl, Gen. Supr.

Marie de la Roche Province (2001): *Providence Heights*, 9000 Babcock Blvd., Allison Park, PA 15101. Tel: 412-931-5241; Fax: 412-635-5416. Sr. Mary Francis Fletcher, C.D.P., Prov. Supr.; Sr. Claudia Ward, C.D.P., Area Asst.-Kingston, MA; Sr. Jacklyn Pritchard, C.D.P., Area Asst.-St. Louis, MO.
Total in Community: 248.
Ministry in the fields of Education; Social Services; Pastoral Ministry; and Health Care Services.
Properties owned and sponsored: La Roche College, Pittsburgh, PA; Providence Heights Alpha School, Allison Park, PA; Kearns Spirituality Center, Allison Park, PA; Providence Connections, Inc.; Providence Family Support Center, Pittsburgh, PA; Providence Villa, Gibsonia, PA; Sisters of Divine Providence of Allegheny County, Allison Park, PA; Divine Providence Foundation, Allison Park, PA; Sisters of Divine Providence Charitable Trust, Allison Park, PA; Room at the Inn, Bridgeton, MO; Sacred Heart School System, Kingston, MA; Congregation of the Sisters of Divine Providence, Kingston, MA; Sisters of Divine Providence of Missouri, Bridgeton, MO, La Posada Providencia, San Bonito, TX.
Represented in the Archdioceses of Boston, Detroit, Kansas City in Kansas, St. Louis, Santa Fe and San Juan and in the Dioceses of Arecibo (PR), Brownsville, Cleveland, Columbus, Erie, Greensburg, Nashville, Orlando, Phoenix, Pittsburgh, Providence, Raleigh, Springfield-Cape Girardeau, Springfield in Illinois, Wheeling-Charleston and Youngstown. Also in the Dominican Republic.

[1000] (C.D.P.)—CONGREGATION OF DIVINE PROVIDENCE, MELBOURNE, KENTUCKY (P)
Founded in France in 1762. First foundation in the United States in 1889.

General Motherhouse: *St. Jean de Bassel*, Fenetrange, France, 57930. Sr. Pascale Kubler, Supr. Gen.

American Provincial House (1889): *St. Anne Convent*, 1000 St. Anne Dr., Melbourne, KY 41059. Tel: 606-441-0679. Sr. Frances E. Moore, C.D.P., Prov. Supr.; Sr. Mary Joan Dohmen, C.D.P., Archivist.
Total number in Province: 147.
Ministry in the field of Academic Education at all levels; Montessori Schools; Home for Working Women; Retreat Center; Religious Education & Pastoral Ministry; Health & Social Services.
Represented in the Archdioceses of Cincinnati, Indianapolis, New York and Washington and in the Dioceses of Covington, Duluth, Lexington, Manchester, Toledo and Wheeling-Charleston. Also in West Africa.

[1010] (C.D.P.)—CONGREGATION OF DIVINE PROVIDENCE, SAN ANTONIO, TEXAS (P)
Founded in France in 1762. First foundation in the United States in 1866.

The Generalate: 515 S.W. 24th St., San Antonio, TX 78207. Tel: 210-434-1866; Fax: 210-568-1050. Sr. Ann Petrus, C.D.P., Supr. Gen.; Sr. Charlotte Kitowski, Archivist; Sr. Madonna Sangalli, C.D.P., Treas. Councilors: Sr. Lourdes Leal, C.D.P.; Sr. Helen Marie Miksch, C.D.P.; Sr. Theresa Anne Billeaud, C.D.P.

Novitiate and Formation: *Formation / Vocation Office*, 515 S.W. 24th St., San Antonio, TX 78207-4600. Tel: 210-434-1866.
Properties owned and/or sponsored: Our Lady of the Lake Retirement Center, San Antonio, TX; Moye Center, Castroville, TX.
Legal Titles & Holdings: Congregation of Divine Providence, Inc.; Providence Trust, San Antonio, TX.
Ministry in all levels of Education; Catechetical Centers; Hospitals, Clinics; Diocesan Offices; Retreat Houses; Spiritual Direction-Counseling; Pastoral; Social Work; Chaplaincies in Public Institutions; Home-Health Care; Administration.
Represented in the Archdioceses of Denver, Galveston-Houston, New Orleans, San Antonio, San Francisco, Seattle and St. Louis and in the Dioceses of Alexandria, Austin, Brownsville, Dallas, Fort Worth, Houma-Thibodaux, La Crosse, Lafayette (LA), Laredo, St. Petersburg, San Angelo, San Jose, Savannah, Victoria and Wichita. Also in Mexico.

[1020] (S.D.R.)—SISTERS OF THE DIVINE REDEEMER (P)
Founded in 1849 at Niederbronn, France. First foundation in the United States on October 6, 1912 at McKeesport.

Generalate: *Suore del Divin Redentore*, Via Casale Piombino 14, Rome, Italy, 00135. Tel: 011-39-06-305-2512. Sr. S. M. Katarina Kristofova, Supr. Gen.

American Province (1922): *Divine Redeemer Motherhouse*, 999 Rock Run Rd., Elizabeth, PA 15037-2613. Tel: 412-751-8600; Fax: 412-751-0355. Sr. M. Monica Kosztolnyik, Archivist; Sr. Rosemary Horvath, S.D.R., Prov. Supr.
Total number in Province: 19.
Legal Titles and Holdings: Sisters of the Divine Redeemer Charitable Trust; Divine Redeemer Health Care Ministries Corp., Elizabeth, PA.
Sisters teach parish CCD Center and own Nursing Home.
Represented in the Archdiocese of Philadelphia and in the Diocese of Pittsburgh.

[1030] (S.D.S.)—SISTERS OF THE DIVINE SAVIOR
Founded in Tivoli, Italy, in 1888. First foundation in the United States in 1895.

General Motherhouse: Viale delle Mura Gianicolensi 67, Rome, Italy Sr. Therezinha Joana Rasera, Supr. Gen.

North American Province: *Sisters of the Divine Savior*, 4311 N. 100th St., Milwaukee, WI 53222-1393. Tel: 414-466-0810; Fax: 414-466-4335. Sr. Carol Thresher, S.D.S., Prov. Supr.; Sr. Susan Staff, S.D.S., Archivist.
Total number in U.S. community: 79.
Ministry in all levels of Education; Pastoral and Social Services; Health Care; and Homes for the Aged.
Properties owned or sponsored: St. Anne's Home for the Elderly; Divine Savior Holy Angels High School, Milwaukee, WI; Divine Savior Healthcare, Inc., Portage, WI.
Represented in the Archdiocese of Milwaukee and in the Dioceses of Birmingham, Green Bay, La Crosse, Madison, Nashville, Phoenix, San Diego and Tucson.

[1040] (C.D.S.)—CONGREGATION OF THE DIVINE SPIRIT (D)
First foundation in Erie, Pennsylvania in 1956.

Motherhouse: 409 W. 6th St., Erie, PA 16507. Tel: 814-455-3590. Mother Patricia O'Connor, Supr. Gen.
Membership: 35.
Sisters serve and staff: Parochial Schools; CCD Activities; Home for Aged; Social Work.
Represented in the Dioceses of Erie and Youngstown.

[1050] (O.P.)—DOMINICAN CONTEMPLATIVE NUNS (P)
(The Nuns of the Orders of Preachers)
Founded in France in 1206. First foundation in the United States in 1880. Monastic contemplative branch of the Order of Preachers. Papal cloister.

Nuns of the Order of Preachers O.P: *Corpus Christi Monastery*, 1230 Lafayette Ave., Bronx, NY 10474. Tel: 718-328-6996; Fax: 718-328-1974. Sr. Maria Pia of the Eucharist, O.P., Prioress.
Total in Community: 11.

Monastery of the Blessed Sacrament: *Nuns of the Order of Preachers*, 29575 Middlebelt, Farmington Hills, MI 48334-2311. Tel: 248-626-8321; Tel: 248-626-8253; Fax: 248-626-8724. Sr. Mary Thomas, O.P., Prioress.
Cloistered Sisters: 31; Extern Sisters: 3.
Nuns of the Order of Preachers (Cloistered Dominican Nuns, Perpetual Adoration)

Monastery of the Angels: *Cloistered Dominican Nuns*, 1977 Carmen Ave., Los Angeles, CA 90068. Tel: 323-466-2186. Mother Mary Martin, O.P., Prioress.
Sisters: 18.
Legal Title: *The Monastery of the Angels.*

Monastery of the Angels: Karachi, Pakistan Sr. Mary Martin, O.P., Prioress.
Sisters: 9.

Queen of Angels Monastery: Bocaue, Bulacan, Philippines Sr. Mary Joseph, O.P., Prioress.
Sisters: 20.

Corpus Christi Monastery: 215 Oak Grove Ave., Menlo Park, CA 94025-3272. Tel: 650-322-1801; Fax: 650-322-6816. Sr. Mary Assumpta, O.P., Prioress.
Cloistered Total Number in Community: 14.

Dominican Nuns O.P: *Monastery of the Mother of God*, 1430 Riverdale St., West Springfield, MA 01089-4698. Tel: 413-736-3639; Fax: 413-736-0850. Sr. Mary St. John, O.P., Prioress.
Total in Community: 16.

Dominican Contemplative Nuns - O.P: *Monastery of Our Lady of the Rosary*, 335 Doat St., Buffalo, NY 14211-2199. Tel: 716-892-0066; Fax: 716-897-1566. Sr. Mary Emmanuel, O.P., Prioress.
Solemnly Professed: 20; Extern Sisters: 3; Simple Vows: 1.
Legal Title: *Dominican Nuns of the Perpetual Rosary.*

Monastery of Our Lady of Grace: 11 Race Hill Rd., Guilford, CT 06437-1099. Tel: 203-457-0599. Sr. Mary Ann, O.P., Prioress.
Total in Community: 30.
Legal Title: *Dominican Nuns of North Guilford, CT Inc.*

Monastery of the Infant Jesus: *Dominican Contemplative Nuns*, 1501 Lotus Ln., Lufkin, TX 75904. Tel: 936-634-4233; Fax: 936-634-2156. Sr. Mary John, O.P., Prioress.
Professed: 26.

Monastery of Our Lady of the Rosary (Rosary Shrine): 543 Springfield Ave., Summit, NJ 07901. Tel: 908-273-1228. Sr. Denise Marie, O.P., Prioress.
Professed Choir Sisters: 13.

Nuns of the Order of Preachers O.P: *Monastery of Mary the Queen*, 1310 W. Church St., Elmira, NY 14905. Tel: 607-734-9506; Fax: 607-734-1452; Web: www.monasteryofmarythequeen.op.org. Sr. Miriam, O.P., Prioress.
Total in Community: 13.

Monastery of the Dominican Nuns of the Perpetual Rosary (Cloistered): 605 14th St. & West St., Union City, NJ 07087-3199. Tel: 201-866-7004. Mother Mary Jordan, O.P., Prioress.
Professed Sisters: 3.

Monastery of the Perpetual Rosary: 1500 Haddon Ave., Camden, NJ 08103. Mother Mary Immaculate Heart, O.P., Prioress.
Professed Nuns: 6.

St. Dominic's Monastery (Contemplative): 2636 Monastery Rd., Linden, VA 22642. Sr. Mary Fidelis, O.P., Prioress.
Nuns: 12.

The Dominican Nuns of the Perpetual Rosary (Cloistered-Contemplative): *Monastery of the Immaculate Heart of Mary*, 1834 Lititz Pike, Lancaster, PA 17601-6585. Tel: 717-569-2104; Fax: 717-569-1598; Email: monlanc@aol.com. Sr. Mary Albert, O.P., Prioress.

Solemnly Professed: 10.

Dominican Monastery of the Perpetual Rosary: 802 Court St., Syracuse, NY 13208. Tel: 315-471-6762. Sr. Bernadette Marie, O.P., Prioress.
Total in Community: 12.
Solemn Vows, Papal enclosure.

Dominican Monastery of St. Jude: 143 County Rd. 20 E., P.O. Box 170, Marbury, AL 36051-0170. Tel: 205-755-1322. Mother Mary Joseph, O.P., Prioress.
Professed Nuns: 5; Novices: 2; Postulants: 1.
Legal Title: *Dominican Nuns of Perpetual Rosary and Adoration.*

[1060] (O.P.)—DOMINICAN CONTEMPLATIVE SISTERS (D)

Cloistered Contemplative

Founded in Calais, France in 1880.

Monastery of the Dominican Sisters of the Perpetual Rosary (Cloistered): 217 N. 68th St., Milwaukee, WI 53213. Tel: 414-258-0579; Email: frannl@wi.rr.com; Web: www.dsopr.org. Mother Miriam Leonard, O.P., Prioress.
Professed Sisters: 10.

[1070] (O.P.)—COLLABORATIVE DOMINICAN NOVITIATE DOMINICAN SISTERS (P)

There are seventeen Congregations of the Dominican Sisters of the Third Order of St. Dominic in the United States. The list of General Motherhouses follows in the order of seniority. If the Congregation is known under a more familiar name, that name is given under the name of the Congregation.

4928 Washington Blvd., St. Louis, MO 63108-1621. Tel: 314-454-0664.

[1070-03] —SINSINAWA DOMINICAN CONGREGATION OF THE MOST HOLY ROSARY (P)

Generalate: *Sinsinawa Dominican Congregation of the Most Holy Rosary*, 585 County Rd. Z, Sinsinawa, WI 53824-9701. Tel: 608-748-4411. Sr. Mary Ellen Gevelinger, O.P., Prioress of the Congregation; Sr. Lois Hoh, O.P., Archivist.
Total in Community: 546.
Ministry in a variety of cultures in Preaching & Evangelization; Elementary, Secondary and Higher Education; Medical, Legal and Social Services; Adult and Religious Education; Diocesan and Parish Administration, Spiritual Direction and Counseling; Rural, Migrant and Native American Services; Writing Research.
Properties owned or Institutions sponsored: Sinsinawa Dominicans, Inc., Dominican University, River Forest, IL; Sinsinawa Housing, Inc., (Academy Apartments), Sinsinawa, WI; Bethlehem Academy, Faribault, MN; Dominican High School, Whitefish Bay, WI; Queen of Peace High School, Burbank, IL; Trinity High School, River Forest, IL; Sinsinawa Nursing, Inc., (St. Dominic Villa), Sinsinawa, WI; Dominican Motherhouse, Sinsinawa, WI; Camp We-Ha-Kee, Winter, WI; Edgewood Campus School; Edgewood High School; Edgewood College, Madison, WI.
Represented in the Archdioceses of Atlanta, Chicago, Denver, Dubuque, Los Angeles, Miami, Milwaukee, Mobile, Omaha, St. Louis, St. Paul-Minneapolis, San Antonio, San Francisco, Santa Fe, Seattle and Washington and in the Dioceses of Albany, Austin, Birmingham, Brownsville, Cheyenne, Dallas, Davenport, Gallup, Gaylord, Grand Rapids, Green Bay, Helena, Honolulu, Jackson, Joliet, Juneau, La Crosse, Madison, Memphis, Nashville, Oakland, Orlando, Owensboro, Palm Beach, Pensacola-Tallahassee, Peoria, Phoenix, Rockford, Sacramento, Saginaw, San Angelo, San Diego, Santa Rosa, St. Augustine, St. Cloud, St. Petersburg, Spokane, Venice and Winona. Also in Bolivia, Italy, Mexico and Trinidad.

[1070-04] —CONGREGATION OF THE MOST HOLY NAME (P)

Generalate: *Dominican Sisters of San Rafael*, 1520 Grand Ave., San Rafael, CA 94901. Tel: 415-453-8303; Fax: 415-453-8367. Sr. Maureen McInerney, O.P.
Total in Community: 117.
Legal Holdings and Titles: San Domenico School, San Anselmo, CA; Santa Sabina Retreat Center, San Rafael, CA; St. Rose Corporation, San Francisco, CA; St. Joseph's Regional Health System; St. Joseph's Housing Corporation, Stockton, CA; St. Mary's Regional Medical Center, Reno, NV; Sisters of St. Dominic, Congregation of the Most Holy Name, San Rafael, CA; Mission Holding Corporation, San Rafael, CA.
Represented in the Archdiocese San Francisco and in the Dioceses of Monterey, Oakland, Reno, Sacramento, San Jose, Santa Rosa and Stockton. Also in Mexico.

Dominican Sisters of San Rafael Convent: 5042 Gadwall Cir., Stockton, CA 95207. Tel: 209-956-6953.

[1070-05] —CONGREGATION OF THE HOLY CROSS (D)

General Motherhouse: *Queen of the Rosary Motherhouse*, Albany Ave., Amityville, NY 11701. Tel: 631-842-6000; Fax: 631-842-0240. Sr. Mary Hughes, O.P., Prioress; Sr. Clare Patrice Farrell, O.P., Archivist.
Total in Community: 496.
Legal Title: *The Sisters of the Order of Saint Dominic.*
Sisters are engaged in the ministry of Education at all levels; Catechetical Schools; Handicapped, Adult and Continuing Education; Hospitals; Homes for the Aged; Residence for Senior Citizens; Spiritual Life Centers; Chaplaincy; Advocacy; Communications; Social Service Institutions; Shelters; Pastoral Services; Prison Ministry; Retreats; Health Services; Ministry to AIDS Victims; Environmental Education Ministry.
Represented in the Archdioceses of Hartford, Newark and New York and in the Dioceses of Albany, Brooklyn, Fort Wayne-South Bend, Kalamazoo, Providence, Rochester, Rockville Centre and Trenton. Also in Puerto Rico and Dominican Republic.

[1070-07] —CONGREGATION OF ST. CECILIA (P)

General Motherhouse: *St. Cecilia Convent*, 801 Dominican Dr., Nashville, TN 37228-1905. Tel: 615-256-5486; Fax: 615-687-3512. Mother Ann Marie Karlovic, O.P., Prioress Gen.; Sr. Marian Sartain, O.P., Archivist and Sec. Gen.
Professed Sisters in Community (183 finally professed; 54 junior professed): 237; Novices: 24; Postulants: 16.
Ministry in the field of Academic Education at all levels.
Legal Holdings and Titles: Aquinas College, Nashville, TN.
Represented in the Archdioceses of Atlanta, Baltimore, Cincinnati, Denver, Houston, New Orleans, St. Louis, St. Paul-Minneapolis and Washington and in the Dioceses of Arlington, Birmingham, Charleston, Joliet in Illinois, Knoxville, Lafayette in Indiana, Memphis, Nashville, Providence and Richmond. Also in Sydney, Australia and Vancouver, Canada.

[1070-09] —CONGREGATION OF ST. CATHERINE OF SIENA (P)

General Motherhouse: *Convent of St. Catherine*, 5635 Erie St., Racine, WI 53402-1900. Tel: 262-639-4100; Fax: 262-639-9702. Sr. Sharon Simon, O.P., Pres.; Sr. Shirley Kubat, Archivist.
Total in Community: 151.
Legal Holdings and Titles: Sisters of St. Dominic, Racine, WI; Dominican College of Racine, Inc., Racine, WI; St. Catherine's High School of Racine, Inc., Racine, WI; Racine Dominican Ministries, Inc., Racine, WI; St. Catherine's Infirmary, Inc., Racine, WI; HOPES Center of Racine, Inc.; Siena Retreat Center, Inc.
Properties sponsored: Franciscan Sisters, Daughters of the Sacred Hearts of Jesus and Mary, Wheaton, IL and the Sisters of St. Dominic, Racine, WI; Catherine Marian Housing, Inc.
Sisters minister in the areas of Elementary, Secondary, Higher and Music-Cultural Education; Adult Education; Religious Education; Administration; Parish and Pastoral Ministry; Prison Ministry; Social Justice; Social Services, Hospital and Health Services; Writing-Research; Hospital Chaplains; Retreats-Prayer Programs; Community Services.
Represented in the Archdioceses of Chicago, Detroit, Milwaukee, St. Louis and Santa Fe and in the Dioceses of Gallup, Green Bay, Jackson, Las Cruces, Las Vegas, Madison, Toledo and Yakima.

[1070-10] —DOMINICAN SISTERS OF SPRINGFIELD, ILLINOIS (P)

General Motherhouse: *Sacred Heart Convent*, 1237 W. Monroe St., Springfield, IL 62704-1680. Tel: 217-787-0481; Fax: 217-787-8169. Sr. Rose Marie Riley, O.P., Prioress Gen.; Sr. Julia Theobald, O.P., Archivist.
Total in Community: 231.
Legal Holdings or Titles: Dominican Sisters of Springfield, Illinois, Inc., Dominican Sisters of Springfield in Illinois Charitable Trust, Springfield, IL; Jubilee Farm, NFP, Springfield, IL; Dominican Literacy Center, Aurora, IL; Dominican Literacy Center, Chicago, IL; Marian Catholic High School, Chicago Heights, IL; Rosary High School, Aurora, IL; Sacred Heart-Griffin High School, Springfield, IL; St. Dominic-Jackson Memorial Hospital, Jackson, MS.
Ministry in Elementary, Secondary Schools and College, Religious & Academic Education; Learning Centers; Hospitals, Nursing Homes, Congregation's Infirmary and Retirement Centers; Retreat & Renewal Center; Administrative Positions in Parishes and Diocesan Offices; Parish Liturgist/Musician & Pastoral Associates; Prison Ministry; Social Services; Foreign Missions.
Represented in the Archdioceses of Chicago, Detroit, and Washington and in the Dioceses of Belleville, Jackson, Joliet, Kansas City-St. Joseph, Peoria, Rockford, and Springfield in Illinois. Also in Peru.

[1070-11] —CONGREGATION OF OUR LADY OF THE ROSARY (D)

General Motherhouse and Novitiate: *Dominican Convent of Our Lady of the Rosary*, 175 Rte. 340, Sparkill, NY 10976. Tel: 845-359-4199. Sr. Mary Murray, O.P., Pres.
Total in Community: 347.
Legal Title: *Dominican Convent of Our Lady of the Rosary.*
Ministry in High Schools and Elementary Schools; Adult Education/Literacy; Parishes; Pastoral; Colleges; Housing and Community Centers; Foreign Missions; Substance Abuse Recovery.
Properties sponsored: Aquinas High School, New York, NY; Albertus Magnus High School, Bardonia, NY; Thorpe Family Residence, Inc., Bronx, NY; One to One Learning Inc., Nyack, NY; Dowling Housing Corp., Sparkill, NY.
Represented in the Archdioceses of Chicago, New York, Newark and St. Louis and in the Dioceses of Brooklyn, Charleston, Great Falls-Billings, Jefferson City, Oakland, Rockville Centre, San Diego, St. Petersburg, Trenton and Wilmington.

[1070-12] —CONGREGATION OF THE QUEEN OF THE HOLY ROSARY (P)

General Motherhouse: *Dominican Convent*, 43326 Mission Blvd., Fremont, CA 94539. Tel: 510-657-2468; Fax: 510-657-1734. Sr. Gloria Marie Jones, Congregational Prioress; Sr. Pauline Bouton, Congregational Sec.
Professed: 210; Novices: 2.
Legal Title: *Dominican Sisters of Mission San Jose, a Corporation, Queen of the Holy Rosary College, a Corporation, St. Catherine's Academy, a Corporation, Anaheim, CA; Immaculate Conception Academy, a Corporation, San Francisco, CA; Flintridge Sacred Heart Academy, a Corporation, La Canada-Flintridge, CA; Pia Backes Support Trust, Fremont, CA.*
The Community is engaged in the Preaching Mission of St. Dominic through ministry in education at all levels, campus ministry, pastoral services, social justice, communications, health services, Congregational services, and full time study.
Represented in the Archdioceses of Los Angeles, San Francisco and St. Louis and in the Dioceses of Oakland, Orange, San Bernardino, San Jose and Tucson. Also in Germany, Mexico, and Guatamala.

[1070-13] —CONGREGATION OF THE MOST HOLY ROSARY (P)

General Motherhouse: 1257 Siena Heights Dr., Adrian, MI 49221. Tel: 517-266-3400; Fax: 517-266-3545. Sr. Attracta Kelly, O.P., Prioress.
Total in Congregation: 778.
Legal Holdings or Titles: Dominican Sisters of Adrian, MI, Inc., Adrian, MI; Camilla Madden Charitable Trust, Adrian, MI; Adrian Dominican Sisters Office of Development, Adrian, MI; Dominican Hospital, Santa Cruz, CA; Dominican Life Center, Adrian, MI; Regina Dominican High School, Wilmette, IL; Rosarian Academy, West Palm Beach, FL; Siena Heights University, Adrian, MI; St. Joseph Academy, Adrian, MI; St. Rose Dominican Hospitals, Henderson, NV; Weber Retreat Center, Adrian, MI.
Sisters minister in the areas of Formal Education - as administrators, teachers and consultants at elementary, secondary, college, state and diocesan levels; Pastoral Ministry - parishes, hospitals and campuses; Religious Education - coordinators and teachers; Social Services - case workers, administrators, counselors, therapists, consultants, care-givers for elderly and staff for retirement centers; Health Services - administrators, nurses, therapists, doctors, physician assistants, psychologists, technologists and dietitians; Business Services - directors, accountants, secretaries, administrative assistants, typists, bookkeepers, office managers, office staff, drivers and housekeeping staff; Spiritual Direction - retreat work, formation, congregation leadership and as diocesan vicars for Religious; Social Justice - coordinators, staff and community organizers; other ministries including research, law, science, public relations, art, communications and full-time study.
Represented in the Archdioceses of Anchorage, Atlanta, Chicago, Cincinnati, Detroit, Galveston-Houston, Indianapolis, Los Angeles, Louisville, Miami, New Orleans, New York, Oklahoma City, Philadelphia, Portland in Oregon; St. Louis, San Antonio, San Francisco, Santa Fe, Seattle and Washington and the Dioceses of Birmingham, Boise, Charleston, Cleveland, Columbus, El Paso, Evansville, Fresno, Fort Wayne-South Bend, Gallup, Gaylord, Green Bay, Harrisburg, Jackson, Joliet, Kalamazoo, Las Vegas, Lansing, Lexington, Marquette, Monterey, Oakland, Orange, Orlando, Palm Beach, Pensacola-Tallahassee, Phoenix, Providence, Pueblo, Richmond, Rockford, Saginaw, St. Petersburg, San Bernardino, San Diego, San Jose, Superior, Toledo, Tucson and Venice. Also in Canada, Dominican Republic, Kenya, Mexico, Philippines and Puerto Rico.

Mission Chapters (1982):

Florida Mission Chapter: 810 N. Olive Ave., West Palm Beach, FL 33401. Tel: 561-832-6521. Sr. Anne Liam Lees, O.P., Chapter Prioress.

Adrian Crossroads Mission Chapter: 1257 Siena Heights Dr., Adrian, MI 49221. Tel: 517-266-4240. Sr. Mary Ellen Youngblood, O.P., Chapter Prioress.

Mid-Atlantic Mission Chapter: P.O. Box 501507, Atlanta, GA 31150. Tel: 678-982-9441. Sr. Mary Priniski, O.P., Chapter Prioress.

Dominican Midwest Mission Chapter: 1515 W. Ogden Ave., La Grange Park, IL 60526. Tel: 708-482-5047. Sr. Patricia Ann Dulka, O.P., Chapter Prioress.

Holy Rosary Mission Chapter: 1257 Siena Heights Dr., Adrian, MI 49221. Tel: 517-266-4107. Sr. Josephine Gaugier, O.P., Chapter Prioress.

Great Lakes Dominican Mission Chapter: 29000 W. 11 Mile Rd., Farmington Hills, MI 48336. Tel: 248-478-4284. Sr. Frances Nadolny, O.P., Chapter Prioress.

Dominican West Mission Chapter: 851 Head St., San Francisco, CA 94132. Tel: 415-504-3525. Sr. Judith Benkert, O.P., Chapter Prioress.

[1070-14] —CONGREGATION OF OUR LADY OF THE SACRED HEART (P)

General Motherhouse: *Marywood*, 2025 E. Fulton St., Grand Rapids, MI 49503. Tel: 616-459-2910; Fax: 616-454-6105. Sr. Nathalie Meyer, O.P., Prioress; Sr. Rose Marie Martin, O.P., Archivist.

Total in Community: 245; Novices: 1.

Legal Holdings or Titles: Sisters of the Order of St. Dominic of Grand Rapids; Marywood Academy; Sisters of St. Dominic of the Congregation of Our Lady of the Sacred Heart Charitable Trust.

Sisters are involved in Academic and Religious Education at all levels; Liturgy; Pastoral Ministry and Administration; Diocesan Offices; Food Service; Health Care; Congregational Services; Social Work; Sabbatical Volunteer; Public Education and Study; Foreign Missions; Justice Advocacy.

Represented in the Archdioceses of Baltimore, Chicago, Detroit, St. Louis and Santa Fe and in the Dioceses of Brooklyn, Cleveland, Colorado Springs, Dallas, Fort Wayne-South Bend, Gaylord, Grand Rapids, Great Falls-Billings, Helena, Kalamazoo, Lansing, Lexington, Oakland, Saginaw, Shreveport and Superior. Also in Peru and Honduras.

[1070-15] —CONGREGATION OF SAINT DOMINIC (D)

General Motherhouse: *Sisters of Saint Dominic of Blauvelt*, 496 Western Hwy., Blauvelt, NY 10913-2097. Tel: 845-359-5600; Fax: 845-359-5773. Sr. Mary Malone, O.P., Pres.

Total in Community: 150.

Sisters serve and staff: Elementary; Secondary; Higher Education; Special Education; Hospital Care; Pastoral Care; Parish Ministry; Retreat Work; Child Care; Neighborhood Services; Services to Migrants; Services to Chemically Dependent.

Represented in the Archdioceses of Newark and New York and in the Dioceses of Orlando, Providence, Rockville Centre, San Bernardino and Trenton.

[1070-17] —CONGREGATION OF ST. CATHERINE DE RICCI (P)

General Motherhouse: *Fanjeaux*, 1750 Ashbourne Rd., Elkins Park, PA 19027-2596. Tel: 215-635-6027. Sr. Carolyn Krebs, O.P., Pres.

Professed Sisters: 72.

Properties owned and/or sponsored: Dominican Retreat House/Convent of Our Lady of Prouille, Elkins Park, PA; St. Dominic Hall, Elkins Park, PA; Dominican Retreat, Immaculate Heart of Mary Convent, McLean, VA; Dominican Retreat House/Our Lady of Grace Convent, Niskayuna, NY; St. Catherine Hall, Elkins Park, PA.

Sisters serve and staff: Religious Education Centers and Parish Services; Hospital; Pastoral Ministry; College; Diocesan Offices; Special Services; Spiritual Direction; Counseling Center; Retreat Houses.

Represented in the Archdioceses of Cincinnati, Detroit, Philadelphia and Santa Fe and in the Dioceses of Albany, Arlington, Biloxi, Camden, Harrisburg, Orlando, Palm Beach, Providence and Raleigh.

[1070-18] —SISTERS OF ST. DOMINIC OF THE AMERICAN CONGREGATION OF THE SACRED HEART OF JESUS (D)

Dominican Motherhouse: 1 Ryerson Ave., Caldwell, NJ 07006. Tel: 973-403-3331; Fax: 973-228-9611. Sr. Arlene Antczak, O.P., Prioress; Sr. Patricia McKearney, O.P., Archivist.

Total in Community: 149.

Properties owned and/or sponsored: Caldwell College, Caldwell, NJ; Mount Saint Dominic Academy, Caldwell, NJ; St. Dominic Academy, Jersey City, NJ; Lacordaire Academy, Upper Montclair, NJ.

Legal Title: *Sisters of St. Dominic of Caldwell, NJ.*

Ministry in Education at all levels; Pastoral Ministry; Health and Human Services.

Represented in the Archdioceses of Newark and Portland in Oregon and in the Dioceses of Lansing, Metuchen, Paterson, Savannah and Trenton.

[1070-19] —DOMINICAN SISTERS OF HOUSTON, TEXAS (CONGREGATION OF THE SACRED HEART) (P)

General Motherhouse & Novitiate: *Dominican Sisters*, 6501 Almeda Rd., Houston, TX 77021. Tel: 713-747-3310; Fax: 713-747-4707. Sr. Carol Mayes, O.P., Prioress.

Total in Community: 80.

Legal Title: *Dominican Sisters of Houston, Texas, Inc. (aka Sacred Heart Convent of Houston).*

Ministry in the field of Academic Education at all levels and parish Ministry.

Properties owned and sponsored: St. Agnes Academy, St. Agnes Academy Foundation, St. Pius X High School, St. Pius X High School Foundation, Inc., The Sacred Heart Convent Retirement Trust.

Represented in the Archdioceses of Galveston-Houston, Indianapolis, Los Angeles, San Antonio and St. Louis and in the Dioceses of Austin, Beaumont, Corpus Christi, Dallas, Houma-Thibodaux, San Bernardino, San Jose and Tyler. Also in Guatemala.

[1070-20] —CONGREGATION OF ST. THOMAS AQUINAS (P)

Motherhouse: *Tacoma Dominican Center*, 935 Fawcett Ave. S., Tacoma, WA 98402-5605. Tel: 253-272-9688; Fax: 253-272-8790. Sr. Sharon Casey, O.P.

Total in Community: 55.

Legal Holdings and Titles: Sisters of St. Dominic, Tacoma Dominican Center; Sisters of St. Dominic - Tacoma Charitable Trust.

Ministry in a variety of missions.

Represented in the Archdiocese of Seattle and in the Dioceses of Fresno, San Diego and Yakima.

[1070-23] —DOMINICAN SISTERS, CONGREGATION OF ST. ROSE OF LIMA (P)

General Motherhouse: *Rosary Hill Home*, 600 Linda Ave., Hawthorne, NY 10532. Tel: 914-769-0114. Mother Mary Francis, O.P., Supr. Gen.

Total in Community: 54.

The work of these sisters is confined entirely to the incurable cancerous poor.

Represented in the Archdioceses of Atlanta, New York and Philadelphia.

[1070-25] —DOMINICAN SISTERS OF ST. CATHERINE OF SIENA (P)

General Motherhouse & Novitiate: 119 Brooks St., Taos, NM 87571. Tel: 575-751-1237; Fax: 575-751-1559. Sr. Susan Anne Snyder, O.P., Prioress.

Total in Community: 8.

Properties owned and/or sponsored: Our Lady of Fatima Villa, Saratoga, CA; Mercy Medical Center, Merced, CA.

Legal Title: *Dominican Sisters of St. Catherine of Siena, Inc.*

Represented in the Archdiocese of Santa Fe and in the Dioceses of Columbus, Fresno and San Jose.

[1070-27] —CONGREGATION OF THE IMMACULATE CONCEPTION (D)

Provincial House: *Immaculate Conception Provincial House*, 9000 W. 81st St., Justice, IL 60458. Tel: 708-458-3040. Mother M. Natalie, O.P., Vicar Prov.; Mother Helena Cempa, O.P., Prov.

Total in Community: 29.

Represented in the Archdioceses of Chicago and Milwaukee and in the Diocese of Little Rock. Also in Canada.

[1070-30] —DOMINICAN SISTERS OF OAKFORD (P)

U.S. Regional Center: *Dominican Sisters of Oakford*, 980 Woodland Ave., San Leandro, CA 94577. Tel: 510-638-2822; Fax: 510-633-9734. Sr. Anna Oven, O.P., Reg. Prioress.

Total in Community: 19.

Properties owned and/or sponsored: 3 residences in California; Formation House, San Leandro, CA; St. Catherine's Convent, Sunnyvale, CA; Our Lady of Oakford Regional Center, San Leandro, CA.

Ministries in Teaching, Spiritual Direction; Massage Therapy; Counseling; Parish Work; Adult Education; Community Outreach; Social Work and Nursing.

Represented in the Dioceses of Oakland, San Bernardino, San Jose and Tucson.

[1100] (O.P.)—DOMINICAN SISTERS OF CHARITY OF THE PRESENTATION OF THE BLESSED VIRGIN (P)

Founded in France in 1696. First foundation in the United States in 1906.

Motherhouse: 15 Quai Portillon, Tours Cedex 2, France, 37081.

Universal total in Congregation: 2527.

Provincial House: 3012 Elm St., Dighton, MA 02715. Tel: 508-669-5425; Tel: 508-669-5433; Tel: 508-669-5023; Fax: 508-669-6521. Sr. Vimala Vadakumpadan, O.P., Major Supr.

Total number in Province: 36.

Ministry in Hospitals; Homes for the Aged; Residence for Working Women and Students; Dispensaries; Education; Pastoral Ministry.

Represented in the Archdiocese of Washington and in the Dioceses of Brownsville, Fall River and Providence. Also in India, Haiti, Honduras, Korea, Peru, Bolivia, Colombia and Mexico.

[1105] (O.P.)—DOMINICAN SISTERS OF HOPE (P)

Founded July 20, 1995, as a merging of three former Congregations: Dominican Sisters of the Congregation of the Most Holy Rosary of Newburgh, NY; Dominican Sisters of the Sick Poor of Ossining, NY and Congregation of Catherine of Siena of Fall River, MA.

General Administrative Offices: *Dominican Sisters of Hope*, 299 N. Highland Ave., Ossining, NY 10562. Tel: 914-941-4420; Fax: 914-941-1125. Sr. Lorelle Elcock, O.P., Prioress.

Total in Community: 201.

Legal Titles and Holdings: Dominican Sisters of Hope Ministry Trust. Sisters of St. Dominic Charitable Trust. Ministry in Religious & Academic Education at all levels; Health, social, community and pastoral services in low income area; Parish service, counseling, retreats and spiritual direction.

Represented in the Archdioceses of Cincinnati, Denver, Hartford, Newark, New York, Oklahoma City and Philadelphia and in the Dioceses of Albany, Bridgeport, Brooklyn, Burlington, Camden, Fall River, Jackson, Manchester, Metuchen, Ogdensburg, Palm Beach, Paterson, Providence, Richmond, Rockville Centre, San Juan, Trenton, Venice and Wheeling.

[1110] (O.P.)—DOMINICAN SISTERS OF OUR LADY OF THE ROSARY AND OF SAINT CATHERINE OF SIENA, CABRA (P)

Founded in Ireland in 1644.

General Motherhouse: *Cabra*, Dublin 7, Ireland

Region of Louisiana established in 1978.

Regional House: Dominican Sisters, Cabra: 1930 Robert E. Lee, New Orleans, LA 70122. Tel: 504-288-1593. Sr. Elizabeth Ferguson, O.P., Reg. Prioress.

Total number in local community: 11.

Ministry in Academic and Religious Education; Parish Ministry; Neighborhood Social Service Agency; Diocesan Tribunal; Prison Ministry; Adult Education; Social Apostolate; Retreats; Spiritual Direction.

Represented in the Archdiocese of New Orleans and in the Dioceses of Fort Worth and Houma-Thibodaux.

[1115] (O.P.)—DOMINICAN SISTERS OF PEACE (P)

Generalate: 2320 Airport Dr., Columbus, OH 43219-2098. Tel: 614-416-1900; Fax: 614-252-7435. Sr. Margaret Ormond, O.P., Prioress.

Total in Community: 587.

Legal Title: *Dominican Sisters of Peace, Inc.*

Properties Owned and/or Sponsored: Albertus Magnus College, New Haven, CT; Cedar Park Place, Great Bend, KS; Clausen Manor, Waterford, MI; Crown Point Ecology Center, Bath, OH; Crystal Spring Center for Ecology, Spirituality & Education, Plainville, MA; Dominican Academy, New York, NY; Dominican Center, Oxford, MI; Fox Manor, Waterford, MI; Heartland Center for Spirituality, Great Bend, KS; Heartland Center for Wholistic Health, Great Bend, KS; Heartland Farm, Pawnee Rock, KS; Lourdes Nursing Home & Rehabilitation Center, Waterford, MI; Martin de Porres Center, Columbus, OH

Mendelson Assisted Living Home, Waterford, MI; Mohun Health Care Center, Columbus, OH; Ohio Dominican University, Columbus, OH; Our Lady of the Elms School, Akron, OH; Rosary Academy Learning Center, Watertown, MA; Rosaryville Spirit Life Center, Ponchatoula, LA; St. Agnes Academy-St. Dominic School, Memphis, TN; St. Catharine College, St. Catharine, KY; St. Catharine Farm, St. Catharine, KY; St. Joseph Hall, Watertown, MA; St. Mary's Retreat House, Oxford, MI; St. Mary's Dominican High School, New Orleans, LA; St. Rose Spirituality House, Waterford, MI; Sansbury Care Center, St. Catharine, KY

Shepherd's Corner, Blacklick, OH; Dominican Learning Center, Columbus, OH; Siena Learning Center, New Britain, CT; Springs Learning Center, New Haven, CT.

Ministry in Diocesan Offices; the field of Academic Education at all levels; Religious Education; Adult Education Programs; Congregational Infirmary; Art and Ecological/Environment; Hospitals; Care of the Elderly; Parish Ministry; Pastoral Care; Justice and Peace Ministry; Retreat Centers and Spiritual Programs; Foreign Missions; Counseling and Canon Law Ministry; Campus Ministry; Social Work; Health Care Ministries; Ministry to Minorities; Housing.

Represented in the Archdioceses of Baltimore, Boston, Chicago, Cincinnati, Denver, Detroit, Hartford, Kansas City in Kansas, Louisville, Milwaukee, New Orleans, New York, Oklahoma City, Omaha, Philadelphia, San Antonio, Seattle and St. Louis and in the Dioceses of Baton Rouge, Brooklyn, Brownsville, Cleveland, Columbus, Davenport, Dodge City, El Paso, Fort Worth, Green Bay, Great Falls-Billings, Grand Island, Gallup, Gary, Houma-Thibodaux, Kansas City-St. Joseph, Lafayette, Manchester, Memphis, Palm Beach, Paterson, Phoenix, Pittsburgh, Providence, Pueblo, Saginaw, Salina, Toledo, Trenton, Tucson, Wheeling-Charleston, Wichita, Worcester, Yakima and Youngstown. Also in Peru, Honduras, Kenya, Nigeria and South Vietnam.

[1120] (O.P.)—DOMINICAN SISTERS OF THE ROMAN CONGREGATION

Founded in France in 1621. First United States foundation in 1904.

General Motherhouse: Rome, Italy Sr. Carmen Lanao, Prioress Gen.

Universal total in Congregation: 413.

U.S. Provincial Office: 123 Dumont Ave., Lewiston, ME 04240-6107. Tel: 207-782-3535; Fax: 207-782-0435. Sr. Monique Belanger, O.P., Prov. Prioress.

Total in Community: 18.

Properties owned and/or sponsored: Retreat House; Residences 3.

Ministry in the field of Religious & Academic Education; Adult Education; Indian Reservation; Pastoral Ministry; Health Care; Social Work.

Represented in the Archdioceses of Chicago and New York and in the Dioceses of Gallup, Phoenix and Portland (In Maine).

[1125] (O.P.)—DOMINICAN SISTERS OF OUR LADY OF THE SPRINGS OF BRIDGEPORT (D)

Founded April 2, 2009 in Bridgeport CT.

Motherhouse: *Sacred Heart Convent*, 21 Schuyler Ave., Stamford, CT 06902-3759. Tel: 203-588-0707; Tel: 203-562-9202; Tel: 203-773-4421. Sr. Melanie Hannigan, O.P., Prioress.

Total in Congregation: 22.

Legal Title: *Dominican Sisters of Our Lady of the Springs of Bridgeport, Inc.*

[1145] (O.P.)—RELIGIOUS MISSIONARIES OF ST. DOMINIC, INC. (P)

General Motherhouse: Via di Val Cannuta 138, Rome, Italy, 00166. Tel: 39-06-66-37-521; Email: dominicas.roma@libero.it. Sr. Elvira Diez, O.P., Prioress Gen.

U.S. Delegation Office: 2237 Waldron Rd., Corpus Christi, TX 78418. Tel: 361-939-8102; Fax: 361-939-8203. Sr. Esperanza H. Seguban, O.P., Delegate of the Gen.

Total in Congregation: 667; Sisters in the U.S: 21.

Represented in the Archdiocese of Los Angeles and in the Diocese of Corpus Christi.

[1150] (E.F.M.S.)—EUCHARISTIC FRANCISCAN MISSIONARY SISTERS (D)

Founded in Mexico in 1943. Mother Maria Gemma de Jesus Aranda, Founderess.

Motherhouse: *Our Lady's Convent*, 943 S. Soto St., Los Angeles, CA 90023. Tel: 323-264-6556.

1421 Cota Ave., Torrance, CA 90501. Tel: 310-328-6725. Mother Rose Seraphim, E.F.M.S., Supr. Gen.; Sr. Miriam Joseph, E.F.M.S., Gen. Sec.

Total in Community: 26.

Legal Title: *Eucharistic Franciscan Missionary Sisters of Los Angeles.*

Sisters serve and staff: The field of Education; Missionary Activities; Catechetics; Social Work; Diocesan and Administration offices.

Represented in the Archdiocese of Los Angeles and in the Dioceses of Stockton and Tyler.

[1170] (C.S.S.F.)—FELICIAN SISTERS (P)

(Congregation of Sisters of St. Felix of Cantalice, of the III Order of St. Francis)

Founded in Poland in 1855. First foundation in the United States in Polonia, Wisconsin in 1874.

Total in North America, Our Lady of Hope Province): 770.

General Motherhouse: Via del Casaletto 540, Rome, Italy, 00151. Sr. Mary Barbara Ann Bosch, C.S.S.F., Min. Gen.

Presentation of the B.V.M. Convent (1874): 36800 Schoolcraft Rd., Livonia, MI 48150. Tel: 734-591-1730; Fax: 734-591-1710; Web: www.feliciansistersna.org. Sr. Mary Christopher Moore, C.S.S.F., Prov. Min.

Professed Sisters: 131.

Properties owned and/or sponsored: Madonna University; Ladywood High School; Montessori Center of Our Lady, Livonia, MI; St. Mary Mercy Hospital, Livonia, MI; St. Joseph Day Care; Presentation Prayer Center, Jackson, MI; Maryville Center, Holly, MI; Angela Hospice Home Care and Inpatient Facility, Marian Professional Building, Livonia, MI; Marywood Nursing Care Center; Inpatient Facility, Marian Professional Bldg.; Marybrook Manor Assisted Living.

Ministry in the field of Academic Education at all levels; Catechetical Center; CCD Programs; Archival and Secretarial Services in Seminary; Diocesan Nursing Home; Pastoral Ministry Programs; DRE Offices; Hospital; Health Care Nursing Homes; Assisted Living; Hospice Inpatient and Home Care Program; Day Care Centers; Retreat Centers; House of Prayer; Senior Clergy Residence.

Represented in the Archdiocese of Detroit and in the Dioceses of Fort Wayne-South Bend, Gaylord, Lansing and Saginaw.

Immaculate Heart of Mary Convent (1900): 600 Doat St., Buffalo, NY 14211. Tel: 716-892-4141; Fax: 716-892-4177; Web: www.feliciansistersna.org. Sr. Mary Christopher Moore, C.S.S.F., Prov. Minister; Sr. Mary Kenneth Mondrala, C.S.S.F., Community Archivist.

Professed Sisters: 166.

Properties owned and/or sponsored: Villa Maria College of Buffalo; Villa Maria Academy.

Ministry in Education on all levels; School for Mentally and Multiply Handicapped; Religious Education Programs; Outreach Centers; Parish Ministries; Social Services; Prison Ministries; Campus Ministries; Diocesan Office.

Represented in the Archdioceses of Los Angeles, Newark and New York and in the Dioceses of Buffalo, Charleston, Syracuse and Rochester. Also in Italy.

Mother of Good Counsel Convent (1910): 3800 W. Peterson Ave., Chicago, IL 60659. Tel: 773-463-3020; Web: www.feliciansistersna.org. Sr. Mary Christopher Moore, C.S.S.F., Prov. Minister.

Professed Sisters: 140.

Ministry in the field of Academic and Religious Education at all levels; Homes for Aged; Independent Living for the Elderly; Assisted Living for the Elderly; Pastoral Ministry; Social Workers; Family Therapists; Day Care Centers; Hospitals; Infirmary for Sisters.

Represented in the Archdioceses of Chicago and Milwaukee and in the Dioceses of Belleville, Green Bay, Joliet and La Crosse.

Immaculate Conception Convent (1913): 260 S Main St., Lodi, NJ 07644-2196. Tel: 973-473-7447; Fax: 973-473-7126; Web: www.feliciansisters.org. Sr. Mary Christopher Moore, C.S.S.F., Prov. Minister; Sr. Mary Virginia Tomasiak, C.S.S.F., Community Archivist; Sr. Rose Marie Smiglewski, Community Archivist; Sr. Mary Jolene Jasinski, C.S.S.F., Treas.

Professed Sisters: 121.

Properties sponsored: Immaculate Conception High School; Felician College; Felician College Day Care Center; Felician School for Exceptional Children, Lodi, NJ; Felician Retreat Center; Our Lady of Grace Home St. Ignatius Nursing Home.

Sisters serve and staff: Colleges; High Schools; Elementary Schools; Hospitals; Home for Aged; Infirmary for Sisters; Day Care Center; School for Exceptional Children; Religious Education; Parish Ministries.

Represented in the Archdioceses of Newark and Philadelphia and in the Dioceses of Metuchen, Paterson, and Wilmington.

Our Lady of the Sacred Heart Convent (1921): 1500 Woodcrest Ave., Coraopolis, PA 15108. Tel: 412-264-2890; Fax: 412-264-7047; Web: www.feliciansistersna.org. Sr. Mary Christopher Moore, C.S.S.F., Prov. Min.

Professed Sisters: 84.

Legal Holdings and Titles: Felician Sisters of Pennsylvania; Our Lady of the Sacred Heart High School.

Ministry in the field of Academic Education at all levels; Religious Education; CCD Centers; Youth and Pastoral Ministry; Home for Mentally Challenged Children & Adults; Infirmary and Home for Aged; Missionary Work.

Represented in the Dioceses of Altoona-Johnstown, Charleston, Greensburg and Pittsburgh.

Our Lady of the Angels Convent (1932): 1315 Enfield St., Enfield, CT 06082-4929. Tel: 860-745-7791; Fax: 860-741-0819; Web: www.feliciansistersna.org. Sr. Mary Christopher Moore, C.S.S.F., Prov. Min.

Professed Sisters: 67.

Ministry in the field of Religious and Academic Education; Pastoral Ministry; Social Services; Healthcare.

Properties owned and sponsored: Enfield Montessori School; Felician Adult Day Care, Enfield, CT; St. Francis Residence, Enfield, CT.

Represented in the Archdiocese of Hartford and in the Dioceses of Albany, Manchester, Portland (In Maine), Providence, Springfield in Massachusetts and Worcester.

Assumption of the B.V.M. Convent (1953): 4210 Meadowlark Ln., S.E., Rio Rancho, NM 87124-1021. Web: www.feliciansistersna.org. Sr. Mary Christopher Moore, C.S.S.F., Prov. Min.

Professed Sisters: 50.

Legal Titles and Holdings: Felician Sisters of the Southwest, Inc.; St. Felix Pantry Inc.

Sisters serve and staff: High Schools; Elementary Schools; Religious Education Centers & Classes; Health Care; Pastoral Care; Food & Clothing Pantry; Youth Ministry; Adult Education; Social Work.

Represented in the Archdioceses of Los Angeles, San Antonio and Santa Fe and in the Diocese of Laredo.

[1180] (O.S.F.)—FRANCISCAN SISTERS OF ALLEGANY, NEW YORK (P)

Founded in the United States in 1859.

General Motherhouse (1859): *St. Elizabeth Motherhouse*, 115 E. Main St., Allegany, NY 14706. Tel: 716-373-0200; Fax: 716-372-5774. Sr. Maureen Avril Chin Fatt, O.S.F., Congregational Min.

Total in Community: 289.

Legal Titles and Holdings: Franciscan Sisters of Allegany, NY, Inc.; Canticle Farm, Inc., Allegany, NY; St. Elizabeth Mission Society, Inc., Allegany, NY; Dr. Lyle F. Renodin Foundation, Inc., Allegany, NY; Franciscan of Center of Tampa, FL, Inc., Tampa, FL; The Dwelling Place of NY Inc., NY.

Ministry to Evangelization in all levels of Education; Health Care; Social Services; Pastoral; Spiritual Ministries and Social Advocacy.

Represented in the Archdioceses of Boston, Miami, Newark, New York, Philadelphia and Washington and in the Dioceses of Buffalo, Camden, Gallup, Metuchen, Palm Beach, Rochester, Rockville Centre, St. Petersburg, Spokane, Springfield in Massachusetts, Syracuse, Trenton and Venice. Also in Bolivia, Brazil and Jamaica.

Jamaica: *Immaculate Conception Convent*, 152 Constant Spring Rd., Box 1654, Kingston, Jamaica Tel: 876-925-6888. Sr. Maureen Clare Hall, O.S.F., Local Min.

Brazil Region: *Convento Mae Admiravel*, C.P. 322, 75001-970 Anapolis, Goias, Brazil Tel: 011-55-62-3333-3803. Sr. Rosimeire Dias Noleto, O.S.F., Regl. Min.

[1190] (S.A.)—FRANCISCAN SISTERS OF THE ATONEMENT (P)

Founded in the United States in 1898.

Motherhouse: *St. Francis Convent-Graymoor*, 41 Old Highland Tpke., Garrison, NY 10524. Tel: 845-424-3623; Fax: 845-424-3298. Sr. Nancy Conboy, S.A., Min. Gen.; Sr. Denise Robillard, S.A., Sec. Gen.

Total in Community: 151.

Properties owned and/or sponsored: St. Francis Convent-Complex, Garrison, NY; Mother Lurana House, Garrison, NY; Washington Retreat House, Washington, D.C.

Represented in the Archdioceses of Boston, New York and Washington and in the Dioceses of Albany, Bridgeport, Burlington, Fresno, Monterey, Norwich, Ogdensburg, Reno, Syracuse and Trenton. Also in Canada, Brazil, Italy, Japan and the Philippines.

[1210] (O.S.F.)—FRANCISCAN SISTERS OF CHICAGO (P)

Founded in Chicago, Illinois in 1894 by Mother Mary Theresa (Josephine Dudzik) Venerable Servant of God.

General Motherhouse: *Our Lady of Victory Convent*, 11400 Theresa Dr., Lemont, IL 60439-2728. Tel: 630-243-3600; Fax: 630-243-3601. Sr. Diane Marie Collins, O.S.F., Gen. Min.

Total in Community: 44.

Properties owned and/or sponsored: Addolorata Villa, Wheeling, IL; St. Anthony Campus, Inc., Crown Point, IN; St. Joseph Village of Chicago, Inc., Chicago, IL; St. Mary of the Woods, Avon, OH; Marian Village, Homer Glen, IL; Mount Alverna Village, Cleveland, OH; Mother Theresa Home, Inc.; Franciscan Village, Lemont, IL; St. Francis House of Prayer; Franciscan Sisters of Chicago Service Corp. Our Lady of Victory Convent, Lemont, IL; Franciscan Community Services, Crown Point, IN; Franciscan Senior Estates, Louisville, KY; St. James Senior Estates, Crete, IL; St. Jude House, Crown Point, IN; The Clare at Water Tower, Chicago, IL; The Village at Victory Lakes, Lindenhurst, IL; University Place, West Lafayette, IN; St. James Senior Estates II, Crete, IL.

Sisters serve and staff: CCD Programs.

Represented in the Archdioceses of Chicago and Louisville and in the Dioceses of Cleveland, Gary, Joliet and Lafayette.

[1230] (O.S.F.)—FRANCISCAN SISTERS OF CHRISTIAN CHARITY (P)

Founded in the United States in 1869.

Motherhouse: *Holy Family Convent*, 2409 S. Alverno Rd., Manitowoc, WI 54220. Tel: 920-682-7728; Fax: 920-682-4195. Sr. Louise Hembrecht, Community Dir.; Sr. Caritas Strodthoff, Community Archivist.

Total in Community: 307.

Properties owned or sponsored: Holy Family Convent, Manitowoc, WI; Holy Family Convent of Franciscan Sisters of Christian Charity, Inc., Manitowoc, WI; Holy Family Memorial, Inc., Manitowoc, WI; The Retirement Trust of the Franciscan Sisters of Christian Charity, Manitowoc, WI; St. Francis Memorial Hospital, West Point, NE; St. Paul Villa, Kaukauna, WI; St. Paul Home, Kaukauna, WI; Silver Lake College, Manitowoc, WI; Franciscan Sisters of Christian Charity Health Care Ministry, Inc., Manitowoc, WI; Holy Family Conservatory of Music, Manitowoc, WI; Chiara Convent, Manitowoc, WI; St. Clare Convent, Manitowoc, WI; St. Francis Convent, Manitowoc, WI; St. Joseph Retirement Community, West Point, NE; Good Samaritan Medical Center, Zanesville, OH.

Represented in the Archdiocese of Omaha and in the Dioceses of Columbus, Green Bay, Jackson, Honolulu, Marquette, Phoenix, Steubenville and Tucson.

[1235] (F.H.M.)—FRANCISCAN SISTERS DAUGHTERS OF MERCY (P)

Franciscanas Hijas de la Misericordia

Founded in Pina, Mallorca, Spain in 1856. First U.S. establishment in 1962.

General Motherhouse: Calle El Nectar, 18, Madrid, Spain, 28022. Sr. Roberta Pauline Aguirre, Supr. Gen.

Universal total in Congregation: 262.

U.S. Regional and House of Formation: 1207 Montopolis Dr., Austin, TX 78741. Tel: 512-385-5090; Tel: 512-389-3411. Sr. Rose Moreno, F.H.M., Reg. Delegate Email: rmfhm@yahoo.com.

Professed Sisters: 6.

Ministry in Catechetical work; Pastoral work; Kindergarten.

Represented in the Diocese of Austin.

[1240] (O.S.F.)—FRANCISCAN SISTERS, DAUGHTERS OF THE SACRED HEARTS OF JESUS AND MARY (P)

Founded in Germany in 1860. First foundation in the United States in 1872.

Generalate: *Via di S. Alessio 24*, Rome, Italy, 00153. Sr. Mary Lou Wirtz, O.S.F., Gen. Dir.

Universal total in Congregation: 670.

St. Clara's Province (1877): *Convent of Our Lady of the Angels, Motherhouse and Novitiate*, P.O. Box 667, Wheaton, IL 60187. Tel: 630-909-6600. Sr. Beatrice Hernandez, O.S.F., Prov. Dir.

Total number in Province: 63.

Legal Holdings and Titles: *Affinity Health System, Menasha, WI; *Franciscan Ministries Community Foundation, Inc., Wheaton, IL; *Marianjoy Foundation, Inc., Wheaton, IL; *Marianjoy, Inc., Wheaton, IL; *Network Health System Inc.; Menasha, WI; *Rehabilitation Medicine Clinic Inc.; Wheaton, IL; *Sartori Health Care Foundation, Inc., Cedar Falls, IA; *Wheaton Franciscan Healthcare - Circle of Life Foundation, Inc.; *Wheaton Franciscan - Elmbrook Memorial Foundation, Inc., Brookfield, WI; *Wheaton Franciscan Healthcare - Foundation for St. Francis and Franklin, Inc.; *Wheaton Franciscan Healthcare - Pharmacy Enterprises and Franciscan Woods Inc.,

Brookfield, WI; *Wheaton Franciscan Healthcare - Southeast Wisconsin, Inc., Milwaukee, WI; *Wheaton Franciscan Medical Group, Inc., Milwaukee, WI; Assisi Homes - Batavia Apartments, Inc., Batavia, IL; Assisi Homes - Colony Park, Inc., Carol Stream, IL; Assisi Homes - Constitution House, Inc., Aurora, IL; Assisi Homes - Jefferson Court, Inc., Milwaukee, WI; Assisi Homes - Kenosha, Inc., Kenosha, WI; Assisi Homes - Saxony, Inc., Kenosha, WI; Assisi Homes of Gurnee, Inc., Gurnee, IL; Assisi Homes of Illinois, Inc., Wheaton, IL; Assisi Homes of Neenah, Inc., Neenah, WI; Canticle Ministries, Inc., Wheaton, IL; Canticle Place, Inc., Wheaton, IL; Catherine Marian Housing, Inc., Racine, WI; Clara Pfaender Fund, Inc., Wheaton, IL; Clare Gardens, Inc., Denver, CO; Clare of Assisi Homes - Westminister, Inc., Westminister, CO; Covenant Foundation, Inc., Waterloo, IA; Covenant Medical Center, Inc., Waterloo, IA

Dayspring Villa, Inc., Denver, CO; Francis Heights, Inc., Denver, CO; Franciscan Health and Education Corporation, Inc., Wheaton, IL; Franciscan Ministries, Inc., Wheaton, IL; Franciscan Seniors, Kenosha, Inc., Kenosha, WI; Franciscan Sisters Charitable Fund of Colorado, Inc., Denver, CO; Marian Housing Center, Inc., Racine, WI; Marian Park, Inc., Wheaton, IL; Marianjoy Rehabilitation Center Auxillary, Wheaton, IL; Marianjoy Rehabilitation Hospital & Clinics, Inc., Wheaton, IL; Mercy Hospital of Franciscan Sisters, Inc., Oelwein, IA; Mercy Medical Center of Oshkosh, Inc., Oshkosh, WI.; O.S.F. Services, Inc., Milwaukee, WI; Ridgeway Place, Inc., Waterloo, IA; Rush Oak Park Hospital Inc., Oak Park, IL; S.E.T. Ministry, Inc., Milwaukee, WI; Sartori Memorial Hospital, Inc., Cedar Falls, IA; St. Catherine's Hospital, Inc., Kenosha, WI; St. Elizabeth Hospital Community Foundation, Inc., Appleton, WI; St. Elizabeth Hospital Inc., Appleton, WI

Starved Rock - LaSalle Manor, Inc., LaSalle, IL; Villa Maria, Inc., Westminster, CO; Villa St. Clare, Inc., Neenah, WI; Wheaton Franciscan Healthcare - All Saints Foundation Inc., Racine, WI; Wheaton Franciscan Healthcare - All Saints, Inc., Racine, WI; Wheaton Franciscan Healthcare - Elmbrook Memorial Inc., Brookfield, WI.; Wheaton Franciscan Healthcare - Iowa, Inc., Waterloo, IA; Wheaton Franciscan Healthcare - St. Francis, Inc., Milwaukee, WI; Wheaton Franciscan - St. Joseph Foundation, Inc., Milwaukee, WI; Wheaton Franciscan, Inc., Milwaukee, WI; *Wheaton Franciscan Healthcare - Terrace at St. Francis, Inc., Milwaukee, WI; Wheaton Franciscan Home Health & Hospice, Inc., Milwaukee, WI; Wheaton Franciscan Services, Inc., Wheaton, IL; Wheaton Franciscan Sisters Religious Charitable Trust, Wheaton, IL; Wheaton Franciscan Sisters Corporation, Wheaton, IL; *Assisi Homes - LaSalle Manor, Inc., Wheaton, IL; *Wheaton Franciscan Health Care - Franklin, Inc., Franklin, WI; *Metro Physicians, Inc., Glendale, WI.

Sisters serve, sponsor and staff: Hospitals; Housing Development; Parish Ministry; Spirituality Center; Corporate Offices; System Ministries Sponsorship of Catholic Hospitals; Long-term Care; Social Services; Wellness; Spiritual Direction; Foreign Mission.

Represented in the Archdioceses of Chicago, Denver, Milwaukee and St. Louis and in the Dioceses of Gary, Green Bay, Joliet and Springfield-Cape Girardeau. Also in Brazil and Italy.

[1250] (F.S.E.)—FRANCISCAN SISTERS OF THE EUCHARIST, INC.

Founded December 2, 1973.

Motherhouse: 405 Allen Ave., Meriden, CT 06451. Tel: 203-238-2243. Team Members: Mother Shaun Vergauwen, F.S.E., Mother Gen.; Mother Miriam Seiferman, Vicar Gen.; Mother Suzanne Gross, F.S.E.; Mother Mary Ann Schmitz, F.S.E.; Mother Agnese Hutchinson, F.S.E.; Mother Barbara Johnson, F.S.E.

Total in Community: 82.

Legal Title: *Franciscan Sisters of the Eucharist, Inc.*

Schools and programs operated under: Franciscan Life Center Network, Incorporated.

Represented in the Archdioceses of Galveston-Houston, Hartford and Portland in Oregon and in the Dioceses of Arlington, Boise, Duluth, and Grand Rapids. Also in Israel, Italy and Latin Patriarchate of Jerusalem.

Generalate: 215 Goodspeed Ave., Meriden, CT 06451. Tel: 203-237-0841.

[1260] (F.H.M.)—FRANCISCAN HANDMAIDS OF THE MOST PURE HEART OF MARY (D)

Founded in the United States in 1916.

General Motherhouse: 15 W. 124th St., New York, NY 10027. Tel: 212-289-5655.

Novitiate: 444 Woodvale Ave., Staten Island, NY 10309. Sr. Maria Goretti, O.P., Congregation Min.; Sr. Loretta Theresa, Dir. Formation; Sr. Jacqueline, Community Archivist.

Total in Community: 23.

Properties owned and/or sponsored: St. Benedict Day Nursery; Camp Saint Edward; Franciscan Handmaids of Mary Novitiate; Franciscan Handmaids of Mary Motherhouse.

Ministry in the field of Education, Social Work and Pastoral Care.

Represented in the Archdiocese of New York.

[1270] (F.H.I.C.)—FRANCISCAN HOSPITALLER SISTERS OF THE IMMACULATE CONCEPTION (P)

Founded in Portugal in 1871.

General Motherhouse: Linda-a-Pastora, Portugal Sr. Maria da Conceição Galvão Ribeiro, Supr. Gen.

U.S. Foundation (1960): *St. Joseph Novitiate*, 300 S. 17th St., San Jose, CA 95112-2245. Tel: 408-998-2896; Fax: 408-998-3407. Sr. Teresa Maria Costa, F.H.I.C., Supr.

Total in Community: 18.

Sisters serve and staff: Parishes; Schools; Hospitals; Social Work.

Represented in the Dioceses of Fresno, Monterey and San Jose.

[1300] (O.S.F.)—FRANCISCAN SISTERS OF THE IMMACULATE CONCEPTION AND ST. JOSEPH FOR THE DYING (D)

Founded in the United States in December, 1919 at San Carlos Parish, Monterey, California.

General Motherhouse: *Ave Maria Convent*, 1249 Josselyn Canyon Rd, Monterey, CA 93940. Tel: 831-373-1216. Sr. Mary Angela Zwolenik.

Total in Community: 1.

Legal Holding: Ave Maria Convalescent Hospital, Monterey, CA.

Represented in the Diocese of Monterey.

[1310] (O.S.F.)—FRANCISCAN SISTERS OF LITTLE FALLS, MINNESOTA (P)

Founded in the United States in 1891.

General Motherhouse: *St. Francis' Convent*, Little Falls, MN 56345. Tel: 320-632-2981. Sr. Beatrice Eichten, O.S.F., Pres.

Total in Community: 162.

Elementary Education; Home Health Care; Hospice Care; Clinics; Religious Education; Parish Ministry; Retreat Ministries; Liturgical Music; Music Center; Ministry to Refugees; Health and Recreation Center; Diocesan Offices; Social Services; Counseling; Spiritual Direction; Consulting; Ministry to the Poor; Ministry to Migrants; Craft Activities; Ministry in Ecology; Social Justice and Nonviolent Activities; Spirituality Farm; Native American Ministry; Hispanic Ministry.

Properties owned or sponsored: St. Francis Music Center; St. Francis Health & Recreation Center; Clare's Well; Sabbath House.

Represented in the Archdioceses of Chicago, Milwaukee, St. Paul-Minneapolis, and San Francisco and in the Dioceses of Brownsville, Jackson, New Ulm, Oakland, St. Cloud, Stockton and Tucson. Also in Ecuador and Mexico.

[1320] (F.M.S.A.)—FRANCISCAN MISSIONARY SISTERS FOR AFRICA (P)

Generalate: *Franciscan Missionary Sisters for Africa*, 34a Gilford Rd., Sandymount, Dublin 4, Ireland Tel: 011-353-1-2838376; Fax: 011-353-1-2602049.

American Headquarters: 172 Foster St., P.O. Box 35095, Brighton, MA 02135. Tel: 617-254-4343; Fax: 617-787-8007. Sr. Nelezinha Carvalho, F.M.S.A.

Total in Community: 7.

Represented in the Archdiocese of Boston.

[1330] (S.F.M.A.)—FRANCISCAN MISSIONARY SISTERS OF ASSISI (P)

General Motherhouse: Via San Francesco, 13, Assisi, Italy, 06081. Sr. Juliana Malama, Mother Gen.

U.S. Vice Province (1961): *St. Francis Convent/Vice Provincial House and Formation House*, 1039 Northampton St., Holyoke, MA 01040. Tel: 413-532-8156; Fax: 413-534-7741. Sr. Theresa Mwelwa, S.F.M.A., Vice Prov. Supr.

Total in Community: 15.

Represented in the Archdiocese of New York and in the Diocese of Springfield in Massachusetts.

[1350] (O.S.F.)—FRANCISCAN SISTERS OF THE IMMACULATE CONCEPTION (P)

Founded in Mexico in 1874. First foundation in the United States in 1926.

Provincial House: 13367 Borden Ave., Unit A, Sylmar, CA 91342-2804. Tel: 818-364-6122; Tel: 818-364-5557; Tel: 818-364-5558; Email: provstclare@verizon.net. Sr. Leticia Rodriguez, O.S.F., Prov. Supr.; Sr. Mary Gabriel De Leon, O.S.F., Community Archivist.

Total in Community: 103.

Legal Holdings and Titles: Franciscan Missionary Sisters of the Immaculate Conception, Inc.; Poverello of Assisi Retreat House, San Fernando, CA; St. Francis Home, Santa Ana, CA; Mother Gertrude Balcazar Home, San Fernando, CA; Provincialate, Sylmar, CA; St. Clare Convent, Sylmar, CA.

Ministry in the field of Education and Religious Education to Children and Adults; Health Care in Hospitals and Home Visitation to the Sick.

Represented in the Archdiocese of Los Angeles and in the Dioceses of Gallup and Orange in California. Also in Mexico.

Novitiate: 11306 Laurel Canyon Blvd., San Fernando, CA 91340.

Novitiate: 8619 Louise Ave., Northridge, CA 91324-3417. Tel: 818-709-7523.

[1360] (M.F.I.C.)—MISSIONARY FRANCISCAN SISTERS OF THE IMMACULATE CONCEPTION (P)

Founded in the United States in 1873 in Belle Prairie, Minnesota.

General Motherhouse: Rome, Italy Sr. Jeanette Gaudet, M.F.I.C., Gen. Min.

Provincialate: *Immaculate Conception Province*, 790 Centre St., Newton, MA 02458-2530. Tel: 617-527-1004; Fax: 617-527-2528. Sr. Donna Driscoll, M.F.I.C., Prov.

Total number in Province: 132.

Represented in the Archdioceses of Boston, Newark and New York and in the Dioceses of Bridgeport, Brooklyn, Providence, Savannah, Syracuse and Venice. Also in Peru and Bolivia.

[1365] (F.M.I.J.)—FRANCISCAN MISSIONARY SISTERS OF THE INFANT JESUS (P)

Founded in Aquila, Italy in 1879 by Sr. Maria Giuseppa Micarelli. First foundation in the United States in 1961.

Generalate: Piazza Nicoloso da Recco 13, Rome, Italy, 00154. Tel: 6-575-8358. Mother Teresa Ferrante, F.M.I.J., Supr. Gen.

U.S. Province and Novitiate: 1215 Kresson Rd., Cherry Hill, NJ 08003. Tel: 856-428-8834; Fax: 856-428-5599; Email: fmijusdel@yahoo.com. Sr. Angela Pia Camillotti, F.M.I.J., Delegate Supr.

Professed Sisters: 16.

Ministries of Evangelization; Education; Health Care; Social-Pastoral Services.

Represented in the Dioceses of Camden and Trenton.

[1370] (F.M.M.)—THE FRANCISCAN MISSIONARIES OF MARY (P)

Founded in India in 1877. First foundation in the United States in 1903.

General Motherhouse: 12 via Giusti, Rome, Italy Sr. Suzanne Phillips, F.M.M., Supr. Gen.

Franciscan Missionaries of Mary-U.S. Province (1920): 3305 Wallace Ave., Bronx, NY 10467-6599. Tel: 718-547-4693; Fax: 718-325-5102; Email: palfmm@aol.com; Web: www.fmmusa.org. Sr. Lois Ann Pereira, F.M.M., Prov.

Total in Province: 115.

Ministry in Educational Projects among Minority Group of Immigrants; Child Care Agencies; Cardiac and General Hospital; General Pediatric Hospital with Rehabilitation Specialty; Chaplaincy; Retreat Work; Day Care for Elderly; Catechetics; Mission Animation & Formation; Home Visiting & Community Development.

Represented in the Archdioceses of Boston, Chicago and New York and in the Dioceses of El Paso, Las Cruces, Providence, Rockville Centre and Savannah.

[1380] (O.S.F.)—FRANCISCAN MISSIONARIES OF OUR LADY (P)

Founded in Calais, France in 1854. First U.S. foundation in Monroe, LA, 1911.

Generalate: Paris, France

Provincial and Novitiate House: *Maryville Convent*, 4200 Essen Ln., Baton Rouge, LA 70809. Tel: 225-926-1627; Fax: 225-925-5268. Sr. Kathleen Cain, O.S.F., Supr.

Total in Community: 19.

Properties owned and sponsored: Our Lady of the Lake Regional Medical Center, Baton Rouge, LA; Ollie Steele Burden Manor, Inc., Baton Rouge, LA; Our Lady of Lourdes Regional Medical Center, Lafayette, LA; St. Francis Medical Center, Monroe, LA; FMOL Health System, Inc., Baton Rouge, LA; Haiti Mission, Inc., Baton Rouge, LA; St. Elizabeth Hospital, Gonzales, LA., Franciscan Health & Wellness.

Represented in the Dioceses of Baton Rouge, Lafayette (LA) and Shreveport.

[1390] (O.S.F.)—FRANCISCAN MISSIONARY SISTERS OF OUR LADY OF SORROWS (D)

Founded in Hunan China in 1939. First United States foundation in 1950.

Community Headquarters: *Our Lady of Peace Retreat House*, 3600 S.W. 170th Ave., Beaverton, OR 97006. Tel: 503-649-7127; Fax: 503-259-9507. Sr. Anne Marie Warren, O.S.F., Supr. Gen.

Total in Community: 42.

Legal Titles and Holdings: Our Lady of Peace Retreat, Beaverton, OR; St. Clare Retreat House, Soquel, CA.

Ministry in religious and academic education; retreat houses, group homes and foreign missions.

Represented in the Archdiocese of Portland in Oregon and in the Diocese of Monterey.

[1400] (F.M.S.C.)—FRANCISCAN MISSIONARY SISTERS OF THE SACRED HEART (P)

Founded in Italy in 1861. First foundation in the U.S. in New York City (1865).

General Motherhouse: Rome, Italy Sr. Paola Dotto, F.M.S.C., Supr. Gen.

St. Francis Province (1869): *Mt. St. Francis*, 250 South St., Peekskill, NY 10566. Tel: 914-737-5409; Fax: 914-736-9614. Sr. Anne Matthew Carlone, F.M.S.C., Prov.

Universal total in Congregation: 680; Total in United States Province: 40.

Legal Title: *Missionary Sisters of the Third Order of St. Francis.*

Ministry in Religious and Academic Education; Health Care for Retired Sisters; Pastoral Ministry; Prison Apostolate; Hospital Ministry.

Represented in the Archdioceses of Newark and New York and in Diocese of Brooklyn.

[1410] (F.M.S.J.)—MILL HILL SISTERS (P)

Franciscan Missionaries of St. Joseph

Founded in 1883. First United States foundation in 1952.

Generalate: *St. Joseph's Convent*, 150 Greenleach Ln., Worsley, Manchester, England, M28 2TS. Sr. Maureen Murphy, F.M.S.J., Community Leader.

American Headquarters: *Franciscan House*, 703 Derzee Ct., Delmar, NY 12054. Tel: 518-512-4362. Sr. Judith Dever, F.M.S.J., Admin.

Total in Community: 2.

Legal Title: *Mill Hill Sisters - New York Charitable Trust.*

Represented in the Dioceses of Albany and Syracuse.

[1415] (F.S.M.)—FRANCISCAN SISTERS OF MARY (P)

Founded in the United States in 1872.

Administrative Offices & Novitiate: *Franciscan Sisters of Mary*, 3221 McKelvey Rd., Ste. 107, Bridgeton, MO 63044-2551. Tel: 314-768-1824; Fax: 314-768-1880. Rose Mary Dowling, F.S.M., Pres.

Total in Community: 100.

Ministry in Hospitals; Skilled Nursing Facilities; Rehabilitation Unit; Woman's Center; Social Services; Pastoral Services; Wholistic Health Services; Consultation Services; Spiritual Direction.

Represented in the Archdioceses of Chicago, Cincinnati, Milwaukee and St. Louis and in the Dioceses of Brownsville, Corpus Christi, Jefferson City, Madison and Springfield-Cape Girardeau.

[1425] (F.S.P.)—FRANCISCAN SISTERS OF PEACE (D)

Sisters of St. Francis of Peace: *Congregation Center*, 20 Ridge St., Haverstraw, NY 10927-1115. Tel: 845-942-2527; Fax: 845-429-8141. Sr. Jeanne Gilligan, F.S.P., Congregation Min.

Total in Community: 59.

Legal Titles and Holdings: Cortlandt Manor, New York, NY; Congregation Center, Haverstraw, NY.

Ministry in Youth; Ministry in Administration & Administrative Services; Education; Catechetical; Social Work; Evangelization; Social Services; Chaplaincies.

Represented in the Archdioceses of Newark, New York and San Francisco and in the Dioceses of Paterson and Tucson.

[1430] (O.S.F.)—FRANCISCAN SISTERS OF OUR LADY OF PERPETUAL HELP (P)

Founded in the United States in 1901.

Motherhouse and Novitiate: *Franciscan Sisters of Our Lady of Perpetual Help*, 335 S. Kirkwood Rd., St. Louis, MO 63122. Tel: 314-965-3700; Fax: 314-965-3710. Sr. Pauline Schwandt, O.S.F., Supr. Gen.

Total in Community: 97.

Legal Holdings and Titles: Tau Center, Kirkwood, MO; Perpetual Help Retirement Corporation, St. Louis, MO.

Ministry in Education: Faith Formation; Parish Ministries: Retreat and Program Directors; Hospital Ministry.

Represented in the Archdioceses of Chicago, Cincinnati, Omaha, Santa Fe and St. Louis, and in the Dioceses of Austin, Belleville, El Paso, Lafayette (IN), Las Cruces, St. Petersburg, Pueblo, Rockford, Rockville Centre, Shreveport and Springfield (IL).

[1440] (S.F.P.)—FRANCISCAN SISTERS OF THE POOR (P)

Founded in Aachen, Germany in 1845. First foundation in the United States in 1858.

Congregational Office: 133 Remsen St., Brooklyn, NY 11201. Tel: 718-643-1919; Fax: 718-643-9710. Sr. Tiziana Merletti, S.F.P., Congregational Min.

Total in Community: 135.

U.S. Area: 60 Compton Rd., Cincinnati, OH 45215. Tel: 513-761-9040; Fax: 513-761-6703. Sr. Joanne Schuster, S.F.P., U.S. Area Councilor.

Congregation sponsors: Franciscan Sisters of the Poor Foundation, Inc., New York, NY; Franciscan at St. Leonard, Centerville, OH; St. Anthony Medical Center, Inc., Columbus, OH.

Represented in the Archdiocese of Cincinnati and in the Diocese of Brooklyn. Also in Italy, Senegal, Brazil and the Philippines.

[1450] (O.S.F.)—FRANCISCAN SISTERS OF THE SACRED HEART (P)

Congregation of the Franciscan Sisters of the Sacred Heart. Founded in Germany 1866. Established in the United States in 1876.

Motherhouse, Novitiate, Postulancy & Portiuncula Center for Prayer: *St. Francis Woods*, 9201 W. St. Francis Rd., Frankfort, IL 60423-8335. Tel: 815-469-4895; Fax: 815-464-3809. Sr. Judith Plumb, O.S.F., Gen. Supr.

Total in Community: 88.

Legal Title: *An Association of Franciscan Sisters of the Sacred Heart; Legal Titles for Health Care entities; Provena Health; St. Anne's Maternity Home; Franciscan Foundation.*

Sisters sponsor: St. Joseph Medical Center, Joliet, IL; St. Joseph Hospital, Elgin, IL; Villa Franciscan, Joliet, IL; Sacred Heart Home, Avilla, IN; LaVerna Terrace, Avilla, IN; St. Anne's Maternity Home, Los Angeles, CA; United Samaritans Medical Center, Logan Campus-Danville, IL; United Samaritans Medical Center, Sager Campus-Danville, IL; Franciscan Foundation, Frankfort, IL.

Sisters serve and staff: Elementary Schools; High School; Religious Education Centers; Neighborhood Health Care Centers; Foreign Mission Centers; Direct Domestic Work at Retreat Houses; Canon Lawyer; Diocesan Offices; Retreat Centers; Clinics, Home Health Agencies, Health Care Systems, Hospitals, Nursing and Retirement Homes; Home for Unwed Mothers; Apartments-Well Elderly; Parish & Youth Ministry; Liturgical Ministry; Social Work; Congregate Care Facility.

Represented in the Archdioceses of Chicago and Los Angeles and in the Dioceses of Fort Wayne-South Bend, Joliet, Peoria, Rockford and Wheeling-Charleston. Also in Brazil.

[1460] (F.S.S.E.)—FRANCISCAN SISTERS OF ST. ELIZABETH (P)

(Suore Franciscane Elisabettine)

First founded in Naples, Italy, 1865. Founded in United States in Newark, New Jersey in 1919.

General Motherhouse: Via Marsico Nuovo 35, Rome, Italy Mother Clara Capaso, Supr. Gen.

Delegate House: 499 Park Rd., Parsippany, NJ 07054. Tel: 973-539-3797. Mother Gina Maria Amico, Delegate Gen.

Total number in the U.S: 56; Total in Community: 300.

Ministry in Day Nurseries; Mission Houses; Elementary Schools and Montessori Schools.

Sister Serve Christ in the person of the poor in Schools & Day Nursery Schools; Catechetical Instruction; Hospitals; Homes for the Poor, Aged and Disabled.

Represented in the Archdiocese of Newark and in the Dioceses of Paterson and St. Petersburg, FL. Also in India, Indonesia, Italy, Panama, Philippines and Africa.

[1470] (F.S.S.J.)—FRANCISCAN SISTERS OF ST. JOSEPH (P)

Founded in the United States in 1897.

General Motherhouse: *Immaculate Conception Convent*, 5229 S. Park Ave., Hamburg, NY 14075. Tel: 716-649-1205; Fax: 716-649-5958. Sr. Ann Marie Hudzina, F.S.S.J., Gen. Min.

Total in Community: 89.

Properties owned and/or sponsored: Immaculata Academy, Hamburg, NY; Marycrest Manor, Livonia, MI.

Ministry in Education; Health Care; Parish Ministries; Social Services.

Represented in the Archdioceses of Baltimore, Detroit and Milwaukee and in the Dioceses of Allentown, Arlington, Buffalo, Springfield in Massachusetts and Trenton.

[1485] (O.S.F.)—FRANCISCAN SISTERS OF ST. PAUL, MN (P)

Franciscan Sisters of the Blessed Virgin Mary of the Holy Angels (Beatae Mariae Virginis Angelorum)

Founded in Germany in 1863. First foundation in the United States in St. Paul in 1923.

General Motherhouse (1863): *St. Marienhaus*, Waldbreitbach, bei Neuwied, Rhine, Germany Sr. Basina Kloos, O.S.F., Supr. Gen.

Universal total in Congregation: 333.

U.S. Foundation: *Franciscan Regional Center*, 1388 Prior Ave. S., Saint Paul, MN 55116. Tel: 651-690-1501; Fax: 651-690-2509. Sr. Mary Lucy Scheffler, O.S.F.

Total in Community: 8.

Represented in the Archdiocese of St. Paul-Minneapolis.

[1500] (F.M.I.)—FRANCISCAN SISTERS OF MARY IMMACULATE OF THE THIRD ORDER OF ST. FRANCIS OF ASSISI (P)

Founded in Switzerland in the 16th Century. First founded in the United States on Aug. 15, 1932 at Amarillo, Texas.

General House: Carrera 81 C No. 24B-20, Barrio Modelia, Bogota, Colombia Sr. Hermana Noemi Quesada, F.M.I., Supr. Gen.

Universal total in Congregation: 578.

St. Francis Convent and Novitiate (1964): *St. Francis Convent (1932)*, 4301 N.E. 18th Ave., Amarillo, TX 79107-7220. Tel: 806-383-5769; Fax: 806-383-6545. Sr. Conchita Carrillo, F.M.I., Local Supr.

Total in Community: 13.

Represented in the Archdiocese of Los Angeles and in the Diocese of Amarillo. Also in Central America.

[1505] (O.S.F.)—ST. FRANCIS MISSION COMMUNITY (P)

Established 1981 in the United States of America in Amarillo, Texas, as an autonomous province of the Franciscan Sisters of Mary Immaculate.

General Motherhouse: *Our Lady of the Angels Convent*, 8202 CR 7700, Wolfforth, TX 79382. Tel: 806-863-4904. Sr. Charlotte Lujan, O.S.F., Prov. Min.

Professed Sisters: 18.

Ministry in the field of Religious and Academic Education at all levels; Parish Work; Pastoral Care in Hospitals.

Properties owned: La Verna Convent, Amarillo, TX; St. Francis Convent, Lubbock, TX; 43 acres of real estate.

Represented in the Archdiocese of Los Angeles and in the Dioceses of Amarillo and Lubbock. Also in Juarez, Mexico.

[1510] (O.S.F.)—SISTERS OF ST. FRANCIS (D)

Sisters of St. Francis of the Mission of the Immaculate Virgin

Canonical union in 2004 with Sisters of the Third Franciscan Order (Syracuse, NY) and Sisters of St. Francis of the Third Order Regular (Williamsville, NY). Now known as Sisters of St. Francis of the Neumann Communities.

[1520] (S.S.F.C.R.-O.S.F.)—SCHOOL SISTERS OF ST. FRANCIS OF CHRIST THE KING (D)

Founded in Maribor, Slovenia in 1869 by Sr. Margareta Pucher. First house in the United States at Kansas City, Kansas, in 1909. U.S. Province established in 1922.

Generalate: Grottaferrata, Italy Sr. M. Klara Simunovic, Supr. Gen.

Universal total in Congregation: 1053.

North American Provincial House: 13900 Main St., Lemont, IL 60439. Tel: 630-257-7495. Sr. Therese Ann Quigney, S.S.F.C.R., Prov. Supr.

Total in Community: 42.

Ministry in Education, Care for Seniors, Parish Ministry; Retreat Ministry.

Properties owned and sponsored: Mount Assisi Convent, Lemont, IL; Mount Assisi Academy, Lemont, IL; Alvernia Manor, Lemont, IL; Our Lady of Angels House of Prayer, Lemont, IL.

Represented in the Archdiocese of Chicago and in the Diocese of Joliet.

[1530] (O.S.F.)—SISTERS OF ST. FRANCIS OF THE CONGREGATION OF OUR LADY OF LOURDES, SYLVANIA, OHIO (P)

Founded in the United States in 1916 at Sylvania, Ohio. Foundation from Rochester, Minnesota.

General Motherhouse: *Convent*, 6832 Convent Blvd., Sylvania, OH 43560-2897. Tel: 419-882-2016; Fax: 419-885-8643; Email: cboratyn@sistersosf.org; Web: www.sistersosf.org. Sr. Diana Lynn Eckel, O.S.F., Congregational Min.

Total number in the Congregation: 180.

Ministry in the field of Religious and Academic Education at all levels; Healthcare; Communications; Media Producing; Counseling; Parish Ministries; Retreat Center; Social Services.

Properties owned and sponsored: Lourdes University, Sylvania, OH; Sylvania Franciscan Health, Sylvania, OH; Franciscan Academy at Lourdes University, Sylvania, OH.

Sponsored Ministries: Franciscan Living Communities, Sylvania, OH, including: St. Leonard, Centerville, OH, St. Leonard Foundation, Providence Care Centers, Sandusky, OH, Providence Care Center, The Commons of Providence, Providence Residential Community Corporation, (Franciscan Properties), Sylvania, OH, Rosary Care Center, Sylvania, OH, Madonna Manor, Villa Hills, KY and Franciscan Care Center, Sylvania, Toledo, OH; Bethany House, Toledo, OH; Sophia Center, Sylvania, OH; St. Joseph Health System, Bryan, TX, including St. Joseph Regional Health Center, Bryan, TX, Grimes St. Joseph Health Center, Navasota, TX, Burleson St. Joseph Health Center, Caldwell, TX, Madison St. Joseph Health Center, Madisonville, TX, St. Joseph Manor, Bryan, TX, Burleson St. Joseph Manor, Caldwell, TX, St. Joseph Foundation, Bryan, TX and Alliance Health Providers of Brazos Valley; and Trinity Health System, Steubenville, OH, including Trinity Medical Center-East, Steubenville, OH, Trinity Medical Center-West, Steubenville, OH; Trinity Health System Foundation, Steubenville, OH; Trinity Hospital Twin City, Dennison, OH.

Represented in the Archdioceses of Cincinnati, Detroit, New Orleans and St. Paul-Minneapolis and in the Dioceses of Austin, Biloxi, Cleveland, Columbus, Fort Wayne-South Bend, Gallup, Lansing, Raleigh, Richmond, St. Cloud, Steubenville, Toledo, Tyler, and Wheeling-Charleston.

[1540] (O.S.F.)—SISTERS OF SAINT FRANCIS, CLINTON, IOWA (P)

Founded in the United States in 1866.

General Motherhouse: *Administrative Center,* 843-13th Ave. N., Clinton, IA 52732-5115. Tel: 563-242-7611; Fax: 563-243-0007. Sr. Janice Cebula, O.S.F., Pres.

Ministry in the field of Academic Education at all levels; Health Care in Centers and Homes for the Aged; Pastoral Ministry; Religious Education and Spiritual Direction; Ministry to the Poor; Disabled; Social Justice & Peace.

Properties and Legal Holdings: The Alverno Health Care Facility; Mount St. Clare Speech and Hearing Center; Sisters of St. Francis, Clinton, IA; Charitable Trust, Clinton, IA; The Canticle, Clinton, IA; Mount Saint Clare Education Foundation.

Represented in the Archdioceses of Chicago, Dubuque and St. Louis and in the Dioceses of Belleville, Davenport, Lafayette (IN), Lexington, Portland, Phoenix, Rockford, San Bernardino, San Diego and Sioux City. Also in Peru.

[1550] (O.S.F.)—SISTERS OF ST. FRANCIS OF THE HOLY CROSS (P)

Founded in Wisconsin in 1881.

Motherhouse and Novitiate: *St. Francis Convent,* 3110 Nicolet Dr., Green Bay, WI 54311-7212. Tel: 920-468-1828; Fax: 920-468-1207. Sr. Donna Koch, O.S.F., Pres.

Total in Community: 66.

Legal Title: *Sisters of St. Francis of the Holy Cross, Inc.*

Ministries in the following areas: Education; Pastoral Ministry and Religious Education; Ministry to the Elderly; Health Care; Hospital Chaplaincy; Retreat Work.

Represented in the Diocese of Green Bay.

[1560] (O.S.F.)—SISTERS OF ST. FRANCIS OF THE HOLY EUCHARIST (D)

Founded in Grimmenstein, Switzerland in 1378. First foundation in the United States in 1892.

Motherhouse, Novitiate and Prayer Center: *St. Francis Convent,* 2100 N. Noland Rd., Independence, MO 64050. Tel: 816-252-1673; Fax: 816-252-5574. Sr. M. Lucy Lang, O.S.F., Sister Servant; Sr. M. Connie Boulch, O.S.F., Vicar.

Total in Community: 16.

Legal Titles: Franciscan Prayer Center, Independence, MO; Sisters of St. Francis of the Holy Eucharist Foundation, Independence, MO.

Ministry in the following areas: Education at all levels; Retreat; Evangelization; Pastoral.

Represented in the Diocese of Kansas City-St. Joseph.

[1570] (O.S.F.)—SISTERS OF ST. FRANCIS OF THE HOLY FAMILY (P)

Founded in Germany in 1864. First foundation in the United States in 1875.

Motherhouse and Novitiate: *Mount St. Francis,* 3390 Windsor Ave., Dubuque, IA 52001-1311. Tel: 563-583-9786; Fax: 563-583-3250. Sr. Nancy Schreck, Pres.; Sr. Veronica Bagenstos, Community Archivist.

Total in Community: 289.

Ministry in the following areas: Academic and Religious Education at all levels; Spirituality and Parish Ministry; Health-Pastoral Care; Diocesan Offices; Social Service-Social Justice and Peace; Food Service-Dietary; Communication Centers; Clerical Work-Business; Administration; Campus Ministry; Music Studios; International Missions.

Properties owned and sponsored: Shalom Retreat Center, Dubuque, IA; Sisters of St. Francis of the Holy Family Charitable Trust, Dubuque, IA.

Represented in the Archdioceses of Chicago, Detroit, Dubuque, Miami, St. Louis, St. Paul-Minneapolis and San Antonio and in the Dioceses of Charleston, Davenport, Des Moines, Fort Wayne-South Bend, Jackson, Joliet, Madison, Manchester, New Ulm, Phoenix, Reno, St. Petersburg, St. Lucia, Santa Rosa, Sioux City, Superior, Toronto, Tulsa, Tyler and Winona. Also in Central America.

[1580] (O.S.F.)—SISTERS OF ST. FRANCIS OF THE IMMACULATE CONCEPTION (D)

Founded in the United States in 1891.

Motherhouse: *Immaculate Conception Convent,* 2408 W. Heading Ave., West Peoria, IL 61604-5096. Tel: 309-674-6168. Sr. Paula Vasquez, Pres.; Sr. Mary Louise Hynd, Archivist.

Total in Community: 37.

Properties owned: Immaculate Conception Convent, Peoria, IL; St. Joseph's Home of Springfield in Illinois.

Represented in the Dioceses of Peoria and Springfield in Illinois.

[1590] (O.S.F.)—SISTERS OF ST. FRANCIS OF THE IMMACULATE HEART OF MARY (HANKINSON, NORTH DAKOTA) (P)

Founded in 1241 in Bavaria. First founded in the United States in 1913 at Collegeville, Minnesota.

General Motherhouse: Dillingen, Germany Sr. Roswitha Heinrich, Supr. Gen.

Province of Hankinson (1928): *Sisters of St. Francis Motherhouse,* Hankinson, ND 58041-0447. Tel: 701-242-7195. Sr. Donna Welder, O.S.F., Prov. Supr.

Professed Sisters: 30.

Legal Holdings or Titles: St. Gerard's Community Nursing Home, Hankinson, ND; St. Anne's Guest Home, Grand Forks, ND.

Ministry in the field of Religious and Academic Education; Health Care in Hospitals; Homes for the Aged.

Represented in the Diocese of Fargo.

[1600] (F.S.G.M.)—SISTERS OF ST. FRANCIS OF THE MARTYR ST. GEORGE (P)

Founded in Thuine, Germany. First United States foundation in 1923.

General Motherhouse: Thuine, Germany Mother Margaretha Maria Brand, F.S.G.M., Supr. Gen.

Provincial Motherhouse: *St. Francis Convent and Novitiate,* 1 Franciscan Way, P.O. Box 9020, Alton, IL 62002-9020. Tel: 618-463-2750; Tel: 618-463-2755. Mother M. Regina Pacis Coury, F.S.G.M., Prov.

Worldwide Total: 1265; Total in American Province: 160.

Properties owned and sponsored: Saint Anthony's Hospital, Alton, IL; St. Francis Day Care Center, Alton, IL; Mother of Good Counsel Home, St. Louis, MO; Saint Clare Hospital, Alton, IL.

Sisters serve and staff: Hospitals; Skilled Nursing Facility; Foreign Missions; Day Care Center; Retirement Homes for the Aged; Grade & High Schools; Retirement Homes for Priests; Archdiocesan Offices.

Represented in the Archdioceses of Kansas City in Kansas, St. Louis and Washington and in the Dioceses of La Crosse, Lincoln, Metuchen, Peoria, Springfield in Illinois, Steubenville and Tulsa. Also in Brazil, Italy and Cuba.

[1630] (O.S.F.)—SISTERS OF ST. FRANCIS OF PENANCE AND CHRISTIAN CHARITY (P)

(aka Sisters of St. Francis of the Holy Name Province)

Founded in Holland in 1835. First foundation in the United States in 1874.

General Motherhouse: Rome, Italy Sr. Deborah Lockwood, O.S.F., Gen. Min.

Universal total in Congregation: 1657.

Holy Name Province (1928): *Sisters of St. Francis,* 4421 Lower River Rd., Stella Niagara, NY 14144. Tel: 716-754-4312; Fax: 716-754-7657. Sr. Edith Wyss, O.S.F., Prov. Minister.

Total in Community: 142.

Legal Holdings: Stella Niagara Education Park, Stella Niagara, NY; Buffalo Academy of the Sacred Heart, Buffalo, NY; Francis Center, Niagara Falls, NY; Sisters of St. Francis of Holy Name Province, Inc., Stella Niagara, NY; Center of Renewal, Stella Niagara, NY.

Ministry in the field of Academic Education at all levels; Foreign Mission Work; Health and Hospital Care; Social Work; Pastoral Ministry.

Represented in the Archdioceses of Cincinnati, Louisville, Miami and Santa Fe and in the Dioceses of Buffalo, Columbus, Palm Beach, Paterson, St. Petersburg, Trenton, and Wheeling-Charleston. Also in Canada.

Sacred Heart Province (1939): 5314 N. Columbine Rd, Denver, CO 80221. Tel: 303-458-6270; Fax: 303-477-4105. Sr. Rita Cammack, O.S.F., Prov. Min.

Total in Community: 46.

Legal Title: Sisters of St. Francis, Denver, Colorado

Legal Holdings or Titles: Casa Chiara, Franciscan Initiatives and Marycrest Campus, Denver, CO; St. Francis Home, (foster care for Native American Children), Manderson, SD; St. Francis Convent and Marian Residence for aged, infirm sisters, Alliance, NE.

Ministry in the following areas: Prayer; Spirituality; Health, human, pastoral Services; Education; Advocacy for peace, justice, social concerns; General, administrative support services.

St. Francis Province (1939): 1330 Brewster Ave., P.O. Box 1028, Redwood City, CA 94062-1312. Tel: 650-369-1725; Fax: 650-369-0845. Sr. Patricia Rayburn, O.S.F., Prov. Min.

Total in Community: 72.

Legal Title: *Sisters of St. Francis of Penance and Christian Charity, OSF.*

Ministry in the following areas: Diocesan Offices; Parish Ministry; Pastoral Ministry; Services Agencies; Hospitals; CCD Centers; ESL; Advocacy.

Represented in the Archdioceses of Los Angeles, San Francisco and Seattle and in the Dioceses of Las Vegas, Oakland, Sacramento and San Jose.

[1640] (O.S.F.)—SISTERS OF ST. FRANCIS OF PERPETUAL ADORATION (P)

Founded in Germany in 1863. First foundation in the United States in 1875.

Generalate: Olpe, Westfalen, Germany Sr. Magdalena Krol, Supr. Gen.

Universal total in Congregation: 460.

Province of the Immaculate Heart of Mary (1875): *Provincial House and Novitiate, St. Francis Convent,* P.O. Box 766, Mishawaka, IN 46546-0766. Tel: 574-259-5427. Sr. M. Angela Mellady, O.S.F., Prov.

Total in Community: 121.

Ministry in the field of Academic Education at all levels; Health Care in Hospitals; Ecclesial Ministry at parish and diocesan level.

Properties owned: Sisters of St. Francis of Perpetual Adoration, Inc.; St. Francis Convent, Mishawaka, IN; University of Saint Francis, Inc., Fort Wayne, IN; Franciscan Alliance Corporate Office, Mishawaka, IN, owns the following: Alverno Clinical Laboratories, Inc., Hammond, IN; Franciscan St. Anthony Health - Crown Point, IN; Franciscan St. Anthony Health - Michigan City; Franciscan St. Elizabeth Health - Crawfordsville; Franciscan St. Elizabeth Health - Lafayette East; Franciscan St. Elizabeth Health - Lafayette Central; Franciscan St. Francis Health - Beech Grove; Franciscan St. Francis Health - Indianapolis; Franciscan St. Francis Health - Mooresville; Franciscan St. James Health - Chicago Heights; Franciscan St. James Health - Olympia Fields; Franciscan St. Margaret Health - Hammond; Franciscan St. Margaret Health - Dyer; Franciscan Alliance Information Services, Beech Grove, IN.

Represented in the Archdioceses of Chicago and Indianapolis and in the Dioceses of Fort Wayne-South Bend, Gary and Lafayette in Indiana.

Province of St. Joseph (March 19, 1932): *Provincial House and Formation House-Mt. St. Francis,* 7665 Assisi Heights, Colorado Springs, CO 80919. Tel: 719-598-5486. Sr. Nadine Heimann, O.S.F., Prov.

Professed Sisters: 58.

Ministry in Education; Hospitals; Homes for the Aged; Parish/Pastoral Ministry; Peace & Justice; Social Ministries; Retreat Centers.

Represented in the Archdioceses of Denver, Los Angeles, Omaha and Santa Fe and in the Dioceses of Colorado Springs, Grand Island, Lincoln, Pueblo and Wichita.

[1650] (O.S.F.)—THE SISTERS OF ST. FRANCIS OF PHILADELPHIA (P)

Founded in the United States in 1855.

Congregational Motherhouse: *Our Lady of Angels Convent,* 609 S. Convent Rd., Aston, PA 19014. Tel: 610-459-4125. Sr. Esther Anderson, O.S.F., Congregational Min.; Sr. Marijane Hresko, O.S.F., Asst. Congregational Min.; Sr. Donna Desien, O.S.F., Congregational Sec.; Sr. Helen Jacobson, O.S.F., Archivist.

Total in Community: 538.

Ministry in Health Care; Eldercare; Academic and Religious Education at all Levels; Specialized Education; Parish Ministry; Social Services; Family Centers; Renewal Centers; Diocesan Offices; Retreat Ministry; National Organizations.

Properties owned: Sisters of St. Francis, Sea Isle City, NJ; Sisters of St. Francis, Aston, PA; Bay House, Tacoma, WA; Marion House, Tacoma, WA; St. Ann Convent, Tacoma, WA; Neumann University, Aston, PA; Assisi House, Aston, PA; Portiuncula Convent, Aston, PA; St. Mary Convent, Langhorne, PA; Franciscan Residence, Langhorne, PA; The Catholic High School of Baltimore, Baltimore, MD; St. Joseph Counseling Center, Spokane, WA; Anna Bachmann House, Aston, PA; Sisters of St. Francis, Aston, PA; Sisters of St. Francis, Aston, PA; Sisters of St. Francis, Wilmington, DE; Sisters of St. Francis of Philadelphia, Canticle House, Philadelphia, PA; Sisters of St. Francis of Philadelphia, TAU Convent, Aston, PA; St. Clare Renewal Center, Aston, PA; Sisters of St. Francis of Philadelphia, Our Lady of the Valley, Aston, PA; Mt. Alvernia Convent, Aston, PA; St. Clare Convent, Trenton, NJ; Sisters of St. Francis of Philadelphia, Mt. St. Francis Convent, Ringwood, NJ; Franciscan Spiritual Center, Ringwood, NJ; Chaplain's Residence, Ringwood, NJ; Caretaker's Residence, Ringwood, NJ; Our Lady of Angels Convent, Ringwood, NJ; St. Clare Convent, Ringwood, NJ; St. Joseph Residence, Ringwood, NJ.

Represented in the Archdioceses of Baltimore, Boston, Hartford, Los Angeles, Mobile, Newark, Philadelphia, Portland in Oregon, San Francisco, Seattle, and Washington and in the Dioceses of Allentown, Arlington, Baker, Birmingham, Camden, Charlotte, Charleston, Cheyenne, Fairbanks, Fresno, Harrisburg, Honolulu, Lexington, Manchester, Oakland, Orlando, Paterson, Pensacola-Tallahassee, Providence, Raleigh, St. Louis, San Bernardino, San Diego, Spokane, Trenton, Venice, Wilmington and Worcester. Also in Ireland, Kenya and Uganda.

[1660] (O.S.F.)—SISTERS OF SAINT FRANCIS OF THE PROVIDENCE OF GOD (P)

Founded in Pittsburgh in 1922.

Generalate: 140 Hamilton Rd., Pittsburgh, PA 15234-2364. Sr. Janet Gardner, O.S.F., Gen. Min.

Motherhouse: *St. Francis Convent,* 3603 McRoberts Rd., Pittsburgh, PA 15234-2398. Tel: 412-882-9911; Fax: 412-885-7210. Sr. J. Lora Dambroski, O.S.F., U.S.A. Prov. Min.

Total Professed: 85.

Ministry in the field of Education; Health Care; Social Service; Pastoral, Parish & Retreat Ministries; Retreat Directors; Prison Chaplains; Foreign Mission work in Brazil & Lithuania.

Properties owned and sponsored: Sisters of St. Francis of the Providence of God; Sisters of St. Francis, Mt. Vernon IL, Inc.; Sisters of St. Francis of the Providence of God Ministries Corporation; St. Francis Academy; Franciscan Child Day Care Center; Franciscan Spirit and Life Center.

Represented in the Archdiocese of Newark and in the Dioceses of Albany, Buffalo, Paterson and Pittsburgh.

[1670] (O.S.F.)—SISTERS OF ST. FRANCIS OF SAVANNAH, MO (P)

Founded in Austria in 1850. Founded in the United States, August 22, 1922.

Provincial House and Novitiate: 908 Franciscan Way, Box 488, Savannah, MO 64485-0488. Tel: 816-324-3179; Fax: 816-324-7264; Web: www.sistersofstfrancis.org. Sr. Christine Martin, O.S.F., Prov. Supr.

Total in Community: 8.

Legal Holdings and Titles: Sisters of St. Francis of Savannah, Inc.; Maintenance and Custodial Care Trust of the Franciscan Sisters of Savannah.

Ministry in rural life issues; Peace and Justice; Pastoral Care; Religious Education; Food Pantry.

Represented in the Diocese of Kansas City-St. Joseph.

[1680] (O.S.F.)—SCHOOL SISTERS OF ST. FRANCIS (P)

Founded in the United States in 1874.

General Motherhouse: 1501 S. Layton Blvd., Milwaukee, WI 53215. Tel: 414-384-4105; Fax: 414-944-6060. Sr. Kathleen Kluthe, O.S.F., Pres.; Sr. Francitta Pazhukkathara, O.S.F., Vice Pres.; Sr. Elsa Paul Chiriyankandath, O.S.F., Vice Pres.; Sr. Rita Eble, O.S.F, Vice Pres.; Sr. Catherine M. Ryan, O.S.F., Treas.; Sr. Charlita Foxhoven, O.S.F., Asst. Treas.; Sr. Corrine Dais, O.S.F., Archivist.

Total in Congregation: 956; Total in U.S: 564.

Properties owned and/or sponsored: St. Joseph Convent, Milwaukee, WI; School Sisters of St. Francis, Inc.

U.S. Province: 1515 S. Layton Blvd., Milwaukee, WI 53215. Tel: 414-384-1515. Provincial Team: Sr. Carol Rigali, O.S.F.; Sr. Deborah Fumagalli, O.S.F.; Sr. Marilyn Ketteler, O.S.F.

Properties owned and sponsored: Alverno College, Milwaukee, WI; Clement Manor, Inc., Greenfield, WI; Maryhill Manor, Niagara, WI; New Cassel, Omaha, NE; Clare Towers I, Milwaukee, WI; Telos, Inc., Milwaukee, WI; St. Clare Management, Inc., Milwaukee, WI; Sacred Heart Center, Milwaukee, WI; St. Joseph Convent, Campbellsport, WI; School Sisters of St. Francis of St. Joseph's Convent, Milwaukee, Wisconsin, Inc.

Sisters serve and staff: Universities, Colleges, Seminaries, High Schools, Grade Schools, Preschools, Adult and Special Education; National and Diocesan Offices; Hospitals and Nursing Homes; School & Parish Musicians; Retreat and Spiritual Direction; Social Ministries; Campus Ministry; Psychotherapy; Home Health Care Service; Religious Education and CCD; Pastoral Ministry; Pastoral Associate; Health Pastoral Care; Retirement Homes.

Represented in the Archdioceses of Chicago, Denver, Dubuque, Milwaukee, New York, Oklahoma City, Omaha and St. Paul-Minneapolis and in the Dioceses of Charlotte, Davenport, Des Moines, El Paso, Grand Island, Green Bay, Jackson, Jefferson City, Joliet, La Crosse, Lexington, Lincoln, Madison, Nashville, Orange, Phoenix, Rockford, San Bernardino, Sioux City, St. Petersburg, Superior, Wheeling-Charleston and Winona.

[1690] (O.S.F.)—SCHOOL SISTERS OF THE THIRD ORDER REGULAR OF ST. FRANCIS UNITED STATES PROVINCE (PITTSBURGH, PA) (P)

Founded in Austria in 1843. First foundation in the U.S. in 1913.

Generalate: Via Nicolo Piccolomini 27, 00165, Rome, Italy Sr. M. Kveta Vinklarkova, O.S.F., Gen. Min.

Motherhouse and Novitiate: *Mount Assisi Convent*, 934 Forest Ave., Bellevue, Pittsburgh, PA 15202. Tel: 412-761-6004; Fax: 412-761-0290. Sr. Bernadine Marie Stemnock, O.S.F., Prov. Min. Tel: 412-761-2855.

Total in Community: 91.

Legal Titles: School Sisters of the Third Order Regular of St. Francis; School Sisters of the Third Order of St. Francis, of Texas.

Ministry in the following areas: the field of academic education at all levels; CCD Centers; Pastoral Ministry; Pastoral Associate; Residence Home for the Elderly; Mission Work; Hospital Ministry; Campus Ministry; Social Ministry.

Represented in the Archdioceses of Newark, Philadelphia and San Antonio and in the Dioceses of Allentown, Erie, Greensburg, Manchester, Metuchen, Pittsburgh, San Angelo, Springfield in Massachusetts and Trenton. Also in South Africa and Rome, Italy.

[1695] (O.S.F.)—SCHOOL SISTERS OF THE THIRD ORDER OF ST. FRANCIS (PANHANDLE, TEXAS) (P)

Founded in Austria, 1723; The Vienna Foundation in 1845. First founded in the United States, 1931.

General Motherhouse: Vienna, Austria

American Center and Novitiate: 119 Franciscan Way, P.O. Box 906, Panhandle, TX 79068. Tel: 806-537-3182. Sr. Jean Maria Lara, O.S.F., Reg. Supr.

Total number in U.S: 24.

Ministry in the following areas: Elementary and High Schools; Faith Formation; Nursing Home; Youth Groups.

Represented in the Diocese of Amarillo.

[1700] (O.S.F.)—SCHOOL SISTERS OF THE THIRD ORDER REGULAR OF ST. FRANCIS (BETHLEHEM, PA) (P)

Founded in Austria, 1843. First founded in the United States, 1913.

General Motherhouse: Via Nicolo Piccolomini 27, Rome, Italy, 00165. Sr. Mary Xavier Bomberger, O.S.F., Gen. Min.

Bethlehem Novitiate: 395 Bridle Path Rd., Bethlehem, PA 18017-3105. Tel: 610-866-2597; Tel: 610-867-8890; Fax: 610-861-7478. Sr. Elaine Hromulak, O.S.F., Prov. Min. Tel: 412-761-2855.

Sisters: 46.

Properties owned and/or sponsored: St. Francis Center for Renewal, Bethlehem, PA.

[1705] (O.S.F.)—THE SISTERS OF ST. FRANCIS OF ASSISI (P)

(Sisters of Penance and Charity)

Founded in the United States in 1849.

General Motherhouse: *St. Francis Convent*, 3221 S. Lake Dr., St. Francis, WI 53235-3799. Tel: 414-744-1160; Fax: 414-744-7193; Web: www.lakeosfs.org. Sr. Florence Deacon, O.S.F., Dir.

Total in Community: 237.

Legal Titles: The Sisters of St. Francis of Assisi, Inc.; The Ongoing Community Support Trust of the Sisters of St. Francis, Inc.; Declaration of Trust of the Franciscan Sisters of Baltimore, Inc.; Sisters of St. Francis of Assisi of New Mexico.

Goals of the Congregation are to bring the healing, teaching, reconciling and liberating power of Jesus into the human situations in which we live and minister; to be in solidarity with the poor through the work of justice and peace; to appreciate and affirm and to encourage the development of each community member and each community apostolate for the sake of full effectiveness in the ministry of the Church; and to work effectively toward implementing co-responsibility, subsidiary and accountability at all levels within the Congregation.

Corporate Ministries: Franciscan Youth Center, Inc., Baltimore, MD; St. Elizabeth School, Inc., Baltimore, MD; Franciscan Center, Inc., Baltimore, MD; St. Ann Center for Intergenerational Care, Inc., Milwaukee, WI; St. Mary's Academy, Inc. (AKA Marian Center for Nonprofits), Milwaukee, WI; Cardinal Stritch University, Inc., Milwaukee, WI; St. Coletta's of Wisconsin, Inc., Jefferson, WI; St. Coletta Wisconsin Charitable Foundation, Inc., Jefferson Charitable Trust, Jefferson, WI; St. Coletta's of Illinois, Palos Park, IL; St. Coletta's of Illinois Foundation, Inc., Palos Park, IL; Cardinal Cushing Centers, Inc., Hanover, MA; Cushing Residence, Inc., Hanover, MA; Cardinal Cushing School Foundation of Hanover Charitable Trust, Hanover, MA; Cardinal Cushing Centers, Inc. Braintree Campus and Braintree St. Coletta, Braintree, MA. Services to the Elderly: Alverno Housing Corporation, Jefferson, WI; Canticle Court, Inc.; Juniper Court, Inc., St. Francis, WI; Canticle and Juniper Courts Foundation, Inc., St. Francis, WI.

Represented in the Archdioceses of Baltimore, Boston, Denver, Dubuque, Milwaukee, San Antonio and Santa Fe and in the Dioceses of Austin, Brownsville, Cheyenne, Des Moines, Gary, Joliet, Kansas City-St. Joseph, La Crosse, Madison, Phoenix, San Diego, Sioux Falls, Superior, Tucson and Tulsa. Also in Mexico and Taiwan.

[1710] (O.S.F.)—CONGREGATION OF THE THIRD ORDER OF ST. FRANCIS OF MARY IMMACULATE, JOLIET, IL (P)

Founded in the United States, Joliet, Illinois, in 1865.

Central Administration Offices: 1433 Essington Rd., Joliet, IL 60432-2873. Tel: 815-725-8735. Sr. Mary Rose Lieb, O.S.F., Pres.; Sr. Marian Voelker, O.S.F., Community Archivist.

Total in Community: 192.

Legal Titles: Congregation of the Third Order of St. Francis of Mary Immaculate, Joliet, IL; Retirement Plan Trust of the Congregation of the Third Order of St. Francis of Mary Immaculate, Joliet, IL.

Sponsored Institutions: Franciscan Learning Center, Joliet Catholic Academy, Our Lady of Angels Retirement Home, University of St. Francis.

Ministry in the following areas: School and Adult Education; Retirement Home; House of Prayer. Also engaged in Religious Education; Social Services; Spiritual Direction; Nursing and Health Services; Hospital and Parish Ministry; Prison Ministry; Hispanic Ministry; Senior Housing.

Represented in the Archdioceses of Boston, Chicago, Cincinnati, Denver, Miami, Milwaukee, Mobile and New York and in the Dioceses of Cleveland, Colorado Springs, Columbus, Fort Wayne-South Bend, Jackson, Joliet, Lansing, Palm Beach, Peoria, Phoenix, St. Cloud, St. Petersburg, Springfield (IL), Stockton, Superior, Toledo, Tucson and Youngstown. Also in Brazil.

[1720] (O.S.F.)—SISTERS OF THE THIRD ORDER REGULAR OF ST. FRANCIS OF THE CONGREGATION OF OUR LADY OF LOURDES (P)

Founded in the United States in 1877.

Administration Center: *Assisi Heights*, 1001 14th St., N.W., Ste 100, Rochester, MN 55901. Tel: 507-282-7441; Fax: 507-282-7762. Sr. Tierney Trueman, O.S.F., Pres./Community Min. Tel: 507-280-2198; Sr. Mary Lonan Reilly, Community Archivist.

Total in Community: 256.

Ministry in the following areas: Education Services; Pastoral Concerns Development; Religious Life Development; Spiritual Life Development; Community Life Development; Social Concerns Development; Business Services; Health Care Services; Support Services.

Properties owned and sponsored: Holy Spirit Retreat Center, Janesville, MN; Assisi Heights, Rochester, MN.

Represented in the Archdioceses of Chicago, Denver, Indianapolis, Milwaukee, St. Paul-Minneapolis, Santa Fe and Washington and in the Dioceses of Columbus, Great Falls-Billings, New Ulm, Oakland, Owensboro, Pueblo, Rockford, St. Cloud, San Bernardino, San Diego, Sioux Falls, Sioux City, Springfield-Cape Girardeau, Superior and Winona. Also in Colombia.

[1730] (O.S.F.)—CONGREGATION OF THE SISTERS OF THE THIRD ORDER OF ST. FRANCIS, OLDENBURG, IN (P)

Founded in U.S., Oldenburg, Indiana in 1851.

General Motherhouse and Novitiate: *Convent of the Immaculate Conception*, Oldenburg, IN 47036. Tel: 812-934-2475. Sr. Barbara Piller, O.S.F., Congregational Min.

Total in Community: 234.

Properties owned and/or sponsored: Marian College, Indianapolis, IN; Oldenburg Academy, Oldenburg, IN.

Sisters serve & staff: Liberal Arts College, Academy, High Schools, Elementary Schools; Navajo, Crow Indian and Cheyenne Missions; Religious Education Centers; Hospital & Parish Ministry; Apostolate of Aging; Diocesan Offices; Retreat & Counseling Ministry; Hispanic Ministry; Justice & Peace Offices; Clerical Staff; Social Services.

Represented in the Archdioceses of Cincinnati, Detroit, Indianapolis, Los Angeles and St. Louis and in the Dioceses of Buffalo, Charleston, Cheyenne, Columbus, Evansville, Gallup, Great Falls-Billings, Lexington, Peoria, Springfield (IL), and Wheeling-Charleston.

[1760] (O.S.F.)—SISTERS OF THE THIRD ORDER OF ST. FRANCIS OF PENANCE AND OF CHARITY (P)

Founded in Tiffin, Ohio in 1869.

General Motherhouse: *St. Francis Convent*, St. Francis Ave., Tiffin, OH 44883. Tel: 419-447-0435; Fax: 419-447-1612. Sr. Jacquelyn Doepker, O.S.F., Community Min.; Robert G. Hauzie, Pres., CEO & Admin. St. Francis Senior Ministries, Inc.; Dr. Dominic Fabrizio, Chm. Bd. Trustees St. Francis Senior Ministries, Inc.; John Haughawout, Chm. St. Francis Senior Ministries Memorial Foundation Board, Inc.

Total in Community: 101.

Legal Title: *Sisters of St. Francis of Tiffin, OH.*

Ministry in the following areas: Ministry to the Aged; Parish Ministry; Retreat and Renewal Centers; Diocese Offices; Health Care; Health-Pastoral Care; Administration; Childcare; Social Justice Outreach.

Properties owned or sponsored: St. Francis Home, Inc., Tiffin, OH; St. Francis Villas, Inc.; St. Francis Senior Ministries Day Care, Inc.; St. Francis Senior Ministries Memorial Foundation Board, Inc.; Friedman Village at St. Francis.

Represented in the Dioceses of Columbus, Lafayette, Lansing, Lexington, Owensboro, Toledo, Wheeling-Charleston and Youngstown. Also in Mexico.

[1770] (O.S.F.)—THE SISTERS OF THE THIRD ORDER OF ST. FRANCIS (EAST PEORIA, ILLINOIS) (P)

Founded in the United States in 1877.

Motherhouse: 1175 St. Francis Ln., East Peoria, IL 61611-1299. Tel: 309-699-7215. Sr. Judith Ann Duvall, O.S.F., Major Supr.

Total in Community: 31.

Properties owned and sponsored: Saint Francis Medical Center, Peoria, IL; St. Joseph Medical Center, Bloomington, IL; St. Mary Medical Center, Galesburg, IL; St. James-John W. Albrecht Medical Center, Pontiac, IL; Saint Anthony Medical Center, Rockford, IL; St. Francis Hospital, Escanaba, MI; OSF Healthcare System, Peoria, IL; OSF Healthcare Foundation, Peoria, IL; Motherhouse, East Peoria, IL; Saint Clare Home, Peoria Heights, IL; Holy Family Medical Center, Monmouth, IL.

Represented in the Dioceses of Marquette, Peoria and Rockford.

[1780] (F.S.P.A.)—CONGREGATION OF THE SISTERS OF THIRD ORDER OF ST. FRANCIS OF PERPETUAL ADORATION (P)

(Franciscan Sisters of Perpetual Adoration)

Founded in the United States in 1849.

Generalate - Motherhouse and Novitiate: *St. Rose Convent*, 912 Market St., La Crosse, WI 54601-4782. Tel: 608-782-5610; Fax: 608-782-6301. Sr. Linda Mershon, F.S.P.A., Pres.; Sr. Mary Ann Gschwind, F.S.P.A., Archivist.

Total in Congregation: 284.

Properties owned and sponsored: St. Anthony Regional Hospital, Inc., Carroll, IA; Viterbo University, Inc., La Crosse, WI; Villa St. Joseph, La Crosse, WI; Franciscan Skemp Healthcare, La Crosse, WI; Clare

Center, Spokane, WA; Franciscan Spirituality Center, La Crosse, WI; Prairiewoods - Franciscan Spirituality Center, Hiawatha, IA; Marywood - Franciscan Spirituality Center, Arbor Vitae, WI; WomanWell, St. Paul, MN.

Represented in the Archdioceses of Agana (GU), Chicago, Denver, Dubuque, Los Angeles, Milwaukee, Portland in Oregon, Santa Fe, Seattle and St. Paul-Minneapolis and in the Dioceses of Colorado Springs, Davenport, El Paso, Green Bay, Jackson, La Crosse, Las Vegas, Madison, Omaha, Peoria, Phoenix, Savannah, Sioux City, Spokane, Superior, Tucson and Winona. Also in Canada, Cameroon, Mexico and Zimbabwe.

[1805] O.S.F.—SISTERS OF ST. FRANCIS OF THE NEUMANN COMMUNITIES (P)

Congregation Offices: 2500 Grant Blvd., Ste. 3, Syracuse, NY 13208. Tel: 315-634-7000; Fax: 315-634-7023; Email: sisters@sosf.org; Web: www.sosf.org.

Total in Community: 489.

Ministry in academic education at all levels; hospitals; religious education & pastoral ministry; retreat houses; rehabilitation center; home for the dying; adult & child day care; diocesan offices; social services; day nurseries; parishes

Sponsored ministries: Nazareth Day Nursery, New York, NY; Hastings Health Systems, Inc., Poughkeepsie, NY; Gingerbread House Day Care & Preschool, Syracuse, NY; St. Joseph's Hospital Health Center, Syracuse, NY; St. Elizabeth Medical Center, Utica, NY; St. Francis Social Adult Day Care Center, Syracuse, NY; Francis House, Syracuse, NY; St. Francis Healthcare System, Honolulu, HI; St. Francis School, Honolulu, HI; Mercy Health & Rehabilitation Center, Auburn, NY; Portiuncula Foundation, Millvale, PA; Mt. Alvernia Day Care & Learning Center, Millvale, PA.

Properties owned: Sisters of St. Francis Centers in Hastings-on-Hudson, Syracuse, Williamsville, Honolulu, HI, Millvale, PA; Stella Maris Retreat Center, Skaneateles, NY, Alverna Heights Spirituality & Nature Center, Fayetteville, NY; Alverna Heights Spirituality-Nature Center, Fayetteville, NY.

Represented in the Archdioceses of Boston, Los Angeles, Newark, New York, Philadelphia and Washington and in the Dioceses of Albany, Altoona-Johnstown, Buffalo, Camden, Charleston, Gallup, Greensburg, Harrisburg, Honolulu, Lubbock, Orange, Orlando, Pittsburgh, Richmond, Rochester, San Diego, Santa Fe, Scranton, St. Petersburg, Syracuse and Trenton. Also in Africa & Peru

[1810] (O.S.F.)—BERNARDINE FRANCISCAN SISTERS (P)

Founded in the United States in 1894.

Congregational Leadership Offices: 450 St. Bernardine St., Reading, PA 19607-1737. Tel: 484-334-6976; Fax: 484-334-6977. Sr. Marilisa Helena da Silva, O.S.F., Congregational Min.

Total in Community: 351.

Total number in the United States: 245.

Ministry in the field of academic education at all levels - preschool to college; religious education of children & adults; hospitals, health & home care; retreat work; social work.

Represented in the Archdioceses of Detroit, Kansas City in Kansas, Los Angeles, Philadelphia, San Antonio, San Juan and Washington and in the Dioceses of Allentown, Bridgeport, Fall River, Metuchen, Richmond, Saginaw, Scranton, Trenton and Worcester. Also in Brazil, Dominican Republic, Liberia and Mozambique.

[1820] (O.S.F.)—HOSPITAL SISTERS OF THE THIRD ORDER REGULAR OF ST. FRANCIS (P)

Founded in Germany in 1844. First foundation in the United States in 1875.

General Motherhouse: *Muenster*, Westphalia, Germany Sr. Sherrey Murphy, O.S.F., Gen. Supr.

American Province (1875): *St. Francis Convent, Motherhouse and Novitiate*, Box 19431, Springfield, IL 62794. Tel: 217-522-3386. Sr. Jomary Trstensky, O.S.F., Prov. Supr.; Sr. Janice Schneider, O.S.F., Prov. Sec. & Contact Person.

Total in Community: 105.

Legal Title: *Hospital Sisters of St. Francis-USA, Inc.*

Properties owned or sponsored: Residence 12; St. Francis Convent, Motherhouse, Novitiate, Springfield, IL; Hospital Sisters Services, Inc., Springfield, IL; Hospital Sisters of St. Francis Foundation, Springfield, IL; Hospital Sisters Health System, Springfield, IL; St. John's Hospital, Springfield, IL; St. John's College of Nursing, Springfield, IL; St. Mary's Hospital, Decatur, IL; St. Anthony Memorial Hospital, Effingham, IL; St. Joseph's Hospital, Highland, IL; St. Francis Hospital, Litchfield, IL; St. Elizabeth's Hospital, Belleville, IL; St. Joseph's Hospital, Breese, IL; St. Mary's Hospital Medical Center, Green Bay, WI; St. Vincent Hospital, Green Bay, WI; Sacred Heart Hospital, Eau Claire, WI; St. Francis Apartments, Eau Claire, WI; St. Nicholas Hospital, Sheboygan, WI; St. Mary's Hospital, Streator, IL; Hospital Sisters Tanzania, Springfield, IL; Hospital Sisters Health Care West, Inc., Chippewa Falls, WI; St. Joseph's Hospital, Chippewa Falls, WI; L.E. Phillips Treatment Center for the Chemically Dependent, Chippewa Falls, WI; Hospital Sisters Mission Outreach, Springfield, IL; Chiara Center, Springfield, IL.

Sisters serve and staff: Hospitals; Home Health Services; Catechetical; Care of Chemically Dependent; Social Ministries; Pastoral Ministries; Overseas Missions.

Represented in the Archdioceses of Chicago and Milwaukee and in the Dioceses of Belleville, Green Bay, La Crosse, Peoria and Springfield in Illinois. Also in Tanzania, Germany and Haiti.

[1830] (R.G.S. - C.G.S.)—THE SISTERS OF THE GOOD SHEPHERD (P)

Congregation of Our Lady of Charity of the Good Shepherd

Founded in France in 1835. First foundation in the United States in Louisville, KY, 1842.

Generalate for the Provinces: *Suore del Buon Pastore*, via Raffaello Sardiello 20, Rome, Italy, 00165. Sr. Brigid Lawlor, Supr. Gen.

Province of Mid-North America (2000): *Province Center*, 7654 Natural Bridge Blvd., St. Louis, MO 63121. Tel: 314-381-3400; Fax: 314-381-7102. Sr. Mary Catherine Massei, R.G.S., Prov.

Professed Apostolic Sisters: 140; Contemplative Sisters: 37.

Legal Title: *Sisters of the Good Shepherd Province of Mid-North America; Pelletier Trust, a Charitable Trust of the Sisters of the Good Shepherd; Sisters of the Good Shepherd Province of Mid-North America Foundation.*

Properties owned and staffed: Good Shepherd Pelletier, Fort Thomas, KY; Sisters of the Good Shepherd of Detroit aka Vista Maria, Dearborn Heights, MI; Good Shepherd Corporation, Scranton, PA aka Lourdesmont Good Shepherd Youth & Family Services, Clarks Summit, PA; CORA Services, Inc., Philadelphia, PA; Good Shepherd Corporation d.b.a. Good Shepherd Neighborhood House, Mediation Program, Philadelphia, PA; House of the Good Shepherd, Baltimore, MD; Good Shepherd Services, Atlanta, GA; Good Shepherd Shelter, Los Angeles, CA; Gracenter, San Francisco, CA; Droste Residence, St. Louis, MO; House of the Good Shepherd of Memphis dba DeNeuville Learning Center, Memphis, TN; House of the Good Shepherd, Chicago, IL; Immaculate Heart Convent, St. Louis, MO; Good Shepherd Provincialate, St. Louis, MO; Home of the Good Shepherd Inc., St. Paul, MN.

Represented in the Archdioceses of Atlanta, Baltimore, Chicago, Detroit, Los Angeles, Louisville, Omaha, Portland in Oregon, Philadelphia, St. Louis, St. Paul-Minneapolis, San Francisco and Washington and in the Dioceses of Columbus, Covington, Gallup, Memphis, Orlando, Scranton and Springfield in Illinois.

Province of New York (1857): *Sisters of the Good Shepherd*, 25-30 21st. Ave., Astoria, NY 11105. Tel: 718-278-1155; Fax: 718-278-1158. Sr. Ellen Kelly, Prov.

Professed Apostolic Sisters: 51; Professed Contemplative Sisters: 26.

Legal Title: *Sisters of the Good Shepherd, Province of New York.*

Legal Holdings or Titles: Sisters of the Good Shepherd, New York, NY; Sisters of the Good Shepherd, Albany, NY; Sisters of the Good Shepherd, Huntington, NY; House of the Good Shepherd in the City of Hartford, Hartford, CT; Good Shepherd Volunteers, Astoria, NY; Madonna Hall, Marlboro, MA; Handcrafting Justice, Inc., Astoria, NY; Maria Droste Services (Madonna Hall); Sisters of the Good Shepherd, Marlboro, MA; Collier Youth Services; Sisters of the Good Shepherd of New Jersey; St. Germaine's Services.

Ministry in Counseling Centers; Social Service Agencies; Special Education Schools; Neighborhood Family Services; Adolescent Residential Programs; Human Services Workshops; Pastoral Ministry; Hospital Chaplaincy.

Programs sponsored: Good Shepherd Services, New York, NY; Maria Droste Services, New York, NY; Handcrafting Justice, Inc.; Collier Youth Services, Wickatunk, NJ; Good Shepherd Volunteers; Maria Drost Services, Quincy, MA.

Represented in the Archdioceses of Boston, Hartford and New York and in the Dioceses of Albany, Brooklyn, Fall River, Rockville Centre and Trenton.

[1840] (G.N.S.H.)—GREY NUNS OF THE SACRED HEART (P)

Generalate, Congregational Offices, Motherhouse: 1750 Quarry Rd., Yardley, PA 19067-3998. Tel: 215-968-4236; Fax: 215-968-6656. Sr. Julia C. Lanigan, G.N.S.H., Pres.; Ms. Eileen Dickerson, Dir. Congregational Advancement Office.

Total in Community: 121.

Properties owned and/or sponsored: Holy Angels Academy, Buffalo, NY; Motherhouse Complex, Yardley, PA.

Sisters staff: College, Secondary and Elementary Education; Hospitals; Nursing Homes; Pastoral Care; Personal Care Home; CCD-Parish Services; Campus Ministry; Prison Ministry; Homeless Housing.

Represented in the Archdioceses of Baltimore, New York and Philadelphia and in the Dioceses of Brooklyn, Buffalo, Charlotte, Ogdensburg, Rochester, Rockville Centre and Trenton. Also in Port-Au-Prince, Haiti.

[1845] (M.G.SP.S.)—GUADALUPAN MISSIONARIES OF THE HOLY SPIRIT (P)

(Misioneras Guadalupanas del Espiritu Santo)

Founded in Morelia, Michoacan, Mexico in 1930 by Rev. Felix de Jesus Rougier, M.Sp.S.

General Motherhouse: Hidalgo #7, Tlalpan 14000, Mexico, D.F., Mexico Mother Juventina Garcia, Supr. Gen.

U.S. Novitiate: 5467 W. 8th St., Los Angeles, CA 90036-3811. Tel: 323-936-0135.

Total Sisters in U.S: 46.

Legal Title: *Missionary Guadalupanas of the Holy Spirit, Inc.*

Ministry in Religious Education; Pastoral and Parish Ministries.

Represented in the Archdioceses of Los Angeles and Miami and in the Dioceses of Birmingham, Houma-Thibodaux, Jackson, Palm Beach, Stockton and Wichita.

[1850] (S.A.C.)—SISTERS OF THE GUARDIAN ANGEL (P)

Founded in Quillan, France in 1839.

General Motherhouse: A vda, del Valle, 42, Madrid 3, Spain Sr. Sagrario Escudero, S.A.C., Supr. Gen.

U.S. Foundation: 1245 S. Van Ness, Los Angeles, CA 90019. Tel: 213-732-7881.

Represented in the Archdiocese of Los Angeles.

[1855] (H.H.C.J.)—CONGREGATION OF THE HANDMAIDS OF THE HOLY CHILD JESUS (P)

Founded in Calabar, Nigeria in 1931 by Sister Mary Charles Magdalen Walker. Obtained Pontifical Status in 1971; first foundation in United States in 1992.

Generalate and Motherhouse: *Handmaids of the Holy Child Jesus - The Generalate, Ifuho*, P.O. Box 155, Ikot Ekpene, Nigeria Tel: 082-775-199. Sr. Leonie-Martha Okaraga, H.H.C.J., Supr. Gen.

North American Mission: *Ancilla Convent*, 3614 Englewood Dr., Pearland, TX 77584. Tel: 281-692-0098; Fax: 281-692-0049; Web: www.hhcjsisters.org. Sr. Caroline Onyeoziri, H.H.C.J., U.S. Supr.; Sr. Felicia Agibi, H.H.C.J., Devel. Dir.

Universal number of Professed Sisters: 805; Professed Sisters in the U.S. and Canada: 60.

Ministry in the field of Education at all levels; Pastoral Work; Health Care services; Women Empowerment; AIDS Education; Special Education; Youth Ministry; Clothing/Counseling Thrift Store.

Represented in the Archdioceses of Galveston-Houston, Mobile and Washington and in the Dioceses of Sacramento and St. Petersburg.

[1860] (H.P.B.)—HANDMAIDS OF THE PRECIOUS BLOOD (P)

Founded in Jemez Springs, New Mexico in 1947.

Motherhouse and Novitiate: *Cor Jesu Monastery*, P.O. Box 90, Jemez Springs, NM 87025. Tel: 575-829-3906. Rev. Mother Marietta, H.P.B., Mother Prioress.

Professed Sisters: 19.

Ministry as Contemplative, Life of Eucharistic Adoration (Perpetual) for the sanctification of priests and for the entire world.

Represented in the Archdioceses of Chicago and Santa Fe.

[1870] (A.C.J.)—THE HANDMAIDS OF THE SACRED HEART OF JESUS (P)

Founded in Spain in 1877. First foundation in the United States in 1926.

General Motherhouse: Via Parre, 16, 00188, Rome, Italy Sr. Inmaculada Fukasawa, Supr. Gen.

Universal total in Congregation: 1159.

Provincial Motherhouse: 616 Coppertown Rd., Haverford, PA 19041-1135. Tel: 610-642-5715; Fax: 610-642-6788; Web: www.acjusa.org. Sr. Dorothy Beck, A.C.J., Prov.

Total in Community: 37.

Properties owned: St. Raphaela Center, Haverford, PA; Ancillae Assumpta Academy, Wyncote, PA; Handmaids of Sacred Heart of Jesus, Philadelphia, PA; facilities in Georgia and Florida.

Sisters serve and staff: Elementary School; Retreat Center; Mission Center; Parish Ministry; CCD; Hispanic Pastoral Ministry; Vietnamese & Cambodian Pastoral Ministry; Mission work.

Represented in the Archdioceses of Atlanta, Miami and Philadelphia.

[1880] (A.R.)—HANDMAIDS OF REPARATION OF THE SACRED HEART OF JESUS (P)

Founded in Messina, Italy in 1918.

U.S. Foundation (1958): *Sacred Heart Villa*, 36 Villa Dr., Steubenville, OH 43953-7129. Tel: 740-282-3801. Sr. Rosalba Putrino, A.R., Supr.

Total number in U.S: 6.

Ministry in Apostolic Work in Religious & Academic Education: Education All Levels; Religious Education; Parish and Diocesan Ministry; CCD Work; Orphanages; Missionary Work in Africa, Brazil and Poland.

Represented in the Dioceses of Arlington and Steubenville. Also in Africa, Brazil, Italy and Poland.

[1890] (H.H.S.)—SOCIETY OF HELPERS (P)

Founded in France in 1856. First foundation in the U.S. in 1892.

Generalate: 16 rue St. J. Baptiste de la Salle, Paris, France, 75006. Sr. Elizabeth Flick, Supr. Gen.

American Provincial Office (1921): 4721 J S. Woodlawn, Chicago, IL 60615. Tel: 773-548-5026. Sr. Mary Ellen Moore, S.H., Prov. Supr.

Total number in U.S. Province: 26.

Legal Title: *Society of the Helpers of the Holy Souls; Helpers of the Holy Souls; Province of the Helpers of the Holy Souls in the United States.*

Represented in the Archdioceses of Chicago, New York, St. Louis and San Francisco and in the Diocese of Charleston.

[1895] (C.S.J.)—HERMANAS CARMELITAS DE SAN JOSE (P)

Founded in El Salvador C.A. in 1916. First foundation in the United States in 2003.

Motherhouse: Final 14 Ave. Norte, Colonia San Antonio Las Palmeras Depto., De La Libertad, El Salvador

Regional House: 141 W. 87th Pl., Los Angeles, CA 90003. Tel: 323-758-6840; Tel: 323-752-2838. Sr. Enedina de Jesus Hernandez, C.S.J., Reg. Supr. US Community.

Total in Congregation: 201; U.S. Community: 4.

Ministry in Pastoral Care: Pastoral assistance in spiritual guidance and counseling; visitation of the sick and elderly; sacramental preparation; religious education for children, youth and/or adults; pastoral visits to the poor; faith formation.

[1900] (H.C.G.)—HERMANAS CATEQUISTAS GUADALUPANAS (P)

Founded in Saltillo, Coahuila, Mexico in 1923. First United States foundation in 1950.

Motherhouse and Novitiate: Saltillo, Coahuila, Mexico

U.S. Address: *Hermanas Catequistas Guadalupanas Convent*, 4110 S. Flores, San Antonio, TX 78214. Tel: 210-532-9344. Sr. Maria Marta Ruiz, H.C.G., Reg. Delegate.

Total number in the U.S: 14.

Represented in the Archdioceses of Oklahoma City and San Antonio and in the Diocese of Fort Worth.

[1910] (H.J.)—HERMANAS JOSEFINAS (P)

General Motherhouse: Condor 336, Col. las Aguilas, Delg. Alvaro Obregon, Mexico, 01710. Mother Isabel Vargas Huante, h.j., Gen. & Supr.

U.S. Address: *Assumption Seminary*, 2600 W. Woodlawn Ave., P.O. Box 28240, San Antonio, TX 78284. Tel: 210-734-0039.

Sisters: 10.

Represented in the Archdioceses of Chicago, Los Angeles and San Antonio and in the Diocese of Joliet in Illinois.

[1920] (C.S.C.)—CONGREGATION OF THE SISTERS OF THE HOLY CROSS (P)

Founded at Le Mans, France in 1841. First foundation in the U.S. in 1843.

General Administration: *Sisters of the Holy Cross Generalate*, 301 Bertrand Hall-Saint Mary's, Notre Dame, IN 46556-5000. Tel: 574-284-5550; Fax: 574-284-5779. Sr. Joan Marie Steadman, C.S.C., Pres.; Sr. Sharlet Ann Wagner, C.S.C., Gen. Sec.

Professed Members: 415; Temporarily Professed: 27; Novices: 15; Candidates: 15.

Legal Title: Sisters of the Holy Cross, Inc.; The Academy of the Holy Cross, Inc., MD; The Corporation of Saint Mary's College, Notre Dame, IN; Holy Cross Ministries of Utah; Society of the Congregation of the Sisters of the Holy Cross, Bangladesh.

Areas and Coordinators:

Angela Area - USA Retired, Notre Dame, IN. Tel: 574-284-5689. Sr. M. John Margaret (Dietzen), C.S.C., Coord.

Area of Africa - Ghana and Uganda Tel: 233-244-753325. Sr. Margaret Mary Nimo, C.S.C., Coord.

Area of Asia - Bangladesh and India. Tel: 88-02-912-9600. Sr. Violet Rodrigues, C.S.C., Coord.

Area of North America - USA & Mexico, Notre Dame, IN, Tel: 574-631-8367. Sr. Ruth Marie Nickerson, C.S.C., Coord.

Area of South America - Brazil and Peru. Tel: 55-71-3011-0223. Sr. Aline Marie Steuer, C.S.C., Coord.

Sisters serve and staff: Colleges; High Schools; Grade Schools; Adult Education Centers; Social Service Centers; Prayer Centers; Counseling Centers; Human Rights Centers; Women's Development Center; Hospitals and other Health Ministries, including Health Systems, Primary Health Care and Long Term Health Care; Parish Ministry; Diocesan Catechetical Services; Other Parish and Diocesan Ministries; Retirement Homes; Senior Citizen Residences; Pastoral Ministry with the Deaf; Correctional Institution.

Represented in the Archdioceses of Baltimore, Chicago, Cincinnati, Indianapolis, Los Angeles, Seattle and Washington and in the Dioceses of Arlington, Austin, Boise, Columbus, Fort Wayne-South Bend, Fresno, Gary, Knoxville, Lafayette in Indiana, Lexington, Oakland, Orange, Palm Beach, Raleigh, Richmond, Sacramento, St. Petersburg, Salt Lake City, and Tucson. Also in Brazil, Peru, Ghana, Uganda, Mexico, Bangladesh and India.

[1930] (C.S.C.)—SISTERS OF HOLY CROSS (P)

Founded in Le Mans, France in 1841. First foundation in Canada in 1847.

General Administration: 905 rue Basile-Moreau, St-Laurent, Montreal, Canada, H4L 4A1. Sr. Kesta Occident, C.S.C., Gen. Animator.

Universal total in Congregation: 580.

American Regional Office: *Sisters of Holy Cross*, 377 Island Pond Rd., Manchester, NH 03109-4811. Tel: 603-622-9504; Fax: 603-622-9782. Sr. Doris E. Gagnon, P.M., Reg. Animator.

Total number in Region: 111.

Ministry in the field of Academic Education at all levels; Religious Education Centers; Social and Family Services; Counselor-Therapist; Parish Ministry; Sabbatical Programs; Clinical leader/nurses; Youth and Hospital Chaplaincies; Administrative Positions; Diocesan Services; Social Work; Elderly Assistance; Holy Cross Family Learning Center assisting immigrants and refugees.

Properties owned: Holy Cross Early Childhood Center, Manchester, NH; St. George Manor, Manchester, NH; Londonderry House, Londonderry, NH; Sisters of the Holy Cross residences at 454 Island Pond Rd., Manchester, NH 03109; 136 Lynwood Ln., Manchester, NH 03109; 113 Wedgewood Ln., Manchester, NH 03109; 377 Island Pond Rd., Manchester, NH; Fairview Rd., R.R. 1, Box 191, Pittsfield, NH 03263; Four units at Crosswoods Path Condos, Merrimack, NH.

Represented the Dioceses of Bridgeport, Burlington, Manchester and St. Petersburg. Also in Burkina Faso, Chile, Haiti, Mali, Peru and Rome.

[1940] (C.H.F.)—CONGREGATION OF THE SISTERS OF THE HOLY FAITH (P)

Founded in Ireland in 1856. First foundation in U.S. in 1953. St. John of God School, 13817 Pioneer Blvd., Norwalk, California, 90650.

Motherhouse: Glasnevin, Dublin II, Ireland

U.S. Region: 12322 S. Paramount Blvd., Downey, CA 90242. Tel: 562-869-6092; Fax: 562-869-4609. Sr. Dolores Madden, C.H.F., Regl. Leader.

Total in Community: 28.

Represented in the Archdioceses of Los Angeles, New Orleans and San Francisco and in the Diocese of Sacramento.

[1950] (S.S.F.)—CONGREGATION OF THE SISTERS OF THE HOLY FAMILY (P)

Founded in New Orleans, Louisiana, in 1842.

Motherhouse: 6901 Chef Menteur Hwy., New Orleans, LA 70126. Tel: 504-241-3088. Sr. Eva Regina Martin, S.S.F., Supr. Gen.

Total in Community: 115.

Ministry in Secondary and Elementary Schools; Day Care Centers; Pastoral and Social Services; Nursing Home and Apartments for the Elderly, Disabled and Handicapped.

Represented in the Archdioceses of Galveston-Houston, New Orleans and Washington and in the Diocese of Lafayette (LA). Also in Belize, Central America.

[1960] (S.H.F.)—SISTERS OF THE HOLY FAMILY (P)

Founded in San Francisco, California, in 1872.

General Motherhouse: P.O. Box 3248, Fremont, CA 94539. Tel: 510-624-4500; Fax: 510-624-4537. Sr. Gladys Guenther, S.H.F., Congregational Pres.

Total in Community: 85.

Properties owned and/or sponsored: St. Elizabeth's Day Home, San Jose, CA.

Ministry in the following areas: Child Care; Developmentally Challenged; Pastoral Care; Social Service Agencies related to Child Protective Services; Hospital Chaplaincy; Parish Administration.

Represented in the Archdioceses of Anchorage, Los Angeles, and San Francisco and in the Dioceses of Fresno, Honolulu, Monterey, Oakland, Reno, Sacramento and Stockton.

[1970] (C.S.F.N.)—SISTERS OF THE HOLY FAMILY OF NAZARETH (P)

Founded in Italy in 1875. First foundation in the United States in 1885.

General Motherhouse: Rome, Italy Mother Jana Zawieja, C.S.F.N., Supr. Gen.

Holy Family Province (1885): 310 N. River Rd., Des Plaines, IL 60016-1211. Tel: 847-298-6760; Fax: 847-803-1941. Sr. Sally Marie Kiepura, C.S.F.N., Prov. Supr.; Sr. Rebecca Sullivan, C.S.F.N., Archivist.

Total number in United States: 332.

Ministry in Academic Education; Hospitals and Health Care; Social Work; Retreat Work; Religious Education; Child Care.

Sponsors: Provena Health Care/Resurrection Health Care.

Represented in the Archdiocese of Chicago.

[1980] (O.S.F.)—CONGREGATION OF THE SERVANTS OF THE HOLY CHILD JESUS OF THE THIRD ORDER REGULAR OF SAINT FRANCIS (P)

Founded in Germany in 1855. First founded in the United States on April 9, 1929, at Staten Island, New York.

General Motherhouse: *Kloster Oberzell*, Wuerzburg, Germany Mother Veridiana Duerr, Supr. Gen.

Regional House: *Servants of the Holy Child Jesus-Villa Maria*, 109 Rte. 156, Yardville, NJ 08620. Tel: 609-585-4660; Fax: 609-585-2759. Sr. M. Antonia Cooper, Reg. Min.

Total in American Region: 16.

Properties owned and/or sponsored: Holy Family Regional House/Villa Maria Sanitarium, Yardville, NJ.

Ministry in Social Work; Health Care; Teaching.

Represented in the Archdiocese of Newark and Dioceses of Metuchen and Trenton.

[1990] (S.N.J.M.)—SISTERS OF THE HOLY NAMES OF JESUS AND MARY (P)

Founded by Blessed Marie Rose Durocher, in Longueuil, Quebec, Canada in 1843. First foundation in the U.S. in 1859.

Generalate: 80, rue Saint-Charles Est, Longueuil, Canada, J4H 1A9. Tel: 450-651-8104. Sr. Catherine Ferguson, Supr.

An international congregation of 1,200 religious women with missions in Lesotho, Nicaragua, Peru and Brazil. Congregational sponsored works include colleges; adult centers; secondary, elementary and preschools; continuing care retirement community and health clinics.

U.S.-Ontario Province: *Provincial Administration*, Box 398, Marylhurst, OR 97036. Tel: 503-675-7100; Fax: 503-675-7136; Web: www.snjmusontario.org. Sr. Mary Ellen Holohan, S.N.J.M., Prov.

Total in Province: 552.

Properties owned and/or sponsored: Academy of the Holy Names, Albany, NY; Academy of the Holy Names, Tampa, FL; Convent, Marylhurst, OR; St. Mary's Academy, Portland, OR; Mary's Woods at Maryhurst, Inc., Marylhurst, OR; Provincial House, Los Gatos, CA; Holy Names University, Oakland, CA; Holy Names High School, Oakland, CA; Ramona Convent Secondary School, Alhambra, CA; Villa Maria del Mar, Santa Cruz, CA; Next Step Learning Center, Oakland, CA; Villa Holy Names, Los Gatos, CA; Convent, Spokane, WA; Holy Names Academy, Seattle, WA; Holy Names Music Center, Spokane, WA; Tutwiler Clinic; Jonestown Family Center for Education and Wellness; Holy Names Heritage Center.

Sisters ministering in works sponsored by other institutions/agencies include Formal Education in Universities, Secondary, Elementary and Preschools; Adult Basic Education/Literacy; Administration in Diocesan Offices; Campus Ministry; Pastoral Ministry; Religious Education, Health Care and Social Services.

Represented in the Archdioceses of Los Angeles, Portland in Oregon, San Francisco, Seattle and Washington and in the Dioceses of Albany, Baker, Jackson, Monterey, Oakland, Orlando, Palm Beach, St. Petersburg, Spokane, Venice and Yakima.

[2000] (C.S.R.)—SISTERS OF THE HOLY REDEEMER (P)

First foundation in the United States on March 19, 1924 in Baltimore, Maryland.

American Province of the Immaculate Conception: 521 Moredon Rd., Huntingdon Valley, PA 19006. Tel: 215-914-4100; Fax: 215-914-4171. Sr. Anne Marie Haas, C.S.R., Prov. Supr.

Legal Holdings and Titles: Holy Redeemer Health Care Corporation and Foundation; Holy Redeemer Health System; Holy Redeemer Hospital and Medical Center; St. Joseph's Manor; The Lafayette-Redeemer; Holy Redeemer Active and Retirement Living Communities; Holy Redeemer Home Care; Holy Redeemer Transitional Care Unit; Holy Redeemer Physician and Ambulatory Services; Redeemer Village & Redeemer Village II; Drueding Center/Project Rainbow; HRH Management Corporation; Convents— Provincialate; Angelus Convent; Emmanuel Convent; St. Elizabeth Convent.

Represented in the Archdioceses of Newark and Philadelphia and in the Dioceses of Camden, Metuchen and Trenton.

[2010] (O.SS.R.)—ORDER OF THE MOST HOLY REDEEMER (P)

(Redemptoristine Nuns)

Founded 1731 by St. Alphonsus de Liguori and Ven. Maria Celeste. (Contemplative). Rule approved 1750 by Pope Benedict XIV. First United States Monastery (1957) Esopus, New York.

Monastery of St. Alphonsus (1960): 200 Liguori Dr., Liguori, MO 63057. Tel: 636-464-1093; Fax: 636-464-9446. Sr. Margaret Eleanor Wilkinson, O.Ss.R., Prioress.

Total in Community: 15.

Properties owned and/or sponsored: Order of the Most Holy Redeemer, Monastery of the Most Holy Redeemer, Thailand.

Represented in the Archdioceses of New York and St. Louis.

Mother of Perpetual Help Monastery: *Redemptoristine Nuns*, P.O. Box 220, Esopus, NY 12429-0220. Tel: 845-384-6533; Fax: 845-384-6654; Email: rednuns.esopus@gamil.com. Sr. Paula Schmidt, O.SS.R., Prioress.
Total in Community: 9; Solemnly Professed Nuns: 8.
Solemn Vows, Papal Enclosure.

[2020] (C.H.S.)—COMMUNITY OF THE HOLY SPIRIT (D)

U.S. Foundation (1970): 6151 Rancho Mission Rd. - #205, San Diego, CA 92108. Tel: 619-584-0809. Sr. Jolene Schmitz, C.H.S.
Total in Community: 13.
Ministry in the field of Education; Health Care; and Social Services.
Represented in the Dioceses of Oakland, Orange, Las Vegas, San Diego, San Jose, Springfield in Illinois and Wichita.

[2030] (C.S.SP.)—SISTERS OF THE HOLY SPIRIT (D)

Founded in the United States 1919; Decree of Establishment 1932.

Motherhouse and Novitiate: 10102 Granger Rd., Cleveland, OH 44125. Sr. Patricia Raelene Peters, C.S.Sp., Supr. Gen.
Total in Community: 8.
Represented in the Diocese of Cleveland.

[2040] (S.H.S.)—SISTERS OF THE HOLY SPIRIT (D)

Founded in the United States in 1913 at Donora, Pennsylvania.

Motherhouse: 5246 Clarwin Ave., Ross Township, Pittsburgh, PA 15229-2208. Tel: 412-931-1917; Fax: 412-931-3711; Email: srshs@verizon.net; Web: www.sistersoftheholyspirit.com. Sr. Grace Fabich, S.H.S., Gen. Supr.
Total in Community: 39.
Facilities owned and staffed: Corporation of Sisters of the Holy Spirit of Pittsburgh; Martina Spiritual Renewal Center Inc.
Sisters serve and staff: Elementary Schools; Religious Education; Health and Social Services; Retreat Services; Child Day Care; Care Facility for the Aged; Pastoral Ministry.
Represented in the Dioceses of Greensburg and Pittsburgh.

[2050] (S.H.SP.)—SISTERS OF THE HOLY SPIRIT AND MARY IMMACULATE (P)

Founded in America in 1893. Papal Approbation 1930; final Approbation, 1938.

General Motherhouse: *Convent of the Holy Spirit and Mary Immaculate*, 300 Yucca St., San Antonio, TX 78203. Tel: 210-533-5149. Sr. Miriam Mitchell, S.H.Sp., Gen. Supr.
Professed Sisters: 79.
Legal Holdings: Holy Spirit Trust; Holy Spirit Motherhouse; Healy Murphy Center, Inc., San Antonio, TX; Mother of Perpetual Help Nursing Home, Brownsville, TX.
Ministry in the following areas: Education; Health Care; Pastoral Ministry; Catechetical Ministry; Social Service; Retreats.
Represented in the Archdioceses of Galveston-Houston, New Orleans and San Antonio and in the Dioceses of Biloxi, Brownsville, Corpus Christi, Dallas, Fort Worth, Houma-Thibodaux, Jackson, Lafayette (LA) and Shreveport. Also in Mexico and Zambia.

[2060] (O.SS.T.)—SISTERS OF THE MOST HOLY TRINITY (P)

Founded in Rome in 1198. First foundation in the United States in 1920.

General Motherhouse: Rome, Italy

Provincial House: *Immaculate Conception Province*, 21281 Chardon Rd., Euclid, OH 44117. Tel: 216-481-8232; Fax: 216-481-6577. Sr. M. Rochelle Guertal, O.SS.T., Reg. Delegate.
Total in Community: 23.
Properties owned and/or sponsored: Our Lady of Lourdes Shrine, Euclid, OH.
Represented in the Archdiocese of Philadelphia and in the Diocese of Cleveland.

[2070] (S.U.S.C.)—HOLY UNION SISTERS (P)

Founded in France in 1826. First foundation in the United States in 1886.

Generalate: Rome, Italy Sr. Carol Regan, S.U.S.C., Supr. Gen.

United States Province: 444 Centre St., P.O. Box 410, Milton, MA 02186-0006. Tel: 617-696-8765; Fax: 617-696-8571. Province Mission Team: Sr. Mary Catherine Burns, S.U.S.C.; Sr. Paula Coelho, S.U.S.C.; Sr. Maryellen Ryan, S.U.S.C.
Total in Community: 99.
Legal Title: *Holy Union Sisters, Inc.*
Sponsored Ministry: Country Day School of the Holy Union, Inc., Groton, MA.
Ministry in the field of Religious and Academic Education; Social Services; Pastoral Care; Pastoral Ministry; Spiritual Renewal; Day Care; Ministry Education; Family Ministry; Nursing; Peace & Justice; Spanish Apostolate; Ministry to the Handicapped; Ministry to Immigrants and Refugees; Clerical & Secretarial services; Diocesan Administrative services.
Represented in the Archdioceses of Baltimore, Boston and New York and in the Dioceses of Albany, Brooklyn, Fall River, Harrisburg, Lexington, Providence, Rockville Centre, and Richmond.

[2080] (G.H.M.S.)—HOME MISSION SISTERS OF AMERICA (D)

(Glenmary Sisters)

Founded July 16, 1952.

Motherhouse: *Glenmary Sisters - Glenmary Center*, P.O. Box 22264, Owensboro, KY 42304-2264. Tel: 270-686-8401. Sr. Sharon Miller, Pres.
Total in Community: 12.
Service to Home Missions.
Represented in the Dioceses of Lexington, Owensboro, Savannah and Springfield Cape-Girardeau.

[2090] (H.V.M.)—SISTERS HOME VISITORS OF MARY (D)

Founded in Detroit, Michigan in 1949.

Motherhouse: 121 E. Boston Blvd., Detroit, MI 48202. Tel: 313-869-2160; Email: homevisitors@att.net.
Total in Community: 22.
Ministry in Urban Parishes; Senior Citizen; Schools and Preschools; Religious Education, RCIA; Clinic; Community Org.
Represented in the Archdiocese of Detroit. Also in Nigeria.

[2100] (C.H.M.)—CONGREGATION OF THE HUMILITY OF MARY (P)

Founded in France in 1854. First United States foundation in 1864.

Motherhouse: *Humility of Mary Center*, Davenport, IA 52804. Sr. Mary Rehmann, C.H.M., Pres.
Total in Community: 115.
Legal Titles: Congregation of the Humility of Mary; Humility of Mary Housing, Inc; Congregation of the Humility of Mary Charitable Trust; New Horizons of Faith; Humility of Mary Shelter, Inc.
Ministry in Schools and Colleges; Religious Education Centers; Migrant Programs; Pastoral Ministry; Social Services; Inner City Programs; Health Services and Ministry to the Elderly.
Represented in the Archdioceses of Chicago, Denver and Los Angeles and in the Dioceses of Davenport, Des Moines, Great Falls-Billings, Jackson, Peoria, Richmond and Rockford. Also in Mexico.

[2110] (H.M.)—SISTERS OF THE HUMILITY OF MARY, INC. (P)

Founded in France in 1854. First foundation in the United States in 1864 at Villa Maria, Lawrence County, Pennsylvania, 16155.

Motherhouse: *Villa Maria Community Center*, P.O. Box 914, Villa Maria, PA 16155-0914. Tel: 724-964-8861; Fax: 724-964-8082. Sr. Susan Schorsten, H.M., Major Supr.; Sr. Joanne Gardner, H.M., Community Archivist.
Total in Community: 165.
Ministry in the field of Academic and Religious Education at all levels; Hospitals and Nursing Home, Assisted Living; Parish and Pastoral Ministries; Publishing of Education Materials; Legal Services; Social Services; Ministry to persons who are Native Americans, Migrants, Hispanics, Haitians and Rural Poor; Housing Ministry to Single Parents, Independent Elderly; Retreat Ministry; Spirituality and Counseling; Advocacy for Eco-justice.
Legal Holdings and Titles: Sisters of the Humility of Mary (Motherhouse), Villa Maria, PA; Sisters of the Humility of Mary Charitable Trust, Villa Maria, PA; Magnificat High School, Rocky River, OH; Villa Montessori Center, Cleveland, OH; The Center for Learning, Villa Maria, PA; Villa Maria Education and Spirituality Center, Villa Maria, PA; Humility of Mary Housing, Inc., Akron, OH; HM Housing Development Corporation, Akron, OH; HM Life Opportunity Services, Akron, OH; Villa Maria Residential Services, Villa Maria, PA.
Represented in the Archdioceses of Baltimore and Cincinnati and in the Dioceses of Arlington, Cleveland, Erie, Grand Island, Lexington, Palm Beach, Pittsburgh, Toledo, Tucson, Wheeling-Charleston and Youngstown. Also in Haiti.

[2120] (R.C.M.)—SISTERS OF THE IMMACULATE CONCEPTION (P)

Founded in Spain in 1892.

General Motherhouse: Princesa 19 y 21, Madrid, Spain, 28008. Mother Maria Luz Martinez, Mother Gen.

U.S. Delegation House (1962): 2230 Franklin, San Francisco, CA 94109. Tel: 415-474-0159. Sr. Encarnacion Ortega, R.C.M., Regl. Supr.; Sr. Angeles Marin, Local Supr.
Represented in the Archdiocese of San Francisco and in the Diocese of Fresno.

[2140] —SISTERS OF THE IMMACULATE CONCEPTION OF THE BLESSED VIRGIN MARY (LITHUANIAN) (P)

Founded in Marijampole, Lithuania in 1918. First foundation in the United States in 1936.

American Headquarters: *Immaculate Conception Convent*, 600 Liberty Hwy., Putnam, CT 06260-2503. Tel: 860-928-7955; Fax: 860-928-1930. Sr. Igne Marijosius, Supr.
Total in Community: 16.
Legal Titles & Holdings: Immaculate Conception Convent; Matulaitis Nursing Home, Putnam, CT; Camp Neringa, Marlboro, VT.
Ministry in Nursing Homes; Retreat House; Catechetical Work in Parishes; Summer Camp for Children and Young Adults.
Represented in the Archdiocese of Chicago and in the Dioceses of Burlington and Norwich. Also in Canada.

[2145] (O.S.A.)—CONGREGATION OF AUGUSTINIAN SISTERS SERVANTS OF JESUS AND MARY (P)

Generalate: via Nomentana 514, Rome, Italy Mother Tessie Bezzina, Gen.

Malta Province: 208 Fleur-de-Lys, B'Kara, Malta Mother Carmen Borg, Mother Prov.

U.S. Foundation: *St. John Convent*, 531 E. Broadway, Brandenburg, KY 40108. Sr. Lydia Falzon, Supr.
Total in Community: 5.
Represented in the Archdiocese of Louisville.

[2150] (I.H.M.)—SISTERS, SERVANTS OF THE IMMACULATE HEART OF MARY (P)

Founded in the United States in 1845.

SSIHM Leadership Council: 610 W. Elm, Monroe, MI 48162-7909. Tel: 734-240-9700; Fax: 734-240-9784. Sr. Joan Mumaw, I.H.M., Interim Pres.
Total in Congregation: 410.
Legal Titles: Marian High School for Young Women, Bloomfield Hills, MI; Visitation North Spirituality Center.
Ministry in Academic and Religious Education at all levels; Pastoral Ministry (parish, healthcare, campus and prison settings); Diocesan and Parish Administration; Peace and Justice; Social Service and Counseling; Spiritual Growth and Development; Overseas Ministries.
Represented in the Archdioceses of Atlanta, Boston, Chicago, Detroit, Galveston-Houston, Louisville, Miami, Milwaukee, Mobile, Oklahoma City, Philadelphia, St. Paul-Minneapolis, San Antonio, San Juan, Santa Fe and Washington and in the Dioceses of Albany, Austin, Cleveland, El Paso, Fort Wayne-South Bend, Joliet, Kansas City-St. Joseph, Lansing, Marquette, Oakland, Orange, Orlando, Palm Beach, Pensacola-Tallahassee, Phoenix, Portland, Raleigh, Richmond, San Diego, Saginaw, St. Augustine, Venice and Wilmington. Also in Canada, Mexico and South Africa.

River House - IHM Spirituality Center: 805 W. Elm Ave., Monroe, MI 48162. Tel: 734-240-5494; Fax: 734-240-5495; Email: riverhouse@ihmsisters.org; Web: www.ihmsisters.org.
Sisters: 3.
Sponsorship of I.H.M. Congregation.

Visitation North Spirituality Center: 7227 Lahser Rd., Bloomfield Hills, MI 48301. Tel: 248-433-0950; Fax: 248-433-0952; Email: visitationnorth@ihmsisters.org; Web: www.visitationnorth.org.
Sisters: 4.
Sponsorship of I.H.M. Congregation.

[2160] (I.H.M.)—SISTERS, SERVANTS OF THE IMMACULATE HEART OF MARY (P)

Founded in 1845. Established in Scranton, Pennsylvania in 1871.

General Motherhouse: *Immaculate Heart of Mary Center*, 2300 Adams Ave., Scranton, PA 18509. Tel: 570-342-6850; Fax: 570-346-5439. Sr. Therese O'Rourke, I.H.M., Pres.
Total in Community: 437.
Properties owned and/or sponsored: IHM Center; Pascucci Family Our Lady of Peace Residence; Our Lady of Grace Center; Manhasset, NY.
Ministry in the field of Academic Education; Hospitals; Early Childhood Education Centers; Spiritual Renewal Center; Directors of Religious Education; Pastoral Ministries; Social Services; Campus Ministry; Volunteer Services; Family Ministry; Drug and Alcohol Counseling; Ministry to Hispanics; Diocesan Offices.
Represented in the Archdioceses of Baltimore, Boston, Detroit, Hartford, Miami, Newark, New York, Philadelphia, Santa Fe and Washington and in the Dioceses of Albany, Allentown, Altoona-Johnstown, Bridgeport, Brooklyn, Camden, Cleveland, Fort Wayne-South Bend, Harrisburg, Jackson, Lexington, Orlando, Paterson, Pittsburgh, Raleigh, Rochester, Rockville Centre, St. Augustine, St. Petersburg, Scranton, Springfield in Massachusetts, Syracuse, Trenton, Wheeling-Charleston and Wilmington. Also in Chile, Guatemala and Peru.

[2170] (I.H.M.)—SISTERS, SERVANTS OF THE IMMACULATE HEART OF MARY (P)

Founded in 1845. Established in West Chester, Pennsylvania in 1872.

General Motherhouse: *Villa Maria House of Studies*, 1140 King Rd., Immaculata, PA 19345. Tel: 610-647-2160; Fax: 610-889-4874. Sr. Lorraine McGrew, I.H.M., Gen. Supr.

Total in Congregation: 862.

Ministry in the field of Academic Education at all levels in the U.S. as well as Peru & Chile; Pastoral Ministry; Literacy Centers; Infirmary work.

Represented in the Archdioceses of Atlanta, Hartford, Miami and Philadelphia and in the Dioceses of Allentown, Camden, Harrisburg, Manchester, Metuchen, Raleigh, Richmond, Savannah and Trenton.

[2180] (I.H.M.)—SISTERS OF THE IMMACULATE HEART OF MARY (P)

Founded in Spain in 1848. First foundation in the United States in 1871.

General Motherhouse: Girona, Spain

U.S. Province: 3820 N. Sabino Canyon Rd., Tucson, AZ 85750-6534. Tel: 520-886-4273. Sr. Alice M. Martinez, Prov. Supr.; Sr. Mary Evelyn Soto, Sec. & Community Archivist.

Total in Community: 20.

Ministry in the field of Academic and Religious Education.

Represented in the Diocese of Tucson.

[2182] (I.H.M.M.)—SISTERS OF THE IMMACULATE HEART OF MARY OF MIRINAE (P)

Founded in 1976 by Rev. Francis Haengman Tiyeng, Mirinae, Diocese of Suwon, Korea, under the motto "Through the Immaculate Heart of Mary to the Most Holy Trinity."

Motherhouse: Mirinae, Korea, South

U.S. Foundation: *Immaculate Heart of Mary Pre School*, 423 South Commonwealth Ave., Los Angeles, CA 90020. Sr. Inviolata Chang, I.H.M.M., Sec.

Properties owned and/or sponsored: Sisters of the Immaculate Heart of Mary of Mirinae, Los Angeles, CA.

Ministry in retreat work, school, youth and care for the aged.

Represented in the Archdiocese of Los Angeles.

[2183] (I.H.M.)—SISTERS OF THE IMMACULATE HEART OF MARY MOTHER OF CHRIST, NIGERIA (P)

Founded in Nigeria, West Africa in 1937. Classified with the Pontifical Institute Right in 1973.

Motherhouse-Immaculate Heart Generalate: P.O. Box 1551, Anambra State, Odoakpu-Onitsha, Nigeria Tel: 234-46-026; Tel: 234-46-485. Mother Mary Dominica Odita, Mother Gen.

Total in Congregation: 827.

U.S.A. Regional House: *Immaculate Heart Convent*, 1209 South Walnut, Freeport, IL 61032. Tel: 815-297-8287. Sr. Mary Nesta Ekene Ezeanya, Reg. Supr.

Total number of Sisters in the U.S: 35.

Legal Title: *The Congregation of the Sisters of the Immaculate Heart of Mary Mother of Christ - Nigeria.*

Ministry in Education; Hospital/Clinic, Pastoral/Social Services; Care of the Aged; Diocesan House Care.

Represented in the Archdioceses of Milwaukee, Seattle and St. Paul-Minneapolis and in the Dioceses of Gallup, Rockford and Syracuse.

[2185] (I.H.M.)—SISTERS OF THE IMMACULATE HEART OF MARY OF WICHITA (D)

Founded in Olot, Spain, in 1848. First foundation in United States in 1871. Wichita foundation in 1979. Canonically established as a religious institute of Diocesan right in 2007.

Motherhouse: 145 S. Millwood St., Wichita, KS 67213. Tel: 316-722-9316. Mother Mary Magdalene O'Halloran, I.H.M., Gen. Supr.

Total in Community: 20.

Apostolate: Contemplation of the Word and the spread of His Message of salvation through the various works and levels of education and retreat work.

Represented in the Diocese of Wichita.

[2187] (I.C.M.)—INCARNATIO-CONSECRATIO-MISSIO (P)

Founded in Vietnam in 1969. First foundation in the United States in 1975.

Motherhouse: 403 Ta Ha, Phuong Loc Tien, Thi Xa Bao Loc, Lam Dong, Vietnam Tel: 011-84-63-862-177.

U.S. Regional House: *Incarnatio-Consecratio-Missio, Inc.*, 5185 Jetsail Dr., Orlando, FL 32812. Tel: 407-658-4124; Fax: 407-658-4124; Email: icmorlando@yahoo.com. Sr. Marie Nguyen, I.C.M., Contact Person.

Universal Membership: 102; Aspirants: 35.

Ministry in the areas of Education; Healthcare; Missionary Outreach; Parish Ministries and Pastoral Care.

Represented in the Dioceses of Baton Rouge and Orlando. Also in Vietnam.

[2190] (C.V.I.)—CONGREGATION OF THE INCARNATE WORD AND BLESSED SACRAMENT (P)

Founded in France in 1625. First foundation in the United States in 1853.

Motherhouse and Novitiate: *Incarnate Word Convent*, 3400 Bradford Pl., Houston, TX 77025-1398. Tel: 713-668-0423. Sr. Lauren Beck, C.V.I., Supr.; Sr. Dympna Lyons, Archivist; Sr. Brendan O'Donnell, Archivist.

Total in Community: 43.

Ministry in the field of Academic Education; Administration; Pastoral Care; Parish Ministry.

Represented in the Archdiocese of Galveston-Houston and in the Diocese of Beaumont.

[2200] (I.W.B.S.)—CONGREGATION OF THE INCARNATE WORD AND BLESSED SACRAMENT (P)

Founded in France in 1625. First founded in the United States in 1853.

Motherhouse and Novitiate: *Incarnate Word Convent*, 1101 N.E. Water St., Victoria, TX 77901-9233. Tel: 361-575-2266; Fax: 361-575-2165. Sr. M. Evelyn Korenek, I.W.B.S., Supr. Gen.; Sr. Mary Virginia Sheblak, I.W.B.S., Community Archivist.

Perpetually Professed: 78; Annually Professed: 1; Novices: 1; Postulants: 1.

Legal Titles: Sisters of the Incarnate Word and Blessed Sacrament, Victoria, Texas, Inc.; Sisters of the Incarnate Word and Blessed Sacrament of Victoria, Texas Medical and Retirement Trust, Victoria, TX.

Ministry in the field of Education; CCD Centers; Hospitals; Pastoral Ministry.

Properties owned or sponsored: Nazareth Academy, Victoria, TX; Blessed Sacrament Academy, San Antonio, TX.

Represented in the Archdiocese of San Antonio and in the Diocese of Victoria. Also in Africa.

[2205] (I.W.B.S.)—SISTERS OF THE INCARNATE WORD AND BLESSED SACRAMENT (P)

Founded in France in 1625. First founded in the United States in 1853.

Motherhouse and Novitiate: *Incarnate Word Convent*, 2930 S. Alameda St., Corpus Christi, TX 78404-2798. Tel: 361-882-5413; Fax: 361-880-4152. Sr. Michelle Marie Kuntscher, I.W.B.S., Supr. Gen.

Sisters: 53.

Legal Titles: Convent Academy of the Incarnate Word; Incarnate Word Academy Foundation; Fannie Bluntzer Nason Renewal Center, Inc., Corpus Christi, TX.

Sisters serve and staff: Private High Schools; Private Kindergartens; Montessori; Private Middle Schools; Parochial and Private Elementary Schools; Other ministries include Religious Education; Hospital Ministry; Vocation Ministry; Prison Ministry; Social Service; Diocesan Offices; Adult Education; General Administration; Retreat Ministry; Parish Ministry.

Represented in the Dioceses of Brownsville, Corpus Christi and Beaumont.

[2210] (S.I.W.)—SISTERS OF THE INCARNATE WORD AND BLESSED SACRAMENT (P)

Founded in France in 1625. First foundation in the United States in 1853.

Motherhouse and Novitiate: 6618 Pearl Rd., Parma Heights, OH 44130-3808. Tel: 440-886-6440. Sr. Mary Rose Kocab, S.I.W., Congregational Leader.

Total in Community: 25.

Ministry includes Evangelization; Elementary and Religious Education; Spiritual Ministry (Retreat and Spiritual Direction); Pastoral Ministry in Parishes, Hospitals and Nursing Homes; Social Service.

Represented in the Diocese of Cleveland.

[2230] (C.I.J.)—CONGREGATION OF THE INFANT JESUS (D)

Founded in France in 1835. First foundation in the United States in 1905.

General Motherhouse: 984 North Village Ave., Rockville Centre, NY 11570. Tel: 516-823-3800; Tel: 516-823-3808; Fax: 516-594-0412. Sr. Dolores Wisniewski, C.I.J., Pres.

Total in Community: 50.

Corporate Title: Nursing Sisters of the Sick Poor Inc.

Ministry in the fields of Nursing; Social Work; Physical Therapy; Pastoral Care; Chaplains; Retreat Work; Parish Ministry; and other works related to Health Services.

Represented in the Dioceses of Brooklyn, Lexington, Portland and Rockville Centre.

[2245] (S.J.S.)—SISTERS OF JESUS THE SAVIOR (P)

Founded in Elele, Nigeria in 1985.

U.S. Foundation: *St. Bartholomew Convent*, 2291 E. Outer Dr., Detroit, MI 48234.

Professed Sisters: 4.

Ministry in Education and Social Assistance.

Represented in the Archdiocese of Detroit.

[2250] (O.S.B.)—CONGREGATION OF BENEDICTINES OF JESUS CRUCIFIED (P)

Founded in France in 1930. First foundation in the United States in Devon, PA in 1955. Second foundation in Newport, RI in 1962. Both foundations merged in Branford, CT in 2001.

General Motherhouse: Brou-sur-Chantereine, France Mother Godefrieda Bouwman, O.S.B., Prioress Gen.

U.S. Foundations: 61 Burban Dr., Branford, CT 06405-4003. Tel: 203-315-9964; Tel: 230-315-0106; Fax: 203-483-5829; Email: monasterygc@juno.com; Web: benedictinesjc.org. Sr. Marie Rita Syn, O.S.B., Prioress; Sr. Marie-Zita Wenker, O.S.B., Vocation Dir.

Total number in the U.S: 17.

Represented in the Archdiocese of Hartford.

[2260] (A.D.)—SISTERS OF THE LAMB OF GOD (D)

Founded in France 1945.

General Motherhouse: *Institute of the Lamb of God*, 85 Rt. du Vieux Saint Marc, Brest, France, 29283. Sr. Marie Francois Piriou, A.D., Supr. Gen.

U.S. Foundation (1958): *House of Formation*, 2063 Wyandotte Ave., Owensboro, KY 42301. Tel: 270-926-8656. Sr. Claire Marle, Supr.; Sr. Audrey Gold, Formation Dir.

Sisters: 11.

[2265] (S.V.)—SISTERS OF LIFE

Founded 1991.

Generalate: 586 McLean Ave., Yonkers, NY 10705. Tel: 914-968-8094; Fax: 914-968-0462. Mother Agnes Mary Donovan, S.V., Supr. Gen.

Legal Title: Sisters of Life, Inc.

Ministry: to advance a sense of the sacredness of human life in all of society by way of missions to 1) vulnerable, pregnant women; 2) providing the faithful a program of retreats and focused retreats of hope and healing for women suffering after abortion; 3) service to the Church through directing diocesan Family Life and Respect Life Offices; and 4) a mission of evangelization bringing the message of the sacredness of human life and the sanctity of human love to all.

Represented in the Archdiocese of New York and in the Diocese of Bridgeport. Also in Archdiocese of Toronto.

[2270] (L.C.M.)—SISTERS OF THE LITTLE COMPANY OF MARY (P)

Founded in England in 1877. First foundation in the United States in 1893.

Generalate: *Little Company of Mary Generalate*, 28 Trinity Crescent, Tooting Bec London, England, SW17 7AE.

Universal total in Congregation: 303; Final Professed Sisters: 290; Temporary Professed Sisters: 6; Novices: 2; Candidates: 5.

Provincial Office: *Province of the Immaculate Conception, The Little Company of Mary*, 9350 S. California Ave., Evergreen Park, IL 60805. Tel: 708-422-0130. Sr. Kathleen McIntyre, L.C.M., Province Leader.

Total in Community: 19.

Ministry in Hospitals and Health Care; Pastoral/Parish areas.

Properties owned: Little Company of Mary Hospital and Health Care Centers, Evergreen Park, IL; Memorial Hospital and Health Care Center, Jasper, IN; Little Company of Mary Health Services (Little Company of Mary Hospital, Torrance, CA and San Pedro Peninsula Hospital, San Pedro, CA).

Represented in the Archdioceses of Chicago and Los Angeles and in the Diocese of Evansville.

[2280] (P.F.M.)—LITTLE FRANCISCANS OF MARY (U.S.)

Founded in the United States in 1889.

General Motherhouse: *Baie St. Paul (Charlevoix)*, Canada Sr. Francoise Duchesne, P.F.M., Supr. Gen.

American Region: 12 Jones St., Apt. 1, Worcester, MA 01604. Tel: 508-755-0878. Sr. Jacquelyn Alix, Reg. Supr.

Total number in Congregation including Canada and the United States: 160.

Represented in the Dioceses of Portland (In Maine) and Worcester.

[2300] (L.S.I.C.)—LITTLE SERVANT SISTERS OF THE IMMACULATE CONCEPTION (P)

Congregatio Sororum Servularum Beatae Mariae Virginis Immaculatae Conceptae)

Founded by Blessed Edmund Bojanowski in Poland on May 3, 1850. First foundation in the United States on December 8, 1926.

General Motherhouse: Stara Wies 460, 36-200 Brzozow, skr. poczt. 66, woj. Podkarpackie, Poland Mother Beata Chwistek, L.S.I.C., Supr. Gen.

Total in Congregation: 1300.

Holy Trinity Province: *Little Servants Sisters of the Immaculate Conception Provincialate-Novitiate*, 1000 Cropwell Rd., Cherry Hill, NJ 08003. Tel: 856-424-1962; Fax: 856-424-5333; Email: lsic.prov@verizon.net; Web: www.littleservantsisters.com. Mother Dorota

Baranowska, L.S.I.C., Supr. Prov.; Sr. M. Philomena Nowicka, L.S.I.C., Vocation Dir.; Sr. Teresa Gradowska, L.S.I.C., Vocation Dir.
Professed Sisters: 72; Postulants: 2; Novices: 1.
Legal Titles: Congregation of the Little Servant Sisters of the Blessed Virgin Mary of the Immaculate Conception (Congregatio Sororum Servularum Beatae Mariae Virginis Immaculatae Conceptae), (Properties owned) Immaculate Conception Convent: Provincialate-Novitiate, Cherry Hill, NJ; Blessed Edmund Early Childhood Education Center, Cherry Hill, NJ; Marian Residence, Cherry Hill, NJ; St. John's Retreat House, Atlantic City, NJ; St. Joseph's Convent, Woodbridge, NJ; St. Joseph's Senior Home (Assisted Living and Nursing Center), Woodbridge, NJ.
Ministry: all levels of Religious Education, Pre-school and Academic Education; Parish Work; Social Work, Hospital Pastoral Care; Visiting Home Nursing Service; Senior Residential Homes; Assisted Living; Skilled Nursing Homes; Retreat House; Prayer Groups & Youth Ministry.
Represented in the Archdioceses of Newark and Philadelphia and in the Dioceses of Camden, Metuchen and Palm Beach. Also in the Philippines.

[2310] (L.S.A.)—LITTLE SISTERS OF THE ASSUMPTION (P)

Founded in France in 1865. First foundation in the United States in 1891.

General Motherhouse: 57 rue Violet, Paris, France, 75015. Sr. Marie Francoise Phelippeau, Supr. Gen.

United States Province: *Little Sisters of the Assumption Provincialate*, 100 Gladstone Ave., Walden, NY 12586. Tel: 845-778-0667; Web: www.littlesisters.org. Sr. Annette Allain, L.S.A., Prov.
Total in Community: 23.
Ministry in Home Health; Community Development Supportive Family Services Located in Poverty Areas; Services are predominantly provided in the Home Setting.
Represented in the Archdioceses of Boston, New York and Philadelphia and in the Diocese of Worcester.

[2315] (L.S.G.)—LITTLE SISTERS OF THE GOSPEL (D)

Founded in 1963 in France by Rev. Rene Voillaume. First foundation in the United States in 1972 in New York.

Generalate: 31 Rue George Politzer, St. Denis, France, 93200. Tel: 1-48233228.

U.S. House: P.O. Box 541355, Mott Haven Sta., Bronx, NY 10454. Tel: 718-402-2092.
Professed Sisters: 70; Novices: 5; Postulants: 5.
Residence: 340 Willis Ave., Bronx, NY, 10454.
Ministry in Prison Ministry; Service to the Poor and Underserved.
Represented in the Archdiocese of New York.

[2330] (L.S.J.)—LITTLE SISTERS OF JESUS (P)

Founded in the Sahara in 1939. First foundation in the United States in 1952.

General Motherhouse: Rome, Italy Sr. Maria Ferrari, Prioress Gen.
Universal total in Congregation: 1235.

U.S. Regional House: 400 N. Streeper St., Baltimore, MD 21224-1230. Tel: 410-327-7823. Sr. Lynn Flear, L.S.J., Reg. Dir.
Total number in U.S: 25.
Represented in the Archdioceses of Anchorage, Baltimore, Chicago and Washington and in the Dioceses of Altoona-Johnstown, Fairbanks and Paterson.

[2331] (L.S.J.M.)—LITTLE SISTERS OF JESUS AND MARY (D)

Founded in the United States in 1974. Sr. Mary Elizabeth, Foundress.

Joseph House: P.O. Box 1755, Salisbury, MD 21802. Tel: 410-543-1645; Fax: 410-742-3390. Sr. Constance R. Ladd, L.S.J.M., Supr. Gen.
Total in Community: 7.
Represented in the Diocese of Wilmington.

[2340] (L.S.P.)—LITTLE SISTERS OF THE POOR (P)

Founded in France in 1839. First foundation in the United States in 1868.

General Motherhouse: *La Tour St. Joseph*, 35190, St. Pern, France Mother Celine de la Visitation, Supr. Gen.

Province of Brooklyn (1868): *Queen of Peace Residence*, 110-30 221st St., Queens Village, NY 11429. Mother Margaret Regina Halloran, L.S.P., Prov.
Total number in Province: 120.
Ministry in Homes for the Aged.
Represented in the Archdioceses of Boston, Hartford, Philadelphia and New York and in the Dioceses of Albany, Brooklyn, Metuchen, Paterson, Providence and Scranton.

Province of Baltimore: *Little Sisters of the Poor*, 601 Maiden Choice Ln., Catonsville, MD 21228-3698. Tel: 410-744-9367; Fax: 410-747-0601. Sr. Loraine Marie Maguire, L.S.P., Prov.
Total number in Province: 106.
Ministry in Homes for the Aged.
Represented in the Archdioceses of Baltimore, Cincinnati, Indianapolis, Mobile and Washington and in the Dioceses of Cleveland, Pittsburgh, Richmond, Toledo and Wilmington.

Province of Chicago: *Little Sisters of the Poor, Chicago Province, Inc.*, 80 W. Northwest Hwy., Palatine, IL 60067-3582. Tel: 847-358-5700; Fax: 847-934-6852. Sr. Maria Christine Lynch, Prov.
Total number in Province: 119.
Ministry in Homes for the Aged.
Represented in the Archdioceses of Chicago, Denver, Los Angeles, Louisville, St. Louis, St. Paul-Minneapolis and San Francisco and in the Dioceses of Evansville, Gallup and Kansas City-St. Joseph.

[2345] (P.O.S.C.)—LITTLE WORKERS OF THE SACRED HEARTS (P)

Founded in Italy in 1892. First foundation in the U.S. in 1948.

General House: Via dei Pamphili 3, Rome, Italy, 00152.

Motherhouse and Novitiate: *Our Lady of Grace Convent*, 635 Glenbrook Rd., Stamford, CT 06906-1409. Tel: 203-348-5531. Sr. Gesuina Gencarelli, P.O.S.C., U.S. Delegate & Supr.
Ministry in Day Care; Catechetics; Preschool.
Represented in the Archdioceses of Philadelphia and Washington and in the Diocese of Bridgeport.

[2350] (S.L.W.)—SISTERS OF THE LIVING WORD (D)

Founded in the United States in 1975.

General Motherhouse: *The Living Word Center*, 800 N. Fernandez Ave. B, Arlington Heights, IL 60004-5336. Tel: 847-577-5972; Fax: 847-577-5980. Leadership Team: Sr. Rita Worm, S.L.W.; Sr. Joel Curcio, S.L.W.
Total in Community: 64.
Ministry in the field of Academic and Religious Education; Health Care; Parish Ministry and Social Services.
Represented in the Archdioceses of Chicago, New Orleans and St. Paul-Minneapolis and in the Dioceses of Alexandria, Cleveland, El Paso, Jackson, Joliet, Lansing, Memphis, Orlando, Rapid City and Sioux City.

[2360] (S.L.)—SISTERS OF LORETTO AT THE FOOT OF THE CROSS (P)

Founded in America in 1812.

General Motherhouse & Novitiate: *Loretto Motherhouse and Novitiate*, Nerinx, KY 40049. Tel: 270-865-5811.

Administrative Office: 4000 S. Wadsworth Blvd, Littleton, CO 80123-1308. Tel: 303-783-0450; Fax: 303-783-0611. Sr. Catherine Mueller, S.L., Pres.
Total in Congregation: 234.
Legal Title: *Loretto Literary and Benevolent Institution.*
Ministry in the field of Academic and Religious Education at all levels; Specialized Education; Health Care-Aging; Community Administration; Pastoral Ministry; Social Justice-Social Service; Administration; Medicine and Nursing; Prayer Retreats; Clerical Offices; Consultants; Spirituality Center.
Represented in the Archdioceses of Baltimore, Chicago, Denver, Galveston-Houston Indianapolis, Louisville, Mobile, St. Louis, Santa Fe and Washington and in the Dioceses of El Paso, Kansas City-St. Joseph, Knoxville, Lexington, Oakland, Orlando, Rockford, San Diego and San Jose.

[2370] (I.B.V.M.)—INSTITUTE OF THE BLESSED VIRGIN MARY (LORETTO SISTERS) (P)

Founded in St. Omer, Belgium, 1609. First foundation in Canada in 1847; in the United States in 1880.

Generalate: *Casa Loreto*, Via Massaua 3, Rome, Italy, 00162. Sr. Marian Moriarty, I.B.V.M., Supr. Gen.
Total in Congregation: 885.

Provincial Office United States: *Loretto Convent*, P.O. Box 508, Wheaton, IL 60187. Tel: 630-665-3814; Fax: 630-653-4886. Sr. Catherine Foley, I.B.V.M., Prov.
Total in Community: 77.
Sisters serve and staff: High Schools; Grammar Schools; Missionary Work; Correspondence School; University; Pastoral Ministry; Adult Education; Social Work; Retreat Ministry; Diocesan Office; Director of Religious Education.
Ministries: Loretta Center; Loretto Early Childhood Center; Loretta Extension Service; Loretta House; Mary Ward Center.
Properties owned: Loretto Development Office; Loretto Convent, Wheaton, IL; Loretto Early Childhood Center, Wheaton, IL; Loretto Center, Wheaton, IL; Houses in California, Arizona and Illinois.
Represented in the Archdiocese of Chicago and Milwaukee and in the Dioceses of Joliet, Marquette, Phoenix and Sacramento.

[2385] (L.H.C.N.T.)—LOVERS OF THE HOLY CROSS NHA TRANG (D)

Founded in Vietnam in 1950. First Foundation in the United States in 2003.

Motherhouse: HT25 Cam Hoa Cam Ranh, Khanh Hoa, Nha Trang, Vietnam

Regional House: 21618 Juan Ave., Hawaiian Gardens, CA 90716. Tel: 562-809-1570; Fax: 562-809-1570. Sr. Mary Men T. Pham, L.H.C.N.T., Rel. Supr.
Total in Congregation: 385; U.S. Community: 5.
Ministry in Pastoral Care: religious education for youth and/or adults, faith formation.

[2390] (L.H.C.)—LOVERS OF THE HOLY CROSS SISTERS (D)

Founded in 1670 in Vietnam by Bishop Pierre Lambert de la Motte. First foundation in the United States in 1976. Established as an autonomous institute of Consecrated Life of Diocesan Right in 1992.

General Motherhouse: *Holy Cross Convent*, 14700 South Van Ness Ave., Gardena, CA 90249. Tel: 310-768-1906; Tel: 310-516-0271; Fax: 310-352-6435. Sr. Thanh Hao Nguyen, L.H.C., Supr. Gen.
Sisters: 61; Novices: 4; Postulants: 2; Aspirants: 10; Oblates: 1.
Legal Title: *Lovers of the Holy Cross Sisters, Inc.*
Represented in the Archdiocese of Los Angeles and in the Dioceses of Orange and San Bernardino.

[2392] (L.H.C.)—LOVERS OF THE HOLY CROSS SISTERS (P)

(Sisters, Lovers of the Holy Cross)

Founded in Vietnam in 1670 by Bishop Pierre Lambert de la Motte. First foundation in the United States in 1975.

U.S. Foundation: *St. Theresa Convent*, 43 Crown Ln., Westbury, NY 11590. Tel: 516-333-9464. Sr. Theresa Nguyen, L.H.C., Supr.
Legal Title: *Sisters, Lovers of the Holy Cross, Inc.*
Represented in the Diocese of Rockville Centre.

[2400] (M.S.)—MARIAN SISTERS OF THE DIOCESE OF LINCOLN (D)

Marycrest Motherhouse: *Catholic Center*, 6765 N. 112th, Waverly, NE 68462. Tel: 402-786-2750; Fax: 402-786-7256. Sr. Jacquelyn Darner, M.S., Major Supr.
Total in Community: 34.
Ministry in the field of Education; Special Education; Health Care; Catechetics; Social Work.
Represented in the Diocese of Lincoln.

[2410] (M.S.C.)—CONGREGATION OF THE MARIANITES OF HOLY CROSS (P)

Founded in France in 1841. First foundation in the United States in 1843.

Congregational Administration Headquarters: 1011 Gallier St., New Orleans, LA 70117. Tel: 504-945-1620; Web: www.marianites.org. Sr. Suellen Tennyson, M.S.C., Congregational Leader.
Total number in North America: 126.
Ministry in Diocesan Administration and Parishes; Social & Health Services; and the field of Education.
Legal Holdings or Titles: Our Lady of Holy Cross Convent, New Orleans, LA; Our Lady of Holy Cross College, New Orleans, LA; Prompt Succor Nursing Home, Opelousas, LA; C'est la Vie (Senior Citizen Independent Living Units), Opelousas, LA; Holy Angels Congregational Center, New Orleans, LA.
Represented in the Archdiocese of New Orleans and in the Dioceses of Alexandria, Austin, Baton Rouge, Camden, Dallas, Houma-Thibodaux, Lafayette (LA), Lake Charles, Manchester, Paterson and Trenton. Also in Bangladesh, France, Canada and Burkina-Faso, Africa.

[2420] (S.M.S.M.)—MARIST MISSIONARY SISTERS (MISSIONARY SISTERS OF THE SOCIETY OF MARY) INC. (P)

Founded in France in 1845-1857. First foundation in the United States in Boston, Massachusetts 1922.

Motherhouse: Via Cassia, 1243, Rome, Italy, 00189.
Universal total in Congregation: 465.

North American Province: *Provincial Office*, 349 Grove St., Waltham, MA 02453-6018. Tel: 781-893-0149; Fax: 781-894-7610. Sr. Judith Sheridan, S.M.S.M., Prov.
Represented in the Archdiocese of Boston and in the Dioceses of Memphis, Oakland, St. Petersburg and San Diego. Also in Jamaica and Africa.

[2430] (S.M.)—MARIST SISTERS/CONGREGATION OF MARY (P)

Founded in France 1824 by Venerable John Claude Colin and Jeanne Marie Chavoin.

Generalate: Via Aurelia 292, Rome, Italy, 00165. Sr. Monica O'Brien, S.M., Congregational Leader.
Universal total in Congregation: 400.

U.S. Foundation (1956): *Marist Sisters - Congregation of Mary*, 9312 S. Kolmar Ave., Oak Lawn, IL 60454. Tel: 708-636-0259. Sr. Linda Sevcik, S.M., Sector Leader.
Total in Community: 15.
Legal Title: *Marist Sisters Inc. 16057 Hauss, Eastpointe, MI, 48021.*
Ministry in Elementary & Adult Education; Pastoral Ministry; Counseling; Pastoral Care in Hospitals; Physical Therapy; Seminary Formation; Social Ministry.
Represented in the Archdioceses of Chicago and Detroit

and in the Dioceses of Laredo and Wheeling-Charleston.

[2440] (S.M.I.)—CATECHIST SISTERS OF MARY IMMACULATE HELP OF CHRISTIANS, INC. (P)

Catechist Sisters of Mary Immaculate, Help of Christians

Founded in India in 1948 by the late Bishop Louis LaRavoire Morrow, Bishop of Krishnagar, India.

General Motherhouse: *Krishnagar*, Nadia Dist., West Bengal, India, 741 101. Sr. Lisette Thuruthimattam, Supr. Gen.

Universal total in Congregation: 610.

U.S. Foundation (1981): *Sisters of Mary Immaculate*, 118 Park Rd., Leechburg, PA 15656. Tel: 724-845-2828. Sr. Jessy George Mullankuzhiyil, S.M.I., Delegation Supr.; Sr. Mercy F. Anchalakal, S.M.I., Supr.

Total in Community: 6.

Legal Holdings and Titles: Bishop Morrow Personal Care Home, Leechburg, PA

[2450] (S.M.P.)—SISTERS OF MARY OF THE PRESENTATION (P)

Founded in France. First foundation in the United States in 1903.

General Motherhouse: *Broons*, 27 Rue de la Barriere, B.P. 31, Broons, France, 22250. Sr. Annick Geffrelot, Supr. Gen.

U.S. Provincial House & Novitiate at Maryvale: 11550 River Rd., Valley City, ND 58072-9620. Tel: 701-845-2864. Sr. Carol Jean Kuntz, Supr. Prov.

Total in Community: 29.

Properties owned and/or sponsored: St. Margaret's Hospital, Spring Valley, IL; Prairieland Home Health Agency, Spring Valley, IL; St. Andrew Health Center, Bottineau, ND; St. Aloisius Medical Center, Harvey, ND; Presentation Medical Center, Rolla, ND; Ave Maria Village, Jamestown, ND; Maryhill Manor, Enderlin, ND; Rosewood on Broadway, Fargo, ND; Villa Maria, Fargo, ND; Sheyenne Care Center, Valley City, ND.

Ministry in the field of Religious and Academic Education at all levels; Parish Ministry; Hospitals and Home Health Agencies.

Represented in the Dioceses of Bismarck, Crookston, Fargo and Peoria.

[2460] (S.M.R.)—SOCIETY OF MARY REPARATRIX (P)

Founded in France in 1857. First foundation in the United States in 1908.

Generalate: *Society Di Maria Riparatrice*, Via dei Lucchesi 3, Rome, Italy, 00187. Sr. Christine Barriere, Supr. Gen.

Total International Membership: 675.

U.S. Region: 17320 Grange Rd., Riverview, MI 48193. Tel: 734-285-4510; Fax: 734-285-8147. Sr. Veronica Blake, S.M.R., Reg. Leadership.

Total in Community: 20.

Represented in the Archdioceses of Detroit, Miami and New York and in the Diocese of Brooklyn.

[2470] (M.M.)—MARYKNOLL SISTERS OF ST. DOMINIC (P)

Founded in New York 1912.

Orientation Program: *Maryknoll Sisters*, Sr. Theresa Kastner, M.M., Co-Dir.; Sr. Shu-Chen Wu, M.M., Co-Dir.

Center: Maryknoll Sisters Center, Maryknoll, NY 10545-0311. Tel: 914-941-7575. Sr. Janice McLaughlin, M.M., Community Pres.; Sr. Rebecca Macugay, M.M., Vice Pres.; Sr. Ann Hayden, M.M., Gen. Sec.; Sr. Bitrina Kirway, M.M., Team Member. Center Coordinators: Sr. Marcelline Yurkovic, M.M.; Sr. Susan Baldus, M.M.; Sr. Patricia Ring, M.M.; Sr. Miedal Stone, M.M.

Total in Congregation: 495.

Legal Titles and Holdings: Maryknoll Sisters of St. Dominic, Inc.; Maryknoll Mission Institute.

Represented in the Archdioceses of Baltimore, Boston, Chicago, Cincinnati, Detroit, Galveston-Houston, Hartford, Los Angeles, Newark, New York, Portland in Oregon, Santa Fe, and Washington and in the Dioceses of Albany, Baker, Brooklyn, Charlotte, Duluth, El Paso, Gallup, Harrisburg, Honolulu, Kansas City-St. Joseph, Norwich, Oakland, Palm Beach, Phoenix, Providence, San Diego and San Jose.

[2480] (M.M.M.)—MEDICAL MISSIONARIES OF MARY (P)

Founded in Nigeria in 1937. First United States Foundation in 1950.

Congregation Centre: *Rosemount*, Booterstown Ave., Blackrock. County Dublin, Ireland Mother Mary Martin, M.M.M., Foundress; Sr. Siobhan Corkery, M.M.M., Congregational Leader.

Medical Missionaries of Mary: 563 Minneford Ave., Bronx, NY 10464-1118. Tel: 718-885-0945; Fax: 718-885-0945; Email: minniefordmmm@verizon.net; Web: www.mmmusa.org. Sr. Jean Clare Eason, M.M.M., Area Leader.

Total in Congregation: 414.

Represented in the Archdioceses of Boston, Chicago and New York and in the Dioceses of Richmond and San Diego.

[2490] (M.M.S.)—MEDICAL MISSION SISTERS (P)

Generalate: London, England Sr. Agnes Lanfermann, M.M.S., Society Coord.

Universal total in Congregation: 600.

North American Headquarters (1925): 8400 Pine Rd., Philadelphia, PA 19111. Tel: 215-742-6100; Fax: 215-342-3948. Sr. Suzanne Maschek, M.M.S., North American Coord.

Total number in North America: 118.

Legal Titles: Society of Catholic Medical Missionaries, Inc.; Society of Catholic Medical Missionaries Generalate, Inc.

Represented in the Archdioceses of Boston, Hartford, Philadelphia, Santa Fe, Seattle and Washington and in the Dioceses of Camden, Harrisburg, Las Cruces, Orange, Palm Beach, Richmond, St. Petersburg, San Diego and Tucson. Also in Mexico.

[2500] (M.S.J.)—MEDICAL SISTERS OF ST. JOSEPH (P)

Founded in Kerala, South India, 1946.

General Motherhouse: *Dharmagiri*, P.O. Kothamangalam, Kerala, India, 686691. Mother Jyohs, Supr. Gen.

U.S. Foundation (1985): *Medical Sisters of Joseph*, 3435 E. Funston, Wichita, KS 67218. Tel: 316-686-4746. Sr. Laly Josony George, M.S.J., Supr.

Total in Congregation: 900.

Ministry as Health Care Apostolates.

Represented in the Diocese of Wichita.

[2510] (M.M.B.)—MERCEDARIAN MISSIONARIES OF BERRIZ (P)

Order originated in Berriz, Spain 1548. Transformed into a missionary institute in 1930 in Spain. First foundation in U.S. in 1946 in Kansas City, MO.

Total Number of Sisters in the Institute: 447.

Generalate: *Mercedarie Missionarie di Berriz*, Viale Polo 10, Rome, Italy, 00198. Tel: 39-068-41-3441. Sr. Amelia Kuwaji, M.M.B., Gen. Coord.

U.S. Regional House: *Mercedarian Missionaries of Berriz*, 2115 Maturanna Dr., #101B, Liberty, MO 64068-7985. Tel: 816-781-8202; Fax: 816-781-8205; Email: mmbus@sbcglobal.net; Web: mmberriz.org. Sr. Sandra Thibodeaux, M.M.B., Reg. Coord.

Total number in Region: 12; Total number in Institute: 447.

Ministries in Health, Pastoral Care and Religious Education.

Property sponsored: Our Lady of Mercy Country Home. Liberty, MO.

Represented in the Diocese of Kansas City-St. Joseph. Also in Japan, Taiwan, Philippines, Guam, Federated States of Micronesia, Republic of Palau, Commonwealth of the Northern Marianas, Peru, Ecuador, Guatemala, Nicaragua, Mexico, Democratic Republic of Congo, Zambia, Spain and Rome, Italy.

[2519] (R.S.M.)—RELIGIOUS SISTERS OF MERCY OF ALMA, MICHIGAN (P)

The Religious Sisters of Mercy of Alma was officially founded on September 1, 1973; Accepted for a foundation in Saginaw Diocese on January 25, 1974; Official pontifical status and approval of Constitutions on June 18, 1982. Final approval of Constitutions May 31, 1991.

Motherhouse and Novitiate: *Religious Sisters of Mercy*, 1965 Michigan Ave., Alma, MI 48801. Tel: 989-463-6035.

Total in Community: 86.

Represented in the Archdioceses of Denver, Portland in Oregon, St. Louis and Washington and in the Dioceses of Knoxville, Lansing, Saginaw, Tulsa and Winona. Also in Australia, Germany and Italy.

[2549] (R.S.M.)—SISTERS OF MERCY (P)

Founded in Ireland in 1831. First foundation in the United States in 1956.

General Motherhouse: *Congregation of the Sisters of Mercy*, 13/14 Moyle Park, Clondalkin, Dublin 22, Ireland Tel: 01-467-3737. Sr. Coirle McCarthy, Supr. Gen.

Total in Congregation: 2770.

U.S. Provincial House: *Sisters of Mercy*, 1075 Bermuda Dr., Redlands, CA 92374. Tel: 909-798-4747; Fax: 909-798-5300. Sr. Rosaline O'Connor, R.S.M., Prov. Supr.

Professed Sisters in U.S. Province: 78.

Legal Title: *Congregation of the Sisters of Mercy-San Bernardino.*

Ministry in the field of Religious Education; Parishes; Social Services; Diocesan Offices

Represented in the Archdioceses of Chicago, Miami and St. Louis and in the Dioceses of Biloxi, Memphis, Mobile, Monterey, Oakland, Orange, Orlando, Palm Beach, Providence, Rapid City, Reno, Sacramento, St. Augustine, San Diego, San Jose, Santa Rosa, San Bernardino, Sioux Falls and Venice.

Sisters of Mercy (1971): 5392 S.W. 33rd Ave., Fort Lauderdale, FL 33312. Tel: 954-989-8291. Sr. Rosaline O'Connor, R.S.M., Prov. Supr.

Total in Community: 4.

Ministry in the field of Education and Parish Work.

Represented in the Archdiocese of Miami.

U.S. Foundation: *St. Joan of Arc*, 500 S.W. 4th Ave., Boca Raton, FL 33432. Tel: 561-368-6655. Sr. Rosaline O'Connor, R.S.M., Prov. Supr.

Professed Sisters: 4.

Represented in the Diocese of Palm Beach.

[2575] (R.S.M.)—SISTERS OF MERCY OF THE AMERICAS (P)

Catherine McAuley founded the Sisters of Mercy in Dublin, Ireland, in 1831. Ten years later, she received confirmation of the Rule by Pope Gregory XVI. In 1843 the Sisters of Mercy established their first U.S.A. foundation in Pittsburgh, followed by various amalgamations. In 1991 the members of the nine provinces of the Union and of 16 other Mercy congregations founded the Sisters of Mercy of the Americas consisting of 25 regional communities.

In 2009, the Sisters of Mercy of the Americas completed a restructuring of the 25 Regional Communities into six communities within the Institute: Caribbean, Central America, South America Community; Mid-Atlantic Community; Northeast Community; New York, Pennsylvania, Pacific West Community; West Midwest Community and South Central Community. The Sisters of Mercy of the Americas are represented in: Argentina, the Bahamas, Belize, Bolivia, Canada, Chile, Guam, Guatemala, Guyana, Haiti, Honduras, Ireland, Jamaica, Panama, Peru, the Philippines, Puerto Rico, South Africa, the United States of America, and West Africa.

Institute Administrative Offices: 8380 Colesville Rd., #300, Silver Spring, MD 20910-6264. Tel: 301-587-0423; Fax: 301-587-0533.

Total in Congregation: 3677.

Legal Title: *Sisters of Mercy of the Americas, Inc.*

Mercy Action, Inc. is separately incorporated to support works directed toward systemic change.

Mercy Volunteer Corps, Inc. is separately incorporated to conduct a volunteer lay ministry program to further the works of mercy.

Conference for Mercy High Education, Inc., is separately incorporated for the purpose of support, coordination and facilitation of the ministry and educational mission of the institutions of higher education recognized by the Sisters of Mercy of the Americas.

Institute Leadership Team Sr. Patricia McDermott, R.S.M., Pres.; Sr. Eileen Campbell, R.S.M.; Sr. Anne Curtis, R.S.M.; Sr. Mary Patricia Garvin, R.S.M., Vice Pres.; Sr. Deborah Troillett, R.S.M.

Sisters of Mercy of the Americas, CCASA (Caribbean, Central America, South America) Community: 8380 Colesville Rd., #300, Silver Spring, MD 20910-6264. Tel: 301-587-0423; Fax: 301-587-0533. Community Leadership Team Sr. Dina Altamiranda, R.S.M., Pres.; Sr. Julie Matthews, R.S.M., Vice Pres.; Sr. Carolee Chanona, R.S.M.; Sr. Patricia Mulderick, R.S.M.

Total in Community: 81.

Legal Title: *Sisters of Mercy of the Americas, CCASA Community, Inc.*

Sisters of Mercy of the Americas, Northeast Community, Inc: 15 Highland View Rd., Cumberland, RI 02864-1124. Tel: 401-333-6333; Fax: 401-333-6450. Community Leadership Team: Sr. Lindora Cabral, R.S.M., Pres.; Sr. Jacqueline Marie Kieslich, R.S.M., Vice Pres.; Sr. Patricia Sullivan, R.S.M.; Sr. Donna Conroy, R.S.M.; Sr. Kathleen Turley, R.S.M.; Gerald Sullivan, COO; Angela Gaffney, Dir. Communications; Sr. Kathleen Pritty, R.S.M., Dir. Justice; Susan Jenkinson, Dir. Ministry; Nancy Bancroft, Assoc. Dir. Ministry; Sr. Ann McGovern, R.S.M., Dir. Vocation & Incorporation; Sr. Patricia Moriarty, R.S.M., Incorporation Minister; Sr. Dale Jarvis, R.S.M., Dir. Vocation & Incorporation; Sr. Eleanor Little, R.S.M., Archivist; Deborah Wallace, Human Resources Mgr.

Vowed Members: 768; Assoc. Members: 393.

Legal Title: *Sisters of Mercy of the Americas-Northeast Community, Inc.*

Ministry in the field of spirituality & retreat work; diocesan & pastoral services; peace & justice initiatives; parish ministry; religious & academic education at all levels; hospitals & health care services/facilities; literacy centers; hospitality houses; nursing homes; social services; counseling services; transitional houses & foreign missionary work.

Sponsored Ministries: Colleges & Universities: Maria College, Albany, NY; Marian Court College, Swampscott, MA; St. Joseph's College, Standish, ME; St. Joseph College, West Hartford, CT; Salve Regina University, Newport, RI.

Secondary Education: Catherine McAuley High School, Portland, ME; Lauralton Hall, Milford, CT; St. Mary Academy, Bay View, PreK-12, Riverside, RI.

Elementary Education: Mater Christi School, Burlington, VT; Mercymount Country Day School, Cumberland, RI; Mount Saint Mary Academy, Manchester, NH.

Hospitals & Health Care Services: St. Peter's Hospital, Albany, NY; St. Peter's Health Care, Albany, NY; St. Peter's Hospital Foundation, Albany, NY; The Community Hospice, Rensselaer, NY; Mercy Cares for Kids, Albany, NY; Our Lady of Mercy Life Center, Guilderland, NY; St. Peters Nursing and Rehabilitation Center, Albany, NY; McAuley Living Services, Albany, NY; Mercy Health System of Maine/Mercy Hospital, Portland, ME; Mercy Community Health System, West Hartford, CT; Saint Mary Home, West Hartford, CT; The McAuley, Inc., West Hartford, CT; Mercy

Community Home Care Services, West Hartford, CT; Warde Health Center, Windham, NH; McAuley Residence, Portland, ME; Gary's House, Portland, ME; Visiting Nurses Association, Portland, ME; Mount Saint Rita Health Centre, Cumberland, RI.
Housing & Shelter: Mercy Housing and Shelter, Hartford, CT; Frances Warde House, Manchester, NH; McAuley Commons, Windham, NH.
Social Services: Circles of Mercy, Albany, NY; McAuley Corporation, Providence, RI; Mercy Connections, Burlington, VT.
Spirituality Centers & Retreat Houses: Mercy Center at Madison, Madison, CT.
Represented in the Archdioceses of Anchorage, Baltimore, Boston, Chicago, Hartford, Miami, Newark, New York, Omaha, Santa Fe, St. Louis, and Washington and in the Dioceses of Albany, Bridgeport, Brooklyn, Burlington, Fall River, Manchester, Norwich, Palm Beach, Pensacola-Tallahassee, Pittsburgh, Portland (ME), Providence, Richmond, St. Augustine, Springfield (MA), Syracuse and Worcester. Also in Belize, Haiti, Honduras and Guatemala.

Institute of the Sisters of Mercy of the Americas, Mid-Atlantic Community, Inc: 273 Willoughby Ave., Brooklyn, NY 11205. Tel: 718-622-5750. Sr. Christine McCann, R.S.M., Pres.
Total in Community: 1072.
Properties owned or sponsored: mercyFirst, Angel Guardian Campus; Mercy Home for Children; Catherine McAuley High School, Brooklyn, NY; mercyFirst, Syosset Campus; Our Lady of Mercy Academy, Syosset
Sisters serve and staff: Elementary and High Schools; Institutions of Higher Education; Child Care Institutions; Pastoral Ministry Programs and Spirituality and Retreat Programs.
Represented in the Archdioceses of Baltimore and Detroit and in the Dioceses of Brooklyn, Orlando and Rockville Centre.

Sisters of Mercy of the Americas (New York, Pennsylvania, Pacific West Community: 625 Abbott Rd., Buffalo, NY 14220. Tel: 716-826-5051; Fax: 716-826-1518; Email: nhoff@mercynyppaw.org; Web: www.mercynyppaw.org.
Total in Community: 463; Associates: 414.
Legal Title: *Sisters of Mercy of the Americas - New York, Pennsylvania, Pacific West Community, Inc.*
Ministry in the fields of spirituality and retreat work, diocesan and pastoral services, peace and justice initiatives, parish ministry; religious and academic education at all levels; hospitals and health care services/facilities, literacy centers, hospitality houses, social services; counseling services; transitional houses and foreign missionary work.
Properties owned sponsored or co-sponsored: Carlow University, Pittsburgh, PA; Mercyhurst College, Erie, PA; Trocaire College, Buffalo, NY; Our Lady of Mercy High School, Rochester, NY; Mercyhurst Preparatory School, Erie, PA; Mt. Mercy Academy, Buffalo, NY; Notre Dame High School, Elmira, NY; The Campus School of Carlow University, Pittsburgh, PA; Mercy Center of the Arts, Erie, PA; Pittsburgh Mercy Health System, Pittsburgh, PA; Holy Cross Hospital, Ft. Lauderdale, FL; Catholic Health System, Buffalo, NY; St. James Mercy Health System, Hornell, NY; Mercy Terrace Apartments, Erie, PA; Mercy Community Services - Rochester dba Mercy Residential Service; Erie DAWN, Inc., Erie, PA; Mercy Center for Women, Erie, PA; Sisters Place, Pittsburgh, PA dba Mercy Outreach Center; Mercy Hilltop Center, Inc. Erie, PA; Mercy Prayer Center, Rochester, NY; Mercy Outreach Ministries Inc.
Represented in the Archdioceses of Miami, San Juan and Washington and in the Dioceses of Bridgeport, Buffalo, Erie, Fall River, MA, Laredo, Orlando, Palm Beach, Phoenix, Pittsburgh, Rochester and Youngstown. Also in the Philippine Islands.
Community Leadership Team Sr. Nancy Hoff, R.S.M., Pres.; Sr. Patricia Prinzing, R.S.M., Vice Pres.; Sr. JoAnne Courneen, R.S.M.; Sr. Guadalupe Lumantas, R.S.M.; Sr. Geraldine Rosinski, R.S.M.

Mid-Atlantic Community, Convent of Mercy: *Convent of the Sisters of Mercy*, 515 Montgomery Ave., Merion Station, PA 19066. Tel: 610-664-6650; Fax: 610-664-3429; Email: info@marcymidatlantic.org.
Vowed Members: 1034; Associates: 940.
Legal Title: *Sisters of Mercy of the Americas, Mid-Atlantic Community, Inc.*
Ministry in the field of religious and academic education at all levels; health care services and facilities; social services; parish and pastoral ministry; spirituality & retreat work; housing; counseling & foreign missionary work.
Sponsored Ministries: Colleges and Universities: Georgian Court University, Lakewood, NJ; Gwynedd Mercy College, Gwynedd Valley, PA: Misericordia University, Dallas, PA; Mt. Aloysius College, Cresson PA.
Secondary Education: Catherine McAuley High School, Brooklyn, NY; Our Lady of Mercy Academy, Syosset, NY; St. Catharine Academy, Bronx, NY; Our Lady of Victory Academy, Dobbs Ferry, NY; Mount Saint Mary Academy, Watchung, NJ; Gwynedd Mercy Academy, Gwynedd Valley, PA; Merion Mercy Academy, Merion, PA; Mercy Vocational High School, Philadelphia, PA; Walsingham Academy, Williamsburg, VA.
Elementary Education: Sisters Academy, Asbury Park, NJ; Waldron Mercy Academy, Merion, PA; Gwynedd Mercy Academy, Gwynedd Valley, PA; Walsingham Academy, Williamsburg, VA.
Special Education: McAuley School for Exceptional Children, Watchung, NJ.
Hospitals & Health Care Services: Mercy Health Partners, Scranton, PA; Mercy Hospital, Scranton, PA; Mercy Special Care Hospital, Naticoke, PA; Mercy Tyler Hospital, Tunkhannock, PA; Mercy Health System of Southeastern PA, Conshohocken, PA; Mercy Philadelphia Hospital, Philadelphia, PA; Mercy Fitzgerald Hospital, Darby, PA; Mercy Suburban Hospital, Norristown, PA; McAuley Hall, Watchung, NJ; Marian Woods, Hartsdale, NY; Mercy Center, Dallas, PA; Mercy Medical Mission, Baltimore, MD; Mercy Care for the Adirondacks, Lake Placid, NY.
Social Services: Mercy Home, Brooklyn, NY; Mercy First, Syosset, NY; Mercy First Angel Guardian Campus, Brooklyn, NY; Mercy Consultation Services, Dallas, PA; Project Remain, Wilkes Barre, PA; Catherine McAuley Center, Scranton, PA; Mercy Institute of Education Development, Dallas, PA; Mercy Center, Asbury Park, NJ; Mercy Center Bronx, NY; The Pines at Mercy Center, Dallas, PA; Dorothy Bennett Center, Brooklyn, NY; Mercy Services, Wilkes Barre, PA.
Spiritual Centers and Retreat Houses: Mount St. Mary House of Prayer, Watchung, NJ; Cranaleith Spiritual Center, Philadelphia, PA; Mercy Consultation Center, Dallas, PA.
Represented in the Archdioceses of Anchorage, Atlanta, Baltimore, Boston, Newark, Philadelphia, St. Louis, New York, San Francisco and Washington and in the Dioceses of Allentown, Altoona-Johnstown, Brooklyn, Camden, Cedar Rapids, Fort Lauderdale, Harrisburg, Hartford, Laredo, Metuchen, Ogdensburg, Paterson, Phoenix, Providence, Richmond, Rockville Centre, Sacramento, Scranton, Tampa, Trenton, Tucson, Wilmington and Worcester. Also in La Paz, Bolivia, Georgetown and Guyana.
Community Leadership Team: Sr. Christine McCann, R.S.M., Pres.; Sr. Patricia Vetrano, R.S.M., Vice Pres.; Sr. Catherine McGroarty, R.S.M., Treas.; Sr. Carol Conly, R.S.M.; Sr. Honora Nicholson, R.S.M.; Sr. Mary Waters, R.S.M.; Ruth Thomas, COO; William DeFeo, Dir. Finance; Debbi DellaPorta, Dir. Communications; Sr. Diane Guerin, R.S.M., Dir. Justice; Sr. Margaret Taylor, R.S.M., Dir. Sponsorship; Sr. Sheila Tynan, R.S.M., Dir. Ministry; Sr. Regina Ward, R.S.M.; Sr. Anne Kappler, R.S.M., Dir. Vocation; Sr. Marguerite Pessagno, R.S.M.; Sr. Therese Condon, R.S.M., Dir. Incorporation; Maureen Skorupa, Archivist.

Sisters of Mercy of the Americas Mid-Atlantic Community: 150 Ridge Rd., Hartsdale, NY 10530. Tel: 914-328-3200; Fax: 914-328-3761. Sr. Patricia Vetrano, R.S.M., Pres.
Total in Community: 999.
Legal Title: *Institue of the Sisters of Mercy of the Americas, Mid-Atlantic Community.*
Ministry in the field of Academic Education at all levels; Health and Child care; Special Education; Social Services; Spirituality and Counseling centers; Catechetical services; Pastoral Ministry.
Properties owned and/or sponsored: St. Catharine Academy, NY; Mercy Center, Bronx, NY.
Represented in the Archdioceses of Hartford, Los Angeles and New York and in the Dioceses of Ogdensburg, Rockville Centre and Worcester.

Sisters of Mercy of the Americas, South Central Community: 101 Mercy Dr., Belmont, NC 28012. Tel: 704-829-5260; Fax: 704-829-5267; Email: info@mercysc.org; Web: www.mercysc.org.
Total in Community: 658.
Legal Title: *Sisters of Mercy of the Americas, South Central Community, Inc.*
Ministry in the following areas: Education: Daycare and Preschool Centers; Elementary Schools; High Schools; Institutions of Higher Education; Special Education; Education Research Programs; Schools for Exceptional Children; Adult Education.
Healthcare: Hospitals; Ambulatory Health Care Center; Long Term Care; Multi-Level Long-Term Care Facility and Health Systems; Urgent Care Centers.
Social Services: Developmental Center for Handicapped Children; Social Work Centers; Care and Counseling; AIDS Ministry.
Retreat/Renewal Centers: Psycho-Spiritual Programs, Conference/Retreat Centers.
Housing: Homes for Aged; Transitional housing for women and children.
Parish Ministry: Pastoral Ministry Programs; Parish ministry; Diocesan ministry.
Properties owned, sponsored or co-sponsored: Alpha Academy, Kingston, Jamaica, WI; Alpha Boys' School, Kingston, Jamaica, WI; Alpha Infant School, Kingston, Jamaica, WI; Alpha Primary School, Kingston, Jamaica, WI; Jessie Ripoll Primary School, Kingston, Jamaica, WI; Mt. St. Joseph Prep School, Manchester, Jamaica, WI; St. John Bosco Children's Home, Manchester, Jamaica, WI; Well of Mercy, Inc. Hamptonville, NC; Holy Angels, Belmont, NC; House of Mercy, Belmont, NC; Catherine's House, Belmont, NC; Sisters of Mercy of NC Foundation, Inc., Charlotte, NC; Sisters of Mercy Services Corporation, Asheville, NC; Mercy Heights Nursery-K, Tamuning, GU; Our Lady of the Pines Retreat Center, Fremont, OH; Mercy Villa Convent, Inc., Murphy Initiative for Justice and Peace, Baltimore, MD; Mount Saint Agnes College; Mercy Villa; Mercy High School, Baltimore, MD; Mount Saint Agnes Theological Center for Women, Baltimore, MD; St. Joseph's Health System, Atlanta (CHE), Atlanta, GA; Marian House, Baltimore, MD; Mount de Sales Academy, Macon, GA; Mercy Medical, Inc. Daphne (CHE), Daphne, AL; St. Mary's Health Care System, Inc. (CHE), Athens, GA; Sisters Academy of Baltimore, Baltimore, MD; The Savannah Institute of the Sisters of Mercy, Inc.; (St. Vincent's Academy), Savannah, GA; Mercy Health Services & (Mercy Medical Center & Stella Maris), Baltimore, MD; St. Joseph's/Candler Health System, Savannah, GA; Catholic Health East, Newtown Square, PA; Mercy Action Marianas, Ltd., Tamuning, GU; Infant of Prague Nursery-K, Mangilao, GU; Academy of Our Lady of Mercy, Inc., Louisville, KY; Assumption High School, Inc.; Louisville, KY; McAuley High School, Inc., Cincinnati, OH; Mother of Mercy High School, Inc., Cincinnati, OH; Mercy Montessori Center, Cincinnati, OH; Mercy Neighborhood Ministries, Cincinnati, OH; Sisters of Mercy of Jamaica, West Indies, Kingston, Jamaica, West Indies; Catholic Healthcare Partners (CHP), Cincinnati, OH; McAuley LLC, Louisville, KY; Mercy Conference and Retreat Center, St. Louis, MO; Our Lady of Wisdom, New Orleans, LA; Mount St. Mary Academy, Little Rock, AR; Mercy Crest Housing, Inc., Barling, AR; Mount Saint Mary High School, Oklahoma City, OK; Arise - Support Center, Alamo, TX; Arise - Muniz, Edinburg, TX; Arise - Las Milpas, Pharr, TX; Arise - South Tower, Alamo, TX; Mercy Housing, Inc., Denver, CO.
Represented in the Archdioceses of Agana (GU), Atlanta, Baltimore, Boston, Cincinnati, Detroit, Louisville, Mobile, New Orleans, New York, Oklahoma City, St. Louis, San Antonio, Seattle and Washington and in the Dioceses of Arlington, Belleville, Biloxi, Birmingham, Brownsville, Caroline Islands, Charlotte, Cleveland, Fort Worth, Jackson, Knoxville, Lansing, Laredo, Las Cruces, Little Rock, Lubbock, Memphis, Metuchen, Nashville, Orlando, Pensacola-Tallahassee, Portland in Maine, Portland in Oregon, Richmond, St. Petersburg, Savannah, Springfield-Cape Girardeau, Toledo, Trenton, Wichita and Wilmington. Also in Jamaica, West Indies and Guyana.
Leadership Team: Sr. Kathy Green, R.S.M., Pres.; Sr. Jane Mary Hotstream, R.S.M., Vice Pres.; Sr. Marie Chin, R.S.M.; Sr. Angela Perez, R.S.M.; Sr. Barbara Wheeley, R.S.M.; Sr. Paulette Williams, R.S.M.

Sisters of Mercy of the Americas, West Midwest Community: 7262 Mercy Rd., Omaha, NE 68124-2389. Tel: 402-393-8225; Fax: 402-393-8145; Email: info@mercywmw.org; Web: www.mercywestmidwest.org. Community Leadership Team: Sr. Judith Frikker, R.S.M., Substitute for Pres. Team Members: Sr. Judith Cannon, R.S.M.; Sr. Michelle Gorman, R.S.M.; Sr. Sheila Megley, R.S.M.; Sr. Kathy Thornton, R.S.M.
Total in Community: 740; Total Number of Associates: 536.
Legal Title: *Sisters of Mercy of the Americas West Midwest Community, Inc.*
Ministry in the following areas: field of spirituality & retreat work; diocesan & pastoral services; peace & justice initiatives; parish ministry; religious & academic education at all levels; hospitals and healthcare services/facilities; literacy centers and programs; hospitality houses; nursing homes; social services; counseling services; transitional houses; foreign ministry work; prison ministry; long-term care facilities for the aged; housing for families and elderly.
Sponsored Ministries (city listed indicates central administrative location of the ministry. Some ministries may have multiple locations): Colleges and Higher Education: Mount Mercy University, Cedar Rapids, IA; Saint Xavier University, Chicago, IL; University of Detroit Mercy, Detroit, MI (co-sponsor); College of Saint Mary, Omaha, NE (affiliated/historical partner). Secondary Education: Cristo Rey High School, Sacramento, CA (co-sponsor); Mercy Education Resource Center, Sacramento, CA; Mercy Education Project, Detroit, MI; Mercy High School, Burlingame, CA; Mercy High School, San Francisco, CA; Mercy High School, Detroit, MI; Mercy High School, Omaha, NE; Mother McAuley Liberal Arts High School, Chicago, IL.
Hospitals & Healthcare Services (city listed indicates central administrative location of the ministry. Some ministries may have multiple locations): Catholic Health Initiatives, Denver, CO (co-sponsor); Catholic Health Ministries/Trinity Health, Novi, MI (participating entity); Catholic Healthcare West, San Francisco, CA (co-sponsor); Mercy Health System of Chicago, Chicago, IL; Mercy Hospital, Iowa City, IA; Mercy Medical Center, Cedar Rapids, IA; Provena Health, Chicago, IL (co-sponsor); Scripps Mercy Chula Vista Hospital, Chula Vista, CA; Scripps Mercy Hospital, San Diego, CA; Elder Care Alliance, Oakland, CA (co-sponsor); and Mercy Retirement and Care Center, Oakland, CA. Mercy Circle, Chicago, IL; Housing & Shelter: Mercy Housing, Inc., Denver, CO (co-sponsor); St. Catherine Residence, Milwaukee, WI; Social Services: Catherine McAuley Center, Cedar Rapids, IA; Development: Mercy Foundation Sacramento, Rancho Cordova, CA; and Mercy Foundation North, Redding, CA. Spirituality/Retreat Centers: Knowles Mercy Spirituality Center, Waterloo, NE; Mercy Center, Auburn, CA; Mercy Center, Burlingame, CA.
Represented in the Archdioceses of Baltimore, Chicago, Denver, Detroit, Dubuque, Hartford, Los Angeles, Louisville, Milwaukee, New York, Omaha, Portland in Oregon, Santa Fe, Seattle, St. Louis, St. Paul-Minneapolis, San Francisco and Washington and in the Dioceses of Altoon-Johnstown, Baton Rouge, Boise, Charleston, Charlotte, Colorado Springs, Davenport, Des Moines, El Paso, Fresno, Gaylord, Grand Rapids, Great Falls-Billings, Helena, Jefferson City, Joliet, Kalamazoo, Kansas City-St. Joseph, Knoxville, Lansing, Laredo, Lexington, Lincoln, Monterey, Oakland, Orange, Peoria, Phoenix, Pueblo, Rockford, Sacramento, Saginaw, San Bernardino, San Diego, San Jose, Sioux City, Springfield-Cape Girardeau, Stockton, Wheeling-Charleston and Winona. Also in Ireland, Peru, South Africa, Sudan, and Uganda.

[2590] (H.M.S.S.)—MERCEDARIAN SISTERS OF THE BLESSED SACRAMENT (P)
(Hermanas Mercedarias del Santisimo Sacramento)

Founded in Mexico in 1910. First foundation in the United States in 1926.

Mercedarian Sisters of the Blessed Sacrament: 227 Keller St., San Antonio, TX 78204. Tel: 210-223-5013; Fax: 210-444-0779.

General Motherhouse: Fernandez Leal #130, Coyoacan, Mexico, 04330. Sr. M. Ma. de la Luz Acosta, H.M.S.S., Supr. Gen.; Sr. Teresa Paz, H.M.S.S., Local Supr.

Regional House: 234 W. Cevallos St., San Antonio, TX 78204. Tel: 210-222-1354.

Professed Sisters in the U.S: 31.

Represented in the Archdiocese of San Antonio and in the Dioceses of Baton Rouge, Cleveland, Corpus Christi and San Diego.

[2600] (R.S.M.)—SISTERS OF MERCY (D)

Founded in the United States in 1960.

General Motherhouse: *Congregation of the Sisters of Mercy*, 13/14 Moyle Park, Convent Rd., Clondalkin, Dublin 22, Ireland Sr. Coirle McCarthy, Supr. Gen.

U.S. Address: *Sacred Heart Convent*, 6240 105th St., Jacksonville, FL 32244. Tel: 904-771-3858. Sr. Patricia O'Hea, Contact Person.

Represented in the Diocese of St. Augustine.

[2630] (S.C.S.C.)—SISTERS OF MERCY OF THE HOLY CROSS (P)

Founded in Switzerland in 1856. First foundation in the U.S. in 1912.

General Motherhouse: Ingenbohl, Switzerland Sr. Marjia Brizar, S.C.S.C., Supr. Gen.

U.S. Provincial Office: *Holy Cross Sisters*, 1400 O'Day St., Merrill, WI 54452. Tel: 715-539-1460; Fax: 715-539-1458. Sr. Celine Goessl, S.C.S.C., Prov.

Total in Community: 33.

Legal Title: Sisters of Mercy of the Holy Cross of Merrill, WI, Inc.; Sponsored Institution: Bell Tower Residence, Inc.

Ministry in the following areas: Schools; Hospitals; Social Ministries and Parishes; Retirement Homes; Adult Education; Campus Ministries; Prison Ministry.

Represented in the Archdioceses of Cincinnati and New Orleans and in the Dioceses of Belleville, La Crosse and Superior.

[2655] (R.S.M.)—DIOCESAN SISTERS OF MERCY OF PORTLAND (D)

Motherhouse: *Diocesan Sisters of Mercy of Portland*, 265 Cottage Rd., South Portland, ME 04106. Tel: 207-767-5804. Sr. Carol Le Tourneau, R.S.M.

[2670] (S.O.L.M.)—SISTERS OF OUR LADY OF MERCY (P)
(Mercedarians)

General Motherhouse: via Ostriana 24, Rome, Italy Mother Igina Caddori, Supr. Gen.

Brooklyn: *Most Precious Blood*, 133 27th Ave., Brooklyn, NY 11214. Sr. Doloretta, Supr.

Sisters: 6.

Represented in the Dioceses of Brooklyn and St. Petersburg.

[2675] (C.F.M.M.)—MINIM DAUGHTERS OF MARY IMMACULATE (P)

Founded in Leon, Guanajuato, Mexico 1886. Came to the United States in 1926.

U.S. Regional House: *Minim Daughters of Mary Immaculate*, 555 Patagonia Hwy., Nogales, AZ 85628. Tel: 520-287-3377; Fax: 520-287-2910. Sr. Rosa Maria Ruiz, C.F.M.M., Reg. Supr.

Total Sisters in the U.S: 17.

Properties owned and/or sponsored: Lourdes Catholic School, Nogales, AZ.

Ministry in Academic and Religious Education and Health Care.

Represented in the Diocese of Tucson.

[2677] (S.M.M.I.)—SISTERS MINOR OF MARY IMMACULATE (D)

First foundation in the United States June 13, 1989. Active- contemplative Franciscan Religious Congregation following the spirituality of St. Maximilian Mary Kolbe, O.F.M.Conv. and St. Terese of Liseux.

Central Motherhouse & Novitiate: Via Germanico 198, Rome, Italy, 00192. Tel: 011-39-06-324-2036. Maria Elisabetta Patrizi, Foundress.

American Headquarters - St. Francis Villa: 305 Washington Blvd., Stamford, CT 06902. Tel: 203-323-4546. Sr. Kathleen Howard, S.M.M.I., U.S. Delegate.

Legal Title: *Sisters Minor of Mary Immaculate.*

Ministry in the field of Academic and Religious Education; Health Care; Pastoral Care; Care to the elderly, youths, widows and immigrants.

Represented in the Archdiocese of Hartford, and in the Diocese of Bridgeport.

[2680] (S.M.)—MISERICORDIA SISTERS (P)

Founded in Canada in 1848. First foundation in the United States in 1887.

General Motherhouse: 12435 Misericorde Ave., Montreal, Canada, H4J 2G3. Tel: 514-332-0550. Sr. Monique Lallier, S.M., Supr.

U.S. Address: 225 Carol Ave., Pelham, NY 10803. Sr. Ellen Hunt, S.M., Supr.

Represented in the Archdiocese of New York.

[2690] (M.C.D.P.)—MISSIONARY CATECHISTS OF DIVINE PROVIDENCE, SAN ANTONIO, TEXAS (P)

Autonomy with Pontifical status granted December 12, 1989.

Administrative House: *St. Andrew's Convent*, 2318 Castroville Rd., San Antonio, TX 78237. Tel: 210-432-0113; Fax: 210-432-1709. Sr. Carmen M. Sanchez, M.C.D.P., Supr.

Total in Community: 38.

Properties owned or sponsored: 4650 Eldridge Ave., San Antonio, TX.

Represented in the Archdioceses of Galveston-Houston and San Antonio and in the Dioceses of Austin, Brownsville, Corpus Christi, Dallas, Dodge City, Fort Worth, Fresno, Grand Island, San Angelo, San Diego and San Jose.

[2700] (M.C.S.H.)—MISSIONARY CATECHISTS OF THE SACRED HEARTS OF JESUS AND MARY (D)

Founded in Mexico City, D.F. in 1918. U.S. foundation in 1943 in Victoria, Texas.

Central House: Mexico City, Mexico Sr. Laura M. Solano, Supr. Gen.

Immaculate Heart of Mary Province: 203 E. Sabine St., Victoria, TX 77901. Tel: 361-570-3332; Fax: 361-570-3377. Sr. Miriam Perez, M.C.S.H., Prov. Supr.

Total number in U.S. Province: 42.

Ministry in Catechetical family ministry in parishes and missions.

Represented in the Archdiocese of Galveston-Houston and in the Dioceses of Fort Worth, Lubbock, Metuchen and Victoria.

[2710] (M.C.)—MISSIONARIES OF CHARITY (P)

Founded in India, 1950.

General Motherhouse: 54A AJC Bose Rd., Kolkata, India, 700016. Sr. M. Prema, M.C., Supr. Gen.

U.S. Foundation & Office (1971): *Missionaries of Charity*, 335 E. 145th St., Bronx, NY 10451. Tel: 718-292-0019. Sr. Rose Clara, M.C., Reg. Supr.

Professed Sisters in Congregation: 5029.

Legal Title: *Missionaries of Charity, Inc.*

Sisters serve and staff: Soup Kitchens; Emergency Shelters for Women; Homes for Unwed Mothers; Shelters for Unwed Mothers; Shelters for Men; Religious Education Programs; After-School and Summer Camp Programs for Children; Homes for AIDS Patients; Prison Ministry; Nursing Homes; Hospital and Shut-in Ministry; Family Counseling and Ministry; Foreign Missionary Work.

Represented in the Archdioceses of Atlanta, Baltimore, Boston, Chicago, Denver, Detroit, Galveston-Houston, Indianapolis, Los Angeles, Miami, New York, Newark, Philadelphia, San Francisco, St. Louis, St. Paul-Minneapolis and Washington and in the Dioceses of Baton Rouge, Bridgeport, Brooklyn, Charlotte, Dallas, Fall River, Gallup, Gary, Lafayette, Lexington, Little Rock, Memphis, Peoria, Phoenix, Sacramento. Spokane and Trenton. Also in Canada, Mexico, Central America and South America.

[2715] (M.CH.R.)—MISSIONARY SISTERS OF CHRIST THE KING FOR POLONIA (P)

Founded in Poland on November 21, 1959 by Father Ignacy Posadzy, TChr. First foundation in the U.S. 1978.

General Motherhouse: *Siostry Misjonarki Chrystusa Krola dla Polonii*, ul. Siostr Misjonarek 10, Poznan, 50, Poland, 61-680. Sr. Edyta Rychel, M.Ch.R., Supr. Gen.

Total in Congregation: 230.

Delegation Superior in the U.S: *Missionary Sisters of Christ the King for Polonia*, 4910 North Menard Ave., Chicago, IL 60630. Tel: 773-481-1831; Fax: 773-545-4171. Sr. Ewa Biniek, M.Ch.R., Supr.; Sr. Gertruda Szymanska, M.Ch.R., Sec.; Sr. Marta Cichon, M.Ch.R., Treas.

Total in Congregation: 198; Professed in U.S. and Canada: 44.

Legal Title: *Missionary Sisters of Christ the King for Polonia.*

Ministry among Polish immigrants and people of Polish heritage.

Represented in the Archdioceses of Chicago, Detroit and Los Angeles and in the Dioceses of Phoenix and San Jose. Also in Toronto, Brampton, Oshawa, Mississauga and Vancouver, Canada.

[2717] (M.D.P.V.M.)—MISSIONARY DAUGHTERS OF THE MOST PURE VIRGIN MARY (P)

Founded in Mexico. First foundation in the United States in the Diocese of Corpus Christi 1916.

General Motherhouse: *Heroe de Nacocariz*, 721 Sur Aguascalientes, Mexico Mother Rita Ramirez, M.D-.P.V.M., Gen. Supr.

Missionary Daughters of the Most Pure Virgin Mary: 919 N. 9th St., Kingsville, TX 78363. Tel: 361-595-1087. Sr. Consuelo Ramirez, M.D.P.V.M., Supr.; Sr. Carmen Villalpando, M.D.P.V.M., Sec.; Sr. Maximina Cruz, M.D.P.V.M., Treas.

Total in Congregation: 419; Present in U.S: 23.

Legal Title: *Missionary Daughters of the Most Pure Virgin Mary.*

Ministry in the field of Religious and Academic Education at the elementary level; Pastoral Ministry.

Represented in the Dioceses of Camden, Corpus Christi and Yakima.

[2720] (M.H.S.H.)—MISSION HELPERS OF THE SACRED HEART (P)

Founded in the United States in 1890.

Mission Helper Center: 1001 W. Joppa Rd., Baltimore, MD 21204. Tel: 410-823-8585; Fax: 410-825-6355. Sr. Loretta Cornell, M.H.S.H., Pres.

Total in Community: 66.

Legal Title: *Institute of Mission Helpers of Baltimore City.*

Represented in the Archdioceses of Baltimore, Boston, Cincinnati, Indianapolis, San Juan (PR), Seattle and Washington and in the Dioceses of Birmingham, Erie, Orlando, Pittsburgh, Rochester, and Tucson. Also in Venezuela.

[2725] (M.S.E.)—MISSIONARY SISTERS OF THE EUCHARIST

Founded in Guatemala, C.A. in 1975. First foundation in the United States in 2001.

Motherhouse: San Andres Semetabaj, Solola, Guatemala Sr. Marta Esperanza Juracan, M.S.E., Supr. Gen.

Total in Community: 51.

Visitation Convent, Magnificat Houses: 3301 San Jacinto St., Houston, TX 77004. Tel: 713-523-8831.

Mailing Address: P.O. Box 88147, Houston, TX 77288-0147. Sr. Maria Chali, M.S.E., Local Supr.

Ministry in parishes, missionary work, health care and social services.

Represented in the Archdiocese of Galveston-Houston.

[2730] (M.S.H.R.)—MISSIONARY SISTERS OF THE HOLY ROSARY (P)

Generalate (1924): 23 Cross Ave., Blackrock County, Dublin, Ireland Sr. Maureen O'Malley, Congregational Leader.

U.S. Regional Headquarters (1954): *Missionary Sisters of the Holy Rosary*, 741 Polo Rd., Bryn Mawr, PA 19010. Tel: 610-520-1974. Sr. Helena McNeill, Reg. Leader.

Total in Community: 382.

Represented in the Archdiocese of Philadelphia.

[2740] (M.S.SP.)—MISSION SISTERS OF THE HOLY SPIRIT (D)

Motherhouse and Novitiate: 1030 N. River Rd., Saginaw, MI 48609. Tel: 989-781-0934. Sr. Margo Tafoya, Pres.

Total in Community: 7.

Legal Title: *Society of the Mission Sisters of the Holy Spirit of the Diocese of Saginaw Holy Spirit Sisters Charitable Trust, Saginaw, MI.*

Ministry in Religious Education at all levels including Developmentally Disabled; Pastoral Ministry.

Represented in the Diocese of Saginaw.

[2750] (I.C.M.)—MISSIONARY SISTERS OF THE IMMACULATE HEART OF MARY (P)

Founded in India in 1897. First foundation in the United States in 1919.

Generalate: Via Filogaso 40, Rome, Italy, 00173. Sr. Saveria Jeganathan, I.C.M., Supr. Gen.

Universal total in Congregation: 716.

American Province: 238 E. 15th St., #5, New York, NY 10003. Tel: 212-677-2959; Tel: 212-260-8567; Fax: 212-475-7455. Sr. Kathryn Vercelling, I.C.M., Prov.

Total in Community: 13.

Missionaries Minister in Education; Catechetical; Pastoral and Social Ministry; Health Care; Ecology; Leprosaria; International Justice and the Promotion of Human Dignity.

Represented in the Archdiocese of New York and in the Diocese of Brownsville. Also in Belgium, Brazil, Burundi, Cameroon, Guatemala, Hong Kong, India, Italy, Philippines, Taiwan, Mongolia, Caribbean Islands, Congo and Senegal.

[2760] (S.M.I.C.)—MISSIONARY SISTERS OF THE IMMACULATE CONCEPTION OF THE MOTHER OF GOD (P)

Founded in Brazil in 1910. First foundation in the United States in 1922.

Generalate: 47 Garden Ave., Woodland Park, NJ 07424. Tel: 973-279-1484. Sr. Livramento Melo de Oliveira, S.M.I.C., Coord. Gen.

U.S. Province (1960): *Provincialate of the Immaculate Conception*, 779 Broadway, Paterson, NJ 07514. Tel: 973-279-3790. Sr. Eleanor Goekler, S.M.I.C., Prov. Coord.

Professed Sisters: 34.

Legal Titles: Missionary Sisters of the Immaculate Conception, Inc.; Province of the Immaculate Conception, Inc.

Sisters serve and staff: Religious Education; Pastoral Ministries; Health and Social Work.

Represented in the Archdioceses of Newark, New Orleans and Santa Fe and in the Dioceses of Austin, Gallup, Paterson, Portland (In Maine) and San Bernardino.

[2770] (M.J.M.J.)—MISSIONARY SISTERS OF JESUS, MARY AND JOSEPH (P)

Founded in Spain in 1942. First foundation in the United States in 1956. Mother Maria Dolores de la Cruz Domingo, Foundress.

Motherhouse: Plaza Inmaculada Concepcion 1, Madrid, Spain, 28019. Sr. Alicia Elizalde, M.J.M.J., Supr. Gen.

Delegation Headquarters: *Mount Thabor Convent*, 12940 Leopard St., Corpus Christi, TX 78410. Tel: 361-241-1955; Fax: 361-241-2271. Sr. Maria Margarita Bitoni, M.J.M.J., Delegation Supr.; Sr. Milagros Tormo, M.J.M.J., Local Supr.

Sisters: 25.

Properties owned and/or sponsored: St. Joseph of the Valley Preschool, El Paso, TX; The Ark Assessment Center & Emergency Shelter for Youth.

Represented in the Archdiocese of San Antonio and in the Dioceses of Corpus Christi and El Paso. Also in Mexico.

[2780] (M.SS.S.)—MISSIONARY SISTERS OF THE MOST BLESSED SACRAMENT (P)

General Motherhouse: Calle Navarro Amandi, 11, Madrid, Spain, 28033. Mother Leonor Gutierreg, Mother Gen.

U.S. Foundation: *Convent of Mary Immaculate*, 1111 Wordin Ave., Bridgeport, CT 06605. Sr. Presentacios Zabala, Prov.

[2790] (M.S.B.T.)—MISSIONARY SERVANTS OF THE MOST BLESSED TRINITY (P)

Founded in the United States in 1912.

Motherhouse-Generalate-Novitiate and Candidacy: 3501 Solly Ave., Philadelphia, PA 19136. Tel: 215-335-7550. Sr. Joan Marie Keller, M.S.B.T., Gen. Custodian.

Total in Community: 139.

Properties owned and sponsored: Blessed Trinity Mother Missionary Cenacle, Philadelphia, PA; Blessed Trinity Shrine Retreat Cenacle, Holy Trinity, AL; Trinita Ecumenical Retreat Center, New Hartford, CT; Mother Boniface Spirituality Center, Philadelphia, PA.

Represented in the Archdioceses of Baltimore, Chicago, Hartford, Newark, Mobile and Philadelphia and in the Dioceses of Birmingham, Brooklyn, Charlotte, Fall River, Gallup, Owensboro, Paterson, Rockville Centre and Wilmington. Also in Puerto Rico, Mexico, and Jamaica.

[2800] (M.S.C.)—MISSIONARY SISTERS OF THE MOST SACRED HEART OF JESUS (OF HILTRUP) (P)

Founded in Germany in 1899. First foundation in the United States in 1908.

Generalate: Via Martiri di Via Fani, 22, Sutri (Viterbo), Italy, 01015. Sr. Mechthild Schnieder, M.S.C.

American Province-Motherhouse (1908): *Sacred Heart Villa*, 51 Seminary Ave., Reading, PA 19605. Tel: 610-929-5751. Sr. Marie Raymond Gazo, M.S.C., Coord.

Total number in U.S. Province: 64.

Legal Title: *Missionary Sisters of the Most Sacred Heart of Jesus, Inc.*

Ministry in Education; Health Care; Home Health Care; Parish Ministry; Pastoral Ministry to people on the move; Prison Ministry; Counseling; Social Ministry; Spiritual Ministry; Care of the Aged.

Properties owned or sponsored: MSC Province Center; Chevalier House, Bethany Convent, Sacred Heart Villa, Reading, PA.

Represented in the Archdioceses of Atlanta, Galveston-Houston and Philadelphia and in the Dioceses of Allentown, Harrisburg, San Bernardino, Syracuse and Venice. Also in Mexico.

MSC Province Center: 2811 Moyers Ln., Reading, PA 19605. Tel: 610-929-5944. Sr. Mary Anne Bigos, M.S.C., Prov.

[2810] (M.S.M.G.)—MISSIONARY SISTERS OF MOTHER OF GOD (D)

(Byzantine Ukrainian Rite-Stamford)

Motherhouse: 711 N. Franklin St., Philadelphia, PA 19123. Tel: 215-627-7808.

U.S. Province: 111 W. North St., Stamford, CT 06902. Tel: 203-323-1237. Sr. Timothea Konyu, M.S.M.G., Treas.

Professed Sisters: 11.

Ministry in the field of Education.

Represented in the Ukrainian Archdiocese of Philadelphia and in the Ukrainian Diocese of Stamford.

[2820] (M.S.O.L.A.)—MISSIONARY SISTERS OF OUR LADY OF AFRICA (P)

(Sisters of Africa)

Founded in Algiers, N. Africa in 1869. First foundation in the United States in 1929.

General Motherhouse: Rome, Italy Sr. Carmen Sammut, Supr. Gen.

Universal total in Congregation: 806.

American Headquarters: 47 West Spring St., Winooski, VT 05404. Tel: 802-655-2395 Ext. 2242. Sr. Marie Heintz, Contact Person.

Total number in U.S: 13.

Represented in the Dioceses of Burlington and Springfield (MA).

[2830] (M.O.M.)—MISSIONARY SISTERS OF OUR LADY OF MERCY (D)

Founded in Piaui, Brazil in 1938. First foundation in the United States at Lackawanna, New York in 1955.

General Motherhouse: Salvador, Bahia, Brazil Mother Raquel de Novais Borges, Supr. Gen.

U.S. Headquarters: *Rainbow K*, 388 Franklin St., Buffalo, NY 14202. Tel: 716-854-5198. Sr. Mary Neves, M.O.M., Supr.

Total in Community: 2.

Represented in the Diocese of Buffalo.

[2840] (M.C.)—POOR CLARE MISSIONARY SISTERS (P)

Founded in Mexico by Mother Maria Ines Teresa Arias.

General Motherhouse: Via Cardinale Garampi 17, Pineta Sachetti, Rome, Italy Mother Julia Meijueiro Morosini, Gen. Supr.

U.S. Foundation: *Regional House and Novitiate*, 1019 N. Newhope, Santa Ana, CA 92703.

Total in Community: 42.

Ministry in Day Nurseries, Schools and Retreat House.

Represented in the Archdiocese of Los Angeles and in the Dioceses of Orange in California and Springfield-Cape Girardeau.

[2850] (C.P.S.)—MISSIONARY SISTERS OF THE PRECIOUS BLOOD (P)

Founded in South Africa on Sept. 8, 1885. First founded in the United States at Princeton, New Jersey on August 15, 1925.

Generalate: *Casa Generalizia*, Suore Missionarie del Preziosissimo Sangue Mariannhill, Via San Giovanni Eudes 93, Rome, Italy, I-00163.

Universal total in Congregation: 889.

North American Province: 1094 Welsh Rd., P.O. Box 97, Reading, PA 19607-0097. Tel: 610-777-1624. Sr. Mary William Verhoeveu, C.P.S., Prov.

Total number in Province: 60.

Represented in the Dioceses of Allentown, Brooklyn and Lexington. Also in Canada.

[2860] (M.S.C.)—MISSIONARY SISTERS OF THE SACRED HEART OF JESUS (P)

(Cabrini Sisters)

Founded in Italy in 1880, by Saint Frances Xavier Cabrini. First foundation in the United States in 1889.

Motherhouse: Viale Cortina D'Ampezzo 269, Rome, Italy, 00135. Sr. Patricia Spillane, M.S.C., Supr. Gen.

Provincial Office: 222 E. 19th St., 5B, New York, NY 10003. Sr. Pietrina Raccuglia, Prov. Supr.

Professed Sisters: 319; Total in Congregation: 346.

Ministry in the field of Education; Hospitals; Nursing Homes; Child Care; Retreat and Shrine Ministries; Parish Ministry.

Represented in the Archdioceses of Chicago, Denver, New Orleans, New York, Philadelphia and Seattle. Also in Argentina, Australia, Brazil, Central America, England, Ethiopia, France, Italy, Mexico, Paraguay, Philippines, Portugal, Siberia, Spain, Switzerland and Swaziland.

[2865] (M.S.C.GPE.)—MISSIONARIES OF THE SACRED HEART OF JESUS AND OUR LADY OF GUADALUPE (P)

National Address: 1212 E. Euclid Ave., Arlington Heights, IL 60004. Tel: 847-255-5616. Sr. Maria del Carmen Sanchez, Local Supr.

Ministry in Schools, Nursing Homes, Seminaries and Foreign Missions.

Represented in the Archdioceses of Boston, Chicago, San Francisco and Washington and in the Diocese of Joliet.

[2880] (S.S.C.)—MISSIONARY SISTERS OF ST. COLUMBAN (P)

(Columban Sisters)

Founded in Ireland in 1922. First foundation in the United States in 1930.

General Motherhouse: Wicklow, Ireland Sr. Ann Gray, S.S.C., Congregational Leader.

U.S. Region: 73 Mapleton St., Brighton, MA 02135-2821. Tel: 617-782-5683; Fax: 617-789-3569. Sr. Margaret Holleran, S.C.C., U.S. Area Coord.

Professed Sisters: 22.

Represented in the Archdioceses of Boston and Los Angeles and in the Diocese of Buffalo.

[2890] (M.S.S.A.)—MISSIONARY SERVANTS OF ST. ANTHONY (D)

Founded in the United States in 1929.

General Motherhouse: 100 Peter Baque Rd., San Antonio, TX 78209-1805. Tel: 210-824-4553. Sr. Mary Ann Domagalski, M.S.S.A., Supr.

Total in Community: 3.

Represented in the Archdiocese of San Antonio.

[2900] (M.S.C.S.)—MISSIONARY SISTERS OF ST. CHARLES BORROMEO (P)

(Scalabrinians)

Founded in Italy in 1895. Began its mission in the United States in 1941 which developed to be the USA Province, Our Lady of Fatima Province USA.

Motherhouse: Via Monte del Gallo 68, Rome, Italy, 00165. Sr. Alda Monica Malvessi, M.S.C.S., Gen. Supr.

Total in Congregation: 735.

Our Lady of Fatima Province, USA & Bishop Scalabrini Community: 1414 N. 37th Ave., Melrose Park, IL 60160. Tel: 708-343-2162; Fax: 708-343-6452. Sr. Marciana Zambiasi, M.S.C.S., Prov. Supr.; Sr. Marissonia Daltoe, M.S.C.S., First Councilor & Treas.; Sr. Elizabeth Pedernal, M.S.C.S., Councilor & Provincial Sec.; Sr. Noemie Digo, M.S.C.S., Councilor & Coordinator of Formation; Sr. Elisete Teresihna Signor, M.S.C.S., Councilor & Coordinator of Apostolate.

Total in Community: 63.

Ministry in the fields of Education; Pastoral Care of the Sick; Catechesis; Social Service; Pastoral Care of Migrants and Refugees.

Represented in the Archdioceses of Boston, Chicago, New York and Washington. Also in Canada, Mexico, the Philippines, India and Indonesia.

[2920] (M.D.)—MOTHERS OF THE HELPLESS (D)

Founded in Malaga, Spain in 1881. Founded in the United States in 1916.

General Motherhouse: Avda. San Jose de la Montana No. 15, Valencia, Spain, 46008. Mother Maria Angeles Villar, Supr. Gen.

U.S. Address: *Sacred Heart Residence*, 432 W. 20th St., New York, NY 10011. Mother Esperanza Fernandez, Supr.

Professed Sisters in U.S: 6.

Properties owned and sponsored: Sacred Heart Residence; San Jose Day Nursery, New York, NY.

Represented in the Archdiocese of New York.

[2930] (I.H.M.)—THE CALIFORNIA INSTITUTE OF THE SISTERS OF THE MOST HOLY AND IMMACULATE HEART OF THE BLESSED VIRGIN MARY (P)

Founded in Spain in 1848. First foundation in the United States in 1871.

Generalate, Novitiate and Retreat House: 3431 Waverly Dr., Los Angeles, CA 90027. Tel: 323-664-3357 Ext. 114. Sr. Catherine Rose, I.H.M., Supr. & Treas.

Professed Sisters: 9.

Properties staffed: Grammar Schools.

Represented in the Archdiocese of Los Angeles.

[2940] (M.H.S.)—SISTERS OF THE MOST HOLY SACRAMENT (P)

Founded in France in 1851. First foundation in the United States in 1872. Pontifical Approbation 1935.

Generalate: *Sisters of the Most Holy Sacrament*, 313 Corona Dr., Lafayette, LA 70503-4757. Tel: 337-981-8475. Sr. Diane Dornan, M.H.S., Major Supr.

Total in Community: 25.

Legal Titles: St. Augustine Trust Fund, Lafayette, LA; Bethany Health Care Center, Lafayette, LA.

Ministry in the field of Education; Homes for the Aged; Pastoral Care.

Represented in the Dioceses of Baton Rouge and Lafayette (LA).

[2950] (N.D.S.)—CONGREGATION OF NOTRE DAME DE SION (P)

Founded in France in 1850. First foundation in the United States in 1892.

Generalate: Rome, Italy Sr. Maureen Cusick, Supr. Gen.

Universal total in Congregation: 535.

Notre Dame de Sion: 3823 Locust St., Kansas City, MO 64109. Tel: 816-531-1374.

Represented in the Archdiocese of Chicago and in the

Dioceses of Brooklyn and Kansas City-St. Joseph.

[2960] (N.D.)—NOTRE DAME SISTERS (P)

Founded in Czechoslovakia, Europe in 1853. First foundation in the United States in 1910.

General Motherhouse: Hradec Kralove, Czech Republic Mother Miriam Baumrukova, N.D., Supr. Gen.

U.S. Provincial Motherhouse: *Notre Dame Convent*, 3501 State St., Omaha, NE 68112-1709. Tel: 402-455-2994; Fax: 402-455-3974. Sr. Celeste Wobeter, N.D., Prov.

Total in Community: 47.

Sisters serve and staff: all levels of academic education; Hispanic Ministry; Pastoral Care; Housing for low income elderly; Social Work; Religious Education; Youth Ministry; Chemical Dependency Counseling; Health Care; TEC; Adult Education; Community Administration and Services.

Represented in the Archdioceses of Denver, Dubuque and Omaha and in the Dioceses of Davenport, Kansas City-St. Joseph, Lincoln, and Pueblo.

[2970] (S.S.N.D.)—SCHOOL SISTERS OF NOTRE DAME (P)

Founded in Germany in 1833. First foundation in the United States in 1847.

General Motherhouse: Rome, Italy Sr. Mary V. Maher, Supr. Gen.

Milwaukee Province (1850); Milwaukee (1983); Mequon (1959): *Milwaukee Office*, 13105 Watertown Plank Rd., Elm Grove, WI 53122-2291. Tel: 262-782-9850; Fax: 262-782-5725. Sr. Mary Anne Owens, S.S.N.D., Prov. Leader.

Total in Community: 1204.

Properties owned and/or sponsored: Mount Mary College, Milwaukee, WI; Notre Dame of Elm Grove, Elm Grove, WI; Our Lady of Mt. Carmel Convent, Mt. Calvary, WI; Our Lady of the Angels (Co-owners).

Legal Titles: School Sisters of Notre Dame, Inc.; School Sisters of Notre Dame at Milwaukee, Wisconsin, Inc. Charitable Trust.

Various ministries to Women, Youth, the Poor, Sick and Elderly; all levels of Academic Education; D.R.E.'s; Pastoral Associates; Volunteer Services.

Represented in the Archdioceses of Agana, Chicago, Detroit, Milwaukee and Seattle and in the Dioceses of Austin, El Paso, Fort Wayne-South Bend, Gallup, Gary, Grand Rapids, Green Bay, Jefferson City, Kansas City-St. Joseph, La Crosse, Laredo, Madison, Marquette, Phoenix, Steubenville, Trenton, Tucson and Wheeling-Charleston.

Atlantic-Midwest Province: *School Sisters of Notre Dame*, 6401 N. Charles St., Baltimore, MD 21212-1099. Tel: 410-377-7774; Fax: 410-377-5363. Sr. Kathleen Cornell, S.S.N.D., Prov. Leader.

Total in Community: 561.

Properties Owned and Legal Titles: School Sisters of Notre Dame in the City of Baltimore; Maria Health Care Center, Inc.; Atlantic-Midwest Province of the School Sisters of Notre Dame, Inc.; The Northeastern Province of the School Sisters of Notre Dame in the State of Connecticut; Lourdes Health Care Center, Inc.; School Sisters of Chicago Province, Inc.; Atlantic-Midwest Province Endowment Trust; SSND Service Corp.; SSND Care, Inc.; SSND Real Estate Holding Corp.; SSND Real Estate Trust; SSND Continuing Care Trust; SSND Charitable Annuity Trust.

Ministries to the Needy and Elderly; Teaching and Administering in the field of Academic Education at all levels; D.R.E.'s and Pastoral Associates.

Represented in the Archdioceses of Baltimore, Boston, Chicago, Hartford, Los Angeles, Miami, Milwaukee, Newark, New York, Philadelphia and Washington and in the Dioceses of Albany, Bridgeport, Brooklyn, Charleston, Charlotte, Grand Rapids, Jackson, Joliet, LaCrosse, Lexington, Manchester, Norwich, Oakland, Orlando, Palm Beach, Paterson, Peoria, Pittsburgh, Providence, Richmond, Rochester, Rockford, Rockville Centre, St. Petersburg, Trenton, Venice, Wheeling-Charleston, Wichita and Wilmington. Also in Rome, Sudan & Switzerland.

Sponsored Corporate Ministries: College of Notre Dame of Maryland; Notre Dame Preparatory School; Institute of Notre Dame, Baltimore, MD; Academy of the Holy Angels, Demarest, NJ; The Caroline Friess Center, Inc.' Academy of Our Lady, Chicago, Inc.; Caroline House, Inc.; School Sisters of Notre Dame Educational Center, Inc.; SisterHouse; Corazon A Corazon, NFP; Notre Dame Learning Center, Inc.

Co-Sponsored Ministries: Sisters Academy of Baltimore, Inc.; Mother Seton Academy, Inc.; Marian House, Incorporated.

Central Pacific Province (1895): *School Sisters of Notre Dame*, 320 E. Ripa Ave., St. Louis, MO 63125. Tel: 314-544-0455; Fax: 314-544-6754. Sr. Mary Anne Owens, S.S.N.D., Prov. Leader.

Total in Community: 1204.

Legal Title: *School Sisters of Notre Dame Central Pacific Province, Inc.; The School Sisters of Notre Dame of Dallas Charitable Trust; School Sisters of Notre Dame at Mankato, Minnesota, Inc. - Charitable Trust; School Sisters of Notre Dame Cooperative Investment Fund; School Sisters of Notre Dame at Milwaukee, Wisconsin, Inc. Charitable Trust; The School Sisters of Notre Dame of St. Louis Caroline Trust.*

Represented in the Archdioceses of Agana, Baltimore, Chicago, Denver, Detroit, Dubuque, Galveston-Houston, Los Angeles, Milwaukee, New Orleans, St. Louis, St. Paul-Minneapolis, San Antonio and San Francisco and in the Dioceses of Amarillo, Austin, Baton Rouge, Belleville, Bismarck, Brownsville, Charlotte, Dallas, Davenport, El Paso, Evansville, Fort Wayne-South Bend, Fort Worth, Fresno, Gallup, Gary, Grand Rapids, Green Bay, Houma-Thibodaux, Jackson, Jefferson City, Kansas City-St. Joseph, La Crosse, Lafayette in Louisiana, Laredo, Madison, Marquette, Monterey, New Ulm, Oakland, Orange, Peoria, Phoenix, Providence, Rapid City, Richmond, Rockford, St. Cloud, San Diego, San Jose, Springfield-Cape Girardeau, Springfield in Illinois, Steubenville, Superior, Tucson, Wheeling-Charleston and Winona. Also in Japan, Nepal, Sierra Leone and Rome, Italy.

Ministries to the Needy and Elderly; Women and Youth; all levels of Academic Education; D.R.E.'s; Pastoral Associates.

Sponsored/Co-Sponsored Ministries: Notre Dame Education Center (NDEC), Canton, MS; Notre Dame of Dallas School; Good Counsel Learning Center, Mankato, MN; Theresa House, Mankato, MN; Notre Dame Middle School Milwaukee, WI; Milwaukee Achiever; Mount Mary College; TYME OUT, Nashotah, WI; Notre Dame High School (Guam); Progressive Education Program, Inc. (PEPI), New Iberia, LA; MORE, St. Paul, MN; East Side Learning Center, St. Paul, MN; Theresa Living Center, St. Paul, MN; Marian Middle School, St. Louis, MO; Notre Dame High School, St. Louis, MO; Notre Dame Preschool, St. Louis, MO.

Mankato Office (1912): *School Sisters of Notre Dame*, 170 Good Counsel Dr., Mankato, MN 56001-3138. Tel: 507-389-4200; Fax: 507-389-4125. Sr. Mary Anne Owens, S.S.N.D., Prov. Leader; Sr. Mary Kay Ash, Community Archivist.

Total in Community: 1204.

Legal Titles: School Sisters of Notre Dame at Mankato, Minnesota, Inc. - Charitable Trust; School Sisters of Notre Dame Cooperative Investment Fund.

Represented in the Archdioceses of Chicago, Dubuque, New Orleans, Seattle, St. Louis, St. Paul-Minneapolis and San Francisco and in the Dioceses of Bismarck, Charleston, Charlotte, New Ulm, Phoenix, Richmond, San Jose, Superior, St. Cloud, and Winona. Also in Nigeria, Ghana, Guatemala, Kenya and Rome, Italy.

Northeast Office (1957): *School Sisters of Notre Dame, Atlantic-Midwest Province*, 345 Belden Hill Rd., Wilton, CT 06897. Tel: 203-762-1220; Fax: 203-762-9434. Sr. Kathleen Cornell, S.S.N.D., Prov. Leader.

Total in Community: 561.

Legal Holdings and Titles: The Northeastern Province of the School Sisters of Notre Dame in the State of Connecticut; Motherhouse and Lourdes Health Care Center, Wilton, CT; Academy of the Holy Angels, Demarest, NJ.

Represented in the Archdioceses of Baltimore, Boston, Chicago, Hartford, Milwaukee, Newark, New York and Washington and in the Dioceses of Albany, Bridgeport, Brooklyn, Brownsville, Grand Rapids, Manchester, Norwich, Palm Beach, Paterson, Phoenix, Providence, Rochester, Rockville Centre, St. Petersburg and Springfield. Also in Chile, Switzerland, Ghana, Guatemala, Paraguay, Peru and Puerto Rico.

Dallas Office (1961): *Notre Dame of Dallas - School Sisters of Notre Dame*, P.O. Box 227275, Dallas, TX 75222. Tel: 214-330-9152; Fax: 214-330-9197. Sr. Mary Anne Owens, S.S.N.D., Prov. Leader.

Total in Community: 1204.

Legal Title: *School Sisters of Notre Dame of Dallas Charitable Trust.*

Represented in the Archdioceses of Galveston-Houston, New Orleans, San Antonio and St. Louis and in the Dioceses of Amarillo, Baton Rouge, Brownsville, Dallas, Davenport, El Paso, Fort Worth, Houma-Thibodaux, Jackson, Lafayette (LA), Laredo and Tucson.

Chicago Office: *School Sisters of Notre Dame, Atlantic Midwest-Province*, 4425 N. Ozanam Ave., Norridge, IL 60706-4507. Tel: 708-583-2402. Sr. Kathleen Cornell, S.S.N.D., Prov. Leader.

Total in Community: 561.

Ministry in the field of Academic, Special and Religious Education; Day Care Centers; Foreign Mission work; Nurses; Pastoral Work; Apostolate of the Aging; Vicar for Women Religious.

Represented in the Archdioceses of Baltimore, Chicago, Los Angeles, Miami, Milwaukee and Washington and in the Dioceses of Joliet, Peoria and Rockford.

[2980] (C.N.D.)—SISTERS OF THE CONGREGATION DE NOTRE DAME (P)

Founded in Canada in 1653. First Foundation in the United States in 1860. American Novitiate established at Bourbonnais, Illinois.

Blessed Sacrament Province: 30 Highfield Rd., Wilton, CT 06897.

Generalate and Motherhouse: 2330 Sherbrooke St., W, Montreal, Canada, H3H 1G8. Sr. Josephine Badali, C.N.D., Congregational Leader.

U.S. Province (1946): *Blessed Sacrament Province*, 30 Highfield Rd., Wilton, CT 06897. Tel: 203-762-4300; Fax: 203-762-4319. Sr. Patricia McCarthy, C.N.D., Prov. Leader.

Total number in the U.S. Province: 139.

Represented in the Archdioceses of Chicago, Hartford, New York and Oklahoma City and in the Dioceses of Albany, Bridgeport, Brooklyn, Charlotte, Joliet, Providence, Rapid City, Richmond, Scranton.

[2990] (S.N.D.)—SISTERS OF NOTRE DAME (P)

Founded in Germany in 1850. First foundation in the United States in 1874.

Generalate: Rome, Italy Sr. Mary Kristin Battles, S.N.D., Supr. Gen.

Universal total in Congregation: 2200.

Cleveland Province (1874): *Notre Dame Educational Center - Provincial Center, Juniorate, & Novitiate*, 13000 Auburn Rd., Chardon, OH 44024-9331. Tel: 440-286-7101; Fax: 440-286-3377. Sr. Margaret Mary Gorman, S.N.D., Prov. Supr.; Sr. M. Patricia Teckman, Prov. Sec.

Total in Community: 337.

Legal Titles: The Corporation of the Sisters of Notre Dame of Chardon, Ohio; The Sisters of Notre Dame Charitable Trust.

Ministry in the field of Academic Education at all levels; Special Education for Exceptional Children; Foreign Mission Work; Religious Education; Pastoral Care; Hospital Chaplaincy; Counseling Ministries; Community Service; Diocesan and National Offices; Pastoral Associate/Minister and D.R.E.; Parish Ministry; Retreat Direction; Spiritual Direction; Hispanic & Refugee Outreach; Ministry to the Sick and Elderly in Hospitals and Nursing Homes; Youth Ministry; Campus Ministry; Writing; Liturgy and Music; Public Defender for Juveniles; Hospice Work; Respite Home for Children; Art Therapy; Social Service; Literacy; Peace and Justice work.

Properties owned and sponsored: Notre Dame Cathedral Latin School, Chardon, OH; Notre Dame Elementary School, Chardon, OH; Notre Dame Pre School, Chardon, OH; Julie Billiart School, Lyndhurst, OH.

Represented in the Archdioceses of Louisville, Miami and Washington and in the Dioceses of Arlington, Cleveland, Orlando, Raleigh, St. Petersburg, St. Augustine, Toledo, Venice and Youngstown. Also in Nicaragua and Tanzania.

Covington Province (1924): *Provincial House and Novitiate of the Sisters of Notre Dame*, 1601 Dixie Hwy., (St. Joseph Heights), Covington, KY 41011. Tel: 859-291-2040; Fax: 859-291-1774. Sr. Marla Monahan, S.N.D., Prov.

Total in Community: 136.

Legal Title: *Sisters of Notre Dame of Covington, KY, Inc.*

Ministry in the field of Education; Hospital and Health Care Services; Child Care.

Properties sponsored and owned: Saint Claire Regional Medical Center, Morehead, KY; St. Charles Care Center and Village, Covington, KY; Notre Academy, Covington, KY; Julie Learning Center, Park Hills, KY.

Represented in the Archdiocese of Cincinnati, Covington and Lexington. Also in Hoima, Uganda and East Africa.

Province of Toledo (1924): *Notre Dame Provincial Center*, 3837 Secor Rd., Toledo, OH 43623. Tel: 419-474-5485. Sr. Mary Delores Gatliff, S.N.D., Prov. Supr.

Total in Community: 224.

Ministry in the field of Academic Education; Special Education for Exceptional Children; Foreign Mission Work; Religious Education, Pastoral Ministry, Vocational School, Health Care Ministry, Counseling Ministry, Community Service, Diocesan Offices, Spiritual Life, Hispanic and Migrant, Campus Ministries, Child Care, Care for Handicapped.

Properties owned and sponsored: Notre Dame Academy; Double ARC; Maria Early Learning Center; Mary Immaculate School; Lial Catholic School; Convent & Renewal Center, Whitehouse, OH; Holy Trinity Mission, Papua, New Guinea.

Represented in the Archdioceses of Chicago, Detroit, Indianapolis, New Orleans and Santa Fe and in the Dioceses of Brooklyn, Charleston, Cleveland, Covington, Fort Wayne-South Bend, Orange, Orlando, St. Augustine and Toledo.

Province of Los Angeles (1961): *Sisters of Notre Dame*, 1776 Hendrix Ave., Thousand Oaks, CA 91360. Tel: 805-496-3243; Fax: 805-379-3616. Sr. Mary Anncarla Costello, S.N.D., Prov. Supr.

Total number in Province: 60.

Legal Titles: Corporation of the Sisters of Notre Dame of Los Angeles; Notre Dame Academy High School; Notre Dame Academy Elementary School, Los Angeles, CA; Notre Dame Center; La Reina High School, Thousand Oaks, CA; Providence House, Long Beach, CA; Notre Dame Learning Center.

Ministry in the field of Education and Parish and Social Ministry; Catechetics; Foreign Mission Work.

Represented in the Archdiocese of Los Angeles.

[3000] (S.N.D.DEN.)—SISTERS OF NOTRE DAME DE NAMUR (P)

Founded in France in 1804. First foundation in the United States in 1840.

Generalate: *Suore di Nostra Signora di Namur*, Via Raffaello Sardiello 20, Rome, Italy, 00165. Tel: 011-39-06-6641-8704. Sr. Teresita Weind, S.N.D.deN., Gen. Moderator.

U.S. Notre Dame Congregational Center: *Congregational Mission Office*, 30 Jeffreys Neck Rd., Ipswich, MA 01938. Tel: 978-356-2159; Fax: 978-356-2118. Sr. Lorraine Connell, S.N.D.deN., Treas.

Boston Province (1973): *Sisters of Notre Dame de Namur*, 351 Broadway, Everett, MA 02149. Tel: 617-387-2500; Fax: 617-387-1303. Prov. Team: Sr. Edie Daly, S.N.D.deN; Sr. Barbara Metz, S.N.D.deN.; Sr.

Maureen Marr, S.N.D.deN.
Total in Community: 197.
Legal Title: *The Boston Province of the Sisters of Notre Dame de Namur, Inc.*
Ministry in the field of Academic Education at all levels; Adult Education Programs; Parish Ministries; Religious Education Programs; and Social Services.
Properties owned and sponsored: Notre Dame Academy, Worcester, MA, Notre Dame Children's Class, Wenham, MA; Notre Dame Education Center, South Boston, MA; St. Patrick School and Education Center, Lowell, MA.
Represented in the Archdioceses of Boston, Hartford, Louisville and Washington and in the Dioceses of Albany, Gallup, Manchester, Orlando, Springfield in Massachusetts and Worcester.

Ipswich Province (1973): *Sisters of Notre Dame de Namur Provincialate*, 30 Jeffrey's Neck Rd., Ipswich, MA 01938. Tel: 978-356-4381; Fax: 978-356-9759. Prov. Admin. Team: Sr. Mary Boretti, S.N.D.deN.; Sr. Mary M. Farren, S.N.D.deN.; Sr. Andrea Walsh, S.N.D.deN.
Total in Community: 132.
Legal Titles: Notre Dame Training School, Inc.; The Sisters of Notre Dame de Namur, Ipswich, MA.
Ministry in all fields of Education; Pastoral Ministry; Health, Social and Community Services; Retreat Work.
Properties owned and sponsored: Academy of Notre Dame, Tyngsboro, MA; Notre Dame Academy, Hingham, MA; Notre Dame Long Term Health Care Facility, Worcester, MA; Notre Dame Education Center, Lawrence, MA; Cuvilly Arts and Earth Center, Ipswich, MA; Notre Dame du Lac, Worcester, MA; St. Julie Billiart Residential Care Center, Ipswich, MA.
Represented in the Archdiocese of Boston and in the Dioceses of Manchester and Worcester.

Connecticut Province (1959): *The Connecticut Province of the Sisters of Notre Dame de Namur, Inc.*, Sisters of Notre Dame de Namur Province Center, 468 Poquonock Ave., Windsor, CT 06095-2473. Tel: 860-688-1832. Prov. Admin. Team: Sr. Mary Rose Crowley, S.N.D.deN.; Sr. Ellen Agritelley, S.N.D.deN.; Sr. Elizabeth McLaughlin, S.N.D.deN.
Total in Community: 97.
Sisters serve and staff: Colleges, High Schools, Grammar Schools; Sisters Engaged in Specialized Educational Programs: Pastoral Ministry and Religious Education, Social Health and Community Services, Diocesan Offices, Spiritual Direction and Adult Basic Education.
Represented in the Archdioceses of Boston, Hartford and Washington and in the Dioceses of Bridgeport, Burlington, Norwich, Providence, Scranton, St. Augustine, Springfield (MA) and Worcester.

Baltimore Province (1934): *Sisters of Notre Dame de Namur, Maryland Province Center*, 1531 Greenspring Valley Rd., Stevenson, MD 21153. Tel: 410-486-5599.
Total in Community: 85.
Properties owned and sponsored: Maryland Province Center, Stevenson, MD; Villa Julie Residence, Stevenson, MD; Maryvale Preparatory School, Brooklandville, MD; Notre Dame Academy, Villanova, PA; Trinity School, Ellicot City, MD; Development Program, Stevenson, MD; Sisters Academy of Baltimore, Inc.
Represented in the Archdioceses of Baltimore, Philadelphia and Washington and in the Dioceses of Atlanta, Brooklyn, Portland (ME), Rockville Centre and Wilmington.
Leadership Team: Sr. Carol Lichtenberg, S.N.D.deN., Provincial; Sr. Judi Clemens, S.N.D.deN.; Sr. Colette Didier, S.N.D.deN.

Chesapeake Province (1990): *Sisters of Notre Dame de Namur Provincial Offices*, 305 Cable St., Baltimore, MD 21210-2511. Tel: 410-243-1993; Fax: 410-243-2279. Administrative Team: Sr. Barbara Ann English, S.N.D.; Sr. Agnes Rose McNally, S.N.D.; Sr. Kathleen O'Brien, S.N.D.; Sr. Mary Margaret Pignone, S.N.D.; Sr. Margaret Shawn Scanlan, S.N.D.; Susan Young.
Total in Community: 66.
Represented in the Archdioceses of Baltimore, Miami, New York, Philadelphia and Washington and in the Dioceses of Arlington, Raleigh, and Wheeling-Charleston. Also in Brazil, Kenya and Dem. Republic of Congo.

Ohio Province (1840): *Sisters of Notre Dame de Namur Provincial House*, 701 E. Columbia Ave., Cincinnati, OH 45215. Tel: 513-761-7636. Sr. Carol Lichtenberg, S.N.D.deN., Provincial.
Total in Community: 160.
Legal Titles: St. Mary's Educational Institute at Cincinnati; Sisters of Notre Dame de Namur - Ohio Province; Sisters of Notre Dame de Namur, Ohio Province, Charitable Trust.
Ministry in the field of Education at all levels; Pastoral Ministry; Administration and Services; Social Services; Communication; Health Care; Community Services.
Represented in the Archdioceses of Boston, Chicago, Cincinnati and Louisville and in the Dioceses of Austin, Buffalo, Columbus, Covington, Phoenix, and Saginaw. Also in Belgium, Brazil, Kenya, Nicaragua, Nigeria, Rome and United Kingdom.

California Province (1851): *Province Center - Sisters of Notre Dame de Namur*, 1520 Ralston Ave., Belmont, CA 94002. Provincial Team: Sr. Louise O'Reilly, S.N.D.deN.; Sr. Georgianna Coonis, S.N.D.deN.; Sr. Maureen Hilliard, S.N.D.deN.; Sr. Virginia Unger, S.N.D.deN.
Total in Community: 122.
Legal Title: *Sisters of Notre Dame de Namur California Province.*
Ministries in the field of Academic Education at all levels; Adult Education Programs; Parish Ministries; Religious Education Programs; Social Services; Diocesan Administration; and Health.
Represented in the Archdioceses of Los Angeles, Portland in Oregon, San Francisco and Seattle and in the Dioceses of Burlington, Des Moines, Monterey, Oakland, Sacramento, San Jose and Stockton.
Properties owned or sponsored: Notre Dame de Namur University, Belmont, CA; Moreland Notre Dame Elementary, Watsonville, CA; Notre Dame Elementary, Belmont, CA; Notre Dame High School, Belmont, CA; Notre Dame High School, San Jose, CA; Cristo Rey, Sacramento, CA. (Co-sponsored with Sisters of Mercy and Jesuits).

Base Communities Province (1989): *Sisters of Notre Dame de Namur Base Communities Province Office:*, 125 Michigan Ave., N.E., Washington, DC 20017-1004. Tel: 202-884-9750. Communications Network Sr. Loreta Jordan, S.N.D.deN.; Sr. Joan Ferraro, S.N.D.deN.; Sr. Marcella Missar, S.N.D.deN.
Total in Province: 37.
Legal Title: *Sisters of Notre Dame de Namur Base Communities, Inc.*
Ministry in Formal Education; Health Care; Social Services/Community Development; Pastoral Ministry.
Represented in the Archdioceses of Baltimore, Boston, Hartford, Philadelphia and Washington and in the Dioceses of Brooklyn, Charleston, Fort Wayne-South Bend, Orlando, Richmond, Rockville Centre and Wilmington.

[3010] (O.S.B.S.)—OBLATE SISTERS OF THE BLESSED SACRAMENT (D)

Founded in 1935 by Rev. Sylvester Eisenman, O.S.B.

Motherhouse: *St. Sylvester's Convent*, 103 Church Dr., P.O. Box 217, Marty, SD 57361. Tel: 605-384-3305. Sr. Inez Jetty, O.S.B.S., Supr.

Kateri Convent: 821 Farlow Ave., Rapid City, SD 57701. Tel: 605-343-6261. Sr. Miriam Shindelar, O.S.B.S., Treas.
Total in Community: 6.
Represented in the Dioceses of Rapid City and Sioux Falls.

[3020] (O.B.T.)—SISTERS OBLATES TO THE BLESSED TRINITY (D)

Founded in Italy in 1923. First foundation in the United States in 1987.

U.S. Generalate & Novitiate: *St. Aloysius Gonzaga Novitiate*, 306 Beekman Rd., P.O. Box 98, Hopewell Junction, NY 12533. Tel: 845-226-5671; Fax: 845-226-5671; Email: Jstab35097@aol.com. Mother Gloria Castro, Supr. Gen.
Total in Community: 40.
Represented in the Archdioceses of New York and San Juan and in the Dioceses of Madison and Ponce. Also in Italy and San Salvador.

[3035] (O.M.O.)—OBLATES OF THE MOTHER OF ORPHANS (P)

Founded in Italy on September 8, 1945.

General Motherhouse: via Amundsen 10, Milano, Italy Sr. Lucilla Passoni, Gen. Supr.
Universal total in Congregation: 200.

U.S. Address: 20 E. 72nd St., New York, NY 10021. Sr. Maria Isabel Reina, O.M.O., Supr.
Total in Community: 3.
Represented in the Archdiocese of New York. Also in Cameroon, Colombia, El Salvador, Guatemala and Italy.

[3040] (O.S.P.)—OBLATE SISTERS OF PROVIDENCE (P)

Founded in the United States in 1829.

General Motherhouse: *Our Lady of Mount Providence Convent*, 701 Gun Rd., Baltimore, MD 21227. Tel: 410-242-8500. Sr. Mary Alexis Fisher, O.S.P., Supr. Gen.; Sr. Mary Clarice Proctor, O.S.P., Asst. Supr. Gen.; Sr. Mary Crescentia Proctor, O.S.P., Sec. Gen.; Sr. Mary Sharon Young, O.S.P., Treas.
Professed Sisters: 69; Serving in Baltimore: 57.
Legal Title: *The Oblate Sisters of Providence of the City of Baltimore.*
Sisters serve as Pastoral Ministry-Associates; in the field of Education; Reading Center; Day Care Centers; Teaching; Counseling; Hispanic & Migrant Ministry.
Represented in the Archdioceses of Baltimore and Miami and in the Diocese of Buffalo. Also in Costa Rica.

[3050] (O.S.H.J.)—OBLATE SISTERS OF THE SACRED HEART OF JESUS (P)

Founded in 1894. First foundation in the United States in 1949.

General Motherhouse: Rome, Italy

American Headquarters: *Villa Maria Teresa*, 50 Warner Rd., Hubbard, OH 44425. Tel: 330-759-9329; Fax: 330-759-7290. Sr. Vittoria Nisi, O.S.H.J., Supr.
Total in Community: 19; Total in Congregation: 300.
Represented in the Diocese of Youngstown.

[3060] (O.S.F.S.)—OBLATE SISTERS OF ST. FRANCIS DE SALES (P)

Founded in France in 1866. First foundation in the United States in 1951.

General Motherhouse: 4 rue des Terrasses, Troyes, France

American Headquarters: *Villa Aviat Convent*, 399 Childs Rd., Childs, MD 21916. Tel: 410-398-3699. Sr. Anne Elizabeth, O.S.F.S., Supr.
Total in Community: 14.
Ministry in the field of Academic and Religious Education.
Represented in the Archdiocese of Philadelphia and in the Dioceses of Arlington and Wilmington.

[3070] (N.A.U.-O.L.C.)—NORTH AMERICAN UNION SISTERS OF OUR LADY OF CHARITY (P)

Founded in Caen, France in 1641, by St. John Eudes. First foundation in the United States in 1855; autonomous houses were federated in 1944 and in 1979 the Union was established.

General Motherhouse and Administrative Centre: 620 Roswell Rd., P.O. Box 340, Carrollton, OH 44615-0340. Tel: 330-627-1641; Fax: 330-627-5789; Email: naucenter@hotmail.com. Sr. Carol Pregno, O.L.C., Supr. Gen.
Total Sisters Membership: 73.
Legal Title: *North American Union of the Sisters of Our Lady of Charity, Inc.*
The primary ministry of the sisters is with the marginalized and wounded, especially women and children: people living with HIV/AIDS, Hispanic ministry and parish ministries, battered women, delinquent girls, nursing homes, human trafficking, both in residential and outreach programs.
Represented in the Dioceses of Dallas, El Paso, Erie, Green Bay, Pittsburgh, San Diego, Steubenville and Wheeling-Charleston. Also in Mexico.

San Diego

North American Union Sisters of Our Lady of Charity: 1930 Illion St., San Diego, CA 92110. Tel: 619-275-0764. Sr. Zita Toto, Local Supr.

Fort Myers

North American Union Sisters of Our Lady of Charity: 2140 Cottage St., Apt. 110, Fort Myers, FL 33901. Tel: 239-337-4550; Email: olcflo@worldnet.att.net. Sr. Mary John Franey, Local Supr.
Dallas Sr. Yolanda Martinez, Local Supr.
Total in Community: 8.
Legal Title: *Sisters of Our Lady of Charity and Refuge.*

El Paso

North American Union of Our Lady of Charity: 415 N. Glenwood Dr., El Paso, TX 79905. Tel: 915-722-0737; Fax: 915-779-2664; Email: mescobar1125@hotmail.com. Sr. Martha P. Escobar, Local Supr.
Legal Title: *North American Sisters of Our Lady of Charity, Inc.*

Erie

North American Union of the Sisters of Our Lady of Charity (1934): 4635 East Lake Rd., Erie, PA 16511. Tel: 814-899-1052; Fax: 814-899-1573; Email: srgentile@hotmail.com. Sr. Catherine Gentile, Local Supr.
Legal Titles: Gannondale Residential Center for Girls, Erie, PA; North American Union Sisters of Our Lady of Charity, Inc.

Green Bay

North American Union of the Sisters of Our Lady of Charity: 2560 Shawano Ave., P.O. Box 10357, Green Bay, WI 54307. Tel: 920-434-8208; Fax: 920-662-0047; Email: sdonna@athenet.net. Sr. Donna Truckey, Local Supr.
Legal Titles: Sisters of Our Lady of Charity of the North American Union, Inc.; McClosky Program, Inc., Green Bay, WI.

Pittsburgh

North American Union of the Sisters of Our Lady of Charity: *Nativity Convent*, 4100 Vinceton St., Pittsburgh, PA 15214. Tel: 412-931-2299; Fax: 412-931-6044. Sr. Sheila Rooney, Local Supr.
Legal Titles: North American Union Sisters of Our Lady of Charity, Inc.; Eudes Institute.

Steubenville

North American Union Sisters of Our Lady of Charity: 620 Roswell Rd., N.W., P.O. Box 158, Carrollton, OH 44615-0158. Tel: 330-627-7647; Fax: 330-627-4415; Email: rosa_olc@hotmail.com. Sr. Rosa Hernandez, Local Supr.
Legal Title: *North American Union Sisters of Our Lady of Charity, Inc.*

Newburgh

North American Union of the Sisters of Our Lady of Charity: 157 Liberty St., Newburgh, NY 12550. Tel: 845-561-4354; Fax: 845-561-4354; Email: marthahmolc@aol.com. Sr. Martha Hernandez, Local

Supr.
Legal Title: *North American Union Sisters of Our Lady of Charity, Inc.*

Wheeling

North American Union Sisters of Our Lady of Charity: 141 Edgington Ln., Wheeling, WV 26003. Tel: 304-242-7070; Fax: 304-242-0042; Email: d.kohlman@frontier.com. Sr. Deana Kohlman, Local Supr.
Legal Title: *North American Union Sisters of Our Lady of Charity, Inc.*

[3072] (R.O.L.C.)—OUR LADY OF CHARITY OF REFUGE (P)

Monastery of Our Lady of Charity of Refuge: 1125 Malvern Ave., Hot Springs National Park, AR 71901. Tel: 501-623-1393; Fax: 501-623-1509. Sr. Theresa Marie Lalancette, R.O.L.C. Supr.
Total in Community: 7.

[3080] (R.C.D.)—SISTERS OF OUR LADY OF CHRISTIAN DOCTRINE (D)

Founded in New York in 1910 for the work of religious education and social service.

Central Office: *Visitation House,* 629 North Midland Ave., Nyack, NY 10960. Tel: 845-512-8663. Sr. Rose T. Vermette, R.C.D., Pres.
Total in Community: 21.
Ministry in the field of Religious Education and Spirituality; Social Work, Nursing and Counseling.
Represented in the Archdiocese of New York.

[3090] (C.L.H.C.)—CONGREGATION OF OUR LADY, HELP OF THE CLERGY (D)
Maryvale Sisters

Founded in the United States in 1961.

Motherhouse: *Maryvale Motherhouse,* 2522 June Bug Rd., Vale, NC 28168. Tel: 704-276-2626. Mother Mary Louis, Supr.
Total in Community: 5.
Represented in the Diocese of Charlotte.

[3100] (R.S.R.)—CONGREGATION OF OUR LADY OF THE HOLY ROSARY (P)

Founded in Rimouski, P.Q., Canada in 1874. First foundation in the United States in 1899.

General Motherhouse: 300 Alle du Rosaire, Rimouski, Canada, G5L 3E3. Tel: 418-724-5940. Sr. Marie-Alma Dube, R.S.R., Supr. Gen.

U.S. Address: *Our Lady of the Holy Rosary,* 25 Portland Ave., Old Orchard Beach, ME 04064. Tel: 207-934-0592; Tel: 207-937-3214. Sr. Maureen Bellerose, R.S.R., Reg.
Total number in the Region: 7.

Our Lady of the Holy Rosary Regional House: 25 Portland Ave., Old Orchard Beach, ME 04064. Tel: 207-934-0592. Sr. Maureen Bellerose, R.S.R., Regional Coord.
Ministry in the fields of Education, Diocesan Ministry, Pastoral Ministry.
Represented in the Diocese of Portland (In Maine).

[3105] (S.O.L.T.)—SISTERS OF THE SOCIETY OF OUR LADY OF THE MOST HOLY TRINITY

Founded in 1958 in New Mexico by Fr. James H. Flanagan. The Society of Our Lady of the Most Holy Trinity is composed of priests, brothers, permanent deacons, sisters, consecrated widows and laity (both single and married). Its members serve on Ecclesial Teams made up of all vocations while living a Marian Trinitarian spirituality.

Motherhouse: P.O. Box 536, Bosque, NM 87006. Tel: 505-861-7175; Fax: 505-864-6776; Email: srannemarie@earthlink.net; Web: www.soltsisters.org. Sr. Anne Marie Walsh, Gen. Sister Servant.
Total number of Sisters in Community: 98.

U.S. Regionalate: P.O. Box 152, Robstown, TX 78380. Tel: 361-287-8090. Sr. Mary Teresa Pacheco, S.O.L.T., American Reg. Sister Servant.
Professed Sisters: 98; Novices: 12; Candidates: 20.
Represented in the Archdioceses of Santa Fe and Seattle and in the Dioceses of Corpus Christi, Fargo, Kansas City-St. Joseph and Laredo.

[3110] (R.C.)—N AMERICAN PROVINCE CONGREGATION OF OUR LADY OF THE CENACLE OF CHICAGO (P)

Founded in France in 1826. First foundation in the United States in 1892.

Generalate: Piazza Madonna del Cenacolo, 15, Rome, Italy, 00136.

North American Province (2000): *Congregation of Our Lady of the Cenacle,* 513 Fullerton Pkwy., Chicago, IL 60614-6428. Tel: 773-528-6300; Fax: 773-549-0554. Sr. Evelyn Jegen, R.C., Prov.
Total in Community: 105.
Properties owned and sponsored: Cenacle Sisters, Hoschton, GA; Cenacle of St. Regis of Flushing, Inc., Ronkonkoma, NY; Cenacle Convent, Inc., Chicago, IL; Cenacle Convent, Inc., Houston, TX; Warrenville Cenacle Retreat House, Warrenville, IL; Religious of Our Lady of the Cenacle of New Brunswick, NJ, Metuchen, NJ; Convent of Our Lady of the Cenacle, Metairie, LA; The Cenacle Convent of Palm Beach Co., Inc., Palm Beach, FL; Ronkonkoma Cenacle, Inc., Rockville Centre, NY; Cenacle Sisters, Gainesville, FL.
Represented in the Archdioceses of Atlanta, Chicago, Denver, Galveston-Houston, New Orleans, New York and St. Louis and in the Dioceses of Fort Wayne-South Bend, Green Bay, Joliet, Metuchen, Palm Beach, Paterson, Rochester, Rockville Centre, St. Augustine, St. Petersburg, and Wheeling-Charleston. Also in Canada.

[3120] (O.L.S.)—SISTERS OF OUR LADY OF SORROWS (P)

Founded in Italy in 1839. First foundation in the United States in 1947.

General Motherhouse: Viale Vaticano 90, Rome, Italy, 00165. Mother Lina Rossi, O.L.S., Supr. Gen.

American Headquarters: *Sisters of Our Lady of Sorrows Convent,* 9894 Norris Ferry Rd., Shreveport, LA 71106. Fax: 318-797-7003. Sr. Carla Bertani, O.L.S., Supr.
Total in Community: 28; Universal total in Congregation: 300.
Ministry in the field of Education; Work with people with mental retardation; Outreach to the poor; Pastoral Ministry; CCD & Adult Education; early childhood education; afterschool art & education program.
Represented in the Dioceses of Alexandria, Lafayette in Louisiana and Shreveport.

[3130] (O.L.V.M.)—OUR LADY OF VICTORY MISSIONARY SISTERS (P)

Founded in the United States in 1922.

Motherhouse: *Victory Noll,* P.O. Box 109, Huntington, IN 46750-0109. Tel: 260-356-0628; Fax: 260-358-1504; Email: victorynoll@olvm.org. Sr. Beatrice Haines, O.L.V.M., Pres.
Total in Community: 103.
Legal Holding: Victory Noll Sisters Community Support Trust.
Represented in the Archdioceses of Chicago, Denver, Dubuque, Los Angeles, San Antonio and Santa Fe and in the Dioceses of Fort Wayne-South Bend, Phoenix, Salt Lake City, San Bernardino, San Diego, Toledo and Tucson.

[3140] (C.S.A.C.)—SISTERS OF THE CATHOLIC APOSTOLATE (PALLOTTINE) (P)

Founded in Italy in 1835. First foundation in the United States in 1889.

General Motherhouse: Via Caio Canuleio 162, Rome, Italy, 00174. Mother M. Serena Cambiaghi, C.S.A.C., Supr. Gen.
Universal total in Congregation: 540.

Provincial Motherhouse in America: *Queen of Apostles Convent,* 98 Harriman Heights Rd., Monroe, NY 10950. Sr. Olivia Reginella, C.S.A.C., Prov. Moderator.
Total in Community: 35.
Ministry in the field of Academic and Religious Education at Elementary and Secondary Levels; Pastoral Services.
Represented in the Archdioceses of Newark and New York.

Provincial: 98 Harriman Heights Rd., Monroe, NY 10950. Tel: 845-492-5080.

[3150] (S.A.C.)—PALLOTTINE MISSIONARY SISTERS - QUEEN OF APOSTLES PROVINCE (P)
(Missionary Sisters of the Catholic Apostolate)

Founded in Rome, Italy in 1838. First founded in the United States in 1912.

General Motherhouse: Rome, Italy Sr. Izabela Swierad, S.A.C., Supr. Gen.

American Provincialate: *Pallottine Renewal Center,* 15270 Old Halls Ferry Rd., Florissant, MO 63034. Tel: 314-837-7100; Fax: 314-837-1041. Sr. Gail Borgmeyer, S.A.C., Prov.; Sr. Marian Ruth Creamer, S.A.C., Archivist.
Total in Community: 680.
Properties owned and/or sponsored: Pallottine Renewal Center, Florissant, MO; St. Mary's Hospital & Convent, Huntington, WV; St. Joseph's Hospital & Convent, Buckhannon, WV; St. Vincent Pallotti Convent, High School & Laurel, MD.
Sisters minister in the fields of Health Care; Child Day Care; Education; Retreat and Renewal Ministry; Social Services; Parish and Pastoral Work.
Represented in the Archdioceses of St. Louis and Washington and in the Diocese of Wheeling-Charleston.

[3160] (P.V.M.I.)—PARISH VISITORS OF MARY IMMACULATE (P)

Founded in New York City in 1920 for family visitation and religious education. A contemplative-missionary community serving the Church by person-to-person evangelization.

Motherhouse and Novitiate: *Marycrest,* P.O. Box 658, Monroe, NY 10949-0658. Tel: 845-783-2251. Sr. Carole Marie Troskowski, Gen. Supr.; Sr. Maria Catherine, Novice Dir.
Total in Community: 58.
Ministry in evangelization, catechetics, & spiritual counseling; liaison for social services.
Represented in the Archdiocese of New York and in the Diocese of Phoenix. Also in Nigeria and Philippines.

[3170] (C.P.)—RELIGIOUS OF THE PASSION OF JESUS CHRIST (P)
(Passionist Nuns)

Founded in Italy in 1771 by St. Paul of the Cross. First foundation in the United States in 1910.

2715 Churchview Ave., Pittsburgh, PA 15227. Tel: 412-881-1155. Mother Joyce Foga, C.P., Supr.
Perpetual Vows: 10.

The Religious of the Passion of Jesus Christ (Contemplative) (1926): *St. Gabriel's Monastery,* 631 Griffin Pond Rd., Clarks Summit, PA 18411. Tel: 570-586-2791; Fax: 570-586-8210. Sr. Teresita Kho, C.P., Supr.
Professed Sisters: 7.
Sisters serve and staff: Retreats and other Programs for Women and Men of all Faiths; Clergy and Religious; Ecumenical Groups; Business and Civic Groups.
Legal Holding: St. Gabriel's Monastery and Retreat Center.

Passionist Nuns (Cloistered Contemplative) (1946): *Passionist Nuns,* 8564 Crisp Rd., Whitesville, KY 42378-9782. Tel: 270-233-4571. Mother Catherine Marie, C.P., Supr.
Professed Nuns: 12; Temporary Vows: 3; Novices: 1.

Passionist Nuns (Contemplative) (1947): *Monastery of the Sacred Passion,* 1151 Donaldson Hwy., Erlanger, KY 41018-1000. Tel: 859-371-8568. Sr. Margaret Mary, C.P., Supr.
Total in Community: 8.
Legal Title: *Passionist Nuns of Covington, KY.*

Passionist Nuns (Cloistered) (1948): *Passionist Monastery,* 15700 Clayton Rd., Ellisville, MO 63011. Tel: 636-527-6867. Mother Mary Salvador, C.P., Supr.
Total in Community: 9.

[3180] (C.P.)—SISTERS OF THE CROSS AND PASSION (P)
(Passionist Sisters)

Founded in 1852. First foundation in the United States in 1924.

Generalate: *Parkmount,* 458 Bury New Rd., Salford, England, M7 4LH. Sr. Maria Angelica Algorta, C.P., Congregational Leader.

Motherhouse-American Provincial Office: One Wright Ln., North Kingstown, RI 02852. Tel: 401-294-3554. Sr. Theresina Scully, C.P., Prov. Leader.
Professed Sisters: 32.
Sisters minister in Retreat Houses; Elementary Education; Hospital Chaplaincy; Parish Ministry; Religious Education; Social Services; Marriage Tribunals.
Properties owned and operated: Our Lady of Calvary Retreat, Farmington, CT.
Represented in the Archdioceses of Hartford and New York and in the Dioceses of Memphis, Norwich, Providence and Rockville Centre. Also in Jamaica, West Indies.

[3190] (A.P.)—NUNS OF THE PERPETUAL ADORATION OF THE BLESSED SACRAMENT (P)

Founded in Rome in 1807. First foundation in the United States in 1925.

El Paso: *Expiatory Shrine of Christ the King and Monastery of Perpetual Adoration,* 145 N. Cotton Ave., El Paso, TX 79901. Tel: 915-533-5323; Email: mary.guadalupe@att.net. Mother Maria Rocio Robles, A.P., Supr.
Sisters: 14.
Represented in the Archdioceses of Anchorage and San Francisco and in the Dioceses of El Paso and Sioux Falls.

San Francisco: *Monastery of Perpetual Adoration,* 771 Ashbury St., San Francisco, CA 94117. Tel: 415-566-2743. Mother Rosalba Maria, A.P., Supr.
Sisters: 13.
Represented in the Archdiocese of San Francisco. Also in Africa, Chile, Italy, Mexico and Spain.

[3195] (A.P.G.)—SISTER OF PERPETUAL ADORATION OF GUADALUPE, INC. (P)

U.S. Foundation: 2403 W. Travis, San Antonio, TX 78207. Tel: 210-227-5546. Mother Ma. Concepcion Quesada A., A.P.G., Gen. Counsel.
Total in Community: 9.

[3200] (SCH.P.)—SISTERS OF THE PIOUS SCHOOLS (P)
(Escolapias)

Founded in Figueras, Spain in 1829.
Universal total in Congregation: 675.

General Motherhouse: Via Crescenzio 77, Rome, Italy, 00193. Mother M. Divina Garcia, Sch.P., Supr. Gen.

U.S. Headquarters (1954): 17601 Nordhoff St.,

Northridge, CA 91325. Tel: 818-885-6265; Fax: 818-718-6752. Sr. Guadalupe Gonzalez, Sch.P.
Total in Community: 8.
Ministry in Religious Education; Parish Schools.
Represented in the Archdiocese of Los Angeles.

[3210] (P.C.P.A.)—POOR CLARES OF PERPETUAL ADORATION (P)

Founded in France, 1854. First foundation in the United States at Cleveland, Ohio, 1921. Poor Clares of Perpetual Adoration, cloistered, contemplative, solemn vows. Object: Perpetual Adoration in spirit of Praise and Thanksgiving and Gospel living. Solemn Exposition day and night. Each monastery is autonomous.

Sancta Clara Monastery (1946): 4200 N. Market Ave., Canton, OH 44714. Tel: 330-492-1171; Fax: 330-492-8657; Web: www.poorclares.org. Mother Magdalen Colson, P.C.P.A., Abbess.
Total in Community: 11.

Adoration Monastery (1921): 4108 Euclid Ave., Cleveland, OH 44103. Tel: 216-361-0783. Mother Mary Thomas, P.C.P.A., Abbess.
Total in Community: 18.

Poor Clares of Perpetual Adoration (1954): *Our Lady of the Most Blessed Sacrament Monastery*, 3900 13th St., N.E., Washington, DC 20017-2699. Tel: 202-526-6808; Fax: 202-526-0678; Email: ourprayer4u@poorclareswdc.org; Web: www.poorclareswdc.org. Mother Mary Angela Perry, P.C.P.A., Abbess.
Total in Community: 5.

Our Lady of the Angels Monastery: *Shrine of the Most Blessed Sacrament*, 3222 County Rd. 548, Hanceville, AL 35077. Tel: 205-271-2917; Fax: 205-795-5702. Mother M. Angelica, P.C.P.A., Abbess Emerita.
Total in Community: 18; Novices: 4; Postulants: 2.
Legal Title: *Our Lady of the Angels Monastery, Inc.*
Represented in the Diocese of Birmingham.

[3220] (P.C.J.)—SISTERS OF THE POOR CHILD JESUS (P)

Founded on February 2, 1844 in Germany. First founded in the United States on July 2, 1924 at Parkersburg, West Virginia.

General Motherhouse: Haus Loreto, Simpleveld, Netherlands Antilles Sr. Maria del Rocio, P.C.J., Supr. Gen.
Universal total in Congregation: 500.

American Region and Novitiate: *In Mohun Health Care Center*, 2340 Airport Dr., Columbus, OH 43219. Joseph D. Scott, Contact Person.
Total in Community: 3.
Ministry in the field of Education.
Represented in the Dioceses of Columbus and Wheeling-Charleston.

[3230] (P.H.J.C.)—POOR HANDMAIDS OF JESUS CHRIST (P)
(The Ancilla Domini Sisters,Inc.)

Founded in Germany in 1851. First foundation in the United States in 1868.

General Motherhouse: Dernbach, Westerwald, Germany Sr. Jolise May, P.H.J.C., Supr. Gen.

American Province-Provincialate: *Convent Ancilla Domini*, 9601 Union Rd., P.O. Box 1, Donaldson, IN 46513. Tel: 574-936-9936; Fax: 574-935-1785. Sr. Nora Hahn, P.H.J.C., Prov. Councilors: Sr. Virginia Kampwerth, P.H.J.C.; Sr. Kathy Haas, P.H.J.C.; Sr. Marlene Ann Lama, P.H.J.C.; Fred Arand, Treas.; Terry Sanders, Vice Pres. Devel.
Professed Sisters: 118.
Ministry in the field of Academic Education at all levels; Healthcare; Parish Ministries; Retreat Ministries; Child Care Institutions; and Retirement Homes.
Properties owned or sponsored: Ancilla Domini College; Convent Ancilla Domini; Bethany Retreat House; St. Henry Convent; Sojourner Truth House; Catherine Kasper Life Center, Inc.; Lindenwood Retreat & Conference Center; Earthworks, Inc.; MoonTree Community, Donaldson, IN; HealthVisions Midwest, Hammond, IN; Poor Handmaids of Jesus Christ Community Support Trust, Donaldson, IN; Poor Handmaids of Jesus Christ Foundation, Inc., Donaldson, IN; Ancilla Systems, Inc., Hobart, IN; Ancilla Domini Convent, Milwaukee, WI; Ancilla Domini Hospitals Self Insurance Trust; St. Catherine Convent, East Chicago, IN; Annunciation Convent, Hoffman Estates, IL; Mary Katherine Convent, Cairo, IL; Marian Convent, Fort Wayne, IN; St. Joseph Community Health Foundation, Ft. Wayne, IN; Catherine Kasper Place, Ft. Wayne, IN; Nazareth Home, East Chicago, IN; Sara House, South Bend, IN.
Represented in the Archdioceses of Chicago, Cincinnati, Indianapolis and Milwaukee and in the Dioceses of Belleville, Fort Wayne-South Bend, Gary, Lafayette in Indiana, Providence, Savannah and Springfield in Illinois. Also in Africa, Brazil, Germany and Mexico.

[3240] (C.J.C.)—POOR SISTERS OF JESUS CRUCIFIED AND THE SORROWFUL MOTHER (D)

Founded in the United States in 1924.

General Motherhouse and Novitiate: *Our Lady of Sorrows Convent*, 261 Thatcher St., Brockton, MA 02302-3997. Sr. Mary Valliere, C.J.C., Gen. Supr.
Total in Community: 20.
Properties owned and/or sponsored: St. Joseph Manor Health Care, Inc; Mater Dei Adult Day Health Program; Our Lady of Sorrows Convent, Brockton, MA; St. Mary's Villa Nursing Home, Elmhurst, PA; St. Mary's Villa Residence, Elmhurst, PA.
Ministry in Nursing Homes; Education Center; Elementary Schools; Assisted Living facilities; and Pastoral Ministry.
Represented in the Archdiocese of Boston.

[3242] (C.S.N.)—THE CONGREGATION OF THE SISTERS OF NAZARETH (P)

Founded in England by Mother St. Basil.

Motherhouse: Hammersmith, London, England, W6 8DB. Sr. St. Hilary, Supr. Gen.

Regional Headquarters: *Nazareth House*, 3333 Manning Ave., Los Angeles, CA 90064. Tel: 310-839-2361. Sr. John Berchmans, Supr.
Professed Sisters: 32.
Legal Title: *The Congregation of the Sisters of Nazareth Mother House U.S.A., Inc.*
Represented in the Archdioceses of Los Angeles and San Francisco and in the Dioceses of Fresno, Madison and San Diego. Also in American Samoa.

[3250] (P.S.S.J.)—POOR SISTERS OF ST. JOSEPH (P)

Founded in Buenos Aires, Argentina in 1880.

General Motherhouse: Pte. Peron 734, 1663 Muniz, Buenos Aires, Argentina Mother Martha S. Guerrero, Mother Gen.

U.S. Foundation: *Casa Belen*, 305 E. Fourth St., Bethlehem, PA 18015. Tel: 610-867-4030.

U.S. Motherhouse: *St. Gabriel Convent*, 4319 Sano St., Alexandria, VA 22312. Tel: 703-354-0395.

Casa Nazareth: 532 Spruce St., Reading, PA 19602. Tel: 610-378-1947.
Total in Community: 11.
Represented in the Dioceses of Allentown and Arlington.

[3260] (C.PP.S.)—SISTERS OF THE PRECIOUS BLOOD (DAYTON, OHIO) (P)

Founded in Switzerland in 1834. First foundation in the United States in 1844.

Generalate: 4000 Denlinger Rd., Dayton, OH 45426. Tel: 937-837-3302; Fax: 937-837-8825. Sr. Joyce Lehman, C.PP.S., Pres.; Sr. Nancy Kinross, C.PP.S., Vice Pres., Councilor & Sec.; Sr. Linda Pleiman, C.PP.S., Councilor; Sr. Cecilia Taphorn, C.PP.S., Councilor; Sr. Mary Yarger, C.PP.S., Councilor; Sr. Noreen Jutte, C.PP.S., Archivist.
Total Membership: 160.
Ministry in Elementary Schools; Pastoral Ministry in Hospitals and Long-term Care Centers; Religious and Adult Education; Homemaking Services in Homes for the Aged; Ethnic Minorities and Marginalized Peoples; Retreat and Music Ministry; Missionary and Volunteer Services.
Properties owned and sponsored: Generalate, Dayton, OH; Salem Heights Convent, Dayton, OH; Maria Stein Center, Maria Stein, OH.
Represented in the Archdioceses of Chicago, Cincinnati and Denver and in the Dioceses of Cleveland, Columbus, Lafayette in Indiana, Lansing, Lexington, Saginaw, San Bernardino and Toledo. Also in Chile and Guatemala.

[3270] (C.PP.S.)—SISTERS OF THE MOST PRECIOUS BLOOD (O'FALLON, MO.) (P)

Founded in Switzerland in 1845. First foundation in the United States in 1870.

General Administration: *St. Mary's Institute of O'Fallon*, 204 N. Main St., O'Fallon, MO 63366-2299. Tel: 636-240-6010; Fax: 636-272-5031. Sr. Fran Raia, C.PP.S., Supr. Gen. General Councilors: Sr. Cecile Gunelson, C.PP.S., Councilor; Sr. Lucy Meissen, C.PP.S., Councilor; Sr. Sandra Barton, C.PP.S., Councilor; Sr. Ellen Orf, C.PP.S., Councilor; Sr. Dory Obermann, Sec.; Sr. Mary Joan Dyer, Community Archivist; Sr. Carmen Schnyder, Treas.
Total in Community: 151.
Ministry in the field of Education; Care of the Elderly; Pastoral and Parish Ministry; Ecclesiastical Art; Foreign Missions; Social Services; Prayer/Presence.
Properties owned: St. Mary's Institute of O'Fallon, O'Fallon, MO; Charitable Trust, Sisters of the Most Precious Blood of O'Fallon, MO; St. Elizabeth Academy, St. Louis, MO; St. Elizabeth Adult Day Care Center, St. Louis, MO; Centers for Professional and Pastoral Services, O'Fallon, MO.
Represented in the Archdioceses of Anchorage, St. Louis and Washington and in the Dioceses of Jefferson City, Springfield in Illinois and Wheeling-Charleston. Also in Bolivia, Peru, Estonia, Finland and Italy.

[3310] (P.M.)—SISTERS OF THE PRESENTATION OF MARY (P)

Founded in France in 1796. First foundation in the United States in 1873.

General Motherhouse: *Presentazione di Maria*, Viale PIO XI, 29 C.P. 104, Castelgandolfo, Italy, 00040. Mother Angele Dion, Supr. Gen.

Inter-Provincial Novitiate: 186 Lowell Rd., Hudson, NH 03051. Tel: 603-880-8186. Sr. Helene Cote, P.M., Dir.

Manchester Province: *Provincial Administration*, 495 Mammoth Rd., Manchester, NH 03104-5494. Tel: 603-669-1080. Sr. Suzanne Bourret, P.M., Prov. Supr.
Total Number in Province: 124.
Properties owned and/or sponsored: Rivier College, Nashua, NH; Presentation of Mary Academy, Hudson, NH; Provincial House; St. Joseph Residence; St. Marie Residence, Manchester, NH; Our Lady of Hope House of Prayer, New Ipswich, NH; Bethany House, Manchester, NH; Presentation of Mary Novitiate, Hudson, NH; Emmanuel House, Woonsocket, RI; Emmaus Convent, Manchester, NH; Adoramus Community, Hudson, NH.
Represented in the Dioceses of Manchester and Providence.

Methuen Province - Provincial Administration: *Sisters of the Presentation of Mary*, 209 Lawrence St., Methuen, MA 01844. Tel: 978-687-1369; Tel: 978-685-0980. Sr. Cecile Plasse, P.M., Prov.
Total number in Province: 93.
Properties owned and/or sponsored: Montessori Day Nurseries; Marie Joseph Spiritual Center, Biddeford, ME; Presentation of Mary Academy, Methuen, MA.
Ministry in High Schools; Elementary Schools; Montessorri Day Nurseries; Religious Instruction Centers; Spiritual Retreat Center.
Represented in the Archdiocese of Boston and in the Dioceses of Portland (In Maine) and Worcester.

[3320] (P.B.V.M.)—SISTERS OF THE PRESENTATION OF THE B.V.M. (P)

Founded in Ireland in 1775. First foundation in San Francisco, CA in 1854.
Represented in the United States in the following Archdioceses and Dioceses.

Dubuque (P)

Mt. Loretto Convent, Motherhouse and Novitiate: 2360 Carter Rd., Dubuque, IA 52001-2997. Tel: 563-588-2008; Fax: 563-588-4463. Sr. Jennifer Rausch, P.B.V.M., Pres.
Total in Community: 117.
Legal Title: *Sisters of the Presentation of the B.V.M., Dubuque, IA.*
Ministry in the field of Religious and Academic Education; Hospital & Prison Chaplaincy; Elder Care; Parish & Campus Ministries; South American Bolivian Mission; Diocesan/Metropolitan Offices; Retreat & Spiritual Direction; Hispanic Ministry; Peace and Justice; Social Services; Internal Community Ministry.
Represented in the Archdioceses of Chicago, Dubuque, Kansas City, KS, Louisville, New Orleans, St. Paul-Minneapolis and Washington and in the Dioceses of Brownsville, Covington, Davenport, Des Moines, Fort Wayne-South Bend, Jackson, Knoxville, La Crosse, Madison, Omaha, Orlando, Rapid City, Sioux City, Sioux Falls, and Winona. Also in Bolivia.

New York (P)

Mt. St. Joseph Administration Center: *Sisters of the Presentation of the Blessed Virgin Mary*, 84 Presentation Way, New Windsor, NY 12553. Tel: 845-564-0513; Fax: 845-567-0219. Sr. Patricia Anastasio, P.B.V.M., Pres.; Sr. Margaret Muller, P.B.V.M., Community Archivist.
Total in Community: 126.
Ministry in the field of Academic Education at all levels; Pastoral Services; Health Care and Social Services.
Represented in the Archdioceses of Boston, Los Angeles, Newark, New Orleans, New York and Washington and in the Dioceses of Brooklyn, Fall River, Norwich, Paterson, Providence and Worcester. Also in Bolivia.

Our Lady of the Presentation Motherhouse: 419 Woodrow Rd., Staten Island, NY 10312. Tel: 718-356-2121. Sr. Rosemary Ward, Congregational Leader.
Professed Sisters: 18.
Ministry in Elementary Schools; University; Campus Ministry; Pastoral Counseling; Adult Education; Healing & Parish Ministry.
Represented in the Archdioceses of New York and Philadelphia and in the Diocese of Sioux Falls.

San Francisco Presentation Congregational Offices: 281 Masonic Ave., San Francisco, CA 94118. Tel: 415-422-5001. Sr. Stephanie Still, P.B.V.M., Pres. Tel: 415-422-5013; Christine Doan, Archivist.
Total in Community: 90.
Legal Title: *Sisters of the Presentation.*
Ministry in the field of Religious and Academic Education at all levels; Parish Ministry; Social and Health Ministry; College and University Teaching; Retreat Work; Church Related Administrative Positions; Missionary Work; Internal Ministry.
Represented in the Archdioceses of Los Angeles and San Francisco and in the Dioceses of Fresno, Oakland, Orange and San Jose.

Albany (P)

St. Colman's Presentation Convent, Motherhouse and Novitiate: Sisters of the Presentation of the Blessed Virgin Mary P.V.B.M., 11 Haswell Rd, Watervliet, NY 12189. Tel: 518-273-4911; Fax: 518-273-3312. Mother Mary Carmel, Supr.
Total in Community: 30.

Ministry in the field of Academic Education; Day Care Center; Child Caring Institution; Resident School for Autistic & Emotionally Disturbed Children; Parish Ministry.
Represented in the Diocese of Albany.

Fargo (P)

Sacred Heart Convent, Motherhouse and Novitiate: *Sisters of Presentation of the Blessed Virgin Mary P.B.V.M.*, 1101 32nd Ave. S., Fargo, ND 58103. Tel: 701-237-4857; Email: president@presentationsisters.com. Sr. Mary Margaret Mooney, P.B.V.M., Pres.; Sr. Maureen Walker, Archivist.
Total in Community: 45.
Sponsored Ministries: Presentation Prayer Center, Fargo, ND; Presentation Center, Fargo, ND; Hughes, Inc., Fargo, ND; The Presentation Sisters Foundation, Fargo, ND; Presentation Partners in Housing; Office of Peace & Justice.
Represented in the Dioceses of Columbus, Fargo, Jackson and New Ulm. Also in Peru.

Sioux Falls (P)

Presentation Convent, Motherhouse and Novitiate: *Sisters of the Presentation of the Blessed Virgin Mary*, 1500 N. Second St., Aberdeen, SD 57401. Tel: 605-229-8419. Sr. Pam Donelan, P.B.V.M., Pres.; Sr. Lois Ann Sargent, Congregation Archivist.
Total in Community: 98.
Ministry in the field of Academic Education; Hospitals; Homes for the Aged; Parish Pastoral Ministry; Hispanic Ministry; Ministry in Zambia, Africa, and Guatamala.
Represented in the Diocese of Sioux Falls.

Worcester (P)

Presentation Convent of the Presentation of the B.V.M: 99 Church St., Leominster, MA 01453. Sr. Patricia Anastasio, P.B.V.M., Pres.
Total in Community: 126.
Sisters staff: Elementary and High School Education; Pastoral Ministry; Social Services; Nursing.
Represented in the Archdioceses of Boston, Los Angeles, Newark, New Orleans, New York and Washington and in the Dioceses of Brooklyn, Fall River, Metuchen, Norwich, Paterson, Providence and Worcester. Also in Bolivia.

[3330] (P.B.V.M.)—UNION OF SISTERS OF THE PRESENTATION OF THE BLESSED VIRGIN MARY (P)

The Congregation of the Presentation was founded in Cork, Ireland, 1775. By decree of the Sacred Congregation for Religious, the Union of Sisters of the Presentation was established in Ireland in 1976. First U.S.A. Province in 1989.

Generalate: Monasterevan Co., Kildare, Ireland Tel: 045-525-335. Sr. Terry Abraham, P.B.V.M., Supr. Gen.; Sr. Antonio Heaphy, P.B.V.M., Provincial; Sr. Vera Butler, P.B.V.M., Asst. Provincial; Sr. Katherine Fennell, P.B.V.M., Treas.

Novitiate: 10843 Gorman Ave., Los Angeles, CA 90059. Tel: 714-220-2861.
Perpetual Profession: 63.
Sisters serve and staff: Elementary, University and Religious Education; Parish Ministry; Retreat Ministry; Health & Hospital Services; Social Services.
Represented in the Archdioceses of Los Angeles, Mobile, New Orleans, San Antonio and San Francisco and in the Dioceses of Biloxi, Jackson, Oakland, Orange, Phoenix, San Bernardino and Tucson.

[3340] (S.P.)—SISTERS OF PROVIDENCE (D)

Founded in Kingston, Canada in 1861. First foundation in the United States in 1873. Became independent, diocesan foundation in 1892.

Administrative Office: 5 Gamelin St., Holyoke, MA 01040-4081. Tel: 413-536-7511; Fax: 413-536-7917; Email: sisters@sisofprov.org. Sr. Kathleen Popko, S.P., Congregation Pres.
Professed Sisters: 47.
Legal Holdings and Titles: Sisters of Providence, Inc., Holyoke, MA; Sisters of Providence Health System, Inc., Springfield, MA; Family Services: Providence Ministries for the Needy, Holyoke, MA; Brightside for Families and Children, Inc., Holyoke, MA; Retreat Center: Genesis Spiritual Life and Conference Center, Inc., Westfield, MA; Mary's Meadow at Providence Place, Inc., Holyoke, MA; Senior Independent Living: Providence Place, Inc., Holyoke, MA; Sponsoring Congregation of Catholic Health East; Sisters of Providence Health System, Inc., Springfield, MA; Hospitals: The Mercy Hospital, Inc.; Mercy Medical Center; The Providence Hospital, Inc.; Providence Behavioral Health Hospital, Holyoke, MA; Sisters of Providence Care Centers, Inc., including: Beaven-Kelley Home, Holyoke, MA; Farren Care Center, Turners Falls, MA; Mount St. Vincent Care Center, Holyoke, MA; Providence Care Center of Lenox, Lenox, MA; Mercy Adult Day Health, Westfield, MA; St. Luke's Home, Springfield, MA; St. Joseph of the Pines, Inc., Southern Pines, NC, including a) Independent Retirement: Belle Meade; Pine Knoll. b) Rehab/Skilled Nursing: The Health Center; Therapy Village. c) Assisted Living: The Coventry. d) Affordable Housing: Providence Place I-IV.
Represented in the Dioceses of Springfield in Massachusetts, Raleigh and Worcester.

[3350] (S.P.)—SISTERS OF PROVIDENCE (P)

Founded in Montreal in 1843. First foundation in the United States in 1856.

General Motherhouse and Novitiate: 12055 rue Grenet, Montreal, Canada, H4J 2J5. Sr. Kathryn Rutan, S.P., Gen. Supr.

Mother Joseph Province (2000): *Sisters of Providence*, 1801 Lind Ave., SW, #9016, Renton, WA 98057-9016. Tel: 425-525-3355; Fax: 425-525-3984; Web: www.sistersofprovidence.net. Sr. Karin Dufault, S.P., Prov. Supr.
Total in Community: 675; Sisters in Province: 146.
Ministerial trusts for women and children; care for the environment; socially responsible investing; repository for history of the Catholic Church in the Northwest; skilled nursing for our senior and disabled sisters from our own and other congregatioins.
Properties, entities and divisions owned or operated: Sisters of Providence-Mother Joseph Province; St. Joseph Residence, Seattle, WA; Mount St. Joseph, Spokane, WA; Providence Pariseau; Sojourner Place, Seattle, WA; Building Bridges, Portland, OR; Providence Archives, Seattle, WA; Sisters of Providence Retirement Trust, Renton, WA.
Represented in the Archdioceses of Portland in Oregon and Seattle and in the Diocese of Spokane.

Novitiate House: 1016 N. Superior St., #4, Spokane, WA 99202-2096. Tel: 509-487-7644; Fax: 509-489-0964. Sr. Margaret Botch, S.P., Novitiate Dir.

Vocation Office: 4800 37th Ave., S.W., Seattle, WA 98126-2724. Tel: 206-923-4028. Sr. Joan Gallagher, S.P., Vocation Dir.

Our Lady of Province: 47 W. Spring St., Winooski, VT 05404. Tel: 802-655-2395; Fax: 802-655-3888. Sr. Carmen Proulx, S.P., Coord.
Total in Community: 24.

Emilie Gamelin Province (2005): *Sisters of Providence*, 47 W. Spring St., Winooski, VT 05404. Tel: 802-655-2395; Fax: 802-655-3888. Sr. Carmen Proulx, S.P., Coord.
Total in Community: 22.

[3360] (S.P.)—SISTERS OF PROVIDENCE OF SAINT MARY-OF-THE-WOODS, INDIANA (P)

Founded in France in 1806. First foundation in the United States in 1840.

General Administration: Sisters of Providence - Owens Hall, Saint Mary Of The Woods, IN 47876-1007. Tel: 812-535-4193; Web: www.sistersofprovidence.org. Sr. Denise Wilkinson, S.P., Gen. Supr.; Sr. Mary Ryan, S.P., Congregation Archivist; Sr. Rosemary Schmalz, S.P., Gen. Sec.
Total number Professed Sisters: 360.
Legal Titles and Sponsored Institutions: Guerin College Preparatory High School, River Grove, IL; *Guerin Outreach Ministries, Inc., Saint Mary-of-the-Woods, IN; Saint Mary-of-the-Woods College, Saint Mary-of-the-Woods, IN; Woods Day Care/Preschool, Inc., St. Mary-of-the-Woods, IN; Providence Self Sufficiency Ministries, Inc., Georgetown, IN; Sisters of Providence Community Support Trust (1969-Foundation to provide support for the aged and infirm members of the Congregation) Indianapolis, IN; Providence Health Care, Inc., St. Mary-of-the-Woods, IN; Providence Cristo Rey High School, Indianapolis, IN.
Ministry in the fields of Education at all levels; Diocesan Offices; Parish and Pastoral Ministry; Health Care and Retirement Facilities; Congregation Administration; Social Services; Therapeutic/Rehabilitative/Mental Health Services.
Represented in the Archdioceses of Baltimore, Boston, Chicago, Cincinnati, Indianapolis, Louisville, Los Angeles, Oklahoma City, Omaha, Portland in Oregon, St. Paul-Minneapolis, San Antonio, Santa Fe and Washington and in the Dioceses of Belleville, Charlotte, Cleveland, Corpus Christi, Duluth, Evansville, Fort Wayne-South Bend, Gary, Joliet, Lafayette (LA), Lafayette in Indiana, La Crosse, Lexington, Manchester, Richmond, San Bernardino, San Diego, Trenton and Venice. Also in China, Singapore and Taiwan.

Area of Taiwan: *Providence University*, 200 Chung Chi Rd., Shalu Districk, Taichung City 43301, Taiwan, Republic of China Tel: 011-886-4-2631-1182. Sr. Norene WU, S.P., Area Rep.
Total in Community: 11.
Ministry in the field of Education; Elderly Care; Opportunity Center for Mentally Handicapped.
Represented in the Archdiocese of Taipei and in the Dioceses of Chiayi, Taichung and Tainan.

[3390] (R.A.)—RELIGIOUS OF THE ASSUMPTION (P)

Founded in France in 1839. Established in the United States in 1919.

Generalate: 17 rue de l'Assomption, Paris, France, 75016.
Universal total in Congregation: 1300.
Represented in 34 countries through Europe, Africa, Asia, North America, Central America and South America.

Administrative Office: 1001 S. 47th St., Philadelphia, PA 19143. Tel: 215-386-2545.

North America Province: *Provincial House*, 11 Old English Rd., Worcester, MA 01609. Tel: 508-793-1954. Sr. Mary Ann Azanza, R.A., Prov. Supr.
Total number in Province: 28.
Ministry in Spiritual Formation; Counseling; Campus Ministry; Pastoral and Social Ministry; Education; Peace and Justice.
Represented in the Archdiocese of Philadelphia and in the Dioceses of Worcester and Las Cruces.

[3400] (R.S.C.)—RELIGIOUS SISTERS OF CHARITY (P)

Founded in Dublin, Ireland in 1815. Sisters in entire Congregation 505.

Motherhouse: *Caritas*, 15 Gilford Rd., Sandymount, Dublin 4, Ireland Sr. Mary Christian, Supr. Gen.

U.S. Headquarters & Novitiate (1953): *Regional Residence*, 10668 St. James Dr., Culver City, CA 90230. Tel: 310-559-0176; Fax: 310-559-3530. Sr. Marsha Moon, R.S.C., Reg. Leader.
Total in U.S. Community: 32.
Represented in the Archdiocese of Los Angeles.

[3410] (R.C.E.)—RELIGIOUS OF CHRISTIAN EDUCATION (P)

Founded in France in 1817. First foundation in the United States in 1905.

General Motherhouse: France

Provincial Residence: 444 Centre St., Milton, MA 02186. Tel: 781-894-2008; Fax: 401-349-4970. Sr. Martha Brigham, R.C.E., Pres.
Total in Community: 14.
Legal Title: *Religious of Christian Education, Inc.*
Ministry in Religious Education Centers; Pastoral Associates; Teaching; Home Care.
Represented in the Archdiocese of Boston and in the Dioceses of Fall River and Springfield in Massachusetts.

[3430] (M.P.F.)—RELIGIOUS TEACHERS FILIPPINI (P)

Founded in Italy in 1692. First foundation in the United States in 1910.

General Motherhouse: *Villa Maria Regina*, Via Stazione Ottavia, 72, Rome, Italy Sr. Nicolina Bandiera, M.P.F., Supr. Gen.

St. Lucy Filippini Province: Villa Walsh, Morristown, NJ 07960-4928. Tel: 973-538-2886. Sr. Betty Jean Takacs, M.P.F., Prov. Supr.; Sr. Mary DeBacco, M.P.F., Community Archivist.
Total in Community: 220.
Ministry in the field of Religious and Academic Education in elementary and secondary schools; Child Care Centers; Parish Ministry; Pastoral Care; Foreign Mission Work; House of Prayer; Retreat House.
Properties owned and sponsored: Villa Walsh, Morristown, NJ; Villa Victoria, Trenton, NJ; St. Joseph by The Sea, South Mantoloking, NJ; St. Joseph Convent, Bristol, CT; Villa Ferretti, Winchester Ctr, CT; Holy Land Convent, Waterbury, CT.
Represented in the Archdioceses of Hartford, Newark, Philadelphia and Santa Fe, and in the Dioceses of Brooklyn, Cleveland, Camden, Metuchen, Orlando, Paterson, Pittsburgh, Providence, Scranton and Trenton.

[3449] (C.V.I.)—RELIGIOUS OF THE INCARNATE WORD (P)

Founded in Lyon, France, in 1625. First foundation in the United States in 1853, in Mexico 1894.

General Motherhouse: Industria #1-Col. Toriello Guerra, Deleg., Tlalpan, Mexico, D.F. 14050. Sr. Margarita Dibildox, C.V.I., Gen. Supr.

U.S. Vice Provincial House: 153 Rainier Ct., Chula Vista, CA 91911. Tel: 619-420-0231. Sr. Camille Crabbe, C.V.I., Vice Prov.
Total in Congregation: 470.
Ministry in Parishes; Schools; Missions and Boarding for Students.
Represented in the Diocese of San Diego. Also in Africa, Argentina, El Salvador, France, Guatemala, Mexico, Spain and Uruguay.

[3450] (R.J.M.)—RELIGIOUS OF JESUS AND MARY (P)

Founded at Lyons, France, 1818. First foundation in the United States in 1877.

Motherhouse: Via Nomentana 325, Rome, Italy Rev. Sr. Angeles Alino, R.J.M., Supr. Gen.
Universal total in Congregation: 1433.

United States Province Provincialate: 125 Michigan Ave., N.E., 4th Fl., Washington, DC 20017. Tel: 202-884-9795; Fax: 202-884-9794. Sr. Eileen C. Reid, R.J.M., Prov.; Sr. Janice Farnham, R.J.M., Archivist.
Total in Community: 90.
Legal Title: *U.S. Province of the Religious of Jesus and Mary, Inc.*
Ministry in the field of Academic and Religious Education; Pastoral Ministry; Social Services; Volunteer Program.
Represented in the Archdioceses of Boston, Los Angeles, New York and Washington and in the Dioceses of Fall River, Manchester, Providence and San Diego. Also in Haiti.

[3460] (R.M.I.)—RELIGIOUS OF MARY IMMACULATE (P)

Founded in Madrid, Spain in 1876.

Mother House: Madrid, Spain

Generalate: Rome, Italy

U.S. Foundation (1954): *Villa Maria*, 719 Augusta St., San Antonio, TX 78215. Tel: 210-226-0025; Fax: 210-226-3305. Sr. Martha Ochoa, R.M.I., Local Supr.
Total in Community: 8.

Headquarters: *Centro Maria*, 539 West 54th St., New York, NY 10019. Tel: 212-581-5273. Sr. Hilda Ramirez, R.M.I., Local Supr.
Total in Community: 8.
Represented in the Archdioceses of New York, San Antonio and Washington.

[3465] (R.S.H.M.)—RELIGIOUS OF THE SACRED HEART OF MARY (P)

Founded in France in 1849. First foundation in the United States in 1877.

Generalate: Via Sorelle Marchisio 41, Rome, Italy, 00168. Sr. Terezinha Cecchin, R.S.C.M., Gen. Supr.
Universal total in Congregation: 900.

Eastern American Province (1907): 50 Wilson Park Dr., Tarrytown, NY 10591. Tel: 914-631-8872. Sr. Kathleen Fagan, R.S.H.M., Prov. Email: kfagan@rshmeap.org.
Total in Community: 193.
Legal Title: *Sisters of the Sacred Heart of Mary.*
Ministries including Education; Pastoral Ministry; Retreat and Spiritual Direction; Health Care and Social Work.
Represented in the Archdioceses of Baltimore, New York and St. Louis and in the Dioceses of Arlington, Brooklyn, Norwich, Oakland, Palm Beach, Richmond, Rockville Centre, Trenton, Venice and Winona. Also in Africa and Europe.

Western American Province (1959): *Religious of the Sacred Heart of Mary R.S.H.M. Provincial Center*, 441 N. Garfield Ave., Montebello, CA 90640-2901. Tel: 323-887-8821; Fax: 323-887-8952. Sr. Mary Genino, R.S.H.M., Prov.
Total number in Province: 62.
Legal Titles or Holdings: Religious of the Sacred Heart of Mary, Western American Province, a California nonprofit corporation, Marymount School, a California nonprofit corporation.
Ministry in the field of Academic Education at all levels; Diverse Pastoral Ministries; Prison Ministry; Justice and Peace Advocacies; Women Shelters; Youths at Risk.
Represented in the Archdioceses of Los Angeles and San Francisco and in the Diocese of San Bernardino. Also in Mexico.

[3470] (S.R.C.M.)—SISTERS OF REPARATION OF THE CONGREGATION OF MARY, INC. (D)

St. Zita's Villa, Monsey, NY 10952. Tel: 845-356-2011. Sr. Maureen Francis, S.R.C.M.
Total in Community: 3.
Represented in the Archdiocese of New York.

[3475] (S.R.)—SISTERS OF REPARATION OF THE SACRED WOUNDS OF JESUS (D)

Founded in 1954 in New York by Mother Mary Rose Therese, S.R. Established in the Diocese of San Diego in 1959. Motherhouse and Novitiate transferred to the Archdiocese of Portland in Oregon in 1973.

General Motherhouse and Novitiate: *Sacred Wounds of Jesus Convent*, 2120 S.E. 24th Ave., Portland, OR 97214. Tel: 503-236-4207; Fax: 503-236-3400; Email: repsrs@comcast.net; Email: MMAngels@comcast.net; Web: www.reparationsisters.org. Mother Mary of the Angels, S.R., Supr.
Sisters: 2; Donne Members: 168.
Legal Title: *Sisters of Reparation of the Sacred Wounds of Jesus, Inc., Portland, OR.*
Ministry in Health Care; Education; Pastoral Animation.
Represented in the Archdiocese of Portland in Oregon.

[3480] (C.R.)—SISTERS OF THE RESURRECTION (P)

Founded in Rome, Italy, in 1891. First foundation in the United States in 1900.

General Motherhouse: Via Marcantonio Colonna 52A, Rome, Italy Rev. Mother Teresa Maria Kreft, C.R., Supr. Gen.
Universal total in Congregation: 450.

Western Province Provincialhouse and Novitiate: 7432 Talcott Ave., Chicago, IL 60631. Tel: 773-792-6363. Sr. Virginia Ann Wanzek, C.R., Prov. Supr.
Total in Community: 42.
Properties owned or sponsored: Resurrection High School; Resurrection Health Care Corporation.
Represented in the Archdioceses of Chicago, Milwaukee and Mobile.

Eastern Province Provincialhouse and Novitiate: *Sisters of the Resurrection*, 35 Boltwood Ave., Castleton On Hudson, NY 12033. Tel: 518-732-2226; Fax: 518-732-2898; Email: crsister@resurrectionsisters.org. Sr. Dolores Stepien, C.R., Prov. Supr.
Total in Community: 35.
Legal Title: *Sisters of the Resurrection, New York, Inc.*
Ministry in Nursing Homes; Elementary Schools; Christian Doctrine Centers; High School for Girls; Preschools; Pastoral Associates.
Represented in the Archdiocese of New York and in the Dioceses of Albany and Trenton.

[3490] (O.S.S.)—RELIGIOUS OF THE ORDER OF THE BLESSED SACRAMENT AND OF OUR LADY (P)

Founded in France in 1639. First foundation in the United States in 1912. The Sisters devote their lives to the perpetual adoration of Christ in the Eucharist.

Blessed Sacrament Monastery: 86 Dromore Rd., Scarsdale, NY 10583-1706. Tel: 914-722-1657. Sr. Mary Veronica, O.S.S., Prioress.
Professed Sisters: 7.

Monastery of Perpetual Adoration (1951): 2798 U.S. 31 N., P.O. Box 86, Conway, MI 49722. Tel: 231-347-0447. Sr. Mary Francis Blackmore, O.S.S., Prioress.
Professed Sisters: 2.
Represented in the Archdiocese of New York and in the Diocese of Gaylord.

[3499] (S.J.S.)—SISTER SERVANTS OF THE BLESSED SACRAMENT (P)

Founded in Mexico in 1904. First foundation in the United States in 1926.

General Motherhouse: Juan Bernardino 650, Guadalajara, Jalisco, Mexico, 45000. Sr. Rosa Maria Sierra Barba, S.J.S., Supr. Gen.

U.S. Province: 3173 Winnetka Dr., Bonita, CA 91902. Tel: 619-267-0720; Fax: 619-267-0920. Sr. Maria Paz Uribe, S.J.S., Prov. Supr.
Total in Community: 56.
Legal Title: *Sister Servants of the Blessed Sacrament, Inc.*
Ministry in the field of Education.
Represented in the Archdiocese of Los Angeles and in the Dioceses of Fresno, Sacramento, San Diego and Monterey.

[3500] (S.S.S.)—SERVANTS OF THE BLESSED SACRAMENT (P)

Founded in France in 1859; First foundation in the United States in 1947.

General Motherhouse: 580 Dufferin, Sherbrooke, Canada, J1H 4N1.

U.S. Address: *Blessed Sacrament Convent*, 101 Silver St., Waterville, ME 04901. Tel: 207-872-7072; Fax: 207-873-2317. Sr. Josephine Roney, S.S.S., Local/Regional Supr.
Total in Community: 16.
Represented in the Dioceses of Portland (In Maine) and Pueblo (Colorado).

[3510] (S.S.C.K.)—CONGREGATION OF SISTER SERVANTS OF CHRIST THE KING (D)

Founded in the United States in 1936.

General Motherhouse: *Loretto Convent*, N. 8114 Co. W.W. Calvary St., Mount Calvary, WI 53057. Tel: 920-753-3211. Sr. Stephen Bloesl, Supr.
Professed Sisters: 6.
Represented in the Archdiocese of Milwaukee and in the Diocese of Fargo.

[3520] (S.S.C.M.)—SERVANTS OF THE HOLY HEART OF MARY (P)

Founded in Paris, France in 1860. First foundation in the United States in 1889.

Generalate: 2029 rue Holy Cross, Montreal, Canada, H4E 2A4. Sr. Louise Payeur, S.S.C.M., Supr. Gen.

United States Region-Holy Family Province: *Provincialate*, 15 Elmwood Dr., Kankakee, IL 60901. Tel: 815-937-2380. Sr. Linda K. Hatton, S.S.C.M., Prov. Supr.
Total number in Region: 37.
Legal Title: *Servants of the Holy Heart of Mary.*
Provena Health.
Ministry in Grammar Schools; Nursing Homes; Health Care; Education; Pastoral Ministry; Parishes; Ministry to the Aged; and Home Missions.
Represented in the Archdiocese of Milwaukee and in the Dioceses of Belleville, Joliet, Peoria and Rockford.

[3530] (S.SP.S.)—MISSIONARY SISTERS SERVANTS OF THE HOLY SPIRIT (P)

Founded in Holland in 1889. First foundation in the United States in 1901.

General Motherhouse: *Convento dello Spirito Santo*, Via Cassia 645, Rome, Italy, 00189. Sr. Maria Theresia Hornemann, S.Sp.S., Supr. Gen.
Universal total in Congregation: 3239.

American Motherhouse (1901): *Convent of the Holy Spirit*, 319 Waukegan Rd., P.O. Box 6026, Techny, IL 60082-6026. Tel: 847-441-0126; Fax: 847-441-5587. Sr. Carol Welp, S.Sp.S., Prov.
Total in Community: 78.
Legal Titles: Arnold Janssen Foundation, Techny, IL; Helena Stollenwerk Foundation, Techny, IL.
Ministry in Schools; Catechetical Work; Parish Ministry & Administration.
Represented in the Archdioceses of Chicago and New York and in the Diocese of Memphis.

[3540] (S.SP.S.DEA.P.)—SISTER-SERVANTS OF THE HOLY SPIRIT OF PERPETUAL ADORATION (P)

Founded in Holland in 1896. First foundation in the United States in 1915. Second foundation in the United States in 1928.

Generalate: Convent of the Most Holy Trinity, Bad Driburg, Germany Mother Maria Elizabeth, S.Sp.S-.deA.P., Supr. Gen.

U.S. House of Formation: *Mount Grace Convent*, 1438 E. Warne Ave., Saint Louis, MO 63107-1015. Tel: 313-381-5686. Sr. Mary Catherine, S.Sp.S.deA.P., Supr.
Professed Sisters: 23.

Convent of Divine Love: 2212 Green St., Philadelphia, PA 19130-3197. Tel: 215-567-0123. Sr. Mary Caritas, S.Sp.S.deA.P., Supr.
Professed Sisters: 22.

Blessed Sacrament Convent: 4105 Ocean Dr., Corpus Christi, TX 78411. Tel: 361-852-6212. Sr. Mary Margaret Friedl, S.Sp.S. de A.P., Supr.
Professed Sisters: 9.

Adoration Convent of Christ the King Church: 1040 S. Cotner Blvd., Lincoln, NE 68510. Tel: 402-489-0765. Sr. Mary Henrita, S.Sp.S.deA.P., Supr.
Professed Sisters: 8.
Represented in the Archdioceses of Lincoln.

[3550] (S.C.I.M.)—SERVANTS OF THE IMMACULATE HEART OF MARY (P)

Good Shepherd Sisters of Quebec

Founded in Canada in 1850. First foundation in the United States in 1882.

Generalate: 2550, rue Marie-Fitzbach, Canada Sr. Theresa Rounds, S.C.I.M., Supr. Gen.
Universal total in Congregation: 472.

Provincial Headquarters: *St. Joseph Province*, 409 Pool St., Biddeford, ME 04005. Tel: 207-282-4976; Fax: 207-282-7376. Sr. Theresa Therrien, S.C.I.M., Prov.
Total in Community: 57.
Ministry in Grammar Schools; Adoption Agency; Group Home for Unmarried Mothers; Youth (Retreat Work); Apostolate to the Elderly; High School Campus Ministry; Prison/Jail Ministry; Home for Women in Transition.
Represented in the Archdiocese of Boston and in the Diocese of Portland (In Maine).

[3560] (S.J.)—SERVANTS OF JESUS (P)

Founded in Detroit, Michigan in 1974.

Headquarters: *Servants of Jesus*, 6055 Weiss, Saginaw, MI 48603. Tel: 989-249-4940.
Total in Community: 17.
Ministries: Diocesan Offices; Parish Ministry; Religious Education; Catholic Schools; Legal Aid; Health Care.
Represented in the Archdiocese of Detroit and in the Dioceses of Grand Rapids, Gaylord and Saginaw.

[3570] (O.S.M.)—MANTELLATE SISTERS, SERVANTS OF MARY OF BLUE ISLAND (P)

Founded in Italy in 1861. First foundation in the United States in 1916.

Generalate and Novitiate: Rome, Italy

U.S. Motherhouse & Novitiate: *Convent of Our Mother of Sorrows*, 13811 S. Western Ave., Blue Island, IL 60406. Tel: 708-385-2103. Sr. Louise Staszewski, O.S.M., Reg. Supr.
Professed Sisters: 12.
Represented in the Archdiocese of Chicago.

[3572] (O.S.M.)—MANTELLATE SISTERS SERVANTS OF MARY OF PLAINFIELD (P)

Founded October 6, 1861 in Treppio, Italy. First founded in the United States 1916.
Universal number of Mantellate Sisters: 392.

Mantellate Sisters Servants of Mary of Plainfield (1977): 16949 S. Drauden Rd., Plainfield, IL 60586-9168. Tel: 815-436-5796. Sr. Louise Staszewski, O.S.M., Reg. Supr.
Sisters: 7.
Ministry in the field of Academic Education; Parish Ministry; Retreats; Social Work; Nursing; Homes for the Aged; Foreign Missions.
Represented in the Archdiocese of Chicago and in the Diocese of Joliet.

[3580] (O.S.M.)—SERVANTS OF MARY (P)

Founded in Italy in the 13th Century. First foundation in the United States in 1893.

General Motherhouse: 1 Brownsea Ct., 160 Clarence Rd., London, England, E58EF. Sr. Marie Therese Connor, O.S.M., Prioress Gen.

American Province (1893): *Provincial Motherhouse, Convent of Our Lady of Sorrows*, 7400 Military Ave., Omaha, NE 68134-3351. Tel: 402-571-2547; Fax: 402-573-6055; Web: osms.org. Sr. Mary Gehringer, O.S.M., Prov.
Total in Community: 82.

Properties owned and/or sponsored: Marian High School, Omaha, NE; Our Lady of Sorrows Convent, Omaha, NE.
Ministry in the field of Religious and Academic Education at all levels; Parishes; Social Service Agencies; Diocesan Offices; Hospital Pastoral Care; Counseling Agencies; Campus Ministry; Hospice; Health Care Services; Medical Research; Consulting; Spiritual Direction; Retreat Work.
Represented in the Archdioceses of Detroit, Omaha and Portland in Oregon and in the Dioceses of Des Moines, Gaylord, Grand Island, Green Bay, Ogdensburg, Sioux City and Tucson.

[3590] (O.S.M.)—SERVANTS OF MARY (SERVITE SISTERS) (D)

Founded in Italy in the 13th Century. First foundation in the United States in 1912.

General Motherhouse: *Servants of Mary*, 1000 College Ave. W., Ladysmith, WI 54848-2199. Tel: 715-532-3364; Fax: 715-532-9611; Web: www.servitesisters.org. Sr. Theresa H. Sandok, O.S.M., Pres.
Total in Community: 61.
Ministry in the fields of Education, Health Care, Pastoral Ministry, Parish Administration, Social Services and Law.
Represented in the Archdioceses of Boston, Chicago, Milwaukee and St. Paul-Minneapolis and in the Dioceses of Joliet, La Crosse, Phoenix, Superior and St. Petersburg.

[3595] (S.S.J.)—SERVANTS OF ST. JOSEPH (P)

Founded in Spain in 1874.

Motherhouse: Salamanca, Spain

General House: Rome, Italy Mother Josefa Somoza, Supr. Gen.

U.S. Address (1957): 203 N. Spring St., Falls Church, VA 22046. Tel: 703-533-8441; Fax: 703-534-9549. Sr. Augustina Temprano.
Total in Community: 7.
Represented in the Diocese of Arlington.

[3600] (S.DEM.)—SISTERS SERVANTS OF MARY (P)

Founded in Madrid, Spain by St. Maria Soledad Torres, August 15, 1851. First foundation in the United States in 1914.
Total Membership 1,700 Sisters.

General Motherhouse: via Antonio Musa 16, Rome, Italy, 00161. Mother Alfonsa Bellido, S.deM., Supr. Gen.

Provincial Motherhouse: 800 N. 18th St., Kansas City, KS 66102. Sr. Carmela Sanz, S.deM., Prov. Supr.; Sr. Claudia Rodriguez, S.deM., Local Supr.; Sr. Silvia Enriguez, S.deM., Community Archivist; Ema Munoz, S.de M., Treas.
Total number in Province: 249.
Represented in the Archdioceses of Kansas City in Kansas, Los Angeles, New Orleans and New York.

[3610] (S.S.M.I.)—SISTERS SERVANTS OF MARY IMMACULATE (P)

Founded in Zuzel, Ukraine on August 28, 1892. Approved by the Holy See, 1932. Arrived in the United States on August 15, 1935 at Stamford, Connecticut.

Generalate: Via Cassia Antica 104, Rome, Italy, 00191. Sr. Theresa Slota, S.S.M.I., Supr. Gen.

Sisters Servants of Mary Immaculate: *Sisters Servants Ln.*, 9 Emmanuel Dr., P.O. Box 9, Sloatsburg, NY 10974-0009. Tel: 845-753-2840. Sr. Kathleen Hutsko, S.S.M.I., Prov. Supr.
Total in Community: 33.
Properties owned and/or sponsored: Immaculate Conception Provincialate & Novitiate; St. Joseph's Home (for the aged); Saint Mary's Villa Spiritual, Cultural and Educational Center, Sloatsburg, NY.
Ministry in the field of Education; Parish and Pastoral ministry; Health Care; Administration; Retreat Ministry; Hospitality; Holy Dormition Pilgrimage; Catechetical; Seminary Library; Youth Ministry.
Represented in the Ukrainian and Byzantine Rite Catholic Dioceses of the United States.

[3615] (E.I.N.)—SERVANTS OF THE IMMACULATE CHILD MARY (ESCLAVAS DE LA INMACULADA NINA) (P)

Founded in Mexico in 1901. First foundation in the United States in 1978.

Motherhouse: *Mother Maria Reina Mula Casas*, Dr. Espina #10, 28019 Madrid, Spain

Provincial House: Matamoros #100, Tlalpan D.F., Mexico, C.P. 14000. Sr. M. Celina Luz Maria Perez Romero, E.W.

U.S. Foundation: 5135 Dartmouth Ave., Los Angeles, CA 90032. Tel: 323-225-3279. Sr. Raquel Diaz, E.I.N., Supr.; Sr. Josefina Lopez, E.I.N.; Sr. Maria del Refugio Carlos, E.I.N.; Sr. Josefina Guzman, E.I.N.

House of Formation: 350 S. Boyle Ave., Los Angeles, CA 90033. Tel: 323-269-7786. Sr. Raquel Diaz, E.I.N., Supr.; Sr. Maria Espindola, E.I.N.; Sr. Petra Lopez, E.I.N.
Total number of Sisters in the U.S: 3.
Ministry in the field of religious education and adult formation in parishes.
Represented in the Archdiocese of Los Angeles.

[3620] (S.S.M.I.)—SISTERS SERVANTS OF MARY IMMACULATE (P)

First founded in Poland in 1878.

General Motherhouse: Mariowka-Opoczynska, Poland Mother Danuta Wrobel, Mother Gen.
Total number of Sisters in the U.S: 33; Universal total in Congregation: 860.

American Province (1935): 1220 Tugwell Dr., Catonsville, MD 21228. Tel: 410-747-1353. Sr. Krystyna Mroczek, Prov. Supr.; Sr. Marianna Danko, Community Archivist.
Total in Community: 33.
Represented in the Archdioceses of Baltimore and Washington and in the Diocese of Cleveland.

[3630] (S.S.C.J.)—SERVANTS OF THE MOST SACRED HEART OF JESUS (P)

Founded in Poland in 1894.

General Motherhouse: 24 Garncarska St., Cracow, Poland Sr. Agnieszka Kijowska, Supr. Gen.

Sister Servants of the Most Sacred Heart of Jesus (1959): *Sacred Heart Province*, 866 Cambria St., Cresson, PA 16630-1713. Tel: 814-886-4223. Mother Jacinta Miryam Hanley, S.S.C.J., Prov. Supr.
Total number in Province: 25; Novices: 1; Aspirants: 2.
Represented in the Archdiocese of Philadelphia and in the Dioceses of Altoona-Johnstown and Wilmington. Also in Mandeville, Jamaica.

[3640] (S.M.G.)—POOR SERVANTS OF THE MOTHER OF GOD (P)

Founded in London, England in 1869. First foundation in the United States in 1947.

General Motherhouse: Maryfield, Roehampton, London, England, S.W. 15. Sr. Mary Whelan, S.M.G., Supr. Gen.

American Foundation: *Maryfield Nursing Home*, 1315 Greensboro Rd., High Point, NC 27260. Tel: 336-886-2444. Sr. Mary O'Duffy, S.M.G., Area Supr.
Total in Community: 5.
Ministry in Hospitals; Nursing Homes.
Represented in the Diocese of Charlotte.

[3658] (S.S.H.J.)—SISTERS OF THE SACRED HEART OF JESUS (P)

Founded in Ragusa, Italy in 1889. First foundation in the United States in 1951.

Generalate House: *Instituto Sacro Cuore di Ragusa*, Via Cassia 1714, Rome, Italy, 00123.
Universal total in Congregation: 610.

Motherhouse: *Instituto Sacro Cuore*, Via Suor Maria Schinina 2, Ragusa, Italy, 97100.

American Headquarters: *Sacred Heart Villa School & Convent*, 5269 Lewiston Rd., Lewiston, NY 14092. Tel: 716-284-8273.
Legal Titles: Sacred Heart Villa School & Convent, Lewiston, NY; Saint Frances Cabrini Nursery and Convent, North Haven, CT.
Ministry in the field of Religious and Academic Education at all levels; Hospitals; Homes for the Aged; Orphanages; Parish Ministry; Youth Ministry; Foreign Missions; Social Services.
Represented in the Archdiocese of Hartford and in the Diocese of Buffalo.

[3660] (S.S.H.J.P.)—SERVANTS OF THE SACRED HEART OF JESUS AND OF THE POOR (P)

Founded in Leon, Gto., Mexico in 1885. First foundation in U.S. in 1907.

Motherhouse: Apartado 92, Puebla, Pue, Mexico, 72000. Tel: 01152-2222-42-18-69. Mother Magdalena Sofia Juarez, Gen. Supr.

U.S. Address: *Sacred Heart Children's Home Convent*, 3310 S. Zapata Hwy., Laredo, TX 78046. Tel: 956-723-3343; Fax: 956-723-3409. Sr. Maria Yolanda Fernandez, S.S.H.J.P., Major Supr.; Mother Maria Teresa Grajeda, S.S.H.J.P., Supr.; Sr. Maria Isidra Valdez, S.S.H.J.P., Admin.
Professed Sisters in U.S: 39.
Ministry in academic and religious education at all levels; Children's Home.
Represented in the Dioceses of Laredo and El Paso.

[3670] (S.S.C.J.)—SISTERS OF THE SACRED HEART OF JESUS OF SAINT JACUT (P)

Founded in France in 1816. First foundation in the United States in 1903.

Generalate: *Villa des Otages*, No. 8 85 rue Haxo, Paris, France, 75020.

Motherhouse: St. Jacut les Pins, Brittany, France, 56220.

USA/Mexico Province (1916): *Provincialate Offices*, 11931 Radium St., San Antonio, TX 78216. Tel: 210-344-7203; Fax: 210-341-0721. Sr. Cecilia Rodriguez, S.S.C.J., Prov.
Total in Community: 38.
Ministry in Education; Pastoral Work; Health Care; Mexico Missions.
Properties owned or sponsored: Mount Sacred Heart School, San Antonio, TX; Casa Angelique; Holy Spirit Convent, San Antonio, TX; Santa Maria Community, San Antonio, TX; St. Joseph's Community, San Antonio, TX; Beth Rachamim Community, San Antonio, TX; Sacred Heart Community, San Antonio, TX; Casa Ste. Emilie, San Antonio, TX; Provincialate Community, San Antonio, TX
Represented in the Archdioceses of Galveston-Houston and San Antonio. Also in Mexico City.

[3680] (S.H.J.M.)—SISTERS OF THE SACRED HEARTS OF JESUS AND MARY (P)

Founded in France in 1866. First foundation in United States in 1953.

Motherhouse: Essex, England

Regional House: 7626 Curry Ave., El Cerrito, CA 94530. Tel: 510-839-5213; Fax: 510-839-5256. Sr. Lorna K. Walsh, S.H.J.M., Team Member.
Universal total in Congregation: 160; U.S. Community: 7.
Ministry in Pastoral Care; Adult Education; Counseling; Children's Faith Formation; Nursing.
Represented in the Dioceses of Oakland and Stockton.

[3690] (SS.CC.)—CONGREGATION OF THE SACRED HEARTS AND OF PERPETUAL ADORATION (P)

Founded in France in 1800 as a Congregation of men and women. Members are consecrated to the Hearts of Jesus and Mary. Special Ministries are Perpetual Adoration, the education of youth, especially the poor, parish work and foreign missions. First Catholic missionaries to Hawaii in 1827: Sisters started Catholic Schools for girls in Hawaii 1859. First foundation in the continental United States in 1908.

Generalate: Via Aurelia 145, Scala C-Int 10-14, Rome, Italy, 00165. Sr. Rosa Maria Ferreiro, SS.CC., Supr. Gen.

Pacific Province: *Sisters of the Sacred Hearts*, 1120 Fifth Ave, Honolulu, HI 96816. Tel: 808-737-5822. Sr. Regina Mary Jenkins, SS.CC., Prov.
Total in Community: 36.
Legal Holdings and Titles: Sisters of the Sacred Hearts Corporation; Regina Pacis Convent; Sacred Hearts Academy Corporation; Saint Anthony Retreat Center Corporation; Malia O Ka Malu Community, Honolulu, HI; Na Leo Ho'onani Community, Honolulu, HI; Paewalani Community, Honolulu, HI; Our Lady of Grace Community, Artesia, NM.

East Coast Region: *Sisters of the Sacred Hearts of Jesus and Mary and of Perpetual Adoration*, 35 Huttleston Ave., Fairhaven, MA 02719-3154. Tel: 508-994-9341. Sr. Muriel Ann Lebeau, SS.CC., Supr.
Total in Community: 3.
Represented in the Diocese of Fall River.

[3710] (C.S.A.)—CONGREGATION OF SISTERS OF SAINT AGNES (P)

Founded in the United States in 1858.

General Motherhouse: *St. Agnes Convent*, 320 County Rd. K, Fond Du Lac, WI 54937-8158. Tel: 920-907-2300; Fax: 920-923-3194. Sr. Joann Sambs, C.S.A., Gen. Supr.; Sr. Diane Bauknecht, C.S.A., Gen. Vicar. Councilors: Sr. Sharon Pollnow, C.S.A.; Sr. Doris Klein, C.S.A.
Total in Congregation: 252.
Ministry in the field of Academic and Religious Education; Hospitals; Homes for Aged; Parish Ministry; Foreign Missions; Social Services; Healthcare.
Properties owned or sponsored: Hazotte Ministries, Inc.; Marian University, Fond du Lac, WI; Agnesian HealthCare of Fond du Lac, WI, Inc.; St. Francis Home, Fond du Lac, WI; Waupun Memorial Hospital, Waupun, WI; The Monroe Clinic, Monroe, WI.
Represented in the Archdioceses of Chicago, Milwaukee, Mobile, New York, and St. Paul-Minneapolis and in the Dioceses of Allentown, Altoona-Johnstown, Columbus, Fort Wayne-South Bend, Gallup, Gary, Green Bay, Jackson, Joliet, Madison, Marquette, Palm Beach, Phoenix, Raleigh, Salina, Toledo, Tucson and Venice. Also in Nicaragua.

[3718] (S.S.A.)—SISTERS OF ST. ANN

Founded in Italy in 1834.

General Motherhouse: V.d. Aldobrandeschi, Rome, Italy, 00163-100. Sr. Ernestine Fernandes, S.S.A., Supr. Gen.
Universal total in Congregation: 1500.

U.S. Delegation (1952): *Mount St. Ann*, 1120 N. Center St., P.O. Box 328, Ebensburg, PA 15931. Tel: 814-472-9354; Fax: 814-472-9354. Sr. Anna Maria Lorenzon, S.S.A., Delegate; Sr. Melany Pereira, S.S.A., Community Archivist.
Total in Community: 9.
Ministry in the field of Education; Retreat Ministry; Foreign Mission; Pastoral Ministry.
Represented in the Dioceses of Altoona-Johnstown and Corpus Christi.

[3720] (S.S.A.)—SISTERS OF SAINT ANNE (P)

Founded in Vaudreuil, Province of Quebec, Canada, 1850. First foundation in the United States in 1866.
Legal Title: *The Community of the Sisters of St. Anne.*

General Motherhouse: 1950 Provost St., H85 1P7, Lachine, Canada Sr. Rita Larivee, Congregational Leader.

Saint Marie Province (1887): 720 Boston Post Rd. E., Marlborough, MA 01752. Tel: 508-481-4934; Fax: 508-481-4939. Provincial Leaders: Sr. Yvette Dargy, S.S.A.; Sr. Pauline Laurence, S.S.A.; Sr. Joanne Dion, S.S.A.
Total number in Province: 103; Total in Community: 518.
Properties owned and/or sponsored: Saint Anne Convent; Mary Martha House, Marlborough, MA; Esther House, Worcester, MA; Marie Esther Health Center, Inc., Marlborough, MA; St. Anne Regional, Worcester, MA.
Ministry in the field of Academic and Religious Education at all levels; Center for Spiritual Renewal; Campus Ministry; Various Apostolates; Retreat Work; Pastoral Ministry; Ministry to the Aged, Shut-ins and the Poor; Assisted Living Nursing; Foreign Ministries.
Represented in the Archdiocese of Boston and in the Dioceses of Fall River, Providence, Springfield in Massachusetts and Worcester.

[3730] (O.S.B.M.)—SISTERS OF THE ORDER OF ST. BASIL THE GREAT (P)
(International Byzantine Rite)

Founded in Cappadocia in the 4th Century by St. Basil the Great and his sister St. Macrina. First foundation in the United States in 1911.

Basilian Generalate: Via San Alessio 26, Rome, Italy, 00153. Sr. Miriam Claire Kowal, O.S.B.M., Gen. Supr.

Philadelphia-Ukrainian Byzantine Rite: *Provincial and Motherhouse*, 710 Fox Chase Rd., Jenkintown, PA 19046. Tel: 215-663-9153; Fax: 215-379-4843. Sr. Dorothy Ann Busowski, O.S.B.M., Prov. Sup.
Solemnly Professed Sisters: 40.
Sponsored Institutions: Manor College; Saint Basil Academy; Basilian Spirituality Center.
Ministry in Education at all levels; Pastoral Ministry.
Represented in the Ukrainian Archdiocese of Philadelphia and in the Ukrainian Dioceses of Chicago, Parma and Stamford.

Pittsburgh Ruthenian Byzantine Rite-Motherhouse and Novitiate: *Mount St. Macrina*, 500 W. Main St., P.O. Box 878, Uniontown, PA 15401. Tel: 724-438-8644. Sr. Seraphim Olsafsky, O.S.B.M., Prov.
Professed Sisters: 61.
Legal Titles: Declaration of the Sisters of the Order of St. Basil the Great Endowment Trust; Declaration of Trust of the Sisters of the Order of St. Basil the Great Community Support Program; Mount St. Macrina Cemetery, Inc., Uniontown, PA.
Sister's serve in Diocesan, Parish and Religious Education Ministry; Health Care; Pastoral Ministry.
Represented in the Byzantine Archdiocese of Pittsburgh and in the Dioceses of Parma, Passaic and Phoenix (Byzantine).

[3735] (C.S.B.)—CONGREGATION OF ST. BRIGID (P)

Founded in Ireland in 1807.

U.S. Foundation (1953): *St. Brigid's Convent*, 5118 Loma Linda Dr., San Antonio, TX 78201. Tel: 210-733-0701. Sr. Anne Drea, C.S.B., Reg. Coord.
Total in Community: 15.
Properties owned and/or sponsored: Regional House.
Pastoral Ministry in Parishes, Detention Center and Hospitals; Academic Education at all levels; Music Ministry.
Represented in the Archdioceses of Boston and San Antonio and in the Diocese of Wilmington.

[3740] (S.S.C.)—SISTERS OF ST. CASIMIR (P)

Founded by Venerable Servant of God, Mother Maria Kaupas in the United States in 1907.

General Motherhouse: 2601 W. Marquette Rd., Chicago, IL 60629. Tel: 773-776-1324; Fax: 773-776-8755. Sr. M. Immacula Wendt, S.S.C., Gen. Supr.; Sr. Margaret Zalot, S.S.C., Gen. Sec.; Sr. Therese Banach, S.S.C., Co-Archivist; Sr. Elaine Kuizinas, S.S.C., Co-Archivist.
Total in Community: 83.
Properties owned and/or sponsored: Maria High School; Holy Cross Hospital, Chicago, IL; Villa Joseph Marie High School, Holland, PA.
Ministry in the field of Academic Education; Foreign Missions; Hospitals; Pastoral Ministry.
Represented in the Archdioceses of Chicago, Philadelphia and San Antonio and in the Diocese of Kalamazoo. Also in Argentina.

[3750] (S.S.CH.)—SISTERS OF ST. CHRETIENNE (P)

Founded in France in 1807. First foundation in the United States in 1903.

General Motherhouse: Metz (Moselle), France, 57000.

Regional Offices: 297 Arnold St., Wrentham, MA 02093-1798. Tel: 508-384-8066; Fax: 508-507-3634. Sr. Agnes Therrien, S.S.Ch., Regional Leader.
Total number in Province: 45.
Properties owned and/or sponsored: St. Chretienne Retirement Residence, Marlborough, MA; Our Lady Thrift Shop, Marlborough, MA; St. Chretienne Residence, Wrentham, MA.
Legal Titles: St. Chretienne Educational Institute, Inc., Marlborough, MA; St. Chretienne Educational Institute Trust Wrentham, MA.
Represented in the Archdiocese of Boston and in the Dioceses of Providence, Portland in Maine and St. Petersburg.

[3760] (O.S.C.)—ORDER OF ST. CLARE
Poor Clares-Poor Clares of the Primitive Observance

Founded in Assisi, Italy in 1212. First permanent foundation in the United States in 1878.
3626 N. 65th Ave., Omaha, NE 68104-3299.
Total in Community: 7.

Monastery of St. Clare: 70 Nelson Ave., Wappingers Falls, NY 12590-1121. Tel: 845-297-1685; Fax: 845-297-7657; Web: www.poorclaresny.com.
Solemnly Professed Sisters: 11; Simply Professed: 1; Postulants: 1.
Assisi, Italy, is called the Motherhouse of the Order, but the Abbess of said Monastery has no jurisdiction over other Communities of Poor Clares. Some Monasteries, such as those at Omaha, Evansville, New Orleans, Memphis, Jamaica Plain, Greenville, Lowell and Spokane, are subject to a Father General and to the Provincial of the Franciscan Province in which the Monastery is located. Monasteries at Aptos, Cleveland, Kokomo, Los Altos Hills, Newport News, Rockford, Roswell and Santa Barbara are Colettines.

St. Clare's Monastery of the Blessed Sacrament O.S.C: 720 Henry Clay Ave., New Orleans, LA 70118. Tel: 504-895-2019. Sr. Charlene Toups, O.S.C., Abbess.
Total in Community: 9.
Cloistered.

Franciscan Monastery of St. Clare O.S.C: 6825 Nurrenbern Rd., Evansville, IN 47712-8518. Tel: 812-425-4396; Web: poorclare.org/evansville. Sr. Jeanne Maffet, O.S.C., Abbess; Sr. Catherine K. Janeway, O.S.C., Vicaress.
Total in Community: 8.

Monastery of St. Clare (1932): 1310 Dellwood Ave., Memphis, TN 38127. Tel: 901-357-6662. Sr. Mary Marguerite, O.S.C., Abbess.
Total in Community: 5.
Solemnly Professed Cloistered.

The Franciscan Monastery of St. Clare: 920 Centre St., Jamaica Plain, MA 02130. Tel: 617-524-1760; Fax: 617-983-5205. Sr. Clare Frances McAvoy, O.S.C., Abbess.
Total in Community: 20.

Monastery of St. Clare O.S.C: 150 White Pine Rd., Chesterfield, NJ 08515. Tel: 609-324-2638; Fax: 609-324-2938. Sr. Miriam Varley, O.S.C., Abbess.
Total in Community: 14.

Franciscan Monastery of Saint Clare: 1271 Langhorne-Newtown Rd., Langhorne, PA 19047-1297. Tel: 215-968-5775; Fax: 215-968-6254. Sr. Evelyn L. Eynon, O.S.C., Abbess.
Total in Community: 11.

Franciscan Monastery of St. Clare, Spokane, Washington: *Poor Clare Nuns*, 4419 N. Hawthorne St., Spokane, WA 99205. Tel: 509-327-4479. Sr. Rita Louise McLean, O.S.C., Abbess; Sr. Colleen Byrne, O.S.C., Vocation Directress.
Professed Nuns: 5.
Solemn Vows, Papal Enclosure Franciscan Province of Santa Barbara. Mother Bentivoglio Federation of Poor Clares.

St. Clare's Monastery: 421 S. Fourth St., Sauk Rapids, MN 56379. Tel: 320-251-3556; Fax: 320-203-7052. Mother Mary Matthew, O.S.C., Abbess.
Total in Community: 18.

St. Clare's Monastery of the Infant Jesus (1953): *Franciscan Poor Clare Nuns*, 8650 Russell Ave. S., Minneapolis, MN 55431-1998. Tel: 952-881-4766. Sr. Frances Getchell, O.S.C., Abbess.
Total in Community: 12.
Legal Title: *Franciscan Poor Clare Nuns.*

Monastery of Poor Clares (1877): *Order of St. Clare-Poor Clare Colettine Nuns P.C.C.*, 3501 Rocky River Dr., Cleveland, OH 44111-2998. Tel: 216-941-2820. Mother Mary Dolores, P.C.C., Abbess.
Total in Community: 18.
Poor Clare Nuns (Colettines), observing the Primitive Rule of St. Clare. Strictly cloistered, Solemn Vows, Perpetual Exposition of the Most Blessed Sacrament.

Franciscan Monastery of St. Clare: *Order of St. Clare*, 1505 Miles Rd., Cincinnati, OH 45231-2427. Tel: 513-825-7177; Fax: 513-825-4071; Email: contactsisters@fuse.net; Web: www.poorclarescincinnati.org. Sr. Ann Bartko, O.S.C., Abbess.
Total in Community: 10.
Solemn vows; papal enclosure.

Corpus Christi Monastery (Solemn Vows, Papal Enclosure): *Poor Clare Colettines P.C.C.*, 2111 S. Main St., Rockford, IL 61102. Tel: 815-963-7343. Sr. Mary Dominica, P.C.C., Abbess.
Total in Community: 20.
Cloistered.

Annunciation Monastery: *Poor Clare Colettines P.C.C.*, 6200 E. Minooka Rd., Minooka, IL 60447-9458.

Monastery of Poor Clares-P.C.C. (1928): 215 E. Los Olivos St., Santa Barbara, CA 93105. Tel: 805-682-7670. Mother Aimee Marie of the Eucharist, Abbess.
Total in Community: 13.

Monastery of St. Clare: 445 River Rd., Andover, MA 01810-4213. Tel: 978-683-7599; Fax: 978-683-6085. Sr. Therese Marie Lacroix, O.S.C., Abbess.
Total in Community: 15.
Cloistered.

Poor Clare Monastery of Our Lady of Guadalupe: 809 E. 19th St., Roswell, NM 88201. Tel: 575-622-0868. Mother M. Angela, Abbess.
Total in Community: 22.
Legal Title: *The Community of Poor Clares of New Mexico, Inc.*
Cloistered.

Poor Clares Immaculate Heart Monastery: 28210 Natoma Rd., Los Altos Hills, CA 94022-3220. Tel: 650-948-2947. Mother Maura, P.C.C., Abbess.
Total in Community: 17.

Monastery of St. Clare: 37 McCauley Rd., Travelers Rest, SC 29690. Tel: 864-834-8015; Fax: 864-834-5402. Sr. Mary Connor, O.S.C., Abbess.
Total in Community: 18.
Cloistered.

Monastery of Poor Clares Colettine P.C.C: 5500 Holly Fork Rd., Barhamsville, VA 23011. Tel: 757-566-1684. Mother Mary Therese, P.C.C., Abbess; Sr. Mary Agnes, P.C.C., Archivist.
Total in Community: 13.
Solemn Vows. Cloistered.

Maria Regina Mater Monastery P.C.C: *Poor Clare Nuns*, 1175 N., 300 W., Kokomo, IN 46901. Tel: 765-457-5743. Mother Miriam, Abbess.
Total in Community: 10; Junior Professed: 1.
Cloistered.

Christ the King Monastery of St. Clare O.S.C: 3900 Sherwood Blvd., Delray Beach, FL 33445. Tel: 561-498-3294. Sr. Leanna Chrostowski, O.S.C., Abbess.
Total in Community: 9.

Monastery of St. Clare of the Immaculate Conception O.S.C: *Poor Clares*, 200 Marycrest Dr., Saint Louis, MO 63129. Tel: 314-846-2618. Mother Mary Leo Hoffmann, O.S.C., Abbess.
Total in Community: 12.
Legal Title: *Nuns of the Order of St. Clare of St. Louis.*

San Damiano Monastery of St. Clare (Solemn Vows, Papal Enclosure): 6029 Estero Blvd., Fort Myers Beach, FL 33931-4325. Tel: 239-463-5599; Fax: 239-463-4993. Sr. Mary Frances Fortin, O.S.C., Abbess.
Cloistered Sisters: 8.

Monastery of St. Clare: P.O. Box 2284, Brenham, TX 77833. Tel: 979-836-2444. Sr. Angela Chandler, O.S.C., Abbess.
Sisters in Community: 2.

Poor Clares of Montana: 3020 18th Ave., S., Great Falls, MT 59405-5167. Tel: 406-453-7891; Fax: 406-453-8689. Sr. Catherine Cook, O.S.C., Abbess.

St. Joseph Monastery of the Poor Clares Colettine, P.C.C: P.O. Box 160, 1671 Pleasant Valley Rd., Aptos, CA 95001-0160. Tel: 831-761-9659. Mother Francis Maria, P.C.C., Abbess.
Total in Community: 12.
(Reform of St. Colette) Daily Exposition of the Most Blessed Sacrament.

Monastery of St. Clare: 4875 Shattuck Rd., Saginaw, MI 48603. Tel: 989-797-0593; Email: sisters@srsclare.com. Sr. Dianne Doughty, O.S.C., Abbess.
Solemnly Professed: 4.

[3765] (O.S.C.CAP.)—CAPUCHIN POOR CLARES (P)

Federation of Our Lady of the Angels in North America (1991): *Monastery of the Blessed Sacrament*, 4201 N.E. 18th St., Amarillo, TX 79107. Tel: 806-383-6771; Fax: 806-383-9877. Mother Theresa Cortes, O.S.C., Pres.

[3770] (O.S.C.)—SISTERS OF ST. CLARE (P)

St. Clare's Convent (Generalate): 63 Harold's Cross Rd., Dublin 6W, Ireland Fax: 011-353-1-496-6388. Sr. Anne Kelly, O.S.C., Abbess Gen.

Santa Clara: 1171 Via Santa Paulo, Vista, CA 92081. Tel: 760-295-0611. Sr. Madeline Fitzgerald, O.S.C., California-Pastoral Coord.; Sr. Lucia Brady, O.S.C., Reg. Supr.-Florida.
Total in Congregation: 125; Total in Guatemala & El Salvador: 21; Total in U.S: 15; Total in England: 15; Total in Ireland: 74.
Ministry in the field of Academic and Religious Education at all Levels; Pastoral & Social Ministry; Retreats; Ministry to the sick, poor and imprisoned.
Represented in the Dioceses of Orange, St. Petersburg, San Bernardino, and San Diego. Also in El Salvador, England, Guatemala, Ireland and Wales.

[3780] (SS.C.M.)—SISTERS OF SAINTS CYRIL AND METHODIUS (P)

Founded in the United States in 1909.

General Motherhouse: Villa Sacred Heart, Danville, PA 17821-1698. Tel: 570-275-3581; Fax: 570-275-5997. Sr. Linda Marie Bolinski, SS.C.M., Gen. Supr.

Total in Community: 86.

Ministry in the field of Education; Parish Ministry and Religious Education; Retreat/Spiritual Direction; Hospital Chaplaincy; Deaf Apostolate; Homes for the Aged; Music Conservatory; Continuing Care Retirement Community.

Properties owned or sponsored: St. Cyril Preschool and Kindergarten; St. Cyril Academy Spiritual Center; Villa Sacred Heart; Maria Hall, Inc.; Maria Joseph Manor, Inc.; The Meadows at Maria Joseph Manor, Inc., Danville, PA; Villa St. Cyril, Highland Park, IL.

Represented in the Archdioceses of Chicago, New York and San Antonio and in the Dioceses of Bridgeport, Charleston, Gary, Harrisburg and Scranton.

[3790] (S.S.D.)—INSTITUTE OF THE SISTERS OF ST. DOROTHY (P)

Founded in Italy in 1834. First foundation in the United States in 1911.

General Motherhouse: Via del Gianicolo 4-a, Rome, Italy, 00165. Sr. Jaci Dutra-Pessoa, S.S.D., Gen. Coord.

Province of United States of America (1920): *Mount Saint Joseph Vice-Provincialate*, 13 Monkeywrench Ln., Bristol, RI 02809-2916. Tel: 401-253-5434. Sr. Dorothy Schwarz, S.S.D., Prov. Coord.

Universal total in Congregation: 1071; Total number in the U.S: 35.

Ministry in the field of Education; Spiritual Life Centers; Hospital Chaplaincies; Social work with immigrants.

Properties owned or sponsored: Villa Fatima, Taunton, MA; Mt. St. Joseph, Bristol, RI; Our Lady of Fatima High School, Warren, RI; St. Dorothy Academy, Staten Island, NY.

[3810] (X.S.)—SOCIETY OF CATHOLIC MISSION SISTERS OF ST. FRANCIS XAVIER, INC. (D)

(Xavier Sisters)

Founded in the United States in 1946.

Convent: 37179 Moravian Dr., Clinton Township, MI 48036. Tel: 586-465-5082; Fax: 586-465-1990. Sr. Mary Agnes Malburg.

Total in Community: 1.

Represented in the Archdiocese of Detroit.

[3820] (C.S.J.B.)—SISTERS OF ST. JOHN THE BAPTIST (P)

Founded in Italy in 1878. First foundation in the United States in 1906.

General Motherhouse: Rome, Italy Sr. Rosaria DiIorio, Supr. Gen.

U.S. Provincial House: 3308 Campbell Dr., Bronx, NY 10465-1358. Tel: 718-518-7820. Sr. Mary Cecile Swanton, C.S.J.B., Prov. Supr.

Total in Community: 90.

Legal Titles and Holdings: Mt. St. John Convent, Purchase, NY; St. John Villa Academy, Staten Island, NY; Providence Rest Nursing Home, Bronx, NY; Mt. St. John Convent, Gladstone, NJ.

Ministry in the field of Education; Health Care for Aged Women & Men; Child Day Care; Pastoral Ministry.

[3830] (C.S.J. OR S.S.J.)—SISTERS OF ST. JOSEPH

The Independent Motherhouses of the Sisters of St. Joseph are represented in the United States in the following Archdioceses and Dioceses:

[3830-01] BOSTON (D)

Motherhouse of the Congregation of the Sisters of St. Joseph of Boston-CSJ (1873): 637 Cambridge St., Brighton, MA 02135. Tel: 617-783-9090; Fax: 617-783-8246. Sr. Mary L. Murphy, C.S.J., Pres.; Sr. Mary Rita Grady, C.S.J., Community Archivist.

Total in Community: 379.

Legal Holdings or Titles: Motherhouse of the Sisters of Saint Joseph of Boston, Brighton, MA; Bethany Health Care Center, Inc., Framingham, MA; Bethany Hill School, Inc., Framingham, MA; St. Joseph Hall, Framingham, MA; Retreat Center, Cohasset, MA; Walnut Park Montessori School, Newton, MA; Jackson School, Newton, MA; Fontbonne Academy, Milton, MA; St. Joseph Preparatory High School, Brighton, MA; Regis College, Weston, MA; Corporation for the Sponsored Ministries of the Sisters of St. Joseph of Boston, Brighton, MA; CSJ Ministries Connection, Inc., Brighton, MA; The Literacy Connection, Brighton, MA.; The Women's Table, Brighton, MA; Casserly House, Roslindale, MA.

[3830-03] ORANGE (P)

Sisters of St. Joseph of Orange - Motherhouse: 480 S. Batavia St., Orange, CA 92868. Tel: 714-744-8121; Fax: 717-744-3165. Sr. Jayne Helmlinger, C.S.J., Gen. Supr.; Sr. Adele Marie Kohummel, C.S.J., Community Archivist.

Total in Community: 150.

Legal Holdings and Titles: Sisters of St. Joseph of Orange; Sisters of St. Joseph Healthcare Foundation, Orange, CA; St. Joseph College, Orange, CA; St. Joseph Health System; St. Joseph Health System Foundation, Orange, CA; St. Jude Hospital, Inc. (dba St. Jude Medical Center); St. Jude Memorial Foundation, Fullerton, CA; St. Joseph Hospital Orange; St. Jude Hospital Yorba Linda, (dba St. Joseph Heritage Healthcare); Yorba Linda, CA; Mission Hospital Regional Medical Center, Mission Viejo, CA; Santa Rosa Memorial Hospital, Santa Rosa, CA; St. Joseph Hospital of Eureka, Eureka, CA; Redwood Memorial Hospital, Fortuna, CA; Redwood Memorial Foundation, Fortuna, CA; Queen of the Valley Hospital of Napa, Napa, CA; St. Mary of the Plains Hospital, Lubbock, TX; St. Mary Medical Center, Apple Valley, CA; St. Joseph Health Ministry.

Ministry in the field of Education; Health & Hospital Services; Pastoral and Social Services.

Represented in the Archdioceses of Los Angeles and San Francisco and in the Dioceses of Orange, San Bernardino, San Diego and Santa Rosa.

[3830-05] ROCKVILLE CENTRE (D)

St. Joseph's Convent - Congregation of the Sisters of Saint Joseph of Brentwood, NY CSJ: Brentwood, NY 11717. Tel: 516-273-4531. Sr. Jean Amore, C.S.J., Pres.; Virginia Dowd, Community Archivist.

Total in Community: 658.

Ministry in the field of Education; Health & Hospital Services; Social Services.

Represented in the Dioceses of Brooklyn and Rockville Centre. Also in Puerto Rico, Dominican Republic and Brazil.

[3830-06] BUFFALO (P)

Generalate - Congregation of the Sisters of St. Joseph SSJ: 10324 Main St., Clarence, NY 14031. Tel: 716-759-6454; Fax: 716-759-6415. Sr. Jean Marie Zirnheld, S.S.J., Pres.; Sr. Eva Amadori, S.S.J., Community Archivist.

Total in Community: 89.

Ministry in the field of Education at all levels; School for Deaf; Youth Ministry; Justice Ministry; Pastoral Ministry; Hospital Chaplaincy; Spirituality Center.

Properties owned or sponsored: Administrative Office; Sisters of St. Joseph Residence.

[3830-09] ERIE (D)

Sisters of St. Joseph SSJ: 5031 W. Ridge Rd., Erie, PA 16506-1249. Tel: 814-836-4100; Fax: 814-836-4278. Sr. Mary Herrmann, S.S.J., Pres.

Total in Community: 116.

Legal Title: *Sisters of St. Joseph of Northwestern PA Inc.*

Ministry in the field of Education at all levels; Social Ministries; Nursing Home; Health Care; Pastoral Work and other Diocesan Ministries.

Institutions sponsored: Saint Vincent Health Center; St. Mary's Home of Erie; Villa Maria Elementary; Sisters of St. Joseph Neighborhood Network, Inc.; St. Patrick's Haven; Erie DAWN; Bethany House.

Represented in the Archdioceses of Chicago and Washington and in the Diocese of Cleveland and Louisville.

[3830-12] OGDENSBURG (D)

Motherhouse of the Society of the Sisters of St. Joseph SSJ: 1425 Washington St., Watertown, NY 13601-4533. Tel: 315-782-3460; Web: www.ssjwatertown.org. Sr. Bernadette Marie Collins, S.S.J., Major Supr.; Sr. Norma Bryant, S.S.J., Community Archivist.

Total in Community: 51.

Ministry in the field of Education at all levels; Parish and Diocesan Administration.

Represented in the Dioceses of Ogdensburg and Syracuse.

[3830-13] PITTSBURGH (P)

Sisters of St. Joseph CSJ - Motherhouse: Sisters of St. Joseph: 1020 State St., Baden, PA 15005. Tel: 724-869-2151; Fax: 724-869-3336. Leadership Team: Sr. Mary Pellegrino, Congregational Moderator; Sr. Carolyn Bodenschatz; Sr. Marguerite Coyne; Sr. Rosanne Oberleitner; Sr. Sally Witt, Community Archivist.

Total in Community: 204.

Properties owned and/or sponsored: Motherhouse and 18 residences.

Ministry in the field of Education; Health Care; Social Services; Spiritual Development; Congregational Services.

Represented in the Archdioceses of Boston, Detroit, Dubuque, Hartford, Miami, New York and Washington and in the Dioceses of Altoona-Johnstown, Arlington, Buffalo, Cheyenne, Erie, Fresno, Greensburg, Jackson, Pittsburgh, Richmond, Tucson and Wheeling-Charleston. Archdiocese of Managua.

[3830-14] ROCHESTER (P)

Sisters of St. Joseph SSJ - Motherhouse: 150 French Rd., Rochester, NY 14618-3822. Tel: 585-641-8100; Fax: 585-641-8524. Sr. Mary Louise Mitchell, Congregational Pres.; Kathleen Urbanic, Archivist.

Total in Community: 257.

Ministry in the field of Education at all levels; Health Care; Pastoral Ministry; Home for Emotionally Disturbed Children; Parish and Diocesan Evangelization; College Campus Ministry; Social Service; Justice and Peace Office; Drug Dependency Programs; Retreats & Spiritual Direction; Prison and Jail Ministry.

Properties owned and sponsored: Nazareth Elementary; Nazareth Convent; St. Joseph's Neighborhood Center; Morning Star.

Sisters sponsor: Home Health Care; Food Kitchen; Health Care Center; Spirituality Center; Domestic and Foreign Missions.

Represented in the Archdioceses of Mobile and St. Louis and in the Diocese of Rochester. Also in Brazil.

[3830-15] SALINA (P)

General Administration Office (1884): *Sisters of St. Joseph of Concordia*, 215 Court St., P.O. Box 279, Concordia, KS 66901. Tel: 785-243-2149. Sr. Marcia Allen, C.S.J., Pres.

Motherhouse (1884): *Sisters of St. Joseph of Concordia CSJ*, 1300 Washington St., P.O. Box 279, Concordia, KS 66901. Tel: 785-243-2113.

Total Sisters in Community: 140.

Legal Titles: Nazareth Convent and Academy Corporation, Concordia, KS; Neighborhood Initiatives, Inc., Concordia, KS; Manna House of Prayer, Concordia, KS; Neighbor to Neighbor, Concordia, KS; St. Mary's Spirituality Center, Silver City, NM.

Ministry in Care for Elderly; Homeless; Education; Parish and Diocesan Evangelization; Social Services; Justice and Peace Offices; Marriage and Family Counseling; Youth Formation; Healthcare; College Campus Ministry; Drug Dependency Programs; Prisons; Consultants; Refugees; Continuous Prayer.

Represented in the Archdioceses of Atlanta, Chicago, Kansas City in Kansas, Omaha and St. Paul-Minneapolis and in the Dioceses of El Paso, Grand Island, Kansas City-St. Joseph, Las Cruces, Phoenix, Rockford, Salina and Wichita. Also in Piaui, Brazil.

[3830-16] SPRINGFIELD (MA) (D)

Motherhouse: *The Congregation of the Sisters of St. Joseph of Springfield (SSJ)-Mont Marie*, 34 Lower Westfield Rd, Holyoke, MA 01040. Tel: 413-536-0853; Fax: 413-533-3275. Maxyne D. Schneider, S.S.J., Pres.; Sherry Enserro, Archivist.

Total in Community: 264.

Legal Holdings and Titles: Mont Marie Child Care Center, Inc.; Mont Marie Health Care Center, Inc.; Mont Marie Senior Residence, Inc., St. Joseph Residence at Mont Marie.

Ministry in the field of Religious & Academic Education; Parish Ministry; Cross-Cultural; Diocesan Administration; Chaplaincy; Health Care, Social Services; Research and Study; Restorative Justice; AIDS Ministry; Creative Arts.

Represented in the Archdiocese of Baltimore and in the Dioceses of Bridgeport, Burlington, Fall River, Lake Charles, Norwich, Providence, Springfield (MA) and Worcester.

[3832] (C.S.J.)—CONGREGATION OF THE SISTERS OF ST. JOSEPH (P)

Legal Holdings: Congregation of the Sisters of St. Joseph Ministries, Inc. d/b/a CSJ Ministries: A.B.L.E. Families, Inc.; Caregiver Companion, Inc.; Christ in the Wilderness, Inc.; Congregation of St. Joseph Ministry Against the Dealth Penalty, Inc.; Dillon Complex for Independent Living, Inc.; Holy Family Childcare & Development Center, Inc.; Nazareth Academy, Inc.; People Program, Inc.; River's Edge, A Place for Reflection and Action, Inc.; St. Joseph Academy, Inc. (Cleveland, OH); St. Joseph's Academy, Inc. (Baton Rouge, LA); SJA Foundation, Inc.*; St. Joseph Adoption Referral Services, Inc. d/b/a St. Joseph Adoption Ministry; St. Joseph Health Initiative, Inc.; St. Joseph Spirituality Center, Inc.; Sheridan Village, Inc. (co-sponsored); Sisters of St. Joseph Charitable Fund, Inc.; Sisters of St. Joseph "Dear Neighbor" Ministries, Inc.; Sisters of St. Joseph Health and Wellness Foundation, Inc.; StepStone, Inc.*; Taller de Jose, Inc.; School and Tutors on Wheels, Inc.

Legal Title: *Congregation of the Sisters of St. Joseph, Inc. d/b/a Congregation of St. Joseph.* 3430 Rocky River Dr., Cleveland, OH 44111-2297. Tel: 216-252-0440; Fax: 216-941-3430; Web: www.csjoseph.org.

Total in Community: 707.

Cleveland Center: 3430 Rocky River Dr., Cleveland, OH 44111-2997. Tel: 216-252-0440; Fax: 216-941-3430.

Legal Titles: Sisters of Saint Joseph; Legal Holdings: Sisters of Saint Joseph Community Support Charitable Trust.

Ministry in the field of Academic and Religious Education at all levels; Parish and Pastoral Ministry; Deaf Apostolate; Parish Team Member; Justice Work; Health Care; Social Services; Radio; Social Concerns; Retreat Work.

Represented in the Archdioceses of Chicago and Washington and in the Dioceses of Cleveland, Youngstown and Venice.

LaGrange Center: 1515 W. Ogden Ave., La Grange Park, IL 60526. Tel: 708-354-9200; Fax: 708-354-9573.

Legal Titles: Sisters of St. Joseph of LaGrange; Legal Holdings: Sisters of St. Joseph of LaGrange Charitable Trust.

Ministry in the field of Education; School Administration; Nursing; Pastoral Care in Hospitals; Nursing Homes; Work with the Elderly; Parish Ministry;

Archdiocesan Administration; Spiritual Direction and Retreats; Administrative Services; Immigration Services.
Represented in the Archdiocese of Chicago and the Dioceses of Joliet, Jackson and Superior.

Medaille Center: 4010 Executive Park Dr., #320, Cincinnati, OH 45241. Tel: 513-761-2888; Fax: 513-761-0088.
Legal Title: *Sisters of St. Joseph of Medaille.*
Ministry in the field of Academic Education at all levels; Health Care; Pastoral Ministry; Religious Education; Foreign Missions; Social Service; Centers for Christian Renewal; Services to the Poor and Minorities; Community Service; Diocesan Offices; Prison Ministry; Ministry Against the Death Penalty; Ministry for Retired-Elderly; Chemical Dependency; Adult Mentally Retarded; Care for Retired Sisters.
Represented in the Archdioceses of Chicago, Cincinnati, New Orleans and St. Paul-Minneapolis and in the Dioceses of Baton Rouge, Crookston, El Paso, Houma-Thibodaux, Rapid City, Superior and Wichita.

Nazareth Center: 3427 Gull Rd., Nazareth, MI 49074. Tel: 269-381-6290; Fax: 269-381-4909.
Legal Titles: The Sisters of St. Joseph of Nazareth; Legal holdings: Ascension Health, Inc. (co-sponsor).
Ministry in the field of Education; Social Services; Parish and Church-related Ministries; Healthcare; Spirituality.
Represented in the Archdioceses of Detroit, Los Angeles, New Orleans and Santa Fe and in the Dioceses of Brooklyn, Fort Wayne-South Bend, Gaylord, Grand Rapids, Kalamazoo, Lafayette (LA), Lafayette in Indiana, Lansing, Lexington, Orange and Saginaw.

Tipton Center: 1440 W. Division Rd., Tipton, IN 46072. Tel: 765-675-4146; Fax: 765-675-7471.
Legal Title: *The Sisters of St. Joseph of Tipton, Indiana, Inc.*
Ministry in the fields of Education, Health Care, Pastoral Ministry, Social Service, Evangelization.
Represented in the Archdioceses of Indianapolis and Louisville and in the Dioceses of Lafayette in Indiana and Lansing.

Wheeling Center: 137 Mount St. Joseph Rd., Wheeling, WV 26003. Tel: 304-232-8160; Fax: 304-232-1404.
Legal Titles: The Sisters of St. Joseph of Wheeling, Inc.; Legal Holdings: Sisters of St. Joseph of Wheeling Foundation, Inc.
Ministry in the following areas: Parish Ministry; Pastoral Services; Elementary, Secondary, College Education; Health Care; Social Services; Spiritual Formation; Direction and Retreat Ministries; Diocesan, Administration and Service.
Represented in the Diocese of Wheeling-Charleston.

Wichita Center: 3700 E. Lincoln, Wichita, KS 67218. Tel: 316-686-7171; Fax: 316-689-4056.
Legal Title: *Sisters of St. Joseph of Wichita, Kansas.*
Ministry in the fields of Religious and Academic Education; Adult Religious Correspondence Courses; Diocesan Program for the Handicapped; Pro-Life Ministry to Women; Home Hospice; Hospital and Clinical Care; Pastoral Ministry; Campus Ministry; Senior Care; Social Services; Transitional Housing; Low Income Senior Housing; Retreat Ministry.
Represented in the Archdiocese of Kansas City in Kansas and in the Dioceses of Dodge City, Grand Island, Kansas City-St. Joseph, Salina and Wichita. Also in Japan.

[3840] (C.S.J.)—SISTERS OF ST. JOSEPH OF CARONDELET (P)

Founded in France in 1650. First foundation in the United States in 1836.

Congregational Offices: 2311 S. Lindbergh Blvd., St. Louis, MO 63131. Tel: 314-966-4048; Fax: 314-966-5041. Congregational Leadership Team for Provinces & Vice Provinces: Sr. Laura Bufano, C.S.J.; Sr. Francine Costello, C.S.J.; Sr. Susan Hames, C.S.J.; Sr. Catherine McNamee, C.S.J.

Province of St. Louis (1836): *St. Joseph's Provincial House*, 6400 Minnesota Ave., St. Louis, MO 63111. Tel: 314-481-8800; Fax: 314-351-3111. Province Leadership Team: Sr. Patricia Clune, C.S.J.; Sr. Pat Giljum, C.S.J.; Sr. Helen Flemington, C.S.J.; Sr. Elizabeth Brown, C.S.J.; Sr. Suzanne Wesley, C.S.J.; Sr. Nancy Corcoran, C.S.J.; Sr. Jean Meier, C.S.J.
Total in Community: 357.
Legal Title: *Sisters of St. Joseph of Carondelet, St. Louis Province.*
Sponsored Institutions: Colleges 2; Academies 2; Institute for the Deaf 1; Long Term Care Facility Co-sponsor 1; Health System Co-sponsor 1.
Ministries in the field of Academic Education; Pastoral Ministries; Diocesan Offices; Health Care; Child Care; Geriatric Care; Foreign Missions; Social Services; Community Services; Special Services; Fine Arts.
Represented in the Archdioceses of Anchorage, Atlanta, Boston, Chicago, Denver, Indianapolis, Kansas City in Kansas, Los Angeles, Mobile, Omaha, St. Louis, St. Paul-Minneapolis and Seattle and in the Dioceses of Belleville, Brownsville, Charleston, Colorado Springs, El Paso, Green Bay, Honolulu, Jackson, Kansas City-St. Joseph, Marquette, Palm Beach, Peoria, San Diego, San Jose, Savannah and Venice.

Province of St. Paul (1851): *St. Joseph's Administration Center*, 1884 Randolph Ave., Saint Paul, MN 55105. Tel: 651-690-7000; Fax: 651-690-7039. Province Leadership Team: Sr. Margaret Gillespie, C.S.J.; Sr. Katherine Rossini, C.S.J.; Sr. Jean Wincek, C.S.J.; Sr. Mary Kraft, C.S.J., Archivist.
Total in Community: 260.
Legal Holdings or Titles: Sisters of St. Joseph of Carondelet.
Ministry in the fields of Education; Health; Social Services; Spirituality.
Represented in the Archdioceses of Baltimore, St. Louis and St. Paul-Minneapolis and in the Dioceses of Brownsville, Charlotte, Fargo, Jackson, New Ulm, St. Cloud and Superior.

Province of Albany (1858): *St. Joseph's Provincial House*, 385 Watervliet-Shaker Rd., Latham, NY 12110-4799. Tel: 518-783-3500; Fax: 518-783-5209; Web: www.csjalbany.org. Province Leadership Team: Sr. Mary Anne Rodgers, C.S.J., Dir.; Sr. Nancy Gregg, C.S.J., First Counselor; Sr. Ann Christi Brink, C.S.J., Exec. Committee; Sr. Charla Commins, C.S.J.; Sr. Mary Jo Tallman, C.S.J.; Sr. Eileen McCann, C.S.J.; Sr. Carol Peston, C.S.J., Prov. Archivist; Rev. Geoffrey D. Burke, Chap.
Total in Community: 388.

Novitiate: 369 Watervliet-Shaker Rd., Latham, NY 12110. Tel: 518-783-3536.
Ministry in the fields of Academic and Special Education at all levels; Hospital and Infirmary Services; Hospital Pastoral Ministries; Parish Ministry and Religious Education; Diocesan Offices; Youth Ministry; Counseling; Retreat and Spiritual Direction; Social and Community Services; Fine Arts.
Represented in the Archdioceses of Cincinnati, Indianapolis, Los Angeles, New York, St. Louis, Seattle and Washington and in the Dioceses of Albany, Birmingham, Brooklyn, Erie, Harrisburg, Honolulu, Kansas City-St. Joseph, Ogdensburg, Palm Beach, Pensacola-Tallahassee, Rochester, Scranton, Shreveport, Spokane and Syracuse. Also in Peru.

Province of Los Angeles (1878): *St. Mary's Provincialate and Carondelet Center*, 11999 Chalon Rd., Los Angeles, CA 90049-1524. Tel: 310-889-2100; Fax: 310-476-8735. Sr. Barbara Anne Stowasser, C.S.J., Prov. Supr.; Sr. Patricia Rose Shanahan, C.S.J., Archivist.
Professed Sisters: 344.
Legal Titles or Holdings: Sisters of St. Joseph in California; Sisters of St. Joseph in Arizona; Sisters of St. Joseph Ministerial Services.
Sisters serve in the fields of Education; Health Services; Social Services; Pastoral Ministry.
Represented in the Archdioceses of Boston, Los Angeles, St. Louis, San Francisco and Seattle and in the Dioceses of Boise, Fresno, Honolulu, Monterey, Oakland, Orange, Phoenix, San Bernardino, San Diego, San Jose, Santa Rosa and Tucson.

Hawaii Vice-Province (1956): *Sisters of St. Joseph of Carondelet, Carondelet Center*, 5311 Apo Dr., Honolulu, HI 96821-1829. Tel: 808-373-8801. Sr. Claudia Wong, C.S.J., Dir.
Professed Sisters: 29.
Legal Title: *Sisters of St. Joseph of Carondelet-Hawaii Vice-Province.*
Ministries include: Elementary and Secondary Schools; Services to the Elderly; Prayer & Spirituality; Administering Diocesan Offices; Religious Education Directors; Social Ministry.
Represented in the Diocese of Honolulu.

[3850] (C.S.J.)—SISTERS OF ST. JOSEPH OF CHAMBERY (P)

Founded in France in 1650. First foundation in United States in 1885.

Generalate: Via del Casaletto, 260, Rome, Italy, 00151. Sr. Sally Hodgdon, C.S.J., Supr. Gen.

Provincial House: *Convent of Mary Immaculate*, 27 Park Rd., West Hartford, CT 06119. Tel: 860-233-5126; Tel: 860-232-8252; Fax: 860-232-4649. Sr. Dolores Lahr, C.S.J., Prov. Supr.
Total in Community: 105.
Legal Title: *The Sisters of St. Joseph Corporation.*
Ministry in the field of Academic and Religious Education at all levels; Social Services; Pastoral and Parish Ministries; Law; Hospitals, Health Care and Prisons; Retreat work and Spiritual Direction.
Represented in the Archdioceses of Hartford and in the Dioceses of Bridgeport, Lexington, Oakland, San Jose and Springfield in Massachusetts.

[3860] (S.J.C.)—SISTERS OF ST. JOSEPH OF CLUNY (P)

Founded in France in 1807.

Generalate: Paris, France Sr. Morag Collins, Supr. Gen.

American Novitiate: *Mary Immaculate Queen Novitiate*, 853 W 7th St., San Pedro, CA 90731. Tel: 310-834-5431. Sr. Genevieve Marie Vigil, S.J.C., Local Coord.

Provincialate: 7 Restmere Ter., Middletown, RI 02842. Tel: 401-846-4757. Sr. Joan Vander Zyden, S.J.C., Prov. of U.S. & Canada.
Professed Sisters in U.S. & Canada: 26.
Legal Title: *Sisters of St. Joseph of Cluny, Inc.*
Ministry in outreach ministry; pastoral work; retreats; healthcare; education.
Represented in the Archdiocese of Los Angeles and in the Dioceses of Newark and Providence. Also in Canada.

[3870] (C.S.J.)—SISTERS OF ST. JOSEPH OF LYONS, FRANCE (P)

Founded in France October 15, 1650. First foundation in United States in 1906 in Jackman, Maine.

General Motherhouse: Lyons, France Sr. Catherine Barange, Supr. Gen.

Maine Province: *Sisters of St. Joseph*, 93 Halifax St., Winslow, ME 04901. Tel: 207-873-4512; Fax: 207-873-1976. Sr. Gilla Dube, C.S.J., Prov.
Total in Community: 29.
Ministry in Catechesis; Holistic Care; Spirituality and Ecology; Pastoral Ministry; Education; Pastoral Care; Mental Health; and Social Work.
Properties owned and sponsored: Mount St. Joseph Holistic Care Community, Waterville, ME.
Represented in the Archdiocese of Los Angeles and in the Dioceses of Manchester and Portland (In Maine).

[3890] (C.S.J.P.)—SISTERS OF ST. JOSEPH OF PEACE (P)

Founded in England 1884. First United States foundation 1885.

Shalom Center: *Sisters of St. Joseph of Peace Generalate, Inc.*, 399 Hudson Ter., Englewood Cliffs, NJ 07632. Tel: 201-568-6348; Fax: 201-568-9880. Sr. Margaret Byrne, C.S.J.P., Congregation Leader; Sr. Teresa Donohue, C.S.J.P., Asst. Congregation Leader; Sr. Kristin Funari, C.S.J.P.; Sr. Anne Hayes, C.S.J.P.; Sr. Coralie Muzzy, C.S.J.P.
Total in Community: 210.
Ministry in the field of Education; Health & Social Services; Religious Education; Parish Ministry, Retreat Ministry, Social & Minority Ministry.
Represented in the Archdioceses of Anchorage, Los Angeles, Newark, New York, Portland in Oregon, San Francisco, Seattle and Washington and in the Dioceses of Camden, Juneau, Metuchen, Paterson, San Diego, Spokane and Yakima. Also in Canada, El Salvador and Haiti.
Sr. Margaret Byrne, C.S.J.P., Congregation Leader; Sr. Teresa Donohue, C.S.J.P., Asst. Congregation Leader.
Total number in the Eastern U.S: 96.
Properties owned or sponsored: St. Joseph's Home for the Blind; St. Ann's Home for The Aged; St. Mary's Residence; St. Joseph's Home; The Nurturing Place (York Street Child Development Center); St. Joseph's School for the Blind; Stella Maris Retreat Center-Water Spirit; The York St. Project; St. Joseph Messenger Office; St. Michael Villa; The Kenmare School.

Wesstern U.S. (1909): *St. Mary's Residence and Novitiate*, 1663 Killarney Way, P.O. Box 248, Bellevue, WA 98009-0248. Tel: 425-467-5400; Fax: 425-462-9760. Sr. Margaret Byrne, C.S.J.P., Congregation Leader.
Total Number in Western U.S: 74.
Corporate Titles: Sisters of St. Joseph of Peace; Sisters of St. Joseph of Peace Charitable Trust, Bellevue, WA.
Properties owned: St. Mary's Residence, Bellevue, WA; Prospect House, Seattle, WA; St. Therese Residence, Seattle, WA; Grace House, Seattle, WA; Alicia Park House, Seattle, WA; Eugene Residence, Eugene, OR; Our Lady of Perpetual Help House, San Diego, CA; Casa Navidad, San Diego, CA.

[3893] (S.S.J.)—SISTERS OF SAINT JOSEPH OF CHESTNUT HILL, PHILADELPHIA (P)

Founded in France in 1650. First foundation in Philadelphia in 1847.

Motherhouse (1847): *Mount St. Joseph Convent*, 9701 Germantown Ave., Philadelphia, PA 19118-2694. Tel: 215-248-7200; Fax: 215-248-7277; Email: msjc@ssjphila.org; Web: www.ssjphila.org. Sr. Anne Patricia Myers, S.S.J., Congregational Pres.; Sr. Patricia Annas, S.S.J., Archivist.
Total in Congregation: 901.
Legal Holdings or Titles: Saint Joseph Villa; Saint Joseph Guild; Bethlehem Retirement Village, Flourtown, PA; Academy Village, McSherrystown, PA; Saint Joseph Housing Corporation; Saint Mary by-the-Sea Convent, Cape May Point, NJ; Cecilian, Philadelphia, PA; Mount Saint Joseph Academy, Flourtown, PA; Norwood-Fontbonne Academy, Philadelphia, PA; Holy Family, Bayonne, NJ; Chestnut Hill College, Philadelphia, PA; Cecilian Village, McSherrystown, PA; SSJ Center for Spirituality, Philadelphia, PA; Saint Joseph Academy, McSherrystown, PA; The Convent of the Sisters of St. Joseph, Chestnut Hill, PA; Elizabeth House, Philadelphia, PA; Saint Joseph Village, McSherrystown, PA; Sisters of Saint Joseph Welcome Center, Philadelphia, PA.
Ministry in the field of Academic and Religious Education at all levels; Institutes for Dependent Children; Pastoral Ministry; Campus Ministry; Care of the Aged; Social Services; Prison Ministry; Health Care; Psychologists; Hospice Ministry; Hospital Chaplaincy; Spiritual Directors; Drug and Alcohol Counselors.
Represented in the Archdioceses of Baltimore, Miami, Newark, New York, Philadelphia, San Antonio and Washington and in the Dioceses of Allentown, Altoona-Johnstown, Arlington, Brooklyn, Camden, Charlotte, Fairbanks, Fort Wayne-South Bend, Harrisburg, Jackson, Metuchen, Paterson, Raleigh, St. Petersburg, Savannah, Trenton, Venice, Wheeling-Charleston and Wilmington. Also in Canada.

[3900] (S.S.J.)—SISTERS OF ST. JOSEPH OF ST. AUGUSTINE, FLORIDA (D)

Founded in France in 1650. First foundation in the United States in 1866. Classified as an American

Congregation in 1899.

Motherhouse (1847): *St. Joseph Convent*, 241 St. George St., P.O. Box 3506, St. Augustine, FL 32085. Tel: 904-824-1752; Email: ssjfl@bellsouth.net. Sr. Ann Kuhn, S.S.J., Gen. Supr.; Sr. Thomas Joseph McGoldrick, S.S.J., Community Archivist.

Total in Community: 82.

Ministry in Hospital-Health Care Services; Social Services; Hospital Pastoral Care; Care of Aged; Academic and Religious Education at all levels; Parish Ministry; Diocesan Office Administration; Architectural Liturgical Design; Retreat Ministry; Ministry to the Handicapped.

Represented in the Archdiocese of Miami and in the Dioceses of Orlando, Palm Beach, Pensacola-Tallahassee, St. Augustine and St. Petersburg.

[3910] (S.J.S.M.)—SISTERS OF ST. JOSEPH OF ST. MARK (D)

Founded in France in 1845. First foundation in the United States in October, 1937.

Generalate: Colmar, France Sr. Sophie Moog, Gen. Supr.

Universal total in Congregation: 249.

General Motherhouse (Cleveland) (1939): 21800 Charden Rd., Euclid, OH 44117-2199. Mother M. Raphael Gregg, Supr. Gen.

Youngstown Diocese: *Sisters of St. Joseph of St. Mark, Community Center*, 2300 Reno Dr., Ste. 319, Louisville, OH 44641. Tel: 330-875-7967. Sr. Edwardine Baznik, S.J.S.M., Supr.

Total number in U.S: 14.

Represented in the Dioceses of Cleveland and Youngstown.

[3920] (S.J.W.)—SISTERS OF ST. JOSEPH THE WORKER (D)

General Motherhouse: *St. William Convent*, 1 St. Joseph Ln., Walton, KY 41094. Mother Mary Christina Murray, S. J.W., Supr. Gen.

Total in Community: 13.

Properties owned and operated: Taylor Manor Nursing Home, Versailles, KY; 16-acre property in Walton, KY: Motherhouse Formation House.

Represented in the Dioceses of Covington and Lexington.

[3930] (SSJ-TOSF)—SISTERS OF ST. JOSEPH OF THE THIRD ORDER OF ST. FRANCIS (P)

Founded in the United States in 1901.

Corporate Office: 1300 Maria Dr., P.O. Box 305, Stevens Point, WI 54481-0305. Tel: 715-341-8457; Fax: 715-341-8830. Sr. Jane Blabolil, S.S.J.-T.O.S.F., Pres.; Sr. Michelle Wronkowski, S.S.J.-T.O.S.F., Vice Pres.; Sr. Dorothy Pagosa, S.S.J.-T.O.S.F., Vice Pres.; Sr. Linda Szocik, S.S.J.-T.O.S.F., Vice Pres.

Total number in the Congregation: 288.

Sponsors: Learning Center; 2 High Schools; Health Care System; Continuing Care Retirement Community.

Ministries in the following areas: Academic Education at all levels; Pastoral Ministry; Health Care Services; Ministry abroad in South America and Puerto Rico; 8th Day Center for Justice; Social Services.

Represented in the Archdioceses of Chicago, Detroit, Hartford, Los Angeles, Milwaukee, St. Paul-Minneapolis, and Washington and in the Dioceses of Arecibo (PR), Cleveland, Fort Wayne-South Bend, Gary, Grand Island, Hartford, Green Bay, Harrisburg, Joliet, Kalamazoo, Knoxville, La Crosse, Lansing, Madison, Norwich, Oakland, Phoenix, Rockford, St. Petersburg, Superior, Toledo and Youngstown. Also in Peru and Brazil.

[3935] (S.S.L.)—THE CONGREGATION OF THE SISTERS OF ST. LOUIS, JUILLY - MONAGHAN (P)

Founded in France in 1842. First foundation in the United States in 1949.

General Motherhouse: Louisville Monaghan, Ireland Sr. Donna Hansen, S.S.L.

Regional House: *Louisville Convent*, 22300 Mulholland Dr., Woodland Hills, CA 91364. Tel: 818-883-1678; Email: sslca4@sistersofsaintlouis.com (Region); Email: sslgen@eircom.net (Institute). Sr. Judith Dieterle, S.S.L.

Finally Professed Sisters: 50.

Legal Title: *Sisters of St. Louis, Juilly-Monaghan, Inc.*

Ministry in the field of Education; Pastoral and Social Ministries.

Represented in the Archdiocese of Los Angeles and in the Dioceses of Orange, Raleigh and San Diego. Also in Brasil.

[3950] (S.S.M.N.)—SISTERS OF SAINT MARY OF NAMUR (P)

Founded in Namur, Belgium, in 1819. First foundation in the United States in 1863.

General Motherhouse: Namur, Belgium Sr. Rejeanne Roussel, Gen. Supr.

Professed 391; Novices 20: 411.

Eastern Province: *Provincial House*, 241 Lafayette Ave., Buffalo, NY 14213-1453. Tel: 716-884-8221; Fax: 716-884-6598. Sr. Caroline Smith, S.S.M.N., Prov. Supr.

Total in Community: 84.

Legal Holdings or Titles: 6 Residences.

Ministry in the field of Religious and Academic Education; Pastoral Ministry; Community Organization; Social Services; Diocesan and Health related services; Refugee Assistance.

Represented in the Dioceses of Bridgeport, Buffalo, Charleston and Savannah. Also in Canada.

Western Province: *Provincial House - Our Lady of Victory Center*, 909 W. Shaw St., Fort Worth, TX 76110. Tel: 817-923-8393. Sr. Patricia St. Marie, Prov.

Total in Community: 44.

Ministry in the field of Religious and Academic Education; Diocesan Offices; Pastoral Ministry; Social Services; Health Care and Missions.

Properties owned or sponsored: Our Lady of Victory Center, Fort Worth, TX; Our Lady of Victory Catholic School, Fort Worth, TX; Sisters of St. Mary of Namur, Fort Worth, TX; Notre Dame Convent; Mercy Convent, Wichita Falls, TX.

Represented in the Dioceses of Dallas and Fort Worth.

[3960] (S.S.M.O.)—SISTERS OF ST. MARY OF OREGON

Founded in Oregon in 1886.

General Motherhouse: *Sisters of St. Mary of Oregon*, 4440 S.W. 148th Ave., Beaverton, OR 97007. Tel: 503-644-9181. Sr. Charlene Herinckx, Supr. Gen.

Total in Congregation: 67.

Ministry in the field of Education; Nursing Homes; and Parish Services.

Properties owned or sponsored: Maryville Nursing Home; SSMO Campus Schools.

Represented in the Archdioceses of Los Angeles and Portland in Oregon and in the Diocese of Helena.

[3980] (S.P.C)—SISTERS OF SAINT PAUL DE CHARTRES (P)

Founded in France in 1696.

General House: 193 Via della Vignaccia, Rome, Italy, 1-00163. Sr. Myriam Kitcharoent, S.P.C., Supr. Gen.

Universal total in Congregation: 4000.

U.S. Province: 1300 County Rd. 492, Marquette, MI 49855-9632. Tel: 906-226-3932. Sr. Gloria J. Schultz, S.P.C., Prov.

Total in Community: 14.

Legal Holding: Bishop Noa Home for Senior Citizens, Escanaba, MI.

Ministry in the field of Academic and Religious Education; Hospital Chaplaincy; Pastoral Ministry.

Represented in the Archdiocese of Washington and in the Diocese of Marquette.

[3990] (S.S.P.C.)—MISSIONARY SISTERS OF ST. PETER CLAVER (P)

Founded in 1894. First Foundation in the United States, 1914.

General House: 16 via dell' Olmata, Rome, Italy, 00184. Sr. Maria Moryl, S.S.P.C., Supr. Gen.

Legal Title: *The Sodality of St. Peter Claver for the African Missions-Missionary Sisters of St. Peter Claver.*

American Headquarters: 225 Century Ave., S., Saint Paul, MN 55125-1155. Tel: 651-738-9704.

Total in Community: 17.

Represented in the Archdioceses of Chicago, St. Louis and St. Paul-Minneapolis.

[4010] (O.S.A.)—SISTERS OF ST. RITA (D)

General Motherhouse: Friedrich-Spee-Str. 32, 97072 Wurzburg, Germany Sr. Rita Maria Kaes, O.S.A., Gen.

Universal total in Congregation: 110.

U.S. Address: *St. Rita's Convent*, 4014 Green Bay Rd., Racine, WI 53404. Tel: 262-639-1766. Sr. Irene Hanika, O.S.A., Supr.

Represented in the Archdiocese of Milwaukee.

[4020] (S.T.J.)—SOCIETY OF ST. TERESA OF JESUS (P)

(Teresian Sisters)

Founded in Spain in 1876. First foundation in the United States in 1910. Total Membership 1,477.

Generalate: Via Valcannuta, 134, Rome, Italy, 00166.

Provincial Office: *St. Francis de Sales Province*, 18080 St. Joseph's Way, Covington, LA 70435-5623. Tel: 985-893-1470; Fax: 985-893-2476.

Formation House: 18158 St. Joseph's Way, Covington, LA 70435-5624. Tel: 985-893-1557. Sr. Martha L. Gonzalez, Community Archivist.

Total in Community: 28.

Properties owned and/or sponsored: St. Teresa's Convent, San Antonio, TX; Henry de Osso Convent, San Antonio, TX; Provincialate, Covington, LA; Blessed Mercedes Prat Convent, New Orleans, LA.

Ministry in the field of Academic Education at all levels; Education in underdeveloped areas; Youth Ministry; Pastoral Ministry.

Represented in the Archdioceses of Miami, New Orleans and San Antonio.

[4030] (S.S.T.V.)—CONGREGATION OF SISTERS OF ST. THOMAS OF VILLANOVA (P)

Founded in France in 1661. First foundation in the United States in 1948.

General Motherhouse: 52 Blvd. d'Argeson, Neuilly-sur-Seine, France, 92200. Tel: 01 47 47 42 20; Fax: 01 47 47 38 00; Email: neuillystv@wanadoo.com; Web: www.congregation-stv.org.

Universal total in Congregation: 175.

Sisters of St. Thomas of Villanova Convent: 76 W. Rocks Rd., Norwalk, CT 06851. Tel: 203-847-2885; Fax: 203-847-3740; Email: sstv_usa@sbcglobal.net; Web: www.saintthomasofvillanova.com. Sr. Marie Lucie Monast, S.S.T.V., Liaison.

Total in Community: 2.

Properties owned and/or sponsored: Notre Dame Convalescent Home.

Represented in the Diocese of Bridgeport.

[4040] (S.U.)—SOCIETY OF ST. URSULA (P)

Founded in Dole, France, in 1606. First foundation in the United States in 1901.

General Motherhouse: St. Cyr-Loire, France Sr. Anne Bayart, S.U., Supr. Gen.

Provincialate: 50 Linwood Rd., Rhinebeck, NY 12572. Tel: 845-876-2341. Sr. Mary Dolan, S.U., Reg. Supr.

Total in Community: 27.

Ministry in the field of Education; Parish Ministry; Spiritual Direction and Retreats.

Represented in the Archdiocese of New York and in the Dioceses of Providence and Raleigh.

[4048] (F.C.J.)—SOCIETY OF THE SISTERS FAITHFUL COMPANIONS OF JESUS (P)

Founded in France in 1820. First founded in the United States in 1895.

General Motherhouse: *Stella Maris Convent*, North Foreland, Braodstairs, Kent, England, CT10 3NR.

Provincial Office: 300 Palmerston Ave., Toronto, Canada, M6J 2J4. Tel: 416-588-1791.

U.S. Provincial Business Office: 324 Cory's Ln., Portsmouth, RI 02871. Tel: 401-683-2222. Sr. Katherine Mary O'Flynn, F.C.J., Supr. Gen.; Sr. Patricia Binchy, F.C.J., Prov.; Sr. Marguerite Goddard, F.C.J., Novice Dir.

Sisters: 16.

[4050] (S.D.S.H.)—SISTERS OF THE SOCIETY DEVOTED TO THE SACRED HEART (D)

Founded in Hungary in 1940.

Motherhouse (1956): 9814 Sylvia Ave., Northridge, CA 91324. Tel: 818-772-9961; Fax: 818-772-2742; Web: www.sacredheartsisters.com. Sr. Jane Stafford, Supr. Gen.

Novitiate House: 10480 Winnetka Ave., Chatsworth, CA 91311. Tel: 818-831-9710; Fax: 818-831-0790; Web: www.sacredheartsisters.com.

Total in Community: 50.

Properties owned and/or sponsored: Sacred Heart Motherhouse, Northridge CA; Heart of Jesus Retreat Center, Santa Ana, CA; Sacred Heart Novitiate, Chatsworth, CA; Sacred Heart Retreat Camp, Big Bear, CA; Sacred Heart Convent, Los Angeles, CA.

Ministry in Parish Religious Education Centers; Catechist Formation Centers; Camp for year-round Retreats and summer Family Retreats Camps; Catechesis; Youth Leadership Programs; Day Retreat Center for Children and Adults; Catechesis in Parochial Schools and Catholic High Schools; "Sacred Heart Kids' Club" Video/DVD Catechesis; Hispanic and Chinese Catechetical Center; Catechetical Programs on Military Bases; Catechetical Missions to Dioceses; Far East Mission in Taiwan; Mission in Hungary.

Represented in the Archdioceses of Los Angeles and St. Louis and the Dioceses of Orange and San Bernardino. Also in Taiwan and Hungary.

[4060] (S.H.C.J.)—SOCIETY OF THE HOLY CHILD JESUS (P)

Founded in England in 1846. First foundation in the United States in 1862.

Motherhouse: Via della Maglianella 379, Rome, Italy, 00166. Sr. Veronica Openibo, S.H.C.J., Society Leader.

American Province: *Provincial Offices*, 1341 Montgomery Ave, Rosemont, PA 19010. Tel: 610-626-1400. Sr. Mary Ann Buckley, S.H.C.J., Prov. Leader; Sr. Helena Mayer, S.H.C.J., Archivist.

Total number in Province: 167.

Ministry in a variety of Educational and Pastoral Work.

Properties owned or sponsored: Connelly School of the Holy Child, Potomac, MD; Cornelia Connelly School, Anaheim, CA; Mayfield Junior School of the Holy Child Jesus; Mayfield Senior School of the Holy Child Jesus, Pasadena, CA; Oak Knoll School of the Holy Child, Summit, NJ; Old Westbury School of the Holy Child, Old Westbury, NY; Rosemont School of the Holy Child, Rosemont, PA; School of the Holy Child, Drexel Hill, PA; School of the Holy Child, Rye, NY; Providence Center, Philadelphia, PA; Cornelia Connelly Center for Education; Holy Child Middle School, New York, NY.

Represented in the Archdioceses of Boston, Chicago, Hartford, Los Angeles, Milwaukee, Newark, New York, Philadelphia, Portland in Oregon and Washington and in the Dioceses of Camden, Charlotte, Orange, Paterson, Rockville Centre, San Diego and Trenton.

[4070] (R.S.C.J.)—SOCIETY OF THE SACRED HEART (P)

Founded in France in 1800. First foundation in the United States in 1818.

Generalate: Via Tarquinio Viper, 16, Rome, Italy, 00152. Sr. Kathleen Conan, Supr. Gen.

United States Provincial House: 4120 Forest Park Ave., St. Louis, MO 63108. Tel: 314-652-1500; Fax: 314-534-6800; Email: provincialhouse@rscj.org. Sr. Paula Toner, R.S.C.J., Prov.; Sr. Carolyn Osiek, R.S.C.J., Prov. Archivist.

Total number in the Province: 349.

Ministry in the field of Religious and Academic Education at all levels; Adult Education; Parish, Pastoral, Social and Health Care Ministries.

Province Corporations: Society of the Sacred Heart, United States Province, Inc.; California Province of the Society of the Sacred Heart, Inc.; Society of the Sacred Heart, Chicago Province, Inc.; Religious of the Sacred Heart, Washington Province, Inc.; Religious of the Sacred Heart, New York Province, Inc.; Ladies of the Sacred Heart, MO; Religious of the Sacred Heart in Massachusetts, Inc.; Network of the Sacred Heart Schools, Inc., 700 N. Third St., St. Charles, MO 63301, Phone: 636-724-7003.

Represented in the Archdioceses of Boston, Chicago, Cincinnati, Detroit, Galveston-Houston, Louisville, Miami, Milwaukee, New Orleans, New York, Omaha, St. Louis, San Francisco, Seattle and Washington and in the Dioceses of Albany, Baton Rouge, Fall River, Fort Wayne-South Bend, Lafayette (LA), Oakland, Portland, San Bernardino, San Diego, San Jose, and Trenton.

[4080] (S.S.S.)—SISTERS OF SOCIAL SERVICE OF LOS ANGELES, INC. (P)

Founded in Hungary. Established in the United States at Los Angeles, California in 1926.

General Motherhouse: 4316 Lanai Rd., Encino, CA 91436. Tel: 818-285-3355; Fax: 818-285-3366. Sr. Rochelle Mitchell, Gen. Dir.

Total in Community: 77.

Legal Titles: Sisters of Social Service of Los Angeles; Sisters of Social Service Support Trust Fund.

Social Service Work in Parishes and in Diocesan Agencies; Leadership Training of Youth and Adults; Summer Camps for Children and Families; Programs for the Elderly; Peace and Justice Work; Religious Education; Settlement Houses; Health Programs; Family Counseling Services; International houses in Mexico, Philippines and Taiwan.

Represented in the Archdioceses of Los Angeles, Portland in Oregon, San Francisco and Seattle and in the Dioceses of Oakland, Sacramento and San Diego.

[4090] (S.S.S.)—SISTERS OF SOCIAL SERVICE OF BUFFALO, INC. (P)

Founded in Budapest, Hungary in 1923; Sr. Margaret Slachta, Foundress.

Generalate: H-1029, Bathori Laszlo u. 10, Budapest, Hungary

U.S. District Residence: 296 Summit Ave., Buffalo, NY 14214-1936. Tel: 716-834-0197; Fax: 716-834-6168. Sr. Teresina Joo, S.S.S., District Moderator; Sr. Agnes Pataki, S.S.S., Gen. Moderator.

Total number in the United States: 14.

Social Work; Parish Ministry; Ministry for Justice and Human Rights; Field of Spirituality.

Represented in the Archdiocese of Miami and in the Diocese of Buffalo.

[4100] (S.S.M.)—SISTERS OF THE SORROWFUL MOTHER (THIRD ORDER OF ST. FRANCIS) (P)

Founded in Italy in 1883. First foundation in the United States in 1889.

General Motherhouse: *Casa Generalizia della Suore dell'Addolorata*, Via Paolo III 7-9, Rome, Italy, I-00165. Sr. M. Teresina Marra, S.S.M., Gen. Supr.

SSM US/Caribbean Provincial Administration: 815 Westhaven Dr., Ste. 100, Oshkosh, WI 54904. Tel: 920-230-2040; Fax: 920-230-2041. Sr. Marilyn Vollmer, S.S.M., Prov. Supr.

Total number in the U.S. Community: 117.

Legal Holding: Sisters of the Sorrowful Mother - Marian Health System, Inc.; Sisters of the Sorrowful Mother - US/Caribbean Province, Inc.

Ministry in the fields of Religious and Academic Education; Nursing Homes; Social Work; Hospitals and Hospital Administration; Pastoral Care.

Represented in the Archdiocese of Milwaukee and in the Dioceses of Green Bay, La Crosse, Paterson, Superior, Tulsa and Wichita. Also in Trinidad, Grenada and Castries, St. Lucia, Port of Spain and Dominican Republic, San Juan de la Maguana, Santiago de los Caballeros.

[4105] —THIRD ORDER REGULAR FRANCISCAN COMMON NOVITIATE

120 N. Elizabeth Ave., Saint Louis, MO 63135-2456. Web: www.newfranciscans.org. Sr. Rosalie Wisniewski, O.S.F.

Total participating congregations: 31.

Ministry in the develpment in each novice of Franciscan spirituality, charism, and prayer.

Represented in the Archdiocese of St. Louis.

[4110] (O.S.U.)—URSULINE NUNS (P)

(Roman Union)

Founded in Italy in 1535. First foundation in the United States New Orleans, Louisiana in 1727.

Generalate: Via Nomentana 236, Rome, Italy, 00162. Mother Cecilia Wang, O.S.U., Prioress Gen.

Eastern Province of the U.S. (1900): *Ursuline Provincialate*, 1338 North Ave., New Rochelle, NY 10804. Tel: 914-712-0060; Fax: 914-712-3134.

Total number in the Province: 115.

Legal Titles: Ursuline Provincialate, Eastern Province of the United States, Inc.; Marian Residence Fund, New Rochelle, NY; OSU Charitable Trust, New Rochelle, NY.

Ministry in the field of Academic Education at all levels; varied Pastoral and Social Services.

Represented in the Archdioceses of New York and Washington and in the Dioceses of Bridgeport, Ogdensburg, Orlando and Wilmington.

Central Province of the U.S: *Ursuline Provincialate*, 353 S. Sappington Rd., Saint Louis, MO 63122. Tel: 314-821-6884; Fax: 314-821-6888. Sr. Diane Fulgenzi, O.S.U., Prov. Prioress.

Total in Community: 111.

Ministry in the field of Religious and Academic Education.

Represented in the Archdioceses of Chicago, Galveston-Houston, New Orleans, St. Louis, St. Paul-Minneapolis and San Antonio and in the Dioceses of Dallas, Laredo, Peoria, Springfield-Cape Girardeau and Springfield (IL).

Western Province U.S. (1932): *Ursuline Provincialate*, 639 Angela Dr., Santa Rosa, CA 95403-1793. Tel: 707-545-6811; Fax: 707-579-8571. Sr. Margaret Johnson, O.S.U., Co-Prov.; Sr. Shirley Ann Garibaldi, O.S.U., Co-Prov.

Total number in the Province: 27.

Ministry in the field of Elementary and Secondary Education; Work with the Eskimos, American Indians, & Hispanics; Parish Ministry; Catechetical Coordinators; Spiritual Direction; Spiritual Growth Center; Counseling Services; Detention Ministry.

Represented in the Archdioceses of Los Angeles and San Francisco and in the Dioceses of Boise, Fairbanks, Great Falls-Billings and Santa Rosa.

Northeastern Province: *Ursuline Provincialate*, 45 Lowder St., Dedham, MA 02026-4200. Tel: 781-326-6219; Fax: 781-326-7296. Sr. Angela Krippendorf, O.S.U., Prov.

Total in Community: 29.

Ministry in the field of Education.

Represented in the Archdiocese of Boston and in the Diocese of Portland (In Maine).

[4120] (O.S.U.)—URSULINE NUNS, OF THE CONGREGATION OF PARIS (P)

Founded in Italy in 1535. First foundation in the United States in New Orleans, Louisiana in 1727.

Motherhouse (1845): *Ursulines of Brown County*, 20860 St. Rte. 251, Fayetteville, OH 45118-9705. Tel: 513-875-2020 Ext. 27; Fax: 513-875-2311; Web: www.ursulinesofbc.org. Sr. Patricia Homan, O.S.U., Supr.

Total in Community: 28.

Legal Title: *St. Ursula Literary Institute; Ursulines of Brown County; Ursuline Academy of Cincinnati, Chatfield College.*

Ministry in the field of Academic Education at all levels; Special Education; Adult Education; Catechetical Instruction; Administration; Retreats; Counseling; Organization Consultation; Social-Inner City & Rural; Senior Services; Campus and Parish Ministry.

Represented in the Archdiocese of Cincinnati and in the Diocese of Toledo.

[4120-01] CINCINNATI (P)

Motherhouse: *Ursulines of Cincinnati, St. Ursula Convent*, 1339 E. McMillan St. (Walnut Hills), Cincinnati, OH 45206. Tel: 513-961-3410. Sr. Mary Jerome Buchert, O.S.U.

Total in Community: 13.

Legal Title: *Ursuline Sisters, Inc.; Ursuline Sisters Charitable Trust.*

Ministry in the field of Academic Education at all levels; Parish and Diocesan Services; Social Services; Communications.

Represented in the Archdiocese of Cincinnati.

[4120-03] LOUISVILLE (P)

Ursuline Sisters of the Immaculate Conception: 3105 Lexington Rd., Louisville, KY 40206. Tel: 502-897-1811; Fax: 502-896-3913. Sr. Lynn Jarrell, O.S.U., Pres.

Total in Community: 110.

Legal Title: *Ursuline Society and Academy of Education aka Ursuline Sisters.*

Ministry in the field of Academic Education; Child Care; Pastoral Ministry; Social Services; Spirituality.

Properties owned and sponsored: Sacred Heart Schools, Louisville, KY.

Represented in the Archdioceses of Baltimore, Cincinnati, Louisville and Philadelphia and in the Dioceses of Charleston, Davenport, Grand Island, Lexington and Wheeling-Charleston.

[4120-04] CLEVELAND (P)

Ursuline Motherhouse and Educational Center: 2600 Lander Rd., Cleveland, OH 44124. Fax: 440-449-3588. Sr. Maureen Grady, O.S.U., Supr. Gen.; Sr. Colette Livingston, O.S.U., Community Archivist.

Total in Community: 185.

Legal Titles: The Ursuline Academy of Cleveland; The Ursuline Sisters of Cleveland.

Ministry in the field of Academic Education at all levels; Parish Ministry; Diocesan Offices; Seminary; Social Service Agency; Hospital and Health Care Ministry; Spiritual Direction and Retreat Ministry; Foreign Mission.

Properties sponsored: Ursuline College; Beaumont High School; Urban Community School; Villa Angela/St. Joseph High School.

Represented in the Archdioceses of Cincinnati, Los Angeles and San Antonio and in the Dioceses of Brownsville, Cleveland, Lexington, Springfield-Cape Girardeau, and Youngstown. Also in El Salvador.

[4120-05] OWENSBORO (P)

Mt. St. Joseph Ursuline Motherhouse: 8001 Cummings Rd., Maple Mount, KY 42356. Tel: 270-229-4103; Fax: 270-229-4127.

Total in Community: 159.

Legal Holdings and Titles: St. Joseph's Female Ursuline Academy; Brescia University, Owensboro, KY; Mount Saint Joseph Conference and Retreat Center, Maple Mount, KY.

Ministry in Colleges; High Schools; Elementary Schools; Parishes; Retreats and Spiritual Direction; Pastoral Care; Health Care; Social Services; Hispanic Outreach; Diocesan Offices.

Represented in the Archdioceses of Kansas City in Kansas, Louisville, Santa Fe, St. Paul Minneapolis and Washington and in the Dioceses of Belleville, Gallup, Kansas City-St. Joseph, Memphis, Owensboro, Shreveport, Springfield-Cape Girardeau and Springfield in Illinois. Also in Chile.

[4120-06] TOLEDO (P)

Ursuline Convent of the Sacred Heart: 4045 Indian Rd., Toledo, OH 43606. Tel: 419-536-9587. Sr. Donna Frey, O.S.U., Gen. Supr.; Sr. Bernarda Breidenbach, O.S.U., Pres./Supr.

Total in Community: 50; Associates: 150.

Legal Title: *Ursuline Convent of the Sacred Heart.*

Ministry in the field of Administration; Religious and Academic Education; Health Care; Counseling Services; Pastoral Ministry; Pastoral Care; Retreat Work; Spiritual Direction; Education in Music; Home Health Care.

Properties owned or sponsored: St. Ursula Academy, Toledo, OH.

Represented in the Archdiocese of Washington and in the Dioceses of Fresno and Toledo. Also in Lima, Peru.

[4120-07] YOUNGSTOWN (P)

Motherhouse: *Ursuline Motherhouse and Educational Center*, 4250 Shields Rd., Canfield, OH 44406. Tel: 330-792-7636. Sr. Nancy Dawson, O.S.U., Gen. Supr.

Total in Community: 52.

Properties owned and/or sponsored: Ursuline Motherhouse; Ursuline Center; Ursuline Preschool & Kindergarten; Beatitude House.

Ministry in the field of Religious and Academic Education at all levels; Parish Ministry; Social Services; Hospital Services; Single Parenting; AIDS Ministry; Preschool; Kindergarten; Nursing Home Service.

Represented in the Dioceses of Cleveland and Youngstown.

[4130] (O.S.U.)—URSULINE SISTERS OF THE CONGREGATION OF TILDONK, BELGIUM (P)

International Congregation

Founded in Italy in 1535 by St. Angela Merici (Ursulines). Congregation of Tildonk founded in Belgium in 1832. First foundation in the United States in Ozone Park, New York, in 1924.

Generalate: Brussels, Belgium Sr. Margaret O'Brien, O.S.U., Gen. Supr.

Ursuline Provincialate: 81-15 Utopia Pkwy., Jamaica, NY 11432. Tel: 718-591-0681. Sr. Catherine Talia, O.S.U., Prov. Supr.

Total in Community: 50.

Properties owned and/or sponsored: St. Ursula Center, Blue Point, NY; Ursuline Provincialate, Jamaica NY.

Ministry in the field of Education in all its aspects; Retreat Work; Chaplaincies.

Represented in the Archdioceses of Hartford and New York and in the Dioceses of Bridgeport, Brooklyn, Burlington and Rockville Centre.

[4155] (M.T.G.)—SISTERS ADORERS OF THE HOLY CROSS (P)

Founded in 1670 in Vietnam by Bishop Pierre Lambert de la Motte. First foundation in the U.S. 1979.

General Motherhouse: *Holy Cross Convent*, 7408 S.E. Alder, Portland, OR 97215. Tel: 503-254-3284. Sr. Mary Trinh Nguyen, M.T.G., Supr.
Sisters: 30.
Represented in the Archdiocese of Portland in Oregon and in the Dioceses of Arlington and Sacramento.

[4160] (V.S.C.)—VINCENTIAN SISTERS OF CHARITY (P)

First foundation in the United States in 1902.

General Motherhouse and Novitiate: *St. Vincent Hill*, 8200 McKnight Rd., Pittsburgh, PA 15237. Tel: 412-364-3000; Fax: 412-364-9055. Sr. Charlene Reebel, V.S.C., Major Supr.
Professed Sisters: 111.
Ministry in the field of Education at all levels; Health Care in Nursing Homes; Child Care Center; Catechetical Centers; Social Apostolates; Pastoral Ministries.
Properties owned or sponsored: Vincentian Child Care Center; Vincentian Academy-Duquesne University Vincentian de Marillac; Vincentian Regency; Vincentian Home, Inc.; Marian Manor, Inc.
Represented in the Archdiocese of Mobile and in Dioceses of Greensburg, Madison, Pittsburgh, Steubenville and Venice. Also in Canada.

[4170] (V.S.C.)—VINCENTIAN SISTERS OF CHARITY (D)

Founded in Bedford in 1928.
5900 Delhi Rd., Mount Saint Joseph, OH 45051.

[4180] (M.P.V.)—RELIGIOUS VENERINI SISTERS (P)

Founded in Italy in 1685. First foundation in the United States in 1909.

General Motherhouse: via Gioachino Belli 31, Rome, Italy Mother Mariateresa Crescini, Supr. Gen.
Universal total in Congregation: 447.

Provincialhouse for the U.S: 23 Edward St., Worcester, MA 01605. Sr. Hilda Ponte, M.P.V., Prov.
Total in Community: 23.
Legal Holdings: Venerini Academy, Worcester, MA.
Ministry in the field of Education; Health Care; Social Services; Parish and Diocesan Ministry; Foreign Missions.
Represented in the Dioceses of Albany and Worcester.

[4190] (V.H.M.)—VISITATION NUNS (P)

Founded in France in 1610. First foundation in the United States in Georgetown, Washington, DC in 1799.

First Federation of North America
Mother Rose Marie Kinsella, V.H.M., Federation Pres.
Listed in the Order of Foundation established.

Monastery of the Visitation (1833): 2300 Springhill Ave., Mobile, AL 36607-3202. Tel: 251-473-2321; Fax: 251-476-9761; Web: www.VisitationMonasteryMobile-.org. Mother Margaret Mary Rumpf, V.H.M., Supr.
Perpetual Vows: 7; Novices: 2.

Monastery of the Visitation: 14 Beach Rd., P.O. Box 432, Tyringham, MA 01264. Tel: 413-243-3995; Fax: 413-243-3543; Email: vistyr@aol.com; Web: www.vistyr.org. Mother Mary Ruth Dolch, Supr.
Total in Community: 18.
Legal Title: *Visitation of Holy Mary.*

Monastery of the Visitation: 12221 Bienvenue Rd., Rockville, VA 23146. Tel: 804-749-4885. Mother Mary Paula Zemienieuski, V.H.M., Supr.
Professed Sisters: 11.
Legal Title: *Visitation of Holy Mary.*

Monastery of the Visitation: 5820 City Ave., Philadelphia, PA 19131-1295. Tel: 215-473-5888. Mother Antoinette Marie Walker, V.H.M., Supr.
Professed Sisters Cloistered: 6.
Legal Title: *Sisters of the Visitation of Philadelphia.*

Monastery of the Visitation (Contemplative): 1745 Parkside Blvd., Toledo, OH 43607-1599. Tel: 419-536-1343; Fax: 419-536-6025; Email: vhm-toledo@toast.net; Web: www.toledovisitation.org. Sr. Sharon Elizabeth Gworek, V.H.M., Supr.
Professed Sisters: 15; In Formation: 7.
Legal Title: *The Contemplative Order of the Visitation of Toledo, Ohio.*

Monastery of the Visitation (Strictly Cloistered): 2055 Ridgedale Dr., Snellville, GA 30078. Tel: 770-972-1060. Sr. Mary Jane Frances Williams, V.H.M., Supr.
Professed Sisters: 10; Postulants: 1.
Legal Title: *Order of the Visitation.*

Second Federation of North America

Monastery of the Visitation of Georgetown: 1500 35th St., N.W., Washington, DC 20007. Tel: 202-337-0305; Fax: 202-965-3845. Mother Mary Berchmans Hannan, Supr.; Sr. Mada-anne Gell, Community Archivist.
Total number in the school community: 483; Total in Community: 21.
Legal Holdings and Titles: Sisters of the Visitation of Georgetown; Georgetown Visitation Preparatory School.

Monastery of the Visitation (1833): 3020 N. Ballas Rd., St. Louis, MO 63131. Tel: 314-625-9260. Sr. Mary Veronica Haronik, V.H.M., Supr.
Total in Community: 12.
Legal Holdings: Visitation Academy of St. Louis County; Monastery of the Visitation, St. Louis, MO.
Ministry in Education.

Monastery of the Visitation (1855): 8902 Ridge Blvd., Brooklyn, NY 11209-5716. Tel: 718-745-5151; Fax: 718-745-3680. Mother Mary Pauline Baulis, V.H.M., Supr.
Professed Sisters: 19.
Legal Title: *Sisters of the Visitation of Brooklyn, NY.*

Monastery of the Visitation: 2455 Visitation Dr., St. Paul, MN 55120. Tel: 651-683-1700. Sr. Mary Denise Villaume, V.H.M., Supr.
Total in Community: 8.
Ministry in Prayer and Education.

[4200] (S.V.M.)—SISTERS OF THE VISITATION OF THE IMMACULATE HEART OF MARY (D)

Founded in France in 1610. First foundation in the United States in 1799.

Visitation Convent: 2950 Kaufmann Ave., Dubuque, IA 52001-1631. Tel: 563-556-2440. Sr. Patricia Clark, S.V.M., Pres.
Total in Community: 5.
Ministry in Higher Education; Adult Education; Parish Ministry.
Represented in the Archdiocese of Dubuque.

[4210] (S.D.V.)—VOCATIONIST SISTERS (P)
(Sisters of the Divine Vocations)

Founded in Italy in 1921. First established in the United States in 1967.

General Motherhouse: *Corso Duca D'Aosta*, 22 Pianura, Naples, Italy, 80126. Sr. Antonietta Colafemina, S.D.V., Supr. Gen.

U.S. Foundation: *Perpetual Help Day Nursery*, 170 Broad St., Newark, NJ 07104. Tel: 973-484-3535. Sr. Perpetua Da Conceicao, S.D.V., Supr.
Total in Community: 6.
Ministry in Nursery Schools & Kindergartens; CCD Program and Parish Services.
Represented in the Archdiocese of Newark.

Sister Joanna Formation House: 88 Brooklake Rd., Florham Park, NJ 07932. Tel: 973-966-9762. Sr. Gelsomina Mosca, Supr.; Sr. Luisa Gargione, Delegate.
Total in Community: 15.
Ministry in Nursery School; Formation House; Religious Education.
Represented in the Archdiocese of Newark and in the Dioceses of Paterson and Metuchen.

[4230] (X.M.M.)—XAVERIAN MISSIONARY SOCIETY OF MARY, INC. (P)

Founded in Italy in 1945. First established in the United States in 1954.

General Motherhouse: *Missionarie Saveriane Di Maria*, Via Omero 4, Parma, Italy Sr. Ines Frizza, X.M.M., Supr. Gen.
Total Membership: 265.

U.S. Headquarters: *Xaverian Missionary Society of Mary*, 242 Salisbury St., Worcester, MA 01609. Tel: 508-757-0514; Email: xavsistersusa@msn.com.
Ministry to Hispanics; Elderly; Families; CCD Programs and Mission Education.
Represented in the Diocese of Worcester.
Sr. Rebeca Sanchez Perez, X.M.M., Supr.

SPECIAL CARE FACILITIES

(For a complete listing refer to the corresponding (Arch)Diocese.)

ALABAMA

Daphne
Archdiocese of Mobile

John McClure Snook Regional Center, 27296 County Rd. 13, Daphne, 36526. Tel: 251-625-2555; Fax: 251-625-2556. (Assisted living Alzheimer community.)

Mobile
Archdiocese of Mobile

Rendu Terrace West, Inc., c/o 6801 Airport Blvd., P.O. Box 850429, Mobile, 36685.

Pelham
Diocese of Birmingham

Contemplative Outreach Birmingham, 106 Red Stick Rd., Pelham, 35124. Tel: 205-991-6964. Email: tschached@bellsouth.net. Web: www.bham.net/cobweb.

ALASKA

Anchorage
Archdiocese of Anchorage

Brother Francis Shelter, 1021 E. Third Ave., Anchorage, 99501. Tel: 907-277-1731. Overnight shelter for homeless men and women.

Covenant House Alaska, 609 F St., Anchorage, 99501. Tel: 907-272-1255; Fax: 907-272-1466. Program for homeless and runaway youth.

AMERICAN SAMOA

Pago Pago
Diocese of Samoa-Pago Pago

Hope House, P.O. Box 596, Pago Pago, AS 96799. Tel: 684-699-2101; Fax: 684-699-6051.

ARIZONA

Phoenix
Diocese of Phoenix

Affordable Services for Seniors, Inc., 1201 E. Thomas Rd., Phoenix, 85014. Tel: 602-285-1800. Email: shastings@fsl.org.

Payson Senior Living, Inc., 1201 E. Thomas Rd., Phoenix, 85014. Tel: 602-285-1800; Fax: 602-285-1838. Email: jgreene@fsl.org. (Pineview Manor Apartments, Payson)

Diocese of Tucson

Valley Center for the Deaf, 5025 E. Washington St., Ste. 114, Phoenix, 85034. Tel: 602-267-1921; Fax: 602-273-1872.

Tucson
Diocese of Tucson

Community Outreach Program for the Deaf, 268 W. Adams, Tucson, 85705. Tel: 520-792-1906; Fax: 520-770-8544.

Immigration Counseling Service, 140 W. Speedway, Ste. 130, Tucson, 85705. Tel: 520-623-0344; Fax: 520-770-8578.

St. Elizabeth's Health Center, 140 W. Speedway, Ste. 100, Tucson, 85705. Tel: 520-628-7871; Fax: 520-770-8528.

ARKANSAS

Little Rock
Diocese of Little Rock

ABBA House, Missionaries of Charity, 1014 S. Oak St., Little Rock, 72204. Tel: 501-666-9718 (Abba House); 501-663-3596 (convent). Home for expectant mothers, homeless women & children.

CALIFORNIA

Chatsworth
Archdiocese of Los Angeles

Rancho San Antonio, 21000 Plummer St., Chatsworth, 91311. Tel: 818-882-6400; Fax: 818-882-6404. Sponsored by Brothers of Holy Cross

Culver City
Archdiocese of Los Angeles

Marycrest Manor (1956) 10664 St. James Dr., Culver City, 90230-5498. Tel: 310-838-2778; 310-838-0016 (Carmelite Sisters); Fax: 310-838-9647; 310-838-0024 (Carmelite Sisters). Email: marycrestocd@yahoo.com. Skilled Nursing Facility attended by priests from Loyola Marymount University.

El Cajon
Diocese of San Diego

St. Madeleine Sophie's Center, 2119 E. Madison Ave., El Cajon, 92019-1111. Tel: 619-442-5129; Fax: 619-442-9651. Email: dturner@stmsc.org. Web: www.stmsc.org.

Hayward
Diocese of Oakland

St. Joseph's Center for Deaf and Hard of Hearing, 25580 Campus Dr., Hayward, 94542-1137. Tel: 510-267-8338 (Voice); 866-977-9920 (Video Phone); Fax: 510-893-0945. Email: rherbst@oakdiocese.org. Web: www.sjcd.org. 2121 Harrison St., Ste. 100, Oakland, 94612-3788.

Lancaster
Archdiocese of Los Angeles

Lancaster Community Shelter, 44611 Yucca Ave., Lancaster, 93534. Tel: 661-945-7524.

Los Angeles
Archdiocese of Los Angeles

Angel Guardian Home for Homeless Disabled Mothers with Minor Children (2000) 1660 Rockwood St., Los Angeles, 90026. Tel: 213-483-6654; Fax: 213-482-0522.

Bethany House, 850 N. Hobart Blvd., Los Angeles, 90029. Tel: 323-665-6937; Fax: 323-664-0754. Email: imas.bethania@hotmail.com.

Convent of the Good Shepherd-Good Shepherd Shelter (1904)Mailing Address: P.O. Box 19487, Los Angeles, 90019. Tel: 323-737-6111; Fax: 323-737-6113. Email: llengel@goodshepherdshelter.org. Web: www.goodshepherdshelter.org. Shelter for Battered Women and Their Children.

Good Shepherd Center for Homeless Women and Children (1984) Languille Emergency Shelter, 267 N. Belmont Ave., Los Angeles, 90026. Tel: 213-250-5241; Fax: 213-250-5073. Email: srjuliamary@sbcglobal.net. Web: www.thegoodshepherdcenter.com. (A Program of Catholic Charities.)

Hawkes Transitional Residence/Women's Village (1998) 1640 Rockwood St., Los Angeles, 90026. Tel: 213-482-0281; Fax: 213-482-0299.

Mother-Child Transitional Residence Administrative Site (1992) 267 N. Belmont Ave., Los Angeles, 90026. Tel: 213-469-6540; Fax: 213-469-0370.

Order of Malta Los Angeles Clinic, Inc., 2222 W. Ocean View, #112, Los Angeles, 90057. Tel: 213-384-4323; Fax: 213-384-4097. Email: freemed112@sbcglobal.net. Primary Health Care for the frail elderly, the working poor and medically underserved children.

St. Anne's, 155 N. Occidental Blvd., Los Angeles, 90026. Tel: 213-381-2931; Fax: 213-381-7804. Email: stannes@stannes.org. Web: www.stannes.org. Residential Treatment Program; Transitional Housing; Mental Health; Family Based Services; Early Learning Center Services for pregnant parent and at risk children and families.

St. Anne's, 155 N. Occidental Blvd., Los Angeles, 90026. Tel: 213-381-2931, Ext. 218; Fax: 213-381-7804. Email: stannes@stannes.org. Web: www.stannes.org. Group Home transitional housing, child care, mental health and family based services for pregnant, parenting teens, their children & families.

St. Joseph's Residence (1957) 1124 W. Adams Blvd., Los Angeles, 90007. Tel: 213-749-9577; Fax: 213-747-6468. Email: divine_providence@sbcglobal.net. Web: www.companyofmary.com.

St. Vincent Senior Citizen Nutrition Program, Inc. aka St. Vincent Meals on Wheels (1977) 2131 W. Third St., Los Angeles, 90057. Tel: 213-484-7778; Fax: 213-484-7276.

Napa
Diocese of Santa Rosa in California

Rainbow House, 1027 Jefferson and 1219 Jefferson St., Ste. 2, Napa, 94559. Tel: 707-224-4403; Fax: 707-224-2889.

Oakland
Diocese of Oakland

St. Joseph's Center for Deaf and Hard of Hearing, 25580 Campus Dr., Hayward, 94542-1137. Tel: 510-267-8338 (Voice); 866-977-9920 (Video Phone); Fax: 510-893-0945. Email: rherbst@oakdiocese.org. Web: www.sjcd.org. 2121 Harrison St., Ste. 100, Oakland, 94612-3788.

Placerville
Diocese of Sacramento

Mother Teresa Maternity Home, 3109 Sacramento St., Placerville, 95667. Tel: 530-295-8006.

San Diego
Diocese of San Diego

Bishop Maher Men's Center (1989) 1501 Imperial Ave., San Diego, 92101. Tel: 619-446-2100; Fax: 619-446-2129. Web: www.neighbor.org. Single men's center - 150 residents.

Joan Kroc Homeless Center (1987) 1501 Imperial Ave., San Diego, 92101. Tel: 619-446-2100; Fax: 619-446-2129. Web: www.neighbor.org. Housing for families & single women (326).

National Aids Foundation dba Josue Homes 3350 E St., San Diego, 92102. Tel: 619-466-4827; Fax: 619-446-2129. Web: www.neighbor.org. Housing for persons with AIDS (38).

Padre Luis Jayme International Outreach, 3350 E St., San Diego, 92101. Tel: 619-446-2100; Fax: 619-446-2129. Providing assistance to colonias, prison ministries and orphanages; earthquakes and flood relief in Mexico.

Paul Mirabile Center--Mirabile Housing Inc. (1994) 1501 Imperial Ave., San Diego, 92101. Tel: 619-446-2100; Fax: 619-446-2129. Emergency housing for 270 men & 80 women; free dining room (4000 meals daily).

Rachel's Women's Center--San Diego, San Diego, 92101. Tel: 619-236-9074.

Toussaint Youth Villages, 1404-5th St., San Diego, 92101. Tel: 619-687-1080; Fax: 619-446-2129. Web: www.neighbor.org. Residential for 35 homeless teens.

Villa Harvey Mandel, 72-17th St., San Diego, 92101. Tel: 619-446-2100; Fax: 619-446-2129. 95 units - Low to moderate income apts.

San Francisco
Archdiocese of San Francisco

Mount St. Joseph-St. Elizabeth (1976) 100 Masonic Ave., San Francisco, 94118. Tel: 415-567-8370; Fax: 415-292-5531. Email: sisterestela@msjse.org. Web: www.msjse.org. Successor Corporation to Mount St. Joseph Home for Girls and St. Elizabeth Infant Hospital. DBA: Epiphany Center

Peter Claver Community, 1340 Golden Gate, San Francisco, 94115. Tel: 415-749-3800; Fax: 415-569-3153. Email: scerreta@cccyo.org. Web: www.cccyo.org.

Rita da Cascia, 1652 Eddy St., #8, San Francisco, 94115. Tel: 415-202-0941; Fax: 415-202-0937. Email: ehammerle@cccyo.org. Web: www.cccyo.org.

The Good Shepherd Gracenter (1986) 1310 Bacon St., San Francisco, 94134. Tel: 415-337-1938; Fax: 415-586-0355. Email: inquiry@gsgracenter.org. Web: www.gsgracenter.org. Residential.

San Jose
Diocese of San Jose in California

The Roman Catholic Welfare Corporation of San Jose, 1150 N. First St., Ste. 100, San Jose, 95112. Tel: 408-983-0168; Fax: 408-983-0296. Email: serventi@dsj.org.

Santa Ana
Diocese of Orange in California

St. Francis Home for the Aged (1944) 1718 W. 6th St., Santa Ana, 92703. Tel: 714-542-0381; Fax: 714-542-4654. Email: stfrancishome@sbcglobal.net. Web: www.st-francis-home.org.

Santa Barbara
Archdiocese of Los Angeles

St. Vincent's (1858) 4200 Calle Real, Santa Barbara, 93110-1454. Tel: 805-683-6381; Fax: 805-967-7508. Email: info@sv-sb.org. Web: www.stvincents-sb.org. For single moms on welfare and/or very low income.

Santa Monica
Archdiocese of Los Angeles

Saint John's Child Study Center, Saint John's Hospital & Health Center, 1339 20th St., Santa Monica, 90404. Tel: 310-829-8921; Fax: 310-829-8455. Affiliated with Saint John's Hospital.

Santa Rosa
Diocese of Santa Rosa in California

Alzheimer's Respite/Resource Center, 987 Airway Ct., Santa Rosa, 95403. Tel: 707-528-8712; Fax: 707-575-4910. P.O. Box 4900, Santa Rosa, 95402.

Saratoga
Diocese of San Jose in California

Our Lady of Fatima Villa, 20400 Saratoga-Los Gatos Rd., Saratoga, 95070. Tel: 408-741-2950; Fax: 408-741-4930. Web: www.fatimavilla.org. Provides skilled nursing rehabilitation services and assisted living facility for aged women and men.

Sonora
Diocese of Stockton

Mother Lode Ombudsman Program Ombudsman Program, Legal Advocacy for Seniors Program, Elder Abuse Prevention Program, Social Security Representative Payee Program, Older Adult Outreach and Engagement Program., 14855 Mono Way, Ste. 101, Sonora, 95370. Tel: 209-532-7632; Fax: 209-532-8448. Email: ktoepel@ccstockton.org.

Spring Valley
Diocese of San Diego

Noah Homes (1983) 12526 Campo Rd., Spring Valley, 91978. Tel: 619-660-6200; Fax: 619-660-1481. Email: m.nocon@noahhomes.org. Web: www.noahhomes.org.

COLORADO

Aurora
Archdiocese of Denver

St. Anna's Home (Congregation of Sisters of Charity of St. Vincent de Paul, Colorado Chapter Inc.), 13901 E. Quincy Ave., Aurora, 80015. Tel: 303-627-2986; Fax: 303-627-2986. Email: st.annashome@hotmail.com.

Canon City
Diocese of Pueblo

Centura Health-Progressive Care Center, 1338 Phay Ave., Canon City, 81212. Tel: 719-285-2540; Fax: 719-285-2256. An operating unit of Catholic Health Initiatives Colorado (an affiliate of Catholic Health Initiatives).

Colorado Springs
Diocese of Colorado Springs

Franciscan Community Counseling, Inc., 7665 Assisi Heights, Colorado Springs, 80919. Tel: 719-955-7008; Fax: 719-598-0346. Email: sharon@stfrancis.org. Web: www.franciscancommunitycounseling.org.

Medalion Retirement Community, 1719 E. Bijou St., Colorado Springs, 80909. Tel: 719-381-1000; Fax: 719-381-4978. An operating unit of Catholic Health Initiatives Colorado. An affiliate of Catholic Health Initiatives.

Namaste Alzheimer Center, 2 Penrose Blvd., Colorado Springs, 80906. Tel: 719-776-6300; Fax: 719-520-9709. An operating unit of Catholic Health Initiatives Colorado. An affiliate of Catholic Health Initiatives; Programs for seniors with Alzheimer's or dementia.

Denver
Archdiocese of Denver

Archdiocesan Family Housing, Inc. (1968) 4045 Pecos St., Ste. A, Denver, 80211. Tel: 303-830-0215; Fax: 303-830-2885. Housing for Low-Income Families.

Archdiocesan Housing, Inc (1968) 4045 Pecos St., Ste. A, Denver, 80211. Tel: 303-830-0215; Fax: 303-830-2885. Email: jrussell@archdiocesanhousing.org. Web: www.archdiocesanhousing.com.

Clare Gardens, Inc. (1972) 2626 Osceola St., Denver, 80212. Tel: 303-433-6268; Fax: 303-455-5359. Web: www.fm-inc.org. Housing Ministry, low-income family units.

Colorado Affordable Catholic Housing Corp. (1991) 4045 Pecos St., Ste. A, Denver, 80211. Tel: 303-830-0215; Fax: 303-830-2885. Web: www.archdiocesanhousing.org.

Decatur Place, Mailing Address: 1999 Broadway, #1000, Denver, 80202. 1155 Decatur St., Denver, 80204. Tel: 303-830-3300; Fax: 303-830-3301. Web: www.mercyhousing.org. Two year single parent transitional housing program.

Holy Cross Village, Inc., 4045 Pecos St., Ste. A, Denver, 80211. Tel: 303-715-3194. Web: www.archdiocesanhousing.org.

Homes for Greeley (1996) 1999 Broadway, Ste. 1000, Denver, 80202. Tel: 303-830-3300; Fax: 303-830-3301. Affordable housing for singles and families.

Housing Management Services, Inc. (1986) 4045 Pecos St., Ste. A, Denver, 80211. Tel: 303-830-0215; Fax: 303-830-2885. Web: www.archdiocesanhousing.org.

Machebeuf Apartments, Inc., 4045 Pecos St., Ste. A, Denver, 80211. Tel: 303-830-0215. Email: jrussell@archdiocesanhousing.org. Web: www.archdiocesanhousing.org. Low income housing for families located in Glenwood Springs, CO.

Mercy Holly Park East, 1999 Broadway, Ste. 1000, Denver, 80202. Tel: 303-830-3300; Fax: 303-830-3301. Affordable housing for singles and families.

Prairie Rose Plaza, 4045 Pecos St., Ste. A, Denver, 80211.

Special Religious Education-Pastoral Care of Developmentally Disabled Persons (1976) (An office of the Archdiocese of Denver), 3101 W. Hillside Pl., Denver, 80219. Tel: 303-934-1999; Fax: 303-935-7795. Religious education of mentally retarded children and adults.

Villa Sierra Madre, Inc., 4045 Pecos St. Ste. A, Denver, 80211. Tel: 303-715-3194. Web: www.archdiocesanhousing.org.

Willow Street Apartments (1996) 1999 Broadway, Ste. 1000, Denver, 80202. Tel: 303-830-3300; Fax: 303-830-3301. Affordable housing for persons with chronic mental illness.

Grand Junction
Diocese of Pueblo

Grand Valley Catholic Outreach, 245 S. 1st St., Grand Junction, 81501. Tel: 970-241-3658; Fax: 970-254-1262. Email: kabland@catholicoutreach.org. Web: www.catholicoutreach.org.

Pueblo
Diocese of Pueblo

Centura Health-Villa Pueblo, 1111 Bonforte Blvd., Pueblo, 81001. Tel: 719-545-5911; Fax: 719-544-1354. An operating unit of Catholic Health Initiatives Colorado (an affiliate of Catholic Health Initiatives).

Westminster
Archdiocese of Denver

Clare of Assisi Homes - Westminster, Inc. (1995) 2451 W. 82 Pl., Westminster, 80031-4099. Tel: 303-412-5771; 303-462-9271 (Corporate). Housing and services for elderly and disabled.

CONNECTICUT

Danbury
Diocese of Bridgeport

The Pope John Paul II Center for Health Care, Inc., 33 Lincoln Ave., Danbury, 06810. Tel: 203-416-1355.

Deep River
Diocese of Norwich

Mount St. John, 135 Kirtland St., Deep River, 06417-1816. Tel: 860-343-1340; Fax: 860-343-1394. Email: decerbod@mtstjohn.org; mckenneyv@mtstjohn.org. Web: www.mtstjohn.org.

Hamden
Archdiocese of Hartford

Clelian Adult Day Center (1988) 261 Benham St., Hamden, 06514-2898. Tel: 203-288-4151; Fax: 203-288-0551. Email: cscaduto@ascjus.org. Web: www.clelianadultdaycenter.com. A day health care facility for the elderly (interdenominational).

Hartford
Archdiocese of Hartford

**Malta House of Care, Inc.*, 19 Woodland St., Ste. 37, Hartford, 06105. Tel: 860-725-0171; Fax: 860-725-0191. Web: www.maltahouseofcare.org. To deliver charitable primary and/or preventative medical health care to the needy uninsured of the Greater Hartford region.

Meriden
Archdiocese of Hartford

Franciscan Family Care Center (1979) 267 Finch Ave., Meriden, 06451. Tel: 203-238-1441; Fax: 203-686-0807. Email: ssuzanne@franciscanhc.org.

West Hartford
Archdiocese of Hartford

Saint Agnes Home, Inc. (1914) 104 Mayflower St., West Hartford, 06110-1425. Tel: 860-521-7516; Fax: 860-521-1756. Email: info@stagneshome.org. Web: www.stagneshome.org. For adolescent single mothers and their infants.

Willimantic
Diocese of Norwich

Holy Family Home and Shelter, Inc., 88 Jackson St., P.O. Box 884, Willimantic, 06226-0884. Tel: 860-423-7719; Fax: 860-423-3770. Email: sisterpeter@holyfamilywillimantic.org. Web: www.holyfamilywillimantic.org.

DELAWARE

New Castle
Diocese of Wilmington

Emmanuel Dining Room, South, 500 Rogers Rd., New Castle, 19720. Tel: 302-577-2951; Fax: 302-652-2576.

Wilmington
Diocese of Wilmington

Andrisani Building (1996) 1801 W. 6th St., Wilmington, 19805. Tel: 302-428-3702; Fax: 302-428-3705.

Angela Merici House (1993) 1105 W. 8th St., Wilmington, 19806-4605. Tel: 302-655-4817. Residence for Sisters of St. Francis.

Benedictine Park, 731 W. 9th St., Wilmington, 19801. Tel: 302-652-5523; Fax: 302-652-1919.

Bethany House (1999) 601 N. Jackson St., Wilmington, 19805-3241. Tel: 302-656-8391. Email: mmatarese@ministryofcaring.org. Permanent housing for women with special needs.

CACFP (Child & Adult Care Food Program), 2604 W. 4th St., Wilmington, 19805. Tel: 302-655-9624; Fax: 302-654-9753.

Emmanuel Dining Room, East, 226 N. Walnut St., Wilmington, 19801-3934. Tel: 302-652-2577; Fax: 302-652-2576.

Emmanuel Dining Room, West (1979) 121 N. Jackson St., Wilmington, 19805-3670. Tel: 302-652-3228; Fax: 302-652-2576.

Francis X. Norton Center (2002) 917 N. Madison St., Wilmington, 19801. Tel: 302-594-9455; Fax: 302-428-3655. Multigenerational community center.

HIV Services, 2601 W. 4th St., Wilmington, 19805. Tel: 302-655-9624; Fax: 302-654-6432. Email: HIVServices@ccwilm.org.

House of Joseph I (1985) 917 N. Madison St., Wilmington, 19801. Tel: 302-652-0904; Fax: 302-594-9472. Email: wnewson@ministryofcaring.org. Shelter for homeless employable men who are seeking employment.

House of Joseph II, 9 W. 18th St., Wilmington, 19802-4833. Tel: 302-594-9473; Fax: 302-594-9494. Email: srjean@ministryofcaring.org. Hospice for people with AIDS.

House of Joseph Transitional Residence (1998) 704 West St., Wilmington, 19801-1523. Tel: 302-652-7968; Fax: 302-594-9472. Email: wnewson@ministryofcaring.org. Transitional residence for employable, formerly homeless persons.

Il Bambino (2002) 903 N. Madison St., Wilmington, 19801. Tel: 302-594-9449; Fax: 302-594-9450. Infant day care program.

Job Placement Center (1985) 1100 Lancaster Ave., Wilmington, 19805-4009. Tel: 302-652-5522; Fax: 302-652-0917. Email: mking@ministryofcaring.org. Employment agency to assist the poor.

Maria Lorenza Longo House (2003) 822 Jefferson St., Wilmington, 19801. Transitional Residence for Families.

Mary Mother of Hope House I (1977) 1103 W. 8th St., Wilmington, 19806. Tel: 302-652-8532; Fax: 302-594-9434. Email: mmatarese@ministryofcaring.org. Emergency shelter for homeless women.

Mary Mother of Hope House II (1983) 121 N. Jackson St., Wilmington, 19805-3670. Tel: 302-652-1935; Fax: 302-594-9475. Emergency shelter for women with children.

Mary Mother of Hope House III (1988) 515 N. Broom St., Wilmington, 19805-3114. Tel: 302-652-0970; Fax: 302-594-9496. Emergency shelter for women with children.

Mary Mother of Hope House Transitional Residence, 818-820 Jefferson St., Wilmington, 19801-1432. Tel: 302-594-9448; Fax: 302-594-9434. Email: mmatarese@ministryofcaring.org. Transitional residence for single women.

Ministry of Caring Distribution Center, 1410 N. Claymont St., Wilmington, 19802-5227. Tel: 302-652-0969; Fax: 302-594-9478.

Ministry of Caring Guild (1990) 506 N. Church St., Wilmington, 19801-4812. Tel: 302-427-9447; Fax: 302-778-5286.

Ministry of Caring, Inc. (1977) 506 N. Church St., Wilmington, 19801-4812. Tel: 302-652-5523; Fax: 302-652-1919. Email: mail@ministryofcaring.org.

Nazareth House I (1998) 106 N. Broom St., Wilmington, 19805-4241. Tel: 302-652-0790; Fax: 302-594-9496.

Nazareth House II (1998) 898 Linden St., Wilmington, 19805-4423. Tel: 302-428-3635; Fax: 302-428-3636. Transitional residence for families.

Nazareth Long Term Housing (1998) 203 N. Jackson St., Wilmington, 19805-3649. Tel: 302-652-5523; Fax: 302-652-1919. Long term housing

Nazareth Long Term Housing (1998) 807 W. 6th St., Wilmington, 19805. Tel: 302-652-5523; Fax: 302-652-1919. Long term housing

Nazareth Long Term Housing, 109-1/2 & 111 N. Jackson St., Wilmington, 19805. Tel: 302-652-5523; Fax: 302-652-1919. Transitional residence for families.

Nazareth Long Term Housing, 207 S. Van Buren St., Wilmington, 19805. Tel: 302-652-5523; Fax: 302-652-1919. Transitional residence for families.

Padre Pio House, 213 N. Jackson St., Wilmington, 19805. Email: wnewson@ministryofcaring.org. Permanent housing for men with special needs.

Pierre Toussaint Dental Office (1995) 830 Spruce St., Wilmington, 19801-4205. Tel: 302-652-8947; Fax: 302-652-8994. Dental office for the homeless.

Sacred Heart Administration, 903 N. Madison St., Wilmington, 19801. Tel: 302-888-1420; Fax: 302-594-9450.

Sacred Heart Convent, 700 W. 9th St., Wilmington, 19801. Tel: 302-692-8532.

Sacred Heart House (1997) 917 N. Madison St., Wilmington, 19801. Tel: 302-428-3652; Fax: 302-428-3655.

Samaritan Outreach (1995) 1410 N. Claymont St., Wilmington, 19802-5227. Tel: 302-594-9476; Fax: 303-594-9478. Social outreach for the homeless.

St. Clare Medical Outreach (1992) 7th & Clayton Sts., Wilmington, 19805-3156. Tel: 302-575-8218. Mobile medical van which provides health services for the poor.

St. Francis Transitional Residence (1995) 103-107 & 111 N. Jackson St., Wilmington, 19805-3648. Transitional living for women and children.

DISTRICT OF COLUMBIA

Washington
Archdiocese of Washington

Lt. Joseph P. Kennedy, Jr., Institute, 801 Buchanan St., N.E., Washington, 20017. Tel: 202-529-7600; Fax: 202-529-2028. Email: gadair@kennedyinstitute.org. Web: www.kennedyinstitute.org. The Lt. Joseph P. Kennedy, Jr., Institute of the Archdiocese of Washington is a private, nonprofit organization providing education, training and employment, therapeutic and residential services to children and adults with developmental disabilities.

**Prison Outreach Ministry* (1982) P.O. Box 51583, Washington, 20091. Tel: 202-347-3218; Fax: 202-347-9217. Email: pomsvb@yahoo.com.

FLORIDA

Boca Raton
Diocese of Palm Beach

Cross International Catholic Outreach, Inc., 2700 N. Military Tr., Boca Raton, 33432. Tel: 561-392-9212, Ext. 104; Fax: 561-367-0564. Email: info@crossinternational.org. Web: www.crosscatholic.org. Mailing Address: P.O. Box 273908, Boca Raton, 33427-3908.

Jacksonville
Diocese of St. Augustine

L'Arche Harbor House (1985) 700 Arlington Rd. N., Jacksonville, 32211. Tel: 904-721-5992; Fax: 904-721-7143. Email: communityleader@bellsouth.net. Web: larchejacksonville.org. A residential community for adults with developmental disabilities and those who choose to share life with them (assistants). We also have an adult day program called the Rainbow Workshop.

Largo
Diocese of St. Petersburg

Bethlehem Centre, Inc., 10895 Hamlin Blvd., Largo, 33774. Tel: 727-596-9394; Fax: 727-596-6792. Senior Center offering programs in Fitness, Exercise, Social, Educational, Music, Art, Computers, and Religious Nature on Tuesday, Wednesday, and Friday. Hot luncheon is available on Tuesday and Friday (Oct.-April).

Miami
Archdiocese of Miami

Camillus Health Concern, Inc. (1984) P.O. Box 012408, Miami, 33101-2408. Tel: 305-374-1065; Fax: 305-373-7431. Web: www.camillus.org. Provides medical, dental, mental health and social services to the homeless and indigent.

Camillus House, Inc. (1960) 336 N.W. 5th St., Miami, 33128. Tel: 305-374-1065, Ext. 308; Fax: 305-372-1402. Email: dr.paul@camillus.org. Web: www.camillus.org. Provides services to the homeless: emergency services, substance abuse rehabilitation, transitional and permanent housing.

Gift of Hope, Missionaries of Charity (1981) 724 N.W. 17th St., Miami, 33136. Tel: 305-326-0032.

Soup Kitchen (1981) Miami. Tel: 305-326-0032.

Women's and Children's Shelter, Miami, 33136. Tel: 305-326-0032.

Panama City
Diocese of Pensacola-Tallahassee

Naomi House, 2941 E. 11th St., Panama City, 32401. Tel: 850-763-0475; Fax: 850-763-2969. Email: cathcharpc@cc.ptdiocese.org. c/o Catholic Charities, 3128 E. 11th St., Panama City, 32401.

St. Barnabas House, 2943 E. 11th St., Panama City, 32401. Tel: 850-763-0475; Fax: 850-763-2969. Email: cathcharpc@cc.ptdiocese.org. c/o Catholic Charities, 3128 E. 11th St., Panama City, 32401.

St. Augustine
Diocese of St. Augustine

Religious Education for Catholic Deaf and Blind, 30 Ocean Ave., St. Augustine, 32084-2813. Tel: 904-825-4272 (Voice/TDD); Fax: 904-825-4348. Email: religiouseduc90@bellsouth.net. Web: www.catholicdeaf.org. Florida School for the Deaf and Blind.

GEORGIA

Atlanta
Archdiocese of Atlanta

Good Shepherd Outreach Center, 2426 Shallowford Ter., Atlanta, 30341. Tel: 770-455-9379; Fax: 770-451-0156.

Our Lady of Perpetual Help Home, 760 Pollard Blvd., S.W., Atlanta, 30315. Tel: 404-688-9515; Fax: 404-588-9568. Web: olphhome.org. Nursing Home for Free Care of Cancer Patients.

Saint Joseph's Mercy Care Services (1985) 424 Decatur St., Atlanta, 30312-1848. Tel: 678-843-8500; Fax: 678-843-8501. Email: aebberwein@sjha.org. Division of Saint Joseph's Health System. Operates Saint Joseph's Mercy Care Services (Atlanta, Georgia). Operates Mercy Senior Care (Rome, Georgia).

Macon
Diocese of Savannah

Nazareth Life Ministries, 538 Orange St., Macon, 31201-2073. Tel: 478-746-9803; Fax: 478-745-0847. Web: faministries.org. Pregnancy Services for birth parents/families/newborn, education & direct services.

HAWAII

Ewa Beach
Diocese of Honolulu

St. Francis Home Care Services, 91-2135 Fort Weaver Rd., Ste 506, Ewa Beach, 96706. Tel: 808-534-0777; Fax: 808-676-1300.

Kalaupapa
Diocese of Honolulu

Kalaupapa Nursing Facility (Molokai), P.O. Box 3333, Kalaupapa, 96742. Tel: 808-567-6911; Fax: 808-567-6916. Operated by the State Dept. of Health for Hansen's Disease Branch.

Lihue
Diocese of Honolulu

St. Francis Home Care Services-Kauai, 4473 Pahee St., Ste. N, Lihue, 96766. Tel: 808-245-6430; Fax: 808-246-8620.

ILLINOIS

Arlington Heights
Archdiocese of Chicago

Northwest Suburban Senior Services, 1801 W. Central, Arlington Heights, 60005. Tel: 847-797-5321; Fax: 847-253-9597.

Calumet City
Archdiocese of Chicago

Josephine P. Argento Senior Center, 1700 N. Memorial Dr., Calumet City, 60409.

Carpentersville
Diocese of Rockford

Provena Family Care, Carpentersville, 2201 Randall Rd., Carpentersville, 60110. Tel: 847-844-7800; Fax: 847-783-0628.

Chicago
Archdiocese of Chicago

Ada S. Niles Adult Day Care, 6717 S. Elizabeth, Chicago, 60639. Tel: 773-488-5400; Fax: 773-488-5878.

Ada S. Niles Senior Center and Adult Day Care Services, 653 W. 63rd St., Chicago, 60621. Tel: 312-745-3307; Fax: 312-745-3330.

Addiction Consultation and Educational Services, 651 W. Lake St., Chicago, 60661. Tel: 312-655-7453.

Archdiocesan AIDS Ministry Office, 651 W. Lake St., Chicago, 60661. Tel: 312-948-6500; Fax: 312-879-0208.

Bishop Edwin M. Conway Residence, 1900 N. Karlov Ave., Chicago, 60639. Tel: 773-252-9941; Fax: 773-525-9946.

Catholic Home Care, Inc., 721 N. La Salle St., Chicago, 60654. Tel: 312-655-7415; Fax: 312-337-2705.

Catholic Office of the Deaf, 3525 S. Lake Park Ave., Chicago, 60653-1402. Tel: 312-534-7899 (Voice); 312-751-8368 (TDD); Fax: 312-534-0394. Email: cathdeafch@archchicago.org. Web: www.deafchurchchicago.parishesonline.com.

Central States Institute of Addiction, 651 W. Lake St., Chicago, 60661. Tel: 312-655-7530; Fax: 312-266-9027.

Children's HealthCare Center, 4015 N. Oak Park Ave., Chicago, 60634. Tel: 773-205-3600; Fax: 773-205-3630.

**Claver House of Renewal, Inc.*, 8514 S. Avalon St., Chicago, 60619. Tel: 773-731-3294. Food pantry, soup kitchen, home-bound senior citizen care, after-school youth recreational programs; mentoring; tutoring and scholarship assistance to elementary and high school graduates continuing studies at Catholic educational institutions. Outreach to the homeless: clothing, toys and basic toiletries for local shelters.

Community Family Service Center, 1100 S. May, Chicago, 60607. Tel: 312-733-5661, Ext. 1467; Fax: 312-733-5211.

Forever Free, 6212 S. Sangamon, Chicago, 60621. Tel: 773-374-8165; Fax: 773-548-4522.

Franciscan Outreach Association, 1645 W. LeMoyne St., Chicago, 60622. Tel: 773-278-6724; Fax: 773-278-7120. Web: www.franoutreach.org. Owns & operates: Marquard Center (dining room for the homeless), Franciscan House of Mary & Joseph (shelter) and a Case Management Program for the homeless in Chicago.

Holbrook Center for Counseling and Psychotherapy, 641 W. Lake St., Chicago, 60661. Tel: 312-655-7719; Fax: 312-655-0678.

Homelessness Prevention Call Center, 721 N. LaSalle St., Chicago, 60610. Tel: 312-698-5070; Fax: 312-655-0678.

House of the Good Shepherd, 1114 W. Grace St., Chicago, 60613. Tel: 773-935-3434; Fax: 773-935-3523. Shelter for abused women with children.

Intact Family Services, 651 W. Lake St., Chicago, 60661. Tel: 312-382-2505; Fax: 312-258-1839.

Jadonal E. Ford Center for Adolescent Parenting, 11255 S. Michigan Ave., Chicago, 60628. Tel: 773-474-7227; Fax: 773-995-0125.

Joseph Cardinal Bernardin Family Shelter Program, 651 W. Lake St., Chicago, 60661. Tel: 312-655-7700; Fax: 773-483-5301.

**L'Arche Chicago*, 2010 W. Carroll Ave., Chicago, 60612. Tel: 312-226-1273; Fax: 708-863-1273 (Call first). Email: larchechicago@sbcglobal.net. Web: www.larchechicago.org. L'Arche is people with and without intellectual disabilities sharing life in communities of faith. Mutual relationships and trust in God is at the heart of our life together.

LOSS (Loving Outreach to Survivors of Suicide), 721 N. LaSalle St., Chicago, 60654. Tel: 312-655-7283; Fax: 312-948-3340.

Maternity/Adoption Services, 651 W. Lake St., Chicago, 60661. Tel: 312-655-7071; Fax: 312-882-1612.

Misericordia/Heart of Mercy Center, 6300 N. Ridge, Chicago, 60660-1017. Tel: 773-973-6300; Fax: 773-973-5214. Web: www.misericordia.com. Children and adults with developmental disabilities.

Mother and Child Food and Nutrition (MAC) Warehouse, 1965 W. Pershing Rd., Chicago, 60608. Tel: 773-523-0299.

Mother and Child Food and Nutrition Program (MAC), 4940 W. Flournoy, Chicago, 60644. Tel: 773-378-3127; Fax: 773-261-0536.

Options for Housing, Inc. f/k/a Shelter for the Homeless, Inc., 721 N. LaSalle St., Chicago, 60610.

Tel: 312-655-7305.

**Port Ministries*, 5013 S. Hermitage Ave., Chicago, 60609. Tel: 773-778-5955; Fax: 773-778-2451. Email: port532857@aol.com. Web: www.portministries.org. A Franciscan outreach to the poor and homeless; mobile soup kitchen, family transitional shelter, GED, ESL, family svcs., neighborhood gym and free clinic.

St. Ailbe Adult Day Care, 9249 S. Avalon, Chicago, 60619. Tel: 773-721-0177; Fax: 773-721-1228.

St. Mary of Providence, 4200 N. Austin Ave., Chicago, 60634. Tel: 773-545-8300; Fax: 773-545-8035. Email: SrRitaB@sbcglobal.net. Developmental training and residential care of developmentally disabled adults.

St. Rose Center, 4911 S. Hoyne Ave., Chicago, 60609. Tel: 773-436-1433; Fax: 773-436-2280. Email: strosecenter@aol.com. Web: www.strosecenter.org. Day Training Program for Developmentally Impaired young adults.

St. Vincent De Paul Residence North Center Senior Satellite, 4040 N. Oakley St., Chicago, 60639. Tel: 312-744-4029; Fax: 312-744-8812.

Villa Guadalupe Senior Services Corporation, 3201 E. 91st St., Chicago, 60617. Tel: 773-933-0344; Fax: 773-933-0827. Organization to provide affordable housing and related services for Senior Citizens in South Chicago.

Women, Infants and Children (WIC) Food and Nutrition Centers Program, 4624 W. Diversey, Chicago, 60639. Tel: 312-951-7672; Fax: 773-205-1271. WIC Warehouse; 4500 W. Chicago Ave., Chicago, IL 60651; WIC Food Centers: 416 E. 43rd St., Chicago, IL 60653; 6202 S. Halsted St., Chicago, IL 60621; 2310 W. Roosevelt Rd., Chicago, IL 60608; 5332 S. Western, Chicago, IL 60609; 3110 W. Armitage, Chicago, IL 60647; 1643 W. Cermak Rd., Chicago, IL 60608; 1734 W. Chicago Ave., Chicago, IL 60622; 3932 W. Madison St., Chicago, IL 60624; 5125 W. Chicago, Chicago, IL 60651; 1802 E. 71st St., Chicago IL 60649; 11255 S. Michigan Ave., Chicago, IL 60628; 4622 W. Diversey Ave., Chicago, IL 60639; 8959 S. Commercial Ave., Chicago, IL 60617; 2400 S. Kedzie Ave., Chicago, IL 60623 and 1106 W. 79th St., Chicago, IL 60620.

Youth and Family Therapeutic Services, 651 W. Lake, Chicago, 60661. Tel: 312-655-7984; Fax: 312-236-5384.

Des Plaines
Archdiocese of Chicago

Maryville Academy, 1150 N. River Rd., Des Plaines, 60016. Tel: 847-294-1999; Fax: 847-824-7277. Web: www.maryvilleacademy.org.

North/Northwest Suburban Family Shelter Program, 1717 N. Rand Rd., Des Plaines, 60016. Tel: 847-376-2100; Fax: 847-390-8214.

Scott Nolan Residential Treatment Center, 555 Wilson Ln., Des Plaines, 60016. Tel: 847-768-5430; Fax: 847-768-5478.

Freeport
Diocese of Rockford

Provena St. Vincent's Community Living Facility and Supported Living Arrangement, 659 E. Jefferson St., Freeport, 61032. Tel: 815-232-6181; Fax: 815-232-6143.

Hampshire
Diocese of Rockford

Provena Family Care, Hampshire, 895 S. State St., Ste. 201, Hampshire, 60140. Tel: 847-683-7099; Fax: 847-683-7104.

Harvey
Archdiocese of Chicago

South Suburban Senior Services and Senior Activity Center, 15300 S. Lexington, Harvey, 60426. Tel: 708-596-2222; Fax: 708-596-6329.

St. Susanna Shelter Apartments, 14926 S. Honore, Harvey, 60426. Tel: 708-331-8211; Fax: 708-339-4398.

Hines
Archdiocese of Chicago

Cooke's Manor Transitional Housing For Men, Bldg. 14 Hines VA Campus, 5th Ave. & Roosevelt Rd., Hines, 60141. Tel: 708-273-6627; Fax: 708-343-4469.

Huntley
Diocese of Rockford

Provena Family Care, Huntley, 12155 Regency Sq. Pkwy., Huntley, 60142. Tel: 847-515-2100; Fax: 847-515-2328.

Kankakee
Diocese of Joliet in Illinois

Lisieux Pastoral Outreach Center, 371 N. St. Joseph Ave., Kankakee, 60901-2741. Tel: 815-939-2913.

Provena St. Mary's Adult Day Center, 1025 N. Washington, Kankakee, 60901. Tel: 815-937-2447; Fax: 815-936-3245. Email: rebecca.barney@provena.org. Web: www.provena.org. 19065 Hickory Creek Dr., #300, Mokena, 60448.

Lake Zurich
Archdiocese of Chicago

Mt. St. Joseph Home, 24955 North Hwy. 12, Lake Zurich, 60047. Tel: 847-438-5050; Fax: 847-438-6313. Email: msjlz@aol.com. Web: mtstjosephhome.com. Intermediate care for developmentally disabled women.

Mokena
Diocese of Joliet in Illinois

Provena Senior Services dba Provena Life Connections 19065 Hickory Creek Dr., Ste. 310, Mokena, 60448-8507. Tel: 708-478-7900; Fax: 708-478-5143. Email: connie.march@provena.org. Web: www.provena.org.

Provena St. Mary's Adult Day Center, 1025 N. Washington, Kankakee, 60901. Tel: 815-937-2447; Fax: 815-936-3245. Email: rebecca.barney@provena.org. Web: www.provena.org. 19065 Hickory Creek Dr., #300, Mokena, 60448.

Momence
Diocese of Joliet in Illinois

Good Shepherd Manor (1971) P.O. Box 260, Momence, 60954. Tel: 815-472-6492; 815-472-3700; Fax: 815-472-2160. Email: gsmanor@mchsi.com. Web: www.goodshepherdmanor.org. Adult Male DD-MR.

Normal
Diocese of Peoria

Homes of Hope, Inc., 401 Pine St., Ste. 1, Normal, 61761. Tel: 309-862-0607; Fax: 309-452-7131. Email: homesofhope1@frontier.com.

Oak Park
Archdiocese of Chicago

Accolade Adult Day Care, 112 S. Humphrey, Oak Park, 60302-2704. Tel: 708-445-1300; Fax: 708-445-9595.

Daughters of the Heart of Mary, 140 N. Euclid Ave., #401, Oak Park, 60302-1684. Tel: 708-386-0190; Fax: 708-383-1327. Email: ephpheta@sbcglobal.net. Web: www.dhmna.org.

Peoria
Diocese of Peoria

Guardian Angel Home, 419 N.E. Madison Ave., Peoria, 61603. Tel: 309-636-7500; Fax: 309-673-3405. Web: www.ccdop.org. Treatment for Abused and Neglected Youth.

Saint Clare Home, 5533 N. Galena Rd., Peoria, 61614. Tel: 309-682-5428; Fax: 309-682-8478. Web: osfhealthcare.org. Skilled nursing facility.

River Forest
Archdiocese of Chicago

Big Sisters, P.O. Box 5728, River Forest, 60305. Tel: 708-488-8893. Web: bigsistersofchicago.org.

Round Lake
Archdiocese of Chicago

Lake County Senior Case Management Services, 116 N. Lincoln, Round Lake, 60073. Tel: 847-546-5733; Fax: 847-546-7114.

Savanna
Diocese of Rockford

Mercy Homecare/Hospice, 1121 N. 5th St., Savanna, 61074. Tel: 815-273-2628; Fax: 815-273-7025. Email: nocj@mercyhealth.com. Web: www.mercyclinton.com.

Springfield
Diocese of Springfield in Illinois

Brother James Court (1975) 2508 St. James Rd., Springfield, 62707. Tel: 217-544-4876; Fax: 217-747-5971. Email: administrator@brotherjamescourt.com. Web: www.brotherjamescourt.com. Residence for Mentally Retarded Male Adults.

St. Clare's Health Clinic, 700 N. 7th St., Ste. A, Springfield, 62702. Tel: 217-523-1474; Fax: 217-523-0194. Web: www.cc.dio.org.

St. John's Breadline, 430 N. Fifth St., Springfield, 62702. Tel: 217-528-6098; Fax: 217-528-3605. Web: www.cc.dio.org.

Tinley Park
Archdiocese of Chicago

St. Coletta's of Illinois, Inc., 18350 Crossing Dr., Tinley Park, 60487. Tel: 708-342-5200; Fax: 708-342-2579. Web: www.stcolettas.com. Sponsored by the Sisters of St. Francis of Assisi. Residential care, education, job training & job placement for developmentally disabled children and adults.

Waukegan
Archdiocese of Chicago

Lake County HIV/AIDS Case Management, 671 S. Lewis, Waukegan, 60085. Tel: 847-782-4144; Fax: 847-782-1030.

Lake County Senior Community Services & Nutrition Program Sites, 671 S. Lewis Ave., Waukegan, 60085. Tel: 847-782-4267; Fax: 847-782-4296.

INDIANA

Crown Point
Diocese of Gary

Franciscan Home Care Services, Inc., 203 Franciscan Dr., Crown Point, 46307. Tel: 219-661-5321; Fax: 219-661-5305. Email: cgrantner@franciscancommunities.com.

East Chicago
Diocese of Gary

Office of Hispanic Ministry (1983) 3814 Grand Blvd., East Chicago, 46312. Tel: 219-397-2125; Fax: 219-397-2168. Email: atorres@dcgary.org. Web: www.dcgary.org.

Hammond
Diocese of Gary

Senior Companion Program, 6919 Indianapolis Blvd., Hammond, 46324. Tel: 219-844-4883; Fax: 219-844-4885.

Spiritual Life/Seimetz Center, 1441 Hoffman St., Hammond, 46327. Tel: 219-932-8321; Fax: 219-932-8321.

Indianapolis
Archdiocese of Indianapolis

A Caring Place - Adult Day Services, c/o Fairview Presbyterian Church, 4609 N. Capitol Ave., Indianapolis, 46208. Tel: 317-466-0015; Fax: 317-475-3093.

Terre Haute
Archdiocese of Indianapolis

Gibault Children's Services, 6401 S. U.S. Hwy. 41, Terre Haute, 47802-0316. Tel: 812-299-1156; Fax: 812-298-3044. Email: gibault@gibault.org. Web: www.gibault.org. Residential treatment facility for males and females between the ages of 8 and 18, sponsored by the Knights of Columbus of Indiana.

St. Ann Community Outreach Services of Terre Haute, 1440 Locust St., Terre Haute, 47807. Tel: 812-232-6832; Fax: 812-232-2442. Email: stannchurch@gmail.com. Mailing Address: 1440 Locust St., Terre Haute, 47807.

IOWA

Clinton
Diocese of Davenport

Arch I, 402 S. Fourth St., Clinton, 52732. Tel: 563-243-3980.

Arch II, 734 Fifth Ave. S., Clinton, 52732. Tel: 563-242-5082.

Arch III, 505 7th Ave. S., Clinton, 52732. Tel: 563-242-8740; Fax: 563-242-8740.

Arch, Inc., Box 0278, Clinton, 52733-0278. Tel: 563-243-9035; Fax: 563-243-7796. Email: bettyk1983@hotmail.com.

Mercy Home Care and Hospice, 638 S. Bluff, Clinton, 52732. Tel: 563-244-3766; Fax: 563-244-3719. Email: meistesk@mercyhealth.com. Web: www.mercyclinton.com.

Des Moines
Diocese of Des Moines

House of Mercy, 1409 Clark St., Des Moines, 50314-1964. Tel: 515-643-6500; Fax: 515-643-6598. Email: tbeveridge@mercydesmoines.org. Web: houseofmercydesmoines.org.

Dubuque
Archdiocese of Dubuque

Caritas Center, 1130 Carmel Dr., Dubuque, 52003-7911. Tel: 563-556-3240. Email: bvmcenter@bvmcong.org. Web: www.bvmcong.org.
Clare House, 3340 Windsor Ave., Dubuque, 52001-1300. Tel: 563-583-9786; Fax: 563-583-6080. Email: info@osfdbq.org. Web: www.osfdbq.org.
Marian Hall Infirmary, 1050 Carmel Dr., Dubuque, 52003. Tel: 563-556-5474; Fax: 563-588-1975. Email: bvmcenter@bvmcong.org. Web: www.bvmcong.org.

Iowa City
Diocese of Davenport

Mercy Outreach Iowa City, Inc., 500 E. Market St., Iowa City, 52245. Tel: 319-339-3540.

KANSAS

Great Bend
Diocese of Dodge City

Heartland Center for Wholistic Health (1988) 1005 Williams, Great Bend, 67530. Tel: 620-793-9067; Fax: 620-793-5817. Email: anita@hcwh.net. Web: www.hcwh.net. Body massage, herbals, chiropractic, natural remedies.

Kansas City
Archdiocese of Kansas City in Kansas

St. Joseph Adoption Referral Service, Inc. (2001) 8160 Parallel Pkwy., Ste. 103, Kansas City, 66112. Tel: 913-299-5222; 800-752-1737; Fax: 913-299-5111. Email: apeacefulblessing@yahoo.com. Web: www.catholicadoption.info.

Wichita
Diocese of Wichita

Guadalupe Clinic, Inc. (1985) 940 S. St. Francis, Wichita, 67211. Tel: 316-264-8974; Fax: 316-262-4938. Email: guadalupe@guadalupeclinic.kscoxmail.com. Web: www.guadalupeclinic.com.
Via Christi Healthcare Outreach Program for Elders, Inc. (HOPE) (2002) 2622 W. Central, Ste. 101, Wichita, 67203. Tel: 316-858-1111; Fax: 316-858-1166. Email: justin.loewen@viachristi.org. Web: www.viachristi.org/villages.
Via Christi Villages, Inc. (1985) 2622 W. Central, Ste. 100, Wichita, 67203. Tel: 316-946-5200; Fax: 316-946-5299. Email: jerry.carley@viachristi.org. Web: www.viachristi.org/villages.

KENTUCKY

Louisville
Archdiocese of Louisville

**Nativity Academy*, 529 E. Liberty St., Louisville, 40202. Tel: 502-855-3300; Fax: 502-562-2192. (Grades 6-8)
Our Lady of Peace, 2020 Newburg Rd., Louisville, 40205. Tel: 502-451-3330; Fax: 502-479-4140. Email: rebecca.kistler@jhsmh.org. Web: www.jhsmh.org. Hospital for Psychiatric Illness.
Pitt Academy, 6010 Preston Hwy., Louisville, 40219. Tel: 502-966-6979; Fax: 502-962-8878. Email: sdowney@pitt.com. Web: www.pitt.com.
Sacred Heart School for the Arts, 3105 Lexington Rd., Louisville, 40206. Tel: 502-897-1816; Fax: 502-896-3927. Email: dthurmond@sacredheartschools.org. Web: www.sacredheartschools.org.
Sacred Heart Village I, Inc. (Senior Housing Apartments), 2110 Payne St., Louisville, 40206. Tel: 502-895-6409; Fax: 502-895-8166.
Sacred Heart Village II, Inc. (Senior Housing Apartments), 2108 Payne St., Louisville, 40206. Tel: 502-895-8085; Fax: 502-895-8039.
Sacred Heart Village III, Inc. (Senior Housing Apartments), 3101 Wayside Dr., Louisville, 40216. Tel: 502-776-5004; Fax: 502-772-7695.
Sacred Heart Village, Inc. dba Sacred Heart Village 2120 Payne St., Louisville, 40206. Tel: 502-895-9425; Fax: 502-357-5549. Mercy Franciscan Health and Housing Services.

LOUISIANA

Alexandria
Diocese of Alexandria

Our Lady of Sorrows Community Homes, 347 Browns Bend Rd., Alexandria, 71303. Tel: 318-487-8897; Fax: 318-487-9987. Email: carlabols@aol.com.
St. Mary's Residential Training School, Inc., P.O. Drawer 7768, Alexandria, 71306. Tel: 318-445-6443; Fax: 318-449-8520. Email: sistercarla@stmarys-rts.org. Web: www.stmarys-rts.org.

Arabi
Archdiocese of New Orleans

St. Bernard Health Center, Inc., 7718 W. Judge Perez, Arabi, 70032. Tel: 504-281-2800; Fax: 504-278-4692.

Baton Rouge
Diocese of Baton Rouge

Chateau Louise, 7565 Bishop Ott Dr., Baton Rouge, 70806. Tel: 225-926-5918. Housing for elderly and handicapped persons.
Maternity & Adoption, 1900 S. Acadian Thruway, Baton Rouge, 70808. Tel: 225-336-8708; Fax: 225-336-8703. Email: adopt@ccdiobr.org. Web: www.adoptbatonrouge.com. Mailing Address: P.O. Box 4785, Baton Rouge, 70821-4785.
Ollie Steele Burden Manor, 4250 Essen Ln., Baton Rouge, 70809-2196. Tel: 225-926-0091; Fax: 225-926-4937. Our Lady of the Lake Regional Medical Center, Our Lady of the Lake Pastoral Care.

Lafayette
Diocese of Lafayette

St. Bernadette Clinic, Lafayette. Tel: 337-264-6292; Fax: 337-261-5276.
St. Joseph Shelter for Men, 425 St. John St., Lafayette, 70501. Tel: 337-233-6816; Fax: 337-233-6829. Web: www.catholicservice.org.

Lake Charles
Diocese of Lake Charles

Our Lady Queen of Heaven Manor, Villa Maria, 3905 Kingston St., Lake Charles, 70605. Tel: 337-478-4780; Fax: 337-474-8822. Email: villamaria@suddenlinkmail.com.

Metairie
Archdiocese of New Orleans

Sisters of Mercy Ministries dba Mercy Family Center Psychological and psychiatric evaluation, counseling and tutorial services., 110 Veterans Memorial Blvd., Ste. 425, Metairie, 70005. Tel: 504-838-8283; Fax: 504-838-9799. Email: sengro@mercyfamilycenter.com. Web: www.mercyfamilycenter.com.

New Orleans
Archdiocese of New Orleans

Baronne Street Transitional Housing/CARE Center (Crisis & Residential Emergency Center), *c/o Catholic Charities*, 1000 Howard Ave., Ste. 1000, New Orleans, 70113-1942. Tel: 504-269-9311.
Boys Hope Girls Hope (1980) Group Homes for Boys and Girls., P.O. Box 19307, New Orleans, 70179-0307. Tel: 504-484-7744; Fax: 504-484-6120. Web: www.bhghnola.org.
Daughters of Charity Services of New Orleans, 3201 S. Carrollton Ave., New Orleans, 70118-4307. Tel: 504-207-3060; Fax: 504-483-6016. Email: jfirstley@dcsno.org.
Jefferson CARE Center, c/o 1000 Howard Ave., Ste. 1000, New Orleans, 70113. Temporary Residence for Homeless Families.
Ocean Avenue, c/o 1000 Howard Ave., Ste. 1000, New Orleans, 70113. Community Home for Developmentally Disabled Adults.
Ozanam Inn Shelter for Homeless Men, 843 Camp St., New Orleans, 70130-3751. Tel: 504-523-1184; Fax: 504-523-1187. Web: www.ozanaminn.org.
Project Lazarus (1986) Residential Program for Persons with AIDS, P.O. Box 3906, New Orleans, 70177-3906. Tel: 504-949-3609; Fax: 504-944-7944. Email: info@projectlazarus.net. Web: www.projectlazarus.net.
Ss. Mary & Elizabeth, c/o 1000 Howard Ave., Ste. 1000, New Orleans, 70113. Community Home for Developmentally Disabled Adults.
St. Jude the Apostle, c/o 1000 Howard Ave., Ste. 1000, New Orleans, 70113. Community Home for Developmentally Disabled Adults.
St. Peter the Fisherman, c/o 1000 Howard Ave., Ste. 1000, New Orleans, 70113. Community Home for Developmentally Disabled Adults.
St. Rosalie, c/o 1000 Howard Ave., Ste. 1000, New Orleans, 70113. Community Home for Developmentally Disabled Adults.
The Apartments at Mater Dolorosa, 1000 Howard Ave., Ste. 100, New Orleans, 70113. Tel: 504-865-7222; Fax: 504-861-9225. 1226 S. Carrollton Ave., New Orleans, 70118. Tel: 504-596-3460; Fax: 504-596-3466. Elderly Affordable Housing

Shreveport
Diocese of Shreveport

St. Catherine Community Center, 7109 Henderson Ave., Shreveport, 71106-7109. Tel: 318-865-9817; Fax: 318-869-2549. Web: www.rc.net/shreveport/stcatherine. 3500 Fairfield Ave., Shreveport, 71104. Afterschool Enrichment, Summer Day Camp, Parenting, Arts, Anger Management, Computers, Teen Mom Mentoring.

Slidell
Archdiocese of New Orleans

Villa Additions Not currently open due to Hurricane Katrina, Gause Blvd. W., Slidell, 70460. Elderly Affordable Housing

MAINE

Biddeford
Diocese of Portland (In Maine)

St. Andre Home, Inc., Admin. Office, 283 Elm St., Biddeford, 04005-3093. Tel: 207-282-3351; Fax: 207-282-8733. Web: www.SaintAndreHome.org. Pregnant and Parenting Young Women, Adoption Services, Infant Foster Care Homes, Emergency Placement; Public Information-Education; Community Outreach Services; Residences in Biddeford, Lewiston, Bangor.

Lewiston
Diocese of Portland (In Maine)

Neighborhood Housing Initiative, Inc., P.O. Box 7291, Lewiston, 04243-7291. Tel: 207-777-8802; Fax: 207-777-8800. Web: www.stmarysmaine.com.
**St. Martin de Porres Residence, Inc.*, Mailing Address: P.O. Box 7227, Lewiston, 04243-7227. 23 Bartlett St., Lewiston, 04243-7227. Tel: 207-786-4690; Fax: 207-786-8866. Email: mdeporres@roadrunner.com.

MARYLAND

Baltimore
Archdiocese of Baltimore

Answers for the Aging, 3310 Benson Ave., Baltimore, 21227-1035. Tel: 410-646-0100; 888-502-7587; Fax: 410-646-0500.
Baltimore City Child and Adolescent Response (Foster/Kinship Care Stabilization Program), 1118 S. Light St., Baltimore, 21230. Tel: 410-727-4800; Fax: 410-727-5853.
Bon Secours Family Support Center, 26 N. Fulton Ave., Baltimore, 21223. Tel: 410-362-3629; Fax: 410-362-3649. Web: www.bonsecours.org/bshsi.
Cherry Hill SeniorLife Center, 606 Cherry Hill Rd., Ste. 201, Baltimore, 21225-1229. Tel: 410-354-5101; Fax: 410-354-5103.
Pastoral Care at the Jenkins Senior Living Community, 3320 Benson Ave., Baltimore, 21227. Tel: 410-646-6513; Fax: 410-646-6541.
Project FRESH Start (Family Relocation, Empowerment, and Self-Help), 228 W. Lexington St., Ste. 220, Baltimore, 21201-3432. Tel: 410-261-6777; Fax: 410-889-0203.
Project SERVE (Service and Education through Residential Volunteer Experience), 228 W. Lexington St., Ste. 220, Baltimore, 21201-3432. Tel: 410-261-6774; Fax: 410-889-0203.
The Neighborhoods at St. Elizabeth Rehabilitation and Nursing Center (Jenkins Memorial Nursing Home, Inc.), 3320 Benson Ave., Baltimore, 21227-1035. Tel: 410-644-7100; Fax: 410-646-6589.
Trinitarian Counseling Services, Inc., 8400 Park Heights Ave., P.O. Box 5719, Baltimore, 21282. Tel: 410-486-5764; Fax: 410-486-0614. Email: treasurer@trinitarians.org.

Princess Anne
Diocese of Wilmington

Seton Center, 30632 Hampden Ave., P.O. Box 401, Princess Anne, MD 21853. Tel: 410-651-9608; Fax: 410-651-1437. Email: setoncenter@ccwilm.org.

Silver Spring
Archdiocese of Washington

Saint Luke Institute, Inc., 8901 New Hampshire Ave., Silver Spring, MD 20903. Tel: 301-445-7970; Fax: 301-422-5400. Email: getinfo@sli.org. Web: www.sli.org. The Institute is a licensed and accredited treatment center for clergy and religious, and a center for education and research.

Timonium
Archdiocese of Baltimore

St. Vincent's Villa Diagnostic Evaluation and Treatment Program, 2600 Pot Spring Rd., Timonium, 21093. Tel: 410-252-4000; Fax: 410-561-8109.

MASSACHUSETTS

Boston
Archdiocese of Boston

Nazareth Residence for Mothers and Children, 91 Regent St., Boston, 02119. Tel: 617-541-0100; Fax: 617-541-8781. Email: nazareth_residence@ccab.org. Home for homeless mothers and children who are HIV positive.

Our Lady's Guild House - Residence for Women, 20 Charlesgate W., Boston, 02215. Tel: 617-536-3000; Fax: 617-536-8508.

St. Helena House, 89 Union Park St., Boston, 02118. Tel: 617-426-2922; Fax: 617-542-3460. Seniors, low income & disabled persons.

St. Mary's Women and Infants Center, 90 Cushing Ave., Boston, 02125. Center for pregnant women.; (See Guidance Centers for more information.)

Braintree
Archdiocese of Boston

Life Resources, Inc., 100 River St., Braintree, 02184. Tel: 781-849-7751; Fax: 781-849-7754. Web: www.liferesourcesinc.org.

Life Resources/Alpha-Omega, 140 Adams St., Braintree, 02184. Tel: 781-848-5510; Fax: 781-380-7565. Web: www.liferesourcesinc.org. A long term residence for 20 adolescent boys.

Brockton
Archdiocese of Boston

Catholic Charities South A Division of Catholic Charities, 686 N. Main St., Brockton, 02301. Tel: 508-587-0815; Fax: 508-580-0837. Email: lisa_lodge@ccab.org. Web: ccab.org.

Cambridge
Archdiocese of Boston

**Youville House, Inc.*, 1573 Cambridge St., Cambridge, 02138-4398. Tel: 617-491-1234; Fax: 617-491-8838. Email: joannecparsons@youvillehouse.org. Web: www.youvilleassistedliving.com. Youville House is an assisted living residence.

Charlton
Diocese of Worcester

Ministry to Retired Priests, 188 Old Worcester Rd., Charlton, 01507. Tel: 508-868-9239; Fax: 508-248-3814.

Holyoke
Diocese of Springfield in Massachusetts

Broderick House, 56 Cabot St., P.O. Box 6269, Holyoke, 01041. Tel: 413-534-7610; Fax: 413-536-1137. SRO (single room occupancy), permanent housing for low income sober men/women.

Kate's Kitchen, 51 Hamilton St., Holyoke, 01040. Tel: 413-532-0233; Fax: 413-536-1137. A community kitchen which provides one meal daily to anyone in need - no questions asked.

Loreto House, 51 Hamilton St., Holyoke, 01041. Tel: 413-533-5909; Fax: 413-536-1137. An around-the-clock shelter for homeless men.

Mary's Meadow at Providence Place, Inc., c/o Sisters of Providence, Inc., 12 Gamelin St., Holyoke, 01040. Tel: 413-536-7511, Ext. 2551; Fax: 413-536-7917.

Providence Ministries for the Needy, Inc., P.O. Box 6269, Holyoke, 01041-6269. Tel: 413-536-9109; Fax: 413-536-1137.

Lakeville
Archdiocese of Boston

Bishop Joseph John Ruocco House, 22 Highland Rd., Lakeville, 02347. Tel: 508-947-2823; Fax: 508-947-0305. Web: liferesourcesinc.org. Short term residence for 16 female adolescents. To provide comprehensive life skill services to residents and their families.

Lawrence
Archdiocese of Boston

**Greater Lawrence Mental Health Center, Inc.*, 30 General St., Lawrence, 01841. Tel: 978-683-3128; Fax: 978-686-7856.

Methuen
Archdiocese of Boston

St. Ann's Home Special Needs School, 100 A. Haverhill St., Methuen, 01844. Tel: 978-682-5276; Fax: 978-688-4932. Email: dgrandbois@st.annshome.org. Web: www.st.annshome.org. Ungraded special needs school for emotionally disturbed and behaviorally disordered children.

St. Ann's Home, Inc., 100A Haverhill St., Methuen, 01844. Tel: 978-682-5276; Fax: 978-688-4932. Email: dgrandbois@st.annshome.org. Web: www.st.annshome.org.

Springfield
Diocese of Springfield in Massachusetts

Diocesan Office for Counseling, Prevention and Victim Services, 65 Elliot St., P.O. Box 1730, Springfield, 01102-1730. Tel: 413-732-3175; 413-452-0624; Fax: 413-452-0618. Web: www.diospringfield.org/MC.html.

Worcester
Diocese of Worcester

Mercy Centre (Developmental Disabilities), 25 W. Chester St., Worcester, 01605-1136. Tel: 508-852-7165; Fax: 508-856-9755. Special Education Day Program and Employment Training Youngsters and Adults with Developmental Disabilities.

Youville House Shelter for Homeless Families, 133 Granite St., Worcester, 01604-4500. Tel: 508-753-3084; Fax: 508-754-0139.

MICHIGAN

Detroit
Archdiocese of Detroit

St. Patrick Senior Center, Inc., 58 Parsons, Detroit, 48201. Tel: 313-833-7080; Fax: 313-833-0128. Web: www.stpatseniorcenter.com.

Fraser
Archdiocese of Detroit

Sanctuary at Fraser Villa (a unit of Trinity Senior Living Communities), 33300 Utica Rd., Fraser, 48026. Tel: 586-293-3300. Email: sliwinsg@trinity-health.org. Web: www.trinityseniorsanctuary.org.

Lake Orion
Archdiocese of Detroit

Guest House Recovery Residence, 444 Nakomis Rd., Lake Orion, 48362. Tel: 248-693-8973; Fax: 248-693-8973.

Guest House for Women Religious, 1720 W. Scripps Rd., Lake Orion, 48360. Tel: 248-391-3100; Fax: 248-393-0186. Web: www.guesthouse.org. A state-licensed and CARF accredited endorsed residential treatment center for Catholic sisters and women in formation.; Central Admissions Office, from U.S. & Canada call: 800-626-6910.

Livonia
Archdiocese of Detroit

**Angela Hospice Home Care, Inc.*, 14100 Newburgh Rd., Livonia, 48154-5010. Tel: 734-464-7810; Fax: 734-779-4601. Email: ahospice@aol.com. Web: www.angelahospice.org.

Marycrest Manor, 15475 Middlebelt Rd., Livonia, 48154. Tel: 734-427-9175; Fax: 734-427-5044. Ownership: Franciscan Sisters of St. Joseph.

Memphis
Archdiocese of Detroit

Sacred Heart Rehabilitation Center, Inc., 400 Stoddard Rd., Box 41038, Memphis, 48041-1038. Tel: 810-392-2167; Fax: 810-392-3385. Treatment for alcoholism and drug dependency to adult men and women. Detox and residential services.

Pontiac
Archdiocese of Detroit

Hispanic Outreach, 76 Williams St., Pontiac, 48341. Tel: 248-338-4250; Fax: 248-335-8130.

Port Huron
Archdiocese of Detroit

Port Huron Mercy Family Care, 2601 Electric Ave., P.O. Box 610669, Port Huron, 48061-0669. Tel: 810-985-1868. (A unit of Trinity Health).

Redford
Archdiocese of Detroit

Holy Cross Family & Community Support Program, 23915 Elmira, Redford, 48239. Tel: 517-423-7556; Fax: 517-423-5442. Email: fboylan@hccsnet.org. Web: www.hccsnet.org. Includes specialized foster care, supervised independent living, in-home family treatment.

Rochester Hills
Archdiocese of Detroit

Sanctuary at Bellbrook (A unit of Trinity Senior Living Communities), 873 W. Avon Rd., Rochester Hills, 48307. Tel: 248-656-6300; Fax: 248-656-8160. Email: lundb@trinity-health.org. Web: www.trinityseniorsanctuary.org.

Royal Oak
Archdiocese of Detroit

Sanctuary at Alexander (A unit of Trinity Senior Living Communities), 718 W. Fourth St., Royal Oak, 48067. Tel: 248-545-0571; Fax: 248-545-9819. Email: goynesb@trinity-health.org. Web: www.trinityseniorsanctuary.org.

Saginaw
Diocese of Saginaw

Queen of Angels Center, 3400 S. Washington, Saginaw, 48601. Tel: 989-755-1971; Fax: 989-755-2780.

Warren
Archdiocese of Detroit

Sanctuary at the Abbey (a unit of Trinity Senior Living Communities), 12250 E. Twelve Mile Rd., Warren, 48093. Tel: 586-751-6200. Email: loriusl@trinity-health.org. Web: www.trinityseniorsanctuary.org.

St. John's Deaf Center, 14057 E. Nine Mile Rd., Warren, 48089. Tel: 586-758-0710 (TDD); 866-281-7108 (VP); 586-774-8476 (Voice); Fax: 586-774-8476.

Waterford
Archdiocese of Detroit

Lourdes Alzheimers Special Care Center, 2400 Watkins Lake Rd., Waterford, 48328. Tel: 248-674-4732; Fax: 248-618-6269. Web: www.lourdescampus.com.

MINNESOTA

Cold Spring
Diocese of St. Cloud

Bethany Home Contact Tim Lieser at Catholic Charities, 13 Eighth Ave. S., Cold Spring, 56320. Tel: 320-685-7899; Fax: 320-685-9808. Email: tlieser@ccstcloud.org. Supervised Living Situation for Persons with Developmental Disabilities.

Mother Teresa Home Contact Catholic Charities, 101 Tenth Ave., Cold Spring, 56320. Tel: 320-685-8626; Fax: 320-685-8626. Supervised Living Situation for Persons with Developmental Disabilities.

St. Anne's Home Contact Catholic Charities, 103 10th Ave. N., Cold Spring, 56320. Tel: 320-685-7898; Fax: 320-685-9819. Supervised Living Situation for Persons with Developmental Disabilities.

St. Luke's Home Contact Catholic Charities, 411 Eighth Ave. N., Cold Spring, 56320. Tel: 320-685-7750. Adults with mild to moderate developmental disabilities.

Fergus Falls
Diocese of St. Cloud

Catholic Charities Intensive Treatment Unit, 1010 Maryland Ln., Fergus Falls, 56537. Tel: 218-739-9325; Fax: 218-739-2242.

Little Falls
Diocese of St. Cloud

St. Camillus Place, 1100 S.E. Fourth St., Little Falls, 56345. Tel: 320-631-5020; Fax: 320-631-5025.

Paynesville
Diocese of St. Cloud

Adult Foster Care for Handicapped Individuals, 1790 W. Mill St., Paynesville, 56362. Tel: 320-243-3750; Fax: 320-243-3718.

St. Cloud
Diocese of St. Cloud

LaPaz Community Inc., Catholic Charities Housing Services, 530 S. 16th St., St. Cloud, 56301. Mailing Address: 157 Roosevelt Rd., Ste. 200, St. Cloud, 56301.

St. Cloud Children's Home of the Diocese of St. Cloud, 1726 Seventh Ave. S., St. Cloud, 56301. Tel: 320-650-1500; Fax: 320-650-1508.

St. Elizabeth Home Contact Tim Lieser at Catholic Charities, 306 15th Ave. N., St. Cloud, 56303. Tel: 320-240-3350. Email: Tlieser@ccstcloud.org. Board and Lodging Home for Functionally Impaired Adults.

St. Francis Home, 1727 Roosevelt Rd., St. Cloud, 56301. Tel: 320-251-7630; Fax: 320-240-8097. Supervised Living Situation for Persons with

Developmental Disabilities.

St. Paul
Archdiocese of St. Paul and Minneapolis

Our House of Minnesota, Inc. I (1975) 1846 Dayton Ave., St. Paul, 55104. Tel: 651-644-6650; Fax: 651-646-1104.

Our House of Minnesota, Inc. II (1975) 1846 Portland, St. Paul, 55104. Tel: 651-644-2411; Fax: 651-646-1104.

Our Lady of Peace Home (1941) 2076 St. Anthony Ave., St. Paul, 55104-5096. Tel: 651-646-2797; Fax: 651-646-7884. Web: www.franciscancare.org.

WomanWell, 1784 La Crosse Ave., St. Paul, 55119-4808. Tel: 651-739-7953; Fax: 651-739-7475. Email: seeking@WomanWell.org. Web: www.womanwell.org.

West St. Paul
Archdiocese of St. Paul and Minneapolis

Saint Paul's Outreach, Inc., 110 Crusader Ave. W., West St. Paul, 55118. Tel: 651-451-6114; Fax: 651-453-0810. Email: info@spoweb.org. Web: www.spoweb.org.

MISSOURI

Blue Springs
Diocese of Kansas City-St. Joseph

St. Mary's Manor (1987) 111 Mock Ave., Blue Springs, 64014. Tel: 816-228-5655; Fax: 816-228-8480. Email: pkelley@carondelet.com. Long term care facility with skilled nursing care and residential care. Sponsored by Sisters of St. Joseph of Carondelet. Managed by Benedictine Health System.

Chesterfield
Archdiocese of St. Louis

St. Joseph Institute for the Deaf, 1809 Clarkson Rd., Chesterfield, 63017-5065. Tel: 636-532-3211 (Voice/TTY); Fax: 636-532-4560. Web: www.sjid.org. School for the Deaf; Auditory-oral day school for hearing-impaired children from birth-8th grade. Early intervention therapy for children 0-5; pre- & elementary school offering intense speech & academic prog.

Creve Coeur
Archdiocese of St. Louis

SSM Rehab, 10101 Woodfield Ln., Ste. 100, Exec. Offices, Creve Coeur, 63132. Tel: 314-768-5300; Fax: 314-768-5355. Web: www.ssmrehab.com. Member of SSM Health Care; For rehabilitation of pediatrics, adolescents and adults.

Florissant
Archdiocese of St. Louis

Child Center - Marygrove (1849) 2705 Mullanphy Ln., Florissant, 63031. Tel: 314-837-1702; Fax: 314-830-6263. Email: hnegri@ccstl.org. Web: www.childcentermarygrove.org. Owned and operated under the auspices of Catholic Charities; Residential treatment for emotionally disturbed males and females (ages 6-21). Special education, therapy and medical services. Overnight emergency care: and crisis nursery males and females (Birth-21). Transitional Services, Apartments, Sequoia House and Drury House. Male and Female (ages 17-21).

St. Elizabeth Adult Day Care Center of Florissant (1994) 1831 N. New Florissant Rd., Florissant, 63033. Tel: 314-838-5005; Fax: 314-838-5005.

Kansas City
Diocese of Kansas City-St. Joseph

Carondelet Manor, 621 Carondelet Dr., Kansas City, 64114. Tel: 816-943-4777; Fax: 816-941-7007. Owned and operated by Carondelet Long Term Care Facilities, Inc. Sponsored by Sisters of St. Joseph of Carondelet and Benedictine Health System.

Lemay
Archdiocese of St. Louis

Catholic Deaf Ministry, 309 Hoffmeister Ave., Lemay, 63125. Email: vbarnhart@archstl.org. Provides Services for Deaf and Hearing Impaired Persons.

Liberty
Diocese of Kansas City-St. Joseph

Immacolata Manor (1981) 2135 Manor Way, Liberty, 64068-9397. Tel: 816-781-4332; Fax: 816-781-8820. Email: info@imanor.org. Residential and day habilitation services for people with developmental disabilities; Operated by the Immacolata Board of Directors.

Normandy
Archdiocese of St. Louis

Maria Droste Residence (1979) 7660 Natural Bridge Rd., Normandy, 63121. Tel: 314-383-5553; Fax: 314-382-1325. Web: goodshepherdsisters.org. For Women in Need.

Springfield
Diocese of Springfield-Cape Girardeau

**McAuley Counseling Services, Inc.*, 2200 E. Sunshine, Ste. 201, Springfield, 65804. Tel: 417-823-0498.

St. John's Mercy Villa, 1100 E. Montclair, Springfield, 65807. Tel: 417-820-8500; Fax: 417-820-8547. Skilled Care of Long Term Nursing Home, for the Aged and Chronically Ill.

St. Louis
Archdiocese of St. Louis

Ascension Health, 4600 Edmundson Rd., St. Louis, 63134. Tel: 314-733-8000; Fax: 314-733-8013. Email: atersigni@ascensionhealth.org. Web: www.ascensionhealth.org.

Ascension Health Alliance, 4600 Edmundson Rd., St. Louis, 63134.

Ascension Health-IS, Inc., 4600 Edmundson Rd., St. Louis, 63134. Tel: 314-733-8000; Fax: 314-733-8013. Email: atersigni@ascensionhealth.org. Web: www.ascensionhealth.org.

Boys Hope/Girls Hope of St. Louis, Inc., 755 S. New Ballas Rd., Ste. 120, St. Louis, 63141. Tel: 314-692-7477; Fax: 314-692-7810. Email: hopestlouis@bhgh.org. Web: www.hopestlouis.org. Residential Care for Adolescent Boys and Girls, Troubled by Family Disruptions, who are Capable of College Preparatory High School Work. Ages 10-18.

Cardinal Ritter Senior Services, 7601 Watson Rd., St. Louis, 63119. Tel: 314-961-8000; Fax: 314-961-1934. Email: swesley@ccstl.org. Web: www.cardinalrittersenorservices.org. Catholic Charities network of agencies provides social services, in home services, residences, adult day care, employment and volunteer services for the elderly.

Carondelet Health System, Inc., 4600 Edmundson Rd., St. Louis, 63134. Tel: 314-733-8000; Fax: 314-733-8013. Email: atersigni@ascensionhealth.org.

Cathedral Tower, 325 N. Newstead Ave., St. Louis, 63108. Tel: 314-367-5500, Ext. 121; Fax: 314-361-5099. Email: tgorski@ccstl.org. Web: www.ccstl.org. Building which houses several agencies of Catholic Charities: Queen of Peace Center; St. Elizabeth Hall; and Peace for Kids, Inc.

Catholic Family Services (1992) 9200 Watson Rd., G101, St. Louis, 63126. Tel: 314-544-3800; 800-652-8055; Fax: 314-843-0552. Provides residential and social services, professional counseling and health care access to families and communities.

Department of Special Education (1950) 4445 Lindell Blvd., St. Louis, 63108. Tel: 314-792-7320; Fax: 314-792-7325. Email: ktichy@archstl.org. Special Education ungraded classrooms at Ascension, and St. John the Baptist. Special Education Schools at Annunziata and the Academy at St. Rose Philippine Duchesne. Special Education Day Care, Preschool and Early Intervention Services at St. Mary's North and St. Mary's South. Special Education Program for children with autism and developmental delays at St. Gemma Center. Special Education services for high school students with disabilities at partner Catholic high schools through St. Joseph's Special Services. Special religious education classes for children and adults with developmental disabilities or major learning disabilities. Psycho-Educational Testing Service. Administrative office for above programs and services.

Father Dempsey's Hotel, Inc., 3427 Washington Ave., St. Louis, 63103. Tel: 314-535-7221; Fax: 314-535-7289. Email: maboussie@archstl.org.

Father Jim's Home, 3427 Washington Ave., St. Louis, 63103. Tel: 314-535-7221; Fax: 314-535-7289. Email: maboussie@archstl.org.

Food and Fuel for Life, 100 N. Jefferson Ave., St. Louis, 63103. Tel: 877-238-3228; 314-881-6000; Fax: 314-531-6712. Email: info@svdpstl.org. Web: www.servingthepoor.org.

Guardian Angel Settlement Association, P.O. Box 2055, St. Louis, 63158-0055. Tel: 314-231-3188; Fax: 314-231-8126. Email: efmurphy@guardianangelsettlement.org. Web: www.guardianangelsettlement.org. Child Care Services and Social Services.

Guardian Angel at Hosea House, 2635 Gravois Ave., St. Louis, 63118. Tel: 314-773-9027; Fax: 314-773-6140.

Queen of Peace Center (1985) 325 N. Newstead Ave., St. Louis, 63108. Tel: 314-531-0511; Fax: 314-531-1458. Email: cneumann@ccstl.org. Comprehensive residential and outpatient behavioral healthcare for addicted women and their children. Specialty in pregnant women, trauma and dually diagnosed. Permanent and transitional housing programs. Licensed by the Department of Mental Health Division of Alcohol and Drug Abuse. Accredited by COA Council on Accreditation.

Rosati Center, 4220-24 N. Grand Ave., St. Louis, 63107. Tel: 314-534-6624; Fax: 314-535-4394. Permanent supportive housing for former homeless single adults. Managed by St. Patrick Center.

Rosati Group Home, Inc., 4218 N. Grand Blvd., St. Louis, 63107. Tel: 314-534-6624; Fax: 314-535-4394. Email: nboland@stpatrickcenter.org. Web: stpatrickcenter.org. Group Home for homeless mentally ill adults. Managed by St. Patrick Center.

Seton Institute, Ascension Health, 4600 Edmundson Rd., P.O. Box 45998, St. Louis, 63164. Tel: 314-733-8286; Fax: 314-733-8013. Email: jimpicciche@ascensionhealth.org. Web: www.setoninstitute.org.

St. Elizabeth Adult Day Care Center (1981) 3401 Arsenal St., St. Louis, 63118. Tel: 314-772-5107; Fax: 314-772-3674. Email: sjamiller@juno.com. Web: www.seadcc.org. Conducted by the Sisters of the Most Precious Blood to Provide Day Care for the Elderly and Handicapped.

St. Martha's Hall, P.O. Box 4950, St. Louis, 63108. Tel: 314-533-1313; Fax: 314-533-2035. Email: stmarthashall@sbcglobal.net. Web: www.saintmarthas.org. Provides Shelter, Advocacy and Support to Abused Women & their Children.

St. Mary's - North, 1724 Redman Ave., St. Louis, 63138. Tel: 314-653-2591; Fax: 314-653-6811. Web: www.archstl.org/education.

St. Mary's - South, 1045 Union Rd., St. Louis, 63123. Tel: 314-631-8231; Fax: 314-631-0015.

St. Mary's Special Services for Exceptional Children (1952)Administrative Office: 4445 Lindell Blvd., St. Louis, 63108. Tel: 314-792-7320; Fax: 314-792-7325. Early Intervention services, day care and Preschool for all children (ages 6 weeks-6years), both with developmental delays and typically-developing, in an inclusionary early childhood center.

St. Philippine Home (1996) 1015 Goodfellow Blvd., St. Louis, 63112. Tel: 314-454-1012; Fax: 314-367-7455. Email: cneumann@ccstl.org. Transitional housing for drug affected homeless city women and their children.

MONTANA

Great Falls
Diocese of Great Falls - Billings

St. Thomas Child and Family Center, 1710 Benefis Ct., Great Falls, 59405. Tel: 406-761-6538; Fax: 406-727-0670. Email: carrie@stthomaskids.org. Web: stthomaskids.org.

NEBRASKA

Lincoln
Diocese of Lincoln

Villa Marie School and Home for the Educable Mentally Handicapped (1964) P.O. Box 80328, Lincoln, 68501. Tel: 402-786-3625; Fax: 402-488-6525.

NEW HAMPSHIRE

Laconia
Diocese of Manchester

Bishop Bradley Senior Living Community, 406 Court St., Laconia, 03246. Tel: 603-524-0466; Fax: 603-527-0884. Email: stf.administrator@nh-cc.org.

Manchester
Diocese of Manchester

St. Joseph Residence (1980) 495 Mammoth Rd., Manchester, 03104-5463. Tel: 603-668-6011; Fax: 603-644-1276. Email: MJMakowski@presmarynh.org. New Hampshire Catholic Charities.

Nashua
Diocese of Manchester

Marguerite's Place, 87 Palm St., Nashua, 03060. Tel: 603-598-1582; Fax: 603-598-7574. Email: balves@margueritesplace.org. Web: www.margueritesplace.org.

NEW JERSEY

Hoboken
Archdiocese of Newark

Good Counsel, Inc. (St. Francis Home), 411 Clinton St., Hoboken, 07030. Tel: 201-798-9059; 201-795-0637; 800-723-8331 (Hotline); Fax: 201-795-0809. Email: cbell@goodcounselhomes.org. Web: www.goodcounselhomes.org; www.postabortionhelp.org. Housing, counseling and referrals for single women who are pregnant or single mothers with children. Counseling for men and women experiencing post abortion stress.

Jersey City
Archdiocese of Newark

Margaret Anna Cusack Care Center, Inc., 537 Pavonia Ave., Jersey City, 07306. Tel: 201-653-8300, Ext. 2152; Fax: 201-653-7705. Email: info@cusackcarecenter.org. Web: www.cusackcarecenter.org. Skilled Nursing Facility for Men & Women.

St. Joseph's Home, 81 York St., Jersey City, 07302. Tel: 201-413-9280; Fax: 201-451-0952. Transitional housing for homeless women and children.

St. Joseph's Home for the Blind (1886) (Skilled nursing facility for men and women), 537 Pavonia Ave., Jersey City, 07306. Tel: 201-653-8300, Ext. 2152; Fax: 201-653-7705. Email: info@cusackcarecenter.org. Web: www.cusackcarecenter.org.

St. Mary's Residence, 240 Washington St., Jersey City, 07302-3806. Tel: 201-432-6289; Fax: 201-451-0952. (Single working women of low income assisted; no children).

Keyport
Diocese of Trenton

Collier House, 386 Maple Pl., Keyport, 07735. Tel: 732-264-3222; Fax: 732-264-3277. Email: pauldes21@verizon.net. Web: www.collieryouthservices.org. Transitional Aging-Out Program for Women 18-21 years old.

Lawrenceville
Diocese of Trenton

Morris Hall/Saint Lawrence, Inc., 2381 Lawrenceville Rd., Lawrenceville, 08648. Tel: 609-896-9500; Fax: 609-895-0242. Email: dhanley@slrc.org. Web: www.slrc.org. St. Lawrence Rehabilitation Center.

Morris Hall/Saint Lawrence, Inc. Morris Hall - St. Joseph's Nursing Center, 1 Bishops' Dr., Lawrenceville, 08648-2050. Tel: 609-896-0006; Fax: 609-896-8037; 609-895-0466. Email: epetroski@morrishall.org. Web: www.morrishall.org. Skilled Nursing Care Facility for the Chronically Ill.

Lodi
Archdiocese of Newark

**The Promise Outreach, Inc.* (1982) Volunteers visit, correspond with, and provide opportunity for spirituality and other basic needs to teens in programs, correctional institutions and centers of rehabilitation., 260 S. Main St., Lodi, 07644. Tel: 973-460-3229; Fax: 973-473-7126. Email: vimsters@aol.com. Web: home.catholicweb.com/thepromiseoutreachinc.

Pompton Lakes
Diocese of Paterson

Pathways Counseling Center, Inc., 16 Pompton Ave., Pompton Lakes, 07442. Tel: 973-835-6337; Fax: 973-616-4688. Email: pegb@pathwayscounseling.org. Web: www.pathwayscounseling.org.

Red Bank
Diocese of Trenton

Collier Group Home, 180 Spring St., Red Bank, 07701. Tel: 732-842-8337; Fax: 732-530-7096. Email: pauldes21@verizon.net. Web: www.collieryouthservices.org. 24 Hour Program-Therapy and Educational Services. Provided Under the Supervision of the Sisters of the Good Shepherd.

Riverside
Archdiocese of New York

Good Counsel, Inc., 116 Heulings Ave., Riverside, NJ 08075. Tel: 856-393-8169; Fax: 856-393-8420.

Wayne
Diocese of Paterson

Bethany Residence, 738 Rte. 23, Wayne, 07470. Tel: 973-628-8109.

Wickatunk
Diocese of Trenton

Collier Services, Collier School, 160 Conover Rd., Wickatunk, 07765. Tel: 732-946-4771; Fax: 732-946-3519. Email: info@collieryouthservices.org. Web: www.collieryouthservices.org. Boys and Girls in grades 6-12.

NEW MEXICO

Albuquerque
Archdiocese of Santa Fe

Casa Angelica (1967) 5629 Isleta Blvd., S.W., Albuquerque, 87105. Tel: 505-877-5763; Fax: 505-873-2786. Email: lturner@casaangelica.org. Web: www.casaangelica.org. Home for developmentally disabled children and young adults.

Good Shepherd Center, Inc., 218 Iron St., S.W., P.O. Box 749, Albuquerque, 87103. Tel: 505-243-2527; Fax: 505-247-2207. Direct Service Agency for the Homeless.

Marie Amadea Shelter for Unwed Mothers (Alternative to Abortion), P.O. Box 708, Albuquerque, 87103. Tel: 505-242-1516; Fax: 505-243-0402. Home for unwed expectant women.

Santa Fe
Archdiocese of Santa Fe

Villa Therese Catholic Clinic, 219 Cathedral Pl., Santa Fe, 87501. Tel: 505-983-8561; Fax: 505-982-7863. Email: vtcc@cnsp.com.

NEW YORK

Albany
Diocese of Albany

Diocesan AIDS Services, 100 Slingerlands St., Albany, 12202. Tel: 518-449-3581; Fax: 518-426-3662.

Emmaus House, 45 Trinity Pl., Albany, 12202. Tel: 518-482-4966. Albany Catholic Worker Community.

Hospitality House Therapeutic Community Inc., 271 Central Ave., Albany, 12206. Tel: 518-434-6468; Fax: 518-434-6302. Email: lbecker@hospitalityhouse.info. A private, not-for-profit, intensive residential treatment program for males, 18 years or older, with a history of drug and/or substance abuse.

Saint Anne Institute, 160 N. Main Ave., Albany, 12206. Tel: 518-437-6500; Fax: 518-437-6555. Email: rriccio@s-a-i.org. Web: www.stanneinstitute.org. Residential and Community-based Preventive Service Center. Regents accredited and certified junior and senior H.S. for the emotionally handicapped and Preschool program for 3-4 year olds who are speech-impaired and emotionally disturbed. Residential care, critical care, and Day Treatment for young women ages 12-18. Family Services, Vocational Training, Sex Abuse Prevention and Juvenile Sex Offender Programs for male and female adolescents in crisis and their families.

St. Peter's Licensed Home Care Agency, 159 Wolf Rd., Albany, 12205. Tel: 518-525-6099; Fax: 518-525-6002. Email: bsmith@stpetershealthcareservices.org.

Allegany
Diocese of Buffalo

St. Elizabeth Motherhouse (1859) 115 E. Main St., Allegany, 14706. Tel: 716-373-0200; Fax: 716-372-5774. Email: fsa@fsallegany.org. Web: www.alleganyfranciscans.org.

Astoria
Diocese of Brooklyn

Peter J. Della Monica Center for Seniors, 23-56 Broadway, Astoria, 11106. Tel: 718-626-1500; Fax: 718-278-4432.

Provincial Office, 25-30 21st Ave., Astoria, 11105. Tel: 718-278-1155.

Steinway Senior Center, 20-43 Steinway St., Astoria, 11105. Tel: 718-728-8472; Fax: 718-278-5301.

Barryville
Archdiocese of New York

New Hope Manor, 35 Hillside Rd., Barryville, 12719. Tel: 845-557-8353; Fax: 845-557-6603. Email: newhopemnr@aol.com. Web: www.newhopemanor.org. See listing in the Miscellaneous section for further details.

Bayside
Diocese of Brooklyn

Bayside Senior Center and Bayside Senior Center Transportation Program, 221-15 Horace Harding Expwy., Bayside, 11364. Tel: 718-225-1144; Fax: 718-229-7320.

Queens Day Habilitation Program, 61-58 Springfield Blvd., Bayside, 11364. Tel: 718-281-0480; Fax: 718-281-0478.

Beacon
Archdiocese of New York

Metropolitan Association of Contemplative Communities, Inc., 89 Hiddenbrooke Dr., Beacon, 12508. Tel: 845-831-5572; Fax: 845-831-5579. Web: macc.catholic.org.

Metropolitan Association of Contemplative Communities, Inc. (1967) 89 Hiddenbrooke Dr., Beacon, 12508. Tel: 845-831-5572; Fax: 845-831-5579. Web: macc.catholic.org.

Blauvelt
Archdiocese of New York

Friends of St. Dominic's Inc., 500 Western Hwy., Blauvelt, 10913. Tel: 845-359-3400; Fax: 845-398-0466. Email: sjm@stdominicshome.org. Web: www.stdominicshome.org/friends.

Saint Dominic's Home (1878) 500 Western Hwy., Blauvelt, 10913. Tel: 845-359-3400; Fax: 845-359-4253. Email: judyk@stdominicshome.org. Web: www.stdominicshome.org.

Bohemia
Diocese of Rockville Centre

Talbot House Alcohol Crisis Center, 30-C Carlough Rd., Bohemia, 11716. Tel: 631-589-4144; Fax: 631-589-3281.

Bronx
Archdiocese of New York

Beacon of Hope House Bronx Congregate Services, 1400 Waters Pl., Bronx, 10461. Tel: 718-892-3494; Fax: 718-892-5507.

East Bronx Supported Housing, 2510 Westchester Ave., Ste. 210, Bronx, 10461. Tel: 718-239-5206; Fax: 718-239-5287.

Good Counsel, Inc., 1157 Fulton Ave., Bronx, 10456. Tel: 718-312-3980, Ext. 10; 800-723-8331 (For Info & Referrals); Fax: 718-312-3991. Email: delores_morgan@gopdcounselhomes.org. Web: www.goodcounselhomes.org.

Highbridge Neighborhood Supported Housing Program, 1484 Nelson Ave., Suite A, Bronx, 10452. Tel: 718-503-8106; Fax: 718-293-0939.

Kolping-on-Concourse, 2916 Grand Concourse, Bronx, 10458. Tel: 718-733-6119. Web: www.kolpingresidence.com. (Catholic Kolping Society New York, Inc.)

Mount St. Ursula Speech Center, 2885 Marion Ave., Bronx, 10458. Tel: 718-584-7679; Fax: 718-584-7954. Email: msuspeech@aol.com.

New York Offices, 853 Longwood Ave., Ste. 202, Bronx, 10459. Tel: 917-645-9100; Fax: 917-645-9095. Web: www.stdominicshome.org.

Saint Dominic's Home - Prevention Program (ASTAAN) Parent Aide Counseling Advocacy Information and Referral., 2345 University Ave., Bronx, 10468. Tel: 718-584-4407; Fax: 718-584-4540. Email: annettet@stdominicshome.org. Web: www.stdominicshome.org.

St. Eleanora's Home for Convalescents (1901) Sisters of Charity Center, 6301 Riverdale Ave., Bronx, 10471. Tel: 718-549-9200, Ext. 261; Fax: 718-884-3013. Email: ghanley@scny.org. Web: scny.org.

TORCH (To Reach Children), 2340 Andrews Ave., Bronx, 10468. Tel: 718-365-7238; Fax: 718-584-3057. Web: www.stdominicshome.org.

Terence Cardinal Cooke Residence, 2467 Bathgate Ave., Bronx, 10458. Tel: 718-367-6990; 718-367-5405 (TTY); Fax: 718-365-2544.

The Clubhouse, 512 Southern Blvd., Bronx, 10455. Tel: 718-993-1078; Fax: 718-993-0216.

Brooklyn
Diocese of Brooklyn

101-105 South Eighth Street Apartments Housing Development Fund Corporation, 191 Joralemon St., Brooklyn, 11201. Tel: 718-722-6050; Fax: 718-722-6096.

161-01 89th Avenue Corp., 191 Joralemon St., Brooklyn, 11201. Tel: 718-262-8190; Fax: 718-739-4331.

176 South Eighth Street Apartments Housing Development Fund Corporation, 191 Joralemon St., Brooklyn, 11201. Tel: 718-722-6050; Fax: 718-722-6096.

72 Lewis Avenue, Apartments Housing Development Fund Corporation, 191 Joralemon St., Brooklyn, 11201. Tel: 718-722-6050.

Advocate for Persons with Disabilities Services, 191 Joralemon St., 7th Fl., Brooklyn, 11201. Tel: 718-722-6232.

Anthonian Hall, Inc., 191 Joralemon St., Brooklyn, 11201. Tel: 718-722-6000; Fax: 718-722-6096.

Bay Ridge Day Habilitation Program, 347 74th St., 2nd Fl., Brooklyn, 11209. Tel: 718-745-7117; Fax: 718-745-3741.

Bellerose Senior HDFC, Inc., 191 Joralemon St., Brooklyn, 11201. Tel: 718-722-6050; Fax: 718-479-6612.

Benson Ridge Senior Services Assistance Center, 6825 5th Ave., Brooklyn, 11220. Tel: 718-236-3205; Fax: 718-837-1957.

Bereavement Services, 191 Joralemon St., 7th Fl., Brooklyn, 11201. Tel: 718-722-6214.

Bethlehem Community HDFC Inc., 191 Joralemon St., Brooklyn, 11201. Tel: 718-722-6000; Fax: 718-722-6045.

Bishop Boardman Senior HDFC, 191 Joralemon St., Brooklyn, 11201. Tel: 718-722-6050; Fax: 718-965-3577.

Bishop Francis J. Mugavero Senior HDFC, 191 Joralemon St., Brooklyn, 11201. Tel: 718-722-6050; Fax: 718-643-6492.

Brooklyn Day Habilitation Program, 177 Livingston Ave., 2nd Fl., Brooklyn, 11201. Tel: 718-797-2020; Fax: 718-237-8958.

Care at Home for the Diocese of Brooklyn, Inc., 269 37th St., Brooklyn, 11232-2409. Tel: 718-907-4711; Fax: 718-965-7010.

Caring Communities Associates HDFC, Inc., 191 Joralemon St., Brooklyn, 11201. Tel: 718-722-6050; Fax: 718-857-5866.

Casa Betsaida HDFC, 191 Joralemon St., Brooklyn, 11201. Tel: 718-722-6000.

Casa Betsaida-Home for people with AIDS, 267 Hewes St., Brooklyn, 11211. Tel: 718-218-7890; Fax: 718-218-8264. Email: cbetsaidainc@aol.com.

Catherine Laboure Special Education Program, Dept. of Educ., 21 Bay 11th St., Brooklyn, 11228. Tel: 718-449-1857; Fax: 718-449-0212. Web: www.dioceseofbrooklyn.org. Program for mentally challenged students ages 5-21 and learning disabled students grades 4-8.

Catherine Sheridan HDFC, Inc., 191 Joralemon St., Brooklyn, 11201. Tel: 718-722-6050; Fax: 718-274-2333.

Catholic Child Care Society, 191 Joralemon St., Brooklyn, 11201. Tel: 718-722-6091; Fax: 718-722-6096.

Catholic Guild for the Blind, Diocese of Brooklyn, Inc., 191 Joralemon St., Brooklyn, 11201. Tel: 718-722-6000; Fax: 718-722-6096.

Circle of Hope Brooklyn and Queens, 2520 Flatbush Ave., Ste. 10, Brooklyn, 11234. Tel: 718-338-4716; Fax: 718-338-5383.

Emmaus of the Diocese of Brooklyn, Inc., 191 Joralemon St., Brooklyn, 11201. Tel: 718-722-6000; Fax: 718-722-6096.

Families Together HDFC, Inc., 191 Joralemon St., Brooklyn, 11201. Tel: 718-722-6000; Fax: 718-722-6045.

Family Home Care Services of Brooklyn and Queens, Inc., 241 37 St., Brooklyn, 11232. Tel: 718-832-0550; Fax: 718-907-8750.

Glenwood Senior Center, 5701 Avenue H, Brooklyn, 11234. Tel: 718-241-7711; Fax: 718-241-1936.

HeartShare Human Services of NY, 12 Metro Tech Center, Brooklyn, 11201. Tel: 718-422-4200. (Formerly Catholic Guardian Society/Diocese of Brooklyn).

Heartshare Wellness Ltd., 177 Livingston Ave. Cellar Level, Brooklyn, 11201. Tel: 718-855-7707; Fax: 718-855-7717.

Holy Spirit Senior HDFC, 191 Joralemon St., Brooklyn, 11201. Tel: 718-722-6050; Fax: 718-854-8521.

Little Flower Children's Services of New York, Corporate Office: 186 Joralemon St., Brooklyn, 11201. Tel: 718-875-3500. Long Island Office: N. Wading River Rd., Wading River, 11792. Tel: 516-929-6200. Queens Office: 89-12 162nd St., Queens, 11439. Tel: 718-526-9150. Long Island Office: N. Wading River Rd., Wading River, NY 11792. Tel: 516- 929-6200.

Mary Immaculate HDFC, Inc., 191 Joralemon St., Brooklyn, 11201. Tel: 718-722-6000; Fax: 718-722-6096.

Mary Immaculate, Inc., 191 Joralemon St., Brooklyn, 11201. Tel: 718-722-6000; Fax: 718-722-6096.

Mary Star of the Sea Senior HFDC, 191 Joralemon St., Brooklyn, 11201. Tel: 718-722-6050; Fax: 718-858-7265.

Mary's Hall, Inc., 191 Joralemon St., Brooklyn, 11201. Tel: 718-722-6000; Fax: 718-722-6096.

Mercy Home for Children (1865) 273 Willoughby Ave., Brooklyn, 11205. Tel: 718-832-1075; Fax: 718-832-7612. Email: info@mercyhomeny.org. Web: www.mercyhomeny.org. Under the sponsorship of the Sisters of Mercy.; Six Intermediate Care Facilities (Residences & Individual Residential Alternatives) for adolescents & adults who are developmentally disabled: Visitation Residence; Harold Warren Residence; de Porres Residence; Littlejohn Residence; Santulli Residence; Kevin Keating Residence; 7 IRA Residences; Chrys Residence; Gail Addeo Residence; Rev. Michael J. McGivney Residence; Augusta Residence, Frank's Residence, and St. Joseph's Residence, Mary E. Casey Residence. Three all day Saturday Recreation Programs, for adolescents and adults with developmental disabilities and children with autism, we offer MSC Services for families and the individuals. In Home Respite Services; James P. Slattery, Mercy Creative Arts Program, Mercy-Mitsui Creative Arts Program.

Mercy Home for Children, 273 Willoughby Ave., Brooklyn, 11205. Tel: 718-832-1075.

MercyFirst, 6301 12th Ave., Brooklyn, 11219. Tel: 718-232-1500; Fax: 718-232-0331. Web: www.mercyfirst.org. Residential services provided in campus and group home settings, including diagnostic/group emergency foster care, non-secure detention, hard to place (JD and clinically intensive), abuse treatment and prevention, mother/child, and OMH programs.; Family Foster Care/Adoption, Aftercare and Preventive Services programs provide services in Nassau, Queens and Brooklyn.

MercyFirst, Brooklyn Office: 6301 12th Ave., Brooklyn, 11219. Long Island Office: 525 Convent Rd., Syosset, NY 11791. Tel: 516-921-0808.

Most Holy Trinity, 157 Graham Ave., Brooklyn, 11206. Tel: 718-963-3956; Fax: 718-963-4028.

Mount Carmel Senior HDFC, 191 Joralemon St., Brooklyn, 11201. Tel: 718-722-6050; Fax: 718-722-6045.

Msgr. John P. O'Brien Senior HDFC, 191 Joralemon St., Brooklyn, 11201. Tel: 718-722-6050; Fax: 718-972-9265.

Narrows Senior Center, 1230 63rd St, Brooklyn, 11219. Tel: 718-232-3211; Fax: 718-232-0512.

Narrows at the Lodge, 7711 18th Ave., Brooklyn, 11214. Tel: 718-621-1081; Fax: 718-621-1407.

Northside Senior Center, 179 N. 6th St., Brooklyn, 11211. Tel: 718-387-2316; Fax: 718-387-3235.

O.L. Loreto Family Housing Development Fund Corporation, 191 Joralemon St., Brooklyn, 11201. Tel: 718-722-6000; Fax: 718-722-6096.

Office of Child Welfare, 191 Joralemon St., Brooklyn, 11201. Tel: 718-722-6091; Fax: 718-722-6096.

Our Lady of Fatima Apartments HDFC, Inc., 191 Joralemon St., Brooklyn, 11201. Tel: 718-722-6050; Fax: 718-507-1214.

Our Lady of Good Counsel, 800-826 Madison St., Brooklyn, 11221. Tel: 718-452-3600; Fax: 718-452-4910.

Partnering with Autistic Citizens (PACT) Day Habilitation Program, 177 Livingston Ave., 2nd Fl., Brooklyn, 11201. Tel: 718-797-2020, Ext. 8051; Fax: 718-237-8958.

Pete McGuinness Senior Center, 715 Leonard St., Brooklyn, 11222. Tel: 718-383-1940; Fax: 718-383-1960.

Pierrepont HDFC, 191 Joralemon St., Brooklyn, 11201. Tel: 718-722-6000; Fax: 718-722-6096.

Pope John Paul II Senior HDFC, 191 Joralemon St., Brooklyn, 11201. Tel: 718-722-6050; Fax: 718-748-4425.

Providence House, Inc. (1979) *Administrative Office*, 703 Lexington Ave., Brooklyn, 11221. Tel: 718-455-0197; Fax: 718-455-0692. Web: www.providencehouse.org.

Queens Rehab Corp., 191 Joralemon St., Brooklyn, 11201. Tel: 718-722-6000; Fax: 718-722-6045.

Restorative Justice, 191 Joralemon St., 7th Fl., Brooklyn, 11201. Tel: 718-722-6113.

Services for Pregnant Women, 191 Joralemon St., 7th Fl., Brooklyn, 11201. Tel: 718-722-6121.

Sheepshead Bay Supportive Services (NORC), 3677 Nostrand Ave. #3-A, Brooklyn, 11229. Tel: 718-769-3579; Fax: 718-769-4155.

**Society of St. Vincent de Paul in Diocese of Brooklyn, Long Island, New York*, Central Office, 191 Joralemon St., Brooklyn, 11201. Tel: 718-625-1400; Fax: 718-625-1421.

South Brooklyn Alzheimer's Adult Care Program, 5701 Avenue H., Brooklyn, 11234. Tel: 718-241-7711; 718-241-1936.

Sr. Lucian Senior HDFC, 191 Joralemon St., Brooklyn, 11201. Tel: 718-722-6050; Fax: 718-381-9407.

Ss. Joachim & Anne Residence, 2720 Surf Ave., Brooklyn, 11224. Tel: 718-714-4800; Fax: 718-714-0874.

St. Brendan Senior HDFC, 191 Joralemon St., Brooklyn, 11201. Tel: 718-722-6050; Fax: 718-645-7180.

St. Francis de Sales School for the Deaf (1960) 260 Eastern Pkwy., Brooklyn, 11225. Tel: 718-636-4573; Fax: 718-636-4577. Email: school@sfdesales.org. Web: www.sfdesales.org. Infant through Elementary Grades (8th Grade).

St. Jerome's Health Services Corp. dba Holy Family Home 1740 84th St., Brooklyn, 11214. Tel: 718-259-8240; Fax: 718-259-9180. Affiliated with Saint Vincent Catholic Medical Centers of New York.

St. Joseph's, 683 Dean St., Brooklyn, 11238. Tel: 718-857-2266; Fax: 718-857-5866.

St. Lucy/St.Patrick HDFC, 191 Joralemon St., Brooklyn, 11201. Tel: 718-722-6050; Fax: 718-722-6045.

St. Paul the Apostle Senior HDFC, 191 Joralemon St., Brooklyn, 11201. Tel: 718-722-6050; Fax: 718-722-6045.

St. Teresa of Avila Senior HDFC, 191 Joralemon St., Brooklyn, 11201. Tel: 718-722-6050.

Sunset Park HFDC, Inc., 191 Joralemon St., Brooklyn, 11201. Tel: 718-722-6050; Fax: 718-871-2407.

Supportive Living Apartments, 1615 8th Ave., Brooklyn, 11226. Tel: 718-930-0820.

The Bay Senior Center, 3643 Nostrand Ave., Brooklyn, 11229. Tel: 718-648-2053; Fax: 718-648-7213.

The David Minkin Residence HDFC, Inc., 191 Joralemon St., Brooklyn, 11201. Tel: 718-722-6050; Fax: 718-438-0052.

The Msgr. Joseph F. Stedman Residence HDFC, 191 Joralemon St., Brooklyn, 11201. Tel: 718-722-6050; Fax: 718-722-6134.

Archdiocese of New York

Kingsborough Intensive Supported Apartment Program, 647 Vanderbilt Ave., Brooklyn, 11238. Tel: 718-398-4556; Fax: 718-398-4807.

Buffalo
Diocese of Buffalo

Catholic Health System Program of All-Inclusive Care for the Elderly, Inc. (CHS PACE), Seton Professional Building, 2121 Main St., Ste. 300, Buffalo, 14214.

St. Francis of Buffalo, Inc. Formerly known as St. Francis Hospital., 291 North St., Buffalo, 14201. Tel: 716-923-4816; Fax: 716-604-1820. Email: cjk@chsbuffalo.org. c/o Catholic Health Systems, 2121 Main St., Ste. 300, Buffalo, 14214.

The Franciscan Center, Inc., 1910 Seneca St., Buffalo, 14210-1842. Tel: 716-822-8017; Fax: 716-822-8537. Web: www.franciscancenterinc.org. Transitional Shelters for Adolescent Males 16-20: Transitional Indep. Living Program, Supported Residence.

Clifton Park
Diocese of Albany

Seton Health at Schuyler Ridge aka Leonard Nursing Home One Abele Dr., Clifton Park, 12065. Tel: 518-371-1400. Email: ssmith@setonhealth.org. Web: schuylerridge.org.

Seton Health at Schuyler Ridge aka Leonard Nursing Home One Abele Dr., Clifton Park, 12065. Tel: 518-371-1400; Fax: 518-371-1240. Email: ssmith@setonhealth.org. Web: schuylerridge.org.

Cornwall
Archdiocese of New York

Contemplative Outreach, Ltd., 10 Landmark Dr., Ste. 117, P.O. Box 208, Cornwall, 12518. Tel: 845-534-5180. Email: office@coutreach.org. Web: www.contemplativeoutreach.org.

East Islip
Diocese of Rockville Centre

Suffolk Hearing & Speech Center, Inc., 369 E. Main St., East Islip, 11730. Tel: 631-376-4001; Fax: 631-376-4208. A diagnostic and treatment center.

Flushing
Diocese of Brooklyn

Alzheimers Adult Day Care, 157-16 65th Ave., Flushing, 11357. Tel: 718-358-3541; Fax: 718-961-4712.

Garrison
Archdiocese of New York

St. Christopher's Inn (1908) Temporary shelter for homeless men. Outpatient chemical dependency services & primary healthcare., 21 Franciscan Way, P.O. Box 150, Garrison, 10524-0150. Tel: 845-335-1000; Fax: 845-335-1017. Email: bdrobach@atonementfriars.org. Web:

www.stchristophersinn-graymoor.org.

Germantown
Diocese of Albany

The Carmelite System, Inc., 646 Woods Rd., Germantown, 12526-5617. Tel: 518-537-7500; Fax: 518-537-7501. Email: xsusansan@carmelitesystem.org. Web: Carmelitesystem.org.

Harrison
Archdiocese of New York

Good Counsel/Daystar Program, 275 North St., Harrison, 10528. Tel: 914-925-9834; 800-723-8331 (Info. & Referrals); Fax: 914-925-9101. Web: www.goodcounselhomes.org; www.postabortionhelp.org.

Hawthorne
Archdiocese of New York

Rosary Hill Home (1901) Free home for incurable cancer patients., Hawthorne, 10532. Tel: 914-769-0114; Fax: 914-769-3916. Web: www.hawthorne.dominicans.org.

Hollis
Diocese of Brooklyn

Project Independence, 183-16 Jamaica Ave., Hollis, 11423. Tel: 718-217-0126; Fax: 718-217-0495.

Southwest Queens Senior Services, 186-16 Jamaica Ave., 2nd Fl., Hollis, 11423. Tel: 718-217-0126; Fax: 718-217-0495.

Holtsville
Diocese of Rockville Centre

Nursing Sisters Home Care, Inc. dba Catholic Home Care 1150 Portion Rd., Holtsville, 11742. Tel: 631-696-1002; Fax: 631-224-8678.

Jackson Heights
Diocese of Brooklyn

Catherine Sheridan Senior Center, 35-24 83rd St., Jackson Heights, 11372. Tel: 718-458-4600; Fax: 718-458-5665.

Jamaica
Diocese of Brooklyn

Hillcrest Senior Center, 168-01B Hillside Ave., Jamaica, 11432. Tel: 718-297-7171; Fax: 718-657-2247.

Lackawanna
Diocese of Buffalo

Baker Victory Services (1851) (formerly known as Baker Hall, Our Lady of Victory Infant Home, St. Joseph Orphanage and St. John's Protectory), 780 Ridge Rd., Lackawanna, 14218. Tel: 716-828-9500; 888-287-1160; Fax: 716-828-9526. Email: webmaster@olv-bvs.org. Web: www.bakervictoryservices.org. Bakery Victory Services assists children, adults and families in need through preventative, outpatient, educational, and residential programs, including international and domestic adoptions, foster care, early childhood education, and a dental clinic, as well as programs for individuals with developmental disabilities and young people who are emotionally, behaviorally, or mentally challenged.

Long Island City
Diocese of Brooklyn

Hour Children (1995) 13-07 37th Ave., Long Island City, 11101. Tel: 718-443-4724; Fax: 718-433-4728. Email: sisterterese@hourchildren.org. Web: www.hourchildren.org.

Long Island City Day Habilitation, 36-40 37th St., Long Island City, 11101. Tel: 718-215-2183; Fax: 718-215-2172.

Montrose
Archdiocese of New York

Kolping-on-Hudson (Catholic Kolping Society New York, Inc.), 95 Montrose Point Rd., Montrose, 10548. Tel: 914-736-0117.

Mount Vernon
Archdiocese of New York

St. Theresa's Residence, 30 S. 10th Ave., Mount Vernon, 10550. Tel: 914-664-5900; Fax: 914-664-6733.

Nesconset
Diocese of Rockville Centre

Cleary Deaf Child Center, Inc. (1925) 301 Smithtown Blvd., Nesconset, 11767. Tel: 631-588-0530 (Voice and TTY); Fax: 631-588-0016. Email: kmorseon@clearyschool.org. Web: www.clearyschool.org. Day School (Infants thru 21 years).

New Rochelle
Archdiocese of New York

Ursuline Social Outreach, Inc. (1996) 138 Centre Ave., New Rochelle, 10805. Tel: 914-633-7298; Fax: 914-633-7393. Email: usoalc@aol.com. Ursuline Outreach sponsors The Adult Learning Center, 138 Centre Ave., New Rochelle, NY 10805.

New York
Archdiocese of New York

Catholic Charities Community Services Beacon of Hope House Division, Catholic Charities, 1011 First Ave., New York, 10022. Tel: 212-371-1000; Fax: 212-421-0021. Email: denise.bauer@archny.org. Web: www.archny.org.

Catholic Charities Department of Housing, Housing Development Institute, Inc., 1011 First Ave., New York, 10022. Tel: 212-371-1000.

Catholic Near East Welfare Association (CNEWA) (1926) 1011 First Ave., New York, 10022. Tel: 212-826-1480; Fax: 212-826-8979. Email: cnewa@cnewa.org. Web: www.cnewa.org.

Centro Maria, Inc. For young students and working women., 539 W. 54th St., New York, 10019. Tel: 212-757-6989; Fax: 212-307-5687. Email: cenmariany@mindspring.com. Web: www.religiosasdemariainmaculada.org.

Cor Mariae, c/o 1011 First Ave., Rm. 1130, New York, 10022. Tel: 212-371-1000, Ext. 2435. Residence for formerly homeless senior women.

Covenant House Under 21 (Runaway and Homeless Youth.), 460 W. 41st St., New York, 10036. Tel: 212-727-4000; Fax: 212-727-4992.

Developmental Disabilities Clinic, 1249 Fifth Ave., New York, 10029. Tel: 212-360-3703; Fax: 212-360-3842. Comprehensive Outpatient medical, therapeutic and educational services. On site and off site OMRDD Article 16 services.

El Carmelo Residence, 249 W. 14th St., New York, 10011. Tel: 212-242-8224; Fax: 212-242-7233.

Emergency Food Services, 1011 First Ave., New York, 10022. Tel: 212-371-1000, Ext. 2481; Fax: 212-317-8719.

Grace Institute, 1233 Second Ave., New York, 10065. Tel: 212-832-7605; Fax: 212-486-2869. Email: info@graceinstitute.org. Web: www.graceinstitute.org.

John A. Coleman School, 590 Avenue of the Americas, New York, 10011. Tel: 646-459-3401; Fax: 646-459-3689. Email: sharon.herl@setonpediatric.org. Web: www.setonpediatric.org.

Kolping Society of New York Men's Residence (Catholic Kolping Society New York, Inc.) (1888) For young Catholic men., 165 E. 88th St., New York, 10128. Tel: 212-369-6647; Fax: 212-987-5652. Email: residence@kolpingny.org.

Lavelle School for the Blind, E. 221st St. and Paulding Ave., New York, 10469. Tel: 718-882-1212; Fax: 718-882-0005. Web: www.lavelleschool.org.

Little Sisters of the Assumption Family Health Service, Inc. (1958) 333 E. 115th St., New York, 10029. Tel: 646-672-5200; Fax: 212-348-8284. Email: gcarter@lsafhs.org.

New York Catholic Deaf Center, St. Elizabeth of Hungry Church, 211 E. 83rd St., New York, 10028. Tel: 212-988-8563 (Voice); 212-988-1903 (TTY); 866-810-3394 (Video Phone); Fax: 212-988-1903. Web: www.deafcathnyc.org.

New York Foundling Charitable Corp., 590 Avenue of the Americas, New York, 10011. Tel: 212-633-9300. Web: www.nyfoundling.org.

SVCMC Health Services Inc., 130 W. 12th St., Ste. 6-E, New York, 10011. Tel: 212-604-7536. Email: estclair@svcmcny.org.

Sacred Heart Residence Working or studying young ladies ages 19-29., 432 W. 20th St., New York, 10011. Tel: 212-929-5790; Fax: 212-924-0891. Email: sacredheartresidence@hotmail.com. Web: www.sacredheartresidence.com.

Sr. Una McCormack Maternity Services, Inc. (1997) 1011 First Ave., New York, 10022. Tel: 212-371-1000, Ext. 2100; Fax: 212-755-4110.

St. Agnes' Residence For students and working women., 237 W. 74th St., New York, 10023. Tel: 212-874-1361.

St. Francis Counseling Center, Inc., 135 W. 31st St., New York, 10001. Tel: 212-736-8500; Fax: 212-736-8545. Web: www.stfrancisnyc.org.

St. Mary's Residence (1913) For students and young working women., 225 E. 72nd St., New York, 10021. Tel: 212-249-6850; Fax: 212-249-4336. Email: St.MarysRes72@aol.com.

The Dwelling Place (1977) For homeless women., 409 W. 40th St., New York, 10018. Tel: 212-564-7887; Fax: 212-695-3642.

The Jeanne d'Arc Residence (1896) 253 W. 24th St., New York, 10011. Tel: 212-989-5952; Fax: 212-691-0257. Email: jdresidence@gmail.com. Women.

The Leo House (1889) Clergy, Sisters & Other Travelers., 332 W. 23rd St., New York, 10011. Tel: 212-929-1010; Fax: 212-366-6801.

Thorpe Family Residence, Inc. (1988) 2252 Crotona Ave., New York, 10457. Tel: 718-933-7312; Fax: 718-933-7311. Email: mdeodati@aol.com. Web: thorpeonline.org.

Ogdensburg
Diocese of Ogdensburg

St. Joseph's Home (1960) 950 Linden St., Ogdensburg, 13669. Tel: 315-393-3780; Fax: 315-393-3847. Email: administrator@stjh.org. Web: www.stjh.org.

Ossining
Archdiocese of New York

Cardinal McCloskey Emergency Residential School (1980) 155 N. Highland Ave., Ossining, 10562. Tel: 914-762-5302; Fax: 914-762-7844.

Dominican Sisters Family Health Service, Inc. (Central Services/Administration) (1974) Community-based, certified, voluntary Home Health Agency and Long Term Home Health Care and AIDS Programs serving all of Westchester, Suffolk and the South Bronx. Unique community outreach programs., 299 N. Highland Ave., Ossining, 10562. Tel: 914-941-1710; Fax: 914-941-0518. Email: VHanrahan@dsfhs.org. Web: www.dsfhs.org.

Ozone Park
Diocese of Brooklyn

Ferrini Welfare League, 98-21 101 Ave., Ozone Park, 11416. Tel: 718-845-0539.

Ozone Park Senior Center, 103-02 101st Ave., Ozone Park, 11416. Tel: 718-847-2100; Fax: 718-847-2166.

Queens
Diocese of Brooklyn

Little Flower Children's Services of New York, Corporate Office: 186 Joralemon St., Brooklyn, 11201. Tel: 718-875-3500. Long Island Office: N. Wading River Rd., Wading River, 11792. Tel: 516-929-6200. Queens Office: 89-12 162nd St., Queens, 11439. Tel: 718-526-9150. Long Island Office: N. Wading River Rd., Wading River, NY 11792. Tel: 516- 929-6200.

Richmond Hill
Diocese of Brooklyn

Woodhaven-Richmond Hill Senior Center, 87-25 118th St., Richmond Hill, 11418. Tel: 718-846-2877; Fax: 718-847-9089.

Rockaway Beach
Diocese of Brooklyn

Seaside Senior Center, 90-01 Rockaway Beach Blvd., Rockaway Beach, 11693. Tel: 718-634-4047; Fax: 718-634-6853.

Roosevelt
Diocese of Rockville Centre

Friends of Mother of Good Counsel Home, Inc., 290 Babylon Tpke., Roosevelt, 11575. Tel: 516-223-1013; Fax: 516-223-4254. Email: ossr290@earthlink.net.

Sloatsburg
Ukrainian Catholic Diocese of Stamford

St. Mary's Villa Spiritual, Cultural & Educational Center, 150 Sisters Servants Ln., P.O. Box 9, Sloatsburg, NY 10974-0009. Tel: 845-753-5100; Fax: 845-753-1956.

Spring Valley
Archdiocese of New York

Good Counsel, Inc., 22 Linden Ave., Spring Valley, 10977. Tel: 845-356-0517; 800-723-8331 (Info & Referrals); Fax: 845-356-0406. Web: www.goodcounselhomes.org; www.postabortionhelp.org.

Springfield Gardens
Diocese of Brooklyn

Martin De Porres Group Homes (1974) 136-25 218th St., Springfield Gardens, 11413. Tel: 718-527-0606; Fax: 718-723-1528. Email: phiro@nyc.rr.com. Web: mdp.org.

Staten Island
Archdiocese of New York

Beacon of Hope House Staten Island Supervised Programs, 777 Seaview Ave., Bldg. D, 2nd Fl., Staten Island, 10305. Tel: 718-980-1072; Fax: 718-980-1077.

Good Counsel, Inc., 38 Wiman Pl., Staten Island, 10305. Tel: 718-727-8266; 800-723-8331 (Info. & Referrals); Fax: 718-447-6625. Web: www.goodcounselhomes.org; www.postabortionhelp.org.

Pax Christi Hospice Hospice Care Services for the terminally ill., 1200 South Ave., Ste. 306, Staten Island, 10314. Tel: 718-876-1022; Fax: 718-876-1803.

Syosset
Diocese of Rockville Centre

MercyFirst (1894) 525 Convent Rd., Syosset, 11791-3864. Tel: 516-921-0808; Fax: 516-921-4542. Email: gmccaffery@mercyfirst.org. Web: www.mercyfirst.org. Residential services provided in campus and group home settings, including diagnostic/group emergency foster care, non secure detention, hard to place (JD and clinically intensive), abuse treatment and prevention, mother/child, and OMH programs.; Family Foster Care/Adoption, Aftercare and Prevention Services programs provide services in Nassau, Queens and Brooklyn.

Syracuse
Diocese of Syracuse

L'Arche of Syracuse, Inc., 920 Spencer St., Syracuse, 13204. Tel: 315-479-8088; Fax: 315-479-8118. Email: larchesyracuse@cnymail.com. Web: www.larchesyracuse.org. A Christian Community concerned with life sharing between persons with a developmental disability and persons who assist them; Homes at 310 Galster Ave, 4550 Cleveland Rd., 211 Croyden Rd., 140 Highland Ave., Syracuse.

Tarrytown
Archdiocese of New York

**Family Home Health Care, Inc.* (Licensed Home Health Care Affiliate), 65 S. Broadway, Tarrytown, 10591. Tel: 914-631-7200; Fax: 914-631-2382. Email: dozure@dsfhs.org.

Utica
Diocese of Syracuse

St. John and St. Joseph Home, Inc., 1408 Genesee St., Utica, 13502. Tel: 315-724-2158; Fax: 315-724-5318.

Valhalla
Archdiocese of New York

Cardinal McCloskey Services (1946) 115 Stevens Ave., Valhalla, 10595. Tel: 914-997-8000; Fax: 914-997-2166. Email: bfinnerty@cardinalmccloskey.org. Web: www.cardinalmccloskeyservices.org. Statistical Information: Sisters 2; Hayden House Capacity: 20, 35 Children Served; Foster Boarding Home Total Assisted: 398; Tappan Group Home Capacity: 8, Total Assisted: 9; Therapeutic Foster Boarding Home: 66 Children Served; General Preventative Services Total Assisted: 875 children/ 365 families; OMH — Family-based Treatment Children Assisted: 9; In Day Care: Site I Capacity: 922 Children Served, Site II: 144 Children Assisted; Site III University Heights: 134 Children Assisted; OPWDD Residence Capacity: 79, 31 Families Assisted; OPWDD Day Habilitation: 18 Consumers Assisted; OPWDD Case Management 99 Consumers Assisted; OPWDD Family Support: 31 Families Assisted; Enhanced Supportive Employment: 4 Consumers Assisted; Medical and Clinical Services: Total Assisted: 728 children.75 families/78 adults; Drop-in-Center: 175 Individuals Served; B2H: 249 Children Served; Rockland Diagnostic: 5 Children Served.

Diocese of Rockville Centre

**Little Flower Children & Family Services of New York* (1929) 2450 N. Wading River Rd., Wading River, 11792-1402. Tel: 631-929-6200; Fax: 631-929-6121. Web: www.LittleFlowerNY.org. Affiliated with the Diocese of Brooklyn. Foster care, adoption & post-adoption svcs., intermediate care facilities, residential treatment center, Special Act school district, family day care, family care for MR/DD clients, foster homes for teen mothers & their babies. Therapeutic foster boarding homes. Eldercare Solutions: Counseling for employees of client organizations.

Watervliet
Diocese of Albany

St. Colman's Home, Watervliet, 12189. Tel: 518-273-4911; Fax: 518-273-3312.

West Park
Archdiocese of New York

St. Cabrini Home (1890)West Park, 12493. Tel: 845-384-6500; Fax: 845-384-6001. Email: info@cabrinihome.com. Web: cabrinihome.com.

White Plains
Archdiocese of New York

RDC Center for Counseling and Human Development, Inc. (1991) 52 N. Broadway, White Plains, 10603. Tel: 914-949-0504; Fax: 914-997-1979. To provide counseling services for laity, religious and clergy. Individual and group counseling are offered as well as marital and family therapy.

Wyandanch
Diocese of Rockville Centre

Gerald J. Ryan Outreach Center, Inc., 1434 Straight Path, Wyandanch, 11798. Tel: 631-643-7591; Fax: 631-643-1871. Email: ryanouthreach@optonline.net.

NORTH CAROLINA

Belmont
Diocese of Charlotte

**Holy Angels Services, Inc.*, 6600 Wilkinson Blvd., Belmont, 28012. Tel: 704-825-4161; Fax: 704-825-0553. Email: info@holyangelsnc.org. Web: www.holyangelsnc.org. Mailing Address: P.O. Box 710, Belmont, 28012. Residential and developmental programs and svcs. for children and adults with mental retardation and physical disabilities.

McAuley Residence ICF/MR Group Homes, Belmont.

Morrow Center, Belmont. (Children 0-20)

Raleigh
Diocese of Raleigh

Catholic Parish Outreach, 2013 N. Raleigh Blvd., Raleigh, 27604. Tel: 919-873-0245; Fax: 919-873-0260. Web: www.cporaleigh.org.

Rosman
Diocese of Charlotte

**Frances Warde Health Service*, 9526 Rosman Hwy., Rosman, 28772. Tel: 828-884-7990; Fax: 828-966-9609. Email: jdewarrsm@juno.com.

NORTH DAKOTA

Dickinson
Diocese of Bismarck

Benedictine Living Communities, Inc. dba Benedict Court (2003) 830 2nd Ave. E., Dickinson, 58601. Tel: 701-456-7242; Fax: 701-456-7250. Email: Jon.frantsvog@bhshealth.org. Web: www.benedict-court.org.

Fargo
Diocese of Fargo

Villa Nazareth dba Friendship, Inc. 801 Page Dr., Fargo, 58103. Tel: 701-235-8217; Fax: 701-235-7538. Email: jeffpederson@catholichealth.net. A community-based facility providing an array of residential, vocational, educational, social and clinical services for children and adults with mental retardation and other developmental disabilities.

Sentinel Butte
Diocese of Bismarck

Home On The Range (1950) 16351 I-94, Sentinel Butte, 58654-9500. Tel: 701-872-3745; Fax: 701-872-3748. Email: jayhotr@gmail.com. Web: www.hotrnd.com.

OHIO

Akron
Diocese of Cleveland

Interval Brotherhood Home Alcohol-Drug Rehabilitation Center (1970) 3445 S. Main St., Akron, 44319. Tel: 330-644-4095; Fax: 330-645-2031. Email: dpfinn@ibh.org. Web: www.ibh.org.

**St. Patrick Manor, Inc. c/o Humility of Mary Housing, Inc.*, 3250 W. Market St., Ste. 204, Akron, 44333. Tel: 330-384-1555; Fax: 330-384-2144. Email: kradigan@hmhousing.org. Web: www.hmhousing.org.

Cincinnati
Archdiocese of Cincinnati

Friars Club, 1615 Vine St., Cincinnati, 45202. Tel: 513-381-5432; Fax: 513-381-7909. Email: atimmons@friarsclubinc.org. Web: www.friarsclubinc.org.

Cleveland
Diocese of Cleveland

Chemical Dependency Services - Midtown Professional Center, 3135 Euclid Ave., Room 202, Cleveland, 44115-2507. Tel: 216-391-2030; Fax: 216-391-8946.

Employment & Training Services - Midtown Professional Center, 3135 Euclid Ave., Room 101, Cleveland, 44115-2507. Tel: 216-426-9870; Fax: 216-426-9932.

Hispanic Senior Center, 7800 Detroit Ave., Cleveland, 44102. Tel: 216-939-3714; Fax: 216-631-3654.

St. Phillip Neri Family Center, 799 E. 82nd St., Cleveland, 44103. Tel: 216-391-4415.

Euclid
Diocese of Cleveland

Rose Mary, The Johanna Grasselli Rehabilitation and Education Center, 19350 Euclid Ave., Euclid, 44117. Tel: 216-481-4823; Fax: 216-481-4154. Web: rose-marycenter.com.

North Lima
Diocese of Youngstown

The Assumption Village, Marian Living Center (Assisted Living Facility), 9800 Market St., North Lima, 44452. Tel: 330-549-0740; Fax: 330-549-0701. Member: Catholic Healthcare Partners and Humility of Mary Health Partners.; Special Care Unit for residents with Alzheimer's or Dementia; Skilled Nursing Unit with Subacute Care Program; Intermediate Care.

Northfield
Diocese of Cleveland

St. Barnabas Villa, Inc. (1985) 9234 Olde Eight Rd., Northfield, 44067. Tel: 330-467-3758; Fax: 330-908-1186. A shared living facility for 11 people over 60 years of age.

Parma
Diocese of Cleveland

CCSC/Parmadale (1925) 6753 State Rd., Parma, 44134. Tel: 440-845-7700; Fax: 440-845-5910. Email: pdale@clevelandcatholiccharities.org. Web: www.clevelandcatholiccharities.org. Specialized Residential Services; Intensive Treatment Services; Chemical Dependency Treatment; Community-Based Family Services; Specialized Foster Care; Outpatient Services; Training and Consultation Services; and Volunteer Program; Adoption Services; Head Start.

Holy Family Home and Hospice (1956) 6707 State Rd., Parma, 44134. Tel: 440-888-7722; Fax: 440-866-6040. Email: info@holyfamilyhome.com. Web: www.holyfamilyhome.com. Inpatient and community-based hospice care.

Poland
Diocese of Youngstown

Hospice of the Valley, Hospice House, 9803 Sharrott Rd, Poland, 44514. Tel: 330-549-5850; Fax: 330-549-5859.

Sandusky
Diocese of Toledo

**Providence Residential Community Corp Apartment and Villa Home Independent Living*, 5000 Providence Dr., Sandusky, 44870. Tel: 419-624-1171; Fax: 419-624-1175. Email: jwindisch@providencecenters.org. Web: www.providencecenters.org.

Tiffin
Diocese of Toledo

St. Francis Home Inc., 182 St. Francis Ave., Tiffin, 44883. Tel: 419-447-2723; Fax: 419-448-1337. Email: ceo@stfrancishome.org. Web: www.stfrancishome.org.

Youngstown
Diocese of Youngstown

Beatitude House (1991) 238 Tod Ln., Youngstown, 44504. Tel: 330-744-3147; Fax: 330-744-3991. Email: info@beatitudehouse.com. Web:

www.beatitudehouse.com. Permanent supportive housing, transitional housing, job preparation, job training, counseling, education and case management for economically disadvantaged women and children.

OKLAHOMA

Oklahoma City
Archdiocese of Oklahoma City

St. Ann's Home, Inc. (1950) 9400 St. Ann's Dr., Oklahoma City, 73162. Tel: 405-728-7888; Fax: 405-728-1302.

PENNSYLVANIA

Ambler
Archdiocese of Philadelphia

St. Mary's Villa for Children and Families, 701 S. Bethlehem Pike, P.O. Box 388, Ambler, 19002-0388. Tel: 215-643-7676; Fax: 215-542-9219. Email: fryer.diana@hfi-pgh.org. Web: www.hfi.org. Family centered organization providing residential care and treatment to youth ages 7-18. St. Mary's is committed to helping children, preserving families and strengthening communities by providing residential treatment and outpatient mental health counseling. It strives to empower children and families to lead responsible lives and develop healthy relationships built on faith, hope and love.

Aston
Archdiocese of Philadelphia

Assisi House, 600 Red Hill Rd., Aston, 19014. Tel: 610-459-8990; Fax: 610-558-5344. Email: JLAMANNA@osfPHILA.org. Web: www.osfphila.org. Home for retired Sisters of St. Francis of Philadelphia.

Audubon
Archdiocese of Philadelphia

St. Gabriel's Hall, Box 7280, Audubon, 19407-7280. Tel: 215-247-2776 (Philadelphia); 610-666-7970 (Audubon); Fax: 610-666-1479. Email: jlavoritano@chs_adphila.org. Offers residential treatment for court-committed delinquent boys, ages 10-18.

Bensalem
Archdiocese of Philadelphia

De La Salle Vocational Day Treatment Center, Box 344, Bensalem, 19020. Tel: 215-464-0344; Fax: 215-638-3767. Email: jlogan@chs-adphila.org. A community based day treatment program for court-committed delinquent boys, ages 15-18.

Bethlehem
Diocese of Allentown

Grace Mansion Personal Care Home of Catholic Senior Housing and Health Care Services, Inc., 1200 Spring St., Bethlehem, 18018. Tel: 610-865-6748; Fax: 610-997-8444. Email: kabruzzese@HFManor.org. Web: www.hfmanor.org. Personal care home for 25 elderly.

Holy Family Apartments of Catholic Housing Corporation of Bethlehem, 330-338 13th Ave., Bethlehem, 18018. Tel: 610-866-4603; Fax: 610-866-1622. Email: hfabeth@epix.net. Catholic housing for the elderly.

Holy Family Manor of Catholic Senior Housing and Health Care Services, Inc. (1963) Holy Family Manor: a division of Catholic Senior Housing and Health Care Services, Inc., 1200 Spring St., Bethlehem, 18018. Tel: 610-865-5595; Fax: 610-997-8454. Email: hkessler@hfmanor.org. Web: www.hfmanor.org. Skilled and intermediate nursing care facility for the aged, chronically ill, or invalid.

Trexler Pavilion, Assisted Living Residence of Catholic Senior Housing and Health Care Services, Inc., 1220 Prospect Ave., Bethlehem, 18018. Tel: 610-868-7776; Fax: 610-865-7775. Email: kabruzzese@HFManor.org. Web: www.hfmpc.org. Personal care/assisted living facility for 23 elderly.

Chester
Archdiocese of Philadelphia

Bernardine Center, 2625 W. Ninth St., Chester, 19013. Tel: 610-497-3225; Fax: 610-497-3659. Email: director@bernardinecenter.org. Web: www.bernardinecenter.org. West Side Brunch, Emergency Food Cupboard, Supercupboard Program, Advocacy, Computer Lab, English as a Second Language (ESL), Computer Classes, Parenting Classes, Anger Management Classes.

Darby
Archdiocese of Philadelphia

Villa Saint Joseph, 1436 Lansdowne Ave., Darby, 19023-1298. Tel: 610-586-8535; Fax: 610-586-2810. Home for aged, infirm and convalescent priests of the Archdiocese of Philadelphia.

Downingtown
Archdiocese of Philadelphia

Guest House at Saint John Vianney Center, 151 Woodbine Rd., Downingtown, 19335. Tel: 610-269-2600; Fax: 610-873-8028. Web: www.sjvcenter.org. An integrated dual diagnosis program, offering specialized treatment for co-occurring mental health and substance abuse disorders for religious and clergy.

St. John Vianney Center, 151 Woodbine Rd., Downingtown, 19335. Tel: 610-269-2600; Fax: 610-518-2020. Web: www.sjvcenter.org. Center for Behavioral Healthcare for Priests, Brothers, and Sisters.

Erie
Diocese of Erie

Gannondale, Inc., 4635 E. Lake Rd., Erie, 16511. Tel: 814-899-7659; Fax: 814-898-4266. Email: gdale@gannondale.org. Web: www.gannondale.org.

St. Patrick Haven, Inc., 147 E. 12th St., Erie, 16501. Tel: 814-454-7219; 814-836-4134; Fax: 814-836-4278.

Harborcreek
Diocese of Erie

Harborcreek Youth Services, 5712 Iroquois Ave., Harborcreek, 16421. Tel: 814-899-7664; Fax: 814-899-3075. Email: jpetulla@hys-erie.org.

Harrisburg
Diocese of Harrisburg

Adoption Services, 939 E. Park Dr., Ste. 103, Harrisburg, 17111. Tel: 717-564-7115; Fax: 717-564-7180.

Hollidaysburg
Diocese of Altoona-Johnstown

Dmitri Manor Priests' Residence, St. Mary's Ln., Hollidaysburg, 16648. Tel: 814-696-4698.

Lancaster
Diocese of Harrisburg

Intensive Day Treatment, 47 S. Mulberry St., Lancaster, 17603. Tel: 717-295-9630; Fax: 717-295-9525.

Meadville
Diocese of Erie

St. James Haven, 169 Walnut St., Meadville, 16335.

New Brighton
Diocese of Pittsburgh

McGuire Memorial (1963) 2119 Mercer Rd., New Brighton, 15066-3437. Tel: 724-843-3400; Fax: 724-847-2004. Email: mcgm@mcguirememorial.org. Web: www.mcguirememorial.org. Residential Facility-Intermediate Care for Developmentally Challenged; Private School, Licensed Adult Training, Community Homes, Employment Option Center.

Philadelphia
Archdiocese of Philadelphia

Casa del Carmen, 4400 N. Reese St., Philadelphia, 19140. Tel: 215-329-5660; Fax: 215-329-6722. Offers emergency crisis social services to the Spanish speaking community in Philadelphia and surrounding areas.

De La Salle-In-Towne Day Treatment Center, 25 S. Van Pelt St., Philadelphia, 19103. Tel: 215-567-5500; Fax: 215-567-6922. Email: cgaus@chs-adphila.org. A community-based day treatment program for court-committed delinquent boys, ages 14-17.

Drueding Center, 413 W. Master St., Philadelphia, 19122. Tel: 215-769-1830; Fax: 215-787-0999. Email: acollins@holyredeemer.com. Web: www.druedingcenter.org. Subsidiary of Holy Redeemer Health System; Provides transitional housing and support services for homeless women with children; daycare is provided for the children.

**Holy Redeemer Home Care and Hospice* Holy Redeemer Support Services, 12265 Townsend Rd., Ste. 400, Philadelphia, 19154. Tel: 215-671-9200; Fax: 215-671-1950. Web: www.holyredeemer.com. Affiliate of Holy Redeemer Health System. Sponsor: Sisters of the Holy Redeemer; Medicare certified home health agency serving patients in their own homes; Medicare certified hospice program serving terminally ill patients and their families.

McAuley House, 1800 Morris St., Philadelphia, 19145. Tel: 215-271-5166; Fax: 215-271-1601.

Mercy Hospice, 334 S. 13th St., Philadelphia, 19107. Tel: 215-545-5153; Fax: 215-545-1872. Provides residential case management and referral services to homeless women, women in recovery who are single or are with their children. Mercy Hospice also provides lunch Monday thru Friday from 12:00 - 12:45 p.m. to homeless women and children. Showers, clothing and the use of a telephone are available on a limited basis.

Mount Nazareth, 2755 Holme Ave., Philadelphia, 19152. Tel: 215-338-8992; Fax: 215-338-8752. Home for retired and infirm sisters.

Norris Square Senior Community Center, 2121 N. Howard St., Philadelphia, 19133. Tel: 215-423-7241; Fax: 215-634-7751.

St. Anne's Senior Community Center, 2607 E. Cumberland St., Philadelphia, 19125. Tel: 215-423-2772; Fax: 215-423-2423.

St. Charles Senior Community Center, 1941 Christian St., Philadelphia, 19146. Tel: 215-790-9530; Fax: 215-790-9765.

St. Francis Inn, 2441 Kensington Ave., Philadelphia, 19125. Tel: 215-423-5845; Fax: 215-423-2289. Email: stfrancisinn@aol.com. Web: www.stfrancisinn.org. Hot meals for the poor.

St. Gabriel's System, Administrative Offices, 227 N. 18th St., Philadelphia, 19103. Tel: 215-665-8777; Fax: 215-665-8821. Email: jlavoritano@chs-adphila.org. Web: www.saintgabrielssystem.org. Administrative and Intake services for residential treatment; Day Treatment for Court-committed delinquent boys, ages 12-17. (See St. Gabriel's Hall, De LaSalle in Towne, De LaSalle Vocational and St. Gabriel's System Reintegration Services and Brother Rousseau Academy).

St. Joachim's Hall Group Home (16 females ages 12-21), 1509 Church St., Philadelphia, 19124. Tel: 215-992-5402; Cell: 267-574-1100; Fax: 215-992-5189.

St. Joan of Arc Hall (16 females ages 12-21), 3556 Frankford Ave., Philadelphia, 19134. Tel: 215-992-5070; Cell: 215-275-4560; Fax: 215-624-8355.

St. John's Hospice for Men, 1221 Race St., Philadelphia, 19107. Tel: 215-563-7763; Fax: 215-563-0108. Web: www.saintjohnshospice.org. Staffed by Catholic Social Services Archdiocese of Philadelphia.

St. Joseph Catholic Home for Children, 222 N. 17th St., Philadelphia, 19103.

St. Joseph's Hall Group Home (12 females ages 12-21), 477 E. Locust Ave., Philadelphia, 19144. Tel: 215-849-1316; Cell: 215-300-2315; Fax: 215-842-0387.

St. Lucy Day School for Children with Visual Impairments and Archbishop Ryan Academy for the Deaf, 4251 L St., Philadelphia, 19124. Tel: 215-289-4220; Fax: 215-289-4229. Email: APLucy01@nni.com. Web: www.slds.org.

St. Mary's Residence, 247 S. 5th St., Philadelphia, 19106. Tel: 215-922-4228; Fax: 215-922-0192.

St. Vincent Homes, Administrative Office Building, 1509 Church St., Philadelphia, 19124. Tel: 215-992-5402; Fax: 215-992-5198. Web: www.stvincenthome.org. Operates the following programs for court adjudicated dependent females ages 12-21 who suffer from abuse and neglect. All facilities are staffed 24/7.

St. Vincent's Services, 222 N. 17th St., Philadelphia, 19103.

Star Harbor Senior Community Center, 4700 Springfield Ave., Philadelphia, 19143. Tel: 215-724-4414; Fax: 215-726-7496.

The Good Shepherd Program of St. John's Hospice, 1225 Race St., Philadelphia, 19107. Tel: 215-569-1101; Fax: 215-569-1622.

Thea Bowman's Women's Center, 2858 Kensington Ave., Philadelphia, 19134. Tel: 215-739-1137. Women's day activity center.

Visitation Homes, 2638 Kensington Ave., Philadelphia, 19125. Tel: 215-425-2080; Fax: 215-425-1412. Residential service program for families making the transition from homelessness to permanent housing. The program offers 18 furnished one to three bedroom apartments and on site case management and life skill services. Referrals come through the City's Office of Emergency Shelter and Services. For a period of up to 2 years, residents are helped to achieve economic self sufficiency and address the other issues which led to their homelessness.

Women of Hope Lombard, 1210 Lombard St.,

Philadelphia, 19147. Tel: 215-732-1341; Fax: 215-732-0659. Residential Facility for chronically mentally ill homeless women.

Women of Hope-Vine, 251 N. Lawrence St., Philadelphia, 19106. Tel: 215-592-9116; Fax: 215-592-0650. Residential facility for chronically mentally ill homeless women.

Phoenixville
Archdiocese of Philadelphia

St. Mary's Franciscan Shelter, 209 Emmett St., Phoenixville, 19460. Tel: 610-933-3097; Fax: 610-917-9845. Email: stmarysfs@verizon.net. Web: stmarysfs.org.

Pittsburgh
Diocese of Pittsburgh

DePaul School for Hearing and Speech (1908) 6202 Alder St., Pittsburgh, 15206. Tel: 412-924-1012; Fax: 412-924-1036. Email: mjmac@depaulinst.com. Web: www.speakmiracles.org. Auditory-Oral day school for children with hearing, speech and language impairments.

Marian Hall Home, Inc. (1970) 934 Forest Ave., Pittsburgh, 15202-1118. Tel: 412-761-1999; Fax: 412-761-2556. Email: marian27@verizon.net. Purpose: to provide programs, facilities, and services, including, but not limited to, residential personal care, and long-term care homes for the elderly, ill, or disabled, including supportive services.

Mercy Outreach Ministries, Inc., 3333 Fifth Ave., Pittsburgh, 15213. Tel: 412-578-6202; Fax: 412-578-6180. Email: fmcdonough@carlow.edu.

Providence Family Support Center (1994) 3113 Brighton Rd., Pittsburgh, 15212-2456. Tel: 412-766-6730; Fax: 412-766-6775. Web: www.providenceconnections.org.

The Community at Holy Family Manor, Inc., 301 Bellevue Rd., Pittsburgh, 15229-2194. Tel: 412-931-6996; Fax: 412-931-7255. Web: chfmanor.org. Programs operating under The Community at Holy Family Manor: Mt. Nazareth Learning Center; Nazareth Housing Services; Holy Family Manor Personal Care Home.

Vincentian Home (1924) 111 Perrymont Rd., Pittsburgh, 15237. Tel: 412-366-5600; Fax: 412-366-1408. Web: www.vcs.org.

Vincentian de Marillac (1943) 5300 Stanton Ave., Pittsburgh, 15206. Tel: 412-361-2833; Fax: 412-361-1237. Email: mcoyne@vcs.org. Catholic, skilled nursing home.

Reading
Diocese of Allentown

Mary's Shelter, 736 Upland Ave., Reading, 19607. Tel: 610-376-1973; Fax: 610-376-5391. Email: dani@marysshelter.org. Web: www.marysshelter.org. A residence for pregnant, homeless young women and teens.

Sacred Heart Villa - Personal Care Community of the Missionary Sisters of the Most Sacred Heart of Jesus (2003) 51 Seminary Ave., Reading, 19605. Tel: 610-929-5751; Fax: 610-929-0762. Email: sacredheart-villa@comcast.com. Web: sacredheartvilla-readingpa.org.

Scranton
Diocese of Scranton

Lourdesmont (1889) 1327 Wyoming Ave., Scranton, 18509. Tel: 570-702-8360; Fax: 570-702-8621. Email: msherman@lourdesmont.org. Web: www.lourdesmont.org.

St. Joseph's Center (1888) 2010 Adams Ave., Scranton, 18509. Tel: 570-342-8379; Fax: 570-342-6080. Web: www.stjosephscenter.org.

Springfield
Archdiocese of Philadelphia

Cardinal Krol Center, 1799 S. Sproul Rd., Springfield, 19064. Tel: 484-475-2467; Fax: 610-543-5387. Web: developmentalprogramsphilly.org. A residential facility for 131 male adults with developmental/intellectual disabilities which provides an environment, both day and residential, that contributes to the individuals own growth and development by fulfilling their potential in the physical, mental, emotional, social, psychological, and spiritual areas of their lives.

Divine Providence Village, 686 Old Marple Rd., Springfield, 19064. Tel: 484-908-6501; Fax: 610-544-1710. Care & specialized training for developmentally disabled females.

Don Guanella School, 1797 S. Sproul Rd., Springfield, 19064-1195. Tel: 484-475-2467; Fax: 610-328-2136. Email: fr.dweber@chs-adphila.org. Web: developmentalprogramsphilly.org. Provides specialized care and residential treatment program for boys with developmental/intellectual disabilities ages 6-21.

Upper Darby
Archdiocese of Philadelphia

Dominican Pastoral Counseling, 131 Copley Rd., Upper Darby, 19082. Tel: 215-635-6027; Fax: 610-352-1947. Email: cealop1@verizon.net. Web: www.elkinsparkop.org.

Warminster
Archdiocese of Philadelphia

Regina Coeli Residence for Priests, 685 York Rd., Warminster, 18974. Tel: 215-441-4642. Home for retired priests of the Archdiocese of Philadelphia.

Wexford
Diocese of Pittsburgh

**St. Anthony School Programs*, 2000 Corporate Dr., Ste. 580, Wexford, 15090. Tel: 724-940-9020; Fax: 724-940-9064. Email: lgeorge@stanthonyschoolprograms.com. Resource rooms for students with special needs in 4 elementary schools, 2 high schools and 1 Post-Secondary Program.

Willow Grove
Archdiocese of Philadelphia

Our Lady of Confidence Day School, Willow Grove. Tel: 215-657-9311; Fax: 215-657-9312. Email: apConf01@nni.com. Web: www.ourladyofconfidence.org. Mentally Challenged.

PUERTO RICO

Bayamon
Archdiocese of San Juan, Puerto Rico

Hogar Del Nino "El Ave Maria Corp." (For Abused Children), Carretera 861, km 2.0, Bo. Pajaros Americanos, Bayamon, 00957. Tel: 787-797-2382; 787-279-3003; Fax: 787-797-2382. Mailing Address: PMS 239, P.O. Box 607061, Bayamon, 00960-7061.

Hogar Escuela Sor Maria Rafaela (Girls with Problems), Carretera 871, km 1.0, Bo. El Volcan, Hato Tejas, Bayamon, 00961. Tel: 787-785-9517; 787-785-1125; Fax: 787-787-5324; 787-779-0449. Email: hogar.sormaria@gmail.com. P.O. Box 3024, Bayamon, PR 00960.

Hogar Fatima (Girls), Ave. Santa Juanita Final, Camino Esteban Cruz, Bayamon, 00961. Fax: 787-780-9763. Email: fatima001@prttc.net. Web: www.osrhogarfatimainc.com. P.O. Box 4228, Bayamon Garden Sta., Bayamon, 00958-4228. Tel: 787-787-2580; Fax: 787-780-9763.

Hogar Santisima Trinidad (Drug Addiction Rehabilitation Home), Lote A y Lote B, km 7.0, Bo Mucarabones, Carr. 861, Toa Alta, 00954. Tel: 787-799-6208; Fax: 787-799-1977. Email: trinita@prtc.net. PMB 326, P.O. Box 607061, Bayamon, 00960-7061.

Bayamon Garden Sta., Bayamon
Archdiocese of San Juan, Puerto Rico

Hogar Fatima (Girls), Ave. Santa Juanita Final, Camino Esteban Cruz, Bayamon, 00961. Fax: 787-780-9763. Email: fatima001@prttc.net. Web: www.osrhogarfatimainc.com. P.O. Box 4228, Bayamon Garden Sta., Bayamon, 00958-4228. Tel: 787-787-2580; Fax: 787-780-9763.

Canovanas
Diocese of Fajardo-Humacao, Puerto Rico

Hogar Teresa Toda (1993) (For Girls), P.O. Box 868, Canovanas, 00729. Tel: 787-886-2060; Fax: 787-886-2075. Email: hteresatoda@aol.com; teresatoda@prtc.net. Web: www.teresatodapr.org. Calle 5-A, R-14, Villa De Loiza, Loiza, 00729. Tel: 787-886-2060; Fax: 787-886-2075.

Dorado
Archdiocese of San Juan, Puerto Rico

Santuario del Espiritu Santo, Box 187, Dorado, 00646-0187. Tel: 787-796-2798; Fax: 787-796-1359. Email: espiritanospr@gmail.com. Web: www.espiritanos.com.

Loiza
Diocese of Fajardo-Humacao, Puerto Rico

Hogar Teresa Toda (1993) (For Girls), P.O. Box 868, Canovanas, 00729. Tel: 787-886-2060; Fax: 787-886-2075. Email: hteresatoda@aol.com; teresatoda@prtc.net. Web: www.teresatodapr.org. Calle 5-A, R-14, Villa De Loiza, Loiza, 00729. Tel: 787-886-2060; Fax: 787-886-2075.

Mayaguez
Diocese of Mayaguez, Puerto Rico

Asylum for the Poor and Aged, Calle Ramon E. Betances 162 Sur., Mayaguez, 00680.

Ponce
Diocese of Ponce, Puerto Rico

Missionaries of Charity (1989)Mailing Address: P.O. Box 32177, Ponce, 00732-2177. Tel: 787-841-5443. *Hna. Selma M.C. (D) Home for the Aged*, 683 Ramos Antonini, El Tuque, Ponce, 00728. Tel: 787-841-5443.

Puerta De Tierra
Archdiocese of San Juan, Puerto Rico

Asylum For The Aged and Infirm (Hogar de Ntra. Sra. de la Providencia), Stop 5, Edif. 205, Puerta De Tierra, 00906-6571. Tel: 787-722-1331; 787-723-2419; 787-724-3574; Fax: 787-725-4308. Mailing Address: P.O. Box 9066571, San Juan, 00906-6571.

Rio Piedras
Archdiocese of San Juan, Puerto Rico

Centro N. Sra. de la Providencia Sisters of Notre Dame., R.F.D. #2, Box 16T, Rio Piedras, 00928. Tel: 787-761-0273.

Centro Santa Luisa (1972) (Services for the Elderly), Carretera 842, Camino Los Romeros km 1.5, Bo. Caimito, Rio Piedras, 00926. Tel: 787-720-2764; Fax: 787-731-7795. Email: centrosantaluisa@yahoo.com. Web: www.geocities.com/centrosantaluisa. Mailing Address: R.R. 6 Box 9492, San Juan, 00926-9492.

San Juan
Archdiocese of San Juan, Puerto Rico

Asylum For The Aged and Infirm (Hogar de Ntra. Sra. de la Providencia), Stop 5, Edif. 205, Puerta De Tierra, 00906-6571. Tel: 787-722-1331; 787-723-2419; 787-724-3574; Fax: 787-725-4308. Mailing Address: P.O. Box 9066571, San Juan, 00906-6571.

Casa La Providencia (Drug Addicted Women), Calle Norzagaray #200, San Juan, 00901. Tel: 787-725-5358; Fax: 787-725-0058. Email: casalaprovidencia@hotmail.com. P.O. Box 9020614, San Juan, 00902-0614.

Casa La Providencia, Inc. Drug Rehabilitation Center, P.O. Box 9020614, San Juan, 00902-0614. Tel: 787-725-5358; Fax: 787-725-0058. Email: casalaprovidencia@hotmail.com. Web: casalaprovidenciapr.org.

Casa de Ninos Manuel Fernandez Juncos (Orphans and Abused Boys) , Calle Villa Verde Esq. Refugio, Pda 11, Miramar, Santurce, 00940. Tel: 787-724-2904; 787-725-6328; Fax: 787-724-0980. P.O. Box 9020163, San Juan, 00902-0163.

Centro De Orientacion Vocacional Nuestra Senora del Consuelo, Floral Park, 20 C. Matienzo Citron, San Juan, 00919. Tel: 787-250-6323; Fax: 787-250-6323. Email: oblahchr@prte.net.

Centro Medico de P.R., Calle 10 #1030, Puerto Nuevo, 00920. Apdo. 347, San Juan, 00936. Tel: 787-763-7272.

Centro Santa Luisa (1972) (Services for the Elderly), Carretera 842, Camino Los Romeros km 1.5, Bo. Caimito, Rio Piedras, 00926. Tel: 787-720-2764; Fax: 787-731-7795. Email: centrosantaluisa@yahoo.com. Web: www.geocities.com/centrosantaluisa. Mailing Address: R.R. 6 Box 9492, San Juan, 00926-9492.

Hogar Carmelitano Julian Bengochea Final (Elderly Retirement Hospice), Calle Julian Bengoechea Final, San Juan, 00924. Tel: 787-769-6510; 787-769-3110; Fax: 787-768-1240.

Hogares Rafaela Ibarra (Orphan or Abused Girls), Urb.San Jose 432 Calle Torrelaguna, San Juan, 00923. Tel: 787-763-1204; Fax: 787-763-6266. Web: www.hogaresrafaelaybarra.com. 432 Calle Torrelaguna, San Juan, 00923-1773.

Politecnico Amigo (For School Dropout Boys), Calle Refugio #960, Pda II, Santurce, 00940. Tel: 787-725-2059; Fax: 787-722-3436. Email: polam@prtc.net. P.O. Box 13204, San Juan, 00908.

Santurce
Archdiocese of San Juan, Puerto Rico

Casa de Ninos Manuel Fernandez Juncos (Orphans and Abused Boys) , Calle Villa Verde Esq. Refugio, Pda 11, Miramar, Santurce, 00940. Tel: 787-724-2904; 787-725-6328; Fax: 787-724-0980. P.O. Box 9020163, San Juan, 00902-0163.

Politecnico Amigo (For School Dropout Boys), Calle

Refugio #960, Pda II, Santurce, 00940. Tel: 787-725-2059; Fax: 787-722-3436. Email: polam@prtc.net. P.O. Box 13204, San Juan, 00908.

Toa Alta
Archdiocese of San Juan, Puerto Rico

Hogar Santisima Trinidad (Drug Addiction Rehabilitation Home), Lote A y Lote B, km 7.0, Bo Mucarabones, Carr. 861, Toa Alta, 00954. Tel: 787-799-6208; Fax: 787-799-1977. Email: trinita@prtc.net. PMB 326, P.O. Box 607061, Bayamon, 00960-7061.

Toa Baja
Archdiocese of San Juan, Puerto Rico

Hogar Divino Nino Jesus, Carretera 854, Km. 3.5, Toa Baja, 00949. Tel: 787-794-0020; Fax: 787-794-3124. Email: divinoninojesus@yahoo.es. P.O. Box 2464, Toa Baja, 00951-2662. (Detox and Tx Residencial)

RHODE ISLAND

Pawtucket
Diocese of Providence

Outreach and Tracking Program, 242 Dexter St., Pawtucket, 02860. Tel: 401-724-8380; Fax: 401-724-8899.

Preserving Families Network, 242 Dexter St., Pawtucket, 02860. Tel: 401-724-8201; Fax: 401-724-8899. 215 Washington St., West Warwick, 02893. 790 Broad St., Providence, 02905.

Providence
Diocese of Providence

Preserving Families Network, 242 Dexter St., Pawtucket, 02860. Tel: 401-724-8201; Fax: 401-724-8899. 215 Washington St., West Warwick, 02893. 790 Broad St., Providence, 02905.

Southern New England Rehabilitation Center, Providence. Tel: 401-456-4500; Fax: 401-456-4501. Web: www.snerc.com. A joint venture of St. Joseph Hospital and Rhode Island Hospital.

West Warwick
Diocese of Providence

Preserving Families Network, 242 Dexter St., Pawtucket, 02860. Tel: 401-724-8201; Fax: 401-724-8899. 215 Washington St., West Warwick, 02893. 790 Broad St., Providence, 02905.

Woonsocket
Diocese of Providence

Woonsocket Outreach Project, 55 Main St., Ste. 1, Woonsocket, 02895. Tel: 401-766-9320; Fax: 401-766-9324.

SOUTH CAROLINA

Johns Island
Diocese of Charleston

Our Lady of Mercy Community Outreach Services, Inc. (1989) 1684 Brownswood Rd., Johns Island, 29455. Tel: 843-559-4109; Fax: 843-559-8819. Email: info@olmoutreach.org. Web: olmoutreach.org. P.O. Box 607, Johns Island, 29457. Tel: 843-559-4109; Fax: 843-558-8819. Sponsored by Sisters of Charity of Our Lady of Mercy.

SOUTH DAKOTA

Manderson
Diocese of Rapid City

St. Francis Home, P.O. Box 122, Manderson, 57756-0122. Tel: 605-455-2077; Fax: 605-455-1680. Email: geraldineosf@aol.com. Home for abandoned and abused children (Licensed) 2-18 years of age. 6 children at a time.

Sioux Falls
Diocese of Sioux Falls

Community Outreach, 231 N. Weber Ave., Sioux Falls, 57103. Tel: 605-331-3935; Fax: 605-336-8924. Email: info@thecommunityoutreach.org.

TENNESSEE

Knoxville
Diocese of Knoxville

Columbus Home, 3227 Division St., Knoxville, 37919. Tel: 865-971-3560; Fax: 865-544-0538.

Memphis
Diocese of Memphis

Shelter, Memphis. Tel: 901-526-5456.

Nashville
Diocese of Nashville

Ladies of Charity Welfare Agency, Inc. (1617) 2212 State St., Nashville, 37203. Tel: 615-327-3430; Fax: 615-321-3312. Email: locwelfare@bellsouth.net.

Mid-Tennessee Rural Outreach Association, 30 White Bridge Rd., Nashville, 37205. Tel: 615-352-3087.

TEXAS

Amarillo
Diocese of Amarillo

Downtown Women's Center, Inc., 409 S. Monroe, Amarillo, 79101. Tel: 806-372-3625; Fax: 806-372-9026. Email: diann@dwcenter.org.

Beaumont
Diocese of Beaumont

Counseling Services, 2780 Eastex Fwy., Beaumont, 77703-4617. Tel: 409-924-4418; Fax: 409-832-0145.

Hospitality Center, 3959 Gulfway Dr., Port Arthur, 77642. Tel: 409-982-4842; Fax: 409-983-7145. 2780 Eastex Fwy., Beaumont, 77703.

El Paso
Diocese of El Paso

Catholic Counseling Services, Inc., 499 St. Matthews St., El Paso, 79907. Tel: 915-872-8424; Fax: 915-872-8425. Email: jcastrellon@elpasodiocese.org.

Fort Worth
Diocese of Fort Worth

Assessment Center of Tarrant, 249 W. Thornhill Dr., Fort Worth, 76115. Tel: 817-534-0814; Fax: 817-531-2996. (Children's Shelter)

Clinical Counseling Department, 249 W. Thornhill Dr., Fort Worth, 76115. Tel: 817-534-0814; Fax: 817-536-1556.

Houston
Archdiocese of Galveston-Houston

Casa Juan Diego (1980) P.O. Box 70113, Houston, 77270. Tel: 713-869-7376; Fax: 713-864-7295. Email: info@cjd.org. Web: www.cjd.org. 4818 Rose, Houston, 77007.

Casa de Esperanza De Los Ninos, Inc. (1982) P.O. Box 66581, Houston, 77266-6581. Tel: 713-529-0639; Fax: 713-529-9179. Email: casa@casahope.org. Web: www.casahope.org. Homes for children in crisis situations, foster care, adoption.

Covenant House Texas, 1111 Lovett Blvd., Houston, 77006. Tel: 713-523-2231; Fax: 713-523-6904. Email: Rgrobinson@covenanthouse.org. Web: www.covenanthousetx.org.

Magnificat Houses Inc. (1968) P.O. Box 25415, Houston, 77265. Tel: 713-520-0461; Fax: 713-520-0461. Email: magnificathouseinc@sbcglobal.net. Web: www.mhihouston.org.

San Jose Clinic (1922) 2615 Fannin, Houston, 77002. Tel: 713-490-2602; Fax: 713-228-2612. Email: leeannkroon@sanjoseclinic.org. Web: www.sanjoseclinic.org.

Santa Maria Hostel, 2605 Parker Rd., Houston, 77093. Tel: 713-691-0900; 713-957-2413; Fax: 713-691-0910. Email: kaustin@santamariahostel.org. Web: www.santamariahostel.org. 2005 Jacquelyn Rd., Houston, 77055. Tel: 713-957-2413; Fax: 713-400-1119. Intensive and supportive residential treatment; housing, shelter and outpatient services (substance abuse) for women ages 18 and above and women with their children. Treatment for co-occurring disorders is also provided.

Port Arthur
Diocese of Beaumont

Hospitality Center, 3959 Gulfway Dr., Port Arthur, 77642. Tel: 409-982-4842; Fax: 409-983-7145. 2780 Eastex Fwy., Beaumont, 77703.

San Angelo
Diocese of San Angelo

Catholic Outreach Services, 410 N. Chadbourne, San Angelo, 76903. Tel: 915-658-4124; Fax: 915-481-0315. Email: cos.margie@verizon.net. Thrift Store Social Services.

San Antonio
Archdiocese of San Antonio

Bro. Charles Andersen Residence, 320 Brahan Blvd., San Antonio, 78215. Tel: 210-223-9117; Fax: 210-223-2081.

Catholic Counseling and Consultation Center, 7711 Madonna, San Antonio, 78216. Tel: 210-377-1133; Fax: 210-377-1230. See Curia Section - Department of Social & Community Services.

Christus Continuing Care dba Christus Homecare 4241 Woodcock Dr., Ste. A-100, San Antonio, 78228. Tel: 210-785-5401; Fax: 210-785-5490. Email: christopher.karam@ChristusHealth.org. Web: www.christushomecare.org.

Guadalupe Home for Homeless Pregnant Women, 1223 S. Trinity St., San Antonio, 78207. Tel: 210-476-0707; Fax: 210-224-7388.

Project Rachel of San Antonio, 9862 Lorene Ln., Ste. 108, San Antonio, 78216. Tel: 210-342-4673; 210-722-4213 (Spanish); (800) 651-HOPE; Fax: 210-341-1572. Email: rachel@anewchoice.org. Web: www.anewchoice.org; www.projectrachelsanantonio.org.

Seton Home, 1115 Mission Rd., San Antonio, 78210. Tel: 210-533-3504; Fax: 210-533-3467. Email: margretstarkey@setonhomesa.org. Web: www.setonhomesa.org.

Visitation House Ministries, 945 W. Huisache, San Antonio, 78201. Tel: 210-735-6910; Fax: 210-738-8794. Web: www.vhmin.org. A nonprofit corporation chartered under the laws of the State of Texas; Provides a two year transitional housing program for homeless women and children and learning center for women.

Splendora
Archdiocese of Galveston-Houston

Shalom Center, Inc. (1980) 13516 Morgan Dr., Splendora, 77372-3121. Tel: 281-399-0520; Fax: 281-399-3366. Email: info@shalomcenterinc.org. Web: www.shalomcenterinc.org. A residential treatment center for priests, brothers and sisters.

UTAH

Ogden
Diocese of Salt Lake City

Catholic Community Services Basic Needs Services - Ogden, 2504 F. Ave., Ogden, 84401. Tel: 801-394-5944; Fax: 801-621-8468. Mailing Address: 2504 F Ave., Ogden, 84401.

Salt Lake City
Diocese of Salt Lake City

Basic Needs Services - Salt Lake Bishop K. Weigand Day Center, 437 W. 200 S., Salt Lake City, 84104. Tel: 801-363-7710; Fax: 801-595-8532.

Basic Needs Services - Salt Lake St. Vincent de Paul Dining Hall, 437 W. 200 S., Salt Lake City, 84104. Tel: 801-363-7710; Fax: 801-595-8532.

Treatment Services - St. Mary's Home for Men, 745 E. 300 S., Salt Lake City, 84102. Tel: 801-328-1894; Fax: 801-328-1895. Residential Substance Abuse Treatment for Adult Males.

VIRGINIA

Lynchburg
Diocese of Richmond

Nott Homes, Inc., 3009-3011 Roundelay Rd., Lynchburg, 24502. Tel: 434-239-0722; Fax: 434-239-1042.

Virginia Beach
Diocese of Richmond

Assisi House, P.O. Box 2400, #159, Virginia Beach, 23450-2400. Tel: 757-450-3671. Email: denibrown@msn.com.

WASHINGTON

Chehalis
Archdiocese of Seattle

Providence Place, 350 S.E. Washington Ave., Chehalis, 98532. Tel: 360-740-8389; Fax: 360-740-6504.

Chewelah
Diocese of Spokane

Providence DominiCare, 110 S. Third St. E., P.O. Box 1070, Chewelah, 99109. Tel: 509-935-4925; Fax: 509-935-4082. Email: joan.sisco@providence.org. Web: www.providence-.org. A home care/personal care service in Stevens, Pierce & Pend Oreille Counties.

Everett
Archdiocese of Seattle

Providence Hospice and Home Care of Snohomish County, 2731 Wetmore Ave., #500, Everett, 98201. Tel: 425-261-4800; Fax: 425-261-4725. Web: www.providence.org/phhc.

Olympia
Archdiocese of Seattle

Providence Mother Joseph Care Center, 3333 Ensign Rd., N.E., Olympia, 98506. Tel: 360-493-4900; Fax: 360-493-4000.

Providence Sound HomeCare and Hospice, 3432 South Bay Rd. N.E., Olympia, 98506. Tel: 800-869-7062; 360-459-8311; Fax: 360-493-4657. Web: www.providence.org.

Seattle
Archdiocese of Seattle

Heritage House at The Market, 1533 Western Ave., Seattle, 98101. Tel: 206-382-4119; Fax: 206-382-0201. Email: charlene.nichols@providence.org.

Martin Luther King. Jr., Day Home Center, 1855 S. Lane St., Seattle, 98144-2907. Tel: 206-328-5670; Fax: 206-325-5922.

Providence Mount St. Vincent, 4831 35th Ave. S., Seattle, 98126. Tel: 206-937-3700; Fax: 206-938-8999. Email: thomas.mitchell@providence.org. Web: www.providence.org/themount.

Providence Peter Claver House, 7101 38th Ave. S., Seattle, 98118. Tel: 206-721-6265; Fax: 206-721-1327. Email: duong.nguyen@providence.org.

Providence Vincent House, 1423 First Ave., Seattle, 98101. Tel: 206-682-9307; Fax: 206-682-0548.

Spokane
Diocese of Spokane

Bernadette Place, Mailing Address: P.O. Box 2253, Spokane, 99210-2253. Tel: 509-326-0547. 925 N. A St., #2, Spokane, 99210-2253. This complex houses twelve developmentally delayed women; 6 units of affordable housing for persons with disabilities and special needs.

Emilie Court Assisted Living (Providence Health & Services-Washington), 34 E. 8th Ave., Spokane, 99202-1202. Tel: 509-474-2550; Fax: 509-474-2618. Email: charlene.longworth@providence.org.

St. Joseph's Counseling Center dba St. Joseph Family Center N. 1016 Superior St., Spokane, 99202-2059. Tel: 509-483-6495; Fax: 509-483-1541. Email: sjfc@sjfconline.org. Web: www.sjfconline.org.

St. Margaret's Shelter, P.O. Box 2253, Spokane, 99210-2253. Tel: 509-624-9788; Fax: 509-624-1461. Emergency and transitional shelter for women & children.

Transitional Living Center, 3128 N. Hemlock, Spokane, 99205. Tel: 509-325-2959; 509-328-6702; Fax: 509-325-8319. Email: ktalbott@help4women.org. Web: www.help4women.org. Housing for homeless women & children.

Transitional Programs for Women, 3104 W. Fort George Wright Dr., Spokane, 99224. Tel: 509-328-6702; Fax: 509-325-9877. Email: dmaurer@help4women.org. Web: www.help4women.org.

Women's Hearth, 920 W. Second Ave., Spokane, 99201. Tel: 509-456-3531; Fax: 509-456-3531. Web: www.help4women.org. A safe place for women at risk.

WEST VIRGINIA

Pineville
Diocese of Wheeling-Charleston

Children's Health Care, Inc., Box 430, Pineville, 24874. Tel: 304-732-7069; Fax: 304-732-7098. Email: ecatters@marshall.edu.

Rhodell
Diocese of Wheeling-Charleston

Rhodell Health Clinic (1975) P.O. Box 158, Rhodell, 25915. Tel: 304-683-4318.

WISCONSIN

Appleton
Diocese of Green Bay

Global Outreach, Inc. (1994) 4815 Whitetail Way, Appleton, 54914. Tel: 920-734-5967. Email: boryczkabb@sbcglobal.net. Web: www.globaloutreachprogram.com.

Chippewa Falls
Diocese of La Crosse

L.E. Phillips Libertas Treatment Center (1977) 2661 County Hwy. I, Chippewa Falls, 54729. Tel: 715-723-5585; 800-680-4578; Fax: 715-726-3504. Email: ddachel@sjcf.hshs.org. Web: www.stjoeschipfalls.com.

Green Bay
Diocese of Green Bay

McClosky Program, Inc., 2560 Shawano Ave., P.O. Box 10357, Green Bay, 54313. Tel: 920-434-8208; Fax: 920-662-0047. A Community based residential facility for women 18 years old and over who are pregnant or in a crisis situation and in need of transitional supervision and guidance. Needs addressed are personal and family problems. Also, shelter offered during crisis or unemployment.

Our Lady of Charity Center, Inc., 2560 Shawano Ave., P.O. Box 10357, Green Bay, 54313. Tel: 920-434-8208; Fax: 920-662-0047.

Kenosha
Archdiocese of Milwaukee

Assisi Homes - Kenosha, Inc. (1994) Independent Housing for Low Income Elderly, 1860 27th Ave., Kenosha, 53140. Tel: 262-551-9821; Fax: 262-551-9843. Web: www.fm-inc.org.

Assisi Homes - Saxony, Inc. (1994) Independent Housing for Low Income Elderly, 1876 22nd Ave., Kenosha, 53140. Tel: 262-551-9005; Fax: 262-551-7586. Web: www.fm-inc.org.

Franciscan Seniors, Kenosha, Inc. (1994) 1920 27th Ave., Kenosha, 53140. Tel: 630-462-9271; 262-551-0989; Fax: 262-551-8683. Web: www.fm-inc.org.

La Crosse
Diocese of La Crosse

Gerard Hall, La Crosse. Tel: 608-791-3985; Fax: 608-791-7802. 8 bed home for women with AODA, MH, or Pregnancy and Parenting Issues.

Madison
Diocese of Madison

Central City Counseling Services, 30 S. Franklin St., Madison, 53703. Tel: 608-256-2358; Fax: 608-256-2350.

Marshfield
Archdiocese of Milwaukee

Ministry Home Care, Inc. (1998) Marshfield. Tel: 715-389-3802; Fax: 715-387-9950.

Milwaukee
Archdiocese of Milwaukee

Assisi Homes - Jefferson Court, Inc. (1993) 415 E. Knapp St., Milwaukee, 53202. Tel: 414-271-5370; Fax: 414-271-5988. Web: www.fm-inc.org.

Daystar, Inc., P.O. Box 2130, Milwaukee, 53201-2130. Tel: 414-385-0334; Fax: 414-385-0336. Email: daystar@daystarinc.org. Web: www.daystarinc.org. Transitional living program for formerly battered women without children, for up to two years.

Eastside Senior Services (1974) 2618 N. Hackett Ave., Milwaukee, 53211. Tel: 414-961-0661; Fax: 414-961-0661. Email: eastside@interfaithmilw.org. Corporate Title: Eastside Senior Services, Inc. - an Interfaith Outreach Program

Sacred Heart Rehabilitation Institute, Inc. (1955) *The Heritage Center*, 2320 N. Lake Dr., Ste. 1700A, Milwaukee, 53211. 2301 N. Lake Dr., Milwaukee, 53211. Fax: 414-270-4869. Ascension Health System.

St. Charles Youth and Family Services, Inc. (1920) 151 S. 84th St., Milwaukee, 53214. Tel: 414-476-3710; Fax: 414-778-5985. Email: scarpenter@stcharlesinc.org. Web: www.stcharlesinc.org.

Wheaton Franciscan Home Health and Hospice, Inc. (1986) 3070 N. 51st St., Ste. 406, Milwaukee, 53210-1661. Tel: 414-874-6161. Web: www.mywheaton.org.

Mount Calvary
Archdiocese of Milwaukee

Cristo Rey Ranch, Inc., 998 Calvary St., Mount Calvary, 53057. Tel: 920-753-2026; 920-753-3211; Fax: 920-753-3100. Email: wbodden@villalorettonh.org; nunbetterfarm@hotmail.com. Provides weekend respite services to families caring for emotionally/behaviorally challenged children and adolescents. Program emphasis on pet therapy. Some day and evening programs thru County Social Services Department.

Oshkosh
Diocese of Green Bay

The Convent Project, Inc., 449 High Ave., Oshkosh, 54901. Tel: 920-233-1894. Email: baker8983@sbcglobal.net. For victims of domestic abuse.

Prairie du Chien
Diocese of La Crosse

Villa Success, Prairie du Chien, 53821. Tel: 608-326-8424; Fax: 608-326-8638. 12 bed halfway house for AODA and AODA outpatient and Detox programs.

Rhinelander
Diocese of Superior

Retired Senior Volunteer Program, 1835 N. Stevens St., Ste. 22, Rhinelander, 54501. Tel: 715-362-1919. Mailing Address: 1416 Cumming Ave., Superior, 54880.

Superior
Diocese of Superior

Retired Senior Volunteer Program, 1416 Cumming Ave., Superior, 54880. Tel: 715-394-4425; Fax: 715-394-5951.

Retired Senior Volunteer Program, 1835 N. Stevens St., Ste. 22, Rhinelander, 54501. Tel: 715-362-1919. Mailing Address: 1416 Cumming Ave., Superior, 54880.

Woodruff
Archdiocese of Milwaukee

Dr. Kate Newcomb Convalescent Center, Inc. (1980) Woodruff. Tel: 715-356-8560; Fax: 715-356-6097.

WYOMING

Casper
Diocese of Cheyenne

Shelter, 324 E. H St., P.O. Box 1557, Casper, 82602. Tel: 307-577-8026; Fax: 307-577-0125.

An Alphabetical List of Diocesan and Religious Priests of the United States

REPORTED TO THE PUBLISHERS FOR THIS ISSUE
(Cardinals, Archbishops, Bishops, Archabbots and Abbots are listed in previous section)

ABBREVIATIONS

A.A. Assumptionists
B.C.S. Brothers of Christian Service
B.G.S. Little Brothers of the Good Shepherd
B.S.O. Basilian Salvatorian Fathers
C.F.A. Alexian Brothers
C.F.C. Congregation of Christian Brothers
C.F.M.M. Brothers of Our Lady, Mother of Mercy
C.F.P. Brothers of the Poor of St. Francis
C.F.R. Franciscan Friars of the Renewal
C.F.X. Brothers of St. Francis Xavier
C.I.C.M. Missionhurst Congregation of the Immaculate Heart of Mary
C.J. Josephite Fathers
C.J.M. Congregation of Jesus and Mary
C.M. Congregation of the Mission
C.M.C. Congregation of Mother Coredemptrix
C.M.F. Claretian Missionaries
C.M.I. Carmelites of Mary Immaculate
C.M.L.M. The Congregation of Maronite Lebanese Missionaries
C.M.M. Congregation of Mananhill Missionaries, Marianhill Fathers & Brothers
C. M.Vd. Mekhitarist Fathers
C.O. Oratorians
C.P. Congregation of the Passion
C.P.M. Congregation of the Fathers of Mercy
C.PP.S. Society of the Precious Blood
C.R. Congregation of the Resurrection
C.R. Theatine Fathers
C.R.I.C. Canons Regular of the Immaculate Conception
C.R.L. Canons Regular of the Lateran
C.R.M. Adorno Fathers
C.R.S. Somascan Fathers
C.R.S.P. Clerics Regular of St. Paul
C.S. Missionaries of St. Charles Scalabrinians
C.S.B. Basilian Fathers
C.S.C. Brothers of the Congregation of Holy Cross
C.S.C. Priests of the Congregation of Holy Cross
C.S.J. Congregation of St. Joseph
C.S.J.B. Congregation of St. John the Baptist
C.S.P. Paulist Fathers
C.S.P.X. Brothers of Saint Pius X
C.S.S. Stigmatine Fathers and Brothers.
C.S.Sp. Congregation of the Holy Spirit
C.SS.R. Redemptorist Fathers
C.S.V. Clerics of St. Viator
D.L.P. Diocesan Labor Priests
Er.Cam. Camaldolese Hermits of the Congregation of Monte Corona
F.C. Brothers of Charity
F.D.P. Sons of Divine Providence
F.F.I. Franciscan Friars of the Immaculate
F.F.S C. Franciscan Brothers of the Holy Cross
F.I.C. Brothers of Christian Instruction
F.J. Congregation of St. John
F.M.M. Brothers of Mercy
F.M.M. Missionary Fraternity of Mary
F.M.S. The Marist Brothers
F.M.S.I. Sons of Mary Missionary Society
F.P.M. Presentation Brothers
F.S.C. Brothers of the Christian Schools
F.S.C.B. Priestly Fraternity of the Missionaries of St. Charles Borromeo, Inc
F.S.E. Brothers of the Holy Eucharist
F.S.P. Brothers of St. Patrick
F.S.R. Brothers of the Congregation of Our Lady of the Holy Rosary
F.S.S.P. Priestly Fraternity of St. Peter
G.H.M. The Glenmary Home Missioners
H.J.D. Los Hermanos de Juan Diego
H.M.C. Hermits of Mount Carmel
I.C. Institute of Charity
I.C. Incarnational Consecration
I.H.M. Brothers of the Immaculate Heart of Mary
I.M.C. Consolata Missionaries
I.S.S.S. Schoenstatt Institute of Secular Priests
L.B.S.F. Little Brothers of Saint Francis
L.C. Legionaries of Christ
M.Afr. Missionaries of Africa
M.C.B.S. Missionary Congregation of the Blessed Sacrament
M.C.C.J. Comboni Missionaries of the Heart of Jesus (Verona)
M.Des. Mercedarios Descalzos
M.E.P. Paris Foreign Mission Society
M.G. Guadalupe Missioners
M.H.M. Mill Hill Missionaries
M.I.C. Congregation of Marians of the Immaculate Conception
M.J. Missionaries of St. Joseph (Mexico)
M.M. Maryknoll
M.S. The Missionaries of Our Lady of La Salette
M.S.A. Missionaries of the Holy Apostles
M.S.C. Missionaries of the Sacred Heart
M.S.F. Congregation of the Missionaries of the Holy Family
M.S.P. Missionaries of St. Paul
M.Sp.S. Missionaries of the Holy Spirit
M.SS.CC. Missionaries of the Sacred Hearts of Jesus and Mary
O.A.R. Order of the Augustinian Recollects
O.Carm. Carmelite Fathers and Brothers
O.Cart. Order of Carthusians
O.C.D. Discalced Carmelite Fathers
O.Cist. Cistercian Fathers
O.C.S.O. The Cistercian Order of the Strict Observance (Trappists)
O.de.M. Order of Our Lady of Mercy
O.F.M. Franciscan Friars
O.F.M-.Cap. The Capuchin Friars
O.F.M-.Conv. Conventual Franciscans
O.H. Hospitaller Brothers of St. John of God
O.I.C. Order of the Imitation of Christ
O.L P. Brothers of Our Lady of Providence
O.M. Minim Fathers
O.Mar. Congregation of Maronite Monks
O.M.I. Oblates of Mary Immaculate
O.M.V. Oblates of the Virgin Mary
O.P. Order of Preachers (Dominicans)
O.Praem. Canons Regular of Premontre
O.R.C. Operarios del Reina de Cristo
O.S.A. The Augustinians
O.S.B. Benedictine Monks
O.S.B-.Cam. Camaldolese Hermits
O S.B.M. Order of St. Basil the Great
O.S.C. Canons Regular of the Order of the Holy Cross
O.S.Cam. Camillian Fathers and Brothers
O.S.F. Congregation of the Religious Brothers of the Third Order Regular of St. Francis
O.S.F. Franciscan Brothers of Christ the King
O.S.F. Franciscan Brothers of the Third Order Regular
O.S.F. Franciscan Missionary Brothers of the Sacred Heart of Jesus
O.S.F.S. Oblates of St. Francis de Sales
O.S.J. Oblates of St. Joseph
O.S.M. Servites
O.S-.P.P.E. Pauline Fathers
O.Ss.S. Brigittine Monks
O.SS.T. Order of the Holy Trinity
P.I.M.E. Pontifical Institute for Foreign Missions
R.C.J. Rogationist Fathers
S.A. Franciscan Friars of the Atonement
S.A.C. Society of the Catholic Apostolate
S.C. Brothers of the Sacred Heart
S.C. Servants of Charity
S.Ch. Society of Christ
Sch.P. Piarist Fathers.
S.C.J. Congregation of the Priests of the Sacred Heart
S.D.B. Salesians of Don Bosco
S.D.S. Society of the Divine Savior
S.D.V. Vocationist Fathers
S.F. Sons of the Holy Family
S.F.M. Scarboro Foreign Missions
S.J. Jesuit Fathers and Brothers
S.M. Society of Mary (Marianists)
S.M. Marist Fathers
S.M.A. Society of African Missions
S.M.M. Montfort Missionaries
S.M.P. Society of Our Mother of Peace
S.O.Cist. Cistercian Monks of the Strict Observance
S.O.L.T. Society of Our Lady of the Most Holy Trinity
s.P. Servants of the Paraclete
S.P.S. St. Patrick Missionary Society
S.S. Society of the Priests of Saint Sulpice
S.S.C. Society of St. Columban
SS.CC. Congregation of the Sacred Hearts of Jesus and Mary
S.S.E. Society of Saint Edmund
S.S.J. St. Joseph's Society of the Sacred Heart
S.S.P. Pauline Fathers and Brothers
S.S.S. Congregation of the Blessed Sacrament
S.S.T. Missionary Society of St. Thomas the Apostle
S.T. Missionary Servants of the Most Holy Trinity
S.X. Xaverian Missionary Fathers
S.V.D. Society of the Divine Word
T.O.R. Third Order Regular of Saint Francis
V.C. Vincentian Congregation (India)
V.D.C. Verbum Dei Community

The letters in parentheses designate the diocese. See the "Diocesan Abbreviations". Letters in brackets designate categories in the Institution Section.

A

A., Jorge *o.s.a.* '96 (PH)[Y] Villanova, PA St. Thomas Monastery.

Aakula, Anthony Swamy '84 (AMA) Bovina, TX St. Ann's; Friona, TX St. Teresa of Jesus.

Aapengnuo, Clement '88 (ARL) Arlington, VA St. Charles Borromeo.

Aaron, Andrew '96 (BAL) Davidsonville, MD Holy Family.

Abad, Jose Antonio P. '82 (AGN) Tumon, GU Blessed Diego Luis de San Vitores Church; Archdiocesan Presbyteral Council.

Abalon, Danilo *s.o.l.t.* '89 (SEA) Seattle, WA St. Alphonsus.

Abalon, Jose Amante M. '01 (NEW) On Duty Outside the Archdiocese.

Abalon, Jose M. (BO) Brockton, MA St. Patrick.

Abalon, Jose Manuel M. '00 (NEW) On Duty Outside the Archdiocese.

Aban, Adolfo A. (DM) Des Moines, IA United States Veterans Hospital.

Aban, Adolfo Aristotle '83 (MO) DEPARTMENT OF VETERANS AFFAIRS HOSPITALS AND CHAPLAINS.

Abaneke, Aloysius '98 (SFE) University Hospital; Albuquerque, NM Our Lady of Fatima.

Abanulo, Athanasius '90 (NSH) Nashville, TN Assumption.

Abara, Lawrence N. '78 (LAF) Breaux Bridge, LA Our Lady of Mercy.

Abarrategui, Leandro *o.f.m.* '54 (SJN) Carolina, PR Santa Clara de Asis.

Abarratelegui, Leanadro *o.f.m.* '68 (SJN).

Abata, Russell J. *c.ss.r.* '57 (NY)[DD] New York, NY Redemptorist Priests and Brothers, C.Ss.R.

Abaukaka, Stephen O. '97 (CHI) Harvey, IL Ascension–St. Susanna.

Abaya, Pascual '96 (HON) Pearl City, HI Our Lady of Good Counsel; Clergy Personnel Board; Presbyteral Council; Vicars Forane.

Abba, Matthew '99 (NY) New York, NY St. Francis de Sales.

Abba, Matthew '94 (NY) Bronx, NY St. Barnabas Hospital.
Abba, Thaer '08 (OLD) Saint Joseph Syriac Catholic Church; Saints Behnam and Sarah Mission.
Abbatiello, Robert *o.f.m.cap.* (NY) New York, NY Good Shepherd.
Abbot, Kerry M. *o.f.m.conv.* '90 (MO) Presbyteral Council; Director of Vocations.
Abbott, Donald S. '73 (CHR) Aiken, SC St. Gerard.
Abbott, Eugene J. '57 (STP) Retired.
Abbott, Gregory E. '07 (STP) Coon Rapids, MN Church of the Epiphany.
Abbott, Kerry *o.f.m.conv.* '90 (MRY)[F] Arroyo Grande St. Joseph Cupertino Province, Provincial Center.
Abbott, William M. *s.j.* '72 (FgM) New York, NY Society of Jesus.
Abdallah, Geoffrey (SAM) Brooklyn, NY Cathedral of Our Lady of Lebanon.
Abdella, Peter *c.s.p.* '85 (LA)[AA] Los Angeles, CA University of California, Los Angeles, University Catholic Center; Los Angeles, CA St. Paul the Apostle.
Abdoo, Louis *i.m.c.* '73 (SB) Riverside, CA St. Francis de Sales.
Abe, John Adam '84 (RIC) Virginia Beach, VA St. Matthew.
Abegg, Victor P. *o.f.m.conv.* '74 (MRY) Pismo Beach, CA St. Paul the Apostle.
Abel, Robert M. '73 (L) Payneville, KY St. Mary Magdalen of Pazzi; Payneville, KY St. Theresa.
Abele, Alan Carl '73 (ANC) Retired.
Abell, Edward '67 (GAL) Houston, TX Retired.
Abella, Ray *o.s.f.s.* '93 (STO) Sonora, CA St. Patrick Church of Sonora (Pastor of); Jamestown, CA Sierra Conservation Center.
Abellan, Jose Antonio Murcia '01 (CHI) Chicago, IL St. James.
Abels, Kevin P. '03 (BRK) Vocations, Office of.
Abercrombie, Jamie M. *c.s.b.* '73 (GAL)[B] Sugar Land, TX Basilian Fathers of Sugarland; [O] Sugar Land Basilian Mission Center.
Abernethy, David S. *c.o.* '94 (PIT)[M] Pittsburgh, PA Congregation of the Oratory of St. Philip Neri; Pittsburgh, PA.
Abert, Richard P. *s.j.* '76 (RC) Pine Ridge, SD Saint Ignatius Loyola; Pine Ridge, SD Holy Rosary/Red Cloud Indian School Inc.; [C] Pine Ridge, SD Jesuit Community of Holy Rosary Mission; Pine Ridge, SD Our Lady of Sorrows.
Abi-Akar, Dany '10 (SAM) Waterbury, CT Our Lady of Lebanon.
Abi-chedid, Elie '85 (SAM) Jacksonville, FL St. Maron Maronite.
Abi-Sarkis, Elias '75 (OLL) Tulsa, OK St. Therese of the Child Jesus Maronite Catholic Church; Presbyteral Council.
Abi-Sarkis, Elias '75 (TLS)[E] Tulsa, OK Saint Francis Hospital; Diocesan Senators.
Abiamiri, Anthony (BAL) Baltimore, MD St. Anthony of Padua; Baltimore, MD Most Precious Blood.
Abiamiri, Vitalis '93 (RVC) Smithtown, NY St. Patrick.
Abiamm, Anthony (BAL)[U] Baltimore, MD Nigeria-Igbo Catholic Community.
Abiera, Frederic *o.a.r.* '03 (NY)[B] Suffern, NY Tagaste Monastery.
Ablanida, Joachim E. '02 (LA) Artesia, CA Holy Family.
Abler, Lawrence E. *o.f.m.cap.* '64 (GB) Menasha, WI St. Patrick.
Ablog, Frederico *s.s.s.* '90 (GAL) Houston, TX St. Paul.
Abmayr, George *s.m.* (CIN)[D] Dayton, OH The University of Dayton; [N] Dayton, OH Marianist Community.
Abog, H. Nestor *c.r.m.* '01 (CHR) Goose Creek, SC Immaculate Conception.
Aboh, Bede C. '88 (KNX) Oak Ridge, TN St. Mary; Presbyteral Council.
Abomo, Paul Tango *s.j.* '07 (CHI)[C] Chicago, IL Jesuit Community at Loyola University Chicago.
Abonce, Jose Gilardo Alvarez *c.o.r.c.* (FWT) Fort Worth, TX Immaculate Heart of Mary.
Aboody, Rt. Rev. Charles '62 (NTN) Presbyteral Council Retired.
Abou, Herve Yepie *s.m.a.* '04 (NEW)[L] Tenafly, NJ Society of African Missions, Provincialate, S.M.A. Fathers.
Aboyi, James *v.c.* '04 (TUC) Superior, AZ Saint Francis of Assisi Roman Catholic Parish - Superior.
Abraham, Anthony '08 (STV)[B] Catholic Charismatic Renewal; Charismatic Movement; St. Thomas, VI Holy Family Parish; St. John, VI Our Lady of Mt. Carmel Parish.
Abraham, Johnson C. '88 (OAK) Priest Representatives - Alameda County.
Abraham, Johnson '88 (OAK) Pleasanton, CA The Catholic Community of Pleasanton.
Abraham, Joseph '90 (RNO) Judicial Vicar/Officialis; Ongoing Formation for Permanent Deacons; Curia; Priest Personnel Board; Reno, NV St. Rose of Lima; Vicar for Clergy.
Abraham, Mathew K. *a.l.c.p.* '99 (SP) Zephyrhills, FL St. Joseph Catholic Church.
Abraham, Thaddeus '91 (BRK) Woodside, NY St. Sebastian.
Abrahamczyk, Kazimierz *s.v.d.* '85 (MEM) Polish Catholic Ministry; Memphis, TN St. John's; Korean Catholic Ministry; [F] Memphis, TN Society of the Divine Word (Chicago Province).
Abrahams, John J. '79 (BAL) Retired.
Abrahim, Jirjis '67 (EST) Eparchial College of Consultors; West Bloomfield, MI St. Thomas Chaldean Catholic Parish.
Abrego, Martin '92 (SJ) Sunnyvale, CA St. Martin.
Abreu, John E. '74 (PRO) Warren, RI St. Thomas the Apostle.
Abruzzese, Rev. Msgr. John A. '74 (BO) On Duty Outside the Archdiocese.
Abruzzese, Joseph A. '90 (PRO) Absent on Leave.
Absalon, Burt H. '01 (RCK) Loves Park, IL St. Bridget.
Abts, John J. *o.f.m.* '90 (FWT)[H] Crowley, TX St. Maximilian Kolbe Friary.
Abts, John *o.f.m.* '84 (FWT)[G] Crowley, TX St. Francis Village, Inc.
Abu-Lail, Samir '94 (NTN) Presbyteral Council; Seattle, WA St. Joseph Mission.
Abuah-Quansah, Francis '76 (LC) Chancellor; Building Commission; Viroqua, WI Annunciation of the Blessed Virgin Mary; Defensor Vinculi; Appointed Members; Consultors.
Abucewicz, Rev. Msgr. John A. '44 (BO) Senior Priests. Retired.
Abugel, Alexander G. '80 (BRK) Long Island City, NY St. Patrick; On Leave/Unassigned.
Abwanda, Joseph Okanda *o.c.d.* '05 (MIL)[P] Milwaukee Provincial Offices - Discalced Carmelites.
Acaba, Jose A. '82 (ARE) Quebradillas, PR San Raphael.
Accardi, Joseph N. '90 (PH) Philadelphia, PA St. Bernard.
Acero, Roman A. '08 (R) Special Assignment.
Acervo, Lee E. '08 (DET) St. Clair Shores, MI St. Joan of Arc.
Acevedo, Antonio '73 (MIA) Retired.
Acevedo, Bertulfo '56 (ARE) Vega-Alta, PR Immaculate Conception of Blessed Virgin Mary Retired.
Acevedo, Edward '97 (MGZ) Las Marias, PR Immaculate Heart of Mary.
Acevedo, Jaime H. '99 (MIA) Miami, FL Mother of Our Redeemer.
Acevedo, Milton '09 (ARL) Woodbridge, VA Our Lady of Angels.
Achadinha, James M. (BO) Cambridge, MA St. Anthony of Padua.
Achbach, Kevin Lee '03 (RC) Philip, SD Sacred Heart; Vocation Program.
Ackah, Jerome Francis '92 (RVC) Oceanside, NY South Nassau Communities Hospital; Freeport, NY Our Holy Redeemer.
Acker, Karl H. '63 (MIL) Retired.
Acker, Thomas S. *s.j.* '63 (DET)[K] Detroit Detroit Province of the Society of Jesus-Provincial Office.
Acker, Thomas S. *s.j.* '63 (Y) Canal Fulton, OH SS. Philip and James.
Ackeret, Dennis '68 (MIL) Eagle, WI St. Theresa; Archdiocesan Consultors; Archdiocesan Council of Priests.
Ackerman, Donald K. '61 (EVN) Retired.
Ackerman, J. Thomas '97 (BIR) Birmingham (Hoover), AL Prince of Peace; Diocesan College of Consultors; Diocesan College of Vicars.
Ackerman, James C. *s.j.* '10 (CLV)[B] University Heights, OH John Carroll Jesuit Community.
Ackerman, Phillip '78 (FAR) Grand Forks, ND Holy Family Church of Grand Forks; Deanery 3.
Ackerman, Raymond K. '91 (OKL) Edmond, OK St. Monica; Council of Priests Archdiocesan; Personnel Committee; Consultors Archdiocesan.
Acklin, Thomas *o.s.b.* '80 (GBG)[H] Latrobe, PA Saint Vincent Archabbey.
Aclan, Alejandro '93 (LA) Pomona, CA St. Madeleine.
Aclan, Alex '93 (LA) San Gabriel Region.
Acob, Augusto '80 (OAK) Livermore, CA St. Charles Borromeo.
Acosta, Francisco '70 (BWN) Brownsville, TX Our Lady of Guadalupe.
Acosta, Jorge E. '02 (NEW) Hackensack, NJ Holy Trinity.
Acosta, Yovanny '96 (BRK) Jackson Heights, NY Our Lady of Fatima.
Acosta-Escobar, Bill John '02 (R) Kinston, NC Holy Spirit Catholic Church.
Acosta-Zunini, Raul *s.d.b.* '67 (LAR) Laredo, TX San Luis Rey.
Acquaro, Philip Anthony *c.s.b.* '70 (GAL)[O] Houston, TX Dillon House Retired.
Acrea, John '62 (DM) Retired.
Acrea, John '62 (STP)[A] St. Paul, MN St. John Vianney Seminary; [C] St. Paul, MN University of St. Thomas.
Acri, John A. '65 (HBG) Lancaster, PA St. Anthony of Padua Retired.
Acton, Rev. Msgr. Sean A. '48 (LA) Retired.
Acton, Rev. Msgr. Thomas M. '57 (LA) Gardena, CA Maria Regina Retired.
Acuna, Jesus '06 (TUC) San Luis, AZ Saint Jude Thaddeus Roman Catholic Parish - San Luis.
Acuna-Delgado, Jesus '06 (TUC) Nogales, AZ San Felipe de Jesus Roman Catholic Parish - Nogales.
Adackapara, Matthew '60 (TR) Retired.
Adain, Dieuseul '98 (NEW) Newark, NJ St. Francis Xavier.
Adajar, Wayne '98 (ORG) Mission Viejo, CA St. Kilian.
Adam, Charles A. '86 (DAV)[A] Davenport, IA St. Ambrose University; [A] Davenport, IA St. Ambrose University; [A] St. Ambrose University.
Adam, Nicholas J. '76 (DAV) Grinnell, IA St. Mary's; Diocesan Consultors; Deans.
Adam, Richard A. '88 (DAV) Davenport, IA Sacred Heart Cathedral.
Adamcik, Bryan F.J. '96 (NEW) Harrington Park, NJ Our Lady of Victories; Part-time Staff/Advocates/ Procurators.
Adamczak, Dawid *s.d.s.* '00 (MET) Great Meadows, NJ Ss. Peter and Paul.
Adamczyk, Lawrence P. '03 (BAL) Westminster, MD St. John; Baltimore, MD St. Ursula.
Adame, Alejandro *c.s.v.* '00 (CHI)[N] Arlington Heights Viatorian Province Center-Clerics of St. Viator.
Adamian, Antoine '70 (OLN) Farmington, MI St. Vartan's.
Adamich, Albert R. '48 (CHI) Evergreen Park, IL Most Holy Redeemer Retired.
Adamko, Rev. Msgr. Cyril A. '53 (Y) Retired.
Adamo, Robert B. '98 (BRK) Brooklyn, NY Immaculate Heart of Mary; Art and Architecture Commission.
Adams, Edmond F. '52 (SC) Retired.
Adams, Rev. Msgr. George J. '50 (STU) Retired.
Adams, Rev. Msgr. George '50 (E) Retired.
Adams, Harry J. '68 (NO) New Orleans, LA Mater Dolorosa.
Adams, James F. '04 (STP) New Market, MN Saint Nickolaus.
Adams, James P. '82 (ATL)[B] Fayetteville, GA Our Lady of Mercy Catholic High School; Special or Other Archdiocesan Assignment.
Adams, James '09 (KAL) Presbyteral Council Members; Presbyteral Council Members; Portage, MI St. Catherine of Siena.
Adams, Joel K. *s.j.* '95 (P)[D] Portland, OR Jesuit High School.
Adams, John E. '69 (WDC) Special Ministries; [W] Washington, DC Community of Christ.
Adams, John Michael '85 (BIR) Birmingham, AL Our Lady of Sorrows.
Adams, Joseph M. *o.s.b.* '09 (GBG)[H] Latrobe, PA Saint Vincent Archabbey.
Adams, Joseph M. *o.s.b.* '09 (MO) Army Reserve Chaplains.
Adams, Rev. Msgr. Michael J. '59 (CHI) Chicago, IL Christ the King; Chicago, IL St. Mary, Star of the Sea Retired.
Adams, Michael J. '06 (TYL) Presbyteral Council; Carthage, TX St. William of Vercelli.
Adams, Rev. Msgr. Michael J. '59 (CHI) Retired.
Adams, Michael T. '68 (MRY) Retired.
Adams, Richard '65 (NY) On Duty Outside the Archdiocese.
Adams, Rodney T. '91 (OM) Omaha, NE St. Patrick (Elkhorn).
Adams, Stephen E. '81 (DEN) Aurora, CO St. Pius X; Deaneries; College of Consultors.
Adams, T. Edmund *o.s.b.* '89 (PRO)[O] Portsmouth, RI Abbey of St. Gregory the Great.
Adams, Terrance *t.o.r.* '67 (WH) Moundsville, WV St. Francis Xavier's.
Adams, Thomas J. '64 (OM) Retired.
Adams, Walter C. '84 (NY) Absent on Sick Leave Retired.
Adams, William *c.ss.r.* '63 (LA) Whittier, CA St. Mary of the Assumption; [P] Whittier, CA Redemptorists of Whittier Retired.
Adams, William '78 (VEN) Fort Myers Beach, FL Ascension.
Adamski, John S. '71 (ATL) Retired.
Adamson, Fredrick J. '95 (PHX) Moderator of the Curia; Vicars General; College of Consultors; Presbyteral Council.
Adamson, Joseph J. '90 (CAM) Deanery Representatives; Glassboro, NJ Mary, Mother of Mercy Parish, Glassboro, N.J.
Adamson, Milton N. *c.s.c.* '66 (PHX) Phoenix, AZ St. Joseph's Hospital; [F] Phoenix, AZ Holy Cross Congregation/Casa Santa Cruz.
Adamson, Milton *c.s.c.* (FTW)[H] Notre Dame Congregation of Holy Cross, United States Province of Priests & Brothers.
Adan, Aurelio '69 (CGS) Diocesan Consultors; Caguas, PR Cathedral Dulce Nombre de Jesus.
Adathiparampil, Thomas '87 (SYM) Fremont, CA St. Mary Syro-Malabar Knanaya Catholic Mission of San Jose.
Adator, Jules *s.m.a.* '05 (PEO) Ottawa, IL St. Francis of Assisi; Ottawa (Naplate), IL St. Mary's.
Adawu, Anthony (BAL) Glen Burnie, MD Holy Trinity.

Addai, Augustine '98 (NY) Yorktown Heights, NY St. Patrick.
Addari, Enzo '76 (LAN)[E] Chelsea, MI St. Louis Center for Exceptional Children & Adults.
Adegboyega, Johnrita '00 (PHX) Chandler, AZ St. Mary Roman Catholic Parish.
Adejoh, Abraham O. '10 (BEL) Mascoutah, IL Holy Childhood of Jesus.
Adejoh, Patrick O. '92 (MO) DEPARTMENT OF VETERANS AFFAIRS HOSPITALS AND CHAPLAINS.
Adekola, Patrick (NY) Spring Valley, NY St. Joseph.
Adeleke, Albert (WDC)[B] Washington, DC St. Joseph's Seminary.
Adelman, Norbert *c.pp.s* '56 (CIN)[N] Carthagena, OH St. Charles Retired.
Adelmann, Edward *o.carm.* '75 (JOL)[L] Darien Carmelite Provincial Office; Darien, IL Provincial Headquarters, Carmelite Provincial Office.
Adhana, Gabre–Tinsaye '47 (GAL)[L] Houston, TX Pope John Paul XXIII Priests' Residence Retired.
Adhav, Satish Baburao '06 (BLX) Kiln, MS St. Matthew the Apostle.
Adhunga, Joseph Okech *a.j.* '91 (NY) New Rochelle, NY Holy Family.
Adibe, Anthony *c.s.sp.* '91 (DM)[D] Des Moines, IA Mercy Medical Center.
Adiletta, David *o.p.* '98 (FgM) New York, NY Province of St. Joseph (Eastern).
Adimakkeel, Joy Joseph '80 (MAR) Bessemer, MI St. Sebastian; Wakefield, MI Immaculate Conception of the Blessed Virgin Mary; [B] Bessemer, MI St. Sebastian Endowment Fund; Vicars Forane.
Adione, Joachim '96 (NY) Bronxville, NY St. Joseph; Lawrence Hospital.
Adiukwu, Richard U. '96 (LKC) Grand Chenier, LA St. Eugene.
Adkins, Howard R. '07 (BR) Independence, LA Mater Dolorosa.
Adolf, Gregory P. '91 (TUC) Sierra Vista, AZ Saint Andrew the Apostle Roman Catholic Parish – Sierra Vista.
Adolfo, Geoffrey '00 (FgM) Boston, MA St. James the Apostle, Inc.
Adongo, Nicholas Olonde *o.c.d.* '07 (MIL)[P] Milwaukee Provincial Offices – Discalced Carmelites.
Adonizio, Joseph J. '56 (SCR) Retired.
Adorno, Anibal '92 (DAL) Dallas, TX St. Augustine Catholic Church.
Adorno, Ivan Martinez '08 (ARE)[A] Arecibo, PR Pontificia Universidad Catholica de Puerto Rico, Recinto de Arecibo.
Adorno, Luis *c.ss.r.* (CGS) Aguas Buenas, PR Church of Tres Santos Reyes.
Adrian, Stephen J. '39 (NU) Retired.
Adrian, Stephen J. '68 (STP) St. Paul, MN St. Matthew.
Adrian, Stephen '39 (PHX) Gilbert, AZ St. Anne Roman Catholic Parish Retired.
Adrians, Rev. Msgr. Thomas M. '67 (PBL) Pueblo, CO Christ the King; Ex Officio; Clergy Assembly; Clergy Personnel; College of Consultors.
Adu, Martin K. '75 (MIA) Miami, FL St. James; Special Assignment.
Adu–Boahen, Peter '03 (ROC) Owego, NY Blessed Trinity; Owego, NY St. Patrick.
Adu–Kwaning, Stephen '84 (NY) Bronx, NY St. Raymond.
Aduaka, Anthony '04 (LEX) Special Assignment.
Adunchezor, Christopher '90 (MO) Army Chaplains.
Aduri, Chinnappa Reddy (NY) Ellenville, NY St. Mary and St. Andrew.
Aduri, Tom '03 (KCK) Meriden, KS St. Aloysius; Perry, KS St. Theresa.
Adversario, Efren F. '89 (MO) Air Force Chaplains.
Adversario, Efren '89 (AGN) On Duty Outside the Archdiocese.
Aelavanthara, Antony '68 (ALX) Powhatan, LA St. Francis of Assisi; College of Consultors.
Aerts, John F. '02 (FAR) Lakota, ND St. Mary's Church of Lakota; Lakota, ND St. Lawrence O'Toole's Church of Michigan; Lakota, ND St. Joseph.
Affelt, Francis *o.f.m.* '52 (FTW)[I] Mishawaka, IN St. Francis Provincialate.
Affelt, Francis *o.f.m.* '52 (GRY)[H] Cedar Lake, IN Our Lady of Lourdes Friary.
Affonso, Alexander '68 (SJ) Morgan Hill, CA St. Catherine of Alexandria.
Affrim, Rev. Msgr. Richard '73 (LA) Pacific Palisades, CA Corpus Christi.
Afful, Samuel Ebulley '83 (BRK) Flushing, NY St. Ann.
Afunugo, Emmanuel *d.d.* '83 (AMA) On Duty Outside the Diocese.
Agaloos, Reinerio '89 (NEW) Elmwood Park, NJ St. Leo's.
Agamba, Clement (TUC) Tucson, AZ Roman Catholic Church of Saint Elizabeth Ann Seton – Tucson.
Agan, Rev. Msgr. Jose '70 (NEW) Retired.
Aganbi, Isaac '79 (NY) Mount Vernon, NY Mount Vernon Hospital.
Agapito, John *c.p.m.* '89 (OWN)[F] Auburn, KY Fathers of Mercy.
Agar, Bartholomew A. *o.praem.* '58 (GB)[J] De Pere, WI St. Norbert Abbey.
Agbagwa, Goddswill (BAL) Glen Burnie, MD Holy Trinity.
Agbagwa, Godswill (BAL)[L] Baltimore, MD The Neighborhoods at St. Elizabeth Rehabilitation and Nursing Center.
Agbasiere, John *s.m.m.m.* '96 (BEL) Mound City, IL St. Patrick; Mound City, IL St. Catherine; Mound City, IL Church of the Immaculate Conception–St. Mary.
Agber, Philip *c.s.sp.* '01 (PH)[F] Bensalem, PA Holy Ghost Preparatory School; [Y] Bensalem, PA Congregation of the Holy Spirit.
Ageas, Cesar R. '83 (SAC) Defenders of the Bond; Citrus Heights, CA Holy Family; Adjutant Judicial Vicar; Judges.
Agele, Comfort *c.s.c.* '04 (FTW)[H] Notre Dame Congregation of Holy Cross, United States Province of Priests & Brothers.
Aggeler, Vincent H. *c.ss.r.* '58 (STL)[O] Liguori, MO St. Clement Health Care Center Retired.
Agi, Lawrence '99 (SD) Scripps Mercy Hospital; San Diego, CA Holy Spirit Catholic Parish; [H] San Diego, CA Scripps Mercy Hospital.
Agila, Angel Vincente '91 (GAL) Galena Park, TX Our Lady of Fatima.
Agirembabazi, Nestorio *a.j.* '90 (NY) Bronx, NY St. Angela Merici.
Agliardo, Michael *s.j.* '94 (CHI)[C] Chicago, IL Jesuit Community at Loyola University Chicago.
Agnese, Sergio Dall *c.s.* '79 (WDC) Riverdale, MD Our Lady of Fatima Parish; Riverdale Park, MD St. Bernard.
Agnew, John C. '90 (POD)[II] New York, NY Prelature of the Holy Cross and Opus Dei; New York.
Agoha, Christopher *s.m.m.m.* '96 (BAK) La Grande, OR Our Lady of the Valley; Board of Education; Defenders of the Bond and Promoters of Justice; Council of Priests and Diocesan Consultors.
Agostinelli, Gianni *c.s.* '86 (ORL) Mount Dora, FL St. Patrick's; Leesburg, FL St. Paul's.
Agostino, Emil *o.carm.* '64 (JOL)[L] Darien Carmelite Provincial Office Retired.
Agostino, Joseph V. *c.m.* '83 (PH)[Y] Philadelphia Congregation of the Mission[Y].
Agostino, Steven J. *s.j.* '93 (Y)[O] Kent, OH Kent State University Newman Center; University Parish Newman Center (Kent State); Kent, OH University Parish Newman Center.
Agresti, Albert A. *s.j.* '94 (BO)[U] Boston The Society of Jesus of New England–Provincial Offices.
Agresti, Frank P. '03 (PAT) Paterson, NJ Our Lady of Pompei; Girl Scouting; Presbyteral Council; Permanent Diaconate Program.
Agu, Hyginus '95 (BGP) Bridgeport, CT St. Andrew.
Agu, Paschalis (CHI)[J] Chicago, IL St. Anthony Hospital.
Agudelo, Carlos A. '98 (BRK) Corona, NY St. Leo.
Agudelo, German Correa '00 (FR) Fall River; Fall River, MA Cathedral of St. Mary of the Assumption.
Agudelo, Gustavo '86 (CAM) Wildwood, NJ Notre Dame de la Mer Parish, Wildwood, N.J.
Agudelo, Luis Henry '11 (NOR) Willimantic, CT St. Joseph.
Agudo, Moises '97 (SFR) San Francisco, CA St. Charles Borromeo; Episcopal Vicar for the Spanish Speaking; Hispanic Ministry.
Agudo, Moises '97 (SFR) On Special Assignment.
Agudo, Teodoro *o.f.m.cap.* '54 (NO) New Orleans, LA St. Theresa of Avila.
Aguera, Jorge *d.c.j.m.* '97 (DEN) Denver, CO Church of the Ascension; [N] Littleton, CO Disciples of the Hearts of Jesus and Mary.
Aguggia, Rev. Msgr. Steven J. '93 (BRK) Middle Village, NY St. Margaret; [V] Flushing, NY Pro Sanctity Movement; Officialis–Judicial Vicar; Committee for Eastern Orthodox–Catholic Relations; [V] Middle Village, NY National Italian Apostolate Conference; Attorneys and Counselors at Canon Law.
Agughara, Fidelis '88 (BUR) Burlington, VT Fletcher Allen Health Care.
Aguilar, Arturo *s.s.c.* '84 (OM)[J] St. Columbans, NE Missionary Society of St. Columban.
Aguilar, Benjamin *o.carm.* '94 (CHI)[D] Chicago, IL; [N] Chicago Carmelite Priory of St. Cyril.
Aguilar, Benjamin *o.carm.* '94 (JOL)[L] Darien Carmelite Provincial Office.
Aguilar, Demetrio I. *s.v.d.* '83 (SB) Beaumont, CA Blessed Kateri Tekakwitha Catholic Community, Inc.
Aguilar, Francis V. '09 (LA) Santa Fe Springs, CA St. Pius X.
Aguilar, Genaro P. *c.s.c.* '83 (SCR)[B] Holy Cross Community.
Aguilar, Genaro P. *c.s.c.* '83 (FTW)[H] Notre Dame Congregation of Holy Cross, United States Province of Priests & Brothers.
Aguilar, Javier '98 (OAK) Livermore, CA St. Michael.
Aguilar, Luis Roberto *o.p.* '92 (SAT)[L] San Antonio, TX Dominican Priory of San Juan Macias.
Aguilar, Rogelio Mur *o.carm.* '56 (MGZ) Anasco, PR St. Anthony Abbot.
Aguilera, Salvador '84 (ELP) On Duty Outside of Diocese; Navy Chaplains.
Aguirre, Ignacio *o.s.b.* '53 (FAJ)[B] Humacao, PR San Antonio Abad Abbey of the Order of St. Benedict.
Aguirre, Jesus (BAL) Lansdowne, MD St. Clement.
Aguirre, Juan Carlos '99 (TUC) Eloy, AZ Saint Helen of the Cross Roman Catholic Church – Eloy.
Aguirre, Nery *o.f.m.* '74 (FgM) New York, NY Franciscan Province of the Immaculate Conception.
Aguirre, Osmar R. '93 (YAK) Prosser, WA Sacred Heart; Diocesan Consultors.
Aguirre, Rosalino *o.r.c.* (PCE) Adjuntas, PR St. Joachim.
Aguirre–Garza, Jesus *o.f.m.* '96 (STL)[O] St. Louis Franciscan Friary of St. Anthony of Padua; U.S. Religious Serving Elsewhere.
Aguste, Jean–Miguel '93 (BRK) Brooklyn, NY St. Jerome.
Agustin, Honesto '82 (RNO) Reno, NV St. Therese Church of the Little Flower.
Agustin, Richard *m.m.* '85 (FgM) Maryknoll, NY MARYKNOLL.
Aguwa, Henry '04 (PBL) La Junta, CO Our Lady of Guadalupe/St. Patrick; Las Animas, CO St. Mary.
Aguwa, Jude '78 (NY) Croton Falls, NY St. Joseph.
Aguzie, Basil *m.s.p.* '98 (AUS) Austin, TX Holy Cross.
Agwu, John Okeke *s.m.m.m.* '04 (FRS) Bakersfield, CA St. Joseph.
Agwuoke, Emmanuel S. *c.s.sp.* (DM) Audubon, IA St. Patrick; Audubon, IA Holy Trinity.
Agyman, Fred '97 (NY) Bronx, NY St. Raymond.
Ahabyona, Titus '97 (OWN) Judges; Owensboro, KY St. Pius Tenth.
Ahanotu, Leonard '94 (TLS) Bixby, OK St. Clement of Rome; Diocesan Senators.
Ahearn, Donald J. '51 (CHI) Chicago, IL St. Juliana Retired.
Ahearn, John F. *m.m.* '73 (FgM) Maryknoll, NY MARYKNOLL.
Ahearn, Richard F. '60 (BO) Senior Priests. Retired.
Ahearn, Thomas A. *m.m.* '68 (NY)[DD] Maryknoll, NY Maryknoll Fathers and Brothers Charitable Trust; [DD] Maryknoll Maryknoll Fathers and Brothers Retired.
Ahern, Bernard '54 (ALB) Retired.
Ahern, Bernie '54 (STA) Jacksonville, FL St. Joseph's.
Ahern, Dennis P. *s.j.* '70 (CIN)[F] Cincinnati, OH St. Xavier High School; [N] Cincinnati, OH Jesuit Community at St. Xavier High School.
Ahern, Rev. Msgr. John B. '54 (NY)[H] New York, NY Holy Name Centre for Homeless Men, Inc.; New York, NY Basilica of St. Patrick's Old Cathedral Retired.
Ahern, John S. '54 (HRT) Retired.
Ahern, John V. '67 (SY) DeWitt, NY Holy Cross.
Ahern, Thomas W. '94 (BRK) Brooklyn, NY St. Augustine.
Ahern, Thomas W. '48 (NOR) Old Lyme, CT Christ the King Retired.
Aherne, James *m.s.* '73 (SPR) Holyoke, MA Immaculate Conception.
Aherne, P. Vincent *c.m.* '52 (STL)[O] St. Louis Vincentian Residence.
Ahiara Kwen, Gabriel A. (BRK) Long Island City, NY Most Precious Blood.
Ahlbach, William J. '62 (SFR) San Mateo, CA St. Matthew.
Ahlemeyer, Richard J. '77 (BRK) Rockaway Beach, NY Saint Camillus–Saint Virgilius.
Ahles, Donald M. '71 (RCK) Sterling, IL St. Mary; Diocesan Consultors.
Ahlin, Robert J. '71 (PIT) Pittsburgh, PA Holy Angels; Judges.
Ahlstrom, Michael P. '69 (CHI) Brookfield, IL St. Barbara; Vicar for the Diaconate Community.
Ahn, Chol–Min '00 (SD) San Diego, CA Saint Columba Catholic Parish.
Ahn, Peter *o.s.b.* '02 (PAT)[N] Newton, NJ St. Paul's Abbey.
Ahn, Simon Hyo–Sung '91 (RIC) Hampton, VA St. Rose of Lima; Hampton, VA Catholic Community of the Korean Martyrs.
Aho, Charles A. '70 (SY) Special Assignment.
Ahoussi, Thomas *s.j.* '10 (BO)[U] Brighton, MA Miguel Pro House.
Ahrens, William B. '51 (STL) Retired.
Ahrensfield, Michael E. '80 (ALN) Lehighton, PA SS. Peter and Paul.
Ahumanda, Jose E. *c.s.c.* '83 (FTW)[H] Notre Dame Congregation of Holy Cross, United States Province of Priests & Brothers.
Ahyuwa, Lawrence David '01 (NY) Bronx, NY St. Gabriel.
Aiardi, Reno *i.m.c.* '65 (SB) San Bernardino, CA Mission Office of the Diocese of San Bernardino; Riverside, CA St. Francis de Sales.
Aichele, Raymond P. '58 (CIN) Retired.
Aidoo, Thomas '85 (RVC) Stony Brook, NY Stony Brook University Hospital; Patchogue, NY Our Lady of Mt. Carmel.
Aiello, Anthony '69 (DM) Retired.
Aiello, Louis F. '77 (SY) Syracuse, NY St. Camillus Health & Rehab Center.

Aigner, Edward M. '72 (WIL) Salisbury, MD St. Francis De Sales; Eastern Correctional Institution.
Aiken, Rev. Msgr. Lloyd '70 (BAL) Baltimore, MD St. Charles Borromeo; Glyndon, MD Sacred Heart; Priest Personnel Board.
Aiken, Richard J. '70 (MIL) Milwaukee, WI St. Sebastian.
Ailer, Gellert Jozsef '06 (WDC) On Duty Outside the Archdiocese.
Aime, Moise '80 (RVC) Lindenhurst, NY Our Lady of Perpetual Help.
Aineto, Louis *s.d.b.* '61 (CHI) Chicago, IL St. John Bosco.
Aita, Mark C. *s.j.* '83 (PH)[C] Jesuit Fathers; [Y] Loyola Center and Manresa Hall.
Aitcheson, William M. '88 (ARL) Chantilly, VA St. Timothy.
Ajanma, Emmanuel '03 (BUR) Elected Members; Barre, VT St. Monica.
Ajemian, David J. '01 (BO) Health Leave.
Ajewole, Michael *m.s.p.* '96 (AUS) Burlington, TX St. Ann; [G] Burlington, TX Missionary Society of St. Paul, MSP; Burlington, TX St. Michael.
Ajoko, Donatus O. '95 (BR)[F] Baton Rouge, LA Our Lady of the Lake Regional Medical Center.
Akalawa, Ambrose '71 (LAF) On Special Assignment.
Akalue, Emmanuel '94 (ORL) Dunnellon, FL St. John the Baptist; African Ministry.
Akamike, Romanus Arinze '89 (SAN) Coleman, TX Sacred Heart; Winters, TX Our Lady of Mt. Carmel.
Akano, Francis '99 (BAK) Council of Priests and Diocesan Consultors; Merrill, OR St. Augustine.
Akao, Michio *s.v.d.* '03 (WDC)[O] Washington, DC Society of the Divine Word/Divine Word House.
Akara, Boniface *c.m.f.* (PHX) Grand Canyon, AZ El Cristo Rey Roman Catholic Parish.
Akeriwe, Raymond A. '03 (LFT) Carmel, IN Our Lady of Mount Carmel.
Akers, Bert *s.j.* '61 (ALN)[A] Wernersville, PA Jesuit Center–Jesuit Community.
Akho, Daniel '90 (HRT) Hartford, CT Cathedral of St. Joseph.
Akin–Otiko, Peter '96 (STA) Palm Coast, FL St. Elizabeth Ann Seton; Defenders of the Bond.
Akiona, Lane *ss.cc.* '81 (HON) Honolulu, HI St. Augustine by the Sea; Members; Presbyteral Council; Members.
Akkalayil, Binoy *o.ss.t.* '05 (BAL) Hanover, MD St. Lawrence Martyr; [Q] Archdiocese of Baltimore, MD – Assigned Elsewhere.
Akordor, Edmund '80 (NO) Jefferson, LA Ochsner Foundation Hospital.
Akoury, Tony (SAM) Somerset, NJ St. Sharbel.
Akpa, Onwuham *o.praem.* '04 (JKS)[E] Raymond, MS Priory of St. Moses the Black; Canton, MS Holy Child Jesus; Canton, MS Sacred Heart.
Akpabio, Felix '78 (RVC) Center Moriches, NY St. John the Evangelist.
Akpan, Godwin B. *s.s.j.* '10 (NO) New Orleans, LA Corpus Christi–Epiphany.
Akpan, Tersur Melchizedek *v.c.* '06 (TUC) Tucson, AZ Our Mother of Sorrows Roman Catholic Parish – Tucson.
Akpanobong, Patrick (SAN) Odessa, TX St. Joseph; Odessa, TX St. Anthony.
Akpoghiran, Peter O. (NO) Metropolitan Tribunal.
Akpunonu, Peter Damian *s.s.l.* '66 (CHI)[A] Mundelein, IL University of St. Mary of the Lake/Mundelein Seminary.
Akpunonu, Raymond (RVC) Dix Hills, NY St. Matthew.
Aksamit, Stanley J. '77 (SPR) Turners Falls, MA Our Lady of Peace; Presbyteral Council.
Akujobi, Stephen '98 (COS)[C] Colorado Springs, CO St. Francis Nursing Center.
Akwue, Francis *c.s.sp.* '71 (MIA) Pompano Beach, FL St. Henry.
Al–Shaikh, Rev. Msgr. Emad Hanna '00 (OLD) El Cajon, CA Saint Joseph Mission; El Cajon, CA Our Mother of Perpetual Help Church.
Alabie, Pierre M. (TR) Hamilton, NJ Our Lady of Sorrows–St. Anthony Parish.
Alagia, Vincent deP. *s.j.* '58 (BAL)[Q] Baltimore, MD Colombiere Jesuit Community.
Alaharasan, V. Antony '65 (NOR) North Stonington, CT St. Thomas More.
Alam, Alam '81 (NTN) Retired.
Alamilla, Guillermo Aguilar *o.f.m.conv.* (AUS) Austin, TX Cristo Rey.
Alamo, Emiliano '64 (PCE) Coamo, PR San Antonio de Padua.
Alapaty, Lourduraj '89 (R) Raleigh, NC Cathedral of the Sacred Heart.
Alappat, Antoo '94 (BIR) Lanett, AL Holy Family.
Alappat, Joy '81 (SYM) Bellwood, IL Mar Thoma Sleeha Cathedral (Chicago).
Alappatt, Joy '81 (SYM) Chaplain to the India Catholic Association (Syro–Malabar Rite); Eparchial Consultors.
Alarcon, Felix '63 (RVC) Retired.
Alarcon, Rev. Msgr. Juan '64 (SFR) South San Francisco, CA St. Augustine Retired.
Alaribe, Felix Okey '98 (TYL)[B] Texarkana, TX Christus Health Ark–La–Tex; [B] Texarkana, TX St. Michael Rehabilitation Hospital.
Alava, Andres *o.a.r.* '63 (LSC) Anthony, NM St. Anthony's; Vicars; Presbyteral Council.
Alava, Basilio S. *o.s.a.* (NY) New York, NY Holy Rosary.
Alayón, Hermenegildo '79 (CGS) Caguas, PR Divino Nino.
Alba, Rev. Msgr. Jose '83 (NEW) Retired.
Alba, Marciano Escobar *c.s.* '95 (PRO) College of Consultors; Council Members.
Albacete, Rev. Msgr. Lorenzo '73 (WDC) On Duty Outside the Archdiocese.
Albaladejo, Juan A. '85 (MET) On Duty Outside the Diocese.
Alban, Arthur P. '87 (GAL) Houston, TX St. Matthew the Evangelist.
Albanese, Charles *o.c.s.o.* '05 (DEN)[N] Snowmass, CO St. Benedict's Monastery.
Albano, Alwyn M. '90 (MO) Army Chaplains.
Albano, Arturo L. '74 (SFR) San Francisco, CA Mission Dolores Basilica.
Albano, Peter J. *c.m.* '68 (BRK)[R] Jamaica, NY Reverend John B. Murray, CM, House.
Albarano, Richard '68 (LA) Burbank, CA St. Francis Xavier.
Albarracin, Diego (HRT) Hartford, CT St. Peter; Hartford, CT Sacred Heart.
Albarracin, Luis '67 (VEN) Lake Placid, FL Communidad Catolica Hispana Santiago Apostol (Santiago Mission); Lake Placid, FL St. James.
Albee, Rev. Msgr. Paul M. '84 (LA) Moorpark, CA Holy Cross; Deanery 4; Archdiocesan Finance Council Members 2011–2012.
Albenesius, Paul M. '97 (OM) Jackson, NE St. Patrick.
Alber, Michael '02 (GR) Grand Rapids, MI St. John Vianney.
Alber, Thomas L. '85 (JC) Marshall, MO St. Peter.
Alberg, Leo W. '91 (LA) Gardena, CA Maria Regina.
Albero, Steven J. *o.praem.* '92 (PH)[B] Paoli, PA Daylesford Abbey; [Y] Paoli, PA Daylesford Abbey; Paoli, PA.
Albers, Austin *o.f.m.* '64 (SFD) Montrose, IL St. Rose of Lima; Teutopolis, IL St. Francis of Assisi; [K] Teutopolis, IL St. Francis Assisi Friary.
Albers, Edwin *o.f.m.* '61 (STL)[O] St. Louis, MO Franciscan Friary of St. Anthony of Padua.
Albers, George *c.pp.s.* '62 (CIN)[N] Carthagena, OH St. Charles Retired.
Albers, James R. *o.s.b.* '00 (KCK)[I] Atchison, KS St. Benedict's Abbey; Atchison, KS.
Albers, Thomas *c.pp.s.* '67 (KC) Nevada, MO St. Mary.
Albert, Andrew *s.m.* '65 (BO) Pastoral Care; [U] Boston, MA Marist Fathers Lourdes Residence; [Z] Boston, MA Marist Fathers Residence; Boston, MA.
Albert, Claude J. '64 (PRT) Diocesan Priests' Benefit Plan – Trustees Retired.
Albert, James R. '86 (PRT) Retired.
Albert, Patrick L. '92 (SCR) Forest City, PA Sacred Heart of Jesus; Pleasant Mount, PA St. Katharine Drexel Parish; Presbyteral Council; Forest City, PA Ascension Parish.
Albertine, Richard P. *m.m.* '66 (FgM) Maryknoll, NY MARYKNOLL.
Alberto, Jose Gerardo *m.sp.s.* '00 (P)[A] Mount Angel, OR Felix Rougier House of Studies; [L] Mount Angel, OR Missionaries of the Holy Spirit, M.Sp.S.
Alberts, Edward T. '75 (NSH) Brentwood, TN Holy Family; Deans.
Albertson, Eric J. '86 (ARL) On Duty Outside the Diocese; Military Chaplains; Army Chaplains.
Albertson, Lawrence '65 (KCK) Bucyrus, KS Queen of the Holy Rosary.
Albietz, Henry F. '74 (CIN) Fayetteville, OH St. Angela Merici; Fayetteville, OH St. Michael.
Albino, Brian E. '79 (FR) Fall River, MA St. Anthony of Padua.
Albino, Rev. Msgr. Ramon E. '84 (MGZ) Aguadilla, PR La Milagrosa; [A] Aquadilla, PR Corpus Christi College.
Albosta, John T. '64 (SCR) Plains, PA SS. Peter and Paul.
Albrecht, Craig L. '95 (SAG) Bay City, MI St. Mary of the Assumption; Diocesan Council of Catholic Women; Territorial Vicars.
Albrecht, James W. '58 (NY)[II] New York, NY Prelature of the Holy Cross and Opus Dei; New York.
Albrecht, Louis Henry '86 (BAK) Retired.
Albrecht, Tomasz (NOR) Niantic, CT St. Agnes.
Albright, Matthew '07 (Y)[F] Warren, OH Upper Campus; Girard, OH St. Rose.
Albright, R. Gerard *s.j.* '58 (DET)[K] Detroit, MI Jesuit Community at the University of Detroit Mercy.
Albright, Robert E. '72 (BAL) Retired.
Alburquerque, Messias '03 (FR) Falmouth, MA St. Patrick's; Vineyard Haven, MA Good Shepherd.
Alcantara, Miguel B. '65 (CHI) Retired.
Alcazar, Emanuel '89 (ELP) El Paso, TX St. Paul the Apostle; Presbyteral Council.
Alcazar, Victor H. '01 (RCK)[J] Rockford, IL Bishop Lane Retreat Center.
Alchouefati, Kamil (SAM) Cary, NC Saint Sharbel Mission.
Alciati, Paul J. '77 (SY) Utica, NY Our Lady of Lourdes; Homer, NY St. Margaret.
Alco, James J. '90 (SCR) Unassigned or Leave of Absence; Falls, PA Church of the Holy Redeemer Retired.
Alcocer, Jose '60 (ELP) El Paso, TX San Jose.
Alcott, Steven Paul *o.p.* '01 (RIC) Charlottesville, VA St. Thomas Aquinas.
Alcuin, William *o.f.m.cap.* '52 (GB)[J] Appleton, WI St. Fidelis Friary Retired.
Alcuino, Miguel '79 (ELP) Fort Davis, TX St. Joseph; Alpine, TX Our Lady of Peace.
Aldaz, Antonio M. '74 (LA) Baldwin Park, CA St. John the Baptist.
Alder, Ronald J. '69 (DET) Retired.
Alderson, John W. *o.f.m.* '66 (BUF)[N] Buffalo, NY St. Patrick Friary.
Aldrich, Louis G. *s.j.* '86 (FgM) Los Gatos, CA Society of Jesus.
Alecio–Rodriguez, Freddy '91 (SJN) On Duty Outside the Archdiocese.
Alejandria, Deogracias *o.s.m.* '97 (P)[L] Portland, OR The Grotto, The National Sanctuary of Our Sorrowful Mother.
Alejo, Francisco *o.f.m.* '96 (PHX) Phoenix, AZ St. Mark Roman Catholic Parish; Phoenix, AZ St. Philip the Deacon Mission, A Quasi–Parish.
Alejunas, Richard *s.d.b.* '89 (NY) Port Chester, NY Our Lady of the Rosary; [CC] Port Chester, NY Don Bosco Community Center of Port Chester, Inc.
Aleksa, Thomas M. '75 (E) Sheffield, PA St. Anthony.
Alello, Michael J. '07 (BR) Labadieville, LA St. Philomena; Board Members; Presbyteral Council.
Alenchery, Joseph '87 (RVC) Centereach, NY Assumption of the Blessed Virgin Mary.
Alengadan, George *s.d.b.* '82 (OAK) Orinda, CA Santa Maria; Deacon Council; Office of Clergy Formation; Presbyteral Council.
Alesandro, Rt. Rev. Msgr. John A. '67 (RVC) Censors of Books.
Alesandro, Rev. Msgr. John A. '66 (RVC) Nassau County Police Department.
Aleska, Thomas M. '75 (E) Warren State Hospital.
Alessandrini, Raniero *c.s.* '57 (LA) Los Angeles, CA St. Peter.
Alessandro, Rev. Msgr. John A. '66 (RVC) Roslyn, NY St. Mary's.
Alex, Boby '94 (BR) St. Amant, LA Holy Rosary.
Alexander, Andrew *s.j.* '79 (OM)[J] Omaha, NE Jesuit Community at Creighton University.
Alexander, Fred *o.c.d.* '82 (MIL) Hubertus, WI St. Mary of the Hill; [P] Hubertus, WI Discalced Carmelite Monastery – Holy Hill Basilica of the National Shrine of Mary, Help of Christians, Holy Hill.
Alexander, Fred *s.o.l.t.* '98 (FAR) St. John, ND St. Benedict's Church of Belcourt; St. John, ND St. John's Church of St. John.
Alexander, Jon *o.p.* '86 (PRO)[O] Providence St. Thomas Aquinas Priory at Providence College.
Alexander, Joseph '73 (LAF) On Leave.
Alexander, Leon F. '66 (WH) Retired.
Alexander, Marc '85 (HON) On Leave of Absence.
Alexandrunas, Albert *o.f.m.cap.* '65 (WH) Belle, WV St. John; [L] Charleston, WV Capuchins–St. Anthony Friary.
Alexius, Vincent *s.v.d.* '03 (BR) Baton Rouge, LA St. Paul the Apostle.
Alfaro, Gustavo A. '02 (NEW) Bergenfield, NJ St. John the Evangelist.
Alfaro, Jose N. '03 (PMB)[A] Boynton Beach, FL St. Vincent de Paul Regional Seminary; On Duty Outside the Archdiocese.
Alfaro, Rev. Msgr. Juan '62 (SAT) San Antonio, TX St. Rose of Lima.
Alfonso, Jairo Ariel *c.s.* '07 (BRK) Brooklyn, NY St. Joseph Patron of the Universal Church.
Alford, Brian C. '11 (SFD) Effingham, IL Sacred Heart; Effingham, IL St. Anthony of Padua; Shumway, IL Annunciation.
Algarin–Rosado, Rodney '01 (SJN) Carolina, PR San Felipe Apostol.
Algarin Lopez, Carlos *o.s.a.* '04 (SJN) Bayamon; Bayamon, PR San Agustin.
Ali, Peter Yakubu '82 (STP) Coon Rapids, MN Church of the Epiphany; Mercy Hospital.
Alicea Rivera, Luis A. '96 (FAJ)[A] Fajardo, PR Colegio Santiago Apostol; Luquillo, PR Madre del Redentor.
Alimaji, Christian A. *m.s.p.* '88 (SAV) Savannah, GA St. Benedict the Moor.
Alimnonu, Anthony (BRK) Brooklyn, NY St. Anselm.
Alindogan, Peter J. '90 (TR) Cinnaminson, NJ St. Charles Borromeo; Defenders of the Bond; Promoter of Justice.
Alindogan, Peter James R. (TR) College of Consultors.
Aliunzi, Robert *a.j.* '91 (PHX) Glendale, AZ St. James Roman Catholic Parish; College of Consultors; Presbyteral Council; Deans.
Alkire, Thomas John *o.carm.* '63 (LA) Los Angeles, CA St. Raphael.

Alkire, Timothy M. '85 (LFT) Lafayette, IN St. Boniface; Officialis; Greater Lafayette Catholic School Board; Presiding Judge; Associate Judges.
Alla, Stanislaus *s.j.* '99 (BO)[U] Newton, MA The Jesuit Community at Boston College.
Allaire, Barry J. '72 (BUF) Awaiting Assignment; Buffalo, NY St. Martin of Tours.
Allam, Show Reddy '94 (JOL) Braidwood, IL Immaculate Conception.
Allard, George L. '60 (PRO)[O] Providence St. John Vianney Residence Retired.
Allard, Rev. Msgr. John C. '75 (PRO) Woonsocket, RI St. Agatha; Woonsocket, RI Precious Blood; [M] Woonsocket, RI Fr. Marot CYO Center.
Allard, John E. *o.p.* '86 (PRO)[O] Providence St. Thomas Aquinas Priory at Providence College.
Allard, Marcel M. '65 (MAN) Manchester, NH Ste. Marie Retired.
Allbright, Brian V. '83 (P) Newport, OR Sacred Heart Parish.
Allega, Ernest '76 (WOR) South Barre, MA St. Thomas–A–Becket.
Allegra, John Christopher '70 (L) Springfield, KY Holy Trinity; [M] St. Catharine, KY Sansbury Care Center, Inc.
Allegretto, William M. *c.m.* '85 (PH)[B] Philadelphia, PA DePaul Novitiate.
Allen, Charles H. *s.j.* '73 (BGP)[B] Fairfield, CT Fairfield University; [O] Fairfield, CT The Fairfield Jesuit Community–Fairfield University.
Allen, David E. '78 (BR) Port Allen, LA Holy Family.
Allen, David G. *s.j.* '79 (BAL)[Q] Baltimore, MD Jesuit Community of Loyola University, Inc.
Allen, Donald *m.m.* '67 (SJ)[M] Los Altos, CA Maryknoll.
Allen, Francis R. *s.j.* '56 (BO)[U] Weston, MA Campion Health Center, Inc.
Allen, Frederick J. *m.m.* '65 (NY)[DD] Retired.
Allen, James F. *o.m.i.* '65 (SAT)[B] San Antonio, TX George Sexton House of Studies.
Allen, John A. '90 (CHL) Greensboro, NC St. Paul the Apostle.
Allen, Joseph P. *o.p.* '67 (HRT) New Haven, CT St. Mary's.
Allen, Joshua '11 (ATL) Graduate Studies.
Allen, Kenneth '04 (NO) Metairie, LA St. Mary Magdalen.
Allen, Loren '94 (SR) Occidental, CA St. Philip.
Allen, Nicholas '08 (NSH) Catholic Youth Office and Search Program; Franklin, TN St. Matthew; [B] Nashville, TN Father Ryan High School.
Allen, Peter '71 (RVC) Retired.
Allen, Philip T. '59 (OG) Adjutant Judicial Vicars; Indian Lake, NY St. Mary's.
Allen, Richard J. '97 (E) Sykesville, PA Assumption of Blessed Virgin Mary; Army National Guard Chaplains; Reynoldsville, PA St. Mary.
Allen, Richard L. '61 (GB) Peshtigo, WI St. Mary Retired.
Allen, Scott W. *f.s.s.p.* '90 (TYL) Tyler, TX St. Joseph the Worker Mission.
Allen, Shawn W. '99 (BO) Billerica, MA St. Theresa of Lisieux.
Allen, Terry '61 (ALX) Retired.
Allende, Rev. Msgr. Santiago Rivera '83 (MGZ) Mayaguez, PR Ascension.
Allender, Raymond '75 (SFR) San Francisco, CA St. Agnes.
Allender, Thomas *s.j.* '71 (SFR)[E] San Francisco, CA St. Ignatius College Preparatory (Coed); [N] San Francisco, CA Jesuit Community at St. Ignatius College Preparatory.
Aller, Domingo *o.s.a.* '61 (SJN) Bayamon, PR Santa Rita de Casia.
Allers, Rodney M. '08 (DUB) Priestly Life and Ministry Committee; Rockwell, IA St. Patrick; Rockford, IA Holy Name; Rockwell, IA Sacred Heart.
Alleyne, Rev. Msgr. Edward D. '60 (CAM) Retired.
Allgaier, Sebastian *o.s.b.* '99 (KC)[J] Conception, MO Conception Abbey; [A] Conception, MO Conception Seminary College.
Alliata, Peter R. '61 (WDC) Retired.
Allie, Stanley J. '58 (ALB) Retired.
Allin, R. Benedict *o.s.b.* '67 (STL) St. Louis, MO St. Anselm; [O] St. Louis, MO The Abbey of St. Mary and St. Louis.
Allison, Rev. Msgr. Bruce R. '61 (E) Erie, PA St. Julia.
Allison, Jeffrey *c.s.c.* '96 (P)[B] University of Portland; [L] Portland, OR Holy Cross Fathers & Brothers, C.S.C. – University of Portland.
Allison, Joseph C. '56 (CIN) Retired.
Allison, Michael P. '91 (E) Grove City, PA Beloved Disciple; Presbyteral Council.
Allman, Matthew T. *c.ss.r.* '73 (PH) Philadelphia, PA St. Peter the Apostle.
Alloggia, Benoit *o.s.b.* '09 (GBG)[H] Latrobe, PA Saint Vincent Archabbey.
Allt, John F. '73 (TUC) Vail, AZ Saint Rita in the Desert Roman Catholic Parish – Vail; Directors.
Almade, Frank D. '78 (PIT) New Castle, PA St. Vitus; New Castle, PA St. Vincent de Paul; Clergy Personnel Board.
Almagno, Romano S. *o.f.m.* '65 (NY)[DD] New York Franciscan Province of the Immaculate Conception.
Almagno, Romano *o.f.m.* '65 (PRO) Providence, RI Cathedral of SS. Peter and Paul.
Almarza, Juan *o.a.r.* '65 (LSC) Anthony, NM St. Anthony's.
Almazan, Leobardo *o.p.* '05 (NO)[R] New Orleans Dominican Friars, Southern Dominican Province of St. Martin de Porres.
Almeida, George F. '65 (FR) Retired.
Almendra, Leoncio T. '60 (NOR) Retired.
Almendras, Joel J. '75 (MRY) Salinas Valley State Prison.
Almeus, Enel '03 (NY) New York, NY Our Lady of Guadalupe at St. Bernard's.
Almonte, Alfred P. *c.s.* '61 (PRO) Johnston, RI Our Lady of Grace.
Almonte, Antonio '97 (NY) New York, NY Our Lady Queen of Martyrs.
Almonte–Mendez, Yunior '05 (NEW) Newark, NJ Cathedral Basilica of the Sacred Heart.
Alobaidi, Joseph *o.p.* '80 (WDC)[B] Washington, DC Dominican House of Studies.
Alonso, Armando '90 (MIA) Sunny Isles Beach, FL St. Mary Magdalen.
Alonso, Ignacio '60 (ARE) Manati, PR La Candelaria.
Alonso, Oscar *sch.p.* '68 (MIA)[D] Fort Lauderdale, FL Cardinal Gibbons High School.
Alookaran, Charles '91 (BIR) Athens, AL St. Paul's.
Alookaran, Joy '80 (BRK) Woodside, NY St. Sebastian.
Alphonse, Anthony '92 (AUS) Dime Box, TX St. Joseph; Dime Box, TX Holy Family Catholic Church – Lexington, Texas.
Alphonse, John Robert (LC) Wausau, WI Church of the Resurrection; Wausau, WI St. Michael.
Alphonse, Justin Nelson *c.p.* '04 (BIR) Fairfield, AL St. Mary's.
Alphonse, Satheesh C. '02 (LAN)[E] Chelsea, MI St. Louis Center for Exceptional Children & Adults.
Alphonso, John '68 (DAL) On Leave of Absence.
Alsola, Felix S. '86 (DET)[H] Southfield, MI Providence Hospital.
Alt, Kenneth G. *c.pp.s.* '78 (CIN) Celina, OH Immaculate Conception of the Blessed Virgin Mary.
Altavilla, Philip A. '92 (SCR) Scranton, PA St. Peter's Cathedral; Moderator of the Curia; Procurator/Advocates; Diocesan Commission on Ecumenism and Inter–Faith Matters; Diocesan Office of Ecumenism; Scouts of America; Scranton, PA The Slovak Catholic Federation (1911); Ex Officio; Vicars General; Diocesan Finance Council; Ex Officio.
Altavista, Salvatore D. *m.s.* '64 (HRT)[L] Hartford, CT Missionaries of LaSalette.
Altenbaugh, Richard L. '60 (PT) Retired.
Altenhofen, Joseph F. '10 (SEA) Vancouver, WA St. Joseph.
Altermatt, Charles K. '08 (DET) Detroit, MI St. Thomas Aquinas.
Altermatt, Gregory M. '76 (HRT) Special and other Archdiocesan Assignment; West Haven, CT Our Lady of Victory; [H] New Haven, CT Hospital of St. Raphael; West Haven, CT St. John Vianney.
Althoff, Arthur J. '55 (STL) Retired.
Altier, Robert J. '89 (STP)[G] Hastings, MN Regina Medical Center; [I] Hastings, MN Regina Retirement Center; Regina Medical Center.
Altine, Richard L. '95 (KAL) Hastings, MI St. Rose of Lima; Scouting Apostolate.
Altman, David *o.c.s.o.* '79 (SLC)[E] Huntsville, UT Abbey of Our Lady of the Holy Trinity of the Order of Cistercians; Huntsville, UT; [A] Huntsville, UT Abbey of Our Lady of the Holy Trinity.
Altman, James F. '07 (LC) Wisconsin Rapids, WI SS. Peter and Paul.
Altman, James T. '08 (LC) Boy Scouts; [C] Wisconsin Rapids, WI Assumption High School; [C] Wisconsin Rapids, WI Assumption Middle School.
Altman, Joseph W. '76 (CHI) Chicago, IL Nativity of Our Lord.
Altmann, Robert T. '62 (LC) Archivist; [H] La Crosse, WI Holy Cross (Seminary) Diocesan Center Retired.
Altrui, Ronald P. '81 (NY) On Duty Outside the Archdiocese; On Leave of Absence.
Altstock, Edward '59 (P) Retired.
Altuna, Javier *s.j.* '66 (LA) Inglewood, CA St. John Chrysostom Retired.
Alvarado, John Paul '88 (MET) South Plainfield, NJ Sacred Heart.
Alvarado, Roberto '89 (ELP) El Paso, TX Holy Family.
Alvarado de Jesus, Jose R. '94 (PCE) Ponce, PR San Conrado.
Alvarado de Jesus, Jose '94 (MO) Army National Guard Chaplains.
Alvares, Jacob *s.a.c.* '97 (FWT) Bridgeport, TX St. John the Baptizer; Decatur, TX Assumption of the Blessed Virgin Mary; Bridgeport, TX St. Mary.
Alvarez, Abel *o.s.a.* '58 (NY) New York, NY Holy Rosary.
Alvarez, Antonio M. '93 (MET) Bernardsville, NJ Our Lady of Perpetual Help.
Alvarez, Carlos A. '01 (PBL) College of Consultors; Deans; Elected.
Alvarez, Carlos '01 (PBL) Pueblo, CO St. Paul the Apostle.
Alvarez, Eduardo *s.j.* '74 (MIA) Miami Dade College–Wolfson Campus; Miami, FL Gesu.
Alvarez, Enrique '03 (SAC) North Highlands, CA St. Lawrence the Martyr.
Alvarez, Fabio A. '04 (ATL) Cumming, GA St. Brendan the Navigator.
Alvarez, Francis *s.j.* '09 (BO)[U] Brighton, MA Alberto Hurtado House.
Alvarez, Fred *s.a.* '61 (NY)[DD] Garrison, NY Franciscan Friars of the Atonement.
Alvarez, Javier *o.f.m.* '89 (FRS) Delano, CA Our Lady of Guadalupe.
Alvarez, John J. '81 (POD)[P] Kirkwood, MO Prelature of the Holy Cross and Opus Dei; Kirkwood.
Alvarez, Jonathan (AGN) Defender of the Bond; Yigo, GU Our Lady of Lourdes.
Alvarez, Jose '03 (MIA) Miami Lakes, FL Our Lady of the Lakes; [D] Miami, FL St. Brendan High School.
Alvarez, Manuel '02 (MIA) Plantation, FL St. Gregory.
Alvarez, Miguel *sch.p.* '61 (PCE) Ponce, PR Our Lady of Mt. Carmel.
Alvarez, Milton *c.m.f.* '77 (LA)[V] Rancho Dominguez, CA Dominguez Seminary Inc.
Alvarez, Nolasco Tamayo '98 (PRO) Providence, RI St. Edward.
Alvarez, Pablo D. *f.s.s.p.* '86 (PCE) On Duty Outside the Diocese.
Alvarez, Perfecto *o.s.a.* '52 (PCE)[B] The Pontifical Catholic University of Puerto Rico.
Alvarez, Perfecto *o.s.a.* '53 (SJN) Bayamon, PR Ntra. Sra. de la Monserrate.
Alvarez, Porfirio '69 (LA) Oxnard, CA St. Anthony.
Alvarez, Ramon '82 (DAL) On Leave of Absence.
Alvarez, Ramon '81 (POD) Guaynabo.
Alvarez, Yuvan Arbey '04 (NEW) Kearny, NJ St. Cecilia's.
Alvarez–Garcia, Julio '75 (WDC) Retired.
Alvarez Hernando, P. Miguel '61 (PCE)[D] Ponce, PR Residencia Santa Marta.
Alvernaz, Dennis '71 (FRS) Retired.
Alves, Eugene L. '61 (BO) Gloucester, MA Our Lady of Good Voyage.
Alves, Francisco *s.j.* '95 (WDC) Potomac, MD Our Lady of Mercy.
Alves, Rev. Msgr. Joseph T. '53 (BO) Senior Priests. Retired.
Alvey, Leonard J. '58 (OWN) Non–Parochial Assignments; [A] Owensboro, KY Brescia University; Judges.
Alvey, Leonard '58 (OWN) Priest Personnel Committee.
Alvizures, Miguel A. '08 (GAL) Houston, TX St. Ambrose.
Alzate, Alberto '77 (LAV) North Las Vegas, NV St. Christopher.
Alzugaray, Rev. Msgr. Joseph '67 (SR) Retired.
Amabile, Patsy L. '73 (CAM) On Duty Outside the Diocese.
Amabisco, Michael A. *o.p.* '10 (SB)[M] Riverside, CA St. Andrew Newman Center; Riverside, CA St. Andrew Newman Center.
Amabisco, Michael Augustine *o.p.* '10 (SB)[I] Riverside, CA St. Vincent Ferrer House.
Amadeo, Michael '92 (DM) Des Moines, IA Holy Trinity; Defenders of the Bond.
Amadi, Christopher C. *s.s.j.* '11 (NO) Reserve, LA Our Lady of Grace.
Amador, Roberto '11 (PAT) Hawthorne, NJ St. Anthony's.
Amaechi, Jerome '94 (SY) North Syracuse, NY St. Rose of Lima.
Amagba, Paschal C. *c.m.f.* '97 (SAT) San Antonio, TX Immaculate Heart of Mary.
Amagba, Paschal *c.m.f.* '97 (LA) Los Angeles, CA Our Lady Queen of Angels Parish.
Amah, Pius '90 (SAC) Sacramento, CA Our Lady of Lourdes.
Amalanathan, Irudayaraj '91 (P) Sublimity, OR St. Boniface; Aumsville, OR St. Mary – Shaw.
Amaldoss, G. '78 (NO) Marrero, LA St. Joachim.
Amalfitano, Joseph A. '63 (PH) Marcus Hook, PA Immaculate Conception.
Amaliri, Paul Obi '00 (TLS) Air Force Reserve Chaplains; On Duty Outside the Diocese.
Amalraj, Arul *o.praem.* '90 (PH) Malvern, PA St. Patrick.
Amalraj, Loyola '81 (NY) New York, NY Epiphany.
Amalraj, Loyola '81 (MIL) Germantown, WI St. Boniface.
Aman, Gerald W. *s.j.* '73 (FgM) New York, NY Society of Jesus.
Amande, Lito D. '03 (RVC) Wantagh, NY St. Frances de Chantal.
Amande, Lito D. '03 (MO) Army National Guard Chaplains.
Amandolare, Rev. Msgr. Ronald J. (PAT) Retired.
Amani, Bernard (FTW)[H] Notre Dame Congregation

of Holy Cross, United States Province of Priests & Brothers.
Amankwa–Danguah, Philip (NY) Bronx, NY St. Barnabas.
Amann, John J. '66 (BRK) Brooklyn, NY Holy Family.
Amann, Steven J. '74 (MIL) Burlington, WI St. Charles.
Amann, William '54 (ROC) Penfield, NY St. Joseph Retired.
Amantia, Damian *t.o.r.* '90 (SP) St. Petersburg, FL St. Mary Our Lady of Grace.
Amar, Joseph P. '74 (SAM)[B] University of Notre Dame Du Lac; On Duty Outside the Diocese.
Amar, Zab '74 (E) Coalport, PA St. Basil the Great; Ramey, PA Holy Trinity.
Amaral, Angelo (TR) Keansburg, NJ St. Ann.
Amaral, Mark '04 (OAK) Pinole, CA St. Joseph.
Amaral, Stephen P. '78 (PRO) Coventry, RI Our Lady of Czenstochowa.
Amaro, Arlindo A. *c.s.sp.* '56 (PRO) Central Falls, RI Immaculate Heart of Mary.
Amasa, Sheldon '90 (TR) Toms River, NJ St. Maximilian Kolbe.
Amato, Antonio '61 (PRT) Retired.
Amato, Frank *s.a.c.* '88 (BRK) Brooklyn, NY Our Lady of the Rosary of Pompeii; Consultors.
Amato, Joseph '59 (ALB) Retired.
Amato, Rev. Msgr. Nicholas P. '70 (BAL) Retired.
Amato, Salvatore J. '69 (BRK) Rego Park, NY Resurrection–Ascension.
Amaya, Hernando Gomez '02 (SAC) Orland, CA St. Dominic.
Ambalathingal, Robert *o.c.d.* '96 (BRK)[Q] Indian Latin Rite Apostolate; Long Island City, NY St. Rita.
Amberger, Frank G. '96 (CIN) Russia, OH St. Remy.
Ambert, Jorge *s.j.* '66 (SJN)[D] San Juan, PR Renovacion Conyugal; Renovacion Conyugal (Fundacion Fernando Martinez Calle, Inc.).
Ambooken, Jose '75 (NY) Bronx, NY St. Margaret Mary.
Ambosta, Dawson '75 (NY) Bronxville, NY St. Joseph.
Ambrogi, James J. '64 (PH) Retired.
Ambrose, John Peter *m.s.f.s.* '98 (KAL) Watervliet, MI St. Joseph.
Ambrose, John Peter *m.s.f.s.* '98 (TYL)[C] Whitehouse, TX The Missionaries of St. Francis de Sales.
Ambrose, Joseph *o.c.d.* '98 (LA) Downey, CA St. Raymond.
Ambrose, Malcolm '72 (LA) Santa Clarita, CA St. Clare.
Ambrosio, Rev. Msgr. Joseph F. '74 (NEW) Newark, NJ Holy Trinity – Epiphany; Newark, NJ Our Lady of Mt. Carmel; Ironbound Deanery 21; Presbyteral Council; Italian Apostolate.
Ambrosy, David J. '85 (DUB)[H] Cedar Rapids, IA Mercy Medical Center–Cedar Rapids; Cedar Rapids, IA St. Pius X; [L] Cedar Rapids, IA Sisters of Mercy of the Americas West Midwest Community, Inc. Sacred Heart Convent.
Ameche, William *s.j.* '81 (SD) San Diego, CA Our Lady of Guadalupe Catholic Parish San Diego.
Amedee, Rev. Msgr. Francis '48 (HT) Retired.
Amen, Maurice E. *c.s.c.* '61 (FTW)[H] Notre Dame Congregation of Holy Cross, United States Province of Priests & Brothers.
Ament, Richard J. '66 (DUB) Maquoketa, IA St. Lawrence.
Amepparambil, John Xaviour '98 (CC) Port Aransas, TX St. Joseph.
Amerando, Jerry '84 (FRS) Easton, CA The Catholic Community of St. Jude and Our Lady of the Assumption.
Amershek, Charles M. '75 (ALT) State College, PA Good Shepherd.
Ames, Gregory '86 (DEN) Northglenn, CO Immaculate Heart of Mary.
Ames, John J. '82 (PH) On Special or Other Archdiocesan Assignment; Conshohocken, PA St. Matthew; [BB] Philadelphia, PA Newman Apostolate for Archdiocese of Philadelphia; Office for Catechetical Formation.
Amesse, Michael J. *o.m.i.* '84 (BWN) Brownsville, TX Immaculate Conception Cathedral; Brownsville Deanery.
Amey, Rev. Msgr. Robert G. '69 (WDC) Rockville, MD St. Mary; Deans; [X] Rockville, MD Archdiocesan Council of Catholic Women.
Amezaga, Louis (LSC) Absent On Leave.
Amezcua, Alfonso '87 (LA) Los Angeles, CA Immaculate Conception.
Amian, Arthur '89 (HON)[C] Honolulu, HI St. Francis Healthcare System of Hawaii; Pearl City, HI Our Lady of Good Counsel.
Amico, Alexander D. '73 (E) Erie, PA St. Paul.
Amico, Charles R. '52 (BUF)[A] East Aurora, NY Christ the King Seminary Retired.
Amico, Francis A. *c.s.b.* '75 (GAL)[O] Sugar Land Basilian Mission Center.
Amidar, Venancio '78 (ORG) Cypress, CA St. Irenaeus.
Amidon, Philip R. *s.j.* '74 (OM) Omaha, NE St. John; [J] Omaha, NE Jesuit Community at Creighton University.
Amiot, Ronald J. *s.j.* '78 (BAL) Towson, MD; [Q] Baltimore, MD Jesuit Community of Loyola University, Inc.; [B] Jesuit Community of Loyola University, Inc.; [Q] Towson, MD Maryland Province of the Society of Jesus.
Amiot, Ronald J. *s.j.* '78 (BO)[U] Boston The Society of Jesus of New England–Provincial Offices.
Amir, Andrews '90 (SFR)[A] Menlo Park, CA St. Patrick Seminary and University.
Amiro, Raymond M. '43 (SFE) Retired.
Amissah, Kofi Ntsiful '79 (ALB) Albany, NY Sacred Heart of Jesus; Menands, NY St. Joan of Arc.
Ammering, Bruce F. '54 (ROC)[L] Rochester, NY Sisters St. Joseph of Rochester Retired.
Amo, Steven '92 (SPR) Feeding Hills, MA Sacred Heart.
Amoako–Attah, Matthew *c.s.sp.* '88 (CIN) Dayton, OH St. Benedict the Moor.
Amobi, Bartholomew '01 (ROC) Webster, NY St. Rita.
Amodio, Francis *o.carm.* '83 (NY)[C] Newburgh, NY Mt. St. Mary College; [GG] Newburg, NY Mt. St. Mary College; [DD] Middletown, NY St. Albert's Priory.
Amora, Eduardo '90 (NY) Staten Island, NY Holy Rosary; Staten Island University Hospital North.
Amora, Silvano B. '77 (TR) Keansburg, NJ St. Ann.
Amoruso, Roberto *f.s.c.b.* '93 (WDC) Lexington, MA; [O] Bethesda, MD Priestly Fraternity of the Missionaries of St. Charles Borromeo, Inc.
Amoruso, Roberto *f.s.c.b.* '93 (BO)[U] Bethesda, MD House of Washington DC.
Amos, Jacob *o.s.b.* '10 (BIR)[E] Cullman, AL St. Bernard Abbey.
Amoy, Roleto B. '11 (YAK) Grandview, WA Blessed Sacrament; Mabton, WA Immaculate Conception.
Ampong, Bernard Osei '97 (ALB) Oneonta, NY St. Mary.
Amrhein, Quentin *c.p.* '53 (BRK)[R] Jamaica, NY Immaculate Conception Monastery Retired.
Amrhein, Robert *o.f.m.conv.* '62 (SY) Binghamton, NY SS. Cyril and Method; Binghamton, NY Holy Trinity.
Amsberry, John '97 (P) Portland, OR Church of St. Joseph the Worker.
Amundsen, Rev. Msgr. Robert L. '69 (DEN) Lafayette, CO Immaculate Conception.
Amy, Rev. Msgr. Peter L. '64 (LA) Sylmar, CA St. Didacus Retired.
Amyot, Andrew J. '64 (OG) Norfolk, NY.
Ana, Eugene Sta. '92 (SD) San Diego, CA Saint John the Evangelist Catholic Parish San Diego; San Diego, CA Saint Vincent de Paul Catholic Parish.
Anaeche, Collins I. '08 (HRT) Southbury, CT Sacred Heart.
Anaele, Ignatius I. '98 (CHI) South Holland, IL St. Jude the Apostle.
Anaeto, Dominic '94 (NOR)[A] Cromwell, CT Holy Apostles College and Seminary.
Anala, Anthony *s.v.d.* (FWT) Fort Worth, TX St. Rita.
Anane, Francis '98 (NY) Mt. Kisco, NY St. Francis of Assisi.
Anania, Alexis *o.f.m.* '58 (PIT) Pittsburgh, PA St. Pamphilus.
Anarado, Ethel '01 (RVC) Mineola, NY Corpus Christi; Mineola, NY Winthrop Hospital.
Anastasia, Thomas '91 (SP) Plant City, FL St. Clement; [L] St. Petersburg, FL St. Clement Housing, Inc.
Anatuanya, Gregory '01 (R) Pinehurst, NC Sacred Heart.
Anawonah, Frederick '95 (BRK) Peninsula Hospital Center; St. John's Episcopal Hospital; Far Rockaway, NY St. Mary Star of the Sea and St. Gertrude.
Anaya–Estrada, Jose–Angel '09 (MIL) Lake Geneva, WI St. Francis de Sales.
Anaya–Maida, Fernando '94 (GAL) Katy, TX St. Bartholomew the Apostle.
Ancharski, John J. '83 (TUC) Leave of Absence.
Ancheril, Jose '86 (BEL) Retired.
Ancona, Rev. Msgr. Gaspar F. '63 (GR) Retired.
Anctil, Peter Claude *o.s.b.* '67 (BUR)[E] Weston, VT Priory of Benedictine Monks.
Andary, John S. '51 (SAM) Retired.
Andebo, Hillary '99 (JC) Jefferson City, MO Immaculate Conception.
Andel, David '95 (SB) Judicial Vicar; Judges; Diocesan Curia; Yucaipa, CA St. Frances Xavier Cabrini; College of Consultors; Elected At–Large Members.
Anderl, Peter J. '01 (FAR) Mantador, ND Sts. Peter & Paul Church of Mantador; Mooreton, ND St. Anthony's.
Anderlonis, Rev. Msgr. Joseph J. '69 (PH) Philadelphia, PA St. George; Vicar for Consecrated Life; On Special or Other Archdiocesan Assignment.
Anders, Rev. Msgr. Arnold '50 (VIC) Retired.
Anders, Rev. Msgr. Arnold (CC)[E] Corpus Christi, TX Mount Carmel Home.
Andersen, Emil (E) Retired.
Anderson, Alexander R. '75 (STL) De Soto, MO St. Rose of Lima.
Anderson, Rev. Msgr. Andrew L. '74 (MIA) Catholic Funeral Directors' Guild; Catholic Lawyers' Guild.
Anderson, Rev. Msgr. Andrew L. '74 (SAM) Judges; On Duty Outside the Archdiocese.
Anderson, Rev. Msgr. Andrew '74 (MIA) Judges; [A] Boynton Beach, FL St. Vincent de Paul Regional Seminary.
Anderson, Arthur T. '58 (CAM) Retired.
Anderson, Arthur (CHI)[N] Chicago, IL St. Peter's Friary.
Anderson, Barg G. '05 (SUP) Somerset, WI St. Anne.
Anderson, Daniel J. *o.f.m.* '76 (CIN)[N] Cincinnati, OH Pleasant Street Friary; Councillors:; [N] Cincinnati, OH St. Francis Seraph Friary.
Anderson, David *s.j.* (SEA)[M] Seattle, WA Arrupe Jesuit Community at Seattle University; [A] Seattle, WA Seattle University.
Anderson, David '83 (STN) Ukiah, CA St. Peter Eastern Catholic Mission.
Anderson, Derek *s.o.l.t.* (PAT) Director of Catechesis as Evangelization; [H] Madison, NJ St. Paul Inside The Walls: The Catholic Center for Evangelization at Bayley–Ellard.
Anderson, Edward C. *c.s.v* '50 (LAV)[C] Las Vegas, NV Clerics of St. Viator Retirement Home.
Anderson, Edward *c.s.v.* '50 (CHI)[N] Arlington Heights Viatorian Province Center–Clerics of St. Viator.
Anderson, Edwin C. '08 (SUP) Spooner, WI St. Catherine; Spooner, WI St. Joseph; Spooner, WI St. Francis De Sales; Presbyteral Council & Diocesan Consultors; Catholic Boy and Girl Scout Chaplain.
Anderson, Gabriel C. '89 (DUB) Dubuque, IA St. Columbkille; Due Process Board.
Anderson, George M. *s.j.* '73 (NY)[DD] New York, NY Jesuit Community of the Immaculate Conception.
Anderson, Rev. Msgr. James B. '78 (GAL)[A] Houston, TX St. Mary's Seminary.
Anderson, James *m.s.a.* '77 (NOR)[G] Cromwell Society of the Missionaries of the Holy Apostles.
Anderson, John C. '93 (SUP) Tomahawk, WI St. Francis of Assisi; Tomahawk, WI St. Mary; East Deanery; Personnel Placement Board.
Anderson, Rev. Msgr. John E. '66 (LSC) Las Cruces, NM Holy Cross; Bishops Administrative Council; Vicar General; Director of Clergy Personnel; Defenders of the Bond; Diocesan Consultors; Presbyteral Council; Clergy Personnel Board; Finance Council; Holy Childhood Association; Propagation of the Faith; Priests Retirement Fund Committee.
Anderson, John R. '96 (ATL) On Leave of Absence.
Anderson, John '96 (ATL) Without Archdiocesan Assignment or Faculties.
Anderson, John (NY)[Z] New York, NY Kateri Residence.
Anderson, Jordan S. *o.praem.* '97 (ORG)[I] Silverado, CA Norbertine Fathers of Orange Inc.
Anderson, Joseph G. '63 (MIL) Retired.
Anderson, Joseph W. '62 (PEO) Retired.
Anderson, Kenneth J. '87 (RCK) DeKalb, IL St. Mary.
Anderson, Kenneth '98 (CHI) Highland Park, IL Immaculate Conception.
Anderson, Kevin '83 (SCL) Braham, MN St. Peter & Paul; Princeton, MN The Church of Christ Our Light Princeton/Zimmerman; Diocesan Consultors.
Anderson, Knute *o.s.b.* '56 (SCL)[I] Collegeville, MN St. John's Abbey, of the Order of St. Benedict.
Anderson, Kurt J. *m.m.* '72 (FgM) Maryknoll, NY MARYKNOLL.
Anderson, Lawrence (PAT) Pompton Lakes, NJ Our Lady of the Assumption.
Anderson, Louis '63 (GR) Retired.
Anderson, Louis '07 (NY) Bronx, NY St. Lucy; Peekskill, NY Assumption.
Anderson, Luke *s.o.cist.* '54 (ALN)[K] New Ringgold, PA Cistercian Monastery; New Ringgold, PA.
Anderson, Michael F. '83 (STP) St. Paul, MN Church of St. Bernard.
Anderson, Patrick S. '10 (CLV) Cleveland Heights, OH Communion of Saints Parish.
Anderson, R. Bentley *s.j.* '96 (NY)[DD] Cardinal Spellman Hall, Jesuit Community.
Anderson, Richard W. *s.j.* '66 (CHI)[D] Chicago, IL St. Ignatius Jesuit Community; [D] Chicago, IL St. Ignatius College Prep.
Anderson, Robert Kevin *o.c.s.o.* '55 (WOR)[N] Spencer, MA St. Joseph's Abbey.
Anderson, Robert S. *o.s.m.* '65 (P)[L] Portland, OR The Grotto, The National Sanctuary of Our Sorrowful Mother.
Anderson, Ronald '72 (DET) Milford, MI St. Mary, Our Lady of the Snows.
Anderson, Shawn Matthew *o.s.b.* '07 (GBG)[H] Latrobe Saint Vincent Archabbey; [H] Latrobe, PA Saint Vincent Archabbey.
Anderson, Stephen A. '86 (E) Western Vicariate.
Anderson, Stephen A. '79 (E) Conneaut Lake, PA Our Lady Queen of the Americas.
Anderson, Steven D. '03 (LAN) Burton, MI Holy Redeemer.
Anderson, Terence '84 (SFS) Huron, SD Holy Trinity.
Anderson, Thomas S. *s.j.* '98 (MIL)[P] Milwaukee, WI Jesuit Community at Marquette University.
Anderson, Thomas '07 (SFS) Westport, SD Sacred Heart of Westport; [H] Aberdeen, SD St. Thomas Aquinas Newman Center.
Anderson, William A. '63 (WH) Retired.

Andert, Thomas *o.s.b.* '75 (SCL)[I] Collegeville, MN St. John's Abbey, of the Order of St. Benedict; Collegeville, MN.
Andinam, Emmanuel '77 (CHR) Lexington, SC Corpus Christi.
Andoh, Godfrey '02 (BLX)[F] Hattiesburg, MS University of Southern Mississippi.
Andonian, Raphael *o.mech.* '65 (OLN) Belmont, MA Holy Cross; Business Chancellor.
Andrade, Bernardino '65 (OAK) Retired.
Andrade, David M. '86 (FR) Fall River, MA Holy Trinity; [B] Fall River, MA Bishop Connolly High School.
Andrade, J. Anthony '92 (STP) St. Paul, MN St. Pascal Baylon.
Andrae, Henry C. '78 (E) Sharon, PA Sacred Heart.
Andraschko, Rev. Msgr. James '59 (SFS) Retired.
Andre, Leonard J. '61 (MIL) Retired.
Andre, Rev. Msgr. Ludwig '57 (SJ) Retired.
Andreano, Rev. Msgr. Michael A. '00 (NEW) Newark, NJ Cathedral Basilica of the Sacred Heart; Presbyteral Council; Vice Chancellor, Secretary to the Archbishop and Director/Master of Ceremonies for Pontifical Liturgies; Vice Chancellor & Secretary to the Archbishop and Director/Master of Ceremonies for Pontifical Liturgies.
Andreassi, Anthony *c.o.* '07 (BRK) Brooklyn, NY St. Boniface; [R] Brooklyn, NY Oratory of Saint Philip Neri, Congregation Pontifical Rite.
Andreassi, Anthony *c.o.* '07 (NY)[E] New York, NY Regis High School.
Andree, Daniel *c.ss.r.* '80 (CHI)[N] Chicago, IL The Redemptorist Fathers of Chicago.
Andree, Daniel *c.ss.r.* '80 (DEN)[N] Denver The Redemptorists/Denver Province.
Andree, John Paul *c.ss.r.* '68 (CHI) Chicago, IL St. Michael in Old Town; [N] Chicago, IL The Redemptorist Fathers of Chicago.
Andrejek, Michael J. '98 (PEO) Oglesby, IL Holy Family.
Andres, Edmundo *c.m.f.* '56 (MET) Perth Amboy, NJ Our Lady of Fatima.
Andres, James *o.f.m.cap.* '63 (DET)[P] Washington, MI Capuchin Retreat.
Andres, Napoleon *m.s.* '85 (HON) Waipahu, HI St. Joseph.
Andres, Timothy *o.carm.* '86 (JOL)[L] Darien Carmelite Provincial Office.
Andrews, Alexander *o.s.b.* '69 (SCL)[I] Collegeville, MN St. John's Abbey, of the Order of St. Benedict.
Andrews, Christopher *o.s.b.* '06 (TLS)[G] Hulbert, OK Our Lady of the Annunciation of Clear Creek Monastery.
Andrews, Daniel R. '01 (OM) Norfolk, NE Sacred Heart.
Andrews, Dave *s.j.* '79 (CI)[C] Kolonia, Pohnpei, FM Jesuit House.
Andrews, Edward *o.s.a.* '59 (CHI)[N] Matteson, IL Austin Friary Retired.
Andrews, Eric *c.s.p.* '95 (LA)[BB] Pacific Palisades, CA Paulist Productions; Los Angeles, CA St. Paul the Apostle.
Andrews, John F. '62 (FR) Retired.
Andrews, John S. '96 (OM) Humphrey, NE St. Francis.
Andrews, Mark W. *s.j.* '92 (CHI)[S] The Jesuit Retreat League of Chicago; [C] Chicago, IL Jesuit Community at Loyola University Chicago.
Andrews, Peter J. '88 (PRO) Tiverton, RI St. Christopher; Tiverton, RI St. Theresa.
Andrey, Roberto A. '83 (SFR) San Bruno, CA St. Robert.
Andrie, Donald A. *c.s.p.* '94 (GR) Campus Ministry; Allendale, MI St. Luke University Parish; [K] Allendale, MI St. Luke University Parish and Catholic Campus Ministry.
Andrino, Guilherme A. *s.v.d.* '07 (TR) Trenton, NJ Blessed Sacrament–Our Lady of the Divine Shepherd Parish.
Andrus, Albin A. '73 (PRT) Portland, ME Our Lady of Hope Parish Retired.
Andrus, Charles *s.s.j.* '76 (NO) New Orleans, LA Blessed Sacrament–St. Joan of Arc; [J] New Orleans, LA St. Augustine High School; [E] New Orleans, LA St. Augustine High School.
Andrus, David L. *s.j.* '79 (NO)[R] Pohnpei, FM Jesuits of Pohnpei.
Andrus, David *s.j.* (CI) Diocesan Consultors; Pohnpei–Kosrae.
Andrus, Richard *s.v.d.* '83 (CHI) Chicago, IL St. Elizabeth.
Andujar, J. Iriarte *o.p.* '86 (PRO)[O] Providence St. Thomas Aquinas Priory at Providence College.
Anello, Robert *m.s.a.* '07 (NOR)[G] Cromwell Society of the Missionaries of the Holy Apostles.
Angel, A. Oliver '01 (BWN) Mission, TX Our Lady of the Holy Rosary; Presiding Judge; Judicial Department and Diocesan Tribunal.
Angel, Fredy A. '05 (SAV) Adel, GA Queen of Peace.
Angel, Jose Rene '93 (BWN) Edinburg, TX Immaculate Conception; San Isidro, TX St. Isidore; Associate Judges; Defenders of the Bond.
Angel, Oliver '01 (LAR) Tribunal.
Angel, Rene '93 (SAT) Defenders of the Bond.
Angeles, Joey F. '00 (BR) Plaquemine, LA St. Joan of Arc; White Castle, LA Our Lady of Prompt Succor.
Angeles, Rodel '92 (CLV) Philippine–American Ministry; Cleveland, OH Cathedral of St. John the Evangelist; [X] Cleveland, OH St. John Cathedral Endowment Trust.
Angelicchio, Paul F. '77 (SY) Rome, NY St. John the Baptist; Rome, NY Transfiguration.
Angelini, Joseph Barry *o.f.m.conv.* (CHL) Winston–Salem, NC Our Lady of Mercy.
Angelini, Joseph '67 (MIA) Retired.
Angell, Charles *s.a.* '60 (NY)[DD] Garrison, NY St. Christopher's Inn; [DD] Garrison, NY St. Christopher's Friary.
Angelle, Rev. Msgr. Robert G. '56 (LAF) Retired.
Angelo, Thomas M. '85 (NOR) On Duty Outside the Diocese; Military Chaplains; Air Force Chaplains.
Angeloni, Michael A. '75 (WIL) Unassigned or Leave of Absence.
Angelov, Rev. Archpriest Kiril '90 (STF) Yonkers, NY St. Michael; Chancellor & Archivist; Diocesan Consultors; New York; Presbyteral Council; Administrative Council; Directors; Ecumenical Commission.
Angelovic, Michael '65 (SEA) Retired.
Angelucci, Patrick *s.d.b.* (NY)[E] New Rochelle, NY Salesian High School.
Angert, James *t.o.r.* '71 (ARL) Herndon, VA St. Joseph.
Angi, Steve J. '85 (CIN) Chancellor; Adjutant Judicial Vicars.
Angi, Steve J. '85 (CIN) Cincinnati, OH St. Louis; Archdiocesan Department Directors; Director; Presbyteral Council.
Angilella, Joseph T. *s.j.* '65 (SJ)[M] Los Gatos, CA Sacred Heart Jesuit Center.
Anginoli, Rev. Msgr. Joseph T. '75 (PAT) Mendham, NJ St. Joseph's; Adjutant Judicial Vicar.
Angkel, Julio '83 (CI)[C] Tunnuk, Chuuk, FM Vicariate Residence; Vocations.
Angken, Julio '83 (CI) Chuuk, FM St. Anthony's.
Anglaaere, Peter '86 (ROC) Hornell, NY Our Lady of the Valley.
Anglada, Julio A. '98 (ARE) Arecibo, PR Church of San Martin de Porres; Arecibo Hospital.
Angles, Rev. Msgr. Sebastian '44 (BRK) Retired.
Anglim, Ronald H. '65 (CHI) Antioch, IL St. Peter Retired.
Anglin, John *o.f.m.* '68 (SP)[N] St. Petersburg, FL St. Anthony Friary.
Angotti, Joseph A. '91 (GRY) La Porte, IN St. Peter.
Anguay, James *ss.cc.* '72 (HON)[D] Honolulu, HI St. Patrick's Monastery.
Angueira, Jose Francisco Quintero '89 (SJN) Bayamon, PR Nuestra Sra. de los Dolores; Diocesan Consultors.
Anguiano, James M. '82 (LA) Clergy Misconduct Oversight Board; Vocations.
Anguiano–Rivera, Jesus G. '09 (SAT) San Antonio, TX St. Luke.
Angulo, Raul '85 (MIA) Miami, FL Mother of Christ.
Ani, Edmund C. '01 (ARL) Falls Church, VA St. James.
Ani, Godwin *s.s.j.* (MOB) Prichard, AL St. James Major.
Anich, Kenneth *s.v.d.* '73 (DUB)[B] Epworth, IA Divine Word College.
Anichini, Albert *m.c.c.j.* '62 (FgM) Cincinnati, OH COMBONI MISSIONARIES (VERONA FATHERS).
Aniekwe, Samuel O. '96 (MO) Army Reserve Chaplains.
Aniello, Frederick M. '79 (HRT) Waterbury, CT Our Lady of Mt. Carmel.
Anifer, Jeffrey R. '67 (DET) Retired.
Aniszczyk, Leon S. '73 (MET) Bound Brook, NJ St. Mary of Czestochowa.
Ankenbrandt, Thomas F. *s.j.* '60 (DET)[K] Clarkston, MI Colombiere Center.
Anklan, Carlos *c.s.* '97 (PMB) Delray Beach, FL Our Lady Queen of Peace.
Ankley, Christopher '09 (KAL) Vocations and Ongoing Formation; Vicksburg, MI St. Martin of Tours.
Annese, Joseph P. '62 (LAV) Retired.
Annese, Lucius *o.f.m.* '58 (NY)[DD] New York Franciscan Province of the Immaculate Conception.
Annie, Rev. Msgr. Frederick P. '78 (WH) Diocesan (Home) Missions; Propagation of the Faith, Pontifical Society for; Vicar General and Moderator of the Curia; Diocesan Consultors; Catholic University, Friends of; Holy Childhood Association; Diocesan and Foreign Missions, Office of; Contacts to Report.
An Ninh, Vincent Nguyen '71 (DET) Detroit, MI Our Lady of Grace Vietnamese Parish.
Annino, Sebastian V. '61 (CAM) Retired.
Annor–Omen, James K. '02 (NY) Yonkers, NY St. Ann.
Annunziato, Michael *ss.cc.* '53 (FR)[F] Fairhaven, MA Damien Residence; [E] New Bedford, MA Sacred Heart Home Retired.
Anonuevo, Salvador '86 (RIC) Bedford, VA Holy Name of Mary; Moneta, VA Resurrection.
Ansaloni, Edmund *o.f.m.* '49 (SP)[N] Clearwater Beach, FL St. Paul Friary.
Ansbro, Rev. Msgr. Francis J. '51 (NY) Peekskill, NY Assumption Retired.
Anschutz, Larry '82 (SFD) Mount Olive, IL Blessed Pope John Paul II.
Anselment, Joseph '61 (ALB) Priests Retirement Board/ Priests Retirement Plan Board Retired.
Ansems, Bruce '05 (KCK) Rossville, KS St. Stanislaus; St. Marys, KS Immaculate Conception; Judges; Defenders of the Bond.
Anslow, Thomas C. *c.m.* '72 (LA)[P] Los Angeles, CA Amat Residence II; Canonical Services, Vicar for; Canonical Services, Vicar for.
Ansomkase, Francis D. '10 (GAL) Houston, TX Our Mother of Mercy.
Anson, Cesar R. '77 (TR) Burlington, NJ The Church of St. Katharine Drexel, Burlington, N.J.
Antal, Andras '68 (CLV) Cleveland, OH St. Elizabeth of Hungary.
Antall, Rev. Msgr. Richard C. '80 (CLV) Cleveland, OH Holy Name.
Antao, Rev. Msgr. John S. '60 (NEW) Retired.
Antczak, John '63 (JOL) Bradley, IL St. Joseph; Kankakee, IL Riverside Medical Center.
Antczak, Robert A. '64 (NEW) Woodcliff Lake, NJ Our Lady Mother of the Church Retired.
Antecini, Claudio '96 (BRK) Brooklyn, NY Visitation of the Blessed Virgin Mary.
Antekeier, Charles R. '62 (GR) Retired.
Antes, Esteban Eugenio D. '93 (RIC) Wytheville, VA St. Mary the Mother of God.
Anthony, Alphonse (TYL) On Duty Outside the Diocese.
Anthony, Angelo *c.pp.s.* '89 (CIN) Dayton, OH Emmanuel; Dayton, OH Holy Trinity; Dayton, OH St. Joseph.
Anthony, Eddy *s.j.* (CI) St. Joseph.
Anthony, Fred Jeffrey '09 (P) Sweet Home, OR St. Helen Catholic Church.
Anthony, Jerold G. '96 (CAM) Vineland, NJ St. Padre Pio Parish, Vineland, N.J.
Anthony, Joseph Pathil '99 (BIS) Williston, ND St. Joseph.
Anthony, Joseph '80 (MO) DEPARTMENT OF VETERANS AFFAIRS HOSPITALS AND CHAPLAINS.
Anthony, Joseph (LAV) On Duty Outside the Diocese.
Anthony, Rev. Msgr. Paul G. '61 (STL) Retired.
Anthonypillai, Gnanapragasm '94 (NY) Bronx, NY Our Lady of Solace.
Anthonysamy, Richard S. *s.j.* '08 (DEN)[N] Denver, CO Xavier Jesuit Center.
Antillon, William R. '79 (RCK) Morrison, IL St. Mary.
Antinarelli, Ronald A. '74 (ROC) Rochester, NY Our Lady of Victory–St. Joseph.
Antiporek, James '81 (JOL) Warrenville, IL St. Irene.
Antoine, James *o.f.m.cap.* '67 (GF) Lodge Grass, MT Our Lady of Loretto.
Antolini, Vincenzo *o.m.v.* '58 (LA) Hawaiian Gardens, CA St. Peter Chanel.
Anton, Ronald J. *s.j.* '83 (GAL) Retired.
Anton, Ronald J. *s.j.* '83 (WDC)[O] Washington, DC The Jesuit Community at Georgetown University.
Anton, William J. '02 (LUB) Lubbock, TX Cathedral Christ the King; [D] Lubbock, TX Christ the King Cathedral School Foundation.
Antone, William *o.m.i.* '80 (WDC) Washington, DC; Washington, DC AMERICAN OBLATE MISSIONS; [O] Washington, DC Provincial Offices of the United States Province of the Missionary Oblates of Mary Immaculate; [O] Washington, DC Oblate Community.
Antone, William *o.m.i.* '80 (LA) Pacoima, CA Mary Immaculate.
Antone, William *o.m.i.* (STP)[S] St. Paul, MN Oblate Media and Communication Corporation.
Antonelle, John N. '06 (NOR)[K] Storrs, CT University of Connecticut; Chaplains; Storrs, CT St. Thomas Aquinas; Members.
Antonelli, Rev. Msgr. Louis '49 (CHK) Rota, MP San Isidro Parish; Presbyteral Council.
Antonelli, Robert *c.s.c.* '65 (P)[B] University of Portland; [L] Portland, OR Holy Cross Fathers & Brothers, C.S.C. – University of Portland.
Antonelli, Robert *c.s.c.* (FTW)[H] Notre Dame Congregation of Holy Cross, United States Province of Priests & Brothers.
Antonellis, Joseph A. '72 (BO) Members; Absent on Leave.
Antoney, Jose Thundathil *c.m.i.* '88 (SPC) Campbell, MO St. Teresa; Campbell, MO St. Ann.
Antonicelli, Rev. Msgr. Charles V. '93 (WDC) Pastoral Center Special Ministries; Episcopal Vicar for Canonical Services; Washington, DC St. Patrick; Judicial Vicars.
Antonik, Jan '03 (VEN) Sarasota, FL St. Thomas More.
Antonucci, Richard J. *o.praem.* '72 (PH)[Y] Paoli, PA Daylesford Abbey; [B] Paoli, PA Daylesford Abbey; Paoli, PA.
Antony, Abraham '95 (SJ) San Jose, CA St. Martin of Tours.
Antony, Albin Roby '86 (NY) Staten Island, NY St. Charles.
Antony, John Britto *c.s.c.* '11 (BUR) Bennington, VT Sacred Heart St. Francis de Sales; North Bennington, VT St. John the Baptist.
Antony, John Francis '91 (NY) Tuckahoe, NY Immaculate Conception.

Antony, John K. '96 (LR) Fayetteville, AR St. Joseph; Huntsville, AR St. John the Evangelist.
Antony, John K. (OKL) Adjutant Judicial Vicars.
Antony, Peter '89 (CC) Riviera, TX Our Lady of Consolation.
Antony, Raju '98 (WH) Wheeling, WV St. Vincent de Paul.
Antony, Sathyan Naduviledath *o.i.c.* (MCE) Valley Stream, NY St. Basil Malankara Catholic Church; Defender of the Bond; Bible Apostolate Director; Elected Members; Priests – Heads of Apostolates.
Antony, Varghese '91 (CC) Corpus Christi, TX Our Lady of the Rosary.
Antonydass, Pichaimuthu *h.g.n.* '00 (PRT) Saco, ME Good Shepherd Parish.
Antos, Paul J. '54 (ALB) Retired.
Antram, Cormac *o.f.m.* '54 (GLP) Radio; St. Michaels, AZ St. Michael.
Antry, Theodore J. *o.praem.* '66 (PH)[Y] Paoli, PA Daylesford Abbey.
Antunez, Roy L. *s.j.* '71 (P) Cottage Grove, OR Our Lady of Perpetual Help; [L] Portland, OR Colombiere Community.
Antunez–Olea, Bardo Fabian '03 (TUC) Morenci, AZ Holy Cross Roman Catholic Church – Morenci.
Antus, Roland '62 (DUL) Retired.
Antweiler, Donald J. '73 (JC) Ministry to Priests; Loose Creek, MO Immaculate Conception; Loose Creek, MO St. Louis.
Antwi, Eric B. '01 (WH) Chester, WV Sacred Heart; New Cumberland, WV Immaculate Conception.
Antwi–Boasiako, Dominic *a.b.* '81 (VIC) Wharton, TX Holy Family.
Anumata, Christopher C. '92 (MO) Army Chaplains.
Anung, Ronelo '92 (NY) Staten Island, NY St. Patrick.
Anuszewski, Albert M. *o.ss.t.* '91 (BAL)[Q] Rome, Italy.
Anuta, Hyginus Chuks '97 (SFE) Tucumcari, NM St. Anne; Vicars Forane (Deans); Presbyteral Council of the Archdiocese of Santa Fe.
Anuzewski, Damian *o.ss.t.* '79 (BAL)[Q] Archdiocese of Washington, DC.
Anweting, Livinus '04 (CHI) Chicago, IL Immaculate Heart of Mary.
Anyaeche, Jude '85 (MO) DEPARTMENT OF VETERANS AFFAIRS HOSPITALS AND CHAPLAINS.
Anyagwa, Donald (HRT) North Haven, CT St. Therese.
Anyama, Vincent C. '09 (DAL) Frisco, TX St. Francis of Assisi; Appointed Members.
Anyamele, Faustinus '06 (DEN) Denver, CO Good Shepherd.
Anyanike, Vitalis E. '02 (OM) Omaha, NE St. Benedict the Moor; Omaha, NE St. Therese of the Child Jesus.
Anyanwu, Celestine '83 (BRK) East Elmhurst, NY St. Gabriel.
Anyanwu, Christopher (PAT) Paterson, NJ St. Joseph Hospital; [K] Paterson, NJ St. Joseph's Hospital and Medical Center.
Anyanwu, Cornelius Kelechi '08 (HRT) Waterbury, CT St. Leo the Great; Waterbury, CT SS. Peter and Paul.
Anyanwu, Innocent '80 (LAV) Las Vegas, NV Holy Family.
Anyikwa, Felix '87 (LKC) Oberlin, LA St. Joan of Arc.
Anziano, James J. '81 (PH) Retired.
Anzoategui, Francisco J. '88 (BO) Framingham, MA St. Stephen.
Anzora, Juan '08 (ATL) Atlanta, GA Immaculate Heart of Mary.
Apassa, Cyril '71 (RNO) Retired.
Apel, John *s.j.* (SPK)[B] Spokane, WA Gonzaga University.
Apfelbeck, Keith B. '99 (LC) Special Assignment.
Apfelbeck, Kurt J. '99 (LC) Leave of Absence.
Apoldite, Dennis A. '78 (TR) Trenton, NJ Sacred Heart; Vicars Forane (Deans).
Apolinar, Moises R. '81 (LA) Los Angeles, CA St. Patrick.
Aponte, Jose *s.j.* '00 (MGZ) Mayaguez, PR Church De El Buen Pastor.
Aponte, Melvin Diaz '02 (PCE) Yauco, PR Santo Domingo de Guzman.
Aponte–Merced, Luis *o.f.m.* '03 (PEO) Peoria, IL St. Joseph; Peoria, IL Sacred Heart.
Aponte Rivera, Eliud '86 (PCE) Ponce, PR Church Santisimo Sacramento.
Apostol, Moises '78 (RCK) Saint Charles, IL St. Patrick.
Apostoli, Andrew D. *c.f.r.* '67 (NY)[A] Yonkers, NY St. Joseph's Seminary; [DD] Yonkers, NY St. Leopold's Friary.
Apparcel, Gregory *c.s.p.* '83 (BRK)[R] Paulist Priests at Paulist Foundations Outside the U.S.
Appelby, Gerald J. '59 (ROC) Henrietta, NY Church of the Good Shepherd; Rush, NY St. Joseph Retired.
Appiah, Kwaku John '98 (KNX) Knoxville, TN All Saints Catholic Church; [A] Knoxville, TN Knoxville Catholic High School.
Appiah–Kubi, Paul Prince *s.v.d.* '07 (SB)[I] Riverside, CA Divine Word Seminary.
Appian, Augustine (NO) New Orleans, LA Blessed Trinity.
Appiasi, Samuel '83 (VIC) Bloomington, TX St. Patrick's; Procurator Advocate.
Appleby, Gerald '59 (ROC) Rochester, NY Guardian Angels.
Applegate, Rev. Msgr. Gary '81 (KCK) Judicial Vicar; Judges; Archdiocesan Consultors.
Applewhite, Mark (RVC) Smithtown, NY St. Catherine of Siena Hospital.
Appleyard, Rev. Msgr. George '68 (SJP) Carnegie, PA Holy Trinity; Consultors; Eparchial Corporation; Central Protopresbytery; Vicar for Religious; Liturgical Commission; Examiners of Clergy; Permanent Deacon Program; Presbyteral Council; Vicar General; Eparchial Convention; Arbitration Board; Presbyters.
Appleyard, Joseph A. *s.j.* '66 (BO)[U] Newton, MA The Jesuit Community at Boston College; Watertown, MA; [U] Watertown, MA The Society of Jesus of New England–Provincial Offices.
Appreh, Francis G. '96 (NSH)[F] Nashville, TN St. Thomas Hospital; Nashville, TN Christ the King.
Apura, Nilo '75 (TR) Trenton, NJ St. Mary Cathedral.
Apuzzo, Pasquale J. '76 (RIC) Chesterfield, VA St. Gabriel; Amelia, VA Good Samaritan.
Aqeas, Cesar R. '83 (SAC) Presbyteral Council.
Aquilera, George '83 (LA) Gardena, CA St. Anthony of Padua.
Aquino, Alexander '74 (SD) Brawley, CA Sacred Heart Catholic Parish Brawley; Brawley, CA Saint Margaret Mary Catholic Parish.
Aquino, Arnel *s.j.* '04 (BO)[U] Brighton, MA Alberto Hurtado House.
Aquino, Francisco '90 (ORL) Deltona, FL Our Lady of the Lakes.
Aquino, Joseph G. *m.s.* '69 (LKC) Sulphur, LA St. Theresa; Presbyteral Council.
Aquino, Rev. Msgr. Oscar A. '62 (NY) Judges; New York, NY St. Lucy.
Aquino, Peter M. '69 (NEW) Livingston, NJ St. Raphael.
Arachi, Grace G. '91 (NEW) Mountainside, NJ Church of Our Lady of Lourdes.
Aracich, Anthony *s.j.* '67 (NEW)[B] Jersey City, NJ Jesuit Center; [L] Jersey City, NJ Jesuits of Saint Peter's College, Inc.; Jersey City, NJ St. Patrick and Assumption/All Saints Church.
Aracil, Javier *s.d.b.* '63 (NY) Port Chester, NY Corpus Christi.
Aracil, Javier '63 (NEW) Elizabeth, NJ St. Anthony's.
Arackal, Bony '93 (SAC) Elk Grove, CA St. Joseph.
Arackal, Joseph J. *v.c.* '67 (SYM) St. Cloud, MN St. Alphonsa Syro–Malabar Catholic Church Minnesota; Saint Cloud, MN.
Arackal, Joseph *v.c.* (SCL)[I] Saint Cloud, MN St. Joseph Province of the Vincentian Congregation.
Aragon, Ramon '50 (SFE) Retired.
Aragon, Salvador *o.f.m.* '55 (SFE)[I] Rio Rancho, NM Felician Sisters; [H] Albuquerque, NM The Province of Our Lady of Guadalupe.
Aram, John '98 (OKL) Ponca City, OK Church of St. Mary.
Arambasick, Dennis *o.f.m.* '85 (HRT) Winsted, CT St. Joseph.
Aramburo, Eugenio '88 (MRY) Los Gatos, CA Christ Child; Administrative Committee Priests' Pension Plan.
Aramburu, Jose A. *m.m.* '84 (NY) Maryknoll, NY; Maryknoll, NY; [DD] Maryknoll Maryknoll Fathers and Brothers.
Aramendi, Juan '91 (POD) Guaynabo.
Aramendi, Juan '91 (SJN)[G] Guaynabo, PR Opus Dei.
Arana, Francisco '64 (SJN)[E] San Juan, PR Centro Medico de P.R.; Carolina, PR Santisima Trinidad.
Arango, Andres *c.j.m.* '95 (PHX) Phoenix, AZ St. Jerome Roman Catholic Parish.
Arango, Andres *eud.* '95 (PHX) Renewal Ministries, Catholic.
Arango, Fabio '66 (MIA)[G] Miami, FL Mercy Hospital.
Arango, Gilberto '75 (STO) Stockton, CA Cathedral of the Annunciation (Pastor of); School of Ministry.
Arango–Medina, Miguel '65 (SAT) Von Ormy, TX St. Peter the Fisherman.
Aranha, George '75 (SJ) Santa Clara, CA St. Clare.
Arano–Ponce, Gerardo '03 (KCK) Roeland Park, KS St. Agnes.
Aransi, John '97 (SP)[J] Tampa, FL St. Joseph's Hospital, Inc.
Araque, Alvaro U. '72 (STO) Stockton, CA St. Gertrude Church (Pastor of).
Arata, Miguel A. '95 (NEW) On Duty Outside the Archdiocese.
Araujo, Arturo *s.j.* '99 (SFR)[N] San Francisco, CA Loyola House Jesuit Community.
Araujo, Manuel *c.p.* (SJN) San Juan, PR Jesus Maestro.
Araujo, Ranieri *s.j.* (CHI)[C] Chicago, IL Jesuit Community at Loyola University Chicago.
Araujo, Robert J. *s.j.* '93 (BO)[U] Boston The Society of Jesus of New England–Provincial Offices.
Araujo, Robert J. *s.j.* '93 (CHI)[C] Chicago, IL Jesuit Community at Loyola University Chicago.
Arauz, Erick E. '85 (SFR) San Francisco, CA Church of the Epiphany.
Aravena, Marcelo '85 (MIL)[T] Waukesha, WI Secular Institute of Schoenstatt Fathers.
Aravena, Marcelo *i.s.p.* (AUS)[G] Austin, TX Schoenstatt Fathers.
Aravindathu, Thadeus J. '83 (SYM) West Nyack, NY Blessed Kunjachan Syro–Malabar Catholic Mission, Staten Island, NY; West Nyack, NY Syro–Malabar Catholic Mission, Rockland.
Arbelaez, Ernesto *s.j.* '56 (LA) Hospital Chaplains.
Arboleda, Dairo H. *o.ss.t.* '03 (PCE) Ponce, PR La Santisima Trinidad; Episcopal Vicar for Sick; Pastoral de la Salud – Hospitales.
Arboleda, Jorge W. '93 (STO) Modesto, CA St. Stanislaus Church (Pastor of).
Arboleda, Vidal '55 (ORL) Retired.
Arboleda–Restrepo, Francisco F. *m.x.y.* (GAL) Houston, TX St. Christopher.
Arboleda Ibarra, Dairo Hernando *o.ss.t.* '03 (PCE)[H] Ponce, PR Pastoral Care of the Sick.
Arbuckle, Matthew J. '11 (LFT) Lafayette, IN St. Lawrence; Lafayette, IN St. Mary Cathedral.
Arcamo, Rev. Msgr. Floro B. '65 (SFR) San Francisco, CA St. Cecilia Retired.
Arce, Aaron *o.p.* '80 (STL)[O] Saint Louis, MO St. Dominic Priory; St. Louis, MO St. Andrew.
Arce, Neil A. '05 (BEA) Anahuac, TX Our Lady of Light; Winnie, TX St. Louis.
Arce, Robert P. '64 (NY) Bronx, NY St. Margaret Mary.
Arce–Flores, Carlos '91 (R) Ex Officio; Office of Hispanic Ministry; Raleigh, NC Our Lady of Lourdes.
Arceneaux, Chester C. '92 (LAF) Diocesan Consultors; Lafayette, LA Cathedral of St. John the Evangelist.
Arceneaux, Jules '90 (LAF) On Leave.
Arceneaux, Louis *c.m.* '66 (NO)[R] New Orleans, LA Congregation of the Mission Western Province (Vincentians).
Archambault, Donald '70 (DET) Detroit, MI Corpus Christi; Archdiocesan Vicars; Presbyteral Council.
Archambault, Rev. Msgr. Henry N. '59 (NOR) Taftville, CT Sacred Heart; College of Consultors; Members; Deans; Lawyers, Guild of Catholic; Judges.
Archambault, James H. '67 (HRT) Retired.
Archambault, Richard L. '55 (NOR)[H] Putnam, CT Holy Spirit Provincial House; Project Northeast.
Archambault, Richard *m.afr.* '73 (FgM)[N] St. Petersburg, FL Missionaries of Africa; Washington, DC; Washington, DC MISSIONARIES OF AFRICA.
Archer, Arthur (NOR) Retired.
Archer, Richard R. *o.p.* '58 (R)[F] Raleigh, NC Dominican Priory.
Archer, Scott '90 (PEO) Fairbury, IL St. John the Baptist.
Archibong, Cosmas P. '88 (MO) DEPARTMENT OF VETERANS AFFAIRS HOSPITALS AND CHAPLAINS.
Archibong, Cosmas (HRT) West Haven, CT V.A. CT Health Care System.
Archibong, Joseph '10 (LR) Fort Smith, AR Immaculate Conception; Fort Smith, AR St. Leo's.
Arcila, David *o.c.d.* '95 (CHI) Mundelein, IL Santa Maria Del Popolo.
Arciniegas, Hector Eduardo Mejia *m.s.c.* '06 (FgM) Aurora, IL MISSIONARIES OF THE SACRED HEART.
Arciniegas, Juan '92 (RCK) Aurora, IL St. Nicholas.
Arciszewski, Gilbert '59 (MIL) Retired.
Arcoleo, Douglas R. '98 (RVC) Freeport, NY Our Holy Redeemer.
Arcosa, Carl Tacuyan '07 (OAK) Brentwood, CA Immaculate Heart of Mary.
Arcuri, Carmen J. '61 (COL) Worthington, OH St. Michael Retired.
Ardagh, Brian '95 (CHI) Lemont, IL St. Alphonsus.
Ardinger, Scott R. '01 (ALN) Orefield, PA St. Joseph The Worker; Office of Worship; Appointed Members; Office of Rite of Christian Initiation of Adults (RCIA).
Ardis, John B. *c.s.p.* '90 (LA) Los Angeles, CA St. Paul the Apostle.
Ardolf, Edward J. '64 (NU) Nicollet, MN St. Paul; New Ulm, MN St. Mary.
Ardolf, Paul C. '49 (STP) Retired.
Ardouin, Rev. Msgr. Beaubrun '93 (NEW) Irvington, NJ St. Leo's; Haitian Apostolate; Members.
Arechiga, Dennis '00 (SAT) San Antonio, TX St. Matthew's.
Arechua, Ramon J. '96 (GAL) Missouri City, TX Holy Family.
Areepparampil, Daison (TR) Red Bank, NJ St. James.
Areiza, Juan F. '08 (ATL) Lawrenceville, GA St. Lawrence.
Arejola, Rodolfo G. '68 (AGN) Tamuning, GU St. Anthony and St. Victor.
Arel, Don *o.m.i.* '64 (OAK)[L] Oakland, CA Missionary Oblates of Mary Immaculate United States Province.
Arella, Rev. Msgr. Gerard '54 (BRK)[R] Douglaston, NY Bishop Mugavero Residence Retired.
Arellano, Edgardo M. '74 (WIL)[L] Dover, DE Secular Institute of the Two Hearts; [J] Dover, DE Oblate Apostles of the Two Hearts; [K] Dover, DE Leaven of the Immaculate Heart of Mary (LIHM).
Arellano, Jesus *c.m.* '73 (NY) New York, NY; New York,

NY Holy Agony; [DD] New York, NY Vincentian Fathers.
Arellano, Josue *c.o.r.c.* '01 (SB)[I] Corona, CA Confraternity of Operarios Del Reino De Cristo, C.O.R.C.
Arellano, Juan *c.p.* (GAL) Galveston, TX Holy Family.
Arellano–Reynoso, Josué *c.o.r.c.* '05 (SB) Corona, CA St. Edward.
Arellano Dedia, P. Ramon '03 (PCE) Jayuya, PR Our Lady of Monserrate.
Arends, Todd '02 (CR) Diocesan Consultors; Moorhead, MN St. Joseph's; [D] Moorhead, MN St. Thomas Aquinas Newman Center.
Arens, John F. '74 (BO)[D] Needham, MA St. Sebastian's School, Inc.
Arens, Patrick O. '00 (WIN) Chatfield, MN St. Mary's; Chatfield, MN St. Patrick; Chatfield, MN St. Columban.
Ares, Francisco J. '83 (BRK) Wyckoff Heights Hospital; Richmond Hill, NY Holy Child Jesus.
Arevalo, Jorge '94 (ATL) Atlanta, GA Cathedral of Christ the King.
Arevalo, Joseph V. '65 (RVC) Babylon, NY St. Joseph.
Arevalos Lupercia, Benjamin '09 (CHI) Waukegan, IL Most Blessed Trinity.
Arflack, Gregory A. '98 (OWN) Absent on Leave.
Argano, Christopher '09 (NY) Monroe, NY Sacred Heart Church.
Argent, Robert W. '55 (STL) Retired.
Argentieri, Nicholas J. '08 (PIT) Pittsburgh, PA Saint Elizabeth of Hungary.
Argentino, Ralph J. '68 (SP) Permanent Diaconate Office; Clearwater, FL Miserere Guild, Inc.; Calvary Catholic Cemetery and Miserere Guild.
Argue, Patrick *ss.cc.* '62 (LA)[P] La Verne, CA Congregation of the Sacred Hearts of Jesus and Mary Retired.
Arguelles, I. Anthony '74 (BLX) Pascagoula, MS Our Lady of Victories; College of Consultors.
Arias, Alfredo '04 (FRS) Corcoran, CA Our Lady of Lourdes.
Arias, Ariel '85 (RNO) Reno, NV St. Therese Church of the Little Flower.
Arias, Gonzalo '00 (NY) Monticello, NY St. Peter.
Arias, Guillermo *s.j.* '72 (MIA)[H] Miami, FL Villa Javier.
Arias, Guillermo '73 (RNO) Sun Valley, NV St. Peter Canisius.
Arias, Guillermo '72 (MIA)[E] Miami, FL Belen Jesuit Preparatory School.
Arias, Hernan '85 (PAT) Morristown, NJ St. Margaret of Scotland; Priestly Life Committee; Vicar for Pastoral Administration; Vocations Board; Pastoral Administration; Morris County Jail.
Arias, Jesus J. '92 (MIA) Miami, FL Good Shepherd; Deans and Deaneries; Appointed by the Archbishop.
Arico, Carl J. '60 (NEW) Bayonne, NJ St. Vincent de Paul Retired.
Aridas, Christopher J. '73 (RVC) Centereach, NY Assumption of the Blessed Virgin Mary.
Arimond, Vincent '55 (DUL) Retired.
Arinze, Paul U. '99 (MAD) Madison, WI St. Dennis; Vocations; Madison; Diocesan Consultors; Appointed.
Aririatu, Samuel '79 (RVC) Port Jefferson, NY St. Charles Hospital, Port Jefferson, New York.
Aristil, Edmond *c.s.sp.* '03 (CHI) Chicago, IL St. William.
Ariza, Campo E. '75 (CGS) Diocesan Consultors; Caguas, PR Cathedral Dulce Nombre de Jesus.
Ariza, Rev. Msgr. Vicente '75 (SJN)[G] Guaynabo, PR Opus Dei.
Arizpe, Samuel '87 (BWN) San Benito Deanery; San Benito, TX St. Theresa; Board Members.
Arkins, Michael *s.s.s.* '73 (SP) Holiday, FL St. Vincent De Paul.
Arlagadda, Joseph '83 (NY) New York, NY St. John the Evangelist.
Arle, David '84 (VEN) Fort Myers, FL St. Vincent de Paul.
Arledge, Joseph H. '97 (OKL) Hennessey, OK St. Joseph's.
Arledge, Thaddaeus R. *o.s.b.* '56 (SEA)[M] Lacey, WA St. Martin's Abbey.
Arlia, William *o.f.m.cap.* '06 (WIL)[J] Wilmington, DE Capuchin Franciscan Friars, St. Francis Renewal Center; [L] Wilmington, DE Secular Franciscan Order; [M] Wilmington, DE St. Francis Renewal Center.
Arlotta, Jack '92 (NY) Highland Falls, NY Sacred Heart of Jesus.
Armamento, Joseph D. '92 (GBG) North Huntingdon, PA St. Agnes.
Armano, Patrick S. '03 (BO) Methuen, MA St. Monica.
Armato, Robert J. '95 (BRK) Art and Architecture Commission; Astoria, NY St. Joseph.
Armbruster, Timothy *c.pp.s.* '01 (KC) Liberty, MO St. James.
Armengol, Jose *c.m.f.* '67 (SJN) Bayamon, PR San Jose.
Armenio, Peter V. '80 (POD)[V] Chicago, IL Prelature of the Holy Cross and Opus Dei; Vicar for the Midwest; Chicago.
Armey, Charles R. '80 (WOR) Worcester, MA Our Lady of Loreto.
Armistead, Rev. Msgr. John M. '71 (STO) Stockton, CA Cathedral of the Annunciation (Pastor of).
Armistead, Rev. Msgr. John '71 (STO) Deans.
Arms, Michael M. '68 (STP) Retired.
Armshaw, Joseph R. *c.ss.r.* '52 (STL)[O] Liguori, MO St. Clement Health Care Center Retired.
Armshaw, Rev. Msgr. Patrick '62 (RVC) Greenlawn, NY St. Francis of Assisi; [L] Bethpage, NY Society of St. Vincent de Paul–Central Council.
Armstrong, Christopher R. '80 (CIN) Cincinnati, OH St. Antoninus; Imprimatur Censors; Judges.
Armstrong, John F. *s.j.* '78 (NO) Saint Louis, MO; [R] New Orleans, LA Jesuit Provincial Office; [C] New Orleans, LA Loyola University New Orleans.
Armstrong, John F. *s.j.* '78 (STL)[O] St. Louis, MO Sacred Heart Jesuit Community; [O] St. Louis, MO The Jesuits of the Missouri Province.
Armstrong, Regis *o.f.m.cap.* '67 (WDC)[C] Catholic University of America, The.
Armstrong, Richard G. '09 (KNX) Christian Formation.
Armstrong, Richard (SJP) Presbyters.
Armstrong, Rev. Msgr. Robert A. '62 (BAL) Baltimore, MD Cathedral of Mary Our Queen; Defender of the Bond Retired.
Armstrong, Rodney J. *s.s.j.* '91 (GAL) Baytown, TX Holy Family.
Arnao, Thomas V. '82 (RVC) Carle Place, NY Church of Our Lady of Hope; Adjutant Judicial Vicar.
Arnaud, Allan '08 (RVC) Seaford, NY Maria Regina.
Arnaud, Michael '75 (LAF) New Iberia, LA Nativity of Our Lady.
Arnberg, Todd '76 (SAG) St. Charles, MI St. Mary; St. Charles, MI Immaculate Conception.
Arnett, Russell L. (MIL) Kansasville, WI St. John the Baptist; Kansasville, WI St. Francis Xavier.
Arnhols, Rev. Msgr. Richard J. '73 (NEW) Bergenfield, NJ St. John the Evangelist; Vicar for Pastoral Life; Members; Presbyteral Council; Vicar for Pastoral Life.
Arnholt, Joseph M. '73 (PH) Philadelphia, PA St. Anne.
Arnister, Rev. Msgr. Edward J. '79 (TR) Belmar, NJ St. Rose; Tribunal Judges; College of Consultors.
Arnold, Chad J. '10 (WCH) Pittsburg, KS Our Lady of Lourdes.
Arnold, Rev. Msgr. Daniel K. '75 (E) Co Directors; Erie, PA St. Mark the Evangelist.
Arnold, Erik J. '99 (BAL) Ellicott City, MD Our Lady of Perpetual Help.
Arnold, John D. *s.j.* '73 (STL)[O] St. Louis, MO Ignatius House.
Arnold, John P. '98 (TUC) Casa Grande, AZ Saint Anthony of Padua Roman Catholic Parish – Casa Grande; Adjutant Judicial Vicar; Diocesan Consultors.
Arnold, Rex A. '04 (OKL) Clinton, OK St. Mary's; Council of Priests Archdiocesan; Region V.
Arnold, Wayne H. '00 (MEM) Bolivar, TN St. Mary Church; Selmer, TN St. Jude the Apostle Catholic Church; Scouting.
Arnold, William L. '80 (COL) Columbus, OH Holy Spirit; Presbyteral Council; Diocesan Judges; Deanery 6: East; Parochial Examiners; Presbyteral Council.
Arnoldt, David L. '68 (WIN) Retired.
Arnone, Alan '80 (SJ) On Leave of Absence.
Arnone, John C. '99 (NO) Saint Bernard, LA St. Bernard; Violet, LA Our Lady of Lourdes.
Arnone, Leo '93 (ALT) Johnstown, PA St. Clare of Assisi; Navy Reserve Chaplains.
Arnoult, Paul '02 (SFR) San Mateo, CA St. Gregory.
Arnout, Eric R. '96 (ALN) Appointed Members; Bethlehem, PA Our Lady of Perpetual Help.
Arnsparger, Roger K. '77 (CHL) Gastonia, NC St. Michael; Education; Diocesan Consultors; Office of Faith Formation.
Arnzen, Mark '05 (SJ) Morgan Hill, CA St. Catherine of Alexandria; Council of Priests; College of Consultors; Ongoing Formation of Clergy.
Arocho, Jose A. '91 (FAJ) Fajardo, PR Santisimo Redentor; Master of Ceremonies.
Arockasaimy, Sengol Rajan (LC) Boyceville, WI St. Luke; Mondovi, WI St. Joseph; Elk Mound, WI St. Joseph.
Arockiadoss, Antony *m.s.c.* '03 (MET) Edison, NJ St. Helena.
Arockiam, Amalraj (LC) Arcadia, WI Holy Family.
Arockiam, Arockiam *s.v.d.* '02 (LAF) Broussard, LA St. Joseph.
Arockiaraj, Christy '95 (SFR)[A] Menlo Park, CA St. Patrick Seminary and University.
Arockiaraj, Inniah Christy '95 (BAL)[K] Baltimore, MD St. Agnes HealthCare, Inc.; [Q] Baltimore, MD St. Mary's Seminary & University.
Arockiasamy, Devaraju '02 (ARL) Manassas, VA Sacred Heart.
Arockiasamy, Joseph '85 (ALB) Granville, NY St. Mary's Roman Catholic Church Roman Catholic Community of Granville.
Arockiasamy, Justin *s.v.d.* (LAF) Lawtell, LA Holy Family; Lawtell, LA St. Ann.
Arockiyasamy, Santhiyagu *m.s.f.s.* '96 (LAN) Flint, MI St. Mary.
Arogyasami, Joseph *i.m.s.* '89 (BR) Albany, LA St. Margaret Queen of Scotland.
Arokiadass, Soosai Arpudam *h.g.n.* '00 (WH) Madison, WV St. Mary, Queen of Heaven.
Arokiam, Santhiyagu *m.s.f.s.* '96 (TYL)[C] Whitehouse, TX The Missionaries of St. Francis de Sales.
Arokiasamy, Kulan–Daisamy '71 (DET) Eastpointe, MI St. Veronica.
Arokiasamy, Saharaj '95 (NY) Staten Island, NY Our Lady Help of Christians.
Arokiaselvam, Nithiyaselvam *m.s.f.s.* '00 (TYL)[C] Whitehouse, TX The Missionaries of St. Francis de Sales.
Arokiaselvam, Nithyaselvam '01 (LAN) Ann Arbor, MI St. Thomas the Apostle.
Arold, Richard J. '67 (NY) Retired.
Arong, Jose *o.m.i.* '66 (OAK) Oakland, CA Sacred Heart; Diocesan Planning Board.
Aronyu, Cuthbert '72 (OAK) Oakland, CA St. Benedict.
Arouje, Lonachan W. '70 (STO) Angels Camp, CA St. Patrick Church of Angels Camp (Pastor of).
Arputham, Michael '78 (NY) Staten Island, NY St. Mary.
Arrambide, Jaime C. *c.ss.r.* '73 (GAL) Houston, TX Holy Ghost.
Arrando, Angelo S. '71 (BGP) Danbury, CT St. Gregory the Great.
Arrazola, Rodrigo A. '01 (HBG) Cornwall, PA Sacred Heart of Jesus.
Arredondo, Francisco *o.f.m.cap.* '10 (NEW) Hackensack, NJ Church of St. Francis of Assisi.
Arrellano, Adondee *m.s.* '03 (HON) Kahului, HI Christ the King.
Arrellano, Mario *o.s.f.* '96 (LA) La Puente, CA St. Joseph.
Arreola, Alberto *o.m.i.* '02 (LA) Pomona, CA Sacred Heart.
Arreola, Luis *c.m.* '64 (LA) Los Angeles, CA Our Lady of the Rosary of Talpa.
Arriaga, Joaquin S. '97 (FRS) Fresno, CA Our Lady of Mt. Carmel.
Arriaga, Jose Jesus '69 (WDC) Gaithersburg, MD St. Rose of Lima.
Arribas, Santiago *c.m.* '66 (SJN)[I] San Juan, PR Servicios Pastorales Paules; Servicios Pastorales Paules; San Juan, PR Jesus Maestro.
Arrieta, Benjamin Zomero *c.m.f.* '11 (CHI)[N] Oak Park Claretian Missionaries USA Eastern Province.
Arrieta, David '62 (SJN) San Juan, PR Nuestra Senora de Lourdes.
Arrieta Correa, Juan Carlos '09 (CHI) Chicago, IL St. Bede the Venerable.
Arriola, Augustin *sch.p.* '60 (LA) Los Angeles, CA Santa Teresita.
Arrizurieta, Candido *c.m.* '54 (NY) New York, NY Holy Agony; [DD] New York, NY Vincentian Fathers; New York, NY.
Arroyave, Jesus Rodrigo '96 (TYL) Tyler, TX Our Lady of Guadalupe; Co Directors.
Arroyave, Jesus '96 (ORL) Haines City, FL St. Ann.
Arroyave, Luis Fernando '88 (TYL) Mount Pleasant, TX St. Michael.
Arroyave, Pastor A. '90 (CGS) Las Piedras, PR San Juan Bautista.
Arroyo, Rev. Msgr. Brigido '61 (AGN) Tamuning, GU St. Anthony and St. Victor; Archdiocesan Presbyteral Council; Catholic Daughters of the Americas; Saint Anthony Parish.
Arroyo, Edward B. *s.j.* '75 (MOB)[I] Mobile, AL Spring Hill College Campus Ministry; [A] Mobile, AL Spring Hill College; Jesuit.
Arroyo, Eric '92 (SR) Windsor, CA Our Lady of Guadalupe.
Arroyo, Mario J. '77 (GAL) Houston, TX St. Cyril of Alexandria.
Arruda, Henry S. '67 (FR) Taunton, MA St. Anthony's; Diocesan Liaison with Portuguese Charismatic Groups.
Arsenault, Rev. Msgr. Edward J. '91 (WDC)[X] Silver Spring, MD Saint Luke Institute, Inc.; On Duty Outside the Diocese.
Arsenault, James M. '89 (RIC) Richmond, VA St. Mary; Glen Allen, VA St. Michael.
Arsenault, Joseph B. *m.m.* '59 (NY)[DD] Maryknoll Maryknoll Fathers and Brothers Retired.
Arsenault, Joseph G. (BO) Abington, MA St. Bridget.
Arsenault, Joseph *s.s.a.* '00 (KCK)[K] Kansas City, KS Society of St. Augustine – Public Association of the Faithful; Judges; Kansas City, KS St. Mary–St. Anthony.
Arseneau, Vernon '72 (JOL) Chebanse, IL SS. Mary and Joseph; Clifton, IL St. Peter's.
Arseneault, David J. '81 (ALT)[I] Huntington, PA Juniata College; Huntingdon, PA Most Holy Trinity; State Correctional Institution.
Arseneault, Rev. Msgr. Edward J. '91 (MAN) Hampton, NH St. Patrick.
Arsenius, '06 (BAK)[B] La Pine, OR Monastery of

Annunciation Hermitage.
Arteaga, Pedro *m.sp.s.* '97 (P)[L] Hillsboro, OR Missionaries of the Holy Spirit, M.Sp.S.
Arteaga, Peter *m.sp.s.* '97 (P) Area Vicars; Hillsboro, OR St. Matthew.
Arter, Ronald L. '61 (COL) Retired.
Arthasseril, Jerome S. '66 (NEW) Verona, NJ Our Lady of the Lake.
Arthur, David J. *c.s.c.* '54 (FR)[A] North Easton, MA Holy Cross Fathers Religious.
Arthur, David J. *c.s.c.* '54 (FTW)[H] Notre Dame Congregation of Holy Cross, United States Province of Priests & Brothers.
Arthur, E. Eugene *s.j.* '66 (COS)[E] Sedalia, CO Sacred Heart Jesuit Community; [G] Sedalia, CO Sacred Heart Jesuit Retreat House.
Arthur, James '83 (LC)[D] Eau Claire, WI Sacred Heart Hospital.
Artmann, Robert J. '64 (MIL) Retired.
Arts, Paul–Louis '64 (SC) Judges Retired.
Artunduaga, Henry '92 (CC) Corpus Christi, TX Nuestra Senora de San Juan de Los Lagos, Madre de la Iglesia.
Arturi, Bradley K. '62 (POD)[II] Overlook Study Center; New Rochelle.
Artuso, Grazioso '64 (BGP) Bridgeport, CT St. Raphael.
Arty, J. Rodolphe *c.s.c.* '94 (JOL) Naperville, IL St. Thomas the Apostle.
Artysiewicz, Chet *g.h.m.* '73 (CIN)[N] Fairfield, OH.
Artzer, James *s.v.d.* '50 (CHI)[N] Techny, IL Divine Word Residence.
Arul, Augustine Peter *m.ss.cc.* '05 (CAM)[H] Pleasantville, NJ Our Lady's Multi–Care Center, Inc.; Linwood, NJ; [L] Linwood, NJ Villa Pieta. Missionaries of the Sacred Hearts of Jesus & Mary.
Arul, John '70 (MRY) Retired.
Arulanandam, John Peter *m.s.f.s.* '01 (DET) White Lake, MI St. Patrick.
Arulanandam, John Peter *m.s.f.s.* '01 (TYL)[C] Whitehouse, TX The Missionaries of St. Francis de Sales.
Arulandu, Thaines '82 (FAR) Edgeley, ND Transfiguration Church of Edgeley; Edgeley, ND Holy Spirit Church of Nortonville.
Arulappa, Devaraj '86 (TYL) Fairfield, TX St. Bernard of Clairvaux.
Arulappa, Luckas *m.s.f.s.* '96 (NSH) Loretto, TN Sacred Heart; Loretto, TN St. Joseph.
Arulappa, Luckas *m.s.f.s.* '96 (TYL)[C] Whitehouse, TX The Missionaries of St. Francis de Sales.
Arulsamy, Ananda Lourdu Raj *o.s.m.* (STL) Affton, MO Seven Holy Founders.
Arulsamy, Arputham '90 (BRK) Brooklyn, NY Our Lady of Angels.
Arumainathan, Antonyra *o.m.i.* '02 (MIA) Miami, FL Christ the King.
Arvay, Alfred S. '58 (NEW) Retired.
Arwady, James Fredrick '10 (DET) Canton, MI St. Thomas a'Becket.
Arwady, Raymond '09 (DET) Grosse Pointe Farms, MI St. Paul Catholic Church.
Arwo–Doqu, Seth N. (RVC) Babylon, NY St. Joseph.
Aryanto, Antonius G. '02 (OAK) El Cerrito, CA St. Jerome.
Arzate, Roman '86 (LA) Canoga Park, CA Our Lady of the Valley.
Arzola, Roberto *o.p.* '74 (SJN) Catano, PR Nuestra Senora del Carmen.
Asagba, Francis Kwame '91 (BRK) Brooklyn, NY St. Catharine of Alexandria.
Asalemo, Asalemo (SPP) Pago Pago, AS St. Peter Chanel–Sa'ilele.
Asalemo, Asalemo '08 (SPP) Pago Pago, AS Church of St. Peter and Paul.
Asante, Augustine N. '98 (VIC) Columbus, TX St. Anthony's.
Asante, Thomas (BRK) Rockaway Beach, NY Saint Camillus–Saint Virgilius.
Asantemungu, Juvenalis '99 (MIL) Wauwatosa, WI St. Jude the Apostle.
Asare, Dominic *s.v.d.* '91 (OAK) Oakland, CA St. Bernard.
Asare, James (BRK) Jamaica, NY St. Bonaventure–St. Benedict the Moor RC Church.
Asare–Dankwah, John '94 (NO) New Orleans, LA Blessed Trinity.
Ascencio, Enrique '88 (MGZ) Moca, PR Our Lady of Monserrate.
Ascencio, Joseph A. '82 (COL) On Duty Outside the Diocese.
Ascheman, Thomas J. *s.v.d.* '82 (FgM) Techny, IL Chicago Province; Techny, IL.
Ascheman, Thomas J. *s.v.d.* '82 (CHI)[N] Techny, IL S.V.D. Funds, Inc.; [N] Techny, IL Society of the Divine Word, Provincial Headquarters–Chicago Prov.
Aschenbrener, Thomas G. '03 (CHI) Chicago, IL Holy Name Cathedral.
Aschenbrenner, George A. *s.j.* '65 (WDC)[O] Washington, DC The Jesuit Community of St. Aloysius Gonzaga.
Aschmann, Karl *c.ss.r.* '50 (ORL)[F] New Smyrna Beach, FL St. Alphonsus Villa–Redemptorist Fathers and Brothers Retired.
Asebius, Anacleto '80 (BRK) Flushing, NY Mary's Nativity.
Asenjo, Jose Maria '65 (GAL) Retired.
Asghedom, Tesfaldet '85 (LA) Los Angeles, CA Sacred Heart.
Ashbaugh, William A. '93 (LAN) Priests' Assignment Commission; Father McGiveny House; Ann Arbor, MI St. Thomas the Apostle; St. Catherine House.
Ashbeck, David K. '68 (GB) On Duty Outside the Diocese.
Ashe, John F. '63 (NOR) Portland, CT St. Mary.
Ashe, Joseph C. '76 (NOR) Groton, CT St. Mary Mother of the Redeemer.
Ashe, Kevin P. '63 (NEW) Retired.
Ashe, Michael B. '59 (CC) Retired.
Ashenbrenner, Robert D. *o.s.f.s.* '54 (WIL)[J] Childs, MD Retirement and Assisted Care Facility Retired.
Ashibuogwu, Michael '00 (PHX) Sun City West, AZ Our Lady of Lourdes Roman Catholic Parish.
Ashkar, Chorbishop Dominic F. '62 (SAM) Washington, DC Our Lady of Lebanon Church.
Ashman, Robert '86 (NY) Yonkers, NY St. Anthony.
Ashmore, Ronald M. '76 (IND) Unassigned.
Ashton, Rev. Msgr. John P. '55 (Y) College of Consultors Retired.
Asia, Thomas F. *m.m.h.c.* '98 (LA) Artesia, CA Holy Family.
Asiedu–Peprah, Martin '87 (BRK) Bayside, NY Sacred Heart of Jesus.
Asih, Paul *m.s.p.* (BIR) Bessemer, AL St. Francis of Assisi.
Asir, Antony '82 (RVC) East Meadow, NY St. Raphael.
Askar, George F. '67 (LFT) Retired.
Asma, Lawrence F. *c.m.* '83 (STL) DePaul Health Center; [O] St. Louis Vincentian Residence; [O] St. Louis, MO Lazarist Residence.
Asma, Lawrence F. *c.m.* '83 (ALB)[L] Albany, NY Vincentian Fathers Residence.
Asmar, Rev. Msgr. Maroun '93 (SAM) Retired.
Assalone, John T. '09 (LAV) Henderson, NV St. Francis of Assisi; Presbyteral Council for the Diocese of Las Vegas; Diocesan Advocates.
Asselin, Jason '06 (FAR) Ecumenical Commission; Devils Lake, ND St. Joseph's Church of Devils Lake.
Assenga, Laurent *a.l.c.p.* '86 (PMB) Royal Palm Beach, FL Our Lady Queen of the Apostles.
Assenmacher, Hugh *o.s.b.* '58 (LR)[A] Subiaco, AR Subiaco Abbey.
Assi, Nicholas '72 (LA) Manhattan Beach, CA American Martyrs.
Assisi, Francis *o.i.c.* (MCE) Representatives of Religious Orders.
Ast, Nicholas K. *o.s.b.* '01 (OKL)[I] Shawnee, OK St. Gregory's Abbey.
Astarita, Joseph J. '03 (NEW) East Rutherford, NJ St. Joseph's.
Astorino, Robert F. *m.m.* '70 (FgM) Maryknoll, NY MARYKNOLL.
Astudillo, Roland '89 (LA) Montebello, CA Our Lady of the Miraculous Medal; Palmdale, CA St. Mary.
Astudillo, Tony P. '73 (LA) Walnut, CA St. Lorenzo Ruiz.
Astuto, Lucian S. '57 (OM) Retired.
Asucan, Julian '00 (BUR) Colchester, VT Holy Cross.
Asuguo, Godwin Nsikan–Ubom '03 (RCK) McHenry, IL St. Patrick.
Asuncion, Leo Alban '79 (OAK) Deanery #10.
Asuncion, Leonardo '79 (OAK) Martinez, CA St. Catherine of Siena.
Atalla, Fadi '07 (OLD) Saint Paul Mission.
Atangana, Edouard '02 (BWN) Pharr, TX St. Frances Xavier Cabrini; Office of Permanent Deacons; Coordinator; Priests' Assignment Board.
Atcher, Joseph *o.carm.* '76 (JOL) Commissary Provincials:; [L] Darien, IL Carmelite Provincial Office; [O] Darien, IL Provincial Office of Lay Carmelites and Scapular Center; [L] Darien, IL St. Simon Stock Priory.
Atem, Henry '08 (ATL) Norcross, GA Saint Patrick.
Aten, Robert L. '79 (STL) Special Assignment; [O] Rocky Mount, MO Contemplative Heart of Mary Hermitage.
Athappilly, Andrews *c.m.i.* '64 (COV) Burlington, KY Immaculate Heart of Mary.
Atherton, Jay John Benedict '11 (ALB) Ballston Spa, NY St. Mary.
Athipozhi, Jacob Shaji *o.s.j.* '08 (FRS) Bakersfield, CA Our Lady of Guadalupe.
Atienza, Abdon *o.s.a.* '61 (MGZ) San German, PR St. Rose of Lima.
Atienza, Brian '02 (SAC) Auburn, CA St. Joseph; Presbyteral Council; Vicars Forane.
Atkin, Timothy *c.i.c.m.* '74 (FgM) Arlington, VA MISSIONHURST.
Atkins, J. Daniel '87 (IND) New Albany, IN Holy Family Catholic Church, New Albany, Inc.
Atkins, James Mary *c.f.r.* '72 (NY)[DD] Yonkers, NY St. Felix Friary; Yonkers, NY Franciscan Friars of the Renewal.
Atkins, James '75 (PRM) On Duty Outside the Diocese Retired.
Atkins, James '75 (PBR) Toronto, OH St. Joseph.
Atkinson, John V. '61 (MEM) Retired.
Ato, Lorenzo '88 (NY) New York, NY St. Brigid; New York, NY St. Emeric; Communications Office (Bureau of Information for the Media).
Atok, George *s.d.b.* '82 (NY)[FF] Stony Point, NY Marian Shrine.
Atok, George *s.d.b.* (NEW) Elizabeth, NJ St. Anthony's.
Atonio, Andrew *m.f.* '91 (SPP) Diocesan Consultors; Director of Propagation of the Faith; Pago Pago, AS Church of the Immaculate Conception.
Atonio, Falaniko '92 (SPP) Faculty Members; Pago Pago, AS Sacred Heart Parish–Pago Pago.
Atoyebi, John B. '94 (CHI) Chicago, IL St. Clotilde; Chicago, IL Holy Angels.
Atraga, Tamiru F. (BO) Abington, MA St. Bridget.
Attak, Cyril '64 (PRM) Allen Park, MI St. Stephen Retired.
Attakruh, John '89 (RVC) Patchogue, NY Brookhaven Memorial Hospital; Patchogue, NY Our Lady of Mt. Carmel.
Attanasio, Raymond V. '58 (MET) Retired.
Attanasio, Scott '95 (NEW) North Arlington, NJ Queen of Peace.
Attard, Joseph '69 (BRK) Brooklyn, NY Most Precious Blood.
Atto, Dennis D. '02 (RCK) Savanna, IL St. John the Baptist; Mount Carroll, IL SS. John and Catherine.
Atuah, Charles *m.s.p.* '90 (BEA) Diocesan College of Consultors; Memorial Hermann Baptist Hospital; Port Arthur, TX Sacred Heart–St. Mary Parish; Presbyteral Council.
Atunzu, Kevin '79 (LR) Fort Smith, AR Christ the King; [B] Fort Smith, AR Trinity Junior High.
Atusameso, Jean–Claude '00 (ARL) Alexandria, VA St. Mary's.
Atwell, Basil *o.s.b.* '02 (BIS) Fort Yates, ND St. Peter – Catholic Indian Mission; Fort Yates, ND St. Philomena; [A] Richardton, ND Assumption Abbey; Fort Yates, ND St. James; Fort Yates, ND St. Elizabeth; Fort Yates, ND Sacred Heart.
Atwine, Lucius *c.s.c.* '97 (FTW)[H] Notre Dame Congregation of Holy Cross, United States Province of Priests & Brothers.
Atwood, Ray E. '94 (DUB) Elma, IA St. Peter; Elma, IA Immaculate Conception; Elma, IA Immaculate Conception; Elma, IA Our Lady of Lourdes; Elma, IA St. Bernard.
Atwood, Ronald E. '84 (OAK) Retired.
Atwood, Ronald J. '69 (COL) Columbus, OH St. Francis of Assisi.
Atwood, Wilbur J. *s.s.j.* '58 (NO)[R] New Orleans, LA The Josephite Faculty House of St. Augustine High School; [E] New Orleans, LA St. Augustine High School; [J] New Orleans, LA St. Augustine High School.
Atzeni, Roberto '88 (ARE) Sabana Hoyos, PR Nuestra Senora de Fatima.
Au, Thomas Y. '79 (LIN) Plattsmouth, NE Church of the Holy Spirit; Advocates; Deaneries and Deans.
Au, Vincent *c.m.c.* '00 (SB) Corona, CA St. Mary Magdalene.
Au, William A. '75 (BAL) Baltimore, MD Shrine of the Sacred Heart.
Aubespin, Francis Borgia *s.v.d.* '65 (GAL) Houston, TX St. Mary of the Purification.
Aubin, Jean P. '01 (BO) Maynard, MA St. Bridget.
Aubin, Rev. Msgr. Joseph G. '55 (OG) Plattsburgh, NY St. Peter Retired.
Aubin, Joseph '61 (LAN) Retired.
Aubin, Pierre *m.s.c.* '58 (OG) Cape Vincent, NY The Catholic Community of Cape Vincent, Rosiere and Chaumont; [F] Watertown, NY Missionaries of the Sacred Heart; [I] Cape Vincent, NY Mission Project Service; Diocesan Consultors; Consultors.
Aubin, Ronald '81 (SP) Land O'Lakes, FL Our Lady of the Rosary; Judicial Vicar; Judges; College of Consultors; [F] Land O Lakes, FL Our Lady of the Rosary Early Childhood Center – Mary's House – ECC; Executive Committee.
Auble, Theodore J. '75 (ROC) Brockport, NY Nativity of the Blessed Virgin Mary.
Aubrey, Robert J. '71 (DM) Retired.
Aubry, Ronald J. '81 (COL) Bolivar, OH Church of the Holy Trinity.
Auby, John R. '94 (MAD) Janesville, WI St. William.
Aucoin, Rev. Msgr. Robert H. '70 (OG) Colton, NY St. Patrick; Potsdam, NY St. Mary; Episcopal Vicar for Catholic Education; Diocesan Consultors; Campus Ministry; Director of Deacon Formation.
Auda, Rev. Msgr. Lawrence '60 (SFD) Gillespie, IL St. Joseph; Gillespie, IL SS. Simon and Jude.
Audet, Arthur J. '85 (HRT) Marlborough, CT St. John Fisher.
Audet, Dennis J. '78 (MAN) Meredith, NH St. Charles Borromeo; Cabinet Secretary for Ministry Formation; Vicars Forane; Secretariat for Ministry Formation; Priest Personnel Board.
Audet, Phil '01 (LAV) Unassigned.

Audette, Albert '93 (BGP) Stamford, CT The Basilica of Saint John the Evangelist Retired.
Audu, John (NY) Kingston, NY St. Mary.
Auer, Benedict L. *o.s.b.* '80 (SEA)[M] Lacey, WA St. Martin's Abbey; [A] Lacey, WA Saint Martin's University.
Auer, Rev. Msgr. John J. '57 (BAL) Severna Park, MD St. John the Evangelist; Jessup, MD Clifton T. Perkins Hospital Retired.
Auer, John '79 (COS) Highlands Ranch, CO St. Mark Catholic Church.
Auer, Joseph E. '57 (CHI) Palos Park, IL; Oak Lawn, IL St. Linus Retired.
Auer, Peter *s.o.l.t.* '93 (MAD) Boscobel, WI Corpus Christi Parish, Boscobel, WI.
Auerbach, Shay W. *s.j.* '99 (RIC) Richmond, VA Sacred Heart.
Aufdermauer, Joseph A. '68 (MIL) New Berlin, WI St. Elizabeth Ann Seton.
Aufieri, Robert J. '74 (NY) Staten Island, NY Holy Rosary; Italian Apostolate, Office of the.
Aufiero, Louis D. '65 (BRK) Flushing, NY Holy Family Retired.
Augenstein, Eric '04 (IND) New Albany, IN Our Lady Of Perpetual Help Catholic Church, New Albany, Inc.; [C] Clarksville, IN Our Lady of Providence Junior – Senior High School.
Auger, George J. *c.s.v.* '61 (CHI)[N] Arlington Heights, IL Viatorian Province Center–Clerics of St. Viator.
Auger, Gerald E. '55 (MAN) Retired.
Auger, Raymond D. '56 (PRT) Retired.
Auguscik, Jerzy *o.f.m. conv.* '93 (HRT) New Britain, CT St. Francis of Assisi.
Augustine, Joseph *h.g.n.* (WH) Weirton, WV Sacred Heart of Mary; Defenders of Bond.
Augustine, Kenneth J. '77 (MIL) Brookfield, WI St. Luke.
Augustine, Liju *c.m.i.* '03 (BRK) Astoria, NY Immaculate Conception.
Augustine, Liju (BRK)[G] Astoria, NY St. John Preparatory School.
Augustine, Rev. Msgr. Roger J. '59 (SC) Sioux City, IA Blessed Sacrament; Priests' Pension Plan – Board of Trustees; Judges Retired.
Augustine, Russell A. '89 (BGP) Ridgefield, CT St. Mary.
Augustine, Sunny *s.j.* '01 (OM)[J] Omaha, NE Jesuit Community at Creighton University.
Augustine, Titus *c.m.i.* '99 (NSH) Brentwood, TN Holy Family.
Augustinowitz, Michael E. '75 (BUR)[G] Montpelier, VT Goddard College (Plainfield); Montpelier, VT St. Augustine.
Augustyn, Boguslaw Adam *c.ss.r.* '93 (MO) Army Reserve Chaplains.
Augustyn, James M. '63 (BUF) Judges; [N] Lackawanna, NY Bishop Head Residence Retired.
Augustyn, Kevin '04 (DEN) Graduate Studies.
Augustyn, Richard H. '76 (BUF) Hospital Chaplains; Buffalo General Hospital.
Aureus, Antonio '77 (DAL) Sherman, TX St. Mary.
Aurilia, John C. *o.f.m.cap.* '66 (SP) Tampa, FL Most Holy Redeemer.
Ausenbaugh, J. Andrew '95 (OWN) Absent on Leave.
Ausperk, Michael D. '89 (CLV) Wadsworth, OH Sacred Heart of Jesus.
Austgen, Robert J. *c.s.c.* '58 (FTW)[B] University of Notre Dame Du Lac; [E] Notre Dame, IN University Health Services; [H] Notre Dame, IN Holy Cross Community, Corby Hall, University of Notre Dame.
Austin, Brian *f.s.s.p.* '09 (VEN) Sarasota, FL Christ the King.
Austin, David M. '03 (RCK) Fulton, IL Immaculate Conception; Albany, IL St. Patrick.
Austin, Jonathan '97 (DAL) Dallas, TX St. Jude Chapel.
Austin, Luke P. '10 (BUR) Unassigned.
Austin, Michael P. '00 (BLX) Moss Point, MS St. Joseph; Deans; Mission Office; Liturgy, Office of; Diocesan Liturgical Commission; Building and Real Estate Committee; Mission Board; Pontifical Association of the Holy Childhood; Propagation of the Faith; Presbyteral Council.
Austin, Stephen E. '84 (TLS) Tulsa, OK Resurrection.
Austin, Walter J. '81 (NO) La Place, LA Ascension of Our Lord; Army National Guard Chaplains.
Austriaco, Nicanor P.G. *o.p.* '04 (PRO)[O] Providence St. Thomas Aquinas Priory at Providence College.
Auth, Clifford H. '99 (SY) Manlius, NY St. Ann; Defender of the Bond; Priests' Personnel Committee.
Auth, James E. '61 (TOL) Advocate; Toledo, OH Regina Coeli; Judges.
Auth, William G. *o.s.f.s.* '69 (TOL)[H] Toledo Oblates of St. Francis de Sales.
Auther, John *s.j.* '90 (PHX) Phoenix, AZ St. Francis Xavier Roman Catholic Parish; [F] Phoenix, AZ Society of Jesus.
Auva'a, Eneliko '91 (SPP) Pago Pago, AS Church of Sacred Heart.
Auve, Rev. Msgr. Perron J. '62 (YAK) Kennewick, WA Holy Spirit; Presbyteral Council Executive Committee.
Avau, Felix A. *c.i.c.m.* '54 (SAT) Retired.
Avella, Alberto '80 (GLP) Grants, NM St. Teresa of Avila; Milan, NM St. Vivian; Milan, NM San Mateo; Milan, NM San Rafael; Priests' Retirement Board; Vicars Forane; Presbyteral Council; Seboyeta, NM Our Lady of Sorrows.
Avella, Robert E. '75 (ARL) Arlington, VA Our Lady of Lourdes.
Avella, Steven M. '79 (MIL) Special Assignment.
Avella, William '50 (RNO) Retired.
Avello, Vicente Salas *o.de.m.* '66 (PCE) Ponce, PR Santuario San Judas Tadeo.
Avendano, Eliseo '10 (SR) Saint Helena, CA St. Helena.
Aveni, Paul J. '98 (BO) Quincy, MA Holy Trinity; Quincy, MA St. Ann.
Avenido, Albert H. '95 (LA) Monterey Park, CA St. Stephen Martyr; Filipino Ministry.
Avenido, Serafin P. '77 (SAN) Odessa, TX St. Anthony; Odessa, TX St. Joseph.
Avestruz, Lester S. '72 (LA) Cedar Sinai Medical Center.
Avicolli, Maurice C. *o.praem.* '68 (PH)[Y] Paoli, PA Daylesford Abbey; Philadelphia, PA St. Edmond.
Avila, Carlos Antonio Massieu '89 (MIA)[N] Coral Gables, FL House of the Divine Will, Inc.
Avila, Dan '01 (FRS) On Special Assignment.
Avila, Daniel '87 (FRS) Fresno, CA St. John Cathedral; Vocations.
Avila, Israel '91 (FRS) Cutler, CA St. Mary.
Avila, Jose Rodolfo Lache '81 (CHR) Camden, SC Our Lady of Perpetual Help.
Avila, Martin Garcia (SAT) San Antonio, TX Holy Trinity.
Avila, Misael '99 (STO) Riverbank, CA St. Frances of Rome Church (Pastor of).
Avila, Saul Garcia *m.s.p.* '08 (SB) Riverside, CA St. John the Evangelist.
Avila, Rev. Msgr. Stephen J. '81 (FR) Mansfield, MA St. Mary's; Diocesan Consultors; Attleboro Deanery; Office for Divine Worship; Television Apostolate.
Avila–Ibarra, Juan Pablo '08 (CHI) Wauconda, IL Transfiguration.
Aviles, Juan A. '03 (MIA) Miami, FL St. Agatha.
Aviles, Mario Alberto *c.o.* '98 (BWN) Hidalgo, TX Sacred Heart; [C] Pharr, TX Oratory Academy of St. Philip Neri; [F] Pharr, TX Pharr Oratory of St. Philip Neri of Pontifical Right; Pharr, TX Oratory Academy of St. Philip Neri; Pharr, TX Oratory – Athenaeum for University Preparation; [B] Pharr, TX Oratory Athenaeum for University Preparation; Pharr, TX.
Aviles, Victor Perez *o.p.* '67 (PCE) Yauco, PR Holy Rosary.
Avis, Rev. Canon William E. *i.c.r.s.s.* '07 (KC) Kansas City, MO Oratory of Old St. Patrick.
Avis, Rev. Canon William E. '07 (STL) St. Louis, MO Oratory of St. Francis de Sales.
Avittappally, Baiju Augustine *m.s.* '01 (ORL) Orlando, FL Good Shepherd.
Avula, Maria Susai J. '80 (TYL) Sulphur Springs, TX St. James.
Avula, Susai '80 (TYL) Deans; Priests' Personnel Board.
Awada, Bechara '03 (OLL) Peoria, IL St. Sharbel Maronite Catholic Church.
Awalt, Rev. Msgr. William J. '47 (WDC) Potomac, MD Our Lady of Mercy Retired.
Award, Richard *c.p.* '81 (FgM) New Rochelle, NY St. Paul of the Cross Province.
Awotwi, Charles K. '11 (SAL) Beloit, KS St. John the Baptist Parish.
Awoyale, Joseph O. '98 (CHI) Chicago, IL St. Clotilde.
Awuafor, Gabriel '91 (NY) Cold Spring, NY Our Lady of Loretto.
Axalan, Romeo J. '97 (MO) Army Reserve Chaplains.
Axe, Thomas R. '60 (CIN) Retired.
Axe, William J. *o.ss.t.* '74 (BAL) Councilors:; [Q] Archdiocese of Los Angeles, CA.
Axe, William *o.ss.t.* '74 (LA) Los Angeles, CA St. Agatha.
Axtmann, David '06 (SFS) Webster, SD Christ the King.
Axtmann, Mark '01 (SFS) Beresford, SD St. Teresa of Avila; Veteran's Hospital.
Ayala, Agustin Mateo '90 (WDC) Washington, DC St. Gabriel; Advocates.
Ayala, Andres '10 (PBL) Monte Vista, CO Holy Name of Mary; Alamosa, CO Sacred Heart; Center, CO St. Francis Jerome; Monte Vista, CO St. Joseph.
Ayala, Daniel '86 (BRK) Rego Park, NY Our Lady of the Angelus.
Ayala, H. Alejandro '06 (CHL) Sylva, NC St. Mary.
Ayala, Ismael N. '10 (WDC) Olney, MD St. Peter.
Ayala, Juan '10 (RCK) Sterling, IL St. Mary.
Ayala, Juan *o.m.i.* '07 (LAR) Laredo, TX Our Lady of Guadalupe.
Ayala, Osvaldo *c.m.* '01 (FgM) Philadelphia, PA Eastern Province.
Ayala, Robert M. '06 (MIA) Fort Lauderdale, FL St. Helen.
Ayang, John M. *s.o.l.t.* '98 (GAL) Houston, TX St. Monica.
Ayathupadam, Joseph '61 (CHL) Retired.
Ayaton, Achilles '79 (ALN) Bethlehem, PA Notre Dame of Bethlehem.
Aydt, Raymond A. '46 (BIS) Grenora, ND St. Boniface.
Aye, Nicodemus Aung Than *m.s.* '04 (FR)[F] Attleboro, MA La Salette Shrine.
Ayem, Alfred A. *s.v.d.* (NO) New Orleans, LA St. Paul the Apostle.
Ayers, Dan '99 (COS)[B] Colorado Springs, CO Penrose Hospital.
Ayers, Eric J. '11 (RIC) Hampton, VA St. Joseph; Fort Monroe, VA St. Mary Star of the Sea; Newport News, VA St. Vincent de Paul.
Ayisu, Stephen '02 (LA) Los Angeles, CA Our Lady of Loretto.
Aylward, Gerald J. *c.s.p.* '53 (NY)[DD] New York, NY Paulist Fathers' Motherhouse Retired.
Aylward, James W. '64 (SFR) Retired.
Aylward, Richard *m.m.* '53 (NY)[DD] Maryknoll Maryknoll Fathers and Brothers Retired.
Aymanathil, Mathew '59 (NEW) Retired.
Ayo, Nicholas *c.s.c.* '59 (FTW)[B] University of Notre Dame Du Lac; [H] Notre Dame, IN Holy Cross Community, Corby Hall, University of Notre Dame.
Ayo, Terencio *s.o.l.t.* '79 (CC)[G] Robstown, TX Society of Our Lady of the Most Holy Trinity.
Ayodi, Benedict *o.f.m.cap* '07 (JC) Montgomery City, MO Immaculate Conception; Martinsburg, MO St. Joseph; Martinsburg, MO Church of the Resurrection.
Ayoob, John '65 (PIT) Retired.
Ayoub, Rev. Msgr. S. Paul '53 (BUF) Retired.
Aytona, Jewel *c.p.m.* (GB)[L] New Franken, WI The Shrine of Our Lady of Good Help, Inc.
Aytona, Joseph *c.p.m.* '10 (OWN)[F] Auburn, KY Fathers of Mercy.
Ayuyu, Isaac M. '86 (CHK) Saipan, MP Cathedral of Our Lady of Mt. Carmel; Director of Worship; Presbyteral Council; Commission on Worship; Main Contact.
Azagbor, Dominic *o.p.* (HBG) Danville, PA Geisinger Medical Center.
Azar, Rt. Rev. John '88 (NTN) Atlanta, GA St. John Chrysostom; Presbyteral Council.
Azar, Nicholas G. '09 (ATL) Atlanta, GA Holy Spirit.
Azar, Rev. Msgr. Peter F. '80 (SAM) Lawrence, MA St. Anthony; Presbyteral Council; Protopresbyters (Deans); College of Consultors; Board of Pastors.
Azaro, Stanley Robert *o.p.* '75 (NY)[DD] New York, NY St. Vincent Ferrer Priory.
Azcoiti, Vicente '56 (BWN) Retired.
Azcona, Jose Luis '89 (AUS) China Spring, TX St. Philip Catholic Church – China Spring, Texas; McGregor, TX St. Eugene Catholic Church – McGregor, Texas; McGregor, TX Our Lady of San Juan Catholic Mission Church – Moody, Texas.
Azhakath, Matthew *o.c.d.* '89 (NY) Phoenicia, NY St. Francis de Sales.
Aziz, George K. *s.j.* '57 (SJ)[M] Los Gatos, CA Sacred Heart Jesuit Center.
Azoon, Philip '94 (NTN) Retired.
Azpericueta, Lucas '69 (FRS) Buttonwillow, CA St. Mary Retired.
Azrak, Albert *c.s.s.* '60 (NY) White Plains, NY Our Lady of Mt. Carmel.
Azuwike, Anthony '01 (MEM) Savannah, TN St. Mary Church.
Azzalin, Gabriele *f.s.c.b.* '05 (DEN) Broomfield, CO Nativity of Our Lord; Lexington, MA; [N] Broomfield, CO Priestly Fraternity of St. Charles Borromeo (F.S.C.B.).
Azzalin, Gabriele *f.s.c.b.* '05 (BO)[U] Broomfield, CO House of Denver.
Azzarto, Anthony J. *s.j.* '69 (NEW)[C] Jersey City, NJ Jesuit Community; [L] Jersey City, NJ Jesuit Community of St. Peter's Prep, Inc.; [B] Jersey City, NJ Jesuit Center; [L] Jersey City, NJ Jesuits of Saint Peter's College, Inc.

B

Baabuge, Martin Atanga '91 (TUC) Clifton, AZ Sacred Heart Roman Catholic Church and St. Mary's Mission – Clifton.
Babcock, David J. *o.f.m.* '53 (FgM) New York, NY Holy Name Province.
Babcock, Rt. Rev. Archimandrite James K. '81 (NTN) Placentia, CA Holy Cross; "Sophia" (A Journal).
Babcock, Timothy F. '68 (DET) Special Assignment; Judges.
Babeu, Gill C. '87 (BGP) Stamford, CT St. Bridget of Ireland.
Babich, Ronald J. '77 (DET) Fraser, MI Our Lady Queen of All Saints.
Babick, Bryan P. '07 (CHR) Divine Worship & Sacraments, Vicar for; Diocesan Master of Ceremonies; Office of Tribunal; Mount Pleasant, SC Christ Our King.
Babicz, Edmund A. '84 (MAN) Center Ossipee, NH St. Joseph; Sanbornville, NH St. Anthony; Carroll County

House of Correction.
Babiczuk, Fred '86 (FR) Fall River, MA Parish of the Good Shepherd.
Babin, Albert C. *c.ss.r.* '52 (STL)[O] Liguori, MO St. Clement Health Care Center.
Babin, Victor '75 (MIA) Hollywood, FL Nativity.
Babineau, Alexis A. *a.a.* '45 (WOR)[N] Worcester, MA Assumptionists (Augustinians of the Assumption).
Babinski, Donald E. '81 (RVC) East Islip, NY St. Mary's.
Babiuch, Thomas '02 (ALB) Fort Edward, NY St. Joseph; Hudson Falls, NY Roman Catholic Community of Hudson Falls/Kingsbury.
Babonas, Alphonse '62 (DET) Farmington, MI Retired.
Babowitch, John F. '96 (PH) Philadelphia, PA St. Barnabas; College of Consultors; Deans; Pastors Review Board; Deans.
Babulu, Francois G. '90 (RIC) Richmond, VA St. Elizabeth.
Bac, Isidore M. Dinh Thanh *c.m.c.* '83 (SPC)[F] Carthage, MO Congregation of the Mother Coredemptrix, United States Assumption Province.
Baca, Al '89 (ORG) Tustin, CA St. Cecilia; Ecumenical and Interreligious Affairs.
Baca, Jamie *c.s.p.* '06 (AUS)[L] Austin, TX University Catholic Center.
Baca, Joseph '01 (FRS) Absent on Sick Leave.
Bacatan, Francisco Sebastian *a.m.* '94 (NY) Scarsdale, NY St. Pius X.
Baccaro, Gaetano T. '85 (SY) Oswego, NY St. Paul; Northern Area Vicar; Board of Diocesan Consultors; Presbyteral Council.
Baccellieri, Joseph '66 (P) Retired.
Bacchi, Lee F. '77 (JOL) Joliet, IL St. Mary Nativity.
Bacchi, Robert A. '77 (CHI) La Grange, IL St. Francis Xavier.
Bacevice, Joseph A. '77 (CLV) Defenders of the Bond; Cleveland, OH St. Casimir.
Bacevicius, John J. *o.f.m.* '62 (PRT)[I] Kennebunk, ME St. Anthony's Friary; Kennebunkport, ME.
Bach, Rev. Msgr. Frank J. '56 (SPK) Retired.
Bach, Gregory J. '99 (COV)[B] Covington, KY Covington Latin School; Vocations Office; Covington, KY Cathedral, Basilica of the Assumption.
Bach, James Nguyen '94 (NO) Avondale, LA Assumption of Mary.
Bach, Lester *o.f.m.cap.* '57 (MAD)[I] Madison, WI San Damiano Friary Retired.
Bachand, Joseph G. *m.s.* '76 (FR)[F] Attleboro, MA La Salette Missionary Association.
Bachand, Joseph G. *m.s.* (HRT) Hartford, CT Missionaries of Our Lady of La Salette; Hartford, CT; [L] Hartford, CT Missionaries of LaSalette Province of Mary, Mother of the Americas.
Bacher, Arthur A. '54 (CLV) Richfield, OH St. Victor; Brunswick, OH St. Colette Retired.
Bachkay, John M. '83 (PIT) Pittsburgh, PA St. Sylvester.
Bachman, Martin E. '09 (CIN) Cincinnati, OH St. James the Greater.
Bachman, Michael J. '84 (BGP) Norwalk, CT St. Ladislaus.
Bachmann, Mark *o.s.b.* '91 (TLS)[G] Hulbert, OK Our Lady of the Annunciation of Clear Creek Monastery.
Bachmeier, A. Bernard '68 (FAR) Retired.
Bachmeier, Brian '97 (FAR) Esmond, ND St. Boniface; Esmond, ND St. William; Esmond, ND Our Lady of Mt. Carmel Church of Balta.
Bachmeier, Mark V. '89 (P) Eugene, OR St. Mary.
Bachmeier, Mark '89 (P) Portland, OR Holy Cross Catholic Church.
Bachner, Daniel '06 (JOL) Wayne, IL Resurrection Catholic Community.
Bachner, James M. '96 (PIT) Pittsburgh, PA St. Catherine of Siena; [C] Mt. Lebanon, PA Seton–LaSalle Catholic High School, Inc.
Bacigalupo, Miguel '07 (JOL)[L] Darien Carmelite Provincial Office.
Bacik, James J. '62 (TOL) Toledo, OH Corpus Christi (University of Toledo); [K] Toledo, OH University of Toledo Campus Ministry; [L] Toledo, OH U.T. Newman Foundation for Student Education and Development.
Bacik, Leonard M. '72 (CLV) Middleburg Heights, OH St. Bartholomew.
Bacino, Ben '75 (PBL) Pueblo, CO St. Mary Help of Christians.
Backer, Dennis J. '07 (STP) Madison Lake, MN Immaculate Conception of Marysburg; Cleveland, MN Church of the Nativity of the Blessed Virgin Mary.
Backes, John J. '73 (NY) Pleasant Valley, NY St. Stanislaus Kostka.
Backherns, Robert *s.m.* '56 (CIN)[N] Dayton, OH Mercy Siena Gardens.
Backiel, Bernard *m.i.c.* '60 (NOR)[G] Thompson, CT Marian Fathers.
Backmann, Albert P. '00 (STP) Retired.
Backous, Timothy *o.s.b.* '86 (SCL)[B] Saint John's University; [D] Collegeville, MN Saint John's Preparatory School; [I] Collegeville, MN St. John's Abbey, of the Order of St. Benedict.
Bacleon, Misael '83 (NY) Bronx, NY St. Ann.
Bacon, Jeffery W. '05 (CIN) Hamilton, OH Queen of Peace.
Bacovin, Rev. Msgr. Ronald J. '66 (TR) Pennington, NJ St. James.
Badawi, Chorbishop Alfred '91 (OLL) Lombard, IL Our Lady of Lebanon Maronite Catholic Church; Presbyteral Council; College of Consultors.
Baddick, Rev. Msgr. Thomas D. '81 (ALN) College of Consultors; Bethlehem, PA Notre Dame of Bethlehem.
Badding, Joseph P. '69 (BUF) Ransomville, NY Immaculate Conception.
Badeaux, James '99 (PSC) Mont Clare, PA St. Michael.
Badeaux, Kevin '84 (BEA) On Leave.
Baden, Robert D. '77 (RC) Retired.
Badenes, Jose Ignacio *s.j.* '93 (LA)[C] Los Angeles, CA Jesuit Community.
Bader, Edward '82 (NY) Marlboro, NY St. Mary.
Bader, Paul A. '61 (CIN) Cincinnati, OH St. Matthias Retired.
Bader, Raed '10 (JOL) Downers Grove, IL St. Mary of Gostyn.
Badger, Arthur A. '53 (TOL) Retired.
Badgerow, Rock J. '79 (GR) Unassigned.
Badgley, Thomas Augustine '87 (NY) White Plains, NY Our Lady of Mt. Carmel.
Badia, Leonard F. '60 (BRK) Retired.
Badilles, Roy Jose '82 (LUB) Snyder, TX Our Lady of Guadalupe.
Badillo, Robert P. *m.id.* '95 (NY) Bronx, NY St. Dominic; Bronx, NY Our Lady of Solace; [DD] Bronx, NY Idente Missionaries – Santa Maria Residence.
Badnerosky, Myron M. '56 (PSC) Levittown, PA Our Lady of Perpetual Help.
Badnerosky, Myron '56 (PSC) Retired.
Badokufa, Joseph B. *s.j.* (BO)[U] Newton, MA The Jesuit Community at Boston College.
Badovsky, Rev. Msgr. Thomas '73 (PEO) Dalzell, IL St. Thomas More.
Badway, Gavin '00 (PMB) West Palm Beach, FL Holy Name of Jesus.
Bae, Constantine Kihyen '85 (LA)[BB] Los Angeles, CA Korean Catholic Renewal Movement of Southern California.
Bae, In hoo (TR) Trenton, NJ The Church of the Korean Martyrs.
Baehr, David J. '64 (VEN) Legion of Mary.
Baehr, David '64 (SY) Retired.
Baek, Augustine *s.d.b.* '95 (NY)[FF] Stony Point, NY Don Bosco Retreat Center and Marian Shrine; [FF] Stony Point, NY Marian Shrine.
Baenziger, Edward J. *c.s.b.* '76 (GAL)[O] Houston, TX Residence of the Basilian Fathers of the University of St. Thomas.
Baer, Campion *o.f.m.cap.* '56 (MIL)[B] Mount Calvary, WI St. Lawrence Seminary; [P] Mount Calvary, WI St. Lawrence Friary.
Baer, Chrysostom Anthony *o.praem* '04 (ORG)[I] Silverado, CA Norbertine Fathers of Orange Inc.; [A] Silverado, CA St. Michael's Norbertine Postulancy, Novitiate and Juniorate.
Baer, Robert W. *c.s.p.* '54 (BRK)[R] Retired Retired.
Baer, Timothy K. '96 (WDC) Clinton, MD St. Mary.
Baer, William J. '96 (STP) Oakdale, MN Transfiguration; Deanery 4.
Baerwald, Jeffrey C. *s.j.* '93 (SJ)[B] Santa Clara, CA Jesuit Community.
Baetzold, Anthony Marie *c.f.r.* '05 (NY) Bronx, NY; [DD] Bronx, NY Saint Lawrence Friary.
Baetzold, Anthony '05 (NEW)[L] Newark, NJ Franciscan Friars of the Renewal.
Baez, Ramon A. '05 (ARL) Notaries; Fairfax, VA St. Leo's.
Baeza, Manuel *m.c.c.j.* '96 (FgM) Cincinnati, OH U.S. Headquarters, Comboni Mission Center.
Bafaro, Michael '53 (WOR) Retired.
Bagadiong, Francisco '65 (SFR) San Francisco, CA St. Anne Retired.
Bagan, T. Francis *o.m.i.* '52 (BO)[X] Tewksbury, MA Immaculate Heart of Mary Residence.
Bagdonis, Raymond *o.carm.* '94 (NY) Middletown, NY Our Lady of Mt. Carmel.
Baggetta, Joseph J. '74 (BO) Boston, MA St. James the Greater; Metro Youth Service Center.
Bagienski, Ronald A. '69 (BUF) Absent on Leave.
Bagnato, James D. *o.praem.* '79 (WIL)[J] Middletown, DE Immaculate Conception Priory of the Canons Regular of Premontre; [J] Middletown, DE Norbertine Fathers of Delaware, Inc.
Baguio, Daniel S. '91 (GAL) Sweeny, TX Our Lady of Perpetual Help.
Bagyinski, Agoston *o.f.m.* '98 (WDC)[B] Silver Spring, MD Holy Name College.
Bahash, James '99 (SD) Presbyteral Council; San Diego, CA Saint Charles Catholic Parish.
Bahena, Rosalino Aguirre *o.r.c.* '03 (PCE) Castaner, PR Our Lady of the Miraculous Medal.
Baher, Kenneth W. *s.j.* '60 (SEA)[C] Tacoma, WA Bellarmine Preparatory School.
Bahhuth, Albert M. '96 (LA) Burbank, CA St. Finbar.
Bahl, Greg E. '06 (DUB) Worship Commission; Monona, IA St. Mary; Monona, IA St. Patrick; Monona, IA St. Bridget.
Bahouamio, Brice '08 (LEX)[F] Versailles, KY Taylor Manor Nursing Home.
Bai, Bonaventure *o.f.m.* '99 (CIN)[C] Cincinnati, OH St. Anthony Shrine, Franciscan Postulancy.
Baiardi, Sereno *o.f.m.* '66 (MIL)[Y] Waterford, WI General Secretariat of the Franciscan Missions, Inc.; Waterford, WI General Secretariat of the Franciscan Missions, Inc.; [P] Burlington, WI Queen of Peace Friary.
Baidoo, Joseph '85 (RVC) Roosevelt, NY Queen of the Most Holy Rosary.
Baidoo, Raphael *o.ss.t.* '77 (VIC) Goliad, TX Immaculate Conception; Presbyteral Council.
Baidoo, Raphael *o.ss.t.* '77 (BAL)[Q] Diocese of Victoria, TX.
Baier, Donald M. '70 (RVC) Coram, NY St. Frances Cabrini.
Baier, William J. '82 (STL) Florissant, MO St. Ferdinand.
Baikauskas, Patrick *o.p.* '08 (LFT)[H] West Lafayette, IN St. Thomas Aquinas Parish and Foundation for Catholic Students Attending Purdue University; West Lafayette, IN St. Thomas Aquinas; Members; Aquinas Educational Foundation, Inc.; Newman Apostolate, Purdue University.
Bailey, Casey *o.c.s.o.* '83 (P)[L] Lafayette, OR The Cistercian (Trappist) Abbey of Our Lady of Guadalupe.
Bailey, Douglas S. *s.d.s.* '77 (ORL)[G] Melbourne, FL Florida Institute of Technology Campus Ministry.
Bailey, Fred K. '83 (ORG) Aliso Viejo, CA Corpus Christi.
Bailey, J. Lawrence '86 (SEA) Gig Harbor, WA St. Nicholas.
Bailey, Paul F. '58 (BO) Plymouth, MA St. Mary; Senior Priests. Retired.
Bailey, Ricardo '03 (ATL) On Leave of Absence; Without Archdiocesan Assignment or Faculties.
Bailey, Robert L. '93 (PRO) Pawtucket, RI St. Maria Goretti.
Bailey, Thomas *o.s.b.* '04 (RCK)[G] Aurora, IL Marmion Abbey.
Bailey, Thomas *o.s.b.* '04 (KC)[A] Conception, MO Conception Seminary College.
Baillargeon, Daniel '07 (PRT) Saco, ME Good Shepherd Parish.
Bailleres, Anthony *l.c.* '81 (MAD)[F] Edgerton, WI Koshkonong Pastoral Center; [I] Edgerton, WI Oaklawn Incorporated.
Bailleres, Anthony *l.c.* '81 (SAC) Sacramento, CA Our Lady of Guadalupe Shrine.
Baima, Thomas A. '80 (CHI)[A] Mundelein, IL University of St. Mary of the Lake/Mundelein Seminary; Mundelein Seminary/University of St. Mary of the Lake; Administrative Council; [A] Mundelein, IL University of St. Mary of the Lake/Mundelein Seminary; [A] Mundelein, IL Ministerial and Continuing Education.
Bain, Andre '04 (BRK) Brooklyn, NY St. Patrick; [D] Brooklyn, NY Campus Ministers and Ministry Centers.
Bain, Daniel '64 (RIC) Retired.
Bain, John '70 (RNO) Retired.
Bain, Kenneth '90 (SFS) Garretson, SD St. Rose of Lima; Garretson, SD St. Joseph the Workman.
Bain, Richard C. '80 (MO) DEPARTMENT OF VETERANS AFFAIRS HOSPITALS AND CHAPLAINS Retired.
Baird, James '93 (DEN) Conifer, CO Our Lady of The Pines.
Baird, Rev. Msgr. Lawrence J. '69 (ORG) Newport Beach, CA Our Lady of Mount Carmel; Diocesan Finance Council.
Bajek, Gerald A. '69 (NEW)[L] Rutherford, NJ St. John Vianney Residence for Priests Retired.
Bajkowski, Dennis W. '71 (CAM) Camden, NJ The Church of Sacred Heart.
Bajor, Wieslaw *c.ss.r.* '95 (MET) Perth Amboy, NJ St. Stephen.
Bajorek, James R. '80 (PH) Absent on Sick Leave.
Bak, Charles *m.s.a.* '09 (NOR)[G] Cromwell Society of the Missionaries of the Holy Apostles; Chester, CT St. Joseph.
Bak, Cheong–il '90 (BUF) Tonawanda, NY St. Andrew Kim.
Bakatu, Sebastien '83 (STP)[A] St. Paul, MN St. John Vianney Seminary; [C] St. Paul, MN University of St. Thomas.
Baker, Rev. Msgr. Andrew R. '91 (ALN) Allentown, PA Cathedral of St. Catharine of Siena.
Baker, Bartley '93 (NEW) Elmwood Park, NJ St. Leo's.
Baker, Brad '00 (JOL) Joliet, IL The Cathedral of St. Raymond.
Baker, David D '07 (BUF) Lackawanna, NY Our Lady of Victory National Shrine.
Baker, Dennis *s.j.* (NY)[E] New York, NY Xavier High School.
Baker, Donald C. '95 (NY) New York, NY Nativity; New

York, NY St. Teresa.
Baker, Donald P. '80 (CHL) Absent On Leave.
Baker, Dwight '09 (BUR) Saint Johnsbury, VT Corpus Christi Parish.
Baker, George (NY) On Leave of Absence.
Baker, Gerald H. '83 (OWN) Morganfield, KY St. Ann.
Baker, Jack H. '93 (DET) Waterford, MI St. Perpetua.
Baker, James E. '63 (DOD) Judge Retired.
Baker, James E. '63 (MO) Judges.
Baker, James H. *s.j.* '69 (STL)[C] Saint Louis University; [O] St. Louis, MO Jesuit Community Corporation at Saint Louis University – Jesuit Hall.
Baker, Jay '92 (HT) Thibodaux, LA St. Joseph Co–Cathedral; Vicar General; Judges; Priests Council; Legal Services; Coordinator; Clergy Personnel; College of Consultors; Diocesan Finance Council.
Baker, John C. '82 (MIA) Key West, FL St. Mary Star of the Sea; Local Chaplain.
Baker, John Sims '94 (NSH) Defenders of the Bond; Vanderbilt; Priest Benefit Foundation; Presbyteral Council.
Baker, Joseph W. '69 (NY) New York, NY Ascension.
Baker, Rev. Msgr. Joseph W. '51 (STL) Retired.
Baker, Joseph (NY) Unassigned.
Baker, Justin J. '99 (BUR) Elected Members; Rutland, VT Christ the King; Wallingford, VT St. Patrick; Diocesan Consultors; Deans.
Baker, Kenneth '84 (CHI) La Grange, IL St. Cletus.
Baker, Nicholas J. '63 (LIN) Minden, NE St. John the Baptist; Deaneries and Deans; Diocesan Area CCD Directors.
Baker, Richard D. (NY) New York, NY St. Malachy's.
Baker, Richard M. *m.m.* '71 (FgM) Maryknoll, NY MARYKNOLL.
Baker, Robert R. *c.s.c.* '70 (FgM) New Rochelle, NY Eastern Brothers Province.
Baker, Robert R. *c.s.c.* '70 (FTW)[H] Notre Dame Congregation of Holy Cross, United States Province of Priests & Brothers.
Baker, Stephen J. *o.s.a.* '90 (PH)[F] Malvern, PA Malvern Preparatory School for Boys; [Y] Rosemont, PA Saxony Hall; [C] Villanova University.
Baker, Thomas E. '89 (LA) Lancaster, CA Sacred Heart; Deanery 8; San Fernando Region.
Baker, W. Pierre '78 (MAN) Nashua, NH Blessed John XXIII Parish; Presbyteral Council.
Baker, William S. '55 (SY) Retired.
Baker, Rev. Msgr. William T. '82 (ALN) Reading, PA St. Paul; Appointed Members.
Bakewell, Donald V. '66 (DUB) Dubuque, IA St. Joseph.
Bakey, Christopher T. '98 (CAM) On Sick Leave.
Bakh, Antoine '88 (OLL) Orange, CA St. John Maron Maronite Catholic Church.
Bakka, Suresh '03 (OWN) Reed, KY St. Augustine; Owensboro, KY St. Peter of Alcantara.
Bakkar, Gabriel Mary *c.f.r.* '07 (NY)[DD] New York, NY St. Joseph's Friary.
Bakke, Lawrence M. '75 (MAD) Monroe, WI St. Clare of Assisi Parish; Personnel Board; Apostolate to the Handicapped.
Bakkelund, Jonathan '11 (RCK) Huntley, IL St. Mary.
Bakker, Richard T. *s.m.a.* '59 (BO) Malden, MA Immaculate Conception.
Bakle, John L. *s.m.* '67 (COL) Cardington, OH Sacred Hearts.
Bakle, John L. *s.m.* '67 (STL)[O] St. Louis Marianists, Province of the United States (Society of Mary).
Bakwaph, Peter '03 (NY) Spring Valley, NY St. Joseph.
Baky, Isidore '72 (MIA) Fort Lauderdale, FL St. Helen; Vietnamese.
Bakyil, Alphonsus *s.o.l.t.* '85 (PHX) Phoenix, AZ Most Holy Trinity Roman Catholic Parish.
Bakyor, Francis (KCK) Lenexa, KS Holy Trinity.
Bala, Paul W. '69 (SAG) Cass City, MI St. Pancratius; Gagetown, MI St. Agatha Retired.
Bala, Pawel '11 (PAT) Mendham, NJ St. Joseph's.
Balabbo, Heherson *c.m.f.* '11 (MET) Perth Amboy, NJ Our Lady of Fatima.
Balagapo, Victorio R. '66 (SFR) San Francisco, CA Visitacion, Church of the Retired.
Balagtas, Rodel G. '91 (LA) Los Angeles, CA Immaculate Heart of Mary.
Balarote, Venancio R. '01 (RIC) Virginia Beach, VA St. Nicholas.
Balas, Christopher *o.f.m.conv.* '57 (TR) Seaside Park, NJ St. Catharine of Siena.
Balas, David *o.cist.* '54 (DAL)[B] University of Dallas; [J] Irving, TX Cistercian Abbey of Our Lady of Dallas.
Balash, Michael D. '87 (Y) Warren, OH St. William; Washington, DC Federation of Diocesan Liturgical Commissions.
Balashowreddy, Salibindla '80 (AMA) Canadian, TX Sacred Heart.
Balasko, George J. '67 (Y) Retired.
Balazs, Richard *c.r.* '65 (CHI) Chicago, IL St. Stanislaus, Bishop and Martyr.
Balazy, Edwin W. '62 (DET) Dearborn Heights, MI St. John the Baptist.
Balbi, Abel E. '82 (SB) Ontario, CA St. George.
Balcerski, Duane *c.s.c.* (FTW)[H] Notre Dame Congregation of Holy Cross, United States Province of Priests & Brothers.
Balcerski, Duane *c.s.c.* '71 (PHX)[F] Phoenix, AZ Holy Cross Congregation/Casa Santa Cruz.
Balchunas, Henry A. '65 (HRT) Wolcott, CT St. Pius X.
Balczeniuk, Mark G. '83 (SCR) Unassigned or Leave of Absence.
Baldacchino, Rev. Msgr. Peter '96 (NEW) On Duty Outside the Archdiocese.
Baldeon Lope, Elvio C. '10 (CHI) Berwyn, IL St. Odilo.
Balderas, Jose Luis '68 (LAR) Laredo, TX Christ the King.
Balderas, Sergio A. '06 (BLX) Vocations; Presbyteral Council; Diberville, MS Sacred Heart.
Balderrama, Sergio '06 (LSC) Las Cruces, NM Holy Cross.
Baldonado, Rev. Msgr. Bonifacio '85 (STO) Modesto, CA Our Lady of Fatima Church (Pastor of).
Baldonado, Luis *o.f.m.* '52 (PHX) Phoenix, AZ St. Mary's Roman Catholic Basilica Retired.
Baldonieri, Thomas F. '90 (CHI) Highwood, IL St. James.
Baldovin, John *s.j.* '75 (BO)[U] Brighton, MA Edmund Campion House.
Balducelli, Roberto *o.s.f.s.* '36 (WIL) Wilmington, DE St. Anthony of Padua.
Balduck, Walter *o.f.m.cap.* '73 (TUC) Mammoth, AZ Blessed Sacrament Roman Catholic Parish – Mammoth.
Baldwin, Bradley C. *t.o.r.* '94 (STP) Brooklyn Park, MN St. Gerard Majella; [J] Brooklyn Park, MN St. Gerard Friary.
Baldwin, Rev. Msgr. Edward J. '55 (DET) Retired.
Baldwin, John F. '59 (CHI) Retired.
Baldwin, Kevin *l.c.* '98 (CHI)[N] Hillside, IL Legion of Christ.
Baldwin, Michael E. '83 (WCH) Pittsburg, KS Our Lady of Lourdes.
Baldwin, Michael '83 (WCH)[B] Pittsburg, KS St. Mary Colgan High School.
Baldwin, Paul C. '97 (DUB) Eldora, IA St. Mary; Iowa Falls, IA St. Mark.
Baldyga, William L. '69 (HRT) Suffield, CT St. Joseph.
Balen, Adilso Luiz *c.s.* '91 (CHI)[N] Oak Park, IL Missionaries of Saint Charles.
Balen, Moacir *c.s.* '77 (ORL) Portuguese/Brazilian Ministry; Winter Garden, FL Resurrection.
Bales, Francis *o.s.b.* '87 (TLS)[G] Hulbert, OK Our Lady of the Annunciation of Clear Creek Monastery.
Bales, Robert '57 (MIL) Retired.
Bales, Rev. Msgr. Thomas E. '74 (RCK) Amboy, IL St. Patrick; Amboy, IL St. Flannen; Amboy, IL St. Mary.
Balestino, Francis P. '60 (ALT) Retired.
Balestrieri, Edward '59 (BEL) Retired.
Balili, Peter D. (BEL) Christopher, IL St. Andrew; Sesser, IL St. Mary.
Balinda, Rev. Msgr. Thadeus '92 (FTW) Culver, IN St. Mary of the Lake.
Balinong, Alfredo *s.j.* '64 (NY) New York, NY Blessed Sacrament.
Balins, Sameem '08 (EST) Chancery Office.
Balint, Rev. Msgr. R. James '61 (DAL) Plano, TX Prince of Peace Retired.
Balint, Stephen J. '65 (BGP) Norwalk, CT St. Ladislaus.
Balistreri, Anthony '93 (SJP) Eastern Protopresbytery; Vicar for Clergy; Presbyteral Council; Personnel Board; Presbyters; Ramey, PA Annunciation B.V.M.
Balizan, Daniel M. '89 (SFE) Raton, NM St. Patrick/St. Joseph; Vicars Forane (Deans); Presbyteral Council of the Archdiocese of Santa Fe.
Balkan, Paschal *o.c.s.o.* '55 (ARL)[H] Berryville, VA Cistercian Abbey of Our Lady of the Holy Cross.
Ball, Raymond A. '87 (MAN) Concord, NH Immaculate Heart of Mary; Catholic Scouting.
Ball, Richard D. '77 (SC) Granville, IA St. Joseph; [B] Granville, IA Spalding Catholic Schools, Inc.; Presbyteral Council; Diocesan Consultors; Deans.
Ball, Wayne L '89 (RIC) Highland Springs, VA St. John the Evangelist; Judges; International Airport; Richmond, VA St. Patrick.
Ballance, Harvey '57 (NEW) Retired.
Ballard, Christopher '10 (SY) Johnson City, NY St. James.
Ballard, Kevin *s.j.* '85 (SJ)[L] Los Altos, CA Jesuit Retreat Center of Los Altos.
Ballard, Mark E. '02 (BO) Marshfield, MA Our Lady of the Assumption.
Ballecer, Robert R. *s.j.* '07 (WDC)[O] Washington, DC Leonard Neale House; Washington, DC.
Ballesteros, Enrique '89 (OAK) Concord, CA Queen of All Saints.
Ballesteros, Jesus '10 (RNO) Carson City, NV St. Teresa of Avila.
Ballesteros, Juan Ignacio '04 (POD) San Juan.
Balleza, John A. '85 (SFR) San Rafael, CA St. Raphael; Council of Priests; College of Consultors.
Ballien, Paul K. '99 (DET) Dearborn Heights, MI St. Linus; Presbyteral Council; Archdiocesan Vicars.
Ballman, Luke R. '01 (ATL) Special or Other Archdiocesan Assignment.
Ballou, Jeffrey A. '01 (SPR) Ware, MA St. Mary's; Air Force Reserve Chaplains.
Balluff, John '88 (JOL) West Chicago, IL St. Mary; Ecumenism; Life and Formation of Clergy.
Balluff, Thomas J. '06 (STP) St. Bonifacius, MN St. Boniface; Delano, MN St. Mary of Czestochowa.
Ballweg, Rev. Msgr. Lawrence F. '40 (RVC) Retired.
Balmeo, Simeon '65 (AGN) Agana, GU Our Lady of the Purification.
Balog, Robert A. '72 (RCK) McHenry, IL St. Mary.
Balser, Edward '56 (JKS) Retired.
Balser, Robert *c.ss.r.* '49 (GR) Grand Rapids, MI St. Alphonsus; [L] Grand Rapids, MI The Society of the Redemptorists of the City of Grand Rapids.
Balskus, Charles '65 (CHI) Chicago, IL St. Mary, Star of the Sea Retired.
Balta, Rev. Msgr. Raymond A. '69 (PBR) Johnstown, PA St. Mary's; Protopresbyters.
Baltes, Gabriel *o.s.b.* '91 (JOL) Lisle, IL St. Joan of Arc.
Baltes, Timothy '76 (SCL) Sartell, MN St. Francis Xavier; Personnel Committee; Diocesan Consultors; Diocesan Planning Council.
Balthazar, Ayala '43 (SJ) Retired.
Balthazar, Rev. Msgr. Norman '63 (SP) Retired.
Baltrus, Michael '07 (NSH) McEwen, TN St. Patrick's; Priest Benefit Foundation.
Baltrusaitis, Gabriel *o.f.m.* '54 (PRT)[I] Kennebunk, ME St. Anthony's Friary; Kennebunkport, ME.
Baltz, Albert G. '70 (BUR) Brandon, VT St. Mary's.
Baltz, David *m.c.c.j.* '67 (FgM) Cincinnati, OH COMBONI MISSIONARIES (VERONA FATHERS).
Baluyot, Michael '97 (BEA) On Leave.
Balwinski, Gerald E. '69 (SAG) Retired.
Balzer, Raymond '49 (FTW) Retired.
Bambenek, Joseph Jerome '10 (STP) St. Paul, MN The Nativity of Our Lord.
Bambenek, Oliver *o.f.m.cap.* '65 (MIL)[B] Mount Calvary, WI St. Lawrence Seminary; [P] Mount Calvary, WI St. Felix Friary.
Bamber, William J. *c.m.* '55 (PH)[Y].
Bambrick, John P. '91 (TR) Toms River, NJ St. Joseph.
Bambrick, John W. '70 (ALN) Ashland, PA St. Joseph; Ashland, PA St. Mauritius; Ashland, PA Our Lady of Good Counsel; Ashland – Court St. Joan of Arc #225.
Bammon, John *o.f.m.conv.* '09 (IND) Terre Haute, IN St. Joseph University Catholic Church, Terre Haute, Inc.
Banach, Henry S. '48 (WOR) Retired.
Banach, Rev. Msgr. Michael '88 (WOR) On Special or Other Diocesan Assignment; On Duty Outside the Diocese.
Banal, Jose Vaughn '96 (LA) Altadena, CA Sacred Heart.
Banas, James T. *c.s.c.* '57 (FTW)[H] Notre Dame Congregation of Holy Cross, United States Province of Priests & Brothers; New Rochelle, NY Eastern Brothers Province.
Banas, Leonard N. *c.s.c.* '52 (FTW)[B] University of Notre Dame Du Lac; [H] Notre Dame, IN Holy Cross Community, Corby Hall, University of Notre Dame.
Banazak, Gregory '85 (DET) Special Assignment.
Banchs, Luis R. *s.e.m.v.* '02 (ARE) Arecibo, PR Our Lady of Guadalupe.
Bancroft, Martin '01 (RVC) Port Jefferson, NY Mather Memorial Hospital; Port Jefferson, NY Infant Jesus.
Bandanadam, Benjamin '94 (OKL) Guymon, OK St. Peter's.
Banden, Joseph W. '69 (STL) Florissant, MO St. Sabina.
Bandico, Marcelino '85 (SD) San Diego, CA Saint Michael Catholic Parish San Diego.
Bandiera, Colombo F. '52 (WH) Retired.
Bandivas, Gemnoli '91 (LAV) Tonopah, NV St. Patrick.
Bandsuch, Mark *s.j.* '00 (LA)[C] Los Angeles, CA Jesuit Community.
Banduku, Charles Mbuyi '98 (MIL) Fox Point, WI St. Eugene.
Banet, Stephen '77 (IND) Indianapolis, IN St. Jude Catholic Church, Indianapolis, Inc.
Bang–Doan, Joseph '74 (GAL)[S] Houston, TX The Catholic Chaplain Corps.
Bangueses, Jose Fernandez '70 (TR) Red Bank, NJ St. Anthony.
Bani, J. Cary '07 (BR) St. Francisville, LA Our Lady of Mount Carmel; Angola, LA Louisiana State Penitentiary.
Baniak, Walter '41 (ALB) Retired.
Banick, Rev. Msgr. Thomas V. '63 (SCR) Wilkes–Barre, PA Our Lady of Fatima Parish; Presbyteral Council.
Banico, Emmanuel Wharren '00 (LA) La Mirada, CA St. Paul of the Cross.
Banigan, Herbert '46 (DEN) Retired.
Baniowski, Thadeusz *s.ch.* '62 (CHI) Chicago, IL Holy Trinity Mission.
Bankemper, Stephen M. '03 (COV)[B] Newport, KY Newport Central Catholic High School; Fort Thomas, KY St. Catherine of Siena.
Banken, Robert L. '68 (STL) Portage Des Sioux, MO St. Francis of Assisi.
Banker, Richard A. '88 (STP) Cottage Grove, MN Church of St. Rita.

Banks, Charles *o.m.i.* '66 (SAT)[K] San Antonio, TX Oblate Madonna Residence; [L] San Antonio, TX Oblate Vocation Office.
Banks, Gary *s.t.* (PAT)[N] Stirling, NJ Shrine of St. Joseph.
Banks, Michael *o.f.m.cap.* '84 (BO)[U] Boston, MA San Lorenzo Friary; [U] Boston, MA San Lorenzo Friary.
Banks, Peter *o.f.m.cap.* '73 (LA) Solvang, CA Old Mission Santa Ines.
Bankston, James '04 (STN) La Mesa, CA St. John the Baptizer.
Bannan, Peter F. '67 (NY) Pelham, NY St. Catharine.
Bannantine, Thomas E. *s.j.* '65 (OM)[J] Omaha, NE Jesuit Community at Creighton University.
Banner, Russell '67 (CLV) Administrative Leave.
Bannes, Timothy L. '07 (STL) Ballwin, MO Holy Infant.
Bannon, Anthony *l.c.* '75 (NY)[HH] Rye, NY Legacy Growth, Inc.
Banos, Felix '58 (ORL) Lakeland, FL St. Joseph's Retired.
Bantz, William '60 (Y) Retired.
Banuelas, Rev. Msgr. Arturo '76 (ELP) El Paso, TX St. Pius X; El Paso, TX San Juan Bautista.
Banye, Anthony '94 (BRK) Brooklyn, NY St. Patrick.
Banzin, Robert S. '64 (CHI) Niles, IL St. John Brebeuf Retired.
Bao, Anthony '48 (OKL) Retired.
Baok, Dominikus *s.v.d.* (WH) Gassaway, WV St. Thomas.
Baptista, Diego '69 (SR) On Duty Outside the Diocese.
Baptista, Diogo '69 (SAC) Ione, CA Mule Creek State Prison; Ione, CA.
Baptiste, Charles J. '96 (PIT) Clairton, PA St. Clare of Assisi.
Baptiste, Eden Jean '83 (RVC) Brentwood, NY St. Anne's; Haitian–American Apostolate.
Baraan, Geoffrey '97 (OAK) Union City, CA St. Anne; Deanery #16.
Barachini, Nello '86 (BGP) Shelton, CT St. Margaret Mary Retired.
Barajas, Abel '96 (MIA) Pompano Beach, FL San Isidro; [N] Pompano Beach, FL Word & Life Catholic Ministry, Inc.; [N] Pompano Beach, FL Ministerio Catolico Verbo y Vida, Inc.; Deans and Deaneries; Appointed by the Archbishop.
Barak, Christopher L. '87 (LIN) Palmyra, NE St. Leo's; Notaries; Commission for Sacred Liturgy and Sacred Music; Office of Religious Education (CCD); Evangelization Committee; Priests' Continuing Education Committee.
Baraki, Tesfamariam '75 (WDC) Washington, DC St. Gabriel; Hospital & Nursing Home Ministries.
Baran, Blaise R. '82 (MET) Washington, NJ St. Joseph.
Baran, Jody '89 (PSC) Passaic, NJ St. Michael Cathedral.
Baran, John P. '84 (BGP) Fairfield, CT St. Anthony of Padua.
Baran, Joseph L. '47 (MIL) Retired.
Baran, Volodymyr '85 (PAT) Paterson, NJ St. Joseph Hospital.
Baran, Volodymyr *c.ss.r.* (PHU) Manassas, VA Annunciation of the Blessed Virgin Mary; Manassas, VA St. John the Baptist.
Baraniak, James T. *o.praem.* '93 (GB) De Pere, WI St. Norbert College; [B] De Pere, WI St. Norbert College; [J] De Pere, WI St. Joseph Priory.
Baraniewicz, Joseph *o.s.f.s.* '57 (TOL)[H] Childs, MD Annecy Hall Retired.
Baraniewicz, Joseph *o.s.f.s.* '57 (WIL)[J] Childs, MD Retirement and Assisted Care Facility Retired.
Baranowski, Arthur R. '68 (DET) Marysville, MI St. Christopher; [T] Marysville, MI National Alliance of Parishes Restructuring into Communities (NAPRC).
Baranowski, David J. '73 (HRT) Rocky Hill, CT St. James; Office for Divine Worship; Special and other Archdiocesan Assignment.
Baranowski, Stanley A. '55 (MIL) Retired.
Baranski, Andrew E. '92 (SY) Priests' Personnel Committee; Syracuse, NY Basilica of the Sacred Heart.
Baranski, Richard *o.f.m.* '06 (FWT)[H] Crowley, TX St. Maximilian Kolbe Friary.
Baransky, Francis J. '79 (ALN) Jim Thorpe, PA St. Joseph.
Barasinski, John B. '81 (GRY) Beverly Shores, IN St. Ann.
Baratelli, David J. '82 (MO) Air Force Reserve Chaplains; Apostleship of the Air.
Baratelli, David J. '82 (PSC) Safe Environment Program.
Barattini, John H. '44 (NO) Retired.
Baraza, Patrick '82 (SPK) Spokane, WA St. Ann.
Barba, Alfredo '09 (FWT) Arlington, TX St. Matthew; Fort Worth, TX St. John the Apostle.
Barbato, Robert A. *o.f.m.cap.* '87 (LA)[B] Santa Ynez, CA San Lorenzo Seminary – Retreat Center; Definitors.
Barbella, John J. '87 (MET) Phillipsburg, NJ St. Philip & St. James.
Barber, Eugene J. *s.j.* '63 (BAL)[Q] Towson Maryland Province of the Society of Jesus; Towson, MD Society of Jesus.
Barber, Hal L. '67 (SFS) Parker, SD St. Christina; Marion, SD Our Lady of Perpetual Help Retired.
Barber, Michael C. *s.j.* '85 (MO) Navy Reserve Chaplains.
Barber, Michael C. *s.j.* '85 (BO)[U] Newton, MA The Jesuit Community at Boston College.
Barber, Michael D. *s.j.* '79 (STL)[C] Arts and Sciences, College of; [C] Philosophy and Letters, College of; [C] Saint Louis University; [O] St. Louis, MO Leo Brown Jesuit Community; [O] St. Louis, MO Sacred Heart Jesuit Community.
Barber, Michael *s.m.* '90 (SAT)[K] San Antonio, TX Marianist Residence: Skilled Nursing.
Barber, Stephen A. *s.j.* '98 (LA)[F] Los Angeles, CA Loyola High School of Los Angeles.
Barbian, Leonard M. '65 (MIL) Retired.
Barbieri, Giusepppe *c.p.* '88 (GAL)[A] Houston, TX St. Mary's Seminary.
Barbieto, Paciano A. (NEW) Kearny, NJ St. Stephen.
Barbone, Joseph F. '72 (NEW) Bayonne, NJ Our Lady of the Assumption.
Barbosa, Cristiano G. Borro '07 (BO) Cambridge, MA St. Anthony of Padua.
Barbosa, Paulo (FR) Fall River, MA Cathedral of St. Mary of the Assumption.
Barbour, Claude–Marie (CHI)[B] Chicago, IL Catholic Theological Union.
Barbour, Hugh C. *o.praem.* '90 (ORG)[A] Silverado, CA St. Michael's Norbertine Postulancy, Novitiate and Juniorate; [I] Silverado, CA Norbertine Fathers of Orange Inc.; Ecumenical and Interreligious Affairs; Silverado, CA.
Barboutz, Paul '09 (PAT) Ringwood, NJ St. Catherine of Bologna.
Barcellona, Thomas J. '95 (CAM) Vocation Advisory Board; Atco, NJ Christ the Redeemer Parish, Atco, N.J.
Barcelos, Robert Elias *o.c.d.* '03 (TUC) Tucson, AZ Saint Margaret Mary Alacoque Roman Catholic Parish – Tucson.
Barcelos, Robert *o.c.d.* '08 (LA) Alhambra, CA St. Therese.
Barch, Howard C. '93 (MO) Navy Reserve Chaplains.
Barch, Howard C. '93 (RCK) Byron, IL St. Mary.
Barcio, Rev. Msgr. Robert G. '47 (E) Erie, PA St. Peter Cathedral Retired.
Barclay, Robert F. '75 (BRK) Ozone Park, NY St. Elizabeth.
Barclift, Richard L. '66 (PEO) Retired.
Barco, Roberto A. '83 (SB) Cathedral City, CA St. Louis.
Barczak, Rene *o.f.m.* '64 (PH)[D] Philadelphia, PA Archbishop Ryan High School; [Y] Philadelphia, PA St. Pius X Residence.
Bardes, Rev. Msgr. George F. '44 (NY)[DD] Bronx, NY John Cardinal O'Connor Residence Retired.
Barfknecht, David *o.s.b.* '89 (HON)[D] Waialua, HI Benedictine Monastery of Hawaii/Retreat Center; Waialua, HI.
Bargola, Cerino O. '84 (MO) Navy Chaplains.
Baribeau, Donald G. *m.s.* '75 (R) Swansboro, NC St. Mildred.
Barica, Daniel *o.f.m.* '99 (LA) Santa Barbara, CA Old Mission Santa Barbara; [P] Santa Barbara, CA Franciscan Friary, Order of Friars Minor (Old Mission).
Baricuatro, J. Michael '10 (SAC) Chico, CA St. John the Baptist.
Barile, Ralph E. '82 (BRK) Long Island City, NY St. Mary.
Barille, Nicholas J. *s.t.* '95 (SB) Coachella, CA Our Lady of Soledad.
Baris, Bernard *m.s.* '69 (FR) Brewster, MA Our Lady of the Cape; [F] Attleboro, MA La Salette Missionary Association.
Barita, Joseph (P) St. Helens, OR St. Frederic.
Barius, Placid *o.f.m.* '43 (PRT)[I] Kennebunk, ME St. Anthony's Friary; Kennebunkport, ME.
Barius, Placidas *o.f.m.* '43 (LIT) Lithuanian Franciscan Province of St. Casimir.
Bariviera, Jefferson O. *c.s.* '09 (MIA) Brazilian and Portuguese Apostolate; Margate, FL St. Vincent.
Barkemeyer, John F. '90 (CHI) Military Chaplains; Army Chaplains.
Barkenquest, Lehr *o.s.f.s.* '64 (LAN) Clarklake, MI St. Rita.
Barker, Brian '94 (BEL) Pinckneyville, IL St. Bruno.
Barker, Jack '92 (SB) Murrieta, CA St. Martha; College of Consultors.
Barker, Rev. Msgr. James '80 (BAL) Forest Hill, MD St. Ignatius.
Barker, Joseph A. '53 (ALB) Priests Retirement Board/ Priests Retirement Plan Board; Troy, NY Our Lady of Victory Retired.
Barker, Joseph '53 (ALB) Retired.
Barker, Richard E. '92 (GAL) Huffman, TX St. Philip the Apostle.
Barker, Ronald A. '75 (BO) Wakefield, MA St. Joseph.
Barkett, James S. '91 (ARL) Fairfax, VA St. Mary of Sorrows.
Barkey, Patrick '90 (PIT) Wildwood, PA St. Catherine of Sweden.
Barkin, Martin F. '77 (PIT) Verona, PA St. Gerard Majella; Penn Hills, PA St. Susanna.
Barlaan, Dwight Dennis G. '97 (SFR) Daly City, CA Our Lady of Perpetual Help.
Barley, Tom '91 (SAN) Judicial Vicar; Diocesan Consultors; Presbyteral Council; San Angelo, TX Cathedral of the Sacred Heart.
Barlow, James P. '73 (SAT) San Antonio, TX St. Luke.
Barman, William '81 (ORG) Lake Forest, CA Santiago de Compostela.
Barmann, Karl *o.s.b.* '65 (KC) Stanberry, MO St. Peter's; [J] Priests Elsewhere; Deans; Presbyteral Council.
Barmasse, Gerald R. *c.s.c.* '76 (FTW)[H] Notre Dame Congregation of Holy Cross, United States Province of Priests & Brothers; New Rochelle, NY Eastern Brothers Province.
Barna, Darek '00 (RCK) Algonquin, IL St. Margaret Mary.
Barna, Dariusz *o.f.m.conv.* (BRK) Brooklyn, NY Most Holy Trinity – Saint Mary.
Barnard, Matthew D. '08 (STL) St. Louis, MO St. Margaret Mary Alacoque.
Barnd, Donald *s.c.j.* '78 (MIL)[P] Franklin Sacred Heart at Monastery Lake.
Barnekow, Kevin '11 (MIL) Waukesha, WI St. William.
Barnes, Christopher M. '10 (E) Greenville, PA St. Michael.
Barnes, David J. '97 (BO) Beverly, MA St. Margaret; Beverly, MA St. Mary Star of the Sea.
Barnes, Gavin *o.s.b.* '52 (IND)[K] Saint Meinrad, IN St. Meinrad Archabbey.
Barnes, James H. '69 (LA) Los Angeles, CA St. Joan of Arc.
Barnes, John G. '52 (DUB) Retired.
Barnes, Patrick Thomas '10 (STP) St. Anthony, MN St. Charles Borromeo; [E] Minneapolis, MN DeLaSalle High School.
Barnes, Thomas C. '87 (COV) Covington, KY Holy Cross.
Barnett, Daniel '00 (SPK) Pasco, WA St. Patrick.
Barnett, James *o.p.* '65 (STL)[O] Saint Louis, MO St. Dominic Priory.
Barnett, Rev. Msgr. Stephen '70 (SFS) Plankinton, SD St. John.
Barnhardt, Bruno *o.s.b.cam.* '66 (MRY)[F] Big Sur, CA New Camaldoli Hermitage.
Barnhart, Victor A. '90 (STL) On Leave of Absence; [V] Lemay, MO Catholic Deaf Ministry.
Barnhill, Robert K. '85 (LIN) Cambridge, NE St. John's; Commission for Sacred Liturgy and Sacred Music; Deaf Ministry; Scouting; Air National Guard Chaplains.
Barno, John R. '06 (NEW) Bayonne, NJ St. Andrew's.
Barnufsky, Stephen *o.f.m.* '76 (TUC) Tucson, AZ San Xavier Mission Roman Catholic Parish – Tucson; Council of Priests; Vicar for Native Americans; Vicars Forane; All Vicars Forane; [E] Tucson, AZ San Xavier Mission Friary.
Barnum, James (RVC) Valley Stream, NY Franklin Medical Center Hospital.
Barnum, Martin '74 (CHI)[A] Mundelein, IL University of St. Mary of the Lake/Mundelein Seminary.
Barnum, Matthew J. '07 (GR) Muskegon, MI St. Mary's; Muskegon, MI St. Jean Baptiste.
Barnwell, Gerald P. '77 (FR) Retired.
Baroma, R. Roy C. '97 (SEA) Snoqualmie, WA Our Lady of Sorrows.
Baron, James '11 (COS) On Duty Outside Diocese.
Baron, Mark *m.i.c.* '04 (WDC)[B] Washington, DC Marian Fathers Scholasticate.
Barona, Jaime '98 (ATL) Gainesville, GA St. Michael.
Barone, Michael C. '08 (NEW) Elizabeth, NJ Trinitas Regional Medical Center.
Barone, Michael J. '75 (TYL) Madisonville, TX St. Elizabeth Ann Seton.
Baroni, Barry J. '79 (ALT) Johnstown, PA Visitation of the B.V.M.
Baronti, David '76 (SPK) On Duty Outside the Diocese.
Barota, Michael '04 (SPA) Ceres, CA St. Matthew's Assyrian–Chaldean Catholic Church.
Barousse, Raphael *o.s.b.* '55 (NO) Mandeville, LA St. Dymphna Catholic Center and Chapel; Mandeville, LA Southeast Louisiana Hospital; [R] St. Benedict, LA St. Joseph Abbey.
Barozzi, Italo '65 (BRK) Flushing, NY St. Mel.
Barr, Brian P. '93 (RVC) Rockville Centre, NY Campus Parish of Long Island; Vocations.
Barr, Brian '93 (BRK)[B] Douglaston, NY Cathedral Seminary Residence of the Immaculate Conception.
Barr, Rev. Msgr. Eric R. '84 (RCK) Durand, IL St. Mary; Special Assignment; Vicars General; Newspaper; Diocesan Consultors.
Barr, Francis J. *o.s.a.* '87 (PH)[Y] Villanova, PA St. Augustine Friary.
Barr, Joseph F. '78 (BAL) Towson, MD Church of the Immaculate Conception; [T] Towson, MD The Immaculate Conception Elementary School Endowment Trust.
Barr, Rev. Msgr. Liam M. '74 (LIN) Lincoln, NE St. Joseph; Deaneries and Deans; Office of Stewardship & Development.

Barr, Mark D. (BO) Malden, MA Immaculate Conception.
Barr, Timothy J. '06 (RCK) Freeport, IL St. Mary; Freeport, IL St. Joseph.
Barragan, Juan Carlos '97 (AMA) Dumas, TX SS. Peter and Paul.
Barragan, Victor D. Marino (BO) Lynn, MA St. Joseph.
Barrameda, Arnel B. '86 (GAL) Crosby, TX Sacred Heart.
Barrand, James R. '89 (HPM) Anchorage, AK Saint Nicholas of Myra.
Barranger, R. Joseph *o.p.* '87 (WDC) Washington, DC St. Dominic Church & Priory.
Barras, Gregory '84 (BLX) Biloxi, MS Cathedral of the Nativity of the Blessed Virgin Mary; Biloxi, MS St. Michael.
Barras, Michael J. '73 (LKC) West Calcasieu Cameron Hospital; Westlake, LA St. John Bosco.
Barras, Robert '80 (GAL) Houston, TX St. Bernadette Soubirous; Southern Vicariate.
Barratt, Anthony M. '85 (ALB) Frankfort, NY Our Lady Queen of Apostles; Ilion, NY Annunciation; Deans; Judges.
Barre, Michael L. *s.s.* '70 (BAL)[A] Baltimore, MD St. Mary's Seminary and University; Baltimore, MD; [Q] Baltimore, MD St. Mary's Seminary & University.
Barreda, Giles *o.f.m.* '61 (FR) Buzzards Bay, MA St. Margaret.
Barrera, Albino F. *o.p.* '93 (PRO)[O] Providence St. Thomas Aquinas Priory at Providence College.
Barrera, Constantino '06 (BEA)[A] Beaumont, TX Monsignor Kelly Catholic High School; Beaumont, TX St. Jude Thaddeus.
Barrera, Fernando '05 (STO) Absent on Leave.
Barrera, Filiberto '98 (OAK) Richmond, CA St. Cornelius.
Barrera, Rev. Msgr. Gustavo '79 (BWN) McAllen–Edinburg Deanery; Promoter of Justice; Defenders of the Bond; College of Consultors; Diocesan Finance Council; McAllen, TX Our Lady of Sorrows.
Barrera, Jose Alberto '92 (SLC) Ogden, UT Saint Joseph LLC 230.
Barrera, Jose Fidel '02 (SLC) Cedar City, UT Christ the King LLC 203.
Barreto, Angel L. Soto '92 (MGZ) San German, PR San German de Auxerre.
Barreto, Roberto '92 (LSC) Hurley, NM Infant Jesus.
Barrett, David A. '97 (STP) New Prague, MN St. Wenceslaus.
Barrett, David S. '64 (GB) Gillett, WI St. John; Suring, WI St. Michael Retired.
Barrett, Edward J. '75 (CHI) Alsip, IL St. Terrence.
Barrett, Rev. Msgr. Francis X. '55 (ALN) Reading, PA Holy Guardian Angels Retired.
Barrett, Gerard *o.m.i.* '64 (SAT)[K] San Antonio, TX Oblate Madonna Residence.
Barrett, James L. '82 (CHI) Chicago, IL St. Margaret Mary; Deans.
Barrett, James L. '56 (KAL) Diocesan Consultors; Presbyteral Council Members; Presbyteral Council Members Retired.
Barrett, John F. '59 (JOL) Retired.
Barrett, John J. '78 (RVC) Wading River, NY St. John Baptist.
Barrett, Joseph '05 (FAR) Jamestown, ND St. James Basilica of Jamestown.
Barrett, Kevin S. '92 (PCE) On Duty Outside the Diocese.
Barrett, Michael J. *s.t.d.* '85 (GAL) Houston, TX Holy Cross Chapel.
Barrett, Michael J. '85 (POD) Houston.
Barrett, Michael '85 (GAL)[N] Houston, TX Opus Dei.
Barrett, Michael '76 (MIL) Wauwatosa, WI St. Bernard.
Barrett, Miles J. '82 (SC) On Duty Outside the Diocese; Navy Chaplains.
Barrett, Miles J. '82 (CAM) Cape May, NJ United States Coast Guard, Command Chaplain's Office.
Barrett, Thomas E. '93 (PMB) Palm Beach Gardens, FL Cathedral of St. Ignatius Loyola; [B] Fort Pierce, FL John Carroll High School, Inc.; Elected Members.
Barrett, Thomas G. '88 (ORL) Ormond Beach, FL St. Brendan.
Barrett, Thomas M. '71 (BEL) Vienna, IL St. Francis de Sales; Vienna, IL St. Paul.
Barrett, Thomas *c.ss.r.* '67 (ROC)[M] Canandaigua, NY Notre Dame Retreat House.
Barrett, Rev. Msgr. Walter C. '75 (RIC) Fort Monroe, VA St. Mary Star of the Sea; Hampton, VA St. Joseph; Newport News, VA St. Vincent de Paul; Regional Vicars.
Barrett, William '59 (ROC) Retired.
Barricks, Robert '94 (P) Absent on Leave.
Barriga, Juan Jose Villa *o.f.m.* '00 (LAR) Hebbronville, TX Our Lady of Guadalupe.
Barrios, Clifford *s.s.s.* '06 (HON) Hilo, HI St. Joseph.
Barrios, Diego *c.m.f.* '42 (LA)[V] Rancho Dominguez, CA Dominguez Seminary Inc.
Barrios, Eduardo *s.j.* '72 (MIA)[E] Miami, FL Belen Jesuit Preparatory School.
Barron, Clemente *c.p.* '70 (SAT)[L] San Antonio, TX Casa Pasionista Guadalupe.
Barron, Dale F. *m.m.* '65 (FgM) Maryknoll, NY MARYKNOLL.
Barron, Gerald *o.f.m.cap.* '66 (LA) Solvang, CA Old Mission Santa Ines.
Barron, John P. *s.j.* '82 (ALN)[A] Wernersville, PA Jesuit Center–Jesuit Community; [N] Wernersville, PA Jesuit Center.
Barron, Robert E. '86 (CHI)[A] Mundelein, IL University of St. Mary of the Lake/Mundelein Seminary.
Barron, Stanley C. '74 (PAT) Priestly Life Committee; Flanders, NJ St. Elizabeth Ann Seton; Paterson, NJ Mission Office.
Barron, William R. '07 (E) Vocation Office; Erie, PA Our Lady of Peace; [C] Erie, PA Cathedral Preparatory School.
Barrons, Brian *m.m.* '84 (FgM) Maryknoll, NY MARYKNOLL.
Barrosa, Julian "Mike" *d.s.* '91 (GAL) Houston, TX St. Augustine.
Barrosa, Michael A. '91 (GAL) International Priest Representative.
Barrow, John A. '80 (PMB) Stuart, FL St. Andrew.
Barrow, Joseph A. '96 (NEW) Lyndhurst, NJ Sacred Heart Retired.
Barruetabena, Felix *c.p.* '52 (SJN) Carolina, PR Santa Gema Galgani.
Barry, David E. *s.j.* '61 (BAL)[Q] Towson Maryland Province of the Society of Jesus.
Barry, David E. *s.j.* '78 (DEN)[N] Denver, CO Xavier Jesuit Center.
Barry, Rev. Msgr. Edward M. '73 (NY) Bronx (Northeast); Bronx, NY St. Barnabas.
Barry, Garrett J. '66 (BO) Randolph, MA St. Mary.
Barry, James D. '61 (NU) Retired.
Barry, James F. '67 (CAM) Retired.
Barry, James J. '69 (BO) Chelsea, MA Our Lady of Grace; Revere, MA St. Mary of the Assumption.
Barry, James (STP) Bloomington, MN St. Edward.
Barry, Rev. Msgr. John F. '61 (LA) Manhattan Beach, CA American Martyrs; Deanery 19; Archdiocesan Finance Council Members 2011–2012.
Barry, John M. '88 (WDC) Bowie, MD St. Edward; [X] Bowie, MD Washington Catholic Charismatic Service Committee.
Barry, John *c.ss.r.* '48 (ORL)[F] New Smyrna Beach, FL St. Alphonsus Villa–Redemptorist Fathers and Brothers Retired.
Barry, Maurice J. '67 (HRT) Windsor, CT St. Gertrude.
Barry, Michael T. '06 (RCK) East Dubuque, IL St. Mary; East Dubuque, IL Nativity of the Blessed Virgin Mary.
Barry, Michael W. *ss.cc.* '64 (LA)[P] La Verne, CA Congregation of the Sacred Hearts of Jesus and Mary.
Barry, Michael *ss.cc.* '64 (SB) Special or Other Diocesan Assignment.
Barry, Rev. Msgr. Patrick (NY) Chappaqua, NY St. John and St. Mary.
Barry, Paul '48 (WDC) Retired.
Barry, Peter J. *m.m.* '65 (FgM) Maryknoll, NY MARYKNOLL.
Barry, Raymond J. '65 (HRT) Retired.
Barry, Robert L. *o.p.* '73 (CHI)[N] Chicago, IL St. Pius V Priory.
Barry, Robert L. *o.p.* '73 (MO) Air National Guard Chaplains.
Barry, Thomas J. '67 (HRT) Farmington, CT St. Patrick.
Barry, William A. *s.j.* '62 (BO)[U] Weston, MA Campion Jesuit Community.
Barszczewski, Rev. Msgr. Francis A. '68 (PH) Retired.
Barta, Ardel H. '63 (DUB) Deanery Representatives; Vinton, IA St. Mary; Walker, IA St. Mary; Vinton, IA Sacred Heart Retired.
Barta, Rev. Msgr. James O. '55 (DUB)[I] Dubuque, IA Marian Hall Infirmary; College of Consultors; Continuing Formation of Priests; Finance Council; Board of Directors/Priest Pension Plan Board of Trustees; Investment Committee; Directors; Defenders of the Bond Retired.
Bartczyszyn, Steven *c.r.* '86 (CHI) Chicago, IL St. Hyacinth Basilica.
Bartek, Valerian '82 (LIN) Trenton, NE St. James; Deaneries and Deans.
Bartek, William C. '61 (OM) Retired.
Bartel, Franklin L. '70 (PHX) Retired.
Bartel, Martin R. *o.s.b.* '85 (GBG) Greensburg, PA St. Benedict; Greensburg, PA St. Bruno; [H] Latrobe, PA Saint Vincent Archabbey.
Bartell, Ernest J. *c.s.c.* '61 (FTW)[B] University of Notre Dame Du Lac; [H] Notre Dame, IN Holy Cross Community, Corby Hall, University of Notre Dame.
Bartelme, James P. '82 (SUP) Barron, WI St. Joseph; Barron, WI St. Peter; Barron, WI St. Boniface.
Barter, Robert '61 (PRM) Clinton Township, MI St. Nicholas; Sacred Liturgy Retired.
Barth, John C. *m.m.* '91 (FgM) Maryknoll, NY MARYKNOLL.
Barth, Michael D. '94 (COV) Morning View, KY St. Matthew; Diocesan Tribunal; Judges.
Barth, Michael *s.t.* '79 (JKS) Camden, MS Sacred Heart; Canton, MS Holy Child Jesus.
Barth, Raymond J. '85 (KAL) Retired.
Barthel, Charles '82 (STL) Manchester, MO Christ, Prince of Peace.
Bartholomew, Michael J. '09 (RVC) Huntington Station, NY St. Hugh of Lincoln.
Bartko, Gerald L. *o.s.f.s.* '66 (BUF)[D] Niagara Falls, NY Niagara Catholic High School; Lockport, NY All Saints.
Bartko, Louis *o.f.m.* '90 (CIN)[N] Cincinnati, OH St. Clement Friary Retired.
Bartkus, Rev. Msgr. Algimantas A. '65 (ALN) On Duty Outside the Diocese; Maspeth, NY St. Stanislaus Kostka.
Bartlett, H. James *s.m.* (CLV)[C] Cleveland, OH Villa Angela–St. Joseph High School; [N] Cleveland, OH Marianist Community; [X] Cleveland, OH Villa Angela–St. Joseph High School Education Endowment Trust.
Bartlett, Richard *c.m.f.* '50 (CHI)[N] Oak Park Claretian Missionaries USA Eastern Province.
Bartley, David J. '70 (BO) Senior Priests. Retired.
Bartley, Denis *s.s.c.* '51 (OM)[J] St. Columbans Missionary Society of St. Columban.
Bartley, Denis *s.s.c.* '51 (PRO)[O] Bristol, RI St. Columban's Retirement House Retired.
Bartnik, James T. '75 (BUF) Retired.
Bartniski, William D. '67 (GAL) Rosenberg, TX St. Wenceslaus Mission; Rosenberg, TX Holy Rosary.
Bartolay, Rolando '08 (OAK) El Cerrito, CA St. John the Baptist.
Bartollotta, Victor W. '90 (ROC) On Duty Outside the Diocese.
Bartolo, Jimmy *s.j.* '97 (BO)[U] Newton, MA The Jesuit Community at Boston College.
Bartolo, Salvador *o.carm.* '52 (JOL)[L] Darien Carmelite Provincial Office.
Bartoloma, James L. '03 (CAM) Judges; Lindenwold, NJ Our Lady of Guadalupe Parish, Lindenwold, N.J.; Vice Chancellors.
Bartolome, Cyrus '07 (BGP) Presbyteral Council; Bethel, CT St. Mary.
Bartolotta, Victor '90 (DAL)[C] Dallas, TX Bishop Lynch High School, Inc.; Dallas, TX St. Thomas Aquinas.
Barton, Michael *m.c.c.j.* '75 (FgM) Cincinnati, OH COMBONI MISSIONARIES (VERONA FATHERS).
Barton, Rev. Msgr. Raymond A. '66 (RIC) Retired.
Bartos, Andrzej A. '83 (CHI) Chicago, IL St. James.
Bartos, Francis J. '54 (PH) Retired.
Bartos, Kris '85 (MIA) Pembroke Pines, FL St. Boniface.
Bartosic, Mark A. '94 (CHI) Cicero, IL St. Frances of Rome; Cicero, IL Our Lady of Charity; Deans.
Bartosz, Andrzej '91 (CHI) Chicago, IL St. Ladislaus.
Bartoszek, Richard '89 (DET) Grosse Pointe, MI Beaumont Hospital; Presbyteral Council.
Bartoul, William '77 (SAM) On Duty Outside the Diocese; Air Force Chaplains.
Bartsch, Ken *o.f.m.conv.* '75 (IND)[J] Mount St. Francis, IN Mount Saint Francis Friary and Retreat Center.
Bartsch, Kenneth W. *o.f.m.conv.* '75 (MO) DEPARTMENT OF VETERANS AFFAIRS HOSPITALS AND CHAPLAINS.
Bartulica, Angelo '08 (KC) Chillicothe, MO St. Columban; Chillicothe, MO St. Joseph's; Deans.
Bartulica, Matthew '10 (KC) Sugar Creek, MO St. Cyril.
Bartylla, Rev. Msgr. James R. '01 (MAD) Vicar General; Diocesan Consultors; Presbyteral Council; Personnel Board; Building Commission; Saint Raphael Society Clergy Retirement Plan; [F] Madison, WI Bishop O'Connor Catholic Pastoral Center; [I] Madison, WI The Catholic Diocese of Madison Foundation, Inc.
Baru, Joseph Uri *o.c.d.* '05 (MIL)[P] Milwaukee Provincial Offices – Discalced Carmelites.
Barusefski, Ronald '89 (PSC) Eparchial College of Consultors; Presbyteral Council.
Barut, Edmundo N. '92 (HON) Honolulu, HI St. Pius X; Honolulu, HI Sacred Heart.
Barut, Joel '97 (HON) Naalehu, HI Sacred Heart; Pahala, HI Holy Rosary.
Barvick, Patrick F. '10 (LIN) Lincoln, NE St. Joseph; Advocates.
Barwig, Regis N. '59 (GB)[J] Oshkosh, WI Community of Our Lady.
Barwin, John G. '80 (E) Wilcox, PA St. Anne Retired.
Baryski, Wojciech *s.ch.* '65 (CHI) Chicago, IL Five Holy Martyrs.
Basa, Francis J. '71 (CLV) Fairlawn, OH St. Hilary.
Basanez, Hector '10 (SJ) Morgan Hill, CA St. Catherine of Alexandria.
Basarab, John G. '79 (PSC) Annandale, VA Epiphany of Our Lord; Syncellus; Eparchial College of Consultors; Presbyteral Council; Members; Evangelization.
Basarte, Aldrin '96 (SAC) College of Consultors; Legion of Mary; Yreka, CA St. Joseph; McCloud, CA St. Joseph; Presbyteral Council; Fort Jones, CA Sacred Heart.

Baseford, Paul '57 (SB) Retired.
Basekela, Cletus '71 (STP) Maplewood, MN St. Jerome.
Bashista, Brian G. '99 (ARL) Arlington, VA Our Lady of Lourdes; Vocations, Office of; Advocates.
Basiimwa, John R. *f.m.h.* '09 (MOB) Mobile, AL Prince of Peace.
Basil, John E. '62 (NEW) Retired.
Basile, Gioacchino '95 (NEW) On Duty Outside the Archdiocese.
Basile, Gioacchino '95 (BRK) East Elmhurst, NY St. Gabriel.
Basilio, Allan '94 (BRK) Astoria, NY Immaculate Conception.
Basinow, Leonard '53 (SAM) Retired.
Basler, Rev. Msgr. Howard B. '58 (BRK) Retired.
Basols, Jose' A. *sch.p.* '68 (PH)[F] Devon, PA Devon Preparatory School; [Y] Devon Piarist Fathers (Order of the Pious Schools).
Ba Son Lam, Philip M. (GAL) Houston, TX St. Elizabeth Ann Seton.
Basquel, Thomas *c.s.sp.* '76 (BRK)[R] Long Island City, NY Holy Ghost Fathers of Ireland; [V] Long Island City, NY World Compassion Link; Long Island City, NY; Councilors.
Basquerizo, Christian Jaramillo '09 (NEW) Union City, NJ Sts. Joseph and Michael.
Bass, Frank B. '03 (BR) Baton Rouge, LA St. Pius X; Baton Rouge, LA St. Isidore the Farmer.
Bass, Michael E. '87 (LR) Little Rock, AR St. Theresa.
Bass, Rev. Msgr. Ricardo E. '74 (DET) Harrison Township, MI St. Hubert; College of Consultors; Presbyteral Council.
Bassaleh, Michel '97 (OLN) Wynnewood, PA St. Mark's Armenian Catholic.
Bassano, Michael *m.m.* '75 (FgM) On Duty Outside the Diocese; Maryknoll, NY MARYKNOLL.
Bassett, Frank W. '00 (NY) Nanuet, NY St. Anthony.
Bassey, Anthony *m.s.p.* '91 (NY) Yonkers, NY St. Bartholomew.
Bassil, Pierre '98 (OLL) Dayton, OH Our Lady of Lebanon Maronite Catholic Mission; Dayton, OH Saint Ignatius of Antioch Maronite Catholic Church; Presbyteral Council.
Basso, Anthony *s.d.v.* '93 (LSC) Carrizozo, NM St. Rita.
Basso, Richard '62 (SEA) Retired.
Bastan, Jose M. Garcia *o.s.a.* '62 (SJN) Bayamon, PR San Juan Bautista de la Salle.
Bastia, Rev. Msgr. Raymond B. '75 (PRO) Providence, RI St. Joseph; Secretary for Planning & Financial Services; Finance Council; Secretariat for Planning and Financial Services; Insurance Commission; Council Members; College of Consultors.
Bastian, James R. '95 (BUF) Air Force Reserve Chaplains; [D] Buffalo, NY St. Joseph's Collegiate Institute; Cheektowaga, NY St. Aloysius Gonzaga.
Bastianelli, Daniel *s.s.j.* '64 (BAL)[Q] Baltimore, MD St. Joseph's Manor.
Bastidas, Alexis '82 (NY) New York, NY Blessed Sacrament.
Bastien, Emmanuel '09 (MIA) Miami, FL Notre Dame d'Haiti.
Bastress, Rev. Msgr. Arthur '51 (BAL) Baltimore, MD St. Alphonsus, Shrine of.
Basulto–Pitol, Marco '00 (TUC) Sierra Vista, AZ Saint Andrew the Apostle Roman Catholic Parish – Sierra Vista.
Basznianin, Richard '84 (TR) Forked River, NJ St. Pius X.
Bataille, Vincent *o.s.b.* (CHI)[A] Mundelein, IL University of St. Mary of the Lake/Mundelein Seminary.
Batch, Thomas A. '76 (SAC) Retired.
Batcha, James J. '85 (PRM) Burton, OH Church of Mariapoch; Eparchial Shrine of the Weeping Madonna of Mariapoch; Sexual Allegation Review Board; Parma, OH Holy Spirit; Presbyteral Council; Eparchial Finance Council; Cantors' Institute Faculty; Office of Evangelization and Missionary Activity; Priest's Pension Board; Stewardship Office; Byzantine Catholic Cultural Center.
Batchelder, George '05 (MRY) Atascadero, CA St. William's.
Batcheldor, C. Joseph '57 (L) Bardstown, KY Basilica of St. Joseph Proto–Cathedral Retired.
Batcho, Robert '88 (STF) Elmira Heights, NY St. Nicholas.
Bateman, John B. '96 (HBG) Deans; Presbyteral Council; Waynesboro, PA St. Andrew; [I] Waynesboro, PA Penn State University, Mont Alto Campus, South Mountain; Air National Guard Chaplains.
Bates, David (SEA)[I] Olympia, WA Providence Mother Joseph Care Center.
Bates, Donald J. *o.s.a.* '60 (JOL) New Lenox, IL St. Jude.
Bates, James R. '63 (LFT) Retired.
Bath, Winston L. '92 (ALB) Hudson, NY Parish of the Holy Trinity; Priests Retirement Board/Priests Retirement Plan Board.
Bathineni, Mohana Rao '01 (GLP) Dulce, NM St. Francis of Assisi.
Batista, Jiobani '93 (VEN) Clewiston, FL St. Margaret.
Batista, Leonel V. (BO) Cambridge, MA St. Anthony of Padua.
Batmomolin, Lukas *s.v.d.* '91 (CHI)[N] Techny, IL Divine Word Residence.
Batsis, Thomas *o.carm.* '70 (LA) North Hollywood, CA St. Jane Frances de Chantal.
Batt, Anthony R. '04 (STU) Carrollton, OH Our Lady of Mercy; Waynesburg, OH St. Mary.
Battafarano, Gregory A. *o.carm.* (PAT) Consulting Psychologists and Experts.
Battafarano, Gregory *o.carm.* '67 (NEW) Bogota, NJ St. Joseph's.
Batterberry, Michael J. '70 (SEA) Retired.
Battersby, Gerard '98 (DET)[A] Detroit, MI Sacred Heart Major Seminary, Inc.
Battiato, Patrick (COS) Retired.
Battisti, Lewis A. '62 (CAM) Retired.
Battle, Rev. Msgr. Lawrence '49 (SB) Retired.
Battolini, Ottaviano *o.f.m.* '43 (FgM) New York, NY Franciscan Province of the Immaculate Conception.
Batts, Peter *o.p.* '81 (PRO)[O] Providence St. Thomas Aquinas Priory at Providence College.
Batule, Rev. Msgr. Robert J. '85 (RVC) Greenlawn, NY St. Francis of Assisi; [A] Huntington, NY Diocesan Seminary of the Immaculate Conception.
Batungbacal, Eugene '10 (GAL) Houston, TX Holy Ghost.
Bature, Anthony '96 (BRK) Brooklyn, NY St. Teresa of Avila.
Batykefer, John J. '90 (PIT) Canonsburg, PA St. Patrick.
Bau, Chau Xuan *c.ss.r.* '62 (LA)[P] Baldwin Park Vietnamese Redemptorist Mission.
Bauer, Carl E. '63 (WH) Retired.
Bauer, Charles A. '78 (MEM) Memphis, TN Holy Rosary.
Bauer, Daniel *s.v.d.* '74 (FgM) Techny, IL.
Bauer, Donald J. '01 (LC) Hillsboro, WI St. Aloysius; Hillsboro, WI St. Jerome.
Bauer, Elmer *c.m.* '93 (PH)[B] Philadelphia, PA St. Vincent's Seminary; Philadelphia, PA; [B] Philadelphia, PA DePaul Novitiate.
Bauer, Elmer *c.m.* '88 (PH)[Y] Philadelphia Congregation of the Mission.
Bauer, Erwin J. '47 (DET) Retired.
Bauer, Rev. Msgr. Henry '48 (KC) Retired.
Bauer, Jacob F. '48 (GI) Retired.
Bauer, John F. '65 (E) Retired.
Bauer, John J. '08 (STP)[A] St. Paul, MN St. John Vianney Seminary; [C] St. Paul, MN University of St. Thomas.
Bauer, John M. '73 (PIT) Carmichaels, PA St. Hugh; Carmichaels, PA Our Lady of Consolation.
Bauer, John M. '79 (STP) Minneapolis, MN The Basilica of St. Mary Co–Cathedral.
Bauer, John *c.ss.r.* (BAL) Baltimore, MD Sacred Heart of Jesus.
Bauer, John (STP) Deanery 13.
Bauer, Karl A. '67 (NY) Yonkers, NY St. Anthony.
Bauer, Richard W. *m.m.* '85 (FgM) Maryknoll, NY MARYKNOLL.
Bauer, Robert A. '87 (DET) Maybee, MI St. Joseph; Carleton, MI St. Patrick.
Bauer, Robert *s.d.b.* '71 (NY)[DD] New Rochelle, NY Salesian Provincial House.
Bauer, Roy R. '59 (SFD) Presbyteral Council Retired.
Bauer, Scott A. '98 (LC) Leave of Absence.
Bauer, Stephan *o.s.c.* '92 (PHX)[F] Phoenix, AZ Crosier Community of Phoenix (Canons Regular of the Order of the Holy Cross); Provincial Councilors.
Bauer, Stephen F. '77 (STL) St. Charles, MO St. Peter.
Bauer, Steven '04 (CHI)[U] Chicago, IL University of Illinois at Chicago – John Paul II Newman Center; Chicago, IL St. Alphonsus.
Bauer, Sylvester W. '42 (SPC) Rural Life Movement Retired.
Bauerle, Bernhard *o.carm.* '64 (JOL)[L] Darien, IL St. Simon Stock Priory; [O] Darien, IL National Shrine of St. Therese; Darien, IL.
Baugh, David G. '57 (CLV) Wickliffe, OH Our Lady of Mount Carmel Retired.
Bauhoff, Rev. Msgr. Richard C. '73 (RVC) Judges for Interdiocesan Tribunal; Priests' Retirement Board.
Baula, Jun '86 (PHX) Mesa, AZ Holy Cross Roman Catholic Parish.
Bauler, Rev. Msgr. Gary P. '67 (LA) Simi Valley, CA St. Peter Claver.
Baum, Matthew '09 (ALT) State College, PA Our Lady of Victory.
Baum, Terrence A. *s.j.* '81 (KC)[D] Kansas City, MO Rockhurst High School; [J] Kansas City, MO Rockhurst Jesuit Community.
Bauman, Dale A. '82 (FTW) Pierceton, IN St. Francis Xavier; Fort Wayne, IN Cathedral of the Immaculate Conception.
Bauman, John '69 (NEW) Retired.
Bauman, Kevin M. '08 (FTW) South Bend, IN Our Lady of Hungary; Our Lady of Hungary.
Bauman, Rodger '82 (STP) Oakdale, MN Guardian Angels.
Baumann, Charles R. *s.j.* '80 (OM)[J] Omaha, NE Jesuit Community at Creighton University.
Baumann, John A. *s.j.* '69 (OAK)[L] Oakland, CA Jesuit Fathers and Brothers; [Q] Oakland, CA PICO National Network.
Baumann, Lawrence L. '64 (PHX) Retired.
Baumann, Richard J. *s.j.* '75 (CHI)[N] Chicago Chicago Province of the Society of Jesus–Provincial Office; Chicago, IL Society of Jesus.
Baumann, Silas *o.f.m.cap.* '51 (GB)[J] Appleton, WI St. Fidelis Friary Retired.
Baumann, Stephen A. '92 (ORL) Longwood, FL Annunciation.
Baumann, Rev. Msgr. Theodore J. '67 (BEL) Retired.
Baumberger, Richard '89 (SFS) Wagner, SD Assumption B.V.M.; Wagner, SD St. John the Baptist.
Baumert, Frank J. '78 (OM) Omaha, NE Holy Name; Age Groups.
Baumgaertner, Rev. Msgr. William L. '46 (STP) Retired.
Baumgartner, Rev. Msgr. A. Thomas '58 (BAL) Baltimore, MD St. Ursula; Baltimore, MD St. Joseph Retired.
Baumgartner, Andrew *o.s.b.* '60 (B)[C] Jerome, ID Monastery of the Ascension.
Baumgartner, Rev. Msgr. David '90 (CR) Adoption Referral/Post Adoption Search; Catholic Campaign for Human Development; Catholic Relief Services; Vicar General & Moderator of the Curia; Information Officer; Promoter of Justice; Diocesan Consultors; Finance Council; Holy Childhood Association; Natural Family Planning; Priests' Council; Priests' Personnel Board; Propagation of the Faith; Diocesan Board of Review for the Protection of Young Children; Catholic Charities; Defenders of the Bond; Chancery Office.
Baumgartner, John H. '63 (MIL) Lyons, WI St. Joseph.
Baumhart, Raymond C. *s.j.* '57 (DET)[K] Clarkston, MI Colombiere Center.
Baur, Joseph A. *o.f.m.* '52 (PHX) Guadalupe, AZ Our Lady of Guadalupe Roman Catholic Parish.
Baura, Arnold B. '02 (HT) Raceland, LA Community of St. Anthony; Raceland, LA St. Hilary of Poitiers.
Bausch, Michael '79 (ROC) Pittsford, NY Church of the Transfiguration.
Bausch, William J. '55 (TR) Retired.
Bauta, Kris (CC) Corpus Christi, TX Most Precious Blood.
Bautista, Efrain '10 (SD) Vista, CA Saint Francis of Assisi Catholic Parish.
Bautista, Gaspar '75 (FRS) Mendota, CA Our Lady of Guadalupe.
Bautista, Jose A. '99 (LA) Navy Chaplains; Military Chaplains.
Bautista, Jose '91 (ORL) Judges; Kissimmee, FL St. Catherine of Siena; Defenders of the Bond.
Bautista, Renato J. '07 (NEW)[A] South Orange, NJ Immaculate Conception Seminary School of Theology; [B] Seton Hall University.
Bautista, Tony *s.s.p.* '05 (Y)[A] Canfield, OH Society of St. Paul.
Bautista–Peráza, Pedro '04 (SPK) Connell, WA St. Vincent; Eltopia, WA St. Paul.
Bautista Benguria, Juan *c.p.* (SJN) Carolina, PR Nuestra Senora de la Piedad.
Bauwens, Thomas E. '87 (OM) Omaha, NE St. Wenceslaus; Consultors; Ex Officio (Consultors).
Bauza, Ricardo '05 (LSC) Las Cruces, NM St. Genevieve; Presbyteral Council; Office of Vocations; Finance Council.
Bava, David '73 (WDC) Washington, DC Holy Redeemer.
Baver, John J. '91 (PIT) Bethel Park, PA St. Germaine.
Baver, Rev. Msgr. William F. '81 (ALN) Bethlehem, PA SS. Simon and Jude; Cemeteries.
Bavinger, Bruce *s.j.* '78 (R) Raleigh, NC St. Raphael the Archangel; [F] Raleigh Jesuit Community.
Bawyn, Anthony E. '82 (SEA) Seattle, WA St. Catherine of Siena; Special Assignment; Judicial Vicar; Judges; Due Process; Presbyteral Council; Seattle, WA Our Lady of the Lake.
Bawyn, Anthony E. '82 (SEA) Catholic Archdiocese of Seattle Clergy Medical Plan Veba Trust; Priests' Pension Plan.
Baxa, Henry '90 (SAL) Abilene, KS St. Andrew Parish; Chapman, KS St. Michael Parish; Moderator.
Baxter, Gregory P. '88 (OM)[P] Omaha, NE Brides of the Victorious Lamb, Inc.
Baxter, Gregory P. '88 (OM) Omaha, NE St. Margaret Mary.
Baxter, M. Shane '03 (BEA) Vocations; [D] Beaumont, TX Lamar University–Catholic Student Center; Vocation Board; Presbyteral Council; Groves, TX Immaculate Conception.
Baxter, Nicholas *o.f.m.* '62 (SAT) San Antonio, TX San Jose y San Miguel.
Baxter, Stephen R. '81 (WCH) Halstead, KS Sacred Heart Parish; Judges; Cursillo (English language); Kansas State Industrial Reformatory.
Baxter, Rev. Msgr. Thomas F. '76 (MAD) Madison, WI Good Shepherd Parish.

Bay, Joseph N. '94 (COL) Columbus, OH Sts. Augustine and Gabriel; Columbus, OH Columbus Vietnamese Catholic Community; Presiding Judges of First Instance.
Bay, Richard '04 (PAT) Catholic Family and Community Services; Clifton, NJ; Clifton, NJ SS. Cyril and Methodius.
Bayard, Michael S. *s.j.* '98 (SEA)[A] Seattle, WA Seattle University; [M] Seattle, WA Arrupe Jesuit Community at Seattle University.
Baybay, Felicito S. '74 (ORL) Candler, FL Immaculate Heart of Mary.
Bayer, Ernest '01 (DEN) Steamboat Springs, CO Holy Name.
Bayer, Lawrence J. '58 (CLV) Parma, OH St. Bridget of Kildare Retired.
Bayer, Peter T. '71 (ROC) St. Ann's Home/Heritage; [F] Rochester, NY St. Ann's Home for the Aged; [F] Rochester, NY St. Ann's Nursing Home Co., Inc.; [F] Rochester, NY Chapel Oaks.
Bayer, Peter '71 (ROC) Rochester, NY Kateri Tekakwitha Roman Catholic Parish.
Bayhi, M. Jeffery '79 (BR) Zachary, LA St. John the Baptist; [L] Baton Rouge, LA Closer Walk Ministries, Inc.
Bayhi, Peter W. *s.j.* '66 (STL)[O] St. Louis, MO Jesuit Community Corporation at Saint Louis University – Jesuit Hall.
Bayim, Cyril '79 (RVC) East Meadow, NY St. Raphael.
Bayle, Stephen (BO)[C] Boston, MA Emmanuel College.
Bayler, Frederick C. '09 (FBK) Fairbanks, AK Immaculate Conception Catholic Church Fairbanks; Hispanic Ministry; [C] Fairbanks, AK Peger Road House.
Baylis, Thomas J. '59 (HRT) Retired.
Baylon, Rafael *s.j.* '05 (MOB)[A] Mobile, AL Spring Hill College.
Bayne, Joseph *o.f.m.conv.* '85 (BUF)[J] Buffalo, NY The Franciscan Center, Inc.; Buffalo Fire Department and Erie County Emergency Services; [N] Athol Springs, NY St. Francis of Assisi Friary.
Baysinger, Leo A. *s.d.b.* '67 (SFR) San Francisco, CA Corpus Christi.
Bayuk, Richard *c.pp.s.* '75 (KC)[A] Liberty, MO Society of the Precious Blood Provincial Offices; [J] Liberty, MO Society of the Precious Blood Provincial Office; [A] Kansas City, MO Gaspar Mission House; Liberty, MO; [N] Liberty, MO St. Gaspar Society.
Baz, Rev. Msgr. Louis '81 (OLL) Detroit, MI St. Maron Maronite Catholic Church.
Bazan, Rev. Msgr. Joaquin '62 (WDC) Retired.
Bazan, Michael J. '84 (ARL) Manassas, VA Sacred Heart.
Bazar, Christopher G. '04 (TOL)[B] Fremont, OH St. Joseph Central Catholic High School; Youth, Young Adult and Campus Ministry; Kelley's Island, OH St. Michael; Put–In–Bay, OH Mother of Sorrows.
Bazar, Ty J. '02 (VIC) Port Lavaca, TX Our Lady of the Gulf.
Bazikila, Ghislain C. '08 (SFR) San Francisco, CA St. Benedict Parish at St. Francis Xavier Church.
Bazyouros, Christopher '03 (LA) Rancho Dominguez, CA St. Albert the Great; Appointed Membership.
Bazzel, Kevin M. '01 (BIR) Tribunal; Chancellor; Diocesan College of Consultors; [H] Birmingham, AL The Chapel of St. Stephen the Martyr Campus Center; Birmingham, AL St. Paul's Cathedral; Priests'/ Presbyteral Council; Diocesan College of Vicars.
Bazzi, Michael J. '64 (SPA) El Cajon, CA St. Peter Chaldean Cathedral.
Bazzoli, Robert L. *o.s.f.s.* '88 (PH) Philadelphia, PA Our Mother of Consolation; Provincial Councilors.
Beach, Rev. Msgr. Francis W. '76 (PH) On Special or Other Archdiocesan Assignment; Gladwyne, PA St. John Baptist Vianney; Office for Stewardship and Development.
Beach, R. Paul '01 (L) Mount Washington, KY St. Francis Xavier; Associate Judges.
Beacom, John F. '37 (OM) Retired.
Beal, John P. '74 (E) On Duty Outside Diocese; Matrimonial Judges.
Beal, John P. '74 (WDC)[C] Catholic University of America, The.
Beale, Kenneth R. '92 (NEW) Military Chaplains; Air Force Chaplains.
Beale, Kenneth (LAV) Military Chaplains.
Bean, E. Gray '03 (BIR) Gadsden, AL St. James.
Beard, Mark B. '09 (BR) Amite, LA St. Helena.
Bearss, James M. '97 (GLD) Gaylord, MI St. Mary Cathedral; Elmira, MI St. Thomas Aquinas; Grayling, MI St. Mary; Gaylord, MI Holy Redeemer.
Beat, Jerome A. '63 (WCH) Cursillo (Spanish language) Retired.
Beath, James D. '79 (CHI) Chicago, IL St. Mary, Star of the Sea; Chicago, IL St. Edward.
Beaton, Kevin J. *s.f.o.* '87 (SAM) Roanoke, VA St. Elias.
Beattie, Rev. Msgr. James T. '61 (WDC) Bethesda, MD St. Bartholomew Retired.
Beatty, James H. '74 (CLV) Avon Lake, OH Holy Spirit.
Beatty, Steven L. '07 (BEL) Equality, IL St. Joseph; Shawneetown, IL St. Patrick; Ridgway, IL St. Joseph; Shawneetown, IL St. Mary.
Beaubien, David W. '93 (WDC) Derwood, MD St. Francis of Assisi.
Beauchamp, E. William *c.s.c.* '82 (FTW)[H] Notre Dame, IN Congregation of Holy Cross, United States Province of Priests & Brothers; [K] Notre Dame, IN Blessed Basil Moreau Endowment Trust.
Beauchamp, Henry *c.ss.r.* '78 (PCE) Guayama, PR St. Anthony of Padua.
Beauchamp, William *c.s.c.* '82 (P)[B] University of Portland; [B] University of Portland; [L] Portland, OR Holy Cross Fathers & Brothers, C.S.C. – University of Portland; Provincial Councilors.
Beauchemin, Ronald A. *m.s.* '68 (FR)[F] Attleboro, MA La Salette Shrine.
Beauclair, Stephen *o.s.b.* '67 (SCL) Richmond, MN SS. Peter and Paul; St. Martin, MN St. Martin; [I] Collegeville, MN St. John's Abbey, of the Order of St. Benedict; Deans.
Beaudet, Christopher J. '00 (STP) Special Assignment.
Beaudin, William L. *o.f.m.* '81 (ALB)[B] Siena College; Provincial Councilors.
Beaudin, William R. '82 (BUR)[G] Middlebury, VT Middlebury College; Middlebury, VT Assumption of the Blessed Virgin Mary; Elected Members; Canon 1742 Panel of Pastors.
Beaudoin, Andrew *s.s.s.* '54 (CLV)[N] Cleveland Congregation of the Blessed Sacrament Provincial House.
Beaudoin, Andrew *s.s.s.* '54 (SP) Spring Hill, FL St. Frances Xavier Cabrini.
Beaudry, David B. '82 (GB) Kimberly, WI Holy Spirit.
Beaulaurier, Brooks F. '08 (YAK) Director of Planned Giving; Development Office/Stewardship; Presbyteral Council Executive Committee; Jail Ministry.
Beaulieu, Kerry '74 (ORG) Newport Beach, CA Our Lady Queen of Angels; Council of Priests.
Beaulieu, Raymond A. '42 (PRO) Retired.
Beaulieu, Richard C. '76 (BO) Winchester, MA St. Mary.
Beaumier, Casey C. *s.j.* '05 (BO)[U] Newton, MA The Jesuit Community at Boston College.
Beaumont, Gregory J. '96 (FRS) Kingsburg, CA Holy Family; Ecumenical Affairs; Scouting.
Beaumont, Richard '58 (FWT) Retired.
Beaupre, R. Bradley *c.s.c.* '68 (ORL) Viera, FL St. John the Evangelist.
Beaupre, R. Bradley R. *c.s.c.* '68 (FTW)[H] Notre Dame Congregation of Holy Cross, United States Province of Priests & Brothers.
Beauregard, Andrew F. *f.p.o.* '08 (BO)[U] Lawrence, MA Franciscans of Primitive Observance; On Duty Outside the Archdiocese.
Beauregard, David N. *o.m.v.* '80 (BO)[B] Boston, MA Our Lady of Grace Seminary; [Z] Boston, MA St. Clement Archdiocesan Eucharistic Shrine.
Beauregard, David *o.m.v.* (SFD) Alton, IL St. Mary's.
Beauregard, James E. '70 (BUR) Retired.
Beausoleil, Charles *o.m.i.* '56 (BO)[X] Tewksbury, MA Immaculate Heart of Mary Residence.
Beausoleil, Kent A. *s.j.* '07 (CIN) Cincinnati, OH St. Robert Bellarmine; [N] Cincinnati, OH Jesuit Community at Xavier University.
Beauvais, David E. '62 (RCK) Retired.
Beaven, Robert W. '68 (CHI) Chicago, IL St. Benedict.
Beaver, Nelson G. '76 (TOL) Lexington, OH Resurrection; Mansfield, OH St. Mary of the Snows; St. Juan Diego Deanery.
Beaver, William A. *o.s.b.* '85 (GBG)[H] Latrobe, PA Saint Vincent Archabbey.
Beavers, Carl '68 (CHY) Rock Springs, WY Holy Spirit Catholic Community; [G] Rock Springs, WY Rock Springs Catholic School Foundation; St. Joseph's Society for Priests (Clergy Mutual Benefit Society); Diocesan Schools Advisory Group.
Bebak, Brian D. '86 (WCH) El Dorado Correctional Facility; El Dorado, KS St. John the Evangelist.
Bebek, Dominic L. '53 (LA) Retired.
Bebek, Dominic (ORG) Retired.
Bebel, Alfred J. '58 (SY) Binghamton, NY Retired.
Becerra, Rafael *c.s.* '95 (GAL) Houston, TX St. Leo the Great.
Becerra, Robert L. '89 (LSC) Santa Clara, NM Santa Clara.
Becerra, Robert L. '89 (NEW) On Duty Outside the Archdiocese.
Becerril, Julian *o.de.m.* '75 (BWN) Alton, TX San Martin de Porres.
Bechamps, Vincent *o.ss.t.* '66 (BAL)[Q] Archdiocese of Philadelphia, PA.
Bechard, Gerard V. '80 (DET) Westland, MI SS. Simon and Jude.
Becher, Albert B. '84 (DAL) Lancaster, TX St. Francis of Assisi.
Becherer, David A. '48 (MOB)[E] Mobile, AL Little Sisters of the Poor, Home For the Aged, Inc. Retired.
Becherer, James R. '54 (CLV) Retired.
Bechill, David '11 (DET) Dearborn, MI Divine Child.
Bechtel, David W. '08 (SCR) Williamsport, PA St. Joseph the Worker; [C] Williamsport, PA Saint John Neumann Regional Academy High School Campus.
Bechtel, James C. '71 (ALN) Tamaqua, PA St. Jerome; Carbon/Schuylkill Serra Club.
Beck, Rev. Msgr. Albert J. '49 (GAL) Retired.
Beck, David J. '67 (TOL) Retired.
Beck, Edward L. *c.p.* '85 (NY)[HH] Pelham, NY Passionist Communications, Inc.; [HH] Pelham, NY Passionist Communications Center; [DD] Pelham Manor, NY St. Vincent's Residence.
Beck, Erwin G. *s.j.* '60 (NY)[DD] New York, NY Murray–Weigel Hall.
Beck, Henry *o.f.m.* '80 (ELP) Catholic Campus Ministry; [I] El Paso, TX Catholic Campus Ministry at University of Texas at El Paso.
Beck, Joseph C. '84 (PIT) Pittsburgh, PA St. Rosalia; Allegheny County, PA Forbes Road Nursing Center; Allegheny County, PA Kane Regional Center – Glen Hazel; Allegheny County, PA Woodhaven Convalescent Center; Allegheny County, PA Health South Hospital of Pittsburgh; Allegheny County, PA Independent Court of Monroeville; Allegheny County, PA Manorcare Health Services North Hills; Forbes Hospice.
Beck, Lawrence J. '88 (LA) On Duty Outside the Archdiocese.
Beck, Lawrence J. '88 (SAC) Jackson, CA St. Patrick's; Jackson, CA Immaculate Conception; Ione, CA Sacred Heart of Jesus.
Beck, R. Patrick '76 (BEA) Military Chaplains; Air Force Chaplains.
Beck, Richard W. '74 (SCR) Hawley, PA Blessed Virgin Mary, Queen of Peace; Presbyteral Council.
Beck, Richard *o.m.i.* '67 (SAT)[K] San Antonio, TX Oblate Madonna Residence.
Beck, Robert L. '66 (DUB) Retired.
Beck, Robert R. '66 (DUB)[L] Dubuque, IA Mt. St. Francis Retired.
Becker, Anthony J. '47 (RCK) Retired.
Becker, Bruno *o.s.b.* '51 (P)[L] St. Benedict, OR Mt. Angel Abbey.
Becker, Charles P. '86 (CHI) Other Assignments.
Becker, Daniel J. '96 (WOR) Warren, MA St. Paul; West Warren, MA St. Stanislaus.
Becker, David R. '66 (ALT) Retired.
Becker, Dennis E. '62 (NU) Retired.
Becker, Donald '67 (BUF) Retired.
Becker, Edward '05 (ORG) La Habra, CA Our Lady of Guadalupe.
Becker, Rev. Msgr. Frederick J. '59 (NY) Bronx, NY St. Lucy; Montefiore Medical Center – North Division.
Becker, John J. '72 (GB) Francis Creek, WI St. Anne; Francis Creek, WI St. Augustine; Mishicot, WI Holy Cross; Priests' Personnel Board; Gillett, WI St. John; Suring, WI St. Michael.
Becker, Joseph P. *o.s.f.s.* '69 (ALN) Lehigh Valley Hospital at Cedar Crest; [B] Center Valley, PA DeSales University; [K] Center Valley, PA Oblates of St. Francis de Sales.
Becker, Rev. Msgr. Michael A. '75 (ALT) Campus Ministry; Lakemont, Altoona, PA St. John the Evangelist; [I] Hollidaysburg, PA Office of Campus Ministry.
Becker, Michael C. '99 (STP)[C] St. Paul, MN University of St. Thomas; [A] St. Paul, MN St. John Vianney Seminary; Saint John Vianney Seminary.
Becker, Nickolas *o.s.b.* '02 (SCL)[I] Collegeville, MN St. John's Abbey, of the Order of St. Benedict.
Becker, Paul D. '73 (BIS) Bismarck, ND Corpus Christi; Presbyteral Council.
Becker, Richard F. '72 (PBL) Trinidad, CO Most Holy Trinity; [E] Trinidad, CO Trinidad Area Catholic Community; Diocesan Council of Catholic Women.
Becker, Robert T. '64 (SFD) Retired.
Becker, Robert '79 (AUS) Georgetown, TX St. Helen.
Becker, Russell C. *o.f.m.* '72 (FgM)[HH] New York, NY Franciscan Missionary Union, Province of the Most Holy Name; New York, NY Holy Name Province; Provincial Councilors:; New York, NY Holy Name Province.
Becker, Thomas G. '80 (SCL) Rice, MN Immaculate Conception.
Becker, Thomas '80 (SCL) Sauk Rapids, MN Annunciation.
Becker, Rev. Msgr. Vincent J. '62 (BUF) Judges Retired.
Becker, William M. '88 (WIN) Plainview, MN St. Joachim's; Censors of Books and Periodicals; Plainview, MN Immaculate Conception.
Beckermann, Julius *o.s.b.* '03 (SCL) Cold Spring, MN St. James; [H] Cold Spring, MN Assumption Home; [H] Cold Spring, MN John Paul Apartments; [H] Cold Spring, MN Assumption Court; [I] Collegeville, MN St. John's Abbey, of the Order of St. Benedict.
Beckfelt, John W. '74 (LC) Retired.
Beckley, Clarence *s.s.c.* '66 (OM)[J] St. Columbans Missionary Society of St. Columban Retired.
Beckley, John *s.m.* (WH)[G] Wheeling, WV Good Shepherd Nursing Home LC.
Beckman, David M. '92 (DUB) Cedar Rapids, IA St. Matthew.
Beckman, Gary L. '95 (DAV) Houghton, IA St. John's; Houghton, IA St. James.
Beckman, Joseph F. '54 (CIN)[B] Cincinnati, OH Mount St. Mary's Seminary of the West Retired.

Beckman, Mark '90 (NSH) Franklin, TN St. Matthew; Presbyteral Council; Clergy Personnel Board.
Beckman, Martin A. '58 (STP) Retired.
Beckman, Richard J. '56 (OKL) Retired.
Beckman, Robert E. *s.j.* '56 (DET)[K] Clarkston, MI Colombiere Center.
Beckmann, Rev. Msgr. Donald M. '70 (RVC) Long Beach, NY St. Ignatius Martyr; Ecumenical & Interreligious Affairs.
Becnel, Rev. Msgr. Terry B. '64 (NO) Norco, LA Sacred Heart of Jesus.
Beczek, Mariusz *o.s.j.* '98 (LA) Co Chairmen; [A] Camarillo, CA St. John's Seminary.
Bedard, Paul *s.d.b.* '65 (SP)[P] Tampa, FL Mary Help of Christians Center.
Bedenikovic, Stephen *o.f.m.* '85 (CHI) Chicago, IL Sacred Heart.
Bedillion, James R. '75 (PIT) West Sunbury, PA St. Alphonsus; Judges.
Bednar, Gerald J. '83 (CLV)[A] Wickliffe, OH St. Mary Seminary and Graduate School of Theology.
Bednar, Martin *o.f.m.* '64 (SP)[N] St. Petersburg, FL St. Anthony Friary.
Bednarik, John F. *o.f.m.cap.* '68 (HBG) Harrisburg, PA St. Francis of Assisi.
Bednark, Walter '47 (SCL) Paynesville, MN St. Margaret's Retired.
Bednarowicz, Andrzej '01 (BUR) Graniteville, VT St. Sylvester.
Bednartz, Rev. Msgr. August C. '52 (BRK)[R] Douglaston, NY Bishop Mugavero Residence Retired.
Bednarz, Jan '72 (SLC) Taylorsville, UT Saint Martin de Porres LLC 236.
Bedore, Donald E. '11 (DOD) Great Bend, KS Prince of Peace Catholic Church of Great Bend, Kansas; Dodge City, KS Cathedral of Our Lady of Guadalupe Catholic Church of Dodge City, Kansas.
Bedoya, Carlos '90 (ORL) Deltona, FL St. Clare.
Bedoya, Dario '91 (TYL) On Duty Outside the Diocese.
Bedoya, Hector '91 (ORG) Santa Ana, CA Immaculate Heart of Mary.
Bedoya, Hugo '56 (BRK) Flushing, NY St. John Vianney Retired.
Bedoya, Martin E. '03 (CHI) Des Plaines, IL St. Mary.
Bedrossian, Armenag '99 (OLN) Glendale, CA St. Gregory Armenian Catholic Church.
Beebe, Rev. Msgr. Charles J. '70 (PEO) Roanoke, IL St. John; Roanoke, IL St. Joseph.
Beebe, David E. '61 (CAM) Retired.
Beeching, Roy T. '74 (GRY) Merrillville, IN St. Joan of Arc; Merrillville, IN Ss. Peter and Paul; Hammond, IN Saint John–Saint Joseph; Priests' Personnel Board; Cemeteries; Council of Catholic Women.
Beeda, Rev. Msgr. Francis J. '61 (SCR) Wilkes Barre, PA Retired.
Beegan, James *m.s.f.* '00 (STL)[N] St. Louis, MO Little Sisters of the Poor, Home for the Aged.
Beek, Alois Van '73 (MIL) Neosho, WI St. Matthew.
Beekman, Carl E. '00 (RCK) Special Assignment; Vocations.
Beekman, Carl E. '00 (RCK) Rockford, IL St. Peter Cathedral.
Beeman, William Daniel '07 (RIC) Norfolk, VA Holy Trinity.
Beerman, Andrew J. '96 (WIN)[A] Winona, MN Immaculate Heart of Mary Seminary; Censors of Books and Periodicals; Additional Diocesan Assignments.
Beers, Ervan *o.f.m.* '55 (FRS) Delano, CA Our Lady of Guadalupe.
Beers, J. Michael (PH)[A] Wynnewood, PA Theological Seminary of St. Charles Borromeo, Overbrook.
Beers, John Michael '79 (MO) Air Force Reserve Chaplains.
Beeson, Rev. Msgr. Lawrence A. '60 (DM) Judges Retired.
Beeson, Terry P. '05 (STP) South St. Paul, MN St. John Vianney.
Beever, Carlton J. '74 (IND) Indianapolis, IN St. Philip Neri Catholic Church, Indianapolis, Inc.; Indianapolis, IN The Church of the Holy Cross, Indianapolis, Inc.
Beezer, Arnold R. *s.j.* '64 (SPK)[J] Spokane, WA Regis Community Retired.
Befort, Daryl '95 (WCH) Wichita, KS St. Francis of Assisi.
Befort, Earl *o.f.m.cap.* '69 (SAL) Hays, KS Our Lady Help of Christians Parish; Catharine, KS St. Catherine Parish; Hays, KS St. Anthony Parish; [A] Hays, KS Thomas More Prep–Marian Alumni Assoc.; [D] Hays, KS St. Joseph's Friary.
Begay, Joseph N. *s.s.j.* '59 (WDC) Washington, DC St. Luke.
Begg, Christopher T. '77 (WDC) Washington, DC St. Joseph on Capitol Hill; Special Ministries; [C] Catholic University of America, The.
Beggane, Thomas (LSC) Absent On Leave.
Beggiani, Chorbishop Seely '61 (SAM)[A] Washington, DC Our Lady of Lebanon Maronite Seminary; Presbyteral Council; Lebanon Commission; Finance Council.
Beggin, Thomas M. '79 (GF) Retired.
Begin, Daniel '75 (CLV) Cleveland Heights, OH Communion of Saints Parish.
Begin, Rev. Msgr. Raymond F. '52 (PRT) Retired.
Begin, Robert T. '64 (CLV) Cleveland, OH St. Colman.
Begley, James J. '82 (RIC) Mechanicsville, VA Church of the Redeemer.
Begley, John J. *s.j.* '62 (BO)[U] Boston The Society of Jesus of New England–Provincial Offices.
Begley, John J. *s.j.* '62 (SCR)[B] Scranton, PA The University of Scranton.
Begley, Thomas B. '60 (SPR) Retired.
Begley, Thomas M. '89 (STL) Retired.
Begly, Mark S. '84 (ALT) Johnstown Deanery; Inter–Faith Minister; Johnstown, PA Our Mother of Sorrows.
Begnaud, Adam *o.s.b.* '96 (NO)[R] St. Benedict, LA St. Joseph Abbey.
Begolly, Rev. Msgr. Michael J. '81 (GBG) New Kensington, PA Mt. St. Peter.
Begue, Joseph E. *c.m.* '55 (STL)[O] St. Louis, MO Lazarist Residence; [V] St. Louis, MO The Vincentian Press Religious Supply.
Behan, George P. '56 (PRO) Retired.
Behan, Harry P. '73 (NU) Retired.
Behan, Hugh F. '64 (JC) Absent on Leave.
Behan, Rev. Msgr. Philip A. '70 (SB) Loma Linda, CA St. Joseph the Worker; Elected Members; Judges.
Behan, Thomas W. *o.s.a.* '58 (SD)[J] San Diego, CA Augustinian Community.
Behay, Vasyl '11 (STF) Communications; Press, Diocesan: "The Sower".
Behen, John *c.pp.s.* '46 (CIN)[N] Carthagena, OH St. Charles Retired.
Behl, Rev. Msgr. Richard A. '66 (MET) Old Bridge, NJ St. Thomas the Apostle; Office of Pontifical Mission Societies; Commission for Pro–Life Action.
Behnen, Robert *o.f.m.* '60 (SFD)[K] Sherman, IL Blessed Giles Friary.
Behnke, John *c.s.p.* '76 (NY)[DD] New York, NY Paulist Fathers' Motherhouse.
Behnke, Robert C. '73 (CHI) Other Assignments.
Behrend, Thomas J. '00 (CLV) Presbyteral Conveners; Presbyteral Council; Wickliffe, OH Our Lady of Mount Carmel.
Behrens, James Stephen *o.c.s.o.* '74 (ATL)[F] Conyers The Monastery of the Holy Spirit.
Behringer, William *s.m.* '60 (SAT)[L] San Antonio, TX Casa Maria Marianist Community.
Beidelman, Patrick J. '98 (IND)[A] Indianapolis, IN Bishop Simon Bruté College Seminary; Indianapolis, IN St. Anthony Catholic Church, Indianapolis, Inc.
Beierwaltes, Charles *c.ss.r.* '67 (MIL)[S] Oconomowoc, WI The Redemptorist Retreat Center.
Beighlie, James T. *c.m.* '79 (STL)[O] St. Louis Vincentian Residence; House Springs, MO Our Lady, Queen of Peace.
Beirne, Gerald E. '62 (PRO) Retired.
Beirne, M. Christen '69 (NEW) Short Hills, NJ St. Rose of Lima.
Beirne, Robert M. '63 (PRO) Providence, RI Assumption of the Blessed Virgin Mary Retired.
Beischel, Thomas *c.pp.s.* '58 (CIN)[N] Carthagena, OH St. Charles Retired.
Beisel, Rev. Msgr. James D. '80 (PH) Warrington, PA St. Robert Bellarmine; Parish Sites and Boundaries, Commission for; Pastors Review Board; Deans; College of Consultors; Deans.
Beitans, John '73 (IND) Archdiocesan Office of Ecumenism; Edinburgh, IN Holy Trinity Catholic Church, Edinburgh, Inc.; Franklin, IN St. Rose of Lima Catholic Church, Franklin, Inc.
Beiter, Eugene J. '64 (LAN) Retired.
Beiter, Robert G. '64 (BUF)[N] Depew, NY Msgr. Conniff Residence Retired.
Beiting, Rev. Msgr. Ralph '49 (LEX) Louisa, KY St. Jude; Father Beiting Appalachian Mission Center.
Beitons, John '73 (IND)[O] Franklin, IN Franklin College.
Bejan, Ciprian '00 (BGP) Greenwich, CT St. Michael the Archangel.
Bejarano, Cesar Rafael *o.f.m.* (NY) Bronx, NY St. Luke.
Bejarano, Ramon '98 (STO) Modesto, CA St. Stanislaus Church (Pastor of); Members at Large.
Bejgrowicz, Joseph J. '70 (NEW) Kenilworth, NJ St. Theresa's; Union North Deanery 23; Members.
Bejo, Lauro *s.o.l.t.* (KC) Kansas City, MO Our Lady of Peace.
Bekala, Mariadas '04 (SCR) Honesdale, PA St. John the Evangelist.
Bekkedahl, Mark '85 (B)[B] Boise, ID Saint Alphonsus Medical Center – Nampa Inc.
Beksha, Francis W. '46 (BO) Senior Priests. Retired.
Belanger, C. Francis *o.p.* '05 (MAN)[K] Hanover, NH Order of Preachers.
Belanger, Daniel R. *c.s.v.* '07 (CHI)[N] Arlington Heights Viatorian Province Center–Clerics of St. Viator.
Belanger, Daniel R. *c.s.v.* '07 (JOL) Bourbonnais, IL St. George.
Belanger, Francis C. *o.p.* '05 (MAN) Hanover, NH St. Denis.
Belanger, Gerald R. '75 (MAN) Peterborough, NH Divine Mercy Parish; College of Consultors; Priest Personnel Board; Presbyteral Council.
Belanger, Thomas G. '06 (CHI) Chicago, IL St. Philip Neri.
Belanggoy, Plutarco *c.i.c.m.* '96 (SAT) San Antonio, TX St. James the Apostle.
Belanich, Giordano '75 (NEW) Fairview, NJ St. John the Baptist; Secaucus, NJ Hudson County Juvenile Correctional Center.
Belardi, Todd *l.c.* '04 (ATL)[C] Cumming, GA Pinecrest Academy, Inc.
Belardi, Todd '04 (MIL) Kenosha, WI St. Mary.
Belauskas, August J. '68 (CHI)[A] Mundelein, IL University of St. Mary of the Lake/Mundelein Seminary.
Belczak, Edward A. '72 (DET) Troy, MI St. Thomas More.
Belczak, Thomas A. '80 (DET) Plymouth, MI St. Kenneth.
Belden, Corey T. '02 (STP) Hamel, MN St. Anne.
Belfield, John '58 (STU) Retired.
Belford, Rev. Msgr. William J. '74 (NY) New York, NY; Archdiocesan Consultors.
Belgarde, George H. *s.j.* '88 (NY)[DD] New York Jesuit Provincial's Office.
Belger, Jeffry W. '03 (DAV) Pella, IA St. Mary's; Scouting; Colfax, IA Immaculate Conception.
Belger, Jeffry W. '03 (DAV) Oskaloosa, IA St. Mary's.
Belgica, Erwin '94 (SP) Temple Terrace, FL Corpus Christi.
Belhumer, Paul N. '61 (PH) Newtown, PA St. Andrew.
Belhumeur, Paul N. *m.s.* '61 (FR) Brewster, MA Our Lady of the Cape.
Beligotti, Richard J. '68 (ROC) Honeoye Falls, NY St. Paul of the Cross; Lima, NY St. Rose.
Beligotti, Robert L. '68 (ROC) Rochester, NY Guardian Angels; Henrietta, NY Church of the Good Shepherd; Rush, NY St. Joseph.
Belinda, Augustine *t.o.r.* '93 (ALT)[G] Loretto, PA St. Francis Friary at Mount Assisi.
Belinsky, Michael T. *c.s.c.* '89 (FTW)[H] Notre Dame Congregation of Holy Cross, United States Province of Priests & Brothers.
Belinsky, Michael T. *c.s.c.* '89 (P)[P] Portland, OR University of Portland; [B] University of Portland; [L] Portland, OR Holy Cross Fathers & Brothers, C.S.C. – University of Portland.
Belisch, Carl L. *c.s.b.* '65 (GAL)[O] Houston, TX Dillon House Retired.
Belisle, Ronald '62 (SEA) Shelton, WA St. Edward.
Belitz, Justin *o.f.m.* '61 (IND) Indianapolis, IN Sacred Heart of Jesus Catholic Church, Indianapolis, Inc.
Belitz, Ronald C. '79 (GB) Green Bay, WI Prince of Peace; College of Consultors; Wausaukee, WI St. Agnes; Wausaukee, WI St. Augustine; Vicariate.
Belizaire, Hilaire '00 (BRK) Brooklyn, NY St. Therese of Lisieux; Art and Architecture Commission.
Belizario, Nelson *o.carm.* '68 (JOL)[L] Darien Carmelite Provincial Office.
Belizario, Nelson *o.carm.* '68 (NY) Bronx, NY St. Simon Stock.
Bell, Brian '70 (PHX) Scottsdale, AZ St. Bernard of Clairvaux Roman Catholic Parish.
Bell, Rev. Msgr. Carl F. '66 (LA) Encino, CA St. Cyril Retired.
Bell, Edward H. '77 (PH) Media, PA Nativity of the Blessed Virgin Mary; Diocesan Priests' Compensation and Benefits Committee.
Bell, Edward M. '64 (WH) Retired.
Bell, Gerald L. '73 (L) Lebanon, KY Holy Name of Mary; Lebanon, KY St. Augustine; Deans.
Bell, Gerard P. *s.j.* '57 (WDC)[X] Silver Spring, MD Apostleship of Prayer; [E] North Bethesda, MD Georgetown Preparatory School.
Bell, Gerard P. *s.j.* '57 (NY)[DD] New York Jesuit Provincial's Office.
Bell, Rev. Msgr. John P. '75 (DAL) Allen, TX Our Lady of Angels; Judicial Vicar; Judicial Vicar.
Bell, Joseph '74 (SPK) Spokane Valley, WA St. John Vianney; Members.
Bell, Richard A. *m.m.* '57 (NY)[DD] Maryknoll Maryknoll St. Teresa's Residence Retired.
Bell, Steven *c.s.p.* '08 (AUS) Austin, TX St. Austin.
Bellafiore, I. Michael *s.j.* '03 (BO)[U] Boston The Society of Jesus of New England–Provincial Offices.
Bellafiore, I. Michael *s.j.* '03 (SCR)[B] Scranton, PA The University of Scranton.
Bellamah, Timothy *o.p.* '98 (WDC)[B] Washington, DC Dominican House of Studies.
Belland, David '87 (SCL) Special Assignment.
Bellantonio, Albert '69 (SCR) Mount Pocono, PA St. Ann; Hispanic Ministry Outreach.
Bellantonio, Albert '69 (BRK) Released from Diocesan Assignment.
Bellefeuille, Albert A. '54 (MAN) Retired.
Bellenoit, George C. '72 (FR) South Yarmouth, MA St. Pius Tenth; Cape Cod Deanery.
Belleque, Thomas '85 (SEA) Bellevue, WA St. Louise.
Bellerive, Joseph V. '86 (ORL) Judges.
Bellerive, Vigny Joseph '86 (ORL) Orlando, FL St. Andrew.

Bellesorte, Anthony R. *o.c.s.o.* '69 (SAC)[A] Vina, CA Abbey of New Clairvaux, Trappist Seminary; [H] Vina, CA Abbey of New Clairvaux, Trappist.
Belletty, Emile Ignatius '78 (LA) Retired.
Bellew, Rev. Msgr. Francis P. '66 (NY) Wappingers Falls, NY St. Mary; Dutchess.
Bellew, Lawrence *c.p.* '53 (BRK)[R] Jamaica, NY Immaculate Conception Monastery Retired.
Belli, Bryan W. '02 (ARL) Stafford, VA St. William of York.
Bellinghausen, David *o.s.b.* '86 (LR)[A] Subiaco, AR Subiaco Abbey; Subiaco, AR.
Bellino, Samuel *s.j.* '88 (SJ)[B] Santa Clara, CA Jesuit Community.
Bellisario, Andrew E. *c.m.* '84 (LA)[V] Montebello, CA DePaul Evangelization Center.
Bellisario, Andrew E. *c.m.* '84 (SJ)[N] Los Altos Hills, CA Daughters of Charity of St. Vincent de Paul, Seton Provincialate.
Bellittiere, David A. '89 (BUF) West Seneca, NY Fourteen Holy Helpers.
Belliveau, Gary J. '85 (MAN) Portsmouth, NH Corpus Christi Parish.
Belliveau, Paul D. *m.m.* '69 (NY)[DD] Maryknoll Maryknoll Fathers and Brothers Retired.
Bello, David *o.p.* '81 (OAK) Antioch, CA Most Holy Rosary.
Bello, Giles *o.f.m.* '55 (PAT)[N] Ringwood, NJ Holy Name Friary, Inc.
Bello, Jorge Luis '03 (MIA) Miami, FL St. Kevin.
Bello, Juan Carlos *t.o.r.* '08 (SAT) San Antonio, TX St. Leonard's.
Bello, Manuel Aznar *c.m.* '66 (MGZ) Mayaguez, PR San Vicente.
Bello, Wilson '98 (NEW) Elizabeth, NJ Immaculate Conception.
Bellonce, Fritzner '06 (MIA) Pompano Beach, FL St. Elizabeth of Hungary Catholic Church.
Belloni, Gianni Soro (ARE) Sabana Hoyos, PR Nuestra Senora de Fatima.
Bellopede, Louis P. '91 (PH) Milmont Park, PA Our Lady of Peace; Ridley Park, PA St. Madeline.
Bellotti, Nicholas V. '10 (NEW) Harrington Park, NJ Our Lady of Victories.
Bellow, Rev. Msgr. Richard '70 (CHL) Diocesan Consultors; Huntersville, NC St. Mark.
Belmonte, John *s.j.* '96 (JOL) Joliet, IL St. Paul the Apostle; Catholic Schools Office.
Belmonte, Luis Gerardo *o.c.d.* '07 (SAT) San Antonio, TX Basilica of the National Shrine of the Little Flower, Our Lady of Mt. Carmel and St. Therese Parish.
Belmontes, Jesus '04 (DAL) Dallas, TX San Juan Diego Parish.
Belogi, James '81 (ALB) Schenectady, NY St. Madeleine Sophie; Schenectady, NY St. Gabriel the Archangel; Priestly Life and Ministry Council.
Beloin, Robert L. '73 (HRT)[Q] New Haven, CT Yale University–St. Thomas More Catholic Center and Chapel; Special and other Archdiocesan Assignment.
Belongea, David *o.f.m.cap.* '59 (GB)[J] Appleton, WI St. Fidelis Friary.
Belongia, Brian S. '05 (GB) Manawa, WI Sacred Heart; Weyauwega, WI SS. Peter and Paul; Priests' Personnel Board; Waupaca, WI St. Mary Magdalene.
Belschner, Wayne L. '95 (BO) East Boston, MA Sacred Heart.
Belsole, Kurt J. *o.s.b.* '78 (GBG)[H] Latrobe Saint Vincent Archabbey; [H] Latrobe, PA Saint Vincent Archabbey.
Belsome, Garland T. '90 (BR) Defenders of the Bond.
Belsome, Gary T. '90 (BR) Gonzales, LA St. Theresa of Avila.
Belsome, Gary (NO)[A] St. Benedict, LA St. Joseph Seminary College.
Belt, David '90 (OM) Fremont, NE St. Patrick.
Beltowski, Andrew '90 (CHI) Chicago, IL St. Barbara.
Beltran, Jacque B. '87 (CHI)[A] Mundelein, IL University of St. Mary of the Lake/Mundelein Seminary.
Beltran, JoAndre '01 (CHI) Chicago, IL Notre Dame de Chicago.
Beltran, Jose J. '11 (SAC) Vacaville, CA St. Joseph.
Beltran, Rafael *c.m.f.* (SJN) Bayamon, PR Santa Maria.
Beltran, Rene Mena *m.div.* '05 (CHI) Chicago Heights, IL St. Paul.
Beltzner, Lucian W. *o.carm.* '63 (NY) Tarrytown, NY Transfiguration.
Belzer, Rev. Msgr. Paul J. '54 (BUF) Retired.
Benacchio, Onorio *c.s.* '50 (VEN) Immokalee, FL Our Lady of Guadalupe.
Benack, Henry I. '51 (RVC) Retired.
Benavente, Rev. Msgr. James L.G. '94 (AGN) Agana, GU Dulce Nombre de Maria Cathedral – Basilica; Archdiocesan College of Consultors; Archdiocesan Finance Council; Archdiocesan Presbyteral Council; Catholic Cemetery Office.
Benda, Frederick J. *s.j.* '72 (DET)[K] Detroit, MI Jesuit Community at the University of Detroit Mercy.
Bendel, Eugene F. '57 (STL) O'Fallon, MO Assumption Retired.
Benden, Stephen *c.ss.r.* (GAL) Houston, TX Holy Ghost.
Bender, Arthur C. *s.j.* '78 (NY)[E] New York, NY Regis High School; [DD] New York, NY St. Ignatius Loyola Residence.
Bender, James *c.pp.s.* '52 (CIN)[N] Dayton Provincial Office of the Cincinnati Province of the Society of the Precious Blood; [N] Carthagena, OH St. Charles Retired.
Bender, Rev. Msgr. Thomas G. '56 (COL) Retired.
Bendik, Rev. Msgr. John J. '67 (SCR) Pittston, PA St. John the Evangelist; Deans; Exeter, PA St. Cecilia; Presbyteral Council.
Bendorf, Richard *o.f.m.* '87 (STL)[O] St. Louis Franciscan Friary of St. Anthony of Padua Retired.
Bendzella, Sylvester J. '59 (ALT) Retired.
Bene, Philip J. '94 (STL) Special Assignment.
Benecki, Stanley '84 (COL) Columbus, OH St. Mary Magdalene; Deaf Apostolate.
Benedetto, James F. '70 (NEW)[L] Caldwell, NJ The Rev. Msgr. James F. Kelley Residence for Retired Priests Retired.
Benedetto, William F. '07 (NEW) Glen Rock, NJ St. Catharine.
Benedict, Joseph '97 (SJ) Special Assignment; Los Altos, CA St. William; Deans; Deacon Formation; Council of Priests.
Benedicto, Benjamin '62 (ORG) Retired.
Beneleit, Edward L. '74 (Y) Canton, OH St. Peter.
Benestad, Rev. Msgr. Thomas J. '70 (ALN) Retired.
Benfatti, Solanus M. *c.f.r.* '06 (NY)[DD] Yonkers, NY St. Leopold's Friary.
Benfatti, Solanus *c.f.r.* '06 (NY)[A] Yonkers, NY St. Joseph's Seminary.
Bengert, Tony '65 (ELP) Absent on Leave.
Bengford, Ronald J. '94 (PRO) Woonsocket, RI Sacred Heart.
Bengochea, Gerardo *s.j.* (RVC) Hempstead, NY Our Lady of Loretto.
Benicewicz, Joseph *o.f.m.conv.* '88 (BAL)[C] Baltimore, MD Archbishop Curley High School; [T] Baltimore, MD Archbishop Curley High School Endowment Trust; [Q] Baltimore, MD Immaculate Heart of Mary Friary.
Beninati, Francis H. *m.m.* '55 (FgM) Maryknoll, NY MARYKNOLL.
Benintende, Joseph '70 (ALB) Oneonta, NY St. Mary; [R] Albany, NY Noonan Community Service Corporation.
Benioff, Edward C. '07 (LA) Hawthorne, CA St. Joseph.
Benish, William '72 (AUS) Retired.
Benitez, Carlos A. '04 (WDC) Priest Council.
Benitez, Edward '66 (ORL) Retired.
Benitez, Gustavo '96 (TUC) Yuma, AZ Saint Francis of Assisi Roman Catholic Parish – Yuma.
Benitez, Ricardo '10 (TR) Riverside, NJ The Church of Jesus, the Good Shepherd, Riverside, N.J.
Benjamin, John J. '93 (SB) Retired.
Benjamin, Joseph C. *s.s.j.* '79 (GAL) Houston, TX St. Francis Xavier.
Benjamin, Matthew '10 (KC) St. Joseph, MO St. Mary's; St. Joseph, MO Seven Dolors.
Benjamin, Robert L. '00 (SR) Ferndale, CA Church of the Assumption.
Benjamine, Anthony '94 (CHR) Yonges Island, SC St. Mary.
Benko, Robert *o.f.m.* '00 (TR) Point Pleasant Beach, NJ St. Peter's.
Benkowski, Gregory '84 (OM) Omaha, NE Holy Ghost.
Benliro, Fernando C. '58 (OM) Retired.
Benn, Walter J. '77 (PH) Philadelphia, PA Mother of Divine Grace.
Bennerfield, Herbert '99 (LAF) Delcambre, LA Our Lady of the Lake; Delcambre, LA Saint Martin de Porres; Diocesan Co Chaplains.
Bennett, Ambrose *o.s.b.* '04 (STL)[F] Creve Coeur, MO St. Louis Priory School; [O] St. Louis, MO The Abbey of St. Mary and St. Louis.
Bennett, Rev. Msgr. Austin P. '49 (BRK)[S] Brooklyn, NY Monastery of the Sisters Adorers of the Precious Blood; Confraternity of the Precious Blood; [S] Brooklyn, NY Confraternity of the Precious Blood; Brooklyn, NY St. Thomas Aquinas Retired.
Bennett, Christopher '90 (SJ) San Jose, CA Santa Teresa; Deans.
Bennett, Rev. Msgr. Donald T. '67 (RVC) Hicksville, NY St. Ignatius Loyola Retired.
Bennett, Rev. Msgr. John F. '71 (RVC) Huntington, NY St. Patrick's.
Bennett, Joseph T. *s.j.* '57 (BO)[D] Boston, MA Boston College High School.
Bennett, Joshua T. '11 (LFT) Kokomo, IN St. Joan of Arc; Kokomo, IN St. Patrick.
Bennett, Michael X. '71 (HBG) On Duty Outside the Diocese.
Bennett, Noel I. '59 (MIA) Retired.
Bennett, Norman S. *c.ss.r.* '71 (BRK) Brooklyn, NY Our Lady of Perpetual Help Basilica.
Bennett, Richard *c.ss.r.* '96 (NY) Bronx, NY Immaculate Conception.
Bennett, Rolland *o.m.i.* '61 (SAT)[K] San Antonio, TX Oblate Madonna Residence.
Bennett, Thomas *l.c.* '91 (PHX) Mesa, AZ Queen of Peace Roman Catholic Parish.
Bennis, Terrence W. '04 (GRY) North Judson, IN Ss. Cyril and Methodius; North Judson, IN All Saints.
Beno, Joseph '57 (P) Retired.
Beno, Patrick C. '04 (GB) De Pere, WI St. Francis Xavier; De Pere, WI St. Mary.
Benoit, Adrian J. '65 (SPR) Retired.
Benoit, Bryan *s.c.j.* '93 (MIL)[P] Hales Corners Priests of the Sacred Heart.
Benoit, Charles J. *o.s.b.* '01 (NO)[R] St. Benedict, LA St. Joseph Abbey; [A] St. Benedict, LA St. Joseph Seminary College.
Benoit, Lloyd F. '90 (LAF) Franklin, LA Assumption B.V.M.
Benoit, Raymond P. '89 (BO) Lowell, MA St. Margaret.
Benoit, Vincent *o.p.* '84 (OAK)[L] Oakland, CA Order of Preachers (Province of the Most Holy Name of Jesus – Western Dominican Province); [L] Oakland, CA Order of Preachers (Province of the Most Holy Name of Jesus – Western Dominican Province).
Benonis, Richard R. '58 (PH) Maggie Valley, NC St. Margaret of Scotland Retired.
Benonis, Richard '52 (SAT) Retired.
Bensman, Gerald E. *s.t.l.* '64 (CIN) Retired.
Bensman, John L. '56 (CIN)[N] Carthagena, OH St. Charles Retired.
Benson, Joseph A. '84 (NO) New Orleans, LA Blessed Francis Xavier Seelos.
Benson, Richard B. *c.m.* '78 (FgM) Earth City, MO Western Province.
Bentil, Augustine Kofi '94 (LC) Hatley, WI St. Ladislaus; Wittenberg, WI St. Joseph.
Bentil, Gabriel '84 (VIC) Inez, TX St. Joseph's; School Board.
Benton, James '73 (LIN) Harvard, NE St. Joseph's; Apostolate to the Spanish Speaking.
Bentz, John C. *s.j.* '04 (SEA)[M] Seattle, WA Jesuit House, Seattle.
Bentz, John C. *s.j.* '04 (P)[L] Portland, OR Jesuit Provincial Office (Society of Jesus, Oregon Prov.).
Benusa, Jeffrey M. '03 (HEL) Plains, MT St. James; Thompson Falls, MT St. William.
Benwell, Rev. Msgr. William '80 (MET) Vicars General; Moderator; Canonical Staff; College of Consultors.
Benya, Edward G. *s.j.* '84 (NO)[R] New Orleans Jesuit Provincial Office.
Benz, Rev. Msgr. David H. '75 (PH) Philadelphia, PA St. Therese of the Child Jesus.
Benz, Gary '99 (BIS) Mohall, ND St. Johns; Mohall, ND St. James; Mohall, ND St. Jerome.
Benz, Gary '99 (FAR) Lansford, ND St. John's Church of Lansford.
Benz, James J. '74 (STL) St. Charles, MO St. Cletus; [V] St. Louis, MO Archdiocesan Stewardship Education Committee.
Benz, Thomas G. *s.j.* '00 (SY)[A] Syracuse, NY Saint Andrew Hall.
Benzmiller, James T. '99 (LC) Leave of Absence.
Benzoni, Martin *o.praem* '81 (LA) Wilmington, CA SS. Peter and Paul.
Beof, Marlon *o.a.r.* '97 (NY)[B] Suffern, NY Tagaste Monastery.
Beof, Marlon *o.a.r.* '97 (LA)[P] Oxnard, CA Order of Augustinian Recollects (O.A.R.), St. Augustine Priory.
Beran, Mark T. '02 (OM) Wayne, NE St. Mary; Age Groups.
Berardi, Rev. Msgr. Ferdinando D. '77 (NY) New Rochelle, NY Holy Family.
Berardi, James J. '59 (CLV) Retired.
Berardi, Thomas '76 (ALB) Lake George, NY Sacred Heart; [Q] Cobleskill, NY State University of New York College of Agricultural & Technology at Cobleskill; Deans; Bolton Landing, NY Blessed Sacrament; Presbyteral Council; Diocesan Board of Consultors; Minister to Active Priests and Priests in Special Circumstances.
Berbary, Richard J. '04 (NEW) Bayonne, NJ St. Henry's.
Berbena, Christopher '80 (OAK) San Leandro, CA Assumption of the Blessed Virgin Mary.
Berberian, David V. '74 (ALB) Judges; Administrative Review Board (Due Process); Administrative Advocate for Priests; Special Assignment; Priests Placement Committee.
Berberian, David V. '74 (ALB) Defender of the Marriage Bond in First Instance; Promoter of Justice.
Berberich, Thomas E. '59 (HRT) Kent, CT Sacred Heart; Appointed.
Bercasio, Rafael '93 (PHX) Phoenix, AZ Corpus Christi Roman Catholic Parish.
Berchmans, Britto '81 (CHI) Park Ridge, IL St. Paul of the Cross; [A] Chicago, IL St. Joseph College Seminary.
Berchmans Antony, John '90 (NEW) Fort Lee, NJ Madonna.
Berchmanz, Anthony '67 (NEW) Military Chaplains.
Bercier, Barry *a.a.* '85 (WOR)[N] Worcester, MA Assumptionists of Assumption College.
Berdis, Donald E. '63 (E) Farrell, PA Our Lady of Fatima–St. Ann.

Berdowicz, Wieslaw *s.ch.* (CHI) Chicago, IL Five Holy Martyrs.
Berdugo, Hernan '83 (SJN) Toa Alta, PR San Esteban, Protomartir.
Berean, Christopher H. '87 (NY) Saugerties, NY St. Mary of the Snow.
Bereda, Stanislaw J. '65 (GLD) Retired.
Berendt, George *p.i.m.e.* '74 (DET)[K] Detroit, MI P.I.M.E. Missionaries.
Berendt, Peter *c.p.* '57 (GAL)[O] Houston, TX Congregation of the Passion, Holy Name Passionist Community and Retreat Center; [Q] Houston, TX Holy Name Retreat Center.
Berens, Cyprian *o.f.m.* '51 (CIN)[M] Cincinnati, OH Archbishop Leibold Home for the Aged; [N] Cincinnati St. Francis Seraph Friary Retired.
Beres, Kevin J. '00 (ARL) Annandale, VA St. Michael.
Beretta, J. Christian *o.s.f.s.* '97 (WIL)[B] Wilmington, DE Salesianum School.
Bereza, Stepan '93 (STF) New Britain, CT St. Josaphat.
Berg, Blaise R. '98 (SAC)[K] Chico, CA St. Thomas Aquinas Newman Center Chico; Chico, CA St. John the Baptist; Vicars Forane.
Berg, Blaise '98 (SAC) Priests' Personnel Board, Diocesan.
Berg, Daniel J. '00 (BIS) Diocesan Corporate Board; Diocesan Finance Council; Flasher, ND St. Theresa the Child Jesus; Flasher, ND St. Lawrence; Flasher, ND St. Gertrude.
Berg, Daniel J. '00 (BIS) Presbyteral Council.
Berg, Donald M. '47 (LC) Retired.
Berg, Peter M. '71 (OG) Newcomb, NY St. Henry; Newcomb, NY St. Therese.
Berg, Ralph *c.m.f.* '64 (FRS) Fresno, CA St. Anthony Claret.
Berg, Richard V. '52 (STP) Retired.
Berg, Richard *c.s.c.* '63 (P)[L] Portland, OR Holy Cross Fathers & Brothers, C.S.C. – University of Portland Retired.
Berg, Richard *c.s.c.* (FTW)[H] Notre Dame Congregation of Holy Cross, United States Province of Priests & Brothers.
Berg, Rev. Msgr. Stephen J. '99 (FWT) Vicar General and Moderator of the Curia; Diocesan Pastoral Council; Consultors; Diocesan Finance Council; Catholic Foundation of North Texas; Diocesan Pastoral Finance Committee; Conduct Review Board; [M] Board of Directors; Presbyteral Council.
Berg, Thomas V. '00 (NY) Yonkers, NY St. Denis; [A] Yonkers, NY St. Joseph's Seminary.
Bergamo, Rev. Msgr. John A. '65 (SCR)[C] East Stroudsburg, PA Notre Dame Jr./Sr. High School; East Stroudsburg, PA St. Matthew; Diocesan Consultors; Presbyteral Council.
Bergbower, Daniel J. '88 (MO) Air National Guard Chaplains.
Bergbower, Daniel '88 (SFD) Military Services.
Bergen, William J. *s.j.* '55 (NY) New York, NY St. Ignatius Loyola; [DD] New York, NY St. Ignatius Loyola Residence.
Berger, Bernard M. '64 (GI) Crawford, NE St. John the Baptist.
Berger, David '06 (VIC) Meyersville, TX SS. Peter & Paul; Cuero, TX Our Lady of Guadalupe; Cuero, TX St. Michael; Presbyteral Council; Catholic Outreach Prison Ministry.
Berger, John G. '67 (NU) Lafayette, MN St. Gregory the Great; Lafayette, MN St. George; St. Peter Regional Treatment Center; [F] Saint Peter, MN St. Peter Regional Treatment Center; Vice–Chancellor; Judicial Vicar (Officialis); On Special or Other Diocesan Assignment.
Berger, John W. '98 (HON) Honolulu, HI Cathedral of Our Lady of Peace.
Berger, Lawrence B. '66 (LC) Consultors; Appointed Members Retired.
Berger, Peter '05 (MIL)[D] Milwaukee, WI Pius XI High School; Special Assignment.
Berger, Robert F. '62 (HBG) Myerstown, PA Mary, Gate of Heaven.
Bergeron, Rev. Msgr. Albert G. '62 (HT) Retired.
Bergeron, C. Paul '81 (LAF) Retired.
Bergeron, David *c.c.* '10 (GAL) Houston, TX Queen of Peace.
Bergeron, Marc H. '70 (FR) Fall River, MA St. Anne's; Procurator–Advocates; Ecumenical Officer.
Bergeron, Michael A. '96 (HT) Houma, LA Annunziata.
Bergeron, Michael '96 (HT)[E] Thibodaux, LA Marian Servants of the Word.
Berggreen, Rev. Msgr. Robert H. '64 (BR) New Roads, LA St. Mary of False River.
Berghammer, Robert J. '49 (MIL) Retired.
Berghout, Paul A. '96 (ARL) Arlington, VA Our Lady of Lourdes; Defenders of the Bond.
Bergin, James *s.v.d.* '69 (DUB)[B] Epworth, IA Divine Word College.
Bergin, John J. *s.v.d.* '67 (BO)[U] Duxbury, MA Society of the Divine Word.
Bergin, John J. *s.j.* '67 (STL)[O] St. Louis, MO De Smet Jesuit High School Community.
Bergin, Karl '04 (ORL) Melbourne, FL Our Lady of Lourdes; [A] Melbourne, FL Central Catholic High School, Inc.; Representative by Age.
Bergin, Paschal '57 (CC) Retired.
Bergin, Patrick A. *m.m.* '59 (NY)[DD] Retired.
Bergin, Rev. Msgr. Thomas J. '61 (NY) Staten Island, NY St. Charles.
Bergkamp, Roger *o.m.i.* '64 (ANC) Pastoral Team:; Pastoral Team:; Pastoral Team.
Bergman, Charles B. '58 (PIT)[M] Pittsburgh, PA St. John Vianney Manor Retired.
Bergman, Eric L. '07 (SCR) On Special or Other Diocesan Assignment; Scranton, PA St. Clare.
Bergman, Richard '55 (DM) Retired.
Bergman, Rev. Msgr. Robert '71 (KCK) Louisburg, KS Immaculate Conception.
Bergner, David J. *s.d.s.* '76 (MO) Navy Reserve Chaplains.
Bergner, David *s.d.s.* '76 (MIL)[P] Milwaukee Salvatorian Provincial Offices; Milwaukee, WI.
Bergner, David *s.d.s.* '76 (FgM) Milwaukee, WI SALVATORIAN MISSIONS.
Bergquist, Patrick D. '90 (FBK) Healy, AK Holy Mary of Guadalupe Catholic Church Healy; Vicar General; Presbyteral Council; Finance Advisory Board.
Bergs, David '76 (LSC) Retired.
Bergsbaken, Dennis L. '78 (GB) Greenleaf, WI St. Clare Corp.
Bergstadt, John P. '68 (GB) Green Bay, WI St. John the Baptist.
Bergstadt, John '68 (GB) Regional Vicars.
Berinti, Benjamin A. *c.pp.s.* '85 (ORL) Directors; [E] Winter Park, FL San Pedro Spiritual Development Center; [F] Winter Park, FL Franciscan Friars, T.O.R., San Pedro Friary; Representative – Religious Priests.
Berinti, Benjamin *c.pp.s.* '85 (CIN)[N] Dayton Provincial Office of the Cincinnati Province of the Society of the Precious Blood; [N] Dayton, OH Provincial Office of the Cincinnati Province of the Society of the Precious Blood.
Beristain, Juan M. '71 (SJN) Levittown, PR Santisima Trinidad.
Berkey, William G. '02 (GBG) Youngwood, PA Holy Cross; [C] Greensburg, PA Greensburg Central Catholic High School/Greensburg Central Catholic Jr. High School.
Berkhout, Frans '97 (SP) Indian Rocks Beach, FL St. Jerome.
Berko–Attah, Abraham '98 (NY) Bronx, NY Christ the King.
Berland, Mark '74 (SAL) Oberlin, KS Sacred Heart Parish; Selden, KS Sacred Heart Parish; Oberlin, KS Immaculate Conception of the Blessed Virgin Mary Parish.
Bermejo, Donardo S. '91 (JC) Shelbina, MO St. Patrick; Shelbina, MO St. Mary.
Bermudez, Alberto '86 (NO) Chateau de Notre Dame Guild; On Special Assignment.
Bermudez, Duverney '10 (NEW) Ho Ho Kus, NJ St. Luke's.
Bermudez, Giovani Romero '99 (BRK) Brooklyn, NY Our Lady of Solace.
Bermudez, Jaime '03 (POD) Ponce.
Bermudez, Jose '80 (SPR) Orange, MA St. Mary.
Bermudez–Hernandez, Mauricio '09 (DEN) Aurora, CO Queen of Peace.
Bermudez Onopa, Jaime '03 (PCE)[G] Ponce, PR Prelature of the Holy Cross and Opus Dei.
Berna, Francis *o.f.m.* '80 (PH)[Y] Philadelphia, PA St. Pius X Residence.
Bernabe, Humberto '75 (LA) Los Angeles, CA Ascension.
Bernacki, William J. *o.p.* '56 (CHI)[D] Oak Park, IL Fenwick High School; [N] Chicago, IL St. Pius V Priory.
Bernadicou, Paul J. *s.j.* '65 (LA)[P] Los Angeles, CA Colombiere House.
Bernal, Edward '87 (SAT) San Antonio, TX St. Benedict.
Bernaola, Javier '85 (SJN)[G] Guaynabo, PR Opus Dei.
Bernaola, Javier '85 (PCE)[G] Ponce, PR Prelature of the Holy Cross and Opus Dei; Ponce.
Bernard, Andre '73 (SR) Retired.
Bernard, George C. *c.s.c.* '49 (P)[L] Portland, OR Holy Cross Fathers & Brothers, C.S.C. – University of Portland Retired.
Bernard, George *c.s.c.* (FTW)[H] Notre Dame Congregation of Holy Cross, United States Province of Priests & Brothers.
Bernard, Lawrence *o.f.m.* '66 (GLP) Gallup, NM St. Francis of Assisi.
Bernardi, Peter J. *s.j.* '87 (CHI)[C] Chicago, IL Jesuit Community at Loyola University Chicago.
Bernardino, Eduardo '91 (SD) Escondido, CA Church of the Resurrection Catholic Parish.
Bernardo, Joseph J. '03 (LIN) Davey, NE St. Mary's; Advocates.
Bernardy, Patrick '60 (GB) Retired.
Bernas, Anthony (PEO) Monmouth, IL Immaculate Conception.
Bernas, Eugene '66 (NEW) Retired.
Bernas, Eugenio F. '80 (CHI) Chicago, IL St. Genevieve.
Bernas, Thomas A. '94 (CHI) Chicago, IL St. Richard.
Bernauer, James W. *s.j.* '75 (BO)[U] Newton, MA The Jesuit Community at Boston College.
Bernauer, James '52 (CR) Retired.
Bernavas, Edison *i.c.* (SP) Spring Hill, FL St. Theresa.
Berndt, Wayne *o.f.m.cap.* '83 (FgM) White Plains, NY The Province of St. Mary of the Capuchin Order.
Bernelli, Rev. Msgr. Matthew '64 (BGP) Bridgeport, CT St. Mary.
Berner, Albert J. '68 (NEW) Verona, NJ Our Lady of the Lake.
Berner, Francis '70 (NO) On Medical Leave of Absence.
Berner, Michael '86 (DM) Logan, IA St. Anne; Missouri Valley, IA St. Patrick.
Bernhardt, Gary *o.f.m.* '99 (SUP) Ashland, WI Our Lady of the Lake Catholic Community; Ashland, WI St. Mary.
Bernier, Michael F. '03 (SPR) Springfield, MA Mary Mother of Hope Parish; Bishop's Commission for Clergy.
Bernier, Paul '00 (FR) Fall River, MA Cathedral of St. Mary of the Assumption.
Bernier, Paul *s.s.s.* '62 (CLV)[N] Cleveland, OH Congregation of the Blessed Sacrament; Highland Heights, OH St. Paschal Baylon.
Bernier, Philip J. *o.f.m.cap.* '01 (CLV)[N] Cleveland, OH St. Paul Friary; Garfield Heights, OH Holy Spirit Parish.
Berning, James C. '91 (WIN) Winona, MN St. Mary's.
Berning, James *s.d.b.* '93 (NY)[FF] Stony Point, NY Marian Shrine; [FF] Stony Point, NY Don Bosco Retreat Center and Marian Shrine.
Bernotas, Robert J. '83 (LFT) Kentland, IN St. Joseph; Members; Kentland, IN St. John the Baptist; Kentland, IN SS. Peter and Paul.
Bernott, Ernest J. '48 (GR) Retired.
Berns, Eric R. '96 (LC) Stratford, WI St. Andrew; Stratford, WI St. Joseph; Deans; St. Joseph's Priest Fund, Inc., (Benevolent Society).
Berny, Paul W. '72 (ATL) Advocates; [B] Roswell, GA Blessed Trinity Catholic High School; College of Consultors; Special or Other Archdiocesan Assignment.
Berran, Donald M. '60 (BRK) South Ozone Park, NY; South Ozone Park, NY Our Lady of Perpetual Help; South Ozone Park, NY Our Lady of Perpetual Help Retired.
Berret, Anthony J. *s.j.* '71 (PH)[C] Jesuit Fathers; [Y] Philadelphia, PA St. Alphonsus House.
Berrette, Hugues '91 (BRK) Brooklyn, NY St. Jerome.
Berrigan, Daniel J. *s.j.* '52 (NY)[DD] New York, NY Jesuit Community of the Immaculate Conception.
Berrio, Augusto *s.j.* '63 (LA) Santa Barbara, CA Our Lady of Sorrows.
Berrio, Ignacio D. '66 (BO) Marlborough, MA Immaculate Conception; Presbyteral Council.
Berrios, Angel '65 (PCE)[H] Penuelas, PR Congregacion San Juan Evangelista; Santa Isabel, PR St. James.
Berrios, Giovanni Perez (SJN) San Juan, PR Nuestra Senora del Carmen.
Berrios, Israel '96 (CGS) Barranquitas, PR San Andres Apostol; [F] Casa del Apostol San Andres; Diocesan Consultors; Priests Senate; Vocations.
Berry, Dennis M. *s.t.* '74 (MOB)[J] Hurtsboro, AL Blessed John XXIII Center; Silver Spring, MD.
Berry, Dennis M. *s.t.* '74 (PT)[E] Tallahassee, FL Missionary Servants of the Most Holy Trinity.
Berry, Michael *o.c.d.* '06 (MIL)[P] Hubertus, WI Discalced Carmelite Monastery – Holy Hill Basilica of the National Shrine of Mary, Help of Christians, Holy Hill.
Berry, William F. '66 (WDC) Retired.
Berryman, Harold L. '58 (GB)[E] New Holstein, WI Divine Savior Catholic Elementary School, Inc.; New Holstein, WI Holy Rosary; New Holstein, WI St. Ann Retired.
Bersabal, Rey '91 (SAC) Vicars Forane; Folsom, CA St. John the Baptist.
Berschied, Paul L. '86 (COV) Southgate, KY St. Therese of the Infant Jesus.
Bertelli, Ameilio James '59 (BO) Senior Priests. Retired.
Bertelli, Mark '06 (SB) Montclair, CA Our Lady of Lourdes.
Bertels, George '55 (KCK) Judges Retired.
Bertels, Henry J. *s.j.* '62 (NY)[DD] Cardinal Spellman Hall, Jesuit Community.
Bertha, Joseph '80 (PSC) Pittston, PA St. Michael; Evangelization; Retirement Plan Board.
Berthelette, Ernest H. '74 (PRO) Providence, RI St. Sebastian.
Bertin, Gerard L. '89 (MAN) Goffstown, NH St. Lawrence.
Bertino, Dominic V. '75 (GRY) Hobart, IN St. Bridget.
Bertiz, Santos B. '93 (NEW) Absent on Leave.
Bertocchi, Luigi *o.s.b.* '70 (SCL)[I] Collegeville, MN St. John's Abbey, of the Order of St. Benedict.
Bertogli, John '77 (DM) Des Moines, IA St. Ambrose Cathedral.

Bertolacci, Caesar *m.c.* '96 (DET)[K] Plymouth, MI Miles Christi.
Bertolotti, David P. '91 (BRK) Woodhull Medical & Mental Health Center; Brooklyn, NY All Saints.
Bertone, Thomas C. *c.s.c.* '98 (FTW)[K] Notre Dame, IN Saint Andre Bessette Continuing Care Trust; [H] Notre Dame, IN Congregation of Holy Cross, United States Province of Priests & Brothers; [A] Notre Dame, IN Moreau Seminary; [H] Notre Dame Congregation of Holy Cross, United States Province of Priests & Brothers.
Bertone, Thomas *c.s.c.* (BGP)[O] Bridgeport, CT Provincial Offices of the Priests and Brothers of Holy Cross, Eastern Province.
Bertoni, Albert *s.m.* '79 (RVC)[D] Uniondale, NY Kellenberg Memorial High School.
Bertoniere, Gabriel *o.c.s.o.* '58 (WOR)[N] Spencer, MA St. Joseph's Abbey.
Bertram, Keith '04 (DUL) Brainerd, MN St. Andrew; Brainerd, MN St. Francis; Brainerd, MN St. Mathias.
Bertram, Michael *o.f.m.cap.* '88 (MIL) Milwaukee, WI St. Francis of Assisi; Milwaukee, WI St. Francis of Assisi; Archdiocesan Council of Priests; Archdiocesan Consultors.
Bertrand, Armand J. '89 (SC) Cherokee, IA Immaculate Conception; Cherokee, IA Holy Name; Presbyteral Council; Deans.
Bertrand, Conley '59 (LAF)[M] Lafayette, LA Come Lord Jesus! Inc.
Bertrand, Emmanuel *o.p.* '58 (L)[L] Louisville, KY St. Louis Bertrand Priory; Louisville, KY St. Louis Bertrand.
Bertrand, Jacob '10 (SD) Chula Vista, CA Saint Rose of Lima Catholic Parish.
Bertrand, Richard D. *s.j.* '79 (BO)[U] Boston The Society of Jesus of New England–Provincial Offices.
Bertrand, Richard D. *s.j.* '79 (PRT) Portland, ME Our Lady of Hope Parish.
Bertrand, Vincent E. '87 (SPC) Buffalo, MO St. William; Adjutant Judicial Vicar; Judges; Conway, MO Sacred Heart; Lebanon, MO St. Francis De Sales.
Berube, Paul W. '60 (BO) Newburyport, MA Immaculate Conception; Senior Priests. Retired.
Berube, Richard N. *s.s.e.* '70 (BUR)[E] Colchester, VT Society of St. Edmund; [A] Colchester, VT St. Michael's College.
Beseau, Steven '95 (KCK)[L] Lawrence, KS St. Lawrence Catholic Campus Center at the University of Kansas and Residence.
Besel, Patrick '06 (BAL) Baltimore, MD St. Mary of the Assumption.
Besendorfer, Ralph L. '59 (STA) Retired.
Beshoner, Sebastian *o.s.b.* '55 (LR)[A] Subiaco, AR Subiaco Abbey.
Beshoner, Seraphim *t.o.r.* '05 (STU)[H] Steubenville, OH Holy Spirit Friary; [A] Steubenville, OH Franciscan University of Steubenville.
Besinga, Dino J. '82 (MO) Army Chaplains.
Bessellieu, Mel '97 (FWT) Consultors; Burleson, TX St. Ann.
Best, Richard '61 (JOL) Retired.
Best, Russell W. '86 (BO) Roxbury, MA St. Patrick; Permanent Disability.
Bestler, Joseph '57 (GB) Retired.
Betances–Torres, Martin '87 (NY) On Leave of Absence.
Betancourt, Cesar '09 (SAT) Helotes, TX Our Lady of Guadalupe.
Betancourt, Homero *s.d.b.* (CGS)[C] Aibonito, PR Casa Salesiana de Retiros.
Betancourt, Jorge R. *o.carm.* '03 (ARE) Ciales, PR Holy Rosary.
Betancourt, Juan Miguel *s.e.m.v.* '01 (STP)[A] Saint Paul, MN The Saint Paul Seminary; St. Paul, MN St. Francis De Sales.
Betancourt Ramirez, Jorge '03 (SJN) Awaiting Assignment.
Betancur, Nelson '75 (PAT) Dover, NJ Sacred Heart; Dover, NJ Our Lady Queen of the Most Holy Rosary.
Betancurt, Rigoberto '83 (SHP) Bossier City, LA Christ the King.
Bethel, Francis *o.s.b.* '83 (TLS)[G] Hulbert, OK Our Lady of the Annunciation of Clear Creek Monastery.
Betley, Michael E. '80 (GB) Stockbridge, WI St. Mary; Sherwood, WI St. John–Sacred Heart; Hilbert, WI St. Mary; Priests' Personnel Board.
Betoni, John P. *o.s.a.* '62 (PH)[C] Villanova University; [Y] Villanova, PA St. Thomas Monastery.
Betrand, Conley '59 (LAF) Retired.
Betrozoff, Larry '73 (MRY) Tres Pinos, CA Retired.
Betschart, Joseph '99 (P) Special Assignment.
Bettendorf, James B. '59 (LAN) Retired.
Betters, John D. '03 (CLV) Euclid, OH SS. Robert & William.
Betti, Frederick G. *s.j.* '90 (BUF)[N] Buffalo, NY Canisius Jesuit Community Inc.; [D] Buffalo, NY Canisius High School.
Betti, Mark J. '96 (R) Clinton, NC Immaculate Conception.
Bettinger, Eugene Joseph *o.carm.* '76 (NEW) Teaneck, NJ Carmelite Chapel of St. Therese; Teaneck, NJ St. Anastasia's.
Bettinger, Mark T. '93 (PBL) Montrose, CO St. Mary; Ecclesiastical Notaries.
Betts, David R. '98 (SCR) Unassigned or Leave of Absence.
Betts, John C. '68 (P) Retired.
Betz, James F. '71 (MO) Diocesan Historian; Army Chaplains; On Duty Outside the Diocese.
Betz, James S. '89 (WDC) Laurel, MD St. Nicholas Retired.
Betz, Kenneth '65 (EVN) Haubstadt, IN St. James.
Betz, Robert '73 (MIL) South Milwaukee, WI Divine Mercy.
Betz, Thomas R. *o.f.m.cap.* '91 (PH) By Election.
Betz, Thomas *o.f.m.cap.* '91 (PH) Chinese Apostolate; Definitors:; Vocations Director:; Philadelphia, PA St. John the Evangelist.
Betzen, James G. *c.pp.s.* '81 (KC)[A] Liberty, MO Society of the Precious Blood Provincial Offices.
Betzen, James G. *c.pp.s.* '81 (JC) Liberty, MO; Sedalia, MO Sacred Heart; Sedalia, MO St. Patrick.
Beuth, William J. *c.pp.s.* '59 (CIN)[N] Dayton Provincial Office of the Cincinnati Province of the Society of the Precious Blood.
Beuther, Richard J. '96 (BRK) Elmhurst, NY St. Bartholomew; Diocesan Consultors.
Beuzer, Vincent *s.j.* '58 (SEA)[C] Tacoma, WA Bellarmine Preparatory School.
Bevacqua, James M. '03 (LA) Glendale, CA Holy Family.
Bevan, James J. '75 (LAV) Retired.
Bevans, Stephen B. *s.v.d.* '71 (CHI)[B] Chicago, IL Catholic Theological Union; [N] Chicago, IL Edward McGuinn, S.V.D. Residence.
Bevenour, Richard F. '57 (DAV) Retired.
Beveridge, John P. '72 (SFD) Collinsville, IL SS. Peter and Paul.
Bevilacqua, Jerome F. *o.s.a.* '65 (SD)[O] San Diego, CA Spirit Ministries; [J] San Diego, CA Augustinian Community.
Bevington, William S. '51 (NSH)[L] Hendersonville, TN Priests Eucharistic League; Judges Retired.
Bevins, John J. '58 (HRT) Waterbury, CT Basilica of the Immaculate Conception.
Beya–Tshingimba, Zacharie '75 (LC) Gays Mills, WI St. Mary; Gays Mills, WI St. Philip.
Beyer, Leroy O. '66 (WH) Retired.
Beyer, Richard J. '81 (DAV)[E] Iowa City, IA Newman Catholic Student Center; Iowa City, IA St. Mary.
Beyette, Paul V. '50 (OG) Retired.
Bezunartea, Rev. Msgr. Herman O. '58 (FRS) Retired.
Biagi, Vincent L. *s.j.* '78 (NY)[DD] New York, NY St. Ignatius Loyola Residence; [DD] New York, NY Society of Jesus, New York Province; New York, NY.
Biain, Jose *o.f.m.* '48 (MIA) Judges.
Bialek, Mark '06 (BAL) Laurel, MD Resurrection of Our Lord.
Bialkowski, David W. '88 (BUF) Absent on Leave.
Bialkowski, Jacek J. '96 (SCR) Mansfield, PA Holy Child.
Bialoncik, Emmanuel *o.f.m.* '73 (BWN) Alamo, TX Resurrection.
Biancalana, Angelo G. *m.c.c.j.* '58 (LA)[BB] Covina, CA Comboni Mission Center.
Bianchi, Raymond S. '52 (TR) Retired.
Bianco, Anthony M. *c.r.s.p.* '51 (ALN)[K] Bethlehem, PA The Barnabite Fathers Barnabite Spiritual Center.
Bianco, Louis A. '05 (BAL) Westminster, MD St. John.
Biase, Justin A. *o.f.m.conv.* '70 (FgM) AMERICAN CONVENTUAL FRANCISCAN MISSIONS; Rensselaer, NY.
Biase, Justin *o.f.m.conv.* '70 (ALB)[A] Rensselaer, NY Conventual Franciscan Friars; [L] Rensselaer, NY Provincialate, Immaculate Conception Friary – Order of Friars Minor Conventual; [R] Rensselaer, NY Franciscans in Collaborative Ministry, Inc.
Biasiotto, Richard *o.f.m.* '64 (ALB)[B] Siena College; [R] Albany, NY St. Francis Chapel.
Biber, Joseph Morton '85 (RIC) Petersburg, VA St. Joseph.
Bichl, William M. *s.j.* '67 (CLV)[B] University Heights, OH John Carroll Jesuit Community.
Bichsel, William *s.j.* '59 (SEA)[C] Tacoma, WA Bellarmine Preparatory School.
Bickel, Timothy C. '92 (MIL) Butler, WI St. Agnes.
Bickett, Anthony '83 (OWN) Hardinsburg, KY St. Romuald; Consultors; Director of Ecumenism; Diocesan Liturgical Committee; Priests' Council.
Bicomong, Sergio '79 (CAM) Fairton, NJ Federal Correctional Institution; Millville, NJ The Parish of All Saints, Millville, N.J.
Bicsko, Stephen C. *c.m.* '70 (BRK)[R] Queens Village, NY DePaul Residence.
Bicz, Marian '88 (RVC) Cutchogue, NY Our Lady of Ostrabrama.
Biczak, Arkad '63 (SFE) Albuquerque, NM St. John the Apostle; Mission Office.
Bida, John A. '73 (NY) Bangall, NY Immaculate Conception; Pine Plains, NY St. Anthony.
Bidawid, Kamal Warda '68 (SPA) Turlock, CA St. Thomas Assyrian–Chaldean Parish; El Dorado Hills, CA Our Lady of Perpetual Help Chaldean/Assyrian Catholic Church.
Bidinger, Bruce M. *s.j.* '86 (PH)[Y] Loyola Center and Manresa Hall; [C] Jesuit Fathers.
Bido, Miguel S. '04 (ARE) Angeles, PR Our Lady of Angels.
Bidwell, Michael L. '89 (CIN) New Carlisle, OH Sacred Heart.
Bidwill, Joseph E. *o.p.* '55 (STP) Minneapolis, MN St. Albert the Great; [J] Minneapolis, MN St. Albert the Great Priory.
Bie, Paul R. '83 (RVC) Medical Leave.
Biebel, Rev. Msgr. William E. '62 (E) Erie, PA St. Peter Cathedral; Northern Vicariate.
Bieberle, Victor '51 (WCH) Retired.
Bieganowski, Ronald *s.j.* '72 (MIL)[P] Milwaukee, WI Jesuit Community at Marquette University.
Biegler, Patrick *m.s.a.* '05 (NOR)[G] Cromwell Society of the Missionaries of the Holy Apostles; Chester, CT St. Joseph.
Biegler, Steven '93 (RC) Piedmont, SD Our Lady of the Black Hills; Vicar General for Temporal Affairs; Diocesan Consultors.
Biegun, Marek (PAT) Unassigned.
Biehl, August *s.m.* '58 (SAT)[K] San Antonio, TX Marianist Residence: Skilled Nursing.
Bielak, Andrew '95 (NY) Manhattan, NY Goldwater Memorial Hospital; New York, NY Our Lady of Peace.
Bielasiewicz, Slawomir '08 (STA) Macclenny, FL St. Mary's; Civil Institutions.
Bielawa, Thomas *s.d.s.* '72 (MIL)[P] Milwaukee Salvatorian Provincial Offices.
Bielecki, Michael H. *o.s.a.* '83 (PH)[Y] Villanova, PA Provincial Offices of the Order of St. Augustine, Province of St. Thomas of Villanova; [Y] Villanova, PA St. Thomas Monastery.
Bielewicz, Harry R. '86 (PIT) Clergy Personnel Board; Secretary for Clergy; Pittsburgh, PA Our Lady of Loreto; Priest Council; Vicar for Clergy Personnel.
Bielonko, Joseph '59 (WOR) Retired.
Bien, Dan '85 (AGN) Dededo, GU Santa Barbara.
Bien, Ysrael '10 (P) Beaverton, OR St. Cecilia.
Bienvenu, Kenneth A. '60 (LAF) St. Martinville, LA St. Martin of Tours Retired.
Bienvenu, Paul G. '92 (LAF) Opelousas, LA Our Lady of Mercy.
Bier, Louis C. '76 (PH) Springfield, PA St. Francis of Assisi; [BB] Philadelphia, PA University of the Sciences in Philadelphia.
Biermann, John G. *s.a.c.* '69 (BAL) Baltimore, MD St. Jude Shrine.
Biernacki, Jacob S. '67 (SPC) Retired.
Biernat, Leon J. '92 (BUF) Lancaster, NY Our Lady of Pompeii.
Biernat, Ryszard S. '09 (BUF) Tonawanda, NY St. Amelia.
Biernat, Wayne C. '04 (SPR) Williamstown, MA SS. Patrick and Raphael; Presbyteral Council.
Biersack, Thomas E. '81 (MIL) Lomira, WI St. Andrew; Mayville, WI St. Mary.
Bierschenk, Stephen W. '76 (DAL) Dallas, TX St. Monica; Personnel Board.
Bierster, Rev. Msgr. Leo N. '52 (HBG) Retired.
Biesinger, Robert J. '56 (BUF)[N] Buffalo, NY Sheehan Residence for Priests Retired.
Biewend, Michael '80 (P) Portland, OR St. Mary Magdalene.
Bigelow, William R. '67 (BUF) Retired.
Biggane, Edward J. *s.m.a.* '58 (NEW)[L] Tenafly, NJ Society of African Missions, Provincialate, S.M.A. Fathers.
Bigirimana, Pascal '97 (CHI) Chicago, IL SS. Peter and Paul.
Bigley, Michael *s.d.s.* (MIL)[P] Greendale, WI.
Biglin, Martin J. '67 (NY) New Rochelle, NY Holy Name of Jesus; Westchester (South Shore).
Bignall, Douglas '93 (DET) Clinton Township, MI St. Thecla; [A] The School of Theology.
Bihr, Rev. Msgr. Louis J. '68 (PAT) Presbyteral Council; College of Consultors; Straight and Narrow, Inc.; Special Assignment.
Bihuniak, Michael J. '90 (MET) Absent on Sick Leave.
Bik, Michael *o.s.b.* '93 (SCL)[I] Collegeville, MN St. John's Abbey, of the Order of St. Benedict.
Bikoma, Rev. Msgr. Edward J. '51 (EST) Retired.
Bilicky, Louis S. '49 (BO) Senior Priests. Retired.
Bilinsky, Rev. Msgr. Canon William M. '65 (STN) Retired.
Bilinsky, Rev. Msgr. William '65 (NO) Retired.
Bill, J. Armand '56 (PRT) Retired.
Bill, Rev. Msgr. Ronald C. '57 (SY) Ecumenical Commission; Fayetteville, NY Immaculate Conception Retired.
Bill, Thomas *c.s.c.* (FTW)[H] Notre Dame Congregation of Holy Cross, United States Province of Priests & Brothers.
Billac, Christopher A. *s.j.* '65 (GAL)[E] Houston, TX Strake Jesuit College Preparatory Inc.
Biller, Andrew *s.v.d.* '61 (MIL)[P] East Troy, WI Divine Word Missionaries Retired.
Biller, Rev. Msgr. Harold N. '70 (ALT) Retired.

Billett, Robert *c.m.f.* '57 (LA)[V] Rancho Dominguez, CA Dominguez Seminary Inc.
Billian, Rev. Msgr. Michael R. '84 (TOL) Toledo, OH Blessed Sacrament; Members; St. Agnes Deanery; Mareda, Inc.
Billiard, Don *o.f.m.* '83 (SFE)[H] Albuquerque, NM The Province of Our Lady of Guadalupe; [L] Albuquerque, NM Anselm Weber Fund; [L] Albuquerque, NM Roger Huser Fund.
Billiard, Don *o.f.m.* '83 (GLP) Pueblo of Acoma, NM San Esteban, Acoma Catholic Indian Mission; Laguna, NM St. Joseph.
Billing, Rev. Msgr. Jerome D. '71 (STL) Chancellor for Canonical Affairs; Promoter of Justice; Archdiocesan Archives; Priests' Purgatorial Society; St. Louis Roman Catholic Theological Seminaries, Inc.; [V] St. Louis, MO St. Louis City Catholic Church Real Estate Corporation; [V] St. Louis, MO St. Louis County Catholic Church Real Estate Corporation; [V] St. Louis, MO Franklin County Catholic Church Real Estate Corporation; [V] St. Louis, MO Jefferson County Catholic Church Real Estate Corporation; [V] St. Louis, MO Lincoln County Church Real Estate Corporation; [V] St. Louis, MO Perry County Catholic Church Real Estate Corporation; [V] St. Louis, MO St. Charles County Catholic Church Real Estate Corporation; [V] St. Louis, MO St. Francois County Catholic Church Real Estate Corporation; [V] St. Louis, MO Ste. Genevieve County Catholic Church Real Estate Corporation; [V] St. Louis, MO Warren County Catholic Church Real Estate Corporation; [V] St. Louis, MO Washington County Catholic Church Real Estate Corporation; St. Louis, MO Basilica of St. Louis, King of France; Defender of the Bond.
Billinger, James J. '83 (WCH) Wichita, KS Holy Savior; Presbyteral Council/College of Consultors; Building Commission.
Billings, Kit '95 (OM)[G] Omaha, NE Archbishop Bergan Mercy Medical Center.
Billman, George '72 (FAR) Retired.
Billote, Dindo '09 (JOL) Naperville, IL St. Raphael.
Billotte, Philip J. '66 (ROC) Retired.
Billotti, Joseph E. *s.j.* '63 (BUF)[N] Buffalo, NY Canisius Jesuit Community Inc.
Billy, Dennis J. *c.ss.r.* '80 (PH)[A] Wynnewood, PA Theological Seminary of St. Charles Borromeo, Overbrook.
Billy, Dennis *c.ss.r.* '80 (NY)[DD] Esopus, NY Redemptorist Priests and Brothers C.Ss.R. (Province of Baltimore).
Bilodeau, Florent '57 (MAN) Retired.
Bilodeau, Leopold J. '73 (BUR) Barre, VT St. Monica; Graniteville, VT St. Sylvester; Elected Members.
Bilodeau, Roger P. '65 (MAN) Nashua, NH St. Joseph The Worker Retired.
Bilot, James D. '92 (DET) Dearborn, MI Divine Child.
Biltz, Maximilian K. '10 (WCH) Wichita, KS Blessed Sacrament.
Bily, John C. '58 (VIC) Weimar, TX St. Michael; Judges.
Bily, Rev. Msgr. Lambert S. '63 (SAT) San Antonio, TX St. Clare.
Bilyk, Ivan '90 (STF) Willimantic, CT Protection of B.V.M.
Bilyk, Stepan '01 (PHU) Shamokin, PA Transfiguration of Our Lord; Shamokin, PA Patronage of the Mother of God.
Binaghi, Maurizio *m.c.c.j.* '99 (CHI)[W] Chicago, IL The Peace Corner, Incorporated; Chicago, IL St. Martin De Porres.
Binder, Mark J. '71 (SPC) Piedmont, MO St. Catherine of Siena.
Bindner, Charles J. '58 (L) Retired.
Binet, Scott *m.i.* '03 (MIL)[P] Milwaukee, WI St. Camillus Delegate House; [Y] Milwaukee, WI Servants of Saint Camillus Disaster Relief Services, Inc.
Bingham, John Marie *o.p.* '10 (OAK)[L] Oakland, CA Order of Preachers (Province of the Most Holy Name of Jesus – Western Dominican Province).
Bingham, John Marie *o.p.* '10 (SAC) Benicia, CA St. Dominic.
Binh Dinh, (Luke M.) Do *c.m.c.* '77 (SPC)[F] Carthage, MO Congregation of the Mother Coredemptrix, United States Assumption Province.
Biniek, Joseph P. '78 (ARL) Retired.
Biniszkiewicz, Rev. Msgr. Leonard E. '63 (BUF)[N] Lackawanna, NY Bishop Head Residence Retired.
Binlayo, Hermes *s.j.* '94 (RNO) Carlin, NV Sacred Heart.
Binlayo, Hermes *s.j.* '02 (RNO) Elko, NV St. Joseph's; Eureka, NV St. Brendan's; Wells, NV St. Thomas Aquinas.
Binsfeld, Douglas '98 (SFS) Florence, SD Blessed Sacrament; Henry, SD St. Henry.
Binsfeld, Steven '79 (SCL) Alexandria, MN St. Mary's; Deans.
Binta, Robert '91 (PHX) Phoenix, AZ St. Paul Roman Catholic Parish.
Biondi, Lawrence H. *s.j.* '70 (STL)[C] Saint Louis, MO Saint Louis University; [O] St. Louis, MO Jesuit Community Corporation at Saint Louis University – Jesuit Hall; [C] Saint Louis University.
Birarelli, Carl A. '58 (CIN) Retired.
Birch, Donald G. '67 (PH) Fallsington, PA St. Joseph the Worker.
Birch, Keith L. '71 (DUB) Monticello, IA Sacred Heart.
Birch, Rev. Msgr. Thomas J. '59 (ALN) Shillington, PA St. John Baptist de la Salle; Douglassville, PA Immaculate Conception Retired.
Bircumshaw, Rev. Msgr. Colin F. '75 (SLC) Vicar General, Vicar for Clergy and Moderator of the Curia; College of Consultors; Finance Council; Board of Directors; Priests' Personnel Board; Board For Ongoing Formation of Priests.
Bird, Stephen J. '76 (OKL) Oklahoma City, OK Church of the Epiphany of the Lord; Special Assignment; Worship and Spiritual Life, Office of.
Bird, Steven '00 (PEO) Rantoul, IL St. Malachy.
Birdsall, Anthony J. '60 (GB) Regional Vicars Retired.
Birdsall, Hugh G. *s.d.s.* '62 (MIL)[P] Greendale, WI; [B] Hales Corners, WI Sacred Heart School of Theology.
Bireley, Robert L. *s.j.* '64 (CHI)[C] Chicago, IL Jesuit Community at Loyola University Chicago.
Biren, Timothy E. '99 (WIN)[I] Mankato, MN St. Thomas More Newman Center, Minnesota State University; Pathways TEC (Teens Encounter Christ).
Birge, Rev. Msgr. George D. '58 (BGP) Retired.
Biriruka, Ernest '81 (MIA) Miramar, FL Blessed John XXIII Church; Non–Incardinated Priests.
Birk, John G. '63 (SPK) Pasco, WA St. Patrick Retired.
Birk, John W. '70 (L) Byzantine Rite Faithful Retired.
Birk, John '63 (SPK) Retired.
Birkel, John B. '96 (LIN) Fairbury, NE St. Michael's.
Birket, Dwight J. '72 (WCH) Lindsborg, KS St. Bridget of Sweden; McPherson, KS St. Joseph; Presbyteral Council/College of Consultors.
Birkle, Rev. Msgr. Walter A. '58 (NY) Retired.
Birkmaier, James '68 (GF) Clerical Benefit Association Retired.
Birmingham, Kevin M. '97 (CHI) Chicago, IL Maternity of the Blessed Virgin Mary.
Birmingham, Robert F. '93 (HRT) Retired.
Birney, Timothy P. '98 (DET) Office of Priestly Vocations.
Biron, Gerald *m.s.* '60 (HRT)[L] Hartford, CT Missionaries of LaSalette.
Biron, Robert G. '74 (MAN) New London, NH Our Lady of Fatima; Priest Personnel Board; Presbyteral Council; College of Consultors.
Biroschak, Robert V. '93 (LA) Retired.
Biroschak, Robert V. '93 (BGP) Judges.
Birungyi, George '75 (RCK) Special Assignment; [D] Elgin, IL Provena Saint Joseph Hospital.
Bisaillon, Rene *m.s.* '59 (HON) Koloa, HI St. Raphael Retired.
Bisbee, Burnell B. *s.j.* '75 (OM)[J] Omaha, NE Jesuit Community at Creighton University.
Bischof, Donald R. '83 (PIT) Fenelton, PA St. John the Evangelist.
Bischoff, Albert J. *s.j.* '56 (CIN)[N] Cincinnati, OH Jesuit Community at Xavier University; [R] Cincinnati, OH Xavier University Dorothy Day Center for Faith & Justice.
Bisharat, Rt. Rev. George Said '93 (NTN) Covina, CA Annunciation Mission.
Bishop, Clifton E. '98 (ALN)[H] Bethlehem, PA Holy Family Manor of Catholic Senior Housing and Health Care Services, Inc.; Allentown, PA Our Lady Help of Christians; Assistants.
Bishop, E. Louis *s.j.* '64 (PHX)[B] Phoenix, AZ Brophy College Preparatory; [F] Phoenix, AZ Society of Jesus.
Bishop, Marc J. '01 (BO) Lowell, MA Ste. Marguerite d'Youville; Lowell, MA St. Rita; Navy Reserve Chaplains.
Bishop, Rev. Msgr. Patrick A. '74 (ATL) Marietta, GA Church of the Transfiguration.
Bishop, Robert *c.m.f.* '71 (LA)[V] Rancho Dominguez, CA Dominguez Seminary Inc.
Bishop, Robert (OLL) Defender of the Bond; Promoter of Justice.
Bishop, Thomas G. '70 (Y) Canton, OH St. Anthony/All Saints Parish.
Bishop, Thomas '75 (CHI) Barrington, IL St. Anne.
Bisig, Josef *f.s.s.p.* '77 (LIN) Denton, NE; [A] Denton, NE Our Lady of Guadalupe Seminary.
Bisignano, Joseph '81 (NY) Yorktown Heights, NY St. Patrick.
Bisoffi, Joseph L. *m.i.* '72 (MIL) Milwaukee, WI; [Y] Wauwatosa, WI St. Camillus Communities, Inc. – House II.
Bissinger, Karl C. '05 (FR) Secretary to the Bishop; Vocations.
Bisson, Andrew R. *o.f.m.* '93 (PRT)[I] Kennebunk, ME St. Anthony's Friary; Kennebunkport, ME.
Bisson, Joseph *s.v.d.* '63 (FgM) Techny, IL.
Bisson, Roger *m.afr.* '55 (FgM)[N] St. Petersburg, FL Missionaries of Africa; Washington, DC; Washington, DC MISSIONARIES OF AFRICA Retired.
Bissonette, James B. '88 (DUL) Duluth, MN St. James; Vicar General; Diocesan Corporate Board; Cemeteries; Promoter of Justice; College of Consultors.
Bissot, Robert H. '57 (GLD) Ossineke, MI St. Gabriel; Harrisville, MI St. Anne; Harrisville, MI St. Raphael; Ossineke, MI St. Catherine; Holy Childhood Pontifical Association; Propagation of the Faith.
Biswas, Tony *ss.cc.* (FR)[F] Fairhaven National Center of the Enthronement.
Biszek, Rev. Msgr. Robert J. '65 (ALN) Bethlehem, PA Holy Infancy.
Bit–shing Chiu, Abraham *o.f.m.* '90 (MET) Chinese Apostolate; New Brunswick, NJ St. Ladislaus.
Bitanga, Rev. Msgr. Fred A. '64 (SFR) San Francisco, CA St. Monica Retired.
Bitchapogu, Anthony '92 (KAL) Dorr, MI St. Stanislaus.
Bitsko, Daniel J. '65 (PSC) Retired.
Bittel, Patrick M. '82 (OWN) Philpot, KY St. William; Knottsville, KY St. Lawrence; Deans; Priests' Council.
Bitterman, John L. *s.s.* '69 (STO) On Duty Outside the Diocese.
Bitterman, John L. *s.s.* '69 (BAL)[Q] Baltimore Society of St. Sulpice, Province of the United States; [M] Baltimore, MD St. Charles Villa.
Bittmenn, David J. '94 (SLC) Orem, UT St. Francis of Assisi LLC 221.
Bittner, Gregory T. '85 (BIR) Members; Tribunal; Birmingham, AL St. Francis Xavier; Priests'/ Presbyteral Council; Diocesan College of Vicars.
Bittner, Wayne W. '64 (MIL) Retired.
Bitz, Al M. '69 (FAR) Jamestown, ND St. Margaret Alacoque; Jamestown, ND St. James Basilica of Jamestown; Jamestown, ND St. Michael; Jamestown, ND St. Mathias Church of Windsor; [I] Jamestown, ND Jamestown College; Deanery 7.
Biven, L. Russell '57 (MOB)[E] Mobile, AL Little Sisters of the Poor, Home For the Aged, Inc. Retired.
Biven, Louis Russell '57 (MOB)[J] Mobile, AL Catholic University, Friends of Retired.
Bixenman, Joseph E. '72 (AMA)[I] Amarillo, TX Roman Catholic Diocese of Amarillo Deposit and Loan Fund; Hereford, TX San Jose.
Bixenman, Rev. Msgr. Joseph '72 (AMA) College of Consultors; Presbyteral Council.
Bizaca, Mate '73 (LA) Los Angeles, CA St. Anthony.
Bizzotto, Giovanni *c.s.* '72 (LA)[B] Sun Valley, CA Scalabrini House of Discernment (Seminary).
Bjerke, Wade E. '10 (SFR) Redwood City, CA St. Pius.
Bjorum, James L. '76 (DET) St. Clair Shores, MI Our Lady of Hope; Judges.
Blacet, Rev. Msgr. William J. '46 (KC) Kansas City, MO Our Lady of Good Counsel; Censor Librorum.
Blach, Leo M. '53 (DEN) Retired.
Black, Frank A. '80 (BRK) Brooklyn, NY St. Laurence.
Black, James P. '88 (COL) Delaware, OH St. Mary.
Blackall, John C. '51 (HRT) Appointed Retired.
Blackall, Randall L. '54 (HRT) Retired.
Blackburn, Michael *o.f.m.* '86 (SPK) Spokane, WA St. Francis of Assisi; Members.
Blackwell, Edward A. '76 (HBG) On Duty Outside the Diocese.
Blackwell, Edward A. '76 (MIA)[C] St. Thomas University.
Blackwell, Michael J. '73 (WDC) Burtonsville, MD Resurrection Parish Retired.
Blackwood, Wallace E. '67 (BO) Nahant, MA St. Thomas Aquinas; Swampscott, MA St. John the Evangelist.
Bladt, Joel S. *s.t.* '61 (SAV) Blakely, GA Holy Family.
Blaes, Donald A. '56 (BEL) Retired.
Blaes, James F. *c.s.c.* '55 (FTW)[H] Holy Cross House Retired.
Blaes, Paul '51 (KC) Retired.
Blaeser, Donald *o.f.m.* '70 (SFD) Quincy, IL St. Francis Solanus; [K] Quincy, IL St. Francis Solanus Friary.
Blaettler, James R. *s.j.* '80 (SFR) San Francisco, CA St. Ignatius; [N] San Francisco, CA Loyola House Jesuit Community.
Blaha, Nicholas (KCK)[B] Topeka, KS Hayden High School.
Blaha, Nicholas '11 (KCK) Topeka, KS Most Pure Heart of Mary.
Blahnik, Jason J. '09 (GB) Wabeno, WI St. Ambrose; Lakewood, WI St. Mary of the Lake.
Blain, Lionel A. '54 (PRO) Retired.
Blaine, James E. '77 (SLC) American Fork, UT Saint Peter LLC 242; American Fork, UT Utah State Prison; Correctional Institution Ministry.
Blaine, Philip *o.f.m.conv.* '63 (NY)[DD] Staten Island, NY St. Francis Friary.
Blair, Guy *s.c.j* (SFS) Chamberlain, SD St. James.
Blair, Rev. Msgr. Raymond O. '60 (MAN) Retired.
Blais, George '90 (ORG) Irvine, CA St. Thomas More.
Blais, Robert L. '63 (PRO) Retired.
Blais, Roland O. '44 (MAN) Retired.
Blake, Andrew P. '63 (RVC) Sag Harbor, NY St. Andrew's Retired.
Blake, Carlyle R. *c.ss.r.* '62 (NY)[DD] New York, NY Redemptorist Priests and Brothers, C.Ss.R.
Blake, David D. *o.f.m.* '95 (BUF)[N] St. Bonaventure, NY St. Bonaventure Friary.
Blake, Gary W. '08 (PEO) Mendota, IL SS. Peter and Paul; Mendota, IL Holy Cross.

Blake, Jerry W. '00 (DUB) Traer, IA St. Paul; Waterloo, IA St. Mary of Mt. Carmel; La Porte City, IA Sacred Heart.
Blake, John Vincent *o.p.* '51 (CHI)[N] Chicago, IL St. Pius V Priory.
Blake, Lawrence R. '99 (STP) Air Force Reserve Chaplains; Waconia, MN St. Joseph.
Blake, Peter M. '84 (STL) St. Louis, MO Our Lady of Sorrows.
Blake, Philip C. *s.j.* '61 (SJ)[M] Los Gatos, CA Sacred Heart Jesuit Center.
Blake, Richard *s.j.* '69 (BO)[U] Newton, MA The Jesuit Community at Boston College.
Blake, Robert '77 (SR) Yountville, CA St. Joan of Arc.
Blake, William B. '63 (SCR)[M] Dunmore, PA Villa St. Joseph Retired.
Blakely, Leonard J. '80 (WIL) Galena, MD St. Dennis.
Blakely, Paige '64 (ORL) Judges Retired.
Blaker, John R. '96 (OAK) Richmond, CA St. David of Wales; Presbyteral Council.
Blanch, Jose Maria *s.f.* '51 (SFE) Santa Cruz, NM Holy Cross.
Blanchard, David *o.carm.* '87 (JOL)[L] Darien Carmelite Provincial Office.
Blanchard, David *o.carm.* '87 (WDC)[B] Washington, DC Whitefriars Hall.
Blanchard, Donald V. '69 (BR) Retired.
Blanchard, Peter R. *s.m.* '67 (WDC)[O] Washington, DC Marist Center.
Blanchet, Leo '86 (MOB) Retired.
Blanchett, Edward H. (TR) Lakewood, NJ St. Mary of the Lake; Cursillo; Riverside, NJ The Church of Jesus, the Good Shepherd, Riverside, N.J.
Blanchette, Melvin C. *s.s.* '73 (WDC)[A] Washington, DC Theological College of the Catholic University of America.
Blanchette, Melvin C. *s.s.* '67 (BAL)[Q] Baltimore Society of St. Sulpice, Province of the United States.
Blanchette, Oliver (Robert) *a.a.* '44 (WOR)[N] Worcester, MA Assumptionists (Augustinians of the Assumption).
Blanchfield, David W. '82 (BGP) Norwalk, CT St. Jerome; Members of the Clergy Personnel Committee; Presbyteral Council; Parochial Examiners.
Blanco, Adalberto (LA) Carpinteria, CA St. Joseph.
Blanco, Gildardo '09 (SJ) San Jose, CA Holy Cross.
Blanco, Gonzalo *o.s.b.* '92 (BIS)[A] Richardton, ND Assumption Abbey; Richardton, ND Assumption Abbey.
Blanco, Ignacio A. *c.m.f.* '51 (SAT) San Antonio, TX Immaculate Heart of Mary.
Blanco, Ildefonso *o.s.a.* '64 (MGZ) Aguada, PR St. Francis of Assisi.
Blanco, John *s.d.b.* '64 (NY)[DD] New Rochelle, NY Salesian Provincial House.
Blanco, Jose A. '77 (LA) On Sick Leave.
Blanco, Joseph '84 (DEN) Retired.
Blanco, Leandro '04 (MIL)[Y] Milwaukee, WI St. Camillus Communities, Inc. – House I.
Blanco, Miguel A. '02 (MIA) Miami, FL St. Brendan.
Blanco, Telesforo R. *o.s.a.* '60 (BEA) Port Arthur, TX Our Lady of Guadalupe.
Blanco, Vincent '90 (ANC) Anchorage, AK Our Lady of Guadalupe; Notaries.
Bland, Thomas A. '74 (SAC) Carmichael, CA St. John the Evangelist.
Blanda, William C. '91 (LAF) Abbeville, LA St. Mary Magdalen.
Blandon, Francisco '96 (SR) Napa, CA St. John the Baptist.
Blaney, Dennis J. '58 (GRY) Sharing Meadows Retired.
Blaney, James *o.m.i.* '65 (JUN) Sitka, AK St. Gregory of Nazianzen.
Blaney, Robert J. '07 (BO) South Boston, MA Gate of Heaven; South Boston, MA St. Brigid.
Blaney, Robert M. '92 (BO) Weymouth, MA St. Jerome; Presbyteral Council.
Blangiardi, B. Jeffrey *s.j.* '86 (BO)[U] Boston The Society of Jesus of New England–Provincial Offices.
Blangiardi, B. Jeffrey *s.j.* '86 (SD) La Jolla, CA Veterans Administration Hospital.
Blank, Matthew '07 (SAC) Truckee, CA Assumption of the Blessed Virgin Mary.
Blank, William H. '87 (NO) Garyville, LA St. Hubert.
Blankenhorn, Bernard *o.p.* '06 (OAK)[L] Oakland Order of Preachers (Province of the Most Holy Name of Jesus – Western Dominican Province).
Blankinship, Calvin L. '96 (B) Fruitland, ID Corpus Christi Catholic Church; Deans; College of Consultors.
Blantz, James R. *c.s.c.* '59 (FTW)[H] Holy Cross House.
Blantz, James R. *c.s.c.* '59 (PHX)[F] Phoenix, AZ Holy Cross Congregation/Casa Santa Cruz.
Blantz, Thomas E. *c.s.c.* '60 (FTW)[B] University of Notre Dame Du Lac; [H] Notre Dame, IN Holy Cross Community, Corby Hall, University of Notre Dame; [H] Notre Dame, IN Congregation of Holy Cross, United States Province of Priests & Brothers.
Blas, Mario W. '83 (MO) DEPARTMENT OF VETERANS AFFAIRS HOSPITALS AND CHAPLAINS.
Blasco, Ignacio '62 (MIA) Retired.
Blaser, John R. '64 (TOL) Retired.
Blasich, Bernard '67 (MIL)[P] Milwaukee, WI St. Camillus Delegate House.
Blasick, George *c.ss.r.* '01 (WIL) Seaford, DE Our Lady of Lourdes.
Blaska, John A. '53 (DET) Retired.
Blasko, Joseph A. '99 (GLD) Beaver Island, MI Holy Cross; Archivist.
Blasko, Zvonko '82 (CLV) Cleveland, OH St. Paul.
Blastic, Michael *o.f.m.* '75 (WDC)[B] Silver Spring, MD Holy Name College.
Blaszczak, Gerald R. *s.j.* '79 (BGP)[V] Fairfield, CT Fairfield University.
Blaszkowski, Andy '08 (STA) Middleburg, FL St. Luke.
Blaszkowski, Remek '05 (STA) Jacksonville, FL Holy Family.
Blaszkowski, Remigiusz '05 (STA) Seminarians; Vocations.
Blattner, Joseph H. '58 (STL) Retired.
Blau, Thomas *o.p.* '99 (COL) Columbus, OH St. Patrick.
Blaufuss, Tony '58 (KCK) Retired.
Blauvelt, Robert '59 (BRK)[R] Douglaston, NY Bishop Mugavero Residence Retired.
Blay, Rev. Msgr. Roberto Garcia '86 (PCE) Mercedita, PR Church of the Resurrection; Vicar General; Diocesan Consultors; Diocesan Board of Administration; Administrator; Committee for Community Planning; Episcopal Vicar for Diocesan Administration.
Blazak, Camillus '51 (BIR) Signal Mountain, TN Retired.
Blazejewski, Richard W. '74 (BUF) Perry, NY St. Isidore.
Blazek, Camilius '51 (KNX)[E] Signal Mountain, TN Alexian Village of Tennessee.
Blazek, David J. '97 (DET) Holly, MI St. Rita; Presbyteral Council; Archdiocesan Vicars.
Blazek, Eugene '76 (HON) On Duty Outside the Diocese.
Blazek, James F. '79 (CHI) Schiller Park, IL St. Maria Goretti.
Blazek, John J. *c.s.c.* '67 (FTW)[H] Holy Cross House.
Blazek, John *c.s.c.* '67 (CLV)[D] Gates Mills, OH Gilmour Academy.
Blazewicz, William J. '59 (LC) Retired.
Blazine, Rev. Msgr. James A. '62 (BEL) Retired.
Blazovich, Victor M. '00 (SPK) Spokane Valley, WA St. Mary.
Bleboo, Lawrence T. '79 (MO) Army Reserve Chaplains.
Blecha, Rev. Msgr. Charles A. '40 (LC) Retired.
Blee, Edward C. *s.m.* '55 (SFR)[N] San Francisco, CA Marist Center of the West Retired.
Bleem, Gerald *o.f.m.* '82 (JOL)[L] Joliet, IL St. John the Baptist Friary; Joliet, IL St. John the Baptist.
Bleeser, Peter '67 (NY)[HH] White Plains, NY Deutschsprachige Katholische Gemeinde New York–German Speaking Catholic Congregation New York.
Bleich, Rev. Msgr. Russell M. '60 (DUB) On Special or Other Archdiocesan Assignment; College of Consultors; Building Commission; Pastoral Council; Ex Officio Members; Vinton, IA St. Mary; Walker, IA St. Mary; Vinton, IA Sacred Heart.
Bleichner, Howard P. '67 (PIT) On Duty Outside the Diocese.
Bleichner, Howard P. *s.s.* '67 (BAL)[Q] Baltimore Society of St. Sulpice, Province of the United States Retired.
Bleichner, Howard P. '67 (SFR)[A] Menlo Park, CA St. Patrick Seminary and University.
Bleiler, William James '66 (CAM) Leesburg, NJ New Jersey State Medium Security Prison Retired.
Blenker, Ambrose J. '62 (LC) Retired.
Blenkle, Joseph A. '90 (NY) Valhalla, NY Holy Name of Jesus.
Blessin, Thomas C. *s.j.* '63 (NY)[DD] New York, NY Murray–Weigel Hall.
Blessing, Gerald J. '05 (STL) Chesterfield, MO Incarnate Word.
Blessing, Howard '76 (LAF) Lafayette, LA Holy Cross.
Blessing, Loren '81 (FRS) Fresno, CA St. Anthony of Padua.
Blessinger, James '64 (EVN) Evansville, IN Corpus Christi.
Blewett, John Patrick '09 (MAD) Sauk City, WI St. Norbert.
Blicharski, Lukasz '11 (MET) Metuchen, NJ Cathedral of St. Francis of Assisi.
Blicharski, Michael *o.cist.* '95 (CHI)[N] Willow Springs, IL Cistercian Fathers, Our Lady Mother of the Church Polish Mission; Argo, IL Our Lady, Mother of the Church Polish Mission.
Blicharz, Dariusz Piotr '91 (BRK) Diocesan Judges; Brooklyn, NY St. Catharine of Alexandria; Attorneys and Counselors at Canon Law.
Blick, Ned J. '92 (WCH) On Duty Outside the Diocese.
Blick, Ned '02 (MO) Army Chaplains.
Blick, Ned '92 (OG) U.S. Army Headquarters.
Blickhan, Donald '74 (SFD) Quincy, IL Illinois Veterans' Home.
Blind, Thomas F. '81 (NEW) Bloomfield, NJ Church of St. Thomas the Apostle; [O] Union, NJ Kean University.
Bline, G. David '98 (CLV) Akron, OH St. Francis de Sales.
Bliss, Rev. Msgr. Michael C. '91 (PEO)[H] East Peoria, IL Saint Francis Medical Center; Vicariates and Vicars; [I] Peoria, IL Saint Clare Home.
Blissert, Richard *c.ss.r.* '56 (FgM) Baltimore Province.
Bliszcz, Michael '87 (SJP) Grand Rapids, MI St. Michael's; On Assignment Outside the Diocese; Presbyters.
Bliven, Edmond '50 (P) Retired.
Blocher, James F. *c.s.b.* '75 (GAL)[E] Houston, TX St. Thomas High School.
Block, John G. '63 (PMB) Retired.
Block, John '63 (ORG) Retired.
Blocklinger, James L. '66 (DUB) Retired.
Blomberg, John F. '59 (STL) Retired.
Blondell, Robert H. '66 (DET) Retired.
Blonski, Joachim '92 (GLP) Show Low, AZ St. Rita; St. Johns, AZ St. John the Baptist; Presbyteral Council; Diocesan Consultors.
Blonski, Joachim '92 (GLP) Priests' Retirement Board.
Blood, Francis J. *o.s.f.s.* (CAM) Camden, NJ The Parish of the Cathedral of the Immaculate Conception, Camden, N.J.
Blood, Rev. Msgr. Francis X. '79 (STL) St. Louis, MO Our Lady of Providence; Holy Childhood, Pontifical Association; Latin American Apostolate, Archdiocese of St. Louis; Pan y Amor; Society for the Propagation of the Faith; New York, NY A. The Pontifical Society for the Propagation of the Faith.
Bloom, Phillip A. '71 (SEA) Monroe, WA St. Mary of the Valley.
Bloomer, Matthew A. '99 (LA)[W] Los Angeles, CA Prelature of the Holy Cross and Opus Dei.
Bloomer, Matthew (POD) Los Angeles.
Bloomfield, Andrew '05 (DET) Absent on Leave.
Bloshchynskyy, Ihor '07 (PHU) Philadelphia, PA St. Josaphat's.
Blostic, Leonard *t.o.r.* '63 (ALT)[G] Hollidaysburg, PA St. Joseph Friary Retired.
Blotsky, Hugo L. *o.s.b.* '88 (BIS)[A] Richardton, ND Assumption Abbey.
Blotsky, Hugo L. *o.s.b.* '88 (CHY) Thermopolis, WY St. Francis.
Blottman, William P. '65 (FR) Retired.
Blount, Anthony *s.o.l.t.* '96 (CC)[G] Robstown, TX Society of Our Lady of the Most Holy Trinity; Robstown, TX St. Anthony.
Blount, Anthony *s.o.l.t.* '96 (CHY)[D] Saint Stephens, WY St. Stephens Mission.
Blout, Daniel L. '86 (GBG) Kittanning, PA St. Mary, Our Lady of Guadalupe; Yatesboro, PA St. Mary.
Blowers, Leslie F. *m.m.* '63 (CIN)[N] Cincinnati, OH The Catholic Foreign Mission Society of America, Inc.
Blowey, David *o.f.m.conv.* '87 (BAL)[Q] Ellicott City Order of Friars Minor Conventual.
Blubaugh, Homer D. '69 (COL) London Correctional Institution; Columbus, OH St. Agnes; Columbus, OH St. Aloysius.
Blue, Peter W. *o.s.b.* '70 (PAT)[N] Newton St. Paul's Abbey; Newton, NJ St. Paul's Abbey.
Bluejacket, David '88 (DEN) Arvada, CO Spirit of Christ.
Bluett, Anthony '69 (ORL) Lake Wales, FL Holy Spirit.
Bluett, James K. '67 (PT) On Leave of Absence.
Bluett, John J. '63 (ORL) Winter Springs, FL St. Stephen.
Blum, John '96 (SP) St. Pete Beach, FL St. John Vianney; Vocations Office; Personnel Board.
Blum, Stephen J. '76 (TOL) Lima, OH St. Charles Borromeo; Delphos, OH St. Patrick.
Blum, William G. *c.s.c.* '65 (FTW)[H] Notre Dame, IN Columba Hall; [H] Notre Dame Congregation of Holy Cross, United States Province of Priests & Brothers; [H] Holy Cross House.
Blume, David '04 (STP) Oak Grove, MN St. Patrick.
Blumenfeld, Donald E. '79 (NEW)[A] South Orange, NJ Immaculate Conception Seminary School of Theology; [B] Seton Hall University; Censores Librorum.
Blumeyer, A. James *s.j.* '63 (KC) Kansas City, MO St. Francis Xavier; [J] Kansas City, MO Rockhurst Jesuit Community.
Blute, Robert H. '56 (BO) Senior Priests. Retired.
Bly, Walter J. '64 (FTW)[C] South Bend, IN Saint Joseph's High School Retired.
Blyman, Robert Y. '70 (RVC) Serving Outside the Diocese.
Blyskosz, Joseph J. '95 (FR) Awaiting Assignment; [F] Fall River, MA Priests' Hostel.
Boachie, Rev. Msgr. John (NY) Congers, NY St. Paul.
Boackle, Paul H. '89 (SAM) Retired.
Boateng–Mensah, Anthony (VIC) Victoria, TX St. Mary's.
Boateng–Mensah, Samanhyia '73 (MO) DEPARTMENT OF VETERANS AFFAIRS HOSPITALS AND CHAPLAINS.
Boateng–Mensah, Semanhyia '73 (PH) Coatesville, PA St. Cecilia; Coatesville, PA Veterans Administration Medical Center.
Bobal, Rev. Msgr. Joseph K. '63 (E) Retired.
Bobbin, Kevin J. '05 (ALN) Schuylkill Haven, PA St. Ambrose.

Bober, Charles S. '72 (PIT) Cranberry Township, PA St. Kilian; [Q] Pittsburgh, PA Priests' Benefit Plan of the Diocese of Pittsburgh; College of Consultors; Priest Council.
Bober, Marjan L. '63 (CAM) Retired.
Boberek, Aurelius *o.s.b.* '57 (IND)[K] Saint Meinrad, IN St. Meinrad Archabbey.
Bobrek, Edwin *o.f.m.* '51 (NY)[DD] New York Franciscan Province of the Immaculate Conception.
Boccaccio, Michael A. '71 (BGP) Norwalk, CT St. Philip; Judges.
Boccafola, Rev. Msgr. Kenneth '63 (RVC) Serving Outside the Diocese.
Boccali, Ronald *p.i.m.e.* '60 (COL) Heath, OH St. Leonard Retired.
Boccardi, Raymond C. '52 (PIT) Retired.
Boccio, Rev. Msgr. Charles P. '61 (BRK) Astoria, NY Immaculate Conception Retired.
Bochanski, Philip G. *c.o.* '99 (PH) Philadelphia, PA St. Francis Xavier; [Z] Philadelphia, PA Sister Servants of the Holy Spirit of Perpetual Adoration (S.Sp-.S.A.P.); [Y] Philadelphia, PA The Philadelphia Congregation of The Oratory of St. Philip Neri.
Bochenek, Joseph G. '71 (BAL) Baltimore, MD St. Brigid.
Bochicchio, Rev. Msgr. Paul L. '71 (PAT) Nutley, NJ Holy Family; [Q] Totowa, NJ The Association of the Marian Apostolate of Mercy, Inc.; Presbyteral Council.
Bochnak, Tomasz '11 (PMB) Boca Raton, FL St. Joan of Arc.
Bochnak, Zenon A. '85 (MO) On Duty Outside the Diocese; Air Force Chaplains.
Bocian, Rev. Msgr. Ronald C. '72 (ALN) Shenandoah, PA St. Mary Magdalen; Shenandoah, PA Annunciation; Shenandoah, PA St. Casimir; Shenandoah, PA St. George; Shenandoah, PA Our Lady of Mt. Carmel; Shenandoah, PA St. Stanislaus; Father Walter Ciszek Prayer League, Inc. (The); Shenandoah, PA St. Stephen.
Bocianowski, Thaddeus Nicholas '71 (BUF) Buffalo, NY St. John Kanty; Buffalo, NY St. Stanislaus.
Bock, Lawrence R. '62 (HRT) Consultors – Canon 1742; Newington, CT Church of the Holy Spirit; College of Consultors; Episcopal Vicars; Ex Officio Members.
Bockskopf, Richard J. '70 (STL) Maryland Heights, MO Holy Spirit.
Boczek, Zenon *s.d.s.* '96 (MET) Port Murray, NJ St. Theodore.
Boczek, Zenon *s.d.s.* '96 (NEW)[L] Verona, NJ The Salvatorian Fathers.
Bodah, Henry J. '78 (PRO) Providence, RI St. Joseph; [R] Providence, RI Brown University.
Bodde, Frederick A. '53 (DET) Retired.
Bodden, Charles J. *o.s.a.* '78 (FgM) Olympia Fields, IL Province of Our Mother of Good Counsel (Midwestern).
Boddie, James R. '78 (STA) Orange Park, FL St. Catherine's; Scouts; Multicultural Ministry.
Bodensteiner, Peter C. '45 (DUB) Retired.
Bodin, Daniel J. '05 (STP) Graduate Studies.
Bodnar, Edward W. *s.j.* '52 (WDC)[O] Washington, DC The Jesuit Community at Georgetown University Retired.
Bodo, Murray L. *o.f.m.* '64 (CIN)[N] Cincinnati, OH Pleasant Street Friary; [U] Cincinnati, OH Franciscans Network.
Bodziak, Charles F. '67 (ALT) St. Michael, PA St. Michael's.
Bodzioch, Michael '11 (DEN) Denver, CO Cathedral Basilica of the Immaculate Conception.
Bodziony, Ralph A. '58 (CLV) Cleveland, OH St. John Cantius Retired.
Boeckman, Scott A. '03 (OKL) Woodward, OK St. Peter's.
Boedy, Thomas *s.j.* '70 (STP) Shakopee, MN St. Mark; Shakopee, MN Church of St. Mary; Shakopee, MN St. Mark; Shakopee, MN St. Mary of the Purification.
Boeff, Dismas *o.s.b.* '76 (CLV)[N] Cleveland Benedictine Order of Cleveland.
Boeglin, John '78 (EVN) Jasper, IN Holy Family; Rural Life Conference.
Boehling, Michael G. '06 (RIC) Vicar for Vocations; Bishop's Administrative Advisory Council.
Boehm, Dustin M. '11 (IND) Indianapolis, IN St. Monica Catholic Church, Indianapolis, Inc.; Richmond State Hospital.
Boehm, Rev. Msgr. James A. '58 (STU) Retired.
Boehm, Michael J. '75 (CHI) Chicago, IL Blessed Sacrament.
Boehm, Michael P. '94 (STL) Washington, MO Our Lady of Lourdes.
Boehman, John *o.f.m.* '59 (CIN)[N] Cincinnati St. Francis Seraph Friary Retired.
Boehme, Arnold *o.c.d.* '68 (MIL)[P] Milwaukee Provincial Offices – Discalced Carmelites.
Boehme, Ferdinand J. '97 (LIN) Wymore, NE St. Mary's.
Boehme, Walter E. *s.j.* '70 (MIL)[P] Milwaukee, WI Arrupe House Jesuit Community.
Boehning, Rev. Msgr. John A. '62 (NY) New York, NY St. Thomas More.
Boekelman, Timothy J. '77 (SC) Carroll, IA Holy Spirit; [C] Carroll, IA St. Anthony Regional Hospital; St. Anthony Regional Hospital; Carroll, IA St. Mary's.
Boel, Joseph H. *s.j.* '59 (DET)[K] Clarkston, MI Colombiere Center.
Boenzi, Joseph *s.d.b.* '79 (OAK)[L] Berkeley Salesians of Don Bosco; [A] Berkeley, CA Dominican School of Philosophy and Theology.
Boes, Clair L. '65 (SC) Retired.
Boes, Edward *s.a.* '98 (NY)[DD] Garrison Franciscan Friars of the Atonement, Minister General Office.
Boes, Marvin '62 (SC) Retired.
Boes, Steven '85 (OM) Boys Town, NE Immaculate Conception B.V.M.
Boesel, Rev. Msgr. James E. '54 (RVC) Hicksville, NY Our Lady of Mercy Retired.
Boettcher, John '91 (SR) On Duty Outside the Diocese.
Boettcher, R. John '91 (COL)[A] Columbus, OH Pontifical College Josephinum.
Boettner, David '94 (KNX) Moderator of the Curia; Moderator of the Curia; Presbyteral Council; Knoxville, TN Cathedral of the Sacred Heart of Jesus; Diocesan Finance Council; Vicars General; Diocesan Consultors; [J] Members of the Corporation.
Boever, Richard *c.ss.r.* '73 (STL)[O] Liguori, MO Liguori Mission House/Redemptorists.
Boever, Richard *c.ss.r.* '73 (PH) Philadelphia, PA St. Peter the Apostle.
Boff, Bernard J. '61 (TOL) Mission of Accompaniment Retired.
Bogacki, Phillip A. '08 (MIL) Brookfield, WI St. John Vianney.
Bogacz, John A. '09 (TR) Toms River, NJ St. Justin.
Bogan, Robert F. '58 (SY) Retired.
Bogda, Rev. Archpriest Dennis M. '67 (PBR) Munhall, PA St. John the Baptist Cathedral; Consultors; Vocations; Revitalization and Renewal Commission.
Bogdan, Rev. Msgr. Leonard A. '60 (KAL) Sun City West, AZ Retired.
Bogdan, Palka *s.d.s.* '92 (NEW)[L] Verona, NJ The Salvatorian Fathers.
Bogert, James '67 (RVC) Retired.
Boghossian, G. Scott '02 (PSC) Linden, NJ St. George's; Respect Life.
Bognanno, Rev. Msgr. Frank E. (DM) Des Moines, IA Christ the King.
Bogniak, Rev. Msgr. Casimir A. '57 (E) Corry, PA St. Thomas The Apostle; Corry, PA St. Elizabeth Retired.
Boguslawski, Steven C. *o.p.* '87 (DET)[T] Washington, DC Operations Office; Consultants.
Boguslawski, Steven C. *o.p.* '87 (WDC)[B] Washington, DC Dominican House of Studies; New York, NY.
Bogusz, Dennis A. '79 (GBG) Mount Pleasant, PA Frick Community Health Center; Connellsville, PA Highlands Hospital & Health Center; Connellsville, PA St. John the Evangelist.
Bohan, Philip *o.f.m.cap.* (NY) New York, NY Good Shepherd.
Bohlin, Rev. Msgr. Thomas G. '97 (POD)[II] New York, NY Prelature of the Holy Cross and Opus Dei; Regional Vicar for the United States; New York.
Bohn, John '97 (JKS) Starkville, MS St. Joseph; [H] Starkville, MS Mississippi State University Catholic Student Association; Approved Advocate and Auditors; Continuing Formation Committee.
Bohner, Allan G. '98 (SR) Retired.
Bohnert, Edward A. '85 (SFR) Belmont, CA St. Mark.
Bohnsack, David *m.c.c.j.* '94 (CHI)[N] Chicago, IL Comboni Missionaries Theologate (M.C.C.J.), Verona Fathers.
Bohnsak, Christopher G. '09 (TOL) Findlay, OH St. Michael the Archangel.
Bohorquez, Carlos M. '99 (SFD) Marine, IL St. Gertrude; Air National Guard Chaplains; Marine, IL St. Elizabeth; Marine, IL St. James.
Bohorquez, Hernan D. '02 (BGP) Leave of Absence.
Bohorquez, Jesus Alberto '01 (MIA) Princeton, FL St. Ann Mission; Christian Family Movement.
Bohorquez, Jesus '01 (MIA) Rural Life Ministry; Naranja and Migrant Ministry.
Bohr, Rev. Msgr. David A. '71 (SCR)[M] Dunmore, PA Villa St. Joseph; Permanent Diaconate Office; Diocesan Office for Continuing Education for Clergy; Diocesan Office for Clergy Formation.
Bohren, Gregory J. '09 (LC) Plover, WI St. Bronislava.
Bohrer, John D. '78 (CAM) Collingswood, NJ Blessed Teresa of Calcutta Parish, Collingswood, N.J.
Boiko, John '87 (AUS) Austin, TX Santa Barbara Catholic Church –Austin, Texas.
Boisaubin, Robert D. '69 (STL) Retired.
Boisvert, Gilbert O. '71 (OG) Altona, NY Holy Angels; Altona, NY St. Louis.
Boisvert, Keith W. '79 (BAL) Frederick, MD St. Katharine Drexel Roman Catholic Congregation, Inc.
Boisvert, Marc *o.m.i.* '84 (FgM) Washington, DC AMERICAN OBLATE MISSIONS.
Boisvert, Ralph '99 (PRT) Retired.
Boisvert, Robert G. '58 (MAN) Retired.
Boivin, Henry P. '57 (BO) Senior Priests. Retired.
Boivin, John P. '76 (CHI) Chicago, IL Holy Name Cathedral.
Bojczuk, Thaddeus J. '73 (CHI) Chicago, IL St. Symphorosa and Seven Sons; Deans.
Boji, Manuel Y. '68 (EST) Vicar General; Eparchial College of Consultors; Diocesan Corporation–The Chaldean Catholic Church of U.S.A.; Sterling Heights, MI Holy Martyrs Chaldean Catholic Church.
Bok, James M. *o.f.m.* '74 (CIN)[N] Cincinnati St. Francis Seraph Friary.
Bok, John *o.f.m.* '62 (CIN) Councillors:; [N] Cincinnati, OH St. Francis Seraph Friary; [N] Cincinnati, OH St. John the Baptist Friary.
Bokenkotter, Thomas '50 (CIN) Cincinnati, OH Assumption of the Blessed Virgin Mary.
Bokinskie, Richard '79 (SAG) Bannister, MI St. Cyril; Chesaning, MI Our Lady of Perpetual Help; Oakley, MI St. Michael; Territorial Vicars.
Bokota, Marek '81 (NEW) Mahwah, NJ Immaculate Heart of Mary.
Boks, Lawrence E. '66 (GLD) Retired.
Boland, Eamonn '69 (DUL) Moose Lake, MN Holy Angels; Moose Lake State Hospital.
Boland, Rev. Msgr. Eugene (PAT) Little Falls, NJ Retired.
Boland, Jeremiah M. '81 (CHI) Chicago, IL Holy Family; Archbishop's Delegate for Extern and International Priests.
Boland, Rev. Msgr. John P. '55 (PH) Defenders of the Bond; Philadelphia, PA St. Christopher Retired.
Boland, Rev. Msgr. John V. '65 (PAT) McAfee, NJ St. Francis de Sales.
Boland, John '75 (GLP) Retired.
Boland, Rev. Msgr. Michael M. '86 (CHI) Chicago, IL Holy Name Cathedral; [G] Administration:; [G] Chicago, IL Mission of the Holy Cross; Health/Hospital Affairs; Administrative Council; Department Directors; Director; Catholic Charities of Chicago.
Boland, Thomas L. '65 (L) Ex Officio; Archdiocesan Examiners Retired.
Bolatete, Ramon '85 (ORL)[G] Lakeland, FL Florida Southern College Newman Center; Lakeland, FL St. Joseph's.
Bolcar, Andrew J. '65 (CAM) Retired.
Bolda, Eugeniusz *s.ch.* '89 (SEA) Tacoma, WA SS. Peter & Paul; Polish Speaking, Ministry to.
Bolderson, John J. '81 (KC) Butler, MO St. Patrick's.
Bolding, Robert '09 (PHX) Phoenix, AZ St. Vincent de Paul Roman Catholic Parish; [A] Phoenix, AZ St. Mary's Roman Catholic High School.
Bolduc, Gerard *o.m.i.* '69 (BEL)[F] Belleville, IL Missionary Oblates of Mary Immaculate – St. Henry's Oblate Residence.
Bolduc, John *s.m.* '70 (FgM) THE SOCIETY OF MARY; Boston, MA.
Bolduc, Marcel *o.m.i.* '39 (BO)[X] Tewksbury, MA Immaculate Heart of Mary Residence.
Bolduc, Richard *o.m.i.* '64 (BO)[X] Tewksbury, MA Immaculate Heart of Mary Residence.
Boles, Joseph M. '65 (SCR)[M] Dunmore, PA Villa St. Joseph Retired.
Boley, Robert *o.carm.* '75 (JOL)[L] Joliet, IL St. Elias Carmelites; [L] Darien Carmelite Provincial Office.
Bolez, Edward C. '74 (ALN) Retired.
Bolger, Anthony '69 (HON) Retired.
Bolger, Jesse L. '07 (BAL) Glen Burnie, MD Crucifixion, Church of the; [T] Glen Burnie, MD The Church of the Good Shepherd Parish Endowment Trust; Air National Guard Chaplains; Glen Burnie, MD Church of the Good Shepherd; Glen Burnie, MD Holy Trinity.
Bolger, John Paul *c.c.* '08 (GAL) Houston, TX Queen of Peace.
Bolger, Michael J. '92 (RCK) Shannon, IL St. Wendelin; [B] Freeport, IL Aquin Central Catholic High School.
Bolger, Rev. Msgr. Richard T. '66 (PH) Willow Grove, PA St. David.
Bolger, Rev. Msgr. William '53 (SD) Retired.
Bolha, Jeremy J. *o.s.b.* '59 (GBG)[H] Latrobe, PA Saint Vincent Archabbey.
Bolieau, Henry G. '72 (NOR) Absent on Leave.
Bolivar, Carlos Alberto '01 (CC) Freer, TX St. Mary.
Boll, John E. '70 (SAC) Archives; Sacramento, CA St. Anthony.
Boll, John *o.p.* '82 (BR) Hammond, LA Holy Ghost.
Boller, Kenneth J. *s.j.* '75 (NY)[E] Bronx, NY Fordham Preparatory School; [DD] Jesuit Community, Kohlmann Hall.
Bolling, Francis Joseph '04 (MOB)[E] Mobile, AL Little Sisters of the Poor, Home For the Aged, Inc. Retired.
Bolling, Joseph M. '91 (MOB) Mobile, AL St. Matthew.
Bollman, Richard W. *s.j.* '69 (CIN) Cincinnati, OH St. Robert Bellarmine; [D] Cincinnati, OH Xavier University; [N] Cincinnati, OH Jesuit Community at Xavier University.
Bolman, Anthony P. '60 (SFE) Retired.
Bolser, Charles G. *c.s.v.* '73 (CHI) Chicago, IL St. Viator; [N] Arlington Heights Viatorian Province Center–Clerics of St. Viator.
Bolser, Robert T. *c.s.v.* '95 (CHI)[N] Arlington Heights Viatorian Province Center–Clerics of St. Viator.
Bolser, Robert T. *c.s.v.* '95 (LAV) Henderson, NV St.

Thomas More.
Bolster, M. Thomas '82 (GR) Hart, MI St. Gregory's.
Bolte, Richard G. '83 (COV) Union, KY St. Timothy.
Bolte, Thomas L. '80 (CIN) Cincinnati, OH St. Teresa of Avila.
Bolton, Bill *s.d.b.* '86 (LA)[V] Rosemead, CA St. Joseph's Salesian Youth Renewal Center.
Bolton, Bill '87 (LA) Ventura, CA Sacred Heart.
Bolton, Norman B. '83 (SPR)[M] Springfield, MA Bay Path College; [M] Chicopee, MA American International College; Ludlow, MA Saint Elizabeth Parish; [M] Springfield, MA Newman Apostolates and Campus Ministries.
Bolton, Paul J. '62 (PRO) Retired.
Boly, Craig *s.j.* '74 (P) Portland, OR St. Pius X[D].
Bomba, Paul M. '77 (WOR) Blackstone, MA St. Theresa.
Bombardier, Dennis P. '68 (SPR) Retired.
Bombardier, Paul A. '82 (SPR) Shelburne Falls, MA St. Joseph's.
Bombera, Alex *t.o.r.* '46 (ALT)[G] Loretto, PA St. Francis Friary at Mount Assisi.
Bomberger, Ray P. *s.s.j.* (BAL) Baltimore, MD St. Peter Claver; Baltimore, MD St. Pius V.
Bommarito, Rev. Msgr. Vincent R. '77 (STL) St. Louis, MO St. Ambrose.
Bona, Joseph F. *s.j.* '72 (DEN)[N] Denver, CO Xavier Jesuit Center.
Bona, Richard '03 (CLV) Translators.
Bonacci, Paul '91 (ROC) Watkins Glen, NY St. Benedict; Watkins Glen, NY St. Mary of the Lake.
Bonadies, Kenneth P. '65 (HRT) Retired.
Bonadio, Joseph J. *s.s.* '64 (BAL)[M] Baltimore, MD St. Charles Villa; Special Assignment; [Q] Baltimore Society of St. Sulpice, Province of the United States Retired.
Bonafed, Joseph E. '92 (GBG) Connellsville, PA Immaculate Conception; Connellsville, PA St. John the Evangelist; Connellsville, PA St. Rita.
Bonanno, Raphael *o.f.m.* '62 (BO)[Z] Boston, MA St. Anthony Shrine.
Bonano, Salvatore *c.m.f.* '43 (LA)[V] Rancho Dominguez, CA Dominguez Seminary Inc. Retired.
Bonar, Clyde A. '84 (ORL) Retired.
Bonarrigo, David *t.o.r.* '78 (ALT)[G] Loretto, PA St. Francis Friary at Mount Assisi.
Bonavitacola, John M. '88 (PH) On Duty Outside the Archdiocese.
Bonavitacola, John '88 (PHX) Tempe, AZ Our Lady of Mt. Carmel Roman Catholic Parish.
Bonczewski, Rev. Msgr. William D. '76 (OLL) Wheeling, WV Our Lady of Lebanon Maronite Catholic Church.
Bond, B. Daniel '84 (RIC) Retired.
Bond, Ernest W. '88 (COS) Retired.
Bond, William D. '99 (OM) Omaha, NE St. Joseph.
Bonderenko, Thomas '80 (BAL) Priests Sick or Absent.
Bondi, Richard A. '74 (SPR) South Hadley, MA St. Theresa of Lisieux.
Bondi, Steven '86 (JOL) Wilmington, IL St. Rose.
Bondy, Alberto P. '86 (DET) Warren, MI St. Anne.
Boneck, Norman D. '62 (LC) Retired.
Boned, Enrique '57 (MIA) Retired.
Bonela, Anthony *m.s.f.s.* '97 (STA) Jacksonville, FL Holy Spirit.
Bonela, Anthony *m.s.f.s.* '97 (TYL)[C] Whitehouse, TX The Missionaries of St. Francis de Sales.
Bonello, Pablo *i.v.e.* '84 (WDC) Mount Rainier, MD St. James.
Bonetti, Henry *s.d.b.* '73 (FgM) New Rochelle, NY SALESIANS OF DON BOSCO.
Boney, Vincent *c.p.* '57 (SCR)[L] Scranton, PA Saint Ann's Passionist Monastery.
Bonfadini, Leo '74 (PBL) Absent on Leave.
Bonfiglio, Gregory R. *s.j.* '94 (SAC)[C] Sacramento, CA Jesuit High School.
Bongard, Joseph W. '86 (PH)[A] Wynnewood, PA Theological Seminary of St. Charles Borromeo, Overbrook; Approved Advocates.
Bongila, Jean Pierre '91 (STP)[C] St. Paul, MN University of St. Thomas.
Boni, Frederick G. '10 (MOB) Mobile, AL St. Dominic Parish, Mobile.
Bonian, Stephen J. *s.j.* '82 (BO)[U] Weston, MA Campion Jesuit Community.
Bonifas, Roger D. '45 (TOL) Cloverdale, OH St. Barbara Retired.
Bonikowski, Leon V. *o.s.f.s.* '65 (FgM)[Y] Philadelphia, PA Father Louis Brisson Residence; Wilmington, DE OBLATES OF ST. FRANCIS DE SALES MISSIONS.
Bonilla, Rev. Msgr. Humberto Lopez '86 (MGZ) Mayaguez, PR Cathedral of Our Lady of Purification.
Bonin, Harold A. '65 (CHI) Chicago, IL St. Jerome Retired.
Bonk, Carl *s.j.* '82 (CLV)[D] Cleveland, OH St. Ignatius High School.
Bonk, Matthew S. *c.ss.r.* '04 (STL) St. Louis, MO St. Alphonsus Liguori.
Bonk, Matthew *c.ss.r* '04 (BR) Baton Rouge, LA St. Gerard Majella.
Bonk, Matthew *c.ss.r.* '04 (DEN)[N] Denver The Redemptorists/Denver Province.
Bonke, James R. '70 (IND) Indianapolis, IN SS. Peter and Paul Cathedral, Indianapolis, Inc.; Indianapolis, IN Christ The King Catholic Church, Indianapolis, Inc.; Defenders of the Bond; Promoter of Justice.
Bonnar, David J. '88 (PIT) Pittsburgh, PA St. Bernard.
Bonneau, Normand *o.m.i.* '76 (WDC)[O] Washington, DC Provincial Offices of the United States Province of the Missionary Oblates of Mary Immaculate; Washington, DC AMERICAN OBLATE MISSIONS.
Bonneau, Ronald *c.ss.r.* '71 (MET) Commission for Hispanic Ministry; Co Directors.
Bonnell, Rev. Msgr. Victor G. '60 (SLC) Retired.
Bonner, Charles E. '65 (PH) Philadelphia, PA St. Cecilia.
Bonner, Michael J. *s.v.d.* '66 (CHI) Wheeling, IL St. Joseph the Worker.
Bonner, Patrick J. *o.s.b.* '59 (PAT)[N] Newton St. Paul's Abbey.
Bonner, Patrick '00 (NY) Manhattan, NY Terence Cardinal Cooke Health Care Center.
Bonner, William J. '67 (LA) Retired.
Bonneville, Lionel E. '63 (SPR) Northampton, MA Veterans Administration Hospital Retired.
Bonnici, John S. '91 (NY) Chester, NY St. Columba; [A] Yonkers, NY St. Joseph's Seminary.
Bonnici, William C. '67 (DET) Retired.
Bonnot, Bernard R. '67 (Y) College of Consultors; Struthers, OH Christ Our Savior Parish; Presbyteral Council.
Bono, James P. '03 (PAT) On Duty Outside the Diocese.
Bono, James P. *i.v.dei* '03 (NY) Suffern, NY Good Samaritan Hospital.
Bono, Jamie (NY)[W] Suffern, NY Good Samaritan Hospital of Suffern.
Bonoan, Tito '80 (OAK)[E] Hayward, CA Moreau Catholic High School.
Bonsignore, Dennis '81 (ROC) Monroe Community Hospital; Strong Health System; Rochester, NY St. Anne; Highland Hospital.
Bonsignore, Mark '95 (HRT)[H] Hartford, CT Saint Francis Hospital and Medical Center.
Bonsor, Jack '74 (SJ) Absent on Sick Leave.
Bonsu, Joseph Osei '99 (ROC) Auburn, NY St. Mary.
Bonvouloir, Philip '54 (WOR) Fiskdale, MA St. Anne's and St. Patrick's.
Bonzagni, Rev. Msgr. John J. '80 (SPR) Lenox Dale, MA St. Vincent de Paul's; Judicial Vicar; Diocesan Diaconate Council; Diocesan Consultors; Bishop's Cabinet.
Book, Matthew '10 (DEN) On Duty Outside the Archdiocese.
Book, Theodore R. '02 (ATL) Liturgical Commission; Office For Divine Worship.
Book, Theodore '02 (ATL)[I] LaGrange, GA LaGrange Jr. College; [I] Atlanta, GA Catholic Center Georgia State University; LaGrange, GA St. Peter.
Booms, Andrew '07 (SAG) Kinde, MI St. Mary–St. Edward; Port Austin, MI St. Michael.
Boone, Scott F. '01 (DUB) On Special or Other Archdiocesan Assignment; [C] Dubuque, IA Loras College.
Boor, Colin J. '50 (WCH) Retired.
Boosel, Brian D. *o.s.b.* '03 (GBG)[H] Latrobe, PA Saint Vincent Archabbey; [H] Latrobe Saint Vincent Archabbey.
Booth, Edward '74 (STA) St. Augustine, FL Cathedral – Basilica of St. Augustine.
Booth, Jim W. '07 (BIR) Birmingham, AL Blessed Sacrament.
Booth, Raymond '57 (ROC) Pittsford, NY St. Louis Retired.
Booth, Stephen R. *m.m.* '86 (NY)[DD].
Boquet, Gregory M. *o.s.b.* '88 (NO)[A] St. Benedict, LA St. Joseph Seminary College; [R] St. Benedict, LA St. Joseph Abbey.
Boquet, Shenan J. '93 (HT) On Duty Outside the Diocese.
Boquet, Shenan J. '93 (ARL)[L] Front Royal, VA Human Life International.
Boras, Kurt D. '86 (CHI) Lemont, IL St. Patrick.
Borawski, Gerald J. '72 (LFT) Monticello, IN Our Lady of the Lakes; Associate Judges.
Borba, Joseph '97 (SB) On Leave of Absence.
Borbely, James A. *s.j.* '76 (ALN)[A] Wernersville, PA Jesuit Center–Jesuit Community; [P] Wernersville, PA ISECP, Inc.
Borbridge, David *s.j.* '63 (MOB)[A] Mobile, AL Spring Hill College.
Borca, Dennis L. '81 (MAR) Retired.
Borcherding, Martin '73 (LAF) Lafayette, LA St. Elizabeth Seton.
Borcic, Rev. Msgr. John J. '76 (STL) St. Louis, MO St. Mary Magdalen; Council of Catholic Youth; Archdiocesan Office of the Permanent Diaconate; Office of Youth Ministry.
Bordeaux, Henry *o.c.d.* '62 (OKL) Oklahoma City, OK Our Lady of Mount Carmel and St. Therese Little Flower.
Bordeleau, Beau–Pierre G. '85 (BRK) Released from Diocesan Assignment.
Bordelon, Kevin P. '05 (LAF) Lafayette, LA Cathedral of St. John the Evangelist.
Bordelon, Kevin '05 (LAF) Seminarians; Vocations; Continuing Formation of Priests.
Bordelon, Rev. Msgr. Roland '50 (ALX) Retired.
Bordenave, Ian G. *o.p.* '00 (GAL) Houston, TX Holy Rosary.
Bordonaro, Joseph C. '89 (PH) Warrington, PA St. Joseph.
Bordonaro, Richard D. '76 (BUF) On Duty Outside the Diocese.
Borek, Derek J. '99 (BO)[A] Brighton, MA St. John Seminary.
Borel, Albert '81 (LKC) Westlake, LA St. John Bosco; Judges; Presbyteral Council.
Borello, Steven '11 (JOL) Clarendon Hills, IL Notre Dame.
Boren, Edward *o.f.m.* '64 (SAT) San Antonio, TX San Jose y San Miguel.
Borer, Robert D. '76 (STU) Cambridge, OH Christ Our Light Parish.
Boretto, Krzysztof '87 (SY) Binghamton, NY Saints John & Andrew; Binghamton, NY Our Lady of Lourdes Memorial Hospital.
Borg, Ronald *c.s.b.* '79 (DET) Detroit, MI St. Bartholomew/St. Rita.
Borgelt, Daniel E. '93 (TOL) Napoleon, OH St. Augustine; Our Lady, Queen of Peace Deanery.
Borgen, Alfonso '98 (LA) Gardena, CA St. Anthony of Padua.
Borger, Rev. Msgr. Marvin G. '91 (TOL) Vicar General; Perrysburg, OH St. Rose; Judges.
Borger, Theodore R. '83 (DAV) Retired.
Borgerding, Terry J. '77 (STL) St. Charles, MO St. Cletus.
Borges, Charles *s.j.* '81 (BAL)[B] Timonium, MD Loyola Graduate Center–Timonium Campus; [Q] Baltimore, MD Jesuit Community of Loyola University, Inc.; [B] Jesuit Community of Loyola University, Inc.
Borges, Jose A. *s.j.* '69 (SJN)[H] San Juan, PR Comunidad Jesuita.
Borges, Laurence J. '59 (BO) Dorchester, MA St. Gregory; Senior Priests. Retired.
Borges, Mario L. '82 (OAK) Castro Valley, CA Transfiguration.
Borges, Robert '04 (FRS) Diocesan Consultors; Clovis, CA Our Lady of Perpetual Help; Vicar Urbanis; Personnel Board.
Borgesen, Ken *o.ss.t.* '87 (BAL)[Q] Diocese of Trenton, NJ.
Borgesen, Kenneth G. *o.ss.t.* '87 (TR) Trenton, NJ The Church of the Incarnation–St. James.
Borgia, Anthony A. '84 (TOL) Toledo, OH St. John the Baptist; Toledo, OH St. Michael the Archangel.
Borgmeyer, Dean '81 (WH) Weirton, WV Sacred Heart of Mary; Weirton, WV St. Joseph the Worker.
Borino, David J. '86 (HRT) Retired.
Borja, Charlito A. '03 (CHK) Presbyteral Council; Knights of Columbus; Rota, MP San Francisco de Borja Parish.
Bork, Vincent D. '95 (ARL) Colonial Beach, VA St. Elizabeth of Hungary.
Borkenhagen, Jason W. '01 (WCH) Parsons, KS St. Patrick; Presbyteral Council/College of Consultors.
Borkowski, Francis '77 (NY) On Leave of Absence.
Borkowski, Mark '96 (DET) Detroit, MI SS. Peter and Paul.
Borkowski, Thomas '81 (KC)[O] Wheaton, IL Wheaton Franciscan Services, Inc.; [N] Lombard, IL Mayslake Ministries, Inc.; On Duty Outside the Diocese.
Borkowski, Tomasz '01 (WOR)[Q] Worcester, MA Worcester Polytechnic Institute.
Borkowski, Walter '85 (SAC) Vallejo, CA St. Basil.
Borlang, Stephen M. '86 (SAC) Vallejo, CA St. Vincent Ferrer.
Bormann, Charles P. '58 (PHX) Retired.
Bormann, Paul D. '85 (SC) Pocahontas, IA Church of the Resurrection; Pocahontas, IA St. Margaret's.
Borno, Saint Charles '04 (BRK) Brooklyn, NY St. Teresa of Avila.
Borntrager, Conrad M. *o.s.m.* '60 (CHI) Chicago, IL Annunciata; [N] Chicago, IL Order of Friar Servants of Mary (Servites) United States of America Province, Inc.; [N] Chicago, IL Annunciata Priory; Chicago, IL.
Boroch, Andrzej '95 (SAG) Marlette, MI St. Elizabeth.
Borodach, Joseph '60 (PBR) Bradenville, PA St. Mary's; Protopresbyters.
Boroughs, Philip L. *s.j.* '78 (WDC)[C] Washington, DC Georgetown University.
Borowiak, David J. '71 (BUF) Cheektowaga, NY St. Philip the Apostle.
Borowiak, Kenneth A. '87 (LIN) Lincoln, NE St. Michael; Bishop Bruskewitz Charity and Stewardship Appeal (DDP); Office of Information and Media; Newspaper.
Borowski, Paul *c.ss.r.* '87 (ALB) Saratoga Springs, NY St. Clement.
Borowski, Raymond *o.f.m. conv.* '61 (HRT) Kensington, CT St. Paul.
Borre, Robert J. '60 (MAD) Retired.
Borrelli, Rev. Msgr. Anthony '54 (COL) Retired.
Borrero, Victor R. *s.e.m.v.* '89 (ARE) Arecibo, PR Our

Lady of Guadalupe.
Borro Barbosa, Cristiano G. '07 (MAN) Brazilian Apostolate.
Borruel, Alberto J. '06 (AUS) Lockhart, TX St. Mary.
Borski, Charles J. *o.m.i.* '70 (GAL) Alvin, TX St. John the Baptist.
Borski, Rev. Msgr. Chester L. '67 (GAL) Kingwood, TX St. Martha; [S] Houston, TX Martha's Kitchen Food Services; Appointees; College of Consultors.
Borski, Jerome *o.s.b.* '92 (PAT)[N] Morristown, NJ St. Mary's Abbey; [O] Convent Station, NJ St. Anne Villa; Morristown, NJ.
Borstelmann, James E. '67 (NY) Kingston, NY St. Colman.
Borsuk, Ronald W. '58 (PBR) Retired.
Bortz, Thomas P. '04 (ALN) Elected Members; [C] Reading, PA Berks Catholic; Shillington, PA St. John Baptist de la Salle.
Boruszewski, Rev. Msgr. Joseph A. '53 (BUF) Retired.
Borzuchowski, John W. '68 (NY) Kingston, NY Immaculate Conception.
Borzych, Alexander J. '80 (MO) Military Chaplains; Navy Chaplains.
Bosack, Albert J. '43 (BUF)[N] Lackawanna, NY Bishop Head Residence Retired.
Bosch, Stan *s.t.* '86 (LA) Los Angeles, CA St. Michael.
Bosch, William J. *s.j.* '60 (SY)[Q] Syracuse, NY Jesuits at LeMoyne, Inc.
Boschert, Hubert G. *s.j.* '68 (OM)[J] Omaha, NE Jesuit Community at Creighton University.
Boschetto, Dan *s.x.* '70 (PAT)[N] Wayne Xaverian Missionary Fathers; Wayne, NJ XAVERIAN MISSIONARY FATHERS.
Boschi, Marcelo *f.d.p.* '95 (BO)[Z] Boston, MA Madonna Queen Shrine.
Bosco, John M. '71 (LAN) Morrice, MI St. Mary.
Bosco, Mark G. *s.j.* '99 (CHI)[C] Chicago, IL Jesuit Community at Loyola University Chicago.
Boscoe, John L. *c.s.b.* '72 (GAL)[O] Sugar Land, TX Basilian Mission Center; [B] Sugar Land, TX Basilian Fathers of Sugarland.
Boscutti, Darrio L. '86 (CHI) Western Springs, IL St. John of the Cross.
Bosken, Robert E. *s.j.* '56 (STL)[O] St. Louis, MO De Smet Jesuit High School Community; [O] St. Louis, MO Jesuit Community Corporation at Saint Louis University – Jesuit Hall Retired.
Boslett, Donald E. '59 (ALT) Retired.
Bosnich, David A. '95 (PBR) Elected Deanery Representatives; Duquesne, PA SS. Peter and Paul.
Bosque, Peter J. '83 (SAC) On Duty Outside the Diocese.
Bosque, Peter '83 (SB) Chino, CA St. Margaret Mary.
Bosse, Dennis *o.f.m.* (NO) New Orleans, LA St. Mary of the Angels.
Bossi, Paul R. '69 (BUF) Buffalo, NY Blessed Sacrament.
Bossi, Stephen E. *c.s.p.* '86 (BRK)[R] Paulist Priests at Paulist Foundations Outside the U.S.
Bossie, Robert W. *s.c.j.* '75 (CHI)[N] SCJ Novitiate.
Bossman, David M. *o.f.m.* '65 (NY)[DD] New York Franciscan Friars, Holy Name Province.
Bosso, Rev. Msgr. Stephen C. '78 (PT) Milton, FL St. Rose of Lima; Seminarian Candidate Review Board; Seminarians, Office of.
Bostwick, John *o.praem.* '76 (GB)[B] St. Norbert College; [J] De Pere, WI St. Joseph Priory.
Bostwick, John '69 (RIC) Unassigned.
Boteju, Bernard '85 (TYL) Priests' Pension Board.
Boteler, William M. *m.m.* '68 (WDC)[B] Washington, DC Maryknoll Fathers and Brothers.
Boteler, William M. *m.m.* '68 (SJ)[M] Los Altos, CA Maryknoll.
Botello, Camillo *m.s.f.* '03 (SAT) New Braunfels, TX Our Lady of Perpetual Help; In Rural Area; Priests Personnel Board; Archdiocesan Presbyteral Council.
Botenhagen, Paul *o.f.m.* '82 (LSC) Mescalero, NM St. Joseph; Presbyteral Council; Priestly Life and Ministry Committee.
Botheroyd, Thomas '00 (JOL) Lombard, IL Sacred Heart.
Botsko, Jerome G. '82 (PBR) Brownsville, PA St. Nicholas; Elected Deanery Representatives.
Botte, Gregory *o.f.m.* '68 (NY)[DD] New York Franciscan Province of the Immaculate Conception.
Botthof, Robert J. *o.p.* '87 (CHI)[N] Chicago Dominicans (Provincial Office); Chicago, IL; [N] Chicago, IL St. Pius V Priory.
Bottino, Rev. Msgr. Dominic J. '78 (CAM) Vice Chancellors; Adjutant Judicial Vicars; Judges; Vineland, NJ Divine Mercy, Vineland, N.J.
Bottino, Rev. Msgr. Edward J. '52 (BRK) Flushing, NY Mary's Nativity Retired.
Botz, Roger *o.s.b.* '60 (SCL)[G] St. Cloud, MN St. Cloud Hospital; [I] Collegeville, MN St. John's Abbey, of the Order of St. Benedict.
Bou, Pedro L. *s.v.d.* '74 (TR) Lakewood, NJ St. Anthony Claret.
Bouchaaya, Georges *m.l.m.* (SAM) Troy, NY St. Ann.
Bouchard, Charles E. *o.p.* '79 (FgM) Chicago, IL Province of St. Albert the Great (Central); Chicago, IL.
Bouchard, Charles E. *o.p.* '79 (CHI)[N] Chicago Dominicans (Provincial Office); [N] Chicago, IL St. Pius V Priory.
Bouchard, Charles E. *o.p.* (NY)[HH] New York, NY St. Thomas Aquinas Foundation.
Bouchard, Denis *f.s.s.p.* '00 (Y) Vienna, OH Queen of the Holy Rosary.
Bouchard, Lucien *o.m.i.* '55 (MIA) Miami, FL Christ the King.
Bouchard, Marcel H. '72 (FR) Nantucket, MA St. Mary's, Our Lady of the Isle; Nantucket.
Bouchard, Rev. Msgr. Paul L. '72 (MAN) Merrimack, NH Our Lady of Mercy; Promoter of Justice; Defenders of the Bond; Presbyteral Council.
Bouchard, Robert P. '84 (PRT) Special or Other Diocesan Assignment.
Bouchard, Thomas '53 (DUL) Retired.
Boucher, Edward F. '60 (SAG) Retired.
Boucher, Edward '60 (GR) Scottville, MI St. Jerome; Custer, MI St. Mary's.
Boucher, Gerard A. '53 (MAN) Retired.
Boucher, Gilmond *o.m.i.* '58 (PMB) Riviera Beach, FL St. Francis of Assisi.
Boucher, Kevin '91 (FAR) Fargo, ND Nativity Church of Fargo.
Boucher, Peter P. '04 (MAN) Newport, NH St. Patrick; Presbyteral Council.
Boucher, Richard R. *m.s.* '60 (HRT)[L] Hartford, CT Missionaries of LaSalette.
Boucher, Roger R. '73 (WOR) On Duty Outside the Diocese.
Boucree, Thaddeus *s.v.d.* '52 (BLX)[D] Bay St. Louis, MS St. Augustine's Residence.
Boudoin, Burt '82 (SD) San Diego, CA Saint Charles Catholic Parish.
Boudreau, C. Paul '83 (NOR) On Duty Outside the Diocese.
Boudreau, George R. *o.p.* '83 (STL)[B] St. Louis, MO Aquinas Institute of Theology.
Boudreau, George '83 (NO)[R] New Orleans Dominican Friars, Southern Dominican Province of St. Martin de Porres.
Boudreau, Paul B. '07 (MAN) Belmont, NH St. Joseph; Presbyteral Council; College of Consultors.
Boudreau, Paul '83 (STO) Mammoth Lakes, CA St. Joseph Church of Mammoth Lakes.
Boudreau, Thomas C. '95 (BO) Avon, MA St. Michael.
Boudreau, Thomas Francis '56 (LA) Retired.
Boudreaux, Claude P. *s.j.* '55 (NO)[R] New Orleans, LA Ignatius Residence Retired.
Boudreaux, John S. '73 (MOB) Mobile, AL Corpus Christi Parish, Mobile.
Boudreaux, Ronald J. *s.j.* '05 (FWT)[J] Lake Dallas, TX Montserrat Foundation, Inc.; [J] Lake Dallas, TX Montserrat Jesuit Retreat House.
Bouffard, Rev. Msgr. James F. '70 (NEW) Westfield, NJ St. Helen.
Bouffier, Robert *s.m.* '74 (HON)[D] Honolulu, HI Chaminade Pohaku Marianist Community.
Boufford, Thomas F. '81 (GR) Ionia, MI SS. Peter and Paul.
Boughton, Michael *s.j.* '79 (BO)[U] Newton, MA The Jesuit Community at Boston College.
Bouhall, William G. '94 (CLV) Brooklyn, OH St. Thomas More; Presbyteral Conveners; College of Consultors; Presbyteral Council.
Boulanger, Gerard J. *m.s.* '73 (FR)[F] Attleboro, MA La Salette Shrine.
Boulet, Marshall '71 (LKC) Elton, LA St. Paul.
Boulette, Rev. Msgr. Michael J. '76 (SAT) College of Consultors; In Rural Area; Kerrville, TX Notre Dame; Archdiocesan Presbyteral Council; Priests Personnel Board; [S] Ingram, TX St. Peter Upon the Water, A Center For Spiritual Direction and Formation.
Bouley, Allan *o.s.b.* '62 (SCL)[I] Collegeville, MN St. John's Abbey, of the Order of St. Benedict.
Boulin, Jean Wesner '04 (PMB) Vero Beach, FL St. Helen.
Boulos, Peter '93 (SAM) Protopresbyters (Deans); Tampa, FL Mission of Sts. Peter & Paul; Presbyteral Council; College of Consultors.
BouMerhi, Rev. Msgr. Jibran '88 (OLL) Warren, MI St. Sharbel Maronite Catholic Church.
Bourcy, Robert Scott '82 (ROC) Mendon, NY St. Catherine of Siena; Priest Consultors.
Bourdon, Norman W. '73 (PRO) Cumberland, RI St. Joan of Arc; Deans.
Bourek, David F. '79 (LIN) Friend, NE St. Joseph's; Advocates; Rural Life Conference.
Bouressa, Donald J. '61 (PRO) Retired.
Bourg, Rodney P. '78 (NO) Deans; Covington, LA Most Holy Trinity.
Bourgault, Ronald L. '63 (BO) Senior Priests. Retired.
Bourgea, Roger *s.m.* '59 (BO) Pastoral Care.
Bourgeois, Bernard W. '95 (BUR)[B] South Burlington, VT Rice Memorial High School; Winooski, VT St. Francis Xavier.
Bourgeois, Donald E. '85 (SY) "The Catholic Sun"; Endicott, NY St. Ambrose.
Bourgeois, Francis L. '61 (LAF) Retired.
Bourgeois, Rev. Msgr. Lloyd '57 (SD) San Diego, CA San Rafael Catholic Parish Retired.
Bourgeois, Louis D. '59 (BO) Senior Priests.; Salem, MA St. James Retired.
Bourgeois, Roger *s.s.s.* '57 (CLV) Highland Heights, OH St. Paschal Baylon; [N] Cleveland, OH Congregation of the Blessed Sacrament.
Bourgeois, Roy L. *m.m.* '72 (NY)[DD].
Bourget, Laurence *o.c.s.o.* '42 (WOR)[N] Spencer, MA St. Joseph's Abbey.
Bourgoin, Raymond *o.m.i.* '66 (FgM) Washington, DC AMERICAN OBLATE MISSIONS.
Bourke, Charles E. '70 (BO) Winthrop, MA St. John the Evangelist.
Bourke, John F. '60 (CAM) Retired.
Bourke, Martin '74 (SEA) Burlington, WA St. Charles; La Conner, WA Sacred Heart; Mount Vernon, WA Immaculate Conception; Sedro Woolley, WA Immaculate Heart of Mary; Mount Vernon, WA Skagit Valley Catholic Churches.
Bourke, Nathaniel J. '59 (GF) Retired.
Bourke, Ulick *s.m.a.* '68 (BO)[U] Dedham, MA African Mission House.
Bourque, Rev. Msgr. Charles J. '62 (BO) Canton, MA St. John the Evangelist; Senior Priests. Retired.
Bourque, Rev. Msgr. Joseph A. '55 (LKC) Retired.
Bourque, Thomas *t.o.r.* '82 (PIT)[M] Pittsburgh, PA Franciscan Friars, T.O.R.
Boursiquot, Jean Gaetan '81 (ORL) Haitian Ministry; Appointed Members.
Bouterie, Thomas '80 (HT) On Duty Outside the Diocese.
Boutin, Emile R. '91 (BO) Walpole, MA Blessed Sacrament.
Bouton, Thomas F. '83 (BO) Health Leave.; Dorchester, MA St. Ambrose.
Boutros, Peter '00 (NTN) Phoenix, AZ St. John of the Desert; Presbyteral Council; Ambassadors.
Bouzi, Quilin *o.m.i.* '07 (BUF) Buffalo, NY Holy Angels; Buffalo, NY Our Lady of Hope.
Bouzigard, Michael A. *s.j.* '01 (NO)[C] New Orleans, LA Loyola University New Orleans; New Orleans, LA; [R] New Orleans, LA Jesuit Provincial Office.
Bova, Eugene R. '57 (BIS) Retired.
Bova Conti, Michael J. '71 (BO) Sudbury, MA Our Lady of Fatima.
Bovard, William R. '64 (PIT)[M] Pittsburgh, PA St. John Vianney Manor Retired.
Bove, Ralph A. '78 (SY) Norwich, NY St. Paul; Norwich, NY St. Bartholomew the Apostle.
Bovee, Brian '81 (RCK) Rockford, IL St. Mary Oratory.
Bovenzi, Robert *c.p.* '85 (GAL)[O] Houston, TX Congregation of the Passion, Holy Name Passionist Community and Retreat Center.
Bowden, John V. '62 (TR)[N] Trenton, NJ Villa Vianney Retired.
Bowden, Lloyd '49 (JOL) Retired.
Bowen, Gerard J. '77 (BAL) Columbia, MD St. John the Evangelist.
Bowen, John W. *s.s.* '49 (BAL)[M] Baltimore, MD St. Charles Villa; [Q] Baltimore Society of St. Sulpice, Province of the United States Retired.
Bowen, Joseph D. '57 (PH) Retired.
Bowens, Lorin M. '74 (MAD) La Valle, WI Holy Family; Lime Ridge, WI St. Boniface; Lime Ridge, WI St. Patrick; Council of Catholic Women.
Bower, Alan '89 (STA) Presbyteral Council; Gainesville, FL St. Patrick Church.
Bower, Lawrence C. '88 (BAK) Navy Reserve Chaplains Retired.
Bowering, Gerhard H. *s.j.* '70 (BGP)[O] Fairfield, CT The Fairfield Jesuit Community–Fairfield University.
Bowers, Phillip T. '64 (LFT) Fishers, IN Holy Spirit Church.
Bowers, Ronald J. '64 (STP) Retired.
Bowers, Ronald J. '64 (SFE) Associate Judges Retired.
Bowes, James J. *s.j.* '66 (NY)[DD] New York, NY Xavier Jesuit Community.
Bowker, Jeffrey *l.c.* '95 (R) Jacksonville, NC Shrine of the Infant of Prague, Church of the Holy Spirit.
Bowlds, Kent '93 (JKS) Cleveland, MS Our Lady of Victories; Rosedale, MS Sacred Heart; [H] Cleveland, MS Delta State University Newman Center; Priests' Council.
Bowler, James M. *s.j.* '74 (BGP)[O] Fairfield, CT The Fairfield Jesuit Community–Fairfield University.
Bowler, Joseph D. *o.s.f.s.* '49 (WIL)[J] Childs, MD Retirement and Assisted Care Facility Retired.
Bowler, Michael J. '57 (CHI) Retired.
Bowles, Rev. Msgr. Richard J. '61 (PT) Retired.
Bowles, William H. '91 (NU) Retired.
Bowles, William H. '91 (MIA) Fort Lauderdale, FL St. John the Baptist.
Bowling, Theodore B. *s.j.* '53 (FgM) Chicago, IL Society of Jesus.
Bowling, William M. '97 (L) Lebanon, KY St. Augustine; Lebanon, KY Holy Name of Mary; Ex Officio.

Bowman, Eric A. '04 (CIN) Cincinnati, OH St. Jude the Apostle.
Bowman, John '65 (SEA) Seattle, WA St. Anne.
Bowman, Ronald P. '82 (ALN) Elected Members.
Bowski, Eugene '77 (GLP) Vanderwagen, NM St. Patrick; Gallup, NM Good Shepherd Catholic Mission; Ramah, NM San Lorenzo.
Boxleitner, Rev. Msgr. J. Jerome '56 (STP) Retired.
Boyack, Kenneth G. *c.s.p.* '79 (WDC)[B] Washington, DC St. Paul's College; [X] Washington, DC Paulist Evangelization Ministries.
Boyalla, Balaji '99 (FWT) Mineral Wells, TX Our Lady of Lourdes.
Boyd, C. Morris '78 (CHL) Asheville, NC Basilica of St. Lawrence.
Boyd, Douglas A. '79 (PIT) Allegheny County, PA Children's Hospital; Allegheny County, PA Magee–Women's Hospital; Allegheny County, PA UPMC Shadyside Hospital; Allegheny County, PA Western Pennsylvania Hospital; Pittsburgh, PA Immaculate Conception–St. Joseph.
Boyd, Ian '63 (NEW)[B] Seton Hall University.
Boyd, James A. '63 (BRK) Retired.
Boyd, James '63 (SD) San Diego, CA Port of San Diego; Apostleship of the Sea.
Boyd, Norman *s.a.* '65 (NY)[DD] Garrison, NY Franciscan Friars of the Atonement.
Boyd, Robert J. '02 (BGP) On Duty Outside the Diocese.
Boyd, Robert *f.s.s.p.* '10 (PAT) Pequannock, NJ Our Lady of Fatima Chapel (Tridentine).
Boyer, Mark G. '76 (SPC) Shell Knob, MO Holy Family; Missionary Apostolate – Society for the Propagation of the Faith.
Boyer, Millard G. '75 (LAF) On Special Assignment.
Boyer, Thomas J. '68 (OKL) Norman, OK Church of St. Mark the Evangelist; Personnel Committee.
Boyer, Wayne M. '87 (JC) Jefferson City, MO St. Francis Xavier; Priestly and Religious Vocations Committee.
Boyhan, J. Patrick *m.s.a.* '77 (NOR)[G] Cromwell Society of the Missionaries of the Holy Apostles.
Boykins, Charles *s.v.d.* '65 (CHI)[N] Techny, IL Divine Word Residence.
Boylan, Martin M. '80 (SCR) Scranton, PA St. Patrick's; Diocesan Consultors; Presbyteral Council.
Boyle, Daniel J. '78 (SPR) Adams, MA Pope John Paul the Great Parish.
Boyle, David (STL)[J] Bridgeton, MO SSM De Paul Health Center Foundation.
Boyle, Dennis P. '73 (PH) Philadelphia, PA St. Jerome.
Boyle, Rev. Msgr. Eugene '46 (SJ) Retired.
Boyle, Rev. Msgr. Francis V. '55 (NY) Staten Island, NY Blessed Sacrament; [DD] Bronx, NY John Cardinal O'Connor Residence Retired.
Boyle, George J. '52 (PH) Retired.
Boyle, Gregory *s.j.* '84 (LA) Los Angeles, CA Dolores Mission.
Boyle, James E. '66 (ROC) Fairport, NY Church of St. John of Rochester of Perinton, New York Retired.
Boyle, James '61 (SEA) Retired.
Boyle, John B. '76 (SCR) Pocono Pines, PA St. Maximilian Kolbe.
Boyle, John J. '97 (MAR) Gwinn, MI St. Anthony.
Boyle, Michael J. *c.m.* '59 (PHX) Phoenix, AZ St. Paul Roman Catholic Parish.
Boyle, Michael '95 (RVC) Ronkonkoma, NY St. Joseph's.
Boyle, Neil *s.s.c.* '43 (FgM) St Columbans, NE House of Post–Graduate Studies.
Boyle, Patrick D. '80 (BRK) Brooklyn, NY Our Lady of Peace.
Boyle, Patrick J. *s.j.* '63 (CHI)[A] Mundelein, IL University of St. Mary of the Lake/Mundelein Seminary.
Boyle, Patrick *o.c.s.o.* '67 (SLC)[E] Huntsville, UT Abbey of Our Lady of the Holy Trinity of the Order of Cistercians.
Boyle, Richard P. *s.j.* '75 (BO)[U] Boston The Society of Jesus of New England–Provincial Offices.
Boyle, Richard P. *s.j.* '75 (TUC)[E] Tucson, AZ Jesuit Community of the Vatican Observatory.
Boyle, Richard *o.s.m.* '84 (SAC) Davis, CA St. James.
Boyle, Rev. Msgr. Robert J. '51 (BO) Senior Priests. Retired.
Boyle, Robert J. '63 (PIT) Finleyville, PA St. Isaac Jogues; Finleyville, PA St. Francis of Assisi; Allegheny County, PA Jefferson Regional Medical Center.
Boyle, Silvan *o.carm.* '48 (PHX)[F] Phoenix, AZ Carmelite Community Retired.
Boyle, Stephen M. '95 (BO) Melrose, MA Incarnation of Our Lord and Savior Jesus Christ.
Boyle, Thomas '56 (PHX) Retired.
Boyle, Valentine *o.carm.* '46 (PHX) Phoenix, AZ; [F] Phoenix, AZ St. Therese Priory.
Bozada, Mark S. '81 (STL) Catawissa, MO St. James; Villa Ridge, MO St. Mary of Perpetual Help.
Bozek, Miroslaw *s.j.* '04 (CHI)[N] Chicago, IL Sacred Heart Mission House.
Bozek, Robert '78 (WDC) Absent On Leave; Bethesda, MD Our Lady of Lourdes.
Bozel, Rev. Msgr. Robert A. '48 (BAL) Retired.
Bozeman, Anthony *s.s.j.* '00 (NO) Board of Directors:; New Orleans, LA St. Raymond–St. Leo the Great.
Boznar, Joseph P. '70 (CLV)[Y] Cleveland, OH St. Vitus Development Corporation; Cleveland, OH St. Vitus.
Bozung, James M. '61 (GR) Retired.
Bozza, Nicholas (PAT) Netcong, NJ St. Michael's; Charismatic Renewal.
Bozzelli, Rev. Msgr. Richard J. '94 (BAL) Glen Burnie, MD Holy Trinity; [T] Glen Burnie, MD The Church of the Good Shepherd Parish Endowment Trust; Glen Burnie, MD Church of the Good Shepherd; Glen Burnie, MD Crucifixion, Church of the.
Bozzo, Kenneth '80 (FRS) Lindsay, CA Sacred Heart.
Braak, Thomas E. '59 (DUB) Retired.
Braaten, James B. '89 (BIS) Bismarck, ND Ascension; Diocesan Corporate Board; Diocesan Finance Council; Vicar for Presbyters; Priests' Benefit Association.
Braathan, Scott *s.o.l.t.* '03 (CC)[G] Robstown, TX Society of Our Lady of the Most Holy Trinity.
Braband, James *s.v.d.* '80 (CHI)[N] Techny, IL Divine Word Residence; [N] Techny, IL Society of the Divine Word, Provincial Headquarters–Chicago Prov.
Brabazon, Kenneth C. '11 (PH) Newtown, PA St. Andrew.
Bracco, Theodore *o.f.m.* '66 (SFD)[K] Teutopolis, IL St. Francis Assisi Friary; Teutopolis, IL St. Francis of Assisi.
Bracke, James *c.s.c.* '80 (FTW)[B] University of Notre Dame Du Lac; [H] Notre Dame, IN Holy Cross Community, Corby Hall, University of Notre Dame.
Bracken, Jerome *c.p.* '68 (BRK)[R] Jamaica, NY Immaculate Conception Monastery.
Bracken, Rev. Msgr. John J. '67 (BRK) Brooklyn, NY Our Lady Help of Christians; Far Rockaway, NY St. Mary Star of the Sea and St. Gertrude.
Bracken, Joseph A. *s.j.* '62 (CIN)[N] Cincinnati, OH Jesuit Community at Xavier University.
Bracken, W. Jerome *c.p.* '68 (NEW)[A] South Orange, NJ Immaculate Conception Seminary School of Theology; [B] Seton Hall University.
Bracken, Walter *s.v.d.* '71 (BLX)[D] Bay St. Louis, MS St. Augustine's Residence.
Bracket, Louis P. '47 (MAR) Retired.
Brackett, Christopher *l.c.* '93 (HRT)[B] Cheshire, CT Novitiate of the Legion of Christ; Thornwood, NY.
Brackin, James D. *s.c.j.* '75 (MIL)[P] Franklin, WI Sacred Heart at Monastery Lake.
Bradbury, Henry M. *c.m.* '59 (BRK)[R] Jamaica, NY Reverend John B. Murray, CM, House.
Braddock, Stephen '98 (MIL)[P] Milwaukee, WI St. Camillus Delegate House.
Braden, Michael *s.j.* '79 (NEW)[B] Jersey City, NJ Jesuit Center; [L] Jersey City, NJ Jesuits of Saint Peter's College, Inc.
Braden, Patrick O. *c.s.b.* '52 (GAL)[O] Houston, TX Residence of the Basilian Fathers of the University of St. Thomas.
Bradford, Richard S. '98 (BO) West Roxbury, MA St. Theresa of Avila; Boston, MA Congregation of Saint Athanasius.
Bradler, Robert C. '62 (ROC)[O] Rochester, NY Holy Childhood Association; The Society for the Propagation of the Faith Retired.
Bradley, Alfred E. *c.ss.r.* '88 (PH) Philadelphia, PA St. Peter the Apostle.
Bradley, Bruce '78 (DAL) At Large Members; Plano, TX St. Elizabeth Ann Seton; Accreditation Board.
Bradley, Charles (PAT) Retired.
Bradley, Ed '75 (OWN) Board Members.
Bradley, Rev. Msgr. Edward G. '66 (NEW)[C] West Orange, NJ Seton Hall Preparatory School; Ex Officio Members; Ministry to Retired Priests; Presbyteral Council.
Bradley, Hugh J. '89 (CAM) On Sick Leave.
Bradley, J. Richard '81 (TLS) Owasso, OK St. Henry.
Bradley, James F. *o.s.f.s.* '61 (TOL)[H] Toledo, OH Retired.
Bradley, James P. '73 (BRK)[K] Brooklyn, NY Advocate for Persons with Disabilities Services.
Bradley, James P. *s.j.* '67 (NO)[R] New Orleans, LA Ignatius Residence.
Bradley, James *s.d.s.* '61 (LA) Whittier, CA St. Bruno.
Bradley, John A. '65 (ORG) Retired.
Bradley, John J. '67 (ALB) Priests Placement Committee.
Bradley, John J. '63 (PH) Philadelphia, PA Sacred Heart of Jesus Retired.
Bradley, John '67 (ALB) Albany, NY Blessed Sacrament; Deans.
Bradley, Joseph A. '91 (SFR) San Mateo, CA St. Gregory; [D] San Mateo, CA Junipero Serra High School (Boys) Retired.
Bradley, Matthew '72 (BO)[W] Scituate, MA Foyer of Charity; Foyer of Charity.
Bradley, Michael '91 (TUC) Leave of Absence.
Bradley, Michael '78 (CHI) Chicago, IL St. Gertrude; Judges.
Bradley, Michael *o.m.i.* '66 (FgM) Washington, DC AMERICAN OBLATE MISSIONS.
Bradley, Michael (SAG) Promoter of Justice.
Bradley, Robert M. '57 (LA) Retired.
Bradley, Valentine J. '06 (ALT) Cresson, PA St. Francis Xavier.
Bradley, Rev. Msgr. William J. '57 (NY) New Rochelle, NY Blessed Sacrament.
Bradlo, Antoni *c.ss.r.* '57 (CHI) Chicago, IL St. Adalbert.
Bradshaw, Alexander H. '85 (ROC) Rochester, NY Our Mother of Sorrows.
Bradshaw, Benjamin P. '06 (MEM) Collierville, TN Church of the Incarnation.
Bradshaw, Jordan *o.p.* '92 (SEA)[P] Seattle, WA University of Washington, Catholic Newman Center; Seattle, WA Blessed Sacrament.
Bradshaw, Paul F. '70 (FTW)[B] University of Notre Dame Du Lac.
Bradshaw, Terry L. '80 (L) College of Consultors; Ex Officio; Prospect, KY St. Bernadette Parish.
Bradtke, Thomas '62 (DEN) Retired.
Brady, Charles '55 (SAC) Sacramento, CA Holy Spirit Retired.
Brady, Daniel J. '61 (CHI) Arlington Heights, IL Our Lady of the Wayside; Mt. Prospect, IL St. Cecilia Retired.
Brady, Daniel O. '84 (RIC) Glen Allen, VA St. Michael.
Brady, Edmund P. '59 (BRK) Retired.
Brady, Edward E. '90 (PH) Philadelphia, PA St. Anne.
Brady, Rev. Msgr. Gerard J. '59 (SR) Napa, CA St. Thomas Aquinas; Parish Priest Consultors.
Brady, James J. '57 (ALN)[J] Bethlehem, PA Holy Family Villa Retired.
Brady, Rev. Msgr. James J. '72 (TR) Brick Town, NJ St. Dominic.
Brady, James J. '53 (MIL) Retired.
Brady, James '06 (LAF) Diocesan Consultors; Opelousas, LA St. Landry; Defenders of the Bond.
Brady, James *s.m.m.* '92 (HRT)[L] Litchfield, CT Montfort Missionaries; [U] Litchfield, CT Lourdes Shrine Guild, Inc.
Brady, Jeremiah A. *s.s.j.* '51 (MOB) Mobile, AL St. Joseph.
Brady, John A. *s.j.* '49 (SJ)[M] Los Gatos, CA Sacred Heart Jesuit Center.
Brady, Rev. Msgr. John B. '55 (WDC) Archdiocesan Chaplain Coordinator/Catholic Committee on Boy Scouts, Girl Scouts & Camp fire Retired.
Brady, John '55 (SFS) Retired.
Brady, Jude W. *o.s.b.* '80 (ALT) Carrolltown, PA St. Benedict's.
Brady, Jude *o.s.b.* '80 (GBG)[H] Latrobe, PA Saint Vincent Archabbey.
Brady, Justin '05 (B) Knights of Columbus; Rupert, ID St. Nicholas; Priest Personnel Commission.
Brady, Michael '01 (STO) Diocesan Finance Council; Manteca, CA St. Anthony Church of Manteca (Pastor of); [A] Modesto, CA Central Catholic High School; Members Appointed.
Brady, Patrick J. '64 (CAM) Northfield, NJ St. Gianna Beretta Molla Parish, Northfield, N.J.
Brady, Patrick J. '93 (PH)[A] Wynnewood, PA Theological Seminary of St. Charles Borromeo, Overbrook.
Brady, Philip W. '43 (BGP) Retired.
Brady, Reginald '93 (DET) Absent on Leave.
Brady, Rev. Msgr. Roger J. '58 (BO) Senior Priests. Retired.
Brady, Theodore E.A. *s.j.* '61 (BAL)[Q] Baltimore, MD Colombiere Jesuit Community.
Brady, Rev. Msgr. Thomas C. '54 (RCK) Vicars General; Diocesan Consultors; Cemeteries Retired.
Brady, Rev. Msgr. Thomas F. '59 (BRK) Brooklyn, NY Good Shepherd Retired.
Brady, Timothy *o.de.m.* '03 (BUF)[N] Le Roy, NY Order of the BVM of Mercy/Mercedarian Friars; Le Roy, NY Our Lady of Mercy; [N] Le Roy, NY St. Raymond Nonnatus Novitiate.
Brady, Vincent M. '95 (PSC) Orlando, FL Holy Dormition.
Brady, William J. '80 (SFR) San Francisco, CA St. Emydius.
Braganca, Socorro *o.c.d.* '03 (NY) New York, NY Our Lady of Victory.
Braganza, Dinesh *s.j.* '01 (BAL)[Q] Baltimore, MD Ferdinand Wheeler Jesuit Community.
Braganza, Simon F. '92 (CHI) Chicago, IL Queen of All Saints Basilica.
Braham, A. '02 (ALN) Bethlehem, PA St. Anne.
Brahm, Harvey '51 (MIL) Retired.
Braida, Ernest E. '64 (DAV) Retired.
Brailsford, William M. '04 (WDC)[M] Washington, DC Little Sisters of the Poor of Washington, D.C., Inc.
Brailsford, William M. (WDC) Office of the Missions.
Brainerd, Winthrop J. '87 (WDC)[M] Washington, DC Cardinal O'Boyle Residence for Priests Retired.
Brajkovich, Thomas R. '61 (PEO) Retired.
Braley, James E. '75 (BO) Plymouth, MA Blessed Kateri Tekakwitha.
Brambilla, Charles A. '70 (STP) Blaine, MN St. Timothy's.
Brambilla, Sigmund *o.f.m.* '55 (NY)[DD] New York Franciscan Province of the Immaculate Conception.
Bramlage, Gregory D. '96 (IND) On Special or Other Archdiocesan Assignment.

Bramlage, James A. '64 (CIN) Judges Retired.
Bramwell, Bevil *o.m.i.* '85 (WDC)[O] Washington, DC Oblate Community.
Bramwell, Bevil *o.m.i.* (ARL)[C] Hamilton, VA The Catholic Distance University.
Branch, Edward B. '74 (ATL)[I] Atlanta, GA Atlanta University Complex–The Catholic Center; Special or Other Archdiocesan Assignment.
Brancich, John A. *f.s.s.p.* '04 (OM) Omaha, NE Immaculate Conception, B.V.M.
Brancolini, Luca '99 (BO)[U] Lexington, MA Priestly Fraternity of the Missionaries of St. Charles Borromeo, Inc.
Brand, Fred '67 (SFE) Retired.
Brand, Frederick '67 (SFE)[H] Abiquiu, NM Monastery of Christ in the Desert.
Brand, William *o.f.m.* '74 (OAK)[L] Oakland, CA Franciscan Friars of California, (Province of St. Barbara).
Brandenberger, Robert J. *c.m.* '52 (PH)[Y].
Brandenhoff, Peter B. '70 (WIN) On Duty Outside the Diocese.
Brandes, John F. '51 (STP) Retired.
Brandl, Mark J. '09 (MIL) Greendale, WI St. Alphonsus.
Brando, Joseph J. '72 (KNX) Gatlinburg, TN St. Mary Retired.
Brandow, Stephen J. '96 (MO) Diocesan, Region 5 & Louisiana Purchase Council Chaplain; Pineville, LA Central Louisiana State Hospital; Pineville, LA Veterans Administration Medical Center; DEPARTMENT OF VETERANS AFFAIRS HOSPITALS AND CHAPLAINS.
Brandstrup, Christian '79 (STA) Absent or Sick Leave.
Brandt, Daniel J. '99 (CHI) Police Department Chaplain.
Brandt, Joseph D. '83 (PH) Glenside, PA St. Luke the Evangelist.
Brandt, Paul C. '84 (PH) Limerick, PA Blessed Teresa of Calcutta.
Brandt, Timothy '09 (GB) Brillion, WI Holy Family.
Brankatelli, Joseph R. '08 (CLV) Parma, OH Holy Family.
Brankin, Anthony J. '75 (CHI) Berwyn, IL St. Odilo.
Brankin, Rev. Msgr. Patrick M. '79 (CHI) On Duty Outside the Archdiocese.
Brankin, Rev. Msgr. Patrick M. '79 (TLS) Special Assignment; Office of Divine Worship; Office of Permanent Diaconate.
Brannan, Patrick P. *s.j.* '63 (PH)[Y] Loyola Center and Manresa Hall.
Brannen, Brett A. '91 (SAV) Statesboro, GA St. Matthew.
Brannigan, John *s.s.c.* '67 (LA) Los Angeles, CA St. Columban.
Brannigan, John *s.s.c.* '67 (OM)[J] St. Columbans Missionary Society of St. Columban.
Bransfield, Christopher '98 (SJ) San Jose, CA St. Martin of Tours; Deans; Building Committee.
Bransfield, J. Brian '94 (PH) Censores Librorum; General Secretary – Elect; Staff; Staff; On Duty Outside the Archdiocese; Staff; Staff Coordinator.
Bransfield, Sean P. '02 (PH)[A] Wynnewood, PA Theological Seminary of St. Charles Borromeo, Overbrook; On Special or Other Archdiocesan Assignment; Assistant Judicial Vicars; The Chancery.
Branson, Bernard E. '59 (KC) Independence, MO St. Ann's.
Branson, Dale A. '97 (TUC) Hayden, AZ Saint Joseph Roman Catholic Parish – Hayden; Diocesan Consultors.
Branson, Keith *c.pp.s.* '00 (JC) Warsaw, MO St. Ann.
Brant, David A. '65 (SEA) Seattle, WA St. James Cathedral Retired.
Brant, Paul W. *s.j.* '77 (R)[F] Raleigh Jesuit Community; Wilson, NC Church of St. Therese.
Brantman, Thomas E. '75 (RCK) Somonauk, IL St. John the Baptist.
Braquet, David J. '94 (ALX) On Duty Outside the Diocese.
Braschoss, Carl *o.praem.* '10 (PH) Paoli, PA St. Norbert; [Y] Paoli, PA Daylesford Abbey; [Y] Paoli, PA Daylesford Abbey.
Brasher, C. John '75 (SFE) Las Vegas, NM Our Lady of Sorrows Church.
Brassard, Leo *a.a.* '69 (BO)[U] Boston Assumptionist Center.
Brassard, Ronald E. '74 (PRO) Cranston, RI Immaculate Conception.
Brasseaux, Joseph *o.s.b.* '10 (LAF)[H] Opelousas, LA Mother of the Redeemer Monastery.
Brassil, Rev. Msgr. James A. '62 (RVC) Retired.
Brassil, Kevin J. '58 (PRO) Retired.
Bratek, Martin *c.r.* '72 (CHI)[D] Chicago, IL Gordon Tech High School.
Brath, John A. '68 (SPC) Retired.
Bratkowski, Allen J. '89 (MIL) Racine, WI St. Edward; Archdiocesan Council of Priests.
Bratus, Walter N. '56 (GBG) Retired.
Braud, Ronald J. '64 (NO) Retired.
Braudis, Joseph M. '77 (ALN)[J] Bethlehem, PA Holy Family Villa Retired.
Brauer, Frank J. '86 (BAL) Hunt Valley, MD Catholic Community of St. Francis Xavier.
Brauer, Mark S. '92 (DET) Farmington, MI Our Lady of Sorrows.
Braukmann, Donald '86 (CR) Bemidji, MN St. Philip's; [D] Bemidji, MN Holy Spirit Newman Center.
Brault, Bernard *s.m.m.* '68 (HRT)[L] Litchfield, CT Montfort Missionaries.
Brault, Gilles '76 (STA) Absent or Sick Leave.
Brault, Laurence V. '77 (WOR) Upton, MA St. Gabriel the Archangel.
Brault, Y. David '77 (WDC) Silver Spring, MD St. John the Baptist; Priest Council.
Braun, Brian *o.f.m.cap.* '60 (MIL)[P] Mount Calvary, WI St. Felix Friary.
Braun, Rev. Msgr. Francis '54 (BUF)[N] Buffalo, NY Sheehan Residence for Priests Retired.
Braun, Gary G. '77 (STL)[T] St. Louis, MO Washington University Newman Centers.
Braun, H. Gerard '85 (FAR) Grand Forks, ND St. Michael's Church of Grand Forks.
Braun, John Joseph *m.afr.* '57 (SP)[N] St. Petersburg, FL Missionaries of Africa; Washington, DC; Washington, DC MISSIONARIES OF AFRICA Retired.
Braun, John S. '87 (SPC) Aurora, MO Sacred Heart; Cassville, MO St. Edward; Monett, MO St. Lawrence.
Braun, Rev. Msgr. Michael '67 (FRS) Bakersfield, CA Our Lady of Perpetual Help; Defenders of the Bond; Finance Committee; Deposit and Loan Fund; [A] Bakersfield, CA Garces Memorial High School.
Braun, Virgil R. '60 (SCL) Eden Valley, MN The Church of the Assumption; Directors.
Braunreuther, Robert J. *s.j.* '65 (BO)[U] Boston The Society of Jesus of New England–Provincial Offices.
Braunreuther, Robert J. *s.j.* '65 (CHI)[C] Chicago, IL Jesuit Community at Loyola University Chicago.
Brausch, Anthony M. '02 (CIN)[B] Cincinnati, OH Mount St. Mary's Seminary of the West; [A] Special Studies Division:; [B] Cincinnati, OH Mount St. Mary's Seminary of the West.
Bravata, Kevin W. '00 (MEM) Millington, TN St. William.
Braverman, John M. *s.j.* '09 (PH)[C] Jesuit Fathers; [Y] Loyola Center and Manresa Hall.
Bravo, Flavio *s.j.* '05 (GAL)[E] Houston, TX Strake Jesuit College Preparatory Inc.
Bravo, Joseph '77 (SFR) Retired.
Bravo, Miguel Angel '06 (DAL) Dallas, TX St. Edward.
Brawner, Frank '05 (LEX) Winchester, KY St. Joseph; Mount Sterling, KY St. Patrick.
Bray, Kevin '67 (FRS) Absent on Sick Leave.
Brazaskas, Robert '66 (TUC) Retired.
Breaker, Donald J. '64 (CIN) Retired.
Bream, James I. '64 (SFS) Retired.
Breault, Charles *o.m.i.* '52 (BO) Chelmsford, MA St. Joseph Cemetery, Inc.
Breault, Charles *o.m.i.* '59 (BO)[U] Lowell, MA St. Eugene House (Residence).
Breault, William F. *s.j.* '62 (SJ)[M] Los Gatos, CA Sacred Heart Jesuit Center.
Breaux, Allen '81 (LAF) Duson, LA St. Benedict the Moor; Duson, LA St. Theresa of the Child Jesus.
Breaux, John G. '04 (LAF) Loreauville, LA St. Joseph.
Breaux, Overton Joseph '68 (LAF) Maurice, LA St. Alphonsus; Defenders of the Bond.
Brecht, David L. *o.s.a.* '65 (DET) Grosse Pointe Park, MI St. Clare of Montefalco; [E] Ray Township, MI Austin Catholic Academy.
Breck, Steven H. '00 (CLV) Bay Village, OH St. Raphael.
Breczinski, Paul '98 (BAL) Bradshaw, MD St. Stephen.
Bredeck, Martin J. *s.j.* '64 (KC)[J] Kansas City, MO Rockhurst Jesuit Community.
Bredemeyer, Ryan '07 (PEO) Washington, IL St. Patrick's.
Breen, Bernard J. '72 (L) Louisville, KY St. Frances of Rome; Louisville, KY St. Leonard.
Breen, Brendan *c.p.* '50 (SCR)[L] Scranton, PA Saint Ann's Passionist Monastery.
Breen, Damian '98 (MET) Bridgewater, NJ St. Bernard of Clairvaux.
Breen, Rev. Msgr. Edward J. '58 (BRK) Jackson Heights, NY Our Lady of Fatima Retired.
Breen, Francis J. *m.m.* '70 (NY)[DD] Maryknoll Maryknoll Fathers and Brothers.
Breen, Gregory '04 (RVC) Garden City, NY St. Joseph's.
Breen, James E. '80 (BGP)[O] Stamford, CT The Catherine Dennis Keefe Queen of the Clergy Retired Priests' Residence Retired.
Breen, James J. '80 (BGP) Retired.
Breen, Joseph P. '61 (NSH) Nashville, TN St. Edward.
Breen, Kenneth *o.de.m.* '85 (SP)[N] St. Petersburg, FL St. Peter Nolasco Residence; Saint Petersburg, FL Cathedral of St. Jude the Apostle.
Breen, Philip M. '65 (NSH) Nashville, TN St. Ann; [L] Nashville, TN Ladies of Charity Welfare Agency, Inc.; Deans; Presbyteral Council; Clergy Personnel Board.
Breen, Robert H. '57 (PH) Retired.
Breidenbach, John '87 (EVN) Evansville, IN St. Theresa.
Breier, Donald P. '69 (PIT) Pittsburgh, PA St. Paul Cathedral; St. Paul Cathedral.
Breier, Rev. Msgr. Henry J. '94 (STL) St. Louis, MO St. Raphael The Archangel.
Breig, Gary R. '78 (STL) Military Chaplains; Air Force Chaplains.
Breighner, Joseph F. '71 (BAL) Baltimore, MD Cathedral of Mary Our Queen; Special Assignment.
Breindel, Charles L. (RIC) Virginia Beach, VA Church of the Ascension.
Breitbach, Richard C. '61 (MIL) Retired.
Brelsford, William J. '70 (LA) Los Angeles, CA Visitation.
Brembah, Philip '98 (FWT) Arlington, TX St. Joseph's.
Bremer, Al '02 (OWN) Sebree, KY St. Michael.
Brenberger, Thomas *c.pp.s.* '66 (CIN)[T] Dayton, OH Community Support Charitable Trust; Maria Stein, OH St. John the Baptist; Maria Stein, OH Most Precious Blood; Maria Stein, OH St. Rose; Maria Stein, OH St. Sebastian.
Brenes–Chaves, Fabio Roy De Jesus '85 (NEW) Elizabeth, NJ Immaculate Heart of Mary and Saint Patrick.
Breneville, Garcia (BO) Lowell, MA Ste. Marguerite d'Youville; Lowell, MA St. Rita.
Brenk, Frederick E. *s.j.* '63 (MIL)[P] Milwaukee, WI Arrupe House Jesuit Community.
Brenkle, Rev. Msgr. John J. '58 (SR) Saint Helena, CA St. Helena; Promoter of Justice; Diocesan Judges.
Brenkus, Pavol '01 (ATL) Peachtree City, GA Holy Trinity.
Brenna, William D. '09 (SUP) Mellen, WI St. George; Mellen, WI Most Precious Blood; Mellen, WI St. Anthony; Mellen, WI Most Holy Rosary; Mellen, WI St. Anne.
Brennan, Anthony V. *m.m.* '61 (FgM) Maryknoll, NY MARYKNOLL.
Brennan, Bernard F. '62 (SFR)[K] San Rafael, CA Nazareth House of San Rafael, Inc. Retired.
Brennan, Brett A. '91 (SAV) Statesboro Deanery.
Brennan, Brian C. '79 (NY) Croton–on–Hudson, NY Holy Name of Mary; Mahopac, NY St. John the Evangelist.
Brennan, Cathal '52 (P) Retired.
Brennan, Rev. Msgr. Dermot R. '56 (NY)[DD] Bronx, NY John Cardinal O'Connor Residence; Yorktown Heights, NY St. Patrick Retired.
Brennan, Edmund J. '82 (ALN) Unassigned.
Brennan, Eugene P. '70 (STL) Lambert – St. Louis International Airport; Florissant, MO St. Sabina Retired.
Brennan, Francis C. *s.j.* '58 (STL)[O] St. Louis, MO Jesuit Community Corporation at Saint Louis University – Jesuit Hall.
Brennan, George P. '68 (STL) DEPARTMENT OF VETERANS AFFAIRS HOSPITALS AND CHAPLAINS Retired.
Brennan, George '75 (ALB) Copake Falls, NY Parish of Our Lady of Hope; Ecumenical and Interreligious Affairs of the Roman Catholic Diocese of Albany, Commission for.
Brennan, Gerard M. '50 (BO) Senior Priests. Retired.
Brennan, James A. *c.ss.r.* '64 (PH) Philadelphia, PA Visitation B.V.M.
Brennan, James F. '55 (BO) Senior Priests. Retired.
Brennan, Rev. Msgr. John A. '56 (TYL) Retired.
Brennan, John D. '70 (PIT) East McKeesport, PA St. Robert Bellarmine.
Brennan, John J. '78 (SPR) Agawam, MA St. John the Evangelist.
Brennan, John P. *s.m.a.* '64 (LA)[A] Camarillo, CA St. John's Seminary.
Brennan, John W. *o.s.f.s.* '65 (WIL)[J] Childs, MD Retirement and Assisted Care Facility Retired.
Brennan, Joseph (Dennis) *o.s.b.* '74 (LA)[P] Valyermo, CA St. Andrew's Abbey.
Brennan, Joseph F. *s.j.* '56 (BO)[U] Weston, MA Campion Health Center, Inc.
Brennan, Joseph F. '59 (LAF) Retired.
Brennan, Joseph T. *o.s.f.s.* '98 (ARL) Reston, VA St. John Neumann.
Brennan, Joseph T. *s.j.* '69 (DET)[K] Clarkston, MI Colombiere Center.
Brennan, Rev. Msgr. Joseph '80 (LA) San Pedro, CA Holy Trinity.
Brennan, Rev. Msgr. Keith R. '84 (PMB)[A] Boynton Beach, FL St. Vincent de Paul Regional Seminary; On Duty Outside the Diocese.
Brennan, Keith *s.d.s.* '70 (MIL)[P] Milwaukee Salvatorian Provincial Offices Retired.
Brennan, Rev. Msgr. Keith '84 (PMB) Judges.
Brennan, Lawrence C. '76 (STL) On Duty Outside the Archdiocese.
Brennan, Lawrence C. '76 (COS) Monument, CO St. Peter; Office of Continuing Formation of Clergy; Office of Permanent Diaconate; Team.
Brennan, Rev. Msgr. Mark E. '76 (WDC) Gaithersburg, MD St. Martin of Tours; Archdiocesan College of Consultors; Priest Council.
Brennan, Matthew '62 (BIR) Retired.
Brennan, Rev. Msgr. Michael J. '71 (BRK) Jackson Heights, NY Our Lady of Fatima; Flushing, NY St.

Andrew Avellino.
Brennan, P. Paul '59 (ROC) Willard, NY Drug Treatment Center; Romulus, NY Five Points Correctional Facility.
Brennan, Patrick A. *o.s.a.* '63 (SB) Upland, CA St. Anthony.
Brennan, Patrick J. '73 (CHI) Other Assignments.
Brennan, Patrick *c.p.* '73 (LA)[P] Sierra Madre, CA Passionist Residence; [V] Sierra Madre, CA Mater Dolorosa Passionist Retreat Center, Inc.
Brennan, Patrick '77 (P) Portland, OR Cathedral of the Immaculate Conception.
Brennan, Patrick '77 (P) College of Consultors; Judicial Vicar; Judges.
Brennan, Paul P. '59 (ROC) Retired.
Brennan, Pierce A. *s.j.* '76 (NY)[DD] Loyola Hall, Jesuit Community.
Brennan, Rev. Msgr. Ralph '57 (AUS) Retired.
Brennan, Rev. Msgr. Robert J. '89 (RVC) Vicar General and Moderator of the Curia; Presbyteral Council; Priests' Personnel Assignment Board; Vicar General; College of Consultors; Long Beach, NY St. Mary of the Isle; Catholic Lawyer's Guild.
Brennan, Robert J. *c.s.c.* '68 (FTW)[H] Notre Dame Congregation of Holy Cross, United States Province of Priests & Brothers.
Brennan, Robert M. '65 (NEW)[L] Rutherford, NJ St. John Vianney Residence for Priests Retired.
Brennan, Ronan P. '50 (SAC) Jackson, CA Immaculate Conception Retired.
Brennan, Rev. Msgr. Seamus F. '72 (MET) Somerville, NJ Immaculate Conception; College of Consultors; Deans.
Brennan, Terrence M. *s.j.* '76 (MIL)[P] Milwaukee, WI Pere Marquette Jesuit Community; [E] Milwaukee, WI Marquette University High School.
Brennan, Terrence P. '99 (SFE) St. Vincent's Hospital.
Brennan, Thomas J. '74 (PH) Coatesville, PA Our Lady of the Rosary.
Brennan, Thomas J. *s.j.* '96 (PH)[C] Jesuit Fathers; [Y] Loyola Center and Manresa Hall.
Brennan, Thomas '89 (LAN) Retired.
Brennan, Thomas '66 (TR) Retired.
Brennan, Timothy J. *o.s.b.* '78 (PAT)[N] Morristown St. Mary's Abbey.
Brennan, Walter G. *s.j.* '60 (FgM) Los Gatos, CA Society of Jesus.
Brennan, William J. '49 (L) Retired.
Brennan, William J. *s.j.* '51 (MIL)[P] Wauwatosa, WI Jesuit Community at St. Camillus.
Brennan, Rev. Msgr. William P. '63 (CAM) Haddonfield, NJ Church of Christ the King, Haddonfield, N.J.; Members.
Brennell, John J. '78 (STL) Imperial, MO St. Joseph.
Brennell, Rev. Msgr. John J. (STL) Archdiocesan Consultors.
Brenner, Raymond '69 (EVN) Jasper, IN St. Joseph; Deans.
Brenner, Rev. Msgr. Thomas R. '61 (HBG) Retired.
Brenny, Kenneth '63 (SCL) Deans Retired.
Brenon, Terence V. '91 (SAN) Abilene, TX St. Vincent Pallotti.
Brensinger, Richard C. '92 (ALN)[O] Kutztown, PA Albright College (Reading); [O] Kutztown, PA Kutztown University (Kutztown).
Brent, James *o.p.* '10 (WDC)[C] Catholic University of America, The; [B] Washington, DC Dominican House of Studies.
Breski, Martin *o.f.m.conv.* '69 (BAL) Ellicott City, MD Franciscan Mission Association, Inc.; Ellicott City, MD Franciscan Mission Association; [Q] Ellicott City Order of Friars Minor Conventual.
Breski, Martin *o.f.m. conv.* (HRT) Kensington, CT St. Paul.
Breslawski, Rev. Msgr. William G. '79 (RVC) Lynbrook, NY Our Lady of Peace; Procurator & Advocates; Presbyteral Council; College of Consultors.
Breslin, Cornelius J. '00 (WIL) Unassigned or Leave of Absence.
Breslin, J. Michael '65 (RIC) Cape Charles, VA St. Charles Borromeo.
Breslin, John B. *s.j.* '73 (NY)[DD] New York, NY Murray–Weigel Hall.
Breslin, Rev. Msgr. John E. '61 (PH) Philadelphia, PA Holy Family Retired.
Breslin, John S. '85 (CHI) Chicago, IL St. Michael the Archangel.
Breslin, John *s.m.m.* '56 (RVC)[N] Bay Shore, NY Montfort Missionaries Retired.
Breslin, Paul *o.f.m.* '88 (FgM) New York, NY Holy Name Province.
Breslin, William E. '74 (DEN) Boulder, CO Sacred Heart of Jesus.
Bresnahan, Edward J. '10 (ARL) Notaries; Fredericksburg, VA St. Mary of the Immaculate Conception.
Bresnahan, James F. *s.j.* '59 (BO)[U] Newton, MA The Jesuit Community at Boston College.
Bresnahan, John E. *o.s.a.* '36 (PH)[Y] Villanova, PA St. Thomas Monastery.
Bresnahan, John J. '60 (CHI) Schiller Park, IL St. Beatrice Retired.
Bresnahan, Richard F. '58 (PEO) Retired.
Bresnahan, Thomas J. '60 (MAN) Retired.
Bresowar, Vincent '11 (BIR) Huntsville, AL Holy Spirit; [A] Huntsville, AL Pope John Paul II Catholic High School.
Brethour, Gary G. '89 (LIN) McCook, NE St. Patrick.
Breton, Albert '54 (SPR) Retired.
Breton, Raymond G. '68 (OAK) Judicial Vicar; Presbyteral Council; Judicial Vicar & Director; Judges; Vicars for Religious; Ex Officio.
Breton, Richard D. '08 (NOR) Uncasville, CT St. John the Evangelist; Quaker Hill, CT Our Lady of Perpetual Help; North Grosvenordale, CT St. Stephen; Oakdale, CT Our Lady of the Lakes.
Bretone, Richard J. '89 (BRK) Ridgewood, NY St. Matthias; [V] Jackson Heights, NY Eternal Flame of Hope Ministries, Inc.
Brett, Frank X. '59 (KNX) Retired.
Brett, Frank '59 (ORL) Indialantic, FL Holy Name of Jesus Retired.
Brett, Stephen F. *s.s.j.* '76 (BAL)[Q] Baltimore, MD St. Joseph's Manor.
Bretzke, James T. *s.j.* '81 (BO)[U] Newton, MA The Jesuit Community at Boston College.
Breu, David L. '73 (NU) Graceville, MN Holy Rosary.
Breu, David '73 (SCL) Browns Valley, MN St. Anthony's.
Breunig, Rudy V. *s.t.* '65 (SAV) Bainbridge, GA St. Joseph's.
Brewczynski, Jacek M. '96 (DET) Absent on Leave.
Brewer, Dexter S. '89 (NSH) Nashville, TN Christ the King; Judicial Vicar; Judges; Presbyteral Council; Priest Benefit Foundation; Diocesan Finance Board; Vicars General; Lay Retirement Administrative Board.
Brewer, Dexter (KNX) Marriage Tribunal.
Brewer, Mark Alan '03 (ROC) Rochester, NY St. Charles Borromeo; Board of Directors.
Brewer, Timothy M. '79 (WOR) Leominster, MA Our Lady of the Lake; Deans; Presbyteral Council.
Brey, Christopher J. '97 (SFD) Beardstown, IL St. Fidelis; Beardstown, IL St. Alexius; Ashland, IL St. Luke; Jacksonville Deanery; Comite Diocesano de Ministerio Hispano – Diocesan Committee for Hispanic Ministry; Coordinator of Hispanic Ministry; Ashland, IL St. Augustine; Presbyteral Council.
Breza, Paul J. '63 (WIN) Retired.
Brezovec, John F. '66 (ALT) Johnstown, PA Memorial Medical Center Lee Campus; [E] Johnstown, PA Good Samaritan Medical Center; Johnstown, PA St. John Gualbert Cathedral; Johnstown, PA Memorial Medical Center; Johnstown, PA Good Samaritan Medical Center.
Brice, Donald '58 (WDC)[M] Washington, DC Cardinal O'Boyle Residence for Priests Retired.
Brice, Rev. Msgr. Frederick J. '69 (MIA) Retired.
Brice, Steven J. '82 (LC) Wausau, WI St. Anne.
Briceland, Alan *s.j.* '63 (BRK) Elmhurst General Hospital.
Briceland, W. Alan *s.j.* '65 (NY)[DD] New York, NY Jesuit Community of the Immaculate Conception.
Brick, Donald *o.c.d.* '00 (MIL)[P] Hubertus, WI Discalced Carmelite Monastery – Holy Hill Basilica of the National Shrine of Mary, Help of Christians, Holy Hill.
Brick, Paul T. *s.d.s.* '63 (SAV) Retired.
Brickler, R. Richard '61 (ROC) Judges Retired.
Brickner, Charles W. '75 (RIC) Woodlawn, VA St. Joseph's.
Brickner, Joseph *l.c.* '04 (HRT)[B] Cheshire, CT Novitiate of the Legion of Christ.
Brickner, Joseph *l.c.* '04 (WDC)[O] Potomac, MD Legionaries of Christ.
Brickner, Ronald J. '92 (TOL) Vermilion, OH St. Mary; St. Vincent dePaul Society.
Bride, Rev. Msgr. Thomas R. '67 (NOR) Old Lyme, CT Christ the King; College of Consultors; Members; Notaries; Advisory Ministry Evaluation Committee.
Bridges, Clarence S. '88 (ALT) Johnstown, PA St. John Gualbert Cathedral.
Bridges, Rev. Msgr. James P. '62 (SAN) Midland, TX St. Stephen's.
Bridgman, Mark M. '96 (OM) Bellevue, NE St. Mary.
Bried, William K. *o.f.m.* '79 (NY) New York, NY St. Stephen of Hungary.
Brieffies, John *m.s.f.* '56 (RIC) West Point, VA; [K] West Point, VA Missionaries of the Holy Family, General Mission Office–M.S.F., Inc.
Brien, Paul J. *m.m.* '60 (FgM) Maryknoll, NY MARYKNOLL.
Brien, Peter C. *m.m.* '60 (FgM) Maryknoll, NY MARYKNOLL.
Brienz, Edward R. '96 (Y) Office of Missions/Evangelization; Youngstown, OH St. Columba Parish; Presbyteral Council.
Brierley, Andrew '08 (PMB) West Palm Beach, FL Holy Name of Jesus.
Briers, Fred *c.r.* '04 (MOB) Montgomery, AL Resurrection Catholic Church.
Bries, Marvin J. '73 (DUB)[F] Guttenberg, IA St. Mary and Immaculate Conception School System; Guttenberg, IA Immaculate Conception; Guttenberg, IA St. Joseph; Guttenberg, IA St. Mary.
Briese, Dominic *o.p.* '96 (OAK)[L] Oakland, CA Order of Preachers (Province of the Most Holy Name of Jesus – Western Dominican Province).
Briese, Llane '10 (ATL) Roswell, GA St. Peter Chanel.
Briese, Michael W. '09 (WDC) Washington, DC Holy Name.
Brietske, Rev. Msgr. Richard C. '62 (TR) Building Commission Retired.
Briffa, Salvino P. '71 (DET) Westland, MI St. Damian; Westland, MI St. Theodore of Canterbury Retired.
Brigandi, Rev. Msgr. Paul A. '54 (SY) Retired.
Brigandi, Stephen J. '97 (RVC) Bayville, NY St. Gertrude's.
Briganti, Phil '73 (ELP) El Paso, TX St. Raphael.
Briganti, Philip J. '73 (PAT) On Duty Outside the Diocese.
Briggman, Michael J. '68 (ALN) Bally, PA Most Blessed Sacrament; [J] Bethlehem, PA Holy Family Villa Retired.
Briggs, Michael J. *m.m.* '76 (FgM) Maryknoll, NY MARYKNOLL.
Brighenti, Kenneth D. '88 (MET) On Duty Outside the Diocese; Navy Reserve Chaplains.
Brighenti, Kenneth D. '88 (BAL)[A] Emmitsburg, MD Mount St. Mary's Seminary.
Brignac, H. L. '83 (NO) Retired.
Brillantes, Edgar B. '80 (HON) Wahiawa, HI Our Lady of Sorrows.
Brillantes, Michael '83 (SFR) San Bruno, CA St. Bruno.
Brimley, Wilfred A. *c.s.p.* '62 (BRK)[R] Retired Retired.
Brincat, George '57 (LA) Retired.
Brindamour, Maurice L. '74 (PRO) Woonsocket, RI Our Lady, Queen of Martyrs; Deans.
Bringas, Daniel '76 (FRS) Wasco, CA State Prison.
Brinker, William *c.s.c.* (FTW)[H] Notre Dame Congregation of Holy Cross, United States Province of Priests & Brothers.
Brinkman, Barry '91 (SAL) Concordia, KS Our Lady of Perpetual Help Parish; Chancellor; Associate Judges; Personnel Board; Lay Review Board–Diocesan Committee Regarding Alleged Cases of Child Sexual Abuse; Ex Officio; Belleville, KS St. Isidore Parish; Belleville, KS St. George Parish; Belleville, KS St. Edward Parish; Catholic Charities Board; Diocesan Administrator.
Brinkman, Gerard *c.ss.r.* '61 (PH) Philadelphia, PA St. Peter the Apostle.
Brinkman, James J. '81 (SUP) New Richmond, WI St. Patrick; New Richmond, WI Immaculate Conception; Board of Directors.
Brinkman, John T. *m.m.* '71 (FgM) Maryknoll, NY MARYKNOLL.
Brinkman, Terence P. '73 (GAL) Baytown, TX St. John the Evangelist; Censor Librorum.
Brinkmann, Charles *c.ss.r.* '56 (NY)[FF] Esopus, NY Mount St. Alphonsus Redemptorist Retreat Center.
Brinkmann, Charles *c.s.s.r.* (HBG)[G] Ephrata, PA St. Clement's Mission House.
Brinkmoeller, David E. '71 (CIN) Dayton, OH St. Helen; Dayton, OH Our Lady of the Immaculate Conception.
Brinn, Adrian J. '68 (SB) Retired.
Brinn, Rev. Msgr. John J. '62 (NY) Poughkeepsie, NY St. Mary.
Brinsmade, John F. '81 (HRT) Plainville, CT Our Lady of Mercy.
Briody, Hugh J. '63 (SUP) Retired.
Briones, Jesus *s.v.d.* '76 (FTW) Fort Wayne, IN St. Patrick; Fort Wayne, IN St. Patrick; Fort Wayne.
Briones, Jose Maria '93 (TLS) Tulsa, OK St. Thomas More; Hispanic Ministry.
Brioni, Luigi *s.x.* '61 (PAT)[N] Wayne Xaverian Missionary Fathers; Wayne, NJ XAVERIAN MISSIONARY FATHERS.
Brioso–Texidor, Luis '93 (MO) DEPARTMENT OF VETERANS AFFAIRS HOSPITALS AND CHAPLAINS.
Brioso Texidor, Luis R. (SJN) San Juan, PR Ntr. Sra. de la Caridad del Cobre.
Briseno, Miguel *o.f.m.conv.* '90 (ELP) El Paso, TX Our Lady of Mt. Carmel.
Briseno, Rev. Msgr. Pedro '81 (BWN) Harlingen, TX Immaculate Heart of Mary.
Brislin, Thomas *c.p.* '68 (FgM) New Rochelle, NY St. Paul of the Cross Province.
Brisotti, William F. '68 (RVC) Wyandanch, NY Our Lady of the Miraculous Medal.
Brissette, Reginald R. '63 (PRT) Westbrook, ME St. Anthony of Padua Parish; Windham, ME Our Lady of Perpetual Help.
Brisson, Robert A. '85 (NY)[II] New York, NY Prelature of the Holy Cross and Opus Dei; New York.
Bristow, David '98 (FWT) Fort Worth, TX St. Mary of the Assumption; Deans.
Brito, Cristiano Aparecido *o.s.b.* '91 (RIC) Virginia Beach, VA St. Gregory the Great.
Brito, Cristiano E. *o.s.b.* '91 (GBG)[H] Latrobe, PA Saint Vincent Archabbey.
Brito, Larry R. '00 (SFE) Ohkay Owingeh, NM San

Juan Bautista; College of Consultors; Ohkay Owingeh, NM Tewa Missions; Presbyteral Council of the Archdiocese of Santa Fe.
Britt, William J. '53 (STL) Retired.
Brittain, Gerald W. '62 (MIL) West Bend, WI Holy Angels.
Britto, Antony *s.a.c.* '88 (GR) Muskegon, MI St. Thomas the Apostle; Muskegon, MI Our Lady of Grace.
Britto, Rev. Msgr. Federico A. '82 (PH) Philadelphia, PA Saint Cyprian.
Britto, John A. *c.s.c.* '11 (FTW)[H] Notre Dame Congregation of Holy Cross, United States Province of Priests & Brothers.
Britto, Sean *c.s.j.* '01 (NEW) Orange, NJ Mt. Carmel.
Brixius, Hilary R. '68 (WIN) Absent on Leave.
Broadhurst, T. Paul *c.s.b.* '60 (ROC)[K] Rochester, NY Basilian Residence.
Brobst, James *o.m.i.* '90 (BEL)[F] Belleville, IL Shrine of Our Lady of the Snows; Councilors.
Brobst, James *o.m.i.* '90 (WDC) Belleville, IL; [O] Washington, DC Provincial Offices of the United States Province of the Missionary Oblates of Mary Immaculate.
Brobst, Richard A. '65 (Y) Retired.
Brocato, John K. '03 (ALX) Military Chaplains; Army Chaplains.
Brocato, Robert S. '95 (SJ) On Duty Outside the Diocese; Special Assignment.
Broccolo, Gerard T. '65 (CHI) Retired.
Brock, David F. '56 (DET) Retired.
Brock, William '91 (DEN) Retired.
Brockett, Norman L. '87 (HRT)[J] West Hartford, CT Saint Mary Home; Special and other Archdiocesan Assignment.
Brockhaus, Rev. Msgr. Edward '64 (SD) Retired.
Brockland, John A. '91 (STL) St. Charles, MO Sts. Joachim and Ann.
Brockland, Robert J. *c.m.* '74 (STL)[O] St. Louis, MO Lazarist Residence.
Brockman, Blaise N. '77 (LA) Arcadia, CA Holy Angels.
Brockman, Rev. Msgr. David D. '90 (R) Diocesan Judges; Vicar General; Diocesan Consultors; Ex Officio.
Brockman, Leon *o.c.s.o.* '55 (SPC)[F] Ava, MO Assumption Abbey (Trappist).
Brockman, Norbert C. *s.m.* '73 (SAT)[C] San Antonio, TX St. Mary's University of San Antonio, Texas.
Brockman, Norbert *s.m.* '73 (SAT)[L] San Antonio, TX Marianist Residence.
Brockmyre, Philip C. '02 (SY) Phoenix, NY St. Stephen.
Brockson, Scott D. '96 (PH) Bridgeport, PA St. Augustine; Swedesburg, PA Sacred Heart.
Broderick, C. Michael '87 (WOR) Whitinsville, MA St. Patrick.
Broderick, James M. '60 (BO) Senior Priests.; Newburyport, MA Immaculate Conception Retired.
Broderick, John W. '89 (SY) Absent on Leave.
Broderick, Leo P. '56 (DET) Retired.
Broderick, Richard '70 (ALB) Special Assignment.
Broderick, Sean A. *c.s.sp.* '65 (MET) Hillsborough, NJ Mary, Mother of God.
Brodersen, Rev. Msgr. Charles F. '48 (OM) Retired.
Brodersen, Steven W. '85 (SC) Presbyteral Council; Halbur, IA Sacred Heart; Halbur, IA St. Augustine's; Halbur, IA Holy Angels.
Brodeski, Rev. Msgr. Aaron R. '98 (RCK) Woodstock, IL St. Mary; [B] Woodstock, IL Marian Central Catholic High School.
Brodeur, Henry C. *m.s.* '66 (FR)[F] Attleboro, MA La Salette Shrine.
Brodeur, Scott N. *s.j.* '90 (BO)[U] Boston The Society of Jesus of New England–Provincial Offices.
Brodeur, Theodore J. '66 (MAR) Brimley, MI St. Francis Xavier; Brimley, MI Blessed Kateri Tekakwitha; Vicars Forane.
Brodniak, Anthony B. *m.m.* '54 (NY)[DD].
Brodnick, Edward J. '76 (COV) Augusta, KY St. Augustine; Brooksville, KY St. James.
Brodnick, Joseph '69 (CLV) Administrative Leave.
Brody, Donald *o.f.m.cap.* '47 (GB)[J] Appleton, WI St. Fidelis Friary Retired.
Brodzeller, Robert E. *s.j.* '63 (MIL)[P] Wauwatosa, WI Jesuit Community at St. Camillus.
Broering, Raymond L. '53 (COV) Administrative Leave Retired.
Brogan, Jared J. '11 (PAT) Morristown, NJ St. Margaret of Scotland.
Brogan, Leo '67 (PHX) Retired.
Brogan, William '68 (NY) Bronx, NY St. Raymond.
Brogus, Albert G. '45 (SCR) Retired.
Brohammer, Ronald '60 (MIA) Retired.
Broheimer, John P. '03 (OM)[B] Elgin, NE Pope John XXIII Central Catholic High School at Elgin; Neligh, NE St. Francis; Tilden, NE Our Lady of Mt. Carmel; [N] Neligh, NE Legion of Mary.
Broker, William H. *c.ss.r.* '49 (STL)[O] Liguori, MO Liguori Mission House/Redemptorists.
Brokman, James P. '97 (DUB) Sumner, IA Immaculate Conception; Fayette, IA St. Francis of Assisi; Clermont, IA St. Peter; West Union, IA Holy Name; Appointed By The Archbishop.
Bromenshenkel, Fintan *o.s.b.* '45 (SCL) Collegeville, MN St. John's Abbey; [I] Collegeville, MN St. John's Abbey, of the Order of St. Benedict.
Bromley, Vincent M. '65 (SUP) Retired.
Brommer, Joshua R. '06 (HBG) Administrative Assistant to the Bishop and Liturgical Coordinator.
Bromwich, James S. '03 (L) On Duty Outside the Archdiocese.
Broniak, Leonard *c.ss.r.* '79 (GAL) Houston, TX Holy Ghost; Deaf Apostolate.
Bronkiewicz, Rev. Msgr. Laurence R. '73 (BGP) Diocesan Censors; Ridgefield, CT St. Mary.
Brookbank, Scott F. *o.f.m.* '08 (PRO)[O] Providence, RI St. Francis Friary; Providence, RI St. Mary.
Brooker, Richard L. *m.m.* '55 (NY)[DD] Retired.
Brooks, Armand L. '97 (FAR) Special Assignment.
Brooks, Bryan V. '93 (TLS) Priests' Personnel Committee.
Brooks, Bryan '93 (TLS) Tulsa, OK Church of the Madalene.
Brooks, Charles R. '65 (GB) Retired.
Brooks, David R. *s.j.* '78 (WDC)[O] Washington, DC The Jesuit Community of St. Aloysius Gonzaga.
Brooks, Jeddie P. '77 (SPR) Monson, MA St. Patrick's; Brimfield, MA St. Christopher's.
Brooks, John E. *s.j.* '59 (WOR)[N] Worcester, MA Jesuits of the Holy Cross, Inc.
Brooks, Michael J. *ss.cc.* '61 (LA)[P] La Verne, CA Congregation of the Sacred Hearts of Jesus and Mary.
Brooks, Robert C. '61 (ARL) Retired.
Brooks, Robert E. '95 (SAC) Tahoe City, CA Corpus Christi.
Brooks, Thomas M. '78 (E) North East, PA St. Gregory Thaumaturgus.
Brooks, Rev. Msgr. William C. '76 (AUS) Austin, TX St. Theresa.
Broom, Edward *o.m.v.* '86 (LA) Hawaiian Gardens, CA St. Peter Chanel.
Broome, William *m.s.a.* '05 (NOR)[G] Cromwell Society of the Missionaries of the Holy Apostles.
Brophy, Edward G. '93 (BRK) Brooklyn, NY St. Edmund.
Brophy, John L. '69 (MIL) Retired.
Brophy, R. Michael *s.j.* '69 (DET)[K] Clarkston, MI Colombiere Center.
Brosk, Steven J. '90 (MO) Military Chaplains; Air Force Reserve Chaplains.
Brosmer, John '05 (EVN) Diocesan Council of Priests; Dale, IN St. Joseph; Santa Claus, IN St. Nicholas.
Brosmer, Thomas J. '69 (COL) Columbus, OH St. Cecilia.
Brosnahan, Bruce C. '01 (TLS) Fairfax, OK Sacred Heart.
Brosnan, Rev. Msgr. Dermot '57 (SAT)[K] San Antonio, TX Padua Place Retired.
Brosnan, Rev. Msgr. Liam P. '59 (SAT) Retired.
Brosnan, Thomas F. '81 (BRK) Bayside, NY Sacred Heart of Jesus.
Brossart, Scott *s.o.l.t.* '00 (FAR) Dunseith, ND St. Michael the Archangel Dunseith; Belcourt, ND St. Ann.
Brost, Corey D. *c.s.v.* '06 (CHI) Arlington Heights, IL; [N] Arlington Heights Viatorian Province Center–Clerics of St. Viator; [D] Arlington Heights, IL St. Viator High School.
Brost, Frederick '56 (SUP) Retired.
Brothersen, Maynard J. '48 (DAV)[J] Davenport, IA St. Vincent Center Retired.
Broudou, Joseph G. '96 (OM) Omaha, NE St. Stephen the Martyr; [M] Crofton, NE St. Joseph Church of Constance Endowment Trust Fund; [M] Crofton, NE St. Rose Church Cemetery Endowment Trust Fund.
Brougher, Douglas C. '62 (NO) New Orleans, LA Touro Infirmary; New Orleans, LA Good Shepherd.
Brouillard, John '56 (P) Retired.
Brouillard, Louis A. (AGN) Retired.
Brouillette, Daniel E. '09 (NO) Destrehan, LA St. Charles Borromeo.
Brouillette, Thomas S. '96 (LIN)[C] Hastings, NE St. Cecilia's Middle School/High School; [L] Hastings, NE St. Cecilia High School Endowment Fund.
Brouillette, Thomas '96 (LIN) Roseland, NE Sacred Heart; Diocesan Consultors; Diocesan Area CCD Directors.
Broussard, A. Rex '66 (LAF) Duson, LA St. Basil.
Broussard, Dennis A. '91 (MAN) Absent on Leave.
Broussard, F. David '93 (LAF) Kaplan, LA Our Lady of the Holy Rosary.
Broussard, Henry J. '72 (LAF) Cankton, LA St. John Berchmans.
Broussard, Hubert C. '52 (HT) Retired.
Broussard, John S. *c.s.b.* '48 (GAL) Manvel, TX Sacred Heart of Jesus.
Broussard, Ken '03 (LAF) Defenders of the Bond; Graduate Studies.
Broussard, Paul '98 (LAF) Rayne, LA St. Leo IV.
Broussard, Richard Dale '00 (LAF) Pine Prairie, LA St. Peter.
Broussard, Rev. Msgr. Ronald '88 (LAF) New Iberia, LA St. Edward.
Broussard, Ted (LAF) Lawtell, LA St. Bridget.
Broussard, Theodore '98 (LAF)[K] Opelousas, LA Cursillo Center; Cursillo.
Broussard, Warren J. *s.j.* '88 (NO)[R] New Orleans, LA Jesuit Provincial Office.
Brouwers, Rev. Msgr. Hans A.L. '78 (PH) Wayne, PA St. Katharine of Siena.
Brovey, Rev. Msgr. Steven L. '91 (CHR) Charleston, SC Cathedral of St. John the Baptist; Charleston, SC St. Mary of the Annunciation.
Brown, Arthur A. '57 (BO) Senior Priests. Retired.
Brown, Avram E. '04 (SAC) Gridley, CA Sacred Heart.
Brown, Benedict J. '74 (L) Springfield, KY Holy Rosary; [A] St. Catharine, KY St. Catharine College.
Brown, Bruce '63 (P) Portland, OR Sacred Heart Retired.
Brown, Charles D. '93 (GR) Holland, MI St. Francis de Sales.
Brown, Charles E. '71 (WDC) Burtonsville, MD Resurrection Parish Retired.
Brown, Charles L. '73 (BRK) On Leave/Unassigned.
Brown, Rev. Msgr. Charles L. '67 (WIL) Wilmington, DE St. John the Beloved; Deans.
Brown, Rev. Msgr. Charles '89 (NY) On Duty Outside the Archdiocese.
Brown, Charles '87 (PSC) Retired.
Brown, Charles '58 (SFE) Retired.
Brown, Charles *s.c.j.* '84 (MIL)[B] Hales Corners, WI Sacred Heart School of Theology; [P] Franklin, WI St. Francis Residence.
Brown, David A. *s.j.* '02 (NO)[R] New Orleans Jesuit Provincial Office.
Brown, David G. *o.s.b.* '75 (CHL)[A] Belmont, NC Belmont Abbey College; [J] Belmont, NC Belmont Abbey.
Brown, David M. *o.s.m.* '48 (CHI) Chicago, IL Assumption of the Blessed Virgin Mary; [N] Chicago, IL Assumption Priory.
Brown, David '07 (P) Eugene, OR St. Paul Catholic Church; Personnel Board.
Brown, Dennis *o.m.v.* '89 (BO)[U] Milton, MA Oblate Residence (St. Joseph House).
Brown, Dom Lawrence *o.s.b.* '84 (BUR)[F] Westfield, VT Monastery of the Immaculate Heart of Mary.
Brown, Douglas T. '06 (CLV) Cleveland, OH Mary Queen of Peace.
Brown, Erin '07 (TR) West Long Branch, NJ St. Jerome.
Brown, Eugene M. '60 (NU) St. Mary's Care Center; [C] Winsted, MN St. Mary's Care Center Retired.
Brown, Everett *s.m.m.* '61 (RVC)[N] Bay Shore, NY Montfort Missionaries.
Brown, Francis Xavier *o.s.b.* '84 (TLS)[G] Hulbert, OK Our Lady of the Annunciation of Clear Creek Monastery.
Brown, George *o.m.i.* '64 (BO)[U] Lowell, MA Missionary Oblates of Mary Immaculate.
Brown, Gerald L. *s.s.* '64 (BAL)[Q] Baltimore Society of St. Sulpice, Province of the United States Retired.
Brown, Gregory *o.f.m.cap.* '04 (WDC)[B] Washington, DC St. Francis Friary–Capuchin College.
Brown, Harold C. *c.pp.s.* '59 (TOL) Liaison Team Priest; [J] Bellevue, OH Sorrowful Mother Shrine; [H] Bellevue Mary Lay Center.
Brown, James E. '72 (TOL) Toledo, OH Our Lady of Perpetual Help; Spiritual Directors.
Brown, James T. '97 (NEW) Bloomfield, NJ Sacred Heart.
Brown, James V. *o.a.r.* '46 (LA)[P] Oxnard, CA Order of Augustinian Recollects (O.A.R.), St. Augustine Priory.
Brown, Jerry W. '01 (OAK) Brentwood, CA Immaculate Heart of Mary.
Brown, Rev. Msgr. John J. '83 (BRK) Belle Harbor, NY St. Francis de Sales; Defenders of the Marriage Bond; Attorneys and Counselors at Canon Law.
Brown, John T. *g.h.m.* '84 (SAV) Swainsboro, GA Holy Trinity.
Brown, Johnathan L. *s.j.* '11 (ELP) El Paso, TX Sacred Heart.
Brown, Joseph A. *s.j.* '72 (MIL)[P] Milwaukee Jesuit Provincial Office, Wisconsin Province.
Brown, Joseph Mary *c.s.j.* '97 (PEO)[K] Princeville, IL Congregation of St. John.
Brown, Joseph *c.pp.s.* '61 (CIN)[N] Carthagena, OH St. Charles Retired.
Brown, Joshua S. '10 (GI) Kearney, NE St. James.
Brown, Keenan Wynn '02 (LAF) Arnaudville, LA St. John Francis Regis; Arnaudville, LA St. Catherine.
Brown, Kenneth A. '77 (STL) Webster Groves, MO Holy Redeemer.
Brown, Kenneth J. '06 (MRY) Arroyo Grande, CA St. Patrick; Diocesan Consultors; Presbyteral Council; Vicars Forane; Diocesan Consultors.
Brown, Lawrence *o.s.b.* '84 (TLS)[G] Hulbert, OK Our Lady of the Annunciation of Clear Creek Monastery.
Brown, Leonard *c.m.f.* '82 (CHI)[N] Oak Park, IL Claretian Missionaries Community Support Trust.
Brown, Leonard *c.m.f.* '82 (ATL)[I] Atlanta, GA Dekalb Community College.
Brown, Lewis E. '67 (ROC) Corning, NY All Saints Retired.

Brown, Matthew F. '63 (SY) Vestal, NY Our Lady of Sorrows; Vestal, NY Binghamton Nursing Homes Retired.
Brown, Matthew J. *o.s.b.* '49 (OKL)[I] Shawnee, OK St. Gregory's Abbey.
Brown, Michael O. '74 (TOL) Toledo, OH St. Clement; College of Consultors.
Brown, Michael R. '89 (ROC) Sonyea, NY Livingston Correctional Facility and Seneca Correctional Facility; Sonyea, NY Groveland Correctional Facility; Auburn, NY St. Hyacinth; Auburn, NY Auburn Correctional Facility.
Brown, Michael '89 (ROC) Auburn, NY St. Francis of Assisi; Auburn, NY Sacred Heart; Auburn, NY St. Hyacinth.
Brown, Ned J. '98 (CIN) Dayton, OH St. Albert the Great.
Brown, Nicholas *s.c.j.* '76 (SAT) San Antonio, TX St. Luke's Baptist Hospital; University Hospital; [L] San Antonio, TX Hospital Ministry House.
Brown, Rev. Msgr. Patrick E. '78 (PAT) Unassigned; Paterson, NJ Cathedral of St. John the Baptist.
Brown, Patrick *o.c.s.o.* '74 (WOR)[N] Spencer, MA St. Joseph's Abbey.
Brown, Phillip J. '89 (BAL)[Q] Baltimore Society of St. Sulpice, Province of the United States.
Brown, Phillip J. *s.s.* '89 (BIS) On Duty Outside the Diocese.
Brown, Phillip J. *s.s.* '89 (WDC)[C] Washington, DC Catholic University of America, The; [C] Catholic University of America, The.
Brown, Richard *s.j.* '58 (SD) San Diego, CA Our Lady of Guadalupe Catholic Parish San Diego.
Brown, Richard '80 (DAL) On Duty Outside the Diocese.
Brown, Rev. Msgr. Robert L. '69 (NOR) Uncasville, CT St. John the Evangelist; Chancellor; College of Consultors; Members; Diocesan Pastoral Council; Notaries; Catholic Relief Services; Advisory Ministry Evaluation Committee.
Brown, Robert P. '63 (SC) Retired.
Brown, Robert W. '66 (ORL) Orlando, FL St. Joseph.
Brown, Rev. Msgr. Robert '69 (NOR) Board of Education.
Brown, Robert *o.s.f.s.* '67 (R) Buxton, NC Our Lady of the Seas.
Brown, Roderick M. *o.p.* '79 (CHI)[N] Chicago, IL St. Pius V Priory.
Brown, Russell D. '04 (MRY) San Luis Obispo, CA San Luis Obispo.
Brown, Shaun S. '94 (NTN) Military Chaplain; Navy Chaplains; Priests Serving Outside the Eparchy.
Brown, Stephan *s.v.d.* '93 (SP)[A] Saint Leo, FL Saint Leo University, Office of Assessment and Institutional Research.
Brown, Stephan *s.v.d.* '93 (ORL) Retired.
Brown, Steven P. '77 (SJ) San Jose, CA St. Maria Goretti; Priests' Retirement Board.
Brown, Theophile W. *o.s.b.* '56 (RIC)[K] Richmond, VA Mary Mother of the Church Abbey; [K] Richmond, VA Mary Mother of the Church Abbey.
Brown, Thomas E. '78 (E) Eldred, PA St. Raphael; Shinglehouse, PA St. Theresa.
Brown, Thomas J. '99 (GR) Muskegon, MI St. Michael's; Muskegon Heights, MI Sacred Heart; Deans.
Brown, Thomas *o.m.i.* '55 (FgM) Washington, DC AMERICAN OBLATE MISSIONS.
Brown, Timothy B. *s.j.* '86 (BAL)[Q] Baltimore, MD Jesuit Community of Loyola University, Inc.; [B] Jesuit Community of Loyola University, Inc.
Brown, Timothy '88 (ROC) Rochester, NY Peace of Christ Roman Catholic Parish of Rochester, NY.
Brown, Victor B. *o.p.* '63 (GAL) Houston, TX Holy Rosary.
Brown, W. P. '80 (PT) Panama City, FL Our Lady of the Rosary.
Brown, Warren A. *o.m.i.* '82 (SAT)[L] San Antonio, TX De Mazenod House; Judges.
Brown, Warren A. *o.m.i.* '82 (CHI)[W] Chicago, IL Oblates for International Pastoral.
Brown, Warren *o.m.i.* '82 (WDC)[O] Washington, DC Provincial Offices of the United States Province of the Missionary Oblates of Mary Immaculate.
Brown, Wilbur J. '04 (LAF) Retired.
Brown, William E. '88 (SFR) Tiburon, CA St. Hilary.
Brown, William P. '80 (PT) Panama City, FL Our Lady Queen of Peace Mission.
Browne, Denis P. *m.m.* '47 (FgM) Maryknoll, NY MARYKNOLL.
Browne, Dennis '79 (SJ) On Leave of Absence.
Browne, Rev. Msgr. George T. '55 (DET) Retired.
Browne, Gerald '81 (MET)[H] Somerset, NJ McCarrick Care Center Retired.
Browne, Rev. Msgr. J. Patrick '67 (SJ) San Jose, CA Cathedral Basilica of St. Joseph; San Jose, CA Five Wounds Portuguese National Church; College of Consultors; Priests' Retirement Board; [O] San Jose, CA San Jose Cathedral Foundation.
Browne, Joseph P. *c.s.c.* '55 (FTW)[H] Holy Cross House Retired.
Browne, Robert M. '61 (BO) Senior Priests. Retired.
Browne, Ronald T. '91 (DET) On Duty Outside the Archdiocese.
Browne, Ronald T. '91 (MAR) Consultors; Ministry Personnel Services, Dept. of; Clergy Support Services; Moderator of the Curia.
Browne, Stanley '81 (GB) Retired.
Browne, William E. '04 (CLV) Parma, OH St. Columbkille.
Brownell, Patrick P. '94 (KNX) Diocesan Consultors; Army National Guard Chaplains.
Brownell, Robert A. '69 (RIC) Richmond, VA St. Peter.
Brownfield, David L. '90 (DAV) Grand Mound, IA Church of St. Philip and James; Delmar, IA St. Patrick's; Delmar, IA St. Anne.
Brownholtz, Andrew C. '01 (PH) Hatfield, PA St. Maria Goretti.
Brownsey, Rev. Msgr. Brian K. '96 (PEO) Vocations Office.
Brownsey, Rev. Msgr. Brian '96 (PEO) Peoria, IL St. Mark's.
Brownstein, Donald P. '81 (COS) Monument, CO St. Peter; Presbyteral Council.
Brozat, Charles *s.a.* '57 (NY)[DD] Garrison, NY Franciscan Friars of the Atonement.
Brozat, Charles *s.a.* '57 (PAT)[N] Ringwood, NJ Holy Name Friary, Inc.
Brozena, Joseph M. '58 (SCR) Retired.
Brozonowicz, Gregory (NOR) Advisory Board.
Brozonowicz, Grzegorz P. '96 (NOR) Old Saybrook, CT St. John; Members; Continuing Education and Formation Commission for the Clergy.
Brozovic, Matthew R. *o.f.m.* '56 (GBG)[H] Uniontown, PA St. Anthony Friary.
Brubaker, Claude '55 (VEN) Retired.
Brubaker, Rev. Msgr. George J. '80 (WIL) Judicial Vicar; Court of First Instance Judges; College of Consultors; Contact; Catholic Relief Services, Inc.
Brubaker, Rev. Msgr. George J. '80 (WIL) Milford, DE St. John the Apostle.
Brubaker, W. Scott '82 (PHX) Mesa, AZ St. Bridget Roman Catholic Parish.
Bruce, Joseph J. *s.j.* '81 (BO)[U] Boston The Society of Jesus of New England–Provincial Offices.
Bruce, Joseph J. *s.j.* '81 (WDC) Chaplains; [O] Washington, DC The Jesuit Community of St. Aloysius Gonzaga.
Bruce, Terry '67 (KC) Kansas City, MO St. Elizabeth's.
Bruch, James A. '65 (SC) Madrid, IA St. Malachy's; Ogden, IA St. John's; Madrid, IA St. John of God; Woodward State Hospital and School.
Bruch, Lynn '86 (SC) Auburn, IA St. Mary's; Lake City, IA St. Mary's; Lake City, IA St. Joseph's.
Bruck, Donald '68 (DM) Retired.
Bruck, Raymond E. '58 (GR) Retired.
Brucker, G. Fredrick '76 (GR) On Special Assignment; Ravenna, MI St. Catherine; Conklin, MI St. Francis Xavier; Conklin, MI St. Joseph's.
Brucker, George W. '56 (ALB) Retired.
Brucksch, James L. '69 (GLD) Retired.
Brucz, James M. *c.s.p.* '74 (PMB)[H] Vero Beach, FL Paulist Fathers Residence.
Brudzynski, Peter F. '50 (BO) Senior Priests. Retired.
Bruecken, Albert *o.s.b.* '77 (KC)[A] Conception, MO Conception Seminary College; [J] Conception, MO Conception Abbey.
Bruemmer, Joseph A. '48 (CIN) Retired.
Bruening, Allen '51 (CLV) Life of Prayer and Penance.
Bruening, Joseph B. '53 (CIN) Retired.
Bruetsch, Joseph J. '70 (LFT) Retired.
Bruggeman, Donald R. '62 (DUB) Retired.
Bruggeman, Sidney B. '09 (GI) U.S. Veterans' Hospital; St. Libory, NE St. Libory's.
Brugger, Rev. Msgr. Robert L. '68 (E) Erie, PA St. George; Finance Council.
Brum, Rev. Msgr. Louis L. '74 (BWN) McAllen, TX Holy Spirit.
Brumleve, Matthew '88 (KC) Kansas City, MO Holy Family.
Brummel, Mark J. *c.m.f.* '60 (CHI)[N] Chicago, IL Claretian Missionaries, St. Jude League, Inc.; [N] Oak Park, IL Claretian Missionaries Community Support Trust; [W] Chicago, IL Villa Guadalupe Senior Services Corporation; Chicago, IL Holy Cross/Immaculate Heart of Mary; Oak Park, IL; [N] Oak Park Claretian Missionaries USA Eastern Province.
Brummel, Thomas *c.m.f.* '59 (CHI)[N] Oak Park, IL Claretian Missionaries USA Eastern Province.
Brummer, Lawrence *o.f.m.* '58 (SAT) San Antonio, TX San Francisco de la Espada.
Brundage, John L. '70 (MET) South River, NJ Corpus Christi.
Brundage, Thomas T. '88 (MIL) On Duty Outside the Archdiocese.
Brundage, Thomas T. '88 (ANC) Judicial Vicar; Diocesan Consultors; Eagle River, AK St. Andrew.
Brundage, Tom '88 (FBK) Defenders of the Bond.
Brune, Meinrad *o.s.b.* '61 (IND)[K] Saint Meinrad, IN St. Meinrad Archabbey.
Brunelle, J. Ernest *m.m.* '59 (NY)[DD] Maryknoll Maryknoll Fathers and Brothers Retired.
Brunelle, Richard *a.a.* '63 (BO)[U] Boston Assumptionist Center.
Brunet, Rev. Msgr. Frederic J. '60 (HT) Chauvin, LA St. Joseph; Finance Officer; Diocesan Finance Council.
Brunet, Jules A. '55 (BR) Retired.
Brunet, Paul J. '11 (SEA) Aberdeen, WA Our Lady of Good Help; Aberdeen, WA St. Mary; Aberdeen, WA SS. Peter and Paul; Aberdeen, WA St. Jerome.
Brunetta, Juan–Diego *o.p.* '01 (NY) New York, NY St. Catherine of Siena.
Brunetta, M. Juan–Diego *o.p.* (RIC) Charlottesville, VA St. Thomas Aquinas.
Brunette, Larry H. '99 (SFD) Absent on Leave.
Bruney, James L. '84 (PIT) Pittsburgh, PA St. Cyril of Alexandria; Defenders of the Bond.
Brungardt, Aloysius '71 (SAL) Junction City, KS St. Francis Xavier Parish.
Bruni, John E. '76 (CAM) Continuing Education & Spiritual Formation of Priests (CESF); Newfield, NJ Our Lady of the Blessed Sacrament, Newfield, N.J.
Brunick, Charles J. *c.s.p.* '70 (P) Portland, OR St. Philip Neri; [Q] Portland, OR Paulist Fathers Catholic Center for Evangelization.
Bruning, David M. (TOL) Procurator–Advocate for Respondents; Associate Judges.
Bruning, David R. '78 (TOL) Wauseon, OH St. Caspar.
Bruning, William '93 (KCK) Topeka, KS Mother Teresa of Calcutta.
Brunkan, Rev. Msgr. Walter L. '56 (DUB) College of Consultors; Greene, IA St. Mary; Greene, IA St. Mary; Deanery Representatives; Directors.
Brunner, John H. '62 (NU) Watkins, MN Church of St. Anthony; Property Committee.
Brunner, Michael *o.s.b.* '05 (STL)[F] Creve Coeur, MO St. Louis Priory School; [O] St. Louis, MO The Abbey of St. Mary and St. Louis.
Brunner, William J. '11 (GB) Antigo, WI St. John; Antigo, WI SS. Mary & Hyacinth; Deerbrook, WI St. Wenceslaus.
Brunner, William *s.s.c.* '62 (OM)[J] St. Columbans Missionary Society of St. Columban.
Brunnert, Edward J. *m.s.* '63 (LKC) Dequincy, LA Our Lady of La Salette.
Brunnert, Jude *m.s.* '64 (LKC) De Ridder, LA St. Joseph's.
Brunnert, Theodore J. '54 (STL) Retired.
Bruno, Anthony J. '68 (HRT) Enfield, CT St. Adalbert's; Wethersfield, CT Connecticut Department of Correction; Special and other Archdiocesan Assignment.
Bruno, John *r.c.j.* '74 (LA) Van Nuys, CA St. Elisabeth; [P] Van Nuys, CA Rogationist Fathers; Van Nuys, CA.
Bruno, Joseph (BRK) Brooklyn, NY St. Therese of Lisieux.
Bruno, Michael J. S. '10 (BRK) Graduate Studies.
Bruno, Robert A. *o.f.m.* '77 (MO) Air Force Chaplains.
Bruno, Robert *o.f.m.* (CIN)[N] Cincinnati St. Francis Seraph Friary.
Bruno, Steven V. '05 (NO) Vocation Office; Serra Club of New Orleans.
Brunovsky, Michael *o.s.b.* '93 (CLV)[D] Cleveland, OH Benedictine High School; [N] Cleveland Benedictine Order of Cleveland.
Brunovsky, Steven K. '92 (CLV) Fairlawn, OH St. Hilary.
Brunsman, Barry *o.f.m.* '56 (OAK)[L] Oakland Franciscan Friars of California, (Province of St. Barbara).
Brunsman, Barry *o.f.m.* '56 (MRY)[H] San Juan Bautista, CA St. Francis Retreat Center.
Brunsman, Barry *o.f.m.* '56 (FRS)[C] Los Banos, CA New Bethany Residential Care and Skilled Nursing Community.
Brunton, Daniel B. '60 (SPR) Retired.
Brusatti, Louis *c.m.* '75 (AUS)[A] St. Edward's University.
Bruse, James C. '84 (ARL) Kilmarnock, VA St. Francis de Sales.
Brusky, David *s.d.s.* '52 (MIL)[P] Milwaukee, WI Salvatorians – Jordan Hall Retired.
Bruso, Robert D. '93 (WOR) Fitchburg, MA St. Anthony of Padua; Hmong Ministry; Presbyteral Council.
Brutus, Ferry '80 (MIA) Miami, FL St. Kevin.
Bryan, Francis E. '62 (IND) Retired.
Bryan, Kevin J. '76 (L) Brandenburg, KY St. John the Apostle; Vine Grove, KY St. Martin of Tours.
Bryan, Paul *c.ss.r.* '59 (HBG)[G] Ephrata St. Clement's Mission House.
Bryant, F. Michael '69 (WDC) Washington, DC Holy Comforter—St. Cyprian; Special Ministries; [X] Washington, DC District of Columbia Detention Facility; [X] Washington, DC Prison Outreach Ministry.
Bryant, Michael '78 (SCR) Scranton, PA Saint John Neumann, Scranton.
Bryce, Edward M. '60 (PIT) Pittsburgh, PA St. Bede.
Bryce, Vincent W. *o.p.* '57 (STL)[O] Saint Louis, MO St. Dominic Priory.
Bryda, Ronald J. '66 (CLV) Litchfield, OH Our Lady Help of Christians Parish.
Bryerton, Robert R. '74 (TUC) Hereford, AZ Retired.
Bryk, John J. '53 (CLV) Retired.
Brylinski, Bruce C. *g.h.m.* '83 (LEX) Grayson, KY Ss.

John & Elizabeth.
Brylinski, Bruce *g.h.m* '83 (COV) Vanceburg, KY Holy Redeemer.
Brylka, Vincent R. '65 (OAK)[K] Oakland, CA Bishop Begin Villa Retired.
Brynda, Rev. Msgr. Gerald J. '57 (TUC) Retired.
Brynes, John *o.s.a.* '55 (PH) Philadelphia, PA St. Nicholas of Tolentine; [Y] Philadelphia, PA Augustinian Community (O.S.A.).
Bryon, Thomas C. '63 (STL) Kirkwood, MO St. Gerard Majella.
Bryson, John H. '50 (MAN) Retired.
Brzeck, Jon '81 (HON) Military Chaplains.
Brzek, Jon J. '81 (PIT) Military Chaplains; Navy Chaplains.
Brzezicki, Zbigniew Canon '88 (STF) Fresh Meadows, NY Annunciation of the B.V.M.
Brzezinski, Andrzej *o.f.m.conv.* '02 (TR) Point Pleasant Beach, NJ St. Peter's.
Brzezinski, Hilary J. *o.f.m.* '76 (BWN) McAllen, TX Sacred Heart.
Brzezinski, Jerome A. '69 (DET) Auburn Hills, MI St. John Fisher Chapel University Parish.
Brzoska, David '00 (CHL) Boone, NC St. Elizabeth.
Brzostowski, Hilary *o.f.m.conv.* '66 (TR) Delran, NJ The Church of the Resurrection, Delran Township, N.J.
Bubel, Robert '04 (NY) New York, NY Cathedral of St. Patrick.
Buby, Bertrand A. *s.m.* '64 (CIN)[D] Dayton, OH The University of Dayton; [N] Dayton, OH Marianist Community Retired.
Bucaria, James A. '72 (SP) Masaryktown, FL St. Mary, Our Lady of Sorrows.
Buccafurni, Ferdinand '58 (PH) Philadelphia, PA St. Donato.
Bucchino, John *o.f.m.* '73 (MAN) Manchester, NH Blessed Sacrament.
Bucci, Michael J. '62 (GBG) Retired.
Bucci, Richard A. '73 (PRO) West Warwick, RI Sacred Heart Church.
Bucciantini, Charles '72 (JKS) Leland, MS St. James; Approved Advocate and Auditors; Trustees.
Bucciantini, Charles '72 (BLX) Trustees.
Bucciarelli, Michael R. '75 (TUC) Benson, AZ The Roman Catholic Parish of Our Lady of Lourdes – Benson; Defenders of the Bond; Council of Priests; Vicars Forane; All Vicars Forane.
Bucciarelli, Robert P. '60 (POD) Chestnut Hill.
Buccicone, Ananias G. *o.s.b.* '93 (GBG)[H] Latrobe, PA Saint Vincent Archabbey.
Buccicone, Ananias *o.s.b.* '93 (ALT) Patton, PA Queen of Peace.
Bucciferro, William *s.d.b.* '83 (NY)[FF] Stony Point, NY Don Bosco Retreat Center and Marian Shrine; [FF] Stony Point, NY Marian Shrine.
Buccilli, Gustavo (NEW)[L] Tenafly, NJ Society of African Missions, Provincialate, S.M.A. Fathers.
Bucek, Timothy P. '76 (GAL) Bellville, TX Sts. Peter & Paul.
Buchanan, Caleb A. '97 (BRK)[Q] West Indian Apostolate; Brooklyn, NY St. Gregory the Great.
Buchanan, Caleb A.P. '97 (BRK) Brooklyn, NY Saint Martin de Porres.
Buchanan, David '93 (BIR) Jasper, AL St. Cecilia.
Buchanan, Donald E. '65 (IND) Retired.
Buchanan, Robert E. '68 (SB) Retired.
Bucher, Mel *o.f.m.* '61 (OAK)[L] Oakland, CA Franciscan Friars of California, (Province of St. Barbara).
Bucher, Otto N. *o.f.m.cap.* '59 (MIL)[B] Hales Corners, WI Sacred Heart School of Theology.
Bucher, Otto N. *o.f.m.cap.* '59 (SUP) Rib Lake, WI Good Shepherd.
Bucher, Rev. Msgr. Philip A. '61 (SPC) Retired.
Bucher, Raymond J. *o.f.m.* '64 (OAK)[N] Danville, CA San Damiano Retreat.
Buchheit, Edward *c.p.* '63 (SCR)[L] Scranton, PA Saint Ann's Passionist Monastery.
Buchheit, Rev. Msgr. Jerome J. '51 (STL) Retired.
Buchholz, Athanasius *o.s.b.* '54 (P)[L] St. Benedict, OR Mt. Angel Abbey.
Buchholz, Canon Denis '04 (MIL) Milwaukee, WI St. Stanislaus.
Buchholz, Samuel James '01 (R) Elizabeth City, NC Holy Family; Deans; Council of Priests.
Buchignani, Rev. Msgr. Peter P. '65 (MEM) Cordova, TN St. Francis of Assisi; Vicar General; Clergy Personnel Board; College of Consultors; Adjutant Judicial Vicar; Presbyteral Council.
Buchignani, Richard G. '62 (NSH) Judges Retired.
Buchlein, Neil R. '98 (WH) Hurricane, WV Catholic Church of the Ascension.
Buchleitner, Donald N. '70 (PIT) Pittsburgh, PA Guardian Angels; Pittsburgh, PA Holy Innocents.
Buchman, Joel R. '91 (LA)[J] San Pedro, CA Providence Little Company of Mary San Pedro Peninsula Hospital Pavilion; [J] San Pedro, CA Providence Little Company of Mary Sub-Acute Center–South Bay.
Buchmeier, Francis X. *s.j.* '73 (FgM) Milwaukee, WI Society of Jesus.
Buchmeier, Robert P. '91 (WDC) La Plata, MD Sacred Heart.
Buchmelter, Brendan '80 (STA) Absent or Sick Leave.
Buchmiller, Ronald J. '69 (SD) Lakeside, CA Our Lady of Perpetual Help Catholic Parish Lakeside; Presbyteral Council; Clergy Personnel Board.
Buck, Frank '85 (ORL) Lakeland, FL St. John Neumann.
Buckalew, Jack '74 (SEA) Tracyton, WA Holy Trinity.
Bucki, John P. *s.j.* '79 (BUF)[N] Buffalo, NY Canisius Jesuit Community Inc.; [Q] Buffalo, NY Canisius College, Campus Ministry Office; [C] Buffalo, NY Canisius College.
Buckius, Walter A. *s.j.* '52 (BAL)[Q] Baltimore, MD Colombiere Jesuit Community.
Buckler, Brendan Joseph '11 (R) Wake Forest, NC St. Catherine of Siena.
Buckles, David J. '88 (LFT) West Lafayette, IN Blessed Sacrament; Special Assignment; Defenders of the Bond; Associate Judges.
Buckles, Luke D. *o.p.* '78 (OAK)[L] Oakland Order of Preachers (Province of the Most Holy Name of Jesus – Western Dominican Province).
Buckley, Brendan P. *o.f.m.cap.* '81 (BO)[U] Jamaica Plain, MA St. Francis of Assisi Friary.
Buckley, Brendan P. *o.f.m.cap.* '81 (LA) Solvang, CA Old Mission Santa Ines.
Buckley, Brendan *o.f.m.cap.* '81 (NY) Goshen, NY St. John the Evangelist.
Buckley, Charles J. *o.s.b.* '70 (OKL)[I] Shawnee, OK St. Gregory's Abbey.
Buckley, Cornelius M. *s.j.* '62 (LA)[C] Santa Paula, CA Thomas Aquinas College.
Buckley, Francis J. *s.j.* '58 (SJ)[M] Los Gatos, CA Sacred Heart Jesuit Center.
Buckley, Frank C. *s.j.* '08 (SFR) San Francisco, CA St. Agnes.
Buckley, Gerald A. *o.p.* '57 (P)[L] Portland, OR Holy Rosary Priory.
Buckley, Gerald J. '57 (SY) The Greater Binghamton Health Center; [Q] Binghamton, NY McDevitt Residence for Retired Priests Retired.
Buckley, Harold P. '53 (RVC) Retired.
Buckley, James B. *f.s.s.p.* '65 (LIN)[A] Denton, NE Our Lady of Guadalupe Seminary; Denton, NE.
Buckley, James F. '59 (FR) Retired.
Buckley, James M. '90 (OM) Omaha, NE St. Patrick.
Buckley, John J. *c.m.* '57 (PH)[Y].
Buckley, John M. *s.j.* '56 (NY)[DD] New York, NY Murray–Weigel Hall.
Buckley, John *s.s.c.* '68 (OM)[J] St. Columbans Missionary Society of St. Columban.
Buckley, John *s.s.c.* '68 (PRO)[O] Bristol, RI St. Columban's Retirement House.
Buckley, Michael J. *s.j.* '62 (SJ)[M] Los Gatos, CA Sacred Heart Jesuit Center.
Buckley, Michael *o.c.d.* '47 (SR)[L] Oakville, CA Carmelite House of Prayer.
Buckley, Thomas E. *s.j.* '70 (OAK)[A] Berkeley, CA Jesuit School of Theology of Santa Clara University (Berkeley, California Campus); [L] Berkeley, CA Jesuit Fathers and Brothers.
Buckley, Thomas J. *s.j.* '74 (WDC)[O] Washington, DC The Jesuit Community at Georgetown University.
Buckley, Thomas R. '76 (ALN) Coopersburg, PA St. Joseph.
Buckley, Thomas W. '55 (BO) Senior Priests. Retired.
Buckley, Timothy J. '92 (PH) Sellersville, PA St. Agnes.
Buckman, Frank (ORG) Retired.
Buckman, Tom '00 (OWN) Paducah, KY St. John the Evangelist; Deans; Priests' Council.
Buckner, Christopher M. '80 (ARL) On Leave of Absence.
Buckner, Mark A. '02 (OWN) Owensboro, KY St. Mary Magdalene; Deans; Priests' Council.
Bucko, Raymond A. *s.j.* '83 (OM)[J] Omaha, NE Jesuit Community at Creighton University.
Bucon, Raymond H. '79 (MO) Army Reserve Chaplains; Dearborn Heights, MI St. Sabina.
Bucsek, Basil '68 (STN) Retired.
Buczyna, Andrew L. '87 (JOL) Leave of Absence.
Buda, Jacek *o.p.* (TUC) Tucson, AZ Saint Thomas More Roman Catholic Newman Parish – Tucson.
Budde, Rev. Msgr. John G. '77 (DET) Davisburg, MI Divine Mercy.
Budde, Todd '01 (MIL) Fredonia, WI Holy Rosary; Random Lake, WI Our Lady of the Lakes.
Budden, William A. '68 (RCK) Retired.
Buddendorff, Kenneth A. *s.j.* '61 (NO)[R] New Orleans, LA Ignatius Residence.
Budenholzer, Francis *s.v.d.* '72 (FgM) Techny, IL.
Budez, Jorge H. '02 (BUF) Absent on Leave.
Budhi, Adrianus *m.s.c.* '89 (SB) Riverside, CA St. Catherine of Alexandria; Riverside, CA Riverside Community Hospital.
Budka, Dennis G. '84 (MIL) Lomira, WI St. Mary; St. Theresa, WI St. Theresa.
Budke, John *l.c.* '01 (CHI)[N] Hillside, IL Legion of Christ.
Budke, Jon *l.c.* '01 (DEN)[S] Centennial, CO LC Pastoral Services Inc.
Budnar, Randy J. '88 (MAD) Darlington, WI Holy Rosary; Deaneries.
Budney, Rev. Msgr. David F. '57 (CAM) Retired.
Budovic, Francis X. *s.j.* '49 (DET)[K] Clarkston, MI Colombiere Center.
Budwick, Rev. Msgr. John J. '64 (NY) Middletown, NY St. Joseph.
Budzikowski, Kenneth A. '80 (CHI) College of Consultors; Vicar for Priests; Evanston, IL St. Mary.
Budzinski, Andrew '10 (FTW) Fort Wayne, IN St. Vincent de Paul.
Buebendorf, Victor J. '64 (NY) Staten Island, NY St. Mary.
Bueche, Charles C. *c.ss.r.* '53 (STL)[O] Liguori, MO St. Clement Health Care Center Retired.
Bueche, William *c.ss.r.* '78 (STP) Brooklyn Center, MN St. Alphonsus; [J] Brooklyn Center, MN Redemptorist Fathers of Hennepin County.
Buechele, Andrew C. *sch.p.* '69 (WDC)[B] Washington, DC Queen of Pious Schools House of Studies–Piarist Fathers.
Buehler, John A. '74 (SY) Utica, NY St. John; Priests' Personnel Committee.
Buelt, Rev. Msgr. Edward '82 (DEN) Foxfield, CO Our Lady of Loreto; College of Consultors.
Buena, Joey R. *c.s.s.* '06 (MRY) Salinas, CA Madonna Del Sasso.
Buenaflor, Evelio '85 (HT) Houma, LA St. Gregory Barbarigo; Priests Council.
Buencamino, Joey (CHY) Rock Springs, WY Holy Spirit Catholic Community.
Buening, Matthew T. '03 (BAL)[T] Ellicott City, MD The St. Paul's Parish Endowment Trust; Ellicott City, MD St. Paul.
Buening, Robert B. '58 (CIN) Cincinnati, OH Corpus Christi Retired.
Bueno, Alberto *t.o.r.* '86 (WDC)[O] Washington, DC St. Louis Friary.
Bueno, Alberto *t.o.r.* '86 (ARL) Herndon, VA St. Joseph.
Bueno, Jaime '88 (CHY) Evanston, WY St. Mary Magdalen.
Buentello, Michael A. *c.s.b.* '95 (GAL)[R] Houston, TX University of St. Thomas Campus Ministry; [O] Houston, TX Residence of the Basilian Fathers of the University of St. Thomas; [C] Houston, TX University of St. Thomas.
Buermann, Eric *o.s.b.* '45 (FAJ)[B] Humacao, PR San Antonio Abad Abbey of the Order of St. Benedict.
Buersmeyer, David A. '80 (DET) Washington, MI SS. John and Paul; Archdiocesan Vicars; Presbyteral Council.
Buerster, Rev. Msgr. James A. '79 (BEL) Germantown, IL St. Boniface; Diocesan Deans.
Buescher, David G. '71 (JC) Retired.
Bueter, Robert *s.j.* '73 (CIN)[N] Cincinnati, OH Jesuit Community at Xavier University.
Buettner, Matthew R. '03 (CHL) Lincolnton, NC St. Dorothy.
Bueya, Emmanuel *s.j.* '05 (BO)[U] Newton, MA The Jesuit Community at Boston College.
Bueza, Ritche '03 (SJ) Milpitas, CA St. John the Baptist.
Buffardi, Joseph G. '76 (PAT) Parsippany, NJ St. Christopher.
Buffer, Thomas J. '91 (COL) Columbus, OH Saint Stephen the Martyr; Censor of Books.
Buffington, Jon '81 (P)[J] Portland, OR Providence Health & Services–Oregon.
Bufogle, Arthur '04 (WH) Kingwood, WV St. Sebastian; Kingwood, WV St. Zita.
Buga, John '99 (ROM) Retired.
Bugarin, Fred '72 (ANC) Anchorage, AK St. Anthony; Diocesan Consultors.
Bugarin, Rev. Msgr. G. Michael '91 (DET) St. Clair Shores, MI St. Joan of Arc; Archdiocesan Vicars; Presbyteral Council; Special Assignment.
Bugas, Joel O. '09 (SFE) Chama, NM St. Patrick; San Jose; Tierra Amarilla, NM Santo Nino.
Bugay, Stephen R. '84 (GBG) Uniontown, PA Nativity of the Blessed Virgin Mary.
Bugayong, Demetrio L. '70 (LA) Carson, CA St. Philomena.
Buggert, Donald W. *o.carm.* '66 (WDC)[B] Washington, DC Whitefriars Hall.
Buggert, Donald W. *o.carm.* '66 (JOL)[L] Joliet, IL St. Elias Carmelites.
Buggert, William (FTW)[B] University of Notre Dame Du Lac.
Bugler, Rev. Msgr. Henry J. '75 (NO) Metairie, LA St. Philip Neri.
Bugman, Rev. Msgr. John H. '52 (BUF) Retired.
Bugner, Joseph *s.v.d.* '63 (CHI)[N] Techny, IL Divine Word Residence.
Bugno, Krzystof *s.d.s.* '85 (SAT)[L] Falls City, TX Salvatorian Fathers Community of Texas.
Bugno, Krzysztof *s.d.s.* '85 (ORL) Titusville, FL St. Teresa.
Buhl, Wilbert L. '60 (GB) Maplewood, WI Retired.
Buhler, Richard O. *s.j.* '70 (STL) St. Louis, MO St. Francis Xavier; [O] St. Louis, MO Jesuit Community Corporation at Saint Louis University – Jesuit Hall.
Buhler, Richard *s.j.* '70 (STL)[C] Saint Louis University.

Buhman, Jay M. '04 (LIN) Advocates; Bellwood, NE St. Peter's.
Buholzer, Robert E. '56 (MAD) Retired.
Buhr, Donald L. '66 (STL) St. Louis, MO Our Lady of the Holy Cross.
Buhr, Eugene S. '54 (LA) Hawthorne, CA St. Joseph Retired.
Buhrman, Donald A. '86 (GI) Spalding, NE St. Michael's; Diocesan Consultors; Personnel Board.
Bui, Dong '92 (JOL) Lisle, IL St. Joan of Arc.
Bui, Dung Quang '02 (STA) Gainesville, FL St. Patrick Church.
Bui, Francis Quyet *s.d.d.* '90 (P) Portland, OR Our Lady of Lavang.
Bui, Francis Ty '75 (LA) Winnetka, CA St. Joseph the Worker.
Bui, Hoang H (GAL) Houston, TX St. Vincent de Paul; Spring, TX Christ the Good Shepherd.
Bui, Joseph T.P. '97 (GAL) Houston, TX Christ, The Incarnate Word.
Bui, Joseph '91 (ORL) Indialantic, FL Holy Name of Jesus.
Bui, Joseph '00 (PHX) Glendale, AZ St. Louis The King Roman Catholic Parish; Priestly Life and Ministry Board.
Bui, Khue Si '01 (BEA) Beaumont, TX St. Joseph.
Bui, Marion J. *o.c.d.* '95 (SAT)[L] San Antonio, TX Discalced Carmelite Fathers of San Antonio; San Antonio, TX Basilica of the National Shrine of the Little Flower, Our Lady of Mt. Carmel and St. Therese Parish.
Bui, Martin Phuoc '11 (ORG) Costa Mesa, CA St. Joachim.
Bui, Minh Cong '01 (ORG) Judges.
Bui, Peter Tam '01 (WOR) Worcester, MA Our Lady of Vilna.
Bui, Phong (TUC) Tucson, AZ Arizona State Prison.
Bui, Tam M. '01 (WOR) Vietnamese Apostolate; Vietnamese Ministry.
Bui, Thaddeus *o.h.* (LA)[K] Ojai, CA St. Joseph's Health and Retirement Center.
Bui, Tho *s.d.b.* '08 (LA)[F] Bellflower, CA St. John Bosco High School.
Bui, Tin Mahn '75 (SFE) Albuquerque, NM Our Lady of Lavang.
Bui, Tuan *c.ss.r.* '97 (DAL) Garland, TX Mother of Perpetual Help.
Bui, Vincent D. *s.s.* '95 (SFR)[A] Menlo Park, CA St. Patrick Seminary and University.
Bui, Vincent D. *s.s.* '95 (BAL)[Q] Baltimore Society of St. Sulpice, Province of the United States.
Bui, Vincent *s.s.* '95 (LAN) On Duty Outside the Diocese.
Buitrago, Alex '67 (DAL) Dallas, TX St. Elizabeth of Hungary.
Buitrago, Luis '67 (DAL) Dallas, TX Parkland Health & Hospital System.
Buitrago, Tarsicio '64 (ARL) Falls Church, VA St. Philip.
Buitron, Luis Segundo '00 (CR) Greenbush, MN Blessed Sacrament.
Bujnak, George A. '65 (PSC) McAdoo, PA St. Michael Retired.
Bukala, Casimir R. *s.j.* '66 (CLV)[B] University Heights, OH John Carroll Jesuit Community.
Bukauskas, Raimundas *o.f.m.* '04 (PRT)[I] Kennebunk, ME St. Anthony's Friary.
Bukowski, Jan *cor* '73 (CHI) Bridgeview, IL St. Fabian.
Bula, Sebastine *v.c.* '04 (TUC) San Manuel, AZ Saint Bartholomew Roman Catholic Parish – San Manuel.
Bulala, Matthew '93 (CHR) Kingstree, SC St. Ann; Lake City, SC St. Philip the Apostle.
Bulfer, Stephen C. '73 (FRS) Mariposa, CA St. Joseph.
Bulger, John '64 (SEA) Retired.
Bulinda, Ernest Livasia '88 (RIC) Norfolk, VA Basilica of St. Mary of the Immaculate Conception.
Bulinski, Marcin J. '07 (CHI) Oak Lawn, IL St. Linus.
Bullene, Richard S. *c.s.c.* '83 (FTW)[B] University of Notre Dame Du Lac; [H] Notre Dame, IN Holy Cross Community, Corby Hall, University of Notre Dame.
Buller, Ruben J. '08 (LKC) Office For Worship; Lake Charles, LA St. Henry; Vocation Recruiters.
Bullman, Rudolph '00 (HEL) Kalispell, MT Risen Christ.
Bullock, Gabriel G. *o.s.b.* '61 (PEO)[A] Peru, IL St. Bede Abbey.
Bullock, John *l.c.* '02 (LA)[P] Arcadia, CA Legionaries of Christ.
Bullock, Scott E. '91 (DUB)[A] Dubuque, IA Seminary of St. Pius X; Dubuque, IA St. Catherine; Bellevue, IA St. Donatus; Dubuque, IA Church of the Nativity; Judicial Vicar; Judicial Vicar; Judges; Seminarians; Seminary Admissions and Advisory Board; Worship Commission; On Special or Other Archdiocesan Assignment.
Bullock, Stewart '06 (BAL) Towson, MD Church of the Immaculate Conception.
Bulwith, Richard E. '67 (CHI)[G] Administration:; [G] Hines, IL Cooke's Manor Transitional Housing For Men; Associate Administrators; Chicago, IL Our Lady of Lourdes.
Bumbar, Rev. Canon Philip '68 (SJP) Carnegie, PA Holy Trinity.
Bumbar, Rev. Archpriest Philip (SJP) Arbitration Board; Presbyters.
Bumbarger, Bruce *m.ss.cc.* '92 (BIR) Clanton, AL Church of the Resurrection.
Bumpus, Rev. Msgr. Harold '63 (SP) Retired.
Bunch, Randall (JC)[B] Jefferson City, MO St. Mary Health Center.
Bunch, Timothy S. '79 (CIN) Cincinnati, OH St. Saviour; Vicarri Foranei (Deans).
Bunda, Roland *s.m.* '67 (HON) Wailuku, HI St. Anthony of Padua.
Bunda, Roland *s.m.* '78 (HON)[D] Wailuku, HI Wailuku Marianist Community.
Bundz, Michael '81 (STF) Personnel Board; Utica, NY St. Michael; Utica, NY St. Volodymyr the Great.
Bunger, Kevin J. '83 (SY) Clinton, NY Church of the Annunciation.
Bungo, Samuel '77 (E) New Bethlehem, PA St. Charles Church.
Buni, Leon Salvador A. '75 (TR) Toms River, NJ St. Joseph.
Bunik, Wasyl '93 (PHU) Warrington, PA Presentation of Our Lord; Warrington, PA St. Anne's.
Bunnell, Adam *o.f.m.conv.* '73 (L) Louisville, KY St. Paul; [A] Bellarmine University.
Bunnell, Thomas J. *s.j.* '74 (YAK) Sunnyside, WA St. Joseph's.
Bunnell, Thomas J. *s.j.* '74 (P)[L] Portland, OR Colombiere Community.
Bunny, Rev. Msgr. J. Michael '65 (LA) Newbury Park, CA St. Julie Billiart Retired.
Bunofsky, Walter *s.v.d.* '60 (DUB)[B] Epworth, IA Divine Word College.
Bunse, Gerald L. '83 (SFD) Farmersville, IL St. Mary; Morrisonville, IL St. Maurice; Raymond, IL St. Raymond.
Bunse, Gerald '83 (SFD) Commission for the Care of Infirm and Retired Priests; Presbyteral Council.
Bunse, Gerald '51 (SFD) Graham Correctional Center.
Bunsic, Albert *o.c.d.* '67 (TUC)[E] Tucson, AZ Discalced Carmelite Friars of St. Margaret Mary's; Tucson, AZ Saint Margaret Mary Alacoque Roman Catholic Parish – Tucson.
Bunyan, Gregory '96 (AMA) Spearman, TX Sacred Heart; Gruver, TX Cristo Redentor.
Buonanno, Vito A. '81 (BRK)[S] Washington, DC Basilica of the National Shrine of the Immaculate Conception; Released from Diocesan Assignment.
Buongirno, Robert F. (NOR) Uncasville, CT St. John the Evangelist; Oakdale, CT Our Lady of the Lakes.
Buono, Carmen '07 (PAT)[C] Denville, NJ Morris Catholic High School; Dover, NJ Sacred Heart.
Buonopane, Gerald '06 (NEW)[B] Seton Hall University.
Buontempo, Giovanni '98 (WDC)[A] Hyattsville, MD Redemptoris Mater Archdiocesan Missionary Seminary.
Buote, Martin L. '60 (FR) Retired.
Bur, George W. *s.j.* '72 (PH)[F] Philadelphia, PA St. Joseph's Preparatory School; [Y] Philadelphia, PA Jesuit Community, Arrupe House.
Burak, Paul C. '72 (CHI) Orland Park, IL St. Michael; College of Consultors.
Burakowski, Wieslaw '92 (NSH) Retired.
Buranosky, Dennis M. '72 (PIT) Bellevue, PA Assumption of the Blessed Virgin Mary on the Beautiful River.
Burasa, James *c.s.c.* '95 (FTW)[H] Notre Dame Congregation of Holy Cross, United States Province of Priests & Brothers.
Burba, Edward A. '75 (CLV) Akron, OH St. Anthony of Padua.
Burbach, Jude *o.s.b.* '53 (KCK)[I] Atchison, KS St. Benedict's Abbey Retired.
Burbank, Foster J. '57 (FR)[A] North Easton, MA Holy Cross Fathers Religious.
Burbank, Foster J. *c.s.c.* '57 (FTW)[H] Notre Dame Congregation of Holy Cross, United States Province of Priests & Brothers.
Burbank, Robert J. '64 (HRT) Branford, CT St. Mary Retired.
Burch, Edward '03 (R) Pinehurst, NC Sacred Heart.
Burch, Francis F. *s.j.* '63 (PH)[Y] Loyola Center and Manresa Hall.
Burch, Thaddeus J. *s.j.* '61 (MIL)[P] Milwaukee, WI Jesuit Community at Marquette University.
Burchell, Richard '75 (CLV) Solon, OH St. Rita.
Burchfield, Michael A. '93 (FRS) Fresno, CA Shrine of St. Therese; On Special Assignment; Judicial Vicar; Tribunal Judges.
Burchill, John P. *o.p.* '65 (PRO) Providence, RI St. Pius V; [O] Providence, RI St. Pius House.
Burckhart, William C. '53 (BO) Westwood, MA St. Denis Retired.
Burda, Andriy (STN) Dearborn Heights, MI Our Lady of Perpetual Help.
Burden, George *s.s.j.* '91 (JKS) Fayette, MS St. Anne; Natchez, MS Holy Family.
Burdess, James J. '88 (ALN) Summit Hill, PA St. Joseph.
Burdick, Thomas J. '84 (SB) Hemet; Appointed Members; Winchester, CA Blessed Teresa of Calcutta Catholic Community, Inc.
Burdzy, Krystian '03 (MET) North Plainfield, NJ St. Joseph.
Burek, Frank J. '71 (CHI) Hickory Hills, IL St. Patricia.
Burgaleta, Claudio M. *s.j.* '92 (NY)[DD] Cardinal Spellman Hall, Jesuit Community.
Burgard, David G. '94 (DET) Wayne, MI St. Mary; Inkster, MI Holy Family Parish.
Burge, Robert '71 (CLV) Retired.
Burger, Edward K. *s.j.* '70 (STL)[O] St. Louis, MO Ignatius House.
Burger, Frank '69 (KCK) Olathe, KS Prince of Peace; Archdiocesan Consultors.
Burger, John *s.s.c.* '73 (FgM) St Columbans, NE U.S. Foundation & Administration.
Burger, Joseph '54 (OKL) Retired.
Burger, Mark J. '80 (CIN) Cincinnati, OH Our Lady of the Visitation.
Burger, Philip G. '83 (HBG) Secretary for Clergy and Consecrated Life; Permanent Diaconate, Office for; Camp Hill, PA Good Shepherd; Consultors, College.
Burger, Rev. Msgr. Raymond '60 (KCK) Defenders of the Bond Retired.
Burger, Robert '48 (KCK) Retired.
Burgess, Yancey O. '10 (WCH)[C] Wichita, KS Via Christi Hospital on North St. Francis.
Burghoff, Theodore H. '55 (STL) Retired.
Burgoon, Charles E. '64 (STL) St. Louis, MO St. Richard; Deaneries/Deans.
Burgos, Adnel T. '89 (BRK) Brooklyn, NY Guardian Angel.
Burgos, Felipe Santiago *c.ss.r.* (SJN) San Juan, PR San Agustin.
Burgos, P. Jorge R. *s.d.b.* (ARE) Orocovis, PR San Juan Bautista.
Burgos, Roman *t.o.r.* '02 (AUS) Waco, TX St. Francis on the Brazos; Waco, TX.
Burgos Brisman, Faustino *c.m.* '87 (SJN) San Juan, PR Sagrado Corazon de Jesus.
Burgoyne, Sidney C. '54 (PH) Retired.
Burian, Rev. Msgr. Ed '65 (SFS) Retired.
Burish, Jesse D. '09 (LC) La Crosse, WI Blessed Sacrament; Appointed Members.
Burk, Robert J. *m.s.a.* '03 (WIL) Georgetown, DE St. Michael the Archangel.
Burk, Robert *m.s.a.* '03 (NOR)[G] Cromwell Society of the Missionaries of the Holy Apostles.
Burkard, Rev. Msgr. Paul J.E. '69 (BUF)[J] Lackawanna, NY Baker Victory Services; Finance Council; Vicars; Lackawanna, NY Our Lady of Victory National Shrine; [S] Lackawanna, NY Our Lady of Victory Homes of Charity.
Burkardt, Donald '58 (GB) Retired.
Burkart, Donald R. '58 (GB) Wausaukee, WI St. Agnes; Wausaukee, WI St. Augustine.
Burkart, James M. '93 (GAL) Houston, TX St. Luke the Evangelist; Liturgical Commission.
Burkart, James '93 (GAL) Priests Personnel Committee.
Burkauskas, Peter M. '79 (PH) Philadelphia, PA St. Andrew.
Burke, Adrian *o.s.b.* '97 (IND)[K] Saint Meinrad, IN St. Meinrad Archabbey.
Burke, Alfred M. *o.s.a.* '57 (FgM)[N] Chicago, IL St. Rita Monastery; Olympia Fields, IL Province of Our Mother of Good Counsel (Midwestern).
Burke, Alfred '69 (NEW) Union, NJ Holy Spirit.
Burke, Christopher R. '86 (PBR) Boardman, OH Infant Jesus of Prague.
Burke, Clement J. '61 (DUB) Retired.
Burke, Donal *o.f.m.cap.* '75 (SFR)[N] Burlingame, CA Capuchin Provincial House.
Burke, Edmund M. '77 (NY) Kingston, NY St. Mary; Kingston, NY St. Peter.
Burke, Edward P. '73 (PH) Philadelphia, PA Cathedral Basilica of SS. Peter and Paul.
Burke, Geoffrey D. '79 (ALB) Latham, NY Our Lady of the Assumption; [M] Latham, NY Provincial House of the Sisters of St. Joseph of Carondelet (Albany Province); Province Leadership Team:; Deans.
Burke, Gilbert J. *o.s.b.* '62 (GBG)[H] Latrobe, PA Saint Vincent Archabbey.
Burke, Gregory '51 (HEL)[E] Butte, MT St. James Health Care, Sisters of Charity of Leavenworth Health System Retired.
Burke, Harry '63 (NY)[E] Bronx, NY Cardinal Hayes High School.
Burke, Herbert '92 (CHL) Forest City, NC Immaculate Conception.
Burke, Rev. Msgr. James A. '56 (NEW) Midland Park, NJ Nativity; Elected Members Retired.
Burke, James C. '64 (ROC) Retired.
Burke, James G. '77 (BO) Westwood, MA St. Denis; Defenders of the Bond; Canonical Affairs Committee.
Burke, Rev. Msgr. James M. '64 (PMB) Assessors; Port St. Lucie, FL St. Lucie; Advocates Retired.
Burke, James *c.ss.r.* '56 (CHR) Sumter, SC Catholic

Community of Sumter; Sumter, SC Catholic Community of Sumter.
Burke, John R. '54 (E) Retired.
Burke, John R. '72 (L) Louisville, KY St. William; Louisville, KY Good Shepherd.
Burke, Joseph F. *s.j.* '78 (BUF)[N] Buffalo, NY Canisius Jesuit Community Inc.; [A] East Aurora, NY Christ the King Seminary.
Burke, Kevin F. *s.j.* '86 (OAK)[A] Berkeley, CA Jesuit School of Theology of Santa Clara University (Berkeley, California Campus); [A] Berkeley, CA Jesuit School of Theology of Santa Clara University (Berkeley, California Campus); [L] Berkeley, CA Jesuit Fathers and Brothers.
Burke, Kevin F. *s.j.* '86 (SJ)[B] Santa Clara University.
Burke, Lawrence A. *o.f.m.* '41 (PAT)[N] Ringwood, NJ Holy Name Friary, Inc.
Burke, Mark J. *s.j.* '93 (BO)[U] Boston The Society of Jesus of New England–Provincial Offices.
Burke, Mark (BRK) Brooklyn, NY St. Francis Xavier.
Burke, Michael A. '76 (PAT) Prospect Park, NJ St. Paul's.
Burke, Rev. Msgr. Michael J. '62 (PH) Primos, PA St. Eugene Retired.
Burke, Michael J. (PAT) Associate Judges; Catholic Family and Community Services.
Burke, Rev. Msgr. Michael L. '74 (MAD) Madison, WI St. Maria Goretti; Diocesan Consultors; Appointed; Personnel Board.
Burke, Michael M. *o.p.* '68 (NO) New Orleans, LA St. Anthony of Padua.
Burke, Michael '50 (CC) Retired.
Burke, Michael *s.c.j.* '63 (MIL)[P] Franklin, WI Sacred Heart at Monastery Lake.
Burke, Paul A. '96 (ATL) Atlanta, GA Holy Spirit.
Burke, Richard *c.p.* '76 (SCR) Consultors:; New Rochelle, NY St. Paul of the Cross Province; New Rochelle, NY; [L] Scranton, PA Saint Ann's Passionist Monastery.
Burke, Richard *c.p* '76 (CHI)[N] Chicago, IL Passionist Provincial Office.
Burke, Robert M. *o.s.a.* '55 (PH)[Y] Villanova, PA St. Thomas Monastery.
Burke, Ronald '72 (HON) Retired.
Burke, Ronald '72 (LSC) Retired.
Burke, Thomas J. *o.ss.t.* '78 (BAL)[A] Baltimore, MD St. Mary's Seminary and University; [Q] Archdiocese of Baltimore, MD – Assigned Elsewhere.
Burke, Thomas J. '01 (PIT) Braddock, PA Good Shepherd; Priest Council; College of Consultors.
Burke, Thomas *c.ss.r.* '81 (CHR) Sumter, SC Catholic Community of Sumter.
Burke, Vincent *s.v.d.* '61 (TR) Techny, IL; [N] Bordentown, NJ Society of the Divine Word.
Burke, William A. '65 (CHI) Retired.
Burke, William A. '65 (CHI) Chicago, IL St. Cajetan.
Burke, Rev. Msgr. William F. '59 (BAL) Baltimore, MD St. Francis of Assisi.
Burke, William F. '75 (MEM) Bartlett, TN Church of The Nativity.
Burke, William T. *s.j.* '78 (DET)[K] Clarkston, MI Colombiere Center.
Burke, William *o.p.* '60 (WDC) Washington, DC St. Dominic Church & Priory.
Burkemper, Robert W. '81 (STL) Overland, MO All Souls.
Burkert, Gerald F. '61 (IND)[I] Beech Grove, IN St. Paul Hermitage Retired.
Burkert, William C. '71 (MIL) Milwaukee, WI Our Lady of Lourdes.
Burkey, Blaine *o.f.m.cap.* '61 (DEN)[N] Denver, CO St. Francis of Assisi Friary; [N] Denver, CO Capuchin Province of Mid–America, Inc.
Burkhalter, Ross C. '94 (OM) Elgin, NE St. Boniface; Elgin, NE St. Bonaventure; [B] Elgin, NE Pope John XXIII Central Catholic High School at Elgin; Deans; Deans.
Burkhard, John *o.f.m.conv.* '67 (WDC)[O] Silver Spring, MD Gemelli House; [B] Silver Spring, MD St. Bonaventure Friary.
Burkhardt, Alan T. '86 (LC) Hatley, WI St. Florian; Schofield, WI St. Agnes.
Burkhardt, Odilo *o.s.b.* '50 (SFS)[F] Marvin, SD Blue Cloud Abbey.
Burkle, Raymond A. '90 (DUB) Holy Cross, IA Holy Trinity; Holy Cross, IA St. Joseph; Holy Cross, IA SS. Peter and Paul; Holy Cross, IA Holy Cross; Holy Cross, IA St. Francis of Assisi; [F] Holy Cross, IA LaSalle Elementary Schools; Deanery Representatives.
Burkley, John T. '70 (CLV) Parkman, OH St. Lucy; Parkman, OH St. Edward.
Burkowski, Paul *c.ss.r.* '87 (ALB) Presbyteral Council; Diocesan Board of Consultors.
Burks, William P. '86 (L) Louisville, KY St. Pius X.
Burkus, John '40 (ELP) Retired.
Burla, Frank J. '63 (NEW) Montclair, NJ Immaculate Conception Retired.
Burnell, Robert J. '70 (CHI) Lyons, IL St. Hugh.
Burnett, Eugene *o.f.m.* '54 (OAK)[L] Oakland, CA Franciscan Friars of California, (Province of St. Barbara).
Burnett, George P. '61 (HRT) Ansonia, CT Assumption Retired.
Burnett, James E. '74 (DAV) On Duty Outside the Diocese; DEPARTMENT OF VETERANS AFFAIRS HOSPITALS AND CHAPLAINS.
Burnett, James E. '74 (MO) National Conference of Veterans Affairs Catholic Chaplains, Inc.; Presbyteral Council.
Burnett, James '68 (JOL) Leave of Absence.
Burnett, James '74 (CHI) Hines V.A. Hospital.
Burnett, Kurt '01 (SFE) Defenders of the Bond.
Burnett, Timothy J. *o.s.b.* '80 (NO) Folsom, LA St. John the Baptist.
Burnett, Travis J. '11 (MOB) Daphne, AL Christ the King Parish, Daphne.
Burnette, John C. '85 (SFD) Decatur, IL Saints James and Patrick Parish.
Burnette, Kurt '89 (HPM) Albuquerque, NM Our Lady of Perpetual Help; College of Consultors; Adjutant Judicial Vicar; Pension Committee; Finance Council.
Burnette, Kurt '89 (LAV) Defender of the Bond; Diocesan Judges.
Burnham, Martin J. '02 (BAL) On Duty Outside the Archdiocese; [Q] Baltimore, MD St. Mary's Seminary & University.
Burnia, Scott A. '88 (SD) El Cajon, CA Saint Louise de Marillac Catholic Parish.
Burnie, James *c.ss.p.* '84 (LR) Hattieville, AR St. Mary.
Burns, Basil David *o.s.b.* '01 (NO)[R] St. Benedict, LA St. Joseph Abbey.
Burns, Charles F. *s.j.* '72 (MIL)[P] Milwaukee Jesuit Provincial Office, Wisconsin Province.
Burns, Claude Thomas '02 (EVN) Evansville, IN Holy Spirit.
Burns, Douglas C. *o.s.f.s.* '99 (ALN)[B] Center Valley, PA DeSales University; [K] Center Valley, PA Oblates of St. Francis de Sales.
Burns, Edward J. '54 (FR) Retired.
Burns, Edward M. '04 (CIN)[R] Fairborn, OH Catholic Campus Ministry.
Burns, Rev. Msgr. G. Thomas '57 (NEW) Retired.
Burns, Gerald H. '69 (BR) Retired.
Burns, Gerald '09 (SEA) Seattle, WA St. Matthew.
Burns, Hugh *o.p.* '82 (NY) Pleasantville, NY Holy Innocents.
Burns, James P. '93 (STP) On Duty Outside the Archdiocese.
Burns, Rev. Msgr. John A. '48 (BRK) Brooklyn, NY Mary Queen of Heaven Retired.
Burns, John M. *o.carm.* '82 (STP)[K] Lake Elmo, MN Carmel of Our Lady of Divine Providence; [J] Lake Elmo, MN Carmelite Hermitage of the Blessed Virgin Mary; Lake Elmo, MN.
Burns, John P. '03 (FRS) Bakersfield, CA Christ the King Retired.
Burns, John R. '90 (PEO) Galva, IL St. John's; Woodhull, IL St. John's; [O] Moline, IL The Order of the Legion of Little Souls of the Merciful Heart of Jesus.
Burns, John '10 (MIL) Wauwatosa, WI Christ King.
Burns, Joseph Clement *o.p.* '54 (CIN)[N] Cincinnati, OH St. Gertrude Priory; Cincinnati, OH St. Gertrude.
Burns, Joseph '60 (CAM) Retired.
Burns, Laurence J. '64 (SC) Retired.
Burns, Rev. Msgr. Lawrence E. '56 (MAN) Retired.
Burns, Lawrence E. '62 (BUF) Blasdell, NY Our Mother of Good Counsel.
Burns, Malcolm J. '85 (RVC) Farmingville, NY Church of the Resurrection.
Burns, Michael J. '58 (SJ) Los Altos, CA St. Simon Retired.
Burns, Michael J. '73 (TR) Bordentown, NJ St. Mary; Legion of Mary.
Burns, Michael *s.d.s.* '05 (MIL)[N] Milwaukee, WI St. Anne's Salvatorian Campus; [P] Milwaukee Salvatorian Provincial Offices.
Burns, Norbert C. *s.m.* '53 (CIN)[D] Dayton, OH The University of Dayton; [N] Dayton, OH Marianist Community Retired.
Burns, Patrick G. '92 (BRK) Jackson Heights, NY Blessed Sacrament.
Burns, Patrick J. *s.j.* '63 (MIL) Milwaukee, WI Society of Jesus; [Y] Milwaukee, WI The Jesuit Partnership; Milwaukee, WI; [P] Milwaukee, WI Jesuit Provincial Office, Wisconsin Province; [P] Milwaukee, WI Arrupe House Jesuit Community.
Burns, Paul D. *c.s.s.* '61 (BO)[X] Waltham, MA Stigmatine Fathers and Brothers.
Burns, Peter *s.j.* '53 (SJ)[M] Los Gatos, CA Sacred Heart Jesuit Center.
Burns, Robert A. *o.p.* '61 (TUC) Tucson, AZ Saint Thomas More Roman Catholic Newman Parish – Tucson; [H] Tucson, AZ University of Arizona.
Burns, Robert O. *s.j.* '57 (OM)[J] Omaha, NE Jesuit Community at Creighton University.
Burns, Thomas J. '54 (SFR) Retired.
Burns, Thomas J. *m.m.* '69 (FgM) Maryknoll, NY MARYKNOLL.
Burns, Thomas *s.c.j.* '65 (SP)[N] Pinellas Park, FL Priests of the Sacred Heart.
Burns, Tom *m.s.c.* '64 (SB) Crestline, CA St. Frances Xavier Cabrini.
Burns, Vincent M. *s.j.* '57 (BO)[U] Weston, MA Campion Health Center, Inc.
Burns, Rev. Msgr. Vincent P. '67 (PH) On Duty Outside the Archdiocese.
Burns, Vincent '67 (JKS) Aberdeen, MS St. Francis of Assisi.
Burns, William L. '85 (HRT) Manchester, CT St. James Retired.
Burr, Jeremiah R. *m.m.* '67 (FgM) Maryknoll, NY MARYKNOLL.
Burr, Stephen '02 (DET)[A] The College of Liberal Arts; Presbyteral Council.
Burr, Thomas E. '73 (RCK) Retired.
Burrascano, Anthony P. *o.s.a.* '79 (FgM)[Y] Villanova, PA Provincial Offices of the Order of St. Augustine, Province of St. Thomas of Villanova; Counselors:; Villanova, PA Province of St. Thomas of Villanova (Eastern); [Y] Ardmore, PA Bellesini Friary.
Burrell, David B. *c.s.c.* '59 (FgM) New Rochelle, NY Eastern Brothers Province.
Burrill, Jeffrey D. '98 (LC) On Duty Outside the Diocese.
Burrows, Michael *o.s.b.* '80 (RCK)[G] Aurora, IL Marmion Abbey.
Burshek, James J. *s.j.* '75 (STL)[O] St. Louis, MO; [S] St. Louis, MO Retreat House.
Burshnick, Frank *s.c.j.* '70 (SP)[N] Pinellas Park, FL Priests of the Sacred Heart.
Burson, James *c.j.m.* '63 (SD) San Diego, CA Blessed Sacrament Catholic Parish.
Burt, Donald X. *o.s.a.* '55 (PH)[Y] Villanova, PA St. Thomas Monastery.
Burt, Michael E. '09 (GR) Remus, MI St. Michael's.
Burtchaell, James *c.s.c.* (FTW)[H] Notre Dame Congregation of Holy Cross, United States Province of Priests & Brothers.
Burton, Charles '80 (KNX) Chattanooga, TN St. Jude.
Burton, Rev. Msgr. John H. '72 (CAM) Vineland, NJ Christ the Good Shepherd Parish, Vineland, N.J.; Liturgical Art and Architectural Commission; Members; Vicars General; Ex Officio Members; Ex Officio Members; Ex Officio Members.
Burton, Rev. Msgr. John H. '72 (CAM)[B] Vineland, NJ Sacred Heart High School; Washington, DC Federation of Diocesan Liturgical Commissions; Consultants.
Burton, Richard T. '03 (BO) Methuen, MA St. Lucy.
Burton, Rev. Msgr. Richard W. '63 (WDC) Retired.
Burton, William L. *o.f.m.* '89 (PMB)[A] Boynton Beach, FL St. Vincent de Paul Regional Seminary.
Burton, William *o.f.m.* '89 (CHI)[N] Chicago, IL St. Peter's Friary.
Burtschi, J. Richard *s.j.* '71 (STL)[O] St. Louis, MO Jesuit Community Corporation at Saint Louis University – Jesuit Hall.
Burusu, Valery '92 (SPC)[D] Joplin, MO Mercy Hospital Joplin; Joplin, MO Joplin Hospital Ministry.
Burwinkel, Elmer J. '84 (IND)[P] Beech Grove, IN Mary's King's Village Schoenstatt Center, Inc.; [I] Beech Grove, IN St. Paul Hermitage Retired.
Bury, Antoni '91 (CHI) Chicago, IL St. Bruno.
Bury, Harold J. '55 (STP) Retired.
Buryadnyk, Mykola '02 (STN) Chicago, IL St. Joseph.
Buryadnyk, Mykola '02 (CHI)[J] Chicago, IL Resurrection Medical Center.
Buryska, James F. '65 (WIN) On Special or Other Diocesan Assignment; [D] Rochester, MN Saint Mary Hospital; Coordinator of Diocesan Health Ministry; Hospitals.
Burzawa, Janusz '86 (SP) St. Petersburg, FL The Mercy of God Polish Mission.
Burzynski, Michael H. '89 (BUF) Legion of Mary; Cheektowaga, NY St. John Gualbert.
Bus, Anthony *c.r.* '84 (CHI) Chicago, IL St. Stanislaus Kostka.
Busch, Arthur '58 (WCH) Retired.
Busch, August '56 (EVN) Retired.
Busch, Joseph '80 (ALB) Queensbury, NY Our Lady of the Annunciation.
Busch, Robert '93 (AMA) Office for the Catholic Schools; [A] Amarillo, TX Holy Cross Catholic Academy; [I] Amarillo, TX Amarillo Catholic School System; [I] Amarillo, TX Amarillo Scholarship Endowment and Assistance Fund.
Busch, Vernon *o.f.m.cap.* '60 (PIT)[M] Pittsburgh, PA St. Augustine Friary.
Busch, Vincent J. *s.s.c.* '74 (FgM) St Columbans, NE House of Post–Graduate Studies.
Buse, Harold J. '77 (OM) Deans; Omaha, NE St. Leo; Deans.
Busemeyer, Louis E. *s.j.* '70 (CHI)[D] Chicago, IL St. Ignatius Jesuit Community.
Busemeyer, Louis *s.j.* '70 (RCK) Aurora, IL St. Rita of Cascia.
Bush, Bernard J. *s.j.* '65 (SJ)[L] Los Altos, CA Jesuit Retreat Center of Los Altos; [M] Los Gatos, CA Sacred Heart Jesuit Center.

Bush, Carson '03 (CHR) Absent On Leave.
Bush, Frederick '51 (ROC) Rochester, NY St. Mark Retired.
Bush, Rev. Msgr. Robert '69 (SAN) Abilene, TX Sacred Heart; Presbyteral Council; Diocesan Consultors.
Bush, Scott '92 (HON) College of Consultors; Ewa Beach, HI Our Lady of Perpetual Help.
Bush, Thomas M. '99 (LIN) Nebraska City, NE St. Joseph's; Advocates.
Bush, William C. '62 (LEX) Nicholasville, KY St. Luke.
Busher, Robert J. '76 (DAV) Wilton, IA St. Mary's; Judges.
Bushmaker, Godfrey E. *o.praem.* '00 (ORG)[I] Silverado, CA Norbertine Fathers of Orange Inc.; Costa Mesa, CA St. John the Baptist.
Bushy, Tim '83 (PHX) Chandler, AZ Chandler Regional Hospital; Gilbert, AZ Mercy Gilbert Medical Center.
Bushy, Timothy F. '83 (CR) On Duty Outside the Diocese.
Bushy, Timothy F. (ORG)[G] Fullerton, CA St. Jude Medical Center.
Busichio, Salvatore A. '60 (R) Raleigh, NC Cathedral of the Sacred Heart.
Busichio, Salvatore '60 (NEW) On Duty Outside the Archdiocese.
Buslon, Arlou '85 (NEW) Leonia, NJ St. John the Evangelist's.
Busobozi, Adolf '97 (SPR) Springfield, MA Mary Mother of Hope Parish.
Bussen, Rev. Msgr. Robert J. '71 (SLC) College of Consultors; Cedar City, UT Christ the King LLC 203.
Bussmann, Frank A. '06 (JC) Fulton, MO St. Jude Thaddeus; V. Mexico; Ministry to Priests; Fulton, MO St. Peter.
Bustamante, Carlos (ATL) Lilburn, GA Our Lady of the Americas.
Bustamante, David '05 (FRS) Porterville, CA St. Anne.
Bustamante, Eduardo A. '11 (NEW) Jersey City, NJ St. Aloysius.
Bustamante, John Christopher '03 (DET) Detroit, MI Assumption Grotto.
Bustamante, Jose Arturo *o.f.m.* '81 (ELP)[B] El Paso, TX Roger Bacon College.
Bustamante, Rolando S. *s.j.* '06 (BO)[U] Newton, MA The Jesuit Community at Boston College.
Busto, George *c.o.* (NOR) Middletown, CT Middlesex Memorial Hospital; Middletown, CT St. Francis of Assisi.
Bustonera, Ian '03 (ORG) Yorba Linda, CA St. Martin de Porres.
Bustos, Javier '01 (MIL) Special Assignment; [B] Hales Corners, WI Sacred Heart School of Theology.
Butcavage, Leonard M. '72 (SCR) Retired.
Butch, Brian T. '93 (TR) Leave of Absence.
Butera, Christopher S. '07 (MO) Military Chaplains; Army Chaplains.
Butera, George J. '68 (BO) Revere, MA St. Anthony of Padua.
Butkowski, Charles M. '11 (CLV) North Royalton, OH St. Albert the Great.
Butler, Allan L. W. '67 (BO) Senior Priests. Retired.
Butler, David A. *o.p.* '57 (WDC) Washington, DC St. Dominic Church & Priory.
Butler, Francis *s.s.j.* '85 (LAF) Church Point, LA Our Mother of Mercy.
Butler, James P. '86 (BO) Senior Priests. Retired.
Butler, James '69 (R) Retired.
Butler, John J. '54 (L) Retired.
Butler, John J. '60 (MO) DEPARTMENT OF VETERANS AFFAIRS HOSPITALS AND CHAPLAINS.
Butler, John M. '72 (GBG) Leckrone, PA Our Lady of Perpetual Help (St. Mary); Masontown, PA All Saints.
Butler, John *s.j.* '00 (BO)[U] Newton, MA The Jesuit Community at Boston College.
Butler, John '60 (HON) On Duty Outside the Diocese.
Butler, Kevin M. '07 (RCK) Elgin, IL St. Thomas More.
Butler, Leo J. '98 (NEW) Norwood, NJ Immaculate Conception.
Butler, Michael A. '85 (R) Greenville, NC St. Gabriel.
Butler, Rev. Msgr. Michael T. '89 (STL) Air Force Chaplains; Military Chaplains.
Butler, Michael '84 (COS) Colorado Springs, CO Holy Apostles; Colorado Springs, CO St. Patrick.
Butler, Norman H. *m.s.* '75 (HRT)[L] Hartford, CT Missionaries of LaSalette.
Butler, Patrick J. '82 (ALB) Clifton Park, NY St. Edward the Confessor; Spiritual Director.
Butler, Patrick '82 (ALB) Priestly Life and Ministry Council.
Butler, Paul F. '87 (RVC) Seaford, NY St. William the Abbot.
Butler, Paul '04 (ALB) Loudonville, NY St. Pius X.
Butler, Rene J. *m.s.* '73 (BUR) The Review Board.
Butler, Rene J. *m.s.* '73 (MAN)[N] Enfield, NH Shrine of Our Lady of La Salette; [K] Enfield, NH Shrine of Our Lady of La Salette.
Butler, Richard J. '62 (BO) Senior Priests. Retired.
Butler, Robert J. '62 (BO) Senior Priests. Retired.
Butler, Robert R. *m.s.* '69 (HRT)[L] Hartford, CT Missionaries of LaSalette.
Butler, Thomas W. '82 (LAN) Otisville, MI St. Francis Xavier.
Butler, Thomas *o.carm.* '50 (TUC)[A] Tucson, AZ Salpointe Catholic High School; [E] Tucson, AZ Carmelite Priory Retired.
Butler, Thomas '82 (LAN) Clio, MI SS. Charles and Helena; Priests' Assignment Commission.
Butler, Timothy A. '88 (MO) Military & VA Chaplains.; Air Force Chaplains.
Butler, Timothy (TUC) Tucson, AZ Christ the King Chapel.
Butler, Victor *s.v.d.* '64 (TR)[N] Bordentown, NJ Society of the Divine Word.
Butler, Vincent E. *s.j.* '63 (NY)[DD] New York, NY Murray–Weigel Hall.
Butor, Walter *o.m.i.* '03 (CR) Ogema, MN Most Holy Redeemer.
Butta, C. Gregory '91 (WDC) Washington, DC St. Francis Xavier.
Butters, Craig M. '83 (ORG) Rancho Santa Margarita, CA San Francisco Solano Church; Liturgical Commission.
Butters, Joseph '65 (JOL) Retired.
Buttersby, Gerard W. '98 (DET) Beverly Hills, MI Our Lady Queen of Martyrs.
Buttner, Michael J. '78 (CHL) Clemmons, NC Holy Family.
Buttner, Michael T. '75 (BAL) Retired.
Buttrick, Dean T. '63 (SUP) Retired.
Butts, James C. *s.d.v.* (BO) Cambridge, MA St. Mary of the Annunciation.
Butz, Joseph *c.ss.r.* '70 (STL)[O] Liguori, MO Liguori Mission House/Redemptorists.
Butz, Robert J. '00 (MAD) De Forest, WI St. Olaf; De Forest, WI St. Joseph.
Buu, Francis X. '74 (NY) New York, NY Immaculate Conception.
Buvala, Andrew G. *o.f.m.* '47 (GLD) Suttons Bay, MI St. Wenceslaus; Suttons Bay, MI Blessed Kateri Tekakwitha; Native American Apostolate.
Buvens, Edward P. *s.j.* '69 (ATL)[H] Atlanta, GA Ignatius House.
Buxkemper, Rev. Msgr. Roland '65 (LUB) Retired.
Buxman, Donald '70 (P) Portland, OR St. Rita; Vicar for Clergy; Clergy; Ex Officio; Clergy Personnel; Board Members.
Buyansky, Timothy *o.s.b.* '69 (CLV)[D] Cleveland, OH Benedictine High School; [N] Cleveland, OH.
Buzga, John P. '59 (E)[K] San Antonio, TX Padua Place Retired.
Buzzelli, Aaron N. *o.s.b.* '77 (GBG)[A] Latrobe, PA St. Vincent Seminary; [H] Latrobe, PA Saint Vincent Archabbey.
Buzzerio, Joseph E. '77 (NEW) Retired.
Bwana, Alfred *c.p.* '06 (CHI)[N] Chicago, IL Passionist Community of St. Vincent Strambi.
Bwayo, Peter K. *a.j.* '89 (MO) DEPARTMENT OF VETERANS AFFAIRS HOSPITALS AND CHAPLAINS.
Bwezani Phiri, Wilfred '96 (CHI) Cicero, IL Our Lady of Charity.
Byabato, Deus–Dedit B. '93 (PEO)[H] Galesburg, IL St. Mary Medical Center.
Byarugaba, George '92 (OAK) Hayward, CA All Saints.
Byarugala, Dismas *a.j.* '03 (CLV) Akron City Hospital; Akron, OH St. Matthew.
Byaruhanga, Frederick K. '89 (MO) DEPARTMENT OF VETERANS AFFAIRS HOSPITALS AND CHAPLAINS.
Byaruhanga, Frederick '89 (LA) Los Angeles, CA St. Joan of Arc.
Byeck, Mitch *o.m.i.* '81 (BUF) Buffalo, NY Our Lady of Hope.
Byekwaso, Celestine '82 (GB) Regional Vicars; Coleman, WI St. Anne Parish Corp.
Byer, James M. '81 (CHL) Taylorsville, NC Holy Trinity.
Byerley, E. Joseph '93 (CAM) Haddon Heights, NJ Church of St. Rose, Haddon Heights, N.J.
Byerley, Timothy E. '85 (CAM)[O] Haddon Heights, NJ Collegium Center for Faith and Culture; Cherry Hill, NJ Holy Eucharist Parish, Cherry Hill, N.J.
Byers, Dohrman W. '74 (CIN) Georgetown, OH St. Mary; Consultors; Ripley, OH St. George; Ripley, OH St. Michael; Presbyteral Council.
Byers, John '95 (LAN) Lansing, MI Immaculate Heart of Mary; [Q] Lansing, MI Catholic Lay Association of the Holy Spirit Oratory.
Byington, Edward J. '70 (FR) Providence, RI St. Augustine Retired.
Bynon, Rev. Msgr. Joseph P. '56 (BRK)[R] Douglaston, NY Bishop Mugavero Residence Retired.
Byomuhangi, Deusdedit '96 (CHI) Calumet Park, IL Seven Holy Founders; Western Springs, IL St. John of the Cross.
Byrd, Charles A. '01 (ATL) Jasper, GA Our Lady of the Mountains.
Byrd, Freddie '88 (OWN) Waverly, KY Sacred Heart; Waverly, KY St. Peter.
Byrne, Rev. Msgr. Albert J. '79 (ALN) Allentown, PA Immaculate Conception.
Byrne, Basil *o.c.s.o.* '76 (WOR)[N] Spencer, MA St. Joseph's Abbey.
Byrne, Bernard M. '06 (SUP) Retired.
Byrne, Bernard P. *m.m.* '56 (SJ)[M] Los Altos, CA Maryknoll.
Byrne, David '88 (WIN) On Special or Other Diocesan Assignment.
Byrne, Edward G. '64 (NY) Ossining, NY St. Ann.
Byrne, Frederick *o.s.b.* '82 (GBG)[H] Latrobe, PA Saint Vincent Archabbey.
Byrne, Frederick *o.s.b.* '82 (WH) Morgantown, WV St. John University Parish, Newman Hall.
Byrne, George '69 (SD) Retired.
Byrne, Glenn F. '75 (BAL) On Duty Outside the Archdiocese.
Byrne, Rev. Msgr. Harry J. '46 (NY) New York, NY Epiphany; [DD] Bronx, NY John Cardinal O'Connor Residence Retired.
Byrne, Harry M. *o.p.* '78 (STL)[B] St. Louis, MO Aquinas Institute of Theology; [O] St. Louis, MO Dominican Community of St. Louis.
Byrne, Hugh A. '62 (BRK)[R] Douglaston, NY Bishop Mugavero Residence Retired.
Byrne, James F. *o.s.f.s.* '60 (CHL) High Point, NC Immaculate Heart of Mary.
Byrne, Joel *o.f.m.* '51 (CIN)[N] Cincinnati, OH St. Clement Friary Retired.
Byrne, John F. *s.s.j.* '66 (BAL)[Q] Baltimore, MD St. Joseph Society of the Sacred Heart House of Central Administration Retired.
Byrne, John M. (NEW) Absent on Leave.
Byrne, Joseph F. '69 (BO) Senior Priests.; Arlington, MA St. Camillus Retired.
Byrne, Joseph L. '54 (HEL) Townsend, MT Holy Cross.
Byrne, Keith '04 (LA) On Active Leave.
Byrne, Laurence *s.d.b.* '52 (SFR)[N] San Francisco, CA Salesian Provincial Residence Retired.
Byrne, Luke J. *s.j.* '65 (KC)[J] Kansas City, MO Rockhurst Jesuit Community.
Byrne, Patrick J. '55 (COL) Retired.
Byrne, Peter D. *s.j.* '75 (P)[L] Portland, OR Jesuit Provincial Office (Society of Jesus, Oregon Prov.); [L] Portland, OR Colombiere Community.
Byrne, Peter J. '84 (NY) Staten Island, NY Immaculate Conception.
Byrne, Rev. Msgr. Raymond J. '57 (NY) Irvington–on–the–Hudson, NY Immaculate Conception.
Byrne, Robert H. '75 (SAG) Frankenmuth, MI Blessed Trinity; Diocesan College of Consultors.
Byrne, Thomas J. *c.s.sp.* '64 (GAL)[O] Houston, TX Congregation of the Holy Spirit, Province of the United States.
Byrne, William D. '94 (WDC) Washington, DC St. Peter; [U] College Park, MD University of Maryland Catholic Student Center; Secretariats; Secretary for Pastoral Ministry and Social Concerns; Pastoral Center Special Ministries.
Byrne, William D. '88 (WIN)[D] Rochester, MN Saint Mary Hospital.
Byrnes, Christopher *o.carm.* '51 (NY)[DD] Middletown, NY St. Albert's Priory.
Byrnes, Rev. Msgr. Donald M. '55 (NO) Retired.
Byrnes, Francis J. '51 (BRK)[R] Douglaston, NY Bishop Mugavero Residence Retired.
Byrnes, James J. '80 (STL) St. Louis, MO Mary, Mother of the Church.
Byrnes, Rev. Msgr. James T. '86 (NY)[E] Goshen, NY John S. Burke Catholic High School.
Byrnes, John D. '94 (ALT) Judicial Vicar; Cresson, PA St. Aloysius; Tribunal.
Byrnes, John W. '47 (BRK)[O] Queens Village, NY Queen of Peace Residence Retired.
Byrnes, Rev. Msgr. Paul A. '62 (BAL) Retired.
Byrnes, Robert R. '67 (GBG) Greensburg, PA Excela Health – Westmoreland Hospital; [K] Greensburg, PA The Bishop William G. Connare Center.
Byrnes, Thomas J. '99 (NY) Monroe, NY Sacred Heart Church.
Byrolly, Bruce '58 (WIL) Retired.
Byron, J. Michael '89 (STP) St. Paul, MN St. Cecilia; [A] Saint Paul, MN The Saint Paul Seminary; [C] St. Paul, MN University of St. Thomas; Censores Librorum.
Byron, William J. *s.j.* '61 (PH)[Y] Loyola Center and Manresa Hall; [C] Jesuit Fathers.
Byron, William '62 (YAK) Goldendale, WA Holy Trinity.
Byrth, Peter *o.carm.* '59 (JOL)[L] Darien Carmelite Provincial Office.
Bzdyra, Stephen H. '79 (HRT) Ansonia–Derby Deanery; Leave of Absence.

C

Cabala, Thomas S. '79 (CHI) Hometown, IL Our Lady of Loretto.
Caballejo, Yuen '06 (ATL) Army Reserve Chaplains; Marietta, GA Cobb County Jail; Special or Other Archdiocesan Assignment; Norcross, GA Mary Our Queen Catholic Church.
Caballero, Francisco '53 (TOL) Retired.
Caban, Carmen '06 (SP)[J] Tampa, FL St. Joseph's Hospital, Inc.

Cabanas, Jaime R. '55 (BWN) Retired.
Cabardo, Donato '99 (NEW) Demarest, NJ Parish of St. Joseph.
Cabasagan, Arbel '07 (SAC) Colusa, CA Our Lady of Lourdes.
Cabasino, Philip A. *c.ss.r.* '47 (BO) Boston, MA Our Lady of Perpetual Help.
Cabell, Barry E. *c.s.c.* '89 (AUS)[G] Austin, TX Brother Andre Residence.
Cabello, Tomas *c.m.f.* (CGS) Caguas, PR Inmaculado Corazon de Maria.
Cabezas, Francisco Javier '79 (NEW) Newark, NJ Northern State Prison.
Cabezas, Richard E. '99 (NEW) Fort Lee, NJ Holy Trinity.
Cabico, Jon '09 (HON) Diocesan Hospital Ministry; Chaplains; Honolulu, HI Co–Cathedral of St. Theresa of the Child Jesus.
Caboboy, Juan '76 (ORG) Garden Grove, CA St. Columban; Council of Priests.
Cabra, M. Arturo '98 (R) Washington, NC Mother of Mercy.
Cabral, Clifford J. '79 (PRO) Pascoag, RI St. Joseph.
Cabral, Fernando A. '86 (PRO) West Warwick, RI St. Anthony.
Cabral, Jeffrey '02 (FR) Judges; Promotor Justitiae; East Taunton, MA Holy Family.
Cabrera, Alberto '99 (MRY) Nipomo, CA St. Joseph; Clergy Life and Ministry Board.
Cabrera, Alberto *c.p.* '65 (BRK)[R] Jamaica, NY Immaculate Conception Monastery.
Cabrera, Encarnacion J. '08 (CC) Alice, TX Our Lady of Guadalupe.
Cabrera, Jose '07 (SAG) Outside the Diocese.
Cabrera, Mario F. '81 (LA) Lynwood, CA St. Emydius.
Cabrera, Rolando '93 (MIA) Southwest Ranches, FL St. Mark.
Cabrera, Sergio '73 (MIA) Retired.
Cabrera–Carranza, Claudio '02 (MRY) King City, CA St. John the Baptist; Vicars Forane.
Cabrerizo, Juan L. *sch.p.* '77 (SJN) San Juan, PR Santisimo Salvador; [B] San Juan, PR Colegio Calasanz.
Cabrisos, Cromwell '78 (ORL) Clermont, FL Blessed Sacrament; Judges.
Cabrita, Paul M. *s.m.* '86 (STP) St. Paul, MN St. Louis King of France.
Cabuenas, Cyrain G. '97 (BUR) Wilmington, VT Our Lady of Fatima.
Caccavale, Charles '81 (BRK) Released from Diocesan Assignment.
Caccavale, Charles '91 (RVC)[A] Huntington, NY Diocesan Seminary of the Immaculate Conception; Censors of Books.
Caccavalle, Pius *o.f.m.cap.* '47 (NEW) Hackensack, NJ Church of St. Francis of Assisi.
Cacciapuoti, Rev. Msgr. Antonio '90 (LA) San Fernando Region; Los Angeles, CA Christ the King; Cardinal McIntyre Fund for Charity Board of Directors.
Cacciapuoti, Rev. Msgr. Antonio '90 (LA) La Canada Flintridge, CA St. Bede the Venerable.
Caceres, Rev. Msgr. Alonso '59 (ORG) Retired.
Caceres, Angel Diaz '76 (SJN)[A] Bayamon Central University.
Caceres, Angel Diaz '76 (ARE) Vega–Alta, PR Santa Ana; Priest's Senate (Consejo Presbiteral).
Caceres, Blas *c.ss.r.* (BAL) Annapolis, MD St. Mary.
Caceres, Jacob Antonio '08 (SAC) Woodland, CA Holy Rosary.
Caceres, Luis Alberto '08 (AUS) Lakeway, TX Church of the Resurrection, Emmaus.
Caceres, Marco A. '67 (MET) New Brunswick, NJ St. John the Baptist; Deans.
Cachat, Leo P. *s.j.* '66 (DET)[P] Bloomfield Hills, MI Manresa Jesuit Retreat House.
Cadalbo, Kenneth *o.f.m.* (CHI)[N] Chicago, IL St. Peter's Friary.
Cadavid, Diego '02 (CHI) Blue Island, IL St. Donatus.
Cadavid, Jose Augusto (ORL) Clermont, FL Blessed Sacrament.
Cadavid–Rivera, Gonzalo '09 (BAL) Cockeysville, MD St. Joseph; On Duty Outside the Archdiocese.
Cadden, Donald R. *s.j.* '58 (SPK)[B] Spokane, WA Gonzaga University.
Caddy, James L. '64 (CLV) Gates Mills, OH St. Francis of Assisi.
Cadena, Lorenzo Gamboa '11 (CHI) Glenview, IL St. Catherine Laboure.
Cadigan, Timothy J. *s.j.* '91 (SCR)[B] Scranton, PA The University of Scranton.
Cadorette, Curtis R. *m.m.* '77 (NY)[DD].
Cadran, Raymond G. *m.s.* '78 (ATL) Marietta, GA St. Ann.
Cadrecha, Robert '04 (SP) Temple Terrace, FL Corpus Christi; Elected Pastors.
Cadusale, Jose '60 (BRK) Rego Park, NY Our Lady of the Angelus; Queens Hospital Center—Pastoral Care Office.
Cadwallader, Simon '97 (FgM) Boston, MA St. James the Apostle, Inc.
Cady, Frank G. '81 (TUC) Tucson, AZ Saint Odilia Roman Catholic Community – Tucson.
Caesar, Floyd '75 (ALN) Weatherly, PA Our Lady of Lourdes Parish; Catholic Daughters of the Americas.
Caesar, Roger J. *s.s.j.* '77 (LA) Los Angeles, CA St. Brigid's.
Cafarelli, Francis T. *c.s.c.* '65 (FTW)[A] Notre Dame, IN Moreau Seminary; [A] Notre Dame, IN Moreau Seminary; [H] Notre Dame Congregation of Holy Cross, United States Province of Priests & Brothers.
Caffrey, Benet W. *o.s.b.* '58 (PAT)[N] Morristown, NJ St. Mary's Abbey.
Caffrey, Gerald *c.m.f.* '80 (PHX) Prescott, AZ United States Veterans Hospital (Prescott); Prescott, AZ Sacred Heart Roman Catholic Parish.
Caffrey, Gerald *c.m.f.* '80 (MO) DEPARTMENT OF VETERANS AFFAIRS HOSPITALS AND CHAPLAINS.
Caffrey, William J. *s.v.d.* '59 (SB)[I] Riverside, CA Divine Word Seminary.
Caffrey, William *s.v.d.* '58 (ORG)[G] Fullerton, CA St. Jude Medical Center.
Cafone, Rev. Msgr. James M. '65 (NEW)[B] Seton Hall University; Censores Librorum; [B] Seton Hall University; Elected Members.
Cagantas, Dennis '95 (NY) Bronx, NY St. Clare of Assisi.
Caggianelli, Gregg '02 (VEN) Fort Myers, FL St. Francis Xavier; Air Force Reserve Chaplains; Presbyteral Council; [F] Fort Myers, FL Villa Francisco.
Caggiano, Kyrin *o.carm.* '62 (JOL)[L] Darien Carmelite Provincial Office Retired.
Cagoco, Eugene E. *d.s.* '97 (GAL)[O] Houston, TX Disciples of Hope (Texas); [O] Houston, TX St. Matthew the Evangelist; [S] Houston, TX The Catholic Chaplain Corps.
Cahalan, Patrick J. *s.j.* '65 (LA)[C] Los Angeles, CA Loyola Marymount University; [C] Los Angeles, CA Jesuit Community.
Cahalane, Rev. Msgr. Thomas '63 (TUC) Tucson, AZ Our Mother of Sorrows Roman Catholic Parish – Tucson; Diocesan Consultors; Ecumenical Commission.
Cahill, Brendan '90 (GAL) Secretariat For Clergy Formation and Chaplaincy Services; Priests Personnel Committee; Elected Members; Secretariat for Clergy Formation and Chaplaincy Services.
Cahill, Clement *c.ss.r.* (HBG)[G] Ephrata, PA St. Clement's Mission House.
Cahill, Daniel '73 (TR) Keansburg, NJ St. Ann.
Cahill, Dennis H. '77 (DUB) Cresco, IA Notre Dame.
Cahill, Edward B. '60 (PH) Retired.
Cahill, J. Donald *s.m.* '61 (STL)[O] St. Louis, MO Cure of Ars Marianist Community Retired.
Cahill, J. Patrick '07 (CHL) Asheville, NC St. Eugene; Charlotte, NC St. Gabriel.
Cahill, James '61 (CHL) Retired.
Cahill, John W. '73 (COV) Hispanic Ministry; Erlanger, KY Cristo Rey.
Cahill, John W. '63 (RCK) Retired.
Cahill, Joseph W. '76 (PRT) Kittery, ME Parish of the Ascension of the Lord.
Cahill, Rev. Msgr. Richard M. '58 (BUF) Retired.
Cahill, Rev. Msgr. Richard '39 (NY) New York, NY National Catholic Community Service.
Cahill, William C. '61 (SY) Special Assignment.
Cahoon, John E. '89 (GAL) Houston, TX St. Cecilia; Promoter of Justice.
Caiazzo, Gregory G. '76 (RIC) Military Chaplains.
Caiazzo, Nicholas '92 (NOR) On Duty Outside the Diocese.
Cain, Dennis R. '79 (DUB) Epworth, IA St. John; Epworth, IA St. Patrick; Epworth, IA St. Joseph; Epworth, IA St. Clement.
Cain, Frederick L. '70 (PIT)[N] Pittsburgh, PA Sisters of St. Francis of the Providence of God; Priest Council; Vicariate 2; College of Consultors; Clergy Personnel Board; Episcopal Vicars.
Cain, Gervase *t.o.r.* '57 (ALT)[G] Loretto, PA St. Francis Friary at Mount Assisi.
Cain, Harry J. *s.j.* '63 (BO)[U] Weston, MA Campion Jesuit Community.
Cain, Rev. Msgr. James E. '50 (STO) Diamond Springs, CA Retired.
Cain, Rev. Msgr. James R. '56 (OM) Omaha Priests Retirement Plan and Trust, The Retired.
Cain, John F. '56 (SC) Spencer, IA Retired.
Cain, Randy N. '88 (CC) Corpus Christi, TX St. Theresa.
Cain, Robert K.C. '95 (TLS) On Duty Outside the Diocese; Navy Reserve Chaplains.
Cain, Stephen *o.f.m.* '74 (OAK)[N] Danville, CA San Damiano Retreat.
Cain, William F. *s.j.* '69 (SJ)[M] Los Gatos, CA Sacred Heart Jesuit Center.
Caindec, Ferdinando '79 (NY) Nanuet, NY St. Anthony.
Cairns, John L. '63 (ALB) Retired.
Cairns, Stephen P. '68 (TOL) Retired.
Cairone, A. Robert '64 (CAM) Retired.
Cal–Ortiz, Rodolfo L. '93 (GAL) Anderson, TX St. Stanislaus; Navasota, TX Christ Our Light.
Calabrese, Charles L. '72 (STU) On Duty Outside the Diocese.
Calabrese, Charles '72 (FWT)[L] Fort Worth, TX Texas Christian University Catholic Community; Youth and Campus Ministry.
Calabrese, Peter M. *c.r.s.p.* '00 (BUF)[B] Youngstown, NY St. Anthony M. Zaccaria Seminary; [S] Youngstown, NY Basilica of the National Shrine of Our Lady of Fatima, Inc.; Youngstown, NY Holy Family.
Calabria, Michael D. *o.f.m.* '03 (BUF)[N] St. Bonaventure, NY St. Bonaventure Friary.
Calabro, John E. '73 (PH) Philadelphia, PA Annunciation B.V.M.
Calabro, Nicholas J. '66 (BGP)[O] Stamford, CT The Catherine Dennis Keefe Queen of the Clergy Retired Priests' Residence Retired.
Calais, Floyd J. '50 (LAF) Retired.
Calamari, Joseph M. *s.s.j.* '45 (BAL)[Q] Baltimore, MD St. Joseph's Manor.
Calasara, Mansuelo '61 (JC) Retired.
Caldarella, James J. '71 (WOR) Princeton, MA Prince of Peace.
Caldas, Rev. Msgr. Constantino R. '51 (BGP) Retired.
Calder, Kenneth J. '60 (BRK) Brooklyn, NY Our Lady of Angels Retired.
Calderon, Cruz '08 (DAL) Dallas, TX Our Lady of Perpetual Help.
Calderon, Jaime '05 (RVC) Westbury, NY St. Brigid.
Calderon, Juan Luis *o.a.r.* '94 (NEW) Union City, NJ Saint Rocco/Saint Brigid; West New York, NJ St. Joseph of the Palisades.
Calderon, Vicente '63 (ELP) Retired.
Calderon, Wilfredo *s.d.b.* '91 (MGZ) San Antonio, PR San Jose Obrero.
Calderone, Joseph D. *o.s.a.* '73 (PH)[C] Villanova University; [Y] Villanova, PA St. Thomas of Villanova Friary.
Calderone, Joseph D. *o.s.a.* '73 (MO) Navy Reserve Chaplains.
Caldognetto, Dominic *s.x.* '66 (MIL)[B] Franklin, WI Xaverian Missionary Fathers College Seminary.
Caldwell, Rev. Msgr. Frank J. *c.s.w.* '81 (RVC) Uniondale, NY St. Martha.
Caldwell, Fred '95 (DAL) Retired.
Caldwell, James A. '03 (TLS) Krebs, OK St. Joseph's.
Caldwell, John A. '70 (L) Pewee Valley, KY St. Aloysius.
Caldwell, Thomas A. *s.j.* '56 (MIL)[P] Milwaukee, WI Jesuit Community at Marquette University.
Caldwell, Rev. Msgr. William '68 (KC) Excelsior Springs, MO St. Ann.
Calegari, Leonard J. '63 (SFR) San Francisco, CA St. Stephen Retired.
Calero, Luis F. *s.j.* '83 (SJ)[B] Santa Clara, CA Jesuit Community.
Calero Gómez, Nomar Jose '91 (MGZ) Lajas, PR Our Lady of the Purification.
Calgaro, John *o.f.m.conv.* '74 (CHI)[N] Chicago Conventual Franciscans of St. Bonaventure Province; Chicago, IL Province of Saint Bonaventure.
Calhoun, Gerald '61 (OWN) Consultors Retired.
Calhoun, Lawrence E. *c.s.c.* '63 (FTW)[H] Notre Dame Congregation of Holy Cross, United States Province of Priests & Brothers.
Calhoun, Michael '02 (PEO)[A] Peru, IL St. Bede Abbey.
Calhoun, Ronald G. '72 (BO) Hudson, MA St. Michael.
Calia, Jeffrey *c.o.* '10 (MET)[I] New Brunswick, NJ The New Brunswick Congregation of the Oratory of St. Philip Neri; New Brunswick, NJ; New Brunswick, NJ St. Peter the Apostle.
Caliba, Jude '94 (NEW) East Orange, NJ Holy Name of Jesus.
Calicchio, Isaac J. *o.f.m.* '56 (HRT) Meriden, CT St. Rose of Lima.
Caligiuri, Rev. Msgr. Angelo M. '58 (BUF)[N] Tonawanda, NY O'Hara Residence; Finance Council Retired.
Caligiuri, Rev. Msgr. Anthony J. '49 (BUF)[N] Tonawanda, NY O'Hara Residence Retired.
Calimeri, Anthony F. '47 (ROC) Retired.
Calise, Rev. Msgr. Joseph P. '80 (BRK) Brooklyn, NY Annunciation of the Blessed Virgin Mary; Brooklyn, NY Our Lady of Mount Carmel Shrine Church.
Calixte, Raymond *s.t.* (PT)[E] Tallahassee, FL Missionary Servants of the Most Holy Trinity.
Calkins, Rev. Msgr. Arthur B. '70 (NO) On Duty Outside the Archdiocese.
Calkins, Rev. Msgr. Arthur B. '70 (STL)[N] Kirkwood, MO St. Agnes Home for the Elderly.
Calkins, Rev. Msgr. Howard W. '67 (NY) Mount Vernon, NY Sacred Heart.
Calkins, Ronald L. '78 (NO) Mandeville, LA Mary, Queen of Peace.
Callaghan, Rev. Msgr. Aloysius R. '71 (ALN) On Duty Outside the Diocese.
Callaghan, Rev. Msgr. Aloysius R. '71 (STP)[C] St. Paul, MN University of St. Thomas; [A] Saint Paul, MN The Saint Paul Seminary; The Saint Paul Seminary School of Divinity; Center for Formation.
Callaghan, Michael J. *c.m.* '76 (BRK)[R] Jamaica, NY Reverend John B. Murray, CM, House.
Callaghan, Michael J. *c.o.* '90 (BRK) Brooklyn, NY St.

Boniface; [R] Brooklyn, NY Oratory of Saint Philip Neri, Congregation Pontifical Rite.
Callaghan, Michael '90 (BAL) On Duty Outside the Archdiocese.
Callaghan, Nicholas E. '04 (NY) Bronx, NY St. Margaret of Cortona.
Callahan, Daniel *s.a.* '87 (NY)[DD] Garrison Franciscan Friars of the Atonement, Minister General Office.
Callahan, David P. '87 (BO) Quincy, MA St. Mary.
Callahan, Francis X. '63 (BAL) Bel Air, MD St. Margaret Retired.
Callahan, Francis X. '49 (HRT) Milford, CT St. Agnes.
Callahan, James A. '73 (PH) Philadelphia, PA Christ the King.
Callahan, James B. '98 (WOR) Leominster, MA St. Anna.
Callahan, James F. '75 (WIN) Worthington, MN St. Mary's.
Callahan, Rev. Msgr. James P. '74 (STL) St. Charles, MO St. Joseph.
Callahan, John J. *s.j.* '70 (BR)[J] Convent, LA Manresa House of Retreats.
Callahan, Joseph F. *c.s.c.* '70 (FR)[A] North Easton, MA Holy Cross Fathers Religious; [H] North Easton, MA Holy Cross Retreat House.
Callahan, Joseph F. *c.s.c.* '70 (FTW)[H] Notre Dame Congregation of Holy Cross, United States Province of Priests & Brothers.
Callahan, Joseph H. '86 (CLV) College of Consultors; Cleveland, OH Our Lady of Lourdes.
Callahan, Joseph W. '66 (PH) Retired.
Callahan, Joseph (CLV)[V] Cleveland, OH Our Lady of Lourdes.
Callahan, Rev. Msgr. Kevin G. '84 (MO) Ellisville, MO St. Clare of Assisi; DEPARTMENT OF VETERANS AFFAIRS HOSPITALS AND CHAPLAINS.
Callahan, Nelson J. '53 (CLV) Bay Village, OH St. Raphael Retired.
Callahan, Richard B. *m.m.* '64 (NY)[DD] Maryknoll Maryknoll Fathers and Brothers; [DD] Maryknoll, NY M.M.A.F. Charitable Trust; [DD] Maryknoll, NY Maryknoll Fathers and Brothers Charitable Trust; [EE] Maryknoll, NY Maryknoll Sisters Charitable Trust; [HH] Maryknoll, NY The Asian Catholic News Fund.
Callahan, Ronan P. *c.p.* '51 (NOR)[A] Cromwell, CT Holy Apostles College and Seminary.
Callahan, Ronan *c.p.* '51 (HRT)[L] West Hartford, CT Holy Family Monastery/Retreat.
Callahan, Rev. Msgr. Steven F. '87 (SD) San Diego, CA Saint Brigid Catholic Parish; Vicar General; Judicial Vicar; Clergy Personnel Board; College of Consultors; Finance Council; Presbyteral Council; Victim Assistance Coordinator.
Callahan, Zachary '58 (RVC) Merrick, NY Curé of Ars Retired.
Callan, Dennis *s.v.d.* '87 (FgM) Techny, IL.
Callan, John *sch.p.* '82 (MIA)[D] Fort Lauderdale, FL Cardinal Gibbons High School.
Callan, Patrick J. '61 (RVC) Point Lookout, NY Our Lady of the Miraculous Medal.
Callanan, Michael G. *m.m.* '60 (LA) Monrovia, CA Annunciation; [P] Monrovia, CA Retired.
Callaway, Donald *m.i.c.* '03 (SPR)[G] Provincial Office.
Calle, Juan de la '54 (PMB) Retired.
Callea, Michael *m.i.c.* '02 (JOL) Yorkville, IL St. Patrick; Plano, IL St. Mary.
Calledo, James '94 (RVC) East Northport, NY St. Anthony of Padua.
Calleja, Rev. Msgr. Guido '53 (MOB) Magnolia Springs, AL St. John the Baptist.
Callery, Peter J. *s.j.* '72 (BR)[J] Convent, LA Manresa House of Retreats.
Callery, William V. '01 (FAR) Retired.
Calles, Rev. Msgr. Robert S. '63 (SFE) Santa Fe, NM The Cathedral Basilica of St. Francis of Assisi Retired.
Callipare, Joseph P. '85 (PT) Vicar for Permanent Deacons and Chairman; Executive Committee of Permanent Deacons; Permanent Deacon Formation Team; Priests' Pension Plan, Board for; Permanent Deacon Formation Board; Office of the Permanent Diaconate and Permanent Deacon Formation.
Callis, Elbert '76 (MEM) Retired.
Caloca–Rivas, Rigoberto *o.f.m.* '82 (OAK)[L] Oakland, CA Franciscan Friars of California, (Province of St. Barbara); [Q] Berkeley, CA Multicultural Institute.
Calovini, Rev. Msgr. Gerald E. '73 (STU) Steubenville, OH Holy Family; Defenders of the Bond; College of Consultors.
Calter, Arthur M. '56 (BO) Senior Priests. Retired.
Caluda, Charles J. '62 (NO) Retired.
Calumba, Faron *c.s.* '79 (HRT) Hamden, CT Our Lady of Mt. Carmel.
Calvario, Fredy '10 (MRY) On Leave.
Calvillo, Ernesto '10 (TLS) Special Assignment.
Calvo, Gabriel '52 (WDC)[B] Washington, DC Diocesan Laborer Priests, House of Studies.
Camacho, Henry A. *o.p.* '60 (HRT) New Haven, CT St. Mary's.
Camacho, Jesus '75 (B) Prison Ministry; Boise, ID St. Mary's.
Camacho, Jesus '06 (SAT) Charlotte, TX St. Rose of Lima.
Camacho, Orlando *c.s.sp.* (ARE) Propagation of Faith; Holy Childhood.
Camacho, Robert '79 (RCK) Special Assignment.
Camacho–Monserrate, Enrique Manuel '07 (SJN) Catholic Charities; Caritas of Puerto Rico; [I] San Juan, PR Caritas de Puerto Rico, Inc.
Camacho–Torres, Jose Orlando *c.s.sp.* '92 (SJN)[F] Dorado, PR Santuario del Espiritu Santo; Propagation of the Faith; Holy Childhood Association.
Camadella, Christian F. *o.f.m.* '56 (PAT)[N] Butler, NJ St. Anthony Friary.
Camaioni, Matthew J. '07 (RCK)[L] DeKalb, IL Newman Foundation for Catholic Students of Northern Illinois University; DeKalb, IL Christ the Teacher, University Parish of Northern Illinois University.
Camara, Michael M. '89 (FR) New Bedford, MA Our Lady of Mt. Carmel; New Bedford, MA St. John the Baptist.
Camarda, Ronald A. '90 (STA) Unassigned.
Camargo, Carlos '06 (B) American Falls, ID Presentation of the Lord.
Camarillo, Joel Arciga '98 (CAM) Camden, NJ St. Joseph Catholic Church, East Camden, N.J. (Pro–Cathedral).
Cambi, Michael '07 (ALB) Stamford, NY Sacred Heart; Priestly Life and Ministry Council.
Cambra, Raymond '77 (FR) Fall River, MA Sacred Heart.
Cameli, Louis J. '69 (CHI) Chicago, IL Holy Name Cathedral.
Camera, Bede G. *o.s.b.* '88 (MAN)[K] Manchester, NH St. Anselm Abbey.
Cameron, Ben *c.p.m.* '97 (OWN)[F] Auburn, KY Fathers of Mercy; Auburn, KY.
Cameron, Hilary J. '64 (PRT) Retired.
Cameron, Lachlan T. '08 (RVC) New Hyde Park, NY Holy Spirit; Massapequa, NY St. Rose of Lima.
Cameron, Peter John *o.p.* (HRT) New Haven, CT St. Mary's.
Cameron, Robert M. '59 (KC) Special Assignment; Holy Childhood Association; Priests' Purgatorial Society; Propagation of the Faith.
Camilleri, Anthony E. '07 (DET) Royal Oak, MI National Shrine of the Little Flower.
Camilleri, Joseph M. '74 (BR) Baton Rouge, LA St. Agnes.
Camilli, E. Michael *m.s.c.* '60 (ALN)[A] Center Valley, PA Sacred Heart Villa, Missionaries of the Sacred Heart.
Caminiti, Antonino '08 (AGN) Asan, GU Nino Perdido Y Sagrada Familia; Nino Perdido Parish (Asan).
Camire, Bernard J. *s.s.s.* '66 (NY) New York, NY St. Jean Baptiste.
Camiring, Paul John T. (WDC) Washington, DC St. Augustine.
Cammisa, James N. '49 (TR)[N] Trenton, NJ St. Lawrence Rehabilitation Center Retired.
Camora, Antonio (BRK)[Q] Apostleship of the Sea; Brooklyn, NY Sacred Hearts of Jesus and Mary and St. Stephen.
Camp, Alfred L. '57 (JKS) Madison, MS St. Francis of Assisi Retired.
Camp, Rev. Msgr. Steven '87 (RVC) Baldwin, NY St. Christopher; Presbyteral Council.
Campagna, Robert M. *o.f.m.* '77 (NY)[DD] New York, NY Franciscan Province of the Immaculate Conception; New York, NY; Definitors.
Campana, Thomas J. '80 (CHI) Chicago, IL Queen of All Saints Basilica.
Campbell, Andrew S. *o.s.b.* '81 (GBG)[H] Latrobe, PA Saint Vincent Archabbey.
Campbell, Bernard J. *o.f.m.cap* '68 (MAN) Manchester, NH St. Anne–St. Augustin; N.H. Prison for Men.
Campbell, Bernard *c.s.p.* '68 (OAK) Berkeley, CA Holy Spirit Parish/Newman Hall.
Campbell, Brian '09 (PMB) Palm Beach Gardens, FL St. Patrick.
Campbell, Donald *c.s.p.* '62 (NY)[DD] New York, NY Paulist Fathers' Motherhouse.
Campbell, Douglas L. '76 (WCH) Judges; [C] Wichita, KS Via Christi Hospital on Harry Street.
Campbell, Dwight '91 (MIL) On Duty Outside the Diocese; Kenosha, WI Our Lady of Mount Carmel.
Campbell, Rev. Msgr. Francis '73 (P) Retired.
Campbell, Gerard J. *s.j.* '51 (WDC)[O] Washington, DC The Jesuit Community at Georgetown University Retired.
Campbell, Howard W. '88 (PIT) Aliquippa, PA Our Lady of Fatima.
Campbell, Rev. Msgr. Hugh P. '61 (PH) Retired.
Campbell, Rev. Msgr. J. Michael '71 (STU) Presbyteral Council; College of Consultors; Vicar for Religious.
Campbell, James C. '06 (E) Port Allegany, PA St. Gabriel the Archangel; Coudersport, PA St. Eulalia.
Campbell, Rev. Msgr. James F. '64 (BUF) Finance Council; Buffalo, NY St. Joseph Cathedral.
Campbell, Joe '99 (KNX) La Follette, TN Our Lady of Perpetual Help.
Campbell, Rev. Msgr. John G. '55 (ORG) Judges Retired.
Campbell, Rev. Msgr. John Michael '71 (STU) Marietta, OH St. Mary's; [L] Marietta, OH Marietta College.
Campbell, Rev. Msgr. John S. '66 (ALN) Northampton, PA Queenship of Mary Parish.
Campbell, Joseph C. '06 (E) Sharon, PA St. Joseph.
Campbell, Joseph '99 (KNX) La Follette, TN Christ the King.
Campbell, Joseph '60 (FAR) Retired.
Campbell, Rev. Msgr. Mark A. '71 (SD) Diocesan Judges; Presbyteral Council; College of Consultors.
Campbell, Rev. Msgr. Mark A. '71 (SD) San Diego, CA Our Mother of Confidence Catholic Parish.
Campbell, Norbert J. '60 (PIT) Wilmerding, PA St. Jude the Apostle.
Campbell, Paul F. '65 (WOR) Dudley, MA St. Anthony.
Campbell, Paul J. '82 (WIL) Chestertown, MD Sacred Heart; Chestertown, MD Washington College; [O] Newark, DE Washington College.
Campbell, Paul *s.j.* '88 (CHI)[N] Chicago, IL Clark Street Jesuit Residence.
Campbell, Peter E. *m.s.c.* '60 (RCK)[G] Aurora, IL Missionaries of the Sacred Heart Community.
Campbell, Robert E. *o.praem.* '08 (SFE) Presbyterian Hospital; [H] Albuquerque, NM Santa Maria de la Vid Priory.
Campbell, Robert J. *m.s.* '58 (HRT)[L] Hartford, CT Missionaries of LaSalette.
Campbell, Roy Edward '07 (WDC) Largo, MD St. Joseph.
Campbell, Shane A. '08 (STP) On Duty Outside the Archdiocese.
Campbell, Shane '08 (BIS) Mandan, ND St. Joseph.
Campbell, Stephen *s.j.* '85 (MOB)[A] Mobile, AL Spring Hill College.
Campbell, Theodore C. '72 (STP) Golden Valley, MN Good Shepherd; Deanery 9.
Campbell, Thomas L. '48 (FR)[A] North Easton, MA Holy Cross Fathers Religious.
Campbell, Thomas L. *c.s.c.* '48 (FTW)[H] Notre Dame Congregation of Holy Cross, United States Province of Priests & Brothers.
Campbell, Wayne '86 (OAK) Moraga, CA St. Monica.
Campbell, William D. '58 (SCR)[M] Dunmore, PA Villa St. Joseph Retired.
Campbell, William G. '63 (FR) Retired.
Campbell, William R. *s.j.* '64 (PRT)[C] Portland, ME Cheverus High School.
Campbell, William W. '52 (BO) Senior Priests. Retired.
Campeaux, Corey '10 (LAF) Lafayette, LA St. Pius X.
Campellone, Joseph G. *o.s.f.s.* '96 (PH)[D] Philadelphia, PA Father Judge High School for Boys; [Y] Philadelphia, PA Father Louis Brisson Residence.
Campi, Vincent L. '45 (WH) Retired.
Campion, Joseph J. '73 (ALN) Whitehall, PA St. John the Baptist.
Campion, Joseph J. *s.s.j.* (LAF) Breaux Bridge, LA St. Francis of Assisi.
Campion, Owen F. '66 (NSH) On Duty Outside the Diocese.
Campion, Thomas B. '52 (HRT) Wethersfield, CT Corpus Christi; Wethersfield, CT Sacred Heart Retired.
Campion, William T. '77 (ALN) Palmerton, PA Sacred Heart; Palmerton Hospital.
Campo, Frank D. '09 (BO) Franklin, MA St. Mary.
Campo, Lance J. '93 (NO) Center of Jesus the Lord; Hispanic Apostolate Pastoral Services; Priests for Life; [T] New Orleans, LA Center of Jesus the Lord.
Campoli, Timothy J. '74 (SPR) Greenfield, MA Blessed Sacrament; Deans.
Campos, Daniel '04 (TLS) Hispanic Ministry; Idabel, OK St. Francis De Sales.
Campos, Miguel *sch.p.* '96 (LA)[P] Los Angeles, CA Piarist Fathers.
Campos, Miguel '98 (FRS) Tipton, CA St. John The Evangelist.
Campos, Pedro '02 (CHI) Chicago, IL St. Kevin.
Campos, Randy Raul '08 (LA) Bell Gardens, CA St. Gertrude.
Campuzano, Guillermo *c.m.* '90 (CHI)[N] Chicago, IL Vincentian Community, Congregation of the Mission, Western Province.
Camuso, Robert '92 (SEA) Shoreline, WA St. Luke.
Can–Vasquez, Gregorio Filipe '88 (GAL) Houston, TX St. Elizabeth Ann Seton.
Canaan, Timothy G. '93 (OG) Campus Ministry; Plattsburgh, NY The Roman Catholic Church of St. John the Baptist.
Canal, Manuel '58 (MRY) Retired.
Canales, Rene L. '06 (CAM) Carney's Point, NJ Saint Gabriel the Archangel Parish, Carneys Point, N.J.
Canales, William '00 (ATL) Gainesville, GA St. Michael.
Canarro, John '01 (SY) Presbyteral Council.
Canary, Rev. Msgr. John F. '69 (CHI) Vicar General; Administrative Council; Vicar General; Chaplaincies/Chaplain Affairs; Chicago, IL Cardinal's Residence; Vice Chairmen; Members.

Canas, Eugene *o.m.i.* '64 (GAL) Cursillos in Christianity; Houston, TX Immaculate Heart of Mary.
Canavan, Edward P. *o.s.f.s.* '64 (TOL)[H] Childs, MD Annecy Hall Retired.
Canavan, Gerald D. '69 (PH) Eddystone, PA St. Rose of Lima.
Canavan, John D. '55 (DET) Retired.
Canavan, Mark P. '71 (CHI) Oak Lawn, IL St. Louis De Montfort.
Canavan, Rev. Msgr. Mitred Martin A. '68 (SJP) Garner, NC SS. Volodymyr and Olha Mission; Presbyters.
Canavera, Lawrence J. '67 (GB) Little Chute, WI St. John Nepomucene.
Canceran, Danilo A. '89 (MET) Old Bridge, NJ St. Thomas the Apostle; Raritan Bay Medical Center–Old Bridge.
Cancino, Francisco J. '10 (SEA) Tacoma, WA St. Ann; Tacoma, WA St. John of the Woods; Tacoma, WA Sacred Heart.
Cancro, Francis T. '81 (CHL) Belmont, NC Queen of the Apostles.
Cancro, Francis '81 (MIA) Judges.
Candalisa, Frank '02 (NO) Metairie, LA St. Christopher the Martyr.
Candela, Rafael '59 (SJN) Retired.
Candelaria, Dino '04 (SFE) Ranchos De Taos, NM San Francisco de Asis.
Candelaria, Ernest *c.s.j.* '58 (LA) Lancaster, CA Blessed Junipero Serra.
Candelas, Ignacio *o.f.m.* '03 (AMA) Amarillo, TX Blessed Sacrament; Amarillo, TX St. Laurence Church.
Candreva, Arthur A. *i.v.dei* '00 (BRK) Middle Village, NY Our Lady of Hope.
Candreva, Rev. Msgr. Thomas D. '63 (RVC) Judges for Interdiocesan Tribunal Retired.
Cane–Gombau, Pere '93 (MIL)[V] Racine, WI Community of St. Paul, Inc.; Special Assignment.
Canela, Jorge '09 (GI) Lexington, NE St. Ann's.
Canepa, Jorge A. *c.s.c.* '56 (FTW)[H] Notre Dame Congregation of Holy Cross, United States Province of Priests & Brothers.
Canete, Hernan '96 (LA) Reseda, CA St. Catherine of Siena.
Canez, Jorge '79 (PHX) Avondale, AZ St. Thomas Aquinas Roman Catholic Parish.
Canfield, Francis E. *s.j.* '67 (CLV)[D] Cleveland, OH St. Ignatius High School.
Canino, Louis *o.f.m.* '69 (CHL)[J] Stoneville, NC Franciscan Friary; [Q] Greensboro, NC Franciscan Center; [M] Stoneville, NC St. Francis Springs Prayer Center.
Canizares, Dwight M. '81 (GAL) Baytown, TX St. Joseph; Northern Vicariate; Area Representatives.
Canjar, John A. '49 (DEN) Retired.
Cann, Hilarion V. '53 (WH) Retired.
Canna, Joseph '70 (LA) Irwindale, CA Our Lady of Guadalupe.
Cannariato, Paul A. '83 (NEW) Closter, NJ St. Mary; Northern Valley Bergen Deanery 2N; Part–time Staff/Advocates/Procurators; Magnificat, A Ministry to Catholic Women.
Canniff, James B. '60 (BO) Malden, MA Immaculate Conception; Senior Priests. Retired.
Canning, Wilfred S. *c.s.b.* '55 (GAL)[O] Houston, TX Dillon House Retired.
Cannoles, Gordon L. *c.ss.r.* '69 (PH) Philadelphia, PA St. Peter the Apostle.
Cannon, Col. Robert R. '78 (VEN) Military Chaplains; Air Force Chaplains.
Cannon, Hugh D. '66 (RVC) East Islip, NY St. Mary's.
Cannon, John '04 (SFE) Chancellor; College of Consultors; Office of Religious; Presbyteral Council of the Archdiocese of Santa Fe; Finance Council.
Cannon, Kenneth V. '97 (BO) Scituate, MA St. Mary of the Nativity.
Cannon, Michael J. '81 (VEN) Lake Placid, FL St. James; Presbyteral Council.
Cannon, Richard E. '86 (MO) Quincy, MA St. John the Baptist; Navy Reserve Chaplains.
Cannon, Thomas *o.m.v.* '11 (SFD) Alton, IL St. Mary's.
Cannuli, Richard G. *o.s.a.* '99 (PH)[C] Villanova University; [Y] Villanova, PA St. Thomas of Villanova Friary.
Canny, Michael '77 (SAC) Mount Shasta, CA St. Anthony; Dunsmuir, CA St. John the Evangelist.
Canny, Stephen '61 (SR) Retired.
Cano, Martin Garcia '00 (PCE) Patillas, PR Inmaculado Corazon de Maria.
Cano, Nicolas *o.s.b.* '97 (BIS)[A] Richardton, ND Assumption Abbey; Richardton, ND Assumption Abbey.
Cano–Ramirez, Andres '09 (KNX) Knoxville, TN Cathedral of the Sacred Heart of Jesus.
Canon, Hector U. (AGN) Malojlo, GU San Isidro.
Canorro, John '01 (SY) Mexico, NY St. Anne, Mother of Mary.
Canova, James C. '01 (RCK) Dundee, IL St. Catherine of Siena; Dundee, IL St. Mary's Mission of Gilberts.
Canoy, Charles '05 (LAN) On Duty Outside the Diocese.
Canterbury, Keith E. '94 (SAC) Weaverville, CA St. Patrick Retired.
Canterna, Charles J. '76 (BAL) Baltimore, MD Maryland Correctional Adjustment Center; Special Assignment; Baltimore, MD Maryland Penitentiary Complex.
Cantley, Rev. Msgr. Michael J. '55 (BRK)[R] Douglaston, NY Bishop Mugavero Residence Retired.
Cantones, Joel P. '81 (NO) Edgard, LA St. John the Baptist.
Cantore, John A. *c.m.* '63 (STL)[O] Perryville, MO Congregation of the Mission.
Cantwell, Edward F. '54 (ALB) Retired.
Cantwell, John '69 (SAC) Placerville, CA St. Patrick's.
Cantwell, Stephen F. *c.m.* '82 (PH)[B] Philadelphia, PA DePaul Novitiate.
Cantwell, William J. *c.s.p.* '56 (PMB)[H] Vero Beach, FL Paulist Fathers Residence.
Canu, John '63 (ELP) El Paso, TX Our Lady of Assumption.
Canuel, Paul E. '66 (FR) Retired.
Canzio, Celestino *o.f.m.* '73 (NY)[DD] New York Franciscan Province of the Immaculate Conception.
Cao, Bill T. '01 (ORG) Anaheim, CA St. Anthony Claret.
Cao, Duy '01 (CHI)[A] Chicago, IL St. Joseph College Seminary.
Cao, John Mary Vu *c.m.c.* '01 (SB)[I] Corona, CA Congregation of the Mother Co–Redemptrix, C.M.C.
Cao, Joseph T. '00 (DEN) Arvada, CO St. Joan of Arc.
Cao, Nghia *c.ss.r.* '05 (SAT)[L] San Antonio, TX Redemptorists of Texas–San Antonio #1.
Cao, Paul '03 (PT) Pensacola, FL Our Lady Queen of Martyrs.
Cao, Paul '01 (CHI)[R] Chicago, IL Kolping Center.
Cao, Peter *c.ss.r.* '04 (BRK) Brooklyn, NY Our Lady of Perpetual Help Basilica.
Cao, Victor *c.s.j.b.* '06 (BRK)[R] Elmhurst, NY Congregation of St. John the Baptist of China; Flushing, NY St. John Vianney.
Cao Phuong Ky, Joseph *s.s., c.m.c.* '59 (SPC)[F] Carthage, MO Congregation of the Mother Coredemptrix, United States Assumption Province.
Cap, Alberto *o.cist.* '11 (NEW) Linden, NJ St. Elizabeth of Hungary.
Capacillo, Euben '75 (ORG) Santa Ana, CA Our Lady of the Pillar.
Capalbo, Kenneth *o.f.m.* '74 (STL)[O] St. Louis Franciscan Friary of St. Anthony of Padua.
Caparas, Allain B. '06 (CAM) Newfield, NJ Our Lady of the Blessed Sacrament, Newfield, N.J.
Capato, Justin *o.s.b.* '80 (PAT)[N] Morristown, NJ St. Mary's Abbey.
Capdepon, Federico '83 (MIA) Miami Shores, FL St. Martha; Deans and Deaneries; Northeast Dade Deanery.
Capdeville, Henri *o.s.b.* '93 (TUC)[E] St. David, AZ Holy Trinity Monastery; Saint David, AZ.
Capeding, Lito J. (MOB) Daphne, AL Shrine of the Holy Cross; Apostleship of the Sea.
Capella, Joseph A. '90 (CAM) Elected Members.
Capella, Joseph P. '90 (CAM) Representatives by Ordination Seniority; Presbyteral Council; Lindenwold, NJ Our Lady of Guadalupe Parish, Lindenwold, N.J.; Members.
Capen, George *o.m.i.* '59 (BEL)[F] Belleville, IL Missionary Oblates of Mary Immaculate – St. Henry's Oblate Residence.
Capetola, Nicholas *c.r.m.* '62 (CHR) Goose Creek, SC Immaculate Conception.
Capewell, Timothy J. '83 (TR) Princeton Jct., NJ Church of St. David the King; Vicars Forane (Deans).
Capik, Rev. Msgr. William J. '54 (MET) Retired.
Capilla, Oscar *l.c.* '07 (HRT)[B] Cheshire, CT Novitiate of the Legion of Christ.
Capitani, Sylvan P. '64 (HBG) New Freedom, PA St. John the Baptist.
Capitolo, Mario L. *s.j.* '59 (SJ)[M] Los Gatos, CA Sacred Heart Jesuit Center.
Capitolo, Paul F. *s.j.* '69 (SJ)[M] Los Gatos, CA Sacred Heart Jesuit Center.
Capizzi, Marc F. '06 (PH) West Chester, PA St. Maximilian Kolbe.
Caplice, Richard L. *s.j.* '64 (NY)[DD] New York, NY Murray–Weigel Hall.
Caplis, Roger J. '58 (CHI) Chicago, IL St. Hilary; Chicago, IL St. Juliana Retired.
Capo, Rafael *sch.p.* '96 (MIA)[L] Miami, FL Southeast Pastoral Institute; [L] Miami, FL SEPI Evangelization and Education Foundation, Inc.; [L] Miami, FL Southeast Regional Office for Hispanic Ministry, Inc.
Capone, Albert L. '80 (BO) Lowell, MA St. Michael.
Capone, Robert '00 (ORG) Huntington Beach, CA St. Vincent de Paul; Council of Priests.
Caponi, Francis J. *o.s.a.* '89 (PH)[C] Villanova University; [F] Malvern, PA Malvern Preparatory School for Boys; [Y] Malvern, PA Augustinian Friars (O.S.A.).
Caporali, Paul M. *s.d.b.* '54 (LA)[V] Rosemead, CA St. Joseph's Salesian Youth Renewal Center.
Caporiccio, Louis *c.p.m.* '97 (OWN) Auburn, KY; [F] Auburn, KY Fathers of Mercy.
Capoverdi, Giacomo D. '97 (PRO) Westerly, RI Immaculate Conception.
Capozzelli, Rev. Msgr. Emmanuel M. '49 (NEW)[L] Caldwell, NJ The Rev. Msgr. James F. Kelley Residence for Retired Priests Retired.
Cappel, Charles H. *m.m.* '44 (NY)[DD] Maryknoll Maryknoll Fathers and Brothers Retired.
Cappelletti, Edward *s.d.b.* '50 (NY)[DD] New Rochelle, NY Salesian Provincial House.
Cappelletti, Joseph '82 (CLV) Retired.
Cappelloni, David P. '86 (SCR) Dunmore, PA SS. Anthony & Rocco Parish.
Cappelloni, Thomas A. '76 (SCR) Hazleton, PA Queen of Heaven, Hazleton.
Capperella, Thomas S. '01 (CAM) Woodbury, NJ Holy Angels Parish, Woodbury, N.J.
Cappleman, Garry J. *o.p.* '03 (SFR)[N] San Francisco, CA St. Dominic Priory; San Francisco, CA St. Dominic.
Cappucci, Chester J. *o.m.i.* '63 (BO)[X] Tewksbury, MA Immaculate Heart of Mary Residence.
Cappuccino, Gregory J. '73 (RVC) Wantagh, NY St. Frances de Chantal; Presbyteral Council.
Caprio, Albert A. *o.p.* '66 (HRT) New Haven, CT St. Mary's Retired.
Caprio, Robert J. *o.f.m.* '63 (BO)[U] Andover St. Francis Friary; [O] Brighton, MA Caritas St. Elizabeth's Medical Center of Boston, Inc.; [U] Boston, MA St. Christopher Friary.
Capriola, David (STV).
Capriolo, Victor R. '71 (MIL) Fond du Lac, WI Holy Family.
Capuano, Brian W. '11 (RIC) Richmond, VA St. Bridget.
Capucci, Giovanni '06 (DEN) Graduate Studies.
Capuci, John M. '90 (BO) Burlington, MA St. Malachy.
Caputo, Ralph J. '75 (BRK) Brooklyn, NY St. Bernard of Clairvaux.
Caputo, Salvatore S. *s.s.c.* '76 (PRO)[O] Bristol, RI St. Columban's Retirement House.
Caputo, Salvatore *s.s.c.* '76 (OM)[J] St. Columbans, NE Missionary Society of St. Columban Retired.
Caraballo, Antonio '81 (ARE) Retired.
Caraballo Galindo, Gerardo E. '09 (MGZ) Mayaguez, PR Nuestra Senora De Fatima.
Carabello, Francis J. '68 (NO) Retired.
Carampatan, Roberto A.R. *s.j.* '04 (BAL)[Q] Baltimore, MD Ferdinand Wheeler Jesuit Community.
Carasala, Arul '94 (KCK) Kelly, KS St. Bede; Seneca, KS SS. Peter and Paul.
Caravia, Santiago Flor '00 (AGN) Hagatna, GU Nuestra Senora de la Paz y Buen Viaje.
Carazo, Jacob *o.f.m.conv.* '04 (OAK) San Pablo, CA St. Paul.
Carbajales, Ignacio '60 (MIA) Retired.
Carballo, Rafael '06 (ATL) Carrollton, GA Church of Our Lady of Perpetual Help.
Carberry, John '81 (SFD) Retired.
Carbine, Rev. Msgr. Francis A. '62 (PH) Philadelphia, PA St. Katherine of Siena Retired.
Carbonaro, Dennis J. '81 (PH) Philadelphia, PA Our Lady of Consolation.
Carbone, Anthony J. '93 (GBG) Latrobe, PA St. John the Evangelist; Judges.
Carbonneau, Robert *c.p.* '78 (NEW)[L] Passionist Archives.
Carbonneau, Robert *c.p.* '78 (BAL)[Q] Baltimore, MD St. Joseph's Passionist Community; Baltimore, MD St. Joseph Passionist Monastery Parish.
Carboy, Daniel *c.ss.r.* '66 (ORL)[F] New Smyrna Beach, FL St. Alphonsus Villa–Redemptorist Fathers and Brothers Retired.
Carcerano, Michael J. '76 (LA) Glendora, CA St. Dorothy.
Carchidi, Rudolph V. *c.s.c.* '55 (FR)[A] North Easton, MA Stonehill College; [A] North Easton, MA Holy Cross Fathers Religious.
Carchidi, Rudolph V. *c.s.c.* '55 (FTW)[H] Notre Dame Congregation of Holy Cross, United States Province of Priests & Brothers.
Cardelli, Rev. Msgr. Daniel E. '57 (OAK)[Q] Oakland, CA Italian Catholic Federation Retired.
Cardenas, Arcangel *s.s.p.* '90 (NY)[B] Staten Island, NY Society of St. Paul.
Cardenas, Eugenio *m.sp.s.* '82 (LA)[A] Camarillo, CA St. John's Seminary.
Cardenas, Hugo G. *i.v.e.* '04 (FR)[L] New Bedford, MA The Institute of the Incarnate Word, Inc.; New Bedford; New Bedford, MA St. Kilian.
Cardenas, Juan Raul '00 (PMB) Stuart, FL St. Joseph.
Cardenas, Marco J. *c.m.f.* '91 (CHI)[N] Oak Park Claretian Missionaries USA Eastern Province; Blue Island, IL St. Benedict.
Cardenas, Prisciliano '50 (SJN) San Juan, PR Francisca Javiera Cabrini.
Cardenas–Robles, Sergio *c.r.* '99 (PBL) Antonito, CO Our Lady of Guadalupe.
Cardenas Bonilla, Jose C. *c.s.* '99 (PRO) Providence, RI Blessed Sacrament.
Cardente, Edward S. '74 (PRO) Providence, RI St. Edward; North Providence, RI St. Anthony; Council Members.
Cardinal, Maurice *m.s.* '50 (SB)[I] Moreno Valley, CA

Missionaries of Our Lady of La Salette, MS.
Cardinale, Kenneth '98 (WOR) North Grafton, MA St. Mary; Grafton, MA St. Philip's.
Cardo, Daniel *s.c.v.* '06 (DEN) Englewood, CO Holy Name.
Cardona, Carlos Garcia '92 (LKC) Kinder, LA St. Philip Neri.
Cardona, George '53 (MIA) Retired.
Cardona, Jorge D. '93 (CGS) Maunabo, PR San Isidro Labrador; Priests Senate.
Cardona, Orlando *c.m.* '97 (PH) Philadelphia, PA St. Vincent de Paul.
Cardona Matta, Jose Miguel '98 (SJN) Puerto Nuevo, PR San Pablo.
Cardone, Anthony F. '11 (WIL) Ocean City, MD St. Luke and St. Andrew.
Cardone, Joseph P. '87 (TOL) Special Assignment; Toledo, OH Our Lady of Lourdes.
Cardone, Thomas A. *s.m.* '85 (RVC)[D] Uniondale, NY Kellenberg Memorial High School; [N] Mineola, NY Provincial Residence and Novitiate; Councilors.
Cardoni, Albert A. *s.j.* '60 (BO)[U] Weston, MA Campion Health Center, Inc.
Cardoso, Carlos A. (BRK) Brooklyn, NY Our Lady of the Rosary of Pompeii.
Cardoso, Carlos *s.a.c.* '05 (NY)[DD] New York, NY Pallottine Fathers.
Cardoso, Reinaldo M. '60 (PRO)[L] Pawtucket, RI Jeanne Jugan Residence Retired.
Cardoso, Roney M. *o.s.a.* '01 (SAT) San Antonio, TX St. Jude.
Cardoza, Edward '57 (SB) Retired.
Cardoza, Manuel '09 (SB) Temecula, CA St. Catherine of Alexandria; Elected Members.
Cardoza, Timothy N. '83 (FRS) Fresno, CA St. Mary Queen of Apostles Catholic Church.
Cardozo, Orlando '02 (DAL)[J] Irving, TX Dominican Priory of St. Albert the Great and Novitiate; Coppell, TX St. Ann.
Cardy, William *o.f.m.* '72 (STL)[J] St. Louis, MO St. Anthony's Medical Center; [O] St. Louis, MO Franciscan Friary of St. Anthony of Padua.
Carek, Peter P. '60 (MIL) Retired.
Carew, Lawrence F. '66 (BGP) Trumbull, CT Christ the King.
Carey, David C. '04 (HRT) Meriden, CT St. Laurent; Meriden, CT Our Lady of Mount Carmel; Appointed Members.
Carey, David M. '62 (BAL) Retired.
Carey, Dennis G. '98 (NOR) Waterford, CT St. Paul; Priests' Retirement Plan Board.
Carey, Gerald P. '98 (PH) Philadelphia, PA St. Paul.
Carey, J. Peter *s.j.* '64 (CIN)[N] Cincinnati, OH Faber Jesuit Community.
Carey, James H. '66 (SY) Pompey, NY Immaculate Conception; Tully, NY St. Leo; Presbyteral Council; Health Care; Lafayette, NY St. Joseph; Syracuse, NY Crouse Irving Memorial Hospital.
Carey, John *o.f.m.cap.* '53 (PIT)[M] Butler, PA St. Mary's Friary.
Carey, Joseph H. *c.s.c.* '69 (FTW)[B] University of Notre Dame Du Lac; [H] Notre Dame, IN Holy Cross Community, Corby Hall, University of Notre Dame; [H] Notre Dame Congregation of Holy Cross, United States Province of Priests & Brothers.
Carey, Rev. Msgr. Leo P. '51 (PAT)[Q] Chester, NJ Nazareth Village Retired.
Carey, Michael *o.p.* '77 (LA) Los Angeles, CA St. Dominic.
Carey, Paul V. '71 (SY) Waterville, NY St. Bernard; Presbyteral Council; Oriskany Falls, NY St. Joseph.
Carey, Raymond '70 (P) Special Assignment.
Carey, Richard T. '65 (WOR) Retired.
Carey, Richard W. '55 (LA) Retired.
Carey, Shawn P. '09 (BO) Assistant Director of the Office of the Deaf Apostolate; Hopkinton, MA St. John the Evangelist.
Carey, Stephen A. '98 (NEW) Fort Lee, NJ Madonna.
Carey, Stephen '62 (CAM) Retired.
Carey, William F. '67 (BGP) Retired.
Carey, William G. '81 (BGP) New Canaan, CT St. Aloysius.
Carfagna, Rev. Msgr. Frank A. '67 (Y) Finance Council; Canton, OH St. Joseph; [Q] Youngstown, OH Catholic Cemeteries of the Diocese of Youngstown, Inc.; Judges.
Cargo, Jason '07 (DAL) Corsicana, TX Immaculate Conception.
Cargo, Thomas '78 (JOL) Winfield, IL St. John the Baptist.
Caridi, Michael A. '94 (PIT) Pittsburgh, PA St. Louise de Marillac.
Carie, Giles *o.f.m.conv.* '61 (ELP) Judges.
Carie, Giles *o.f.m.conv.* '61 (LSC) Judges.
Cariglio, Rev. Msgr. Michael J. '70 (Y) Youngstown, OH Our Lady of Mt. Carmel; Youngstown, OH St. Anthony; College of Consultors; Department of Canonical Services; Judicial Vicar; Presbyteral Council.
Carignan, Armand *o.m.i.* '53 (FgM) Washington, DC AMERICAN OBLATE MISSIONS.
Carignan, Ronald *o.m.i.* '59 (SAT)[K] San Antonio, TX Oblate Madonna Residence.
Carina, Chester H. '85 (MET) Matawan, NJ Most Holy Redeemer; Holy Name Society.
Carini, James P. '65 (NOR) Tolland, CT St. Matthew; Members; Deans; District Spiritual Advisors; Liturgical Commission; Advisory Board.
Carkenord, David '62 (FTW) Waterloo, IN St. Michael the Archangel.
Carkhuff, Thomas *o.s.c.* '76 (SCL)[I] Onamia, MN Crosier Priory.
Carl, Scott M. '00 (STP)[C] St. Paul, MN University of St. Thomas; [A] Saint Paul, MN The Saint Paul Seminary; Hamel, MN St. Anne; Loretto, MN SS. Peter and Paul; Hamel, MN St. Thomas the Apostle.
Carles, Alexander J. '88 (MET) Somerville, NJ Immaculate Conception.
Carleton, Robert J. *m.m.* '64 (SJ)[M] Los Altos, CA Maryknoll.
Carley, Patrick F. '69 (SLC) West Jordan, UT Saint Joseph the Worker LLC 232.
Carlin, Bernard *c.ss.r.* '78 (GR) Grand Rapids, MI St. Alphonsus; [L] Grand Rapids, MI The Society of the Redemptorists of the City of Grand Rapids.
Carlin, John T. '76 (CLV) Parma, OH St. Charles Borromeo.
Carlin, Warren *o.carm.* '58 (JOL)[L] Darien Carmelite Provincial Office Retired.
Carlino, Richard A. '79 (ALB) Schenectady, NY St. Anthony; Schenectady, NY St. John the Evangelist.
Carlo, Cyprian '73 (LA) Ventura, CA Sacred Heart.
Carlo, Edgar '97 (MGZ) Hormigueros, PR El Salvador.
Carlo, Joseph C. '63 (BUF)[N] Tonawanda, NY O'Hara Residence Retired.
Carlo, Raymond J. '87 (CHR) Garden City, SC St. Michael; Presbyteral Council.
Carlone, Carmen A. '69 (CAM) Retired.
Carlos, Joseph P. *o.f.m.* '75 (SFD) Dieterich, IL St. Isidore the Farmer Church; [K] Teutopolis, IL St. Francis Assisi Friary.
Carlos, Miguel '95 (LAN) On Leave of Absence.
Carlsen, James F. '00 (MOB) Belle Fontaine, AL St. Philip Neri; Coden, AL St. Michael the Archangel.
Carlson, Alex Bernard '10 (STP) Coon Rapids, MN Church of the Epiphany.
Carlson, Curtis *o.f.m.cap.* '95 (KCK) Lawrence, KS St. John the Evangelist; [I] Lawrence, KS St. Conrad Friary.
Carlson, Rev. Msgr. George F. '66 (BO) West Roxbury, MA Holy Name; Elected.
Carlson, Gregory I. *s.j.* '74 (OM)[J] Omaha, NE Jesuit Community at Creighton University.
Carlson, James R. '73 (SAG) Saginaw, MI St. John Vianney; Ecumenism Ministry.
Carlson, Kenneth F. '98 (MO) Army Chaplains; Military Chaplains.
Carlson, Michael A. '07 (HRT) Waterbury, CT Blessed Sacrament; Waterbury, CT Shrine of Saint Anne for Mothers.
Carlson, Paul '10 (PEO)[B] Peoria, IL Peoria Notre Dame High School; Peoria, IL St. Jude.
Carlson, Richard D. '69 (NEW) Montclair, NJ St. Peter Claver.
Carlson, Robert D. '63 (GAL) Retired.
Carlson, Sally '77 (OM)[G] Omaha, NE Archbishop Bergan Mercy Medical Center.
Carlson, Steven V. '96 (R) Wilmington, NC Christ the King; Wilmington, NC St. Mark.
Carlton, Maurice T. '68 (MET) High Bridge, NJ St. Joseph.
Carman, Bernard '80 (BRK) Brooklyn, NY Our Lady of the Rosary of Pompeii.
Carmichael, Eugene *s.j.* '73 (CIN)[N] Cincinnati, OH Jesuit Community at Xavier University.
Carmichael, John F. '97 (BO) Marshfield, MA St. Ann by the Sea.
Carmody, Emeric *o.carm.* '54 (JOL)[L] Darien Carmelite Provincial Office Retired.
Carmody, James F. '70 (WOR) Northbridge, MA St. Peter.
Carmody, James P. '63 (RVC) Retired.
Carmody, Lawrence W. '90 (COS) Security, CO St. Dominic.
Carmody, Michael J. '83 (GAL) Humble, TX St. Mary Magdalene.
Carmody, Stephen F. *o.p.* '81 (COL) Somerset, OH St. Joseph's; Somerset, OH Holy Trinity.
Carmola, Michael J. '64 (SY) Special Assignment; Laymen & Laywomen Retreat Movements Retired.
Carmona, Henry '78 (B) Boise, ID Cathedral of St. John the Evangelist; Judicial Vicar; Judges.
Carmona, Hugo '85 (PRO) Woonsocket, RI All Saints Parish.
Carnecer, Ryan Z. *c.i.c.m.* '11 (R) Wendell, NC St. Eugene.
Carneiro, Denis '68 (CHI) Buffalo Grove, IL St. Mary.
Carnes, Matthew E. *s.j.* '03 (SJ)[B] Santa Clara, CA Jesuit Community.
Carnes, Matthew E. *s.j.* '03 (WDC)[O] Washington, DC The Jesuit Community at Georgetown University.
Carnes, Valerie (KNX)[E] Signal Mountain, TN Alexian Village of Tennessee.
Carnevale, Michael *o.f.m.* '61 (NY) New York, NY St. Francis of Assisi.
Carney, Angus N. *o.s.a.* '43 (PH)[Y] Villanova, PA St. Thomas Monastery.
Carney, Bryan J. '07 (BRK) N.Y. Hospital Medical Center of Queens.
Carney, Bryan J. '07 (BRK) Flushing Hospital and Medical Center.
Carney, Edward '63 (PEO) Retired.
Carney, James R. *s.j.* '56 (NY)[DD] New York, NY Murray–Weigel Hall.
Carney, John F. '91 (SFE) Los Alamos, NM Immaculate Heart of Mary.
Carney, John J. '63 (BAL) Retired.
Carney, John J. *c.m.* '82 (FgM) Philadelphia, PA Eastern Province.
Carney, Joseph T. '68 (MIA) Miami Springs, FL Blessed Trinity.
Carney, Lawrence D. '07 (WCH) Wellington, KS St. Anthony/St. Rose.
Carney, Rev. Msgr. Patrick J. '55 (NY) Hartsdale, NY Sacred Heart.
Carney, Robert E. '91 (TUC) Tucson, AZ Saint Francis de Sales Roman Catholic Parish – Tucson.
Carney, Thomas *m.s.c.* '54 (ALN)[A] Center Valley, PA Sacred Heart Villa, Missionaries of the Sacred Heart.
Caro, Eddie *o.f.m.* (SJN)[C] Sabana Seca, PR Post–Noviciado San Jose Obrero.
Caro, Luis A. *c.ss.r.* '75 (BRK) Brooklyn, NY Our Lady of Perpetual Help Basilica.
Caro, Robert V. *s.j.* '70 (LA)[C] Los Angeles, CA Loyola Marymount University; [C] Los Angeles, CA Jesuit Community.
Carola, Joseph A. *s.j.* '93 (NO)[R] New Orleans Jesuit Provincial Office.
Carolan, Craig G. '91 (BWN) On Assignment Outside the Diocese.
Carolan, Craig (SAG) Merrill, MI Sacred Heart; Merrill, MI St. Patrick.
Carolan, Emmet '62 (SAT) San Antonio, TX Holy Family; Judges.
Carolan, John J. '51 (CHI) Oak Park, IL St. Catherine of Siena–St. Lucy Retired.
Carolin, Joseph C. '66 (HBG) South Mountain, PA Restoration Center.
Caroluzza, Rev. Msgr. Thomas '58 (RIC) Virginia Beach, VA Retired.
Caro Morales, Jorge L. '89 (MGZ) Sabana Grande, PR Church of San Isidro.
Caron, Antonin R. '69 (PRT) Retired.
Caron, David G. *o.p.* '89 (NO)[R] Metairie, LA Dominican Friars, Southern Dominican Province of St. Martin de Porres; [R] Metairie, LA Southern Dominican Foundation; [U] Metairie, LA Southern Dominican Foundation; New Orleans, LA St. Dominic.
Caron, Eduardo *c.s.sp.* '57 (SJN)[F] Dorado, PR Santuario del Espiritu Santo.
Caron, Gerard J. '94 (PRO) Harrisville, RI St. Theresa of the Child Jesus; College of Consultors; Council Members.
Caron, Rev. Msgr. Marc B. '89 (PRT) Personnel Board; Diocesan Consultors; Liturgical Commission; Lewiston, ME Prince of Peace Parish.
Caron, Paul A. '83 (FR) Mattapoisett, MA St. Anthony's; Marion, MA St. Rita's.
Caronan, John *o.praem.* '94 (ORG)[I] Silverado, CA Norbertine Fathers of Orange Inc.; Defender of the Bond.
Carongay, Jovito B. '92 (BRK) Elmhurst, NY Ascension.
Carosella, Jerome A. '63 (VEN) Boca Grande, FL Our Lady of Mercy; Pension Plan Board of Trustees (Archdiocese of Miami/Diocese of Venice).
Carota, Peter '97 (STO) Ripon, CA St. Patrick Church of Ripon (Pastor of).
Carotenuto, Anthony M. '68 (TR) Red Bank, NJ St. Anthony; College of Consultors.
Carpender, John W. '53 (DUB) Retired.
Carpenter, Brian Kumar '09 (ROC) Rochester, NY Peace of Christ Roman Catholic Parish of Rochester, NY.
Carpenter, Edward C. '95 (ELP) El Paso, TX St. Joseph's; Advocates.
Carpenter, Sean G. '09 (SCR) Brodheadsville, PA Our Lady Queen of Peace.
Carpenter, Todd *o.f.m.* '99 (WIL) Wilmington, DE St. Paul's.
Carpentier, Normand E. '71 (PRT) Diocesan Review Board; Diocesan Priests' Benefit Plan – Trustees; Personnel Board; Brunswick, ME All Saints Parish.
Carpentier, Robert A. '67 (PRO) Absent on Leave.
Carpinelli, Vincent G. '71 (CAM) Retired.
Carr, Alton *c.ss.r.* '60 (SAT)[L] San Antonio, TX Redemptorists of Texas–San Antonio #1; San Antonio, TX St. Gerard Majella.
Carr, Andrew *c.ss.r.* '55 (BAL) Baltimore, MD Sacred Heart of Jesus.
Carr, Brandon '72 (BAL) Glen Burnie, MD Holy Trinity Retired.
Carr, Brendan '72 (BAL) Retired.
Carr, David W. '80 (PMB)[B] West Palm Beach, FL

Cardinal Newman High School, Inc.
Carr, Dom Elias *can. reg.* '99 (RVC) Glen Cove, NY St. Rocco.
Carr, Ephrem *o.s.b.* '67 (IND)[K] Saint Meinrad St. Meinrad Archabbey.
Carr, Eugene R. '63 (SCR) Retired.
Carr, Gary M. '82 (SPC) Leave of Absence.
Carr, Rev. Msgr. James A. '55 (CAM) Retired.
Carr, James P. *s.j.* '92 (BO) Towson, MD; [W] Gloucester, MA Eastern Point Retreat House; [U] Boston The Society of Jesus of New England–Provincial Offices.
Carr, James P. *s.j.* '92 (SY)[A] Syracuse, NY Saint Andrew Hall.
Carr, James V. '69 (RIC) Retired.
Carr, Joseph A. '06 (PIT) Ambridge, PA Good Samaritan; Baden, PA St. John the Baptist.
Carr, Mark A. *s.j.* '05 (MIL)[P] Milwaukee, WI Pere Marquette Jesuit Community; [E] Milwaukee, WI Marquette University High School.
Carr, Michael '68 (CHY) Guernsey, WY St. Anthony's; Torrington, WY St. Rose; College of Consultors; Lusk, WY St. Leo's; Ex Officios, Voting; Judges; Wyoming Women's Center (Correctional Facility); [G] Torrington, WY Catholic Charities of Wyoming, Inc.; Vicar General; Presbyteral Council; Diocesan Pastoral Council; Stewardship Committee.
Carr, Neil J. *s.j.* '51 (NY)[DD] New York, NY Murray–Weigel Hall.
Carr, Raymond J. *s.m.* '63 (WDC)[O] Washington, DC Marist Center Retired.
Carr, Raymond *s.m.* '63 (WH)[G] Wheeling, WV Good Shepherd Nursing Home LC.
Carr, Richard T. '01 (ARL) Front Royal, VA St. John the Baptist.
Carr, Robert J. (BO) Somerville, MA St. Benedict.
Carr, Walter '92 (AUS) Retired.
Carr, Rev. Msgr. William H. '69 (RIC) Richmond, VA St. Bridget.
Carr, Rev. Msgr. William '59 (WCH) Retired.
Carrano, David A. '10 (MAD) Waunakee, WI St. John the Baptist.
Carrano, Michael A. '70 (BRK) Middle Village, NY Our Lady of Hope; Assignment Board.
Carranza, Fernando '95 (NEW) On Duty Outside the Archdiocese.
Carranza, Fernando '95 (DAL)[A] Dallas, TX The Redemptoris Mater House of Formation.
Carranza, Manuel Fragoso '05 (TUC) Parker, AZ Sacred Heart Roman Catholic Parish – Parker.
Carranza, Riz J. '80 (LA) Santa Maria, CA St. Mary of the Assumption.
Carrara, Christopher C. '94 (OG) Deans; Committee on Assignments; Lowville, NY St. Hedwig; Lowville, NY St. Mary; Lowville, NY St. Peter.
Carraro, David '10 (MAD) Waunakee, WI St. Mary of the Lake.
Carraro, Francesco '95 (NEW) On Duty Outside the Archdiocese.
Carre, Joseph P. Edwidge '83 (NSH) Nashville, TN Church of the Most Holy Name.
Carreiro, Walter A. '95 (BO) Cambridge, MA St. Anthony of Padua; Vicariate IV; Portuguese.
Carrella, Eugene J. '84 (NY) Staten Island, NY St. Adalbert.
Carreon, Noe '92 (DEN) Denver, CO Holy Rosary; Denver, CO Our Lady of Grace.
Carreon, Regidor '75 (PHX) Sun Lakes, AZ St. Steven Roman Catholic Parish Retired.
Carrero, Angel Dario *o.f.m.* '95 (SJN) Sabana Seca, PR San Jose Obrero; [A] Bayamon Central University.
Carrier, Mark F. '99 (ARL) Alexandria, VA St. Louis.
Carrier, Michael J. '95 (WIL) Wilmington, DE Church of the Holy Child; Office of Worship; Catholic Scouting Program.
Carrier, Paul E. *s.j.* '77 (BO)[U] Weston, MA Campion Jesuit Community.
Carriero, John P. *s.j.* '63 (ROC)[B] Rochester, NY McQuaid Jesuit High School.
Carrigan, Thomas C. '60 (SAC) Retired.
Carrigg, George A. '57 (BO) Dorchester, MA St. Christopher.
Carrigg, William J. '56 (BO) Senior Priests. Retired.
Carrillo, Rev. Msgr. Arsenio S. '56 (TUC) Retired.
Carrillo, Arthur *c.p.* '70 (CHI)[N] Chicago, IL Stauros U.S.A.; [N] Chicago, IL Passionist Missions of India; [N] Chicago, IL Passionist Missions, Inc.; Chicago, IL Holy Cross Province (Western); [N] Chicago, IL Passionist Community–Immaculate Conception Community.
Carrillo, Ron *s.f.* '74 (SFE) Chimayo, NM Holy Family.
Carrillo, Sergio '82 (MIA) Retired.
Carrington, Richard J. '76 (NEW) Union City, NJ Sts. Joseph and Michael; Holy Name Federation.
Carrion, Michael J. '77 (BAL) Judge.
Carrion, Michael W. '77 (BAL) Baltimore, MD Immaculate Heart of Mary; [T] Baltimore, MD The Immaculate Heart of Mary School Endowment Trust; [U] Crownsville, MD Holy Name Society (Union).
Carrion, Patrick '82 (BAL) Baltimore, MD Holy Cross; Baltimore, MD St. Mary, Star of the Sea; Permanent Deacon Formation Program; [A] Baltimore, MD St. Mary's Seminary and University; Baltimore, MD Our Lady of Good Counsel.
Carrol, Michael '67 (LA) Newbury Park, CA St. Julie Billiart.
Carrola, Rudy T. '88 (SAT) San Antonio, TX St. John Berchmans.
Carroll, Rev. Msgr. Aidan M. '63 (LA) Valinda, CA St. Martha; [D] La Puente, CA Bishop Amat Memorial High School.
Carroll, Alban *s.a.* '55 (NY)[DD] Garrison, NY Franciscan Friars of the Atonement.
Carroll, Brian '62 (JKS) Jackson, MS St. Richard of Chichester.
Carroll, Daniel *o.carm.* '60 (CHI)[D] Chicago, IL; [N] Chicago, IL Carmelite Priory of St. Cyril Retired.
Carroll, Daniel *o.carm.* '60 (JOL)[L] Darien Carmelite Provincial Office.
Carroll, Edward E. '50 (MIL) Retired.
Carroll, Edward G. '67 (BO) Permanent Disability.
Carroll, Emmett H. *s.j.* '62 (SEA) Bainbridge Island, WA St. Cecilia; [M] Seattle, WA Arrupe Jesuit Community at Seattle University.
Carroll, Emmett *o.f.m.conv.* '54 (TR) Seaside Park, NJ St. Catharine of Siena.
Carroll, Francis P. *s.s.c.* '62 (PRO) St Columbans, NE House of Post–Graduate Studies; [O] Bristol, RI St. Columban's Retirement House.
Carroll, Francis *s.s.c.* '62 (OM)[J] St. Columbans Missionary Society of St. Columban.
Carroll, George A. *s.j.* '58 (SJ)[M] Los Gatos, CA Sacred Heart Jesuit Center.
Carroll, J. Alfred *s.j.* '59 (SPK)[B] Spokane, WA Gonzaga University.
Carroll, James J. '56 (NEW) Retired.
Carroll, James M. '68 (BO) Senior Priests. Retired.
Carroll, James *o.f.m.* '79 (PSC) Mahanoy City, PA St. Mary's; [A] Sybertsville, PA Holy Dormition Friary; Eparchial College of Consultors; Presbyteral Council.
Carroll, John A. *s.s.j.* '66 (WDC) Washington, DC Incarnation.
Carroll, Rev. Msgr. John J. '66 (PAT) Kinnelon, NJ Our Lady of the Magnificat; Presbyteral Council; Associate Judges.
Carroll, John J. *s.j.* '55 (FgM) New York, NY Society of Jesus.
Carroll, John R. (BO) Woburn, MA St. Anthony of Padua.
Carroll, Rev. Msgr. Joseph A. '74 (SD)[O] San Diego, CA Catholic Committee on Scouting Retired.
Carroll, Joseph '55 (HON) Retired.
Carroll, Keith M. '09 (HBG) Chambersburg, PA Corpus Christi.
Carroll, Michael A. '72 (SAC) Auburn, CA St. Teresa of Avila Parish.
Carroll, Rev. Msgr. Michael J. *c.m.* '77 (PH)[B] Philadelphia, PA St. Vincent's Seminary; [Y] Philadelphia Congregation of the Mission.
Carroll, Michael J. *c.m.* '77 (FgM) Philadelphia, PA Eastern Province; Philadelphia, PA.
Carroll, Rev. Msgr. Michael J. '61 (PH) Wayne, PA St. Katharine of Siena; Office for Ecumenical and Interreligious Affairs Retired.
Carroll, Michael J. *c.m.* '77 (PH) Philadelphia, PA Immaculate Conception.
Carroll, Michael '70 (GB) Absent on Leave, Sick or Disabled.
Carroll, Norman P. '93 (WIL) Wilmington, DE St. Elizabeth; Deans.
Carroll, Patrick '53 (NY) Retired.
Carroll, Rev. Msgr. Ralph E. '58 (NO) Retired.
Carroll, Rev. Msgr. Robert B. '63 (PAT) Highland Lakes, NJ Our Lady of Fatima.
Carroll, Robert C. *o.carm.* (TUC)[E] Tucson, AZ Carmelite Priory.
Carroll, Rev. Msgr. Robert J. '75 (PH) West Chester, PA St. Maximilian Kolbe.
Carroll, Roger '63 (STP) Retired.
Carroll, Sean *s.j.* (TUC)[I] Nogales, AZ Kino Border Initiative.
Carroll, Thomas R. *sch.p.* '70 (LEX)[B] Martin, KY The Piarist School; [G] Martin, KY Piarist Fathers.
Carroll, William R. '70 (BO) Marian Devotions; Melrose, MA St. Mary of the Annunciation.
Carroll, William *s.j.* '69 (SJ)[M] Los Gatos, CA Sacred Heart Jesuit Center.
Carrozza, Andrew P. '90 (NY) Yonkers, NY St. Ann.
Carrozzo, Anthony M. *o.f.m.* '66 (NY) New York, NY St. Francis of Assisi.
Carruthers, Rev. Msgr. Michael '91 (MIA) Coral Gables, FL St. Augustine; University of Miami.
Carscallen, Rev. Msgr. Edward C. '47 (TUC) Retired.
Carson, Michael '98 (SJ) San Jose, CA Queen of Apostles; Priests' Retirement Board.
Carson, Robert E. *o.praem.* '46 (GB)[J] De Pere, WI St. Norbert Abbey.
Carson, Rev. Msgr. Stanley B. '79 (ALT) Altoona Deanery; Altoona, PA Sacred Heart.
Cartagena, Antonio '85 (CGS) Gurabo, PR San Jose; Vicar General; Diocesan Consultors; Priests Senate.
Cartagenas, Tito Jesus '10 (SJ) San Jose, CA Holy Family.
Cartaya, Pedro *s.j.* '67 (MIA)[E] Miami, FL Belen Jesuit Preparatory School; [H] Miami, FL Villa Javier.
Carten, Thomas F. *c.s.c.* '79 (SCR)[B] Holy Cross Community.
Carten, Thomas F. *c.s.c.* '79 (FTW)[H] Notre Dame Congregation of Holy Cross, United States Province of Priests & Brothers.
Carter, Augustine W. *o.carm.* '51 (LA)[P] Encino, CA Our Lady of Mount Carmel Priory.
Carter, Daniel E. '79 (SFR) San Francisco, CA Our Lady of Lourdes.
Carter, Francis T. '86 (HRT) New Haven, CT St. Bernadette.
Carter, H. Todd '11 (TR) Hamilton, NJ Our Lady of Sorrows–St. Anthony Parish.
Carter, J. David '05 (KNX) Vocations; Presbyteral Council; Vice Chancellor; Knoxville, TN All Saints Catholic Church.
Carter, Rev. Msgr. James A. '66 (CHR) Mount Pleasant, SC Christ Our King.
Carter, James C. *s.j.* '58 (NO)[C] New Orleans, LA Loyola University New Orleans.
Carter, John T. '70 (BAL) Williamsport, MD St. Augustine Retired.
Carter, Rev. Msgr. John T. '49 (E) Retired.
Carter, Kevin E. '86 (NEW) Jersey City, NJ St. Nicholas; Our Lady of Fatima First Saturday Family; Members.
Carter, Mark *o.f.m. cap.* '92 (PIT)[M] Butler, PA St. Mary's Friary; Cabot, PA St. Joseph; Butler, PA St. Mary of the Assumption.
Carter, Martin *s.a.* '75 (NY)[DD] Garrison, NY Franciscan Friars of the Atonement.
Carter, Roy (SY) The Greater Binghamton Health Center.
Carter, Stephen *o.f.m.cap.* '82 (FgM) Pittsburgh, PA Province of St. Augustine.
Carter, Stephen *o.f.m. cap.* '80 (SJN) San Juan, PR San Francisco de Asis.
Carton, A. Richard '93 (PAT) Stirling, NJ St. Vincent de Paul; Sussex County Jail.
Carton, Rev. Msgr. William J. '59 (TR)[N] Trenton, NJ Villa Vianney Retired.
Cartwright, Christopher M. *s.j.* '80 (SJ)[B] Santa Clara, CA Jesuit Community.
Carty, John A. *s.j.* '59 (FgM) Watertown, MA Society of Jesus.
Carucci, David P. '95 (MOB) Montgomery, AL St. Peter; Montgomery, AL St. Bede the Venerable Catholic Church; Montgomery, AL St. John the Baptist; [I] Montgomery, AL Alabama State University Newman Center.
Carusi, Angelo N. '98 (PRO) Providence, RI Blessed Sacrament; Providence, RI Our Lady of Mt. Carmel; Catholic Scouting–Boy Scouts, Girl Scouts, Camp Fire.
Caruso, Daniel J. '94 (SY) Syracuse, NY Our Lady of Pompei/St. Peter.
Caruso, Michael P. *s.j.* '82 (CHI)[D] Chicago, IL St. Ignatius College Prep; [D] Chicago, IL St. Ignatius Jesuit Community.
Caruso, Philip J. '78 (NY) New Rochelle, NY St. Joseph.
Caruso, Robert J. '80 (PHX) Mesa, AZ All Saints Roman Catholic Parish; Defenders of the Bond.
Carvajal, Rev. Msgr. Felipe N. '68 (PAT) Passaic, NJ St. Nicholas Retired.
Carvajal, Raul H. '65 (MRY) Retired.
Carvajal–Basto, Tomas *c.r.* '09 (PBL) Elected; Pueblo, CO Holy Family.
Carvajal–Salazer, Gabriel S. '10 (CHL) Hickory, NC St. Aloysius.
Carvajol, Jorge Arturo (DAL) Dallas, TX Santa Clara.
Carvalho, Antonio '93 (COL) Columbus, OH Holy Name of Jesus.
Carvalho, Gordian '85 (HON) Honolulu, HI St. Pius X; Honolulu, HI Sacred Heart.
Carvalho, Joaquim *o.s.b.* '82 (KCK)[I] Atchison, KS St. Benedict's Abbey.
Carven, John W. *c.m.* '60 (PH)[B] Philadelphia, PA St. Vincent's Seminary[Y].
Carver, Dennis J. '94 (BLX) Pass Christian, MS Holy Family Parish; Deans; Personnel Board; Vocations; Presbyteral Council; College of Consultors; CDB Seminarian Education, Inc.
Carver, Joseph P. *s.j.* (SEA)[M] Seattle, WA Jesuit House, Seattle.
Carver, Joseph *s.j.* (HEL) Missoula, MT St. Francis Xavier.
Carvill, Michael *f.s.c.b.* '90 (DEN) Broomfield, CO Nativity of Our Lord; Lexington, MA; [N] Broomfield, CO Priestly Fraternity of St. Charles Borromeo (F.S.C.B.).
Carvill, Michael *f.s.c.b.* '90 (BO)[U] Broomfield, CO House of Denver.
Carville, John '63 (BR) Retired.
Cary, Liam '92 (P) College of Consultors.
Cary, Robert M. *c.s.p.* '84 (MEM) Memphis, TN St. Augustine.
Cary, William J. '58 (SUP) Retired.
Casabon, Luis '61 (MIA) Retired.

Casadia, James A. '01 (CAM) Glassboro, NJ Mary, Mother of Mercy Parish, Glassboro, N.J.
Casagram, Michael *o.c.s.o.* '82 (L)[L] Trappist, KY Abbey of Our Lady of Gethsemani, of the Order of Cistercians of the Strict Observance.
Casale, Charles B. '69 (FRS) Retired.
Casale, Charles '69 (PHX) Gilbert, AZ St. Anne Roman Catholic Parish.
Casale, Rev. Msgr. Franklyn M. '67 (MIA)[C] St. Thomas University.
Casale, Rev. Msgr. Franklyn M. '67 (NEW) On Duty Outside the Archdiocese.
Casaleggio, David E. '81 (LAV) Las Vegas, NV St. Anne; Las Vegas, NV St. Joan of Arc; Presbyteral Council for the Diocese of Las Vegas.
Casari, Michael T. '95 (WIL) Retired.
Casarotto, Secondo *c.s.* '66 (BUF) Buffalo, NY St. Anthony of Padua.
Casavantes, Carlos S. *f.s.s.p.* (B) Coeur d'Alene, ID St. Joan of Art Chapel; Coeur d'Alene, ID St. Joan of Arc.
Casazza, Rev. Msgr. David J. '43 (NEW) River Edge, NJ St. Peter the Apostle Retired.
Cascino, Marion *o.f.m.* '49 (NY)[DD] New York Franciscan Province of the Immaculate Conception.
Cascione, James R. *c.ss.r.* '83 (NY) New York, NY Most Holy Redeemer.
Casciotti, James A. *s.j.* '78 (BAL)[U] Baltimore, MD Radio Mass of Baltimore, Inc.; Towson, MD; [Q] Towson, MD Maryland Province of the Society of Jesus; [Q] Baltimore, MD Colombiere Jesuit Community.
Case, Frank *s.j.* '69 (SPK)[B] Spokane, WA Gonzaga University.
Case, Lowell D. *s.s.j.* '80 (BR) New Roads, LA St. Augustine.
Case, Richard *s.j.* '75 (SPK) Spokane, WA St. Aloysius; Members; [B] Spokane, WA Gonzaga University.
Casellas Rivera, Ramon J. *o.f.m.cap.* (SJN)[H] San Juan, PR The Viceprovince of Saint John the Baptist, Puerto Rico, of the Order Friars Minor Capuchin; Catechetics; San Juan, PR San Antonio.
Caserta, Angelo C. '45 (CIN) Piqua, OH St. Boniface Retired.
Caserta, Charles W. '54 (CIN) Retired.
Caserta, Rev. Msgr. Thomas G. '79 (BRK) Brooklyn, NY St. Bernadette; Presbyteral Council.
Casey, Anthony C. '58 (BRK)[O] Queens Village, NY Queen of Peace Residence Retired.
Casey, Christopher J. '07 (BO) Methuen, MA Our Lady of Good Counsel.
Casey, David J. *s.j.* '69 (SY)[Q] Syracuse, NY Jesuits at LeMoyne, Inc.
Casey, Denis '57 (TLS)[E] Tulsa, OK Saint Francis Hospital Retired.
Casey, Diarmid *c.s.sp.* '69 (SFR) Millbrae, CA St. Dunstan.
Casey, Donald A. '65 (SB) Retired.
Casey, Donald A. '43 (LAV) Henderson, NV St. Peter the Apostle Retired.
Casey, Edward J. '79 (PH) Broomall, PA St. Pius X; [D] Radnor, PA Archbishop John Carroll High School.
Casey, James R. '00 (PH)[D] Philadelphia, PA Roman Catholic High School for Boys; Collingdale, PA St. Joseph.
Casey, Rev. Msgr. John F. '54 (BRK) Queens Village, NY Our Lady of Lourdes Retired.
Casey, Rev. Msgr. John H. '57 (CAM) Retired.
Casey, John J. *m.m.* '56 (NY)[DD] Maryknoll Maryknoll Fathers and Brothers.
Casey, John P. *m.m.* '56 (NY)[DD] Retired.
Casey, John W. '45 (SCR) Retired.
Casey, John *s.a.c.* '67 (FWT) Weatherford, TX St. Stephen.
Casey, Joseph H. *s.j.* '49 (BO)[U] Weston, MA Campion Health Center, Inc.
Casey, Kevin P. *s.j.* '72 (SD) Santee, CA Guardian Angels Catholic Parish.
Casey, M. Joseph *s.j.* '67 (CIN) Cincinnati, OH St. Francis Xavier.
Casey, Noah J. '76 (IND) Priests' Personnel Board; Archdiocesan Cathedral; Indianapolis, IN SS. Peter and Paul Cathedral, Indianapolis, Inc.
Casey, Patrick L. '65 (NU) Retired.
Casey, Patrick P. '97 (DET) Canton, MI St. Thomas a'Becket; Presbyteral Council; Archdiocesan Vicars.
Casey, Patrick T. *o.m.i.* '80 (JUN) Juneau, AK Cathedral of the Nativity of The Blessed Virgin Mary; Port Chaplains.
Casey, Peter J. '68 (BO) Milton, MA St. Agatha.
Casey, Richard L. '65 (BO) Littleton, MA St. Anne.
Casey, Robert E. '87 (BO) South Boston, MA St. Brigid; South Boston, MA Gate of Heaven; Vicariate II.
Casey, Robert G. '94 (CHI) Brookfield, IL St. Barbara.
Casey, Thomas J. *o.s.a.* '69 (PH)[Y] Villanova, PA St. Thomas Monastery.
Casey, Thomas Joseph *s.j.* '57 (STL)[O] St. Louis, MO Jesuit Community Corporation at Saint Louis University – Jesuit Hall.
Casey, William *c.p.m.* '91 (OWN)[F] Auburn, KY Fathers of Mercy; Auburn, KY.
Cash, Richard '89 (OWN) Bardwell, KY St. Charles; Bardwell, KY St. Denis.
Cashen, Michael E. '91 (TLS) Tulsa, OK St. Catherine.
Cashin, James '65 (SAT) Comfort, TX Sacred Heart.
Cashman, Christopher T. '89 (BRK) Brooklyn, NY St. Mary Star of the Sea.
Cashman, James *o.s.c.* '48 (SCL)[I] Onamia Crosier Priory.
Cashman, Jeremiah '55 (LC) Cornell, WI Holy Cross.
Casillas, Rafael '72 (LA) Los Angeles, CA St. Joseph.
Casillas, Richard *s.v.d.* '97 (LA) Los Angeles, CA Our Lady of Loretto.
Casimir, Benjamin *c.s.* '03 (VEN) Immokalee, FL Our Lady of Guadalupe.
Casimiro, Angelo *m.i.c.* '11 (MIL) Kenosha, WI St. Peter.
Casipong, Guillermo *c.i.c.m.* '07 (SAT)[H] San Antonio, TX Christus Santa Rosa Health Care Corporation; San Antonio, TX Santa Rosa Hospital System.
Casper, Paul *s.c.j.* '57 (MIL)[P] Franklin, WI Sacred Heart at Monastery Lake.
Cassar, Edward A. '69 (BRK) Brooklyn, NY Our Lady of Grace.
Cassar, Julian '77 (BAK) Baker, OR Cathedral of St. Francis De Sales.
Cassato, Rev. Msgr. David L. '72 (BRK) Brooklyn, NY St. Athanasius; Parish Services Corp.; Police Department; Board of Directors; Diocesan Insurance Committee.
Cassem, Ned H. *s.j.* '70 (BO)[U] Weston, MA Campion Jesuit Community.
Casserly, Eugene D. '69 (PT) Vicars Forane; Defender of the Bond.
Cassese, Anthony J. '77 (CLV) Cleveland, OH St. Jerome.
Cassidy, Bernard F. *s.j.* '63 (SJ)[M] Los Gatos, CA Sacred Heart Jesuit Center.
Cassidy, Rev. Msgr. Charles C. (PAT) Retired.
Cassidy, Daniel J. '78 (CHI) Chicago, IL Saint Ita.
Cassidy, Felix F. *o.p.* '54 (SFR) San Francisco, CA St. Dominic; [N] San Francisco, CA St. Dominic Priory.
Cassidy, Francis J. '59 (LA) Monrovia, CA Immaculate Conception Retired.
Cassidy, James M. '61 (CLV) Ashland, OH St. Edward; Litchfield, OH Our Lady Help of Christians Parish Retired.
Cassidy, James W. '90 (NY) Staten Island, NY Our Lady of Good Counsel.
Cassidy, James '78 (STP) Minneapolis, MN St. Joan of Arc.
Cassidy, John M. '58 (CHI) Retired.
Cassidy, Rev. Msgr. John T. '79 (PT) Pensacola, FL St. Thomas More; Priests' Pension Plan, Board for.
Cassidy, John V. '69 (LC) Retired.
Cassidy, Kevin W. '60 (MAD) Sun City, AZ Retired.
Cassidy, Rev. Msgr. Martin J. '57 (MIA) Retired.
Cassidy, Matthew J. *s.j.* '99 (FgM) New York, NY Society of Jesus.
Cassidy, Richard '67 (DET) Special Assignment.
Cassidy, Terry A. '84 (PEO) Peoria, IL St. Ann; Cursillo Program.
Cassidy, Theodore *s.m.* '68 (CLV) Cleveland, OH St. Aloysius – St. Agatha.
Cassidy, Thomas *s.c.j.* '71 (MIL)[P] Hales Corners, WI Priests of the Sacred Heart; [P] Franklin, WI Sacred Heart at Monastery Lake.
Cassieri, Achilles *o.f.m.cap.* '52 (NY)[B] Beacon, NY St. Lawrence of Brindisi Friary.
Cassin, Rev. Msgr. Andrew J. '54 (WDC) Waldorf, MD St. Peter Retired.
Cassista, Fernand *m.s.* '65 (FR)[F] Attleboro, MA La Salette Shrine; [H] Attleboro, MA La Salette Retreat Center.
Casstevens, Jennifer (BO)[CC] Cambridge, MA The Youville House, Inc.
Castaldi, Joseph '63 (NOR) Fishers Island, NY Our Lady of Grace; New London, CT St. Joseph; Defenders of the Bond; Priests' Retirement Plan Board.
Castanada, Heibar '94 (MRY) Hollister, CA Sacred Heart/St. Benedict Catholic Community.
Castanas, Edilberto S. '11 (OAK) Pinole, CA St. Joseph.
Castaneda, Brian '99 (LA) Los Angeles, CA Cathedral of Our Lady of the Angels; Our Lady of the Angels Region; Office of the Archbishop.
Castaneda, Jose '10 (GB) Green Bay, WI St. Bernard; Green Bay, WI St. Philip the Apostle.
Castaneda, Luis J. *o.c.d.* '03 (SAT)[L] San Antonio, TX Discalced Carmelite Fathers of San Antonio; San Antonio, TX; San Antonio, TX Basilica of the National Shrine of the Little Flower, Our Lady of Mt. Carmel and St. Therese Parish.
Castaneda, Luis *o.c.d.* '03 (OKL) Oklahoma City, OK Our Lady of Mount Carmel and St. Therese Little Flower.
Castaneda, Mario '95 (PMB) West Palm Beach, FL St. John Fisher.
Castaneda, Rev. Msgr. Oscar F. '87 (MIA) Hialeah, FL St. John the Apostle; [N] Hialeah, FL Opus Caritatis Corp.
Castaneda, Rev. Msgr. Oscar '87 (MIA) Deans and Deaneries.
Castaneda, Severiano '71 (LA) Los Angeles, CA San Francisco Church.
Castano, Jairo *s.d.s.* '66 (LAF) On Special Assignment; Lafayette, LA St. Jules.
Castano Fernandez, Rafael '88 (ATL) Hartwell, GA Sacred Heart of Jesus.
Casteel, Michael J. '84 (SPC) Benton, MO St. Denis; Benton, MO St. Lawrence.
Castejon, Antonio Garcia '81 (SJN) Police Chaplains.
Castellino, Albert J. *c.ss.r.* '62 (STL)[O] Liguori, MO Liguori Mission House/Redemptorists.
Castelow, Ralph T. '89 (WIL) Wilmington, DE St. John the Beloved.
Caster, Gary C. '92 (PEO) On Duty Outside the Diocese.
Caster, Gary C. (SPR)[M] Williamstown, MA.
Castillo, Alexander Q. '11 (OAK) Fremont, CA Our Lady of Guadalupe.
Castillo, Carlos C. *c.m.f.* '73 (LA) Hospital Chaplains; [V] Rancho Dominguez, CA Dominguez Seminary Inc.
Castillo, Eduardo (POD) Miami.
Castillo, Eduardo '02 (MIA)[M] Miami, FL Prelature of the Holy Cross and Opus Dei.
Castillo, Francisco '67 (BWN) Mission, TX Our Lady of St. John of the Fields.
Castillo, Gustavo '01 (LA) Azusa, CA St. Frances of Rome; San Gabriel Region.
Castillo, Javier del '05 (POD) Chicago.
Castillo, Jose '80 (SD) San Ysidro, CA Our Lady of Mt. Carmel Catholic Parish San Ysidro.
Castillo, Miguel Gonzalez '06 (YAK) Youth/Young Adult Hispanic Ministry.
Castillo, Miguel '58 (NY) Haverstraw, NY St. Peter.
Castillo, Paulino Matus *o.f.m.conv.* '88 (ATL) Lithia Springs, GA St. John Vianney.
Castillo, Pedro '85 (AUS) Lampasas, TX St. Mary of the Immaculate Conception; Lampasas, TX Good Shepherd.
Castillo, Rene R. '89 (MO) Rocky Mount, VA Francis of Assisi; Salem, VA Salem VA Medical Center; Roanoke, VA St. Gerard; DEPARTMENT OF VETERANS AFFAIRS HOSPITALS AND CHAPLAINS.
Castillo, Ricardo '03 (CHI) Chicago, IL St. Bronislava; Chicago, IL Immaculate Conception of the Blessed Virgin Mary.
Castillo, Richard '83 (PT) On Leave of Absence.
Castillo, Rolo B. '92 (RIC) Waynesboro, VA St. John the Evangelist.
Castillo, Ruben Dario (PAT) Paterson, NJ Cathedral of St. John the Baptist.
Castillo, Santos '04 (JOL) Kankakee, IL St. Teresa.
Castillo, Ysidro Valero '73 (SJN) San Juan, PR San Miguel Arcangel.
Castillo DelGadillo, Guillermo '74 (BIR) Birmingham, AL St. Joseph's.
Castle, Nathan *o.p.* '85 (SJ) Stanford, CA Catholic Community at Stanford.
Castles, Patrick J. '69 (TR) Allentown, NJ St. John.
Castoldi, Heitor *c.s.* '05 (NY) Mount Vernon, NY Our Lady of Victory.
Castor, Timothy William '01 (RC) Lead, SD St. Patrick's.
Castori, Michael T. T. *s.j.* '90 (SJ)[B] Santa Clara, CA Jesuit Community.
Castrillo, Jesus Saez *o.de.m.* '69 (PCE) Ponce, PR La Merced.
Castrillo, Jesus *c.m.f.* '49 (LA) El Monte, CA Our Lady of Guadalupe.
Castro, Alberto '79 (MGZ) Diocesan Board of Administration.
Castro, Angel '08 (LA) Los Angeles, CA Cathedral of Our Lady of the Angels.
Castro, Antonio '84 (GAL) Deer Park, TX St. Hyacinth.
Castro, Carlos Eduardo (AMA) Stratford, TX St. Joseph's.
Castro, Dominic Joseph '98 (MRY)[I] Monterey, CA; Special Assignment.
Castro, Geronimo *m.s.* '99 (HON) Makawao, HI St. Joseph.
Castro, Geronimo *m.s.* '92 (HON) Members.
Castro, John G. *o.m.i.* '62 (SAT)[D] San Antonio, TX Antonian College Preparatory High School; [L] San Antonio, TX.
Castro, Mario A. '00 (BWN) Board Members; Brownsville, TX Church of the Good Shepherd.
Castro, Mario Lopez '10 (ATL) Atlanta, GA The Basilica of the Sacred Heart of Jesus.
Castro, Oscar M. '93 (GAL) Pasadena, TX St. Pius the Fifth; Central Vicariate.
Castro, Patrick *o.f.m.cap.* '88 (AGN)[F] Agana Heights, GU St. Fidelis Friary; Archdiocesan Presbyteral Council.
Castro, Robert '85 (SR) Imola, CA Napa State Hospital.
Castro, Rogelio Banvelas '90 (CHI) Calumet Park, IL Seven Holy Founders.
Castronovo, Edmund A. '76 (SY) Verona, NY Our Lady of Good Counsel.
Caswell, Thomas C. '66 (SPK) Archivist; Members Retired.
Catagnus, James N. '70 (PH) Philadelphia, PA St. Ambrose.

Catalana, Mark '91 (SJ) San Jose, CA St. Thomas of Canterbury.
Catalano, James *o.s.j.* '63 (MRY) Davenport, CA St. Vincent De Paul; [F] Shrine of St. Joseph.
Catallo, Sylvester *o.f.m.cap.* '54 (NY)[B] Beacon, NY St. Lawrence of Brindisi Friary.
Catanach, Richard '88 (LSC) Priests Retirement Fund Committee; Defenders of the Bond; Vicars; Presbyteral Council; Clergy Personnel Board; Priestly Life and Ministry Committee; Mesilla, NM Basilica of San Albino.
Catania, Thomas M. '74 (BRK) Richmond Hill, NY Holy Child Jesus.
Catanise, Joseph R. '82 (ROC) Hilton, NY St. Leo.
Cataudo, Anthony I. *o.p.* '60 (CAM)[L] Camden, NJ Dominican Sisters of the Perpetual Rosary Chaplain's Residence; [M] Camden, NJ Monastery of the Dominican Nuns of the Perpetual Rosary.
Catella, Anthony '10 (ALX) Leesville, LA St. Michael.
Catena, Paul G. '07 (ALB) Margaretville, NY Sacred Heart; Presbyteral Council; Diocesan Board of Consultors; Albany, NY Christ the King.
Catoir, John T. '60 (PAT)[Q] Chester, NJ Nazareth Village; [Q] Passaic, NJ St. Jude Media Ministries; Associate Judges Retired.
Caton, Scott '11 (ROC) Rochester, NY Blessed Sacrament; Rochester, NY St. Boniface; Rochester, NY St. Mary.
Catt, Gregoire *s.j.* '11 (BO)[U] Brighton, MA Alberto Hurtado House.
Catucci, Thomas F. '82 (SY) Kirkwood, NY St. Joseph; Kirkwood, NY St. Mary; Kirkwood, NY St. Joseph; Kirkwood, NY Our Lady of Lourdes.
Catungal, Mario T. *o.c.d.* '04 (MO) Air Force Chaplains.
Caul, Robert F. '61 (PRO) North Providence, RI Mary, Mother of Mankind Retired.
Cauley, Thomas F. '81 (PMB) Port St. Lucie, FL Holy Family.
Caulfield, John P. '03 (WDC) Mechanicsville, MD Immaculate Conception.
Caulfield, John '59 (ORL) Lakeland, FL St. Joseph's.
Caulfield, Sean '49 (B) Retired.
Cauterucci, Francis J. '90 (PH) Philadelphia, PA Our Lady of Mt. Carmel.
Cavagnaro, John A. '75 (CAM) Collings Lakes, NJ Church of Our Lady of the Lakes, Collings Lakes, N.J.
Cavagnaro, Mark R. '70 (CAM) Blackwood, NJ Our Lady of Hope Parish, Blackwood, N.J.
Cavagnuolo, Salvatore F. '67 (HRT) Yalesville, CT Our Lady of Fatima.
Cavalcante, Jose M. (HRT) Hartford, CT St. Lawrence O'Toole; Waterbury, CT St. Stanislaus Kostka.
Cavalier, Robert C. '72 (NO) Abita Springs, LA St. Jane de Chantal.
Cavalier, Wayne A. *o.p.* '93 (SAT)[L] San Antonio, TX Dominican Priory of San Juan Macias.
Cavalli, Victor *o.p.* '48 (SAC) Benicia, CA St. Dominic Retired.
Cavalluzzi, Kevin P. '93 (BRK) Brooklyn, NY The Cathedral–Basilica of St. James; [D] Brooklyn, NY Campus Ministers and Ministry Centers; Brooklyn, NY St. Brendan.
Cavanagh, Brian M. '58 (LA) Covina, CA Sacred Heart Retired.
Cavanagh, David J. '85 (BO)[T] Cambridge, MA Opus Dei, Prelature of the Holy Cross and Opus Dei; Cambridge.
Cavanagh, Gerald F. *s.j.* '64 (DET)[K] Detroit, MI Jesuit Community at the University of Detroit Mercy.
Cavanagh, James '80 (LA) On Sick Leave.
Cavanagh, Joseph A. *s.j.* '62 (CI)[C] Kolonia, Pohnpei, FM Jesuit House.
Cavanaugh, Brian *t.o.r.* '82 (STU)[A] Steubenville, OH Franciscan University of Steubenville; [H] Steubenville, OH Holy Spirit Friary.
Cavanaugh, Daniel J. '66 (PH) Media, PA Nativity of the Blessed Virgin Mary Retired.
Cavanaugh, Harry M. *c.pp.s.* '54 (CIN)[N] Carthagena, OH St. Charles Retired.
Cavanaugh, James K. '51 (Y) Retired.
Cavanaugh, John '90 (FAR) Reynolds, ND Our Lady of Perpetual Help Church of Reynolds; Thompson, ND St. Jude's Church of Thompson.
Cavanaugh, Kevin P. '86 (HRT) Manchester, CT St. James; Hartford Vicariate; Army National Guard Chaplains; Manchester, CT Assumption.
Cavanaugh, Michael T. *o.s.f.s* '76 (MO) DEPARTMENT OF VETERANS AFFAIRS HOSPITALS AND CHAPLAINS.
Cavanaugh, Michael *o.s.f.s.* '76 (WH) Martinsburg, WV St. Joseph's.
Cavanaugh, Thomas J. '03 (PH) Philadelphia, PA St. Matthew.
Cavazos–Gonzales, Gilberto *o.f.m.* '85 (CHI)[B] Chicago, IL Catholic Theological Union; [N] Chicago, IL Holy Spirit Friary, Order of Friars Minor.
Caveglia, Patrick *o.s.b.* '94 (KC)[A] Conception, MO Conception Seminary College; [J] Conception, MO Conception Abbey; [N] Conception, MO The St. Benedict Education Foundation; President's Council.
Cavellier, Richard '79 (DET) Auburn Hills, MI Sacred Heart.
Caverly, Rev. Msgr. J. Bernard '65 (SP) St. Petersburg, FL St. Raphael Retired.
Caverly, Rev. Msgr. Patrick J. '61 (ORL) Retired.
Caverte, Rolando A. '62 (SFR) San Francisco, CA Church of the Epiphany Retired.
Cavey, Donald J. '76 (RIC) Hampton, VA VA Medical Center; DEPARTMENT OF VETERANS AFFAIRS HOSPITALS AND CHAPLAINS.
Caviedes, Victor '99 (VEN) Hispanic, Migrant and Spanish Speaking Apostolates; Sebring, FL St. Catherine.
Caviglia, Caesar J. '55 (LAV) Retired.
Cavitt, Arthur J. '02 (STL) St. Louis, MO St. Elizabeth, Mother of John the Baptist; [V] St. Louis, MO St. Charles Lwanga Center.
Cavoto, Joseph F. *s.a.* '80 (NY) New York, NY St. Francis of Assisi; [DD] Garrison, NY Franciscan Friars of the Atonement.
Cawley, John *c.m.* '65 (LA)[A] Camarillo, CA St. John's Seminary.
Cawley, Martin *o.c.s.o.* '61 (P)[L] Lafayette, OR The Cistercian (Trappist) Abbey of Our Lady of Guadalupe.
Cawley, Patrick '70 (GR) Retired.
Cawley, Thomas *c.m.* '57 (KC)[J] Independence, MO Vincentian Parish Mission Center.
Cawley, William M. '73 (HBG) On Duty Outside of the Diocese; York, PA St. Patrick; [A] York, PA York Catholic High School.
Cayer, John B. '96 (PT) Crestview, FL Our Lady of Victory.
Cayetano, Alvin *s.o.l.t.* '95 (PHX) Camp Verde, AZ St. Frances Cabrini Roman Catholic Parish.
Caylor, Dennis J. '75 (CIN) Springfield, OH St. Joseph; Springfield, OH St. Raphael; Vicarri Foranei (Deans); Defenders of the Bond.
Cazares Haro, Salvador A. '00 (TUC) Leave of Absence.
Cazayoux, Clair M. *s.j.* '62 (NO)[R] New Orleans, LA Ignatius Residence Retired.
Cazenavette, Joseph E. '05 (NO) Mandeville, LA Our Lady of the Lake Roman Catholic Church; Legion of Mary.
Cebula, Joseph '75 (ALB) Waterford, NY St. Mary's Church.
Cebula, Thomas W. '68 (Y) Massillon, OH St. Barbara.
Cebulka, Peter *c.o.* '93 (MET)[I] New Brunswick, NJ The New Brunswick Congregation of the Oratory of St. Philip Neri; [N] New Brunswick, NJ Catholic Center at Rutgers University; New Brunswick, NJ St. Peter the Apostle.
Cecero, John J. *s.j.* '89 (NY)[DD] New York, NY Jesuit Community at Fordham University; [DD] Cardinal Spellman Hall, Jesuit Community.
Cecil, Bruce *c.s.c.* (FTW)[H] Notre Dame Congregation of Holy Cross, United States Province of Priests & Brothers.
Cecil, Bruce *c.s.c* '92 (OAK)[L] Berkeley, CA Priests of the Congregation of Holy Cross.
Cecil, Ivo E. '54 (L) Retired.
Cecil, Patrick G. '78 (CHI) Chicago, IL St. Mary of the Woods.
Cedolia, Robert J. '78 (PIT) Pittsburgh, PA St. Anne.
Cedro, Michael '04 (NY) Croton Falls, NY St. Joseph; New City, NY St. Augustine.
Ceja, Miguel R. '90 (SB) San Bernardino, CA Our Lady of Hope Catholic Community, Inc.
Cejas, Orlando *s.d.b.* (CGS)[C] Aibonito, PR Casa Salesiana de Retiros.
Cejudo, Serafin '56 (GAL) Retired.
Celano, Freddy '87 (TYL) Malakoff, TX Mary, Queen of Heaven Church; Athens, TX St. Edward Church; Gun Barrel City, TX St. Jude.
Celano, Rev. Msgr. Joseph G. '87 (MET) Bridgewater, NJ St. Bernard of Clairvaux; Episcopal Vicars.
Celano, Leo J. *o.praem.* '72 (ORG)[I] Silverado, CA Norbertine Fathers of Orange Inc.
Celentano, Christopher '08 (SY) Presbyteral Council; Central Square, NY St. Michael; Brewerton, NY St. Agnes.
Celeste, Charles R. '80 (ALB) Leave of Absence.
Celiano, Alfred V. '53 (NEW)[B] Seton Hall University Retired.
Celichowski, John *o.f.m.cap.* '93 (FgM) Detroit, MI Province of St. Joseph; Detroit, MI.
Celichowski, John *o.f.m.cap.* '93 (DET)[K] Detroit, MI Provincialate; [K] Detroit St. Bonaventure Friary.
Celichowski, John *o.f.m.cap.* '93 (NY)[DD] White Plains, NY Capuchin Friars of North America.
Celino, Anthony C. '97 (ELP) Judges; El Paso, TX Santa Lucia; Ex Officio Members; Moderator of the Curia; Priests' Retirement and Disability Plan; Missions Office/Propagation of the Faith/Catholic Relief Services; Diocesan Tribunal; Priests' Personnel Advisory Committee; Finance Council; Vicars General.
Celis Quintero, Marco A. '09 (NEW) Summit, NJ St. Teresa's.
Cella, John *o.f.m.* '78 (MIL)[Y] Franklin, WI Franciscan Pilgrimage Programs, Inc.; [P] Provincial Offices of the Franciscan Friars, Assumption BVM Province, Inc.; Judges for Second Instance; Provincial Councilors:; [B] Hales Corners, WI Sacred Heart School of Theology.
Cellini, Ronald R. '79 (CHR) Deans; Personnel Committee; Vicar for Priests; Seminary Admissions Board; Bluffton, SC St. Gregory the Great; College of Consultors; Presbyteral Council; Curia.
Celso, B. Thomas '79 (ROC) Unassigned.
Celuch, Martin '03 (Y) Poland, OH Holy Family; Judges.
Cely, Alfonso '01 (ORL) Ocala, FL Blessed Trinity.
Cely, Manuel '05 (BIS)[A] Richardton, ND Assumption Abbey.
Cembor, Thomas M. '79 (NEW) Montclair, NJ Mountainside Hospital; Montclair, NJ Our Lady of Mt. Carmel.
Cement, Blaine (LAF) Evangeline, LA St. Joseph.
Cencula, Leonard T. '63 (STU) Retired.
Cenefeldt, Harry E. '54 (TR)[N] Trenton, NJ Villa Vianney Retired.
Centeno, Yader F. *sch.p.* '96 (MIA) Miami Shores, FL St. Rose of Lima.
Centina, Gilbert Luis R. *o.s.a.* (NY) New York, NY Holy Rosary.
Centner, David J. *o.c.d.* '71 (MIL) Milwaukee, WI St. Florian.
Cera, James B. '64 (MIL) Retired.
Cerank, Gerald A. '72 (OG) Mooers Forks, NY St. Joseph; Mooers Forks, NY St. Ann.
Ceranowski, Albert B. '64 (TOL) Retired.
Ceranowski, Gerald L. '67 (TOL) Retired.
Cerbone, James *s.d.b.* '80 (NEW)[L] Ramsey, NJ Don Bosco Prep Salesian Residence; [C] Ramsey, NJ Don Bosco Preparatory High School.
Cerezo, Alberto F. '60 (YAK) Retired.
Ceriello, Joseph A. '78 (BRK) Brooklyn, NY Queen of All Saints.
Cerio, Frank '86 (ORL) Deltona, FL Our Lady of the Lakes.
Cerkas, John W. '70 (GB) Retired.
Cermak, Michael Gilmary *m.m.a.* '95 (SAM)[B] Petersham, MA Maronite Monks of Adoration Most Holy Trinity Monastery.
Cerniglia, George *s.m.* '69 (HON)[D] Honolulu, HI Center Marianist Community; [A] Honolulu, HI Chaminade University of Honolulu.
Cernoch, Gerard '64 (VIC) Bay City, TX Our Lady of Guadalupe.
Cerny, George F. '64 (CHI) Chicago, IL St. Bartholomew Retired.
Cerpich, Richard J. '61 (MIL) Sheboygan, WI St. Peter Claver Retired.
Cerratos, Ramon *s.x.* '99 (FgM)[N] Wayne Xaverian Missionary Fathers; Wayne, NJ XAVERIAN MISSIONARY FATHERS.
Cerretto, Michael P. *c.s.b.* '69 (LSC) Director of Deacon Formation; Las Cruces, NM Cathedral of the Immaculate Heart of Mary; [B] Las Cruces, NM Basilian Fathers; Agua Viva Editorial Advisory Board.
Cerrone, Michael J. '81 (SAV) Retired.
Cerullo, Fritz J. *o.s.a.* (BO) Andover, MA St. Augustine.
Cervantes, Fidel '55 (ELP) Retired.
Cervantes, Leo (RIC) Retired.
Cervantes, Luis Cananza *m.c.c.j.* '75 (LA) Los Angeles, CA Holy Cross.
Cervenak, Andrew '78 (TR) Retired.
Cervero, Joseph '89 (BGP) Redding Ridge, CT St. Patrick.
Cervine, Keith '09 (MET)[N] New Brunswick, NJ Catholic Center at Rutgers University; Office of Vocations; Hopelawn, NJ.
Cervini, Rev. Msgr. John '68 (RVC) Serving Outside the Diocese.
Cervinski, Paul '61 (BIS) Retired.
Cerwonka, Clarence J. '61 (PBL) Retired.
Cerwonka, Clarence J. '61 (SY) Maine, NY Most Holy Rosary.
Cesa, Dean '98 (CHL) Sapphire, NC St. Jude; Highlands, NC Our Lady of the Mountains.
Cesanek, Damian *o.f.m.* '69 (CIN)[N] Cincinnati, OH St. Francis Seraph Friary.
Cesaro, Nicholas J. '54 (HRT) Newington, CT St. Mary Retired.
Cesarone, Jeffrey T. *o.praem* '94 (CAM) Atlantic City, NJ St. Michael's Church, Atlantic City, N.J.
Cespedes, Carlos J. '75 (MIA)[K] Miami, FL National Shrine of Our Lady of Charity.
Cespedes, Jorge A. '11 (MEM) Memphis, TN Church of the Holy Spirit.
Cespedes–Segura, Jorge A. '11 (MEM) Graduate Studies.
Cessario, Romanus *o.p.* '71 (BO)[A] Brighton, MA St. John Seminary.
Cesta, James M. '74 (SY) Utica, NY St. Mary of Mt. Carmel/Blessed Sacrament.
Cestaro, Joseph A. '62 (BRK) Retired.
Ch'e, James '54 (AGN) Tamuning, GU St. Anthony and St. Victor.
Cha, Simeon Ho Chan (CHI) Des Plaines, IL St. Paul Chong Hasang.

Chaanine, George '96 (LAV) Administrative Leave.
Chaaya, Sami *m.l.m.* '06 (OLL)[A] Houston, TX The Congregation of Maronite Lebanese Missionaries.
Chaaya, Sami *m.l.m.* '06 (OKL) Norman, OK Church of St. Mark the Evangelist.
Chaback, Rev. Msgr. Michael J. '70 (ALN) Permanent Diaconate Office; Northampton, PA Queenship of Mary Parish.
Chabak, Rev. Msgr. Robert M. '72 (NEW) Retired.
Chabala, Brian J. '77 (DET) Rochester Hills, MI St. Irenaeus.
Chabot, Peter L. *m.m.* '65 (CIN)[N] Cincinnati, OH The Catholic Foreign Mission Society of America, Inc.
Chabot, Robert A. *s.s.s.* '66 (GAL) Houston, TX Corpus Christi.
Chabot, Roger P. '65 (PRT) Retired.
Chabwine, Guillaume (Billy) Birhashwirwa *s.j.* '11 (OAK)[L] Berkeley, CA Jesuit Fathers and Brothers.
Chachlowski, Marek '82 (NEW) Berkeley Heights, NJ Church of the Little Flower.
Chackaleckel, Davis *m.s.f.s.* '80 (NSH) Columbia, TN St. Catherine.
Chackaleckel, Davis *m.s.f.s.* '80 (TYL)[C] Whitehouse, TX The Missionaries of St. Francis de Sales.
Chacko, Antony '97 (STO) Oakdale, CA St. Mary of the Annunciation Church (Pastor of).
Chacko, Chanlis '04 (PH) Indian Apostolate, Syro Malankara Rite; Philadelphia, PA Our Lady of Mt. Carmel.
Chacko, Jose Brahmakulam '87 (BIR) Birmingham, AL Our Lady Queen of the Universe.
Chacko, Joseph Ampatt '77 (SHP) Bossier City, LA Mary, Queen of Peace.
Chacko, Joseph C. '68 (MET) U.S. Veterans Medical Center.
Chacko, Rev. Msgr. Joseph C. '68 (MO) DEPARTMENT OF VETERANS AFFAIRS HOSPITALS AND CHAPLAINS.
Chacko, Joseph P. '94 (WIN) On Special or Other Diocesan Assignment; [D] Rochester, MN Saint Mary Hospital.
Chacko, Joseph P. *i.m.s.* '80 (HT) Thibodaux, LA St. Joseph Co–Cathedral; Amelia, LA St. Andrew.
Chacko, Joseph T. '84 (NY) New York, NY Holy Family.
Chacko, Joy T. '92 (TR) Marlboro, NJ St. Gabriel.
Chacko, Philip '85 (FAR) Bisbee, ND Holy Rosary; Rolette, ND Sacred Heart; Willow City, ND Notre Dame de la Victoire Church of Willow City.
Chacko, Sebastian V. '76 (HON) Honolulu, HI Holy Family.
Chacko, Tom '95 (WH) Spencer, WV Holy Redeemer.
Chacko, Vincent *i.m.s.* '80 (AUS) Bertram, TX Holy Cross; Burnet, TX Our Mother of Sorrows.
Chacon, Frank '89 (GLP) Winslow, AZ St. Joseph's; Winslow, AZ Madre de Dios; Presbyteral Council; Diocesan Consultors.
Chacon, Gilbert M. *s.j.* '73 (SJ)[M] Los Gatos, CA Sacred Heart Jesuit Center.
Chacon, Jaime H. '04 (YAK) Mabton, WA Immaculate Conception; Diocesan Consultors; Hispanic Ministries/ Hispanic Ministry Formation; Grandview, WA Blessed Sacrament; Presbyteral Council Executive Committee.
Chacon, Jorge '74 (NEW) Elizabeth, NJ Immaculate Conception.
Chacon, William '91 (BRK) Brooklyn, NY All Saints.
Chadwick, Brian D. '01 (GRY) Bishop's Council of Priests; Judicial Vicar; Judges; Charismatic Apostolate; Merrillville, IN St. Andrew.
Chadwick, John J. '95 (NEW) Office of Divine Worship; Mahwah, NJ Immaculate Conception; [A] South Orange, NJ Immaculate Conception Seminary School of Theology; [B] Seton Hall University.
Chadwick, Lawrence A. '75 (RVC) Dix Hills, NY St. Matthew.
Chae, Dong–Ho '89 (COS) Colorado Springs, CO St. Andrew Kim Quasi Parish.
Chaffman, Rev. Msgr. Charles J. '84 (LA) Los Angeles, CA Christ the King; Judicial Vicar; Judges.
Chahinian, Krikor '98 (OLN) Glendale, CA St. Gregory Armenian Catholic Church.
Chaker, Victor '03 (NOR) District Spiritual Advisors; Coventry, CT St. Mary; Courage Chaplain; Courage Chaplain; Courage Chaplain.
Chakian, Joy '78 (DET) Troy, MI Beaumont Hospital; Rochester, MI Crittendon Hospital.
Chakkiath, Janil Joseph *o.ss.t.* '08 (BAL)[Q] Assigned in India.
Chalackal, A. David *c.m.i.* '88 (MET) Piscataway, NJ Our Lady of Fatima; [G] New Brunswick, NJ Saint Peter's University Hospital.
Chalackal, Poulose *o.ss.t.* '05 (BAL)[Q] Assigned in India.
Chalany, Robert '52 (WH) Retired.
Chalbhagam, George *c.m.i.* '86 (SAL) Mankato, KS Sacred Heart Parish; Mankato, KS St. Theresa Parish; Smith Center, KS St. Mary Parish.
Chalissery, Joy '90 (BIR) Huntsville, AL Our Lady Queen of the Universe.
Chalkey, Andrew G. *o.m.i.* '56 (BEL)[F] Belleville, IL Missionary Oblates of Mary Immaculate – St. Henry's Oblate Residence.
Challancin, James '68 (MAR) Ishpeming, MI St. Joseph; Republic, MI St. Augustine.
Challinor, Michael F. '91 (NY) Bronx, NY St. Mary Star of the Sea.
Challman, Stephen G. '96 (NY) Staten Island, NY Holy Rosary.
Chalmers, H. Edward '79 (WOR) Worcester, MA St. Stephen's; Diocesan College of Consultors.
Chalupa, Fred '73 (AUS) Retired.
Chalupka, Anzelm *o.s.p.p.e.* (NY) Yonkers, NY St. Casimir.
Chamberlain, Francis P. *s.j.* '68 (FgM) Chicago, IL Society of Jesus.
Chamberlain, Robert F. '57 (GI) Retired.
Chamberlain, Rev. Msgr. Robert J. '64 (DM) Retired.
Chamberlain, Tom '70 (AUS) Temple, TX St. Matthew; Temple, TX Our Lady of Guadalupe Catholic Church – Temple, Texas.
Chamberland, Gary S. *c.s.c.* '98 (FTW)[H] Notre Dame Congregation of Holy Cross, United States Province of Priests & Brothers.
Chamberland, Gary *c.s.c.* '98 (P)[P] Portland, OR University of Portland; [B] University of Portland; [L] Portland, OR Holy Cross Fathers & Brothers, C.S.C. – University of Portland.
Chamberlin, Gregory D. *o.s.b.* '65 (IND)[K] Saint Meinrad St. Meinrad Archabbey.
Chamberlin, Gregory *o.s.b.* '65 (EVN) Evansville, IN St. Benedict Cathedral.
Chamberlin, Jim F. '86 (OKL) Norman, OK Church of St. Mark the Evangelist.
Chamberlin, Rev. Msgr. Mark '68 (CC) Deans; College of Consultors; Presbyteral Council; Judges; Portland, TX Our Lady of Mount Carmel.
Chambers, Francis E. '78 (PH)[Y] Villanova, PA St. Thomas Monastery.
Chambers, Francis *o.s.a.* '78 (PH)[C] Villanova University.
Chambers, Henry G. '65 (BO) Millis, MA St. Thomas the Apostle.
Chambers, James E. *s.j.* '55 (DET)[K] Clarkston, MI Colombiere Center.
Chambers, James *s.j.* '55 (CHI) Chicago, IL John H. Stroger, Jr. Hospital of Cook County.
Chambers, Thomas E. *c.s.c.* '61 (FTW)[H] Notre Dame Congregation of Holy Cross, United States Province of Priests & Brothers; Members.
Chambers, Thomas E. *c.s.c.* '61 (NO)[U] Metairie, LA Willwoods Community; New Orleans, LA Good Shepherd.
Chamblain, Joseph *o.s.m.* '84 (CHI)[N] Chicago, IL Assumption Priory; Chicago, IL Assumption of the Blessed Virgin Mary.
Champagne, Michael '94 (LAF)[M] Lafayette, LA Community of Jesus Crucified.
Champakara, Pathros '08 (SYM) Brandon, FL Sacred Heart Syro–Malabar Knanaya Catholic Church (Tampa).
Champigny, Richard *o.carm.* '65 (PMB) Boca Raton, FL St. Jude.
Champigny, Thomas R. '81 (SPR) On Sabbatical.
Champlin, Michael A. *o.p.* '66 (SUP)[H] Webster, WI Thomas More Center for Preaching and Prayer, Inc.
Champlin, William E. '93 (WOR) Westminster, MA St. Edward the Confessor; St. Vincent dePaul Society—.
Champoli, Daniel '09 (BRK) Graduate Studies.
Champoux, Thomas C. '67 (YAK) Clergy Personnel Board; Richland, WA Christ the King; Defenders of the Bond; Diocesan Coordinator for Health Affairs; St. Vincent de Paul Society.
Chan, Paul '50 (NY)[HH] New York, NY Chinese Catholic Information Center.
Chan–A–Sue, Andrew '00 (MIA) Miramar, FL St. Bartholomew.
Chanama, Oliver '80 (NY) East Elmhurst, NY George Vierno Center; New York, NY Holy Innocents.
Chanas, Stefan '96 (NY) New York, NY St. John Nepomucene.
Chanassery, Johnson *o.c.d.* '99 (BRK) Brooklyn, NY St. John the Evangelist.
Chancler, Joseph *t.o.r.* '83 (ALT)[A] Loretto, PA St. Francis University.
Chandler, Anthony L. '89 (L) LaGrange, KY Immaculate Conception; Defenders of the Bond.
Chaney, Robert E. '88 (SAV) Savannah, GA Resurrection of Our Lord; Director of African American Ministry.
Chang, Augustine '11 (LA) San Pedro, CA Holy Trinity.
Chang, Benedict '63 (SFR) San Francisco, CA Star of the Sea Retired.
Chang, Cornelius P. *o.s.b.* '62 (GBG)[H] Latrobe Saint Vincent Archabbey; [H] Latrobe, PA Saint Vincent Archabbey.
Chang, John O. (TR) Lakewood, NJ St. Mary of the Lake.
Chang, Joseph *o.s.b.* '57 (JOL)[L] Lisle, IL St. Procopius Abbey; Lisle, IL.
Changwoo, Ambrosius Yoo (TUC) Korean Catholic Community.
Chap, Robert W. *c.m.* '66 (FgM) Earth City, MO Western Province.
Chapa, Emilio Landeros '08 (TUC) Tucson, AZ Saint Augustine Cathedral Roman Catholic Parish – Tucson.
Chapa, Robert J. *s.o.l.t.* '07 (MO) Navy Chaplains.
Chapdelaine, Gerard E. *s.j.* '66 (SEA)[C] Tacoma, WA Bellarmine Preparatory School; [C] Tacoma, WA Bellarmine Preparatory School.
Chapel, Rev. Msgr. Joseph R. '92 (NEW)[A] South Orange, NJ Immaculate Conception Seminary School of Theology; [A] South Orange, NJ Immaculate Conception Seminary School of Theology[B].
Chapin, Daniel L. '72 (OG) Croghan, NY St. Stephen; Ecumenical Commission.
Chapman, Lawrence J. '77 (MIL) Twin Lakes, WI St. John the Evangelist; East Troy, WI St. Peter; New Munster, WI St. Alphonsus.
Chapman, Michael L. '69 (OKL) Oklahoma City, OK Holy Angels; Region I–A; Priests' Retirement Trust Fund.
Chapman, Robert J. '67 (PH) Narberth, PA St. Margaret.
Chappell, Arthur B. *o.s.a.* '69 (PH)[Y] Villanova, PA St. John Stone Friary.
Chappell, James T. '67 (DUB) Retired.
Chappetto, Rev. Msgr. Raymond F. '71 (BRK) Floral Park, NY Our Lady of the Snows; Diocesan Consultors; Vicar for Clergy, Consecrated Life and Apostolic Organizations; Assignment Board.
Chappidi, Rajasekhar '98 (LR) McGehee, AR St. Mary; Monticello, AR St. Mark; Monticello, AR Holy Child Church.
Charboneau, Marion *o.s.b.* '06 (KCK)[I] Atchison, KS St. Benedict's Abbey; [A] Atchison, KS Benedictine College.
Charbonneau, Damian M. *o.s.m.* '50 (CHI) Chicago, IL Assumption of the Blessed Virgin Mary; [N] Chicago, IL Assumption Priory.
Charbonneau, Roger L. '71 (BUR) Propagation of the Faith; Defenders of the Bond; National Shrine of the Immaculate Conception, Washington; Enosburg Falls, VT St. John the Baptist; Notaries; Sheldon Springs, VT St. Anthony.
Charbonnet, Clayton "Beau" '03 (NO) New Orleans, LA St. Andrew the Apostle.
Charelus, Ronel *s.m.m.* '95 (RVC) Westbury, NY St. Brigid.
Charest, Glenn '77 (ORL) Winter Park, FL St. Margaret Mary.
Charest, Roger M. *s.m.m.* '42 (RVC)[N] Bay Shore, NY Montfort Missionaries Retired.
Charland, George A. '60 (WOR) East Brookfield, MA St. John the Baptist.
Charland, Paul A. '71 (PRO) Retired.
Charlebois, Rev. Msgr. Robert L. '57 (GRY) Retired.
Charles, Jean Gabriel (BO) Dorchester, MA St. Matthew.
Charles, Patrick '06 (MIA) Miami, FL Our Lady of Lourdes.
Charles, Robes C. '99 (MIA) Fort Lauderdale, FL St. Clement.
Charles, Wismick Jean *s.m.m.* '95 (RVC) Westbury, NY St. Brigid.
Charlot, Lucien '61 (BRK) Brooklyn, NY St. Augustine Retired.
Charlton, Robert *ss.cc.* '88 (BWN) Edinburg, TX Sacred Heart.
Charlton, Terrence P. *s.j.* '76 (FgM) Chicago, IL Society of Jesus.
Charm, Robert '77 (OAK) Retired.
Charman, Eugene J. '71 (HRT) Cheshire, CT St. Thomas Becket; Waterbury Vicariate.
Charnley, George '76 (DET) Novi, MI St. James.
Charnoki, Rev. Msgr. William G. '65 (GBG) Ligonier, PA Holy Trinity; Judges.
Charpentier, Alfred *o.m.i.* '71 (FgM) Washington, DC AMERICAN OBLATE MISSIONS.
Charron, Jason '08 (SJP) Presbyters.
Chase, Kenneth M. '84 (DET) Canton, MI Resurrection.
Chase, Lee P. '93 (ROC) Absent on Leave.
Chase, Martin *s.j.* '91 (NY)[DD] Cardinal Spellman Hall, Jesuit Community.
Chase, Maurice '53 (SD) Retired.
Chase, P. Geoffrey *o.s.b.* '59 (PRO)[O] Portsmouth, RI Abbey of St. Gregory the Great.
Chase, Raymond C. '78 (BAL)[J] Timonium, MD St. Vincent's Villa; Special Assignment; Baltimore, MD St. Charles Borromeo.
Chassaniol, Warren F. '65 (HT) Retired.
Chateau, Ixon '06 (BO) Beverly, MA St. Margaret; Beverly, MA St. Mary Star of the Sea.
Chateau, Paul F. '66 (DET) Oak Park, MI Our Lady of Fatima.
Chau, Pedro Bismarck '08 (NEW) Garfield, NJ Our Lady of Mt. Virgin.
Chaupetta, Victor *m.s.* '70 (FR)[F] Attleboro, MA La Salette Shrine.
Chauvin, Gregory '97 (LAF) Lydia, LA St. Nicholas.
Chavajay, Juan (MGZ) Mayaguez, PR Sacred Heart.
Chavannes, Jacques Eddy '85 (PRO) Providence, RI St.

Michael the Archangel; Providence, RI Rhode Island Hospital.
Chavarria, Horacio '66 (BWN) Harlingen, TX Our Lady of the Assumption.
Chavarria, Jerome L. *c.ss.r.* '84 (ORL)[F] New Smyrna Beach, FL Redemptorist Fathers of the Vice Province of Richmond; New Smyrna Beach, FL Retired.
Chavarria, John '11 (CC) Kingsville, TX St. Gertrude; Kingsville, TX St. Thomas Aquinas, Catholic Center (Texas A&M University Kingsville).
Chavenia, Nestor '94 (TR) Keyport, NJ St. Joseph.
Chavez, Arturo '91 (SB) Retired.
Chavez, Carlos '84 (SFE) Clovis, NM Sacred Heart.
Chavez, Frank '76 (SAN) Midland, TX Our Lady of San Juan de Los Lagos.
Chavez, Johnny Lee '76 (SFE) Albuquerque, NM Sangre de Cristo.
Chavez, Jose Luis *c.ss.r.* '84 (LA) Whittier, CA St. Mary of the Assumption; [P] Whittier, CA Redemptorists of Whittier.
Chavez, Jose M. '98 (GI) Elm Creek, NE Immaculate Conception.
Chavez, Jose '96 (MRY) On Leave.
Chavez, Luis N. '91 (TUC) Retired.
Chavez, Manuel '96 (SR) Calistoga, CA Our Lady of Perpetual Help; Deans; Board of Consultors; Priests' Council; Vocations.
Chavez, Patrick J. '68 (SFE) Retired.
Chavez, Ricardo A. '63 (OAK) Retired.
Chavez, Rigoberto *s.t.* '08 (SB) Coachella, CA Our Lady of Soledad.
Chavez, Vincent P. '91 (SFE) Albuquerque, NM St. Therese of the Infant/Jesus Shrine of the Little Flower.
Cheah, Joseph *o.s.m.* '92 (HRT) Avon, CT St. Ann's.
Cheatham, Louis W. '45 (GBG)[G] Greensburg, PA Neumann House Retired.
Cheble, Michel '02 (NTN) Warren, MI Our Lady of Redemption.
Checchia, Jose *c.ss.r.* '63 (CGS) Aguas Buenas, PR Church of Tres Santos Reyes.
Checchio, Rev. Msgr. James F. '92 (CAM) On Duty Outside the Diocese.
Check, Paul N. '97 (BGP) Norwalk, CT St. Mary.
Check, Ronald '07 (PH) Graduate Studies.
Checon, Amarilho *s.j.* '57 (BRK) Queens Village, NY Our Lady of Lourdes.
Cheesman, Robert *c.ss.r.* (NY)[DD] New York, NY Redemptorist Priests and Brothers, C.Ss.R.
Chelena, Thomas '68 (PRM) Absent on Leave.
Chelich, James A. '76 (GR) Grand Rapids, MI St. Thomas the Apostle.
Cheline, Paschal *o.s.b.* '64 (P)[A] St. Benedict, OR Mount Angel Seminary; [L] St. Benedict, OR Mt. Angel Abbey.
Chellaian, Lawrence '92 (TYL)[B] Texarkana, TX Christus Health Ark–La–Tex; [B] Texarkana, TX St. Michael Rehabilitation Hospital.
Chellakandathil, Tomy *c.m.i.* '96 (JOL) Aurora, IL Our Lady of Mercy.
Chemazar, Blase *o.f.m.* '53 (CHI)[N] Lemont, IL The Slovene Franciscan Fathers, Order of Friars Minor, Commissariat of the Holy Cross; [S] Lemont, IL St. Mary's Retreat House; Lemont, IL.
Chemino, Scott '93 (ALX) Cheneyville, LA St. Joseph; Vicar General; Echo, LA St. Francis de Sales; Administrator and Assessor, Code of Pastoral Conduct; Judges; Ex Officio; Louisiana Interchurch Council; College of Consultors.
Chen, Anthony K. '52 (CHI) Retired.
Chen, Paul Feng '07 (OAK) Chinese Pastoral Center; Union City, CA Our Lady of the Rosary.
Chen, Peter Tianzhi (BAL) Catonsville, MD St. Mark.
Chen, Tommy '08 (VIC) Respect Life–Pro Life; Hallettsville, TX Sacred Heart; Hallettsville, TX St. John the Baptist.
Chen, Vincent P. '57 (MET) Phillipsburg, NJ St. Philip & St. James.
Chenault, Richard A. '08 (BIR) Tuscaloosa, AL St. Francis of Assisi University Parish; Diocesan College of Vicars; Vocations.
Chenevy, Anthony *s.s.p.* '58 (Y)[A] Canfield, OH Society of St. Paul.
Cheney, Craig I. '03 (MAN) Coos County House of Corrections; Vicars Forane; Colebrook, NH North American Martyrs Parish.
Cheney, James W. '95 (MO) Air National Guard Chaplains.
Cheney, James '95 (FAR) Fargo, ND St. Paul's Newman Church of Fargo; [H] Fargo, ND St. Paul's Newman Church of Fargo.
Cheng, Jian (Joseph) '03 (NEW) Absent on Leave.
Chenier, Michael D. '09 (MAR) Menominee, MI Resurrection; Menominee, MI Holy Spirit.
Chenot, Paul *c.p.* '72 (BRK) Creedmoor Psychiatric Center; [R] Jamaica, NY Immaculate Conception Monastery.
Cheon, Joachim '01 (FRS) Bakersfield, CA San Clemente Mission Parish.
Chepaitis, Peter *o.f.m.* '72 (ALB) Special Assignment; [N] Middleburgh, NY Bethany Ministries.
Chepelskyy, Vasyl '10 (PSC) White Plains, NY St. Nicholas of Myra.
Cheplic, Rev. Msgr. Peter A. '72 (NEW)[L] Rutherford, NJ St. John Vianney Residence for Priests Retired.
Chepponis, James J. '85 (PIT) Pittsburgh, PA St. John Capistran; Music, Office for.
Cherayath, Davis '72 (SYM) Oklahoma City, OK Holy Family Syro–Malabar Catholic Church Oklahoma.
Cheri, Fernand *o.f.m.* (NO)[U] Montz, LA Lyke Foundation.
Cheri, Fernand *o.f.m.* '78 (SFD)[B] Quincy, IL Quincy University.
Cheri, Fernand *o.f.m.* '79 (SFD)[K] Quincy, IL Holy Cross Friary.
Chermeil, Tony '91 (VEN) West Collier County; Fort Myers, FL St. Francis Xavier.
Chern, James N. '99 (NEW) Campus Ministry; [O] Upper Montclair, NJ Newman Catholic Center at Montclair State University.
Chernetzki, Michael '11 (RCK) Geneva, IL St. Peter.
Cherolikal, John '74 (LUB) Snyder, TX St. Elizabeth's.
Cherrez, Ornoldo '97 (LA) Valinda, CA St. Martha.
Cherry, Athanasius C. *o.s.b.* '68 (GBG)[H] Latrobe, PA Saint Vincent Archabbey.
Cherry, Richard W. *s.j.* '69 (FgM) Chicago, IL Society of Jesus.
Cherubini, Perry A. '85 (CAM) Deanery Representatives; Absecon, NJ Church of Saint Elizabeth Ann Seton, Absecon, N.J.; Elected Members; Members.
Cherup, Rev. Msgr. Michael A. '81 (PT) Fort Walton Beach, FL St. Mary Church; Vicars Forane; Priests' Pension Plan, Board for.
Cheruparambil, Francis *v.c.* '82 (TR) Keyport, NJ Holy Family.
Chervanek, Gregory *o.f.m.cap.* '79 (BAL)[Q] Cumberland, MD The Friary.
Chervenak, Gregory *o.f.m.cap.* (BAL) Cumberland, MD Our Lady of the Mountains, Roman Catholic Congregation, Inc.
Chervenak, Stephen M. '60 (PIT) White Oak, PA St. Angela.
Chesney, Michael *s.j.* '91 (MIA)[H] Miami, FL Villa Javier; [E] Miami, FL Belen Jesuit Preparatory School.
Chethipuzha, Varghese I. '69 (NY) New City, NY St. Augustine.
Chettiyath, Shoby Mathew '06 (SPC) Joplin, MO St. Peter The Apostle; Lamar, MO St. Mary.
Chevalier, Martin '83 (DM) On Duty Outside the Diocese.
Chevalier, Thomas H. '80 (ALB) Voorheesville, NY St. Matthew.
Chew, Randolph G. '71 (PRO) Portsmouth, RI St. Barnabas; Deans.
Chewning, Seraphim John '93 (PBR) Retired.
Chia, Luis P. '59 (GAL) Retired.
Chiang, John B. '53 (NY) Retired.
Chiang, Rev. Msgr. Joseph '59 (NEW)[L] Rutherford, NJ St. John Vianney Residence for Priests Retired.
Chiantella, David M. '82 (R) Raleigh, NC Our Lady of Lourdes.
Chiapa–Villarreal, Hector '06 (DEN) Roggen, CO Sacred Heart.
Chiaramonte, Anthony J. '65 (ALB) Special Assignment; Office; Members.
Chiaravalle, Dominic M. '65 (PH) Chadds Ford, PA St. Cornelius.
Chiarello, Leonir Mario '95 (NY)[HH] New York, NY Scalabrini International Migration Network.
Chiarilli, Rev. Msgr. Patrick S. '61 (CAM) Clayton, NJ Retired.
Chiarinoti, Juan Carlos '86 (BAK) Milton Freewater, OR St. Francis of Assisi.
Chica, Esterminio '06 (NEW) Elizabeth, NJ St. Mary of the Assumption.
Chichetto, James W. *c.s.c.* '68 (FR)[A] North Easton, MA Stonehill College; [A] North Easton, MA Holy Cross Fathers Religious.
Chichetto, James W. *c.s.c.* '68 (FTW)[H] Notre Dame Congregation of Holy Cross, United States Province of Priests & Brothers.
Chidiac, Bakhos '91 (OLL) Lakewood, CO St. Rafka Maronite Catholic Church.
Chidiac, Fady *s.j.* '11 (OAK)[L] Berkeley, CA Jesuit Fathers and Brothers.
Chidozie, Marcus '93 (DAL) Commerce, TX St. Joseph.
Chieffo, Rev. Msgr. Ralph J. '75 (PH) Media, PA St. Mary Magdalen.
Chiesa, Robert E. *s.j.* '68 (FgM) Los Gatos, CA Society of Jesus.
Chiffriller, Edward J. *s.s.j.* '74 (BAL)[Q] Baltimore, MD St. Joseph Society of the Sacred Heart House of Central Administration.
Chiffriller, Edward *s.s.j.* '74 (BR) Baton Rouge, LA St. Francis Xavier.
Chigbo, Kenneth '96 (NY) Valhalla, NY Westchester Medical Center; Sleepy Hollow, NY The Magdalene.
Chikawe, Hugh '71 (SP) Tampa, FL St. Peter Claver.
Chikezie, Emmanuel '89 (BEA)[B] Beaumont, TX CHRISTUS Health Southeast Texas – CHRISTUS Hospital – St. Elizabeth.
Chikweto, Timothy C. *s.s.* '03 (BAL)[Q] Baltimore Society of St. Sulpice, Province of the United States.
Chilagorom, Desmond '79 (RVC) Smithtown, NY St. Patrick.
Child, John F. '59 (DET) Dearborn, MI Sacred Heart Retired.
Childs, Guy A. '00 (ALB) South Glens Falls, NY St. Michael the Archangel.
Chilen, Rev. Msgr. Michael D. '69 (CC) Retired.
Chiles, Richard P. *o.praem.* '87 (JKS) Raymond, MS Immaculate Conception; [E] Raymond, MS Priory of St. Moses the Black.
Chillog, Thomas A. '84 (STU) St. Clairsville, OH St. Mary's; [L] St. Clairsville, OH Ohio University – Eastern; Auditors; Defenders of the Bond; Presbyteral Council; College of Consultors; Priests Personnel Board; Continuing Education of Priests; Health Panel of the Clergy; Vicar for Priests.
Chilson, Elbert '78 (DEN) Aurora, CO St. Therese.
Chilson, Richard *c.s.p.* '72 (SFR) San Francisco, CA Old St. Mary's Cathedral Retired.
Chilufya, Lewis B. *s.s.* '00 (BAL)[Q] Baltimore Society of St. Sulpice, Province of the United States.
Chimera, Angelo M. '69 (BUF) Buffalo, NY All Saints.
Chimiak, Rev. Msgr. Karl A. '80 (WDC) Deans; Valley Lee, MD St. George.
Chin, Donald J. *o.f.m.* '67 (FgM) New York, NY Holy Name Province.
Chinaka, Emmanuel '93 (ALX) Alexandria, LA Our Lady of Prompt Succor.
Chinchar, Gerald T. *s.m.* '82 (CIN)[D] Dayton, OH The University of Dayton; [N] Dayton, OH Marianist Community; [R] Dayton, OH University of Dayton Campus Ministry.
Chinchilla, Ricardo *c.j.m.* '93 (SD) Carlsbad, CA Saint Patrick Catholic Parish Carlsbad.
Ching, Herbert '47 (HON) Retired.
Ching, Philip '09 (DET) Utica, MI St. Lawrence.
Chingandu, Pedro *m.s.* '96 (ATL) Smyrna, GA St. Thomas the Apostle.
Chininis, Thomas '83 (MAN) Diocesan Review Board.
Chinnacode, Peter Pramonte *c.s.s.* '94 (BO)[U] Waltham, MA Stigmatine Fathers & Brothers Provincial House.
Chinnaiah, Bellamkonda (AMA) Amarillo, TX St. Francis.
Chinnapa, John Britto *m.s.f.s.* (DET) Gibraltar, MI St. Victor.
Chinnappa, Ambrose (TYL) Mount Vernon, TX Sacred Heart.
Chinnappa, Johnbritto *m.s.f.s.* '97 (TYL)[C] Whitehouse, TX The Missionaries of St. Francis de Sales.
Chinnappan, Benjamin '88 (CHI) Hines V.A. Hospital; DEPARTMENT OF VETERANS AFFAIRS HOSPITALS AND CHAPLAINS.
Chinnappan, Peter '85 (DAL) Dallas, TX All Saints.
Chinnici, Joseph P. *o.f.m.* '72 (OAK)[A] Berkeley, CA Franciscan School of Theology; [A] Berkeley, CA Franciscan School of Theology; [L] Berkeley, CA Franciscan Friars (Province of St. Barbara).
Chinyanwa, Smart H. *s.s.* '01 (BAL)[Q] Baltimore Society of St. Sulpice, Province of the United States.
Chiodo, Rev. Msgr. Frank '76 (DM) Des Moines, IA St. Anthony's.
Chiola, Richard L. '72 (SFD) Chicago, IL National Organization for Continuing Education of Roman Catholic Clergy, Inc. (NOCERCC); Springfield, IL St. Frances Cabrini; Ongoing Formation of Clergy.
Chiola, Richard L. '72 (CHI)[T] Chicago, IL National Organization for Continuing Education of Roman Catholic Clergy, Inc.
Chipson, Joseph (BIS) Hettinger, ND Sacred Heart; Hettinger, ND Sacred Heart; Hettinger, ND Holy Trinity.
Chirackal, Francis *c.m.i.* '92 (SAC) Sacramento, CA St. Mary.
Chiraphurathel, Felix *o.praem.* '72 (TYL) Atlanta, TX St. Catherine of Siena Church.
Chirayath, Chummar *o.s.j.* '78 (FRS) Bakersfield, CA Our Lady of Guadalupe.
Chirayath, Joseph Vadake '75 (TLS) Hugo, OK St. Agnes; Hugo, OK Immaculate Conception.
Chircop, Manuel J. *c.s.b.* '77 (DET) Detroit, MI Ste. Anne de Detroit.
Chiriaco, William J. '86 (PH) Media, PA St. Mary Magdalen; [D] Springfield, PA Cardinal O'Hara High School.
Chirichella, Vincent G. '07 (BRK) Whitestone, NY St. Luke.
Chirichiello, Richard *o.s.b.* '95 (GBG)[H] Latrobe, PA Saint Vincent Archabbey.
Chirichiello, Richard o.s.b. (RIC) Chincoteague Island, VA St. Andrew the Apostle.
Chirico, Peter F. *s.s.* '56 (BAL)[Q] Baltimore Society of St. Sulpice, Province of the United States Retired.
Chirico, Peter *s.s.* '56 (SEA) Retired.
Chirovsky, Rt. Rev. Andriy '80 (STN) Tucson, AZ St. Michael.
Chirovsky, Ivan (SJP) Pittsburgh, PA St. John the Baptist; Liturgical Commission; St. Josaphat Sacerdotal Society; Arbitration Board; Presbyters.

Chishimba, Adrian (AUS) Austin, TX St. John Neumann.
Chisholm, Gregory C. *s.j.* '93 (BO)[U] Boston The Society of Jesus of New England–Provincial Offices.
Chisholm, Gregory *s.j.* (NY) New York, NY St. Charles Borromeo; Manhattan (Central Harlem).
Chisholm, Thomas *o.s.b.* '89 (JOL)[L] Lisle, IL St. Procopius Abbey; Lisle, IL.
Chittattukkara, Shiju *s.d.v.* '07 (BUR) Derby Line, VT St. Edward; Newport, VT St. Mary Star of the Sea.
Chitteth, Biju (BIS) Crosby, ND St. Patrick; Crosby, ND St. Luke; Crosby, ND St. John the Baptist.
Chittooparamban, Biju *c.m.* '98 (BRK)[R] Brooklyn, NY St. John the Baptist Rectory.
Chiusano, Louis *o.f.m.cap.* '57 (FgM) White Plains, NY The Province of St. Mary of the Capuchin Order.
Chizmar, Rev. Msgr. John G. '75 (ALN) Lake Harmony, PA St. Peter the Fisherman; Vicars Forane.
Chladek, Melchior *o.cist.* '55 (DAL)[J] Irving, TX Cistercian Abbey of Our Lady of Dallas.
Chlebo, John C. '80 (CLV) Rocky River, OH St. Christopher.
Chleborad, Gerald '60 (CHY) Retired.
Chlopecki, Robert J. '74 (BEL) Retired.
Chmiel, Bronislaw '69 (CHI) Chicago, IL St. Pancratius.
Chmiel, Gerald J. '70 (TOL) Members Retired.
Chmielecki, Janusz *o.f.m.conv.* (BO) South Boston, MA Our Lady of Czestochowa.
Chmielewski, Francis J. '73 (BUF) Buffalo, NY St. Bernard.
Chmielewski, Philip J. *s.j.* '81 (LA)[C] Los Angeles, CA Jesuit Community.
Chmil, John J. '95 (SCR) Wellsboro, PA St. Peter's.
Chmura, Gary '78 (CLV) Cleveland, OH Our Lady of Peace; Northcoast Behavioral Healthcare System North Campus; Northfield, OH Northcoast Behavioral Healthcare System South.
Chmura, Julian '64 (DET) Retired.
Chmurski, Marek '95 (FR) New Bedford, MA St. Lawrence Martyr.
Cho, Hong–Ray Peter '11 (NEW) Kenilworth, NJ St. Theresa's.
Cho, James Hooyeon '06 (NEW) Maplewood, NJ St. Andrew Kim.
Cho, Minhyun '99 (NEW) Maplewood, NJ St. Andrew Kim; Korean Apostolate.
Choate, Lawrence M. *o.s.m.* '78 (CHI) Chicago, IL St. Francis of Assisi; [N] Berwyn, IL Servants of Mary (Servite) Development Office; Chicago, IL; Chicago, IL; [N] Chicago, IL Order of Friar Servants of Mary (Servites) United States of America Province, Inc.; [N] Chicago, IL Monastery of Our Lady of Sorrows.
Choc, Pedro *o.s.b.* '90 (SFS)[F] Marvin, SD Blue Cloud Abbey.
Chocarro, Antonio (CGS) Retired.
Chochol, Ronald C. '64 (STL) Special Assignment; [Q] St. Louis, MO Mother of Good Counsel Home.
Chodakowski, Ireneusz *m.i.c.* '78 (SPR)[G] On Duty Outside of House.
Chodakowski, Ireneusz *m.i.c.* '78 (MIL) Kenosha, WI St. Peter.
Chodkowski, Grzegorz '03 (WOR) Webster, MA St. Joseph Basilica.
Chodzynski, Jacek *o.c.d.* '88 (GRY)[H] Munster, IN Discalced Carmelite Fathers Monastery.
Chodzynski, Jacek *o.c.d.* '88 (CHI) Chicago, IL St. Camillus.
Choe, James Bong–Won '77 (LA) Los Angeles, CA Holy Trinity.
Choi, DaeJe *s.j.* '03 (LA) Los Angeles, CA St. Agnes.
Choi, Henry Sung Gee '93 (SEA) Koreans, Ministry to; Fife, WA St. Paul Chong Hasang Personal Parish.
Choi, Jae Peter (IND) Indianapolis, IN St. Lawrence Catholic Church, Lawrence, Inc.
Choi, Yong Hoon *s.s.c.* '01 (OM)[J] St. Columbans Missionary Society of St. Columban.
Choiniere, John Marie *m.m.a.* '95 (SAM)[B] Petersham, MA Maronite Monks of Adoration Most Holy Trinity Monastery.
Chojda, Arthur *o.c.d.* '03 (STA)[H] Bunnell, FL Discalced Carmelite Fathers of Florida.
Chojnacki, Anthony *o.f.m.* '68 (GB)[J] Pulaski, WI Friary.
Chojnacki, Anthony *o.f.m.* '68 (GRY)[H] Cedar Lake, IN Our Lady of Lourdes Friary.
Chojnacki, Bernard '09 (VEN) On Administrative Leave.
Chojnacki, Gerald J. *s.j.* '73 (NY)[DD] New York, NY Xavier Jesuit Community; [HH] New York, NY Centro Altagracia de Fe y Justicia, Inc. (Altagracia Center of Faith and Justice, Inc.).
Cholewa, Gregory T. *o.m.i.* '76 (CHI)[N] Chicago, IL The Oblate House of Theology.
Cholewa, Gregory *o.m.i.* '76 (WDC)[O] Washington, DC Provincial Offices of the United States Province of the Missionary Oblates of Mary Immaculate.
Chompoochan, Weerasak (Lee) '06 (OAK) Pleasanton, CA The Catholic Community of Pleasanton.
Chong, Joseph Hyue *s.d.b.* '98 (SP) Tampa, FL Mary Help of Christians; [P] Tampa, FL Mary Help of Christians Center.
Chong, Peter L. '92 (OAK) Oakland, CA St. Theresa of the Infant Jesus (The Little Flower).
Chong, Sammy *s.j.* '07 (BO)[U] Newton, MA The Jesuit Community at Boston College.
Chontos, Joseph '82 (KCK) Special Assignment.
Choo, Thomas *ss.cc.* '69 (HON) Honolulu, HI St. Patrick; [D] Honolulu, HI St. Patrick's Monastery.
Choolakkal, Dixon *c.r.s.* '08 (MAN)[H] Allenstown, NH Pine Haven Boys Center; Nashua, NH Immaculate Conception.
Choong, Norbert '84 (AMA) Retired.
Choorackunnel, John V. *c.m.i.* '64 (TLS)[E] Tulsa, OK Saint Francis Hospital; Special Assignment.
Choorathottiyil, Paul A. '95 (CHI) Chicago, IL St. Mary of the Lake.
Choquet, Alexei H. '83 (CHL) On Duty Outside the Diocese.
Choquette, David P. '98 (NOR) Pomfret, CT Most Holy Trinity; Continuing Education and Formation Commission for the Clergy; District Spiritual Advisors.
Choquette, David '98 (NOR) Putnam, CT St. Mary Church of the Visitation.
Chorey, Robert '02 (RNO) Fernley, NV St. Robert Bellarmine; Diocesan Board of Consultors; Seminary Board; Presbyteral Council; Lists of Deans; Liturgy Commission; Vocations Team.
Chorikavunkal, Joseph '75 (LUB) Spur, TX St. Mary.
Chorpenning, Joseph F. *o.s.f.s.* '79 (PH)[C] Jesuit Fathers; [Y] Wyndmoor, PA Villa de Sales Oblate Residence.
Chortos, Donald '66 (PIT) Retired.
Chortos, George F. '64 (PIT) Monaca, PA St. John the Baptist; Monongahela, PA St. Damien of Molokai Parish.
Chouinard, Lionel G. '65 (PRT) Lisbon Falls, ME Holy Trinity; Sabattus, ME Our Lady of the Rosary.
Choutapalli, Joseph '90 (SAN) San Angelo, TX St. Margaret; Carlsbad, TX St. Therese of the Child Jesus; Priests' Personnel Board; Deans.
Chovanec, Paul R. '72 (GAL) Houston, TX St. Justin Martyr.
Chow, Louis Y. '89 (HRT) Retired.
Chow, Luke L. '54 (PH) Retired.
Chowning, Daniel *o.c.d.* '88 (MIL)[P] Hubertus, WI Retreat Center.
Chowning, Michael *o.f.m.* '68 (LEX) Hazard, KY Mother of Good Counsel; [K] Hazard, KY Father Farrell Spiritual Life Center; College of Consultors.
Chretien, Richard L. '67 (FR) Fall River, MA Notre Dame de Lourdes; Fall River, MA Our Lady of the Immaculate Conception.
Chripko, Vladimir *c.o.* '95 (NY) Tappan, NY Our Lady of the Sacred Heart; [HH] Sparkill, NY New York Oratory of St. Philip Neri, Inc.
Chrisman, Michael '11 (PBL) Vocations; Center, CO St. Francis Jerome; Monte Vista, CO St. Joseph; Alamosa, CO Sacred Heart; Monte Vista, CO Holy Name of Mary.
Chrismer, Mark A. '09 (STL) Wildwood, MO St. Alban Roe.
Christ, John P. *o.s.c.* '65 (DET) Royal Oak, MI St. Dennis.
Christ, John *o.s.c.* '65 (PHX)[F] Phoenix, AZ Crosier Community of Phoenix (Canons Regular of the Order of the Holy Cross).
Christensen, Brian Patrick '99 (RC) Timber Lake, SD Holy Cross; Deaneries.
Christensen, Brian '99 (RC) Continuing Education of Clergy; Director of Ongoing Formation.
Christensen, Christian *i.s.p.* '71 (AUS)[G] Austin, TX Schoenstatt Fathers.
Christensen, Christian *i.s.s.s.* '71 (MIL)[T] Waukesha, WI Secular Institute of Schoenstatt Fathers.
Christensen, Dana Robert '05 (SFS) Dimock, SD SS. Peter and Paul.
Christensen, Joseph *f.m.i.* '97 (FAR)[E] Minto, ND Saint Gianna's Home Inc.; Special Assignment.
Christensen, Lawrence *c.m.* '84 (DEN)[N] Denver, CO Congregation of the Mission Western Province: De Paul House; Denver, CO Church of the Risen Christ.
Christensen, Michael R. '79 (LIN) Lincoln, NE St. Peter.
Christensen, William *s.m.* '73 (STL)[O] St. Louis Marianists, Province of the United States (Society of Mary).
Christenson, Christian *i.s.p.* (AUS) Austin, TX St. Paul.
Christian, George G. *o.p.* '55 (L) Louisville, KY St. Louis Bertrand; [L] Louisville, KY St. Louis Bertrand Priory.
Christian, Lawrence J. '83 (SAT) San Antonio, TX St. Francis of Assisi.
Christian, Robert *o.p.* '76 (OAK)[L] Oakland Order of Preachers (Province of the Most Holy Name of Jesus – Western Dominican Province).
Christiana, Michael *s.j.* (IND)[D] Indianapolis, IN Brebeuf Jesuit Preparatory School, Inc.
Christiansen, Andrew J. *s.j.* '72 (NY)[DD] New York, NY "America;" Residence and publication office of the America Press; [HH] New York, NY America Press, Inc.
Christiansen, Cal '08 (SEA) Longview, WA St. Rose de Viterbo.
Christman, Rev. Msgr. Bernard E. '59 (OG) Judges Retired.
Christman, Rev. Msgr. Bernard '59 (ORL) Indialantic, FL Holy Name of Jesus Retired.
Christman, John *s.s.s.* '11 (CHI) Chicago, IL Blessed Sacrament.
Christman, John *s.s.s.* '11 (CLV)[N] Cleveland Congregation of the Blessed Sacrament Provincial House.
Christofferson, Kevin '97 (HEL) Helena, MT Santo Tomas; On Duty Outside the Diocese.
Christopher, Brian J. *s.j.* '09 (FgM) St. Louis, MO Society of Jesus.
Christopher, Brian J. *s.j.* '09 (STL)[O] St. Louis, MO The Jesuits of the Missouri Province; Saint Louis, MO.
Christopher, Christian *s.s.s.* '83 (NY) Manhattan, NY Lenox Hill Hospital; New York, NY St. Jean Baptiste.
Christopher, Mark '62 (ORL) Sanford, FL All Souls Retired.
Christopher, Mark '57 (PMB) Retired.
Christopher, Patrick J. '91 (STL) Ellisville, MO St. Clare of Assisi.
Christudasl, Velanmarukudiyil *o.s.b.* '86 (TR) Brick, NJ Visitation.
Christy, Timothy '92 (MET) Flemington, NJ St. Magdalen de Pazzi.
Christy, William H. *c.s.sp.* '92 (FgM) Bethel Park, PA CONGREGATION OF THE HOLY SPIRIT.
Chriszt, Dennis *c.pp.s.* '82 (CIN) Cincinnati, OH Church of the Resurrection.
Chrobot, Leonard F. '64 (FTW) South Bend, IN St. Hedwig; South Bend, IN St. Patrick.
Chrusciel, Bogumil '68 (NEW) Newark, NJ St. Stanislaus.
Chrysostom, Francis X. '60 (LA)[J] Inglewood, CA Daniel Freeman Memorial Hospital.
Chryst, Robert D. '68 (SY) Syracuse, NY St. Anthony of Padua; Spanish Apostolate.
Chrzan, John P. '03 (CHI) Park Ridge, IL St. Paul of the Cross.
Chrzastek, Brian *o.p.* '92 (WDC)[B] Washington, DC Dominican House of Studies.
Chu, Joseph Ly Quy '02 (DM) Des Moines, IA Church of St. Peter Vietnamese Catholic Community.
Chu, Peter M.Q. *s.j.* '68 (SJ)[D] San Jose, CA Bellarmine College Preparatory.
Chu, Peter Ngoc Thanh '55 (GAL)[L] Houston, TX Pope John Paul XXIII Priests' Residence Retired.
Chu, Quang Vinh '91 (ORG) Huntington Beach, CA St. Mary's by the Sea.
Chua, Freddie T. '98 (LA) Tujunga, CA Our Lady of Lourdes.
Chubirko, Michael *s.d.b.* '60 (SP)[P] Tampa, FL Mary Help of Christians Center.
Chudy, Carl S. *s.x.* '86 (PAT)[N] Wayne, NJ Xaverian Missionary Fathers; Wayne, NJ XAVERIAN MISSIONARY FATHERS.
Chukwu, Donatus '93 (CHI) Chicago, IL St. Margaret Mary; [J] Chicago, IL Saint Joseph Hospital.
Chukwu, Kenneth '95 (LA)[J] Burbank, CA Providence Saint Joseph Medical Center; [J] Tarzana, CA Providence Tarzana Medical Center; Hospital Chaplains.
Chukwube, Stanislaus '88 (RVC) West Islip, NY Our Lady of Lourdes.
Chukwuleta, Daniel '91 (FTW) Fort Wayne, IN St. Joseph Hospital.
Chukwuma, Francis '96 (FTW) Bluffton, IN St. Joseph; First Court of Judges; Appeal Court Judges.
Chumo, Augustine '98 (ROC) Lyons, NY St. Michael; Clyde, NY St. John the Evangelist.
Chun, Francis '63 (P) Retired.
Chun, Glen *s.j.* '08 (CHI)[D] Chicago, IL St. Ignatius Jesuit Community.
Chung, Alex '88 (LA) Los Angeles, CA St. Gregory Nazianzen.
Chung, Anthony '71 (SFR) Retired.
Chung, Brian '00 (LA) Cursillo Movement.
Chung, Eugene *o.c.s.o.* '06 (ROC)[K] Piffard, NY Abbey of the Genesee.
Chung, Francis '93 (AUS) Austin, TX St. Andrew Kim Taegon Korean Catholic Church.
Chung, Hee Ook '76 (LAV) Las Vegas, NV St. Paul Jung–Ha–Sang.
Chung, John Mary '11 (SFR) Menlo Park, CA The Church of the Nativity.
Chuong, Joseph Doan Huy '64 (GAL)[O] New Caney, TX Congregation of the Mother Coredemptrix Retired.
Church, Rev. Msgr. James F. '58 (SAC) Propagation of the Faith; Sacramento, CA St. Rose.
Church, Timothy A. '95 (DAL) Allen, TX St. Jude.
Church, Wenceslaus '59 (CHI)[N] Chicago, IL St. Peter's Friary.
Churchwell, Rev. Msgr. Stephen T. '76 (ATL) Special or Other Archdiocesan Assignment; Adjutant Judicial Vicars; Board of Directors.
Chwalek, John '48 (SPR) Retired.
Chwalek, Kazimierz *m.i.c.* '87 (SPR)[G] Stockbridge,

MA Congregation of Marian Fathers of The Immaculate Conception of the Most Blessed Virgin Mary; Stockbridge, MA; [G] Provincial Office.
Chwalek, Kazimierz *m.i.c.* '87 (LIT) Marian Province of Mary Mother of Mercy.
Chwieroth, Edward J. '50 (PH) Bensalem, PA Retired.
Chycinski, Gregory A. '71 (MIL) Milwaukee, WI Blessed Savior Parish.
Chylewski, Rev. Msgr. Anthony '52 (SD) Retired.
Chylinski, Keith J. '07 (PH) North Wales, PA Mary, Mother of the Redeemer.
Chylko, Gerard H. *c.ss.r.* '79 (WDC)[O] Washington, DC Holy Redeemer College.
Ciaccio, Accursio *f.s.c.b.* (DEN) Lexington, MA; [N] Broomfield, CO Priestly Fraternity of St. Charles Borromeo (F.S.C.B.); Broomfield, CO Nativity of Our Lord.
Ciaccio, Accursio *f.s.c.b.* '08 (BO)[U] Broomfield, CO House of Denver.
Ciampaglio, Rev. Msgr. Joseph A. (PAT) Diocesan Council of Catholic Women.
Ciampaglio, Rev. Msgr. Joseph M. (PAT) Retired.
Ciancimino, David S. *s.j.* '88 (NY) New York, NY; [DD] New York, NY Society of Jesus, New York Province; New York, NY Society of Jesus; [DD] New York, NY Xavier Jesuit Community.
Ciandella, Roch *o.f.m.* '72 (NY)[FF] Wappingers Falls, NY Mt. Alvernia Retreat House.
Ciano, Kenneth J. '95 (IND) Retired.
Ciappi–Azcorra, Angel L. '98 (SJN) Diocesan Consultors; Legion of Mary; Vicar of Development; San Juan, PR Cristo Redentor.
Ciaramitaro, James M. *o.f.m.conv.* (RCK) Rockford, IL St. Anthony of Padua.
Ciaramitaro, Rev. Msgr. Victor P. '72 (MEM) Memphis, TN St. Michael's; Clergy Personnel Board; College of Consultors; Judges; Presbyteral Council.
Ciaravolo, Ronald '54 (NY) Retired.
Ciardiello, Bruno *o.f.m.* '45 (NY)[DD] New York, NY Padua Friary Retired.
Ciaston, Krzysztof D. '07 (CHI) Chicago, IL St. Tarcissus.
Ciavaglia, Julio M. *c.r.s.p.* '66 (BUF)[B] Youngstown, NY St. Anthony M. Zaccaria Seminary; [S] Youngstown, NY Basilica of the National Shrine of Our Lady of Fatima, Inc.
Ciba, Thomas J. '74 (NEW) Jersey City, NJ Our Lady of Czestochowa.
Cibangu, Sylvain '95 (SEA) Everett, WA Immaculate Conception; Everett, WA Our Lady of Perpetual Help.
Cibelli, Ernest W. '09 (BAL)[T] Cockeysville, MD St. Joseph, Texas Endowment Trust.
Ciccarino, Christopher M. '96 (NEW)[B] Seton Hall University; [A] South Orange, NJ Immaculate Conception Seminary School of Theology; [A] South Orange, NJ Immaculate Conception Seminary School of Theology.
Ciccolini, Samuel R. '69 (CLV) Akron, OH Immaculate Conception.
Ciccone, Joe *c.s.p.* '89 (COL)[I] Columbus, OH Campus Ministry.
Ciccone, Mark *s.j.* '85 (LA)[J] Burbank, CA Providence Saint Joseph Medical Center; [P] Los Angeles, CA Colombiere House; Hospital Chaplains; Hospital Chaplains.
Ciccone, Michael *o.p.* '75 (COL)[A] Columbus, OH Pontifical College Josephinum; [A] Columbus, OH Pontifical College Josephinum.
Cicerale, Rev. Msgr. Charles W. '75 (MET) Woodbridge, NJ St. James; College of Consultors; Deans.
Cicero, Christopher '10 (Y) Youngstown, OH St. Christine.
Cichon, Michael W. '85 (NY) Staten Island, NY Assumption/St. Paul; Staten Island, NY St. Paul.
Cicinato, Michael '76 (MRY) San Luis Obispo, CA Nativity of Our Lady.
Cid, Roberto M. '07 (MIA) Pax Catholic Communications; Miami, FL Corpus Christi; Secretary; Appointed by the Archbishop.
Ciemiega, Wieslaw *o.f.m.conv.* '93 (BO) South Boston, MA Our Lady of Czestochowa.
Cieniewicz, Donald W. '83 (ALN) Hamburg, PA St. Mary.
Cienik, Kenneth *s.a.* '77 (NY)[DD] Garrison, NY Franciscan Friars of the Atonement.
Ciesla, Marek '82 (DEN) Denver, CO St. Joseph Polish.
Ciesla, Walter M. '81 (GRY) Michigan City, IN St. Stanislaus Kostka; Blue Army; Bishop's Council of Priests.
Cieslak, William M. *o.f.m.cap.* '73 (OAK)[Q] Board of Directors.
Cieslak, William *o.f.m.cap.* '73 (CHI)[N] Chicago, IL St. Clare Friary.
Cieslewicz, Vincent P. '94 (E) Mount Jewett, PA St. Joseph; Smethport, PA St. Elizabeth; Bradford, PA Federal Correction Institution.
Cieslik, R. Dale '82 (L) Louisville, KY St. Elizabeth Ann Seton; Archivist; Priest Personnel Commission.
Cieslikowski, Thomas J. '88 (HRT) New Britain, CT St. Jerome; New Britain, CT St. Maurice.
Ciferni, Andrew D. *o.praem.* '68 (PH)[B] Paoli, PA Daylesford Abbey; [Y] Paoli, PA Daylesford Abbey.
Cifuentes, Patricio Gallego '79 (PCE) Patillas, PR Inmaculado Corazon de Maria.
Cigan, John J. '74 (PSC) Danbury, CT St. Nicholas; Retirement Plan Board; Peekskill, NY SS. Peter and Paul.
Cihak, John '98 (P) On Duty Outside the Archdiocese.
Cilano, Richard J. '05 (BUF) United Memorial Medical Center; Pavilion, NY Mary Immaculate.
Cilia, Rev. Msgr. Francis V. '79 (SJ) Special Assignment; [O] San Jose, CA Roman Catholic Seminary Corporation of San Jose; Roman Catholic Seminary Corporation; Vicar General and Moderator of the Curia; Vicar for Clergy; College of Consultors; Roman Catholic Welfare Corporation; Office of the Vicar for Clergy; Diocesan Clergy Personnel Board; Priests' Retirement Board; Council of Priests; Building Committee; Lay Retirement Board; Bishop's Cabinet; Ongoing Formation of Clergy.
Cilibraise, Michael '08 (GR) Greenville, MI St. Charles Borromeo; Presbyteral Council.
Cilinski, Robert C. '79 (ARL) Manassas, VA All Saints; Deans; Diocesan Consultors.
Cima, Jose '58 (SB) Retired.
Cima, Thomas E. '67 (CHI) Deans; Chicago, IL St. Michael the Archangel.
Cimbala, Edward G. '88 (PSC) Hillsborough Township, NJ St. Mary's; Protosyncellus–Vicar General and Moderator of the Curia; Priesthood & Diaconate Formation Programs.
Cimerman, Krizolog *o.f.m.* '73 (NY) New York, NY St. Cyril; Councilors.
Cimino, Michael '86 (SFE) Albuquerque, NM Our Lady of the Assumption.
Cimpl, Charles L. '78 (SFS) Sioux Falls, SD St. Michael; Vicar General; Tribunal Judges; Diocesan Consultors; Presbyteral Council; Personnel Board.
Cincinnati, Anthony '87 (WH) Priests' Health and Retirement Association; Diocesan Consultors; Episcopal Vicar for Clergy; Permanent Diaconate Formation; Contacts to Report; [H] Wheeling, WV Welty Trust, Inc.; Wheeling, WV St. Joseph's Cathedral.
Cindric, John R. '74 (GBG)[K] Greensburg, PA The Bishop William G. Connare Center.
Cingle, Martin A. '73 (ALT) Nanty–Glo, PA St. Mary's.
Cini, Rev. Msgr. J. Thomas '68 (WIL) Vicar General for Administration and Moderator of the Curia; Diocesan Planning; Diocesan Real Estate Committee; Catholic Ministry to the Elderly; College of Consultors; Diocesan Building Committee; Public Affairs Advisory Committee; Catholic Diocese of Wilmington, Inc.; Catholic Ministry to the Elderly, Inc.; Catholic Press of Wilmington, Inc.; Catholic Charities, Inc.; Catholic Youth Organization, Inc.; Children's Home, Inc.; Seton Villa, Inc.; Siena Hall, Inc.; Delawareans United for Education; Wilmington, DE St. Ann.
Cink, James J. '85 (MOB) Mobile, AL St. Dominic Parish, Mobile; Victim Assistance Coordinator; Archdiocesan Consultors.
Cinnante, Justin S. '07 (NY)[E] White Plains, NY Archbishop Stepinac High School.
Cinque, Stephen J. '81 (NEW) Washington Township, NJ Our Lady of Good Counsel.
Cinquegrani, Bruce '79 (MEM) Director for Worship & Spiritual Life; Rites and Sacraments; Institute for Liturgy and Spirituality.
Cinquegrani, David *c.p.* '96 (HRT)[P] West Hartford, CT Holy Family Passionist Retreat Center; Commission for Priests' Retreats; [L] West Hartford, CT Holy Family Monastery/Retreat.
Cinquegrani, R. Bruce '79 (MEM) Memphis, TN St. Brigid.
Cinson, Victor '74 (STU) Minerva, OH St. Francis Xavier; Minerva, OH St. Gabriel the Archangel.
Cintron, Angel L. (CGS) Juncos, PR Inmaculada Concepcion.
Cintron, Angel Luis '91 (FAJ) Catechetical Vicar; Vocations.
Cintron, Frederick '87 (BRK) Brooklyn, NY St. Catharine of Alexandria.
Cintron, Segismundo '89 (PCE) Yauco, PR St. Martin de Porres; [B] The Pontifical Catholic University of Puerto Rico; Police Chaplains.
Cintron Gonzalez, Kevin '11 (CGS) Caguas, PR Cathedral Dulce Nombre de Jesus.
Cintron Ortiz, Angel L. '91 (FAJ) Fajardo, PR Cathedral Santiago Apostol.
Cintula, Francis M. '65 (CHL) Retired.
Cio, Robert J. '74 (NEW) Summit, NJ Overlook Hospital; Apostleship of the Sea; Hackensack, NJ Holy Trinity.
Cioch, Gregory '00 (DEN) Fort Collins, CO St. Elizabeth Ann Seton; Deaneries.
Cioffi, Alfred '85 (MIA) Hialeah, FL Immaculate Conception.
Cioffi, Alfred '85 (PH)[CC] Philadelphia, PA National Catholic Bioethics Center.
Cioffi, Phillip F. '81 (CHI) Chicago, IL Our Lady of Mount Carmel.
Cioffi, Ronald J. '69 (TR) Keyport, NJ St. Joseph.
Ciolek, Dominik *s.j.* '07 (OAK)[L] Berkeley, CA Jesuit Fathers and Brothers.
Ciomek, Christopher '98 (CHI)[A] Mundelein, IL University of St. Mary of the Lake/Mundelein Seminary.
Cionca, Calin '00 (NEW) Absent on Leave.
Cioppa, John A. *m.m.* '59 (FgM) Maryknoll, NY MARYKNOLL.
Cioppi, Martin T. '81 (PH) King of Prussia, PA Mother of Divine Providence.
Ciordia, Jose Antonio '61 (NEW) Union City, NJ St. Augustine's.
Ciordia, Pedro M. '61 (LA) Retired.
Ciorra, Anthony J. '73 (NY)[HH] New York, NY Voluntas Dei USA.
Ciotola, Rev. Msgr. Romano '65 (COL) Columbus, OH Our Lady of Victory.
Ciotoli, Vincent J. '76 (ALB) Schenectady, NY Our Lady Queen of Peace.
Cipagauta, Uriel Salamanca '87 (BEL) Cobden, IL St. Joseph.
Cipar, Daniel '61 (Y) Retired.
Cipolla, Richard G. '84 (BGP) Norwalk, CT St. Mary.
Cipot, Edwin H. '00 (NY) Staten Island, NY Holy Child.
Cippel, Rev. Msgr. John A. '60 (SP) Brandon, FL Church of the Nativity Retired.
Cipriani, Peter A. '04 (BGP) Trumbull, CT St. Theresa; [C] Fairfield, CT Notre Dame Catholic High School.
Cipriano, Joseph F. '59 (SCR)[M] Dunmore, PA Villa St. Joseph Retired.
Cipriano, Robert P. '87 (SFR) Sausalito, CA St. Mary Star of the Sea Retired.
Ciranni, Salvatore *r.c.j.* '55 (FRS) Sanger, CA St. Mary; Sanger, CA Retired.
Cirata, David J. '06 (TOL) Walbridge, OH St. Jerome; Members.
Cirba, Richard J. '89 (SCR) Pittston, PA St. John the Evangelist.
Circe, Scott M. '05 (ORL)[G] Orlando, FL Catholic Campus Ministry at the University of Central Florida; Oviedo, FL Most Precious Blood Catholic Church; Catholic Campus Ministry at University of Central Florida.
Cirera, Arsenio G. '89 (SFR) Belmont, CA Immaculate Heart of Mary.
Ciriaco, Dominic G. '99 (NEW) Dumont, NJ St. Mary's.
Cirignani, Anthony *o.f.m.* '83 (GB) Green Bay, WI SS. Peter and Paul.
Cirilli, Matthew R. '64 (PIT) Retired.
Cirillo, Nicholas A. '95 (BGP) New Fairfield, CT St. Edward the Confessor; [A] Stamford, CT St. John Fisher Seminary Residence; [C] Stamford, CT Trinity Catholic High School.
Cirino, Andre *o.f.m.* '67 (NY)[DD] Mount Vernon, NY St. Bernardine of Siena Friary.
Ciriza, Jesus M. *m.ss.cc.* '59 (SJN) Bayamon, PR Santiago Apostol.
Cirone, Theodore *c.m.f.* '55 (CHI)[N] Chicago, IL Claret House.
Cirujeda, Pablo '03 (MIL) Special Assignment; [V] Racine, WI Community of St. Paul, Inc.
Ciryak, Michael A. '98 (FR) Swansea, MA Saint Francis of Assisi; Bristol Community College; [K] Fall River, MA Bristol Community College Newman Center; Director.
Ciscar, Tomas *o.carm.* '78 (ARE) Morovis, PR Nuestra Senora del Carmen.
Ciscar, Tomas *o.carm.* '78 (MGZ) Anasco, PR St. Anthony Abbot.
Cisco, Bede *o.s.b.* '78 (IND)[K] Saint Meinrad, IN St. Meinrad Archabbey; [A] Saint Meinrad, IN Saint Meinrad School of Theology.
Cisek, Herman W. *m.m.* '65 (CHI)[N] Chicago, IL Maryknoll Fathers & Brothers.
Cisek, Herman W. *m.m.* '65 (NY)[DD] Maryknoll Maryknoll Fathers and Brothers.
Cisetti, Joseph '91 (KC) Permanent Diaconate.
Cisewski, John '71 (NO) New Orleans, LA St. Katharine Drexel.
Ciski, Michael *t.o.r.* '00 (FWT) Arlington, TX St. Maria Goretti.
Cisneros, Daniel '03 (SAT) San Antonio, TX Our Lady of Perpetual Help.
Cisneros, Mario M. *s.j.* '04 (BO)[U] Newton, MA The Jesuit Community at Boston College.
Cisneros, Ramon '99 (ORG) Santa Ana, CA St. Anne's.
Cisneros, Richard Mederich Marcelino '98 (NY) Bronx, NY St. Peter and St. Paul.
Ciszkowski, Slawomir '00 (NY) Ossining, NY St. Augustine.
Citero, Samuel *o.carm.* '84 (NEW) Cresskill, NJ St. Therese of Lisieux.
Citino, Angelo R. '77 (PH) Warminster, PA Nativity of Our Lord.
Citro, Anthony M. '94 (GLD) Traverse City, MI Immaculate Conception.
Ciuba, Rev. Msgr. Edward J. '59 (NEW) Upper Saddle River, NJ Church of the Presentation; Censores Librorum Retired.
Ciupek, James D. '97 (BUF) Council of Priests; Alden, NY St. John the Baptist.

Ciurpita, John '89 (PHU) Presbyteral Council; Chester, PA Holy Ghost; Clifton Heights, PA SS. Peter and Paul.
Civille, John R. '66 (CIN) Middletown, OH Holy Family.
Cizik, Ladis '87 (PIT) Allegheny County, PA Beverly Manor Nursing Home; Hamilton Hills Personal Care; Allegheny County, PA Ladies of the Grand Army Republic (LGAR); Allegheny County, PA Manorcare Health Services Monroeville; Allegheny County, PA Presbyterian Seniorcare Westminister Place; Seneca Manor Assisted Living; Sunrise Assisted Living; Seneca Place; Pittsburgh, PA Our Lady of Joy; Golden Living Center Monoreville.
Clagett, Rev. Msgr. Carl P. '55 (COL) Retired.
Clair, John J. '82 (CHI)[L] Chicago, IL Misericordia/ Heart of Mercy Center.
Clancy, "Ray" '74 (AUS) Retired.
Clancy, Rev. Msgr. Douglas P. '71 (HRT) Suburban Hartford Deanery; West Hartford, CT St. Brigid; West Hartford, CT St. Helena.
Clancy, Richard F. '91 (BO)[AA] Cambridge, MA Massachusetts Institute of Technology Catholic Community; Campus Ministry; Massachusetts Institute of Technology.
Clancy, Richard F. (BO) Dorchester, MA St. Gregory.
Clancy, Robert E. '74 (CLV) Cleveland, OH St. Vincent de Paul.
Clancy, Timothy R. *s.j.* '89 (SPK)[B] Spokane, WA Gonzaga University; Nine Mile Falls, WA Our Lady of the Lake.
Clanton, Bruce *s.d.s.* '78 (MIL)[P] Milwaukee Salvatorian Provincial Offices.
Clapham, Bruce '95 (MO) DEPARTMENT OF VETERANS AFFAIRS HOSPITALS AND CHAPLAINS.
Clapsaddle, Harlan '77 (RCK) Retired.
Clarin, Rolando *o.s.c.* '93 (LA) Valinda, CA St. Martha.
Clark, Anthony '79 (LSC) Retired.
Clark, Anthony *s.v.d.* '85 (MEM)[F] Memphis, TN Society of the Divine Word (Chicago Province); African American Catholics; Memphis, TN St. Joseph's; Director Multicultural Ministries.
Clark, Augustine '97 (ORL) Orlando, FL St. Charles Borromeo.
Clark, Dana '01 (SAL) Colby, KS Sacred Heart Parish; Catholic Charities Board.
Clark, David '84 (P) On Duty Outside the Archdiocese.
Clark, Rev. Msgr. Dennis R. '66 (SD) Retired.
Clark, Douglas K. '76 (SAV) Port Wentworth, GA Our Lady of Lourdes; Censor Librorum; College of Consultors; Diocesan Worship Commission.
Clark, Rev. Msgr. Eugene V. '51 (NY)[HH] New York, NY Friends of American Art in Religion, Inc.
Clark, Howard T. '57 (WIL) Retired.
Clark, J. Michael '95 (OWN) Utica, KY St. Anthony; Judicial Vicar.
Clark, James B. '95 (BO) Unassigned.
Clark, James E. '96 (ALB) Round Lake, NY Corpus Christi; Catholic Deaf Ministry.
Clark, James M. '11 (MEM) Bartlett, TN St. Ann.
Clark, James P. '52 (NY) Bronx, NY St. Frances of Rome Retired.
Clark, James W. '84 (GBG) Uniontown, PA Uniontown Hospital; Republic, PA Madonna of Czestochowa.
Clark, John F. *c.m.* '70 (STL)[O] St. Louis, MO Lazarist Residence.
Clark, John W. *s.j.* '59 (LA)[P] Culver City, CA Ignatius House, The Novitiate of the California Province, Society of Jesus.
Clark, John W. *s.j.* '59 (SJ)[M] Los Gatos, CA Sacred Heart Jesuit Center.
Clark, John *c.m.* (EVN)[F] Evansville, IN Daughters of Charity of St. Vincent de Paul – Mater Dei House.
Clark, Joseph J. '96 (ARL) Annandale, VA St. Michael.
Clark, Joseph L. '76 (RIC) Retired.
Clark, Keith *o.f.m.cap.* '65 (GB)[M] Appleton, WI Monte Alverno Retreat & Spirituality Center.
Clark, Lucian *c.p.* '65 (NEW)[L] "Compassion" Magazine; [L] Union City, NJ Congregation of the Passion (Passionists)–St. Michael's Residence; [L] Passionist Volunteers, International.
Clark, Luke *o.p.* '04 (RIC) Charlottesville, VA St. Thomas Aquinas; Lay Fraternity of St. Dominic.
Clark, Mark *c.m.f.* '03 (SPC)[F] Springfield, MO Claretians Missionaries' Residence–Villa Claret.
Clark, Matthew R. *o.s.b.* '87 (NO)[R] St. Benedict, LA St. Joseph Abbey; [A] St. Benedict, LA St. Joseph Seminary College; [A] St. Benedict, LA St. Joseph Seminary College.
Clark, Patrick S. '61 (SEA) Seattle, WA St. Patrick.
Clark, Paul M. '03 (HBG) Dauphin, PA St. Matthew, Apostle and Evangelist; Promoter of Justice; Defenders of the Bond.
Clark, Peter A. *s.j.* '92 (PH)[C] Jesuit Fathers; [Y] Loyola Center and Manresa Hall.
Clark, Peter J. '02 (LAN) Williamston, MI St. Mary; [R] Lansing, MI Charismatic Renewal Diocesan Service Committee; Vicar for Charismatic Communities.
Clark, Peter (PAT) Clifton, NJ St. Brendan.
Clark, Ray '91 (OWN) Non–Parochial Assignments; Society for the Propagation of the Faith; Holy Childhood Association; Serra Club.
Clark, Richard '93 (MRY) Retired.
Clark, Robert J. '99 (CHI) La Grange, IL St. Cletus; Deans.
Clark, Robert J. *o.s.b.* '87 (MO) Navy Reserve Chaplains.
Clark, Robert *s.s.c.* '65 (OM)[J] St. Columbans Missionary Society of St. Columban.
Clark, Steven E. '90 (NY) Mt. Kisco, NY St. Francis of Assisi.
Clark, Thomas F. *s.j.* '81 (BO)[U] Boston The Society of Jesus of New England–Provincial Offices.
Clark, Thomas F. *s.j.* '81 (BR) Baton Rouge, LA Immaculate Conception.
Clark, Thomas R. '62 (L) Retired.
Clark, Timothy *o.c.s.o.* '80 (P)[L] Lafayette, OR The Cistercian (Trappist) Abbey of Our Lady of Guadalupe.
Clark, Timothy '80 (SEA) Seattle, WA Our Lady of the Lake.
Clark, Vernon F. '80 (CHY) Cody, WY St. Anthony; Vicars Forane.
Clark, Vernon '80 (CHY) Presbyteral Council.
Clark, William A. *s.j.* '93 (WOR)[N] Worcester, MA Jesuits of the Holy Cross, Inc.
Clark, William A. *s.j.* '93 (CHI)[C] Chicago, IL Jesuit Community at Loyola University Chicago.
Clark, William *o.m.i.* '55 (BEL)[F] Belleville, IL Missionary Oblates of Mary Immaculate – St. Henry's Oblate Residence.
Clarke, Brian J.T. '07 (SCR) Scranton, PA St. Peter's Cathedral; [C] Dunmore, PA Holy Cross High School.
Clarke, Brian J.W. '02 (SCR) Ex Officio; Vicars General; Diocesan Finance Council; Scranton, PA St. Peter's Cathedral; Ex Officio; Chief Canonical Counsel.
Clarke, David M. *s.j.* '64 (DEN)[B] Denver, CO Regis University; [N] Denver, CO Regis Jesuit Community (The Jesuits at Regis University).
Clarke, Fergus *o.f.m.* '73 (FgM) Washington, DC COMMISSARIAT OF THE HOLY LAND.
Clarke, Rev. Msgr. James A. '70 (Y) North Canton, OH St. Paul.
Clarke, Rev. Msgr. James T. '38 (SCR) Retired.
Clarke, James '81 (LA)[A] Camarillo, CA St. John's Seminary; Spirituality Commission.
Clarke, Jeremy *s.j.* '02 (BO)[U] Newton, MA The Jesuit Community at Boston College.
Clarke, Rev. Msgr. John A. '59 (CAM) Retired.
Clarke, Kevin T. *s.j.* '73 (P)[J] Portland, OR Providence Health & Services–Oregon.
Clarke, Mark *c.m.f.* '03 (LA)[V] Rancho Dominguez, CA Dominguez Seminary Inc.
Clarke, Mark *c.m.f.* '03 (SPC)[J] Springfield, MO Catholic Campus Ministry O'Reilly Catholic Student Center, Missouri State University, Drury University, Ozarks Technical Community College; [B] Springfield, MO Springfield Catholic High School.
Clarke, Peter '63 (CHR) Gloverville, SC Our Lady of the Valley Retired.
Clarke, Ransford '11 (NY) New York, NY St. Joseph of the Holy Family.
Claro, Carlos Luis *c.s.v.* '98 (CHI)[N] Arlington Heights Viatorian Province Center–Clerics of St. Viator.
Claro, Mario R. '67 (WH) Franklin, WV St. Elizabeth Ann Seton.
Clary, Brian M. '97 (BO) Brookline, MA St. Mary of the Assumption; Vicariate I; Priests' Recovery Program.
Clary, Michael '77 (KC) Lees Summit, MO Holy Spirit; Deans.
Class, Michael D. *s.j.* '90 (MIL)[P] Milwaukee, WI Jesuit Community at Marquette University.
Classen, Joseph '03 (STL) On Duty Outside the Archdiocese.
Classen, Joseph '03 (ANC) Kodiak, AK St. Mary's.
Classick, Bede *o.s.b.* '67 (SEA)[M] Lacey, WA St. Martin's Abbey; [A] Lacey, WA Saint Martin's University.
Clauder, J. Gibbs '73 (MAD) Leave of Absence.
Claudio, Miguel '06 (CGS) Catholic Youth; Priests Senate.
Clausen, Rev. Msgr. William J. '62 (RCK) Retired.
Claverla, Ray (CC)[D] Corpus Christi, TX CHRISTUS Spohn Hospital Corpus Christi – Shoreline.
Clavero, Jose M. *sch.p.* '64 (NY) New York, NY Annunciation; [DD] New York, NY Calasanzian Fathers (Piarists).
Clavey, W. James (CHI) Chicago, IL St. Bride.
Clavijo, Manuel A. '05 (WOR) St. Peter.
Clavijo, Manuel (WOR) Worcester, MA St. Peter; [Q] Paxton, MA Anna Maria College.
Clavin, M. Oliver '70 (SPC) Kelso, MO St. Augustine; Scott City, MO St. Joseph.
Clavin, Nicholas P. '73 (SD) San Diego, CA Saint Gregory the Great Catholic Parish.
Clay, Catesby '07 (LEX) Lawrenceburg, KY St. Lawrence.
Clay, Chris '07 (LEX) Priests' Retirement Committee.
Clay, Christopher R. '98 (SCR) Unassigned or Leave of Absence.
Clay, David J. *s.s.c.* (FgM) St Columbans, NE House of Post–Graduate Studies.
Clay, John C. '51 (STP) St. Paul, MN St. Stanislaus.
Clay, Rev. Msgr. Michael G. '80 (R) Council of Priests; Clayton, NC St. Ann.
Clayton, Barry '11 (KCK) Lenexa, KS Holy Trinity.
Clayton, Daniel '68 (DAL) Dallas, TX Methodist Dallas Medical Center; Dallas, TX Methodist Charlton Medical Center.
Clayton, Rev. Msgr. Murray '56 (SHP) Retired.
Cleary, Christopher *c.p.* '86 (BRK)[R] Jamaica, NY Immaculate Conception Monastery.
Cleary, Dennis W. *m.m.* '77 (FgM) Maryknoll, NY MARYKNOLL.
Cleary, Donald M. '71 (OM) North Bend, NE St. Charles Borromeo; Snyder, NE St. Leo.
Cleary, Donald R. '68 (KC) Retired.
Cleary, Edward L. *o.p.* '57 (PRO)[O] Providence St. Thomas Aquinas Priory at Providence College.
Cleary, Gerard M. '61 (BLX) Gulfport, MS St. John the Evangelist Retired.
Cleary, Herbert J. *s.j.* '68 (BO)[S] South Boston, MA Marian Manor; [D] Boston, MA Boston College High School; [U] Weston, MA Campion Health Center, Inc.
Cleary, Hugh W. *c.s.c.* '73 (FTW)[H] Notre Dame Congregation of Holy Cross, United States Province of Priests & Brothers.
Cleary, Hugh *c.s.c.* '73 (FR)[A] North Easton, MA Stonehill College; [A] North Easton, MA Holy Cross Fathers Religious.
Cleary, James L. *o.f.m.cap.* '70 (LA) Los Angeles, CA St. Lawrence of Brindisi.
Cleary, Rev. Msgr. Kevin '48 (FRS) Retired.
Cleary, Paul '74 (SAT) LaCoste, TX Our Lady of Grace; Defenders of the Bond.
Cleary, Philip C. '79 (CHI) Missionary Work.
Cleary, William M. *o.s.a.* '61 (PH)[Y] Villanova, PA St. Thomas Monastery.
Cleary, William '61 (WDC) Washington, DC St. Mary, Mother of God.
Cleary, William '04 (NY) Graduate Studies.
Cleary, William *c.ss.r.* '62 (SEA)[M] Seattle, WA The Redemptionist Society of Washington; Seattle, WA Sacred Heart of Jesus.
Cleaton, C. Thomas '75 (CLV) Avon, OH St. Mary of the Immaculate Conception.
Cleator, Gerard B. *o.p.* '65 (CHI) Chicago, IL Province of St. Albert the Great (Central); Chicago, IL; [N] Chicago, IL St. Pius V Priory.
Cleaveland, Raymond '06 (SEA) Seattle, WA Christ the King; Deans; Presbyteral Council.
Clegg, Thomas E. '90 (IND) Jeffersonville, IN Sacred Heart Catholic Church, Jeffersonville, Inc.; Jeffersonville, IN St. Augustine Catholic Church, Jeffersonville, Inc.
Clegg, Timothy '71 (LFT) On Duty Outside the Diocese.
Clemens, Bailey '98 (BAK) Pendleton, OR St. Mary; Council of Priests and Diocesan Consultors.
Clemens, John W. '72 (CHI)[W] Chicago, IL The Aquin Guild; Rosemont, IL Our Lady of Hope.
Clemens, Neal C. '01 (MO) Air Force Chaplains.
Clemens, Neal '01 (OAK) Deacon Council; Clergy Services.
Clement, Frederick *m.ss.cc.* '94 (CAM)[L] Linwood, NJ Villa Pieta. Missionaries of the Sacred Hearts of Jesus & Mary; Linwood, NJ.
Clement, Philip Dac '08 (SP) Tampa, FL Incarnation.
Clement, Richard H. '85 (ALN) Shillington, PA St. John Baptist de la Salle.
Clement, Thomas '95 (SFS) Herreid, SD St. Michael.
Clement, Youssef *b.s.o.* (NTN) Methuen, MA Basilian Salvatorian Order.
Clemente, Joseph J. '81 (SY) East Syracuse, NY St. Matthew.
Clemente, Michael '55 (ALB) Retired.
Clemente, Santiago Rubio (NY) Bronx, NY St. Brendan.
Clemente, Vincent L. '76 (VEN) Arcadia, FL St. Paul.
Clementich, LeRoy E. *c.s.c.* '57 (FTW)[H] Notre Dame Congregation of Holy Cross, United States Province of Priests & Brothers.
Clements, Charles '62 (MIA) Retired.
Clements, Daniel A. '54 (NSH) Retired.
Clements, George H. '57 (CHI) Retired.
Clements, Robert '90 (PHX) Tempe, AZ All Saints Roman Catholic Newman Center; [H] Tempe, AZ Arizona State University.
Clements, Thomas P. '55 (CHL) Retired.
Clemo, Ronald C. *s.j.* '67 (SJ)[M] Los Gatos, CA Sacred Heart Jesuit Center.
Clemons, Delma '66 (OWN) Retired.
Clennon, Raymond *o.carm.* '67 (CHI) Gurnee, IL St. Paul the Apostle.
Cleofe, Edgar (RIC) West Point, VA Our Lady of the Blessed Sacrament.
Clerkin, Robert J. '80 (RVC) Glen Head, NY St. Paul the Apostle; Presbyteral Council; Priests' Retirement Board.
Clerkin, Thomas J. *c.s.p.* '85 (LA) Los Angeles, CA St. Paul the Apostle; Torrance, CA L.A. County–Harbor–U.C.L.A. Medical Center.
Clermont, John *o.f.m.cap.* '53 (NY) White Plains, NY The Province of St. Mary of the Capuchin Order; New York, NY St. John the Baptist.

Cleto, Jorge L. *o.s.a.* '08 (MIA)[H] Miami Gardens, FL Casa San Lorenzo.
Cletus, Jerome Ugochukwu *s.s.j.* '11 (BEA) Beaumont, TX Blessed Sacrament; Beaumont, TX Our Mother of Mercy.
Cletus, Sales T. (Ranjan) '84 (AUS) Temple, TX St. Mary.
Cleu, Paul '74 (OAK) Retired.
Cleves, Simeon *o.f.m.* '55 (CIN)[N] Cincinnati, OH St. Francis Seraph Friary.
Cleves, Rev. Msgr. William F. '78 (COV) Newport, KY Holy Spirit.
Click, Patrick R. '71 (LFT) Fishers, IN St. Louis de Montfort.
Clifford, Donald P. '61 (BO) Senior Priests. Retired.
Clifford, James *o.s.a.* '72 (P)[L] Myrtle Creek, OR Augustinian Community; [J] Medford, OR Providence Health & Services–Oregon.
Clifford, Jerome *s.c.j.* '61 (MIL)[P] Hales Corners Priests of the Sacred Heart.
Clifford, Joseph G. '89 (VEN) Fort Myers, FL St. Columbkille.
Clifford, Leo *o.f.m.* '46 (PAT)[N] Ringwood, NJ Holy Name Friary, Inc.
Clifford, Michael J. '60 (GB) Retired.
Clifford, Paul T. (BO) Hopkinton, MA St. John the Evangelist.
Clifford, Peter C. '76 (ROC) Fairport, NY Church of St. John of Rochester of Perinton, New York; Newly Ordained Priests.
Clifford, Richard J. *s.j.* '66 (BO)[B] Chestnut Hill, MA The Ecclesiastical Faculty at Boston College; [U] Brighton, MA Noel Chabanel House.
Clifford, Richard L. *m.m.* '53 (FgM) Maryknoll, NY MARYKNOLL.
Clifford, Richard (FTW)[B] University of Notre Dame Du Lac.
Clifford, Thomas F. *s.j.* '81 (WDC)[E] Washington, DC Gonzaga College High School; [O] Washington, DC The Jesuit Community of St. Aloysius Gonzaga; Washington, DC St. Aloysius.
Clifton, James F. *s.j.* '88 (OM) Omaha, NE St. Frances Cabrini; [J] Omaha, NE Jesuit Community at Creighton University.
Clinch, Craig J. '11 (LIN) Wahoo, NE St. Wenceslaus; Advocates.
Clinch, Kevin D. '83 (TUC)[H] Casa Grande, AZ Central Arizona College, Holy Family Newman Center.
Cline, Brian James '10 (Y) Canton, OH St. Michael the Archangel.
Cline, Martin E. '05 (OG) Fort Covington, NY St. Mary; Fort Covington, NY St. Patrick; Fort Covington, NY St. Joseph.
Clinton, Donald E. '90 (MAN) Manchester, NH Sacred Heart of Jesus; Manchester, NH Ste. Marie.
Clinton, Kevin I. '74 (STP) New Prague, MN St. Wenceslaus.
Clisch, Norman A. '65 (MAR) Retired.
Clody, Rev. Msgr. Albert W. '65 (BUF) Retired.
Clogan, Paul M. '99 (PRT) Retired.
Cloherty, Francis J. '62 (BO) Quincy, MA St. Ann.
Cloherty, John J. '60 (SFR) Retired.
Cloherty, Thomas '74 (DAL) Personnel Board; Plano, TX Prince of Peace.
Cloney, Michael W. '68 (SR) McKinleyville, CA Christ the King; Deans; Board of Consultors; Priests' Council.
Clooney, Rev. Archpriest David '64 (PHU) Northampton, PA St. John the Baptist.
Cloquet, Victor '50 (SEA) Retired.
Clore, Victor '65 (DET) Detroit, MI Christ the King; [T] Detroit, MI Dominican Center for Religious Development.
Close, Frederick J. '01 (WDC) Washington, DC St. Anthony; Charismatic Renewal Regional Service Committee; Archdiocesan College of Consultors; Priest Council.
Close, John L. '82 (MO) Navy Reserve Chaplains.
Close, John '82 (ALB) New Lebanon, NY Immaculate Conception.
Cloud, Charles W. '89 (TUC) Florence, AZ Assumption of the Blessed Virgin Mary Roman Catholic Parish – Florence.
Clough, Wulfstan F. *o.s.b.* '96 (GBG)[H] Latrobe, PA Saint Vincent Archabbey.
Clougherty, Paul L. '60 (BO) Senior Priests. Retired.
Cloutier, Roland C. '66 (NOR) Somersville, CT All Saints; Members; Advisory Board.
Cloutier, Ronald F. '72 (GAL) Harris County Jail; Correctional Ministries (Jail Chaplains); Houston, TX All Saints.
Cloutier, Timothy '83 (STP) Judicial Vicar.
Clovis, Stephen M. '89 (MO) Navy Reserve Chaplains.
Clovis, Stephen '89 (P) Corvallis, OR St. Mary.
Clovis, Steve '89 (P)[P] Corvallis, OR Trinity Court (Student Housing).
Clubb, Ronald E. *s.t.p.* '86 (STP) Retired.
Clune, Malachy *o.p.* '60 (SJN)[C] San Juan, PR Fraternidad San Antonio.
Clutario, Reynaldo *s.o.l.t.* '93 (PHX) Camp Verde, AZ St. Frances Cabrini Roman Catholic Parish; Mayer, AZ St. Joseph Roman Catholic Mission, A Quasi–Parish.
Clyne, Rev. Msgr. Vincent F. '45 (NY) Retired.
Co, Anthony '05 (PEO) Champaign, IL St. John's Catholic Chapel; [M] Champaign, IL St. John's Catholic Newman Center at the University of Illinois, Urbana–Champaign.
Coady, Frank '76 (SAL) Salina, KS St. Elizabeth Ann Seton Parish; Art and Architecture Commission; Director Adult Faith Formation; Office of Liturgy; Office of Deacons.
Coady, John '59 (GF) Retired.
Coakley, John P. *s.j.* '70 (DET)[K] Clarkston, MI Colombiere Center.
Coakley, Patrick *m.s.c.* '86 (AUS) Austin, TX St. Catherine of Siena.
Coan, Gregory S. '03 (WDC) Newburg, MD Holy Ghost.
Coates, John T. '45 (PH) Retired.
Coates, Roderick J. D. *s.s.j.* (NO) Reserve, LA Our Lady of Grace.
Cobb, Gerald T. *s.j.* '81 (P)[L] Portland, OR Jesuit Provincial Office (Society of Jesus, Oregon Prov.); [L] Portland, OR Colombiere Community.
Cobb, Richard E. *s.j.* '62 (SJ)[D] San Jose, CA Bellarmine College Preparatory.
Cobel, Lawrence F. '73 (BUF) Springville, NY St. Aloysius; West Valley, NY St. John the Baptist.
Cobenas, Pedro A. '92 (LA) La Puente, CA St. Louis of France.
Coble, Scott *s.j.* '79 (SPK)[B] Spokane, WA Gonzaga University.
Cobona, Kusitino '84 (LAN) Mason, MI St. James.
Cobos, J. Abelardo '03 (GAL) Houston, TX Our Lady of Mt. Carmel.
Coby, Thomas W. '73 (RVC) Medford, NY St. Sylvester; Riverhead, NY St. John the Evangelist.
Cocca, Stephen M. '96 (WDC) Absent On Leave.
Cocco, William T. '04 (WIL) Wilmington, DE Christ Our King; [A] Wilmington, DE St. Mark's High School.
Cochran, George L. *o.p.* '62 (PRO)[O] Providence St. Thomas Aquinas Priory at Providence College.
Cochran, Paul M. *s.j.* '94 (SPK)[J] Spokane, WA Regis Community.
Cochran, Paul W. '88 (LFT) Associate Judges.
Cochran, Ronald '01 (SD) El Cajon, CA The Church of Saint Luke Catholic Parish.
Cocio, Carlos '83 (TUC) Administrative Leave of Absence.
Cockayne, John E. '85 (HRT) Retired.
Cocozza, Dennis E. '75 (NEW) Absent on Leave.
Cocucci, Joseph M.P.R. '96 (WIL) Wilmington, DE Cathedral of St. Peter; Office of Priestly and Religious Vocations and Seminarians and Newly Ordained; Diocese of Wilmington – Serra Club Information.
Coda, Joseph F. '63 (NEW)[L] Rutherford, NJ St. John Vianney Residence for Priests Retired.
Codd, Rev. Msgr. Kevin A. '79 (SPK)[N] Pullman, WA "St. Thomas More Catholic Student Center" – Washington State University.
Coddaire, Louis '78 (SR) Retired.
Code, Sean K. '93 (ALT) Cemetery Commission; Fallentimber, PA St. Thomas Aquinas; Fallentimber, PA St. Joan of Arc.
Codega, John C. '99 (PRO) Riverside, RI St. Brendan; Council Members.
Codori, Joseph B. '00 (PIT) Pittsburgh, PA Madonna del Castello.
Cody, Aelred *o.s.b.* '57 (IND)[K] Saint Meinrad, IN St. Meinrad Archabbey.
Cody, Daniel '62 (STA) Jacksonville, FL St. Joseph's; Diocesan Consultors; Family Life, Diocesan Center for; Presbyteral Council.
Cody, Henry P. '58 (HRT) West Hartford, CT The Church of St. Timothy.
Cody, Rev. Msgr. John K. '73 (COL) Columbus, OH St. Christopher; Adjutant Judicial Vicar; Presiding Judges of First Instance; Priests Personnel Board.
Cody, John R. *c.ss.r.* '81 (TR)[R] Long Branch, NJ San Alfonso Retreat House.
Cody, John *c.ss.r.* '81 (DEN)[N] Denver The Redemptorists/Denver Province.
Cody, Kevin W. '93 (MO) Military Chaplains; Air Force Chaplains.
Cody, Thomas '68 (STA) Retired.
Coe, Austin J. '85 (MO) Army Reserve Chaplains.
Coe, Austin '85 (HON) Military Chaplains.
Coelho, Adilso *c.o.* '01 (CHR)[E] Rock Hill, SC Oratory of St. Philip Neri, Congregation of the Oratory of Pontifical Rite; York, SC Divine Saviour.
Coelho, Blaise (CHI) Tinley Park, IL St. George.
Coelho, Brian Alick '07 (WDC) Landover Hills, MD St. Mary's Catholic Church; Rockville, MD St. Elizabeth.
Coelho, Gabriel P. '78 (CC) Tivoli, TX Our Lady of Guadalupe; Corpus Christi, TX Corpus Christi Cathedral.
Coelho, Oscar '08 (SFE) Espanola, NM Sacred Heart; Presbyteral Council of the Archdiocese of Santa Fe.
Coelho, Paul *s.j.* '88 (OM)[J] Omaha, NE Jesuit Community at Creighton University; Milwaukee, WI.
Coelho, Paul *s.j.* '88 (MIL)[P] Milwaukee, WI Jesuit Provincial Office, Wisconsin Province.
Coelho–Harguindeguy, Rev. Msgr. John '67 (FRS) Lemoore, CA St. Peter Prince of Apostles.
Coello, Demetrio *s.d.b.* '60 (ARE) Orocovis, PR San Juan Bautista.
Coen, Rev. Msgr. Charles P. '68 (NY) Red Hook, NY St. Christopher.
Coenen, Thomas '77 (DM) Council Bluffs, IA Corpus Christi.
Coens, Frank *o.f.m.* '73 (SHP) West Monroe, LA St. Paschal; Vicars Forane; Ex Officio Members.
Coerber, Joseph H. '66 (MIL) New Holstein, WI St. Mary; Fond du Lac, WI St. John the Baptist.
Coerver, Richard V. '76 (STL) Washington, MO St. Ann; Washington, MO St. Gertrude.
Coerver, Rev. Msgr. Robert M. '80 (DAL) Dallas, TX St. Rita; Pastors Consultors; Censor Librorum; Deans.
Coffaro, Nicholas F. '08 (SAG) Linwood, MI St. Anne.
Coffas, William '04 (ROC) Office of Vocations; Rochester, NY St. Thomas More; Rochester, NY Our Lady Queen of Peace; [K] Rochester, NY Becket Hall.
Coffey, Brian *m.h.m.* '72 (NY) Suffern, NY Good Samaritan Hospital; Suffern, NY Sacred Heart.
Coffey, James Brian *m.h.m.* '72 (NY)[DD] Hartsdale, NY Mill Hill Fathers Residence.
Coffey, John P. '73 (CHR) Absent On Leave.
Coffey, Joseph L. '96 (MO) Military Chaplains; Navy Chaplains.
Coffey, Michael J. '91 (CAM) Cherry Hill, NJ Holy Eucharist Parish, Cherry Hill, N.J.
Coffey, Peter *s.d.s.* '68 (MIL)[P] Milwaukee Salvatorian Provincial Offices Retired.
Coffey, Stephen G. *o.s.b.* '07 (MRY)[F] San Luis Obispo, CA Men's Residence.
Cogan, James J. '04 (VEN) Port Charlotte, FL St. Charles Borromeo.
Cogan, William B. *s.j.* '55 (NY)[DD] New York, NY Murray–Weigel Hall.
Coghlan, Rev. Msgr. Brian '63 (ORG) Seal Beach, CA Holy Family Retired.
Coghlan, John '74 (MOB) Citronelle, AL St. Thomas; Mount Vernon, AL St. Cecilia.
Cohan, Dennis J. '74 (NEW) Clark, NJ St. Agnes.
Cohea, Victor H. '80 (NO)[S] New Orleans, LA Sisters of the Holy Family Motherhouse, S.S.F.; [U] New Orleans, LA Pan African Roman Catholic Clergy Conference; Members At Large:; New Orleans, LA St. Maria Goretti.
Coicedo, Horacio Florez '89 (SAT) San Antonio, TX St. Alphonsus.
Coine, Robert E. '76 (WIL) Easton, MD SS. Peter and Paul.
Coiro, Gregory *o.f.m.cap.* '82 (SFR)[B] San Francisco, CA Capuchin Franciscan Order San Buenaventura Friary; San Francisco, CA St. Francis of Assisi, National Shrine.
Coiro, Mark J. '94 (BO) Holliston, MA St. Mary; Presbyteral Council.
Cokonougher, Brian K. '99 (DET) Port Huron, MI Holy Trinity.
Cokus, Rev. Msgr. Joseph J. '58 (LA) Retired.
Colacicco, Rev. Msgr. Gerardo J. '82 (NY) Hopewell Junction, NY St. Columba.
Colacino, John A. *c.pp.s.* '80 (ROC)[K] Rochester, NY Missionaries of the Precious Blood.
Colagreco, Michael A. '77 (PH) Lenni, PA St. Francis de Sales.
Colaj, Rene Otzoy *o.s.b.* '82 (RCK)[G] Aurora, IL Marmion Abbey.
Colamaria, Francis A. '01 (BRK) Richmond Hill, NY Holy Child Jesus.
Colamarino, Dennis J. '73 (PIT) Duquesne, PA St. Joseph; Duquesne, PA Christ the Light of the World; Defenders of the Bond.
Colangelo, Dominic *o.p.* (DAL) Plano, TX Prince of Peace.
Colankin, Dimitrij '76 (AUS) Cameron, TX St. Monica.
Colapietro, Peter M. '76 (NY) New York, NY Holy Cross; New York Sanitation Department.
Colaresi, Robert E. *o.carm.* '67 (JOL)[L] Darien, IL St. Simon Stock Priory; [N] Darien, IL Carmelite Spiritual Center; [O] Darien, IL Society of the Little Flower; Councilors.
Colarusso, Darin V. '06 (BO) Reading, MA St. Athanasius.
Colasito, Francisco '99 (PHX) Phoenix, AZ St. Theresa Roman Catholic Parish.
Colaste, Sherwin S. '06 (SAC) Rio Vista, CA St. Joseph; Presbyteral Council.
Colasurdo, Peter '77 (STA) Retired.
Colautti, Federico '92 (DEN)[A] Denver, CO Redemptoris Mater House of Formation.
Colavechio, Xavier G. *o.praem.* '55 (GB)[J] De Pere, WI St. Norbert Abbey.
Colberg, Rev. Msgr. James Philip '55 (LA) Santa Maria, CA St. Mary of the Assumption Retired.
Colbert, Richard K. *s.m.* '64 (WDC)[O] Washington, DC Marist Center Retired.
Colborn, Francis R. '63 (LA) Retired.

Colchin, Stephen E. '84 (FTW) New Haven, IN St. Louis.
Cole, Barry '82 (CHI)[V] Chicago, IL Midtown Residence.
Cole, Basil *o.p.* '66 (CIN) Cincinnati, OH St. Gertrude; [N] Cincinnati, OH St. Gertrude Priory.
Cole, G. Barry '82 (POD) Urbana; Oak Park.
Cole, James J. '71 (BGP)[P] Monroe, CT Sisters of the Holy Family of Nazareth, C.S.F.N.
Cole, Rev. Msgr. Raymond L. '72 (MET) Hillsborough, NJ St. Joseph.
Cole, Robert F. '72 (MAN) Priest Personnel Board.
Cole, Robert F. '71 (MAN) Wolfeboro, NH St. Katharine Drexel; Presbyteral Council.
Cole, Robert J. '72 (CLV) Oberlin, OH Sacred Heart; Oberlin, OH Mercy Allen Hospital.
Cole, Robert J. '06 (RIC) Virginia Beach, VA St. John the Apostle Church.
Cole, Vincent P. *m.m.* '71 (FgM) Maryknoll, NY MARYKNOLL.
Colella, David *o.ss.t* '57 (BAL)[Q] In Residence – Holy Trinity Monastery Baltimore.
Colello, Michael A. '01 (PRO) Providence, RI Cathedral of SS. Peter and Paul; Bishop's Office & Chancery Office.
Coleman, Rev. Msgr. Brian P. '63 (GB) Vice–Chancellor; Adjutant Judicial Vicars; Judges Retired.
Coleman, C. Michael '67 (KC) Special Assignment; Judge, Adjutant Judicial Vicar; Archivist.
Coleman, Christopher C. '06 (CIN) Consultors; Dayton, OH St. Anthony of Padua; Presbyteral Council.
Coleman, Christopher L. '94 (BRK) Members At Large:; Brooklyn, NY Saint Martin de Porres.
Coleman, Christopher (NO)[U] New Orleans, LA Pan African Roman Catholic Clergy Conference.
Coleman, Donald E. '74 (SD) Carlsbad, CA Saint Elizabeth Seton Catholic Parish.
Coleman, Ed '86 (P) Scio, OR Our Lady of Lourdes; Stayton, OR Immaculate Conception; Area Vicars.
Coleman, Gerald D. *s.s.* '68 (SFR) Redwood City, CA St. Pius.
Coleman, Gerald D. *s.s.* '68 (BAL)[Q] Baltimore Society of St. Sulpice, Province of the United States.
Coleman, Gerald J. '78 (TLS)[E] Tulsa, OK St. John Medical Center, Inc.; Special Assignment.
Coleman, Rev. Msgr. James G. '62 (HRT) Waterbury, CT SS. Peter and Paul; Episcopal Vicars; Waterbury, CT St. Leo the Great; Ex Officio Members; Archbishop's Annual Appeal; College of Consultors; Consultors – Canon 1742 Retired.
Coleman, James Montini '99 (MOB) Retired.
Coleman, James '76 (COL) Columbus, OH Our Lady of the Miraculous Medal.
Coleman, James '73 (P) Yamhill, OR St. John.
Coleman, John A. '67 (SFR)[N] San Francisco, CA Loyola House Jesuit Community; San Francisco, CA St. Ignatius.
Coleman, John J. '54 (NY) Retired.
Coleman, John K. '71 (SFR) Retired.
Coleman, John R. '88 (PHX) Chandler, AZ St. Andrew the Apostle Roman Catholic Parish.
Coleman, John R. '50 (SFR) East Palo Alto, CA St. Francis of Assisi Retired.
Coleman, John *o.carm.* '78 (LA)[P] Encino, CA Our Lady of Mount Carmel Priory.
Coleman, Rev. Msgr. John '50 (SJ) Retired.
Coleman, Michael A. '81 (JC) Moberly, MO St. Pius X; Teens Encounter Christ (TEC).
Coleman, Paul '03 (OAK) Danville, CA St. Isidore.
Coleman, Rev. Msgr. Robert F. '78 (NEW)[A] South Orange, NJ Immaculate Conception Seminary School of Theology; [B] School of Theology; [B] Seton Hall University.
Coleman, Robert J. '87 (JOL) Retired.
Coleman, Robert P. '78 (CHI) Other Assignments.
Coless, Gabriel M. *o.s.b.* '57 (PAT)[N] Morristown, NJ St. Mary's Abbey.
Coletta, Rev. Msgr. Thomas J. '63 (PAT) Clergy Personnel Office; Paterson, NJ Our Lady of Victories.
Coletti, Arnold F. '62 (BO) Lexington, MA Sacred Heart; Presbyteral Council.
Coley, James E. '47 (TR)[N] Trenton, NJ St. Lawrence Rehabilitation Center Retired.
Colgan, Arthur J. *c.s.c.* '73 (FTW)[H] Notre Dame Congregation of Holy Cross, United States Province of Priests & Brothers.
Colgan, John '48 (SP) Retired.
Colgan, John (LSC) Retired.
Colgan, Richard J. *c.s.p.* '79 (WDC)[B] Washington, DC St. Paul's College.
Colgan, Thomas A. *s.j.* '75 (BUF)[N] Buffalo, NY Canisius Jesuit Community Inc.; [Q] Buffalo, NY Canisius College, Campus Ministry Office.
Colgan, Rev. Msgr. Thomas J. '49 (RVC) Northport, NY St. Philip Neri Retired.
Colgan, Tobias *o.s.b.* '82 (IND)[K] Saint Meinrad, IN St. Meinrad Archabbey; [A] Saint Meinrad, IN Saint Meinrad School of Theology.
Colhour, David *c.p.* '94 (L)[L] Louisville, KY Sacred Heart Retreat; Louisville, KY St. Agnes.
Colibraro, Daniel '56 (CHY) Retired.
Colibraro, Philip '57 (CHY) Retired.
Colicchio, Damian '62 (NEW)[B] Lodi, NJ Lodi Campus.
Colicchio, Ralph M. '67 (HRT) New Haven, CT St. Anthony; New Haven, CT St. Michael.
Colin, Alberto '09 (SAT) Kerrville, TX Notre Dame.
Colina, Jose '89 (SP) Dunedin, FL Our Lady of Lourdes.
Coll, Eduardo *i.v.e.* '88 (PH) Philadelphia, PA St. Veronica.
Coll, Jerome B. *s.j.* '59 (PH)[Y] Loyola Center and Manresa Hall.
Coll, John J. *s.j.* '56 (BAL)[Q] Baltimore, MD Colombiere Jesuit Community.
Coll, Rev. Msgr. Robert J. '59 (ALN) Bethlehem, PA Assumption B.V.M. Retired.
Collado, Domingo '93 (BRK) Jamaica, NY Presentation of the Blessed Virgin Mary.
Collard, Bruce W. '80 (MAN) Nashua, NH St. Christopher; [L] Manchester, NH St. George Manor.
Coller, Jerome *o.s.b.* '59 (SCL)[I] Collegeville, MN St. John's Abbey, of the Order of St. Benedict.
Colleran, James A. '63 (CHI) Retired.
Collet, John *o.m.i.* '67 (SAT)[A] San Antonio, TX Assumption Seminary.
Colletta, Ralph V. '61 (CLV) Retired.
Collette, Rev. Msgr. Richard '52 (WOR) Retired.
Colletti, Arnold F. (BO) Lexington, MA St. Brigid.
Colletti, Peter '84 (CLV) Independence, OH St. Michael.
Colletti, Richard M. '78 (WIN) Winona, MN Cathedral of the Sacred Heart; Winona, MN St. Casimir's; Vicar General; Chancellor; Diocesan Board of Administration; Vicar General; Chancellor; Ex Officio; Archives; Victim Assistance Coordinator; [I] Winona, MN St. Thomas Aquinas Newman Center; Priest Assignments Committee; Diocesan Consultors; Finance Council; Deposit and Loan Board; Priests' Pension Board; Diocese of Winona Incardination Board; Misconduct Issues; Diocesan Review Board; Permanent Deacons.
Collier, Joseph '58 (SD) Retired.
Colligan, James P. *m.m.* '55 (LA)[P] Los Angeles, CA Retired.
Colling, Paul J. '87 (GI) Lexington, NE St. Ann's; Hispanic Ministry; Priests' Advisory Board (Presbyteral Council); CEC (Catholics Encounter Christ); Diocesan Consultors.
Collini, Rev. Msgr. Celsus O. '47 (BRK) Retired.
Collins, Austin I. *c.s.c.* '82 (FTW)[B] University of Notre Dame Du Lac; [H] Notre Dame, IN Holy Cross Community, Corby Hall, University of Notre Dame.
Collins, Carl '91 (HT) Houma, LA Our Lady of the Most Holy Rosary; Priests Council; Terrebonne Deanery; College of Consultors.
Collins, Charles E. '72 (BO) Cambridge, MA St. John the Evangelist.
Collins, Charlie I. '82 (WIN) Rochester, MN St. Pius X; Propagation of the Faith.
Collins, Christopher S. *s.j.* '06 (OM)[J] Omaha, NE Jesuit Community at Creighton University.
Collins, Chuck '05 (PT) Blountstown, FL St. Francis of Assisi; Chattahoochee, FL Holy Cross Parish; Florida State Hospital.
Collins, Corwin *o.s.b.* '57 (SCL)[I] Collegeville, MN St. John's Abbey, of the Order of St. Benedict.
Collins, Daniel J. '58 (CHI) Chicago, IL St. Mary of the Lake Retired.
Collins, David J. *s.j.* '98 (WDC)[O] Washington, DC The Jesuit Community at Georgetown University.
Collins, Denis E. *s.j.* '69 (LA) Santa Barbara, CA Our Lady of Sorrows.
Collins, Edward A. '68 (PAT)[K] Paterson, NJ St. Joseph's Hospital and Medical Center; Paterson, NJ St. Joseph Hospital.
Collins, Edwin J. '54 (RVC) Retired.
Collins, George E. *s.j.* '10 (BGP)[O] Fairfield, CT The Fairfield Jesuit Community–Fairfield University; [B] Fairfield, CT Fairfield University.
Collins, James B. '04 (MO) Army National Guard Chaplains.
Collins, James J. '64 (PH) Philadelphia, PA Saint Martha; [C] Philadelphia, PA Holy Family University; On Special or Other Archdiocesan Assignment.
Collins, James M. *s.j.* '58 (BO)[U] Weston, MA Campion Health Center, Inc.
Collins, James M. '95 (CHL) Newton, NC St. Joseph.
Collins, James R. '68 (CIN) Retired.
Collins, James R. '81 (PRO) Cranston, RI St. Matthew.
Collins, John E. *c.s.p.* '70 (NY)[DD] New York, NY Paulist Fathers' Motherhouse.
Collins, John M. '79 (CHI) Chicago, IL St. John de la Salle.
Collins, John Michal '69 (LA) On Active Leave.
Collins, John P. '72 (PH) Yeadon, PA St. Louis.
Collins, John *c.ss.r.* '87 (PH)[C] Gwynedd Valley, PA Gwynedd–Mercy College.
Collins, John '79 (CHI) College of Consultors; Vicar for Priests; Commission on the Mission and Life of Diocesan Priests.
Collins, John '98 (LA) Burbank, CA St. Robert Bellarmine.
Collins, Kevin A. *o.m.i.* '82 (GAL) Houston, TX Immaculate Conception.
Collins, Kevin S. *c.m.* '85 (LA)[P] Montebello, CA DePaul Evangelization Center.
Collins, Lawrence '77 (CHI) Des Plaines, IL St. Mary.
Collins, Leonard J. *c.s.c.* '69 (FTW) South Bend, IN St. Adalbert; South Bend, IN St. Augustine.
Collins, Michael J. '67 (BR) Baton Rouge, LA St. Jude the Apostle Retired.
Collins, Michael T. *o.praem.* '78 (PH)[Y] Paoli, PA Daylesford Abbey.
Collins, Neil J. '58 (NEW)[L] Rutherford, NJ St. John Vianney Residence for Priests Retired.
Collins, Patrick '64 (PEO) Retired.
Collins, Raymond F. '59 (PRO) Retired.
Collins, Raymond *c.ss.r.* (BO) Boston, MA Our Lady of Perpetual Help.
Collins, Richard '04 (FWT) Henrietta, TX St. Jerome; Henrietta, TX St. Mary; Henrietta, TX St. William; Henrietta, TX St. Joseph.
Collins, Robert C. *s.j.* '67 (NY)[DD] New York, NY "America;" Residence and publication office of the America Press.
Collins, Seamus *o.p.* '58 (SP) Hudson, FL St. Michael the Archangel.
Collins, Stephen L. '83 (E) Bradford, PA St. Francis of Assisi; Lewis Run, PA Our Mother of Perpetual Help Retired.
Collins, Terrence '71 (R) Retired.
Collins, Thomas E. '92 (NY)[E] White Plains, NY Archbishop Stepinac High School.
Collins, Thomas S. '92 (PT) Santa Rosa Beach, FL Christ the King Mission; Santa Rosa Beach, FL St. Rita.
Collins, Thomas '92 (NY) White Plains, NY Burke Rehabilitation Center.
Collins, Rev. Msgr. Timothy '58 (NY) New York, NY Our Lady of the Rosary; [DD] Bronx, NY John Cardinal O'Connor Residence Retired.
Collins, Vincent *o.c.s.o.* '72 (ARL)[H] Berryville, VA Cistercian Abbey of Our Lady of the Holy Cross.
Collins, Rev. Msgr. William A. '61 (BAL) Randallstown, MD Holy Family Retired.
Collins, William B. '74 (PAT) Hamburg, NJ St. Jude the Apostle.
Collins, William F. '65 (CAM) Retired.
Collins, Rev. Msgr. William J. '60 (NY) Livingston Manor, NY St. Aloysius.
Collins, William P. '56 (RCK) Retired.
Collins, William *m.s.c.* '67 (SAT) San Antonio, TX Immaculate Conception; [L] San Antonio, TX Missionaries of the Sacred Heart; Sectional Leadership Team.
Collison, Craig A. '78 (SC) Sioux City, IA Sacred Heart; Presbyteral Council.
Collogan, Robert '82 (JOL) Leave of Absence.
Collopy, Rev. Msgr. John C. '56 (BAL) Lutherville Timonium, MD Retired.
Collucci, Bennett *o.f.m.cap.* '57 (SAL)[D] Victoria, KS St. Fidelis Friary.
Collum, Patrick '92 (NO) Bogalusa, LA Annunciation Catholic Church.
Colnaghi, Andrew *o.s.b.cam.* '79 (MRY)[F] Big Sur New Camaldoli Hermitage.
Colnaghi, Andrew '79 (OAK)[L] Berkeley, CA Incarnation Monastery, Camaldolese Benedictines.
Colohan, Edward A. '61 (BGP)[O] Stamford, CT The Catherine Dennis Keefe Queen of the Clergy Retired Priests' Residence Retired.
Colom, Marti '00 (MIL)[V] Racine, WI Community of St. Paul, Inc.; On Duty Outside the Archdiocese.
Coloma, Redentor *s.d.b.* '99 (OAK)[L] Berkeley Salesians of Don Bosco.
Colombo, Ronald A. '72 (GB) Denmark, WI St. James; Denmark, WI All Saints; De Pere, WI St. Mary; Kellnersville, WI St. Joseph; Denmark, WI Holy Trinity Mission.
Colombo, Stefano *f.s.c.b.* '99 (BO)[U] Lexington, MA Priestly Fraternity of the Missionaries of St. Charles Borromeo, Inc.; Lexington, MA.
Colominas, Octavio '02 (MIA) On Leave.
Colon, Alberto Diaz '85 (ARE) Priest's Senate (Consejo Presbiteral); Defenders of the Bond.
Colon, Angel '95 (CGS) Caguas, PR Nuestra Senora de la Providencia; Priests Senate.
Colon, Jackson '90 (CHI) Chicago, IL St. Ignatius.
Colon, Jorge *c.ss.r.* (SJN) San Juan, PR San Agustin.
Colon, Jose '01 (ARE) Vega Baja, PR Parroquia de San Martin de Porres.
Colon, Juan J. (CGS) Naranjito, PR San Miguel Arcangel.
Colon, Luis A. *s.e.m.v.* '81 (ARE) Vicar General; Diocesan Consultors; Priest's Senate (Consejo Presbiteral); Arecibo, PR Our Lady of Guadalupe.
Colon, Rene A. (ARE) Arecibo, PR Our Lady of Guadalupe.
Colon, Vincent A. '50 (STP) Retired.
Colopelnic, Vasile '04 (STF) Spring Valley, NY SS. Peter and Paul; Presbyteral Council; Catechetics; Religious Education.
Colosimo, Felix R. '65 (SY) New Hartford, NY Our Lady of the Rosary.

Colpitts, Albert B. '73 (PRT) Limerick, ME St. Matthew.
Colter, Dennis J. '66 (DUB) Cedar Falls, IA St. Patrick; Directors Retired.
Colton, Gary P. '68 (HON) Lahaina, HI Maria Lanakila; Presbyteral Council.
Colucci, Bennett '57 (SAL) Retired.
Colvin, Andrew '02 (MO) Navy Chaplains; Military Services.
Colwell, Michael P. '94 (SAT) Defenders of the Bond.
Colwell, Rev. Msgr. Michael P. '94 (AMA) Marriage Encounter; Promoter of Justice; [I] Amarillo, TX Project Solidarity; [I] Amarillo, TX Marriage Encounter; College of Consultors; [I] Amarillo, TX Pope John Paul II House of Discernment; Borger, TX St. John the Evangelist.
Coman, Christopher M. '08 (SAG) Standish, MI Resurrection of the Lord.
Comandini, Glenn J. '86 (MET) Basking Ridge, NJ St. James; Theological Commission.
Comboy, Richard *s.j.* '69 (STL)[O] St. Louis, MO Jesuit Community Corporation at Saint Louis University – Jesuit Hall.
Combs, Gordon *o.f.m.cap.* '64 (HON) Members; Honolulu, HI Cathedral of Our Lady of Peace Retired.
Combs, J. Derran *o.f.m.* '94 (JOL) Joliet, IL St. John the Baptist; [A] Joliet, IL University of St. Francis; [L] Joliet, IL St. John the Baptist Friary.
Combs, Ronald P. '03 (CIN) Dayton, OH St. Henry.
Combs, William H. '04 (SAT)[S] San Antonio, TX Brothers of the Beloved Disciple; San Antonio, TX St. Mary Magdalen.
Comeau, Ronald R. '71 (LFT) On Duty Outside the Diocese.
Comeaux, Nathan A. '11 (LAF) Eunice, LA St. Anthony of Padua; Eunice, LA Annunciation of the B.V.M.
Comellas, Wilfredo T. '03 (SCR) On Duty Outside the Diocese.
Comer, John P. '64 (STL) Retired.
Comer, Michael E. '80 (COV) Deans; Burlington, KY Immaculate Heart of Mary; Diocesan Consultors.
Comerford, Christopher J. '96 (SFD) Granite City, IL St. Elizabeth.
Comerford, Christopher '96 (SFD) Comite Diocesano de Ministerio Hispano – Diocesan Committee for Hispanic Ministry.
Comerford, John J. *o.carm.* '77 (JOL)[L] Joliet, IL St. Elias Carmelites.
Comerford, Patrick '69 (LA)[J] Santa Monica, CA Saint John's Health Center; [L] Santa Monica, CA Saint John's Child Study Center, Saint John's Hospital & Health Center; Hospital Chaplains; Hospital Chaplains.
Comesanas, Raul E.L. '77 (NEW) Newark, NJ St. Thomas Aquinas.
Comeskey, John H. '56 (SY) Utica, NY St. Elizabeth Hospital; [M] Utica, NY St. Elizabeth Medical Center Retired.
Comesky, Clement *o.f.m.* '55 (FgM) New York, NY Holy Name Province.
Comesky, Clement *o.f.m.* '55 (SP)[N] St. Petersburg, FL St. Anthony Friary.
Comiskey, Rev. Msgr. James '50 (LUB) Kansas City, MO Retired.
Comiskey, John P. '60 (NY)[E] Staten Island, NY Monsignor Farrell High School.
Comisky, John *c.s.c.* '68 (FgM) St Columbans, NE House of Post–Graduate Studies.
Commyn, James E. '86 (DET) St. Clair Shores, MI St. Lucy.
Como, Denis R. *s.j.* '66 (BO)[U] Weston, MA Campion Health Center, Inc.
Comparan, Jose Luis '03 (DUB) Waterloo, IA Queen of Peace.
Compentente, Virgilio '67 (NY) Yonkers, NY Immaculate Conception.
Complo, Daniel C. '54 (DET) Retired.
Compton, Matthew Ross '04 (CHI) Chicago, IL Holy Name Cathedral.
Comstock, Douglas G. '67 (OG) Diocesan Consultors; Alexandria Bay, NY St. Cyril of Alexandria (Catholic Community of Alexandria).
Comtois, Norman *o.m.i.* '73 (BO)[U] Lowell, MA Missionary Oblates of Mary Immaculate.
Conahan, Rev. Msgr. John J. '62 (PH) Retired.
Conard, James A. *m.m.* '56 (FgM) Maryknoll, NY MARYKNOLL.
Conard, Ray J. '55 (GB) Retired.
Conaty, Charles '88 (CAM) Retired.
Conboy, Michael F. '62 (ROC) Auburn, NY St. Hyacinth Retired.
Concannon, Stephen F. '64 (PRT) Retired.
Concannon, Stephen F. '64 (MAN) Hampton, NH Our Lady of the Miraculous Medal.
Concepcion, Mervin P. '03 (SAC) Tulelake, CA Holy Cross; Weed, CA Holy Family; Vicars Forane.
Concha, Alfonso J. '76 (PH) On Duty Outside the Archdiocese.
Concha, Augusto M. '72 (PH) Bristol, PA St. Mark.
Concordia, George L. *o.p.* '58 (WDC) Washington, DC St. Dominic Church & Priory.
Concordia, George Lawrence *o.p.* '58 (NY)[HH] New York, NY Dominican Shrine of St. Jude, Inc.
Concordia, Stephen P. *o.s.b.* '95 (GBG)[H] Latrobe, PA Saint Vincent Archabbey.
Conde, Francis Enrico '74 (PAT) Paterson, NJ St. Joseph Hospital.
Conde, Norberto '89 (GAL) Houston, TX Our Lady of Sorrows.
Conde, Ramon (PCE) San Judas Tadeo.
Conde, Thomas P. '87 (CHI) Chicago, IL Christ the King; Deans.
Condon, Daniel J. '81 (ROC) Chancellor; Chancellor and Director of the Department of Legal Services; College of Consultors; Board of Directors; Vicar for Religious; Pension Committee (Lay and Priests); Priest Consultors.
Condon, Denis '78 (CHI) La Grange Park, IL St. Louise de Marillac.
Condon, Edwin D. '61 (BO) Senior Priests.; Presbyteral Council; Pastoral Care of Clergy Retired.
Condon, Gerald A. '56 (DUB) Retired.
Condon, Gerald W. '55 (BAK) Northern; Heppner, OR St. Patrick's.
Condon, Liam '63 (ALB) Cambridge, NY St. Patrick.
Condon, Sean '57 (ORG) Newport Beach, CA Our Lady of Mount Carmel Retired.
Condon, Rev. Msgr. T. Mark '89 (PAT) Little Falls, NJ Our Lady of the Holy Angels; Theological Commission; Deans; Defenders of the Bond; Office of Worship and Spirituality; Liturgical Commission.
Condon, Thomas M. *o.p.* '88 (MEM) Memphis, TN St. Peter Church; [F] Memphis, TN The Dominican Friars of Memphis, Inc.; Presbyteral Council.
Condon, William F. '54 (RIC) Retired.
Condon, William G. *c.s.c.* '61 (MO) Navy Reserve Chaplains.
Condon, William G. *c.s.c.* '61 (FR)[F] North Dartmouth, MA Holy Cross Residence; [F] North Dartmouth, MA St. Joseph's Hall Retired.
Condon, William G. *c.s.c.* '61 (FTW)[H] Notre Dame Congregation of Holy Cross, United States Province of Priests & Brothers.
Condori Puma, Delfin (NY) New York, NY St. Paul.
Condorson, Alfonso R. '95 (MET) Iselin, NJ St. Cecelia.
Condron, Robert F. '69 (HRT) Ansonia, CT Assumption.
Conelly, Marcos A. '03 (ARE) Arecibo, PR Our Lady of Guadalupe.
Conen, Paul F. *s.j.* '57 (DET)[K] Clarkston, MI Colombiere Center.
Conesa, Rev. Msgr. Diego '57 (STA) Retired.
Confer, Thomas B. *o.p.* '73 (BUF)[O] Buffalo, NY Monastery of Our Lady of the Rosary.
Congdon, John '00 (FRS) On Duty Outside the Diocese.
Congdon, Robert J. '87 (BO) Brookline, MA St. Mary of the Assumption.
Congote, Gregory *o.s.b.* '11 (OM)[J] Elkhorn, NE Mount Michael Benedictine Abbey; [C] Elkhorn, NE Mount Michael Benedictine School.
Congro, Basil P. '78 (CHR) Absent On Leave.
Conheeney, Thomas P. '55 (NEW) Bayonne, NJ St. Mary Star of the Sea Retired.
Coning, Jeffrey J. '97 (COL) New Philadelphia, OH Sacred Heart.
Conka, Francis *c.o.* '98 (NY) Tappan, NY Our Lady of the Sacred Heart.
Conka, Frantisek *c.o.* '98 (NY)[HH] Sparkill, NY New York Oratory of St. Philip Neri, Inc.
Conkle, Francis *s.t.* '78 (WDC)[O] Adelphi, MD Father Judge Missionary Cenacle.
Conlan, Rev. Msgr. F. Allan '54 (SCR) Retired.
Conlan, Timothy *o.p.* '67 (FgM)[L] Oakland Order of Preachers (Province of the Most Holy Name of Jesus – Western Dominican Province); Oakland, CA Province of the Holy Name (Western Dominican Province).
Conlan, Walter J. *s.j.* '76 (BO)[U] Newton, MA The Jesuit Community at Boston College.
Conley, Brian J. *s.j.* '01 (WDC)[L] Washington, DC Georgetown University Hospital; [O] Washington, DC The Jesuit Community at Georgetown University.
Conley, Brian J. *s.j.* '01 (BO)[U] Boston The Society of Jesus of New England–Provincial Offices.
Conley, Charles '74 (MIL) Wauwatosa, WI St. Jude the Apostle.
Conley, John E. *c.s.c.* '79 (FTW)[B] University of Notre Dame Du Lac; [H] Notre Dame, IN Holy Cross Community, Corby Hall, University of Notre Dame.
Conley, John P. '93 (SFR) Retired.
Conley, John *s.j.* '83 (BAL)[B] Jesuit Community of Loyola University, Inc.
Conley, John *c.p.* '76 (CHI)[N] Chicago, IL Passionist Community of St. Vincent Strambi; [N] Chicago, IL Passionist Provincial Office.
Conley, Lawrence J. '67 (PRT) Vicars Forane; Portland, ME Cathedral of the Immaculate Conception Retired.
Conley, Martin P. '57 (OM) Retired.
Conley, Rev. Msgr. Peter V. '64 (BO) Norfolk, MA St. Jude; Elected.
Conley, Rory T. '89 (WDC) Special Ministries; Bryantown, MD St. Mary.
Conley, Roy H. '61 (PIT)[M] Pittsburgh, PA St. John Vianney Manor Retired.
Conley, Seraphin J. *t.o.r.* '61 (ORL)[F] New Smyrna Beach, FL Villa Madonna Retired.
Conlin, Daniel C. '90 (STP) Special Assignment.
Conlin, Matthew *o.f.m.* '45 (PAT)[N] Ringwood, NJ Holy Name Friary, Inc.
Conlon, Anthony J. '62 (WH) Retired.
Conlon, Arthur F. '54 (TR) Retired.
Conlon, Christopher W. *s.m.* '66 (CIN)[D] Dayton, OH The University of Dayton; [N] Dayton, OH Marianist Community.
Conlon, Colmbanus '59 (ORG) Retired.
Conlon, James P. '02 (LAN) Westphalia, MI St. Mary.
Conlon, James '64 (OAK)[B] Holy Names University.
Conlon, Philip J. '55 (MAD) Forsyth, MO Our Lady of the Ozarks Retired.
Conlon, Richard W. '64 (BRK) Flushing, NY Mary's Nativity.
Conlon, Timothy *o.s.c.* '79 (PHX)[F] Phoenix, AZ Crosier Provincial House Province of St. Odilia.
Conlon, Timothy *c.m.* (GLP) St. Johns, AZ San Rafael; St. Johns, AZ St. John the Baptist.
Conn, James J. *s.j.* '74 (BO)[U] Newton, MA The Jesuit Community at Boston College.
Conn, James J. *s.j.* '74 (BAL) Canonical & Theological Consultants to the Archbishop.
Connaghan, Daniel H. '90 (HRT) Retired.
Connall, Darrin '92 (SPK) Spokane, WA Cathedral of Our Lady of Lourdes; Vocation Director.
Connaughton, James '50 (MIA) Retired.
Connaughton, Rev. Msgr. Lawrence M. '70 (NY) New York, NY St. Stephen and Our Lady of the Scapular; New York, NY Chapel of the Sacred Hearts of Jesus and Mary.
Connealy, Gerald A. '87 (OM) Stanton, NE St. Peter.
Connell, Rev. Msgr. Andrew F. '51 (BO) Senior Priests. Retired.
Connell, James C. '87 (MIL) Vice Chancellor.
Connell, James E. '87 (MIL) Sheboygan, WI St. Clement; Sheboygan, WI Holy Name; Judges for Second Instance; Special Assignment.
Connell, John Andrew '81 (PAT) Randolph, NJ Resurrection.
Connell, John F. '62 (WOR) Retired.
Connell, John M. '85 (LR) Springdale, AR St. Raphael; Diocesan Consultors.
Connell, Kevin *s.j.* (SPK)[D] Spokane, WA Gonzaga Preparatory School.
Connell, Loren *o.f.m.* '76 (CIN)[M] Centerville, OH St. Leonard; [U] Centerville, OH St. Leonard Faith Community; [N] Cincinnati St. Francis Seraph Friary.
Connell, Mark J. '86 (NY)[HH] Chappaqua, NY Newburgh San Miguel Program.
Connell, Martin T. *s.j.* '94 (FgM) Chicago, IL Society of Jesus; [K] Detroit Detroit Province of the Society of Jesus–Provincial Office.
Connell, Patrick J. '92 (DET) Berkley, MI Our Lady of La Salette.
Connell, Rev. Msgr. William J. '76 (Y) Poland, OH Holy Family; Judges; Presbyteral Council.
Connell, William '75 (MAD) Clinton, WI St. Stephen.
Connelly, Rev. Msgr. Christopher D. '93 (SPR) Springfield, MA St. Michael's Cathedral; Vicar General and Moderator of the Curia; Bishop's Commission for Clergy; Bishop's Cabinet; Diocesan Consultors; Massachusetts Catholic Conference; Judges; Presbyteral Council; Diocesan Pastoral Council.
Connelly, Donald F. '58 (WIN) Retired.
Connelly, Edward C. '65 (BAL) Crofton, MD St. Elizabeth Ann Seton.
Connelly, Fidelis *c.p.* '50 (PMB)[H] North Palm Beach, FL Our Lady of Florida Spiritual Center.
Connelly, Rev. Msgr. James E. '55 (PH) Philadelphia, PA St. Monica Retired.
Connelly, Rev. Msgr. James N. '49 (BUF)[N] Tonawanda, NY O'Hara Residence Retired.
Connelly, James *c.s.c.* (FTW)[H] Notre Dame Congregation of Holy Cross, United States Province of Priests & Brothers.
Connelly, John J. '50 (BO) Newton, MA Sacred Heart; Dorchester, MA St. Ann.
Connelly, Laurence D. (GAL) Retired.
Connelly, Mark J. '87 (WIL) Lewes, DE St. Jude The Apostle.
Connelly, Peter *o.s.b.* '87 (WOR)[N] Still River, MA Benedictine Monks, St. Benedict Abbey.
Conner, Jacob Scott '10 (LKC) Lake Charles, LA St. Margaret; Presbyteral Council; [A] Lake Charles, LA St. Louis Catholic High School.
Conner, James *o.c.s.o.* '57 (L)[L] Trappist, KY Abbey of Our Lady of Gethsemani, of the Order of Cistercians of the Strict Observance.
Conner, Michael P. '85 (GLD) Kingsley, MI St. Mary.
Conner, Paul M. *o.p.* '67 (PRO)[O] Providence St. Thomas Aquinas Priory at Providence College.
Conner, Steven '94 (NEW) Ridgefield, NJ St. Matthew's; Southeast Bergen Region Deanery 6.
Conners, Quinn *o.carm.* '71 (WDC)[B] Washington, DC

Whitefriars Hall; Councilors.
Connerton, Rev. Msgr. Barry R.L. '70 (PRO) Providence, RI St. Augustine; Deans.
Connery, J. Thomas '63 (ALB) Priests Retirement Board/Priests Retirement Plan Board Retired.
Connery, Sean P. *o.s.f.s.* '71 (WIL) Elsmere, DE Veteran's Hospital; [B] Wilmington, DE Salesianum School.
Connery, Sean P. *o.s.f.s.* '71 (MO) DEPARTMENT OF VETERANS AFFAIRS HOSPITALS AND CHAPLAINS.
Connery, Thomas '83 (ORL) DeLand, FL St. Peter's Church; [G] Deland, FL Stetson University Catholic Campus Ministry.
Connery, Thomas '63 (ALB) Glenville, NY Immaculate Conception.
Connole, Marlin J. '68 (SEA) Retired.
Connolly, Andrew P. '56 (RVC) Patchogue, NY Retired.
Connolly, Brennan *o.f.m.* '56 (PAT)[N] Ringwood, NJ Holy Name Friary, Inc.
Connolly, Brian W. '55 (PIT) Retired.
Connolly, Charles B. *s.j.* '74 (BO)[U] Boston, MA Loyola House.
Connolly, Rev. Msgr. Clement J. '64 (LA) South Pasadena, CA Holy Family Retired.
Connolly, Edward B. '66 (ALN) Girardville, PA St. Joseph; Girardville, PA St. Vincent de Paul; Girardville – Court St. Cecilia #1529.
Connolly, Gerard M. *t.o.r.* '69 (ALT)[G] Hollidaysburg, PA St. Joseph Friary.
Connolly, James M.T. '78 (ALN) Military Chaplains.
Connolly, James P. '54 (NY) New York, NY St. John the Evangelist; Holy Name Society Archdiocesan Union of New York.
Connolly, Jerry '67 (GF) Retired.
Connolly, John G. '63 (BO) Senior Priests. Retired.
Connolly, John J. '94 (BO) Dorchester, MA St. Brendan; Boston, MA Holy Trinity.
Connolly, John T. '78 (PAT) Clifton, NJ Sacred Heart; Clifton, NJ SS. Cyril and Methodius; Deans; Advocates.
Connolly, Joseph F. *t.o.r.* '68 (VEN) Sarasota, FL Our Lady Queen of Martyrs.
Connolly, Joseph M. *c.s.s.* '57 (BO)[X] Waltham, MA Stigmatine Fathers and Brothers Retired.
Connolly, Joseph *s.v.d.* '60 (BO)[U] Duxbury, MA Society of the Divine Word.
Connolly, Joseph *t.o.r.* '68 (VEN) College of Consultors; Venice Diocesan Council of Catholic Women.
Connolly, K. Scott '95 (SEA) Bellingham, WA Assumption.
Connolly, Kevin '85 (WIN) Deans; Elected At–Large Representatives; Priest Assignments Committee; Diocesan Consultors.
Connolly, Kevin '85 (WIN) Rochester, MN Resurrection.
Connolly, Leo L. '81 (COL) Columbus, OH St. Cecilia; Deanery 5: West; Presbyteral Council; Diocesan Judges; Parochial Examiners.
Connolly, Mark '57 (BGP)[W] Greenwich, CT Clemons Productions, Inc.; Communications Retired.
Connolly, Michael C. *o.s.f.s.* '74 (WIL)[B] Wilmington, DE Salesianum School.
Connolly, Michael J. *s.j.* '68 (SPK)[B] Spokane, WA Gonzaga University.
Connolly, Michael J. *s.j.* '68 (BO)[U] Boston The Society of Jesus of New England–Provincial Offices.
Connolly, Michael '78 (NY)[DD] Yonkers, NY St. Clare Friary.
Connolly, Rev. Msgr. Neil A. '58 (NY) New York, NY St. Mary.
Connolly, Patrick *s.j.* '66 (LA)[C] Los Angeles, CA Jesuit Community.
Connolly, Paul '83 (DAV) DeWitt, IA St. Joseph's; Diocesan Consultors.
Connolly, Peter *c.ss.r.* (STP) Brooklyn Center, MN St. Alphonsus; [J] Brooklyn Center, MN Redemptorist Fathers of Hennepin County.
Connolly, Robert P. '79 (PIT) Burgettstown, PA Our Lady of Lourdes.
Connolly, Thomas '00 (SPK) Spokane, WA St. Charles.
Connolly, William J. *s.j.* '56 (BO)[U] Weston, MA Campion Health Center, Inc.
Connor, Brian P. '89 (LIN) Lincoln, NE North American Martyrs.
Connor, Charles P. '90 (SCR) On Duty Outside the Diocese; Censor Librorum; Diocesan Historian.
Connor, Charles P. (BAL)[A] Emmitsburg, MD Mount St. Mary's Seminary.
Connor, Gerald T. '54 (ROC) Retired.
Connor, J. Patrick '61 (NSH) Presbyteral Council Retired.
Connor, James L. *s.j.* '59 (BAL)[Q] Baltimore, MD Jesuit Community of Loyola University, Inc.
Connor, James '78 (HEL) Polson, MT Immaculate Conception; Ronan, MT Sacred Heart; Presbyteral Council; Personnel Board; [E] Polson, MT St. Joseph Medical Center.
Connor, John F. '64 (NEW) Newark, NJ Our Lady of Good Counsel Retired.
Connor, John M. *c.ss.r.* '65 (TR)[R] Long Branch, NJ San Alfonso Retreat House.
Connor, John *c.p.* '84 (PMB)[H] North Palm Beach, FL Our Lady of Florida Spiritual Center.
Connor, John *c.s.c.* (FTW)[H] Notre Dame Congregation of Holy Cross, United States Province of Priests & Brothers.
Connor, John '01 (DET)[F] Clarkston, MI Everest Academy.
Connor, Kevin T. '87 (MAN) Absent on Leave.
Connor, Martin P. '64 (BO)[CC] Hanover, MA League of Catholic Women of the Archdiocese of Boston; Hanover, MA St. Mary of the Sacred Heart; Senior Priests. Retired.
Connor, Martin *l.c.* '01 (ATL)[F] Alpharetta, GA Norcross Pastoral Center, Inc.
Connor, Patrick L. '83 (ROC) Addison, NY The Catholic Parish of Saints Isidore and Maria Torribia.
Connor, Patrick *s.v.d.* '57 (TR)[N] Bordentown, NJ Society of the Divine Word.
Connor, Robert A. (POD) South Orange.
Connor, Sean M. '01 (BO) Dorchester, MA St. Ann.
Connor, Vincent '71 (SB) Corona, CA Retired.
Connor, William Joseph '66 (LA) Retired.
Connors, Cletus *o.s.b.* '72 (SCL) Cold Spring, MN St. Boniface; [I] Collegeville, MN St. John's Abbey, of the Order of St. Benedict.
Connors, Edmund P. '66 (NY) Katonah, NY St. Mary of the Assumption.
Connors, Francis E. '73 (BUR) Island Pond, VT St. James the Greater.
Connors, John E. '01 (SPR) Northampton, MA Saint Elizabeth Ann Seton; Presbyteral Council.
Connors, John '01 (SPR)[M] Springfield, MA Smith College.
Connors, Martin *o.p.* '51 (NY)[EE] Hawthorne, NY Motherhouse & Novitiate of the Sisters of St. Dominic, Congregation of St. Rose of Lima.
Connors, Michael *c.s.c.* '84 (FTW)[B] University of Notre Dame Du Lac; [H] Notre Dame, IN Holy Cross Community, Corby Hall, University of Notre Dame.
Connors, Richard P. '79 (PH) Philadelphia, PA Nativity of the Blessed Virgin Mary.
Connors, Robert L. '71 (BO) Vicariate II; Watertown, MA St. Patrick; Presbyteral Council.
Connors, Rev. Msgr. Terrence L. '75 (MAD) Sun Prairie, WI St. Albert the Great; Elected; Personnel Board.
Conoboy, Shawn '06 (Y) Campbell, OH St. John the Baptist; Campbell, OH St. Joseph the Provider; Campbell, OH St. Lucy; Campbell, OH St. Rose of Lima.
Conole, Robert W. '91 (BO) Haverhill, MA Sacred Hearts.
Conoscenti, Frederick M. '65 (BUF) Retired.
Conover, James (TR) Freehold, NJ St. Rose of Lima.
Conrad, John F. '63 (GB) Retired.
Conrad, Sebastian *m.s.f.s.* '90 (TYL)[C] Whitehouse, TX The Missionaries of St. Francis de Sales.
Conrad, Simon *o.f.m.cap.* '46 (SAL)[D] Victoria, KS St. Fidelis Friary Retired.
Conroy, Donald B. '64 (WDC)[X] Washington, DC National Institute for the Family.
Conroy, Francis M. '64 (BO) Newton, MA Corpus Christi – St. Bernard; Senior Priests. Retired.
Conroy, J. Peter *s.j.* '71 (NY)[DD] Cornwall, NY Jogues Retreat Center.
Conroy, James R. *s.j.* '78 (BAL)[U] Baltimore, MD Ignatian Volunteer Corps.
Conroy, James *s.j.* '78 (BO) Towson, MD; [U] Newton, MA The Jesuit Community at Boston College.
Conroy, Kevin M. '82 (CLV) Released from Diocesan Assignment.
Conroy, Kevin M. '68 (FgM) Maryknoll, NY MARYKNOLL.
Conroy, Patrick J. *s.j.* '83 (WDC)[O] Washington, DC Leonard Neale House.
Conroy, Philip M. '64 (BO) Senior Priests. Retired.
Conry, Austin '65 (MOB) Coden, AL St. Rose of Lima.
Conry, Roy *o.carm.* '56 (TUC)[E] Tucson, AZ Carmelite Priory Retired.
Consani, Robert E. '59 (KAL) Kalamazoo, MI St. Monica.
Consani, Robert E. '63 (KAL) Retired.
Consemino, Angelo R. '84 (LUB) Floydada, TX St. Mary Magdalen.
Conserva, Stephen *o.m.i.* '74 (WDC)[O] Washington, DC Provincial Offices of the United States Province of the Missionary Oblates of Mary Immaculate.
Considine, James F. '02 (MET) Piscataway, NJ St. Frances Cabrini.
Considine, Matthew J. *s.m.m.* '77 (BRK)[R] Ozone Park, NY Montfort Missionaries Provincialate (Missionaries of the Company of Mary); Ozone Park, NY; Ozone Park, NY St. Mary Gate of Heaven.
Considine, William *s.m.m.* '73 (HRT)[U] Litchfield, CT Lourdes Shrine Guild, Inc.; [L] Litchfield, CT Montfort Missionaries; Counselors.
Consiglio, Cyprian *o.s.b.cam.* '98 (MRY)[F] Big Sur, CA New Camaldoli Hermitage.
Constant, Van '93 (HT) Army National Guard Chaplains; Gibson, LA Most Blessed Sacrament Faith Community.
Constantin, Rodrigue '03 (OLL) Mendota Heights, MN Holy Family Maronite Catholic Church.
Constantine, Bennett P. '58 (LAN) Eaton Rapids, MI St. Peter.
Constantine, Cyprian G. *o.s.b.* '77 (GBG)[A] Latrobe, PA St. Vincent Seminary; [H] Latrobe, PA Saint Vincent Archabbey.
Contadino, Eugene *s.m.* '70 (CIN) Cincinnati, OH St. Francis de Sales; [N] Cincinnati, OH De Sales Crossings Marianist Community.
Contardi, Michael *o.de.m.* '60 (CLV) Cleveland, OH St. Rocco.
Conte, James W. '48 (NY) Retired.
Conte, John P. '58 (ALN)[J] Bethlehem, PA Holy Family Villa Retired.
Conte, Rev. Msgr. John P. '64 (HRT) Consultors – Canon 1742; Madison, CT St. Margaret; Episcopal Vicars; College of Consultors; Ex Officio Members.
Contell, Andres Codoner '08 (NEW) Newark, NJ St. Columba's.
Conterno, Austin *s.d.b.* '48 (SFR) San Francisco, CA SS. Peter and Paul.
Conti, John P. '46 (NY) Retired.
Conti, Vincent G. *s.j.* '01 (WDC)[E] Washington, DC Gonzaga College High School; [O] Washington, DC The Jesuit Community of St. Aloysius Gonzaga.
Contons, Rev. Msgr. Albert J. '48 (BO) Senior Priests. Retired.
Contons, Rev. Msgr. Albert '48 (LIT) Lithuanian R. Catholic Priests' League of America.
Contran, Sergio *m.c.c.j.* '50 (LA)[BB] Covina, CA Comboni Mission Center.
Contreras, Arnulfo '05 (KC) Kansas City, MO Holy Cross.
Contreras, David '93 (AMA) Childress, TX Holy Angels; Memphis, TX Sacred Heart.
Contreras, David '93 (AMA) Advocates; Priests' Pension Plan Retirement Committee.
Contreras, Humberto E. '91 (RVC) Freeport, NY Our Holy Redeemer.
Contreras, Marcos A. Cepeda *m.n.m.* (ARE) Camuy, PR Our Lady of Asumption.
Contreras, Wilfredo '03 (MIA) Miami Beach, FL St. Patrick.
Contreras Tribaldo, Carlos Alberto (SJN) Trujillo Alto, PR Exaltacion de la Santa Cruz; [B] Trujillo Alto, PR Santa Cruz.
Conva, Matthias T. '62 (NEW) Paramus, NJ Our Lady of the Visitation Retired.
Converse, Brian J. '91 (NOR) Gales Ferry, CT Our Lady of Lourdes; Army National Guard Chaplains.
Converset, John Michael *m.c.c.j.* '71 (NEW) Newark, NJ St. Lucy's; [L] Montclair, NJ Comboni Missionaries of the Heart of Jesus (Verona Fathers).
Convertino, David I. *o.f.m.* (PAT)[Q] Paterson, NJ St. Anthony's Guild.
Convery, Paul C. *c.o.* '84 (PH)[Y] Philadelphia, PA The Philadelphia Congregation of The Oratory of St. Philip Neri; Philadelphia, PA St. Francis Xavier.
Conway, David '52 (WDC) Retired.
Conway, Dennis *m.c.c.j.* '68 (CHI)[N] La Grange Park, IL Comboni Missionaries.
Conway, Edward *o.f.m.cap.* '98 (NY) New York, NY St. John the Baptist.
Conway, Gerald W. '56 (WIN) Retired.
Conway, James '65 (SAT) Castroville, TX St. Louis.
Conway, Rev. Msgr. Jeffrey '73 (NY) Staten Island, NY Our Lady Star of the Sea.
Conway, John E. *m.m.* '73 (FgM) Maryknoll, NY MARYKNOLL.
Conway, Rev. Msgr. John L. '56 (GBG) Retired.
Conway, John T. '00 (ATL) Blue Ridge, GA St. Anthony.
Conway, Rev. Msgr. John T. '77 (PH) North Wales, PA Mary, Mother of the Redeemer.
Conway, John '69 (SFE) Retired.
Conway, Michael J. *s.d.b* (SP)[T] St. Petersburg, FL The Salesian Society of St. Petersburg, Inc.
Conway, Rev. Msgr. Michael '60 (PAT) Retired.
Conway, Michael *o.ss.t.* '73 (BAL)[Q] Diocese of Las Vegas, NV.
Conway, Michael *s.d.b.* '92 (SP)[B] St. Petersburg, FL St. Petersburg Catholic High School, Inc.
Conway, Michael *o.ss.t.* '73 (LAV) Las Vegas, NV St. Francis de Sales.
Conway, Richard C. '63 (BO) Dorchester, MA St. Peter; Dorchester, MA Blessed Mother Teresa of Calcutta; Dorchester, MA St. Ambrose; Dorchester, MA Holy Family.
Conway, Richard T. '83 (BO) Andover, MA St. Robert Bellarmine.
Conway, Robert R. '04 (CHL) Charlotte, NC St. Matthew.
Conway, Robert *c.pp.s.* '53 (CIN)[N] Carthagena, OH St. Charles Retired.
Conway, Thomas E. *o.f.m.* (TR) Brant Beach, NJ St. Francis of Assisi.
Conway, Thomas S. '86 (BLX) Hattiesburg, MS St. Thomas Aquinas; University of Southern Mississippi; [F] Hattiesburg, MS University of Southern Mississippi; Defenders of the Bond; Deans; Campus Ministry; Trustees; Presbyteral Council.

Conway, Thomas '86 (JKS) Trustees.
Conway, Thomas *o.f.m.* '05 (WDC)[B] Silver Spring, MD Holy Name College.
Conway, William '77 (JOL) Downers Grove, IL Divine Savior.
Conwell, Joseph *s.j.* (SPK)[B] Spokane, WA Gonzaga University.
Conwill, Giles '73 (SD) On Duty Outside the Diocese.
Conwill, Giles '73 (NO)[C] New Orleans, LA Xavier University of Louisiana.
Conyard, James R. *s.j.* '62 (SPK)[B] Spokane, WA Gonzaga University.
Conyers, Richard *c.s.c.* '69 (CHI) Chicago, IL Queen of All Saints Basilica; [D] Niles, IL Notre Dame College Prep.
Conyers, Richard *c.s.c.* (FTW)[H] Notre Dame Congregation of Holy Cross, United States Province of Priests & Brothers.
Coogan, Roch A. *o.f.m.* '54 (SP)[N] St. Petersburg, FL St. Anthony Friary Retired.
Coogan, Roch A. *o.f.m.* '54 (NY)[DD] New York Franciscan Friars, Holy Name Province Retired.
Coogan, Rev. Msgr. Thomas '97 (RVC) Bay Shore, NY St. Patrick's; Islip Deanery; Presbyteral Council.
Cook, Adrian L. '72 (MOB) Brewton, AL St. Maurice.
Cook, Brian J. '85 (CHL) Winston–Salem, NC St. Leo the Great.
Cook, Damien '99 (OM) Omaha, NE St. Peter; Deans; Deans.
Cook, Daniel '90 (GR) Faculties Suspended.
Cook, Rev. Msgr. Douglas '94 (ORG) Orange, CA Cathedral of the Holy Family; Judicial Vicar; Judges; Council of Priests; Consultors; Special Assignment; Office of Canonical Services.
Cook, Edward J. '67 (MIL) Milwaukee, WI Congregation of the Great Spirit.
Cook, John Joseph Mary *f.i.* '02 (SY)[Q] Maine, NY Mount St. Francis Hermitage, Inc.
Cook, Joseph T. '86 (CHI) Chicago Heights, IL St. Kieran.
Cook, Kevin A. '01 (FR) East Taunton, MA Holy Family; Vocations.
Cook, Michael J. '73 (WIL) Newark, DE Holy Family.
Cook, Michael L. *s.j.* '66 (SPK)[B] Spokane, WA Gonzaga University.
Cook, Rev. Msgr. Paul G. '59 (BAL) Cockeysville, MD St. Joseph; [T] Cockeysville, MD St. Joseph, Texas Endowment Trust.
Cook, Philip C. *o.s.a.* '97 (CHI)[N] Chicago, IL St. Augustine Friary.
Cook, Robert J. '65 (LC) Genoa, WI St. Charles Borromeo Retired.
Cook, Robert P. '03 (B) Vocations.
Cook, Robert P. '03 (B) Boise, ID Sacred Heart.
Cook, Robert W. '00 (CHY)[B] Lander, WY Wyoming Catholic College.
Cook, Robert *o.f.m.conv.* (PEO) Peoria, IL Holy Family.
Cook, Stephen M. '97 (KC) Kansas City, MO St. Peter's; Finance Council.
Cook, Thomas E. '97 (WIN) Moderator of the Curia; Wabasha, MN St. Felix; Wabasha, MN St. Agnes.
Cook, Thomas S. '88 (LA) Lompoc, CA La Purisima Concepcion.
Cook, Timon *o.f.m.* '50 (SFE)[H] Albuquerque, NM The Province of Our Lady of Guadalupe Retired.
Cook, Timothy R. '83 (STL) Ferguson, MO Blessed Teresa of Calcutta.
Cook, William G. '88 (NEW) East Orange, NJ Holy Name of Jesus.
Cooke, Christopher R. '06 (PH) Philadelphia, PA St. Martin of Tours; By Election.
Cooke, Rev. Msgr. Colman M. '65 (SP) Retired.
Cooke, Vincent M. *s.j.* '67 (NY)[DD] New York, NY St. Ignatius Loyola Residence.
Cookson, Edmund L. *m.m.* '65 (FgM) Maryknoll, NY MARYKNOLL.
Cool, Brian '93 (ROC)[N] Rochester, NY Catholic Newman Community at the University of Rochester; [N] Eastman School of Music Catholic Students Organization.
Cooley, John Edward '48 (LA) Retired.
Cooley, Stephen *o.carm.* '67 (LA)[P] Encino, CA Our Lady of Mount Carmel Priory.
Coolong, Raymond *s.m.* (SP) Tampa, FL Our Lady of Perpetual Help.
Coon, David N. '93 (SPC) Poplar Bluff Hospital Ministry; Doniphan, MO St. Benedict; Poplar Bluff, MO Sacred Heart.
Coon, John Clancy '01 (BEA) Diocesan College of Consultors; Port Arthur, TX St. James.
Coonan, Joseph A. '11 (WOR).
Coonan, Matthew M. '11 (FTW) Elkhart, IN St. Vincent de Paul.
Coonan, Robert J. '65 (SPR) Hatfield, MA Our Lady of Grace Parish; Deans.
Coonan, Terrence '11 (FTW)[C] South Bend, IN Saint Joseph's High School.
Cooney, David *s.d.s.* '67 (NSH) McMinnville, TN St. Catherine; Smithville, TN St. Gregory.
Cooney, Dennis J. '74 (VEN) Lehigh Acres, FL St. Raphael; Respect Life Department.
Cooney, Francis C. *m.s.* '69 (HRT) Hartford, CT Our Lady of Sorrows; [L] Hartford, CT Our Lady of Sorrows Rectory.
Cooney, Gerald '50 (FWT) Retired.
Cooney, Rev. Msgr. James J. '64 (BRK)[R] Douglaston, NY Bishop Mugavero Residence Retired.
Cooney, John M. '62 (HRT) Watertown, CT St. John the Evangelist; Waterbury Vicariate; Cursillo Movement, Archdiocesan Director of.
Cooney, Michael N. '75 (DET) Mount Clemens, MI St. Peter; Archdiocesan Vicars; Presbyteral Council; Advocates.
Cooney, Patrick *o.s.b.* '91 (MO) Air National Guard Chaplains.
Cooney, Patrick *o.s.b.* '91 (IND)[A] Saint Meinrad, IN Saint Meinrad School of Theology; [K] Saint Meinrad, IN St. Meinrad Archabbey; Defenders of the Bond.
Cooney, Robert F. *c.s.v.* '57 (CHI)[N] Arlington Heights, IL Viatorian Province Center–Clerics of St. Viator.
Cooney, Rev. Msgr. Roger P. '70 (COV) Fort Thomas, KY St. Thomas.
Cooney, Romaeus *o.carm.* '58 (ALB) Troy, NY Holy Trinity; Troy, NY St. Joseph.
Cooney, Sean K. '59 (ORL) Retired.
Cooney, Stephen A. '76 (LIN) Health Care Facilities.
Cooney, Theophane *c.p.* '52 (BRK) Jamaica, NY Immaculate Conception; [R] Jamaica, NY Immaculate Conception Monastery.
Cooney, Thomas *c.s.c.* (FTW)[H] Notre Dame, IN Congregation of Holy Cross, United States Province of Priests & Brothers.
Cooney, Xavier *s.v.d.* '83 (WH) Summersville, WV St. John The Evangelist.
Cooper, David E. '70 (MIL) Milwaukee, WI St. Matthias.
Cooper, Donald A. '53 (NEW) Retired.
Cooper, Donald J. '63 (E) Retired.
Cooper, James W. '80 (LIN) Osceola, NE St. Vincent Ferrer; Advocates.
Cooper, Jeffrey *c.s.c.* (FTW)[H] Notre Dame Congregation of Holy Cross, United States Province of Priests & Brothers.
Cooper, Jeffrey *c.s.c.* '94 (P)[B] University of Portland; [L] Portland, OR Holy Cross Fathers & Brothers, C.S.C. – University of Portland.
Cooper, John A. '80 (LIN)[E] Lincoln, NE Bonacum House Retired.
Cooper, Joseph M. '95 (MAN) Hudson, NH St. Kathryn; Priest Personnel Board.
Cooper, Leo '43 (KCK) Retired.
Cooper, Mark A. *o.s.b.* '76 (MAN)[K] Manchester, NH St. Anselm Abbey.
Cooper, Michael W. *s.j.* '73 (CHI)[N] Chicago Chicago Province of the Society of Jesus–Provincial Office.
Cooper, Michael *s.j.* '73 (SP)[A] Saint Leo, FL Saint Leo University, Office of Assessment and Institutional Research.
Cooper, Patrick E. '91 (CHR) Mauldin, SC St. Elizabeth Ann Seton.
Cooper, Robert T. '07 (NO) Covington, LA St. Peter.
Cooper, Ronald C. '83 (CIN) Priests On Administrative Leave.
Cooper, Warren L. '71 (NO) Deans; Ministry to Sick Priests; Blue Army of Our Lady of Fatima; River Ridge, LA St. Matthew the Apostle; On Special Assignment.
Coopmans, Joseph R. *o.praem.* '81 (GB)[J] De Pere, WI St. Norbert Abbey.
Copeland, Leonard R. *o.c.d.* '67 (MIL)[H] West Allis, WI Mary Queen of Saints Catholic Academy; West Allis, WI Holy Assumption.
Copeland, Leonard *o.c.d.* '67 (BO)[U] Boston, MA Carmelite Monastery.
Copeland, Robert F. '99 (LAN) Flint, MI St. Pius X.
Copelin, Boniface T. *o.s.b.* '08 (OKL)[I] Shawnee, OK St. Gregory's Abbey.
Copenhaver, John L. '88 (LIN) McCook, NE St. Patrick.
Copp, Rodney J. '73 (BO) Waltham, MA St. Charles Borromeo; Trustees; Pontifical Society of Saint Peter the Apostle; Promoter of Justice; Defenders of the Bond; Canonical Affairs Committee; [CC] Braintree, MA Pontifical Mission Societies in the Archdiocese of Boston.
Coppenrath, Rev. Msgr. Leonard A. '53 (BO) Senior Priests. Retired.
Coppinger, Edmund '59 (OAK) Richmond, CA St. Cornelius Retired.
Coppinger, John W. *s.a.* '72 (NY)[DD] Garrison, NY Franciscan Friars of the Atonement; [DD] Garrison, NY St. Christopher's Friary.
Coppola, Anthony '02 (SP) Pinellas Park, FL Sacred Heart.
Coppola, Vincent J. *c.s.c.* '01 (BUR) West Rutland, VT St. Bridget; West Rutland, VT St. Stanislaus Kostka.
Coppola, Vincent J. *c.s.c.* '01 (FTW)[H] Notre Dame Congregation of Holy Cross, United States Province of Priests & Brothers.
Cops, Augustin *o.f.m.cap.* '86 (MAD)[I] Madison, WI San Damiano Friary Retired.
Copsey, Robert A. '78 (SAC) Galt, CA St. Christopher.
Coral, Jose Tineo *c.s.c.* '07 (FTW)[H] Notre Dame Congregation of Holy Cross, United States Province of Priests & Brothers.
Corali, Serafino A. '47 (RVC)[N] Amityville, NY St. Pius X Residence Retired.
Corbally, Christopher *s.j.* '76 (TUC)[E] Tucson, AZ Jesuit Community of the Vatican Observatory.
Corbelli, Vincent F. *m.m.* '60 (FgM) Maryknoll, NY MARYKNOLL.
Corbett, Eugene J. *s.j.* '62 (SJ) Santa Clara Valley Medical Center; [M] Los Gatos, CA Sacred Heart Jesuit Center.
Corbett, John B. '56 (PIT) Pittsburgh, PA Retired.
Corbett, John Dominic *o.p.* '80 (WDC)[B] Washington, DC Dominican House of Studies.
Corbett, John F. '95 (NEW) Apostleship of the Sea; Elizabeth, NJ Our Lady of Fatima.
Corbett, Michael E. '54 (PBL) Retired.
Corbett, Robert L. '51 (STL) Retired.
Corbett, Rev. Msgr. W. Joseph '95 (ATL) Special or Other Archdiocesan Assignment; College of Consultors; Vicars General; Board of Directors.
Corbin, Raymond G. '04 (BUF) Cheektowaga, NY Infant of Prague; Roswell Park Memorial Institute.
Corbino, Thomas A. '72 (JOL) Lombard, IL St. Pius X.
Corbley, Timothy L. *i.v. dei* '93 (COS) Woodland Park, CO Teller County Catholic Community.
Corbo, Alfred P. '56 (CHI) Franklin Park, IL St. Gertrude Retired.
Corces, Pedro M. '88 (MIA) Miami, FL St. Timothy.
Corcione, Michael *o.f.m.* '01 (NY)[DD] St. Peter Friary.
Corciulo, Rev. Msgr. Cosimo '56 (SB) Retired.
Corcoran, Anthony J. *s.j.* (NO)[R] New Orleans Jesuit Provincial Office.
Corcoran, Brian '72 (SD) Encinitas, CA Saint John the Evangelist Catholic Parish Encinitas.
Corcoran, Edward G. '56 (CHI) Retired.
Corcoran, Frank '54 (JKS) Greenville, MS St. Joseph Retired.
Corcoran, John J. '55 (RVC) Center Moriches, NY St. John the Evangelist Retired.
Corcoran, Kevin J. (SY) Cazenovia, NY St. James.
Corcoran, Kevin '88 (SY)[T] Cazenovia, NY Cazenovia College Newman Center.
Corcoran, Kevin (PAT) Priest Secretary to the Bishop; Vice Chancellors.
Corcoran, Lawrence E. *s.j.* '63 (BO)[U] Weston, MA Campion Health Center, Inc.
Corcoran, Michael (BRK) Brooklyn, NY St. Ignatius.
Corcoran, Shawn D. (COL) Presbyteral Council.
Corcoran, Shawn D. '00 (COL) Chancellor; Columbus, OH St. Joseph Cathedral; College of Consultors; Bishop's Council; Diocesan Finance Council.
Corcoran, Stanley D. '90 (DAL) Retired.
Corcoran, T. Kevin '99 (PAT) Vocations Board; Special Assignment.
Corcoran, Thomas B. '98 (BO) Chelmsford, MA St. Mary.
Corcoran, William T. '81 (CHI) Oak Lawn, IL St. Linus; Deans.
Cordani, Raymond T. '11 (SPR) Holyoke, MA St. Jerome; Holyoke, MA Our Lady of Guadalupe.
Cordell, Hyacinth Marie *o.p.* '11 (PRO) Providence, RI St. Pius V; [O] Providence, RI St. Pius House.
Cordeno, Peter (ORL) Orlando, FL Holy Family.
Corder, Stephen *s.j.* '01 (ORG)[H] Orange, CA Loyola Institute for Spirituality; [I] Anaheim, CA Manresa Jesuit Residence.
Cordero, Carlos *o.s.a.* '99 (SJN)[C] Bayamon, PR Seminario Agustiniano Sto. Tomas De Villanueva; Bayamon, PR Ntra. Sra. de la Monserrate.
Cordero, Rev. Msgr. Faustino '71 (BRK) Brooklyn, NY St. Rocco.
Cordero, Martin G. '99 (LSC) Charismatic Renewal Liaisons; Jal, NM St. Cecilia; Diocesan Consultors; Presbyteral Council.
Cordero, Mert '74 (NEW) Ridgewood, NJ Our Lady of Mount Carmel; Ridgewood, NJ Valley Hospital.
Corderro, Luis '98 (STO) Turlock, CA Sacred Heart Church of Turlock (Pastor of).
Cordery, Robert J. '80 (MO) Air Force Reserve Chaplains.
Cordery, Robert J. '80 (BO) Military & VA Chaplains.
Cordes, Christopher L. '95 (JC) Kirksville, MO Mary Immaculate; IV. Kirksville; Board of Trustees; Priestly and Religious Vocations Committee; Senators.
Cordes, John '03 (KCK) Topeka, KS Our Lady of Guadalupe.
Cordier, Michael L. '02 (CIN) Milford, OH St. Elizabeth Ann Seton.
Cordisco, Philip *o.ss.t.* '60 (BAL)[Q] Diocese of Trenton, NJ.
Core, Jeffrey '11 (SPK) Walla Walla, WA Assumption of the Blessed Virgin Mary; Walla Walla, WA St. Francis of Assisi; Walla Walla, WA St. Patrick.
Coreas, Edwin A. '92 (GAL) Houston, TX Our Lady of St. John; Defenders of the Bond.
Corel, Joseph S. '00 (JC) Cursillo Movement; Ministry Formation; Priestly and Religious Vocations Committee.
Coria, Hector '11 (SAC) Carmichael, CA Our Lady of

the Assumption.
Coric, Christopher *o.f.m.conv.* '71 (BUF) Veterans Hospital; Lackawanna, NY Our Lady of Bistrica.
Coriden, James A. '57 (GRY) On Duty Outside the Diocese.
Corigliano, Anthony M. *c.s.s.* '55 (SPR) Springfield, MA Our Lady of Mt. Carmel.
Corkery, Daniel '55 (ALX) Hessmer, LA St. Martin of Tours Retired.
Corkery, Raymond *o.carm.* '59 (JOL)[K] Darien, IL Carmelite Carefree Retirement Village Retired.
Corl, Ronald *c.p.* '66 (DET)[P] Detroit, MI St. Paul of the Cross Passionist Retreat; [K] Detroit, MI St. Paul of the Cross Community, Congregation of the Passion.
Corley, Joseph M. '75 (PH) Darby, PA Blessed Virgin Mary.
Corley, Malachy *o.c.s.o.* '55 (ATL)[F] Conyers, GA The Monastery of the Holy Spirit.
Corley, Theodosius *o.f.m.cap.* '74 (NY) Yonkers, NY Sacred Heart.
Cormack, James *c.m.* '76 (STL) St. Louis, MO St. Catherine Laboure; Society of St. Vincent de Paul, Council of St. Louis.
Cormack, Michael J. '54 (SAC) Roseville, CA St. Rose of Lima Retired.
Cormier, Gregory P. '83 (LAF) Baldwin, LA Sacred Heart; Charenton, LA Immaculate Conception.
Cormier, Leo G. '57 (BO) Senior Priests. Retired.
Cormier, Michael Robert '00 (SP) Port Richey, FL St. James the Apostle; Vicars Forane.
Cormier, Robert J. '82 (NEW) Newark, NJ St. Rose of Lima; Newark, NJ Northern State Prison.
Cormier, Roger C. '61 (BO) Senior Priests. Retired.
Cormier, William N. '71 (WOR) Douglas, MA St. Denis.
Cornea, Sergiu '96 (ROM) Aurora, IL Ss. Peter and Paul Church.
Corneille, Cecil C. '95 (MO) Army National Guard Chaplains.
Corneille, Cecil '95 (STV) On Duty Outside the Diocese.
Cornejo, Martin *o.f.m.* '01 (LSC) Garfield, NM San Isidro.
Cornejo, Quirino H. '91 (SAN) Fort Stockton, TX St. Agnes; Sanderson, TX St. James; Fort Stockton, TX St. Joseph's.
Cornejo, Vincent C. '56 (MET) Retired.
Cornejo–Castillero, Justino '05 (NEW)[A] Kearny, NJ Redemptoris Mater Archdiocesan Missionary Seminary.
Corneli, Luis R. *s.s.* '91 (BAL)[Q] Baltimore, MD St. Mary's Seminary & University.
Cornelia, Jose D. *d.s.* '99 (PHX) Scottsdale, AZ St. Bernadette Roman Catholic Parish.
Cornelio, Noel *p.i.m.e.* '03 (DET)[K] Detroit, MI P.I.M.E. Missionaries.
Cornelius, Jeffrey L. '04 (CLV) Absent on Leave.
Cornelius, Leonard *o.f.m.* '69 (PIT)[M] Pittsburgh, PA Holy Family Friary.
Cornelius, Rev. Msgr. William R. '58 (STU) Retired.
Cornell, Richard P. (BO) Ashland, MA St. Cecilia.
Cornely, Francis J. '48 (PH) Retired.
Cornett, David '85 (STU) Nelsonville, OH Holy Cross; Nelsonville, OH St. Mary of the Hills; [L] Nelsonville, OH Hocking Technical College; Presbyteral Council; College of Consultors.
Cornish, Ron '68 (KCK) Retired.
Cornwell, Malcolm *c.p.* '69 (SCR)[L] Scranton, PA Saint Ann's Passionist Monastery.
Corominas, John *c.m.f.* '49 (LA)[V] Rancho Dominguez, CA Dominguez Seminary Inc.
Corona, Andrew J. '93 (GRY) Portage, IN Nativity of Our Savior.
Corona, Dominic '10 (SP) St. Petersburg, FL St. Raphael; Elected Parochial Vicars.
Corona, Enrique '07 (PAT) Office of Multicultural Ministries; Chester, NJ St. Lawrence the Martyr.
Corona, Hector Miguel *m.sp.s.* '05 (SB) Indio, CA Our Lady of Perpetual Help.
Corona, John '71 (RNO) Retired.
Corona, Rev. Msgr. Michael J. '68 (MET) Raritan, NJ The Catholic Church of St. Ann; Department of Education; Catholic Scouting Apostolate; College of Consultors.
Coronado, Genero '51 (LA) Retired.
Coronado, Victorino B. *c.i.c.m.* '55 (CAM) Williamstown, NJ Our Lady of Peace Parish, Monroe Township, N.J.
Coronado–Arrascue, Rev. Msgr. Ricardo '90 (COS) Judicial Vicar and Chancellor; Judicial Vicar; Vicar for Religious; Presbyteral Council; Judicial Vicar and Chancellor; Chancellor and Judicial Vicar; College of Consultors; Team.
Coroztieta, Jose Madoz '53 (SJN) Retired.
Corpora, Joseph *c.s.c.* '84 (FTW)[H] Notre Dame Congregation of Holy Cross, United States Province of Priests & Brothers; [B] University of Notre Dame Du Lac; [H] Notre Dame, IN Holy Cross Community, Corby Hall, University of Notre Dame.
Corr, Rev. Msgr. John F. '51 (PAT) Retired.
Corradi, Frank '85 (LC)[D] Chippewa Falls, WI St. Joseph's Hospital.
Corrado, Dennis M. *c.o.* '70 (BRK) Brooklyn, NY St. Boniface; [R] Brooklyn, NY Oratory of Saint Philip Neri, Congregation Pontifical Rite; Brooklyn, NY.
Corral, Arturo '98 (LA) Los Angeles, CA St. Thomas the Apostle.
Corral, Jose M. '79 (SFR) San Francisco, CA St. Finn Barr; [S] Tiburon, CA Catholic Charismatic Movement.
Corral, Jose '66 (LA) Pasadena, CA St. Andrew.
Corral, Roberto *o.p.* '88 (OAK) Antioch, CA Most Holy Rosary.
Corrales, Alirio '78 (LAR) Laredo, TX Santa Margarita de Escocia; Ex Officio Members.
Corrales, Dominador F. '85 (SFR) San Mateo, CA St. Bartholomew.
Corrales–Diaz, Roger A. '02 (CHI) Berwyn, IL St. Leonard.
Correa, Fabio Correa '97 (OAK) Brentwood, CA Immaculate Heart of Mary.
Correa, Gino *o.f.m.* '76 (SFE)[H] Albuquerque, NM The Province of Our Lady of Guadalupe; Albuquerque, NM.
Correa–Garcia, Luis Norberto '04 (SJN) San Juan, PR Santa Maria de Los Angeles; Adjunct Vicars; Judges.
Correa–Roballo, Victor '89 (CHI) Chicago, IL St. Mary, Star of the Sea.
Corredor, Gustavo '91 (CHR) Batesburg–Leesville, SC St. John of the Cross.
Correia, Edward E. '68 (FR) Fall River, MA St. Joseph's; Fall River, MA St. Michael.
Correio, Bruce '85 (LA) Santa Barbara, CA St. Raphael.
Correz, Steven '00 (LA) Ventura, CA Our Lady of the Assumption.
Corriere, Basil *e.c.* '87 (STU)[H] Bloomingdale, OH Holy Family Hermitage.
Corrigan, Allen F. '82 (CLV) Richfield, OH St. Victor.
Corrigan, George C. *o.f.m.* '07 (SP) Tampa, FL Sacred Heart.
Corrigan, Gregory M. '86 (WIL) Wilmington, DE Wilmington Hospital; KAIROS Ministries, Inc.; Wilmington, DE Parish of the Resurrection.
Corrigan, Rev. Msgr. Hugh J. '63 (NY) Yonkers, NY Immaculate Conception; Yonkers, NY Our Lady of the Rosary.
Corrigan, J. David *s.j.* '65 (STL)[O] St. Louis, MO Jesuit Community Corporation at Saint Louis University – Jesuit Hall.
Corrigan, Michael T. (GAL) Retired.
Corriveau, Ernest *m.s.* '64 (LKC) Sulphur, LA St. Theresa.
Corriveau, Michel G. *c.p.m.* '05 (FR) Sturdy Memorial Hospital.
Corriveau, Real *o.m.i.* '61 (FgM) Washington, DC AMERICAN OBLATE MISSIONS.
Corriveau, Roger R. *a.a.* '74 (WOR)[N] Worcester, MA Assumptionists of Assumption College.
Corry, Francis J. '74 (NY) Bronx, NY St. Frances of Rome.
Corso, Charles W. *c.s.c.* '75 (FTW)[H] Notre Dame Congregation of Holy Cross, United States Province of Priests & Brothers.
Cortes, Antonio '96 (MRY) On Leave.
Cortes, Ariel '96 (TYL) Whitehouse, TX Prince of Peace; Deans; Priests' Personnel Board; Diocesan Christian Initiation Team; Presbyteral Council.
Cortes, Jesse '63 (LAV) Las Vegas, NV St. Bridget Roman Catholic Church.
Cortes, Jose Maria *f.s.c.b.* '95 (WDC) Lexington, MA; [O] Bethesda, MD Priestly Fraternity of the Missionaries of St. Charles Borromeo, Inc.
Cortes, Jose Maria *f.s.c.b.* '95 (BO)[U] Bethesda, MD House of Washington DC.
Cortes, Oscar '94 (RCK) McHenry, IL Church of Holy Apostles.
Cortes, Raul '62 (LA) Reseda, CA St. Catherine of Siena.
Cortes, Victor '96 (POD) Delray Beach.
Cortes, Victor '96 (MIA)[M] Miami, FL Prelature of the Holy Cross and Opus Dei.
Cortes, Victor '96 (PMB)[G] Delray Beach, FL Prelature of the Holy Cross and Opus Dei.
Cortes–Campos, Roberto J. '02 (WDC) Washington, DC Our Lady Queen of the Americas.
Cortese, Francis X. *o.praem.* '62 (PH)[Y] Paoli, PA Daylesford Abbey.
Cortese, Patrick S. '48 (SCR) Retired.
Cortese, Richard A. '82 (MEM) Memphis, TN St. James.
Cortez, Edil Calero *s.j.* (CHI)[C] Chicago, IL Jesuit Community at Loyola University Chicago.
Cortez, Fernando '77 (OAK) Hayward, CA All Saints.
Cortez, Jose '73 (TYL) Jacksonville, TX Our Lady of Guadalupe; Rusk, TX Hodge Unit and Skyview Unit, Texas Department of Criminal Justice; Auditor.
Cortez, Ramiro *o.m.i.* '70 (GAL) Houston, TX Immaculate Heart of Mary.
Cortinovis, Charles '09 (WDC) Rockville, MD St. Raphael.
Coruna, Roberto '77 (MET) Bloomsbury, NJ Church of the Annunciation; Filipino Apostolate.
Coryer, Francis J. '82 (OG) Charismatic Renewal.
Corzo, Wilson O. '98 (FTW) Ligonier; Ligonier, IN St. Patrick.
Corzo, Wilson '98 (FTW) Presbyteral Council.
Cos, Rafael '82 (MIA) Hialeah, FL St. John the Apostle.
Cosby, Rev. Msgr. R. Roy '54 (ARL) Retired.
Coschignano, Joseph C. '69 (RVC) Bellmore, NY St. Barnabas the Apostle.
Cosentino, Jack '70 (FAR) Venice, FL Epiphany Cathedral Retired.
Cosgrove, Edward *c.ss.r.* '55 (STL)[O] Liguori, MO St. Clement Health Care Center.
Cosgrove, Francis J. '65 (JKS) Meridian, MS St. Patrick; Meridian, MS St. Joseph; East Mississippi State Hospital; Priests' Council; Diocesan Consultors; Approved Advocate and Auditors.
Cosgrove, Jerome P. '63 (SC) Judges; Presbyteral Council Retired.
Cosgrove, Joseph J. '92 (BAL) Edgewater, MD Our Lady of Perpetual Help.
Cosgrove, Rev. Msgr. Joseph '60 (LA) Retired.
Cosgrove, William B. '74 (NY)[HH] Scarsdale, NY Catholic Charismatic Renewal Office; Canon 1742 Panel of Pastors; Charismatic Renewal Office; New City, NY St. Augustine.
Cosgrove, William P. '99 (BIS) Retired.
Cosgrove, William P. '99 (TUC) Patagonia, AZ Saint Therese of Lisieux Roman Catholic Parish – Patagonia.
Cosgrove, William '55 (ROC) Retired.
Cosmic, John J. '90 (OG) Carthage, NY St. James Minor Retired.
Coss, John *f.m.s.i.* '56 (BO)[B] Framingham, MA Sylva Maria; Framingham, MA.
Cossavella, Anthony J. '81 (PH) West Chester, PA St. Agnes.
Cossette, Raymond '55 (DUL) Retired.
Costa, Anthony J. '90 (PH)[A] Wynnewood, PA Theological Seminary of St. Charles Borromeo, Overbrook.
Costa, Caetano F. '64 (RVC) Deer Park, NY SS. Cyril and Methodius.
Costa, Carl A. *m.m.* '71 (FgM) Maryknoll, NY MARYKNOLL.
Costa, David A. '85 (FR) North Attleboro, MA St. Mary's; North Attleboro, MA Sacred Heart; [B] Attleboro, MA Bishop Feehan High School.
Costa, Edson Fernando '05 (NEW) West Orange, NJ Our Lady of Lourdes.
Costa, Eugene *o.de.m.* '74 (BUF)[N] Le Roy, NY Order of the BVM of Mercy/Mercedarian Friars; [N] Le Roy, NY St. Raymond Nonnatus Novitiate.
Costa, Gabriel B. '79 (NEW)[B] Seton Hall University; Minister for Priests.
Costa, Lucas Torrell deAlmeida *o.s.b.* '67 (GBG)[H] Latrobe Saint Vincent Archabbey; [H] Latrobe, PA Saint Vincent Archabbey.
Costa, Thomas C. '78 (RVC) Hicksville, NY Our Lady of Mercy; Procurator & Advocates.
Costa, Thomas E. '05 (FR) Cape Cod Hospital.
Costales, Frederick A. *m.s.* '02 (SB)[I] Moreno Valley, CA Missionaries of Our Lady of La Salette, MS.
Costantino, Joseph S. *s.j.* '87 (NY) New York, NY St. Francis Xavier; [DD] New York, NY Xavier Jesuit Community.
Costanza, Jared J. '99 (PRO) Bristol, RI St. Elizabeth.
Costanzo, John J. '64 (PBL) Retired.
Costello, Andrew *c.ss.r.* '65 (BAL) Annapolis, MD St. Mary.
Costello, Bernard B. '63 (PIT)[M] Pittsburgh, PA Cardinal Dearden Center Retired.
Costello, Brian L. '00 (SFR) San Francisco, CA Star of the Sea; Archdiocesan Board of Education.
Costello, Coleman J. '67 (BRK)[R] Douglaston, NY Bishop Mugavero Residence; Flushing, NY St. Mel Retired.
Costello, Daniel F. '98 (CHI) Chicago, IL St. Thomas of Canterbury.
Costello, David '95 (FgM) Boston, MA St. James the Apostle, Inc.
Costello, David *o.c.d.* '62 (SR)[L] Oakville, CA Carmelite House of Prayer.
Costello, David '95 (BO)[U] Boston, MA The Society of St. James the Apostle, Inc.
Costello, Edward *o.f.m.conv.* '61 (NY)[DD] Staten Island, NY St. Francis Friary.
Costello, Frank B. *s.j.* '52 (SPK)[B] Spokane, WA Gonzaga University Retired.
Costello, James J. *s.j.* '66 (STL) St. Louis, MO St. Francis Xavier; [O] St. Louis, MO Jesuit Community Corporation at Saint Louis University – Jesuit Hall.
Costello, James *s.j.* '66 (STL)[C] Saint Louis University.
Costello, John F. '96 (VEN) Venice, FL Epiphany Cathedral.
Costello, John J. '89 (BRK) Released from Diocesan Assignment; Jamaica, NY St. Nicholas of Tolentine.
Costello, John J. *c.s.sp.* '54 (PIT)[O] Bethel Park, PA The Spiritan Center.
Costello, Rev. Msgr. John M. '72 (STL) Kirkwood, MO St. Peter.
Costello, John M. *s.j.* '84 (NY)[DD] New York, NY Murray–Weigel Hall; [E] Bronx, NY Fordham Preparatory School.

Costello, Mark Joseph *o.f.m.cap.* '91 (CHI)[N] Chicago, IL St. Clare Friary; Detroit, MI.
Costello, Robert B. '53 (BO) Senior Priests. Retired.
Costello, Robert T. *s.j.* '63 (STL)[O] St. Louis, MO Jesuit Community Corporation at Saint Louis University – Jesuit Hall.
Costello, Ted '85 (SP) Clearwater, FL St. Michael The Archangel.
Costello, Vincent F. '76 (CHI) Deerfield, IL Holy Cross.
Costello, William J. '64 (CHI) Retired.
Costello, William M. '74 (FR) Seekonk, MA Our Lady of Mt. Carmel.
Coster, Henry G. *s.j.* '59 (ALN)[A] Wernersville, PA Jesuit Center–Jesuit Community.
Costigan, Christopher M. '08 (RVC) Levittown, NY St. Bernard.
Costigan, George (PAT) Retired.
Costigan, James P. *c.p.m.* '02 (OWN)[F] Auburn, KY Fathers of Mercy.
Costigan, Rev. Msgr. P. James '68 (SAV) Savannah, GA St. Peter the Apostle Church; Savannah Deanery.
Costigan, Richard F. *s.j.* '64 (STL)[O] St. Louis, MO Jesuit Community Corporation at Saint Louis University – Jesuit Hall.
Cotant, Charles *c.ss.r.* '41 (FgM) Denver, CO Denver Province.
Cote, David P. '68 (PRT) Madawaska, ME Notre Dame du Mont Carmel Parish; Van Buren, ME Saint Peter Chanel Parish.
Cote, Duaine '62 (FAR)[I] Fargo, ND Cursillo Movement; Fargo, ND Sts. Anne & Joachim Church of Fargo Retired.
Cote, E. Joseph '69 (BAL)[R] Baltimore, MD The School Sisters of Notre Dame Atlantic–Midwest Province.
Cote, E. Joseph J. '69 (BAL) Special Assignment.
Cote, Gerald M. '56 (TUC) Retired.
Cote, Mark '04 (JOL) Wheaton, IL St. Michael.
Cote, Norman J. '58 (OG) Retired.
Cote, Normand C. '58 (OG) Rouses Point, NY St. Joseph; Plattsburgh, NY The Roman Catholic Church of St. John the Baptist Retired.
Cote, Paul E. '71 (PRT) Special or Other Diocesan Assignment.
Cotone, Michael *o.s.c.* '74 (PHX)[F] Phoenix, AZ Crosier Provincial House Province of St. Odilia.
Cotta, Rev. Msgr. Myron J. '87 (FRS) On Special Assignment; Diocesan Consultors; Finance Committee; Holy Childhood Association; Personnel Board; The Society for the Propagation of the Faith/The Society of St. Peter Apostle; Continuing Formation of Priests; Diocesan Administrator.
Cotta, Rev. Msgr. Myron '87 (FRS) Deposit and Loan Fund.
Cotter, George C. *m.m.* '60 (NY)[DD] Maryknoll Maryknoll Fathers and Brothers.
Cotter, John F. '80 (SAG) Territorial Vicars; Gladwin, MI Sacred Heart.
Cotter, Lawrence E. '52 (OG) Defenders of the Bond; Censor Librorum Retired.
Cotter, Pius *o.f.m.cap.* '88 (GB) Brussels, WI St. Francis–St. Mary Parish.
Cotter, Raymond C. '86 (GLD) Acme, MI Christ the King.
Cotter, Robert L. '47 (OG) Judges Retired.
Cotter, Vincent '83 (OAK) Concord, CA St. Agnes.
Cotton, Charles E. '73 (COL) Columbus, OH St. Elizabeth.
Cottrell, James '68 (SP) Retired.
Coucelo, Andres '68 (MIA) Retired.
Coughlan, Rev. Msgr. Michael J. '52 (SD) Retired.
Coughlan, Robert '90 (SFE) Retired.
Coughlin, Bernard J. *s.j.* '55 (SPK)[B] Spokane, WA Gonzaga University.
Coughlin, Rev. Msgr. Daniel P. '60 (CHI) Retired.
Coughlin, Edward J. *s.j.* '74 (NY)[DD] Cornwall, NY Jogues Retreat Center.
Coughlin, James K. *s.j.* '99 (ROC)[B] Rochester, NY McQuaid Jesuit High School.
Coughlin, John C. *o.f.m.* '02 (BUF)[P] West Clarksville, NY Mount Irenaeus, Franciscan Mountain Retreat & Holy Peace Friary; [Q] St. Bonaventure, NY St. Bonaventure University.
Coughlin, John J. *o.f.m.* (FTW)[B] University of Notre Dame Du Lac.
Coughlin, John *o.f.m.* '83 (NY)[DD] New York Franciscan Friars, Holy Name Province.
Coughlin, Kenneth F. '90 (LAN) Grand Blanc, MI Holy Family.
Coughlin, Paul E. '66 (PRT) Retired.
Coughlin, Paul F. '91 (BO) Medford, MA St. Raphael.
Coughlin, Thomas '77 (HON) On Duty Outside the Diocese.
Coughlin, Thomas *o.p.miss.* '77 (SAT) Deaf and Hard of Hearing Ministry; [B] San Antonio, TX Dominican Missionaries for the Deaf Apostolate House of Studies; [S] San Antonio, TX Deaf Ministry of San Antonio; Deaf Community.
Coughlin, Thomas *o.m.i.* '70 (LA) San Fernando, CA St. Ferdinand.
Coughlin, William D. '66 (BO) Wakefield, MA Most Blessed Sacrament; Members.
Couhig, Michael D. *c.s.c.* '80 (FTW)[H] Notre Dame Congregation of Holy Cross, United States Province of Priests & Brothers.
Couhig, Michael *c.s.c.* '80 (AUS) Austin, TX St. Ignatius Martyr.
Coulter, Gary '99 (LIN) Ashland, NE St. Mary's; Catholic Lawyers Guild; Promoters Justitiae; Defensores Vinculi.
Coulter, Lawrence W. '86 (GI) Priests' Pension and Welfare Board Retired.
Coulthard, Gregory *s.d.s.* '67 (GB)[J] New Holstein, WI Salvatorian Public Relations.
Coulthard, Gregory *s.d.s.* '67 (FgM) Milwaukee, WI SALVATORIAN MISSIONS.
Counce, Paul D. '79 (BR) Baton Rouge, LA St. Joseph Cathedral; Judicial Vicar; College of Consultors; Presbyteral Council.
Courier, Rick L. '85 (MAR) Escanaba, MI St. Thomas the Apostle; Escanaba, MI St. Anthony.
Cournoyer, Alfred C. '85 (SPR) On Duty Outside the Diocese.
Cournoyer, Michael R. '98 (ALB) Leave of Absence.
Courteau, Allen *o.m.i.* '76 (FgM) Washington, DC AMERICAN OBLATE MISSIONS.
Courtemanche, Normand L. '65 (PRO) Retired.
Courtney, Patrick E. '87 (LFT) Unassigned.
Courtney, Scott M. '00 (LIN) Steinauer, NE St. Anthony; Advocates.
Courtright, Lawrence P. '61 (TLS) Retired.
Courtright, Raymond P. '92 (FAR) Fargo, ND St. Anthony of Padua's Church of Fargo; Continuing Education of Priests.
Courville, Carl James '74 (GAL) Pearland, TX St. Helen.
Courville, Rev. Msgr. J. Douglas '76 (LAF) Berwick, LA St. Stephen.
Courville, Robert '63 (LAF) Retired.
Coury, Charles *c.ss.r.* '76 (FgM) Baltimore Province.
Coury, Paul *c.ss.r.* '72 (TUC)[G] Tucson, AZ Redemptorist Society of Arizona Redemptorist Renewal Center.
Coury, Philip J. *c.m.* '71 (STL)[O] St. Louis, MO Lazarist Residence.
Cousens, Dennis L. '77 (L) Radcliff, KY St. Christopher.
Cousineau, Robert H. *s.j.* '60 (NY)[DD] Loyola Hall, Jesuit Community.
Cousins, John P. *o.f.m.cap.* '76 (COS)[H] Colorado Springs, CO Catholic Center at the Citadel; [E] Colorado Springs, CO Solanus Casey Friary.
Couterier, David *o.f.m.cap.* (BO) Pastoral Planning.
Coutinha, Paul *s.a.c.* '82 (DET)[K] Redford, MI Society of the Catholic Apostolate–Indian Province of the State of Michigan.
Coutinho, Absalom (PAT) Retired.
Couto, Nelson '79 (NY) Croton–on–Hudson, NY Holy Name of Mary.
Couto, Robert '96 (MAN) Londonderry, NH St. Jude.
Couture, Jeffrey W. '10 (BGP) New Fairfield, CT St. Edward the Confessor.
Couture, Paul E. *s.s.e.* '56 (BUR)[E] Colchester, VT Society of St. Edmund.
Couture, Roger *o.m.i.* '55 (NOR)[G] Willimantic, CT Missionary Oblates of Mary Immaculate; [I] Willimantic, CT Immaculata Retreat House.
Couture, Roland '53 (BO)[U] Lowell, MA Andre Garin Retirement Residence.
Couturier, David B. *o.f.m.cap.* (BO)[U] Jamaica Plain, MA St. Francis of Assisi Friary.
Couturier, George M. '81 (HRT) Glastonbury, CT St. Dunstan.
Covarrubias, Raul R. '83 (B) Idaho Falls, ID Blessed John Paul II Parish; Priest Retirement Committee; College of Consultors; Deans; Priest Personnel Commission.
Covarrubias–Pina, Salomon '91 (YAK) White Salmon, WA St. Joseph.
Coveney, James B. '64 (ALT) Retired.
Coveny, Richard C. '56 (BUF)[N] Lackawanna, NY Bishop Head Residence Retired.
Cover, Phillip B. '70 (LFT) On Duty Outside the Diocese.
Covert, Derek Scott '07 (LKC) On Duty Outside the Diocese.
Covert, Kevin (KAL) Dowagiac, MI Holy Maternity of Mary.
Covington, Charles L. '85 (AUS) Ecumenism.
Covington, Larry '85 (AUS) Austin, TX St. Louis.
Covos, Ruben '06 (SAN) Military Chaplains; Air Force Chaplains.
Cowan, George R. '65 (BRK)[R] Douglaston, NY Bishop Mugavero Residence Retired.
Cowan, Steven '99 (RIC) Unassigned.
Coward, Robert *c.p.* '68 (CHI)[N] Chicago Passionist Provincial Office.
Cowart, Conrad '96 (STA) Starke, FL St. Edward.
Cowell, Raymond '57 (CHI) Retired.
Cower, D. Craig '54 (RC) Retired.
Cowie, Donald *s.m.* '61 (SAT)[F] San Antonio, TX Central Catholic High School; [L] San Antonio, TX Central Catholic Marianist Community.
Cowles, James '86 (RIC) Gloucester, VA St. Therese, the Little Flower.
Cowles, Kristopher '11 (SFS) Pierre, SD SS. Peter and Paul.
Cox, Alan B. '76 (LFT) Retired.
Cox, Alonzo Q. '10 (BRK) Rosedale, NY St. Clare.
Cox, Bernard '91 (IND) Danville, IN Mary. Queen of Peace Catholic Church, Danville, Inc.
Cox, Christopher *c.s.c.* '99 (FTW)[H] Notre Dame Congregation of Holy Cross, United States Province of Priests & Brothers; [H] Notre Dame Congregation of Holy Cross, United States Province of Priests & Brothers.
Cox, Rev. Msgr. Craig A. '78 (LA) Co Chairmen; [A] Camarillo, CA St. John's Seminary.
Cox, Rev. Msgr. David D. '81 (JC) Jefferson City, MO Immaculate Conception; Diocesan Consultors; Priestly and Religious Vocations Committee.
Cox, Francis '50 (WCH) Retired.
Cox, Rev. Msgr. Gregory A. '76 (LA) Los Angeles, CA St. Anastasia; [X] Los Angeles, CA Catholic Charities of Los Angeles, Inc.; [X] Los Angeles, CA Central Administrative Offices; Executive Director; Members; [BB] Los Angeles, CA Opus Caritatis, Inc.; Cardinal McIntyre Fund for Charity Board of Directors.
Cox, Rev. Msgr. Gregory (SAC)[N] Sacramento, CA Catholic Charities of California, Inc.
Cox, James M. '98 (PH) Philadelphia, PA Holy Cross; Philadelphia, PA St. Madeleine Sophie.
Cox, Rev. Msgr. James '51 (NY) Retired.
Cox, John T. *o.m.i.* '87 (MIA) Miami, FL Holy Redeemer.
Cox, Joseph C. '46 (MAD) Retired.
Cox, Joseph *o.s.b.* '91 (IND)[K] Saint Meinrad, IN St. Meinrad Archabbey.
Cox, Michael '10 (FRS) Merced, CA Our Lady of Mercy/St. Patrick's; Planada, CA Sacred Heart.
Cox, Paul '54 (ALB) Warrensburg, NY St. Cecilia; Ministers to Retired Priests Retired.
Coy, Richard D. '00 (MEM) College of Consultors; Presbyteral Council Retired.
Coy, William J. *m.m.* '55 (NY)[DD] Maryknoll Maryknoll Fathers and Brothers Retired.
Coyle, Arthur M. (BO) Ex Officio; Merrimack Region; Lowell, MA St. Rita; College of Consultors; Presbyteral Council.
Coyle, Dan '89 (FRS) Bakersfield, CA Sacred Heart.
Coyle, Rev. Msgr. Edward J. '80 (ALN) Bally, PA Most Blessed Sacrament; Army National Guard Chaplains.
Coyle, Eugene P. '54 (BRK)[R] Douglaston, NY Bishop Mugavero Residence Retired.
Coyle, Patrick J. *s.m.* '45 (SFR)[N] San Francisco, CA Marist Center of the West Retired.
Coyle, Patrick P. *ss.cc.* '61 (LA)[P] La Verne, CA Congregation of the Sacred Hearts of Jesus and Mary Retired.
Coyle, Rev. Msgr. Robert J. '91 (RVC) Mineola, NY Corpus Christi; Navy Reserve Chaplains.
Coyle, Thomas J. '70 (MAD) Jefferson, WI St. John the Baptist; Sullivan, WI St. Mary Help of Christians; Jefferson, WI St. Lawrence.
Coyne, Edwin J. '62 (BGP) Retired.
Coyne, Emmett A. '66 (MAN) Retired.
Coyne, Rev. Msgr. George R. '59 (STU) Presbyteral Council; College of Consultors Retired.
Coyne, Gregory '89 (POD)[V] Washington, DC Tenley Study Center; Washington.
Coyne, James P. '75 (SEA) Covington, WA St. John the Baptist; Deans; Presbyteral Council.
Coyne, Liam '98 (ATL) Fort Oglethorpe, GA St. Gerard Majella.
Coyne, Martin P. *s.j.* '66 (FgM) Chicago, IL Society of Jesus.
Coyne, Rev. Msgr. Michael J. '55 (CAM) Retired.
Coyne, Robert F. *m.m.* '83 (FgM) Maryknoll, NY MARYKNOLL.
Coyne, Ronald D. '73 (BO) Randolph, MA St. Mary.
Coyte, Thomas '74 (DEN) Denver, CO Holy Cross.
Coz, Richard T. *s.j.* '58 (SJ)[M] Los Gatos, CA Sacred Heart Jesuit Center.
Cozzens, Andrew H. '97 (STP)[A] Saint Paul, MN The Saint Paul Seminary; [C] St. Paul, MN University of St. Thomas.
Cozzens, Donald '65 (CLV) Retired.
Cozzi, Phillip M. '06 (ARL) Presbyteral Council.
Cozzini, Robert P. '60 (NEW)[L] Caldwell, NJ The Rev. Msgr. James F. Kelley Residence for Retired Priests Retired.
Cozzubbo, Gregory P. *c.m.* '84 (PH) Philadelphia, PA Immaculate Conception; [B] Philadelphia, PA St. Vincent's Seminary; [Y] Philadelphia Congregation of the Mission; Philadelphia, PA Eastern Province; Philadelphia, PA.
Crabb, John T. *s.j.* '79 (BO)[U] Boston The Society of Jesus of New England–Provincial Offices.
Crabb, John T. *s.j.* '79 (PRT)[H] Portland, ME Mercy Hospital.
Crable, John M. '53 (OG) Retired.
Craddock, Joseph F. '04 (PRO) Providence, RI Rhode Island Hospital; Cranston, RI St. Mark.

Crafts, George A. (POD) Providence; Cambridge.
Crafts, George '65 (PRO)[N] Providence, RI Prelature of the Holy Cross and Opus Dei.
Crager, Richard '85 (NEW) Elizabeth, NJ St. Anthony's.
Crager, Richard *s.d.b.* '85 (NY)[FF] Stony Point, NY Don Bosco Retreat Center and Marian Shrine.
Crahen, Daniel *o.m.i.* '71 (BO) Lowell, MA St. Patrick.
Craig, Anthony John '11 (DUL) Hibbing, MN Blessed Sacrament.
Craig, Bruce *s.d.b.* '74 (SP) Tampa, FL Mary Help of Christians; [P] Tampa, FL Mary Help of Christians Center.
Craig, Christopher A. '93 (IND) Madison, IN Prince of Peace Catholic Church, Madison, Inc.; Madison, IN Most Sorrowful Mother of God Catholic Church, Vevay, Inc.; [O] Madison, IN Hanover College; [C] Madison, IN Shawe Memorial Junior–Senior High School.
Craig, Dale *s.o.l.t.* '97 (CC)[G] Robstown, TX Society of Our Lady of the Most Holy Trinity.
Craig, David '96 (ATL) On Duty Outside the Archdiocese.
Craig, David '96 (LA) VA Long Beach Healthcare System.
Craig, Donald R. '74 (CHI) Chicago, IL St. Mary of Perpetual Help.
Craig, John V. *s.j.* '77 (STL)[O] St. Louis, MO De Smet Jesuit High School Community.
Craig, John V. *s.j.* '77 (KC)[J] Kansas City, MO Rockhurst Jesuit Community.
Craig, Patrick H. '05 (KAL) Decatur, MI Holy Family.
Craig, Paul *o.f.m.cap.* '66 (FgM) Detroit, MI Province of St. Joseph; [K] Detroit St. Bonaventure Friary.
Craig, Richard J. '61 (BO) Senior Priests. Retired.
Craig, Robert N. *o.f.m.cap.* '67 (MO) DEPARTMENT OF VETERANS AFFAIRS HOSPITALS AND CHAPLAINS.
Craig, Robert *o.f.m.cap.* '67 (PIT)[M] Pittsburgh, PA St. Augustine Friary; University Drive; H.J. Heinz III (Aspinwall); VA Pittsburgh Health Care System.
Craig, Rod L. '77 (FRS) Visalia, CA St. Mary; Visalia, CA Holy Family; Visalia, CA St. Thomas the Apostle.
Craig, Thomas '82 (FWT) Arlington, TX St. Vincent de Paul; Mission Council; Society for the Propagation of the Faith; Priests' Pension Plan Trustees; Holy Childhood Association; Mission Council; Presbyteral Council; Mission Outreach.
Craig, William R. *o.praem.* '55 (PH)[Y] Paoli, PA Daylesford Abbey.
Cramblitt, Rev. Msgr. Richard E. '72 (BAL) Hydes, MD St. John the Evangelist.
Cramer, David W. '91 (SCR) Great Bend, PA St. Lawrence; Susquehanna, PA St. Martin of Tours; Legion of Mary; Susquehanna, PA St. John the Evangelist.
Cramer, Donald W. '01 (HBG) Sunbury, PA St. Monica.
Cramer, Harry N. '84 (WH) Bridgeport, WV All Saints.
Cramer, Joseph '77 (KCK) Gardner, KS Divine Mercy; Archdiocesan Council of Catholic Women (ACCW).
Cramer, Terry A. '99 (ARL) Alexandria, VA Blessed Sacrament.
Cramer, William N. '77 (PAT) Absent on Leave.
Crane, Mark W. '05 (TR) Manalapan, NJ St. Thomas More.
Crane, Matthew '11 (SCL) St. Cloud, MN St. Anthony of Padua; St. Cloud, MN Holy Spirit; St. Cloud, MN St. John Cantius.
Crane, Rev. Msgr. Thomas E. '57 (BUF) Censors—Board of Diocesan Censors of Books and Vigilance for the Faith; [N] Tonawanda, NY O'Hara Residence Retired.
Cranor, Bernard *o.s.b.* '62 (SFE)[H] Abiquiu, NM Monastery of Christ in the Desert.
Crasta, Rudy '89 (LUB) Presbyteral Council; Diocesan Pastoral Liturgy Commission; Levelland, TX St. Michael's.
Crawford, Rev. Msgr. C. Slade '65 (PT) Retired.
Crawford, Cyril K. *o.s.b.* '07 (NO)[R] St. Benedict, LA St. Joseph Abbey.
Crawford, Douglas Y. '07 (NY) Poughkeepsie, NY St. Martin de Porres.
Crawford, John G. '63 (CLV) Parma, OH St. Francis de Sales Retired.
Crawford, Larry P. '66 (IND) Indianapolis, IN St. Gabriel the Archangel Catholic Church, Indianapolis, Inc.
Crawford, Richard E. '75 (PEO) Retired.
Crawford, Robert F. *m.m.* '61 (FgM) Maryknoll, NY MARYKNOLL.
Crawley, Richard *o.f.m.cap.* '10 (BUR) Pittsford, VT St. Alphonsus Liguori; Rutland, VT St. Peter.
Cray, David G. *s.s.e.* '72 (BUR) Charlotte, VT Our Lady of Mount Carmel; Hinesburg, VT St. Jude the Apostle.
Craycroft, Bernard L. '57 (L) Retired.
Creagan, Michael '97 (STP) West St. Paul, MN St. Joseph.
Creagan, Robert F. '88 (KAL) Portage, MI St. Catherine of Siena; Knights of Columbus; Diocesan Historian/Archivist; Pilgrimages.
Creagh, Kevin G. *c.m.* '96 (BUF)[N] Niagara University, NY Vincentian Community at Niagara University; [Q] Niagara University, NY Niagara University; [C] Niagara University, NY Niagara University.
Creagh, Richard C. '76 (CHI) Chicago, IL St. Gabriel.
Crean, Hugh F. '62 (SPR) Retired.
Creane, Anthony '56 (SPR) Retired.
Creary, Rev. Msgr. J. Edwin '73 (MEM) Germantown, TN Our Lady Of Perpetual Help; Defenders of the Bond.
Creason, Richard H. '67 (STL) St. Louis, MO Most Holy Trinity.
Creed, Peter M. '67 (RIC) Norge, VA St. Olaf, Patron of Norway.
Creed, Peter '67 (SY) On Duty Outside the Diocese.
Creed, William E. *s.j.* '71 (CHI)[C] Chicago, IL Jesuit Community at Loyola University Chicago.
Creeden, Brendan D. *o.s.b.* '78 (CHI)[N] Chicago, IL Monastery of the Holy Cross.
Creedon, Gerard '68 (ARL) Dale City, VA Holy Family.
Creedon, Joseph D. '68 (PRO) Kingston, RI Christ the King; [R] Kingston, RI University of Rhode Island Catholic Center.
Creegan, Kevin G. '01 (PEO) DePue, IL St. Mary's.
Cregan, David A. *o.s.a.* '99 (PH)[Y] Villanova, PA Fray de Leon Community; [C] Villanova University.
Cregan, Francis A. *o.a.r.* '95 (NY) Bronx, NY St. John's.
Cregan, John C. '87 (ARL) Alexandria, VA Blessed Sacrament; Bishop's Delegate for Retired Priests and Permanent Diaconate; Deans; Permanent Diaconate; Clergy Personnel Board.
Cregan, John J. '61 (CLV) Retired.
Cregan, Mark T. *c.s.c.* '83 (FR)[A] North Easton, MA Stonehill College; [A] North Easton, MA Holy Cross Fathers Religious; Prov. Councilors.
Cregan, Mark T. *c.s.c.* '83 (FTW)[H] Notre Dame Congregation of Holy Cross, United States Province of Priests & Brothers.
Crehan, Lawrence F. '74 (PH) Ardsley, PA Queen of Peace.
Crehan, Matthias J. *o.f.m.* '75 (MO) DEPARTMENT OF VETERANS AFFAIRS HOSPITALS AND CHAPLAINS.
Crehan, Matthias *o.f.m.* '75 (CIN)[N] Cincinnati St. Francis Seraph Friary.
Crehan, Matthias *o.f.m.* '75 (PHX) Phoenix, AZ United States Veterans Affairs Medical Center.
Creider, Philip B. '77 (OKL) Navy Chaplains; Special Assignment.
Creighton, Bernard R. *o.f.m.* '67 (PAT)[N] Butler, NJ St. Anthony Friary.
Creighton, Rev. Msgr. Edward '47 (SD) Retired.
Creighton, James J. *s.j.* '60 (CHI)[D] Chicago, IL St. Ignatius Jesuit Community; [J] Maywood, IL Loyola University Medical Center.
Creighton, Matthew E. *s.j.* '57 (DET)[K] Clarkston, MI Colombiere Center.
Cremaldi, Angelo '60 (LAF) Retired.
Cremin, Michael *s.a.c.* '83 (DET) Wyandotte, MI St. Elizabeth; Wyandotte, MI St. Joseph; Wyandotte, MI St. Patrick.
Cremins, John J. '69 (BRK) Forest Hills, NY Our Lady of Mercy Retired.
Cremonie, Louis D. '72 (HRT) Manchester, CT Manchester Memorial Hospital; Special and other Archdiocesan Assignment; East Hartford, CT St. Christopher.
Creson, Michael '87 (KNX) Chattanooga, TN Our Lady of Perpetual Help.
Crespin, George E. '62 (OAK) Richmond, CA St. Cornelius Retired.
Crespo, Charles '01 (STV) Carenage, VI Chapel of St. Anne; Hispanic Ministry; Diocesan Newspaper; [B] St. Thomas, VI Hispanic Ministry.
Cressman, Richard *s.d.b.* '80 (BO)[M] Salesian Staff.
Cretella, Joseph J. '10 (HRT) Tariffville, CT St. Bernard.
Crevcoure, Stuart '01 (TLS) Stillwater, OK St. John the Evangelist Parish and Newman Center; [I] Stillwater, OK St. John's University Parish and Catholic Student Center; Campus Ministry.
Crewe, Ronald O. '63 (MIL) Racine, WI St. Joseph; Racine, WI Sacred Heart Congregation.
Crews, Clyde F. '73 (L)[A] Bellarmine University.
Crews, John S. '71 (SR)[G] Sonoma, CA Hanna Boys Center; Diocesan Judges.
Cribben, Andrew G. *o.praem.* '94 (GB) Green Bay, WI St. Willebrord.
Cribben, Rev. Msgr. Philip J. '62 (PH) Newtown Square, PA St. Anastasia.
Cribbin, Austin J. '56 (BAK) Retired.
Cricchio, Santo *o.f.m.conv.* '91 (MO) Navy Reserve Chaplains.
Cricchio, Santo *o.f.m.conv.* (BRK) Brooklyn, NY Most Holy Trinity – Saint Mary.
Crilly, James F. *c.s.v.* '56 (CHI)[N] Arlington Heights, IL Viatorian Province Center–Clerics of St. Viator.
Crilly, Marc *o.s.b.* '93 (WOR)[N] Still River, MA Benedictine Monks, St. Benedict Abbey.
Crimmins, Rev. Msgr. Michael (NY) New York, NY St. Gregory.
Crino, Patrick M. (TUC) Tucson, AZ Saints Peter and Paul Roman Catholic Parish – Tucson; O.F.C. Members; Council of Priests; Vicars Forane; All Vicars Forane; Diocesan Building Committee.
Criqui, J. Kenneth '63 (KC) Carrollton, MO St. Mary's; Consultors; Deans.
Criscitelli, Anthony M. *t.o.r.* '80 (STP) Minneapolis, MN St. Bridget; [J] Minneapolis, MN St. Bridget Friary.
Criscuolo, Rev. Msgr. Salvatore A. '78 (WDC) Washington, DC St. Patrick; Special Ministries.
Crisman, James H. '01 (DEN) Director; Lakewood, CO Our Lady of Fatima.
Crisostomo, Abraham *o.f.m.conv.* '96 (CHI)[N] Chicago Conventual Franciscans of St. Bonaventure Province; Chicago, IL Province of Saint Bonaventure.
Crisostomo, Armando S. '93 (NEW) Jersey City, NJ St. Joseph.
Crisostomo, Michael '96 (AGN) Hagatna, GU Immaculate Heart of Mary; Catholic Campus Ministry, Newman Center, University of Guam; [H] Hagatna, GU Office of Youth, Young Adult & Campus Ministry; Archdiocesan Presbyteral Council; Youth and Young Adults Ministry.
Crisp, Michael L. '97 (SUP) Iron River, WI St. Peter; Iron River, WI St. Florian; Iron River, WI St. Michael; Iron River, WI SS. Peter and Paul.
Crisp, Robert R. '75 (DAL) On Leave of Absence.
Crispo, Roderick A. *o.f.m.* '55 (BO)[B] Chestnut Hill, MA Redemptoris Mater Archdiocesan Missionary Seminary.
Crispo, Roderick *o.f.m.* '55 (NY)[DD] Mount Vernon, NY St. Bernardine of Siena Friary; [DD] New York Franciscan Province of the Immaculate Conception.
Criste, Ambrose *o.praem.* '08 (ORG)[A] Silverado, CA St. Michael's Norbertine Postulancy, Novitiate and Juniorate; [I] Silverado, CA Norbertine Fathers of Orange Inc.
Cristina, Mark Mary *m.v.f.a.* '03 (BIR)[E] Birmingham, AL Franciscan Missionaries of the Eternal Word, A Public Association of the Christian Faithful.
Cristler, Richard F. '00 (TLS) Collinsville, OK St. Therese Church and Diocesan Eucharistic Shrine of Saint Therese.
Cristobal, Daniel *o.f.m.cap.* '59 (AGN)[H] Agana, GU Secular Franciscans.
Critch, Gerard F. '89 (VEN) Naples, FL St. Peter the Apostle; Presbyteral Council.
Crivello, Peter A. '93 (MRY) Monterey, CA Cathedral of San Carlos Borromeo; Special Assignment; Vicar General; Diocesan Consultors; Diocesan Consultors; Presbyteral Council.
Crkva, Odilo *o.s.b.* '53 (JOL)[L] Lisle, IL St. Procopius Abbey; Lisle, IL.
Croak, Rev. Msgr. David P. '66 (DEN) Retired.
Croak, Thomas *c.m.* '65 (CHI)[N] Chicago, IL Vincentian Community, Congregation of the Mission, Western Province.
Croce, Albert A. *c.s.c.* '50 (FR)[F] North Dartmouth, MA Holy Cross Residence Retired.
Croce, Albert A. *c.s.c.* '50 (FTW)[H] Notre Dame Congregation of Holy Cross, United States Province of Priests & Brothers.
Crochet, Barry F. '93 (LAF) New Iberia, LA Our Lady of Prompt Succor.
Crocker, John R. *s.j.* '61 (CHI)[D] Chicago, IL St. Ignatius Jesuit Community.
Croell, Benedict *o.p.* '98 (WDC)[B] Washington, DC Dominican House of Studies.
Croft, J. George *o.m.i.* '44 (BO) Tewksbury, MA St. William.
Crofut, Robert J. '72 (BGP) Norwalk, CT St. Thomas the Apostle; Parochial Examiners; Priest Vocation Advisory Board; Presbyteral Council.
Croghan, James P. *s.j.* '85 (NY)[E] New York, NY Regis High School; [DD] New York, NY Xavier Jesuit Community.
Croghan, John P. '75 (SY) Clinton, NY St. Mary; [T] Clinton, NY Hamilton College Newman Center.
Croglio, James C. '80 (BUF)[D] Buffalo, NY St. Joseph's Collegiate Institute.
Crohan, Robert F. *m.m.* '62 (NY)[DD] Retired.
Croisetiere, David N. '77 (SD) San Diego, CA Our Lady of Refuge Catholic Parish; Promoter of Justice.
Croke, Alfred M. '63 (NY) Livingston Manor, NY St. Aloysius; [DD] Bronx, NY John Cardinal O'Connor Residence Retired.
Crombie, Francis H. '68 (SPR) Springfield, MA St. Patrick's.
Cromley, Nathan *c.s.j.* '07 (PEO)[K] Princeville, IL Congregation of St. John.
Cron, Steven D. '78 (GR) Wyoming, MI St. Joseph The Worker.
Cronauer, Patrick T. *o.s.b.* '84 (GBG)[H] Latrobe, PA Saint Vincent Archabbey; [A] Latrobe, PA St. Vincent Seminary.
Crone, Patrick H. '71 (CIN) Cincinnati, OH St. Veronica Retired.
Crone, Terence '02 (ATL) Toccoa, GA St. Mary; Deans; Deans.
Cronen, James *o.s.b.* '54 (ROC)[K] Pine City, NY Mount Saviour Monastery; Pine City, NY.
Cronin, Daniel C. '55 (NOR) Columbia, CT St. Columba.

Cronin, Edward J. '80 (CHI) Chicago, IL St. Jane de Chantal.
Cronin, Harry C. *c.s.c.* '62 (FTW)[H] Notre Dame Congregation of Holy Cross, United States Province of Priests & Brothers.
Cronin, Harry *c.s.c.* '62 (OAK)[L] Berkeley, CA Priests of the Congregation of Holy Cross.
Cronin, James J. '62 (HRT) Milford, CT St. Mary.
Cronin, Joseph R. '98 (HRT) West Haven, CT Our Lady of Victory; West Haven, CT St. John Vianney.
Cronin, Kevin M. *o.f.m.* '74 (PAT)[N] Butler, NJ St. Anthony Friary; [N] Franciscan Ministry of the Word.
Cronin, Michael J. '73 (CHI) Chicago, IL St. Edward.
Cronin, Michael J. '95 (WIN) Winona, MN Cathedral of the Sacred Heart; Winona, MN St. Casimir's.
Cronin, Rev. Msgr. Patrick '67 (SAT) San Antonio, TX Prince of Peace.
Cronin, Peadar *ss.cc.* '72 (LA)[D] La Verne, CA Damien High School; San Dimas, CA Holy Name of Mary; [P] La Verne, CA Congregation of the Sacred Hearts of Jesus and Mary.
Cronin, Peter J. *s.s.c.* '54 (BUF)[M] Silver Creek, NY St. Columbans on the Lake, Home for the Aged.
Cronin, Peter *s.s.c.* '54 (OM)[J] St. Columbans Missionary Society of St. Columban.
Cronin, Richard F. *o.s.b.* '66 (PAT)[N] Morristown, NJ St. Mary's Abbey.
Cronin, Richard '60 (JC) Retired.
Cronin, Robert J. *s.o.l.t.* '83 (FAR) Belcourt, ND St. Ann; Belcourt, ND St. Ann.
Cronin, Robert W. '52 (NOR) Censor of Books Retired.
Cronin, Rev. Msgr. Sylvester J. '88 (MET) Department of Stewardship and Development; College of Consultors; Metuchen, NJ Cathedral of St. Francis of Assisi.
Cronin, Thomas '69 (KC) Retired.
Cronin, Rev. Msgr. Timothy P. '85 (STL) Crestwood, MO St. Elizabeth of Hungary.
Cronin, William *m.i.* '76 (MIL)[Y] Wauwatosa, WI St. Camillus Communities, Inc. – House II.
Cronk, James F. '69 (DET) Bloomfield Hills, MI St. Owen.
Cronkleton, Thomas E. '86 (CHY) Judicial Vicar; Cheyenne, WY Holy Trinity; College of Consultors; Ex Officios, Voting; Judicial Vicar; Judges; St. Joseph's Society for Priests (Clergy Mutual Benefit Society); Presbyteral Council.
Cronogue, Michael P. *s.s.e.* '77 (BUR)[E] Colchester, VT Society of St. Edmund; Colchester, VT SOCIETY OF ST. EDMUND; Colchester, VT; Colchester, VT Society of St. Edmund.
Cronogue, Michael *s.s.e.* '77 (NOR)[L] Mystic, CT St. Edmund's of Connecticut, Inc.
Crook, David G. '81 (BEL) Retired.
Crooker, Robert W. *c.s.b.* '53 (GAL)[O] Houston, TX Residence of the Basilian Fathers of the University of St. Thomas.
Crookston, James F. '71 (ALT) Johnstown, PA St. John Gualbert Cathedral.
Crookston, Michael J. '80 (GBG) Uniontown, PA St. John The Evangelist; Bishop's Priests Council.
Crosara, Lawrence *s.x.* '58 (MIL)[B] Franklin, WI Xaverian Missionary Fathers College Seminary.
Crosby, Rev. Msgr. Charles E. '56 (MAN) Hampton, NH St. Patrick Retired.
Crosby, Dan *o.f.m.cap.* '64 (LC)[G] Marathon City, WI St. Anthony Spirituality Center.
Crosby, Michael *o.f.m.* '64 (STL)[S] Dittmer, MO Il Ritiro–The Little Retreat.
Crosby, Michael *o.f.m.cap.* '66 (MIL) Milwaukee, WI St. Benedict the Moor.
Crosby, Neil A. '81 (CLV) Cuyahoga Falls, OH St. Eugene; Cuyahoga Falls, OH Fallsview Mental Health Center.
Crosby, Theodore A. '00 (OG) Ellenburg, NY St. Edmund; Lyon Mountain, NY St. Bernard.
Crosby, Vincent R. *o.s.b.* '72 (GBG)[H] Latrobe, PA Saint Vincent Archabbey.
Crosier, Rev. Msgr. Raymond '75 (AMA) Priests' Pension Plan Retirement Committee.
Cross, Michael L. '62 (MRY) Felton, CA St. John's; Administrative Committee Priests' Pension Plan.
Cross, Robert A. '52 (CHI) Oak Park, IL Ascension Retired.
Cross, William D. '85 (STU) Judicial Vicar; Wintersville, OH Blessed Sacrament; Wintersville, OH Our Lady of Lourdes.
Cross, William H. '74 (CIN) Cincinnati, OH St. Margaret – St. John Parish.
Crosse, Charles G. '53 (SEA) Lakewood, WA St. John Bosco Retired.
Crossen, Jason '00 (DAV) Muscatine, IA SS. Mary and Mathias of Muscatine; Columbus Junction, IA St. Joseph.
Crosser, Raymond G. '56 (ALT) Retired.
Crossin, John W. *o.s.f.s.* '76 (WDC)[B] Washington, DC Deshairs Community–Oblates of St. Francis de Sales Residence; Washington, DC Annunciation.
Crossmyer, Robert *c.p.* '88 (BIR) Birmingham, AL Holy Family; [I] Birmingham, AL Congregation of the Passion: Holy Family Community, Inc.
Crosthwaite, Alejandro *o.p.* '98 (OAK)[L] Oakland Order of Preachers (Province of the Most Holy Name of Jesus – Western Dominican Province).
Croteau, Roger H. '67 (MAN) Derry, NH Holy Cross; Advocates.
Crotty, Christopher *c.p.m.* '01 (OWN)[F] Auburn, KY Fathers of Mercy.
Crotty, Columban *ss.cc.* '58 (WDC) Seat Pleasant, MD St. Margaret.
Crotty, John M. '47 (NY)[DD] Bronx, NY John Cardinal O'Connor Residence Retired.
Crowe, George W. '65 (PH) Retired.
Crowe, Hugh '58 (LA) Los Angeles, CA St. Ann Retired.
Crowe, Raymond *o.m.i.* '54 (BO)[X] Tewksbury, MA Immaculate Heart of Mary Residence.
Crowe, William R. '08 (LA) Simi Valley, CA St. Peter Claver.
Crowley, Cale J. *s.s.* '69 (BAL)[Q] Baltimore Society of St. Sulpice, Province of the United States.
Crowley, Cale J. *s.s.* '69 (GF) On Duty Outside of the Diocese.
Crowley, Daniel J. '68 (BO) Senior Priests.; Middleborough, MA Sacred Heart Retired.
Crowley, Dennis J. '89 (PAT) Morristown, NJ Assumption of the Blessed Virgin Mary; Morristown, NJ Morristown Memorial Hospital.
Crowley, Edmund G. '70 (MAN) Hooksett, NH Holy Rosary; Suncook, NH St. John the Baptist; Air National Guard Chaplains.
Crowley, James M. '87 (CHR) Greenwood, SC Our Lady of Lourdes.
Crowley, John A. '61 (PMB) Delray Beach, FL; Vero Beach, FL St. John of the Cross Retired.
Crowley, John C. '03 (PH) Doylestown, PA Our Lady of Mount Carmel.
Crowley, Joseph P. '06 (HRT)[D] West Hartford, CT Northwest Catholic High School; New Britain, CT St. Joseph's; New Britain, CT St. Peter.
Crowley, Patrick J. *ss.cc.* '72 (LA)[P] La Verne, CA Congregation of the Sacred Hearts of Jesus and Mary.
Crowley, Paul G. *s.j.* '92 (SJ)[B] Santa Clara, CA Jesuit Community.
Crowley, R. Kevin '68 (MET) Retired.
Crowley, Richard P. '64 (BO) Middleborough, MA Sacred Heart.
Crowley, Thomas F. '76 (WDC) Waldorf, MD Our Lady Help of Christians.
Crowley, William C. '74 (B) Coeur d'Alene, ID St. Thomas; Adjutant Judicial Vicars; Judges.
Crowley, William F. *c.s.sp.* '49 (PIT)[B] Pittsburgh, PA Duquesne University of the Holy Spirit; [O] Bethel Park, PA The Spiritan Center Retired.
Crozzoletto, Provvido *m.c.c.j.* '70 (NEW)[L] Montclair, NJ Comboni Missionaries of the Heart of Jesus (Verona Fathers); Newark, NJ St. Lucy's.
Crucet, Jose '88 (PMB) West Palm Beach, FL St. Juliana.
Crumbley, Charles W. '67 (Y) Warren, OH St. James.
Crummy, Michael E. '86 (MET) Hillsborough, NJ Mary, Mother of God.
Crump, Michael Edward *s.o.l.t.* '09 (CC) Robstown, TX St. Anthony; [G] Robstown, TX Society of Our Lady of the Most Holy Trinity.
Cruz, Alexander '91 (NEW) West New York, NJ St. Joseph of the Palisades.
Cruz, Bernardo '10 (DET) Presbyteral Council.
Cruz, Camilo E. '10 (NEW) Upper Montclair, NJ St. Cassian.
Cruz, Cecilio de la (SJN)[F] Rio Piedras, PR Hermanitas de los Ancianos Desamparados Hogar Santa Teresa Jornet de Caspey Inc.
Cruz, Rev. Msgr. David '86 (LUB) Lubbock, TX Our Lady of Grace; [A] Lubbock, TX Office for Cursillo Movement; Cursillo Movement.
Cruz, Domingo '73 (HT) Schriever, LA St. Bridget.
Cruz, Eric '02 (NY) Graduate Studies.
Cruz, Fidel '05 (NY) New York, NY Our Lady of Lourdes.
Cruz, Francisco '87 (CHR) Joanna, SC St. Boniface; Newberry, SC St. Mark; [H] Gaffney, SC Limestone College.
Cruz, Gilbert J. '81 (SJN) Retired.
Cruz, Gilbert '81 (LA) Altadena, CA Sacred Heart.
Cruz, Gustavo '74 (LAV) Las Vegas, NV Prince of Peace; Presbyteral Council for the Diocese of Las Vegas; Priests' Pension Board.
Cruz, Hector J. *s.m.* '77 (BWN) Brownsville, TX San Felipe de Jesus; San Pedro, TX San Pedro.
Cruz, Hector *sch.p.* '04 (PCE)[C] Coto Laurel, PR Colegio Ponceno.
Cruz, James A. '05 (NY) New York, NY; Secretary to the Archbishop.
Cruz, Johnny *o.ss.t.* '91 (PCE) Ponce, PR La Santisima Trinidad.
Cruz, Jose Gabrie Rodriguez '98 (CHR) Johns Island, SC Church of the Holy Spirit.
Cruz, Jose '07 (LA) Los Angeles, CA Immaculate Conception.
Cruz, Luciano '86 (PAT) Paterson, NJ St. Therese.
Cruz, Luis A. *sch.p.* (NY)[DD] New York, NY Calasanzian Fathers (Piarists); New York, NY Annunciation.
Cruz, Ramon Macoy *c.f.i.c.* '98 (COL) Hospital Ministry.
Cruz, Rev. Msgr. Remberto '49 (SJN) Retired.
Cruz, Robert Joel '96 (HT) Thibodaux, LA Our Lady of Prompt Succor; Pontifical Societies for the Propagation of the Faith.
Cruz, Saul E. '92 (RCK) DeKalb, IL St. Mary; Special Assignment.
Cruz, Victor '01 (FWT) Gainesville, TX St. Mary.
Cruz–Davila, Carlos D. '80 (SJN) San Juan, PR Cristo Rey; [E] San Juan, PR Doctor's Community Hospital; [E] San Juan, PR Centro Medico de P.R.
Cruz–Gonzalez, Luis A. (SJN) San Juan, PR Jesus Mediador.
Cruz–Ramirez, Bernardo '10 (DET) Pontiac, MI St. Damien of Molokai Parish.
Cruzada, Efren (CC)[D] Corpus Christi, TX CHRISTUS Spohn Hospital Corpus Christi – Memorial.
Cruz Collazo, Jose A. *o.f.m. cap.* '83 (SJN) San Juan, PR San Francisco de Asis.
Cruz Garcia, Edwin A. '95 (SJN) Bayamon, PR La Resurreccion del Senor.
Cruz Gonzalez, Gil '48 (SJN) Retired.
Cryan, James F. *o.s.f.s.* '65 (TOL) Toledo, OH Gesu; [H] Toledo, OH Provincial Residence.
Cryan, John J. '81 (NEW) Jersey City, NJ Our Lady of Mercy; Jersey City, NJ Church of Our Lady of Sorrows; Jersey City South Deanery 12; Archdiocesan Judges.
Cryans, Andrew W. '75 (MAN) Durham, NH St. Thomas More; [O] Durham, NH St. Thomas More Catholic Student Center at the University of New Hampshire.
Csaszar, James C. '99 (COL) Corning, OH St. Bernard; New Lexington, OH Church of the Atonement; New Lexington, OH St. Patrick; New Lexington, OH St. Rose of Lima; Deanery 8: Muskingum–Perry; Parochial Examiners; Presbyteral Council.
Csete, Ivan L. '81 (NY) Forestburgh, NY St. Thomas Aquinas.
Csizmar, Richard A. '68 (BUF) Vicars; Clergy Personnel Board; Albion, NY Holy Family.
Cuadrado, Angel *o.de.m.* '86 (PCE) Ponce, PR Santuario San Judas Tadeo.
Cuadrado, Hector F. *c.m.f.* '91 (SJN) Bayamon, PR San Jose; Bayamon, PR Santa Maria.
Cuadros, Jesus '66 (BRK) Brooklyn, NY Holy Family–Saint Thomas Aquinas.
Cuario, Bruno '91 (PHX) Williams, AZ St. Joseph's Roman Catholic Parish; Seligman, AZ St. Francis Roman Catholic Parish; Ashfork, AZ St. Anne Roman Catholic Mission, A Quasi–Parish.
Cuarto, Jonathan '05 (SJ) San Jose, CA St. Victor.
Cubas–Ramirez, Franklin *s.m.* '89 (SB) Rancho Cucamonga, CA Our Lady of Mount Carmel.
Cucarella, Diego Ramon Sarrio *m.afr.* '01 (WDC) Washington, DC; Washington, DC MISSIONARIES OF AFRICA; [O] Washington, DC Missionaries of Africa.
Cuccaro, John J. '79 (PBR) Hermitage, PA St. Michael; Elected Deanery Representatives.
Cuccia, Salvatore H. *o.praem.* '66 (GB) De Pere, WI St. Norbert College; [J] De Pere, WI St. Norbert Abbey; [B] De Pere, WI St. Norbert College.
Cudak, Emil '74 (CHI) Chicago, IL St. Bruno.
Cudden, Jerome *o.p.* '07 (LA) Los Angeles, CA St. Dominic.
Cuddigan, John D. *s.j.* '62 (OM)[J] Omaha, NE Jesuit Community at Creighton University.
Cuddihy, Rev. Msgr. William '56 (SD) Retired.
Cuddy, Rev. Msgr. John J. '53 (SAV) Retired.
Cuddy, Michael J. *o.p.* '07 (PRO)[B] Providence, RI Providence College; [O] Providence St. Thomas Aquinas Priory at Providence College.
Cuddy, Rev. Msgr. William F. (BO) Beverly, MA St. John the Evangelist.
Cudnik, Chester C. '48 (CLV) Retired.
Cuellar, Ernesto Vargas (CHI) Chicago, IL Our Lady of Tepeyac.
Cuenca, Fernando *o.m.v.* '84 (LA) Hawaiian Gardens, CA St. Peter Chanel.
Cuenin, Walter H. '70 (BO)[AA] Waltham, MA Brandeis University Catholic Chaplaincy; Brandeis University; Allston, MA St. Anthony of Padua.
Cuevas, Alberto R. '98 (SFR) Menlo Park, CA St. Anthony.
Cuevas, Diego O. '03 (MAD) University Hospitals; [F] Madison, WI Bishop O'Connor Catholic Pastoral Center.
Cuevas, Fernando *c.s.* '02 (CHI) Melrose Park, IL Our Lady of Mount Carmel.
Cuevas, Henan '11 (CHI) Evanston, IL St. Athanasius.
Cuevas, Jose Luis '74 (LA) Long Beach, CA St. Athanasius.
Cuevas, Randy M. '82 (BR)[K] Hammond, LA St. Albert the Great Catholic Student Center; Board Members; Continuing Formation for the Clergy.
Cuevas, Wilson '81 (ELP) El Paso, TX Corpus Christi; Ex Officio Members; St. Matthew; Priests' Personnel Advisory Committee.

Cuff, John P. *m.m.* '69 (FgM) Maryknoll, NY MARYKNOLL; Chicago, IL.
Culbertson, Terry Ruth (SY) Syracuse, NY Upstate University Hospital.
Culhane, Alberic *o.s.b.* '57 (SCL)[I] Collegeville, MN St. John's Abbey, of the Order of St. Benedict.
Culkin, Rev. Msgr. Francis J. '44 (SY) Rome, NY St. Mary's–St. Peter's Retired.
Culkin, Michael J. (HBG) Lancaster, PA St. John Neumann.
Culkin, Michael '78 (WDC) On Duty Outside the Archdiocese.
Cull, Rev. Msgr. Lawrence W. '69 (NEW) Ramsey, NJ St. Paul Retired.
Cullen, Anthony F. '75 (SPR) Springfield, MA Holy Cross.
Cullen, Bernard J. *o.c.s.o.* '48 (DUB)[K] Peosta, IA New Melleray Abbey, Order of Cistercians of the Strict Observance.
Cullen, Christopher M. *s.j.* '94 (NY)[DD] Cardinal Spellman Hall, Jesuit Community.
Cullen, Daniel *s.m.a.* '47 (NEW)[L] Tenafly, NJ Society of African Missions, Provincialate, S.M.A. Fathers.
Cullen, Donald '71 (KCK) Overland Park, KS Queen of the Holy Rosary.
Cullen, Harold '68 (TR) Deal, NJ St. Mary of the Assumption; West Long Branch, NJ St. Jerome.
Cullen, Hugh G. '75 (GAL) Houston, TX St. Mark the Evangelist.
Cullen, Rev. Msgr. J. Peter '67 (BGP) Greenwich, CT St. Michael the Archangel; Vicars General; Presbyteral Council; Finance Council; Priest Vocation Advisory Board; Diocesan Consultors.
Cullen, John J. '99 (BUF) Council of Priests; Canaseraga, NY St. Mary.
Cullen, Kevin L. *s.j.* '86 (STL)[O] St. Louis, MO The Jesuits of the Missouri Province.
Cullen, Patrick P. '68 (BIR) Bessemer, AL St. Aloysius Church; [I] Bessemer, AL St. Aloysius Educational Foundation; Diocesan College of Consultors; Apostolate with Mentally Retarded Persons; Priests'/Presbyteral Council; Diocesan College of Vicars.
Cullen, Patrick *s.p.s.* '52 (NEW)[L] Cliffside Park, NJ St. Patrick's Missionary Society Retired.
Cullen, Paul M. *o.s.m.* '65 (CHI) Chicago, IL Annunciata; [N] Chicago, IL Annunciata Priory.
Cullen, Robert J. '05 (BO) Quincy, MA St. John the Baptist.
Cullen, William '48 (JOL) Retired.
Cullen, William '83 (JKS) Retired.
Culler, Eric J. '08 (TOL) New Washington, OH St. Bernard; Willard, OH St. Francis Xavier.
Culley, Brian *c.m.f.* '84 (CHI)[N] Chicago, IL Barbastro House (Claretian Candidate House).
Culligan, Kevin *o.c.d.* '63 (BO)[U] Boston, MA Carmelite Monastery.
Culligan, Martin J. *c.m.* '57 (STL)[O] St. Louis, MO Lazarist Residence Retired.
Culligan, Michael A. '59 (SR) Petaluma, CA St. James.
Cullinane, Brian *o.f.m.* '71 (BO)[Z] Boston, MA St. Anthony Shrine.
Cullinane, Briant *o.f.m.conv.* '57 (ALB) Special Assignment.
Cullinane, Briant *o.f.m.conv.* '58 (R)[F] Elon, NC Conventual Franciscans; Burlington, NC Blessed Sacrament.
Cullinane, Jeremiah J. '59 (WH) Retired.
Cullinane, John F. *p.e.* '56 (BRK) Rockaway Point, NY Blessed Trinity Roman Catholic Church Retired.
Cullings, David Ronald '67 (P)[C] Eugene, OR Marist Catholic High School Retired.
Culloty, John P. '72 (BO) Norwood, MA St. Timothy; Vicariate IV.
Culnane, William R. '60 (SCR)[M] Dunmore, PA Villa St. Joseph Retired.
Culotta, Joachim *o.p.* '64 (STL) Judicial Vicar; [O] Saint Louis, MO St. Dominic Priory.
Culotta, Joseph G. '83 (BIR) Birmingham, AL St. Mark the Evangelist; Diocesan College of Consultors; Priests'/Presbyteral Council; Diocesan College of Vicars.
Culotta, Rev. Msgr. Salvador J. '53 (BEA) Retired.
Culver, Garry '64 (DM) Retired.
Culver, James A. '55 (SY) Retired.
Culver, Richard J. '85 (OAK) Bay Point, CA Our Lady, Queen of the World; Deanery #12; Diocesan Finance Council.
Cumberland, Matthew T. '92 (LA) La Puente, CA St. Joseph.
Cummings, Brian J. *s.s.e.* '96 (BUR)[A] Colchester, VT St. Michael's College; [E] Colchester, VT Society of St. Edmund; [H] Isle La Motte, VT St. Anne's Shrine; Councilors:; Board Members.
Cummings, Rev. Msgr. Carl F. '75 (BAL) Pasadena, MD St. Jane Frances de Chantal.
Cummings, Charles J. '68 (SCR) Retired.
Cummings, Charles J. *o.c.s.o.* '71 (SLC)[A] Huntsville, UT Abbey of Our Lady of the Holy Trinity; [E] Huntsville, UT Abbey of Our Lady of the Holy Trinity of the Order of Cistercians.
Cummings, Gabriel '84 (SAV) St. Marys, GA Our Lady Star of the Sea.
Cummings, Rev. Msgr. George '43 (SP) Citrus Springs, FL St. Elizabeth Ann Seton Retired.
Cummings, John J. '88 (LFT) Reynolds, IN St. Joseph.
Cummings, Jose Emilio '77 (SJN) San Juan, PR Catedral de San Juan Bautista; [D] San Juan, PR Santa Ana Chapel.
Cummings, Juniper *o.f.m.conv.* '50 (STP)[J] Prior Lake, MN St. Joseph Cupertino Friary; [M] Prior Lake, MN Franciscan Retreats.
Cummings, Leo P. '64 (SCR)[M] Dunmore, PA Villa St. Joseph.
Cummings, Marilyn '97 (SP)[J] Tampa, FL St. Joseph's Hospital, Inc.
Cummings, Maurice H. *o.carm.* '71 (DOD) Ashland, KS St. Joseph Catholic Church of Ashland, Kansas.
Cummings, McLean A. '98 (BAL) On Duty Outside the Archdiocese.
Cummings, McLean (BAL) Ellicott City, MD Our Lady of Perpetual Help.
Cummings, Patrick J. '78 (GAL)[S] Houston, TX The Catholic Chaplain Corps.
Cummings, Paul J. '55 (LAN) Retired.
Cummings, Thomas W. *s.j.* '69 (STL)[F] St. Louis, MO St. Louis University High School, George H. Backer Memorial; [O] Saint Louis, MO St. Louis University High School Jesuit Community.
Cummings, Timothy '08 (SP) Scouting Office, Boys; Tampa, FL St. Paul; Elected Parochial Vicars.
Cummings–Espada, Rev. Msgr. Jose E. '72 (SJN) Diocesan Consultors; Subcommission for Sacred Art.
Cummins, Anthony O. '65 (SAT) Boerne, TX St. Peter the Apostle.
Cummins, Charles T. '68 (SLC) Ogden, UT Saint Florence Catholic Community LLC 254; Ogden, UT Saint Joseph LLC 230; [G] Ogden, UT Weber State University, Newman Center.
Cummins, Joseph V. *c.m.* '72 (PH) Philadelphia, PA St. Francis of Assisi.
Cummins, Michael E. '95 (KNX)[I] Johnson City, TN ETSU–Catholic Center; East Tennessee State University; Vocation Discernment Office.
Cummins, Michael E. '95 (KNX) Vocations; Presbyteral Council.
Cummins, Michael J. *c.m.* '77 (BRK)[R] Queens Village, NY DePaul Residence.
Cummins, Robert L. '86 (RIC) Mathews, VA Church of Francis de Sales; Topping, VA Church of the Visitation.
Cuneo, Rev. Msgr. J. James '67 (BGP) Stratford, CT Holy Name of Jesus; Catholic Lawyers; Adjutant Judicial Vicar.
Cuneo, James J. '63 (DEN) Retired.
Cunha, Egionor '92 (MO) Navy Reserve Chaplains.
Cunnane, Rev. Msgr. Jarlath '77 (LA) Encino, CA Our Lady of Grace.
Cunnane, Michael A. '61 (SD) Clergy Personnel Board; Santee, CA Guardian Angels Catholic Parish Retired.
Cunneen, Rev. Msgr. Sean R. '67 (NEW) Scotch Plains, NJ Immaculate Heart of Mary.
Cunney, Henry M. '59 (BO) Senior Priests. Retired.
Cunniff, Charles *c.s.p.* '83 (COL)[I] Columbus, OH Campus Ministry.
Cunniff, Vincent '53 (P) Retired.
Cunningham, Donald M. *s.j.* '64 (STL)[O] St. Louis, MO Jesuit Community Corporation at Saint Louis University – Jesuit Hall.
Cunningham, Douglas D. '87 (MO) Marathon, NY St. Stephen; Whitney Point, NY The Catholic Community of St. Stephen–St. Patrick; Air National Guard Chaplains.
Cunningham, Gerard M. '93 (ORL) Lady Lake, FL St. Timothy.
Cunningham, James B. '87 (BUF) Buffalo, NY St. Teresa.
Cunningham, James K. '95 (BRK) Brooklyn, NY Holy Name.
Cunningham, James *c.s.s.* '50 (BO)[X] Waltham, MA Stigmatine Fathers and Brothers Retired.
Cunningham, John D. *s.j.* '05 (CHI)[C] Chicago, IL Jesuit Community at Loyola University Chicago.
Cunningham, John F. '74 (PHX) Retired.
Cunningham, John H. '65 (ALX) Retired.
Cunningham, John Vianney *t.o.r.* '70 (ORL)[E] Winter Park, FL San Pedro Spiritual Development Center.
Cunningham, John (BAL) Bel Air, MD St. Margaret.
Cunningham, Rev. Msgr. Joseph C. '71 (PH) Retired.
Cunningham, Joseph L. '63 (BRK) Bellerose, NY St. Gregory the Great.
Cunningham, Joseph L. '56 (MIL) Retired.
Cunningham, Leonard A. *o.c.s.o.* '50 (CHR)[E] Moncks Corner, SC Mepkin Abbey.
Cunningham, Lloyd (Samuel) *s.v.d.* '81 (FTW) Fort Wayne, IN St. Patrick.
Cunningham, Mark '99 (ALB) Herkimer, NY St. Francis de Sales; Mohawk, NY Blessed Sacrament.
Cunningham, Michael '86 (OAK) Concord, CA Queen of All Saints.
Cunningham, Nicholas J. '79 (TOL) Plymouth, OH St. Joseph; Shelby, OH Most Pure Heart of Mary.
Cunningham, Rev. Msgr. Peter J. '56 (MOB)[E] Mobile, AL Little Sisters of the Poor, Home For the Aged, Inc. Retired.
Cunningham, Robert W. *s.j.* '55 (FgM) Los Gatos, CA Society of Jesus.
Cunningham, Vianney *t.o.r.* '70 (ORL)[F] Winter Park, FL Franciscan Friars, T.O.R., San Pedro Friary.
Cunningham, Vincent P. *s.m.m.* '60 (RVC)[N] Bay Shore, NY Montfort Missionaries Retired.
Cuny, W. Timothy *o.s.a.* '70 (KAL)[E] Douglas, MI Order of St. Augustine; Douglas, MI St. Peter.
Cuomo, Rocco A. '64 (TR) Retired.
Cupp, Edwin F. '69 (WH) Retired.
Cupple, Gerard J. '85 (DET) Lincoln Park, MI St. Henry.
Cupps, David W. '09 (RIC) Portsmouth, VA Church of the Holy Angels; Portsmouth, VA Church of the Resurrection; Portsmouth, VA St. Paul; Chesapeake, VA St. Mary.
Curalli, Joseph M. *c.ss.r.* '78 (STL)[O] Liguori, MO Liguori Mission House/Redemptorists.
Curbelo, Luis *s.e.m.v.* '94 (STP) St. Paul, MN St. Francis De Sales.
Curci, Rev. Msgr. Richard G. '72 (GBG)[K] Greensburg, PA The Bishop William G. Connare Center.
Curesky, Mark *o.f.m.conv.* '75 (NOR) Cromwell, CT St. John.
Curiel, James A. *o.c.d.* '95 (SAT) San Antonio, TX Basilica of the National Shrine of the Little Flower, Our Lady of Mt. Carmel and St. Therese Parish; [L] San Antonio, TX Discalced Carmelite Fathers of San Antonio.
Curley, Augustine J. *o.s.b.* '88 (NEW)[L] Newark, NJ Newark Abbey; Newark, NJ.
Curley, Rev. Msgr. Joseph K. '62 (RVC) Priests' Retirement Board Retired.
Curley, Patrick K. '08 (NY) Fishkill, NY Church of St. Mary, Mother of the Church.
Curley, Patrick '70 (JKS) Vicksburg, MS St. Michael.
Curley, Terence P. '72 (BO) Senior Priests. Retired.
Curley, Thomas J. '70 (NY) Red Hook, NY St. Christopher; Tivoli, NY St. Sylvia.
Curnutte, William G. '82 (SLC) Retired.
Curran, Anthony T. '83 (ATL) Retired.
Curran, Anthony '72 (ALB) Schenectady, NY St. John the Evangelist; Albany County Nursing Home; Special Assignment.
Curran, Brendan A. *o.p.* '01 (CHI) Chicago, IL St. Pius V; [N] Chicago, IL Dominican Community.
Curran, Charles E. '58 (ROC) On Duty Outside the Diocese.
Curran, Francis D. '50 (CLV) Willoughby, OH Immaculate Conception Retired.
Curran, Francis T. '69 (GI) Retired.
Curran, Rev. Msgr. Hugh D. '54 (NY) Retired.
Curran, Rev. Msgr. James P. '63 (CAM) Gloucester, NJ St. Mary's Church, Gloucester.
Curran, Rev. Msgr. James P. '63 (CAM) Parent–Teachers Association.
Curran, James *o.m.i.* '83 (LA) San Gabriel, CA San Gabriel Mission.
Curran, John F. *s.j.* '59 (CI)[C] Kolonia, Pohnpei, FM Jesuit House; Vicar General; Finance Committee; Notaries.
Curran, John F. *s.j.* '59 (NY)[DD] New York, NY Murray–Weigel Hall.
Curran, John M. *o.m.i.* '78 (FgM) Pacoima, CA Mary Immaculate; Washington, DC AMERICAN OBLATE MISSIONS.
Curran, John W. *o.f.m.conv.* '71 (ELP) El Paso, TX Our Lady of Mt. Carmel.
Curran, Joseph L. '76 (BO) Watertown, MA Sacred Heart.
Curran, Rev. Msgr. Michael J. '81 (BRK) Rockaway Point, NY Blessed Trinity Roman Catholic Church.
Curran, Oliver '76 (RNO) Zephyr Cove, NV Our Lady of Tahoe.
Curran, Oliver '76 (GLP) On Duty Outside of Diocese.
Curran, Patrick '01 (STO) San Andreas, CA St. Andrew Church of San Andreas (Pastor of).
Curran, Paul E. '59 (BO) Senior Priests. Retired.
Curran, Rev. Msgr. Paul F. '57 (PH) Springfield, PA Holy Cross Retired.
Curran, Peter *o.m.i.* '71 (FgM) Washington, DC AMERICAN OBLATE MISSIONS.
Curran, Richard G. '76 (BO) Chelmsford, MA St. John the Evangelist.
Curran, Robert F. *s.j.* '74 (SFR)[N] San Francisco, CA Jesuit Community at St. Ignatius College Preparatory.
Curran, Thomas B. *o.s.f.s.* '84 (KC)[B] Kansas City, MO Rockhurst University; [J] Kansas City, MO Rockhurst Jesuit Community.
Curran, Vincent J. '98 (HRT) East Hartford, CT St. Christopher; Manchester Deanery.
Curran, William J. '69 (CHI) Tinley Park, IL St. George.
Curran, William *m.afr.* '66 (FgM) Washington, DC MISSIONARIES OF AFRICA.
Currans, Clement W. '74 (SC) Emmetsburg, IA Holy Family; Ruthven, IA Sacred Heart.
Current, Maurice H. '80 (LIN) Beaver Crossing, NE

Sacred Heart; Adjutant Judicial Vicars; Commission for Sacred Liturgy and Sacred Music; Ecumenical Affairs, Commission for; Priests' Continuing Education Committee.
Currie, Charles A. '59 (SY) Endicott, NY St. Ambrose.
Currie, Charles L. *s.j.* '63 (WDC)[O] Washington, DC Leonard Neale House.
Currie, John A. '97 (BO) Holbrook, MA St. Joseph.
Currie, Joseph A. *s.j.* '68 (ALN)[A] Wernersville, PA Jesuit Center–Jesuit Community; [N] Wernersville, PA Jesuit Center.
Currin, John M. '98 (DET) Romulus, MI St. Aloysius.
Curry, Andrew '08 (FTW) Fort Wayne, IN Our Lady of Good Hope.
Curry, Frederic F. '49 (TUC) Tucson, AZ Saint Joseph Roman Catholic Parish – Tucson Retired.
Curry, James J. *s.j.* '74 (NY)[E] New York, NY Loyola School; [DD] New York, NY St. Ignatius Loyola Residence.
Curry, Rev. Msgr. Joseph M. '86 (MET) Office of Ministry to Priests; Spotswood, NJ Immaculate Conception.
Curry, Richard J. *s.j.* '09 (WDC)[O] Washington, DC The Jesuit Community at Georgetown University.
Curry, Robert S. *s.j.* '64 (PH)[Y] Merion Station St. Alphonsus House.
Curry, Stephen M. *o.s.a.* '96 (CAM)[C] Richland, NJ St. Augustine Preparatory School; Richland, NJ.
Curry, Terrence M. *s.j.* '77 (WOR)[N] Worcester, MA Jesuits of the Holy Cross, Inc.
Curry, Thomas P. *o.s.b.* '03 (GBG) Latrobe, PA St. Vincent Basilica; [H] Latrobe, PA Saint Vincent Archabbey.
Curso, Manuel '72 (SFR) Colma, CA Holy Angels.
Curtin, Eugene P. '56 (BO) Senior Priests. Retired.
Curtin, James '69 (JOL) Lockport, IL St. Dennis.
Curtin, Martin *o.f.m.cap.* (RVC) East Patchogue, NY St. Joseph the Worker.
Curtin, Vincent C. *s.j.* '68 (CHL) Mooresville, NC St. Therese; [J] Mooresville, NC Jesuit Community.
Curtis, Bonaventure J. *o.s.b.* '10 (GBG)[H] Latrobe, PA Saint Vincent Archabbey.
Curtis, Howard *o.c.s.o.* '57 (P)[L] Lafayette, OR The Cistercian (Trappist) Abbey of Our Lady of Guadalupe.
Curtis, John C. '84 (LEX) Carlisle, KY Shrine of Our Lady of Guadalupe; Paris, KY Annunciation of the Blessed Virgin Mary; HIV/AIDS Ministry.
Curtis, Joseph C. '69 (CHI) Indian Creek, IL St. Mary of Vernon.
Curtiss, Donald J. '71 (ROC) Clifton Springs, NY St. Dominic; Clifton Springs, NY St. Felix/St. Francis Parish Cluster.
Curtsinger, George '52 (FWT) Retired.
Cusack, Rev. Msgr. Francis V. '54 (MOB) Retired.
Cusack, Rev. Msgr. John J. '71 (PAT) Military Chaplains.
Cusack, John J. *c.m.* '45 (PH)[Y].
Cusack, Rev. Msgr. John J. (TUC) Tucson, AZ Christ the King Chapel.
Cusack, Thomas *s.s.c.* '62 (LA)[P] Los Angeles, CA Columban Fathers, Procure House.
Cusack, Thomas *s.s.c.* '62 (OM)[J] St. Columbans Missionary Society of St. Columban.
Cusatis, Girard J. '63 (PH) Drexel Hill, PA St. Andrew Retired.
Cuschieri, Rev. Msgr. Albert '61 (DAL) Retired.
Cush, John P. '98 (BRK) Censors of Books; [B] Elmhurst, NY Cathedral Preparatory Seminary of the Immaculate Conception; Brooklyn, NY St. Saviour.
Cushing, Matthew A. '09 (COV)[B] Maysville, KY St. Patrick High School; Maysville, KY St. Patrick.
Cushing, Robert A. '78 (SAV) Cordele, GA St. Theresa.
Cushing, Vincent de Paul *o.f.m.* '63 (WDC)[O] Silver Spring, MD Gemelli House; [B] Silver Spring, MD Holy Name College.
Cushing, Walter F. '56 (ROC) Retired.
Cushing, Walter '56 (ROC) Rochester, NY Kateri Tekakwitha Roman Catholic Parish Retired.
Cusick, Eugene G. '64 (PH) Retired.
Cusick, John C. '70 (CHI) Chicago, IL Old St. Patrick's; Young Adult Ministry/Singles; Archdiocesan Council of Catholic Men.
Cusick, Kevin M. '92 (WDC) Benedict, MD St. Francis de Sales.
Cusick, Thomas H. '64 (DET) Belleville, MI St. Anthony.
Cusick, Timothy S. '00 (STA) Presbyteral Council.
Cusick, Timothy '00 (STA) Jacksonville, FL Holy Family.
Cusimano, Joseph Gabriel *o.s.b.* '76 (SFE)[H] Abiquiu, NM Monastery of Christ in the Desert.
Cusimano, Salvatore J. '49 (BUF)[N] Tonawanda, NY O'Hara Residence Retired.
Custer, Edward O. *m.m.* '72 (FgM) Maryknoll, NY MARYKNOLL.
Custer, John S. '83 (PSC) Westbury, NY Resurrection; Westbury, NY St. Andrew the Apostle; Evangelization.
Custodio, Rinaldo B. '62 (STP) Deanery 18 Retired.
Cutcher, Anthony E. '99 (CIN) St. Marys, OH Holy Rosary; Presbyteral Council.
Cutler, Shawn W. '05 (BGP) Greenwich, CT St. Michael the Archangel.
Cutrara, Vincent *c.s.* '57 (CIN) Cincinnati, OH Sacred Heart.
Cutrone, Dominick F. '55 (BRK) Brooklyn, NY Our Lady of Grace Retired.
Cwiekowski, Bruce '79 (P)[J] Portland, OR Providence Health & Services–Oregon.
Cwiekowski, Frederick J. *s.s.* '62 (SFR)[A] Menlo Park, CA St. Patrick Seminary and University.
Cwiekowski, Frederick J. *s.s.* '62 (HRT) On Duty Outside the Archdiocese.
Cwiekowski, Frederick J. *s.s.* '62 (BAL)[Q] Baltimore Society of St. Sulpice, Province of the United States Retired.
Cwik, Tom *s.j.* '00 (DEN) Denver, CO St. Ignatius Loyola; [N] Denver, CO Society of Jesus – St. Ignatius Loyola Jesuit Community.
Cybulski, David '09 (DET) Presbyteral Council; Farmington, MI Our Lady of Sorrows.
Cyktor, Ronald L. '00 (GBG) Brady's Bend, PA St. Patrick.
Cylwicki, Albert W. *c.s.b.* '60 (ROC)[K] Rochester, NY Basilian Residence.
Cymbor, Rev. Msgr. John A. '50 (STU) Retired.
Cymerman, Alexander B. *o.f.m.conv.* '65 (SPR) Holyoke, MA Our Lady of the Cross.
Cyr, Joel R. '71 (PRT) Benedicta, ME St. Benedict's; East Millinocket, ME Christ the Divine Mercy Parish.
Cyr, John '02 (PEO) Tolono, IL St. Patrick's.
Cyr, L. Chanel '53 (PRT) Retired.
Cyr, L. Philip '69 (PRT) St. Agatha, ME Our Lady of the Valley.
Cyr, Lawrence *c.pp.s.* '44 (CIN)[N] Carthagena, OH St. Charles Retired.
Cyr, Myles *o.m.i.* '54 (PRT) Lincoln, ME St. Mary.
Cyr, Richard E. '60 (DET) Retired.
Cyr, Roger *o.m.i.* '59 (PRT) Howland, ME St. Leo The Great; Lincoln, ME St. Mary.
Cyr, Terrence *o.carm.* '75 (JOL)[L] Darien Carmelite Provincial Office.
Cyr, William '71 (SPR) North Adams, MA Saint Elizabeth of Hungary Parish; Office of Lay Ministry Formation; [M] Springfield, MA Massachusetts College of Liberal Arts.
Cyscon, Peter J. '73 (CHI) Bridgeview, IL St. Fabian.
Cyscon, Philip E. '84 (CHI) Chicago, IL Holy Innocents.
Cyvas, Matthew '41 (ALB) Retired.
Cyza, Mark L. '04 (LIN) Advocates; Nebraska City, NE St. Benedict's; Apostolate to the Spanish Speaking; Diocesan Consultors; Legion of Mary; [C] Nebraska City, NE Lourdes Central Catholic Schools.
Czabala, Teodor '98 (PHU) Sayre, PA Ascension of Our Lord.
Czabala, Theodor (STF) Johnson City, NY Sacred Heart Ukrainian Catholic Church; Presbyteral Council.
Czachor, Richard E. '77 (SCR) Tannersville, PA Our Lady of Victory; Diocesan Consultors; Presbyteral Council.
Czahur, John P. '77 (TR) Mount Holly, NJ Sacred Heart; Censores Librorum.
Czaicki, Franciszek *o.c.d.* '97 (GRY)[H] Munster, IN Discalced Carmelite Fathers Monastery.
Czaja, Blaise *c.p.* '64 (SAC)[H] Citrus Heights, CA Christ the King Passionist Retreat Center.
Czaja, Joseph S. '46 (Y) Retired.
Czajkowski, Andrew A. '74 (LAN) Burton, MI Blessed Sacrament; Davison, MI St. John the Evangelist; Regional Vicars.
Czajkowski, Richard S. *m.m.* '61 (FgM) Maryknoll, NY MARYKNOLL.
Czapinski, Richard J. '58 (PIT) Retired.
Czapla, Bruce *o.f.m.* '03 (MAN) Derry, NH St. Thomas Aquinas.
Czapla, Donald J. '03 (DUB) Marshalltown, IA St. Henry.
Czarcinski, Edward A. '88 (MET) Milltown, NJ Our Lady of Lourdes.
Czarkowski, Joseph R. '74 (E) Tidioute, PA St. John.
Czarnecki, Andrew '98 (DET) Woodhaven, MI Our Lady of the Woods.
Czarnecki, Rev. Msgr. Anthony S. '66 (WOR) Webster, MA St. Joseph Basilica; Defenders of the Bond; Deans; Presbyteral Council; Polish Ministry.
Czarnecki, Edward R. '66 (BUF) Defenders of the Bond; Blasdell, NY Our Mother of Good Counsel.
Czarnecki, Eryk '01 (CHI) Franklin Park, IL St. Gertrude.
Czarnecki, Mark '96 (GAL) Huntsville, TX St. Thomas the Apostle.
Czarnecki, Stanislaw *s.j.* '97 (CHI)[N] Chicago, IL Sacred Heart Mission House; [N] Chicago, IL Jan Beyzym Society, Inc.
Czarnota, Paul '03 (DET) Roseville, MI St. Angela.
Czarnota, Stanislaus '56 (LAN) Retired.
Czartorynski, David F. '84 (MO) On Duty Outside the Diocese; DEPARTMENT OF VETERANS AFFAIRS HOSPITALS AND CHAPLAINS.
Czaster, Herman *o.f.m.conv.* '65 (BRK) Elmhurst, NY St. Adalbert.
Czech, Edward M. '73 (CLV) Cleveland, OH Holy Name Retired.
Czeck, Thomas *o.f.m.conv.* (OAK)[L] Castro Valley, CA Conventual Franciscans (Province of St. Joseph of Cupertino).
Czelusniak, Donald '78 (ALB) Gloversville, NY Church of the Holy Spirit; Deans.
Czemerda, Edward M. '87 (PIT)[M] Pittsburgh, PA St. John Vianney Manor.
Czerniak, Ryszard *s.ch.* '00 (CHI) Burbank, IL St. Albert the Great.
Czerwinski, James W. *o.f.m.* '77 (PAT) Butler, NJ St. Anthony; [N] Butler, NJ St. Anthony Friary.
Czerwinski, James W. *o.f.m.* '77 (NY)[DD] New York Franciscan Friars, Holy Name Province.
Czerwonka, Paul G. '03 (LC) Plum City, WI St. John the Baptist; Plum City, WI St. Joseph.
Czerwonka, Piotr *s.a.c.* '89 (VEN) Sarasota, FL St. Martha.
Czok, Robert W. '66 (BRK) Brooklyn, NY St. Anthony of Padua–St. Alphonsus Retired.
Czudek, Jan '99 (BRK) Forest Hills, NY Our Lady Queen of Martyrs.
Czyzewski, Michael *o.s.p.p.e.* '04 (PH)[Y].
Czyzewski, Michal *o.s.p.p.e.* '04 (NY) Yonkers, NY St. Casimir.
Czyzynski, John *s.c.j.* '63 (CHI)[N] SCJ Novitiate.

D

D'Abele, Peter *s.m.m.* '75 (BRK)[R] Ozone Park, NY Montfort Missionaries Provincialate (Missionaries of the Company of Mary); Ozone Park, NY St. Mary Gate of Heaven.
D'Achille, Arnold V. '59 (DET) Retired.
D'Aco, Joseph '99 (FAR) Cando, ND Sacred Heart Church of Cando; Cando, ND St. Vincent de Paul Church of Leeds.
D'Addezio, Rev. Msgr. Louis A. '61 (PH) Philadelphia, PA St. Patrick Retired.
D'Agostino, Carl L. '59 (CLV) Independence, OH St. Michael; Cleveland, OH Holy Redeemer Retired.
D'Agostino, Francesco *c.s.* '10 (DAL) Irving, TX St. Luke.
D'Agostino, Joseph '41 (ALB) Retired.
D'Agostino, Rodolfo *r.c.j.* '64 (LA) Van Nuys, CA St. Elisabeth; [P] Van Nuys, CA Rogationist Fathers; Van Nuys, CA.
D'Albro, Thomas G. '73 (BRK) Belle Harbor, NY St. Francis de Sales.
D'Alessandro, Benedict J. *o.f.m.* '66 (NY)[DD] New York, NY Padua Friary Retired.
D'Alliessi, Daniel '04 (NY) Washington, DC St. Mary, Mother of God; Graduate Studies.
D'Almeida, Edward P. '09 (LR) De Queen, AR St. Barbara.
D'Alonzo, Alfred F. *c.s.c.* '53 (FTW)[H] Notre Dame Congregation of Holy Cross, United States Province of Priests & Brothers.
D'Ambrosia, Peter J. '85 (PRO) Warwick, RI St. Rita.
D'Amico, Carmen A. '82 (PIT) Meadow Lands, PA Our Lady of the Miraculous Medal.
D'Amico, Frank A. '87 (STL) Wentzville, MO St. Patrick.
D'Amico, Joseph A. '95 (NEW) Jersey City, NJ St. Aloysius; Archdiocesan Judges; Presbyteral Council.
D'Andrea, Edward R. '73 (RVC) Blue Point, NY Our Lady of the Snow.
D'Andrea, Steven D. '97 (NEW) Wallington, NJ Most Sacred Heart of Jesus.
D'Angelico, Rev. Msgr. Anthony J. '74 (PH) Southampton, PA Our Lady of Good Counsel.
D'Angelo, Anthony *s.d.b.* '67 (BIR) Birmingham, AL Holy Rosary.
D'Angelo, Donald S. '68 (SFR) Retired.
D'Angelo, Joseph '68 (RVC) Nassau County Police Department; North Merrick, NY Sacred Heart; Chaplains of the Nassau County Police Department.
D'Angelo, Paul R. '09 (VEN) Naples, FL St. William.
D'Angelo, Thomas P. '84 (NY) Pastoral Life Conference.
D'Angelo, Thomas (NY) Bronx, NY St. Theresa of the Infant Jesus.
d'Anjou, John R. *s.j.* '72 (PRT) Portland, ME Our Lady of Hope Parish.
d'Anjou, John R. *s.j.* '72 (BO)[U] Boston The Society of Jesus of New England–Provincial Offices.
D'Anjou, Lawrence C. '00 (OAK) Confraternity of Eucharistic Devotion (CEDDO); Dublin, CA St. Raymond.
D'Antonio, John A. '73 (SP) St. Petersburg, FL Holy Cross; Incardination Committee.
D'Antonio, Ronald M. '77 (BRK) Brooklyn, NY St. Athanasius.
D'Aquila, Ulysses L. '04 (SFR) Redwood City, CA Our Lady of Mount Carmel.
D'Arpino, John A. '11 (BO) Bridgewater, MA St. Thomas Aquinas.
d'Auby, Phillip *s.m.* '61 (SFR)[N] San Francisco, CA Marist Center of the West Retired.

D'Aurora, Joseph A. '73 (RIC) Lexington, VA St. Patrick; Navy Reserve Chaplains.

D'Aversa, Robert *t.o.r.* '76 (ORL) Mount Dora, FL St. Patrick's; Vicar for Religious.

D'Costa, Maxy *s.f.x.* '96 (P) Milwaukie, OR St. John the Baptist; Area Vicars.

D'Cruz, Ferreolus '59 (ALX) Tallulah, LA St. Edward; College of Consultors.

D'Cruz, Michael *o.f.m.* '57 (NY)[DD] New York Franciscan Province of the Immaculate Conception.

D'Cunha, Theodore *s.a.c.* '90 (DET) Livonia, MI St. Priscilla.

D'Emma, Gregory J. '70 (MO) Military Chaplains; Army Chaplains.

D'Eon, Earl '89 (PHX) Retired.

d'Escoto, Miguel F. *m.m.* '61 (NY)[DD] Maryknoll Maryknoll Fathers and Brothers Retired.

D'heedene, Walter O. *c.i.c.m.* '67 (SAT) San Antonio, TX Sacred Heart.

D'Imperio, Robert J. '07 (CAM) Galloway, NJ The Church of the Assumption.

D'Incecco, Alfred '75 (NY) Absent on Sick Leave.

D'Mello, John '73 (PMB) West Palm Beach, FL St. Ann.

D'Mello, Norbert *c.s.c.* '90 (SUP) Clear Lake, WI St. John; Glenwood City, WI St. John the Baptist; Glenwood City, WI St. Bridget; Presbyteral Council & Diocesan Consultors.

D'Onofrio, Joseph J. '05 (BO) Unassigned.

D'Ostilio, Silvio *c.s.sp.* '54 (LR) Center Ridge, AR St. Joseph.

D'Silva, Joseph R. '67 (MO) DEPARTMENT OF VETERANS AFFAIRS HOSPITALS AND CHAPLAINS.

D'Silva, Percival L. '64 (WDC) Washington, DC Blessed Sacrament, Shrine of the Most; Kensington, MD Holy Redeemer Retired.

D'Souza, Claude J. '65 (RVC) Retired.

D'Souza, Gerard *o.c.s.o.* '01 (ROC)[K] Piffard, NY Abbey of the Genesee.

D'Souza, Gilbert P. '73 (BGP) Norwalk, CT St. Joseph.

D'Souza, Maurice *c.s.c.* '77 (CLV) Cleveland, OH Veterans Administration Hospitals, Brecksville V.A.

D'Souza, Michael '77 (NSH) Nashville, TN Assumption; Nashville, TN St. Pius X.

D'Souza, Peter '79 (LUB) Presbyteral Council.

D'Souza, Robert '73 (FTW) Fort Wayne, IN St. Jude; Fort Wayne, IN Parkview Memorial Hospital; Clergy Retirement Board; Retired Clergy Committee.

D'Souza, Sudhir '95 (BGP) Norwalk, CT St. Matthew.

D'Souza, Sylvester (KCK) Hiawatha, KS St. Ann.

D'Souza, William '76 (GF) Broadus, MT St. David; Diocesan Consultors; Priests' Council.

Dabash, G. Adrian *o.p.* '71 (PRO)[O] Providence St. Thomas Aquinas Priory at Providence College.

Dabney, Philip *c.ss.r.* '78 (BO) Boston, MA Our Lady of Perpetual Help.

Dabria, Jerry J. '55 (NO) Retired.

Dabrowski, George J. *c.m.* '58 (HRT)[L] Manchester DePaul Provincial Residence Retired.

Dabrowski, James O. '84 (CAM) Berlin, NJ Saint Simon Stock Parish, Berlin, N.J.; Deanery Representatives.

Dabrowski, Klemens *s.ch.* '87 (MIA) Pompano Beach, FL Our Lady of Czestochowa Mission; Polish – (Our Lady of Czestochowa Polish Mission); Appointed by the Archbishop.

Dabruzzi, James S. '53 (SUP) Retired.

Dacechen, Mario *o.s.b.m.* '88 (STN) Warren, MI St. Josaphat.

Dacey, Donald '53 (DET) Retired.

Dachauer, Andrew C. *s.j.* '64 (SJ)[M] Los Gatos, CA Sacred Heart Jesuit Center.

DaCorte, Allan *o.f.m.* '77 (STL)[O] St. Louis Franciscan Friary of St. Anthony of Padua.

Da Costa, Darrell '97 (BRK) Corona, NY St. Paul the Apostle.

DaCosta, Lee '73 (BWN) Weslaco, TX St. Joan of Arc.

da Cunha, Domingos M. '71 (PRO) Cumberland, RI Our Lady of Fatima.

Dada, Jacek A. '92 (CHI) Calumet City, IL St. Andrew the Apostle.

Dadatt, Gelso '98 (PH) Portuguese and Brazilian Apostolates; Philadelphia, PA St. Martin of Tours.

Dadey, Neil R. '81 (ALT) Northern Deanery; Bellefonte, PA St. John the Evangelist's; Spring Mills, PA Blessed Kateri Tekakwitha.

Daelemans, Bert *s.j.* '08 (OAK)[L] Berkeley, CA Jesuit Fathers and Brothers.

Daffron, Justin *s.j.* '05 (CHI)[C] Chicago, IL Jesuit Community at Loyola University Chicago.

Daganta, Felizardo J. *o.a.r.* '88 (LA) Montebello, CA St. Benedict.

Dagelen, Anthony L. *s.j.* '65 (MIL)[P] Wauwatosa, WI Jesuit Community at St. Camillus.

Dagher, Rt. Rev. George *b.s.o.* '43 (NTN) Methuen, MA Basilian Salvatorian Order; Methuen, MA Retired.

Dagit, Rick D. '86 (DUB) Colo, IA St. Gabriel; Colo, IA St. Patrick; Colo, IA St. Joseph; Colo, IA St. Mary.

Dagle, Harold F. '59 (ALN) DEPARTMENT OF VETERANS AFFAIRS HOSPITALS AND CHAPLAINS; Lebanon, PA Assumption of the Blessed Virgin Mary Retired.

Dagle, Harold '58 (HBG) Lebanon, PA Veterans Administration Hospital.

Dagle, Thomas W. '02 (WH) Hinton, WV Sacred Heart; Hinton, WV St. Patrick.

Dagnoli, Albert *ss.cc.* '68 (FR)[F] Fairhaven, MA Damien Residence.

Daguplo, Genaro '84 (TR) Hamilton, NJ St. Raphael–Holy Angels Parish.

Daher, Richard '95 (OLD) Parossie Notre Dame de L'Assomption.

Dahl, Henry J. '96 (FR) Auditors Retired.

Dahl, Philip *o.cart.* '65 (BUR)[E] Arlington, VT Carthusian Foundation in America, Inc., Charterhouse of the Transfiguration.

Dahlberg, Daniel J. '67 (SUP) Retired.

Dahlby, Charles '77 (SFD) Retired.

Dahlheimer, Ronald W. '59 (STP) Retired.

Dahlinger, James H. *s.j.* '91 (SY)[Q] Syracuse, NY Jesuits at LeMoyne, Inc.

Dahlke, Robert W. *s.j.* '65 (NY)[DD] New York, NY Murray–Weigel Hall.

Dahm, Charles W. *o.p.* '64 (CHI)[N] Chicago, IL Dominican Community; Chicago, IL St. Pius V.

Dahm, Paul J. '62 (RVC) Retired.

Dahms, Paul G. '58 (MO) DEPARTMENT OF VETERANS AFFAIRS HOSPITALS AND CHAPLAINS.

Dahms, Paul '58 (RC) Retired.

Dai, Ba Thai *s.v.d.* '05 (FgM) Techny, IL.

Daiber, Rev. Msgr. Sean J. '67 (CAM) On Duty Outside the Diocese.

Daigle, Christopher '78 (TLS) Pawhuska, OK Immaculate Conception.

Daigle, David A. '03 (MO) Navy Chaplains.

Daigle, David (BGP) On Duty Outside the Diocese.

Daigle, Eugene *c.ss.r.* '72 (ORL)[F] New Smyrna Beach, FL St. Alphonsus Villa–Redemptorist Fathers and Brothers Retired.

Daigle, Gregory J. '93 (BR) Lakeland, LA Immaculate Conception; Board Members.

Daigle, Karl J. '97 (SHP) Shreveport, LA St. Joseph; Advocates; Church Vocations Board & Vocations Office.

Daigle, Robert E. '63 (HPM) Retired.

Daigle, Roland *o.f.m.cap.* '84 (FgM) White Plains, NY The Province of St. Mary of the Capuchin Order.

Daigle, Steven '89 (DUL) Cursillo Movement; Biwabik, MN St. John; Hoyt Lakes, MN Queen of Peace; Aurora, MN Holy Rosary.

Dailey, Gary M. '85 (SPR) Vocations; Newman Apostolate and Campus Ministry.

Dailey, Joseph E. '77 (DET) Lake Orion, MI Christ the Redeemer.

Dailey, Stanley L. (Stash) '08 (COL) Deanery 3: North High; Worthington, OH St. Michael; Presbyteral Council.

Dailey, Thomas F. *o.s.f.s.* '87 (ALN)[B] Center Valley, PA DeSales University; [K] Center Valley, PA Oblates of St. Francis de Sales.

Dailey, William R. *c.s.c.* '01 (FTW)[H] Notre Dame Congregation of Holy Cross, United States Province of Priests & Brothers; [B] University of Notre Dame Du Lac; [H] Notre Dame, IN Holy Cross Community, Corby Hall, University of Notre Dame.

Daily, Gary '85 (SPR)[M] Amherst, MA The Newman Catholic Center; [M] Amherst, MA University of Massachusetts.

Daily, Vincent E. '58 (BO) Dorchester, MA St. Gregory; Senior Priests. Retired.

Dair, Richard J. '80 (ARL) Retired.

Daise, Richard '10 (SAL) Ellis, KS St. Mary Parish.

Daisy, George '97 (LAN) Lansing, MI Immaculate Heart of Mary.

Dakes, John T. '87 (WDC) Leonardtown, MD St. Aloysius.

Dakin, Kenneth M. '88 (SAT) Hondo, TX St. John the Evangelist.

Dalbello, Americo '73 (CHI) Chicago, IL Transfiguration of Our Lord.

Dalbon, Luis '47 (CGS)[C] Aibonito, PR Casa Salesiana de Retiros.

Daleo, Joseph P. '71 (BEA) Eastern Vicariate; Orange, TX St. Mary.

Dalessandro, Dennis G. '83 (HBG) Berwick, PA St. Joseph's.

Daley, Brian E. *s.j.* '70 (CHI)[N] Chicago Chicago Province of the Society of Jesus–Provincial Office.

Daley, Brian *s.j.* '70 (FTW)[B] University of Notre Dame Du Lac; [K] South Bend, IN Jesuit Community.

Daley, Daniel P. '70 (GLP) Quemado, NM Sacred Heart; Pinetop, AZ St. Mary of the Angels; Ecumenical Affairs in Arizona, Arizona Ecumenical Council; Springerville, AZ St. Peter.

Daley, E. Raymond *o.p.* '52 (NY)[DD] New York, NY St. Vincent Ferrer Priory.

Daley, Rev. Msgr. Ernest J. '55 (E) Episcopal Delegate for Retired Priests; Members Retired.

Daley, Francis E. '66 (BO) Lakeville, MA Saints Martha and Mary.

Daley, Frederick D. '74 (SY) Syracuse, NY All Saints.

Daley, Jacques de Paul *o.s.b.* '71 (GBG) Latrobe, PA Excela Health – Latrobe Area Hospital; [H] Latrobe, PA Saint Vincent Archabbey; [I] Greensburg, PA Benedictine Nuns; [J] Greensburg, PA St. Emma Retreat House.

Daley, James D. '54 (ALB) Delmar, NY St. Thomas the Apostle Retired.

Daley, Joseph A. '68 (CHY) Retired.

Dalimpuo, Felix '93 (ROC) Newark, NY St. Michael.

Dalin, Jonathan J. '09 (PH) Collegeville, PA St. Eleanor.

Dall, Lincoln '08 (JKS) Belzoni, MS All Saints; Yazoo City, MS St. Mary; Yazoo City, MS St. Francis; Priests' Council.

Dallas, Benjamin '02 (SAV) Vidalia, GA Sacred Heart.

Dallen, James '69 (SAL) Retired.

Dallmeier, Michael *o.f.m.* '63 (SD)[J] Oceanside, CA Old Mission San Luis Rey.

Dalpiaz, Alex *c.s.* '56 (MIA) Brazilian and Portuguese Apostolate.

Dalpiaz, Alexander P. *c.s.* '56 (MIA) Margate, FL St. Vincent.

Dalpiaz, Gino *c.s.* '51 (CHI)[N] Chicago, IL Scalabrini House of Theology; Chicago, IL Santa Maria Addolorata.

Dalseth, Gerald '64 (SCL) Pierz, MN St. Michael's; Pierz, MN St. Joseph's.

Dalton, Brendan '69 (MIA) Hollywood, FL St. Bernadette; [D] Southwest Ranches, FL Archbishop Edward A. McCarthy High School.

Dalton, Donald T. '60 (STL) Retired.

Dalton, George R. '84 (PIT) Cranberry Township, PA St. Ferdinand.

Dalton, James E. *o.s.f.s.* (PH) Newtown Square, PA St. Anastasia; [D] Philadelphia, PA Father Judge High School for Boys.

Dalton, James '68 (SEA) Arlington, WA Immaculate Conception.

Dalton, John Bryan '70 (MIA) Deerfield Beach, FL St. Ambrose.

Dalton, Rev. Msgr. John W. '58 (DUB) Retired.

Dalton, Michel *o.f.m.cap.* '78 (HON) Vicars Forane; Ewa, HI Immaculate Conception Church; Bishops Administrative Advisory Council; Clergy Personnel Board; Implementation Commission of Diocesan Road Map for Pastoral Program and Facility Needs; Presbyteral Council.

Dalton, Robert *g.h.m.* '62 (CIN)[N] Cincinnati Headquarters of Glenmary Home Missioners Retired.

Dalupang, Arturo O. '95 (CHR) Hilton Head Island, SC Holy Family.

Daly, Anthony C. *s.j.* '72 (STL)[C] Saint Louis University; [O] St. Louis, MO Jesuit Community Corporation at Saint Louis University – Jesuit Hall.

Daly, Bartholomew *m.h.m.* '62 (NY) New York, NY Our Lady of Peace; [DD] Hartsdale, NY Mill Hill Fathers Residence; Hartsdale, NY.

Daly, Rev. Msgr. Charles W. '51 (HRT)[A] In Res. at the Archbishop Daniel A. Cronin Retirement Residence at St. Thomas Seminary Retired.

Daly, Christopher H. '60 (NY)[DD] Bronx, NY John Cardinal O'Connor Residence Retired.

Daly, David *l.c.* '01 (ATL)[F] Alpharetta, GA Norcross Pastoral Center, Inc.

Daly, Denis E. *s.j.* '64 (STL)[C] Saint Louis University; [O] St. Louis, MO Jesuit Community Corporation at Saint Louis University – Jesuit Hall.

Daly, Rev. Msgr. Desmond '66 (SP) Retired.

Daly, Edwin J. *s.j.* '59 (FgM) Chicago, IL Society of Jesus.

Daly, Francis J. *s.j.* '72 (CIN)[F] Cincinnati, OH St. Xavier High School; [N] Cincinnati, OH Jesuit Community at St. Xavier High School.

Daly, J. Daniel *s.j.* '92 (STL)[O] St. Louis, MO The Jesuits of the Missouri Province; Saint Louis, MO; [O] St. Louis, MO Sacred Heart Jesuit Community.

Daly, Jerome R. '87 (ARL) Retired.

Daly, John J. '58 (HRT) North Haven, CT St. Barnabas Retired.

Daly, John J. '59 (LA) Los Angeles, CA Holy Trinity Retired.

Daly, John P. *s.j.* '56 (MIL)[P] Wauwatosa, WI Jesuit Community at St. Camillus.

Daly, John R. *s.j.* '63 (DEN)[N] Denver, CO Xavier Jesuit Center.

Daly, John V. *s.j.* '66 (FgM) Milwaukee, WI Society of Jesus.

Daly, Joseph V. *c.m.* '60 (BRK)[R] Jamaica, NY St. Vincent's House.

Daly, Manus P. '65 (JC) Retired.

Daly, Peter J. '86 (WDC) Prince Frederick, MD St. John Vianney.

Daly, Raymond '52 (NY) Judges.

Daly, Richard L. '58 (BEL) Retired.

Daly, Robert J. *s.j.* '63 (BO)[U] Newton, MA The Jesuit Community at Boston College; Watertown, MA; [U] Watertown, MA The Society of Jesus of New England–Provincial Offices.

Daly, Robert L. '41 (NEW) Retired.

Daly, Shawn T. '95 (HRT) Meriden, CT St. Joseph; Meriden, CT St. Mary; New Haven Vicariate; Meriden Deanery; College of Consultors.

Daly, Simeon *o.s.b.* '48 (IND)[K] Saint Meinrad, IN St. Meinrad Archabbey.
Daly, Timothy P. '96 (ORL) Daytona Beach, FL Basilica of Saint Paul; [G] Daytona Beach, FL.
Daly, Vincent M. '71 (BRK) South Ozone Park, NY Our Lady of Perpetual Help.
Dam, LoXuan *m.m.* '00 (FgM) Maryknoll, NY MARYKNOLL.
Damboise, Aaron L. '08 (PRT) Caribou, ME Parish of the Precious Blood; [M] Portland, ME University of Maine at Presque Isle.
Damhorst, Joseph *s.j.* '68 (FgM) St. Louis, MO Society of Jesus.
Damian, Lawrence P. '71 (BUF) Depew, NY Blessed Mother Teresa of Calcutta.
Damian, Rinaldo '88 (MO) DEPARTMENT OF VETERANS AFFAIRS HOSPITALS AND CHAPLAINS.
Damian, Ronald '88 (WOR) On Duty Outside the Diocese.
Damico, Rodney M. '92 (COL) Columbus, OH Corpus Christi; Columbus, OH St. Ladislas; Columbus, OH St. Mary Church.
Damien, Paul (SAM) Easton, PA Our Lady of Lebanon.
Damis, Frank J. '84 (NY) Kingston, NY St. Joseph.
Dammay, Dante U. '77 (STO) Manteca, CA St. Anthony Church of Manteca (Pastor of).
Dammeir, James L. '79 (MIL) Retired.
Damoah, Francis *s.v.d.* '10 (JKS) Jackson, MS Holy Family; Jackson, MS Holy Ghost.
Damron, Robert '83 (LEX) Prestonsburg, KY St. Martha; Salyersville, KY St. Luke.
Dan, Bernard '04 (ROC) Geneseo, NY St. Luke the Evangelist Roman Catholic Church Society of Livingston County.
Danaher, Rev. Msgr. Mortimer '53 (STA) Retired.
Danaher, Philip M. '83 (JOL) Addison, IL St. Philip The Apostle.
Danaher, Thomas E. *s.m.* '62 (SJ)[M] Los Altos, CA Maryknoll.
Danber, Bernard R. *o.s.a.* '86 (CHI)[J] Chicago, IL Holy Cross Hospital; Chicago, IL St. Rita of Cascia.
Dance, Kevin *c.p.* (NEW)[L] Union City, NJ Congregation of the Passion (Passionists)–St. Michael's Residence.
Danczyk, Mark J. '92 (MIL) Caledonia, WI St. Louis.
Danda, Sean R. '09 (IND)[O] Indianapolis, IN University of Indianapolis Newman Center; Indianapolis, IN St. Barnabas Catholic Church, Indianapolis, Inc.
Dande, Benjamin *m.s.f.s.* '01 (DOD) Jetmore, KS St. Lawrence Catholic Church of Jetmore, Kansas; Jetmore, KS St. Anthony Catholic Church of Hanston, Kansas.
Dande, Benjamin *m.s.f.s.* '01 (TYL)[C] Whitehouse, TX The Missionaries of St. Francis de Sales.
Dandelet, James D. '54 (WIN) Retired.
Dandeneau, Stephen J. '11 (PRO) Bristol, RI Our Lady of Mount Carmel; [R] Bristol, RI Roger Williams University.
Dandurand, Douglas E. '82 (STP) Deephaven, MN St. Therese.
Dandurand, Michael G. '97 (TOL)[K] Bowling Green, OH Bowling Green State University Campus Ministry; Bowling Green, OH St. Thomas More University Parish; Youth, Young Adult and Campus Ministry.
Dane, James E. '83 (MOB) Orange Beach, AL St. Thomas by the Sea; Holy Childhood Association; Pontifical Mission Societies of the United States.
Dane, John '91 (LEX) Retired.
Danek, Michael *c.r.* '86 (JOL) Westmont, IL Holy Trinity.
Danel, Joseph B. *s.j.* '52 (FgM)[L] Portland Jesuit Provincial Office (Society of Jesus, Oregon Prov.); Portland, OR Society of Jesus.
Danella, Francis W. *o.s.f.s.* '73 (CAM) Cape May, NJ The Church of Our Lady Star of the Sea, Cape May.
Dang, Bernadine *c.m.c.* '02 (VEN) Fort Myers, FL Blessed Pope John XXIII.
Dang, Chin Van '83 (RIC) Military Chaplains; Navy Chaplains.
Dang, Ha Dinh '05 (BGP) Bridgeport, CT St. Augustine Cathedral.
Dang, Hai Duc '99 (GAL) New Caney, TX St. John of the Cross.
Dang, Joseph *s.v.d.* '93 (BEA) Beaumont, TX St. Pius X.
Dang, Quy *s.v.d.* '09 (TR)[N] Bordentown, NJ Society of the Divine Word.
Dang, Thomas Thien *o.s.b.* '93 (P)[L] St. Benedict, OR Mt. Angel Abbey.
Dang, Vincent H. '95 (SCR) Wyoming, PA St. Frances Cabrini.
Dang, Vincent Tinh '08 (SJ) Los Altos, CA St. Nicholas.
Dang Ha, Dominic Thuy '84 (SLC) Salt Lake City, UT Our Lady of Perpetual Help LLC 261.
Dango, Enno *c.p.* '10 (DET)[K] Detroit, MI St. Paul of the Cross Community, Congregation of the Passion.
Daniel, John C. '92 (SFE) College of Consultors; Albuquerque, NM St. Jude Thaddeus.
Daniele, Anthony J. '56 (BO) Senior Priests. Retired.
Danielewicz, Noel *o.f.m.conv.* (HRT)[M] Enfield Convent.
Danielewicz, Noel '76 (SPR) Chicopee, MA St. Stanislaus Basilica.
Daniels, Desmond '89 (GAL) Katy, TX St. Bartholomew the Apostle.
Daniels, Jerrell Michael '01 (JKS) Serving Outside the Diocese.
Daniels, Joel *o.f.m.cap.* '67 (NY)[DD] Yonkers, NY St. Clare Friary.
Daniels, John W. '36 (GRY) Retired.
Daniels, Joseph E. '90 (PRT) Vicars Forane; Waterville, ME Corpus Christi Parish.
Daniels, Lawrence *o.c.d.* '65 (MIL)[P] Milwaukee Provincial Offices – Discalced Carmelites.
Daniels, Leo Francis *c.o.* '65 (BWN) Pharr, TX St. Jude Thaddeus; [F] Pharr, TX Pharr Oratory of St. Philip Neri of Pontifical Right; Pharr, TX; [C] Pharr, TX Oratory Academy of St. Philip Neri; [B] Pharr, TX Oratory Athenaeum for University Preparation.
Daniels, Paul A. '57 (MIL) Retired.
Danielsen, Thomas *c.ss.r.* '64 (GR) Grand Rapids, MI St. Alphonsus.
Danielson, Charles R. '92 (BUR) Cambridge, VT St. Mary; Underhill Center, VT St. Thomas; Canon 1742 Panel of Pastors.
Danielson, Daniel E. '63 (OAK) Piedmont, CA Corpus Christi; Presbyteral Council Retired.
Danielson, Harold *s.d.b.* '66 (SFR) San Francisco, CA SS. Peter and Paul.
Danielson, Thomas *c.ss.r.* '64 (GR)[L] Grand Rapids, MI The Society of the Redemptorists of the City of Grand Rapids.
Danik, Daniel A. '48 (NEW) Bloomfield, NJ Sacred Heart; Serra Club of West Essex Retired.
Daniszewski, Rev. Msgr. Alfred '45 (MAN) Manchester, NH St. Hedwig.
Dankosa, Jacob '04 (DAL) Richardson, TX St. Joseph.
Dankoski, Francis '09 (STU)[J] Hopedale, OH The Order of the Sacred and Immaculate Hearts of Jesus and Mary.
Danneker, David L. '82 (HBG) Elizabethtown, PA St. Peter; [I] Elizabethtown, PA Elizabethtown College; Catholic Physicians League.
Danneker, Edward A.J. '64 (ATL) Atlanta, GA Holy Cross Retired.
Danner, Brian J. '95 (SC) Mapleton, IA St. Mary's.
Danner, James L. '74 (MEM) Retired.
Danner, Michael A. '65 (GR) Retired.
Danos, Dean F. '80 (HT) Upper Lafourche Deanery; Thibodaux, LA St. Genevieve.
Danos, Dean '80 (HT) Priests Council.
Dansak, Thomas J. '73 (PIT) SCI Pittsburgh.
Danso, Daniel A. '85 (VIC) Cuero, TX St. Michael; Cuero, TX Our Lady of Guadalupe.
Danso, Thomas '83 (BR)[F] Baton Rouge, LA Our Lady of the Lake Regional Medical Center.
Dant, J. Nicholas '77 (IND) Indianapolis, IN Our Lady of Lourdes Catholic Church, Indianapolis, Inc.; Indianapolis, IN St. Bernadette Catholic Church, Indianapolis, Inc.
Dant, Nicholas J. '77 (IND) Archdiocesan Judges.
Dante, Neal F. '64 (CAM) Retired.
Danter, Albert F. '43 (STL) Retired.
Dantinne, Gary J. '68 (GB) Retired.
Danylo, Rev. Archpriest Bohdan '96 (STF)[A] Stamford, CT Ukrainian Catholic Seminary Inc. St. Basil College; Presbyteral Council; Vocations; Liturgical Commission.
Danyluk, Richard J. *ss.cc.* '75 (LA) San Dimas, CA Holy Name of Mary; [P] La Verne, CA Congregation of the Sacred Hearts of Jesus and Mary.
Danzi, Rocco C. *s.j.* '00 (NEW)[L] Jersey City, NJ Jesuits of Saint Peter's College, Inc.
Danzi, Rocco C. *s.j.* '89 (NEW)[B] Jersey City, NJ Jesuit Center.
Dao, Anthony C. *o.p.* '82 (SB) Montclair, CA Our Lady of Lourdes; West End; Appointed Members.
Dao, Joseph Nam H. '00 (CHI) Highland Park, IL Immaculate Conception.
Dao, Ngo Van *c.ss.r.* '86 (LA)[P] Baldwin Park Vietnamese Redemptorist Mission.
Dao, Simon *c.m.c.* '05 (KC)[A] Conception, MO Conception Seminary College.
Dao, Thanh X. '03 (SEA) Vietnamese, Ministry to; Seattle, WA Vietnamese Martyrs Personal Parish.
Daoust, Joseph P. *s.j.* '69 (DET)[K] Detroit Detroit Province of the Society of Jesus–Provincial Office.
Daprile, James M. '76 (Y) Aurora, OH Our Lady of Perpetual Help.
Darbouze, Joseph '55 (NY) Bronx, NY St. Raymond.
Darbouze, Rev. Msgr. Rollin '69 (BRK) Retired.
Darcy, Brendan *s.m.a.* '67 (NEW)[L] Tenafly, NJ Society of African Missions, Provincialate, S.M.A. Fathers; Tenafly, NJ.
Darcy, David M. '94 (SPR) Chicopee, MA Holy Name of Jesus; Bishop's Commission for Clergy; Deans.
Darcy, James F. '66 (BO) Senior Priests. Retired.
Darcy, Rev. Msgr. John J. '79 (PRO) Providence, RI St. Sebastian.
Darcy, Michael J. *c.o.* '02 (PIT)[M] Pittsburgh, PA Congregation of the Oratory of St. Philip Neri.
Darcy, Michael P. '00 (WIL) Catholic Scouting Program; Hockessin, DE St. Mary of the Assumption.
Dargan, Peter S. '61 (HRT) Orange, CT Holy Infant.
Dargis, Andre E. '67 (WOR) Retired.
Dargis, Andre '67 (PHX) Scottsdale, AZ St. Patrick Roman Catholic Parish.
Daries, Joseph *c.m.f.* '56 (LA)[V] Rancho Dominguez, CA Dominguez Seminary Inc.
Darilek, Rev. Msgr. Dennis '73 (SAT) Seguin, TX St. James.
Darin, David M. '91 (BEL) Belleville, IL St. Luke; Diocesan Liturgical Commission; Belleville, IL St. Teresa of the Child Jesus.
Darling, George E. '84 (GR) Grand Rapids, MI Blessed Sacrament; Clergy Fund.
Darling, William G. '73 (ROC) Weedsport, NY Our Lady of the Snow.
Darmawanto, Irtikandik *o.carm.* '08 (WDC)[B] Washington, DC Whitefriars Hall.
Darnell, Lawrence T. *o.m.v.* '82 (LA) Hawaiian Gardens, CA St. Peter Chanel.
Darow, Robert G. '63 (CHI) Chicago, IL St. Hilary Retired.
DaRoza, George *s.s.c.* '85 (OM)[J] St. Columbans Missionary Society of St. Columban.
Darragh, John J. '69 (HEL) Hamilton, MT St. Francis.
Darragh, John '69 (HEL) Presbyteral Council; Diocesan Consultors.
Dasari, Joseph Jojayya '97 (BGP) Danbury, CT St. Joseph.
Dascenzo, Joseph J. '58 (PIT) Ellwood City, PA Holy Redeemer Parish Retired.
Daschbach, Richard *s.v.d.* '64 (FgM) Techny, IL.
Dash, Alan J. '67 (R) Retired.
Dash, George J. *o.f.m.cap.* '92 (NY) Beacon, NY Fishkill Correctional Facility; East Elmhurst, NY Anna M. Kross Center; Prison Apostolate.
Da Silva, A. Paul '98 (MET) Legion of Mary.
DaSilva, Antonio F. '88 (NEW) Newark, NJ Our Lady of Fatima.
da Silva, Antonio L. *s.d.v.* '83 (NEW) Newark, NJ St. Michael's.
DaSilva, Arlindo Paul '98 (MET) Piscataway, NJ Our Lady of Fatima.
da Silva, Darci Donizetti (BO) Rockland, MA Holy Family.
Da Silva, Jose Carlos '92 (BRK)[Q] Brazilian Apostolate; Long Island City, NY St. Rita.
da Silva, Rev. Msgr. Joseph '72 (B) Boise, ID Risen Christ Catholic Community; Vicars General; Ex Officio; Priest Personnel Commission; Ecumenical Commission; Ex Officio; Finance Council.
Das Neves, Antonio '61 (SB) Sun City, CA St. Vincent Ferrer.
Dass, Ajith Kumar *ss.cc.* '06 (FR)[F] Fairhaven National Center of the Enthronement.
Dass, Joseph '89 (LA) Alhambra, CA All Souls.
Dassanayake, Vincent Paul (NY) Pawling, NY St. John the Evangelist.
Datko, James *o.m.i.* '51 (DUL) Duluth, MN Holy Family.
Dattilo, Anthony A. '90 (STL) Apple Creek, MO St. Joseph; Perryville, MO St. Maurus; Deaneries/Deans.
Dattilo, Anthony M. '84 (CIN) Cincinnati, OH St. Catharine of Siena.
Datzman, Harold L. *o.s.b.* '65 (PEO) Peru, IL St. Joseph's; [A] Peru, IL St. Bede Abbey.
Daugherty, Daniel L. '94 (TYL) Gun Barrel City, TX St. Jude.
Daugherty, Patrick *c.p.* '02 (PMB)[H] North Palm Beach, FL Our Lady of Florida Spiritual Center.
Daugherty, Rev. Msgr. Scott '83 (FRS) Porterville, CA St. Anne.
Dauphinais, Louis Marie *m.m.a.* '70 (SAM)[B] Petersham, MA Maronite Monks of Adoration Most Holy Trinity Monastery; Petersham, MA.
Dauphine, Marc Rene '09 (MRY) Watsonville, CA St. Patrick.
Dauses, Jeffrey S. '90 (BAL) Annapolis, MD St. Andrew by the Bay; [T] Annapolis, MD St. Andrew by the Bay Endowment Trust.
Dauss, Francis '48 (SP) Retired.
Dautremont, Charles R. '60 (GR) Grand Rapids, MI St. Dominic.
Davadilla, Joel '88 (FRS) Tehachapi, CA St. Malachy.
Davalos, Rev. Msgr. Carlos '78 (SAT) In Metropolitan Area; Priests Personnel Board; Helotes, TX Our Lady of Guadalupe; College of Consultors; Archdiocesan Presbyteral Council.
Davalos, Juan Pablo '07 (BWN) Santa Rosa, TX St. Mary; [K] Santa Rosa, TX Boy Scouts.
Davantes, Carlo B. '79 (MO) Navy Reserve Chaplains.
Davanzo, Joseph V. '97 (RVC) Commack, NY Christ the King; Priests' Retirement Board.
Dave, Kyle V. '01 (NO) Lacombe, LA Sacred Heart.
Davenport, Christopher M. '61 (PRO) Retired.
Davenport, Clement A. '48 (SFR) Retired.
Davern, Rev. Msgr. Robert B. '51 (SY)[Q] Syracuse, NY Tommy Coyne Residence Dillon Hall Retired.
Davern, Timothy R. '78 (PHX) Censor Librorum; Presbyteral Council; Diocesan Judges.

Davern, Timothy '78 (PHX) Priests' Assurance Association; Tempe, AZ Holy Spirit Roman Catholic Parish.
Davey, Edward M. '53 (PAT)[Q] Chester, NJ Nazareth Village Retired.
Davich, Rev. Msgr. George '62 (SLC) Retired.
David, Angelo '11 (SJ) San Jose, CA Queen of Apostles.
David, Craig '96 (MO) DEPARTMENT OF VETERANS AFFAIRS HOSPITALS AND CHAPLAINS.
David, Craig '96 (LA) Veterans Affairs Medical Center.
David, George '71 (ROM) Roebling, NJ St. Mary; Trenton, NJ St. Basil; Finance Council; College of Consultors; Protosyncellus; Director of Vocations; Trenton Deanery.
David, Jamin S. '08 (BR) Baton Rouge, LA St. Aloysius; Judges.
David, Jamin (NO)[A] St. Benedict, LA St. Joseph Seminary College.
Davidowich, Glenn M. '89 (PSC) Leave of Absence.
Davidson, John '64 (EVN) Evansville, IN St. Anthony.
Davidson, Michael F. *s.j.* '09 (BO)[U] Newton, MA The Jesuit Community at Boston College.
Davies, Daniel *o.p.* '58 (NY) Pleasantville, NY Holy Innocents.
Davies, Julian A. *o.f.m.* '60 (ALB)[B] Siena College.
Davies, Maximos '06 (ROM)[A] St. Nazianz, WI Holy Resurrection Monastery.
Davies, Steven E. '77 (SFR) Retired.
Davignon, Charles P. '56 (BUR) Retired.
Davignon, Philip A. '62 (FR) Osterville, MA Our Lady of the Assumption.
Davila, Alexis '84 (SD) San Diego, CA Saint Jude Shrine of the West Catholic Parish.
Davila, Andres (ARE) On Duty Outside the Diocese.
Davila, Rafael R. *m.m.* '58 (GAL)[A] Houston, TX St. Mary's Seminary; [O] Houston Maryknoll Fathers and Brothers.
Davila, Reinaldo I. '90 (ARE) Arecibo, PR Cathedral of San Felipe Apostol.
Davila, Rito '05 (AUS) Buda, TX Santa Cruz.
Davin, Neil W. *c.p.* '52 (MET)[I] Somerset, NJ Maria Regina Residence; Canonical Staff.
Davin, Neil *c.p.* '52 (BRK)[R] Jamaica, NY Immaculate Conception Monastery.
Davin, William *c.p.* '56 (PIT)[M] Pittsburgh, PA St. Paul of the Cross Monastery.
Davino, Michael J. '86 (CHR) Absent On Leave.
Davis, Anthony K.A. '85 (SEA) Enumclaw, WA Sacred Heart of Jesus.
Davis, Augustine *o.s.b.* '59 (IND)[K] Saint Meinrad, IN St. Meinrad Archabbey.
Davis, Christopher J. '98 (CHL) Greensboro, NC Our Lady of Grace.
Davis, Christopher *o.s.b.* '58 (PRO)[O] Portsmouth, RI Abbey of St. Gregory the Great.
Davis, Clement T. '70 (IND) Columbus, IN St. Bartholomew Catholic Church, Columbus, Inc.; Archdiocesan Judges.
Davis, Clyde F. *m.m.* '63 (SJ)[M] Los Altos, CA Maryknoll.
Davis, Clyde F. *m.m.* '63 (NY)[DD].
Davis, Cyprian *o.s.b.* '56 (IND)[A] Saint Meinrad, IN Saint Meinrad School of Theology; [K] Saint Meinrad, IN St. Meinrad Archabbey.
Davis, D.G. "Skip" '98 (E) Fryburg, PA St. Michael.
Davis, Daniel C. *o.p.* '94 (SFE) ALBQ: Aquinas Newman Center; [K] Albuquerque, NM St. Thomas Aquinas (Newman Center) University Parish; Albuquerque, NM St. Thomas Aquinas University Parish.
Davis, Edward V. *m.m.* '61 (FgM) Maryknoll, NY MARYKNOLL.
Davis, Ernest P. '02 (KC) Priestly Life and Ministry; Kansas City, MO St. Therese Little Flower; Administrative Committee.
Davis, F. Hampton (LAF) Lafayette, LA Our Lady Queen of Peace.
Davis, Gary G. '75 (L) Louisville, KY St. Athanasius.
Davis, Henry *s.s.j.* '93 (BEA) Beaumont, TX Blessed Sacrament; Beaumont, TX Our Mother of Mercy; Presbyteral Council.
Davis, Jacob '99 (YAK) East Wenatchee, WA Holy Apostles.
Davis, John B. *o.p.* '66 (WDC) Washington, DC St. Dominic Church & Priory.
Davis, John E. '69 (FAR) Retired.
Davis, John P. '63 (PRT) Retired.
Davis, Joseph P. '72 (PAT) Unassigned.
Davis, Karl *o.m.i.* '05 (OAK) Oakland, CA Sacred Heart.
Davis, Kenneth *o.f.m.conv.* '86 (IND)[J] Mount St. Francis, IN Mount Saint Francis Friary and Retreat Center.
Davis, Kirk *o.s.a.* '09 (SD)[C] San Diego, CA St. Augustine High School; [J] San Diego, CA Augustinian Community.
Davis, Leo D. '64 (SPK)[J] Spokane, WA Regis Community.
Davis, Mark E. '96 (TOL) Bowling Green, OH St. Aloysius.
Davis, Michael J. '87 (PH) Croydon, PA St. Thomas Aquinas.
Davis, Michael W. '90 (MIA) Coral Gables, FL Little Flower.
Davis, Noel '62 (LAR) Encinal, TX Immaculate Heart of Mary.
Davis, Richard P. '63 (LR) Bigelow, AR St. Elizabeth; Bigelow, AR St. Boniface; Bigelow, AR St. Francis of Assisi Church.
Davis, Richard *t.o.r.* '80 (STU) Presbyteral Council; [A] Steubenville, OH Franciscan University of Steubenville; [H] Steubenville, OH Holy Spirit Friary.
Davis, Terrence '69 (SJ) Retired.
Davis, Thomas R. '83 (R) Hope Mills, NC Good Shepherd.
Davis, Rev. Msgr. Wilbur '64 (ORG) Newport Beach, CA Our Lady Queen of Angels Retired.
Davis, William E. *o.s.f.s.* '82 (WIL)[J] Wilmington Wilmington–Philadelphia Province of the Oblates of St. Francis de Sales; [J] Wilmington, DE DeSales House.
Davis, William F. *o.s.f.s.* '61 (WDC)[B] Washington, DC Oblates of St. Francis de Sales.
Davis, William F. *o.s.f.s.* '61 (WIL)[B] Wilmington, DE Salesianum School.
Davis, William Tom *o.s.a.* '10 (LA) Ojai, CA St. Thomas Aquinas.
Davis, William *o.m.i.* '60 (LAR) Laredo, TX San Francisco Javier.
Davison, Andreas R. '07 (BO) Marlborough, MA Immaculate Conception.
Davison, Ben '92 (SD) El Cajon, CA Saint Kieran Catholic Parish.
Davison, Donald *c.pp.s.* '80 (CIN)[N] Dayton Provincial Office of the Cincinnati Province of the Society of the Precious Blood.
Davison, Donald *c.pp.s.* '80 (LFT) Rensselaer, IN St. Augustine.
Davison, Timothy L. '85 (TLS) Tulsa, OK SS. Peter and Paul; Diocesan Senators; Diocesan Consultors.
DaVola, Rev. Msgr. F. Robert '67 (BWN) Retired.
Davoren, Stephen V. '96 (LA) Ventura, CA Our Lady of the Assumption; Santa Barbara Region.
Davy, Andy *m.i.c.* '09 (JOL) Plano, IL St. Mary.
Davy, Kavungal Lonappan *c.m.i.* '96 (COV) Carrollton, KY St. John the Evangelist.
Daw, Timothy M. '91 (CLV) Rocky River, OH St. Christopher.
Daw, Victor *o.m.m.* '86 (OLL) Ann Arbor, MI; [A] Ann Arbor, MI Maronite Order of the Blessed Virgin Mary.
Dawis, Ralph '54 (NY) Staten Island, NY Richmond University Medical Center; Staten Island, NY Richmond University Medical Center/Bayley Seton Campus.
Dawley, Robert (RVC) Melville, NY Good Shepherd Hospice (Nassau).
Dawson, Rev. Msgr. James D. '54 (LIN)[E] Lincoln, NE Bonacum House; Evangelization Committee Retired.
Dawson, Richard '81 (PT) Bonifay, FL Blessed Trinity; De Funiak Springs, FL St. Margaret.
Dawson, Wayne '98 (MRY) Salinas, CA Madonna Del Sasso.
Dawson, William A. *s.j.* '58 (BAL)[Q] Baltimore, MD Colombiere Jesuit Community.
Dawson, William F. '54 (DAV)[A] St. Ambrose University Retired.
Day, Charles J. '81 (CHR) Retired.
Day, Dennis C. '76 (B) Sandpoint, ID St. Joseph's; College of Consultors; Deans.
Day, James R. *o.ss.t.* '72 (BAL)[Q] Archdiocese of Philadelphia, PA.
Day, James R. *o.s.s.t.* '72 (WDC)[E] Hyattsville, MD De Matha Catholic High School.
Day, James Richard '96 (NO) Gretna, LA St. Joseph.
Day, Jeffrey '99 (DET) Farmington Hills, MI St. Fabian; Ecumenical/Interfaith Relations.
Day, Jerome J. *o.s.b.* '95 (MAN) Manchester, NH St. Raphael; [K] Manchester, NH St. Anselm Abbey.
Day, John P. *c.p.* '72 (CHI)[N] Chicago Passionist Provincial Office.
Day, John Patrick *c.p.* '72 (STL) Sullivan, MO Church of the Holy Martyrs of Japan.
Day, Martin *o.f.m.conv.* '91 (IND)[J] Mount St. Francis, IN Province of Our Lady of Consolation, Inc.
Day, Martin *o.f.m.conv.* '91 (SAT)[B] San Antonio, TX San Damiano Friary, Prenovitiate House of Formation; [L] San Antonio, TX San Damiano Friary.
Day, Michael '71 (SJ) On Leave of Absence.
Day, Wilfred E. '67 (IND) Floyds Knobs, IN St. John the Baptist Catholic Church, Starlight, Inc.; Deaneries and Deans.
Day, William F. '86 (GLP) Retired.
Daya, John *o.f.m.cap.* '78 (PH) Philadelphia, PA St. John the Evangelist.
Daz, Rev. Msgr. Rudolph A. '54 (SLC) Retired.
Daza, Diego '98 (POD) Washington.
Daza, Wilmer de Jesus '99 (DAL)[M] Dallas, TX Nuestra Senora del Pilar Land & Development Trust; Dallas, TX Nuestra Senora del Pilar.
DeAdder, James W. '55 (BO) Senior Priests. Retired.
De Agostini, Claudio *c.s.j.* '58 (LA) San Pedro, CA St. Peter.
DeAguilar, Arturo '97 (CHL) Absent On Leave.
De Alba, Ricardo *m.sp.s.* '81 (LA) Hacienda Heights, CA St. John Vianney.
de Almeida, Filipe R.J. *o.s.b.* '00 (GBG)[H] Latrobe, PA Saint Vincent Archabbey.
DeAmato, Norbert *o.f.m.* '48 (BO) Cambridge, MA St. Francis of Assisi; [U] Boston, MA St. Christopher Friary Retired.
Dean, Frederic D. '65 (PRO)[O] Providence St. John Vianney Residence Retired.
Dean, Gregory '54 (CC) Retired.
Dean, Harry '96 (AUS) Priestly Life and Formation Committee; Vicar for Clergy; Ex Officio.
Dean, John T. '72 (SPR)[M] Westfield, MA Westfield State College Retired.
Dean, Joseph R. *s.c.j.* '84 (RC)[C] Lower Brule, SD SCJ Community House; Lower Brule, SD St. Mary's.
Dean, Joseph *s.c.j.* '84 (MIL)[P] Hales Corners, WI Priests of the Sacred Heart.
Dean, Joseph *s.c.j.* '84 (SFS) Fort Thompson, SD St. Joseph; Lower Brule, SD Immaculate Conception.
Dean, Justin Damian (MOB) On Leave from the Archdiocese.
Dean, Mark *o.m.i.* '83 (BEL)[H] Belleville, IL King's House Retreat and Renewal Center.
Dean, Prentice C. '10 (NSH) Springfield, TN Our Lady of Lourdes.
Dean, William E. '76 (PH) Philadelphia, PA Sacred Heart of Jesus.
de Anda, James R. '05 (OM) South Sioux City, NE St. Michael.
Deane, J. Peter *s.j.* '66 (DET)[K] Clarkston, MI Colombiere Center.
Deane, Rev. Msgr. Joseph '59 (AUS) Retired.
de Angel, Miguel A. '05 (CGS) Yabucoa, PR Santos Angeles Cutodios.
DeAngelis, Mark J. '88 (BO) Framingham, MA St. Bridget.
De Angelis, Sante *o.f.m.* '62 (MIL)[Y] Waterford, WI General Secretariat of the Franciscan Missions, Inc.
DeAngelis, Sante *o.f.m.* '59 (MIL)[P] Burlington, WI Queen of Peace Friary.
DeAngelo, Jude *o.f.m.conv.* (WDC)[C] Washington, DC Catholic University of America, The.
DeAntoniis, Paul J. *o.praem* '63 (PH)[Y] Paoli, PA Daylesford Abbey; [S] Darby, PA Mercy Fitzgerald Hospital.
Dear, John S. *s.j.* '93 (BAL)[Q] Baltimore, MD Ferdinand Wheeler Jesuit Community.
Deardorff, Joseph F. *c.pp.s.* '82 (CIN)[N] Dayton Provincial Office of the Cincinnati Province of the Society of the Precious Blood.
Dearhammer, John W. '91 (CHI) Schaumburg, IL Church of the Holy Spirit; Deans.
de Armas, Alexio Jose *o.c.d.* '58 (PCE) Ponce, PR San Jose.
De Arruda Zamith, Rt. Rev. Joaquim F. *o.s.b.* '00 (GBG)[H] Latrobe, PA Saint Vincent Archabbey Retired.
Deary, John F. *o.s.a.* '66 (VEN) Cape Coral, FL Saint Katharine Drexel.
Deas, Rev. Msgr. George T. '51 (BRK)[R] Douglaston, NY Bishop Mugavero Residence Retired.
DeAscanis, Michael '04 (BAL) Baltimore, MD St. Agnes; Baltimore, MD St. William of York.
Dease, Dennis J. '69 (STP)[C] St. Paul, MN University of St. Thomas.
Deasey, Ken '87 (LA) Holy Childhood Association.
Deasio, August J. '75 (STU) Retired.
Deasy, Jeremiah '67 (BIR) Tuscaloosa, AL Holy Spirit; [I] Tuscaloosa, AL The Harrison Family Endowment Trust for the Benefit of Holy Spirit School; Diocesan College of Consultors; Priests'/Presbyteral Council; Diocesan College of Vicars.
Deasy, Kenneth '87 (LA) Los Angeles, CA St. Brendan.
Deasy, Rev. Msgr. Timothy J. '58 (MOB) Retired.
Deasy, Wayman P. *m.m.* '59 (NY)[DD] Maryknoll Maryknoll Fathers and Brothers; [DD] Maryknoll, NY Maryknoll Fathers and Brothers Charitable Trust.
Deatrick, John D. '66 (L) Retired.
Deaver, Stephen F. '59 (GI) Council of Catholic Women, Diocesan Retired.
DeAvila, Rafael '74 (SFR) San Bruno, CA St. Bruno.
Debany, Edgar J. *s.j.* '84 (BAL)[Q] Towson Maryland Province of the Society of Jesus; Towson, MD Society of Jesus.
DeBellis, John A. '85 (NY) Carmel, NY St. James the Apostle.
DeBellis, Peter '97 (ROC) Absent on Leave.
Debes, Donald *o.f.m.cap.* '70 (FgM) Denver, CO Province of Mid–America.
DeBiase, William *o.f.m.* '66 (PH)[Y] Philadelphia, PA Order of Friars Minor of the Province of the Most Holy Name.
Debicki, John P. '64 (POD) Washington.
Debicki, John '64 (WDC)[V] Washington, DC Prelature of the Holy Cross and Opus Dei; [G] Potomac, MD The Heights School.
DeBisschop, James P. '88 (PEO) Coal Valley, IL St. Maria Goretti; Orion, IL Mary, Our Lady of Peace.

Debitetto, Ronald E. '63 (WOR) Retired.
DeBlanc, Rev. Msgr. Jefferson J. '77 (LAF) Church Point, LA Our Lady of the Sacred Heart.
De Blas, Alonso *o.f.m.* '64 (PHX)[G] Scottsdale, AZ Franciscan Renewal Center, Inc. (Casa de Paz Y Bien); Scottsdale, AZ Our Lady of the Angels Conventual Church.
de Blas, Mariano *l.c.* '72 (LA)[P] Arcadia, CA Legionaries of Christ.
DeBlase, Dominic *s.d.b.* '61 (WDC) Washington, DC Nativity.
DeBlase, Dominic *s.d.b.* '61 (NY)[FF] Stony Point, NY Don Bosco Retreat Center and Marian Shrine.
DeBlasio, Dominck A. '40 (PIT) Retired.
DeBlasio, Ernie '88 (MEM) Memphis, TN Church of the Resurrection; College of Consultors; Presbyteral Council.
DeBlock, Matthew '08 (RCK)[K] Elgin, IL St. Edward Central Catholic High School Education Foundation.
Debo, William D. '95 (JC) Hermann, MO St. George; Rhineland, MO Church of the Risen Savior; Senators.
DeBoe, Stanley W. *o.ss.t.* '83 (BAL)[Q] Diocese of Victoria, TX.
DeBoe, Stanley *o.ss.t.* '83 (VIC) Victoria, TX Our Lady of Sorrows; Presbyteral Council.
DeBona, Guerric *o.s.b.* '86 (IND)[A] Saint Meinrad, IN Saint Meinrad School of Theology; [K] Saint Meinrad, IN St. Meinrad Archabbey; Officers.
De Brito Alves, Joseph '67 (BGP) Bridgeport, CT Our Lady of Fatima.
de Bruijn, Johan *o.cart.* '91 (BUR)[E] Arlington, VT Carthusian Foundation in America, Inc., Charterhouse of the Transfiguration.
DeBruycker, James R. '82 (STP) Minneapolis, MN St. Joan of Arc.
Debski, Joseph E. '64 (MIL) Retired.
Dec, Ignatius (Allen) *m.m.a.* '84 (SAM)[B] Petersham, MA Maronite Monks of Adoration Most Holy Trinity Monastery.
Decaen, Ramon E. '00 (LIN) Lincoln, NE Cristo Rey; Advocates; Apostolate to the Spanish Speaking.
Decal, Wilfredo '77 (HT) Cut–Off, LA Sacred Heart.
De Candia, Anthony '07 (R) Raleigh, NC Doggett Center at Aquinas House.
DeCandia, Anthony '01 (R)[I] Raleigh, NC Doggett Center for Catholic Campus Ministry at Aquinas House.
de Cardenas, Rev. Msgr. Javier Garcia '85 (NY)[II] New York, NY Prelature of the Holy Cross and Opus Dei; New York.
DeCarlo, Philip J. '55 (PIT) Retired.
DeCarlo, Thomas M. '69 (DM)[E] Johnston, IA Bishop Drumm Retirement Center.
De Carlo Mena, Francisco '50 (SJN) Retired.
DeCarolis, Joseph R. '59 (HRT) Retired.
DeCarolis, Vito C. '54 (HRT) Retired.
Decasa, George '78 (SD) Holtville, CA Saint Joseph Catholic Parish Holtville.
De Celles, John C. '96 (ARL) Springfield, VA St. Raymond of Penafort.
Decewicz, Michael W. '78 (PIT) Sharpsburg, PA Saint Juan Diego Parish.
Dechant, Leo *c.s.j.* '80 (LA) Lancaster, CA Blessed Junipero Serra.
Dechant, Paul *o.s.f.s.* '90 (CHL) Kernersville, NC Holy Cross.
Dechering, Rev. Msgr. Anton '62 (SP) St. Petersburg, FL Blessed Trinity; Scouting Office, Girls.
Decipeda, Raymond *m.m.h.c.* '91 (LA) Artesia, CA Holy Family.
Deck, Allan F. *s.j.* '76 (WDC)[O] Washington, DC Leonard Neale House.
Deck, Marion *t.o.r.* '69 (ALT)[G] Loretto, PA St. Francis Friary at Mount Assisi.
Decker, Chris (NO)[A] St. Benedict, LA St. Joseph Seminary College.
Decker, Christopher J. '07 (BR) St. James, LA St. James; Vacherie, LA St. Philip; Presbyteral Council.
Decker, Douglas A. '78 (OG) Tupper Lake, NY St. Alphonsus – Holy Name of Jesus; Advocates; Air National Guard Chaplains.
Decker, Jonathan *m.m.j. m.j.* '76 (OLL) Portland, OR Saint Sharbel Maronite Catholic Church; [D] Portland, OR Oblates of Jesus, Mary & Joseph.
Decker, Lawrence J. '84 (ALB) Amsterdam, NY St. Joseph–St. Michael–Our Lady of Mount Carmel.
Decker, Neil F. *s.j.* '58 (BO)[U] Weston, MA Campion Health Center, Inc.
Decker, Raymond G. '58 (SFR) Retired.
Decker, Robert L. '83 (OG) Harrisville, NY St. Francis Solanus; Star Lake, NY St. Hubert; Campus Ministry.
Deckman, Peter '64 (ROC) Retired.
DeClippel, Ludo *c.j.* '68 (LA) Santa Barbara, CA Holy Cross; Santa Maria, CA.
DeClue, Richard '07 (CHL) Charlotte, NC St. Patrick Cathedral.
DeCola, Vincent P. *s.j.* '88 (NY)[DD] New York, NY "America;" Residence and publication office of the America Press.
DeConcilliis, Anthony J. *c.s.c.* '67 (FTW)[H] Notre Dame Congregation of Holy Cross, United States Province of Priests & Brothers.
DeCosta, George '64 (HON) Retired.
DeCosta, Joseph F. '90 (NOR) Killingworth, CT St. Lawrence.
DeCoste, Wade '03 (ALX) On Duty Outside the Diocese.
Decoteau, Vernon P. '75 (SPR) Belchertown, MA St. Francis of Assisi; Diocesan Commission for the Liturgy.
DeCrans, Joseph '84 (CR) Deans; Ada, MN St. Joseph's; Priests Retirement Board of Trustees.
DeCrans, William '08 (CR) Deans; Hallock, MN St. Patrick's.
de Cristobal, Fernando '65 (GRY) Retired.
Dede, Paul M. '64 (IND) Retired.
de Dios, Alfredo *o.a.r.* '60 (ORG)[I] Santa Ana, CA Augustinian Recollects; Santa Ana, CA Our Lady of Guadalupe.
de Dios Oliveros, Juan '99 (ATL) Dalton, GA St. Joseph.
DeDomenico, Dominic *o.p.* '66 (OAK)[L] Oakland, CA Order of Preachers (Province of the Most Holy Name of Jesus – Western Dominican Province); [Q] Oakland, CA Dominican Community Support Charitable Trust; [L] Oakland, CA Order of Preachers (Province of the Most Holy Name of Jesus – Western Dominican Province); Oakland, CA.
De Dominici, Lorenzo '46 (LA) San Pedro, CA Mary, Star of the Sea Retired.
Dee, Rev. Msgr. Dacian '56 (SP) Promoter of Justice; Defenders of the Bond Retired.
Deegan, James *o.m.i.* '70 (STP)[M] Buffalo, MN Christ the King Retreat Center.
Deegan, John E. *o.s.a.* '61 (PH)[Y] Villanova, PA St. John Stone Friary; Counselors.
Deehan, Robert J. '83 (BO) Duxbury, MA Holy Family; Ex Officio.
Deehr, Anselm *s.t.* '90 (WDC)[O] Adelphi, MD Father Judge Missionary Cenacle.
Deeke, Von C. '03 (BEL) Diocesan Pastoral Council; Belleville, IL St. Augustine of Canterbury.
Deeker, Geoffrey J. *c.s.s.* '60 (SPR) Diocesan Commission for the Liturgy; Pittsfield, MA St. Joseph's.
Deeley, Rev. Msgr. Robert P. '73 (BO) Vicar General and Moderator of the Curia; Vicars General; Ex Officio; [CC] Braintree, MA Caritas Christi Retirement Plan and Trust; Ex Officio; Health Benefit Trust, Insurance and Pension Trusts, Caritas Christi Retirement Plan; Chair; Boston, MA Cathedral of the Holy Cross; College of Consultors; Members.
Deely, John *o.m.i.* '70 (FgM) Washington, DC AMERICAN OBLATE MISSIONS.
Deely, Thomas (Martin) *c.ss.r.* '65 (NY)[FF] Esopus, NY Mount St. Alphonsus Redemptorist Retreat Center.
Deeney, Charles J. *o.m.i.* '71 (ORL) Apopka, FL St. Francis of Assisi.
Deering, Rev. Msgr. Mark '53 (AUS) Retired.
Deering, Michael J. '02 (BIR) Gardendale, AL St. Elizabeth Ann Seton; Diocesan College of Consultors; Priests'/Presbyteral Council; Diocesan College of Vicars.
Dees, Elliott Richard '11 (CHI) Glenview, IL Our Lady of Perpetual Help.
Deevy, Edward '62 (ALX) Absent on Leave.
Defayette, Jeffrey M. '88 (WDC) Lanham, MD St. Matthias Apostle.
DeFazio, Vincent G. '92 (SFE) Retired.
DeFelice, Jonathan P. *o.s.b.* '74 (MAN)[B] Manchester, NH Saint Anselm College; [K] Manchester, NH St. Anselm Abbey.
Deffenbaugh, Joseph T. '79 (Y) On Duty Outside the Diocese.
Deffenbaugh, Terry A. *o.s.a.* '75 (CHI)[N] Matteson, IL Austin Friary.
DeFolco, Jay '85 (SEA) Snohomish County Jail.
DeFolco, Joseph '85 (SEA) Snohomish, WA St. Michael; Lake Stevens, WA Holy Cross Parish.
DeForest, Matthew J. '09 (ARL) Falls Church, VA St. Anthony's.
DeForge, Michael W. '79 (BUR) Canon 1742 Panel of Pastors; Shelburne, VT St. Catherine of Siena; Deans; [G] Northfield, VT Norwich Newman Apostolate.
De Francisco, Joseph '75 (DAV)[A] St. Ambrose University.
DeFrancisco, Joseph '75 (BEA) On Duty Outside the Diocese.
De Franco, Anthony '38 (ALB) Schenectady, NY St. Anthony Retired.
DeFrange, Jonathan M. *o.s.b.* '78 (NO)[R] St. Benedict, LA St. Joseph Abbey; Covington, LA St. Benedict.
DeFronzo, Anthony P. '81 (PSC) Special or Other Diocesan Assignment.
de Gaal, Emery '00 (CHI)[A] Mundelein, IL University of St. Mary of the Lake/Mundelein Seminary.
DeGaetano, Louis J. '79 (BRK) Flushing, NY St. Kevin.
Degagne, Richard E. '82 (FR) East Freetown, MA St. John Neumann.
DeGaris, Herbert P. '91 (NY) Bronxville, NY St. Joseph.
Degen, Jerome A. '59 (SC) Retired.
Degenhardt, Gervase *o.f.m.cap.* '58 (PIT)[M] Pittsburgh, PA St. Augustine Friary; [N] Pittsburgh, PA Sisters of St. Francis of the Neumann Communities, Western Pennsylvania Region.
DeGeorge, Salvatore *o.m.i.* '65 (GAL) Houston, TX St. Patrick; Central Vicariate.
DeGerolami, Michael '74 (SAT) San Antonio, TX St. Timothy's.
Degeyter, Edward '70 (LAF) Retired.
DeGiacomo, Albert J. '08 (LEX) Lexington, KY The Newman Center, Holy Spirit; [L] Lexington, KY The Newman Center Holy Spirit Parish University of Kentucky.
DeGiovine, Christopher '77 (ALB) Special Assignment; [B] Albany, NY The College of Saint Rose; Priestly Life and Ministry Council.
Deglaire, Pierre L. *c.s.sp.* '70 (SB) Highland, CA St. Adelaide.
Degnan, Charles *s.s.c.* '43 (OM)[J] St. Columbans Missionary Society of St. Columban.
Degnan, Charles *s.s.c.* '43 (PRO)[O] Bristol, RI St. Columban's Retirement House Retired.
Degnan, Rev. Msgr. Henry B. '48 (PH) Norristown, PA St. Paul Retired.
Degnan, James F. '55 (BO) Senior Priests. Retired.
DeGracia Yadao, Rolando Rosendo '11 (NEW) Summit, NJ St. Teresa's.
DeGrand, Robert L. '80 (SFD) Effingham, IL St. Mary Help of Christians; Sigel, IL Sacred Heart; Sigel, IL St. Mary of the Assumption; Sigel, IL St. Michael the Archangel; Presbyteral Council.
DeGrassa, James R. '10 (PH) Penndel, PA Our Lady of Grace.
DeGrocco, Rev. Msgr. Joseph '88 (RVC) Presbyteral Council; College of Consultors; [A] Huntington, NY Diocesan Seminary of the Immaculate Conception.
DeGrood, Donald E. '97 (STP) Forest Lake, MN St. Peter.
DeGroot, Francis J. '93 (MAR) Escanaba, MI St. Anne; Advocates; Vicars Forane.
DeGroot, Ignatius *o.f.m.* '64 (TUC) Topawa, AZ San Solano Missions Roman Catholic Parish – Topawa.
DeGroot, Kenneth *o.praem.* (GB)[J] De Pere, WI St. Joseph Priory.
DeGuzman, Dennis U. '91 (OM) Military Chaplains.
De Guzman, Dennis '91 (MO) Air Force Chaplains.
Deh, Christopher '84 (RVC) Shoreham, NY St. Mark.
De Heredia, Agnel '80 (SFR) South San Francisco, CA All Souls.
De Herrera, Christopher *o.s.* '97 (PCE) Penuelas, PR Sacred Heart; [H] Penuelas, PR Oblates of Wisdom.
Dehetre, Mark '93 (LAN) On Leave of Absence.
Dehne, Carl A. *s.j.* '70 (STL)[O] St. Louis, MO Jesuit Community Corporation at Saint Louis University – Jesuit Hall.
DeHondt, Ronald '73 (DET) St. Clair Shores, MI St. Margaret of Scotland.
Deibel, David L. '83 (SR)[L] Napa, CA Provincialate Community.
Deibel, David L. '83 (SAC) Judges.
Deibel, David L. (CHY) Defenders of the Bond.
Deibel, David '83 (MRY) Special Assignment.
Deichert, Joseph '84 (BIS) On Duty Outside the Diocese; Air Force Chaplains.
Deichert, Joseph '84 (HON) Military Chaplains.
Deig, Robert A. '50 (EVN) Retired.
Deikel, Jeffrey '76 (LA) Covina, CA Sacred Heart.
Deimeke, L. Edward '75 (ALB) Priests Placement Committee; Leadership Team.
Deis, Dennis *o.m.i.* '65 (SFS) Rosholt, SD St. John the Baptist.
Deisch, Raymond J. '62 (RC) Retired.
Deister, Charles C. '63 (STL)[Q] Saint Louis, MO School Sisters of Notre Dame.
Deitch, Richard S. '86 (SFR) Retired.
Deitelhoff, Bernard H. '57 (MAD) Retired.
Deiters, James E. '91 (BEL) O Fallon, IL St. Clare; Diocesan Consultors.
Deiters, James R. '91 (BEL) Formation of Priests.
Deiters, Robert M. *s.j.* '58 (FgM) Chicago, IL Society of Jesus.
Deitz, Christopher *o.f.m.conv.* '85 (MRY)[F] Arroyo Grande, CA St. Joseph Cupertino Province, Provincial Center; Arroyo Grande, CA; [F] Arroyo Grande, CA St. Joseph Cupertino Friary.
Deitzer, Gerald E. *c.m.* '55 (PH)[Y].
De Jesus, Dwight '85 (ALX) Simmesport, LA Christ the King.
de Jesus, Hector Bruno '85 (TYL) Gilmer, TX St. Francis of Assisi.
De Jesus, Rev. Msgr. Herminio '69 (PCE)[B] The Pontifical Catholic University of Puerto Rico; Chancellor; Diocesan Consultors.
de Jesus, Orlando (CGS) Diocesan Tribunal of Caguas.
DeJesus Colon, Jose Daniel *c.m.f.* (SJN) Bayamon, PR Santa Maria.
de Jesus Gomez, Orlando '86 (CGS) Cidra, PR Nuestra Senora del Carmen.
de Jesus Reynaga, Jose '04 (FRS) Merced, CA Sacred Heart.
de Jesus Viera, Rev. Msgr. Herminio (PCE) Cofradia

Sagrado Corazon; Movimiento Juan XXIII; Movimiento Sacerdotal Mariano.
de Jong, Jan *s.c.j.* '64 (MIL)[B] Hales Corners, WI Sacred Heart School of Theology; [P] Hales Corners, WI Priests of the Sacred Heart.
DeJulio, David '90 (SP) Tampa, FL St. Mark the Evangelist.
DeJulio, Robert J. '72 (NY) Pelham Manor, NY Our Lady of Perpetual Help.
Deka, Robbie '07 (GLD) Special Assignment.
Deka, Robbie '07 (HON) Kapaa, HI St. Catherine.
Dekaa, Thomas T. '82 (TUC) Kearny, AZ Infant Jesus of Prague Roman Catholic Parish – Kearny.
Dekat, Carl '53 (KCK) Wamego, KS St. Joseph Retired.
Dekat, Earl '66 (KCK) Horton, KS St. Leo; Horton, KS St. Mary.
Deken, John C. '72 (STL) New Haven, MO St. Paul; New Haven, MO Assumption.
DeKeyser, Andrew '10 (LFT) Lafayette, IN St. Mary Cathedral; Lafayette, IN St. Lawrence.
Dekrem, Bruno '92 (RVC) Massapequa, NY St. Rose of Lima.
de la Calle, Juan '54 (PMB) Indiantown, FL Holy Cross.
de la Cruz, Jenaro *o.c.d.* (DAL) Dallas, TX St. Mary of Carmel.
de la Cruz, Juan '57 (ATL) Snellville, GA St. Oliver Plunkett.
Delacruz, Leandro '83 (TR) Hamilton, NJ St. Raphael–Holy Angels Parish.
Dela Cruz, Manuel C. *m.s.* '90 (HON) Honolulu, HI St. Anthony.
de la Cruz, Martin '01 (BWN) San Benito, TX St. Ignatius.
De la Cruz, Nicolas *c.r.l.* '08 (ARE) Hatillo, PR Our Lady of Mt. Carmel.
De la Cruz, Perlito '03 (SAC) Williams, CA Sacred Heart.
DeLa Cruz, Vicente '90 (HT) Judicial Vicar; Judges; Houma, LA Cathedral of St. Francis De Sales.
DeLacy, Stephen P. '04 (PH) Schwenksville, PA St. Mary; [D] Royersford, PA Pope John Paul II High School.
deLadurantaye, Paul F. '88 (ARL) Arlington, VA Cathedral of St. Thomas More; Diocesan Judges; Catholic Education, Office of Catechetics; Liturgy, Office of Sacred.
Delaere, Paul *c.i.c.m.* '43 (FgM) Arlington, VA MISSIONHURST.
Delahanty, Patrick D. '69 (L) Louisville, KY St. Martin de Porres; Executive Director; Louisville, KY St. Augustine.
Delahunty, Richard A. '65 (ORG) Laguna Woods, CA St. Nicholas.
Delahunty, Thomas P. '55 (SAC) Retired.
De La Iglesia, Narciso (SJN) San Juan, PR San Juan Bosco.
de Laire, Georges F. '97 (MAN) On Duty Outside the Diocese.
del Almeida, Felipe R.J. *o.s.b.* '07 (GBG)[H] Latrobe Saint Vincent Archabbey.
de la Madrid, James Gil *m.ss.cc.* '97 (SJN) San Juan, PR San Juan M. Vianney.
DeLand, Robert J. '73 (SAG) Freeland, MI St. Agnes; Judicial Vicar; Judges.
Delaney, Brian '75 (LA) Montebello, CA Our Lady of the Miraculous Medal; Norwalk, CA St. Linus.
Delaney, Charles A. *c.s.c.* '49 (FTW)[H] Notre Dame Congregation of Holy Cross, United States Province of Priests & Brothers; New Rochelle, NY Eastern Brothers Province.
Delaney, Rev. Msgr. Dennis M. '76 (STL) St. Louis, MO St. John the Apostle and Evangelist; Catholic Cemeteries of St. Louis.
Delaney, Donald *s.d.b.* '76 (NO) Harvey, LA St. John Bosco.
Delaney, Rev. Msgr. Howard L. '40 (PBL) Retired.
Delaney, James *c.s.sp.* '54 (BRK)[R] Long Island City, NY Holy Ghost Fathers of Ireland; [V] Long Island City, NY World Compassion Link Retired.
Delaney, James *c.s.sp.* '54 (NEW) Jersey City, NJ St. Aloysius.
Delaney, John J. '62 (NY) Retired.
Delaney, John W. (BO) North Andover, MA St. Michael; Vicariate III.
Delaney, Rev. Msgr. John W. '64 (MIA) Retired.
Delaney, John '81 (FTW) South Bend, IN St. Jude Church; Advisory Board; South Bend, IN Sacred Heart of Jesus (Lakeville).
Delaney, Larry '90 (CR) East Grand Forks, MN Sacred Heart; Priests' Personnel Board.
Delaney, Lawrence '67 (LAN)[M] De Witt, MI St. Francis Retreat Center.
Delaney, Matthew S. '51 (LA) Retired.
Delaney, Rev. Msgr. Michael J. '85 (SCR) Scranton, PA St. Paul's.
DeLaney, Michael M. *c.s.c.* '87 (FgM) New Rochelle, NY Eastern Brothers Province.
DeLaney, Michael *c.s.c.* (FTW)[H] Notre Dame Congregation of Holy Cross, United States Province of Priests & Brothers; [H] Notre Dame Congregation of Holy Cross, United States Province of Priests & Brothers.
Delaney, Thomas '57 (JKS) Crystal Springs, MS St. John the Evangelist.
Delaney, Thomas *o.m.i.* '60 (FgM) Washington, DC AMERICAN OBLATE MISSIONS.
Delaney, William I. '61 (RVC) Retired.
Delaney, William J. *c.pp.s.* '63 (LA) Los Angeles, CA St. Agnes.
Delaney, William J. '54 (NY) New York, NY Holy Innocents; [DD] Bronx, NY.
Delaney, William K. *s.j.* '85 (LA)[P] Los Angeles, CA Colombiere House; [BB] Burbank, CA SCRC (Southern California Renewal Communities).
Delange, Maurice '71 (COV) Retired.
del Angel, Jesus '00 (FRS) Adjutant Judicial Vicar; On Special Assignment; Fresno, CA Shrine of St. Therese.
Delano, Kenneth J. '60 (FR) Retired.
de la Pena, Cosme R. '92 (CAM) International Priests Representatives; Absecon, NJ Church of Saint Elizabeth Ann Seton, Absecon, N.J.
De La Pena, Ericson *o.f.m.conv.* '08 (SY) Syracuse, NY Assumption B.V.M.
De la Pena, Jose Manuel '00 (NEW) Bayonne, NJ St. Mary Star of the Sea.
De La Pena, Ordanico '98 (NEW) Hoboken, NJ Our Lady of Grace and Saint Joseph Parish.
DeLaPena, Richard '82 (NY) Castle Point, NY V.A. Hudson Valley Healthcare.
De la Pena, Uldarico '82 (MO) Kingston, NY St. Joseph; DEPARTMENT OF VETERANS AFFAIRS HOSPITALS AND CHAPLAINS.
de la Puebla, Tomàs *c.m.* '49 (MGZ) Mayaguez, PR San Vicente Retired.
Delargy, Torlach C. '66 (SFR)[R] San Francisco, CA Prelature of the Holy Cross and Opus Dei.
Delargy, Torlach (POD) San Francisco.
De La Riva, John *o.f.m.cap.* '99 (MO) DEPARTMENT OF VETERANS AFFAIRS HOSPITALS AND CHAPLAINS.
De La Riva, John *o.f.m.cap.* '99 (LA) Los Angeles, CA St. Lawrence of Brindisi.
de la Rosa, Frank '78 (SJN)[E] Carolina, PR Hospital Universitario de Puerto Rico.
De la Rosa, Jose Luis '84 (SAT) Selma, TX Our Lady of Perpetual Help.
de la Rosa, Roger *s.j.* '03 (STL)[O] St. Louis, MO Leo Brown Jesuit Community.
de la Rosa, Roger *s.j.* '03 (SFR)[N] San Francisco, CA Loyola House Jesuit Community.
De la Rosa, Roland '95 (SFR) South San Francisco, CA Mater Dolorosa.
de la Rosa Peguero, Frank '78 (SJN) Carolina, PR San Francisco de Asis.
Delarue, Louis '75 (BEA) Retired.
de la Torre, Bartholomew *o.p.* '67 (FgM) Oakland, CA Province of the Holy Name (Western Dominican Province).
dela Torre, Bartholomew *o.p.* '67 (OAK)[L] Oakland Order of Preachers (Province of the Most Holy Name of Jesus – Western Dominican Province).
de la Torre, Carlos V. '81 (GAL) Houston, TX St. Cecilia.
de la Torre, Jorge '97 (FRS) Arvin, CA St. Thomas the Apostle.
de la Torre Carrillo, Sergio '10 (CHI) Chicago, IL Good Shepherd.
Delauney, Herbert C. '75 (LAF) Absent on Sick Leave.
De Laura, Felice J. '63 (BRK) Retired.
DeLay, Dominic *o.p.* '93 (LA) Los Angeles, CA St. Dominic.
Delay, Donald R. '83 (BO) Walpole, MA St. Mary; Presbyteral Council.
Delbel, James A. '81 (OG) Champlain, NY St. Mary.
del Bosque, Alejandro *l.c.* '87 (SAT) Converse, TX St. Monica.
Del Bove, Stefano *s.j.* '03 (CHI)[C] Chicago, IL Jesuit Community at Loyola University Chicago.
Delcambre, Michael L. '05 (LAF) Cecilia, LA St. Joseph; Cecilia, LA St. Rose of Lima.
Del Carmen, Leo '91 (LA) Canoga Park, CA Our Lady of the Valley.
del Castillo, F. Javier '05 (CHI)[V] Chicago, IL Prelature of the Holy Cross and Opus Dei.
DelConte, Eugene *o.s.a.* '55 (PH) Philadelphia, PA St. Rita of Cascia.
DelDuca, John A. '68 (CAM) Elected Members; Blackwood, NJ Our Lady of Hope Parish, Blackwood, N.J.
DeLeers, Stephen V. '84 (MIL) Retired.
DeLeeuw, John '44 (LAF) Retired.
Delendick, Rev. Msgr. John '77 (BRK) Brooklyn, NY St. Jude Shrine Church; Fire Department; Diocesan Real Estate Board.
DeLeo, Roy James '69 (NEW) Elizabeth, NJ St. Genevieve's Retired.
DeLeon, Benedict '80 (SAC) South Lake Tahoe, CA St. Theresa; Priests' Personnel Board, Diocesan.
DeLeon, Eddie (HRT)[Q] New Haven, CT Yale University–St. Thomas More Catholic Center and Chapel.
de Leon, Edward T. *o.m.i.* '80 (SAN) Midland, TX Our Lady of Guadalupe; Diocesan Liturgical Commission.
de Leon, Emmanuel Tolosa (RIC) Farmville, VA Church of the Nativity; Farmville, VA St. Theresa; Blackstone, VA Immaculate Heart of Mary; Meherrin, VA Sacred Heart.
DeLeon, Esteban *s.v.d.* (RIC) Virginia Beach, VA Star of the Sea.
de Leon, Jose A. '81 (CGS) Vocations; Barranquitas, PR Church of St. Anthony of Padua.
DeLeon, Jose Raul '08 (WDC) Takoma Park, MD Our Lady of Sorrows.
DeLeon, Juancho G. '94 (NEW) Bloomfield, NJ St. Valentine; North Essex Deanery 16.
DeLeon, Marco Tulio '01 (PMB) Jensen Beach, FL St. Martin de Porres.
De Leon, Michael '95 (LAR) Laredo, TX Divine Mercy.
de Leon, Michael *a.m.* (NY) Scarsdale, NY St. Pius X.
DeLeon, Robert E. *c.s.c.* '85 (ALB) Albany Medical Center Hospital; [L] Valatie, NY St. Joseph Center; Special Assignment.
DeLeon, Robert E. *c.s.c.* '85 (FTW)[H] Notre Dame Congregation of Holy Cross, United States Province of Priests & Brothers.
DeLerno, Christian W. '11 (NO) Metairie, LA St. Edward the Confessor.
DeLerno, Kevin T. '09 (NO) Metairie, LA St. Christopher the Martyr.
Delfra, Louis A. *c.s.c.* '04 (FTW)[B] University of Notre Dame Du Lac; [H] Notre Dame, IN Holy Cross Community, Corby Hall, University of Notre Dame.
Delgadillo, Salvador (SEA) Immigration & Customs Enforcement.
Delgado, Alfonso *ss.cc.* '95 (GAL) Houston, TX Prince of Peace.
Delgado, Alvaro H. '02 (STO) Stockton, CA St. Edward Church (Pastor of).
Delgado, Camilo Garcia '08 (B) St. Anthony, ID Mary Immaculate.
Delgado, Enrique '96 (MIA) Weston, FL St. Katharine Drexel.
Delgado, Jose Manuel *c.m.* '04 (FgM) Philadelphia, PA Eastern Province.
Delgado, Joseph '95 (SJ) On Leave of Absence.
Delgado, Juan R. Mora '92 (ARE) Adjutant Judges.
Delgado, Lenin *c.ss.r.* '91 (NY) New York, NY Most Holy Redeemer.
Delgado, Leslie N. '55 (LA) Los Angeles, CA Our Lady of Guadalupe Sanctuary.
Delgado, Ruben '90 (BWN) Elsa, TX Sacred Heart; College of Consultors.
Delgado–Diaz, Rafael *o.p.* (SJN) Trujillo Alto, PR San Bartolome.
Del Giudice, Carl '81 (CHL) Brevard, NC Sacred Heart.
Delich, David L. *o.p.* '63 (STL)[O] Saint Louis, MO St. Dominic Priory.
Deliman, Rev. Msgr. Edward M. '73 (PH) Bensalem, PA Our Lady of Fatima.
de Lira, Noel R. '99 (BAL)[Q] Baltimore, MD St. Mary's Seminary & University.
de Lira, Noel '00 (SFR)[A] Menlo Park, CA St. Patrick Seminary and University.
Delis, Robert *s.d.b.* '79 (MO) Navy Chaplains.
Delis, Robert *s.d.b.* '79 (SFR)[N] San Francisco, CA Salesian Provincial Residence.
Delis, Robert '79 (HON) Military Chaplains.
Delisi, Anthony *o.c.s.o.* '54 (ATL)[F] Conyers, GA The Monastery of the Holy Spirit.
Delisle, Eric T. '03 (MAN) Southern N.H. Regional Medical Center; St. Joseph Hospital; Nashua, NH Immaculate Conception.
DeLisle, Henri A. *o.m.i.* '58 (MAN)[K] Colebrook, NH Shrine of Our Lady of Grace.
Dell, Robert '90 (SEA) Retired.
Dell'Anno, Anthony V. '69 (BRK) Brooklyn, NY St. Edmund Retired.
Dellaert, Brian M. '05 (DUB) Van Horne, IA St. John; Van Horne, IA St. Paul; Van Horne, IA St. Michael; Van Horne, IA Immaculate Conception; Van Horne, IA St. Patrick.
Dellagiovanna, Mariano N. '07 (NEW) On Duty Outside the Archdiocese.
Dellagiovanna, Mariano N. (GLD) Empire, MI St. Philip Neri.
Della Neve, Louis '52 (BUF) Retired.
De Llano, Domingo '68 (CC) Retired.
Della Pietra, Douglas '96 (ROC) Absent on Leave.
Dellaporte, Dominic '85 (NEW) Hoboken, NJ St. Ann's.
Dellinger, Jonathan '05 (DEN) Wray, CO St. Andrew the Apostle; Yuma, CO St. John the Evangelist.
Dello Russo, Albert '10 (PMB) Stuart, FL St. Joseph.
Dello Russo, John F. *o.s.a.* '87 (BO) Lawrence, MA St. Mary of the Assumption.
Dellos, Richard E. '68 (SY) Utica, NY St. Joseph and St. Patrick.
Dell'Oro, Italo *c.r.s.* '82 (GAL) Houston, TX Christ the King; Priests Personnel Committee; Director of Ministry to Priests.
Delmonte, Albert L. '69 (ROC) Pittsford, NY St. Louis Retired.
Delmore, Eugene P. *s.j.* '69 (SEA) Tacoma, WA St. Rita of Cascia; [C] Tacoma, WA Bellarmine Preparatory School.

de Loera, Marco A. '11 (WCH) Wichita, KS St. Elizabeth Ann Seton.
del Olmo, Alberto *s.j.* (NY) New York, NY St. Elizabeth.
Del Olmo, Jose '92 (VEN) Hispanic, Migrant and Spanish Speaking Apostolates.
DeLong, Allen *s.m.* '77 (STL)[O] St. Louis Marianists, Province of the United States (Society of Mary).
Delonnay, Lawrence '75 (DET) Waterford, MI Our Lady of the Lakes.
DeLora, John '94 (NY) Staten Island University Hospital North; Staten Island, NY Staten Island University Hospital South.
DeLorenzo, John R. '76 (SY) Jordan, NY St. Patrick.
DeLorme, R. Daniel '57 (SY) Jamesville, NY Retired.
de los Reyes, Joel '75 (AGN) Cursillo in Christianity; Dededo, GU Santa Barbara.
De Los Rios, Enrique '00 (LA) Los Angeles, CA St. Alphonsus.
De Los Santos, Rev. Msgr. Jorge '91 (DEN) Denver, CO Assumption of the Blessed Virgin Mary; Vicar for Hispanic Ministry; Vicar for Hispanic Ministry; College of Consultors.
Delos Santos, Joshua M. *f.i.* '09 (FR)[F] New Bedford, MA Marian Friary of Our Lady, Queen of the Seraphic Order.
DeLoza, Jose '87 (YAK) On Duty Outside the Diocese.
Del Prete, Rev. Msgr. Frank G. '77 (NEW) Saddle River Borough, NJ St. Gabriel the Archangel; Archdiocesan Judges; Metropolitan Tribunal.
Del Priore, John *s.j.s.* '08 (MAD) Platteville, WI St. Augustine University Parish; Platteville, WI St. Mary.
Del Priore, Kenneth '83 (SD) Escondido, CA Church of the Resurrection Catholic Parish.
Del Rosario, Anulfo *c.m.* (SJN) San Juan, PR Jesus Maestro.
del Rosario, Jaime *o.m.i.* '95 (SAT)[L] San Antonio, TX Joseph Gerard House.
del Rosario, Mark *s.s.s.* '80 (HON) Honolulu, HI Star of the Sea; Members.
del Toro, Alejandro '07 (RCK) DeKalb, IL Christ the Teacher, University Parish of Northern Illinois University; [L] DeKalb, IL Newman Foundation for Catholic Students of Northern Illinois University.
Del Toro, Jose L. *t.o.r.* '95 (MO) Air Force Chaplains.
DelToro, José Jaime *c.s.b.* '08 (DET) Detroit, MI Ste. Anne de Detroit.
DeLuca, Anthony G. '53 (PIT) Retired.
DeLuca, David *m.s.c.* '66 (OG)[F] Watertown, NY Missionaries of the Sacred Heart.
DeLuca, Paul F. '81 (CIN) Cincinnati, OH Nativity of Our Lord.
DeLuca, Stephen J. '65 (BGP) Greenwich, CT Greenwich Hospital; Riverside, CT St. Catherine of Siena.
DeLucia, Gerald M. '78 (Y) Boardman, OH St. Charles Borromeo.
DeLucia, Gerald '78 (Y)[C] Youngstown, OH Cardinal Mooney High School.
DeLucia, Vincent G. *o.p.* (HRT) New Haven, CT St. Mary's.
De Luney, Gerald C. '69 (SB) Corona, CA Corpus Christi.
Delva, Jean M. '07 (BRK) Queens Village, NY SS. Joachim and Anne.
Del Valle, Tomas '79 (SJN) On Duty Outside the Archdiocese.
DelValle, Tomas (NY) New York, NY St. Columba.
Delvard, Quesnel *s.d.b.* '03 (PMB) Lake Worth, FL Sacred Heart.
Del Vecchio, Joseph F. *s.s.j.* '36 (WDC) Washington, DC St. Luke.
DelVecchio, Rev. Msgr. Michael E. '54 (BUF) Retired.
Delzell, David G. '50 (TR) Retired.
Delzingaro, Richard M. *c.r.s.p.* '96 (BUF)[S] Youngstown, NY Basilica of the National Shrine of Our Lady of Fatima, Inc.; [B] Youngstown, NY St. Anthony M. Zaccaria Seminary.
DeMaio, Dominic *o.p.* '08 (ANC) Hispanic Ministry; Anchorage, AK Holy Family Cathedral.
DeMaio, Joseph *o.carm.* '65 (ROC)[B] Rochester, NY McQuaid Jesuit High School; [K] Rochester, NY Whitefriars Priory.
Deman, Shane '08 (SC) Fort Dodge, IA Holy Trinity Parish of Webster County.
DeMan, Thomas *o.p.* '62 (P)[N] McKenzie Bridge, OR St. Benedict Lodge Dominican Retreat & Conference Center.
Demarais, Garvin J. '81 (OG) Black River, NY St. Paul; Black River, NY St. Rita; Advocates; Plattsburgh, NY St. Mary of the Lake.
DeMarco, David G. *s.j.* '05 (RC)[C] Pine Ridge, SD Jesuit Community of Holy Rosary Mission; Pine Ridge, SD Holy Rosary/Red Cloud Indian School Inc.
DeMarco, Peter A. '60 (BGP) Deaf, Apostolate for; [O] Stamford, CT The Catherine Dennis Keefe Queen of the Clergy Retired Priests' Residence Retired.
DeMartinis, Michael G. '97 (E) Erie, PA Mount Calvary; [C] Erie, PA Cathedral Preparatory School.
De Martinis, Robert '86 (ALB) Amsterdam, NY St. Stanislaus.
DeMartino, Robert J. '92 (ARL) Stafford, VA St. William of York.
DeMattia, John '68 (PAT) Dover, NJ St. Mary's; Deans.
deMayo, Martin P. '03 (BGP) Stratford, CT St. Mark; Stamford, CT Sacred Heart.
Demecais, Genaro C. '82 (FRS) Fresno, CA St. Helen.
Demek, Martin H. '75 (BAL) Baltimore, MD Corpus Christi.
Demers, Francis L. *o.m.i.* '55 (MAN) Diocesan Judges.
Demers, Francis *o.m.i.* '55 (BO)[X] Tewksbury, MA Immaculate Heart of Mary Residence.
Demers, Gerard A. *s.m.* '59 (BO) Boston, MA Our Lady of Victories.
Demers, Normand J. '58 (PRO) Retired.
Demers, Paul R. *s.c.* '81 (MAN)[B] Nashua, NH Rivier College.
Demers, Richard D. '83 (OG) Absent on Sick Leave, Disabled.
Demers, Wilfred G. '59 (MAN) Retired.
Demets, Laurent *f.s.s.p.* '00 (LR)[K] North Little Rock, AR Priestly Fraternity of St. Peter.
DeMeulemeester, Patrick '95 (PEO) Granville, IL Sacred Heart Of Jesus; Granville, IL St. Patrick's.
DeMeulenaere, Martin *o.s.b.* '73 (KC) Maryville, MO St. Gregory Barbarigo; [J] Priests Elsewhere.
Deming, Robert N. '58 (KC) Retired.
Demkiv, Ivan '92 (PHU) Philadelphia, PA Immaculate Conception of Blessed Virgin Mary, Cathedral; College of Archeparchial Consultors; Presbyteral Council; Protopresbyters (Deans).
Demko, James J. '82 (PSC) Beaver Meadows, PA SS. Peter and Paul.
Demkovich, Rev. Msgr. John J. '65 (PAT) Associate Judges; Paterson, NJ Mission Office; Legion of Mary; Clifton, NJ SS. Cyril and Methodius Retired.
Deml, Francis S. '57 (DEN) Retired.
Demmer, Donald L. '75 (DET) Troy, MI St. Alan; Birmingham, MI St. Columban.
Demo, John M. '88 (OG) Willsboro, NY Catholic Community of St. Philip of Jesus of Willsboro (1909) & St. Joseph of Essex (1872).
DeMolen, Richard '98 (RNO) Retired.
de M Pereira, Luciano J. '54 (FR) Somerset, MA St. John of God Retired.
Dempsey, Dennis '80 (STP) Northfield, MN St. Dominic.
Dempsey, Edward M. '67 (NOR) Absent on Leave; Members.
Dempsey, Rev. Msgr. James '56 (BEA) Retired.
Dempsey, John G. '64 (STL) Arnold, MO Immaculate Conception Retired.
Dempsey, Nicholas '71 (SD) San Diego, CA Saint Therese of Carmel Catholic Parish.
Dempsey, Rev. Msgr. Patrick E. '97 (WDC) Bowie, MD Sacred Heart.
Dempsey, Richard J. '58 (CHI) Evergreen Park, IL Most Holy Redeemer Retired.
Dempsey, Rev. Msgr. Robert J. '80 (CHI) Northfield, IL St. Philip the Apostle; College of Consultors.
Dempsey, Sean *s.j.* '08 (LA)[C] Los Angeles, CA Jesuit Community.
Dempsey, Terrence E. *s.j.* '85 (STL)[C] Saint Louis University; [O] St. Louis, MO Jesuit Community Corporation at Saint Louis University – Jesuit Hall.
Dempsey, Terrence E. *s.j.* '85 (NY)[DD] Cardinal Spellman Hall, Jesuit Community.
Dempsey, Rev. Msgr. Thomas J. '61 (RCK) Retired.
Dempsey, Rev. Msgr. Thomas J. '62 (STL) St. Louis, MO St. Joan of Arc Retired.
Demse, Thomas P. '76 (MIL) Milwaukee, WI St. Gregory The Great.
Demuth, Rev. Msgr. George R. '46 (SCR) Retired.
Demuth, Paul E. '68 (GB) Green Bay, WI St. Elizabeth Ann Seton.
Dene, Charles J. '58 (ALN) Shenandoah, PA Annunciation.
Denemark, Emil J. *s.j.* '81 (MO) Milwaukee, WI Society of Jesus; Army Reserve Chaplains.
De Nguyen–Dang, Thomas '82 (ORG) Tustin, CA St. Cecilia.
Denha, Suleiman '59 (EST) Eparchial College of Consultors Retired.
Denig, Philip P. '85 (DEN) On Duty Outside the Archdiocese.
Denig, Stephen J. *c.m.* '75 (BUF)[N] Niagara University, NY Vincentian Community at Niagara University; [C] Niagara University, NY Niagara University; [G] Niagara Falls, NY Catholic Academy of Niagara Falls.
Deniger, Joseph L. *c.s.sp.* '58 (SB) Hemet, CA Our Lady of the Valley.
DeNigris, Emanuele '05 (WDC) Germantown, MD Mother Seton Parish; On Duty Outside the Archdiocese; [B] Chestnut Hill, MA Redemptoris Mater Archdiocesan Missionary Seminary.
DeNinno, Dale E. '78 (PIT) Pittsburgh, PA Saint Elizabeth of Hungary.
DeNinno, Louis L. '76 (PIT) Pittsburgh, PA Holy Wisdom; Matrimonial Concerns, Office for; Matrimonial Concerns, Office for; Judges.
Denk, Kurt *s.j.* '07 (BO)[U] Newton, MA The Jesuit Community at Boston College.
Denk, Michael J. '07 (CLV) Amherst, OH St. Joseph.
Denn, James J. *c.s.c.* '61 (FTW)[H] Notre Dame Congregation of Holy Cross, United States Province of Priests & Brothers.
Dennehy, John D. '81 (NEW)[B] Seton Hall University.
Dennehy, Martin J. '51 (BGP) Retired.
Dennemann, Thomas J. '73 (CIN) Cincinnati, OH St. Ann.
Dennerlein, John L. '74 (JOL) Retired.
Denning, John F. *c.s.c.* '87 (FR)[A] North Easton, MA Stonehill College; [A] North Easton, MA Holy Cross Fathers Religious.
Denning, John F. *c.s.c.* '87 (FTW) Prov. Councilors:; [H] Notre Dame Congregation of Holy Cross, United States Province of Priests & Brothers.
Denning, John F. *c.s.c.* '87 (FTW)[H] Notre Dame Congregation of Holy Cross, United States Province of Priests & Brothers.
Dennis, Jack *s.j.* (BAL)[S] Baltimore, MD Loyola University.
Dennis, John J. *o.s.f.s.* '45 (WIL)[J] Childs, MD Retirement and Assisted Care Facility Retired.
Dennis, John M. *s.j.* '86 (BAL)[Q] Baltimore, MD Jesuit Community of Loyola University, Inc.; [B] Jesuit Community of Loyola University, Inc.
Dennis, Patrick '78 (B) Retired.
Dennis, Peter K. *ss.cc.* '62 (LA)[P] La Verne, CA Congregation of the Sacred Hearts of Jesus and Mary.
Dennis, Sam *o.s.b.* '57 (SFE)[H] Pecos, NM Our Lady of Guadalupe Abbey.
Dennis, Thomas J. '92 (SFD) Absent on Leave.
Dennis, Tyler '09 (RC) Rapid City, SD Blessed Sacrament.
Dennison, Arthur '73 (MIA) Retired.
Dennison, Frederick J. '73 (IND) Retired.
Denniston, John '79 (RVC) Serving Outside the Diocese; New Hyde Park, NY Notre Dame.
Denny, Charles J. '69 (TOL) Retired.
Denny, John T. *o.s.a.* '90 (PH) Bryn Mawr, PA Our Mother of Good Counsel; [Y] Bryn Mawr, PA Augustinians Friars (O.S.A.).
Denny, Thomas F. *s.j.* '68 (NY)[DD] New York, NY St. Ignatius Loyola Residence.
Deno, Rev. Msgr. Lawrence M. '59 (OG) Cadyville, NY St. James Church.
DeNoble, Augustine *o.s.b.* '55 (P)[L] St. Benedict, OR Mt. Angel Abbey.
Denron, Christopher J. *s.j.* '01 (CHI)[N] Chicago, IL Miguel Pro Jesuit Community.
Densmore, Anthony M. '04 (DAL) Kaufman, TX St. Ann; Seagoville, TX Federal Correctional Institution.
Dente, Thomas A. '93 (NEW) Members; Office of Divine Worship; Maplewood, NJ St. Joseph's; Scotch Plains, NJ St. Bartholomew.
Dentici, Rev. Msgr. Thomas '53 (DEN) Steamboat Springs, CO Holy Name Retired.
Dentinger, Roy E. '50 (L) Retired.
Denzer, Joseph W. '68 (BRK)[R] Douglaston, NY Bishop Mugavero Residence Retired.
De Oca, Jose Monte '96 (NEW) Paramus, NJ Our Lady of the Visitation.
De Oliveira, Alvaro *o.s.j.* '70 (SCR)[A] Pittston, PA St. Joseph's Oblate Seminary.
de Oliveira, Pedro *o.f.m.conv.* '00 (SPR) Chicopee, MA St. Stanislaus Basilica.
DePalma, Michael '03 (SFE) Corrales, NM San Ysidro; Vocations; Presbyteral Council of the Archdiocese of Santa Fe.
De Pascale, Daniel '61 (ALB) Retired.
DePasquale, Leonard D. *i.m.c.* '71 (SB) Appointed Members; San Bernardino; San Bernardino, CA St. Bernardine.
Depatie, Donald L. '78 (PRO) Cumberland, RI St. Aidan.
DePaula, Christobal '02 (MIA) Miami, FL St. Joachim.
de Paulo, Craig (SJP) On Leave; Presbyters.
Depcik, Michael (DET)[Q] Warren, MI St. John's Deaf Center.
Depeaux, Bernard F. '50 (BUR) Retired.
De Peaux, Rowland C. *o.praem.* '51 (GB)[J] De Pere, WI St. Joseph Priory.
DePew, Daniel R. '85 (GR) Spring Lake, MI St. Mary's.
DePeyster, Aaron '04 (DET) Dearborn, MI St. Sebastian.
Depinet, Robert L. *m.m.* '61 (NY)[DD] Maryknoll Maryknoll Fathers and Brothers Retired.
DePinto, Basil '58 (OAK) Piedmont, CA Corpus Christi Retired.
Depman, Rev. Msgr. Francis J. '81 (PH) West Grove, PA Assumption B.V.M.; Avondale, PA St. Rocco.
Deponai, Joseph J. '83 (NY) Nanuet, NY St. Anthony.
De Porter, Arnold W. '63 (WDC) Retired.
DePra, Italo '51 (P) Retired.
DePrinzio, Kevin *o.s.a.* '04 (PH)[Y] Villanova, PA Provincial Offices of the Order of St. Augustine, Province of St. Thomas of Villanova; [C] Villanova University; [Y] Ardmore, PA Bellesini Friary.
DeProfio, Rev. Msgr. Louis A. '56 (BGP) Diocesan Consultors; Retired Priests; Presbyteral Council; [O] Stamford, CT The Catherine Dennis Keefe Queen of

the Clergy Retired Priests' Residence Retired.
DeProspero, Nicholas '70 (PSC) Pottstown, PA St. John the Baptist.
Deptula, Rev. Msgr. Stanley L. '96 (PEO) Peoria, IL St. Mary's Cathedral; Peoria, IL St. Bernard's; Peoria, IL St. Peter's; [O] Peoria, IL Archbishop Fulton J. Sheen Foundation; Vice Chancellors; Liturgy, Churches and Chapels; Divine Worship, Office of; Assistant Directors.
DeRammelaere, Bruce A. '06 (DAV) Burlington, IA SS. John & Paul.
DeRamos, Fidel '64 (WDC) Retired.
de Ranitz, Richard *o.p.* '70 (CHI)[N] Chicago Dominicans (Provincial Office).
Derasmo, John '81 (RVC) Seaford, NY St. James.
Derbish, Michael *o.f.m.* '62 (SJP) Presbyters Retired.
Derda, Christopher '06 (KAL) Augusta, MI St. Ann; Presbyteral Council Members; Presbyteral Council Members; Vocations and Ongoing Formation.
Derenne, Karin (GB)[G] Appleton, WI St. Elizabeth Hospital, Inc.; [G] Oshkosh, WI Mercy Medical Center of Oshkosh, Inc.
Deresienski, Stanley *s.s.e.* (MOB)[G] Selma, AL Edmundite Fathers.
Derfus, Kenneth J. '56 (MIL) Retired.
Derise, Mark '97 (LAF) New Iberia, LA Our Lady of Perpetual Help; Knights of Columbus.
DeRiso, John M. *c.s.c.* '02 (FTW) South Bend, IN St. Joseph; [H] Notre Dame Congregation of Holy Cross, United States Province of Priests & Brothers; Catholic School Board.
De Ritis, Gilbert J. *m.m.* '54 (NY)[DD] Maryknoll Maryknoll Fathers and Brothers Retired.
Derivan, Rev. Msgr. Thomas B. '72 (NY) Bronx, NY St. Helena.
Derivaux, Donald F. '55 (JKS) Retired.
Dermody, Thomas '62 (SAC) Retired.
Dermond, Rev. Msgr. John K. '68 (TR) Episcopal Council; Assistant Chancellor; Judicial Vicar; [N] Trenton, NJ Villa Vianney.
Dermott, William R. '82 (MO) Military Chaplains; Navy Chaplains.
Dernbach, Rev. Msgr. Arthur '53 (P) Retired.
Dernek, Richard J. '70 (WIN) Lake City, MN St. Mary's of the Lake; Lake City, MN St. Patrick of West Albany.
DeRoche, Wilfred L. '65 (OG) Retired.
De Rosa, Francis M. '97 (ARL) Colonial Beach, VA St. Elizabeth of Hungary.
Derosa, Vincent '08 (WDC) Silver Spring, MD St. Bernadette.
DeRose, Martin '88 (ALB) Hagaman, NY St. Stephen.
DeRosia, Volney J. '03 (MAN) Epping, NH St. Joseph; Rockingham County House of Corrections; Auditors.
Derosier, Edmond M. '73 (BO) Ayer, MA St. Mary; Shirley, MA St. Anthony of Padua.
DeRouchey, Gary K. '02 (SFS) Milbank, SD St. Lawrence.
DeRouen, Rev. Msgr. Keith J. '83 (LAF) Office of Worship; Opelousas, LA Our Lady Queen of Angels.
DeRouen, Robert R. *s.j.* '54 (DEN)[N] Denver, CO Xavier Jesuit Center.
Derpich, Nikola *l.c.* '06 (PRO)[E] Wakefield, RI Immaculate Conception Academy, Inc.; [G] Warwick, RI Overbrook Academy at Our Lady of Providence Center.
Derrane, Mark G. '95 (BO) Lynn, MA Sacred Heart.
Derrera, Ferdinand *s.j.* '61 (LAF) Grand Coteau, LA St. Charles Borromeo.
Derry, Daniel '63 (SJ) Gilroy, CA St. Mary.
Dery, Henry R. '48 (HRT)[A] In Res. at the Archbishop Daniel A. Cronin Retirement Residence at St. Thomas Seminary Retired.
Dery, Peter '99 (VIC) Port Lavaca, TX Our Lady of the Gulf.
Dery Gbaalo, Peter '99 (BRK) Brooklyn, NY St. Columba.
Derzack, Rev. Msgr. Thomas A. '76 (ALN) Walnutport, PA St. Nicholas; College of Consultors; Scranton, PA The Slovak Catholic Federation (1911).
DeSa, Walter *o.s.f.s.* '65 (FgM) Wilmington, DE OBLATES OF ST. FRANCIS DE SALES MISSIONS.
DeSalvo, Donald D. '69 (RCK) Retired.
DeSalvo, William '88 (JOL) Hinsdale, IL St. Isaac Jogues; Deans.
DeSanctis, Peter A. '79 (BRK) Released from Diocesan Assignment.
DeSanctis, Peter (RVC) Shelter Island Heights, NY Our Lady of the Isle.
DeSandre, John G. '64 (TR) Retired.
De Santi, Bruno *c.s.j.* '51 (LA) San Pedro, CA St. Peter.
De Santiago–Carreon, Rito '11 (MEM) Memphis, TN St. Michael's.
DeSantis, Rev. Msgr. Joseph A. '75 (ALN) Reading, PA Sacred Heart; Appointed Members.
DeSantis, Linus *o.f.m.conv.* '71 (SY)[T] Syracuse, NY Syracuse University, St. Thomas More Foundation, Inc.; Syracuse, NY Assumption B.V.M.
DeSanto, Joseph A. '54 (NY) Nanuet, NY St. Anthony Retired.
Desaulniers, Richard P. '70 (PRO) Manville, RI St. James; Council Members.
Desch, Paul *o.f.m.* '56 (CIN)[N] Cincinnati, OH St. John the Baptist Friary.
Deschamps, Wilfred H. '90 (MAN) Greenville, NH Sacred Heart of Jesus; Jaffrey, NH St. Patrick; Greenville, NH Sacred Heart; Cursillo.
DeSciose, Michael C. '75 (PBL) Parkview Hospital.
Descoteaux, Lee R. '07 (RVC) Priests' Personnel Assignment Board; Deer Park, NY SS. Cyril and Methodius.
Des Forges, Edmond *o.f.m.conv.* '77 (CHI)[N] Libertyville, IL Marytown, Our Lady of Fatima Friary.
Desharnais, Gary L. '00 (YAK) Yakima, WA Holy Family.
Deshautelle, Blake Paul '07 (ALX) Vocations and Seminarians; Woodworth, LA Congregation of Mary, Mother of Jesus Roman Catholic Church, Woodworth, Louisiana; [I] Alexandria, LA Louisiana State University at Alexandria.
DeSiano, Francis P. *c.s.p.* '72 (WDC)[B] Washington, DC St. Paul's College; [X] Washington, DC Paulist Evangelization Ministries.
Desiderio, Frank *c.s.p.* '82 (BO)[N] Boston, MA Paulist Center; [Z] Boston, MA Chapel of the Holy Spirit.
DeSilva, L. Praxid '69 (NY) Briarcliff Manor, NY St. Theresa.
DeSilva, Lionel A. *c.s.p.* '59 (NY) Roosevelt Site; [DD] New York, NY Paulist Fathers' Motherhouse.
DeSimone, David A. '87 (NY) Poughkeepsie, NY Vassar Brothers Hospital.
Desimone, Nicholas '10 (WOR) Charlton City, MA St. Joseph's.
DeSimone, Russell J. *o.s.a.* '51 (PH).
DeSimone, Thomas '06 (NY) White Plains, NY Our Lady of Sorrows.
Desir, Jean Hugues '04 (ORL) Clermont, FL St. Faustina Catholic Church.
Desjardins, George A. '59 (MAN) Retired.
Desjardins, James M. *s.j.* '77 (FgM)[Q] Towson Maryland Province of the Society of Jesus; Towson, MD Society of Jesus.
Deskevich, Andrew J. '97 (PBR) Warren, OH SS. Peter and Paul's; [B] Warren, OH Infant of Prague Manor; Revitalization and Renewal Commission; Communications.
DeSloover, A. Robert '74 (TOL) Retired.
Desmarais, Paul E. '79 (PRO) Carolina, RI St. Mary.
Desmond, David A. '02 (SFS) Hartford, SD St. George; [C] Sioux Falls, SD O'Gorman High School; Diocesan Consultors; Presbyteral Council.
Desmond, Hubert E. '58 (BO) Senior Priests. Retired.
Desmond, Rev. Msgr. Joseph E. '47 (MAN) Retired.
Desmond, Joseph L. '74 (MET)[I] Somerset, NJ Maria Regina Residence; Absent on Sick Leave.
Desmond, Rev. Msgr. Michael J. '71 (NEW) Caldwell, NJ St. Aloysius; Elected Members.
Desmond, Nicholas R. '84 (CHI) Chicago, IL St. Aloysius; Chicago, IL St. Stephen, King of Hungary; Deans.
DeSocio, John A. '78 (ROC) Navy Reserve Chaplains; Elmira, NY St. Mary.
Desormeaux, J. Scott '91 (LAF) Abbeville, LA St. Mary Magdalen.
Desormeaux, Roland *c.s.* '82 (PMB) Delray Beach, FL Our Lady of Perpetual Help Mission.
DesOrmeaux, Scott '91 (LKC) On Duty Outside the Diocese.
de Sousa, Anderson Luis '09 (LAF) Lafayette, LA Immaculate Heart of Mary.
DeSousa, John C. '11 (NEW) Lodi, NJ St. Francis de Sales.
DeSouza, Carl '66 (RIC) Retired.
de Souza, Owen '70 (LA) On Sick Leave.
DesRochers, Emery N. *m.s.* '48 (HRT)[L] Hartford, CT Missionaries of LaSalette.
Desrochers, Rev. Msgr. Timothy H. '64 (MAR) Retired.
Des Rosiers, Denis A. '69 (OAK) Walnut Creek, CA St. Stephen.
DesRosiers, N. Wilfrid *s.s.j.* '55 (BAL)[Q] Baltimore, MD St. Joseph Society of the Sacred Heart House of Central Administration Retired.
Desrosiers, Paul H. '75 (NO) New Orleans, LA University of New Orleans; New Orleans, LA Transfiguration of the Lord.
Desrosiers, Philip J. '66 (BO) Senior Priests. Retired.
DesRosiers, Ronald G. *s.m.* '63 (DET)[K] Livonia, MI Marist Fathers & Brothers Community.
DesRuisseaux, Charles E. '60 (MAN) Presbyteral Council; Ecumenical and Interreligious Affairs; College of Consultors Retired.
Desruisseaux, G. Frantz '78 (BGP) Norwalk, CT St. Joseph; Episcopal Vicar for Haitians; Promoter of Justice; Priest Vocation Advisory Board.
Desso, Leo C. '79 (ANC) Retired.
DeStefano, Salvatore '08 (NY) Larchmont, NY SS. John and Paul.
DeStephano, Mark T. *s.j.* '88 (NEW)[B] Jersey City, NJ Jesuit Center; [L] Jersey City, NJ Jesuits of Saint Peter's College, Inc.; [Q] South Orange, NJ U.S. Catholic China Bureau.
Deston, David C. '09 (FR) South Yarmouth, MA St. Pius Tenth.
DeSutter, Mark A. '82 (PEO) Clergymen's Aid, Inc.; Morton, IL Blessed Sacrament.
DeTaVo, Peter *s.v.d.* '87 (CHI)[N] Techny, IL Divine Word Residence.
Determan, Joseph *o.p.* '51 (SAT) San Antonio, TX Methodist Hospital; [L] San Antonio, TX Dominican Priory of San Juan Macias.
Deters, Frederick J. *s.j.* '67 (IND)[D] Indianapolis, IN Brebeuf Jesuit Preparatory School, Inc.; [G] Beech Grove, IN Franciscan St. Francis Health.
Deters, Gregory J. '87 (DET) St. Clair, MI St. Mary.
Detig, Joseph *s.v.d.* '62 (TR)[N] Bordentown, NJ Society of the Divine Word.
Detisch, John J. '88 (E) Erie, PA Sacred Heart; Deans.
Detisch, Scott P. '87 (E) Fairview, PA Holy Cross; The Bishop's Theological Advisory Committee; Presbyteral Council.
De Tommaso, Louis D. *o.f.m.* '54 (NY)[DD] New York, NY Padua Friary Retired.
DeTore, Richard *c.m.f.* (ATL) Stone Mountain, GA Corpus Christi.
Detscher, Rev. Msgr. Alan F. '71 (BGP) Riverside, CT St. Catherine of Siena.
Dettenwanger, Dennis '64 (CIN) Retired.
Dettmer, Alfred J. '56 (GRY) Retired.
Dettmer, David J. '80 (BRK) Whitestone, NY St. Luke.
Deutsch, Rev. Msgr. Daniel J. '94 (RCK) Batavia, IL Holy Cross; Bishop's Secretary for Retired Priests; Diocesan Consultors; Deans; Clergy Relief Society, Priests' Retirement Committee.
Deutsch, George E. '57 (TR) Retired.
Deutsch, Marvin *m.m.* '57 (SJ)[M] Los Altos, CA Maryknoll.
Deutsch, Paul *s.j.* '90 (NO)[R] New Orleans, LA Jesuit Provincial Office.
Deutsch, Paul (JC)[B] Jefferson City, MO St. Mary Health Center.
Deutsch, Timothy '94 (DUL) Crosby, MN St. Joseph; Crosby, MN St. Joseph.
Devadhasan, Antony Das S. '99 (NY) Staten Island, NY St. Charles.
Devanapalle, George '95 (NY) Kingston, NY St. Joseph.
Devane, John F. *s.j.* '52 (BO)[U] Weston, MA Campion Health Center, Inc.
Devaraj, Chinnappan M. *o.f.m.* '94 (PMB)[F] West Palm Beach, FL Lourdes–Noreen McKeen Residence for Geriatric Care.
Devaraj, Peter *s.a.c.* '81 (RVC) Bridgehampton, NY Queen of the Most Holy Rosary; Presbyteral Council; Sag Harbor, NY St. Andrew's.
Devasagayam, Susai Antony (NY) Bronx, NY St. Frances de Chantal.
Deveau, Adhemar *o.m.i.* '52 (BO)[U] Lowell, MA Andre Garin Retirement Residence.
Deveau, Daniel R. '75 (MAN) Groveton, NH St. Marguerite d'Youville Parish.
DeVeer, Richard S. (BO) Weymouth, MA St. Francis Xavier.
DeVelis, Mark–Joseph *o.c.d.* (BO)[U] Boston, MA Carmelite Monastery.
Dever, Dennis A. '60 (BO) Medford, MA St. Clement.
Dever, James T. *o.s.f.s.* '73 (TR) Riverton, NJ Sacred Heart.
Dever, Rev. Msgr. William '65 (MIA) Fort Lauderdale, FL St. Helen.
Devera, Percival P. '91 (ORL) Kissimmee, FL Holy Redeemer.
Devereaux, Martin C. '54 (PMB) Retired.
Devereaux, Thomas W. '68 (SR) Cloverdale, CA St. Peter's; Ecumenical and Interreligious Affairs.
Devereux, James A. *s.j.* '58 (PH)[Y] Loyola Center and Manresa Hall.
Devereux, Peter *l.c.* '99 (ATL)[K] Alpharetta, GA Home and Family, Inc.; [F] Alpharetta, GA Legionaries of Christ, Incorporated.
Devereux, Raymond P. '68 (CHI) Schiller Park, IL St. Beatrice Retired.
Devereux, Simon *l.c.* '10 (HRT)[B] Cheshire, CT Novitiate of the Legion of Christ.
de Verteuil, Jack '89 (FBK) Leave of Absence.
de Verteuil, Jack (B) St. Maries, ID St. Mary Immaculate.
Devery, Thomas P. '77 (NY) Priest Personnel, Office of; Pastoral Life Conference; Priest Personnel Board.
Devett, Aaron *o.s.b.* '75 (RCK)[G] Aurora, IL Marmion Abbey.
Devett, Aaron *o.s.b.* '75 (SUP) Woodruff, WI Holy Family.
DeViese, James R. '09 (WH) Follansbee, WV St. Anthony; [O] Bethany, WV St. John Fisher Catholic Chapel; Judges.
de Villa, Camilo '92 (PHX) Mesa, AZ Christ the King Roman Catholic Parish.
DeVille, George T. '57 (PIT) Muse, PA Holy Rosary.
DeVille, William H. '62 (COL) Retired.
Devin, John C. *c.ss.r.* '49 (BO) Boston, MA Our Lady of Perpetual Help.
Devine, Charles F. '65 (SB) Idyllwild, CA Retired.
Devine, Daniel P. '65 (PH) Drexel Hill, PA St. Charles Borromeo.
Devine, Donald G. *s.j.* '65 (NY)[E] Bronx, NY Fordham

Preparatory School; [DD] Jesuit Community, Kohlmann Hall.
Devine, Finbarr Columba '70 (LA) Retired.
Devine, James T. '60 (BRK)[R] Douglaston, NY Bishop Mugavero Residence Retired.
Devine, Joseph T. '80 (HRT) Hartford, CT St. Lawrence O'Toole; Hartford Vicariate.
Devine, Kevin A. *c.s.p.* '56 (NY)[DD] New York, NY Paulist Fathers' Motherhouse.
Devine, Rev. Msgr. Michael F. '57 (SP) Clearwater, FL St. Brendan Retired.
Devine, Patrick A. '69 (HBG) Retired.
Devine, Paul '63 (OAK) Retired.
Devine, Richard J. *c.m.* '55 (BRK)[R] Queens Village, NY DePaul Residence.
Devine, Stephen M. '64 (FRS) Hanford, CA Immaculate Heart of Mary.
Devine, Terry '85 (OWN) Uniontown, KY St. Agnes.
Devine, Thomas J. *o.a.r.* '68 (NEW) Union City, NJ St. Augustine's.
Devine, William B. '58 (SC) Retired.
Devine, William D. '73 (BO) Bridgewater, MA St. Thomas Aquinas.
Devine, William J. '48 (CHI) Evergreen Park, IL Most Holy Redeemer Retired.
Devine, William P. '52 (DUB) Retired.
Deviney, Raymond L. '59 (SCR) Retired.
deVinney, Jesus Guerra *o.p.* '69 (FgM) Metairie, LA St. Martin de Porres Province (Southern Dominican Province).
Devino, Terrence P. *s.j.* '87 (BO)[U] Newton, MA The Jesuit Community at Boston College.
Deviny, Edward *c.p.* '66 (SCR)[L] Scranton, PA Saint Ann's Passionist Monastery.
Devis, Sanjai *v.c.* '97 (CAM) Sewell, NJ Church of the Holy Family, Washington Township; International Priests Representatives.
De Vita, James C. '57 (RVC) Retired.
Devito, Darius *o.f.m.cap.* '57 (NY)[DD] Yonkers, NY St. Clare Friary.
DeVito, Michael C. '76 (HRT) Suffield, CT Sacred Heart; Enfield Deanery.
Devlin, David J. *o.s.f.s.* '77 (R) Durham, NC Holy Infant.
Devlin, Francis X. *o.s.a.* '73 (CAM)[C] Richland, NJ St. Augustine Preparatory School; Richland, NJ.
Devlin, James E. '72 (BRK) Brooklyn, NY Good Shepherd; Diocesan Consultors.
Devlin, Joseph D. *s.j.* '66 (BO)[U] Weston, MA Campion Health Center, Inc.
Devlin, Joseph P. '91 (PH) Philadelphia, PA St. Bridget; [BB] Philadelphia, PA Philadelphia University.
Devlin, Kevin '54 (OKL) Retired.
Devlin, Mark '79 (TR) Keyport, NJ Holy Family.
Devlin, Philip T. *c.s.c.* '56 (FTW)[H] Instituto de Estudios Aymaras; New Rochelle, NY Eastern Brothers Province.
Devlin, Raymond A. *s.j.* '55 (SJ)[M] Los Gatos, CA Sacred Heart Jesuit Center.
Devlin, Vianney *o.f.m.* '55 (BO)[X] Boston, MA Saint Anthony Residence Retired.
DeVolder, Philip '80 (FTW) Warsaw, IN Sacred Heart.
Devorak, James W. '72 (NU) Granite Falls, MN St. Andrew; Montevideo, MN St. Joseph; Priests' Council.
Devore, Daniel B. '79 (MO) DEPARTMENT OF VETERANS AFFAIRS HOSPITALS AND CHAPLAINS.
Devore, Daniel B. '79 (BGP) On Duty Outside the Diocese.
DeVore, John C. *m.s.f.s.* '86 (ATL)[F] Snellville, GA The Missionaries of St. Francis De Sales.
Devore, John *m.s.f.s.* '86 (TYL)[C] Whitehouse, TX The Missionaries of St. Francis de Sales.
Devot, Paul *s.j.* '72 (LA) Santa Barbara, CA Our Lady of Sorrows.
DeVous, Phillip W. '04 (COV) Crescent Springs, KY St. Joseph.
DeVries, Thomas D. '89 (MIL)[A] St. Francis, WI Saint Francis de Sales Seminary; Special Assignment.
Devron, Christopher *s.j.* (CHI)[D] Chicago, IL Christ the King Jesuit College Preparatory School.
Dewaele, Joseph *c.i.c.m.* '49 (ARL)[H] Arlington, VA Missionhurst, C.I.C.M.–Central House and Provincialate.
DeWalt, Rev. Msgr. Homer C. '50 (E)[I] Canton, OH House of Loreto Retired.
Dewan, Wilfred F. *c.s.p.* '53 (BRK)[R] Retired; Flushing, NY St. Andrew Avellino Retired.
Dewan, William G. '86 (JOL) Shorewood, IL Holy Family; Vicar for Priests.
Dewane, Daniel '71 (GB) Retired.
DeWane, E. Thomas *o.praem.* '58 (MO) DEPARTMENT OF VETERANS AFFAIRS HOSPITALS AND CHAPLAINS.
Dewane, Rev. Msgr. John B. '62 (GB) Appleton, WI; Marinette, WI Holy Family Retired.
deWater, Joseph M. '67 (NO) On Duty Outside the Archdiocese.
Dewes, John W. '65 (CHI) Barrington, IL St. Anne Retired.
DeWitt, David D. '84 (PIT) Pittsburgh, PA Incarnation of the Lord; Pittsburgh, PA Risen Lord.
Dewitt, Phil (GB)[G] Oshkosh, WI Mercy Medical Center of Oshkosh, Inc.
Deye, Walter C. *s.j.* '75 (FgM) Chicago, IL Society of Jesus; Chicago, IL Society of Jesus.
Deye, Walter C. *s.j.* '75 (DET)[K] Chicago, IL Detroit Province of the Society of Jesus–Provincial Office.
Deye, Walter C. *s.j.* '75 (CHI)[N] Chicago, IL Chicago Province of the Society of Jesus–Provincial Office; [W] Chicago, IL Jesuit International Missions, Inc.; [N] Chicago, IL Clark Street Jesuit Residence.
DeYoung, Thomas J. '83 (GR) Retired.
Deziel, William *o.s.c.* '97 (STP) North Saint Paul, MN St. Peter.
Dhabliwala, Neil '08 (ATL)[I] Dahlonega, GA North Georgia College; Dahlonega, GA St. Luke; Special or Other Archdiocesan Assignment.
Dhanwar, Walter *i.m.s.* '91 (AUS) Lott, TX Church of the Visitation.
Dhein, William A. '02 (LC) Eau Claire, WI Sacred Heart of Jesus–St. Patrick; [C] Eau Claire, WI Regis Middle School; [C] Eau Claire, WI Regis High School; Consultors; Navy Reserve Chaplains; Appointed Members.
Dhondt, Edward F. '69 (LFT) Anderson, IN St. Ambrose; Associate Judges Retired.
Diachak, Rev. Msgr. Robert (PAT) Chester, NJ Retired.
Diachek, Rev. Msgr. Robert M. '71 (PAT)[Q] Chester, NJ Nazareth Village.
Diala, Innocent Onwukwe '91 (BAK) Chiloquin, OR Our Lady of Mt. Carmel.
Diamond, David E. '83 (PH) Jenkintown, PA Immaculate Conception.
Diamond, Matthew J. '71 (BRK) Flushing, NY St. Andrew Avellino Retired.
Dianda, Carl F. '59 (WDC) Washington, DC St. Francis de Sales; [J] Bethesda, MD Ladies of Charity.
Dias, D. Francis '71 (NY) Staten Island, NY Our Lady Help of Christians.
Dias, John F. *c.s.c.* '63 (FR)[F] North Dartmouth, MA St. Joseph's Hall; [F] North Dartmouth, MA Holy Cross Residence Retired.
Dias, John F. *c.s.c.* '63 (FTW)[H] Notre Dame Congregation of Holy Cross, United States Province of Priests & Brothers.
Dias, Rosimar '02 (JOL) Naperville, IL Sts. Peter and Paul.
Dias da Costa, Josias *o.s.b.* '86 (KCK)[I] Atchison, KS St. Benedict's Abbey.
Diaz, Alberto '85 (ARE) Arecibo, PR Church of Sagrado Corazon de Jesus.
Diaz, Alberto (SJN) Clergy Social Security (Prevision Social del Clero).
Diaz, Alejandro '11 (WDC) Gaithersburg, MD St. Martin of Tours.
Diaz, Alvaro '73 (CAM) Ocean City, NJ Saint Damien Parish, Ocean City, N.J.
Diaz, Alvaro '45 (SJN) Retired.
Díaz, Angel R. '85 (ARE) Priest's Senate (Consejo Presbiteral).
Diaz, Angel '76 (ARE) Bajadero, PR La Milagrosa.
Diaz, Cesar Jaime Guzman '96 (AUS) Austin, TX San Francisco; Austin, TX San Juan Diego Mission of Dolores – Stony Point.
Diaz, Claudio '00 (CHI) Arlington Heights, IL Mision San Juan Diego.
Diaz, Dairo E. '01 (HRT) Appointed Members; Hartford, CT St. Peter; Hartford, CT Sacred Heart.
Diaz, David '79 (CGS) Comerio, PR Santo Cristo de la Salud.
Diaz, Edwin '98 (NY) New York, NY St. Thomas More.
Diaz, Eleazar '11 (YAK) Yakima, WA St. Paul Cathedral.
Diaz, Erno (NY) Staten Island, NY St. Margaret Mary; [HH] New York, NY Chapel San Lorenzo Ruiz (Philippine Pastoral Center).
Diaz, Francisco G. '77 (MIA) Miami, FL Prince of Peace.
Diaz, Francisco '87 (FRS) Delano, CA Kern Valley State Prison.
Diaz, Gilbert M. '94 (KNX) Chattanooga, TN St. Stephen; Presbyteral Council.
Diaz, Gonzalo '63 (MGZ) On Special Assignment.
Diaz, Gonzalo '52 (SJN)[G] Guaynabo, PR Opus Dei.
Diaz, Rev. Msgr. Gonzalo '63 (MGZ) Vicar General; Diocesan Consultors.
Diaz, Rev. Msgr. Gonzalo '63 (PCE) Mayaguez.
Diaz, Gonzalo '52 (POD) Guaynabo.
Diaz, Rev. Msgr. Heberto M. '89 (BWN) Catholic Foundation of the Rio Grande Valley Board; Office of the Chancellor; Moderator of the Curia/Brownsville/San Juan; College of Consultors; Campaign for Human Development; [K] Brownsville, TX Catholic Foundation of the Rio Grande Valley; [D] Executive Board:; Ex Officio Members; Priests' Assignment Board; Members; Brownsville, TX Mary, Mother of the Church.
Diaz, Hector '82 (MO)[E] San Juan, PR Centro Medico de P.R.; DEPARTMENT OF VETERANS AFFAIRS HOSPITALS AND CHAPLAINS.
Diaz, Hernando '71 (SLC) College of Consultors; Deans.
Diaz, Hernando '71 (SLC) Milford, UT Saint Bridget LLC 217.
Diaz, J. Glenn '87 (SP) Tampa, FL St. Paul.
Diaz, Jaime *o.p.* '00 (NO)[R] New Orleans Dominican Friars, Southern Dominican Province of St. Martin de Porres.
Diaz, Jose–Juan Cardona (SJN) San Juan, PR San Juan de La Cruz.
Diaz, Joseph A. '94 (HON) Kapolei, HI St. Jude.
Díaz, José Matías '89 (WDC)[A] Hyattsville, MD Redemptoris Mater Archdiocesan Missionary Seminary.
Diaz, Martin '78 (SLC) Midvale, UT Saint Therese of the Child Jesus LLC 246; Deans; Team; Presbyteral Council.
Diaz, Michael '73 (SD) Oceanside, CA Saint Mary, Star of the Sea Catholic Parish.
Diaz, Oscar '94 (SR) Priests' Council; Hispanic Ministry; Parish Priest Consultors; Cotati, CA St. Joseph.
Diaz, P. Angel (PCE) Yauco, PR Holy Rosary.
Diaz, Raul '97 (FRS) Dinuba, CA St. Catherine of Siena.
Diaz, Thomas K. '81 (SR) Santa Rosa, CA Star of the Valley; Vocations; Santa Rosa, CA Holy Spirit.
Diaz, Tony *c.m.f.* '95 (LA) San Gabriel, CA San Gabriel Mission.
Diaz–Amaya, Alex '06 (ARL) Falls Church, VA St. Anthony's.
Diaz–Diaz, Francisco Javier *s.j.* (WDC)[O] Washington, DC The Jesuit Community at Georgetown University.
Diaz–Llamas, Salvador *m.n.m.* '89 (SAT) Del Rio, TX Our Lady of Guadalupe.
Diaz–Munoz, Javier A. '98 (TR) Trenton, NJ St. Joseph.
Diaz De Leon, Juan Ramon '72 (SR) Special Assignment.
Díaz Delgado, Rafael (SJN) Catano, PR Nuestra Senora del Carmen.
Diaz Vilar, J. Juan *s.j.* '69 (NEW)[L] Jersey City, NJ Jesuits of Saint Peter's College, Inc.
DiBacco, John V. '67 (WH) Morgantown, WV St. Mary.
DiBardino, Anthony R. '76 (CAM) Continuing Education & Spiritual Formation of Priests (CESF); Mullica Hill, NJ Catholic Community of the Holy Spirit, Mullica Hill, N.J.
Dibble, Michael '60 (NY) Retired.
Dibble, Michael (OAK) Pleasant Hill, CA Christ the King.
Dibeashi, Ignatius '89 (SD) Campo, CA Saint Adelaide of Burgundy Catholic Parish.
DiBiccaro, Dominic M. '04 (HBG) Columbia, PA St. Peter.
DiBuo, Roger F. '89 (WIL) Bear, DE St. Elizabeth Ann Seton.
Dichey, Byron '09 (SEA) Elma, WA St. Joseph.
DiCicco, Mario *o.f.m.* (CHI)[N] Chicago, IL St. Peter's Friary.
Dick, Gregory M. *o.praem.* '96 (ORG)[A] Silverado, CA St. Michael's Norbertine Postulancy, Novitiate and Juniorate; [I] Silverado, CA Norbertine Fathers of Orange Inc.
Dick, John '96 (DAL) Ennis, TX Epiphany (Quasi Parish); Ennis, TX St. John Nepomucene.
Dickenson, William R. '89 (CLV) Released from Diocesan Assignment.
Dickie, Rev. Msgr. John A. '56 (SD) San Diego, CA Saint Mary Magdalene Catholic Parish Retired.
Dickinson, Andrew '06 (SFS) White, SD St. Paul; [H] Brookings, SD Pius XII Student Center.
Dickinson, John "Jack" '11 (PRT) Waterville, ME Corpus Christi Parish.
Dickinson, John (Jack) '11 (PRT)[M] Waterville, ME Colby College; [M] Waterville, ME Thomas College.
Dickinson, William '89 (PH)[CC] Wayne, PA Catholic Leadership Institute; King of Prussia, PA Mother of Divine Providence.
Dickman, Richard C. '93 (LC) Kendall, WI St. Patrick; Kendall, WI St. Joseph; Kendall, WI St. John the Baptist; Appointed Members.
Dickmann, Louis H. '59 (COV) Retired.
Dicks, Thomas '87 (NY) Goshen, NY St. John the Evangelist.
Dicks, Tom (NY)[Q] Bronx, NY District Council of the Bronx.
Dickson, Norman *s.j.* '54 (GLD) Kalkaska, MI St. Aloysius; Kalkaska, MI St. Mary of the Woods.
Dicristina, Frank T. '86 (SB) Phelan, CA Blessed Junipero Serra; Wrightwood, CA Our Lady of the Snows.
Didier, Jacques R. *m.e.p.* '53 (SFR)[N] San Francisco, CA Paris Foreign Mission Society Residence; San Francisco, CA.
Didita, Gabriel '11 (ROM) Chesterland, OH Most Holy Trinity; Cleveland, OH St. Helena.
Didone, Matthew *c.s.* '67 (BRK)[R] Jamaica, NY Saint Charles House of Studies.
Didone, Matthew '67 (NY)[HH] New York, NY Trust for the Center for Migration Studies in New York.
Diebel, Thomas '79 (LUB) Retired.
Dieckhaus, Anthony W. '62 (PH) Retired.
Dieckhaus, Joseph C. '74 (PH) Exton, PA SS. Philip and

James; Deans; Archdiocesan Judges; Deans.
Dieckmann, Rev. Msgr. Michael '74 (STL) Fenton, MO St. Paul; Archdiocesan Consultors.
Diederich, Donald F. '58 (RVC) Retired.
Diederichs, Carl E. '02 (MIL) Milwaukee, WI All Saints.
Diedrick, Charles T. '78 (CLV) Lagrange, OH St. Mary; College of Consultors; Associate Judges; Presbyteral Council; Presbyteral Conveners.
Diegel, Rev. Msgr. Ron L. '75 (TYL) Deans; Presbyteral Council.
Diegel, Rev. Msgr. Ronald L. '75 (TYL) College of Consultors; Priests' Pension Board; Priests' Personnel Board; Holly Lake Ranch, TX Holy Spirit Church.
Diegelman, Robert W. '93 (R) Retired.
Diehl, Dennis P. '74 (BAL) Fulton, MD St. Francis of Assisi.
Diehm, Noah J. '11 (DUB) Dyersville, IA Basilica of St. Francis Xavier; Earlville, IA St. Joseph; New Vienna, IA St. Boniface; Dyersville, IA SS. Peter and Paul; Worthington, IA St. Paul.
Dieker, James P. '93 (DOD) Liberal, KS St. Anthony of Padua Catholic Church of Liberal, Kansas; Satanta, KS St. Alphonsus Catholic Church of Satanta, Kansas; Deans.
Diekhans, Joseph '65 (GF) Chester, MT St. Mary; Personnel Board; Chester, MT Our Lady of Ransom.
Diekhoff, Bernard *c.pp.s.* '47 (CIN)[N] Carthagena, OH St. Charles Retired.
Diem, Joseph '85 (BO) Medford, MA St. Joseph.
Diemand, James E. '68 (SPR) DEPARTMENT OF VETERANS AFFAIRS HOSPITALS AND CHAPLAINS Retired.
Diemer, Michael *m.j.* (TOL) Willard, OH St. Francis Xavier; Eastern Office.
Diem Phuc Le, Simon M. *c.m.c.* '03 (SPC) Springfield, MO Immaculate Conception; Billings, MO St. Joseph.
Dien, Tran Gia '08 (LA)[P] Baldwin Park, CA Vietnamese Redemptorist Mission.
Dienert, Robert T. '62 (LR)[G] Little Rock, AR St. John Manor Retired.
Dienert, Robert T. (OKL) Judges.
Dien Nguyen, Raymond M. *c.m.c.* '88 (SPC)[F] Carthage, MO Congregation of the Mother Coredemptrix, United States Assumption Province.
Dieringer, James J. '58 (P) Retired.
Diermeier, Joseph G. '78 (LC) Marathon City, WI Nativity of the Blessed Virgin Mary; Promoter of Justice; Vicars General; Ex Officio; Consultors.
Diesbourg, Raymond *m.s.c.* '74 (RCK)[G] Aurora, IL Missionaries of the Sacred Heart Community.
Diesbourg, Raymond *m.s.c.* '74 (FgM) Aurora, IL; Aurora, IL MISSIONARIES OF THE SACRED HEART.
Diesen, Edwin Bryan '07 (GLP) Milan, NM St. Vivian; Milan, NM San Mateo; Milan, NM San Rafael; Grants, NM St. Teresa of Avila.
Diesta, V. Henry M. (RIC) Newport News, VA St. Jerome.
Dieter, Thomas M. '83 (JOL) On Duty Outside the Diocese; DEPARTMENT OF VETERANS AFFAIRS HOSPITALS AND CHAPLAINS.
Dieter, Xavier L. *o.c.s.o.* '58 (DUB)[K] Peosta, IA New Melleray Abbey, Order of Cistercians of the Strict Observance.
Dietlein, Damian *o.s.b.* '57 (IND)[A] Saint Meinrad, IN Saint Meinrad School of Theology.
Dietlein, Damian *o.s.b.* '57 (BIS)[A] Richardton, ND Assumption Abbey.
Dietlein, Raymond *o.s.b.* '54 (BIS)[A] Richardton, ND Assumption Abbey Retired.
Dietrich, Christopher *o.f.m.cap.* '59 (NY) Yonkers, NY Sacred Heart.
Dietrich, Douglas D. '96 (LIN) Lincoln, NE St. Mary; Permanent Deacon Continuing Education Committee; Ecumenical Affairs, Commission for.
Dietrich, John J. '92 (BAL)[A] Emmitsburg, MD Mount St. Mary's Seminary.
Dietrich, John J. '93 (HRT) On Duty Outside the Archdiocese.
Dietrich, Severin *o.f.m.conv.* '53 (TR)[M] Yardville, NJ Villa Maria Sanitarium.
Dietsch, William '71 (EVN) Retired.
Dietz, Rev. Msgr. Conrad R. '57 (BRK)[B] Douglaston, NY Cathedral Seminary Residence of the Immaculate Conception; [R] Douglaston, NY Bishop Mugavero Residence Retired.
Dietz, Donald *o.m.i.* '57 (CHI)[O] Lake Villa, IL Handmaids of the Precious Blood.
Dietz, Donald *o.m.i.* '57 (WDC)[O] Washington, DC Provincial Offices of the United States Province of the Missionary Oblates of Mary Immaculate.
Dietz, Elias *o.c.s.o.* '03 (L)[L] Trappist, KY Abbey of Our Lady of Gethsemani, of the Order of Cistercians of the Strict Observance; Trappist, KY.
Dietz, Joseph '87 (NY) Sleepy Hollow, NY The Magdalene.
Dietz, Rev. Msgr. Norbert J. '49 (STL) Retired.
Dietzenbach, Rev. Msgr. John A. '80 (BAL) Ellicott City, MD Resurrection.
Dietzler, William J. '69 (MIL) Retired.
Diez, Rev. Msgr. Antonio '59 (SP) Spanish Speaking Spiritual Moderator Retired.
Diez, Jose L. *o.s.a.* '72 (MGZ) Diocesan Consultors; Parish Priests Consultors.
Diez, Oscar '68 (DAL) Retired.
DiFazio, Silverio '10 (STA) Jacksonville, FL St. Paul's.
Diffley, Patrick J. '63 (BRK) Retired.
DiFilippo, John V. *o.s.f.s.* '45 (PH)[Y] Philadelphia, PA Father Louis Brisson Residence Retired.
DiFiore, John *s.d.b.* '97 (NO) Harvey, LA St. Rosalie.
DiFolco, Thomas P. '83 (CIN) Cincinnati, OH St. Michael; Priestly Formation.
Digal, Danilo C. '78 (NO) Chalmette, LA Our Lady of Prompt Succor; Deans.
DiGeronimo, Michael A. '76 (WOR) Advocates; Sutton, MA St. Mark.
DiGiacamo, James J. *s.j.* '56 (NY)[DD] New York, NY Murray–Weigel Hall.
Di Giovanni, Rev. Msgr. Stephen M. '77 (BGP) Stamford, CT The Basilica of Saint John the Evangelist.
DiGiralamo, Gerald *s.a.* '81 (BO)[N] Brockton, MA Chapel of Our Savior–Catholic Pastoral and Information Center; [U] Brockton, MA Chapel of Our Savior; [Z] Brockton, MA Chapel of Our Saviour.
DiGiralamo, Gerald *s.a.* '81 (NY)[DD] Brockton, MA Chapel of Our Savior.
DiGirolamo, Dante '48 (NEW) Retired.
DiGirolamo, Rev. Msgr. Paul A. '83 (PH) Philadelphia, PA Old St. Mary's; Judicial Vicar; Diocesan Priests' Compensation and Benefits Committee.
DiGiulio, Richard S. '69 (BUF) Charismatic Renewal Program; Advocates; [N] Depew, NY Msgr. Conniff Residence Retired.
Dignan, Eamon '59 (WDC) Hollywood, MD St. John Francis Regis Retired.
Dignan, Thomas L. '57 (BIS) Retired.
Di Gregorio, Michael F. *o.s.a.* '73 (FgM) Villanova, PA Province of St. Thomas of Villanova (Eastern).
DiGuglielmo, Anthony J. '03 (PH) Graduate Studies.
DiIanni, Albert *s.m.* '60 (BO)[Z] Boston, MA Marist Fathers Residence.
DiIannl, Albert *s.m.* '60 (BO)[U] Boston, MA Marist Fathers Lourdes Residence.
DiIorio, Michael C. '77 (PH) Levittown, PA St. Michael the Archangel.
Dike, Anthony O. (GLP) Holbrook, AZ Our Lady of Guadalupe.
Dikete, Fidele O. '02 (SAT) San Antonio, TX Our Lady of Good Counsel; In Metropolitan Area; Archdiocesan Presbyteral Council; Priests Personnel Board.
Di Lella, Alexander A. *o.f.m.* '55 (WDC)[C] Catholic University of America, The Retired.
DiLella, Alexander A. *o.f.m.* '55 (SP)[N] St. Petersburg, FL St. Anthony Friary.
DiLella, Rev. Msgr. Christopher C. '79 (PAT) Wayne, NJ Our Lady of the Valley; Wayne, NJ Holy Cross.
DiLella, Rev. Msgr. Christopher C. (PAT) Apostleship of Prayer; Priests Eucharistic League.
Di Lella, Mario *o.f.m.* '53 (SP)[N] St. Petersburg, FL St. Anthony Friary Retired.
DiLeo, Anthony '64 (SB) Retired.
Dilg, Donald W. *c.s.c.* '75 (COS)[E] Cascade, CO Holy Cross Novitiate.
Dilg, Donald W. *c.s.c.* '75 (FTW)[H] Notre Dame Congregation of Holy Cross, United States Province of Priests & Brothers.
Dilger, Basil *o.s.b.* '61 (FgM) Marvin, SD Blue Cloud Abbey.
Dilger, Donald '59 (EVN) Retired.
Diliberto, Peter J. '43 (LA)[P] Montebello, CA DePaul Evangelization Center; [V] Montebello, CA DePaul Evangelization Center Retired.
Dilion, Joseph A. '46 (HRT) Retired.
Dilipy, Basilio '94 (CI) Chuuk, FM Holy Family Church; [C] Tunnuk, Chuuk, FM Vicariate Residence.
Dill, Edwin *s.t.* '59 (WDC)[O] Adelphi, MD Father Judge Missionary Cenacle.
Dillabough, Rev. Msgr. Daniel J. '74 (SD)[B] San Diego, CA University of San Diego; Defenders of the Bond; College of Consultors; Finance Council; Presbyteral Council.
Dillane, Maurice '63 (SAT) Retired.
Dillard, Daniel C. '09 (OWN) Hopkinsville, KY SS. Peter and Paul; Elkton, KY St. Susan; Guthrie, KY Sts. Mary & James.
Dillard, Steven C. *s.j.* '86 (WDC)[O] Washington, DC Leonard Neale House.
Dillard, William '98 (SD) San Diego, CA Saint John the Evangelist Catholic Parish San Diego; San Diego, CA Saint Vincent de Paul Catholic Parish; Spiritual Direction for Candidates and Priests; Spiritual Direction for Candidates and Priests; [A] San Diego, CA St. Francis De Sales Center.
Dillenburg, Rev. Msgr. James E. '65 (GB) Retired.
Dillinger, Joseph A. '96 (SC) Breda, IA St. John the Baptist; Breda, IA Our Lady of Mt. Carmel; Breda, IA St. Bernard's.
Dillingham, Charles C. '73 (WIL) Hockessin, DE St. Mary of the Assumption.
Dillon, Ciarian *o.m.i.* '54 (OAK) Crockett, CA St. Rose of Lima.
Dillon, David *o.carm.* '65 (JOL)[K] Darien, IL Carmelite Carefree Retirement Village Retired.
Dillon, Dennis T. *s.j.* '69 (LAN) Ann Arbor, MI St. Mary Student Parish; [J] Ann Arbor, MI Detroit Province of the Society of Jesus – Jesuit Residence.
Dillon, Rev. Msgr. Desmond P. '41 (YAK) Kennewick, WA St. Joseph's Retired.
Dillon, Rev. Msgr. Edward J. '67 (ATL) Atlanta, GA Holy Spirit; Advisory Board on Sexual Abuse of Minors; Archdiocesan Judges; [K] Atlanta, GA The Solidarity Association.
Dillon, Edward J. *o.f.m.* '55 (SP)[N] St. Petersburg, FL St. Anthony Friary Retired.
Dillon, Edward J. (PAT) Retired.
Dillon, Edward J. '60 (ROC) Geneseo, NY St. Luke the Evangelist Roman Catholic Church Society of Livingston County; [N] Geneseo, NY State University College at Geneseo (Geneseo), Newman Catholic Community at the Interfaith Center Retired.
Dillon, Geoffrey R. *s.j.* '83 (SFR)[N] San Francisco, CA Loyola House Jesuit Community.
Dillon, J. Thomas '11 (PT) Pensacola, FL Holy Spirit; Pensacola, FL St. John the Evangelist.
Dillon, Jeffry T. '81 (BRK) Springfield Gardens, NY Christ the King; South Ozone Park, NY St. Clement Pope; Springfield Gardens, NY St. Mary Magdalene.
Dillon, Jerome V. '77 (MO) Military Chaplains; Navy Chaplains.
Dillon, John J. '98 (WDC) Hyattsville, MD St. Mark; Deans; Priest Council; Archdiocesan College of Consultors.
Dillon, John T. *s.j.* '63 (DET)[K] Clarkston, MI Colombiere Center.
Dillon, Kevin J. '03 (RVC) Williston Park, NY St. Aidan's Church.
Dillon, Kevin M. '00 (HRT) Plantsville, CT St. Aloysius.
Dillon, Michael J. '61 (SAC) Rocklin, CA SS. Peter and Paul Retired.
Dillon, Richard J. '61 (NY) On Duty Outside the Archdiocese.
Dillon, Robert W. '97 (NY) Staten Island, NY St. John Neumann; Staten Island, NY St. Joseph, St. Thomas.
Dillon, Thomas J. '59 (GI) Retired.
DiLorenzo, Thomas A. '79 (BO) Winthrop, MA Holy Rosary.
DiLoreto, Anthony '54 (B) Retired.
DiLuzio, James M. *c.s.p.* '93 (NY)[DD] New York, NY Paulist Fathers' Motherhouse.
Dimaranan, Vitaliano *s.d.b.* (AGN)[B] Hagatna, GU The Father Duenas Memorial School.
DiMarco, Rev. Msgr. Abel A. '56 (PCE)[B] The Pontifical Catholic University of Puerto Rico; Sacred Music Commission.
DiMarco, Anthony J. '06 (NOR) Pomfret, CT Most Holy Trinity.
DiMarco, Anthony '06 (NOR) Putnam, CT St. Mary Church of the Visitation.
DiMaria, Peter J. '93 (PH) Royersford, PA Sacred Heart.
DiMaria, Sean E. '05 (BUF)[G] Wellsville, NY Immaculate Conception School of Allegany County; Vicars; Wellsville, NY Immaculate Conception; Alfred, NY SS. Brendan and Jude; Almond, NY Blessed Sacrament; Belmont, NY Holy Family of Jesus, Mary & Joseph; Bolivar, NY St. Mary.
Di Marzio, Vito *r.c.j.* '75 (LA) Sanger, CA; [P] Van Nuys, CA Rogationist Fathers; Van Nuys, CA St. Elisabeth; Van Nuys, CA.
DiMascola, Charles J. '81 (SPR) Turners Falls, MA Our Lady of Czestochowa.
DiMattei, Robert A. '91 (BAL) Baltimore, MD St. Athanasius; Baltimore, MD St. Rose of Lima.
DiMauro, John C. *o.f.m.* '56 (BO)[U] Andover St. Francis Friary; [U] Boston, MA St. Christopher Friary Retired.
DiMauro, Rev. Msgr. Joseph V. '67 (CAM) Appointed Members; Members; Woodbury, NJ Holy Angels Parish, Woodbury, N.J.
Di Mauro, Joseph *s.a.* '78 (NY)[DD] Garrison, NY Franciscan Friars of the Atonement.
Dimic, Milan '85 (BGP) Easton, CT Notre Dame (of Easton).
Dimler, G. Richard *s.j.* '63 (BAL)[Q] Baltimore, MD Colombiere Jesuit Community.
Dinan, Dennis M. '92 (NY) Cornwall–on–Hudson, NY St. Thomas of Canterbury.
DiNardo, Daniel A. '66 (CAM) Bridgeton, NJ The Parish of the Holy Cross, Bridgeton, N.J.
DiNardo, Lawrence A. '74 (PIT) Pittsburgh, PA Holy Wisdom; Director, Department for Canon and Civil Law Services; Judges; Canon and Civil Law Services, Dept. for; Canonical Services, Office for; Health Care Liaison, Office of the; Diocesan Review Board; Vicar for Canonical Services; Promoter of Justice; Priest Council; Vicar for Canonical Services.
DiNardo, Mark A. '58 (CLV) Cleveland, OH St. Patrick; Presbyteral Conveners; Presbyteral Council.
Dinda, John J. '62 (PH) Retired.
Dindorf, Meinrad *o.s.b.* '58 (SCL)[H] St. Cloud, MN St.

Benedict's Senior Community; [I] Collegeville, MN St. John's Abbey, of the Order of St. Benedict.
Dineen, Michael P. '49 (MIL) Retired.
Dineen, William *c.pp.s.* '66 (CIN)[N] Carthagena, OH St. Charles Retired.
Dinelli, William J. '61 (SAC) Retired.
Dinello, John E. '85 (PIT) Pittsburgh, PA Immaculate Conception–St. Joseph; Army Reserve Chaplains.
Dineros, Santiago A. '55 (RVC) Retired.
Dinga, William '75 (RIC) Retired.
Dinguis, George L '05 (BRK) Jackson Heights, NY Our Lady of Fatima.
Dinguis, Jorge '06 (TYL) On Duty Outside the Diocese.
Dinguis, Jorge '06 (BRK) Long Island City, NY Most Precious Blood; Long Island City, NY St. Patrick.
Dinh, (Anselm M.) Can Vuong *c.m.c.* '77 (SPC)[F] Carthage, MO Congregation of the Mother Coredemptrix, United States Assumption Province.
Dinh, Chien *s.v.d.* '08 (GAL) Houston, TX St. Mary of the Purification.
Dinh, Domininc Hai *c.ss.r.* '95 (DAL)[J] Dallas, TX St. John Neumann Formation House.
Dinh, Felix Mary Luan Viet *c.m.c.* '89 (SB)[I] Corona, CA Congregation of the Mother Co–Redemptrix, C.M.C.
Dinh, Hai D. '08 (DAV) Vicar for Vietnamese.
Dinh, Hai Duc '08 (DAV)[M] Davenport, IA Vietnamese Catholic Community of Our Lady of Mong Trieu; Davenport, IA Sacred Heart Cathedral.
Dinh, Hao '93 (SJ) San Jose, CA Holy Family; Special Assignment.
Dinh, Hoan '07 (ROC) Geneva, NY Our Lady of Peace Roman Catholic Church of Geneva, NY.
Dinh, Hoan *o.f.m.* '06 (WDC)[B] Silver Spring, MD Holy Name College.
Dinh, Hung M. *m.m.* '08 (FgM) Maryknoll, NY MARYKNOLL.
Dinh, Joseph Huy Quang *c.s.sp.* '10 (GAL) Houston, TX St. Benedict the Abbot; [B] Houston, TX Holy Ghost Fathers and Brothers.
Dinh, Joseph Long '00 (CHL) Eden, NC St. Joseph of the Hills.
Dinh, Joseph Thien *s.c.j.* '02 (GAL) Houston, TX Our Lady of Guadalupe.
Dinh, Ky Ngoc *s.v.d.* '08 (SB)[I] Riverside, CA Divine Word Seminary.
Dinh, Quang Duc *s.v.d.* '92 (CHI)[N] Techny, IL Divine Word Residence; [N] Chicago, IL Divine Word Theologate.
Dinh, Tran Thuc '61 (OAK) San Leandro, CA St. Felicitas Retired.
Dinh, Tri M. *s.j.* '00 (LA) Los Angeles, CA Dolores Mission.
Dinh, Trung Hoa *s.j.* '06 (BO)[U] Newton, MA The Jesuit Community at Boston College.
Dinh, Van '02 (MO) Military Chaplains; Air Force Chaplains.
Dinh, Victor T. '03 (FRS) Fresno, CA St. Genevieve; Fresno, CA Veterans Administration Medical Center; Community Regional Medical Center.
Dinh, Vo Tran Gia *a.a.* '11 (WOR)[N] Worcester, MA Assumptionists of Assumption College.
Dinh–Van–Thiep, Philip '83 (GB) Green Bay, WI St. Matthew.
Dinh Hau, Vincent Nguyen '09 (SAC)[H] Walnut Grove, CA Monastery of Chau Son Sacramento.
Dinh Van, Anton Quang '04 (SAT) San Antonio, TX San Francesco di Paola (Italian).
Dini, Tekle '73 (SR) Willits, CA St. Anthony of Padua.
DiNigris, Emmanuelle (MIA)[B] Hialeah, FL Redemptoris Mater Seminary.
Dininni, Nicholas J. '93 (PH) Coatesville, PA St. Cecilia.
Diniz, Rev. Msgr. Pedro D. '71 (BGP) Danbury, CT St. Peter.
Dinkel, Harvey *o.f.m.cap.* '61 (SAL)[C] Hays, KS St. John's Hays; [C] Victoria, KS St. John's Victoria; [D] Victoria, KS St. Fidelis Friary.
Dinkha, Samuel '80 (SPA) North Hollywood, CA St. Paul Assyrian–Chaldean Catholic Parish.
Dinkha, Chorbishop Samuel '80 (LA) North Hollywood, CA St. Paul Assyrian–Chaldean.
Dinkins, Rev. Msgr. Jack M. '63 (GAL) Katy, TX Epiphany of the Lord.
Dinneen, James J. *s.j.* '60 (NEW)[C] Jersey City, NJ Jesuit Community.
DiNoia, Joseph Augustine *o.p.* '70 (WDC) On Duty Outside the Archdiocese.
DiNola, Leonard J. '58 (NY)[DD] Bronx, NY Retired.
Dinovo, Anthony A. '01 (COL) Kenton, OH Immaculate Conception.
Dinsdale, Samuel '03 (SLC) Team; Tooele, UT St. Marguerite LLC 235; Liturgical Commission.
Dio, Jacob D. *m.s.f.s.* (TYL)[C] Whitehouse, TX The Missionaries of St. Francis de Sales.
Dio, Jacob *m.s.f.s.* '04 (NSH) Murfreesboro, TN St. Rose of Lima.
Diogo, Louis M. '46 (PRO) Providence, RI St. Joseph Retired.
Dioka, Jude T. '80 (LC) Custer, WI Immaculate Conception; Amherst, WI St. James; Amherst, WI St. Mary of Mount Carmel.
Diokno, Rev. Msgr. Rolando V. '70 (GAL) Houston, TX Notre Dame.
Diomartich, Rev. Msgr. Felix S. '37 (LA) Retired.
Dion, Richard H. '99 (MAN) Manchester, NH St. Anthony of Padua.
Dionisio, Romeo '84 (PHX) Tempe, AZ Church of the Resurrection Roman Catholic Parish; Mesa, AZ Banner Desert Medical Center.
Dionne, Adrian L. *o.p.* '49 (WDC) Washington, DC St. Dominic Church & Priory.
Dionne, Francis '81 (MO) DEPARTMENT OF VETERANS AFFAIRS HOSPITALS AND CHAPLAINS Retired.
Dionne, J. Joseph *c.ss.r.* (CHL) Concord, NC St. James.
Dionne, Rene *m.afr.* '61 (FgM) Washington, DC MISSIONARIES OF AFRICA.
DiOrio, John R. '99 (PH) Philadelphia, PA Stella Maris.
Diorio, Ralph A. '57 (WOR) On Special or Other Diocesan Assignment; Apostolate for Healing.
Di Pasquale, Donald J. '62 (NEW)[L] Caldwell, NJ The Rev. Msgr. James F. Kelley Residence for Retired Priests Retired.
DiPerri, James M. '88 (BO) Waltham, MA Our Lady, Comforter of the Afflicted; [A] Weston, MA Blessed John XXIII National Seminary.
Diphe, Juan M. '76 (HEL) Military Chaplains.
DiPietro, Leroy A. '70 (PIT) Retired Priests, Delegate for; Pittsburgh, PA St. Athanasius.
Dipre, Gilio L. '55 (E)[B] Erie, PA Gannon University Retired.
DiRaimando, Domenico *m.sp.s.* (P)[L] Banks, OR Missionaries of the Holy Spirit, M.Sp.S.
Direen, John '01 (OAK) Berkeley, CA St. Joseph The Worker; Chaplains.
DiRenzo, Michael J. '70 (STU) On Duty Outside the Diocese.
Dirkx, Dennis A. '72 (MIL) Whitefish Bay, WI Holy Family; Shorewood, WI St. Robert.
Dirscherl, Denis A. *s.j.* '67 (CIN)[N] Cincinnati, OH Jesuit Community at St. Xavier High School.
Dirscherl, Denis A. *s.j.* '67 (CHI)[N] Chicago Chicago Province of the Society of Jesus–Provincial Office.
Di Russo, Anthony '63 (MAN) Retired.
DiSalvatore, Remo *o.f.m.cap.* '97 (CHL) Charlotte, NC St. Thomas Aquinas.
DiSalvatore, Remo *o.f.m.cap.* '97 (NEW) Definitors:; [L] Union City, NJ Capuchin Friars – Province of the Sacred Stigmata of St. Francis.
Dischler, Raymond J. '73 (MAD) Poynette, WI St. Thomas; Poynette, WI St. Joseph; Deaneries.
DiSciacca, Joseph V. '73 (HRT) Bristol, CT St. Joseph; Special and other Archdiocesan Assignment; Waterbury Vicariate; Office of Ministry for Priests; Ex Officio.
Disco, Bernard *o.s.b.* '06 (MAN)[K] Manchester, NH St. Anselm Abbey.
DiSenso, Gerard '53 (NY)[DD] Bronx, NY John Cardinal O'Connor Residence Retired.
Diskin, Michael L. '77 (PHX) Glendale, AZ St. Louis The King Roman Catholic Parish; Assistant Chancellor; College of Consultors; Catholic Cemeteries; Ecumenical and Interreligious Affairs; Presbyteral Council.
Diskin, Michael '77 (PHX) Priests' Assurance Association.
DiSpigno, Francis J. *o.f.m.* '96 (NY)[DD] New York Franciscan Friars, Holy Name Province.
DiSpigno, Francis *o.f.m.* '96 (BUF)[N] St. Bonaventure, NY St. Bonaventure Friary; [Q] St. Bonaventure, NY St. Bonaventure University; [C] St. Bonaventure University.
DiSpigno, Gennaro J. '81 (RVC) Bellport, NY Mary Immaculate; South Brookhaven Deanery; Presbyteral Council.
Dissek, Jerome M. '69 (BUF) Retired.
DiStefano, Joseph '84 (ORG) Absent on Sick Leave.
DiStefano, Salvatore '03 (NEW)[D] Summit, NJ The Oratory Catholic Preparatory School.
Distefano, Simeon C. *o.f.m.* '63 (NY)[DD] New York Franciscan Province of the Immaculate Conception.
Dister, John E. *s.j.* '62 (CLV)[B] University Heights, OH John Carroll Jesuit Community.
Distor, Leo *s.s.c.* '96 (OM)[J] St. Columbans Missionary Society of St. Columban.
Distor, Leo *s.s.c.* '96 (CHI)[N] Chicago, IL Columban Fathers Theologate.
DiTaddeo, Alessandro '54 (CHI) Chicago, IL St. Francis Borgia.
Ditenhafer, John A. '61 (STL) Ladue, MO Church of the Annunziata Retired.
Ditillo, James J. *s.j.* '74 (ALN)[A] Wernersville, PA Jesuit Center–Jesuit Community.
DiTomasso, Peter *m.ss.cc.* '06 (CAM)[L] Linwood, NJ Villa Pieta. Missionaries of the Sacred Hearts of Jesus & Mary; Linwood, NJ.
Di Tomo, Christopher P. '11 (RCK) Crystal Lake, IL St. Elizabeth Ann Seton.
Dittberner, Jerome M. *s.t.d.* '64 (STP) Retired.
Dittmeier, Charles R. '70 (L) On Duty Outside the Archdiocese; Maryknoll, NY MARYKNOLL.
Dittmer, Antonio '97 (WIN)[A] Winona, MN Immaculate Heart of Mary Seminary; Additional Diocesan Assignments.
Ditto, Anthony W. '90 (GBG) Donegal, PA St. Raymond of the Mountains; Donegal, PA St. Boniface.
Ditullio, Brian '06 (PAT) Swartswood, NJ Our Lady of Mt. Carmel.
DiTullio, Peter S. *s.d.c.* '68 (PRO) East Providence, RI Sacred Heart.
DiUlio, Albert J. *s.j.* '74 (TUC)[E] Tucson, AZ Jesuit Community of the Vatican Observatory.
Diurczak, Eugene '68 (NEW) Linden, NJ Holy Family.
Diver, Patrick *s.d.b.* (NEW) Elizabeth, NJ St. Anthony's.
Divine, Finbarr '70 (LA) Whittier, CA St. Gregory the Great Retired.
Divis, Daniel O. '79 (CLV) Lorain, OH Mary Mother of God.
Divis, M. James '76 (LIN)[A] Seward, NE St. Gregory the Great Seminary; Deaneries and Deans; Censores Librorum; Ecumenical Affairs, Commission for; Commission on Alcohol and Drug Abuse.
Dixey, Edward *o.s.a.* '57 (PH)[Y] Villanova, PA St. Augustine Friary.
Dixon, David C. '57 (PIT)[M] Pittsburgh, PA St. John Vianney Manor Retired.
Dixon, Francis F. *o.carm.* '76 (NY)[GG] New Rochelle, NY Iona College; Tarrytown, NY Transfiguration.
Dixon, Isadore (WDC) Hyattsville, MD St. Jerome.
Dixon, J. Isidore '64 (WDC) Retired.
Dixon, James M. *s.j.* '73 (CHI)[N] Chicago, IL Woodlawn Jesuit Community.
Dixon, James R. '70 (NO) Retired.
Dixon, Jeremy *c.m.* (STO) Patterson, CA Sacred Heart Church of Patterson (Pastor of).
Dixon, Jerome A. '57 (PIT) Pittsburgh, PA Retired.
Dlabal, Norbert '72 (SAL) Goodland, KS Our Lady of Perpetual Help Parish; Goodland, KS Holy Ghost Parish; Board of Trustees; College of Consultors.
Dlugos, Raymond F. *o.s.a.* '83 (BO)[C] Our Mother of Good Counsel Monastery.
Dlugos, Raymond F. *o.s.a.* '83 (PH)[C] Villanova, PA Villanova University; Counselors.
Dmoch, Paul '76 (NY) Washingtonville, NY St. Mary.
Do, Andrew Mary Sang Linh *c.m.c.* '83 (SB)[I] Corona, CA Congregation of the Mother Co–Redemptrix, C.M.C.
Do, Andy H. *c.s.sp.* (GAL) Houston, TX St. Benedict the Abbot.
Do, Rev. Msgr. Dominic Dinh '80 (SJ) San Jose, CA St. Maria Goretti.
Do, Hee Chan '98 (JOL) Darien, IL Our Lady of Korean Martyrs Mission.
Do, James Long Hai *c.m.c.* '10 (SPC) Springfield, MO Cathedral of St. Agnes.
Do, Joseph Chung Van *o.p.* '95 (GAL) Houston, TX Our Lady of Lavang Church.
Do, Joseph Toan '04 (MIL)[B] Hales Corners, WI Sacred Heart School of Theology.
Do, Nho Duy '66 (LR)[G] Little Rock, AR St. John Manor Retired.
Do, Peter Quan '02 (L) Louisville, KY St. Bartholomew; Ex Officio.
Do, Peter *o.p.* '09 (SLC) Salt Lake City, UT Saint Catherine of Siena LLC 218; [G] Salt Lake City, UT University of Utah, Newman Center.
Do, Timothy T. '10 (SB) Riverside, CA Our Lady of Perpetual Help.
Do, Tuan Anh '00 (CIN) Priests On Personal Leave.
Do, Tung Minh '04 (L) On Duty Outside the Archdiocese.
Do, Vien Van '90 (PEO) Wyoming, IL St. John the Baptist; Wyoming, IL St. Patrick; Wyoming, IL St. Dominic's.
Do, Vincentius Toan '07 (BRK)[Q] Chinese Apostolate–Brooklyn; Brooklyn, NY St. Rosalia–Regina Pacis.
Doai, Dang Kim *c.m.* '08 (BRK)[R] Jamaica, NY Reverend John B. Murray, CM, House.
Doan, (Mark M.) Bau Quang *c.m.c.* '77 (SPC)[F] Carthage, MO Congregation of the Mother Coredemptrix, United States Assumption Province.
Doan, John Baptist Minh *o.p.* '03 (GAL) Houston, TX Our Lady of Lavang Church.
Doan, Peter Khoi Anh Hoang *s.d.d.* '09 (P) Portland, OR Our Lady of Lavang.
Doan Nguyen, Joseph Tan *o.f.m.* '86 (STL)[O] St. Louis Franciscan Friary of St. Anthony of Padua.
Do Ba Ai, Joseph *c.m.c.* '51 (SPC)[F] Carthage, MO Congregation of the Mother Coredemptrix, United States Assumption Province.
Do Ba Cong, James *c.m.c.* '61 (SPC)[F] Carthage, MO Congregation of the Mother Coredemptrix, United States Assumption Province.
Dobbin, Edmund J. *o.s.a.* '62 (PH)[C] Villanova University; [Y] Villanova, PA St. Thomas Monastery.
Dobbins, Michael J. '99 (ARL) Winchester, VA Sacred Heart of Jesus.
Dobbs, Jeffrey L. '08 (WIN) Fulda, MN St. Gabriel's; Fulda, MN Immaculate Heart of Mary; Fulda, MN St. Anthony's.

Dober, Edward J. '76 (LA) Norwalk, CA St. John of God.
Dobes, Rev. Msgr. George E. '68 (CHI) On Duty Outside the Archdiocese.
Dobes, Rev. Msgr. George E. '68 (WDC) Advocates.
Dobihal, Robert F. '50 (STP) Retired.
Dobosiewciz, Leon W. '46 (Y) Retired.
Dobosiewicz, Rev. Msgr. Leo '46 (ORL) Lake Wales, FL Holy Spirit Retired.
Dobosz, Jerzy George '95 (TYL) On Duty Outside the Diocese.
Dobosz, Jerzy '95 (SAG) Kawkawlin, MI St. Valentine; Kawkawlin, MI Sacred Heart.
DoBranski, John V. '89 (BAL) Priests Sick or Absent.
Dobrosky, John M. '83 (TR) Leave of Absence.
Dobrowolski, Rev. Archpriest Thomas '88 (STN) Retired.
Dobrowski, Peter P. '71 (PHX) Bullhead City, AZ St. Margaret Mary Roman Catholic Parish; Defenders of the Bond; Dolan Springs, AZ Our Lady of the Desert Mission, A Quasi–Parish.
Dobrzenski, Francis G. '77 (MAR) Lake Linden, MI St. Joseph; Consultors.
Dobrzynski, Martin J. '84 (GRY) Schererville, IN St. Michael; Priests' Personnel Board; Bishop's Council of Priests.
Dobson, Christopher *t.o.r.* '78 (ALT)[A] Loretto, PA St. Francis University; [I] Loretto, PA St. Francis University (Loretto).
Dobson, Gregory J. '83 (BUF)[G] Olean, NY Southern Tier Catholic School; Vicars; Olean, NY St. Mary of the Angels.
Docabo, Ranulfo D. '93 (NEW) Union, NJ St. Michael's.
Docabo, Ranulfo '93 (NY) Staten Island, NY St. Patrick.
Do Carmo Araujo, Rosenilton '02 (ATL) Atlanta, GA St. Jude.
Dockendorf, Ronald '82 (SCL) Grey Eagle, MN St. Joseph's; Grey Eagle, MN St. John the Baptist.
Dockerill, Walter '60 (PMB) Retired.
Doctor, Daniel E. '06 (KAL) Coldwater, MI St. Charles Borromeo; Florence Crane Correctional Facility for Women; Lakeland Correctional Facility for Men.
Doctor, John *o.f.m.* '76 (SFD)[B] Quincy, IL Quincy University; [K] Quincy, IL Holy Cross Friary.
Doda, Eugene J. '77 (MIL) Waterford, WI St. Thomas Aquinas.
Dodd, Michael A. '00 (TLS) Broken Arrow, OK St. Anne.
Dodd, Michael A. (OKL) Judges.
Dodd, Michael *s.s.c.* '61 (OM)[J] St. Columbans, NE Missionary Society of St. Columban; Religious Orders.
Dodd, Ronald '05 (PEO) Campus, IL Sacred Heart; Odell, IL St. Paul's.
Dodds, Michael J. *o.p.* '77 (OAK) Berkeley, CA St. Mary Magdalen; [A] Berkeley, CA Dominican School of Philosophy and Theology.
Dodge, Edwin J. *o.s.a.* '57 (CHI)[N] Chicago, IL St. Rita Monastery.
Dodge, Terry '05 (FAR) Wahpeton, ND St. John's Church of Wahpeton.
Dodo, Wilfred Y. (NY) Staten Island, NY Holy Child.
Dodrai, Alexius '97 (FTW) Fort Wayne, IN St. Patrick.
Dodson, James C. '11 (BUR) Rutland, VT Christ the King; [B] Rutland, VT Mount St. Joseph Academy – Rutland Catholic Schools; Wallingford, VT St. Patrick.
Doerfler, John F. '91 (GB)[O] Green Bay, WI Sacred Heart Seminary Corporation; Chancellor; Priests' Personnel Board; Cecil, WI St. Martin; Special Assignment; College of Consultors; Vicars General; Ex Officio.
Doerfler, Rev. Msgr. Marvin G. '59 (SAT) Canyon Lake, TX St. Thomas the Apostle.
Doerger, Berard *o.f.m.* '61 (SFE) Pena Blanca, NM Nuestra Senora De Guadalupe.
Doerhoff, Rev. Msgr. Dennis E. '76 (STL) Creve Coeur, MO St. Monica.
Doering, Christopher E. '98 (MO) Army Chaplains.
Doering, Christopher '98 (CHI) Military Chaplains.
Doerner, David L. *s.a.* '60 (NY)[DD] Garrison, NY Franciscan Friars of the Atonement Retired.
Doerr, Brian M. '98 (LFT) On Duty Outside the Diocese.
Doerr, Brian M. '98 (BAL)[A] Emmitsburg, MD Mount St. Mary's Seminary.
Doerr, Richard J. '93 (LFT) Carmel, IN Our Lady of Mount Carmel; [I] Carmel, IN Our Lady of Mount Carmel Parochial School.
Doerre, Edmund J. '63 (LC) Trempealeau, WI St. Mary; Trempealeau, WI St. Bartholomew.
Doersching, Lawrence *s.m.* '73 (MIA)[E] Hollywood, FL Chaminade–Madonna College Preparatory.
Doffing, Gordon M. '60 (STP) Retired.
Dogali, Michael F. '92 (BGP) Fairfield, CT St. Pius X; Danbury, CT St. Joseph.
Dogaru, Alin Nadir '00 (ROM) East Chicago, IN St. Nicholas; Communications Director.
Dogaru, Alin '00 (CHI)[J] Maywood, IL Loyola University Medical Center.
Doheny, Thomas R. '58 (MAD) Retired.
Doherty, Cathal *s.j.* '10 (BO)[U] Brighton, MA Noel Chabanel House.
Doherty, Charles '58 (CC) Retired.
Doherty, D. G. *o.p.* '57 (FgM) New York, NY Province of St. Joseph (Eastern).
Doherty, Daniel J. *s.s.* '94 (SCR) On Duty Outside the Diocese.
Doherty, Daniel J. *s.s.* '94 (BAL)[A] Baltimore, MD St. Mary's Seminary and University; [Q] Baltimore Society of St. Sulpice, Province of the United States.
Doherty, Donald J. *m.m.* '62 (NY)[DD] Retired.
Doherty, Edward C. *m.s.a.* '69 (NOR)[G] Cromwell, CT Society of the Missionaries of the Holy Apostles.
Doherty, Edward C. *o.s.a.* '57 (PH)[Y] Villanova, PA St. Thomas Monastery.
Doherty, Glennon C. '78 (STL) On Leave of Absence.
Doherty, Henry F. '56 (BO) Senior Priests. Retired.
Doherty, James J. *c.s.c* (FR) Taunton; Taunton, MA St. Mary's.
Doherty, James J. *c.s.c.* '78 (FTW)[H] Notre Dame Congregation of Holy Cross, United States Province of Priests & Brothers.
Doherty, James '72 (GLD) Suttons Bay, MI St. Gertrude; Suttons Bay, MI St. Michael the Archangel.
Doherty, John R. '64 (NEW) Bayonne, NJ St. Andrew's Retired.
Doherty, Louis *c.p.* '57 (L)[L] Louisville, KY Sacred Heart Retreat.
Doherty, Michael *o.f.m.* '76 (LA)[V] Malibu, CA Serra Retreat; Definitors.
Doherty, Rev. Msgr. Patrick J. '55 (BWN) Retired.
Doherty, Patrick J. '59 (MAD) Retired.
Doherty, Paul J. '95 (WOR) On Administrative Leave of Absence.
Doherty, Raymond J. *s.s.e.* '58 (BUR)[E] Colchester, VT Society of St. Edmund; [A] Colchester, VT St. Michael's College.
Doherty, Robert G. *s.j.* '60 (BO)[U] Weston, MA Campion Jesuit Community.
Doherty, Robert J. '70 (BO) Senior Priests. Retired.
Dohman, William '73 (B) Retired.
Dohman, William '73 (STN) Retired.
Dohner, Stephen J. '76 (CLV) Medina, OH Holy Martyrs.
Dohogne, David J. '92 (SPC) Dexter, MO Sacred Heart; Campbell, MO St. Teresa; Campbell, MO St. Ann; Region IX; Co Directors; Office of Worship; Liturgical Commission.
Doiron, David E. '69 (WOR) Paxton, MA St. Columba.
Doktorczyk, Steve '05 (ORG) Special Assignment.
Dolan, Daniel D. *m.m.* '54 (NY)[DD] Maryknoll Maryknoll Fathers and Brothers Retired.
Dolan, Edward *s.s.c.* '58 (OM)[J] St. Columbans, NE Missionary Society of St. Columban Retired.
Dolan, Edward *s.s.c.* '58 (PRO)[O] Bristol, RI St. Columban's Retirement House.
Dolan, Gerald M. *o.f.m.* '56 (SP)[N] St. Petersburg, FL St. Anthony Friary Retired.
Dolan, Guthrie '11 (DM) Des Moines, IA St. Anthony's.
Dolan, Hugh '57 (PT) Retired.
Dolan, James L. *o.p.* '60 (FgM) Metairie, LA St. Martin de Porres Province (Southern Dominican Province).
Dolan, James Linus *o.p.* '60 (NO)[R] New Orleans Dominican Friars, Southern Dominican Province of St. Martin de Porres.
Dolan, James W. '75 (PIT) Butler, PA St. Michael the Archangel; Butler, PA St. Peter.
Dolan, Jarlath '74 (LA) Westlake Village, CA St. Maximilian Kolbe.
Dolan, John P. '89 (SD) Chula Vista, CA Saint Rose of Lima Catholic Parish; Vicars Forane.
Dolan, John R. *m.s.* '79 (FR) Brewster, MA Our Lady of the Cape.
Dolan, Joseph K. '60 (BRK) Brooklyn, NY St. Bernadette Retired.
Dolan, Joseph M. '92 (WOR) Fitchburg, MA St. Bernard Parish at St. Camillus de Lellis; [Q] Fitchburg, MA Fitchburg State College (Fitchburg).
Dolan, Joseph V. *s.j.* '52 (NY)[DD] Loyola Hall, Jesuit Community.
Dolan, Joseph '60 (BRK) Retired.
Dolan, Laurence *o.f.m.* '65 (SD)[J] Oceanside, CA Old Mission San Luis Rey.
Dolan, Leo A. '52 (STP) Retired.
Dolan, Rev. Msgr. Leo M. '60 (SAT) San Antonio, TX St. Helena.
Dolan, Mark A. '76 (STL) Overland, MO Our Lady of the Presentation.
Dolan, Michael F. '97 (WDC) Retired.
Dolan, Michael J. '96 (HRT)[Q] Hartford, CT University of Hartford Newman Center; Special and other Archdiocesan Assignment; [A] Bloomfield, CT St. Thomas Seminary; Vocations; [Q] Hartford, CT Trinity College Chapel.
Dolan, Rev. Msgr. Neal T. '64 (SD) Poway, CA Saint Michael Catholic Parish Poway.
Dolan, Patrick G. '71 (JC) Laurie, MO Shrine of St. Patrick.
Dolan, Patrick J. '78 (L) Liberty, KY St. Bernard; Ex Officio; Army National Guard Chaplains; Defenders of the Bond.
Dolan, Patrick '95 (DEN) Denver, CO Most Precious Blood.
Dolan, Paul '84 (RVC) Port Jefferson, NY Infant Jesus.
Dolan, Peter C. '54 (PMB) Port St. Lucie, FL St. Lucie Retired.
Dolan, Raymond '56 (B) Retired.
Dolan, Robert L. *s.j.* '73 (FgM) Chicago, IL Society of Jesus.
Dolan, Thomas D. '51 (BRK)[R] Douglaston, NY Bishop Mugavero Residence Retired.
Dolan, Timothy E. '83 (STP) Deanery 10; Mound, MN Our Lady of the Lake.
Dolan, Walter *o.f.m.* '61 (CLV)[N] Brooklyn, OH St. Anthony of Padua Friary.
Dolan, William S. *s.j.* '82 (SY)[Q] Syracuse, NY Jesuits at LeMoyne, Inc.; [T] Syracuse, NY LeMoyne College Campus Ministry.
Dolce, Linus *o.s.b.* '10 (STL)[F] Creve Coeur, MO St. Louis Priory School; [O] St. Louis, MO The Abbey of St. Mary and St. Louis.
Dolce, Thomas Joseph T.J. '09 (GAL) Kingwood, TX St. Martha.
Dolciamore, Rev. Msgr. John V. '52 (CHI)[A] Mundelein, IL University of St. Mary of the Lake/Mundelein Seminary; Westchester, IL Divine Providence Retired.
Dolciamore, Rev. Msgr. John V. '52 (VEN) Judicial Vicar; Judges.
Dolcic, Maurus *t.o.r.* '99 (WDC) Washington, DC Providence Hospital; [O] Washington, DC St. Louis Friary; [L] Washington, DC Providence Hospital.
Doldan, Felipe '58 (CAM) Woodbury Heights, NJ Infant Jesus Parish, Woodbury Heights, N.J.
Dolehide, John R. *o.p.* '47 (CHI)[N] Chicago, IL St. Pius V Priory.
Dolejsi, Bryan '06 (SEA)[B] Burien, WA John F. Kennedy Catholic High School; Seminarian Services; Vocations; Special Assignment.
Dolezal, Richard R. '76 (MIL) Retired.
Dolezal, Thomas '70 (KCK) Olathe, KS Prince of Peace Retired.
Dolinic, Louis S. '66 (BUF)[N] Depew, NY Msgr. Conniff Residence Retired.
Dolinksi, Pawel *s.d.s.* '97 (MET) Great Meadows, NJ Ss. Peter and Paul.
Dolinski, Pawel *s.d.s.* '97 (NEW)[L] Verona, NJ The Salvatorian Fathers.
Doll, Donald A. *s.j.* '68 (OM)[J] Omaha, NE Jesuit Community at Creighton University.
Dollard, Mark E. '91 (MAN) Berlin, NH Good Shepherd; Gorham, NH Holy Family; Northern New Hampshire Correctional Facility; Presbyteral Council.
Dollen, Bernard '53 (ROC) Retired.
Dollins, Randy '07 (DEN) Deaneries; Frisco, CO St. Mary.
Domagas, Reynaldo '87 (NY) Manhattan, NY New York Downtown Hospital – New York Infirmary; New York, NY Our Lady of Victory.
Domandich, Anthony '58 (SEA) Retired.
Domas, John R. '50 (SB) Retired.
Domaszewicz, Chester '78 (VEN) LaBelle, FL Our Lady Queen of Heaven.
Dombroski, Dean W. '64 (GB) Peshtigo, WI St. Mary; Porterfield, WI SS. Joseph & Edward Retired.
Dombrow, Rev. Msgr. William A. '70 (PH)[T] Darby, PA Villa Saint Joseph; [W] Ventnor, PA Villa St. Joseph by the Sea; Department Retired Clergy; On Special or Other Archdiocesan Assignment.
Dombrowski, Francis *o.f.m.cap.* '59 (MIL)[S] South Milwaukee, WI The Dwelling Place.
Dombrowski, John *o.f.m.* '84 (JOL) Joliet, IL St. John the Baptist; [L] Joliet, IL St. John the Baptist Friary; Councilors.
Dombrowski, Ronald J. '72 (SAG) Saginaw, MI St. John the Baptist; Saginaw, MI St. Josaphat; Saginaw, MI St. Matthew.
Dombrowski, Stanley J. *o.s.f.s.* '83 (VEN) Fort Myers, FL St. Cecilia; Presbyteral Council.
Dombrowski, Steven G. '89 (CHI) Mt. Prospect, IL St. Raymond de Penafort.
Dombrowski, Timothy '73 (LAN)[G] Ann Arbor, MI St. Joseph Mercy Hospital.
Dome, Thomas J. *c.r.i.c.* '98 (LA) Santa Paula, CA St. Sebastian; [B] Santa Paula, CA Canons Regular of the Immaculate Conception, (C.R.I.C.) Dom Grea House (House of Formation); [P] Santa Paula, CA Canons Regular of the Immaculate Conception.
Domec, Rev. Msgr. Charles C. '56 (GAL) The Woodlands, TX Sts. Simon and Jude.
Domek, Kazimierz '73 (SP) Tampa, FL Blessed Sacrament.
Domfang, Martin–Claude *s.j.* '06 (MIL)[P] Milwaukee, WI Jesuit Community at Marquette University.
Domfeh–Boateng, Joseph '95 (NY) Bedford, NY St. Patrick.
Domhoff, Ronald J. '72 (L) Louisville, KY St. Peter the Apostle Parish.
Domin, Rev. Msgr. Edward R. '88 (ALN) Reading, PA St. Catharine of Siena.
Domin, John M. '50 (P) Retired.
Domingo, Alberto *c.m.f.* '79 (LA)[V] Rancho Dominguez, CA Dominguez Seminary Inc. Retired.

Domingo, Santiago '65 (LAR) Laredo, TX Santo Nino.
Domingue, Kenneth J. '91 (LAF) Leonville, LA St. Leo the Great; Leonville, LA St. Catherine.
Dominguez, Jesus '02 (RCK) Elgin, IL St. Joseph.
Dominguez, Juan Rumin *o.f.m.* '95 (MIA)[K] Miami, FL National Shrine of Our Lady of Charity; Archicofradia Nuestra Senora de la Caridad (Spanish).
Dominguez, Julio '03 (CHL) Lenoir, NC St. Francis of Assisi; Diocesan Consultors.
Dominguez, Oscar Martin (BO) East Boston, MA Our Lady of the Assumption.
Dominguez, Ramon '00 (FR) On Duty Outside the Diocese.
Dominguez, Ramon *y.a.* '00 (ARL)[L] McLean, VA Youth Apostles Institute, An Association of Christian Faithful.
Dominguez, Vincent '02 (SFE) Pecos, NM St. Anthony of Padua.
Dominiak, Thomas M. '61 (GLD) Retired.
Dominic, Francis J. '52 (MAD) Retired.
Dominic, Johny (NY) New York, NY St. Agnes.
Dominic, Joseph *s.a.c.* '80 (MIL)[P] Milwaukee, WI Pallotti House; Hartford, WI St. Lawrence; Allenton, WI Resurrection.
Dominic, Michael M. '88 (MO) Army Reserve Chaplains.
Dominic, Sunny '94 (SC) Fort Dodge, IA Holy Trinity Parish of Webster County.
Dominik, Kevin J. '88 (PIT) Pittsburgh, PA St. Winifred.
Dominik, Stanley J. '58 (GRY) Whiting, IN Immaculate Conception; Whiting, IN Sacred Heart; Whiting, IN St. Adalbert; Whiting, IN St. John the Baptist Retired.
Dominique, Todd M. '94 (TOL) Defiance, OH St. John the Evangelist.
Domme, Edward C. '79 (SFE) Albuquerque, NM Our Lady of the Assumption; Presbyteral Council of the Archdiocese of Santa Fe; Finance Council.
Dommer, Ian *o.s.b.* '79 (SCL)[I] Collegeville, MN St. John's Abbey, of the Order of St. Benedict.
Domond, Osner *c.m.* (PCE) Ponce, PR San Vicente–Cantera.
Dompke, Ramon *c.ss.r.* '64 (CHI)[N] Glenview, IL The Redemptorists of Glenview, Illinois.
Domurat, Thomas S. '79 (BO) East Boston, MA Most Holy Redeemer.
Don, Sextus '79 (FTW) Wabash, IN St. Bernard.
Donaghey, John *s.v.d.* '54 (CHI)[N] Techny, IL Divine Word Residence.
Donaghey, Patrick H.M. '85 (ATL) Lilburn, GA St. Stephen the Martyr.
Donaghy, Thomas J. '79 (BAL) Ellicott City, MD St. Paul Retired.
Donahoe, Patrick *t.o.r.* '74 (ALT)[A] Loretto, PA St. Francis University.
Donahoe, Patrick *t.o.r.* '74 (ARL) Herndon, VA St. Joseph.
Donahoe, Rev. Msgr. Thomas '54 (SC) Retired.
Donahue, Aidan N. '86 (HRT) Bloomfield, CT Sacred Heart; Ecumenical Affairs, Commission for; Special and other Archdiocesan Assignment; Tariffville, CT St. Bernard.
Donahue, Rev. Msgr. Brian G. '83 (FAR) Military Chaplains.
Donahue, Brian G. '83 (MO) Army Reserve Chaplains.
Donahue, Rev. Msgr. Brian '83 (NY) West Point, NY Catholic Chapel of the Most Holy Trinity.
Donahue, Cecil J. *o.s.b.* '54 (MAN)[K] Manchester, NH St. Anselm Abbey.
Donahue, Charles *c.s.p.* '05 (KNX) Knoxville, TN Blessed John XXIII University Parish/Catholic Center; [I] Knoxville, TN UT–Knoxville, Newman Foundation, Inc.; University of Tennessee–Knoxville; Presbyteral Council; Diocesan Consultors.
Donahue, Denis M. '90 (ARL) Falls Church, VA St. Philip.
Donahue, Eugene *s.j.* '70 (GB)[M] Oshkosh, WI Jesuit Retreat House.
Donahue, John A. *s.j.* '79 (FgM) Los Gatos, CA Society of Jesus.
Donahue, John G. '60 (STP) Retired.
Donahue, John R. *s.j.* '64 (BAL)[Q] Baltimore, MD Jesuit Community of Loyola University, Inc.
Donahue, John '06 (PIT) Glenshaw, PA St. Mary of the Assumption.
Donahue, L. Scott '82 (CHI) Chicago, IL St. Robert Bellarmine; [H] Chicago, IL Mission of Our Lady of Mercy–Mercy Home for Boys and Girls.
Donahue, Martin P. '61 (WOR) Deans Retired.
Donahue, Richard T. '68 (BO) On Duty Outside the Archdiocese.
Donahue, Scott (CHI) Mercy Home for Boys and Girls; [G] Chicago, IL Mercy Home for Boys & Girls.
Donahue, Stephen D. '86 (IND) Aurora, IN St. Mary Immaculate Conception Catholic Church, Aurora, Inc.
Donahue, William H. *c.s.c.* '49 (FTW)[H] Notre Dame Congregation of Holy Cross, United States Province of Priests & Brothers Retired.
Donahue, William P. '70 (GBG) Latrobe, PA St. Rose.
Donahue, William P. '86 (SR) Napa, CA St. Apollinaris; Advocates.
Donahugh, Donald E. '62 (RCK) Active Outside the Diocese.
Donajkowski, Charles G. '91 (GLD) East Tawas, MI Holy Family; Hale, MI St. Pius X; Oscoda, MI Sacred Heart; Members of the College of Consultors; Whittemore, MI St. James.
Donald, John R. *s.j.* '72 (FgM) Los Gatos, CA Society of Jesus.
Donald, Michael L. '72 (STL) Creve Coeur, MO St. Monica.
Donaldson, Raymond J. *s.j.* '05 (R) Durham, NC Holy Cross; [F] Raleigh Jesuit Community.
Donaldson, Thomas J. '68 (LC) Personnel Council Retired.
Donaldson, Thomas *c.ss.r.* '77 (CHI)[N] Chicago, IL The Redemptorist Fathers of Chicago; Chicago, IL St. Michael in Old Town.
Donarski, Richard *o.c.s.o.* '86 (ATL)[F] Conyers, GA The Monastery of the Holy Spirit.
Donat, Robert J. '66 (SB) Retired.
Donatelli, Gino *s.j.* '81 (LEX) Lexington, KY Cathedral of Christ the King.
Donato, John P. *c.s.c.* '91 (FTW)[H] Notre Dame Congregation of Holy Cross, United States Province of Priests & Brothers.
Donato, John *c.s.c.* '91 (P)[L] Portland, OR Holy Cross Fathers & Brothers, C.S.C. – University of Portland; [B] University of Portland.
Dondanville, Joseph '95 (PEO) Kickapoo (Edwards), IL St. Mary of Kickapoo.
Dondapati, John N. *a.l.c.p./o.s.s.* '88 (CHI) Chicago, IL Our Lady of Mount Carmel.
Donehue, Ambrose *o.f.m.* '51 (ALB)[B] Siena College; [R] Albany, NY St. Francis Chapel.
Donelan, Jeb S. '11 (ARL) Manassas, VA All Saints.
Donellan, Rev. Msgr. Thomas J. '56 (BAL) Hunt Valley, MD Catholic Community of St. Francis Xavier.
Donellen, Rev. Msgr. Thomas J. '56 (BAL) Retired.
Doner, Roy '81 (SAC) Oroville, CA St. Thomas the Apostle.
Dong, Quang Minh '91 (OAK) On Duty Outside the Diocese.
Dong, Quang Minh '91 (LAV) Las Vegas, NV Our Lady of La Vang.
Donia, John E. '07 (PH)[D] Philadelphia, PA Archbishop Ryan High School; Feasterville, PA Assumption B.V.M.
Donio, Frank S. *s.a.c.* '94 (WDC)[B] West Hyattsville, MD Pallottine Seminary at Green Hill.
Donio, Thomas S. '95 (CAM) Hammonton, NJ Saint Mary of Mount Carmel Parish, Hammonton, N.J.
Donish, Peter M. '70 (PSC) Retirement Plan Board; Hazleton, PA St. Mary's; Presbyteral Council; Freeland, PA St. Mary's; McAdoo, PA St. Michael.
Donlan, Paul A. '62 (POD) Los Angeles.
Donlan, Paul A. '62 (LA)[W] Los Angeles, CA Prelature of the Holy Cross and Opus Dei.
Donley, Christopher D. '11 (PIT) Graduate Studies.
Donlon, James I. '75 (ALB) Special Assignment; Vicar Judicial; Judges; Bishop's Delegate for Marriage Dispensations; Presbyteral Council; Diocesan Board of Consultors.
Donlon, James W. '65 (PH) Media, PA Nativity of the Blessed Virgin Mary Retired.
Donnarumma, Francesco '05 (NEW) On Duty Outside the Archdiocese.
Donnarumma, Francesco '05 (PCE) Penuelas, PR St. Joseph.
Donnay, David N *o.s.c.* '01 (PHX)[F] Phoenix, AZ Crosier Community of Phoenix (Canons Regular of the Order of the Holy Cross).
Donnelly, Eamonn *s.v.d.* '70 (LA) Los Angeles, CA Our Lady of Lourdes.
Donnelly, Rev. Msgr. Edward J. '54 (RVC) Valley Stream, NY Holy Name of Mary Retired.
Donnelly, Eugene F. '48 (BRK) Jackson Heights, NY Our Lady of Fatima Retired.
Donnelly, J. Patrick *s.j.* '65 (MIL)[P] Milwaukee, WI Jesuit Community at Marquette University.
Donnelly, Joseph T. '71 (HRT) Southbury, CT Sacred Heart; Suburban Waterbury Deanery.
Donnelly, Joseph–Benedict *o.c.s.o.* '43 (P)[L] Lafayette, OR The Cistercian (Trappist) Abbey of Our Lady of Guadalupe.
Donnelly, Rev. Msgr. Lawrence Edward '49 (LA) Retired.
Donnelly, Michael *s.s.c.* '63 (OM)[J] St. Columbans Missionary Society of St. Columban.
Donnelly, P. Martin '64 (TOL) Retired.
Donnelly, Robert W. *m.m.* '59 (NY)[DD] Maryknoll Maryknoll Fathers and Brothers Retired.
Donnelly, Robert '91 (ALB) Retired.
Donnelly, Sean J. '82 (CLV) Madison, OH Immaculate Conception.
Donnelly, Stephen H. '97 (RVC) Huntington, NY St. Patrick's.
Donnelly, Thomas F. *m.m.* '57 (SJ)[M] Los Altos, CA Maryknoll.
Donnelly, Thomas '61 (RNO) Retired.
Donnelly, Timothy *o.s.b.* '65 (LR) Winslow, AR Our Lady of the Ozarks Shrine; Van Buren, AR St. Michael.
Donnelly, William F. *s.j.* '63 (SJ)[B] Santa Clara, CA Jesuit Community.
Donnelly, William J. *m.m.* '65 (CHI)[N] Chicago, IL Maryknoll Fathers & Brothers.
Donnelly, William P. '64 (PH) Retired.
Donnelly, William '71 (JOL) Oakbrook Terrace, IL Ascension of Our Lord.
Donnelly, William '64 (ROC) Retired.
Dono, Abram E. *s.t.* '64 (TUC) Tucson, AZ Blessed Kateri Tekakwitha Roman Catholic Missions Parish – Tucson; [I] South Tucson, AZ Blessed Kateri Tekakwitha Parish Center.
Donoghue, Denis G. *s.j.* '05 (BGP)[O] Fairfield, CT The Fairfield Jesuit Community–Fairfield University.
Donoghue, Henry Thomas *o.p.* '57 (WDC)[B] Washington, DC Dominican House of Studies.
Donoghue, Patrick '82 (P) Portland, OR St. Anthony.
Donoghue, Paul *s.m.* '68 (STL)[O] St. Louis Marianists, Province of the United States (Society of Mary).
Donoher, Edward (TOL)[G] Oregon, OH Sacred Heart Home.
Donohoe, Rev. Msgr. Edward '50 (STO) Diamond Springs, CA Retired.
Donohoe, Patrick K. '82 (CC) Corpus Christi, TX Holy Family; Presbyteral Council.
Donohoe, Peter '50 (SFD) Retired.
Donohoe, Richard E. '84 (BIR) Annual Catholic Charities Appeal; Diocesan College of Vicars.
Donohoe, Stephen S. '92 (MO) Chelmsford, MA St. Mary; Navy Reserve Chaplains; Presbyteral Council.
Donohoe, Thomas E. '62 (RVC) Long Beach, NY St. Mary of the Isle; [N] Amityville, NY St. Pius X Residence Retired.
Donohoe, Thomas P. '52 (BO) Carlisle, MA St. Irene.
Donohoo, Daniel B. '86 (IND) Indianapolis, IN SS. Peter and Paul Cathedral, Indianapolis, Inc.; Archdiocesan Judges.
Donohoo, Lawrence J. '85 (BAL)[A] Emmitsburg, MD Mount St. Mary's Seminary.
Donohue, Edward J. *o.f.m.* '56 (PAT)[N] Butler, NJ St. Anthony Friary.
Donohue, James *c.r.* '83 (BAL)[B] Emmitsburg, MD Mount Saint Mary's University.
Donohue, John J. '48 (CHI) Chicago, IL St. Edward Retired.
Donohue, John J. '73 (NEW) Bloomfield, NJ St. Valentine; Belleville, NJ Clara Maass Medical Center.
Donohue, John J. *s.j.* '59 (WOR)[N] Worcester, MA Jesuits of the Holy Cross, Inc.
Donohue, Michael F. '75 (NOR) Building Commission.
Donohue, Michael T. '75 (NOR) East Lyme, CT St. Matthias; Deans; Campaign for Human Development; Navy Reserve Chaplains; Members; College of Consultors.
Donohue, Paul *m.c.c.j.* '75 (NEW) Newark, NJ St. Lucy's; [L] Montclair, NJ Comboni Missionaries of the Heart of Jesus (Verona Fathers).
Donohue, Peter M. *o.s.a.* '79 (PH)[C] Villanova, PA Villanova University; [Y] Villanova, PA Fray de Leon Community.
Donohue, Raymond A.J. '85 (BUF) Retired.
Donoso, Fermin J. *c.s.c.* '67 (FTW)[H] Notre Dame Congregation of Holy Cross, United States Province of Priests & Brothers.
Donoughe, Patrick *t.o.r.* (ALT)[I] Loretto, PA St. Francis University (Loretto).
Donovan, Bernard Thomas '05 (MO) Springfield, IL St. Aloysius; Air National Guard Chaplains; Presbyteral Council.
Donovan, Charles *c.ss.r.* '72 (CHR) Sumter, SC Catholic Community of Sumter.
Donovan, Daniel E. *c.m.* '42 (PH)[Y].
Donovan, Dennis *s.d.b.* '83 (SP)[P] Tampa, FL Mary Help of Christians Center; [N] Tampa, FL Salesians of Don Bosco; [R] Tampa, FL Mary Help of Christians Camp.
Donovan, Edward *c.s.p.* '59 (LA) Los Angeles, CA St. Paul the Apostle Retired.
Donovan, J. Michael '65 (SY) Retired.
Donovan, J. Paul '58 (TLS) Owasso, OK St. Henry Retired.
Donovan, James J. '87 (CHI) Diocesan Priests' Placement Board; Chicago, IL St. Barnabas.
Donovan, John L. '54 (BO) Senior Priests. Retired.
Donovan, John P. '86 (SY) Johnson City, NY St. James; Adjutant Judicial Vicar.
Donovan, Joseph J. *m.m.* '79 (LA)[P] Los Angeles, CA Maryknoll Fathers and Brothers.
Donovan, Kevin G. '88 (HRT) East Haven, CT St. Clare; Branford, CT St. Elizabeth.
Donovan, Michael A. '62 (DET) Roseville, MI St. Donald.
Donovan, Michael '04 (NEW) Franklin Lakes, NJ Most Blessed Sacrament.
Donovan, Michael *o.de.m.* (CLV)[N] Cleveland, OH Mercedarians; Cleveland, OH Our Lady of Mount Carmel.

Donovan, Michael (PAT)[C] Wayne, NJ De Paul Catholic High School.
Donovan, Patrick *o.s.m.* '55 (ORG) Fullerton, CA St. Juliana Falconieri; [M] Fullerton, CA California State University Fullerton, Newman Center.
Donovan, Patrick *c.s.sp.* '57 (SFR) Millbrae, CA St. Dunstan.
Donovan, Paul A. *s.j.* '56 (PH)[Y] Loyola Center and Manresa Hall.
Donovan, Richard R. '58 (RVC) Malverne, NY Our Lady of Lourdes Retired.
Donovan, Richard *o.f.m.* '85 (BO)[U] Andover St. Francis Friary.
Donovan, Robert C. '70 (FR) Retired.
Donovan, Thomas F. '57 (LAV) Diocesan Judges.
Donovan, Rev. Msgr. Walter J. '44 (ATL) Retired.
Donovan, William G. '94 (PH) Diocesan Priests' Compensation and Benefits Committee; [A] Wynnewood, PA Theological Seminary of St. Charles Borromeo, Overbrook.
Donovan, Rev. Msgr. William '50 (SY) Retired.
Donton, Joseph P. '91 (PEO) Ottawa, IL St. Patrick's.
Doody, Cyril F. '57 (BRK) Brooklyn, NY St. Mark Retired.
Doody, Michael J. *s.j.* '78 (BGP)[O] Fairfield, CT The Fairfield Jesuit Community–Fairfield University; [B] Fairfield, CT Fairfield University; [V] Fairfield, CT Fairfield University.
Doody, Rev. Msgr. Peter J. '71 (PAT) Wayne, NJ Annunciation; Minister to Priests.
Doogan, James A. *s.j.* '98 (SAC)[K] Sacramento, CA Newman Catholic Community at Sacramento State.
Dool, Franz C. '11 (CLV) Gates Mills, OH St. Francis of Assisi.
Doolan, Vincent P. '80 (BO) Quincy, MA St. Joseph.
Dooley, Rev. Msgr. Joseph P. '56 (ALN) Retired.
Dooley, Kevin F. '84 (MAD) Evansville, WI St. Paul; Footville, WI St. Augustine.
Dooley, Matthew R. '09 (NEW) River Edge, NJ St. Peter the Apostle; [O] Hoboken, NJ Catholic Campus Ministry at Stevens Institute of Technology.
Dooley, Michael D. *s.j.* '85 (NO)[R] New Orleans, LA Jesuit Provincial Office; New Orleans, LA Immaculate Conception; New Orleans, LA.
Dooley, Peter C. '76 (RVC) Northport, NY St. Philip Neri; Priests' Retirement Board.
Dooley, Thomas V. '91 (DM) Avoca, IA St. Mary, Mediatrix of All Graces; Avoca, IA St. Patrick; Des Moines, IA St. Anthony's.
Dooling, Patrick '82 (MRY) Monterey, CA Cathedral of San Carlos Borromeo; Clergy Life and Ministry Board; Presbyteral Council.
Dooner, William B. '70 (PH) Penndel, PA Our Lady of Grace; Diocesan Priests' Compensation and Benefits Committee.
Do Quang Chau, Peter '73 (NSH) Vietnamese Ministry.
Dora, Rev. Msgr. Peter A. '72 (ATL) Defenders of the Bond.
Dora, Rev. Msgr. Peter P. '67 (BGP) Stamford, CT Stamford Hospital.
Dorairaj, Peter J. *s.s.s.* '99 (GAL) Houston, TX Corpus Christi; [S] Houston, TX The Catholic Chaplain Corps.
Doran, Austin C. '78 (LA) San Gabriel, CA St. Anthony.
Doran, Brian D. '71 (LA) Long Beach, CA St. Anthony Retired.
Doran, Edward E. *o.s.a.* '61 (PH)[Y] Villanova, PA St. Thomas Monastery.
Doran, Edward P. '84 (BRK) Brooklyn, NY St. Charles Borromeo.
Doran, James *o.s.b.* '00 (WOR)[N] Still River, MA Benedictine Monks, St. Benedict Abbey.
Doran, Rev. Msgr. John E. '72 (NEW) Members; Presbyteral Council; Members; Vicar General, Moderator of the Curia and Chancellor; [Q] Newark, NJ CatholiCare, Inc.; [Q] Newark, NJ New Jersey Caritas Corporation, Inc.; Newark, NJ Cathedral Basilica of the Sacred Heart; New Energies – Archdiocesan Implementation Team.
Doran, Rev. Msgr. John E. '66 (WOR) Leominster, MA St. Leo; Members.
Doran, Joseph A. '10 (GAL) Houston, TX St. Jerome.
Doran, Joseph *s.d.b.* '66 (NY)[FF] Stony Point, NY Marian Shrine; [FF] Stony Point, NY Don Bosco Retreat Center and Marian Shrine.
Doran, Robert M. *s.j.* '69 (MIL)[P] Milwaukee, WI Jesuit Community at Marquette University.
Dorantes, Manuel '10 (CHI) Chicago, IL St. Clement.
Dorcey, Joseph *c.ss.r.* '79 (DEN)[N] Denver The Redemptorists/Denver Province.
Dore, M.J. Bernard '82 (PRO) Foster, RI St. Paul the Apostle.
Dore, Robert '89 (JKS) Columbus, MS Annunciation; West Point, MS Immaculate Conception; [H] Columbus, MS Mississippi University for Women Student Center.
Dore, Thomas M. '61 (CHI) Oak Park, IL St. Giles; Chicago, IL St. Pascal Retired.
Dore, Timothy *o.f.m.conv.* (BRK) Brooklyn, NY Most Holy Trinity – Saint Mary.
Dorff, Francis W. *o.praem.* '60 (SFE)[H] Albuquerque, NM Santa Maria de la Vid Priory.
Dorgan, Gerard L. '58 (BO) Danvers, MA St. Mary of the Annunciation.
Dorgan, John J. '65 (RIC) Retired.
Dorhauer, Robert '63 (STL) Florissant, MO Sacred Heart.
Dorin, Robert R. *s.j.* '67 (BO)[D] Boston, MA Boston College High School.
Doriot, Thomas E. '49 (FTW) Retired.
Doris, John A. '75 (SCR) Dunmore, PA Our Lady of Mount Carmel Parish; Presbyteral Council.
Dormer, David J. '77 (SCR) Military Chaplains.
Dormido, Arecio P. '83 (NY) Fishkill, NY Downstate Correctional Facility.
Dorn, John *o.ss.t.* '81 (BAL)[Q] In Residence – Holy Trinity Monastery Baltimore.
Dorn, Louis E. '72 (JC) Louisiana, MO St. Joseph; Senators; Mediation and Arbitration Board; [F] Jefferson City, MO Catholic Charities of Central and Northern Missouri.
Dorn, Rupert *o.f.m.cap* '51 (MAD)[I] Madison, WI San Damiano Friary Retired.
Dorn, Thomas E. '03 (CIN) Fort Recovery, OH Mary Help of Christians; Fort Recovery, OH St. Peter; Fort Recovery, OH St. Joseph; Fort Recovery, OH St. Paul.
Dornak, Melvin '92 (AUS) Llano, TX Holy Trinity Catholic Church – Llano, Texas; Llano, TX St. Joseph.
Dornbos, William '68 (HEL) Special Assignments; Butte, MT Holy Spirit.
Dorner, Joseph E. '95 (GB) Marinette, WI Holy Family; Regional Vicars.
Dorner, William E. '07 (PIT) Evans City, PA St. Matthias; Zelienople, PA St. Gregory.
Dorney, Rev. Msgr. Dennis C. '67 (TLS) Priests' Personnel Committee; Tulsa, OK Church of St. Mary; [J] Tulsa, OK Priest Retirement Trust of the Roman Catholic Diocese of Tulsa; Vicar General; Ex Officio; Diocesan Consultors; Seminary Board.
Dorney, Rev. Msgr. James J. '58 (NY) Staten Island, NY St. Peter; [F] Staten Island, NY Seton Foundation for Learning, Inc.; Staten Island.
Dorniak, Joseph *o.f.m.conv.* '79 (BAL)[Q] Ellicott City, MD Friary of St. Joseph Cupertino; [M] Baltimore, MD St. Joseph's Nursing Home.
Doroin, Elias E. '64 (GAL) Retired.
Dorpe, Ray Van *c.m.* '82 (STL)[O] St. Louis, MO Lazarist Residence.
Dorr, James F. *c.m.* '58 (BRK)[R] Jamaica, NY Reverend John B. Murray, CM, House.
Dorrill, Rev. Msgr. James F. '60 (MOB) Retired.
Dorrmann, William J. '55 (CIN) Harrison, OH St. John the Baptist Retired.
Dorsch, Henry L. '68 (SPR) Southwick, MA Our Lady of the Lake; Presbyteral Council.
Dorsch, Larry W. '75 (WH) Weirton, WV St. Paul's.
Dorsel, John F. '61 (R) Retired.
Dorsey, Dan *g.h.m.* '78 (CIN)[N] Fairfield, OH.
Dorsey, Garrett D. '59 (PIT) Allison Park, PA St. Ursula.
Dorsey, Joseph A. *c.s.c.* '57 (FTW)[H] Notre Dame Congregation of Holy Cross, United States Province of Priests & Brothers; New Rochelle, NY Eastern Brothers Province.
Dorsey, Patrick *s.j.* '96 (CHI)[C] Chicago, IL Jesuit Community at Loyola University Chicago.
Dorson, James E. '77 (RIC) Retired.
Dorsonville, Mario E. '85 (WDC)[I] Washington, DC Spanish Catholic Center, Inc./Division of Immigrant and Refuge Services; Priest Council; Archdiocesan College of Consultors.
Dorta, Juan Manuel *s.j.* '55 (MIA)[E] Miami, FL Belen Jesuit Preparatory School; [H] Miami, FL Villa Javier; [H] Belen Jesuit Alumni Association.
Dorton, John '70 (DM) Panama, IA St. Mary of the Assumption; Westphalia, IA St. Boniface; Advocates; Portsmouth, IA St. Mary.
Dorula, Douglas E. '02 (GBG) New Kensington, PA Mt. St. Peter.
Dorvil, Pierre A *s.m.m.* '84 (SP) Tampa, FL Epiphany of Our Lord.
Dorwart, William D. *c.s.c.* '80 (MO) Navy Chaplains.
Dorwart, William *c.s.c.* (FTW)[H] Notre Dame Congregation of Holy Cross, United States Province of Priests & Brothers.
Dory, Michael '76 (GB) Military Chaplains.
Dosch, Leander *o.c.s.o.* '50 (SLC)[E] Huntsville, UT Abbey of Our Lady of the Holy Trinity of the Order of Cistercians.
Dosch, Michael *o.p.* '05 (COL) Columbus, OH St. Patrick.
Doscher, Joseph *s.c.j.* '73 (SP)[N] Pinellas Park, FL Priests of the Sacred Heart Retired.
Dosh, Mark B. '58 (STP) Excelsior, MN St. John the Baptist; Censores Librorum.
Doskey, Rev. Msgr. Clinton J. '54 (NO) New Orleans, LA St. Pius X; Adjutant Judicial Vicars; Archdiocesan Consultors Retired.
dos Reis, Antonio Jose '82 (SJ) San Jose, CA Five Wounds Portuguese National Church.
Dos Reis, Jose Q. '64 (PRO)[O] Providence St. John Vianney Residence.
dos Reis, Jose Q. '64 (PRO) Providence, RI Rhode Island Hospital; [C] Warwick, RI Bishop Hendricken High School.
dos Remedios, Francis *o.s.b.* '82 (BIS)[A] Richardton, ND Assumption Abbey Retired.
dos Santos, Antonio *c.s.s.* '00 (SAC) Special Assignment; West Sacramento, CA Holy Cross; Sacramento, CA St. Elizabeth.
dos Santos, Egidio Alves (BO) Cape Verdean; Roxbury, MA St. Patrick; Brockton, MA St. Edith Stein.
dos Santos, Jose A.F. '53 (FR) Retired.
Dos Santos, Joseph E.S. '10 (NEW) Portugese Apostolate; Elizabeth, NJ Our Lady of Fatima.
Dos Santos, Kenneth *m.i.c.* '10 (SPR)[G] The National Shrine of The Divine Mercy.
Dos Santos, Stephen *c.pp.s.* '06 (CIN) Englewood, OH St. Paul.
Dos Santos, Tarcisio *s.d.b.* '89 (NY) Port Chester, NY Our Lady of the Rosary.
Dosyak, Mykhaylo (STF) Syracuse, NY St. John the Baptist.
Dotson, Rev. Msgr. Paul J. '68 (LA) Redondo Beach, CA St. Lawrence Martyr.
Doty, Craig A. '97 (LIN) Wilber, NE St. Wenceslaus; Vicars For Religious; Adjutant Judicial Vicars.
Doucet, David A. '69 (BO) Stow, MA St. Isidore.
Doudican, James '48 (CHY) Cheyenne, WY Holy Trinity Retired.
Dougher, James P. '03 (SCR) Throop, PA Blessed Sacrament Parish; Olyphant, PA Holy Cross Parish.
Dougherty, C. Peter '61 (LAN) Retired.
Dougherty, Damien *o.f.m.* '75 (STL)[O] St. Louis, MO Franciscan Friary of St. Anthony of Padua.
Dougherty, Daniel J. '70 (PH) Retired.
Dougherty, Denis *o.s.b.* '56 (SPC) Springfield, MO St. Joseph's.
Dougherty, Edward C. *s.j.* '72 (WDC) Port Tobacco, MD St. Ignatius.
Dougherty, Edward M. *m.m.* '79 (FgM) Maryknoll, NY; Maryknoll, NY; [DD] Maryknoll Maryknoll Fathers and Brothers.
Dougherty, Eugene J. '53 (PIT)[M] Pittsburgh, PA St. John Vianney Manor Retired.
Dougherty, Hugh J. '69 (PH) Pottstown, PA St. Thomas More.
Dougherty, James R. '68 (BEL) Retired.
Dougherty, James '67 (JOL) Glen Ellyn, IL St. Petronille.
Dougherty, John J. *c.s.c.* '94 (P) Portland, OR Holy Redeemer.
Dougherty, John *c.s.c.* (FTW)[H] Notre Dame Congregation of Holy Cross, United States Province of Priests & Brothers.
Dougherty, Joseph V. '05 (E) Galeton, PA St. Bibiana; Presbyteral Council.
Dougherty, Rev. Msgr. Paul V. '80 (PH) Huntingdon Valley, PA St. Albert the Great.
Dougherty, Stephen J. '73 (PH) Narberth, PA St. Margaret; [A] Wynnewood, PA Theological Seminary of St. Charles Borromeo, Overbrook.
Dougherty, Terrence *o.c.d.* '63 (BO)[U] Boston, MA Carmelite Monastery.
Dougherty, Terrence *o.c.d.* (WOR) Worcester, MA Our Lady of the Angels.
Dougherty, William J. *c.s.p.* '63 (BRK)[R] Retired Retired.
Dougherty, William N. *o.s.f.s.* '65 (ARL) Reston, VA St. John Neumann.
Dougherty, William '63 (TUC) Tucson, AZ Saint Pius X Roman Catholic Parish – Tucson Retired.
Doughterty, Charles T. *c.p.* '68 (SFE) Albuquerque, NM St. John the Apostle.
Doughtery, Edward M. '79 (STP)[J] Bloomington, MN Maryknoll Fathers and Brothers, Catholic Foreign Mission Society of America.
Doughty, Rees W. '94 (NY) Nyack, NY St. Ann.
Douglas, David M. '65 (LFT) Retired.
Douglas, Gordon W. '68 (SEA) Retired.
Douglas, John *c.p.* '81 (BRK) Jamaica, NY Immaculate Conception.
Douglas, Norman '74 (CLV) Akron, OH St. Bernard – St. Mary Parish.
Douglass, Vincent *c.ss.r.* '66 (ORL)[F] New Smyrna Beach, FL St. Alphonsus Villa–Redemptorist Fathers and Brothers Retired.
Doussan, Rev. Msgr. Douglas A. '60 (NO) New Orleans, LA St. Gabriel the Archangel.
Dove, Thomas J. *c.s.p.* '61 (SFR) San Francisco, CA Old St. Mary's Cathedral Retired.
Dover, Edward R. '85 (LA) La Crescenta, CA St. James the Less; Deanery 6; Montrose, CA Holy Redeemer.
Dovick, Robert E. '53 (CHI) Palos Heights, IL Incarnation Retired.
Dovzhuk, Mykola '91 (STN) Houston, TX Protection of the Mother of God.
Dow, Emanuel *c.ss.r.* '86 (LA) Hospital Chaplains.
Dowalgo, Mitchell G. *c.s.b.* '82 (LSC) Las Cruces, NM St. Albert the Great Newman Parish; [B] Las Cruces, NM Basilian Fathers.
Dowalgo, Mitchell *c.s.b.* '82 (LSC) Campus Ministry;

Presbyteral Council.
Dowd, Barry G. '82 (BUR) On Duty Outside the Diocese.
Dowd, Barry '82 (ORL) Orlando, FL Basilica of the National Shrine of Mary Queen of the Universe.
Dowd, Brian P. '91 (BRK) Long Island City, NY Queen of Angels.
Dowd, James '56 (P) Retired.
Dowd, John *c.ss.r.* '61 (CHI)[N] Chicago, IL The Redemptorist Fathers of Chicago Retired.
Dowd, Robert A. *c.s.c.* '94 (FTW)[B] University of Notre Dame Du Lac; [H] Notre Dame, IN Holy Cross Community, Corby Hall, University of Notre Dame; Members.
Dowd, Thomas M. '54 (GI) Retired.
Dowd, William J. '67 (NEW) Special Assignment in the Archdiocese.
Dowdel, Lawrence J. '91 (LA) On Sick Leave.
Dowdell, Aaron M. *o.ss.t.* '74 (BAL)[Q] In Residence – Holy Trinity Monastery Baltimore.
Dowdell, Rev. Msgr. Joseph M. '63 (BUF) Lakewood, NY Sacred Heart.
Dowdell, Thomas '71 (OKL) Ardmore, OK St. Mary.
Dowdle, David P. '79 (CHI) Western Springs, IL St. John of the Cross.
Dower, Daniel P. *s.t.l.* '84 (TYL) Overton, TX Moore, B. (BM), TX Dept. of Criminal Justice; Nacogdoches, TX Sacred Heart; Kilgore, TX Christ the King.
Dowling, Edward T. *s.j.* '69 (NY)[DD] Loyola Hall, Jesuit Community.
Dowling, Finbarr *o.s.b.* '68 (STL) Marthasville, MO St. Ignatius Loyola; [O] St. Louis, MO The Abbey of St. Mary and St. Louis.
Dowling, John C. '51 (NEW) Retired.
Dowling, John J. *o.s.a.* '68 (FgM) Olympia Fields, IL Province of Our Mother of Good Counsel (Midwestern); Chicago, IL St. Turibius.
Dowling, John R. '83 (KNX) Fairfield Glade, TN St. Francis of Assisi.
Dowling, Joseph K. '80 (NSH) Centerville, TN Christ the Redeemer; Hohenwald, TN Holy Trinity; Hohenwald, TN St. Cecilia; Air Force Reserve Chaplains.
Dowling, Joseph *o.m.i.* '07 (ANC) Pastoral Team:; Pastoral Team:; Pastoral Team.
Dowling, Kevin '80 (NSH)[L] Nashville, TN Diocesan Council of Catholic Women.
Dowling, Lawrence R. '91 (CHI) Chicago, IL St. Agatha; Deans; College of Consultors.
Dowling, Ray '61 (AUS) Retired.
Dowling, Raymond '61 (GB) Retired.
Dowling, Sean P. '09 (BUR)[G] Poultney, VT Green Mountain College; Middletown Springs, VT St. Anne; Poultney, VT St. Raphael; The Blue Army (World Apostolate of Fatima).
Dowling, Timothy '93 (PAT) Parsippany, NJ St. Ann.
Downes, Rev. Msgr. Stephen N. '66 (LA) Santa Barbara, CA Our Lady of Mount Carmel.
Downey, Christopher J. '09 (AUS)[L] College Station, TX St. Mary's Catholic Center; Copperas Cove, TX Holy Family.
Downey, David C. '03 (PMB) Vero Beach, FL St. John of the Cross.
Downey, Donald *j.c.l.* '81 (CC) Corpus Christi, TX St. Michael the Archangel Latin Mass Community.
Downey, Kevin J. *o.f.m.* '82 (ARL) Triangle, VA St. Francis of Assisi.
Downey, Michael '72 (SAC) Fairfield, CA Holy Spirit.
Downie, Arley T. '88 (GLP) Retired.
Downing, Andrew N. *s.j.* '07 (FTW)[K] South Bend, IN Jesuit Community.
Downing, Andrew N. *s.j.* '07 (BO)[U] Boston The Society of Jesus of New England–Provincial Offices.
Downing, Andrew N. *s.j.* '07 (CHI)[N] Chicago Chicago Province of the Society of Jesus–Provincial Office.
Downing, Charles H. '65 (PRO) West Warwick, RI St. Joseph.
Downs, Gregory Todd '91 (LAF) Absent on Sick Leave.
Downs, James A. '70 (PIT) Hillsville, PA Christ the King; Pulaski, PA St. James.
Downs, James E. *m.s.a.* '02 (WIL) Georgetown, DE St. Michael the Archangel.
Downs, James *m.s.a.* '02 (NOR)[G] Cromwell Society of the Missionaries of the Holy Apostles.
Downs, John L. '55 (OG) Retired.
Downs, L. James '66 (WDC) Retired.
Downs, R. Bruce '94 (PHX) Glendale, AZ St. Helen Roman Catholic Parish.
Downs, Walter *m.s.c.* '58 (SB) Palm Springs, CA St. Theresa.
Downs, Walter *m.s.c.* '58 (ALN) Nazareth, PA Holy Family.
Dowsey, Gary '80 (SP) Dunedin, FL Our Lady of Lourdes; Elected Pastors.
Doyen, Mitchell S. '91 (STL) St. Louis, MO St. Simon the Apostle; [E] St. Louis, MO Saint Mary's High School.
Doyle, Alan T. *m.m.* '64 (FgM) Maryknoll, NY MARYKNOLL.
Doyle, Brendan '63 (JC) Jefferson City, MO Immaculate Conception; [A] Jefferson City, MO Helias Catholic High School; Vice–Chancellors; Judicial Vicar.
Doyle, Charles E. '53 (GRY) Retired.
Doyle, Dennis J. '65 (STL) Shrewsbury, MO St. Michael.
Doyle, Dennis M. '92 (STL) Adjutant Judicial Vicars; Judges; [A] St. Louis, MO Kenrick School of Theology; [A] St. Louis, MO Cardinal Glennon College.
Doyle, Donald '53 (ALB) Retired.
Doyle, Edward F. '64 (JC) Retired.
Doyle, Eugene '76 (SCL) Becker, MN Immaculate Conception; Big Lake, MN Our Lady of the Lake; Mora, MN St. Mary's; Mora, MN St. Kathryn's; Presbyteral Council; Diocesan Planning Council.
Doyle, Francis J. *o.s.a.* '70 (FgM) Villanova, PA Province of St. Thomas of Villanova (Eastern).
Doyle, Francis W. '10 (JC) Jefferson City, MO St. Peter.
Doyle, Rev. Msgr. James F. '59 (NY) Bronxville, NY St. Joseph.
Doyle, Rev. Msgr. James Michael '57 (SFS) Retired.
Doyle, James '61 (LKC) Lake Charles, LA St. Theodore; Defenders of the Bond.
Doyle, James '49 (ROC) Retired.
Doyle, Rev. Msgr. Jerald A. '69 (BGP) Stratford, CT Our Lady of Grace; Episcopal Vicar for Administration; Judicial Vicar; Diocesan Consultors; Presbyteral Council; Priest Vocation Advisory Board.
Doyle, John J. '58 (JOL) Crest Hill, IL St. Ambrose; Crest Hill, IL St. Anne.
Doyle, John L. '52 (BO) Senior Priests. Retired.
Doyle, John '52 (DUL) Virginia, MN Sacred Heart; Virginia, MN Holy Spirit; Virginia, MN Sacred Heart Retired.
Doyle, Joseph C. '72 (NEW) Fair Lawn, NJ St. Anne's; Presbyteral Council.
Doyle, Joseph M. *s.s.j.* '68 (NO)[R] New Orleans, LA The Josephite Faculty House of St. Augustine High School.
Doyle, Kenneth '66 (ALB) Albany, NY Parish of Mater Christi; Chancellors; Presbyteral Council; Public Information.
Doyle, Kevin '08 (SFS) Hoven, SD St. Anthony of Padua.
Doyle, Lawrence Michael *o.s.m.* '65 (CHI)[N] Chicago, IL Assumption Priory.
Doyle, Mathias *o.f.m.* '62 (BO) Presbyteral Council.
Doyle, Matthias *o.f.m.* '62 (ALB)[B] Siena College.
Doyle, Michael A. '94 (TYL) On Duty Outside the Diocese.
Doyle, Michael J. '85 (MO) Navy Reserve Chaplains.
Doyle, Rev. Msgr. Michael J. '59 (CAM) Camden, NJ The Church of Sacred Heart; Deanery Representatives.
Doyle, Michael M. '89 (NU) Redwood Falls, MN St. Catherine; Building Committee.
Doyle, Michael *o.s.m.* '65 (CHI) Chicago, IL Assumption of the Blessed Virgin Mary.
Doyle, N. Brendan '89 (ATL) On Leave of Absence; Without Archdiocesan Assignment or Faculties.
Doyle, Oliver '78 (GF) Great Falls, MT St. Ann's Cathedral.
Doyle, Patrick '75 (IND) Indianapolis, IN Nativity of Our Lord Jesus Christ Catholic Church, Indianapolis, Inc.; Priests' Personnel Board.
Doyle, Paul F. *c.s.c.* '77 (FTW)[B] University of Notre Dame Du Lac; [H] Notre Dame, IN Holy Cross Community, Corby Hall, University of Notre Dame.
Doyle, Philip R. '48 (NY) Retired.
Doyle, Rev. Msgr. Seamus '56 (MIA) Miami Shores, FL St. Rose of Lima.
Doyle, Thomas D. '82 (BUF) Clarence, NY Our Lady of Peace; Wende Correctional Facility.
Doyle, Thomas J. '08 (RCK) Woodstock, IL St. Patrick; [B] Woodstock, IL Marian Central Catholic High School; Special Assignment.
Doyle, Thomas P. *o.p.* '71 (CHI)[N] Chicago Dominicans (Provincial Office).
Doyle, Thomas P. *c.s.c.* '98 (FTW)[B] University of Notre Dame Du Lac; [B] University of Notre Dame Du Lac; [H] Notre Dame, IN Holy Cross Community, Corby Hall, University of Notre Dame.
Doyle, Thomas R. '62 (DAV) Retired.
Doyle, Thomas V. '84 (BRK) Brooklyn, NY St. Thomas Aquinas.
Doyle, Rev. Msgr. Thomas '54 (LA) La Crescenta, CA Retired.
Doyle, Thomas *s.j.* (TOL)[L] Toledo, OH Saint John's Jesuit High School Foundation.
Doyle, Rev. Msgr. Vincent J. '65 (NEW) Retired.
Doyne, David A. '56 (PH) Retired.
Drab, John P. '46 (RVC)[N] Amityville, NY St. Pius X Residence Retired.
Drabek, Howard E. '91 (GAL) League City, TX St. Mary; Air Force Reserve Chaplains.
Drabik, Richard *m.i.c.* '60 (SPR)[G] Stockbridge, MA Congregation of Marian Fathers of The Immaculate Conception of the Most Blessed Virgin Mary.
Dragga, Thomas M. '83 (CLV)[A] Wickliffe, OH Borromeo Seminary; [A] Wickliffe, OH St. Mary Seminary and Graduate School of Theology; [Y] Wickliffe, OH Center for Pastoral Leadership Services, Inc.
Dragon, Joseph W. '78 (PH) Secane, PA Our Lady of Fatima.
Drake, Timothy A. '71 (RIC) Clintwood, VA St. Joseph; Norton, VA St. Anthony; Big Stone Gap, VA Sacred Heart; Jonesville, VA Church of the Holy Spirit.
Drapeau, Benoit *c.j.m.* '59 (PHX) Phoenix, AZ St. Jerome Roman Catholic Parish; Presbyteral Council.
Draper, Andrew *t.o.r* '88 (STU)[A] Steubenville, OH Franciscan University of Steubenville; [H] Steubenville, OH Holy Spirit Friary.
Draugialis, Josef '63 (LA) Los Nietos, CA Our Lady of Perpetual Help.
Draves–Arpaia, Cornelius '79 (PHX) On Leave.
Draves–Arpaia, Neil '79 (ALB) Northville, NY St. Francis of Assisi; Broadalbin, NY St. Joseph.
Drea, Michael E. '04 (BO) Cambridge, MA St. Paul; [AA] Cambridge, MA Harvard Catholic Center; Pilgrimages; Harvard University.
Dreasen, Rev. Msgr. John R. '79 (RVC) East Northport, NY St. Anthony of Padua; Huntington Deanery; East Northport, NY St. Anthony of Padua.
Dreckman, Philip F. *s.j.* '62 (STP)[J] Minneapolis, MN Markoe House Jesuit Community.
Dreese, Rev. Msgr. John J. '59 (COL) Diocesan Judges Retired.
Dreffein, Larry *o.f.m.* '76 (JOL)[K] Oak Brook, IL Mayslake Annex II, NFP.
Dreger, Rev. Msgr. Francis X. '51 (PH) Retired.
Dreher, Daniel A. '08 (AMA) Catholic Student Center at West Texas A & M University; [H] Canyon, TX Catholic Student Center at West Texas A & M University; Amarillo, TX St. Thomas the Apostle; Advocates.
Dreher, John D. '64 (PRO) Woonsocket, RI St. Agatha Retired.
Dreiling, Gerald G. *c.pp.s.* '58 (CIN)[N] Dayton Provincial Office of the Cincinnati Province of the Society of the Precious Blood.
Dreiling, Rev. Msgr. Raymond C. '75 (FRS) Visalia, CA St. Thomas the Apostle; Visalia, CA Holy Family; Diocesan Consultors; Vicars Forane; Personnel Board; Visalia, CA St. Mary.
Dreisbach, Charles V. '59 (BAK) Retired.
Drendel, Ralph J. *s.j.* '53 (SJ)[M] Los Gatos, CA Sacred Heart Jesuit Center.
Drennan, Jimmy David '96 (SAT) Spring Branch, TX St. Joseph.
Drennan, Lawrence J. '61 (BO) Senior Priests. Retired.
Drennan, Rev. Msgr. William A. '55 (STL) Wildwood, MO St. Alban Roe Retired.
Drennen, Christopher J. *o.s.a.* '83 (PH)[Y] Malvern, PA Augustinian Friars (O.S.A.).
Drenzek, Peter C. '69 (MIL) Retired.
Dressler, Paul *o.f.m.cap.* '99 (WDC)[B] Washington, DC St. Francis Friary–Capuchin College.
Dressler, Philip J. '61 (CHI) Chicago, IL St. Juliana Retired.
Dressman, James J. *s.j.* '61 (BO)[U] Weston, MA Campion Health Center, Inc.
Dressman, Richard E. '72 (CIN) Cincinnati, OH St. Aloysius–on–the–Ohio; Cincinnati, OH St. Simon the Apostle.
Dressman, Robert C. *s.j.* '55 (DET)[K] Clarkston, MI Colombiere Center.
Dreves, Mark '95 (LEX) Lexington, KY Cathedral of Christ the King; Vicar General; Secretariat of the Vicar General.
Drew, Andrew *o.f.m.cap.* '61 (NY)[DD] Yonkers, NY St. Clare Friary Retired.
Drew, Geoffrey D. '04 (CIN) Liberty Township, OH St. Maximilian Kolbe.
Drewniak, Stanley '78 (JOL) Lockport, IL St. John Vianney.
Drexel, John *o.m.i.* '62 (FgM) Washington, DC AMERICAN OBLATE MISSIONS.
Drexler, Harold J. '55 (DUB) Retired.
Driesch, David A. '82 (PIT) Pittsburgh, PA Our Lady of Joy.
Drilling, Peter J. '67 (BUF)[A] East Aurora, NY Christ the King Seminary; [A] East Aurora, NY Christ the King Seminary; Council of Priests; Consultors, College of; Censors—Board of Diocesan Censors of Books and Vigilance for the Faith.
Drinane, Gerald A. *s.j.* '62 (FgM) Chicago, IL Society of Jesus.
Driscoll, Arthur J. '52 (BO) Senior Priests. Retired.
Driscoll, Daniel '76 (HEL) Whitehall, MT St. Teresa of Avila.
Driscoll, Donald '64 (NY) Retired.
Driscoll, Rev. Msgr. Eugene J. '70 (LUB) Lubbock, TX Holy Spirit; Priests Personnel Board; Defender of the Bond; Defender of the Bond–Appeal; Presbyteral Council; Diocesan Building Commission; Vicar General.
Driscoll, James A. *o.p.* '54 (PRO)[O] Providence St. Thomas Aquinas Priory at Providence College.
Driscoll, Jeremy *o.s.b.* '81 (P)[L] St. Benedict, OR Mt. Angel Abbey.
Driscoll, John P. '47 (FR) Retired.
Driscoll, John '54 (JOL) Romeoville, IL St. Andrew the Apostle Retired.
Driscoll, Joseph J. '79 (BO) On Duty Outside the Archdiocese.

Driscoll, Michael A. '68 (MET) Retired.
Driscoll, Michael '76 (FTW)[B] University of Notre Dame Du Lac; Liturgical Commission.
Driscoll, Michael '77 (HEL) On Duty Outside the Diocese; Consultant.
Driscoll, Michael *o.carm.* '67 (PMB) Boca Raton, FL St. Jude; Elected Members.
Driscoll, Patrick R. '04 (MOB) Montgomery, AL Church of the Holy Spirit; Group III; Archdiocesan Consultors.
Driscoll, Paul G. '64 (RVC) Retired.
Driscoll, Richard A. '55 (BO) Senior Priests. Retired.
Driscoll, Richard *s.d.s.* '65 (MIL)[P] Milwaukee Salvatorian Provincial Offices.
Driscoll, Samuel *o.f.m.cap.* '50 (CLV)[N] Cleveland, OH St. Paul Friary.
Driscoll, Rev. Msgr. Thomas J. '61 (BGP) Easton, CT Notre Dame (of Easton); Vicars General; Judges; Diocesan Censors; Diocesan Consultors; Presbyteral Council; Finance Council; Priest Vocation Advisory Board.
Driscoll, Timothy Paul '99 (FR) Taunton, MA Annunciation of the Lord.
Driscoll, William D. '55 (NEW) Retired.
Drobach, William *s.a.* '88 (NY)[AA] Garrison, NY St. Christopher's Inn; [DD] Garrison, NY St. Christopher's Inn; [DD] Garrison, NY St. Christopher's Friary.
Drobin, Paul J. '66 (SY)[T] Utica, NY Newman Center at SUNY Institute of Technology; [T] Utica, NY Utica College Newman Center.
Drobinski, Joseph J. '75 (WIL) Wilmington, DE St. Matthew.
Droessler, Chad M. '10 (MAD) Madison, WI St. Maria Goretti.
Droessler, Jeffrey A. '09 (ORG) Fountain Valley, CA Holy Spirit.
Droessler, Joseph '95 (ORG) Westminster, CA Blessed Sacrament.
Droessler, Wayne J. '69 (DUB) Coggon, IA St. Joseph; Central City, IA St. Stephen; Coggon, IA St. John the Evangelist; Anamosa, IA St. Patrick.
Drofych, Mykola '08 (STF) Kenmore, NY St. John the Baptist.
Drogon, Greg (PAT) Medical Leave.
Droll, Rev. Msgr. Larry J. '73 (SAN) Priests' Personnel Board; Presbyteral Council; Vicar General; Defensores Vinculi; Diocesan Consultors; Board of Directors; Midland, TX St. Ann's; Priests' Pension Plan.
Drolshagen, Jerry *s.o.l.t.* '04 (CC)[G] Robstown, TX Society of Our Lady of the Most Holy Trinity.
Drongowski, Stanley *o.p.* '79 (IND) Bloomington, IN St. Paul Catholic Center, Bloomington, Inc.
Droski, Norman P. '64 (GR) Coopersville, MI St. Michael's Retired.
Drouin, Marc B. '90 (MAN) Belknap County House of Corrections; Laconia, NH St. Andre Bessette.
Drouncheck, Anthony M. '89 (ALN) Catasauqua, PA Annunciation B.V.M.–St. Mary's.
Drozak, Lukasz *c.ss.r.* '06 (MET) Perth Amboy, NJ St. Stephen.
Drozd, Henry J. '62 (DAL) Retired.
Drozd, Henry J. '62 (SAV) Retired.
Drozd, Marian '91 (MET) South Amboy, NJ Sacred Heart.
Drozdovsky, Michael '92 (SJP) Parma, OH Pokrova Ukrainian Catholic Parish; Presbyters.
Drozdzik, Roch T. '96 (R) Absent on Leave.
Droze, D. Anthony '85 (CHR) North Myrtle Beach, SC Our Lady Star of the Sea; Presbyteral Council.
Drucker, James N. '78 (PSC) Leave of Absence Retired.
Druggan, Dennis *o.f.m.cap.* '84 (MIL)[P] Mount Calvary, WI St. Lawrence Friary; [B] Mount Calvary, WI St. Lawrence Seminary.
Drummond, Alexander R. '94 (ARL) Great Falls, VA St. Catherine of Siena.
Drummond, Elsyn J. '54 (NOR) Retired.
Drummy, John A. '71 (SUP) Amery, WI St. Joseph; Balsam Lake, WI Our Lady of the Lakes; Southwest Deanery; Personnel Placement Board.
Drury, Dennis G. '82 (GB) Denmark, WI St. Therese de Lisieux; Denmark, WI St. Isidore the Farmer.
Drury, George *s.j.* '52 (BO)[U] Newton, MA The Jesuit Community at Boston College.
Drury, Michael J. '74 (PAT) Long Valley, NJ St. Luke.
Drury, Michael '84 (HEL) Cut Bank, MT St. Margaret; Shelby, MT St. William; Valier, MT St. Francis; Diocesan Consultors; Presbyteral Council.
Drury, Robert '79 (OWN) Franklin, KY St. Mary.
Drutowski, Robert J. '79 (MIL) Pewaukee, WI Queen of Apostles.
Drybka, Krzysztof *o.s.p.p.e.* (NOR) Rockville, CT St. Joseph.
Drywal, Justin *o.s.b.* '98 (CLV) Broadview Heights, OH Assumption.
Drzaic, Frank '62 (LA) Los Angeles, CA Our Lady of Loretto.
Drzal, Stanislaw *s.ch.* '69 (DET) Sterling Heights, MI Our Lady of Czestochowa.
Duaime, Jeffrey T. *c.s.sp.* '86 (PH)[F] Bensalem, PA Holy Ghost Preparatory School; [Y] Bensalem, PA Congregation of the Holy Spirit; Councilors.
Duane, Robert J. '53 (NY) Ardsley, NY Our Lady of Perpetual Help; [DD] Bronx, NY John Cardinal O'Connor Residence Retired.
Duarte, J. Scott '78 (RIC) Quinton, VA St. Elizabeth Ann Seton; Vicar for the Causes of Saints.
Dube, Gregory P. '07 (PRT) Portland, ME Cathedral of the Immaculate Conception; Portland, ME St. Louis; Portland, ME Maine Medical Center; Portland, ME St. Christopher's; Portland, ME St. Peter's; Portland, ME Sacred Heart/St. Dominic.
Dube, Marcel *o.carm.* '54 (VEN) Englewood, FL St. Francis of Assisi.
Dubell, Rev. Msgr. James H. '65 (TR) Medford, NJ St. Mary of the Lakes.
Dubert, James W. '98 (DUB)[N] Ames, IA St. Thomas Aquinas Church and Catholic Student Center (Iowa State University); Ames, IA St. Thomas Aquinas Church (and Catholic Student Center); Gilbert, IA SS. Peter and Paul.
Dubi, Leonard A. '68 (CHI) Calumet City, IL St. Victor.
Dubitsky, Roman '65 (PHU) Retired.
Dublinski, Steve '85 (SPK) Vicar General; Members; Diocesan Pastoral Council; Diocesan Liturgical Commission; [A] Spokane, WA Bishop White Seminary.
Dublinski, Steven L. '85 (SPK) Bishop White Seminary.
Dubois, Rev. Msgr. Andrew '95 (PRT) Guardian; Diocesan Consultors; Staff; Diocesan Finance Council; Personnel Board; Special or Other Diocesan Assignment; Ex Officio; Vicars General; Moderator of the Curia; Director of Chaplaincies; Department of Administrative & Ministerial Services; Hospital Chaplaincy; Portland, ME St. Peter's.
Dubois, Rev. Msgr. Charles J. '64 (LKC) Lake Charles, LA St. Theodore.
DuBois, David J. '80 (GAL) Pattison, TX Sacred Heart.
DuBois, Francis J. '70 (ALB) Latham, NY St. Ambrose.
Dubois, Patrick '04 (VEN) Defenders of the Bond; Venice, FL Our Lady of Lourdes.
DuBois, Rev. Msgr. William '48 (SP) Retired.
Dubovici, Rt. Rev. Mitred Archpriest Mihai '94 (STF) Bridgeport, CT Protection of B.V.M.; [A] Stamford, CT Ukrainian Catholic Seminary Inc. St. Basil College; Vice Econome; Notary Publics; Presbyteral Council; Administrative Council; Priests' Benevolent Association.
Dubriske, Edward J. *s.s.e.* '64 (BUR)[E] Colchester, VT Society of St. Edmund; Colchester, VT SOCIETY OF ST. EDMUND.
Dubrouillet, James N. '97 (CHR) Orangeburg, SC Holy Trinity; Orangeburg, SC St. Andrew.
Dubuisson, William *o.m.i.* '55 (SAT)[K] San Antonio, TX Oblate Madonna Residence.
Duc, Dominic Tran Minh '90 (PH) East Lansdowne, PA St. Cyril of Alexandria.
Ducaji, John '54 (JOL) Wheaton, IL St. Mark.
Ducci, Alex '61 (STA) Retired.
Duc Do, Tan Peter *o.f.m.* '02 (CLV)[N] Brooklyn, OH St. Anthony of Padua Friary.
Ducette, Rev. Msgr. John I. '62 (BUF) Apostleship of the Sea Retired.
Duch, Robert G. '64 (PIT) Retired.
Duchaine, Rev. Msgr. R. Mark '78 (SC) Judicial Vicar; Judges; Diocesan Finance Council; Presbyteral Council; Diocesan Consultors; Priests' Pension Plan – Board of Trustees; Vicar General; Catholic School Foundation of the Diocese of Sioux City; Priests' Personnel Board.
DuCharme, Paul '55 (GB) Retired.
DuChez, Daniel B. (LC) Retired.
Duchnowicz, Arthur F. '01 (GLD) Posen, MI St. Casimir; Rogers City, MI St. Ignatius.
Duchschere, Paul C. '90 (FAR) Fargo, ND Sts. Anne & Joachim Church of Fargo.
Ducle, Rico '06 (CAM) Continuing Education & Spiritual Formation of Priests (CESF); Pennsauken, NJ Mary, Queen of All Saints, Pennsauken, N.J.
Duc Minh, Joseph N. '61 (LA) Retired.
Duc Ngo, (John Damas. M.) Voung *c.m.c.* '91 (SPC)[F] Carthage, MO Congregation of the Mother Coredemptrix, United States Assumption Province.
Ducre, Kennon Y. '83 (ELP) El Paso, TX All Saints.
Duda, Pawel '98 (STA) Jacksonville, FL Christ the King.
Duda, Rafal P. '11 (OAK) Rodeo, CA St. Patrick.
Duda, Robert '84 (JOL) Villa Park, IL St. John the Apostle.
Dudak, Rev. Msgr. George A. '56 (PAT)[Q] Chester, NJ Nazareth Village Retired.
Dudash, Derrick F. '74 (GRY) Hebron, IN St. Helen.
Dudek, Bernard *o.f.m. conv.* '54 (BAL) Baltimore, MD St. Clement Mary Hofbauer.
Dudek, Stanislaus *o.f.m. conv.* '87 (HRT) New Britain, CT Sacred Heart of Jesus.
Dudek, Stanislaw '62 (BUF)[N] Depew, NY Msgr. Conniff Residence Retired.
Dudek, Stephen S. '84 (GR) Grand Rapids, MI Holy Name of Jesus; On Special Assignment; [L] Grand Rapids, MI The Society For The Propagation Of The Faith.
Dudkevych, Andriy '95 (PHU) Passaic, NJ St. Nicholas.
Dudkiewicz, Stanley '52 (SY) Retired.
Dudley, James *m.s.c.* '56 (SAT)[L] San Antonio, TX Missionaries of the Sacred Heart.
Dudo, Michael '08 (CAM) Galloway, NJ The Church of the Assumption.
Dudo, Nicholas '08 (CAM) Egg Harbor City, NJ St. Nicholas' Church, Egg Harbor City; Representatives by Ordination Seniority; Vocation Advisory Board.
Dudziak, Rev. Msgr. Paul M. '69 (WDC) Gaithersburg, MD St. Rose of Lima; Priest Council.
Dudzik, Dariusz '95 (NOR) Groton, CT Sacred Heart.
Dudzik, Jozef W. '00 (BUF) Clymer, NY Christ Our Hope.
Dudzinski, Andrew J. '96 (LFT) Muncie, IN St. Mary.
Dudzinski, Brian A. '97 (LFT) Fishers, IN St. John Vianney Parish; Members.
Dudzinski, Paul L. '86 (ARL) Alexandria, VA St. Louis.
Dudzinski, Theodore C. '97 (LFT) Kokomo, IN St. Joan of Arc; Kokomo, IN St. Patrick; Office of the Permanent Diaconate.
Due, Rev. Msgr. J. Michael '00 (COV) Diocesan Consultors; Religious; Vicar General.
Duell, James S. '82 (CIN) Troy, OH St. Patrick.
Duenas, Jaime H. '50 (NY) Bronx, NY Nativity of Our Blessed Lady Retired.
Duenas, Jose Luis *o.a.r.* '59 (ELP) El Paso, TX Guardian Angel.
Dueñas, Manuel '07 (NEW) Bergenfield, NJ St. John the Evangelist.
Duerr, Rt. Rev. Gregory *o.s.b.* '64 (P)[L] St. Benedict, OR Mt. Angel Abbey; Saint Benedict, OR.
Duesdieker, Robert W. '80 (JC) Boonville, MO SS. Peter and Paul; Fayette, MO St. Joseph; Defenders of the Bond; Personnel Board.
Duesman, Rev. Msgr. Jerome P. '68 (DAL) Irving, TX Holy Family of Nazareth; Building Commission.
Duesman, Rev. Msgr. Leon '65 (DAL) Defensor Vinculi.
Duesterhaus, Michael R. '91 (ARL) Navy Reserve Chaplains; Woodbridge, VA Our Lady of Angels.
Duet, Jared (HT) Administrative Leave.
Duet, Jerod '08 (HT) Houma, LA St. Bernadette.
Dueweke, Robert *o.s.a.* '79 (ELP) Permanent Diaconate Office; Tepeyac Institute.
Duff, Daniel Joseph '07 (LFT) Westfield, IN St. Maria Goretti.
Duff, John J. '77 (NY) Pawling, NY St. John the Evangelist.
Duff, Paul J. *c.s.c.* '55 (FTW)[H] Notre Dame Congregation of Holy Cross, United States Province of Priests & Brothers.
Duffe, Stephen J. '96 (NEW) Washington Township, NJ Our Lady of Good Counsel.
Duffeck, David A. '06 (GB) Absent on Leave, Sick or Disabled.
Duffell, John P. '69 (NY) New York, NY Ascension.
Duffey, Joseph A. '52 (PH)[Y] Villanova, PA St. Thomas Monastery Retired.
Duffner, Paul A. *o.p.* '40 (P) Portland, OR Holy Rosary Parish & Dominican Priory; [L] Portland, OR Holy Rosary Priory Retired.
Duffner, Ralph J. '56 (SPC) Chaffee, MO St. Ambrose; Priests' Mutual Benefit Society; Advance, MO St. Joseph; Oran, MO Guardian Angel Retired.
Dufford, Robert J. *s.j.* '73 (DM) Atlantic, IA St. Timothy; Atlantic, IA Our Lady Of Grace.
Dufford, Robert J. *s.j.* '73 (OM)[J] Omaha, NE Jesuit Community at Creighton University.
Duffy, Darrell G. '05 (BUF) Jamestown, NY St. James.
Duffy, Donald '59 (NO) Lafitte, LA St. Anthony Retired.
Duffy, Rev. Msgr. Francis J. '70 (PAT) Morris Plains, NJ St. Virgilius.
Duffy, Rev. Msgr. Francis X. '49 (NY) Cornwall–on–Hudson, NY St. Thomas of Canterbury; [DD] Bronx, NY John Cardinal O'Connor Residence Retired.
Duffy, George '63 (MIA) Retired.
Duffy, Hugh E. *o.s.f.s.* '60 (WIL)[J] Childs, MD Retirement and Assisted Care Facility Retired.
Duffy, Hugh P. *s.j.* '68 (SEA)[A] Seattle, WA Seattle University; [M] Seattle, WA Arrupe Jesuit Community at Seattle University.
Duffy, Hugh '66 (PMB) Okeechobee, FL Sacred Heart.
Duffy, James D. *s.m.* '79 (ATL) Atlanta, GA Our Lady of the Assumption; Deans; Deans.
Duffy, James F. *s.j.* '06 (WDC)[O] Washington, DC The Jesuit Community at Georgetown University.
Duffy, James H. '56 (MIL) Special Assignment.
Duffy, John F. *c.s.p.* '75 (BRK)[R] Paulist Priests at Paulist Foundations Outside the U.S.
Duffy, Joseph P. *s.j.* '57 (BO)[U] Newton, MA The Jesuit Community at Boston College.
Duffy, Jude *o.f.m.cap.* '58 (NY)[B] Beacon, NY St. Lawrence of Brindisi Friary.
Duffy, Lawrence *s.m.* '75 (FgM) THE SOCIETY OF MARY.
Duffy, Michael A. *o.f.m.* '71 (PH)[Q] Philadelphia, PA St. Francis Inn; [Y] Philadelphia, PA Order of Friars Minor of the Province of the Most Holy Name.
Duffy, Michael M. '76 (RIC) Mineral, VA St. Jude; Judges; Adjutant Judicial Vicar.
Duffy, Patrick D. '74 (CIN) On Special and Archdiocesan Assignment.

Duffy, Patrick '81 (SFE) Retired.
Duffy, Paul J. *m.m.* '79 (FgM) Maryknoll, NY MARYKNOLL.
Duffy, Raymond '68 (FRS) Retired.
Duffy, Richard *o.f.m.* '58 (FgM) Saint Louis, MO Sacred Heart Province.
Duffy, Thomas J. '66 (PH) Retired.
Duffy, Rev. Msgr. Thomas M. '53 (WDC) Washington, DC Our Lady of Victory Retired.
Dufner, Dan '96 (YAK) Moses Lake, WA Our Lady of Fatima; Moses Lake, WA Queen of All Saints.
Dufner, Daniel G. '96 (YAK) Diocesan Finance Council; Clergy Personnel Board.
Dufner, Thomas W. '83 (STP) St. Louis Park, MN Holy Family.
Dufour, David W. '94 (NO) Kenner, LA Divine Mercy.
Dufour, George J. '70 (BO) Salem, MA St. Anne.
DuFour, Louis C. '58 (BO) Senior Priests. Retired.
DuFrange, Jonathan (NO)[A] St. Benedict, LA St. Joseph Seminary College.
Dufresne, Oliver J. '45 (STP) Retired.
Dufresne, Vincent J. '83 (BR) Paulina, LA St. Michael the Archangel; Paulina, LA Most Sacred Heart of Jesus; Paulina, LA St. Joseph; Promoter of Justice; Defenders of the Bond.
Dufresne, Vincent (NO)[A] St. Benedict, LA St. Joseph Seminary College.
Duga, Bernard '99 (NEW) Hackensack, NJ Hackensack University Medical Center.
Dugal, James *c.pp.s.* '56 (CIN)[N] Carthagena, OH St. Charles Retired.
Dugan, J. Thomas '70 (E) Erie, PA St. Jude the Apostle.
Dugan, James L. *s.j.* '73 (NY)[DD] New York, NY St. Ignatius Loyola Residence; New York, NY St. Ignatius Loyola.
Dugan, James M. '89 (ALT) Meyersdale, PA SS. Philip and James; Somerset, PA State Correctional Institution; Somerset, PA State Correctional Institution, Laurel Highlands.
Dugan, Paul J. *s.j.* '56 (BUF)[N] Buffalo, NY Canisius Jesuit Community Inc.
Dugan, T. Michael '88 (DAL) Deans; Dallas, TX St. Elizabeth of Hungary; Pastors Consultors.
Dugan, Thomas P. *c.s.b.* '60 (GAL)[O] Sugar Land Basilian Mission Center.
Dugan, William M. '49 (SPK) Retired.
Dugandzic, Peter '95 (RVC) Valley Stream, NY Blessed Sacrament.
Dugandzic, Peter '95 (NY)[A] Yonkers, NY St. Joseph's Seminary.
Dugas, Jerome A. '62 (BR) Retired.
Dugas, Scott '77 (HT) Administrative Leave.
Dugas, Scott '77 (JKS) Mound Bayou, MS St. Gabriel; Clarksdale, MS St. Elizabeth; Clarksdale, MS Immaculate Conception.
Dugas, Willard '77 (LAF) Retired.
Dugay, Anthony *s.v.d.* '62 (FgM) Techny, IL.
Duggan, Edmund Brendan *c.s.sp.* '75 (BRK)[Q] Irish Apostolate; Woodside, NY Blessed Virgin Mary, Help of Christians.
Duggan, Eugene F. '46 (SFR) Sausalito, CA St. Mary Star of the Sea Retired.
Duggan, John J. '56 (PRO) Coventry, RI SS. John and Paul Retired.
Duggan, Joseph P. '64 (VEN) Retired.
Duggan, Kevin F.X. '98 (SEA) Sammamish, WA Mary, Queen of Peace.
Duggan, Kevin P. '87 (MET) Jamesburg, NJ St. James the Less.
Duggan, Kevin *s.m.* '86 (MRY) Campus Ministry Department; [I] San Luis Obispo, CA California State Polytechnic Institute/Cuesta College; [F] San Luis Obispo, CA Society of Mary (Marists)–S.M.
Duggan, Michael A. *m.m.* '59 (NY)[DD] Maryknoll Maryknoll Fathers and Brothers.
Duggan, Nicholas '62 (SAC) Retired.
Duggan, Oliver '71 (SEA) Seattle, WA St. Catherine of Siena; Seattle, WA Assumption.
Duggan, Paul O'Donnell '70 (PAT) Pompton Plains, NJ Our Lady of Good Counsel.
Duggan, Robert D. '69 (WDC) Retired.
Duggan, Robert J. *c.s.b.* '64 (GAL)[B] Sugar Land, TX Basilian Fathers of Sugarland.
Duggan, Sean B. *o.s.b.* '88 (NO)[R] St. Benedict, LA St. Joseph Abbey.
Duggan, Sean *o.s.b.* '88 (BUF) Westfield, NY St. Dominic.
Duggimpudi, Jaya Prathap '99 (BIR) Birmingham, AL Our Lady of Sorrows.
Duggins, Dominic R. *g.h.m.* '74 (CIN)[N] Fairfield, OH; [T] Fairfield, OH Glenmary Home Missioners Charitable Trust; Cincinnati, OH.
Dugue, Nerva W. '93 (NEW) Absent on Leave.
Duhaime, James H. '61 (PRO) Retired.
Duhaime, John N. '71 (WH) Retired.
Duhe, Thomas P. '78 (BR) Baton Rouge, LA St. Thomas More; Presbyteral Council; College of Consultors.
Duhon, Edward J. '07 (LAF) Broussard, LA Sacred Heart of Jesus.
Dukart, George '59 (BIS) Retired.
Duke, Rev. Msgr. Charles J. '47 (NO) Retired.
Duke, Jerome J. '68 (CLV) Cleveland, OH Our Lady of Angels; Associate Judges.
Dukehart, C. Henry *s.s.* '43 (BAL)[Q] Baltimore Society of St. Sulpice, Province of the United States Retired.
Dukehart, Claude H. *s.s.* '43 (BAL)[M] Baltimore, MD St. Charles Villa Retired.
Dukeley, Boris '98 (SJP) Presbyters Retired.
Duker, Rev. Msgr. Russell A. *s.e.o.d.* '70 (PBR) Pittsburgh, PA Holy Spirit; Protosyncellus; Consultors; Priests' Pension Board; Pittsburgh, PA St. Pius X.
Dukowski, James G. *o.m.i.* '67 (FgM) Washington, DC AMERICAN OBLATE MISSIONS.
Dulaney, William R. '73 (BRK) Bellerose, NY St. Gregory the Great.
Dulek, Lawrence V. '73 (MIL) On Leave.
Duling, Daniel J. '11 (WCH) Wichita, KS St. Thomas Aquinas.
Dullahan, Robert J. '57 (ALN)[A] Wernersville, PA Jesuit Center–Jesuit Community.
Dullea, Denis '61 (ATL) Retired.
Dullea, John F. *s.j.* '59 (SJ)[M] Los Gatos, CA Sacred Heart Jesuit Center.
Dulli, Brian '08 (MAD) Graduate Studies.
Dulock, Vincent *c.s.b.* '69 (GAL)[B] Sugar Land, TX Basilian Fathers of Sugarland.
Duma, Rev. Msgr. Gregory '64 (ROM) College of Consultors; Canton Deanery Retired.
Dumag, Peter '92 (HON) Vocations Director; Honolulu, HI Co–Cathedral of St. Theresa of the Child Jesus.
Dumais, George J. *s.j.* '71 (HEL) Missoula, MT St. Francis Xavier; Special Assignments.
Dumais, Paul H. '04 (PRT) Windham, ME Our Lady of Perpetual Help; Bridgton, ME St. Joseph.
Dumais, Steven *s.d.b.* '78 (NY)[DD] New Rochelle, NY Salesian Provincial House; New Rochelle, NY.
Duman, Charles J. '52 (SFS) Retired.
Dumas, Emile E. *m.m.* '67 (NY)[DD].
Dumas, John Gerald '10 (DET) Macomb, MI St. Isidore.
Dumas, Terrence J. '88 (MO) Ann Arbor, MI St. Francis of Assisi; DEPARTMENT OF VETERANS AFFAIRS HOSPITALS AND CHAPLAINS Retired.
Dumenko, Oleksandr '01 (PHU) Millville, NJ St. Nicholas; Toms River, NJ St. Stephen's.
Duminiak, John J. '60 (ALN)[J] Bethlehem, PA Holy Family Villa Retired.
Dumm, Demetrius R. *o.s.b.* '47 (GBG)[H] Latrobe, PA Saint Vincent Archabbey.
Dummer, Anthony *o.m.i.* '84 (SFS) Sisseton, SD St. Catherine; Sisseton, SD St. Peter.
Dumont, C. Peter '71 (MAN) Presbyteral Council; College of Consultors Retired.
Dumont, Gerald '80 (BRK) Brooklyn, NY Our Lady of Miracles.
Dumont, Jacob *l.c.* '08 (CHI)[N] Hillside, IL Legion of Christ.
Dumoulin, Marcel L. '61 (PRT) Retired.
Dumphrey, Joseph C. *o.s.f.s.* '64 (BUF) Lockport, NY St. John the Baptist.
Dumphy, Charles '55 (WOR) Retired.
Dumpson, Roland J. '83 (NY) Retired.
Dunavan, Thomas B. '98 (LIN) Tecumseh, NE St. Andrew's; Lincoln, NE Nebraska Penal Complex; Apostolate to the Spanish Speaking.
Dunbar, Francis '55 (ALB) Retired.
Duncan, Andrew D. '93 (CHY) College of Consultors.
Duncan, Andrew '93 (CHY) Torrington, WY St. Rose.
Duncan, Rev. Msgr. Edward J. '41 (PEO)[M] Champaign, IL St. John's Catholic Newman Center at the University of Illinois, Urbana–Champaign; Champaign, IL St. John's Catholic Chapel Retired.
Duncan, Rev. Msgr. John C. '60 (LFT) Carmel, IN Our Lady of Mount Carmel; Associate Judges.
Duncan, Rev. Msgr. Joseph P. '89 (PH) Bensalem, PA St. Charles Borromeo.
Duncan, Rev. Msgr. Joseph (IND)[I] Indianapolis, IN St. Augustine Home, Little Sisters of the Poor.
Duncan, Rev. Msgr. William H. '90 (GR) Byron Center, MI St. Sebastian's; On Special Assignment; Vicar General/Moderator of the Curia; College of Consultors; Moderator of the Curia; Diocesan Finance Council Membership.
Duncanson, Rev. Msgr. Richard F. '71 (SD) San Diego, CA Mission San Diego De Alcala Catholic Parish.
Duncanson, Rev. Msgr. Richard '71 (SD) Vicars Forane; Censores Librorum.
Duncklee, Lawrence T. '80 (RVC) Procurator & Advocates.
Dundon, Luke R. '11 (ARL) Falls Church, VA St. Philip.
Dundon, Robert W. *s.j.* '69 (FgM) Milwaukee, WI Society of Jesus.
Dunfee, Dirk J. *s.j.* '97 (KC)[J] Kansas City, MO Rockhurst Jesuit Community.
Dunfee, James M. '84 (STU) Mingo Junction, OH St. Agnes; Censores Librorum; Judges; Deans.
Dung, Ha Quoc *c.ss.r.* '10 (LA)[P] Baldwin Park, CA Vietnamese Redemptorist Mission.
Dung, Nguyen Quoc *c.ss.r.* '05 (LA)[P] Baldwin Park Vietnamese Redemptorist Mission.
Dung, Peter Ngo Duc (OAK) Bay Point, CA Our Lady, Queen of the World.
Dunghe, Adelino P. *s.j.* '95 (SY)[Q] Syracuse, NY Jesuits at LeMoyne, Inc.
Dunham, Larry C. *o.f.m.* '74 (SFE)[H] Albuquerque, NM The Province of Our Lady of Guadalupe.
Dunkle, Brian P. *s.j.* '09 (FTW)[K] South Bend, IN Jesuit Community.
Dunkle, Brian P. *s.j.* '09 (CHI)[N] Chicago Chicago Province of the Society of Jesus–Provincial Office.
Dunkley, George '70 (SD) San Marcos, CA Saint Mark Catholic Parish.
Dunkley, George '70 (WOR) On Duty Outside the Diocese.
Dunlap, Christopher J. '06 (STL) Ballwin, MO Holy Infant.
Dunlap, William (TR) Atlantic Highlands, NJ St. Agnes; Highlands, NJ Our Lady of Perpetual Help.
Dunleavy, Thomas J. '75 (PH) Philadelphia, PA St. Anselm; College of Consultors; Pastors Review Board; Deans; Deans.
Dunleavy, Thomas J. *m.m.* '75 (FgM) Maryknoll, NY MARYKNOLL.
Dunmyer, Raymond A. '76 (BIR) Montevallo, AL St. Thomas the Apostle; [H] Montevallo, AL University of Montevallo.
Dunn, Bob '85 (CC) Corpus Christi, TX Most Precious Blood; Personnel Board – Priests.
Dunn, Charles J. *s.j.* '55 (WOR)[N] Worcester, MA Jesuits of the Holy Cross, Inc.
Dunn, Christopher J. *o.f.m.* '82 (FgM) New York, NY Holy Name Province.
Dunn, Rev. Msgr. Donald F. '61 (COS) Retired.
Dunn, Edmond J. '72 (DAV) Oxford, IA St. Peter's; Oxford, IA St. Mary's; [A] St. Ambrose University Retired.
Dunn, Rev. Msgr. Edward C. '43 (TOL) Retired.
Dunn, Gerald R. '57 (MAN) Gonic, NH St. Leo Retired.
Dunn, Harold *m.s.a.* '78 (NOR)[G] Cromwell Society of the Missionaries of the Holy Apostles.
Dunn, Jerome *o.f.m.cap.* '68 (PIT)[M] Pittsburgh St. Augustine Friary.
Dunn, John F. '54 (DET) Retired.
Dunn, Laurence J. '68 (CHI) Lake Forest, IL St. Patrick.
Dunn, Lawrence *m.i.c.* '87 (WDC)[B] Washington, DC Marian Fathers Scholasticate.
Dunn, Michael G. '03 (TR) Burlington, NJ The Church of St. Katharine Drexel, Burlington, N.J.
Dunn, Michael L. '94 (BGP) Weston, CT St. Francis of Assisi.
Dunn, Richard B. '80 (SY) Military Chaplains; Hamilton, NY St. Mary.
Dunn, Rev. Msgr. Richard F. '58 (BRK)[R] Douglaston, NY Bishop Mugavero Residence Retired.
Dunn, Robert M. '92 (NY)[Z] Bronx, NY Jeanne Jugan Residence.
Dunn, Stephen '71 (SD) Retired.
Dunn, Rev. Msgr. William A. '65 (COL) Logan, OH St. John; College of Consultors.
Dunn, William S. '06 (BO) West Roxbury, MA St. John Chrysostom.
Dunne, Dermot J. '00 (OM) On Duty Outside the Archdiocese.
Dunne, Dermot '00 (SP) St. Pete Beach, FL St. John Vianney.
Dunne, George W. *s.s.s.* '82 (ORL) Winter Springs, FL St. Stephen.
Dunne, Gerald *o.s.f.s.* '77 (WIL)[J] Wilmington, DE DeSales House.
Dunne, Gerard *s.s.c.* '67 (OM)[J] St. Columbans Missionary Society of St. Columban.
Dunne, James M. '61 (BRK) Rockaway Beach, NY Saint Camillus–Saint Virgilius Retired.
Dunne, John S. *c.s.c.* '54 (FTW)[B] University of Notre Dame Du Lac; [H] Notre Dame, IN Holy Cross Community, Corby Hall, University of Notre Dame.
Dunne, Rev. Msgr. Joseph A. '42 (NY)[DD] Bronx, NY Retired.
Dunne, Mark '02 (TYL) Longview, TX St. Mary.
Dunne, Patrick J. '70 (NY) Hopewell Junction, NY St. Denis.
Dunne, Rev. Msgr. Peter F. '44 (OM) Boys Town, NE Immaculate Conception B.V.M. Retired.
Dunne, Raymond A. *s.j.* '50 (DET)[K] Clarkston, MI Colombiere Center.
Dunne, Thomas *s.d.b.* '72 (NY)[DD] New Rochelle, NY Salesian Cooperators of St. John Bosco; [DD] New Rochelle, NY Salesian Provincial House; New Rochelle, NY; New Rochelle, NY SALESIANS OF DON BOSCO.
Dunning, James Patrick '63 (ORG) Retired.
Dunnivan, John '53 (KCK) Retired.
Dunphy, James R. *m.s.* '57 (STL)[O] LaSalette Spirituality Center.
Dunphy, Larry *o.f.m.* '60 (OAK)[L] Oakland, CA Franciscan Friars of California, (Province of St. Barbara).
Dunphy, Richard W. *s.j.* '73 (COS)[E] Sedalia, CO Sacred Heart Jesuit Community; [G] Sedalia, CO Sacred Heart Jesuit Retreat House.
Dunphy, Robert J. '65 (CAM) Retired.
Dunphy, Thomas R. '58 (CLV) Valley City, OH St. Martin of Tours.
Dunson, Donald '82 (CLV)[A] Wickliffe, OH Borromeo

Seminary; [A] Wickliffe, OH St. Mary Seminary and Graduate School of Theology.

Dunston, Allen *o.p.* '78 (SFR)[N] San Francisco, CA St. Dominic Priory.

Dunyo, Andrew (BRK) Brooklyn, NY St. Mark.

Duoba, John *m.i.c.* '46 (NOR)[G] Bros. & Priests Elsewhere.

Duong, Cu Minh '87 (MOB) Mobile, AL St. Monica; Vicar for Vietnamese Affairs.

Duong, Duc '00 (BEA) Port Arthur, TX St. Catherine of Siena.

Duong, James Duc H. '01 (CHL) Greensboro, NC St. Benedict.

Duong, Paul '74 (SJ) San Jose, CA Christ the King; Diocesan Clergy Personnel Board.

Duong, Tien H. '01 (CHL) Franklin, NC St. Francis of Assisi.

Duong, Tri Minh *c.m.* '05 (BRK)[R] Jamaica, NY Reverend John B. Murray, CM, House.

Duplissey, James Joshe '09 (LSC) Vicars; Deming, NM Holy Family; Presbyteral Council.

DuPont, Arthur J. '54 (HRT) Appointed; Wallingford, CT Resurrection Retired.

Dupont, Bernard *o.p.* '68 (WDC)[B] Washington, DC Dominican House of Studies.

Dupre, Matthew C. '98 (BR) Brusly, LA St. John the Baptist; College of Consultors; Presbyteral Council.

Dupre, Stephane *f.s.s.p.* (COS) Security, CO Immaculate Conception Parish.

DuPreez, Frank V. '86 (LR) North Little Rock, AR St. Patrick; North Little Rock, AR St. Mary.

Duprey, Rev. Msgr. Dennis J. '70 (OG) Plattsburgh, NY St. Peter; Advocates.

Dupuis, Philip '51 (LAN) Retired.

DuQuesnay, Damian *o.s.b.* '46 (SP)[N] Saint Leo, FL St. Leo Abbey.

Duquet, Heribert *m.e.p.* '39 (SFR)[K] San Francisco, CA Home for the Aged of the Little Sisters of the Poor; [N] San Francisco, CA Paris Foreign Mission Society Residence Retired.

Duquette, Don Bosco *o.f.m.cap.* '64 (NOR) Middletown, CT St. Pius X Retired.

Duquette, Roy H. '58 (SPR) Retired.

Dura, Eduardo '77 (SFR) San Francisco, CA St. Patrick.

Durack, Jerome F. *s.j.* '60 (FgM) Chicago, IL Society of Jesus.

Duraisamy, Johnbosco (CHR) Sullivan's Island, SC Stella Maris.

Duran, Jorge '75 (SAT) On Leave.

Duran, Juan Pablo '11 (HRT)[B] Cheshire, CT Novitiate of the Legion of Christ.

Duran, Said '95 (TYL) On Duty Outside the Diocese.

Duran–Ortega, Alfonso *o.de m.* '98 (SB) Riverside, CA Our Lady of Guadalupe Shrine.

Durand, Donald '58 (P) Retired.

Durant, Thomas M. '76 (SY) Whitesboro, NY St. Anne; Whitesboro, NY St. Paul.

Durante, Charles '94 (RNO) Carson City, NV St. Teresa of Avila; Vicar General; Diocesan Board of Consultors; Finance Council; Seminary Board; Presbyteral Council; Priest Personnel Board; Life, Peace & Justice Commission; Curia.

Durazo, Marco Antonio '07 (LA) Graduate Studies.

Durbin, John G. '79 (R) Hampstead, NC St. Jude the Apostle.

Durchholz, Jack J. '95 (EVN) Clergy Personnel Board; Ferdinand, IN St. Ferdinand.

Durette, Mathias D. *o.s.b.* '93 (MAN)[K] Manchester, NH St. Anselm Abbey.

Durette, Robert *o.m.i.* '60 (FgM) Washington, DC AMERICAN OBLATE MISSIONS.

Durham, DePorres C. *o.p.* '90 (CHI)[D] Oak Park, IL Fenwick High School; [N] River Forest, IL St. Thomas Aquinas Priory.

Durham, Neil *s.d.s.* '82 (MIL)[P] Milwaukee, WI Salvatorians – Jordan Hall Retired.

Durian, Ariel *c.s.* '05 (LA) Sun Valley, CA Our Lady of the Holy Rosary.

Durig, D. Kent '93 (WH) Stonewood, WV Our Lady of Perpetual Help.

Duris, Lawrence M. '69 (CHI) Chicago, IL St. Ailbe.

Durkee, David R. '80 (CLV) Uniontown, OH Queen of Heaven.

Durken, Daniel *o.s.b.* '56 (SCL)[I] Collegeville, MN St. John's Abbey, of the Order of St. Benedict.

Durkin, Daniel '73 (FTW) Fort Wayne, IN St. Henry; Fort Wayne, IN Sacred Heart.

Durkin, Edward J. *s.j.* '75 (BUF)[N] Buffalo, NY Canisius Jesuit Community Inc.; [E] Buffalo, NY The NativityMiguel Middle School of Buffalo.

Durkin, Eugene F. '49 (CHI) Retired.

Durkin, James J. '68 (CAM)[H] Cherry Hill, NJ St. Mary's Catholic Home, Cherry Hill, N.J.

Durkin, John F. '99 (ATL) Duluth, GA St. Monica.

Durney, Charles W. '63 (PH) Retired.

Duron, Adan Sandoval '06 (CHI) Cicero, IL Our Lady of the Mount.

Durr, Edmund J. '65 (SY) Retired.

Durso, Michael H. *s.j.* '66 (STL)[O] St. Louis, MO De Smet Jesuit High School Community.

Duru, Hippolytus '97 (NEW) Livingston, NJ St. Barnabas Medical Center; West Orange, NJ Our Lady of Lourdes; Bronx, NY St. Francis Xavier; Bronx, NY North Central Bronx Hospital; Jacobi Medical Center.

Dury, Daniel J. '10 (COL) Westerville, OH St. Paul the Apostle.

Duschl, Frederick J. '65 (TOL) Retrouvaille Retired.

Dusecina, Regis J. '73 (PBR) Greensburg, PA St. Nicholas of Myra.

Dushack, Rev. Msgr. Douglas L. '72 (MAD) Middleton, WI St. Bernard.

Dusheck, Leo *s.v.d.* '61 (TR)[N] Bordentown, NJ Society of the Divine Word.

Dussan, Luis *c.m.f.* '49 (SAT) San Antonio, TX Immaculate Heart of Mary Retired.

Duster, Charles *s.s.c.* '61 (CHI) Council:; [N] Chicago, IL Columban Fathers Mission Center.

Duster, Charles *s.s.c.* '61 (OM)[J] St. Columbans Missionary Society of St. Columban.

Duston, Allen Robert *o.p.* '78 (SFR)[S] San Francisco, CA Shrine of St. Jude Thaddeus; San Francisco, CA St. Dominic.

Duston, Allen *o.p.* '78 (OAK)[L] Oakland, CA Order of Preachers (Province of the Most Holy Name of Jesus – Western Dominican Province).

Duston, Thomas L. '92 (MAN) Deaf Ministry; Henniker, NH St. Theresa; Hillsborough, NH St. Mary; Pastoral Council; Public Policy Commission; Presbyteral Council.

Dusza, Donald W. '83 (ALT) Bedford, PA St. Thomas.

Dutel, Gilbert J. '70 (LAF) Lafayette, LA St. Edmond.

Dutkiewicz, Eugene M. *s.j.* '61 (MIL)[P] Milwaukee, WI Jesuit Provincial Office, Wisconsin Province; Milwaukee, WI; [P] Milwaukee, WI Jesuit Community at Marquette University.

Dutra, David '07 (STO) Stockton, CA St. George Church (Pastor of); Members at Large.

Dutra, Luis C. '55 (LAF)[H] Lafayette, LA De La Salle Christian Brothers Retired.

Dutram, Charles J. '58 (WOR) Retired.

DuVall, W. Scott '09 (RCK) Huntley, IL St. Mary.

Duvelius, Dennis M. '96 (IND) Tell City, IN St. Paul Catholic Church, Tell City, Inc.; Deaneries and Deans; Tell City, IN St. Mark's Catholic Church, Perry County, Inc.

DuWell, Ralph '00 (ORL) Longwood, FL Church of the Nativity.

Dux, John H. '73 (STA) Retired.

Duyka, Stephen J. '97 (TYL) Rusk, TX Sacred Heart; Rusk, TX Hodge Unit and Skyview Unit, Texas Department of Criminal Justice.

Duyshart, Edwin C. '84 (LA) Los Angeles, CA St. Ignatius of Loyola.

Dvorak, Donald *o.p.* '63 (DAL)[J] Irving, TX Dominican Priory of St. Albert the Great and Novitiate; [L] Irving, TX University of Dallas–Campus Ministry.

Dvorak, Donald *o.p.* '63 (DAL) Irving, TX Church of the Incarnation.

Dvorak, Franklin A. '70 (OM) Deans; Deans; Omaha, NE St. Elizabeth Ann.

Dvorak, Gerald '79 (STP) Richfield, MN St. Peter.

Dvorscak, James '76 (JOL) Mokena, IL St. Mary Church.

Dwomoh, Charles O. '86 (VIC) Defenders of the Bond; Hungerford, TX St. John the Baptist; Diocesan Consultors; Presbyteral Council.

Dworak, Joseph J. '65 (ALB) Retired.

Dworak, Joseph '65 (ALB) Priests Retirement Board/ Priests Retirement Plan Board Retired.

Dworak, Walter W. '72 (PIT) Pittsburgh, PA St. Philip.

Dwyer, Arthur J. *m.m.* '49 (SJ)[M] Los Altos, CA Maryknoll.

Dwyer, Daniel P. *o.f.m.* '88 (ALB)[B] Siena College.

Dwyer, David P. *c.s.p.* '00 (NY)[DD] New York, NY Paulist Fathers' Motherhouse.

Dwyer, Rev. Msgr. Donald M. '79 (NY) Rye, NY Resurrection.

Dwyer, Edwin C. '11 (SAG) Midland, MI Blessed Sacrament.

Dwyer, Eugene F. *s.j.* '59 (DET)[K] Clarkston, MI Colombiere Center.

Dwyer, James *s.s.c.* '58 (PRO)[O] Bristol, RI St. Columban's Retirement House.

Dwyer, James *s.s.c.* '58 (OM)[J] St. Columbans Missionary Society of St. Columban.

Dwyer, John A. '74 (WOR) Lunenburg, MA St. Boniface.

Dwyer, John F. '56 (NY) Tappan, NY Our Lady of the Sacred Heart Retired.

Dwyer, Robert D. '62 (SY) Retired.

Dwyer, Thomas P. *o.s.a.* '58 (PH)[Y] Villanova, PA St. Thomas Monastery.

Dwyer, Timothy *s.m.* '68 (CAM)[N] Cape May Point, NJ Marianist Family Retreat Center.

Dyachok, Petro '89 (STN) San Francisco, CA Immaculate Conception Catholic Church; Santa Clara, CA St. Volodymyr Ukrainian Catholic Mission.

Dybas, Richard W. '59 (ALB) Retired.

Dye, David M. '92 (ATL) Norcross, GA Mary Our Queen Catholic Church.

Dye, Robert M. '91 (TLS) Hispanic Ministry; Tulsa, OK St. Francis Xavier Church and Diocesan Marian Shrine & Expiatory Temple of Our Lady of Guadalupe.

Dyer, Francis X. *o.p.* '69 (CHI)[N] Chicago Dominicans (Provincial Office).

Dyer, Gene J. '85 (CHI) Chicago, IL St. Thecla.

Dyer, George J. '53 (CHI) Wadsworth, IL St. Patrick Retired.

Dyer, Hugh Vincent *o.p.* '08 (HRT)[Q] Hamden, CT Catholic Community at Quinnipiac University; New Haven, CT St. Mary's.

Dyer, James W. '97 (STL) Farmington, MO St. Joseph.

Dyer, Joseph '74 (JKS) Forest, MS St. Michael; Forest, MS St. Michael; [H] Forest, MS East Central Community College Newman Center; Priests' Council.

Dyer, Kevin B. *s.j.* '10 (DEN)[D] Aurora, CO Regis Jesuit High School Corporation; [N] Centennial, CO Regis High Jesuit Community.

Dyer, Raymond E. '46 (PRO) Retired.

Dyer, Thomas P. '69 (Y)[C] Louisville, OH St. Thomas Aquinas High School; [P] Louisville, OH St. Thomas Aquinas High School Endowment Fund.

Dyer, Rev. Msgr. Timothy J. '74 (LA) Our Lady of the Angels Region; Members.

Dygert, C. Joseph '11 (COS) Parker, CO Ave Maria.

Dygula, Rafal '96 (LA) Los Angeles, CA Our Lady of the Bright Mount.

Dykas, Benjamin '71 (ALT) Retired.

Dylag, Rev. Msgr. Michael R. '65 (GBG) Retired.

Dymek, Janusz '01 (BRK) Brooklyn, NY Guardian Angel.

Dymek, Mariusz *o.s.p.p.e.* '02 (BUF) Buffalo, NY Corpus Christi.

Dymowski, Thomas H. *o.ss.t.* '80 (SAT) Special Assignment.

Dymowski, Thomas *o.ss.t* '85 (SAT)[L] San Antonio, TX Trinitarian Residence.

Dymowski, Tom *o.ss.t.* '85 (BAL)[Q] Archdiocese of San Antonio, TX.

Dynek, Wieslaw A. '74 (MO) Army Chaplains.

Dyrwal, Justin *o.s.b.* '98 (CLV)[N] Cleveland, OH.

Dysinger, Luke *o.s.b.* '86 (LA)[P] Valyermo, CA St. Andrew's Abbey; Co Chairmen; [A] Camarillo, CA St. John's Seminary.

Dytkowski, Louis M. '60 (BGP) Retired.

Dzengeleski, Martin G. (BO) Watertown, MA St. Patrick.

Dziadek, Vladimir '82 (SP) Tampa, FL St. Joseph.

Dziak, Theodore A. *s.j.* '83 (NO)[C] New Orleans, LA Loyola University New Orleans.

Dziak, Theodore A. *s.j.* '83 (BO)[U] Boston The Society of Jesus of New England–Provincial Offices.

Dziedziak, Robert T. '05 (VEN) Sarasota, FL St. Patrick.

Dziedzic, Gerald H. '74 (HRT) Terryville, CT Immaculate Conception; Terryville, CT St. Casimir; Appointed Members; College of Consultors.

Dzieglewicz, John T. *s.j.* '83 (NY)[DD] Cardinal Spellman Hall, Jesuit Community.

Dziekan, Wayne H. '94 (GLD) Justice and Peace.

Dzielak, Rev. Msgr. Thomas L. '63 (RCK) Rock Falls, IL St. Andrew; Tampico, IL St. Mary; Deans; Council of Catholic Women, Diocesan; Ecumenism, Office of; Pro Synodal Judges.

Dzien, Joseph Duc '83 (NO) Des Allemands, LA St. Gertrude; Paradis, LA St. John the Baptist.

Dzien, Marek (STA) St. Augustine, FL San Sebastian.

Dzieszko, Thaddeus '88 (CHI) Chicago, IL St. Constance; [T] Chicago, IL Catholic League for Religious Assistance to Poland.

Dzikowski, Piotr *s.ch.* '87 (P) Portland, OR St. Stanislaus.

Dziob, Rev. Msgr. Michael W. '42 (PRO)[O] Providence St. John Vianney Residence Retired.

Dziordz, Walter *m.i.c.* '84 (JOL) Darien, IL Our Lady of Peace.

Dziorek, Anthony *c.r.* '75 (CHI) Chicago, IL St. Stanislaus, Bishop and Martyr.

E

Eagan, Joseph F. *s.j.* '53 (MIL)[P] Wauwatosa, WI Jesuit Community at St. Camillus.

Eagan, William J. *s.j.* '75 (BGP)[O] Fairfield, CT The Fairfield Jesuit Community–Fairfield University; [E] Fairfield, CT Fairfield College Preparatory School.

Eagle, Raphael *t.o.r.* '67 (FWT) Councilors:; Fort Worth, TX St. Patrick Cathedral.

Eale, Francois–Xavier '00 (HRT) Orange, CT Holy Infant.

Earl, John '94 (RCK) Aurora, IL Holy Angels.

Earl, Marcellus R. *o.c.s.o.* '63 (ROC)[K] Piffard, NY Abbey of the Genesee.

Earl, Patrick F. *s.j.* '74 (CHL) Charlotte, NC St. Peter.

Earl, Patrick *s.j.* (CHL)[J] Mooresville, NC Jesuit Community.

Earley, James *c.p.* '57 (BRK)[R] Jamaica, NY Immaculate Conception Monastery Retired.

Earley, Jerome *o.c.d.* '95 (DAL)[H] Dallas, TX Mount Carmel Center; [J] Dallas, TX Mt. Carmel Center.

Earley, Phillip B. '74 (BO) Wilmington, MA St. Dorothy; Wilmington, MA St. Thomas of Villanova; Catholic Charities Senior Management.
Earls, John Patrick *o.s.b.* '65 (SCL)[I] Collegeville, MN St. John's Abbey, of the Order of St. Benedict.
Early, Francis J. '85 (WDC) Bushwood, MD Sacred Heart.
Early, William F. '68 (BRK) Retired.
Earner, Rev. Msgr. Thomas '62 (SP) Retired.
Earthedath, Sebastian *m.s.t.* '86 (SP) New Port Richey, FL Our Lady Queen of Peace.
Earthman, Michael G. '07 (GAL)[A] Houston, TX St. Mary's Seminary.
East, Rev. Msgr. Raymond G. '81 (WDC) Washington, DC St. Teresa of Avila.
Easterling, William T. '82 (LA) Covina, CA Sacred Heart.
Eastman, Patrick W. '84 (TLS) Retired.
Easton, Rev. Msgr. Frederick C. '66 (IND) Retired.
Easton, Rev. Msgr. Frederick '66 (IND) Adjunct Vicars Judicial.
Easton, Rev. Msgr. William H. '70 (DET) Presbyteral Council; Royal Oak, MI National Shrine of the Little Flower; [D] Royal Oak, MI Shrine Catholic High School & Academy; Archdiocesan Vicars.
Eaton, John *o.f.m.* '78 (NSH) Nashville, TN St. Vincent de Paul; Councilors:; [H] Nashville, TN Franciscan Friars.
Eaton, Matthew '10 (CHI)[J] Maywood, IL Loyola University Medical Center.
Ebach, Aloys *c.pp.s.* '74 (KC)[A] Kansas City, MO Gaspar Mission House; Kansas City, MO Sacred Heart–Guadalupe.
Ebarb, Walter E. '62 (SHP) Retired.
Ebarb, Walter '62 (SAT) San Antonio, TX Retired.
Ebben, Bertrand E. *o.p.* '59 (R)[F] Raleigh, NC Dominican Priory.
Ebbesmier, John '78 (PHX) Youngtown, AZ Church of St. Joachim & St. Anne Roman Catholic Parish.
Ebejer, Lino P. '91 (WH) Retired.
Ebel, Stephen P. '70 (DAV) Knoxville, IA St. Anthony's; Melcher, IA Sacred Heart.
Eberhart, Lewis '04 (LAN) University of Michigan Hospitals/Pastoral Dept.
Eberle, Paul '05 (BIS) Hague, ND St. Mary; Strasburg, ND Sts. Peter and Paul; Strasburg, ND St. Michael.
Eberle, Richard *o.s.f.s.* '82 (LAN) Hudson, MI Sacred Heart; Manitou Beach, MI St. Mary on the Lake.
Ebert, Douglas '09 (STP) Chaska, MN Guardian Angels.
Ebert, James A. '09 (ALB) Presbyteral Council; Diocesan Board of Consultors; Cohoes, NY Holy Trinity.
Ebert, Mark S. '76 (STL) Park Hills, MO Immaculate Conception.
Ebey, Carl F. *c.s.c.* '72 (FTW)[B] University of Notre Dame Du Lac; [H] Notre Dame, IN Holy Cross Community, Corby Hall, University of Notre Dame.
Ebker, Daniel '06 (PEO) Canton, IL St. Mary's; Lewistown, IL St. Mary's.
Eble, James E. *m.m.* '88 (FgM) Maryknoll, NY MARYKNOLL.
Eblen, James '64 (SEA) Special Assignment; Theological Resources; Judges Retired.
Ebner, Patrick '04 (AUS) Bryan, TX St. Anthony; Bryan, TX San Salvador.
Ebright, James A. '05 (CHL) Charlotte, NC St. Patrick Cathedral.
Ebrom, Robert L. '71 (CHI) Elk Grove Village, IL Queen of the Rosary.
Ebron, Jose Erlito '93 (NEW) Kenilworth, NJ St. Theresa's.
Ebulueme, Theophilus '95 (NSH) Clarksville, TN Immaculate Conception.
Eburuche, Eugene *s.m.m.m.* '65 (SB) Chino, CA California Institute for Men; Chino, CA St. Margaret Mary.
Ebuziem, Cajetan '96 (LFT)[E] Lafayette, IN Emmaus House; [C] Lafayette, IN Franciscan St. Elizabeth Health–Lafayette Central.
Ecandon, Luis '06 (DEN) Denver, CO St. Mary Magdalene.
Eccleston, John '55 (SCL) Retired.
Echavarria, Carlos A. '10 (HRT) Torrington, CT St. Francis of Assisi; Torrington, CT St. Mary; Torrington, CT Sacred Heart; Torrington, CT St. Peter.
Echavarria, Henry Wilson Rodriguez *c.h.s.* '95 (CHR) Greenwood, SC Our Lady of Lourdes; Greer, SC Blessed Trinity.
Echavarria, Juan David '11 (WOR) Whitinsville, MA St. Patrick.
Echekwu, Kyrian C. '92 (BRK) Elmhurst, NY Ascension.
Echert, John P. '87 (MO) South St. Paul, MN Holy Trinity; Air National Guard Chaplains.
Echevarria, Wilfredo *o.ss.t.* '81 (ARE) Isabela, PR St. Anthony.
Echeverria, Miguel *o.a.r.* '61 (LSC) Chaparral, NM St. Thomas More Church.
Echeverria, Pedro Faustino '84 (PCE) Aguirre, PR Sacred Heart.
Echevia, Les Suberi '61 (RCK) Retired.
Eck, Ivan C. '51 (WCH) Mount Hope, KS St. Rose; Mount Hope, KS St. Joseph; Mount Hope, KS St. Louis.
Eck, John E. *c.s.v.* '63 (CHI)[N] Arlington Heights Viatorian Province Center–Clerics of St. Viator.
Eck, John E. *c.s.v.* '63 (JOL) Kankakee, IL St. Patrick.
Eck, Reinhard C. '50 (WCH) Andale, KS St. Joseph.
Eckart, Frank K. '69 (TOL) Members Retired.
Eckberg, Joseph A. '00 (WCH) Hutchinson, KS Church of the Holy Cross.
Ecker, Rev. Msgr. John A. '58 (YAK) Yakima, WA St. Paul Cathedral; Vicar General; Diocesan Consultors; Ecumenical Liaison; Diocesan Finance Council; Clergy Personnel Board; Presbyteral Council Executive Committee; Lay Advisory Board.
Ecker, Rev. Msgr. Robert J. '51 (BRK) Retired.
Eckerman, Felix *s.v.d.* '47 (CHI)[N] Techny, IL Divine Word Residence.
Eckermann, Rev. Msgr. Charles H. '56 (SY) Retired.
Eckert, John C. '72 (PH) Morrisville, PA Holy Trinity.
Eckert, John J. '10 (CHL) Greensboro, NC Our Lady of Grace.
Eckert, Sidney J. '66 (DET) Retired.
Eckert, Thomas J. *c.s.c.* '02 (PHX)[J] Goodyear, AZ St. John Vianney School Development Fund.
Eckert, Tom *c.s.c.* '02 (PHX) Goodyear, AZ Saint John Vianney Roman Catholic Parish.
Eckert, William F. '64 (CAM) Retired.
Eckinger, Ambrose *o.p.* '81 (WIL) Newark, DE St. Thomas More Oratory; Catholic Campus Ministry; Newark, DE University of Delaware; [O] Newark, DE Catholic Campus Ministry, Univ. of Delaware.
Eckley, Michael P. '91 (OM) Omaha, NE St. Pius X.
Eckman, Mark A. '85 (PIT) Pittsburgh, PA St. Thomas More; College of Consultors; Clergy Personnel Board; Priest Council; Members.
Eckroth, Leonard A. '58 (BIS) Retired.
Eckroth, Richard *o.s.b.* '52 (SCL)[I] Collegeville, MN St. John's Abbey, of the Order of St. Benedict.
Eckstein, Francis J. '58 (IND) Retired.
Eco, Roy V. '80 (ORL) Filipino Ministry; Ocala, FL Blessed Trinity; Representative – Secular Priests Not Incardinated.
Edakkulathoor, Joseph *c.m.i.* '89 (COV) Falmouth, KY St. Francis Xavier.
Edamattan, Thomas '66 (RVC) Huntington, NY St. Patrick's; Huntington, NY Huntington Hospital.
Edassery, Davies *s.a.c.* '88 (MIL)[P] Milwaukee, WI Pallotti House; [N] Wauwatosa, WI St. Camillus Health Center, Inc.
Edathumparambil, Binu *m.s.f.s.* '00 (TYL)[C] Whitehouse, TX The Missionaries of St. Francis de Sales.
Edathumparambil, Binu *m.s.f.s.* '00 (STL) Manchester, MO St. Joseph.
Edayadiyil, Jose *v.c.* '73 (SCL) Isanti, MN St. Elizabeth Ann Seton; [I] Saint Cloud, MN St. Joseph Province of the Vincentian Congregation.
Eddy, Corbin '68 (MAR) Retired.
Eddy, William A. '75 (CHI) Chicago, IL St. Hilary.
Edeh, Charles (WDC) Hyattsville, MD St. Jerome.
Edelen, Luke A. *o.s.b.* '80 (NEW)[L] Newark, NJ Newark Abbey; Archdiocesan Commission of Christian Unity; [O] Jersey City, NJ New Jersey City University, Gilligan Student Union.
Edelen, M. Daniel '08 (LEX) West Liberty, KY Prince of Peace.
Edelen, Thomas '01 (TYL) On Duty Outside the Diocese.
Eden, Timothy *s.m.* '77 (HON)[D] Honolulu, HI Center Marianist Community; [G] Honolulu, HI Our Lady the Mystical Rose Chapel.
Edens, William L. *c.s.p.* '81 (OAK) Berkeley, CA Holy Spirit Parish/Newman Hall.
Eder, Donald '54 (LAN) Retired.
Eder, Donald '60 (LFT) Retired.
Ederer, John A. '77 (SAG) Retired.
Edgerly, Leo J. '84 (OAK) Piedmont, CA Corpus Christi; Cursillo Movement; Pastoral Leadership Placement Board (PLPB).
Edison, John '95 (NY) Harrison, NY St. Gregory the Great.
Ediza, Manuel '79 (SD) San Diego, CA Saint Michael Catholic Parish San Diego; Presbyteral Council.
Edlefsen, Frederick H. '01 (ARL)[K] Fredericksburg, VA University of Mary Washington; Fredericksburg, VA St. Mary of the Immaculate Conception.
Edmunds, Garret *o.f.m.* '82 (FgM) Oakland, CA St. Barbara Province.
Edmunds, Garrett *o.f.m.* '82 (OAK) Washington, DC; [L] Oakland Franciscan Friars of California, (Province of St. Barbara).
Edmunds, Garrett *o.f.m.* '82 (FgM) Washington, DC COMMISSARIAT OF THE HOLY LAND; [O] Washington, DC Franciscan Monastery USA Inc.; [O] Washington, DC Commissariat of the Holy Land, Franciscan Monastery – Mount St. Sepulchre.
Edmunds, John S. *s.t.* '76 (FgM) Silver Spring, MD MISSIONARY SERVANTS OF THE MOST HOLY TRINITY; Silver Spring, MD; Silver Spring, MD Missionary Servants of the Most Holy Trinity (Trinity Missions).
Edmunds, John S. *s.t.* '76 (WDC)[O] Silver Spring, MD Missionary Servants of the Most Holy Trinity; [O] Riverdale, MD Holy Spirit Missionary Cenacle.
Edney, Mark *o.p.* '97 (NO)[U] Metairie, LA International Dominican Foundation; New Orleans, LA St. Dominic.
Edogwo, Linus V. '86 (NEW) Newark, NJ St. Mary's.
Edomobi, Eustace '75 (NEW) Maplewood, NJ St. Joseph's.
Eduarte, Edmund P. '93 (GAL) Freeport, TX St. Mary: Star of the Sea.
Eduvala, Andre *o.f.m.cap.* '04 (AGN)[F] Agana Heights, GU St. Fidelis Friary.
Edwards, Brice *c.p.* '70 (SCR)[L] Scranton, PA Saint Ann's Passionist Monastery.
Edwards, Charles A. '86 (SFD) Highland, IL St. Paul.
Edwards, Cyril D. '84 (SCR) Scranton, PA Mary, Mother of God Parish.
Edwards, Dale '83 (FWT) Retired.
Edwards, David A. '02 (BEA) Diocesan College of Consultors; Beaumont, TX St. Jude Thaddeus.
Edwards, Guy F. '85 (OG) Dannemora, NY St. Joseph.
Edwards, J. Daniel '94 (LAF) Lafayette, LA St. Jules.
Edwards, James T. '76 (STL) Retired.
Edwards, John H. *s.j.* '54 (DAL)[D] Dallas, TX Jesuit College Preparatory School.
Edwards, Michael W. '79 (PMB) Vero Beach, FL St. Helen; Propagation of the Faith & Missionary Cooperative Plan; Assessors; Consultors; Ex Officio; Vicars Forane.
Edwards, Philip *o.s.b.* '67 (LA)[P] Valyermo, CA St. Andrew's Abbey; [V] Valyermo, CA St. Andrew's Abbey Retreat Center (All Groups).
Edwards, Robert R. '81 (Y) Leetonia, OH St. Patrick; Salem, OH St. Paul; Charismatic Prayer Group.
Edwards, Tom J. '90 (OAK)[K] Oakland, CA Bishop Begin Villa.
Edyk, Rev. Msgr. Eugene '61 (DET) Retired.
Effiong, Noel *m.s.p.* '89 (RVC) West Hempstead, NY St. Thomas, the Apostle.
Efiong, Emmanuel '89 (CHR) Pickens, SC Holy Cross.
Efodigbue, Ayo E. *m.s.p.* '94 (BR) Donaldsonville, LA St. Catherine of Siena; Presbyteral Council.
Eftink, Rev. Msgr. Edward M. '66 (SPC) Retired.
Eftink, Glenn A. '93 (SPC) Charleston, MO St. Henry; Sikeston, MO St. Francis Xavier's.
Egan, Arthur B. '57 (CLV) Avon, OH St. Mary of the Immaculate Conception Retired.
Egan, Brennan *o.f.m.* (FR)[F] Onset, MA St. Joseph Friary–Franciscan Friars.
Egan, Rev. Msgr. Eugene E. '54 (WIN) Retired.
Egan, Gerard P. '65 (CHI) Other Assignments.
Egan, Harvey D. *s.j.* '69 (BO)[U] Newton, MA The Jesuit Community at Boston College.
Egan, Patrick '66 (LAN)[P] Ann Arbor, MI Catholic Men's Movement.
Egan, Patrick *o.s.b.* '08 (BIR) Cullman, AL Sacred Heart; [E] Cullman, AL St. Bernard Abbey.
Egan, Philip '82 (KC) Clinton, MO Holy Rosary; Deans.
Egan, Robert J. *s.j.* '62 (SEA)[M] Seattle, WA Arrupe Jesuit Community at Seattle University.
Egan, Robert John *s.j.* '73 (SJ)[M] Los Gatos, CA Sacred Heart Jesuit Center.
Egan, Robert M. *c.s.v.* '78 (CHI)[D] Arlington Heights, IL St. Viator High School; [N] Arlington Heights Viatorian Province Center–Clerics of St. Viator.
Egan, Thomas F. '75 (WOR) Leominster, MA Holy Family of Nazareth.
Egan, Thomas R. *m.m.* '64 (FgM) Maryknoll, NY MARYKNOLL.
Egargo, Fernando '92 (RVC) West Hempstead, NY St. Thomas, the Apostle.
Egbe, Paul '95 (MOB) Ozark, AL St. John.
Egbeji, Jude '89 (NY) Sleepy Hollow, NY St. Teresa of Avila.
Egbers, James B. '96 (COV) Alexandria, KY St. Mary of the Assumption.
Eggert, Rev. Msgr. Francis '58 (SFE) Albuquerque, NM Our Lady of Fatima; College of Consultors; Presbyteral Council of the Archdiocese of Santa Fe.
Egging, Martin L. '93 (GI) Loup City, NE St. Josaphat's; Ravenna, NE Our Lady of Lourdes; Diocesan Consultors.
Eggleston, Earl '96 (SD) San Diego, CA Our Lady of Angels Catholic Parish; Liturgy and Spirituality.
Eggleton, Christopher T. '88 (FgM) Metairie, LA St. Martin de Porres Province (Southern Dominican Province).
Eggleton, Christopher T. *o.p.* '88 (NO) New Orleans, LA St. Anthony of Padua; [R] Metairie, LA Dominican Friars, Southern Dominican Province of St. Martin de Porres; [R] Metairie, LA Southern Dominican Foundation; [U] Metairie, LA Southern Dominican Foundation.
Eggleton, Christopher T. *o.p.* (NY)[HH] New York, NY St. Thomas Aquinas Foundation.
Eghiabumhe, Fabian '04 (NY) Beacon, NY St. John the Evangelist.
Egitto, Philip J. '88 (ORL) Daytona Beach, FL Our Lady of Lourdes.
Egloff, Adolph '40 (EVN) Retired.
Ego, Anthony M. '85 (PEO) Milan, IL St. Ambrose.

Egubuogu, Martin (BRK) Elmhurst, NY Ascension.
Eguiarte, Enrique A. *o.a.r.* '85 (NEW) Centro Guadalupe.
Eguiguren, Jose Martin *s.s.s.* '61 (CGS) Caguas, PR Santisimo Sacramento.
Eguino, Desiderio *o.p.* '78 (MIA) Miami, FL St. Dominic; [H] Miami, FL Dominican Fathers of Miami, Inc.
Ehalt, William L. '99 (IND) Spencer, IN St. Jude Catholic Church, Spencer, Inc.
Ehiahuruike, Stephen *s.d.v.* '04 (NEW) Palisades Park, NJ St. Nicholas.
Ehiemere, Michael '81 (CHY) Sheridan, WY Holy Name.
Ehinack, Benedict '10 (OAK) Oakland, CA St. Lawrence O'Toole–St. Cyril of Jerusalem.
Ehli, Joshua J. '09 (BIS) Dickinson, ND Queen of Peace Church; [C] Dickinson, ND Trinity High School.
Ehmke, Matthew '70 (STP) New Hope, MN St. Therese Care Center & Residence.
Ehr, Donald J. *s.v.d.* '55 (CHI) Chicago, IL St. Anselm.
Ehrhardt, Joseph B. *o.f.m.* '67 (FgM) New York, NY Holy Name Province.
Ehrich, John D. '00 (PHX) Phoenix, AZ St. Thomas the Apostle Roman Catholic Parish; Presbyteral Council; Defenders of the Bond; Medical Ethics Board.
Ehrman, Dale W. '90 (LFT) Cicero, IN Sacred Heart of Jesus; Vicar for Clergy; [I] Noblesville, IN Hamilton County Catholic High School Corporation, Blessed Theodore Guerin High School; Associate Directors.
Ehrman, Terrence P. *c.s.c.* '00 (FTW)[H] Notre Dame Congregation of Holy Cross, United States Province of Priests & Brothers.
Ehwald, Joseph A. '62 (COL) Retired.
Eichenberger, Thomas P. '76 (MIL) Mequon, WI St. Francis Borgia.
Eichenseer, Rev. Msgr. Donald W. '61 (BEL) Defensores Vinculi Retired.
Eichhoff, Paul E. '70 (TLS) Diocesan Senators.
Eichhoff, Paul '70 (TLS) Claremore, OK St. Cecilia; Diocesan Consultors.
Eichhurst, Franklin (Duane) *o.f.m.cap.* '57 (TUC) Tucson, AZ Saint John the Evangelist Roman Catholic Parish – Tucson.
Eichner, Philip K. *s.m.* '66 (RVC)[D] Uniondale, NY Kellenberg Memorial High School.
Eichor, Barnabas *o.f.m.cap.* (SAL) Hays, KS St. Joseph Parish.
Eickhoff, Jeffrey R. '95 (LIN)[A] Seward, NE St. Gregory the Great Seminary; Pro Life.
Eickhoff, Matthew '89 (LIN) Brainard, NE Holy Trinity; Commission for Sacred Liturgy and Sacred Music; Engaged Encounter; Evangelization Office; Evangelization Committee; Family Life Office; Marriage Encounter; Natural Family Planning; PREP; Teens Encounter Christ (TEC); Ecumenical Affairs, Commission for.
Eickhoff, Stephen '10 (JOL) Hinsdale, IL St. Isaac Jogues.
Eid, Elie '07 (NTN) Plymouth, MI St. Michael.
Eifler, John G. '61 (L) Retired.
Eikhuemelo, Bernadine '96 (STA) Jacksonville, FL St. Joseph's.
Eilen, Allan Paul '09 (STP) Edina, MN Our Lady of Grace.
Eilerman, Craig R. '87 (COL) Lancaster, OH St. Mary.
Eilers, Brian Joseph '04 (AUS)[L] San Marcos, TX Texas State University, H.L. Grant Catholic Student Center.
Eilers, Brian '04 (AUS) San Marcos.
Eilert, Rev. Msgr. Edward J. '64 (NEW)[L] Rutherford, NJ St. John Vianney Residence for Priests Retired.
Eimer, Frank J. '58 (L) Retired.
Eiroa, Andres '88 (POD)[D] Mayaguez, PR Opus Dei (Prelature of the Holy Cross and Opus Dei); Mayaguez.
Eis, Charles R. '66 (SPK) Retired.
Eisele, Francis X. '54 (RVC) East Rockaway, NY St. Raymond's.
Eisele, James F. '88 (LAN) Grand Ledge, MI St. Michael.
Eisele, Paul F. '68 (SC) Alton, IA St. Mary's; Hospers, IA St. Anthony's.
Eisemann, Frederick F. '53 (ROC) Rochester, NY Holy Cross Retired.
Eisweirth, Thomas C. '74 (Y) Warren, OH Blessed Sacrament.
Eivers, Rev. Msgr. Michael J. '55 (MIA) Retired.
Ejaidu, Cyril Ngbede '95 (AUS) Waco, TX St. John the Baptist.
Ejike, John '78 (FAR) Rugby, ND St. Theresa, Little Flower Church of Rugby.
Ejimadu, Festus N. '93 (DET) Farmington, MI St. Gerald.
Ejimofor, Francis *s.s.sp.* '90 (TOL)[F] Toledo, OH Mercy Medical Center St. Vincent.
Ejimofor, Joseph '77 (LR) Benton, AR Our Lady of Fatima.
Ejiofo, Lawrence O. (MAN) Dartmouth–Hitchcock Medical Center.
Ekada, Santulino *o.c.d.* '03 (MIL)[P] Milwaukee Provincial Offices – Discalced Carmelites.
Ekaitis, Timothy M. '07 (MAR) Norway, MI St. Mary; Vulcan, MI St. Barbara.
Ekanem, Peter Cimbert '98 (NY) Garnerville, NY St. Gregory Barbarigo.
Ekdahl, Kenneth W. '91 (TR) Keyport, NJ Jesus the Lord.
Eke, Anselm *m.s.p.* '92 (BEA) Orange, TX St. Therese.
Eke, Casimir *c.s.sp.* '74 (CHI) Blue Island, IL St. Isidore.
Eke, Peter O. '97 (GLD) Onaway, MI St. Monica; Onaway, MI St. Paul; Adjutant Judicial Vicar.
Eke, Rafael E. '01 (SAT) Army Chaplains; Military Chaplains.
Ekechukwu, Alexander *c.s.sp.* '73 (MIA) Miami, FL St. Agatha; FIU–University Park; Nigerian Apostolate.
Ekeh, Paul '97 (PBL) Rocky Ford, CO St. Peter.
Ekekwe, Kenneth '00 (BUR) Bethel, VT Our Lady of the Valley Parish.
Ekemgba, Fidelis '81 (SCR)[H] Williamsport, PA Divine Providence Hospital of the Sisters of Christian Charity.
Ekenachi, Donatus '83 (LA) Santa Clarita, CA Our Lady of Perpetual Help.
Ekeocha, James M. '07 (AUS) Temple, TX St. Luke; Associate Directors.
Ekete, Damian '95 (NY) Bronx, NY Holy Spirit.
Ekiert, Ireneusz *o.ss.t.* '00 (BAL)[Q] Diocese of Trenton, NJ.
Ekiert, Ireneusz *o.ss.t* '00 (TR)[T] West Long Branch, NJ Catholic Center at Monmouth University; Asbury Park, NJ Our Lady of Mt. Carmel.
Ekka, Alexuis '81 (JC) Palmyra, MO St. Joseph.
Ekka, Louis T. '89 (LAN) Flushing, MI St. Robert; Montrose, MI Good Shepherd.
Ekka, Ranjan Prekash *t.o.r.* '99 (WH) Moundsville, WV St. Francis Xavier's.
Ekpo, Joseph '86 (CHI) Bellwood, IL St. Simeon; [D] Oak Park, IL Fenwick High School.
Ekwoanya, John C. '97 (NU) Kandiyohi, MN St. Patrick; Kandiyohi, MN St. Thomas More.
Ekwugha, Francis X. '82 (BAK) Council of Priests and Diocesan Consultors; Board of Education; Bend, OR St. Francis of Assisi.
El–Khalli, Georges Y. '81 (SAM) Religious Education; Presbyteral Council; Protopresbyters (Deans); College of Consultors; Jamaica Plain, MA Our Lady of the Cedars of Lebanon.
Elam, Raymond R. *o.s.a.* '70 (HON) Hawi, HI Sacred Heart.
Elambasseril, George '92 (SYM) Southfield, MI St. Thomas Syro–Malabar Catholic Church, Detroit.
Elambassery, Xavier '66 (SJP) Latrobe, PA Assumption of B.V.M.; Arbitration Board; Presbyters.
Elamparayil, Joseph *o.c.d.* '96 (ARL) Falls Church, VA St. James.
Elamparayil, Joseph '96 (SYM) Darnestown, MD St. Jude Syro–Malabar Catholic Mission of Northern Virginia; Falls Church, VA St. Alphonsa Syro–Malabar Mission of Richmond.
Elanjileth, J. Matthew '45 (PIT) Retired.
Elanjimattathil, Michael *c.m.i.* '96 (SAL) Oakley, KS St. Joseph Parish; Oakley, KS St. Paul Parish.
Elavunkal, Thomas *c.m.i.* '97 (SHP) Shreveport, LA St. Joseph.
Elayidathamadam, Mathew *m.s.f.s.* '96 (TYL)[C] Whitehouse, TX The Missionaries of St. Francis de Sales.
El Basha, Assaad *m.l.m.* '92 (OLL) Lewisville, TX Our Lady of Lebanon Maronite Catholic Church; [A] Houston, TX The Congregation of Maronite Lebanese Missionaries.
Elbert, Kevin P. '10 (CLV) Hudson, OH St. Mary.
Elbert, William '73 (MIA) North Miami Beach, FL St. Lawrence; Spiritual Moderators.
Elder, Gregory '06 (SB) Ecumenical Office; Murrieta, CA St. Martha.
Elder, John W. *s.j.* '65 (BO)[U] Weston, MA Campion Health Center, Inc.
Elder, Leonard F. *s.c.j.* '96 (JKS) Holly Springs, MS St. Joseph; [E] Nesbit, MS St. Michael Community House.
Elder, William S. '81 (NY) New York, NY Our Lady of Good Counsel; Judicial Vicar; Judges.
Eldred, Richard W. '99 (IND) Bedford, IN St. Vincent de Paul Catholic Church, Bedford, Inc.; Mitchell, IN St. Mary of the Assumption Catholic Church, Mitchell, Inc.
Eldredge, Richard *t.o.r.* '78 (FWT) Diocesan Pastoral Council; Colleyville, TX Good Shepherd; Consultors.
Eldridge, Darren J. '07 (LAF) Chataignier, LA Our Lady of Mount Carmel; Eunice, LA St. Mathilda.
Eldridge, Francis *s.a.* '77 (LA) Los Angeles, CA St. Odilia.
Eldridge, Francis *s.a.* '77 (NY)[DD] Garrison Graymoor Ecumenical and Interreligious Institute.
Eldridge, Richard *t.o.r.* '78 (FWT) Presbyteral Council.
Eldringhoff, John P. '68 (KC) Retired.
Elejalde, Manuel *c.p.* '49 (SJN) Carolina, PR Nuestra Senora de la Piedad.
Eles, Joseph '65 (PSC) Retired.
Elewaut, Thomas J. '86 (LA) Ventura, CA San Buenaventura Mission.
Elford, Hugh Ricardo *c.ss.r.* '64 (TUC)[G] Cortaro, AZ Redemptorist Society of Arizona Desert House of Prayer.
Elhajj, Simon '10 (SAM) Carnegie, PA Our Lady of Victory.
Eli, Jude *o.p.* '76 (OAK)[L] Oakland, CA Order of Preachers (Province of the Most Holy Name of Jesus – Western Dominican Province); Oakland, CA.
Eli, Jude *o.p.* '76 (LA) Los Angeles, CA St. Dominic.
Elia, Chorbishop Faouzi '77 (OLL) Peoria, IL St. Sharbel Maronite Catholic Church; [F] Saint Louis, MO Eparchial Endowments; Pastoral Center; College of Consultors; Office for Immigration; Presbyteral Council.
Elia, Victor *c.m.* '57 (NY) New York, NY Holy Agony; [DD] New York, NY Vincentian Fathers; New York, NY.
Eliaona, David *c.s.c.* '08 (FTW)[A] Notre Dame, IN Moreau Seminary.
Elias, Benjamin '97 (BRK) Brooklyn, NY St. Mary Mother of Jesus.
Elias, Mario '93 (SD) San Diego, CA Saint Columba Catholic Parish.
Elias–Haddix, Ralph *o.c.d.* '98 (MIL) Milwaukee, WI St. Florian.
Elie, Matthew '05 (BEL) Belleville, IL Blessed Sacrament.
Elis, Patrick H. '69 (BUF) Absent on Leave.
Elis, Tomas Alfonso '70 (LA) Retired.
Eliscar, Joseph LaMartine *m.s.* '10 (ATL) Marietta, GA St. Ann.
Elizardo, Pedro T. '01 (CC) Office of Worship.
Elizardo, Pedro (Pete) T. '01 (CC) Corpus Christi, TX Corpus Christi Cathedral.
Elizondo, Ernesto '00 (AUS) Manor, TX St. Joseph.
Elizondo, Ruben *o.m.i.* '62 (FgM) Washington, DC AMERICAN OBLATE MISSIONS.
Elizondo, Virgil '63 (SAT)[A] San Antonio, TX Assumption Seminary; San Antonio, TX St. Rose of Lima.
Elizondo, Virgilio P. (FTW)[B] University of Notre Dame Du Lac.
Elkhoury, Armando '04 (OLL) Eparchial Webmaster.
El Khoury, Pierre '98 (OLL)[A] Houston, TX The Congregation of Maronite Lebanese Missionaries; Houston, TX Our Lady of the Cedars Maronite Catholic Church.
Elkin, Rev. Msgr. Frederic F. '77 (SY) Military Chaplains Retired.
Elko, Joseph M. '70 (HRT) New Haven, CT Saint Martin de Porres.
Eller, Hugh *o.f.m.* '53 (PAT)[N] Butler, NJ St. Anthony Friary.
Ellerman, Thomas E. *s.m.* '67 (OAK)[L] Berkeley, CA Marist Fathers and Brothers.
Ellias, John J. '64 (ALT) Retired.
Ellickal, Saji *m.c.b.s.* '00 (MEM) Memphis, TN St. Louis.
Elliot, Joseph *c.ss.r.* '49 (STL)[O] Liguori, MO St. Clement Health Care Center Retired.
Elliot, Thomas *c.s.c.* '67 (BGP)[P] Wilton, CT Lourdes Health Care Center, Inc.
Elliot, Rev. Msgr. William '60 (CLV) Retired.
Elliott, Patrick H. '00 (SLC) Ogden, UT Holy Family LLC 205.
Elliott, Roger *c.p.* '58 (SCR)[L] Scranton, PA Saint Ann's Passionist Monastery.
Elliott, Ron '73 (OM)[G] Omaha, NE Archbishop Bergan Mercy Medical Center.
Elliott, Ronald J. '02 (KC) Blue Springs, MO St. John La Lande; Consultors; Permanent Diaconate.
Elliott, Thomas A. '99 (LR) North Little Rock, AR Immaculate Conception.
Elliott, Thomas F. *c.s.c.* '67 (FTW)[H] Notre Dame Congregation of Holy Cross, United States Province of Priests & Brothers.
Elliott, Thomas *c.s.c.* '67 (BGP)[P] Wilton, CT School Sisters of Notre Dame.
Elliott, Timothy P. '82 (STL) Lake Saint Louis, MO Saint Gianna.
Elliott, Trumie C. '88 (L) Springfield, KY St. Dominic.
Elliott, W. Gregg '00 (TLS) Retired.
Elliott, William J. *s.j.* '61 (WDC)[E] North Bethesda, MD Georgetown Preparatory School.
Elliott, Rev. Msgr. William '60 (SD) Retired.
Elliott, Zachary *o.f.m.* '08 (SP) Tampa, FL Sacred Heart.
Ellis, Alfred J. *o.s.a.* '63 (ALB) Troy, NY St. Augustine.
Ellis, John H.R. '91 (VEN) Retired.
Ellis, Kail C. *o.s.a.* '67 (PH)[C] Villanova University; [Y] Villanova, PA St. John Stone Friary.
Ellis, Matthew '88 (DET) Shelby Twp., MI St. Therese of Lisieux.
Ellison, Joseph T. '95 (SB) Murrieta, CA St. Martha.
Ellorin, Raymund '91 (HON) Honokaa, HI Our Lady of Lourdes.
Ellos, William J. *s.j.* '68 (MIL)[P] Milwaukee Jesuit Provincial Office, Wisconsin Province.
Elmer, Gregory *o.s.b.* '76 (LA)[P] Valyermo, CA St. Andrew's Abbey.
Elmer, John *o.f.m.conv.* '73 (IND) Clarksville, IN St.

Anthony of Padua Catholic Church, Clarksville, Inc.; [K] Mount St. Francis, IN Development Office.
Elmer, Richard J. *c.s.b.* '57 (DET)[E] Novi, MI Catholic Central High School.
Elmer, Timothy S. '73 (SY)[F] Syracuse, NY Bishop Joseph T. O'Keefe, Inc.; [U] Syracuse, NY David W. Barry Foundation; Chancellor; Management Team; Presbyteral Council; Judicial Vicar; Vicar for Administration; Building Commission; Clerical Fund Society of the Roman Catholic Diocese of Syracuse; Priests' Personnel Committee; [U] Syracuse, NY Grimes Foundation; Board of Diocesan Consultors; Finance Committee; Contact; Special Assignment; Administration; Syracuse, NY Blessed Sacrament.
Elorriaga, Javier *o.ss.t.* '68 (SJN) Bayamon, PR Ascension Del Senor.
Elsasser, Thomas G. '88 (CLV) Mentor, OH St. Mary of the Assumption.
Elsbernd, James H. '90 (CIN) On Special and Archdiocesan Assignment; Hamilton, OH St. Joseph.
Elser, William '86 (LR) Hot Springs Village, AR Sacred Heart of Jesus.
Elshoff, Matthew G. *o.f.m.cap.* '82 (SFR)[N] Burlingame, CA Capuchin Provincial House.
Elshoff, Matthew *o.f.m.cap.* '82 (NY)[DD] White Plains, NY Capuchin Friars of North America.
Elskamp, Frederick J. '62 (JC) Diaconate Office; California, MO Annunciation; Tipton, MO St. Andrew.
Elsner, Martin L. *s.j.* '62 (SAT)[A] San Antonio, TX Assumption Seminary.
Elston, Joseph G. '85 (SCR)[C] Wilkes–Barre, PA Holy Redeemer High School; On Special or Other Diocesan Assignment; Ministry with Deaf and Hard of Hearing.
Elue, Callistus I. (GB) Green Bay, WI St. Patrick; Green Bay, WI Annunciation of the Blessed Virgin Mary; Green Bay, WI St. Joseph; Green Bay, WI St. Jude.
Elukunnel, Joseph Dominic *s.a.c.* '80 (MIL)[P] Milwaukee, WI Pallotti House.
Eluvathingal, Jose *s.a.c.* '85 (MIL)[P] Milwaukee, WI Pallotti House.
Ely, Peter B. *s.j.* '69 (SEA)[A] Seattle, WA Seattle University; [M] Seattle, WA Arrupe Jesuit Community at Seattle University.
Elyse, Esteker *s.m.m.* '64 (MIA) Miami, FL St. Mary's Cathedral.
Elzi, Joseph *c.m.* '52 (CHL) Charlotte, NC Our Lady of Guadalupe Church.
Emagalit, Zeverin '72 (NY)[W] Poughkeepsie, NY St. Francis Hospital; Poughkeepsie, NY St. Francis Hospital.
Emanuel, John '92 (TUC) Retired.
Emanuel, Steve (OM)[B] Bellevue, NE Daniel J. Gross Catholic High School of Omaha.
Emechete, Innocent '72 (MO) Navy Reserve Chaplains.
Emechete, Innocent '72 (SB) Victorville, CA Federal Corrections Institute.
Emeh, Augustine '90 (BRK) Lutheran Medical Center.
Emeh, Martin C. (BAL)[U] Baltimore, MD African Conference of Catholic Clergy & Religious in the United States, Inc.
Emeh, Martins '02 (RCK) Geneva, IL St. Peter; Vice Chancellor; Special Assignment.
Emeli, Edwin '88 (TUC)[D] Tucson, AZ Carondelet St. Mary's Hospital.
Emelu, Maurice (CLV) Cleveland, OH Our Lady of Peace.
Emen, Austin (BRK) Brooklyn, NY Holy Name.
Emerick, Stephen J. '58 (CIN) Retired.
Emerson, George F. '56 (BO) Norwood, MA St. Timothy; Senior Priests.; Presbyteral Council; College of Consultors Retired.
Emery, Rev. Msgr. Robert E. '87 (NEW) South Orange, NJ Our Lady of Sorrows; Adjutant Judicial Vicar; Presbyteral Council; Metropolitan Tribunal; Archdiocesan Judges.
Emezie, Charles '83 (SFS)[D] Aberdeen, SD Avera St. Luke's; [D] Aberdeen, SD Avera St. Luke's.
Emille, Cyprien (NY) Bronx, NY Our Lady of Grace.
Emmanuel, Joseph A. '81 (NY) Tuxedo, NY Our Lady of Mt. Carmel.
Emmons, Rayford E. '74 (PH) Philadelphia, PA Our Lady of Hope.
Empereur, James L. *s.j.* '65 (SAT) San Antonio, TX St. Matthew's.
Emrisek, Gene *o.f.m.cap.* '68 (DEN) Denver, CO Sacred Heart; [N] Denver, CO San Antonio Friary.
Emusa, Peter '97 (LAF) Carencro, LA Our Lady of the Assumption; Scott, LA Saint Martin de Porres.
Encarnacion, Ramon (SJN)[G] Guaynabo, PR Opus Dei.
Encinares, Rev. Msgr. Cesar E. '77 (SB) Redlands, CA The Holy Name of Jesus Catholic Community, Inc.
Endejan, John '57 (MIL) Retired.
Enderle, Gilbert *c.ss.r.* '62 (STL)[O] Liguori, MO Liguori Mission House/Redemptorists.
Enderle, Gilbert *c.ss.r.* '62 (DEN)[N] Denver The Redemptorists/Denver Province.
Enderlin, R. E. '69 (PEO) Retired.
Enderlin, Ronald '69 (PEO) Lacon, IL Immaculate Conception.
Endiape, Dario '93 (MET) Milltown, NJ Our Lady of Lourdes.
Endres, David J. '09 (CIN)[B] Cincinnati, OH Mount St. Mary's Seminary of the West.
Endres, Gilbert J. '52 (STP) Retired.
Endres, James F. '82 (PH)[T] Warminster, PA Regina Coeli Residence for Priests; On Special or Other Archdiocesan Assignment.
Endres, John C. *s.j.* '76 (OAK)[A] Berkeley, CA Jesuit School of Theology of Santa Clara University (Berkeley, California Campus); [L] Berkeley, CA Jesuit Fathers and Brothers.
Endres, William '69 (ROC) Scottsville, NY St. Mary of the Assumption; Strong Health System; East Rochester, NY St. Jerome; Caledonia, NY St. Columba; Churchville, NY St. Vincent De Paul.
Endress, James '60 (EVN) Retired.
Ene, Herbert '97 (MEM) Memphis, TN St. Paul The Apostle.
Eneh, Barry C. '91 (MO) DEPARTMENT OF VETERANS AFFAIRS HOSPITALS AND CHAPLAINS.
Enelichi, Alphonsus I. *m.s.p.* '90 (GAL) Barrett Station, TX St. Martin de Porres.
Enemali, Aloysius (BRK) Hollis, NY St. Gerard Majella.
Engbarth, David R. '76 (RCK) Aurora, IL Our Lady of Good Counsel.
Engebretson, Aaron *s.j.* (SEA)[C] Tacoma, WA Bellarmine Preparatory School.
Engel, Paul *o.f.m.cap.* '64 (NY)[DD] White Plains, NY St. Conrad Friary.
Engel, Paul '55 (ALB) Delanson, NY Our Lady of Fatima Retired.
Engelbrecht, Rev. Msgr. Henry H. '68 (NO) New Orleans, LA Ochsner Baptist Medical Center.
Engelbrecht, S. Stephen '00 (PEO) Andalusia, IL St. Patrick Church.
Engelhardt, Charles F. *o.s.f.s.* '77 (PH)[Y] Wyndmoor, PA Villa de Sales Oblate Residence.
Engelhardt, Rev. Msgr. Herbert G. '40 (BUF) Retired.
Engelhart, Henry R. '63 (BEL) Retired.
Engels, Richard J. '60 (WIN) Retired.
Engen, Bruce '89 (DUL) Pine River, MN Our Lady of Lourdes Retired.
Engh, Michael E. *s.j.* '81 (SJ)[B] Santa Clara University.
England, Barry C. '68 (FTW) Mishawaka, IN St. Bavo.
Engle, Richard F. '56 (COL) Zaleski, OH St. Sylvester Retired.
Engler, Clarence A. *m.m.* '59 (FgM) Maryknoll, NY MARYKNOLL.
Engler, Ernest J. '51 (DUB) Retired.
Engler, John Chapin '07 (WH) White Sulphur Springs, WV St. Catherine of Siena; White Sulphur Springs, WV St. Charles Borromeo.
Engler, Simon Mary *t.o.r.* '49 (ALT)[G] Loretto, PA St. Francis Friary at Mount Assisi.
Englert, Michael *o.f.m.conv.* '89 (PMB) Port St. Lucie, FL St. Lucie.
English, James M. *s.j.* '66 (PH)[Y] Loyola Center and Manresa Hall.
English, Joseph *o.f.m.cap.* '90 (AGN) Agana Heights, GU Our Lady of the Blessed Sacrament; [F] Agana Heights, GU St. Fidelis Friary; Archdiocesan Presbyteral Council.
English, Paul F. (ROC)[K] Rochester, NY Basilian Fathers.
English, Robert K. '88 (OM) Omaha, NE Mary Our Queen.
English, Rev. Msgr. Tobias P. '63 (LA) Pasadena, CA St. Andrew Retired.
English, William J. '60 (BO) Senior Priests.; Waltham, MA Our Lady, Comforter of the Afflicted Retired.
English, Rev. Msgr. William J. '69 (WDC) Potomac, MD Our Lady of Mercy.
Enke, Rev. Msgr. Paul P. '72 (COL) Granville, OH St. Edward the Confessor.
Enlow, Rev. Msgr. Leo J. '75 (SFD) Quincy, IL St. Peter.
Enman, Frederick *s.j.* '88 (BO)[U] Newton, MA The Jesuit Community at Boston College.
Enneking, Marvin '91 (SCL) Greenwald, MN St. Andrew's; Greenwald, MN St. John's; Melrose, MN St. Mary's; Greenwald, MN St. Michael's; Adjutant Judicial Vicar; Judges; Deans.
Enneking, Thomas A. *o.s.c.* '84 (FgM)[F] Phoenix, AZ Crosier Provincial House Province of St. Odilia; Phoenix, AZ CROSIER FATHERS MISSIONS; Phoenix, AZ.
Enneking, Thomas *o.s.c.* '84 (CHI)[N] Chicago, IL Crosier Community of Chicago.
Ennis, Timothy *o.carm.* '02 (ALB) Troy, NY St. Joseph.
Ennis, William '64 (ORL) Orlando, FL Holy Family.
Enoh, Uwem '10 (OWN) Paducah, KY Rosary Chapel; Paducah, KY St. Francis de Sales.
Enright, Edward J. *o.s.a.* '73 (BO)[C] Our Mother of Good Counsel Monastery.
Enright, James C. '69 (BUF) Retired.
Enright, Michael P. '84 (CHI) Chicago, IL St. Paul.
Enright, Thomas M. '66 (CHI) Niles, IL Our Lady of Ransom.
Enriquez, Alex '85 (TR) Hopewell, NJ St. Alphonsus.
Enriquez, David '06 (FRS) Orange Cove, CA St. Isidore the Farmer.
Enriquez, Juan '80 (LA) Lynwood, CA St. Philip Neri.
Enriquez, Miguel '08 (DEN) Aurora, CO St. Therese.
Enriquez, Rean F. '93 (MO) Navy Chaplains.
Ensey, Eric S. '95 (SCR) Unassigned or Leave of Absence.
Enslin, John *s.j.* '11 (WOR)[N] Worcester, MA Jesuits of the Holy Cross, Inc.
Enslow, Batholomew *s.s.j.* '49 (BLX) Pass Christian, MS Our Mother of Mercy.
Ensman, Raymond E. '66 (TOL) Retired.
Enverga, Edgardo *c.r.m.* '86 (CHR) Moncks Corner, SC St. Philip Benizi.
Enyan–Boadu, Peter '84 (ROC) Rochester, NY St. Lawrence.
Enyiaka, Canice '07 (PBL) Delta, CO St. Michael.
Enzeani, Fidelis (NY) Nyack, NY St. Ann.
Enzler, Rev. Msgr. John J. '73 (WDC) Staff; Vicar of Development.
Enzler, Rev. Msgr. John '73 (WDC)[I] Washington, DC Catholic Charities of the Archdiocese of Washington, Inc.; [I] Washington, DC The Catholic Charities Foundation of the Archdiocese of Washington.
Enzweiler, Rev. Msgr. Donald A. '87 (COV) Covington, KY Holy Cross.
Enzweiler, Raymond N. '06 (COL)[A] Columbus, OH Pontifical College Josephinum; [A] Columbus, OH Pontifical College Josephinum.
Ephraim, John B. '99 (RVC) Roslyn, NY St. Francis Hospital.
Eppenbrock, Donald '59 (SAG) Port Sanilac, MI St. Mary Retired.
Epperley, Wayne *c.s.sp.* '83 (SB) Hemet, CA Our Lady of the Valley.
Epperson, Frank '01 (SR) Ukiah, CA St. Mary of the Angels; Deans; Board of Consultors; Priests' Council; Clergy Personnel Committee.
Epping, Robert L. *c.s.c.* '70 (COS) Colorado Springs, CO Sacred Heart; Metro–South Deanery (Colorado Springs); Presbyteral Council; College of Consultors; Vicars Forane.
Era, John *c.m.* (CHI)[N] Chicago DePaul Vincentian Residence.
Eraly, Mathew '75 (MO) DEPARTMENT OF VETERANS AFFAIRS HOSPITALS AND CHAPLAINS.
Eraly, Mathew '87 (NEW) East Orange, NJ Veterans Administration Hospital.
Eraly, Matthew '75 (NEW) Livingston, NJ St. Philomena.
Erb, Francis J. '54 (ROC) Retired.
Erbacher, Joseph F. '72 (EVN) Loogootee, IN St. John; Loogootee, IN St. Martin; Loogootee, IN St. Joseph; Loogootee, IN St. Mary's; Defender of the Bond; Diocesan Council of Priests.
Erbacher, William J. '87 (ARL) On Leave of Absence.
Erbland, Philip N. *m.m.* '66 (NY)[DD] Maryknoll Maryknoll Fathers and Brothers.
Ercolano, Anthony S. '73 (BRK) On Leave/Unassigned.
Erdei, Joseph J. *o.s.b.m.* '58 (PSC)[A] Matawan, NJ Basilian Fathers of Mariapoch.
Erdeljac, Frank G. '83 (PIT) Retired.
Erdle, Thomas M. '55 (ROC) Retired.
Erdlen, Harry J. *o.s.a.* '57 (PH)[F] Malvern, PA Malvern Preparatory School for Boys.
Erdlen, Harry J. *o.s.a.* '57 (PH)[Y] Malvern, PA Augustinian Friars (O.S.A.).
Erestain, Alfonso E. '64 (MO) DEPARTMENT OF VETERANS AFFAIRS HOSPITALS AND CHAPLAINS.
Erhart, Henry J. *s.j.* '55 (PH)[Y] Loyola Center and Manresa Hall.
Ericksen, Matthew '09 (SAV) Augusta, GA St. Joseph.
Erickson, David '98 (CHY) Lander, WY Holy Rosary; St. Joseph's Society for Priests (Clergy Mutual Benefit Society).
Erickson, John Paul '06 (STP) Worship.
Erickson, Matthew *o.p.* '90 (WDC)[B] Washington, DC Dominican House of Studies.
Erickson, Philip Lee '95 (L) Louisville, KY Our Lady of Mount Carmel; Louisville, KY St. Thomas More; Adjutant Judicial Vicar.
Erickson, Richard M. '85 (MO) Air Force Reserve Chaplains.
Erickson, Robert E. *c.s.v.* '67 (CHI)[N] Arlington Heights, IL Viatorian Province Center–Clerics of St. Viator.
Erickson, Robert J. '58 (SB) Elected Members Retired.
Erickson, Robert L. *s.j.* '74 (GF) Hays, MT St. Paul's Indian Mission.
Erikson, Richard M. '85 (BO) Presbyteral Council; West Roxbury, MA Holy Name; Trustees.
Erlander, Michael '68 (STP) Retired.
Erlenbush, Ryan '09 (GF) Miles City, MT Sacred Heart; Diocesan Pastoral Council.
Ermatinger, Cliff O. '97 (MIL) Milwaukee, WI St. Anthony of Padua.
Ermatinger, Roderick (HEL) Kalispell, MT St. Matthew.

Ermer, James '78 (FAR) Casselton, ND St. Thomas; Casselton, ND St. Leo's Church of Casselton.
Ermis, Norman '83 (SAT) San Antonio, TX St. Margaret Mary.
Ernest, Bryan D. '82 (GI) Ogallala, NE St. Luke's; Personnel Board; Priests' Advisory Board (Presbyteral Council).
Ernest, Matthew S. '04 (NY) Graduate Studies; Scarsdale, NY Immaculate Heart of Mary.
Ernst, Anthony '98 (EVN) Fort Branch, IN Holy Cross; Haubstadt, IN SS. Peter and Paul; Diocesan Council of Priests; Fort Branch, IN St. Bernard.
Ernst, Jeff *o.f.m.cap.* '96 (SAL) Victoria, KS St. Fidelis Parish; Victoria, KS St. Ann Parish; Victoria, KS St. Boniface Parish; [D] Victoria, KS St. Fidelis Friary.
Ernst, Rev. Msgr. Norbert A. '72 (STL) St. Louis, MO St. Margaret Mary Alacoque.
Ernst, Stephen T. *s.t.* '86 (WDC)[O] Adelphi, MD Father Judge Missionary Cenacle.
Ernst, William W. '64 (IND) Retired.
Ernster, James M. '55 (MIL) Retired.
Ernster, Milo L. '55 (WIN) Retired.
Ernstmann, Rev. Msgr. Mark C. '51 (SPC) Springfield, MO Cathedral of St. Agnes Retired.
Erondu, Isaac Emeka '93 (BWN) San Benito, TX Our Lady, Queen of the Universe.
Erpelding, Edward '66 (FTW) Avilla, IN St. Mary of the Assumption.
Erpelding, Michael J. '89 (SC) Sioux City, IA St. Boniface; Sioux City, IA St. Joseph; Judges; Adjutant Judicial Vicar.
Erps, James *s.j.* '80 (LA)[C] Los Angeles, CA Jesuit Community.
Erps, James (LA)[AA] Los Angeles, CA Loyola Marymount University.
Erralcalde, P. Javier *o.de.m.* '56 (PCE) Ponce, PR Santuario San Judas Tadeo.
Errasti, Mariano *o.f.m.* '50 (SJN) San Juan, PR Resurreccion del Senor.
Errecalde, Javier *o.de.m.* '54 (SJN) San Juan, PR Nuestra Senora de la Merced.
Ertle, Thomas J. *o.p.* '56 (PRO)[O] Providence St. Thomas Aquinas Priory at Providence College.
Ertzbischoff, Edmond L. '76 (LAN) Ypsilanti, MI St. Joseph.
Eruaga, Donald *m.s.p.* '00 (NY) Yonkers, NY St. Bartholomew.
Eruo, Basil '99 (JC) Jefferson City, MO St. Peter.
Ervin, Mark W. '90 (WDC) Germantown, MD Mother Seton Parish; Charlotte Hall, MD St. Mary.
Erving, James C. *o.m.i.* '00 (BWN) Port Isabel, TX Our Lady Star of the Sea.
Erwin, Michael J. '98 (MIL) Beaver Dam, WI St. Katharine Drexel.
Erwin, Patrick O. '68 (PAT) Absent on Leave.
Ery, Sunder '00 (SFD) Effingham, IL Sacred Heart; Effingham, IL St. Anthony of Padua; Shumway, IL Annunciation.
Esarey, Brian G. '04 (IND) Leopold, IN St. Augustine Catholic Church, Leopold, Inc.; St. Croix, IN Holy Cross Catholic Church, St. Croix, Inc.; Saint Meinrad, IN St. Martin of Tours Catholic Church, Siberia, Inc.
Escalante, Agustin '88 (LAR) Zapata, TX Our Lady of Lourdes.
Escalante, Augustin '88 (SFR) On Duty Outside the Archdiocese.
Escalante, Jose Manuel '10 (WH)[O] Shepherdstown, WV Good Shepherd Catholic Campus Ministry Center; Charles Town, WV St. James.
Escalante, Peter '78 (SD) San Diego, CA Saint Joseph Cathedral Catholic Parish; Clergy Personnel Board; Presbyteral Council.
Escalante, Ronald S. '95 (ARL) Purcellville, VA St. Francis de Sales.
Escanilla, Elias F. '84 (HON) Paia, HI Holy Rosary.
Escano, Marco (P) Junction City, OR St. Rose of Lima; Junction City, OR St. Helen.
Escano, Mariano Regalado '09 (P) Eugene, OR St. Mary.
Escario, Edison (NEW) Bayonne, NJ St. Mary Star of the Sea.
Esch, Aaron J. '09 (MIL) Mequon, WI Lumen Christi; Archdiocesan Council of Priests.
Esch, Eugene *o.s.b.* '54 (B)[C] Jerome, ID Monastery of the Ascension.
Eschbach, Victor J. '72 (PH) Parkesburg, PA Our Lady of Consolation.
Eschweiler, Edward R. '48 (MIL) Retired.
Esclanda, Derrick '99 (DAL)[I] Irving, TX Opus Dei.
Esclanda, Derrick '99 (POD) Oak Park.
Escobar, Agustin '87 (ORG) Orange, CA St. Norbert.
Escobar, Joseph A. '88 (PRO) Providence, RI Our Lady of the Rosary.
Escobar Felix, Francisco Javier '98 (SB) Mecca, CA Sanctuary of Our Lady of Guadalupe.
Escobedo, Armando '64 (BWN) Retired.
Escobedo, Gilberto '00 (ORG) Costa Mesa, CA St. Joachim.
Escribano, Pedro '88 (MAD) Sauk City, WI St. Norbert; Sauk City, WI Divine Mercy Parish.
Escurel, Armando P. '79 (SD) San Diego, CA Saint Rita Catholic Parish.
Eseke, Anthony M. '96 (STA) Gainesville, FL St. Augustine.
Esenther, Keith J. *s.j.* '71 (FgM) Chicago, IL Society of Jesus; [N] Chicago Chicago Province of the Society of Jesus–Provincial Office.
Esguerra, Bernadino '87 (TR) Brick Town, NJ Epiphany; Lakewood, NJ St. Mary of the Lake.
Esguerra, Martin *m.id.* (NY) Bronx, NY Santa Maria.
Esker, Karl *c.ss.r.* '76 (FgM) Baltimore Province.
Esker, Karl *c.ss.r.* (NEW) Newark, NJ St. James.
Eskind, Rev. Msgr. Jace F. '87 (LKC) Lake Charles, LA Immaculate Conception Cathedral; Diocesan Board of Administration; Vicar Judicial; Judges; Diocesan Consultors; Presbyteral Council; Office For Worship.
Esmilla, Efren V. '93 (PH) Philadelphia, PA Our Lady of Hope; Filipino Apostolate.
Esmond, William '55 (ALB) Retired.
Espadas, Miguel Angel '09 (MEM) Memphis, TN Church of the Resurrection.
Espaillat, Joseph '03 (NY) Yonkers, NY St. Peter.
Esparza, Erik L. '08 (SB) Rancho Cucamonga, CA Sacred Heart; Elected At–Large Members.
Esparza, Jose Luis *f.n.* '99 (DAL) Garland, TX Good Shepherd.
Espejel, Rene *c.s.b.* '87 (LSC)[B] Las Cruces, NM Basilian Fathers; Las Cruces, NM Cathedral of the Immaculate Heart of Mary.
Espelage, Arthur J. *o.f.m.* '71 (VEN) Venice, FL Our Lady of Lourdes; Judicial Vicar.
Espelage, Arthur *o.f.m.* '71 (CIN)[N] Cincinnati St. Francis Seraph Friary; Cincinnati, OH.
Espelage, Thomas '70 (CIN) Cincinnati, OH St. John the Evangelist.
Espeleta, Bonifacio G. '84 (SFR) Daly City, CA St. Andrew.
Espenilla, Silverio '89 (SD) San Marcos, CA Saint Mark Catholic Parish.
Esper, Abraham L. '85 (SY) Chadwicks, NY St. Patrick–St. Anthony.
Esper, John C. '83 (DET)[T] Detroit, MI Detroit Catholic Charismatic Renewal Center; Madison Heights, MI St. Vincent Ferrer.
Esper, Joseph M. '82 (DET) Lakeport, MI St. Edward's on the Lake.
Esper, Thomas '51 (DET) Retired.
Espinal, Alberto '97 (NY) Ossining, NY St. Ann.
Espinal, David '02 (BRK) On Leave/Unassigned.
Espinel, Luis *o.p.* '59 (SJN)[A] Bayamon Central University.
Espino, Jose '83 (MIA) Hialeah, FL San Lazaro; Northwest Dade Deanery.
Espinosa, Anthony L. '96 (OM) Ralston, NE St. Gerald.
Espinosa, Boris (CGS) San Lorenzo, PR Sagrado Corazon de Jesus y 12 Apostoles.
Espinosa, Carlos '85 (LSC) Alamogordo, NM Immaculate Conception.
Espinosa, David F. '98 (BRK) On Leave/Unassigned.
Espinosa, Donald *a.a.* '71 (BO)[U] Boston, MA Assumptionist Center; [U] Boston Assumptionist Center.
Espinosa, Eduardo *o.f.m.* '04 (GLP) Presbyteral Council; Diocesan Consultors; St. Michaels, AZ St. Michael.
Espinosa, Gabriel D. '07 (VIC) Presbyteral Council; Wharton, TX Our Lady of Mt. Carmel.
Espinoza, Adalberto '10 (DET) Royal Oak, MI National Shrine of the Little Flower.
Espinoza, Galo *o.a.r.* '92 (LA) Los Angeles, CA Cristo Rey.
Espinoza, Martin '11 (MET) Spotswood, NJ Immaculate Conception.
Espinoza, Pedro '02 (MRY) Castroville, CA Our Lady of Refuge; Defenders of the Bond.
Espona Jimenez, Juan (PCE) On Duty Outside the Diocese.
Esposito, Alberto '01 (STA) Flagler Beach, FL Santa Maria Del Mar.
Esposito, Anthony '56 (Y) Retired.
Esposito, Augustine M. *o.s.a.* '79 (PH)[F] Malvern, PA Malvern Preparatory School for Boys.
Esposito, Charles P. '99 (GBG) Kent, PA Church of the Good Shepherd.
Esposito, Rev. Msgr. Ernest T. '67 (BGP)[W] Trumbull, CT St. Joseph's Manor; District Spiritual Directors; Fairfield, CT St. Pius X Retired.
Esposito, Juan '08 (WDC) Auditors.
Esposito, Lawrence J. '76 (WOR) Linwood, MA Good Shepherd.
Esposito, Luigi '64 (BAL) Baltimore, MD Our Lady of Pompei; Baltimore, MD.
Esposito, Mario *o.carm.* '77 (ALB)[M] Germantown, NY Postulation Office; Middletown, NY.
Esposito, Mario *o.carm.* '77 (NY)[DD] Middletown, NY Carmelite Friars (North American Province of St. Elias).
Esposito, Ralph J. '67 (LR) Retired.
Esposito, Samuel J. '78 (PIT) Vicariate 3; Episcopal Vicars; Priest Council; College of Consultors; Clergy Personnel Board.
Esposito, Stanislao '03 (WIL) Ocean City, MD St. Mary, Star of the Sea.
Esposito, Thomas *o.cist.* '11 (DAL)[J] Irving, TX Cistercian Abbey of Our Lady of Dallas.
Esposito, William C. '58 (SY) Retired.
Esposito–Garcia, Juan '08 (WDC) Hyattsville, MD St. Mark; Pastoral Center Special Ministries.
Esquerra, Martin I. '08 (NY)[DD] Bronx, NY Idente Missionaries – Santa Maria Residence.
Esquivel, Carlos *o.s.j.* '83 (FRS) Madera, CA St. Joachim; Advocates.
Esquivel, Giovanni Ruiz '00 (CGS)[B] San Lorenzo, PR Casa Charlie Rodriguez; [E] San Lorenzo, PR Diocesan Shrine Our Lady of Mount Carmel.
Esquivel, Rev. Msgr. John '68 (FRS) Reedley, CA St. Anthony of Padua; Diocesan Consultors; Vicars Forane; Personnel Board.
Ess, Thomas '66 (CHI)[N] Chicago, IL St. Peter's Friary.
Esseff, Rev. Msgr. John A. '53 (SCR)[M] Dunmore, PA Villa St. Joseph Retired.
Esselman, Thomas E. *c.m.* '80 (FgM)[O] St. Louis, MO Vincentian Residence; [O] St. Louis, MO Vincentian Residence; Earth City, MO Western Province.
Essen, Peter Von *o.f.m.cap.* '56 (FgM) White Plains, NY The Province of St. Mary of the Capuchin Order.
Esser, James *o.f.m.* '67 (GB)[J] Wausaukee, WI Villa Alverna.
Esser, Paul M. '57 (MIL) Retired.
Essex, Rev. Msgr. Donald S. '73 (WDC) Bethesda, MD St. Jane Frances de Chantal; Priest Retirement Fund of the Archdiocese of Washington, Inc.
Essig, Edward J. '94 (ALN) New Philadelphia, PA Holy Cross Parish.
Essig, Herbert '74 (JOL) Bolingbrook, IL St. Francis of Assisi.
Essling, Harold W. *c.s.c.* '78 (AUS)[G] Austin, TX Brother Andre Residence.
Essman, Ronald '80 (DET) Clinton Township, MI St. Paul of Tarsus.
Essuon, James (NY) Staten Island, NY St. Clare.
Esswein, Michael J. '98 (STL) Kirkwood, MO St. Peter.
Estabrook, Kevin E. '09 (CLV) Parma, OH St. Columbkille.
Estacio, Jeffrey '11 (LEX) Lexington, KY Mary, Queen of the Holy Rosary.
Estada, Julio '59 (MIA)[G] Miami, FL Mercy Hospital.
Estadilla, Lino *o.m.v.* '06 (BO)[B] Boston, MA Oblate Provincialate.
Estaris, Michael J. '10 (SAC) Rancho Cordova, CA St. John Vianney.
Esteban, Pedro Antonio '85 (LA) Los Angeles, CA St. Aloysius Gonzaga.
Estensoro, Jose '60 (ARE) Retired.
Estepa, Isaias '94 (CC) Odem, TX Sacred Heart.
Estephan, Andre S. *m.l.m.* '90 (OLL) Houston, TX Our Lady of the Cedars Maronite Catholic Church; [A] Houston, TX The Congregation of Maronite Lebanese Missionaries.
Estes, Dan *s.o.l.t.* '99 (CC)[G] Robstown, TX Society of Our Lady of the Most Holy Trinity; [F] Corpus Christi, TX Queen of Peace Retreat Center.
Estevez, Leobardo Almazan *o.p.* '05 (FgM) Metairie, LA St. Martin de Porres Province (Southern Dominican Province).
Estibalez, Inocencio '52 (SP) Retired.
Estilette, Grady J. '63 (LAF) Retired.
es Tillore, Mark Martin B. '93 (TLS) Tulsa, OK St. Bernard of Clairvaux.
Estiverne, Saint–Martin (BRK) Brooklyn, NY St. Matthew.
Estiverne, St. Martin '97 (BRK) Downstate Medical Center; Maimonides Medical Center of Brooklyn.
Estok, Edward T. '85 (CLV) North Royalton, OH St. Albert the Great.
Estok, Edward T. '85 (CLV) College of Consultors; Presbyteral Council.
Estoque, Justino (HT) Dulac, LA Holy Family.
Estorque, Roger O. '85 (GAL) Houston, TX St. Dominic.
Estrada, Augustin '90 (SAT)[A] San Antonio, TX Assumption Seminary.
Estrada, Enrique J. '93 (MIA) Miami, FL St. Raymond.
Estrada, Hector Diaz '82 (SJN)[E] San Juan, PR VA Medical Center.
Estrada, Ignacio *s.v.d.* '03 (ORG)[G] Fullerton, CA St. Jude Medical Center.
Estrada, Ignacio *s.v.d.* '03 (SB)[I] Riverside, CA Divine Word Seminary.
Estrada, J. Manuel '86 (SFR) San Francisco, CA St. Peter.
Estrada, Jorge L. '07 (CHI) Chicago, IL Our Lady of Mercy.
Estrada, Rafael A. '05 (SAV) Baxley, GA Good Shepherd.
Estrada, Richard *c.m.f.* '78 (LA) Los Angeles, CA Our Lady Queen of Angels Parish.
Estrada, Sabino '72 (BRK) Retired.
Esty, Gregory L. '75 (STP) St. Paul Park, MN St. Thomas Aquinas.
Esukpa, Emmanuel *m.s.p.* '92 (GAL) Houston, TX St. Peter the Apostle.
Ethen, Jeffrey D. '88 (SCL) Belgrade, MN St. Francis De Sales; Brooten, MN St. Donatus; Elrosa, MN SS.

Peter and Paul; Navy Reserve Chaplains; Presbyteral Council.
Etheredge, F. William '83 (RCK) Special Assignment; [B] Aurora, IL Aurora Central Catholic High School.
Etienne, Bernard T. '93 (EVN) Diocesan Council of Priests; Special Assignment; Vicar General; Diocesan Consultors; Deans; Ex Officio; Evansville, IN Holy Rosary.
Etienne, Zachary J. '04 (EVN) Evansville, IN Good Shepherd.
Etim, Idongesit A. '09 (WIL) New Castle, DE Our Lady of Fatima.
Etlinger, Peter J. *c.s.b.* '47 (ROC) Rochester, NY Kateri Tekakwitha Roman Catholic Parish.
Ettensohn, John M. *o.m.i.* '89 (BEL)[F] Belleville, IL Missionary Oblates of Mary Immaculate – St. Henry's Oblate Residence.
Ettlinger, Gerard H. *s.j.* '66 (NY)[DD] New York Jesuit Provincial's Office.
Ettner, Wilhelm J. '93 (ARL) Woodstock, VA St. John Bosco.
Ettolil, Sebastian *m.c.b.s.* '68 (MAR) Ewen, MI Sacred Heart; Watersmeet, MI Immaculate Conception; Watersmeet, MI Lac Vieux Desert Reservation.
Etuale, Kolio '03 (SPP) Pago Pago, AS Church of the Holy Cross; Director of Vocations; Faculty Members; Auditors; Diocesan Consultors.
Etuale, Viane '90 (SPP) Vicar General of Diocese; Pago Pago, AS Christ the King; Diocesan Consultors; Diocesan Pastoral Council; Faculty Members; Judges.
Etxeandia, Jesus *c.p.* (ARE) Lares, PR St. Joseph.
Etxeandia Ormaetzea, Jesús *c.p.* '59 (SJN) Carolina, PR Nuestra Senora de la Piedad.
Etzel, Peter J. *s.j.* '94 (RC)[C] Howes, SD Kino Jesuit Community; [E] Howes, SD The Diocese of Rapid City Mahpiya na Maka Okogna; Permanent Diaconate Program, Sioux Spiritual Center.
Euk, Vincent '86 (NY) On Duty Outside the Archdiocese.
Euker, John T. '74 (GBG) Apollo, PA St. James the Greater; East Vandergrift, PA Our Lady, Queen of Peace.
Eurico, Francisco '94 (HRT) Waterbury, CT Our Lady of Fatima.
Euvrard, Scott A. '94 (BO) Sharon, MA Our Lady of Sorrows.
Evancho, George '64 (PBR) Retired.
Evancho, Robert '79 (PSC) Saint Petersburg, FL St. Therese; Syncellus.
Evangelista, Romeo '02 (MRY) Pacific Grove, CA St. Angela Merici Church.
Evangelisto, Louis Anthony '54 (HRT) Retired.
Evanick, Michael '60 (PRM) Retired.
Evanish, Robin '83 (PIT) Carnegie, PA St. Elizabeth Ann Seton.
Evanko, Joseph J. '91 (SCR) Mountain Top, PA St. Jude; Wapwallopen, PA Our Lady Help of Christians; Presbyteral Council.
Evanofski, Bernard P. '86 (VEN) Sarasota, FL Incarnation.
Evans, Edward '80 (WDC) Retired.
Evans, G. William '78 (TR)[N] Trenton, NJ Villa Vianney.
Evans, George P. '77 (BO) Weston, MA St. Julia; Elected; Presbyteral Council.
Evans, George *s.s.s.* '57 (CLV)[N] Cleveland Congregation of the Blessed Sacrament Provincial House; [N] Richfield, OH Regina Health Center.
Evans, James L. '94 (AUS) Retired.
Evans, John R. '09 (RCK) Batavia, IL Holy Cross.
Evans, John '80 (FAR) On Duty Outside the Diocese.
Evans, John '80 (WIN)[D] Rochester, MN Saint Mary Hospital.
Evans, John *o.p.* '04 (SLC) Riverton, UT Saint Andrew Catholic Church LLC 233.
Evans, Ken '86 (NEW) Cliffside Park, NJ Epiphany.
Evans, Larry '01 (NEW) Ridgefield Park, NJ St. Francis of Assisi.
Evans, Larry '01 (NEW) Archdiocesan Stewardship Advisory Committee.
Evans, Michael A. *s.j.* '83 (WDC)[X] Washington, DC Jesuit Refugee Service; [O] Washington, DC Leonard Neale House.
Evans, Michael J. '92 (LA) Arcadia, CA Holy Angels.
Evans, Richard A. '82 (CLV) Parma, OH Holy Family.
Evans, Robert T. '03 (STL) Webster Groves, MO Annunciation.
Evans, Wilfred F. '68 (SY) Syracuse, NY Veterans Administration Hospital Retired.
Evans, William G. '78 (TR) Leave of Absence.
Evans, William Morris '81 (CHL) Retired.
Evans–Campos, Raphael Blake '10 (WDC) Rockville, MD Shrine of St. Jude.
Evanson, Robert '91 (SEA) Seattle, WA Our Lady of Fatima; First Hills Hospital.
Evard, Paul A. '61 (IND) Retired.
Evardoni, Luis '99 (GAL) Houston, TX St. Matthew the Evangelist.
Evardoni, Luis Paolo Agostino V. *d.s.* '99 (GAL)[O] Houston, TX St. Matthew the Evangelist.
Eve, Paul W. '82 (L) Jamestown, KY Holy Redeemer; Jamestown, KY Holy Spirit.
Evenson, Dennis D. '67 (STP) Retired.
Everding, Richard F. '66 (STL) Retired.
Everett, Willis E. '90 (COL) On Duty Outside the Diocese; DEPARTMENT OF VETERANS AFFAIRS HOSPITALS AND CHAPLAINS.
Evernden, Michael *c.s.p.* '74 (P) Portland, OR St. Philip Neri; [Q] Portland, OR Paulist Fathers Catholic Center for Evangelization; Area Vicars.
Evers, Leonard M. '68 (GB) Cecil, WI St. Martin; Shawano, WI Sacred Heart.
Evers, Linus *c.pp.s.* '71 (CIN)[N] Carthagena, OH St. Charles Retired.
Evers, Rev. Msgr. Paul C. '54 (WIN) Retired.
Evers, Paul H. '80 (HON) On Duty Outside the Diocese.
Evers, Robert B. '60 (GRY) Retired.
Eversley, Garth *o.carm.* '03 (NY)[DD] Middletown, NY St. Albert's Priory; [DD] Middletown, NY Office of Lay Carmelites.
Eversole, Paul M. '95 (ARL) Spotsylvania, VA St. Matthew.
Everson, Joseph M. *m.m.* '99 (FgM) Maryknoll, NY MARYKNOLL.
Everts, Donald E. '95 (GB) Green Bay, WI Annunciation of the Blessed Virgin Mary; Green Bay, WI St. Joseph; Green Bay, WI St. Jude; Green Bay, WI St. Patrick.
Ewen, Sharbel *o.s.b.* '88 (SD)[J] Oceanside, CA Prince of Peace Abbey.
Ewenteang, Tatieru *m.s.c.* (CI) Chuuk, FM Mortlock.
Ewers, Paul J. *m.c.c.j.* '65 (CHI) Chicago, IL St. Martin De Porres.
Ewert, J. Michael *o.f.m.* '59 (SFD)[K] Teutopolis, IL St. Francis Assisi Friary; Teutopolis, IL St. Francis of Assisi.
Ewing, Matt J. *o.carm.* '54 (LA)[P] Encino, CA Our Lady of Mount Carmel Priory.
Extejt, John I. *o.s.f.s.* '85 (TOL)[C] Toledo, OH St. Francis de Sales High School; [H] Toledo, OH.
Extejt, Thomas J. '73 (TOL) Columbus Grove, OH St. Anthony of Padua; Procurator–Advocate for Respondents; Associate Judges.
Exume, Gilbert '08 (ATL) Johns Creek, GA St. Brigid.
Eybel, John W. *m.m.* '70 (CHI) Chicago, IL; [N] Chicago, IL Maryknoll Fathers & Brothers.
Eyerman, Matthew '95 (CHI) Chicago, IL St. Malachy + Precious Blood.
Eyman, Bryan R. '85 (PRM) Marblehead, OH St. Mary; Presbyteral Council; Ohio; Building Commission.
Ezaki, Bernard J. '88 (ALN) Bethlehem, PA Notre Dame of Bethlehem; [C] Bethlehem, PA Bethlehem Catholic High School.
Ezama, Ruffino *m.c.c.j.* '94 (CIN)[N] Cincinnati, OH Comboni Missionaries (Verona Fathers)–Comboni Mission Center.
Ezama, Rufino *m.c.c.j.* '94 (CHI)[W] Chicago, IL The Peace Corner, Incorporated.
Eze, Cyprian '88 (LAF) On Special Assignment; Lafayette, LA Cathedral of St. John the Evangelist.
Ezeanokwasa, Jude '89 (MIA) Judges.
Ezeatu, Mike Steve '94 (CAM) Collingswood, NJ Most Precious Blood Parish, Collingswood, N.J.
Ezeh, Christian '95 (STO) Stockton, CA St. Mary of the Assumption Church (Pastor of).
Ezeh, Christopher O. '94 (MO) DEPARTMENT OF VETERANS AFFAIRS HOSPITALS AND CHAPLAINS.
Ezeh, Gabriel I. '94 (BWN) La Feria, TX St. Francis Xavier.
Ezeh, Gabriel U. *s.m.m.m.* '05 (BAK) La Grande, OR Our Lady of the Valley.
Ezeh, Raphael *m.s.p.* (CHI) Chicago, IL Corpus Christi.
Ezeibekwe, Samuel '79 (FAR) Pisek, ND Sts. Peter & Paul Church of Bechyne; Pisek, ND St. Joseph's Church of Lankin; Pisek, ND St. John Nepomucene's Church of Pisek.
Ezeigbo, Pius '99 (SAT) Brackettville, TX St. Mary Magdalen.
Ezeihuona, Puschal O. (GAL) Houston, TX St. Gregory the Great.
Ezeiruaku, Vitus '96 (SFE) Penasco, NM San Antonio de Padua; Vicars Forane (Deans); Dixon, NM St. Anthony; Presbyteral Council of the Archdiocese of Santa Fe.
Ezekwe, Anthony I. (BRK) Flushing, NY St. Michael.
Ezenwa, Hilary '96 (RVC) Bethpage, NY New Island Hospital.
Ezenwa, Hipolitus I. *s.m.m.m.* (GAL) Dickinson, TX Shrine of the True Cross.
Ezenwachi, Ferdinand (BAL) Columbia, MD St. John the Evangelist.
Ezeoke, Benedict '96 (CHI) Melrose Park, IL Sacred Heart; [J] Chicago, IL St. Anthony Hospital.
Ezeoke, Christopher '91 (BRK) South Ozone Park, NY St. Anthony of Padua.
Ezeonyeka, Aloysius *o.s.b.* '02 (LA) Azusa, CA St. Frances of Rome.
Ezeonyido, John Paul '03 (ATL) Lilburn, GA St. Stephen the Martyr.
Ezeugwa, Romanus *m.s.p.* (MOB) Tuskegee Institute, AL St. Joseph; [I] Tuskegee Institute, AL Tuskegee University Newman Center.
Ezhanikkatt, Vincent '84 (SYM) Morgantown, WV St. Mary Syro–Malabar Catholic Mission Pittsburgh, PA.
Ezop, Dwight M. '97 (LAN) De Witt, MI St. Jude; [R] FAITH Magazine.
Ezratty, John *m.c.* '02 (DET)[K] Plymouth, MI Miles Christi.
Ezuma, Jude '11 (GAL) Houston, TX Co–Cathedral of the Sacred Heart.
Ezurike, Paschal '95 (P) Oregon City, OR St. Philip Benizi.

F

Faber, Emmet N. '55 (LC) Retired.
Fabian, Andrew C. *o.p.* '56 (WIN) Additional Diocesan Assignments.
Fabian, John V. '68 (DET) Retired.
Fabian, John *o.p.* '59 (CHI) River Forest, IL St. Vincent Ferrer.
Fabian, John '68 (MAR)[H] Paradise, MI Companions of Christ the Lamb.
Fabiano, Philip *o.f.m.cap.* '64 (NY) New York, NY St. John the Baptist.
Fabing, Robert J. *s.j.* '74 (SJ)[L] Los Altos, CA Jesuit Retreat Center of Los Altos; [O] Los Altos, CA Jesuit Institute for Family Life.
Fabish, Rapael A. *o.p.* '53 (CHI)[N] Chicago, IL St. Pius V Priory.
Fabj, Frank T. '84 (GAL) Houston, TX St. Frances Cabrini.
Fabre, Jacques E. *c.s.* '86 (ATL) Forest Park, GA San Felipe de Jesus.
Fabre, Richard '73 (LAF) St. Martinville, LA St. Rita.
Facci, John *s.a.c.* '71 (ALB) Retired.
Fackler, Neil E. '98 (CHI) Chicago, IL St. Robert Bellarmine.
Facura, Joseph C. '68 (RIC) Retired.
Fadallan, Elbert A. '80 (MO) Air Force Chaplains.
Fadok, Christopher *o.p.* '10 (SEA) Seattle, WA Blessed Sacrament.
Fador, Francis R. '96 (HRT) Sharon, CT St. Bridget; Sharon, CT St. Bernard.
Fadrowski, Rev. Msgr. William J. '87 (NEW) North Arlington, NJ Queen of Peace; Priest Personnel Policy Board.
Faesser, Arthur A. '76 (GI) Sidney, NE St. Patrick's.
Fafinski, Donald S. '66 (BUF) Retired.
Fagan, Christopher B. '09 (LA) Culver City, CA St. Augustine.
Fagan, Rev. Msgr. Emmet '55 (BRK)[K] Brooklyn, NY Ecclesial Consultants, Inc.
Fagan, Rt. Rev. Msgr. Emmet '55 (RVC) Priests' Retirement Board.
Fagan, George V. '69 (COS) Limon, CO Our Lady of Victory; Defender of the Bond; Eastern Deanery; Vicars Forane; College of Consultors.
Fagan, George V. (PBL) Defensores Vinculi.
Fagan, John E. *s.j.* '83 (WOR)[N] Worcester, MA Jesuits of the Holy Cross, Inc.
Fagan, Joseph K. '67 (BO)[A] Weston, MA Blessed John XXIII National Seminary; Senior Priests. Retired.
Fagan, Paul R. *c.p.* '86 (NY)[DD] Pelham Manor, NY St. Vincent's Residence.
Fagan, Rev. Msgr. Robert Emmet (RVC) Retired.
Fagan, Robert R. '58 (ALN)[J] Bethlehem, PA Holy Family Villa Retired.
Fagin, Gerald M. *s.j.* '69 (NO)[C] New Orleans, LA Loyola University New Orleans.
Fagone, Benedict *o.f.m.conv.* '67 (SPR) Chicopee, MA St. Anthony of Padua.
Fahey, Rev. Msgr. Charles J. '58 (BRK)[K] Brooklyn, NY Ecclesial Consultants, Inc.; [DD] Loyola Hall, Jesuit Community; On Duty Outside the Diocese.
Fahey, Edward J. '89 (WIL) Nursing Homes; Wilmington, DE St. Helena.
Fahey, Rev. Msgr. Gerard '51 (SR) Santa Rosa, CA Star of the Valley; Cemeteries.
Fahey, James L. '59 (BO) Senior Priests. Retired.
Fahey, James W. '70 (FR) Retired.
Fahey, John H. '61 (WH) Retired.
Fahey, John M. '54 (TUC) Retired.
Fahey, John Peter '84 (LA) Retired.
Fahey, Michael A. *s.j.* '64 (BO)[U] Newton, MA The Jesuit Community at Boston College.
Fahey, Robert E. *s.m.* '53 (SFR)[N] San Francisco, CA Marist Center of the West Retired.
Fahey, Thomas C. '47 (FTW)[I] Huntington, IN Victory Noll—Motherhouse of Our Lady of Victory Missionary Sisters Retired.
Fahey, Thomas C. '47 (CHY) Retired.
Fahey–Guerra, John P. *c.ss.r.* '96 (CHI)[N] Chicago, IL Redemptorist Theology Residence.
Fahnestock, John *m.s.c.* '71 (SB) Hesperia, CA Holy Family.
Fahrbach, Paul A. '84 (TOL) Bellevue, OH St. Gaspar del Bufalo; Attica, OH Our Lady of Hope.
Faiella, William W. *c.s.c.* '79 (FTW)[H] Notre Dame Congregation of Holy Cross, United States Province of Priests & Brothers.
Faiella, William W. *c.s.c.* '79 (PHX)[F] Phoenix, AZ Holy

Cross Congregation/Casa Santa Cruz; Scottsdale, AZ St. Bernard of Clairvaux Roman Catholic Parish.
Fain, John M. '03 (LAN) Lansing, MI Resurrection.
Faiola, Fabio '08 (AGN) Agana, GU Our Lady of Guadalupe.
Faiola, Rev. Msgr. Samuel J. '49 (BUF) Censors—Board of Diocesan Censors of Books and Vigilance for the Faith Retired.
Faiola, Thomas *o.f.m.cap.* '85 (NY) New York, NY Our Lady of Sorrows.
Fairbanks, Gregory J. '90 (PH) On Duty Outside the Archdiocese.
Fairbanks, Patrick A. *s.j.* '00 (CHI)[D] Chicago, IL St. Ignatius College Prep; [N] Chicago, IL Chicago Province of the Society of Jesus–Provincial Office; Chicago, IL; Detroit, MI; [D] Chicago, IL St. Ignatius Jesuit Community.
Fairbanks, Patrick A. *s.j.* '00 (DET)[K] Chicago, IL Detroit Province of the Society of Jesus–Provincial Office.
Fairchild, Rev. Msgr. Edward '59 (COL) Retired.
Fairman, Derek '06 (ALT) Johnstown, PA St. Benedict's.
Fairman, Timothy J. '88 (CHI) Ingleside, IL St. Bede.
Fait, Thomas G. '74 (MIL) Personal Leave.
Faix, William R. *o.s.a.* '63 (FgM) Villanova, PA Province of St. Thomas of Villanova (Eastern).
Fajardo, Ricardo '87 (NY) Bronx, NY Holy Spirit.
Fajella, Francis *m.s.a.* '82 (NOR)[G] Cromwell Society of the Missionaries of the Holy Apostles.
Faker, Dennis A. '08 (LFT) Crawfordsville, IN St. Bernard.
Falara, Arkadiusz '06 (CHI) Palos Heights, IL Incarnation.
Falardeau, Ernest R. *s.s.s.* '56 (NY) New York, NY St. Jean Baptiste.
Falbo, Samuel J. '60 (LAV) Italian Catholic Federation; Las Vegas, NV St. Anthony of Padua.
Falbo, Samuel '60 (SFE) Retired.
Falco, Frank M. *o.s.m.* '67 (CHI) Chicago, IL; [N] Chicago, IL Order of Friar Servants of Mary (Servites) United States of America Province, Inc.
Falco, Frank *o.s.m.* '67 (ORG) Fullerton, CA St. Juliana Falconieri; [I] Fullerton, CA Servite Fathers and Brothers.
Falco, Ronald G. '81 (WOR) Office of Ongoing Priestly Formation; Worcester, MA St. George.
Falcone, Emilio '57 (RCK) Active Outside the Diocese Retired.
Falcone, Mark D. *o.praem* '66 (GB)[J] De Pere, WI St. Norbert Abbey.
Falcone, Sebastian '51 (ROC)[A] Rochester, NY St. Bernard's School of Theology & Ministry Retired.
Fale, Emmanuel (BAL) Baltimore, MD Immaculate Heart of Mary.
Faletoi, Konelio '92 (HON) Kailua–Kona, HI St. Michael The Archangel; College of Consultors; Vicars Forane; Presbyteral Council; Clergy Personnel Board.
Faliskie, Edmund *c.ss.r.* '91 (BRK)[R] Brooklyn, NY Redemptorist Fathers of New York, Inc.–Baltimore Province.
Falk, Gerald R. '59 (GB) Retired.
Falk, Robert *s.d.b.* '63 (FgM) New Rochelle, NY SALESIANS OF DON BOSCO.
Falkenhan, Pierre M. '80 (PIT) Donora, PA Our Lady of the Valley.
Falkenthal, Thomas W. '75 (CHI) Retired.
Falla, Gustavo A. '96 (BGP) Bridgeport, CT St. Augustine Cathedral; Episcopal Vicar for Hispanics; Priest Vocation Advisory Board.
Faller, Rodel '08 (BEA) Beaumont, TX St. Anne.
Falletta, Frank J. '66 (ROC) Rochester, NY St. Lawrence.
Falletta, Joseph '72 (ALB) Stuyvesant, NY Church of St. Joseph; Presbyteral Council; Diocesan Board of Consultors.
Fallgren, Matthew '01 (RC) Eagle Butte, SD All Saints.
Fallon, Daniel R. '76 (CHI) Chicago, IL St. Cornelius.
Fallon, James *s.s.j.* '68 (JKS) Fayette, MS St. Anne; Natchez, MS Holy Family.
Fallon, John C. '71 (ATL) Atlanta, GA Holy Spirit; Prison Apostolate.
Fallon, John F. '58 (BO) Senior Priests. Retired.
Fallon, John J. '46 (BO) Senior Priests. Retired.
Fallon, John P. '95 (FAR) Absent on Leave.
Fallon, John P. *o.s.f.s.* '60 (STO)[A] Stockton, CA St. Mary's High School; Diocesan Finance Council.
Fallon, John '69 (BIR) Birmingham (Hoover), AL Prince of Peace.
Fallon, Joseph '96 (NY) Walden, NY Most Precious Blood.
Fallon, Marc F. *c.s.c.* '91 (FR) Taunton; [A] North Easton, MA Holy Cross Fathers Religious.
Fallon, Marc F. *c.s.c.* '91 (FTW)[H] Notre Dame Congregation of Holy Cross, United States Province of Priests & Brothers.
Fallon, Vince *ss.cc.* '91 (RNO)[F] Reno, NV University of Nevada, Newman Community; Reno, NV Our Lady of Wisdom; Diocesan Board of Consultors; Presbyteral Council.
Fallon, Vincent *ss.cc.* '91 (LA)[P] La Verne, CA Congregation of the Sacred Hearts of Jesus and Mary.
Fallone, Thomas H. '02 (PAT) Boonton, NJ Our Lady of Mount Carmel.
Falotico, Ronald S. '69 (CAM) Hammonton, NJ Saint Mary of Mount Carmel Parish, Hammonton, N.J.
Falsey, James E. '72 (SAG) AuGres, MI St. Mark; Territorial Vicars.
Falter, John *c.pp.s.* '61 (CIN)[N] Dayton Provincial Office of the Cincinnati Province of the Society of the Precious Blood; [N] Carthagena, OH St. Charles Retired.
Falusczak, James G. '96 (E) Kersey, PA St. Boniface.
Falzon, Angelo *o.f.m.* '84 (FgM) New York, NY Franciscan Province of the Immaculate Conception.
Fama, Lawrence J. '92 (NEW) Maywood, NJ Our Lady Queen of Peace.
Famania, Edison *c.m.* '94 (FgM) Philadelphia, PA Eastern Province.
Fambrini, Robert *s.j.* '79 (SD) San Diego, CA Our Lady of Guadalupe Catholic Parish San Diego.
Familar, Rex '93 (ORL) Orlando, FL St. John Vianney.
Famiyeh, Emmanuel '90 (LC) Alma Center, WI Immaculate Conception; Black River Falls, WI St. Joseph; Melrose, WI St. Kevin.
Fana, Elmon Hernandez (ARE) Manati, PR Nuestra Senora del Mar.
Fanale, James F. *c.s.v.* '69 (CHI)[N] Arlington Heights Viatorian Province Center–Clerics of St. Viator.
Fanale, James *c.s.v.* '69 (JOL) St. Anne, IL St. Anne.
Fane, Kevin R. *o.p.* '69 (CHI) River Forest, IL St. Vincent Ferrer; [J] Chicago, IL Resurrection Medical Center.
Fanelli, Charles V. '71 (CHI) Chicago, IL St. Thomas More; [W] Chicago, IL Italian Catholic Federation.
Fanelli, James G. '56 (HRT)[A] In Res. at the Archbishop Daniel A. Cronin Retirement Residence at St. Thomas Seminary Retired.
Fangman, James E. '63 (SC) Carroll, IA Retired.
Fangman, Robert M. '54 (SC) Retired.
Fangman, Thomas M. '92 (OM) Omaha, NE Sacred Heart; [N] Omaha, NE Christian Urban Education Service.
Fangmann, Frederick C. '63 (DUB) Retired.
Fanning, John (NY) On Leave of Absence.
Fanning, Patrick F. *ss.cc.* '83 (FR)[F] Fairhaven National Center of the Enthronement.
Fannon, Noel '61 (BLX) Retired.
Fano, Frank J. '11 (NEW) Westfield, NJ St. Helen.
Fanous, Antonios (BRK) Brooklyn, NY Holy Name.
Fanous, Sherif S.I. '98 (BRK) Methodist Hospital; [Q] Arabic Speaking Apostolate.
Fanrak, James M. '71 (LR) Deans; Harrison, AR Mary, Mother of God; Yellville, AR St. Andrew Church; Presbyteral Council.
Fanta, Thomas G. '88 (CLV) Shaker Heights, OH St. Dominic; [X] Shaker Heights, OH St. Dominic Endowment Fund.
Fanucci, Santino J. '58 (SCR)[M] Dunmore, PA Villa St. Joseph Retired.
Faour, George '91 (NEW) Orange, NJ St. John's; Central Essex Deanery 17.
Farace, Frederick A. '55 (HBG) Retired.
Faraci, Douglas F. '69 (BUF) Retired.
Faraci, Francis '59 (LAN) Otisville, MI St. Francis Xavier Retired.
Farana, Mario P. '71 (SFR) San Francisco, CA St. Paul; Deans.
Farano, Michael A. '68 (ALB) Special Assignment; Vicar General and Moderator of the Curia; Propagation of the Faith–Pontifical Society; Presbyteral Council; Loudonville, NY St. Pius X.
Farao, John *o.f.m.conv.* '88 (MRY) California Men's Colony West; California Men's Colony East; Pismo Beach, CA St. Paul the Apostle.
Farbolin, Alberic R. *o.c.s.o.* '02 (DUB)[K] Peosta, IA New Melleray Abbey, Order of Cistercians of the Strict Observance.
Fardellone, Emil *s.d.b.* '44 (NO)[D] Marrero, LA Archbishop Shaw High School.
Fares, Lawrence T. '50 (DET) Retired.
Faretra, Albert M. '86 (BO) Bellingham, MA St. Blaise.
Farfaglia, Salvatore James '87 (CC) Corpus Christi, TX Our Lady of Guadalupe.
Farfan, Carlos *p.e.s.* (STP)[A] St. Paul, MN St. John Vianney Seminary; St. Paul, MN St. Mark; [A] St. Paul, MN St. John Vianney Seminary.
Farge, William J. *s.j.* '78 (NO)[C] New Orleans, LA Loyola University New Orleans.
Farhat, Vincent '10 (SAM) Philadelphia, PA St. Maron.
Faria, Carl M.D. '88 (MRY) Archives.
Farias, Joseph G. '75 (PAT) Convent Station, NJ St. Thomas More.
Farias, Joseph *s.d.b.* '64 (SFR)[N] San Francisco, CA Salesian Provincial Residence.
Faricy, Robert L. *s.j.* '62 (MIL)[P] Milwaukee, WI Jesuit Community at Marquette University.
Farina, Carlo A. *s.j.* '64 (SJ)[M] Los Gatos, CA Sacred Heart Jesuit Center.
Faris, Chorbishop John D. '76 (SAM) Utica, NY St. Louis Gonzaga.
Farke, Rodney '72 (SFS) Brookings, SD St. Thomas More; Tribunal Judges; Cursillo; Presbyteral Council.
Farland, Rev. Msgr. George A. '68 (SPR) Springfield, MA Sacred Heart; Bishop's Commission for Clergy; Deans; Clergy Counseling Service; Vicars for the Clergy.
Farland, Norman '66 (ORL) Wahneta, FL Our Lady of Guadalupe.
Farleo, Brennan–Joseph *o.f.m.conv.* '86 (NY)[DD] Staten Island, NY St. Francis Friary.
Farley, Bernard C. '68 (PH)[V] Philadelphia, PA St. John Neumann Nursing Home; On Special or Other Archdiocesan Assignment.
Farley, James W. '65 (PRO) Retired.
Farley, John B. '93 (PBL) Grand Junction, CO Immaculate Heart of Mary; College of Consultors; Deans; Elected.
Farley, John *s.v.d.* '60 (BO)[U] Duxbury, MA Society of the Divine Word.
Farley, Leo O. '54 (NEW)[L] Caldwell, NJ The Rev. Msgr. James F. Kelley Residence for Retired Priests; Newark, NJ Essex County Correctional Facility Retired.
Farley, Leslie A. '93 (LR) Springdale, AR St. Raphael.
Farley, Louis '11 (KC) Kansas City, MO St. John Francis Regis.
Farley, Patrick '05 (PHX) Carefree, AZ Our Lady of Joy Roman Catholic Parish; Advocates.
Farley, Thomas J. '02 (PRT) Retired.
Farmer, J. Kevin '92 (BAL) On Duty Outside the Archdiocese; Glen Burnie, MD Holy Trinity.
Farmer, Rev. Msgr. James P. '79 (BAL) Westminster, MD St. John; Courage.
Farmer, Rev. Msgr. Michael L. '95 (MOB) On Leave from the Archdiocese.
Farmer, Regis M. '73 (PIT) Wildwood, PA St. Catherine of Sweden; College of Consultors; Priest Council.
Farmer, Terrence '03 (PRM) Columbus, OH St. John Chrysostom; Young Adults; Presbyteral Council.
Farnan, Donald P. '87 (KC) Kansas City, MO St. Thomas More; Consultors; Deans; Administrative Committee.
Farnan, James B. '00 (PIT) Beaver Falls, PA St. Philomena; [P] New Brighton, PA Geneva College; Beaver Falls, PA Divine Mercy.
Farnum, David E. *c.s.p.* '00 (NY)[DD] New York, NY Paulist Fathers' Motherhouse.
Faroh, Paul *o.f.m.conv.* '85 (TOL) Carey, OH Our Lady of Consolation, Basilica–National Shrine.
Faron, Wieslaw *s.j.* '06 (CHI)[N] Chicago, IL Sacred Heart Mission House.
Farrar, Brandon '06 (KCK) Baldwin, KS Annunciation; Osage City, KS St. Francis of Assisi.
Farre, Raymond *sch.p.* '53 (LA) Los Angeles, CA Santa Teresita.
Farrell, Bernard P. '65 (BLX) Ocean Springs, MS St. Elizabeth Ann Seton; Catholic Housing Board; Personnel Board.
Farrell, David E. *c.s.c.* '68 (FgM) New Rochelle, NY Eastern Brothers Province.
Farrell, David E. *c.s.c.* '68 (FTW)[H] Notre Dame Congregation of Holy Cross, United States Province of Priests & Brothers.
Farrell, Dennis J. '73 (BRK) Holy Name Society; Brooklyn, NY Resurrection.
Farrell, Rev. Msgr. Francis '55 (BLX) Biloxi, MS Our Lady of Fatima Retired.
Farrell, George A. '96 (MET) North Plainfield, NJ St. Joseph.
Farrell, Gerald J. *m.m.* '57 (FgM) Maryknoll, NY MARYKNOLL.
Farrell, James M. '75 (IND) Indianapolis, IN St. Andrew the Apostle Catholic Church, Indianapolis, Inc.; Indianapolis, IN St. Pius X Catholic Church, Indianapolis, Inc.; Retreat & Renewal Ministries and Fatima Retreat House; [J] Indianapolis, IN Our Lady of Fatima Retreat House, Inc.
Farrell, John E. '62 (BO) Lynnfield, MA Our Lady of the Assumption; Vicariate I.
Farrell, John J. *o.s.a.* '59 (PH)[C] Villanova University; [Y] Villanova, PA St. Thomas Monastery Retired.
Farrell, Joseph J. '74 (TR) New Egypt, NJ The Church of the Assumption.
Farrell, Joseph L. '95 (PH) Philadelphia, PA St. Leo.
Farrell, Joseph L. *o.s.a.* '91 (PH)[C] Villanova University; [Y] Ardmore, PA Bellesini Friary; Counselors.
Farrell, Kevin R. '65 (JOL) Wood Dale, IL Holy Ghost.
Farrell, Kurt P. '98 (WIN) St. Charles, MN Holy Redeemer; St. Charles, MN St. Charles Borromeo; St. Charles, MN St. Aloysius.
Farrell, Lawrence *o.p.* '71 (SB)[I] Riverside, CA St. Vincent Ferrer House.
Farrell, Lawrence '01 (KAL) Kalamazoo, MI St. Monica; Advocates; Holy Childhood Association and Propagation of the Faith; Missions; Vicars Forane.
Farrell, Michael A. '70 (ORL) Merritt Island, FL Divine Mercy Catholic Community.
Farrell, Michael J. *s.s.j.* '60 (BAL)[Q] Baltimore, MD St. Joseph's Manor.
Farrell, Michael J. '11 (BO) Amesbury, MA Holy Family; Amesbury, MA Star of the Sea.

Farrell, Patrick J. *o.c.d.* '62 (MIL)[P] Hubertus, WI Discalced Carmelite Monastery – Holy Hill Basilica of the National Shrine of Mary, Help of Christians, Holy Hill.

Farrell, Rev. Msgr. Patrick '60 (JKS) Vicksburg, MS St. Paul; Diocesan Consultors; Approved Advocate and Auditors; Trustees.

Farrell, Rev. Msgr. Patrick (BLX) Trustees.

Farrell, Philip N. '93 (PIT) Vicariate 4; Priest Council; College of Consultors; Clergy Personnel Board; Episcopal Vicars.

Farrell, Richard T. '84 (ROC) Elmira, NY Blessed Sacrament Roman Catholic Church of Elmira, NY; Elmira, NY Elmira Correctional Facility, Center and Camp Monterey; Pine City, NY Southport Correctional Facility.

Farrell, Richard '84 (ROC)[N] Elmira, NY Elmira College.

Farrell, Richard *c.m.f.* '52 (CHI)[N] Oak Park, IL Claretian Missionaries USA Eastern Province.

Farrell, Robert J. '80 (CIN) Mason, OH St. Susanna.

Farrell, Robert *s.j.* '64 (BO)[U] Newton, MA The Jesuit Community at Boston College.

Farrell, Ronald J. '00 (CHR) Georgetown, SC St. Mary Our Lady of Ransom; Georgetown, SC St. Cyprian.

Farrell, Seamus J. '67 (OAK) Hayward, CA St. Bede; Consultors; Presbyteral Council.

Farrell, Thomas J. '92 (GB) Appleton, WI St. Pius X.

Farrell, Thomas P. '82 (LEX) Danville, KY SS. Peter & Paul; College of Consultors; Bluegrass West.

Farrell, Timothy W. '89 (GLP) Farmington, NM Sacred Heart; Priests' Retirement Board.

Farrell, Walter L. *s.j.* '47 (DET)[P] Bloomfield Hills, MI Manresa Jesuit Retreat House.

Farrelly, Paul *o.s.b.* '10 (SD)[J] Oceanside, CA Prince of Peace Abbey.

Farrelly, Terence J. '50 (ORL) Rockledge, FL St. Mary's Retired.

Farren, John Aquinas *o.p.* '64 (NY)[DD] New York, NY St. Catherine of Siena Priory; New York, NY St. Catherine of Siena.

Farris, William *o.f.m.* '77 (CIN)[E] Cincinnati, OH Roger Bacon High School; [T] Cincinnati, OH Roger Bacon High School Endowment; Councillors:; [N] Cincinnati, OH St. Clement Friary.

Farrugia, David J. *o.p.* '60 (OAK) Berkeley, CA St. Mary Magdalen; Deanery #6.

Farrugia, Mario *s.j.* '83 (PH)[C] Jesuit Fathers; [Y] Philadelphia, PA St. Alphonsus House.

Farrugia, William C. '63 (BRK) Astoria, NY St. Joseph Retired.

Farry, John A. '65 (CHI) Chicago, IL St. Andrew Retired.

Farry, John J. '67 (PH) Levittown, PA Queen of the Universe.

Farsaci, Francis A. *o.s.a.* '64 (PH)[Y] Villanova, PA St. Thomas Monastery.

Fasano, Eric R. '02 (RVC) Inwood, NY Our Lady of Good Counsel; Diocesan Judge.

Fasano, Jerome W. '77 (ARL) Front Royal, VA St. John the Baptist.

Fasching, Jeffery A. '97 (SPC) Ava, MO Immaculate Heart of Mary; On Duty Outside the Diocese; Mountain Grove, MO Sacred Heart.

Fasching, Jeffery '97 (SPC) Springfield, MO Cathedral of St. Agnes.

Fasching, Jeffrey A. '97 (SPC) Springfield Hospital Ministry.

Fasciglione, Massimo S. '74 (CAM) Ocean City, NJ Saint Damien Parish, Ocean City, N.J.

Fasline, Anthony '62 (Y) Retired.

Fasnacht, Matthew J. '07 (WIN) Stewartville, MN St. Bridget's; Stewartville, MN St. Bernard's; Appointed Members.

Faso, Charles '67 (CHI)[N] Chicago, IL St. Peter's Friary.

Fassero, Jonathan *o.s.b.* '78 (IND)[A] Saint Meinrad, IN Saint Meinrad School of Theology; [K] Saint Meinrad, IN St. Meinrad Archabbey; [A] Indianapolis, IN Bishop Simon Bruté College Seminary.

Fassett, Edward S. *s.j.* '88 (WDC)[O] Washington, DC Leonard Neale House; Washington, DC.

Fata, Joseph A. '68 (Y) Boardman, OH St. Luke.

Fater, Rev. Msgr. Douglas '70 (SAT) Retired.

Fath, Robert '07 (FBK) North Pole, AK St. Nicholas Catholic Church North Pole; Presbyteral Council.

Fatooh, Rev. Msgr. Charles G. '85 (MRY) Cayucos, CA St. Joseph.

Faucher, Eugene J. '51 (CHI) Arlington Heights, IL St. Edna; Morton Grove, IL St. Martha Retired.

Faucher, W. Thomas '71 (B) Boise, ID St. Mary's; Judges.

Faugno, Valerian *o.f.m.* '58 (ALB)[A] Catskill, NY St. Anthony Friary.

Faul, Charles J. '80 (RIC) Tabb, VA Blessed Kateri Tekakwitha.

Faulhaber, Gregory M. '79 (BUF) Defenders of the Bond; [A] East Aurora, NY Christ the King Seminary; [A] East Aurora, NY Christ the King Seminary.

Faulk, Kendal '10 (LAF) Rayne, LA St. Joseph.

Faulk, Peter A. '06 (ALX) Alexandria, LA St. Francis Xavier Cathedral; Alexandria, LA Rapides Regional Medical Center.

Faulkner, Joseph J. '05 (LIN) Hastings, NE St. Michael's; Advocates.

Faulstich, Paul J. *s.j.* '68 (CHI)[N] Chicago, IL Chicago Province of the Society of Jesus–Provincial Office.

Fauser, Steven W. '03 (HBG) Danville, PA State Hospital; Danville, PA St. Joseph.

Faust, Gary J. '78 (STL) Lemay, MO St. Bernadette.

Faust, Louis J. '74 (WDC) Brandywine, MD St. Michael; Germantown, MD Mother Seton Parish.

Faustner, William J. '76 (COL) Columbus, OH St. Timothy.

Fausz, Kevin P. *c.m.* '91 (SAT) In Metropolitan Area; Archdiocesan Presbyteral Council; Priests Personnel Board; San Antonio, TX Holy Redeemer; [D] San Antonio, TX St. Gerard Catholic High School.

Favazza, Robert D. '09 (MEM) Brownsville, TN St. John Church; Jackson, TN St. Mary Church.

Fawcett, Rev. Msgr. Henry F. '64 (SD) College of Consultors; Presbyteral Council Retired.

Fawls, Daniel J. '97 (BUF) Medina, NY Holy Trinity.

Fay, David E. '64 (CIN) Cincinnati, OH St. Gabriel; Judges.

Fay, Gregory J. '76 (STA) Jacksonville, FL San Jose.

Fay, William J. '64 (PIT) Retired.

Fay, Rev. Msgr. William J. (BO) College of Consultors.

Fay, Rev. Msgr. William P. '74 (BO) Brighton, MA St. Columbkille.

Fayle, Vaughn *o.f.m.* (CHI)[N] Chicago, IL St. Peter's Friary.

Faylona, Joey '03 (SAN) Andrews, TX Our Lady of Lourdes.

Fayos, Javier *l.c.* '97 (SAT)[G] San Antonio, TX Rolling Hills Academy, Inc.

Fazio, Cosimo R. '48 (NY) New Rochelle, NY St. Joseph Retired.

Fazio, Paul *o.f.m.conv.* '74 (OAK)[L] Castro Valley, CA Conventual Franciscans (Province of St. Joseph of Cupertino).

Fazolini, Leandro *s.f.* '11 (WDC)[B] Silver Spring, MD Holy Family Seminary.

Fazolini, Leandro (BAL) Columbia, MD St. John the Evangelist.

Feather, Ronald Joseph '11 (AUS) Austin, TX St. Vincent de Paul.

Feccia, August *c.s.* '62 (CHI) Melrose Park, IL St. Charles Borromeo.

Fecher, Rev. Msgr. Vincent '50 (SAT)[K] San Antonio, TX Padua Place Retired.

Fechner, Erich A. '92 (STL) St. Louis, MO St. Simon the Apostle; [V] St. Louis, MO Archdiocesan Stewardship Education Committee.

Fecht, Geoffrey *o.s.b.* '88 (SCL)[I] Collegeville, MN St. John's Abbey, of the Order of St. Benedict.

Fecko, Leonard J. '89 (CIN) On Special and Archdiocesan Assignment.

Fecteau, Raymond L. '72 (WDC) Darnestown, MD Our Lady of the Visitation; Irving, TX National Catholic Committee on Scouting Executive Committee (1934).

Fedak, Dennis Z. '98 (PH) Philadelphia, PA Nativity of the Blessed Virgin Mary; Philadelphia, PA Our Lady Help of Christians.

Fedak, Paul C. '98 (FR) North Easton, MA Immaculate Conception.

Fedders, William '68 (LEX) Special Assignment.

Fedek, Robert M. '05 (CHI) Chicago, IL Our Lady of Victory; College of Consultors.

Fedele, Giuseppe '05 (NEW) On Duty Outside the Archdiocese.

Federico, Cesidio J. '62 (WH) Retired.

Federline, Thomas A. '85 (GBG) Greensburg, PA St. Paul; Diocesan Ecumenical Office.

Feders, Joseph *o.s.b.* '99 (SCL) Saint Joseph, MN St. Joseph's; [I] Collegeville, MN St. John's Abbey, of the Order of St. Benedict; Diocesan Consultors; Presbyteral Council.

Federspiel, Nicholas '04 (RCK) South Beloit, IL St. Peter.

Fedewa, Eric '11 (DET) Troy, MI St. Anastasia.

Fedewa, Matthew '58 (LAN) Retired.

Fedewa, Rev. Msgr. Sylvester L. '54 (LAN) Cursillo Retired.

Fedigan, James J. *s.j.* '65 (NY)[DD] Loyola Hall, Jesuit Community.

Fedigan, James (BRK) Jackson Heights, NY Our Lady of Fatima.

Fedor, Gregory F. '83 (Y) Austintown, OH St. Joseph; College of Consultors.

Fedor, Lawrence L. *o.s.b.* '65 (MIL)[P] Benet Lake, WI St. Benedict's Abbey.

Fedor, Mark Q. '72 (CLV) Cleveland, OH St. Mel; Promoters of Justice.

Fedor, Robert P. '61 (E) Retired.

Fedora, Joseph *m.m.* '84 (FgM) Maryknoll, NY MARYKNOLL.

Fee, James M. *o.m.i.* '71 (BUF) Buffalo, NY Holy Angels.

Fee, John *ss.cc.* (FR)[F] Fairhaven, MA Damien Residence.

Feehan, Stephen S. '62 (NEW) Retired.

Feehily, John W. '73 (OKL) Moore, OK St. Andrew the Apostle Catholic Church.

Feela, Paul F. '78 (STP) St. Paul, MN Church of Lumen Christi.

Feeley, Paul *o.carm.* '53 (NY) New York, NY St. John the Martyr Retired.

Feely, Rev. Msgr. James B. '58 (GB) Hortonville, WI SS. Peter and Paul; Priests' Personnel Board Retired.

Feely, Thomas H. *s.j.* '75 (NY) New York, NY; Watertown, MA; [DD] New York, NY Society of Jesus, New York Province; [DD] New York, NY Xavier Jesuit Community; Towson, MD.

Feely, Thomas J. *s.j.* '75 (BO)[U] Watertown, MA The Society of Jesus of New England–Provincial Offices.

Feeney, Christopher P. '10 (NOR) Old Saybrook, CT St. John.

Feeney, John J. '54 (PRT) Retired.

Feeney, Joseph J. *s.j.* '65 (PH)[C] Jesuit Fathers; [Y] Loyola Center and Manresa Hall.

Feeney, Kevin J. '77 (CHI)[A] Mundelein, IL University of St. Mary of the Lake/Mundelein Seminary.

Feeney, Robert T. '86 (PH) Philadelphia, PA Sacred Heart of Jesus.

Feeney, Thomas M. '48 (PH) Retired.

Feeney, Rev. Msgr. Thomas P. '79 (CC) Office of the Bishop; Diaconate Formation Screening Committee; Tribunal; Judges; Canonical Affairs; Judicial Vicar; Presbyteral Council.

Feeney, William P. '72 (PIT) Judges; Washington, PA Immaculate Conception; Priest Council.

Fegan, Joseph Peter *o.p.* '01 (WDC)[B] Washington, DC Dominican House of Studies.

Fehn, Jerome W. '78 (MO) Army National Guard Chaplains.

Fehn, Jerry '78 (STP) Fairview–Southdale Hospital; Methodist Hospital.

Fehrenbacher, Henry '48 (SCL) Retired.

Fehring, Fabian *o.f.m.cap.* '53 (GF) Hardin, MT St. Joseph.

Feierfeil, Gerald F. '67 (SC) Continuing Education for Priests Retired.

Feigh, Jason R. '11 (E) Erie, PA Our Lady of Peace.

Feil, Carl *o.s.m.* '61 (ORL) Melbourne, FL Our Lady of Lourdes Retired.

Feild, Rev. Msgr. Martin E. '59 (BAL) Taneytown, MD St. Joseph; Priest Personnel Board.

Feiss, Hugh *o.s.b.* '66 (B)[C] Jerome, ID Monastery of the Ascension.

Feit, Matthias '56 (PHX)[G] Phoenix, AZ Mount Claret Roman Catholic Retreat Center Retired.

Fekete, George J. '65 (GR) Retired.

Feketie, Michael J. '57 (NEW) Plainfield, NJ St. Mary Retired.

Felago, John F. *m.m.* '68 (SJ)[M] Los Altos, CA Maryknoll.

Felczak, Leonard J. '44 (CHI) Chicago, IL St. Tarcissus Retired.

Feld, Norbert F. *s.s.c.* '49 (PRO)[O] Bristol, RI St. Columban's Retirement House Retired.

Feld, Norbert *s.s.c.* '49 (OM)[J] St. Columbans Missionary Society of St. Columban.

Feldcamp, Rev. Msgr. William J. '65 (SCR) Scranton, PA St. Clare; Diocesan Consultors; Deans; Scranton, PA St. Paul's; Presbyteral Council.

Feldhaus, Rev. Msgr. Eugene A. '46 (BRK) Little Neck, NY; [R] Douglaston, NY Bishop Mugavero Residence Retired.

Feldhaus, Thomas F. '76 (CIN) Priests On Administrative Leave.

Feldkamp, Angelo J. *o.praem.* '68 (GB)[J] De Pere, WI St. Norbert Abbey.

Feldmeier, Russell J. *m.m.* '80 (FgM) Maryknoll, NY MARYKNOLL.

Felice, John M. *o.f.m.* '68 (NY) New York, NY St. Francis of Assisi.

Felice–Pace, Albert *o.p.* '60 (LAV) St. Thomas Aquinas Catholic Newman Community at UNLV; [E] Las Vegas, NV St. Thomas Aquinas Catholic Newman Community at UNLV; [C] Las Vegas, NV Dominican Rectory, Fra Angelico House.

Felices, Rev. Msgr. Fernando B. '82 (SJN) World Apostolate of Fatima.

Felices–Sanchez, Rev. Msgr. Fernando B. '82 (SJN) Censor Librorum; Spiritual Directors.

Feliciano, Abraham *s.d.b.* '05 (WDC) Washington, DC Nativity.

Felicitas, Godofredo '82 (BRK) Bayside, NY St. Robert Bellarmine; [Q] Filipino Apostolate.

Felipe, Marvin P. *s.d.b.* '92 (SFR) San Francisco, CA St. Anne.

Felipe, Matias *o.m.i.* '56 (SAT)[K] San Antonio, TX Oblate Madonna Residence.

Felix, Bernard H. '92 (DOD) Scott City, KS St. Joseph Catholic Church of Scott City, Kansas; Dighton, KS St. Theresa Catholic Church of Dighton, Kansas; Presbyteral Council.

Felix, Eduardo Logiste *o.p.* '10 (MEM)[F] Memphis, TN The Dominican Friars of Memphis, Inc.; Memphis, TN St. Peter Church.

Felix, Paul G. '90 (GAL) Dickinson, TX Shrine of the

True Cross; Southern Vicariate; Area Representatives.
Felix, William P. '81 (LC) Boyd, WI Sacred Heart of Jesus–St. Joseph; Stanley, WI Holy Family; [M] Boyd, WI Institute of St. Joseph.
Feliz, Normando '75 (VEN) Retired.
Felker, Joseph F. '73 (SB) Riverside, CA St. Thomas the Apostle.
Fell, Rev. Msgr. John N. '88 (MET) Bernardsville, NJ Our Lady of Perpetual Help; [L] Bernardsville, NJ Sacred Heart Chapel; Episcopal Vicars.
Fell, Timothy J. '99 (BAL) Priests Sick or Absent.
Fellenz, Ralph *o.f.m.cap.* '68 (GB)[J] Appleton, WI St. Fidelis Friary Retired.
Feller, Richard J. '53 (CHI) South Holland, IL Holy Ghost Retired.
Feller, Robert M. *o.praem.* '55 (GB)[J] De Pere, WI St. Norbert Abbey.
Fellrath, Frank W. '89 (MET) Edison, NJ Our Lady of Peace.
Felt, James W. *s.j.* '56 (SJ)[B] Santa Clara, CA Jesuit Community.
Felt, Richard R. '69 (PHX) Mesa, AZ Holy Cross Roman Catholic Parish; College of Consultors; Presbyteral Council; Deans.
Felter, Francis J. *m.m.* '69 (FgM) Maryknoll, NY MARYKNOLL.
Feltes, Victor C. '09 (LC)[C] Marshfield, WI Columbus High School; [C] Marshfield, WI Columbus Catholic Middle School; Marshfield, WI St. John the Baptist; Marshfield, WI Christ the King.
Feltman, Philip S. '66 (TOL) Retired.
Feltman, Thomas M. '01 (FAR) Fargo, ND Nativity Church of Fargo.
Felton, Daniel J. '81 (GB) Newton, WI St. Thomas the Apostle; Priests' Personnel Board; Manitowoc, WI St. Francis of Assisi; Appointed Members; Vicars General; College of Consultors.
Feltz, John G. '73 (BUR) Army National Guard Chaplains; Defenders of the Bond; Fairfax, VT St. Luke; Milton, VT St. Ann; Notaries.
Feltz, Joseph E. '79 (PIT) Prospect, PA St. Christopher at the Lake.
Feltz, Joseph M. '02 (IND) Brownsburg, IN St. Malachy Catholic Church, Brownsburg, Inc.
Feltz, Thomas '85 (LA) Encino, CA Our Lady of Grace.
Felux, Jonathan W. '09 (SAT) San Antonio, TX Our Lady of Grace; Office of the Archbishop; [A] San Antonio, TX Assumption Seminary.
Feminelli, John '87 (CC) Retired.
Fenelon, David '70 (DM) Retired.
Fenger, Guy '77 (MIA) Retired.
Fenili, J. Robert *c.ss.r.* '62 (CHI)[N] Chicago, IL Redemptorist Theology Residence.
Fenlon, Brian '75 (PHX) Special Assignment Retired.
Fenlon, John P. '70 (SY) Syracuse, NY St. Patrick; Syracuse, NY St. Brigid and St. Joseph.
Fenlon, Thomas '61 (NY) Bronx, NY St. Augustine; Bronx, NY Our Lady of Victory; Bronx, NY Vernon C. Bain Center.
Fennell, Joseph G. *s.j.* '45 (BO)[U] Weston, MA Campion Health Center, Inc.
Fennell, Patrick A. *o.s.b.* '89 (PEO)[A] Peru, IL St. Bede Abbey.
Fenner, Eric *o.f.m.conv.* '46 (TR) Seaside Park, NJ St. Catharine of Siena.
Fennessy, Rev. Msgr. James J. '68 (ATL) Atlanta, GA St. Jude.
Fennessy, James '02 (ROC) Waterloo, NY St. Patrick; Waterloo, NY St. Mary.
Fennessy, Joseph H. '56 (HBG) Retired.
Fennessy, Keith G. '84 (NY) New York, NY St. Columba.
Fennessy, Peter J. *s.j.* '70 (DET)[P] Bloomfield Hills, MI Manresa Jesuit Retreat House.
Fenske, Donald J. '58 (CHI) Calumet City, IL Our Lady of Knock Retired.
Fenstermaker, James E. *c.s.c.* '84 (FR) South Easton, MA Holy Cross.
Fenstermaker, James E. *c.s.c.* '84 (FTW)[H] Notre Dame Congregation of Holy Cross, United States Province of Priests & Brothers.
Fenton, Joe *s.m.* '94 (LA)[AA] Claremont, CA Claremont Colleges.
Fenton, Joseph *s.m.* '72 (WDC)[O] Washington, DC Marist Center.
Fenton, Lawrence E. '63 (GI) Retired.
Fenton, Patrick '08 (TYL) Trinity, TX Most Holy Trinity.
Fenzl, Roderick R. *o.praem.* '55 (GB)[J] De Pere, WI St. Norbert Abbey.
Ferdinand, Cruz Cruz '05 (PCE) Villalba, PR Our Lady of Mt. Carmel.
Ference, Damian J. '03 (CLV)[A] Wickliffe, OH Borromeo Seminary.
Ferguson, Gary M. '71 (TOL) Archbold, OH St. Peter; Fayette, OH Our Lady of Mercy.
Ferguson, James A. '85 (ALX) Defender of the Bond and Promoter of Justice; Alexandria, LA St. Francis Xavier Cathedral; College of Consultors; Elected Members.
Ferguson, James J. *c.s.c.* '64 (PHX)[F] Phoenix, AZ Holy Cross Congregation/Casa Santa Cruz; Glendale, AZ St. Helen Roman Catholic Parish.
Ferguson, Justin R. '06 (SAV) Grovetown, GA St. Teresa of Avila; Presbyteral Council.
Ferguson, Michael B. (RIC) Virginia Beach, VA Church of the Holy Apostles.
Ferguson, Paul Anthony '02 (EVN) Evansville, IN Holy Redeemer.
Ferguson, Peter A. '90 (GAL) Retired.
Ferguson, Robert *f.s.s.p.* '02 (LIN)[A] Denton, NE Our Lady of Guadalupe Seminary.
Ferguson, Thomas P. '94 (ARL) Alexandria, VA Good Shepherd; Diocesan Judges; Episcopal Vicar for Faith Formation and Director of the Diaconate Formation Program; Diaconal Formation Program.
Ferguson, William J. '06 (COL) Buckeye Lake, OH Our Lady of Mt. Carmel; Diocesan Commission for Ecumenical and Interreligious Affairs.
Ferland, Martin *m.m.a.* '95 (SAM)[B] Petersham, MA Maronite Monks of Adoration Most Holy Trinity Monastery.
Ferland, Thomas J. '87 (PRO) Pawtucket, RI St. Teresa of the Child Jesus.
Ferlita, Ernest *s.j.* '62 (NO) Retired.
Fermeglia, Charles S. '88 (SFR) Half Moon Bay, CA Our Lady of the Pillar.
Fermeglia, Charles '88 (BRK) Released from Diocesan Assignment.
Fernan, Matthew F. '89 (NY) Hastings–on–Hudson, NY St. Matthew.
Fernandes, Babasino '75 (LKC) Jennings, LA St. Lawrence; Elton, LA St. Joseph's.
Fernandes, Cosme S. '95 (NY) Bronx, NY St. Martin of Tours.
Fernandes, Cyril '88 (FTW) Fort Wayne, IN St. John the Baptist.
Fernandes, David A. '97 (PH) Roslyn, PA St. John of the Cross.
Fernandes, Earl K. '02 (CIN) Imprimatur Censors; [A] Cincinnati, OH The Athenaeum of Ohio; [B] Cincinnati, OH Mount St. Mary's Seminary of the West; [B] Cincinnati, OH Mount St. Mary's Seminary of the West.
Fernandes, George S. '87 (SB) Upland, CA St. Joseph.
Fernandes, John '77 (OAK) Retired.
Fernandes, Jose Manuel '59 (NEW) Elizabeth, NJ Our Lady of Fatima.
Fernandes, Lourdino '69 (FTW) Monroeville, IN St. Rose of Lima.
Fernandes, Mauro N. de Souza *o.s.b.* '84 (GBG)[H] Latrobe Saint Vincent Archabbey; [H] Latrobe, PA Saint Vincent Archabbey.
Fernandes, Patrick O. '83 (BUF) Buffalo General Hospital.
Fernandes, Peter *s.f.x.* '99 (CHI) Chicago, IL St. Timothy.
Fernandes, Roque A.D. '69 (LA) Azusa, CA St. Frances of Rome Retired.
Fernandes, Socorro *s.a.c.* '99 (DET) Redford, MI Our Lady of Loretto.
Fernandes, Stephen *o.f.m.cap.* '10 (BAL)[Q] Cumberland, MD The Friary; Cumberland, MD Our Lady of the Mountains, Roman Catholic Congregation, Inc.
Fernandes, Sydney '79 (HON) Honolulu, HI SS Peter and Paul.
Fernandez, Agostino *o.s.b.* '06 (CHL)[J] Belmont, NC Belmont Abbey.
Fernandez, Agustin Estrada '00 (SAT) San Antonio, TX St. Vincent de Paul.
Fernandez, Altaire '00 (LA) Granada Hills, CA St. John Baptist de la Salle.
Fernandez, Archelito '93 (TLS) Bartlesville, OK St. James.
Fernandez, Cesar A. '95 (LA) La Puente, CA St. Louis of France; On Sick Leave.
Fernandez, Rev. Msgr. Daniel (ARE) Seminary Board and Vocation Program.
Fernandez, Eduardo C. *s.j.* '92 (OAK)[A] Berkeley, CA Jesuit School of Theology of Santa Clara University (Berkeley, California Campus); [L] Berkeley, CA Jesuit Fathers and Brothers.
Fernandez, Edward P. '70 (DAL) Retired.
Fernandez, Emmanuel '79 (LAF) Erath, LA St. John.
Fernandez, Fabio Jose '04 (CAM) Glassboro, NJ St. Bridget's Catholic Church, Glassboro, N.J.
Fernandez, Felipe *o.s.a.* '71 (SJN) Bayamon, PR San Agustin.
Fernandez, Francis X. *o.f.m.cap.* '58 (FWT) Fort Worth, TX Our Lady of Guadalupe; Cursillo Center.
Fernandez, Frank '79 (PHX) Retired.
Fernandez, Gerardo '91 (SD) Calexico, CA Our Lady of Guadalupe Catholic Parish Calexico.
Fernandez, Gustavo D. *s.j.* '67 (FgM) Los Gatos, CA Society of Jesus.
Fernandez, Jose A. '60 (BGP) Retired.
Fernandez, Julio '57 (MGZ) Censor Librorum; Religious Consultor; Religious Coordinator.
Fernandez, Luis J. '71 (NO) Retired.
Fernandez, Rev. Msgr. Manuel '62 (ORL) Retired.
Fernandez, Marcellus '68 (B) Retired.
Fernandez, Peter '95 (DOD) Garden City, KS St. Dominic Catholic Church of Garden City, Kansas; Ingalls, KS St. Stanislaus Catholic Church of Ingalls, Kansas.
Fernandez, Rafael *o.f.m.* '87 (FgM) New York, NY Franciscan Province of the Immaculate Conception.
Fernandez, Ricardo *c.m.* (ARE) Manati, PR Sagrada Familia.
Fernandez, Romualdo *c.m.f.* '53 (SJN) Bayamon, PR San Antonio Maria Claret.
Fernandez, Samuel *o.c.d.* '07 (CGS) Caguas, PR San Jose.
Fernandez, Simine G. *o.ss.t.* '04 (BAL)[Q] Assigned in India.
Fernandez–Diaz, Mariano *s.t.* '05 (FAJ) Luquillo, PR San Jose.
Fernandez Martinez, Jose *o.de.m.* (SJN) San Juan, PR Nuestra Senora de la Merced.
Fernandez Minguez, Serapio '50 (ARE) Retired.
Fernandez Torres, Ismael *o.p.* (SJN) Bayamon, PR Invencion de la Santa Cruz.
Fernando, Antony '85 (CR) Mahnomen, MN St. Michael's Parish.
Fernando, Augustine '64 (RVC) Farmingdale, NY St. Kilian.
Fernando, Bernard '65 (NEW) Retired.
Fernando, Camillus '80 (BAK) Vale, OR St. Patrick.
Fernando, Cresus '82 (NY) Suffern, NY Sacred Heart.
Fernando, G. Peter (B) Priest River, ID St. Catherine's.
Fernando, Gamini E. '71 (NY) Poughkeepsie, NY Holy Trinity; Stormville, NY Green Haven Correctional Facility; Prison Apostolate.
Fernando, Joachim '62 (BRK) Retired.
Fernando, Joseph Paul '62 (RVC) Long Beach, NY St. Ignatius Martyr; Long Beach, NY Long Beach Memorial Medical Center.
Fernando, Lionel '87 (SAN) Sonora, TX St. Ann's.
Fernando, Peter Damian '70 (LA) Ventura, CA San Buenaventura Mission.
Fernando, Polycarp '78 (FTW) Fort Wayne, IN St. Vincent de Paul.
Fernando, Roger M. '75 (P) Florence, OR St. Mary, Our Lady of the Dunes; Reedsport, OR St. John the Apostle.
Fernando, Simon '60 (RVC) Retired.
Fernando, Susil '87 (LKC) Vinton, LA St. Joseph; Diocesan Consultors; Vocation Recruiters.
Fernando, Rev. Msgr. Venantius M. '61 (NEW) Hillside, NJ Christ the King.
Fernando–Diaz, Luis *s.t.* '10 (MOB) Fort Mitchell, AL St. Joseph; Sacramental Ministers.
Ferone, John M. *s.j.* '83 (CIN)[N] Cincinnati, OH Faber Jesuit Community.
Ferraioli, Rev. Msgr. Frank B. '61 (PAT) Parsippany, NJ St. Christopher Retired.
Ferraioli, Joseph *o.m.i.* '77 (SD) Chula Vista, CA Most Precious Blood Catholic Parish.
Ferrante, Frank *c.m.f.* '70 (LA)[V] Rancho Dominguez, CA Dominguez Seminary Inc.
Ferrara, Alberto A. *c.s.b.* '00 (GAL)[O] Sugar Land Basilian Mission Center.
Ferrara, Angelus '90 (NTN) Leave of Absence.
Ferrara, Charles F. '90 (STL) Lemay, MO St. Martin of Tours.
Ferrara, Giorgio *p.i.m.e.* '86 (DET)[T] Detroit, MI PIME Foster Parents–Adoptions at a Distance; [K] Detroit, MI P.I.M.E. Missionaries.
Ferrara, John *o.m.v.* '82 (BO)[U] Milton, MA Oblate Residence (St. Joseph House).
Ferrara, Joseph R. '77 (CAM) Margate City, NJ Holy Trinity Parish, Margate, N.J.
Ferrarese, Rev. Msgr. Fernando A. '77 (BRK)[K] Brooklyn, NY Italian Board of Guardians; Astoria, NY Immaculate Conception.
Ferrari, Rev. Msgr. Steven A. '80 (BRK) Brooklyn; Assignment Board; Brooklyn, NY Immaculate Heart of Mary.
Ferraro, Joseph A. '90 (NEW) Newark, NJ St. Anthony's; Members; Presbyteral Council.
Ferraro, Rev. Msgr. Joseph '67 (OAK) Retired.
Ferraro, Michael M. '68 (BO) Lynn, MA St. Mary.
Ferraro, Pat '92 (Y) Streetsboro, OH St. Joan of Arc; Presbyteral Council.
Ferraro, Ronald A. '60 (HRT) Waterbury, CT Our Lady of Lourdes; Waterbury, CT St. Lucy.
Ferraro, Vincent J. '70 (BUF) Kenmore, NY St. Andrew.
Ferras, Jesus '04 (MIL)[T] Waukesha, WI Secular Institute of Schoenstatt Fathers.
Ferras, Jesus *i.s.p.* '04 (AUS) Office of Youth, Young Adult and Campus Ministry; [G] Austin, TX Schoenstatt Fathers.
Ferrazoli, Henry R. '61 (NEW) Retired.
Ferrecchia, Leonard *c.s.s.* '55 (BO)[X] Waltham, MA Stigmatine Fathers and Brothers Retired.
Ferreira, Alfonse *o.f.m.* '72 (BO)[U] Lynn, MA Franciscan Community (Province of Immaculate Conception); [U] Lynn, MA "The Listening Place" (Counseling Center); The Listening Place; The Listening Place; The Listening Place.
Ferreira, James (NY) Staten Island, NY St. Teresa.
Ferreira, Jose S. '56 (BO) Senior Priests. Retired.

Ferreira, Joseph A. '59 (OAK)[K] Oakland, CA Bishop Begin Villa Retired.
Ferreira, Manuel P. '60 (FR) Retired.
Ferrence, John J. *o.s.a.* '52 (PH)[Y] Villanova, PA St. Thomas Monastery.
Ferrer, Antonio '98 (NY) Staten Island, NY St. Joseph.
Ferrer, Charles M. '64 (CHI) Chicago, IL St. Mary of the Angels; [V] Chicago, IL Midtown Residence; Chicago.
Ferrer, Christopher '01 (AUS) Judicial Vicar; Diocesan Tribunal Judges; Hutto, TX St. Patrick; Ex Officio.
Ferrer, Gonzalo '81 (AUS) Retired.
Ferrer, Jorge *s.j.* '77 (MGZ) Mayaguez, PR Church De El Buen Pastor.
Ferrer, Melchor *s.d.b.* '74 (NY) New York, NY St. Rose of Lima; Manhattan, NY New York Presbyterian Hospital.
Ferrer, Michael M. *s.d.b.* '74 (NY) Manhattan, NY New York Presbyterian–Columbia Medical Center.
Ferretti, Samuel J. '74 (SCR) Scranton, PA St. Lucy's; Scranton, PA SS. Peter and Paul; Deans.
Ferri, Gregory J. '98 (BAL) Special Assignment.
Ferrick, Michael P. '99 (E) St. Marys, PA Queen of the World; [F] St. Marys, PA Elk County Catholic High School; [F] Saint Marys, PA St. Marys Catholic Middle School; [F] Saint Marys, PA St. Marys Catholic Elementary School.
Ferrick, Raymond J. '77 (PRO) Barrington, RI Holy Angels.
Ferrie, Francis '65 (NO) New Orleans, LA Mater Dolorosa Retired.
Ferrier, Francis V. *s.j.* '61 (BR) Special Assignment.
Ferrier, Ronald J. '68 (PH) Philadelphia, PA St. Katherine of Siena.
Ferrigan, Robert '61 (CHI) Winnetka, IL Sacred Heart Retired.
Ferris, Aaron R. '09 (GR) Grand Rapids, MI Sacred Heart of Jesus.
Ferris, Carl A. '55 (GI) Retired.
Ferris, Luke A. '11 (GB) Oshkosh, WI St. Raphael the Archangel; Winneconne, WI St. Mary; Omro, WI St. Mary.
Ferris, Robert M. '01 (CHL) Hickory, NC St. Aloysius.
Ferris, Thomas B. '63 (PIT) Retired.
Ferris, Timothy F. '03 (TOL) Bluffton, OH St. Mary; [B] Lima, OH Central Catholic High School; Delphos, OH St. John the Evangelist; Procurator–Advocate for Respondents; Associate Judges.
Ferrito, Rev. Msgr. Joseph L. (PAT) Retired.
Ferro, Ralph '71 (RVC) New Hyde Park, NY Holy Spirit; East Meadow, NY Nassau County Correctional Center; Chaplains.
Ferry, James P. '06 (NEW)[O] Teaneck, NJ Fairleigh Dickinson Univ.–Teaneck Campus; River Edge, NJ St. Peter the Apostle.
Ferry, James T. *m.m.* '56 (FgM) Maryknoll, NY MARYKNOLL.
Ferry, James '84 (FR) Fall River, MA Espirito Santo.
Ferry, Rev. Msgr. John T. '84 (NY) Central Westchester; Scarsdale, NY Immaculate Heart of Mary.
Fesen, Thomas A. '99 (TR) Hamilton Square, NJ St. Gregory the Great.
Feser, Victor *o.s.b.* '64 (BIS)[A] Richardton, ND Assumption Abbey; [B] Bismarck, ND University of Mary.
Fesniak, Mark '03 (PHU) Minersville, PA Nativity of B.V.M.; Minersville, PA St. Nicholas.
Fesniak, Mark (PHU) Presbyteral Council.
Fessio, Joseph D. *s.j.* '72 (SFR)[N] San Francisco, CA Jesuit Community at St. Ignatius College Preparatory.
Fest, Donald M. *s.s.j.* '76 (BAL) Baltimore, MD St. Veronica.
Fesuh, Tesfay Woldemarian '88 (WDC)[X] Washington, DC Ethiopian and Eritrean Catholic Mission, USA.
Fesuh, Tesfaye (WDC) Washington, DC Blessed Sacrament, Shrine of the Most.
Fetcho, John E. '64 (SY) Retired.
Fetscher, James F. '68 (MIA) Fort Lauderdale, FL St. Sebastian; Appointed by the Archbishop.
Fetscher, James '68 (MIA)[J] Pinecrest, FL Morning-Star Renewal Center, Inc.
Fetters, Donald G. *c.s.c.* '76 (FgM) New Rochelle, NY Eastern Brothers Province.
Feucht, Urban C. '55 (SEA)[M] Lacey, WA St. Martin's Abbey.
Feudjio, Rev. Msgr. Jerome '90 (STV) Vicar for Clergy and Religious; Charlotte Amalie, VI Cathedral of Sts. Peter and Paul; Diocesan Consultors; Vocations; Catholic Television Network (CTN); Prison Ministry.
Feusahrens, Frederick J. '72 (RIC) Retired.
Fevlo, Anthony *s.m.a.* '98 (BO)[U] Dedham, MA African Mission House.
Fey, Albert *c.pp.s.* '46 (CIN)[N] Carthagena, OH St. Charles Retired.
Fey, George *c.pp.s.* '43 (CIN)[N] Carthagena, OH St. Charles Retired.
Fey, Thomas J. '70 (ALX) Retired.
Fiala, Timothy R. '96 (CHI) Hillside, IL St. Domitilla; [A] Chicago, IL St. Joseph College Seminary.
Fiala, Vit *o.f.m.* '98 (Y) Definitors:; Youngstown, OH; [J] Youngstown, OH Mt. Alverna Friary.
Fiala, Vit *o.f.m.* (NY)[DD] Mount Vernon, NY Franciscan Mission Associates.
Fialkowski, Edward R. '78 (CHI) Arlington Heights, IL Our Lady of the Wayside; College of Consultors; Deans.
Fialkowski, Thomas M. '66 (E) Directors Retired.
Fiano, Guy *o.carm.* '83 (PMB) Boca Raton, FL St. Jude.
Fice, Joseph J. *s.j.* '72 (SJ)[L] Los Altos, CA Jesuit Retreat Center of Los Altos.
Ficek, Ryszard '98 (RVC) Floral Park, NY Our Lady of Victory.
Fichteman, William L. '81 (L) Archdiocesan Examiners Retired.
Fichter, Stephen J. '00 (NEW) Haworth, NJ Sacred Heart.
Fichter, Stephen J. (WDC)[X] Washington, DC CARA, Center for Applied Research in the Apostolate.
Fichtner, Rev. Msgr. Robert C. '55 (BO) Senior Priests. Retired.
Fickel, William *s.s.s.* '81 (CLV)[N] Cleveland, OH Congregation of the Blessed Sacrament; Highland Heights, OH St. Paschal Baylon.
Fickes, Daniel R. '91 (CLV) Garfield Heights, OH St. Therese.
Ficorilli, Chad R. *o.s.b.* '79 (GBG)[H] Latrobe, PA Saint Vincent Archabbey.
Ficorilli, Chad R. *o.s.b.* '79 (ALT) Nicktown, PA St. Nicholas.
Fictum, Robert A. '78 (MIL) Ripon, WI St. Catherine of Siena.
Fidalgo, Federico '63 (CC) Retired.
Fider, William '66 (DUL) Duluth, MN St. Joseph; Duluth, MN St. Lawrence.
Fiebelkorn, Daniel F. '97 (BUF) Silver Creek, NY Our Lady of Mt. Carmel.
Fiedler, Donald J. '59 (DOD) Retired.
Fiedler, Rev. Msgr. Kenneth J. '71 (MAD) Madison, WI Our Lady, Queen of Peace; [H] Madison, WI Saint Martin House; Deaneries.
Fiedler, Loyd *s.v.d.* '70 (FgM) Techny, IL.
Fiedler, Tomasz *s.j.* '11 (BO)[U] Brighton, MA Walter Ciszek House.
Fiedurek, Jan *t.chr* (WDC) Silver Spring, MD Our Lady Queen of Poland and Saint Maximilian Kolbe; [X] Silver Spring, MD Friends of John Paul II Foundation.
Field, Eugene J. '94 (NEW) Paramus, NJ Our Lady of the Visitation; Boy Scouts of America/Catholic Committee on Scouting.
Field, Michael J. '82 (CAM) Wildwood, NJ Notre Dame de la Mer Parish, Wildwood, N.J.
Fields, Rev. Archpriest John M. '86 (PHU) Deacon Formation; [D] Philadelphia, PA Ascension Manor, Inc.; College of Archeparchial Consultors; Presbyteral Council; Protopresbyters (Deans); Frackville, PA St. Michael's; Board Members; Frackville, PA St. John the Baptist.
Fields, Robert H. '82 (JC) I. Columbia; Brunswick, MO St. Boniface; Brunswick, MO St. Raphael.
Fields, Stephen M. *s.j.* '86 (WDC)[O] Washington, DC The Jesuit Community at Georgetown University.
Fields, William Dominic *o.p.* '91 (L) Louisville, KY St. Louis Bertrand; [L] Louisville, KY St. Louis Bertrand Priory.
Fier, Brian J. '89 (STP) Bloomington, MN St. Edward.
Fierro, Rev. Msgr. David G. '76 (ELP) El Paso, TX St. Matthew; Vicar for Clergy; Defenders of the Bond; Finance Council; Ex Officio Members; Priests' Personnel Advisory Committee.
Fierros, Rick '78 (FRS) Delano, CA St. Mary of the Miraculous Medal.
Fifagrowicz, Joseph G. '62 (BUF) Eggertsville, NY St. Benedict Retired.
Figaredo, Tarsicio Gotay *o.carm.* '73 (SJN) San Juan, PR Santa Teresita Del Nino Jesus; San Juan–Santurce; Subcommission for Popular Piety.
Figel, Terence *o.m.i.* '64 (DUL) Duluth, MN Holy Family.
Figge, Urban *o.m.i.* '57 (BEL)[F] Belleville, IL Missionary Oblates of Mary Immaculate – St. Henry's Oblate Residence.
Figlia, Sidney *s.d.b.* '68 (SP)[P] Tampa, FL Mary Help of Christians Center.
Figliola, Nicholas J. '64 (RVC) Sayville, NY St. Lawrence the Martyr.
Figliozzi, Rev. Msgr. Richard M. '79 (RVC) Elmont, NY St. Vincent de Paul; Franklin Square, NY St. Catherine of Sienna.
Figueiredo, Rev. Msgr. Anthony J. '94 (NEW) On Duty Outside the Archdiocese.
Figueredo, Sergio *s.j.* '60 (MIA) Miami, FL Gesu.
Figueroa, Alberto (SJN) San Juan, PR Santa Luisa de Marillac.
Figueroa, Edward *o.m.i.* '60 (FgM) Washington, DC AMERICAN OBLATE MISSIONS.
Figueroa, Honecimo '99 (MO) Army National Guard Chaplains; On Assignment Outside the Diocese.
Figueroa, Jose I. '96 (DAL) Dallas, TX Blessed Sacrament.
Figueroa, Ruben C. *o.f.m.* '70 (TYL) Hispanic Ministry Advisory Council.
Figueroa, Tomas Galarza '86 (MGZ) San German, PR San German de Auxerre.
Figueroa–Esquer, Francisco J. '01 (OAK) Bishop's Representative for Catholic Charismatics (Spanish); Oakland, CA St. Jarlath.
Figueroa–Esquer, Francisco '01 (OAK) Chaplains.
Figurelli, Nicholas G. '82 (NEW)[B] Seton Hall University; Absent on Leave.
Filacchione, Rev. Msgr. Marc J. '80 (NY) New York, NY Our Lady of Victory; New York Fire Department; Hospital Apostolate, Office of the.
Filardi, Rev. Msgr. Edward J. '94 (WDC) Bethesda, MD Our Lady of Lourdes; Priest Council.
Filary, Richard M. '82 (SAG) Bay City, MI St. Stanislaus Kostka; Judges.
Filice, Francis P. '79 (SFR)[K] San Rafael, CA Nazareth House of San Rafael, Inc. Retired.
Filice, Peter F. *s.j.* '71 (LA)[F] Los Angeles, CA Loyola High School of Los Angeles.
Filipkowski, Peter '86 (PAT) Mountain Lakes, NJ St. Catherine of Siena.
Filippelli, John L.M. *s.s.j.* '57 (WDC)[B] Washington, DC St. Joseph's Seminary.
Filippello, Michael A. '00 (PH) Jamison, PA St. Cyril of Jerusalem.
Filippini, Renato *s.x.* '97 (PAT)[N] Wayne Xaverian Missionary Fathers; Wayne, NJ XAVERIAN MISSIONARY FATHERS.
Filipski, Raymond R. '75 (NEW) Bergenfield, NJ St. John the Evangelist.
Fillion, Normand A. *o.m.i.* '50 (BO)[X] Tewksbury, MA Immaculate Heart of Mary Residence.
Fillion, Stephen '79 (SAG) Bay City, MI Our Lady of the Visitation.
Fillman, G. Allan '77 (TOL) Paulding, OH Divine Mercy Parish; St. Maximilian Kolbe Deanery.
Filmanski, Francis E. '53 (RVC) Retired.
Filmer, Eric R. '04 (SAV) Moultrie, GA Immaculate Conception.
Filmyer, Bernard G. *s.j.* '52 (BAL)[Q] Baltimore, MD Colombiere Jesuit Community.
Filut, David C. '68 (MIL) Retired.
Fimian, Kevin J. '96 (ARL) Notaries; Annandale, VA St. Michael.
Finamore, Robert A. '70 (WDC) Retired.
Finch, Joseph E. '58 (ALB)[M] Germantown, NY St. Teresa's Motherhouse.
Finch, Joseph E. '58 (OM) Retired.
Finch, Raymond J. *m.m.* '76 (FgM) Maryknoll, NY MARYKNOLL.
Fincutter, John F. *s.v.d.* '50 (MIL)[P] East Troy, WI Divine Word Missionaries Retired.
Fincutter, Patrick *s.v.d.* '55 (MIL)[P] East Troy, WI Divine Word Missionaries Retired.
Finder, James '91 (JC) Cuba, MO St. Francis; Cuba, MO Holy Cross; Cuba, MO St. Michael.
Findikyan, Michael (FTW)[B] University of Notre Dame Du Lac.
Findlan, Rev. Msgr. Joseph G. '38 (PIT)[M] Pittsburgh, PA St. John Vianney Manor Retired.
Finegan, Rev. Msgr. Gerard '67 (VEN) Longboat Key, FL St. Mary Star of the Sea; Presbyteral Council; College of Consultors.
Finegan, Lawrence J. '70 (SFR) Retired.
Finelli, Jay A. '92 (PRO) Tiverton, RI Holy Ghost; Council Members.
Finelli, Rev. Msgr. Victor F. '89 (ALN) Allentown, PA St. Francis of Assisi; Judges.
Finelli, Victor '89 (LEX) Associate Judges.
Fineo, Richard '02 (FAR) Cooperstown, ND Sacred Heart Church of Aneta; Cooperstown, ND St. George; Cooperstown, ND St. Olaf; Cooperstown, ND St. Lawrence; Diocesan College of Consultors.
Fineran, A. Gerard *s.j.* '50 (NO)[R] New Orleans Jesuit Provincial Office.
Finerty, Bernard *o.f.m.cap.* '61 (BAL)[Q] Cumberland, MD The Friary; Cumberland, MD Our Lady of the Mountains, Roman Catholic Congregation, Inc.
Finerty, D. Bryan '59 (PRO) Retired.
Finerty, Raymond J. *o.p.* '71 (LA)[AA] Los Angeles, CA Occidental College, Catholic Campus Ministry.
Finerty, Raymond *o.p.* '71 (SB) Riverside, CA St. Andrew Newman Center; [M] Riverside, CA St. Andrew Newman Center; [I] Riverside, CA St. Vincent Ferrer House.
Fink, Rev. Msgr. Charles R. '76 (RVC)[A] Huntington, NY Diocesan Seminary of the Immaculate Conception.
Fink, Frederick T. '61 (NU) Retired.
Fink, John L. '67 (IND) Bradford, IN St. Michael Catholic Church, Bradford, Inc.
Fink, John L. '69 (IND) Depauw, IN St. Bernard Catholic Church, Frenchtown, Inc.; Depauw, IN St. Joseph Catholic Church, Marengo, Inc.
Fink, John '71 (MIA) Catholic Charismatic Services—Archdiocese of Miami Retired.
Fink, Joseph '83 (STP) Watertown, MN Immaculate Conception.
Fink, Peter E. *s.j.* '69 (NY)[DD] New York, NY Xavier Jesuit Community; New York, NY St. Francis Xavier.
Fink, Philip *o.f.m.cap.* '77 (PIT)[M] Pittsburgh, PA St.

Augustine Friary.
Finlan, Robert T. '94 (ALN) Frackville, PA St. Ann; Frackville, PA Annunciation B.V.M.; Frackville, PA St. Joseph; Elected Members; College of Consultors; Frackville – Court St. James #1029.
Finlay, Joseph F. '57 (STA) Retired.
Finley, James F. '63 (BRK) Military Chaplains Retired.
Finley, James F. '63 (TUC) Yuma, AZ MCAS Chapel.
Finley, John Thomas '75 (LAF) On Special Assignment.
Finley, William '81 (ORL) Retired.
Finn, Daniel J. '72 (BO) Dorchester, MA St. Ambrose; Dorchester, MA St. Mark; Presbyteral Council.
Finn, David C. '03 (RCK) Special Assignment; Sterling, IL Sacred Heart; North Aurora, IL Blessed Sacrament Catholic Church.
Finn, Dominick F. *o.s.f.s.* '56 (PH)[Y] Philadelphia, PA Father Louis Brisson Residence.
Finn, Edward S. '52 (SCR) On Special or Other Diocesan Assignment Retired.
Finn, Firmin *o.f.m.conv.* '55 (ALB)[J] Latham, NY Our Lady of Hope Residence; [L] Rensselaer, NY Provincialate, Immaculate Conception Friary – Order of Friars Minor Conventual; Special Assignment.
Finn, Gregory T. *o.s.j.* '89 (SCR) Hazleton, PA Annunciation, Hazelton.
Finn, John A. *o.s.f.s.* '62 (WIL)[J] Wilmington, DE DeSales House.
Finn, John P. '81 (NO) Retired.
Finn, Joseph P. '98 (LIN) Lincoln, NE St. Mary; Health Care Facilities.
Finn, Michael E. '77 (SCR) Lake Ariel, PA St. Thomas More.
Finn, Rev. Msgr. Peter G. '65 (NY) Staten Island, NY Blessed Sacrament; [H] New York, NY The Ladies of Charity of the Catholic Charities of the Archdiocese of New York; [F] Staten Island, NY Seton Foundation for Learning, Inc.; Staten Island.
Finn, Robert E. *s.j.* '91 (CHI) Chicago, IL John H. Stroger, Jr. Hospital of Cook County; [N] Chicago, IL Woodlawn Jesuit Community.
Finn, Seamus P. *o.m.i.* '76 (WDC)[O] Washington, DC Provincial Offices of the United States Province of the Missionary Oblates of Mary Immaculate; [O] Washington, DC Oblate Community.
Finn, William P. *c.m.* '48 (PH)[Y].
Finnegan, Charles *o.f.m.* '58 (BO)[Z] Boston, MA St. Anthony Shrine.
Finnegan, Gerald F. *s.j.* '67 (BO)[U] Boston The Society of Jesus of New England–Provincial Offices.
Finnegan, Gerald F. *s.j.* '67 (PRO) Woonsocket, RI St. Charles.
Finnegan, J. Kevin '96 (STP) Faribault, MN Divine Mercy Catholic Church.
Finnegan, John P. '54 (CHI) Indian Creek, IL St. Mary of Vernon Retired.
Finnegan, John S. '56 (SY) Baldwinsville, NY St. Elizabeth Ann Seton.
Finnegan, Joseph '65 (HEL) Retired.
Finnegan, Kevin H. '90 (GLP) Crownpoint, NM St. Paul; Promoter of Justice; Chancellor; Defenders of the Bond; Vicars Forane; Presbyteral Council.
Finnegan, Kevin '96 (STP) Shieldsville, MN St. Patrick; Kenyon, MN St. Michael.
Finnegan, Robert K. *o.praem.* '52 (GB)[J] De Pere, WI St. Norbert Abbey; [O] De Pere, WI Canons Regular of Magnovarad, Ltd.; [O] De Pere, WI Norbertine Generalate, Inc.; Bishop's Finance Council.
Finnegan, William J. '57 (CHI) Orland Park, IL St. Michael; Orland Park, IL Our Lady of the Woods Retired.
Finnell, John H. '78 (WH) South Charleston, WV Blessed Sacrament.
Finnell, Terrell '92 (KC) Kansas City, MO St. Monica.
Finnerty, Rev. Msgr. D. Joseph '63 (BRK) Flushing, NY St. Kevin.
Finnerty, Rev. Msgr. James J. '55 (NEW) Jersey City, NJ St. Paul's Retired.
Finnerty, Joseph G. '61 (NOR) Retired.
Finnerty, Rev. Msgr. Joseph L. '57 (SD) Poway, CA Saint Michael Catholic Parish Poway Retired.
Finnerty, Vincent H. *c.m.* '79 (CHL) Charlotte, NC Our Lady of Guadalupe Church.
Finnestad, Jerald L.C. '80 (FAR) Lisbon, ND St. Vincent's Church of Gwinner; Lisbon, ND St. Aloysius Church of Lisbon.
Finney, Donald T. '94 (PMB) Jupiter, FL St. Peter.
Finney, Peter P. '10 (NO) Metairie, LA St. Clement of Rome.
Finnigan, Francis *c.p.* (FgM) New Rochelle, NY St. Paul of the Cross Province.
Finnigan, John B. '61 (MAN) Suncook, NH St. John the Baptist Retired.
Finno, James '72 (CHI) Tinley Park, IL St. Stephen, Deacon and Martyr.
Finsterbach, Thomas P. *s.j.* '76 (SJ)[M] Los Gatos, CA Sacred Heart Jesuit Center.
Finucan, J. Thomas '55 (LC) Retired.
Fiore, Arthur B. '75 (WIL) Newark, DE St. John the Baptist–Holy Angels.
Fiore, John J. *c.s.b.* '57 (GRY)[H] Merrillville, IN Basilian Fathers Residence Retired.
Fiore, Joseph A. '70 (BUF) Darien Center, NY Immaculate Heart of Mary.
Fiore, Peter A. *o.f.m.* '55 (ALB)[B] Siena College.
Fiorelli, Lewis S. *o.s.f.s.* '70 (ARL) Vienna, VA Our Lady of Good Counsel.
Fiorillo, Antimo M. '43 (NY)[DD] Bronx, NY Retired.
Fiorino, Alfred L. *s.j.* '60 (NY)[DD] Loyola Hall, Jesuit Community.
Fiorino, Dominic J. '61 (NEW)[L] Caldwell, NJ The Rev. Msgr. James F. Kelley Residence for Retired Priests Retired.
Firestone, Thomas '78 (LAN) Flint, MI St. John Vianney; [Q] Fenton, MI Alma Redemptoris Mater; College of Consultors; Presbyteral Council.
Firko, Frank A. '77 (PBR) McKees Rocks, PA Holy Ghost.
Firmin, Daniel F. '04 (SAV) Savannah, GA Cathedral of St. John the Baptist; Catholic Relief Services; Mission Cooperative Appeal; Chancellor; Chancery; Tribunal Judges; Staff.
Firpo, John A. '77 (ROC) Rochester, NY St. Charles Borromeo; Board of Directors.
Fischer, Adrian *o.f.m.* '75 (SHP) Monroe, LA Little Flower of Jesus.
Fischer, Andrew C. '82 (PIT) Moon Township, PA St. Margaret Mary.
Fischer, Barry J. *c.pp.s.* '73 (CIN)[N] Dayton Provincial Office of the Cincinnati Province of the Society of the Precious Blood.
Fischer, Benedict *o.s.b.* '07 (BIS)[B] Bismarck, ND University of Mary; [A] Richardton, ND Assumption Abbey.
Fischer, Brian J. '79 (CHI) Chicago, IL St. Gregory, the Great.
Fischer, Brian R. '03 (STL) Master of Ceremonies; Office of Youth Ministry; Special Assignment.
Fischer, Charles H. '71 (KAL) Bangor, MI Sacred Heart of Jesus; Advocates.
Fischer, Charles '90 (FAR) Fargo, ND St. Mary's Cathedral of Fargo; Special Assignment.
Fischer, Clarence L. '61 (HON) Members.
Fischer, Rev. Msgr. Don L. '67 (DAL) Retired.
Fischer, Eugene '65 (SD) Retired.
Fischer, G. William *o.s.f.s.* '69 (E)[L] Erie, PA Saint Mary's Home of Erie.
Fischer, Harold *o.m.i.* '00 (BEL)[F] Belleville, IL Shrine of Our Lady of the Snows.
Fischer, Henry J. '71 (BEL) Bartelso, IL St. Cecilia.
Fischer, Hilary *m.s.c.* '57 (SB) Anza, CA Sacred Heart.
Fischer, James J. *s.j.* '55 (ROC)[B] Rochester, NY McQuaid Jesuit High School.
Fischer, John M. '63 (E) Girard, PA Retired.
Fischer, John P. '76 (CIN) Judges.
Fischer, John '86 (SFS) Vermillion, SD St. Agnes.
Fischer, Jonathan *o.s.b.* '61 (STP)[G] St. Paul, MN HealthEast St. Joseph's Hospital; St. Joseph's Hospital.
Fischer, Jonathan *o.s.b.* '61 (SCL)[I] Collegeville, MN St. John's Abbey, of the Order of St. Benedict.
Fischer, Kenneth J. '71 (CHI) River Forest, IL St. Luke.
Fischer, Mark F. '95 (ATL) Jackson, GA Saint Mary, Mother of God Catholic Church.
Fischer, Norman '00 (LEX) Lexington, KY St. Peter Claver.
Fischer, Richard O. '76 (MO) Air Force Reserve Chaplains; Southern; Klamath Falls, OR St. Pius X; Health and Retirement Board.
Fischler, James *c.i.c.m.* '76 (SAT) Priests Personnel Board; Del Rio, TX Sacred Heart; In Rural Area; Archdiocesan Presbyteral Council.
Fisette, Carl B. '06 (PRO) Vocations; [A] Providence, RI Seminary of Our Lady of Providence; Narragansett, RI St. Thomas More.
Fisette, Kevin R. '81 (PRO) Absent on Leave.
Fish, Alfred H. '77 (OG) St. Regis Falls, NY Church of the Holy Cross; St. Regis Falls, NY St. Ann.
Fish, Justin '05 (DUL)[G] Cloquet, MN Educational Endowment Trust, Queen of Peace Church; Cloquet, MN Holy Family; Cloquet, MN Queen of Peace; College of Consultors.
Fish, Michael *o.s.b.cam.* '78 (MRY)[F] Big Sur, CA New Camaldoli Hermitage.
Fishel, Gregory *s.d.b.* '89 (CHI) Chicago, IL St. John Bosco.
Fisher, A. J. '56 (BAK) Retired.
Fisher, Albert '81 (BIR) On Duty Outside the Diocese.
Fisher, Albert '81 (SAV) Special Assignment.
Fisher, Andrew J. '98 (ARL) Annandale, VA St. Ambrose; Vocations, Office of.
Fisher, Bernard *s.v.d.* '45 (CHI)[N] Techny, IL Divine Word Residence.
Fisher, Clarence L. '61 (HON) Members; Diocesan Ecumenical Commission Retired.
Fisher, David E. '86 (LAN) Owosso, MI St. Joseph; Priests' Assignment Commission.
Fisher, David T. *s.j.* '53 (SJ)[M] Los Gatos, CA Sacred Heart Jesuit Center.
Fisher, David '84 (OLL) Cincinnati, OH St. Anthony of Padua Maronite Catholic Church.
Fisher, Donald C. '61 (PIT) Retired.
Fisher, Edward K. '92 (MEM) Memphis, TN Blessed Sacrament.
Fisher, John P. '76 (CIN) Medical Leave of Absence.
Fisher, John *o.s.f.s.* '88 (ALN)[B] Center Valley, PA DeSales University; [K] Center Valley, PA Oblates of St. Francis de Sales.
Fisher, John *o.s.f.s.* '88 (PH)[Y] Philadelphia, PA Father Louis Brisson Residence.
Fisher, Kyle *c.ss.r.* '63 (STL)[O] St. Louis, MO Redemptorist Fathers.
Fisher, Leo *c.f.r.* (PAT)[N] Paterson, NJ Saint Michael's Friary.
Fisher, Martin J. '86 (ALB) Greenwich, NY St. Joseph; Schuylerville, NY Notre Dame–Visitation; Presbyteral Council; Diocesan Board of Consultors.
Fisher, Martin '51 (GF) Retired.
Fisher, Rev. Msgr. Michael W. '90 (WDC) Secretariats; Archdiocesan College of Consultors; Priest Council; Pastoral Center Special Ministries; Hyattsville, MD St. Mark; Secretariat for Ministerial Leadership and Vicar for Clergy.
Fisher, Paul R. '95 (HBG) Harrisburg, PA Our Lady of the Blessed Sacrament.
Fisher, Raymond A. '71 (TOL) Retired.
Fisher, Robert D. '80 (DEN) Englewood, CO All Souls.
Fisher, Robert J. '92 (DET) Utica, MI St. Lawrence.
Fisher, Robert *s.v.d.* '65 (SB)[I] Riverside, CA Divine Word Seminary.
Fisher, Roe '02 (STA) Absent or Sick Leave.
Fisher, Terry '85 (FTW) Mishawaka, IN St. Joseph; Presbyteral Council.
Fisher, William F. *o.s.f.s.* '61 (DET) Monroe, MI St. Anne; Monroe, MI St. Joseph.
Fisher, William '93 (KCK) Ottawa, KS Sacred Heart.
Fishwick, Joseph '75 (MIA) Retired.
Fiske, Jack *c.ss.r.* (BAL) Baltimore, MD Our Lady of Fatima.
Fister, Daniel '09 (LEX) Pikeville, KY St. Francis of Assisi.
Fister, Stephen J. '82 (P)[N] Gold Hill, OR St. Rita's Retreat Center.
Fitch, John '02 (VEN) Venice, FL Epiphany Cathedral.
Fittin, Edward Seton *o.s.b.* '93 (PAT)[N] Morristown, NJ St. Mary's Abbey.
Fitts, Robert L. *s.j.* '69 (SPK)[J] Spokane, WA Regis Community.
Fitz, James *s.m.* '74 (CIN)[D] Dayton, OH The University of Dayton.
Fitz, James *s.m.* '74 (CIN)[N] Dayton, OH Marianist Community.
Fitz–Henry, Edward '85 (MRY) On Leave.
Fitz–Patrick, David M. '79 (MO) Military Chaplains; Air Force Chaplains.
Fitzgerald, Allan *o.s.a.* '67 (PH) Rosemont, PA St. Thomas of Villanova Parish; [C] Villanova University.
Fitzgerald, Brendan '00 (NY) New York, NY Chapel of the Sacred Hearts of Jesus and Mary; New York, NY Chapel of the Sacred Hearts of Jesus and Mary.
Fitzgerald, Christopher *i.c.* '58 (SP) Seffner, FL St. Francis of Assisi Retired.
Fitzgerald, David E. *s.a.* '65 (R) Apex, NC St. Andrew the Apostle.
Fitzgerald, David T. *s.p.* '78 (SFE)[H] Jemez Springs, NM Our Lady of Lourdes; Jemez Springs, NM Our Lady of the Assumption.
Fitzgerald, David *s.a.* '65 (NY)[DD] Garrison Graymoor Ecumenical and Interreligious Institute.
Fitzgerald, David *s.p.* '78 (STL)[V] Dittmer, MO Servants of the Paraclete Missouri Generalate Corporation.
Fitzgerald, Edmund H. '57 (PRO) Retired.
Fitzgerald, Rev. Msgr. Edmund J. '68 (FR) Somerset, MA St. Thomas More; Diocesan Consultors; Fall River Deanery; Diocesan Health Facilities.
Fitzgerald, Edward T. '59 (SPR) Ware, MA All Saints.
Fitzgerald, Edward W. '95 (CHR) Hanahan, SC Divine Redeemer; Defenders of the Bond.
Fitzgerald, Edward '95 (CHR) Diaconate, Office of.
Fitzgerald, George R. *c.s.p.* '65 (SFR) San Francisco, CA Old St. Mary's Cathedral.
Fitzgerald, Howard E. '78 (DM) Glenwood, IA Our Lady of the Holy Rosary; Advocates.
Fitzgerald, Rev. Msgr. J. Terrence '62 (SLC) College of Consultors; Promoter of Justice; Administrative Assistant to the Bishop Retired.
Fitzgerald, James E. *s.j.* '66 (MIL)[P] Wauwatosa, WI Jesuit Community at St. Camillus.
Fitzgerald, John B. '55 (LA) Retired.
Fitzgerald, John E. '57 (PH) Philadelphia, PA St. Anselm Retired.
Fitzgerald, John E. '63 (STO) Twain Harte, CA All Saints Church (Pastor of); Deans.
Fitzgerald, Rev. Msgr. John G. '62 (LA) Lompoc, CA Our Lady Queen of Angels.
Fitzgerald, John J. *o.s.a.* '41 (PH)[Y] Villanova, PA St. Thomas Monastery.
Fitzgerald, John J. '58 (RVC) Setauket, NY St. James Retired.
FitzGerald, Rev. Msgr. John L. '67 (BAL) Special

Assignment; [U] Baltimore, MD Stella Maris Seafarers' Center.
Fitzgerald, John P. '74 (PIT) Conway, PA Our Lady of Peace; Air National Guard Chaplains.
Fitzgerald, Joseph *c.m.* '05 (FgM) Philadelphia, PA Eastern Province.
Fitzgerald, Joseph '07 (RVC)[C] Hicksville, NY Holy Trinity Diocesan High School; Syosset, NY St. Edward Confessor.
FitzGerald, Kevin T. *s.j.* '88 (WDC)[O] Washington, DC The Jesuit Community at Georgetown University.
Fitzgerald, M. Durkin *c.ss.r.* '49 (STL)[O] Liguori, MO St. Clement Health Care Center Retired.
Fitzgerald, Paul J. *s.j.* '92 (BGP)[B] Fairfield, CT Fairfield University; [O] Fairfield, CT The Fairfield Jesuit Community–Fairfield University.
Fitzgerald, R. Martin '89 (R) On Duty Outside the Diocese.
Fitzgerald, R. Martin '89 (MO) Air Force Chaplains.
Fitzgerald, R. Patrick *o.f.m.* '61 (NY) New York, NY St. Francis of Assisi.
Fitzgerald, Raymond R. *s.j.* '91 (NO)[E] New Orleans, LA Jesuit High School; [J] New Orleans, LA Jesuit High School; [U] New Orleans, LA 124 Airline Drive, Inc.; [R] New Orleans, LA Jesuit Provincial Office.
Fitzgerald, Richard W. (BO) Wellesley, MA St. Paul.
Fitzgerald, Robert H. *s.j.* '66 (MIL)[P] Wauwatosa, WI Jesuit Community at St. Camillus.
Fitzgerald, Thomas J. '75 (PAT) Clifton, NJ St. Clare.
Fitzgerald, Thomas P. '66 (STP) Centerville, MN St. Genevieve.
Fitzgerald, Thomas *s.s.s.* '64 (SP) Holiday, FL St. Vincent De Paul.
Fitzgerald, Timothy *c.p.* '56 (PIT)[M] Pittsburgh, PA St. Paul of the Cross Monastery; [O] Pittsburgh, PA St. Paul of the Cross Retreat Center.
Fitzgerald, Timothy (DM) Altoona, IA SS. John and Paul.
Fitzgerald, Rev. Msgr. William F. '50 (TR)[N] Trenton, NJ Villa Vianney Retired.
Fitzgerald, William J. '58 (OM) Retired.
Fitzgerald, Rev. Msgr. William '57 (KAL) Vicar for Clergy Retired.
Fitzgibbon, Edmond J. '59 (STL) Retired.
Fitzgibbons, John A. '68 (PH) Retired.
Fitzgibbons, John P. *s.j.* '85 (MIL)[P] Milwaukee, WI Jesuit Community at Marquette University.
Fitzgibbons, Peter L. '84 (MO) Albemarle, NC Our Lady of the Annunciation; Military Chaplains; Army Reserve Chaplains.
Fitzhenry, Stephen *o.p.* (COL)[H] Columbus, OH Mohun Health Care Center.
Fitzmaurice, James '84 (ALB) Albany, NY Christ the King; Presbyteral Council; Diocesan Board of Consultors.
Fitzmaurice, Rev. Msgr. V. Paul '73 (GBG) North Huntingdon, PA St. Agnes.
Fitzmyer, Joseph A. *s.j.* '51 (PH)[Y] Loyola Center and Manresa Hall.
Fitzpatrick, Bede *o.f.m.* '55 (FgM) New York, NY Holy Name Province.
Fitzpatrick, Daniel J. *s.j.* '66 (NY)[HH] New York, NY Brooklyn Prep Alumni Association; [HH] Bronx, NY Metro New York Christian Life Communities, Inc.; [B] Bronx, NY Ciszek Hall.
Fitzpatrick, Rev. Msgr. Donnelly J. '63 (PEO) Retired.
Fitzpatrick, Edward J. '70 (DAV)[E] Iowa City, IA Newman Catholic Student Center; [J] Iowa City, IA O'Keefe Hall; Judges.
Fitzpatrick, Edward T. *o.s.f.s.* '74 (CAM) Cape May, NJ The Church of Our Lady Star of the Sea, Cape May.
Fitzpatrick, Gerald J. *s.j.* '71 (WDC)[R] Faulkner, MD Loyola Retreat House.
Fitzpatrick, James M. '84 (FR) Absent on Sick Leave.
Fitzpatrick, James M. '71 (SAG) Retired.
Fitzpatrick, Rev. Msgr. John E. '70 (PAT) Oak Ridge, NJ St. Thomas, the Apostle.
Fitzpatrick, John P. '60 (BO) Senior Priests. Retired.
Fitzpatrick, John P. '52 (STP) Retired.
Fitzpatrick, Joseph F. *s.j.* '65 (NY)[DD] New York, NY Murray–Weigel Hall.
Fitzpatrick, Mallick J. *s.j.* '60 (NY)[E] Bronx, NY Fordham Preparatory School; [DD] Loyola Hall, Jesuit Community.
Fitzpatrick, Michael J. '83 (PH) Honey Brook, PA St. Peter.
Fitzpatrick, Michael J. *s.j.* '77 (BAK) Pendleton, OR St. Andrew's Indian Mission.
Fitzpatrick, Michael J. '03 (FR) East Sandwich, MA Corpus Christi.
Fitzpatrick, Michael *s.j.* '77 (SPK)[O] Spokane, WA Kateri Northwest Ministry Institute.
Fitzpatrick, Paul E. *s.m.* '77 (BO)[A] Weston, MA Blessed John XXIII National Seminary.
Fitzpatrick, Paul K. '98 (LA) San Marino, CA Saints Felicitas and Perpetua; Cardinal McIntyre Fund for Charity Board of Directors.
Fitzpatrick, Paul *s.m.* '77 (HON)[D] Honolulu, HI Marianist Hall Community.
Fitzpatrick, R. Michael '71 (OM) Omaha, NE St. Stanislaus; Promoter of Justice; Defenders of the Bond; Consultors; Finance Council; Ex Officio (Consultors).
Fitzpatrick, Robert J. '54 (CHI) Ingleside, IL St. Bede Retired.
Fitzpatrick, Robert J. '73 (STP) Roseville, MN St. Rose of Lima.
Fitzpatrick, Robert *o.m.i.* '71 (FgM) Washington, DC AMERICAN OBLATE MISSIONS.
Fitzpatrick, Thomas J. *s.j.* '68 (MAN) Salem, NH Saints Mary and Joseph.
Fitzpatrick, Thomas J. *s.j.* '68 (BO)[U] Boston The Society of Jesus of New England–Provincial Offices.
Fitzpatrick, Thomas P. '61 (SY) Syracuse, NY Our Lady of Lourdes.
Fitzpatrick, Thomas '04 (SFS) Sioux Falls, SD St. Joseph Cathedral; Sioux Falls, SD Our Lady of Guadalupe.
Fitzpatrick, Vincent (FAR) Special Assignment.
Fitzsimmons, Donald J. *c.s.v.* '60 (CHI)[N] Arlington Heights, IL Viatorian Province Center–Clerics of St. Viator.
Fitzsimmons, Rev. Msgr. Eugene J. '60 (CAM) Retired.
Fitzsimmons, Gerald J. *s.m.m.* '75 (BRK) Ozone Park, NY St. Mary Gate of Heaven; Presbyteral Council.
Fitzsimmons, J. Thomas '62 (CIN) Eaton, OH Visitation of the Blessed Virgin Mary; Eaton, OH St. John the Evangelist.
Fitzsimmons, Rev. Msgr. Richard '56 (PEO) Retired.
Fitzsimmons, Robert P. *o.p.* '55 (WDC) Washington, DC St. Dominic Church & Priory.
Fitzsimmons, Rev. Msgr. Thomas B. '62 (CAM) Retired.
Fitzsimons, Patrick '01 (LEX) Nicholasville, KY St. Luke.
Fiuk, Rev. Canon Stanislaw '90 (SAT) La Vernia, TX St. Ann.
Fix, Joseph J. '68 (GR) Evart, MI Sacred Heart; Evart, MI St. Agnes; Deans.
Fix, Robert H. '53 (CHR) Retired.
Fixsen, Patrick '07 (PEO) Cherry, IL St. Patrick's; Cherry, IL Holy Trinity.
Flach, Carl '58 (P) Retired.
Flach, James A. '86 (SFD) Wood River, IL Holy Angels.
Flach, Rev. Msgr. Thomas D. '71 (BEL) Marion, IL St. Joseph; Defensores Vinculi.
Flack, Robert S. *s.j.* '74 (CHI)[S] The Jesuit Retreat League of Chicago.
Fladung, Charles J. '92 (DAV) Keota, IA Holy Trinity; Sigourney, IA St. Mary's.
Flagg, Wayne N. '88 (VIC) New Ulm, TX SS. Peter and Paul; Alleyton, TX St. Roch.
Flaherty, Charles *s.s.c.* '50 (OM)[J] St. Columbans Missionary Society of St. Columban Retired.
Flaherty, Daniel J. '54 (DEN) Louisville, CO St. Louis Retired.
Flaherty, Edward F. *s.j.* '65 (DEN)[N] Denver, CO Xavier Jesuit Center.
Flaherty, Frederick R. *m.s.* '57 (HRT)[L] Hartford, CT Missionaries of LaSalette.
Flaherty, Rev. Msgr. James J. '80 (PT) Pensacola, FL Holy Spirit; Pensacola, FL St. John the Evangelist; Judicial Vicar; Judges; College of Consultors; Administrative Council; Department of Pastoral Ministry; Continuing Education & Formation.
Flaherty, James P. *s.j.* '92 (MIL)[G] Milwaukee, WI Nativity Jesuit Middle School, Inc.; [P] Milwaukee, WI Jesuit Community at Marquette University.
Flaherty, John R. '90 (DUB) Manchester, IA St. Mary; [E] Manchester, IA St. Paul School of Religion; Manchester, IA Immaculate Conception; Ryan, IA St. Patrick; Priestly Life and Ministry Committee.
Flaherty, Kevin H. *s.j.* '83 (CHI)[N] Chicago Chicago Province of the Society of Jesus–Provincial Office.
Flaherty, Kevin H. *s.j.* '83 (FgM) Chicago, IL Society of Jesus.
Flaherty, Leon *c.pp.s.* '61 (CIN)[N] Dayton Provincial Office of the Cincinnati Province of the Society of the Precious Blood.
Flaherty, Leon *c.pp.s.* '61 (GRY) Whiting, IN St. John the Baptist.
Flaherty, Malachy *o.c.s.o.* '60 (SLC)[E] Huntsville, UT Abbey of Our Lady of the Holy Trinity of the Order of Cistercians.
Flaherty, Malachy *o.f.m.cap.* (RVC) Melville, NY Long Island Developmental Center.
Flaherty, Michael T. '73 (CIN) Retired.
Flaherty, Richard C. *o.f.m.* '82 (BO)[Z] Boston, MA St. Anthony Shrine.
Flaherty, William J. '52 (CHI) Winnetka, IL SS. Faith, Hope and Charity; Flossmoor, IL Infant Jesus of Prague Retired.
Flajole, John Paul *o.f.m.* '64 (GAL) Galveston, TX Holy Family.
Flamm, Paul M. *c.ss.p.* '99 (FgM) Bethel Park, PA CONGREGATION OF THE HOLY SPIRIT.
Flammia, Paul G. '96 (BO) Wilmington, MA St. Thomas of Villanova; Wilmington, MA St. Dorothy.
Flanagan, Brian '98 (PMB) Palm Beach Gardens, FL St. Patrick.
Flanagan, Damian '91 (MIA) Coral Gables, FL Little Flower.
Flanagan, David J. '87 (MAD) Benton, WI St. Patrick; Cuba City, WI St. Rose of Lima.
Flanagan, Edward R. '88 (MET) Monroe Township, NJ Nativity of Our Lord.
Flanagan, Edward *o.f.m.* '64 (WDC)[O] Washington, DC Franciscan Monastery USA Inc.
Flanagan, James D. '71 (NY) Bronx, NY Holy Family.
Flanagan, James E. *c.s.s.* '50 (BO)[X] Waltham, MA Stigmatine Fathers and Brothers Retired.
Flanagan, James W. '61 (DUB) Retired.
Flanagan, James '08 (ATL) McDonough, GA St. James the Apostle.
Flanagan, John B. '97 (PH)[D] Philadelphia, PA Roman Catholic High School for Boys; Philadelphia, PA St. Bridget.
Flanagan, John J. '74 (SAT) San Antonio, TX St. Jerome; In Metropolitan Area; Archdiocesan Presbyteral Council; Priests Personnel Board.
Flanagan, John P. '59 (SY) Utica, NY St. John Retired.
Flanagan, Michael J. *m.s.* '60 (HRT)[L] Hartford, CT Missionaries of LaSalette.
Flanagan, Rev. Msgr. Michael T. '65 (JC) Columbia, MO Our Lady of Lourdes; Episcopal Vicars; Diocesan Consultors; Personnel Board; Ex Officio Members; Finance Committee; Board of Trustees.
Flanagan, Michael '10 (LEX) Berea, KY St. Clare; [L] Berea, KY St. Clare Church–Berea College; Priests' Retirement Committee.
Flanagan, Rev. Msgr. P. Kevin '59 (PAT) Clifton, NJ; Clifton, NJ St. Philip the Apostle Retired.
Flanagan, Rev. Msgr. Patrick J. '56 (SAT) Retired.
Flanagan, Patrick S. *c.m.* (BRK)[R] Jamaica, NY Reverend John B. Murray, CM, House.
Flanagan, Rev. Msgr. Sean B. '59 (LA) Retired.
Flanagan, Rev. Msgr. Thomas J. '49 (BRK) Retired.
Flanagan, Thomas J. '74 (SC) Milford, IA St. Joseph's.
Flanagan, William F. '64 (JC) Retired.
Flanigan, Rev. Msgr. Gerald A. '51 (DET) Retired.
Flanigan, James F. *c.s.c.* '62 (FTW)[B] University of Notre Dame Du Lac; [H] Notre Dame, IN Holy Cross Community, Corby Hall, University of Notre Dame.
Flanigan, Rev. Msgr. Thomas P. '69 (PH) Lansdale, PA Corpus Christi.
Flannagan, Bruce G. '78 (BO) Danvers, MA St. Richard of Chichester.
Flannery, John *o.p.* '60 (OAK)[L] Oakland, CA Order of Preachers (Province of the Most Holy Name of Jesus – Western Dominican Province).
Flannery, Kevin L. *s.j.* '87 (DET)[K] Detroit Detroit Province of the Society of Jesus–Provincial Office.
Flannery, Michael '97 (ALB) Fort Ann, NY St. Ann; Whitehall, NY Our Lady of Hope; Great Meadows Correctional Institution.
Flannery, Rev. Msgr. Michael '64 (JKS) Madison, MS St. Francis of Assisi; Office of Vicar General; Promoter of Justice; Defenders of the Bond; Diocesan Consultors.
Flannery, Patrick R. '97 (NEW) Caldwell, NJ St. Aloysius.
Flannery, Robert B. '73 (BEL) Carbondale, IL St. Francis Xavier; Carterville, IL Church of the Holy Spirit; Diocesan Deans; Ecumenical and Interreligious Affairs.
Flater, Gerald *o.m.i.* '57 (BO)[X] Tewksbury, MA Immaculate Heart of Mary Residence.
Flatley, Brian M. '66 (BO) Arlington, MA Saint Agnes.
Flatoff, Alfred *s.d.b.* (NEW)[C] Ramsey, NJ Don Bosco Preparatory High School; [L] Ramsey, NJ Don Bosco Prep Salesian Residence.
Flattery, John J. '55 (PEO) Retired.
Flavin, James *o.m.i.* '63 (BO)[U] Tewksbury, MA Oblate World/Missionary Association of Mary Immaculate; [X] Tewksbury, MA Immaculate Heart of Mary Residence.
Flavin, John E. '60 (CHI) Glenview, IL Our Lady of Perpetual Help Retired.
Flax, Myron *o.f.m.cap.* '64 (SAL)[D] Victoria, KS St. Fidelis Friary Retired.
Fleck, David G. '75 (EVN) Vincennes, IN St. Vincent de Paul; Judges; Diocesan Consultors; Diocesan Council of Priests; Deans; Vincennes, IN St. John the Baptist; Petersburg, IN SS. Peter and Paul.
Fleck, John W. '59 (TOL) Retired.
Fleck, Kenneth J. '76 (CHI) Tinley Park, IL St. George.
Fleckenstein, John D. '02 (KAL) Presbyteral Council Members; Presbyteral Council Members; Battle Creek, MI St. Philip; Cemeteries; Education; Diocesan Finance Council; Vicar for Education.
Fleckenstein, Robert W. '10 (PIT) Wexford, PA St. Alphonsus.
Flecky, Michael J. *s.j.* '77 (OM)[J] Omaha, NE Jesuit Community at Creighton University.
Fleischhacker, John J. *o.s.c.* '61 (SCL)[I] Onamia, MN Crosier Priory.
Fleischman, Richard J. '68 (MIL) Belgium, WI St. Mary; Fredonia, WI Holy Rosary; Random Lake, WI Our Lady of the Lakes.
Fleischmann, George R. '56 (MIL) Retired.
Fleiter, Robert V. '61 (STL) Retired.
Fleming, Alfred J. *m.m.* '67 (NY)[DD] Retired.
Fleming, Austin H. '73 (BO) Concord, MA Holy Family.
Fleming, Brendan '52 (P) Retired.

Fleming, Daniel J. '96 (ATL) Newnan, GA St. Mary Magdalene; Deans.
Fleming, David L. *s.j.* '65 (STL)[O] St. Louis, MO Ignatius House.
Fleming, David '90 (DM) Council Bluffs, IA St. Patrick; Diocesan Consultors.
Fleming, Dennis J. *c.s.c.* (FTW)[H] Notre Dame Congregation of Holy Cross, United States Province of Priests & Brothers.
Fleming, George '94 (ALB) Troy, NY Transfiguration Parish.
Fleming, James J. *s.j.* '95 (BO)[U] Boston The Society of Jesus of New England–Provincial Offices.
Fleming, James J. *s.j.* '95 (WH)[A] Wheeling, WV Wheeling Jesuit University.
Fleming, Jeffrey M. '92 (HEL) Missoula, MT Christ the King; [G] Missoula, MT University of Montana; Personnel Board; Defenders of the Bond; Members.
Fleming, John M. '61 (CAM) Retired.
Fleming, John W. '96 (MAN) Auditors; Finance Council; Manchester, NH Parish of the Transfiguration.
Fleming, Joseph W. '74 (ALT) Chest Springs, PA St. Monica's; Dysart, PA St. Augustine.
Fleming, Martin M.P. '52 (STP) Retired.
Fleming, Raymond H. '82 (ROC) Rochester, NY Emmanuel Church of the Deaf of the Diocese of Rochester; Rochester, NY St. Monica.
Fleming, Rodger P. '07 (STL) St. Louis, MO St. Clement.
Fleming, T.J. '85 (SAG) New Lothrop, MI St. Michael.
Fleming, Terence K. '67 (ROC) On Duty Outside the Diocese.
Fleming, Rev. Msgr. Terrance L. '73 (LA) Los Angeles, CA St. Brendan; Deanery 14; Members; Propagation of the Faith; Our Lady of the Angels Region; Mission Office.
Fleming, Thomas '55 (JOL) Retired.
Fleming, Wess (SY) Syracuse, NY Elmcrest Children's Center.
Flemming, James K. '86 (VEN) Retired.
Flens, Daniel A. '89 (CHI) Chicago, IL Cardinal's Residence; Office of the Archbishop.
Fletcher, Luke Mary *c.f.r.* '03 (NY)[DD] New York, NY St. Joseph's Friary.
Fletcher, Patrick '85 (PCE) On Duty Outside the Diocese.
Fleury, Colonel Joseph M. *s.m.* '84 (WDC)[O] Washington, DC Marist Center.
Fleury, Joseph M. *s.m.* '84 (MO) Army Chaplains.
Flickinger, Don D. '64 (FRS) Retired.
Flickinger, Robert E. '75 (KAL) Advocates; South Haven, MI St. Basil; Presbyteral Council Members.
Flint, Edward A. *s.j.* '69 (DET)[K] Clarkston, MI Colombiere Center.
Flint, James *o.s.b.* '83 (JOL) Lisle, IL; [L] Lisle, IL St. Procopius Abbey.
Flisk, Louden–Hans W. '01 (FAR) Retired.
Fliss, James W. '75 (BUF) Farnham, NY St. Anthony's.
Fliss, Paul J. '92 (MIL) Fox Point, WI St. Eugene; Whitefish Bay, WI St. Monica.
Fliss, Richard L. '66 (LC) On Duty Outside the Diocese Retired.
Floch, W. Roy '77 (SPK) Spokane, WA St. Paschal.
Flock, Robert H. '82 (LC) Foreign Missions.
Floeder, John P. '07 (STP) Graduate Studies; [A] Saint Paul, MN The Saint Paul Seminary.
Floersh, Philip M. *c.m.* '62 (STL)[O] St. Louis Vincentian Residence; [O] Perryville, MO Congregation of the Mission.
Flood, Augustine A. *o.s.b.* '64 (GBG)[H] Latrobe, PA Saint Vincent Archabbey.
Flood, Charles J. *o.ss.t.* '90 (BAL)[Q] Diocese of Trenton, NJ.
Flood, Charles J. *o.ss.t.* '90 (TR) Asbury Park, NJ Our Lady of Mt. Carmel; Jersey Shore Medical Center.
Flood, David *o.f.m.* '58 (BUF)[N] St. Bonaventure, NY St. Bonaventure Friary.
Flood, Eric *f.s.s.p.* '00 (SCR)[L] Elmhurst Twp., PA Priestly Fraternity of St. Peter (F.S.S.P.), North American District Headquarters; Elmhurst Twp., PA.
Flood, Francis *o.s.b.* '93 (NEW)[L] Newark, NJ Newark Abbey.
Flood, Rev. Msgr. J. Michael '68 (PH)[BB] Glenside, PA Arcadia University.
Flood, James F. '62 (CLV)[M] Fairlawn, OH St. Edward Home; [M] Fairlawn, OH St. Edward Home.
Flood, Matthew C. *s.j.* '61 (NY)[DD] Loyola Hall, Jesuit Community.
Flood, Maurice *o.c.s.o.* '91 (ARL)[H] Berryville, VA Cistercian Abbey of Our Lady of the Holy Cross.
Flood, Maurice *o.c.s.o.* '91 (SR)[M] Whitethorn, CA Our Lady of the Redwoods Abbey.
Flood, Paul '90 (ATL) Johns Creek, GA St. Benedict.
Flood, Rev. Msgr. Peter J. '69 (TR) Retired.
Flood, Rev. Msgr. William J. '57 (BRK) BMT Holy Name Society; Bayside, NY Our Lady of the Blessed Sacrament Retired.
Flor, Carlos F. '97 (BO) Revere, MA Immaculate Conception.
Flor, Carlos '97 (NEW) On Duty Outside the Archdiocese.
Flora, Carmel *o.f.m.cap.* '53 (FgM) Detroit, MI Province of St. Joseph; [K] Detroit St. Bonaventure Friary.
Flora, Giandomenico M. '06 (NEW) On Duty Outside the Archdiocese.
Flora, Giandomenico '06 (BGP) Bridgeport, CT St. Raphael.
Florcnosos, Absolon '98 (BUR) Hardwick, VT Mary Queen of All Saints Parish.
Florczyk, Franciszek '81 (CHI) Tinley Park, IL St. George.
Florczyk, Walter '62 (SY) Retired.
Florea, Eugene '07 (PHX)[G] Black Canyon City, AZ Our Lady of Silence Hermitage: A House of Prayer for Priests.
Florek, Rev. Msgr. Frederick J. '64 (SD) Retired.
Florek, Richard T. *o.f.m.conv.* '72 (PMB) Boynton Beach, FL St. Mark.
Florek, Thomas W. *s.j.* '86 (DET)[K] Detroit, MI Jesuit Community at the University of Detroit Mercy.
Florek, Thomas (FTW)[B] University of Notre Dame Du Lac.
Florenciani, Javier Aquino '06 (MGZ) Rosario, PR Our Lady of Rosary.
Flores, Alejandro F. '09 (BWN) Brownsville, TX Mary, Mother of the Church.
Flores, Alejandro '09 (JOL) Leave of Absence.
Flores, Amadito '10 (PAT) Paterson, NJ St. Anthony's.
Flores, Antonio *c.r.* '05 (DEN) Fort Collins, CO Holy Family; [N] Denver, CO The Theatine Fathers.
Flores, Arthur *o.m.i.* '92 (SAT)[S] San Antonio, TX Oblate Missions; [L] San Antonio, TX Missionary Oblates of Mary Immaculate; Councilors.
Flores, Arthur *o.m.i.* '92 (WDC)[O] Washington, DC Provincial Offices of the United States Province of the Missionary Oblates of Mary Immaculate.
Flores, Benjamin '93 (ELP) El Paso, TX Blessed Sacrament.
Flores, Efrain '91 (ORG) Westminster, CA Blessed Sacrament; Clergy Personnel Board.
Flores, Francisco '00 (B) Caldwell, ID Our Lady of the Valley; [F] Caldwell, ID The College of Idaho; Priest Personnel Commission; Priest Retirement Committee.
Flores, Gabriel '85 (SFR) San Francisco, CA St. Charles Borromeo.
Flores, Guillermo Martinez *m.s.p.* '02 (SB) Fontana, CA St. Joseph.
Flores, Guillermo *m.sp.s.* '03 (LA) Oxnard, CA Our Lady of Guadalupe Parish.
Flores, Hilario *sch.p.* '10 (LA) Los Angeles, CA Our Lady Help of Christians (Maria Auxiliadora).
Flores, Javier *s.d.v.* '08 (NEW) Newark, NJ St. Michael's.
Flores, Jesus '85 (ROC) Office of Migrant Ministry.
Flores, Jose Siesquen '88 (SPR) Springfield, MA Blessed Sacrament; Springfield, MA All Souls.
Flores, Juan M. '98 (YAK) Zillah, WA Resurrection; Toppenish, WA St. Aloysius.
Flores, Juan Manuel '03 (YAK) Diocesan Commission on Public Worship.
Flores, Juan Manuel '03 (FRS) Exeter, CA Sacred Heart.
Flores, Lee A. '85 (GAL) Rosenberg, TX Our Lady of Guadalupe.
Flores, Luzvimindo '79 (ANC) Big Lake, AK Corp. of Our Lady of the Lake Church.
Flores, Miguel '94 (FRS) Bakersfield, CA St. Joseph.
Flores, Orlando '11 (CHI) Berwyn, IL St. Mary of Celle.
Flores, Ramiro '95 (OAK) Richmond, CA St. Mark.
Flores, Raymond J. '05 (LSC) Hatch, NM Our Lord of Mercy; Office of Vocations; Clergy Personnel Board; Presbyteral Council; Priestly Life and Ministry Committee; Diocesan Consultors.
Flores, Richard '84 (FWT) Fort Worth, TX St. Peter The Apostle.
Flores, Roberto *s.v.d.* '96 (OAK) Oakland, CA St. Bernard.
Flores–Alva, Luis M. '06 (BAK) Madras, OR St. Patrick.
Flores Alferez, Juan M. '98 (YAK) Diocesan Commission for the Catechumenate.
Florez, Andrew '93 (NY) Rosendale, NY St. Peter.
Florez, Carlos A. '11 (TR) Middletown, NJ St. Mary.
Florez, Hernan '05 (DEN) Frederick, CO St. Theresa.
Florez, Juan Rommel Perez *o.f.m.* '11 (JOL)[L] Joliet, IL St. John the Baptist Friary.
Florez, Luis '59 (STA) Retired.
Florez–Ardilla, Carlos '03 (MIL) Milwaukee, WI Prince of Peace/Principe de Paz; Milwaukee, WI St. Vincent de Paul; Milwaukee, WI St. Hyacinth.
Flori, David J. '86 (DAL) Richardson, TX St. Paul the Apostle.
Floridi, Nicholas A. '00 (PHX) Phoenix, AZ St. Joan of Arc Roman Catholic Parish.
Florido, Robert '79 (MO) DEPARTMENT OF VETERANS AFFAIRS HOSPITALS AND CHAPLAINS.
Florio, Philip A. *s.j.* '01 (NY)[GG] Bronx, NY Fordham University at Rosehill; [DD] Cardinal Spellman Hall, Jesuit Community.
Florvil, Thelamaque (NY) New York, NY St. Catherine of Genoa.
Flott, Phil '02 (GI) Scottsbluff, NE Our Lady of Guadalupe.
Flowers, Thomas A. '77 (WIL) Smyrna, DE St. Polycarp; Delaware Home & Hospital for the Chronically Ill; Catholic Charismatic Renewal.
Floyd, Ronnie Paul '08 (FR) Wareham, MA St. Patrick's; Tobey Hospital.
Fluet, Gregoire J. '82 (NOR) Moodus, CT St. Bridget of Kildare; Deans; Archivist; [A] Cromwell, CT Holy Apostles College and Seminary; Members; Director and Chaplain; Board of Education.
Fluetsch, John P. '91 (FRS) Wasco, CA St. John the Evangelist.
Flum, Martin '01 (STU)[H] Bloomingdale, OH Holy Family Hermitage.
Flusche, Vincent '90 (LR)[D] Fort Smith, AR St. Edward Mercy Medical Center.
Flynn, Arthur C. '52 (BO) Senior Priests. Retired.
Flynn, Brian L. '03 (BO) Lynn, MA St. Mary.
Flynn, Brian *o.f.m.* '60 (PAT)[N] Ringwood, NJ Holy Name Friary, Inc.
Flynn, Charles P. '69 (DUL) Eveleth, MN Resurrection; Gilbert, MN St. Joseph.
Flynn, Dennis *s.v.d.* '61 (SD) San Diego, CA Saint Catherine Laboure Catholic Parish.
Flynn, Edmund *o.c.s.o.* '70 (ARL)[H] Berryville, VA Cistercian Abbey of Our Lady of the Holy Cross.
Flynn, Francis J. '69 (OG) Constable, NY The Catholic Community of Constable, Westville and Trout River; Constable, NY St. Bridget's Oratory.
Flynn, George R. '56 (BO) Senior Priests. Retired.
Flynn, George '56 (FgM) Boston, MA St. James the Apostle, Inc.
Flynn, J. Joseph *o.f.m.cap.* (NY)[C] New Rochelle, NY The College of New Rochelle.
Flynn, James B. '64 (WOR) Southborough, MA St. Matthew; [B] Worcester, MA Holy Name Central Catholic Junior/Senior High School.
Flynn, James E. '55 (L) Retired.
Flynn, James E. '67 (CHI) Deans.
Flynn, James F. '67 (CHI) Chicago, IL Holy Name of Mary; Chicago, IL Sacred Heart Mission of Holy Name of Mary.
Flynn, James R. *o.s.a.* '72 (PH)[F] Malvern, PA Malvern Preparatory School for Boys; [Y] Malvern, PA Augustinian Friars (O.S.A.).
Flynn, James '06 (FWT) Pilot Point, TX St. Thomas Aquinas.
Flynn, James '73 (SJ)[L] Los Altos, CA Jesuit Retreat Center of Los Altos.
Flynn, John C. '55 (NY)[DD] Bronx, NY.
Flynn, John F. *o.s.a.* (KAL) Douglas, MI St. Peter; [E] Douglas, MI Order of St. Augustine Retired.
Flynn, John J. *s.j.* '69 (SJ)[M] Los Gatos, CA Sacred Heart Jesuit Center.
Flynn, John Joseph *o.f.m.cap.* (NY)[GG] New Rochelle, NY College of New Rochelle.
Flynn, John L. *s.j.* '64 (SJ)[M] Los Gatos, CA Sacred Heart Jesuit Center.
Flynn, John R. *o.s.a.* '71 (MIL)[P] Racine, WI Augustinian Novitiate; Racine, WI St. Rita.
Flynn, Rev. Msgr. John '52 (TYL) Candidates Approved as Canonical Advocates for Marriage Cases; Lufkin, TX St. Patrick School Retired.
Flynn, Joseph *o.f.m.cap.* '66 (NY)[DD] White Plains, NY St. Conrad Friary.
Flynn, Lawrence W. *m.m.* '87 (NY)[DD] Maryknoll Maryknoll Fathers and Brothers Retired.
Flynn, Mark F. '72 (HRT) Marlborough, CT St. John Fisher.
Flynn, Matthew *o.c.s.o.* '58 (WOR)[N] Spencer, MA St. Joseph's Abbey.
Flynn, Michael E. '77 (CHI) Chicago, IL St. Daniel the Prophet.
Flynn, Michael F. '91 (BGP) Trumbull, CT St. Theresa.
Flynn, Michael J. '94 (PT) On Duty Outside the Diocese; [A] Boynton Beach, FL St. Vincent de Paul Regional Seminary.
Flynn, Rev. Msgr. Michael P. '71 (RVC) Farmingdale, NY St. Kilian.
Flynn, Michael *o.carm.* '60 (CHI) Chicago, IL Nativity of Our Lord.
Flynn, Michael *o.carm.* '61 (JOL)[L] Darien Carmelite Provincial Office.
Flynn, Patrick *c.ss.r.* '69 (BAL) Annapolis, MD St. Mary.
Flynn, Paul *o.s.a.* '82 (ORG) San Clemente, CA Our Lady of Fatima.
Flynn, Rev. Msgr. Sean P. '75 (TR) Sea Girt, NJ St. Mark.
Flynn, Stephen A. '08 (CLV) Solon, OH St. Rita; Presbyteral Council; Presbyteral Conveners.
Flynn, Thomas A. '60 (CLV) North Olmsted, OH St. Clarence Retired.
Flynn, Rev. Msgr. Thomas M. '58 (CAM) Retired.
Flynn, Thomas P. '60 (DET) Retired.
Flynn, Thomas '61 (HEL) On Duty Outside the Diocese.
Flynn, William J. '64 (NOR) Taftville, CT Sacred Heart Retired.
Flynn, William J. *s.s.* '59 (SCR)[M] Dunmore, PA Villa St. Joseph Retired.

Flynn, William J. *s.s.* '59 (BAL)[Q] Baltimore Society of St. Sulpice, Province of the United States Retired.
Fobare, Scott D. '87 (OG) Port Henry, NY Catholic Community of Moriah; Committee for the Continuing Education of Clergy; Diocesan Consultors.
Foelker, James *o.m.i.* '55 (CC) Sarita, TX Our Lady of Guadalupe.
Fogal, Joseph B. '75 (WIN) Rochester, MN SS. Peter and Paul; Rochester, MN Pax Christi; Priest Assignments Committee.
Fogarty, Austin '81 (ATL) Newnan, GA St. George.
Fogarty, Declan *o.s.a.* '59 (SB) Norco, CA St. Mel.
Fogarty, Gerald P. *s.j.* '70 (WDC)[O] Washington, DC The Jesuit Community at Georgetown University; Towson, MD.
Fogarty, James '54 (SLC) Retired.
Fogarty, John (PIT)[B] Pittsburgh, PA Duquesne University of the Holy Spirit.
Fogarty, John *c.s.sp.* '81 (PIT)[M] Bethel Park, PA Congregation of the Holy Spirit Province of the United States; [M] Bethel Park, PA Holy Spirit Fathers and Brothers Provincialate; [Q] Bethel Park, PA Spiritan Support Trust; Bethel Park, PA; Province of the United States; Bethel Park, PA CONGREGATION OF THE HOLY SPIRIT; Priest Council.
Fogarty, Joseph A. *o.p.* '59 (CHI)[N] Chicago, IL St. Pius V Priory.
Fogarty, Rev. Msgr. Noel '57 (MIA) Members Retired.
Fogarty, Rev. Msgr. Paul '67 (ATL) Decatur, GA St. Thomas More.
Fogarty, Thomas *s.s.p.* '57 (Y)[A] Canfield, OH Society of St. Paul.
Fogle, Bruce '83 (OWN) Earlington, KY Holy Cross; Dawson Springs, KY Resurrection; Earlington, KY Immaculate Conception.
Fogliasso, John P. '11 (WCH) Wichita, KS Church of the Magdalen.
Foglio, John '61 (LAN) Retired.
Fohlin, Paul *o.c.d.* '72 (BO)[U] Boston, MA Carmelite Monastery.
Fohn, Kurt M. '01 (CHL) Statesville, NC St. Philip the Apostle.
Foisy, Leonard R. '57 (MAN) Retired.
Folbrecht, Robert A. '75 (LA) L.A. County Fire Dept.; Covina, CA St. Louise de Marillac.
Folchetti, John T. '74 (TR) Lincroft, NJ St. Leo the Great.
Folda, Rev. Msgr. John T. '89 (LIN)[A] Seward, NE St. Gregory the Great Seminary; Notaries; Vicars For Religious; Censores Librorum; Catholic Physicians Guild; Members; Diocesan Health Ministries, Inc.; Diocesan Housing Ministries, Inc.; Priests' Continuing Education Committee.
Foley, Augustine E. *o.s.b.* '89 (NO)[A] St. Benedict, LA St. Joseph Seminary College; [R] St. Benedict, LA St. Joseph Abbey; [A] St. Benedict, LA St. Joseph Seminary College.
Foley, Brendan P. '55 (HT) Retired.
Foley, Daniel R. '60 (SPR) Springfield, MA St. Michael's Cathedral Retired.
Foley, Daniel R. '60 (SPR) Judges; Promoter of Justice; Presbyteral Council.
Foley, David M. '72 (MEM) Retired.
Foley, Dennis *c.ss.r.* '61 (TR)[R] Long Branch, NJ San Alfonso Retreat House.
Foley, Edward *o.f.m.cap.* (CHI)[B] Chicago, IL Catholic Theological Union; Detroit, MI.
Foley, Edwin *c.ss.r.* '47 (BAL) Baltimore, MD Our Lady of Fatima.
Foley, Francis P. '84 (MO) Military Chaplains; Navy Chaplains.
Foley, George '58 (FWT) Mansfield, TX St. Jude.
Foley, Gerald J. '59 (GB) Appointed Members Retired.
Foley, Jerome P. '84 (SFR) San Francisco, CA St. James.
Foley, John B. *s.j.* '72 (STL)[C] Saint Louis University; [O] St. Louis, MO Jesuit Community Corporation at Saint Louis University – Jesuit Hall.
Foley, John J. *c.s.p.* (BRK)[R] Jamaica Estates, NY Paulist Fathers – Generalate.
Foley, Rev. Msgr. John Kieran '59 (LA) Montrose, CA Holy Redeemer Retired.
Foley, John P. *s.j.* '67 (CHI) Chicago, IL St. Procopius; [N] Chicago, IL Miguel Pro Jesuit Community.
Foley, John P. *s.j.* '59 (CHI)[W] Chicago, IL Cristo Rey Network.
Foley, John '74 (WOR) Diocesan Building Commission Members; Shrewsbury, MA St. Anne.
Foley, Joseph P. *c.m.* '68 (BRK)[R] Queens Village, NY DePaul Residence.
Foley, Marc *o.c.d.* '81 (WDC)[B] Washington, DC Discalced Carmelite Friars.
Foley, Matthew E. '89 (CHI) Army Chaplains; Military Chaplains.
Foley, Rev. Msgr. Matthew F. '56 (BRK) Retired.
Foley, Matthew *o.f.m.conv.* '09 (BAL)[Q] Baltimore, MD Immaculate Heart of Mary Friary; [C] Baltimore, MD Archbishop Curley High School.
Foley, Michael G. '86 (CHI) Orland Park, IL St. Michael.
Foley, Rev. Msgr. Michael G. '70 (WOR) Westborough, MA St. Luke the Evangelist.
Foley, Michael '70 (PT) Tallahassee, FL Good Shepherd; College of Consultors.
Foley, Patrick '72 (PT) Pensacola, FL St. Joseph.
Foley, Peter J. '67 (PH) Retired.
Foley, Richard L. *o.s.a.* '60 (BO) Andover, MA St. Augustine.
Foley, Thomas C. '57 (BO) Senior Priests.; Quincy, MA St. Ann Retired.
Foley, Thomas F. '77 (SFR) San Francisco, CA Old St. Mary's Cathedral.
Foley, Thomas S. '86 (BO) Parish Life and Leadership; Ex Officio; Presbyteral Council; Quincy, MA St. John the Baptist.
Foley, Timothy M. '65 (STL) University City, MO Christ the King.
Foley, Walter W. '76 (ATL) Retired.
Foley, William B. *s.j.* '77 (BO)[U] Weston, MA Campion Jesuit Community.
Foley, William E. '79 (WDC) Upper Marlboro, MD Saint Mary of the Assumption; Deans; [J] Washington, DC The Washington Cursillo Movement.
Foley, Rev. Msgr. William J. '67 (NY) Stony Point, NY Immaculate Conception.
Foley, William (BAL) Aberdeen, MD St. Joan of Arc.
Folger, Benedict *ss.cc.* '57 (FR)[F] Fairhaven, MA Damien Residence.
Folino, Frank *o.f.m.* '05 (SHP)[F] Ruston, LA E. Donn Piatt Catholic Student Center at Louisiana Tech University; Ruston, LA St. Thomas Aquinas.
Follmann, Roland F. *o.s.a.* '60 (TLS)[B] Tulsa, OK Cascia Hall Preparatory School.
Follmar, A. Joseph '59 (LC) Greenwood, WI St. Mary Help of Christians; Greenwood, WI Holy Family.
Folsey, William David *o.p.* '60 (PRO)[O] Providence St. Thomas Aquinas Priory at Providence College.
Folsom, Cassian *o.s.b.* '84 (IND)[K] Saint Meinrad St. Meinrad Archabbey.
Folsom, Paul '65 (SCL) Retired.
Folsom, William P. '91 (MOB) Retired.
Foltyn, Rev. Msgr. Emilian '64 (AUS) Jarrell, TX Holy Trinity Catholic Church – Corn Hill, Texas; Rural Life.
Foltz, Rev. Msgr. Michael H. '89 (CR) Adjutant Judicial Vicar; Finance Council; Diocesan Consultors; Moorhead, MN St. Joseph's; Priests' Personnel Board.
Folzenlogen, John N. *s.j.* '65 (GAL)[E] Houston, TX Strake Jesuit College Preparatory Inc.
Folzenlogen, Joseph D. *s.j.* '71 (CIN)[U] Cincinnati, OH Claver Jesuit Ministry; [N] Cincinnati, OH Faber Jesuit Community.
Fonck, Benet *o.f.m.* '72 (JOL)[K] Joliet, IL Our Lady of Angels Retirement Home.
Fonck, Benet *o.f.m.* '72 (CHI)[N] Countryside, IL St. Gratian Friary, Franciscan Friars.
Fones, Michael S. *o.p.* '92 (TUC)[H] Tucson, AZ University of Arizona Retired.
Fones, Michael *o.p.* '92 (OAK)[L] Oakland, CA Order of Preachers (Province of the Most Holy Name of Jesus – Western Dominican Province); [L] Oakland, CA Order of Preachers (Province of the Most Holy Name of Jesus – Western Dominican Province); [A] Berkeley, CA Dominican School of Philosophy and Theology; [A] Berkeley, CA Dominican School of Philosophy and Theology.
Fong, Franklin *o.f.m.* '06 (OAK)[A] Berkeley, CA Franciscan School of Theology; Definitors:; [L] Berkeley, CA Franciscan Friars (Province of St. Barbara).
Fonscea, Joaquin Mayorqa (SJN) San Juan, PR Santos Pedro y Pablo los Apostoles.
Fonseca, Erwin A. *c.s.c.* '91 (FTW)[H] Notre Dame Congregation of Holy Cross, United States Province of Priests & Brothers.
Fonseca, Rev. Msgr. Harvey '92 (FRS) Livingston, CA St. Jude Thaddeus.
Fonseca, Joseph *c.ss.r.* (CHL) Concord, NC St. James.
Fonseca, Luis '09 (SAV) Valdosta, GA St. John the Evangelist.
Fonseca, Oscar D. '07 (MO) Air Force Reserve Chaplains.
Fonseca, Oscar D. '69 (NEW) West New York, NJ St. Joseph of the Palisades.
Fonseca, Rolando '94 (ELP) Advocates; Presbyteral Council; Marfa, TX St. Mary's.
Fonseka, Matthew '69 (NEW) Saddle Brook, NJ St. Philip the Apostle.
Fontaine, David A. *o.carm.* '79 (SAC) Fairfield, CA Our Lady of Mount Carmel,.
Fontana, Alphonso R. '97 (HRT) Bristol, CT St. Anthony.
Fontana, Charles S. '69 (DET) Dearborn, MI St. Clement.
Fontana, Glenn J. '92 (PEO) Lincoln, IL Holy Family.
Fontana, John M. *o.s.m.* '78 (CHI)[N] Chicago, IL Order of Friar Servants of Mary (Servites) United States of America Province, Inc.; Chicago, IL.
Fontanella, Andrew J. '56 (HBG) Retired.
Fontanella, Paul C. '02 (SCR) Williamsport, PA St. Ann; Presbyteral Council.
Fontanini, Chris '97 (DM) Earling, IA St. Joseph; Defiance, IA St. Peter.
Fontenot, Anthony M. '01 (LKC) Jennings, LA Immaculate Conception; Deans; Diocesan Consultors; Presbyteral Council.
Fonti, Joseph G. '92 (BRK) Ministerial Development Program; [B] Douglaston, NY Cathedral Seminary Residence of the Immaculate Conception; Spiritual Director of the Cathedral Seminary Residence; Office of Priestly Life & Ministry.
Foote, Job J. *o.s.b.* '89 (GBG)[H] Latrobe, PA Saint Vincent Archabbey.
Foote, Job *o.s.b.* '89 (MO) Navy Reserve Chaplains.
Foppiano, Michael '07 (BAL) Severna Park, MD St. John the Evangelist.
Foppiano, Steven E. '02 (SAC) Roseville, CA St. Clare.
Foradori, V. David '86 (E) Du Bois, PA St. Joseph; Du Bois, PA St. Michael.
Foran, Peter '74 (LA) Westlake Village, CA St. Jude.
Forbes, Eric *o.f.m.cap.* '90 (AGN)[F] Agana Heights, GU St. Fidelis Friary; Archdiocesan College of Consultors; Archdiocesan Presbyteral Council.
Forbes, John J. '91 (R) Raleigh, NC Our Lady of Lourdes.
Forbes, Richard L. '67 (CAM) Retired.
Forbidussi, John E. '94 (PIT) Richeyville, PA St. Agnes.
Forcelle, Joseph '80 (SFS) Tyndall, SD St. Leo.
Forcier, Richard–Jacob *o.f.m.conv.* '86 (BAL)[U] Ellicott City, MD Fr. Justin Ministry Fund, Inc.; [Q] Ellicott City Order of Friars Minor Conventual.
Forcier, Robert H. '03 (PRO) Cranston, RI St. Paul.
Ford, Christopher M. '87 (HRT) Branford, CT St. Mary; Defender of the Bond; Judges.
Ford, Harold LeRoy '49 (LA) Long Beach, CA St. Joseph Retired.
Ford, Rev. Msgr. J. Joseph '67 (PRT) Diocesan Consultors; Diocesan Priests' Benefit Plan – Trustees; Personnel Board; Yarmouth, ME Parish of the Holy Eucharist.
Ford, John T. *c.s.c.* '59 (FTW)[H] Notre Dame Congregation of Holy Cross, United States Province of Priests & Brothers.
Ford, John T. *c.s.c.* '59 (WDC)[C] Catholic University of America, The.
Ford, Lawrence D. *o.f.m.* '96 (NY) New York, NY Holy Name of Jesus.
Ford, Michael F. *s.j.* '75 (BO)[U] Cohasset, MA Bellarmine House; [U] Newton, MA The Jesuit Community at Boston College.
Ford, Michail *o.p.* '10 (LFT) West Lafayette, IN St. Thomas Aquinas; [H] West Lafayette, IN St. Thomas Aquinas Parish and Foundation for Catholic Students Attending Purdue University.
Ford, Nevin *o.f.m.* '54 (LA)[P] Santa Barbara, CA Franciscan Friary, Order of Friars Minor (Old Mission).
Ford, Rev. Msgr. Robert A. '44 (NY)[DD] Bronx, NY John Cardinal O'Connor Residence Retired.
Ford, Ryan T. '11 (MAR) Marquette, MI St. Peter Cathedral.
Ford, William A. '82 (STO) Diamond Springs, CA Retired.
Fordjour, Gabriel Adansi (SY) Binghamton, NY St. Paul.
Forester, Raymond L. '66 (WIL) Rehoboth Beach, DE St. Edmond.
Forgach, Carl J. '60 (Y) Retired.
Forge, Michael D. '97 (DAL) Dallas, TX Mary Immaculate; At Large Members.
Forget, Timothy W. '02 (OM) Clarkson, NE SS. Cyril and Methodius; Leigh, NE St. Mary.
Forintos, Bradley '91 (DET) Trenton, MI St. Joseph.
Foriska, John M. '70 (GBG) Jeannette, PA Sacred Heart; Jeannette, PA Ascension; Bishop's Priests Council.
Forlani, Joseph *m.c.c.j.* '58 (LA)[BB] Covina, CA Comboni Mission Center.
Forlano, Albert (STF) Catechetics.
Forlano, Philip M. '03 (PH) Lansdale, PA St. Stanislaus.
Forler, Christopher A. '08 (EVN) Chrisney, IN St. Martin; Rockport, IN St. Bernard.
Forliti, John E. '62 (STP) Retired.
Forman, Bruce H. '74 (STL) St. Louis, MO Sts. Peter and Paul.
Forman, Patrick J. '89 (BUR) Elected Members; Catholic Daughters of The Americas; Saint Johnsbury, VT Corpus Christi Parish; Deans.
Fornasari, Archimede *m.c.c.j.* '50 (CHI)[N] Chicago, IL Comboni Missionaries Theologate (M.C.C.J.), Verona Fathers.
Forner, Craig W. '75 (SFR) Redwood City, CA St. Matthias.
Forni, John V. '77 (ROC) Rochester, NY St. John the Evangelist.
Forno, R. Adam '87 (ALB) Rensselaer, NY Parish of St. John the Evangelist and St. Joseph's.
Forrest, Stephen '04 (MIL)[Y] Kenosha, WI St. Mark Latin American Center; Kenosha, WI St. Mark.
Forrest, Thomas *c.ss.r.* '54 (WDC)[O] Washington, DC Holy Redeemer College.
Forrey, William C. '90 (HBG) Deans; Presbyteral Council; Carlisle, PA Saint Patrick.

Forsen, Rev. Msgr. James '79 (LA) Vocations; Los Angeles, CA St. Columbkille.
Forsman, David '01 (DUL) Aitkin, MN St. James; Aitkin, MN Our Lady of Fatima; Aitkin, MN Holy Family.
Forst, Aloysius A. '49 (STL) Retired.
Forst, Rev. Msgr. Charles J. '49 (STL) Retired.
Forst, Rev. Msgr. Charles '45 (STL) St. Louis, MO St. Mark Retired.
Forst, Rev. Msgr. Robert M. '51 (ALN) Allentown, PA Our Lady Help of Christians; Elected Members Retired.
Forster, Francis P. *o.s.b.* '64 (CHL)[J] Belmont, NC Belmont Abbey.
Forster, Rev. Msgr. William J. '54 (BO) Senior Priests. Retired.
Forsyth, Kevin J. '86 (HRT) Naugatuck, CT St. Vincent Ferrer.
Forsythe, Daniel A. '09 (PBR) Irving, TX St. Basil the Great.
Forsythe, Patrick Don Bosco '04 (BIR) Tuscumbia, AL Our Lady of the Shoals.
Forte, Anthony J. *s.j.* '83 (BO)[U] Boston The Society of Jesus of New England–Provincial Offices.
Forte, Anthony '91 (NEW) Newark, NJ Our Lady of Mt. Carmel.
Forte, John Paul *o.p.* '93 (SD)[N] San Diego, CA University of California at San Diego (Campus Ministry).
Fortenberry, Jerome *c.m.* '55 (STL)[O] Perryville, MO Congregation of the Mission.
Fortener, Kenneth R. '69 (L) Howardstown, KY St. Ann; Associate Judges; New Hope, KY St. Vincent de Paul.
Fortier, Joel '69 (JOL) Naperville, IL St. Thomas the Apostle; [D] Naperville, IL All Saints Catholic Academy.
Fortier, Theodore L. *a.a.* '53 (WOR)[N] Worcester, MA Assumptionists (Augustinians of the Assumption).
Fortin, John R. *o.s.b.* '76 (MAN)[K] Manchester, NH St. Anselm Abbey.
Fortin, Philip '00 (PT) Port St. Joe, FL St. Joseph.
Fortin, Richard A. '62 (WOR) Millbury, MA Assumption.
Fortin, Robert *a.a.* '58 (WOR)[N] Worcester, MA Assumptionists (Augustinians of the Assumption).
Fortman, Anthony *c.pp.s.* (TOL) Glandorf, OH St. John the Baptist.
Fortman, Anthony *c.pp.s.* '01 (CIN)[N] Dayton Provincial Office of the Cincinnati Province of the Society of the Precious Blood.
Fortner, Mark *s.c.j.* (MIL)[P] Franklin, WI Sacred Heart at Monastery Lake.
Fortney, Kenneth E. '79 (HEL) Whitefish, MT St. Charles Borromeo.
Fortuna, Joseph J. '80 (CLV) Euclid, OH Our Lady of the Lake Parish.
Fortuna, Joseph (CLV) Cleveland, OH Euclid Hospital.
Fortuna, Stanley *c.f.r.* '90 (NY)[DD] Bronx, NY Our Lady of the Angels Friary; [HH] Bronx, NY Francesco Productions Inc.
Fortunato, Anthony M. *o.de.m.* '67 (CLV) Cleveland, OH Our Lady of Mount Carmel; [N] Cleveland, OH Mercedarians.
Fortunato, Vincent *o.f.m.cap.* '80 (NEW) Hoboken, NJ St. Ann's.
Fortunio, Carlo '85 (NEW) West New York, NJ Holy Redeemer; West New York, NJ Our Lady of Libera; North Hudson Deanery 8.
Foschiatto, Edi *s.x.* '81 (PAT) Wayne, NJ XAVERIAN MISSIONARY FATHERS; [N] Wayne Xaverian Missionary Fathers.
Foshage, Nathanael *o.s.b.* '68 (OM)[J] Elkhorn, NE Mount Michael Benedictine Abbey.
Foshage, Nathanael *o.s.b.* '68 (PBL) Ouray, CO St. Daniel the Prophet; Ouray, CO St. Patrick; Telluride, CO St. Patrick.
Foshage, Ronald B. *m.s.* '75 (BEA) Northern Vicariate; Jasper, TX St. Michael; Jasper, TX Our Lady of La Salette Mission; Jasper, TX St. Raymond Mission.
Fosnot, James '94 (RIC) Richmond, VA St. Augustine Retired.
Fossa, Leandro '07 (GAL) Houston, TX St. Leo the Great.
Fosselman, Albert M. '60 (RNO) Judges Retired.
Fosselman, Rev. Msgr. John Anthony '42 (LA) Retired.
Foster, Clyde K. '75 (CLV) Chagrin Falls, OH Holy Angels.
Foster, Dominic *t.o.r.* '05 (STU)[A] Steubenville, OH Franciscan University of Steubenville; [H] Steubenville, OH Holy Spirit Friary.
Foster, Edward '51 (DUL) Retired.
Foster, James A. '72 (ALX) Natchitoches, LA Immaculate Conception.
Foster, James J. '80 (STL) New Haven, MO Holy Family.
Foster, James K. *c.s.c.* '95 (FTW)[B] University of Notre Dame Du Lac; [H] Notre Dame, IN Holy Cross Community, Corby Hall, University of Notre Dame.
Foster, John F. *s.j.* '68 (SEA)[A] Seattle, WA Seattle University; [M] Seattle, WA Arrupe Jesuit Community at Seattle University.
Foster, John J. M. '91 (WDC)[C] Catholic University of America, The.
Foster, John J.M. '91 (STO) On Duty Outside the Diocese; Judges.
Foster, John Mary *f.j.* '87 (SAT) Special Assignment.
Foster, Jonathan D. *o.f.m.* '60 (JOL)[N] Lombard, IL Mayslake Ministries, Inc.
Foster, Joseph R. '91 (BO) Medford, MA St. Francis of Assisi.
Foster, Rev. Msgr. Michael S. '80 (BO) Tribunal Court.
Foster, Reginald *o.c.d.* '66 (MIL)[P] Milwaukee Provincial Offices – Discalced Carmelites.
Foster, Thomas J. '86 (DUL)[C] Duluth, MN St. Mary's Medical Center; [G] Duluth, MN St. Mary's Medical Center.
Foster, Thomas J. '82 (MO) Air National Guard Chaplains.
Foster, Thomas W. *s.j.* '72 (SJ)[M] Los Gatos, CA Sacred Heart Jesuit Center.
Fostner, Jay J. *o.praem.* '88 (GB)[B] De Pere, WI St. Norbert College; [B] St. Norbert College.
Fosu, Rev. Msgr. Dominic K. A. '94 (COV) Crescent Springs, KY St. Joseph.
Foudy, Rev. Msgr. John T. '40 (SFR) Retired.
Foudy, Thomas F. '67 (MIA) Pompano Beach, FL St. Coleman; Northeast Broward Deanery.
Fountain, Dennis '81 (LSC) Absent On Leave.
Fountain, Michael *o.f.m.cap.* '73 (MIL)[Y] Milwaukee, WI House of Peace.
Fournier, Denis *o.s.b.* '60 (BIS)[A] Richardton, ND Assumption Abbey.
Fournier, Peter J. '09 (FR) Hyannis, MA St. Francis Xavier's; Cape Cod Hospital.
Fournier, William '73 (DUL) On Duty Outside the Diocese.
Foutts, Patrick D. *o.praem.* '93 (ORG)[H] Silverado, CA St. Michael's Summer Camp.
Foutts, Patrick *o.praem* '93 (LA) Wilmington, CA SS. Peter and Paul.
Fowler, Rev. Msgr. Eugene A. '48 (NY) Lake Katrine, NY St. Catherine Laboure Retired.
Fowler, J. Richard '91 (HRT) Bristol, CT Bristol Hospital.
Fowler, John W. '53 (DAL) Retired.
Fowler, Joseph M. '61 (L) Retired.
Fowler, Michael *o.f.m.* '76 (STL) St. Louis, MO St. Anthony of Padua.
Fowlkes, Eric L. '89 (NSH) Hendersonville, TN Our Lady of the Lake.
Fox, Anthony *o.f.m.conv.* '82 (DET)[K] Dearborn Heights, MI All Saints Friary.
Fox, Brian P. *s.s.j.* '91 (GAL) Houston, TX Our Mother of Mercy; Houston, TX Our Lady Star of the Sea.
Fox, Charles D. '06 (DET) Office of the Archbishop.
Fox, Daniel A. '82 (LA) Woodland Hills, CA St. Bernardine of Siena.
Fox, Daniel *o.f.m.cap.* (SAG) Sanford, MI St. Agnes.
Fox, Donal R. *o.s.b.* '66 (PAT)[N] Morristown, NJ St. Mary's Abbey.
Fox, Gabriel '74 (GLD) Retired.
Fox, George W. '61 (MAD) Retired.
Fox, James E. '74 (DEN) Denver, CO Good Shepherd; Deaneries.
Fox, James R. '90 (DEN) Craig, CO Saint Michael; Meeker, CO Holy Family.
Fox, John J. '60 (BUF) Retired.
Fox, Joseph E. *o.p.* (TOL) Assessors.
Fox, Martin E. '03 (CIN) Piqua, OH St. Boniface; Piqua, OH St. Mary.
Fox, Martin F. '65 (GB) Retired.
Fox, Melvin E. '63 (GR) Retired.
Fox, Rev. Msgr. Patrick '52 (SD) Retired.
Fox, Richard E. '92 (SCR) Hunlock Creek, PA Our Lady of Mount Carmel.
Fox, Richard '85 (SFS) Sioux Falls, SD Christ the King.
Fox, Robert J. '59 (GF) Retired.
Fox, Robert L. '01 (CHY) Casper, WY Our Lady of Fatima; [G] Torrington, WY Catholic Charities of Wyoming, Inc.; Presbyteral Council.
Fox, Sean P. '53 (SEA) Mountlake Terrace, WA St. Pius X.
Fox, Thomas E. '60 (LFT) Remington, IN Sacred Heart.
Fox, Thomas *o.f.m.* '62 (JOL)[L] Joliet, IL St. John the Baptist Friary.
Fox, Thomas *o.f.m.* '62 (SFD) Quincy, IL St. Francis Solanus; [K] Quincy, IL St. Francis Solanus Friary; Comite Diocesano de Ministerio Hispano – Diocesan Committee for Hispanic Ministry.
Foxen, David K. *m.s.c.* '97 (SB) Palm Springs, CA Our Lady of Solitude; Palm Springs, CA Our Lady of Guadalupe.
Foxhoven, H. Christopher '04 (STU) Marietta, OH St. Mary's.
Foy, Timothy J. '11 (STL) Dardenne Prairie, MO Immaculate Conception.
Foye, Thomas M. '55 (NEW) Bayonne, NJ St. Andrew's Retired.
Foynes, Rev. Msgr. Aiden '61 (SP) Clearwater, FL St. Cecelia Retired.
Fracaro, Mark A. '67 (JOL) Minooka, IL St. Mary.
Frade, Paulo '97 (NEW) Newark, NJ St. Aloysius.
Fraenzle, Wilfred '64 (LEX) Retired.
Fragelli, Canon Henry *i.c.* '08 (OAK) Oakland, CA St. Margaret Mary.
Fragelli, Canon Henry '08 (SJ) Santa Clara, CA Oratory of Our Mother of Perpetual Help.
Fragomeni, Richard '75 (ALB) On Duty Outside the Diocese; Special Assignment.
Fragomeni, Richard '75 (CHI)[B] Chicago, IL Catholic Theological Union.
Fraher, Joseph P. '50 (CHY) Retired.
Fraher, Kevin *c.ss.r.* (STL)[O] Liguori, MO St. Clement Health Care Center.
Fraher, Leonard W. '56 (SUP) Retired.
Fraile, Mariano *o.c.d.* '47 (PCE) Ponce, PR San Jose.
Fraile, Tomas *c.r.* '63 (DEN) Denver, CO St. Cajetan.
Frain, Brian *s.j.* '02 (ROC)[B] Rochester, NY McQuaid Jesuit High School.
Fraini, Frederick D. '08 (WOR) Gardner, MA Sacred Heart of Jesus.
Frambes, John *o.f.m.* '79 (WIL) Wilmington, DE St. Paul's; Wilmington, DE St. Joseph's R.C. Church of Wilmington, Inc.
Franca, Hugo '04 (OAK) San Lorenzo, CA St. John the Baptist.
Francavilla, Rt. Rev. Joseph F. '68 (NTN) McLean, VA Holy Transfiguration.
Francavilla, Rt. Rev. Joseph '68 (NTN) Protopresbyters; College of Eparchial Consultors; Presbyteral Council.
France–Kelly, Kenneth A. *o.p.* '81 (NY)[DD] New York, NY St. Catherine of Siena Priory.
Franceschini, Mark *o.s.m.* '59 (DEN) Denver, CO Our Lady of Mount Carmel.
Franceschini, Rev. Msgr. Philip J. '66 (NY) Staten Island, NY Our Lady of Pity.
Francesco, Richard G. '87 (NEW) On Duty Outside the Archdiocese.
Francesco, Richard (HEL) Helena, MT St. Mary.
Francez, James *m.c.c.j.* '57 (FgM) Cincinnati, OH COMBONI MISSIONARIES (VERONA FATHERS).
Franchomme, Emilio '04 (DEN) Johnstown, CO St. John the Baptist.
Francik, Gerard C. '87 (BAL) Fallston, MD St. Mark.
Francik, Jerry (BAL) Priest Personnel Board.
Francis, Bernard C. '69 (NO) Hahnville, LA Our Lady of the Holy Rosary.
Francis, Daniel *c.ss.r.* '91 (NY)[HH] Bronx, NY Perpetual Help Center.
Francis, Daniel *c.ss.r.* (BAL)[U] Annapolis, MD Redemptorist Office for Mission Advancement; Annapolis, MD St. Mary.
Francis, Rev. Msgr. Eugene (GAL) Retired.
Francis, George '85 (SP)[J] Tampa, FL St. Joseph's Hospital, Inc.
Francis, John '90 (BRK) Woodhaven, NY St. Thomas Apostle.
Francis, Joseph A. '78 (NY) New York, NY St. Monica.
Francis, Mark R. *c.s.v.* '82 (CHI)[N] Arlington Heights Viatorian Province Center–Clerics of St. Viator.
Francis, Mathew '91 (KCK) Easton, KS St. Joseph–St. Lawrence.
Francis, R. Peter '80 (MO) DEPARTMENT OF VETERANS AFFAIRS HOSPITALS AND CHAPLAINS.
Francis, Sean M. '04 (PIT) Lawrence County, PA Almira Home; Lawrence County, PA Belvedere Residence, Inc.; Lawrence County, PA Golden Hill Nursing, Inc.; Lawrence County, PA Haven Convalescent Home; Lawrence County, PA Highland Hall Care Center; Lawrence County, PA Hillview Manor; Lawrence County, PA Castle Manor; Lawrence County, PA Cedar Manor; Lawrence County, PA Majors Manor; New Castle, PA St. Vitus; Jameson Hospital North Campus; Edison Manor Nursing & Rehab; New Castle, PA St. Vincent de Paul.
Francis, Sunny *s.v.d.* '88 (CHI)[N] Techny, IL Divine Word Residence.
Francisco, Joey '93 (BRK) Brooklyn, NY Our Lady Help of Christians.
Francisco, Ramon J. '96 (HON) Waihee, HI St. Ann.
Franciscus, Thomas *c.ss.r.* '65 (FRS) Tribunal Judges.
Franck, James E. *c.pp.s.* '64 (CIN)[N] Dayton Provincial Office of the Cincinnati Province of the Society of the Precious Blood.
Franck, James *c.pp.s.* '64 (OAK) Newark, CA St. Edward.
Franck, John J. *c.pp.s.* '67 (LA) Los Angeles, CA St. Agnes.
Franck, John *c.pp.s* '67 (CIN)[N] Dayton Provincial Office of the Cincinnati Province of the Society of the Precious Blood.
Franco, Federico M. *o.s.m.* '89 (ELP) El Paso, TX Our Lady of Sorrows.
Franco, Rev. Msgr. Hilary '55 (NY) Ossining, NY St. Augustine.
Franco, Joseph E. '04 (MO) DEPARTMENT OF VETERANS AFFAIRS HOSPITALS AND CHAPLAINS; Bronx, NY Sacred Heart.
Franco, Juan '08 (OAK) San Leandro, CA St. Leander.
Franco, Maurilio *m.g.* '66 (LA) Los Angeles, CA St. Paul.

Franco, Robert J. '82 (CLV) Catholic Renewal Ministries; North Ridgeville, OH St. Peter.
Franco, Rodolfo '99 (BWN) Brownsville, TX The Parish of the Lord of Divine Mercy.
Franco, Ronald A. *c.s.p.* '95 (NY) New York, NY St. Paul the Apostle.
Franco, Ronald A. *c.s.p.* '95 (KNX) Knoxville, TN Immaculate Conception; Knoxville, TN Calvary Cemetery; Cemeteries.
Franco Henao, Luis Fernando (ARL) Springfield, VA St. Bernadette.
Francois, Ducasse '98 (PMB) Fellsmere, FL Our Lady of Guadalupe Mission; Sebastian, FL St. Sebastian.
Francois, Jean Augustin '90 (BRK) Brooklyn, NY Holy Family.
Francois, Marc Arthur (NEW) Jersey City, NJ St. Patrick and Assumption/All Saints Church.
Francois, Yves '05 (PMB) Wellington, FL St. Rita.
Franczek, J. August '48 (GLD) Retired.
Franey, John A. '63 (PH) Retired.
Frank, Chrysostom '85 (DEN) Denver, CO St. Elizabeth of Hungary.
Frank, Edward R. '57 (SAV) Retired.
Frank, Gerald W. '70 (BWN) San Juan, TX St. John the Baptist; Pharr Deanery; [K] Mercedes, TX La Merced Charitable Trust.
Frank, Paul G. '04 (LIN) Red Cloud, NE Sacred Heart; Advocates.
Frank, Richard C. *m.m.* '53 (FgM) Maryknoll, NY MARYKNOLL.
Frank, Richard W. '72 (JC) Glasgow, MO St. Mary; Slater, MO St. Joseph.
Frank, Thomas R. *s.s.j.* '78 (WDC) Washington, DC Our Lady of Perpetual Help.
Frank, Thomas R. *s.s.j.* '78 (BAL)[Q] Baltimore, MD St. Joseph Society of the Sacred Heart House of Central Administration.
Frank, Rev. Msgr. Thomas '70 (AUS) Austin Central.
Frank, Tom '70 (AUS) Austin, TX San Jose.
Franken, William F. '88 (BAL) Baltimore, MD Our Lady of Hope.
Frankenberger, William J. *c.s.b.* '62 (GAL) Houston, TX St. Anne.
Franklin, Claude W. '97 (SAM) New Castle, PA St. John the Baptist.
Franklin, David W. '85 (BGP) Danbury, CT St. Joseph.
Franklin, Mark '02 (SHP) Minden, LA St. Paul; Priests' Retirement Board.
Franklin, Osvaldo (NY) Yonkers, NY Our Lady of Fatima; Yonkers, NY Immaculate Conception.
Frankman, Greg '81 (SFS) De Smet, SD St. Thomas Aquinas.
Franko, George M. '50 (Y) Retired.
Franko, John *o.m.i.* '67 (GAL) Alvin, TX St. John the Baptist.
Frankovich, Francis A. *c.c.* '68 (GAL)[S] Houston, TX Catholic Charismatic Center; Houston, TX Queen of Peace.
Frankovich, Lawrence *o.f.m.* '66 (MIL) West Allis, WI St. Augustine.
Frankowski, Miroslaw *s.ch.* '98 (DET) Hamtramck, MI St. Florian.
Franks, Donald E. '79 (COL) Columbus, OH Corpus Christi; Columbus, OH St. Ladislas; Columbus, OH St. Mary Church.
Franks, T. Becket *o.s.b.* '86 (JOL)[L] Lisle, IL St. Procopius Abbey.
Franks, Thomas *o.f.m.cap.* '08 (NY) New York, NY St. John the Baptist.
Fransco, Peter J. '58 (SC) Retired.
Fransiscus, Thomas J. *c.ss.r.* '65 (LAV) Diocesan Judges; Diocesan Advocates; Promoter of Justice.
Fransiscus, Thomas *c.ss.r.* '65 (RNO) Adjutant Judicial Vicar; Diocesan Board of Consultors; Dayton, NV St. Ann; Presbyteral Council; Lists of Deans.
Fransiscus, Thomas *c.ss.r.* '65 (DEN)[N] Denver The Redemptorists/Denver Province.
Fransiscus, Tom *c.ss.r.* '65 (RNO) Virginia City, NV St. Mary's in the Mountains.
Frantz, Henry *c.pp.s.* '54 (CIN)[N] Carthagena, OH St. Charles Retired.
Franxman, Thomas W. *s.j.* '64 (COV) Fort Mitchell, KY Blessed Sacrament.
Franz, Paul R. '66 (BO) Senior Priests. Retired.
Franz, S. Michael '69 (CLV) Cleveland, OH St. Stephen.
Franzinell, Benjamin '50 (LAV) Retired.
Franzman, Thomas R. '70 (CHI)[A] Mundelein, IL University of St. Mary of the Lake/Mundelein Seminary; [A] Mundelein, IL University of St. Mary of the Lake/Mundelein Seminary; [A] Mundelein, IL Conference Center; Mundelein Seminary/University of St. Mary of the Lake.
Frapaul, Sam *o.f.m.cap.* '78 (PAT) Passaic, NJ St. Mary Hospital; [K] Passaic, NJ St. Mary's Hospital.
Frappier, Rev. Msgr. George L. '56 (PRO) Retired.
Frascadore, Henry C. '59 (HRT) Retired.
Fraser, Bernard '00 (DET) Absent on Leave.
Fraser, Christopher J. '01 (PHX) College of Consultors; Judicial Vicar; Presbyteral Council; Priests' Assurance Association.
Fraser, Daniel J. '99 (TOL) Retired.
Fraser, Donald D. '74 (B) Retired.
Fraser, Gerald C. '72 (BO) Permanent Disability.
Fraser, James F. '65 (BRK) Flushing, NY Holy Family Retired.
Fraser, John '96 (NY) Hawthorne, NY Holy Rosary.
Fraser, Michael B. '75 (NO) On Administrative Leave.
Fraszczak, Zbigniew *s.v.d.* (SB) San Bernardino, CA St. Anthony.
Fratt, Gregory '98 (HT) Morgan City, LA Sacred Heart of Jesus.
Fratts, Ralph J. '60 (ROC) Retired.
Frausto, Jorge *o.f.m.* '86 (ELP)[B] El Paso, TX St. Anthony's School of Theology.
Frawley, Gerard *s.a.c.* '68 (DET) Wyandotte, MI; Ortonville, MI St. Anne.
Frawley, John P. '44 (CHI) Chicago, IL St. Thomas More Retired.
Frawley, Patrick J. '78 (BRK) Jackson Heights, NY Our Lady of Fatima; Released from Diocesan Assignment.
Frayna, Ramon '86 (AUS) Rockdale, TX St. Joseph.
Frazer, Christopher '07 (SAC) Folsom, CA St. John the Baptist; Presbyteral Council.
Frazer, Edward J. *s.s.* '61 (BAL)[M] Baltimore, MD St. Charles Villa; [Q] Baltimore Society of St. Sulpice, Province of the United States Retired.
Frazer, Edward J. *s.s.* '61 (GF) Retired.
Frazer, J. Francis '75 (PIT) Clarksville, PA St. Thomas; Greene County, PA State Correctional Institute at Greene.
Frazer, Joseph '84 (AUS) Retired.
Frazier, Lawrence K. '71 (BAL) Buckeystown, MD St. Joseph–on–Carrollton Manor.
Frazier, William B. *m.m.* '56 (NY)[DD] Maryknoll Maryknoll Fathers and Brothers.
Frechette, Christopher *s.j.* '99 (BO)[U] Brighton, MA Miguel Pro House.
Frechette, Leo L. '55 (MAN) Retired.
Frechette, Rt. Rev. Paul G. '78 (NTN) Worcester, MA Our Lady of Perpetual Help; Continuing Education of Clergy Office.
Frechette, Paul *s.m.* '76 (WDC)[O] Washington, DC Marist Center.
Frechette, Richard *c.p.* '79 (FgM) New Rochelle, NY St. Paul of the Cross Province.
Frechette, Thomas A. '86 (FR) Attleboro Falls, MA St. Mark's.
Frecker, Rev. Msgr. A. Anthony '72 (COL) Canal Winchester, OH Pope John XXIII.
Frederici, David C. '01 (FR)[K] Centerville, MA Cape Cod Campus Ministry; University of Massachusetts Dartmouth; Cape Cod Campus Ministry; Catholic Scouting Program; [K] North Dartmouth, MA UMass Dartmouth Campus Ministry; St. Luke's Hospital; North Dartmouth, MA St. Julie Billiart.
Frederick, Curt J. '75 (MIL) Archdiocesan Consultors; Waukesha, WI St. William; Judges for Second Instance; Archdiocesan Council of Priests.
Frederick, Joseph B. '56 (MIL) Retired.
Frederick, Rev. Msgr. Lawrence A. '66 (LR)[B] Little Rock, AR Catholic High School.
Frederick, Robert A. '00 (ATL) Cumming, GA St. Brendan the Navigator.
Fredericks, James L. '77 (SFR) On Duty Outside the Archdiocese.
Fredericks, James '77 (LA)[C] Los Angeles, CA Jesuit Community.
Fredericks, Michael '87 (MO) Air Force Reserve Chaplains; Colton, CA Immaculate Conception.
Frederico, Charles A. *s.j.* '06 (BO) Watertown, MA; [U] Watertown, MA The Society of Jesus of New England–Provincial Offices.
Frederico, Charles A. *s.j.* '06 (NY)[DD] New York, NY "America;" Residence and publication office of the America Press; [DD] New York, NY Society of Jesus, New York Province.
Free, Daniel *c.p.* '52 (BRK)[R] Jamaica, NY Immaculate Conception Monastery Retired.
Free, Henry *c.p.* '58 (BRK)[R] Jamaica, NY Immaculate Conception Monastery Retired.
Freed, Eric '90 (SR) Eureka, CA St. Bernard; [J] Arcata, CA Newman Community, Humboldt State University.
Freed, Eric '90 (SFR) Japanese Mission.
Freedy, Joseph M. '08 (PIT) Priestly Vocations, Office for; Priest Council.
Freeh, Vincent T. *m.s.c.* '59 (OG)[F] Watertown, NY Missionaries of the Sacred Heart.
Freeman, James '65 (DM) Retired.
Freeman, John A. '73 (PH) Ardmore, PA St. Colman Retired.
Freeman, Joseph '05 (SD) Encinitas, CA Saint John the Evangelist Catholic Parish Encinitas.
Freeman, Justin *o.de.m.* '11 (CLV) Metro Health Medical Center & Rehabilitation Center; Cleveland, OH St. Rocco.
Freeman, Roland P. '67 (DEN)[G] Denver, CO Special Religious Education–Pastoral Care of Developmentally Disabled Persons.
Freemesser, Paul J. '59 (ROC) Rochester, NY St. Theodore Retired.
Freer, Douglas '07 (TR) Episcopal Council; Vicar.
Fregapane, Rev. Msgr. Mercurio A. '51 (HBG) Retired.
Freiburger, Jason '07 (FTW) Ecumenism; Chaplains; Fort Wayne, IN Cathedral of the Immaculate Conception; Presbyteral Council; Vice Chancellor; Assistant to the Bishop–Fort Wayne.
Freidburger, Jason (FTW)[C] Fort Wayne, IN Bishop Dwenger High School.
Freiermuth, Harry '59 (MRY) Retired.
Freihofer, Michael A. '87 (MO) Air Force Reserve Chaplains.
Freihofer, Michael '06 (DEN) Granby, CO St. Anne.
Freitag, Patrick '96 (SEA) Mercer Island, WA St. Monica.
Freitas, Daniel L. '49 (FR) Retired.
Freitas, Patrick '65 (HON) Haiku, HI St. Rita.
Fremgen, Edward George '92 (LA) Retired.
French, D. James *s.j.* '75 (RVC) Oceanside, NY St. Anthony.
French, Donald J. '76 (HRT) Hamden, CT Blessed Sacrament.
French, James R. '78 (STL) Villa Ridge, MO St. John the Baptist.
French, John F. '54 (ALB) Retired.
French, Michael D. *s.j.* '46 (STL)[C] Saint Louis University.
French, Michael D. *s.j.* '75 (STL)[O] St. Louis, MO Jesuit Community Corporation at Saint Louis University – Jesuit Hall.
French, Raymond D. *c.s.sp.* '91 (PIT)[B] Pittsburgh, PA Duquesne University of the Holy Spirit; [P] Pittsburgh, PA Duquesne University.
French, Robert E. '63 (RIC) Retired.
French, Rev. Msgr. Thomas A. '49 (SAT)[K] San Antonio, TX Incarnate Word Retirement Community; [M] San Antonio, TX Incarnate Word Retirement Community Inc. Retired.
French, Thomas *s.m.* '97 (STL) St. Louis, MO Our Lady of the Pillar; [O] St. Louis, MO Marianist Community, Our Lady of the Pillar Parish.
French, Walter V. '65 (NEW) Retired.
Frenier, Steven *o.f.m.conv.* '82 (BAL)[Q] Companions Evangelization & Mail Order Office.
Frenoy, Fortune C. *s.m.* '54 (WDC)[O] Washington, DC Marist Center Retired.
Frerichs, Glenn K. '00 (WIN) Appointed Members.
Frerker, Jack W. '63 (BEL) Retired.
Freson, Kenan *o.f.m.* '67 (CIN)[C] Cincinnati, OH St. Anthony Shrine, Franciscan Postulancy; [T] Cincinnati, OH Community Support Charitable Trust; Councillors.
Freund, Joseph *c.ss.r.* '66 (NY)[DD] New York, NY Redemptorist Priests and Brothers, C.Ss.R.; [FF] Esopus, NY Mount St. Alphonsus Redemptorist Retreat Center.
Frey, Rev. Msgr. Andrew F. '48 (BR) Retired.
Frey, Rev. Msgr. Francis '58 (SAN) Retired.
Frey, Jerome V. '50 (LAF)[M] Lafayette, LA Community of Jesus Crucified Retired.
Frey, Rev. Msgr. John T. '70 (CAM) Deanery Representatives; Amicus; Avalon, NJ St. Brendan the Navigator Parish, Avalon, N.J.
Freyer, Timothy '89 (ORG) Anaheim, CA St. Boniface; [G] Fullerton, CA St. Jude Medical Center; Clergy Personnel Board.
Frez, Joseph S. '10 (SLC) Kearns, UT Saint Francis Xavier LLC 222.
Frias, Rev. Msgr. Carlos '60 (ELP) Retired.
Frias, Luciano *c.m.* '01 (SJN) San Juan, PR San Vicente de Paul.
Frias, Martin '03 (PBL) Aguilar, CO St. Anthony; Walsenburg, CO Sacred Heart; Walsenburg, CO St. Mary.
Frias, Ramon *o.f.m.cap.* '72 (NY) New York, NY St. John the Baptist.
Frias, Rev. Msgr. Santiago C. '59 (RIC) Retired.
Friberg, Daniel '62 (STP) Retired.
Fride, Edward O. '86 (LAN) Ann Arbor, MI Christ the King.
Friebel, Rick *c.pp.s.* '78 (CIN) Montezuma, OH Our Lady of Guadalupe.
Fried, Francis L. '68 (STP) Roseville, MN Corpus Christi.
Friedel, John (J.) F. '86 (SPC) Joplin, MO St. Peter The Apostle; Vocations–Seminarians; Diocesan Consultors; Presbyteral Council; [J] Joplin, MO Newman Club, Missouri Southern State University; Campus Ministries; Lamar, MO St. Mary.
Friedel, Robert E. '57 (CLV) Twinsburg, OH SS. Cosmas and Damian Retired.
Friedell, John C. '54 (DUB) Retired.
Friedell, Ronald G. '66 (DUB)[I] Dubuque, IA Clare House Retired.
Friedl, Erwin J. '71 (CHI) Melrose Park, IL Sacred Heart.
Friedl, Rev. Msgr. Francis P. '43 (DUB) Retired.
Friedl, Thomas '92 (CR) Boy Scouts; Park Rapids, MN St. Peter the Apostle; Priests' Council; Pastoral Leadership Program Board.
Friedley, Craig '07 (PHX) Tempe, AZ Our Lady of Mt. Carmel Roman Catholic Parish; Queen Creek, AZ Our Lady of Guadalupe Roman Catholic Parish.

Friedman, Cecil H. '50 (SC) Retired.
Friedman, Daniel L. '72 (BEL) Aviston, IL St. Francis of Assisi.
Friedman, Gregory *o.f.m.* '76 (CIN) Cincinnati, OH St. Francis Seraph; [N] Cincinnati, OH Pleasant Street Friary; [N] Cincinnati, OH St. Francis Seraph Friary.
Friedrich, James '89 (SFS) Woonsocket, SD St. Joseph; Woonsocket, SD St. Wilfrid; Defenders of the Matrimonial Bond.
Friedrich, Lawrence '47 (SFS) Retired.
Friedrichs, Richard M. '70 (PRO) Warwick, RI St. Catherine.
Friedrichsen, Timothy A. '84 (SC) Presbyteral Council; Denison, IA St. Rose of Lima; Denison, IA St. Ann's; Denison, IA St. Marys; Denison, IA St. Boniface.
Friel, Daid M. '11 (PH) Philadelphia, PA St. Anselm.
Friel, John F. '70 (TUC) Yuma, AZ Saint John Neumann Roman Catholic Church – Yuma.
Friel, Mark M. '63 (BUF)[N] Buffalo, NY Sheehan Residence for Priests Retired.
Friend, Rev. Msgr. R. Scott '87 (LR) Vicar General; Diocesan Consultors; Monsignor James E. O'Connell Diocesan Seminarian Fund, Inc.; Vocations; Clergy Personnel Advisory Board (Diocesan); Presbyteral Council.
Frient, Lawrence '84 (Y) Niles, OH Our Lady of Mt. Carmel.
Fries, Richard R. *m.m.* '76 (FgM) Maryknoll, NY MARYKNOLL.
Frigo, Martin A. *o.praem.* '49 (WIL)[J] Middletown, DE Immaculate Conception Priory of the Canons Regular of Premontre.
Frigo, William *o.f.m. cap.* '63 (MAD)[I] Madison, WI San Damiano Friary Retired.
Frilot, Rev. Msgr. Eugene P. '55 (LA) Glendale, CA Church of the Incarnation Retired.
Frink, Thomas J. (MAN) Salem, NH Saints Mary and Joseph.
Frinsko, Donald S. *t.o.r.* '79 (STU)[H] Steubenville, OH Holy Spirit Friary; [A] Steubenville, OH Franciscan University of Steubenville.
Frisch, Carl '95 (SAT)[F] San Antonio, TX St. Anthony Catholic High School.
Frisch, Kenneth J. '78 (MAD) Highland, WI SS. Anthony and Philip; Montfort, WI St. Thomas; Personnel Board.
Frisch, Michael F. *o.praem.* '97 (GB)[J] De Pere, WI St. Norbert Abbey.
Frisch, Ralph *s.t.* (PAT)[N] Stirling, NJ Shrine of St. Joseph.
Frische, Emile *m.h.m.* '70 (NY) New York, NY St. Malachy's; Coordinator for Special & Pastoral Ministries; [DD] Hartsdale, NY Mill Hill Fathers Residence.
Friske, Joseph P. '62 (SAG) Outside the Diocese Retired.
Frison, Theodore '72 (P) Absent on Leave.
Frisoni, Matthew H. '05 (ALB) Special Assignment.
Frister, Jerome '57 (JUN) Retired.
Fritsch, Albert *s.j.* '67 (LEX) Ravenna, KY St. Elizabeth of Hungary; Stanton, KY Our Lady of the Mountains.
Fritsch, Michael C. '85 (IND) Bloomington, IN St. John the Apostle Catholic Church, Bloomington, Inc.; Deaneries and Deans.
Fritz, Henry H. *o.s.b.* '52 (PEO)[A] Peru, IL St. Bede Abbey Retired.
Fritz, Rev. Msgr. John C. '00 (RCK) Chancellor; Secretary to the Bishop & Diocesan Master of Ceremonies; Cemeteries.
Fritz, Rev. Msgr. John '00 (RCK) Special Assignment.
Fritz, Peter *o.f.m.* '50 (SFD)[K] Sherman, IL Blessed Giles Friary.
Fritz, Richard A. '75 (KAL) Bronson, MI St. Mary's.
Fritz, Robert J. '75 (CAM) North Cape May, NJ The Parish of Saint John Neumann, North Cape May, N.J.
Fritzen, James C. '69 (SY) Liverpool, NY Christ the King.
Frizzell, Lawrence E. '62 (NEW)[B] Seton Hall University.
Froehle, Charles L. '63 (STP) Minneapolis, MN Our Lady of Lourdes.
Froehlich, James P. *o.f.m.cap.* '82 (WDC) Washington, DC Shrine of the Sacred Heart; [A] Washington, DC Theological College of the Catholic University of America.
Froehlich, Rev. Msgr. Mark J. '69 (STU) Barnesville, OH Assumption; Barnesville, OH St. Mary's; Judges.
Froelich, Canice *o.f.m.cap.* '47 (SAL) Hays, KS St. Joseph Parish; [D] Hays, KS St. Joseph's Friary.
Frohlich, Attila '01 (EVN) On Leave.
Froidurot, Michel '78 (SD) Poway, CA Saint Gabriel Catholic Parish.
Fromageot, Robert *f.s.s.p.* '01 (LIN)[A] Denton, NE Our Lady of Guadalupe Seminary; [L] Lincoln, NE St. Francis of Assisi Church.
Fromholzer, Francis J. '58 (ALN) Retired.
Fronckowiak, Dennis F. '77 (BUF) Tonawanda, NY St. Timothy.
Fronczak, Dennis A. '75 (BUF) Vicars; Defenders of the Bond; Holland, NY St. Joseph.
Fronek, Randy '05 (RCK) Aurora, IL Holy Angels.
Fronk, Christopher S. *s.j.* '97 (MO) Navy Chaplains.
Fronk, Christopher S. *s.j.* '97 (BAL)[Q] Towson Maryland Province of the Society of Jesus.
Fronske, Edward *o.f.m.* '67 (GLP) Cibecue, AZ St. Catherine; Whiteriver, AZ St. Francis.
Frontiero, Rev. Msgr. Anthony R. '91 (MAN) Manchester, NH St. Joseph Cathedral.
Frost, Arthur *c.ss.r.* '41 (LA) Whittier, CA St. Mary of the Assumption; [P] Whittier, CA Redemptorists of Whittier Retired.
Frost, John M. '87 (DM) Harlan, IA St. Michael; [A] Harlan, IA Elementary School: Shelby County Catholic School.
Frost, Rev. Msgr. Stephen A. '77 (FRS) Bakersfield, CA Christ the King.
Frost, Rev. Msgr. Stephen '77 (RNO) Judges.
Frost, Thomas *o.f.m.* '60 (MRY)[F] San Miguel, CA Novitiate House for the Franciscan Friars, O.F.M.; [F] San Miguel, CA Franciscan Friars, O.F.M.; San Miguel, CA San Miguel.
Frozena, Kenneth R. '60 (GB) Retired.
Frueh, Robert '63 (BRK) Kingsboro Psychiatric Center; Brooklyn, NY St. Saviour.
Fruge, Rev. Msgr. Donald J. '72 (GAL) Retired.
Frundt, Oscar H. '56 (WIL) Retired.
Frutades, Alfredo *i.v.e.* '01 (PHX) Phoenix, AZ Immaculate Heart of Mary Roman Catholic Parish; Phoenix, AZ St. Anthony Roman Catholic Parish.
Fruth, Paul '74 (DUL) McGregor, MN Our Lady of Fatima; McGregor, MN Holy Family; Diocesan Deans; Council of Catholic Women.
Fry, James Q. '79 (ORG) Retired.
Fry, Wallace Blake '07 (ELP) El Paso, TX Our Lady of Assumption.
Fryar, James A. *f.s.s.p.* '04 (VEN) Sarasota, FL Christ the King.
Fryar, James *f.s.s.p.* '04 (ORL) Retired.
Fryar, Rev. Msgr. Thomas S. '78 (DEN) Denver, CO Cathedral Basilica of the Immaculate Conception; College of Consultors; Moderator of the Curia; Archdiocesan Finance Council; Moderator of the Curia.
Fryda, William *m.m.* '88 (FgM) Maryknoll, NY MARYKNOLL.
Frydrych, Jerszy *s.ch.* '85 (SD) San Diego, CA St. Maximilian Kolbe Mission.
Fryer, Rev. Msgr. Patrick L. '73 (WH) Martinsburg, WV St. Joseph's.
Fu, Joseph '60 (NEW) Retired.
Fuccile, Dominic G. '66 (NEW) Retired.
Fucheck, Robert '66 (ORL) Retired.
Fuchs, Eric W. '04 (NEW) Bayonne, NJ St. Vincent de Paul.
Fuchs, John *s.j.* '75 (SEA)[C] Tacoma, WA Bellarmine Preparatory School.
Fuchs, Moritz A. '55 (SY) Retired.
Fucinaro, Rev. Msgr. Thomas J. '89 (LIN) On Duty Outside the Diocese.
Fuemmeler, James R. '58 (JC) Retired.
Fuenmayor, Jose Maria '84 (DEN)[A] Denver, CO Redemptoris Mater House of Formation.
Fuentes, Enrique *o.c.d.* (SD) El Cajon, CA Our Lady of Grace Catholic Parish.
Fuentes, Theo *c.m.f.* '51 (LA) San Gabriel, CA San Gabriel Mission.
Fuentes Rodriguez, Jose '45 (SJN) Retired.
Fuentez, Trinidad '78 (ELP) El Paso, TX Queen of Peace; Defenders of the Bond.
Fuertes, Agustin '02 (DAL) Dallas, TX Blessed Sacrament.
Fugee, Michael '94 (NEW) Propagation of the Faith; Society of St. Peter the Apostle; Holy Childhood Association; Missionary Union of Priests & Religious; Rochelle Park, NJ Sacred Heart; Part–time Staff/Advocates/Procurators.
Fugini, Francis *o.f.m.cap.* '54 (PIT)[M] Pittsburgh, PA St. Augustine Friary.
Fugle, James L. '08 (BUF) Getzville, NY St. Pius X.
Fugolo, Joseph *c.s.* '67 (NY)[HH] New York, NY American Committee on Italian Migration, Inc.
Fuhrman, Bruno *o.s.b.* '54 (LR)[A] Subiaco, AR Subiaco Abbey.
Fuhrman, Rev. Msgr. Robert J. '81 (NEW) On Duty Outside the Archdiocese.
Fuhrmann, Nicholas *o.s.b.* '54 (LR)[A] Subiaco, AR Subiaco Abbey.
Fuino, Crispin *o.f.m.conv.* '48 (TR) Point Pleasant Beach, NJ St. Peter's Retired.
Fukes, Gary M. '88 (MO) Military Chaplains; Army Chaplains.
Fukes, James *o.f.m.conv.* '98 (R) Siler City, NC St. Julia; [F] Pittsboro, NC Our Lady of Guadalupe Friary.
Fuks, Mariusz K. '08 (SAV) Columbus, GA St. Anne.
Fulcher, Titus '96 (CHR) Office of Child Protection Services.
Fulco, William J. *s.j.* '66 (LA)[C] Los Angeles, CA Jesuit Community.
Fuld, Charles '86 (SD) "Southern Cross"—(Diocesan Newspaper) Retired.
Fuld, Chuck '86 (LA) State Chaplain.
Fulgenzi, Mario A. *o.s.b.* '68 (GBG)[H] Latrobe, PA Saint Vincent Archabbey.
Fulgenzi, Mario '68 (RIC) Virginia Beach, VA St. Gregory the Great.
Fullam, Rev. Msgr. T. Dominick '94 (BLX) Biloxi, MS St. Mary; Vicar General; Defenders of the Bond; Catholic Foundation–Diocese of Biloxi; Catholic Housing Board; Finance Council; Insurance Committee; Catholic University, Friends of; Moderator of Curia; College of Consultors; Personnel Board; Presbyteral Council.
Fullam, Rev. Msgr. Vincent F. '65 (BRK) Legion of Mary; Astoria, NY Immaculate Conception Retired.
Fuller, Jon D. *s.j.* '90 (BO)[D] Boston, MA Boston College High School.
Fuller, Michael J.K. '97 (RCK)[A] Mundelein, IL University of St. Mary of the Lake/Mundelein Seminary; Special Assignment.
Fuller, Neil *s.v.d.* '69 (SB) Corona, CA St. Matthew.
Fuller, Orlando R. '75 (MO) Army Chaplains.
Fuller, Orlando R. (SAL) Fort Riley, KS Fort Riley Catholic Community.
Fuller, Rev. Msgr. Robert D. '56 (TUC) Tucson, AZ Saint Frances Cabrini Roman Catholic Parish – Tucson; Directors; [I] Tucson, AZ St. Frances Cabrini Foundation, Inc.
Fuller, Samuel *o.f.m.cap.* '08 (NOR) Middletown, CT St. Pius X.
Fuller, Timothy M. '93 (OKL) Midwest City, OK St. Philip Neri; Archdiocesan Finance Council; Master of Ceremonies; Air National Guard Chaplains.
Fullerton, Daniel J. '91 (MO) Navy Chaplains.
Fullerton, Daniel '91 (SCR) Military Chaplains.
Fullmer, Hugh '72 (JOL) Aurora, IL Our Lady of Mercy.
Fullum, John J. '67 (BRK) East Glendale, NY Sacred Heart.
Fullum, Rev. Msgr. Vincent '65 (BRK) Diocesan Consultors.
Fulton, Rev. Msgr. David I. '67 (MET) Baptistown, NJ Our Lady of Victories.
Fulton, Rev. Msgr. David I. (BAL)[A] Baltimore, MD St. Mary's Seminary and University; [A] Baltimore, MD St. Mary's Seminary and University.
Fulton, Rev. Msgr. David I. (PH)[A] Wynnewood, PA Theological Seminary of St. Charles Borromeo, Overbrook.
Fulton, David L. '02 (OM) Fordyce, NE St. Joseph; Fordyce, NE St. John the Baptist; Fordyce, NE St. Boniface; [M] Fordyce, NE Cemetery Endowment for St. Boniface Church.
Fulton, Eugene J. '67 (PSC)[FF] Larchmont, NY Trinity Retreat; On Duty Outside Diocese.
Fulton, Eugene J. '67 (NY) Spiritual Development, Office of.
Fulton, Kenneth S. '50 (TLS) Retired.
Fulton, Patrick W. *c.s.b.* '97 (GAL)[E] Houston, TX St. Thomas High School.
Fulton, Robert P. '04 (LA) Covina, CA St. Louise de Marillac.
Fulton, Rev. Msgr. Robert W. '62 (MOB) Gulf Shores, AL Our Lady of the Gulf.
Fulton, Terry A. '94 (SAC) Sacramento, CA St. Maria Goretti.
Funaro, Rev. Msgr. Joseph A. '65 (BRK) Forest Hills, NY Our Lady Queen of Martyrs.
Funesti, Peter K. '88 (NEW) Midland Park, NJ Nativity.
Funk, David J. *o.f.m.cap.* '68 (GB)[J] Appleton, WI St. Joseph Friary; Appleton, WI St. Joseph; Appleton, WI St. Mary.
Funk, Rev. Msgr. David R. '74 (COL) Reynoldsburg, OH St. Pius X.
Funk, Peter C. '64 (PH) On Duty Outside the Archdiocese.
Funk, Peter C. '64 (BEA) Commission for Continuing Education of Clergy & Religious; [E] Beaumont, TX Holy Family Retreat Center.
Funk, Peter *o.s.b.* '04 (CHI)[N] Chicago, IL Monastery of the Holy Cross.
Funk, Virgil C. '63 (RIC) Retired.
Funke, Gerald '80 (B) Nampa, ID St. Paul's; Adjutant Judicial Vicars; Judges; St. Vincent de Paul Society.
Funke, Rev. Msgr. Richard P. '60 (DUB) Defenders of the Bond Retired.
Funke, Ronald R. *s.j.* '68 (SEA)[M] Seattle, WA Arrupe Jesuit Community at Seattle University.
Funtila, Aloysius '83 (CHI) Waukegan, IL St. Anastasia.
Furdzik, Pawel P. *o.c.d.* '95 (CHI) Chicago, IL St. Camillus.
Furdzik, Pawel *o.c.d.* '95 (GRY)[H] Munster, IN Discalced Carmelite Fathers Monastery.
Furey, J. Barry '71 (BGP) Fairfield, CT Our Lady of the Assumption; Vicariate III (Fairfield, Easton, West Bridgeport); Parochial Examiners; Presbyteral Council.
Furey, John *c.ss.r.* '60 (BO) Boston, MA Our Lady of Perpetual Help.
Furey, Matthew J. '99 (NY) Bronx, NY St. Francis Xavier.

Furey, Thomas J. '73 (PH) Springfield, PA St. Francis of Assisi.
Furfaro, Virgil '73 (SFE) Retired.
Furlan, Gerard *s.x.* '58 (BO)[U] Holliston, MA Xaverian Missionaries.
Furlan, Michael J. '75 (CHI) Oak Lawn, IL St. Germaine.
Furlong, Aidan M. *a.a.* '53 (WOR)[N] Worcester, MA Assumptionists (Augustinians of the Assumption).
Furlong, J. Daryl '66 (MAD) Retired.
Furlong, Richard V. '72 (BUF) On Duty Outside the Diocese.
Furlong, Rev. Msgr. Thomas D. '60 (OM) Bellevue, NE St. Matthew The Evangelist Church of Bellevue Retired.
Furman, Henry P. '02 (BUR)[G] Castleton, VT Castleton State College; Castleton, VT St. John the Baptist; Castleton, VT St. Paul.
Furnari, Casper J. '68 (BRK) Flushing, NY Holy Family.
Furnari, Salvatore C. *s.a.c.* '05 (BAL) Baltimore, MD St. Leo.
Furrell, Reynold '98 (ORG) Ladera Ranch, CA Holy Trinity.
Furrevig, Edward G. '67 (NEW) Retired.
Furtado, Al *c.s.sp.* '64 (SFR) Belmont, CA St. Mark.
Furtado, Jose '97 (SP)[J] St. Petersburg, FL St. Anthony's Hospital, Inc.
Fusco, Albin *o.f.m.* '61 (ALB)[A] Catskill, NY St. Anthony Friary.
Fusco, Christopher (MET) Canonical Staff.
Fusco, Mark *s.j.* '11 (WDC)[O] Washington, DC The Jesuit Community at Georgetown University.
Fusco, Thomas M. '85 (RVC) Syosset, NY St. Edward Confessor.
Fuselier, Karl '94 (LKC) On Leave.
Fuss, Edward F. *s.m.* '89 (WDC)[O] Washington, DC Marist Center Retired.
Fussner, Donald T. '60 (NY) New York, NY St. Peter Retired.
Futie, Richard F. '82 (BGP) Defenders of the Bond; Stamford, CT Sacred Heart.
Futter, Volker *o.s.b.* '69 (OM)[M] Schuyler, NE Benedictine Mission House Endowment Trust; [J] Schuyler, NE Benedictine Mission House; Schuyler, NE.
Fynn, Isaac A. '79 (TUC) Tucson, AZ St. Joseph's Hospital; [D] Tucson, AZ Carondelet St. Joseph's Hospital.

G

Gaa, David *o.f.m.* '98 (SD)[J] Oceanside, CA Old Mission San Luis Rey; [M] Oceanside, CA Old Mission San Luis Rey Retreat.
Gaalaas, Rev. Msgr. Patrick J. '72 (TLS) Diocesan Consultors; Priests' Personnel Committee; Seminary Board; Ecumenism; Tulsa, OK St. Bernard of Clairvaux.
Gabage, John B. '07 (WIL) Wilmington, DE St. Elizabeth.
Gabel, Emanuel '57 (DEN) Retired.
Gabel, Martin M. '68 (JOL) Homer Glen, IL St. Bernard.
Gabela, Jose Luis Diez *o.s.a.* '72 (MGZ) Aguada, PR St. Francis of Assisi.
Gaberle, Jiri '89 (MIL) Special Assignment.
Gabet, George *f.s.s.p.* '97 (FTW) Fort Wayne, IN Sacred Heart.
Gabin, John D. '75 (PH) Springfield, PA Holy Cross.
Gabler, Michael J. *o.s.b.* '08 (GBG)[H] Latrobe, PA Saint Vincent Archabbey.
Gabler, Michael *o.s.b.* (RIC) Virginia Beach, VA St. Gregory the Great.
Gabor, Pavel *s.j.* '04 (TUC)[E] Tucson, AZ Jesuit Community of the Vatican Observatory.
Gaborit, Mauricio *s.j.* '78 (FgM) St. Louis, MO Society of Jesus.
Gaboury, Victor *s.s.c.* '57 (OM)[J] St. Columbans Missionary Society of St. Columban Retired.
Gaboury, Victor *s.s.c.* '57 (PRO)[O] Bristol, RI St. Columban's Retirement House Retired.
Gabriel, Abelardo *s.v.d.* '06 (CHI) Chicago, IL St. Anselm.
Gabriel, Eduardo *o.p.* '92 (NO) New Orleans, LA St. Anthony of Padua.
Gabriel, John B. '98 (MO) Army Chaplains.
Gabriel, John D. '87 (NEW) Vocations Office; Presbyteral Council; Emmaus House of Discernment; Director of Vocations; Members.
Gabriel, John *m.s.* '91 (ATL) Marietta, GA St. Ann.
Gabriel, Michael A. '84 (CHI) Chicago, IL St. Josaphat.
Gabriel, Paul *o.f.m.conv.* '05 (R) Burlington, NC Blessed Sacrament; [F] Elon, NC Conventual Franciscans.
Gabriel–Maisonet, Guillermo '11 (TYL) Clarksville, TX St. Joseph; Paris, TX Our Lady of Victory.
Gabrielli, Ted *s.j.* '96 (LA) Los Angeles, CA Dolores Mission.
Gabrielli, Theodore E. *s.j.* '96 (FgM) Los Gatos, CA; Los Gatos, CA Society of Jesus.
Gabrielli, Theodore *s.j.* '96 (SJ)[O] Los Gatos, CA California Jesuit Missions.
Gabrus, Alois '72 (STL)[O] St. Louis, MO Franciscan Friary of St. Anthony of Padua.
Gabuzda, Richard J. '81 (OM)[O] Omaha, NE Institute for Priestly Formation; On Duty Outside the Diocese.
Gacad, Manuel *m.j.* '78 (LA)[P] Los Angeles, CA Missionaries of Jesus, Inc.; Los Angeles, CA St. Kevin; Los Angeles, CA Precious Blood.
Gaddy, Rev. Msgr. James '65 (LKC) Lake Charles, LA Our Lady Queen of Heaven.
Gaddy, Kenneth F. *c.ss.r.* '88 (FgM) Baltimore Province.
Gadenz, Pablo T. '96 (TR) On Duty Outside the Diocese; Censores Librorum.
Gadenz, Pablo T. '96 (NEW)[B] Seton Hall University; [A] South Orange, NJ Immaculate Conception Seminary School of Theology.
Gadient, Peter J. '45 (LIN) Retired.
Gadziala, Timothy '94 (ATL) On Duty Outside the Archdiocese.
Gaeke, Thomas M. '75 (CIN) Medical Leave of Absence.
Gaelens, Albert R. *c.s.b.* '60 (GAL)[E] Houston, TX St. Thomas High School.
Gaesser, Ronald E. '61 (ROC) Auburn, NY Holy Family Retired.
Gaeta, Bernard N. '73 (Y) Advocates; Judges; Struthers, OH Christ Our Savior Parish.
Gaeta, David R. '80 (SLC) On Duty Outside the Diocese.
Gaeta, Rev. Msgr. Francis X. '63 (RVC)[N] Amityville, NY St. Pius X Residence Retired.
Gaetano, Francis M. *s.a.c.* '48 (NEW) Fairview, NJ Our Lady of Grace.
Gaetano, Rev. Msgr. Lewis F. '73 (Y) Canton, OH Christ the Servant Parish.
Gaffey, Eugene F. '69 (PRT)[M] Portland, ME University of Maine at Machias; Machias, ME Saint Peter the Fisherman Parish.
Gaffey, Rev. Msgr. James P. '60 (SR) Diocesan Judges Retired.
Gaffey, Kevin P. '57 (SFR) Retired.
Gaffigan, Charles A. '62 (ALB) Retired.
Gaffigan, William J. '64 (ALB) Retired.
Gaffney, Brian R. *c.o.* '05 (PH)[Y] Philadelphia, PA The Philadelphia Congregation of The Oratory of St. Philip Neri; Philadelphia, PA St. Francis Xavier.
Gaffney, Christopher *o.f.m.* (MAN) Derry, NH St. Thomas Aquinas.
Gaffney, David F. '00 (PRO)[C] Warwick, RI Bishop Hendricken High School; [A] Providence, RI Seminary of Our Lady of Providence; College of Consultors; Seminary of Our Lady of Providence; Council Members.
Gaffney, Edward M. *o.p.* '49 (HBG)[H] Lancaster, PA Dominican Nuns of the Perpetual Rosary, Incorporated.
Gaffney, Francis P. '64 (CAM) Swedesboro, NJ St. Clare of Assisi Parish, Gibbstown, N.J. Retired.
Gaffney, J. Michael '73 (OG) Massena, NY The Catholic Community of St. Mary's & St. Joseph's.
Gaffney, John H. *o.s.a.* '45 (TLS)[B] Tulsa, OK Cascia Hall Preparatory School.
Gaffney, John *s.o.l.t.* '09 (CHY) Saint Stephens, WY St. Stephen's; [D] Saint Stephens, WY St. Stephens Mission.
Gaffney, Michael (OG) Committee on Assignments.
Gaffney, Patrick D. *c.s.c.* '74 (FTW)[B] University of Notre Dame Du Lac; [H] Notre Dame, IN Holy Cross Community, Corby Hall, University of Notre Dame.
Gaffney, William *c.ss.r.* '60 (TR)[R] Long Branch, NJ San Alfonso Retreat House.
Gaffny, David J. '57 (NSH) Dover, TN St. Francis of Assisi.
Gaffny, David J. '06 (NSH) Clarksville, TN Immaculate Conception.
Gaffny, David '57 (NSH) Deans.
Gagala, John '58 (DET) Retired.
Gagan, Charles R. *s.j.* '68 (SFR) San Francisco, CA St. Ignatius; [N] San Francisco, CA Loyola House Jesuit Community; [P] San Francisco, CA Catholic Charities CYO of the Archdiocese of San Francisco.
Gagan, Phillip R. '79 (STA) Retired.
Gage, George '79 (ROM) Boardman, OH St. Mary; College of Consultors.
Gage, Philip S. *s.m.* '69 (WDC)[O] Washington, DC Marist Center.
Gaggawala, Paul O. *a.j.* '80 (ALN)[P] Shenandoah, PA Apostles of Jesus; [P] Northampton, PA Apostles of Jesus.
Gaglia, Fred R. '63 (SB) Retired.
Gagliano, Philip J. '76 (NY) Ardsley, NY Our Lady of Perpetual Help.
Gagliardi, Richard '62 (OAK) Retired.
Gagliardo, Anthony F. '61 (BUF) Retired.
Gaglione, John R. '76 (BUF) Air Force Reserve Chaplains; Snyder, NY Christ the King; Finance Council.
Gaglioni, Joseph B. *c.s.sp.* '64 (SB)[I] Hemet, CA Congregation of the Holy Spirit Retired.
Gagne, Donald *s.m.* '54 (PRT) Lewiston, ME Central Maine Medical Center.
Gagne, Marc R. '85 (MAN) Dover, NH Parish of the Assumption; Vicars Forane.
Gagne, Roger C. '75 (PRO) Warwick, RI St. Peter.
Gagne, Ronald G. *m.s.* '71 (FR)[F] Attleboro, MA La Salette Shrine.
Gagne, Ronald '66 (DUL) Retired.
Gagne, Walter *s.a.* '71 (NY)[DD] Garrison, NY Franciscan Friars of the Atonement.
Gagnepain, John F. *c.m.* '62 (SPC) Ecumenism; Diocesan Director of Continuing Formation of Clergy; Presbyteral Council.
Gagnepain, John F. *c.m.* '62 (STL)[O] Perryville, MO Congregation of the Mission.
Gagnier, John F. '78 (ROC) Rochester, NY Holy Name of Jesus.
Gagnon, Andre J. '57 (MAN) Retired.
Gagnon, Daniel *o.m.i.* '87 (FgM) Washington, DC AMERICAN OBLATE MISSIONS.
Gagnon, Herve *o.m.i.* '45 (BO)[U] Lowell, MA St. Eugene House (Residence) Retired.
Gagnon, Joseph A. '61 (DET) Retired.
Gagnon, Leo G. '72 (MAN) Richmond, VA Retired.
Gagnon, Mariano *o.f.m.* '57 (FgM) New York, NY Holy Name Province.
Gagnon, Raymond E. '72 (MAN) Franklin, NH St. Paul; Tilton, NH St. Mary of the Assumption.
Gagnon, Richard *s.d.s.* '65 (NSH) Smyrna, TN St. Luke.
Gagnon, Ronald P. '56 (TUC) Retired.
Gago, Jose *o.m.i.* '56 (SAT)[K] San Antonio, TX Oblate Madonna Residence.
Gahagan, William H. '70 (KNX) Helenwood, TN St. Jude Parish; Norris, TN St. Joseph; Clinton, TN St. Therese.
Gahan, James L. '68 (STL) St. Charles, MO Sts. Joachim and Ann; [E] St. Charles, MO Duchesne High School.
Gahan, Timothy M. '07 (CHR) Spartanburg, SC St. Paul the Apostle.
Gaiardo, Martin J. '70 (SCR) Retired.
Gaines, G. Timothy '87 (DEN) Louisville, CO St. Louis.
Gaitan, Jose Alexander *c.m.f.* '11 (CHI)[N] Oak Park Claretian Missionaries USA Eastern Province.
Gaitan, Ramon *o.a.r.* '60 (NY)[B] Suffern, NY Tagaste Monastery.
Gaitley, Michael *m.i.c.* '10 (SPR)[G] Stockbridge, MA Association of Marian Helpers, Marian Helpers Center.
Gajardo, Leonardo J. *s.s.* '06 (BAL)[A] Baltimore, MD St. Mary's Seminary and University; [Q] Baltimore, MD St. Mary's Seminary & University.
Gajda, Piotr J. '55 (CC) Military Chaplains; Air Force Chaplains.
Gajdos, Rev. Msgr. T. George '70 (MIL) Wauwatosa, WI Christ King; Archdiocesan Consultors; Archdiocesan Council of Priests.
Gajdzinski, Norman A. '63 (CLV) Garfield Heights, OH St. Therese Retired.
Gajettan, Jesu Alangaram Ronald (MOB) Elberta, AL St. Bartholomew.
Gajewski, Rev. Msgr. Chester A. '50 (SCR)[M] Dunmore, PA Villa St. Joseph Retired.
Gajewski, Robert S. '07 (NEW) Cranford, NJ St. Michael's.
Galambos, Stephen *o.f.m.* '96 (NY)[DD] New York Franciscan Province of the Immaculate Conception.
Galan, Jose M. '65 (PCE) Mercedita, PR Church of the Sacred Heart.
Galan, Victor Aurelio Vargas (SJN) San Juan, PR Nuestra Senora de la Esperanza; Santurce, PR Doctors Community Hospital.
Galang, Jose '78 (SJ) Saratoga, CA Church of the Ascension.
Galant, Andrzej *s.ch.* '81 (MIL) Milwaukee, WI SS. Cyril and Methodius; Milwaukee, WI St. Maximilian Kolbe.
Galarneault, Thomas '07 (DUL) Bigfork, MN Our Lady of the Snows; Bigfork, MN St. Catherine; Bigfork, MN St. Michael.
Galarza, Edison *o.c.c.s.s.* '99 (STP) Minneapolis, MN SS. Cyril & Methodius.
Galasso, Michael S. '71 (HRT) East Hartford, CT Blessed Sacrament.
Galaz, Jesse C. '81 (LA) Paramount, CA Our Lady of the Rosary.
Galazka, Symeon '10 (SFE)[H] Pecos, NM Our Lady of Guadalupe Abbey.
Galea, Michael A. '80 (BR) Sorrento, LA St. Anthony of Padua; Sorrento, LA St. Anne.
Galeano, John J. '02 (NEW) Lodi, NJ St. Francis de Sales; South Kearny, NJ Hudson County Correctional Center; Archdiocesan Stewardship Advisory Committee.
Galeano, Juan Pablo '09 (HON) Kailua–Kona, HI St. Michael The Archangel.
Galek, Peter '83 (CHI) Rolling Meadows, IL St. Colette.
Galens, Jeffrey R. '90 (NY) Rhinebeck, NY The Good Shepherd.
Galetto, Paul W. *o.s.a.* '82 (PH)[C] Villanova, PA Villanova University; [Y] Villanova, PA St. Thomas of Villanova Friary.
Gali, Arockiaraj (SAN) Garden City, TX St. Lawrence.
Galic, Rev. Msgr. Bernard J. '70 (FTW) Yoder, IN St. Aloysius; Budget Committee; Vocation Office.
Galic, Josip N. *o.f.m.* '66 (CHI)[N] Chicago, IL St. Anthony's Friary.

Galido, Ariel *m.s.c.* '04 (MI) Cathedral of the Assumption; Prefecture Consultors.
Galier, Victor A. '98 (ATL) Atlanta, GA St. Anthony of Padua; Judges.
Galinada, Michael–Dwight Colin '78 (ORG) Brea, CA St. Angela Merici; Council of Priests.
Galipeau, Roland J. '64 (SPR) Retired.
Galivan, James F. '81 (CHI) Other Assignments.
Gall, Jacob M. '62 (FTW) Retired.
Gallagher, Adrian *o.f.m.conv.* '92 (HBG) Coal Township, PA Our Lady of Hope; Trevorton, PA St. Patrick.
Gallagher, Anthony (TOL) Retired.
Gallagher, Brian *s.s.c.* '52 (PRO)[O] Bristol, RI St. Columban's Retirement House Retired.
Gallagher, Brian *s.s.c.* '52 (OM)[J] St. Columbans Missionary Society of St. Columban.
Gallagher, Cathal *s.s.c.* '74 (SFS) Armour, SD St. Paul the Apostle.
Gallagher, Cathal *s.s.c.* '74 (OM)[J] St. Columbans Missionary Society of St. Columban.
Gallagher, Charles A. *s.j.* '58 (NEW)[B] Jersey City, NJ Jesuit Center; [L] Jersey City, NJ Jesuits of Saint Peter's College, Inc.
Gallagher, Charles G. '44 (CHI) La Grange, IL St. Cletus Retired.
Gallagher, Charles M. '10 (WDC) Rockville, MD St. Mary.
Gallagher, Charles R. *s.j.* '10 (BO)[U] Newton, MA The Jesuit Community at Boston College.
Gallagher, Cyrus *o.f.m.cap.* '65 (COS)[E] Colorado Springs, CO Solanus Casey Friary.
Gallagher, Cyrus *o.f.m. cap.* '67 (COS)[H] Colorado Springs, CO Catholic Center at the Citadel.
Gallagher, Daniel B. '99 (GLD) Special Assignment.
Gallagher, Daniel J. '51 (PH) Retired.
Gallagher, Daniel '65 (JKS) Cursillo Movement; [C] Jackson, MS St. Dominic–Jackson Memorial Hospital.
Gallagher, David F. *c.s.s.* '59 (BO)[X] Waltham, MA Stigmatine Fathers and Brothers Retired.
Gallagher, Dennis J. *o.s.a.* '65 (PH)[C] Villanova University; [Y] Villanova, PA St. Thomas Monastery.
Gallagher, Dennis *a.a.* '78 (WOR)[A] Worcester, MA Assumption College; [N] Worcester, MA Assumptionists of Assumption College; Councilors.
Gallagher, Edward L. '53 (BO) Senior Priests. Retired.
Gallagher, Edward *s.a.* '71 (NY)[DD] Garrison Franciscan Friars of the Atonement, Minister General Office Retired.
Gallagher, Francis M. '64 (PH) Retired.
Gallagher, Francis (PEO) On Leave of Absence.
Gallagher, Gregory Robert *o.m.i.* '92 (CHI)[W] Chicago, IL Oblates for International Pastoral.
Gallagher, Gregory *o.m.i.* '92 (WDC)[O] Washington, DC Provincial Offices of the United States Province of the Missionary Oblates of Mary Immaculate; [O] Washington, DC Oblate Community.
Gallagher, James E. '87 (RIC) Appomattox, VA Our Lady of Peace; Hurt, VA St. Victoria; Lynchburg, VA Holy Cross.
Gallagher, James R. '65 (CHI)[J] Evergreen Park, IL Little Company of Mary Hospital and Health Care Centers Retired.
Gallagher, James T. *c.s.c.* '07 (FTW)[A] Notre Dame, IN; [H] Notre Dame Congregation of Holy Cross, United States Province of Priests & Brothers; [B] University of Notre Dame Du Lac; [H] Notre Dame, IN Holy Cross Community, Corby Hall, University of Notre Dame.
Gallagher, John E. '59 (BO) Senior Priests. Retired.
Gallagher, Rev. Msgr. John Gerald '57 (CAM) Retired.
Gallagher, John J. '55 (BAL) Retired.
Gallagher, John M. '71 (GB) Retired.
Gallagher, John P. '80 (DAV) Defenders of the Bond Retired.
Gallagher, John P. '57 (PH) Retired.
Gallagher, John P. '68 (PIT) Cranberry Township, PA St. Ferdinand.
Gallagher, John Peter '92 (IND) Lawrenceburg, IN St. Lawrence Catholic Church, Lawrenceburg, Inc.
Gallagher, John R. '93 (WH) Vienna, WV St. Michael.
Gallagher, Rev. Msgr. John '55 (NY) Harrison, NY Saint Vincent's Westchester.
Gallagher, John '92 (PMB) Released from Diocesan Assignment.
Gallagher, John *m.i.* '81 (WOR)[N] Whitinsville, MA St. Camillus Community.
Gallagher, John '81 (MIL)[P] Milwaukee, WI St. Camillus Delegate House.
Gallagher, John *o.f.m.cap.* (NOR) Middletown, CT St. Pius X.
Gallagher, Kevin J. '02 (PH) Lafayette Hill, PA St. Philip Neri; Vocation Office for Diocesan Priesthood.
Gallagher, Kevin M. '98 (NY) Pine Bush, NY The Infant Saviour.
Gallagher, Kevin P. '83 (ALN) Mahanoy City, PA Blessed Teresa of Calcutta Parish.
Gallagher, Laurence *c.ss.r.* '03 (LA) Norwalk, CA St. John of God.
Gallagher, Maurice O. '50 (PBL) Retired.
Gallagher, Michael J. '69 (WIL) On Duty Outside the Diocese.
Gallagher, Michael J. '66 (SD) El Cajon, CA Our Lady of Grace Catholic Parish.
Gallagher, Michael S. *s.j.* '84 (NO)[R] New Orleans Jesuit Provincial Office.
Gallagher, Otmar *o.f.m.cap.* '48 (PIT)[M] Pittsburgh, PA St. Augustine Friary Retired.
Gallagher, Rev. Msgr. Patrick J. '70 (MOB) Dothan, AL St. Columba; [I] Dothan, AL George C. Wallace Jr. Community College Newman Center; Vicars Forane.
Gallagher, Patrick *o.f.m.conv.* '65 (ALB) Fonda, NY St. Cecilia; Tribes Hill, NY Sacred Heart.
Gallagher, Paul V. '63 (RIC) Retired.
Gallagher, Paul '82 (STL)[S] Dittmer, MO Il Ritiro–The Little Retreat.
Gallagher, Philip P. '78 (LAN) Retired.
Gallagher, Richard '36 (SEA) Retired.
Gallagher, Richard '72 (TR) Leave of Absence.
Gallagher, Richard '60 (SEA) Regional Justice Center Retired.
Gallagher, Robert A. '77 (STU) Little Hocking, OH St. Ambrose.
Gallagher, Rev. Msgr. Robert J. '73 (LA) North Hollywood, CA St. Charles Borromeo; Deanery 7; Members; Archdiocesan Finance Council Members 2011–2012.
Gallagher, Roger P. '54 (WDC) Retired.
Gallagher, Simeon *o.f.m.cap.* '71 (DEN)[N] Denver, CO St. Francis of Assisi Friary.
Gallagher, Simon P. *o.s.b.* '73 (PAT) Morris Plains, NJ Greystone Park Psychiatric Hospital; [N] Morristown, NJ St. Mary's Abbey.
Gallagher, Steven P. '11 (JUN) Ketchikan, AK Holy Name.
Gallagher, Rev. Msgr. Thomas G. '68 (RVC) Retired.
Gallagher, Thomas J. '61 (CLV) Retired.
Gallagher, Thomas M. *o.f.m.* '82 (HRT) Hartford, CT St. Patrick–St. Anthony.
Gallagher, Thomas P. *o.s.f.s.* '67 (PH)[Y] Wyndmoor, PA Villa de Sales Oblate Residence.
Gallagher, Timothy M. *o.m.v.* '79 (BO)[B] Boston, MA Our Lady of Grace Seminary.
Gallagher, Timothy '09 (ATL) Conyers, GA St. Pius X.
Gallagher, Tom *s.j.* '61 (SPK)[B] Spokane, WA Gonzaga University.
Gallagher, William E. '46 (SEA) Retired.
Gallagher, William G. '53 (RVC) Retired.
Gallagher, William J. '47 (WOR) Retired.
Gallagher, Rev. Msgr. William J. '69 (BUF) Orchard Park, NY St. John Vianney; Finance Council.
Gallant, Jon–Paul '78 (FR) Attleboro, MA St. Theresa of the Child Jesus.
Gallardo, David '84 (LA) Pico Rivera, CA St. Mariana de Paredes.
Gallardo, Joseph *o.a.r.* '94 (NEW)[L] West Orange, NJ Augustinian Recollects.
Gallarelli, George A. *s.j.* '62 (BGP)[E] Fairfield, CT Fairfield College Preparatory School; [O] Fairfield, CT The Fairfield Jesuit Community–Fairfield University.
Gallaro, George D. '72 (NTN) Priests Serving Outside the Eparchy.
Gallaro, George D. '72 (PBR) Vicar for Canonical Services; Judicial Vicar; [A] Pittsburgh, PA Byzantine Catholic Seminary of SS. Cyril and Methodius.
Gallas, John '05 (STP) Loretto, MN SS. Peter and Paul; Hamel, MN St. Thomas the Apostle.
Gallatin, Joseph G. '97 (STP)[F] Eagan, MN Faithful Shepherd Catholic School; Mendota, MN St. Peter.
Gallatin, Paul H. '58 (OKL) Oklahoma City, OK Retired.
Galle, Maciej '08 (CHI) Chicago, IL St. Constance; Defenders of the Bond.
Gallego, Jose M. *o.m.* '57 (SJN) San Juan, PR Ntra. Sra. de Fatima.
Gallegos, David *o.s.m.* '66 (ORG) Fullerton, CA St. Philip Benizi.
Gallegos, Joseph *c.r.* '69 (PBL) Durango, CO Sacred Heart.
Gallegos, Stephen *c.m.* (GLP) Kayenta, AZ Our Lady of Guadalupe; Tuba City, AZ St. Jude.
Gallegos, Valentine '09 (SAT) San Antonio, TX St. Matthew's.
Gallen, Francis H. '47 (PH) Retired.
Gallen, John J. *s.j.* '63 (NY)[DD] New York, NY Murray–Weigel Hall.
Gallen, John '69 (HT) Thibodaux, LA Christ The Redeemer.
Gallenbach, Thomas E. '58 (LAV) Las Vegas, NV St. Joseph, Husband of Mary.
Gallenbach, Thomas '58 (SFD) On Duty Outside the Diocese.
Gallenstein, Joseph A. '90 (COV) Taylor Mill, KY St. Anthony; [B] Covington, KY Covington Catholic High School.
Gallerini, Philip G. '62 (SPR) Retired.
Galles, Rev. Msgr. Francis A. '52 (WIN) Retired.
Gallia, Andrew R. '62 (SCR) Retired.
Galligan, Charles H. '87 (PRO) Pawtucket, RI St. Edward.
Galligan, James L. *o.s.a.* '50 (PH)[Y] Villanova, PA St. Thomas Monastery.
Gallinger, Carl '89 (CHY) Laramie, WY St. Paul's Newman Center; [F] Laramie, WY St. Paul's Newman Center, University Catholic Community (University of Wyoming); College of Consultors; Vicars Forane; Defenders of the Bond; Presbyteral Council; Stewardship Committee.
Gallipeau, Mark T. '06 (WH) Marlinton, WV St. John Neumann.
Gallipoli, Mario *c.p.* '61 (BRK)[R] Jamaica, NY Immaculate Conception Monastery.
Gallivan, Rev. Msgr. David M. '66 (BUF) Buffalo, NY Holy Cross.
Gallo, Dennis '85 (MRY) Soledad, CA Our Lady of Solitude.
Gallo, Gerardo D. '85 (NEW) Elizabeth, NJ Blessed Sacrament.
Gallo, Manuel *s.d.b.* '10 (NEW)[C] Ramsey, NJ Don Bosco Preparatory High School; [L] Ramsey, NJ Don Bosco Prep Salesian Residence.
Gallo, Regis *o.f.m.* '62 (ALB)[A] Catskill, NY St. Anthony Friary.
Gallo, Vincent '60 (BRK) Retired.
Gallus, David *o.s.c.* '66 (SCL)[I] Onamia, MN Crosier Priory.
Galluzzo, James '90 (P) Retired.
Galonek, David B. '96 (WOR) Presbyteral Council; West Brookfield, MA Sacred Heart of Jesus; Deans; West Brookfield, MA St. Mary's.
Galos, Artemio '85 (DET) Sterling Heights, MI St. Michael.
Galovich, George '71 (STL) Retired.
Galt, Ronald '92 (CHI)[J] Maywood, IL Loyola University Medical Center; Chicago, IL Immaculate Conception of the Blessed Virgin Mary; Chicago, IL St. Joseph.
Galuppi, Michael '07 (SY) Endicott, NY Our Lady of Good Counsel.
Galvan, Alfred '65 (LSC) Ruidoso, NM St. Eleanor; Vicars; Presbyteral Council.
Galvan, John *s.j.* '99 (LA)[C] Los Angeles, CA Jesuit Community.
Galvez, Elias *o.f.m.* '56 (FgM) Oakland, CA St. Barbara Province.
Galvez, Elias *o.f.m.* '56 (OAK)[L] Oakland Franciscan Friars of California, (Province of St. Barbara).
Galvez, Jesus Manuel *o.f.m. conv.* '91 (OAK) Hayward, CA St. Bede.
Galvez, Mariano Martínez *o.m.i.* '84 (SJN) San Juan, PR Nuestra Sra. de Guadalupe.
Galvez, Miguel *s.j.s.* '01 (MAD) Muscoda, WI St. John Nepomucene.
Galvez–Orellana, Jose Antonio (LR) Rogers, AR St. Vincent de Paul.
Galvez–Pineda, Rafael I. '06 (NEW) Westwood, NJ St. Andrew's.
Galvin, Garrett *o.f.m.* '00 (OAK)[A] Berkeley, CA Franciscan School of Theology; [L] Berkeley, CA Franciscan Friars (Province of St. Barbara).
Galvin, Gregory P. '94 (NOR) Storrs, CT St. Thomas Aquinas; Seminarian Advisory Board; Vocation; [K] Storrs, CT University of Connecticut; Members.
Galvin, James Gerard '94 (SAT) San Antonio, TX San Juan Capistrano.
Galvin, James M. '51 (LA)[V] Santa Barbara, CA St. Mary's Seminary Center.
Galvin, John P. '68 (WDC)[C] Catholic University of America, The; On Duty Outside the Archdiocese.
Galvin, John *s.m.* '63 (FgM) THE SOCIETY OF MARY.
Galvin, Thomas J. '82 (PIT) Pittsburgh, PA St. John the Baptist.
Galvin, William J. *m.m.* '56 (FgM) Maryknoll, NY MARYKNOLL.
Galyo, Rev. Msgr. John M. '54 (PH) Retired.
Gama, Armando Gomez *c.s.* (BO) Everett, MA St. Anthony of Padua.
Gama, Manuel Baeza *m.c.c.j.* '96 (CIN)[N] Cincinnati, OH Comboni Missionaries (Verona Fathers)–Comboni Mission Center.
Gamache, Barry J. '81 (PRO) Bristol, RI St. Mary.
Gamallo, Edito '75 (NEW) Newark, NJ St. Anthony's.
Gamas, Giovanni '07 (SAC) Woodland, CA Holy Rosary.
Gamba, Jose I. '86 (NEW) Fairview, NJ St. John the Baptist; Hispanic Apostolate.
Gambaro, Giampiero *o.f.m.cap.* '90 (NY)[DD] White Plains, NY Capuchin Friars International, Inc.; [DD] White Plains, NY St. Francis of Assisi Foundation.
Gambatese, Angelus *o.f.m.* '59 (NY) New York, NY St. Stephen of Hungary; [HH] New York, NY Shrine of St. Jude, Inc.
Gamber, Matthew T. *s.j.* '95 (CHI)[N] Chicago Chicago Province of the Society of Jesus–Provincial Office.
Gamber, William K. '64 (STP) Retired.
Gambet, Daniel G. *o.s.f.s.* '57 (ALN)[B] Center Valley, PA DeSales University; [K] Center Valley, PA Oblates of St. Francis de Sales.
Gamboriko, Elias Rinaldo *a.j.* '99 (SFS) Sioux Falls, SD St. Josephine Bakhita Catholic Church.
Gambro, John M. *o.p.* '57 (CHI)[N] Chicago, IL St. Pius V Priory.

Gamel, Robert E. '90 (FRS) Los Banos, CA St. Joseph.
Gameros, Ignacio L. '81 (TUC) Retired.
Gamez, Francisco J. '03 (SFR) San Francisco, CA Cathedral of St. Mary (Assumption).
Gamez, Rigoberto '94 (CHI) Defenders of the Bond; Advocates.
Gamez, Steven A. '08 (SAT) San Antonio, TX St. Philip of Jesus.
Gamez–Alfonso, Rigoberto '95 (CHI) Chicago, IL Our Lady of Tepeyac.
Gamm, David B. '72 (COV) Florence, KY St. Paul.
Gamm, Joseph *c.m.f.* '45 (LA)[V] Rancho Dominguez, CA Dominguez Seminary Inc.
Gammad, Engelberto '84 (SJ) Council of Priests; Judges; Special Assignment; Adjutant Judicial Vicar; Diocesan Clergy Personnel Board.
Gamrot, Jaroslaw '91 (WDC) Chaptico, MD Our Lady of the Wayside.
Gancarz, Eugeniusz '71 (SP) Riverview, FL Resurrection.
Gancayco, Richard K. '92 (WDC) Washington, DC St. Benedict the Moor.
Ganci, William Philip '09 (PT) Vocations, Office of; Tallahassee, FL Good Shepherd.
Gancila, Joseph A. '01 (BRK) Brooklyn, NY St. Bernadette.
Gandara, Juan Luis '67 (LAF) New Iberia, LA Sacred Heart of Jesus; On Special Assignment.
Gang, Dennis *t.o.r.* '76 (STU)[A] Steubenville, OH Franciscan University of Steubenville; [H] Steubenville, OH Holy Spirit Friary.
Gangolu, Babu *s.a.c.* '92 (SP) St. Petersburg, FL St. Paul.
Ganiel, Joseph F. '83 (CAM) Runnemede, NJ Holy Child Parish, Runnemede, N.J.
Ganley, Thomas P. '85 (MET)[H] Somerset, NJ McCarrick Care Center; [I] Somerset, NJ Maria Regina Residence; Robert Wood Johnson University Hospital.
Gann, Seán J. '94 (RVC) Chaplains of the Suffolk County Police Department; Kings Park, NY St. Joseph's.
Gannon, Bernard J. '71 (CAM) Retired.
Gannon, Brian P. '97 (BGP) Trumbull, CT St. Theresa.
Gannon, Daniel J. *s.j.* '68 (RC)[C] Pine Ridge, SD Jesuit Community of Holy Rosary Mission; Pine Ridge, SD Holy Rosary/Red Cloud Indian School Inc.
Gannon, Dismas *o.c.s.o.* '50 (P)[L] Lafayette, OR The Cistercian (Trappist) Abbey of Our Lady of Guadalupe.
Gannon, Donald C. *s.j.* '76 (RVC) Oceanside, NY St. Anthony.
Gannon, George J. '02 (BAL) Baltimore, MD Sacred Heart of Mary; [T] Baltimore, MD The Sacred Heart of Mary Cemetery Continuing Care Trust.
Gannon, James *o.f.m.* '87 (MIL) Franklin, WI; [C] Milwaukee, WI Cardinal Stritch University; [P] Provincial Offices of the Franciscan Friars, Assumption BVM Province, Inc.
Gannon, Josephjude C. '04 (BRK) Hollis, NY St. Gerard Majella; [D] Brooklyn, NY Campus Ministers and Ministry Centers.
Gannon, Patrick J. '60 (LA) Retired.
Gannon, Patrick '76 (NO) Avondale, LA St. Bonaventure; Waggaman, LA Our Lady of the Angels.
Gannon, William Robert *o.p.* '53 (NY)[DD] New York, NY St. Vincent Ferrer Priory.
Ganshert, Rev. Msgr. Daniel T. '74 (MAD) Watertown, WI St. Bernard; Watertown, WI St. Henry; Diocesan Consultors; Appointed.
Ganss, Karl P. '68 (RCK) Elburn, IL St. Gall.
Gantley, Donald M. *o.s.m.* '59 (CHI)[N] Chicago, IL Monastery of Our Lady of Sorrows.
Gantley, Mark J. '91 (SY) Bainbridge, NY St. John the Evangelist.
Gantley, Mark J. '91 (HON) Promoter of Justice; Defender of the Bond.
Ganuza, Felix *sch.p.* (PCE) Ponce, PR Our Lady of Mt. Carmel.
Ganz, Richard H. *s.j.* '84 (P)[L] Portland, OR Colombiere Community.
Ganza, Jean Baptiste *s.j.* '05 (SEA)[M] Seattle, WA Arrupe Jesuit Community at Seattle University.
Gappa, Herbert T. *m.m.* '68 (NY)[DD] Maryknoll Maryknoll Fathers and Brothers Retired.
Gaquit, Teodulo '70 (HON) Honolulu, HI St. Anthony; Diocesan Hospital Ministry; Chaplains.
Garamendi, Martin *o.m.* '52 (SJN) San Juan, PR Ntra. Sra. de Fatima.
Garand, J. Douglas '01 (TOL) Toledo, OH St. Catherine of Siena; Members.
Garanzini, Michael J. *s.j.* '80 (CHI)[C] Chicago, IL President's Office; [C] Chicago, IL Jesuit Community at Loyola University Chicago.
Garatea, Juan M. '59 (B) Retired.
Garavel, Andrew J. *s.j.* '92 (BO)[U] Boston The Society of Jesus of New England–Provincial Offices.
Garavel, Andrew J. *s.j.* '92 (SJ)[B] Santa Clara, CA Jesuit Community.
Garaventa, Louis *s.j.* '76 (NY)[E] New York, NY Xavier High School.
Garavito, David (KCK) Overland Park, KS Holy Cross.
Garbaciak, Dariusz *s.v.d.* '96 (CHI)[N] Techny, IL Divine Word Residence; [N] Techny, IL Blessed Arnold Charitable Trust; [N] Techny, IL DWTCRE Charitable Trust; [N] Techny, IL S.V.D. Funds, Inc.; Techny, IL; [N] Techny, IL Society of the Divine Word, Provincial Headquarters–Chicago Prov.; [W] Techny, IL Divine Word Techny Community Corporation.
Garbacz, Casimir *s.v.d.* (CHI) Ethnic Offices.
Garbacz, Kazimierz *s.v.d.* '70 (CHI)[N] Techny, IL Divine Word Residence.
Garbacz, Marcin Stanislaw '04 (RC) Faith, SD St. Joseph; [E] McLaughlin, SD Priest Retirement and Aid Association/Pension Plan Board.
Garbarino, Joseph J. '83 (PAT) Graduate Studies; Clifton, NJ St. Clare.
Garbin, Raymond '63 (JOL) Elmhurst, IL Immaculate Conception.
Garbo, Francis Mark P. '90 (SFR) San Mateo, CA St. Timothy.
Garces, Francis *o.f.m.cap.* '66 (FWT) Fort Worth, TX Our Lady of Guadalupe.
Garcia, Abraham R. *m.g.* '82 (LA)[P] Los Angeles, CA Guadalupe Missioners Procure.
Garcia, Albert *ss.cc.* '69 (HON)[D] Kaneohe, HI Sacred Hearts Center.
Garcia, Alfredo '02 (COS) Colorado Springs, CO Our Lady of Guadalupe.
Garcia, Alfredo *ss.cc.* '63 (BWN) Edinburg, TX Sacred Heart.
Garcia, Alonzo M. '05 (TUC) Tucson, AZ Our Lady Queen of All Saints Roman Catholic Parish – Tucson.
Garcia, Andres '93 (PH) Kennett Square, PA St. Patrick; Avondale, PA St. Rocco.
Garcia, Andrey '08 (SJ) San Jose, CA St. Leo the Great.
Garcia, Antonio '81 (SJN) Carolina, PR Ntra. Sra. Del Carmen.
Garcia, Antonio *o.m.* (CGS) Cayey, PR Nuestra Senora de la Asuncion.
Garcia, Armand D. '05 (PH) Philadelphia, PA Immaculate Heart of Mary.
Garcia, Rev. Msgr. Avelino R. '68 (SP) Beverly Hills, FL Our Lady of Grace.
Garcia, Camilo '00 (STO) Manteca, CA St. Anthony Church of Manteca (Pastor of).
Garcia, Daniel E. '88 (AUS) Austin, TX St. Vincent de Paul; College of Consultors; Austin North; Presbyteral Council.
Garcia, David '75 (SAT) College of Consultors; Archdiocesan Presbyteral Council; San Antonio, TX Old Spanish Missions; Future Evangelization Program for the Missions with Archbishop Gustavo Garcia–Siller; San Antonio, TX Purisima Concepcion; San Antonio, TX Purisima Concepcion.
Garcia, Dennis M. '00 (SFE) Albuquerque, NM San Felipe de Neri; Judicial Vicar; Judicial Vicar; Delegate for Matrimonial Dispensations; Albuquerque, NM San Ignacio.
Garcia, Eduardo H. '90 (CC) Retired.
Garcia, Eliseo *o.s.a.* '57 (MGZ) San German, PR St. Rose of Lima.
Garcia, Emilio '57 (ORL) Retired.
Garcia, Enrique Granados '09 (MEM) Jackson, TN St. Mary Church.
Garcia, Erlin Yoan (GRY) Hammond, IN St. Margaret Mary.
Garcia, Esau '87 (ORL) Deans; Orlando, FL Holy Cross; Censor of Books; Ex Officio Members.
Garcia, Francisco Gius '95 (RVC) Wantagh, NY St. Frances de Chantal.
Garcia, Francisco J. '06 (DEN) Loveland, CO St. John the Evangelist.
Garcia, Francisco *o.f.m.cap.* '78 (PCE)[H] Ponce, PR Albergue La Providencia para El Bienestar Social, Inc.
Garcia, Gabriel *o.f.m.* '99 (AMA) Amarillo, TX St. Laurence Church.
Garcia, George A. '73 (MIA) Coconut Grove, FL St. Hugh.
Garcia, Guillermo C. '75 (LA) Co Chairmen.
Garcia, Hector *o.carm.* '94 (MGZ) Anasco, PR St. Anthony Abbot.
Garcia, Hector *c.ss.r.* (CGS)[B] Aguas Buenas, PR Casa Cristo Redentor.
Garcia, Hignio '99 (SD) Lemon Grove, CA Saint John of the Cross Catholic Parish.
Garcia, Isidor *c.m.f.* '54 (LA)[V] Rancho Dominguez, CA Dominguez Seminary Inc.
Garcia, J. Isidore *o.m.i.* '64 (GAL) Houston, TX St. Patrick.
Garcia, J. Jesus '98 (LA) Los Angeles, CA St. Alphonsus.
Garcia, Jacinto '97 (DAL) Dallas, TX St. Rita.
Garcia, Jaime A. '08 (PRO) Providence, RI St. Charles Borromeo; Council Members.
Garcia, James L. '70 (SFR) San Francisco, CA St. Anthony of Padua.
Garcia, Jesus A. '94 (SJN) San Juan, PR San Jorge.
Garcia, Jesus '09 (DEN) Edwards, CO St. Clare of Assisi.
Garcia, Jorge A. '08 (SB) Loma Linda, CA Loma Linda University Medical Center; Redlands, CA The Holy Name of Jesus Catholic Community, Inc.; Appointed Members.
Garcia, Jorge E. (B) Buhl, ID Immaculate Conception.
Garcia, Jose Cruz Mendez *c.o.r.c.* '07 (SB)[I] Corona, CA Confraternity of Operarios Del Reino De Cristo, C.O.R.C.
Garcia, Jose L. (ARE) Retired.
Garcia, Jose Luis '00 (BWN) Brownsville, TX Christ the King; Board Members.
Garcia, Jose '52 (MIA) Retired.
Garcia, Rev. Msgr. Juan F. '67 (SPR) Springfield, MA All Souls; Springfield, MA Blessed Sacrament; Presbyteral Council.
Garcia, Juan L. *d.l.p.* '70 (SB)[A] Grand Terrace, CA Blessed Junipero Serra House of Formation; Blessed Junipero Serra House of Formation; [I] Grand Terrace, CA Diocesan Laborer Priests, DLP.
Garcia, Rev. Msgr. Juan '67 (SPR) Procurator–Advocate; Diocesan Consultors.
Garcia, Justiniano '98 (SJN)[G] Guaynabo, PR Opus Dei.
Garcia, Lino Ayala *c.s.* (BO) Framingham, MA St. Tarcisius.
Garcia, Louis '93 (STO) Stockton, CA St. Mary of the Assumption Church (Pastor of).
Garcia, Luis F. '11 (GR) Grand Rapids, MI St. John Vianney.
Garcia, Rev. Msgr. Luis Javier '76 (BWN) Pharr, TX St. Margaret Mary.
Garcia, Luis '97 (MIA) Pompano Beach, FL St. Coleman.
Garcia, Manuel '75 (SJN)[E] San Juan, PR Centro Medico de P.R.
Garcia, Marcelino *s.j.* '70 (MIA)[H] Miami, FL Villa Javier; Comunidad de Vida Cristiana, Regina Mundi, South Florida Region; Encuentros Familiares y Casa Manresa (Spanish); [E] Miami, FL Belen Jesuit Preparatory School.
Garcia, Marcial I. '95 (VEN) College of Consultors; Palmetto, FL Holy Cross Church.
Garcia, Mario *o.f.m.cap.* '88 (DAL)[J] Dallas, TX Capuchin Franciscan Friars, Vice Province of Texas; Dallas, TX Our Lady of Lourdes; Dallas, TX.
Garcia, Martin '99 (STO) Modesto, CA Our Lady of Fatima Church (Pastor of).
Garcia, Michael A. *o.p.* '81 (CHI) River Forest, IL St. Vincent Ferrer.
Garcia, Michel '04 (MIA) On Leave.
Garcia, Miguel A. *c.ss.r.* (SJN) San Juan, PR San Agustin.
Garcia, Millan '62 (SFE) Retired.
Garcia, Nelson *s.j.* '67 (MIA)[J] Miami, FL John Paul II Retreat House; [E] Miami, FL Belen Jesuit Preparatory School; [H] Miami, FL Villa Javier.
Garcia, Rev. Msgr. Otto L. '73 (BRK) Jackson Heights, NY St. Joan of Arc; Diocesan Judges; Attorneys and Counselors at Canon Law.
Garcia, Patrick Kenny Q. '89 (AGN) Yigo, GU Our Lady of Lourdes.
Garcia, Rev. Msgr. Pedro F. '64 (MIA) Retired.
Garcia, Pedro '65 (GR) Retired.
Garcia, Philip *o.f.m.* '82 (MRY)[F] San Juan Bautista, CA Franciscan Friars; [H] San Juan Bautista, CA St. Francis Retreat Center.
Garcia, Porfirio *o.m.i.* '08 (LA) Pacoima, CA Mary Immaculate.
Garcia, Rafael *s.j.* '93 (SFE) Albuquerque, NM Immaculate Conception; Presbyteral Council of the Archdiocese of Santa Fe.
Garcia, Rev. Msgr. Ramon V. '55 (SAT)[K] San Antonio, TX Padua Place.
Garcia, Raul Valencia '03 (TUC) Tucson, AZ Saint Monica Roman Catholic Parish – Tucson.
Garcia, Rev. Msgr. Raymond '55 (SAT) Retired.
Garcia, Raymundo '74 (TYL) Lufkin, TX St. Patrick; Presbyteral Council.
Garcia, Reynaldo A. *s.j.* '76 (DET)[P] Bloomfield Hills, MI Manresa Jesuit Retreat House.
Garcia, Rizalimo P. *c.m.* '99 (NY) Staten Island, NY St. Joseph, St. Thomas.
García, Rodolfo '97 (DAL) Vocations.
Garcia, Rolando G. '86 (MIA) Miami, FL St. Agatha; FIU–University Park.
Garcia, Ruben *o.c.d.* '97 (SAT) San Antonio, TX St. Cecilia.
Garcia, Salomon '09 (ATL) Winder, GA St. Matthew.
Garcia, Saul A. *m.s.p.* '02 (LA) Los Angeles, CA Our Lady of Solitude.
Garcia, Sebastian J. '07 (NEW) On Duty Outside the Archdiocese.
Garcia, Selvin *f.m.m.* '01 (MIL) Beaver Dam, WI St. Katharine Drexel.
Garcia, Severiano *c.m.f.* '50 (SJN) Bayamon, PR San Jose.
Garcia–Ferrer, Eduardo '93 (CHI) Hanover Park, IL St. Ansgar.
Garcia–Icedo, Mario '78 (PHX) Cashion, AZ St. William Roman Catholic Parish.
Garcia–Miro, Sergio '78 (MIA) Retired.

Garcia–Ramirez, Pedro '92 (AUS) Pflugerville, TX St. Elizabeth.
Garcia–Rosales, Nelson '67 (MIA) Agrupacion Catolica Universitaria (ACU).
Garcia–Tunon, Guillermo *s.j.* '00 (MIA)[E] Miami, FL Belen Jesuit Preparatory School; [H] Miami, FL Villa Javier.
Garcia Almodovar, Angel L. '03 (ALN) Allentown, PA Sacred Heart of Jesus.
Garcia Arias, Rev. Msgr. Justiniano '98 (POD) Regional Vicar for Puerto Rico; Guaynabo.
Garcia Echevarria, Roberto (PCE) Coto Laurel, PR Retired.
Garcia Flores, Efren Fergus '02 (SAC) Burney, CA St. Francis of Assisi.
Garcia Revilla, Lazaro '10 (LA) Pico Rivera, CA St. Mariana de Paredes.
Garcon, Barthelemy *s.m.m.* (ORL) Ocala, FL St. Jude's Catholic Community.
Gardin, Rev. Msgr. Vernon E. '71 (STL) Richmond Heights, MO Immacolata; Richmond Heights, MO Immacolata; [H] St. Louis, MO Department of Special Education; [H] St. Louis, MO St. Mary's – South; Archdiocesan Consultors.
Gardiner, Christopher B. '68 (MAR) Munising, MI Sacred Heart of Jesus.
Gardiner, James K. '69 (GLD) Bellaire, MI St. Luke; East Jordan, MI St. Joseph; Elected Members.
Gardiner, James *s.a.* '69 (NY)[DD] Garrison, NY Franciscan Friars of the Atonement; [DD] Garrison Franciscan Friars of the Atonement, Minister General Office.
Gardiner, Richard E. '67 (WDC) Retired.
Gardner, Clement G. '67 (ALT) Juniata Deanery; Hollidaysburg, PA St. Michael's.
Gardner, Daniel '78 (KCK) Kansas City, KS All Saints; [J] Kansas City, KS Cathedral of St. Peter.
Gardner, Giles *c.ss.r.* '39 (FgM) Baltimore Province.
Gardner, Rev. Msgr. Glenn D. '70 (DAL) Forney, TX St. Martin of Tours; Adjutant Judicial Vicars; College of Consultors; Censor Librorum; Deans.
Gardner, Jerome J. '79 (CIN) Cincinnati, OH Church of the Assumption; Cincinnati, OH St. Margaret Mary.
Gardner, Royal J. '51 (SPR) Retired.
Gardner, Thomas J. '10 (PH) Philadelphia, PA St. Christopher.
Gardner, William M. '92 (PEO) Peru, IL St. Mary; Peru, IL St. Valentine.
Gardocki, Patrick M. *o.f.m.* '81 (MO) DEPARTMENT OF VETERANS AFFAIRS HOSPITALS AND CHAPLAINS; Navy Reserve Chaplains.
Gardocki, Patrick *o.f.m.* '81 (BUF) Veterans Hospital; Cheektowaga, NY St. John Gualbert.
Gardocki, Thomas F. '65 (WIL) Retired.
Gardon, Emmanuel *c.p.* '50 (PMB)[H] North Palm Beach, FL Our Lady of Florida Spiritual Center.
Gareau, Timothy W. '88 (CLV) Bay Village, OH St. Raphael.
Gargani, Francis *c.ss.r.* (BRK)[R] Brooklyn, NY Redemptorist Fathers of New York, Inc.–Baltimore Province.
Gargotta, Anthony '01 (PIT) Monroeville, PA St. Bernadette; [P] Monroeville, PA Community College of Allegheny County – Boyce Campus; Priest Council.
Garibaldi, Anthony *o.f.m.* '76 (SAC) Sacramento, CA St. Francis of Assisi.
Gariepy, Andre M. '58 (WOR) Retired.
Gariepy, Robert E. '63 (WOR) Retired.
Gariepy, Thomas P. *c.s.c.* '74 (FR)[A] North Easton, MA Stonehill College; [A] North Easton, MA Holy Cross Fathers Religious.
Gariepy, Thomas P. *c.s.c.* '74 (FTW)[H] Notre Dame Congregation of Holy Cross, United States Province of Priests & Brothers.
Garinger, Grant S. *s.j.* '97 (MIL)[P] Milwaukee, WI Jesuit Community at Marquette University.
Gariolo, Joseph M. *c.r.s.p.* '50 (BUF)[B] Youngstown, NY St. Anthony M. Zaccaria Seminary.
Garisto, James A. '77 (NY) Poughkeepsie, NY St. Peter.
Garkowski, John '66 (BRK) South Ozone Park, NY Our Lady of Perpetual Help.
Garland, Reynolds *o.f.m.* '60 (LEX) Jackson, KY Holy Cross; Mountain East.
Garneau, James F. '84 (R) Council of Priests; Mount Olive, NC St. Mary of the Angels; Diocesan Consultors; Home Mission Society of the Diocese of Raleigh; Deans; Office of Permanent Diaconate.
Garner, D. Andrew '01 (OWN) Bowling Green, KY St. Joseph; Consultors; Priest Personnel Committee; Priests' Council; Vocations Office.
Garner, Dominic Mary *m.f.v.a.* '04 (BIR)[E] Birmingham, AL Franciscan Missionaries of the Eternal Word, A Public Association of the Christian Faithful.
Garner, Joel P. *o.praem.* '65 (SFE)[H] Albuquerque, NM Santa Maria de la Vid Priory; [L] Albuquerque, NM Norbertine Community of New Mexico, Inc.; Albuquerque, NM Our Lady of Most Holy Rosary.
Garner, Kirby '77 (AUS) Defenders of the Bond; Buda, TX Santa Cruz.
Garner, Steven M. '09 (DUB) Dubuque, IA Holy Spirit.
Garnica, Antonio *m.s.c.* '79 (LA)[P] Cudahy, CA Misioneros del Sagrado Corazon y Santa Maria de Guadalupe; Deanery 17; San Pedro Region; Vice Chairman.
Garnica, Luis Felipe Rodriguez '97 (SJN) Guaynabo, PR Cristo Salvador.
Garnier, David W. '08 (GAL) Spring, TX St. Ignatius of Loyola.
Garon, Robert E. J. '05 (LA) Sylmar, CA St. Didacus.
Garone, Thomas *o.f.m.* '73 (NY)[FF] Wappingers Falls, NY Mt. Alvernia Retreat House.
Garr, T. Mattingly *s.j.* '75 (FgM) Chicago, IL Society of Jesus.
Garrahy, Michael '51 (WCH) Retired.
Garramone, Dominic M. *o.s.b.* '92 (PEO)[A] Peru, IL St. Bede Abbey; [C] Peru, IL St. Bede Academy; Peru, IL.
Garrett, Benton Lee '06 (WDC) Military Chaplains; Navy Chaplains.
Garrett, John C. '04 (TR) Barnegat, NJ St. Mary.
Garrett, Patrick Stuart '09 (GAL) Boy and Girl Scouts; Spring, TX St. Edward.
Garrett, Scott '03 (ANC) Wasilla, AK Sacred Heart; Defenders of the Bond; Big Lake, AK Corp. of Our Lady of the Lake Church; Talkeetna, AK St. Bernard; Dillingham, AK Holy Rosary.
Garrett, Scott '03 (FBK) Defenders of the Bond.
Garrido, Alejandro '92 (CHI) Chicago, IL Providence of God.
Garrido, Mariano '79 (LA) Los Angeles, CA St. Teresa of Avila.
Garrigan, Gerard *o.s.b.* '89 (STL) St. Louis, MO St. Anselm; [O] St. Louis, MO The Abbey of St. Mary and St. Louis.
Garrione, Robert '89 (ALX) Alexandria, LA Christus St. Frances Cabrini Hospital; Alexandria, LA St. Francis Xavier Cathedral.
Garrison, G. Matthew '04 (LR) Little Rock, AR Cathedral of St. Andrew.
Garrity, Charles *o.c.d.* '66 (SR)[L] Oakville, CA Carmelite House of Prayer.
Garrity, Francis D. '56 (BO) Senior Priests. Retired.
Garrity, Rev. Msgr. G. Patrick '76 (KNX) Knoxville, TN St. John Neumann; Deans of the Diocese; Presbyteral Council; Diocesan Consultors; Ministries of the Cumberland Mtn. Deanery; Priestly Life and Ministry; Episcopal Vicar for Priests.
Garrity, Rev. Msgr. Paul V. '73 (BO) Norwood, MA St. Catherine of Siena; Trustees.
Garrity, Robert M. '81 (RCK) Active Outside the Diocese.
Garrity, Sean M. *c.s.b.* '88 (LSC)[B] Las Cruces, NM Basilian Fathers.
Garrote, Sancho E. '76 (NY) Bronx, NY North Central Bronx Hospital.
Garrote, Sancho G. '76 (NY) Jacobi Medical Center; Bronx, NY St. Brendan.
Garrott, William P. *o.p.* '94 (L)[L] Louisville, KY St. Louis Bertrand Priory; Louisville, KY St. Louis Bertrand; College of Consultors; Ex Officio.
Garrou, Dennis '11 (DEN) Evergreen, CO Christ the King.
Garry, Peter J. '68 (RVC) Southold, NY St. Patrick's.
Garry, Ron '83 (RC)[E] McLaughlin, SD Priest Retirement and Aid Association/Pension Plan Board; McLaughlin, SD St. Bonaventure's; McLaughlin, SD St. Bernard; McLaughlin, SD Standing Rock Reservation.
Garst, Charles C. *o.s.f.s.* '83 (PH) Philadelphia, PA St. Dominic.
Gartland, Daniel B. '82 (LFT) Lafayette, IN St. Mary Cathedral; Lafayette, IN St. Lawrence; Deans; Diocesan Consultors; Members.
Gartland, James G. *s.j.* '93 (CHI)[D] Chicago, IL Cristo Rey Jesuit High School, Inc.; [N] Chicago, IL Miguel Pro Jesuit Community.
Gartland, Rev. Msgr. R. Vincent '81 (TR) Episcopal Council; Lawrenceville, NJ St. Ann.
Gartner, Charles A. '58 (RVC) Homestead, FL; [N] Amityville, NY St. Pius X Residence Retired.
Garvey, Rev. Msgr. Francis J. '59 (NU) Grove City, MN Church of Our Lady.
Garvey, James W. '76 (PIT) Retired.
Garvey, John F. *s.j.* '74 (NY)[DD] New York, NY St. Ignatius Loyola Residence.
Garvey, John M. *m.s.* '53 (HRT)[L] Hartford, CT Missionaries of LaSalette.
Garvey, Michael '71 (Y) Mantua, OH St. Joseph.
Garvey, Roderick *c.ss.r.* '49 (STL)[O] Liguori, MO St. Clement Health Care Center Retired.
Garvey, Thomas J. '57 (STP) Retired.
Garvin, Rev. Msgr. Joseph P. '73 (PH) Philadelphia, PA St. Christopher.
Garvin, Thomas R. *s.j.* '58 (SPK)[J] Spokane, WA Regis Community Retired.
Gary, Paul '84 (CHL) Charlotte, NC St. Luke; Diocesan Consultors.
Garza, Amador '85 (BWN) San Juan, TX Basilica of Our Lady of San Juan del Valle–National Shrine; Board Members; Priests' Assignment Board; [I] San Juan, TX The Basilica of Our Lady of San Juan del Valle–National Shrine.
Garza, Charlie '10 (AUS) Austin, TX San Jose.
Garza, David '07 (SFS) Sioux Falls, SD Our Lady of Guadalupe.
Garza, Juan G. '02 (WCH) Newton, KS Our Lady of Guadalupe; Kansas State Industrial Reformatory.
Garza, Roberto '96 (MIA)[A] Miami, FL St. John Vianney College Seminary; Catholic Charities of the Archdiocese of Miami, Inc.; Consultors; Ex Officio.
Garzarelli, Santo R. '61 (PH) Retired.
Garzon, Fabio H. '86 (KAL) Fennville, MI San Felipe de Jesus; Hartford, MI Immaculate Conception; Presbyteral Council Members; Presbyteral Council Members.
Gaskin, Grantley DaCosta '06 (WDC) Military Chaplains; Army Chaplains.
Gasnick, Roy *o.f.m.* '60 (SP)[N] St. Petersburg, FL St. Anthony Friary Retired.
Gaspar, Antony J. '98 (LA) Rowland Heights, CA St. Elizabeth Ann Seton.
Gaspar, Jonathan M. '04 (BO) Divine Worship and Spiritual Life; Boston, MA Cathedral of the Holy Cross.
Gaspar, Joseph Antony Panimayakumar '84 (NY) Staten Island, NY Our Lady Star of the Sea.
Gasparik, Francis *o.f.m.cap.* '86 (NY) New York, NY St. John the Baptist; [DD] White Plains, NY St. Conrad Friary; White Plains, NY The Province of St. Mary of the Capuchin Order; White Plains, NY.
Gasparin, Giampietro *c.s.j.* '79 (LA)[D] Lancaster, CA Paraclete High School; Lancaster, CA Blessed Junipero Serra.
Gasparini, Louis *m.c.c.j.* '66 (CIN) Archdiocesan Office of Hispanic Ministry.
Gaspeny, Peter J. '83 (SAG) Midland, MI Blessed Sacrament; Diocesan Presbyteral Council; Territorial Vicars; Diocesan College of Consultors.
Gass, Michael W. '77 (DEN) Denver, CO Notre Dame.
Gastalver, Alfredo '76 (SJN)[G] Guaynabo, PR Opus Dei.
Gastalver, Alfredo '76 (POD) Guaynabo.
Gaston, Rev. Msgr. James T. '70 (GBG) Lower Burrell, PA St. Margaret Mary; Deaneries; Bishop's Priests Council; College of Deans.
Gately, R. Troy '89 (GAL) Houston, TX St. John Vianney.
Gately, Robert E. '52 (COL) Retired.
Gathenya, John '86 (ROC) Auburn, NY Holy Family.
Gathungu, John (B) McCall, ID Our Lady of the Lake.
Gatlin, Bernard '68 (LA) Fillmore, CA St. Francis of Assisi.
Gatlin, Jeffrey D. '00 (L) Louisville, KY SS. Simon and Jude; Louisville, KY Most Blessed Sacrament.
Gatman, Ronald P. *o.s.b.* '79 (SAV)[B] Savannah, GA Benedictine Military School; [D] Savannah, GA The Benedictine Priory.
Gatman, Ronald *o.s.b.* '79 (GBG)[H] Latrobe, PA Saint Vincent Archabbey.
Gatschet, Fred '93 (SAL)[G] Hays, KS Comeau Catholic Campus Center; [A] Hays, KS Thomas More Prep–Marian.
Gattari, Valentine A. '54 (DET) Retired.
Gatti, Daniel J. *s.j.* '72 (NY)[DD] New York, NY "America;" Residence and publication office of the America Press.
Gatto, Joseph C. '83 (BUF)[A] East Aurora, NY Christ the King Seminary; Williamsville, NY St. Gregory the Great.
Gatto, Reynold J. *s.j.* '68 (SJ)[M] Los Gatos, CA Sacred Heart Jesuit Center.
Gatto, Rev. Msgr. Vincent S. '55 (WDC) Rockville, MD St. Raphael Retired.
Gatzak, John P. '75 (HRT) Special and other Archdiocesan Assignment; Office of Radio and Television; Waterbury, CT Blessed Sacrament; Office of WJMJ–FM.
Gau, Davind H. *s.j.* '62 (MIL)[P] Wauwatosa, WI Jesuit Community at St. Camillus.
Gauchat, Eric *o.f.m.cap.* '92 (BAL)[Q] Cumberland, MD The Friary; Frostburg, MD St. Michael; Midland, MD St. Joseph; Westernport, MD St. Peter; Cumberland, MD Our Lady of the Mountains, Roman Catholic Congregation, Inc.
Gauci, Albert *o.f.m.* '71 (FgM) New York, NY Franciscan Province of the Immaculate Conception.
Gauci, John *c.ss.r.* '59 (BRK) Brooklyn, NY Our Lady of Perpetual Help Basilica.
Gaudet, Joseph A. '57 (BO) Senior Priests. Retired.
Gaudio, Dean A. '03 (TR) Brick Town, NJ St. Dominic.
Gaudio, Robert '74 (ROC) North Chili, NY St. Christopher; [N] Rochester, NY Roberts Wesleyan College c/o St. Christopher Church.
Gaudreau, Bernard E. '75 (BUR) Canon 1742 Panel of Pastors; South Burlington, VT St. John Vianney; Elected Members; Diocesan Consultors.
Gaudreau, James E. '69 (BO) Lynn, MA St. Joseph.
Gaudreault, Lucien *s.v.d.* '88 (MIL)[P] East Troy, WI Divine Word Missionaries.
Gaughan, Joseph '94 (FTW) Fort Wayne, IN Most Precious Blood; Presbyteral Council; Catholic School Board.
Gaughan, Rev. Msgr. Patrick '68 (STU) Athens, OH Christ the King University Parish; Athens, OH St. Paul's; Deans; Priests Personnel Board.
Gaughan, Thomas E. *c.s.c.* '87 (FTW)[B] University of

Notre Dame Du Lac; [H] Notre Dame, IN Holy Cross Community, Corby Hall, University of Notre Dame.
Gaul, Richard G. '68 (DUB) College of Consultors; Manchester, IA St. Mary; Manchester, IA Immaculate Conception; Ryan, IA St. Patrick.
Gaul, Thomas J. '73 (R) Hope Mills, NC Good Shepherd Retired.
Gaulin, Frederick J. *c.m.* '50 (PH)[Y].
Gaumond, Paul J. '74 (NOR) Essex, CT Our Lady of Sorrows; District Spiritual Advisors.
Gaunt, Thomas P. *s.j.* '81 (WDC)[O] Washington, DC The Jesuit Community at Georgetown University.
Gaus, Rev. Msgr. Arnold L. '59 (ALT) Ebensburg, PA Holy Name.
Gauthier, Donald F. '75 (MAN) Intervale, NH Our Lady of the Mountains.
Gauthier, Ernest '62 (KC) Retired.
Gauthier, John C. '65 (PHX) Retired.
Gauthier, Lawrence T. '55 (MAR) Catholic Relief Services; Holy Childhood Association; Propagation of the Faith Retired.
Gauthreaux, Rev. Msgr. L. Earl '56 (NO) New Orleans, LA St. Maria Goretti; Judges.
Gautreau, Henry W. '79 (BR) Catholic Charismatic Renewal Retired.
Gautreaux, Francis *c.ss.r.* '50 (FgM) Denver, CO Denver Province.
Gauvin, Maurice O. '86 (FR) Westport, MA St. George's.
Gavaler, Campion P. *o.s.b.* '59 (GBG)[H] Latrobe, PA Saint Vincent Archabbey.
Gavancho, Juan C. '07 (CHI) Chicago, IL St. Thomas More.
Gavin, Carney E. '65 (BO) Brighton, MA St. Columbkille.
Gavin, Emmett *o.carm.* '87 (NEW) Teaneck, NJ St. Anastasia's.
Gavin, James R. *o.f.m.cap.* '65 (NY) New York, NY Good Shepherd.
Gavin, John F. *s.j.* '11 (WOR)[N] Worcester, MA Jesuits of the Holy Cross, Inc.
Gavin, Patrick *o.carm.* '97 (PHX) Phoenix, AZ St. Agnes Roman Catholic Parish.
Gavin, Robert A. *o.f.m.* '59 (NY) New York, NY St. Francis of Assisi.
Gavin, Thomas M. *s.j.* '75 (NY)[FF] Staten Island, NY Mount Manresa Jesuit Retreat House.
Gaviola, Raul R. '95 (NEW) Dumont, NJ St. Mary's.
Gaviria, Jesus A. '06 (PAT) Madison, NJ St. Vincent Martyr.
Gaviria, Omar Bedoya '94 (PCE)[B] The Pontifical Catholic University of Puerto Rico.
Gavit, James F. '54 (SAG) Retired.
Gavit, Steven M. '97 (SAG) Hemlock, MI St. Mary.
Gavitt, J. Duane '84 (SCR) Freeland, PA Our Lady of the Immaculate Conception.
Gavotto, Robert W. *o.s.a.* '64 (SD)[J] San Diego, CA Augustinian Community; [C] San Diego, CA St. Augustine High School.
Gawienowski, John '00 (SPR)[M] Amherst, MA University of Massachusetts; Absent on Leave.
Gawlik, Jerzy *s.v.d.* '81 (CHI) Wheeling, IL St. Joseph the Worker.
Gawlowski, Michael R. '02 (DET) Warren, MI St. Clement; Warren, MI St. Teresa of Avila; Absent on Leave.
Gawlowski, Paul *o.f.m.conv.* '99 (SFR) San Francisco, CA St. Paul of the Shipwreck.
Gawronski, Gerald '01 (LAN) Ann Arbor, MI St. Patrick.
Gawronski, Marc A. '91 (DET) Monroe, MI St. Mary; Archdiocesan Vicars; Presbyteral Council.
Gawronski, Raymond T. *s.j.* '86 (BAL)[Q] Towson Maryland Province of the Society of Jesus.
Gawrych, Andrew *c.s.c.* '08 (FTW)[A] Notre Dame, IN Moreau Seminary; [A] Notre Dame, IN Moreau Seminary; [A] Notre Dame, IN.
Gawrylewski, Patrick M. *o.f.m.* '76 (GB) Green Bay, WI St. Mary of the Angels; Hortonville, WI St. Denis; Hortonville, WI St. Patrick; [J] Wausaukee, WI Villa Alverna.
Gay, G. Gregory *c.m.* '80 (FgM) Philadelphia, PA Eastern Province.
Gay, G. Gregory *c.m.* '70 (PH)[Y].
Gay, James A. '59 (BGP) Retired.
Gayam, Francis '78 (SR)[F] Santa Rosa, CA Santa Rosa Memorial Hospital; Healdsburg, CA St. John the Baptist.
Gayarre, Eugenio '61 (ARE) Arecibo, PR Church of Christ the King.
Gaydos, Anthony M. *o.s.m.* '48 (SPC) Ironton, MO Ste. Marie Du Lac.
Gaydosik, David A. '87 (STU) Presbyteral Council; Priests Personnel Board.
Gaydosik, David L. '87 (STU) Woodsfield, OH St. John the Baptist; Woodsfield, OH St. Sylvester; Woodsfield, OH St. John Bosco Mission; Catholic Rural Life.
Gaynor, James E. *c.pp.s.* '67 (CIN)[N] Dayton Provincial Office of the Cincinnati Province of the Society of the Precious Blood.
Gaytan, Jose Alfredo *s.o.l.t.* '82 (LAR) Laredo, TX St. Frances Cabrini.
Gaytan Ramirez, Rodolfo '02 (CHI) Chicago, IL Saint Ita.
Gayton, John J. '86 (WIL) Claymont, DE Holy Rosary.
Gayton, John J. *m.i.c.* '86 (MO) Navy Reserve Chaplains.
Gaza, J. Patrick '68 (GRY) Gary, IN SS. Monica–St. Luke; Gary, IN St. Mark; Bishop's Council of Priests.
Gazdowicz, Krzysztof '04 (SP) Spring Hill, FL St. Frances Xavier Cabrini.
Gazzingan, Mark '07 (SJ) Los Altos, CA St. Simon; Council of Priests.
Gazzingan, Michael '03 (SJ) San Jose, CA St. Maria Goretti.
Geaney, John J. *c.s.p.* '64 (GR) Evangelization; Grand Rapids, MI Cathedral of St. Andrew.
Geaney, John *c.s.p.* '62 (GR)[L] Grand Rapids, MI Catholic Information Center.
Geany, Nash P. (NY) Stewart Field.
Gearhart, Edwin F. '73 (CIN) Springfield, OH St. Teresa of the Child Jesus; Adjutant Judicial Vicars.
Gearhart, James '77 (JC)[B] Jefferson City, MO St. Mary Health Center.
Gearhart, Lawrence M. '03 (CIN) Mechanicsburg, OH St. Michael; Mechanicsburg, OH Immaculate Conception.
Gearheard, William '94 (LAF) On Leave.
Gearing, Barry T. '00 (CLV) Berea, OH St. Adalbert.
Geary, Brian A. '98 (RCK) Belvidere, IL St. James.
Geary, Edward P. '64 (BO) Senior Priests. Retired.
Geary, Patrick G. '56 (DUB) Retired.
Gebbia, Gregory V. *o.f.m.* '86 (NEW) Jersey City, NJ St. John the Baptist; [C] Newark, NJ Christ the King Preparatory School of Newark, N.J., Corp.
Gebelein, Gary M. '74 (STL) St. Louis, MO St. Francis of Assisi.
Gebhard, Robert L. '87 (BUF)[A] East Aurora, NY Christ the King Seminary.
Gebhardt, Paul L. '91 (CIN) Cincinnati, OH St. Vivian.
Gebremichael, Abayneh (BO) Eritrean; Ethiopian.
Geditz, Roger '69 (SFS) Geddes, SD St. Ann Retired.
Gedvila, Izidorius '48 (GF) Retired.
Gee, Daniel N. '95 (ARL) Alexandria, VA St. Rita.
Gee, John F. '53 (WOR) Auburn, MA North American Martyrs; [R] Auburn, MA Kateri Tekakwitha Development, Inc.
Geelan, Thomas E. '62 (SC) Retired.
Geer, Steve '06 (P) Portland, OR St. Therese of the Child Jesus; Finance Council.
Geers, Frank *o.f.m.* '58 (CIN)[C] Cincinnati, OH St. Anthony Shrine, Franciscan Postulancy.
Geers, Harold *o.f.m.* '60 (CIN)[N] Cincinnati St. Francis Seraph Friary.
Geffrard, Yves '01 (PMB) Haitian Ministry; Fort Pierce, FL Notre Dame Mission.
Geger, Barton T. *s.j.* '01 (DEN)[N] Denver, CO Regis Jesuit Community (The Jesuits at Regis University).
Gegotek, Tadeusz '91 (BEL) Military Chaplains; Navy Chaplains.
Gehl, Rev. Msgr. James C. '74 (LA) Granada Hills, CA St. Euphrasia.
Gehl, James E. '69 (SY) Cicero, NY Sacred Heart.
Gehling, Kenneth B. '62 (DUB)[H] Mason City, IA Mercy Medical Center–North Iowa; Deans.
Gehring, Robert P. '66 (GRY) Retired.
Gehringer, Andrew N. '00 (ALN) Allentown, PA St. Paul; Elected Members; Advocates; Office of Hispanic Affairs.
Geib, David Willis *o.p.* '67 (P)[N] McKenzie Bridge, OR St. Benedict Lodge Dominican Retreat & Conference Center.
Geib, Harry F. *s.j.* '92 (WH)[A] Wheeling, WV Wheeling Jesuit University.
Geiger, Angelo Mary *f.i.* '91 (NOR)[G] Griswold, CT Marian Friary of Our Lady of Guadalupe; Griswold, CT.
Geiger, Bernard *o.f.m.conv.* '59 (CHI)[N] Chicago Conventual Franciscans of St. Bonaventure Province.
Geiger, Rt. Rev. Archimandrite Damon '71 (NTN) Akron, OH St. Joseph; Liturgical Commission.
Geiger, Rev. Msgr. James A. '50 (COL) Diocesan Judges Retired.
Geiger, Michael A. '02 (TOL) Shelby, OH Sacred Heart of Jesus; Crestline, OH St. Joseph.
Geilenkirchen, Jude '73 (DEN) Rifle, CO St. Mary Retired.
Geinzer, Eugene M. *s.j.* '74 (FgM) Towson, MD Society of Jesus; [Q] Towson Maryland Province of the Society of Jesus.
Geinzer, John A. '67 (PIT) Allegheny County, PA Little Sisters of the Poor; [J] Pittsburgh, PA Little Sisters of the Poor Home for the Aged.
Geinzer, Patrick *c.p.* '95 (PIT)[M] Pittsburgh, PA St. Paul of the Cross Monastery; [O] Pittsburgh, PA St. Paul of the Cross Retreat Center.
Geis, John F. '64 (IND) Napoleon, IN St. Maurice Catholic Church, Napoleon, Inc.; Greensburg, IN Immaculate Conception Catholic Church, Millhousen, Inc.; Greensburg, IN St. Denis Catholic Church, Jennings County, Inc. Retired.
Geiser, Allen A. '90 (GB) Retired.
Geisinger, Robert J. *s.j.* '91 (CHI)[N] Chicago Chicago Province of the Society of Jesus–Provincial Office.
Geissler, Robert '47 (NY) Montgomery, NY Holy Name of Mary Retired.
Geiszel, John I. *s.j.* '57 (SJ)[M] Los Gatos, CA Sacred Heart Jesuit Center.
Geitner, John E. *m.m.* '53 (FgM) Maryknoll, NY MARYKNOLL.
Geleney, Joseph F. '01 (AUS) Waco, TX St. Mary of the Assumption.
Gelfant, Michael L. '05 (BRK) Brooklyn, NY St. Finbar.
Gelfenbien, Gary Paul '71 (ALB) Chatham, NY St. James.
Gelfer, Peter *o.h.* '80 (SB) Apple Valley, CA St. Mary Medical Center.
Gelfer, Peter *o.h.* '80 (LA) Hospital Chaplains.
Gelido, Manuel T. '79 (WH) Nitro, WV Christ the King; Nitro, WV Holy Trinity; Nitro, WV St. Patrick.
Gelinas, Rene *m.s.* '60 (HRT)[L] Hartford, CT Missionaries of LaSalette.
Gelinas, Robert James '05 (NEW) Navy Chaplains; Military Chaplains.
Gellel, Lawrence *s.j.* '54 (BRK) Astoria, NY St. Joseph.
Geller, Charles H. '73 (BEL) Special Assignment.
Gelsomino, Rev. Msgr. Peter (NY) Port Chester, NY Sacred Heart of Jesus.
Gelson, James N. *s.j.* '60 (BAL)[Q] Towson Maryland Province of the Society of Jesus.
Gelthaus, Harry J. '85 (L) Louisville, KY St. Stephen, Martyr.
Gelthaus, Lawrence J. '88 (L) Edmonton, KY Christ the Healer; Ex Officio.
Gembala, Joseph J. '87 (DET) Sterling Heights, MI St. Malachy.
Gemme, Stephen M. '02 (WOR) Northboro, MA St. Bernadette.
Gemza, Richard J. '95 (BGP) Greenwich, CT St. Mary.
Genabia, Joel S. '03 (SAC) Chico, CA Our Divine Savior; Presbyteral Council.
Gendreau, Claude R. '93 (PRT) Special or Other Diocesan Assignment.
Gendreau, Michael P. '90 (PRT) Special or Other Diocesan Assignment.
Gendreau, Richard R. '69 (FR) Swansea, MA St. Louis de France.
Gendron, Michael E. '95 (MAN) Auburn, NH St. Peter; Advocates.
Genello, Patrick J. '83 (SCR) Hazleton, PA Holy Rosary.
Genereux, Wayne C. *o.de.m.* '97 (SP) Tampa, FL St. Mary.
Generose, Rev. Msgr. Anthony J. '99 (SCR) Glen Lyon, PA Corpus Christi; Mocanaqua, PA St. Mary, Our Lady of Perpetual Help; Episcopal Vicar for Administrative Canonical Processes & Judicial Vicar; Mocanaqua, PA St. Martha.
Geneta, Elpidio M. '95 (WH) Williamson, WV Sacred Heart; Judges.
Geng, Dennis *o.c.d.* '89 (MIL)[P] Milwaukee Provincial Offices – Discalced Carmelites.
Gengaro, Nicholas S. '81 (NEW)[B] Seton Hall University.
Geniesse, Joseph F. *c.s.c.* '57 (AUS)[G] Austin, TX Brother Andre Residence Retired.
Genilla, Bruno L. '83 (HON) Kula, HI Our Lady Queen of the Angels.
Genito, Joseph A. *o.s.a.* '75 (PH) Philadelphia, PA St. Rita of Cascia; [CC] Philadelphia, PA National Shrine of Saint Rita of Cascia.
Genovese, Anthony M. *o.s.a.* '73 (PH)[Y] Villanova, PA Provincial Offices of the Order of St. Augustine, Province of St. Thomas of Villanova; Villanova, PA Province of St. Thomas of Villanova (Eastern); [Y] Villanova, PA St. Thomas Monastery; [C] Villanova, PA Villanova University.
Genovese, Seamus D. '75 (OAK) Oakland, CA Our Lady of Lourdes.
Genovesi, James.(LC) On Special Assignment.
Genovesi, Vincent J. *s.j.* '69 (PH)[C] Jesuit Fathers; [Y] Loyola Center and Manresa Hall.
Gensler, Harry J. *s.j.* '74 (CLV)[B] University Heights, OH John Carroll Jesuit Community.
Gentile, Carl J. '60 (PIT) Pittsburgh, PA St. John Fisher Retired.
Gentile, Robert A. '03 (SPR) Holyoke, MA Blessed Sacrament; Bishop's Commission for Clergy; Deans; Presbyteral Council; Diocesan Consultors.
Gentile, Thomas E. '73 (L) Ex Officio; Louisville, KY Mary Queen of Peace Parish.
Gentili, Rev. Msgr. Joseph P. '87 (PH) Doylestown, PA Our Lady of Guadalupe.
Gentleman, Gerard J. '97 (RVC) Hicksville, NY Holy Family; Presbyteral Council.
Gentleman, John W. '87 (BO) Manchester by the Sea, MA St. John the Baptist; Manchester by the Sea, MA Sacred Heart.
Genua, Ronald L. '65 (HRT) Retired.
Genuardi, Gasper A. '68 (PH) Conshohocken, PA SS. Cosmas and Damian.
Genuario, Rev. Msgr. William A. '56 (BGP) Judges; [O] Stamford, CT The Catherine Dennis Keefe Queen of the Clergy Retired Priests' Residence Retired.

Geo, Patrick '93 (FRS) Rosamond, CA St. Mary of the Desert.
Geoghegan, James *o.c.d,* '60 (SJ)[M] San Jose, CA Carmelite Monastery, Novitiate.
Geoghegan, John F. '45 (STL) Retired.
George, Abraham K. *m.c.b.s.* '16 (NY) Poughkeepsie, NY St. Martin de Porres.
George, Abraham Karott *m.c.b.s.* '95 (MIL)[P] Kenosha, WI Missionary Congregation of the Blessed Sacrament, Inc., Zion Province.
George, Rev. Msgr. Alexander C. '65 (LA) Retired.
George, Benny *c.m.i.* '88 (LA) Burbank, CA St. Francis Xavier.
George, Binoy '08 (BRK) East Glendale, NY Sacred Heart.
George, Rev. Msgr. David M. '76 (SAM) On Sabbatical.
George, Francis M. '87 (LAN) Howell, MI St. John The Baptist.
George, Gary *c.ss.r.* '92 (OLL) Saint Louis, MO St. Raymond Maronite Catholic Cathedral; Office of Youth Ministries; Presbyteral Council; College of Consultors; Personnel Board.
George, Gary (SAM) Youth Ministry Office.
George, George C. '86 (AUS) Chaplains of the Military; DEPARTMENT OF VETERANS AFFAIRS HOSPITALS AND CHAPLAINS.
George, George C. '86 (SYM) Helotes, TX St. Thomas Syro–Malabar Catholic Mission of San Antonio.
George, J. Clark '56 (ALT) Retired.
George, Jacob C. '97 (WDC) Landover Hills, MD Syro–Malankara Mission.
George, James '70 (HRT) Watertown, CT St. John the Evangelist.
George, John Kutty '97 (SYM) Sacramento, CA Infant Jesus Syro–Malabar Catholic Mission of Sacramento, CA.
George, Jose '77 (SP) Valrico, FL St. Stephen.
George, Rev. Msgr. Joseph S. '62 (LA) Retired.
George, Lloyd *s.j.* '73 (BAL)[D] Baltimore, MD Loyola Blakefield; [Q] Baltimore, MD Jesuit Community of Loyola University, Inc.
George, Madhu '98 (TUC) Tucson, AZ Our Mother of Sorrows Roman Catholic Parish – Tucson.
George, Mark *s.j.* '98 (CLV)[D] Cuyahoga Falls, OH Walsh Jesuit High School.
George, Patrick *t.o.r.* '55 (ALT)[G] Loretto, PA St. Francis Friary at Mount Assisi.
George, Rejimon *c.m.i.* '03 (BEA) Port Arthur, TX St. Therese the Little Flower of Jesus.
George, Richard E. '95 (PMB) Fort Pierce, FL Notre Dame Mission; Fort Pierce, FL St. Anastasia; Elected Members.
George, Robert J. '95 (ALN)[C] Easton, PA Notre Dame High School; Bethlehem, PA Sacred Heart of Jesus.
George, Robert J. '76 (PIT)[N] Pittsburgh, PA Sisters of Mercy of the Americas – New York, Pennsylvania, Pacific West Community.
George, Sebastian K. *c.m.i.* '80 (STA) Branford, FL San Juan Mission; High Springs, FL St. Madeleine Sophie Parish.
George, Sojan *h.g.n.* '00 (FWT) Wichita Falls, TX Our Lady Queen of Peace.
George, William L. *s.j.* '73 (WDC) Archdiocesan Tuition Assistance Fund; [O] Washington, DC The Jesuit Community at Georgetown University.
George–Obilonu, Kingsley (GLP) Springerville, AZ St. Peter.
Georgekutty, Ponnachan '83 (NY) Patterson, NY Sacred Heart.
Georgia, John J. '75 (HRT) Consultors – Canon 1742; Wallingford, CT Resurrection.
Georgis, Pieter '00 (SPA) Perris, CA St. Hormizdah Mission.
Gephart, John B. '46 (L)[L] Louisville, KY Bishop David Apartments Retired.
Gera, Francis '64 (PSC) Retired.
Geraci, Anthony J. '75 (CIN) South Charleston, OH St. Charles Borromeo; Yellow Springs, OH St. Paul.
Geraghty, Rev. Msgr. Martin T. '64 (BRK) Bayside, NY St. Robert Bellarmine.
Gerald, John J. '82 (SC) Sioux Rapids, IA Sacred Heart; Sioux Rapids, IA St. Joseph; Royal, IA St. Louis.
Gerathy, Rev. Msgr. Kenneth A. '54 (NY)[DD] Bronx, NY Retired.
Gerber, Anthony J. '11 (STL) Imperial, MO St. Joseph.
Gerber, Brian C. '08 (MAR) Hancock, MI Resurrection.
Gerber, Martin '76 (ORL) Orlando, FL Basilica of the National Shrine of Mary Queen of the Universe.
Gerdes, Harry J. '62 (CIN) Retired.
Gerend, Lawrence '76 (GB) Retired.
Gerg, Joseph U. *o.s.b.* '65 (GBG)[H] Latrobe, PA Saint Vincent Archabbey.
Gergel, Stephen J. '62 (ALT) Retired.
Gergel, Stephen J. '62 (SAV) Retired.
Gergen, Michael J. *s.d.b.* '79 (LAR) Laredo, TX San Luis Rey.
Gerhard, John J. *s.j.* '49 (NY)[DD] New York, NY Murray–Weigel Hall.
Gering, Kenneth *o.f.m.conv.* '58 (IND)[J] Mount St. Francis, IN Mount Saint Francis Friary and Retreat Center.
Geris, Thierry '09 (SJ) Ongoing Formation of Clergy.
Gerken, Theodore J. '57 (ALB) Hudson, NY Parish of the Holy Trinity; Columbia County Jail Retired.
Gerl, Robert '79 (LAN) On Duty Outside the Diocese.
Gerlach, Dominic *c.pp.s.* '50 (CIN)[N] Carthagena, OH St. Charles Retired.
Gerlach, John *o.p.* '63 (MAD)[G] Sinsinawa, WI Dominican Motherhouse.
Gerlach, Matthew J. '96 (TLS) Propagation of the Faith; Vocations; Tulsa, OK St. Pius X; Seminary Board.
Gerlach, Michael J. '82 (PH) West Chester, PA SS. Simon and Jude.
Gerlach, William Peter '04 (FAR) Forman, ND St. Mary; Oakes, ND St. Charles Church of Oakes.
Gerlich, Robert S. *s.j.* '73 (NO)[C] New Orleans, LA Loyola University New Orleans.
Gerlock, Stanley J. '60 (SY) Broome County Jail; [Q] Binghamton, NY McDevitt Residence for Retired Priests Retired.
Germain, Levelt '02 (NY) Bronx, NY Our Lady of Grace.
Germaine, Kenneth *s.d.b.* '67 (BIR) Birmingham, AL Holy Rosary.
German, Brian (MIA) FIU–University Park.
German, Michael J. '68 (NEW) River Edge, NJ St. Peter the Apostle.
Germann, Lauren '78 (SCL) Elk River, MN The Church of St. Andrew; Deans; Diocesan Corporate Board; Diocesan Education Council.
Gerosa, Julian *c.r.s.* '78 (GAL) Houston, TX Christ the King.
Gerres, Daniel W. '66 (WIL) Wilmington, DE St. Elizabeth Retired.
Gerrety, James P. '57 (COV) Retired.
Gerritts, John R. '91 (SUP) Rhinelander, WI St. John; Presbyteral Council & Diocesan Consultors; Rhinelander, WI Nativity of Our Lord; Board of Directors.
Gerrity, Raymond J. '45 (CHI) Retired.
Gersbach, Karl A. *o.s.a.* '61 (PH)[Y] Villanova, PA St. Thomas Monastery.
Gerth, John H. '93 (SP) St. Petersburg, FL St. Joseph.
Gerth, John '93 (SP)[F] Saint Petersburg, FL Immaculate Conception Early Childhood Center.
Gerth, Kenneth *m.c.c.j.* '65 (CIN)[N] Cincinnati, OH Comboni Missionaries (Verona Fathers)–Comboni Mission Center.
Gerth, Kenneth *m.c.c.j.* '64 (SP)[J] Tampa, FL St. Joseph's Hospital, Inc.
Gerum, Jerome G. '50 (LC) Retired.
Gerut, William F. *s.j.* '67 (OM)[J] Omaha, NE Jesuit Community at Creighton University.
Gerut, William F. *s.j.* '67 (DM)[J] Griswold, IA Creighton University Retreat Center.
Gervacio, Adrian R. '67 (HON) Honolulu, HI Our Lady of the Mount.
Gervasio, Rev. Msgr. Thomas N. '82 (TR) College of Consultors; Hamilton, NJ Our Lady of Sorrows–St. Anthony Parish.
Gessner, Glenn *o.f.m.cap.* '60 (FgM) Detroit, MI Province of St. Joseph.
Gessner, Glenn *o.f.m.cap.* '60 (DET)[K] Detroit St. Bonaventure Friary.
Gesty, John *o.f.m.cap.* '66 (PIT)[M] Allison Park, PA St. Conrad Friary.
Gesy, Lawrence J. '75 (BAL) Retired.
Getchel, Richard '76 (GB) De Pere, WI St. Francis Xavier; De Pere, WI St. Mary; Adjutant Judicial Vicars; Regional Vicars; Judges.
Getigan, Bernardito '85 (SAN) Odessa, TX Holy Redeemer.
Getsinger, Ronald A. '68 (WH) Retired.
Getsy, John *o.f.m.cap.* '66 (PIT) Rochester, PA St. Cecilia.
Gettinger, Rev. Msgr. Robert J. '64 (STL) St. Louis, MO St. Augustine.
Getz, Joseph J. *o.s.a.* '51 (PH)[Y] Villanova, PA St. Thomas Monastery.
Getz, Rev. Msgr. Robert L. '61 (LSC) Episcopal Vicar for Clergy and Personnel; Diocesan Consultors; Clergy Personnel Board; Priests Retirement Fund Committee Retired.
Geurtz, Gary '81 (FWT) Retired.
Geyer, Kenneth A. *o.s.b.* '53 (CHL)[J] Belmont, NC Belmont Abbey.
Geyman, Donald R. '96 (GLD) Traverse City, MI St. Patrick; Director of Vocations.
Ghaby, Jean '92 (NTN) Utica, NY St. Basil.
Ghanoum, Rt. Rev. Exarch Gabriel *b.s.o.* '93 (NTN) Delray Beach, FL St. Nicholas; Continuing Education of Clergy Office; Order of St. Nicholas; Victim Assistance Coordinator; College of Eparchial Consultors.
Ghazarian, Tavit (OLN) Tujunga, CA Mekhitarist School.
Ghebray, Araia Ghiday (WDC) Washington, DC Kidane–Mehret Ge'ez Rite Catholic Church.
Gherardi, Marc *o.s.f.s.* '08 (VEN) Naples, FL St. Ann.
Ghezzi, Giancarlo *p.i.m.e.* '84 (PAT)[N] Wayne, NJ P.I.M.E. Missionaries Residence.
Ghezzi, Giancarlo '84 (DET)[K] Detroit, MI P.I.M.E. Missionaries.
Ghezzi, Richard G. '86 (SCR)[K] Wilkes–Barre, PA Little Flower Manor of the Diocese of Scranton; [K] Wilkes–Barre, PA St. Therese Residence; Wilkes–Barre, PA Our Lady of Hope Parish.
Ghiloni, Mark V. '83 (COL) London, OH St. Patrick.
Ghio, John J. '80 (STL) Webster Groves, MO Annunciation Retired.
Ghiorso, David A. '81 (SFR) San Carlos, CA St. Charles; Serra Club of San Francisco (Downtown); On Special Assignment; Office of Vocations; College of Consultors.
Ghisalberti, Giacomo G. '70 (R) Retired.
Ghozairan, Poulos '75 (SPA) Las Vegas, NV St. Barbara Assyrian–Chaldean Catholic Church.
Ghyselinck, Mark R. *c.s.c.* '88 (FTW)[H] Notre Dame Congregation of Holy Cross, United States Province of Priests & Brothers.
Ghyselinck, Mark *c.s.c.* '88 (P)[B] University of Portland; [L] Portland, OR Holy Cross Fathers & Brothers, C.S.C. – University of Portland.
Giachino, Valeriano *s.s.p.* '57 (LA)[P] Los Angeles, CA The Society of St. Paul; Los Angeles, CA.
Giacinti, Gaston *i.v.e.* '05 (DAL) Dallas, TX St. Bernard of Clairvaux.
Giacomini, Salvatore H. *s.d.b.* '51 (SFR) San Francisco, CA SS. Peter and Paul.
Gialogo, Rev. Msgr. Agustin '73 (STO) Stockton, CA St. Michael Church of Stockton (Pastor of).
Giamello, Anthony '05 (WIL) Wilmington, DE St. John the Beloved; New Castle, DE; Air National Guard Chaplains.
Giammona, Rev. Msgr. John J. '59 (GR) Retired.
Giampietro, Anthony E. *c.s.b.* '93 (GAL)[O] Houston, TX Residence of the Basilian Fathers of the University of St. Thomas.
Giandurco, Rev. Msgr. Joseph R. '87 (NY) Suffern, NY Sacred Heart; Canon 1742 Panel of Pastors; [HH] Cause:; [A] Yonkers, NY St. Joseph's Seminary.
Gianelli, Gene E. '70 (HRT) Consultors – Canon 1742; Woodbridge, CT Church of the Assumption; New Haven Vicariate; West Shore Line Deanery.
Giangiacomo, Tosello *c.s.sp.* '48 (ARE) Orocovis, PR Our Lady of Fatima.
Giannamore, Rev. Msgr. Anthony J. '56 (STU) Retired.
Giannamore, Pete A. '95 (WH)[O] Bethany, WV St. John Fisher Catholic Chapel; [O] West Liberty, WV West Liberty State College, St. Thomas Aquinas Campus Ministry; Follansbee, WV St. Anthony.
Gianni, Vincent J. '70 (BO) Wakefield, MA St. Florence.
Giannini, Stephen W. '93 (IND) Deacons' Personnel Board.
Giannini, Stephen W. '93 (IND) Assistant Chancellor; Priests' Personnel Board; Vicariate for Clergy and Parish Life Coordinators: Formation and Personnel; Personnel: Priests and Parish Life Coordinators; Archdiocesan Judges; Terre Haute, IN Sacred Heart of Jesus Catholic Church, Terre Haute, Inc.; Board of Consultors.
Giannitelli, Michael C. '91 (NOR) Durham, CT Notre Dame; Middlefield, CT St. Colman; Seminarian Advisory Board.
Giannone, Ronald *o.f.m.cap.* '90 (WIL) Wilmington, DE Sacred Heart; [G] Wilmington, DE Ministry of Caring, Inc.; [J] Wilmington, DE St. Felix Friary; [K] Wilmington, DE Monastery of St. Veronica Giuliani; Union City, NJ.
Giannone, Ronald *o.f.m.cap.* '90 (NEW)[L] Union City, NJ Capuchin Friars – Province of the Sacred Stigmata of St. Francis.
Gianola, William '62 (CHY) Retired.
Giaquinto, Albert C. '48 (NOR) Retired.
Giaquinto, Albert C. *s.s.* '48 (BAL)[M] Baltimore, MD St. Charles Villa; [Q] Baltimore Society of St. Sulpice, Province of the United States Retired.
Giardina, Robert J. '76 (PRO) West Warwick, RI SS. Peter and Paul.
Giardino, Andrew *o.f.m.* '62 (HRT) Hartford, CT St. Patrick–St. Anthony.
Giardino, Louis '75 (BIR) Judges; Huntsville, AL Good Shepherd.
Gibas, Robert G. '62 (Y) Judges Retired.
Gibbeaut, Wayne *o.f.m.* '83 (SFE)[H] Albuquerque, NM The Province of Our Lady of Guadalupe.
Gibbeaut, Wayne *o.f.m.* (GLP) Pueblo of Acoma, NM San Esteban, Acoma Catholic Indian Mission; Laguna, NM St. Joseph.
Gibbons, Donald Patrick '91 (SFD) Grafton, IL St. Patrick; Jerseyville, IL St. Francis Xavier; Presbyteral Council.
Gibbons, Edward '97 (VEN) Cape Coral, FL St. Andrew.
Gibbons, Ian R. *s.j.* '06 (KC)[D] Kansas City, MO Rockhurst High School; [J] Kansas City, MO Rockhurst Jesuit Community.
Gibbons, James *o.m.i.* '69 (FgM) Washington, DC AMERICAN OBLATE MISSIONS.
Gibbons, John J. '58 (NEW) Bayonne, NJ Saint Michael and Saint Joseph Retired.
Gibbons, John M. '89 (ALN) Reading, PA St. Margaret.
Gibbons, John M. '56 (DEN) Retired.
Gibbons, John Michael '10 (ALT) Altoona, PA Cathedral

of the Blessed Sacrament.
Gibbons, Rev. Msgr. John '60 (TR) Retired.
Gibbons, John *o.f.m.* '01 (OAK) Oakland, CA St. Barbara Province; [L] Oakland Franciscan Friars of California, (Province of St. Barbara).
Gibbons, Joseph Marie of Jesus *m. carm.* '10 (CHY)[D] Powell, WY Monks of the Most Blessed Virgin Mary of Mt. Carmel.
Gibbons, Rev. Msgr. Robert C. '81 (SP) St. Petersburg, FL St. Paul; Judges; College of Consultors; Executive Committee; [T] Saint Petersburg, FL Partners with Haiti, Inc.; Elected Pastors.
Gibbons, Thomas F. *m.m.* '48 (NY)[DD] Retired.
Gibbs, Donald J. *o.s.b.* '05 (MIL)[P] Benet Lake, WI St. Benedict's Abbey.
Gibbs, Phillip G. '94 (DUB) Decorah, IA St. Benedict; Deanery Representatives; Priests' Council; Priestly Life and Ministry Committee.
Gibino, Joseph R. '81 (BRK) Whitestone, NY Holy Trinity.
Gibney, Robert G. '54 (NEW)[L] Caldwell, NJ The Rev. Msgr. James F. Kelley Residence for Retired Priests Retired.
Gibowski, Boguslaw T. '69 (PRO) Retired.
Gibson, Beryl '96 (SAL) Retired.
Gibson, Brendan *s.j.c.* '05 (CHI) Chicago, IL St. John Cantius; [P] Chicago, IL Canons Regular of Saint John Cantius.
Gibson, Bruno *o.p.* '60 (OAK) Berkeley, CA St. Mary Magdalen.
Gibson, Christopher *c.p.* '75 (CHI)[N] Chicago, IL Passionist Community of St. Vincent Strambi.
Gibson, James *c.r.* '79 (CHI)[N] Chicago Provincial Office of the Congregation of the Resurrection.
Gibson, John *s.d.b.* '70 (OAK) Berkeley, CA St. Ambrose.
Gibson, Rev. Msgr. Lawrence J. '55 (LA) Retired.
Gibson, Robert J. '58 (SCR) Unassigned or Leave of Absence.
Gibson, Stephen C. *c.s.c.* '70 (FTW)[H] Notre Dame Congregation of Holy Cross, United States Province of Priests & Brothers.
Gibson, Stephen G. '81 (GRY) East Chicago, IN St. Mary; Hammond, IN St. Margaret Mary.
Gibson, Thomas '93 (PEO) Moline, IL Sacred Heart.
Gick, Francois *s.j.* '80 (BO)[U] Boston The Society of Jesus of New England–Provincial Offices.
Gideon, Peter M. '76 (COL) Lancaster, OH St. Mark.
Gideon, Stephen G. '97 (NSH) Gallatin, TN St. John Vianney.
Giedgaudas, Francis *o.f.m.* '47 (PRT)[I] Kennebunk, ME St. Anthony's Friary; Kennebunkport, ME.
Giel, John '78 (ORL) Leesburg, FL St. Paul's; Deans; Judges; Ex Officio Members.
Gielow, Richard *c.m.* '70 (KC)[J] Independence, MO Vincentian Parish Mission Center; Saint Louis, MO Ladies of Charity of the United States of America (LCUSA).
Gier, Rev. Msgr. Gregory A. '67 (TLS) Tulsa, OK Holy Family Cathedral.
Giera, Craig Anthony '10 (DET) Clawson, MI Guardian Angels.
Giermek, Joachin *o.f.m.conv.* '69 (BAL)[Q] Ellicott City, MD Order of Friars Minor Conventual.
Giese, Samuel C. '85 (WDC) Landover Hills, MD St. Mary's Catholic Church; Army National Guard Chaplains.
Giesen, Cal '47 (FWT)[H] Crowley, TX St. Maximilian Kolbe Friary.
Giesige, Randy P. '98 (TOL) Defiance, OH St. Mary.
Giesing, Rev. Msgr. Anthony '55 (SD) Retired.
Giesler, Michael E. '79 (STL)[P] Kirkwood, MO Prelature of the Holy Cross and Opus Dei; Kirkwood.
Gietl, Joseph A. '73 (GAL) Spring, TX St. Edward; Northern Vicariate; College of Consultors; Appointees.
Gietzen, Albin J. '56 (GLD) Retired.
Gigante, Louis R. '59 (NY) Retired.
Gigantiello, Rev. Msgr. Jamie J. '95 (BRK) Brooklyn, NY Mary Queen of Heaven; Secretariat for Development.
Giggi, Rev. Msgr. J. Robert '53 (BO) Natick, MA St. Linus.
Giglio, Michael E. '94 (ORL) Retired.
Gigliotti, James *t.o.r.* '80 (FWT) Arlington, TX St. Maria Goretti.
Gigliotti, Vincent J. '76 (GBG) Belle Vernon, PA St. Anne.
Gignac, Francis T. *s.j.* '67 (WDC)[C] Catholic University of America, The; [O] Washington, DC The Jesuit Community at Georgetown University.
Gikenyi, Mark '11 (P) Milwaukie, OR St. John the Baptist.
Gikonyo, David Kamau *i.m.c.* '97 (MET)[I] Somerset, NJ Consolata Society for Foreign Missions.
Gil, Fernando '88 (ORL) Judicial Vicar; Director of Tribunal; Judges.
Gilb, Rev. Msgr. Eugene A. '57 (LA) Rancho Palos Verdes, CA St. John Fisher Retired.
Gilbaugh, Eric C. '05 (HEL) Three Forks, MT Holy Family.
Gilbert, Dennis M. '71 (MRY) On Leave.
Gilbert, Rev. Msgr. Donald J. '68 (MAN) Diocesan Review Board; Judicial Vicar.
Gilbert, John Mary '03 (LC)[M] Boyd, WI Institute of St. Joseph.
Gilbert, Patrick N. '01 (MAN) Nashua, NH Blessed John XXIII Parish.
Gilbert, Paul T. '01 (MAN)[L] Concord, NH Monastery of Discalced Carmelites; Henniker, NH St. Theresa; Concord Hospital; Hillsborough, NH St. Mary.
Gilbert, Philip F. *c.pp.s.* '60 (LFT)[A] Rensselaer, IN Saint Joseph's College.
Gilbert, Robert J. '98 (CHI) Chicago, IL St. Joachim.
Gilbert, Thomas R. '05 (BRK) Brooklyn, NY Our Lady of Guadalupe.
Gilbertson, Lee C. '63 (SPR) Retired.
Gilbo, Robert *c.s.c.* '67 (FgM) New Rochelle, NY Eastern Brothers Province.
Gilbo, Roberto M. *c.s.c.* '67 (FTW)[H] Notre Dame Congregation of Holy Cross, United States Province of Priests & Brothers.
Gilborges, Anthony *o.s.f.s.* '89 (VEN) Fort Myers, FL Our Lady of Light.
Gilchrist, Rev. Msgr. John J. '57 (NEW) Harrison, NJ Holy Cross Retired.
Gilday, Robert J. '75 (IND) Adjunct Vicars Judicial; Indianapolis, IN St. Therese of the Infant Jesus Catholic Church, Indianapolis, Inc.
Gilde, Lothar M. '06 (LIN) Advocates; McCook, NE St. Patrick.
Gildea, Arthur *c.ss.r.* '67 (BAL) Baltimore, MD Our Lady of Fatima.
Gildea, John J. '66 (BRK) Elmhurst, NY St. Bartholomew; Brooklyn, NY Holy Family.
Gile, Honesto D. '87 (SFR) Olema, CA Sacred Heart.
Gile, Joseph M. '88 (WCH)[A] Wichita, KS Newman University; Ongoing Formation of the Clergy Committee; Wichita, KS Blessed Sacrament.
Gilg, Rev. Msgr. James E. '66 (OM) Omaha, NE St. Mary Magdalene; Catholic Schools Office; Age Groups.
Giljum, Stephen P. '03 (STL) O'Fallon, MO Assumption.
Gill, David H. *s.j.* '67 (BO)[U] Boston The Society of Jesus of New England–Provincial Offices.
Gill, David H. *s.j.* '67 (OAK)[A] Berkeley, CA Jesuit School of Theology of Santa Clara University (Berkeley, California Campus); [L] Berkeley, CA Jesuit Fathers and Brothers; Oakland, CA St. Patrick.
Gill, G. Dennis '83 (PH) Philadelphia, PA Cathedral Basilica of SS. Peter and Paul; Office for Divine Worship; On Special or Other Archdiocesan Assignment.
Gill, Ilyas *o.f.m.* '93 (BRK)[Q] Pakistani Apostolate; Brooklyn, NY Mary Queen of Heaven.
Gill, Joseph C. *s.j.* '59 (MIL)[P] Wauwatosa, WI Jesuit Community at St. Camillus.
Gill, Michael J. '66 (NOR) Norwichtown, CT Sacred Heart.
Gill, Rev. Msgr. Richard '56 (BUF) Retired.
Gill, Richard *l.c.* '91 (NY) Brewster, NY St. Lawrence O'Toole.
Gill, Rev. Msgr. William J. '55 (RVC) Southold, NY; Southampton, NY Sacred Hearts of Jesus and Mary Retired.
Gilleece, Rev. Msgr. Thomas E. '67 (NY) Chappaqua, NY St. John and St. Mary.
Gillelan, Robert M. '89 (HBG) York, PA Immaculate Conception of the Blessed Virgin Mary; Deans; Presbyteral Council.
Gillelan, Robert M. '99 (HBG) Consultors, College.
Gillen, George D. '71 (NEW) Elizabeth, NJ St. Genevieve's; Presbyteral Council.
Gillen, Rev. Msgr. James G. '52 (WDC) Retired.
Gillen, Rev. Msgr. John J. '45 (NY) Retired.
Gillen, Kevin *o.p.* '00 (NY) New York, NY St. Joseph.
Gillen, Niles *o.carm.* '56 (VEN) Englewood, FL St. Raphael.
Gillen, Peter D. '78 (BRK) Woodside, NY Corpus Christi; On Leave/Unassigned.
Giller, Roderic *o.s.b.* '62 (KCK)[I] Atchison, KS St. Benedict's Abbey; Bendena, KS St. Benedict; Troy, KS St. Charles; Wathena, KS St. Joseph.
Gilles, Brian *c.ss.r.* '03 (STP) Brooklyn Center, MN St. Alphonsus; [J] Brooklyn Center, MN Redemptorist Fathers of Hennepin County.
Gilles, Rev. Msgr. Richard W. '94 (LC) Tomah, WI St. Mary (Immaculate Conception); Warrens, WI St. Andrew; Deans; Pastoral Council.
Gilles, Thomas C. '67 (CLV) Parma, OH St. John Bosco Retired.
Gillespie, Barnabas *o.s.b.* '80 (IND) Tell City, IN St. Michael Catholic Church, Cannelton, Inc.; Tell City, IN St. Pius V Catholic Church, Troy, Inc.; [K] Saint Meinrad St. Meinrad Archabbey; Tell City, IN St. Paul Catholic Church, Tell City, Inc.
Gillespie, Edward F. '57 (RCK) Retired.
Gillespie, Francis J. '72 (CHR) Hardeeville, SC St. Anthony.
Gillespie, Francis P. *s.j.* '72 (ALN)[A] Wernersville, PA Jesuit Center–Jesuit Community.
Gillespie, Francis T. '59 (ALN)[J] Bethlehem, PA Holy Family Villa Retired.
Gillespie, Hugh '06 (BRK) Ozone Park, NY St. Mary Gate of Heaven.
Gillespie, Jerome F. '82 (BO) Awaiting Assignment.; Charlestown, MA St. Mary – St. Catherine of Siena.
Gillespie, John D. '72 (STA) St. Augustine, FL San Sebastian.
Gillespie, John '95 (R) Lumberton, NC St. Francis De Sales.
Gillespie, Joseph P. *o.p.* '70 (STP) Minneapolis, MN St. Albert the Great; [J] Minneapolis, MN St. Albert the Great Priory.
Gillespie, Joseph '50 (PHX) Retired.
Gillespie, Kevin *s.j.* '86 (CHI)[C] Chicago, IL School of Social Work; [C] Chicago, IL Jesuit Community at Loyola University Chicago.
Gillespie, Martin Joseph '00 (BLX) Columbia, MS Holy Trinity; Industrial and Training School.
Gillespie, Philip '10 (CHR) Simpsonville, SC St. Mary Magdalene.
Gillespie, Thomas E. '72 (MAD) Hollandale, WI Immaculate Conception; Hollandale, WI St. Patrick; Hollandale, WI Holy Redeemer; Elected.
Gillespie, Thomas J. *o.s.f.s.* '60 (VEN) Naples, FL St. Ann.
Gillespie, Thomas L. '10 (PIT) Butler, PA St. Paul; Butler, PA St. Wendelin.
Gillespie, Thomas M. '68 (BO) North Reading, MA St. Theresa of Lisieux.
Gillespie, Thomas '61 (SB) Retired.
Gillespie, Thomas *o.s.b.* '64 (SCL)[I] Collegeville, MN St. John's Abbey, of the Order of St. Benedict.
Gilley, Charles F. *i.v.dei.* '96 (BRK) Long Island City, NY St. Patrick.
Gillgannon, Michael '58 (KC) Mission Duty.
Gillick, Lawrence D. *s.j.* '72 (OM)[J] Omaha, NE Jesuit Community at Creighton University.
Gilligan, Adrian *o.s.a.* '68 (PH)[Y] Villanova, PA St. Thomas Monastery.
Gilligan, James M. *m.m.* '55 (NY)[DD] Maryknoll Maryknoll Fathers and Brothers Retired.
Gilligan, Michael J. '69 (CHI) Other Assignments; [W] South Holland, IL American Catholic Press.
Gillin, Thomas P. '74 (PH)[F] Bryn Mawr, PA Country Day School of the Sacred Heart; Springfield, PA St. Kevin; Secane, PA Our Lady of Fatima.
Gillis, David C. '79 (ALN) On Duty Outside the Diocese.
Gillis, David C. '79 (ORL) DeBary, FL St. Ann's.
Gillis, Ralph J. '59 (GB) Crandon, WI St. Joseph.
Gillis, Ronald S. '67 (BAL)[A] Emmitsburg, MD Mount St. Mary's Seminary.
Gillis, Ronald S. (POD) Reston.
Gillmeyer, Patrick S. *o.s.b.* '03 (RCK)[G] Aurora, IL Marmion Abbey; Aurora, IL Annunciation of the Blessed Virgin Mary.
Gillon, James A. *s.j.* '74 (FgM) Watertown, MA Society of Jesus.
Gil Londono, William A. '00 (LA) Paramount, CA Our Lady of the Rosary.
Gills, Thomas '86 (BAL) Military Chaplains; Air Force Chaplains.
Gillum, William *o.f.m.cap.* '76 (PIT) Rochester, PA St. Cecilia; [M] Beaver, PA St. Fidelis Friary; Beaver County, PA McGuire Memorial Home.
Gilman, Leonard *o.carm.* '98 (NEW) Tenafly, NJ Our Lady of Mount Carmel.
Gilmartin, Rev. Msgr. John D. '72 (RVC) Centerport, NY Our Lady Queen of Martyrs.
Gilmartin, Paul P. *s.j.* '62 (BO)[U] Weston, MA Campion Health Center, Inc.
Gilmore, Alan *o.c.s.o.* '70 (L)[L] Trappist, KY Abbey of Our Lady of Gethsemani, of the Order of Cistercians of the Strict Observance.
Gilmore, Lawrence *s.d.b.* '84 (FgM) New Rochelle, NY SALESIANS OF DON BOSCO.
Gilmore, Vincent O. *o.praem.* '90 (ORG)[I] Silverado, CA Norbertine Fathers of Orange Inc.; Tustin, CA St. Cecilia.
Gilmour, James *c.ss.r.* '72 (MET) Co Directors; Commission for Hispanic Ministry.
Gilmour, Robert G. *c.s.c.* '68 (FgM) New Rochelle, NY Eastern Brothers Province.
Gilroy, Robert G. *s.j.* '97 (BO)[U] Weston, MA Campion Jesuit Community.
Gilsdorf, Daniel C. '60 (GB) Retired.
Gilsdorf, Gordon J. '49 (GB) Special Assignment; Censores Librorum.
Gilsenan, Rev. Msgr. John P. '56 (WCH) Wichita, KS St. Catherine of Siena; Presbyteral Council/College of Consultors; Promoters of Justice; Defenders of the Bond.
Gilsenan, Michael J. *ss.cc.* '65 (SB)[I] Chino Hills, CA Congregation of the Sacred Hearts of Jesus & Mary, SS.CC.; Chino Hills, CA St. Paul the Apostle.
Gilson, Michael C. *s.j.* '02 (SAC)[H] Carmichael, CA Sacramento Jesuit Community; [C] Sacramento, CA Jesuit High School.
Gimeno, Rev. Msgr. Fabian G. '60 (ORL) Retired.
Gimeno, Jose A. *sch.p.* '89 (NY) New York, NY Annunciation; [DD] New York, NY Calasanzian Fathers (Piarists).

Gimpl, Carl '55 (P) Judges; [P] Monmouth, OR Western Oregon University (Monmouth).
Gimpl, Rev. Msgr. Carl '55 (P) Independence, OR St. Patrick Church.
Ginel, Robert J. '78 (NY) Bronx, NY Holy Cross.
Ging, Regis B. *m.m.* '66 (FgM) Maryknoll, NY MARYKNOLL.
Gingras, Dennis C. '90 (HRT) Unassigned.
Gingras, Jerome R. '78 (ALB) Glenville, NY Immaculate Conception.
Gins, Paul M. *o.s.m.* '75 (CHI)[N] Chicago, IL Order of Friar Servants of Mary (Servites) United States of America Province, Inc.; [N] Fullerton, CA Servite Vocation Director; Chicago, IL.
Gins, Paul M. *o.s.m.* '75 (ORG) Fullerton, CA St. Juliana Falconieri.
Ginther, Lawrence P. '46 (WIN) Retired.
Ginther, Richard M. '83 (IND) Deaneries and Deans.
Ginther, Richard '83 (IND) Terre Haute, IN St. Patrick Catholic Church, Terre Haute, Inc.; Terre Haute, IN St. Margaret Mary Catholic Church, Terre Haute, Inc.
Ginty, Rev. Msgr. Thomas M. '85 (HRT) Forestville, CT St. Matthew; Waterbury Deanery.
Gioeli, Leonard '05 (VEN) Naples, FL St. John the Evangelist.
Gion, Chad '02 (BIS) Mandan, ND Spirit of Life; Mandan, ND St. Martin; Associate Judges; Mandan, ND St. Anthony; Priests' Personnel Board.
Gionet, Urbain J. '51 (WOR) Retired.
Gioppato, Alfonso *o.m.i.* '64 (SAT) Nixon, TX St. Joseph's; Smiley, TX St. Philip Benizi.
Giordani, Rev. Msgr. Mark J. '69 (PAT) Paterson, NJ Cathedral of St. John the Baptist; Passaic County Jail.
Giordano, John C. '67 (MET) Retired.
Giordano, Joseph *c.i.c.m.* '72 (ARL)[H] Arlington, VA Missionhurst, C.I.C.M.–Central House and Provincialate.
Giordano, Pasquale T. *s.j.* '72 (FgM) New York, NY Society of Jesus.
Giorno, Stephen J. *s.t.* '86 (NEW) Jersey City, NJ Christ, the King.
Giovanoni, Peter M. '01 (WDC) Washington, DC Our Lady Queen of Peace.
Gipson, Rev. Msgr. Robert W. '62 (LA) Retired.
Giraldo, Alonso Escobar '84 (PCE) Arroyo, PR Our Lady of Mt. Carmel.
Giraldo, Jesus Antonio '02 (KNX) Lenoir City, TN St. Thomas the Apostle.
Girard, Charles A. *s.m.* '66 (ATL)[C] Atlanta, GA Marist School.
Girardin, Peter T. '60 (BO) Senior Priests. Retired.
Girnius, Charles F. *m.m.* '44 (NY)[DD] Retired.
Giroir, Rev. Msgr. Frank J. '81 (NO) Parish Sites & Boundaries Committee; Serra Club of West St. Tammany; Madisonville, LA St. Anselm.
Girone, Joseph D. '83 (NEW) East Newark, NJ St. Anthony's; Harrison, NJ Holy Cross.
Girone, Joseph F. *o.s.a.* '81 (NY) Bronx, NY St. Nicholas of Tolentine.
Girotti, John W. '02 (GB) College of Consultors.
Girotti, John W. '02 (GB) Clintonville, WI St. Rose; Green Bay, WI St. Francis Xavier Cathedral; Clintonville, WI St. Mary; Green Bay, WI St. John.
Girouard, Robert J. '59 (PRT) Retired.
Giroux, Garry B. '76 (OG) Brasher Falls, NY St. Patrick; Brasher Falls, NY St. Lawrence; Advocates; [H] Brasher Falls, NY St. Patrick's Cemetery Association of Brasher Falls, N.Y.
Giroux, Harry E. '76 (OG) Absent on Sick Leave, Disabled Retired.
Giroux, Joseph W. '00 (OG) Malone, NY Notre Dame.
Giroux, Peter *f.p.o.* '98 (BO)[U] Lawrence, MA Franciscans of Primitive Observance; On Duty Outside the Archdiocese.
Giroux, Regis J. '70 (SPR) Absent on Leave.
Giroux, Richard M. '69 (MAN) Retired.
Giroux, William P. '80 (BUR) Burlington, VT St. Mark's.
Girres, Edward M. '79 (SC) Deans; Presbyteral Council; Algona, IA St. Cecelia.
Girzone, Joseph '55 (ALB) Retired.
Gismondi, Carl N. *f.s.s.p.* '02 (SCR)[L] Elmhurst Twp., PA Priestly Fraternity of St. Peter (F.S.S.P.), North American District Headquarters; Elmhurst Twp., PA.
Gismondi, Carl *f.s.s.p.* '02 (SD) San Diego, CA Saint Anne Catholic Parish.
Gitau, Paul '94 (ROC) Webster, NY St. Paul.
Gits, Douglas J. '53 (WIN) Retired.
Gitter, Paul '93 (STP)[C] St. Paul, MN University of St. Thomas; [A] St. Paul, MN St. John Vianney Seminary.
Gittins, Anthony *c.s.sp.* '67 (CHI)[B] Chicago, IL Catholic Theological Union.
Gittons, Gordon (DM) Retired.
Gitzen, Patrick *o.m.i.* '75 (FgM) Washington, DC AMERICAN OBLATE MISSIONS.
Giudice, Anthony *o.f.m.cap.* '54 (SP) Tampa, FL Most Holy Redeemer.
Giudice, Francis J. '56 (PRO) Providence, RI St. Charles Borromeo; Westerly, RI St. Pius X Retired.
Giuffre, Carmelo '07 (MIL) Milwaukee, WI St. Charles Borromeo.
Giuffre, Frank A. '97 (PH)[A] Wynnewood, PA Theological Seminary of St. Charles Borromeo, Overbrook.
Giuliani, John B. '60 (BGP)[N] West Redding, CT The Benedictine Grange Retired.
Giuliani, John P. *c.o.* '80 (CHR) Fort Mill, SC St. Philip Neri; [E] Rock Hill, SC Oratory of St. Philip Neri, Congregation of the Oratory of Pontifical Rite.
Giuliani, Scott *s.o.l.t.* '09 (PBL) Capulin, CO St. Joseph.
Giuliano, Anthony J. '84 (NY) Dover Plains, NY St. Charles Borromeo.
Giuliano, Carmen *s.a.* '61 (NY)[DD] Garrison, NY Franciscan Friars of the Atonement.
Giuliano, Steven B. '80 (WIL) Middletown, DE St. Joseph; Deans.
Giulietti, Julio *s.j.* '79 (BO)[U] Boston The Society of Jesus of New England–Provincial Offices.
Giulietti, Julio *s.j.* '72 (FgM) Watertown, MA Society of Jesus.
Giunta, Jose *i.v.e.* '91 (SJ) Santa Clara, CA Our Lady of Peace; [A] Santa Clara, CA Shrine of Our Lady of Peace.
Giusta, Rev. Msgr. Frank J. '63 (ATL) Special or Other Archdiocesan Assignment Retired.
Gizler, John B. '02 (PIT) Butler, PA Holy Sepulcher.
Gjengdahl, Nels H. '07 (STP) Special Assignment.
Gjergji, Nue '73 (DET) Southfield, MI Our Lady of Albanians.
Gjonaj, Damien *o.s.b.* '00 (DET)[B] Oxford, MI St. Benedict Monastery.
Glab, Joseph *c.r.* '75 (CHI) Schaumburg, IL St. Matthew.
Glab, Stephen *c.r.* '82 (RCK) Woodstock, IL Resurrection.
Glabik, Peter S. '07 (PAT) On Duty Outside the Diocese.
Glabik, Peter S. '07 (DET)[A] Orchard Lake, MI SS. Cyril and Methodius Seminary.
Glabinski, Janusz '86 (LAR) Rio Bravo, TX Santa Rita de Casia.
Glabinski, Jozef '89 (LAR) Crystal City, TX Sacred Heart.
Glackin, Thomas J. '68 (VEN) Retired.
Glade, Albert G. *o.p.* '72 (CHI)[N] Chicago Dominicans (Provincial Office).
Gladstone, James J. *s.j.* '66 (MIL) Milwaukee, WI; [P] Milwaukee, WI Jesuit Community at Marquette University.
Glahn, Carl '52 (OWN) Retired.
Glancy, Christopher J. *c.s.v.* '93 (CHI)[N] Arlington Heights Viatorian Province Center–Clerics of St. Viator; Chicago, IL St. Viator.
Glandorf, Ken (DUB)[H] Cedar Rapids, IA Mercy Medical Center–Cedar Rapids.
Glanzmann, Edward J. *o.s.b.* '79 (CHI)[N] Chicago, IL Monastery of the Holy Cross.
Glapiak, Edward '61 (WIL) Retired.
Glaros, Matthew J. '99 (MO) Military Chaplains; Air Force Chaplains.
Glaser, Kenneth J. '00 (DUB) Associate Directors; Recently Ordained Program; [N] Cedar Falls, IA St. Stephen the Witness Catholic Student Center, University of Northern Iowa; On Special or Other Archdiocesan Assignment; Christian Initiation Advisory Committee; Priestly Life and Ministry Committee.
Glaser, Lawrence A. *o.c.s.o.* '58 (SAC)[A] Vina, CA Abbey of New Clairvaux, Trappist Seminary; [H] Vina, CA Abbey of New Clairvaux, Trappist.
Glasgow, Dennis T. *s.j.* '84 (LAN) Ann Arbor, MI St. Mary Student Parish; [J] Ann Arbor, MI Detroit Province of the Society of Jesus – Jesuit Residence.
Glasgow, Mark W. '62 (PIT) Homestead, PA St. Maximilian Kolbe; Military Chaplains; Highland Drive; VA Pittsburgh Health Care System.
Glasgow, Robert K. '85 (MAN) Military Chaplains.
Glasgow, Robert K. '85 (MO) Army Chaplains.
Glasgow, Rev. Msgr. T. Gaspard '69 (NO) Retired.
Glass, James M. *o.s.b.* '04 (RIC)[K] Richmond, VA Mary Mother of the Church Abbey; Richmond, VA St. Edward The Confessor.
Glass, Robert H. *c.s.b.* '74 (GAL)[E] Houston, TX St. Thomas High School.
Glass, Senan *o.f.m.cap.* '57 (PH) Philadelphia, PA St. John the Evangelist.
Glassmire, David R. '94 (BUF) Batavia, NY Ascension.
Glastetter, Donald A. '65 (STL) Wentzville, MO St. Patrick.
Glastetter, Michael J. *o.f.m.conv.* '99 (MIL) Milwaukee, WI Basilica of St. Josaphat.
Glavin, Leonard *o.f.m.cap.* '54 (NY) New York, NY St. John the Baptist Retired.
Glavin, Patrick *o.f.m.cap.* '08 (MAN) Manchester, NH St. Anne–St. Augustin.
Gleason, Carl *s.d.s.* '56 (MIL)[P] Milwaukee, WI Salvatorians – Jordan Hall Retired.
Gleason, Jack '95 (TLS) Tulsa, OK Church of St. Mary; Diocesan Senators; Diocesan Consultors; Seminary Board.
Gleason, Joseph F. '87 (PH)[A] Wynnewood, PA Theological Seminary of St. Charles Borromeo, Overbrook.
Gleason, Laurence J. '96 (PH) West Chester, PA St. Agnes.
Gleason, Rev. Msgr. Paul D. '47 (PRT) Retired.
Gleason, Richard J. '67 (LA) Culver City, CA St. Augustine.
Gleason, William T. '66 (PBL) Pueblo, CO St. Joseph; Avondale, CO Sacred Heart; Pueblo, CO St. Therese.
Gleba, William P. '58 (SY) Retired.
Gleeson, Edward D. '69 (CHI) Lemont, IL St. James at Sag Bridge.
Gleeson, Martin J. *o.p.* '98 (NO) New Orleans, LA St. Dominic.
Gleeson, Michael '75 (LA) Long Beach, CA St. Cornelius.
Gleeson, Stephen J. '63 (BGP) Trumbull, CT St. Stephen; Nurses, Council of Catholic.
Gleeson, Thomas F. *s.j.* '68 (PH)[Y] Loyola Center and Manresa Hall.
Gleissner, Leopold *o.f.m.cap.* '52 (GB)[J] Appleton, WI St. Fidelis Friary Retired.
Gleixner, Joseph *m.s.c.* '65 (RCK)[G] Aurora, IL Missionaries of the Sacred Heart Community.
Glenn, Rev. Msgr. Michael G. '90 (DEN)[A] Denver, CO Saint John Vianney Theological Seminary; College of Consultors; Saint John Vianney Theological Seminary.
Glenn, Nicholas '98 (STN)[A] Eagle Harbor, MI Holy Transfiguration Skete.
Glennon, Bertin *s.t.* '71 (KNX) Chattanooga, TN Basilica of Sts. Peter and Paul.
Glennon, James G. *o.s.a.* '52 (PH)[Y] Villanova, PA St. Thomas Monastery.
Glennon, Thomas *s.s.c.* '79 (OM)[J] St. Columbans Missionary Society of St. Columban.
Glepko, Robert J. '76 (CLV) Lorain, OH Nativity of the Blessed Virgin Mary.
Gliatta, Ronald *o.f.m.* '77 (NY)[DD] New York Franciscan Province of the Immaculate Conception.
Glinkowski, Raphael K. *o.s.p.p.e.* '62 (GBG) Kittanning, PA Armstrong County Hospital; [H] Kittanning, PA Pauline Fathers Monastery.
Glisson, Nicholas '79 (OAK) Oakland, CA St. Lawrence O'Toole–St. Cyril of Jerusalem.
Glockner, David *g.h.m.* '66 (CIN)[N] Cincinnati Headquarters of Glenmary Home Missioners Retired.
Glockner, Michael W. *c.s.c.* '70 (FTW)[H] Notre Dame Congregation of Holy Cross, United States Province of Priests & Brothers.
Glogowski, John F. '71 (SFR) Retired.
Glorie, Rev. Msgr. John W. '60 (MIA) Retired.
Glorioso, Charles '95 (SHP) Bossier City, LA Christ the King; Priests' Retirement Board; Church Vocations Board & Vocations Office.
Gloss, John C. '03 (MET) Colonia, NJ St. John Vianney.
Glosser, Rev. Msgr. William F. '84 (ALN) Saint Clair, PA St. Clare of Assisi Parish.
Gloudeman, Francis M. *o.praem.* '91 (ORG)[I] Silverado, CA Norbertine Fathers of Orange Inc.
Gloudeman, Robert J. '64 (MIL) Retired.
Glover, Donald F. *m.m.* '70 (NY)[DD] Maryknoll Maryknoll Fathers and Brothers Retired.
Glover, Francis N. *s.j.* '58 (FgM) New York, NY Society of Jesus.
Glover, Jason A. *s.t.l.* '02 (E)[B] Erie, PA Gannon University.
Glover, Mark '08 (SPR) Springfield, MA St. Catherine of Siena.
Glover, S. Matthew '04 (PRO)[R] Kingston, RI University of Rhode Island Catholic Center.
Glovik, Rev. Msgr. Karl L. '61 (DUB) Retired.
Gluc, Vincent *o.f.m.conv.* '79 (BAL)[Q] Baltimore, MD Immaculate Heart of Mary Friary; [C] Baltimore, MD Archbishop Curley High School.
Glueckert, Leopold *o.carm.* '68 (WDC)[B] Washington, DC Whitefriars Hall.
Glynn, Canon Thomas '64 (STN) Chicago, IL St. Joseph.
Glynn, Edward *s.j.* '67 (BAL)[Q] Baltimore, MD Colombiere Jesuit Community.
Glynn, Francis M. '70 (BO) Allston, MA St. Anthony of Padua.
Glynn, Joseph *c.s.sp.* '76 (SFR) Millbrae, CA St. Dunstan; Long Island City, NY.
Glynn, Martin G. '78 (PAT) Denville, NJ St. Mary's.
Glynn, Robert *s.j.* '91 (FgM) Los Gatos, CA Society of Jesus.
Glynn, Seamus A. '58 (ORG) Anaheim, CA San Antonio de Padua Del Cañon Church Retired.
Glynn, Thomas Joseph '54 (LA) Long Beach, CA Our Lady of Refuge Retired.
Glynn, Rev. Msgr. William F. '47 (BO) Senior Priests. Retired.
Gmerek, Ronald E. '71 (E) Erie, PA Our Mother of Sorrows.
Gnall, Julian '55 (HPM) Retired.
Gnanaraj, Michael '76 (BWN) Brownsville, TX Valley Baptist Health Systems–Brownsville; Brownsville, TX Valley Regional Medical Center; Brownsville, TX

Christ the King.
Gnanaraj, Sengole Thomas '07 (IND) Guilford, IN St. John the Baptist Catholic Church, Dover, Inc.
Gnansegaram, Francis '84 (RVC) Franklin Square, NY St. Catherine of Sienna.
Gnarackatt, Joseph '67 (TR) Brick Town, NJ St. Dominic.
Gniewyk, Eugene '90 (NEW) Fairfield, NJ St. Thomas More.
Gnirk, Lloyd A. '78 (OM) Valley, NE St. John; [B] Omaha, NE Roncalli Catholic High School of Omaha.
Gnoinski, Piotr '05 (CHI) Chicago, IL St. Francis Borgia; Streamwood, IL St. John the Evangelist.
Gobbo, Paolo '94 (SJ) San Jose, CA St. Patrick.
Gober, Christopher M. '00 (CHL) Spruce Pine, NC St. Lucien; Vocations; Linville, NC St. Bernadette.
Gobitas, Rev. Msgr. Gerald E. '75 (ALN) Chancellor; Secretary to the Bishop; Secretariat for Clergy; Priest Personnel Office; College of Consultors; Ex Officio Members; Holy Family Villa for Priests.
Goblirsch, Robert P. '60 (NU) Ortonville, MN St. James; Ortonville, MN St. John; Ortonville, MN St. Joseph; Board of Trustees for Pension Plan for Priests.
Gockel, Guido *m.h.m.* '69 (NY)[HH] New York, NY Catholic Near East Welfare Association (CNEWA).
Goda, Paul J. *s.j.* '66 (SJ)[B] Santa Clara, CA Jesuit Community.
Godagotti, Arogyaiah '99 (FAR) Jamestown, ND St. James Basilica of Jamestown.
Godecker, Jeffrey H. '69 (IND) Indianapolis, IN Christ The King Catholic Church, Indianapolis, Inc.; [O] Indianapolis, IN Butler University.
Godenciuc, Iura '94 (STF) New Haven, CT St. Michael.
Godenciuc, Vasile '81 (STF) Staten Island, NY Holy Trinity.
Godfrey, Donal *s.j.* '92 (SFR)[N] San Francisco, CA Loyola House Jesuit Community.
Godfrey, Joseph J. *s.j.* '69 (PH)[C] Jesuit Fathers; [Y] Philadelphia, PA St. Alphonsus House.
Godfrey, Timothy S. *s.j.* '85 (WDC)[O] Washington, DC The Jesuit Community at Georgetown University.
Godic, Frank G. '73 (CLV) Cleveland, OH Immaculate Conception.
Godin, Normand J. '73 (PRO) Providence, RI St. Agnes.
Godina, Juan Manuel '07 (YAK) Wapato, WA St. Peter Claver; Natural Family Planning Advisory Committee; Natural Family Planning; Respect Life Committee; Social Justice and Human Life Commission.
Godinez, Alejandro (NSH) Shelbyville, TN St. William.
Godinez, Eulices '08 (LEX) Hispanic Ministry.
Godinez, Francisco H. '10 (B) Coeur d'Alene, ID St. Pius X.
Godinez, Librado '05 (NY) Bronx, NY St. Thomas Aquinas.
Godinez, Rodolfo '91 (STA) Williston, FL Holy Family; Hispanic Charismatic Renewal.
Godleski, David A. *s.j.* '98 (WDC)[O] Washington, DC Leonard Neale House.
Godley, Patrick '53 (SEA) Retired.
Goebel, Joseph A. '50 (CLV) Euclid, OH SS. Robert & William Retired.
Goebel, Robert A. *s.j.* '63 (SPK)[J] Spokane, WA Regis Community Retired.
Goebel, Robert W. '74 (CIN) Cincinnati, OH St. Therese, The Little Flower.
Goeckner, Jeffrey H. '95 (SFD) Edwardsville, IL St. Boniface; Alton Deanery; Comite Diocesano de Ministerio Hispano – Diocesan Committee for Hispanic Ministry.
Goedde, Bernard C. '72 (BEL) Nashville, IL Our Lady of Perpetual Help; Pinckneyville, IL St. Mary Magdalen; Office of Youth Ministry.
Goedert, Robert A. *o.p.* '51 (CHI)[N] Chicago, IL St. Pius V Priory.
Goedert, William O. '55 (CHI) Oak Lawn, IL St. Germaine Retired.
Goehring, Rev. Msgr. Raymond J. '64 (LAN) Lansing, MI Resurrection; Tribunal Judges.
Goehring, Rev. Msgr. Raymond (LAN) Retired.
Goeke, James F. *s.j.* '88 (STL)[C] Saint Louis University; [O] St. Louis, MO Bellarmine House of Studies.
Goellen, Richard M. '63 (FAR) Retired.
Goergen, David *m.afr.* '69 (FgM) Washington, DC MISSIONARIES OF AFRICA.
Goergen, Donald *o.p.* '75 (STL)[O] Saint Louis, MO St. Dominic Priory; [B] St. Louis, MO Aquinas Institute of Theology.
Goergen, Michael A. '62 (CHI) Chicago, IL St. Bartholomew; Chicago, IL St. Robert Bellarmine Retired.
Goering, Rev. Msgr. Joseph P. '00 (FAR) Moderator of the Curia; Vicar General; Vicar for Clergy; Corporate Board; Diocesan Finance Council; Arbitration & Conciliation Board; Diocesan College of Consultors.
Goerner, James E. '93 (PH) Upper Darby, PA St. Laurence.
Goertz, Rev. Msgr. Alois J. '48 (SAT)[K] San Antonio, TX Casa De Padres Retired.
Goertz, Bernard C. '52 (AUS) Retired.
Goertz, Howard '77 (AUS) Luling, TX St. John the Evangelist.
Goertz, Jonathan '10 (RIC) Tappahannock, VA St. Timothy.
Goertz, Rev. Msgr. Victor '52 (AUS) Retired.
Goethals, Gregory M. *s.j.* '88 (LA)[F] Los Angeles, CA Loyola High School of Los Angeles.
Goettemoeller, Leonard *c.pp.s* '49 (CIN)[N] Carthagena, OH St. Charles Retired.
Goetz, Donald R. '68 (L) Louisville, KY St. Brigid; Louisville, KY St. James; Defenders of the Bond.
Goetz, Gerald E. *s.j.* '73 (MIL)[P] Milwaukee, WI Jesuit Community at Marquette University.
Goetz, J. Raymond '81 (OWN) Owensboro, KY St. Alphonsus.
Goetz, Joseph W. '60 (CIN) Retired.
Goetz, Martin G. '92 (DAV) Kalona, IA Holy Trinity; Riverside, IA St. Mary of the Assumption; Riverside, IA St. Joseph.
Goff, William P. *c.m.* '66 (PH)[Y].
Gofigan, Paul M. '04 (AGN) Dededo, GU Santa Barbara; El Shaddai (PPFI), Prayer Partner International, Guam Chapter.
Goggin, Cornelius J. '56 (MAN) Retired.
Goggin, John T. '64 (NU) On Duty Outside the Diocese.
Goggins, James K. '94 (DEN) Lakewood, CO St. Bernadette; Deaneries.
Goguen, Rev. Msgr. Francis T. '66 (WOR) Leominster, MA St. Cecilia; Diocesan College of Consultors; Deans.
Gohlke, Nathan '08 (JOL) Leave of Absence.
Gohm, Robert S. '75 (SAG) Bay City, MI Holy Trinity.
Gohring, William '84 (ORL) Special Assignment.
Goin, James A. '92 (OKL) Norman, OK St. Thomas More University Parish.
Goins, James A. '92 (OKL)[K] Norman, OK Campus Ministry for the Archdiocese of Oklahoma City; Campus Ministry, Department of.
Gojuk, Peter P. *o.m.v.* '81 (BO)[B] Boston, MA Our Lady of Grace Seminary; [A] Brighton, MA St. John Seminary.
Golas, Eugene S. '55 (GR) Retired.
Golas, John S. '81 (HRT) Consultors – Canon 1742; Unionville, CT St. Mary; Hartford Vicariate.
Golasinski, Rev. Msgr. James L. '58 (GAL) Houston, TX Annunciation.
Golba, Gregorz '97 (PAT) Sparta, NJ Our Lady of the Lake.
Gold, William '65 (SD) Retired.
Goldade, Leo *o.s.b.m.* '72 (RVC)[N] Glen Cove, NY St. Josaphat's Monastery, Novitiate and Retreat House.
Goldade, Leo *o.s.b.m.* '72 (STF)[B] Glen Cove, NY Basilian Fathers Novitiate of the Order of St. Basil the Great.
Goldasich, Mark '81 (KCK) Tonganoxie, KS Sacred Heart; Newspaper "The Leaven".
Goldbach, Edmund *o.f.m.conv.* '65 (IND) Terre Haute, IN St. Benedict Catholic Church, Terre Haute, Inc.
Goldbach, Peter D. *c.m.* '44 (BRK)[R] Jamaica, NY Reverend John B. Murray, CM, House.
Goldberg, James M. '76 (GBG) Slickville, PA St. Sylvester.
Golden, Edward '61 (ROC) Retired.
Golden, James '48 (DUL) Retired.
Golden, Patrick '96 (RIC) Richmond, VA Cathedral of the Sacred Heart.
Golden, Paul L. *c.m.* '65 (DEN)[N] Denver, CO Congregation of the Mission Western Province: De Paul House.
Golding, Edward '88 (ALB) Delhi, NY St. Peter; Walton, NY St. John the Baptist.
Goldrick, Timothy J. '72 (FR) North Dighton, MA St. Nicholas of Myra Parish.
Gole, Joseph '43 (MIL)[B] Hales Corners, WI Sacred Heart School of Theology; [P] Franklin Sacred Heart at Monastery Lake.
Golemba, Rev. Msgr. Roman '75 (STF) Fall River, MA St. John–the–Baptist; Woonsocket, RI St. Michael.
Golias, Rev. Msgr. Andrew J. '70 (PH) Norristown, PA St. Teresa of Avila.
Goliath, J. Charles *o.s.f.s.* '03 (ALN)[K] Center Valley, PA Oblates of St. Francis de Sales.
Golini, Ronald '68 (NTN) Leave of Absence.
Golish, Robert *m.m.* '53 (NY)[DD] Retired.
Golka, James R. '94 (GI) North Platte, NE St. Patrick; Ongoing Formation for Clergy and Liturgy; Personnel Board.
Golla, Yesu *h.g.n.* '03 (WH) Logan, WV St. Francis of Assisi; Man, WV St. Edmund.
Gollapalli, Alphonse '89 (LR) Nashville, AR St. Martin Church; Hope, AR Our Lady of Good Hope.
Gollatz, Ronald J. '72 (CHI) Wauconda, IL Transfiguration.
Gollob, Timothy A. '58 (DAL) Dallas, TX VA – North Texas Health Care System; Dallas, TX Holy Cross.
Gollob, Timothy A. '58 (SAT) Defenders of the Bond.
Golombek, Rev. Msgr. Robert K. '65 (BUF) Retired.
Goloran, Mauricio O. '84 (LA) Valinda, CA St. Martha.
Golueke, Thomas J. '77 (BAL) Priests Sick or Absent.
Golyzniak, Gregory '98 (COS) Colorado Springs, CO St. Joseph's.
Goman, Ralph J. '64 (STP) Retired.
Gomes, Benedict '69 (KCK) Leawood, KS Curé of Ars.
Gomes, Christopher (BO) Peabody, MA Our Lady of Fatima.
Gomes, Herman *ss.cc.* '78 (HON) Vicars Forane; Kaneohe, HI St. Ann; Presbyteral Council; Clergy Personnel Board.
Gomes, John A. '69 (FR) South Dartmouth, MA St. Mary's.
Gomes, Martin *ss.cc.* '69 (FR)[F] Fairhaven National Center of the Enthronement.
Gomes, Robert M. '66 (CAM) Retired.
Gomes, Ronald A. '87 (BO) Senior Priests. Retired.
Gomes, Stanley '95 (NEW)[B] Seton Hall University; [B] Seton Hall University; Adjunct Clergy Personnel; Ex Officio Members.
Gomes, William J. '69 (RVC) Elmont, NY St. Boniface.
Gomez, Anselmo *c.ss.r.* (WOR) Brazilian Ministry.
Gomez, Anthony J. '98 (LA) Norwalk, CA St. Linus.
Gomez, Aurelio Yanez '74 (NEW) Hillside, NJ St. Catherine of Siena.
Gomez, Carlos '03 (PHX) Phoenix, AZ St. Augustine Roman Catholic Parish.
Gomez, Cesar '98 (WIL) Georgetown, DE St. Michael the Archangel.
Gomez, Edmund '93 (SB) Perris, CA St. James.
Gomez, Edmundo '69 (NY) Bronx, NY St. Helena.
Gomez, Eduardo '07 (BWN)[A] Brownsville, TX The Saint Joseph and Saint Peter Seminary; Olmito, TX Our Heavenly Father.
Gomez, Edwin A. '05 (WOR) Westborough, MA St. Luke the Evangelist; St. Luke.
Gomez, Emerito *o.f.m.* '82 (OAK)[L] Oakland Franciscan Friars of California, (Province of St. Barbara).
Gómez, Enrique '77 (CGS) Las Piedras, PR Inmaculada Concepcion.
Gomez, F. Augustin Anda (BO) Billerica, MA St. Theresa of Lisieux.
Gomez, Francisco *o.m.i.* '07 (FgM) Washington, DC AMERICAN OBLATE MISSIONS.
Gomez, Francisco '09 (BGP) Darien, CT St. John.
Gomez, Frank '61 (BWN) Retired.
Gomez, Gustavo '01 (YAK) Cowiche, WA St. Juan Diego; Charismatic Renewal, Spanish.
Gomez, Rev. Msgr. Henry '58 (LA) Retired.
Gomez, Humberto '88 (SAC) Vacaville, CA St. Mary; Priests' Personnel Board, Diocesan.
Gomez, Jerry A. '93 (CAM) Haddon Heights, NJ Church of St. Rose, Haddon Heights, N.J.
Gomez, John J. '07 (BGP) Bridgeport, CT St. Augustine Cathedral.
Gomez, John Jairo '09 (TYL) Graduate Studies.
Gomez, Jorge A. '04 (BWN) Brownsville, TX Holy Family; [A] Brownsville, TX The Saint Joseph and Saint Peter Seminary; Office of the Chancellor; [J] Brownsville, TX University of Texas at Brownsville/Texas Southmost College (UTB/TSC).
Gomez, Jose Roberto '92 (NO) Metairie, LA Our Lady of Divine Providence.
Gomez, Jose '95 (AMA) Amarillo, TX Our Lady of Guadalupe; Advocates.
Gomez, Juan Fernando (CC) Mathis, TX Sacred Heart; Corpus Christi, TX Holy Family.
Gomez, Rev. Msgr. Leo '63 (GLP) Retired.
Gomez, Rev. Msgr. Leo '63 (SFE) Retired.
Gomez, Lorenzo *l.c.* '73 (DET)[T] Clarkston, MI Clarkston Pastoral Center, Inc.; [T] Bloomfield Hills, MI Logos, Inc. (Michigan); [P] Oxford, MI Queen of the Family Retreat Center.
Gomez, Lorenzo *s.d.v.* (PAT) Paterson, NJ St. Gerard Majella; Paterson, NJ St. Michael the Archangel.
Gomez, Miguel '81 (MIA) Hialeah, FL Santa Barbara.
Gomez, Miguel '02 (MRY) On Leave.
Gomez, Orlando Perez *o.s.b.* '01 (RCK)[G] Aurora, IL Marmion Abbey.
Gomez, Orlando '97 (SAC) Roseville, CA St. Rose of Lima.
Gomez, Otoniel J. '90 (PRO) Central Falls, RI Holy Spirit Parish.
Gomez, Rafael '73 (BRK) Woodhaven, NY St. Thomas Apostle; Ozone Park, NY St. Elizabeth.
Gomez, Ramon '85 (OAK) Hayward, CA St. Clement; Deanery #17.
Gomez, Roberto '09 (SJ) San Jose, CA St. Maria Goretti.
Gomez, Romulo Cesar '84 (RVC) Central Islip, NY St. John of God.
Gomez, Silvestre *o.p.* '97 (SJN) Bayamon, PR Santo Domingo de Guzman; Bayamon, PR Nuestra Senora del Perpetuo Socorro.
Gomez, Walter '80 (MO) Air National Guard Chaplains.
Gomez–Baca, Walter S. '80 (SJN) Military Services; Guaynabo–Puerto Nuevo; San Juan, PR San Juan Evangelista.
Gomez–Medina, Oscar '02 (SAC) Presbyteral Council; Sacramento, CA All Hallows; Sacramento, CA St. Peter; College of Consultors.
Gomez–Sosa, Mauricio (SAT) San Antonio, TX St. Agnes.
Gomez del Valle, Jorge *m.sp.s.* '73 (SEA) Mill Creek, WA St. Elizabeth Ann Seton.
Gomez Soto, Oscar Fernando *c.s.b.* '10 (GAL)[O] Sugar Land Basilian Mission Center.

Gómez Urias, Ceferino '65 (SJN) Catano, PR Nuestra Senora del Carmen.
Gomide, Tomaz '71 (RVC) Mineola, NY Corpus Christi.
Gomolski, Joseph T. '81 (WIL) Retired.
Gomori, Mark A. '06 (HPM) Las Vegas, NV St. Gabriel the Archangel.
Gomori, Mark '06 (LAV) Las Vegas, NV St. Elizabeth Ann Seton; Auditors; Pension Committee; Diocesan Advocates.
Goncalves, Miguel Alvamir '95 (BO)[Z] Boston, MA Madonna Queen Shrine.
Gonchar, John Joseph *o.f.m.* '56 (GBG)[H] Uniontown, PA St. Anthony Friary.
Gonda, Gerard *o.s.b.* '80 (CLV)[N] Cleveland, OH; [D] Cleveland, OH Benedictine High School.
Gondek, Albert J. *o.s.f.s.* '66 (CHL) Lexington, NC Our Lady of the Rosary.
Gonderinger, Gerald E. '74 (OM) West Point, NE St. Aloysius; West Point, NE St. Boniface; West Point, NE St. Anthony; West Point, NE Assumption B.V.M.
Gonet, Charles F. '58 (SPR) Retired.
Goni, Galadima G. '72 (SPR) Haydenville, MA Our Lady of the Hills.
Goni, Joaquin *o.a.r.* '40 (LA)[P] Oxnard, CA Order of Augustinian Recollects (O.A.R.), St. Augustine Priory.
Goni, Paul *o.a.r.* '51 (LA)[P] Oxnard, CA Order of Augustinian Recollects (O.A.R.), St. Augustine Priory.
Gonsalves, Anil *o.f.m. cap.* (WH)[L] Charleston, WV Capuchins–St. Anthony Friary; Charleston, WV St. Anthony.
Gonsalves, Israel *o.c.d.* '96 (DEN) Centennial, CO St. Thomas More.
Gonsalves, Joseph *o.f.m.* '11 (GLP) Gallup, NM St. Francis of Assisi.
Gonsalves, Valerian '90 (TLS) Durant, OK St. William.
Gonser, Richard A. '62 (CLV) North Ridgeville, OH St. Julie Billiart.
Gonyo, Lance M. '93 (ROC) Spencerport, NY St. John the Evangelist.
Gonzales, Adam Gregory *o.c.d.* '05 (SB)[L] Redlands, CA El Carmelo Retreat House; [I] Redlands, CA Discalced Carmelites, OCD.
Gonzales, Rev. Msgr. Gabriel '84 (LA) Los Angeles, CA St. Anastasia.
Gonzales, George '71 (SB) Judges Retired.
Gonzales, Loren '89 (PHX) Peoria, AZ St. Charles Borromeo Roman Catholic Parish.
Gonzales, Rev. Msgr. Loreto '78 (LA) Long Beach, CA St. Barnabas.
Gonzales, Randy *c.i.c.m.* '04 (ARL)[H] Arlington, VA Missionhurst, C.I.C.M.–Central House and Provincialate.
Gonzales, Richard '98 (CC) Beeville, TX St. Joseph.
Gonzales, Robert A. '78 (TUC) On Duty Outside the Diocese.
Gonzales, Ronald *s.j.* '03 (SAT) San Antonio, TX Our Lady of Guadalupe.
Gonzales, Vidal '09 (PAT) Succasunna, NJ St. Therese.
Gonzales–Cabrera, Javier '08 (SB) Fontana, CA Kaiser Permanente Hospital.
Gonzalez, Alvaro Pio '03 (PT) Gulf Breeze, FL Saint Sylvester.
Gonzalez, Angel '52 (FRS) Retired.
Gonzalez, Anthony '92 (LA) Santa Monica, CA St. Clement.
Gonzalez, Anthony '93 (NY) Staten Island, NY St. Rita.
Gonzalez, Antonio '50 (FRS) Retired.
Gonzalez, Aquilino D. *o.s.a.* '72 (FgM) Villanova, PA Province of St. Thomas of Villanova (Eastern).
Gonzalez, Arnold J. *c.m.f.* '58 (LA) San Gabriel, CA San Gabriel Mission.
Gonzalez, Arturo M. *o.s.m.* '91 (ELP) El Paso, TX Our Lady of Sorrows.
Gonzalez, Avelino A. '06 (WDC) Washington, DC St. Joseph on Capitol Hill; Office for Ecumenical and Interreligious Affairs.
González, Carlos *s.f.m.* '04 (MGZ) Mayaguez, PR Our Lady of Mt. Carmel.
Gonzalez, Carlos *s.d.w.* '70 (ORL) Retired.
Gonzalez, Charles G. *s.j.* '67 (WDC)[C] Washington, DC Georgetown University; [O] Washington, DC The Jesuit Community at Georgetown University.
Gonzalez, Cristobal Guardado '85 (LA) Rancho Dominguez, CA St. Albert the Great.
Gonzalez, Daniel '92 (TYL) On Duty Outside the Diocese.
Gonzalez, Daniel '92 (SUP) Butternut, WI Immaculate Conception; Park Falls, WI St. Francis of Assisi; Park Falls, WI St. Anthony of Padua.
Gonzalez, Domingo N. '64 (ORL) Lakeland, FL Church of the Resurrection Retired.
Gonzalez, Eliseo *o.a.r.* '03 (NY) Bronx, NY St. John's.
Gonzalez, Elkin '08 (TLS) On Duty Outside the Diocese.
Gonzalez, Emilio '88 (SEA) Lynden, WA St. Joseph.
Gonzalez, Fernando '95 (BWN) Brownsville, TX St. Luke.
Gonzalez, Francisco Javier Garcia '80 (R) Raleigh, NC Cathedral of the Sacred Heart.
Gonzalez, George A. '87 (BWN) Brownsville, TX Jail Ministry; Harlingen, TX Our Lady of the Assumption.
Gonzalez, George G. '67 (SAT) Military Chaplains.
Gonzalez, Geronimo '11 (DEN) Longmont, CO St. John the Baptist.
Gonzalez, Gonzalo *o.s.a.* '49 (SJN) Bayamon, PR San Agustin.
Gonzalez, Ivan '01 (RVC) Shoreham, NY St. Mark.
Gonzalez, J. Eduardo '81 (DAL) Appointed Members; Dallas, TX Cathedral–Santuario de Guadalupe; College of Consultors; At Large Members.
Gonzalez, Jaime '90 (VEN) Fort Myers, FL Jesus the Worker Mission (Jesus Obrero); Fort Myers, FL San Jose Mission.
Gonzalez, Jesus (SJN)[E] San Juan, PR Hospital Hima San Pablo; [E] San Juan, PR Centro Medico de P.R.; Bayamon, PR Santa Elena.
Gonzalez, John Alex '02 (R) Burgaw, NC St. Joseph.
Gonzalez, Jorge L. *s.d.b.* '89 (SJN) Catano, PR San Francisco de Sales.
Gonzalez, Jose Antonio '91 (VEN)[I] Lake Placid, FL Campo San Jose; Deans; Hispanic, Migrant and Spanish Speaking Apostolates; Juventud Hispana (Hispanic Youth Outreach); Sebring, FL St. Catherine; Presbyteral Council.
Gonzalez, Jose de Jesus '08 (B) Blackfoot, ID St. Bernard's.
Gonzalez, Jose Duvan (ATL) Cedartown, GA St. Bernadette.
Gonzalez, Jose G. '54 (SP) St. Petersburg, FL St. Raphael Retired.
Gonzalez, Jose Luis '98 (P) Gresham, OR St. Anne.
Gonzalez, Jose Navarro *m.g.* '75 (LA) Los Angeles, CA St. Paul.
Gonzalez, Jose '69 (SR) Santa Rosa, CA Resurrection.
Gonzalez, Jose (MIL) Milwaukee, WI St. Adalbert; Milwaukee, WI St. Rafael the Archangel.
Gonzalez, Juan Francisco '94 (LA) South El Monte, CA Epiphany.
Gonzalez, Juan J. *s.m.* '82 (BRK) Brooklyn, NY St. Francis of Assisi–St. Blaise.
Gonzalez, Juan Jose *m.sp.s.* '00 (P)[L] Banks, OR Missionaries of the Holy Spirit, M.Sp.S.
Gonzalez, Juan Jose Saliva '90 (PCE) Arroyo, PR Our Lady of Mt. Carmel.
Gonzalez, Juan Rolando *o.f.m.cap.* (MGZ) Aguada, PR Santuario Protomartires de la Concepcion.
Gonzalez, Juan *c.pp.s.* '76 (GRY) East Chicago, IN Our Lady of Guadalupe.
Gonzalez, Julio A. Vera '98 (MGZ) Moca, PR Our Lady of Monserrate.
Gonzalez, Julio Angel '98 (MO) Army National Guard Chaplains.
Gonzalez, Julio *s.f.* '00 (SFE) Chimayo, NM Holy Family.
Gonzalez, Julio '09 (LA) North Hollywood, CA St. Charles Borromeo.
Gonzalez, Lauro *m.n.m.* '94 (DAL) Dallas, TX St. Pius X.
Gonzalez, Lorenzo '03 (RCK) Rockford, IL St. Edward.
Gonzalez, Lorenzo '01 (VEN) Moore Haven, FL St. Joseph the Worker.
Gonzalez, Luis O. '00 (NEW) Newark, NJ St. Augustine's; Newark, NJ St. Columba's.
Gonzalez, Luis P. '94 (NEW) Plainfield, NJ St. Mary.
Gonzalez, Marco A. '06 (AMA) Tulia, TX Church of the Holy Spirit.
Gonzalez, Marcos '94 (LA) Advisory Members to the Commission; Inglewood, CA St. John Chrysostom.
Gonzalez, Mario *o.s.a.* '58 (SJN) Bayamon, PR Ntra. Sra. de la Monserrate; [C] Bayamon, PR Seminario Agustiniano Sto. Tomas De Villanueva.
Gonzalez, Mario '55 (VEN) Retired.
Gonzalez, Miguel A. '98 (ORL) Orlando, FL St. John Vianney; Chairman–Elect; Ex Officio Members; Vicars for Clergy.
Gonzalez, Miguel '06 (YAK) Ephrata, WA St. Rose of Lima; Presbyteral Council Executive Committee.
Gonzalez, Octavio '01 (PCE) Penuelas, PR St. Joseph.
Gonzalez, Octavio '01 (NEW) On Duty Outside the Archdiocese.
Gonzalez, Orestes '86 (POD) Washington.
Gonzalez, P. Carlos '04 (MGZ)[C] Mayaguez, PR Comunidad Belen.
Gonzalez, P. Juis *o.f.m.cap.* '98 (PCE) Ponce, PR Santa Teresita.
Gonzalez, Primitivo '62 (LA) Maywood, CA St. Rose of Lima.
Gonzalez, Rafael J. *c.r.l.* '93 (ARE) Corozal, PR La Milagrosa.
Gonzalez, Ramon *o.p.* '09 (SAT)[P] San Antonio, TX St. Anthony Catholic Student Center at U.T.S.A. 1604 Campus; [L] San Antonio, TX Dominican Priory of San Juan Macias.
Gonzalez, Rev. Msgr. Ricardo '57 (NEW) Orange, NJ St. John's Retired.
Gonzalez, Rodolfo (R) Robbins, NC Saint Juan Diego.
Gonzalez, Rudolph F. '87 (NY) Spring Valley, NY St. Joseph.
Gonzalez, Salvador *o.m.i.* '04 (NOR)[I] Willimantic, CT Immaculata Retreat House; Members; [G] Willimantic, CT Missionary Oblates of Mary Immaculate.
Gonzalez, Salvador '01 (FRS) Fresno, CA St. John Cathedral.
Gonzalez, Tomas '01 (SJN)[C] Rio Piedras, PR Seminario Mayor Regional San Juan Bautista.
Gonzalez–Alba, Rogelio '11 (SB) Riverside, CA Our Lady of Perpetual Help.
Gonzalez–Ballesteros, Rodolfo '88 (TR) Sea Girt, NJ St. Mark.
Gonzalez–Gaytan, Jose Enrique '03 (CHL) Boonville, NC Divine Redeemer (Divino Redentor).
Gonzalez–Gonzalez, Tomas '01 (SJN) Cursillos De Cristiandad.
Gonzalez–Hernandez, Marco Antonio '07 (R) Wilmington, NC St. Mark; Wilmington, NC Christ the King.
Gonzalez–Martinez, Eduardo '98 (DAL)[A] Dallas, TX The Redemptoris Mater House of Formation.
Gonzalez–Medina, Ruben *c.m.f.* (SJN) "El Visitante".
Gonzalez–Torres, Marcos A. '06 (MAN) College of Consultors; Presbyteral Council; Nashua, NH St. Aloysius of Gonzaga.
Gonzalez Chao, Luis '58 (SJN) Retired.
Gonzalez Pola, Antonio '63 (SJN)[A] Bayamon Central University.
Gonzalo, Andrew B. '94 (WDC) Oxon Hill, MD St. Columba.
Good, Daniel F. '10 (MOB) Mobile, AL St. Mary.
Goode, Francis *o.p.* '87 (P) Eugene, OR St. Thomas More Church.
Goode, James *o.f.m.* '72 (FgM)[DD] New York, NY St. Clare Friary; Definitors:; [DD] New York, NY Franciscan Province of the Immaculate Conception; New York, NY Franciscan Province of the Immaculate Conception.
Goode, Rev. Msgr. Joseph J. '73 (PAT) Long Valley, NJ St. Mark the Evangelist; Canonical Advisor; Deans; Catholic Deaf Society; Long Valley, NJ Our Lady of the Mountain.
Goode, Lawrence C. '64 (SFR) East Palo Alto, CA St. Francis of Assisi; [S] East Palo Alto, CA Legion of Mary.
Goode, Michael *c.pp.s.* '79 (KC)[N] Liberty, MO St. Gaspar Society; [J] Liberty, MO Precious Blood Center.
Goode, William F. '60 (WDC) Bowie, MD Ascension Retired.
Goodly, Timothy '93 (LKC) Cameron, LA Our Lady Star of the Sea; Cameron, LA Sacred Heart of Jesus; Diocesan Consultors.
Goodman, Julian '66 (RIC) Retired.
Goodman, Leo M. '91 (HBG) Lancaster, PA Assumption of the Blessed Virgin Mary.
Goodrow, David C. (BO) Natick, MA St. Patrick.
Goodrum, James R. '57 (LFT) Associate Judges Retired.
Goodson, Todd Michael '02 (IND) Indianapolis, IN St. Monica Catholic Church, Indianapolis, Inc.
Goodwin, Calvin R. *f.s.s.p.* '79 (LIN)[A] Denton, NE Our Lady of Guadalupe Seminary; Denton, NE.
Goodwin, Christopher P. '04 (LIN) Advocates; Weston, NE St. John Nepomucene; Presbyteral Council.
Goodwin, James '97 (FAR) Larimore, ND St. Stephen's Church of Larimore; Presbyteral Council; Judges.
Goodwin, Owen F. *ss.cc.* '54 (FR)[F] Fairhaven, MA Damien Residence Retired.
Goodwin, Patrick '69 (OAK) On Medical Leave.
Goodwin, Raymond M. '69 (WOR) Portuguese Ministry; Milford, MA St. Mary of the Assumption.
Goodwin, Robert T. '57 (MAN) Retired.
Goodwin, Thomas L. '85 (CC) On Special Assignment; [I] Corpus Christi, TX Journey to Damascus, Inc.; Ingleside, TX Our Lady of the Assumption.
Goodyear, Robert *s.t.* '75 (JKS) Philadelphia, MS Holy Rosary.
Gooley, Laurence L. *s.j.* '65 (P) Rockaway, OR St. Mary by the Sea.
Goolsby, Gregory D. '93 (ATL) Alpharetta, GA St. Thomas Aquinas; Judges.
Goopio, Jose Rodriguez *s.v.d.* '73 (SB)[I] Riverside, CA Divine Word Seminary.
Gootee, Jason E. '99 (ALX)[I] Natchitoches, LA Northwestern State University; Natchitoches, LA Holy Cross.
Gootee, Paul *s.v.d.* '55 (FgM) Techny, IL.
Gopaul, Antonius P. '97 (BRK) Brooklyn, NY St. Thomas Aquinas.
Goraieb, Charles '91 (PHX) Mesa, AZ Queen of Peace Roman Catholic Parish; Mesa, AZ St. Timothy Roman Catholic Parish; Members.
Gorczyca, Andrzej *m.i.c.* '74 (SPR)[G] Stockbridge, MA Congregation of Marian Fathers of The Immaculate Conception of the Most Blessed Virgin Mary.
Gorczyca, Grzegorz P. '05 (CHI) Palatine, IL St. Theresa.
Gordinier, William J. '58 (ROC) Retired.
Gordon, Charles *c.s.c.* '87 (FTW)[H] Notre Dame Congregation of Holy Cross, United States Province of Priests & Brothers.
Gordon, Charles *s.t.* '67 (FgM) Silver Spring, MD MISSIONARY SERVANTS OF THE MOST HOLY TRINITY.
Gordon, Charles *c.s.c.* '87 (P)[B] University of Portland;

[L] Portland, OR Holy Cross Fathers & Brothers, C.S.C. – University of Portland.
Gordon, Dennis *f.s.s.p.* '08 (SD) San Diego, CA Saint Anne Catholic Parish.
Gordon, Gerald R. *s.j.* '60 (SPK)[B] Spokane, WA Gonzaga University Retired.
Gordon, Gerald *t.o.r.* '69 (FWT) Fort Worth, TX St. Andrew.
Gordon, Gerard '88 (RVC) Chaplains of the Nassau County Police Department; Nassau County Police Department.
Gordon, Rev. Msgr. Gregory W. '88 (LAV) On Duty Outside the Diocese.
Gordon, Jacob A. '06 (TOL) Delphos, OH St. John the Evangelist.
Gordon, James E. '81 (RIC) Richmond, VA Church of the Epiphany.
Gordon, James *i.c.* '69 (SP) Seminole, FL Blessed Sacrament.
Gordon, James *f.s.s.p.* '04 (KCK)[E] Maple Hill, KS St. John Vianney Preparatory School.
Gordon, Rev. Msgr. John B. '85 (MET) Perth Amboy, NJ Our Lady of Hungary; Perth Amboy, NJ La Asuncion; [A] South Amboy, NJ Cardinal McCarrick High School; Deans.
Gordon, John F. '88 (NEW) Nutley, NJ Holy Family.
Gordon, John J. *o.m.i.* '01 (SAT) San Antonio, TX St. Mary.
Gordon, Joseph A. '71 (SFR) Retired.
Gordon, Kevin M. '83 (SUP) On Special or Other Diocesan Assignment; Presbyteral Council & Diocesan Consultors; Diocesan Coordinator of Health Affairs; Personnel Placement Board; Bayfield, WI Holy Family; Cornucopia, WI St. Ann; Bayfield, WI St. Joseph; Bayfield, WI St. Francis; Washburn, WI St. Louis.
Gordon, Terrence *f.s.s.p.* (OM) Omaha, NE Immaculate Conception, B.V.M.
Gore, Aidan *o.s.b.* '11 (SFE)[H] Pecos, NM Our Lady of Guadalupe Abbey.
Gore, William R. *o.s.f.s.* '69 (FgM)[J] Wilmington, DE DeSales House; Wilmington, DE OBLATES OF ST. FRANCIS DE SALES MISSIONS.
Gorecho, Welthy '99 (WIL)[J] Dover, DE Oblate Apostles of the Two Hearts.
Gorena, Pedro *o.ss.t.* (SJN) Bayamon, PR Ascension Del Senor; [F] Toa Alta, PR Hogar Santisima Trinidad.
Gorges, Bernard X. '95 (WCH) Chanute, KS St. Patrick; Chanute, KS St. Joseph.
Gorges, Peter '68 (JUN) Diocesan Consultors Retired.
Gorham, Francis X. *o.m.i.* '58 (BO)[X] Tewksbury, MA Immaculate Heart of Mary Residence.
Gori, Peter G. *o.s.a.* (BO) Andover, MA St. Augustine; Court Advocate/Respondent; Canonical Affairs Committee; Presbyteral Council.
Goring, Mark J. '02 (GAL)[S] Houston, TX Catholic Charismatic Center.
Gorka, Thaddeus '88 (PH) Philadelphia, PA St. Adalbert.
Gorman, Charles '54 (GF) Retired.
Gorman, Cyril *o.s.b.* '90 (SCL)[I] Collegeville St. John's Abbey, of the Order of St. Benedict.
Gorman, Edward M. *o.p.* '92 (MO) Navy Reserve Chaplains.
Gorman, Rev. Msgr. Francis P. '59 (NY) Sleepy Hollow, NY St. Teresa of Avila.
Gorman, James P. '73 (PH) Philadelphia, PA Nativity of the Blessed Virgin Mary.
Gorman, James '81 (STP) Special Assignment.
Gorman, John E. *s.d.s.* '69 (MIL)[P] Milwaukee Salvatorian Provincial Offices.
Gorman, John '58 (SB) Retired.
Gorman, Joseph F. '55 (HRT) Waterbury, CT St. Leo the Great Retired.
Gorman, Kevin D. *o.s.b.* '51 (PEO)[A] Peru, IL St. Bede Abbey Retired.
Gorman, Michael J. '80 (LC) Special Assignment; Vicars General; Ecclesiastical Notaries; Diocesan Judges; Ex Officio; St. Joseph's Priest Fund, Inc., (Benevolent Society); [H] La Crosse, WI Holy Cross (Seminary) Diocesan Center; Moderator of the Curia; Consultors.
Gorman, Richard F. '82 (NY)[E] Bronx, NY Cardinal Spellman High School; Prison Apostolate.
Gorman, Robert G. '80 (MET) Old Bridge, NJ St. Ambrose; Charismatic Movement.
Gorman, Rody Ignatius '55 (LA) Huntington Park, CA St. Matthias Retired.
Gorman, Thomas J. '59 (TOL) Retired.
Gorman, William A. '73 (ALB) Dolgeville, NY St. Joseph; Newport, NY St. John the Baptist.
Gorman, William N. '76 (MOB) Dauphin Island, AL St. Edmund–by–the–Sea.
Gormley, Brendan '07 (NY) Bronx, NY St. Barnabas.
Gormley, Charles E. '51 (PH) Bala Cynwyd, PA St. Matthias Retired.
Gormley, George *s.v.d.* '07 (BLX)[D] Bay St. Louis, MS Southern Province of St. Augustine – Provincial Offices; Bay Saint Louis, MS; [D] Bay St. Louis, MS St. Augustine's Residence.
Gormley, Gerard '85 (SR) Arcata, CA St. Mary's; Clergy Personnel Committee.
Gormley, James W. '54 (PH) Retired.
Gormley, Kevin '64 (JC) Marshall, MO St. Peter.
Gormley, Raymond P. '92 (CAM) Deanery Representatives; Runnemede, NJ Holy Child Parish, Runnemede, N.J.
Gormley, William J. *c.m.* '49 (PH)[Y].
Gorney, Joseph *c.ss.r.* '51 (ORL)[F] New Smyrna Beach, FL St. Alphonsus Villa–Redemptorist Fathers and Brothers Retired.
Gorny, Ed *g.h.m.* '68 (CIN)[N] Cincinnati Headquarters of Glenmary Home Missioners Retired.
Gorny, Edward V. *g.h.m.* '68 (SAV) Retired.
Gorny, Tomasz '10 (SPR) Greenfield, MA Holy Trinity.
Gorospe, Paterno '66 (NEW) Teaneck, NJ Holy Name Hospital; [F] School of Nursing.
Gorowski, Roman *c.m.* '72 (HRT) Derby, CT St. Michael the Archangel.
Gorsic, Gregor '97 (JOL) Romeoville, IL St. Andrew the Apostle.
Gorski, Eugene F. *c.s.c.* '60 (FTW)[B] University of Notre Dame Du Lac; [H] Notre Dame, IN Holy Cross Community, Corby Hall, University of Notre Dame.
Gorski, Rev. Msgr. J. Donald '59 (CHR) Retired.
Gorski, John F. *m.m.* '63 (FgM) Maryknoll, NY MARYKNOLL.
Gorski, John J. '64 (CLV) Avon, OH Holy Trinity Retired.
Gorski, Lawrence E. '75 (CHI) Chicago, IL Our Lady of Grace.
Gorski, Robert E. '80 (MAN) Manchester, NH St. Pius X; College of Consultors; Priest Personnel Board; Propagation of the Faith; Moderator of the Curia; Presbyteral Council; Real Estate Board; Staff.
Gorski, Terrence *o.f.m.* '75 (BWN) La Grulla, TX Holy Family.
Gorton, Timothy J. '82 (PRO) Woonsocket, RI St. Agatha; Woonsocket, RI Precious Blood.
Gosciniak, Dariusz '92 (HRT) New Britain, CT Holy Cross.
Gosma, Robert D. '59 (MIL) Retired.
Gosnell, David H. '65 (GRY) Bishop's Council of Priests Retired.
Gosnell, Stephen D. '78 (BAL)[K] Baltimore, MD Mercy Health Services Inc.; Special Assignment.
Gosselin, Andre L. *s.m.* '64 (WDC)[O] Washington, DC Marist Center.
Gosselin, Fernand L. *m.m.* '70 (NY)[DD] Retired.
Gosselin, Rev. Msgr. Homer P. '69 (SPR) Episcopal Vicars; Ludlow, MA Saint Elizabeth Parish; Presbyteral Council.
Gosselin, Joseph *m.s.* '65 (ORL) Orlando, FL Blessed Trinity.
Gosselin, Larry *o.f.m.* '81 (MRY)[F] San Miguel, CA Novitiate House for the Franciscan Friars, O.F.M.; [H] San Miguel, CA San Miguel Retreat House; [F] San Miguel, CA Franciscan Friars, O.F.M.; San Miguel, CA San Miguel.
Gosselin, Rt. Rev. Lawrence '76 (NTN) Presbyteral Council.
Gosselin, Richard R. '59 (BO) Senior Priests. Retired.
Gossett, Michael '11 (STU) St. Clairsville, OH St. Mary's.
Gossman, John A. '71 (DUB) Marion, IA St. Joseph; Mount Vernon, IA St. John the Baptist; Springville, IA St. Isidore; Anamosa, IA St. Patrick; Deans.
Goth, Dennis J. '84 (LFT) Muncie, IN St. Lawrence.
Gothie, George J. '67 (PAT) Hopatcong, NJ St. Jude's.
Gothman, August '93 (CR) Warroad, MN St. Mary's; Commission on Building and Planning; Commission on Liturgy, Sacred Music and Art; Pastoral Office of Worship/RCIA.
Gotimer, Rev. Msgr. James E. '53 (BRK) Retired.
Gott, Camillus *o.f.m.conv.* '77 (IND)[J] Mount St. Francis, IN Province of Our Lady of Consolation, Inc.
Gott, Camillus *o.f.m.conv.* (FTW)[H] Mishawaka, IN St. Francis of Assisi Novitiate.
Gotta, Paul A. '06 (HRT) Broad Brook, CT St. Catherine; East Windsor, CT St. Philip's.
Gottemoeller, Mark '76 (IND) Mooresville, IN St. Thomas More Catholic Church, Mooresville, Inc.
Gottschalk, David *o.f.m.cap.* '69 (DEN)[N] Denver, CO St. Francis of Assisi Friary.
Gottschalk, Matthew *o.f.m.cap.* '53 (MIL)[Y] Milwaukee, WI House of Peace.
Gotwalt, Joseph F. '65 (HBG) Hanover, PA St. Joseph; Deans.
Goudreau, George W. '48 (PRT) Retired.
Goudreau, Rev. Msgr. Joseph L. '63 (PRT) Retired.
Goudreau, Paul '60 (SP) Retired.
Gouger, John E.P. *c.ss.r.* '65 (GAL) Houston, TX Holy Ghost.
Gouin, Joseph O. '65 (MAR) Kingsford, MI American Martyrs.
Gould, Clayton '81 (LR) Dardanelle, AR St. Augustine.
Gould, Rev. Msgr. James C. *s.j.* '74 (MI) Former Prelate.
Gould, Rev. Msgr. James C. *s.j.* (MI).
Gould, James C. *s.j.* '74 (FgM) New York, NY Society of Jesus.
Gould, James R. '81 (ARL) Warrenton, VA St. John the Evangelist.
Gould, Lawrence *s.a.c.* '76 (MO) DEPARTMENT OF VETERANS AFFAIRS HOSPITALS AND CHAPLAINS.
Gould, Lawrence *s.a.c.* '76 (SFR) San Francisco, CA St. Monica; Veterans' Hospital.
Gould, Louis J. '62 (WOR) Retired.
Gould, Michael *m.m.* '54 (NY)[DD] Retired.
Gould, Shawn '10 (CHI) Chicago, IL St. Alphonsus.
Goulding, Laurence *g.h.m.* '62 (CIN)[N] Cincinnati Headquarters of Glenmary Home Missioners Retired.
Gouldrick, John W. *c.m.* '69 (FgM) Philadelphia, PA Eastern Province.
Gouldrick, John W. *c.m.* '69 (BUF)[N] Niagara University, NY Vincentian Community at Niagara University; [C] Niagara University, NY Niagara University.
Goulet, Daniel R. '07 (MO) Military Chaplains; Army Chaplains.
Goulet, Raymond O. '57 (BO) Senior Priests. Retired.
Goulet, Xavier *o.f.m.conv.* (TOL) Carey, OH Our Lady of Consolation, Basilica–National Shrine.
Gournas, John Victor '10 (R) New Bern, NC St. Paul.
Gousse, Paul M. '99 (MAN) Gonic, NH St. Leo; Rochester, NH Our Lady of the Holy Rosary.
Gouthro, Arthur *s.a.* '69 (NY)[DD] Garrison Franciscan Friars of the Atonement, Minister General Office.
Governale, Russell *o.f.m.conv.* '88 (BRK) Elmhurst, NY St. Adalbert; Definitors:; Presbyteral Council.
Govin, Lazarus J. '08 (MIA) Fort Lauderdale, FL St. Clement.
Govindu, Balaswamy '77 (SR) Point Arena, CA St. Aloysius.
Govorchin, Vincent '55 (SLC) Retired.
Gow, John '08 (RCK) Dixon, IL St. Patrick.
Gowen, Daniel '89 (TR) Avon By The Sea, NJ St. Elizabeth.
Gower, James M. '53 (PRT) Retired.
Gower, Peter J. '84 (PRO) Warren, RI St. Mary of the Bay.
Goyette, Giles R. *m.m.a.* '82 (SAM)[B] Petersham, MA Maronite Monks of Adoration Most Holy Trinity Monastery.
Goyo, Jimwell '89 (DAL) Dallas, TX St. James.
Gozaloff, Rev. Msgr. Paul J. '56 (WDC) Retired.
Graap, Augustine *o.carm.* '66 (NY) Otisville, NY Otisville Correctional Facility; Poughkeepsie, NY Hudson River Psychiatric Center.
Graap, Augustine *o.carm.* (NY) Poughkeepsie, NY Our Lady Health of the Sick; Prison Apostolate.
Grab, Michael J. '77 (HBG) Enola, PA Our Lady of Lourdes.
Grabert, Colman *o.s.b.* '65 (IND)[K] Saint Meinrad, IN St. Meinrad Archabbey.
Grabish, Rev. Msgr. John J. '72 (ALN) Allentown, PA Sacred Heart of Jesus.
Grabner, Donald *o.s.b.* '54 (KC)[A] Conception, MO Conception Seminary College; [J] Conception, MO Conception Abbey.
Grabner, Eugene W. '59 (WCH) Retired.
Grabner, Kenneth E. *c.s.c.* '60 (FTW)[H] Notre Dame, IN Holy Cross Village; [H] Notre Dame Congregation of Holy Cross, United States Province of Priests & Brothers.
Grabowski, Dennis '76 (Y) Retired.
Grabowski, Eugene M. '89 (R) Retired.
Grabowski, Walter P. '81 (BUF) Eden, NY Immaculate Conception; North Collins, NY Holy Spirit.
Grabowsky, Rev. Msgr. Myron '67 (PHU) Shenandoah, PA St. Nicholas; Shenandoah, PA St. Michael's.
Grabrian, Dennis '70 (COS) On Duty Outside Diocese.
Grabrian, John '70 (DEN) Lakewood, CO Christ on the Mountain Parish.
Grace, Edward D. '67 (CHI) Chicago, IL Queen of All Saints Basilica; Vicars for Senior Priests.
Grace, Gerald '65 (PMB) Advocates; Highland Beach, FL St. Lucy; Consultors; Elected Members.
Grace, Hugh R. '64 (NY) Wesley Hills, NY St. Boniface.
Grace, James N. '59 (CHI) Retired.
Grace, John A. '79 (RIC) Blacksburg, VA St. Mary.
Grace, John J. '48 (SAC) South Lake Tahoe, CA St. Theresa Retired.
Grace, John J. '50 (CHI) Chicago, IL St. Tarcissus Retired.
Grace, John M. '88 (MAN) Nashua, NH Parish of the Resurrection.
Grace, John *o.s.a.* '62 (ORG) Special Assignment.
Grace, Joseph W. '53 (MO) U.S. Veteran's Hospital; DEPARTMENT OF VETERANS AFFAIRS HOSPITALS AND CHAPLAINS Retired.
Grace, Peter *c.p.* '72 (BRK)[R] Jamaica, NY Immaculate Conception Monastery.
Grace, Thomas A. *c.m.* '64 (STL)[O] Perryville, MO Congregation of the Mission.
Gracey, John '93 (FRS) Bishop, CA Our Lady of Perpetual Help.
Gracz, Rev. Msgr. Henry C. '65 (ATL) Atlanta, GA Shrine of the Immaculate Conception; Advocates; Vicars for Clergy.
Graczyk, Carl *o.f.m.* '73 (PH) Philadelphia, PA St. Jerome; [Y] Philadelphia, PA St. Pius X Residence.
Graczyk, Randolph *o.f.m.cap.* '68 (GF) Pryor, MT St.

Charles Borromeo Church.
Graden, John L. *o.s.f.s.* '76 (BUF)[S] Stella Niagara, NY DeSales Resources and Ministries, Inc.; Niagara Falls, NY Holy Family of Jesus, Mary and Joseph.
Gradilone, Rev. Msgr. Thomas J. '50 (BRK)[R] Douglaston, NY Bishop Mugavero Residence Retired.
Grady, Bernard C. '68 (DUB) Hampton, IA St. Patrick; Hampton, IA St. Mary; Deans; Stewardship Committee.
Grady, Brian D. '00 (RCK) Vicar for Clergy and Religious; Ministry to Priests Program; Priest Personnel; Crystal Lake, IL St. Elizabeth Ann Seton; Special Assignment.
Grady, Francis *s.s.c.* '63 (OM)[J] St. Columbans Missionary Society of St. Columban Retired.
Grady, Francis *s.s.c.* '63 (PRO)[O] Bristol, RI St. Columban's Retirement House.
Grady, John P. *m.m.* '55 (NY)[DD] Retired.
Grady, Michael '94 (MIA) Fort Lauderdale, FL St. Jerome.
Grady, Peter W. '53 (FAR) Retired.
Graebe, Brian '11 (NY) LaGrangeville, NY Blessed Kateri Tekakwitha.
Graef, Rev. Msgr. Franz '57 (SHP) Judges; Censor of Books Retired.
Graehler, Kenneth '63 (EVN) Retired.
Graf, Gary M. '84 (CHI) Chicago, IL St. Gall.
Graf, Henry C. '49 (PH) Retired.
Graf, James W. '72 (L) Raywick, KY St. Francis Xavier Church; Lebanon, KY St. Charles.
Graf, Rev. Msgr. John W. '74 (PH) Absent on Sick Leave.
Graf, Paul '82 (LFT)[C] Lafayette, IN Franciscan St. Elizabeth Health–Lafayette Central.
Graf, William E. '60 (ROC) Censores Librorum; Staff; Ministry to Priests Retired.
Graff, Francis C. '65 (PIT) Retired.
Graff, Joseph P. '76 (GLD) Harbor Springs, MI Holy Cross; Harbor Springs, MI St. Ignatius; Harbor Springs, MI Holy Childhood of Jesus; Cross Village, MI St. Nicholas; Ecumenical and Interreligious Affairs, Delegate for.
Graff, Timothy G. '85 (NEW) Archdiocesan Commission on Justice and Peace; Department of Human Concerns; Youth and Young Adult Ministries; Archdiocesan Girl Scouts; [N] Kearny, NJ Archdiocesan Youth Retreat Center; Harrison, NJ Holy Cross; Public Policy Committee of the New Jersey Catholic Conference; Elected Members.
Graffis, Joseph T. '71 (L) Louisville, KY St. Edward.
Grafsky, George J. '71 (STP) Le Sueur, MN St. Anne.
Graham, Edgar *s.j.* '54 (PH)[Y] Loyola Center and Manresa Hall.
Graham, George Nelson (LC) New Lisbon, WI Our Lady of the Lake; New Lisbon, WI St. Paul.
Graham, Rev. Msgr. George P. '52 (RVC) Levittown, NY St. Bernard; Censors of Books; Priests' Retirement Board Retired.
Graham, J. David '91 (MEM) Memphis, TN St. Anne's; College of Consultors; Presbyteral Council.
Graham, James G. '66 (PIT) Pittsburgh, PA St. Lawrence O'Toole.
Graham, Rev. Msgr. James J. '73 (PH) Havertown, PA St. Denis; Defenders of the Bond.
Graham, James K. '93 (SJ) San Jose, CA St. Elias; San Jose, CA St. John Vianney.
Graham, Jerry D. *s.j.* '00 (B) DeSmet, ID Sacred Heart.
Graham, John J. '90 (BO) Arlington, MA Saint Agnes.
Graham, Rev. Msgr. John K. '74 (NY) Bronx, NY St. Raymond; Canon 1742 Panel of Pastors.
Graham, Michael J. *s.j.* '88 (CIN)[D] Cincinnati, OH Xavier University; [N] Cincinnati, OH Jesuit Community at Xavier University.
Graham, Rev. Msgr. Neil '59 (NY) White Plains, NY St. John the Evangelist.
Graham, Rev. Msgr. Thomas A. '62 (BRK) Rosedale, NY St. Pius X.
Graham, Walter F. *c.m.* '49 (PH)[Y].
Graham, William C. '76 (DUL)[A] Duluth, MN College of St. Scholastica.
Graham, Rev. Msgr. William P. '65 (CAM) Retired.
Graham, William *o.f.m.cap.* (BAL) Judicial Vicar; Baltimore, MD St. Ambrose; [Q] Baltimore, MD St. Ambrose Friary.
Grajales, David Vargas '02 (SJN) Trujillo Alto, PR San Francisco de Asis.
Grajeda, Miguel Angel '97 (MRY) Watsonville, CA St. Patrick; Clergy Personnel Board; Vicar for Hispanic Clergy.
Grajek, Lawrence '57 (SB) Retired.
Grala, Paul *s.o.l.t.* (SEA) Sedro Woolley, WA Immaculate Heart of Mary.
Gralapp, Robert W. '64 (SC) Manning, IA Sacred Heart; Manning, IA Sacred Heart.
Gramaje, Arthur *c.m.f.* '94 (PHX) Prescott, AZ Sacred Heart Roman Catholic Parish.
Gramata, Raymond C. '70 (E) Bradford, PA St. Bernard.
Grambow, Arnold J. '69 (MAR) Retired.
Gramigna, Francis J. '64 (CAM) Retired.
Gramlich, Anthony *m.i.c.* '02 (SPR)[G] Stockbridge, MA Association of Marian Helpers, Marian Helpers Center.
Grams, Rev. Msgr. Douglas L. '87 (NU) New Ulm, MN St. Mary; Vicar General; Associate Judges; College of Consultors; Committee on Parishes; Corporate Board; Priest Personnel; Priest Personnel Board; Bishop's Delegate in Matters Pertaining to Sexual Misconduct; Board of Trustees for Pension Plan for Priests; On Special or Other Diocesan Assignment; Priests' Council.
Gramza, Ronald J. '73 (MIL) Racine, WI St. Richard of Chichester; [Y] Racine, WI NewBridges, Ltd.
Granadino, David F. '81 (LA) On Administrative Leave.
Granado, Jason '08 (AGN) Agat, GU Our Lady of Mount Carmel.
Granados, Carlos E. '88 (ARE) Vega Baja, PR N.S. de la Providencia.
Granados, John J. '98 (BRK) Brooklyn, NY St. Rosalia–Regina Pacis.
Granados, Jorge '05 (YAK) Mattawa, WA Our Lady of the Desert.
Granata, Rev. Msgr. Joseph P. '75 (RVC) Huntington Station, NY St. Hugh of Lincoln; Presbyteral Council.
Granato, John *s.m.* '06 (HRT) Torrington, CT St. Francis of Assisi; Torrington, CT St. Mary; Torrington, CT St. Peter; Torrington, CT Sacred Heart.
Granato, Rev. Msgr. Joseph J. '55 (NEW) Newark, NJ St. Lucy's Retired.
Grande, Kenneth J. '78 (BRK) Brooklyn, NY St. Nicholas; Brooklyn, NY St. Francis of Paola; Brooklyn, NY St. Cecilia.
Grandon, Douglas '08 (PEO) On Duty Outside the Diocese.
Grandon, Douglas '08 (DEN) Denver, CO Church of the Risen Christ.
Grandpre, Louis '61 (DET) Retired.
Grandstrand, Charles P. '66 (NEW) Bergen Pascack Valley Deanery 2P.
Graner, Thomas '94 (FAR) Rugby, ND St. Mary's Church of Knox; Rugby, ND St. Theresa, Little Flower Church of Rugby; Rural Life.
Graney, William F. '71 (WIL) Wilmington, DE Parish of the Resurrection.
Granfield, Patrick *o.s.b.* '57 (WDC)[C] Catholic University of America, The; [O] Washington, DC St. Anselm's Abbey Retired.
Granger, Sean '07 (MIL) Racine, WI St. Lucy; Racine, WI St. Joseph.
Granillo, Paul C. '97 (SB) On Leave of Absence.
Granito, Mark E. '98 (SFE) Tijeras, NM Holy Child.
Grankauskas, Paul M. '00 (ARL) Reston, VA St. Thomas a Becket.
Grankowski, Zbigniew '83 (DET) Detroit, MI St. Cunegunda; Dearborn, MI St. Barbara.
Granstrand, Charles P. '66 (NEW) Park Ridge, NJ Our Lady of Mercy.
Grant, Benedict *f.p.o.* '08 (BO)[U] Lawrence, MA Franciscans of Primitive Observance; On Duty Outside the Archdiocese.
Grant, James A. '66 (PH) Bala Cynwyd, PA St. Matthias.
Grant, Jeffery A. '82 (SFD) Springfield, IL Blessed Sacrament; Board of Catholic Education.
Grant, Paul G. '84 (POD) New Rochelle.
Grant, Paul '84 (NY)[II] Overlook Study Center.
Grant, Robert J. '93 (HRT) Thomaston, CT St. Thomas.
Grant, Robert L. '80 (DAV)[A] St. Ambrose University; Blue Grass, IA St. Andrew.
Grant, Robert '84 (DM) On Duty Outside the Diocese.
Grant, W. Douglas '80 (PRO) On Duty Outside the Diocese.
Grant, William D. '86 (LIN) Apostolate to the Spanish Speaking.
Grant, William David '86 (LIN) Evangelization Committee; Lincoln, NE Cristo Rey.
Grant, Zachary '56 (NY)[DD] Yonkers, NY St. Clare Friary.
Grantz, Leon *c.p.* '46 (L)[L] Louisville, KY Sacred Heart Retreat.
Granzotto, Peter *s.d.b.* '57 (NY) Port Chester, NY Corpus Christi.
Grapes, Jesse (RIC)[B] Richmond, VA Benedictine High School of Richmond, Inc.
Grappoli, Frank B. *s.x.* '63 (PAT)[N] Wayne, NJ Xaverian Missionary Fathers; Wayne, NJ XAVERIAN MISSIONARY FATHERS.
Grasher, Al '86 (SPK) Deer Park, WA St. Mary Presentation; Members.
Grasing, John '88 (WIL) Middletown, DE St. Joseph.
Grass, Aloysius P. *c.m.* '51 (PH)[Y].
Grassel, Martin *o.s.b.* '04 (P)[L] St. Benedict, OR Mt. Angel Abbey; [Q] St. Benedict, OR The Abbey Foundation of Oregon.
Grasselli, Rev. Msgr. Renato '94 (NEW)[A] Kearny, NJ Redemptoris Mater Archdiocesan Missionary Seminary; Members; [P] Kearny, NJ Eucharistic Shrine of the Adorable Face of Jesus.
Grassi, Dominic J. '73 (CHI) Chicago, IL St. Gertrude.
Grassi, Timothy J. '00 (WH) Thomas, WV St. Thomas Aquinas.
Grassl, Joseph A. '50 (LC) Mosinee, WI St. Francis Xavier; Mosinee, WI St. John the Baptist.
Grasso, Aldo *o.s.j.* '44 (MRY)[F] Shrine of St. Joseph.
Grasso, Anthony R. *c.s.c.* '78 (SCR)[B] Holy Cross Community.
Grasso, Anthony R. *c.s.c.* '78 (FTW)[H] Notre Dame Congregation of Holy Cross, United States Province of Priests & Brothers.
Grasso, Joseph A. *c.pp.s.* '91 (MO) DEPARTMENT OF VETERANS AFFAIRS HOSPITALS AND CHAPLAINS.
Grasso, Joseph *c.pp.s.* '91 (ALB) Veterans' Administration Hospital.
Grasso, Richard '63 (PAT) On Duty Outside the Diocese.
Grathwohl, John M. '55 (KAL) Retired.
Gratkowski, Eugene W. '67 (CHI) River Grove, IL St. Cyprian.
Grattaroti, Robert A. '62 (WOR) Charlton City, MA St. Joseph's; Cursillo.
Grauls, Paul *s.d.b.* '62 (WDC) Washington, DC Nativity.
Grave, Miguel de Peralta '96 (ATL) Special or Other Archdiocesan Assignment.
Graven, Thomas J. '68 (STU) Maynard, OH St. Joseph; Maynard, OH St. Stanislaus.
Graves, Robert *s.d.w* '87 (ORL) Retired.
Grawe, Michael *o.f.m.* '70 (STL)[O] St. Louis, MO Franciscan Friary of St. Anthony of Padua.
Gray, Daniel J. '76 (PRO) Portsmouth, RI St. Anthony.
Gray, Edward J. *c.ss.r.* '58 (ORL) New Smyrna Beach, FL Sacred Heart.
Gray, Howard J. *s.j.* '55 (WDC)[O] Washington, DC The Jesuit Community at Georgetown University.
Gray, James C. '88 (STL) Maplewood, MO Immaculate Conception; Barnes – Jewish Hospital.
Gray, Rev. Msgr. Jason A. '97 (PEO) Judges; Peoria, IL St. Vincent De Paul; Judicial Vicar.
Gray, John W. '58 (PRO) Retired.
Gray, John '86 (PT) Retired.
Gray, Joseph B. '09 (KAL) Albion, MI St. John the Evangelist.
Gray, Jude J. *o.s.b.* '68 (MAN)[K] Manchester, NH St. Anselm Abbey.
Gray, Michael '08 (LFT) Lafayette, IN St. Lawrence.
Gray, Peter W. *s.s.* '79 (BAL)[Q] Baltimore Society of St. Sulpice, Province of the United States.
Gray, Rev. Msgr. Philip A. '60 (SCR)[M] Dunmore, PA Villa St. Joseph Retired.
Gray, Richard *m.s.s.a.* (BAL) Westernport, MD St. Peter.
Gray, Richard (BAL) Frostburg, MD St. Michael; Frostburg, MD St. Ann; Midland, MD St. Joseph; [T] Frostburg, MD St. Michael School Endowment Trust.
Gray, Robert B. '57 (L) Louisville, KY St. Elizabeth of Hungary; Louisville, KY St. Therese Retired.
Gray, Robert '88 (SJ) On Leave of Absence.
Gray, S. Matthew '11 (CHR) Columbia, SC St. Joseph.
Gray, Sherman '70 (BGP) Leave of Absence.
Graziadio, Rev. Msgr. Domenick T. '66 (RVC) Plainview, NY St. Pius X; Judges for Interdiocesan Tribunal.
Graziano, Gerard J. '61 (NEW) Hackensack, NJ Immaculate Conception.
Graziano, J. Damien '67 (JOL) Missions Office/Propagation of the Faith Retired.
Graziano, Peter N. '63 (FR) Retired.
Grazulis, Antanas *s.j.* '78 (LIT) Lithuanian Jesuit Province.
Grazulis, Antanas *s.j.* '78 (CHI)[N] Lemont, IL Baltic Jesuits Advancement Office.
Grazulis, Antanas *s.j.* (GRY) Beverly Shores, IN St. Ann.
Grbavac, Charbel R. *o.praem.* '06 (ORG) Council of Priests; [I] Silverado, CA Norbertine Fathers of Orange Inc.
Grbes, Jozo *o.f.m.* '93 (CHI) Chicago, IL St. Jerome.
Greaney, Thomas M. *o.s.m.* '70 (CHI)[N] Chicago, IL Monastery of Our Lady of Sorrows.
Greatorex, Robert W. '57 (LC)[I] Stevens Point, WI St. Joseph Motherhouse Retired.
Greaves, Gerald F. '74 (NEW) Livingston, NJ St. Raphael; Part–time Staff/Advocates/Procurators.
Greaves, John G. '58 (PRO) Retired.
Greb, John '06 (PHX) Phoenix, AZ St. Joseph Roman Catholic Parish.
Greb, Michael P. *o.f.m.cap.* '89 (PIT) Pittsburgh, PA Our Lady of the Angels.
Grecco, Robert J. '93 (PIT) Pittsburgh, PA Sacred Heart.
Grecia, Rholando '98 (HT) Larose, LA Our Lady of the Rosary; Cut–Off, LA Sacred Heart.
Greco, Anthony F. '79 (WIL) Retired.
Greco, Evan *o.f.m.* (PAT)[L] Totowa, NJ St. Joseph's Home for the Elderly.
Greco, Michael *o.f.m.cap.* '06 (BRK)[R] Brooklyn, NY St. Michael's Friary.
Greco, Raymond *o.s.b.* '63 (MRY)[F] San Luis Obispo, CA Men's Residence Retired.
Greco, Robert *o.carm.* '55 (NY) Middletown, NY Our Lady of Mt. Carmel.
Greeley, Andrew M. '54 (CHI) Retired.
Greeley, Rev. Msgr. Joseph F. '74 (LA) Lakewood, CA

St. Pancratius.
Green, Austin E. *o.p.* '53 (NO) Retired.
Green, Bernard *s.d.s.* '73 (PHX) Tempe, AZ Our Lady of Mt. Carmel Roman Catholic Parish.
Green, Charles C. '95 (WDC) Retired.
Green, David E. '88 (PRO) East Providence, RI St. Martha.
Green, Fred J. *s.j.* '58 (FgM) Los Gatos, CA Society of Jesus.
Green, Rev. Msgr. Gerard L. '56 (BUF) Retired.
Green, Gregory A. *c.s.c.* '62 (FTW)[B] University of Notre Dame Du Lac; [H] Notre Dame, IN Holy Cross Community, Corby Hall, University of Notre Dame.
Green, John '10 (DEN) Centennial, CO St. Thomas More.
Green, Matthew E. *l.c.* (BO) Gloucester, MA Holy Family.
Green, Michael R. *o.s.b.* '70 (DET)[K] Detroit, MI St. Sylvester Monastery; [B] Oxford, MI St. Benedict Monastery; Oxford, MI.
Green, Romuald *o.f.m.* '55 (WDC) Washington, DC; [O] Washington, DC Franciscan Monastery USA Inc.
Green, Ronald L. '96 (MRY) Santa Cruz, CA Star of the Sea.
Green, Ronald L. *m.m.* '85 (NY)[DD] Maryknoll Maryknoll Fathers and Brothers.
Green, Ronald Lee *m.m.* '85 (ALB) Worcester, NY St. Joseph.
Green, Rev. Msgr. Thomas J. '63 (BGP) On Duty Outside the Diocese; [C] Catholic University of America, The.
Green, Thomas P. *s.j.* '61 (NY) New York, NY St. Aloysius.
Green, Thomas P. *s.j.* '61 (BUF) Buffalo, NY St. Michael.
Green, William H. '63 (SUP) Retired.
Greene, Daniel '58 (YAK) Retired.
Greene, Gordon L. '94 (KAL) Otsego, MI St. Margaret.
Greene, John C. '85 (GLD) Special Assignment.
Greene, John L. '76 (SFR) San Francisco, CA St. Monica; San Francisco, CA Our Lady of Fatima Byzantine Catholic Church; San Francisco Fire Department.
Greene, Michael M. '79 (BRK) On Leave/Unassigned.
Greene, Michael *c.p.* '82 (BRK)[T] Jamaica, NY Bishop Molloy Retreat House; [R] Jamaica, NY Immaculate Conception Monastery.
Greene, Padraig '76 (OAK) Pleasanton, CA The Catholic Community of Pleasanton.
Greene, Rev. Msgr. Richard '65 (LAF) New Iberia, LA Sacred Heart of Jesus; Ecumenism.
Greene, Thomas P. *s.j.* '07 (FgM)[X] Washington, DC Jesuit Missions, Inc.; [X] Washington, DC Jesuit Social and International Ministries–National Office; Washington, DC National Headquarters; Washington, DC.
Greene, Rev. Msgr. William L. '50 (BR) Judges Retired.
Greenfield, David J. '08 (MAD) Pardeeville, WI St. Andrew; Pardeeville, WI St. Mary of the Most Holy Rosary; Pardeeville, WI Holy Family Parish.
Greenfield, James J. *o.s.f.s.* '90 (WDC)[U] Washington, DC George Washington Univ. Newman Center; Wilmington, DE.
Greenfield, James J. *o.s.f.s.* '90 (WIL) Wilmington, DE Oblates of St. Francis de Sales (O.S.F.S.); [P] Wilmington, DE Brisson Fund; [J] Wilmington, DE Wilmington–Philadelphia Province of the Oblates of St. Francis de Sales.
Greenhalgh, Donald C. '84 (ARL) Arlington, VA St. Ann.
Greenlaw, Martin F. '68 (SFR) Retired.
Greenleaf, Daniel P. '95 (PRT) Special or Other Diocesan Assignment.
Greenleaf, Daniel (WDC)[A] Washington, DC Theological College of the Catholic University of America.
Greenough, Patrick *o.f.m.conv.* '87 (CHI)[N] Chicago, IL Conventual Franciscans of St. Bonaventure Province; [P] Libertyville, IL Marytown, U.S. National Center of the Militia of the Immaculata Movement; Chicago, IL Province of Saint Bonaventure; Chicago, IL; [N] Libertyville, IL Marytown, Our Lady of Fatima Friary.
Greenway, George G. '87 (SPR) Retired.
Greenway, George G. '87 (SAV) Retired.
Greenwell, Charles C. '82 (SAN) San Angelo, TX Holy Angels; Defensores Vinculi.
Greenwell, Joseph M. *c.ss.r* '48 (STL)[O] Liguori, MO St. Clement Health Care Center Retired.
Greenwell, Michael A. *o.carm.* '79 (SFR) San Francisco, CA St. Teresa; St. Mary's Medical Center; [J] San Francisco, CA St. Mary's Medical Center.
Greer, Bradley '09 (STU)[F] Steubenville, OH Trinity Medical Center, West; Hospitals; Steubenville, OH Triumph of the Cross; Steubenville, OH Holy Name Cathedral; Priests Personnel Board; Assistant Directors.
Greer, G. Michael '81 (COV) Covington, KY St. John.
Greer, Michael '75 (MIA) Lauderdale–by–the–Sea, FL Assumption Church; Deans and Deaneries; Archdiocesan Council of Catholic Women; Worship & Spiritual Life Commission; Appointed by the Archbishop.
Grega, Bernard F. '62 (ALT) Colver, PA Holy Family.
Grega, Rudolf *f.s.s.p.* '06 (RIC) Richmond, VA St. Joseph.
Gregoire, Jocelyn *c.s.sp.* '86 (PIT)[B] Pittsburgh, PA Duquesne University of the Holy Spirit.
Gregoire, Paul L. '55 (MAN) Retired.
Gregoire, Wilfrid G. '56 (PRO) Retired.
Gregor, Robert M. *c.p.m.* '00 (L)[D] Louisville, KY Holy Angels Academy, Inc.
Gregorek, Joseph C. '65 (E)[B] Erie, PA Gannon University; Deans.
Gregorek, Stan M. '66 (PIT) Cecil, PA St. Mary; [Q] Pittsburgh, PA Cursillo Movement–Diocese of Pittsburgh.
Gregori, Emidio O. '58 (BGP) Retired.
Gregorio, Robert J. '68 (CAM) Somers Point, NJ St. Joseph's Church, Somers Point, N.J.
Gregoris, Nicholas L. '97 (SCR) On Duty Outside the Diocese.
Gregory, James T. '99 (HRT) Oakville, CT St. Mary Magdalen; [D] Waterbury, CT Sacred Heart High School.
Gregory, Kenneth '73 (ALB) Grafton, NY Parish of Our Lady of the Snow; Albany Medical Center Hospital; Special Assignment; [G] Watervliet, NY St. Colman's Home.
Gregory, Lourduraj Gally (SLC) Salt Lake City, UT Saint Patrick LLC 241; Salt Lake City, UT Veterans Administration Hospital.
Gregory, Peter A. '73 (SPR) Pittsfield, MA St. Charles.
Gregory, Rev. Msgr. Robert S. '69 (KC) Consultors; Deans; Finance Council; Kansas City, MO Cathedral of Immaculate Conception.
Grehl, Paul F. *o.s.f.s.* '60 (LAN) Manitou Beach, MI St. Mary on the Lake; [B] Jackson, MI Lumen Christi Catholic High School.
Greig, Rev. Msgr. Harry D. '76 (LKC) Lake Charles, LA St. Mary of the Lake; Defenders of the Bond.
Greig, Rev. Msgr. Kenneth R. '67 (BEA) Diocesan College of Consultors; Diocesan Judges; Groves, TX Immaculate Conception; Groves, TX St. Peter the Apostle.
Grein, Blane *o.f.m.* '62 (GLP) Chinle, AZ Our Lady of Fatima; Lukachukai, AZ St. Isabel; Ministry Formation Program.
Greiner, James A. '63 (OKL) Mustang, OK Church of the Holy Spirit.
Greiner, Robert '93 (BAK) Council of Priests and Diocesan Consultors; Prineville, OR St. Joseph.
Greisen, Thomas A. '82 (OM) Omaha, NE St. Rose; Servant Minister.
Greiten, Gregory J. '92 (MIL) Milwaukee, WI St. Bernadette.
Greiwe, Edward *o.s.c.* '64 (SCL)[I] Onamia, MN Crosier Priory.
Grek, Richard *c.r.* '67 (CHI) Park Ridge, IL Mary, Seat of Wisdom.
Greka, Rev. Msgr. David '62 (AMA) Retired.
Grelak, Andrew T. '71 (BO) Chelsea, MA St. Stanislaus.
Grell, Loras K. '96 (LIN) Lawrence, NE Sacred Heart; Diocesan Area CCD Directors.
Grellinger, R. Michael '62 (MIL) Retired.
Grembocki, Joseph L. '71 (ALN) Slatington, PA Assumption B.V.M.
Gremillion, Rick '98 (ALX) Catholic Relief Services; [H] Alexandria, LA Catholic Charities and Special Ministries; Tioga, LA Immaculate Heart of Mary; Director of Catholic Charities and Special Ministries.
Gremmels, John '91 (FWT) On Leave of Absence.
Grenache, Claude *a.a.* '66 (BO)[U] Boston, MA Assumptionist Center; Bentley College.
Grendler, Albert O. '59 (SC) Retired.
Grenham, John P. '80 (NO) Slidell, LA Our Lady of Lourdes.
Grenier, Louis L. *s.j.* '49 (FgM) Watertown, MA Society of Jesus.
Grennan, James '44 (SAL) Retired.
Grennan, Larry '66 (SAL) Board of Trustees.
Grennan, Lawrence E. '66 (SAL) Clay Center, KS Saints Peter and Paul Parish; Clay Center, KS St. Anthony Parish.
Grennon, John *o.c.d.* '97 (MIL)[P] Hubertus, WI Retreat Center.
Grenon, Paul R. '78 (PRO) Coventry, RI SS. John and Paul; Deans.
Gres–Gayer, Jacques '69 (WDC)[C] Catholic University of America, The.
Greschel, Mark '01 (CHI) Military Chaplains; Army Chaplains.
Greskiewicz, Joseph A. '69 (SCR) Plains, PA SS. Peter and Paul; Diocesan Building Commission.
Gresko, Gregory *o.s.b.* '05 (RIC)[K] Richmond, VA Mary Mother of the Church Abbey.
Greskoviak, Neri *o.f.m.* '63 (PEO) Metamora, IL St. Mary of Lourdes.
Greskowiak, David '09 (FRS) Bakersfield, CA St. Francis of Assisi.
Gresock, Thomas G. '85 (BUF) Retired.
Gretchko, A. Edward '72 (PBR) Massillon, OH St. Nicholas.
Gretchko, A. Edward '72 (Y) Massillon, OH Saint Mary; [P] Massillon, OH National Shrine of St. Dymphna.
Gretz, James R. '94 (PIT) Worship Commission; Worship, Dept. for; Pittsburgh, PA SS. Simon and Jude.
Grevatch, William N. '64 (LC) Wausau, WI St. Michael; Consultors; Wausau, WI Church of the Resurrection; Ex Officio.
Greving, Daniel M. '97 (SC) Merrill, IA Assumption Church; Merrill, IA St. Joseph's; Priests' Personnel Board.
Grewe, Michael W. '79 (OM) Gretna, NE St. Patrick; Vicar General; Consultors; Finance Council; Cemeteries; Ex Officio (Consultors).
Grey, Michael T. *c.s.sp* '79 (GAL)[A] Houston, TX St. Mary's Seminary.
Greytak, William '56 (HEL) Boulder, MT St. Catherine; Boulder River School and Hospital.
Grib, Philip J. *s.j.* '72 (CHI) Chicago, IL St. Eugene; [D] Chicago, IL St. Ignatius Jesuit Community.
Grib, Robert I. *s.j.* '72 (CHI)[D] Chicago, IL St. Ignatius Jesuit Community; Chicago, IL St. Francis Borgia.
Gribbin, Rev. Msgr. Robert C. '47 (HBG) Abbottstown, PA Immaculate Heart of Mary Retired.
Gribble, G. Michael '81 (COL) Columbus, OH St. Joseph Cathedral; Diocesan Judges; Priests Continuing Education.
Gribble, Richard E. *c.s.c.* '89 (FR)[A] North Easton, MA Stonehill College; [A] North Easton, MA Holy Cross Fathers Religious.
Gribble, Richard E. *c.s.c.* '89 (FTW)[H] Notre Dame Congregation of Holy Cross, United States Province of Priests & Brothers.
Gribbon, Michael C. '81 (BRK) Rockaway Point, NY Blessed Trinity Roman Catholic Church.
Gribik, John '89 (SJP) Ford City, PA St. Mary; Jeannette, PA St. Demetrius; Presbyters.
Grice, Edward M. '80 (MO) Army Reserve Chaplains; Westwego, LA Our Lady of Prompt Succor.
Gricius, Aurelijus *o.f.m.* '96 (PRT)[I] Kennebunk, ME St. Anthony's Friary.
Gricoski, Thomas *o.s.b.* '10 (IND)[K] Saint Meinrad St. Meinrad Archabbey.
Grieco, Frank M. '01 (RVC) East Northport, NY St. Anthony of Padua.
Grieco, John '11 (POD) Chicago.
Grieco, Michael S. '83 (LA) Oxnard, CA Santa Clara.
Grieco, Rev. Msgr. Nicholas V. '59 (BGP)[O] Stamford, CT The Catherine Dennis Keefe Queen of the Clergy Retired Priests' Residence Retired.
Grieman, Gerald G. '79 (STP) Retired.
Griener, George E. *s.j.* '73 (OAK)[A] Berkeley, CA Jesuit School of Theology of Santa Clara University (Berkeley, California Campus); [L] Berkeley, CA Jesuit Fathers and Brothers.
Gries, Andrew *o.c.s.o.* '59 (ARL)[H] Berryville, VA Cistercian Abbey of Our Lady of the Holy Cross.
Gries, Eugene *o.praem.* '68 (SFE)[H] Albuquerque, NM Santa Maria de la Vid Priory.
Gries, Jason '04 (EVN) Vincennes, IN Sacred Heart; Special Assignment; Associate Directors; Bicknell, IN St. Philip Neri.
Gries, Jeremy M. '09 (IND) Rushville, IN St. Mary Catholic Church, Rushville, Inc.
Griesbach, Rev. Msgr. John '76 (FRS) On Special Assignment; [F] Three Rivers, CA St. Anthony's Retreat Center; St. Anthony Retreat Center.
Griesbach, Seamus P. '07 (PRT) Bangor, ME Saint Paul the Apostle Parish.
Griesedieck, Rev. Msgr. Edmund O. '65 (STL)[A] St. Louis, MO Kenrick School of Theology; [V] St. Ann, MO St. Louis Catholic Charismatic Renewal; Charismatic Renewal Retired.
Griesemer, Edward *s.c.j.* '57 (MIL)[W] West Allis, WI Milwaukee Archdiocesan Holy Name Union; [P] Franklin, WI Sacred Heart at Monastery Lake.
Griesgraber, Paul Gerard '06 (LA) Reseda, CA St. Catherine of Siena; Van Nuys, CA St. Bridget of Sweden.
Griffey, M. Brendan '74 (JC) Columbia Catholic Hospital Ministry; Milan, MO St. Mary.
Griffin, Carter H. '04 (WDC) Vocations for Men; Pastoral Center Special Ministries; Priest Council; Blessed John Paul II Seminary; [A] Washington, DC Blessed John Paul II Seminary.
Griffin, Charles R. '56 (COL) Chillicothe, OH St. Peter; Chillicothe, OH Ross Correctional Institution Retired.
Griffin, David G. '66 (BUF) Retired.
Griffin, David R. *o.s.b.* '76 (ALT)[I] University Park, PA Penn State University, University Park; [J] University Park, PA Penn State Catholic Community.
Griffin, David R. *o.s.b.* '76 (GBG)[H] Latrobe, PA Saint Vincent Archabbey.
Griffin, Edward V. *o.s.a.* '49 (PH)[Y] Villanova, PA St. Thomas Monastery.
Griffin, James C. '82 (RIC) Virginia Beach, VA Catholic Church of St. Mark.
Griffin, John C. '77 (MRY) Carmel, CA San Carlos Borromeo Basilica; Advocates; Contact Persons.
Griffin, John '72 (SR) Rohnert Park, CA St. Elizabeth Seton.
Griffin, Joseph J. *o.s.f.s.* '56 (WIL)[J] Childs, MD

Retirement and Assisted Care Facility Retired.
Griffin, Joseph M. '82 (SAG) Argyle, MI St. Joseph; Ubly, MI St. Columbkille; Ubly, MI St. John the Evangelist.
Griffin, Michael J. '49 (MAN) Retired.
Griffin, Michael '90 (SFS) Pierre, SD SS. Peter and Paul; Communications Office – "Bishop's Bulletin"; Personnel Board.
Griffin, Michael *o.c.d.* '50 (MIL)[P] Hubertus, WI Discalced Carmelite Monastery – Holy Hill Basilica of the National Shrine of Mary, Help of Christians, Holy Hill.
Griffin, Patrick E. '67 (STP) Retired.
Griffin, Patrick J. *c.m.* '79 (NY)[C] Staten Island, NY St. John's University Staten Island Campus.
Griffin, Patrick J. *c.m.* '79 (BRK)[R] Jamaica, NY Reverend John B. Murray, CM, House.
Griffin, Robert E. *s.j.* '61 (SJ)[M] Los Gatos, CA Sacred Heart Jesuit Center.
Griffin, Thomas A. *s.j.* '58 (NO)[R] New Orleans, LA Ignatius Residence Retired.
Griffin, Thomas E. *o.s.a.* '83 (DET) Grosse Pointe Park, MI St. Clare of Montefalco.
Griffin, Thomas *o.s.a.* '83 (MO) Navy Reserve Chaplains.
Griffin, Thomas (LA)[J] Los Angeles, CA St. Vincent Medical Center.
Griffin–Smolenski, Thomas J. *s.j.* '00 (LA)[P] Los Angeles, CA Colombiere House.
Griffin–Smolenski, Tomas *s.j.* '00 (LA) Hospital Chaplains.
Griffith, Daniel F. '02 (STP) College of Consultors; [C] St. Paul, MN University of St. Thomas.
Griffith, Darragh '97 (ATL) Marietta, GA Holy Family.
Griffith, Sidney H. '65 (WDC)[C] Catholic University of America, The; [O] Riverdale, MD Holy Spirit Missionary Cenacle.
Griffith, Sydney '61 (BAL) Glen Burnie, MD Holy Trinity.
Griffith, Thomas *s.v.d.* '69 (BO)[U] Duxbury, MA Society of the Divine Word.
Griffiths, Charles L. '05 (TR) Trenton, NJ Divine Mercy Parish.
Griffiths, John M. '76 (CHI) Chicago, IL Queen of Angels; Judges.
Griffiths, John (WIN) Defenders of the Bond.
Griffiths, John (CHY) Defenders of the Bond.
Griffiths, Thomas *c.p.* '57 (BRK)[R] Jamaica, NY Immaculate Conception Monastery Retired.
Griffiths, Thomas *s.v.d.* (BO) Presbyteral Council.
Grifone, Fabian *o.f.m.* '54 (NY) New York, NY Most Precious Blood.
Grigassy, Daniel P. *o.f.m.* '77 (PAT) Paterson, NJ St. Bonaventure.
Grigus, John P. *o.f.m.conv.* '89 (PEO) Peoria, IL Holy Family.
Grile, Harry *c.ss.r.* '68 (FgM) Denver, CO; Denver, CO Denver Province.
Grile, Harry *c.ss.r.* '68 (DEN)[N] Denver, CO The Redemptorists/Denver Province.
Grile, Patrick *c.ss.r.* '71 (GR)[L] Grand Rapids, MI The Society of the Redemptorists of the City of Grand Rapids; Grand Rapids, MI St. Alphonsus.
Grilliot, Joseph J. *c.pp.s* '11 (LA) Los Angeles, CA St. Agnes.
Grilliot, Thomas J. '76 (CIN) Piqua, OH St. Mary Retired.
Grimaldi, Joseph A. '90 (HON) Retired.
Grimaldi, Joseph A. '90 (MO) Defenders of the Bond.
Grimaldi, Joseph R. '83 (BRK) Brooklyn, NY St. Mark; Diocesan Consultors; Brooklyn, NY St. Margaret Mary; Diocesan Real Estate Board.
Grimaldi, Robert B. *s.j.* '68 (FgM) Los Gatos, CA Society of Jesus.
Grimalia, Rev. Msgr. Vincent J. '68 (SCR) On Special or Other Diocesan Assignment; [K] Wilkes–Barre, PA Saint Luke's Villa.
Grimard, Rocky *o.m.i.* '91 (SAT)[C] Oblate School of Theology; [N] San Antonio, TX Oblate Renewal Center; Retreats, Men.
Grimes, John C. '00 (MET) Old Bridge, NJ St. Ambrose.
Grimes, John J. (BO) Dover, MA Most Precious Blood; Sherborn, MA St. Theresa of Lisieux.
Grimes, Price D. '88 (OKL) Absent on Sick Leave.
Grimes, Raymond P. '55 (PBL) Retired.
Grimes, Robert R. *s.j.* '84 (NY)[C] Bronx, NY Fordham University; [DD] Cardinal Spellman Hall, Jesuit Community.
Grimm, John S. '02 (WIL) Associate Directors; New Castle, DE Holy Spirit.
Grimm, John S. '02 (NEW) Censores Librorum.
Grimm, Robert *s.j.* '76 (SEA)[M] Seattle, WA Arrupe Jesuit Community at Seattle University.
Grimm, William J. *m.m.* '77 (FgM) Maryknoll, NY MARYKNOLL.
Grimme, D. Timothy '77 (ALT) Altoona, PA St. Therese of the Child Jesus.
Grimmer, James A. '54 (BUF) Retired.
Griner, William S. '61 (L) Priest Personnel Commission Retired.
Grinnell, Horace H. '74 (ARL) Arlington, VA St. Charles Borromeo.
Grinnen, Jack *t.o.r.* '72 (ALT)[G] Loretto, PA St. Francis Friary at Mount Assisi.
Grinsell, John *s.d.b.* '71 (NEW) Orange, NJ Our Lady of the Valley.
Grippe, Louis A. '69 (SCR) Hazleton, PA Church of the Most Precious Blood.
Grippo, Robert F. '72 (NY) Bronx, NY St. Theresa of the Infant Jesus; Canon 1742 Panel of Pastors.
Gripshover, Ronald J. '96 (ARL) Fredericksburg, VA St. Patrick; Advocates.
Grise, Clifford J. '45 (BGP)[O] Stamford, CT The Catherine Dennis Keefe Queen of the Clergy Retired Priests' Residence Retired.
Grispino, Frank *s.m.* '56 (DET)[K] Livonia, MI Marist Fathers & Brothers Community.
Grissom, Joel *s.m.* '03 (BWN) Brownsville, TX San Felipe de Jesus.
Griswold, Edward J. '73 (TR) On Duty Outside the Diocese.
Griswold, Edward '73 (BAL)[A] Baltimore, MD St. Mary's Seminary and University; [A] Baltimore, MD St. Mary's Seminary and University.
Grix, Robert *o.f.m.cap.* (PAT)[N] Ringwood, NJ Holy Name Friary, Inc.
Grizzelle–Reid, Paul *s.c.j.* '72 (MIL)[P] Hales Corners, WI Priests of the Sacred Heart.
Grizzelle–Reid, Paul *s.c.j.* '72 (STA) Middleburg, FL St. Luke.
Groarke, Francis P. '73 (PH) Glen Mills, PA St. Thomas the Apostle.
Grob, Jeffrey S. '92 (CHI) Elmwood Park, IL St. Celestine; Associate Vicars.
Grochowski, Bernard J. '63 (WOR) Retired.
Grodecki, Henry *c.m.* '75 (SPC) Neosho, MO St. Canera.
Groden, Michael F. '65 (BO) Senior Priests. Retired.
Grodnicki, Robert S. '88 (TR) College of Consultors; Toms River, NJ St. Luke.
Groeschel, Benedict J. *c.f.r.* '59 (BRK)[M] Brooklyn, NY St. Francis Home for Boys.
Groeschel, Benedict J. *c.f.r.* '59 (NEW)[J] Hoboken, NJ Good Counsel, Inc. (St. Francis Home); [J] Hoboken, NJ Good Counsel, Inc.
Groeschel, Benedict Joseph *c.f.r.* '59 (NY)[A] Yonkers, NY St. Joseph's Seminary; [DD] Bronx, NY Franciscan Friars of the Renewal; [FF] Larchmont, NY Trinity Retreat; [FF] Larchmont, NY St. Francis Retreat, Inc.; [R] Spring Valley, NY Good Counsel, Inc.; [HH] Cause:; [HH] Larchmont, NY The Oratory of Divine Love, Inc.; [HH] Bronx, NY Franciscan Renewal Ministries, Inc.
Grogan, Gerald P. '60 (VEN) Retired.
Grogan, J. Clyde '68 (BEL) Red Bud, IL St. Patrick.
Grogan, Richard P. *s.j.* '73 (NY)[DD] New York, NY Murray–Weigel Hall.
Grogan, Todd '90 (CIN) Cincinnati, OH Annunciation of the Blessed Virgin Mary.
Grogan, Vincent B. *o.f.m.* '63 (PAT)[N] Butler, NJ St. Anthony Friary; Advocates; Provincial Councilors.
Grogan, William E. '83 (PH) Philadelphia, PA All Saints.
Grogan, William P. '76 (CHI) Chicago, IL St. Ignatius; Health/Hospital Affairs; Bio Ethics Commission.
Groh, Christopher '79 (JOL) Joliet, IL St. Mary Magdalene.
Grohe, Eugene J. *c.ss.r.* '50 (NY) Esopus, NY Sacred Heart; [DD] Esopus, NY Redemptorist Priests and Brothers C.Ss.R. (Province of Baltimore).
Groher, Robert C. '66 (GB) Retired.
Grollmes, Eugene E. *s.j.* '64 (STL)[O] St. Louis, MO Jesuit Community Corporation at Saint Louis University – Jesuit Hall.
Grollmes, Eugene *s.j.* '64 (STL)[C] Saint Louis University.
Gromadzki, Michael '01 (MET) Clinton, NJ Immaculate Conception.
Gromadzki, Stanley G. '89 (MET) South River, NJ St. Mary of Ostrabrama.
Gron, Ryszard '88 (CHI) Chicago, IL St. Constance.
Groncki, Rev. Msgr. Richard F. '66 (NEW) Members; Paramus, NJ Church of the Annunciation.
Grondin, Charles R. '03 (PRO) East Greenwich, RI Our Lady of Mercy.
Groner, Eric *s.v.d.* '96 (BEA) Cleveland, TX St. Mary.
Groner, John W. '71 (JC) St. Robert, MO St. Jude; St. Robert, MO St. Robert Bellarmine.
Gronert, Stephen F. '86 (WCH) Eureka, KS Sacred Heart; Eureka, KS St. John; Eureka, KS St. Teresa of Avila.
Gronski, Peter '71 (STF)[F] Stamford, CT Missionary Sisters of Mother of God.
Groody, Daniel G. *c.s.c.* '93 (FTW)[B] University of Notre Dame Du Lac; [H] Notre Dame, IN Holy Cross Community, Corby Hall, University of Notre Dame; Consultants.
Groover, Henry *o.p.* '92 (AUS)[G] Austin, TX Dominican Friars of Austin.
Gros, Edwin L. *s.j.* '80 (ELP) El Paso, TX Sacred Heart.
Gros, Paul A. '09 (BR) Paulina, LA St. Michael the Archangel; Paulina, LA Most Sacred Heart of Jesus; Paulina, LA St. Joseph; Presbyteral Council.
Grosch, Robert D. '74 (GF) Billings, MT St. Patrick Co–Cathedral; Judicial Vicar; Clerical Benefit Association; Holy Cross Cemetery (Billings).
Grosch, Robert (HEL) Promoter of Justice.
Groshek, Rev. Msgr. Richard '62 (LAN) Vicar General Retired.
Grosko, Joseph R. '59 (PIT) West Mifflin, PA St. Agnes; West Mifflin, PA Holy Trinity.
Gross, Barry R. '75 (WDC)[E] Olney, MD Our Lady of Good Counsel High School.
Gross, Barry '75 (LFT) On Duty Outside the Diocese.
Gross, Brian P. '10 (BIS) Bismarck, ND Cathedral of the Holy Spirit.
Gross, David C. '10 (GR) Big Rapids, MI St. Mary's; Big Rapids, MI St. Paul's Campus Parish.
Gross, Donald L. '59 (LFT) Ambia, IN St. Mary; Fowler, IN Sacred Heart of Jesus; Deans; Defenders of the Bond; Members; Diocesan Consultors.
Gross, G. Robert '07 (DUB)[A] Dubuque, IA Seminary of St. Pius X; Deanery Representatives; Dubuque, IA Church of the Nativity; Seminarians; Seminary Admissions and Advisory Board.
Gross, Gary L. '83 (MO) Army Chaplains.
Gross, Gary '83 (LIN) On Duty Outside the Diocese.
Gross, Gerard *o.c.s.o.* '78 (ATL)[F] Conyers, GA The Monastery of the Holy Spirit.
Gross, James '99 (FAR) Velva, ND Sts. Peter & Paul Church of Karlsruhe; Velva, ND St. Cecilia's Church of Velva.
Gross, Joseph J. *o.ss.t* '70 (BAL)[Q] In Residence – Holy Trinity Monastery Baltimore.
Gross, Kenneth A. '71 (DM) Greenfield, IA St. John; Massena, IA St. Patrick.
Gross, Lawrence F. '66 (ROC) Retired.
Gross, Lee W. '87 (ARL) On Duty Outside the Diocese.
Gross, Lee W. '87 (BAL)[A] Emmitsburg, MD Mount St. Mary's Seminary.
Gross, Matthew *o.f.m.cap.* '61 (DEN)[N] Denver, CO St. Francis of Assisi Friary.
Gross, Ralph C. '70 (MIL) Dousman, WI St. Bruno; Archdiocesan Consultors; Archdiocesan Council of Priests.
Gross, Richard C. '62 (NU) Retired.
Gross, Richard J. '63 (FAR) Retired.
Gross, Richard K. *s.j.* '76 (BO)[U] Boston The Society of Jesus of New England–Provincial Offices.
Gross, Stephen *o.f.m.conv.* '69 (MRY)[F] Arroyo Grande, CA St. Joseph Cupertino Province, Provincial Center.
Gross, Steve *o.f.m.conv.* '69 (LA) Hermosa Beach, CA Our Lady of Guadalupe.
Gross, Thomas L. '75 (HON) Kailua, HI St. John Vianney.
Gross, Rev. Msgr. Val '63 (FAR) Fargo, ND Holy Spirit Church of Fargo Retired.
Grossenburg, Tony '99 (RC) Lemmon, SD St. Mary's.
Grossi, Anthony J. *o.s.b.* '99 (GBG)[H] Latrobe, PA Saint Vincent Archabbey.
Grosskopf, Albert A. *s.j.* '83 (SFR) San Francisco, CA St. Ignatius; [N] San Francisco, CA Loyola House Jesuit Community.
Grosso, James D. '79 (BGP) Stamford, CT St. Leo.
Grote, Alan W. '82 (GBG) Legion of Mary; New Kensington, PA St. Joseph; New Kensington, PA St. Mary of Czestochowa.
Groth, Rev. Msgr. Ronald '69 (LKC) Lake Charles, LA Sacred Heart of Jesus; Presbyteral Council; Lake Charles, LA Immaculate Heart of Mary; Diocesan Consultors; Development Office.
Grous, Rev. Msgr. Albin J. '87 (PH) Drexel Hill, PA St. Andrew.
Grove, Kevin G. *c.s.c.* '10 (FTW)[H] Notre Dame Congregation of Holy Cross, United States Province of Priests & Brothers.
Grove, Stanley *m.s.a.* '00 (HRT) Waterbury, CT Basilica of the Immaculate Conception.
Grove, Stanley *m.s.a.* '00 (NOR)[G] Cromwell Society of the Missionaries of the Holy Apostles.
Grovenburg, Gregg *s.j.* '88 (NO)[C] New Orleans, LA Loyola University New Orleans.
Grover, David A. '83 (CAM) Swedesboro, NJ St. Clare of Assisi Parish, Gibbstown, N.J.; Deanery Representatives; Consultants.
Grover, Peter *o.m.v.* '90 (BO)[B] Boston, MA Our Lady of Grace Seminary; [Z] Boston, MA St. Clement Archdiocesan Eucharistic Shrine.
Groves, Edmund '49 (PHX) Retired.
Grubb, Paul *s.j.* '08 (P)[D].
Grubba, Dale W. '66 (MAD) Princeton, WI St. James; Princeton, WI St. John the Baptist; Deaneries.
Gruben, John A. *o.a.r.* '74 (LA) Montebello, CA St. Benedict.
Gruben, John *o.a.r.* '74 (NY)[B] Suffern, NY Tagaste Monastery.
Gruber, Rev. Msgr. Aloys Conrad '67 (STO) Oakdale, CA St. Mary of the Annunciation Church (Pastor of).
Gruber, Anthony P. '70 (NOR) Retired.
Gruber, Eric J. '91 (ALN) Catasauqua, PA St. Andrew; Catasauqua, PA St. Lawrence the Martyr.
Gruber, Kevin W. '80 (RVC) Bohemia, NY St. John

Nepomucene.
Gruber, Mark F.X. *o.s.b.* '83 (GBG)[H] Latrobe, PA Saint Vincent Archabbey.
Grubisch, Rev. Msgr. Donald W. '53 (WIN) Diocese of Winona Incardination Board Retired.
Gruden, William J. '79 (SAG) Bay City, MI St. James; Territorial Vicars.
Grudowski, Rev. Msgr. Robert J. '61 (PH) Holland, PA St. Bede the Venerable Retired.
Gruenbauer, Hans H. '76 (CIN) On Special and Archdiocesan Assignment.
Gruenes, Bernard '98 (SCL) Office of Diaconate Retired.
Grullon, Carlos Manuel '07 (PCE) Guayanilla, PR Immaculate Conception.
Grummer, James E. *s.j.* '82 (MIL)[P] Milwaukee Jesuit Provincial Office, Wisconsin Province.
Grumsey, Dennis *o.f.m.conv.* '86 (BAL) Baltimore, MD St. Casimir.
Grundhaus, Rev. Msgr. Roger L. '66 (CR) Judicial Vicar; Priests' Council; Chancery Office Retired.
Grundowski, Francis M. '71 (ALN) Retired.
Grunewald, Bernard *er.o.l.s* '77 (OLL)[D] Philippi, WV Our Lady of Solitude Maronite Hermitage, Inc. Retired.
Grunow, Stephen E. '97 (CHI) Lake Forest, IL St. Mary.
Grupczynski, Gerald *s.ch.* '88 (LAV) Presbyteral Council for the Diocese of Las Vegas; Las Vegas, NV Our Lady of Las Vegas.
Gruska, Artur '04 (LA) Fillmore, CA St. Francis of Assisi.
Gruver, David '85 (ORG) Lake Forest, CA Santiago de Compostela.
Gryga, Theodore '64 (SY) Military Chaplains.
Gryszko, Alojzy *s.d.b.* '72 (LA) Paramount, CA Our Lady of the Rosary.
Grytner, Eugene *s.d.s.* '79 (ORL) Bartow, FL St. Thomas Aquinas.
Grytner, Eugeniusz *s.d.s.* '79 (SAT)[L] Falls City, TX Salvatorian Fathers Community of Texas.
Grytsyuk, Volodymyr '06 (SJP) Solon, OH Protection B.V.M.; Presbyters.
Grzelak, Thaddeus A. '65 (BRK) Retired.
Grzymski, Donald *o.f.m.conv.* '80 (BAL) Baltimore, MD St. Clement Mary Hofbauer; [U] Owings Mills, MD Knights of Columbus.
Gschwend, James P. *s.j.* '65 (CHI)[S] The Jesuit Retreat League of Chicago.
Guadagnoli, Michael '97 (DAL) Deans; Dallas, TX St. Pius X; Personnel Board.
Guadarrama, Edgar *o.s.a.* '11 (LAR) Laredo, TX St. Vincent de Paul.
Guagliardo, Salvatore J. '59 (RCK) Retired.
Guaipo, Jose Gregorio '88 (SJN) Guaynabo, PR Santa Rosa de Lima.
Gualano, Kevin M. '04 (ALN) Orefield, PA St. Joseph The Worker.
Gualtieri, Raymond A. '64 (PIT) Retired.
Guanchez, Omar '09 (SCL) Greenwald, MN St. Michael's; Greenwald, MN St. Andrew's; Greenwald, MN St. John's; Melrose, MN St. Mary's.
Guardiola, Louis *c.p.m.* '01 (OWN)[F] Auburn, KY Fathers of Mercy.
Guarino, Rt. Rev. Msgr. Charles A. '67 (RVC) Promoter of Justice; Defenders of the Bond Retired.
Guarino, Mario *f.d.p.* '81 (NY) New York, NY St. Ann.
Guarino, Thomas G. '77 (NEW)[A] South Orange, NJ Immaculate Conception Seminary School of Theology; [B] Seton Hall University; Censores Librorum.
Guarnieri, Richard '71 (NY) Bronx, NY St. Clare of Assisi.
Guarnizo, Jhon '03 (STA) Crescent City, FL St. John the Baptist; Presbyteral Council; Multicultural Ministry.
Guarnizo, Marcel '98 (WDC) Gaithersburg, MD St. John Neumann.
Guarracino, Ralph '54 (BRK) Retired.
Guastella, Luke *o.f.m.cap.* '55 (NY)[B] Beacon, NY St. Lawrence of Brindisi Friary.
Guastella, Rev. Msgr. Richard J. '72 (NY) Staten Island, NY St. Clare.
Guatiua, Javier '10 (MIL)[H] Milwaukee, WI Holy Wisdom Academy; [V] Racine, WI Community of St. Paul, Inc.; Milwaukee, WI Blessed John Paul II Parish.
Guay, Robert F. '73 (PIT) Judges; Priest Council; [N] Pittsburgh, PA Motherhouse, Sisters of the Holy Spirit (S.H.S.); Vicariate 1; College of Consultors; Clergy Personnel Board; Episcopal Vicars.
Guba, Michael '65 (NEW) Garfield, NJ Church of Our Lady of Sorrows.
Gubbels, Wayne '71 (DM) Adel, IA St. John.
Gubbins, John '70 (MIA) Retired.
Gubbins, William B. '55 (CHI) Orland Hills, IL St. Elizabeth Seton; Chicago, IL St. John Berchmans Retired.
Gubbiotti, Jeffrey '04 (HRT) West Haven, CT St. Louis.
Gubernat, Michael E. '77 (NEW) Nutley, NJ St. Mary's.
Guberovic, Zeljko J. '06 (NEW) On Duty Outside the Archdiocese.
Guberovic, Zeljko J. (GLD) Empire, MI St. Philip Neri.
Guckin, Matthew W. '99 (PH)[D] Downingtown, PA Bishop Shanahan High School; Downingtown, PA St. Joseph.
Gudalefsky, Adam B. *m.m.* '59 (FgM) Maryknoll, NY MARYKNOLL.
Gudewicz, John L. '70 (PIT) Pittsburgh, PA All Saints.
Gudipalli, Ravi '00 (LR) Huntsville, AR St. John the Evangelist; Fayetteville, AR St. Joseph.
Gudipalli, Thomas '03 (GI) Mitchell, NE St. Theresa's.
Guenter, Frank (GAL) Retired.
Guenther, Daniel C. '82 (SC) Sioux City, IA Immaculate Conception.
Guenther, Rev. Msgr. Donald E. '62 (NEW) West Orange, NJ St. Joseph's; Elected Members Retired.
Guentner, Francis J. *s.j.* '47 (STL)[O] St. Louis, MO Jesuit Community Corporation at Saint Louis University - Jesuit Hall.
Guentner, Hugh M. *o.s.m.* '91 (DEN) Denver, CO Our Lady of Mount Carmel.
Guererro, Larry '83 (STO) Modesto, CA St. Joseph Church of Modesto (Pastor of).
Guerin, Louis T. '87 (PMB)[K] Diocese of Palm Beach Health Plan Trust; [A] Boynton Beach, FL St. Vincent de Paul Regional Seminary; Released from Diocesan Assignment.
Guerin, Peter J. *o.s.b.* '63 (MAN)[K] Manchester, NH St. Anselm Abbey; Manchester, NH.
Guerin, William A. *o.s.f.s.* '57 (PH)[Y] Wyndmoor, PA Villa de Sales Oblate Residence.
Guerini, Ademir *c.s.* (BO) Somerville, MA St. Anthony of Padua.
Guerra, Alcibiades *c.m.* '90 (FgM) Philadelphia, PA Eastern Province.
Guerra, Aroldo '54 (NY) New York, NY Incarnation.
Guerra, Jose Sobarzo '04 (RNO) Winnemucca, NV St. Paul.
Guerra, Juan Gabriel *l.c.* '91 (ATL)[F] Alpharetta, GA Norcross Pastoral Center, Inc.
Guerra, Ricardo V. *o.m.i.* '78 (SAT) San Antonio, TX San Juan De Los Lagos Shrine.
Guerra, Robert F. '00 (VIC) Eagle Lake, TX Parish of the Nativity; Presbyteral Council.
Guerra–Mayaudon, Gerardo *o.p.* '69 (AUS)[G] Austin, TX Dominican Friars of Austin.
Guerreiro, Clarence L. *ss.cc.* '70 (HON) Honolulu, HI St. Patrick; [D] Honolulu, HI St. Patrick's Monastery.
Guerreiro, Clyde L. *ss.cc.* '76 (HON) Kalaupapa, HI St. Francis; Kaunakakai, HI Saint Damien of Molokai Church; Members.
Guerrera, Richard P. *s.j.* '73 (FgM) Watertown, MA Society of Jesus.
Guerrera, Rev. Msgr. Vittorio '91 (HRT) Hartford, CT St. Luke.
Guerrero, Abraham '98 (TUC) Tucson, AZ Saint Monica Roman Catholic Parish - Tucson.
Guerrero, Felix Leon *o.f.m.cap.* '86 (AGN)[F] Agana Heights, GU St. Fidelis Friary; Notary; Confraternity of Christian Mothers.
Guerrero, Jose Ma. (ARE) On Duty Outside the Diocese.
Guerrero, Joseph Ricardo *m.j.* '85 (LA)[P] Los Angeles, CA Missionaries of Jesus, Inc.
Guerrero, Juan Carlos Ruiz *o.f.m* (CHI)[N] Chicago, IL St. Peter's Friary.
Guerrero, Robert '92 (SB) Chino, CA Our Lady of Guadalupe.
Guerrero, Toribio C. '96 (LAR) Laredo, TX St. Peter The Apostle; Cursillo Movement.
Guerrero–Almanza, J. Jesus *o.s.a.* '98 (GAL) Pasadena, TX St. Juan Diego.
Guerrette, William J. '55 (BO) Senior Priests. Retired.
Guerrini, Brian *ss.cc.* '08 (LA)[P] La Verne, CA Congregation of the Sacred Hearts of Jesus and Mary.
Guerrini, Brian '08 (LSC) Artesia, NM Our Lady of Grace; Members.
Guerrini, Roderic M. '63 (LA) Retired.
Guertin, Donald F. *c.s.c.* '64 (FTW)[H] Notre Dame Congregation of Holy Cross, United States Province of Priests & Brothers.
Guesnier, Rene *o.s.b.* '61 (DOD) Seward, KS St. Francis Xavier Catholic Church of Seward, Kansas.
Guessetto, Robert J. *o.s.a.* '79 (FgM) Villanova, PA Province of St. Thomas of Villanova (Eastern).
Guest, Richard M. '94 (ARL) Ashburn, VA St. Theresa.
Guevara, Alfonso M. '77 (BWN) McAllen, TX St. Joseph the Worker; Board Members.
Guevara, Jose Maria '68 (LAR) Laredo, TX St. Jude; College of Consultors.
Guevara, Manuel '10 (PAT) Paterson, NJ Cathedral of St. John the Baptist; Auditors.
Guevara, Miguel H. '67 (GI) Retired.
Guevin, Benedict M. *o.s.b.* '85 (MAN)[K] Manchester, NH St. Anselm Abbey; Lay Ministry Formation Commission.
Guffey, David L. *c.s.c.* (FTW)[H] Notre Dame Congregation of Holy Cross, United States Province of Priests & Brothers.
Guffey, David *c.s.c.* '91 (LA) Santa Monica, CA St. Monica.
Guglielmelli, Michael V. '70 (NEW) Hoboken, NJ St. Francis.
Guglielmi, Donald A. '84 (BGP) Stratford, CT St. Mark.
Guglielmo, Alan F. '68 (NEW) Secaucus, NJ Immaculate Conception Retired.
Gugliotta, Francis *s.x.* '52 (FgM) Wayne, NJ XAVERIAN MISSIONARY FATHERS.
Gugliotta, Kevin A. '96 (NEW) Scotch Plains, NJ St. Bartholomew.
Guianan, Francisco *s.o.l.t.* (KC) Kansas City, MO Our Lady of Peace.
Guiao, Raymond P. *s.j.* '90 (CHI)[N] Chicago, IL Clark Street Jesuit Residence; [N] Chicago, IL Chicago Province of the Society of Jesus–Provincial Office.
Guiao, Raymond P. *s.j.* '99 (DET)[K] Chicago, IL Detroit Province of the Society of Jesus–Provincial Office.
Guichard, Benoit *f.s.s.p.* '04 (PAT) Pequannock, NJ Our Lady of Fatima Chapel (Tridentine).
Guida, Amedeo G. '85 (SY) Solvay, NY St. Cecilia; Syracuse, NY Our Lady of Peace.
Guido, Joseph J. *o.p.* '81 (PRO)[O] Providence St. Thomas Aquinas Priory at Providence College; [B] Providence, RI Providence College.
Guido, Luis '07 (SB) Indio, CA Our Lady of Perpetual Help.
Guido, Paul *o.f.m.* '66 (ALB)[A] Catskill, NY St. Anthony Friary.
Guido, Thomas J. '87 (PT) Miramar Beach, FL Church of the Resurrection; Orders & Ministries, Commission for.
Guidon, Pat *o.m.i.* '50 (SAT)[L] San Antonio, TX Oblate Benson Residence (Southwest Area).
Guidon, Patrick *o.m.i.* '50 (SAT)[G] San Antonio, TX St. Anthony's School.
Guidry, Joseph *s.v.d.* '57 (CHI)[N] Techny, IL Divine Word Residence.
Guidry, Michael '91 (LAF) Minister to Priests.
Guidry, Michael '71 (LAF) Morrow, LA St. Peter.
Guidry, Mitchell '97 (LAF) On Special Assignment.
Guijarro, Rev. Msgr. Mario (SJN) Hermandad N. Sra. De La Caridad; [B] Guaynabo, PR Colegio San Pedro Martir.
Guijarro de Corzo, Rev. Msgr. Mario A. '78 (SJN) Guaynabo, PR San Pedro Martir de Verona.
Guilbeau, Aubrey V. '82 (LKC) Sulphur, LA Immaculate Conception of the B.V.M.; Deans; Diocesan Consultors; Deaf Apostolate; Presbyteral Council.
Guilbeau, Jeremy Aquinas *o.p.* '02 (NY)[DD] New York St. Vincent Ferrer Priory.
Guilbert, Norman J. '97 (BGP) Bridgeport, CT St. Patrick Church.
Guillemette, Robert C. '01 (MAN) Absent on Leave.
Guillen, Fernando E. '90 (NEW) Medical Leave.
Guillen, Omar Oswaldo *s.d.b.* '02 (PMB) Belle Glade, FL St. Philip Benizi.
Guillen, Randy '96 (NEW) Santa Ana, CA St. Anne's; On Duty Outside the Archdiocese.
Guillen, Robert '70 (WDC) Washington, DC Holy Name.
Guillen–Santoyo, Patricio '57 (SB) Retired.
Guillen–Vega, Henry '10 (P) Salem, OR St. Joseph.
Guillermo–Cordoba, Luis '00 (ATL) Lilburn, GA Our Lady of the Americas.
Guillory, Brad D. '09 (LAF) Parks, LA St. Joseph.
Guillory, Joshua P. '07 (LAF) Ville Platte, LA Sacred Heart of Jesus; Ville Platte, LA St. Joseph; Graduate Studies.
Guillot, Rev. Msgr. Leo '56 (BR) Baton Rouge, LA St. Louis, King of France Retired.
Guillot, Raymond J. '00 (NO) Kenner, LA Our Lady of Perpetual Help.
Guilmain, Roland *a.a.* '53 (BO)[U] Boston, MA Assumptionist Center.
Guilmette, Leo *o.m.i.* '63 (FgM) Washington, DC AMERICAN OBLATE MISSIONS.
Guimon, Michael M. *o.s.m.* '70 (OAK) Alta Bates Campus of the Alta Bates Summit Medical Center; Herrick Campus of the Alpha Bates Summit Medical Center; [L] Berkeley, CA Servites.
Guimond, John *o.f.m. cap.* '83 (DET)[P] Washington, MI Capuchin Retreat.
Guinan, Frank '66 (PMB) Retired.
Guinan, Michael D. *o.f.m.* '64 (OAK)[A] Berkeley, CA Franciscan School of Theology; [L] Berkeley, CA Franciscan Friars (Province of St. Barbara).
Guinan, Michael '53 (GF) Retired.
Guiney, John *s.m.a.* '61 (JOL) Retired.
Guiry, Robert W. '60 (BRK) On Leave/Unassigned.
Guise, Cyril *o.c.d.* '59 (MIL)[P] Hubertus, WI Discalced Carmelite Monastery - Holy Hill Basilica of the National Shrine of Mary, Help of Christians, Holy Hill.
Guitron, Steven '94 (LA) Pacoima, CA Guardian Angel.
Guk, Vincent '86 (TR) Eatontown, NJ St. Dorothea.
Gula, Richard M. *s.s.* '73 (BAL)[Q] Baltimore Society of St. Sulpice, Province of the United States; Baltimore, MD.
Gula, Richard *s.s.* (E) On Duty Outside Diocese.
Gulash, George M. '92 (ALT) Windber, PA SS. Cyril and Methodius.
Gulino, Stephen S. '97 (NOR) District Spiritual Advisors; Jewett City, CT St. Mary; Preston, CT St.

Catherine of Siena; Voluntown, CT St. Thomas the Apostle.
Guljas, Andrew *c.s.c.* '68 (FTW)[H] Notre Dame Congregation of Holy Cross, United States Province of Priests & Brothers.
Gulley, Anthony D. '56 (ALB) Albany, NY Blessed Sacrament Retired.
Gulley, James '81 (ALB) Retired.
Gullo, Joseph A. '86 (BUF) Council of Priests; Arcade, NY St. Mary.
Gully, Bernard L. '62 (SAN) Priests' Personnel Board; Presbyteral Council; Cursillos de Cristiandad; Deans; Big Spring, TX Holy Trinity Parish.
Gumapo, Polycarpo (Pol) R. '70 (SAC) Citrus Heights, CA Holy Family.
Gumataotao, Agustin *o.f.m.cap.* '82 (AGN) Sinajana, GU Saint Jude Thaddeus; [F] Agana Heights, GU St. Fidelis Friary; Archdiocesan Presbyteral Council.
Gumbert, Kenneth R. *o.p.* '85 (FR) Fall River, MA Notre Dame de Lourdes.
Gummersheimer, Gary P. '79 (BEL) Murphysboro, IL St. Andrew.
Gumprecht, Thomas *s.a.* '68 (NY)[DD] Garrison Graymoor Ecumenical and Interreligious Institute.
Gumprecht, Thomas *s.a.* '68 (R) Apex, NC St. Andrew the Apostle.
Gunderson, Gerald T. '76 (CHI) Park Ridge, IL Mary, Seat of Wisdom.
Gundrum, Lyle *o.f.m.cap.* '67 (CHI) Chicago, IL St. Simon the Apostle.
Gunn, Rev. Msgr. James L. '77 (MAD) Waunakee, WI St. John the Baptist; Waunakee, WI St. Mary of the Lake; Vicar for Priests.
Gunning, Eugene L. '55 (SCR) Retired.
Gunningham, John '07 (SB) Loma Linda, CA Loma Linda University Medical Center.
Gunnoud, James B. '59 (HRT) Retired.
Gunter, David W. '09 (BO) Methuen, MA St. Monica.
Gunti, Charles *o.f.m.* '68 (SAT) San Antonio, TX San Jose y San Miguel.
Gunwall, Kurtis L. '08 (FAR) Permanent Diaconate; Vocation Director.
Guppenberger, August '61 (CIN)[N] Cincinnati Headquarters of Glenmary Home Missioners Retired.
Gural, Marion A. '56 (BRK) Retired.
Gurath, Guy G. '64 (MIL) Retired.
Gurdak, Joseph *o.f.m.cap.* '70 (MAN) Manchester, NH St. Anne–St. Augustin; Manchester Hispanic Parish Ministry.
Gurgul, Walter *m.i.c.* '60 (SPR)[G] Stockbridge, MA Congregation of Marian Fathers of The Immaculate Conception of the Most Blessed Virgin Mary.
Gurka, Gerald J. '80 (SCR) St. John the Baptist.
Gurnee, William H. '00 (WDC) Pastoral Center Special Ministries; [A] Washington, DC Blessed John Paul II Seminary.
Gurnick, Michael K. '98 (CLV) Secretary; Cleveland, OH Cathedral of St. John the Evangelist.
Gurovich, Rev. Archpriest Daniel '74 (PHU) Presbyteral Council; Bethlehem, PA St. Josaphat's; Adjunct Judicial Vicars; Priests Beneficial Fund.
Gurrieri, John A. '67 (BRK)[R] Douglaston, NY Bishop Mugavero Residence Retired.
Gurtler, Gary *s.j.* '79 (BO)[U] Newton, MA The Jesuit Community at Boston College.
Gurtner, Mark A. '96 (FTW) Fort Wayne, IN Our Lady of Good Hope; On Special Assignment; Pro–Synodal Judges; Judicial Vicar; Consultors; Budget Committee; Presbyteral Council; Liturgical Commission; Tribunal; First Court of Judges; Appeal Court Judges; Sacred Art and Architecture Committee.
Gurtubay, Ramon *c.p.* '80 (SJN)[C] Dorado, PR Estudiantado Pasionista.
Gurumombe, Emmanuel *s.j.* '03 (BO)[U] Newton, MA The Jesuit Community at Boston College.
Gurzynski, Rev. Msgr. James C. '63 (AMA) Defenders of the Bond Retired.
Gusiora, Alphonsus '83 (PCE) On Duty Outside the Diocese.
Gusmer, Rev. Msgr. Charles W. '66 (NEW) Cedar Grove, NJ St. Catherine of Siena; New Providence, NJ Our Lady of Peace; Office of Divine Worship; Members Retired.
Gusmer, Rev. Msgr. Charles W. '66 (NEW) Censores Librorum.
Gusmer, Charles '66 (NEW) Retired.
Gussoni, Lino '44 (NY) Retired.
Gustafson, Christopher M. '95 (CHI) Niles, IL Our Lady of Ransom.
Guste, Placid *s.m.p.* '61 (SPC)[F] Marionville, MO The Society of Our Mother of Peace, Sons of Our Mother of Peace.
Guste, Placid *s.m.p.* '61 (STL)[O] High Ridge, MO Society of Our Mother of Peace; [S] High Ridge, MO Society of Our Mother of Peace at Mary the Font Solitude.
Gustin, Clement N. *o.s.c.* '55 (SCL)[I] Onamia, MN Crosier Priory.
Gutgsell, Michael F. '74 (OM) Defenders of the Bond; Officers; Omaha, NE St. Cecilia Cathedral; Consultors; Ex Officio (Consultors).
Gutgsell, Stephen J. '84 (OM) Fort Calhoun, NE St. John the Baptist.
Guth, Edward L. *s.j.* '60 (NY)[DD] New York, NY Murray–Weigel Hall.
Guthneck, Peter E. '71 (GF) Box Elder, MT St. Margaret Mary; Vicars Forane; Diocesan Consultors; Priests' Council.
Guthridge, Timothy *c.pp.s.* '97 (KC)[C] St. Joseph, MO Bishop LeBlond High School.
Guthrie, Douglas '77 (GAL) Houston, TX St. Michael.
Guthrie, John G. '90 (BIS) Bismarck, ND Cathedral of the Holy Spirit; Vicar General; Diocesan Corporate Board; Diocesan Finance Council; Presbyteral Council; Moderator of the Curia.
Guthrie, Raymond P. '84 (PEO) Ottawa, IL St. Columba.
Gutierrez, Alfonso '85 (SAV) Tifton, GA Our Divine Saviour.
Gutierrez, Alvin P. '61 (PIT) Retired.
Gutierrez, Celestino '64 (VEN) Hispanic, Migrant and Spanish Speaking Apostolates; Sarasota, FL St. Jude.
Gutierrez, David *t.o.r.* '92 (SAT) San Antonio, TX St. Leonard's.
Gutierrez, Francisco '01 (YAK) Yakima, WA Holy Redeemer.
Gutierrez, Franco '65 (SJN) Trujillo Alto, PR Maria Llena de Gracia.
Gutierrez, Gilberto '73 (PAT) Passaic, NJ Our Lady of Fatima.
Gutierrez, Guido '08 (CHI) Chicago, IL St. Michael the Archangel.
Gutierrez, Ismael '04 (OAK) Concord, CA St. Francis of Assisi; Pastoral Leadership Placement Board (PLPB).
Gutierrez, Javier *s.f.* '91 (SFE) Santa Cruz, NM Holy Cross.
Gutierrez, Jeronimo '81 (SJ) San Jose, CA Christ the King.
Gutierrez, Jose Luis '08 (STO)[G] Stockton, CA St. John Vianney House of Formation; Vocations; Stockton, CA Presentation Church (Pastor of).
Gutierrez, Jose '73 (STP) Retired.
Gutierrez, Jose '76 (CC)[D] Corpus Christi, TX.
Gutierrez, Juan Antonio *o.f.m.* '97 (LSC) Roswell, NM St. John the Baptist.
Gutierrez, Juan Rogelio '07 (BWN) San Juan, TX Basilica of Our Lady of San Juan del Valle–National Shrine; [I] San Juan, TX The Basilica of Our Lady of San Juan del Valle–National Shrine.
Gutierrez, Luis '98 (JOL) Addison, IL St. Joseph.
Gutierrez, Manuel *f.n.* '09 (DAL) Garland, TX Good Shepherd.
Gutierrez, Michael D. '93 (LA) Baldwin Park, CA St. John the Baptist.
Gutierrez, Oscar *m.d.m.* '96 (PHX) Tempe, AZ Holy Family Roman Catholic Parish; Tempe, AZ St. Martin de Porres Roman Catholic Parish; Phoenix, AZ St. Edward Confessor Roman Catholic Parish.
Gutierrez, Rogelio '09 (YAK) Wenatchee, WA St. Joseph's.
Gutirerrez, Jose '76 (CC) On Special Assignment.
Gutmann, David '83 (P) Beaverton, OR Holy Trinity.
Gutmann, Donald '91 (P) Newberg, OR St. Peter; Area Vicars.
Gutowski, Edmund *c.m.* '60 (HRT)[L] Manchester, CT DePaul Provincial Residence.
Gutowski, Matthew J. '88 (OM) Springfield, NE St. Joseph; Censor Librorum.
Gutting, James G. '75 (E) Erie, PA St. Mary of the Immaculate Conception; Deans; Priest Personnel Board; Inner–City Outreach; Presbyteral Council.
Gutting, John C. '54 (LA) Retired.
Guyer, James B. *s.j.* '72 (DEN)[N] Denver, CO Regis Jesuit Community (The Jesuits at Regis University).
Guz, Edmund F. '55 (CHI) Burnham, IL Mother of God Retired.
Guz, Leonard J. '55 (JOL) Retired.
Guzaldo, John Michael '06 (AUS) Waco, TX St. Louis.
Guzik, Michael A. '03 (MIL)[P] Milwaukee, WI Jesuit Community at Marquette University.
Guzinski, Joseph D. *c.p.* '51 (BRK)[R] Jamaica, NY Immaculate Conception Monastery.
Guzman, Agustin *c.o.* '11 (CHR)[E] Rock Hill, SC Oratory of St. Philip Neri, Congregation of the Oratory of Pontifical Rite.
Guzman, Agustin *c.o.* '11 (CHR) Rock Hill, SC St. Mary.
Guzman, Alfonso *o.f.m.* '71 (SJN) Sabana Seca, PR San Jose Obrero.
Guzman, Alfonso *o.f.m.* '71 (SP)[N] St. Petersburg, FL St. Anthony Friary.
Guzman, Armando '86 (SEA)[B] Seattle, WA Bishop Blanchet High School.
Guzman, Bandilio *s.j.* (SJN) Rio Piedras, PR Academia San Ignacio de Loyola; [B] San Juan, PR Academia San Ignacio de Loyola; Maranatha House of Prayer.
Guzmán, Baudilio *s.j.* '91 (SJN) San Juan, PR San Ignacio de Loyola; [H] San Juan, PR Comunidad Jesuita.
Guzman, David *o.c.d.* '10 (LA) Alhambra, CA St. Therese.
Guzman, Javier Uribe *m.n.m.* '58 (SAT) Del Rio, TX Our Lady of Guadalupe.
Guzman, Jesus Aguirre '89 (BAL) Glen Burnie, MD Holy Trinity.
Guzman, Juan Jose *o.a.r.* '08 (ORG) Santa Ana, CA Our Lady of Guadalupe.
Guzman, Juan Santa '85 (SJN) for Education; Vicar for Education; Carolina, PR Santo Cristo de la Agonia.
Guzman, Julian *s.d.s.* '68 (WDC)[B] Silver Spring, MD Salvatorian Community.
Guzman, Luiz *o.f.m.* '10 (SD) Oceanside, CA Mission San Luis Rey Catholic Parish.
Guzman, Mark A. '08 (SEA) Marysville, WA St. Mary.
Guzman, Miguel *c.r.* '06 (DEN) Denver, CO Our Lady of Guadalupe.
Gúzman, Salvador '00 (DAL) Van Alstyne, TX Holy Family; McKinney, TX St. Michael; At Large Members.
Guzman, Walter F. '02 (HBG) Lebanon, PA St. Benedict the Abbot.
Guzman Alfaro, Alfonso *o.f.m.* '71 (FgM) New York, NY Holy Name Province.
Guzman Alfaro, Alfonso *o.f.m.* '71 (SJN) Secretary to the Archbishop; Vicar of Religious.
Guzman Quintana, Pedro J. '10 (PCE) Juana Diaz, PR St. Raymond Nonato.
Gveric, Drago *o.f.m.* (SJ) San Jose, CA St. Mary of the Assumption.
Gwiazda, Francis A. '69 (PH) Philadelphia, PA St. Laurentius.
Gwinner, David E. '84 (COL) Westerville, OH St. Paul the Apostle.
Gwozdz, John P. '86 (HRT) Glastonbury, CT St. Paul; South Glastonbury, CT St. Augustine.
Gwozdz, Thomas L. *s.b.d.* '75 (NO)[A] St. Benedict, LA St. Joseph Seminary College; [A] St. Benedict, LA St. Joseph Seminary College.
Gwudz, John S. '72 (NOR) On Duty Outside the Diocese.
Gyamfi, Paul M. '88 (BRK) Ozone Park, NY Nativity of the Blessed Virgin Mary.
Gyan, Eric V. '86 (BR) Prairieville, LA St. John the Evangelist.
Gyan–Obeng, Simon (NY) Nyack, NY St. Ann.
Gye–Chun, John (B) Lee '97 (WIL) Korean Catholics; Korean Catholic Community, Inc.
Gyhra, Richard A. '99 (LIN) On Duty Outside the Diocese.
Gyure, William Louis '91 (TUC) Payson, AZ Saint Philip the Apostle Roman Catholic Church – Payson.
Gyure, William '91 (NEW) Retired.
Gyves, Peter W. *s.j.* '08 (NEW)[B] Jersey City, NJ Jesuit Center; [L] Jersey City, NJ Jesuits of Saint Peter's College, Inc.; [B] Jersey City, NJ St. Aedan's: St. Peter's College Church.

H

Ha, Alex H. '93 (ORG) Irvine, CA St. Thomas More.
Ha, Dominic Vinh Van '93 (CHI) Chicago, IL St. Henry.
Ha, Hieu Minh '00 (ATL) Army Chaplains; Military Chaplains.
Ha, Louis Pham *c.m.c.* '94 (FWT) Fort Worth, TX Christ the King.
Ha, Peter '74 (LA) North Hills, CA Our Lady of Peace.
Ha, Simon Hyung–Min '92 (PH) Springfield, PA Holy Cross; Korean Apostolate.
Ha, Tae–su Michael *s.j.* (ATL) Doraville, GA Korean Martyrs Catholic Church.
Ha, Thomas Do Thanh '63 (ORG) Retired.
Haag, Michael B. '05 (SFD) Greenup, IL St. Charles Borromeo; Greenup, IL Christ the King; Marshall, IL St. Mary.
Haag, Ralph L. *c.s.c.* '04 (FTW)[B] University of Notre Dame Du Lac; [H] Notre Dame, IN Holy Cross Community, Corby Hall, University of Notre Dame.
Haag, Theodore *o.f.m.* '79 (CLV)[D] Parma, OH Padua Franciscan High School; [N] Brooklyn, OH St. Anthony of Padua Friary.
Haake, Chris G. '97 (PEO) Earlville, IL St. Teresa of Avila.
Haake, Gregory P. *c.s.c.* '07 (FTW)[H] Notre Dame Congregation of Holy Cross, United States Province of Priests & Brothers.
Haake, Gregory P. *c.s.c.* '07 (FTW)[H] Notre Dame Congregation of Holy Cross, United States Province of Priests & Brothers.
Haake, Gregory P. *c.s.c.* '07 (SFR) Menlo Park, CA St. Raymond.
Haaland, Byron *s.c.j.* '77 (MIL)[P] Franklin, WI St. Joseph's at Monastery Lake.
Haarer, Eric '01 (PBL)[H] Crestone, CO Spiritual Life Institute of America, Inc.
Haas, Dietrich A. '67 (MIL)[T] Waukesha, WI Schoenstatt Fathers.
Haas, Joseph H. '59 (MIL) Retired.
Haas, Julian *o.f.m.cap.* '64 (DEN)[N] Denver, CO St. Francis of Assisi Friary.
Haas, Lawrence W. '63 (FAR) Retired.
Haas, Robert L. '62 (TOL) Retired.
Haas, Roger *o.f.m.conv.* '69 (PAT) Clifton, NJ St. John Kanty.
Haase, Albert *o.f.m.* '83 (CHI)[N] Chicago, IL Holy Spirit Friary, Order of Friars Minor; [N] Countryside,

IL St. Gratian Friary, Franciscan Friars.
Haase, Howard G. '83 (MIL) Waukesha, WI St. Mary; [H] Waukesha, WI Waukesha Catholic School System, Inc.
Hababag, Jimmy '82 (PMB) Boca Raton, FL St. Joan of Arc.
Habash, Andrwos '05 (OLD) North Hollywood, CA Jesus Sacred Heart Church.
Habash, Safaa '99 (OLD) Farmington Hills, MI Saint Toma Church; Sterling Heights, MI Christ the King Mission.
Habash, Chorbishop Yousif '75 (LA) North Hollywood, CA Sacred Heart Syriac Catholic Parish.
Habchi, Nabil *o.m.m.* '02 (OLL)[A] Ann Arbor, MI Maronite Order of the Blessed Virgin Mary; Ann Arbor, MI.
Haber, Thomas N. '01 (BGP) Leave of Absence.
Haberkorn, Timothy A. '92 (KCK) Topeka, KS Sacred Heart–St. Joseph.
Haberman, C. Robert '75 (PBL) On Duty Outside the Diocese.
Haberman, Clayton J. '50 (WIN) Retired.
Haberman, Robert '75 (SFR)[C] San Rafael, CA Dominican University of California.
Habetz, Thomas E. '01 (LAF) Lafayette, LA St. Genevieve.
Habib, Fadi '04 (EST) Warren, MI Our Lady of Perpetual Help.
Habiger, Rev. Msgr. James D. '51 (WIN) Retired.
Habiger, Matthew *o.s.b.* '68 (KCK)[I] Atchison, KS St. Benedict's Abbey.
Habing, Paul '80 (SFD) Springfield, IL St. Katharine Drexel; Comite Diocesano de Ministerio Hispano – Diocesan Committee for Hispanic Ministry.
Habison, Gerhart '76 (LA) Torrance, CA Nativity.
Hablewitz, James A. '67 (GB) Little Chute, WI St. John Nepomucene; Vicariate.
Haby, Gerald *s.m.* '69 (SAT)[L] San Antonio, TX Central Catholic Marianist Community Retired.
Haby, Marie–Elie '96 (DET) Detroit, MI Our Lady Queen of Angels; Archdiocesan Vicars; Detroit, MI St. Stephen–Mary Mother of the Church; Presbyteral Council.
Hache, Yvon '88 (ORL) Barefoot Bay, FL St. Luke.
Hachey, Paul J. *s.m.* '84 (ATL) Special or Other Archdiocesan Assignment; [C] Atlanta, GA Marist School; Judicial Vicar.
Hacin, Patricio Antonio *f.s.c.b.* '11 (WDC)[O] Bethesda, MD Priestly Fraternity of the Missionaries of St. Charles Borromeo, Inc.
Hack, Michael A. '70 (CHI) Judicial Vicar; Judges; Chicago, IL Notre Dame de Chicago.
Hack, Michael A. '70 (KAL) Defender of the Bond.
Hack, Rev. Msgr. Michael A. (RCK) Defenders of the Bond.
Hack, Thomas '55 (GR) Retired.
Hackel, Daniel H. '02 (LC) Colby, WI St. Bernard; Colby, WI St. Mary Help of Christians; Colby, WI St. Louis; Owen, WI Holy Rosary; Deans.
Hackel, Robert *s.m.* '65 (FWT)[H] Fort Worth, TX Society of Mary.
Hackenmueller, Jerome B. '69 (STP) Retired.
Hackert, Eugene C. '51 (NU) Retired.
Hackett, James F. '68 (L) Louisville, KY Our Mother of Sorrows.
Hackev, Louis *o.s.b.* '85 (IND)[K] Saint Meinrad St. Meinrad Archabbey.
Hackman, Marvin R. '71 (CIN) Retired.
Hadberg, Dennis C. '72 (E) On Leave of Absence.
Haddad, Norman A. *o.p.* '61 (WDC) Washington, DC St. Dominic Church & Priory; [O] Washington, DC Center for Assisted Living.
Haddad, Wayne M. '97 (MO) On Duty Outside the Diocese; Navy Chaplains.
Hadden, Robert F. '09 (CIN) Dayton, OH St. Peter.
Hadden, Rev. Msgr. Thomas P. '58 (R) Diocesan Judges Retired.
Hadel, Richard E. *s.j.* '65 (STL)[O] St. Louis, MO; [S] St. Louis, MO Retreat House.
Haden, Kyle E. *o.f.m.* '97 (NY)[DD] New York Franciscan Friars, Holy Name Province.
Haden, Kyle *o.f.m.* '97 (NY) New York, NY St. Stephen of Hungary.
Hadley, Christopher M. *s.j.* '09 (MIL)[P] Milwaukee, WI Arrupe House Jesuit Community.
Hadnagy, John Raphael *o.f.m.conv.* '90 (TOL) Upper Sandusky, OH Transfiguration of the Lord; Carey, OH Our Lady of Consolation, Basilica–National Shrine.
Hadusek, Paul J. '69 (NU) Retired.
Hadyka, Richard J. '67 (CAM) Retired.
Haefeli, Joaquin C. '51 (LA) Retired.
Haefling, Maurice C. *o.s.b.* '94 (KCK)[I] Atchison, KS St. Benedict's Abbey; Canon City, CO.
Haefling, Maurice C. *o.s.b.* '94 (PBL)[H] Florence, CO Trinity Ranch Conference & Renewal Center, Inc.
Haefner, Douglas J. '83 (MET) Somerset, NJ St. Matthias.
Haemmerle, Gerald R. '67 (CIN) Dayton, OH St. Charles Borromeo; Judges.
Haesaert, William F. *c.s.v.* '80 (LAV) Las Vegas, NV St. Viator; Presbyteral Council for the Diocese of Las Vegas; [C] Las Vegas, NV Clerics of St. Viator Retirement Home.
Haesaert, William F. *c.s.v.* '80 (CHI)[N] Arlington Heights Viatorian Province Center–Clerics of St. Viator.
Hafeman, Harry G. '76 (GB) Green Bay, WI SS. Peter and Paul; Special Assignment.
Hafemann, George '99 (NY) Port Jervis, NY Immaculate Conception.
Haffey, Thomas P. '69 (HEL) Butte, MT Holy Spirit; Butte, MT St. Ann; Director for Ministry to Priests; Associate Judges; Deaneries; Continuing Formation of the Clergy; Personnel Board; Butte, MT St. John the Evangelist.
Haffey, Thomas P. '69 (HEL) Presbyteral Council; Diocesan Consultors.
Hafner, Gerard '62 (ROC) Retired.
Haft, Ronald C. '07 (CIN) Hamilton, OH St. Peter in Chains.
Hagan, Aelred *o.c.s.o.* '89 (CHR)[E] Moncks Corner, SC Mepkin Abbey.
Hagan, Rev. Msgr. Charles H. '70 (PH) Doylestown, PA Our Lady of Mount Carmel.
Hagan, Harry *o.s.b.* '86 (IND)[A] Saint Meinrad, IN Saint Meinrad School of Theology; [K] Saint Meinrad, IN St. Meinrad Archabbey.
Hagan, James '69 (SFR) On Duty Outside the Archdiocese.
Hagan, Paul '82 (LFT) Unassigned.
Hagan, Robert A. *s.j.* '72 (NO) New Orleans, LA Holy Name of Jesus.
Hagan, Robert P. *o.s.a.* '03 (PH)[C] Villanova University; [Y] Rosemont, PA Saxony Hall.
Hagan, Thomas *o.s.f.s.* '69 (FgM) Wilmington, DE OBLATES OF ST. FRANCIS DE SALES MISSIONS.
Hagan, Vincent J. '66 (RVC) Retired.
Hagarman, Vincent A. *s.j.* '54 (DET)[K] Clarkston, MI Colombiere Center.
Hagearty, Charles B. '59 (HRT) Retired.
Hagedorn, Thomas J. '71 (CLV) Retired.
Hagelin, Bradley R. '11 (SEA) Tacoma, WA St. Charles Borromeo.
Hagemann, John *o.s.b.* '75 (OM)[J] Elkhorn, NE Mount Michael Benedictine Abbey.
Hagen, Gerald A. '91 (SUP) Phillips, WI St. Paul the Apostle; Phillips, WI St. Therese of Lisieux; Phillips, WI St. John the Baptist; Presbyteral Council & Diocesan Consultors.
Hagen, John J. *o.s.a.* '57 (PH)[C] Villanova University; [Y] Villanova, PA St. Thomas Monastery.
Hagen, Joseph B. *o.f.m.* '46 (STL)[O] St. Louis, MO Franciscan Friary of St. Anthony of Padua.
Hagendorf, Thomas A. *o.praem.* '63 (GB) Green Bay, WI Holy Cross.
Hager, Raymond D. '97 (STL) Elsberry, MO Sacred Heart.
Hager, Van Allen *i.m.c.* '73 (MET)[I] Somerset, NJ Consolata Society for Foreign Missions.
Hagerman, James W. '86 (MET) Parlin, NJ St. Bernadette.
Hagerty, Rev. Msgr. John B. '55 (E) Episcopal Delegate for Retired Priests; Erie, PA Blessed Sacrament; Members Retired.
Haggar, Rt. Rev. Exarch Joseph S. '66 (NTN) Lincoln, RI St. Basil the Great; Woonsocket, RI St. Elias; Defender of the Bond and Promoter of Justice; Protopresbyters; College of Eparchial Consultors; Presbyteral Council; Finance Council.
Haggerty, Donald F. '89 (NY) Censors Librorum.
Haggerty, Donald '89 (NY) On Duty Outside the Archdiocese.
Haggerty, Shaun Thomas '09 (SFS) Aberdeen, SD Sacred Heart.
Haggerty, Rev. Msgr. Thomas M. '64 (BRK) Brooklyn, NY Our Lady of Mount Carmel Shrine Church; Alcoholism Committee; Lake Orion, MI National Catholic Council on Alcoholism and Related Drug Problems, Inc. Retired.
Haggerty, Thomas '79 (RVC) East Meadow, NY St. Raphael; Procurator & Advocates.
Haggins, Martin *o.f.m.cap* '64 (SFR)[B] San Francisco, CA Capuchin Franciscan Order San Buenaventura Friary.
Hagileiram, John S. *s.j.* '85 (CI) Yap, FM St. Ignatius; Diocesan Consultors; Yap; New York, NY Society of Jesus.
Haglof, Anthony *o.c.d.* '71 (BO)[U] Boston, MA Carmelite Monastery.
Hagstrom, Thomas '93 (SFD) Quincy, IL St. Anthony of Padua; Priests' Personnel Board.
Hahn, Bernardine '43 (STL)[O] St. Louis, MO Franciscan Friary of St. Anthony of Padua.
Hahn, Dominic D. '80 (SEA) Vancouver, WA St. James.
Hahn, Francis *o.m.i.* '72 (FgM) Washington, DC AMERICAN OBLATE MISSIONS.
Hahn, Gerald T. '79 (NEW) Northvale, NJ St. Anthony's.
Hahn, James David '61 (SCL) Cambridge, MN Christ the King.
Hahn, Peter I. '02 (HBG) Presbyteral Council; Lancaster, PA St. Leo the Great; Consultors, College.
Hahn, Raymond W. '74 (E) Erie, PA Our Lady of Mt. Carmel.
Hahn, Scott R. '03 (WDC) Camp Springs, MD St. Philip the Apostle; Priest Council.
Hahn, William P. '04 (COL) Chillicothe, OH St. Peter; Waverly, OH St. Mary, Queen of the Missions.
Hahr, Karl A. '04 (BUR) Knights of Columbus; Richford, VT All Saints.
Hai, Dinh Minh *c.ss.r.* '95 (LA)[P] Baldwin Park Vietnamese Redemptorist Mission.
Hai, Nguyen Tat *c.ss.r.* '95 (LA)[P] Baldwin Park Vietnamese Redemptorist Mission.
Haider, Craig '06 (SD) On Duty Outside the Diocese.
Haider, Craig '06 (GLD) Oscoda, MI Sacred Heart; East Tawas, MI Holy Family.
Haig, Frank R. *s.j.* '60 (BAL)[Q] Baltimore, MD Jesuit Community of Loyola University, Inc.; [B] Jesuit Community of Loyola University, Inc.
Haight, Roger D. *s.j.* '67 (NY)[DD] New York, NY "America;" Residence and publication office of the America Press.
Hain, Rev. Msgr. Raymond B. '48 (LIN)[E] Lincoln, NE Bonacum House Retired.
Haines, Jeffrey R. '85 (MIL) Milwaukee, WI Cathedral of St. John the Evangelist; Archdiocesan Consultors; Archdiocesan Council of Priests.
Haines, Kevin J. '87 (LFT) Westfield, IN St. Maria Goretti.
Haiss, Maurice *s.t.* '56 (WDC)[O] Adelphi, MD Father Judge Missionary Cenacle.
Hajduk, Rev. Msgr. Edward J. '53 (NEW)[L] Rutherford, NJ St. John Vianney Residence for Priests Retired.
Hakala, Thomas *o.carm.* '78 (JOL)[L] Darien Carmelite Provincial Office.
Hake, Rev. Msgr. James E. '60 (SAL) Lincoln, KS St. Joseph Parish; Lincoln, KS St. Patrick Parish; Defender of the Bond; College of Consultors; Personnel Board; Art and Architecture Commission; Ex Officio; Consultors.
Halabura, Stephen J. '61 (ALN)[J] Bethlehem, PA Holy Family Villa Retired.
Haladej, Peter '02 (Y) East Liverpool, OH Holy Trinity Parish; Presbyteral Council.
Haladus, Victorian *o.f.m.* '61 (SFD)[K] Sherman, IL Blessed Giles Friary.
Halaiko, David J. '67 (CLV) Akron, OH Nativity Of the Lord Jesus.
Halbing, William J. '82 (NEW) Newark, NJ St. Antoninus.
Halborg, John T. '80 (NY)[HH] New York, NY St. Ansgar Scandinavian Catholic League Retired.
Halbur, Kenneth '09 (DM) Council Bluffs, IA Corpus Christi; [C] Council Bluffs, IA Saint Albert Catholic Schools.
Haldane, Richard S. '92 (B) Cottonwood, ID Assumption; Cottonwood, ID St. Anthony's; Cottonwood, ID St. Mary's.
Haldas, Piotr *s.d.s.* (NEW) Garfield, NJ St. Stanislaus Kostka.
Hale, Robert *o.s.b.cam.* '66 (MRY)[F] Big Sur, CA New Camaldoli Hermitage.
Haley, James A. *c.s.p.* '68 (NY)[DD] New York, NY Paulist Fathers' Motherhouse.
Haley, James A. *c.s.p.* '68 (BRK)[R] Paulist Priests at Paulist Foundations Outside the U.S.
Haley, Thomas '78 (STL) Saint Louis, MO Our Lady of the Rosary.
Halfacre, Rev. Msgr. Philip '91 (PEO) Vicariates and Vicars; Censor Librorum; Streator, IL St. Michael the Archangel Church.
Halfmann, Rev. Msgr. Curtis T. '59 (LUB) Retired.
Halfpenny, Rev. Msgr. Patrick F. '75 (DET) Grosse Pointe Farms, MI St. Paul Catholic Church.
Halka, Frantisek A. '98 (ALT) Army Chaplains; Military Chaplains.
Halkovic, Thomas M. *c.s.c.* '71 (FR)[A] North Easton, MA Stonehill College; [A] North Easton, MA Holy Cross Fathers Religious.
Halkovic, Thomas M. *c.s.c.* '71 (FTW)[H] Notre Dame Congregation of Holy Cross, United States Province of Priests & Brothers.
Hall, Adrian B. '64 (NO) Retired.
Hall, Charles D. '79 (GR) Holland, MI Our Lady of the Lake.
Hall, Conan *s.a.* '74 (NY)[DD] Garrison, NY St. Francis of Assisi Novitiate.
Hall, Daniel R. *c.s.v.* '88 (CHI)[N] Arlington Heights Viatorian Province Center–Clerics of St. Viator.
Hall, Douglas C. '79 (OM) Omaha, NE Christ the King.
Hall, Eric '01 (WH) Parkersburg, WV St. Francis Xavier's; Parkersburg, WV St. Monica's.
Hall, Howard B. '62 (BR) Retired.
Hall, Howard *o.f.m.* '53 (LA)[P] Santa Barbara, CA Franciscan Friary, Order of Friars Minor (Old Mission).
Hall, James W. '70 (ELP) El Paso, TX St. Thomas Aquinas; Judges.
Hall, John F. '55 (DET) Presbyteral Council Retired.
Hall, John M. '80 (IND) Martinsville, IN St. Martin of

Tours Catholic Church, Martinsville, Inc.; French Lick, IN Our Lady of the Springs Catholic Church, French Lick, Inc.; French Lick, IN Our Lord Jesus Christ the King Catholic Church, Paoli, Inc.
Hall, Joseph S. '85 (L) Retired.
Hall, Martin J. '52 (RVC) Levittown, NY St. Bernard Retired.
Hall, Michael *o.s.b.* '65 (WDC)[O] Washington, DC St. Anselm's Abbey.
Hall, Michael '10 (TR) Bayville, NJ St. Barnabas; Censores Librorum.
Hall, R. Eric '01 (WH) Presbyteral Council.
Hall, Ralph T. *o.p.* '55 (PRO)[O] Providence St. Thomas Aquinas Priory at Providence College Retired.
Hall, Richard R. *o.m.i.* '93 (SAT) San Antonio, TX San Juan De Los Lagos Shrine.
Hall, Robert C. '79 (ALT) Conemaugh, PA Church of the Transfiguration.
Hall, Robert '85 (HEL) Butte, MT Butte Catholic Community North; Butte, MT Immaculate Conception; Butte, MT St. Joseph; Butte, MT St. Patrick; [G] Butte, MT Montana College of Mineral Science and Technology; Presbyteral Council; Diocesan Consultors.
Hall, Rodney '91 (SAC) Retired.
Hall, Roger L. *o.f.m.* '03 (HRT)[L] Waterbury, CT St. Michael Rectory; Waterbury, CT St. Michael.
Hall, Sidney '57 (SAC) Retired.
Hall, Timothy J. '06 (WIN) Adrian, MN St. Adrian; Lismore, MN St. Anthony's; Adrian, MN Our Lady of Good Counsel; Lismore, MN St. Kilian.
Hall, Warren R. '89 (NEW)[D] Jersey City, NJ Hudson Catholic Regional High School; [B] Seton Hall University.
Halladay, Paul A. '00 (MO) On Leave for Military; Army Chaplains.
Hallahan, Kenneth P. '75 (CAM) Campaign for Human Development; Blackwood, NJ Our Lady of Hope Parish, Blackwood, N.J.
Hallahan, Timothy J. '57 (SPR) Retired.
Hallahan, William *o.m.i.* '59 (OAK)[L] Oakland, CA Missionary Oblates of Mary Immaculate United States Province.
Hallee, Roger *o.m.i.* '63 (FgM) Washington, DC AMERICAN OBLATE MISSIONS.
Hallegado, Salvador Den '03 (CHI) Chicago, IL St. Genevieve.
Halleman, John L. '55 (STL) Retired.
Haller, Jeffery *o.f.m.* (STL)[O] St. Louis Franciscan Friary of St. Anthony of Padua.
Halleron, James E. '97 (TOL) Montpelier, OH Sacred Heart; Bryan, OH St. Patrick.
Hallett, Garth L. *s.j.* '59 (STL)[O] St. Louis, MO Jesuit Community Corporation at Saint Louis University – Jesuit Hall.
Halley, James L. '04 (LA) Long Beach, CA St. Joseph; San Pedro Region.
Halligan, Damian O. *s.j.* '67 (RVC)[P] Manhasset, NY St. Ignatius Jesuit Retreat House, Inisfada.
Halligan, John J. *s.j.* '61 (FgM) New York, NY Society of Jesus.
Halligan, Raymond Ferrer *o.p.* '60 (NY)[DD] New York, NY St. Vincent Ferrer Priory.
Hallin, Rev. Msgr. Albert W. '61 (PEO) Ivesdale, IL St. Joseph's; Seymour, IL St. Boniface; Vicariates and Vicars; Commission for Ecumenism; Thomasboro, IL St. Elizabeth of Hungary.
Hallinan, Edward J. '83 (PH) Wallingford, PA St. John Chrysostom.
Hallinan, Mark C. *s.j.* '95 (NY) Staten Island, NY St. Mary of the Assumption; Staten Island, NY Our Lady of Mt. Carmel–St. Benedicta.
Hallissey, LaSalle Sean *o.p.* '79 (SAC) Benicia, CA St. Dominic.
Hallock, Addison *m.s.a.* '74 (NOR)[A] Cromwell, CT Holy Apostles College and Seminary; [G] Cromwell, CT Society of the Missionaries of the Holy Apostles; Cromwell, CT Missionaries of the Holy Apostles, Society of the; Cromwell, CT.
Halloran, James F. '43 (COS) Retired.
Halloran, Rev. Msgr. John C. '62 (PRO) Retired.
Halloran, Joseph H. '47 (COS) Retired.
Halloran, Joseph '53 (ALB) Retired.
Halloran, Paul F. '53 (WIN) Retired.
Hallsten, Thomas J. '90 (PHX) Tempe, AZ Holy Spirit Roman Catholic Parish; Scenic, AZ La Santisima Trinidad Mission, A Quasi–Parish.
Halphen, Jude '94 (LAF) New Iberia, LA St. Peter; Marriage and Family Life Ministry.
Halpin, Don *o.f.m.conv.* '72 (IND)[J] Mount St. Francis, IN Mount Saint Francis Friary and Retreat Center.
Halpin, Joseph A. '79 (TR) Retired.
Halpin, Joseph W. *m.m.* '52 (FgM) Maryknoll, NY MARYKNOLL.
Halsema, Douglas G. '00 (PT) Pensacola, FL St. Paul; Independent Review Board; Permanent Deacon Formation Board; Permanent Deacon Formation Team.
Halstead, James R. *o.s.a.* '76 (CHI) Evanston, IL St. Nicholas.
Halstead, John (TOL)[F] Tiffin, OH Mercy Hospital of Tiffin.
Halter, Robert *c.ss.r.* '70 (DEN)[N] Denver, CO The Redemptorists/Denver Province; Denver, CO.
Halus, Robert E. '82 (PBR) Perryopolis, PA St. Nicholas.
Halvey, William *s.v.d.* '76 (CHI)[N] Techny, IL Divine Word Residence.
Halvorson, Richard '04 (KCK) Holy Childhood Association; Pontifical Mission Societies in the United States; Archdiocesan Council on Finances; Paola, KS Holy Trinity.
Ham, Rev. Msgr. Jerome '68 (PEO) Diocesan College of Consultors Retired.
Hamaday, Ronald A. *o.s.a.* '78 (CAM)[C] Richland, NJ St. Augustine Preparatory School; Richland, NJ.
Hamaday, Ronald A. *o.s.a.* '78 (MO) Navy Reserve Chaplains.
Hamak, William '92 (SFS) Mobridge, SD St. Joseph.
Hambach, Lawrence *s.v.d.* '61 (FgM) Techny, IL.
Hambrough, Rev. Msgr. Patrick K. '85 (STL) St. Louis, MO St. Mark.
Hamel, J. Thomas *s.j.* '58 (WOR)[N] Worcester, MA Jesuits of the Holy Cross, Inc.
Hamel, James A. '92 (MO) Military Chaplains; Air Force Chaplains.
Hamel, Joseph L. *m.m.* '85 (FgM) Maryknoll, NY MARYKNOLL.
Hamel, Philip N. '85 (FR) New Bedford, MA St. Joseph–St. Therese.
Hamel, Robert F. '83 (STP) Retired.
Hamernik, Peter P. '56 (WOR) Retired.
Hamill, Gregory J. '94 (PH) Oxford, PA Sacred Heart; [BB] Oxford, PA Lincoln University.
Hamill, William A. *o.s.a.* '68 (TLS)[B] Tulsa, OK Cascia Hall Preparatory School.
Hamilton, Daniel E. '72 (ARL) On Leave of Absence.
Hamilton, Rev. Msgr. Daniel S. '58 (RVC) Lindenhurst, NY Our Lady of Perpetual Help Retired.
Hamilton, Donald Joseph *o.c.s.o.* '46 (SPC)[F] Ava, MO Assumption Abbey (Trappist).
Hamilton, Edward A. '59 (ORL) Retired.
Hamilton, James J. '53 (PRO) Retired.
Hamilton, James '58 (CC) Judges Retired.
Hamilton, John W. '70 (BUR)[D] Rutland, VT St. Joseph/Kervick Residence Retired.
Hamilton, Mark M. '94 (L) Louisville, KY St. Martha.
Hamilton, Stephen V. '99 (OKL) Kingfisher, OK SS. Peter and Paul; Region IX; Council of Priests Archdiocesan; Defenders of the Bond.
Hamilton, Terence J. '73 (CIN) Cincinnati, OH St. Martin of Tours; Consultors; Presbyteral Council.
Hamilton, Thomas M. '88 (SFR) San Francisco, CA St. Gabriel; Young Ladies' Institute.
Hamilton, Thomas *o.f.m.conv.* '82 (OAK)[L] Castro Valley, CA Conventual Franciscans (Province of St. Joseph of Cupertino).
Hamilton, William J. *s.j.* '63 (BO)[U] Weston, MA Campion Health Center, Inc.
Hamlet, Mark '10 (AUS) San Marcos, TX St. John the Evangelist.
Hamlet, Ralph '62 (RIC) Retired.
Hamlett, Christopher M. '82 (E) Greenville, PA St. Michael.
Hamm, David A. *s.t.* '75 (BLX) Pass Christian, MS Most Holy Trinity Parish.
Hamm, M. Dennis *s.j.* '70 (OM)[J] Omaha, NE Jesuit Community at Creighton University.
Hamm, Thomas F. '00 (STU)[L] Gallipolis, OH Rio Grande University.
Hamm, Thomas F. '00 (STU) Gallipolis, OH St. Louis; [M] Gallipolis, OH RCIA; Diocesan Director of Ecumenism; RCIA.
Hammelman, William *o.s.b.* '71 (P) Silverton, OR St. Paul; [L] St. Benedict, OR Mt. Angel Abbey.
Hammer, James *o.f.m.cap.* '65 (NOR) Middletown, CT St. Pius X.
Hammer, Jefferson J. '60 (NY) Retired.
Hammer, Michael J. '69 (MIL) Retired.
Hammer, William D. '80 (L) Bardstown, KY Basilica of St. Joseph Proto–Cathedral; Deans; Fairfield, KY St. Michael; Priests' Council.
Hammerl, Rev. Msgr. Leo E. '44 (BUF)[N] Tonawanda, NY O'Hara Residence Retired.
Hammerschmitt, Clemens '73 (PMB) Lake Worth, FL St. Matthew; [K] Palm Beach Gardens, FL Diocesan Council of Catholic Women; Council of Catholic Women.
Hammerstein, Harold *o.s.b.* '48 (IND)[K] Saint Meinrad St. Meinrad Archabbey.
Hammes, Anderson L. *c.s.* '10 (CHI) Melrose Park, IL St. Charles Borromeo.
Hammes, Greg '07 (KCK) Sabetha, KS St. Augustine.
Hammes, Gregory '07 (KCK) Sabetha, KS Sacred Heart; Sabetha, KS St. James.
Hammett, Peter E. *o.s.b.* '72 (NO)[R] St. Benedict, LA St. Joseph Abbey; Franklinton, LA Holy Family.
Hammond, Charles '76 (SAG) Sandusky, MI St. Joseph.
Hammond, David '10 (ALB) Schenectady, NY Our Lady Queen of Peace.
Hammond, Gerard E. *m.m.* '60 (FgM) Maryknoll, NY MARYKNOLL.
Hammond, H. Martin '73 (BAL) Baltimore, MD St. Isaac Jogues.
Hammond, John *o.s.b.* '50 (BUR)[E] Weston, VT Priory of Benedictine Monks.
Hammond, Joseph '89 (KNX) Morristown, TN St. Patrick.
Hammond, Mark J. '89 (COL) Mt. Vernon, OH St. Vincent de Paul; Deanery 9: Knox Licking; Presbyteral Council; Presbyteral Council; Defenders of the Bond; Health Affairs Department (Hospitals); Parochial Examiners.
Hamon, Victor '93 (TYL) Diboll, TX Our Lady of Guadalupe.
Hampe, Rev. Msgr. Raymond A. '54 (STL) St. Charles, MO St. Peter; St. Charles, MO St. Joseph Health Center; [J] St. Charles, MO SSM St. Joseph Health Center Retired.
Hamperzonian, Jerry '70 (SD) On Duty Outside Diocese; San Diego, CA Blessed Sacrament Catholic Parish.
Hampsch, John *c.m.f.* '52 (LA)[V] Rancho Dominguez, CA Dominguez Seminary Inc.
Hamrogue, John M. *c.ss.r.* '63 (PH) Philadelphia, PA St. Peter the Apostle.
Han, Jae Sang (NSH) Korean Catholic Community of St. Joseph.
Han, Jinwook '10 (NEW) Saddle Brook, NJ Church of Korean Martyrs.
Han, Maryjoseph Kwangseog (HON) Honolulu, HI Korean Catholic Community.
Han, Seung Hoon (R) Fayetteville, NC St. Andrew Kim.
Han, Thomas '83 (LA) West Covina, CA St. Christopher.
Han, Young Seung J. '98 (SB) Riverside, CA St. Andrew Kim Korean Community.
Hanbury, Rev. Msgr. Kevin M. '72 (NEW) Livingston, NJ St. Philomena; [B] Seton Hall University; Office of the Superintendent of Schools/Vicariate for Education; Presbyteral Council; Vicar for Education and Superintendent of Schools; Members.
Hancock, Rev. Msgr. George '47 (OWN) Retired.
Hand, Dennis M. '75 (GRY) On Duty Outside the Diocese.
Hand, John D. '98 (PH) Philadelphia, PA St. Francis de Sales.
Hand, Kenneth J. '72 (BRK) On Leave/Unassigned.
Hand, Raymond *o.f.m.cap.* '62 (NY)[DD] Yonkers, NY St. Clare Friary.
Hand, Robert T. '97 (SAV) Retired.
Handal, Ephrem '03 (NTN) McLean, VA Holy Transfiguration.
Handges, Rev. Msgr. William E. '64 (ALN) Coplay, PA St. Peter.
Handrahan, John B. *s.j.* '58 (BO)[U] Weston, MA Campion Health Center, Inc.
Handwerker, Rev. Msgr. Valentine N. '74 (MEM) Memphis, TN Cathedral of the Immaculate Conception; [C] Memphis, TN Immaculate Conception Cathedral School.
Hanefeldt, Joseph G. '84 (OM) On Duty Outside the Archdiocese.
Hanel, Charles T. '83 (MIL) Hubertus, WI St. Gabriel.
Haney, John R. '61 (PIT) Pittsburgh, PA St. Gabriel of the Sorrowful Virgin; Clergy Personnel Board; Priest Council.
Haney, Michael *o.f.m.* '74 (GLD) Indian River, MI Cross in the Woods Catholic Shrine.
Haney, T. Ronald '58 (HBG) New Cumberland, PA St. Theresa of the Infant Jesus Retired.
Haney, William *o.f.m.* '84 (MRY)[F] San Juan Bautista, CA Franciscan Friars; [H] San Juan Bautista, CA St. Francis Retreat Center.
Hanh, Joseph Phan Trong '70 (KC) Kansas City, MO Church of the Holy Martyrs.
Hanhauser, Martin *o.f.m.* (PAT)[N] Ringwood, NJ Holy Name Friary, Inc.
Hanic, John D. '83 (CHL) North Wilkesboro, NC St. John Baptist de LaSalle.
Hanic, Jonathan '67 (CHL) Absent On Leave.
Hanifan, Mark '07 (RNO) Respect Life Commission; Reno, NV St. Albert the Great.
Hanifin, Michael P. '87 (ORG) Yorba Linda, CA Santa Clara de Asis; Boy Scouts/Girl Scouts; Irving, TX National Catholic Committee on Scouting Executive Committee (1934).
Hanincik, Frank A. '08 (PSC) New Britain, CT Holy Trinity; Trumbull, CT St. John the Baptist.
Hankee, Robert Jason '02 (IND) Corydon, IN St. Joseph Catholic Church, Corydon, Inc.; Corydon, IN Most Precious Blood Catholic Church, New Middleton,Inc.; Corydon, IN St. Peter Catholic Church, Elizabeth, Inc.
Hankiewicz, Edward A. '79 (GR) On Special Assignment; Tribunal Office; Lowell, MI St. Mary's.
Hanking, Brendan *o.praem.* (ORG)[D] Silverado, CA St. Michael's Preparatory School.
Hankins, Brendan R. *o.praem.* '11 (ORG)[I] Silverado, CA Norbertine Fathers of Orange Inc.
Hankomoone, Cornelius *s.s.* '96 (BAL)[Q] Baltimore Society of St. Sulpice, Province of the United States.
Hanks, Gregory '89 (AUS) Wimberley, TX St. Mary.
Hanks, Sebastian J. *o.s.p.p.e.* '81 (GBG)[H] Kittanning,

PA Pauline Fathers Monastery.
Hankus, David J. '84 (JOL) Oswego, IL St. Anne; Deans.
Hanley, Rev. Msgr. Andrew W. '40 (SD) Retired.
Hanley, Christopher '08 (WIL) Bethany Beach, DE St. Ann.
Hanley, Daniel F. '05 (ARL) Secretary to the Bishop; Vocations, Office of.
Hanley, Dennis P. '81 (HRT) Military Chaplains.
Hanley, Foster *o.carm.* '63 (TUC)[A] Tucson, AZ Salpointe Catholic High School; [E] Tucson, AZ Carmelite Priory.
Hanley, Gerald T. '73 (RNO) Retired.
Hanley, James R. *s.j.* '58 (SJ)[M] Los Gatos, CA Sacred Heart Jesuit Center.
Hanley, John A. *o.s.f.s.* '86 (ALN)[B] Center Valley, PA DeSales University; [K] Center Valley, PA Oblates of St. Francis de Sales; [O] Center Valley, PA DeSales University (Center Valley).
Hanley, John P. '94 (PAT) Paterson, NJ St. Casimir's; Auditors; Natural Family Planning Retired.
Hanley, John W. *o.m.i.* '70 (NOR)[I] Willimantic, CT Immaculata Retreat House; [G] Willimantic, CT Missionary Oblates of Mary Immaculate.
Hanley, John '56 (PHX)[G] Phoenix, AZ Mount Claret Roman Catholic Retreat Center Retired.
Hanley, Rev. Msgr. Joseph F. '68 (CHR) Presbyteral Council.
Hanley, Rev. Msgr. Joseph F. '68 (CHR) North Charleston, SC St. John; Charleston, SC Blessed Sacrament; College of Consultors; Deans; Personnel Committee.
Hanley, Thomas E. '65 (WIL) Retired.
Hanley, William '69 (ORL) Retired.
Hanlon, Berard J. *o.f.m.* '63 (FgM) New York, NY Holy Name Province.
Hanlon, Capistran *o.f.m.* '60 (ALB)[B] Siena College.
Hanlon, Edward J. '86 (WOR) South Grafton, MA St. James.
Hanlon, Francis *o.s.f.s.* '76 (VEN) Fort Myers, FL St. Cecilia.
Hanlon, Kevin J. *m.m.* '89 (NY)[DD] Maryknoll Maryknoll Fathers and Brothers.
Hanlon, Robert M. *s.j.* '64 (BO)[U] Boston The Society of Jesus of New England–Provincial Offices.
Hanly, Denis J. *m.m.* '59 (FgM) Maryknoll, NY MARYKNOLL.
Hanly, Michael A. '67 (NEW) Verona, NJ Our Lady of the Lake.
Hann, Gregory B. '99 (NEW) Absent on Leave.
Hann, Michael *c.i.c.m.* '73 (ARL)[H] Arlington, VA Missionhurst, C.I.C.M.–Central House and Provincialate.
Hanna, Dominique '07 (SAM) Atlanta, GA St. Joseph's Maronite Church; Vocations.
Hanna, George *s.d.b.* '66 (WDC) Washington, DC Nativity.
Hanna, Jack H. *c.s.b.* '74 (GAL)[E] Houston, TX St. Thomas High School.
Hannafey, Francis T. *s.j.* '93 (BGP)[B] Fairfield, CT Fairfield University; [O] Fairfield, CT The Fairfield Jesuit Community–Fairfield University.
Hannafin, Steven J. '01 (RVC) New Hyde Park, NY Notre Dame.
Hannah, Raymond *s.v.d.* '60 (TR)[N] Bordentown, NJ Society of the Divine Word.
Hannan, Gabriel *s.t.* '55 (WDC)[O] Adelphi, MD Father Judge Missionary Cenacle.
Hannan, James E. *o.s.a.* '44 (SD)[J] San Diego, CA Augustinian Community.
Hannan, James G. '81 (BRK) On Leave/Unassigned.
Hannan, John K. '55 (SAC) Sacramento, CA St. Philomene Retired.
Hannan, John *s.m.* '68 (FgM) THE SOCIETY OF MARY.
Hannappel, Joseph A. '84 (GI) Kearney, NE St. James; Diocesan Consultors; Personnel Board.
Hanneke, Rev. Msgr. Richard E. '76 (STL) Office of Priests' Personnel and Continuing Formation of Priests; St. Louis, MO St. Stephen, Protomartyr.
Hanneman, Dennis A. '72 (OM) Bellevue, NE St. Mary.
Hannes, David A. '83 (PRM) Flushing, MI St. Michael; Presbyteral Council; Judges.
Hannick, Anthony S. '58 (YAK) Retired.
Hannigan, John T. '76 (MO) Navy Chaplains; Military Chaplains.
Hannigan, Raymond (HEL) Retired.
Hannon, James J. '57 (RVC) Retired.
Hannon, James J. '52 (RVC)[N] Amityville, NY St. Pius X Residence Retired.
Hannon, Rev. Msgr. James W. '88 (BAL) Special Assignment; Clergy Personnel, Division of; Baltimore, MD Cathedral of Mary Our Queen.
Hannon, John M. '60 (BO) Hanson, MA St. Joseph the Worker.
Hannon, Ken *o.m.i.* '72 (SAT)[C] Oblate School of Theology; [L] San Antonio, TX De Mazenod House.
Hannon, Michael '47 (ORL) Retired.
Hannon, Patrick *c.s.c.* '89 (P)[B] University of Portland; [L] Portland, OR Holy Cross Fathers & Brothers, C.S.C. – University of Portland.
Hannon, Richard T. '93 (GLD) Retired.
Hannon, Robert J. '79 (Y) Canton, OH St. Therese Little Flower Retired.
Hannon, W. *c.s.c.* (FTW)[H] Notre Dame Congregation of Holy Cross, United States Province of Priests & Brothers.
Hanouille, Roger M. *o.s.a.* '59 (PH)[Y] Villanova, PA St. Thomas Monastery.
Hanowsky, Rev. Canon Andrew '88 (SJP) Cleveland, OH Ss. Peter and Paul; Administrative Council; Consultors; St. Josaphat Sacerdotal Society; Presbyters.
Hanrahan, Denis G. '59 (OKL) Retired.
Hanrahan, Edward J. *s.j.* '61 (BO)[U] Weston, MA Campion Health Center, Inc.
Hanrahan, John W. '55 (L) Retired.
Hanrahan, William P. '69 (NEW) Military Chaplains.
Hanrahan, William '69 (ANC) Diocesan Consultors; Notaries.
Hansen, John R. *s.m.p.* '81 (SPC)[F] Marionville, MO The Society of Our Mother of Peace, Sons of Our Mother of Peace.
Hansen, Lawrence H. '68 (NU) Retired.
Hansen, Michael H. (NEW) Retired.
Hansen, Stephen '06 (KC) Grandview, MO Coronation of Our Lady.
Hanser, F. Patrick *c.m.* '70 (DAL)[J] Dallas, TX Congregation of the Mission, Western Province.
Hanson, Rev. Msgr. Donald M. '71 (RVC) East Hampton, NY Most Holy Trinity.
Hanson, Rev. Msgr. James E. '61 (STL) Retired.
Hanson, John Henry *o.praem.* '06 (ORG)[I] Silverado, CA Norbertine Fathers of Orange Inc.; [D] Silverado, CA St. Michael's Preparatory School; [A] Silverado, CA St. Michael's Norbertine Postulancy, Novitiate and Juniorate.
Hanson, Richard N. '75 (CHL) Unassigned.
Hanson, Rev. Msgr. William A. '72 (RVC) Port Jefferson Station, NY St. Gerard Majella; North Brookhaven Deanery.
Hanudel, Francis A. *o.f.m.* (NY) New York, NY St. Anthony of Padua.
Hanus, Thomas J. '66 (AUS) Retired.
Hanwell, John J. *s.j.* '91 (BGP)[E] Fairfield, CT Fairfield College Preparatory School; [O] Fairfield, CT The Fairfield Jesuit Community–Fairfield University.
Hao, William T. '09 (ATL) Dunwoody, GA All Saints.
Hapanowicz, Arthur R. '56 (SY) New Hartford, NY St. John the Evangelist.
Hapka, Jerome A. *s.a.c.* '55 (MIL)[P] Milwaukee, WI Pallotti House.
Harahan, Rev. Msgr. Robert E. '74 (NEW) Wyckoff, NJ St. Elizabeth.
Harak, G. Simon *s.j.* '79 (MIL)[P] Milwaukee, WI Jesuit Community at Marquette University.
Harak, G. Simon *s.j.* '79 (BO)[U] Boston The Society of Jesus of New England–Provincial Offices.
Haran, F. Ignatius '59 (SAC) Folsom, CA St. John the Baptist; [N] Sacramento, CA The Parochial Fund, Inc.; Members Retired.
Haran, James E. '44 (BUF) Retired.
Harbaugh, James *s.j.* '76 (SEA)[C] Tacoma, WA Bellarmine Preparatory School; Tacoma, WA St. Leo the Great.
Harbaugh, Paul E. '74 (BEL) Leave of Absence.
Harbaugh, Russell D. '04 (MEM) Bartlett, TN St. Ann; College of Consultors; Presbyteral Council.
Harbour, Gerald G. '73 (PRO) Pawtucket, RI St. John the Baptist.
Harbour, Linn S. '86 (MOB) On Leave for Military.
Harburg, Nathan E. '11 (SAG) Port Austin, MI St. Michael; Kinde, MI St. Mary–St. Edward.
Harcarik, Bernard M. '63 (PIT) Pittsburgh, PA Prince of Peace.
Harder, Kenneth J. '96 (TLS) Stillwater, OK St. Francis Xavier; Judges; Adjutant Judicial Vicar.
Hardesty, Ernest L. '75 (LR)[I] Russellville, AR St. Leo the Great University Parish; Presbyteral Council; Russellville, AR St. Leo the Great University Parish; Atkins, AR Assumption B.V.M.
Hardesty, Matthew T. '11 (L) Elizabethtown, KY St. James; White Mills, KY St. Ignatius; Ex Officio; Elizabethtown, KY St. Ambrose.
Hardiman, Rev. Msgr. Michael J. '78 (BRK) Woodside, NY St. Sebastian.
Hardin, Boniface *o.s.b.* '59 (IND)[K] Saint Meinrad St. Meinrad Archabbey.
Hardin, John S. *o.f.m.* '86 (SFR) Oakland, CA; San Francisco, CA St. Boniface.
Hardin, John *o.f.m.* '82 (OAK)[L] Oakland, CA Franciscan Friars of California (Province of St. Barbara); [Q] Oakland, CA Province of Saint Barbara Fraternal Care Trust.
Harding, Ignatius *o.f.m.* '72 (FgM) New York, NY Holy Name Province.
Harding, Pius X *o.s.b.* '93 (P)[L] St. Benedict, OR Mt. Angel Abbey; [N] St. Benedict, OR Mount Angel Abbey Retreat House.
Hardon, John *s.j.* '47 (WDC)[X] Kensington, MD Inter Mirifica.
Hardy, J. Patrick '06 (SUP) Winter, WI St. Peter; Winter, WI Sacred Heart.
Hardy, Joseph F. '65 (CHI) Evergreen Park, IL Most Holy Redeemer.
Hardy, L. Richard '06 (PAT) Parsippany, NJ St. Peter the Apostle.
Haremza, Shawn T. '00 (WIN) Rochester, MN Resurrection.
Haren, Thomas A. '73 (CLV) Garfield Heights, OH St. Monica; Holy Name Societies, Cleveland Diocesan Union.
Harfmann, John G. *s.s.j.* '62 (NO) New Orleans, LA Corpus Christi–Epiphany.
Hargaden, Kevin J. '99 (ATL) Tyrone, GA St. Matthew; Advocates; Vicars for Clergy.
Harger, Bruce E. '01 (NEW) Hillsdale, NJ St. John the Baptist.
Hargesheimer, Thomas J. '68 (WIN) Diocesan Consultors; Winona, MN St. Stanislaus; Deans; Council of Catholic Women; Winona, MN St. John Nepomucene.
Hargreaves, Henry G. *s.j.* '47 (SPK)[J] Spokane, WA Regis Community.
Harhager, John H. *s.m.* '79 (ATL)[C] Atlanta, GA Marist School.
Harkins, Conrad *o.f.m.* '61 (STU)[A] Steubenville, OH Franciscan University of Steubenville; [H] Steubenville, OH Holy Spirit Friary.
Harkins, Evan '10 (KC) Kansas City, MO St. Therese Parish.
Harkins, John M. '65 (PH) Philadelphia, PA St. Ambrose.
Harkins, Michael J. '79 (BO) Newton, MA Mary Immaculate of Lourdes.
Harkins, Simon *f.s.s.p.* '10 (SCR)[D] Elmhurst Twp., PA St. Gregory's Academy; [L] Elmhurst Twp., PA Priestly Fraternity of St. Peter (F.S.S.P.), North American District Headquarters.
Harkrader, Edward O. '69 (PEO) Retired.
Harlow, Lance W. '93 (BUR) Richmond, VT Our Lady of the Holy Rosary; Charismatic Renewal; Williston, VT Immaculate Heart of Mary.
Harlow, Sean R. *o.carm.* '69 (NY) New York, NY St. John the Martyr.
Harman, Paul F. *s.j.* '68 (WOR)[N] Worcester, MA Jesuits of the Holy Cross, Inc.
Harman, Peter C. '99 (SFD) Springfield, IL St. Katharine Drexel; Springfield, IL Cathedral of the Immaculate Conception.
Harmening, Adrian W. *o.s.b.* '55 (RIC)[K] Richmond, VA Mary Mother of the Church Abbey.
Harmless, William J. *s.j.* '87 (OM)[J] Omaha, NE Jesuit Community at Creighton University.
Harmon, Alban *c.p.* '58 (BAL)[Q] Baltimore, MD St. Joseph's Passionist Community; Baltimore, MD St. Joseph Passionist Monastery Parish.
Harmon, Barry J. '90 (SFD) Arcola, IL St. John the Baptist; Tuscola, IL Forty Martyrs; Comite Diocesano de Ministerio Hispano – Diocesan Committee for Hispanic Ministry.
Harmon, John '93 (DM) Urbandale, IA St. Pius X.
Harms, Rev. Msgr. William C. '65 (NEW) New Energies – Archdiocesan Implementation Team; Berkeley Heights, NJ Church of the Little Flower Retired.
Harnan, James A. *m.s.c.* '64 (SAT) Stonewall, TX St. Francis Xavier; [L] San Antonio, TX Missionaries of the Sacred Heart.
Harness, H. Robert '82 (DAV) Davenport, IA Holy Family.
Harnett, Brendan G. '73 (PRT) Wells, ME Holy Spirit Parish.
Harnett, Edward F. '58 (CHI) Wilmette, IL St. Francis Xavier Retired.
Harnett, Rev. Msgr. Timothy '56 (SD) Retired.
Harney, Thomas C. '62 (GF) Laurel, MT St. Anthony.
Harnischfeger, William '93 (PHX) Retired.
Haro–Palos, Arturo '99 (ATL) Cleveland, GA St. Paul the Apostle; Blairsville, GA St. Francis of Assisi.
Harold, Rev. Msgr. Thomas J. '91 (RVC) Garden City, NY St. Anne; Belmont Deanery.
Harpe, David L. '94 (GR) Faculties Suspended.
Harpel, John *s.v.d.* '44 (CHI)[N] Techny, IL Divine Word Residence.
Harper, John H. '87 (GB) Green Bay, WI Nativity of Our Lord.
Harpole, Ryan '11 (OWN) Paducah, KY St. Thomas More.
Harr, Gerald J. '62 (GI) Gering, NE Christ the King.
Harr, Richard *o.m.i.* '52 (BO)[X] Tewksbury, MA Immaculate Heart of Mary Residence.
Harren, Robert C. '66 (SCL) St. Stephen, MN St. Stephen's; Promoter Justitiae; Censores Librorum.
Harrer, Ronald *o.m.i.* '70 (STP)[J] St. Paul, MN Oblate Residence; Regions Medical Center.
Harrigan, Maurice D. '96 (LA) Los Angeles, CA Holy Trinity.
Harrigan, Philip K. *s.j.* '56 (BO)[U] Weston, MA Campion Health Center, Inc.
Harriman, Rev. Msgr. Michael D. '68 (SFR) San Francisco, CA St. Cecilia; College of Consultors; Apostleship of the Sea.
Harrington, Brian J. '67 (FR) Retired.
Harrington, Daniel J. *s.j.* '71 (BO)[U] Brighton, MA

Isaac Jogues House.
Harrington, Donald J. *c.m.* '73 (BRK)[C] Queens, NY St. John's University; [R] Jamaica, NY St. Vincent's House.
Harrington, Donald J. *c.m.* '73 (NY)[C] Staten Island, NY St. John's University Staten Island Campus.
Harrington, Ignatius '82 (NTN) Westerville, OH Holy Resurrection; Zanesville, OH Holy Trinity; Continuing Education of Clergy Office.
Harrington, James J. '53 (BO) Senior Priests. Retired.
Harrington, Jay M. *o.p.* '85 (COL)[A] Columbus, OH Pontifical College Josephinum.
Harrington, Jay (COL)[A] Columbus, OH Pontifical College Josephinum.
Harrington, Jeremy *o.f.m.* '59 (CIN)[T] Cincinnati, OH Community Support Charitable Trust; Washington, DC Commissariat of the Holy Land; Washington, DC; [N] Cincinnati St. Francis Seraph Friary.
Harrington, Jeremy *o.f.m.* '59 (FgM)[O] Washington, DC Franciscan Monastery USA Inc.; Washington, DC COMMISSARIAT OF THE HOLY LAND; [O] Washington, DC Commissariat of the Holy Land, Franciscan Monastery – Mount St. Sepulchre.
Harrington, John P. '66 (BRK) Astoria, NY St. Joseph.
Harrington, John P. '04 (FR) Awaiting Assignment.
Harrington, Rev. Msgr. Joseph D. '56 (HEL) Friends of The Catholic University; Episcopal Vicar for Senior Status Priests; Diocesan Finance Council Retired.
Harrington, Kevin J. '75 (FR) New Bedford, MA St. Francis of Assisi.
Harrington, Rev. Msgr. Kieran E. '01 (BRK) Brooklyn, NY St. Joseph; Office of Communications & Public Policy; Office of Legislative Affairs; Secretariat for Communications.
Harrington, Mark '79 (PHX) Anthem, AZ St. Rose Philippine Duchesne Roman Catholic Parish; New River, AZ Good Shepherd Mission, A Quasi–Parish; Black Canyon City, AZ St. Philip Benizi Roman Catholic Mission, A Quasi–Parish.
Harrington, Michael C. (BO) Vocations; Dedham, MA St. Mary.
Harrington, Rev. Msgr. Robert J. '71 (NEW) Elizabeth, NJ St. Mary of the Assumption; Archdiocesan Judges.
Harrington, Rev. Msgr. Russell J. '79 (LAF) Church Point, LA Assumption of the Blessed Virgin Mary; Chancellor & Vicar for Priests; Vicar for Priests; Diocesan Consultors; Secretariat of Religious Personnel.
Harrington, Rev. Msgr. Thomas J. '64 (FR) Defenders of the Bond Retired.
Harris, Alfred J. '94 (WDC) Washington, DC St. Mary, Mother of God.
Harris, Anton T. *s.j.* '75 (NY)[DD] Cardinal Spellman Hall, Jesuit Community.
Harris, Arlen *o.f.m.cap.* '08 (NY) New York, NY Good Shepherd; Allen Pavilion–Columbia Presbyterian.
Harris, Daniel E. *c.m.* '74 (STL)[B] St. Louis, MO Aquinas Institute of Theology; [O] St. Louis, MO Lazarist Residence.
Harris, David G. '06 (GAL) Hempstead, TX St. Katherine Drexel.
Harris, David W. '08 (L) Pewee Valley, KY St. Aloysius.
Harris, Edwin B. *s.j.* '75 (SJ)[D] San Jose, CA Bellarmine College Preparatory; Los Gatos, CA.
Harris, Gerald P. '79 (SUP) Hammond, WI Immaculate Conception; River Falls, WI St. Bridget; Presbyteral Council & Diocesan Consultors.
Harris, Glenn '92 (PEO) Rapids City, IL St. John the Baptist.
Harris, Rev. Msgr. Jack D. '74 (LR) West Memphis, AR St. Michael; West Memphis, AR Sacred Heart Church; Deans.
Harris, Rev. Msgr. James E. '85 (LAR) Laredo, TX St. John Neumann.
Harris, Julian P. '91 (PMB) Boynton Beach, FL St. Thomas More.
Harris, Rev. Msgr. Martin P. '55 (WDC) Hollywood, MD St. John Francis Regis Retired.
Harris, Michael B. '89 (SCR) Unassigned or Leave of Absence.
Harris, Raymond L. '94 (BAL) Priests Sick or Absent.
Harris, Rev. Msgr. Richard D. '93 (CHR) Columbia, SC St. Joseph; Finance Council; Building & Renovation Advisory Committee; Investment Council; College of Consultors; Sites & Boundaries Committee; Personnel Committee; Vicar General's Office; Seminary Admissions Board; Presbyteral Council; Priest Retirement Committee; Curia.
Harris, Rev. Msgr. Robert M. '59 (BRK)[M] Brooklyn, NY St. Vincent's Services, Inc.; [K] Brooklyn, NY St. Vincent's Services, Inc.; Released from Diocesan Assignment.
Harris, Robert '96 (DM) Des Moines, IA All Saints.
Harris, Scott T. *m.m.* '78 (NY)[DD].
Harris, Steven J. '80 (PH) Archdiocesan Judges.
Harris, Timothy *t.o.r.* '06 (ARL) Herndon, VA St. Joseph.
Harris, Whitney G. '80 (LKC) On Leave.
Harris, William R. '78 (SEA) Shoreline, WA St. Mark.
Harris, Xavier J. *o.f.m.* '48 (OAK)[L] Oakland Franciscan Friars of California, (Province of St. Barbara).
Harrison, Brian W. *o.s.* '85 (PCE) On Duty Outside the Diocese.
Harrison, Brian W. *o.s.* '85 (STL)[U] Saint Louis, MO Oblates of Wisdom Study Center.
Harrison, Rev. Msgr. Craig F. '87 (FRS) Bakersfield, CA St. Francis of Assisi; Buttonwillow, CA St. Mary; [D] Bakersfield, CA Catholic Charities, Diocese of Fresno; Diocesan Consultors; Vicars Forane; Personnel Board; Taft, CA St. Mary.
Harrison, Eugene *c.ss.r* '01 (NO) New Orleans, LA St. Alphonsus; New Orleans, LA St. Mary's Assumption; New Orleans, LA St. Mary's Chapel.
Harrison, George E. '68 (FR) East Sandwich, MA Corpus Christi.
Harrison, James '55 (ATL) Lawrenceville, GA St. Marguerite D'Youville.
Harrison, Jeffrey D. *s.j.* '87 (FgM) St. Louis, MO Society of Jesus.
Harrison, Jeffrey D. *s.j.* '87 (DEN)[D] Aurora, CO Regis Jesuit High School Corporation; [N] Centennial, CO Regis High Jesuit Community.
Harrison, John *c.ss.r.* '67 (BAL) Annapolis, MD St. Mary.
Harrison, Patrick C. '91 (OM) Omaha, NE St. Joan of Arc.
Harrison, Patrick C. (GI) Promoter Justitiae.
Harrison, Robert '64 (NY)[E] Bronx, NY Cardinal Hayes High School.
Harrison, Robert *c.s.s.r.* '05 (HBG)[G] Ephrata, PA St. Clement's Mission House; Ephrata, PA Mother of Perpetual Help.
Harrison, Timothy A. '91 (BO) Vicariate IV; Newburyport, MA Immaculate Conception.
Harrison, William S. '72 (PH) Cheltenham, PA St. Joseph; Cheltenham, PA Presentation of Blessed Virgin Mary.
Harrity, Rev. Msgr. Dennis '60 (DET) Retired.
Harrity, Patrick V. *c.m.* '68 (STL)[O] Perryville, MO Congregation of the Mission.
Harrity, Patrick V. *c.m.* '68 (CHI)[N] Chicago, IL Vincentian Community, Congregation of the Mission, Western Province.
Harrold, John J. '92 (GBG) Herminie, PA St. Edward.
Harrold, Rev. Msgr. Michael '50 (VIC) Victoria, TX Our Lady of Victory Cathedral; Diocesan Consultors; Victoria Deanery; Presbyteral Council; Judges; Priests' Personnel Board.
Harry, William *o.carm.* '83 (TUC)[A] Tucson, AZ Salpointe Catholic High School; [E] Tucson, AZ Carmelite Priory.
Harshaw, Albert E. '73 (CAM) Collingswood, NJ Blessed Teresa of Calcutta Parish, Collingswood, N.J.
Hart, Brian '63 (SEA) Retired.
Hart, Charles *o.f.m.* '79 (SFD)[K] Springfield, IL Our Lady of Angels Friary.
Hart, Rev. Msgr. E. James '96 (FWT) Consultors; Keller, TX St. Elizabeth Ann Seton; Vicar for Special Projects.
Hart, Gregory G. '84 (LR) Tontitown, AR St. Joseph.
Hart, James '65 (KC) Retired.
Hart, Jean F. *s.o.l.t.* '90 (CC) Corpus Christi, TX St. Anselm Anglican Use Community; [G] Robstown, TX Society of Our Lady of the Most Holy Trinity.
Hart, John B. '60 (SLC) Retired.
Hart, Rev. Msgr. John E. '81 (PAT) Morristown, NJ Assumption of the Blessed Virgin Mary; Associate Judges; Presbyteral Council; College of Consultors; Theological Commission.
Hart, Jonathan '96 (FgM) Boston, MA St. James the Apostle, Inc.
Hart, Joseph A. '73 (ROC) Rochester, NY Our Lady Queen of Peace; Rochester, NY St. Thomas More; Vicars General; Moderator of the Pastoral Center; Censores Librorum; Board of Directors; Pension Committee (Lay and Priests); Priest Consultors.
Hart, Rev. Msgr. Kevin T. '74 (WDC) Rockville, MD St. Patrick; Advocates; Priests Retirement Board.
Hart, Paul S. '89 (NO) New Orleans, LA St. Andrew the Apostle.
Hart, Philip W. *c.s.p.* '73 (BRK)[R] Retired Retired.
Hart, Richard J. '01 (SAV) Dublin, GA Immaculate Conception.
Hart, Richard *o.f.m.cap.* '55 (MIL)[P] Milwaukee, WI St. Conrad Friary.
Hart, Robert H. '00 (STP) Inver Grove Heights, MN Church of St. Patrick; Executive Director; College of Consultors.
Hart, Rolland A. '64 (OG) Retired.
Hart, Ronald '71 (JOL)[K] Naperville, IL St. John Vianney Villa.
Hart, Thomas J. '74 (SC) West Bend, IA St. Mary's; West Bend, IA SS. Peter and Paul.
Hart, Thomas Joseph '07 (LR) North Little Rock, AR Immaculate Heart of Mary.
Hart, Thomas M. *o.s.b.* '88 (GBG)[H] Latrobe, PA Saint Vincent Archabbey.
Hart, William H. '58 (CAM) Retired.
Harte, Rev. Msgr. F. Joseph '61 (ORL) Retired.
Harte, Paul D. '76 (CAM) Representatives by Ordination Seniority; Elected Members; Consultants; Carney's Point, NJ Saint Gabriel the Archangel Parish, Carneys Point, N.J.
Harten, Dennis *o.s.a.* '75 (VEN) Naples, FL St. Elizabeth Seton.
Hartenbach, William *c.m.* '64 (STL)[O] St. Louis, MO Vincentian Residence; [O] St. Louis, MO Lazarist Residence.
Harter, Michael G. *s.j.* '74 (STL) Saint Louis, MO; [V] St. Louis, MO Review for Religious.
Hartford, Kevin F. '04 (WOR) North Brookfield, MA St. Joseph.
Hartgen, Rev. Msgr. Dennis T. '73 (ALN) Reading, PA Holy Guardian Angels; Vicars Forane.
Hartgen, William E. *s.s.* '76 (BAL)[Q] Baltimore Society of St. Sulpice, Province of the United States Retired.
Harth, John M. '87 (SPC) Region VII; Jackson, MO Immaculate Conception.
Hartigan, Dennis P. '80 (TOL) Toledo, OH Historic Church of Saint Patrick; Toledo, OH Immaculate Conception; [B] Toledo, OH Central Catholic High School; Blessed Teresa of Calcutta Deanery.
Hartin, Patrick '71 (SPK)[A] Spokane, WA Bishop White Seminary; Ecumenical Relations.
Hartlage, Albert J. '56 (L) Fairfield, KY St. Michael Retired.
Hartle, Thomas R. *o.f.m.* '79 (PAT)[N] Butler, NJ St. Anthony Friary.
Hartle, Thomas R. *o.f.m.* '71 (BO)[X] Boston, MA Saint Anthony Residence.
Hartlein, Rev. Msgr. Jerome D. '58 (BEL) Mascoutah, IL Holy Childhood of Jesus; Building Commission, Chancery Office.
Hartley, Matthew '06 (DEN) Greeley, CO St. Peter.
Hartley, Paul M. '81 (JC) Kahoka, MO St. Michael the Archangel; Kahoka, MO The Shrine of St. Patrick; Appointed Members.
Hartling, Charles W. '79 (NEW) Rutherford, NJ Church of St. Mary Retired.
Hartman, Augustine *o.p.* '66 (SEA) Seattle, WA Blessed Sacrament.
Hartman, Glenn R. '76 (CAM) Lakeland, NJ Camden County Hospital at Lakeland; [O] Berlin, NJ Mater Ecclesiae Mission.
Hartman, Raymond S. '68 (COV) Covington, KY Mother of God.
Hartman, Rev. Msgr. Thomas '71 (RVC) Chaplains of the Nassau County Police Department.
Hartmann, Rev. Msgr. John F. '53 (BRK) Madison, CT Retired.
Hartmann, Joseph A. '78 (DEN) Estes Park, CO Our Lady of the Mountains.
Hartmann, Paul B.R. '94 (MIL)[Y] Waukesha, WI St. Thomas More Lawyers Society of Wisconsin; Special Assignment; Judicial Vicar; Judges for First Instance; Judges for Second Instance; Office for Marital Reconciliation–Separation; Archdiocesan Court of Equity; [D] Waukesha, WI Catholic Memorial High School.
Hartmann, Richard A. '73 (DET) Flat Rock, MI St. Roch.
Hartnett, Daniel F. *s.j.* '74 (CHI) Waukegan, IL Most Blessed Trinity.
Hartnett, James '72 (ORG) Judges; Seal Beach, CA Holy Family.
Hartnett, Patrick (TYL) Mount Pleasant, TX St. Michael.
Hartnett, Rev. Msgr. Robert L. '79 (BAL) Baltimore, MD Our Lady of Mount Carmel; Executive Director.
Hartrich, Kurt *o.f.m.* '66 (CHI) Chicago, IL St. Peter's; [W] Chicago, IL S.F.V., Inc.; [N] Chicago, IL St. Peter's Friary.
Hartsfield, John H. '01 (BIR) Oneonta, AL Corpus Christi; Priests'/Presbyteral Council.
Hartshorn, Christopher '94 (DM) Winterset, IA St. Joseph; [J] Des Moines, IA Roman Catholic Pastoral Center Foundation; Vicar General; Diocesan Consultors; Diocesan Corporation Board; Priests' Pension Fund Society; Winterset, IA St. Patrick; [J] Des Moines, IA Endowment for Educational Excellence.
Hartwell, James W. '02 (BUF) Warsaw, NY St. Michael.
Hartz, Gerald A. '59 (SC) Retired.
Hartzer, John '54 (IND) Retired.
Hartzler, Joseph *s.m.* '87 (SJ)[M] Cupertino, CA The Marianist Center.
Harvey, Charles K. '52 (WCH) Retired.
Harvey, David W. '68 (LAN) Fenton, MI St. John the Evangelist; Gaines, MI St. Joseph.
Harvey, Frederick R. '00 (BIS) Minot, ND St. Therese the Little Flower.
Harvey, James P. '96 (KNX) Greeneville, TN Notre Dame.
Harvey, John A. '66 (PIT) Retired.
Harvey, John D. *o.f.m.cap.* '72 (PIT) Pittsburgh, PA Our Lady of the Angels.
Harvey, John F. *o.s.f.s.* '44 (NY)[HH] New York, NY Courage International, Incorporated.
Harvey, John L. '86 (CHI) Riverdale, IL St. Mary Queen of Apostles.
Harvey, L. Warren '88 (LR) Pine Bluff, AR St. Joseph; Holy Cross.
Harvey, Michael K. '99 (BO) Haverhill, MA All Saints.
Harvey, Michael L. *o.f.m.* '89 (ORG) Huntington Beach,

CA SS. Simon and Jude; Consultors; Council of Priests.
Harvey, Peter J. *o.s.f.s.* '60 (WIL)[J] Childs, MD Retirement and Assisted Care Facility Retired.
Harvey, Warren '88 (LR) Deans; Diocesan Council for Black Catholics; [B] Pine Bluff, AR St. Joseph Catholic Jr./Sr. High School; Presbyteral Council; Diocesan Consultors.
Harvey, Wilfred *o.m.i.* '63 (BO)[U] Lowell, MA Missionary Oblates of Mary Immaculate.
Hascall, John S. *o.f.m.cap.* '67 (MAR) Sault Sainte Marie, MI Holy Family Mission; Sault Sainte Marie, MI St. Isaac Jogues Mission; Sault Sainte Marie, MI St. Isaac Jogues.
Haschka, Jonathan *s.j.* '75 (MIL)[P] Wauwatosa, WI Jesuit Community at St. Camillus.
Haschke, Jonathan J. '09 (LIN) Lincoln, NE Blessed Sacrament; Advocates.
Hascinger, Philip S. '72 (LFT) Grissom, IN Grissom Air Force Base, St. Michael's Chapel.
Haselhorst, Rev. Msgr. Vincent '57 (BEL) Retired.
Hasenkamp, Robert '63 (KCK) Retired.
Hasenoehrl, Chase R. '10 (B) Boise, ID Risen Christ Catholic Community.
Hasey, Adam '50 (FAR) Retired.
Hasieber, Joseph S. '73 (ALX) Retired.
Haskamp, Gregory '93 (KC) Smithville, MO Church of the Good Shepherd.
Haske, Henry B. *s.j.* '57 (SCR)[D] Scranton, PA Scranton Preparatory School; [B] Scranton, PA The University of Scranton.
Haskin, Jay C. '67 (BUR) Lisle, IL The National Catholic Risk Retention Group, Inc. Retired.
Haslach, Stephen *c.p.* '54 (BRK)[R] Jamaica, NY Immaculate Conception Monastery.
Hasler, Clifford P. *m.s.* '71 (HRT)[L] Hartford, CT Missionaries of LaSalette.
Haspedis, George '56 (SPK) Spokane, WA St. Peter Retired.
Hasse, Benjamin J. '09 (MAR) On Duty Outside the Diocese.
Hasser, David Joseph '07 (LFT) Zionsville, IN St. Alphonsus; Vocation Director.
Hassett, James F. '75 (BUF) Barker, NY Our Lady of the Lake.
Hasso, Bede J. *o.s.b.* '57 (GBG)[H] Latrobe, PA Saint Vincent Archabbey.
Hasso, Daniel *c.m.* '97 (CHI)[N] Chicago DePaul Vincentian Residence.
Hast, James C. *o.f.m.cap.* '77 (DET)[K] Detroit, MI St. Mary's Friary; [T] Detroit, MI Solanus Casey Center.
Hastings, Eric F. '05 (DUL) Judicial Vicar; Censor of Books; Vice Chancellor; Duluth, MN St. Benedict.
Hastings, Joel '99 (DUL) Proctor, MN St. Rose; Proctor, MN St. Philip Neri; Department of Liturgy.
Hastings, Scott A. '08 (OM) Norfolk, NE Sacred Heart; Madison, NE St. Leonard of Port Maurice.
Hastrich, Rev. Msgr. George M. '50 (MAD) Retired.
Hastrich, George M. '50 (RCK)[M] Saint Charles, IL Queen of Americas Guild.
Hatcher, John *s.j.* '74 (RC) St. Francis, SD St. Charles Borromeo; St. Francis, SD St. Francis Mission/ Rosebud Educational Society; [C] Howes, SD Kino Jesuit Community; Rosebud, SD St. Bridget.
Hatcher, Rev. Msgr. William C. '71 (NEW) Springfield, NJ St. James the Apostle; Commission for the Men's Apostolate.
Hater, Robert J. '59 (CIN) Cincinnati, OH St. Clare Retired.
Hatfield, James H. '10 (COL) Deanery 10: Tuscarawas–Holmes–Coshocton; Dover, OH St. Joseph.
Hathaway, Christopher *f.s.s.p.* '01 (RC) Rapid City, SD Cathedral of Our Lady of Perpetual Help.
Hathaway, Edward C. '91 (ARL) Chantilly, VA St. Veronica.
Hatrick, Brian M. '79 (BUF) Retired.
Hattie, Eugene F. *s.j.* '53 (FgM) Chicago, IL Society of Jesus.
Hatton, Ronald J. '95 (PSC) Lansford, PA St. John the Baptist.
Hattrup, Theobald *o.f.m.* '56 (CIN)[N] Cincinnati St. Francis Seraph Friary Retired.
Hauber, Douglas L. '89 (JOL) Herscher, IL St. Margaret Mary; Irwin, IL St. James The Apostle; Bonfield, IL Sacred Heart.
Hauck, Herbert C. '64 (STL) Retired.
Hauck, Herbert '64 (PHX) Carefree, AZ Our Lady of Joy Roman Catholic Parish.
Hauer, Joseph L. '81 (DUB)[G] Dubuque, IA Holy Family Catholic Schools; Dubuque, IA Church of the Resurrection; Judges; Finance Council.
Hauer, Maurus *o.f.m.conv.* '45 (IND)[J] Mount St. Francis, IN Mount Saint Francis Friary and Retreat Center.
Haugan, Daniel C. '03 (STP) Saint Paul, MN Holy Spirit.
Haugen, John S. '84 (DUB) On Special or Other Archdiocesan Assignment; Worship Office; Church Design/Renovation Commission.
Haugh, John '61 (DAL) Retired.
Haughey, John C. *s.j.* '61 (WDC)[O] Washington, DC Woodstock Jesuit Community; [X] Washington, DC Woodstock Theological Center; [O] Washington, DC The Jesuit Community at Georgetown University.
Haughney, Rev. Msgr. William J. '47 (MET)[I] Somerset, NJ Maria Regina Residence Retired.
Haupt, Lloyd '54 (SCL) Retired.
Haus, Robert A. *s.j.* '55 (BUF)[N] Buffalo, NY Canisius Jesuit Community Inc. Retired.
Hauser, Albert J. '81 (OG) Morristown, NY The Roman Catholic Community of Morristown, Hammond and Rossie; Advocates; Apostleship of Prayer; Priests' Eucharistic League.
Hauser, Albert *o.s.b.* '60 (KCK) Axtell, KS St. Michael; Summerfield, KS Holy Family; [I] Atchison, KS St. Benedict's Abbey.
Hauser, Gerald B. '45 (MIL) Retired.
Hauser, John G. '71 (BRK) On Leave/Unassigned.
Hauser, Nathanael *o.s.b.* '83 (SCL)[I] Collegeville, MN St. John's Abbey, of the Order of St. Benedict.
Hauser, Richard J. *s.j.* '68 (OM)[J] Omaha, NE Jesuit Community at Creighton University.
Hausladen, Robert T. '01 (IND) Terre Haute, IN St. Ann Catholic Church, Terre Haute, Inc.; [C] Indianapolis, IN Father Thomas Scecina Memorial High School; [C] Indianapolis, IN Bishop Chatard High School; Indianapolis, IN St. Matthew Catholic Church, Indianapolis, Inc.
Hausmann, Leo '92 (RC) Wall, SD St. Patrick's; Officialis.
Hausmann, William C. *s.j.* '66 (SPK)[B] Spokane, WA Gonzaga University.
Haut, Rev. Msgr. Vincent J. '68 (STA) Jacksonville, FL Blessed Trinity; Diocesan Consultors; Deans.
Hautz, Roland *g.h.m.* '53 (RIC) Gate City, VA St. Bernard.
Hauwert, Gerardus *i.v.e.* '11 (SJ) Santa Clara, CA Our Lady of Peace.
Havel, Elias *m.m.a.* '95 (SAM)[B] Petersham, MA Maronite Monks of Adoration Most Holy Trinity Monastery.
Havel, Gregory G. '90 (WIN) La Crescent, MN Holy Cross; La Crescent, MN The Church of the Crucifixion.
Havens, James A. '79 (MOB) Mobile, AL St. Vincent de Paul.
Havey, Lee *c.p.* '06 (SCR)[L] Scranton, PA Saint Ann's Passionist Monastery.
Haviland, William T. '62 (HBG) Retired.
Havrilka, Joseph '05 (SFD) Ramsey, IL St. Joseph; Vandalia, IL Mother of Dolors.
Havron, Daniel *o.f.m.* '77 (ALN)[M] Easton, PA St. Francis Retreat House; [K] Easton, PA St. Francis Friary.
Havron, Daniel *o.f.m.* '77 (CIN)[C] Cincinnati, OH St. Anthony Shrine, Franciscan Postulancy.
Hawes, Rev. Msgr. Cletus J. '52 (DUB)[E] Calmar, IA Christian Family School of Religion; Ossian, IA St. Francis de Sales; Ossian, IA Our Lady of Seven Dolors.
Hawes, Donald J. '53 (DUB)[F] Calmar, IA Calmar–Festina–Spillville Catholic School; Spillville, IA St. Wenceslaus; Calmar, IA St. Aloysius.
Hawes, Roger '01 (VIC) Presbyteral Council; Cuero Deanery; Yorktown, TX Holy Cross; Priests' Personnel Board.
Hawk, Patrick *c.ss.r.* '69 (TUC)[G] Tucson, AZ Redemptorist Society of Arizona Redemptorist Renewal Center.
Hawk, Vincent J. '02 (CLV) Ministers; Presbyteral Council; Loudonville, OH St. Peter; Presbyteral Conveners; [W] Loudonville, OH University of Ashland; Loudonville, OH Kettering–Mohican Area Medical Center.
Hawken, Michael '94 (KCK) Shawnee, KS St. Joseph.
Hawker, James '63 (CHL) Retired.
Hawkes–Teeples, Steven B. *s.j.* '93 (FgM) St. Louis, MO Society of Jesus.
Hawkins, Allan R.G. '94 (FWT) Arlington, TX Church of St. Mary the Virgin.
Hawkins, Charles '78 (PMB) Boca Raton, FL Ascension.
Hawkins, Donald A. *s.j.* '76 (NO) Ecumenical Officer; New Orleans, LA Holy Name of Jesus.
Hawkins, John *o.s.c.* '66 (SCL)[I] Onamia, MN Crosier Priory.
Hawkins, Robert F. '75 (PRO) Barrington, RI St. Luke.
Hawkins, Thomas J. D. '70 (KC) Higginsville, MO St. Mary's.
Hawley, Benjamin B. *s.j.* '00 (LAN) Ann Arbor, MI St. Mary Student Parish; [N] Ann Arbor, MI St. Mary Student Parish; [J] Ann Arbor, MI Detroit Province of the Society of Jesus – Jesuit Residence.
Hawley, Gerard L. '92 (SCR) Unassigned or Leave of Absence.
Hawthorne, Patrick J. '82 (WOR) Manchaug, MA St. Anne.
Hawver, Carl *o.f.m.* '74 (IND) Oldenburg, IN Holy Family Catholic Church, Oldenburg, Inc.; [L] Oldenburg, IN Motherhouse of the Congregation of the Sisters of the Third Order of St. Francis.
Hay, John N. '07 (WCH) Wichita, KS St. Paul Parish; [I] Wichita, KS St. Paul Newman Center (Wichita State University).
Hay, Rev. Msgr. Theodore H. *s.t.l.* '55 (MOB) Retired.
Hay, W. Michael '92 (CIN) Cincinnati, OH St. Aloysius Gonzaga.
Hayatsu, Richard K. '65 (SEA) Seattle, WA St. Francis of Assisi; Federal Way, WA St. Theresa.
Haycock, Anthony J. '72 (SEA) Seattle, WA St. Mary; [Q] Seattle, WA Catholic Seamen's Club Retired.
Haycock, Donald J. *c.s.c.* '58 (FTW)[H] Notre Dame Congregation of Holy Cross, United States Province of Priests & Brothers.
Hayde, Rev. Msgr. Ronald '81 (RVC) Medical Leave.
Hayden, Charles (NEW)[L] Newark, NJ Newark Abbey.
Hayden, Hilary *o.s.b.* '56 (WDC)[O] Washington, DC St. Anselm's Abbey.
Hayden, James P. '91 (GLD) Elected Members; Traverse City, MI Immaculate Conception Retired.
Hayden, Johnrose '95 (LUB) Retired.
Hayden, Joseph F. '63 (L) Retired.
Hayden, Joseph J. *s.j.* '70 (BAL)[Q] Baltimore, MD Colombiere Jesuit Community.
Hayden, Joseph M. '48 (CAM) Retired.
Hayden, Joseph M. '48 (ORL) Retired.
Hayden, Michael M. *o.c.s.o.* '54 (ROC)[K] Piffard Abbey of the Genesee.
Hayden, Michael T. '85 (SUP) Boulder Junction, WI St. Anne; Boulder Junction, WI St. Rita; Boulder Junction, WI St. Mary.
Hayden, Patrick T. '90 (STL) On Duty Outside the Archdiocese.
Hayden, Robert L. '70 (RVC) Seaford, NY St. William the Abbot.
Hayden, Ted *s.m.a.* '58 (FgM) Tenafly, NJ SOCIETY OF AFRICAN MISSIONS.
Hayden, Terence '77 (NO) Gretna, LA Ochsner Medical Center, West Bank; New Orleans, LA Holy Spirit.
Hayden, Thomas E. *s.m.a.* '58 (NEW)[L] Tenafly, NJ Society of African Missions, Provincialate, S.M.A. Fathers.
Haydinger, Christian J. '76 (RIC) Ashland, VA St. Ann.
Haydock, Kenneth '80 (SEA) Edmonds, WA Holy Rosary.
Hayduk, Rev. Archpriest Michael '77 (PRM) Parma, OH Saint John the Baptist, Cathedral; Syncellus for Doctrine and Worship; Presbyteral Council; Eparchial Pastoral Council; Eparchial Consultors; Sacred Liturgy; Cantors' Institute Faculty; Seminary Education Formation Board.
Hayek, Herbert C. *o.p.* '71 (CHI) River Forest, IL St. Vincent Ferrer.
Hayek, Rev. Msgr. Sami '59 (SAM) Retired.
Hayek, Rev. Msgr. Stanley J. '59 (DUB) Building Commission; Directors Retired.
Hayer, James '89 (PSC) Wilkes–Barre, PA St. Mary's; Syncellus; Communications and Telecommunications; Eparchial Newspaper; Building and Properties Commission.
Hayes, Bonaventure *o.f.m.* '67 (PAT)[N] Ringwood, NJ Holy Name Friary, Inc.
Hayes, Brian '92 (SD) El Cajon, CA Holy Trinity Catholic Parish.
Hayes, Dennis J. '86 (NO) New Orleans, LA St. Rita Catholic Church.
Hayes, Dennis J. '76 (SY) Marietta, NY Corpus Christi.
Hayes, Edward A. *m.m.* '59 (FgM) Maryknoll, NY MARYKNOLL.
Hayes, Edward '58 (KCK) Retired.
Hayes, Finbarr *o.p.* '57 (OAK)[L] Oakland, CA Order of Preachers (Province of the Most Holy Name of Jesus – Western Dominican Province).
Hayes, Gary '90 (OWN) Absent on Leave.
Hayes, Gerard C. '60 (HT) Retired.
Hayes, James A. *s.s.j.* '55 (BAL)[Q] Baltimore, MD St. Joseph Society of the Sacred Heart House of Central Administration; [Q] Baltimore, MD St. Joseph's Manor Retired.
Hayes, James M. *s.j.* '85 (WOR)[N] Worcester, MA Jesuits of the Holy Cross, Inc.
Hayes, James *s.s.s.* '77 (NY) New York, NY St. Andrew.
Hayes, Jerry *s.j.* '07 (LA)[F] Los Angeles, CA Loyola High School of Los Angeles.
Hayes, John H. '87 (ROC) Honeoye, NY St. Mary, Our Lady of the Hills; Livonia, NY St. Matthew Catholic Church Society.
Hayes, John J. '60 (CLV) Cleveland, OH Immaculate Conception Retired.
Hayes, Lawrence *o.f.m.* (R) Durham, NC Immaculate Conception.
Hayes, Leo J. '61 (BEL) Ava, IL St. Elizabeth; Ava, IL St. Ann; Ava, IL St. Joseph.
Hayes, Martin E. '84 (OWN) Leitchfield, KY St. Elizabeth of Hungary; Leitchfield, KY St. Paul.
Hayes, Maurice C. *o.f.m.conv.* '69 (ELP) El Paso, TX Our Lady of Mt. Carmel; El Paso, TX Our Lady of the Valley.
Hayes, Rev. Msgr. Paul J. '48 (NEW) New Providence, NJ Our Lady of Peace Retired.
Hayes, Robert E. '71 (SJ) Defender of the Bond; Ongoing Formation of Clergy; Special Assignment.
Hayes, Robert '71 (MRY) Defenders of the Bond.
Hayes, Samuel '83 (CHY) Rawlins, WY St. Joseph's;

Vicars Forane; Defenders of the Bond.
Hayes, Stephen Dominic *o.p.* '88 (COL) Zanesville, OH St. Thomas Aquinas.
Hayes, Terrence M. '72 (STP) Minneapolis, MN Our Lady of Victory.
Hayes, Thomas J. '73 (ALB) Delmar, NY St. Thomas the Apostle; Members; Priestly Life and Ministry Council.
Hayes, Thomas *o.p.* '59 (SFR)[K] San Francisco, CA Home for the Aged of the Little Sisters of the Poor; [N] San Francisco, CA St. Dominic Priory Retired.
Hayes, Thomas *o.m.i.* '64 (BEL)[E] Belleville, IL Our Lady of the Snows Apartment Community Retirement Home; [F] Belleville, IL Missionary Oblates of Mary Immaculate – St. Henry's Oblate Residence.
Hayes, Timothy M. '85 (COL) Columbus, OH St. Timothy; Deanery 2: Northwest; Presbyteral Council; Diocesan Judges; Parochial Examiners.
Hayes, William E. *s.j.* '58 (P)[D].
Hayes, Zachary *o.f.m.* '59 (SFD)[K] Sherman, IL Blessed Giles Friary.
Hayman, Robert W. '66 (PRO) Providence, RI Cathedral of SS. Peter and Paul Retired.
Hayn, Carl H. *s.j.* '47 (SJ)[B] Santa Clara, CA Jesuit Community.
Haynes, Mark J. '85 (PH) Havertown, PA Annunciation B.V.M.
Haynes, Scott *s.j.c.* '07 (CHI) Chicago, IL St. John Cantius; [P] Chicago, IL Canons Regular of Saint John Cantius.
Hays, Henry Bryan *o.s.b.* '62 (SCL)[I] Collegeville, MN St. John's Abbey, of the Order of St. Benedict.
Hays, John S. '93 (SP) Ridge Manor, FL St. Anne.
Hays, Kevin W. '77 (CHI) Missionary Work.
Hays, Kevin '77 (FgM) Boston, MA St. James the Apostle, Inc.
Hays, Richard Rex *c.m.* '93 (STO) Patterson, CA Sacred Heart Church of Patterson (Pastor of).
Hays, Timothy '96 (SPK) Colbert, WA St. Joseph; Members.
Hayward, William *m.i.c.* '89 (MIL) Kenosha, WI Our Lady of the Holy Rosary.
Hazard, Rev. Msgr. Michael D. '72 (KAL) Kalamazoo, MI St. Joseph; Vicar General; Diocesan Consultors; Presbyteral Council Members; Presbyteral Council Members.
Hazebrouck, Maurice L. '45 (PRO) Retired.
Hazel, Robert L. '66 (STP) Retired.
Hazel, Terrence J. '75 (Y) Scouting, Diocesan Office; Canfield, OH St. Michael; Defenders of the Bond; Physically and Developmentally; Deaf and Hearing Impaired.
Hazelton, James '61 (HEL) Retired.
Hazewski, Eugene J. '59 (NEW)[L] Rutherford, NJ St. John Vianney Residence for Priests Retired.
Hazuka, Jeremy L. '97 (LIN) Morse Bluff, NE St. George; [C] Wahoo, NE Bishop Neumann Jr.–Sr. High School; Legion of Mary.
Hazzard, William M. '63 (WIL) Wilmington, DE St. Matthew Retired.
Hazzouri, Alex J. '57 (SCR)[M] Dunmore, PA Villa St. Joseph Retired.
Head, Bernard '53 (IND) Saint Mary Of The Woods, IN St. Mary–of–the–Woods Catholic Church, Inc. Retired.
Headley, Donald J. '58 (CHI) Chicago, IL St. Mary of the Woods; Chicago, IL Our Lady of Mercy Retired.
Headley, William '64 (SD)[B] University of San Diego.
Heagerty, John J. '54 (SY) Retired.
Heagerty, Kevin *o.f.m.cap.* '61 (FgM) Detroit, MI Province of St. Joseph.
Heagerty, Kevin *o.f.m.cap.* '61 (DET)[K] Detroit St. Bonaventure Friary.
Heagle, John L. '65 (LC) On Duty Outside the Diocese.
Healey, Bernard A. '95 (PRO) Albion, RI St. Ambrose; Government Liaison; Newspaper.
Healey, Charles J. *s.j.* '65 (BO)[D] Boston, MA Boston College High School; [U] Newton, MA The Jesuit Community at Boston College.
Healey, Edward J. '87 (FR) West Harwich, MA Holy Trinity.
Healey, Fergus *o.f.m.* '54 (BO)[Z] Boston, MA St. Anthony Shrine.
Healey, John E. '70 (MAN) St. Joseph Hospital; Nashua, NH St. Patrick; Southern N.H. Regional Medical Center.
Healey, Joseph G. *m.m.* '66 (FgM) Maryknoll, NY MARYKNOLL.
Healey, Kenneth *s.m.* '70 (BO)[D] Reading, MA Austin Preparatory School.
Healey, William B. '55 (SCR)[M] Dunmore, PA Villa St. Joseph; Priests' Retirement Advisory Board Retired.
Healy, Cornelius J. '66 (SFR) Ross, CA St. Anselm.
Healy, Daniel H. '01 (MET)[M] Oxford, NJ The Anawim Community.
Healy, Daniel (ROC)[O] Corning, NY Anawim Community Center.
Healy, Gabriel *ss.cc.* '57 (FR)[F] Fairhaven, MA Damien Residence Retired.
Healy, George *c.s.sp.* '53 (SB)[I] Hemet, CA Congregation of the Holy Spirit Retired.
Healy, Rev. Msgr. Gerard M. '61 (MAD) Stoughton, WI St. Ann.
Healy, J. Cletus *s.j.* '51 (MIL)[P] Wauwatosa, WI Jesuit Community at St. Camillus.
Healy, Jack *o.carm.* '70 (ROC)[B] Rochester, NY McQuaid Jesuit High School; [K] Rochester, NY Whitefriars Priory.
Healy, James E. '72 (KC) Blue Springs, MO St. Robert Bellarmine.
Healy, James F. '66 (NY) Yonkers, NY St. Paul the Apostle.
Healy, John J. '66 (SAC) AIDS, Ministry to; Hospitals, Diocesan Liaison for Catholic.
Healy, John '41 (SR) Retired.
Healy, Kieran Jeremiah *o.p.* '61 (P)[N] McKenzie Bridge, OR St. Benedict Lodge Dominican Retreat & Conference Center.
Healy, Michael J. '70 (SFR) San Francisco Police Department; San Mateo, CA St. Bartholomew.
Healy, Patrick F. *o.m.i.* '47 (BO)[X] Tewksbury, MA Immaculate Heart of Mary Residence; Pastoral Care.
Healy, Patrick *s.s.j.* (MOB) Mobile, AL Most Pure Heart of Mary; Religious.
Healy, Rev. Msgr. Peter C. '53 (LA) Burbank, CA St. Robert Bellarmine Retired.
Healy, Stephen M. '85 (BO) Monponsett, MA Our Lady of the Lake.
Healy, Terence P. '62 (ALB) Richfield Springs, NY St. Joseph the Worker.
Healy, Thomas F. *s.j.* '65 (SPK)[J] Spokane, WA Regis Community.
Healy, Thomas I. '52 (CHI) Chicago, IL Our Lady of Mount Carmel; [W] Chicago, IL St. Bonaventure Oratory Retired.
Healy, Thomas J. '66 (BRK) Corona, NY Our Lady of Sorrows.
Healy, Thomas '67 (SAV) Augusta, GA St. Joseph; Promoter of Justice.
Healy, William P. '66 (PHX) Scottsdale, AZ St. Patrick Roman Catholic Parish Retired.
Healy, William *o.c.d.* '46 (MIL)[P] Milwaukee Provincial Offices – Discalced Carmelites Retired.
Heames, Denis M. (SAG) Outside the Diocese.
Heaney, John F. '57 (PRO) Retired.
Heaney, John J. *s.j.* '52 (NO)[R] New Orleans, LA Ignatius Residence.
Hearn, Philip A. '66 (SY) Rome, NY St. Mary's–St. Peter's; Eastern Area Vicars; Board of Diocesan Consultors; Presbyteral Council.
Hearne, William '11 (CHR) Garden City, SC St. Michael.
Hearty, Joseph *f.s.s.p.* '03 (DEN) Littleton, CO Our Lady of Mount Carmel.
Heaslip, Andrew J. '09 (LIN) Hastings, NE St. Cecilia's; Advocates.
Heath, Christopher '88 (ORG) Dana Point, CA St. Edward the Confessor; Council of Priests.
Hebda, Martin J. '67 (CHI)[J] Chicago, IL Mercy Hospital and Medical Center.
Hebda, Michael J. '96 (SAC) Winters, CA St. Anthony.
Hebden, W. Scott '99 (CHI)[A] Mundelein, IL University of St. Mary of the Lake/Mundelein Seminary.
Heberlein, Kenneth '71 (GAL) Retired.
Hebert, Adrien T. *c.s.sp.* '58 (FgM) Bethel Park, PA CONGREGATION OF THE HOLY SPIRIT.
Hebert, Daniel J. '79 (ANC) Anchorage, AK St. Patrick.
Hebert, David B. '11 (LAF) Scott, LA Sts. Peter and Paul.
Hebert, Earl '52 (SPR) Retired.
Hebert, Gerard A. '81 (FR) East Falmouth, MA St. Anthony's; Defenders of the Bond.
Hebert, Rev. Msgr. J. Gaston '60 (LR) Presbyteral Council; Clergy Personnel Advisory Board (Diocesan).
Hebert, John M. '51 (LIN) Retired.
Hebert, Joseph Elmo *m.afr.* '63 (SP)[N] St. Petersburg, FL Missionaries of Africa; Washington, DC; Washington, DC MISSIONARIES OF AFRICA Retired.
Hebert, Oliver J. *t.o.r.* '71 (PBR) Northern Cambria, PA St. John the Baptist; Patton, PA SS. Peter and Paul.
Hebert, Rev. Msgr. Ray P. '52 (NO) Retired.
Hebert, Ronald '65 (SD) San Diego, CA Sacred Heart Catholic Parish San Diego.
Hebert, T. J. '49 (LAF) Retired.
Hebl, Rev. Msgr. John H. '61 (MAD) Retired.
Hechenberger, Gerald R. '96 (BEL) Smithton, IL St. John the Baptist; Leave of Absence.
Heck, Quintin T. '00 (MO) Special Assignment; DEPARTMENT OF VETERANS AFFAIRS HOSPITALS AND CHAPLAINS.
Heck, Thomas A. '76 (VEN) Port Charlotte, FL St. Charles Borromeo.
Heck, Thomas '76 (VEN)[F] Port Charlotte, FL St. Charles Housing I, Inc.; [F] Port Charlotte, FL St. Charles Housing II, Inc.
Heckathorne, Brad *o.f.m.conv.* '81 (BGP) Danbury, CT Sacred Heart of Jesus.
Heckel, Guerric Frederick A. '66 (CHR)[E] Moncks Corner, SC Mepkin Abbey.
Hecker, Rev. Msgr. Lawrence A. '58 (NO) Retired.
Hecktor, Brian E. '08 (STL) Chesterfield, MO Ascension.
Hector de la Vega, J. '77 (DOD) Liberal, KS St. Anthony of Padua Catholic Church of Liberal, Kansas.
Hedderman, James A. '95 (BIR) Russellville, AL Good Shepherd Church.
Hederman, James J. *s.j.* '99 (BO)[U] Boston The Society of Jesus of New England–Provincial Offices.
Hederman, James J. *s.j.* '99 (NY)[DD] Jesuit Community, Kohlmann Hall; [DD] New York, NY Society of Jesus, New York Province.
Hederman, Kevin F. '75 (STL) On Leave of Absence.
Hedges, John P. '87 (DET) New Boston, MI St. Stephen.
Hedrick, John H. '70 (MAD) Beloit, WI St. Jude; Beloit, WI St. Thomas the Apostle; Elected.
Hedrick, Rev. Msgr. Kenneth J. '73 (NO) Metairie, LA St. Angela Merici; Worship Office; Liturgical Commission.
Hedz, Bohdan '10 (STF) Rochester, NY St. Josaphat; Holy Name Societies.
Heeg, Lawrence M. '57 (GRY) Retired.
Heekin, John M. '63 (PAT) Retired.
Heelan, Patrick A. *s.j.* '58 (WDC)[O] Washington, DC The Jesuit Community at Georgetown University.
Heemrood, Jan *o.m.i.* '45 (SAT)[K] San Antonio, TX Oblate Madonna Residence.
Heenan, Michael F. '55 (RVC) Retired.
Heerdink, Eugene '51 (EVN) Spanish Speaking Ministry Retired.
Heese, Henry '61 (CC) Retired.
Heet, Donald J. *o.s.f.s.* '76 (WDC)[B] Washington, DC Deshairs Community–Oblates of St. Francis de Sales Residence; Officers; Provincial Councilors:; Provincial Staff.
Heffern, Colman *o.s.b.* '76 (SFE)[H] Pecos, NM Our Lady of Guadalupe Abbey.
Heffernan, Henry G. *s.j.* '62 (WDC)[O] Washington, DC The Jesuit Community of St. Aloysius Gonzaga.
Heffernan, James F. '50 (BRK) Retired.
Heffernan, John J. *o.f.m.* '89 (ARL) Triangle, VA St. Francis of Assisi.
Heffernan, Joseph A. '65 (FRS) Retired.
Heffernan, Raymond '57 (SEA) Friday Harbor, WA St. Francis Retired.
Heffernan, Robert G. '63 (HRT) Hamden, CT St. Stephen.
Heffner, Carroll '61 (NO) Retired.
Heffron, William *ss.cc.* '68 (FR)[F] Fairhaven, MA Damien Residence.
Hefner, Rev. Msgr. Helmut A. '69 (LA) Woodland Hills, CA St. Mel; Appointed Membership.
Heft, James L. *s.m.* '73 (LA)[BB] Los Angeles, CA The Institute for Advanced Catholic Studies.
Heft, James *s.m.* '73 (STL)[O] St. Louis Marianists, Province of the United States (Society of Mary).
Hegarty, Frederick J. *m.m.* '53 (FgM) Maryknoll, NY MARYKNOLL.
Hegarty, Michael P. '95 (CAM) Retired.
Hegedusich, William '06 (WDC) Absent On Leave.
Hegenbarth, Robert S. '56 (LC) Bangor, WI St. Mary; West Salem, WI St. Leo the Great.
Hegnauer, Edward Anthony '09 (WDC) Clinton, MD Church of St. John the Evangelist.
Hegyi, Martin S. *s.j.* '63 (NY)[HH] Bronx, NY Saint Jutta Foundation, Inc.; [DD] New York, NY Murray–Weigel Hall.
Heher, Rev. Msgr. Michael '78 (ORG) Staff; Clergy Personnel Board; Vicar General; Moderator of the Curia; Council of Priests; Consultors; Land Advisory Board; Diocesan Finance Council; Special Assignment; Seal Beach, CA St. Anne's.
Hehir, J. Bryan '66 (BO) Catholic Charitable Bureau of the Archdiocese of Boston, Inc.; Catholic Relief Services; Wellesley, MA St. John the Evangelist.
Hehman, Lawrence W. '65 (LEX) Priests' Retirement Committee Retired.
Hehn, Robert E. '63 (DEN) Rifle, CO St. Mary.
Heiar, Rev. Msgr. Donald J. '00 (MAD) Madison, WI St. Thomas Aquinas; Military Chaplains.
Heiar, Donald Joseph '00 (MO) Air National Guard Chaplains.
Heiar, James *s.v.d.* '70 (DUB)[B] Epworth, IA Divine Word College.
Heiar, James *s.v.d.* '70 (BO)[U] Duxbury, MA Society of the Divine Word.
Heidecke, Albert J. '93 (JOL) Deans; Manteno, IL St. Joseph.
Heidenblut, Gregory *o.s.a.* '04 (SD)[O] San Diego, CA The Bellesini Foundation; [O] San Diego, CA The Tagaste Foundation.
Heidenblut, Gregory *o.s.a.* '04 (LA)[F] Ojai, CA Villanova Preparatory School in California.
Heidenreich, Robert J. '69 (CHI) Winnetka, IL Sacred Heart.
Heidenrich, Peter J. '77 (CHI) Chicago, IL St. Walter.
Heidgen, Warren *o.s.b.* '60 (BIS)[A] Richardton, ND Assumption Abbey.
Heidt, Charles A. '59 (BIS) Priests' Benefit Association Retired.
Heidt, Ed *c.s.b.* '76 (LSC) Las Cruces, NM Cathedral of the Immaculate Heart of Mary; [B] Las Cruces, NM

Basilian Fathers.
Heier, Thomas *c.m.m.* '58 (DET)[K] Vocation Office; Dearborn Heights, MI.
Heier, Vergil *c.m.m.* '63 (DET)[K] Vocation Office.
Heikkala, Gregory R. '91 (MAR) Special Assignment; Champion, MI Sacred Heart; Ishpeming, MI St. John the Evangelist; Republic, MI St. Augustine; Vocation Office.
Heil, John P. *s.s.d.* '74 (STL) Special Assignment.
Heil, John P. *s.s.d.* '74 (WDC)[C] Catholic University of America, The.
Heille, Gregory J. *o.p.* '75 (STL)[B] St. Louis, MO Aquinas Institute of Theology; [O] St. Louis, MO Dominican Community of St. Louis.
Heilman, Richard M. '88 (MAD) Mount Horeb, WI St. Ignatius; Cross Plains, WI St. Mary of Pine Bluff; Appointed; Diocesan Consultors.
Heim, Edward L. '71 (STL) Augusta, MO Immaculate Conception.
Heim, John P. *s.j.* '65 (CIN)[N] Cincinnati, OH Jesuit Community at St. Xavier High School; Reading, OH Sts. Peter and Paul.
Heim, Joseph A. *m.m.* '61 (NY)[DD] Maryknoll Maryknoll Fathers and Brothers Retired.
Heim, Joseph A. *m.m.* (PH) Phoenixville, PA St. Ann Retired.
Heim, Michael J. '82 (PH) Philadelphia, PA St. Dominic.
Heiman, Andrew '05 (WCH) Cherryvale, KS St. Francis Xavier's; Independence, KS St. Andrew.
Heiman, Lawrence *c.pp.s.* '43 (CIN)[N] Carthagena, OH St. Charles Retired.
Heimer, Michael G. '71 (GRY) Walkerton, IN St. Anthony of Padua; Walkerton, IN St. John Kanty.
Heimerman, Francis D. '44 (DUB) Retired.
Heimos, Robert L. '67 (STL) Retired.
Hein, John '63 (RVC) Hewlett, NY St. Joseph's Retired.
Heina, Steven '82 (SAL) Ellsworth, KS St. Bernard Parish; Ellsworth, KS St. Ignatius Loyola Parish; Holy Childhood, Pontifical Association; Propagation of the Faith.
Heine, Michael *o.f.m.conv.* '90 (BAL)[Q] Companions Evangelization & Mail Order Office.
Heineman, Rev. Msgr. Donald P. '47 (DUB) Retired.
Heinen, Francis A. '59 (NEW)[L] Caldwell, NJ The Rev. Msgr. James F. Kelley Residence for Retired Priests; Scotch Plains, NJ Immaculate Heart of Mary Retired.
Heinen, Miles J. *c.m.* '82 (PH)[B] Philadelphia, PA DePaul Novitiate.
Heinen, Virgil O. '60 (SUP) Retired.
Heines, Timothy '94 (DAL) Richardson, TX St. Joseph.
Heiney, Lawrence W. '75 (CHL) Winston–Salem, NC St. Benedict the Moor.
Heinlein, Gregory (RVC) Massapequa Park, NY Our Lady of Lourdes.
Heinlein, Rev. Msgr. John T. '61 (RVC) Mastic Beach, NY St. Jude Retired.
Heinrich, Harold D. '56 (HRT) Retired.
Heinsz, Vernon R. *s.j.* '73 (KC)[J] Kansas City, MO Rockhurst Jesuit Community.
Heintz, Andrew J. '05 (ARL) Notaries; Alexandria, VA Queen of Apostles.
Heintz, Daniel '54 (SY) North Syracuse, NY St. Rose of Lima Retired.
Heintz, James *m.afr.* (SP)[N] St. Petersburg, FL Missionaries of Africa.
Heintz, Rev. Msgr. Michael W. '93 (FTW) South Bend, IN St. Matthew Cathedral; [B] University of Notre Dame Du Lac; Consultors; Censor Librorum; Liturgical Commission; Inter City Catholic League; Pro–Synodal Judges.
Heintz, Robert L. '49 (SFD) Retired.
Heintzelman, Edward F. '84 (CAM) Mays Landing, NJ St. Vincent de Paul Parish, Mays Landing, N.J.
Heintzelman, Gerard T. '59 (HBG)[F] Danville, PA Maria Hall, Inc. Retired.
Heinz, David C. '77 (PEO) Bartonville, IL St. Anthony.
Heinz, John *o.f.m.conv.* '93 (RNO) Diocesan School Board; Reno, NV St. Thomas Aquinas Cathedral; Reno, NV St. Therese Church of the Little Flower.
Heinz, Rev. Msgr. Martin G. '94 (RCK) Aurora, IL Holy Angels.
Heinz, Robert P. '80 (CHI) Northbrook, IL St. Norbert.
Heinz, Walter E. '62 (STU) Retired.
Heinze, Arthur G. '69 (MIL) Retired.
Heinzel, Thomas R. '75 (HON) Retired.
Heis, Clarence G. '82 (CIN) On Special and Archdiocesan Assignment.
Heise, Bert *o.f.m.* '57 (CIN)[N] Cincinnati St. Francis Seraph Friary.
Heiser, James '05 (CHY) Sheridan, WY Holy Name; Vicars Forane; Diocesan Schools Advisory Group; Advocates; College of Consultors.
Heiser, W. Charles *s.j.* '53 (STL)[C] Saint Louis University; [O] St. Louis, MO Jesuit Community Corporation at Saint Louis University – Jesuit Hall Retired.
Heisig, James *s.v.d.* '69 (FgM) Techny, IL.
Heisler, John F. '99 (ARL) On Duty Outside the Diocese; [A] Columbus, OH Pontifical College Josephinum.
Heisler, John '99 (COL)[A] Columbus, OH Pontifical College Josephinum.
Heithoff, James H. '77 (GI) Personnel Board; Ainsworth, NE St. Pius X.
Heiting, R. Paul '87 (WIN)[A] Winona, MN Immaculate Heart of Mary Seminary; Judicial Officers; Misconduct Issues; Additional Diocesan Assignments; Diocesan Review Board.
Heitkamp, Samuel '67 (SAT) Retired.
Heitke, Lawrence R. '67 (MAD) Retired.
Heitz, Louis S. '57 (LFT) Retired.
Heitz, Warren *o.s.b.* '66 (IND)[K] Saint Meinrad, IN St. Meinrad Archabbey.
Heitzman, Clarence J. '56 (COV) Southgate, KY St. Therese of the Infant Jesus.
Hejdak, Andrew '84 (CC) Woodsboro, TX St. Therese, The Little Flower.
Hejna, Lewis E. '81 (SPC) Springfield, MO Immaculate Conception; Billings, MO St. Joseph.
Helbing, Brendan *o.s.b.* '65 (OKL)[I] Shawnee, OK St. Gregory's Abbey.
Helfrich, P. Frederick '71 (ROC) Webster, NY Holy Spirit.
Helfrich, Paul D. *b.h.* '00 (BO) Boston University; On Duty Outside the Archdiocese.
Helfrich, Peter G. '76 (OG) Absent on Sick Leave, Disabled.
Helfrich, Thomas J. *o.s.f.s.* '78 (LAN)[N] Adrian, MI Siena Heights University; Parr Hwy. Correctional Facility (Consolidated with Gus Harrison).
Heller, Rev. Msgr. Christopher J. '79 (RVC) Babylon, NY St. Joseph; Babylon Deanery.
Heller, James '68 (SAG) Saginaw, MI St. Stephen.
Hellmann, Rev. Canon Andreas '00 (GB)[O] Green Bay, WI Oratory of St. Joseph.
Hellmann, Rev. Msgr. Donald F. '53 (COV) Florence, KY St. Paul; Diocesan Consultors; Priest Personnel; Judges Retired.
Hellmann, Wayne *o.f.m.conv.* '67 (IND)[J] Mount St. Francis, IN Mount Saint Francis Friary and Retreat Center; [J] Mount St. Francis, IN Province of Our Lady of Consolation, Inc.
Hellstrom, Christopher '88 (DEN) Denver, CO Blessed Sacrament.
Hellwig, Carl '06 (PMB) Port St. Lucie, FL St. Elizabeth Ann Seton.
Hellwig, Lee W. '86 (HRT) Military Chaplains; Navy Chaplains.
Helly, Victor J. *s.j.* '54 (FgM) New York, NY Society of Jesus.
Helmick, Raymond G. *s.j.* '63 (BO) West Roxbury, MA St. Theresa of Avila; [U] Newton, MA The Jesuit Community at Boston College.
Helmick, Rev. Msgr. William M. '62 (BO) West Roxbury, MA St. Theresa of Avila; Trustees.
Helmin, Virgil A. '75 (SCL) Clear Lake, MN St. Marcus; Judicial Vicar; Notaries; Diocesan Priests Pension Plan Trustees.
Helmin, Virgil '75 (SCL) Foley, MN St. Lawrence's; Judges.
Helmin, Virgil '75 (CR) Defenders of the Bond.
Helmlinger, Peter '04 (CIN) Cincinnati, OH St. Matthias; Cincinnati, OH Our Lady of the Rosary.
Helms, Michael L. '90 (DOD) Deerfield, KS Christ the King Catholic Church of Deerfield, Kansas; Lakin, KS St. Anthony of Padua Catholic Church of Lakin, Kansas; Syracuse, KS St. Raphael Catholic Church of Syracuse, Kansas.
Helms, Walter '69 (DAV) Coralville, IA St. Thomas More; [M] Coralville, IA St. Thomas More New Season Charitable Trust.
Helmueller, John '01 (SFS) Flandreau, SD SS. Simon and Jude; Spanish–Speaking Apostolate.
Helou, Nadim *m.l.m.* (SAM) Uniontown, PA St. George.
Helwig, Alan R. '58 (WDC) Retired.
Helwig, Paul C. '74 (HBG) Camp Hill, PA Good Shepherd.
Heman, Richard J. '67 (STL) Retired.
Hemann, David '85 (SC) Holstein, IA Our Lady of Good Counsel; Ida Grove, IA Sacred Heart; Odebolt, IA St. Martin's.
Hemann, Everett '71 (DUB) Retired.
Hemann, Rev. Msgr. John W. '60 (DUB) Retired.
Hemann, Maurice *o.m.i.* '50 (FgM) Washington, DC AMERICAN OBLATE MISSIONS.
Hemann, Melvin D. '59 (DUB) Marriage Retorno Retired.
Hemauer, Gilbert *o.f.m.cap.* (GB)[J] Appleton, WI St. Fidelis Friary Retired.
Hemberger, Kent A. '88 (WCH) Andover, KS St. Vincent de Paul; Building Commission.
Hemberger, Rev. Msgr. Robert E. '70 (WCH) Ongoing Formation of the Clergy Committee.
Hemberger, Rev. Msgr. Robert E. '70 (WCH) Victim Assistance Coordinator; [F] Wichita, KS Wichita Center, Congregation of the Sisters of St. Joseph; Vicar General; Moderator of the Diocesan Curia; Director of Diocesan Planning; Presbyteral Council/ College of Consultors; Judges; Building Commission; Finance Council; Health Affairs – Diocesan Liaison.
Hembrow, William '60 (SFD) Jerseyville, IL St. Mary; Jerseyville, IL Holy Ghost.
Hemm, Thomas *c.pp.s.* '78 (CIN) Saint Henry, OH St. Bernard; Saint Henry, OH St. Aloysius; Saint Henry, OH St. Francis; Saint Henry, OH St. Henry; Saint Henry, OH St. Wendelin; [N] Dayton Provincial Office of the Cincinnati Province of the Society of the Precious Blood; Provincial Council.
Hemmelgarn, Larry J. *c.pp.s.* '84 (CIN)[N] Dayton, OH Provincial Office of the Cincinnati Province of the Society of the Precious Blood; [N] Dayton Provincial Office of the Cincinnati Province of the Society of the Precious Blood.
Hemmer, Joseph *o.f.m.* '54 (FBK) Kaltag, AK St. Teresa Catholic Church; Saint Louis, MO Sacred Heart Province; Presbyteral Council; Consultors.
Hemmerle, R. Joseph '67 (L) Loretto, KY Holy Cross; St. Francis, KY St. Francis of Assisi.
Hemmerling, Henry L. '66 (MET) Retired.
Hemp, Lawrence '67 (LUB) Retired.
Hemrick, Eugene F. '63 (JOL) Retired.
Hemrick, Eugene '63 (WDC) Washington, DC St. Joseph on Capitol Hill.
Hemsing, John D. '88 (MIL)[A] St. Francis, WI Saint Francis de Sales Seminary; Archdiocesan Consultors; Special Assignment; Archdiocesan Council of Priests.
Henault, James A. *m.s.* '80 (ATL) Snellville, GA St. Oliver Plunkett.
Henault, John *o.m.i.* '63 (FgM) Washington, DC AMERICAN OBLATE MISSIONS.
Henchal, Rev. Msgr. Michael J. '73 (PRT) South Portland, ME St. John the Evangelist; Scarborough, ME St. Maximilian Kolbe; Cape Elizabeth, ME St. Bartholomew; Vicars General; Promoter of Justice; Associate Judges; Diocesan Consultors; South Portland, ME Church of the Holy Cross; Ex Officio Members; [M] Portland, ME Southern Maine Community College; Staff.
Henchey, Joseph *c.s.s.* '56 (NY)[A] Yonkers, NY St. Joseph's Seminary; White Plains, NY Our Lady of Mt. Carmel.
Hencier, John Gregory *c.m.f.* '72 (LA)[V] Rancho Dominguez, CA Dominguez Seminary Inc.
Hendel, Lawrence '77 (SJ) San Jose, CA St. Anthony.
Henderson, Christopher '94 (SAM) Retired.
Henderson, Donald '70 (PEO) Clergymen's Aid, Inc.; Peoria, IL St. Vincent De Paul.
Henderson, James B. *o.c.s.o.* '60 (DUB)[K] Peosta, IA New Melleray Abbey, Order of Cistercians of the Strict Observance.
Henderson, John A. '87 (JC) Perry, MO St. William.
Henderson, John '84 (P) Vocations.
Henderson, Robert J. '65 (COV)[I] Edgewood, KY St. Elizabeth Edgewood Retired.
Henderson, Timothy J. '04 (STL) St. Louis, MO St. Gabriel the Archangel.
Hendren, Lucian '63 (SFE) Retired.
Hendrick, Christianus '98 (RC)[C] Lower Brule, SD SCJ Community House; Lower Brule, SD St. Mary's.
Hendrick, Christianus *s.c.j.* '98 (SFS) Fort Thompson, SD St. Joseph; Lower Brule, SD Immaculate Conception.
Hendrick, Rev. Msgr. Frank J. '54 (ARL) Retired.
Hendrick, Rev. Msgr. Matthew D. '85 (R) Retired.
Hendricks, Clare '63 (GRY) On Duty Outside the Diocese.
Hendricks, Edward S. '77 (BAL) On Duty Outside the Archdiocese.
Hendricks, Rev. Msgr. Joseph M. '72 (COL) Dublin, OH St. Brigid of Kildare; [K] Columbus, OH Diocesan Retirement Community Corp.; [G] Columbus, OH The Villas at St. Therese Independent Living, Inc.; [G] Columbus, OH The Villas at St. Therese Assisted Living, Inc.
Hendricks, Theodore J. '65 (GB) Black Creek, WI St. Mary; Bonduel, WI St. Lawrence.
Hendrickson, D. Scott *s.j.* '08 (FgM) St. Louis, MO Society of Jesus.
Hendrickson, Daniel *s.j.* '94 (NY)[DD] New York, NY Xavier Jesuit Community.
Hendrickson, Rev. Msgr. Michael D. '01 (MO) San Jose, CA St. Victor; Navy Reserve Chaplains; Council of Priests.
Hendry, Rev. Msgr. Owen J. '60 (NEW) North Caldwell, NJ Notre Dame Retired.
Hendry, Simon J. *s.j.* '77 (DET)[K] Detroit, MI Jesuit Community at the University of Detroit Mercy.
Heneghan, James A. '83 (CHI) Chicago, IL Immaculate Heart of Mary.
Heneghan, Jarlath '55 (SEA) Retired.
Heneghan, John F. '55 (YAK) Judges Retired.
Henehan, Patrick '98 (PEO) Peoria, IL St. Jude.
Henehan, Thomas P. *m.m.* '65 (FgM) Maryknoll, NY MARYKNOLL.
Henery, Ronald Eugene *o.p* '78 (NY)[DD] New York St. Vincent Ferrer Priory.
Heney, David '78 (LA) Thousand Oaks, CA St. Paschal Baylon.
Hengle, John R. '68 (CLV) Tallmadge, OH Our Lady of Victory; Associate Judges.

Henke, Donald E. '93 (STL)[A] St. Louis, MO Kenrick School of Theology; [D] St. Louis, MO Paul VI Institute of Catechetical and Pastoral Studies.
Henke, Rev. Msgr. James '66 (SAT) Judges Retired.
Henkels, Edmund *o.s.b.* '59 (WDC)[O] Washington, DC St. Anselm's Abbey.
Henkle, Charles *o.f.m.conv.* '97 (SAV) Brunswick, GA St. Francis Xavier.
Henley, Earl *m.s.c.* '69 (SB) Native American Ministry; San Jacinto, CA St. Joseph Mission.
Henn, William *o.f.m.cap.* '78 (PIT)[M] Pittsburgh, PA St. Augustine Friary.
Hennecke, William '07 (SPC) Leopold, MO St. John; [B] Cape Girardeau, MO Notre Dame Regional High School.
Hennelly, Michael F. '91 (PH) Levittown, PA Queen of the Universe.
Hennen, David R. '05 (STP) Buffalo, MN St. Francis Xavier.
Hennen, Joseph '67 (HON) Hilo, HI Malia Puka O' Kalani (Mary Gate of Heaven).
Hennen, Thomas Joseph '04 (DAV) Presbyteral Council; Vocations; [J] Davenport, IA St. Vincent Center.
Hennessey, Daniel F. '02 (BO) Vocations; Waltham, MA St. Mary.
Hennessey, John E. '67 (CHI) Libertyville, IL St. Joseph.
Hennessey, John J. *c.ss.r.* (BO) Boston, MA Our Lady of Perpetual Help.
Hennessey, Joseph M. '88 (BO) Associates; Weston, MA St. Julia.
Hennessey, Lawrence R. '71 (CHI)[A] Mundelein, IL University of St. Mary of the Lake/Mundelein Seminary; [W] Mundelein, IL Civitas Dei Foundation.
Hennessey, Rev. Msgr. William J. '61 (MIA) Retired.
Hennessy, Brian P. '99 (PH) Office of the Archbishop; On Special or Other Archdiocesan Assignment.
Hennessy, Rev. Msgr. Douglas '63 (PEO) Bloomington, IL Holy Trinity; Clergymen's Aid, Inc.
Hennessy, James W. '61 (WIN) Retired.
Hennessy, John A. *s.j.* '69 (MIL)[P] Wauwatosa, WI Jesuit Community at St. Camillus.
Hennessy, John '78 (FWT) Fort Worth, TX St. John the Apostle.
Hennessy, Joseph I. '63 (PHX) Retired.
Hennessy, Thomas J. '96 (ATL) Special or Other Archdiocesan Assignment.
Henning, James P. *o.f.m.conv.* '82 (PEO) Clinton, IL St. John the Baptist Catholic Church; Farmer City, IL Sacred Heart.
Henning, Michael L. '74 (STL) Saint Louis, MO Holy Name of Jesus.
Henning, Phillip D. '93 (SAT) Floresville, TX Sacred Heart.
Henning, Rev. Msgr. Richard G. '92 (RVC)[A] Huntington, NY Diocesan Seminary of the Immaculate Conception.
Henninger, George '85 (VIC) Victoria, TX Holy Family of Joseph, Mary & Jesus.
Henninger, Mark *s.j.* '78 (WDC)[O] Washington, DC The Jesuit Community at Georgetown University.
Hennington, Bruce M. '68 (MAD) Retired.
Henrich, Steven *o.s.c.* '74 (PHX)[F] Crosiers Serving Abroad.
Henrick, John C. '62 (NSH) Antioch, TN St. Ignatius of Antioch; Defenders of the Bond; Presbyteral Council; Priest Benefit Foundation.
Henricksen, Rev. Msgr. Francis C. '55 (DAV) Promoters of Justice; Vicar for Religious; Vicar for Clergy Retired.
Henriot, Peter J. *s.j.* '70 (FgM) Portland, OR Society of Jesus.
Henriquez, Genaro '99 (BWN) Pharr, TX St. Anne, Mother of Mary.
Henritzy, Elias A. *o.p.* '92 (L)[L] Louisville, KY St. Louis Bertrand Priory; Louisville, KY St. Louis Bertrand.
Henry, Charles W. *o.s.b.* '53 (NEW)[L] Newark, NJ Newark Abbey.
Henry, Donald H. '71 (VEN) Sarasota, FL St. Thomas More.
Henry, Earl J. *o.s.b.* '64 (GBG)[H] Latrobe, PA Saint Vincent Archabbey.
Henry, James R. '71 (MRY) Salinas, CA Madonna Del Sasso; Vicars Forane; Diocesan Consultors; Diocesan Consultors; Presbyteral Council.
Henry, James *s.v.d.* '59 (LA)[D] Lakewood, CA Saint Joseph High School.
Henry, James '71 (MRY) San Juan Bautista, CA San Juan Bautista.
Henry, Jeffrey F. (SAC) Vallejo, CA St. Vincent Ferrer.
Henry, Joseph P. '58 (PRO) Retired.
Henry, Joseph *m.s.f.s.* (TYL)[C] Whitehouse, TX The Missionaries of St. Francis de Sales.
Henry, Lawrence J. *c.s.c.* '61 (FTW)[H] Notre Dame Congregation of Holy Cross, United States Province of Priests & Brothers.
Henry, Leo G. '55 (PIT) Retired.
Henry, Matthew '10 (PHX) Phoenix, AZ SS. Simon and Jude Roman Catholic Cathedral; [A] Phoenix, AZ Bourgade Catholic High School.
Henry, Patrick J. (CHI) Oak Lawn, IL St. Catherine of Alexandria.
Henry, Paul J. '70 (BAL) Special Assignment.
Henry, Paul J. '68 (ORL) Orlando, FL Basilica of the National Shrine of Mary Queen of the Universe; Vicars for Clergy.
Henry, Paul J. '70 (MO) DEPARTMENT OF VETERANS AFFAIRS HOSPITALS AND CHAPLAINS.
Henry, Paul '68 (ORL) Ex Officio Members; Tourism Ministry.
Henry, Perry *c.m.* '83 (STL)[O] Earth City, MO Congregation of the Mission Western Province (Vincentians).
Henry, Perry *c.m.* '83 (FgM) Earth City, MO Western Province; Earth City, MO.
Henry, Peter J. '68 (ORL) DeBary, FL St. Ann's.
Henry, Robert P. '79 (NY) Scarsdale, NY Immaculate Heart of Mary.
Henry, Terence *t.o.r.* '76 (STU)[A] Steubenville, OH Franciscan University of Steubenville; [H] Steubenville, OH Holy Spirit Friary.
Henry, William F. '84 (JKS) Jackson, MS St. Therese; Charismatic Renewal; Personnel Board.
Henseler, J. Thomas '63 (PEO) On Duty Outside the Diocese.
Henseler, J. Thomas '63 (SFD) Mount Sterling, IL Holy Family; Mount Sterling, IL St. Thomas; Mount Sterling, IL Western Illinois Correctional Center.
Henseler, Philip E. '00 (CHI) Other Assignments.
Hensell, Eugene *o.s.b.* '69 (IND)[A] Saint Meinrad, IN Saint Meinrad School of Theology; [K] Saint Meinrad, IN St. Meinrad Archabbey.
Henson, Darren '01 (KCK) On Leave of Absence.
Henson, Joel '93 (LA)[A] Camarillo, CA St. John's Seminary; Appointed Membership.
Henson, Paul *o.carm.* '02 (LA)[F] Encino, CA Crespi Carmelite High School; [P] Encino, CA Our Lady of Mount Carmel Priory.
Hensy, Patrick E. *c.s.p.* '78 (LA) Los Angeles, CA St. Paul the Apostle Retired.
Hentges, James *o.s.c.* '76 (PHX)[F] Crosiers Serving Abroad.
Hentz, Otto H. *s.j.* '68 (WDC)[O] Washington, DC The Jesuit Community at Georgetown University.
Hentzner, John T. '45 (MIL) Retired.
Henyk, Christopher '08 (Y) Presbyteral Council; Warren, OH Blessed John Paul II Parish.
Henz, Kenneth W. '51 (CIN) Retired.
Heon, Charles *o.m.i.* '64 (BO)[X] Tewksbury, MA Immaculate Heart of Mary Residence.
Hepburn, Timothy M. '93 (ATL) Vocations; Permanent Diaconate; Special or Other Archdiocesan Assignment.
Hephner, John J. '59 (GB) Wausaukee, WI St. Agnes; Wausaukee, WI St. Augustine; Armstrong Creek, WI St. Stanislaus Kostka; Goodman, WI St. Joan of Arc Retired.
Hepnar, Bede '57 (GB)[J] Green Bay, WI St. Mary of the Angels Friary.
Hepnar, Bede *o.f.m.* '57 (MIL)[P] Burlington, WI Queen of Peace Friary.
Hepner, Ernest C. '61 (CLV) Retired.
Heppe, Patrick E. '77 (MIL) Special Assignment; Archbishop's Executive Council; Vicars General; Vicar for Ordained and Lay Ecclesial Ministry; Archdiocesan Consultors; Archdiocesan Council of Priests.
Heppen, Michael J. *c.s.c.* '63 (FTW)[H] Holy Cross House.
Heppler, Jeremy *o.s.b.* '10 (KCK)[I] Atchison, KS St. Benedict's Abbey.
Her, Chundo '94 (SAC) Sacramento, CA St. Jeong–Hae Elizabeth.
Hera, Marianus Pale *s.v.d.* '04 (WDC)[O] Washington, DC Society of the Divine Word/Divine Word House.
Herald, Robert '89 (AUS) Waco, TX St. Joseph.
Heras, Rev. Msgr. Michael '84 (CC) Personnel Board – Priests; Corpus Christi, TX Our Lady of Perpetual Help.
Heraty, John T. '67 (RCK) Retired.
Herba, Stanislaw '64 (SLC) Park City, UT Saint Mary of the Assumption LLC 238.
Herbein, Rev. Msgr. John J. '74 (E) Franklin, PA St. Patrick.
Herbek, Rev. Msgr. Adrian F. '59 (LIN) Building Commission; Members Retired.
Herbek, Rev. Msgr. Adrian F. '59 (LIN)[E] Lincoln, NE Bonacum House Retired.
Herber, Alvin *c.pp.s.* '50 (CIN)[N] Carthagena, OH St. Charles Retired.
Herber, John *c.pp.s.* '68 (CIN)[N] Carthagena, OH St. Charles.
Herber, Stanley J. '64 (IND) Connersville, IN St. Gabriel Catholic Church, Connersville, Inc.; Knightstown, IN St. Rose of Lima Catholic Church, Knightstown, Inc.; Liberty, IN St. Bridget Catholic Church, Liberty, Inc.; New Castle, IN St. Anne Catholic Church, New Castle, Inc.; Deaneries and Deans.
Herberger, Edward *s.v.d.* '60 (CHI)[N] Techny, IL Divine Word Residence.
Herberger, Roy T. '68 (BUF) Sheehan Memorial Emergency Hospital; Buffalo, NY SS. Columba–Brigid.
Herbers, Simon *c.p.* '50 (GAL)[O] Houston, TX Congregation of the Passion, Holy Name Passionist Community and Retreat Center.
Herbert, Eugene '81 (LA) Monrovia, CA Annunciation.
Herbert, G. Paul '86 (WDC) Fort Washington, MD St. Ignatius; Pastoral Center Special Ministries; Promoters of Justice; Defenders of the Bond; Air Force Reserve Chaplains.
Herbert, G. Paul '86 (MO) Judges; Defenders of the Bond.
Herbert, John J. '83 (BUR)[D] Rutland, VT Loretto/Kervick Home Retired.
Herbert, Rev. Msgr. Leo P. '67 (ATL) Retired.
Herbert, Michael J. '05 (RIC) Lebanon, VA Good Shepherd; St. Paul, VA St. Therese.
Herbst, Robert M. *o.f.m.conv.* '91 (OAK) Adjutant Judicial Vicars; Judges; Vicars for Religious; Consultors; Court of Second Instance; Alameda, CA St. Barnabas.
Herbst, Thomas *o.f.m.* '92 (SD)[J] Oceanside, CA Old Mission San Luis Rey.
Herbster, Rev. Msgr. Kenneth J. '63 (NEW) North Caldwell, NJ Notre Dame Retired.
Hercek, Joseph R. '72 (MRY) Retired.
Hercik, Terry A. '80 (GBG) Coral, PA Our Lady of the Assumption.
Herda, Jerome '90 (MIL) Whitefish Bay, WI St. Monica; Fox Point, WI St. Eugene.
Heredia, Juan Victor '91 (BWN) Raymondville, TX St. Anthony.
Hereford, Thomas D. '85 (JC) Absent on Leave.
Hereley, Peter J. *o.p.* '63 (CHI) River Forest, IL St. Vincent Ferrer; [T] River Forest, IL American Friends of the Ecole Biblique.
Hereshko, David M. '00 (HBG) Mechanicsburg, PA St. Joseph; [A] Camp Hill, PA Trinity High School.
Herff, Jerome *c.m.* '67 (LA) Los Angeles, CA St. Vincent De Paul.
Hergenroeder, Charles *c.ss.r.* '73 (WIL) Seaford, DE Our Lady of Lourdes.
Hergenrother, John C. '66 (CHI) Judges; Other Assignments; La Grange Park, IL St. Louise de Marillac.
Herhenrerder, Peter V. '59 (SCR) Retired.
Heria, Fernando '96 (MIA) Judges; Miami, FL St. Brendan.
Herian, Kenneth J. *s.j.* '55 (MIL) Milwaukee, WI Gesu Parish; [P] Milwaukee, WI Jesuit Community at Marquette University.
Heric, William '81 (SEA) Redmond, WA St. Jude; Duvall, WA Holy Innocents.
Herle, Clifford *o.f.m.* '55 (LSC) Tularosa, NM St. Francis de Paula.
Herlihy, Rev. Msgr. Daniel J. '67 (MET) Episcopal Vicars; Highland Park, NJ Transfiguration of the Lord Parish.
Herlihy, Neil '05 (ATL) The Rock, GA St. Peter the Rock.
Herlong, Theophilus L. '58 (LKC) Advocates Retired.
Herman, Charles A. '97 (FTW) South Bend, IN St. John the Baptist; South Bend, IN Holy Family.
Herman, Jean–Pierre (KC) Kansas City, MO Oratory of Old St. Patrick.
Herman, John *c.s.c.* (FTW)[H] Notre Dame Congregation of Holy Cross, United States Province of Priests & Brothers.
Herman, Norbert H. '88 (SAT) Runge, TX St. Anthony's; Kenedy, TX Our Lady Queen of Peace.
Herman, Robert D. '60 (WIN) Medford, MN Christ the King; Medford, MN Corpus Christi Retired.
Herman, William J. '00 (DET) Harper Woods, MI Our Lady Queen of Peace.
Hermann, Rev. Msgr. Carlton P. '52 (SFS) Retired.
Hermanns, Mel *o.f.m.cap.* '64 (CHI) Chicago, IL Our Lady Gate of Heaven.
Hermes, Alphonsus B. *o.praem.* '01 (ORG)[D] Silverado, CA St. Michael's Preparatory School; [I] Silverado, CA Norbertine Fathers of Orange Inc.
Hermes, Rev. Msgr. Daniel J. '69 (RCK) Crystal Lake, IL St. Thomas the Apostle; Diocesan Consultors.
Hermes, Rev. Msgr. Eustace '41 (VIC) Retired.
Hermes, Joseph H. *m.m.* '62 (FgM) Maryknoll, NY MARYKNOLL.
Hermes, Michael '91 (KCK)[B] Kansas City, KS Bishop Ward High School; Leawood, KS Church of the Nativity.
Hermes, Richard C. '98 (SP)[C] Tampa, FL Jesuit High School.
Hermes, Thomas W. '82 (KC) Montrose, MO Immaculate Conception; Consultors.
Hermoso, Rev. Msgr. Seth F. '67 (GAL) Houston, TX St. John Neumann; Ethnic Vicars.
Hernandez, Alfred Ricardo '66 (SAT) Military Chaplains.
Hernandez, Alfred Z. *c.s.c.* '03 (FTW)[H] Notre Dame Congregation of Holy Cross, United States Province of Priests & Brothers.
Hernandez, Alfred '82 (LA) Torrance, CA Nativity.
Hernandez, Rev. Msgr. Alfred '55 (LA) Retired.
Hernandez, Alfredo '92 (PMB) West Palm Beach, FL St. Juliana; Ex Officio; Vicars Forane.
Hernandez, Angelo J. '93 (PH) On Special or Other

Archdiocesan Assignment; Chester, PA Saint Katharine Drexel.
Hernandez, Anselmo *l.c.* '01 (MO) Army Chaplains.
Hernandez, Rev. Msgr. Anthony '95 (BRK)[V] Brooklyn, NY Casa Betsaida–Home for people with AIDS; Chancellor; Diocesan Consultors; Presbyteral Council; Brooklyn, NY Transfiguration; Vicar for Canonical Affairs; Assignment Board.
Hernandez, Anthony '00 (HPM) Los Gatos, CA St. Basil the Great; Director of Religious Education.
Hernandez, Anthony (OAK) On Duty to Byzantine Ministry in the Diocese.
Hernandez, Antonio X. '92 (SAT) On Leave; Sabinal, TX St. Patrick's.
Hernandez, Antonio *c.ss.r.* '67 (CGS) Aguas Buenas, PR Church of Tres Santos Reyes.
Hernandez, Apolinar '90 (SR) On Leave.
Hernandez, Ariel '03 (CAM) Bridgeton, NJ The Parish of the Holy Cross, Bridgeton, N.J.
Hernandez, Benito A. *c.r.* '03 (DEN) Denver, CO Our Lady of Guadalupe.
Hernandez, Bernardo Lozano '01 (CHI) Chicago, IL St. Francis de Sales.
Hernandez, Bernardo *c.m.* '63 (ARE) Manati, PR Sagrada Familia.
Hernandez, Bradford '08 (AUS) Austin, TX St. Julia.
Hernandez, Edgardo Lopez '83 (MGZ) Sabana Grande, PR Church of San Isidro.
Hernandez, Edwin R. '83 (CGS) Cayey, PR San Esteban Protomartir.
Hernandez, Eliseo *c.o.r.c.* '82 (SB) Barstow, CA St. Joseph; Barstow, CA St. Philip Neri; Trona, CA St. Madeleine Sophie Barat; [I] Corona, CA Confraternity of Operarios Del Reino De Cristo, C.O.R.C.; Appointed Members.
Hernandez, Enrico '96 (SJ) On Leave of Absence.
Hernandez, Eric *m.n.m.* (DAL) Dallas, TX St. Philip.
Hernandez, Esteban '87 (BWN) Los Fresnos, TX St. Cecilia.
Hernandez, Fernando A. '90 (NY) Newburgh, NY St. Patrick.
Hernandez, Fidel *o.a.r.* '98 (LA) Oxnard, CA Mary Star of the Sea; [P] Oxnard, CA Order of Augustinian Recollects (O.A.R.), St. Augustine Priory.
Hernandez, Francis G. *s.j.* '63 (SAC)[C] Sacramento, CA Jesuit High School.
Hernandez, Francis G. *s.j.* '63 (SJ)[M] Los Gatos, CA Sacred Heart Jesuit Center.
Hernandez, Francisco J. '90 (LAR) Laredo, TX San Agustin Cathedral.
Hernandez, Francisco J. '94 (MIA) Hialeah, FL Immaculate Conception.
Hernandez, Francisco J. '90 (YAK) On Duty Outside the Diocese Retired.
Hernandez, Francisco '95 (CGS)[B] Aibonito, PR Casa Manresa; Priests Senate; Formacion Diac. Permanentes.
Hernandez, Gerardo *c.ss.r.* (CGS) Aguas Buenas, PR Church of Tres Santos Reyes.
Hernandez, Rev. Msgr. Gonzalo Diaz '63 (MGZ) Hormigueros, PR Shrine of Our Lady of Monserrate; Chancellor; Diocesan Board of Administration; Parish Priests Consultors.
Hernandez, Ivan '09 (FRS) Bakersfield, CA St. Philip the Apostle.
Hernandez, J. Trinidad *c.o.r.c.* (SB)[I] Corona, CA Confraternity of Operarios Del Reino De Cristo, C.O.R.C.
Hernandez, Jaime B. '03 (WDC) Clinton, MD Church of St. John the Evangelist.
Hernandez, Jaime *o.f.m.* '11 (AMA) Amarillo, TX St. Laurence Church.
Hernandez, Jimmy '83 (ARE) Retired.
Hernandez, Jorge *o.f.m.* '98 (P) Portland, OR Ascension; [L] Portland, OR Ascension Friary.
Hernandez, Jose A. '60 (SFE) Tome, NM Immaculate Conception.
Hernandez, Jose Luis '99 (SPK) Spokane, WA Cathedral of Our Lady of Lourdes; Rosalia, WA St. Catherine of Alexandria; Rosalia, WA Holy Rosary; Saint John, WA Our Lady of Perpetual Help; Rosalia, WA Sacred Heart; Spokane, WA St. Joseph.
Hernandez, Jose Reynaldo (DM) Des Moines, IA Our Lady of the Americas.
Hernandez, Rev. Msgr. Joseph F. '81 (LA) Los Angeles, CA St. Teresa of Avila; Vice Chancellor; Cardinal McIntyre Fund for Charity; Continuing Formation for Clergy; ACC Liaison to Brothers' Council; Continuing Formation; Cardinal McIntyre Fund for Charity Board of Directors.
Hernandez, Juan Pedro '89 (PT) Tallahassee, FL Blessed Sacrament.
Hernandez, Juan Ramon *c.ss.r.* '80 (CGS) San Lorenzo, PR Nuestra Senora de la Mercedes.
Hernandez, Lawrence C. *o.ss.t.* '78 (BAL)[Q] Archdiocese of Washington, DC.
Hernandez, Manuel Santiago '85 (PCE) Catholic Youth Organization.
Hernandez, Manuel '96 (CC) Retired.
Hernandez, Miguel A. '02 (ORG) Anaheim, CA St. Anthony Claret.
Hernandez, Nils '04 (DUB) Clarion, IA St. John; Eagle Grove, IA Sacred Heart; Belmond, IA St. Francis Xavier; Deanery Representatives; Worship Commission.
Hernandez, Oscar *m.j.* (GAL) Houston, TX St. Stephen.
Hernandez, Pablo A. '06 (L) Hodgenville, KY Our Lady of Mercy.
Hernandez, Pedro '89 (ARE) Vega Alta, PR Our Lady of Mt. Carmel.
Hernandez, Ramon '73 (SP) Tampa, FL St. Mary Retired.
Hernandez, Ricardo '00 (RCK) Rockford, IL St. Patrick.
Hernandez, Ricardo '98 (SJN) Clergy Social Security (Prevision Social del Clero).
Hernandez, Victor '06 (TYL) Grand Saline, TX St. Celestine; Emory, TX St. John the Evangelist Church; Diocesan Liturgical Commission.
Hernandez–Ayala, Jose Luis '06 (ATL) Clarkesville, GA St. Mark.
Hernandez–Barron, J. Asuncion F. '09 (SB) Riverside, CA St. John the Evangelist.
Hernandez–Gomez, Francisco J. '01 (SAC) Vocations.
Hernandez Morales, Ricardo '98 (SJN) Spiritual Director.
Hernandez Ralat, Edwin '01 (SJN) Graduate Studies.
Hernandez Velez, Daniel Enrique '03 (MGZ) Mayaguez, PR Church of the Resurrection; Vocations.
Hernando, Ciro '90 (KCK) Kansas City, KS Our Lady of Unity.
Hernando, Henry L. '67 (LA)[BB] San Pedro, CA Apostleship of the Sea, Catholic Maritime Ministry; Apostleship of the Sea.
Hernando, Jose L. '62 (MIA) Key Biscayne, FL St. Agnes.
Hernandoz Baeza, Martin E. '96 (DEN) Fort Morgan, CO St. Helena.
Herne, Robert G. '47 (CHI) Palos Hills, IL Sacred Heart; Northbrook, IL Our Lady of the Brook Retired.
Herold, Anthony J. '79 (DAV) Burlington, IA SS. John & Paul; Personnel Board; Deans.
Heron, J. Thomas '78 (PH) Conshohocken, PA St. Matthew.
Herondi, Fernandes de Araujo *s.x.* '76 (PAT) Wayne, NJ XAVERIAN MISSIONARY FATHERS; [N] Wayne Xaverian Missionary Fathers.
Herpin, Rev. Msgr. Michael '66 (LAF) On Leave.
Herpin, Wayne D. *s.j.* '74 (LSC) Alamogordo, NM St. Jude.
Herr, Kenneth H. '68 (EVN) Evansville, IN St. Boniface.
Herrador, Blas P. '52 (GAL) Houston, TX Resurrection.
Herrea, Henry Erazo '98 (DAL) Dallas, TX Cathedral–Santuario de Guadalupe.
Herrejon–Lopez, Armando '07 (ATL) Marietta, GA Holy Family; Atlanta, GA St. Jude.
Herrera, Anthony W. '91 (OAK) Hayward, CA All Saints.
Herrera, David '89 (SAN) San Angelo, TX St. Mary's.
Herrera, Edward '91 (LSC) Absent On Leave.
Herrera, Rev. Msgr. Emigdio '77 (LA) Lynwood, CA St. Emydius; Santa Maria, CA St. John Neumann.
Herrera, Enrique '96 (MRY) Greenfield, CA Holy Trinity; Presbyteral Council.
Herrera, Francisco '67 (ELP) Presbyteral Council Retired.
Herrera, Jorge '03 (RNO) Yerington, NV Holy Family; Hawthorne, NV Our Lady of Perpetual Help; Priest Personnel Board; Seminary Board; Vocations Team.
Herrera, Jose Francisco '88 (BRK) Woodside, NY Corpus Christi; Richmond Hill, NY Our Lady of the Cenacle; Jamaica, NY St. Pius V.
Herrera, Jose G. '89 (MO) Army Chaplains.
Herrera, Jose M. '09 (YAK) Yakima, WA St. Joseph Parish.
Herrera, Jose '89 (STV) On Duty Outside the Diocese.
Herrera, Juan '11 (WOR) Unassigned.
Herrera, Manuel Victor (NY) Bronx, NY Our Lady of Grace.
Herrera, Pedro E. *c.s.v.* '80 (CHI)[N] Arlington Heights Viatorian Province Center–Clerics of St. Viator.
Herrera, Roberto '08 (ATL) Alpharetta, GA St. Thomas Aquinas.
Herrera, Ruben '06 (RCK) Aurora, IL Our Lady of Good Counsel.
Herrero, Rev. Msgr. Nicolas '59 (FRS) Retired.
Herres, Rev. Msgr. Joseph W. '72 (LA) Baldwin Park, CA St. John the Baptist.
Herring, James B. *o.praem.* (GB) Judges.
Herring, James B. *o.praem.* '02 (GB)[A] De Pere, WI St. Norbert Abbey; [J] De Pere, WI St. Norbert Abbey; [O] De Pere, WI NORBERT & CO.; De Pere, WI.
Herman, Gilbert P. '49 (DOD) Retired.
Herrmann, Francis R. *s.j.* '74 (BO)[U] Newton, MA The Jesuit Community at Boston College.
Herrmann, James (STP) Crystal, MN St. Raphael.
Herrmann, Richard J. '44 (LC) Retired.
Herrmann, Robert W. '58 (PIT) Retired.
Herron, Rev. Msgr. Denis M. '73 (BRK) Woodside, NY St. Teresa.
Herron, Francis X. '55 (PH) Retired.
Herron, Jack B. '74 (FAR) Military Chaplains.
Herron, John B. '74 (MO) Army Chaplains.
Herron, Rev. Msgr. Joseph P. '62 (CAM) Retired.
Hersey, Bryan L. '98 (SEA) Everett, WA Immaculate Conception; Everett, WA Our Lady of Perpetual Help; Presbyteral Council; Deans.
Hertel, James R. (PAT) Retired.
Hertel, John *o.carm.* '53 (JOL)[K] Darien, IL Carmelite Carefree Retirement Village Retired.
Hertel, Joseph *o.f.m.* '66 (SP)[N] St. Petersburg, FL St. Anthony Friary.
Hertges, Donald A. '07 (DUB) Preston, IA St. Joseph; Maquoketa, IA St. Lawrence; Maquoketa, IA Sacred Heart.
Hertzfeld, Adam L. '02 (TOL) Toledo, OH St. Joan of Arc.
Hervey, Paul '95 (SP) Knights of Columbus Retired.
Herzing, Joseph '99 (SCL) Perham, MN Holy Cross; Perham, MN St. Henry's; Diocesan Consultors.
Herzog, John M. '56 (DUB) Retired.
Herzog, Lawrence A. '80 (STL) Richmond Heights, MO Little Flower.
Herzog, Mark J. '79 (TOL) Oregon, OH St. Ignatius; Members; Diocesan Council of Catholic Women (DCCW).
Herzstein, Joseph M. *c.s.sp.* '63 (FgM) Bethel Park, PA CONGREGATION OF THE HOLY SPIRIT.
Hesburgh, Theodore M. *c.s.c.* '43 (FTW)[H] Holy Cross House.
Heskamp, Charles *s.v.d.* '58 (TR)[N] Bordentown, NJ Society of the Divine Word.
Hesketh, John E. *o.s.b.* '94 (PAT)[N] Morristown, NJ St. Mary's Abbey.
Heskin, Thomas *o.s.m.* '55 (CHI)[N] Berwyn, IL St. Bonfilius Priory; Riverside, IL St. Mary.
Hesko, Daniel C. '84 (TR) Middletown, NJ St. Catherine.
Heslin, Rev. Msgr. James J. '54 (STA) Retired.
Heslin, Rev. Msgr. Philip J. '57 (SUP) Retired.
Heslin, Sean '67 (ORL) Cocoa Beach, FL Church of Our Saviour; Deans; Ex Officio Members.
Hess, Daniel K. '11 (CIN) Sidney, OH Holy Angels; [E] Sidney, OH Lehman Catholic High School.
Hess, James D. *o.carm.* '76 (PBR) North Huntingdon, PA St. Stephen's.
Hess, Larry J. '79 (ALN) Reading, PA St. Anthony of Padua; Charismatic Renewal; Catholic Men of Good News (CMOGN).
Hess, Michael N. '71 (DM) West Des Moines, IA Sacred Heart.
Hess, Rev. Msgr. Michael (DM) Priests' Pension Fund Society.
Hess, Stephen *s.j.* '95 (NEW)[B] Jersey City, NJ Jesuit Center; [L] Jersey City, NJ Jesuits of Saint Peter's College, Inc.
Hesse, Anthony R. '01 (NU) Winsted, MN Holy Trinity; College of Consultors; Worship Committee; Priests' Council.
Hesse, Paul A. '91 (CC) Corpus Christi, TX St. Pius X.
Hesse, Thomas '63 (KCK) Retired.
Hessel, Gerald J. '67 (MIL) Retired.
Hesseling, Jason E. '00 (MAD) Military Chaplains.
Hesseling, Jason E. '73 (MO) Army Chaplains.
Hessian, Roger J. '61 (STP) Retired.
Hession, Anthony '99 (FAR) Fargo, ND St. Mary's Cathedral of Fargo.
Hession, Mark R. '84 (FR) Centerville, MA Our Lady of Victory; Auditors; Continuing Education of the Clergy; Diocesan Council of Catholic Nurses.
Hessling, Ambrose B. *o.s.b.* '57 (PEO)[A] Peru, IL St. Bede Abbey Retired.
Hessling, Daniel '04 (JOL) Momence, IL St. Patrick.
Hester, John '59 (SJ) Stanford Medical Center.
Heter, Bernard P. '74 (NY) Cornwall–on–Hudson, NY St. Thomas of Canterbury.
Hetland, John G. '11 (CHI) Chicago, IL St. Barnabas.
Hetzler, Leo A. *c.s.b.* '55 (ROC)[K] Rochester, NY Basilian Residence.
Heuberger, Joseph '70 (P) Salem, OR St. Vincent de Paul; Building Commission.
Heuberger, Mark L. '80 (VEN) Bradenton, FL SS. Peter and Paul the Apostles.
Heumann, Carl J. *s.j.* '92 (STL)[F] St. Louis, MO St. Louis University High School, George H. Backer Memorial; [O] Saint Louis, MO St. Louis University High School Jesuit Community.
Heuschkel, Regis *o.p.* '50 (Y) Youngstown, OH St. Dominic.
Heusel, Daniel '00 (STU) Bellaire, OH St. John; Neffs, OH Sacred Heart; Auditors; Notaries; Presbyteral Council; College of Consultors; Assistant Directors; Defenders of the Bond.
Heuser, James *s.d.b.* '84 (NEW)[L] Ramsey, NJ Don Bosco Prep Salesian Residence; [C] Ramsey, NJ Don Bosco Preparatory High School.
Hever, Rev. Msgr. Thomas '62 (PHX) Scottsdale, AZ Our Lady of Perpetual Help Roman Catholic Parish.
Hevern, Vincent W. *s.j.* '76 (SY)[Q] Syracuse, NY Jesuits at LeMoyne, Inc.
Hevia, Todd O. '67 (PT) Retired.
Hewe, Manuel '97 (HON) Clergy Personnel Board;

West Honolulu; Members; Members; Episcopal Vicar for Clergy; Office of Clergy – Diocesan Screening Committee; Implementation Commission of Diocesan Road Map for Pastoral Program and Facility Needs; Bishops Administrative Advisory Council; Honolulu, HI Cathedral of Our Lady of Peace; Presbyteral Council.
Hewes, James E. '74 (ROC) Rochester, NY St. Jude the Apostle; Rochester, NY St. Helen; Rochester, NY Holy Ghost.
Hewes, Robert S. '78 (MO) Air Force Reserve Chaplains; Dix Hills, NY St. Matthew.
Hewes, Russell L. '01 (OKL) Ada, OK St. Joseph; [K] Ada, OK East Central State University; Region III.
Hewett, Alfred J. '56 (CAM) Haddon Heights, NJ Church of St. Rose, Haddon Heights, N.J. Retired.
Hewitt, Anthony '99 (VEN) Defenders of the Bond; Auditors; Sarasota, FL St. Jude.
Hewitt, Kenneth R. (PAT) Retired.
Hewitt, Matthew A. '04 (SC) Le Mars, IA St. James.
Heyd, James F. '89 (CHI) Other Assignments; Skokie, IL St. Lambert.
Heyd, Joseph J. *o.s.b.* '56 (PEO)[A] Peru, IL St. Bede Abbey Retired.
Heyer, Bryan '04 (VIC) Palacios, TX St. Anthony's.
Heying, John '00 (RC) Buffalo, SD St. Anthony.
Heyman, George P. '81 (ROC) Priests' Sabbatical Committee; Fairport, NY Church of the Resurrection; [A] Rochester, NY St. Bernard's School of Theology & Ministry.
Heyman, Jerome M. *o.s.a.* '61 (JOL) Homer Glen, IL Our Mother of Good Counsel.
Heymen, Richard '56 (GB) Retired.
Heyrosa, Alfredo '83 (SD) El Cajon, CA Holy Trinity Catholic Parish.
Hezel, Francis X. *s.j.* '69 (CI)[A] Pohnpei, FM Micronesian Seminar; [C] Kolonia, Pohnpei, FM Jesuit House.
Hezel, Francis X. *s.j.* '69 (RVC) Oceanside, NY St. Anthony.
Hezel, Kenneth J. *s.j.* '66 (FgM) New York, NY Society of Jesus.
Hezel, Kenneth J. *s.j.* '66 (AGN) Archdiocesan College of Consultors; Archdiocesan Presbyteral Council; [F] Tamuning, GU Society of Jesus Micronesia.
Hezel, Kenneth J. *s.j.* '66 (CI)[C] Manresa Jesuit House.
Hezel, Kenneth J. *s.j.* '66 (CHK) Saipan, MP San Jude Parish; Presbyteral Council.
Hibner, Cyprian *o.carm.* '67 (TUC)[A] Tucson, AZ Salpointe Catholic High School; [E] Tucson, AZ Carmelite Priory Retired.
Hibner, Jerome H. '64 (BEL) Retired.
Hicarte, Mateo H. '53 (LA) Los Angeles, CA Immaculate Heart of Mary Retired.
Hickel, Rev. Msgr. John J. '55 (STL) St. Paul, MO St. Paul.
Hickey, Christopher J. '94 (BO) Hanover, MA St. Mary of the Sacred Heart.
Hickey, Daniel J. '59 (BO) Malden, MA Sacred Hearts.
Hickey, Dennis W. *c.s.p.* '76 (NY)[DD] New York, NY Paulist Fathers' Motherhouse Retired.
Hickey, George W. '73 (PRT) Hallowell, ME Sacred Heart.
Hickey, Gregory J. '79 (PH) Boothwyn, PA St. John Fisher.
Hickey, James F. '68 (BO) Rockland, MA Holy Family.
Hickey, Jerome J. *o.c.s.o.* '59 (ATL)[F] Conyers, GA The Monastery of the Holy Spirit Retired.
Hickey, Rev. Msgr. John '81 (AMA) Retired.
Hickey, Joseph W. '56 (NY) DEPARTMENT OF VETERANS AFFAIRS HOSPITALS AND CHAPLAINS; Castle Point, NY V.A. Hudson Valley Healthcare Retired.
Hickey, Kieran *o.f.m.* '49 (GB)[J] Appleton, WI St. Fidelis Friary Retired.
Hickey, Michael '62 (VEN) Retired.
Hickey, Thomas E. '70 (CHI) Glenview, IL Our Lady of Perpetual Help.
Hickey, Thomas F. *c.ss.r.* '54 (BRK) Brooklyn, NY Our Lady of Perpetual Help Basilica.
Hickey, Thomas W. '10 (HRT) Glastonbury, CT St. Paul; South Glastonbury, CT St. Augustine.
Hickey, Timothy J. *c.ss.p.* '99 (ARL) Arlington, VA Our Lady, Queen of Peace.
Hickie, J. Noel '67 (P)[J] Eugene, OR Sacred Heart Medical Center; On Duty Outside the Diocese.
Hickin, Michael '97 (FAR) On Duty Outside the Diocese.
Hickl, Robert *o.m.i.* '79 (FgM) Washington, DC AMERICAN OBLATE MISSIONS.
Hickman, J. Stephen '82 (RIC) Retired.
Hickman, J. Stephen '82 (SFE) Retired.
Hicks, Alfred J. *s.j.* '66 (FgM) Watertown, MA Society of Jesus.
Hicks, Boniface *o.s.b.* '04 (GBG)[H] Latrobe, PA Saint Vincent Archabbey.
Hicks, Francis J. '00 (LA) Los Angeles, CA St. Basil's; Ex Officio.
Hicks, Francis '00 (LA) Clergy, Vicar for; Assistant Vicar Clergy.
Hicks, Ronald A. '94 (CHI)[A] Mundelein, IL University of St. Mary of the Lake/Mundelein Seminary; [A] Mundelein, IL University of St. Mary of the Lake/ Mundelein Seminary; Mundelein Seminary/University of St. Mary of the Lake.
Hicks, Steven '82 (SAN) Military Chaplains; Navy Chaplains.
Hidaka, Ronald E. *s.j.* '74 (FgM) Portland, OR Society of Jesus.
Hiebl, Charles J. '62 (LC) Athens, WI St. Anthony de Padua; Athens, WI St. Thomas; Appointed Members.
Hien, Joachim L. '74 (SPK) Spokane, WA St. Anthony; Vietnamese Apostolate.
Higdon, Francis B. *m.m.* '67 (FgM) Maryknoll, NY MARYKNOLL.
Higgens, Peter '56 (AUS) Retired.
Higginbotham, Matthew P. '94 (LAF) Crowley, LA Immaculate Heart of Mary.
Higginbotham, Robert P. '75 (BLX) Diberville, MS Sacred Heart; Personnel Board.
Higgins, Brian J. '99 (ATL) Dawsonville, GA Christ the Redeemer Catholic Church.
Higgins, Charles J. '75 (BO) Clerk.
Higgins, Charles J. '75 (BO) Kingston, MA St. Joseph; Newton, MA Mary Immaculate of Lourdes; [BB] Braintree, MA Massachusetts Catholic Self–Insurance Group, Inc.; Vicariate IV.
Higgins, Donald *c.s.s.* '64 (BO)[X] Waltham, MA Stigmatine Fathers and Brothers Retired.
Higgins, Rev. Msgr. E. Edward '57 (PEO) Retired.
Higgins, Edward F. '54 (GBG) Retired.
Higgins, Edward J. '76 (PSC) Philadelphia, PA Holy Ghost; South Pennsylvania Protopresbyterate; Commission for Ecumenism; Presbyteral Council; Levittown, PA Our Lady of Perpetual Help.
Higgins, Francis C. '68 (SAV) Retired.
Higgins, Rev. Msgr. Grant J. '56 (BUF) Retired.
Higgins, Jerome *o.f.m.cap.* '54 (MIL)[B] Mount Calvary, WI St. Lawrence Seminary; [P] Mount Calvary, WI St. Lawrence Friary Retired.
Higgins, John F. *m.s.* '72 (HRT)[L] Hartford, CT Missionaries of LaSalette.
Higgins, John J. *s.j.* '66 (BGP)[O] Fairfield, CT The Fairfield Jesuit Community–Fairfield University.
Higgins, John J. '96 (NY) Peekskill, NY Assumption.
Higgins, John '01 (BEL) Leave of Absence.
Higgins, John '81 (LA) Downey, CA St. Raymond.
Higgins, Rev. Msgr. Joseph P. '58 (MAD) Retired.
Higgins, Rev. Msgr. Laurence E. '53 (SP) Tampa, FL St. Lawrence Retired.
Higgins, Leonard H. '82 (TLS) McAlester, OK St. John.
Higgins, Michael *c.p.* '70 (CHI)[N] Chicago, IL Province Development Office; [N] Chicago, IL Passionist Community–Immaculate Conception Community.
Higgins, Michael *o.carm.* '68 (TUC)[E] Tucson, AZ Carmelite Priory Retired.
Higgins, Patrick G. '10 (CC) Corpus Christi, TX St. Patrick.
Higgins, Peter '56 (VIC) Retired.
Higgins, Raymond (DM) Stuart, IA All Saints; Diocesan Consultors; Stuart, IA St. John.
Higgins, Robert F. '05 (CHR) Ridgeland, SC St. Anthony.
Higgins, Thomas M. '85 (PH) Philadelphia, PA Holy Innocents; Interparochial Cooperation, Commission for; Deans; Deans.
Higgs, Donald X. '88 (WH) Wheeling–Charleston Diocesan Council of Catholic Women; Elkins, WV St. Brendan; Vicars Forane; Coalton, WV St. Patrick Church.
Highberger, Donald E. *s.j.* '81 (STL)[O] St. Louis, MO Jesuit Community Corporation at Saint Louis University – Jesuit Hall.
Highberger, Donald *s.j.* '81 (STL)[C] Saint Louis University.
Highberger, Rev. Msgr. George '61 (PHX) Wickenburg, AZ St. Anthony of Padua Roman Catholic Parish; Congress, AZ Good Shepherd of the Desert Mission.
Highet, Iain R. '11 (HRT) Harwinton, CT Immaculate Heart of Mary; New Hartford, CT Immaculate Conception.
Highfill, Brian H. '74 (NO) Retired.
Hight, Michael '82 (RC) Retired.
Hightower, Craig *s.j.* '04 (SPK)[B] Spokane, WA Gonzaga University.
Hightower, Oliver Lee '61 (SEA) Lakewood, WA St. John Bosco.
Higley, Rev. Msgr. Gregory L. '81 (JC) Holts Summit, MO St. Andrew; Vicar General; Moderator of the Curia; Adjutant Judicial Vicar; Diocesan Consultors; Personnel Board; Ex Officio Members; Finance Committee; Board of Trustees; Priestly and Religious Vocations Committee.
Higuera, Federico '82 (BEL) Anna, IL St. Mary.
Higuera, Francisco '01 (YAK) On Duty Outside the Diocese.
Higuera, Francisco '01 (MAD) Dane, WI St. Michael; Lodi, WI St. Patrick.
Hiland, Gerard P. '85 (CIN) Batavia, OH Holy Trinity; Owensville, OH St. Louis; Owensville, OH St. Philomena; Batavia, OH St. Ann.
Hilander, Augustine *o.p.* '08 (ANC) Anchorage, AK Holy Family Cathedral.
Hilbert, J. Robert *s.j.* '56 (MIL)[P] Wauwatosa, WI Jesuit Community at St. Camillus.
Hilbert, Joseph C. '52 (HBG) Lancaster, PA St. Joseph Retired.
Hilbert, Michael P. *s.j.* '83 (NY)[DD] New York Jesuit Provincial's Office.
Hildebrandt, Henry F. '87 (DOD) Ness City, KS Sacred Heart Catholic Church of Ness City, Kansas; Ness City, KS St. Aloysius Catholic Church of Ransom, Kansas; Presbyteral Council.
Hilden, Michael J. *o.s.a.* '73 (FgM) Villanova, PA Province of St. Thomas of Villanova (Eastern).
Hilderbrand, H. Michael '76 (IND) Floyds Knobs, IN St. Mary–of–the–Knobs Catholic Church, Floyds Knobs, Inc.; Priests' Personnel Board.
Hilderbrand, Ryan Paul '09 (EVN) Evansville, IN Christ the King.
Hilferty, John G. '78 (ALN)[G] Allentown, PA Sacred Heart Hospital.
Hilfiker, Robert G. '87 (NY) New Windsor, NY St. Joseph.
Hilgartner, Richard B. '95 (BAL) On Duty Outside the Archdiocese; Staff.
Hilgeman, Edward J. '52 (STL) Spiritual Directors Retired.
Hilgeman, James L. *m.m.* '65 (NY)[DD] Maryknoll Maryknoll Fathers and Brothers Retired.
Hilgendorf, Patrick J. '97 (DAV) Ottumwa, IA St. Patrick's; Deans.
Hilgert, John *c.p.* '75 (SAC)[H] Citrus Heights, CA Christ the King Passionist Retreat Center.
Hilinski, Joseph T. '74 (CLV) Diocesan Interfaith Commission; Continuing Education for Formation of Ministers.
Hilinski, Joseph '74 (CLV) Eastlake, OH St. Justin Martyr.
Hill, Allan J. '83 (HRT) Waterbury, CT Our Lady of Loreto; Waterbury, CT St. Stanislaus Kostka.
Hill, Rev. Msgr. Charles E. '64 (LA) Retired.
Hill, Clifton *c.s.sp.* '65 (BR) Baton Rouge, LA St. Agnes.
Hill, Donald M. '94 (L) Louisville, KY St. Raphael the Archangel.
Hill, Edward T. '60 (BAL) Retired.
Hill, Eric J. '00 (ATL) Flowery Branch, GA Prince of Peace.
Hill, Eric '00 (ATL) Advocates.
Hill, Frederick '67 (RVC) Smithtown, NY St. Patrick; Smithtown, NY St. Catherine of Siena Hospital.
Hill, George H. '68 (NY)[GG] Bronx, NY Manhattan College; Bronx, NY St. Gabriel.
Hill, George H. '68 (WOR) On Duty Outside the Diocese.
Hill, Patrick J. '68 (LA) Canonical Services Coordinator.
Hill, Rev. Msgr. Philip W. '70 (MO) Military Chaplains; Army Chaplains.
Hill, Rev. Msgr. Robert Cary '66 (WDC) Garrett Park, MD Holy Cross.
Hill, Scott *o.m.i.* '79 (OAK) Oakland, CA Sacred Heart.
Hill, W. Paul '64 (WDC) Retired.
Hill, William '06 (CHY) St. Joseph's Society for Priests (Clergy Mutual Benefit Society); Vocation Office; Presbyteral Council.
Hiller, Everett J. '54 (RCK) Retired.
Hilley, Stephen J. '79 (MIA) Key Largo, FL St. Justin Martyr.
Hillier, David A. '76 (TR) On Duty Outside the Diocese.
Hillier, David A. (HBG)[I] Shippensburg, PA Shippensburg University; Shippensburg, PA Our Lady of the Visitation.
Hillier, John '88 (NOR)[A] Cromwell, CT Holy Apostles College and Seminary.
Hillyard, Matthew J. *o.s.f.s.* '91 (CAM) Continuing Education & Spiritual Formation of Priests (CESF); Camden, NJ The Parish of the Cathedral of the Immaculate Conception, Camden, N.J.; Appointed Members.
Hils, Damian J. '95 (COV) Bellevue, KY Divine Mercy; Dayton, KY St. Bernard.
Hilt, Ronald H. '09 (ROM) Aurora, IL St. George.
Hilton, Francis G. *s.j.* '92 (BAL)[Q] Baltimore, MD Jesuit Community of Loyola University, Inc.; [B] Jesuit Community of Loyola University, Inc.
Hilton, Hank *s.j.* '92 (BAL)[B] Timonium, MD Loyola Graduate Center–Timonium Campus.
Hilton, John L. '82 (DEN) Aspen, CO St. Mary.
Himawan, Ignatius *m.s.f.* '92 (SAT) New Braunfels, TX Holy Family.
Himes, Kenneth *o.f.m.* '76 (BO)[U] Newton, MA The Jesuit Community at Boston College.
Himes, Michael J. '72 (BRK) Released from Diocesan Assignment.
Himes, Robert P. '58 (YAK) Grand Coulee, WA St. Henry's; Coulee City, WA St. Patrick's.
Himmelsbach, James R. '77 (STP) Minneapolis, MN Annunciation.
Himsworth, Raymond J. '62 (PH) Retired.
Hincapie, Lisimaco (ARE) Sabana Hoyos, PR Inmaculado Corazon de Maria.

Hinch, Rev. Msgr. Lawrence E. '59 (BRK)[R] Douglaston, NY Bishop Mugavero Residence Retired.
Hincks, Michael *o.r.c.* '98 (DET)[K] Grosse Pointe, MI Order of Canons Regular of the Holy Cross.
Hinde, Peter *o.carm.* '52 (JOL)[L] Darien Carmelite Provincial Office; Darien, IL Provincial Headquarters, Carmelite Provincial Office.
Hindel, Richard *o.s.b.* '47 (IND)[K] Saint Meinrad, IN St. Meinrad Archabbey.
Hindelang, Joseph C. *s.m.* '78 (DET)[D] Pontiac, MI Notre Dame Preparatory School and Marist Academy.
Hinders, Joseph *c.pp.s.* '63 (CIN)[N] Carthagena, OH St. Charles Retired.
Hinders, Joseph *c.pp.s.* (COL) Columbus, OH St. James–the–Less.
Hindley, Robert J. *o.s.f.s.* '58 (FgM) Wilmington, DE OBLATES OF ST. FRANCIS DE SALES MISSIONS.
Hindman, John '75 (SB) On Leave of Absence.
Hinds, William H. '87 (COV) Williamstown, KY St. William; [R] Fort Mitchell, KY Mission Share.
Hindsley, Leonard P. '84 (FR) Westport, MA St. John the Baptist.
Hiner, Jason '11 (SPK) Spokane, WA St. Thomas More.
Hines, George C. '04 (BO) Wrentham, MA St. Mary; Elected.
Hines, Hugh *o.f.m.* '60 (NY) New York, NY St. Francis of Assisi.
Hines, J. William '72 (WDC) Rockville, MD Shrine of St. Jude.
Hinfey, Donald J. *s.j.* '63 (FgM) New York, NY Society of Jesus.
Hinkley, Michael F.X. *s.t.d.* '91 (HRT) Medical Leave.
Hinnebusch, John Frederick *o.p.* '50 (WDC)[B] Washington, DC Dominican House of Studies.
Hinnen, James W. '71 (MAD) Mineral Point, WI Congregation of St. Mary–St. Paul; Judges.
Hinni, Thomas R. *c.m.* '63 (STL)[O] St. Louis, MO Lazarist Residence.
Hinojal, Ricardo *o.a.r.* '62 (LSC) Las Cruces, NM Our Lady of Health; [B] Mesilla, NM Augustinian Recollect Fathers.
Hinojos, Jaime '02 (DET) Detroit, MI St. Gabriel.
Hinojosa, Damian '87 (NO) Marrero, LA Immaculate Conception.
Hinojosa, Jose Alfredo '04 (ELP) Presidio, TX Santa Teresa de Jesus.
Hinojosa, P. Nolasco '96 (LAR) Laredo, TX Holy Family.
Hinojosa, Rafael '09 (YAK) Kennewick, WA St. Joseph's.
Hinrichsen, Rev. Msgr. Carl D. '55 (NEW) Park Ridge, NJ Our Lady of Mercy Retired.
Hinsvark, John '66 (FBK) Retired Retired.
Hinton, Frederick M. '70 (BUF) Retired.
Hinton, John T. '73 (NO) New Orleans, LA Mater Dolorosa.
Hintz, Rev. Msgr. David R. '86 (LIN)[L] Lincoln, NE Calvary Cemetery and Mausoleum; Cemeteries; [A] Seward, NE St. Gregory the Great Seminary.
Hippee, Rev. Msgr. Michael E. '73 (MAD) Madison, WI St. Bernard; Judicial Vicar; Judges; Appointed; Building Commission.
Hipskind, J. Timothy *s.j.* '00 (DET)[K] Detroit, MI Jesuit Community at the University of Detroit Mercy.
Hipsley, Milton A. '70 (BAL) Retired.
Hipwell, Patrick J. '77 (STP) St. Paul, MN The Nativity of Our Lord; Deanery 2; College of Consultors.
Hiramatsu, Joseph *s.a.* '82 (NY)[DD] Garrison Franciscan Friars of the Atonement, Minister General Office.
Hire, Richard '70 (FTW) Syracuse, IN St. Martin de Porres; Diocesan Council of Catholic Women.
Hirniak, Mark '98 (STF) Notary.
Hirsch, Rev. Msgr. Clinton F. '45 (EVN) Retired.
Hirsch, Joseph W. '86 (LC) Special Assignment; [A] La Crosse, WI Holy Cross Seminary House of Formation; [H] La Crosse, WI Holy Cross (Seminary) Diocesan Center; Ex Officio.
Hirt, Alan *o.f.m.* '77 (CIN) Cincinnati, OH Holy Name; Cincinnati, OH St. Monica–St. George Parish Newman Center; [R] Cincinnati, OH University of Cincinnati Newman Center.
Hirten, Timothy J. '93 (BRK) Air Force Chaplains; Military Chaplains.
Hirtz, Daniel J. '73 (SPC) Salem, MO Sacred Heart; Region V.
Hislop, Edward '73 (HEL) Missoula, MT Blessed Trinity Parish; Presbyteral Council; Diocesan Consultors; Deaneries; Liturgical Commission.
Hissey, L. Pierre '66 (PHX) Sun Lakes, AZ St. Steven Roman Catholic Parish; Priests' Assurance Association.
Hissrich, John E. '86 (PIT) Pittsburgh, PA Nativity.
Hitch, David '68 (DAV) Tipton, IA St. Mary's.
Hitchcock, Martin B. '51 (BGP) Retired.
Hitchens, Robert '94 (PHU) Washington, DC Ukrainian Catholic National Shrine of the Holy Family; College of Archeparchial Consultors; Protopresbyters (Deans); Archeparchial Seminary Advisory and Admissions Board; Presbyteral Council; [A] Washington, DC St. Josaphat Seminary.
Hite, Gregory R. '81 (TOL) Mansfield, OH St. Peter; Judges.
Hite, Jordan F. *t.o.r.* '70 (MO) Defenders of the Bond.
Hite, Jordan *t.o.r.* '70 (BAL) Baltimore, MD St. Wenceslaus; Baltimore, MD St. Ann.
Hite, Jordan *t.o.r.* '70 (HBG) Diocesan Judges; Harrisburg, PA St. Catherine Laboure.
Hite, Richard B. *m.s.a.* '70 (WH)[E] Old Fields, WV Holy Spirit Hermitage.
Hite, Richard *m.s.a.* '70 (NOR)[G] Cromwell Society of the Missionaries of the Holy Apostles.
Hitpas, Joseph H. *o.m.i.* '65 (WDC)[O] Washington, DC Provincial Offices of the United States Province of the Missionary Oblates of Mary Immaculate; [O] Washington, DC Oblate Community; [X] Washington, DC Archdiocese of Cotabato.
Hitpas, Joseph *o.m.i.* '65 (CHI)[W] Chicago, IL Oblates for International Pastoral.
Hitpas, Rev. Msgr. William J. '67 (BEL) O Fallon, IL St. Nicholas.
Hjelstrom, Timothy '07 (DEN) Akron, CO St. Joseph.
Hladik, Dusan '83 (CHI) Brookfield, IL Czech Mission of Saints Cyril and Methodius.
Hladni, Mirko '71 (CLV) Cleveland, OH St. Paul; Judges in Second Instance.
Hlavaty, Kirby '99 (VIC) Priests' Personnel Board; Shiner, TX SS. Cyril and Methodius; Diocesan Consultors; Presbyteral Council.
Hlond, Waclaw *c.m.* '55 (HRT) Ansonia, CT St. Joseph Retired.
Hlubik, Joseph G. '93 (TR) Trenton Psychiatric Hospital; Jobstown, NJ St. Andrew's Church, Jobstown.
Hmircik, Donald A. '56 (MIL) Retired.
Hnatkivskyy, Vasyl (STN) Denver, CO Transfiguration of Our Lord.
Hnatyshyn, Rev. Canon Robert '64 (SJP) Presbyters Retired.
Ho, Antonio *c.s.j.b.* '95 (LA)[BB] Monterey Park, CA Congregation of St. John the Baptist.
Ho, Antonius *c.s.j.b.* '95 (BRK) Elmhurst, NY Our Lady of China Chapel; [Q] Chinese Apostolate–Queens; [R] Elmhurst, NY Congregation of St. John the Baptist of China; [R] Elmhurst, NY Our Lady of China Chapel; Flushing, NY St. John Vianney.
Ho, David Liang *o.s.b.* '09 (GBG)[H] Latrobe Saint Vincent Archabbey; [H] Latrobe, PA Saint Vincent Archabbey.
Ho, Joseph Khanh '90 (BEA) Western Vicariate; Diocesan College of Consultors; Diocesan Judges; Mont Belvieu, TX Holy Trinity; Presbyteral Council.
Ho, M. Justin Cong Huu *o.cist.* '06 (SB)[I] Lucerne Valley, CA The Cistercian Congregation of the Holy Family, St. Joseph Monastery.
Ho, Nicholas '79 (SAC) West Sacramento, CA Our Lady of Grace.
Ho, Thomas *c.ss.r.* '10 (DAL) Garland, TX Mother of Perpetual Help.
Ho, Thuc Si '04 (SJ) Santa Clara, CA St. Lawrence, the Martyr; College of Consultors.
Ho, Viet Peter '00 (ORG) Santa Ana, CA Christ Our Savior Cathedral; Adjutant Judicial Vicars; Special Assignment.
Ho, Xuan *s.v.d.* '03 (FgM) Techny, IL.
Hoa, Vincent Liem Tran Van *o.cist.* (PAT)[N] Morristown St. Mary's Abbey.
Hoag, Michael *s.j.* (BGP) Norwalk, CT St. Jerome.
Hoag, Timothy S. '95 (RC) Belle Fourche, SD St. Paul; Spearfish, SD St. Joseph; Deaneries.
Hoagland, Victor *c.p.* '59 (NEW)[L] Union City, NJ Congregation of the Passion (Passionists)–St. Michael's Residence; [L] Passionist Press, Inc.
Hoak, Jack W. *o.f.m.* '75 (MO) Navy Reserve Chaplains.
Hoak, Jack *o.f.m.* '75 (NY)[DD] New York Franciscan Province of the Immaculate Conception.
Hoak, Jack *o.f.m.* '75 (HRT) Meriden, CT St. Rose of Lima; Appointed Members.
Hoan, Basil P. '77 (TYL) Retired.
Hoan, Michael Mai Khai '72 (ORG) Santa Ana, CA St. Barbara Catholic Church.
Hoang, Dat '03 (GAL) Seminarian Support; Vocations Office.
Hoang, Doan T. *s.j.* '97 (LA) Los Gatos, CA; [P] Culver City, CA Ignatius House, The Novitiate of the California Province, Society of Jesus.
Hoang, Dominic Hung '90 (OKL) Oklahoma City, OK St. Andrew Dung–Lac.
Hoang, Francis Dang *s.j.* '95 (LA) West Covina, CA St. Christopher.
Hoang, John Minh Toan '68 (GAL) Retired.
Hoang, John '08 (VEN) Sarasota, FL St. Martha.
Hoang, Joseph Duc '04 (ORG) Stanton, CA St. Polycarp.
Hoang, Joseph Vien *s.d.b.* '83 (NO) Harvey, LA St. John Bosco.
Hoang, Joseph Viet '94 (SD) San Diego, CA Saint Rita Catholic Parish.
Hoang, Joseph '99 (P) Absent on Leave.
Hoang, Khanh '94 (HON) Honolulu, HI Cathedral of Our Lady of Peace; Hilo, HI Malia Puka O' Kalani (Mary Gate of Heaven).
Hoang, Linh *o.f.m.* '09 (ALB)[B] Siena College.
Hoang, Peter Thien Van *o.p.* '72 (GAL) Houston, TX Our Lady of Lourdes.
Hoang, Petrus B. '96 (P) Portland, OR St. Stephen.
Hoang, Phuong V. '89 (SEA) Port Orchard, WA St. Gabriel.
Hoang, Son Linh '03 (PMB) Port St. Lucie, FL St. Bernadette.
Hoang, Tat–Thang *c.ss.r.* '06 (NY) Bronx, NY Immaculate Conception.
Hoang, Thang *s.v.d.* '04 (DUB)[B] Epworth, IA Divine Word College.
Hoang, Thuan V. '97 (SFR) San Francisco, CA Visitacion, Church of the; Promoter of Justice; On Special Assignment; Defenders of the Bond.
Hoar, Leo James '66 (SPR) Retired.
Hoar, Richard J. *s.j.* '56 (BUF) Buffalo, NY St. Michael.
Hoar, Thomas F.X. *s.s.e.* '78 (NOR)[I] Mystic, CT St. Edmund's Retreat; [L] Mystic, CT St. Edmund's of Connecticut, Inc.; Groton, CT U.S. Submarine Base–New London.
Hoare, Liam *s.p.* '68 (STL)[O] Saint Louis, MO Servants of the Paraclete; [S] Dittmer, MO Vianney Renewal Center; Cedar Hill, MO; [V] Dittmer, MO Servants of the Paraclete Missouri Generalate Corporation.
Hoare, Patrick T. '07 (CHL) Charlotte, NC St. John Neumann.
Hoare, Richard '69 (BRK) South Ozone Park, NY St. Teresa of Avila.
Hoat, Rochus Vu Dinh *c.m.c.* '60 (SPC)[F] Carthage, MO Congregation of the Mother Coredemptrix, United States Assumption Province.
Hoatson, Robert M. '97 (NEW) Absent on Leave.
Hoban, Michael *s.s.c.* '70 (FgM) St Columbans, NE House of Post–Graduate Studies.
Hoban, Rev. Msgr. Thomas E. '60 (ALN) Retired.
Hobbes, Thomas F. '56 (SY)[Q] Binghamton, NY McDevitt Residence for Retired Priests Retired.
Hobbs, Rev. Msgr. James V. '57 (BAL) Retired.
Hober, Raymond *s.v.d.* '60 (PIT)[M] Pittsburgh, PA Society of The Divine Word.
Hobert, James M. '85 (TUC) Ministry to Priests Program.
Hobert, James '85 (TUC) Tucson, AZ Sacred Heart Roman Catholic Parish – Tucson.
Hobson, J. Mark '86 (CLV) Solon, OH Resurrection of Our Lord.
Hobson, Michael A. (BO) Middleton, MA St. Agnes; Presbyteral Council.
Hochheim, William A. '60 (STA) Retired.
Hochreiter, Robert S. '68 (SCR) Military Chaplains.
Hochstatter, Theodore '80 (PEO) On Duty Outside the Diocese.
Hock, Neal J. '11 (GI) On Duty Outside the Diocese.
Hockman, Richard C. *c.s.c.* '80 (SCR)[B] King's College; [B] Holy Cross Community.
Hockman, Richard C. *c.s.c.* '80 (FTW)[H] Notre Dame Congregation of Holy Cross, United States Province of Priests & Brothers.
Hoderny, Thomas S. '79 (E) Du Bois, PA St. Catherine.
Hodge, Rev. Msgr. William A. '74 (CAM) Deanery Representatives; Atlantic City, NJ Church of St. Nicholas, Atlantic City, N.J.; Delegate for Inter–Parochial Affairs; Diocesan Finance Council.
Hodges, Gabriel *o.s.b.* '06 (IND)[K] Saint Meinrad, IN St. Meinrad Archabbey.
Hodges, Leo '86 (ORL) Palm Bay, FL Our Lady of Grace.
Hodges, Robert *o.praem.* '74 (ORG) Costa Mesa, CA St. John the Baptist.
Hodges, Ronald E. '06 (DAV) Pella, IA St. Mary's; Oskaloosa, IA St. Mary's.
Hodgson, William M. '79 (SPC) Carthage, MO St. Ann; Secretariat for Cursillo; Diocesan School Board; Charismatic Prayer Groups.
Hodnett, John J. *c.m.* '59 (PH)[Y].
Hoeberechts, Dwight *o.m.i.* '97 (CR) Waubun, MN St. Frances Cabrini; Waubun, MN St. Anne; Waubun, MN St. Ann.
Hoebing, Philibert *o.f.m.* '50 (SFD)[B] Quincy, IL Quincy University; [K] Quincy, IL Holy Cross Friary Retired.
Hoeck, Andreas '92 (DEN) Denver, CO Cathedral Basilica of the Immaculate Conception.
Hoeffner, Robert J. '73 (ORL) Palm Bay, FL St. Joseph.
Hoefgen, Francis *o.s.b.* '79 (SCL)[I] Collegeville, MN St. John's Abbey, of the Order of St. Benedict.
Hoefler, David J. '02 (SFD)[D] Effingham, IL St. Anthony High School; Effingham, IL Sacred Heart; Effingham Deanery; Priests' Personnel Board; Effingham, IL St. Anthony of Padua; Shumway, IL Annunciation.
Hoefler, Robert '85 (DM)[J] West Des Moines, IA St. Francis of Assisi Roman Catholic School Foundation; West Des Moines, IA St. Francis of Assisi.
Hoegerl, Carl W. *c.ss.r.* '50 (BRK)[R] Brooklyn, NY Redemptorist Fathers of New York, Inc.–Baltimore Province; Brooklyn, NY.
Hoehn, Daniel '04 (JOL) Peotone, IL St. Paul the Apostle; Manhattan, IL St. Patrick.

Hoelke, Augustine *o.cist.* '10 (DAL)[J] Irving, TX Cistercian Abbey of Our Lady of Dallas.
Hoelsken, Mark *s.j.* '91 (SPK) Wellpinit, WA St. Philip Benizi; Wellpinit, WA Sacred Heart; Wellpinit, WA Our Lady of Lourdes.
Hoene, Robert E. *s.j.* '53 (MIL)[P] Wauwatosa, WI Jesuit Community at St. Camillus.
Hoening, Gerald '52 (DAV) Retired.
Hoerburger, Henry R. '43 (LC) Elk Mound, WI St. Joseph Retired.
Hoernig, Alphonse X. *c.m.* '56 (STL)[O] Perryville, MO Congregation of the Mission.
Hoerning, Richard P. '73 (RVC) Rocky Point, NY St. Anthony of Padua.
Hoerter, James '06 (RC) Rapid City, SD Cathedral of Our Lady of Perpetual Help.
Hoeser, Jerome G. '63 (LC) Eau Galle, WI St. Henry.
Hoesing, Kenneth F. '97 (LIN) Dawson, NE St. Mary's; Diocesan Area CCD Directors.
Hoesing, Paul C. '02 (OM) Vocations Office; Omaha, NE St. Margaret Mary.
Hoesli, Frederick Damien *o.p.* '64 (NY)[DD] New York St. Vincent Ferrer Priory.
Hoewischer, Harry E. *s.j.* '57 (DEN)[N] Denver, CO Xavier Jesuit Center.
Hoey, James F. '65 (WOR) Spencer, MA Mary, Queen of the Rosary.
Hofer, Kenneth Andrew *o.p.* '02 (WDC)[B] Washington, DC Dominican House of Studies.
Hoff, Wilfred G. *o.p.* '47 (CHI)[N] Chicago, IL St. Pius V Priory.
Hoffa, Allen J. '09 (ALN) Office of Youth and Young Adult Ministry; Allentown, PA St. Thomas More.
Hoffenkamp, Robert A. '89 (JOL) Carol Stream, IL Corpus Christi.
Hoffer, Steven R. '05 (LAV) Building Committee; Henderson, NV St. Francis of Assisi.
Hoffman, Charles '63 (GB) Retired.
Hoffman, Daniel R. '09 (E) On Duty Outside Diocese.
Hoffman, David J. '96 (GB) Freedom, WI St. Nicholas; De Pere, WI Immaculate Conception; Oneida, WI St. Joseph.
Hoffman, Dennis H. '70 (DUL) Nashwauk, MN Mary Immaculate; Nashwauk, MN St. Mary; Marble, MN St. Mary; Nashwauk, MN St. Cecilia's; Nashwauk, MN St. Kevin; Coleraine, MN St. Joseph.
Hoffman, Dennis L. '90 (DAV) Farmington, IA St. Boniface; West Point, IA St. Mary of the Assumption.
Hoffman, Emmett G. '53 (GF) Retired.
Hoffman, Francis T. '90 (BGP) Office for the Continuing Education of Clergy.
Hoffman, Frank J. '92 (CHI)[V] Chicago, IL Prelature of the Holy Cross and Opus Dei; Chicago.
Hoffman, Henry J. '03 (BGP) New Fairfield, CT St. Edward the Confessor.
Hoffman, James A. *o.f.m.* '67 (CHI)[N] Chicago, IL St. Peter's Friary.
Hoffman, James A. '67 (SUP) Retired.
Hoffman, John R. '75 (CHI) La Grange, IL St. Francis Xavier.
Hoffman, Joseph M. '79 (BRK) Brooklyn, NY St. Barbara; Fire Department.
Hoffman, Mark A. '90 (E) Erie, PA St. Jude the Apostle.
Hoffman, Michael J. '05 (GRY) Valparaiso, IN St. Paul.
Hoffman, Michael *s.d.s.* '82 (MIL)[P] Milwaukee Salvatorian Provincial Offices.
Hoffman, Paul '10 (LC) Wisconsin Rapids, WI Our Lady, Queen of Heaven; [C] Wisconsin Rapids, WI Assumption Middle School; [C] Wisconsin Rapids, WI Assumption High School.
Hoffman, Philip '64 (GB) Retired.
Hoffman, Raniero *o.s.b.cam.* '75 (MRY)[F] Big Sur, CA New Camaldoli Hermitage; Big Sur, CA.
Hoffman, Rev. Msgr. Robert B. '62 (RCK) Retired.
Hoffman, Robert E. *m.m.* '60 (FgM) Maryknoll, NY MARYKNOLL.
Hoffman, Robert M. *c.s.c.* '47 (FTW)[H] Holy Cross House Retired.
Hoffman, Robert '56 (PEO) Retired.
Hoffman, Steven B. (STP) Clearwater, MN St. Luke.
Hoffman, Thomas W. *s.j.* '76 (LSC) Alamogordo, NM St. Jude.
Hoffman, Thomas '80 (CHI) Zion–Beach Park, IL Our Lady of Humility.
Hoffman, William A. '80 (GB) Appleton, WI St. Therese.
Hoffman, Rev. Msgr. William G. '61 (ATL) Retired.
Hoffmann, Andrew W. '74 (SC) Dedham, IA St. Joseph's; Coon Rapids, IA Annunciation.
Hoffmann, Charles G. '63 (GB) Antigo, WI SS. Mary & Hyacinth; Phlox, WI St. Joseph–Holy Family Parish.
Hoffmann, Christopher '87 (MO) Air Force Reserve Chaplains.
Hoffmann, Christopher '87 (ORL) Port Orange, FL Our Lady of Hope.
Hoffmann, Edward '61 (PIT) Retired.
Hoffmann, Francis T. '90 (BGP) Riverside, CT St. Catherine of Siena; Vicariate I (Stamford, Darien, Glenbrook, Greenwich, Byram, Riverside); Presbyteral Council.
Hoffmann, Frank '71 (RNO) Retired.
Hoffmann, Henry '03 (BGP) Brookfield, CT St. Joseph.
Hoffmann, Lawrence R. '71 (DM) Des Moines, IA St. Theresa of the Child Jesus; Defenders of the Bond; Diocesan Consultors.
Hofmann, Charles A. *s.j.* '66 (CIN)[N] Cincinnati, OH Faber Jesuit Community.
Hofmann, Raymond *c.r.* '56 (L)[L] Louisville, KY Villa Pacis, Resurrectionist Retirement Home; Louisville, KY.
Hofmann, Rev. Msgr. Thomas X. '77 (CHR) Canonical Consultant; Office of Tribunal.
Hofschulte, Charles L. *c.j.* '71 (LA) Santa Maria, CA St. Louis de Montfort; Deanery 1; [P] Santa Maria, CA American Region of the Josephite Fathers Charitable Trust.
Hofstede, John '75 (STP) Minneapolis, MN Abbott–Northwestern Hospital; Minneapolis, MN Minneapolis Children's Hospital.
Hofstetter, Rev. Msgr. Robert J. '54 (KNX) Newport, TN Good Shepherd; Deans of the Diocese; Diocesan Consultors; Censor Librorum; Ministries of the Five Rivers Deanery; Presbyteral Council.
Hogan, Rev. Msgr. Daniel M. '53 (STL) O'Fallon, MO St. Barnabas.
Hogan, Gary *c.r.* '86 (CHI)[N].
Hogan, Gary *c.r.* (STL)[O] St. Louis, MO Congregation of the Resurrection.
Hogan, George G. (BO) North Andover, MA St. Michael.
Hogan, James J. '61 (HEL) Retired.
Hogan, John A. '57 (GRY) Retired.
Hogan, John F. '88 (SY) Oswego, NY St. Mary of the Assumption; Hannibal, NY Our Lady of the Rosary.
Hogan, John J. *o.m.i.* '65 (BO) Tewksbury, MA St. William.
Hogan, John P. *o.f.m.* '75 (BO)[Z] Boston, MA St. Anthony Shrine.
Hogan, John *s.s.c.* '62 (ORG)[H] Westminster, CA Korean Catholic Ministry; [I] Westminster, CA Columban Fathers.
Hogan, John *s.s.c.* '62 (PRO)[O] Bristol, RI St. Columban's Retirement House.
Hogan, John *s.s.c.* '62 (OM)[J] St. Columbans Missionary Society of St. Columban.
Hogan, Joseph F. '88 (MET) Retired.
Hogan, Joseph T. '88 (PEO) Champaign, IL St. Mary's; Urbana, IL St. Patrick's.
Hogan, Michael '65 (ALB) Schenectady, NY St. Joseph.
Hogan, Phil D. *o.f.m.* '62 (CHI)[D] Chicago, IL Hales Franciscan High School, Inc.; [N] Chicago, IL Holy Spirit Friary, Order of Friars Minor.
Hogan, Ralph R. '52 (PRO)[O] Providence St. John Vianney Residence Retired.
Hogan, Richard '86 (DET) Absent on Leave.
Hogan, Robert C. *s.j.* '64 (FgM) New York, NY Society of Jesus.
Hogan, Robert E. '83 (SAT)[S] San Antonio, TX Brothers of the Beloved Disciple; San Antonio, TX St. Mary Magdalen.
Hogan, Sean M. *c.s.sp.* '67 (PIT)[B] Pittsburgh, PA Duquesne University of the Holy Spirit; [B] School of Health Sciences.
Hogan, Rev. Msgr. Terence '80 (MIA) Miami, FL St. Mary's Cathedral; Ex Officio; Director; Celebration and Rite Committee; Office of Ecumenical and Inter–Faith Relations.
Hogan, Thomas J. *s.j.* '65 (STL)[O] St. Louis, MO Jesuit Community Corporation at Saint Louis University – Jesuit Hall.
Hogan, Timothy A. '66 (L) Retired.
Hogan, Timothy D. '82 (DET) Office for Clergy and Consecrated Life; Presbyteral Council.
Hogan, Timothy J. '82 (SC) Sanborn, IA St. Cecilia's; Sanborn, IA Sacred Heart.
Hogan, Verne F. '57 (COV) Flemingsburg, KY St. Charles; May's Lick, KY St. Rose of Lima.
Hogan, William A. '66 (GF) Retired.
Hogarty, Paul '48 (PT) Retired.
Hoge, James *o.s.b.* '43 (SP)[N] Saint Leo, FL St. Leo Abbey.
Hohenbrink, Rev. Msgr. Michael G. '74 (TOL) Findlay, OH St. Michael the Archangel; St. Francis of Assisi Deanery.
Hohenstein, Robert J. '68 (ALB) Schenectady, NY Our Lady of Mt. Carmel; Moderators; Priests Placement Committee.
Hohenwarter, Norman C. '96 (HBG) Lancaster, PA St. Anne.
Hohl, Alan *o.c.s.o.* '63 (SLC)[E] Huntsville, UT Abbey of Our Lady of the Holy Trinity of the Order of Cistercians.
Hohlmayer, Louis R. '53 (CIN) Retired.
Hohman, George R. *s.j.* '58 (WH)[A] Wheeling, WV Wheeling Jesuit University.
Hohman, Steve '10 (OWN) Bowling Green, KY Holy Spirit.
Hohosha, Ihor '07 (SJP) Aliquippa, PA Ss. Peter and Paul; McKees Rocks, PA St. John the Baptist; Alternates.
Hohosho, Ihor (SJP) Presbyteral Council; Presbyters.
Hoi, Joseph '84 (JC) Edina, MO St. Joseph; Memphis, MO St. John; Edina, MO St. Aloysius.
Hoisington, Thomas M. '95 (WCH) Respect Life and Social Justice Office; Colwich, KS St. Mark; [K] Wichita, KS Father Kapaun Guild.
Hokanson, Richard P. '74 (CHL) Absent on Medical Leave.
Hoke, John R. '76 (HBG) On Duty Outside the Diocese; Navy Chaplains.
Hoke, Thomas R. (HBG) York, PA St. Rose of Lima.
Holbrook, James A. '10 (STL) Fenton, MO St. Paul.
Holbrook, William M. '70 (CHI) Chicago, IL St. Monica Retired.
Holbrook, William M. '70 (LFT) Retired.
Holbus, Brian T. '81 (MIL) Milwaukee, WI St. Roman.
Holcomb, Joseph T. '80 (BRK) Flushing, NY St. Andrew Avellino.
Hold, William '77 (SAC) Retired.
Holden, James T. '62 (MOB) Retired.
Holden, James T. '62 (BUR) Readsboro, VT St. Joachim.
Holden, Robert A. '62 (TOL) Retired.
Holder, Thomas '95 (KC) Lees Summit, MO Our Lady of the Presentation.
Holdren, Benjamin P. '07 (LIN) Lincoln, NE St. Thomas Aquinas; [I] Lincoln, NE University of Nebraska, Newman Club; Vocations; Advocates.
Holeda, Timothy Michael '11 (PT) Tallahassee, FL Blessed Sacrament.
Holian, John P. '63 (NEW) Retired.
Holicky, Gregory '72 (GRY)[D] Hammond, IN Franciscan St. Margaret Health – Hammond.
Holihan, John W. '49 (NY)[DD] Bronx, NY Retired.
Holinga, Rev. Msgr. Thomas P. '74 (SFD) Springfield, IL St. Joseph; Commission for the Care of Infirm and Retired Priests.
Holl, James E. '48 (STP) Retired.
Holl, Kermit *o.s.c.* '90 (SCL)[I] Onamia, MN Crosier Priory; Provincial Councilors.
Holland, Cajetan *c.s.c.* '79 (ORL) Retired.
Holland, Cajetan *c.s.c.* '79 (FTW)[H] Notre Dame Congregation of Holy Cross, United States Province of Priests & Brothers.
Holland, Daniel F. '65 (ROC) Spencerport, NY St. John the Evangelist Retired.
Holland, Edward T. '97 (CLV) Stow, OH Holy Family.
Holland, Francis M. '52 (BUR) Retired.
Holland, Rev. Msgr. George T. '48 (PBL) Retired.
Holland, James P. '98 (PIT) Moon Township, PA St. Margaret Mary.
Holland, Jeremiah *ss.cc.* '67 (LA)[P] La Verne, CA Congregation of the Sacred Hearts of Jesus and Mary.
Holland, Kilian '56 (SD) Retired.
Holland, Matthew *s.j.* (SEA)[C] Tacoma, WA Bellarmine Preparatory School.
Holland, Paul D. *s.j.* '80 (BGP)[B] Fairfield, CT Fairfield University; [E] Fairfield, CT Fairfield College Preparatory School; [O] Fairfield, CT The Fairfield Jesuit Community–Fairfield University.
Holland, Stanley *t.o.r.* '96 (SP) Tampa, FL St. Patrick.
Hollas, Eric *o.s.b.* '75 (SCL)[I] Collegeville, MN St. John's Abbey, of the Order of St. Benedict.
Holleman, John L. '81 (MOB) Semmes, AL Holy Name of Jesus.
Hollenbach, David *s.j.* '71 (BO)[U] Newton, MA The Jesuit Community at Boston College.
Holler, Martin J. '66 (STU)[L] Athens, OH Christ the King University Parish – Ohio University Retired.
Holleran, Rev. Msgr. J. Warren '52 (SFR) Retired.
Holleran, Leo C. *m.s.* (ATL) Winder, GA St. Matthew.
Holleran, Michael K. '79 (NY) New York, NY Notre Dame.
Holleran, Rev. Msgr. Warren '52 (SFR) Censor Librorum.
Hollfelder, Eugene F. '68 (MAD) Middleton, WI St. Peter's; Cross Plains, WI St. Martin of Tours Retired.
Holliday, John J. *c.m.* '05 (BAL) Emmitsburg, MD St. Joseph; [Q] Emmitsburg, MD Vincentian House.
Hollis, Keith *o.s.a.* '02 (BO)[AA] North Andover, MA Merrimack College Campus Ministry Center; [C] North Andover, MA Merrimack College.
Hollis, Mark L. '72 (CLV)[A] Wickliffe, OH St. Mary Seminary and Graduate School of Theology.
Holloran, Michael J. '82 (CIN) Dayton, OH St. Adalbert; Dayton, OH Holy Cross; Dayton, OH Our Lady of the Rosary; Dayton, OH St. Stephen.
Holloway, David L. '82 (KC) Kansas City, MO St. Bernadette's; Presbyteral Council; Deans.
Holloway, Gerald '98 (BIR) Tuscaloosa, AL St. Francis of Assisi University Parish; [H] Tuscaloosa, AL Diocesan Campus Ministry Office; [H] Tuscaloosa, AL University of Alabama in Tuscaloosa.
Holloway, James P. '70 (WDC) Retired.
Holloway, James '70 (SAV) Retired.
Holloway, Thomas B. '99 (PEO) Bushnell, IL St. Bernard; Bushnell, IL St. Augustine; [M] Macomb, IL St. Francis of Assisi Newman Center.
Hollowell, John J. '09 (IND) Brownsburg, IN St. Malachy Catholic Church, Brownsburg, Inc.; [C] Indianapolis, IN Cardinal Ritter High School.
Holly, Dennis *g.h.m.* '64 (NSH) Lafayette, TN Holy Family.
Holly, Dennis *g.h.m.* '64 (OWN) Scottsville, KY Christ the King.

Holly, John *o.f.m.cap* '80 (MIL)[B] Mount Calvary, WI St. Lawrence Seminary; [P] Mount Calvary, WI St. Lawrence Friary.
Hollywood, Patrick J. *o.m.i.* '60 (BO)[Z] Lowell, MA Andre Garin Residence.
Holmberg, J. Michael '73 (FWT) Frisco, TX Holy Cross.
Holmer, James J. '76 (TOL) Health Leave.
Holmes, Albert '93 (SCL) Special Assignment.
Holmes, Del *g.h.m.* '63 (CIN)[N] Cincinnati Headquarters of Glenmary Home Missioners Retired.
Holmes, Emmett P. *s.j.* '59 (CLV)[D] Cuyahoga Falls, OH Walsh Jesuit High School.
Holmes, Rev. Msgr. Kevin D. '84 (MAD) Madison, WI Cathedral Parish of St. Raphael; Diocesan Consultors; Appointed.
Holmes, Paul A. '81 (NEW)[B] Seton Hall University; [B] Seton Hall University.
Holmes, Raymond M. '65 (NEW) Hasbrouck Heights, NJ Corpus Christi.
Holmes, Stephen '00 (ARL) Annandale, VA St. Ambrose.
Holmes, Thomas '91 (ALB) Middleburgh, NY Parish of Our Lady of the Valley; Deans; Cobleskill, NY St. Vincent de Paul.
Holoubek, K. William '97 (LIN) Sutton, NE St. Mary's; Holy Childhood, Pontifical Association; Missionary Union of the Clergy; Propagation of the Faith.
Holoubek, Roger '69 (MIA) Dania Beach, FL St. Maurice.
Holpp, Lawrence V. '62 (PIT) Bobtown, PA St. Ignatius of Antioch.
Holquin, Rev. Msgr. Arthur A. '74 (ORG) San Juan Capistrano, CA Mission Basilica – San Juan Capistrano; Council of Priests; Judges; Consultors; Liturgical Commission; Building and Renovation Committee of the Liturgical Commission.
Holroyd, Patrick '74 (ARL) Vienna, VA St. Mark.
Holscher, Raymond T. *s.j.* '72 (FgM) New York, NY Society of Jesus.
Holt, Paul–Stephen '72 (WDC) Retired.
Holt, William Alexander *o.p.* '76 (NY) Pleasantville, NY Holy Innocents; New York, NY; [DD] New York, NY St. Vincent Ferrer Priory.
Holterhoff, Edward G. '70 (PAT) On Duty Outside the Diocese.
Holterhoff, Edward J. '70 (MRY) Cayucos, CA St. Joseph; Morro Bay, CA St. Timothy.
Holtgrewe, Donald E. *o.f.m.* '63 (CIN)[N] Cincinnati St. Francis Seraph Friary.
Holthaus, Paul G. '70 (BAL) Retired.
Holtman, Rev. Msgr. Elmer '64 (AUS) College of Consultors; Presbyteral Council Retired.
Holtman, Jeffry '85 (SFD) Granite City, IL Holy Family.
Holtman, William Jeffry *s.f.o.* '85 (SFD) Presbyteral Council; Madison, IL St. Mary and St. Mark.
Holtmann, Christopher F. '00 (STL) Hillsboro, MO Church of the Good Shepherd.
Holtschneider, Dennis H. *c.m.* '89 (CHI)[C] Chicago, IL De Paul University; [N] Chicago DePaul Vincentian Residence.
Holtschneider, Dennis H. *c.m.* '89 (PH)[Y].
Holtz, Albert T. *o.s.b.* '69 (NEW)[L] Newark, NJ Newark Abbey.
Holtz, Dominic M. *o.p.* '06 (CHI)[N] Chicago Dominicans (Provincial Office).
Holtz, Robert '03 (TR) Maple Shade, NJ Our Lady of Perpetual Help.
Holtz, Vernon A. *o.s.b.* '62 (GBG)[H] Latrobe, PA Saint Vincent Archabbey.
Holtzinger, William '00 (P) Grants Pass, OR St. Anne.
Holtzman, Jerome '57 (SFS) Retired.
Holup, James '59 (JOL) Ashkum, IL Assumption of the Blessed Virgin Mary.
Holway, Craig T. '10 (STL) Webster Groves, MO Mary, Queen of Peace.
Holy, Richard C. '08 (GRY) Munster, IN St. Thomas More.
Holz, Robert A. '08 (RVC) Baldwin, NY St. Christopher.
Holzer, Claudio *c.s.* '86 (CHI) Deans; Melrose Park, IL Our Lady of Mount Carmel.
Holzhauser, J. Joseph '82 (SFS) Aberdeen, SD St. Mary; Personnel Board.
Holzhauser, John J. '82 (MO) Army National Guard Chaplains.
Holzmann, Michael '88 (RVC)[C] West Islip, NY St. John the Baptist.
Homa, Richard M. '73 (CHI) Orland Hills, IL St. Elizabeth Seton.
Hombach, Leo J. *s.j.* '61 (SJ)[M] Los Gatos, CA Sacred Heart Jesuit Center.
Homes, Dennis '72 (BAK) Retired.
Homes, Ronald G. '93 (LIN) Bruno, NE St. Anthony.
Homic, Russell '11 (SFS) Sioux Falls, SD St. Joseph Cathedral.
Hommel, George W. '66 (NY) Phoenicia, NY St. Francis de Sales; Woodstock, NY St. John; Ulster; Canon 1742 Panel of Pastors.
Hommrich, Thomas A. '63 (L) Retired.
Homrich, Eugene *c.s.c.* '55 (FgM) New Rochelle, NY Eastern Brothers Province.
Honan, Eugene D. '67 (SPR) South Hadley, MA St. Patrick's Retired.
Honeygoskey, Stephen *o.s.b.* '75 (GBG)[H] Latrobe, PA Saint Vincent Archabbey.
Honhart, Mark A. '80 (SCR) Unassigned or Leave of Absence.
Honkomp, Clinton P. *o.p.* '88 (DEN) Denver, CO St. Dominic; [N] Denver, CO Dominican Friars.
Honold, Thomas G. '87 (MIA) Retired.
Honor, Michael P. '69 (MO) Army Chaplains.
Honorio, Gregorio S. *m.s.* '95 (HON) Waipahu, HI St. Joseph; Presbyteral Council.
Hont, Leon *o.s.b.* '80 (GBG) Crabtree, PA St. Bartholomew; [H] Latrobe, PA Saint Vincent Archabbey.
Hontiveros, Romeo (NY) New York, NY Our Lady of Victory.
Hood, Carl J. '86 (MEM) Memphis, TN St. Therese the Little Flower; Continuing Education for Clergy.
Hood, Jared M. *s.j.s.* '06 (MAD) Sauk City, WI St. Norbert; Appointed; Sauk City, WI Divine Mercy Parish.
Hood, Rev. Msgr. Mervin J. '54 (SC) Retired.
Hoog, Eric *c.ss.r.* (BAL) Annapolis, MD St. Mary.
Hook, Stephen E. '03 (BAL) Priest Personnel Board; Baltimore, MD St. Ursula.
Hoolahan, Michael *c.p.* '61 (CHI)[N] Chicago, IL Province Finance Office.
Hoolahan, Michael *c.p.* '61 (LA)[P] Sierra Madre, CA Passionist Residence; [V] Sierra Madre, CA Mater Dolorosa Passionist Retreat Center, Inc.
Hoon Gyeom Kim, John '92 (HRT) Wethersfield, CT Sacred Heart.
Hooper, J. Leon *s.j.* '75 (WDC)[O] Washington, DC Woodstock Jesuit Community; [X] Washington, DC Woodstock Theological Center; [O] Washington, DC The Jesuit Community at Georgetown University.
Hooper, Robert K. '70 (PAT)[Q] Chester, NJ Nazareth Village Retired.
Hoorman, Albert F.H. '67 (PHX) Phoenix, AZ Corpus Christi Roman Catholic Parish.
Hoover, Brett C. *c.s.p.* '97 (LA) Los Angeles, CA St. Paul the Apostle.
Hoover, Conrad '89 (CHL) Retired.
Hoover, Gary *o.s.b.* '83 (CLV)[D] Cleveland, OH Benedictine High School; [N] Cleveland, OH; Cleveland, OH.
Hoover, James '60 (SAL)[E] Concordia, KS Sisters of St. Joseph of Concordia; [H] Concordia, KS Nazareth Convent & Academy Corporation Retired.
Hoover, John P. '76 (CHL) Special Assignment.
Hoover, Matthew N. '95 (COL) Dover, OH St. Joseph; College of Consultors; Newcomerstown, OH St. Francis de Sales.
Hopcus, Daniel R. '64 (IND)[L] Saint Mary Of The Woods, IN Sisters of Providence General Administration.
Hope, Abbott J. '54 (CAM) Retired.
Hope, Donald E. '76 (SLC) East Carbon, UT Good Shepherd LLC 204; Helper, UT Saint Anthony of Padua Catholic Church LLC 216; Price, UT Notre Dame de Lourdes LLC 207; Deans; Presbyteral Council; Priests' Personnel Board.
Hopefl, Gregory J. '76 (SUP) Stone Lake, WI St. Ignatius; Stone Lake, WI St. Francis of Solanus; Stone Lake, WI St. Philip; Holy Childhood Association; Propagation of the Faith.
Hopka, Jack '79 (SAT) Judges.
Hopka, John '79 (DAL) Plano, TX St. Mark the Evangelist.
Hopkins, Rev. Msgr. John P. '78 (WIL) Newark, DE St. Margaret of Scotland; College of Consultors; Priests' Council; Priests' Continuing Formation Committee.
Hopkins, John *l.c.* '91 (WDC)[X] Bethesda, MD Alpha Omega, Inc.; [O] Potomac, MD Legionaries of Christ.
Hopkins, John *l.c.* '91 (BAL)[U] Crownsville, MD Springhill Center for Family Development.
Hopkins, Michael *c.ss.r.* '63 (NY)[DD] New York, NY Redemptorist Priests and Brothers, C.Ss.R.
Hopkins, Peter *l.c.* '91 (DAL)[J] Irving, TX Legionaries of Christ.
Hopkins, Richard J. '44 (GF) Retired.
Hopmeir, Ronald J. '91 (STL) Saint Louis, MO Sts. Mary and Joseph Chapel; St. Louis, MO St. Stephen, Protomartyr.
Hopp, Raymond '65 (BAK) Retired.
Hopp, Thomas R. (CIN) Priests Commended to a Life of Prayer and Penance.
Hoppe, Arthur '47 (SCL) Freeport, MN St. Rose of Lima Retired.
Hoppe, Lawrence '60 (GBG)[G] Greensburg, PA Neumann House.
Hoppe, Leslie *o.f.m.* '71 (MIL)[P] Provincial Offices of the Franciscan Friars, Assumption BVM Province, Inc.
Hoppe, Rev. Msgr. Ronald C. '58 (ALX) Retired.
Hoppe, Sean *o.s.b.* '82 (IND)[K] Saint Meinrad, IN St. Meinrad Archabbey.
Hoppe, William M. '78 (BRK) Defenders of the Marriage Bond; Attorneys and Counselors at Canon Law.
Hoppe, William M. '78 (BRK) Corona, NY St. Leo; Promoters of Justice.
Hoppenjans, Terence E. '55 (LEX) Paintsville, KY St. Michael Catholic Church.
Hopper, Jeffrey G. '06 (L) Bardstown, KY St. Monica; Bardstown, KY St. Thomas; Ex Officio.
Hopper, Thomas W. '04 (GAL) Conroe, TX Sacred Heart.
Hopping, John Paul '85 (STL) Saint Louis, MO Our Lady of Guadalupe.
Hoppough, Gregory J. *c.s.s.* '74 (BO)[A] Weston, MA Blessed John XXIII National Seminary; [U] Waltham, MA Bertoni Hall – Formation House.
Hora, Robert J. '83 (BUF) Boston, NY St. John the Baptist.
Horak, Rev. Msgr. Donald E. '63 (STU) Retired.
Horak, Mark F. *s.j.* '94 (WDC) Washington, DC Holy Trinity.
Horan, Brendan *s.j.* '93 (CHI)[C] Chicago, IL Jesuit Community at Loyola University Chicago.
Horan, George E. '72 (LA) Los Angeles, CA Sacred Heart; Los Angeles, CA Office of Restorative Justice; Los Angeles, CA L.A. Men's Central Jail; Restorative Justice.
Horan, Gerald M. *o.s.m.* '82 (ORG) Office for Faith Formation; Fullerton, CA St. Philip Benizi; Membership; Vicar for Faith Formation; Catholic Schools and Parish Faith Formation; Staff; Special Assignment.
Horan, Gerald M. *o.s.m.* '82 (CHI) Chicago, IL; [N] Chicago, IL Order of Friar Servants of Mary (Servites) United States of America Province, Inc.
Horan, John '46 (SEA) Retired.
Horan, Mike '80 (SAT) San Antonio, TX Holy Spirit.
Horan, Ray '68 (ATL) Retired.
Horan, Terence J. '68 (SFR) Retired.
Horan, Thomas A. '62 (ALN) Ashland, PA Our Lady of Good Counsel Retired.
Horan, Thomas C. *o.m.i.* '94 (SFD)[A] Godfrey, IL Immaculate Heart of Mary Novitiate.
Horan, Thomas '73 (ALN)[J] Bethlehem, PA Holy Family Villa Retired.
Horan, Timothy E. '79 (ROC) Webster, NY Holy Trinity; Office of Vocations.
Horanzy, Joseph M. '59 (SCR)[M] Dunmore, PA Villa St. Joseph Retired.
Horath, George B. '63 (MAD) Fennimore, WI St. Mary; Fennimore, WI St. Lawrence O'Toole.
Horath, James R. '73 (SUP) Retired.
Horath, William G. '75 (SUP) Three Lakes, WI St. Kunegunda; Three Lakes, WI St. Theresa; Defender of the Bond.
Horejsi, Jeffrey P. '91 (NU) Fairfax, MN St. Andrew; Franklin, MN Sacred Heart; Gibbon, MN St. Willibrord; Winthrop, MN St. Francis de Sales; Finance Council; Social Concerns Committee.
Horgan, John E. '72 (WOR) Ashburnham, MA St. Denis; Ashburnham, MA St. Anne.
Horgan, Joseph E. '53 (PRO) Retired.
Horgan, Timothy J. '55 (NEW) Retired.
Horgas, Robert '91 (E) Morrisdale, PA St. Agnes.
Horihan, Robert S. '02 (WIN) Censors of Books and Periodicals.
Horkan, Edward R. '03 (ARL) Falls Church, VA St. James; Catholic Scouting Information; Advocates.
Horley, Ray J. '58 (CLV)[M] Cleveland, OH Little Sisters of the Poor Retired.
Horn, Francis J. *o.s.a.* '75 (CAM)[C] Richland, NJ St. Augustine Preparatory School.
Horn, John P. *s.j.* '85 (STL)[O] St. Louis, MO Jesuit Community Corporation at Saint Louis University – Jesuit Hall.
Horn, John *s.j.* (STL) Kenrick–Glennon Seminary; Cardinal Glennon College; [A] St. Louis, MO Kenrick School of Theology.
Horn, Joseph K. *o.praem.* '81 (ORG)[I] Silverado, CA Norbertine Fathers of Orange Inc.
Horn, Joseph R. '97 (DET) Archdiocesan Vicars; Memphis, MI Holy Family; Presbyteral Council.
Hornacek, Joseph F. '66 (MIL) Archdiocesan Consultors; Archdiocesan Council of Priests Retired.
Hornat, Stephen *s.s.e.* '76 (MOB)[I] Selma, AL Marion Institute Newman Center; [G] Selma, AL Edmundite Fathers; Orrville, AL Immaculate Conception; Selma, AL Our Lady Queen of Peace.
Horner, Timothy *o.s.b.* '53 (STL)[O] St. Louis, MO The Abbey of St. Mary and St. Louis.
Hornes, Charlie (CC)[D] Corpus Christi, TX CHRISTUS Spohn Hospital Corpus Christi – Shoreline.
Hornicak, John Joseph '03 (JOL) South Wilmington, IL Sacred Heart; South Wilmington, IL St. Lawrence.
Hornick, Joseph R. '05 (SCR) Dushore, PA Immaculate Heart of Mary Parish.
Horning, Edward '04 (SD) El Centro, CA Saint Mary Catholic Parish El Centro.
Horning, Roy Theodore '01 (LAN) Flushing, MI St. Robert.
Horning, Roy '01 (LAN) Montrose, MI Good Shepherd; Priests' Assignment Commission.
Hornung, Eugene H. '03 (SUP) Retired.
Horowski, Janusz '95 (CHI)[N] Techny, IL Divine Word Residence.
Horrigan, Kevin P. '70 (BO) Senior Priests. Retired.
Horrigan, Rev. Msgr. Leo R. '59 (DEN) Retired.

Horrigan, Phil (JOL)[N] Lombard, IL Mayslake Ministries, Inc.
Horrigan, Sean '98 (GAL) Houston, TX Christ the Redeemer; Area Representatives.
Horton, Geoffrey '08 (PEO) Hoopeston, IL St. Anthony Church; [B] Danville, IL Schlarman Academy.
Horton, W. Peter '79 (PIT)[B] Pittsburgh, PA La Roche College; [P] Pittsburgh, PA Office for Campus Ministry; Campus Ministry, Office for; [P] Pittsburgh, PA La Roche College.
Horvat, Francis '58 (KCK) Kansas City, KS St. John the Baptist.
Horvath, Arpad *s.j.* '07 (ATH) "A Sziv".
Horvath, Gerlac A. *o.praem.* '46 (ORG)[I] Silverado, CA Norbertine Fathers of Orange Inc. Retired.
Horvath, Pius L. *o.s.b.* '53 (SFR)[N] Portola Valley, CA Woodside Priory.
Horzen, Bernard A. *o.s.b.* '53 (PEO)[A] Peru, IL St. Bede Abbey Retired.
Hosak, Peter J. '83 (PSC) Phillipsburg, NJ SS. Peter and Paul; Bethlehem, PA SS. Peter and Paul; Syncellus; Lansford, PA St. John the Baptist.
Hosak, Peter J. *m.s.* (ALN)[C] Bethlehem, PA Bethlehem Catholic High School.
Hose, Samuel '91 (AUS) Lakeway, TX Church of the Resurrection, Emmaus; Presbyteral Council; College of Consultors.
Hosey, P. Keith '56 (LFT) Retired.
Hosie, James J. *s.j.* '65 (BO)[D] Boston, MA Boston College High School.
Hosie, Stanley W. *s.m.* '46 (WDC)[O] Washington, DC Marist Center Retired.
Hosinski, Thomas *c.s.c.* '73 (P)[B] University of Portland; [L] Portland, OR Holy Cross Fathers & Brothers, C.S.C. – University of Portland.
Hosinski, Thomas *c.s.c.* (FTW)[H] Notre Dame Congregation of Holy Cross, United States Province of Priests & Brothers.
Hosko, George H. *c.s.b.* '68 (GAL)[O] Houston, TX Residence of the Basilian Fathers of the University of St. Thomas.
Hosler, Gregory '01 (PSC) East Brunswick, NJ Nativity of Our Lord.
Hospodar, Robert J. '78 (PSC) New York, NY St. Mary's; Syncellus; Chancellor; Eparchial College of Consultors; Promoter of Justice; Respect Life; Eparchial Historian; Retirement Plan Board; White Plains, NY St. Nicholas of Myra; Presbyteral Council.
Hospodar, Robert '78 (NY) Promoter of Justice; Defenders of the Bond.
Hossan, Rev. Msgr. John B. '53 (BGP) Retired.
Host, Dick '74 (GR) Grand Rapids, MI St. Mary's.
Hostetter, Larry '87 (OWN) Non–Parochial Assignments; [A] Owensboro, KY Brescia University; Committee for Education.
Hostettler, Paul A. '50 (KNX) Retired.
Hostettler, Paul (NSH) Nashville, TN St. Mary Villa Parish Community.
Hostios, Jaime E. '07 (CAM) Atlantic City, NJ Our Lady, Star of the Sea, Atlantic City, N.J.
Hotard, Rev. Msgr. Howard H. '55 (NO) Retired.
Hotovy, Dennis W. '57 (LIN) Retired.
Hottinger, Paul '75 (JOL) Naperville, IL St. Margaret Mary; [D] Naperville, IL All Saints Catholic Academy.
Hottinger, Theodore J. *s.j.* '63 (WIN) Retrouvaille.
Hottle, Maximilian J. *o.f.m.* '61 (LSC) Tularosa, NM St. Francis de Paula.
Hottovy, Jamie S. '99 (LIN) Orleans, NE St. Mary's; Advocates; Building Commission.
Hotze, John V. '93 (WCH) Presbyteral Council/College of Consultors; Judicial Vicar; Judges; [K] Wichita, KS Father Kapaun Guild.
Hotze, John V. '93 (DOD) Judicial Vicar.
Houck, Gregory *o.carm.* '92 (JOL) Councilors:; [L] Darien Carmelite Provincial Office.
Houde, Daniel *o.ss.t.* '87 (BAL)[Q] Diocese of Trenton, NJ.
Houde, Daniel *o.ss.t.* '87 (TR) Trenton, NJ The Church of the Incarnation–St. James.
Hougan, Andrew C. '01 (RCK) Sandwich, IL St. Paul the Apostle.
Hough, J. Patrick *s.j.* '11 (SFE) Albuquerque, NM Immaculate Conception.
Hough, Roger '64 (SAL) Retired.
Houghton, Rev. Msgr. Francis J. '51 (NEW) Retired.
Houlahan, Richard A. *o.m.i.* '58 (SAT)[K] San Antonio, TX Oblate Madonna Residence.
Houle, Andre *o.m.i.* '52 (BO)[X] Tewksbury, MA Immaculate Heart of Mary Residence.
Houle, Michael '79 (STA)[A] Jacksonville, FL Bishop Kenny High School, Inc.; Episcopal Vicar for Development and Finance; Special Assignment; [A] St. Augustine, FL St. Joseph's Academy, Inc.; Jacksonville, FL Holy Rosary; Educational Services.
Houle, Roger A. '77 (PRO) North Scituate, RI St. Joseph; Deans; Senior Priest Advisor.
Houle, Thomas R. *o.f.m.cap.* '78 (BUR) Proctor, VT St. Dominic; Rutland, VT St. Peter.
Houlihan, John J. '64 (GF) Retired.
Houlihan, Michael K. '79 (LIN) Hastings, NE St. Michael's; Advocates; Deaneries and Deans.
Houlihan, Ralph D. *s.j.* '65 (STL)[F] St. Louis, MO St. Louis University High School, George H. Backer Memorial; [O] Saint Louis, MO St. Louis University High School Jesuit Community.
Houlis, Paul C. '11 (NEW) Verona, NJ Our Lady of the Lake.
Hourican, John J. '05 (MEM) Covington, TN St. Alphonsus Church.
Hourigan, Michael '66 (MIA) Age Group III; Lighthouse Point, FL St. Paul the Apostle.
Hourihan, Raymond B. '87 (CHL) Retired.
House, Christopher A. '02 (SFD) Auburn, IL Holy Cross; Virden, IL St. Patrick; Virden, IL Sacred Heart; Liturgical Ministry: Liturgical Leadership; Office for Vocations; Advisory Board.
House, Richard M. '92 (YAK) Naches, WA St. John.
Householder, Paul C. '73 (PIT) Aliquippa, PA St. Titus.
Houser, Michael J. '08 (STL) Special Assignment.
Houser, Samuel E. '76 (HBG) York, PA St. Patrick.
Housey, Walter L. *c.m.* '56 (LA)[P] Santa Barbara, CA St. Mary's Evangelization Center; [V] Santa Barbara, CA St. Mary's Seminary Center Retired.
Houston, James A. '68 (WOR) Northboro, MA St. Rose of Lima.
Houston, Michael *c.ss.r.* '98 (FgM) Baltimore Province; Brooklyn, NY AMERICAN REDEMPTORIST FATHERS.
Houston, Michael *c.ss.r.* (TOL) Lima, OH St. Gerard.
Hovanec, Craig M. '03 (CLV) Lorain, OH St. Peter.
Hovley, Vincent E. *s.j.* '69 (COS)[E] Sedalia, CO Sacred Heart Jesuit Community; [G] Sedalia, CO Sacred Heart Jesuit Retreat House.
Howard, Anthony *o.f.m. conv.* '84 (MRY)[F] Arroyo Grande St. Joseph Cupertino Province, Provincial Center.
Howard, Arthur '06 (KAL) Bridgman, MI Our Lady Queen of Peace.
Howard, Bryan J. '11 (NO) Marrero, LA The Visitation of Our Lady.
Howard, C. Donald *s.a.* '72 (ARL) Sterling, VA Christ the Redeemer.
Howard, Clarence J. '61 (L) Retired.
Howard, David G. '06 (CIN) Reading, OH Sts. Peter and Paul.
Howard, Dennis J. '90 (LAN) Fowler, MI Most Holy Trinity; Regional Vicars.
Howard, Edward F. *s.j.* '66 (BO)[U] Weston, MA Campion Jesuit Community.
Howard, Evan Arthur *o.f.m.* '55 (OAK)[N] Danville, CA San Damiano Retreat Retired.
Howard, Rev. Msgr. James J. '52 (PH) Retired.
Howard, John *c.j.m.* '67 (SD) Solana Beach, CA Saint James Catholic Parish; [J] Solana Beach, CA The Eudists, Congregation of Jesus and Mary.
Howard, Joseph '89 (SHP) Bossier City, LA Christ the King.
Howard, Joseph (HBG) Harrisburg, PA St. Catherine Laboure.
Howard, Kenneth J. *s.s.j.* '87 (GAL) Houston, TX Our Mother of Mercy.
Howard, Phillip R. *c.s.sp.* '79 (NY) New York, NY St. Mark the Evangelist.
Howard, Randy '01 (OWN) Leitchfield, KY St. Joseph's; Leitchfield, KY St. John the Evangelist; Deans; Priests' Council.
Howard, Rev. Msgr. Robert E. '62 (LA) Retired.
Howard, Theodore J. '65 (RVC) Shoreham, NY St. Mark.
Howard, Rev. Msgr. Vincent '47 (LAN) Retired.
Howarth, Joseph E. '80 (PH) Philadelphia, PA Resurrection of Our Lord; Approved Advocates.
Howe, Edward *c.r.* '10 (JOL) Morris, IL Immaculate Conception of the Blessed Virgin Mary.
Howe, J. Norbert '56 (TOL) Retired.
Howe, Robert J. '94 (SAG) Bad Axe, MI Sacred Heart; Rapson, MI St. Joseph.
Howe, Timothy A. *s.j.* '98 (CIN)[F] Cincinnati, OH St. Xavier High School; [N] Cincinnati, OH Jesuit Community at St. Xavier High School.
Howell, Charles W. '98 (LEX) Frankfort, KY Good Shepherd.
Howell, David F. '78 (LAN) Brighton, MI St. Mary Magdalen Church.
Howell, David W. '65 (BGP)[O] Stamford, CT The Catherine Dennis Keefe Queen of the Clergy Retired Priests' Residence Retired.
Howell, Michael J. '67 (KAL) Retired.
Howell, Rev. Msgr. Michael '74 (CC) Robstown, TX St. Thomas the Apostle; Presbyteral Council; Judges.
Howell, Patrick J. *s.j.* '72 (SEA)[A] Seattle, WA Seattle University; Presbyteral Council; [M] Seattle, WA Arrupe Jesuit Community at Seattle University.
Howell, Stephen H. '74 (SFR) Belmont, CA Immaculate Heart of Mary; [E] Belmont, CA Notre Dame High School (Girls).
Hower, William J. '64 (MAD) Retired.
Howes, Marc C. '04 (LAV) Las Vegas, NV St. Joseph, Husband of Mary; Board of Trustees.
Howley, Rev. Msgr. Edward J. '47 (BGP) New Milford, CT Retired.
Howley, Vincent de Paul '97 (NY) Hopewell Junction, NY St. Denis.
Howley, Vincent DePaul (NY) Carmel, NY St. James the Apostle.
Howren, John T. '95 (ATL) Lilburn, GA St. John Neumann.
Hoye, Rev. Msgr. Daniel F. '72 (FR) Mashpee, MA Christ The King; Defenders of the Bond.
Hoye, Justin E. '06 (KC) Kansas City, MO St. Patrick; Presbyteral Council.
Hoye, Ronald J. *c.m.* '91 (CHI)[N] Chicago DePaul Vincentian Residence.
Hoyek, Gaby '05 (OLL) Livonia, MI St. Rafka Maronite Catholic Mission; Warren, MI St. Sharbel Maronite Catholic Church.
Hoyer, Michael '80 (MIA) Plantation, FL St. Gregory.
Hoying, David A. *c.pp.s.* '83 (LFT) Bryant, IN Holy Trinity; Members.
Hoying, John *c.pp.s.* '62 (CIN)[N] Carthagena, OH St. Charles Retired.
Hoying, Mark *c.pp.s.* (TOL) Continental, OH St. John the Baptist; Kalida, OH St. Michael.
Hoying, Vincent *c.pp.s.* '58 (CIN)[N] Carthagena, OH St. Charles Retired.
Hoyles, Monte J. '06 (TOL) Ecclesiastical Notary; Delegate of the Bishop; Toledo, OH Queen of the Most Holy Rosary Cathedral; Ex Officio Members; Chancellor and Moderator of the Curia.
Hoynes, Richard '88 (LA) Los Angeles, CA St. Francis Xavier Chapel.
Hoyng, William *c.pp.s.* '61 (CIN)[N] Carthagena, OH St. Charles Retired.
Hoyos, Jose Eugenio '84 (ARL) Spanish Apostolate.
Hoyos, Jose Eugenio '84 (ARL) Falls Church, VA St. Anthony's.
Hoyt, Stephen M. *o.f.m.cap.* '92 (CHL) Charlotte, NC St. Thomas Aquinas.
Hoyt, Stephen *o.f.m.cap.* (PAT)[K] Passaic, NJ St. Mary's Hospital.
Hoyumpa, Santiago '09 (GLD) Cadillac, MI St. Ann; Lake City, MI St. Theresa; Lake City, MI St. Stephen.
Hrebenko, Pawel M. '04 (BGP) Presbyteral Council; Priest Vocation Advisory Board.
Hreha, James D. '87 (WIL) Lewes, DE St. Jude The Apostle.
Hrezo, Paul '03 (STU) On Duty Outside the Diocese.
Hrezo, Paul '00 (COL)[A] Columbus, OH Pontifical College Josephinum; [A] Columbus, OH Pontifical College Josephinum.
Hribsek, Aloysius J. '49 (BGP)[O] Stamford, CT The Catherine Dennis Keefe Queen of the Clergy Retired Priests' Residence Retired.
Hricko, Michael A. *s.j.* '73 (PH)[Y] Loyola Center and Manresa Hall.
Hritsko, William A. '98 (COL) Coshocton, OH Sacred Heart.
Hritz, Paul J. '53 (CLV) Cleveland, OH St. Malachi Retired.
Hrubiak, Rev. Archpriest Dennis M. '70 (PRM) Presbyteral Council.
Hrubiak, Rev. Archpriest Dennis M. '70 (PRM) Fairview Park, OH St. Mary Magdalene; Chancellor; Eparchial Consultors; Cantors' Institute Faculty; Office of Vocations; Seminary Education Formation Board; Priest's Pension Board.
Hruska, Eugene P. '58 (GF) Retired.
Hruska, Timothy W. '96 (MAR) Grand Marais, MI Holy Rosary Church.
Hrydziuszko, Michael '95 (DET) Macomb, MI St. Isidore.
Hrynkiw, Wasyl '91 (STF) Hempstead, NY St. Vladimir.
Hrynuck, Rev. Msgr. Stephen '38 (PHU) Retired.
Hsu, Peter '57 (BEL) Retired.
Htun, Francis Than '02 (SFR) Burmese Ministry; San Francisco, CA St. Finn Barr.
Huan, Joseph Van Tran '73 (RIC) Retired.
Huar, Ralph '81 (STP) Long Lake, MN St. George.
Huard, Jeffrey H. '94 (STP)[C] St. Paul, MN University of St. Thomas; [A] Saint Paul, MN The Saint Paul Seminary.
Huard, Leo *o.carm.* '65 (JOL)[L] Darien Carmelite Provincial Office.
Hubba, Rev. Msgr. David C. '74 (NEW)[A] South Orange, NJ Seton Hall University College Seminary; [B] Seton Hall University; Presbyteral Council.
Hubbard, J. Randall '90 (L) Louisville, KY Epiphany.
Hubbard, Jeffrey A. '05 (OG) On Duty Outside the Diocese.
Hubbard, Jeffrey A. '05 (BAL)[Q] Baltimore, MD St. Mary's Seminary & University.
Hubbard, Lawrence E. '68 (STP) Retired.
Hubbard, William '08 (ORG) La Habra, CA Our Lady of Guadalupe.
Hubbert, Joseph G. *c.m.* '77 (BUF)[N] Niagara University, NY Vincentian Community at Niagara University; [C] Niagara University, NY Niagara University.
Hubbs, Timothy L. '84 (MO) On Duty Outside the Diocese; Army Chaplains.
Hubbs, Timothy L. '84 (MO) Presbyteral Council.
Huber, Rev. Msgr. Daniel R. '50 (PBL) Retired.
Huber, Henry P. '02 (DUB) Gilbertville, IA Immaculate

Conception; Gilbertville, IA St. Joseph; Vocation Awareness Advisory Committee; [G] Gilbertville, IA Don Bosco High School.
Huber, John B. *c.s.b.* '92 (DET)[E] Novi, MI Catholic Central High School.
Huber, Kevin R. '91 (GRY) Michigan City, IN Queen of All Saints; Bishop's Council of Priests; Priestly Life.
Huber, Larry T. '95 (STL) Wentzville, MO St. Joseph.
Huber, Rev. Msgr. Mark D. '94 (LIN) Denton, NE St. Mary's; Diocesan Consultors; Officialis; Presbyteral Council; Deaneries and Deans; Building Commission; Priests' Continuing Education Committee.
Huber, Matthew P. '87 (HEL) Associate Judges; Stevensville, MT St. Mary.
Huber, Richard *m.s.c.* '59 (OG) Cape Vincent, NY Cape Vincent Correctional Facility; [F] Watertown, NY Missionaries of the Sacred Heart.
Huber, Vincent J. '64 (STU) Judges; Priests' Retirement Board; Vicar for Retired Priests; Wintersville, OH Blessed Sacrament Retired.
Hubert, Raymond P. '58 (PMB) Delray Beach, FL Emmanuel Retired.
Hubertus, Rev. Msgr. Albert '50 (SAT)[K] San Antonio, TX Casa De Padres; Judges Retired.
Huberty, Mark A. '96 (STP) Maplewood, MN Presentation of the Blessed Virgin Mary.
Huberty, Ronald V. '90 (NU) Ivanhoe, MN SS. Peter & Paul; Ivanhoe, MN St. Genevieve; Ivanhoe, MN St. Dionysius; Ivanhoe, MN St. John Cantius; Committee on Parishes; Priest Personnel Board.
Hubmann, William G. *c.pp.s.* '79 (CHI)[J] Chicago, IL Saints Mary and Elizabeth Medical Center.
Huck, Chuck '06 (CR) Deans; Red Lake Falls, MN St. Joseph's; Priests' Personnel Board.
Huckaby, John B. '11 (LKC) Lake Charles, LA Our Lady Queen of Heaven.
Hudak, Mark J. *o.f.m.* '93 (CIN)[E] Cincinnati, OH Roger Bacon High School; [N] Cincinnati, OH Pleasant Street Friary.
Hudak, Ralph '77 (CLV) Cleveland, OH Immaculate Heart of Mary.
Hudak, Richard E. '68 (CLV) Lorain, OH St. Anthony of Padua.
Hudak, Thomas R. '73 (SCR) Unassigned or Leave of Absence.
Hudepohl, Howard *o.f.m.* '54 (CIN)[N] Cincinnati, OH St. Clement Friary.
Hudert, John P. *m.m.* '62 (NY)[DD] Maryknoll Maryknoll St. Teresa's Residence[DD] Retired.
Hudgins, David '01 (LAN) Adrian, MI St. Joseph; Brooklyn, MI St. Joseph Shrine; College of Consultors; Priests' Assignment Commission.
Hudgins, James C. '98 (ARL)[D] Arlington, VA Bishop Denis J. O'Connell High School; Fredericksburg, VA St. Jude.
Hudock, Paul A. '98 (WH) Vocations, Office of; Priest–Secretary for Bishop.
Hudson, Dan (LA)[J] Torrance, CA Providence Little Company of Mary Medical Center Torrance; Providence Little Company of Mary Medical Center.
Hudson, John Paul '11 (AUS) Austin, TX Sacred Heart.
Hudzan, Volodymyr '93 (STN) Chicago, IL St. Nicholas Ukrainian Catholic Cathedral.
Hudziak, Jerome M. '64 (MIL)[B] Hales Corners, WI Sacred Heart School of Theology; Archdiocesan Consultors; Archdiocesan Council of Priests Retired.
Huebner, Terrance J. '74 (MIL) Racine, WI St. Paul the Apostle.
Huebsch, Rev. Msgr. Joseph R. '50 (FAR) Retired.
Huegelmeyer, Charles T. *m.m.* '51 (NY)[DD] Retired.
Huehlefeld, Matthew H. '96 (VIC) Hallettsville Deanery; Yoakum, TX St. Joseph; Diocesan Tribunal.
Huehlefeld, Matthew H. '96 (VIC) Judicial Vicar.
Huemmer, David '10 (LFT) Kokomo, IN St. Patrick; Kokomo, IN St. Joan of Arc.
Huerga Teruelo, Alvaro (PCE)[B] The Pontifical Catholic University of Puerto Rico.
Huerta, Enrique '86 (LA) Pico Rivera, CA St. Francis Xavier.
Huerta, Juan *s.s.p.* '86 (NY)[B] Staten Island, NY Society of St. Paul.
Huerta, Ubaldo Rogue '08 (WIN) Rochester, MN St. Francis of Assisi.
Huertas, Alvaro '81 (MIA) Miami, FL St. Thomas the Apostle.
Huertas–Colon, Rev. Msgr. Ivan L. '93 (SJN)[C] Rio Piedras, PR Seminario Mayor Regional San Juan Bautista; San Juan Bautista Regional Seminary.
Huertas–Colon, Rev. Msgr. Ivan Luis '93 (SJN) Vicar for Vocations.
Huesca, Omar A. '81 (MIA) Retired.
Huesing, Paul D. *c.s.p.* '82 (WDC)[B] Washington, DC St. Paul's College.
Huete, Francis W. *s.j.* '82 (DAL)[D] Dallas, TX Jesuit College Preparatory School.
Huff, Thomas M. (LC) Eastman, WI St. Wenceslaus; Seneca, WI St. Patrick; Deans; Wauzeka, WI Sacred Heart.
Huffman, David L. '72 (STU) Ironton, OH St. Joseph; Ironton, OH St. Lawrence; Ironton, OH St. Mary; [K] Franklin Furnace, OH Our Lady of Fatima Shrine.
Huffman, Timothy J. '93 (STU) Lowell, OH St. Henry; Lowell, OH Our Lady of Mercy; Presbyteral Council.
Huffstetter, Stephen *s.c.j.* '89 (SFS)[B] Chamberlain, SD St. Joseph Indian School.
Hug, James E. *s.j.* '72 (WDC)[O] Washington, DC Leonard Neale House; [X] Washington, DC Center of Concern.
Huggins, Scott '01 (JOL) Elmhurst, IL Visitation.
Huggins, William A. '67 (SPC) Retired.
Hughes, Anthony '93 (LAV) Pahrump, NV Our Lady of the Valley.
Hughes, Barnabas B. *o.f.m.* '53 (LA)[P] Encino, CA Our Lady of Mount Carmel Priory.
Hughes, Brian C. '81 (SC) Building Commission; Diocesan Consultors; Presbyteral Council; Spirit Lake, IA St. Mary's.
Hughes, Charles J. '74 (BO) Lowell, MA St. Anthony of Padua.
Hughes, Charles *g.h.m.* '54 (CIN)[N] Cincinnati Headquarters of Glenmary Home Missioners Retired.
Hughes, Charles *g.h.m.* '54 (SAV) Augusta, GA St. Mary on the Hill Retired.
Hughes, Christopher '98 (SFS) Redfield, SD St. Bernard.
Hughes, Dennis E. '75 (SP) Incardination Committee; Trinity, FL St. Peter the Apostle Catholic Church in Trinity, Inc.
Hughes, Derek '86 (MRY) Corralitos, CA Holy Eucharist; Respect Life.
Hughes, Edward R. '58 (RCK) Retired.
Hughes, Francis J. '80 (BRK) Brooklyn, NY St. Columba.
Hughes, James F. '52 (PH) Retired.
Hughes, James L. '81 (BRK) Brooklyn, NY St. Sylvester.
Hughes, Rev. Msgr. John Charles '49 (LA) Camarillo, CA St. Mary Magdalen Retired.
Hughes, John Jay '54 (STL) University City, MO Christ the King Retired.
Hughes, John *m.s.* '53 (WOR) Fitchburg, MA St. Joseph's.
Hughes, John '94 (BEA) Beaumont, TX St. Jude Thaddeus.
Hughes, Joseph B. '67 (BAL) Retired.
Hughes, Joseph W. '70 (TR) Leave of Absence.
Hughes, Kenneth J. *s.j.* '66 (BO)[U] Brighton, MA Alberto Hurtado House.
Hughes, Mark F. '82 (WDC) Kensington, MD Holy Redeemer; Priest Council.
Hughes, Michael J. *o.s.a.* '75 (VEN) Bokeelia, FL Our Lady of the Miraculous Medal.
Hughes, P.J. (FgM) Boston, MA St. James the Apostle, Inc.
Hughes, Peter *c.s.sp.* '61 (FAR) Special Assignment; Fargo, ND St. Anthony of Padua's Church of Fargo.
Hughes, Raymond E. '02 (TR) Toms River, NJ St. Maximilian Kolbe; Spring Lake, NJ St. Catharine.
Hughes, Rev. Msgr. Richard A. '52 (WDC) Forestville, MD Mt. Calvary Retired.
Hughes, Robert E. '90 (CAM) Officers; Liturgical Art and Architectural Commission; Chancellor; Ex Officio Members; Ex Officio Members; Sewell, NJ Church of the Holy Family, Washington Township; Ex Officio Members; The Church of the Holy Spirit, Atlantic City, N.J.
Hughes, Robert E. *s.m.* '59 (CIN)[N] Dayton, OH Marianist Community.
Hughes, Robert W. '68 (MAD) Johnson Creek, WI St. Mary Magdalene; Lake Mills, WI St. Francis Xavier.
Hughes, Ronald J. '82 (SCR) Old Forge, PA Prince of Peace Parish, Old Forge.
Hughson, D. Thomas *s.j.* '71 (MIL)[P] Milwaukee, WI Arrupe House Jesuit Community.
Hughson, Robert S. '79 (BUF) Niagara Falls, NY St. Vincent de Paul; Vicars.
Hugli, Richard H. '95 (MO) Defenders of the Bond.
Hugo, Joseph Gaspar D. '94 (BRK) Astoria, NY Immaculate Conception.
Hugo, William *o.f.m. cap.* '80 (CHI)[N] Chicago, IL St. Clare Friary.
Huguley, Vernon '93 (BIR) Adamsville, AL St. Patrick's; Diocesan College of Vicars; Birmingham, AL St. Stanislaus.
Huhn, Thomas J. *m.s.* '69 (HRT)[L] Hartford, CT Our Lady of Sorrows Rectory; Hartford, CT Our Lady of Sorrows.
Hulko, Joseph D. '67 (ALN)[J] Bethlehem, PA Holy Family Villa Retired.
Hull, Francis M. *s.s.j.* '57 (ARL) Alexandria, VA St. Joseph's.
Hull, Rev. Msgr. Michael F. '93 (NY) New York, NY Guardian Angel; New York, NY Our Lady of Loreto; Censors Librorum; [A] Yonkers, NY St. Joseph's Seminary.
Hullinger, Jon '99 (KCK) Topeka, KS Mater Dei.
Hullinger, Ty S. '04 (BAL) Baltimore, MD St. Dominic; Cumberland, MD Federal & State Correctional Facilities; Baltimore, MD St. Anthony of Padua; Baltimore, MD Most Precious Blood.
Hullings, Clifford '61 (SPK) Retired.
Hulot, Vincent *o.s.b.* '97 (TLS)[G] Hulbert, OK Our Lady of the Annunciation of Clear Creek Monastery.
Hulscher, Alfred J. *o.s.b.* '60 (SEA)[M] Lacey, WA St. Martin's Abbey; Lacey, WA.
Hulshof, David F. '82 (SPC) Cape Girardeau, MO St. Vincent de Paul; Diaconate (Permanent); Advocates for the Respondent; Presbyteral Council; Diocesan Lay Endowment Board; Diocesan Council of Catholic Women (DCCW); Diocesan Consultors.
Hultberg, William J. *o.s.f.s.* '62 (WIL)[J] Wilmington Wilmington–Philadelphia Province of the Oblates of St. Francis de Sales.
Hultquist, Thomas H. '76 (WOR) Barre, MA St. Joseph.
Humbrecht, Rev. Msgr. T. Allen '72 (KNX) Soddy Daisy, TN Holy Spirit Catholic Church; [K] Knoxville, TN Diocesan Council of Catholic Women; Diocesan Consultors; Ecumenism; [K] Chattanooga, TN Ladies of Charity; Presbyteral Council.
Hume, Kenneth '63 (P) Retired.
Humenay, Robert L. '69 (MO) Air National Guard Chaplains.
Humitz, Rev. Msgr. Robert S. '60 (DET) Retired.
Hummel, Donald K. '78 (NEW) Clark, NJ St. Agnes; Continuing Education and Formation of Priests; Office of the Permanent Diaconate.
Hummel, Kenneth J. '98 (PEO) Raritan, IL Church of St. Patrick; On Duty Outside the Diocese.
Hummel, Kenneth (CIN) Dayton, OH St. Peter.
Hummer, Lawrence L. '73 (COL) Chillicothe, OH St. Mary; Chillicothe, OH Chillicothe Correctional Institution.
Humphrey, Arthur F. '75 (NEW) Little Ferry, NJ St. Margaret of Cortona; South Central Bergen Deanery 5.
Humphrey, Delos A. *m.m.* '54 (FgM) Maryknoll, NY MARYKNOLL.
Humphrey, Steven (BEL) Retired.
Humphries, Ryan P. '05 (ALX) College of Consultors; Campti, LA Nativity of The Blessed Virgin Mary; Elected Members; Deans.
Humphrys, Richard A. '57 (SB) Bloomington, CA St. Charles Borromeo.
Hund, Francis '82 (KCK) Leawood, KS Church of the Nativity.
Hund, Joseph *o.f.m.* '89 (CIN)[N] Cincinnati St. Francis Seraph Friary.
Hund, William *c.s.c.* '60 (P)[L] Portland, OR Holy Cross Fathers & Brothers, C.S.C. – University of Portland Retired.
Hund, William *c.s.c.* (FTW)[H] Notre Dame Congregation of Holy Cross, United States Province of Priests & Brothers.
Hundt, Rev. Msgr. George F. '81 (PAT) Madison, NJ St. Vincent Martyr; Presbyteral Council; Defenders of the Bond; College of Consultors.
Hundt, Rev. Msgr. Robert P. '61 (LC) Judicial Vicar; Diocesan Judges; [H] La Crosse, WI Holy Cross (Seminary) Diocesan Center.
Hundt, Robert P. (DEN) Metropolitan Judges.
Huneger, Rev. Msgr. Richard '73 (P) Oregon City, OR St. John the Apostle; College of Consultors; Diaconate Office.
Hung, Bernard Nguyen '97 (AUS) Kingsland, TX St. Charles Borromeo Catholic Church – Kingsland, Texas; Horseshoe Bay, TX Our Lady of the Lake.
Hung, Le Trong *c.ss.r.* '08 (LA)[P] Baldwin Park Vietnamese Redemptorist Mission.
Hung, Peter '67 (CHI) Indochinese Catholic Center Retired.
Hung, Pham Quoc *c.ss.r.* '94 (LA)[P] Baldwin Park, CA Vietnamese Redemptorist Mission; [BB] Baldwin Park, CA The Redemptorist Vietnamese Mission Corporation.
Hung, Tran Duy '05 (ATL) Holy Vietnamese Martyrs.
Hung, Trinh Peter '65 (CHI) Chicago, IL St. Thomas of Canterbury.
Hung Le, Francis *o.p.* '04 (P) Portland, OR Holy Rosary Parish & Dominican Priory; [L] Portland, OR Holy Rosary Priory.
Hung Long Tran, Francis M. *c.m.c.* '99 (SPC)[F] Carthage, MO Congregation of the Mother Coredemptrix, United States Assumption Province.
Hunh, Thomas J. *m.s.* (LKC) Sulphur, LA Our Lady of Prompt Succor.
Hunke, Norman F. '73 (OM) Gretna, NE St. Charles Borromeo; Consultors; Ex Officio (Consultors).
Hunkler, Jerome '83 (FAR) Steele, ND St. Francis de Sales; Steele, ND St. Paul; Steele, ND St. Mary's Church of Medina.
Hunstiger, Thomas '65 (STP) Retired.
Hunt, Dennis M. (LIN) Aurora, NE St. Mary's.
Hunt, Doug '92 (PBL) Ignacio, CO St. Ignatius Parish.
Hunt, Henry Clay '09 (SAT) Del Rio, TX St. Joseph's.
Hunt, Rev. Msgr. James A. '55 (BRK)[R] Douglaston, NY Bishop Mugavero Residence Retired.
Hunt, James M. '83 (GI) Broken Bow, NE St. Joseph's; Procurator; Advocates; Priests' Advisory Board (Presbyteral Council).
Hunt, John W. '68 (PRO) Cumberland, RI St. Joseph.
Hunt, Kevin *o.c.s.o.* '79 (WOR)[N] Spencer, MA St. Joseph's Abbey.
Hunt, Rev. Msgr. Luke '67 (PT) Gulf Breeze, FL St. Ann; Vicar General; Building & Renovation, Diocesan Commission for; Finance, Diocesan Commission

for; Knights of Columbus; Priests' Pension Plan, Board for; College of Consultors; Administrative Council.
Hunt, Mark J. '85 (PH) On Special or Other Archdiocesan Assignment; Fallsington, PA St. Joseph the Worker; [C] Philadelphia, PA Holy Family University; [A] Wynnewood, PA Theological Seminary of St. Charles Borromeo, Overbrook.
Hunt, Mark '01 (NSH) Nashville, TN Holy Rosary; Diocesan Finance Board; Priest Benefit Foundation.
Hunt, Richard D. *s.j.* '71 (OAK)[L] Berkeley, CA Jesuit Fathers and Brothers.
Hunt, Robert *c.pp.s.* '54 (CIN)[N] Dayton Provincial Office of the Cincinnati Province of the Society of the Precious Blood.
Hunt, Robert '54 (ORL) Retired.
Hunter, Alan M. '77 (SFD) Kincaid, IL St. Rita; Stonington, IL Holy Trinity; Taylorville, IL St. Mary.
Hunter, Alan '77 (SFD) Commission for the Care of Infirm and Retired Priests.
Hunter, Eric '72 (SP) Clearwater, FL St. Brendan; Personnel Board.
Hunthausen, John F. '52 (HEL) Retired.
Hunthausen, John M. *s.j.* '70 (STL)[O] St. Louis, MO Jesuit Community Corporation at Saint Louis University – Jesuit Hall; [A] St. Louis, MO Kenrick School of Theology.
Huntimer, Donald W. *c.s.v.* '59 (CHI)[N] Arlington Heights, IL Viatorian Province Center–Clerics of St. Viator.
Huntzinger, Rev. Msgr. Ralph J. '50 (COL) Retired.
Huon, Phan Phat *c.ss.r.* '53 (LA)[P] Baldwin Park Vietnamese Redemptorist Mission.
Huong, Joseph '01 (SAC) Sacramento, CA St. Anne.
Hur, Chan Rhan '98 (OAK)[L] Berkeley Salesians of Don Bosco.
Hurbanczuk, Adam '91 (HRT) Hartford, CT SS. Cyril and Methodius.
Hurd, R. Scott '00 (WDC) Special Ministries; Pastoral Center Special Ministries.
Hurd, R. Scott (POC) Vicar General.
Hurd, Robert E. *s.j.* '91 (CIN)[N] Cincinnati, OH Jesuit Community at Xavier University.
Hurd, Scott '00 (WDC) Executive Director, Permanent Diaconate.
Hurd, Steven F. *s.j.* '80 (CHI)[N] Chicago Chicago Province of the Society of Jesus–Provincial Office.
Hurd, Timothy C. '92 (SHP) Zwolle, LA St. Joseph; Vicars Forane; Advocates; Diocesan Liturgy Commission; College of Consultors; Ex Officio Members.
Hurkes, Charles *o.m.i.* '58 (WDC)[O] Washington, DC Oblate Community.
Hurlbert, James F. '90 (CHI) Chicago, IL St. Alphonsus.
Hurley, Brendan *s.j.* '93 (BAL)[Q] Towson Maryland Province of the Society of Jesus.
Hurley, Brian K. '02 (DET) Temperance, MI St. Anthony.
Hurley, Rev. Msgr. Daniel J. '59 (RVC) Massapequa, NY St. Rose of Lima Retired.
Hurley, Rev. Msgr. Edward '70 (DM) Vicar for Finance; Priests' Pension Fund Society; Des Moines, IA St. Joseph's.
Hurley, George '55 (JOL) Retired.
Hurley, Gerard '76 (JKS) Flowood, MS St. Paul; Continuing Formation Committee; Personnel Board.
Hurley, John E. *c.s.p.* (BAL) Consultants; Baltimore, MD Cathedral of Mary Our Queen; Department of Evangelization.
Hurley, John J. *o.s.f.s.* '68 (FgM)[J] Wilmington, DE DeSales House; Wilmington, DE OBLATES OF ST. FRANCIS DE SALES MISSIONS; Wilmington, DE Oblates of St. Francis de Sales (O.S.F.S.).
Hurley, John J. '56 (CHI) Arlington Heights, IL St. Edna Retired.
Hurley, John W. '74 (CHI) Prospect Heights, IL St. Alphonsus Liguori.
Hurley, John '82 (WDC) Washington, DC St. Matthew Cathedral Retired.
Hurley, Rev. Msgr. Leonard F. '58 (WDC) Special Ministries; Hospital & Nursing Home Ministries; [M] Washington, DC Cardinal O'Boyle Residence for Priests; [X] Washington, DC Carroll Manor Nursing & Rehabilitation Center; Cardinal O'Boyle Residence for Priests.
Hurley, Michael *o.p.* '07 (SAC) Benicia, CA St. Dominic.
Hurley, Patrick M. *o.s.b.* '76 (PAT)[J] Morristown, NJ St. Mary's Abbey Retreat Center; [N] Morristown, NJ St. Mary's Abbey.
Hurley, Paul K. '95 (MO) Military & VA Chaplains.; Army Chaplains.
Hurley, Phillip R. *s.j.* '08 (MIL)[P] Milwaukee, WI Jesuit Community at Marquette University; [Y] Milwaukee, WI Apostleship of Prayer.
Hurley, Sean Patrick *f.p.o.* '11 (BO)[U] Lawrence, MA Franciscans of Primitive Observance.
Hurley, Steven P. '03 (WIL) Wilmington, DE St. Thomas the Apostle; Chancery Office; Priests' Council; Chancellor.
Hurley, Thomas J. '93 (CHI) Chicago, IL Old St. Patrick's.
Hurrell, Johnathan *ss.cc.* '05 (HON) Waialua, HI St. Michael.
Hurst, Paul F. '77 (CIN) Springfield, OH St. Bernard.
Hurst, Thomas R. *s.s.* '73 (ALB) On Duty Outside the Diocese.
Hurst, Thomas R. *s.s.* '73 (BAL)[A] Baltimore, MD St. Mary's Seminary and University; [Q] Baltimore Society of St. Sulpice, Province of the United States; [A] Baltimore, MD St. Mary's Seminary and University.
Hurtado, Mauricio '10 (SAC) Fair Oaks, CA St. Mel.
Hurtado, Tomas '04 (ORL) Apopka, FL St. Francis of Assisi.
Hurtado–Badillo, Domingo '93 (CHI)[J] Hoffman Estates, IL St. Alexius Medical Center.
Hurtado–Olazo, Marco '02 (NEW) Union, NJ Holy Spirit.
Hurtuk, Joseph *s.m.* '74 (STP) St. Paul, MN St. Louis King of France.
Huse, Charles F. *o.a.r.* '61 (NEW)[L] West Orange, NJ Augustinian Recollects.
Huse, Ralph G. *s.j.* '75 (STL)[O] St. Louis, MO Jesuit Community Corporation at Saint Louis University – Jesuit Hall.
Huse, Robert *o.a.r.* '56 (LA)[P] Oxnard, CA Order of Augustinian Recollects (O.A.R.), St. Augustine Priory.
Huser, Jeremy S. '11 (WCH) Wichita, KS St. Francis of Assisi.
Hushen, Mark A. *o.s.f.s.* '91 (WIL)[J] Childs, MD Retirement and Assisted Care Facility; [J] Wilmington Wilmington–Philadelphia Province of the Oblates of St. Francis de Sales.
Huske, Leonard G. '56 (CHI) Retired.
Hussey, Daniel C. '85 (GLP) On Duty Outside of Diocese.
Hussey, Daniel '85 (RNO) Elko, NV St. Joseph's; Lists of Deans; Diocesan Board of Consultors; Presbyteral Council.
Hussey, Edmund M. '58 (CIN) Retired.
Hussey, Gerald W. '78 (PRO) Little Compton, RI St. Catherine of Siena; Tiverton, RI St. Madeleine Sophie.
Hussey, Michael *o.m.i.* '60 (BEL)[F] Belleville, IL Missionary Oblates of Mary Immaculate – St. Henry's Oblate Residence.
Hussey, Robert M. *s.j.* '00 (R) Raleigh, NC St. Raphael the Archangel; [F] Raleigh Jesuit Community; Towson, MD; Council of Priests.
Hussli, Edward J. '67 (MIL) Retired.
Husted, Richard *o.f.m.* (PAT) Pompton Lakes, NJ Our Lady of the Assumption.
Huston, Richard '95 (SD) San Diego, CA Good Shepherd Catholic Parish Retired.
Huszti, Michael J. '75 (PRM) On Duty Outside the Diocese; Cantors' Institute Faculty; Judges.
Huszti, Michael '76 (PBR)[D] Uniontown, PA Monastery and Novitiate of the Sisters of St. Basil the Great; Pro–Synodal Judges.
Hut, Clemens '36 (EVN) Retired.
Hutcherson, Bartholomew J. *o.p.* '97 (TUC) Tucson, AZ Saint Thomas More Roman Catholic Newman Parish – Tucson; [H] Tucson, AZ University of Arizona.
Hutcherson, Bartholomew J. *o.p.* '97 (OAK)[L] Oakland, CA Order of Preachers (Province of the Most Holy Name of Jesus – Western Dominican Province).
Hutchins, James '67 (PH) Broomall, PA St. Pius X.
Hutchins, Michael *s.v.d.* (DM) On Special Assignment.
Hutchinson, Ronald D. '94 (GR) Jenison, MI Holy Redeemer; On Special Assignment; Vocations Office.
Hutchison, William J. *s.j.* '66 (STL) St. Louis, MO St. Matthew, Apostle; [O] St. Louis, MO St. Matthew Jesuit Community.
Hutmacher, Robert '79 (CHI)[N] Chicago, IL St. Peter's Friary.
Hutsko, Basil '79 (PRM) Merrillville, IN St. Michael; Presbyteral Council; Priest's Pension Board.
Hutsko, Joseph '79 (HPM) Fontana, CA St. Nicholas; College of Consultors; Youth.
Hutsko, Rev. Archpriest Michael '84 (PHU) Mount Carmel, PA Assumption of B.V.M.; Board Members; Mount Carmel, PA SS. Peter and Paul.
Hutter, John S. '92 (PH) Phoenixville, PA St. Mary of the Assumption.
Hutton, Leon '80 (LA)[A] Camarillo, CA St. John's Seminary.
Hutzler, James '80 (AMA)[C] Panhandle, TX St. Joseph's Home for Retired Priests Retired.
Huvane, James H. *m.m.* '70 (CLV)[N] Cleveland, OH Maryknoll Fathers & Brothers; Cleveland, OH.
Huyen, Leo Vu Dinh *c.m.c.* '94 (ROC) Rochester, NY St. Helen.
Huyett, Gerald T. *s.j.* '73 (NY)[DD] New York, NY Jesuit Community of the Immaculate Conception.
Huyn, Mark M. Nguyen Thanh *c.m.c.* (FWT) Wichita Falls, TX Immaculate Conception of Mary.
Huynh, Andrew (ORG) Retired.
Huynh, Joseph Dinh C. '67 (PH) Philadelphia, PA St. Thomas Aquinas.
Huynh, Peter Loi '02 (SJ) San Jose, CA St. Patrick; Ongoing Formation of Clergy.
Huynh, Viet Tan '93 (PT) Madison, FL St. Vincent de Paul; Madison, FL St. Margaret.
Huy Quang Vu, John M. *c.m.c.* '85 (SPC)[F] Carthage, MO Congregation of the Mother Coredemptrix, United States Assumption Province.
Huy Quyen, Nguyen '73 (JOL) Glen Ellyn, IL Queenship of Mary.
Hvozdovic, Andrew S. '87 (SCR) Sayre, PA Epiphany Parish; Deans; Pilgrimages.
Hwang, Andrew *o.f.m.* (NY) New York, NY St. Francis of Assisi.
Hwang, Matthias Seon Ki '88 (SJ) Sunnyvale, CA Holy Korean Martyrs.
Hwang, Paul '01 (NEW) Fort Lee, NJ Holy Trinity.
Hy, Hilary Tran–Khac '57 (WDC) Silver Spring, MD Our Lady of Vietnam Retired.
Hyatt, Donald F. *c.s.b.* '68 (LSC) Truth or Consequences, NM Our Lady of Perpetual Help; [B] Las Cruces, NM Basilian Fathers.
Hyatt, John R. *s.j.* '77 (NY) Staten Island, NY St. Mary of the Assumption; Staten Island, NY Our Lady of Mt. Carmel–St. Benedicta.
Hyatt, Martin A. *b.s.o.* '84 (NTN) Methuen, MA Seminary of St. Basil the Great; Methuen, MA Basilian Salvatorian Order; Methuen, MA.
Hybner, Joseph '63 (VIC) Flatonia, TX SS. Cyril and Methodius; Flatonia, TX Sacred Heart.
Hyclak, Walter J. '69 (CLV) Olmsted Falls, OH St. Mary of the Falls; College of Consultors.
Hyde, Gregory J. *s.j.* '98 (DET)[P] Bloomfield Hills, MI Manresa Jesuit Retreat House.
Hyde, Mark *s.d.b.* '81 (NY)[HH] New Rochelle, NY Salesian Missions, Inc.; New Rochelle, NY SALESIANS OF DON BOSCO.
Hyde, Robert P. '88 (MO) DEPARTMENT OF VETERANS AFFAIRS HOSPITALS AND CHAPLAINS.
Hyde, Robert P. '88 (SY) Promoters of Justice; Syracuse, NY St. Margaret.
Hykavy, Roman *o.s.b.m.* '94 (STN) Hamtramck, MI Immaculate Conception of B.V.M.
Hyl, Robert J. '63 (BGP) Stamford, CT Holy Spirit.
Hyland, James M. '81 (CHI) Evergreen Park, IL Most Holy Redeemer.
Hyland, Rev. Msgr. John M. '68 (DAV)[J] Davenport, IA St. Vincent Center; Finance Council; Vicar General and Moderator of the Curia; Diocesan Consultors; Diocesan Corporate Board; Pastoral Services; Notaries.
Hyman, David L. *o.f.m.* '60 (ATL) Special or Other Archdiocesan Assignment; [I] Athens, GA University of Georgia – Catholic Student Center; Athens, GA Catholic Student Center at The University of Georgia.
Hyman, Robert A. '61 (TUC) Retired.
Hyman, Robert (GLP) McNary, AZ St. Anthony.
Hymel, Ray A. '87 (NO) Pearl River, LA SS. Peter and Paul.
Hynes, Aidan '81 (PMB) Hobe Sound, FL St. Christopher; Ex Officio; Vicars Forane.
Hynes, Rev. Msgr. Christopher J. '92 (NEW)[B] Seton Hall University; Assistant to the Archbishop for Public Affairs.
Hynes, Gerald *c.p.* '51 (BAL) Baltimore, MD St. Ursula Retired.
Hynes, James P. '49 (PRO)[O] Providence St. John Vianney Residence Retired.
Hynes, James '73 (SAT) San Antonio, TX Our Lady of the Angels.
Hynes, John F. '55 (DAV) Retired.
Hynes, John M. '65 (WIL) Wilmington, DE St. Catherine of Siena.
Hynes, Rev. Msgr. Richard P. '72 (CHI) Chicago, IL Nativity of Our Lord; Department Directors; Department of Parish Life and Formation; Administrative Council.
Hynes, Thomas J. *c.m.* '59 (BRK)[R] Brooklyn, NY St. John the Baptist Rectory.
Hynes, Rev. Msgr. William '49 (SR) Sebastopol, CA St. Sebastian Retired.
Hynous, David M. *o.p.* '59 (CHI) Judges; [N] Chicago, IL St. Pius V Priory.
Hynous, David *o.p.* '59 (JOL) Judges.
Hypolite, Douglas *s.j.* '80 (SP)[C] Tampa, FL Jesuit High School.

I

Iacona, Francesco *c.m.f.* '02 (CHI)[N] Oak Park Claretian Missionaries USA Eastern Province.
Iaconis, Anthony '97 (RVC) Islip Terrace, NY St. Peter the Apostle.
Iacovacci, Rev. Msgr. Nicholas J. '51 (PRO) Warwick, RI St. Peter Retired.
Iacovone, Angelo *c.p.* '46 (BRK)[R] Jamaica, NY Immaculate Conception Monastery Retired.
Iannizzotto, Christopher J. *o.carm.* '08 (NY) Bronx, NY St. Simon Stock.
Iannone, Raphael *o.f.m.cap.* '64 (NY)[DD] New Paltz, NY St. Joseph Friary; New Paltz, NY St. Joseph.
Ianotti, Pascal '61 (ALB) Retired.
Iantosca, August P. (BRK) Creedmoor Psychiatric Center; Queens Village, NY Incarnation.
Ianucci, Thomas '94 (MO) Navy Chaplains.

Iaquinta, Patsy J. '70 (WH) Retired.
Iaquinto, Richard *o.s.b.* '68 (BUR)[E] Weston, VT Priory of Benedictine Monks; Weston, VT.
Iaquinto, Robert '81 (NEW) Retired.
Iasiello, Louis V. *o.f.m.* '78 (SP)[N] St. Petersburg, FL St. Anthony Friary.
Iasiello, Louis V. *o.f.m.* '78 (COL)[A] Columbus, OH Pontifical College Josephinum; [A] Columbus, OH Pontifical College Josephinum.
Iaucci, Thomas '94 (RIC) Military Chaplains.
Ibach, Michael J. '73 (YAK) Judicial Vicar; Judges; Diocesan Consultors; Yakima, WA Holy Family.
Ibach, William D. *s.j.* '59 (BO)[U] Weston, MA Campion Jesuit Community.
Ibanga, Francis *m.s.p.* '86 (CHI) Chicago, IL St. Kilian.
Ibarra, Arnold '00 (SAT)[A] San Antonio, TX Assumption Seminary.
Ibarra, Brando '99 (PAT) Passaic, NJ St. Anthony of Padua; Spanish Cursillos.
Ibarra, Manuel '98 (LSC) Lovington, NM St. Thomas Aquinas; Clergy Personnel Board.
Ibarra, Martin D. '07 (CHI) Chicago, IL St. Agnes of Bohemia.
Ibarra, Martin *o.f.m.* '08 (OAK) Oakland, CA St. Elizabeth; [L] Oakland, CA Franciscan Friars of California, (Province of St. Barbara).
Ibay, Eulalio (Yul) P. '98 (CC) Corpus Christi, TX Our Lady Star of the Sea.
Ibe, Bartholomew '98 (ALX) Evergreen, LA Little Flower.
Ibe, Ignatius A. *s.m.m.m.* '03 (ALX) Marksville, LA Holy Ghost.
Ibe, Santus K. '00 (MAD) Ridgeway, WI St. Bernadette.
Ibe, Titus (HRT) West Haven, CT St. Paul's.
Ibebuike, Chuma P. '79 (LR) Russellville, AR St. John.
Ibeh, Eliseus *m.s.p.* '89 (AUS) Florence, TX Santa Rosa.
Ibeh, Valentine U. '91 (NY) Mount Vernon, NY St. Ursula.
Ibekwe, Anthony (GB) Appleton, WI St. Bernadette; Appleton, WI Sacred Heart.
Ibemere, Julian '98 (OWN) Owensboro, KY St. Pius Tenth.
Ibok, Augustine *s.m.p.* '07 (SPC)[F] Marionville, MO The Society of Our Mother of Peace, Sons of Our Mother of Peace.
Idagbo, Osang *c.m.* '05 (BEL) Waterloo, IL SS. Peter and Paul; Waterloo, IL Immaculate Conception.
Idler, Peter M. '97 (CAM) On Duty Outside the Diocese.
Idra, Augustine *a.j.* '97 (KNX)[A] Chattanooga, TN Notre Dame High School; Chattanooga, TN St. Stephen.
Idyu, Matthias '92 (JOL)[I] Kankakee, IL Provena St. Mary's Hospital.
Idzik, George '73 (NEW) Retired.
Ifele, Andrew '89 (SFE) Questa, NM St. Anthony.
Iffert, John C. '97 (BEL) Diocesan Deans; Mount Vernon, IL St. Mary; Diocesan Finance Council.
Iffert, Wilbert J. '52 (BEL) Retired.
Ifionu, Bartholomew *s.m.m.m.* '04 (BAK) John Day, OR St. Elizabeth.
Ifkovits, Edward M. *s.j.* (BAL) Baltimore, MD St. Ignatius Church.
Igboanugo, Francis (BRK) Flushing, NY St. Mel.
Igboanusi, Gerald "Chi" '08 (OM) Omaha, NE St. Elizabeth Ann; [B] Omaha, NE Roncalli Catholic High School of Omaha.
Iglesias, Clement '58 (BEA) Retired.
Iglesias, Fernando Gonzalez '56 (LA) Retired.
Ignacio, Alejandro '74 (FRS) Fresno, CA Sacred Heart.
Ignacio, Roberto '00 (TR) Riverton, NJ Sacred Heart.
Ignasik, Slawomir '00 (JOL) Itasca, IL St. Peter the Apostle.
Ignaszak, Michael A. '84 (MIL)[H] Milwaukee, WI Holy Wisdom Academy; Milwaukee, WI Blessed John Paul II Parish.
Igoe, Martin S. '62 (BGP) District Spiritual Directors Retired.
Igrobay, Manuel D. '89 (SFR) Colma, CA Holy Angels.
Igwe, Paschal '96 (DET) Farmington Hills, MI Botsford Hospital.
Igwenwanne, Fidelis '90 (PHX) Phoenix, AZ Banner Good Samaritan Medical Center.
Igweonu, Romanus '92 (BUR) Ludlow, VT Annunciation of the Blessed Virgin Mary.
Igwilo, Peter C. '92 (PH) Norwood, PA St. Gabriel.
Iheaka, Emmanuel K. '90 (MO) DEPARTMENT OF VETERANS AFFAIRS HOSPITALS AND CHAPLAINS.
Iheaka, Emmanuel K. '90 (PH) Coatesville, PA Veterans Administration Medical Center; Honey Brook, PA St. Peter.
Iheanaho, Kenneth '90 (TLS) Tulsa, OK St. Augustine's; Tulsa, OK St. Monica's.
Ihedioha, Hilary A. '85 (SAN) Brady, TX St. Patrick's.
Ihedoro, Christian *c.m.f.* '66 (LA)[V] Rancho Dominguez, CA Dominguez Seminary Inc.
Iheke, Uche G. *s.m.m.m.* '98 (MO) Army Chaplains.
Ihemedu, Emmanuel I. '06 (HRT) Hartford Deanery; Hartford, CT St. Justin; Hartford, CT St. Michael.
Ihewulezi, Cajetan *c.ss.p.* (STL) Saint Louis, MO Sts. Teresa and Bridget.
Ihm, Gregory S. '10 (MAD) Waunakee, WI St. John the Baptist; Waunakee, WI St. Mary of the Lake.
Ihnatowicz, Janusz '62 (GAL)[O] Houston, TX Residence of the Basilian Fathers of the University of St. Thomas.
Ihrie, Bernard R. '55 (WDC) Retired.
Ihuoma, Alphonsus '96 (PBL) La Junta, CO Our Lady of Guadalupe/St. Patrick; Las Animas, CO St. Mary.
Ihuoma, Stanley K. *s.s.j.* (BAL) Baltimore, MD St. Francis Xavier.
Ijeoma, John Vianney '88 (MO) Army Chaplains.
Ijere, Ignatius (GRY)[D] Dyer, IN St. Margaret Mercy Healthcare Centers, South Campus.
Ikalowych, Jerry '08 (SJP) Conyers, GA Mother of God; Presbyters.
Ikanga, Jean Ngeyeye *s.v.d.* (DET)[K] Detroit, MI Jesuit Community at the University of Detroit Mercy.
Ikataere, John *m.s.c.* '72 (CI) Chuuk, FM Mortlock.
Ike, Anthony '94 (STA) Switzerland, FL San Juan Del Rio.
Ike, Roberto M. '94 (JC) Westphalia, MO St. Anthony of Padua.
Ikemelu, Hyacinth I. '99 (BRK) Brooklyn, NY St. Fortunata.
Ikeocha, Ikechukwu '00 (LA) Whittier, CA St. Gregory the Great.
Ikhane, Irenaeus '01 (NY) Beacon, NY St. John the Evangelist.
Ikwuegbu, Charles E. '95 (HRT) West Hartford, CT St. Brigid; West Hartford, CT St. Helena.
Ilango, Xavier '88 (CR) Callaway, MN Assumption; Frazee, MN Sacred Heart; Vocations; Priests' Council.
Ilano, Jovencio '96 (RIC) Retired.
Ilechukwu, Pius N. '80 (FTW) Walkerton, IN St. Patrick.
Ilgen, Timothy W. '03 (SEA) Centralia, WA St. Mary; Chehalis, WA St. Joseph; Pe Ell, WA St. Joseph; Toledo, WA St. Francis Xavier; Winlock, WA Sacred Heart.
Ililau, John Paul '90 (CI) Palau, PW St. John Baptist; [C] Manresa Jesuit House.
Illikattil, Mathew (KAL) Mattawan, MI St. John Bosco.
Illo, Joseph P. '91 (STO) Modesto, CA St. Joseph Church of Modesto (Pastor of); Deans.
Ilnicki, Theodosius (Roman) *o.s.b.m.* '88 (RVC)[N] Glen Cove, NY St. Josaphat's Monastery, Novitiate and Retreat House.
Ilnicki, Theodosius *o.s.b.m.* '88 (STF) Judge; [B] Glen Cove, NY Basilian Fathers Novitiate of the Order of St. Basil the Great.
Ilokaba, Damian O. '86 (MO) Army Chaplains.
Imamshah, Harold '90 (ALX) Colfax, LA St. Joseph.
Imana, Vincent Musaby '96 (SFR) San Francisco, CA Star of the Sea.
Imbarrato, Stephen '05 (SFE) Bernalillo, NM Our Lady of Sorrows.
Imbelli, Robert P. '66 (NY) On Duty Outside the Archdiocese; Newton, MA Sacred Heart.
Imberi, Anthony '62 (SFS) Retired.
Imbroll, Gregory E. *o.f.m.* '57 (NY)[DD] New York Franciscan Province of the Immaculate Conception.
Imfeld, Thomas J. '59 (LEX) Retired.
Imgrund, Norman P. '64 (ALT) Retired.
Imhangbe, Osayamen Samson '99 (NY) Bronx, NY Holy Rosary.
Imholte, Otto *s.s.c.* '63 (FgM) St Columbans, NE House of Post–Graduate Studies.
Iminga, Wilfredo *m.s.* '92 (HON) Waipahu, HI St. Joseph.
Imming, Donald '60 (SFS) Retired.
Imo, Cletus '91 (SB) Rancho Cucamonga, CA Sacred Heart.
Imokhai, Charles '68 (NY) New Rochelle, NY Blessed Sacrament.
Imoru, Godwin (LAF) Crowley, LA St. Theresa.
Inbaraj, Victor '95 (LC) Chippewa Falls, WI Holy Ghost; Chippewa Falls, WI St. Bridget.
Incardona, Victor *m.i.c.* (SPR)[G] Stockbridge, MA Congregation of Marian Fathers of The Immaculate Conception of the Most Blessed Virgin Mary.
Ince, Michael W. '64 (STP) Elysian, MN St. Andrew; Waterville, MN Holy Trinity.
Ince, Owen F. '00 (NEW) On Duty Outside the Archdiocese; Newark, NJ Our Lady of Good Counsel.
India, Stephen J. *c.m.* '49 (PH)[Y].
Infanger, Frank '02 (JOL) Leave of Absence.
Infante, Angel *t.o.r.* '08 (FWT) Fort Worth, TX All Saints.
Infante, Joseph '94 (RNO) Reno, NV St. Albert the Great.
Infante, Richard A. '92 (PIT) Pittsburgh, PA Our Lady of Grace; Diocesan Development Board.
Ingalls, Fred D. '74 (BUF) Retired.
Ingels, Gregory G. '74 (SFR) Retired.
Ingels, Kyle Thomas '05 (WDC) Bowie, MD Ascension.
Ingemie, Dominic '67 (ALB) Saratoga Springs, NY St. Peter; Deans.
Ingham, G. Nicholas *o.p.* '81 (PRO)[O] Providence St. Thomas Aquinas Priory at Providence College.
Ingham, Rev. Msgr. Jeffrey A. '75 (R) Southern Pines, NC St. Anthony of Padua; Deans; Diocesan Consultors; Council of Priests.
Inghilterra, Vincent J. '72 (TR) Retired.
Inghilterra, Vincent '72 (STU)[A] Steubenville, OH Franciscan University of Steubenville; [H] Steubenville, OH Holy Spirit Friary.
Ingiyimbere, Fidele *s.j.* '09 (BO)[U] Newton, MA The Jesuit Community at Boston College.
Inglot, Mark '81 (LAN) East Lansing, MI St. John the Evangelist Church and Student Center; East Lansing, MI St. Thomas Aquinas; [N] East Lansing, MI St. John the Evangelist Church and Student Center.
Ingold, Michael L. '91 (GB) Neenah, WI St. Margaret Mary.
Ingram, Brian '90 (RVC) Sayville, NY St. Lawrence the Martyr; Priests' Personnel Policy Board.
Ingram, Walter Y. (Mike) '02 (SAV) Grovetown, GA St. Teresa of Avila.
Inigo Monreal, Juan Javier *c.m.* '61 (PCE)[B] The Pontifical Catholic University of Puerto Rico.
Inman, Robert D. '03 (YAK) On Duty Outside the Diocese.
Innes, Ben R. *o.f.m.* '84 (P) Portland, OR Ascension; [L] Portland, OR Ascension Friary.
Innocenti, Mark '99 (SCL) Little Falls, MN Holy Family; Little Falls, MN Our Lady of Lourdes; Advocates.
Innocenzi, Rev. Msgr. James G. '76 (TR) Titusville, NJ St. George; Vice Chancellors; Associate Judicial Vicars.
Inserra, John J. '03 (BGP) Greenwich, CT St. Mary.
Intal, Arlan G. *m.s.* '05 (SB) Moreno Valley, CA St. Patrick.
Intal, Arlan *m.s.* '06 (SB)[I] Moreno Valley, CA Missionaries of Our Lady of La Salette, MS.
Intovigne, Raymond D. '64 (NOR) Co–Directors; Coventry, CT St. Mary.
Intranuovo, Ralph *s.c.j.* '83 (SP)[N] Pinellas Park, FL Priests of the Sacred Heart.
Introini, Rev. Msgr. Elso C. (PAT) Retired.
Inverso, Leon J. '85 (TR)[N] Trenton, NJ Villa Vianney.
Inwang, Augustine Etemma *m.s.p.* '90 (BAL)[K] Baltimore, MD Mercy Health Services Inc.; Baltimore, MD Transfiguration Catholic Community.
Inyanwachi, Edward S. '94 (SFR) Menlo Park, CA St. Raymond.
Iodice, Ciro *o.f.m.* '72 (NY)[DD] New York Franciscan Province of the Immaculate Conception.
Iorio, Peter J. '93 (KNX) Johnson City, TN St. Mary.
Iott, Martin *o.p.* '70 (GAL) Houston, TX Holy Rosary.
Iovino, Paul '61 (PAT) Retired.
Ipolito, Pascal D. '70 (BUF) West Falls, NY St. George.
Ippolito, Robert F. *m.s.* '73 (R) Shallotte, NC St. Brendan the Navigator.
Irace, Dominic P. '75 (ARL) Retired.
Irarrazaval, Diego *c.s.c.* (FTW)[H] Notre Dame Congregation of Holy Cross, United States Province of Priests & Brothers.
Irawan, Paulus Bambang *s.j.* '10 (BO)[U] Brighton, MA Francis Xavier House.
Ireland, Dave R. '83 (CLV) South Euclid, OH Sacred Heart of Jesus Parish.
Irish, Robert '92 (LAN) On Duty Outside the Diocese.
Irizarry, Alan M. '83 (MO) On Duty Outside the Diocese; Army Chaplains.
Irizarry, Elvin A. '97 (ARE) Utuado, PR Our Lady of Sorrows.
Irizarry Roman, Elvin A. '97 (ARE) Prison Services.
Irizzary, Jose Fernando *o.f.m.cap.* '01 (SJN)[C] Rio Piedras, PR Fraternidad Santa Maria de Los Angeles.
Iroh, Anthony '94 (BRK) Brooklyn, NY St. Dominic.
Iromenu, Anthony '95 (FRS) Wofford Heights, CA St. Jude.
Ironuma, Donatus '94 (SPR)[D] Springfield, MA CHE – The Mercy Hospital, Inc.; Springfield, MA Mary Mother of Hope Parish.
Iroot, Francis *a.j.* (NY) New York, NY St. Cecilia.
Irrgang, Kenneth E. '68 (NU) Retired.
Irudamoney, Arul Joseph '91 (BIS) Glen Ullin, ND Sacred Heart of Jesus; Glen Ullin, ND St. Joseph; Hebron, ND St. Clement (Oratory).
Irudayaraj, Arokiasamy Madhichetty '01 (LR) Wynne, AR St. Peter; Wynne, AR St. Mary Church.
Irudayaraj, Arul Pragasam *s.v.d.* '06 (SB) Riverside, CA Queen of Angels.
Irudayaraj, Nalazala '93 (SCR) Olyphant, PA Holy Cross Parish; Throop, PA Blessed Sacrament Parish.
Irvin, Charles '67 (LAN) Promoter of Justice Retired.
Irving, Alfred E. '71 (PRT) Retired.
Irving, G. Peter '83 (LA) Long Beach, CA Holy Innocents.
Irwin, Den '01 (MOB)[I] Troy, AL St. Martin Catholic Newman Center.
Irwin, James W. *c.s.c.* '65 (FTW)[H] Notre Dame Congregation of Holy Cross, United States Province of Priests & Brothers.
Irwin, Joseph F. '62 (NY) Mamaroneck, NY Most Holy Trinity.
Irwin, Joseph M. '05 (OKL) Enid, OK St. Francis

Xavier; Council of Priests Archdiocesan; Region VII.
Irwin, Rev. Msgr. Kevin W. '71 (WDC) On Duty Outside the Archdiocese; [C] Catholic University of America, The.
Irwin, Michael Den '01 (MOB) Troy, AL St. Martin of Tours; Priests' Eucharistic League.
Irwin, Patrick F. '59 (MAN) Retired.
Irwin, Rev. Msgr. Patrick '69 (SP) Clearwater, FL St. Cecelia; Incardination Committee.
Irwin, Robert C. (B) Soda Springs, ID Good Shepherd Catholic Community.
Irwin, Robert '78 (FAR) Advocates; Auditor.
Isaac, Dominic '87 (PH) Apostleship of the Sea; Philadelphia, PA St. William; Pakistani Apostolate.
Isaac, Makarios F. *m.m.* '88 (FgM) Maryknoll, NY MARYKNOLL.
Isaac, Monica '10 (CHI)[J] Maywood, IL Loyola University Medical Center.
Isaac, Tariq (HBG) Lancaster, PA St. Joseph.
Isaacon, James E. *s.j.c.* '04 (CHI) Volo, IL St. Peter.
Isaacson, James *s.j.c.* '04 (CHI)[P] Chicago, IL Canons Regular of Saint John Cantius.
Isacsson, Alfred *o.carm.* '58 (NY) Middletown, NY Our Lady of Mt. Carmel.
Ischay, Matthew A. '75 (CLV) Administrative Leave.
Ishida, Michael L. '06 (SPK) Wilbur, WA St. Joseph; Wilbur, WA Sacred Heart.
Ishmael, Keith E. '03 (ALX) Jena, LA St. Mary.
Isidor, Rahab '06 (SPC) Webb City, MO Sacred Heart.
Isinta, Christopher D. '04 (NEW) Roseland, NJ Our Lady of the Blessed Sacrament.
Isla, Elias (NY) New York, NY St. Jude.
Isla Chavez, Mario Genaro '04 (PCE) Juana Diaz, PR St. Raymond Nonato.
Isopo, Dominic '80 (ALB) Schenectady, NY St. Luke; Priestly Life and Ministry Council.
Issac, Jose '75 (RNO) Sparks, NV Holy Cross Catholic Community.
Issing, Daniel J. *c.s.c.* '90 (SCR)[B] Holy Cross Community.
Issing, Daniel J. *c.s.c.* '90 (FTW)[H] Notre Dame Congregation of Holy Cross, United States Province of Priests & Brothers.
Isukala, Ananda R. '98 (CHI) Northbrook, IL Our Lady of the Brook.
Iszezuck, Cyril *o.s.b.m.* '89 (STF) New York, NY St. George; Sodalities, B.V.M.
Ittiyappara, Mathew '67 (SR) Retired.
Itube, Rene J. '64 (SFR) Deans.
Itukulapati, Joji '88 (SFS) Faulkton, SD St. Thomas the Apostle.
Iturbe, Rene *s.m.* '74 (SFR) San Francisco, CA Notre Dame des Victoires; Boston, MA; College of Consultors.
Iturrieta, Pablo Daniel Munoz *i.v.e.* '06 (WDC) Mount Rainier, MD St. James.
Iturrizaga, Johnny C. *c.m.v.* '97 (ARE) Sabana Hoyos, PR Nuestra Senora de Fatima.
Itzaina, John *s.d.b.* '74 (SFR) San Francisco, CA SS. Peter and Paul.
Iulio, Vaiula '06 (SPP) Pago Pago, AS Christ the King; Pago Pago, AS Sts. Peter & Paul.
Ivan, Nicholas '56 (PRM) Retired.
Ivanov, Mykola '05 (PHU) Pottstown, PA SS. Peter and Paul; Pottstown, PA St. Michael's; Defender of the Bond.
Ivans, Joseph *o.c.d.* '53 (GRY)[H] Munster, IN Discalced Carmelite Fathers Monastery.
Ivany, Mark '08 (WDC) Bowie, MD St. Pius X.
Ivers, Rev. Msgr. Leslie J. '79 (NY) New York, NY Epiphany.
Ivers, Victor J. '45 (CHI) Retired.
Ivey, David J. '86 (AUS) Brenham, TX St. Mary of the Immaculate Conception; Vandenberg Air Force Base.
Ivory, Rev. Msgr. Thomas P. '64 (NEW) West Orange, NJ St. Joseph's Retired.
Iwan, Janusz '76 (DET) Detroit, MI St. Hyacinth.
Iwaniec, Wieslaw '86 (SAT) Uvalde, TX Sacred Heart.
Iwanowski, Thomas B. '75 (NEW) New Milford, NJ St. Joseph's; Office of Divine Worship.
Iwasiw, Nestor '93 (PHU) Presbyteral Council; Archeparchial Seminary Advisory and Admissions Board; Olyphant, PA SS. Cyril and Methodius; Procurator/Advocate.
Iweh, Emmanuel '84 (SEA) Snohomish, WA St. Michael; Snohomish County Jail.
Iwele, Gode *o.m.i.* (NY) New York, NY St. Andrew.
Iwu, Ifeanyi '90 (PAT) Denville, NJ St. Clare Hospital.
Iwu, Pius Ajunwa '77 (LR) Stuttgart, AR Holy Rosary; Presbyteral Council; Stuttgart, AR SS. Cyril and Methodius; [K] Stuttgart, AR Holy Rosary Catholic School "Vision 2000" Educational Trust Fund.
Iwuala, Ishamel O. '87 (NY) Bronx, NY Bronx–Lebanon Hospital Center; Bronx, NY Our Lady of Victory.
Iwuala, Peter O. '09 (NEW) Bloomfield, NJ Sacred Heart.
Iwuc, Anthony D. '53 (PRO)[O] Providence St. John Vianney Residence Retired.
Iwuchukwu, Azuka (WDC)[L] Washington, DC Georgetown University Hospital.
Iwuchukwu, Azuka '87 (WIL) Elsmere, DE Veteran's Hospital.
Iwuchukwu, Azuka '87 (MO) DEPARTMENT OF VETERANS AFFAIRS HOSPITALS AND CHAPLAINS.
Iwuji, Luke '97 (DET) Dearborn, MI Oakwood Hospital; [H] Livonia, MI St. Mary Mercy Hospital.
Iwuji, Matthew C. '74 (AUS) Austin, TX Sacred Heart.
Iwuji, Matthew C. '74 (SAT) Defenders of the Bond.
Iwuji, Paulinus *s.m.m.m.* '01 (AUS) Austin, TX Seton/Brackenridge Hospital.
Iwuoha, Anastasius (SLC) Sandy, UT Saint Thomas More Catholic Church LLC 248.
Iwuoha, Kevin '97 (SFE) Arroyo Seco, NM La Santisima Trinidad.
Izac, Andre C. (WDC) On Duty Outside the Archdiocese.
Izaguirre, Jorge R. *c.s.c.* '97 (FTW)[H] Notre Dame Congregation of Holy Cross, United States Province of Priests & Brothers.
Izen, Michael J. '05 (STP) Crystal, MN St. Raphael.
Izer, Rt. Rev. Wesley W. '77 (HPM) Gilbert, AZ St. Thomas the Apostle; Finance Officer; Chancellor; College of Consultors; Finance Council; Building and Sacred Arts Commission; Pension Committee; Personnel Board; Ecclesiatical Notaries.
Izral, John '56 (BLX) Retired.
Izral, John '56 (SJP) Arnold, PA St. Vladimir; Presbyters.
Izuka, Emmanuel '97 (SFE) Cimarron, NM Immaculate Conception Church; Springer, NM St. Joseph.
Izyk, Andrew '74 (CHI) Chicago, IL St. Monica.
Izzo, Brian A. '98 (PH) Brookhaven, PA Our Lady of Charity.
Izzo, D. Dominic *o.p.* '94 (FgM) New York, NY Province of St. Joseph (Eastern).
Izzo, David Dominic *o.p.* '94 (NY)[HH] New York, NY The Dominican Foundation of Dominican Friars, Province of St. Joseph, Inc.; [HH] New York, NY St. Jude Dominican Missions; New York, NY; New York, NY St. Joseph; [HH] Dominican Mission Secretariat.
Izzo, Dominic *o.p.* '94 (WDC)[X] Washington, DC Rosary Shrine of St. Jude; New York, NY Dominican Mission Secretariate.
Izzo, Januarius *o.f.m.* '62 (NY)[DD] New York Franciscan Province of the Immaculate Conception.
Izzo, Januarius *o.f.m.* '48 (BO)[U] Boston, MA St. Christopher Friary Retired.

J

Jablonske, William (LC)[D] Chippewa Falls, WI St. Joseph's Hospital Retired.
Jablonski, Edward J. '96 (PH) On Special or Other Archdiocesan Assignment; Downingtown, PA St. Joseph; [W] Downingtown, PA Catholic Health Care Services–Villa Saint Martha; [V] Downingtown, PA St. Martha Manor.
Jablonski, Joseph *m.s.c.* '76 (RCK)[G].
Jablonski, Rev. Msgr. William W. '63 (RVC)[N] Amityville, NY St. Pius X Residence Retired.
Jabo, Scott W. '90 (E)[C] Erie, PA Villa Maria Academy; Erie, PA St. James; [C] Erie, PA Erie Catholic Preparatory School; [C] Erie, PA Cathedral Preparatory School.
Jabusch, Willard F. '56 (CHI)[W] Wilmette, IL Musica Pacis Retired.
Jach, Edward M. *s.m.* '64 (CIN) Presbyteral Council; [N] Dayton, OH Mercy Siena Support Community.
Jacinto, Marty Borbon '01 (NEW) Jersey City, NJ Our Lady of Mercy.
Jack, Cuthbert A. *o.s.b.* '90 (GBG)[H] Latrobe, PA Saint Vincent Archabbey.
Jack, Cuthbert A. *o.s.b.* '90 (PBR) Homer City, PA St. Mary's Holy Protection.
Jack, Duane C. '67 (PEO) Colona, IL St. Patrick's.
Jack, J. Robert '92 (CIN)[B] Cincinnati, OH Mount St. Mary's Seminary of the West.
Jackiewicz, Frederick W. '71 (TR) Leave of Absence.
Jacklin, Richard '84 (JOL) Kankakee, IL Shapiro Development Center; Bonfield, IL Sacred Heart.
Jackovic, George V. '46 (PIT) Retired.
Jackson, James M. '75 (WIL) Bear, DE St. Elizabeth Ann Seton.
Jackson, James R. *m.m.* '58 (FgM) Maryknoll, NY MARYKNOLL.
Jackson, James *f.s.s.p.* '85 (DEN) Littleton, CO Our Lady of Mount Carmel.
Jackson, Joseph M. '74 (CHI) Chicago, IL St. Ignatius.
Jackson, Lawrence J. '60 (DET) Retired.
Jackson, Richard '10 (CHR) Florence, SC St. Anthony.
Jackson, Robert H. '84 (CLV) Norton, OH Prince of Peace; Presbyteral Council; Presbyteral Conveners.
Jacob, Abraham M. '80 (CHI) Chicago, IL Our Lady of Victory; [J] Chicago, IL Our Lady of the Resurrection Medical Center.
Jacob, Abraham Mutholathu '80 (SYM) Vicar General (Syncellus); St. Paul, MN Syro–Malabar Knanaya Catholic Mission of Minnesota.
Jacob, Anthony J. *o.s.b.* '65 (JOL)[L] Lisle, IL St. Procopius Abbey; Lisle, IL.
Jacob, Jerome J. '92 (CHI) Arlington Heights, IL St. Edna.
Jacob, Jose *s.m.m.* '86 (RVC)[N] Bay Shore, NY Montfort Missionaries.
Jacob, Leonardo M. '88 (RCK) Elizabeth, IL St. Mary; Hanover, IL St. John the Evangelist.
Jacob, Lijoy *o.carm* '04 (WDC)[B] Washington, DC Whitefriars Hall.
Jacob, Matthew *d.s.* '07 (PHX) Gilbert, AZ St. Mary Magdalene Roman Catholic Parish.
Jacob, Roy (BRK)[R] Brooklyn, NY Carmelites of Mary Immaculate, Inc.; Brooklyn, NY St. Anthony of Padua–St. Alphonsus.
Jacobi, Arthur '81 (DET) Retired.
Jacobi, Joseph A. '91 (OKL) Oklahoma City, OK St. Eugene's; Council of Priests Archdiocesan.
Jacobs, Charles E. '86 (HRT) Hartford, CT Holy Trinity.
Jacobs, Gilbert H. *o.praem.* '55 (GB)[J] De Pere, WI St. Norbert Abbey.
Jacobs, Richard A. (PAT) Retired.
Jacobs, Richard M. *o.s.a.* '83 (JOL)[L] New Lenox, IL Augustinian Friary.
Jacobs, Richard *o.s.a.* '76 (PH)[C] Villanova University.
Jacobs, William '03 (KAL) Benton Harbor, MI Ss. John & Bernard; Diocesan Finance Council; Vicars Forane.
Jacobson, Clifford '96 (CHY) Clergy Continuing Education Grants; Gillette, WY St. Matthew's.
Jacobson, Gary '65 (P) Retired.
Jacobson, James *s.j.* (SPK)[J] Spokane, WA Regis Community.
Jacobus, Michael J. '08 (MAR) Ontonagon, MI Holy Family; Ontonagon, MI St. Mary; White Pine, MI St. Jude.
Jacquel, John B. '83 (E) Erie, PA Holy Rosary; Erie, PA St. John the Baptist.
Jacquemin, George '72 (CIN) Cincinnati, OH St. Clare; Vicarri Foranei (Deans).
Jacques, Alfred '60 (PRT) Retired.
Jacques, Donald W. '53 (PRT) Retired.
Jacques, Ernest J. *s.j.* '66 (NO)[R] New Orleans, LA Ignatius Residence.
Jacques, Eugene F. '80 (NO) Metairie, LA St. Catherine of Siena.
Jacques, Geto '99 (NEW) Elizabeth, NJ Our Lady of Most Holy Rosary/St. Michael.
Jacques, Michael P. *s.s.e.* '82 (NO) New Orleans, LA St. Peter Claver; Deans; Archdiocesan Consultors.
Jacques, Roger N. '78 (BO) Health Leave.
Jacunski, Robert D. '56 (NEW)[L] Caldwell, NJ The Rev. Msgr. James F. Kelley Residence for Retired Priests Retired.
Jadin, Samuel D. *o.praem.* '55 (GB)[K] Manitowoc, WI Holy Family Convent of Franciscan Sisters of Christian Charity.
Jadotte, Jean '06 (MIA) Miramar, FL St. Bartholomew.
Jadwisiak, Edmund '79 (PRM) Retired.
Jaeb, Maurus P. *o.s.b.* '95 (OKL) Del City, OK St. Paul, Apostle; [I] Shawnee, OK St. Gregory's Abbey.
Jaeger, David *o.f.m.* '86 (FgM) Washington, DC COMMISSARIAT OF THE HOLY LAND.
Jaeger, David Maria A. *o.f.m.* '86 (SAT) Judges.
Jaeger, James P. '86 (ROC) Hammondsport, NY St. Gabriel; Bath, NY St. Mary; Air National Guard Chaplains.
Jaeger, Louis M. '73 (DUB) Lay Formation Advisory Board; American Martyrs Retreat House Advisory Board; [G] Waterloo, IA Columbus High School; Waterloo, IA Sacred Heart; [G] Waterloo, IA Cedar Valley Catholic Schools; Priestly Life and Ministry Committee.
Jaeger, Rev. Msgr. Robert E. '90 (COS) Colorado Springs, CO Saint Paul; Vicar General; Vicar for Clergy; Presbyteral Council; College of Consultors; Vicar General; Vicar General.
Jaffe, Joel D. '03 (ARL)[D] Fairfax, VA Paul VI Catholic High School.
Jagdfeld, Lawrence *o.f.m.* '75 (CHI)[N] Cicero, IL San Damiano Friary Order of Friars Minor.
Jagela, Walter M. '94 (WH) Absent on Leave.
Jagerstatter, Victor '06 (B) Weiser, ID St. Agnes.
Jagielski, James J. '77 (DET) Retired.
Jagodensky, Joe *s.d.s.* '80 (MIL)[N] Milwaukee, WI Alexian Village of Milwaukee, Inc.; [P] Milwaukee Salvatorian Provincial Offices.
Jagodzinski, Charles *o.f.m.conv.* (CHL)[L] Winston–Salem, NC Wake Forest University and Winston–Salem University; Winston–Salem, NC Our Lady of Mercy.
Jagodzinski, Rev. Msgr. John J. '62 (PH) Broomall, PA St. Pius X.
Jagoe, Bede R. *o.p.* '60 (CHI)[N] River Forest, IL St. Thomas Aquinas Priory.
Jagudilla, Julian S. *o.f.m.* '08 (NEW) Wood Ridge, NJ Our Lady of the Assumption.
Jakel, Pat Gerald '85 (SFD) Troy, IL St. Jerome.
Jakobiak, Arthur '56 (SFE) Retired.
Jakopac, George I. '00 (ALT) New Baltimore, PA St. John the Baptist.
Jakopac, George I. '00 (BAL) On Duty Outside the Archdiocese.
Jaksina, Edward S. '55 (HRT) Seymour, CT Good Shepherd.
Jakub, John T. '02 (TR) Neptune, NJ Holy Innocents.

Jakub, Joseph A. '06 (TR)[B] Lawrenceville, NJ Notre Dame High School; [T] Trenton, NJ Emmaus House, Rider University; [T] Hamilton Township, NJ Mercer County Community College; Catholic Campaign for Human Development.

Jakubauskas, Richard A. '99 (WOR) Petersham, MA St. Peter; Athol, MA St. Francis; Athol, MA Our Lady Immaculate; Members.

Jakubco, Bernard *m.s.c.* '64 (PT) Perry, FL Immaculate Conception.

Jakubik, Richard '93 (CHI) Wilmette, IL St. Francis Xavier; Associate Administrators.

Jakubowicz, Greg *o.f.m.* '04 (ALB)[B] Loudonville, NY Siena College; [B] Siena College; [Q] Loudonville, NY Siena College.

Jakubowski, Allen F. '75 (LC) Durand, WI St. Mary's Assumption; Durand, WI Holy Rosary; Durand, WI Sacred Heart of Jesus; Personnel Council.

Jalbert, Edward *c.j.* '87 (LA)[B] Santa Maria, CA St. Joseph Seminary (Josephite Fathers' Novitiate); [D] Santa Maria, CA St. Joseph High School.

Jalbert, Jason Y. '03 (MAN) Masters of Ceremonies; Vocations Office; Office for Worship; Real Estate Board.

Jalbert, Robert A. *m.m.* '79 (NY)[DD] Maryknoll Maryknoll Fathers and Brothers.

Jallas, Robert J. '84 (SFD) Springfield, IL St. Agnes.

Jamail, Rev. Msgr. Michael A. '60 (BEA) Vicar General and Moderator of the Curia; Diocesan College of Consultors; Promoter of Justice; Defender of Bond; Psychologists for the Tribunal; Beaumont, TX St. Anne; Presbyteral Council.

Jambon, Jeffery '01 (NO) Abita Springs, LA St. Jane de Chantal; On Special Assignment.

James, David J. '91 (SY) Syracuse, NY Veterans Administration Hospital.

James, David John '91 (MO) DEPARTMENT OF VETERANS AFFAIRS HOSPITALS AND CHAPLAINS.

James, Rev. Msgr. David L. '96 (ALN) Whitehall, PA Holy Trinity; Promoter of Justice; Advocates; Vocations Office; College of Consultors; Appointed Members; Defenders of the Bond; Vice Chancellor.

James, Rev. Msgr. Joseph W. '57 (LUB)[B] Slaton, TX Our Lady of Mercy Retreat Center Retired.

James, Joy *o.s.h.* '01 (GAL) Houston, TX St. Vincent de Paul; [O] Missouri City, TX The Society of the Oblates of Sacred Heart.

James, Saji *m.s.t.* '98 (SP) New Port Richey, FL Our Lady Queen of Peace.

James, Thomas *s.v.d.* '69 (LAF) Lafayette, LA Immaculate Heart of Mary.

James, V. Warwick '80 (SJ) Los Altos, CA St. Simon.

James, Rev. Msgr. William R. '54 (MOB) Retired.

Jameson, Rev. Msgr. W. Ronald '68 (WDC) Washington, DC St. Matthew Cathedral; Deans; Archdiocesan Sacred Arts Committee; Commission on Sacred Art and Architecture.

Jamieson, Andrew '88 (TR) Tabernacle, NJ Holy Eucharist.

Jamison, Dale *o.f.m.* '74 (PHX) Sacaton, AZ St. Peter; Native American Ministry, Office of; Laveen, AZ St. John The Baptist.

Jamnicky, John A. '72 (CHI) Old Mill Creek, IL St. Raphael the Archangel.

Jamros, Daniel P. *s.j.* '76 (BO)[U] Boston The Society of Jesus of New England–Provincial Offices.

Jamros, Daniel P. *s.j.* '76 (BUF)[N] Buffalo, NY Canisius Jesuit Community Inc.

Jamroz, Sigmund S. *m.m.* '66 (FgM) Maryknoll, NY MARYKNOLL.

Janaczek, Joseph P. '71 (BUF) Falconer, NY St. Patrick; Falconer, NY Our Lady of Loreto.

Janak, Gary W. '88 (VIC) Chancellor; Diocesan Consultors; El Campo Deanery; Judges; Priests' Personnel Board; Propagation of the Faith, Holy Childhood Association; Mission Cooperative Plan; Victim Assistance Coordinators; Presbyteral Council; El Campo, TX St. Philip the Apostle.

Janas, Camillus *o.f.m.* '59 (CHI)[N] Chicago, IL Holy Name Friary; Niles, IL St. Isaac Jogues.

Janasik, Daniel R. '09 (MIL) Mequon, WI St. Francis Borgia.

Jancarz, Janusz Jay '83 (VEN) Parrish, FL Saint Frances Xavier Cabrini.

Janczak, Krzysztof '05 (CHI) Niles, IL St. John Brebeuf.

Jandaczek, Peter '99 (OKL) Duncan, OK Assumption.

Jandernoa, Ronald L. '94 (MET) Blairstown, NJ St. Jude; College of Consultors; Deans.

Janeczek, Vladimir '59 (GRY) Hammond, IN St. Casimir Retired.

Janelli, Rev. Msgr. Anthony '64 (FRS) Visalia, CA St. Thomas the Apostle; Visalia, CA Holy Family; Visalia, CA St. Mary Retired.

Janes, David A. '83 (SFS) Retired.

Janes, David '75 (P) Retired.

Janette, Paul '63 (MIL) Retired.

Janezic, Lawrence R. *o.f.m.* '78 (IND) Indianapolis, IN Sacred Heart of Jesus Catholic Church, Indianapolis, Inc.

Janicki, Carl F. '94 (PH) Flourtown, PA St. Genevieve; On Special or Other Archdiocesan Assignment.

Janicki, Laurian *o.f.m.* '64 (PSC)[A] Sybertsville, PA Holy Dormition Friary; Sybertsville, PA Assumption B.V.M. Province.

Janiga, Bruce G. '83 (NEW)[C] West Orange, NJ Seton Hall Preparatory School.

Janiga, Joseph '45 (DET) Retired.

Janik, Anthony F. *o.f.m.* '70 (GRY)[D] Crown Point, IN Franciscan St. Anthony Health – Crown Point; [H] Cedar Lake, IN Our Lady of Lourdes Friary; Provincial Councilors.

Janik, Bruno '66 (CHI) Retired.

Janik, Leszek T. '92 (NOR) Vicar General; Diocesan Pastoral Council; Diocesan Finance Council; Advisory Board; Seminarian Advisory Board; Norwich, CT SS. Peter and Paul; College of Consultors; Presbyteral Council; Judges.

Janise, Johnathan J. '11 (LAF) Carencro, LA St. Peter.

Janish, Rev. Msgr. James '69 (SAT) Judges; Macdona, TX Our Lady Queen of Heaven; Von Ormy, TX Sacred Heart; College of Consultors; Archdiocesan Presbyteral Council.

Janiszeski, Joseph J. *t.o.r.* '78 (PIT) Pittsburgh, PA St. Matthew.

Janiunas, Albin F. '48 (BO) Senior Priests. Retired.

Jank, Tadeusz '96 (NEW) Linden, NJ St. Theresa of the Child Jesus.

Janko, John *s.d.b.* '78 (NEW)[C] Ramsey, NJ Don Bosco Preparatory High School; [L] Ramsey, NJ Don Bosco Prep Salesian Residence.

Jankowiak, Patrick M. '92 (SAG) Mount Pleasant, MI St. Joseph the Worker.

Jankowski, James *o.f.m. conv.* '99 (LAV) Las Vegas, NV St. Elizabeth Ann Seton.

Jankowski, James *o.f.m.cap.* (LAV) Presbyteral Council for the Diocese of Las Vegas.

Jankowski, Peter G. '96 (JOL) Joliet, IL St. Patrick.

Jankowski, Richard '92 (SP) Spring Hill, FL St. Frances Xavier Cabrini; Diocesan Finance Council.

Jankowski, Stanislaw *c.r.* '94 (CHI) Chicago, IL St. Hedwig.

Jankowski, Valentine M. *o.f.m.conv.* '61 (LSC) Carlsbad, NM San Jose; Loving, NM Our Lady of Grace; Vicars; Diocesan Consultors; Presbyteral Council.

Jann, Francis J. '47 (BUF) Rushford, NY St. Mark Retired.

Janoch, Edward J. '00 (CLV) Northfield, OH St. Barnabas.

Janocha, Carl William '91 (OKL) Elk City, OK St. Matthew's.

Janoski, Steven A. '88 (SFD)[B] Springfield, IL Benedictine University at Springfield; Special or Other Diocesan Assignment.

Janovec, James J. '64 (GI) Wood River, NE St. Mary's.

Janowiak, Paul A. *s.j.* '84 (OAK)[L] Berkeley, CA Jesuit Fathers and Brothers; [A] Berkeley, CA Jesuit School of Theology of Santa Clara University (Berkeley, California Campus).

Janowiak, Paul *s.j.* '84 (OAK)[A] Berkeley, CA Jesuit School of Theology of Santa Clara University (Berkeley, California Campus).

Janowicz, Barney J. '57 (SAG) Retired.

Janowicz, Richard '80 (STN) Springfield, OR Nativity of the Mother of God; Diocesan Consultors; Personnel Board; South–West.

Janowski, Lawrence *o.f.m.* '73 (CHI)[N] Chicago, IL Holy Name Friary.

Janowski, Michael S. '03 (GLD) Lake Leelanau, MI St. Mary; Members of the College of Consultors.

Janowski, Rock J. '64 (LA) Retired.

Janowski, Stan *o.f.m.* '66 (MIL)[P] Burlington, WI Queen of Peace Friary.

Janowski, Wesley '93 (LC) Cazenovia, WI St. Anthony de Padua; Richland Center, WI Nativity of the Blessed Virgin Mary; Cazenovia, WI Sacred Heart.

Jansch, Ronald *o.f.m.cap.* '50 (MIL)[P] Mount Calvary, WI St. Lawrence Friary Retired.

Jansen, Anthony *s.m.* '54 (CIN)[N] Dayton, OH Marianist Community.

Jansen, Raymond L. '99 (LIN) Ulysses, NE Immaculate Conception.

Jansen, William J. *m.c.c.j.* '66 (CIN)[N] Cincinnati, OH Comboni Missionaries (Verona Fathers)–Comboni Mission Center.

Janski, Jerome J. '50 (STP) Retired.

Janson, Christian A. *s.m.* '73 (SAT)[L] San Antonio, TX Holy Rosary Marianist Community; In Metropolitan Area; Archdiocesan Presbyteral Council; Priests Personnel Board; San Antonio, TX Holy Rosary.

Janssen, Henri *o.m.i.* '43 (SAT)[K] San Antonio, TX Oblate Madonna Residence.

Janton, Anthony W. '77 (PH) Abington, PA Our Lady Help of Christians.

Janus, Mark–David *c.s.p.* '79 (NEW)[L] Mahwah, NJ Paulist Fathers – Paulist Press; [Q] Mahwah, NJ Paulist Press.

Janus, Mark–David *c.s.p.* '79 (NY)[DD] New York, NY Paulist Fathers' Motherhouse.

Januszkiewicz, Henry '62 (WDC) Retired.

Janvier, Paul '00 (TR) Asbury Park, NJ Holy Spirit.

Janze, John E. '75 (ORG) Irvine, CA St. Thomas More; Council of Priests; Consultors.

Jao, Radmar '11 (SFR) San Francisco, CA St. Agnes.

Jaques, Domingos '47 (OAK) Retired.

Jaramillo, Ernesto '11 (LA) Encino, CA Our Lady of Grace.

Jaramillo, Jose G. *m.g.* '80 (SB) Highland, CA St. Adelaide; Special or Other Diocesan Assignment.

Jaramillo, Leonardo '92 (PAT) Clifton, NJ St. Paul.

Jaramillo, Luis '60 (SFE) Retired.

Jaramillo, Misael '01 (PAT) Paterson, NJ Blessed Sacrament; Paterson, NJ Our Lady of Lourdes.

Jaramillo, Oscar '90 (B) Emmett, ID Sacred Heart.

Jaramillo, Pablo *o.f.m.cap.* '08 (FWT) Fort Worth, TX Our Lady of Guadalupe.

Jaramillo, Peter *s.s.a.* '81 (KCK)[K] Kansas City, KS Society of St. Augustine – Public Association of the Faithful; Kansas City, KS Holy Family; Kansas City, KS St. Mary–St. Anthony; Kansas City, KS St. John the Baptist.

Jaramillo, Peter '81 (MO) Army National Guard Chaplains.

Jaranilla, Roberto '96 (LA) Pomona, CA St. Joseph.

Jarboe, Rev. Msgr. J. Bruce '86 (BAL) Baltimore, MD Cathedral of Mary Our Queen.

Jarecki, Michael S. '44 (OG) Retired.

Jarmoluk, Rev. Msgr. Joseph F. '84 (RCK) Spring Grove, IL St. Peter.

Jaron, Glenn Giovanni *m.s.p.* '91 (SAC) Fort Jones, CA Sacred Heart; Yreka, CA St. Joseph.

Jaros, Joseph P. '56 (TOL) Judges Retired.

Jarosch, Eugene H. *s.a.c.* '51 (MIL)[P] Milwaukee, WI St. Vincent Community.

Jarosewic, Daniel '71 (CHI) Homewood, IL St. Joseph.

Jarosz, Peter '89 (JOL) Lombard, IL Christ the King; [O] Joliet, IL The Upper Room Crisis Hotline (TURCH).

Jarosz, Stanley '65 (MET) Helmetta, NJ Holy Trinity.

Jaroszeski, Paul A. '76 (STP) Ramsey, MN St. Katharine Drexel.

Jarreau, Niel *s.j.* '56 (ATL)[H] Atlanta, GA Ignatius House.

Jarrell, Stephen T. '73 (IND) Indianapolis, IN Christ The King Catholic Church, Indianapolis, Inc.

Jarret, Peter A. *c.s.c.* '92 (FTW)[A] Notre Dame, IN Moreau Seminary; [H] Notre Dame, IN Congregation of Holy Cross, United States Province of Priests & Brothers; Provincial Councilors:; Members; [A] Notre Dame, IN Moreau Seminary.

Jarret, Peter C. *c.s.c.* (FTW)[K] Notre Dame, IN Father Edward Sorin Trust.

Jarvis, Edward A. *s.j.* '54 (PH)[Y] Loyola Center and Manresa Hall.

Jarvis, Paul '04 (STP) Rosemount, MN St. Joseph.

Jarzombek, Casimir '60 (VIC) Bay City, TX Holy Cross Retired.

Jarzombek, Dennis '79 (SAT) Stockdale, TX St. Mary.

Jasany, Robert J. '79 (CLV) Cleveland, OH St. John Nepomucene; Presbyteral Conveners.

Jasilek, Bartlomiej *s.v.d.* '09 (LAF) Opelousas, LA Holy Ghost.

Jasinski, Andrew '98 (FAR) Diocesan College of Consultors; Catholic Education and Formation.

Jasinski, Andrew '98 (FAR) West Fargo, ND Holy Cross Church of West Fargo.

Jasinski, Rev. Msgr. Anthony J. '49 (BUF)[N] Lackawanna, NY Bishop Head Residence Retired.

Jasinski, Raymond J. '54 (CHI)[M] Justice, IL Rosary Hill Home Retired.

Jaskierny, Joseph '11 (RCK) Cary, IL SS. Peter & Paul.

Jaskot, Rev. Msgr. Robert J. '98 (BAL) Middletown, MD Holy Family Catholic Community; [A] Baltimore, MD St. Mary's Seminary and University.

Jaskowiak, Wojciech B. '03 (NEW) On Duty Outside the Archdiocese.

Jaskowiak, Wojciech B. '03 (AGN) Merizo, GU San Dimas and Our Lady of the Rosary; Merizo, GU San Dionisio; [A] Yona, GU Redemptoris Mater Archdiocesan Missionary Seminary.

Jaskula, Edward *c.r.* '55 (CHI)[D] Chicago, IL Gordon Tech High School.

Jaskulski, Bronislaus *o.f.m.* '46 (MIL)[P] Burlington, WI Queen of Peace Friary.

Jaskulski, George *o.f.m.* '55 (CLV)[N] Garfield Heights, OH Marymount Convent; [O] Garfield Heights, OH Marymount Congregational Home; [M] Garfield Heights, OH Village at Marymount.

Jaskulski, Nathan *o.f.m.* '61 (GB)[K] Manitowoc, WI Holy Family Convent of Franciscan Sisters of Christian Charity.

Jaskulski, Nathan *o.f.m.* '61 (CHI)[N] Chicago, IL Holy Name Friary.

Jasmin, Arsene (WDC) Washington, DC Shrine of the Sacred Heart.

Jasney, Robert J. '79 (CLV) Presbyteral Council.

Jasper, Frank *o.f.m.* '73 (CIN)[C] Cincinnati, OH St. Anthony Shrine, Franciscan Postulancy; [N] Cincinnati, OH St. Francis Seraph Friary.

Jasper, John '00 (BAK) Retired.

Jasper, Louis H. '51 (COV) Retired.

Jaspers, David Leo '09 (P) Springfield, OR St. Alice.

Jaspers, J. Dennis '66 (CIN) Cincinnati, OH All Saints; Presbyteral Council; Consultors.
Jasso, Jaroslav *c.m.* '93 (CHI)[N] Chicago DePaul Vincentian Residence.
Jasso, Stephen *t.o.r.* '65 (FWT) Fort Worth, TX All Saints; Diocesan School Advisory Council; Mission Council.
Jastrab, David J. '75 (PIT) Sewickley, PA St. Mary.
Jaszczuk, Radoslaw *c.ss.r.* '91 (CHI) Cicero, IL St. Mary of Czestochowa.
Jaszek, Stanislaw '88 (FBK) Presbyteral Council; Pilot Station, AK St. Charles Spinola Catholic Church Pilot Station; Consultors.
Jaume, John *c.r.* '66 (NY) Plattekill, NY Our Lady of Fatima.
Jauregui, Luke '05 (SD) Chula Vista, CA Saint Pius X Catholic Parish Chula Vista.
Java, Miguel B. '73 (LA) Guadalupe, CA Our Lady of Guadalupe; La Puente, CA St. Louis of France.
Javier, Francisco (NEW) South Kearny, NJ Hudson County Correctional Center.
Javier, Nazareno '98 (BRK) On Leave/Unassigned.
Jawa, Stanley *s.v.d.* (LAF) Opelousas, LA Holy Ghost; St. Martinville, LA Notre Dame de Perpetuel Secours.
Jawidzik, Edward M. '81 (TR) Freehold, NJ St. Robert Bellarmine.
Jaworowski, Rev. Msgr. Anthony E. '44 (PH) Retired.
Jaworowski, Grzegorz '93 (HRT) Derby, CT St. Jude.
Jayachandra, Hermanagild '68 (DEN) Boulder, CO St. Martin de Porres.
Jayaraj, M. Jones '83 (TYL) Frankston, TX St. Charles Borromeo.
Jayasuriya, Jerome '61 (DAL) Retired.
Jayasuriya, Jerome '61 (FWT) Albany, TX Jesus of Nazareth; Breckenridge, TX Sacred Heart.
Jayr, Canon Benoit '92 (MIL) Milwaukee, WI St. Stanislaus.
Jazdzewski, Brian J. '99 (LC) Fountain City, WI St. Lawrence; Waumandee, WI St. Boniface; Fountain City, WI Immaculate Conception.
Jazmin, Romeo D. '85 (RIC) Chesapeake, VA Prince of Peace.
Jazmines, Vicente F. '79 (OG) Ogdensburg, NY St. Lawrence Psychiatric Center; Ogdensburg, NY St. Mary's Cathedral.
Jazon, Yvans '07 (CAM) Atlantic City, NJ St. Monica's Catholic Church, Atlantic City, N.J.
Jean, Agapit H. '95 (MAN) Merrimack, NH St. John Neumann; Vicars Forane.
Jean, Aland *c.i.c.m.* '02 (ORL) Titusville, FL St. Teresa.
Jean, Antonio '99 (VEN) Bradenton, FL SS. Peter and Paul the Apostles.
Jean, Franky '93 (MIA) North Miami, FL Holy Family.
Jean, Lesly '83 (MIA) Appointed by the Archbishop; Miami, FL St. Thomas the Apostle.
Jean, Thony Roody '99 (ATL) Without Archdiocesan Assignment or Faculties; On Leave of Absence.
Jean–Louis, Arlin *o.m.i.* (BO) Cambridge, MA St. John the Evangelist; Brockton, MA Christ the King.
Jean–Mary, Reginald '01 (MIA) Miami, FL Notre Dame d'Haiti; Haitians.
Jean–Philippe, Jean Claude '88 (MIA) Hollywood, FL Nativity.
Jean–Pierre, Norbert '07 (PMB) West Palm Beach, FL Holy Name of Jesus.
Jeanfreau, James J. '92 (NO) Kenner, LA St. Jerome; Pontifical Mission Societies/Holy Childhood Association/Propagation of the Faith; Missionaries of St. Therese.
Jean Paul, Souvenir *s.m.* '97 (BRK) Kings County Hospital Center.
Jeanty, Chanel '04 (MIA) Vicar General; Chancellors.
Jeanty, Chanel '04 (MIA) Youth and Young Adult Ministry; Archdiocesan Vocations Review Board; Consultors; Judges; Ex Officio.
Jeanty, Succes (BO) Chelsea, MA St. Rose of Lima.
Jecewicz, Jerome '75 (BRK) Long Island City, NY St. Raphael.
Jednaki, P. Gregorz '08 (NOR) Norwich, CT St. Patrick Cathedral.
Jedrychowski, Janusz '95 (STF) Hudson, NY St. John the Baptist; Hudson, NY St. Nicholas.
Jedrzejewski, Richard '74 (BUF) Buffalo, NY Assumption.
Jeffers, Robert A. '54 (NY) New York, NY Our Lady of the Rosary Retired.
Jeffrey, C. James '59 (FAR) Retired.
Jeffrey, Donald *m.s.* '64 (WDC)[O] Washington, DC La Salette Formation Community.
Jeffrey, George A. '65 (SCR)[M] Dunmore, PA Villa St. Joseph Retired.
Jeffrey, James '59 (BEL) Retired.
Jeffries, Brian E. '73 (HRT) Canaan, CT St. Joseph; Canaan, CT Immaculate Conception.
Jekielek, Steven A. '11 (BUF) Tonawanda, NY St. Christopher.
Jelinek, Anthony (MIL)[N] Kenosha, WI St. Joseph's Home and Rehabilitation Center.
Jendrek, Michael J. '87 (BAL) Ijamsville, MD St. Ignatius of Loyola.
Jendrysik, Mark '85 (JOL) Naperville, IL St. Raphael; Cursillo.
Jenga, Fred *c.s.c.* (FTW)[H] Notre Dame Congregation of Holy Cross, United States Province of Priests & Brothers.
Jenik, Rev. Msgr. John J. '70 (NY) Bronx, NY Our Lady of Refuge; Bronx (Northwest); Archdiocesan Consultors; Priests Council of the Archdiocese of New York.
Jenkins, Aaron M. '08 (IND) Lawrenceburg, IN St. Teresa Benedicta of the Cross, Bright, Inc.
Jenkins, Alan *s.v.d.* '73 (SB) San Bernardino, CA Our Lady of the Rosary Cathedral.
Jenkins, J. Wayne '72 (L) Louisville, KY St. Albert the Great; Ex Officio.
Jenkins, John I. *c.s.c.* '83 (FTW)[B] University of Notre Dame Du Lac; [B] University of Notre Dame Du Lac; [H] Notre Dame, IN Holy Cross Community, Corby Hall, University of Notre Dame.
Jenkins, John M. '60 (CLV) Akron, OH St. Paul; Painesville, OH St. Mary Retired.
Jenkins, Joseph A. '86 (WDC) Mitchellville, MD Holy Family.
Jenkins, Rev. Msgr. Ron '89 (AUS) On Duty Outside the Diocese.
Jenkins, Rev. Msgr. Ronny E. '89 (DAL) Defensor Vinculi.
Jenkins, Rev. Msgr. Ronny (BAL) Canonical & Theological Consultants to the Archbishop.
Jenkins, Walter E. *c.s.c.* (FTW)[H] Notre Dame Congregation of Holy Cross, United States Province of Priests & Brothers.
Jenkins, Walter *c.s.c.* (BRK)[G] Flushing, NY Holy Cross High School.
Jenkins, Wayne *s.c.j.* '77 (MIL)[P] Hales Corners, WI Priests of the Sacred Heart.
Jenne, Walter H. '70 (CLV) Brecksville, OH St. Basil the Great.
Jennett, Rev. Msgr. Michael J. '74 (LA) Santa Barbara, CA San Roque; Santa Barbara Region.
Jenniges, Leonard J. '48 (NU) Retired.
Jennings, Henry J. '62 (BO) Somerville, MA St. Joseph.
Jennings, John A. '50 (SEA) Retired.
Jennings, Rev. Msgr. Joseph '43 (MOB) Retired.
Jennings, Michael T. '69 (KNX) Rogersville, TN St. Henry; Sneedville, TN St. James the Apostle.
Jennings, Paul F. '74 (WIL) Chester, MD St. Christopher; Deans.
Jennings, Thomas J. '69 (WIN) Luverne, MN St. Catherine's; Diocesan Consultors; Elected Deanery Representatives; Luverne, MN St. Mary's.
Jennings, Tommie '88 (SD) San Diego, CA Christ the King Catholic Parish; San Diego, CA Saint John the Evangelist Catholic Parish San Diego.
Jennings, William E. '40 (WIL) Retired.
Jenniskens, Thomas J. *s.j.* '56 (NO)[R] New Orleans, LA Ignatius Residence Retired.
Jennrich, Michael *o.f.m.* '87 (FgM) Saint Louis, MO Sacred Heart Province.
Jensen, Daniel P. *m.m.* '62 (NY)[DD] Retired.
Jensen, Jens–Peter (Jay) '01 (TUC) Sahuarita, AZ Roman Catholic Parish of San Martin De Porres – Sahuarita.
Jensen, Joseph *o.s.b.* '54 (WDC)[C] Catholic University of America, The; [O] Washington, DC St. Anselm's Abbey; [X] Washington, DC Catholic Biblical Association.
Jensen, Larry '88 (SAM) Waterville, ME St. Joseph.
Jenson, Glen T. '95 (STP) Minneapolis, MN Holy Cross; Minneapolis, MN St. Anthony of Padua; Minneapolis, MN St. Hedwig.
Jenuwine, David '09 (SAG) Saginaw, MI Cathedral of Mary the Assumption.
Jeon, Andrew Soo Hong '91 (JOL) Itasca, IL St. Andrew Kim.
Jeon, Dong Hyuk '01 (DET) Northville, MI St. Andrew Kim Korean Catholic Church.
Jerabek, Bryan W. '08 (BIR) Huntsville, AL Holy Spirit.
Jerek, John '88 (Y) Lowellville, OH Our Lady of the Holy Rosary; College of Consultors; Office of Vocations; Office of Clergy Services; Department of Clergy and Religious Services; Presbyteral Council.
Jeremiah, Ian '08 (BGP) Presbyteral Council; New Canaan, CT St. Aloysius.
Jerge, Lawrence A. *c.s.c.* '68 (FR) South Easton, MA Holy Cross.
Jerge, Lawrence A. *c.s.c.* '68 (FTW)[H] Notre Dame Congregation of Holy Cross, United States Province of Priests & Brothers.
Jerome, Louis R. '88 (NY) Staten Island, NY Sacred Heart; Archdiocesan Consultors.
Jerse, William M. '80 (CLV) Adjunct Judicial Vicars; Middleburg Heights, OH St. Bartholomew.
Jervis, Rev. Msgr. Paul W. '73 (BRK) Brooklyn, NY Saint Martin de Porres.
Jeselnick, Stephen E. '77 (E) Retired.
Jesionowski, Richard A. '68 (BUF) Cheektowaga, NY Our Lady Help of Christians.
Jeske, Richard *o.f.m.* '59 (STL) St. Louis, MO St. Anthony of Padua; [O] St. Louis, MO Franciscan Friary of St. Anthony of Padua.
Jesuraj, M. Maria Salethu *h.g.n.* (LEX) Louisa, KY St. Jude.
Jesusmaria, Marcelo de *c.r.* '04 (CHI) Chicago, IL St. Hedwig.
Jette, Mark R. '72 (HRT) West Haven, CT St. Lawrence; West Haven, CT St. Paul's.
Jewison, Harry P. '54 (WIN) Retired.
Jezierski, John '08 (LFT) Lafayette, IN St. Lawrence.
Jiang, Joseph Xiu Hui '10 (STL) St. Louis, MO Cathedral Basilica of Saint Louis; Archdiocesan Master of Ceremonies.
Jicha, John J. '95 (BAL) Williamsport, MD St. Augustine; Boonsboro, MD St. James Boonsboro Roman Catholic Congregation, Inc.
Jimenez, Adrian N. '87 (ARE) Arecibo, PR Cathedral of San Felipe Apostol; Cathedral of San Felipe Apostol.
Jimenez, Alvaro '84 (ORL) Orlando, FL St. Charles Borromeo.
Jimenez, David J. '95 (YAK) Judges; Selah, WA Our Lady of Lourdes; Adjutant Judicial Vicar.
Jimenez, Diego A. '11 (HRT) Hartford, CT St. Augustine.
Jimenez, Eloy (FTW) Plymouth, IN St. Michael; Plymouth.
Jimenez, Emilio B. '99 (CC) Bishop's Office; Personnel Board – Priests; Vicar for Priests; [B] Corpus Christi, TX Holy Family Catholic School; Presbyteral Council.
Jimenez, Fernando '09 (FTW) Goshen, IN St. John the Evangelist; Goshen.
Jimenez, Francisco '88 (ARE) Retired.
Jimenez, John T. '98 (SFR) San Francisco, CA St. Peter.
Jimenez, Jose Carmelo '99 (OWN) Owensboro, KY SS. Joseph and Paul.
Jimenez, Jose Luis *o.a.r.* '59 (ORG) Santa Ana, CA St. Barbara Catholic Church Retired.
Jimenez, Jose Orlando Cheverria '97 (CHR) North Myrtle Beach, SC Our Lady Star of the Sea.
Jimenez, Jose Pio *c.m.* '68 (FgM) Philadelphia, PA Eastern Province.
Jimenez, Ryan P. (CHK).
Jimenez, Ryan '03 (CHK) Saipan, MP Cathedral of Our Lady of Mt. Carmel; Chancellor; Presbyteral Council; Diocesan Publications Office; Electronic Media; Cursillo Movement; Superintendent of Catholic Schools; Commission on Heritage Cultural of the Church.
Jimenez, Victorino (ARE) Retired.
Jimenez–Londono, Fredy A. '93 (PRO) Absent on Leave.
Jimenez Lopez, Jose Ramon *c.o.r.c.* (SJN) San Juan, PR Nuestra Senora del Pilar.
Jimenez Ortiz, Adrian N. '87 (ARE) Vicar of Diocesan Pastoral Affairs; Priest's Senate (Consejo Presbiteral).
Jin, Francisco Ho Seok '11 (LA) West Covina, CA St. Christopher.
Jindra, Frank E. '84 (OM) Omaha, NE St. Anthony; Omaha, NE SS. Peter and Paul; [L] Elkhorn, NE Apostolic Sodales.
Jirak, John F. '02 (WCH) Wichita, KS Blessed Sacrament; Ongoing Formation of the Clergy Committee.
Jirovsky, Lee T. '06 (LIN) Hastings, NE St. Cecilia's; Advocates; [C] Hastings, NE St. Cecilia's Middle School/High School.
Joaquin, Joseph M. '81 (BGP) Danbury, CT St. Peter Retired.
Job, John R. '11 (NEW) Franklin Lakes, NJ Most Blessed Sacrament.
Jocson, Edgardo P. '01 (NEW) Cranford, NJ St. Michael's.
Jocson, Salvador '57 (SFR) Retired.
Joda, Robert J. *s.j.* '58 (MIL)[P] Milwaukee, WI Jesuit Community at Marquette University.
Joensen, William M. '89 (DUB)[A] Dubuque, IA Seminary of St. Pius X; [C] Loras College; Medical–Moral Commission; [C] Dubuque, IA Loras College.
Joerger, Robert H. *c.p.* '77 (NY)[DD] Pelham Manor, NY St. Vincent's Residence; [HH] New Rochelle, NY St. Paul's Benevolent, Educational and Missionary Institute, Inc.
Joerger, Robert *c.p.* '77 (FgM) New Rochelle, NY St. Paul of the Cross Province; New Rochelle, NY.
Johansen, Robert J. '01 (KAL) Three Rivers, MI Immaculate Conception.
John, Arun *i.m.s.* '92 (BR) Baton Rouge, LA Our Lady of Mercy.
John, Cyriac '93 (CC) Ben Bolt, TX St. Peter Mission.
John, Jacob '02 (PH) Philadelphia, PA St. Dominic.
John, Jacob (MCE) Nominated Members.
Johnon, Phillip (CAM)[Q] Glassboro, NJ Rowan University.
Johns, Thomas W. '78 (CLV) Mentor, OH St. John Vianney.
Johnson, Andrew R. '04 (SFR) On Special Assignment; San Francisco, CA St. Thomas More.
Johnson, Andrew '91 (FR) Charlton Memorial Hospital.
Johnson, Arthur D. *o.s.a.* '63 (PH) Rosemont, PA St. Thomas of Villanova Parish.
Johnson, Arthur M. *s.a.* '77 (ARL) Sterling, VA Christ the Redeemer.
Johnson, Bernard M. *o.praem.* '81 (ORG)[I] Silverado, CA Norbertine Fathers of Orange Inc.

Johnson, Brian A. '97 (OWN) Clarkson, KY St. Augustine; Clarkson, KY St. Anthony; Clarkson, KY St. Benedict.
Johnson, Brian J. *c.ss.r.* '86 (KC)[J] Kansas City, MO Redemptorists Fathers of Kansas City, Missouri; [N] Kansas City, MO Our Lady of Perpetual Help Charitable Trust; Kansas City, MO Our Lady of Perpetual Help.
Johnson, Carl D. '78 (NY) Port Ewen, NY Presentation of the Blessed Virgin Mary.
Johnson, Carl '77 (LEX) Special Assignment.
Johnson, Charles K. *o.p.* '06 (NO) New Orleans, LA Tulane Catholic Center; New Orleans, LA St. Anthony of Padua.
Johnson, Charles W. '94 (AUS) Navy Chaplains; Chaplains of the Military.
Johnson, Christopher *o.p.* '60 (NY)[DD] New York, NY St. Catherine of Siena Priory.
Johnson, Christopher *o.c.d.* '93 (NY) Port Chester, NY Our Lady of Mercy.
Johnson, Cyril '94 (TR) Keyport, NJ St. Joseph.
Johnson, Daniel E. '51 (HRT) Diocesan Labor Institute Retired.
Johnson, David P. '89 (OWN) Whitesville, KY St. Mary of the Woods.
Johnson, David W. *s.j.* '69 (OAK)[L] Berkeley, CA Jesuit Fathers and Brothers.
Johnson, Doug '83 (SFS) Retired.
Johnson, Edward D. '55 (PRO) Retired.
Johnson, Rev. Msgr. Edward Joseph '58 (LA) Retired.
Johnson, Eric Matthew '02 (IND) Nashville, IN St. Agnes Catholic Church, Nashville, Inc.; Priestly and Religious Vocations.
Johnson, Francis P. '60 (HRT) West Hartford, CT St. Helena Retired.
Johnson, Gary W. *o.f.m.conv.* '00 (SAT)[B] San Antonio, TX San Damiano Friary, Prenovitiate House of Formation; [L] San Antonio, TX San Damiano Friary.
Johnson, George '98 (CC) George West, TX St. George.
Johnson, Gerald '04 (SFE) Retired.
Johnson, H. Thomas '78 (DET) Shelby Twp., MI St. Kieran.
Johnson, Henry Joseph '57 (LA) Retired.
Johnson, Howard J. '54 (MIL) Retired.
Johnson, Howard '60 (WDC)[B] Washington, DC St. Joseph's Seminary Retired.
Johnson, James B. '80 (SP) Inverness, FL Our Lady of Fatima; [R] Floral City, FL Our Lady of Good Counsel Camp; Our Lady of Good Counsel Camp; Air Force Reserve Chaplains; Appointed Members; Personnel Board; College of Consultors.
Johnson, James '60 (Y) Retired.
Johnson, James '00 (SEA) Seattle, WA Our Lady of Fatima.
Johnson, James *o.f.m. cap.* '68 (LA)[B] Santa Ynez, CA San Lorenzo Seminary – Retreat Center.
Johnson, James '00 (SEA) Special Assignment.
Johnson, James *o.f.m.cap.* '68 (OAK)[L] Saint Conrad Friary.
Johnson, Jeff G. '92 (MAR) Marquette, MI Marquette General Hospital; Marquette, MI St. Christopher.
Johnson, Jeffrey C. *s.j.* '11 (NO) New Orleans, LA Immaculate Conception.
Johnson, Jerome A. '86 (MET) Iselin, NJ St. Cecelia.
Johnson, Joachim *o.c.s.o.* '02 (L)[L] Trappist, KY Abbey of Our Lady of Gethsemani, of the Order of Cistercians of the Strict Observance.
Johnson, Rev. Msgr. John G. '74 (COL) Hilliard, OH St. Brendan; Presiding Judges of First Instance.
Johnson, John J. '66 (STL) St. Louis, MO St. James the Greater.
Johnson, John R. '72 (SAG) Saginaw, MI SS. Peter and Paul.
Johnson, John R. '07 (SAV) On Duty Outside the Diocese.
Johnson, John R. '11 (L) Louisville, KY Holy Spirit.
Johnson, Joseph R. '98 (STP) St. Paul, MN Cathedral of Saint Paul; Censores Librorum.
Johnson, Kevin '87 (PT) Tallahassee, FL St. Louis; Vicars Forane.
Johnson, Lawrence M. '83 (BAL) Special Assignment; [M] Timonium, MD Stella Maris.
Johnson, Lawrence P. '76 (MO) On Duty Outside the Diocese; Navy Chaplains.
Johnson, Lyle '76 (LIN) Lincoln, NE St. John the Apostle.
Johnson, Marcus '02 (LKC) Lake Charles, LA Immaculate Heart of Mary; [A] Lake Charles, LA St. Louis Catholic High School; Deans; Diocesan Consultors; Vocation Recruiters; Presbyteral Council.
Johnson, Maxwell E. '78 (FTW)[B] University of Notre Dame Du Lac.
Johnson, Michael *o.f.m.* '02 (WDC) Silver Spring, MD St. Camillus; Priest Council.
Johnson, Michael '09 (STP) New Brighton, MN St. John the Baptist.
Johnson, Rev. Msgr. Oliver F. '62 (AUS) Retired.
Johnson, Patrick D. *c.s.p.* '74 (MO) Navy Reserve Chaplains.
Johnson, Paul J. *o.p.* '59 (STP) Minneapolis, MN St. Albert the Great; [J] Minneapolis, MN St. Albert the Great Priory.
Johnson, Peter '91 (CHY) Buffalo, WY St. John the Baptist.
Johnson, Rev. Msgr. Philip '64 (FWT) Fort Worth, TX Holy Family.
Johnson, Phillip M. '10 (CAM) Rowan University; Glassboro, NJ St. Bridget's Catholic Church, Glassboro, N.J.
Johnson, Richard *c.p.* '51 (CHI)[N] Chicago Passionist Provincial Office.
Johnson, Rijo *s.d.v.* (PAT) Paterson, NJ St. Gerard Majella; Paterson, NJ St. Michael the Archangel.
Johnson, Rev. Msgr. Robert K. '90 (WOR) Office for Divine Worship; Worcester, MA St. Paul Cathedral; Deans; Diocesan Building Commission Members; Presbyteral Council.
Johnson, Rev. Msgr. Robert '51 (DAL) Retired.
Johnson, Robert *s.v.d.* '92 (FgM) Techny, IL.
Johnson, Robert '09 (PT) Niceville, FL Christ Our Redeemer.
Johnson, Terrance '94 (CHI) Park Forest, IL St. Irenaeus.
Johnson, Thomas '78 (DET) College of Consultors; Presbyteral Council.
Johnson, Timothy A. '93 (SC) Carroll, IA St. Mary's; St. Anthony Regional Hospital; [C] Carroll, IA St. Anthony Regional Hospital; Board of Education; Carroll, IA Holy Spirit.
Johnson, Timothy K. '71 (OAK) Oakland, CA St. Leo the Great; Deanery #2.
Johnson, Timothy '01 (FAR) Oriska, ND St. Agatha's Church of Hope; Oriska, ND St. Bernard's Church of Oriska; Oriska, ND Sacred Heart Church of Sanborn.
Johnson, Rev. Msgr. W. Robert '51 (FWT)[G] Crowley, TX St. Francis Village, Inc. Retired.
Johnson, Walter W. *m.m.* '53 (NY)[DD] Retired.
Johnson, William B. '83 (OAK) Contra Costa Regional Medical Center and VA Administrative Skilled Nursing Center; Walnut Creek Campus of John Muir Memorial Hospital; DEPARTMENT OF VETERANS AFFAIRS HOSPITALS AND CHAPLAINS.
Johnson, William T. *s.j.* '91 (OM)[J] Omaha, NE Jesuit Community at Creighton University.
Johnston, Christian R. '05 (KAL) Wayland, MI SS. Cyril and Methodius; Wayland, MI St. Therese of Lisieux; Vicars Forane.
Johnston, German Bartolome Vasquez '93 (TUC) Wellton, AZ Saint Joseph the Worker Roman Catholic Parish – Wellton.
Johnston, Jeffrey (RVC) Medical Leave.
Johnston, Kenneth J. '68 (CAM) Mantua, NJ R.C. Church of the Incarnation, Township of Mantua, New Jersey.
Johnston, Michael O. '70 (NSH) Nashville, TN St. Henry.
Johnston, Michael '96 (P) Dallas, OR St. Philip; Judges.
Johnston, Paul *s.o.l.t.* '03 (CC)[G] Robstown, TX Society of Our Lady of the Most Holy Trinity.
Johnston, Robert F. '71 (SAT) Retired.
Johnstone, Brian *c.s.s.r.* '58 (WDC)[C] Catholic University of America, The.
Johnstone, Brian *c.ss.r.* '64 (WDC)[O] Washington, DC Holy Redeemer College.
Johri, Mauro *o.f.m.cap.* (FgM) AMERICAN CAPUCHIN MISSIONS.
Joly, Henry L. '58 (ALT) Retired.
Joly, Michael D. '94 (PAT) On Duty Outside the Diocese.
Joly, Michael '94 (RIC) Yorktown, VA St. Joan of Arc.
Jonas, Lawrence A. *s.j.* '59 (MIL) Milwaukee, WI Gesu Parish; [P] Wauwatosa, WI Jesuit Community at St. Camillus.
Joncas, J. Michael (FTW)[B] University of Notre Dame Du Lac.
Joncas, Jan Michael '69 (STP)[C] St. Paul, MN University of St. Thomas.
Jonczyk, Dariusz J. '97 (PRO) Central Falls, RI St. Joseph; Woonsocket, RI St. Stanislaus.
Jones, Anthony '89 (OWN) Owensboro, KY The Immaculate.
Jones, Brandon H. '08 (CHL) Andrews, NC Holy Redeemer.
Jones, C. Gregory *c.s.v.* '96 (CHI)[N] Chicago, IL Viatorian Residence; [N] Arlington Heights Viatorian Province Center–Clerics of St. Viator.
Jones, Carleton Parker *o.p.* (BAL) Baltimore, MD SS. Philip and James.
Jones, Charles F. '63 (KC) Retired.
Jones, Clarence Edward *c.o.* '94 (SEA) Seattle, WA Our Lady of Mount Virgin.
Jones, Daniel J. '97 (DET) Special Assignment; [A] The School of Theology.
Jones, David A. '89 (CHI) Chicago, IL St. Benedict the African (East); Deans.
Jones, David J. *m.m.* '62 (NY)[DD] Maryknoll Maryknoll Fathers and Brothers Retired.
Jones, Donald R. '86 (PIT) Retired.
Jones, Edward T. '03 (PT) Crawfordville, FL St. Elizabeth Ann Seton; Lanark Village, FL Sacred Heart of Jesus.
Jones, Felix (NY) New York, NY St. Agnes.
Jones, Glenn '08 (SFE) Clayton, NM St. Francis Xavier.
Jones, Herbert J. *o.carm.* '60 (BO)[Z] Peabody, MA St. Theresa Carmelite Chapel; Presbyteral Council; [U] Peabody, MA Our Lady of the Scapular Priory.
Jones, Herbert *o.f.m.* '77 (SAT) San Antonio, TX San Francisco de la Espada.
Jones, J. Overton '64 (CAM) Retired.
Jones, James *o.f.m.* '76 (SP)[N] St. Petersburg, FL St. Anthony Friary Retired.
Jones, John E. '59 (L) Retired.
Jones, Joseph F. *c.ss.r.* '73 (BRK) Brooklyn, NY; [R] Brooklyn, NY Redemptorist Fathers of New York, Inc.–Baltimore Province.
Jones, Joseph R. *c.p.* '65 (SCR) Scranton, PA St. Ann's Basilica Parish; [L] Scranton, PA Saint Ann's Passionist Monastery.
Jones, Kenneth '69 (NEW) Plainfield, NJ St. Mary Retired.
Jones, Mark R. '92 (MIL) Racine, WI St. Lucy.
Jones, Martin J. '94 (NOR) Delegate for Evangelization in Hispanic Ministry; Norwich, CT St. Mary; Delegate for Evangelization in Hispanic Ministry.
Jones, Michael K. '92 (BGP) Shelton, CT St. Lawrence.
Jones, Michael P. *o.f.m.* '01 (NY)[DD] New York Franciscan Friars, Holy Name Province.
Jones, Michael T. '85 (MO) Bowie, MD St. Pius X; Air Force Reserve Chaplains; Priest Council.
Jones, Michael *o.f.m.* (PAT) Butler, NJ St. Anthony.
Jones, Neil G. *m.s.* '72 (ATL) Snellville, GA St. Oliver Plunkett.
Jones, Paul W. '96 (JC) Retired.
Jones, Ralph O. '03 (CC) Fulton, TX Stella Maris Chapel.
Jones, Rev. Msgr. Raymond N. '59 (DEN) Retired.
Jones, Richard S. '88 (PIT) Coraopolis, PA St. Joseph.
Jones, Rick L. '90 (SPC) Branson, MO Our Lady of the Lake; Forsyth, MO Our Lady of the Ozarks; Diocesan Development Fund; Priests' Mutual Benefit Society.
Jones, Robert J. *c.m.* '69 (LA) Los Angeles, CA St. Camillus Center for Spiritual Care; [P] Montebello, CA DePaul Evangelization Center; [V] Montebello, CA DePaul Evangelization Center.
Jones, Robert J. *s.j.* '70 (SPK) Inchelium, WA St. Michael's Mission; [J] Spokane, WA Regis Community.
Jones, Robert M. *s.v.d.* '68 (BO)[U] Duxbury, MA Society of the Divine Word; Norfolk County Correctional Facility.
Jones, Robert S. '60 (SY) Special Assignment.
Jones, Robert W. '92 (RCK) Sugar Grove, IL St. Katharine Drexel Parish.
Jones, Robert *c.m.* '67 (LA) LAC + USC Medical Center.
Jones, Ronald A. '73 (RCK) Retired.
Jones, Scott *s.d.s.* '04 (MIL)[P] Milwaukee Salvatorian Provincial Offices; Consultors:; [B] Hales Corners, WI Sacred Heart School of Theology.
Jones, Thomas J. *c.s.c.* '72 (FTW) Notre Dame, IN Sacred Heart; [H] Notre Dame Congregation of Holy Cross, United States Province of Priests & Brothers; [B] University of Notre Dame Du Lac; [H] Notre Dame, IN Holy Cross Community, Corby Hall, University of Notre Dame.
Jones, Rev. Msgr. William H. '47 (DEN) Retired.
Jones, William P. '69 (ALN) Retired.
Jones, William R. '67 (SY) Syracuse, NY Crouse Irving Memorial Hospital; Syracuse, NY The Cathedral of the Immaculate Conception.
Jong, Lyndon A. '91 (MO) Army Chaplains.
Jong–A–Kiem, Walter '03 (OM) Omaha, NE St. Vincent de Paul.
Jonientz, Bernard '63 (SEA) Retired.
Jonikas, Gintaras '89 (DET) Detroit, MI St. Anthony; Southfield, MI Divine Providence.
Joppa, Mark J. '07 (STP) Forest Lake, MN St. Peter.
Jorda, Mario Busquets '58 (MIA)[N] Miami, FL Peruvian Mission, Inc.
Jordain, Floyd McCoy '84 (MGZ) Hormigueros, PR Shrine of Our Lady of Monserrate.
Jordan, Brian *o.f.m.* '83 (WDC)[B] Silver Spring, MD Holy Name College.
Jordan, Daniel J. '99 (BUR) Judicial Vicar; Judges; Catholic Golden Age; Burlington, VT Christ the King–St. Anthony.
Jordan, Francis G. '60 (DOD) Ingalls, KS St. Stanislaus Catholic Church of Ingalls, Kansas Retired.
Jordan, Rev. Msgr. Harry J. '61 (CAM)[L] Cherry Hill, NJ Sacred Heart Residence for Priests, Inc.; Representative for Retired Priests; [L] Cherry Hill, NJ Sacred Heart North; [L] Cherry Hill, NJ Sacred Heart South Retired.
Jordan, Rev. Msgr. John J. '69 (SCR) Roaring Brook Twp., PA St. Eulalia.
Jordan, John M. '83 (PIT) Absent on Sick Leave; [M] Pittsburgh, PA Cardinal Dearden Center.
Jordan, Rev. Msgr. John W. (WDC)[X] Washington, DC Foundation for the Nativity & Miguel Schools.
Jordan, Joseph A. *o.s.a.* '58 (PH)[Y] Villanova, PA St. Thomas Monastery.
Jordan, Maryon C. *o.s.b.* '83 (MO) DEPARTMENT OF

VETERANS AFFAIRS HOSPITALS AND CHAPLAINS.
Jordan, Michael *s.o.l.t.* '83 (CC)[G] Robstown, TX Society of Our Lady of the Most Holy Trinity.
Jordan, Milton E. '72 (WDC) Retired.
Jordan, Patrick (ORL) Retired.
Jordan, Regis *o.c.d.* '64 (WDC)[B] Washington, DC Discalced Carmelite Friars; [X] Washington, DC Spiritual Life.
Jordan, Salvador R. *s.j.* '77 (WDC)[O] Washington, DC The Jesuit Community at Georgetown University.
Jordan, Thomas *o.carm.* '70 (FgM) Darien, IL Provincial Headquarters, Carmelite Provincial Office; [L] Darien Carmelite Provincial Office.
Jorden, James A. '83 (PT) Retired.
Jorgensen, Alan P. '05 (KAL) Allegan, MI Blessed Sacrament.
Joseph, Alex '94 (NY) New York, NY St. Peter.
Joseph, Antony A. '75 (CHI) Evanston, IL St. Mary.
Joseph, Augustine '90 (OAK) San Leandro, CA St. Felicitas.
Joseph, Augustine *m.s.f.s.* '04 (KNX)[D] Signal Mountain, TN Alexian Village Health Care Center; [E] Signal Mountain, TN Alexian Village of Tennessee.
Joseph, Charles Heston '94 (NY) Poughkeepsie, NY Vassar Brothers Hospital; Poughkeepsie, NY St. Mary.
Joseph, Cidouane C. '11 (HRT) Hartford, CT St. Patrick–St. Anthony.
Joseph, Cidouane C. *o.f.m.* '11 (NY)[DD] New York Franciscan Friars, Holy Name Province.
Joseph, Dominic '93 (SYM) Norcross, GA Holy Family Syro–Malabar Knanaya Catholic Church (Atlanta); Norcross, GA St. Anthony Syro–Malabar Knanaya Catholic Church (San Antonio).
Joseph, Francis A. *o.c.d.* '79 (STO) Tracy, CA St. Bernard Church (Pastor of).
Joseph, Gasparraj Valentine (LC) Mauston, WI St. Patrick.
Joseph, George '99 (AUS) Elgin, TX Sacred Heart; Bastrop/Lockhart; Presbyteral Council; College of Consultors.
Joseph, George '94 (NEW) Bayonne, NJ Saint Michael and Saint Joseph.
Joseph, Irudamoney Arul '91 (BIS) Hebron, ND St. Ann.
Joseph, Jacob *c.m.i.* '83 (CHR) North Augusta, SC Our Lady of Peace.
Joseph, James *s.d.b.* '91 (GI) Gordon, NE St. Leo's.
Joseph, Jean–Ronald '93 (VEN) On Administrative Leave.
Joseph, Jiang *s.j.* '08 (BO)[U] Newton, MA The Jesuit Community at Boston College.
Joseph, Jimmy *v.c.* '97 (SCL) Little Falls, MN Sacred Heart; Randall, MN St. James; Little Falls, MN St. Stanislaus; [I] Saint Cloud, MN St. Joseph Province of the Vincentian Congregation.
Joseph, Joseph K. '83 (GI) Grand Island, NE Blessed Sacrament.
Joseph, Joy *t.o.r.* '95 (FWT) Fort Worth, TX St. Patrick Cathedral.
Joseph, Lawrence '84 (LA) Glendora, CA St. Dorothy.
Joseph, Mamachan *c.m.i.* '86 (SAN) Fort Stockton, TX St. Agnes; Fort Stockton, TX St. Joseph's.
Joseph, Rev. Msgr. Milam J. '64 (DAL) College of Consultors; Episcopal Vicar; Diocesan Judges; Episcopal Vicar; Ex Officio Members.
Joseph, Paul Chemplamparampil *c.m.i.* '83 (NY) White Plains, NY St. John the Evangelist.
Joseph, Peter *h.g.n.* '01 (LEX) Lancaster, KY St. William; Lancaster, KY St. Sylvester.
Joseph, Pham M. *c.m.* (DAL) Dallas, TX St. Peter Vietnamese.
Joseph, Reji *c.m.i.* '05 (NY) Stony Point, NY Immaculate Conception.
Joseph, Sajeev *o.ss.t.* '08 (BAL)[Q] Assigned in India.
Joseph, Saju Puthenpurackal '99 (WH) Fairmont, WV St. Anthony; Monongah, WV Holy Spirit.
Joseph, Saju '94 (SJ) Special Assignment; Los Gatos, CA St. Mary of the Immaculate Conception; Judges.
Joseph, Satish Antony '94 (CIN) Dayton, OH Our Lady of the Immaculate Conception; Dayton, OH St. Helen.
Joseph, Theophilus '74 (BRK) Brooklyn, NY St. Ephrem.
Joseph, Thomas P. '80 (HON) Aiea, HI St. Elizabeth; College of Consultors; Members.
Joseph, Thomas '05 (STP) Carver, MN St. Nicholas.
Joseph, Tomy P. *m.s.f.s.* '94 (NSH) Madison, TN St. Joseph.
Joseph, Tomy *m.s.f.x.* '98 (BIS) Foxholm, ND St. Mary; Glenburn, ND St. Philomena.
Joseph, V. Arul '78 (LC) Stevens Point, WI St. Casimir.
Joseph, Valentine (LC) Lyndon Station, WI St. Mary.
Joseph, Varkey V. '79 (LC) Elmwood, WI Sacred Heart.
Joseph, Vijayan '80 (KNX) Pigeon Forge, TN Holy Cross.
Joseph, Vincent Ezhanikatt '84 (WH) Morgantown, WV St. Luke the Evangelist.
Joseph, Vincent *v.c.* '85 (FTW) South Bend, IN Holy Family; South Bend, IN St. John the Baptist.
Joseph, Vio O. *s.a.c.* '79 (COL) Chillicothe, OH Veteran's Affairs Medical Center.
Joseph, Vio O. *s.a.c.* '79 (MO) DEPARTMENT OF VETERANS AFFAIRS HOSPITALS AND CHAPLAINS.
Joseph, William '62 (PT) Retired.
Joseph, William '62 (ORL) Retired.
Joslyn, James W. '73 (CHI) Retired.
Joslyn, James '73 (MO) Presbyteral Council.
Josoma, Stephen S. (BO) Dedham, MA St. Susanna.
Jost, Aloys *o.f.m.* '80 (SHP) Hispanic Ministry and Immigration Services.
Jost, C. Thomas *s.j.* '68 (DEN)[N] Denver, CO Xavier Jesuit Center.
Jost, Edward F. '96 (BUF) North Tonawanda, NY St. Jude the Apostle.
Josten, Paul '87 (SFS) Howard, SD St. Agatha.
Jovanovic, Rev. Msgr. Robert P. '61 (STL) St. Charles, MO St. Elizabeth Ann Seton.
Jowdy, Albert W. '84 (ATL) Lawrenceville, GA St. Lawrence; Judges; Deans; College of Consultors.
Joy, Laurence '60 (LA) Retired.
Joy, William P. (BO) Mattapan, MA St. Angela Merici; Dorchester, MA St. Matthew.
Joyce, Brian T. '63 (OAK) Pleasant Hill, CA Christ the King; Presbyteral Council.
Joyce, Daniel R.J. *s.j.* '01 (PH)[C] Jesuit Fathers; [Y] Loyola Center and Manresa Hall.
Joyce, Rev. Msgr. David J. '68 (SPR) Episcopal Vicars; Bishop's Commission for Clergy; Diocesan Consultors; Presbyteral Council; Cursillo Movement; Diocesan Pastoral Council; Springfield, MA Holy Name; Vicars for the Clergy.
Joyce, Donald J. *o.m.i.* '58 (SAT)[K] San Antonio, TX Oblate Madonna Residence.
Joyce, Edward *c.pp.s.* '56 (CIN)[N] Dayton Provincial Office of the Cincinnati Province of the Society of the Precious Blood; [N] Carthagena, OH St. Charles Retired.
Joyce, Gerald P. '61 (CHI) Westchester, IL Divine Infant Retired.
Joyce, James F. *s.j.* '75 (NY)[DD] New York, NY Murray–Weigel Hall.
Joyce, James K. '72 (SPR) Pittsfield, MA Sacred Heart.
Joyce, James M. '48 (SFS) Worldwide Marriage Encounter Retired.
Joyce, John J. '89 (BEL) Okawville, IL St. Barbara; Albers, IL St. Bernard; Damiansville, IL St. Damian.
Joyce, John M. '54 (ORG) Irvine, CA St. John Neumann Retired.
Joyce, Kevin P. '80 (SJ) Campbell, CA St. Lucy; Council of Priests.
Joyce, Kevin '01 (OM) Omaha, NE St. Pius X.
Joyce, Michael P. *c.m.* '76 (STL)[O] St. Louis, MO Lazarist Residence.
Joyce, Michael P. *c.m.* '76 (MEM) Chief Pastoral Officer; Presbyteral Council; Judicial Vicar; Chief Pastoral Officer; Clergy Personnel Board.
Joyce, Michael S. *o.f.m.* '67 (PRO)[O] Providence, RI St. Francis Friary.
Joyce, Michael *o.f.m.cap.* '85 (CLV) Pittsburgh, PA; [A] Wickliffe, OH Borromeo Seminary.
Joyce, Michael '63 (OAK) Retired.
Joyce, Rev. Msgr. Peter M. '92 (CAM) Marmora, NJ The Parish of St. Maximilian Kolbe, Marmora, N.J.
Joyce, Peter '83 (WOR) St. Mary; Southbridge, MA Blessed John Paul II.
Joyce, Randal *c.p.* '50 (DET)[K] Detroit, MI St. Paul of the Cross Community, Congregation of the Passion.
Joyce, Raymond '62 (WCH) Retired.
Joyce, Thomas *c.p.* '69 (BRK)[R] Jamaica, NY Immaculate Conception Monastery Retired.
Joyce, Thomas *c.m.f.* '59 (CHI)[N] Chicago, IL Barbastro House (Claretian Candidate House); Chicago, IL Nativity of Our Lord.
Joyce, Timothy J. '59 (BO)[U] Hingham, MA Glastonbury Abbey.
Joyce, William F. '60 (BO) Readville, MA St. Anne.
Jozefiak, Greg '92 (PEO) East Moline, IL St. Anne; Silvis, IL Our Lady of Guadalupe.
Jozefiak, Matthew *c.pp.s.* (TOL) Ottawa, OH SS. Peter and Paul.
Jozwiak, Lawrence W. '87 (GAL) Houston, TX Co–Cathedral of the Sacred Heart; Metropolitan Tribunal.
Jozwiak, Richard '59 (SAG) Retired.
Jozwiak, Ronald J. '79 (DET) West Bloomfield, MI Prince of Peace; Judges.
Ju, Yong Don '94 (RVC) Woodbury, NY Holy Name of Jesus.
Juan, Dennis R. '98 (ATL) Griffin, GA Sacred Heart.
Juan, Francisco *s.d.b.* (CGS)[C] Aibonito, PR Casa Salesiana de Retiros.
Juan, Marcial '66 (LA) Glendale, CA Holy Family.
Juan, Vincent R. '03 (SAC) Judges; Defenders of the Bond.
Juarez, Hector Montoya '09 (SAC) Vallejo, CA St. Vincent Ferrer.
Juarez, Lawrence '75 (CIN) Cincinnati, OH Old St. Mary.
Juarez, Lucio '91 (LA) Oxnard, CA Santa Clara.
Juarez, Mario '09 (ORG) Dana Point, CA St. Edward the Confessor.
Juarez, Miguel Angel Gusatvo Ruiz '06 (SPK) Walla Walla, WA Assumption of the Blessed Virgin Mary; Walla Walla, WA St. Francis of Assisi; Walla Walla, WA St. Patrick.
Juarez, Robert Jesus '80 (LA) On Administrative Leave.
Juarez, Rudolph T. '80 (DAV) Vicar for Hispanics; Iowa City, IA St. Patrick's; Judges; Diocesan Consultors.
Juchniewicz, Leon '80 (SAC) Elk Grove, CA Good Shepherd Catholic Church.
Judd, Augustine *o.p.* '96 (WDC)[U] Washington, DC American University Catholic Community; [B] Washington, DC Dominican House of Studies.
Judd, Peter A. *o.p.* (PRO) Providence, RI St. Pius V.
Judd, Stephen P. *m.m.* '78 (FgM) Maryknoll, NY MARYKNOLL.
Judd, Timothy '56 (LUB) Retired.
Jude, Robert J. '49 (STP) Retired.
Judge, Anthony *c.ss.r.* '79 (CHI) Chicago, IL St. Michael in Old Town; [N] Chicago, IL The Redemptorist Fathers of Chicago.
Judge, James G. '72 (BUF) Council of Priests; Buffalo, NY St. Martin of Tours; Buffalo, NY St. Thomas Aquinas; [G] Buffalo, NY South Buffalo Catholic School.
Judge, Rev. Msgr. John G. '69 (NEW) Retired.
Judge, Philip G. *s.j.* '93 (NY)[E] New York, NY Regis High School; [DD] New York, NY St. Ignatius Loyola Residence.
Judge, Robert K. *s.j.* '65 (BAL)[Q] Baltimore, MD Colombiere Jesuit Community.
Judge, Russell R. '78 (JC) Vandalia, MO Sacred Heart.
Judge, Timothy M. '79 (PH) Diocesan Priests' Compensation and Benefits Committee; Navy Reserve Chaplains; On Special or Other Archdiocesan Assignment; [Z] Huntingdon Valley, PA Sisters of the Holy Redeemer Provincialate.
Judie, John T. '87 (L) Louisville, KY Christ the King; Louisville, KY Immaculate Heart of Mary; Ex Officio.
Judy, Albert G. *o.p.* '62 (CHI) River Forest, IL St. Vincent Ferrer.
Judy, Albert G. *o.p.* '62 (CHI) Chicago, IL St. Ferdinand.
Judy, Myron *o.carm.* '63 (JOL)[L] Darien Carmelite Provincial Office; Councilors.
Juelfs, Daniel '73 (RC) Eagle Butte, SD All Saints; Vicar General; Diocesan Consultors.
Juenker, Rev. Msgr. Paul R. '45 (BUF) Retired.
Juettner, Mark R. '79 (STP) Bayport, MN St. Charles.
Jugan, Joseph J. '58 (PBR) Canonsburg, PA St. Michael; Protopresbyters.
Jugenheimer, James R. '87 (GB) Vicariate; College of Consultors.
Jugenheimer, James R. '87 (GB) Oshkosh, WI Most Blessed Sacrament.
Juhas, John J. '75 (CLV) Retired.
Juhl, Dennis D. '73 (DUB) Cedar Rapids, IA St. Ludmila; Church Design/Renovation Commission.
Juknialis, Joseph J. '69 (MIL) Eden, WI Shepherd of the Hills (Good Shepherd).
Juleen, Stuart '77 (SAT) San Antonio, TX St. Brigid.
Julian, Mario F. *o.f.m.* '81 (ALB) Troy, NY St. Anthony of Padua (Shrine Church).
Julien, Eddy '67 (RVC) Elmont, NY St. Boniface.
Julien, Roland M. '65 (STA) Gainesville, FL St. Patrick Church; [L] Gainesville, FL Spirit Radio of North Florida, Inc.
Julito, (SAC) Downieville, CA Immaculate Conception.
Junak, Jacek *c.r.* '95 (RCK) Johnsburg, IL St. John the Baptist.
Juncer, Bartholomew *s.j.c.* '08 (CHI) Chicago, IL St. John Cantius; [P] Chicago, IL Canons Regular of Saint John Cantius.
Jung, Cheol Hyun (SAV) Augusta, GA St. Joseph.
Jung, Dominic *c.pp.s.* (BO) Korean.
Jung, Jerome L. '93 (POD) Berkeley.
Jung, Jerome L. '93 (OAK)[P] Berkeley, CA Opus Dei.
Jung, Joseph B. '56 (PH) Retired.
Jung, Michael *o.s.b.* '63 (BR) Baton Rouge, LA St. Agnes; Baton Rouge, LA Baton Rouge General Medical Center.
Jung, Michael *o.s.b.* '63 (NO)[R] St. Benedict, LA St. Joseph Abbey.
Jungmann, William '03 (DEN) Holyoke, CO St. Patrick.
Juniet, Paul *o.f.m.* '66 (SFE) Jemez Pueblo, NM San Diego Indian Missions.
Junio, Joven T. *m.s.* '86 (SB)[I] Moreno Valley, CA Missionaries of Our Lady of La Salette, MS; Moreno Valley, CA St. Christopher.
Junius, Richard *o.m.i.* '56 (FgM) Washington, DC AMERICAN OBLATE MISSIONS.
Junker, Nicholas G. '08 (BEL) Du Quoin, IL Sacred Heart of Jesus.
Jupin, Alan D. '62 (ALB) Retired.
Jura, Jacek A. '04 (CHI) Glenview, IL Our Lady of Perpetual Help; Wilmette, IL St. Joseph.
Juracek, Joseph *o.f.m.* '83 (NY) Obernburg, NY St. Mary.
Juran, Michael P. '76 (BUF) Absent on Leave.
Jurcak, Lawrence '81 (CLV) Parma, OH St. John Bosco;

Adjunct Judicial Vicars; Presbyteral Council; Presbyteral Conveners.
Jurchak, Benedict *t.o.r.* '11 (STU)[H] Steubenville, OH Holy Spirit Friary.
Jurejewicz, Hubert '09 (PAT)[P] Haledon, NJ William Paterson University of New Jersey.
Jurek, Daniel J. '73 (BEL) Prairie du Rocher, IL St. Joseph; Diocesan Consultors; Diocesan Deans; Modoc, IL St. Leo; Big Muddy River Correctional Center; Waterloo, IL St. Patrick.
Jurewicz, Francis Z. '59 (PIT) Retired.
Jurgelonis, Joseph J. '73 (WOR) East Templeton, MA Holy Cross; Templeton Developmental Center; Deans; Presbyteral Council; Otter River, MA St. Martin Mission.
Jurgensmeier, Charles *s.j.* '88 (CHI)[C] Chicago, IL Jesuit Community at Loyola University Chicago.
Juric, Ante *o.f.m.* '72 (SJ) San Jose, CA St. Mary of the Assumption.
Juric, Jakov '00 (GLP) On Duty Outside of Diocese.
Jurisich, Melvin A. *o.f.m.* '70 (OAK)[Q] Oakland, CA Province of Saint Barbara Fraternal Care Trust.
Jurisich, Melvin A. *o.f.m.* '70 (LA)[V] Malibu, CA Serra Retreat.
Jurjewicz, Hubert (PAT) Vocations Office; [A] Boonton, NJ Domus Bartimaeus.
Jurkiewicz, Andrzej '83 (ORL) Orlando, FL St. Joseph; Polish Ministry.
Jurkovich, Robb M. '04 (MAR) Vicars Forane; Menominee, MI Resurrection; Menominee, MI Holy Spirit.
Jurkowski, Joseph V. '58 (CAM) Retired.
Jurkus, Alan F. '70 (MIL) Greendale, WI St. Alphonsus; Archdiocesan Council of Priests.
Juroszek, Robert S. '05 (MO) CIVIL AIR PATROL.
Jurzyk, Marek '91 (JOL) Naperville, IL Sts. Peter and Paul.
Jusino, P. Luis (MGZ) Moca, PR Our Lady of Monserrate.
Just, Felix N.W. *s.j.* '91 (ORG)[I] Anaheim, CA Manresa Jesuit Residence; [H] Orange, CA Loyola Institute for Spirituality.
Justavino, Teodoro *c.m.* '90 (FgM) Philadelphia, PA Eastern Province.
Justice, Joseph Charles '75 (ORG) Absent on Sick Leave.
Juszczak, John W. *c.ss.r.* '88 (MO) Air Force Chaplains.
Juszczak, John *c.ss.r.* (STV) Christiansted, VI Church of the Holy Cross.
Jutt, Anthony J. '51 (SPR) Retired.
Jutte, Edgar *c.pp.s.* '62 (CIN)[N] Dayton Provincial Office of the Cincinnati Province of the Society of the Precious Blood.
Jutton, David J. '66 (SY) Retired.
Juza, Philip J. '95 (SUP) Hayward, WI St. Joseph; South Central Deanery; Pastoral Consultors; Personnel Placement Board.
Juzix, Richard *o.f.m.* '75 (LA) Los Angeles, CA St. Francis of Assisi.
Juzix, Richard *o.f.m.* '75 (ORG) Huntington Beach, CA SS. Simon and Jude.

K

Kabagambe, Evarist '03 (TR) Neptune, NJ Holy Innocents.
Kabali, Joseph '96 (MET) Flemington, NJ St. Magdalen de Pazzi; Hunterdon Medical Center.
Kabango, Jean–Marie *o.f.m.* '99 (WDC) Silver Spring, MD St. Camillus.
Kabat, Robert J. '79 (GB) Seymour, WI St. John; Judicial Vicar; Bonduel, WI St. Lawrence; Judges; Seymour, WI St. Sebastian.
Kaberia, Silvio '83 (RIC) Virginia Beach, VA St. Luke.
Kabiru, Francis '07 (DUL) Walker, MN Sacred Heart; Walker, MN St. Agnes.
Kabot, Damian *s.v.d.* '02 (LA) Los Angeles, CA St. John, The Evangelist.
Kacalo, Robert C. '06 (MIL) Union Grove, WI St. Robert Bellarmine; Kansasville, WI St. Mary–Dover.
Kacerguis, Edward '82 (ALB)[Q] Troy, NY The Rensselaer Newman Foundation; [Q] Troy, NY University Parish of Christ Sun of Justice.
Kachappilly, Xavier *o.ss.t.* '08 (BAL)[Q] Assigned in India.
Kachel, Czeslaw L. '57 (PRO)[O] Providence St. John Vianney Residence Retired.
Kachel, Steven J. '95 (LC) Onalaska, WI St. Patrick.
Kachuba, Rt. Rev. Mitred Archpriest John S. '74 (PRM) Euclid, OH St. Stephen; Ex Officio; Protosyncellus; Presbyteral Council; Eparchial Pastoral Council; Eparchial Finance Officer; Eparchial Consultors; Office of Religious Education; Seminary Education Formation Board; Priest's Pension Board.
Kachuba, Samuel S. '08 (BGP) Fairfield, CT St. Pius X.
Kachur, Oleh '03 (SJP) On Assignment Outside the Diocese; Presbyters.
Kachurka, Edward M. '89 (BRK) Flushing, NY St. Ann.
Kacinko, Elmer A. '61 (GBG) Retired.
Kacprzak, Stanley '85 (ROC) Penn Yan, NY Our Lady of the Lakes Catholic Community; [N] Penn Yan, NY Keuka College c/o St. Michael's Church.
Kaczkowski, Conrad J. *s.m.* '68 (SAT)[C] San Antonio, TX St. Mary's University of San Antonio, Texas Retired.
Kaczmarczyk, Pawel '03 (DET) Absent on Leave.
Kaczmarek, David *t.o.r.* '06 (ORL)[F] Winter Park, FL Franciscan Friars, T.O.R., San Pedro Friary; [E] Winter Park, FL San Pedro Spiritual Development Center.
Kaczmarek, Rev. Msgr. James A. '69 (MAR) Iron Mountain, MI Immaculate Conception of the Blessed Virgin Mary; Veterans Administration Center.
Kaczmarek, Peter '69 (RVC) Greenlawn, NY St. Francis of Assisi.
Kaczmarek, Thaddeus J. '71 (GBG) Murrysville, PA Mother of Sorrows; Finance Council.
Kaczorowski, Edward J. '58 (WIL) Bear, DE Retired.
Kaczorowski, Rev. Msgr. James T. '73 (CHI) Chicago, IL Queen of Angels; Deans.
Kaczowka, Julian *s.ch.* '88 (JOL) Joliet, IL St. Mary Nativity; Joliet, IL Holy Cross.
Kaczynski, Krzysztof '93 (MET) Milford, NJ St. Edward the Confessor.
Kadambukatt, Ambrose Joseph *o.c.d.* '98 (LA) Hospital Chaplains; [J] Lynwood, CA St. Francis Medical Center.
Kadambukatt, Ambrose *o.c.d.* '98 (LA) Hospital Chaplains.
Kadaprayil, Joseph *s.d.b.* '78 (GI) Mullen, NE St. Mary's.
Kadavil, Antony '67 (MOB) Grand Bay, AL St. John Baptist.
Kaddo, Chorbishop Joseph F. '72 (SAM) Fall River, MA St. Anthony of the Desert; Presbyteral Council.
Kaddo, Chorbishop Joseph (OLL) Order of St. Sharbel.
Kadera, Thomas R. '87 (CHY) Wheatland, WY St. Patrick's; Air Force Reserve Chaplains; Adjutant Judicial Vicar; Adjutant Judicial Vicar; Judges.
Kaderabek, Matthew *l.c.* '03 (CHI)[N] Hillside, IL Legion of Christ.
Kadlec, Jared '97 (FAR) Kindred, ND St. Maurice; Horace, ND St. Benedict's Church of Wild Rice; Judges.
Kado, Paul '06 (FRS) Ridgecrest, CA St. Ann.
Kadrmas, Christopher J. '00 (BIS) Minot, ND St. Leo.
Kadukappillil, Thomas '91 (SYM) Somerset, NJ St. Thomas Syro–Malabar Catholic Church (East Millstone).
Kadukunnel, Jose *c.m.i.* '86 (JOL) Paxton, IL St. Mary.
Kadungamparambil, Josep Augustine '87 (RVC) Merrick, NY Curé of Ars.
Kaduthodil, Abraham '81 (CHI) Forest Park, IL St. Bernardine; [M] Northlake, IL Villa Scalabrini Nursing and Rehabilitation Center.
Kadylo, Vasyl '03 (STF) Brooklyn, NY St. Nicholas.
Kaech, Paul A. '06 (SEA) Raymond, WA St. Lawrence; Seaview, WA St. Mary.
Kaeding, Robert F. '73 (TR) Monmouth Beach, NJ Church of the Precious Blood; On Duty Outside the Diocese.
Kaelin, Dennis J. '76 (NEW) Rahway, NJ Divine Mercy Parish.
Kafara, Andrew '85 (SAT) Pearsall, TX Immaculate Heart of Mary.
Kafor, James O. '02 (SJ) San Jose, CA Five Wounds Portuguese National Church.
Kagan, Rev. Msgr. David D. '75 (RCK) Special Assignment.
Kagere, Guy '03 (BAL)[K] Baltimore, MD Good Samaritan Hospital; [L] Baltimore, MD Belvedere Green at Good Samaritan.
Kaggwa, Denis '04 (SFE) Ohkay Owingeh, NM San Juan Bautista.
Kagoma, Clement '97 (NEW) Newark, NJ St. John's.
Kagoma, Clement (NY) Buchanan, NY St. Christopher.
Kagoo, Edwin '80 (AUS) College Station, TX St. Thomas Aquinas.
Kahan, Paul *s.v.d.* '99 (BLX)[D] Bay St. Louis, MS Southern Province of St. Augustine – Provincial Offices.
Kahan, Paul *s.v.d.* '99 (FWT) Fort Worth, TX St. Rita.
Kaharuza, Bruno T. '97 (CHI) Chicago, IL SS. Peter and Paul.
Kahle, George G. *c.s.c.* '53 (FTW)[H] Holy Cross House.
Kahle, Jason J. '09 (TOL) Sandusky, OH St. Mary; [D] Sandusky, OH Sandusky Central Catholic School.
Kahlhamer, Bernard '59 (SCL) Retired.
Kahlich, Daniel P. '66 (VIC) La Grange, TX Holy Rosary; La Grange, TX SS. Peter and Paul.
Kahmann, Kevin James '10 (COV) Erlanger, KY Mary, Queen of Heaven.
Kahrs, Lee J. '65 (GB) Defenders of the Bond; Casco, WI St. Peter–St. Hubert; Maplewood, WI St. Mary Retired.
Kahumburu, Joseph '83 (NY) Mamaroneck, NY Most Holy Trinity.
Kaicher, Edward '80 (SD) Vista, CA Saint Francis of Assisi Catholic Parish.
Kaichiramattathil, Stephen *s.a.c.* '96 (MIL)[P] Milwaukee, WI Pallotti House.
Kail, Chorbishop Michael J. '74 (OLL) College of Consultors; Office of Liturgy; Presbyteral Council; Protopresbyters; Board of Pastors; Youngstown, OH St. Maron Maronite Catholic Church; Personnel Board.
Kaim, Phillip '03 (MO) Active Outside the Diocese; Air Force Chaplains.
Kaimann, Gerald J. '70 (JC) Brookfield, MO Immaculate Conception; Brunswick, MO St. Raphael; Marceline, MO St. Bonaventure; Milan, MO St. Mary; Brunswick, MO St. Boniface.
Kain, Rev. Msgr. Peter V. '65 (BRK) Brooklyn, NY St. Ephrem; Presbyteral Council; Parish Services Corp.; Board of Directors; Diocesan Insurance Committee; Diocesan Consultors.
Kainikunnel, George *s.d.b.* '96 (OAK)[L] Berkeley Salesians of Don Bosco.
Kairouz, Elie G. '01 (SAM) Williamsville, NY St. John Maron.
Kairu, James Kimani '94 (OAK) Richmond, CA St. David of Wales.
Kais, Paul D. '02 (POD)[N] Houston, TX Opus Dei; Vicar for Texas; Houston.
Kaiser, Gary Edward '06 (EVN) Clergy Personnel Board; Jasper, IN Precious Blood; Diocesan Consultors.
Kaiser, Lawrence B. '73 (DEN) Denver, CO Guardian Angels.
Kaiser, Lawrence H. '64 (DET) Retired.
Kaiser, Rev. Msgr. Ralph L. '54 (KC) Buckner, MO Church of the Santa Fe.
Kaithackal, Sebastian D. *c.m.i.* '81 (MET) Woodbridge, NJ St. James; John F. Kennedy Medical Center.
Kajoh, Robert T. *m.s.p.* (GAL) Houston, TX St. Philip Neri.
Kakareka, Joseph R. '72 (SCR) Sugar Notch, PA Holy Family Parish.
Kakascik, Rev. Msgr. Edward '55 (STU) Retired.
Kakaty, Rt. Rev. Edward '72 (NTN) Waterford, CT St. Ann.
Kakkuzhiyil, John *s.d.b.* '86 (GI) Valentine, NE St. Nicholas.
Kako, Fawaz *c.ss.r.* '10 (CHI)[N] Glenview, IL The Redemptorists of Glenview, Illinois.
Kala, Paul '10 (SFD) Highland, IL St. Paul.
Kalabat, Frank '95 (EST) West Bloomfield, MI St. Thomas Chaldean Catholic Parish; Eparchial College of Consultors; Diocesan Corporation–The Chaldean Catholic Church of U.S.A.
Kalachalil, Roy Kurian *o.ss.t.* '08 (BAL)[Q] Assigned in India.
Kalaj, Frederik '01 (DET) Erie, MI St. Joseph.
Kalam, Thomas *c.m.i.* '69 (NSH) Shelbyville, TN St. William; [K] Liberty, TN Carmel Center of Spirituality; Presbyteral Council.
Kalamaja, Theodore M. *s.j.* '67 (NO) New Orleans, LA Orleans Parish Criminal Sheriff's Office Community Correctional Center; [R] New Orleans, LA Ignatius Residence.
Kalampatt, George '81 (AMA) Umbarger, TX St. Mary's; Happy, TX Holy Name of Jesus.
Kalamuzi, Ivan '05 (COV) Maysville, KY St. Patrick.
Kalappura, George *c.m.i.* '60 (BEA) Beaumont, TX St. Anthony Cathedral Basilica; Convalescent Home Ministry.
Kalarickal, Joseph *m.s.t.* '90 (SP) New Port Richey, FL Our Lady Queen of Peace.
Kalarickal, Luka U. *m.s.f.s.* '88 (TYL)[B] Tyler, TX Trinity Mother Frances Health System; [C] Whitehouse, TX The Missionaries of St. Francis de Sales.
Kalas, Ronald N. '59 (CHI) Park Ridge, IL Mary, Seat of Wisdom; Deans Retired.
Kalata, Dominik P. '65 (ALN) Allentown, PA St. John the Baptist; Allentown, PA SS. Peter and Paul.
Kalathil, Francis Osana *o.c.d.* '79 (LA) Downey, CA St. Raymond.
Kalathil, Josely Dhyan *i.m.s.* '89 (LR) Scranton, AR St. Ignatius; Scranton, AR St. Meinrad Church; Scranton, AR SS. Peter and Paul.
Kalaw, Teodoro *c.r.m.* '05 (CHR)[H] Spartanburg, SC Converse College, Wofford College, USC – Upstate; Spartanburg, SC Jesus Our Risen Savior.
Kalayil, Roy Jacob (CC) Aransas Pass, TX St. Mary, Star of the Sea.
Kalb, Howard E. *s.j.* '54 (OM)[J] Omaha, NE Jesuit Community at Creighton University.
Kalchik, Paul J. '99 (CHI) Chicago, IL Resurrection.
Kalck, Michael V. '74 (CHI) Chicago, IL Holy Rosary.
Kalema, Josephat Kato '85 (NEW) Newark, NJ The Parish of the Transfiguration.
Kalema, Mark '88 (CHI) Chicago, IL Our Lady of Peace.
Kaler, Adolph *o.m.i.* '57 (SAT)[K] San Antonio, TX Oblate Madonna Residence.
Kalert, David *o.m.i.* '64 (SAT)[L] San Antonio, TX De Mazenod House.
Kaley, Richard *o.f.m.conv.* (STP) Bloomington, MN St. Bonaventure; [J] Bloomington, MN St. Bonaventure Friary.
Kalich, Patrick J. '94 (GRY) Crown Point, IN St. Mary.
Kalicky, John E. *c.pp.s.* '61 (GRY) Whiting, IN St. John the Baptist; Whiting, IN St. Adalbert; Whiting, IN Immaculate Conception; Whiting, IN Sacred Heart.
Kalil, Gordon '94 (SR) Napa, CA St. John the Baptist;

Priests' Council.
Kalin, William A. '59 (LIN)[E] Lincoln, NE Bonacum House Retired.
Kalina, Isaac *o.s.b.* '89 (LA)[P] Valyermo, CA St. Andrew's Abbey.
Kalinowski, Dariusz '99 (FR) Graduate Studies.
Kalinowski, Joseph J. '79 (MO) On Duty Outside Diocese; Army Chaplains.
Kalinowski, Loren M. '75 (SAG) Mount Pleasant, MI Sacred Heart.
Kalinowski, Ryszard *s.v.d.* '74 (LAF) Lafayette, LA Immaculate Heart of Mary.
Kalinski, Eugene E. '60 (GB)[J] Oshkosh, WI Community of Our Lady.
Kalisch, Jonathan *o.p.* '03 (MAN)[K] Hanover, NH Order of Preachers; [O] Hanover, NH The Catholic Student Center at Dartmouth, Aquinas House, Aquinas at Dartmouth, Inc.
Kalist, Pancrose '88 (NY) Staten Island, NY Our Lady, Queen of Peace.
Kalista, Timothy D. '03 (CLV) Chardon, OH St. Mary.
Kalita, Thomas M. '74 (WDC) Olney, MD St. Peter.
Kaliyadan, William V. *m.s.* '94 (MAN) Lebanon, NH Sacred Heart; Vicars Forane.
Kaliyadan, William *m.s.* '94 (HRT)[L] Hartford, CT Missionaries of LaSalette Province of Mary, Mother of the Americas.
Kalkman, Richard '56 (SCL) Retired.
Kall, Anthony *o.f.m.conv.* '71 (ALB)[R] Rensselaer, NY Assisi in Albany, Inc.
Kallabat, Stephen H. '66 (EST) Oak Park, MI Mar Addai Chaldean Parish; Eparchial College of Consultors; Eparchial Tribunal.
Kalladan, Joseph K. '69 (GAL) Sugar Land, TX St. Thomas Aquinas.
Kallaher, Timothy S. '72 (CIN) Cincinnati, OH St. John the Baptist; Judges; Presbyteral Council; Consultors.
Kallarackal, Lijo *o.s.b.silv.* (STL) Eureka, MO Sacred Heart.
Kallarackal, Sebastian *c.m.i.* '77 (SHP) Monroe, LA Our Lady of Fatima; [F] Monroe, LA Catholic Campus Ministry at the University of Louisiana at Monroe.
Kallock, Michael J. *c.s.p.* '73 (CHI) Chicago, IL Old St. Mary.
Kallookalam, Joseph *c.m.i.* '71 (SHP) Shreveport, LA St. Pius X.
Kallukalam, Jose '72 (STA) Fernandina Beach, FL St. Michael's.
Kallumady, Thomas '73 (NY) New York, NY Holy Innocents.
Kallumkalkudy, George *c.m.i.* '76 (STP) Kilkenny, MN St. Canice; Montgomery, MN Most Holy Redeemer.
Kalluvilayil, Job (GAL) Houston, TX St. Thomas More.
Kalluvilayil, Job (MCE) Houston, TX St. Peter's Malankara Catholic Church; Elected Members; Youth Apostolate Director; Priests – Heads of Apostolates.
Kalmon, Aaron P. '10 (SUP) Bayfield, WI Holy Family; Cornucopia, WI St. Ann; Bayfield, WI St. Joseph; Bayfield, WI St. Francis; Washburn, WI St. Louis; Presbyteral Council & Diocesan Consultors.
Kalombo, Jean Rene '95 (OWN) Fordsville, KY St. John the Baptist; Morgantown, KY Holy Trinity.
Kalonga, Simon '84 (DEN) Denver, CO Cure D'Ars.
Kalousieh, George '81 (OLN) Little Falls, NJ Sacred Heart.
Kalscheuer, Henry N. '59 (MAD) Retired.
Kalscheuer, Roger '80 (OM) Omaha, NE St. James.
Kalscheur, Gregory *s.j.* '01 (BO)[U] Newton, MA The Jesuit Community at Boston College.
Kaltenbach, Victor J. '62 (SFD) Greenville, IL St. Lawrence.
Kaltreider, Carl E. '79 (CHL) Marion, NC Our Lady of the Angels.
Kalu, Clement '84 (NY) Staten Island, NY Richmond University Medical Center.
Kalu, Clement '84 (NY) Staten Island, NY Richmond University Medical Center/Bayley Seton Campus.
Kalu, Samuel Joseph '95 (LFT) Associate Judges; [E] Lafayette, IN Emmaus House.
Kalungi, John *a.j.* '89 (NY) Bronx, NY St. Angela Merici.
Kaluza, Michael C. '07 (STP) Belle Plaine, MN Our Lady of the Prairie.
Kamanzi, Pascal K. *s.x.* (CHI) Chicago, IL St. George.
Kamas, John A. *s.s.s.* '75 (NY) New York, NY St. Francis de Sales.
Kamas, John *s.s.s.* '75 (CLV)[N] Cleveland Congregation of the Blessed Sacrament Provincial House.
Kamau, Francis *f.m.h.* '00 (SHP) Shreveport, LA St. Mary of the Pines.
Kamber, Kenneth L. '53 (L) Retired.
Kambitsch, Larry '69 (MRY) Tres Pinos, CA Immaculate Conception.
Kamienski, Gabriel *s.d.s.* '82 (SAT) Bandera, TX St. Stanislaus; [L] Falls City, TX Salvatorian Fathers Community of Texas.
Kamiensky, Joseph J. *s.j.* '77 (NY)[DD] Jesuit Community, Kohlmann Hall; [E] Bronx, NY Fordham Preparatory School.
Kaminski, Dariusz K. '91 (PAT) Deans; Deacon Internship Program; Paterson, NJ St. Stephen's.
Kaminski, Edward J. *c.s.c.* '75 (PHX) Phoenix, AZ Our Lady of the Valley Roman Catholic Parish; Glendale, AZ St. Raphael Roman Catholic Parish.
Kaminski, Edward J. *c.s.c.* '75 (FTW)[H] Notre Dame Congregation of Holy Cross, United States Province of Priests & Brothers.
Kaminski, Frank T. *s.j.* '76 (WDC)[R] Faulkner, MD Loyola Retreat House.
Kaminski, Louis T. '77 (SCR) Army National Guard Chaplains; Old Forge, PA Prince of Peace Parish, Old Forge; Presbyteral Council.
Kaminski, Mark P. '01 (SY)[S] Syracuse, NY Christ the King Retreat House.
Kaminski, Stephen J. '91 (CLV) Wickliffe, OH Our Lady of Mount Carmel; Concord, OH Tri Point Medical Center; Willoughby, OH Lake Health Hospital, Willoughby Campus.
Kaminsky, Joseph T. '61 (HRT) Retired.
Kammen, Paul A. '07 (STP) Delano, MN St. Peter; Delano, MN St. Joseph.
Kammer, Alfred C. *s.j.* '76 (NO)[C] New Orleans, LA Loyola University New Orleans.
Kammerer, James '97 (SAT) On Leave.
Kammerer, Joseph '98 (LA) Manhattan Beach, CA American Martyrs.
Kammerer, Raymond '64 (CIN) Waynesville, OH St. Augustine.
Kammerer, Richard F. '80 (RVC) Deer Park, NY SS. Cyril and Methodius; Hicksville, NY Our Lady of Mercy.
Kampschneider, Daniel J. '79 (OM) Omaha, NE St. Vincent de Paul.
Kamundo, Leopold '87 (ALB) Schenectady, NY St. John the Evangelist.
Kanagarajan, Lourdusamy '93 (DUL) Sandstone, MN Sacred Heart; Sandstone, MN St. Joseph; Sandstone, MN St. Luke.
Kanai, Charles '95 (MO) Army Reserve Chaplains.
Kanavalil, Joseph Thomas *c.m.i.* '98 (SFE) Santa Rosa, NM St. Rose of Lima.
Kandathikudy, Jos '71 (SYM) Bronx, NY St. Thomas Syro–Malabar Catholic Church (Bronx).
Kandathiparambil, Joseph John '94 (BIS) Garrison, ND St. Nicholas; Garrison, ND Immaculate Conception; Garrison, ND Sacred Heart.
Kandathiparampil, Joseph '63 (WIL) Retired.
Kandrac, Antone *o.f.m.conv.* '57 (ALB) Nassau, NY St. Mary; [L] Rensselaer, NY Franciscan Mission House; [L] Rensselaer, NY Provincialate, Immaculate Conception Friary – Order of Friars Minor Conventual.
Kandt, Gregory '90 (RIC) Charlottesville, VA Church of the Incarnation.
Kandyuk, Valeriy '90 (STN) Detroit, MI St. John the Baptist.
Kane, Brian P. '00 (LIN) Mead, NE St. James; [C] Wahoo, NE Bishop Neumann Jr.–Sr. High School; Army National Guard Chaplains; [L] Wahoo, NE Bishop Neumann High School Endowment Fund.
Kane, Edward R. P. '78 (BRK) Brooklyn, NY Holy Family.
Kane, Farrell J. *o.carm.* '65 (CHI) Gurnee, IL St. Paul the Apostle.
Kane, George J. '51 (CHI) Schaumburg, IL Church of the Holy Spirit Retired.
Kane, Rev. Msgr. James D. '58 (SY)[Q] Binghamton, NY McDevitt Residence for Retired Priests Retired.
Kane, James E. '51 (DEN) Retired.
Kane, James J. '71 (ALB) Ravena, NY St. Patrick.
Kane, James '71 (ALB) Ecumenical and Interreligious Affairs of the Roman Catholic Diocese of Albany, Commission for.
Kane, John E. *c.m.* '70 (MOB) Opelika, AL St. Mary Church; Hispanic Apostolate.
Kane, John '69 (SP) Retired.
Kane, Joseph M. '70 (BO) Senior Priests. Retired.
Kane, Joseph P. *s.j.* '68 (NY)[DD] New York, NY Murray–Weigel Hall.
Kane, Rev. Msgr. Joseph T. '62 (PH) Retired.
Kane, Joseph '67 (EVN) Retired.
Kane, Michael '80 (PSC) Coconut Creek, FL Our Lady of the Sign.
Kane, Philip M. '88 (JC) Pilot Grove, MO St. Joseph.
Kane, Terence '68 (ATL) Retired.
Kane, Thomas A. *c.s.p.* '75 (BRK)[R] On Special Assignment in the U.S.
Kane, Rev. Msgr. Thomas A. '52 (WDC) Retired.
Kane, Rev. Msgr. Thomas S. '67 (RVC) Retired.
Kane, Timothy J. '82 (DET) Detroit, MI St. Gregory the Great; Detroit, MI Church of the Madonna; Highland Park, MI St. Benedict.
Kane, Rev. Msgr. William J. '60 (WDC) Retired.
Kanfush, Philip M. *o.s.b.* '00 (GBG)[H] Latrobe, PA Saint Vincent Archabbey.
Kang, Jeoung Keun '90 (ALB) Korean Catholic Apostolate of Albany.
Kang, Paul '91 (NY) On Leave of Absence.
Kang–Gun Lee, Vincent '94 (SFR) San Francisco, CA St. Michael Korean Catholic Church; Korean Catholic Ministry.
Kanga, Florent *s.a.c.* '04 (MIL)[P] Milwaukee, WI Pallotti House.
Kania, Donald A. '09 (SUP) Superior, WI St. Anthony; Lake Nebagamon, WI St. Anthony.
Kania, Marcin '10 (TR) Lincroft, NJ St. Leo the Great.
Kaniampadickal, Sebastian '00 (SYM) Garland, TX St. Thomas the Apostle Catholic Church/Dallas (Syro–Malabar).
Kanicki, Philip A. '85 (RIC) Navy Chaplains; Unassigned.
Kaniparampil, James *c.m.i.* '98 (STA) Jacksonville Beach, FL St. Paul's.
Kaniseli, Soane T. '87 (SAC) Sacramento International Airport; Sacramento, CA Divine Mercy; Special Assignment.
Kanjirathumkal, Albert Francis *h.g.n.* (FWT) Megargel, TX St. Mary; [H] Seymour, TX Heralds of Good News Mother Theresa Province, Inc.; Wichita Falls, TX Sacred Heart.
Kannai, Niby *c.m.i.* '05 (COV) Elsmere, KY St. Henry.
Kannampuzha, Jose J. '92 (TYL) Lufkin, TX St. Andrew.
Kanonik, Stephen F. '82 (CHI) Deans; Chicago, IL St. Juliana.
Kantner, William R. '75 (MEM) Memphis, TN St. James.
Kantor, Rev. Msgr. Adolph A. '43 (SY) Retired.
Kantor, Robert Joseph '98 (MO) Navy Reserve Chaplains.
Kantor, Robert '98 (VEN) Presbyteral Council; Naples, FL St. Agnes; Deans; Planning and Development Committee.
Kantz, Robert J. '01 (CAM) Defenders of the Bond; Woodbury, NJ Holy Angels Parish, Woodbury, N.J.
Kanu, Clement '03 (NY) Bronx, NY St. Benedict.
Kanzic, Gerald (PAT) On Duty Outside the Diocese.
Kanzik, Gerald (PIT) Allegheny County, PA Mercy Health System of Pittsburgh–Pittsburgh Mercy Hospital.
Kao, Paulus '59 (LSC) Bayard, NM Our Lady of Fatima; Hurley, NM Infant Jesus.
Kapa, Benedict E. '00 (WH) Fort Ashby, WV Annunciation of Our Lord; Fort Ashby, WV St. Anthony; Romney, WV Our Lady of Grace.
Kapfer, Leon *s.j.* '53 (SPK)[J] Spokane, WA Regis Community.
Kapinus, Augustine *o.f.m.conv.* '58 (TR) Seaside Park, NJ St. Catharine of Siena.
Kapitan, John J. *o.f.m.* '95 (PBR) Pleasant City, OH St. Michael the Archangel.
Kapitan, John *o.f.m.* '95 (PRM)[C] Dayton, OH St. Barbara Prayer Community.
Kapitz, Donald '73 (SFE) Retired.
Kaplan, Jan F. '67 (CHI) Argo, IL St. Blasé.
Kappalumakkel, Mathew T. '89 (HRT) Washington Depot, CT Our Lady of Perpetual Help.
Kappe, John H. '71 (GAL) Hitchcock, TX Our Lady of Lourdes.
Kappes, Christiaan W. '02 (IND) Graduate Studies.
Kappes, Joseph B. *s.j.* '77 (CHL) Mooresville, NC St. Therese.
Kappes, Joseph B. *s.j.* '77 (MIL) Milwaukee, WI Gesu Parish; [P] Milwaukee, WI Jesuit Community at Marquette University.
Kappler, Stephan '94 (OAK) Study Leave.
Kappler, Stephan (STP) Burnsville, MN Church of the Risen Savior.
Kapral, Richard J. '70 (SY) Oneida, NY St. Joseph; Oneida, NY St. Patrick.
Kapron, Alan '94 (PSC) Leave of Absence.
Kapushion, Rev. Msgr. Marvin J. '56 (PBL) Rye, CO St. Aloysius; Judicial Expert Retired.
Kapusnak, Joseph '66 (PBR) Leisenring, PA St. Stephen; Revitalization and Renewal Commission.
Kapustka, Gerald *o.m.i.* '65 (FgM) Washington, DC AMERICAN OBLATE MISSIONS.
Karalus, Peter J. '97 (BUF) Lake View, NY Blessed John Paul II; Council of Priests; Consultors, College of.
Karam, Hanna '01 (SAM) Wilkes–Barre, PA St. Anthony + St. George.
Karam, Peter '88 (OLL) Cleveland, OH St. Maron Maronite Catholic Church; Victim Assistance Coordinator; Office of Protection of Minors; College of Consultors.
Karamitis, Dennis R. *s.j.* '75 (CHI) Chicago, IL Notre Dame de Chicago.
Karanauskas, Tomas '98 (LA) Los Angeles, CA St. Casimir.
Karani, Stephen '93 (ROC) Wayland, NY Holy Family Catholic Community.
Karas, Stephen '65 (Y) Retired.
Karasek, Edward '87 (AUS) West, TX St. Mary, Church of the Assumption; [M] Clerical Endowment Fund; Waco.
Karava, Norbert *o.f.m.cap.* '80 (MO) Navy Chaplains.
Karban, Roger R. '64 (BEL) Renault, IL Our Lady of Good Counsel.
Karcher, Jerome T. '83 (ORG) Huntington Beach, CA St. Vincent de Paul.
Karcsinski, Joseph J. '79 (BGP) Monroe, CT St. Jude.
Karczewski, Julian A. '74 (CAM) Swainton, NJ Retired.

Kardas, Stanislaw (SY) Syracuse, NY Basilica of the Sacred Heart.
Kardian, Richard S. *m.m.* '56 (NY)[DD] Retired.
Kardong, Terrence *o.s.b.* '63 (BIS)[A] Richardton, ND Assumption Abbey.
Kardzis, Christopher '84 (TOL) Sandusky, OH Holy Angels.
Kardzis, Krzysztof (TOL) Procurator–Advocate for Respondents; Associate Judges.
Karels, Ambrose G. '59 (KC) Retired.
Karempelis, Daniel *m.s.a.* '94 (NOR)[G] Cromwell, CT Society of the Missionaries of the Holy Apostles.
Karenbauer, Richard P. '70 (GBG) United, PA St. Florian; Holy Name Society.
Karepin, James M. *o.p.* '90 (CHI)[N] Chicago, IL St. Pius V Priory.
Karepin, James M. *o.p.* '90 (STN) Personnel Board; Eparchial Ecumenical Officer.
Karg, Rev. Msgr. William C. '57 (E) Oil City, PA St. Stephen.
Karg, William D. '64 (CLV) Akron, OH St. Sebastian Retired.
Kargul, A. Waine '67 (HRT) Plantsville, CT Mary Our Queen.
Kari, Arnold '77 (RC) Sturgis, SD St. Francis of Assisi.
Kariamadam, Jose *c.m.i.* '74 (NSH) Fayetteville, TN St. Anthony; [K] Liberty, TN Carmel Center of Spirituality; Deans.
Karikunnel, Joseph (NY) Staten Island, NY St. Clare.
Karimadam, Jose *c.m.i.* '74 (NSH) Pulaski, TN Immaculate Conception.
Karimatton, Joseph (NY) Larchmont, NY St. Augustine.
Kariu, James K. '94 (OAK) Kenyan Community.
Kariuki, Alphonsus '86 (MET) Edison, NJ St. Matthew the Apostle.
Karkees, Rev. Msgr. Polis '61 (SPA) El Cajon, CA St. Peter Chaldean Cathedral.
Karl, Kevin '69 (OWN) Absent on Leave.
Karl, Robert J. '57 (PBR) Erie, PA SS. Peter and Paul; Revitalization and Renewal Commission; Girard, PA SS. Cyril and Methodius.
Karle, William J. '72 (SCR) Deans; Bear Creek, PA St. Elizabeth.
Karlen, Donald H. '64 (SY) Forestport, NY St. Patrick; Presbyteral Council.
Karls, Victor *c.ss.r.* '70 (STL)[O] Liguori, MO Liguori Mission House/Redemptorists.
Karma, Gregorz O. (SJN) Carolina, PR Ntra. Sra. de Fatima.
Karmanocky, Bernard *o.f.m.* '73 (ALT) Johnstown, PA St. Therese of the Child Jesus; Councilors.
Karnik, George W. '58 (DUB) CEW Advisory Board Retired.
Karnish, Robert '66 (GI) Kimball, NE St. Joseph's.
Karns, David W. '74 (ALN) Port Carbon, PA St. Stephen.
Karomi, Khalid '90 (OLD) Paroisse Saint Ephrem.
Karoor, Isaac M. '69 (BAL) Retired.
Karpiey, Daniel J. '59 (HRT)[A] In Res. at the Archbishop Daniel A. Cronin Retirement Residence at St. Thomas Seminary Retired.
Karpinski, Jerzy *s.j.* '76 (CHI)[N] Chicago, IL Sacred Heart Mission House.
Karpyn, Gregory R. '87 (ALN) Allentown, PA St. Paul; Reading Hospital and Medical Center; Allentown, PA Manor Care Nursing Home; Macungie, PA Lehigh Center Nursing Home; Macungie, PA Lehigh Commons Personal Care Home; Reading, PA Sacred Heart.
Karris, Robert *o.f.m.* '65 (CHI)[N] Chicago, IL St. Peter's Friary.
Karris, Robert *o.f.m.* '65 (BUF)[N] St. Bonaventure, NY St. Bonaventure Friary.
Kartje, John F. '02 (CHI)[U] Evanston, IL Northwestern University, Sheil Center.
Karuhn, Robert J. '65 (GB) Retired.
Karuvelil, George *s.j.* '89 (WDC)[O] Washington, DC Woodstock Jesuit Community.
Karvelis, Francis V. '49 (HRT) Retired.
Karwacki, Bart *o.f.m.conv.* '75 (NOR) Cromwell, CT St. John.
Karwacki, Francis J. '83 (HBG) Mount Carmel, PA Our Lady of Mount Carmel; Charismatic Renewal.
Karwin, John J. *s.j.* '67 (BO)[U] Weston, MA Campion Health Center, Inc.
Karwowski, Edmund K. '87 (HRT) Windsor, CT St. Gabriel.
Karwowski, Ephrem *o.f.m.cap.* '88 (NOR) Middletown, CT St. Pius X.
Kasanziki, Pascal *s.x.* '94 (CHI)[N] Chicago, IL Xaverian Missionaries (S.X.).
Kaschenbach, Rev. Msgr. Arthur J. '51 (SCR) West Hazleton, PA Holy Name of Jesus Parish Retired.
Kasel, Randal J. '05 (STP) Pine Island, MN St. Michael; Zumbrota, MN St. Paul.
Kasela, Adam J. '01 (SAV) Savannah, GA Most Blessed Sacrament.
Kaserow, John M. *m.m.* '69 (NY)[DD] Maryknoll Maryknoll Fathers and Brothers.
Kaseta, Peter *o.f.m.cap.* '67 (PRT) Yarmouth, ME Parish of the Holy Eucharist.
Kash, Robert J. '52 (CHI) Bridgeview, IL St. Fabian Retired.
Kashangaki, David *c.s.c.* '99 (FTW)[H] Notre Dame Congregation of Holy Cross, United States Province of Priests & Brothers.
Kashen, David *o.f.m.conv.* (NOR) Members; Stafford Springs, CT St. Edward.
Kashmer, George B. '58 (GRY) Retired.
Kasinskas, Clement *c.p.* '57 (SCR)[L] Scranton, PA Saint Ann's Passionist Monastery.
Kasinski, James J. '66 (BUF) Retired.
Kasiyan, Andriv '02 (STF) Lackawanna, NY Our Lady of Perpetual Help.
Kasiyan, Ihor '92 (SJP) Parma, OH St. Andrew; Administrative Council; Alternates; Presbyters.
Kaska, E. William '69 (DAV)[J] Iowa City, IA O'Keefe Hall; State University of Iowa Hospital.
Kaskie, Brian '92 (JKS) McComb, MS St. Alphonsus; Continuing Formation Committee; Approved Advocate and Auditors; Chatawa, MS St. Teresa; Personnel Board; Priests' Council.
Kaslyn, Robert J. *s.j.* '85 (WDC)[C] Washington, DC Catholic University of America, The; [O] Washington, DC The Jesuit Community of St. Aloysius Gonzaga.
Kasparek, John A. '69 (PMB) Palm City, FL Holy Redeemer.
Kasper, John *o.s.f.s.* '79 (OAK) Lafayette, CA St. Perpetua; Deanery #9.
Kasperczuk, Marek '99 (CHI) Chicago, IL Holy Innocents; Bishop Abramowicz Seminary; Seminary Formation House–Bishop Abramowicz Seminary.
Kasperek, David D. '63 (GB) Green Bay, WI SS. Edward and Isidore.
Kasprick, Roger *o.s.b.* '59 (SCL)[I] Collegeville, MN St. John's Abbey, of the Order of St. Benedict.
Kasprzak, John F. '75 (BUF) Lackawanna, NY Queen of Angels.
Kasprzyk, James H. '65 (BUF) Retired.
Kasprzyk, Rev. Msgr. Leon J. '61 (MET)[H] Somerset, NJ McCarrick Care Center Retired.
Kasputis, Thomas R. '76 (CHI) Chicago, IL St. Rene Goupil.
Kass, Thomas G. *c.s.v.* '77 (CHI)[N] Chicago, IL Viatorian Residence; [N] Arlington Heights Viatorian Province Center–Clerics of St. Viator.
Kassis, Daniel F. '81 (GLP) On Duty Outside of Diocese.
Kasteel, Rev. Msgr. Ben '64 (LUB) Retired.
Kasten, Edward F. '54 (MIL) Retired.
Kastenholz, John P. *o.praem.* '65 (GB)[J] De Pere, WI St. Norbert Abbey; [O] De Pere, WI NORBERT & CO.; De Pere, WI; Hortonville, WI St. Denis; Hortonville, WI St. Patrick.
Kastenholz, Nicholas E. '02 (STL) University City, MO Our Lady of Lourdes; Judges; Adjutant Judicial Vicars.
Kaster, Alfred D. '60 (DUL) On Duty Outside the Diocese.
Kastigar, James J. '82 (CHI) Chicago, IL St. Mary of the Lake.
Kastigar, John J. '52 (CHI) Retired.
Kastl, Gary '07 (TLS) On Duty Outside the Diocese.
Kastner, Edwin H. '51 (BEL) Retired.
Kasu, Show Reddy '92 (BIR) Winfield, AL Holy Spirit.
Kasuboski, Walter *o.f.m.cap.* '74 (FgM) Detroit, MI Province of St. Joseph; [K] Detroit St. Bonaventure Friary.
Kasule, Gerald *c.s.sp.* '06 (SD) Escondido, CA Saint Mary Catholic Parish Escondido.
Kasun, Paul L. *o.s.b.* '94 (OM)[J] Schuyler, NE Benedictine Mission House.
Kasza, Rev. Msgr. John C. '93 (DET)[A] Orchard Lake, MI SS. Cyril and Methodius Seminary; Special Assignment.
Kaszczak, Rev. Archpriest Ivan '85 (STF) Presbyteral Council; Air Force Reserve Chaplains; [A] Stamford, CT Ukrainian Catholic Seminary Inc. St. Basil College; Stamford, CT Holy Protection of the Mother of God; Chaplain to the Ukrainian Scouts Plast Organization; Censor.
Kasznel, Richard C. '65 (STL) Saint Mary, MO Immaculate Conception.
Katanga, Wenceslaus '03 (FAR) Wishek, ND St. David; Wishek, ND St. Patrick; Wishek, ND St. Andrew's Church of Zeeland.
Katcher, Eugene '92 (DET) Roseville, MI Sacred Heart.
Katende, Fulgentius *c.s.c.* '91 (FTW)[H] Notre Dame Congregation of Holy Cross, United States Province of Priests & Brothers.
Kathawa, Anthony '10 (EST) Southfield, MI Our Lady of Chaldeans Cathedral, Mother of God Chaldean Parish; Eparchial College of Consultors.
Katoa, Sione Malakai '98 (SFR) Tongan Ministry; San Mateo, CA St. Timothy.
Katompa, Zephyrin Kabengele '98 (NEW) Elizabeth, NJ Our Lady of Most Holy Rosary/St. Michael.
Katricak, Kenneth J. *o.s.b.* '83 (CLV)[N] Cleveland Benedictine Order of Cleveland.
Katsouros, Stephen *s.j.* '98 (SFR)[N] San Francisco, CA Loyola House Jesuit Community.
Kattakkara, Joseph *c.m.i.* '89 (BEA) Convalescent Home Ministry; Beaumont, TX St. Anthony Cathedral Basilica.
Kattookkaran, Elson *m.s* '05 (NOR) Danielson, CT St. James.
Kattuthara, Joseph Anson '01 (SYM) Dayton, KY Blessed Chavara Syro–Malabar Catholic Church Cincinnati, OH.
Katz, Jerome A. '71 (SY) Retired.
Katz, Roger L. '89 (DUB) Retired.
Katzenberger, Scott *c.ss.r.* '97 (LA) Whittier, CA St. Mary of the Assumption; [P] Whittier, CA Redemptorists of Whittier.
Katziner, Stephen F. '74 (PH) Bensalem, PA Saint Ephrem.
Kauchak, Justin *o.p.* '66 (NO)[R] Metairie, LA Dominican Friars, Southern Dominican Province of St. Martin de Porres; [R] Metairie, LA Southern Dominican Foundation; [U] Metairie, LA Southern Dominican Foundation; Metairie, LA; New Orleans, LA St. Anthony of Padua.
Kaucheck, Kenneth R. '76 (DET) Absent on Leave.
Kauffman, Dennis *c.s.b.* '79 (DET)[E] Novi, MI Catholic Central High School.
Kauffman, Niles J. *o.f.m.cap.* '58 (MIL)[P] Milwaukee, WI St. Conrad Friary.
Kauffman, William B. '90 (WIL) Unassigned or Leave of Absence; DEPARTMENT OF VETERANS AFFAIRS HOSPITALS AND CHAPLAINS.
Kauffmann, James '76 (RIC) Richmond, VA Saint Benedict; Nocturnal Adoration Society.
Kaufman, Harry J. '02 (BO) German; Somerville, MA St. Catherine of Genoa.
Kaufman, Kent R. '93 (TOL) Rossford, OH All Saints; Members; Members.
Kaufman, William C. '74 (PH) Philadelphia, PA St. Richard; Diocesan Priests' Compensation and Benefits Committee; Deans; Deans.
Kaukus, Edwin J. '57 (BUF) Retired.
Kaul, John L. '75 (DET) On Duty Outside the Archdiocese.
Kaump, Joey '05 (MEM) Quest; Leadership Camp; Voyage.
Kaump, Richard J. '04 (MEM) Camden, TN St. Mary Church; College of Consultors; Presbyteral Council.
Kauth, Matthew K. '00 (CHL) Graduate Studies.
Kautzky, Zachary '10 (DM)[C] West Des Moines, IA Dowling Catholic High School; Des Moines, IA St. Augustin's.
Kautzman, Jerome G. '59 (BIS)[G] Bismarck, ND Emmaus Place Retired.
Kauvaetupu, Lomano *m.s.c.* (CI) Chuuk, FM Holy Cross.
Kavanagh, Aelred *o.s.b.* '94 (NO)[R] St. Benedict, LA St. Joseph Abbey.
Kavanagh, Rev. Msgr. Edward J. '48 (SAC) Sacramento, CA St. Rose; Diocesan Council of Catholic Women Retired.
Kavanagh, James F. '64 (LA) Redondo Beach, CA St. James Retired.
Kavanagh, Kevin J. '83 (COL) Columbus, OH Our Lady of Peace; College of Consultors; Diocesan Judges.
Kavanaugh, John J. '57 (WIL) Berlin, MD St. John Neumann Roman Catholic Church Retired.
Kavanaugh, John P. '48 (SFR) Knights of Malta Retired.
Kavanaugh, John *s.j.* '71 (STL)[C] Saint Louis University; [O] St. Louis, MO Jesuit Community Corporation at Saint Louis University – Jesuit Hall.
Kavanaugh, Kieran *o.c.d.* '55 (WDC)[B] Washington, DC Discalced Carmelite Friars; [X] Washington, DC Institute of Carmelite Studies and ICS Publications.
Kavanaugh, Michael J. '85 (SAV) Macon, GA Holy Spirit; Ecumenism and Interreligious Affairs; Presbyteral Council.
Kavcak, John P. *m.s.c.* '73 (SB) Palm Springs, CA Our Lady of Solitude; Palm Springs, CA Our Lady of Guadalupe.
Kaveney, Thomas J. '47 (CHI) Berwyn, IL St. Odilo Retired.
Kavipurayidam, Mathew *t.o.r.* '75 (FWT) Carrollton, TX St. Catherine of Siena; Mission Council.
Kavishe, Apolinary *a.j.* '98 (PRT) Bangor, ME Eastern Maine Medical Center; Bangor, ME Saint Paul the Apostle Parish.
Kavookjian, Rev. Msgr. Perry J. '87 (FRS) Advocates.
Kavookjian, Rev. Msgr. Perry '87 (FRS) Personnel Board; Bakersfield, CA St. Elizabeth Ann Seton.
Kavumkal, Sebastian *m.s.t.* '79 (MAR) Sault Sainte Marie, MI Holy Name of Mary; Sault Sainte Marie, MI Sacred Heart.
Kavungal, Jose '82 (COV) Alexandria, KY St. Mary of the Assumption.
Kawa, Rev. Msgr. Robert J. '69 (STU) Beverly, OH St. Bernard; [M] Beverly, OH Marriage Encounter; Deans; Priests Personnel Board.
Kawai, Thomas '91 (PHX) Lake Havasu City, AZ Our Lady of the Lake Roman Catholic Parish.
Kawalec, Pawel '95 (VEN) Palmetto, FL Holy Cross Church.
Kawamura, Peter *o.s.b.* '88 (SCL)[I] Collegeville St. John's Abbey, of the Order of St. Benedict.

Kawecki, Andrew M. '80 (GBG) Fairchance, PA SS. Cyril and Methodius; Fairchance, PA St. Hubert.
Kawka, Frederick J. '64 (SAG) Shepherd, MI St. Vincent De Paul; Diocesan College of Consultors Retired.
Kay, Colin Adrian '05 (NEW) Fair Lawn, NJ St. Anne's.
Kay, Joseph *m.afr.* '48 (SP)[N] St. Petersburg, FL Missionaries of Africa; Washington, DC; Washington, DC MISSIONARIES OF AFRICA Retired.
Kayajan, Daniel R. *c.s.c.* '97 (SP) Dade City, FL St. Rita; Vicars Forane.
Kayajan, Daniel R. *c.s.c.* '97 (FTW)[H] Notre Dame Congregation of Holy Cross, United States Province of Priests & Brothers.
Kayammakal, Thomas '80 (SFE) Ribera, NM San Miguel Del Vado; Villanueva, NM Our Lady of Guadalupe.
Kayatta, Francis P. '80 (MO) Narragansett, RI St. Mary, Star of the Sea; Air Force Reserve Chaplains; College of Consultors; Officers.
Kayiwa, Julius '62 (PHX) Bullhead City, AZ St. Margaret Mary Roman Catholic Parish.
Kaylor, Lee '81 (SFR) Retired.
Kayrouz, Rev. Msgr. Victor '64 (OLL) Retired.
Kayser, DeWayne '98 (SFS) Bowdle, SD St. Augustine; Presbyteral Council.
Kayser, Leonard '59 (SFS) Retired.
Kayser, Robert J. '52 (RVC)[N] Amityville, NY St. Pius X Residence Retired.
Kaywell, Jerome P. '91 (VEN) Punta Gorda, FL Sacred Heart.
Kaza, Rev. Msgr. Charles A. '72 (E) Brockway, PA Holy Cross; Brockway, PA St. Tobias; Eastern Vicariate; Administrative Cabinet; College of Consultors; Finance Council; Vicars General; Presbyteral Council.
Kazadi, Andre *c.i.c.m.* '03 (SAT) San Antonio, TX St. Patrick.
Kazarnowicz, Anthony S. '75 (MO) Army Chaplains; Military Chaplains.
Kazibwe, John C. '03 (RIC) Clarksville, VA St. Catherine of Siena; South Boston, VA St. Paschal Baylon; South Hill, VA Good Shepherd.
Kazista, Rev. Msgr. Francis G. '66 (WDC) Silver Spring, MD St. Andrew Apostle Retired.
Kazmierczak, Carl M. '55 (MIL) Retired.
Keahi, Christopher *ss.cc.* '65 (HON) Kaneohe, Oahu, HI; [D] Kaneohe, HI Congregation of the Sacred Hearts of Jesus and Mary (Hawaii Province SS.CC.); [D] Kaneohe, HI Sacred Hearts Center; Members.
Kealey, Edward J. '89 (RVC) Retired.
Kealy, Sean *c.s.sp.* '65 (PIT)[B] Pittsburgh, PA Duquesne University of the Holy Spirit.
Kean, Brian M. '08 (PH) Downingtown, PA St. Joseph.
Kean, Brian '10 (CHI) Oak Lawn, IL St. Germaine.
Kean, James F. '97 (DET)[T] Pontiac, MI Mt. Hope Catholic Cemetery Association; Pontiac, MI St. Damien of Molokai Parish.
Keane, Aquinas *o.c.s.o.* '73 (WOR)[N] Spencer, MA St. Joseph's Abbey; [P] Spencer, MA St. Joseph Abbey.
Keane, Denis J. '63 (GF) Red Lodge, MT St. Agnes.
Keane, Rev. Msgr. Dennis P. '71 (NY) Crestwood, NY Church of the Annunciation.
Keane, Rev. Msgr. James P. '45 (SFR) Retired.
Keane, James T. '55 (LFT) Muncie, IN St. Mary.
Keane, John F. '65 (BO) Senior Priests. Retired.
Keane, John J. '62 (HRT) Retired.
Keane, John J. '62 (PIT) Retired.
Keane, Michael F. '90 (NY) Harriman, NY St. Anastasia; [EE] Monroe, NY Queen of Apostles Convent; Canon 1742 Panel of Pastors.
Keane, Patrick A. '03 (R) Newton Grove, NC Our Lady of Guadalupe.
Keane, Patrick J. *o.s.a.* '52 (SD)[J] San Diego, CA Augustinian Community.
Keane, Philip S. *s.s.* '67 (BAL)[Q] Baltimore Society of St. Sulpice, Province of the United States Retired.
Keane, Philip S. *s.s.* '67 (SY) Syracuse, NY St. Charles Borromeo; On Duty Outside the Diocese.
Keane, Robert E. '78 (STP) Retired.
Keane, Robert L. *s.j.* '78 (MO) Navy Chaplains.
Keane, Robert L. *s.j.* '78 (BO)[U] Boston The Society of Jesus of New England–Provincial Offices.
Keane, Rev. Msgr. Vincent A. '58 (BRK) Apostleship of Prayer; [R] Douglaston, NY Bishop Mugavero Residence Retired.
Keaney, Francis *s.s.c.* '65 (PRO)[O] Bristol, RI St. Columban's Retirement House Retired.
Keaney, Francis *s.s.c.* '65 (OM)[J] St. Columbans Missionary Society of St. Columban.
Keaney, John B. *m.m.* '55 (NY)[DD] Retired.
Kearney, A. Damian *o.s.b.* '56 (PRO)[O] Portsmouth, RI Abbey of St. Gregory the Great.
Kearney, Christopher *o.f.m.cap.* '68 (SFR)[B] San Francisco, CA Capuchin Franciscan Order San Buenaventura Friary.
Kearney, Daniel S. '87 (NY) New York, NY St. Elizabeth.
Kearney, John T. '83 (NY) Lake Katrine, NY St. Catherine Laboure.
Kearney, Joseph A. '67 (SCR) Wilkes–Barre, PA St. Benedict Parish; Wilkes–Barre, PA Geisinger Wyoming Valley Hospital.
Kearney, Michael J. '82 (BO) Saugus, MA Blessed Sacrament; Saugus, MA St. Margaret.
Kearney, Timothy E. '96 (BO) Haverhill, MA All Saints; Haverhill, MA Sacred Hearts.
Kearns, Adam '54 (TR)[N] Trenton, NJ Villa Vianney Retired.
Kearns, Edward A. '63 (MET) Retired.
Kearns, Edward T. '77 (PH) Philadelphia, PA St. Dominic.
Kearns, John P. '88 (BO) Charlestown, MA St. Mary – St. Catherine of Siena.
Kearns, Lawrence *c.ss.r.* '65 (FgM) Baltimore Province.
Kearns, Owen *l.c.* '83 (HRT)[B] Cheshire, CT Novitiate of the Legion of Christ.
Kearns, Thomas '60 (KCK) Retired.
Keating, Carroll J. *s.j.* '61 (SJ)[M] Los Gatos, CA Sacred Heart Jesuit Center.
Keating, Earl *c.p.* '58 (SCR)[L] Scranton, PA Saint Ann's Passionist Monastery.
Keating, Edward C. *o.f.m.* '58 (SP) Tampa, FL St. Lawrence Retired.
Keating, Edward J. '94 (HBG) Selinsgrove, PA St. Pius X; Selinsgrove, PA Selinsgrove Center; [I] Selinsgrove, PA Susquehanna University Catholic Campus Ministry.
Keating, James R. *o.s.a.* '84 (PH) Philadelphia, PA St. Nicholas of Tolentine; [Y] Philadelphia, PA Augustinian Community (O.S.A.).
Keating, John R. *s.j.* '61 (NY)[DD] Loyola Hall, Jesuit Community.
Keating, Joseph R. '57 (LC) Retired.
Keating, Michael J. '02 (STP)[C] St. Paul, MN University of St. Thomas; Deanery 16.
Keating, Michael P. '97 (OM) Columbus, NE St. Bonaventure.
Keating, Patrick J. '05 (BRK) Catholic Migration Services, Inc.; Graduate Studies.
Keating, Thomas *o.c.s.o.* '49 (DEN)[N] Snowmass, CO St. Benedict's Monastery.
Keating, Timothy G. *s.m.* '85 (ATL)[F] Atlanta, GA; Atlanta, GA.
Keating, Timothy G. *s.m.* '85 (WDC)[B] Washington, DC Marist College, Provincialate of the Marist Society in the USA.
Keating, Timothy *c.ss.r.* '66 (ALB) Saratoga Springs, NY St. Clement.
Keck, Barnabas *o.f.m.cap.* '51 (NY) New Paltz, NY St. Joseph; [DD] New Paltz, NY St. Joseph Friary.
Keck, Edward '73 (COL) Retired.
Keck, Robert J. *s.j.* '60 (NY)[DD] New York, NY Jesuit Community of the Immaculate Conception.
Kedati, Andreas A. *s.v.d.* '00 (LKC) Iowa, LA St. Raphael.
Kedjierski, Walter F. '02 (RVC) Center Moriches, NY St. John the Evangelist; Procurator & Advocates.
Kedzierski, Casimir '60 (PIT) Glassport, PA Queen of the Rosary.
Kee, Rev. Msgr. James S. '95 (MOB) Judicial Vicar; Archdiocesan Consultors; Mobile, AL St. Catherine of Siena.
Keebler, Paul J. '66 (SY) Retired.
Keebler, William '91 (PEO) Rushville, IL St. Rose.
Keech, William J. *o.s.f.s.* '57 (WIL)[J] Wilmington, DE DeSales House.
Keefe, Bernard A. '63 (BGP) New Canaan, CT St. Aloysius Retired.
Keefe, Charles R. '76 (MIL)[N] Milwaukee, WI Milwaukee Catholic Home; Special Assignment; [K] Milwaukee, WI Columbia St. Mary's Hospital Milwaukee, Inc.
Keefe, Daniel G. '83 (HRT) Hamden, CT St. Joan of Arc; New Haven Vicariate; Hamden–North Haven Deanery; College of Consultors.
Keefe, Daniel T. '54 (OG) Retired.
Keefe, Donald J. *s.j.* '62 (NY)[DD] Loyola Hall, Jesuit Community.
Keefe, Francis J. '58 (PRO)[O] Providence St. John Vianney Residence Retired.
Keefe, Gerald E. '47 (STP) Retired.
Keefe, Jeffrey *o.f.m.conv.* '52 (SY) Syracuse, NY Assumption B.V.M.
Keefe, John J. '68 (LIN) Crete, NE Sacred Heart; Apostolate to the Spanish Speaking.
Keefe, John P. *c.s.c.* '59 (PHX)[F] Phoenix, AZ Holy Cross Congregation/Casa Santa Cruz; Tempe, AZ St. Margaret Roman Catholic Parish.
Keefe, John *c.s.c.* (FTW)[H] Notre Dame Congregation of Holy Cross, United States Province of Priests & Brothers.
Keefe, Joseph L. '71 (WIN) Retired.
Keefe, Thomas H. *m.m.* '55 (NY)[DD] Retired.
Keeffe, Anthony J. '63 (SY) Retired.
Keegan, James M. *s.j.* '71 (BO)[U] Weston, MA Campion Health Center, Inc.
Keegan, John E. *m.m.* '60 (NY)[DD] Maryknoll Maryknoll Fathers and Brothers Retired.
Keegan, John W. *s.j.* '69 (BO)[U] Boston The Society of Jesus of New England–Provincial Offices.
Keegan, John W. *s.j.* '69 (MAN) Milford, NH St. Patrick.
Keegan, Martin P. *m.m.* '65 (NY)[DD] Maryknoll Maryknoll Fathers and Brothers Retired.
Keegan, Terence *o.p.* '68 (PRO)[O] Providence St. Thomas Aquinas Priory at Providence College.
Keehan, Terence M. '86 (CHI) Inverness, IL Holy Family.
Keehner, John '93 (Y) Youngstown, OH St. Columba Parish; Judges.
Keel, Edwin L. *s.m.* '70 (WDC)[O] Washington, DC Marist Center.
Keelen, Kevin J. '91 (TR) Bayville, NJ St. Barnabas; College of Consultors; Vicars Forane (Deans).
Keeley, Isaac *o.c.s.o.* '92 (WOR)[N] Spencer, MA St. Joseph's Abbey.
Keeling, Paul M. *c.r.s.p.* '75 (BUF)[B] Youngstown, NY St. Anthony M. Zaccaria Seminary; [S] Youngstown, NY Basilica of the National Shrine of Our Lady of Fatima, Inc.
Keena, James *c.ss.r.* '57 (CHI) Chicago, IL St. Michael in Old Town.
Keenan, Alexander J. '76 (BO) East Boston, MA Most Holy Redeemer; Health Leave.
Keenan, Basil *o.s.b.* '67 (OKL) Seminole, OK Immaculate Conception; [I] Shawnee, OK St. Gregory's Abbey.
Keenan, Rev. Msgr. Desmond R. '49 (R) Retired.
Keenan, E.T. (TR)[N] Trenton, NJ Villa Vianney.
Keenan, Eugene '71 (TR) Retired.
Keenan, Francis X. *c.p.* '61 (CHI)[N] Chicago, IL Passionist Community–Immaculate Conception Community.
Keenan, James F. *s.j.* '69 (NY)[G] New York, NY Nativity Mission Center, Inc.; New York, NY; [DD] New York, NY Society of Jesus, New York Province; [DD] New York, NY Xavier Jesuit Community.
Keenan, James R. '99 (RCK) Elgin, IL St. Mary.
Keenan, James *s.j.* '82 (BO)[U] Newton, MA The Jesuit Community at Boston College.
Keenan, Rev. Msgr. John C. '51 (ORG) Retired.
Keenan, John *s.s.s.* '69 (HON) Kaneohe, HI St. Ann.
Keenan, Joseph F. '84 (PIT) Pittsburgh, PA St. Pio of Pietrelcina Parish.
Keenan, Joseph *s.t.* '79 (PAT)[N] Stirling, NJ Shrine of St. Joseph.
Keenan, Rev. Msgr. Patrick J. '69 (NY) Cortlandt Manor, NY St. Columbanus.
Keenan, Thomas E. '55 (MAN) Retired.
Keenan, Thomas L. '63 (PRO) Retired.
Keenan, Vincent P. *s.s.j.* '52 (BAL)[Q] Baltimore, MD St. Joseph's Manor.
Keenan, William R. *o.f.m.* '56 (FgM) New York, NY Holy Name Province.
Keene, James H. *s.j.* '73 (LA)[C] Los Angeles, CA Jesuit Community.
Keene, Kenneth R. '95 (PIT) McKees Rocks, PA Holy Trinity.
Keene, Mark A. '84 (COV) Fort Wright, KY St. Agnes; Deans; Priests' Retirement Committee.
Keene, Warren '81 (STA) Jacksonville, FL Immaculate Conception.
Keener, Robert J. '95 (MO) Navy Chaplains; Military Chaplains.
Keeney, Charles P. '78 (BRK)[D] Brooklyn, NY Campus Ministers and Ministry Centers; Brooklyn, NY St. Augustine.
Keeney, Timothy E. '96 (RIC) Bristol, VA St. Anne.
Keenoy, John A. '87 (STL) Pacific, MO St. Bridget Church.
Keese, John H. '74 (LA) Rowland Heights, CA St. Elizabeth Ann Seton.
Keewa, James *c.ss.r.* '57 (CHI)[N] Chicago, IL The Redemptorist Fathers of Chicago.
Keferl, Francis J. '73 (CIN) Vandalia, OH St. Christopher.
Keffer, Robert F. '68 (WDC) Burtonsville, MD Resurrection Parish.
Keffer, Robert '96 (MAD)[G] Prairie du Sac, WI Valley of Our Lady Monastery; Sparta, WI.
Keffler, Leopold *o.f.m.conv.* '63 (IND)[B] Indianapolis, IN Marian University; [P] Indianapolis, IN Mount Saint Francis Sanctuary, Inc.
Kegley, Jeffrey '96 (TR) Charismatic Renewal; Hamilton, NJ St. Raphael–Holy Angels Parish.
Kehew, Donal R. '63 (PRO) Providence, RI St. Joseph Retired.
Kehoe, Charles B. '73 (BRK) Retired.
Kehoe, Rev. Msgr. Daniel J. '39 (PH) Sharon Hill, PA Holy Spirit Retired.
Kehoe, James P. '70 (MO) Evanston, IL St. Joan of Arc; Navy Reserve Chaplains.
Kehoe, Joseph F. '66 (SY) Durhamville, NY St. Francis; Munnsville, NY St. Therese of the Infant Jesus.
Kehoe, Mark '99 (MET) Phillipsburg, NJ Warren Hospital; Phillipsburg, NJ St. Philip & St. James.
Kehoe, Richard J. *c.m.* '57 (PH)[Y].
Kehres, Franklin P. '68 (TOL) Norwalk, OH St. Paul; Members; Members.
Keigher, Bernard '74 (TR) Lakehurst, NJ St. John.
Keighron, Robert E. '06 (BRK) Howard Beach, NY St. Helen.
Keikati, Youssef '85 (SFR) San Francisco, CA St. Thomas More.

Keiser, Jerome F. '71 (STP) Lakeland, MN St. Francis Of Assisi.
Keiser, Raymond W. '70 (BIR) Retired.
Keiter, Adam '08 (WCH) Pittsburg, KS Our Lady of Lourdes; [I] Pittsburg, KS St. Pius X Newman Center (Pittsburg State University).
Keiter, James E. '01 (OM) Fremont, NE St. Patrick.
Keitz, Bernard Lawrence *o.p.* '54 (NY)[DD] New York, NY St. Vincent Ferrer Priory.
Keke, Kenneth *s.s.j.* '10 (LA) Los Angeles, CA St. Brigid's.
Kelash, David '94 (PHX) Cottonwood, AZ Immaculate Conception Roman Catholic Parish; Presbyteral Council.
Kelber, Vincent *o.p.* '07 (P) Portland, OR Holy Rosary Parish & Dominican Priory; [L] Portland, OR Holy Rosary Priory.
Kelchak, Joseph M. '50 (SUP) Retired.
Keleher, Rev. Msgr. J. Patrick '68 (BUF)[Q] Amherst, NY State University of New York at Buffalo (North Campus) Newman Center.
Keleta, Neguse Fesseha '84 (SEA) Mercer Island, WA St. Monica.
Keliher, Michael P. *c.s.v.* '76 (LAV) Henderson, NV St. Thomas More.
Keliher, Michael P. *c.s.v.* '76 (CHI)[N] Arlington Heights Viatorian Province Center–Clerics of St. Viator.
Kelleher, Cornelius '56 (DUL) Hinckley, MN St. Joseph; Hinckley, MN St. Patrick; Diocesan Deans.
Kelleher, James R. *s.o.l.t.* '96 (CC)[G] Robstown, TX Society of Our Lady of the Most Holy Trinity.
Kelleher, John P. *o.s.b.* '89 (BO)[U] Hingham, MA Glastonbury Abbey.
Kelleher, John P. *o.s.b.* '89 (FR) North Falmouth, MA St. Elizabeth Seton; Pocasset, MA St. John the Evangelist.
Kelleher, Lawrence A. '93 (GLD) Retired.
Kelleher, Mark A. '96 (WIL) Centreville, MD Our Mother of Sorrows.
Kelleher, Michael '65 (BLX) Pascagoula, MS Sacred Heart.
Kelleher, Robert J. '06 (SCR) Plymouth, PA All Saints.
Kelleher, Timothy J. '71 (BO) Walpole, MA Blessed Sacrament.
Kelleher, Walter T. *m.m.* '56 (NY)[DD] Retired.
Kellen, Elmer W. '50 (WIN) Retired.
Keller, Brendan '60 (MOB) Retired.
Keller, Gerald J. '65 (CLV) Berea, OH St. Adalbert Retired.
Keller, Herbert B. *s.j.* '81 (SCR)[B] Scranton, PA The University of Scranton; [D] Scranton, PA Scranton Preparatory School.
Keller, J. Rod '54 (ORG) Retired.
Keller, John D. *o.s.a.* '64 (SD)[J] San Diego, CA Augustinian Community; Counselors.
Keller, John R. '54 (ORG) Huntington Beach, CA St. Bonaventure Retired.
Keller, John T. '74 (GAL) Houston, TX Prince of Peace.
Keller, John *o.s.a.* (SD)[B] Center for Christian Spirituality.
Keller, Ken '69 (AMA) Nazareth, TX Holy Family; [I] Amarillo, TX Holy Family Parish of Nazareth, Texas Endowment Foundation.
Keller, Lawrence E. '47 (STP) Retired.
Keller, Matthew A. '02 (GLP) Gallup. Cure of Ars House of Discernment; Propagation of the Faith; Vocations; Priests' Retirement Board.
Keller, Neil J. '55 (CIN) Retired.
Keller, Paul J. *c.m.f.* '96 (LA) Temple City, CA; [V] Los Angeles, CA Tepeyac House.
Keller, Paul *o.p.* '93 (CIN) New York, NY; Cincinnati, OH St. Gertrude; [B] Cincinnati, OH Mount St. Mary's Seminary of the West; [N] Cincinnati, OH St. Gertrude Priory.
Keller, Robert J. '74 (MO) Harper Woods, MI St. Peter the Apostle; Air Force Reserve Chaplains.
Keller, Robert L. '67 (CIN) Cincinnati, OH Resurrection of Our Lord.
Keller, Robert *o.p.* '83 (DEN) Denver, CO St. Dominic; [N] Denver, CO Dominican Friars.
Keller, Theodore A. '46 (LEX) Lexington, KY St. Peter Retired.
Keller, Thomas G. '97 (STL) Florissant, MO St. Angela Merici.
Keller, Thomas W. '58 (LR) Carlisle, AR St. Rose of Lima Church; England, AR Holy Trinity Church.
Keller, Thomas '84 (B) Weiser, ID St. Agnes.
Keller, Thomas *m.s.c.* '55 (ALN)[A] Center Valley, PA Sacred Heart Villa, Missionaries of the Sacred Heart.
Kellerman, Raymond C. '73 (CIN) Cincinnati, OH Holy Trinity Church; Judges.
Kelley, Aloysius P. *s.j.* '62 (NY)[DD] Cardinal Spellman Hall, Jesuit Community.
Kelley, Arnold E. '56 (BO) Senior Priests.; Haverhill, MA All Saints Retired.
Kelley, Charles F. *s.j.* '84 (BO)[U] Boston The Society of Jesus of New England–Provincial Offices.
Kelley, Clark T. *o.s.f.s.* '64 (STO)[A] Stockton, CA St. Mary's High School.
Kelley, Daniel '95 (FWT) Chancellor; Arlington, TX St. Joseph's; Consultors; North Texas San Benito, Inc.
Kelley, David F. '88 (WIL) Bethany Beach, DE St. Ann; Deans; College of Consultors.
Kelley, David *o.s.a.* '73 (ALB) Waterford, NY St. Mary of the Assumption.
Kelley, Donald *s.s.c.* '62 (OM)[J] St. Columbans Missionary Society of St. Columban Retired.
Kelley, Edward J. '66 (MAN) Presbyteral Council Retired.
Kelley, Edward J. '68 (PRO) On Duty Outside the Diocese; Army Chaplains.
Kelley, Rev. Msgr. Francis H. '68 (BO) Roslindale, MA Sacred Heart; Presbyteral Council.
Kelley, Joel *o.s.b.* '66 (SB) San Bernardino, CA St. Bernardine Medical Center.
Kelley, John E. '61 (WOR) Presbyteral Council Retired.
Kelley, John '91 (AUS) Marlin, TX Sacred Heart; Marlin, TX St. Joseph.
Kelley, Joseph J. '87 (PH) Philadelphia, PA St. Monica.
Kelley, Laurence E. '60 (BO) Senior Priests. Retired.
Kelley, Michael A. '00 (PRO) Coventry, RI St. Vincent de Paul.
Kelley, Michael J. '75 (WDC) Washington, DC St. Martin of Tours.
Kelley, Omer C. '49 (GB)[G] Antigo, WI Langlade Hospital – Hotel Dieu of St. Joseph of Antigo Wisconsin Retired.
Kelley, Richard J. '72 (MAN) Nashua, NH St. Christopher.
Kelley, Robert E. '79 (WOR) Worcester, MA Our Lady of Lourdes Retired.
Kelley, Rev. Msgr. Thomas J. '51 (PH) Philadelphia, PA St. Matthew Retired.
Kelley, Thomas L. '88 (MAD) Cross Plains, WI St. Francis Xavier; Personnel Board; Deaneries.
Kelley, William H. *c.s.c.* '70 (BUR) Bennington, VT Sacred Heart St. Francis de Sales; North Bennington, VT St. John the Baptist.
Kelley, William H. *c.s.c.* '70 (FTW)[H] Notre Dame Congregation of Holy Cross, United States Province of Priests & Brothers.
Kelley, William *s.j.* '85 (SJ)[D] San Jose, CA Bellarmine College Preparatory.
Kellick, John W. '52 (GAL) Retired.
Kelliher, Michael M. *s.j.* '67 (SEA)[A] Seattle, WA Seattle University; [M] Seattle, WA Arrupe Jesuit Community at Seattle University.
Kellner, Winfried '63 (ROC) Rochester, NY Our Mother of Sorrows Retired.
Kellogg, Michael '02 (SCL) Bowlus, MN St. Stanislaus Kostka; Upsala, MN St. Edward's; Freeport, MN St. Francis of Assisi; Upsala, MN St. Mary; Diocesan Planning Council.
Kelly, Albert P. '72 (MOB) Elmore, AL Our Lady of Guadalupe.
Kelly, Andrew E. '70 (DAV) Mechanicsville, IA St. Mary's.
Kelly, Anthony *s.a.c.* '59 (NY) New York, NY Our Lady of Mt. Carmel.
Kelly, Augustine G. *o.s.b.* '88 (MAN)[K] Manchester, NH St. Anselm Abbey.
Kelly, Brendan R.J. '05 (LIN) Advocates.
Kelly, Brian F. '77 (SCR) Military Chaplains.
Kelly, Charles F. '64 (MET)[I] Somerset, NJ Maria Regina Residence Retired.
Kelly, Charles M. '07 (NEW) North Arlington, NJ Queen of Peace.
Kelly, Charles '99 (SAC) Rancho Cordova, CA St. John Vianney; Presbyteral Council.
Kelly, Columba *o.s.b.* '58 (IND)[A] Saint Meinrad, IN Saint Meinrad School of Theology; [K] Saint Meinrad, IN St. Meinrad Archabbey.
Kelly, Daniel A. '87 (PAT) Wayne, NJ Immaculate Heart of Mary.
Kelly, Daniel J. '56 (LC) Retired.
Kelly, Daniel L. '72 (RIC) Amherst, VA St. Francis of Assisi; Lovingston, VA St. Mary.
Kelly, Darrell C. *s.v.d.* '05 (JKS) Jackson, MS Holy Ghost; [H] Jackson, MS Tougaloo College Newman Center; Jackson, MS Holy Family.
Kelly, David A. *c.pp.s.* '82 (CIN)[N] Dayton Provincial Office of the Cincinnati Province of the Society of the Precious Blood.
Kelly, David A. *c.pp.s.* '82 (CHI)[W] Chicago, IL Kolbe House; [W] Chicago, IL Precious Blood Ministry of Reconciliation.
Kelly, David C. *m.m.* '57 (NY)[DD] Maryknoll Maryknoll Fathers and Brothers Retired.
Kelly, David (NO)[A] New Orleans, LA Notre Dame Seminary Graduate School of Theology.
Kelly, Donald F. '63 (ALB) Retired.
Kelly, E. Francis '67 (SCR)[K] Scranton, PA Home for Aged of the Little Sisters of the Poor, Holy Family Residence.
Kelly, Edward C. '90 (PH) Springfield, PA Holy Cross.
Kelly, Edward E. '65 (MEM) Retired.
Kelly, Edward J. '68 (PH) Norristown, PA Visitation B.V.M.
Kelly, Edward M. '68 (MIA) Coral Springs, FL St. Elizabeth Ann Seton.
Kelly, Eugene L. *o.s.f.s.* '65 (WIL)[J] Childs, MD Retirement and Assisted Care Facility Retired.
Kelly, Rev. Msgr. Francis D. '63 (WOR) On Duty Outside the Diocese.
Kelly, Francis E. '55 (PH) Retired.
Kelly, Francis '57 (LA) Retired.
Kelly, Francis (PAT) West Milford, NJ St. Joseph.
Kelly, Frank F. '77 (GF) Retired.
Kelly, George F. *c.ss.r.* '59 (ORL)[F] New Smyrna Beach, FL St. Alphonsus Villa–Redemptorist Fathers and Brothers Retired.
Kelly, Gerald E. *m.m.* '67 (GAL)[O] Houston, TX Maryknoll Fathers and Brothers.
Kelly, Gerard P. *c.m.* '82 (CHI)[N] Chicago, IL Vincentian Community, Congregation of the Mission, Western Province; Associate Administrators.
Kelly, Gregory W. '08 (SCR) Kingston, PA St. Ignatius Loyola, Kingston.
Kelly, Gregory '82 (DAL) Ex Officio Members; Vicar for Clergy; Pastors Consultors; College of Consultors; Personnel Board; Priest Personnel; Accreditation Board; I. Vicar for Clergy.
Kelly, J. Patrick *o.f.m.* '71 (NY)[DD] New York Franciscan Friars, Holy Name Province.
Kelly, Rev. Msgr. James A. '82 (SFR)[R] San Francisco, CA Prelature of the Holy Cross and Opus Dei.
Kelly, Rev. Msgr. James A. (POD) Menlo Park.
Kelly, Rev. Msgr. James G. '62 (BUF) Buffalo, NY St. Margaret; Clergy Personnel Board.
Kelly, Rev. Msgr. James J. '60 (BRK) Brooklyn, NY St. Brigid.
Kelly, James J. '83 (LA) Covina, CA Sacred Heart.
Kelly, James J. '50 (PH) Plymouth Meeting, PA Epiphany of Our Lord Retired.
Kelly, James M. *c.m.* '53 (BRK)[O] Bayside, NY Ozanam Hall of Queens Nursing Home, Inc.; [R] Jamaica, NY Reverend John B. Murray, CM, House.
Kelly, Rt. Rev. Msgr. James P. '62 (RVC) Priests' Retirement Board; Rockville Centre, NY St. Agnes Cathedral Retired.
Kelly, James Patrick *o.f.m.* '71 (BO)[Z] Boston, MA St. Anthony Shrine.
Kelly, James T. '92 (BO) Billerica, MA St. Andrew.
Kelly, James *g.h.m.* '48 (CIN)[N] Cincinnati Headquarters of Glenmary Home Missioners Retired.
Kelly, James *o.f.m.* '78 (CLV)[N] Brooklyn, OH St. Anthony of Padua Friary.
Kelly, James *s.j.* '03 (BAL)[Q] Baltimore, MD Jesuit Community of Loyola University, Inc.; [B] Jesuit Community of Loyola University, Inc.
Kelly, Joel *o.s.b.* '66 (SCL)[I] Collegeville St. John's Abbey, of the Order of St. Benedict.
Kelly, John D. '86 (ARL) Clifton, VA St. Andrew the Apostle; Deans.
Kelly, John E. '73 (BO) Stoughton, MA St. James.
Kelly, John E. '87 (BUF) Military Chaplains; Navy Chaplains.
Kelly, John F. '84 (PT) Gulf Breeze, FL Saint Sylvester.
Kelly, John J. '64 (BLX) Retired.
Kelly, John J. '87 (PH) Drexel Hill, PA St. Bernadette.
Kelly, John J. *s.j.* '74 (PH)[Y] Loyola Center and Manresa Hall.
Kelly, John J. *o.s.f.s.* '71 (R) Fayetteville, NC St. Elizabeth Ann Seton.
Kelly, John L. '54 (BAL) Glen Burnie, MD Church of the Good Shepherd; Catonsville, MD St. Mark Retired.
Kelly, John P. '45 (BO) Senior Priests. Retired.
Kelly, John R. '68 (R) Retired.
Kelly, John T. '61 (ALB) Memorial Hospital; Special Assignment.
Kelly, John Thomas *s.j.* '74 (WDC)[R] Faulkner, MD Loyola Retreat House.
Kelly, John *s.c.a.* '72 (DET)[K] Wyandotte, MI Pallottine Missionary Center (Irish Province).
Kelly, Jonathan '11 (STP) Lakeville, MN All Saints.
Kelly, Jordan James *o.p.* '03 (NY) New York, NY St. Catherine of Siena; [DD] New York, NY St. Catherine of Siena Priory.
Kelly, Joseph J. '78 (NY) Bronx, NY St. Anthony.
Kelly, Joseph L. *c.s.sp.* '50 (PIT)[O] Bethel Park, PA The Spiritan Center.
Kelly, Rev. Msgr. Joseph P. '66 (SCR)[P] Tunkhannock, PA Camp St. Andrew; [Q] Scranton, PA St. Francis of Assisi Kitchen; Catholic Social Services; Hispanic Ministry Outreach; Plymouth, PA All Saints.
Kelly, Joseph '78 (BRK)[B] Douglaston, NY Cathedral Seminary Residence of the Immaculate Conception.
Kelly, Justin J. *s.j.* '66 (DET)[E] Detroit, MI Loyola High School.
Kelly, Kenneth W. '79 (KCK) Mission, KS St. Pius X.
Kelly, Kevin J. '02 (PH) North Wales, PA St. Rose of Lima; [D] Wyncote, PA Bishop McDevitt High School.
Kelly, Kevin *c.o.* '06 (MET)[I] New Brunswick, NJ The New Brunswick Congregation of the Oratory of St. Philip Neri; New Brunswick, NJ St. Peter the Apostle; New Brunswick, NJ St. Joseph.
Kelly, Leonard H. *m.s.f.* '57 (SAT)[K] San Antonio, TX Padua Place.
Kelly, Martin '65 (FgM) Boston, MA St. James the Apostle, Inc.
Kelly, Maurus *o.f.m.* '56 (LA)[P] Santa Barbara, CA

Franciscan Friary, Order of Friars Minor (Old Mission).
Kelly, Michael D. '76 (SFS) Groton, SD St. Elizabeth Ann Seton.
Kelly, Rev. Msgr. Michael E. '66 (NEW)[C] West Orange, NJ Seton Hall Preparatory School; Liaison to the Irish Community.
Kelly, Michael J. '82 (PH) Hilltown, PA Our Lady of the Sacred Heart.
Kelly, Michael J. R. '10 (ARL) Alexandria, VA St. Mary's; Notaries.
Kelly, Michael M. '81 (SR) Sonoma, CA St. Francis Solano; Parish Priest Consultors.
Kelly, Michael *ss.cc.* '63 (FR)[F] Fairhaven, MA Damien Residence.
Kelly, Michael '73 (STO) Personnel Board; Lockeford, CA St. Joachim Church of Lockeford (Pastor of); Deans; Members at Large.
Kelly, Patrick J. '48 (BO) Woburn, MA St. Charles Borromeo; Senior Priests. Retired.
Kelly, Patrick *s.j.* '99 (SEA)[A] Seattle, WA Seattle University; [M] Seattle, WA Arrupe Jesuit Community at Seattle University.
Kelly, Patrick *s.m.a.* '74 (NEW)[L] Tenafly, NJ Society of African Missions, Provincialate, S.M.A. Fathers.
Kelly, Paul J. '74 (OG) Saranac Lake, NY St. Bernard; Saranac Lake, NY St. Paul; Lake Clear, NY St. John in the Wilderness; Tupper Lake, NY Sunmount Developmental Center.
Kelly, Paul Maurice '47 (LA) Retired.
Kelly, Paul '83 (SC) Denison, IA St. Boniface; Denison, IA St. Rose of Lima; Denison, IA St. Marys; Denison, IA St. Ann's.
Kelly, Paul *s.c.j.* '77 (MIL)[P] Franklin, WI St. Joseph's at Monastery Lake.
Kelly, Randy J. '94 (SAG) Saginaw, MI St. Thomas Aquinas; Territorial Vicars.
Kelly, Rev. Msgr. Raymond J. '61 (BRK)[K] Brooklyn, NY District Council of Kings; [R] Douglaston, NY Bishop Mugavero Residence; Long Island City, NY St. Patrick Retired.
Kelly, Raymond M. '49 (PRO) Retired.
Kelly, Richard J. '88 (NEW) Ramsey, NJ St. Paul.
Kelly, Robert D. '00 (PRM) Mentor–on–the–Lake, OH St. Michael; Lakewood, OH St. Gregory the Theologian; Mentor–on–the–Lake, OH St. Andrew the Apostle.
Kelly, Robert G. *s.j.* '57 (NY)[DD] New York, NY Murray–Weigel Hall.
Kelly, Robert J. '74 (ALT) Holy Childhood; Propagation of the Faith; Philipsburg, PA SS. Peter and Paul; Catholic Relief Services & Foreign Mission Outreach.
Kelly, Robert L. '77 (SY) Rome, NY St. Paul; Presbyteral Council.
Kelly, Robert *s.v.d.* '86 (CHI)[N] Techny, IL Divine Word Residence.
Kelly, Robert *o.p.* '89 (LAN)[K] Adrian, MI Motherhouse of the Sisters of St. Dominic, Congregation of the Most Holy Rosary.
Kelly, Stephen M. *s.j.* '90 (OAK)[L] Oakland, CA Jesuit Fathers and Brothers.
Kelly, Thomas D. '77 (MO) Air Force Reserve Chaplains.
Kelly, Thomas E. *o.f.m.* '62 (PAT)[N] Butler, NJ St. Anthony Friary.
Kelly, Thomas E. J. *s.j.* '79 (STL)[C] Saint Louis University; [O] St. Louis, MO Jesuit Community Corporation at Saint Louis University – Jesuit Hall Retired.
Kelly, Thomas F. '56 (PEO) Retired.
Kelly, Thomas J. '68 (ALB) Ballston Spa, NY St. Mary.
Kelly, Thomas J. '86 (HRT) Orange, CT Holy Infant.
Kelly, Thomas M. '90 (BIR) Birmingham, AL St. Peter the Apostle; [I] Birmingham, AL St. Peter's Endowment Foundation.
Kelly, Thomas N. '10 (VEN) Naples, FL St. John the Evangelist.
Kelly, Rev. Msgr. Thomas R. '67 (NY) Larchmont, NY St. Augustine.
Kelly, Timothy J. '99 (TYL) Flint, TX St. Mary Magdalene Church; Presbyteral Council.
Kelly, Tom (MRY) Special Assignment.
Kelly, Tony *s.a.c.* '59 (NY)[DD] New York, NY Pallottine Fathers.
Kelly, Vincent J. '57 (SY) Retired.
Kelly, Rev. Msgr. Vincent T. '56 (MIA) Fort Lauderdale, FL St. John the Baptist; [D] Fort Lauderdale, FL St. Thomas Aquinas High School.
Kelly, William A. '59 (STA) Jacksonville Beach, FL St. Paul's; Vicar General; Diocesan Consultors; Presbyteral Council; Finance Council; Building Commission.
Kelly, William J. *s.j.* '54 (MIL)[P] Milwaukee, WI Jesuit Community at Marquette University.
Kelly, William J. *o.praem.* '05 (PH)[Y] Paoli, PA Daylesford Abbey.
Kelly, Rev. Msgr. William M. '47 (SY) Retired.
Kelly, William T. '78 (GAL) Plantersville, TX St. Mary Retired.
Kelly, William T. (BO) Dedham, MA St. Mary.
Kelly, William *s.d.s.* '79 (NSH) Lewisburg, TN St. John the Evangelist.
Kelly, William *o.praem.* '05 (CAM) Bridgeton, NJ The Parish of the Holy Cross, Bridgeton, N.J.
Kelpsas, A. *m.i.c.* '53 (JOL) Retired.
Kelpsas, Jaunius '94 (CHI) Chicago, IL Nativity of the Blessed Virgin Mary.
Kelso, Francis E. '61 (MAN) Retired.
Kelso, Ronald *s.s.c.* '73 (FgM) St Columbans, NE House of Post–Graduate Studies.
Keltos, Adam *o.f.m.conv.* '62 (SY) Syracuse, NY Assumption B.V.M.
Kelty, Edward J. *o.s.* '89 (PCE) On Duty Outside the Diocese.
Kelty, Rev. Msgr. Leo A. '60 (TR) Retired.
Kemayou, Louis '92 (STV) Carenage, VI Chapel of St. Anne.
Kemberling, Andrew '88 (DEN) Centennial, CO St. Thomas More.
Kemeter, Robert '72 (PSC) Somerset, NJ SS. Peter and Paul.
Kemme, Allen M. '91 (SFD) Newton, IL St. Thomas the Apostle; Ste. Marie, IL St. Mary.
Kemme, Rev. Msgr. Carl A. '86 (SFD) Sherman, IL St. John Vianney; [N] Springfield, IL Catholic Care Center, Inc.; Corporate Board Members; Board of Catholic Education; Lay Employees' Pension Plan Administrative Committee; Commission for Buildings and Property; Moderator of the Curia; Priests' Personnel Board; Consultants; Diocesan Health Insurance Program Committee; [N] Springfield, IL Diocesan Care Management, Inc.; Comite Diocesano de Ministerio Hispano – Diocesan Committee for Hispanic Ministry; Office of the Vicar General; Bishop's Cabinet; Ex Officio.
Kemner, Kieran *o.f.m.* '53 (CHI)[N] Countryside, IL St. Gratian Friary, Franciscan Friars.
Kemo, Rev. Msgr. Kurt H. '83 (STU) Wintersville, OH Blessed Sacrament; Wintersville, OH Our Lady of Lourdes; Child Protection Review Board; Presbyteral Council; Priests Personnel Board; Diocesan Finance Council; College of Consultors; Victim Assistance Coordinator; Diocesan Administrator.
Kemp, Christopher J. '11 (SUP) Ladysmith, WI St. Mary; Ladysmith, WI St. Francis of Assisi; Ladysmith, WI St. Mary of Czestochowa; Ladysmith, WI Our Lady of Sorrows; Ladysmith, WI St. Anthony de Padua; Ladysmith, WI SS. Peter and Paul.
Kemp, Raymond B. '67 (WDC) Special Ministries; [X] Washington, DC Woodstock Theological Center.
Kemp, Thomas L. '52 (BUF) Retired.
Kempa, Rev. Msgr. Stanislaw (BO) Lowell, MA Holy Trinity.
Kemper, Jeffrey M. '79 (CIN) Vicarri Foranei (Deans); Harrison, OH St. John the Baptist.
Kemper, John C. *s.s.* '83 (HBG) On Duty Outside the Diocese.
Kemper, John C. *s.s.* '83 (BAL)[Q] Baltimore Society of St. Sulpice, Province of the United States; [U] Baltimore, MD Mother Seton House on Paca Street, Inc.
Kempf, Joseph G. '80 (STL) O'Fallon, MO Assumption.
Kempf, William G. '84 (STL) Normandy, MO St. Ann; [T] St. Louis, MO University of Missouri, St. Louis, Catholic Newman Center.
Kempfirl, Fred '65 (NY) Milton, NY St. James.
Kempinger, Stephen *c.s.c.* '01 (FTW)[A] Notre Dame, IN Moreau Seminary; [A] Notre Dame, IN Moreau Seminary.
Kempski, Leonard J. '66 (WIL) Liaison for Non–Christian Religions; Claymont, DE Holy Rosary Retired.
Kenaston, Perry '99 (JUN) Haines, AK Sacred Heart; Diocesan Consultors.
Kendall, Jeffrey A. '97 (CHR) Walterboro, SC St. Anthony.
Kendall, R. Daniel *s.j.* '70 (SFR)[N] San Francisco, CA Loyola House Jesuit Community.
Kendall, R. Daniel *s.j.* '70 (MIL)[Y] Milwaukee, WI Theological Studies, Inc.
Kendzierski, James *o.f.m.* '81 (GRY)[H] Cedar Lake, IN Our Lady of Lourdes Friary.
Kendzierski, James *o.f.m.* '82 (FTW)[I] Mishawaka, IN Our Lady of the Angels Convent.
Kendzierski, Norbert V. '64 (DET) Farmington Hills, MI St. Colman.
Kenealy, John J. *s.j.* '58 (FgM) Chicago, IL Society of Jesus.
Kenefick, Paul F. '56 (HRT)[A] In Res. at the Archbishop Daniel A. Cronin Retirement Residence at St. Thomas Seminary Retired.
Kenehan, David A. *o.s.f.s.* '74 (MO) Army Chaplains.
Kenkel, Benedict J. '53 (DM) Retired.
Kenkel, Leonard A. '60 (DM) Retired.
Kenlon, Knute *o.f.m.cap.* '58 (NY)[EE] Pelham, NY Sisters of St. Francis of the Neumann Communities; [DD] Yonkers, NY St. Clare Friary.
Kenna, Daniel T. *o.f.m.* '73 (NY) New York, NY Holy Name of Jesus.
Kenna, Joseph J. '67 (YAK) On Duty Outside the Diocese Retired.
Kenna, Joseph R. '99 (ARL) Annandale, VA Holy Spirit.
Kennard, George V. *s.j.* '50 (SJ)[M] Los Gatos, CA Sacred Heart Jesuit Center.
Kenneally, Rev. Msgr. John A. '69 (SAV) Finance Council; Clergy Personnel; Valdosta–Brunswick Deanery; College of Consultors; St. Simons Island, GA St. William; Vicars General.
Kenneally, William G. '61 (CHI) Chicago, IL St. Barnabas; Chicago, IL St. Gertrude Retired.
Kennealy, John H. '04 (WDC) Lexington Park, MD Immaculate Heart of Mary.
Kennealy, Thomas P. *s.j.* '62 (CIN)[N] Cincinnati, OH Jesuit Community at Xavier University.
Kennedy, Alex '90 (TLS) Grove, OK St. Elizabeth; Vinita, OK Holy Ghost.
Kennedy, Andrew '63 (BIR) Birmingham, AL Our Lady of Lourdes.
Kennedy, Arthur L. '67 (BO)[A] Brighton, MA St. John Seminary.
Kennedy, Bernard *o.f.m.* '88 (CHI) Provincial Councilors:; [N] Chicago, IL St. Joseph Interprovincial Post–Novitiate Formation House.
Kennedy, Charles J. '66 (PH) Philadelphia, PA Cathedral Basilica of SS. Peter and Paul; On Special or Other Archdiocesan Assignment.
Kennedy, David W. '97 (OWN) Oak Grove, KY St. Michael the Archangel.
Kennedy, Rev. Msgr. David '53 (GAL) Defenders of the Bond Retired.
Kennedy, Edward J. '68 (PH) On Special or Other Archdiocesan Assignment; Darby, PA Blessed Virgin Mary; [V] Darby, PA St. Francis Country House.
Kennedy, Ernest E. '56 (CHR) Retired.
Kennedy, Francis M. '64 (SPR) Bishop's Commission for Clergy Retired.
Kennedy, Glenn (RVC) Leave of Absence.
Kennedy, Rev. Msgr. J. Nevin '58 (MET)[I] Somerset, NJ Maria Regina Residence Retired.
Kennedy, Rev. Msgr. James M. '54 (SY) North Syracuse, NY St. Rose of Lima.
Kennedy, Jerrold F. '66 (OAK) Alameda, CA St. Philip Neri–St. Albert the Great Retired.
Kennedy, John D. '93 (SHP) Retired.
Kennedy, John F. '63 (NEW) Retired.
Kennedy, John F. *m.m.* '55 (NY)[DD].
Kennedy, Rev. Msgr. John J. '49 (STL) Retired.
Kennedy, John V. *c.m.* '49 (PH)[Y].
Kennedy, John '56 (SFD) Retired.
Kennedy, Joseph P. '73 (WDC) Retired.
Kennedy, Joseph *s.j.* '55 (BAL)[Q] Baltimore, MD Colombiere Jesuit Community.
Kennedy, Kevin (SFR) Redwood City, CA St. Pius; Sequoia Hospital.
Kennedy, Laurence W. '57 (SY) Retired.
Kennedy, Leo R. *m.m* '59 (NY)[DD] Maryknoll Maryknoll Fathers and Brothers Retired.
Kennedy, Leo *o.f.m.conv.* '90 (SAV) Brunswick, GA St. Francis Xavier.
Kennedy, Malcolm M. '61 (POD)[II] New Rochelle, NY; New York.
Kennedy, Michael E. *s.j.* '77 (LA) Sylmar, CA Barry J. Nidorf Juvenile Hall.
Kennedy, Michael J. *c.m.* '51 (PH)[Y].
Kennedy, Oliver *s.s.c.* '47 (OM)[J] St. Columbans Missionary Society of St. Columban.
Kennedy, Patrick A. '77 (STP) Eden Prairie, MN Pax Christi.
Kennedy, Patrick J. '53 (DEN) Retired.
Kennedy, Patrick J. R. '70 (NO) Retired.
Kennedy, Patrick '59 (SP) Clearwater, FL St. Cecelia Retired.
Kennedy, Paul M. '77 (PH) Philadelphia, PA St. Katherine of Siena.
Kennedy, Richard C. '73 (ORG) Santa Ana, CA St. Barbara Catholic Church.
Kennedy, Richard *m.s.c.* '67 (OG) Watertown, NY Our Lady of the Sacred Heart; [F] Watertown, NY Missionaries of the Sacred Heart.
Kennedy, Robert E. *s.j.* '65 (NEW)[B] Jersey City, NJ Jesuit Center; [L] Jersey City, NJ Jesuits of Saint Peter's College, Inc.
Kennedy, Robert J. '74 (ROC) Rochester, NY Blessed Sacrament; Rochester, NY St. Boniface; Liturgical Commission; Rochester, NY St. Mary.
Kennedy, Robert R. '66 (BO) South Boston, MA St. Monica–St. Augustine.
Kennedy, Robert T. '59 (NY) Retired.
Kennedy, Russell F. '75 (NOR) Willington, CT St. Jude; Ashford, CT St. Philip the Apostle.
Kennedy, T. Frank *s.j.* '76 (BO)[U] Newton, MA The Jesuit Community at Boston College.
Kennedy, Thaddeus J. *o.c.s.o.* '58 (DUB)[K] Peosta, IA New Melleray Abbey, Order of Cistercians of the Strict Observance.
Kennedy, Thomas R. *c.m.* '64 (PH)[Y].
Kennedy, Thomas '07 (FWT) Clifton, TX Holy Angels; Hillsboro, TX Our Lady of Guadalupe; Presbyteral Council.
Kennedy, Victor P. '77 (NEW) Jersey City, NJ Parish of the Resurrection; Jersey City Downtown Deanery 11.
Kennedy, W. Henry *s.j.* '52 (DET)[K] Clarkston, MI Colombiere Center.

Kennedy, William M. '87 (BO) Military & VA Chaplains.; Navy Chaplains.
Kennedy, William M. '71 (CIN) Retired.
Kennedy–Warley, David G. '57 (BUR) Retired.
Kennehan, John P. '62 (OG) On Duty Outside the Diocese.
Kennehan, John P. (STL) St. Louis, MO St. Richard; St. Louis, MO Mercy Hospital St. Louis.
Kennelley, James J. '70 (E) Mercer, PA Immaculate Heart.
Kennelly, Daniel '77 (BGP) Retired.
Kennelly, Michael F. *s.j.* '46 (NO) Retired.
Kennelly, Stephen '69 (SAN) Retired.
Kenney, Rev. Msgr. Albert A. '94 (PRO) Vicars General; Secretary for Diocesan Administration; Vicars General; Moderator of the Curia; Officers; Secretariat for Diocesan Administration; Finance Council; Barrington, RI St. Luke.
Kenney, Brian A. '02 (L) Shepherdsville, KY St. Benedict; Shepherdsville, KY St. Aloysius; Priest Personnel Commission.
Kenney, C. Douglas '99 (BAL) Bel Air, MD St. Margaret.
Kenney, Francis J. *s.m.* '49 (CIN)[N] Dayton, OH Mercy Siena Woods, Nursing Care.
Kenney, Gerard J. '97 (LUB) Lubbock, TX St. John Neumann; Diocesan Council of Catholic Women; Priests' Pension Board.
Kenney, Rev. Msgr. Jeremiah F. '72 (BAL) Retired.
Kenney, Kevin T. '94 (STP) St. Paul, MN Our Lady of Guadalupe; Vicar for Latinos.
Kenney, Mark G. *s.m.* '79 (WDC)[O] Washington, DC Marist Center.
Kenney, Paul C. *s.j.* '72 (BO)[U] Weston, MA Campion Jesuit Community.
Kenney, Peter J. *s.s.j.* '44 (BAL)[Q] Baltimore, MD St. Joseph's Manor.
Kenney, Sean W. '91 (MET) Warren, NJ Our Lady of the Mount.
Kenney, Timothy *s.m.* '82 (STL)[O] St. Louis, MO Cure of Ars Marianist Community.
Kenney, William J. '56 (STP) Retired.
Kenney, William J. *c.s.p.* '51 (BRK)[R] Retired Retired.
Kenny, Donald '66 (JOL) Retired.
Kenny, Eugene '53 (DOD) Retired.
Kenny, Gregory D. *c.m.f.* '59 (ATL) Stone Mountain, GA Corpus Christi.
Kenny, John F. *o.s.f.s.* '69 (WIL)[J] Childs, MD Retirement and Assisted Care Facility Retired.
Kenny, John J. *c.s.p.* '58 (GR) Evangelization.
Kenny, Joseph H. *o.p.* '50 (FgM) Chicago, IL Province of St. Albert the Great (Central).
Kenny, Joseph P. *o.p.* '63 (CHI)[N] Chicago Dominicans (Provincial Office).
Kenny, Paul *s.s.c.* (RVC) Syosset, NY St. Edward Confessor.
Kenny, Peter *s.s.c.* '58 (LA)[P] Los Angeles, CA Columban Fathers, Procure House.
Kenny, Peter *s.s.c.* '58 (OM)[J] St. Columbans Missionary Society of St. Columban.
Kenny, Pierce *c.ss.r.* '69 (BRK) Brooklyn, NY Our Lady of Perpetual Help Basilica.
Kenny, Robert J. '03 (SEA) Seattle, WA St. Paul; Seattle, WA St. Edward; Seattle, WA St. George.
Kenny, Stephen K. '91 (MEM) Somerville, TN St. Philip the Apostle.
Kenny, Thomas A. '46 (NEW) Retired.
Kenny, Thomas J. *s.j.* '09 (BO)[D] Boston, MA Boston College High School.
Kenny, Rev. Msgr. Walter F. '54 (NY) Larchmont, NY St. Augustine Retired.
Kenny, William J.M. '71 (LAV) Las Vegas, NV Christ the King; Las Vegas, NV Holy Spirit Catholic Church.
Kenshol, Joseph W. '73 (GR) Sand Lake, MI Mary Queen of Apostles; Deans; Presbyteral Council.
Kent, Daniel '63 (MIA) Retired.
Kent, James *o.f.m.conv.* '91 (IND)[J] Mount St. Francis, IN Province of Our Lady of Consolation, Inc.; [K] Mount St. Francis, IN Provincial Headquarters, Our Lady of Consolation Province, Conventual Franciscans; Mount Saint Francis, IN Province of Our Lady of Consolation.
Keohan, Edward M. '59 (BO) Senior Priests.; Salem, MA Immaculate Conception Retired.
Keohane, Daniel G. '78 (BRK)[R] Douglaston, NY Bishop Mugavero Residence Retired.
Keohane, Daniel T. '78 (SFR) Absent on Leave.
Keohane, Donal '68 (LA) Los Angeles, CA St. Martin of Tours.
Keohane, Donal '68 (SAV) Retired.
Keolker, Richard F. '63 (YAK) On Duty Outside the Diocese.
Keon, James J. *c.s.b.* '52 (GAL)[O] Houston, TX Residence of the Basilian Fathers of the University of St. Thomas.
Keough, Joseph F. '96 (HRT) Newington, CT St. Mary.
Keppel, Timothy F. *c.r.* '77 (SB)[I] Apple Valley, CA Congregation of the Resurrection, CR; Apple Valley, CA Our Lady of the Desert; Chicago, IL; Lucerne Valley, CA St. Paul; Elected At–Large Members.
Keppel, Timothy *c.r.* '77 (CHI)[N].
Keppens, Gustaaf M. *s.j.* '61 (WDC)[L] Washington, DC Georgetown University Hospital; [O] Washington, DC The Jesuit Community at Georgetown University.
Keppler, Rev. Msgr. John F. '60 (BRK)[R] Douglaston, NY Bishop Mugavero Residence Retired.
Kerbawy, Kevin '76 (SAG) Bay City, MI Holy Trinity; Bay City, MI St. Hedwig.
Kerber, John V. '58 (STL) Festus, MO Our Lady.
Kerber, Joseph P. '88 (SFD) Glen Carbon, IL St. Cecilia.
Kerber, Justin *c.p.* '72 (R) Greenville, NC St. Peter's; Deans; Council of Priests.
Kerby, Robert '70 (NTN) Retired.
Kerestes, Michael '89 (PSC) Beltsville, MD St. Gregory of Nyssa; Retirement Plan Board.
Kerestus, Thomas J. '69 (ALN) Retired.
Kereszty, Roch *o.cist.* '60 (DAL)[J] Irving, TX Cistercian Abbey of Our Lady of Dallas.
Kerin, Rev. Msgr. Joseph A. '57 (CHL) Charlotte, NC Retired.
Kerin, Michael J. *g.h.m.* (R) Windsor, NC Catholic Community of Bertie County.
Kerkemeyer, Carl '02 (TLS) Miami, OK Sacred Heart.
Kerketta, George '81 (BWN) Raymondville, TX Our Lady of Guadalupe.
Kerketta, Jerome *s.j.* '09 (OAK)[L] Berkeley, CA Jesuit Fathers and Brothers.
Kerketta, Pankratius '85 (LAN) Lansing, MI Resurrection.
Kermra, David J. *f.s.s.p.* (B) Coeur d'Alene, ID St. Joan of Art Chapel.
Kern, Rev. Msgr. Crosby W. '65 (NO) New Orleans, LA Cathedral – Basilica of St. Louis King of France; New Orleans, LA Shrine of St. Lazarus of Jerusalem; Newspaper; Old Ursuline Convent.
Kern, John R. '68 (MIL) Milwaukee, WI St. Catherine.
Kern, Martin F. '94 (ALN) Boyertown, PA St. Columbkill; Cursillo Movement.
Kernan, Rev. Msgr. Eugene J. '49 (CAM) Retired.
Kernan, William A. '93 (SD) San Diego, CA Saint Charles Borromeo Catholic Parish; San Diego, CA San Diego Airport.
Kerner, Terrence D. '72 (DET) Dearborn, MI St. Martha; Dearborn, MI St. Joseph.
Kerns, John '85 (P) Portland, OR St. Juan Diego Catholic Church; Continuing Education for Clergy; College of Consultors.
Kerper, Michael '85 (MAN) Nashua, NH St. Patrick; Advocates; Public Policy Commission; Presbyteral Council.
Kerr, Cherubin F. *o.s.a.* '44 (PH)[Y] Villanova, PA St. Thomas Monastery.
Kerr, John W. '98 (LR) Leave of Absence.
Kerr, Robert '95 (KC) Kansas City, MO St. Catherine of Siena.
Kerr, Robert '84 (STA) Absent or Sick Leave.
Kerr, Seamus '60 (YAK) Ephrata, WA St. Rose of Lima Retired.
Kerrigan, Bernard A. '48 (WIN)[F] Wabasha, MN St. Elizabeth's Health Care Center Retired.
Kerrigan, James P. '70 (WOR) Rutland, MA St. Patrick; Advocates.
Kerrigan, Rev. Msgr. Joseph J. '90 (MET) New Brunswick, NJ Sacred Heart; Catholic Relief Services.
Kerrigan, Michael F. '64 (DEN) Idaho Springs, CO St. Paul.
Kerrigan, Michael P. *c.s.p.* '87 (NY) Blauvelt, NY St. Catharine.
Kerschen, Leon J. '62 (WCH) Retired.
Kerscher, Francis '55 (GB) Retired.
Kersgieter, Paul J. '45 (STL) Retired.
Kerst, Patrick '90 (SPK) Walla Walla, WA Assumption of the Blessed Virgin Mary; Walla Walla, WA St. Francis of Assisi; Walla Walla, WA St. Patrick; Continuing Education of Priests; Members.
Kersten, Edward J. *o.s.a.* '56 (CHI) Chicago, IL St. Rita of Cascia.
Kersten, Jay J. '98 (MO) On Duty Outside the Diocese; Navy Chaplains.
Kersten, John *s.v.d.* '40 (CHI)[N] Techny, IL Divine Word Residence.
Kersten, Kevin F. *s.j.* '72 (OM)[J] Omaha, NE Jesuit Community at Creighton University.
Kertys, Martin *c.o.* '95 (NY) Tappan, NY Our Lady of the Sacred Heart; [HH] Sparkill, NY New York Oratory of St. Philip Neri, Inc.
Kertz, Leo *o.m.i.* '63 (FgM) Washington, DC AMERICAN OBLATE MISSIONS.
Kertz, Rev. Msgr. Raymond N. '67 (MAD) Retired.
Kerul'–Kmec, Miron '90 (PRM) Barberton, OH St. Nicholas.
Kerwan, Francis T. '43 (HRT) Enfield, CT Holy Family.
Kerwin, Art *o.p.* '84 (GAL) Houston, TX Holy Rosary.
Kerze, William F. '69 (LA) Malibu, CA Our Lady of Malibu.
Kesicki, Michael T. '88 (E)[A] Erie, PA St. Mark's Seminary; [B] Erie, PA Gannon University; [N] Erie, PA Holy Family Monastery; The Bishop's Theological Advisory Committee; St. Mark Seminary.
Kesicki, Timothy P. *s.j.* '94 (FgM) Detroit, MI; Chicago, IL Society of Jesus; Chicago, IL Society of Jesus.
Kesicki, Timothy P. *s.j.* '94 (DET)[K] Chicago, IL Detroit Province of the Society of Jesus–Provincial Office; Chicago, IL.
Kesicki, Timothy P. *s.j.* '94 (CHI)[N] Evanston, IL Canisius House.
Kesicki, Timothy P. *s.j.* '73 (CIN)[U] Cincinnati, OH St. Xavier Church Property Corporation.
Kesicki, Timothy P. *s.j.* '94 (CHI)[N] Chicago, IL Chicago Province of the Society of Jesus–Provincial Office.
Kessel, Gerald *o.f.m.cap.* '82 (DET)[P] Washington, MI Capuchin Retreat.
Kessing, Bernardine *o.f.m.* '60 (BO)[X] Boston, MA Saint Anthony Residence Retired.
Kessinger, David R. *o.s.b.* '58 (CHL)[J] Belmont, NC Belmont Abbey.
Kessler, Mathew *c.ss.r.* '91 (STL)[V] Liguori, MO Redemptorist Fathers.
Kessler, Mathew *c.ss.r.* '91 (DEN)[N] Denver The Redemptorists/Denver Province.
Kessler, Thomas '84 (CHL) Monroe, NC Our Lady of Lourdes.
Kessler, Thomas '75 (EVN) Mount Vernon, IN St. Matthew; Mount Vernon, IN St. Philip; New Harmony, IN Holy Angels.
Kessler, William Thomas '74 (COL) Lancaster, OH St. Bernadette; Censor of Books; Bremen, OH St. Mary.
Kessler, William '99 (SFD) Edwardsville, IL St. Mary; Presbyteral Council.
Kester, Kevin A. '81 (LA) La Canada Flintridge, CA St. Bede the Venerable.
Kester, William J. '70 (STL) Maryland Heights, MO St. John Bosco Retired.
Kestermeier, Charles T. *s.j.* '75 (OM)[J] Omaha, NE Jesuit Community at Creighton University.
Kestler, Theodore E. *s.j.* '75 (FBK) St. Marys, AK Church of the Nativity Catholic Church St. Marys; [E] Bethel, AK Brother Joe Prince Jesuit Community; Office of Native Permanent Diaconate; [E] St. Marys, AK Native Ministry Training Program.
Ketcham, Rev. Msgr. Gregory K. '94 (PEO) Champaign, IL St. John's Catholic Chapel; [M] Champaign, IL St. John's Catholic Newman Center at the University of Illinois, Urbana–Champaign.
Ketcham, Robert W. '08 (RVC) Valley Stream, NY Holy Name of Mary.
Kettelberger, John A. *c.m.* '78 (BRK)[R] Jamaica, NY St. Vincent's House.
Ketteler, Ronald M. '61 (COV) Ecumenism.
Kettenring, Michael J. '01 (NO) Marrero, LA The Visitation of Our Lady.
Ketter, Daniel '08 (ATL) Atlanta, GA St. Jude.
Keulman, Kenneth P. '69 (NO)[C] New Orleans, LA Loyola University New Orleans.
Keulman, Kenneth P. '69 (SJ) On Leave of Absence.
Keveny, M. Valentine (WDC) Rockville, MD St. Mary.
Keville, Joseph F. '96 (BO) Malden, MA Immaculate Conception.
Kew, Larry J. '66 (GRY) Hammond, IN St. Catherine of Siena.
Key, Oren W. *s.j.* '53 (SFE) Albuquerque, NM Immaculate Conception.
Key, Paul R. '07 (TYL) Nacogdoches, TX Nacogdoches, St. Mary's Chapel, Stephen F. Austin State University; [E] Nacogdoches, TX St. Mary's Catholic Campus Ministry; Young Adult/Campus Ministries; West Central Deanery.
Key, William W. '75 (MIL)[W] Whitewater, WI Cursillos in Christianity; Waukesha, WI St. Joseph.
Keyes, Jeffrey R. *c.pp.s.* '91 (OAK) Newark, CA St. Edward.
Keyes, Jeffrey R. *c.pp.s.* '91 (CIN)[N] Dayton Provincial Office of the Cincinnati Province of the Society of the Precious Blood.
Keyes, Patrick *c.ss.r.* '89 (NY) Bronx, NY Immaculate Conception.
Keyes, Paul T. '63 (BO) North Andover, MA St. Michael.
Keyes, Thomas E. '73 (BO) Ipswich, MA Our Lady of Hope.
Keymont, Walter F. '80 (BO) East Bridgewater, MA St. John the Evangelist.
Keys, Rev. Msgr. Thomas J. '70 (SR) On Leave.
Kezmarsky, Kenneth E. '86 (PIT) Springdale, PA St. Alphonsus.
Khachan, Chorbishop Bernard C. '60 (OLL) Retired.
Khachan, Charles H. *m.l.m.* '99 (OLL) San Antonio, TX St. George Maronite Catholic Church; [A] Houston, TX The Congregation of Maronite Lebanese Missionaries.
Khai Vu, Joseph '96 (NEW) Elizabeth, NJ St. Genevieve's.
Khalil, Naim *b.s.o.* '90 (NTN) Brooklyn, OH St. Elias; Presbyteral Council.
Khan, Joseph Nguyen '63 (DAV) Retired.
Khanh, Alberto O. *o.cist.* (PAT)[N] Morristown St. Mary's Abbey.
Kharuk, Wasyl '92 (PHU) Presbyteral Council; Board Members; Washington, DC Ukrainian Catholic National Shrine of the Holy Family; [A] Washington, DC St. Josaphat Seminary.

Khdmyn, Eugene (Andriy) *o.s.b.m.* '10 (RVC)[N] Glen Cove, NY St. Josaphat's Monastery, Novitiate and Retreat House.
Khin, Theodore '99 (WCH) Council Grove, KS St. Rose; Council Grove, KS St. Anthony of Padua.
Khoi, Jim Ngo Huang *c.m.c.* (FWT) Fort Worth, TX Our Lady of Fatima.
Khomyn, Eugene *o.s.b.m.* (STF)[B] Glen Cove, NY Basilian Fathers Novitiate of the Order of St. Basil the Great.
Khong, Ambrose *c.s.j.b.* '08 (BRK)[R] Elmhurst, NY Congregation of St. John the Baptist of China.
Khoueiry, Joseph '00 (SAM) Dover, NH St. George.
Khoury, Ghattas '90 (OLL) Phoenix, AZ St. Joseph Maronite Catholic Church.
Khoury, Rev. Msgr. James T. '75 (SAM) Retired.
Khue, Thomas '91 (OAK) Fremont, CA Holy Spirit.
Kiarie, Joseph M. *s.j.* (BO)[U] Newton, MA The Jesuit Community at Boston College.
Kibby, Patrick J. '84 (NSH) Old Hickory, TN St. Stephen; Presbyteral Council.
Kibirige, Charles '98 (LAN)[D] Ann Arbor, MI Spiritus Sanctus Academy.
Kibler, Gary R. '71 (BUF) Swormville, NY St. Mary.
Kibler, Joshua *c.o.* '09 (PIT)[P] Pittsburgh, PA Carnegie–Mellon University; [P] Pittsburgh, PA University of Pittsburgh; [M] Pittsburgh, PA Congregation of the Oratory of St. Philip Neri; [P] Pittsburgh, PA Chatham College.
Kichak, Francis J. *c.s.sp.* '54 (PIT)[O] Bethel Park, PA The Spiritan Center.
Kichak, Francis *c.s.sp.* '54 (SB)[I] Hemet, CA Congregation of the Holy Spirit Retired.
Kickham, Robert T. (BO)[CC] Braintree, MA Caritas Christi Retirement Plan and Trust; Boston, MA Cathedral of the Holy Cross.
Kidaagen, Baiju *v.c.* '01 (COV)[C] Villa Hills, KY Villa Madonna Academy High School; Edgewood, KY St. Pius X.
Kidd, William J. *s.j.* '63 (MIL)[P] Milwaukee, WI Jesuit Community at Marquette University.
Kidder, Rev. Msgr. James C. '67 (SAC) El Dorado Hills, CA Holy Trinity.
Kiddy, Curtis A. '92 (MIA) Miami Gardens, FL Visitation.
Kidner, M. Paul *o.s.b.* '58 (STL)[F] Creve Coeur, MO St. Louis Priory School; [O] St. Louis, MO The Abbey of St. Mary and St. Louis.
Kidney, Rev. Msgr. Liam J. '68 (LA) Pacific Palisades, CA Corpus Christi.
Kidney, Timothy '71 (SJ) Mountain View, CA St. Joseph Retired.
Kiedinger, Daniel J. '91 (LC) Leave of Absence.
Kiefer, Joel '04 (SD) San Diego, CA Saint Anne Catholic Parish.
Kiefer, John D. '70 (LFT) Fishers, IN St. Louis de Montfort.
Kiefer, Robert '91 (SJ) San Jose, CA St. Frances Cabrini.
Kiefer, Thomas P. '81 (SPC) Cape Girardeau, MO Cathedral of St. Mary of the Annunciation; Vice Chancellor; Judicial Vicar; Priests' Mutual Benefit Society; Diocesan Consultors; Judges.
Kiefer, William J. '58 (SB) Retired.
Kieffer, Charles G. '80 (PHX) Phoenix, AZ St. Mark Roman Catholic Parish; Phoenix, AZ St. Theresa Roman Catholic Parish; Diocesan Judges; Deans; Phoenix, AZ St. Philip the Deacon Mission, A Quasi–Parish.
Kieffer, John L. *s.j.* '68 (LEX) Monticello, KY St. Peter; [J] Mount Vernon, KY Appalachia Science in the Public Interest.
Kieffer, Joseph '04 (SAL) Beloit, KS St. John the Baptist Parish; College of Consultors.
Kieffer, Lawrence J. '50 (MAD) Retired.
Kieffer, Merlin '60 (SAL) Manhattan, KS Seven Dolors of the Blessed Virgin Mary Parish Retired.
Kieffer, Robert '69 (SCL) Morris, MN Assumption of the Blessed Virgin Mary.
Kieffer, Thomas A. *orat.* '65 (MRY)[F] Monterey, CA Oratorian Community–Congregation of the Oratory of Pontifical Right; [K] Monterey, CA Newman Institute for Historical and Religious Studies.
Kiel, William J. '93 (GBG) Indiana, PA St. Bernard of Clairvaux.
Kielb, John T. '75 (TR)[N] Trenton, NJ Villa Vianney; Leave of Absence.
Kielbasa, Richard '59 (SC) Retired.
Kielhorn, Justin *l.c.* '07 (HRT)[B] Cheshire, CT Novitiate of the Legion of Christ.
Kieliszewski, Jan M. '73 (MIL) Milwaukee, WI St. Augustine of Hippo.
Kielkowski, Andrzej *s.d.s.* '81 (NEW)[L] Verona, NJ The Salvatorian Fathers.
Kielkowski, Andzej C. *s.d.s.* '81 (CAM) Haddonfield, NJ St. Joseph the Worker Parish, Haddon Township, N.J.
Kieltyka, Robert '58 (MOB) Retired.
Kiely, Benedict C. '94 (BUR) Office of Continuing Education for Clergy; Stowe, VT Blessed Sacrament; Deans.
Kiely, Brian R. '78 (BO) Natick, MA St. Patrick.
Kiely, Cornelius '67 (FgM) Boston, MA St. James the Apostle, Inc. Retired.
Kiely, Thomas P. '88 (NY) Cortlandt Manor, NY Holy Spirit.
Kiely, Thomas R. '03 (CAM) Richard Stockton College of New Jersey; Elected Members; [Q] Pomona, NJ Richard Stockton College of New Jersey; Avalon, NJ St. Brendan the Navigator Parish, Avalon, N.J.
Kiem, Anthony '46 (PT) Retired.
Kiene, Joachim *o.f.m.conv.* '64 (IND) Veterans' Administration Hospital.
Kiene, Joseph *o.f.m.conv.* '64 (MO) DEPARTMENT OF VETERANS AFFAIRS HOSPITALS AND CHAPLAINS.
Kienzle, Jerome C. '72 (MIL) Sick Leave.
Kiepura, Kenneth '69 (CHI) Libertyville, IL St. Joseph.
Kieran, John C. '67 (ATL) Conyers, GA St. Pius X.
Kieran, Richard A. '65 (ATL) On Leave of Absence; Without Archdiocesan Assignment or Faculties.
Kiernan, Edward J. '54 (BRK) Retired.
Kiernan, James W. '62 (DM) Retired.
Kiernan, Joseph *o.f.m.* '69 (PAT)[N] Ringwood, NJ Holy Name Friary, Inc.
Kiernan, Michael F. '73 (SAC) Sacramento, CA Cathedral of the Blessed Sacrament; [E] Sacramento, CA St. Patrick Children's Home, Inc.; [L] Sacramento, CA Catholic Charities of Sacramento, Inc.; [L] Sacramento, CA Catholic Social Service of Sacramento; [L] Marysville, CA Grand Council, Catholic Ladies Relief Society of the Diocese of Sacramento; Director of Social Services; Vicars Forane; Catholic Charities of Sacramento, Inc.; Ecumenical & Interreligious Affairs; Department of Social Services.
Kiernan, Rev. Msgr. R. Donald '49 (ATL) Judges.
Kiernan, Robert J. *o.s.b.* '60 (BUR)[E] Weston, VT Priory of Benedictine Monks.
Kiernan, Thomas '48 (SY) Retired.
Kiesel, James P. '95 (BAL) Crofton, MD Church of the Holy Apostles; Priest Personnel Board.
Kiesel, Leo C. '63 (EVN) Retired.
Kieselbach, Joseph '61 (CR) Retired.
Kiesling, John F. *s.a.* '68 (NY)[DD] Garrison, NY St. Christopher's Inn; [DD] Garrison, NY St. Christopher's Friary.
Kieta, Stephen J. *s.j.* '08 (BO)[U] Newton, MA The Jesuit Community at Boston College.
Kieton, Dennis J. '85 (PRO) Cumberland, RI Our Lady of Fatima; Council Members.
Kiff, Herbert J. '95 (NO) Harahan, LA St. Rita.
Kiffmeyer, James G. '85 (CIN) Cincinnati, OH Holy Family.
Kifolo, Patrick J. *o.s.f.s.* '07 (WIL)[B] Wilmington, DE Salesianum School.
Kiggins, Roy '64 (ROC) Retired.
Kightlinger, Jon T. '03 (BAL) Priests Sick or Absent.
Kigozi, Denis S. '91 (COL) Columbus, OH St. Thomas the Apostle; Deanery 1: Center–South Columbus.
Kigozi, Denis '91 (COL) Parochial Examiners.
Kihm, Frederick C. '93 (STU) Flushing, OH St. Paul's; Lafferty, OH St. Mary.
Kihm, Peter J. '81 (NY) Poughkeepsie, NY Our Lady of Mt. Carmel.
Kihneman, Rev. Msgr. Louis F. '77 (CC) Office of the Bishop; College of Consultors; Diaconate Formation Screening Committee; Finance Council; Presbyteral Council; Vicar General; Building Commission; Personnel Board – Priests; Corpus Christi, TX Corpus Christi Cathedral.
Kikoba, Athanasius '04 (SJ) Mountain View, CA St. Athanasius.
Kilasara, Thomas '85 (NO) Slidell, LA St. Margaret Mary; Slidell, LA Greenbriar Nursing & Convalescent Home; Slidell, LA Guest House of Slidell Nursing Home; Slidell, LA Trinity Neurologic Rehabilitation Center at Slidell.
Kilbride, Eugene M. '59 (HRT) West Hartford, CT St. Helena Retired.
Kilburg, Jack *m.s.f.* '79 (SAT) Seguin, TX Our Lady of Guadalupe.
Kilburn, Clay *c.m.* (GLP) Keams Canyon, AZ St. Joseph's Indian Mission; Vicars Forane; Presbyteral Council.
Kilcarr, Stephen M. '56 (NEW)[C] West Orange, NJ Seton Hall Preparatory School Retired.
Kilcawley, Sean P. '05 (LIN) Advocates; Graduate Studies.
Kilcline, Francis I. '81 (LFT) Peru, IN St. Charles Borromeo; Deans; Members; Diocesan Consultors.
Kilcomons, Richard '06 (PAT) Morris Plains, NJ St. Virgilius.
Kilcourse, George A. '76 (L)[A] Bellarmine University.
Kilcoyne, Patrick '75 (SJ) Retired.
Kilcoyne, Terence T. '76 (WOR) Harvard, MA Holy Trinity; Advocates.
Kileo, Albert *a.l.c.p.* '92 (SLC) Roosevelt, UT Saint Helen LLC 224; Vernal, UT Saint James the Greater LLC 227.
Kiley, Francis *o.f.m.conv.* '54 (CHI)[N] Chicago Conventual Franciscans of St. Bonaventure Province.
Kiley, J. Cletus '74 (CHI) On Duty Outside the Archdiocese.
Kiley, John A. '66 (PRO) Ecumenical Officer Retired.
Kiley, John G. '70 (BO) Gloucester, MA Holy Family.
Kiley, Philip *s.j.* '71 (BO)[U] Newton, MA The Jesuit Community at Boston College.
Kiley, Phillip C. '78 (CHI) Chicago, IL St. George.
Kiley, Raymond P. '96 (BO) Quincy, MA Sacred Heart.
Kilgallen, John J. *s.j.* '65 (CHI)[C] Chicago, IL Jesuit Community at Loyola University Chicago.
Kilgallon, John J. '69 (PH) Southampton, PA Our Lady of Good Counsel.
Kilian, Waldemar A. '87 (MO) Navy Reserve Chaplains; Military Chaplains.
Kilianski, Edward *s.c.j.* '83 (MIL)[P] Hales Corners, WI Priests of the Sacred Heart.
Kilianski, Edward *s.c.j.* '83 (GAL) Houston, TX Our Lady of Guadalupe.
Kilidjian, Vincent *m.s.a.* '68 (NOR)[G] Cromwell Society of the Missionaries of the Holy Apostles.
Kilkelly, Timothy *m.m.* '90 (FgM) Maryknoll, NY MARYKNOLL.
Kill, Donald *s.s.c.* '72 (FgM) St Columbans, NE House of Post–Graduate Studies.
Kill, Robert J. '71 (TOL) Defiance, OH St. Michael; Defiance, OH St. Isidore.
Killackey, Cyprian *o.c.d.* '52 (TUC) Tucson, AZ Saint Margaret Mary Alacoque Roman Catholic Parish – Tucson; [E] Tucson, AZ Discalced Carmelite Friars of St. Margaret Mary's.
Killeen, John C. '59 (CAM) Retired.
Killeen, John P. '57 (CC) Retired.
Killeen, Rev. Msgr. Michael F. '59 (LA) Rowland Heights, CA St. Elizabeth Ann Seton Retired.
Killeen, Thomas *o.m.i.* '58 (ANC) Cordova, AK St. Joseph.
Killeen, William E. '75 (CHI) La Grange, IL St. Francis Xavier.
Killeen, William J. '59 (HRT) Retired.
Killian, Anthony J. '08 (ARL) Advocates; Alexandria, VA Blessed Sacrament.
Killian, Wayne E. '84 (ALN) Bethlehem, PA Holy Ghost; [O] Bethlehem, PA Lehigh University (Bethlehem); [O] Bethlehem, PA Moravian College (Bethlehem).
Killilea, Patrick *ss.cc.* '69 (FR) Fairhaven, MA St. Mary's.
Kilmurray, Fintan J. '77 (BLX) Wiggins, MS St. Francis Xavier; Army National Guard Chaplains.
Kilolelo, Ignas L. '00 (OAK) Oakland, CA St. Leo the Great.
Kilpatrick, Andrew W. '96 (SCR) Unassigned or Leave of Absence.
Kilpatrick, John J. '61 (SCR)[M] Dunmore, PA Villa St. Joseph Retired.
Kilroy, Brendan K. *s.p.s.* '62 (NEW)[C] Ramsey, NJ Don Bosco Preparatory High School; [L] Cliffside Park, NJ St. Patrick's Missionary Society.
Kilroy, Cornelius A. *o.p.* '61 (STP) Minneapolis, MN St. Albert the Great; [J] Minneapolis, MN St. Albert the Great Priory.
Kilroy, Paul E. '70 (BO)[AA] Weston, MA Regis College Office of Campus Ministry; Allston, MA St. Anthony of Padua.
Kilty, Cornelius F. *o.s.f.s.* '69 (PH) Philadelphia, PA Mater Dolorosa.
Kilumanga, Raphael '71 (SP) St. Petersburg, FL Holy Cross.
Kilumbu, Claudes '94 (MO) Army Chaplains.
Kilumbu, Jean Claude (OG) U.S. Army Headquarters.
Kilzer, James *o.s.b.* '98 (BIS)[A] Richardton, ND Assumption Abbey.
Kim, Adrian *c.p.* '02 (FRS) Clovis, CA Our Lady of Perpetual Help; Community Medical Center, Clovis.
Kim, Alapaki '82 (HON) Nanakuli, HI St. Rita; Diocesan Pastoral Council; Presbyteral Council.
Kim, Alex K. '91 (ORG)[H] Anaheim, CA St. Thomas Korean Catholic Center.
Kim, Alfonso *m.m.* '97 (FgM) Maryknoll, NY MARYKNOLL.
Kim, Andrew M. '98 (BRK) Brooklyn, NY St. Anselm.
Kim, Bede '07 (MET) Highland Park, NJ Transfiguration of the Lord Parish.
Kim, Bosco *o.s.b.* '71 (PAT)[N] Newton, NJ St. Paul's Abbey.
Kim, Carlos C. '93 (BO) On Duty Outside the Archdiocese.
Kim, Charles Sim Teck *s.j.* (STP)[J] Minneapolis, MN Markoe House Jesuit Community.
Kim, Chongkuk Carlos '93 (LA) Los Angeles, CA St. Alphonsus.
Kim, Chrysostom *o.s.b.* '60 (SCL)[I] Collegeville, MN St. John's Abbey, of the Order of St. Benedict.
Kim, Dominic '90 (OAK) Korean Pastoral Center.
Kim, Dominic '91 (DAL) Dallas, TX St. Andrew Kim.
Kim, Dong Kyum '07 (NEW) Demarest, NJ Parish of St. Joseph.
Kim, Dong–Jin Samuel '08 (BRK) Flushing, NY St. Paul Chong Ha–Sang Roman Catholic Chapel.
Kim, Donghoon '08 (SEA) Seattle, WA St. Andrew Kim Personal Parish.

Kim, Francis K. *o.f.m.* '96 (NY)[DD] New York, NY All Saints Friary; [HH] New York, NY Franciscan Missionary Charities, Inc.; New York, NY All Saints.
Kim, Jerome (SLC) Salt Lake City, UT Saint Ambrose LLC 214.
Kim, Jinsu Lawrence '00 (OKL) Oklahoma City, OK Korean Martyrs.
Kim, Jiwan A. *o.f.m.conv.* '93 (LA) Ventura, CA San Buenaventura Mission.
Kim, John Bosco *o.s.b.* (FgM) Newton, NJ St. Paul's Abbey.
Kim, Jong–Sup (PIT) Chaplain to Korean Catholic Community.
Kim, Joseph S. '90 (LAN) Lansing, MI St. Andrew Dung–Lac Retired.
Kim, Joseph Sy '90 (LAN)[O] Blessed Sacrament Educational Trust Fund.
Kim, Joseph Y. '74 (BAL) Baltimore, MD Holy Korean Martyrs.
Kim, Joseph *o.f.m.* '06 (NY) New York, NY All Saints.
Kim, Joseph '10 (SJ) San Jose, CA Holy Spirit; Council of Priests.
Kim, Joseph *o.f.m.cov.* '11 (RNO) Reno, NV St. Thomas Aquinas Cathedral.
Kim, Joseph *o.f.m.* '06 (WDC)[B] Silver Spring, MD Holy Name College.
Kim, Joseph (AUS) Franklin, TX St. Francis of Assisi.
Kim, Jung Yeon '05 (NO) Metairie, LA Hanmaum Korean Catholic Chapel; Hanmaum Korean Catholic Chapel.
Kim, Jungha '08 (ARL) Fairfax, VA St. Paul Chung.
Kim, Jungsoo '03 (NEW) Demarest, NJ Parish of St. Joseph.
Kim, Juntack (John) (AUS) Austin, TX St. Mary Cathedral.
Kim, Mary Joseph *o.cart.* '92 (BUR)[E] Arlington, VT Carthusian Foundation in America, Inc., Charterhouse of the Transfiguration.
Kim, Nam J. *s.s.* '90 (BAL)[Q] Baltimore Society of St. Sulpice, Province of the United States.
Kim, Nam J. *s.s.* '90 (SFR) Menlo Park, CA St. Anthony.
Kim, Nam Joseph '90 (ELP) On Duty Outside of Diocese.
Kim, Peter Sang Yun *s.d.b.* '02 (NY)[FF] Stony Point, NY Marian Shrine; [FF] Stony Point, NY Don Bosco Retreat Center and Marian Shrine.
Kim, Samuel *o.s.b.* '95 (PAT)[N] Newton, NJ St. Paul's Abbey; Newton, NJ.
Kim, Seung–Je Pancratius '06 (BRK) Flushing, NY St. Paul Chong Ha–Sang Roman Catholic Chapel.
Kim, Silvester (BAL) Baltimore, MD St. Thomas Aquinas.
Kim, Stefano Young–hoon *s.j.* '10 (ATL) Doraville, GA Korean Martyrs Catholic Church.
Kim, Steve '11 (SJ) San Jose, CA St. John Vianney.
Kim, Sung Heum (John) '91 (CAM) Absecon, NJ St. Andrew Kim Korean Catholic Mission, Inc.; Westville Grove, NJ St. Yi Yun Il John Korean Catholic Mission.
Kim, Tu–Jin Paul *c.p.* '00 (CHI)[N] Chicago Passionist Provincial Office.
Kim, Tu–Jin Paul *c.p.* '00 (RVC) Great Neck, NY St. Aloysius.
Kim, Yeongmin '11 (NEW) Ramsey, NJ St. Paul.
Kim, Youngcheol '93 (CHL) Korean Catholic Cultural Center.
Kimani, Muthumbi wa *s.j.* '07 (STL)[O] St. Louis, MO Jesuit Community Corporation at Saint Louis University – Jesuit Hall.
Kimaryo, Simon (CLV)[K] Parma, OH Holy Family Home and Hospice.
Kim Ban, Albert M. P. *c.m.c.* '03 (SPC)[F] Carthage, MO Congregation of the Mother Coredemptrix, United States Assumption Province.
Kime, David W. '97 (GRY) La Porte, IN St. Joseph; Deans; Bishop's Council of Priests; Consultors; Priests' Personnel Board.
Kimel, Alvin '06 (NEW) On Duty Outside the Archdiocese.
Kimes, John Paul '00 (OLL) Special Assignment.
Kimes, John Paul '00 (SAM) Judges.
Kimeu, Titus Waita *o.c.d.* '01 (MIL)[P] Milwaukee Provincial Offices – Discalced Carmelites.
Kimla, James E. '76 (MIL) Wauwatosa, WI St. Joseph Congregation; Whitefish Bay, WI Holy Family.
Kimm, Gregory C. '87 (SJ) Cupertino, CA St. Joseph of Cupertino.
Kimminau, Bernard '94 (LIN) David City, NE St. Mary's.
Kimminau, Irenaeus *o.f.m.* '49 (SFD)[K] Quincy, IL Holy Cross Friary Retired.
Kimmons, Steven E. *s.j.* '94 (CHI)[C] Chicago, IL Jesuit Community at Loyola University Chicago.
Kimtis, Kevin J. '11 (TR) Lawrenceville, NJ St. Ann.
Kinane, Gerard P. '73 (NO) On Administrative Leave.
Kinane, William P. '57 (SAC) Retired.
Kinast, Robert L. '68 (ATL) On Duty Outside the Archdiocese; On Leave of Absence; Without Archdiocesan Assignment or Faculties.
Kincl, Robert L. '67 (AUS) Diocesan Tribunal Judges.
Kindall, John J. *s.j.* '57 (SPK)[J] Spokane, WA Regis Community.
Kindangen, George *c.m.i.* '92 (BEA) Orange, TX St. Helen.
Kindel, Joseph C. '04 (CIN) On Special and Archdiocesan Assignment; Centerville, OH St. Francis of Assisi.
Kinderman, Dennis *c.pp.s.* '67 (CIN)[N] Dayton Provincial Office of the Cincinnati Province of the Society of the Precious Blood.
Kinderman, Dennis *c.pp.s.* '67 (CHI)[W] Chicago, IL Precious Blood Ministry of Reconciliation.
Kindon, W. Frederick '74 (PH) New Hope, PA St. Martin of Tours.
Kinerk, Edward *s.j.* '72 (COS)[E] Sedalia, CO Sacred Heart Jesuit Community; [G] Sedalia, CO Sacred Heart Jesuit Retreat House.
King, Andrew '96 (NY)[A] Yonkers, NY Cathedral Prep Program; [A] Yonkers, NY St. Joseph's Seminary.
King, Arthur *o.m.i.* '59 (BUF) Buffalo, NY Holy Angels.
King, Brian Madison '97 (LKC)[B] Lake Charles, LA CHRISTUS Health Southwestern Louisiana.
King, Brian '00 (PMB) Episcopal Secretary; Liturgy.
King, Bruce *i.c.* '85 (PEO) Farmington, IL St. Matthew's.
King, Chad '10 (PHX)[A] Phoenix, AZ Xavier College Preparatory Roman Catholic High School; Scottsdale, AZ Our Lady of Perpetual Help Roman Catholic Parish; Priests' Assurance Association.
King, Donald E. '74 (Y) Canton, OH St. Michael the Archangel.
King, Edward L. '55 (BO) Senior Priests. Retired.
King, Francis *o.c.s.o.* '58 (P)[L] Lafayette, OR The Cistercian (Trappist) Abbey of Our Lady of Guadalupe.
King, Gerald J. *t.o.r.* '71 (FgM) Loretto, PA THIRD ORDER REGULAR MISSIONS.
King, Gregory C. '76 (LA) Hawthorne, CA St. Joseph.
King, Howard J. '63 (E) Retired.
King, James B. *c.s.c.* '88 (FTW)[B] University of Notre Dame Du Lac; [H] Notre Dame, IN Holy Cross Community, Corby Hall, University of Notre Dame.
King, James E. '71 (PBL) Pueblo, CO Holy Rosary; Pueblo, CO Our Lady of the Meadows; Vicar General; College of Consultors; Finance; Finance Advisory Council; Clergy Benefit Society of the Diocese of Pueblo, Inc.; Ex Officio.
King, James H. '11 (CAM) Continuing Education & Spiritual Formation of Priests (CESF); Woodbury Heights, NJ Infant Jesus Parish, Woodbury Heights, N.J.
King, James J. *s.j.* '63 (CLV)[D] Cuyahoga Falls, OH Walsh Jesuit High School.
King, Rev. Msgr. James P. '46 (BRK)[R] Douglaston, NY Bishop Mugavero Residence Retired.
King, James W. '91 (BRK) Brooklyn, NY Assumption of the Blessed Virgin Mary.
King, James *c.s.c.* '88 (FTW)[B] University of Notre Dame Du Lac.
King, Jeffrey '87 (GLP) Reserve, NM Santo Nino; Catholic Committee on Scouting.
King, Jeremy *o.s.b.* '76 (IND)[K] Saint Meinrad, IN St. Meinrad Archabbey.
King, John R. *m.m.* '53 (NY)[DD] Maryknoll Maryknoll Fathers and Brothers Retired.
King, John *o.m.i.* '54 (BO)[U] Lowell, MA Missionary Oblates of Mary Immaculate.
King, John '48 (PEO) Retired.
King, Larry '89 (GR) Portland, MI St. Patrick's; Deans; College of Consultors.
King, Leo *ss.cc.* '45 (FR)[F] Fairhaven, MA Damien Residence Retired.
King, Martin '96 (P) On Duty Outside the Archdiocese; Air Force Chaplains.
King, Michael J. '77 (WDC) Owings, MD Jesus the Good Shepherd; Deans.
King, Nicholas '66 (ORL) Rockledge, FL St. Mary's; Representative by Age.
King, Norman A. '88 (RNO) Sparks, NV Immaculate Conception.
King, Paul Stephen '10 (SFS) Sioux Falls, SD St. Lambert.
King, Philip J. '49 (BO) Senior Priests. Retired.
King, Stephen *o.f.m.conv.* '96 (BAL)[Q] Ellicott City Order of Friars Minor Conventual.
King, Thomas F. '64 (LA) Los Angeles, CA St. Anastasia Retired.
King, Thomas J. *o.f.m.* '93 (SFR) San Francisco, CA St. Boniface.
King, Thomas M. '73 (CIN) Cincinnati, OH Guardian Angels.
King, Thomas *c.s.c.* '69 (FTW)[H] Notre Dame Congregation of Holy Cross, United States Province of Priests & Brothers.
King, Thomas *c.s.c.* '69 (KAL) Niles, MI St. Mark.
King, Rev. Msgr. William J. '83 (HBG) Contact; Mechanicsburg, PA St. Elizabeth Ann Seton; Mechanicsburg, PA St. Elizabeth Ann Seton; Vicar General; Moderator of the Curia; Youth Protection Program.
King, William J. (SAM) Promoter of Justice.
King, William M. *s.j.* '64 (WDC)[C] Washington, DC Georgetown University.
Kingery, Michael G. '99 (ATL) Roswell, GA St. Andrew.
Kingery, Patrick J. '93 (ATL) Rome, GA St. Mary.
Kingery, Victor *o.f.m.* '49 (SFD)[K] Sherman, IL Blessed Giles Friary.
Kingori, James *i.m.c.* '87 (BUF)[N] Williamsville, NY Consolata Fathers.
Kingsbury, John *c.ss.r.* '80 (WDC)[O] Washington, DC Holy Redeemer College.
Kingsley, Richard M. '83 (TUC) Tucson, AZ Corpus Christi Roman Catholic Parish – Tucson; [I] Tucson, AZ Parish Pooled Investment Trust.
Kingsley, S. Thomas '03 (CHR) Charleston, SC Church of the Nativity.
Kinh, Ignatius Nguyen Dai *c.m.c.* (STP)[S] Minneapolis, MN Queen Anne Communities; Minneapolis, MN Church of St. Anne – St. Joseph Hien.
Kiniry, Rev. Msgr. Lawrence R. '65 (GBG)[G] Greensburg, PA Neumann House.
Kinkel, Rev. Msgr. Robert J. '70 (DEN) College of Consultors; Edwards, CO St. Clare of Assisi.
Kinkopf, John J. '57 (CLV) Chagrin Falls, OH St. Joan of Arc Retired.
Kinn, James W. '57 (CHI) Mundelein, IL Santa Maria Del Popolo Retired.
Kinnally, Robert M. '05 (BGP)[A] Stamford, CT St. John Fisher Seminary Residence; Office of Vocations; [A] Stamford, CT St. John Fisher Seminary Residence; Presbyteral Council; Westport, CT Church of the Assumption; Priest Vocation Advisory Board.
Kinnaman, Leroy G. '73 (LFT) Tipton, IN St. John the Baptist.
Kinnane, James F. '63 (HRT) Special and other Archdiocesan Assignment; Judges; Office for Religious; Adjutant Judicial Vicar; Newington, CT Church of the Holy Spirit.
Kinney, Donald *o.c.d.* '88 (SJ)[M] San Jose, CA Carmelite Monastery, Novitiate.
Kinney, George R. '63 (STP) Retired.
Kinney, James J. '98 (SUP) Solon Springs, WI St. Anthony of Padua; Solon Springs, WI St. Mary; Solon Springs, WI St. Pius X; Pastoral Consultors.
Kinney, John M. '76 (MO) Military Chaplains; Air Force Chaplains.
Kinney, Leo '92 (FAR) Harwood, ND St. William; Hillsboro, ND St. Rose of Lima's Church of Hillsboro.
Kinney, M. Eugene '84 (MIL) On Duty Outside the Archdiocese.
Kinney, M. Eugene '84 (LAV) Las Vegas, NV Holy Family.
Kinney, Matthew '10 (AUS) Kyle, TX St. Anthony Marie De Claret.
Kintanar, Chris '05 (SD) Alpine, CA Queen of Angels Catholic Parish.
Kinter, John P. '67 (WDC) Washington, DC St. Thomas More; Hospital & Nursing Home Ministries.
Kintiba, George '96 (WDC)[D] Washington, DC Archbishop Carroll High School.
Kintiba, Georges *s.v.d.* '96 (WDC)[O] Washington, DC Society of the Divine Word/Divine Word House.
Kinyua, Linus '96 (DET) Wyandotte, MI St. Patrick.
Kinzler, Dale H. '74 (FAR) Devils Lake, ND St. Joseph's Church of Devils Lake; [I] Devils Lake, ND Marriage Encounter; Deanery 5; Healthcare Director.
Kinzler, Herman *o.carm.* (NEW) Englewood, NJ St. Cecilia's.
Kinzler, Herman *o.carm.* '08 (JOL) Glendale Heights, IL St. Matthew.
Kiocha, Milton *a.j.* (CLV) Akron General Hospital; Akron, OH St. Matthew.
Kipfer, David M. '88 (PEO) Ottawa, IL St. Columba.
Kiplagat, Anthony '93 (KCK) Olathe, KS Prince of Peace.
Kipper, Nicholas A. '06 (LIN) Advocates; Lincoln, NE St. Michael; Newspaper.
Kiran, Ravi '04 (GLP) Zuni, NM St. Anthony, Our Lady of Guadalupe; Diocesan Superintendent of Catholic Schools.
Kiratu, Ngugi Bernard '10 (ORL) Lakeland, FL Church of the Resurrection.
Kirby, Daniel J. '94 (DM) Council Bluffs, IA Corpus Christi; On Special Assignment; Seminarians.
Kirby, Donald J. *s.j.* '72 (SY)[Q] Syracuse, NY Jesuits at LeMoyne, Inc.
Kirby, Edward A. '61 (PT) Retired.
Kirby, Gerald S. '84 (NOR) St. Mary Church – Spanish Apostolate; Norwich, CT St. Mary; Norwich.
Kirby, Jeffrey '07 (CHR) Scouting Programs; Seminary Admissions Board; Vocations; The Drexel House – Catholic Residence for Men.
Kirby, Jim '96 (DM) Carlisle, IA St. Elizabeth Seton.
Kirby, John *s.v.d.* '71 (CHI)[N] Techny, IL Divine Word Residence.
Kirby, Louis *o.s.b.* '48 (KCK)[I] Atchison, KS St. Benedict's Abbey.
Kirby, Mark *o.s.b.* '86 (TLS) Special Assignment; [G] Tulsa, OK Monastery of Our Lady of the Cenacle.
Kirby, Martin F. '67 (BRK) Retired.
Kirby, Robert F. '59 (FR) Retired.
Kirby, Shane L. '04 (SCR) Williamsport, PA St. Joseph the Worker; Deans; Presbyteral Council.

Kirby, Thomas M. '57 (PIT)[N] Elizabeth, PA Divine Redeemer Motherhouse Retired.
Kirch, Jeffrey S. *c.pp.s.* '04 (LFT)[A] Rensselaer, IN Saint Joseph's College.
Kirch, Jeffrey *c.pp.s.* '04 (CIN)[N] Dayton, OH Provincial Office of the Cincinnati Province of the Society of the Precious Blood; [N] Dayton Provincial Office of the Cincinnati Province of the Society of the Precious Blood; Dayton, OH Society of the Precious Blood; Provincial Council:; [N] Dayton Provincial Office of the Cincinnati Province of the Society of the Precious Blood.
Kirchgessner, Christopher A. *o.s.b.* '80 (CHL)[J] Belmont, NC Belmont Abbey.
Kirchhoefer, Thomas A. '98 (MO) Military Chaplains; Army Chaplains.
Kirchner, Donnell *c.ss.r.* '66 (STL)[O] Liguori, MO Liguori Mission House/Redemptorists.
Kirchner, James A. '63 (NEW) Retired.
Kirchner, Peter K. '93 (SCL) Glenwood, MN Sacred Heart; Glenwood, MN St. Bartholomew's; Directors; Presbyteral Council.
Kirigia, Lazarus (DM)[D] Corning, IA Alegent Health Mercy Hospital; Corning, IA St. Patrick's; Lenox, IA St. Patrick.
Kirila, Michael '87 (ROM) Retired.
Kirk, Rev. Msgr. Albert E. '68 (MEM) Memphis, TN Church of the Holy Spirit; College of Consultors; Presbyteral Council.
Kirk, David R. '83 (MO) Military Chaplains; Army Chaplains.
Kirk, James T. '86 (WIL) Wilmington, DE St. Mary Magdalen.
Kirk, John L. '70 (NSH) Catholic Charismatic Renewal; Spring Hill, TN Church of the Nativity.
Kirk, Rev. Msgr. Raymond '59 (SD) Retired.
Kirk, Rev. Msgr. Thomas D. '69 (MEM) Brownsville, TN St. John Church; Jackson, TN St. Mary Church; Dean of the Jackson Deanery.
Kirk, William S. '72 (PH) Philadelphia, PA Our Lady of Calvary.
Kirke, Eugene K. '62 (BO) Senior Priests. Retired.
Kirkham, Richard '11 (FWT) Denton, TX Immaculate Conception.
Kirkhoff, Gerald J. '69 (IND) Priests' Personnel Board; Vicariate for Advocacy to Priests; Indianapolis, IN Good Shepherd Roman Catholic Church, Indianapolis, Inc.; Board of Consultors.
Kirkness, Michael D. '77 (GF) On Duty Outside of the Diocese.
Kirkness, Michael D. '77 (LA) Federal Correctional Institution.
Kirkpatrick, James W. '08 (BUF) Cheektowaga, NY St. Philip the Apostle.
Kirlin, Bernard G. '71 (MIA) Sunny Isles Beach, FL St. Mary Magdalen.
Kirrane, James A. '46 (BRK) Retired.
Kirsch, Gerard D. *o.s.b.* '70 (SEA)[M] Lacey, WA St. Martin's Abbey; [A] Lacey, WA Saint Martin's University.
Kirsch, Myron M. *o.s.b.* '73 (GBG)[H] Latrobe, PA Saint Vincent Archabbey.
Kirsch, Patrick V. '81 (SB) Alta Loma, CA St. Peter & St. Paul.
Kirschman, Andrew R. *s.j.* '11 (DEN)[N] Denver, CO Regis Jesuit Community (The Jesuits at Regis University).
Kirtz, Raymond R. *o.m.i.* '58 (STP)[M] Buffalo, MN Christ the King Retreat Center.
Kirwen, Michael C. *m.m.* '63 (FgM) Maryknoll, NY MARYKNOLL.
Kirwin, George *o.m.i.* '58 (WDC)[O] Washington, DC Oblate Community.
Kirwin, John D. '66 (ALB) Ministers to Retired Priests Retired.
Kirwin, Michael J. '76 (SCR) Scott Twp., PA St. John Vianney; Clifford, PA St. Pius X.
Kirwin, Peter *o.f.m.* '81 (PHX)[G] Scottsdale, AZ Franciscan Renewal Center, Inc. (Casa de Paz Y Bien); Scottsdale, AZ Our Lady of the Angels Conventual Church.
Kirwin, Rev. Msgr. Robert J. '45 (RVC) Williston Park, NY St. Aidan's Church Retired.
Kis–Horvath, Pascal *o.cist.* '57 (DAL)[J] Irving, TX Cistercian Abbey of Our Lady of Dallas.
Kisala, Robert *s.v.d.* '85 (FgM) Techny, IL.
Kiselica, John J. '84 (DET) Special Assignment.
Kiser, Karl *s.j.* '97 (DET)[E] Detroit, MI University of Detroit Jesuit High School and Academy.
Kish, Carl '62 (Y) Cortland, OH St. Robert Bellarmine Parish.
Kish, Jerome '98 (JOL) Downers Grove, IL St. Joseph.
Kish, Leslie P. '97 (B) Lewiston, ID All Saints Catholic Parish – Our Lady of Lourdes Church; [F] Lewiston, ID Lewis Clark State College; Lewiston, ID All Saints Catholic Parish – St. Stanislaus Church; College of Consultors; Deans; Lewiston, ID All Saints Catholic Parish – St. James Church.
Kish, Matthew J. '43 (GRY) Retired.
Kish, Michael A. '65 (MIA) Pinecrest, FL St. Louis; Miami Dade College–Kendall Campus; Police Chaplains.
Kishe, Venance Max '97 (CHR) Charleston, SC Blessed Sacrament.
Kiss, Barnabas G. *o.f.m.* '78 (ATH) Delegate in North America; American Hungarian Catholic Priests' Association (USA).
Kiss, Barnabas G. *o.f.m.* '78 (DET) Detroit, MI Holy Cross.
Kissane, Maurice J. '64 (CHI) Retired.
Kissane, Michael *o.carm.* '86 (NY)[DD] Middletown, NY Brandsma Priory.
Kissane, Michael *o.carm* '86 (PMB) Boca Raton, FL St. Jude.
Kissel, Anthony '73 (EVN) On Duty Outside the Diocese.
Kissel, Anthony '73 (SP)[A] Saint Leo, FL Saint Leo University, Office of Assessment and Institutional Research.
Kissel, Francis J. *s.m.* '71 (ATL)[C] Atlanta, GA Marist School.
Kissel, Ignatius M. *o.s.m.* '65 (P)[L] Portland, OR The Grotto, The National Sanctuary of Our Sorrowful Mother.
Kissell, Terrence '78 (DEN) Aurora, CO St. Michael the Archangel.
Kissinger, Rodney T. *s.j.* '53 (NO)[R] New Orleans, LA Ignatius Residence Retired.
Kissling, John M. '53 (DUB) Retired.
Kissner, Mark *o.c.d.* '10 (SB)[I] Redlands, CA Discalced Carmelites, OCD; [L] Redlands, CA El Carmelo Retreat House.
Kist, Harold W. '74 (CIN) Russells Point, OH St. Mary of the Woods; Presbyteral Council Retired.
Kistler, Leonard A. *c.pp.s.* '61 (CIN)[N] Carthagena, OH St. Charles Retired.
Kistner, Hilarion *o.f.m.* '55 (CIN)[N] Cincinnati, OH St. Francis Seraph Friary.
Kita, John M. '98 (SCR) Elkland, PA St. Thomas the Apostle.
Kitchin, George R. '70 (BLX) Gulfport, MS St. James; Charismatic Renewal.
Kitenge, Denis '87 (SP)[J] Tampa, FL St. Joseph's Hospital, Inc.
Kitheka, Joseph Charles (PEO) Peoria, IL St. Mark's.
Kithuri, Elias K. '03 (CHI) Chicago, IL St. Ignatius.
Kitsmiller, Robert J. '04 (COL) West Jefferson, OH SS. Simon and Jude.
Kitt, William J. '43 (CLV) Elyria Township, OH St. Vincent de Paul Retired.
Kitten, Marvin *s.j.* '65 (MOB)[A] Mobile, AL Spring Hill College; [I] Mobile, AL Spring Hill College Campus Ministry.
Kittock, Francis R. '55 (STP) Deanery 18; College of Consultors Retired.
Kituli, Christopher '10 (CHI) Oak Forest, IL St. Damian.
Kitz, Raphael *o.c.d.* '59 (LR)[A] Little Rock, AR Marylake – Carmelite Novitiate.
Kitzhaber, Keith '08 (LC) Loyal, WI St. Anthony of Padua.
Kitzke, Timothy L. '89 (MIL) Milwaukee, WI Old St. Mary; Milwaukee, WI Our Lady of Divine Providence; Milwaukee, WI Three Holy Women Catholic Parish; Milwaukee, WI SS. Peter and Paul.
Kivel, Joseph G. '61 (STP) Retired.
Kiwale, Methodius S. *a.l.c.p.* '96 (SFR) San Francisco, CA St. John of God.
Kiwan, Naji (SAM).
Kiwanuka, Deogratias '91 (PEO)[H] Bloomington, IL OSF St. Joseph Medical Center.
Kiwus, John *c.ss.r.* (NY)[DD] Esopus, NY Redemptorist Priests and Brothers C.Ss.R. (Province of Baltimore).
Kizewski, Justin '08 (LC)[C] Chippewa Falls, WI McDonell Central Catholic High School; Chippewa Falls, WI Holy Ghost; Chippewa Falls, WI St. Bridget.
Kizhakedan, John *c.m.i.* '74 (BEL) Waterloo, IL St. Patrick; Walsh, IL St. Pius V; Special Assignment.
Kizhakkedam, Augustine *o.c.d.* '84 (SYM) Apex, NC Lourdes Matha Syro–Malabar Catholic Church (North Carolina).
Kizhakumpurath, Philip Thomas *m.s.f.s.* '87 (TYL)[C] Whitehouse, TX The Missionaries of St. Francis de Sales.
Kizhakumpurath, Philip Thomas *m.s.f.s.* (NY) Yonkers, NY St. Paul the Apostle.
Kizis, Kenneth G. '59 (SCR)[M] Dunmore, PA Villa St. Joseph Retired.
Kizito, John Fisher '02 (FAR) Ellendale, ND St. Helena's Church of Ellendale; Ellendale, ND St. Patrick.
Klaas, Gregory '67 (SR)[G] Sonoma, CA Hanna Boys Center.
Klaers, Marvin J. '50 (STP) Retired.
Klag, Michael A. '03 (WCH) Winfield, KS St. Mary; Winfield, KS Holy Name.
Klaiber, Jeffrey L. *s.j.* '74 (FgM)[N] Chicago Chicago Province of the Society of Jesus–Provincial Office; Chicago, IL Society of Jesus.
Klajbor, Richard J. '79 (CHI) Chicago, IL Our Lady, Mother of the Church.
Klak, Jan Piotr '79 (SAT) San Antonio, TX St. Anthony Mary Claret; [C] Oblate School of Theology.
Klamut, Charles '99 (PEO)[M] Champaign, IL St. John's Catholic Newman Center at the University of Illinois, Urbana–Champaign; Champaign, IL St. John's Catholic Chapel.
Klanichka, Volodymyr '01 (PHU) Wilmington, DE St. Nicholas.
Klapperich, Giles R. *o.p.* '53 (CHI)[N] Chicago, IL St. Pius V Priory.
Klapps, William J. '58 (WIL) Wilmington, DE St. Matthew Retired.
Klarer, Michael E. '79 (MO) Monroe, WI St. Clare of Assisi Parish; Navy Reserve Chaplains; Medical Leave of Absence.
Klasek, Stephen A. '83 (NSH) Manchester, TN St. Mark; Tullahoma, TN St. Paul the Apostle; Defenders of the Bond; Priest Benefit Foundation; Clergy Personnel Board; Diocesan Planning.
Klasinski, George '51 (KCK) Retired.
Klasinski, Stanley J. '77 (CLV) Lyndhurst, OH St. Clare.
Klassen, Roger *o.s.b.* '66 (SCL) Freeport, MN Sacred Heart; New Munich, MN Immaculate Conception; Freeport, MN St. Rose of Lima; [I] Collegeville, MN St. John's Abbey, of the Order of St. Benedict; Personnel Committee; Defensor Vinculi.
Klatka, Joseph S. '67 (MAN) Retired.
Klauck, Michael '94 (BIR) Absent on Leave.
Klauck, Rev. Msgr. Peter N. '55 (GB) Retired.
Klauck, Stanley B. '46 (MIL) Retired.
Klauer, Gary *o.f.m.conv.* '75 (MRY)[F] Arroyo Grande, CA St. Joseph Cupertino Province, Provincial Center.
Klauer, Gary *o.f.m.conv.* '75 (OAK) San Pablo, CA St. Paul; Deanery #7.
Klaus, John Mark *t.o.r.* '99 (VEN) Liturgical Commission; Sarasota, FL Our Lady Queen of Martyrs; Department of Worship.
Kleas, Rev. Msgr. Milam '51 (GAL) Houston, TX St. Maximilian Kolbe Retired.
Kleba, Gerald J. '67 (STL) St. Louis, MO St. Cronan.
Kleber, Cecil *o.f.m.* '50 (SFE)[H] Albuquerque, NM The Province of Our Lady of Guadalupe.
Klecha, Joseph A. *m.m.* '69 (SJ)[M] Los Altos, CA Maryknoll.
Klecha, Joseph A. *m.m.* '69 (NY)[DD] Maryknoll Maryknoll Fathers and Brothers Retired.
Kleczewski, Kieran '78 (PHX) Avondale, AZ St. Thomas Aquinas Roman Catholic Parish; Worship and Liturgy, Office of; Avondale, AZ St. Michael Roman Catholic Parish; Deans; Priestly Life and Ministry Board.
Kleczka, Lukasz *s.d.s.* '99 (GRY)[H] Merrillville, IN Salvatorian Fathers (Society of the Divine Savior).
Klee, Joseph C. '01 (COL) Columbus, OH Sacred Heart.
Klees, Raymond F. '73 (CHI)[D] Niles, IL Notre Dame College Prep.
Kleffman, James '60 (DM) Council Bluffs, IA Retired.
Kleiber, Kenneth R. '68 (MO) Other Assignments; DEPARTMENT OF VETERANS AFFAIRS HOSPITALS AND CHAPLAINS.
Kleiber, Kenneth '68 (PHX) Phoenix, AZ United States Veterans Affairs Medical Center.
Klein, Charles F. '59 (BAL) Baltimore, MD St. Rose of Lima.
Klein, Charles R. '59 (BAL) Retired.
Klein, David F. *s.j.* '71 (SAC)[C] Sacramento, CA Jesuit High School; [H] Carmichael, CA Sacramento Jesuit Community.
Klein, David J. '90 (CAM)[T] Blackwood, NJ Pius X Spiritual Life Center; Judicial Vicar; Judicial Vicar; Vocation Advisory Board; Members; Judges.
Klein, David O. *c.s.b.* '70 (MO) DEPARTMENT OF VETERANS AFFAIRS HOSPITALS AND CHAPLAINS.
Klein, David O. *c.s.b.* '70 (LSC)[B] Las Cruces, NM Basilian Fathers.
Klein, Dennis D. '66 (BRK) On Leave/Unassigned.
Klein, Donald L. '65 (DUB) Personnel Advisory Board; Retired Priests' Representatives Retired.
Klein, Douglas M. '96 (SC) Rock Valley, IA St. Mary's; Sioux Center, IA Christ the King.
Klein, Eugene M. '74 (WIN) On Special Assignment.
Klein, George W. '59 (CHI) Northfield, IL St. Philip the Apostle; Chicago, IL St. Monica Retired.
Klein, Gregory L. *o.carm.* '75 (VEN) Osprey, FL Our Lady of Mount Carmel.
Klein, J. Leo *s.j.* '64 (CIN)[N] Cincinnati, OH Jesuit Community at Xavier University.
Klein, James J. '02 (COS) Colorado Springs, CO Divine Redeemer.
Klein, James T. '78 (CLV) Parma, OH St. Charles Borromeo.
Klein, John J. '70 (PAT)[Q] Chester, NJ Nazareth Village Retired.
Klein, John P. '78 (LAN) Lansing, MI St. Gerard; Regional Vicars.
Klein, John '02 (JOL) Bensenville, IL St. Charles Borromeo.

Klein, John '78 (LAN) Priests' Assignment Commission.
Klein, Lawrence J. '84 (BWN) Harlingen, TX St. Anthony.
Klein, Leonard R. '06 (WIL) Wilmington, DE Wilmington Hospital; St. Thomas More Society; Regina Coeli Society; Wilmington, DE St. Mary of the Immaculate Conception; Wilmington, DE St. Patrick; Office for Pro Life Activities.
Klein, Louis S. '81 (BUF) Cheektowaga, NY Queen of Martyrs.
Klein, Martin L. '91 (RVC) Glen Cove, NY St. Patrick's.
Klein, Pascal L. '87 (DOD) LaCrosse, KS Holy Trinity Catholic Church of Timken, Kansas; LaCrosse, KS St. Michael Catholic Church of LaCrosse, Kansas; Liebenthal, KS St. Joseph Catholic Church of Liebenthal, Kansas.
Klein, Peter J. '74 (WIN) Janesville, MN St. Ann's; Janesville, MN St. Joseph's; Priest Assignments Committee.
Klein, Pius *o.s.b.* '74 (EVN)[F] Ferdinand, IN Sisters of St. Benedict of Ferdinand, IN, Inc., Monastery Immaculate Conception.
Klein, Pius *o.s.b.* '74 (IND)[K] Saint Meinrad, IN St. Meinrad Archabbey.
Klein, Terrance W. '84 (COL) On Duty Outside the Diocese.
Kleiner, James '67 (DEN) Retired.
Kleiner, Robert *m.c.c.j.* '71 (LA) Los Angeles, CA Holy Cross.
Kleinfehn, Walter J. '60 (DUB) Retired.
Kleinheinz, Joseph L. '54 (SUP) Retired.
Kleinhenz, John H. *s.j.* '52 (DET)[K] Clarkston, MI Colombiere Center.
Kleinmann, Dennis W. '93 (ARL) Alexandria, VA St. Mary's.
Kleinschmidt, John '02 (FAR) Minto, ND Sacred Heart Church of Minto; Minto, ND St. Stanislaus Church of Warsaw; Deanery 4.
Kleinschmidt, Sylvester '50 (SCL) Retired.
Kleinstuber, Joseph J. '64 (WDC) Retired.
Kleinwachter, John '77 (CR) Roseau, MN Sacred Heart; Priests' Personnel Board.
Kleissler, Rev. Msgr. Thomas A. '57 (NEW) Special Assignment in the Archdiocese; [Q] Plainfield, NJ RENEW International; Renew International Retired.
Klem, Daniel N. '83 (RIC) Norfolk, VA Sacred Heart.
Klem, Robert J. *c.s.b.* '56 (GAL)[O] Sugar Land, TX Basilian Mission Center; [B] Sugar Land, TX Basilian Fathers of Sugarland.
Klemash, Dennis *o.f.m.cap.* '90 (HBG) York, PA St. Joseph.
Klemme, Dennis C. '57 (VEN) Judges.
Klemme, Dennis C. '57 (MIL)[Q] Pewaukee, WI Carmel of the Mother of God; Judges for Second Instance Retired.
Klemme, Robert '91 (LFT) Oxford, IN St. Patrick; Oxford, IN St. Charles.
Klemmer, Marvin J. '66 (BIS) Pro-Synodal Judges; [G] Bismarck, ND Emmaus Place Retired.
Klemmer, Marvin (BIS) Retired.
Klepac, Rev. Msgr. Kenneth J. '58 (MOB) Mobile, AL St. Joan of Arc; Associate Judges.
Klepac, Richard *s.o.l.t.* '06 (DET) Detroit, MI Holy Redeemer.
Kleppner, Joseph J. '71 (PIT) Aliquippa, PA St. Frances Cabrini; Theological Commission.
Klettner, Frederick J. '65 (DET) Retired.
Kletzel, Thomas P. '83 (PH) East Norriton, PA St. Titus.
Klevence, John P. '85 (WIL) New Castle, DE St. Peter the Apostle.
Klikunas, Bruce J. *o.s.m.* '72 (OAK)[L] Berkeley, CA Servites Retired.
Klim, Vincent '89 (PAT)[Q] Chester, NJ Nazareth Village Retired.
Klima, James A. '76 (COL) Pickerington, OH Seton Parish.
Klimczyk, Jan (John) '81 (FTW) Albion, IN Blessed Sacrament.
Klimczyk, Leon F. *s.j.* '79 (STP)[J] Minneapolis, MN Markoe House Jesuit Community.
Kline, Donald J. '95 (PHX) Phoenix, AZ St. Joan of Arc Roman Catholic Parish; [J] Phoenix, AZ Cursillo Movement; Members.
Kline, Donald '95 (PHX) Presbyteral Council.
Kline, Edwin J. *c.s.b.* '56 (DET)[E] Novi, MI Catholic Central High School.
Kline, John J. '47 (CLV) Retired.
Kline, Robert J. '04 (RVC) Center Moriches, NY St. John the Evangelist; Lindenhurst, NY Our Lady of Perpetual Help.
Kline, Rev. Msgr. Roy F. '51 (ALT) Altoona, PA Cathedral of the Blessed Sacrament Retired.
Klingeisen, Richard H. '72 (GB) Regional Vicars; Diocesan Health Services; Manitowoc, WI St. Francis of Assisi.
Klingele, Brian '02 (KCK) Garnett, KS Holy Angels; Greeley, KS St. John the Baptist; Legion of Mary.
Klinger, Charles F. '83 (COL) Westerville, OH St. Paul the Apostle; Parochial Examiners; Deanery 4: Northland; Presbyteral Council; Diocesan Judges.
Klinger, Rev. Msgr. Nevin J. (SAM) Advocates.
Klingler, Donald P. '61 (KAL) Diocesan Council of Catholic Women (D.C.C.W.) Retired.
Klingler, John *s.c.j.* '67 (MIL)[P] Franklin, WI Sacred Heart at Monastery Lake.
Klingler, Ronald M. '65 (Y) Canton, OH St. John the Baptist.
Klink, Anthony G. '58 (MIL) Retired.
Klink, Eugene A. '63 (LC) Eau Claire, WI Immaculate Conception; Consultors; Ex Officio.
Klink, Kenneth J. '66 (MAD) Retired.
Klink, Peter J. *s.j.* '81 (RC)[C] Pine Ridge, SD Jesuit Community of Holy Rosary Mission; Pine Ridge, SD Holy Rosary/Red Cloud Indian School Inc.
Klintworth, William P. *s.j.* '61 (FgM) New York, NY Society of Jesus.
Klinzing, Rev. Msgr. Thomas J. '71 (PMB) Judicial Vicar; Judges; Consultors; Ex Officio; Palm Beach, FL St. Edward.
Klismet, Kurt J. *o.ss.t.* '02 (BAL) Councilors:; [Q] In Residence – Holy Trinity Monastery Baltimore; Mount Airy, MD St. Michael.
Klister, Rev. Msgr. Roy M. '69 (GB) Green Bay, WI Annunciation of the Blessed Virgin Mary; Green Bay, WI St. Joseph; Green Bay, WI St. Jude; Green Bay, WI St. Patrick.
Klizek, Duane R. '82 (BUF) Niagara Falls, NY Holy Family of Jesus, Mary and Joseph; [M] Lewiston, NY Our Lady of Peace, Inc.
Kloak, David G. '78 (MO) Military Chaplains; Navy Chaplains.
Klobuka, John *s.m.* '78 (HON)[D] Wailuku, HI Wailuku Marianist Community.
Klocek, Andrzej Wojciech '89 (BRK) Bayside, NY St. Josaphat.
Klockeman, John A. '00 (STP)[A] Saint Paul, MN The Saint Paul Seminary; [C] St. Paul, MN University of St. Thomas.
Kloda, Marshall J. '89 (PH) On Special or Other Archdiocesan Assignment.
Kloepfer, John S. '53 (JOL) Retired.
Kloepfer, John S. '53 (RIC) Retired.
Klores, Stanley P. '82 (NO) New Orleans, LA St. Patrick.
Klos, Joseph '80 (BUF) Judges; Snyder, NY Christ the King.
Klos, Michael E. '00 (LC) Cashton, WI Sacred Heart of Jesus; Cashton, WI St. Augustine of Hippo; Cashton, WI Nativity of the Blessed Virgin Mary.
Kloskowski, Rev. Msgr. Stanley E. '58 (CAM) Retired.
Kloss, Anthony *o.s.b.* '91 (WOR)[N] Still River, MA Benedictine Monks, St. Benedict Abbey.
Kloster, David (BGP) On Duty Outside the Diocese.
Kloster, George M. '68 (CHL) Murphy, NC St. William.
Klosterman, Timothy Clement '08 (LA) Santa Monica, CA St. Monica.
Kloton, Michael J. '87 (SCR) Wilkes-Barre, PA St. Andre Bessette Parish.
Klotter, Frederick W. '96 (L) Louisville, KY St. Martin of Tours; Promoter of Justice; Ex Officio.
Kluba, Zbigniew '73 (PAT) Morristown, NJ Morristown Memorial Hospital.
Klucinec, Benedict *m.s.a.* '87 (NOR)[G] Cromwell Society of the Missionaries of the Holy Apostles.
Klucinec, Benedict *m.s.a.* '87 (PT) Panama City, FL St. Dominic.
Klug, Richard L. '51 (CIN) Imprimatur Censors; Judges Retired.
Kluge, Stephen *o.f.m.* '01 (TR) Brant Beach, NJ St. Francis of Assisi.
Kluk, Richard (HEL) Harlowton, MT St. Joseph; White Sulphur Springs, MT St. Bartholomew.
Klump, Gregory S. '98 (STL) Ste. Genevieve, MO Ste. Genevieve.
Klunk, David '09 (ORG) Newport Beach, CA Our Lady Queen of Angels.
Klunk, Timothy '79 (BAL) Baltimore, MD Our Lady of Victory.
Klusman, Christopher L. '11 (MIL) Milwaukee, WI St. Roman; Ministry to the Deaf and Hard of Hearing.
Kmiec, Roman *c.m.* '86 (HRT) New Haven, CT St. Stanislaus.
Knab, George *o.m.i.* '67 (WDC)[O] Washington, DC Provincial Offices of the United States Province of the Missionary Oblates of Mary Immaculate.
Knapek, John A. *s.j.* '57 (DET)[K] Clarkston, MI Colombiere Center.
Knapik, Andrew G. '57 (ALT) Retired.
Knapik, Andrew '78 (CLV) Cleveland, OH Immaculate Heart of Mary.
Knapp, Charles '63 (TUC) Defenders of the Bond Retired.
Knapp, Eric J. *s.j.* '04 (CIN) Cincinnati, OH St. Francis Xavier; [U] Cincinnati, OH St. Xavier Church Property Corporation; Presbyteral Council.
Knapp, Gerard J. *c.ss.r.* '75 (BAL) Baltimore, MD Sacred Heart of Jesus.
Knapp, James G. *s.j.* '81 (STL)[F] St. Louis, MO St. Louis University High School, George H. Backer Memorial; [O] Saint Louis, MO St. Louis University High School Jesuit Community; [O] St. Louis, MO Jesuit Community Corporation at Saint Louis University – Jesuit Hall.
Knapp, John M. (NY) Bronx, NY St. Gabriel.
Knapp, Rev. Msgr. Kenneth R. '63 (EVN) Evansville, IN Christ the King; Evansville, IN St. Theresa; Clergy Personnel Board.
Knapp, Rev. Msgr. Richard '55 (SFR)[K] San Rafael, CA Nazareth House of San Rafael, Inc. Retired.
Knappik, Richard *c.s.s.r.* '58 (HBG)[G] Ephrata, PA St. Clement's Mission House.
Knauer, Rev. Msgr. Paul F. '64 (PAT) Chester, NJ St. Lawrence the Martyr.
Knauf, Randall *o.f.m.cap* '91 (MIL)[P] Milwaukee, WI St. Conrad Friary.
Kneafsey, Rev. Msgr. Cornelius T. '58 (BRK) South Richmond Hill, NY St. Benedict Joseph Labre Retired.
Kneeland, David L. '06 (MAN) Lincoln, NH St. Joseph.
Kneemiller, William C. '99 (DAV) Hills, IA St. Joseph's; Lone Tree, IA St. Mary's; Nichols, IA St. Mary's; Army Reserve Chaplains.
Kneifl, Rodney V. '85 (OM) Platte Center, NE St. Joseph; Platte Center, NE St. Michael; [N] Platte Center, NE Servants of the Heart of the Father; Platte Center, NE St. Stanislaus.
Kneip, Paschal N. *o.s.b.* '51 (GBG)[H] Latrobe, PA Saint Vincent Archabbey.
Knepper, Daniel J. '70 (DUB) Dubuque, IA St. Raphael Cathedral; Worship Commission; Dubuque, IA St. Patrick.
Knepper, Timothy *c.pp.s* '03 (CIN)[N] Carthagena, OH St. Charles.
Knerr, Joseph '80 (ORG) Huntington Beach, CA St. Bonaventure; Council of Priests.
Knestout, Mark D. '98 (WDC) Washington, DC St. Matthew Cathedral; Pastoral Center Special Ministries; Office of Worship.
Knickerbocker, Knick '09 (SAN) Junction, TX St. Theresa of the Child Jesus.
Knies, Jerome G. *o.s.a.* '62 (MIL)[P] Racine, WI Augustinian Novitiate; Racine, WI St. Rita.
Knight, David B. '61 (MEM) Retired.
Knight, Dennis '77 (LEX) Priests' Retirement Committee.
Knight, Rev. Msgr. Jeffrey N. '88 (STL) Ste. Genevieve, MO St. Joseph.
Knight, Robert '83 (STL) St. Clair, MO St. Clare.
Knipe, Michael J. '88 (TLS) Muskogee, OK Saint Joseph Church; Judicial Vicar; Judges; Diocesan Senators.
Knippel, Kenneth P. '76 (MIL) Brookfield, WI St. John Vianney.
Knippenberg, Robert E. '00 (VIC) Victoria, TX Holy Family of Joseph, Mary & Jesus; School Board.
Knipper, Daniel J. '67 (DUB) Lansing, IA St. Pius Oratory Retired.
Knittel, Kilian J. '60 (CHI) Chicago, IL St. Columba Retired.
Knoblach, Thomas '87 (SCL) St. Cloud, MN Holy Spirit; St. Cloud, MN St. Anthony of Padua; St. Cloud, MN St. John Cantius; Directors; Health Ministry.
Knoebel, Thomas L. '69 (MIL)[B] Hales Corners, WI Sacred Heart School of Theology Retired.
Knoll, Charles *o.f.m.cap.* '54 (PIT)[M] Pittsburgh St. Augustine Friary.
Knoll, Jerome E. *c.s.c.* '60 (FTW)[B] University of Notre Dame Du Lac; [H] Notre Dame Congregation of Holy Cross, United States Province of Priests & Brothers; [H] Notre Dame, IN Holy Cross Community, Corby Hall, University of Notre Dame.
Knoll, Lester *o.f.m.cap.* '64 (CLV)[A] Wickliffe, OH Borromeo Seminary.
Knoll, Urban H. '69 (STL) Retired.
Knop, Andrew *o.m.i.* (BO) Tewksbury, MA St. William.
Knopik, Andrew J. '83 (BEL) Nashville, IL St. Ann.
Knopik, John '11 (SCL) Elk River, MN The Church of St. Andrew.
Knopp, Benjamin *o.f.m.conv.* '55 (L) Louisville, KY St. Paul.
Knopp, John '78 (ELP) Absent on Leave.
Knotek, Michael P. '96 (CHI) Chicago, IL St. Columbanus; College of Consultors.
Knott, J. Ronald '70 (IND) On Duty Outside the Archdiocese; [A] Saint Meinrad, IN Saint Meinrad School of Theology.
Knott, William P. '59 (RCK) Retired.
Knox, James '51 (PRT) Retired.
Knox, Sean Vincent '01 (PT) Military Chaplains; Air Force Chaplains.
Knox, Rev. Msgr. Stephen J. '89 (RCK) Huntley, IL St. Mary; Diocesan Consultors.
Knudsen, Ronald '72 (SEA) Mountlake Terrace, WA St. Pius X.
Knueven, Gerald E. '68 (TOL) Retired.
Knueven, Rev. Msgr. Harold L. '58 (IND) Retired.
Knuffman, Donald E. '65 (SFD) Retired.
Knurek, Dennis A. '77 (BGP) Retired.
Knusel, Frank '89 (P) Retired.
Knusel, Frank '73 (HPM) Portland, OR St. Irene Byzantine Catholic Church.
Ko, Benedict *m.s.c.* '05 (MIL)[Y] Milwaukee, WI The

Korean Catholic Community of Milwaukee; Milwaukee, WI St. Mary Magdalen.
Ko, Moo–Chan Benedict *m.s.c.* '04 (RCK)[G].
Kobak, David *o.f.m.* '03 (IND) Oldenburg, IN Holy Family Catholic Church, Oldenburg, Inc.
Kobasuk, Maxim *o.s.b.m.* '77 (STF)[A] Stamford, CT Ukrainian Catholic Seminary Inc. St. Basil College; Diocesan Consultors; Diaconate, Permanent; Liturgical Commission; Presbyteral Council.
Kobbeman, Rev. Msgr. Gerald P. '66 (RCK) Pro Synodal Judges; Deans Retired.
Kobe, Robert S. '79 (ELP) El Paso, TX Christ The Savior; Adjutant Vicars; Judges.
Kobel, Stanley *o.f.m.cap.* '96 (CHL) Charlotte, NC St. Thomas Aquinas.
Kobida, Vincent F. '80 (MIL) Milwaukee, WI St. Margaret Mary.
Kobos, Martin *o.f.m.conv.* '76 (HBG) Shamokin, PA Mother Cabrini.
Kobti, Rev. Msgr. Labib '75 (SFR) San Francisco, CA St. Thomas More; St. Thomas More Society; [Q] San Francisco, CA Newman Center, San Francisco State University; Arab–American Catholic Ministry; San Francisco State Univ., Newman Center.
Kobus, Boguslaw '92 (PAT) Franklin, NJ Immaculate Conception.
Kobus, Damian M. *o.s.m.* '49 (P)[L] Portland, OR The Grotto, The National Sanctuary of Our Sorrowful Mother Retired.
Kobuszewski, Thomas P. '64 (SY) Syracuse, NY Transfiguration.
Koch, David J. '69 (GB) Denmark, WI All Saints; Denmark, WI Holy Trinity Mission; [G] Green Bay, WI St. Mary's Hospital–Medical Center; Special Assignment; Denmark, WI St. James; Kellnersville, WI St. Joseph.
Koch, Donald J. '60 (STL) Retired.
Koch, Edward H. '01 (RVC) Saint James, NY SS. Philip and James.
Koch, Eugene R. '59 (DM) Advocates Retired.
Koch, George J. *s.j.* '59 (SJ)[M] Los Gatos, CA Sacred Heart Jesuit Center.
Koch, Ivor '84 (FWT) Catholic Women, Council of.
Koch, Jason *l.c.* '03 (KC) Kansas City, MO St. Anthony; Kansas City, MO Holy Cross.
Koch, Joseph A. *c.v.* '82 (MO) Navy Chaplains.
Koch, Kevin '85 (CHY) Cheyenne, WY Holy Trinity.
Koch, Mariusz Casimir *c.f.r.* '69 (NY)[HH] Bronx, NY Franciscan Mission Outreach, Inc.
Koch, Mariusz *c.f.r.* '69 (NEW)[L] Newark, NJ Franciscan Friars of the Renewal.
Koch, Michael R. '53 (GB)[I] Green Bay, WI The McCormick Memorial Home for the Aged Retired.
Koch, Paul M. '61 (DM) Retired.
Kochan, Frederick A. '55 (WIL) Retired.
Kochanowicz, Piotr *s.j.* '98 (CHI)[N] Chicago, IL Sacred Heart Mission House.
Kocher, Donald '63 (JOL) Lisle, IL St. Joan of Arc Retired.
Kocherla, Sundar Raj '76 (JOL) Glen Ellyn, IL St. Petronille.
Kocherry, Varghese *c.ss.r.* '62 (PH) Philadelphia, PA St. Peter the Apostle.
Kochery, Peter '70 (TR) Manalapan, NJ St. Thomas More.
Kochery, Rev. Msgr. Peter (MCE) Manalapan, NJ St. Thomas Malankara Catholic Church; Vicar General; Vicar General.
Kochery, Rev. Msgr. Peter (MCE) Seminary Formation Director; Ex Officio Members; Ex Officio Members; Members; Public Relations Office.
Kochu, Paul '74 (SP)[F] Palm Harbor, FL St. Luke Early Childhood Center; Propagation of the Faith; Palm Harbor, FL St. Luke the Evangelist.
Kochuparambil, Johnson *o.s.j.* '91 (SCR) Hazleton, PA Annunciation, Hazelton.
Kochuparambil, Jose Matthew *o.s.b.* '97 (LUB) Officialis.
Kochuparambil, Jose '97 (LUB) Idalou, TX St. Philip Benizi.
Kochuparathanathu, Augustine *v.c.* (FTW) Huntington, IN SS. Peter and Paul.
Kochupurackal, Abraham *c.m.i.* (STP) Bloomington, MN Nativity of the Blessed Virgin Mary.
Kochupurackal, Santy *m.s.f.s.* '95 (TYL)[C] Whitehouse, TX The Missionaries of St. Francis de Sales.
Kochupurackal, Sebastian *c.m.i.* '75 (HRT) Bristol, CT St. Gregory the Great.
Kocik, Francis W. '76 (SY) On Duty Outside the Diocese; Binghamton, NY St. Mary of the Assumption; Binghamton, NY St. Paul.
Kocik, Thomas M. '97 (FR) Fall River, MA Santo Christo.
Kociolek, Charles J. *c.s.c.* '79 (SCR)[B] Holy Cross Community.
Kociolek, Charles J. *c.s.c.* '79 (FTW)[H] Notre Dame Congregation of Holy Cross, United States Province of Priests & Brothers.
Kocurek, Antonin (BRK)[Q] Czech/Slovak Apostolate.
Kodakarakaran, Paul '75 (TLS) Special Assignment; [E] Tulsa, OK Saint Francis Hospital.
Kodakassery, Thomas *o.s.b.* '76 (FTW) North Manchester, IN St. Robert Bellarmine.
Koday, Mishael J. '08 (BWN) McAllen, TX Our Lady of Sorrows.
Koehl, Keith '97 (AUS) On Duty Outside the Diocese.
Koehl, Keith '97 (DAL)[A] Irving, TX Holy Trinity Seminary.
Koehler, John '65 (SEA) Retired.
Koehler, Jon C. '74 (BR) St. Amant, LA Holy Rosary.
Koehler, Kenneth '72 (DEN) Westminster, CO St. Mark; Deaneries.
Koehler, Steven C. '82 (DET) Sterling Heights, MI St. Rene Goupil.
Koehr, Louis '87 (BEL) Retired.
Koelker, Harry H. '68 (DUB) Oelwein, IA Sacred Heart; Fairbank, IA Immaculate Conception.
Koelsch, John '56 (B) Gooding, ID St. Elizabeth's; Shoshone, ID St. Peter's Retired.
Koen, Stephen A. '58 (BO) Senior Priests. Retired.
Koenig, Paul *o.f.m.cap.* '93 (FgM) Detroit, MI Province of St. Joseph; [K] Detroit St. Bonaventure Friary.
Koenig, Rev. Msgr. William E. '83 (RVC) Rockville Centre, NY St. Agnes Cathedral; Rockville Centre Deanery.
Koenigsfeld, James F. '68 (PBL) Durango, CO St. Columba.
Koenigsknecht, William J. '68 (LAN) Retired.
Koeninger, Francis F. '79 (STL) Hawk Point, MO St. Mary.
Koeplin, John P. *s.j.* '91 (SFR)[N] San Francisco, CA Loyola House Jesuit Community; [S] San Francisco, CA Sisters of the Presentation Community Support Trust Fund.
Koesel, Douglas H. '78 (CLV) Cleveland, OH Blessed Trinity Parish.
Koester, Timothy J. '83 (MO) Navy Chaplains; Military Chaplains.
Koesterer, David L. *s.j.* '64 (STL)[O] St. Louis, MO Jesuit Community Corporation at Saint Louis University – Jesuit Hall.
Koeth, Stephen M. *c.s.c.* '07 (FTW)[H] Notre Dame Congregation of Holy Cross, United States Province of Priests & Brothers.
Koetter, David A. '07 (SAV) Savannah, GA St. James.
Koetter, Rev. Msgr. Paul D. '77 (IND) Indianapolis, IN Holy Spirit Catholic Church, Indianapolis, Inc.; Board of Consultors; Deaneries and Deans; Priests' Personnel Board.
Koeune, August '84 (CHY) Casper, WY Saint Patrick's; Vicars Forane; [G] Casper, WY St. Anthony Tri–Parish School Foundation.
Koeune, George '95 (CHI) Chicago, IL St. Eugene.
Kofi, Samuel (NY) Millbrook, NY St. Joseph.
Kofitse, Ted K. '84 (BO) Hanover, MA St. Mary of the Sacred Heart.
Kofski, James W. *m.m.* '91 (WDC)[B] Washington, DC Office of Justice and Peace; Maryknoll, NY MARYKNOLL.
Kogut, Daniel J. '11 (LAN)[B] Flint, MI Luke M. Powers Catholic High School; Swartz Creek, MI St. Mary.
Kohapural, Augustine J. *t.o.r.* (FWT) Carrollton, TX St. Catherine of Siena.
Koharchik, Edward *c.s.p.* '05 (AUS) Dripping Springs, TX St. Martin de Porres; Presbyteral Council.
Koharchik, George D. '74 (ALT) Mount Union, PA St. Catherine of Siena.
Kohler, Edward '77 (HEL) Browning, MT Church of the Little Flower; Deaneries.
Kohler, Girard J. *c.s.sp.* '63 (PIT)[M] Bethel Park, PA Holy Spirit Fathers and Brothers Provincialate; [O] Bethel Park, PA The Spiritan Center.
Kohler, Lawrence A. *m.s.* '61 (LKC) Sulphur, LA Our Lady of LaSalette.
Kohler, Peter D. *m.s.* '68 (HRT)[L] Hartford, CT Missionaries of LaSalette.
Kohler, Russell E. '73 (DET)[Q] Detroit, MI Pope John XXIII Hospitality House; [Q] Onsted, MI St. Patrick's Retreat; Detroit, MI Most Holy Trinity; [Q] Harrisville, MI The Oratory.
Kohler, William (Guillo) *c.ss.r.* '83 (TUC) Tucson, AZ Tucson Medical Center; Tucson, AZ Roman Catholic Church of Saint Elizabeth Ann Seton – Tucson.
Kohler, William E. '67 (MIL) Muskego, WI St. Leonard Congregation; Archdiocesan Council of Priests; Archbishop's Executive Council.
Kohler, William F. '55 (PIT) Retired.
Kohler, William J. (MIL) Moderator of the Curia; Vicars General.
Kohlerman, Charles W. *c.s.c.* '63 (FTW)[A] Notre Dame, IN Moreau Seminary; [A] Notre Dame, IN Moreau Seminary; [H] Notre Dame, IN Congregation of Holy Cross, United States Province of Priests & Brothers.
Kohli, Charles F. '61 (RVC) Retired.
Kohlmann, Vernon *s.d.v.* '98 (PAT) Florham Park, NJ; [N] Florham Park, NJ Father Justin Vocationary; Florham Park, NJ.
Kohls, Rev. Msgr. Eugene C. '57 (STA) Vicar for Senior Priests Retired.
Kohner, David W. '90 (STP) Archdiocesan Council on Catholic Women; Little Canada, MN St. John of Little Canada.
Kohrman, Glenn '92 (FTW) Elkhart, IN St. Vincent de Paul; Elkhart.
Kohut, David *o.f.m.* '79 (CIN)[N] Cincinnati, OH St. Clare Friary.
Kohut, Rev. Msgr. Joseph J. '62 (BGP)[O] Stamford, CT The Catherine Dennis Keefe Queen of the Clergy Retired Priests' Residence Retired.
Koilparampil, Augustine '64 (OAK) Livermore, CA St. Michael; VA Palo Alto Health Care System Home Livermore Division.
Kokeram, Sudash J. '99 (NEW) Military Chaplains; Army Chaplains.
Kokoria, Saimon *m.s.c.* '09 (MI) Majuro, MH Holy Rosary; Prefecture Consultors.
Kokose, Pius Eusebius *c.s.sp.* '98 (CHI) Posen, IL St. Stanislaus Bishop and Martyr.
Kolaj, Frane '87 (DET) Rochester Hills, MI St. Paul Albanian Catholic Community.
Kolakowski, Robert B. '02 (MET) Lambertville, NJ St. John the Evangelist; Canonical Staff; Associate Judicial Vicar.
Kolarec, William T. *s.j.* '69 (MIL)[P] Wauwatosa, WI Jesuit Community at St. Camillus.
Kolasa, Stanley *ss.cc.* '70 (FR)[H] Wareham, MA Sacred Hearts Retreat Center.
Kolb, Jim *c.s.p.* '76 (P) Portland, OR St. Elizabeth of Hungary; Portland, OR Oregon Health Sciences University.
Kolb, Joseph C. '53 (OKL) Retired.
Kolb, Joseph E. *s.j.* '63 (WH)[A] Wheeling, WV Wheeling Jesuit University.
Kolb, Michael R. *s.j.* '82 (MIL)[P] Milwaukee, WI Arrupe House Jesuit Community.
Kolberg, Lawrence R. '68 (ORG) Retired.
Kolcun, Stephen J. '46 (PBR) Retired.
Kolczaski, Richard '55 (PEO) Retired.
Kolde, Steven J. '00 (CIN) Cincinnati, OH St. John Neumann.
Kolencheril, Varghese '86 (CC) Edroy, TX Our Lady of Guadalupe Mission.
Kolenski, Robert D. '62 (LAN) Retired.
Kolesar, Rev. Msgr. John C. '64 (STU) Adena, OH St. Casimir's; Adena, OH St. Adalbert; Diocesan Director of Cemeteries; Council Members.
Kolf, Gerald S. '95 (POD) Washington.
Kolf, Gerald S. '95 (WDC)[G] Potomac, MD The Heights School; [V] Washington, DC Tenley Study Center.
Kolibas, Kenneth R. '94 (MET) Raritan, NJ St. Joseph.
Kolinovsky, Sebastian *c.p.* '51 (SCR)[L] Scranton, PA Saint Ann's Passionist Monastery.
Kolinski, Dennis *s.j.c.* '04 (CHI)[P] Chicago, IL Canons Regular of Saint John Cantius.
Kolitsos, Andrew '94 (ROM) On Loan to Other Diocese (Eparches).
Kolitsos, Andrew '94 (PBR) Newton Falls, OH St. Michael.
Kolla, Edward R. '01 (CAM) Ocean City, NJ Saint Damien Parish, Ocean City, N.J.
Kollannur, John (VIC) Victoria, TX Our Lady of Lourdes.
Kollapallil, Kurian *m.s.f.s.* '95 (LAN) Fenton, MI St. John the Evangelist.
Kollapallil, Kurian *m.s.f.s.* '97 (TYL)[C] Whitehouse, TX The Missionaries of St. Francis de Sales.
Kollar, Anton *o.carm.* '51 (JOL)[L] Darien Carmelite Provincial Office.
Kollar, Rene M. *o.s.b.* '74 (GBG)[H] Latrobe, PA Saint Vincent Archabbey.
Kollasch, Merle F. '64 (SC) Retired.
Kollath, Robert '97 (GB)[L] Chilton, WI St. Peregrine Shrine; Chilton, WI Good Shepherd; Kiel, WI SS. Peter and Paul; New Holstein, WI Holy Rosary; New Holstein, WI St. Ann; College of Consultors; Appointed Members.
Koller, Michael '04 (KCK) Lenexa, KS Holy Trinity; Archdiocesan Consultors.
Koller, Thomas *o.c.d.* '90 (SJ)[M] San Jose, CA Carmelite Monastery, Novitiate.
Kolling, James L. '65 (LA) Los Angeles, CA Visitation Retired.
Kollithanath, Philip '84 (CHL) Asheboro, NC St. Joseph.
Kollman, Paul V. *c.s.c.* '91 (FTW)[B] University of Notre Dame Du Lac; [H] Notre Dame, IN Holy Cross Community, Corby Hall, University of Notre Dame.
Kollross, Dennis D. '81 (SFD) Mattoon, IL Immaculate Conception.
Kolmaga, Jan *o.s.p.p.e.* '82 (PH)[Y] Doylestown, PA.
Kolo, Vincent F. '95 (PIT) Pittsburgh, PA Immaculate Conception–St. Joseph; Allegheny County, PA UPMC Shadyside Hospital.
Kolodziej, Jack *o.s.f.s.* '99 (PH)[D] Philadelphia, PA Father Judge High School for Boys; [Y] Philadelphia, PA Father Louis Brisson Residence.
Kolodziej, Ludwik '94 (BRK) Brooklyn, NY Our Lady of Consolation.
Kolodziej, Ludwik *s.d.s.* (NEW)[L] Verona, NJ The Salvatorian Fathers.
Kolodziej, Michael *o.f.m.conv.* '70 (ATL) Jonesboro, GA

St. Philip Benizi.
Kolodziej, Ryszard '96 (R) Castle Hayne, NC St. Stanislaus.
Kolodziejczyk, Sebastian J. '99 (LC) Foreign Missions.
Kolodziejski, Karl *o.f.m.conv.* '78 (ALT) Hooversville, PA Holy Family.
Kolp, Rev. Msgr. James '50 (Y) Retired.
Kolson, Lawrence F. '74 (BAL) Bradshaw, MD St. Stephen.
Kolton, Stanislaus J. '46 (CAM) Retired.
Kolumber, Denis A. *m.s.* '67 (HRT)[L] Hartford, CT Missionaries of LaSalette.
Kolzow, Andrew *o.p.* '58 (DAL)[J] Irving, TX Dominican Priory of St. Albert the Great and Novitiate.
Komar, John E. '64 (NEW)[L] Rutherford, NJ St. John Vianney Residence for Priests Retired.
Komatz, David *o.praem* '75 (CHI)[N] Chicago, IL Premonstratensian Fathers and Brothers (Norbertines).
Kombarakkaran, Joshi Antony *o.ss.t.* '11 (BAL)[Q] Assigned in India.
Kombo, Honore M. '90 (HRT) Seymour, CT St. Augustine.
Kommer, Venard *o.f.m.* '46 (JOL) Clarendon Hills, IL Notre Dame.
Kommers, Thomas M. '80 (STP) Red Wing, MN Church of St. Joseph.
Komo, George '09 (DM) West Des Moines, IA St. Francis of Assisi; [C] Council Bluffs, IA Saint Albert Catholic Schools.
Komonchak, Joseph A. '64 (WDC)[C] Catholic University of America, The Retired.
Komorowski, Louis A. *o.s.f.s.* '56 (LAN) Adrian, MI St. Mary of Good Counsel.
Komperda, Pawel '06 (CHI)[A] Chicago, IL St. Joseph College Seminary.
Kon, Placyd *o.f.m.* '96 (CLV) Cleveland, OH St. Stanislaus; [N] Cleveland, OH St. Stanislaus Friary.
Koncik, Michael *c.ss.r.* '82 (NY) East Elmhurst, NY Eric M. Taylor Center; East Elmhurst, NY Otis Bantum Correctional Center; Cincinnati, OH American Catholic Correctional Chaplains Association; [DD] New York, NY Redemptorist Priests and Brothers, C.Ss.R.; Manhattan, NY Gracie Square.
Konda, Bernard '67 (JUN) Retired.
Kondeja, Stanley '62 (RVC) Southampton, NY Our Lady of Poland.
Konderla, David '95 (AUS)[L] College Station, TX St. Mary's Catholic Center; College Station, TX St. Mary; Presbyteral Council; College of Consultors.
Kondik, Curtis L. '00 (MO) Army Chaplains; Military Chaplains.
Kondik, Curtis '00 (OG) U.S. Army Headquarters.
Kondzielski, Thaddeus T. '67 (E) Edinboro, PA St. Philip.
Kondziolka, Ronald L. '76 (CHI)[J] Chicago Heights, IL Franciscan St. James Health.
Konen, Lyle *c.ss.r.* '61 (SEA) Minimum Security Unit; Special Offenders Center; [M] Seattle, WA The Redemptionist Society of Washington; Monroe Correctional Complex; Seattle, WA Sacred Heart of Jesus; Washington State Reformatory.
Konen, Lyle *c.ss.r.* '61 (SEA) King County Jail.
Konerman, Edward H. *s.j.* '58 (CHI)[N] Chicago Chicago Province of the Society of Jesus–Provincial Office.
Konerman, Gregory J. '93 (CIN) Urbana, OH Sacred Heart (St. Paris); Urbana, OH St. Mary; Consultors; Presbyteral Council.
Konicki, William C. '78 (WOR) Hopedale, MA Sacred Heart of Jesus.
Konieczka, Edward J. '63 (SAG) Bay City, MI St. Hyacinth.
Konieczny, Stan J. '06 (BEL) Smithton, IL St. John the Baptist.
Konka, Balaswamy '95 (OKL) Edmond, OK St. John the Baptist.
Konka, Rayappa '89 (LIN) Lincoln, NE St. Patrick's.
Konkel, Eugene J. *s.s.* '57 (SFR)[A] Menlo Park, CA St. Patrick Seminary and University.
Konkel, Eugene J. *s.s.* '57 (MIL) Retired.
Konkel, Eugene J. *s.s.* '57 (BAL)[Q] Baltimore Society of St. Sulpice, Province of the United States Retired.
Konkel, Joseph D. *o.p.* '70 (GAL) Houston, TX Holy Rosary.
Konkler, Paul Jerome *o.c.s.o.* '68 (SAC)[A] Vina, CA Abbey of New Clairvaux, Trappist Seminary; [H] Vina, CA Abbey of New Clairvaux, Trappist.
Konkol, Robert *o.f.m.* '94 (GB) Sturgeon Bay, WI SS. Peter and Paul; Sturgeon Bay, WI St. Joseph.
Kono, Mario '91 (VEN) North Fort Myers, FL St. Therese.
Konold, Lon *o.m.i.* '77 (STP)[M] Buffalo, MN Christ the King Retreat Center.
Konopa, Brian D. '98 (LC) Eau Claire, WI St. Olaf; Deans.
Konopa, Robert *o.f.m.* '91 (JKS) Greenwood, MS St. Francis of Assisi.
Konopacky, Joseph R. '82 (LC) Leave of Absence.
Konopelski, Louis *s.d.b.* (NO)[D] Marrero, LA Archbishop Shaw High School; [H] Marrero, LA Archbishop Shaw Junior High School.
Konopik, Michael J. '07 (SFR) San Bruno, CA St. Robert.
Konopka, Edward F. '45 (DET) Retired.
Konopka, Edward M. '60 (NOR) Retired.
Konopka, Thomas E. '90 (ALB) Colonie, NY St. Clare; Special Assignment.
Konopka, Thomas E. '90 (ALB) Office.
Konrad, Erwin '89 (JC) Retired.
Konrade, Jarett '05 (SAL) Boy Scouts; Priests' Continuing Formation Committee; Office of Priestly Vocations; Office of Priestly Vocations; College of Consultors; Wilson, KS St. Wenceslaus Parish; Wilson, KS St. Mary Parish; Wilson, KS St. Joseph Parish.
Konz, Gregory N. P. *s.j.* '90 (WDC)[O] Washington, DC Leonard Neale House.
Konzen, Joel M. *s.m.* '79 (ATL)[C] Atlanta, GA Marist School.
Koo, Matthew '88 (SJ) San Jose, CA St. Leo the Great; Santa Clara, CA Chinese Catholic Community Retired.
Kookoothe, Neil P. '95 (CLV) North Olmsted, OH St. Clarence.
Koons, Rev. Msgr. Thomas P. '97 (ALN) Allentown, PA St. Francis of Assisi; [L] Coopersburg, PA Carmelite Monastery; Judges; Vicar for Religious.
Koons, Thomas P. '97 (LEX) Associate Judges.
Koopman, Dennis *o.f.m.* '70 (CHI)[N] Countryside, IL St. Gratian Friary, Franciscan Friars.
Koopman, Joseph M. '01 (CLV)[A] Wickliffe, OH St. Mary Seminary and Graduate School of Theology.
Koopmann, Robert *o.s.b.* '81 (SCL)[B] Saint John's University; [I] Collegeville, MN St. John's Abbey, of the Order of St. Benedict.
Koos, Rev. Msgr. Gerald J. '66 (E) Erie, PA Our Mother of Sorrows Retired.
Kopacek, Jerry F. '88 (DUB) Courage; Waterloo, IA St. Edward; Deans; Review Board for the Protection of Minors.
Kopacz, Joseph R. '77 (SCR) Mount Pocono, PA St. Bernadette; Mount Pocono, PA Most Holy Trinity Parish; Mount Pocono, PA St. Ann; Hispanic Ministry Outreach; Priests' Retirement Advisory Board.
Kopacz, K. S. '95 (FAR) Judicial Vicar; Presiding Judge; Special Assignment.
Kopacz, KS *j.c.l.* (FAR) West Fargo, ND Blessed Sacrament Church of West Fargo.
Kopacz, Mark W. '92 (WIL) Unassigned or Leave of Absence.
Kopacz, Rev. Msgr. Matthew S. '63 (BUF) Retired.
Kopacz, Stephen A. '72 (NEW) Cedar Grove, NJ St. Catherine of Siena.
Kopaczynski, Germain *o.f.m.conv.* '74 (PMB) Boynton Beach, FL St. Mark.
Kopchik, Martin *m.s.f.s.* '86 (ATL)[F] Snellville, GA The Missionaries of St. Francis De Sales.
Kopczewski, Linus E. *o.f.m.* '65 (MIL)[N] Milwaukee, WI St. Ann Rest Home.
Kopczynski, Tadeusz '89 (DEN) Fort Collins, CO Blessed John XXIII.
Kopec, Chester C. *o.p.* '63 (SB) Retired.
Kopec, Christopher A. '93 (WIL) Military Chaplains.
Kopec, Edward S. '92 (PEO) Toluca, IL St. Ann's.
Kopec, Jerome E. '79 (BUF) Williamsville, NY SS. Peter and Paul.
Kopec, Krzysztof A. '93 (MO) Army Chaplains.
Kopec, Krzysztof (TUC) Fort Huchuca, AZ Fort Huchuca Army Post.
Kopec, Rajmund '92 (MO) Military Chaplains; Army Chaplains.
Kopel, Jerome '77 (SFS) Gettysburg, SD Sacred Heart.
Koper, Rev. Msgr. Francis B. '71 (WIL) On Duty Outside the Diocese.
Koper, Rev. Msgr. Francis '71 (DET)[A] Orchard Lake, MI SS. Cyril and Methodius Seminary.
Koper, Ryszard '78 (BRK) Maspeth, NY Holy Cross.
Koperski, Matthew J. '04 (GI) Personnel Board; Vocations; [D] Kearney, NE University of Nebraska at Kearney Newman Apostolate.
Kopfensteiner, Thomas R. '81 (STL) On Duty Outside the Archdiocese.
Kopil, Michael J. '08 (GRY) Vocations; Schererville, IN St. Michael.
Kopinski, Rev. Msgr. Richard P. '64 (RVC) Glen Head, NY St. Hyacinth; Judges for Interdiocesan Tribunal.
Koplik, Rev. Msgr. William J. '62 (NEW) Ridgefield, NJ St. Matthew's Retired.
Koplinka, Steven '79 (PRM) Cleveland, OH St. Mary; Syncellus for Clergy and Religious; Presbyteral Council; Eparchial Pastoral Council; Sacred Liturgy; Seminary Education Formation Board.
Kopp, Rev. Msgr. Richard M. '69 (SY) Western Area Vicars; Board of Diocesan Consultors; Presbyteral Council; Vicar for Priests; Building Commission; Finance Committee; Priest Personnel; Special Assignment; Priests' Personnel Committee.
Kopp, Thomas A. (BO) Presbyteral Council.
Koppala, Leo Charles '94 (WIN) Blue Earth, MN SS. Peter and Paul's; Blue Earth, MN St. Mary's.
Koppes, Albert P. *o.carm.* '59 (JOL)[L] Darien Carmelite Provincial Office.
Koppes, Albert P. *o.carm.* '59 (LA)[C] Los Angeles, CA Jesuit Community; [C] Los Angeles, CA Loyola Marymount University.
Kopystynski, A. Rafal *c.m.* (HRT)[L] Manchester, CT DePaul Provincial Residence.
Korabik, Joseph *c.r.* '38 (CHI)[D] Chicago, IL Gordon Tech High School.
Korba, Rev. Msgr. Frank '66 (PRM) Munster, IN Saint Nicholas; Eparchial Consultors; Midwest; Associates; Catechetical Board.
Korban, Janusz '97 (RC) Rapid City, SD Blessed Sacrament.
Korbelak, John J. '74 (NEW) Hillsdale, NJ St. John the Baptist.
Korchinsky, Leonard '60 (STN) Mishawaka, IN St. Michael; Eparchial Office of Religious Education & Catechesis.
Korcsmar, John *c.s.c.* '74 (PHX) Goodyear, AZ Saint John Vianney Roman Catholic Parish.
Korcz, Krzysztof '94 (WOR) Athol, MA Our Lady Immaculate; Petersham, MA St. Peter; Athol, MA St. Francis.
Korda, J. James '79 (Y) Catholic Television Network of Youngstown (CTNY).
Kordas, Edward J. '68 (CLV) Hudson, OH St. Mary; Associate Judges.
Kordek, Frank *o.f.m.* '72 (SUP) Hurley, WI St. Mary of the Seven Dolors; Saxon, WI St. Ann.
Kordsmeier, Rev. Msgr. John '49 (LR)[G] Little Rock, AR St. John Manor; Defenders of the Bond Retired.
Korenek, Gregory E. '93 (VIC) Bay City, TX Holy Cross; Judges.
Koressel, James '69 (EVN) All Saints; Montgomery, IN St. Peter; Clergy Personnel Board; Deans; Diocesan Consultors.
Korf, Joseph '74 (SCL) Staples, MN St. Michael's; Staples, MN Sacred Heart; Advocates; Deans; Diocesan Corporate Board.
Korie, Ikechi *o.p.* '96 (CHR) Greenville, SC St. Mary.
Kornacki, Thomas J. *o.f.m.* '77 (FgM) New York, NY Holy Name Province.
Kornath, Edwin M. '84 (MIL) Kewaskum, WI St. Michael; Kewaskum, WI Holy Trinity; Archdiocesan Council of Priests.
Kornmeyer, Thomas E. '90 (OG) Evans Mills, NY St. Mary.
Korogi, Dale J. '83 (STP) Minneapolis, MN Christ the King.
Korpi, Wilson I. '08 (ARL) Burke, VA Church of the Nativity; Notaries.
Korte, Owen W. '81 (OM) Ralston, NE St. Gerald.
Korte, William L. '83 (JC) New Cambria, MO St. Mary of the Angels; Salisbury, MO St. Joseph; Legion of Mary.
Kortendick, Steven J. '85 (MAD) Columbus, WI St. Jerome; Doylestown, WI St. Patrick; Elected.
Korth, David M. '92 (OM) Homer, NE St. Cornelius; Winnebago, NE St. Joseph; Our Lady of Fatima; Winnebago, NE St. Augustine's; [M] Winnebago, NE FEATHERS; Deans; Deans.
Kos, Donald *o.f.m.conv.* '61 (BAL)[Q] Ellicott City Order of Friars Minor Conventual.
Kos, Sebastian K. '10 (HRT) Hamden, CT St. Rita.
Kos, Stanislaw '96 (RCK) Scales Mound, IL Holy Trinity; Galena, IL St. Mary.
Kosak, Rev. Msgr. Michael F. '70 (STV) Kingshill, VI Church St. Ann; [B] Lumen 2000/Caribbean Region; Diocesan Consultors; Caribbean Catholic Network (CCN); Communications Coordinator.
Kosaka, Paulo R. *o.f.m.cap.* '84 (HON) Kaneohe, HI Our Lady of Mt. Carmel.
Kosanke, Rev. Msgr. Charles G. '85 (DET)[T] Orchard Lake, MI American Friends of the Vatican Library; Bloomfield Hills, MI St. Regis.
Kosanke, Rev. Msgr. Charles '85 (DET)[N] Detroit, MI Catholic Charities of Southeast Michigan.
Kosasih, Benny *ss.cc.* '02 (HON) Kaneohe, HI St. Ann.
Kosatka, Leonard *c.p.* '59 (L)[L] Louisville, KY Sacred Heart Retreat.
Kosch, Leo D. '93 (LIN) Prague, NE St. John's; Commission for Sacred Liturgy and Sacred Music; Victim Assistance Coordinator; Diocesan Area CCD Directors.
Kosciesza, Bogumil '94 (WDC) Wheaton, MD St. Catherine Laboure.
Kosciesza, Bogumil (DUL) Retired.
Kosco, William "Billy" J. '00 (PHX) Buckeye, AZ Saint Henry Roman Catholic Parish; Presbyteral Council.
Kosek, Robert B. *c.r.s.p.* '89 (ALN)[K] Bethlehem, PA The Barnabite Fathers Barnabite Spiritual Center.
Kosem, Frank P. '70 (CLV) Elyria, OH St. Jude.
Koser, Albert C. '59 (PIT)[M] Pittsburgh, PA St. John Vianney Manor Retired.
Koser, Rudolph J. '74 (GBG) Clymer, PA Church of the Resurrection.
Koshko, Dennis '75 (HON) Vicars Forane; Honolulu, HI Holy Trinity; College of Consultors; Clergy Personnel Board; Presbyteral Council; Office of Clergy Priest Retirement Committee.
Koshyk, Ihor '05 (STN) Chicago, IL SS. Volodymyr and Olha.

Koshyk, Ihor (CHI)[J] Chicago, IL Saints Mary and Elizabeth Medical Center.
Kosicki, Bohdan W. '50 (DET) Retired.
Kosicki, George *c.s.b.* '54 (ROC)[K] Rochester Basilian Residence.
Kosinski, Stephen D. '81 (GRY) Hammond, IN All Saints.
Kosisko, Richard J. '85 (GBG) Mount Pleasant, PA St. Pius X; Mount Pleasant, PA Visitation of the Blessed Virgin Mary; Judges; Bishop's Priests Council.
Kosler, Timothy '71 (VIC) Schulenburg, TX St. John The Baptist; Schulenburg, TX Nativity of the Blessed Virgin Mary; Schulenburg, TX St. Rose of Lima; Diocesan Consultors; Schulenburg Deanery; Presbyteral Council; Defenders of the Bond; Priests' Personnel Board.
Kosmicki, Raymond M. '68 (GI) St. Paul, NE SS. Peter and Paul; Priests' Advisory Board (Presbyteral Council).
Kosmoski, David B. '83 (MET) Avenel, NJ St. Andrew.
Kosmowski, Gary J. '90 (MAN) Hampton, NH Our Lady of the Miraculous Medal.
Kosnac, Benjamin '93 (DET) Sterling Heights, MI SS. Cyril and Methodius.
Kosowicz, Wojciech '65 (LAR) Laredo, TX St. Patrick; Finance Council.
Kosse, Gerald C. '76 (WIN) Pipestone, MN St. Leo's; Pipestone, MN St. Martin's; Advocates; Pipestone, MN St. Joseph's.
Kosse, Theodore C. '71 (CIN) Peebles, OH St. Mary Queen of Heaven; West Union, OH Holy Trinity.
Kostek, John S. '72 (NY) Staten Island, NY St. John Neumann.
Kostelnik, Rev. Msgr. Kevin J. '82 (LA) Los Angeles, CA Cathedral of Our Lady of the Angels.
Kostelz, Richard F. '52 (JOL) Cabery, IL St. Joseph Retired.
Koster, Dale F. '54 (SC) Retired.
Koster, Kenneth J. '76 (SFS) Kranzburg, SD Holy Rosary; Tribunal Judges.
Kosterman, Richard A. '93 (GLD) Retired.
Kostiuk, Stepan '06 (CHI)[M] Niles, IL Saint Andrew Life Center; [M] Park Ridge, IL Resurrection Nursing and Rehabilitation Center; [J] Des Plaines, IL Holy Family Medical Center; Chicago, IL SS. Volodymyr and Olha.
Kostka, Leonard J. *c.pp.s.* '40 (LFT)[A] Rensselaer, IN Saint Joseph's College Retired.
Kostrzomb, Stanley '77 (NEW) Lyndhurst, NJ St. Michael's.
Kosty, Robert J. '74 (WDC) Port Tobacco, MD St. Ignatius Loyola; Port Tobacco, MD St. Catherine of Alexandria.
Kostyk, Jaroslaw (STF) Directors.
Kostyk, Marian '90 (STF) Amsterdam, NY St. Nicholas; Amsterdam, NY St. Nicholas; Personnel Board.
Kostyk, Yaroslaw (STF) Campbell Hall, NY St. Volodymyr; Campbell Hall, NY St. Andrew's; Administrative Council.
Kostyuk, Volodymyr '98 (PHU) Jenkintown, PA St. Michael the Archangel.
Koszarek, Rev. Msgr. Paul P. '54 (GB) Laona, WI St. Norbert; Laona, WI St. Hubert Mission; Armstrong Creek, WI St. Stanislaus Kostka; Goodman, WI St. Joan of Arc; Laona, WI St. Leonard Retired.
Koszarek, Robert J. '74 (SUP) Eagle River, WI St. Peter the Fisherman.
Koszyk, Dariusz '04 (RVC) Copiague, NY Our Lady of the Assumption; Hicksville, NY Our Lady of Mercy; Oyster Bay, NY St. Dominic's.
Koszyk, Severyn J. *s.a.c.* '59 (BUF)[N] North Tonawanda, NY Society of the Catholic Apostolate.
Kot, Luke C. *o.c.s.o.* '48 (ATL)[F] Conyers, GA The Monastery of the Holy Spirit Retired.
Kotara, James A. '76 (SAT) Defenders of the Bond; San Antonio, TX St. Thomas More.
Kotas, Adam '10 (SR) Sonoma, CA St. Francis Solano.
Kotecki, Ronald E. '72 (MIL) Milwaukee, WI Immaculate Conception.
Koterski, Joseph W. *s.j.* '92 (NY)[DD] Cardinal Spellman Hall, Jesuit Community; [A] Yonkers, NY St. Joseph's Seminary.
Koterski, Joseph W. *s.j.* (WDC)[X] Washington, DC Fellowship of Catholic Scholars.
Kotlanger, Michael J. *s.j.* '78 (SFR)[E] San Francisco, CA St. Ignatius College Preparatory (Coed); [N] San Francisco, CA Jesuit Community at St. Ignatius College Preparatory.
Kotlarczyk, Mark E. '88 (SB) Wildomar, CA St. Frances of Rome.
Kotlarz, Robert J. '69 (DET) Detroit, MI Our Lady Queen of Heaven; Detroit, MI St. Raymond–Our Lady of Good Counsel.
Kotlinski, Bede *o.s.b.* '84 (CLV)[D] Cleveland, OH Benedictine High School; [N] Cleveland, OH; Translators.
Kotlinsky, Eugene *c.m.* (BGP) Stamford, CT Holy Name of Jesus.
Kotnis, Gregory M. '56 (PHX) Retired.
Kottackal, Paul '74 (NEW) Garfield, NJ Church of Our Lady of Sorrows.
Kottackal, Paul '74 (SYM) Garfield, NJ Syro–Malabar Catholic Mission of Garfield.
Kottana, Kishore '09 (TOL) Maumee, OH St. Joseph.
Kottar, Michael T. '94 (CHL) Shelby, NC St. Mary's.
Kottaram, Mathew '63 (RVC) Retired.
Kottarathil, Benny '07 (STO) Modesto, CA St. Joseph Church of Modesto (Pastor of).
Kottas, Charles '70 (DM) Council Bluffs, IA St. Peter.
Kottayil, Joseph '79 (MIA)[A] Miami, FL St. John Vianney College Seminary.
Kottenstette, William P. '73 (JC)[D] Kirksville, MO Catholic Newman Center, Truman State University.
Kouba, Charles J. '51 (CHI) Retired.
Koury, James '92 (NTN) Leave of Absence.
Koury, Rev. Msgr. Joseph A. '50 (JKS) Retired.
Koury, Joseph J. '77 (PRT) Bridgton, ME St. Joseph; Gorham, ME St. Anne; Windham, ME Our Lady of Perpetual Help; Associate Judges; Westbrook, ME St. Anthony of Padua Parish.
Koury, Joseph N. '07 (LEX) Beattyville, KY Queen of All Saints.
Koury, Joseph (NTN) Judges.
Koutnik, Jerome '99 (RCK) Crystal Lake, IL St. Thomas the Apostle.
Kouts, Michael '91 (SJP) Brooksville, FL St. Andrew; Presbyters.
Kovacevich, Steve '86 (ROM) Unassigned.
Kovach, John '65 (PRM) Retired.
Kovacic, Rev. Msgr. Anthony '47 (CHL) Retired.
Kovacik, Jozef '98 (ALT) Tyrone, PA St. Matthew.
Kovacik, Mark S. '07 (DEN) Denver, CO St. Anthony of Padua.
Kovacs, Matthew *o.cist.* '57 (DAL)[J] Irving, TX Cistercian Abbey of Our Lady of Dallas.
Kovalcin, John A. '81 (STL) On Duty Outside the Archdiocese.
Kovalik, George J. '47 (STP) Retired.
Kovalyshin, Severyn '00 (SJP) North Port, FL Entrance of B.V.M. into the Temple (St. Mary's); Presbyters.
Kovanis, Joel '94 (SP) Sun City Center, FL Prince of Peace.
Kovarik, Peter '91 (RC) Custer, SD St. John the Baptist; Hot Springs, SD St. Anthony of Padua.
Kovash, Russell P. '09 (BIS) Beach, ND St. John the Baptist; [F] Sentinel Butte, ND Home On The Range; Beach, ND St. Mary (Medora); Beach, ND St. Mary's Golva; Priests' Personnel Board; Priests' Benefit Association.
Kovatch, Thomas G. '07 (IND) Bloomington, IN St. Charles Borromeo Catholic Church, Bloomington, Inc.
Kowal, Jacek L. '09 (MEM) Bartlett, TN St. Ann.
Kowalczyk, Adolph M. '88 (BUF) Orchard Park, NY Our Lady of the Sacred Heart.
Kowalczyk, Joseph W. *m.m.* '61 (SJ)[M] Los Altos, CA Maryknoll.
Kowalczyk, Miroslaw *f.d.p.* '88 (BO) East Boston, MA St. Joseph–St. Lazarus; [S] East Boston, MA Don Orione Nursing Home.
Kowalczyk, Sigismund C. '56 (DET) Retired.
Kowalczyk, Thomas M. '67 (SAG) Retired.
Kowalczyk, Thomas (SAG) AuGres, MI St. Mark.
Kowalewski, John A. *o.s.f.s.* '77 (WIL)[J] Childs, MD Retirement and Assisted Care Facility; Wilmington, DE OBLATES OF ST. FRANCIS DE SALES MISSIONS.
Kowalik, Jacek '79 (VEN) Military Chaplains; Air Force Reserve Chaplains.
Kowalske, Kevin J. '95 (MIL) Newburg, WI Holy Trinity.
Kowalski, Aleksy (PAT) Theological Commission.
Kowalski, Alfred J. '51 (NEW) Kenilworth, NJ St. Theresa's Retired.
Kowalski, Eric '93 (CHL) Mt. Airy, NC Holy Angels.
Kowalski, George '56 (DET) Retired.
Kowalski, Janusz '89 (LC) Rothschild, WI St. Therese of the Child Jesus.
Kowalski, Kazimierz A. (NY) New York, NY Our Lady of Good Counsel.
Kowalski, Lawrence T. '69 (OKL) Retired.
Kowalski, Matthew *o.s.b.* '87 (SFS)[F] Marvin, SD Blue Cloud Abbey.
Kowalski, Matthew *o.s.b.* '87 (CHI) Lake Forest, IL St. Mary.
Kowalski, Wladyslaw J. '51 (SUP) Mosinee, WI St. John the Baptist Retired.
Kowatch, Thomas '85 (CLV) North Ridgeville, OH St. Julie Billiart.
Kownacki, Raymond F. '60 (BEL) Retired.
Koyickal, Joseph *s.a.c.* '80 (MIL) Milwaukee, WI; [P] Milwaukee, WI Pallotti House.
Koyickal, Thomas '70 (PT) Cantonment, FL St. Jude Thaddeus.
Koys, Thomas R. '85 (CHI) Chicago, IL Immaculate Conception.
Kozacheson, Roman *o.f.m.cap* '61 (BAL)[Q] Baltimore, MD St. Ambrose Friary; Baltimore, MD St. Ambrose.
Kozak, David J. '83 (ALN) Defenders of the Bond; Reading, PA St. Peter the Apostle; Elected Members.
Kozak, Lawrence F. '04 (PH) Philadelphia, PA Our Lady of Calvary.
Kozak, Remigius A. '54 (BLX) Retired.
Kozak, Richard J. '67 (CHI) Homewood, IL St. Joseph.
Kozak, Timothy J. '04 (STU) Pomeroy, OH Sacred Heart; Propagation of the Faith.
Kozanko, Andrzej J. '00 (FR) Awaiting Assignment; [F] Fall River, MA Priests' Hostel.
Kozar, Rev. Msgr. John E. '71 (NY)[HH] New York, NY Catholic Near East Welfare Association (CNEWA); Propagation of the Faith, National Office; New York, NY B. The Society of St. Peter Apostle; New York, NY C. The Pontifical Missionary Union.
Kozar, Rev. Msgr. John E. '71 (PIT) On Duty Outside the Diocese.
Kozar, Joseph F. *s.m.* '77 (CIN) Troy, OH St. Patrick; [D] Dayton, OH The University of Dayton; [N] Dayton, OH Marianist Community.
Kozar, Petro (STN) Sacramento, CA St. Andrew the Apostle.
Kozen, Bert S. '63 (MO) Army National Guard Chaplains.
Kozen, Bert S. '82 (SCR) Jersey Shore, PA Immaculate Conception of the Blessed Virgin Mary; Williamsport, PA St. Luke.
Kozhaya Akoury, Tanios '82 (SAM) Advocates.
Kozhippadan, Santhosh George *o.ss.t.* (TR) Trenton, NJ The Church of the Incarnation–St. James.
Kozhippandan, Santhosh George *o.ss.t.* '07 (BAL)[Q] Diocese of Trenton, NJ.
Koziczuk, Andrzej A. '79 (SAC) Isleton, CA St. Therese's; Walnut Grove, CA St. Anthony.
Kozina, Vladimir '45 (OAK) Retired.
Koziol, John *o.f.m.conv.* '88 (ATL) Jonesboro, GA St. Philip Benizi; Deans; Deans.
Koziol, Ryszard Andrzej '97 (CC) Bishop, TX St. James.
Koziol, Stanley N. '58 (BGP) Retired.
Koziola, Marcin '05 (VEN) Fort Myers, FL Blessed Pope John XXIII.
Koziolkiewicz, Piotr '07 (NEW) Summit, NJ St. Teresa's.
Kozlowski, John C. *o.p.* (MO) Assessors.
Kozlowski, John Chrysostom *o.p.* '10 (WDC)[B] Washington, DC Dominican House of Studies.
Kozlowski, Joseph P. '49 (RVC) Glen Head, NY St. Hyacinth Retired.
Kozlowski, Lukasz '09 (SY) Greene, NY Immaculate Conception; Greene, NY St. Joseph.
Kozlowski, Theodore '58 (GR) Grand Rapids, MI Our Lady of Sorrows; Deans; College of Consultors.
Kozminski, Andrew *s.a.c.* '88 (VEN) Sarasota, FL St. Martha.
Kozoil, Micah E. '76 (GBG) Brownsville, PA St. Peter; Brownsville, PA St. Cecilia.
Kozub, Tomasz '93 (CC) Corpus Christi, TX St. Thomas More Parish.
Kozyra, Oscar *o.de.m.* '73 (SP)[N] St. Petersburg, FL St. Peter Nolasco Residence; [S] St. Petersburg, FL Eckerd College – Catholic Campus Ministry.
Krach, Joseph W. '57 (BAL) Retired.
Kracke, Cole '11 (STP) Hastings, MN St. Elizabeth Ann Seton.
Kraeger, David *t.o.r.* '68 (FWT) St. Boniface; Windthorst, TX St. Mary.
Kraemer, Edwin '55 (SCL) Retired.
Kraemer, John A. '57 (RCK) Retired.
Kraeszig, Charles J. '52 (IND) Retired.
Krafft, Joseph M. '02 (NO)[A] New Orleans, LA Notre Dame Seminary Graduate School of Theology.
Krafinski, Thomas S. *c.m.* '68 (PH)[Y].
Kraft, Philip G. '62 (SFD) Retired.
Kraft, Thomas *o.p.* '84 (FgM) New York, NY Province of St. Joseph (Eastern).
Kraft, William '86 (STO) Lodi, CA St. Anne Church (Pastor of).
Krah, James B. '71 (PIT) Retired.
Krahenbuhl, Gary L. '84 (MAD) Beloit, WI Our Lady of the Assumption; Elected.
Krahman, Philip G. '72 (STL) Old Monroe, MO Immaculate Conception; St. Peters, MO All Saints.
Kraig, Robert J. '72 (CLV) Strongsville, OH St. John Neumann.
Kraizyi, Melecio (STF) Long Island City, NY Holy Cross.
Krajcovic, Bernard '56 (STU) Retired.
Krajewski, Joseph A. '73 (MET) New Brunswick, NJ St. Joseph.
Krajewski, Paul A. (PAT) Retired.
Krajnak, Jozef *s.d.b.* '91 (NEW) West New York, NJ St. Joseph of the Palisades.
Krajnik, Paul A. '50 (CLV) Retired.
Kraker, Joseph H. '64 (CLV) Akron, OH St. Vincent.
Kraker, Lames J. '65 (SUP) Retired.
Kraljic, John R. '69 (NY)[E] Bronx, NY Cardinal Spellman High School.
Kralka, Joseph Ihor *o.s.b.m.* '08 (STN) Hamtramck, MI Immaculate Conception of B.V.M.
Krall, Jack '63 (P) Retired.
Krall, Kenneth R. *s.j.* '71 (SPK)[B] Spokane, WA Gonzaga University.
Kralovich, Louis W. '60 (TR) Toms River, NJ St. Luke; Tribunal Judges Retired.
Kramarz, Andreas *l.c.* '03 (HRT)[B] Cheshire, CT

Novitiate of the Legion of Christ.
Kramberg, Donald F. '74 (OG) Dannemora, NY St. Joseph; Redford, NY Church of the Assumption.
Kramer, Carl '52 (SAL) Hays, KS Retired.
Kramer, Daniel J. *c.m.* '47 (PH)[Y].
Kramer, Gary J. '93 (PH) Hatboro, PA St. John Bosco.
Kramer, George '62 (JC) Retired.
Kramer, James F. '68 (CLV) Copley, OH Guardian Angels.
Kramer, Lawrence '60 (FTW) Fort Wayne, IN St. Elizabeth Ann Seton; Appeal Court Judges.
Kramer, Mark A. *s.j.* '05 (FgM) St. Louis, MO Society of Jesus.
Kramer, Richard R. '66 (RCK) Retired.
Kramer, Scott T. *c.pp.s.* '90 (CIN)[T] Dayton, OH Community Support Charitable Trust.
Kramer, Scott *c.pp.s.* '90 (COL) Columbus, OH St. James–the–Less; Council for Religious.
Kramer, Thomas E. '58 (BIS) Presbyteral Council; [G] Bismarck, ND Emmaus Place Retired.
Kramer, Thomas J. '77 (DET) Dearborn Heights, MI St. Mel.
Kramer, William *c.pp.s.* '44 (CIN)[N] Carthagena, OH St. Charles Retired.
Kramis, Joseph '57 (SEA) Retired.
Kramlich, Lloyd *s.d.s.* '58 (MIL)[P] Milwaukee Salvatorian Provincial Offices.
Kramper, James V. '73 (OM) Ewing, NE St. John The Baptist; Ewing, NE St. Peter de Alcantara; Council of Catholic Women, Archdiocesan.
Krantz, Ernest *c.pp.s.* '76 (CIN)[N] Dayton Provincial Office of the Cincinnati Province of the Society of the Precious Blood.
Krantz, Robert V. '78 (SFS) Humboldt, SD St. Ann; Montrose, SD St. Patrick; Personnel Board.
Kranyc, Andrew G. '87 (WH) Absent on Leave.
Kranz, Stephen *o.s.b.* '55 (BIS) Mandaree, ND St. Anthony; [A] Richardton, ND Assumption Abbey; Mandaree, ND St. Joseph.
Krapfl, Gary F. '72 (DUB) Retired.
Krasevac, Edward *o.p.* '77 (OAK) Antioch, CA Most Holy Rosary; [A] Berkeley, CA Dominican School of Philosophy and Theology.
Krasic, Ljubo *o.f.m.* (CHI)[N] Chicago, IL St. Anthony's Friary.
Krasman, James *o.f.m.* '86 (MIL)[P] Burlington, WI Queen of Peace Friary.
Krastel, Francis W. '54 (WDC)[U] St. Mary's City, MD St. Mary's College Campus Ministry.
Krastel, Joseph *c.ss.r.* (BAL) Annapolis, MD St. Mary.
Krasulski, Andrew '98 (SJP) Presbyters; Johnstown, PA St. John the Baptist.
Kraszewski, Thomas P. '97 (Y) Niles, OH St. Stephen; Mineral Ridge, OH St. Mary.
Kratz, Alexander *o.f.m.* '99 (DET) Detroit, MI St. Aloysius.
Kratz, Conrad J. *o.praem.* '73 (GB)[A] De Pere, WI St. Norbert Abbey; [J] De Pere, WI St. Joseph Priory; [M] De Pere, WI Norbertine Center for Spirituality; De Pere, WI.
Kraus, David H. '67 (DOD) Promoter of Justice; Defender of the Bond; Presbyteral Council Retired.
Kraus, Leonard E. *s.j.* '72 (STL)[O] St. Louis, MO; [S] St. Louis, MO Retreat House.
Kraus, Philip D. *s.j.* '75 (STL)[O] St. Louis, MO Jesuit Community Corporation at Saint Louis University – Jesuit Hall.
Kraus, Stephen '75 (ROC) Rochester, NY St. Theodore.
Kraus, Rev. Msgr. Theodore W. '63 (OAK) Orinda, CA Santa Maria.
Kraus, William *o.f.m.cap.* '73 (FgM) Denver, CO Province of Mid–America; [N] Denver, CO San Damiano Friary.
Krause, Bruce J. *c.m.* '82 (BUF)[C] Niagara University, NY Niagara University; [N] Niagara University, NY Vincentian Community at Niagara University; [Q] Niagara University, NY Niagara University.
Krause, Edward C. *c.s.c.* '66 (FTW)[H] Notre Dame Congregation of Holy Cross, United States Province of Priests & Brothers.
Krause, Edward *c.s.c.* '66 (E)[B] Erie, PA Gannon University; The Bishop's Theological Advisory Committee.
Krause, Edward *c.s.c.* '40 (STL)[V] St. Louis, MO Central Bureau of the C.C.V.A.
Krause, Joseph A. '68 (TUC) Judge Retired.
Krauth, Lothar '73 (GF) Great Falls, MT Our Lady of Lourdes.
Krautsack, Blaise R. *o.praem.* '74 (PH)[Y] Paoli, PA Daylesford Abbey.
Krawczenko, Artur '03 (SY) New York Mills, NY Church of Sacred Heart and St. Mary.
Krawontka, Stephen A. '77 (SCR) Scranton, PA St. Patrick's.
Kraynak, Nicholas '59 (PSC) Retired.
Kraynak, William B. '81 (Y) Canton, OH St. Joan of Arc; Presbyteral Council.
Krebill, Dan (GF) Montana Association of Churches.
Krebs, Bruce D. '78 (BIS) Minot, ND Our Lady of Grace; Pro–Synodal Judges; Presbyteral Council.
Krebs, Rev. Msgr. Donald H. '55 (CR) Retired.
Krebs, Rev. Msgr. Henry L. '60 (E) Clearfield, PA St. Francis.
Krebs, John F. '57 (CHI) Ingleside, IL St. Bede Retired.
Krebs, Paul F. '57 (COV) Retired.
Krebs, Peter *s.t.* '69 (PAT)[N] Stirling, NJ Shrine of St. Joseph.
Kreckel, Robert G. '54 (ROC) Penfield, NY St. Joseph Retired.
Kredel, Thomas E. '72 (PIT) New Brighton, PA Holy Family.
Kredensor, Daniel M. '08 (PH) Havertown, PA St. Denis.
Kreder, Mark '03 (TR) Toms River, NJ St. Justin.
Kreder, Michael J. '85 (NEW) Rutherford, NJ Church of St. Mary; Archdiocesan Stewardship Advisory Committee.
Kreher, Albert E. '65 (BEL) Retired.
Kreidler, Rodney A. '05 (CLV) Ashland, OH Samaritan Hospital; Ashland, OH St. Edward.
Kreidler, Thomas W. '77 (CIN) Cincinnati, OH Immaculate Heart of Mary.
Kreilein, Philip '74 (EVN) Evansville, IN Resurrection; Diocesan Council of Priests.
Kreilein, Ronald '07 (EVN) Diocesan Council of Priests; Ireland, IN Annunciation of the Blessed Virgin Mary.
Kreimer, Richard *g.h.m.* '79 (CIN)[N] Cincinnati Headquarters of Glenmary Home Missioners Retired.
Kreinheder, Gregory J. '07 (SY) Oswego, NY St. Joseph; Oswego, NY St. Stephen the King.
Kreiser, Thomas L. '94 (NY) Yorktown Heights, NY St. Patrick.
Kreitinger, Todd '00 (BIS) Dickinson, ND St. Patrick.
Krekelberg, Rev. Msgr. Richard G. '73 (LA) Sierra Madre, CA St. Rita; Deanery 10.
Krekelberg, William '70 (ORG) Irvine, CA St. Thomas More; Archivist; Special Assignment.
Kremen, Timothy M. *o.s.m.* '61 (DEN)[J] Denver, CO Little Sisters of the Poor.
Kremer, John R. '59 (DUB) Delhi, IA St. John; Hopkinton, IA St. Luke; Deans.
Kremer, Philip *o.s.b.* '57 (RCK)[G] Aurora, IL Marmion Abbey.
Kreml, Curt *o.f.m.conv.* (WDC)[B] Silver Spring, MD St. Bonaventure Friary.
Kremmell, William T. '66 (BO) Pax Christi USA; Senior Priests. Retired.
Kremp, Bruno *o.f.m.* '65 (CIN)[K] Cincinnati, OH Mercy Hospitals West; [N] Cincinnati, OH St. John the Baptist Friary.
Krempa, Adam J. '90 (BUR) Retired.
Krempa, Stanley J. '70 (ARL) Winchester, VA Sacred Heart of Jesus.
Krempel, Matthew *o.f.m.* '74 (PHX) Kingman, AZ St. Mary Roman Catholic Parish.
Krenik, Michael J. '84 (STP) Special Assignment.
Krenik, Thomas '77 (STP) Burnsville, MN Church of the Risen Savior.
Krenzke, John W. '57 (COS) Retired.
Kresak, Stephen A. '05 (PIT) McKeesport, PA Corpus Christi Parish.
Kresinski, Daniel J. '70 (E) Farrell, PA St. Adalbert; Sharon, PA St. Anthony.
Kress, Dennis '99 (KNX) Elizabethton, TN St. Elizabeth; Mountain City, TN St. Anthony of Padua Catholic Church.
Kret, John A. *o.s.a.* '61 (JOL)[L] New Lenox, IL Augustinian Friary; [C] New Lenox, IL Providence Catholic High School.
Kretowicz, Antoni '87 (RCK) Aurora, IL St. Peter.
Krettek, Daniel F. '78 (DM) Elkhart, IA St. Mary/Holy Cross; [H] Des Moines, IA Emmaus House; Judges; Charismatic Renewal Liaison.
Krettek, G. Thomas *s.j.* '82 (MIL)[P] Milwaukee, WI Arrupe House Jesuit Community.
Kretz, James C. '91 (PEO) Retired.
Kreul, Ron *o.p.* '78 (JC) Columbia, MO Our Lady of Lourdes.
Kreutz, William H. *s.j.* '69 (FgM) New York, NY Society of Jesus.
Kreutzer, Dan '98 (OWN) Cloverport, KY St. Rose; Irvington, KY Holy Guardian Angels.
Kribs, Charles R. '51 (BEL) Retired.
Kribs, Don Richard '61 (LA) Retired.
Kricek, Henry C. '80 (CHI) Wilmette, IL St. Joseph; [A] Chicago, IL St. Joseph College Seminary.
Krick, Howard K. '58 (PH) Retired.
Krieg, Charles F. *c.m.* '63 (BAL) Emmitsburg, MD St. Joseph; [Q] Emmitsburg, MD Vincentian House.
Krieg, Rev. Msgr. Gerard C. '53 (ROC) Pittsford, NY St. Louis; Pittsford, NY; Defender of the Bond Retired.
Krieg, Thomas J. '92 (LC)[K] Menomonie, WI Newman Center of Stout; Deans; Menomonie, WI St. Joseph.
Kriegel, Rev. Msgr. Henry A. '70 (E) Erie, PA St. Hedwig; Erie, PA St. Patrick.
Kriegshauser, J. Laurence *o.s.b.* '69 (STL)[O] St. Louis, MO The Abbey of St. Mary and St. Louis.
Krier, John P. '69 (SPK) On Duty Outside of the Diocese; Medical Lake, WA St. Anne.
Krier, John '69 (SPK) Medical Lake, WA Mary Queen of Heaven.
Krile, Stephen L. '83 (COL) Millersburg, OH St. Peter.
Kriley, Victor *o.f.m.cap.* '64 (PIT)[M] Pittsburgh St. Augustine Friary.
Krill, Jude Michael *o.f.m.conv.* '83 (PH)[C] Aston, PA Neumann University.
Krill, Jude Michael *o.f.m.conv.* (ATL) Lithia Springs, GA St. John Vianney.
Krill, Philip D. (STL) Maryland Heights, MO Holy Spirit.
Krisak, Anthony F. '75 (WDC)[X] Washington, DC Paulist Evangelization Ministries.
Krisak, Anthony F. *s.s.* '75 (TR) On Duty Outside the Diocese.
Krisanda, Stephen J. *m.s.* '60 (ORL) Orlando, FL Good Shepherd.
Krische, James J. '91 (BRK) Brooklyn, NY St. Cecilia; Army Reserve Chaplains; Military Chaplains; Bellerose, NY St. Gregory the Great.
Krische, Rev. Msgr. Vincent E. '64 (KCK) Retired.
Kriski, Frank *c.ss.r.* '63 (KC) Kansas City, MO Our Lady of Perpetual Help; [J] Kansas City, MO Redemptorists Fathers of Kansas City, Missouri.
Krisman, Ronald '73 (ORL) On Duty Outside the Diocese.
Kriss, Aaron J. '91 (PIT) Tarentum, PA Holy Martyrs.
Kriss, Zigford J. '58 (HRT) West Hartford, CT St. Helena Retired.
Kristancic, Dennis J. '83 (CLV) Strongsville, OH St. John Neumann.
Kristofak, Terence J. *c.p.* '69 (HRT)[P] West Hartford, CT Holy Family Passionist Retreat Center; [L] West Hartford, CT Holy Family Monastery/Retreat.
Kristy, Mark *o.c.d.* '85 (SR)[L] Oakville, CA Carmelite House of Prayer.
Krivak, John A. '82 (ALN)[O] Allentown, PA The Newman Center; [O] Allentown, PA Cedar Crest College (Allentown); [O] Allentown, PA Muhlenberg College (Allentown).
Kriz, Dennis *o.s.m.* '99 (CHI) Chicago, IL Annunciata; [N] Chicago, IL Annunciata Priory.
Krizner, William R. '79 (CLV) Brunswick, OH St. Colette.
Krlis, William F. '68 (BRK) Diocesan Real Estate Board; Long Island City, NY Most Precious Blood; Diocesan Consultors; Long Island City, NY St. Patrick.
Kroeger, James H. *m.m.* '75 (FgM) Maryknoll, NY MARYKNOLL.
Kroeger, John '72 (CIN) On Special and Archdiocesan Assignment.
Kroeger, Timothy '90 (LFT) Lebanon, IN St. Joseph.
Kroes, Ralph S. *m.m.* '58 (NY)[DD] Retired.
Kroger, Daniel *o.f.m.* '73 (CIN)[U] Cincinnati, OH St. Anthony Messenger; [U] Cincinnati, OH St. Anthony Messenger Press and Franciscan Communications; [C] Cincinnati, OH St. Anthony Shrine, Franciscan Postulancy.
Kroger, John H. '55 (COV) Bellevue, KY Divine Mercy; [I] Edgewood, KY St. Elizabeth Edgewood; Vicar for Retired Priests; Bellevue, KY Retired.
Krogman, David '81 (SFS) Sioux Falls, SD St. Mary; [D] Sioux Falls, SD Avera McKennan; Diocesan Consultors; Presbyteral Council.
Krogman, Philip J. '60 (MAD) Green Lake, WI Our Lady of the Lake.
Krol, Boleslaus '61 (DET) Detroit, MI St. Louis the King.
Krol, Marek '95 (COS) Elizabeth, CO Our Lady of the Visitation.
Krolczyk, David B. '72 (CHI) Sauk Village, IL St. James.
Krolh, Jan (SJN) Carolina, PR Cristo Rey.
Kroll, Anthony '61 (SCL) Retired.
Kroll, Miroslaw K. '99 (NEW) Linden, NJ St. Theresa of the Child Jesus.
Kroll, Robert J. *s.j.* '99 (WDC)[O] Washington, DC The Jesuit Community of St. Aloysius Gonzaga.
Kromholtz, Bryan *o.p.* '00 (OAK) Oakland, CA; [L] Oakland, CA Order of Preachers (Province of the Most Holy Name of Jesus – Western Dominican Province); [A] Berkeley, CA Dominican School of Philosophy and Theology; [L] Oakland, CA Order of Preachers (Province of the Most Holy Name of Jesus – Western Dominican Province).
Kronkowski, Leonard J. '55 (GRY) Retired.
Kropac, Robert J. '82 (CLV) Concord Twp., OH St. Gabriel.
Kropf, Richard '58 (GLD)[G] Johannesburg, MI Stella Maris Hermitage.
Kropf, Richard '58 (LAN) On Duty Outside the Diocese.
Kropiwnicki, Henry '58 (FR) Retired.
Kropp, Steven *o.f.m.cap.* '04 (MIL) Mount Calvary, WI St. Isidore Congregation; Archdiocesan Council of Priests; [P] Mount Calvary, WI St. Felix Friary.
Kros, Donald M. '59 (OM) Retired.
Krosfield, George '70 (ALX) Dupont, LA Immaculate Conception.
Krosnicki, Thomas *s.v.d.* '66 (WDC)[O] Washington, DC Society of the Divine Word/Divine Word House.
Krotec, Rt. Rev. Mitred Archpriest Ivan '70 (STN) Chicago, IL SS. Volodymyr and Olha.
Krotkiewicz, Luke '83 (DET) Warren, MI Henry Ford

Macomb Hospital.
Krouse, Dennis '68 (SD)[B] University of San Diego.
Krozser, John J. '56 (NEW) Retired.
Kruc, James '89 (RIC) Philadelphia, PA Retired.
Krueger, Robert '56 (P) Portland, OR St. Francis of Assisi Retired.
Kruesuwan, John Bosco Prasit '99 (FRS) Visalia, CA Holy Family; Visalia, CA St. Mary; Visalia, CA St. Thomas the Apostle.
Krug, Clement M. *c.ss.r.* '65 (NEW) Newark, NJ St. James; Brazilian Apostolate.
Krug, Clement *c.ss.r.* '65 (FgM) Baltimore Province.
Krugel, Stephen A. '88 (HRT) Enfield, CT Willard–Cybulski Correction Institute; Cheshire, CT Cheshire Correctional Institution; Suffield, CT Macdougall – Walker Correctional Institute; Special and other Archdiocesan Assignment.
Kruger, Brent A. *c.s.c.* '97 (FTW)[H] Notre Dame Congregation of Holy Cross, United States Province of Priests & Brothers.
Kruger, Brent A. *c.s.c.* '97 (OAK)[L] Berkeley, CA Priests of the Congregation of Holy Cross.
Krulak, Michael '84 (PSC) New Port Richey, FL St. Anne's.
Krull, Michael G. '86 (MET) Hopelawn, NJ Our Lady of the Most Holy Rosary; Perth Amboy, NJ Holy Spirit.
Krumm, John E. '76 (CIN) Jamestown, OH St. Augustine; Xenia, OH St. Brigid.
Krummert, Gary W. '02 (PIT) Bentleyville, PA Ave Maria.
Krupa, Stephen T. *s.j.* '88 (CHI)[C] Chicago, IL Jesuit Community at Loyola University Chicago.
Krupa, Thomas '71 (ALB) Castleton On Hudson, NY Sacred Heart; Advocates; Deans; Priestly Life and Ministry Council.
Krupich, Thomas J. '88 (FAR) Fessenden, ND St. Augustine's Church of Fessenden; Fessenden, ND St. Patrick's Church of Hurdsfield; Fessenden, ND Holy Family.
Krupka, Michael '77 (SJP) Wheeling, WV Our Lady of Perpetual Help; Consultors; Presbyters; Personnel Board.
Krupnik, Marion I. '54 (HRT) Retired.
Krupp, Albert A. '65 (CLV) Senior Priests; Bay Village, OH St. Raphael.
Krupp, Joseph J. '98 (LAN) East Lansing, MI St. Thomas Aquinas; East Lansing, MI St. John the Evangelist Church and Student Center; [N] East Lansing, MI St. John the Evangelist Church and Student Center.
Kruse, Anthony J. '11 (DUB) Deanery Representatives; Marion, IA St. Joseph.
Kruse, David B. '94 (BAL) Military Chaplains; Air Force Chaplains.
Kruse, Rev. Msgr. James E. '96 (PEO) East Peoria, IL St. Monica Church; Vicars General; Adjutant Judicial Vicar; Assistant Directors; Finance Council (Canon 492).
Kruse, Phillip F. '81 (DUB)[G] Bellevue, IA Bellevue Area Elementary School; Dubuque, IA St. Catherine; Bellevue, IA St. Donatus; Springbrook, IA SS. Peter and Paul; Bellevue, IA St. Joseph; Deans; [G] Bellevue, IA Marquette High School; Vocation Awareness Advisory Committee.
Kruse, Robert J. *c.s.c.* '58 (FR)[A] North Easton, MA Holy Cross Fathers Religious.
Kruse, Robert J. *c.s.c.* '58 (FTW)[H] Notre Dame Congregation of Holy Cross, United States Province of Priests & Brothers.
Krutcik, Stanley F. '80 (WOR) Worcester, MA St. Christopher.
Krutewicz, Jan '00 (JOL) Elmhurst, IL Visitation.
Kruthaupt, Timothy J. '07 (GBG) Clymer, PA Church of the Resurrection; Indiana, PA Indiana Hospital; St. Thomas More Society for Lawyers.
Krutzik, Norman '57 (GB) Retired.
Krylowicz, Mark J. '91 (CHI) Chicago, IL St. Anthony of Padua.
Krymski, Christopher M. *o.s.m.* '83 (CHI) Chicago, IL Our Lady of Sorrows, Basilica of; Chicago, IL; [N] Chicago, IL National Shrine of St. Peregrine, O.S.M.; [N] Chicago, IL Order of Friar Servants of Mary (Servites) United States of America Province, Inc.; [N] Chicago, IL Monastery of Our Lady of Sorrows.
Krynen, Joseph G. '46 (PHX) Tempe, AZ Church of the Resurrection Roman Catholic Parish Retired.
Krysa, Czeslaw M. '80 (BUF) Worship, Office Of; [A] East Aurora, NY Christ the King Seminary; Finance Council; Buffalo, NY St. Casimir Oratory.
Krystosek, Glenn A. '07 (SCL) Paynesville, MN St. Margaret's; Paynesville, MN St. Louis; Paynesville, MN St. Agnes.
Krystosek, Robert H. '56 (GI) Retired.
Kryszkiewicz, Pawel '93 (CAM) Camden, NJ St. Joseph's Catholic Church, Camden, N.J.
Kryvokulsky, Oleh '98 (STN) Chicago, IL SS. Volodymyr and Olha.
Kryzwda, Leonard *c.r.* '65 (SB) Lake Arrowhead, CA Our Lady of the Lake; Running Springs, CA St. Anne in the Mountains.
Krzanowski, Lukasz *m.s.* '91 (SPR) Westfield, MA Holy Trinity.
Krzemien, Filip *o.cist.* '04 (CHI)[N] Willow Springs, IL Cistercian Fathers, Our Lady Mother of the Church Polish Mission.
Krzewinski, Charles *o.m.i.* '52 (SAT)[K] San Antonio, TX Oblate Madonna Residence.
Krzyston, Stanley '85 (TR) Yardville, NJ St. Vincent de Paul.
Krzywda, Jerzy '89 (LAR) Carrizo Springs, TX Our Lady of Guadalupe; Ex Officio Members.
Krzywda, Leonard *c.r.* '65 (SB)[I] Lake Arrowhead, CA.
Krzywicki, Lance P. '83 (PT) Military Chaplains.
Krzyzaniak, Timothy D. '91 (LAN) Manchester, MI St. Mary.
Krzyzanowski, Casimir *m.i.c.* '56 (WDC)[B] Washington, DC Marian Fathers Scholasticate.
Krzyzopolski, Al '50 (SFS) Tribunal Judges Retired.
Kselman, John J. *s.s.* '67 (TR) On Duty Outside the Diocese.
Kselman, John S. *s.s.* '67 (BAL)[Q] Baltimore Society of St. Sulpice, Province of the United States.
Kselman, John S. *s.s.* '67 (SFR)[A] Menlo Park, CA St. Patrick Seminary and University.
Ksiazek, Karol J. '10 (BGP) Trumbull, CT St. Theresa.
Ku, Theodore John Baptist *o.p.* '99 (WDC)[B] Washington, DC Dominican House of Studies.
Kub, Francis Q. '65 (CHI) Associate Vicars; Chicago, IL St. Simon the Apostle.
Kuba, William M. '62 (E) East Brady, PA St. Eusebius.
Kubacki, Rev. Msgr. William J. '78 (TOL) Toledo, OH Queen of the Most Holy Rosary Cathedral; Vicar for Priests; Continuing Formation for Priests; Deacon Formation.
Kubajak, James '77 (PRM) Northwood, OH St. Michael the Archangel; Ex Officio; Great Lakes; Defender of the Bond; Promoter of Justice; Presbyteral Council.
Kubala, Daniel I. '76 (MIA) Miami, FL St. Thomas the Apostle; Consultors; Chairman; West Dade Deanery.
Kubart, Rev. Msgr. Francis E. '41 (OM) Omaha Priests Retirement Plan and Trust, The Retired.
Kubat, Christopher K. '99 (LIN) Apostolate of Suffering; Catholic Social Services; Diocesan Housing Ministries, Inc.; [K] Lincoln, NE Catholic Social Services.
Kubat, Christopher (GI) Charities.
Kubeck, John C. '65 (MIL)[O] Brookfield, WI Prelature of the Holy Cross and Opus Dei Layton Study Center; Brookfield.
Kubiak, Joseph *o.f.m.cap.* '74 (MET) Colonia, NJ St. John Vianney.
Kubicki, James M. *s.j.* '83 (MIL)[Y] Milwaukee, WI Apostleship of Prayer; [P] Milwaukee, WI Jesuit Community at Marquette University.
Kubina, Eugene *t.o.r.* '53 (ALT)[G] Hollidaysburg, PA St. Bernardine Monastery Retired.
Kubinski, Scott M. '84 (ROC) Priest Consultors.
Kubinski, Scott '84 (ROC) Elmira, NY Christ the Redeemer.
Kubisa, Jan '82 (GAL) Houston, TX St. Joseph.
Kubishyn, Ivan '79 (SJP) Presbyters; Apopka, FL St. Mary's.
Kubista, Paul Basil '10 (STP) Chanhassen, MN St. Hubert.
Kubrak, Wladyslaw Z. '06 (BRK) Ridgewood, NY St. Matthias.
Kuca, Stanislaw '91 (CHI) Orland Hills, IL St. Elizabeth Seton.
Kucer, Peter *m.s.a.* '03 (NOR)[G] Cromwell Society of the Missionaries of the Holy Apostles.
Kucer, Peter *m.s.a.* '03 (HRT) Waterbury, CT Basilica of the Immaculate Conception.
Kucera, David G. '98 (DUB) Church Design/Renovation Commission; Reinbeck, IA Holy Family Church, Reinbeck, Iowa.
Kucera, Edward C. '73 (GAL) Plantersville, TX St. Mary.
Kucera, Edward J. *o.s.b.* '53 (JOL)[L] Lisle, IL St. Procopius Abbey; Lisle, IL.
Kucera, Jeremy G. '04 (NU) Ghent, MN St. Eloi; Minneota, MN St. Edward.
Kuchar, Joseph *s.a.c.* '05 (BAL) Baltimore, MD St. Jude Shrine.
Kuchar, Michael W. '80 (LAN) Goodrich, MI St. Mark the Evangelist.
Kucharczyk, Dennis H. '85 (SAG) Caro, MI Sacred Heart; Navy Reserve Chaplains.
Kucharski, Steven M. '77 (MAN) Keene, NH Mary, Queen of Peace Parish; Presbyteral Council; Keene, NH Parish of the Holy Spirit.
Kuchera, Michael J. *s.j.* '87 (BAL)[Q] Towson Maryland Province of the Society of Jesus.
Kuczborski, Joseph '82 (PMB) Retired.
Kuczmanski, Gregory M. '75 (BWN) Mission, TX St. Paul.
Kuczynski, Edward P. '77 (PH) On Special or Other Archdiocesan Assignment; Philadelphia, PA St. Charles Borromeo.
Kuczynski, James H. *m.s.* '73 (HRT) Hartford, CT; [L] Hartford, CT Missionaries of LaSalette Province of Mary, Mother of the Americas.
Kuczynski, James H. *m.s.* '73 (ATL) Smyrna, GA St. Thomas the Apostle.
Kuczynski, Kazimierz '76 (NEW) Jersey City, NJ St. Ann's.
Kuder, Donald E. *c.s.b.* '63 (GAL)[O] Houston, TX Dillon House Retired.
Kuder, Stephen R. *s.j.* '73 (SPK)[B] Spokane, WA Gonzaga University.
Kudilil, James '63 (FRS) Retired.
Kudilil, Joseph '66 (JOL) Rockdale, IL St. Joseph Church.
Kudiyiruppil, John '84 (SYM) Longwood, FL St. Mary Syro–Malabar Catholic Mission (Orlando).
Kudiyiruppilulaltannan, John '84 (ORL) Longwood, FL Church of the Nativity.
Kudleychuk, Bohdan (STN) St. Joseph, MO St. Joseph's; Omaha, NE St. George's; Omaha, NE Assumption of B.V.M.
Kuebler, A.M. Seamus '75 (WDC) On Duty Outside the Archdiocese.
Kuehler, Rev. Msgr. Norbert '55 (AMA) Retired.
Kuehnemund, Thomas '93 (DET) Emmett, MI Our Lady of Mount Carmel; Yale, MI Sacred Heart.
Kuehner, John *c.ss.r.* '03 (CHI) Chicago, IL St. Michael in Old Town; [N] Chicago, IL The Redemptorist Fathers of Chicago.
Kuehner, Rev. Msgr. Ralph J. '50 (WDC) Derwood, MD St. Francis of Assisi Retired.
Kuffel, Thomas '89 (LIN) Exeter, NE St. Stephen's; [L] Mc Cool Junction, NE Camp Kateri; Diocesan Area CCD Directors.
Kuffner, Patrick J. '02 (MET) Middlesex, NJ Our Lady of Mount Virgin; Deans.
Kugler, Michael '89 (GLP) On Duty Outside of Diocese.
Kuhlmann, John L. '68 (BUF) Retired.
Kuhlmann, Steven F. *o.p.* '92 (MAD) Madison, WI Blessed Sacrament.
Kuhn, Aaron J. '07 (SCL) Special Assignment.
Kuhn, Christopher J. '97 (RCK) Galena, IL St. Mary; Galena, IL St. Michael; Scales Mound, IL Holy Trinity.
Kuhn, Christopher *c.s.c.* (FTW)[H] Notre Dame Congregation of Holy Cross, United States Province of Priests & Brothers.
Kuhn, Dennis R. '82 (CHL) Absent On Leave.
Kuhn, George J. '64 (NY) Yonkers, NY St. Joseph Parish.
Kuhn, James G. '71 (MAD) Janesville, WI St. Patrick.
Kuhn, Matthew '10 (SCL) St. Cloud, MN St. Michael; Waite Park, MN St. Joseph's.
Kuhn, Michael F. *y.a.* '97 (ARL)[L] McLean, VA Youth Apostles Institute, An Association of Christian Faithful.
Kuhn, Michael F. '97 (FR) On Duty Outside the Diocese.
Kuhn, Richard W. '53 (DUB)[F] Farley, IA Seton Catholic Schools; Peosta, IA St. John the Baptist Church of Peosta, Iowa.
Kuhn, Richard *s.m.* (BAL)[Q] Baltimore, MD Society of Mary (Marianists).
Kuhn, Thomas A. '67 (CIN) Priests On Administrative Leave.
Kuhneman, Timothy '06 (RIC) Virginia Beach, VA Holy Spirit.
Kuhns, Howard *c.s.c.* (FTW)[H] Notre Dame Congregation of Holy Cross, United States Province of Priests & Brothers.
Kuhns, James '61 (SPK) Retired.
Kuhr, William '67 (GB) Retired.
Kuizon, Antonio '77 (NEW) Scotch Plains, NJ Immaculate Heart of Mary.
Kujawa, Andrzej *s.d.s* '08 (BRK) Brooklyn, NY Our Lady of Consolation.
Kujawinski, Matthew J. '03 (E) Meadville, PA St. Agatha.
Kujovsky, Rev. Msgr. Thomas J. '57 (HBG) Catholic History and Archives, Office of; Presbyteral Council Retired.
Kukatla, Jones '83 (CAM)[H] Vineland, NJ Bishop McCarthy Residence; Vineland, NJ Divine Mercy, Vineland, N.J.
Kukielka, Zbigniew '11 (NEW) Linden, NJ St. John the Apostle.
Kuklich, Stepan '95 (BUF) Millard Fillmore Suburban Hospital; Lakeview Shock Incarceration Correctional Facility.
Kukulka, Janusz *s.t.l.* '85 (HRT) Derby, CT St. Mary the Immaculate Conception.
Kulacz, Sean R. '09 (BGP) Bridgeport, CT St. Augustine Cathedral.
Kulah, Henry N. '84 (CHR) Charleston, SC St. Patrick; Charleston, SC Our Lady of Mercy.
Kulak, Joseph F. '66 (RCK) Retired.
Kulandairajan, S. '78 (NY) Shrub Oak, NY Saint Elizabeth Ann Seton.
Kulas, Francis J. *m.s.* '54 (HRT) Rocky Hill, CT Veterans' Home and Hospital.
Kulas, John *o.s.b.* '57 (SCL)[I] Collegeville, MN St. John's Abbey, of the Order of St. Benedict.
Kulas, William J. '74 (WIN) Blooming Prairie, MN St. Columbanus; Blooming Prairie, MN Sacred Heart;

Associate Judges; Priests' Pension Board.
Kulathinal, Jose J. *c.m.i.* '92 (STA) Jacksonville, FL St. Matthew's; Diocesan Consultors; Presbyteral Council; Deans; Cursillos de Cristiandad.
Kulathingal, Francis *o.ss.t.* '09 (BAL)[Q] Assigned in India.
Kulathumkal, Babu *h.g.n.* '96 (OWN) Hardin, KY St. Henry; Cadiz, KY St. Stephen.
Kulavich, John J. '83 (SCR)[K] Dallas, PA Mercy Center Nursing Unit, Inc.
Kulbicki, Timothy A. *o.f.m.conv.* '86 (BAL)[A] Baltimore, MD St. Mary's Seminary and University.
Kulbicki, Timothy *o.f.m.conv.* '86 (BAL) Baltimore, MD St. Casimir; [A] Baltimore, MD St. Mary's Seminary and University.
Kulbis, Augustine M. *o.s.m.* '58 (CHI)[N] Chicago, IL Monastery of Our Lady of Sorrows.
Kulczynski, Jason '89 (PH) Lansdowne, PA St. Philomena; [D] Philadelphia, PA SS. John Neumann and Maria Goretti Catholic High School.
Kulesa, Daniel J. '62 (Y) Judges Retired.
Kulhawik, Frank '40 (CR) Retired.
Kulick, Larry J. '92 (GBG) Greensburg, PA Our Lady of Grace; Catholic Business and Professional Women's Association; Office for Clergy Vocations.
Kulick, Michael '09 (SJP) Parma, OH St. Josaphat Cathedral; Presbyters.
Kulig, Rev. Msgr. Anthony J. '61 (NEW)[B] Seton Hall University; [A] South Orange, NJ Immaculate Conception Seminary School of Theology.
Kulig, Krzysztof A. '07 (CHI) Arlington Heights, IL St. James.
Kuligowski, Peter J. '97 (ALT) Absent on Leave.
Kuligowski, Peter '97 (ALX) St. Joseph, LA St. Joseph; Deans; Appointed Members.
Kulik, Rev. Msgr. Alexander T. '54 (SCR)[M] Dunmore, PA Villa St. Joseph Retired.
Kulik, Francis J. '69 (SCR) Unassigned or Leave of Absence.
Kull, John J. *o.f.m.* '66 (PAT)[N] Butler, NJ St. Anthony Friary.
Kull, Martin R. '76 (BRK) Brooklyn, NY St. Anselm.
Kulleck, Rev. Msgr. Donald R. '54 (SD) Chula Vista, CA Saint Pius X Catholic Parish Chula Vista Retired.
Kulleck, Thomas G. '74 (BWN) Associate Judges; Office of the Chancellor; Brownsville, TX Our Lady of Good Counsel.
Kuller, Thomas J. *s.j.* '90 (BAL)[Q] Baltimore, MD Ferdinand Wheeler Jesuit Community.
Kullmann, Charles *c.s.p.* '78 (AUS) Austin, TX St. Austin.
Kulma, Ryszard '02 (GAL) Katy, TX St. Edith Stein.
Kulwicki, Raymond J. *c.s.sp.* '56 (PIT)[O] Bethel Park, PA The Spiritan Center.
Kulwiec, Richard *o.m.i.* '81 (LAR) Eagle Pass, TX St. Joseph.
Kumai, Felix K. '86 (NY) Army Chaplains; West Point, NY Catholic Chapel of the Most Holy Trinity.
Kumar, Joseph Nirmal '87 (CC) Corpus Christi, TX Holy Family.
Kumarthusseril, Joy *m.f.* '88 (OAK) Alameda, CA St. Philip Neri–St. Albert the Great.
Kumbakeel, Boby Kurian *o.ss.t.* '08 (BAL)[Q] Diocese of Trenton, NJ.
Kumbakkeel, James *o.s.b.* '86 (FTW) Fort Wayne, IN St. Charles Borromeo.
Kumbalaprampil, Xavier '66 (SAV) Retired.
Kumblumkal, Jose *c.m.i.* '90 (TYL) Jefferson, TX Immaculate Conception; Jefferson, TX St. Paul of Tarsus Mission.
Kumi, Matthew '99 (DOD) Garden City, KS St. Mary Catholic Church of Garden City, Kansas.
Kummer, John R. '72 (CIN) Retired.
Kummer, William '75 (FTW) Plymouth, IN St. Michael; Clergy Retirement Board; Presbyteral Council; Retired Clergy Committee.
Kummerer, Timothy M. '83 (TOL) Bascom, OH SS. Patrick & Andrew; New Riegel, OH All Saints.
Kumo, Michael (BO) Kenyan.
Kumplam, Chacko K. '80 (HRT) Milford, CT St. Mary.
Kumse, John M. '79 (CLV) Cleveland, OH St. Mary; [Y] Cleveland, OH Cleveland Slovenian Community Center.
Kuna, Lech '73 (HRT)[J] Enfield, CT The Home for the Aged of the Little Sisters of the Poor.
Kuna, Vincent A. *c.s.c.* '09 (COS) Colorado Springs, CO Sacred Heart.
Kuna, Vincent A. *c.s.c.* '09 (FTW)[H] Notre Dame Congregation of Holy Cross, United States Province of Priests & Brothers.
Kunat, Bartosz T. '11 (BLX).
Kunath, Thomas '85 (TR) Barnegat, NJ St. Mary.
Kunco, Edward J. '69 (PIT) Cranberry Township, PA St. Ferdinand.
Kunderevych, Orest '98 (PHU) Edwardsville, PA St. Vladimir's; Mount Carmel, PA SS. Peter and Paul.
Kunigonis, Mark S. '00 (PH) Philadelphia, PA Holy Spirit.
Kunisch, Robert *c.pp.s.* '56 (TOL)[H] Bellevue Mary Lay Center; [J] Bellevue, OH Sorrowful Mother Shrine.
Kunisch, William J. '02 (HON) Vicars Forane; Honolulu, HI Co–Cathedral of St. Theresa of the Child Jesus; Presbyteral Council; College of Consultors.
Kunisch, William '02 (HON) Clergy Personnel Board; Members; Office of Worship; Ex Officio.
Kunkel, A. Henry '70 (BAL) Pylesville, MD St. Mary.
Kunkel, Albert A. '57 (CLV)[M] Akron, OH Francesca Residence; [O] Akron, OH Provincial Motherhouse and Novitiate of the Daughters of Divine Charity; Norton, OH Prince of Peace.
Kunkel, Charles *o.s.c.* '67 (SCL)[I] Onamia, MN Crosier Priory.
Kunkel, George C. '77 (CIN) Cincinnati, OH St. Vincent Ferrer.
Kunkel, James E. '73 (PIT) Turtle Creek, PA St. Colman; Judges.
Kunkel, Ronald T. '00 (CHI)[A] Mundelein, IL University of St. Mary of the Lake/Mundelein Seminary.
Kunkel, Steven '01 (PHX) Mesa, AZ Christ the King Roman Catholic Parish; Priests' Assurance Association.
Kunkle, Albert A. '57 (CLV) Retired.
Kunnakkattuthara, Rev. Msgr. Zacharias S. '75 (TYL) Palestine, TX Sacred Heart; Palestine, TX Powledge Unit, Texas Department of Criminal Justice; Tennessee Colony, TX Coffield Unit, Texas Department of Hodge Unit and Skyview Unit, Texas Department of Criminal Justice; Tennessee Colony, TX Gurney Unit; Tennessee Colony, TX Michael Unit; College of Consultors; Deans; Priests' Pension Board; Priests' Personnel Board.
Kunnalakattu, Peter '84 (CHI)[J] Elk Grove Village, IL Alexian Brothers Medical Center.
Kunnaseril, John Joseph *i.m.s.* '80 (BR) Livonia, LA St. Frances Xavier Cabrini; Grosse Tete, LA St. Joseph; Grosse Tete, LA Immaculate Heart of Mary.
Kunnath, Matthew '60 (NEW) Nutley, NJ St. Mary's Retired.
Kunnath, Sebastian '73 (NEW) Paramus, NJ Our Lady of the Visitation.
Kunnathu, Varghese *m.c.b.s.* '74 (VIC) Wharton, TX Holy Family.
Kunnel, Lawrence K. '60 (TR) Retired.
Kunnel, Thomas *s.d.b.* '83 (NY) Tappan, NY Our Lady of the Sacred Heart.
Kunnel, Thomas *t.o.r.* (DM) Imogene, IA St. Patrick; Red Oak, IA St. Mary.
Kunninu, Sibi *ms* '02 (LKC) Sulphur, LA Our Lady of Prompt Succor.
Kunnumpuram, Paul *m.s.f.s.* '76 (ALX) Deville, LA St. John the Baptist.
Kunnumpuram, Paul *m.s.f.s.* '76 (TYL)[C] Whitehouse, TX The Missionaries of St. Francis de Sales.
Kunst, Richard '98 (DUL) Auditor; Department of Vocations and Priestly Formation; Duluth, MN St. John; Duluth, MN St. Joseph.
Kuntz, Donald B. '41 (DET) Retired.
Kuntz, Kenneth E. '77 (DAV) Clinton, IA Jesus Christ, Prince of Peace; Diocesan Consultors; Deans.
Kunz, David C. '80 (LC) Personnel Council; Ex Officio; International Priests; Special Assignment.
Kunz, Eric J. '08 (STL) Oakville, MO Queen of All Saints.
Kunz, Francis P. '49 (WIN) Retired.
Kunz, James H. '73 (WIN) On Special or Other Diocesan Assignment; [D] Rochester, MN Saint Mary Hospital.
Kunz, John M. '76 (WIN) Mankato, MN St. John the Baptist.
Kunz, Thomas W. '04 (PIT) Graduate Studies.
Kunze, Robert W. '74 (NEW) Retired.
Kunzman, Richard T. '63 (CAM) Retired.
Kuolt, Benedict J. '47 (NY)[DD] Bronx, NY John Cardinal O'Connor Residence Retired.
Kuper, Raymond L. '64 (EVN) Judges Retired.
Kupisz, Julian '74 (FAR) Retired.
Kupka, Marek S. '01 (PRO) Providence, RI St. Adalbert.
Kupke, Rev. Msgr. Raymond J. '73 (PAT) Hawthorne, NJ St. Anthony's; Archivist; Theological Commission.
Kuppe, Paul *o.f.m.cap.* '70 (PH) Philadelphia, PA Our Lady of the Blessed Sacrament.
Kuras, Alexander A. '69 (DET) Westland, MI Church of the Divine Savior.
Kurash, Stanley J. '71 (SCR) Unassigned or Leave of Absence.
Kurber, Robert '60 (ORL) Retired.
Kurc, Slawomir '95 (CHI) Chicago, IL St. Daniel the Prophet.
Kurdziel, Dennis M. '75 (ALT) Priests on Medical Leave.
Kurgan, Charles *o.carm.* '65 (PHX)[F] Phoenix, AZ St. Therese Priory; Phoenix, AZ.
Kurgan, John J. '04 (SY) Vestal, NY Binghamton Nursing Homes; Vestal, NY Our Lady of Sorrows; Presbyteral Council; Priests' Personnel Committee.
Kuriakose, John (MCE) Fathers' Forum Director; Priests – Heads of Apostolates.
Kuriakose, Thomas '83 (HT) Montegut, LA St. Charles Borromeo.
Kurian, Santy M. *m.s.f.s.* '95 (GAL) Sugar Land, TX St. Laurence.
Kuriappilly, Johnson '90 (BIS) Beulah, ND St. Joseph; Hazen, ND St. Martin.
Kurilec, Robert E. '68 (SB) Retired.
Kurimay, Michael D. *s.j.* '73 (MIL)[P] Wauwatosa, WI Jesuit Community at St. Camillus.
Kurimsky, Frank M. '86 (PIT) Oakmont, PA St. Irenaeus.
Kurkowski, Innocent *o.f.m.conv.* '56 (BUF)[N] Athol Springs, NY St. Maximilian Kolbe Friary Retired.
Kurnath, Joseph G.M. '91 (HRT) Lakeville, CT St. Mary.
Kuroly, James A. '07 (BRK) Graduate Studies; Hollis, NY St. Gerard Majella.
Kuroly, James A. '06 (BRK)[B] Elmhurst, NY Cathedral Preparatory Seminary of the Immaculate Conception.
Kurovsky, Andrew '85 (SCR) Unassigned or Leave of Absence.
Kurowski, Canon Andrzej *s.a.c.* '76 (BRK) Brooklyn, NY St. Frances de Chantal.
Kurpel, Yaroslav '93 (PHU) Philadelphia, PA Christ the King.
Kurpios, Szymon *sch.p.* (HRT) New Britain, CT Holy Cross.
Kurps, Jack *s.c.j.* '77 (JKS)[I] Walls, MS Sacred Heart League; [I] Walls, MS Sacred Heart Southern Missions Housing Corporation; [I] Walls, MS Sacred Heart Southern Missions, Inc.; [E] Nesbit, MS St. Michael Community House.
Kurt, Allan J. '55 (DUB) Retired.
Kurtenbach, Harold R. '60 (GI) Charismatic Renewal; DEPARTMENT OF VETERANS AFFAIRS HOSPITALS AND CHAPLAINS Retired.
Kurtyka, Rev. Msgr. Edward J. '71 (PAT) Prospect Park, NJ St. Paul's; Judicial Vicar.
Kurtz, James *o.f.m. cap.* (WH) Charleston, WV St. Anthony; Elkview, WV Our Lady of the Hills; [L] Charleston, WV Capuchins–St. Anthony Friary.
Kurtz, Jeffrey A. '90 (MAR) Crystal Falls, MI Guardian Angels.
Kurtzke, John *c.s.c.* (FTW)[H] Notre Dame Congregation of Holy Cross, United States Province of Priests & Brothers.
Kurucz, Frank A. '98 (CHI) Chicago, IL St. Cajetan.
Kurumbel, Joseph *o.s.b.* '76 (LUB) Lamesa, TX St. Margaret Mary; Vicars Forane; Lamesa, TX St. Margaret Mary.
Kurutz, Joseph V. '59 (PIT) Bethel Park, PA Retired.
Kuruvila, Prince '92 (CC) Orange Grove, TX St. John of the Cross.
Kuruvilla, Baby V. '90 (HT) Thibodaux, LA St. Lawrence the Martyr.
Kuruvilla, Prince '92 (SYM) Orange Grove, TX St. Alphonsa Syro–Malabar Catholic Mission Austin, TX.
Kurwicki, Rev. Msgr. Robert A. '85 (JC) Jefferson City, MO St. Joseph Cathedral; Personnel Board; Senators; Vice–Chancellors.
Kury, Ignatius '06 (SJP) Akron, OH Holy Ghost; Akron, OH St. Nicholas; Consultors; St. Josaphat Sacerdotal Society; Presbyters.
Kurylowicz, Martin '79 (GR) Faculties Suspended.
Kuryvial, George *o.m.i.* '58 (BEL)[F] Belleville, IL Missionary Oblates of Mary Immaculate – St. Henry's Oblate Residence.
Kurz, Andrew J. '02 (LIN) Doniphan, NE St. Ann's; Doniphan, NE Sacred Heart; Advocates.
Kurz, Rev. Msgr. Michael A. '75 (RCK) Special Assignment; Judicial Vicar.
Kurz, William S. *s.j.* '70 (MIL)[P] Milwaukee, WI Jesuit Community at Marquette University.
Kurzaj, Rev. Msgr. Franciszek '76 (SAT) San Antonio, TX St. Paul; College of Consultors; Archdiocesan Presbyteral Council.
Kurzak, John F. '75 (SC) On Duty Outside the Diocese.
Kurzawa, Ronald '64 (DET) Retired.
Kurzawinski, Zygmunt '03 (WDC) Waldorf, MD St. Peter.
Kurzyna, Andrew E. '74 (NY) Buchanan, NY St. Christopher; Verplanck, NY St. Patrick.
Kurzynski, James '03 (LC) Fall Creek, WI St. Raymond of Penafort.
Kus, Robert J. '98 (R) Wilmington, NC St. Mary; Holy Childhood Pontifical Association; Pontifical Mission Societies in the United States.
Kus, Sebastian *o.f.m.* '57 (GB)[J] Pulaski, WI Friary.
Kusa, Daniel K. '03 (CHI) Chicago, IL St. Priscilla.
Kuse, Rev. Msgr. Michael '67 (SFD) Quincy Deanery; Commission for the Care of Infirm and Retired Priests; Quincy, IL Blessed Sacrament; Presbyteral Council.
Kusek, Wojciech *c.ss.r.* '04 (MET) Manville, NJ Sacred Heart of Jesus.
Kushnir, Volodymyr '09 (STN) Chicago, IL St. Joseph.
Kusi, Gordon P. '95 (BRK) Jamaica, NY St. Bonaventure–St. Benedict the Moor RC Church; Presbyteral Council.
Kusibab, Justin *o.f.m.conv.* '87 (DET)[K] Dearborn Heights, MI All Saints Friary.

Kusibab, Miroslaw *c.s.m.a.* '91 (NEW) Cliffside Park, NJ Epiphany.
Kusmirek, Mark '77 (TYL) Rusk, TX Hodge Unit and Skyview Unit, Texas Department of Criminal Justice; Deans; Priests' Personnel Board; Presbyteral Council; Jacksonville, TX Our Lady of Sorrows.
Kuss, Allen R. '84 (BIS) On Duty Outside the Diocese.
Kuss, Allen '84 (STP)[A] Saint Paul, MN The Saint Paul Seminary.
Kusugh, Richard '04 (TUC) Yuma, AZ Immaculate Conception Roman Catholic Parish & Guadalupe Mission – Yuma.
Kusy, Jerzy '86 (CLV) Perry, OH St. Cyprian.
Kutch, Joseph P. '88 (SCR) Unassigned or Leave of Absence.
Kutch, Peter *o.f.m.cap.* '66 (CHI)[N] Chicago, IL St. Clare Friary.
Kutiuk, Casimir '57 (GB) Retired.
Kutlesa, Zvonimir *o.f.m.* '66 (CHI)[N] Chicago, IL St. Anthony's Friary.
Kutner, Rev. Msgr. Raymond W. '64 (BRK) Retired.
Kutsch, Eugene C. '51 (DUB) Retired.
Kuttiyanickal, Thomas *s.a.c.* '77 (MIL)[P] Milwaukee, WI Pallotti House.
Kuttiyanickal, Thomas *s.a.c.* '77 (CHI)[J] Evanston, IL Saint Francis Hospital; Evanston, IL Divine Liturgy–Ascension Church.
Kuttner, David '09 (SPK) Oroville, WA Immaculate Conception; Oroville, WA Holy Rosary.
Kutubebi, Frederick K.A. '97 (SR) American Canyon, CA Holy Family; [F] Napa, CA Queen of the Valley Medical Center.
Kutubebi, Frederick '96 (RVC) Glen Cove, NY North Shore University Hospital at Glen Cove.
Kutys, Rev. Msgr. Daniel J. '80 (PH) West Chester, PA SS. Peter and Paul; Deans; College of Consultors; Pastors Review Board; Diocesan Priests' Compensation and Benefits Committee; Deans.
Kutz, Lawrence A. (POD) Reston.
Kutzner, Roger '90 (JOL) Joliet, IL St. Joseph.
Kuupuo, Severo '91 (LA) Walnut, CA St. Lorenzo Ruiz.
Kuykendall, Andrew '78 (WCH) Wichita, KS St. Peter the Apostle.
Kuykendall, Henry '86 (EVN) Evansville, IN Nativity; Deaf Ministry.
Kuykendall, Thomas S. '94 (YAK) Wenatchee, WA St. Joseph's; Diocesan Commission on Public Worship; Ministry & Education Center; Presbyteral Council Executive Committee.
Kuzara, Yuri (George) J. *c.pp.s.* '78 (TOL)[H] Bellevue Mary Lay Center; [J] Bellevue, OH Sorrowful Mother Shrine.
Kuzhichalil, Joseph (NY) Pearl River, NY St. Margaret of Antioch.
Kuzhikottayil, John *s.d.b.* '82 (HRT) Branford, CT St. Mary.
Kuzhippallil, George (PAT) Retired.
Kuzhupil, Joseph *m.s.f.s.* '85 (KNX) Signal Mountain, TN St. Augustine.
Kuzhupil, Joseph *m.s.f.s.* '85 (TYL)[C] Whitehouse, TX The Missionaries of St. Francis de Sales.
Kuzia, Anthony F. *c.m.* '76 (MAN) Pelham, NH St. Patrick.
Kuzinskas, Rev. Msgr. John A. '52 (CHI) Vicars for Senior Priests Retired.
Kuzinskas, Rev. Msgr. John A. '52 (CHI) Chicago, IL Nativity of the Blessed Virgin Mary Retired.
Kuzma, Rev. Archpriest Mykhailo '81 (STN) Palatine, IL Immaculate Conception; Diocesan Consultors; Personnel Board; Chicago; Presbyteral Council.
Kuzma, Mykhailo '81 (CHI)[J] Hoffman Estates, IL St. Alexius Medical Center.
Kuzmeski, Charles H. '75 (SPR) Granby, MA Immaculate Heart of Mary.
Kuzmich, Rev. Msgr. John M. '65 (FTW) Fort Wayne, IN St. Vincent de Paul; Presbyteral Council; Clergy Retirement Board; Retired Clergy Committee.
Kuzniewski, Anthony J. *s.j.* '79 (WOR)[N] Worcester, MA Jesuits of the Holy Cross, Inc.
Kuznik, Robert '98 (RVC) Riverhead, NY St. Isidore's; Presbyteral Council.
Kvedas, Leonard J. '61 (HRT) Beacon Falls, CT St. Michael; Waterbury Vicariate.
Kwak, Peter Hoin '81 (ARL) Fairfax, VA St. Paul Chung.
Kwang–Sung, An '89 (ANC) Korean Ministry; Anchorage, AK Corp. of St. Andrew Kim Parish of the Korean Community.
Kwatera, Michael *o.s.b.* '77 (SCL)[I] Collegeville, MN St. John's Abbey, of the Order of St. Benedict.
Kwebuza, Silverino *a.j.* '99 (ALX) Hessmer, LA St. Martin of Tours; Marksville, LA Our Lady of Lourdes.
Kwiatek, Piotr *o.f.m.cap* '00 (PH) Philadelphia, PA St. John the Evangelist.
Kwiatkowski, Dawid '11 (SAV) Macon, GA St. Joseph.
Kwiatkowski, Joseph '06 (NEW) Glen Rock, NJ St. Catharine.
Kwiatkowski, Mike '78 (SPK) Otis Orchards, WA St. Joseph.
Kwiatkowski, Paul M. '64 (TOL)[B] Toledo, OH Central Catholic High School Retired.
Kwiatkowski, Richard P. '72 (NEW) Leonia, NJ St. John the Evangelist's.
Kwiatkowski, Robert M. '83 (HRT) Woodbury, CT St. Teresa.
Kwiatkowski, Sylvester '89 (SAC) Downieville, CA Immaculate Conception; Grass Valley, CA St. Patrick; Priests' Personnel Board, Diocesan; Nevada City, CA St. Canice.
Kwiecien, John S. '76 (BUF) Collins Correctional Facility; Angola, NY Most Precious Blood.
Kwiecien, Mark *o.carm.* '80 (CHI)[D] Chicago, IL.
Kwiecien, Michael E. *o.carm.* '80 (SFR) Kaiser Hospital San Francisco; San Francisco, CA St. Teresa.
Kwiecien, Michael *o.carm.* '80 (CHI)[N] Chicago Carmelite Priory of St. Cyril.
Kwiecien, Wojciech '79 (CHI) Argo, IL St. Blasé.
Kwofie, Emmanuel '97 (BWN) Weslaco, TX Knapp Medical Center; Edinburg, TX Doctor's Hospital at Renaissance; Elsa, TX Sacred Heart.
Kwoka, Edward '78 (TR) Trenton, NJ Divine Mercy Parish.
Ky, Joseph T. *s.s.* '59 (BAL)[Q] Baltimore Society of St. Sulpice, Province of the United States Retired.
Ky, Joseph T. *s.s.* '59 (HON) Retired.
Kyabuta, Jean Baptiste '88 (NSH) Decherd, TN Good Shepherd; Univ. of South–Sewanee.
Kyara, Bernard '96 (CHR) Columbia, SC St. Peter.
Kyaw, Firmin '83 (DOD) Kiowa, KS St. John the Apostle Catholic Church of Kiowa, Kansas; Medicine Lodge, KS Holy Rosary Catholic Church of Medicine Lodge, Kansas; Sharon, KS St. Boniface Catholic Church of Sharon, Kansas.
Kyazze, Richard *c.s.c.* '03 (FTW)[H] Notre Dame Congregation of Holy Cross, United States Province of Priests & Brothers.
Kyeah, Barnabas (LC) Marathon, WI Sacred Heart; Mosinee, WI St. Patrick.
Kyebasuuta, John '98 (LA) Panorama City, CA St. Genevieve.
Kyere, John '01 (HRT) East Hartford, CT St. Mary; East Hartford, CT St. Isaac Jogues; East Hartford, CT St. Rose.
Kyeremeh, George (NY) Highland, NY St. Augustine.
Kyfes, Robert J. '77 (CHI) Chicago, IL St. John Fisher.
Kyle, Eric F. *o.f.m.* '52 (PAT)[N] Ringwood, NJ Holy Name Friary, Inc.
Kynam, Victor '07 (GR) Lake Odessa, MI St. Edward's; Saranac, MI St. Anthony.
Kyrpczak, James A. '96 (MET) Phillipsburg, NJ St. Philip & St. James.
Kysely, Andrew T. '07 (GB) Combined Locks, WI St. Paul.
Kysiak, Marek (PAT) Totowa, NJ St. James of the Marches.
Kyte, Michael G. *o.p.* '87 (CHI)[N] Chicago, IL St. Pius V Priory; River Forest, IL St. Vincent Ferrer.
Kythe, Jay K. '02 (STP) Cannon Falls, MN St. Pius V; Miesville, MN St. Joseph.
Ky Truong, Augustine M. *c.m.c.* '11 (SPC)[F] Carthage, MO Congregation of the Mother Coredemptrix, United States Assumption Province.

L

L'Arche, Jeffrey '75 (ALB)[J] Albany, NY Teresian House; [P] Altamont, NY La Salette Shrine; Special Assignment.
L'Estrange, Peter *s.j.* '79 (WDC)[O] Washington, DC The Jesuit Community at Georgetown University.
L'Heureux, Ernest L. '62 (PRT) Retired.
L'Heureux, William D. '91 (OM) Genoa, NE St. Rose of Lima; Genoa, NE SS. Peter and Paul; Silver Creek, NE St. Lawrence.
Laba, Gerald *c.p.* '73 (PIT)[M] Pittsburgh, PA St. Paul of the Cross Monastery; [O] Pittsburgh, PA St. Paul of the Cross Retreat Center; Priest Council.
Labacevich, Ihar '06 (PRM) Minneapolis, MN St. John the Baptist.
LaBaff, Arthur J. '66 (OG) Clayton, NY St. Mary's of Clayton; Clayton, NY St. John the Evangelist; Deans; Diocesan Consultors; Committee on Assignments.
Labaire, Steven M. '87 (WOR) Deans; Presbyteral Council; Uxbridge, MA St. Mary's.
Labak, Joseph L. '77 (CLV) Wadsworth, OH Sacred Heart of Jesus.
Labaka, Francisco *o.f.m.* (SJN) Carolina, PR Santa Clara de Asis.
Labaky, Mansour (OLL)[F] Saint Louis, MO Our Lady of Smiles Orphanage.
Labarda, Nathaniel C. '93 (HRT) Milford, CT St. Mary.
LaBarge, Christopher W. '85 (WIL) Salisbury, MD St. Francis De Sales.
Labarre, Renald D. '60 (PRT) Retired.
Labat, Dennis C. '74 (NU) Springfield, MN St. Raphael; On Special or Other Diocesan Assignment; Riverbend TEC (Together Encounter Christ); Priest Personnel Board; Pastoral Administrators.
LaBat, Sean J. '99 (SJP) Raleigh, NC St. Basil The Great Mission; Presbyters.
Labat, Sean (NTN) South Bend, IN St. John of Damascus.
LaBauve, J. Joel '70 (BR) Napoleonville, LA St. Anne; Napoleonville, LA Assumption of the Blessed Virgin Mary.
Labbe, Clifton *s.v.d.* '69 (BEA) Diocesan College of Consultors; Livingston, TX St. Martin de Porres Mission; Livingston, TX St. Joseph.
Labbe, Donavan J. '97 (LAF) Patterson, LA St. Joseph.
Labbe, Jason M. '01 (BR) Leave.
Labbe, Wilfred P. '99 (PRT)[M] Orono, ME University of Maine; Newman Apostolate; Old Town, ME Parish of the Resurrection of the Lord; Campus Ministry.
Labella, Robert '54 (CLV) Retired.
LaBelle, Jeffrey T. *s.j.* '88 (MIL)[P] Milwaukee, WI Jesuit Community at Marquette University.
LaBelle, Joseph *o.m.i.* '92 (SAT)[C] Oblate School of Theology; [L] San Antonio, TX De Mazenod House.
LaBelle, Patrick L. *o.p.* '65 (SFR) San Francisco, CA St. Dominic.
LaBelle, Patrick *o.p.* '65 (OAK)[L] Oakland, CA Order of Preachers (Province of the Most Holy Name of Jesus – Western Dominican Province).
LaBelle, Patrick *o.p.* '65 (SFR)[N] San Francisco, CA St. Dominic Priory.
Labinski, Jacek W. '83 (TR) Trenton, NJ St. Hedwig; College of Consultors.
Labinsky, Paul '81 (PHU) Retired.
Labita, Francis J. '49 (BRK)[R] Douglaston, NY Bishop Mugavero Residence Retired.
Labo, Timothy P. '86 (ORL) Kissimmee, FL Holy Redeemer.
Laboe, Timothy A. '99 (DET) Graduate Studies.
Labonte, Richard H. '70 (WOR) Retired.
LaBonte, Roger A. *m.afr.* '62 (FgM) Washington, DC MISSIONARIES OF AFRICA.
Labonte, Youville *m.afr.* '52 (SP)[N] St. Petersburg, FL Missionaries of Africa; Washington, DC; Washington, DC MISSIONARIES OF AFRICA Retired.
Laboon, Joseph D. '57 (PIT) Retired.
Labor, Jesus G. '83 (SFR) Pacifica, CA Good Shepherd.
Laborde, Lucas '05 (P) Portland, OR St. Patrick; [P] Portland, OR Portland State University Newman Center.
Labosky, James M. '79 (R) Chapel Hill, NC St. Thomas More.
LaBove, M. Keith '81 (LAF) Lafayette, LA St. Patrick; Hospitals.
Labrador, Rene '91 (DOD) Garden City, KS St. Dominic Catholic Church of Garden City, Kansas; Ingalls, KS St. Stanislaus Catholic Church of Ingalls, Kansas; Presbyteral Council.
LaBranch, Derek R. P. '07 (SAC) Weaverville, CA St. Patrick; Air Force Reserve Chaplains.
LaBrecque, Frederick '67 (CHR) Retired.
LaBree, Paul '03 (PRT) Special or Other Diocesan Assignment.
Labrie, Jean–Paul '82 (PRT) Personnel Board; Caribou, ME Parish of the Precious Blood; Vicars Forane.
LaBrie, Joseph *s.j.* '97 (LA)[C] Los Angeles, CA Loyola Marymount University; [C] Los Angeles, CA Jesuit Community.
Labrie, Ray J. '03 (MAN) Litchfield, NH St. Francis of Assisi; Manchester, NH St. Catherine of Siena.
Labrie, Robert G. '64 (BO) Pastoral Care; Salem, MA St. James.
LaBuda, David E. *m.m.* '71 (NY)[DD] Maryknoll Maryknoll Fathers and Brothers.
LaBurt, Brian R. '86 (SAV) Columbus, GA Our Lady of Lourdes; [G] Columbus, GA Our Lady of Lourdes; Finance Council.
Labus, Gregory T. '06 (BWN) Mercedes, TX Our Lady of Mercy; Weslaco Deanery.
LaCanne, Stephen J. '76 (STP) Minneapolis, MN St. Leonard of Port Maurice; St. Joseph's Hospital; [G] St. Paul, MN HealthEast St. Joseph's Hospital; HealthEast, Inc. & HealthEast Hospice; Deanery 17.
La Casa, Vicente Paz en '66 (PBL) Westcliffe, CO Our Lady of the Assumption.
LaCasse, Andre–Joseph *o.p.* '92 (CIN) Cincinnati, OH St. Gertrude; [N] Cincinnati, OH St. Gertrude Priory.
Lacasse, Eugene *o.c.s.o.* '54 (WOR)[N] Spencer, MA St. Joseph's Abbey.
LaCasse, James *s.j.* '74 (FRS)[A] Bakersfield, CA Garces Memorial High School.
Lacasse, Roland *s.m.* '60 (BO)[U] Boston, MA Marist Fathers Lourdes Residence; [Z] Boston, MA Marist Fathers Residence.
LaCaze, Rev. Msgr. J. Carson '57 (SHP) Ecumenism and Interreligious Affairs; Shreveport, LA St. John Berchmans Cathedral.
Lacerna, Rodolfo '68 (ELP) Van Horn, TX Our Lady of Fatima.
Lacey, Joseph P. *s.j.* '71 (BAL) Woodstock, MD St. Alphonsus Rodriguez.
Lacey, Michael '78 (OAK) San Lorenzo, CA St. John the Baptist.
Lacey, Robert Edward '05 (SFS) Dakota Dunes, SD Blessed Teresa of Calcutta Catholic Church.
Lacfenmier, James *c.s.c.* (FTW)[H] Notre Dame, IN Congregation of Holy Cross, United States Province

of Priests & Brothers.
LaChance, Matthew G. '03 (TLS) Cushing, OK SS. Peter and Paul; Cushing, OK St. John.
LaChance, Roger '67 (B) Coeur d'Alene, ID St. Pius X; [F] Coeur d'Alene, ID North Idaho College; Catholic Scouts.
LaChapelle, Hector *m.s.* '68 (R) Shallotte, NC St. Brendan the Navigator.
Lache Avila, Jose Rodolfo '81 (CHR) Columbia, SC Our Lady of the Hills.
Lachendro, Vincent *o.f.m.conv.* '63 (FgM)[Q] Ellicott City Order of Friars Minor Conventual; Ellicott City, MD Province of Saint Anthony of Padua.
Lachica, Jose P. '02 (MO) Army Chaplains.
Lachner, Anton '68 (STP) Retired.
Lachowicz, Francis B. '60 (PIT) Retired.
Lachowitzer, Charles V. '90 (STP) Eagan, MN St. John Neumann.
Lachowitzer, Charles (STP) Appointees; Regional Vicars.
Lack, Chris '90 (CIN) Cincinnati, OH St. Dominic.
Lackenmier, James R. *c.s.c.* '64 (FR)[K] North Easton, MA Wheaton College Newman Center; Wheaton College; Provincial Councilors:; [A] North Easton, MA Holy Cross Fathers Religious.
Lackenmier, James *c.s.c.* '64 (FTW)[H] Notre Dame Congregation of Holy Cross, United States Province of Priests & Brothers.
Lacki, Marek *o.s.p.p.e.* '06 (PH)[Y].
Lackie, Dan *o.f.m.* '96 (ORG)[I] Huntington Beach, CA Franciscan Friars.
Lackie, Daniel *o.f.m.* '96 (OAK)[L] Oakland, CA Franciscan Friars of California (Province of St. Barbara).
Lackland, Anthony F. '06 (DAL) Vocations; Dallas, TX Christ the King.
Lackner, Bede *o.cist.* '52 (DAL)[J] Irving, TX Cistercian Abbey of Our Lady of Dallas.
Lackner, Joseph *s.m.* '72 (HON)[D] Honolulu, HI Center Marianist Community.
LaCombe, Terrence '87 (GB) Military Chaplains.
LaCorte, Richard '87 (FAR) Grand Forks, ND Holy Family Church of Grand Forks.
Lacovic, Lawrence L. '69 (ALT) Northern Cambria, PA Prince of Peace.
Lacre, Cormac '03 (SAC) Corning, CA Immaculate Conception.
LaCroix, Charles '05 (FAR)[A] Fargo, ND Shanley High School and Sullivan Middle School; Special Assignment; Fargo, ND Sts. Anne & Joachim Church of Fargo.
Lacroix, Daniel W. '88 (FR) Hyannis, MA St. Francis Xavier's; Auditors.
Lacroix, Maurice R. '53 (MAN) DEPARTMENT OF VETERANS AFFAIRS HOSPITALS AND CHAPLAINS Retired.
LaCroix, Robert A. '98 (DET) Novi, MI Holy Family.
Lacroix, Stephen A. *c.s.c.* '08 (FTW)[A] Notre Dame, IN Old College; [A] Notre Dame, IN Moreau Seminary; [B] University of Notre Dame Du Lac; [H] Notre Dame, IN Holy Cross Community, Corby Hall, University of Notre Dame.
LaCroix, Wilfred L. *s.j.* '69 (STL)[O] St. Louis, MO Jesuit Community Corporation at Saint Louis University – Jesuit Hall Retired.
LaCrosse, James *s.m.* '67 (WH) Paden City, WV Mater Dolorosa.
Lacruz, Cecilio *sch.p.* '59 (PCE) Ponce, PR Our Lady of Mt. Carmel.
LaCuesta, Don A. '06 (DET) Garden City, MI St. Dunstan.
Lacy, Aidan '93 (PMB) Released from Diocesan Assignment.
Laczko, Rev. Msgr. T. Ansgar '60 (WDC) Retired.
Ladamus, Robert G. '70 (HRT) Retired.
Ladd, John O. '79 (GLD) Retired.
Ladda, Paul '93 (BUF) Buffalo, NY Holy Cross.
Ladish, Robert W. '53 (HRT) Retired.
Ladkau, William D. '84 (CHR) Columbia, SC Good Shepherd.
Ladzinski, Rev. Msgr. Casimir H. '62 (TR) Episcopal Council; Ocean County; Bay Head, NJ Sacred Heart.
Laenen, Henry A. *o.m.i.* '52 (GAL) Alvin, TX St. John the Baptist.
Laenen, Joseph C. *o.praem.* '51 (PH)[Y] Paoli, PA Daylesford Abbey; [S] Darby, PA Mercy Fitzgerald Hospital.
LaFache, Anthony '68 (SY) Utica, NY St. Anthony of Padua; Utica, NY St. Elizabeth Hospital.
La Femina, Rev. Msgr. Anthony A. '61 (VEN) Retired.
Laferrera, Rev. Msgr. John J. '73 (NEW) Presbyteral Council; Holy Name Federation; Absent on Leave.
Laferrera, Robert G. '88 (NEW) Roseland, NJ Our Lady of the Blessed Sacrament.
Laferty, Charles P. *o.s.a.* '53 (PH)[C] Villanova University; [Y] Villanova, PA St. Thomas Monastery.
Lafey, Kevin *o.carm* '72 (JOL) Glendale Heights, IL St. Matthew.
Lafferty, Owen J. '66 (NY) New York, NY Holy Innocents.
Laffey, Matthew T. *o.s.b.* '00 (ALT)[I] University Park, PA Penn State University, University Park; [J] University Park, PA Penn State Catholic Community.
Laffey, Matthew T. *o.s.b.* '00 (GBG)[H] Latrobe, PA Saint Vincent Archabbey.
LaFlamme, Julien J. '58 (BUR) Retired.
Laflamme, Steven '09 (DUL) Brainerd, MN St. Andrew; Brainerd, MN St. Francis; Brainerd, MN St. Mathias.
LaFleur, Paul J. '85 (LAF) Breaux Bridge, LA St. Bernard.
Lafond, Donald E. '62 (MAN) Catholic Medical Center Retired.
Lafontaine, James F. *s.j.* '87 (PRT)[I] Portland, ME St. Ignatius Residence (The Jesuits of Maine); [M] Portland, ME; Members; Portland, ME Our Lady of Hope Parish.
LaFontaine, Paul A. '72 (STP) St. Anthony, MN St. Charles Borromeo.
Laforet, Albert '02 (AUS) Austin, TX St. Mary Cathedral; Presbyteral Council.
LaForge, Paul *s.v.d.* '58 (DUB)[B] Epworth, IA Divine Word College.
Laframboise, Ross '03 (FAR) Napoleon, ND St. Philip's Church of Napoleon; Diocesan College of Consultors; Deanery 8.
La Fratta, William '63 (RIC) Retired.
LaFreniere, Thomas '09 (PMB) Palm Springs, FL St. Luke; Vocations; Vocations; Seminarians.
Lafrenz, James '54 (ELP) Retired.
Lagace, Raymond R. *o.f.m.* '59 (PRT) Togus, ME Togus VA Medical Center.
Lagace, Raymond R. *o.f.m.* '59 (MO) DEPARTMENT OF VETERANS AFFAIRS HOSPITALS AND CHAPLAINS.
Lagan, Hugh *s.m.a.* '90 (BO)[U] Dedham, MA African Mission House.
Lager, John *o.f.m.cap.* '79 (DEN)[N] Denver, CO St. Francis of Assisi Friary; Denver, CO; [N] Denver, CO Capuchin Province of Mid–America, Inc.
Lagges, Rev. Msgr. Patrick R. '77 (CHI)[U] Chicago, IL University of Chicago Calvert House; Judges; [B] Chicago, IL Catholic Theological Union.
Lagges, Patrick R. '77 (TUC) Promoter of Justice – Penal Cases.
Laghezza, Pasquale V. *ss.cc.* '60 (NY) New York, NY New York City Veterans Administration Hospital.
Laghezza, Pasquale V. *ss.cc.* '60 (LA)[P] La Verne, CA Congregation of the Sacred Hearts of Jesus and Mary.
Lagiovane, John M. '92 (NY)[E] Poughkeepsie, NY Our Lady of Lourdes High School; [E] Poughkeepsie, NY Our Lady of Lourdes High School; Archdiocesan Consultors; Hyde Park, NY Regina Coeli.
Lago, Danilo *s.x.* '77 (PAT)[N] Wayne Xaverian Missionary Fathers; Wayne, NJ XAVERIAN MISSIONARY FATHERS.
Lago, William J. (TR)[T] Trenton, NJ Bede House, College of New Jersey; Campus Ministries.
Lagoa, Raul M. '79 (FR) Somerset, MA St. John of God.
Lagodinski, Dale '72 (FAR) Wahpeton, ND St. John's Church of Wahpeton; [H] Wahpeton, ND State College of Science Newman Student Parish; Deanery 1.
La Goe, John P. '61 (GR) Retired.
Lagomarsino, John *s.s.c.* '70 (OM)[J] St. Columbans Missionary Society of St. Columban.
La Grutta, George '10 (NY) Port Jervis, NY Immaculate Conception.
Laguerre, Jean G. '95 (BRK) The Mount Sinai Hospital of Queens.
Laguna–Vargas, Enrique *o.carm.* '90 (JOL)[L] Darien Carmelite Provincial Office.
Lagunas, Ascencion Rea *o.r.c.* '08 (STO) Ceres, CA St. Jude Church (Pastor of).
Lagunilla, Ariel R. '06 (SAN) Rowena, TX St. Boniface; Rowena, TX St. Joseph's; Miles, TX St. Thomas.
Laguros, Mario '96 (SR) Clearlake, CA Our Lady, Queen of Peace.
Lagututta, Nunzio J. '78 (SJ) On Leave of Absence.
Lah, Peter *s.j.* '95 (STL)[O] St. Louis, MO Leo Brown Jesuit Community.
Lahart, Daniel K. *s.j.* '94 (GAL)[E] Houston, TX Strake Jesuit College Preparatory Inc.; Elected Members; [S] Houston, TX Strake Jesuit Retreat and Leadership Center, Inc.
Lahens, Albert '95 (MIA) Pembroke Pines, FL St. Edward.
Lahey, Piers M. '82 (SFR) San Carlos, CA St. Charles.
LaHood, Thomas G. '00 (WDC) Leonardtown, MD Our Lady's; Gaithersburg, MD St. John Neumann.
Lahoud, Rev. Msgr. Joseph F. '59 (SAM) Retired.
Lahrs, Carey T. *s.d.s.* '72 (MIL)[P] Milwaukee Salvatorian Provincial Offices.
Lai, Doan Van '73 (SD) San Diego, CA Holy Spirit Catholic Parish.
Laible, Jeffrey G. '88 (PEO) Lincoln, IL Holy Family; Lincoln, IL Logan Correctional Center; Lincoln, IL St. Patrick; Air National Guard Chaplains.
Laicha, Michael '89 (HBG)[F] Danville, PA Holy Family Convent and Infirmary.
Laing, Vincent Thu '87 (SAL) New Almelo, KS St. Joseph Parish; Norton, KS St. Francis of Assisi Parish.
Laird, Kenneth W. '75 (BR) Retired.
Laird, Martin L. '08 (ALX) Mansura, LA St. Paul the Apostle; Hispanic Ministry.
Laird, Martin S. *o.s.a.* '90 (PH)[Y] Rosemont, PA Saxony Hall.
Laird, Martin *o.s.a.* '90 (PH)[C] Villanova University; [Y] Villanova, PA St. Thomas Monastery.
Laird, Peter A. '97 (STP)[S] West St. Paul, MN Saint Paul's Outreach, Inc.; Office of Vicar General and Moderator of the Curia; Ex Officio; Archbishop's Commission on Bio–Medical Ethics; Archdiocesan Finance Council (AFC); College of Consultors; Members of the Corporation; Board of Directors.
Laird, William F. '75 (ROC) Censores Librorum; Palmyra, NY The Parish of St. Katharine Drexel.
Lajack, Edward F. '68 (CLV) Absent on Sick Leave.
Lajack, Jerome M. '66 (CLV) Retired.
Lajiness, Todd '95 (DET)[A] Detroit, MI Sacred Heart Major Seminary, Inc.
Lajo, Saturnino *o.m.i.* '63 (SAT)[R] San Antonio, TX Oblate Lourdes Grotto Shrine of the Southwest, Tepeyac de San Antonio; [S] San Antonio, TX Oblate Missions.
Lajoie, Roland A. *s.m.* '74 (WDC)[O] Washington, DC Marist Center.
Lakers, John J. *o.f.m.* '58 (SFD)[B] Quincy, IL Quincy University Retired.
Lakra, Albert '87 (BAK) Pendleton, OR St. Mary.
Lakra, Nonatus '91 (LAN) Owosso, MI St. Paul.
Lakra, Prabhu '02 (LAN) Howell, MI St. Joseph.
Laksana, Albertus Bagus *s.j.* '03 (LA)[C] Los Angeles, CA Jesuit Community.
Laliberte, George G. '56 (HRT) Retired.
LaLiberte, Nathan '11 (STP) Anoka, MN St. Stephen.
Laliberte, Rev. Msgr. Robert '73 (FAR) Censor Librorum Retired.
Lalli, Tony B. *s.x.* '66 (BO)[U] Holliston, MA Xaverian Missionaries.
Lally, Brendan G. *s.j.* '77 (PH)[C] Jesuit Fathers; [Y] Loyola Center and Manresa Hall.
Lally, Rev. Msgr. Dennis M. '65 (GB) New London, WI St. Patrick; Priests' Personnel Board.
Lally, Joachim *c.s.p.* '65 (BRK)[R] Retired Retired.
Lally, Martin '78 (DEN) Aurora, CO Queen of Peace.
Lally, Owen *c.p.* '59 (BRK)[R] Jamaica, NY Immaculate Conception Monastery.
Lally, Owen *c.p.* '59 (NY)[HH] Jamaica, NY The Fellowship of the Beloved Disciple.
Lalonde, Venant *o.f.m.* '54 (SP)[N] St. Petersburg, FL St. Anthony Friary Retired.
Lalor, Thomas '66 (JKS) Priests' Council; Tupelo, MS St. James; Diocesan Consultors.
Lam, Hoang Chi '06 (DET) St. Clair Shores, MI St. Joan of Arc.
Lam, John *s.d.b.* '71 (LA) Los Angeles, CA St. Bridget's Chinese Catholic Church; [P] Los Angeles, CA Dominic Savio Salesian Residence.
Lam, Peter Vu '04 (SD) Oceanside, CA Tri City Hospital; Vista, CA Saint Francis of Assisi Catholic Parish.
Lam, Thao '08 (GAL) Houston, TX St. Cecilia.
Lama, Michael '84 (SB) On Leave of Absence.
Lamanna, Alfred '49 (ALB) Retired.
Lamanna, Thomas J. *s.j.* '97 (P)[A] Portland, OR Jesuit Novitiate of Sheridan Orgeon.
LaMar, Joseph P. *m.m.* '83 (NY)[DD] Maryknoll Maryknoll Fathers and Brothers Retired.
LaMartina, Liborio J. *s.j.* '67 (BAL)[Q] Towson, MD Maryland Province of the Society of Jesus; Towson, MD; [Q] Baltimore, MD Colombiere Jesuit Community.
Lamas, Rodolfo '80 (SJN) Caguas, PR Divino Nino Jesus; Subcommission for Sacred Art.
LaMazza, Carmen G. *m.m.* '55 (SJ)[M] Los Altos, CA Maryknoll.
Lamb, Bruce *o.f.m.conv.* (OAK)[L] Castro Valley, CA Conventual Franciscans (Province of St. Joseph of Cupertino).
Lamb, Gary E. '83 (MEM) Lexington, TN St. Andrew the Apostle.
Lamb, Louis J. '61 (OKL) Retired.
Lamb, Matthew L. '62 (MIL) On Duty Outside the Archdiocese.
Lamb, Patrick H. '83 (ALN) Bethlehem, PA Notre Dame of Bethlehem.
Lamb, Paul T. '96 (FR) Retired.
Lamb, Thomas J. '71 (BO)[T] Cambridge, MA Opus Dei, Prelature of the Holy Cross and Opus Dei; [T] Newton, MA Prelature of the Holy Cross and Opus Dei.
Lamb, Thomas '71 (POD) New Rochelle.
Lamb, Wes '81 (SAV) Springfield, GA St. Boniface Church.
Lambelho, Jose Fernando '84 (LA) Cursillo Movement.
Lamberson, Bryan '00 (L) Jewish Hospital; Louisville, KY St. Peter the Apostle Parish.
Lambert, Cornelius F. '83 (CAM) Avalon, NJ St. Brendan the Navigator Parish, Avalon, N.J. Retired.
Lambert, Curtis '74 (CHI) Prospect Heights, IL St.

Alphonsus Liguori.
Lambert, James J. '80 (PT) Retired.
Lambert, James L. *s.j.* '66 (LAF) Grand Coteau, LA St. Charles Borromeo.
Lambert, John C. '84 (SCR) Regional Episcopal Vicars; Conyngham, PA St. John Bosco; Ex Officio; Schools.
Lambert, Louis *s.j.* '66 (ELP) El Paso, TX Sacred Heart.
Lambert, Paul Francis '09 (PT) Gulf Breeze, FL St. Ann.
Lambert, Peter S. '79 (DUL) Floodwood, MN Immaculate Conception; Floodwood, MN St. Louis; Floodwood, MN St. Mary.
Lambert, Peter '72 (MIA) Miami Lakes, FL Our Lady of the Lakes.
Lambert, Richard D. '80 (CR) Commission on Building and Planning; Thief River Falls, MN St. Bernards; Priests' Council.
Lambert, Richard I. '75 (PBR) Youngstown, OH Assumption of the Blessed Virgin; Consultors; Protopresbyters.
Lambert, Timothy J. '92 (MET) On Duty Outside the Diocese.
Lambeth, K. Michael '94 (TR) Little Egg Harbor Twp, NJ St. Theresa.
Lambour, Stephen *c.s.c.* '55 (ORL) Retired.
Lambro, Edward (PAT) Secretariat for Catholic Charities; Special Assignment.
Lamela, Juan *c.m.* '62 (PCE) Ponce, PR La Milagrosa.
Lamendola, Salvatore R. '90 (GBG) Avonmore, PA St. Matthew; Slickville, PA St. Sylvester; Avonmore, PA St. Ambrose.
LaMere, Cletus *s.d.s.* '48 (MIL)[P] Milwaukee, WI Salvatorians – Jordan Hall Retired.
Lamica, Alan J. '78 (OG) Malone, NY Barehill Correctional Facility; [G] Our Lady of the Adirondacks Community; Advocates; Malone, NY Franklin Correctional Facility; Malone, NY Upstate Correctional Facility.
Lamirez, Robert '95 (NEW) Rahway, NJ Divine Mercy Parish.
Lamitie, Robert O. '57 (OG) Retired.
Lamm, Timothy J. *o.s.b.* '54 (SEA)[M] Lacey, WA St. Martin's Abbey.
Lamm, William *s.j.* '44 (SCR)[B] Scranton, PA The University of Scranton.
Lammeier, Francis G. '55 (CIN) Retired.
Lammers, Rev. Msgr. Donald W. '66 (JC) Eldon, MO Sacred Heart; Personnel Board.
Lammers, Ralph A. '63 (OM) Retired.
Lammert, Edward *o.f.m.* '58 (CIN)[N] Cincinnati, OH St. John the Baptist Friary.
LaMoine, Gary '81 (CR) Barnesville, MN Assumption; Priests Retirement Board of Trustees; Finance Council; Priests' Council.
Lamonde, Rev. Msgr. Joseph R. '74 (PIT) McKees Rocks, PA Holy Trinity; Institutional Ministries; Clergy Personnel Board.
LaMontagne, Bernard L. '63 (PRO) On Duty Outside the Diocese.
Lamore, Victor E. '80 (OG) Dannemora, NY Clinton Correctional Facility; Ray Brook, NY Adirondack Correctional Facility.
LaMorte, Joseph P. '81 (MO) Garnerville, NY St. Gregory Barbarigo; Poughkeepsie, NY Holy Trinity; Air National Guard Chaplains; Priests Council of the Archdiocese of New York.
LaMorte, Richard '66 (NY)[GG] Poughkeepsie, NY Marist College.
Lamothe, C. Romeo '48 (WOR) Retired.
Lamothe, Daniel O. '62 (MAN) Cheshire County House of Corrections; Vicars Forane; Keene, NH Mary, Queen of Peace Parish; Keene, NH Parish of the Holy Spirit.
Lamothe, Donat R. *a.a.* '62 (WOR)[N] Worcester, MA Assumptionists of Assumption College.
LaMothe, Philip R. '55 (BUR) Retired.
Lamoureux, Matthew *m.i.c.* '05 (SPR)[G] Provincial Office.
Lamoureux, Matthew *m.i.c.* '05 (JOL) Provincial Councilors:, Yorkville, IL St. Patrick; Plano, IL St. Mary.
Lamoureux, Richard E. *a.a* '71 (WOR)[N] Worcester, MA Assumptionists of Assumption College.
Lamoureux, Richard *a.a.* '71 (BO)[U] Boston Assumptionist Center.
Lamoureux, Roger E. *o.m.i.* '83 (BO)[U] Lowell, MA Missionary Oblates of Mary Immaculate.
Lamoureux, Roger J. *o.m.i.* '59 (NOR) Willimantic, CT St. Mary; Defenders of the Bond.
Lamourt, Ivan (NEW)[C] Newark, NJ Saint Benedict's Preparatory School.
Lamp, Edward '82 (SP) Retired.
Lampe, Stephen J. '82 (MIL) Special Assignment.
Lampert, Robert E. '65 (STL) Retired.
Lampert, Robert E. '65 (SAT) Retired.
Lampert, Vincent '91 (IND) Board of Consultors; Greenwood, IN SS. Francis and Clare of Assisi Catholic Church, Greenwood, Inc.; Archdiocesan Judges.
Lamping, Thomas E. '84 (CHI) Summit, IL St. Joseph.
Lampitt, Robert '08 (PEO) Champaign, IL St. Matthew; [B] Champaign, IL High School of St. Thomas More.
Lamprea, Gefford C. '00 (SPC) Leave of Absence.
Lampron, Alfred J. '75 (PAT) Wharton, NJ St. Bernard's.
Lampron, Maurice W. '63 (MAN) Retired.
Lamy, Raymond J. '81 (MAN) Absent on Leave.
Lamy, Robert E. *c.m.* '51 (STL)[O] Perryville, MO Congregation of the Mission.
Lan, Augustine Pham Van '63 (CLV) Vietnamese–American Apostolate.
Lanahan, Daniel J. *o.f.m.* '62 (PAT)[N] Butler, NJ St. Anthony Friary.
Lancaster, Leo '54 (WOR) Shrewsbury, MA St. Mary's.
Lancaster, Robert '99 (SFE) Moriarty, NM Estancia Valley Catholic Parish.
Lancellotti, Vincent A. '68 (NY)[DD] Bronx, NY John Cardinal O'Connor Residence Retired.
Landa, Florencio *c.p.* '63 (SJN) Carolina, PR Nuestra Senora de la Piedad.
Landa, Sal (ORG)[G] Fullerton, CA St. Jude Medical Center.
Landa, Salvador '94 (ORG) Buena Park, CA St. Pius V.
Landauer, Joseph P. '78 (POD) Chicago.
Landauer, Joseph P. '78 (CHI) Chicago, IL St. Mary of the Angels; [V] Chicago, IL Midtown Residence.
Landenwitch, Shawn R. '09 (CIN) Cincinnati, OH St. Ann.
Lander, Mark C. '00 (SB) On Leave of Absence.
Landewe, Robert A. '59 (SPC) Springfield, MO St. Joseph's Retired.
Landeza, Jayson J. '87 (OAK) San Leandro, CA St. Felicitas.
Landgraff, Thomas A. *o.s.f.s.* '64 (TOL)[H] Toledo, OH.
Landi, Lodovico Joseph '90 (SFR) San Francisco, CA St. Cecilia.
Landicho, Rey D. '97 (WH) Morgantown, WV St. John University Parish, Newman Hall.
Landis, Christopher P. '11 (PH) Newtown Square, PA St. Anastasia.
Landis, Gabriel *o.s.b.* '04 (KCK) Atchison, KS St. Joseph; [I] Atchison, KS St. Benedict's Abbey; Atchison, KS St. Patrick.
Lando, Camillo *c.s.* '66 (PRO) Providence, RI St. Bartholomew; Providence, RI Holy Ghost.
Landolfi, Paul J. *s.m.* (BRK)[K] Rockaway Park, NY St. John's Residence & School for Boys.
Landrau–Roman, Jose A. '90 (SJN) Instructors.
Landreau, Edward Joseph '57 (LA) Azusa, CA St. Frances of Rome Retired.
Landreville, Norbert B. '58 (MAR) Retired.
Landry, Bartholomew K. *c.s.p.* '07 (SFR) San Francisco, CA Old St. Mary's Cathedral.
Landry, Charles R. '83 (BR) St. Gabriel, LA St. Gabriel the Archangel; Presbyteral Council.
Landry, Clint '11 (FBK) Fairbanks, AK Sacred Heart Cathedral Catholic Church Fairbanks; [C] Fairbanks, AK Kobuk Center.
Landry, Francis *c.p.* '76 (SCR) Scranton, PA St. Ann's Basilica Parish; [L] Scranton, PA Saint Ann's Passionist Monastery.
Landry, Gary S. *c.m.* '73 (LA)[V] Montebello, CA DePaul Evangelization Center.
Landry, Leroy *o.m.i.* (BO)[U] Lowell, MA Andre Garin Retirement Residence.
Landry, Michael Keith '08 (LAF) Abbeville, LA St. Anne.
Landry, Oneil Anthony '47 (LAF) Retired.
Landry, Philip G. '88 (NO) Deans; New Orleans, LA St. Francis of Assisi.
Landry, Ralph James '62 (LAF) Retired.
Landry, Richard B. *m.s.* '69 (PH) Newtown, PA St. Andrew.
Landry, Roger J. '99 (FR) New Bedford, MA St. Anthony of Padua's; Diocesan Newspaper.
Landry, Thomas '83 (WOR) On Medical Leave of Absence.
Landsberger, Nicholas '61 (SCL) Little Falls, MN Holy Family; Little Falls, MN St. Mary; Directors.
Landsberger, Robert '57 (SCL) Holdingford, MN St. Columbkille's Retired.
Landwerlen, Paul E. '54 (IND) Shelbyville, IN St. Vincent De Paul Catholic Church, Shelby County, Inc.; Greensburg, IN Immaculate Conception Catholic Church, Millhousen, Inc.; Greensburg, IN St. Denis Catholic Church, Jennings County, Inc.
Lane, Brian '89 (RC) Rapid City, SD Blessed Sacrament; Rapid City, SD St. Rose of Lima; Diocesan Consultors; Presbyteral Council; Diocesan Finance Council.
Lane, Edmund C. *s.s.p.* '64 (NY)[B] Staten Island, NY Society of St. Paul; Staten Island, NY.
Lane, Rev. Msgr. Frank P. '67 (COL) Diocesan Judges Retired.
Lane, Rev. Msgr. Frank '67 (CIN)[B] Cincinnati, OH Mount St. Mary's Seminary of the West; [B] Cincinnati, OH Mount St. Mary's Seminary of the West.
Lane, George A. *s.j.* '67 (CHI)[N] Chicago, IL Woodlawn Jesuit Community.
Lane, James M. '07 (HPM) San Luis Obispo, CA Saint Anne; Secretary for the Presbyteral Council & The College of Consultors.
Lane, John Thomas *s.s.s.* '92 (CLV) Highland Heights, OH St. Paschal Baylon; [N] Cleveland, OH Congregation of the Blessed Sacrament; Presbyteral Council.
Lane, Mark J. *c.o.* '83 (BRK) Brooklyn, NY St. Boniface; [R] Brooklyn, NY Oratory of Saint Philip Neri, Congregation Pontifical Rite.
Lane, Rev. Msgr. Mark Richard '74 (RIC) Vicar for Clergy; Bishop's Administrative Advisory Council; Vicar General & Moderator of the Curia.
Lane, Michael '74 (JOL) Joliet, IL St. Jude; Deans.
Lane, Robert C. '69 (STL) O'Fallon, MO St. Barnabas.
Lane, Thomas J. '90 (BAL)[A] Emmitsburg, MD Mount St. Mary's Seminary.
Lane, Thomas V. '64 (YAK) Yakima, WA Holy Family Retired.
Lane, Timothy R. *c.j.* '95 (LA)[B] Santa Maria, CA St. Joseph Seminary (Josephite Fathers' Novitiate).
Lane, William '50 (SEA) Retired.
Lanergan, James F. '61 (BO) Senior Priests. Retired.
Lanese, John '73 (ALB) Albany, NY St. Francis of Assisi Parish.
Lanese, Pasquale *o.m.i.* '53 (BWN) Brownsville, TX Immaculate Conception Cathedral Retired.
Lang, Arnold *s.v.d.* '53 (CHI)[N] Techny, IL Divine Word Residence.
Lang, Brian E. '98 (SY) Syracuse, NY St. Ann; Syracuse, NY St. Charles Borromeo.
Lang, Rev. Msgr. Charles E. '65 (DUB)[C] Dubuque, IA Loras College Retired.
Lang, Charles F. '75 (CIN) Fairborn, OH Mary Help of Christians.
Lang, Frederick *c.pp.s.* '54 (CIN)[N] Carthagena, OH St. Charles Retired.
Lang, Henry A. '46 (BRK) Bayside, NY St. Robert Bellarmine Retired.
Lang, Hugh J. '56 (PIT) Pittsburgh, PA St. Anne Retired.
Lang, James P. '75 (SY) Special Assignment; Board of Diocesan Consultors; Management Team; Presbyteral Council; Vicar for Parishes; Boy Scouts/Girl Scouts; Building Commission; Priests' Personnel Committee; Liverpool, NY Immaculate Heart of Mary.
Lang, James Paul '75 (Y) Hanoverton, OH St. Philip Neri; Lisbon, OH St. George; Hanoverton, OH St. John.
Lang, Joseph R. *m.m.* '52 (NY)[DD] Retired.
Lang, Joseph '65 (CLV) Life of Prayer and Penance.
Lang, Joseph '05 (DET) Royal Oak, MI National Shrine of the Little Flower.
Lang, Leonard P. '75 (TR) Leave of Absence.
Lang, Michael P. '92 (TR) Millstone Township, NJ St. Joseph.
Langa, Daniel J. '09 (PIT) Pittsburgh, PA St. Thomas More; Priest Council.
Langan, John P. *s.j.* '72 (WDC)[O] Washington, DC The Jesuit Community at Georgetown University.
Langan, Thomas '59 (HBG) Retired.
Langan, Vincent F. '60 (SCR) Retired.
Langan, William J.P. '77 (SCR) Honesdale, PA St. John the Evangelist; Navy Reserve Chaplains.
Langdon, Robert H. '56 (NEW)[L] Rutherford, NJ St. John Vianney Residence for Priests Retired.
Lange, Donald F. '70 (MAD) Retired.
Lange, George O. '57 (WOR) Retired.
Lange, John J. *m.m.* '58 (FgM) Maryknoll, NY MARYKNOLL.
Lange, John W. *s.j.* '61 (SCR)[B] Scranton, PA The University of Scranton.
Lange, Joshua L. '09 (COV) Cold Spring, KY St. Joseph.
Lange, Milton R. '52 (LR) Retired.
Lange, Robert A. '86 (ARL) Arlington, VA Our Lady of Lourdes Retired.
Lange, Ronald *s.v.d.* '71 (FgM) Techny, IL.
Lange, Steven J. '02 (RCK) Rochelle, IL St. Patrick.
Lange, Timothy J. '61 (OM) Retired.
Lange, William S. '92 (PH) Aston, PA St. Joseph.
Langelier, Rev. Msgr. Gerald J. '61 (BRK) Forest Hills, NY Our Lady of Mercy Retired.
Langenbrunner, Norman W. '77 (CIN) Judges.
Langenbrunner, Norman '70 (CIN) Retired.
Langenderfer, Carl J. *o.f.m.* '71 (CIN) Presbyteral Council; [C] Cincinnati, OH St. Anthony Shrine, Franciscan Postulancy.
Langenderfer, Max *o.f.m.* '73 (CIN)[N] Cincinnati St. Francis Seraph Friary.
Langenfeld, Thomas G. *c.s.v.* '60 (CHI)[N] Arlington Heights Viatorian Province Center–Clerics of St. Viator.
Langenkamp, August *s.v.d.* '57 (CHI)[N] Techny, IL Divine Word Residence.
Langford, Terry L. '96 (L) Louisville, KY St. Lawrence.
Langford, Terry L. (CHI) Hines V.A. Hospital.
Langhans, Victor E. '84 (HEL) Retired.
Langhans, Victor '84 (MI) Blessed Sacrament.
Langhorst, Randall L. '92 (LIN) Seward, NE St. Vincent de Paul.
Langille, Justin '80 (SD) San Diego, CA Immaculate Conception Catholic Parish.
Langley, Barry J. *o.f.m.* '94 (BO)[Z] Boston, MA St.

Anthony Shrine.
Langley, Terence *s.c.j.* '79 (JKS) Olive Branch, MS Queen of Peace.
Langlois, Charles '96 (LAF) New Iberia, LA St. Peter.
Langlois, Frederick M. '91 (HRT) New Milford, CT Our Lady of the Lakes; [U] New Milford, CT Our Lady of the Lakes Corporation.
Langlois, John Albert *o.p.* '91 (NY)[DD] New York, NY St. Vincent Ferrer Priory; New York, NY.
Langlois, William A. '74 (GR) Grand Haven, MI St. Patrick – St. Anthony.
Langone, Robert *s.a.* '89 (NY)[DD] Brockton, MA Chapel of Our Savior.
Langone, Robert *s.a.* '89 (BO)[N] Brockton, MA Chapel of Our Savior–Catholic Pastoral and Information Center; [U] Brockton, MA Chapel of Our Savior; [Z] Brockton, MA Chapel of Our Saviour.
Langsch, Gerold M. '72 (MIL)[T] Waukesha, WI Schoenstatt Fathers.
Langsdorf, Karl *s.p.s.* '72 (CHI)[N] Chicago, IL St. Patrick's Missionary Society; Saratoga, CA.
Langsfeld, Rev. Msgr. Paul J. '77 (WDC) Washington, DC St. Stephen Martyr; Priest Council; Archdiocesan College of Consultors.
Langston, Micheas *o.s.b.* '65 (IND)[K] Saint Meinrad St. Meinrad Archabbey.
Langton, Bernard F. *o.p.* '69 (PRO)[O] Providence St. Thomas Aquinas Priory at Providence College.
Lanik, Hank (TYL)[E] Tyler, TX Catholic Campus Ministry of Tyler.
Lanik, Robert H. (Hank) (TYL) Vice Chancellor.
Lanik, Robert H. (Hank) (TYL) Gladewater, TX St. Theresa of the Infant Jesus; Pastoral Ministries; Young Adult/Campus Ministries.
Lankeit, John '06 (PHX) Phoenix, AZ SS. Simon and Jude Roman Catholic Cathedral; College of Consultors; Presbyteral Council.
Lankford, Michael G. '92 (MO) On Duty Outside the Diocese; DEPARTMENT OF VETERANS AFFAIRS HOSPITALS AND CHAPLAINS.
Lannan, James '11 (STP) West St. Paul, MN St. Joseph; [E] Maplewood, MN Hill–Murray School.
Lanning, Michael J. '78 (CLV) Fairview Park, OH St. Angela Merici.
Lannon, Paul A. *c.s.p.* '66 (BRK)[R] Paulist Priests at Paulist Foundations Outside the U.S.
Lannon, Timothy R. *s.j.* '77 (OM)[A] Omaha, NE Creighton University; [J] Omaha, NE Jesuit Community at Creighton University.
LaNoue, Bertrand *o.s.b.* '52 (KCK)[I] Atchison, KS St. Benedict's Abbey.
Lanoue, Marc L. '09 (BAL) Glyndon, MD Sacred Heart.
Lantigua, Ramon Fco. Garcia '01 (PCE)[H] Coto Laurel, PR Diocesan Fathers of Schoenstatt–Santuary of Schoenstatt.
Lantry, Jerome *o.c.d.* '46 (LA) Alhambra, CA St. Therese.
Lantry, Stephen C. *s.j.* '81 (SEA) Tacoma, WA St. Leo the Great; [C] Tacoma, WA Bellarmine Preparatory School.
Lantsberger, James *o.m.i.* '57 (SR) Imola, CA Napa State Hospital.
Lantsberger, John '76 (SFS) Watertown, SD Holy Name; Tribunal Judges; Personnel Board.
Lantz, Rev. Msgr. David S. '78 (SFD) Springfield, IL Christ The King; Office for the Diaconate; Office for Ministry Formation.
Lantz, Gary *s.c.j.* '78 (SFS) Retired.
Lanuevo, Edwin C. '94 (NY) Staten Island, NY Our Lady of Pity.
Lanuevo, Victor '75 (MO) On Duty Outside the Diocese; Army Chaplains.
Lanza, Daniel A. *m.m.* '59 (NY)[DD] Retired.
Lanza, Steven M. '81 (CHI) Tinley Park, IL Saint Julie Billiart.
Lanzaderas, Francisco (NY) Staten Island, NY Blessed Sacrament.
Lanzalaco, Joseph M. *c.s.b.* '87 (ROC)[K] Rochester, NY Basilian Residence; [N] Rochester, NY St. John Fisher College.
Lanzrath, Curt *o.f.m.* '54 (CIN)[N] Cincinnati St. Francis Seraph Friary Retired.
Lanzrath, John P. '88 (WCH) Presbyteral Council/ College of Consultors; Ongoing Formation of the Clergy Committee; Chancellor; Finance Council.
Lap, Gilbert D. '03 (RVC) West Babylon, NY Our Lady of Grace.
LaPalme, Paul M. '97 (WOR) Millbury, MA St. Brigid; Deans; Presbyteral Council.
La Pan, Kenneth *t.o.r.* '52 (ALT)[G] Hollidaysburg, PA St. Bernardine Monastery Retired.
LaPastina, Cyprian P. '97 (BGP) Stamford, CT St. Gabriel.
LaPata, Richard C. *o.p.* '59 (CHI)[D] Oak Park, IL Fenwick High School; [N] River Forest, IL St. Thomas Aquinas Priory.
La Patka, Gerald '56 (DUL) Retired.
Lapauw, Joseph A. *c.i.c.m.* '73 (R) Wendell, NC St. Eugene.
La Paz, Rev. Msgr. Gabriel '78 (NY) New York, NY Incarnation; Manhattan (North).
Lape, Lydell T. '90 (OM) Columbus, NE St. Anthony.
Lape, Steven W. '99 (ROC) Caledonia, NY St. Columba; Churchville, NY St. Vincent De Paul; Scottsville, NY St. Mary of the Assumption.
Lapensky, John G. '77 (STP) Veseli, MN Most Holy Trinity.
Lapera, John M. '84 (SCR) Clarks Green, PA St. Gregory; Diocesan Consultors; Diocesan Office for Parish Life; Office of Pastoral Planning; [F] Clarks Summit, PA St. Gregory Early Childhood Center; Ex Officio.
Laperle, Theodore R. '54 (WOR) Retired.
LaPlante, Bob J. '95 (CR) Detroit Lakes, MN St. Mary of the Lakes; Lake Park, MN St. Francis Xavier's.
La Plante, David W. '78 (MIL) Hartford, WI St. Kilian.
LaPlante, David W. '78 (OM) On Duty Outside the Archdiocese.
LaPlante, Eugene *a.a.* '58 (WOR)[N] Worcester, MA Assumptionists (Augustinians of the Assumption) Retired.
Laplante, Jean–Paul '50 (BUR) Retired.
LaPlante, Joseph A. '54 (WIN) Retired.
LaPlante, Roland M. '62 (HRT)[A] In Res. at the Archbishop Daniel A. Cronin Retirement Residence at St. Thomas Seminary Retired.
LaPlante, Roland M. '56 (HRT) Retired.
Lapointe, Donald R. '67 (SPR) Building Commission; Holy Childhood Association; Propagation of the Faith Retired.
Lapointe, Donald R. '67 (SPR) Psychological Consultants.
La Pointe, Jacques *o.f.m.* '97 (PRT) Madawaska, ME Notre Dame du Mont Carmel Parish; Van Buren, ME Saint Peter Chanel Parish.
LaPointe, John G. '72 (PRO) Johnston, RI St. Robert Bellarmine.
LaPointe, Laurence A.M. '70 (NOR) Willimantic, CT St. Joseph; [K] Willimantic, CT Campus Ministry; [K] New London, CT Connecticut College; College of Consultors; Deans; Campus Ministry; New London; Willimantic; Censor of Books; Members.
Lapomarda, Vincent A. *s.j.* '64 (WOR)[N] Worcester, MA Jesuits of the Holy Cross, Inc.
Lapommeray, Rodnev '11 (BRK) Brooklyn, NY Our Lady of Angels.
LaPone, Arthur '76 (JOL) Leave of Absence.
LaPorta, Ross Anthony '51 (BAL) Retired.
LaPorte, Gerard B. *c.ss.r.* '65 (NO) New Orleans, LA St. Alphonsus.
Laporte, Paul J. '65 (PRO) Retired.
Lappe, Derek J. '00 (SEA) Bremerton, WA Our Lady, Star of the Sea; Presbyteral Council; Deans.
Lapuebla, Enrique C. *m.s.* '80 (HON) Kekaha, HI St. Theresa.
Laquerre, Jean Gerard (BRK) Long Island City, NY Most Precious Blood.
Lara, Fernando Alvarez *s.j.* '09 (SEA)[A] Seattle, WA Seattle University; [M] Seattle, WA Arrupe Jesuit Community at Seattle University.
Lara, Rev. Msgr. James C. '57 (SP) Brandon, FL Church of the Nativity Retired.
Lara, Jose Rafael '99 (LA) Los Angeles, CA Presentation of Mary Parish.
Lara, Josue '94 (RCK) Carpentersville, IL St. Monica.
Lara, Santiago G. '72 (LA)[P] Los Angeles, CA Guadalupe Missioners Procure.
LaRaia, Joseph P. '46 (BO) Senior Priests. Retired.
Laramie, Joseph *s.j.* '11 (BO)[U] Brighton, MA Edmund Campion House.
Laranjinha, Armindo Simao *s.d.b.* (PAT)[O] Haledon, NJ Institute of the Daughters of Mary Help of Christians.
Lardner, Gerald V. *s.s.* '67 (BAL)[Q] Baltimore Society of St. Sulpice, Province of the United States Retired.
Largaespada, Luis Roger '09 (MIA) Miami, FL Our Lady of Lourdes.
Large, John J. '75 (PH) Philadelphia, PA St. Joan of Arc; Philadelphia, PA Mater Dolorosa.
Largent, Jeffery A. '84 (FTW) South Bend, IN St. Therese, Little Flower.
Largente, Laurent '59 (SJ) Retired.
Larger, Raymond E. '77 (CIN) Pastoral Council Secretariat; Cincinnati, OH St. Peter in Chains Cathedral.
Larion, Steven '06 (SD) Lemon Grove, CA Saint John of the Cross Catholic Parish; Presbyteral Council.
Lariviere, Robert D. '78 (PRT) Diocesan Priests' Benefit Plan – Trustees; Sanford, ME Saint Therese of Lisieux Parish.
Larkin, Rev. Msgr. Alexander C. '67 (SJ) Retired.
Larkin, Brian '11 (DEN) Northglenn, CO Immaculate Heart of Mary.
Larkin, Joseph M. '57 (SY) Minetto, NY Our Lady of Perpetual Help.
Larkin, Kevin John '59 (LA) Sherman Oaks, CA St. Francis de Sales Retired.
Larkin, Michael J. '59 (STA) Jacksonville, FL Prince of Peace.
Larkin, Patrick '57 (WCH) Retired.
Larkin, Rev. Msgr. Robert W. '73 (NY) Bronx, NY Visitation; Canon 1742 Panel of Pastors.
Larko, Ronald P. '82 (PBR) Uniontown, PA St. John the Baptist.
Larmore, Donald E. '63 (GI) Retired.
Larocca, Christopher *o.c.d.* (SEA) Stanwood, WA St. Cecilia.
LaRocca, Frank *s.j.* '98 (BUF)[N] Buffalo, NY Canisius Jesuit Community Inc.
LaRocca, John J. *s.j.* '75 (CIN)[N] Cincinnati, OH Jesuit Community at Xavier University.
Laroche, Christopher J. '85 (MO) Air Force Reserve Chaplains.
Laroche, Leonidas B. '61 (BUR) Fairfield, VT St. Patrick.
Laroche, Victor E. *o.p.* '02 (R)[F] Raleigh, NC Dominican Priory.
LaRoche, Victor *o.p.* '02 (SAT)[H] San Antonio, TX Christus Santa Rosa Health Care Corporation.
Larochelle, Maurice R. '87 (MAN) Manchester, NH Ste. Marie; Manchester, NH Sacred Heart of Jesus.
LaRocque, Rev. Msgr. Richard P. '63 (NOR) College of Consultors; Members; Auditor/Assessors; Stonington, CT St. Mary.
Laroga, Wilbert A. '05 (HON) Honolulu, HI Star of the Sea.
LaRosa, John J. '81 (PH) Philadelphia, PA St. Bartholomew.
LaRosa–Lopez, Manuel '96 (GAL) Richmond, TX St. John Fisher.
LaRousse, William J. *m.m.* '80 (FgM) Maryknoll, NY MARYKNOLL.
Larran, Francisco *o.s.a.* '50 (MGZ) San German, PR St. Rose of Lima.
Larrea, Hector '94 (NEW) Union City, NJ Sts. Joseph and Michael.
Larrea, Luis E. *m.f.e.* '77 (TYL) College of Consultors; Hispanic Ministry Advisory Council; Priests' Personnel Board; Presbyteral Council.
Larrea, Luis Eduardo *m.f.e.* '77 (TYL) Tyler, TX St. Peter Claver.
Larrivee, Leo J. *s.s.* '77 (BAL) Catonsville, MD Our Lady of the Angels Catholic Community; [Q] Baltimore Society of St. Sulpice, Province of the United States.
Larrivee, Leo J. *s.s.* '77 (SEA) On Duty Outside the Archdiocese.
Larroque, Rev. Msgr. H. Alexandre '55 (LAF)[I] Lafayette, LA Discalced Carmelites; Vicars General; Promoter of the Justice; Judges; Diocesan Consultors.
Larry, Anthony J. *o.s.f.s.* '67 (WIL)[J] Childs, MD Retirement and Assisted Care Facility Retired.
Larsen, Kevin J. '93 (ARL) Springfield, VA St. Bernadette.
Larsen, Matthew '09 (SPK) Spokane Valley, WA St. Mary; Members.
Larson, Jan '68 (SEA) Retired.
Larson, Lawrence A. '77 (BGP) Westport, CT Church of the Assumption.
Larson, Paul '79 (DUL) Deer River, MN St. Augustine; Deer River, MN St. Mary.
Larson, Ryan '07 (JOL) Leave of Absence.
Larussa, Raymond '74 (COL) Powell, OH St. Joan of Arc.
Las, Stefan '88 (PAT) Passaic, NJ Holy Rosary.
Las, Wlodzimierz R. *s.d.s.* '86 (BRK) Brooklyn, NY Our Lady of Consolation.
LaSalle, Donald *s.m.m.* '83 (BRK)[R] Ozone Park, NY Montfort Missionaries Provincialate (Missionaries of the Company of Mary).
Lascelle, Roger L. '77 (DEN) Minturn, CO St. Patrick.
Lascelles, William A. '73 (PBR) Ernest, PA St. Jude Thaddeus; Clymer, PA St. Anne.
Lasch, Rev. Msgr. Kenneth E. '62 (PAT) Retired.
Lasecki, Daniel J. '64 (MIL) Retired.
LaSelva, Giacomo *o.f.m.* '10 (NY)[DD] New York Franciscan Province of the Immaculate Conception.
Lasheras, Antonio *o.a.r.* '62 (ELP) El Paso, TX Saint Therese of the Little Flower Parish; Ex Officio Members; St. Paul; Priests' Personnel Advisory Committee; El Paso, TX Augustinian Recollect Fathers; El Paso, TX.
Laska, William M. '88 (E) Brookville, PA Immaculate Conception.
Laske, Kenneth S. '58 (CHI) Retired.
Laskowski, Keith R. '02 (ALN) Easton, PA St. Jane Frances de Chantal; Advocates.
Laskowski, Norbert F. '79 (NEW)[L] Caldwell, NJ The Rev. Msgr. James F. Kelley Residence for Retired Priests Retired.
Lasky, Michael *o.f.m.conv.* '00 (BGP)[V] Danbury, CT Newman Center at Western CT State University.
Lasky, Michael *o.f.m.conv.* '00 (NY)[HH] New York, NY Franciscans International, Inc.
Lasota, Stanislaw *c.r.* (CHI) Chicago, IL St. Hyacinth Basilica.
Lasrado, Francis '80 (RVC) Holbrook, NY Good Shepherd; Port Jefferson, NY Infant Jesus.
Lasrado, Max '92 (RCK) Sublette, IL Our Lady of Perpetual Help; West Brooklyn, IL St. Mary; Amboy, IL St. Patrick.
Last, Carl A. '69 (MIL) Retired.
Lastimosa, Philip Neri *o.cist.* '10 (DAL)[J] Irving, TX

Cistercian Abbey of Our Lady of Dallas.
Lastiri, Jean–Michael '85 (FRS) Oakhurst, CA Our Lady of the Sierra; Worship and Evangelization.
Lasuba, John Lugala '93 (WIN) Rochester, MN St. John the Evangelist.
Laszewski, Richard G. *m.m.* '51 (SJ)[M] Los Altos, CA Maryknoll.
Latcovich, Mark A. '81 (CLV)[A] Wickliffe, OH St. Mary Seminary and Graduate School of Theology.
Lathem, Rev. Msgr. E. Christopher '65 (CHR) Summerville, SC St. John the Beloved.
Lathrop, Robert '01 (DAV) Keokuk, IA All Saints.
Latkowski, Waldemar *c.ss.r.* '97 (MET) Perth Amboy, NJ St. Stephen; Perth Amboy, NJ Our Lady of the Rosary of Fatima; Perth Amboy, NJ St. Mary.
La Torre, Anthony '97 (SFR) San Francisco, CA St. Philip the Apostle.
Latosynski, Roger '84 (PT) Apalachicola, FL St. Patrick.
Latour, Charles L. *o.p.* '02 (NO)[D] Covington, LA Archbishop Hannan High School.
Latre, Rev. Msgr. Angel '54 (MGZ) Moca, PR Our Lady of Monserrate.
Latronico, Philip F.A. '86 (NEW)[Q] Rutherford, NJ The Community of God's Love; Archdiocesan Commission of Christian Unity; Archdiocesan Commission for Interreligious Affairs; The Community of God's Love.
Latsko, Andrew J. '92 (PH)[W] Elverson, PA St. Mary of Providence Center.
Latsko, Andrew '92 (CHL) Retired.
Lattner, Stephen E. *o.s.b.* '07 (MIL)[P] Benet Lake, WI St. Benedict's Abbey; Benet Lake, WI.
Latus, Charles J. '68 (ROC) Webster, NY St. Rita.
Latzko, Frank J. '84 (CHI) Chicago, IL St. Teresa of Avila.
Lau, Ignatius '58 (ORG) Santa Ana, CA Immaculate Heart of Mary Retired.
Lau, John *o.m.i.* '91 (FgM) Washington, DC AMERICAN OBLATE MISSIONS.
Lau, Michael '61 (P) Retired.
Laubach, Barnabas *o.s.b.* '52 (SCL)[I] Collegeville St. John's Abbey, of the Order of St. Benedict.
Laubacker, Jerome P. *o.de.m.* '74 (CLV) Cleveland, OH Our Lady of Mount Carmel; [N] Cleveland, OH Mercedarians.
Laubenthal, Allan R. '61 (CLV) Associate Judges Retired.
Lauden, Edward J. '05 (NO) Des Allemands, LA St. Gertrude; Paradis, LA St. John the Baptist.
Lauder, Robert E. '60 (BRK) Released from Diocesan Assignment.
Laudick, John R. '64 (TOL) Retired.
Lauducci, James V. '57 (SY) Retired.
Laudwein, James R. *s.j.* '62 (P)[L] Portland, OR Colombiere Community.
Lauenstein, Gary *c.ss.r.* '71 (DEN)[N] Denver The Redemptorists/Denver Province.
Lauer, Douglas J. '94 (COV) Cynthiana, KY St. Edward; Deans.
Lauer, Eugene F. '61 (PIT) Priest Council Retired.
Lauerman, James P. '70 (FAR) Grafton, ND Sacred Heart Church of Oakwood; Grafton, ND St. Thomas Church of St. Thomas.
Laughery, Kevin '83 (SFD) New Berlin, IL Visitation B.V.M.; New Berlin, IL Sacred Heart of Jesus; New Berlin, IL Sacred Heart of Mary; New Berlin, IL St. Sebastian; Office for Tribunal Services.
Laughlin, James J. '91 (BO) Wayland, MA St. Ann; Wayland, MA St. Zepherin; Canonical Affairs Committee; Wayland, MA Good Shepherd Parish.
Laughlin, Joseph R. *s.j.* '57 (BO)[U] Weston, MA Campion Health Center, Inc.
Laughlin, Rev. Msgr. Martin T. '52 (DUB) Retired.
Launderville, Dale *o.s.b.* '79 (SCL)[I] Collegeville, MN St. John's Abbey, of the Order of St. Benedict.
Laurance, John D. *s.j.* '70 (MIL)[P] Milwaukee, WI Jesuit Community at Marquette University.
Laurent, Edward *o.f.m.cap.* '64 (PIT)[M] Pittsburgh, PA St. Augustine Friary.
Laurent, Jean Sterling '02 (MIA)[G] Miami, FL Mercy Hospital.
Laurenzo, James '69 (DM) Retired.
Lauretti, George F. '56 (HRT) Retired.
Lauri, John F. '73 (NY) Mount Vernon, NY SS. Peter and Paul.
Laurick, Richard *c.s.c.* (FTW)[H] Notre Dame Congregation of Holy Cross, United States Province of Priests & Brothers.
Laurinaitis, Saulius P. '48 (COL) Hilliard, OH St. Brendan Retired.
Lauriola, Guglielmo *o.f.m.* '53 (SFR) San Francisco, CA St. Anthony of Padua.
Lause, James *o.f.m.* '98 (CHI)[N] Chicago, IL St. Joseph Interprovincial Post–Novitiate Formation House.
Lause, Richard L. *c.m.* '77 (STL)[O] St. Louis, MO Lazarist Residence.
Lautermilch, David J. '62 (TOL) Retired.
Lautz, Boniface *o.s.b.* '60 (B)[C] Jerome, ID Monastery of the Ascension.
Lauzon, Kris C. '91 (OG) Au Sable Forks, NY Catholic Community of Holy Name and St. Matthew.
Lavagetto, Xavier M. *o.p.* '96 (SFR) San Francisco, CA St. Dominic; [N] San Francisco, CA St. Dominic Priory.
Lavagetto, Xavier *o.p.* '96 (OAK)[L] Oakland, CA Order of Preachers (Province of the Most Holy Name of Jesus – Western Dominican Province).
Lavallee, Michael N. '05 (WOR) Worcester, MA St. George.
LaVallee, Pierre A. '61 (BUR) Retired.
LaValley, Rev. Msgr. Richard G. '64 (BUR) Deans; Vicar for Clergy; [G] Northfield, VT Norwich Newman Apostolate; Winooski, VT St. Francis Xavier.
LaVan, Kenneth G. '58 (STP) Retired.
Lavan, Michael G. '06 (RCK) Dundee, IL St. Catherine of Siena; Dundee, IL St. Mary's Mission of Gilberts.
Lavann, Jason '06 (MIL) Personal Leave.
Lavarone, Kenneth *o.f.m.* '79 (OAK)[L] Oakland, CA Franciscan Friars of California (Province of St. Barbara); [L] Berkeley, CA Franciscan Friars (Province of St. Barbara).
Lavaroni, Rino '67 (NEW) Retired.
Lavastida, Jose I. '87 (NO)[A] New Orleans, LA Notre Dame Seminary Graduate School of Theology.
Lavelle, Donald *c.m.f.* '46 (LA)[V] Rancho Dominguez, CA Dominguez Seminary Inc.
Lavelle, Edward R. '63 (HBG) Defenders of the Bond; Middletown, PA Seven Sorrows of the Blessed Virgin Mary.
Lavelle, John–Michael '00 (Y) Ravenna, OH Immaculate Conception; Council for Catechesis.
Lavelle, Raymond E. '57 (COL) Retired.
Lavely, Charles J. *c.s.c.* '65 (FTW)[H] Notre Dame Congregation of Holy Cross, United States Province of Priests & Brothers.
Laver, Eugene F. (PIT) Pittsburgh, PA Prince of Peace.
LaVerde, Calogero N. '68 (CAM) Turnersville, NJ The Church of Saints Peter and Paul, Washington Township, N.J.
Laverde Saldarriaga, Luis Fernando '89 (BRK) Brooklyn, NY St. Rita.
LaVerghetta, Rev. Msgr. Richard D. '86 (TR) Episcopal Council; Marlton, NJ St. Joan of Arc.
Laverone, Kenneth J. *o.f.m.* '79 (MRY) Special Assignment; Judicial Vicar; Judges.
Laverty, Seamus '68 (SEA) Tacoma, WA St. Patrick.
Laverty, Tod *o.f.m.* '72 (DET) Detroit, MI St. Patrick; Detroit, MI St. Aloysius.
Laviano, Vincent A. *o.f.m.* '74 (NY) New York, NY St. Francis of Assisi.
Lavich, David *o.c.s.o.* '73 (WOR)[N] Spencer, MA St. Joseph's Abbey.
Lavigne, Maurice D. '68 (MAN) Rye Beach, NH St. Theresa.
Lavilla, Rafael *o.s.j.* '05 (MRY) Santa Cruz, CA Shrine of St. Joseph Guardian of the Redeemer; [F] Shrine of St. Joseph.
Lavin, Bernard C. '79 (PRO) Lincoln, RI St. Jude.
Lavin, Rev. Msgr. James M. '45 (STP) Saint Paul, MN Retired.
Lavin, John J. '64 (PRO) Retired.
Lavin, Thomas *o.f.m.conv.* '87 (NOR) Stafford Springs, CT St. Edward.
Lavin, Wayne Patrick '71 (CAM) Retired.
LaVoie, Joseph '64 (SFE) Retired.
Lavoie, Merle L. '68 (SPR) Retired.
Lavoie, Michel J. *m.afr.* '70 (WDC) Washington, DC; [O] Washington, DC Missionaries of Africa; Washington, DC MISSIONARIES OF AFRICA Retired.
LaVoie, Raymond J. '00 (HBG) Appointed; Vocations, Office for; Steelton, PA Prince of Peace; Army National Guard Chaplains; [A] Harrisburg, PA Bishop McDevitt High School of Harrisburg; Consultors, College.
Lavoie, Rene G. '51 (PRT) Retired.
Lavoie, Richard *m.s.* '64 (STL)[O] LaSalette Spirituality Center.
Lavoie, Rev. Msgr. Robert G. '53 (PRT)[G] Waterville, ME Mt. St. Joseph Holistic Care Community Retired.
Lavorgna, John L. '06 (HRT) East Haven, CT Our Lady of Pompeii; Litchfield Deanery.
Lawe, Pius *s.v.d.* '05 (JKS) Greenville, MS Sacred Heart.
Lawler, Bruce A. '80 (SC) Schaller, IA St. Joseph's; Storm Lake, IA St. Mary's; [G] Storm Lake, IA St. Mary's Foundation of Storm Lake, Iowa; Priests' Personnel Board; Priests' Pension Plan – Board of Trustees; Catholic School Foundation of the Diocese of Sioux City.
Lawler, David '62 (IND) Indianapolis, IN St. Christopher Catholic Church, Indianapolis, Inc.
Lawler, Rev. Msgr. Joseph A. '61 (BEL) Retired.
Lawler, Rev. Msgr. Robert L. '56 (OG) Madrid, NY St. John the Baptist; Waddington, NY St. Mary; Diocesan Consultors; Committee on Assignments.
Lawler, Rev. Msgr. Terrance M. '74 (MET) Alpha, NJ St. Mary.
Lawler, Thomas A. *s.j.* '99 (MIL)[Y] Milwaukee, WI The Jesuit Partnership; Milwaukee, WI Society of Jesus; Milwaukee, WI; [P] Milwaukee, WI Arrupe House Jesuit Community; [P] Milwaukee, WI Jesuit Provincial Office, Wisconsin Province.
Lawler, William J. '72 (WIL) Cambridge, MD St. Mary Refuge of Sinners; Liaison for Evangelization.
Lawless, George P. *o.s.a.* '56 (FgM) Villanova, PA Province of St. Thomas of Villanova (Eastern).
Lawless, Joseph *m.s.f.* '71 (CC) Corpus Christi, TX St. Joseph.
Lawless, P. Brendan '64 (JC) Retired.
Lawless, Thomas '07 (ALB) Little Falls, NY Holy Family; Members; Herkimer, NY St. Anthony–St. Joseph.
Lawlor, Brendan '55 (SP) Retired.
Lawlor, David T. *o.praem.* '71 (PH)[Y] Paoli, PA Daylesford Abbey.
Lawlor, Edward J. *s.s.j.* '40 (BAL)[Q] Baltimore, MD St. Joseph's Manor Retired.
Lawlor, J. Michael '73 (BO) Hamilton, MA St. Paul; Presbyteral Council.
Lawlor, James F. '63 (ROC) Rochester, NY St. Anne Retired.
Lawlor, Mark S. '95 (CHL) Charlotte, NC St. Vincent de Paul; Propagation of the Faith.
Lawlor, Rev. Msgr. Timothy F. '43 (SB) Ontario, CA St. George Retired.
Lawrence, Andrew F. '00 (MO) Army Chaplains.
Lawrence, Andrew '00 (DUB) Military Chaplains.
Lawrence, David '97 (JOL) Bolingbrook, IL St. Dominic.
Lawrence, David *s.j.* '74 (OAK) Concord, CA St. Bonaventure.
Lawrence, James A. '70 (BUR) Fair Haven, VT Our Lady of Seven Dolors.
Lawrence, John M. '76 (SAC) Redding, CA St. Joseph.
Lawrence, Kenneth F. '60 (HBG) Columbia, PA Holy Trinity; Deans; Presbyteral Council; Consultors, College.
Lawrence, Rev. Msgr. Kevin C. '87 (PH) Philadelphia, PA St. Malachy.
Lawrence, Martin E. '03 (SFS) Salem, SD St. Mary.
Lawrence, Michael S. '73 (ALN) Retired.
Lawrence, Neal Henry *o.s.b.* '60 (FgM) Collegeville, MN St. John's Abbey.
Lawrence, Peter '99 (SPA) El Cajon, CA St. Michael Chaldean Catholic Church; San Diego, CA Mar Addai Mission.
Lawrence, Richard T. '68 (BAL) Baltimore, MD St. Vincent de Paul.
Lawrence, Rev. Msgr. Robert E. '66 (HBG) Bloomsburg, PA St. Columba.
Lawrence, Rev. Msgr. Robert E. '67 (SB) Defender of the Bond Retired.
Lawrence, William *f.s.s.p.* (LIN)[A] Denton, NE Our Lady of Guadalupe Seminary.
Lawrenz, Jaroslaw Robert *c.m.* '87 (BRK) Brooklyn, NY St. Stanislaus Kostka.
Lawryniuk, Lawrence *o.s.b.m.* '64 (STF) Bronx, NY St. Mary Protectress.
Lawson, Douglas J. '62 (R) Retired.
Lawson, Harold F. '59 (BO) Senior Priests. Retired.
Lawson, Meinrad J. *o.s.b.* '67 (GBG)[H] Latrobe, PA Saint Vincent Archabbey.
Lawson, Meinrad *o.s.b.* '67 (E) St. Marys, PA St. Mary; Presbyteral Council.
Lawson, Theodore L. *c.ss.r.* (STL)[O] Liguori, MO St. Clement Health Care Center.
Lawson, Walter G. '03 (BRK) Corona, NY Our Lady of Sorrows.
Lawton, Robert B. *s.j.* '81 (WDC)[O] Washington, DC The Jesuit Community at Georgetown University.
Layden, Christopher A. '01 (PEO) Peoria, IL St. Bernard's; Peoria, IL St. Peter's.
Layton, Richard *o.c.s.o.* '82 (P)[L] Lafayette, OR The Cistercian (Trappist) Abbey of Our Lady of Guadalupe.
Layton, Thomas Michael '09 (P) Waldport, OR St. Anthony.
Laz, Medard P. '69 (CHI) Other Assignments; [W] La Grange Park, IL Joyful Again.
Lazar, John E. '80 (BRK) On Leave/Unassigned.
Lazar, Maria '01 (BUR) Bellows Falls, VT St. Charles.
Lazarek, Mariusz '04 (SAT) Panna Maria, TX Immaculate Conception of the Blessed Virgin Mary.
Lazaro de La Fe, P. *o.c.d.* (MIA)[H] Miami Gardens, FL Discalced Carmelite Friars of Miami, Inc.
Lazarra, Alexis '10 (HT) Houma, LA St. Bernadette.
Lazarski, Marvin I. '62 (MIL) Special Assignment; Spiritual Director.
Lazo, Alonzo *s.m.m.* '07 (BRK)[R] Ozone Park Montfort Missionaries Provincialate (Missionaries of the Company of Mary).
Lazo, Johnny Laura '94 (WIL) Milford, DE St. John the Apostle.
Lazzarato, Mauro *c.s.* '86 (CHI)[N] Chicago, IL Scalabrini House of Theology.
Lazzeroni, Gary F. '07 (SEA) Vancouver, WA St. Joseph.
Le, Anthony Duc *s.v.d.* '06 (FgM) Techny, IL.
Le, Ben '98 (LA) Los Angeles, CA St. Martin of Tours.
Le, Duy T. '11 (ORG) Seal Beach, CA St. Anne's.
Le, Hoang V. '99 (BO) Lexington, MA St. Brigid; Vietnamese; Lexington, MA Sacred Heart.
Le, Hoang Viet '61 (TLS) Retired.
Le, Hung Viet '01 (TLS) Hartshorne, OK Holy Rosary.

Le, James Vinh '87 (KAL) Mendon, MI St. Edward.
Le, John Hung *s.v.d.* '04 (FgM) Techny, IL.
Le, Joseph Hung *c.ss.r.* '08 (DAL)[J] Dallas, TX St. John Neumann Formation House.
Le, Joseph Thu '03 (GAL) Houston, TX St. Christopher.
Le, Justin '09 (SJ) Milpitas, CA St. Elizabeth; [O] San Jose, CA Catholic Professionals.
Le, Khoa T. '06 (RVC) Massapequa, NY St. Rose of Lima.
Le, Lam T. '04 (GR) Big Rapids, MI St. Paul's Campus Parish; Big Rapids, MI St. Mary's.
Le, Nhat Hong '05 (CHI) Mt. Prospect, IL St. Raymond de Penafort.
Le, Peter Quang (OKL) Defenders of the Bond.
Le, Peter Tai '98 (HT) Grand Isle, LA Our Lady of the Isle.
Le, Peter Tuan '06 (DAL) Duncanville, TX Holy Spirit.
Le, Quoc *c.s.sp.* '10 (FgM) Bethel Park, PA CONGREGATION OF THE HOLY SPIRIT.
Le, Thai '08 (LA) Thousand Oaks, CA St. Paschal Baylon.
Le, Trieu Ngoc '42 (PIT) Retired.
Le, Trinh *c.s.sp.* '07 (FgM) Bethel Park, PA CONGREGATION OF THE HOLY SPIRIT.
Le, Tuan *s.j.* '99 (CHI)[C] Chicago, IL Jesuit Community at Loyola University Chicago; [J] Maywood, IL Loyola University Medical Center.
Le (Peter), Hung Van *c.m.* '08 (BRK)[R] Jamaica, NY Reverend John B. Murray, CM, House.
Lea, Joseph P. '04 (PH) Military Chaplains; Army Chaplains.
Leach, Gregory '80 (DM) Des Moines, IA St. Mary of Nazareth.
Leach, Jerome '76 (SFR) Absent on Leave.
Leach, Rev. Msgr. Phillip '85 (R) Retired.
Leach, Thomas F. '73 (BRK) Brooklyn, NY Our Lady of Grace; Presbyteral Council; Assignment Board.
Leach, Rev. Msgr. William J. '58 (STL) St. Louis, MO St. Margaret Mary Alacoque Retired.
Leahey, Patrick R. '77 (ALT) Absent on Leave.
Leahy, Anthony M. '55 (CHI) Chicago, IL St. Barnabas Retired.
Leahy, Edwin D. *o.s.b.* '72 (NEW)[L] Newark, NJ Newark Abbey; [C] Newark, NJ Saint Benedict's Preparatory School; [C] Newark, NJ Saint Benedict's Preparatory School.
Leahy, Juvenal F. *o.f.m.* '58 (FgM) New York, NY Holy Name Province.
Leahy, Liam '72 (TUC) Tucson, AZ Saint Mark Roman Catholic Parish – Tucson.
Leahy, Maurice J. '55 (SB) Retired.
Leahy, William P. *s.j.* '78 (BO)[C] Chestnut Hill, MA Boston College; [U] Newton, MA The Jesuit Community at Boston College; [B] Chestnut Hill, MA The Ecclesiastical Faculty at Boston College.
Leake, Jerome L. '68 (RCK) Aurora, IL St. Joseph.
Leake, Stephen *s.d.b.* '00 (NEW)[L] Orange, NJ The Salesian Community.
Lealofi, Rev. Msgr. Etuale '69 (SPP) Fatuoaiga Multipurpose Cultural and Pastoral Center; Adjunct Judicial Vicar; Diocesan Consultors; Pago Pago, AS St. Joseph the Worker Futiga.
Leary, Albert R. '54 (BIS) Retired.
Leary, Daniel P. '97 (WDC) Silver Spring, MD St. Andrew Apostle.
Leary, Donald G. '51 (WIN) Retired.
Leary, James F. '68 (HRT) Hartford Vicariate; West Hartford, CT St. Peter Claver.
Leary, James P. *o.f.m.cap.* '70 (GB) Appleton, WI St. Joseph; [J] Appleton, WI St. Joseph Friary; Appleton, WI St. Mary.
Leary, Rev. Msgr. Patrick '76 (LAV) Presbyteral Council for the Diocese of Las Vegas; CEO; Board of Trustees; [F] Las Vegas, NV Catholic Charities of Southern Nevada.
Leary, Richard *c.p.* '46 (BRK)[R] Jamaica, NY Immaculate Conception Monastery Retired.
Lease, James E. '06 (HBG) Hanover, PA St. Joseph; [A] York, PA York Catholic High School.
Leatham, Gerald '65 (LUB) Brownfield, TX St. Anthony's; Priests Personnel Board; Vicar of Priests.
Leatherby, Jeremy P. '06 (SAC) Sacramento, CA Presentation of the Blessed Virgin Mary; Presbyteral Council.
Leavins, Brice A. *o.f.m.* '69 (WOR) Auditor; Judges.
Leavins, Brice *o.f.m.* '69 (PRO) Providence, RI Our Lady of Lourdes; Judges.
Leavitt, Robert F. *s.s.* '68 (BAL)[A] Baltimore, MD St. Mary's Seminary and University; [Q] Baltimore, MD St. Mary's Seminary & University.
Leavitt, Robert F. *s.s.* '68 (HRT) On Duty Outside the Archdiocese.
Lebanowski, Gerald *m.s.* '59 (MIL)[P] Twin Lakes, WI La Salette Missionaries.
Lebar, Ivan M. *t.o.r.* '58 (WH) Keyser, WV Assumption.
Lebdowicz, Jan Krzystof '80 (NEW) Plainfield, NJ The Parish of St. Bernard and St. Stanislaus.
LeBeau, Philip A. '93 (PAT) Deans; Lincoln Park, NJ St. Joseph's.
Lebel, Jean–Paul *s.d.b.* '66 (FgM) New Rochelle, NY SALESIANS OF DON BOSCO.
Lebel, Maurice T. '67 (PRT) Retired.
Lebiedz, Bernard V. *o.s.b.* '59 (LAF)[H] Opelousas, LA Mother of the Redeemer Monastery.
LeBlanc, Alvin J. '82 (HRT) Bristol Deanery.
LeBlanc, Alvin J. '82 (HRT) Bristol, CT St. Ann; Judges.
LeBlanc, Charles R. '79 (NOR) North Grosvenordale, CT St. Joseph; North Grosvenordale, CT St. Stephen; Deans; Council of Catholic Women; Diocesan Commission for Ecumenical and Interreligious Affairs; Members.
LeBlanc, Christopher '10 (PT) Florida State University; Tallahassee, FL Co–Cathedral of St. Thomas More.
Le Blanc, Clyde *s.j.* '75 (BR)[J] Convent, LA Manresa House of Retreats.
LeBlanc, Daniel *o.m.i.* '78 (WDC)[O] Washington, DC Oblate Community.
LeBlanc, Daniel *o.m.i.* (NY)[HH] New York, NY International Catholic Organizations Information Center, Inc.
LeBlanc, Etienne '71 (HT) Retired.
LeBlanc, Harold E. '61 (BO) Woburn, MA St. Joseph.
LeBlanc, James L. '96 (CHR) Priest Retirement Committee.
LeBlanc, James L. '96 (CHR) Myrtle Beach, SC St. Andrew; Family Life Services; [J] Myrtle Beach, SC St. Elizabeth Ann Seton High School Association.
LeBlanc, Keith P. '96 (BO) Unassigned.
LeBlanc, Leo A. '74 (MAN) Plymouth, NH Holy Trinity Parish.
LeBlanc, Leo–Paul J. '79 (WOR) Winchendon, MA Immaculate Heart of Mary.
LeBlanc, Omer *c.j.m.* '61 (SD) El Cajon, CA Our Lady of Grace Catholic Parish.
LeBlanc, Paul J. (NY) Bronx, NY St. Joan of Arc.
LeBlanc, Steven C. '77 (LAF) Lafayette, LA St. Pius X.
LeBleu, Wayne '95 (LKC) Lake Charles, LA Christ the King; Propagation of the Faith & Holy Childhood Association; Relief Services Catholic; Pastoral Services, Catholic.
LeBoeuf, Gerard '93 (DET)[D] Madison Heights, MI Bishop Foley Catholic High School; Clawson, MI Guardian Angels.
LeBourgeois, Rev. Msgr. Louis P. '61 (NO) Retired.
Le Bouteiller des Haries, Philippe *o.s.b.* '95 (TLS)[G] Hulbert, OK Our Lady of the Annunciation of Clear Creek Monastery.
Lebrun, Raymond A. *o.m.i.* '68 (WDC)[O] Washington, DC Oblate Community; [S] Washington, DC Basilica of the National Shrine of the Immaculate Conception.
LeCaptain, Douglas E. '93 (GB) Oshkosh, WI St. Raphael the Archangel; Regional Vicars; Omro, WI St. Mary; Winneconne, WI St. Mary; Priests' Personnel Board.
Lech, Waclaw L. *o.c.d.* '74 (CHI) Chicago, IL St. Camillus.
Lech, Waclaw L. *o.c.d.* '74 (GRY)[H] Munster, IN Discalced Carmelite Fathers Monastery.
Lechnar, William J. '97 (GBG) Indiana, PA St. Thomas More University Parish; Office for Planning.
Lechner, Peter *s.p.* '68 (STL)[V] Dittmer, MO Servants of the Paraclete Missouri Generalate Corporation.
Lechner, Rev. Msgr. Roger A. '66 (SD) San Diego, CA Holy Spirit Catholic Parish.
Lechtenberg, Rev. Msgr. Edward W. '51 (DUB) Retired.
Lecias, J. Michael O. '10 (WH) Beckley, WV St. Francis De Sales.
Leckie, Michael J. '76 (PRO) Hope Valley, RI St. Joseph.
LeClair, Richard J. *c.ss.p.* '51 (PIT)[O] Bethel Park, PA The Spiritan Center.
LeClaire, H. Fred *c.m.f.* '87 (PHX) Chino Valley, AZ St. Catherine Laboure Roman Catholic Mission, A Quasi–Parish; Advocates.
LeClaire, Karl *s.d.s.* '86 (MIL)[P] Milwaukee Salvatorian Provincial Offices.
Leclerc, Thomas L. *m.s.* '80 (BO) Cambridge, MA St. John the Evangelist.
LeCompte, Glenn '86 (HT) Houma, LA St. Lucy; Thibodaux, LA St. Luke; Continuing Education of the Clergy–Ministry to Priests Program; Worship; Ecumenism.
Lecomte, Gerard *c.j.m.* '78 (LA) Chatsworth, CA St. John Eudes.
LeCours, Sylva P. '47 (NOR) Retired.
Lecumberri, Rufino '54 (NY) Bronx, NY Sacred Heart.
Leddy, Leonard '59 (AUS) Retired.
Leder, Dennis M. *s.j.* '76 (FgM) New York, NY Society of Jesus.
Ledermann, Paul F. '63 (OG) Retired.
Ledesma, Salvador '99 (STO) Newman Apostolate; Members by Age Group.
Ledet, Rev. Msgr. Donald '63 (HT) Retired.
Ledford, John S. '75 (WH) Charles Town, WV St. James.
Ledoux, Albert H. '87 (ALT) Gallitzin, PA St. Demetrius.
Ledoux, Damien C. '05 (MAN) Absent on Leave.
LeDoux, Jerome G. *s.v.d.* '57 (FWT) Fort Worth, TX Our Mother of Mercy.
Ledoux, Louis Vernon '52 (LAF) Retired.
Ledoux, Mark '99 (LAF) Carencro, LA St. Peter.
Ledoux, Michael Dominic W. *o.f.m.* '86 (ALB)[A] Catskill, NY St. Anthony Friary.
Ledoux, William J. '93 (PRO) Pawtucket, RI St. Mary of the Immaculate Conception; Deans.
LeDuc, Roger D. '60 (FR) Retired.
Ledwidge, Brendan '55 (LAN) Retired.
Ledwith, Harry '74 (TUC) Tucson, AZ Saint Pius X Roman Catholic Parish – Tucson.
Ledwon, Jacob C. '72 (BUF) Council of Priests; [Q] Buffalo, NY State University of New York at Buffalo (Main St. South Campus); Buffalo, NY St. Joseph–University; Consultors, College of.
Lee, Andrew H. (NY) Bronx, NY St John Nam.
Lee, Andrew Kyung C. '83 (ORL) Orlando, FL St. Ignatius Kim Korean Mission.
Lee, Andrew Kyung–Chul '83 (ORL) Korean Ministry.
Lee, Andrew T. '11 (BO) Weymouth, MA Sacred Heart.
Lee, Anthony S. '97 (LA)[A] Camarillo, CA St. John's Seminary.
Lee, Bernard *s.m.* '67 (SAT)[L] San Antonio, TX Ligustrum Marianist Community.
Lee, Bongmoon '93 (MIA) Korean.
Lee, Cha Yong (Paul) (TR) Eatontown, NJ Immaculate Conception.
Lee, Chul Ho (R) New Hill, NC St. Ha–Sang Paul Jung.
Lee, Rev. Msgr. David M. '68 (BUF)[A] East Aurora, NY Christ the King Seminary; Buffalo, NY Our Lady of Charity.
Lee, Dominic Savio '94 (SFR) San Mateo, CA St. Matthew.
Lee, Eugene '04 (ORG)[H] Anaheim, CA St. Thomas Korean Catholic Center; Liturgical Commission.
Lee, Gabriel '97 (BRK) Flushing, NY St. Paul Chong Ha–Sang Roman Catholic Chapel.
Lee, Gerard *o.f.m.* '71 (ALB)[B] Siena College; [R] Albany, NY St. Francis Chapel.
Lee, Gitae (CHL) Korean Catholic Cultural Center.
Lee, Gyo Jeong Joseph *c.p.* '05 (AUS) Harker Heights, TX St. Paul Chong Hasang.
Lee, Huengwoo '04 (CIN)[U] Cincinnati, OH St. Andrew Kim Korean Catholic Community.
Lee, J.M. Gregory '10 (WIL) Newark, DE St. John the Baptist–Holy Angels.
Lee, Jae Hyeong (Luke) '01 (CHK) Saipan, MP Korean Catholic Community.
Lee, Jae (Luke) Hyeong '01 (CHK) Presbyteral Council.
Lee, Jaehwa John '07 (PH)[BB] Newtown Square, PA Tri–College Newman Cluster–Bryn Mawr, Haverford and Swarthmore Colleges; On Special or Other Archdiocesan Assignment; Newtown Square, PA St. Anastasia.
Lee, James E. '75 (SEA) Olympia, WA St. Michael; Deans; Presbyteral Council.
Lee, Jeffrey E. '92 (TR) Episcopal Council; Expansion and Restructuring Commission; Trenton, NJ Our Lady of the Angels Parish; Mercer County.
Lee, John Michael *c.p.* '72 (BRK)[T] Jamaica, NY Bishop Molloy Retreat House; [R] Jamaica, NY Immaculate Conception Monastery.
Lee, John R. *c.s.b.* '56 (ROC)[K] Rochester, NY Basilian Residence.
Lee, John Sungwoong '11 (CLV) Medina, OH St. Francis Xavier.
Lee, John T. Matthew '93 (WDC) Absent On Leave.
Lee, John '11 (LA) Redondo Beach, CA St. James.
Lee, Rev. Archimandrite Joseph (Richard) '72 (PHU)[E] Washington, DC Monastery of the Holy Cross.
Lee, Joseph C. '91 (DAL) Duncanville, TX Holy Spirit.
Lee, Joseph P. '57 (LA) Retired.
Lee, Joseph '55 (CHI) Retired.
Lee, Joseph *f.s.s.p.* (LIN)[A] Denton, NE Our Lady of Guadalupe Seminary.
Lee, Joshua Peter '89 (LA) Pico Rivera, CA St. Hilary.
Lee, Keun–Soo '95 (BR) Morganza, LA St. Ann.
Lee, Matthew K. '09 (CIN) Botkins, OH St. Lawrence; Wapakoneta, OH St. Joseph; Botkins, OH Immaculate Conception.
Lee, Michael J. *o.praem.* '70 (PH) Paoli, PA St. Norbert; [Y] Paoli, PA Daylesford Abbey.
Lee, Michael *s.j.* '96 (LA)[C] Los Angeles, CA Jesuit Community.
Lee, Michael '11 (PAT) Morristown, NJ St. Margaret of Scotland.
Lee, Patrick J. '76 (CHI) Chicago, IL Immaculate Conception of the Blessed Virgin Mary; Chicago, IL St. Joseph.
Lee, Patrick J. *s.j.* '78 (P)[L] Portland, OR Jesuit Provincial Office (Society of Jesus, Oregon Prov.); [L] Portland, OR Colombiere Community.
Lee, Patrick J. '68 (SAC) Elk Grove, CA St. Joseph Retired.
Lee, Patrick J. *s.j.* '78 (FgM) Portland, OR Society of Jesus; Portland, OR.
Lee, Paul D. '83 (WDC) Washington, DC Epiphany; Priest Council.
Lee, Paul Kyung '06 (NEW) Fort Lee, NJ Madonna.
Lee, Raphael '08 (NEW) Saddle River Borough, NJ St. Gabriel the Archangel.
Lee, Robert Anthony '93 (PEO) Atkinson, IL St. Anthony's.

Lee, Roy '86 (MIL) Personal Leave; Board of Directors.
Lee, Sang Yil '92 (AUS) Retired.
Lee, Sebastian *s.s.p.* '05 (NY)[B] Staten Island, NY Society of St. Paul.
Lee, Terence J. *m.h.m.* '57 (NY)[DD] Hartsdale, NY Mill Hill Fathers Residence.
Lee, Rev. Msgr. Thaddeus (PAT) Retired.
Lee, Thomas M. '53 (PRT) Retired.
Lee, William J. *s.s.* '46 (BAL)[Q] Baltimore Society of St. Sulpice, Province of the United States Retired.
Lee, Yong Huyk '01 (GAL) Houston, TX St. Andrew Kim.
Lee, Young Chang '01 (PHX) Chandler, AZ St. Columba Kim Roman Catholic Mission, A Quasi Parish.
Leeuw, Daniel R. '57 (FTW) Veterans Administration Hospital; [F] Avilla, IN Provena LaVerna Terrace Retired.
Leeuw, Daniel R. '57 (MO) DEPARTMENT OF VETERANS AFFAIRS HOSPITALS AND CHAPLAINS.
Lefebure, Leo D. '78 (WDC) Other Assignments; Washington, DC Our Lady of Victory.
Lefebvre, Rev. Msgr. Gerald M. '56 (BR) Judges Retired.
Lefebvre, James '59 (ALB) Albany, NY St. Mary; Advocates; Priests Retirement Board/Priests Retirement Plan Board Retired.
Lefebvre, Robert R. *m.m.* '57 (NY)[DD] Maryknoll Maryknoll Fathers and Brothers Retired.
Lefebvre, Simon P. *c.s.v.* '56 (CHI)[N] Arlington Heights Viatorian Province Center–Clerics of St. Viator.
LeFevre, Rev. Msgr. Michael C. '82 (DET) Presbyteral Council; Highland Park, MI St. Benedict; Detroit, MI St. Gregory the Great; Detroit, MI Church of the Madonna; Detroit, MI Cathedral, Church of the Most Blessed Sacrament; Archdiocesan Vicars.
LeFevre, Robert J. '66 (ALB) Saratoga Springs, NY St. Peter Retired.
Leffler, Richard J. '78 (MAD) Potosi, WI SS. Andrew and Thomas.
LeFleur, R. Keith '76 (SAG) Retired.
Lefor, Jason '99 (FAR) Grand Forks, ND St. Thomas Aquinas Newman Church of Grand Forks; [H] Grand Forks, ND St. Thomas Aquinas Newman Church of Grand Forks.
LeFort, David R. '98 (ALB) East Greenbush, NY St. Mary.
LeFrois, Rev. Msgr. Marvin '49 (SAV) Valdosta, GA St. John the Evangelist Retired.
Legal, Wilfred A. *o.s.b.* '94 (GAL) Humble, TX St. Mary Magdalene.
Legarra, Francisco J. *o.a.r.* '74 (NEW) Union City, NJ Holy Family; [L] Union City, NJ Augustinian Recollects, St. Nicholas of Tolentine Monastery.
Legarreta, Felipe '93 (JOL) Bloomingdale, IL St. Isidore.
Legarski, Anthony J. '83 (ALT) Hollidaysburg, PA St. Mary's; Altoona, PA Veterans Medical Center.
Legaspi, Alex L. '76 (SFR) Daly City, CA St. Andrew; Navy Reserve Chaplains.
Legaspi, Dennis L. '93 (SB) Appointed Members; Desert Hot Springs, CA St. Elizabeth of Hungary.
Legaspi, Fulgencio Paul '89 (MO) Navy Reserve Chaplains.
Legaspy, Dennis L. '93 (SB) Low Desert.
LeGault, Michael *m.s.a.* '71 (NOR)[G] Cromwell, CT Society of the Missionaries of the Holy Apostles.
Legault, Michel *m.s.a.* '71 (NOR)[A] Cromwell, CT Holy Apostles College and Seminary.
Leger, Austin '62 (LAF) Retired.
Leger, G. Robert '71 (SJ) Sunnyvale, CA Church of The Resurrection; Pastoral Resource Committee for Ministry to Gay and Lesbian Catholics.
Leger, Jeffrey P. '97 (L) Louisville, KY Guardian Angels.
Leger, Laurie L. *m.s.* '54 (WOR) Fitchburg, MA St. Joseph's.
Leger, Steven L. '86 (BEA) Bridge City, TX St. Henry; Presbyteral Council; Diocesan Judges.
Legerski, John '81 (B) On Duty Outside the Diocese.
Legerski, John '81 (RNO)[A] Reno, NV Bishop Manogue Catholic High School, a Nevada non–profit corporation; On Special Assignment.
Lego, William E. *o.s.a.* '83 (CHI) Chicago, IL St. Turibius.
Lehane, Brian J. *s.j.* '97 (DET)[E] Detroit, MI University of Detroit Jesuit High School and Academy.
Leheny, Rev. Msgr. Bernard M. '66 (LA) Long Beach, CA St. Bartholomew; Cardinal McIntyre Fund for Charity Board of Directors; Deanery 20.
Lehman, Charles (TUC)[D] Tucson, AZ Carondelet St. Joseph's Hospital.
Lehman, John J. (MAR) Retired.
Lehman, Rev. Msgr. Joseph P. '80 (RIC) Roanoke, VA Our Lady of Nazareth.
Lehman, Paul J. '54 (NEW) Couples for Christ; Bukas–Loob Sa Diyos Community (BLD) (Open to the Spirit of God); Newark, NJ St. Antoninus Retired.
Lehmkuhl, Gerhardt B. *s.j.* '74 (STL)[O] St. Louis, MO Jesuit Community Corporation at Saint Louis University – Jesuit Hall.
Lehner, John *o.s.f.s.* '70 (TOL)[H] Toledo, OH.
Lehnerd, Frank M. '58 (Y) Retired.
Lehnert, Brian '00 (PMB) Wellington, FL St. Therese de Lisieux.
Lehning, Thomas J. '70 (ARL) Clifton, VA St. Clare of Assisi.
Lehocky, Rev. Msgr. Leigh A. '68 (CHR) Columbia, SC St. Peter.
Lehr, James W. *m.m.* '53 (NY)[DD] Maryknoll Maryknoll Fathers and Brothers Retired.
Lehrberger, James *o.cist.* '76 (DAL)[B] University of Dallas; [J] Irving, TX Cistercian Abbey of Our Lady of Dallas.
Leibenguth, Gerald T. *o.s.b.* '72 (BO)[U] Hingham, MA Glastonbury Abbey.
Leibham, David '87 (AUS) Franklin, TX St. Francis of Assisi; Hearne, TX St. Mary.
Leibrecht, Robert G. '58 (STL) Retired.
Leidich, Kevin A. *s.j.* '82 (SAC)[C] Sacramento, CA Jesuit High School; [H] Carmichael, CA Sacramento Jesuit Community.
Leies, John A. *s.m.* '56 (SAT)[C] San Antonio, TX St. Mary's University of San Antonio, Texas; [L] San Antonio, TX Marianist Residence; Catholic Physicians Guild.
Leif, Gregory P. '78 (WIN) Caledonia, MN St. Mary; Caledonia, MN St. Patrick's.
Leigh, David J. *s.j.* '68 (SEA)[A] Seattle, WA Seattle University; [M] Seattle, WA Arrupe Jesuit Community at Seattle University.
Leighton, Rev. Msgr. Donald E. '62 (PH) Gladwyne, PA St. John Baptist Vianney.
Lein, Lambert *s.v.d.* '00 (LAF) Lafayette, LA St. Anthony.
Leinen, Ronald *m.s.c.* '57 (ALN)[A] Center Valley, PA Sacred Heart Villa, Missionaries of the Sacred Heart.
Leininger, Charles A. *s.j.* '53 (DAL)[D] Dallas, TX Jesuit College Preparatory School.
Leininger, William '56 (SJ) Retired.
Leiphon, Donald A. '68 (FAR) Retired.
Leise, Gerald '74 (OM) Emerson, NE Sacred Heart; Pender, NE St. John.
Leise, Leo V. *s.j.* '94 (SFE) Albuquerque, NM Immaculate Conception.
Leisen, Leo '54 (SCL) Retired.
Leisen, Richard '56 (SCL) Diocesan Priests Pension Plan Trustees; Legion of Mary Retired.
Leising, Edmund *o.m.i.* '46 (FgM) Washington, DC AMERICAN OBLATE MISSIONS.
Leising, Rev. Msgr. Frederick D. '71 (BUF) Williamsville, NY Nativity of the Blessed Virgin Mary; Finance Council.
Leising, John J. '69 (BUF) Williamsville, NY Nativity of the Blessed Virgin Mary.
Leising, Robert *o.m.i.* '90 (BEL)[F] Belleville, IL Shrine of Our Lady of the Snows.
Leisy, Christian *o.s.b.* '88 (SFE)[H] Abiquiu, NM Monastery of Christ in the Desert.
Leitem, Leon *o.f.m.cap.* '57 (HBG) Harrisburg, PA St. Francis of Assisi.
Leiting, Robert L. '67 (SC) Retired.
Leitner, Rev. Msgr. John E. '55 (KC) Presbyteral Council Retired.
Leitner, Thomas Aquinas *o.s.b.* '92 (OM)[J] Schuyler, NE Benedictine Mission House.
Leiweke, Robert W. *s.j.* '58 (MIL)[P] Wauwatosa, WI Jesuit Community at St. Camillus.
Le Jacq, Peter M. *m.m.* '87 (NY)[DD] Maryknoll Maryknoll Fathers and Brothers.
LeJeune, Ronald J. '71 (TOL) Retired.
Lek, Basil L. '04 (NEW) On Duty Outside the Archdiocese.
Leke, Charles '82 (SP) Inverness, FL Our Lady of Fatima.
Leland, Thomas '99 (WCH) Erie, KS St. Ambrose; St. Paul, KS St. Francis.
Leliaert, Richard M. '67 (DET) Redford Township, MI St. Robert Bellarmine.
Lelo, Albert *c.i.c.m.* (SAT) Poteet, TX St. Philip Benizi.
Leloczky, Julius *o.cist.* '61 (DAL)[J] Irving, TX Cistercian Abbey of Our Lady of Dallas.
Lelonis, Richard M. '71 (PIT)[N] Pittsburgh, PA Mount Assisi Convent; Judges; Matrimonial Concerns, Officefor; Matrimonial Concerns, Office for.
Lemaine, Calonge '89 (BRK) Brooklyn, NY Our Lady of Miracles.
Lemaster, Scott '85 (DAV) Charlotte, IA Assumption and St. Patrick's; Charlotte, IA Ss. Mary and Joseph; Charlotte, IA Immaculate Conception.
Lemautu, Faitau '11 (SPP) Pago Pago, AS Cathedral of the Holy Family.
Lemay, Donald H. '89 (RIC) Richmond, VA St. Edward The Confessor.
LeMay, Donald *o.s.b.* '57 (SCL)[I] Collegeville, MN St. John's Abbey, of the Order of St. Benedict.
Lemay, Jean M. '75 (MAN) Manchester, NH St. Joseph Cathedral; Catholic Medical Center.
LeMay, John R. *o.s.m.* '84 (CHI)[N] Chicago, IL Monastery of Our Lady of Sorrows; Chicago, IL Our Lady of Sorrows, Basilica of.
Lemay, Larry '99 (BEL) Leave of Absence.
Lembo, Richard '75 (WOR) Gilbertville, MA St. Aloysius.
Lemence, Daniel *s.o.l.t.* '05 (PHX) Phoenix, AZ Most Holy Trinity Roman Catholic Parish.
Le Mieux, Thomas A. '59 (MIL) Retired.
Lemire, Paul W. '89 (WOR) Shrewsbury, MA St. Anne.
Lemkuhl, David A. '79 (CIN) Cincinnati, OH St. Anthony; Cincinnati, OH St. Margaret – St. John Parish.
Lemlin, Timothy J. '78 (PRO) West Warwick, RI Christ the King.
Lemme, Christopher *t.o.r.* '98 (ARL) Luray, VA Our Lady of the Valley.
Lemoi, Paul R. '75 (PRO) West Warwick, RI Our Lady of Good Counsel; Army National Guard Chaplains.
Lemoine, Russell J. '70 (ALX) Retired.
Lemon, Rev. Msgr. Clement P. '64 (WIL) Wilmington, DE Immaculate Heart of Mary; Vicar for Priests; College of Consultors.
Lemor, Kiskama *c.s.sp.* '00 (ORL) Cocoa Beach, FL Church of Our Saviour.
Lemos, Thomas *c.s.c.* '74 (FTW) South Bend, IN St. Adalbert; South Bend, IN St. Casimir; [H] Notre Dame Congregation of Holy Cross, United States Province of Priests & Brothers; South Bend.
Lemus, Raul '02 (SR) Sebastopol, CA St. Sebastian; Clergy Personnel Committee.
Lenaghan, J. Jordan *o.p.* '95 (COL) Columbus, OH St. Patrick.
Lenane, Rev. Msgr. William '50 (SJ) Retired.
Lencewicz, Leonard *o.f.m.* '63 (NY)[DD] New York Franciscan Friars, Holy Name Province.
Lencewicz, Leonard *o.f.m.* '63 (SP)[N] St. Petersburg, FL St. Anthony Friary.
Lenchak, Timothy *s.v.d.* '70 (DUB)[B] Epworth, IA Divine Word College.
Lendacky, Francis G. '61 (PH) Philadelphia, PA St. Agnes–St. John Nepomucene; Legion of Mary.
Lendvai, John B. '94 (PIT) West Mifflin, PA Holy Spirit; [P] West Mifflin, PA Community College of Allegheny County – South Campus.
Lenehan, Claude T. *o.f.m.* '55 (PAT)[N] Butler, NJ St. Anthony Friary.
Lenehan, Vincent '54 (SAC) Retired.
Lengerich, Bob J. '07 (FTW) Bremen, IN St. Dominic; Bremen.
Lengerich, Rev. Msgr. Vincent L. '48 (CIN)[N] Carthagena, OH St. Charles; Judges Retired.
Lengwin, Ronald P. '66 (PIT) Pittsburgh, PA St. Mary of Mercy; General Secretary; Diocesan Finance Council; Building Commission; Ecumenical and Interfaith Commission; Mission Office; Pilgrimage Office; Public and Community Affairs, Office for; Society for the Propagation of the Faith; Priest Council; Clergy Personnel Board; Vicars General; College of Consultors.
Lenihan, Daniel F. *o.c.s.o.* '55 (DUB)[K] Peosta, IA New Melleray Abbey, Order of Cistercians of the Strict Observance.
Lenihan, Rev. Msgr. John J. '53 (STA) Retired.
Lenk, Dominic *o.s.b.* '98 (STL)[O] St. Louis, MO The Abbey of St. Mary and St. Louis; [F] Creve Coeur, MO St. Louis Priory School.
Lenneman, Marc J. '06 (HEL)[A] Helena, MT Carroll College; Presbyteral Council; Diocesan Consultors; Borromeo Pre–Seminary Program; Vocations Office; [B] Helena, MT Carroll College; Personnel Board.
Lennon, James M. '58 (JOL) Retired.
Lennon, Peter F. '55 (NEW)[B] Seton Hall University Retired.
Lennon, Raymond T. *s.v.d.* '64 (TR)[N] Bordentown, NJ Society of the Divine Word.
Lenoci, Dominick J. '95 (NEW) Emerson, NJ Church of the Assumption.
Lenti, Arthur *s.d.b.* '50 (OAK)[A] Berkeley, CA Dominican School of Philosophy and Theology; [L] Berkeley Salesians of Don Bosco.
Lentine, Peter S. '50 (DET) Detroit, MI St. Philomena.
Lentini, James S. '03 (WIL)[A] Magnolia, DE St. Thomas More Academy; Censor of Books; Dover, DE Holy Cross.
Lentz, Frank (VIC) Retired.
Lentz, Gerald J. *s.j.* '60 (SJ)[M] Los Gatos, CA Sacred Heart Jesuit Center.
Lentz, Lawrence D. *c.s.v.* '81 (CHI) Arlington Heights, IL; [N] Arlington Heights, IL Viatorian Province Center–Clerics of St. Viator.
Lenz, Daniel *o.s.b.* '85 (OM)[C] Elkhorn, NE Mount Michael Benedictine School; [J] Elkhorn, NE Mount Michael Benedictine Abbey; Religious Orders.
Lenz, David *o.f.m.conv.* '86 (IND)[J] Mount St. Francis, IN Mount Saint Francis Friary and Retreat Center.
Lenz, Frank '69 (MAR) Retired.
Lenz, Rev. Msgr. Paul A. '49 (ALT) Retired.
Lenzini, Donald J. '51 (BEL) Retired.
Lenzner, George '57 (GB) Retired.
Leo, Arthur R. '85 (NY) Absent on Sick Leave.
Leon, Bartholomew *o.s.b.* '85 (SAM) Greer, SC St. Rafka Maronite Mission.
Leon, Carlos '98 (ORG) Santa Ana, CA Immaculate Heart of Mary.

Leon, David '05 (SD) UCSD Medical Center; La Mesa, CA Little Flower Haven; [I] La Mesa, CA Little Flower Haven; San Diego, CA Nazareth House.
Leon, Francisco *o.s.a.* '78 (LAR) Laredo, TX Holy Redeemer; Priests Personnel Board; Ex Officio Members.
Leon, Gregorio '88 (LAV) Las Vegas, NV St. Anne.
Leon, Hector (BGP) Danbury, CT Our Lady of Guadalupe.
Leon, Jose M. '81 (OAK) Union City, CA Our Lady of the Rosary; Presbyteral Council.
Leon, Raguiel Rodriguez '08 (FAJ) Humacao, PR Concathedral Dulce Nombre de Jesus.
Leon, Victor *o.s.j.* '00 (SCR) Hazleton, PA Annunciation, Hazelton; Hispanic Ministry Outreach.
Leon–Angulo, Marcos '03 (R) Whiteville, NC Sacred Heart; Deans; Office of African Ancestry Ministry and Evangelization; Council of Priests.
Leon–Valencia, Rafael A. '04 (R) Fayetteville, NC St. Patrick.
Leonard, Albert P. '89 (SCR) Unassigned or Leave of Absence.
Leonard, Daniel '94 (DEN) Denver, CO Christ the King.
Leonard, Derek '96 (FgM) Boston, MA St. James the Apostle, Inc.
Leonard, Edwin M. '84 (CLV) Parma, OH St. Charles Borromeo.
Leonard, Eugene A. '66 (CHR) Retired.
Leonard, Francis B. '50 (BO) Chelmsford, MA St. John the Evangelist; Senior Priests. Retired.
Leonard, John E. '65 (RIC) Retired.
Leonard, John F. '55 (BO) Senior Priests. Retired.
Leonard, John J. *s.j.* '50 (NY)[DD] New York, NY Murray–Weigel Hall.
Leonard, John J. *o.f.m.* '96 (HRT) Hartford, CT St. Patrick–St. Anthony.
Leonard, John (NTN) Retired.
Leonard, Matthew '98 (MO) Black Mountain, NC St. Margaret Mary; DEPARTMENT OF VETERANS AFFAIRS HOSPITALS AND CHAPLAINS.
Leonard, Michael '91 (CHI) Chicago, IL St. Tarcissus.
Leonard, Peter J. *o.s.f.s.* '86 (ALN)[B] Center Valley, PA DeSales University; [K] Center Valley, PA Oblates of St. Francis de Sales.
Leonard, Raymond J. '90 (MET) On Duty Outside the Diocese.
Leonard, Samuel *i.v.e.* '04 (SJ) Santa Clara, CA Our Lady of Peace.
Leonard, Sebastian *o.s.b.* '57 (HRT)[E] New Milford, CT Canterbury School.
Leonard, Sebastian *o.s.b.* '57 (IND)[K] Saint Meinrad St. Meinrad Archabbey.
Leonard, Rev. Msgr. Thomas P. '56 (NY) New York, NY Holy Trinity; Manhattan (West).
Leonard, William T. '69 (BO) Waltham, MA St. Jude; Pastoral Care.
Leonards, Martin C. '66 (LAF) Duson, LA St. Theresa of the Child Jesus; Duson, LA St. Benedict the Moor.
Leone, Arthur '56 (NY) New York, NY St. Peter Retired.
Leone, James M. '60 (BRK) Retired.
Leone, Richard D. *o.s.f.s.* '59 (WIL)[J] Childs, MD Retirement and Assisted Care Facility Retired.
Leone, William B. '74 (ROC) East Rochester, NY St. Jerome.
Leonelli, Louis *c.f.r.* '09 (NY)[DD] Bronx, NY Franciscan Friars of the Renewal.
Leong, Francis J. *m.m.* '87 (NY)[DD] Retired.
Leong, Herman '91 (OAK) Judges.
Leong, Herman '91 (HON) Defender of the Bond.
Leon Guerrero, Felixberto C. *o.f.m.cap.* '86 (AGN) Mangilao, GU Santa Teresita.
Leonhardt, Douglas J. *s.j.* '69 (MIL)[P] Milwaukee, WI Jesuit Community at Marquette University.
Leonhardt, Louis J. '56 (DAV) DEPARTMENT OF VETERANS AFFAIRS HOSPITALS AND CHAPLAINS Retired.
Leonhardt, Robert *o.f.m.* '59 (FWT)[H] Crowley, TX St. Maximilian Kolbe Friary.
Leopold, David C. '82 (BGP) Georgetown, CT Sacred Heart.
Leopold, Martin J. '01 (SAT) Ecumenical Affairs; San Antonio, TX St. John The Evangelist; Ecumenical Relations; Administrative Assistant to the Archbishop; Administrative Services Department; Priests Personnel Board; Moderator of the Curia & Director of Administration; Archdiocesan Presbyteral Council; [H] San Antonio, TX San Fernando Health Care Centre of San Antonio; Lay Pension Plan Committee.
Leota, Niko F. '87 (LA) Carson, CA St. Philomena.
LePage, Bradley *t.o.r.* '03 (STU)[A] Steubenville, OH Franciscan University of Steubenville; [H] Steubenville, OH Holy Spirit Friary.
Lepak, Przemyslaw '06 (PRO) Riverside, RI St. Brendan.
Lepak, Roy C. '62 (STP) Special Assignment Retired.
Lepine, Steven M. '06 (MAN) Charlestown, NH All Saints Parish.
Le Quang Thanh, Nicolas (SAC)[H] Walnut Grove, CA Monastery of Chau Son Sacramento.
Lequin, Thomas '77 (PRT) Farmington, ME St. Joseph's; Jay, ME St. Rose of Lima; [M] Farmington, ME University of Maine at Farmington; Pastoral Associates.
Lery, Bruce J. *s.m.* '87 (SFR) San Francisco General Hospital; [N] San Francisco, CA Marist Center of the West.
Lesak, William P. '75 (NEW) Military Chaplains.
Lescher, Raymond C. '63 (JOL) Joliet, IL Sacred Heart.
Lesczynski, James J. '64 (LC) Retired.
Leser, Rev. Msgr. William J. '63 (LA) Retired.
Leser, Chorbishop William J. '62 (SLC) Murray, UT Saint Jude.
Leser, Chorbishop William '63 (OLL) Murray, UT Saint Jude Maronite Catholic Church; Judicial Vicar.
Leshney, Michael F. '73 (CIN) Bethel, OH St. Mary; New Richmond, OH St. Peter.
LeSieur, Rev. Msgr. David '76 (LR) Deans; Continuing Education for the Clergy; Minister to Priests; Rogers, AR St. Vincent de Paul; Clergy Personnel Advisory Board (Diocesan); Presbyteral Council; Diocesan Consultors.
Lesigues, Lope '90 (NEW) Upper Saddle River, NJ Church of the Presentation.
Leskovar, Richard J. '68 (ALB) Delmar, NY St. Thomas the Apostle; Ministers to Retired Priests; Priests Retirement Board/Priests Retirement Plan Board Retired.
Leslie, Patrick J. '69 (SR) Santa Rosa, CA Star of the Valley; Sonoma Developmental Center.
Lesniak, David '91 (DET) Dearborn, MI St. Alphonsus.
Lesniak, Richard D. '66 (MAD) Retired.
Lesnick, John F. '78 (BAL) Special Assignment; Emmitsburg, MD Our Lady of Mount Carmel.
Lesniewski, Stephen F. '93 (CHI) Chicago, IL Epiphany.
Lesniowski, Stanley '70 (PAT) Passaic, NJ St. Joseph's.
Lesousky, John *c.r.* '56 (L)[L] Louisville, KY Villa Pacis, Resurrectionist Retirement Home; Louisville, KY.
Lessard, Eugene R. '59 (PRO) North Scituate, RI St. Joseph Retired.
Lessard, Gerard *o.p.* '84 (WDC) Washington, DC St. Dominic Church & Priory.
Lessard, Leo '60 (GB) Retired.
Lessard–Thibodeau, John G. '92 (SPR) On Sabbatical.
Lesseps, Roland J. *s.j.* '65 (NO)[R] New Orleans, LA Ignatius Residence Retired.
Lester, John E. '59 (TOL) Retired.
Lester, John J. '62 (NEW) Scotch Plains, NJ St. Bartholomew Retired.
Lester, Thomas '57 (OAK) San Leandro, CA St. Leander Retired.
Leszczynski, Jacek K. *o.f.m.conv.* '98 (R)[F] Elon, NC Conventual Franciscans; Burlington, NC Blessed Sacrament.
Letendre, Theodore *f.i.c.* '97 (PRT)[I] Alfred, ME Notre Dame Institute; [I] Notre Dame Spiritual Center; [L] Alfred, ME Notre Dame Retreat & Spiritual Center.
Leto, Nelo A. '54 (DM) Retired.
Letoile, Kenneth R. *o.p.* '74 (WDC)[B] Washington, DC Dominican House of Studies.
Letona, Robert M. '09 (LC)[C] Stevens Point, WI St. Peter Middle School; [C] Stevens Point, WI Pacelli High School; Chippewa Falls, WI St. Charles Borromeo.
Letourneau, Daniel J. '06 (OKL) Perry, OK St. Rose of Lima.
Letourneau, Daniel '06 (OKL)[B] Oklahoma City, OK Bishop McGuinness Catholic High School.
Letourneau, Larry '00 (SAL) Clyde, KS St. John the Baptist Parish; Board of Trustees; Aurora, KS St. Peter Parish; Clyde, KS St. Mary Parish.
LeTran, Benjamin T. '05 (BO) Haverhill, MA Sacred Hearts.
Letteer, Michael C. '96 (HBG) Harrisburg, PA Cathedral Parish of St. Patrick.
Lettic, Edward P. '73 (WOR) Lancaster, MA Immaculate Conception.
Lettre, Raymond '88 (SP) Retired.
Leurck, Raymond J. '67 (CIN) Shandon, OH St. Aloysius.
Leute, Charles J. *o.p.* '69 (FAR) Fort Totten, ND St. Jerome's Church of Crow Hill; Fort Totten, ND Seven Dolors; Fort Totten, ND Christ the King Church of Tokio; Fort Totten, ND Christ the King – Tokio; Fort Totten, ND Seven Dolors Indian Mission.
Leuthardt, Henry '10 (RVC) Ronkonkoma, NY St. Joseph's.
Leva, Stephen F. '88 (PH) Philadelphia, PA St. Timothy.
Levandusky, Edward '65 (PHU) Retired.
LeVasseur, Giles '84 (WH) Moorefield, WV Epiphany of the Lord; Petersburg, WV St. Mary's.
LeVasseur, Lawrence A. *c.s.c.* '51 (SAT)[L] San Antonio, TX Holy Cross Community.
LeVecke, John R. *s.j.* '84 (ORG) Anaheim, CA San Antonio de Padua Del Cañon Church.
LeVecke, John *s.j.* '84 (LA)[P] Culver City, CA Ignatius House, The Novitiate of the California Province, Society of Jesus.
Leveille, Andre E. *c.s.c.* '78 (FTW)[H] Notre Dame, IN Holy Cross Community, Corby Hall, University of Notre Dame; [B] University of Notre Dame Du Lac.
Leveille, Rudolph J. '57 (PRT) Retired.
Leven, Marvin F. '59 (OKL) Special Assignment; [L] Okarche, OK New Leaven Ministries Foundation; Charismatic Renewal Retired.
Levenhagen, Robert J. '57 (DUB) Retired.
Levens, Robert J. *s.j.* '81 (BO)[U] Weston, MA Campion Jesuit Community; [U] Weston, MA Campion Health Center, Inc.
Levesque, Gerald A. '64 (PRT) Retired.
Levesque, Joseph L. *c.m.* '67 (BUF)[N] Niagara University, NY Vincentian Community at Niagara University; [C] Niagara University, NY Niagara University.
Levesque, Robert G. *o.m.i.* '60 (MAN)[K] Colebrook, NH Shrine of Our Lady of Grace.
Levesque, Roger J. '59 (FR) Fall River, MA St. Anne's Retired.
Levesque, Sylvio J. '55 (PRT) Retired.
Levine, Joseph '10 (BAK) Bend, OR St. Francis of Assisi; Jordan Valley, OR St. Bernard; Ontario, OR Blessed Sacrament.
Levis, Robert J. '48 (E) Retired.
Levitt, Donald L. '79 (PEO) Moline, IL Christ the King.
Levko, John J. *s.j.* '78 (SCR)[B] Scranton, PA The University of Scranton.
Levra, Ronald W. '07 (SUP) Retired.
Levreault, Raymond G. '05 (SAV) Douglas, GA St. Paul's; Catholic Cemetery.
Levri, Fid *g.h.m.* '67 (CIN)[N] Cincinnati Headquarters of Glenmary Home Missioners Retired.
Levy, Michael *o.m.i.* '57 (SAT)[K] San Antonio, TX Oblate Madonna Residence.
Lewandowski, Andrew *o.f.m.* '76 (STL)[O] St. Louis, MO Franciscan Friary of St. Anthony of Padua.
Lewandowski, Andrew *c.r.* '89 (RCK) Richmond, IL St. Joseph.
Lewandowski, Bruce *c.ss.r.* '94 (PH) Philadelphia, PA Visitation B.V.M.; By Election; Vicar for Cultural Ministries.
Lewandowski, David J. '55 (HRT) Retired.
Lewandowski, Dennis '85 (JOL) Naperville, IL Holy Spirit Catholic Community.
Lewandowski, Donald R. *o.s.a.* '69 (JOL) New Lenox, IL St. Jude.
Lewandowski, Glen *o.s.c.* '74 (PHX)[F] Crosiers Serving Abroad.
Lewandowski, John '96 (FAR) Retired.
Lewandowski, Leonard A. '77 (PH) Philadelphia, PA St. Josaphat.
Lewandowski, Michael *o.f.m.conv.* '75 (ALT) Davidsville, PA St. Anne.
Lewandowski, Raymond H. '85 (DET) Garden City, MI St. Raphael the Archangel.
Lewandowski, Richard P. '74 (WOR) Retired.
Lewandowski, Ronald C. '95 (CHI) Old Mill Creek, IL St. Raphael the Archangel Retired.
Lewandowski, Theodore V. '98 (RCK) Retired.
Lewandowski, Thomas J. '00 (PIT) New Castle, PA St. Camillus; [P] New Castle, PA Westminster College.
Lewanski, Gary J. '82 (CHI) Other Assignments.
Lewett, George *o.f.m.* '88 (FgM) Washington, DC COMMISSARIAT OF THE HOLY LAND.
Lewicki, Roman B. *s.j.* '65 (FgM) Chicago, IL Society of Jesus.
Lewinski, Cassian *o.p.* '69 (LAV)[C] Las Vegas, NV Dominican Rectory, Fra Angelico House; Las Vegas, NV St. Joseph, Husband of Mary.
Lewinski, Ronald J. '72 (CHI) Mundelein, IL St. Mary of the Annunciation; Deans; [W] Mundelein, IL Foundation for Adult Catechetical Teaching Aids; Frassati Catholic Academy.
Lewis, Alexander Joseph '85 (LA) North Hills, CA Our Lady of Peace; On Sick Leave.
Lewis, Billy '09 (OKL)[C] Oklahoma City, OK Mount St. Mary High School.
Lewis, Clyde A. '64 (OG) Rouses Point, NY St. Joseph; Rouses Point, NY St. Patrick; Committee on Assignments.
Lewis, David C. '04 (BO) Peabody, MA St. Adelaide.
Lewis, David J. '66 (GB) New London, WI Most Precious Blood; Hortonville, WI SS. Peter and Paul.
Lewis, David '90 (CI)[C] Tunnuk, Chuuk, FM Vicariate Residence.
Lewis, Dennis J. '75 (MIL) Milwaukee, WI St. Michael; Milwaukee, WI St. Rose.
Lewis, Dwight P. '11 (SEA) Olympia, WA St. Michael.
Lewis, Emmanuel (FWT) Frisco, TX Holy Cross.
Lewis, Eric Anthony '69 (LA)[J] West Covina, CA Citrus Valley Medical Center, Queen of the Valley Campus; La Puente, CA St. Louis of France; Hospital Chaplains; Hospital Chaplains.
Lewis, Rev. Msgr. Gerald L. '61 (R) New Bern, NC St. Paul Retired.
Lewis, Harry J. '50 (SCR) Retired.
Lewis, James B. (FTW)[B] University of Notre Dame Du Lac.
Lewis, James V. *s.j.* '69 (DET)[K] Clarkston, MI Colombiere Center.
Lewis, James *o.carm.* '83 (JOL)[L] Darien Carmelite Provincial Office.
Lewis, Jeffrey '11 (SPK) Spokane, WA Cathedral of Our Lady of Lourdes.
Lewis, Lawrence J. *m.m.* '75 (NY)[DD] Maryknoll Maryknoll Fathers and Brothers.

Lewis, Leo T. '60 (STL) Retired.
Lewis, Mark *s.j.* '91 (NO)[R] New Orleans, LA Jesuit Provincial Office; New Orleans, LA; New Orleans, LA Immaculate Conception.
Lewis, Ryan P. '99 (OM) Omaha, NE St. Thomas More; Ecumenical Officer; Judges.
Lewis, Walter G. '79 (RIC) Powhatan, VA St. John Neumann.
Lewis, William M. '09 (OKL) Oklahoma City, OK Sacred Heart.
Lewkiewicz, Richard '68 (BRK) Brooklyn, NY Our Lady of Angels.
Lewon, Michal '08 (CHI) Riverside, IL St. Mary.
Lexa, Robert '70 (GB) Retired.
Ley, Philip *o.f.m.conv.* '84 (SAT)[L] San Antonio, TX San Damiano Friary.
Ley, Phillip *o.f.m.conv.* '57 (SAT)[B] San Antonio, TX San Damiano Friary, Prenovitiate House of Formation.
Ley, Richard J. '71 (ARL) Woodstock, VA St. John Bosco.
Ley, Theodore *s.m.* '59 (LA)[F] Marianist Community.
Leyba, John Paul '02 (DEN) Westminster, CO Holy Trinity.
Leykam, Rev. Msgr. John J. '72 (STL) Archdiocesan Consultors; Deaneries/Deans; Ladue, MO Church of the Annunziata.
Leykam, Lambert *o.f.m.* '56 (FWT)[H] Crowley, TX St. Maximilian Kolbe Friary.
Leyland, Thomas J. '65 (TOL) Retired.
Leyrita, Norbert '63 (GR) Retired.
Lhoposo, Jean–Pierre Swamunu *c.i.c.m.* '04 (CHL) Hamlet, NC St. James.
Li, Dong Min (Paul) '07 (HON) Kahuku, HI St. Roch; Presbyteral Council.
Liable, Adrian *o.s.b.* '58 (OM)[J] Elkhorn, NE Mount Michael Benedictine Abbey.
Lianjiang, Bai (BRK) Brooklyn, NY St. Agatha's.
Liaugminas, Andrew '10 (CHI) Park Ridge, IL Mary, Seat of Wisdom.
Libaire, Nathan '81 (SFE) Santa Fe, NM St. John the Baptist.
Libanati, Ciro '62 (SB) Victorville, CA St. Joan of Arc.
Libasci, Peter A. (MAN)[Q] Gilmanton Iron Works, NH Camp Bernadette (Girls); Presbyteral Council; Pastoral Council; Finance Council; Diocesan Bureau of Housing; [Q] Gilmanton Iron Works, NH Camp Fatima.
Libby, Donald L. '05 (GLD) Maple City, MI St. Rita–St. Joseph; Members of the College of Consultors; Cedar, MI Holy Rosary.
Libby, Richard A. '99 (CC) Alice, TX St. Joseph.
Libens, John F. *s.j.* '70 (CLV)[D] Cleveland, OH St. Ignatius High School.
Libera, Thomas A. '69 (CHI) Evanston, IL St. Athanasius.
Liberatore, David D. '60 (CLV) Brecksville, OH St. Basil the Great.
Liberman–Ormaza, Antonio '85 (DAL) Ennis, TX St. John Nepomucene; Ennis, TX Epiphany (Quasi Parish).
Liberty, Donald *c.ss.r.* '61 (STL)[O] Liguori, MO St. Clement Health Care Center Retired.
Liberty, Robert S. '03 (DET) Absent on Leave.
Libiszewski, Dominik Pawel *o.s.p.p.e.* '07 (NY) New York, NY St. Stanislaus Bishop and Martyr.
Libone, John '80 (DAL) Deans; Dallas, TX St. Thomas Aquinas; Adjutant Judicial Vicars; College of Consultors.
Librandi, Michael A. '78 (RCK)[F] Rockford, IL Provena Cor Mariae Center Retired.
Librea, Raphael B. '35 (OM) Retired.
Licanda, Sam '94 (OKL) Okarche, OK Holy Trinity.
Licari, John J. '02 (PT) Pensacola, FL St. Anne's.
Licari, Jonathan *o.s.b.* '76 (SCL) Diocesan Planning Council; [I] Collegeville, MN St. John's Abbey, of the Order of St. Benedict; Defensor Vinculi.
Licciardi, Fred *c.pp.s.* '82 (CIN)[N] Dayton Provincial Office of the Cincinnati Province of the Society of the Precious Blood.
Licciardi, Fred *c.pp.s.* '82 (CHI) Barrington, IL St. Anne.
Licciardi, Giuseppe '67 (DET) Detroit, MI Holy Family.
Lichtenthal, Rev. Msgr. James J. '63 (BUF) Retired.
Lichter, Mark '92 (SFS) Yankton, SD Sacred Heart; Personnel Board.
Lickman, Peter '68 (PSC) Miami, FL St. Basil; Syncellus; Eparchial College of Consultors; Presbyteral Council.
Lickteig, Anthony E. '10 (WDC) Bethesda, MD Little Flower.
Lickteig, Anthony '54 (KCK) Louisburg, KS Retired.
Lickteig, Bernard *o.carm.* '46 (JOL)[L] Darien Carmelite Provincial Office.
Licznerski, Henry *c.r.* '92 (SB) Blythe, CA St. Joan of Arc; [I] Blythe, CA.
Liddy, Rev. Msgr. Richard M. '63 (NEW)[B] Seton Hall University.
Liderbach, Daniel P. *s.j.* '73 (DET)[K] Clarkston, MI Colombiere Center.
Liebert, William *s.v.d.* '57 (CHI)[N] Techny, IL Divine Word Residence Retired.
Lieberth, Joseph '68 (CLV) Administrative Leave.
Liebhardt, Kevin M. '74 (CLV) Eastlake, OH St. Justin Martyr; [F] Eastlake, OH St. Mary Magdalene–St. Justin Martyr School, Inc.; Presbyteral Council.
Liebler, Thomas R. '81 (SFD) Bethalto, IL Our Lady Queen of Peace.
Liebner, David M. '60 (ALN) Girardville, PA St. Vincent de Paul Retired.
Liebner, James *s.v.d.* '85 (FgM) Techny, IL.
Liebscher, Arthur F. *s.j.* '84 (SJ)[B] Santa Clara, CA Jesuit Community.
Liekhus, James C. '05 (STP) Hopkins, MN St. John the Evangelist; Hopkins, MN St. Joseph's.
Liem, Vincent *o.cist.* '10 (NEW) Linden, NJ St. Elizabeth of Hungary.
Lienert, Rev. Msgr. Charles '68 (P) Portland, OR St. Andrew; Area Vicars; Personnel Board.
Lienhard, Joseph T. *s.j.* '71 (NY)[A] Yonkers, NY St. Joseph's Seminary; [DD] Cardinal Spellman Hall, Jesuit Community.
Lies, C. Jarrod '01 (WCH) Viola, KS St. John; Office of Faith Formation.
Lies, David J. '98 (WCH) Derby, KS St. Mary Catholic Church; [K] Derby, KS Engaged Encounter.
Lies, Eric *o.s.b.* '45 (IND)[K] Saint Meinrad, IN St. Meinrad Archabbey.
Lies, James M. *c.s.c.* '97 (FTW)[H] Notre Dame Congregation of Holy Cross, United States Province of Priests & Brothers.
Lies, James *c.s.c.* '97 (P)[B] University of Portland; [L] Portland, OR Holy Cross Fathers & Brothers, C.S.C. – University of Portland.
Lies, William M. *c.s.c.* '94 (FTW)[B] University of Notre Dame Du Lac; [H] Notre Dame, IN Holy Cross Community, Corby Hall, University of Notre Dame; Provincial Councilors:; [H] Notre Dame, IN Congregation of Holy Cross, United States Province of Priests & Brothers.
Lieser, Gregory '63 (SCL) Defensor Vinculi; Deans; Catholic Women, Council of Retired.
Lieser, Vincent '67 (SCL) St. Cloud, MN St. Michael; Waite Park, MN St. Joseph's.
Liewer, David F. '74 (OM) Ponca, NE St. Peter; Ponca, NE St. Joseph.
Lifrak, Richard L. *ss.cc.* '95 (BWN) Board Members; Edinburg, TX Sacred Heart.
Ligato, Anthony F. '95 (ALB) Wynantskill, NY St. Jude the Apostle; Priestly Life and Ministry Council; Presbyteral Council; Diocesan Board of Consultors.
Ligenza, Rafal '11 (VEN) Bradenton, FL St. Joseph.
Ligeti, Angelus *o.f.m.* '79 (DET) Detroit, MI Holy Cross.
Ligeza, Jan A. '03 (STA) Unassigned.
Ligeza, Kazimierz '90 (STA) Gainesville, FL Queen of Peace.
Lightner, Michael '05 (MIL)[X] Milwaukee, WI St. Catherine of Alexandria Catholic Campus Ministry Center, Inc.; Special Assignment; Directors.
Ligonde, Jean–Marie Fritz '89 (VEN) Naples, FL St. Finbarr; Haitian Ministry; Lee County; Presbyteral Council.
Ligory, Joseph '83 (NY) Bronx, NY St. Helena.
Ligot, Andres C. '92 (SJ) Judicial Vicar; Judicial Vicar; Special Assignment; Saratoga, CA Church of the Ascension.
Liguori, Christopher '03 (STA) Jacksonville, FL St. Patrick.
Liistro, Frank J. '74 (WOR) Retired.
Lijewski, Thomas F. '70 (MIL) Port Washington, WI St. Peter of Alcantara; Saukville, WI Immaculate Conception; Port Washington, WI St. Mary.
Lijewski, Timothy M. '93 (CHR) Conway, SC St. James.
Lijo, Thomas *c.m.i.* '05 (SHP) Monroe, LA St. Matthew.
Lill, Kenneth J. '91 (TOL) Fremont, OH Sacred Heart.
Lillpopp, Michael '05 (MO) West Springfield, MA St. Frances Xavier Cabrini Parish; Air Force Reserve Chaplains.
Lilly, Robert A. *m.m.* '62 (NY)[DD] Retired.
Lilly, Robert M. *m.m.* '60 (FgM) Maryknoll, NY MARYKNOLL.
Lilly, Thomas C. '03 (ANC) Anchorage, AK St. Elizabeth Ann Seton; Vicar General; Diocesan Consultors; Air Force Reserve Chaplains; Unalaska, AK Corp. of St. Christopher By the Sea Church; Director of Seminarians.
Lim, Candido *s.j.* '69 (SJ)[M] Los Gatos, CA Sacred Heart Jesuit Center.
Lim, Carmelo Rey '95 (HON) Waianae, HI Sacred Heart; Members.
Lim, Joseph (NY) Rye, NY Resurrection.
Lim, Marc '07 (OM) Omaha, NE Mary Our Queen.
Lim, Roque G. '06 (BAL) Baltimore, MD St. Joseph.
Lima, John H. '63 (OAK) Retired.
Lima, Vivian B. '85 (LA) Woodland Hills, CA St. Mel.
Limmer, George A. '64 (BAL) Retired.
Limpiado, Edwin *c.s.s.* (MRY) Youth and Young Adult Ministry; Presbyteral Council; Carmel, CA San Carlos Borromeo Basilica.
Linago, Deogracias '64 (NY) Staten Island, NY Staten Island University Hospital South.
Linakis, William *s.a.* '77 (NY)[DD] Garrison Franciscan Friars of the Atonement, Minister General Office.
Linares, Jose R. '86 (MGZ) Cabo Rojo, PR St. Michael.
Lincoln, Daniel L. '84 (L) Vine Grove, KY St. John the Baptist; Vine Grove, KY St. Brigid.
Lincoln, Howard A. '91 (SB) Palm Desert, CA Christ of the Desert; Palm Desert, CA Sacred Heart; Elected At–Large Members.
Lincon, Joseph B. (TYL) Longview, TX St. Anthony.
Lincon, Joseph '89 (BGP) On Duty Outside the Diocese.
Lind, Rev. Msgr. Joseph G. '65 (BO) Senior Priests.; Wellesley, MA St. Paul Retired.
Lind, Thomas *s.c.j.* '58 (JKS)[E] Nesbit, MS St. Michael Community House.
Lindblad, Karl–Albert '87 (MO) Military Chaplains; Navy Chaplains.
Lindemann, Gene E. '83 (BIS) Bismarck, ND St. Mary; Judicial Vicar; Presbyteral Council; Office of Worship.
Lindemann, Gene '83 (BIS) Pro–Synodal Judges.
Linden, Emmet *c.p.* '51 (L)[L] Louisville, KY Sacred Heart Retreat.
Linden, John '07 (LAN) Department of Formation and Lay Ministry; Director of Seminarians; Joseph H. Albers Trust Fund for Diocesan Vocations; Emmaus House.
Linden, Michael D. *s.j.* '80 (BO)[U] Watertown, MA The Society of Jesus of New England–Provincial Offices; Presbyteral Council; Watertown, MA Society of Jesus.
Linden, Michael J. *s.j.* '80 (FgM) Watertown, MA; Watertown, MA Society of Jesus.
Linden, Phillip J. *s.s.j.* '69 (NO) Gray, LA St. Nicholas of Myra Byzantine Catholic Mission.
Linden, Phillip J. *s.s.j.* '69 (PBR) New Orleans, LA St. Nicholas of Myra Mission.
Lindenfelser, Timothy M. '94 (STA) Elkton, FL St. Ambrose; St. Augustine, FL St. Augustine Diocesan Cemeteries; Judicial Vicar.
Linder, Rev. Msgr. William J. '63 (NEW) Newark, NJ St. Rose of Lima.
Lindle, Lawrence H. '59 (L)[P] Louisville, KY Perpetual Eucharistic Adoration; [P] Louisville, KY World Apostolate of Fatima (Blue Army); [P] Louisville, KY Sacred Heart Apostolate; [P] Louisville, KY Archdiocesan Marian Committee; Sacred Heart Enthronement Center Retired.
Lindley, Philip '83 (AMA) Unassigned.
Lindner, Jerold W. *s.j.* '76 (SJ)[M] Los Gatos, CA Sacred Heart Jesuit Center.
Lindner, Thomas F. '95 (LC) Stevens Point, WI Newman University Parish; [K] Stevens Point, WI Newman University Parish; Deans.
Lindsay, Michael P. '87 (MO) Defenders of the Bond; Army National Guard Chaplains.
Lindsay, Michael '87 (LSC) Priests Retirement Fund Committee.
Lindsay, Stewart M. *o.s.f.s.* '74 (BUF)[K] Lewiston, NY Mount St. Mary's Hospital of Niagara Falls; Niagara Falls, NY Holy Family of Jesus, Mary and Joseph.
Lindsey, John '10 (JOL) Downers Grove, IL St. Joseph.
Lindsey, Robert *c.ss.r.* '09 (KC)[J] Kansas City, MO Redemptorists Fathers of Kansas City, Missouri; Kansas City, MO Our Lady of Perpetual Help.
Lindstrom, Michael *s.v.d.* '82 (FgM) Techny, IL.
Linebach, Martin A. '87 (L) Louisville, KY St. Patrick; Ex Officio; Ecumenical and Interreligious Relations Officer.
Linehan, Dennis M. *s.j.* '72 (PH) Philadelphia, PA Old St. Joseph's Retired.
Linehan, Maurice F. *m.s.* '52 (HRT)[L] Hartford, CT Missionaries of LaSalette.
Linehan, Michael '71 (CC) Retired.
Linehan, Stephen J. '75 (BO) Westwood, MA St. Margaret Mary.
Lingan, Joseph E. *s.j.* '90 (WDC)[O] Washington, DC The Jesuit Community at Georgetown University.
Lingao, Deogracias (NY) Staten Island, NY Sacred Heart.
Lingle, Brent C. '07 (SC) Department of Formation and Ministry; Sioux City, IA Cathedral of the Epiphany; Building Commission; Presbyteral Council.
Linhares, William P. *t.o.r., u.f.* '84 (WH)[D] Kearneysville, WV Priest Field Pastoral Center; Vicars Forane; Councilors.
Linhares, William P. *t.o.r.* '84 (ALT)[G] Hollidaysburg, PA Province Econome's Office.
Lininger, Paul *o.f.m.conv.* (WDC)[O] Silver Spring, MD Gemelli House.
Link, David T. '08 (GRY) Retired.
Link, David '91 (OAK)[K] Oakland, CA Bishop Begin Villa; Bishop's Representative for Eastern Rite Catholics.
Link, Fred *o.f.m.* '70 (CIN) Cincinnati, OH St. Clement; [N] Cincinnati, OH St. Clement Friary.
Link, Frederick G. '69 (CAM) Haddonfield, NJ St. Joseph the Worker Parish, Haddon Township, N.J.
Link, Mark J. *s.j.* '60 (DET)[K] Clarkston, MI Colombiere Center.
Link, Matthew B. *c.pp.s* (SFR) Tiburon, CA St. Hilary.
Linkchorst, William J. '73 (ALN) Tamaqua, PA SS. Peter and Paul.
Linn, Matthew L. *s.j.* '73 (STP)[J] Minneapolis, MN

Markoe House Jesuit Community.
Linnan, John E. *c.s.v.* '61 (CHI)[N] Arlington Heights Viatorian Province Center–Clerics of St. Viator.
Linnan, Roger J. '62 (SC) Hawarden, IA St. Mary's; Directors; Presbyteral Council; Akron, IA St. Patrick.
Linnane, Brian F. *s.j.* '86 (BO)[U] Boston The Society of Jesus of New England–Provincial Offices.
Linnane, Brian F. *s.j.* '86 (BAL)[B] Timonium, MD Loyola Graduate Center–Timonium Campus; [Q] Baltimore, MD Jesuit Community of Loyola University, Inc.; [B] Baltimore, MD Loyola University in Maryland; [B] Jesuit Community of Loyola University, Inc.
Linnebur, Leroy '61 (WCH) Retired.
Linnebur, Michael '08 (WCH)[A] Wichita, KS Newman University.
Linowski, Eugene R. '57 (PRM) Retired.
Lins, James R. '64 (MAD) Retired.
Linse, Henry *c.s.s.* '48 (BO)[X] Waltham, MA Stigmatine Fathers and Brothers Retired.
Linsky, Gary S. '95 (MO) Military Chaplains; Air Force Chaplains.
Linsler, Christopher E. '78 (ROC) Horseheads, NY St. Mary Our Mother.
Linster, Rev. Msgr. Joseph B. '69 (RCK) Saint Charles, IL St. Patrick; Deans.
Linton, Edward *o.s.b.* '91 (CHI) Chicago, IL St. James.
Linton, Edward *o.s.b.* '91 (IND)[K] Saint Meinrad St. Meinrad Archabbey.
Lintz, Charles *s.s.c.* '70 (OM)[J] St. Columbans, NE Missionary Society of St. Columban; Omaha, NE Our Lady of Guadalupe – St. Agnes Parish.
Lintzenich, Stephen P. '74 (EVN) Evansville, IN St. John the Apostle; Evansville, IN St. Joseph; Evansville, IN St. Mary; Clergy Personnel Board; Judges; Diocesan Council of Priests; Special Assignment; Diocesan Consultors.
Linzmaier, Eric G. '00 (LC) Durand, WI St. Mary's Assumption; Durand, WI Holy Rosary; Durand, WI Sacred Heart of Jesus.
Lioi, Frank E. '67 (ROC) Auburn, NY St. Mary.
Lion, William J. '58 (CHI) Oak Lawn, IL St. Catherine of Alexandria Retired.
Lionelli, Anthony J. '72 (NEW) Montclair, NJ Our Lady of Mt. Carmel.
Lipareli, Michael A. '80 (PH) Philadelphia, PA Veterans Administration Medical Center.
Lipareli, Michael A. '80 (MO) DEPARTMENT OF VETERANS AFFAIRS HOSPITALS AND CHAPLAINS.
Lipiec, Bartholomew W. '83 (BUF) Depew, NY St. Martha.
Lipinski, Edward J. '71 (CAM) Turnersville, NJ The Church of Saints Peter and Paul, Washington Township, N.J.
Lipinski, Paul M. '73 (RCK) Special Assignment; [B] Rockford, IL Boylan Central Catholic High School.
Lipka, Wieslaw '65 (KAL) Kalamazoo, MI St. Monica.
Lipnicki, Thomas P. '78 (NEW) Oakland, NJ Our Lady of Perpetual Help; Northwest Bergen Region Deanery 1; Cursillo Movement.
Liporace, Francisco *i.v.e.* '93 (CHI) Chicago, IL St. Francis of Assisi.
Lipp, John F. *o.s.a.* '54 (PH)[Y] Villanova, PA St. Thomas Monastery.
Lippert, Donald F. *o.f.m.cap* '85 (WDC)[X] Washington, DC Spanish Catholic Center.
Lippert, Donald *o.f.m.cap.* '85 (FgM) Pittsburgh, PA Province of St. Augustine.
Lippert, Paul R. '61 (MIL) Retired.
Lippold, John L. '57 (BAL) Retired.
Lipps, Rev. Msgr. Frank J. '68 (NO) Slidell, LA Our Lady of Lourdes.
Lipps, Lewis J. *s.j.* '52 (DET)[K] Clarkston, MI Colombiere Center.
Lippstock, Paul E. '78 (DUB) Britt, IA St. Patrick; Forest City, IA St. Patrick; Garner, IA St. Wenceslaus; Forest City, IA St. James; Garner, IA St. Boniface; Forest City, IA St. Patrick; Military Chaplains.
Lippstock, Paul Eldon '78 (MO) Army National Guard Chaplains.
Liprie, James *o.s.b.* '83 (LAF)[H] Opelousas, LA Mother of the Redeemer Monastery.
Lipscomb, John B. (SP)[P] Lutz, FL Bethany Center, Inc.
Lipscomb, William W. '97 (GLD) Members of the College of Consultors.
Liptak, Rev. Msgr. David Q. '53 (HRT) Hartford, CT Cathedral of St. Joseph; Special and other Archdiocesan Assignment; [A] Cromwell, CT Holy Apostles College and Seminary; Newspaper; Censor Librorum.
Liptak, Edward *s.d.b.* '59 (SFR) San Francisco, CA Corpus Christi.
LiPuma, Rev. Msgr. David G. '87 (BUF) Secretary to Diocesan Bishop and Vice Chancellor; [N] Buffalo, NY Bishop's Residence.
Lira, Juan Pineda *m.s.c.* '77 (FRS) Huron, CA St. Frances Cabrini; Avenal, CA St. Joseph.
Lis, Albert *o.f.m.* '86 (MIL)[N] Greenfield, WI Clement Manor Health Center; [Y] Greenfield, WI Clement Manor Retirement Community; [P] Provincial Offices of the Franciscan Friars, Assumption BVM Province, Inc.
Lis, John S. '73 (SPR) Agawam, MA St. John the Evangelist Retired.
Lis, Pawel '03 (DET)[A] Orchard Lake, MI SS. Cyril and Methodius Seminary.
Lisante, Rev. Msgr. James P. '81 (RVC) Massapequa Park, NY Our Lady of Lourdes.
Lisbeth, Michael *s.m.* '80 (CIN)[N] Dayton, OH Marianist Community, Novitiate.
Lischwe, Bruno V. *c.ss.r.* '52 (STL)[O] Liguori, MO St. Clement Health Care Center.
Liscinsky, Steven *l.c.* '02 (MAN)[A] Center Harbor, NH Immaculate Conception Apostolic School.
Lisik, Paul A. '81 (GBG) Greensburg, PA Our Lady of Grace; College of Consultors.
Liska, Richard A. '70 (MIL) Oak Creek, WI St. Stephen.
Lisowski, Edward E. '64 (MIL) Retired.
Lisowski, Lawrence M. '84 (CHI) Lemont, IL SS. Cyril and Methodius.
Lisowski, William J. '50 (CHI) Chicago, IL St. Florian; Chicago, IL St. Ladislaus Retired.
Liss, Robert C. '62 (STL) Richwoods, MO St. Stephen.
Lisson, Edwin *s.j.* '69 (STL)[C] Saint Louis University; [O] St. Louis, MO Jesuit Community Corporation at Saint Louis University – Jesuit Hall.
List, John E. '85 (LEX) Judicial Vicar; Lexington, KY St. Peter.
Liston, Rev. Msgr. Daniel P. '85 (SPR) Springfield, MA St. Michael's Cathedral; Vicar for Canonical Affairs and Chancellor; Judges; Bishop's Commission for Clergy; Bishop's Cabinet; Diocesan Consultors; Presbyteral Council.
Liston, Paul F. '58 (WDC)[X] Washington, DC Catholic Historical Society of Washington; [M] Washington, DC Cardinal O'Boyle Residence for Priests Retired.
Liszewski, Francis A. '69 (NOR) Retired.
Liszewski, Peter B. '78 (NOR) Westbrook, CT St. Mark; Continuing Education and Formation Commission for the Clergy.
Litak, Czeslaw (STL) Saint Louis, MO St. Agatha Parish, Polish Roman Catholic Church.
Litavec, Edward S. '60 (PIT) Pittsburgh, PA Sacred Heart Retired.
Litcheck, Michael P. '71 (SCR) Retired.
Literal, Peter (BAL) Baltimore, MD Cathedral of Mary Our Queen.
Literski, Rev. Msgr. Roy E. '53 (WIN) Tucson, AZ Retired.
Litke, Jared Austin *o.p.* '11 (WDC)[B] Washington, DC Dominican House of Studies.
Litot, Rev. Msgr. Edward F. '47 (GRY) Judges Retired.
Littelmann, Edward J. '69 (TOL) College of Consultors; Spiritual Directors Retired.
Little, Rev. Msgr. Anthony B. '82 (ALT) Newry, PA St. Patrick's.
Little, John '88 (ALN) Pottsville, PA St. Patrick.
Littlefield, Philaret '87 (NTN) Milwaukee, WI St. George; Protopresbyters; Associated Melkite Charities; College of Eparchial Consultors; Presbyteral Council.
Litwack, Joshua E. '00 (TLS) Wilburton, OK Sacred Heart.
Litwin, Rev. Msgr. Paul A. '79 (BUF) The Diocese of Buffalo, N.Y.; Chancellor; [N] Buffalo, NY Bishop's Residence; [A] East Aurora, NY Christ the King Seminary; Finance Council.
Litzau, Richard *o.p.* '05 (CHI)[N] Chicago Dominicans (Provincial Office).
Litzau, Richard *o.p.* '05 (SFE)[K] Albuquerque, NM St. Thomas Aquinas (Newman Center) University Parish; Albuquerque, NM St. Thomas Aquinas University Parish.
Litzner, Corey J. '04 (MAR) Stephenson, MI Precious Blood Church; Consultors; Menominee, MI Holy Redeemer.
Liu, Daniel '08 (AUS) Associate Directors; Presbyteral Council.
Liu, Peter T. '60 (RVC) Ronkonkoma, NY St. Joseph's Retired.
Liu, Pius *o.f.m.* '53 (FgM) New York, NY Holy Name Province.
Liuzzi, Kenneth J. '75 (DEN) Denver, CO St. Francis de Sales.
Liuzzi, Peter J. *o.carm.* '65 (LA) North Hollywood, CA St. Jane Frances de Chantal.
Liuzzo, Vincent *o.f.m.cap.* '49 (PAT) Passaic, NJ Our Lady Of Mt. Carmel.
Lively, Gregory '01 (HEL) Eureka, MT Our Lady of Mercy.
Lively, Joseph A. '57 (BUR) Retired.
Livigni, Salvatore '61 (BAL) Baltimore, MD St. Michael Retired.
Livigni, Salvatore '61 (BAL) Office of Pastoral Service for Senior and Retired Clergy.
Livingston, Benedict *s.p.* '72 (STL)[O] Saint Louis, MO Servants of the Paraclete.
Livingston, James T. '90 (STP) North Memorial Hospital.
Livingston, James '91 (DET) Absent on Leave.
Livingston, James (DM) Des Moines, IA St. Augustin's.
Livingstone, Benedict *s.p.* '72 (STL)[S] Dittmer, MO Vianney Renewal Center; [V] Dittmer, MO Servants of the Paraclete Missouri Generalate Corporation.
Livingstone, James W. '03 (SFR) Retired.
Livojevich, Ronald '70 (KCK) Retired.
Lizalde, Jesus '93 (GAL) Baytown, TX Our Lady of Guadalupe.
Lizama, Sergio *s.a.c.* '06 (MIL)[P] Milwaukee, WI Pallotti House; Burlington, WI St. Charles.
Lizarraga, Candido *rr.t.c.* '41 (SJN)[F] Santurce, PR Casa de Ninos Manuel Fernandez Juncos.
Lizarralde, Jose *c.p.* '69 (MGZ) San Sebastian, PR San Sebastian Martir.
Lizcano, Otoniel '99 (BGP) Danbury, CT St. Gregory the Great.
Lizewski, John M. '99 (WOR) Worcester, MA Christ the King.
Lizinczyk, Tadeusz '98 (PH)[Y].
Lizio, John R. '57 (BO) Senior Priests. Retired.
Lizor, Rev. Msgr. Joseph S. '58 (BAL) Edgemere, MD St. Luke.
Llamas, Rodolfo D. '93 (SAC) Elk Grove, CA St. Joseph.
Llambias, Martin '73 (SJN)[G] Guaynabo, PR Opus Dei; San Juan.
Llanos, Philip S. '78 (LA) Military Chaplains.
Lleo, Pedro '76 (MIA) Retired.
LLona, German *o.ss.t.* '61 (ARE) Isabela, PR Our Lady of Mount Carmel.
Llorente, Ignacio '09 (P) Corvallis, OR St. Mary; [P] Corvallis, OR Newman Center at Oregon State University (Corvallis).
Lloyd, C. Todd '11 (BR) Baton Rouge, LA Christ the King; [K] Baton Rouge, LA Christ the King Parish and Catholic Center.
Lloyd, James B. *c.s.p.* '48 (NY)[DD] New York, NY Paulist Fathers' Motherhouse Retired.
Lloyd, Patrick *s.c.j.* '69 (GB) Appointed Members; Tigerton, WI St. Mary; Tigerton, WI St. Mary; Tigerton, WI St. Anthony; Tigerton, WI Holy Family–St. William.
Lloyd, Philip P. '78 (GAL) Houston, TX St. Theresa.
Lloyd, Robert J. *m.m.* '62 (NY)[DD] Maryknoll Maryknoll Fathers and Brothers Retired.
Llywelyn, Dorian *s.j.* '90 (LA)[C] Los Angeles, CA Jesuit Community.
Loaiza, Jorge H. '98 (RCK) Elgin, IL St. Mary; Saint Charles, IL St. Patrick.
Lobacz, James E. '79 (MIL) Special Assignment.
Lobato, Nicanor '61 (VEN) Retired.
Lobaton, Jose Ruben *o.f.m.* '73 (TYL) Wills Point, TX St. Luke.
Lobert, Richard C. '75 (BAL) On Duty Outside the Archdiocese.
Lobert, Richard C. '75 (LAN)[B] Ann Arbor, MI Father Gabriel Richard High School.
LoBianco, Rev. Msgr. Francis R. '54 (NEW) Retired.
LoBianco, Paschal *s.v.d.* '50 (CHI)[N] Techny, IL Divine Word Residence.
LoBianco, Richard J. '79 (CHI) Norridge, IL Divine Savior.
LoBiondo, Gasper F. *s.j.* '68 (WDC)[O] Washington, DC Woodstock Jesuit Community; [X] Washington, DC Woodstock Theological Center; [O] Washington, DC The Jesuit Community at Georgetown University.
Lobo, Benjamin '63 (GF) Retired.
Lobo, Joseph *s.j.* '97 (OAK)[L] Berkeley, CA Jesuit Fathers and Brothers.
Lobo, Raul Venust '62 (NO) Retired.
Lobo, Simon C. *c.c.* '09 (DET) Youth, Young Adults and Campus Ministries; Detroit, MI St. Scholastica.
Lobo, Stanley M. '65 (NEW) Palisades Park, NJ St. Michael's Retired.
Lobon, Simon *c.ss.sp.* '90 (DET) Detroit, MI St. Mary.
Loc, Paul '08 (NY) Bronx, NY Immaculate Conception.
Loch, Killian (Kev) *o.s.b.* '79 (SCR) On Duty Outside the Diocese.
Lock, Bertram *ss.cc.* '89 (HON) Waialua, HI St. Michael.
Lockard, Rev. Msgr. David A. '75 (ALT) State College, PA Our Lady of Victory.
Locke, James E. '61 (PH) Retired.
Lockey, Paul E. '87 (GAL) Houston, TX St. Elizabeth Ann Seton.
Lockman, James *o.f.m.* (OAK)[Q] Board of Directors.
Lockman, Rev. Msgr. V. James '67 (WDC) Washington, DC Annunciation.
Lockulu, Jean Paulin '95 (JUN) Craig, AK St. John by the Sea; Diocesan Consultors.
Lockwood, Gregory J. '88 (KC) Kansas City, MO Christ the King; Special Assignment; Vocation Office.
Lococo, Donald J. *c.s.b.* '90 (ROC)[K] Rochester, NY Basilian Residence.
Loda, Mauro *s.x.* '99 (FgM)[N] Wayne Xaverian Missionary Fathers; Wayne, NJ XAVERIAN MISSIONARY FATHERS.
Lodge, John G. '73 (CHI)[A] Mundelein, IL University of St. Mary of the Lake/Mundelein Seminary; [A] Mundelein, IL University of St. Mary of the Lake/Mundelein Seminary.

Lodge, Richard J. '69 (CAM) Collingswood, NJ Most Precious Blood Parish, Collingswood, N.J.
Lodi, George C. '74 (NY) Shrub Oak, NY Saint Elizabeth Ann Seton.
Lody, John '62 (Y) Retired.
Loeb, Karl E. '95 (BUF) Attica, NY SS. Joachim & Anne.
Loebl, Jeffrey R. *s.j.* '82 (MIL)[P] Wauwatosa, WI Jesuit Community at St. Camillus.
Loecke, Douglas J. '89 (DUB) Cascade, IA St. Patrick; Investment Committee; Cascade, IA St. Peter; Cascade, IA St. Matthias; Cascade, IA Sacred Heart; Judges; Directors.
Loecker, Craig J. '92 (OM) Omaha, NE St. Philip Neri; Omaha, NE Blessed Sacrament.
Loegering, Leonard '73 (FAR) Milnor, ND St. Arnold's Church of Milnor; Wyndmere, ND St. John the Baptist.
Loehr, Charles D. '47 (MIL) Retired.
Loehr, James P. '67 (MIL) Retired.
Loehrlein, Richard A. *s.m.* '61 (STL)[O] St. Louis Marianists, Province of the United States (Society of Mary).
Loeper, David J. '83 (ALN) Pottsville, PA St. John the Baptist.
Loeper, Rev. Msgr. Richard J. '50 (ALN) Douglassville, PA Immaculate Conception; Bethlehem, PA Holy Ghost Retired.
Loera, Abel '03 (LA) Los Angeles, CA Mother of Sorrows; Los Angeles, CA St. Malachy.
Loesch, Robert (ALB) Ecumenical and Interreligious Affairs of the Roman Catholic Diocese of Albany, Commission for.
Loew, James H. *o.s.b.* '97 (GBG) Vandergrift, PA St. Gertrude; [H] Latrobe, PA Saint Vincent Archabbey.
Lofgren, Eric '93 (SAC) Lincoln, CA St. Joseph.
Loftin, Don '94 (AUS) Lago Vista, TX Our Lady of the Lake Catholic Church – Lago Vista, Texas.
Lofton, Rev. Msgr. Edward D. '82 (CHR) Summerville, SC St. Theresa the Little Flower; Continuing Education for Priests; Bishop's Missionary Support Committee; Holy Childhood Association; Propagation of the Faith; Priest Retirement Committee.
Lofton, James J. '61 (ALN) Retired.
Loftus, David C. '94 (LA) Northridge, CA Our Lady of Lourdes.
Loftus, John Allan *s.j.* '74 (BO)[U] Newton, MA The Jesuit Community at Boston College; Newton, MA St. Ignatius Loyola.
Loftus, Kenneth G. *s.j.* '91 (BO) Newton, MA St. Ignatius Loyola; [U] Newton, MA The Jesuit Community at Boston College.
Loftus, Rev. Msgr. Padraic '62 (LA) Retired.
Loftus, Robert A. '91 (WOR) Leicester, MA St. Joseph; Leicester, MA St. Pius X.
Loftus, Steven P. '02 (PEO) Rock Island, IL St. Mary; Rock Island, IL Sacred Heart; Rock Island, IL St. Joseph's; [B] Rock Island, IL Alleman High School.
Loftus, Thomas *c.ss.r.* '57 (HBG)[G] Ephrata, PA St. Clement's Mission House Retired.
Logan, Aidan (Arthur H.) *o.c.s.o.* '85 (WOR)[N] Spencer, MA St. Joseph's Abbey.
Logan, Rev. Msgr. Daniel B. '63 (STA) Ponte Vedra Beach, FL Our Lady Star of the Sea; Associate Judges.
Logan, Gary '93 (SR) Retired.
Logan, Hugh *s.m.a.* (WDC) Bethesda, MD St. Bartholomew.
Logan, James J. '59 (LC) Retired.
Logan, Rev. Msgr. James T. '54 (FRS) Diocesan Consultors Retired.
Logan, Jerry '79 (PEO) Rock Island, IL St. Pius X.
Logan, John *o.carm.* '64 (NY)[DD] Middletown, NY St. Albert's Priory; Middletown, NY Our Lady of Mt. Carmel.
Logan, William R. '69 (RVC) West Islip, NY Consolation Nursing Home.
LoGatto, Joseph J. '57 (PAT) Retired.
Loggiodice, Omar '09 (ATL) Athens, GA St. Joseph.
Logrip, Rev. Msgr. Joseph L. '72 (PH)[V] Lansdale, PA St. Mary Manor.
Logsdon, L. Peter *c.s.c.* '68 (AUS) New Rochelle, NY Eastern Brothers Province; [G] Austin, TX Brother Andre Residence.
Logsdon, Wilfrid *o.f.m.conv.* '59 (SAV) Brunswick, GA St. Francis Xavier.
Logue, Charles D. '48 (BO) Senior Priests. Retired.
Logue, Mark '73 (BAL) West River, MD Our Lady of Sorrows.
Lohan, Louis '71 (BLX) Long Beach, MS St. Thomas the Apostle; College of Consultors; Presbyteral Council.
Lohan, William P. (BO) Wrentham, MA St. Mary.
Lohr, Charles H. *s.j.* '61 (NY)[DD] New York, NY Murray–Weigel Hall.
Lohrmeyer, Kenneth P. '70 (SAL) Minneapolis, KS Immaculate Conception of the Blessed Virgin Mary Parish; Judicial Vicar–Officialis; Associate Judges; Minneapolis, KS St. Mary Parish.
Lohse, Edward M. '89 (E) On Duty Outside Diocese.
Loi, Nguyen '68 (OM) Omaha, NE Our Lady of Fatima Catholic Community.
Loiacono, James A. *o.m.i.* '79 (LAR) Eagle Pass, TX Our Lady of Refuge; Ex Officio Members.
LoJacono, Joseph *i.v.e.* '09 (WIN) Mankato, MN SS. Peter and Paul's.
Lojek, Robert J. '03 (CHI) Chicago, IL St. William; Deans.
Lokanga, Daniel '86 (BUR) St. Albans, VT Holy Angels.
Lolio, Rev. Msgr. John W. '70 (PRO) East Greenwich, RI Our Lady of Mercy; Deans.
Lomasiewicz, Donald E. '62 (GR) Grand Rapids, MI St. Isidore.
Lomax, Mark '80 (NO) Slidell, LA St. Luke the Evangelist; Deans.
Lombard, Richard J. '53 (SHP) Shreveport, LA St. Joseph; Advocates.
Lombard, Roy A. '47 (WH) Retired.
Lombardi, Gary '69 (SR) Petaluma, CA St. Vincent de Paul.
Lombardi, John J. '92 (BAL) Hancock, MD St. Peter's; St. Vincent de Paul Society.
Lombardi, Joseph L. *s.j.* '75 (PH)[C] Jesuit Fathers; [Y] Loyola Center and Manresa Hall.
Lombardi, Nicholas D. *s.j.* '72 (NY)[DD] Cardinal Spellman Hall, Jesuit Community.
Lombardi, Thomas '75 (FTW) Fort Wayne, IN St. Joseph.
Lombardo, Francis *o.f.m.conv.* '71 (BUF)[N] Athol Springs, NY St. Francis of Assisi Friary; Williamsville, NY St. Gregory the Great.
Lombardo, Gerard Michael '86 (NEW) Bayonne, NJ Saint Michael and Saint Joseph.
Lombardo, Joseph A. '85 (TUC) Tucson, AZ Roman Catholic Church of Saint Elizabeth Ann Seton – Tucson.
Lombardo, Michael D. '78 (PAT) Wayne, NJ Our Lady of Consolation.
Lombardo, Nicholas E. *o.p.* '04 (WDC)[B] Washington, DC Dominican House of Studies; [C] Catholic University of America, The.
Lombardo, Robert *c.f.r.* '90 (NY)[DD] New York, NY St. Joseph's Friary.
Lomeli, Pastor Hermosillo *m.s.c.* '79 (FRS) Earlimart, CA St. Jude Thaddeus.
Lomello, Lucian B. *s.d.b.* '48 (LA)[P] Los Angeles, CA Dominic Savio Salesian Residence Retired.
Lomibao, Conrado (NY) Bronx, NY Our Lady of Mercy.
Lomica, Frank A. '02 (DEN) Brush, CO St. Mary.
LoMonaco, Lawrence M. '02 (CHL) Waynesville, NC St. John the Evangelist.
Lonardo, Alfred C. '63 (PRO) Retired.
Loncar, Stephen *o.f.m.conv.* '88 (GRY) Gary, IN St. Joseph The Worker.
Lonchyna, Taras '77 (PHU) Silver Spring, MD Holy Trinity; Pro–Life and Family Ministry.
Loncle, John '05 (ROC) Fairport, NY Assumption of the Blessed Virgin Mary.
Londono, Hugo Leon *m.s.c.* '03 (CHI) Chicago, IL St. Joseph.
Londono, Hugo Leon *m.s.c.* '03 (RCK)[G].
Londono, Hugo '62 (ORL) Retired.
Londono, Hugo '11 (MIL) Milwaukee, WI St. Hyacinth; Milwaukee, WI Prince of Peace/Principe de Paz; Milwaukee, WI St. Vincent de Paul.
Londono Zuluaga, Edwin Albeiro '07 (SJN) Vocations Promoter; Spiritual Directors.
Lone, Henry Saw '94 (SAL) Hill City, KS Immaculate Heart of Mary Parish; Damar, KS St. Joseph Parish.
Lonek, Stephen C. '76 (WIL) Secretary, MD Our Lady of Good Counsel.
Lonergan, David W. '61 (HRT) Retired.
Lonergan, J. Barry '66 (ALB) Retired.
Lonergan, Lester *m.h.m.* '62 (NY)[DD] Hartsdale, NY Mill Hill Fathers Residence Retired.
Lonergan, Michael J. '93 (PH) Bensalem, PA St. Elizabeth Ann Seton.
Long, Anthony Vu Khac '92 (RCK) DeKalb, IL St. Mary; Special Assignment.
Long, Daniel '94 (CHI) Chicago, IL Epiphany.
Long, David P. '02 (PAT) Absent on Leave.
Long, Galen '91 (SAL) Plainville, KS Sacred Heart Parish; Plainville, KS St. Thomas Parish.
Long, Garrett J. *s.m.* '76 (RVC)[D] Mineola, NY Chaminade High School (Boys); [N] Mineola, NY Provincial Residence and Novitiate; Mineola, NY.
Long, J. William '89 (R) Ahoskie, NC St. Charles Borromeo.
Long, James T. '63 (BEL) Retired.
Long, Jeffrey D. '06 (SFD) Pierron, IL Immaculate Conception; Pierron, IL St. Nicholas; Jacksonville, IL Jacksonville Correctional Center; Commission for the Care of Infirm and Retired Priests; Priests' Personnel Board.
Long, John R. '89 (SUP) Gilman, WI SS. Peter and Paul; Gilman, WI St. Michael; Gilman, WI St. Stanislaus; Gilman, WI St. John the Apostle.
Long, John '61 (JC) Retired.
Long, John '78 (STP) Brooklyn Park, MN St. Vincent de Paul.
Long, Joseph J. *c.s.c.* '59 (ORL)[F] Cocoa Beach, FL Congregation of Holy Cross, United States Province Retired.
Long, Joseph J. *c.s.c.* '59 (SCR)[B] Wilkes–Barre, PA King's College Retired.
Long, Joseph J. *c.s.c.* '59 (FTW)[H] Notre Dame Congregation of Holy Cross, United States Province of Priests & Brothers.
Long, Mark J. '07 (TUC) Tucson, AZ Saint Ambrose Roman Catholic Parish – Tucson.
Long, Matthew Tyler '09 (SHP) Monroe, LA Jesus the Good Shepherd.
Long, Melvin '66 (SAL) Retired.
Long, Nathan '08 (LKC) Clergy Formation; Scouting; Vocation Recruiters.
Long, Nguyen Phi *c.ss.r.* '03 (LA)[P] Baldwin Park Vietnamese Redemptorist Mission.
Long, Richard E. '90 (BRK)[D] Brooklyn, NY Campus Ministers and Ministry Centers; Brooklyn, NY St. Cecilia.
Long, Stuart '07 (HEL) Health Leave.
Long, Thomas E. *c.s.v.* '69 (CHI)[N] Chicago, IL Viatorian Residence; [N] Arlington Heights Viatorian Province Center–Clerics of St. Viator.
Long, Thomas '91 (GB)[O] Green Bay, WI Teens Encounter Christ (TEC), Green Bay Chapter; Newton, WI St. Thomas the Apostle.
Long, Vincent P. '69 (SY) Hinckley, NY St. Ann; Holland Patent, NY St. Leo; Marcy, NY Marcy Correctional Facility; Oneida, NY Mohawk Correctional Facility.
Long, W. Thomas '91 (GB) Vicar for Ministers; Special Assignment; Ex Officio; Priests' Personnel Board.
Longalong, Patrick H. O. '08 (BRK) Floral Park, NY Our Lady of the Snows.
Longanga, Emery '94 (SP) Valrico, FL St. Stephen.
Longbucco, John L. '90 (MAR) Lanse, MI The Most Holy Name of Jesus–Blessed Kateri Tekakwitha; Baraga, MI St. Ann; L'Anse, MI Sacred Heart; Baraga, MI The Most Holy Name of Jesus–Blessed Kateri Tekakwitha.
Longchamps, Adrien R. '75 (MAN)[L] Manchester, NH Monastery of the Precious Blood; Elliott Hospital.
Longe, James '07 (SPR) Longmeadow, MA St. Mary's.
Longenecker, Dwight '06 (CHR) Greenville, SC Our Lady of the Rosary.
Longo, Robert *o.f.m.cap.* '85 (CAM) Retired.
Longobucco, Robert '98 (ALB) Schenectady, NY St. Helen; Office of Evangelization, Catechesis and Family Life.
Longoria, Jose Delacruz *m.n.m.* '96 (ELP) Clint, TX San Lorenzo.
Longtin, Lucien F. *s.j.* '65 (ALN)[N] Wernersville, PA Jesuit Center; [A] Wernersville, PA Jesuit Center–Jesuit Community.
Longua, Rev. Msgr. Paul A. '61 (PAT) Retired.
Longua, Thomas *f.s.s.p.* '03 (DAL) Irving, TX Mater Dei Personal Parish.
Long Vu, Michael *s.v.d.* '06 (BEA) Dayton, TX St. Joseph the Worker; Dayton, TX St. Anne Mission.
Lonzo, Anthony P. '05 (COL) Dennison, OH Immaculate Conception.
Looby, Christopher J. '01 (OG) Brushton, NY St. Mary's Church; Brushton, NY St. Augustine.
Looby, John J. '66 (OG) Chateaugay, NY Catholic Community of Burke and Chateaugay; Deans; Diocesan Consultors.
Loomis, Rev. Msgr. Richard A. '76 (LA) On Administrative Leave.
Loomis, Richard P. '52 (WIN) Austin, MN St. Edward's Retired.
Loomis, Thomas A. '92 (WIN) Adams, MN Sacred Heart; Adams, MN St. John's; Adams, MN Queen of Peace; Adams, MN St. Peter's; Finance Council; Priest Assignments Committee.
Looney, Daniel A. '71 (SAC) Priests' Personnel Board, Diocesan; Sacramento, CA Holy Spirit.
Looney, Joseph E. '67 (HRT) Bethlehem, CT Church of the Nativity.
Looney, Mathew D. '58 (NEW) Retired.
Looney, Thomas P. *c.s.c.* '87 (FTW)[H] Notre Dame Congregation of Holy Cross, United States Province of Priests & Brothers.
Loos, Frederick C. '63 (SAG) Retired.
Lopardo, Vito R. '55 (BEL) Retired.
Lopatesky, Rev. Msgr. Raymond M. '75 (PAT)[Q] Chester, NJ Nazareth Village; Clergy Personnel Office.
Lopera, Rafael I. *c.s.b.* '94 (GAL)[O] Sugar Land Basilian Mission Center.
Loperfido, Ernest '59 (Y) Retired.
Lopes, Richard A. *o.f.m.cap* '82 (MO) DEPARTMENT OF VETERANS AFFAIRS HOSPITALS AND CHAPLAINS.
Lopes, Richard *o.f.m.cap.* '82 (SFR)[N] Burlingame, CA Capuchin Provincial House.
Lopes, Rev. Msgr. Steven J. *s.t.l.* '01 (SFR) On Duty Outside the Archdiocese.
Lopes, Thomas C. '65 (FR) Retired.
Lopez, Abel '56 (SJ) Retired.
Lopez, Agustin *sch.p.* '57 (SJN)[B] San Juan, PR Colegio Calasanz; San Juan, PR Santisimo Salvador.
Lopez, Agustin '11 (WDC) Rockville, MD St. Raphael.
Lopez, Alberto '87 (SJN) Trujillo Alto, PR San Pio X.

Lopez, Alejandro *o.f.m.conv.* '03 (MIL) Milwaukee, WI Basilica of St. Josaphat.
Lopez, Alfred A. *o.p.* '84 (CHI)[N] River Forest, IL St. Thomas Aquinas Priory.
Lopez, Alvaro M. '86 (STO) Stockton, CA St. Mary of the Assumption Church (Pastor of).
Lopez, Angel *c.ss.r.* '79 (CGS) San Lorenzo, PR Nuestra Senora de la Mercedes.
Lopez, Anthony '08 (NSH) Antioch, TN Our Lady of Guadalupe.
Lopez, Antonio Garnica *m.s.c.* '79 (LA) Cudahy, CA Sagrado Corazon y Santa Maria de Guadalupe.
Lopez, Antonio *f.s.c.b.* '95 (BO) Lexington, MA; [U] Bethesda, MD House of Washington DC.
Lopez, Antonio *f.s.c.b.* (WDC) Lexington, MA; [O] Bethesda, MD Priestly Fraternity of the Missionaries of St. Charles Borromeo, Inc.
Lopez, Armando *o.f.m.* '90 (MRY)[F] San Juan Bautista, CA Franciscan Friars.
Lopez, Arturo *o.f.m.* (SFR) San Francisco, CA St. Boniface.
Lopez, Benigno '62 (CGS) Cayey, PR Nuestra Senora de la Merced.
Lopez, Bruce '88 (PEO) Monticello, IL St. Michael; Monticello, IL St. Philomena.
Lopez, Camilo '93 (NEW) Emerson, NJ Church of the Assumption.
Lopez, Carlos A. (BO) Roxbury, MA St. Patrick.
Lopez, Carlos A. (ARE) On Duty Outside the Diocese.
Lopez, Carlos *o.s.b.* '02 (LA)[P] Valyermo, CA St. Andrew's Abbey.
Lopez, Rev. Msgr. Daniel '63 (FRS) Retired.
Lopez, Edilberto '97 (ELP) Priests' Retirement and Disability Plan; El Paso, TX St. Luke.
Lopez, Eduardo *c.m.* '70 (GAL) Houston, TX St. Charles Borromeo.
Lopez, Efrain (SJN)[F] Puerta De Tierra, PR Asylum For The Aged and Infirm.
Lopez, Elpidio (TYL) Alto, TX Venerable Antonio Margil; Jacksonville, TX Our Lady of Sorrows.
Lopez, Enrique '93 (LSC) Deming, NM St. Ann's; Promoter of Justice; Clergy Personnel Board; Presbyteral Council; Diocesan Consultors.
Lopez, Erick *o.f.m.* '11 (WDC) Silver Spring, MD St. Camillus.
Lopez, Erick *o.f.m.* '11 (NY)[DD] New York Franciscan Friars, Holy Name Province.
Lopez, Ernesto '06 (LUB) Director of Vocations; Diocesan Pastoral Liturgy Commission.
Lopez, Fabian '99 (NY) New York, NY Our Lady of Lourdes; Archdiocesan Consultors.
Lopez, Felipe '59 (NEW) Hispanic Curia of Hudson County; Fairview, NJ St. John the Baptist; [L] Rutherford, NJ St. John Vianney Residence for Priests Retired.
Lopez, Fernando A. '11 (TR) Jackson, NJ St. Aloysius.
Lopez, Francisco *m.n.m.* '99 (ELP) Clint, TX San Lorenzo.
Lopez, Frank '93 (ELP) El Paso, TX St. Frances Xavier Cabrini Parish; Diocesan Building Committee; Ex Officio Members; Our Lady of Guadalupe; Priests' Personnel Advisory Committee.
Lopez, Gabriel Maduro '59 (ARE) Promoter of Justice.
Lopez, Rev. Msgr. Gerard M. '91 (SB) Office of the Vicar General/Moderator of the Curia; Ex Officio Member; Diocesan Curia; College of Consultors; Ex Officio.
Lopez, Gustavo '90 (HRT) New Britain, CT St. Ann; New Britain, CT St. Mary's.
Lopez, Gustavo '95 (LFT) Lafayette, IN St. Boniface.
Lopez, Gustavo *o.s.j.* '09 (FRS) Madera, CA St. Joachim.
Lopez, Hector '10 (FRS) Fresno, CA St. John Cathedral.
Lopez, Jairo '94 (AUS) Goldthwaite, TX St. Peter; Marble Falls, TX St. John the Evangelist; San Saba, TX St. Mary; Lampasas/Marble Falls.
Lopez, James F. '04 (DET) St. Clair Shores, MI St. Isaac Jogues.
Lopez, Javier *sch.p.* '78 (SJN) San Juan, PR Santisimo Salvador.
Lopez, Jesus Francisco '96 (CC) Taft, TX Immaculate Conception.
Lopez, Joel '03 (RCK) Rockford, IL St. Bernadette.
Lopez, Johnson '11 (RCK) Woodstock, IL St. Mary.
Lopez, Jose E. '95 (BRK) Brooklyn, NY Holy Spirit.
Lopez, Jose Jesus '08 (PHX) Glendale, AZ Our Lady of Perpetual Help Roman Catholic Parish.
Lopez, Jose M. (ARE) On Duty Outside the Diocese.
Lopez, Jose Maria *o.c.d.* '57 (MIL)[P] Milwaukee Provincial Offices - Discalced Carmelites.
Lopez, Jose '94 (JKS) Retired.
Lopez, Jose '94 (BRK) Brooklyn, NY St. Rose of Lima.
Lopez, Jose '11 (PAT) Passaic, NJ Assumption of the Blessed Virgin Mary; Passaic, NJ St. Nicholas.
Lopez, Joseph A. '02 (CC) Office of the Bishop; College of Consultors; Presbyteral Council; Judges; Chancellor; Seminary Formation & Vocations; Bishop's Office-;Finance Council; Priest Secretary to the Bishop; Newspaper "The South Texas Catholic"; Corpus Christi, TX Our Lady of Perpetual Help.
López, José Refugio *s.s.p.* '83 (LA)[P] Los Angeles, CA The Society of St. Paul.
Lopez, Juan Carlos '03 (AUS) Kyle, TX St. Anthony Marie De Claret; Presbyteral Council; College of Consultors.
Lopez, Juan J. '89 (ARE) On Duty Outside the Diocese.
Lopez, Juan M. '62 (MIA) Miami, FL SS. Peter and Paul.
Lopez, Juan M. '08 (SFR) San Mateo, CA St. Matthew.
Lopez, Karlos (CGS)[F] Caguas, PR Movimiento Juan XXIII.
Lopez, Kharlosg '77 (FAJ) Humacao, PR Maria Reina de la Paz.
Lopez, Leonardo '11 (PAT) Stirling, NJ St. Vincent de Paul.
Lopez, Lionel '96 (BWN) On Assignment Outside the Diocese.
Lopez, Lionel '96 (MIA)[E] Miami, FL Belen Jesuit Preparatory School; [H] Miami, FL Villa Javier.
Lopez, Luis A. *c.p.* (ARE) Lares, PR St. Joseph.
Lopez, Luis E. *c.s.v.* '95 (CHI)[N] Arlington Heights Viatorian Province Center–Clerics of St. Viator.
Lopez, Marco T. '97 (SLC) Park City, UT Saint Mary of the Assumption LLC 238.
Lopez, Mariano H. '11 (ELP) El Paso, TX St. Patrick Cathedral.
Lopez, Mario *o.carm.* '76 (BO)[Z] Peabody, MA St. Theresa Carmelite Chapel; [U] Peabody, MA Our Lady of the Scapular Priory.
Lopez, Mauricio '92 (SAT) Converse, TX St. Monica; [S] San Antonio, TX The World Apostolate of Fatima.
Lopez, Nestor (GRY) Hammond, IN St. Casimir.
Lopez, P. Harry '86 (MGZ) Aguadilla, PR St. Charles Borromeo.
Lopez, P. Ramon *o.f.m.cap.* '76 (PCE) Ponce, PR Santa Teresita.
Lopez, Pedro J. '81 (LA) Deanery 18; Santa Fe Springs, CA St. Pius X; Members; Appointed Membership.
Lopez, Ramon '08 (NY) New York, NY St. Rose of Lima.
Lopez, Renato *s.s.* '86 (BAL)[A] Baltimore, MD St. Mary's Seminary and University; [Q] Baltimore, MD St. Mary's Seminary & University; [A] Baltimore, MD St. Mary's Seminary and University.
Lopez, Rev. Msgr. Richard J. '73 (ATL)[B] Atlanta, GA St. Pius X Catholic High School; Special or Other Archdiocesan Assignment.
Lopez, Richard '89 (ELP) Absent on Leave.
Lopez, Romualdo *c.r.s.* '07 (GAL) Houston, TX Assumption.
Lopez, Sergio '98 (OAK) Judges; Vocations.
Lopez, Severino *c.m.f.* '44 (CHI) Chicago, IL Our Lady of Guadalupe; [N] Oak Park Claretian Missionaries USA Eastern Province.
Lopez, Stephen Maria *o.p.* '10 (OAK)[L] Oakland, CA Order of Preachers (Province of the Most Holy Name of Jesus – Western Dominican Province).
Lopez, Stephen Maria *o.p.* '10 (SFR) San Francisco, CA St. Dominic; [N] San Francisco, CA St. Dominic Priory.
Lopez, Varghese *s.j.* '11 (BO)[U] Brighton, MA Alberto Hurtado House.
Lopez, Walter Suarez '96 (SJ) San Jose, CA Sacred Heart of Jesus.
Lopez–Bolanos, Eddy E. '09 (PRO) Coventry, RI SS. John and Paul.
Lopez–Cardinale, Alejandro '91 (NEW)[Q] Plainfield, NJ RENEW International; Elizabeth, NJ Blessed Sacrament; Pastoral Services Team.
Lopez–Flores, Antonio *o.praem* '02 (ORG) Santa Ana, CA St. Anne's.
Lopez–Restrepo, Eugenio '84 (SAC) Sacramento, CA St. Charles Borromeo.
Lopez Aponte, Nelson '91 (FAJ) Vieques, PR Inmaculada Concepcion.
Lopez Figueroa, Rev. Msgr. Alberto '87 (SJN) for Pastoral Affairs; Vicar for Pastoral Affairs; Diocesan Consultors.
Lopez Vega, Jose Antonio '92 (PCE) Coto Laurel, PR Our Lady of Mt. Carmel.
LoPinto, Rev. Msgr. Alfred P. '70 (BRK)[K] Brooklyn, NY Catholic Charities; Vicar for Human Services; Howard Beach, NY St. Helen; [K] Brooklyn, NY O.L. Loreto Family Housing Development Fund Corporation; [K] Brooklyn, NY O.L. Loreto Family Housing Development Fund Corporation.
LoPresti, Carl '97 (PEO) Chenoa, IL St. Joseph's; Colfax, IL St. Joseph's.
Lopresti, Julio *i.v.e.* '96 (BGP) Bridgeport, CT St. George; [O] Bridgeport, CT Instituto Verbo Encarnado.
Lopresti, Marcelo R. *i.v.e.* '02 (PH) Philadelphia, PA St. Hugh of Cluny.
Lorance, Douglas '84 (SJP) Lyndora, PA St. Michael; Presbyters.
Lord, David *m.i.c.* '91 (SPR)[G] Stockbridge, MA Congregation of Marian Fathers of The Immaculate Conception of the Most Blessed Virgin Mary.
Lord, Robert J. '60 (HRT) Retired.
Lordemann, Francis W. '72 (OM) West Point, NE Assumption B.V.M.; West Point, NE St. Aloysius; West Point, NE St. Boniface; West Point, NE St. Anthony.
Lorden, Demetrio '70 (SP) Wimauma, FL Our Lady of Guadalupe Mission.
Lorei, Brian '09 (ATL) Decatur, GA St. Thomas More.
Loremus, Gabriel (BO) Lynn, MA St. Mary.
Lorenc, Henryk '80 (MO) Army Chaplains.
Lorente, Jose '65 (MET)[M] Stewartsville, NJ Society of Jesus Christ the Priest; New Brunswick, NJ Our Lady of Mt. Carmel.
Lorente, Manuel '68 (MET)[M] Stewartsville, NJ Society of Jesus Christ the Priest; New Brunswick, NJ Our Lady of Mt. Carmel.
Lorentsen, Michael *o.f.m.conv.* '94 (WDC)[B] Silver Spring, MD St. Bonaventure Friary.
Lorenz, Bernard A. '85 (LIN) Imperial, NE St. Patrick's; Diocesan Area CCD Directors.
Lorenz, John F. '54 (DM)[G] Des Moines, IA Institute of the Heart of Jesus Retired.
Lorenz, Matthais E. '69 (CHI) On Duty Outside the Archdiocese.
Lorenz, Richard J. *s.a.c.* '60 (MIL)[P] Milwaukee, WI St. Vincent Community.
Lorenzana, Elias *o.m.* (CGS) Cayey, PR Nuestra Senora de la Asuncion.
Lorenzetti, Rev. Msgr. Dino J. '53 (BUF)[N] Tonawanda, NY O'Hara Residence Retired.
Lorenzo, Andy Puga '03 (TYL) Nacogdoches, TX Sacred Heart.
Lorenzo, Avelino *s.d.b.* '60 (LA) Bellflower, CA St. Dominic Savio.
Lorenzo, Eduardo '66 (LAN) Retired.
Lorenzo, Elias R. *o.s.b.* '89 (PAT)[N] Morristown St. Mary's Abbey.
Lorenzo, Joseph F. *o.f.m.* '76 (NY) New York, NY St. Anthony of Padua.
Lorenzo, Juan '93 (VEN) Charismatic Renewal.
Lorenzo, Juan '97 (VEN) LaBelle, FL Our Lady Queen of Heaven.
Lorenzo–Puga, Andy '03 (MIA) Sunrise, FL All Saints.
Lorenzoni, Larry *s.d.b.* '51 (SFR)[N] San Francisco, CA Salesian Provincial Residence Retired.
Lorfanfant, Ernest P. *s.m.* '68 (RVC)[N] Mineola, NY Provincial Residence and Novitiate.
Lorge, Felix P. '50 (SPK) Retired.
Lorig, Douglas E. '84 (PHX) Scottsdale, AZ St. Maria Goretti Roman Catholic Parish; Members.
Lorig, Jeffrey '04 (OM) O'Neill, NE St. Patrick.
Lorilla, Willy O. (AGN) Piti, GU Assumption of Our Lady.
Lorimer, Daniel S. '04 (WCH) On Duty Outside the Diocese; Army Chaplains.
Lorio, Rev. Msgr. Joseph O. '54 (NO) Retired.
Lorkowski, Robert A. '77 (CLV) Parma, OH St. Anthony of Padua.
Lorrain, Matthew P. '86 (BR) Defenders of the Bond; Serra Clubs; Vocations.
Los, Waldemer P. *s.j.* (SY)[Q] Syracuse, NY Jesuits at LeMoyne, Inc.
Losarcos, Javier '51 (NEW) Newark, NJ St. Benedict's Retired.
Lo Sasso, John *o.f.m.cap.* '89 (NY) Bronx, NY Immaculate Conception.
LoSasso, John *o.f.m.cap.* '89 (NY)[DD] New York, NY Immaculate Conception Friary.
LosBanes, Hermes '86 (MO) Army Chaplains.
Lo Schiavo, John J. *s.j.* '55 (SFR)[N] San Francisco, CA Loyola House Jesuit Community.
Loseke, Jeffery S. '00 (OM) Hartington, NE St. Michael; Hartington, NE Holy Trinity; [B] Hartington, NE Cedar Catholic High School; Air Force Reserve Chaplains.
Losh, Joseph F. '64 (COL) Retired.
Loskarn, George '65 (BAL) Retired.
Losoya, Jose E. *c.o.* '91 (BWN) Pharr, TX St. Jude Thaddeus; [F] Pharr, TX Pharr Oratory of St. Philip Neri of Pontifical Right; [B] Pharr, TX Oratory Athenaeum for University Preparation; Pharr, TX Oratory – Athenaeum for University Preparation; [C] Pharr, TX Oratory Academy of St. Philip Neri; Pharr, TX Oratory Academy of St. Philip Neri.
Lossing, Larry '84 (ORL) Orlando, FL St. Joseph Retired.
Lostritto, Paul *o.f.m.* '96 (BO)[Z] Boston, MA St. Anthony Shrine.
Loterte, Samuel E. *s.s.s.* '91 (HON) Hilo, HI St. Joseph.
Lothamer, James W. *s.s.* '68 (BAL)[Q] Baltimore Society of St. Sulpice, Province of the United States.
Lothamer, James '68 (LAN) Retired.
Lotz, Ezekiel *o.s.b.* '00 (P)[L] St. Benedict, OR Mt. Angel Abbey.
Lotz, Ezekiel *o.s.b.* (B)[C] Jerome, ID Monastery of the Ascension.
Lotz, Robert J. '73 (MIL) Sheboygan Falls, WI Blessed Trinity; Kohler, WI St. John Evangelist; Archdiocesan Council of Priests.
Louapre, Albert C. *s.j.* '60 (ATL)[H] Atlanta, GA Ignatius House.
Loubriel, Harry '05 (MIA)[C] St. Thomas University; Campus Ministry; St. Thomas University; Miami Gardens, FL Visitation.
Loucks, Thomas '77 (B) Kellogg, ID St. Rita's; Wallace, ID St. Alphonsus.
Loughery, Robert L. *c.s.c.* '89 (FTW)[H] Notre Dame Congregation of Holy Cross, United States Province

of Priests & Brothers; [B] University of Notre Dame Du Lac; [H] Notre Dame, IN Holy Cross Community, Corby Hall, University of Notre Dame.
Loughlin, Rev. Msgr. William J. '69 (BGP) Pilgrimages, Office of Diocesan; [O] Stamford, CT The Catherine Dennis Keefe Queen of the Clergy Retired Priests' Residence Retired.
Loughman, Rev. Msgr. Kenneth M. '58 (NY) Retired.
Loughnane, Rev. Msgr. James J. '61 (LA) Diamond Bar, CA St. Denis; Deanery 12; Chairman.
Loughnane, John B. '88 (MAN) Pittsfield, NH Our Lady of Lourdes.
Loughney, Gregory F. '11 (SCR) Mount Pocono, PA St. Bernadette; Mount Pocono, PA Most Holy Trinity Parish; Mount Pocono, PA St. Ann.
Loughran, James *s.a.* '89 (NY)[DD] New York, NY Atonement Friars; [DD] New York, NY Graymoor Ecumenical and Interreligious Institute.
Loughran, John J. *o.s.f.s.* '80 (LAN) Toledo, OH; Deerfield, MI Light of Christ Parish.
Loughrey, Vivian '97 (MIA) Miramar, FL Blessed John XXIII Church.
Louis, Jean Woady '91 (VEN) Bradenton Beach, FL St. Bernard; Manatee and Hardee Counties.
Louis, Rev. Msgr. John H. '62 (SCR) Defenders of the Bond; [M] Dunmore, PA Villa St. Joseph Retired.
Louis, John *o.m.i.* '43 (BEL)[F] Belleville, IL Missionary Oblates of Mary Immaculate – St. Henry's Oblate Residence Retired.
Louis, Kevin C. '89 (LC) Spring Valley, WI Sacred Heart of Jesus.
Louis, Olin Pierre '09 (SJN) Santurce, PR Hospital Del Nino San Jorge; San Juan, PR San Mateo; [E] Santurce, PR San Jorge's Children Hospital.
Louis, Pascal '83 (BRK) Brooklyn, NY Holy Innocents.
Lourdusamy, Joseph '95 (TYL) Chireno, TX Our Lady of Lourdes; Nacogdoches, TX Immaculate Conception – Moral.
Lourduswami, Augustine '92 (SCR) East Stroudsburg, PA St. Matthew.
Louwagie, Vicente *o.m.i.* '68 (SAT)[C] Oblate School of Theology.
Louzon, Bede *o.f.m.cap.* '85 (DET) Hazel Park, MI St. Mary Magdalen.
Lovas, Donald J. '63 (WIN) Retired.
Lovat, Rene *s.x.* '57 (PAT)[N] Wayne Xaverian Missionary Fathers; Wayne, NJ XAVERIAN MISSIONARY FATHERS.
Love, John W. '90 (LA) Goleta, CA St. Mark University Parish; [AA] Goleta, CA University of California Santa Barbara; Air National Guard Chaplains.
Love, Lester E. *s.j.* '91 (OAK)[L] Oakland, CA Jesuit Fathers and Brothers.
Lovell, Allen B. '02 (CAM) Gibbsboro, NJ St. Andrew the Apostle's R.C. Church, Gibbsboro, N.J.
Lovell, John '07 (ARL) Springfield, VA St. Raymond of Penafort.
Lover, Lawrence E. *c.ss.r.* '51 (BRK)[R] Brooklyn, NY Redemptorist Fathers of New York, Inc.–Baltimore Province; Brooklyn, NY.
Lovett, Gerald F. '59 (SEA) Retired.
Lovrencic, Athanasius *o.f.m.* '48 (CHI)[N] Lemont, IL The Slovene Franciscan Fathers, Order of Friars Minor, Commissariat of the Holy Cross; Councilors.
Lovric, Ivan (NY) Crestwood, NY Church of the Annunciation.
Lowchy, Gregory '01 (R) Wilson, NC Church of St. Therese.
Lowe, Bryan K. '01 (BIR) Anniston, AL Sacred Heart of Jesus; Priests'/Presbyteral Council.
Lowe, Frank E. '85 (MO) Air Force Chaplains; On Duty Outside The Diocese.
Lowe, Philip J. '82 (PH) On Special or Other Archdiocesan Assignment; Chadds Ford, PA St. Cornelius.
Lowe, Russell P. '92 (CLV) Cleveland, OH St. Leo the Great.
Lowery, Brian S. *o.s.a.* '67 (FgM) Villanova, PA Province of St. Thomas of Villanova (Eastern).
Lowery, James T. *m.s.* '55 (HRT)[L] Hartford, CT Missionaries of LaSalette.
Lowery, Martin J. *m.m.* '68 (NY)[DD] Maryknoll Maryknoll Fathers and Brothers.
Lowery, Rev. Msgr. Philip A. '76 (TR) Red Bank, NJ St. James.
Lowery, Shaun *o.s.f.s.* '09 (TOL) Toledo, OH Gesu.
Lowery, Stephen *c.o.* '09 (PIT)[P] Pittsburgh, PA Carnegie–Mellon University; [P] Pittsburgh, PA Chatham College; [M] Pittsburgh, PA Congregation of the Oratory of St. Philip Neri; [P] Pittsburgh, PA University of Pittsburgh.
Lowery, Wilfred *c.ss.r.* '49 (STP) Brooklyn Center, MN St. Alphonsus; [J] Brooklyn Center, MN Redemptorist Fathers of Hennepin County.
Lowie, Richard J. '69 (GR) Retired.
Lowisz, Myron *o.f.m.* '60 (GRY)[F] Crown Point, IN Franciscan Communities at St. Anthony Campus; [H] Cedar Lake, IN Our Lady of Lourdes Friary.
Lowney, Jeremiah (HEL) Retired.
Lowrey, Robert *o.m.v.* '78 (BO)[U] Milton, MA Oblate Residence (St. Joseph House); [Z] Boston, MA St. Francis Chapel.
Lowry, Matthew '08 (PHX) Flagstaff, AZ Holy Trinity Newman Center; [H] Flagstaff, AZ Holy Trinity Catholic Newman Center; Vocations Office.
Lowry, Nolan '10 (TYL) Centerville, TX St. Leo the Great; Hilltop Lakes, TX St. Thomas More; Graduate Studies; Respect Life Program.
Loya, Daniel J. '66 (PBR) East Pittsburgh, PA St. Mary's.
Loya, John F. '74 (CLV)[A] Wickliffe, OH Borromeo Seminary.
Loya, Joseph *o.s.a.* '79 (PH)[C] Villanova University; [Y] Rosemont, PA Saxony Hall.
Loya, Mario *o.carm.* '04 (JOL)[L] Darien Carmelite Provincial Office.
Loya, Thomas '82 (PRM) Homer Glen, IL Annunciation Byzantine Catholic Church; Syncellus for Parishes and Laity; Presbyteral Council; Eparchial Pastoral Council; Office of Youth Ministry; Respect Life Office.
Loyson, Michael '92 (DET) St. Clair Shores, MI St. Lucy; Defenders of Bond.
Lozada, Enrique Francisco, Garcia '07 (CHI) Franklin Park, IL St. Gertrude.
Lozano, Freddy '85 (RVC) Patchogue, NY Our Lady of Mt. Carmel.
Lozano, Rev. Msgr. Jose '65 (PCE) Juana Diaz, PR St. Raymond Nonato; Diocesan Consultors; Parish Priests Consultors.
Lozano, Juan Antonio Hernandez (DM) Des Moines, IA Christ the King; Des Moines, IA St. Anthony's; Des Moines, IA Basilica of Saint John.
Lozano, Roland *c.m.f.* '75 (LA) Los Angeles, CA Our Lady Queen of Angels Parish.
Lozaro, Americo '10 (DAL) Garland, TX Good Shepherd.
Lozier, Donald G. *o.m.i.* '60 (BO)[U] Lowell, MA Andre Garin Retirement Residence; Lowell, MA Holy Family.
Lozier, Timothy R. '88 (STA) Jacksonville, FL Most Holy Redeemer; Presbyteral Council; Cursillos de Cristiandad.
Lozinski, Rev. Msgr. Eugene L. '72 (NU) Morgan, MN St. Joseph (Oratory); Morgan, MN St. Michael; Sleepy Eye, MN St. Mary; Board of Trustees for Pension Plan for Priests; On Special or Other Diocesan Assignment; Bishop's Delegate for the Permanent Diaconate; Chancellor; Associate Judges; Corporate Board; Priest Personnel Board; Diocesan Council of Catholic Women; College of Consultors; Priests' Council.
Lozinski, Robert W. *c.s.c.* '73 (PSC) Dunmore, PA St. Michael.
Lozinski, Robert W. *c.s.c.* '73 (FTW)[H] Notre Dame Congregation of Holy Cross, United States Province of Priests & Brothers.
Lu, Joe *o.f.m.* (MRY)[F] San Miguel, CA Franciscan Friars, O.F.M.
Luamanu, Setefano T. '92 (SPP) Auditors.
Luan, Nguyen Truong '98 (LA)[P] Baldwin Park Vietnamese Redemptorist Mission.
Lubeley, Rev. Msgr. Richard J. '49 (STL) Retired.
Luberti, Richard *c.ss.r.* '79 (DET) Maybee, MI St. Joseph.
Lubic, Robert T. '96 (GBG) Perryopolis, PA St. John the Baptist; Smock, PA St. Hedwig; [C] Connellsville, PA Geibel Catholic Junior–Senior High School.
Lubinsky, Michael '78 (SAV) Augusta, GA Church of the Most Holy Trinity.
Lubowa, Francis Muteesasira '02 (SP) Judges; Beverly Hills, FL Our Lady of Grace.
Lubrano, Joseph *s.d.s.* '74 (MIL)[P] Greendale, WI.
Lubrano, Robert '85 (RVC) Medical Leave.
Luca, Edward J. '54 (CLV) Sheffield, OH St. Teresa of Avila; Judges in Second Instance Retired.
Luca, Rev. Msgr. Joseph L. '70 (BAL) Clarksville, MD St. Louis.
Lucas, Christopher D. '85 (PH)[D] Fairless Hills, PA Conwell–Egan Catholic High School; Levittown, PA Immaculate Conception B.V.M.
Lucas, Edward M. '61 (PBR) Weirton, WV St. Mary's.
Lucas, George J. *c.s.c.* '72 (FTW)[H] Notre Dame Congregation of Holy Cross, United States Province of Priests & Brothers.
Lucas, James W. '00 (GB) Appleton, WI St. Thomas More.
Lucas, Jayaselanraj '96 (TYL) Henderson, TX St. Jude; Bradshaw State Facility, Texas Department of Criminal Justice.
Lucas, Jeffrey '65 (E) Sharon, PA St. Stanislaus Kostka–Holy Trinity.
Lucas, Rev. Msgr. John J. '65 (E) Warren, PA Holy Redeemer.
Lucas, John P. '68 (CHI) Oak Park, IL St. Edmund; Provincial Court of Appeals; [W] Chicago, IL Court of Appeals–Province of Chicago.
Lucas, John P. (STN) "New Star" – Eparchial Newspaper.
Lucas, John '66 (STN) Chicago, IL St. Michael's.
Lucas, Kevin '08 (PEO)[M] Peoria, IL Newman Foundation at Bradley University & Illinois Central College; Peoria, IL St. Mark's.
Lucas, Lawrence E. '59 (NY) New York, NY Our Lady of Lourdes.
Lucas, Robert F. '02 (PH) Drexel Hill, PA St. Bernadette.
Lucas, Robert *c.m.* '74 (CHI)[N] Chicago, IL Vincentian Community, Congregation of the Mission, Western Province.
Lucas, Robert *c.m.* (JOL)[I] Joliet, IL Provena Saint Joseph Medical Center.
Lucas, Theodore '84 (CLV) Willowick, OH St. Mary Magdalene.
Lucas, Thomas M. *s.j.* '85 (SFR)[N] San Francisco, CA Loyola House Jesuit Community.
Lucas, William P. '90 (BIR) Trussville, AL Holy Infant of Prague; Diocesan College of Consultors; Priests'/Presbyteral Council; Diocesan College of Vicars.
Lucasinsky, Raymond *c.m.m.* '62 (DET)[K] Vocation Office.
Lucatero, Heliodoro '86 (SPK) On Duty Outside the Diocese.
Lucatero, Heliodoro '86 (SAT) Office of Worship; San Antonio, TX St. Michael.
Lucavei, Januario *o.s.b.m.* '00 (STF) Long Island City, NY Holy Cross.
Lucchetti, Luis R. '97 (LA) Monrovia, CA Immaculate Conception; El Monte, CA Nativity.
Lucero, Edward F. '08 (TUC) Solomon, AZ Our Lady of Guadalupe Roman Catholic Parish – Solomon; Council of Priests; Vicars Forane; Safford, AZ Saint Rose of Lima Roman Catholic Parish – Safford; All Vicars Forane.
Lucero, Jose *s.d.b.* '03 (SFR) San Francisco, CA Corpus Christi.
Lucero, Rev. Msgr. Leo '60 (SFE) Retired.
Lucero, Lorenzo '56 (ELP) Retired.
Lucey, Beatus T. *o.s.b.* '59 (PAT)[N] Morristown, NJ St. Mary's Abbey.
Lucey, Gregory F. *s.j.* '64 (WDC)[X] Washington, DC Association of Jesuit Colleges and Universities; [O] Washington, DC Leonard Neale House.
Lucey, Paul T. *s.j.* '48 (BO)[U] Weston, MA Campion Health Center, Inc.
Lucey, Walter D. '98 (NEW)[B] Seton Hall University; [A] South Orange, NJ Immaculate Conception Seminary School of Theology.
Lucey, William F. '51 (BO) Senior Priests.; Pastoral Care Retired.
Lucht, Shannon G. '01 (BIS) Belfield, ND St. Bernard; South Heart, ND St. Mary; Belfield, ND SS. Peter and Paul; Associate Judges; Presbyteral Council.
Lucia, Douglas J. '89 (OG) Canton, NY St. Mary; Adjutant Judicial Vicars; Department of Worship; Diocesan Consultors; Committee on Assignments; Episcopal Vicar for Worship and Priestly Formation; Canton, NY Newman Ministry of St. Mary's Parish: Newman Center; Campus Ministry.
Luciana, Rev. Msgr. Lawrence J. '63 (WH) Huntington, WV St. Joseph's.
Luciano, Edmund A. '09 (MET) Raritan, NJ The Catholic Church of St. Ann.
Luciano, William J. '83 (NY) Priests Council of the Archdiocese of New York; Yonkers, NY Christ the King.
Lucid, Philip *s.j.* '55 (SPK)[J] Spokane, WA Regis Community Retired.
Lucido, John '73 (ELP) Kermit, TX St. Thomas & St. Joseph; Monahans, TX St. John the Apostle and Evangelist; Ex Officio Members; St. Mark and St. Luke; Priests' Personnel Advisory Committee.
Luck, Robert O. '62 (LA) Retired.
Lucree, Rev. Msgr. Lawrence A. '60 (SAV) Retired.
Luczak, Andrew E. '70 (CHI) Niles, IL St. Isaac Jogues.
Luczak, Jay R. '92 (TUC) Miami, AZ Our Lady of the Blessed Sacrament Roman Catholic Church – Miami; Council of Priests; Vicars Forane; All Vicars Forane.
Luczak, Thomas *o.f.m.* '70 (BWN) McAllen, TX Sacred Heart; Vicar for Religious.
Luczycki, Rev. Msgr. Matthew C. '45 (SY) Oneida, NY St. Joseph Retired.
Ludden, John J. '97 (VEN) Naples, FL St. John the Evangelist; Presbyteral Council; Vicar for Priests; Continuing Education of Clergy; Propagation of the Faith/Mission Cooperative Program.
Ludescher, Kenneth F. '61 (STP) Retired.
Ludvik, John J. '71 (SEA) Buckley, WA St. Aloysius.
Ludwick, Edmond '97 (CI) Chuuk, FM Holy Cross; [C] Tunnuk, Chuuk, FM Vicariate Residence.
Ludwig, Alexander '58 (SCL) Retired.
Ludwig, Eugene M. *o.f.m.cap.* '71 (SFR)[N] Burlingame, CA Capuchin Provincial House.
Ludwig, Eugene *o.f.m.cap.* '71 (OAK)[A] Berkeley, CA Dominican School of Philosophy and Theology.
Ludwig, John P. '74 (DM) Saint Marys, IA Assumption; Advocates; Priests' Pension Fund Society; Norwalk, IA St. John the Apostle Church.
Ludwig, Thomas K. '87 (KC) St. Joseph, MO Our Lady of Guadalupe.
Ludwig, Thomas '87 (MO) Air National Guard Chaplains.
Ludwikoski, James E. '73 (KCK) Shawnee, KS Good Shepherd.

Luebbert, Philip '10 (KC) Blue Springs, MO St. John La Lande.
Luebking, Rev. Msgr. Thomas A. '71 (TR) Spring Lake, NJ St. Catharine.
Lueckenotte, Daniel I.J. '90 (JC) VII. Sedalia/Lake Ozark; Hermitage, MO St. Bernadette; Camdenton, MO St. Anthony.
Lueras, Charles R. *c.r.i.c.* '81 (LA) Santa Paula, CA Our Lady of Guadalupe; [P] Santa Paula, CA Canons Regular of the Immaculate Conception.
Luerman, John H. '56 (IND) Retired.
Luevano, Rafael '81 (ORG) Orange, CA Cathedral of the Holy Family; Special Assignment.
Luft, Matthew *o.s.b* '05 (SCL)[I] Collegeville, MN St. John's Abbey, of the Order of St. Benedict.
Lugger, William R. '89 (LAN) Lansing, MI St. Casimir; Worship Commission.
Lugo, Camillo '70 (RVC) Copiague, NY Our Lady of the Assumption.
Lugo, Joseph W. '62 (PAT) Retired.
Lugo, Lawrence *a.m.* (TUC) Tucson, AZ Saint Joseph Roman Catholic Parish – Tucson.
Lui, Gabriel '79 (LA) Monterey Park, CA St. Thomas Aquinas; On Active Leave.
Lui, Tovia '83 (LA) Torrance, CA St. Catherine Laboure.
Luis, Raymond Rodriquez *s.a.* '09 (NY)[DD] Garrison Franciscan Friars of the Atonement, Minister General Office.
Luisi, Joseph G. '83 (PIT) Monroeville, PA North American Martyrs.
Luiten, Gary '92 (FAR) Grafton, ND St. Luke's Church of Veseleyville; Park River, ND St. Mary; Diocesan College of Consultors.
Luiz, Gary M. *c.p.p.s.* '77 (RNO) Defenders of the Bond.
Lukac, Thomas M. '63 (GBG) Retired.
Lukachinsky, Jerome A. '88 (CLV) Garfield Heights, OH St. Monica Retired.
Lukas, Andrew F. '58 (WH) Retired.
Lukas, Joseph S. '46 (BO) Senior Priests. Retired.
Lukas, Martin C. *o.s.f.s.* '80 (TOL)[H] Toledo, OH Provincial Residence; Toledo, OH Gesu.
Lukaschek, Ernest C. *m.m.* '64 (NY)[DD] Maryknoll Maryknoll Fathers and Brothers.
Lukaszewski, Stanley P. '79 (TR) Manasquan, NJ St. Denis; Vicars Forane (Deans).
Lukati, Willy Frank *c.s.c.* (FTW)[H] Notre Dame Congregation of Holy Cross, United States Province of Priests & Brothers.
Luke, Eugene *o.s.b.* '61 (LR) Paris, AR St. Joseph.
Luke, Francis '98 (BGP) Brookfield, CT St. Marguerite Bourgeoys.
Lukefahr, Oscar *c.m.* '66 (STL)[O] Perryville, MO Congregation of the Mission; [V] Perryville, MO Catholic Home Study Service.
Lukehart, Frederick '63 (Y) Serra Club of Mahoning County; Catholic Women, Diocesan Council of Retired.
Lukenda, Raymond T. '56 (NEW) Retired.
Lukianiuk, Andrzej '86 (BRK) Rockaway Beach, NY St. Rose of Lima; On Leave/Unassigned.
Lukka, Antony '95 (MAR) Lanse, MI The Most Holy Name of Jesus–Blessed Kateri Tekakwitha; Baraga, MI The Most Holy Name of Jesus–Blessed Kateri Tekakwitha; Baraga, MI St. Ann; L'Anse, MI Sacred Heart.
Lukose, Abraham (MCE) New Hyde Park, NY St. Chrysostom Malankara Catholic Church; Secretary; Notary; Liturgy Director; Elected Members; Priests – Heads of Apostolates.
Lukoskie, Raymond M. '58 (PEO) Retired.
Luksza, Mariusz G. '04 (NEW) Garfield, NJ St. Stanislaus Kostka.
Lukyamuzi, Joseph M. *o.s.b.* '81 (RIC)[K] Richmond, VA Mary Mother of the Church Abbey.
Lule, John '81 (RC) McLaughlin, SD St. Bonaventure's; McLaughlin, SD St. Bernard; McLaughlin, SD Standing Rock Reservation.
Lule, Mugagga '95 (LAV) Vocations; Henderson, NV St. Peter the Apostle; [F] Las Vegas, NV Serra House.
Lulf, Ken '99 (SFS) Yankton, SD St. Benedict.
Luljak, Louis P. '61 (MIL) Retired.
Lulko, Leo T. '65 (DET) Highland, MI Church of the Holy Spirit.
Lum, Donald (STA) Jacksonville, FL Assumption.
Lumbre, Roger S. '86 (WCH) Arma, KS St. Joseph; Girard, KS St. Michael.
Luminais, Rev. Msgr. J. Anthony '54 (NO) Retired.
Lumpe, Michael J. '04 (COL) Columbus, OH St. Catharine.
Lumsden, Patrick L. '96 (DAV) Albia, IA St. Patrick's; Lovilia, IA St. Peter's; Melrose, IA St. Patrick's.
Luna, Barrera *m.s.a.* '87 (NOR)[G] Cromwell, CT Society of the Missionaries of the Holy Apostles.
Luna, Ignacio '65 (BWN) San Benito, TX St. Benedict.
Luna, Jonathan Dela *s.j.* (WDC)[O] Washington, DC The Jesuit Community at Georgetown University.
Luna, Rev. Msgr. Lambert J. '78 (SFE) Albuquerque, NM Saint Joseph on the Rio Grande; Vicar–General; College of Consultors; Presbyteral Council of the Archdiocese of Santa Fe; Finance Council.
Luna, Luis G. Belmonte *o.c.d.* '07 (SAT)[L] San Antonio, TX Discalced Carmelite Fathers of San Antonio.
Luna, Luis *m.s.a.* '87 (NOR)[A] Cromwell, CT Holy Apostles College and Seminary.
Luna, Nicolas *e.c.* '64 (STU)[H] Bloomingdale, OH Holy Family Hermitage.
Lund, Donald J. '69 (CHI) Chicago, IL Good Shepherd Retired.
Lundberg, Bjorn C. '06 (ARL) Notaries; Fredericksburg, VA St. Mary of the Immaculate Conception.
Lundberg, Jan *o.c.d.* '93 (LA) Alhambra, CA St. Therese.
Lundberg, Jan *o.c.d.* '93 (P)[Q] Mount Angel, OR Carmelite House of Studies; [L] Mount Angel, OR Discalced Carmelite Friars (OCD).
Lundberg, John W. '60 (TLS) Retired.
Lundemba, Emmanuel *s.j.* '11 (BO)[U] Brighton, MA Isaac Jogues House.
Lundgren, Erik Carl Martin '10 (STP) Faribault, MN Divine Mercy Catholic Church; Kenyon, MN St. Michael; Shieldsville, MN St. Patrick.
Lundgren, Stephen A. '79 (DUB) Edgewood, IA St. Mark; Medical–Moral Commission; Deanery Representatives; Edgewood, IA St. Patrick.
Lundy, George F. *s.j.* '78 (NO)[C] New Orleans, LA Loyola University New Orleans; New Orleans, LA Holy Name of Jesus.
Lundy, James P. *c.ss.r.* '47 (NY)[DD] New York, NY Redemptorist Priests and Brothers, C.Ss.R.
Lungay, Jose Roel G. '84 (NO) Slidell, LA St. Genevieve.
Luniw, Paul '82 (STF) Diocesan Consultors; Judicial Vicar; Hartford; Presbyteral Council; Terryville, CT St. Michael.
Luniw, Paul (PHU) Adjunct Judicial Vicars.
Lunness, John A. '04 (WIL) Rehoboth Beach, DE St. Edmond.
Lunney, William H. '94 (SPR) Holyoke, MA St. Jerome; Holyoke, MA Our Lady of Guadalupe; Presbyteral Council.
Lunsford, Keith '92 (KCK) Archdiocesan Pastoral Council; Prairie Village, KS St. Ann.
Lunsford, Rev. Msgr. Robert D. '60 (LAN) Retired.
Luo, Matteo *o.f.m.conv.* '59 (BAL)[Q] Ellicott City Order of Friars Minor Conventual.
Luong, (Francis Xavier M.) Tri Van *c.m.c.* '83 (SPC)[F] Carthage, MO Congregation of the Mother Coredemptrix, United States Assumption Province.
Luong, Andrew (ARL) Alexandria, VA Queen of Apostles.
Luong, Duc *c.s.sp.* '04 (FgM) Bethel Park, PA CONGREGATION OF THE HOLY SPIRIT.
Luong, Tri M. '94 (HBG) Mechanicsburg, PA St. Elizabeth Ann Seton.
Luongo, Anthony V. (BO) Norwood, MA St. Catherine of Siena.
Luongo, John '78 (ORG) Retired.
Luoni, Christopher '05 (Y) Office of Vocations; Youngstown State University.
Lupico, Samuel '65 (BAL) Baltimore, MD St. Pius X Retired.
Lupo, David *ss.cc.* '91 (FR)[H] Wareham, MA Sacred Hearts Retreat Center.
Lupo, Robert L. '08 (PRT) Auburn, ME Immaculate Heart of Mary Parish; Norway, ME Blessed Teresa of Calcutta Parish.
Lupton, Brendan P. '05 (CHI) Other Assignments.
Lusch, Daniel J. *s.j.* '62 (BO)[U] Boston The Society of Jesus of New England–Provincial Offices.
Lusch, Daniel J. *s.j.* '62 (BUF)[N] Buffalo, NY Canisius Jesuit Community Inc.
Luschen, Timothy D. '88 (OKL) Oklahoma City, OK St. Charles Borromeo; Council of Priests Archdiocesan; Consultors Archdiocesan.
Lusembo, Matthias '81 (RIC) Norfolk, VA Christ the King.
Lusik, William A. '97 (NEW) Absent on Leave.
Lusk, Craig '08 (KAL) New Buffalo, MI St. Mary of the Lake.
Lusoski, Thomas J. '57 (CLV) Retired.
Lussier, Bonaventure *o.c.d.* '75 (WH)[L] Hinton, WV Monastery of Christ on the Mountain.
Lussier, Louis *m.i.* '90 (MIL)[P] Milwaukee, WI St. Camillus Delegate House; [Y] Wauwatosa, WI St. Camillus Health System, Inc.; [Y] Wauwatosa, WI St. Camillus Ministries, Inc.; [Y] Wauwatosa, WI San Camillo, Inc.; [Y] Wauwatosa, WI Order of St. Camillus Foundation, Inc.
Lussier, Louis *o.s.cam.* '90 (SAV) Sylvania, GA Our Lady of the Assumption.
Lussier, Robert *o.s.b.* '92 (SFE)[H] Pecos, NM Our Lady of Guadalupe Abbey; [I] Santa Fe, NM Discalced Carmelite Monastery.
Lusson, David R. '80 (SUP) Cumberland, WI Sacred Heart of Jesus Church; Cumberland, WI St. Anthony Abbot; Cumberland, WI St. Ann; Board of Directors.
Lustan, Ariel G. '94 (TUC) Sierra Vista, AZ Our Lady of the Mountains Roman Catholic Parish – Sierra Vista; [H] Safford, AZ Eastern Arizona Junior College; Defenders of the Bond.
Luther, Benjamin F. '64 (OWN) Central City, KY St. Joseph; Deans; Legion of Mary; Priests' Council.
Lutjen, George J. '68 (BRK) Retired.
Lutmer, Joseph H. '46 (CIN) Retired.
Lutz, Bernard A. '63 (EVN) Diocesan Council of Priests; Diocesan Consultors Retired.
Lutz, Donald J. '70 (BUF) Buffalo, NY Our Lady of Perpetual Help.
Lutz, Frederick J. '73 (SPC) Springfield, MO Retired.
Lutz, Rev. Msgr. George C. '62 (NEW) Retired.
Lutz, Gerald J. '56 (PIT) Butler, PA St. Paul Retired.
Lutz, Herman '58 (IND)[I] Beech Grove, IN St. Paul Hermitage Retired.
Lutz, Rev. Msgr. James M. '58 (SY) Retired.
Lutz, Joseph L. '87 (RCK) Retired.
Lutz, Kevin F. '78 (COL) Columbus, OH Holy Family.
Lutz, Thomas '93 (NY) Patterson, NY Sacred Heart.
Luu, Khien *s.v.d.* '92 (DUB)[B] Epworth, IA Divine Word College.
Lux, Joseph W. *s.j.* '71 (BUF)[N] Buffalo, NY Canisius Jesuit Community Inc.; [D] Buffalo, NY Canisius High School.
Lux, Thomas J. '85 (LIN) Holdrege, NE All Saints; Diocesan Council of Catholic Women.
Luyet, Gregory T. '95 (LR) Adjutant Judicial Vicar; Judges; Fort Smith, AR Immaculate Conception; Fort Smith, AR St. Leo's; Clergy Personnel Advisory Board (Diocesan); Presbyteral Council; Diocesan Consultors; Deans.
Lwin, Paw Tun '02 (KC) On Duty Outside the Diocese.
Lwin, Paw '02 (ORG) Laguna Niguel, CA St. Timothy.
Lybarger, Curtis F. '77 (STP) Plymouth, MN St. Mary of the Lake.
Lyden, Dennis P. '63 (STU) Retired.
Lydon, John E. *o.p.* '99 (NO) New Orleans, LA St. Anthony of Padua.
Lydon, John J. *o.s.a.* '84 (FgM) Villanova, PA Province of St. Thomas of Villanova (Eastern).
Lydon, Leo B. '50 (WH) Retired.
Lydon, Michael J. '84 (STL) Affton, MO St. Dominic Savio.
Lydon, Michael '74 (SP) New Port Richey, FL St. Thomas Aquinas; [F] New Port Richey, FL St. Thomas Aquinas Early Childhood Center.
Lyle, Rev. Msgr. Dennis J. '91 (CHI)[A] Mundelein, IL University of St. Mary of the Lake/Mundelein Seminary; Mundelein Seminary/University of St. Mary of the Lake; [A] Mundelein, IL University of St. Mary of the Lake/Mundelein Seminary.
Lyle, John W. *o.s.f.s.* '85 (MO) Navy Chaplains.
Lyman, Edward P. '67 (SCR) Swoyersville, PA Holy Name/St. Mary's; Swoyersville, PA Holy Trinity.
Lynam, John '00 (PIT) Pittsburgh, PA Madonna del Castello.
Lynam, Michael John (PIT) Pittsburgh, PA Word of God.
Lynam, Robert G. '84 (MET) Kendall Park, NJ St. Augustine of Canterbury; Deans.
Lynch, Antone '81 (BLX) Retired.
Lynch, Brian T. '06 (STP) Stillwater, MN St. Mary; Stillwater, MN St. Michael.
Lynch, Charles E. *c.s.b.* '58 (GAL) Manvel, TX Sacred Heart of Jesus.
Lynch, Cornelius B. '54 (PRO) Retired.
Lynch, Daniel C. '48 (SC) Retired.
Lynch, Daniel *s.m.a.* '73 (WDC)[O] Takoma Park, MD Lay Missionary Program.
Lynch, Dennis J. '68 (LC)[D] Stevens Point, WI St. Michael's Hospital of Stevens Point, Inc.
Lynch, E. Patrick *c.ss.r.* '69 (STV) Frederiksted, VI Church of St. Patrick; Diocesan Consultors; Catholic Schools Office.
Lynch, E. Patrick *c.ss.r* '69 (FgM) Baltimore Province.
Lynch, Edward C. *s.j.* '64 (NY)[DD] New York, NY Murray–Weigel Hall.
Lynch, Rev. Msgr. Edward J. '57 (BAL) Towson, MD Church of the Immaculate Conception Retired.
Lynch, Francis A. *c.m.* '50 (PH)[Y].
Lynch, Francis '57 (BRK) Retired.
Lynch, Frank M. (BRK) Long Island City, NY Our Lady of Mount Carmel.
Lynch, Gerard F. *o.ss.t.* '74 (PH) Bristol, PA St. Ann.
Lynch, Gerard *o.ss.t.* '74 (BAL)[Q] Diocese of Trenton, NJ.
Lynch, Gregory A. *s.j.* '03 (WOR)[N] Worcester, MA Jesuits of the Holy Cross, Inc.
Lynch, James M. *m.m.* '74 (FgM) Maryknoll, NY MARYKNOLL.
Lynch, Jeremiah W. *s.j.* '03 (CHI)[C] Chicago, IL Jesuit Community at Loyola University Chicago.
Lynch, John E. *c.s.p.* '51 (WDC)[B] Washington, DC St. Paul's College; [C] Catholic University of America, The Retired.
Lynch, John J. '65 (NY) Woodbourne, NY Immaculate Conception.
Lynch, John S. '63 (E) Retired.
Lynch, John W. (NY) Ellenville, NY St. Mary and St. Andrew.
Lynch, John *m.afr.* '62 (WDC)[O] Washington, DC Missionaries of Africa; Washington, DC MISSIONARIES OF AFRICA; Washington, DC Retired.
Lynch, Joseph P. '53 (CHI) Burbank, IL St. Albert the Great Retired.

Lynch, Joseph *s.m.* '64 (STL)[O] St. Louis Marianists, Province of the United States (Society of Mary).
Lynch, Kevin A. *c.s.p.* '53 (NEW)[L] Mahwah, NJ Paulist Fathers – Paulist Press; [Q] Mahwah, NJ Paulist Press.
Lynch, Kevin A. *c.s.p.* '53 (NY)[DD] New York, NY Paulist Fathers' Motherhouse.
Lynch, Leo A. '93 (ALT) Roaring Spring, PA St. Thomas More.
Lynch, Leo X. '56 (BO) Senior Priests. Retired.
Lynch, Michael J. '82 (BRK) Brooklyn, NY Annunciation of the Blessed Virgin Mary.
Lynch, Michael J. '82 (TR) Highlands, NJ Our Lady of Perpetual Help.
Lynch, Michael J. *s.j.* '93 (BAL) Towson, MD Society of Jesus; [Q] Towson Maryland Province of the Society of Jesus.
Lynch, Michael '89 (MIA) Catholic Fire Service Ministry; Deerfield Beach, FL St. Ambrose.
Lynch, Michael '88 (BRK) Brooklyn, NY Our Lady of Mount Carmel Shrine Church.
Lynch, Patrick J. *s.j.* '72 (BUF)[N] Buffalo, NY Canisius Jesuit Community Inc.
Lynch, Patrick *c.s.c.* (FTW)[A] Notre Dame, IN Moreau Seminary; [H] Notre Dame Congregation of Holy Cross, United States Province of Priests & Brothers.
Lynch, Peter J. '99 (BGP) Trumbull, CT St. Catherine of Siena.
Lynch, Robert *o.f.m.* '43 (PAT)[N] Ringwood, NJ Holy Name Friary, Inc.
Lynch, Shane M. '01 (OG) Old Forge, NY St. Anthony of Padua; Old Forge, NY St. Bartholomew; Old Forge, NY St. William.
Lynch, Stephen P. '77 (BRK)[D] Brooklyn, NY Campus Ministers and Ministry Centers; Brooklyn, NY St. Michael.
Lynch, Stephen *o.f.m.* '55 (PAT)[N] Butler, NJ St. Anthony Friary.
Lynch, T. Patrick *s.j.* '61 (NY)[DD] New York, NY Murray–Weigel Hall.
Lynch, Thomas A. '92 (NY) Bronx, NY Our Lady of Angels.
Lynch, Thomas F. '71 (BGP) Stratford, CT St. James.
Lynch, Thomas P. *o.p.* '86 (DEN)[N] Denver, CO Dominican Friars; Denver, CO St. Dominic; Lafayette, CO Immaculate Conception.
Lynch, William J. *s.j.* '48 (CHL)[J] Mooresville, NC Jesuit Community.
Lynes, James F. '79 (GAL) Clute, TX St. Jerome.
Lynes, John G. '87 (MOB) Mobile, AL Little Flower.
Lyness, Stephen J. '98 (ATL) Special or Other Archdiocesan Assignment; Norcross, GA Mary Our Queen Catholic Church.
Lyng, Rev. Msgr. Edward F. '58 (SD) Retired.
Lynn, William D. *s.j.* '54 (ALN)[A] Wernersville, PA Jesuit Center–Jesuit Community.
Lyon, Rev. Msgr. Gerald F. '49 (SC) Retired.
Lyon, Joseph A. '50 (L) Retired.
Lyons, Edward D. '62 (CAM) Retired.
Lyons, Rev. Msgr. Frederick J. '52 (ALX) Retired.
Lyons, James A. '94 (PH) Philadelphia, PA St. John the Baptist; [BB] Philadelphia, PA Roxborough Memorial School of Nursing.
Lyons, Rev. Msgr. James M. '88 (HBG) Deans; Steelton, PA Prince of Peace.
Lyons, James *o.m.i.* '61 (FgM) Washington, DC AMERICAN OBLATE MISSIONS.
Lyons, John F. '46 (Y) Retired.
Lyons, John J. '80 (SAV) Savannah, GA Sacred Heart of Jesus.
Lyons, John P. '88 (TUC) Special Assignment; Judicial Vicar; Council of Priests; Vicars Forane; All Vicars Forane; Tucson, AZ Saint Thomas the Apostle Roman Catholic Parish – Tucson.
Lyons, John R. *m.s.a.* '05 (HRT) Waterbury, CT Basilica of the Immaculate Conception.
Lyons, John R. *m.s.a.* '05 (NOR)[G] Cromwell Society of the Missionaries of the Holy Apostles.
Lyons, John T. '74 (PH) Ambler, PA St. Anthony of Padua.
Lyons, John '73 (CLV) Cleveland, OH Our Lady of Angels.
Lyons, John *d.m.v.* '84 (SAC) Sacramento, CA St. Stephen the First Martyr Parish.
Lyons, Lawrence '54 (MIA) Retired.
Lyons, Michael J. '70 (DUL) Silver Bay, MN St. Mary; Two Harbors, MN Holy Spirit.
Lyons, Michael P. '96 (BGP) Presbyteral Council.
Lyons, Michael '96 (VIC) Ganado, TX Assumption of the B.V.M.; Edna Deanery; Presbyteral Council; Defenders of the Bond; Priests' Personnel Board; Diocesan Consultors.
Lyons, Patrick J. '45 (LIN)[E] Lincoln, NE Bonacum House Retired.
Lyons, Patrick M. '70 (CHI) Calumet City, IL Our Lady of Knock.
Lyons, Peter A. *t.o.r.* '66 (BAL) Baltimore, MD St. Ann; Baltimore, MD St. Wenceslaus; Councilors.
Lyons, Richard J. '74 (MET) North Plainfield, NJ St. Joseph; Judicial Vicar.
Lyons, Robert *s.j.* '77 (SPK)[B] Spokane, WA Gonzaga University.
Lyons, Timothy V. *c.m.* '86 (PH) Philadelphia, PA St. Francis of Assisi.
Lyons, Timothy *o.f.m.* '82 (ATL) Lithia Springs, GA St. John Vianney.
Lyons, Rev. Msgr. William J. '56 (STL) Special Assignment.
Lytle, Gerald A. '60 (HBG) Retired.
Lyttle, Eugene '93 (DUL) Retired.

M

M., Cesar Vega (YAK) Yakima, WA Holy Family; Clergy Personnel Board.
Ma, Peter '55 (NY) New York, NY St. Mary Retired.
Maag, Ronald E. '78 (BAK) Western; Director of Campaign for Human Development; Priests' Continuing Education Committee; Hood River, OR Immaculate Conception; Health and Retirement Board.
Maassen, Jeffrey A. '97 (STL) Arnold, MO St. David.
Mabango, Ashiono Anthony '95 (PAT) Absent on Leave.
Mabon, Rev. Msgr. Thomas K. '57 (ALT) Retired.
Macabalo, Ponciano *o.f.m.* '77 (MIL) Waterford, WI General Secretariat of the Franciscan Missions, Inc.; [Y] Waterford, WI General Secretariat of the Franciscan Missions, Inc.; [P] Burlington, WI Queen of Peace Friary.
Macabio, Arnel *m.s.* '03 (SB)[I] Moreno Valley, CA Missionaries of Our Lady of La Salette, MS.
Macalintal, Dionisio '63 (SD) National City, CA Saint Mary Catholic Parish National City; Filipino.
Macatangay, Francis M. '99 (GAL)[A] Houston, TX St. Mary's Seminary.
MacAulay, Gerard '59 (OKL) Defenders of the Bond Retired.
Macaulay, Neil *o.m.i.* '63 (SJN) San Juan, PR Nuestra Sra. de Guadalupe.
Macaya, Miguel '65 (LSC) Dona Ana, NM Our Lady of the Purification.
MacCandless, William J. *o.s.b.* '58 (NO)[R] St. Benedict, LA St. Joseph Abbey.
MacCarthy, John P. *o.praem.* '69 (GB)[J] De Pere St. Norbert Abbey.
MacCarthy, Joseph T. '97 (BO) Plymouth, MA St. Mary.
MacCarthy, Justin H. '64 (ORG) La Habra, CA Our Lady of Guadalupe.
mac Carthy, Liam J. '68 (SAC) Coordinator for Retired Priests; Priests' Personnel Board, Diocesan Retired.
MacCarthy, Timothy '60 (ORG) Laguna Woods, CA St. Nicholas Retired.
MacDonald, Adam *s.v.d.* '00 (CHI)[N] Techny, IL Divine Word Residence.
MacDonald, Adam *s.v.d.* '00 (DUB)[B] Epworth, IA Divine Word College.
MacDonald, Rev. Msgr. Arthur F. '52 (GLP) Retired.
Macdonald, Colin '81 (SAC) Retired.
MacDonald, Fabian '77 (SEA) Seattle, WA Immaculate Conception.
MacDonald, Hugh J. '64 (HRT) North Haven, CT St. Barnabas.
MacDonald, James H. '67 (SFR) Retired.
MacDonald, Kevin M. *c.ss.r.* '91 (FgM) Baltimore Province.
MacDonald, Kevin (STV) Frederiksted, VI Church of St. Patrick.
MacDonald, Paul V. '59 (BO) Senior Priests. Retired.
MacDonald, Sebastian *c.p.* '58 (CHI)[N] Chicago, IL Passionist Community of St. Vincent Strambi.
MacDonald, Timothy E. '00 (LAN) Jackson, MI Queen of the Miraculous Medal; Michigan Center, MI Our Lady of Fatima.
MacDonald, Timothy I. *s.a.* '67 (NY)[DD] Garrison, NY Franciscan Friars of the Atonement, Minister General Office; [DD] New York, NY Atonement Friars; General Council.
MacDonald, Vincent *s.c.j.* '58 (MIL)[P] Franklin Sacred Heart at Monastery Lake.
MacDonough, Richard B. *s.s.* '60 (BAL)[Q] Baltimore Society of St. Sulpice, Province of the United States Retired.
MacDonough, Richard *s.s.* '60 (PRT) Retired.
MacDougall, James L. *o.s.a.* '59 (MIA)[C] St. Thomas University; [H] Miami Gardens, FL Casa San Lorenzo.
Mace, John D. *s.j.* '68 (MIL)[P] Milwaukee Jesuit Provincial Office, Wisconsin Province; Milwaukee, WI Society of Jesus.
MacEntee, Francis J. *s.j.* '54 (SCR)[B] Scranton, PA The University of Scranton.
MacEwen, Michael W. (BO) Marlborough, MA Immaculate Conception; Vicariate I.
Macey, James R. '07 (BIR) Jacksonville, AL St. Charles Borromeo; [H] Jacksonville, AL Jacksonville State University.
Macfarlane, Rev. Msgr. John F. '66 (WDC) Rockville, MD St. Elizabeth.
MacGabhann, Kevin '63 (PMB) Retired.
MacGee, James *o.m.i.* '57 (PRT) Howland, ME St. Leo The Great.
MacGillivray, John J. *c.m.* '76 (FgM) Philadelphia, PA Eastern Province.
Machado, Dayan '10 (SP) Tampa, FL St. Lawrence.
Machado, Domingos A. *o.a.r.* '95 (LA) Montebello, CA St. Benedict; West Orange, NJ.
Machado, Johnson J. '05 (CC) Benavides, TX Santa Rosa de Lima.
Machado, Jose '93 (WCH) Wichita, KS Our Lady of Perpetual Help.
Machain, David B. '52 (PH) Philadelphia, PA St. Bernard Retired.
Machalski, Thomas C. '85 (BRK) Released from Diocesan Assignment.
Machalski, Thomas C. (DET)[A] Orchard Lake, MI SS. Cyril and Methodius Seminary.
Machamire, Cuthbert (CC)[D] Corpus Christi, TX CHRISTUS Spohn Hospital Corpus Christi – Shoreline.
Machar, Jerome J. *o.c.s.o.* '75 (ROC)[K] Piffard, NY Abbey of the Genesee; Piffard, NY.
Machira, Paul (SY) Binghamton, NY St. Thomas Aquinas; Binghamton, NY St. Patrick.
Machnik, Theodore F. '91 (COL) Circleville, OH St. Joseph; Deanery 12: Chillicothe; Presbyteral Council; Parochial Examiners.
Macho, George S. '53 (NEW) Retired.
Machozi, Vincent *a.a.* '94 (BO)[U] Boston, MA Assumptionist Center.
Machuca, Ricardo *s.j.* (TUC)[I] Nogales, AZ Kino Border Initiative.
Maciag, Waldemar '97 (ORL) Leesburg, FL St. Paul's.
Macias, Alonso E. (BO) Vocations; Jamaica Plain, MA St. Thomas Aquinas; Roxbury, MA St. Mary of the Angels; Jamaica Plain, MA Our Lady of Lourdes.
Macias, Frank '94 (SAT) San Antonio, TX St. Leo.
Macias, Fray Jorge *o.f.m.cap.* (SJN).
Macias, Gabino Olivia (BO) Waltham, MA St. Mary.
Macias, Salvador '82 (OAK) Fremont, CA Corpus Christi.
Maciej, David '80 (SCL) Lastrup, MN Holy Cross; Lastrup, MN St. John Nepomuk; Directors; Koinonia Program of Central Minnesota; Presbyteral Council.
Maciejewski, Norbert F. '69 (DET) Retired.
Maciejewski, Tadeusz *c.m.* '88 (BRK) Brooklyn, NY SS. Cyril and Methodius.
MacInnes, Colin '70 (FgM) Boston, MA St. James the Apostle, Inc.
MacInnis, John E. (BO) Peabody, MA St. Thomas the Apostle; Vicariate II; Designated; Peabody, MA St. John the Baptist.
MacInnis, Michael *o.f.m./i.c.* (BO) Boston, MA St. Leonard of Port Maurice.
MacIntyre, Frederick H. '92 (WDC) Washington, DC St. Patrick Retired.
MacIssac, Charles S. *o.s.* '83 (PCE) On Duty Outside the Diocese Retired.
Mack, John P. '85 (BUF) Air Force Reserve Chaplains; On Duty Outside the Diocese.
Mack, Joseph W. '89 (CHL) Reidsville, NC Holy Infant.
Mack, Rev. Msgr. Thomas E. '78 (PEO) Cullom, IL St. John's; Pontiac, IL St. Mary's; Vicariates and Vicars.
MacKay, Arthur T. (BO) Woburn, MA St. Charles Borromeo.
Macke, Richard J. '54 (SC) Retired.
MacKenzie, John B. '00 (MAN) Lancaster, NH Gate of Heaven.
MacKenzie, William M. '66 (BO) Senior Priests. Retired.
Mackert, Albert J. '61 (CLV) Cleveland, OH Immaculate Conception Retired.
Mackey, Alan C. '00 (BIR) Scottsboro, AL St. Jude.
Mackey, James '61 (ALB) Troy, NY St. Michael the Archangel Retired.
Mackin, Kevin *o.f.m.* (NY)[C] Newburgh, NY Mt. St. Mary College.
MacKinnon, Donald *c.ss.r.* '59 (OAK)[L] Berkeley, CA Redemptorist Fathers (Denver Province); Kmhmu/Laotian Pastoral Center.
Mackle, Daniel E. '80 (PH)[A] Wynnewood, PA Theological Seminary of St. Charles Borromeo, Overbrook; Philadelphia, PA St. Patrick.
Macklin, Eckley *s.o.l.t.* '95 (CHY) Saint Stephens, WY St. Stephen's; [D] Saint Stephens, WY St. Stephens Mission.
Mackowski, Richard M. *s.j.* '61 (DET)[K] Clarkston, MI Colombiere Center.
MacLean, Thomas S. '02 (LIN) Advocates; Health Care Facilities; Lincoln, NE Nebraska Penal Complex; Building Commission.
MacLellan, Iain G. *o.s.b.* '87 (MAN)[K] Manchester, NH St. Anselm Abbey.
MacLennan, Donald B. '67 (DET) Retired.
MacLeod, Malcolm *m.ss.cc.* '87 (CAM) Linwood, NJ The Church of Our Lady of Sorrows, Linwood, N.J.; Linwood, NJ.
MacMahon, Craig *o.m.v.* '90 (LA) Hawaiian Gardens, CA St. Peter Chanel.
MacMahon, Rev. Msgr. Eamon '47 (MRY) Retired.
Mac Mahon, Michael '66 (BIR) Huntsville, AL Holy Spirit; Diocesan College of Consultors; Priests'/Presbyteral Council; Diocesan College of Vicars.
MacMahon, Patrick '69 (SPK) Davenport, WA Immaculate Conception; Harrington, WA St. Francis of Assisi; Davenport, WA St. Michael.

MacMaster, Thomas A. *o.c.s.o.* '57 (DUB)[K] Peosta, IA New Melleray Abbey, Order of Cistercians of the Strict Observance.
MacMillan, Donald A. *s.j.* '72 (BO)[U] Newton, MA The Jesuit Community at Boston College.
MacMillan, Len '91 (B) Meridian, ID Holy Apostles.
MacNamara, Robert C. '51 (ROC) Elmira, NY St. Mary Retired.
MacNeil, Paul D. '89 (CHR) Beaufort, SC St. Peter.
MacNew, James '69 (PH)[C] Philadelphia, PA Holy Family University.
Maco, Stephen L. '76 (ALN) Bangor, PA Our Lady of Good Counsel.
Macora, Athanasius *o.f.m.* '92 (FgM) Washington, DC COMMISSARIAT OF THE HOLY LAND.
Macoskie, Melvin H. '55 (MIL) Retired.
Macoy, Jose '60 (HON) Hana, HI St. Mary.
MacPhaidin, Bartley J. *c.s.c.* '63 (FTW)[H] Notre Dame Congregation of Holy Cross, United States Province of Priests & Brothers.
MacPherson, Damian *s.a.* '78 (NY)[DD] Garrison Franciscan Friars of the Atonement, Minister General Office.
MacPherson, Stephen E.C. '86 (SR) On Leave.
Macpherson, Walter '86 (CIN) Retired.
MacQuarrie, John D. '78 (CIN) West Milton, OH Transfiguration.
MacRory, Camillus *o.f.m.cap.* '51 (SFR) Definitors:; [N] Burlingame, CA Capuchin Provincial House Retired.
Macsherry, Hugh *o.f.m.* '09 (CAM) Camden, NJ St. Anthony of Padua Roman Catholic Church, Camden, N.J.
Mactutis, Peter '06 (SEA) Lakewood, WA St. Frances Cabrini.
MacVeigh, Donal T. *s.j.* '72 (NEW)[B] Jersey City, NJ Jesuit Center; [L] Jersey City, NJ Jesuits of Saint Peter's College, Inc.
MacVeigh, Michael C. '56 (PIT)[M] Pittsburgh, PA St. John Vianney Manor Retired.
MacWade, Joseph A. *s.j.* '61 (FgM) Watertown, MA Society of Jesus.
Madalaimuthu, Kulandairaj '93 (MET) Baptistown, NJ Our Lady of Victories.
Madanu, Anthaiah *s.v.d.* '92 (LA) Los Angeles, CA St. John, The Evangelist.
Madanu, Joseph (Jo Joppa) *m.f.* '02 (GLP) Grants, NM St. Teresa of Avila; Milan, NM St. Vivian; Milan, NM San Mateo; Milan, NM San Rafael.
Madanu, Santosh *h.g.n.* '01 (LEX) Jenkins, KY St. George.
Madathil, Sojan Anthony (BRK)[R] Brooklyn, NY Carmelites of Mary Immaculate, Inc.
Madathiparambil, Vinod '98 (SYM) Eparchial Consultors; Procurator, Chancellor & Secretary to Bishop.
Madathummuriyil, Sebastian *m.c.b.s.* '98 (MIL)[P] Kenosha, WI Missionary Congregation of the Blessed Sacrament, Inc., Zion Province.
Madavana, Martin *i.c.* '09 (SP) Seffner, FL St. Francis of Assisi.
Madden, Benjamin F. *o.f.m. cap.* (WH)[L] Charleston, WV Capuchins–St. Anthony Friary; Charleston, WV St. Anthony.
Madden, Rev. Msgr. Brendan P. '51 (PAT)[Q] Chester, NJ Nazareth Village Retired.
Madden, Rev. Msgr. Edward T. '52 (DEN) Retired.
Madden, J. Thomas '53 (SFR) Retired.
Madden, James J. *m.m.* '60 (NY)[DD] Maryknoll Maryknoll Fathers and Brothers.
Madden, James P. *c.s.c.* '57 (ALB)[L] Valatie, NY St. Joseph Center.
Madden, James P. *c.s.c.* '57 (FTW)[H] Notre Dame Congregation of Holy Cross, United States Province of Priests & Brothers.
Madden, John F. '84 (WOR) Worcester, MA St. John's.
Madden, John J. *s.j.* '69 (SAV) Special Assignment.
Madden, John P. '86 (Y) McDonald, OH Our Lady of Perpetual Help.
Madden, John R. '70 (SAV) Pine Mountain, GA Christ the King Church.
Madden, Rev. Msgr. John R. '59 (SY) Retired.
Madden, Joseph *o.f.m.conv.* '62 (R)[F] Pittsboro, NC Our Lady of Guadalupe Friary; Apex, NC St. Andrew the Apostle.
Madden, Michael J. '95 (BGP) Leave of Absence.
Madden, Michael '75 (EVN) Bloomfield, IN Holy Name; Advocates; Diocesan Council of Priests; Linton, IN St. Peter; Diocesan Consultors.
Madden, Patrick J. '83 (MOB) Robertsdale, AL St. Patrick.
Madden, Patrick J. '74 (SHP) Greco Institute; Grambling, LA St. Benedict the Black; Hodge, LA St. Lucy.
Madden, Stephen J. '88 (BO) Foxborough, MA St. Mary.
Madden, Thomas F. '76 (NY) Haverstraw, NY St. Peter; Canon 1742 Panel of Pastors.
Madden, Rev. Msgr. Thomas G. '55 (NEW) North Arlington, NJ Queen of Peace; [L] Rutherford, NJ St. John Vianney Residence for Priests Retired.
Madden, Thomas J. *s.j.* '57 (LAF)[J] Grand Coteau, LA Jesuit Spirituality Center (St. Charles College).
Madden, Thomas '81 (SP) Clearwater, FL St. Cecelia.
Madden, William T. *m.m.* '58 (NY)[DD] Maryknoll Maryknoll Fathers and Brothers; [HH] Maryknoll, NY Friends of St. Maria Goretti, U.S.A., Inc. Retired.
Maddineni, Ananda Prasad *m.s.f.s.* '96 (STA) Jacksonville, FL Holy Spirit.
Maddock, Andrew *s.j.* '85 (HEL) St. Ignatius, MT St. Ignatius Mission; Presbyteral Council.
Maddock, George *o.f.m.cap.* '64 (FgM)[F] Agana Heights, GU St. Fidelis Friary; White Plains, NY The Province of St. Mary of the Capuchin Order.
Maddock, Jay T. '75 (FR)[J] Fall River, MA Diocesan Catholic Youth Organization; Judges; Catholic Youth Organization; Fall River, MA Holy Name.
Maddock, Laurence F. '56 (CHI)[A] Chicago, IL St. Joseph College Seminary; Chicago, IL Saint Ita Retired.
Madej, Paul D. '90 (SY) Military Chaplains; Army Chaplains.
Madel, Samuel Tanios *m.l.m.* (OLL)[A] Houston, TX The Congregation of Maronite Lebanese Missionaries.
Madel, Samuel '91 (OLL) West Covina, CA St. Jude Maronite Catholic Church.
Mader, George L. '59 (NEW)[L] Caldwell, NJ The Rev. Msgr. James F. Kelley Residence for Retired Priests Retired.
Mader, Joseph E. '67 (IND) Retired.
Mader, Stan P. '92 (STP) Hampton, MN St. Mathias; Vermillion, MN St. John the Baptist; Deanery 6; New Trier, MN St. Mary.
Madera, Juan '08 (FRS) Absent on Sick Leave.
Madey, Louis '68 (MO) Navy Reserve Chaplains; On Duty Outside the Diocese.
Madeya, Gregory *b.h.s.* '08 (SJP) McKeesport, PA St. John the Baptist; Presbyters.
Madhichetti, Anthony '00 (GI) Mitchell, NE St. Theresa's.
Madi–Okin, Charles '07 (BO) Somerville, MA St. Joseph.
Madigan, Arthur R. *s.j.* '77 (BO)[U] Newton, MA The Jesuit Community at Boston College.
Madigan, Daniel A. *s.j.* '83 (WDC)[X] Washington, DC Woodstock Theological Center; [O] Washington, DC The Jesuit Community at Georgetown University; [O] Washington, DC Woodstock Jesuit Community.
Madigan, Daniel '64 (SAC) Clarksburg, CA St. Joseph.
Madigan, Henry *o.f.m.conv.* '56 (ALB)[L] Rensselaer, NY Provincialate, Immaculate Conception Friary – Order of Friars Minor Conventual.
Madigan, John C. '74 (SEA) Seattle, WA Holy Rosary; Seattle, WA Our Lady of Mount Virgin; Deans; Presbyteral Council.
Madigan, Rev. Msgr. John J. '54 (WDC) Silver Spring, MD Our Lady of Grace Retired.
Madigan, John R. *o.m.i.* '77 (BEL)[J] Belleville, IL Missionary Association of Mary Immaculate–Missionary Oblates of Mary Immaculate; [F] Belleville, IL Shrine of Our Lady of the Snows.
Madigan, Kevin '70 (NY) New York, NY St. Peter.
Madigan, Patrick S. *s.j.* '83 (NO)[R] New Orleans Jesuit Provincial Office.
Madike, Sebastian Chukwudi (BO) Brighton, MA St. Columbkille.
Madison, Martin *s.a.* '62 (NY)[DD] Garrison, NY Franciscan Friars of the Atonement.
Madley, Rev. Msgr. Jeffrey J. '76 (RVC) Southampton, NY Sacred Hearts of Jesus and Mary.
Madori, Peter J. '69 (NY) Wurtsboro, NY St. Joseph.
Madrid, Moises (BRK) Flushing, NY St. Michael.
Madrigal, Hector '87 (AMA) Advocates; Ex Officio; Vicars Forane; Amarillo, TX St. Joseph's.
Madrigal, Ildefonso M. '57 (LA) Retired.
Madsen, Rev. Msgr. John W. '66 (BUF)[N] Depew, NY Msgr. Conniff Residence Retired.
Madu, Anthony '93 (RVC) Rockville Centre, NY Mercy Medical Center; Malverne, NY Our Lady of Lourdes.
Madu, Cletus '78 (LA) Los Angeles, CA Mother of Sorrows.
Madu, Ferdinand E. '86 (MO) Army Chaplains.
Madu, Omumuawuike *c.m.f.* '96 (NY) Manhattan, NY New York Presbyterian Hospital.
Maduakor, Casmir (CHR) Myrtle Beach, SC St. Andrew.
Madukkakuzhy, Emmanuel '90 (SYM) Bellwood, IL Mar Thoma Sleeha Cathedral (Chicago).
Madumelu, Jerome '94 (RVC) West Islip, NY Good Samaritan Hospital Medical Center.
Maduri, John '87 (BRK) Brooklyn, NY Most Precious Blood; Nocturnal Adoration Society.
Maduro, P. Gabriel '59 (ARE) Arecibo, PR Cathedral of San Felipe Apostol; Defenders of the Bond; Susoni Hospital.
Madus, Rev. Msgr. Peter P. '68 (SCR) Peckville, PA Sacred Heart of Jesus.
Maduzia, Norbert J. '82 (GAL) Spring, TX St. Ignatius of Loyola; Building and Planning Commission.
Maechler, Edmund Francis '49 (LA) Retired.
Maekawa, Steven *o.p.* '98 (OAK)[L] Oakland, CA Order of Preachers (Province of the Most Holy Name of Jesus – Western Dominican Province); [L] Oakland, CA Order of Preachers (Province of the Most Holy Name of Jesus – Western Dominican Province).
Maes, Allen J. *o.m.i.* '68 (BEL)[F] Belleville, IL Missionary Oblates of Mary Immaculate – St. Henry's Oblate Residence.
Maes, Anthony G. *o.praem.* '82 (SFE)[B] Albuquerque, NM St. Pius X High School; [H] Albuquerque, NM Santa Maria de la Vid Priory.
Maes, Clarence '87 (SFE) Albuquerque, NM Sacred Heart; Presbyteral Council of the Archdiocese of Santa Fe.
Maes, Clark B. '95 (STL) Bloomsdale, MO St. Agnes; Bloomsdale, MO St. Lawrence.
Maes, John J. '67 (DOD) Diocesan Finance Council; College of Consultors Retired.
Maestri, William F. '77 (NO) New Orleans, LA Cathedral – Basilica of St. Louis King of France; On Special Assignment; Archives and Records (Archdiocesan).
Maffei, Vincent R. '64 (BO) Randolph, MA St. Mary; Senior Priests. Retired.
Maffeo, Michael T. '91 (RVC) Ronkonkoma, NY St. Joseph's; Priests' Personnel Assignment Board.
Maga, Glenn *c.p.* (ATL) Atlanta, GA St. Paul of the Cross.
Magabe, Benedict *c.pp.s.* '06 (CIN) Saint Henry, OH St. Bernard; Saint Henry, OH St. Aloysius; Saint Henry, OH St. Francis; Saint Henry, OH St. Henry; Saint Henry, OH St. Wendelin; [N] Dayton, OH Provincial Office of the Cincinnati Province of the Society of the Precious Blood.
Magallanes, Manuel *o.s.b.* '76 (OKL)[I] Shawnee, OK St. Gregory's Abbey.
Magallanes, Oscar '10 (TUC) San Luis, AZ Saint Jude Thaddeus Roman Catholic Parish – San Luis; Yuma, AZ Immaculate Conception Roman Catholic Parish & Guadalupe Mission – Yuma.
Magallenes, Alejandro '69 (LA)[B] Santa Ynez, CA San Lorenzo Seminary – Retreat Center.
Magallon, Ernesto '98 (BWN) Board Members; Edcouch, TX St. Theresa of the Infant Jesus.
Magaña, Alberto O. '01 (YAK) Special Assignment.
Magana, Edgar *o.f.m.* '02 (SJ) San Jose, CA Our Lady of Guadalupe.
Magana, Emilio A. '07 (SD) Calipatria, CA Saint Patrick Catholic Parish Calipatria.
Magana, Jose L. '98 (LA) Long Beach, CA St. Anthony.
Magana, Salvador '06 (WIL) Wilmington, DE St. Catherine of Siena.
Magararu, Richard *s.m.m.* '94 (BRK)[R] Ozone Park, NY Montfort Missionaries Provincialate (Missionaries of the Company of Mary); Ozone Park, NY St. Mary Gate of Heaven.
Magary, Thomas A. '66 (STU) Retired.
Magat, Geronimo A. '02 (ARL) Stafford, VA St. William of York.
Magbanua, Celso '01 (CHK) Legion of Mary at Kristo Rai Parish/Mother Refuge of Sinners, Praesidium; Diocesan Publications Office; Kristo Rai Parish; Mount Carmel School, Inc. (Saipan); Presbyteral Council.
Magbanua, Rev. Msgr. Mario '65 (DAL) Dallas, TX St. James.
Magdaleno, Ricardo '89 (FRS) Children's Hospital Central California; Kaiser Permanente Medical Center; Fresno, CA St. Anthony of Padua.
Magdaong, Joseph '98 (LA) Downey, CA Our Lady of Perpetual Help.
Magdaraog, Vicente '96 (TR) Howell, NJ St. Veronica.
Magee, George P. *o.s.a.* '68 (PH)[Y] Villanova, PA St. Thomas Monastery.
Magee, Rev. Msgr. Michael K. '91 (PH)[A] Wynnewood, PA Theological Seminary of St. Charles Borromeo, Overbrook.
Magee, Patrick F. '70 (TR) Retired.
Magee, Patrick '81 (FR) On Duty Outside the Diocese.
Magee, Patrick *f.l.h.f.* '81 (PAT) Paterson, NJ St. Casimir's.
Magee, Raphael M. *f.i.* '98 (FR)[F] New Bedford, MA Marian Friary of Our Lady, Queen of the Seraphic Order.
Magel, John E. '60 (L) Retired.
Mager, Martin J. *o.s.b.* '63 (SFR)[N] Portola Valley, CA Woodside Priory; Portola Valley, CA.
Maghinay, Jose '92 (STO) Stockton, CA Presentation Church (Pastor of).
Maghinay, Joseph '74 (STO) Filipino Pastoral Ministry; Members Appointed.
Maghsoudi, Aron M. '06 (ALT) Williamsburg, PA St. Joseph; Cresson, PA State Correctional Institution; Huntingdon, PA State Correctional Institution.
Magiera, Michael W. *f.s.s.p.* '05 (IND) Indianapolis, IN Our Lady of the Most Holy Rosary Catholic Church, Indianapolis, Inc.
Maginnis, Andrew F. *s.j.* '52 (SJ)[M] Los Gatos, CA Sacred Heart Jesuit Center.
Maginnis, Edward L. *s.j.* '53 (STL)[O] St. Louis, MO Jesuit Community Corporation at Saint Louis University – Jesuit Hall.
Maginot, Michael L. '83 (GRY) Merrillville, IN St. Stephen, Martyr.
Maginot, Richard J. '50 (CHI) Prospect Heights, IL St. Alphonsus Liguori Retired.

Magnan, Oscar G. '63 (NEW)[B] Jersey City, NJ Jesuit Center; [L] Jersey City, NJ Jesuits of Saint Peter's College, Inc.
Magnano, Paul A. '67 (SEA) Seattle, WA Christ Our Hope Personal Parish; Seattle, WA St. Peter; College of Consultors.
Magnaye, Carlo Benjamin *m.f.* '96 (AUS) Mexia, TX St. Mary; Mexia, TX State School.
Magner, Kevin P. '03 (STP) Anoka, MN St. Stephen.
Magner, Richard P. *s.j.* (SEA)[M] Seattle, WA Jesuit House, Seattle.
Magni, Daniel M. '78 (BO) Senior Priests. Retired.
Magnuson, Sean R. '06 (STP) Military Chaplains; Army Chaplains.
Mago, Israel E. '07 (MIA) Doral, FL Our Lady of Guadalupe; Confraternity of Our Lady of Chiquinquira.
Magoon, R. Dale '60 (GLD) Mancelona, MI St. Anthony of Padua.
Magpayo, Teodoro P. '89 (SFR) Daly City, CA Our Lady of Mercy.
Magraw, Rev. Msgr. Daniel E. '75 (E) Erie, PA Blessed Sacrament; Presbyteral Council; College of Consultors; Members.
Maguire, Connell J. '45 (PH) Retired.
Maguire, Daniel J. '69 (SFR) Retired.
Maguire, Enda J. '59 (STO) Diamond Springs, CA Retired.
Maguire, Francis X. *c.m.* '78 (PH)[Y].
Maguire, Robert *o.cist.* '76 (DAL)[B] University of Dallas; [J] Irving, TX Cistercian Abbey of Our Lady of Dallas.
Maguire, Seamus J. '53 (WH) Retired.
Maguire, Thomas H. '76 (BO) Norwell, MA St. Helen Mother of the Emperor Constantine.
Maguire, Thomas J. '69 (SAC) Alcoholism Advisory Board; Folsom, CA St. John the Baptist Retired.
Maguire, William *c.p.* (HRT)[L] West Hartford Holy Family Monastery/Retreat.
Magwaza, Thulani D. '89 (CHI) Chicago, IL St. Sabina.
Mahalic, Philip A. '83 (LFT) Military Chaplains.
Mahalic, Philip A. '75 (MO) Army Reserve Chaplains.
Mahan, Terrance L. *s.j.* '54 (LA)[C] Los Angeles, CA Jesuit Community.
Mahaney, Hilary F. '69 (CHI) Chicago, IL St. Mary of the Angels; [V] Chicago, IL Midtown Residence; Chicago.
Mahar, Christopher M. '04 (PRO)[A] Providence, RI Seminary of Our Lady of Providence; Seminary of Our Lady of Providence.
Mahar, James (BRK)[D] Brooklyn, NY Campus Ministers and Ministry Centers.
Mahar, Raymond J. '58 (BUF)[N] Buffalo, NY Sheehan Residence for Priests Retired.
Maher, Arthur '54 (JOL) Retired.
Maher, Charles E. '60 (PRO) Retired.
Maher, Daniel J. '62 (ALB) Retired.
Maher, Edmund J. '88 (PH)[CC] Philadelphia, PA Catholic League For Persons With Disabilities Retired.
Maher, Edward J. '81 (CAM) Cherry Hill, NJ St. Mary's R.C. Church, Delaware Township, N.J.
Maher, Francis '54 (JOL) Retired.
Maher, Francis '54 (COS) Colorado Springs, CO St. Joseph's Retired.
Maher, J. David '71 (JC) Russellville, MO St. Michael; Jefferson City, MO St. Peter; Personnel Board.
Maher, James J. *c.m.* '90 (BRK)[C] St. John's University; [R] Jamaica, NY St. Vincent's House.
Maher, James Joseph '92 (LA) Retired.
Maher, Jerry '94 (MRY)[I] Santa Cruz, CA Cabrillo College; [I] Santa Cruz, CA University of California at Santa Cruz; Campus Ministry Department; Santa Cruz, CA Holy Cross.
Maher, John L. *s.j.* '74 (FgM) St. Louis, MO Society of Jesus.
Maher, John T. *c.m.* '81 (PH)[Y].
Maher, Michael L. '48 (SAG) Retired.
Maher, Michael N. *ss.cc.* '63 (SB) Cathedral City, CA St. Louis.
Maher, Michael N. *ss.cc* '63 (LA)[P] La Verne, CA Congregation of the Sacred Hearts of Jesus and Mary.
Maher, Michael W. *s.j.* '86 (SPK)[B] Spokane, WA Gonzaga University.
Maher, P. Brent '11 (BR) Baton Rouge, LA St. George.
Maher, Patrick '71 (LUB) Plainview, TX St. Alice.
Maher, Patrick '53 (MOB) Dothan, AL St. Columba Retired.
Maher, Raymond V. *o.carm.* '97 (MO) DEPARTMENT OF VETERANS AFFAIRS HOSPITALS AND CHAPLAINS.
Maher, Rev. Msgr. Robert E. '71 (BWN) Edinburg, TX St. Joseph; Vicar General; Ex Officio Members; College of Consultors; [E] San Juan, TX San Juan Nursing Home, Inc.; [D] Executive Board.
Maher, Robert G. '57 (WIN) Retired.
Maher, Robert *o.f.m.cap.* '74 (HON) Waimanalo, HI St. George.
Maher, Ryan J. *s.j.* '97 (WDC)[O] Washington, DC The Jesuit Community at Georgetown University.
Maher, Ryan L. '05 (COV) Covington, KY St. Benedict; Diocesan Consultors; Deanery Pastoral Council; Initiation; Office of Worship.
Maher, Sean M. '09 (BO) Duxbury, MA Holy Family.
Maher, T. Patrick '02 (GLD) West Branch, MI Holy Family; West Branch, MI St. Joseph; Members of the College of Consultors; Prescott, MI St. Stephen of Hungary.
Maher, Thomas F. '47 (CHI) Chicago, IL St. Genevieve Retired.
Maher, Thomas F. '94 (TR) Whiting, NJ St. Elizabeth Ann Seton.
Maher, Thomas *o.m.i.* '57 (FgM) Washington, DC AMERICAN OBLATE MISSIONS.
Maher, William *o.m.i.* '66 (FgM) Washington, DC AMERICAN OBLATE MISSIONS.
Mahler, Clyde '99 (HT) Houma, LA Maria Immacolata; Knights of Columbus.
Mahler, Rev. Msgr. Frank E. '56 (ARL) Retired.
Mahlmann, Raymond '85 (GLP) Defenders of the Bond; Ecumenical Affairs in New Mexico; Farmington, NM St. Mary's.
Mahon, Ambrose J. '58 (STP) Retired.
Mahon, Rev. Msgr. Dennis '70 (NEW)[B] Seton Hall University.
Mahon, Rev. Msgr. Gerald A. '71 (WIN) Rochester, MN St. John the Evangelist.
Mahon, Joseph F. *c.s.p.* '56 (NY)[DD] New York, NY Paulist Fathers' Motherhouse Retired.
Mahon, Leo T. '51 (CHI) Chicago, IL St. Mary of the Woods Retired.
Mahon, Rev. Msgr. Leo T. '51 (CHI) Retired.
Mahon, M. Shawn '88 (BAL) Priests Sick or Absent.
Mahon, William A. '92 (NEW) New Providence, NJ Our Lady of Peace.
Mahone, Casey B. '89 (WH) Clarksburg, WV Immaculate Conception.
Mahone, Michael '80 (RNO) Reno, NV Our Lady of the Snows; Seminary Board; Vocations Team; Priest Personnel Board; Diocesan Board of Consultors; Presbyteral Council.
Mahoney, Bernard '53 (AUS) Retired.
Mahoney, Brian E. '95 (BO) Dracut, MA St. Francis of Assisi; Vicariate II.
Mahoney, Daniel C. '70 (GBG) Latrobe, PA Holy Family; Deaneries; Bishop's Priests Council; College of Deans.
Mahoney, Daniel J. '56 (BO) Charlestown, MA St. Francis de Sales.
Mahoney, Gerard J. *o.s.f.s.* '80 (WIL) Wilmington, DE St. Anthony of Padua.
Mahoney, James M. '92 (BO) Abington, MA St. Bridget; Elected.
Mahoney, Rev. Msgr. James T. (PAT) Chatham, NJ Corpus Christi; Vicar General and Moderator of the Curia; Presbyteral Council; Finance Council; College of Consultors; [Q] Wayne, NJ Consortium of Catholic Schools of the Roman Catholic Diocese of Paterson, Inc.; [Q] Sparta, NJ The Catholic Academy of Sussex County, Inc.
Mahoney, Rev. Msgr. John E. '72 (BRK) Jackson Heights, NY Our Lady of Fatima.
Mahoney, John J. '90 (MAN) Diocesan Judges; Manchester, NH Parish of the Transfiguration; Defenders of the Bond.
Mahoney, John '90 (BUR) Judges.
Mahoney, Joseph P. '57 (WOR) Worcester, MA St. Stephen's.
Mahoney, Kevin J. '81 (STL) Retired.
Mahoney, Mark A. '86 (BO) Topsfield, MA St. Rose of Lima.
Mahoney, Maurice J. *o.s.a.* '60 (FgM) Villanova, PA Province of St. Thomas of Villanova (Eastern).
Mahoney, Michael *o.f.m.cap.* '74 (SFR) Burlingame, CA Our Lady of Angels.
Mahoney, Rev. Msgr. Neil J. '70 (NEW) Newark, NJ St. John's; Newark, NJ St. Patrick's Pro–Cathedral.
Mahoney, Peter '61 (BRK)[K] Brooklyn, NY Catholic Charities; Brooklyn, NY Assumption of the Blessed Virgin Mary.
Mahoney, Richard J. '58 (STP) Coates, MN St. Agatha Retired.
Mahoney, Robert J. '55 (KC) Retired.
Mahoney, Shaun L. '91 (PH)[A] Wynnewood, PA Theological Seminary of St. Charles Borromeo, Overbrook; St. Charles Borromeo Seminary; College of Consultors; By Appointment.
Mahoney, Thomas A. '98 (BO) Belmont, MA St. Joseph; Boston, MA St. Cecilia.
Mahoney, Thomas D. '65 (CLV) Retired.
Mahoney, Thomas E. '68 (WOR) Advocates; Upton, MA St. Gabriel the Archangel.
Mahonge, Augustine '09 (CHI) Des Plaines, IL St. Zachary.
Mahony, John '58 (SP) Retired.
Mahowald, Rev. Msgr. Richard J. '55 (SFS) Retired.
Mai, Dan T. *s.j.* '03 (P)[L] Portland Jesuit Provincial Office (Society of Jesus, Oregon Prov.).
Mai, Khoa Luong '05 (LA) Rancho Palos Verdes, CA St. John Fisher.
Mai, Peter Vong '04 (OAK)[L] Saint Conrad Friary.
Mai, Trung Thanh *s.v.d.* '05 (DUB)[B] Epworth, IA Divine Word College.
Mai–Chi–Than, Joseph M. '57 (PEO) Retired.
Maibusch, Henry *o.s.a.* '54 (MIL) Racine, WI St. Rita.
Maichen, Richard F. '54 (DUB) Retired.
Maida, Thaddeus S. '58 (PIT) Retired.
Maier, John '90 (DM) Leavenworth, KS Retired.
Maier, Joseph *c.ss.r.* '65 (FgM) Denver, CO Denver Province.
Maier, Paul '70 (RIC) Abingdon, VA Christ the King; Marion, VA St. John the Evangelist Church.
Maiers, Brennan *o.s.b.* '63 (SCL)[I] Collegeville, MN St. John's Abbey, of the Order of St. Benedict.
Maikowski, Thomas R. '76 (MO) Defenders of the Bond; Air Force Reserve Chaplains.
Maikowski, Thomas '76 (GLP) Page, AZ Immaculate Heart of Mary.
Mailadiyil, Augustine '75 (SP) Sun City Center, FL Prince of Peace.
Maillet, Paul A. *s.s.* '01 (BAL) Special Assignment; [Q] Baltimore Society of St. Sulpice, Province of the United States.
Maillet, Paul A. *s.s.* '01 (SFR)[A] Menlo Park, CA St. Patrick Seminary and University.
Mailloux, Thomas Bernard *c.s.b.* '50 (GAL) Houston, TX St. Anne Retired.
Maina, Paul T. '98 (PH) Philadelphia, PA Incarnation of Our Lord.
Mainardi, Donald G. '64 (ORL) Viera, FL St. John the Evangelist Retired.
Mainza, Peter C. *a.j.* '89 (ALN)[P] Shenandoah, PA Apostles of Jesus.
Mainzer, James S. '87 (WCH) Newton, KS St. Mary; Legion of Mary.
Maione, Francis T. '65 (NEW) Retired.
Mair, Robert G. '65 (CHI) Glenview, IL St. Catherine Laboure Retired.
Maisano, Richard J. '69 (PH) Avondale, PA St. Gabriel of the Sorrowful Mother.
Maiser, Raymond *c.ss.r.* '64 (SEA)[M] Seattle, WA The Redemptionist Society of Washington; Seattle, WA Sacred Heart of Jesus.
Maisog, Alberic *o.c.s.o.* '00 (SPC)[F] Ava, MO Assumption Abbey (Trappist); [A] Ava, MO Assumption Novitiate (Trappists).
Maison, Gabriel '78 (VIC) Promoter of Justice; Moulton, TX St. Joseph's; Flatonia, TX St. Mary's; Permanent Diaconate Program.
Maison, John Bosco '96 (ORL) Port Orange, FL Epiphany.
Maisonet–Ortiz, Rev. Msgr. Tomas '45 (SJN) Retired.
Maivelett, Bruce A. *s.j.* '88 (PH)[F] Philadelphia, PA St. Joseph's Preparatory School; [Y] Philadelphia, PA Jesuit Community, Arrupe House.
Maiza, Jesus Maria *s.s.s.* '67 (CGS) Caguas, PR Santisimo Sacramento.
Maj, George C. *s.a.c.* '58 (BUF)[N] North Tonawanda, NY Society of the Catholic Apostolate.
Maj, Jerzy *o.s.p.p.e.* (ORL) Summerfield, FL St. Mark the Evangelist.
Majalla, Roc *s.a.c.* '92 (GR) Fremont, MI St. Michael.
Majarucon, Rev. Msgr. Jon F. '84 (LA) Oxnard, CA Santa Clara; Deanery 3; Santa Barbara Region.
Majchrowski, Anthony P. '44 (LAN) Flint, MI All Saints.
Majerus, Daniel '57 (SCL) Retired.
Majewski, Edmund W. *s.j.* '83 (NEW)[B] Jersey City, NJ Jesuit Center; [L] Jersey City, NJ Jesuits of Saint Peter's College, Inc.
Majewski, Francis *o.f.m.cap.* '64 (PAT)[N] Ringwood, NJ Holy Name Friary, Inc.
Majewski, Joseph B. '67 (RIC) Retired.
Majewski, Mariusz '08 (B) Twin Falls, ID St. Edward The Confessor.
Majic, Timothy *o.f.m.* '39 (CHI)[N] Chicago, IL St. Anthony's Friary.
Majikas, David J. '97 (CLV) Barberton, OH St. Augustine; Barberton, OH Barberton Citizens Hospitals.
Majka, Frank A. *s.j.* '74 (MIL)[P] Milwaukee, WI Jesuit Community at Marquette University.
Majka, Frank A. *s.j.* '74 (OAK)[L] Berkeley, CA Jesuit Fathers and Brothers.
Majka, George '72 (MAN) Claremont, NH St. Joseph.
Majka, Philip S. '65 (ARL) Chicago, IL National Conference of Catholic Airport Chaplains (NCCAC); Falls Church, VA St. James.
Major, Charles M. '59 (SY) Retired.
Major, Peter *m.h.m.* '68 (NY)[DD] Hartsdale, NY Mill Hill Fathers Residence.
Major, Steven P. '87 (LIN) Beatrice, NE St. Joseph's.
Major, Thomas J. '91 (SCR) Shohola, PA St. Ann's; Lords Valley, PA St. John Neumann.
Majoros, Rev. Msgr. George A. '79 (PH) Secane, PA Our Lady of Fatima.
Majoros, Stephen R. '57 (TOL) Retired.
Majstorovic, Ivica *o.f.m.* '00 (CHI) Chicago, IL Blessed Alojzije Stepinac Croatian Mission; [N] Chicago, IL Croatian Franciscan Fathers; Councilors.
Maka, Tomek '01 (DET) Ira Township, MI Immaculate Conception.

Makacinas, Stanley *o.carm.* '70 (JOL)[L] Darien Carmelite Provincial Office.
Makar, Paul J. '10 (PHU) Office of Vocations; Special Assignment.
Makarewicz, Rev. Msgr. Marion J. '87 (JC) Argyle, MO St. Aloysius; Vienna, MO Holy Guardian Angels; Vienna, MO Visitation of the Blessed Virgin Mary; VI. Rolla; Ministry to Priests.
Maki, George S. '88 (MAR) Watersmeet, MI Immaculate Conception.
Makori, Raphael A. '97 (CHI) Chicago, IL St. Joachim.
Makos, Jason M. '05 (BO) Whitman, MA Holy Ghost.
Makothakat, John M. '62 (SAT) San Antonio, TX; [C] Oblate School of Theology; Judges Retired.
Makowski, Douglas T. '66 (CLV) Parma, OH St. Anthony of Padua Retired.
Makowski, Lee J. *o.s.a.* '80 (PH)[C] Villanova University; [Y] Villanova, PA St. Thomas Monastery.
Makowski, Tomasz '93 (PMB) West Palm Beach, FL Mary Immaculate.
Makranyi, Steven F. '69 (LAN) Retired.
Maksvytis, Jerome J. '74 (MAD) Berlin, WI All Saints.
Maksym, Kevin M. '01 (SAG) Midland, MI Assumption of the Blessed Virgin Mary.
Maksymowicz, Rev. Msgr. John H. '70 (BRK) Released from Diocesan Assignment.
Makwali, Silvester *c.s.c.* '98 (FTW)[H] Notre Dame Congregation of Holy Cross, United States Province of Priests & Brothers.
Makwali, Silvester (P)[L] Portland Holy Cross Fathers & Brothers, C.S.C. – University of Portland.
Malabad, Antonio R. '53 (RIC) Retired.
Malacari, Carmen '93 (CHL) Denver, NC Holy Spirit.
Malachowski, Christopher *o.s.* '58 (PCE) On Duty Outside the Diocese.
Malacrida, Mario *m.c.c.j.* '87 (CHI)[N] Chicago, IL Comboni Missionaries Theologate (M.C.C.J.), Verona Fathers.
Malagesi, Robert P. *m.ss.cc.* '07 (HBG)[J] Fairfield, PA Missionaries of the Sacred Hearts of Jesus & Mary House of Studies; Fairfield, PA Immaculate Conception of the Blessed Virgin Mary; Fairfield, PA St. Rita.
Malagesi, Robert *m.ss.cc.* '07 (CAM)[L] Linwood, NJ Villa Pieta. Missionaries of the Sacred Hearts of Jesus & Mary.
Malagon, Eduardo '00 (GRY) Cursillos in Christianity; Lake Station, IN St. Francis Xavier.
Malagon, Julio Cesar Sanchez '09 (AGN)[A] Yona, GU Redemptoris Mater Archdiocesan Missionary Seminary.
Malagreca, Rev. Msgr. Joseph P. '76 (BRK) Brooklyn, NY Holy Cross; Renouveau Charismatique of the Diocese of Brooklyn; Renovacion Carismatica of the Diocese of Brooklyn.
Malai, Dominic '90 (SR) Napa, CA St. Apollinaris.
Malain, Rev. Msgr. Dan '66 (BEA) Nederland, TX St. Charles Borromeo; Presbyteral Council.
Malanowski, Rev. Msgr. Thaddeus F. '47 (NOR) Retired.
Malanowski, Rev. Msgr. Thaddeus F. '47 (BGP)[O] Stamford, CT The Catherine Dennis Keefe Queen of the Clergy Retired Priests' Residence.
Malanyaon, Joven (TOL) Western Office.
Malarz, Andrew '92 (VEN) Cape Coral, FL St. Andrew.
Malatesta, Christopher A. '93 (SPR) Dalton, MA St. Agnes; [L] Goshen, MA Holy Cross Camp Grounds; Diocesan Consultors; Deans; Presbyteral Council.
Malave, Jason A. '97 (CHI) Chicago, IL St. Bartholomew.
Malave, Will–Roger '86 (HRT) Waterbury, CT St. Patrick Retired.
Malaver, Daniel '03 (WDC) Silver Spring, MD St. Michael.
Malavolti, Nathan *t.o.r.* '05 (ALT)[A] Loretto, PA St. Francis University.
Malayil, Thomas (MCE) Philadelphia, PA St. Jude Malankara Catholic Church; Mothers' Forum Director; Elected Members; Priests – Heads of Apostolates.
Malcolm, Lawrence J. '70 (CHI) Oak Lawn, IL St. Gerald.
Malczuk, Dariusz '03 (SAC) Rocklin, CA SS. Peter and Paul.
Malczyk, Joseph *c.r.* '69 (CHI)[D] Chicago, IL Gordon Tech High School.
Maldari, Donald C. *s.j.* '85 (SY)[Q] Syracuse, NY Jesuits at LeMoyne, Inc.
Maldonado, Angel M. *o.s.m.* '79 (ELP) El Paso, TX St. Ignatius of Loyola.
Maldonado, Edward *o.f.m.cap.* '83 (ARE) Utuado, PR San Miquel; Priest's Senate (Consejo Presbiteral).
Maldonado, Fernando '02 (SPK) Special Ministry.
Maldonado, Francisco '90 (TUC) Rio Rico, AZ Most Holy Nativity of Our Lord Jesus Christ Roman Catholic Parish – Rio Rico; Green Valley, AZ Our Lady of the Valley Roman Catholic Parish – Green Valley.
Maldonado, Fredy Cesar *s.j.* '92 (BGP)[O] Fairfield, CT The Fairfield Jesuit Community–Fairfield University; [B] Fairfield, CT Fairfield University.
Maldonado, Leonardo '64 (RCK) Elgin, IL St. Joseph.
Maldonado, Roberto *l.d.* '06 (PCE)[H] Orocovis, PR Santuario Nuestra Senora del Encuentro con Dios – Hilasterio Masculino.
Malecki, John J. '48 (ALB) Office Retired.
Malekunnel, Shinu Mathew *o.ss.t.* '09 (BAL)[Q] Assigned in India.
Malene, Rev. Msgr. Robert M. '72 (E) West Middlesex, PA Good Shepherd; Western Vicariate; Administrative Cabinet; College of Consultors; Presbyteral Council.
Malesic, Edward C. '87 (HBG) York Haven, PA Holy Infant; Judicial Vicar; Appointed; Judicial Vicar; Consultors, College.
Maleszyk, Mieczyslaw "Mitch" '00 (SAC) Paradise, CA St. Thomas More.
Maletta, Sammie L. '80 (GRY) St. John, IN St. John the Evangelist.
Maletz, Leo J. '73 (ALN) Minersville, PA St. Matthew the Evangelist.
Malewski, Christian '09 (KC) Harrisonville, MO Our Lady of Lourdes.
Mali, Joseph '88 (NY)[W] Poughkeepsie, NY St. Francis Hospital; Poughkeepsie, NY St. Francis Hospital.
Malia, Thomas R. '84 (BAL)[K] Baltimore, MD Mercy Health Services Inc.; Special Assignment; Lansdowne, MD St. Clement.
Maliakkal, Varghese '85 (IND) Indianapolis, IN St. Michael the Archangel Catholic Church, Indianapolis, Inc.
Malick, Kevin M. '07 (NY) Tuckahoe, NY Immaculate Conception.
Maliekal, Cyriac '71 (HRT) Milford, CT Christ the Redeemer.
Maliekal, George '01 (SP)[J] Tampa, FL St. Joseph's Hospital, Inc.
Maliekal, Jose *m.s.f.s.* '74 (ATL)[F] Snellville, GA The Missionaries of St. Francis De Sales.
Malin, Delbert J. '58 (LC) Special Assignment; Ex Officio Retired.
Malin, Donald P. '03 (PBL) Pagosa Springs, CO Immaculate Heart of Mary; Liaison; Pagosa Springs, CO Pope John Paul II Parish.
Malin, Gary J. '86 (CLV) Chagrin Falls, OH St. Joan of Arc.
Malinowski, Rev. Msgr. John C. '63 (AUS)[F] Bryan, TX St. Joseph Regional Health Center Retired.
Malinowski, Rev. Msgr. John '63 (AUS) Bryan/College Station Retired.
Malinowski, Stanley J. '54 (PEO) Rantoul, IL St. Malachy; Thomasboro, IL St. Elizabeth of Hungary Retired.
Malitz, George M. '97 (PSC) Leave of Absence.
Maliwa, Festus '02 (TLS) Bartlesville, OK St. John's.
Malkiewicz, Stephen E. *o.f.m.* '69 (MIL)[B] Hales Corners, WI Sacred Heart School of Theology; [P] Provincial Offices of the Franciscan Friars, Assumption BVM Province, Inc.
Malkov, Leonid *c.ss.r.* '90 (PHU) Newark, NJ St. John the Baptist.
Mallaghan, Thomas P. *c.m.* '60 (PH)[Y].
Mallak, Mark S. '88 (NU) Defender of the Bond; Members; Morgan, MN St. Michael.
Mallari, Arturo O. '07 (RCK) Freeport, IL St. Thomas Aquinas.
Mallavarapu, Kasparaj '84 (FBK) Fairbanks, AK St. Raphael Catholic Church Fairbanks; Chaplains of Public Institutions.
Mallea, Jorge M. *c.s.c.* '94 (FTW)[H] Notre Dame Congregation of Holy Cross, United States Province of Priests & Brothers.
Mallen, Santiago *c.ss.r.* '47 (CGS) San Lorenzo, PR Nuestra Senora de la Mercedes.
Mallet, Rev. Msgr. Charles J. '55 (LAF) Retired.
Mallet, W. Curtis '92 (LAF) Lafayette, LA St. Genevieve; Vicars General; Judges; Diocesan Consultors.
Mallett, James K. '66 (NSH) General Counsel; Judges; Censor Librorum Retired.
Mallett, James '66 (KNX)[I] Chattanooga, TN Newman Foundation of Chattanooga, Inc.; University of Tennessee–Chattanooga.
Mallett, Raymond *o.f.m.conv.* '76 (LA) Hermosa Beach, CA Our Lady of Guadalupe.
Mallette, Daniel J. '57 (CHI) Chicago, IL St. Margaret of Scotland Retired.
Malley, Francis '01 (SFE) Cerrillos, NM St. Joseph.
Malley, James B. *s.j.* '64 (BO)[U] Weston, MA Campion Health Center, Inc.
Malley, John *o.carm.* '56 (JOL)[O] Darien, IL Carmelite Mission Office; Councilors.
Malley, John *o.carm.* '56 (TUC)[A] Tucson, AZ Salpointe Catholic High School; [E] Tucson, AZ Carmelite Priory; Darien, IL Mission Office, Carmelite Missions.
Malley, Kenneth '97 (SP) Lutz, FL St. Timothy; [F] Lutz, FL St. Timothy Catholic Early Childhood Learning Center; Vicars Forane; Personnel Board.
Malley, Raymond *s.m.* '68 (SJ)[M] Cupertino, CA The Marianist Center.
Malley, Vernon *o.carm.* '59 (TUC)[A] Tucson, AZ Salpointe Catholic High School; [E] Tucson, AZ Carmelite Priory Retired.
Malley, William J. *s.j.* '64 (FgM) New York, NY Society of Jesus.
Mallia, Joseph '92 (DET) Allen Park, MI St. Frances Cabrini; Archdiocesan Vicars; Presbyteral Council.
Mallick, Andrew '83 (ORL) Ocala, FL Our Lady of the Springs.
Mallick, Marcus '05 (DEN) Boulder, CO Sacred Heart of Mary.
Mallin, Peter *o.f.m.conv.* '90 (LA) Hospital Chaplains; Hermosa Beach, CA Our Lady of Guadalupe; [J] Torrance, CA Providence Little Company of Mary Medical Center Torrance; Hospital Chaplains.
Mallo, Walter *i.v.e.* '90 (DAL) Dallas, TX St. Bernard of Clairvaux; Dallas, TX Doctors Hospital.
Mallon, Elias D. *s.a.* '71 (NY)[DD] New York, NY Atonement Friars; [DD] Garrison, NY Franciscan Friars of the Atonement, Minister General Office; General Council.
Mallonee, Robert *s.v.d.* '67 (BO)[U] Duxbury, MA Society of the Divine Word.
Malloy, Rev. Msgr. David J. '83 (MIL) Lake Geneva, WI St. Francis de Sales; General Secretary; Staff; Consultants; Staff.
Malloy, Edward A. *c.s.c.* '70 (FTW)[H] Notre Dame, IN Holy Cross Community, Corby Hall, University of Notre Dame; [B] University of Notre Dame Du Lac.
Malloy, Francis X. '85 (MO) Air Force Reserve Chaplains; On Duty Outside the Archdiocese; DEPARTMENT OF VETERANS AFFAIRS HOSPITALS AND CHAPLAINS.
Malloy, John *s.d.b.* '50 (OAK)[E] Richmond, CA Salesian High School.
Malloy, Joseph J. '70 (BGP) Stamford, CT St. Clement of Rome.
Malloy, Michael B. '76 (OM) Battle Creek, NE St. Patrick's.
Malloy, Richard G. *s.j.* '88 (SCR)[B] Scranton, PA The University of Scranton.
Malloy, Stephen J. '96 (BO) Health Leave.; Weymouth, MA St. Albert the Great.
Malloy, Thomas *o.s.f.s.* '67 (R) Fayetteville, NC St. Ann.
Malloy, William E. '73 (CHI) Chicago, IL St. Barnabas.
Mally, Edward J. *s.j.* '61 (NY)[DD] New York Jesuit Provincial's Office.
Mallya, Sabas '91 (PMB) Jupiter, FL St. Peter.
Mallya, Stephen *a.j.* (Y)[K] Canton, OH Sancta Clara Monastery.
Malm, Raymond B. '76 (PRO) Newport, RI St. Joseph.
Malnar, Rev. Msgr. Matthew G. (LC) Retired.
Malnar, Rev. Msgr. Matthew '66 (AMA) Retired.
Malnar, Stan '72 (HEL) Special Assignments.
Malo, Richard C. '87 (PRT) Greenville, ME Holy Family; Jackman, ME St. Anthony; Vicars Forane.
Malone, Rev. Msgr. Alan '59 (PHX) Retired.
Malone, Rev. Msgr. Bernard G. '50 (LR)[G] Little Rock, AR St. John Manor Retired.
Malone, Daniel L. '07 (MAR)[E] Iron Mountain, MI Monastery of the Holy Cross.
Malone, Edward T. (BO) Reading, MA St. Agnes.
Malone, Rev. Msgr. Francis I. '77 (LR) Little Rock, AR Christ the King; Judicial Vicar; Diocesan Consultors; Deans; Hospitals; Propagation of the Faith; Chancellor for Ecclesial Affairs; Clergy Personnel Advisory Board (Diocesan); Presbyteral Council.
Malone, H. Patrick '69 (MO) Veterans Administration Hospital; DEPARTMENT OF VETERANS AFFAIRS HOSPITALS AND CHAPLAINS Retired.
Malone, John M. '67 (STP)[C] St. Paul, MN University of St. Thomas.
Malone, John S. *c.s.sp.* '65 (MO) DEPARTMENT OF VETERANS AFFAIRS HOSPITALS AND CHAPLAINS.
Malone, John (RVC) Northport, NY Veteran's Administration Hospital.
Malone, Michael T. *c.s.sp.* '65 (PRO)[B] Newport, RI Salve Regina University.
Malone, Patrick J. *s.j.* '01 (OM) Omaha, NE St. John; [J] Omaha, NE Jesuit Community at Creighton University.
Malone, Rev. Msgr. Richard '62 (PH) Upper Darby, PA St. Laurence.
Maloney, Bernard M. *o.f.m.cap.* '69 (NY) New Paltz, NY St. Joseph; [DD] New Paltz, NY St. Joseph Friary.
Maloney, Daniel *o.s.b.* '68 (BIS)[A] Richardton, ND Assumption Abbey; [B] Bismarck, ND University of Mary; [H] Bismarck, ND Annunciation Monastery.
Maloney, Edward J. '55 (CHI) Retired.
Maloney, Francis G. '60 (R) Retired.
Maloney, Rev. Msgr. J. Christopher '66 (NY) Yonkers, NY St. John the Baptist.
Maloney, James F. *c.m.f.* '60 (CHI)[N] Oak Park Claretian Missionaries USA Eastern Province.
Maloney, James G. '71 (CLV) Norton, OH St. Andrew the Apostle.
Maloney, John P. '66 (BRK) Retired.
Maloney, Rev. Msgr. John W. '75 (BRK) Brooklyn, NY St. Anselm.
Maloney, Joseph L. '91 (PH) Pottstown, PA St. Aloysius.
Maloney, Joseph *o.f.m.cap.* '58 (DET)[K] Detroit St. Bonaventure Friary.
Maloney, Kevin '05 (SY) Canastota, NY St. Agatha.

Maloney, Patrick H. *c.s.c.* '54 (FTW)[B] University of Notre Dame Du Lac; [H] Notre Dame Congregation of Holy Cross, United States Province of Priests & Brothers; [H] Notre Dame, IN Holy Cross Community, Corby Hall, University of Notre Dame.
Maloney, Richard *s.d.s.* '69 (WDC)[B] Silver Spring, MD Salvatorian Community.
Maloney, Robert P. *c.m.* '66 (PH)[Y].
Maloney, Robert S. *s.x.* '57 (BO)[U] Holliston, MA Xaverian Missionaries.
Maloney, Rufino *o.f.m.conv.* '59 (ALB)[L] Rensselaer, NY Provincialate, Immaculate Conception Friary – Order of Friars Minor Conventual.
Maloney, Rev. Msgr. Thomas F. '68 (BUF) Finance Council; Tonawanda, NY St. Amelia.
Maloney, Thomas J. '65 (SCR) Pittston, PA Our Lady of the Eucharist Parish.
Maloney, Thomas P. '70 (RVC) Retired.
Maloney, Wilfred F. '55 (PH) Retired.
Maloney, William J. '48 (E) Retired.
Malovetz, Rev. Msgr. Gregory E. S. '83 (MET) Skillman, NJ St. Charles Borromeo.
Maloy, Dale '54 (PEO) Retired.
Maltese, James L. (NOR) On Duty Outside the Diocese.
Maltese, James L. '65 (RVC) Stony Brook, NY Stony Brook University Hospital; Saint James, NY SS. Philip and James.
Malthaner, John P. '93 (E)[C] Oil City, PA Venango Catholic High School; Priest Personnel Board.
Malvey, Killian *o.s.b.* '73 (SEA)[M] Lacey, WA St. Martin's Abbey; [A] Lacey, WA Saint Martin's University.
Malvey, Seamus *o.c.s.o.* '86 (L)[L] Trappist, KY Abbey of Our Lady of Gethsemani, of the Order of Cistercians of the Strict Observance.
Malyarchuk, Roman '95 (STF) Riverhead, NY St. John the Baptist.
Malzacher, Craig S. '08 (MIA) Coral Springs, FL St. Andrew.
Mamba, Maurice (NY) New York, NY Corpus Christi.
Mamich, Joseph R. '06 (CLV) Strongsville, OH St. Joseph; Presbyteral Council.
Mammarella, Dominick '53 (HBG) Retired.
Mamo, Nathan '78 (HON) On Duty Outside the Diocese.
Mamo, Nathan '78 (RNO) Gardnerville, NV St. Gall.
Mampilly, Joy '84 (NY) Staten Island, NY St. Ann.
Manahan, Christopher J. *s.j.* '03 (STP)[B] St. Paul, MN Jesuit Novitiate.
Manahan, John J. *s.m.* '68 (SAT)[L] San Antonio, TX Marianist Residence.
Manahan, Reynaldo '95 (SD) Pala, CA Mission San Antonio de Pala Catholic Parish.
Manahan, Thomas C. *s.j.* '95 (MIL)[P] Milwaukee, WI Jesuit Community at Marquette University; [E] Milwaukee, WI Marquette University High School.
Manakatt, Mathew '78 (PH) Huntingdon Valley, PA St. Albert the Great.
Manakatt, Mathew '78 (SYM) Huntingdon Valley, PA Syro–Malabar Knanaya Catholic Mission of Greater Philadelphia.
Manakkatt, Mathew '78 (PH) Indian Apostolate–Knanayan Comm. Syro–Malabar Rite.
Manalel, Mathew '72 (KAL) Battle Creek, MI St. Jerome.
Manalili, Feliciano *o.c.s.o.* '62 (CHR)[E] Moncks Corner, SC Mepkin Abbey.
Manalo, Pantaleon O. '63 (RIC)[E] Portsmouth, VA Bon Secours Maryview Medical Center.
Manalo, Rosendo R. '94 (OAK) Fremont, CA St. Joseph (Old Mission San Jose).
Manalo, Vincent P. *c.s.p.* '00 (SFR) San Francisco, CA Old St. Mary's Cathedral.
Manano, Grace '96 (CAM) Swedesboro, NJ St. Clare of Assisi Parish, Gibbstown, N.J.
Manappuram, Joseph '69 (GAL) Spring, TX St. James the Apostle.
Manarchuck, Joseph J. '78 (SCR) Wyalusing, PA Our Lady of Perpetual Help Parish; Wyalusing, PA St. Joachim.
Manase, Michael '77 (HT) Thibodaux, LA St. Charles Borromeo.
Manatt, Timothy T. *s.j.* '07 (STP)[E] Minneapolis, MN Cristo Rey Jesuit High School – Twin Cities; [S] Minneapolis, MN Cristo Rey Corporate Internship Program – Twin Cities.
Mancha, George '87 (SJ) Santa Clara, CA St. Justin.
Manchapilly, George *c.m.i.* '71 (BLX) Bay St. Louis, MS St. Ann.
Manchas, Lawrence L. '78 (GBG) Clymer, PA Church of the Resurrection; Deaneries; College of Consultors; Bishop's Priests Council; College of Deans.
Manchester, Roman R. '05 (PRO) Warwick, RI St. Kevin.
Mancini, Rev. Msgr. Anthony '78 (PRO) Providence, RI Cathedral of SS. Peter and Paul; Deans.
Mancini, Domenic '76 (PIT) Imperial, PA St. Columbkille.
Mancini, Rev. Msgr. James E. '66 (LR) Charismatic Movement; [G] Little Rock, AR St. John Manor Retired.
Mancini, John *o.s.f.s.* '80 (SAG) Saginaw, MI SS. Simon and Jude; Saginaw, MI St. Christopher.
Mancini, Joseph A. '01 (NEW) Kearny, NJ St. Stephen; Newark, NJ Cathedral Basilica of the Sacred Heart; Members.
Mancini, Marc A. '92 (PAT) Vocations Board; Succasunna, NJ St. Therese; College of Consultors; Vice Chancellors; Associate Judges.
Mancini, Nicholas '75 (Y) Louisville, OH Sacred Heart of Mary.
Mancini, Robert *o.s.f.s.* '77 (ARL) Reston, VA St. John Neumann.
Mancuso, Anthony J. '83 (SJ) San Jose, CA St. John Vianney.
Mancuso, Dennis J. '96 (BUF) Cuba, NY Our Lady of the Angels; Belmont, NY St. Patrick; Fillmore, NY St. Patrick.
Mancuso, Henry '75 (LKC) Retired.
Mancuso, Rev. Msgr. Joseph A. '64 (KC) Retired.
Mancuso, Luke *o.s.b.* '83 (SCL)[I] Collegeville, MN St. John's Abbey, of the Order of St. Benedict.
Mandac, Elmer '96 (SD) Valley Center, CA Saint Stephen Catholic Parish.
Mandagiri, Jojaiah *m.s.f.s.* '95 (KCK) Atchison, KS Corpus Christi; Nortonville, KS St. Joseph; Nortonville, KS St. Mary's Immaculate Conception.
Mandagiri, Jojaiah *m.s.f.s.* '95 (TYL)[C] Whitehouse, TX The Missionaries of St. Francis de Sales.
Mandala, Michael J. *s.j.* '77 (LA) Los Angeles, CA Blessed Sacrament.
Mandala, Michael *s.j.* '77 (LA)[D] Los Angeles, CA Verbum Dei High School; [F] In Res.
Mandala, Michael *s.j.* (OAK)[Q] Oakland, CA PICO National Network.
Mandapati, Lourdumar Reddy '97 (SUP) Lac du Flambeau, WI St. Anthony of Padua; Manitowish Waters, WI Our Lady Queen of Peace; Mercer, WI St. Isaac Jogues and Companions.
Mandato, Kieran '87 (NY) Military Chaplains; Navy Chaplains.
Mandato, Pio *f.m.h.j.* '85 (SCR)[L] Laceyville, PA Franciscan Missionary Hermits of St. Joseph.
Mandel, Brian L. '94 (NU) Willmar, MN St. Mary.
Manderfield, Paul G. '60 (MAR) Panama Mission Fund.
Manderfield, R.P. Geraldo (MAR) Retired.
Mandile, John J. *s.j.* '57 (BO)[U] Weston, MA Campion Health Center, Inc.
Manding, Benito O. '64 (SJ) Retired.
Manding, Benito (SY) Endicott, NY St. Ambrose.
Mandock, Patrick H. '72 (GBG) Retired.
Mandoli, Richard *o.c.d.* '92 (SJ)[M] San Jose, CA Carmelite Monastery, Novitiate.
Mandry, Stephen (GAL) Retired.
Manenti, Rene *c.s.* '02 (NY)[DD] Staten Island, NY Scalabrinian Missionaries.
Manerowski, Joseph '95 (ALB) Glens Falls, NY St. Mary.
Maney, Robert L. '51 (MIL) Retired.
Manfred, Donald J. '67 (OG) Massena, NY Church of Sacred Heart and St. Lawrence; Diocesan Consultors.
Mangalath, Augustine A. (MCE) Chancellor; Ex Officio Members; Secretaries; Members; Members; Spring Valley, NY St. Peter's Malankara Catholic Church; Chancellor; Finance Officer; Exarchate Webteam.
Mangalath, Augustine '79 (HRT) West Haven, CT St. Paul's; [H] New Haven, CT Hospital of St. Raphael.
Mangalath, Jaison *s.v.d.* '99 (LAF) Opelousas, LA Holy Ghost.
Mangampo, Gil '91 (GLP) On Leave of Absence.
Mangan, Rev. Msgr. Charles '89 (SFS) Marian Apostolate.
Manganello, Rev. Msgr. Salvatore '82 (BUF) Due Process; Judicial Vicar; Judges; Buffalo, NY St. Louis.
Mangano, Charles N. '90 (RVC) Merrick, NY Curé of Ars.
Mangat, B. Thomas *c.m.i.* '89 (SAL) Hoxie, KS St. Frances Cabrini Parish; Hoxie, KS St. Martin Parish.
Manger, Daniel *o.s.b.cam.* '85 (MRY)[F] Big Sur, CA New Camaldoli Hermitage.
Manger, Rev. Msgr. William '62 (BEA) Southeast Texas ACTS Mission Chapter; Central Vicariate; Charismatic Prayer Renewal; Beaumont, TX St. Anne.
Mangiafico, Paul J. '70 (HRT) Medical Leave.
Mangiafico, Paul '70 (SP) St. Petersburg, FL Holy Family.
Mangiaracina, Cayet N. *o.p.* '64 (BR) Hammond, LA Holy Ghost; Ponchatoula, LA St. Joseph.
Mangiaracina, George *o.c.d.* '93 (MIL)[B] Hales Corners, WI Sacred Heart School of Theology.
Mangieri, Thomas '01 (PAT) Mountain Lakes, NJ St. Catherine of Siena.
Mangini, Richard A. '67 (OAK) Concord, CA St. Bonaventure.
Mangini, Richard '67 (OAK) Deanery #11.
Manglaviti, Leo M. *s.j.* '99 (BO)[A] Weston, MA Blessed John XXIII National Seminary; [U] Weston, MA Campion Health Center, Inc.
Mango, Louis A. *c.s.c.* '65 (ORL)[F] Cocoa Beach, FL Congregation of Holy Cross, United States Province.
Mangum, Peter B. '90 (SHP) Shreveport, LA St. John Berchmans Cathedral; Judicial Vicar; Judges; Presbyteral Council; Diocesan Liturgy Commission; [A] Shreveport, LA Loyola College Prep; College of Consultors.
Mani, David Lazar (RVC) Northport, NY Veteran's Administration Hospital.
Mani, David '64 (SEA) Veterans Administration Medical Center.
Mani, L. David '64 (MO) DEPARTMENT OF VETERANS AFFAIRS HOSPITALS AND CHAPLAINS.
Maniamkerry, Mathew *o.ss.t.* '84 (BAL)[Q] Assigned in India.
Maniangat, Joseph '64 (STA) Retired.
Maniangattu, George '89 (ORL) Ocala, FL Our Lady of the Springs.
Manickam, Peter M. '81 (LC) Marshfield, WI Corpus Christi; Marshfield, WI Sacred Heart of Jesus.
Manickathan, Jose Souru *c.f.i.c.* '06 (COL) Hospital Ministry; Columbus, OH Holy Cross.
Manickathan, Paulose '98 (WH) Welch, WV St. Peter.
Manickathan, Thomas Paulose *h.g.n.* (WH) Gary, WV Our Lady of Victory; Powhatan, WV Sacred Heart.
Manikuttiyil, Kurian '90 (PT) Crestview, FL Our Lady of Victory.
Manimala, Thomas '95 (SAN) Presbyteral Council; Odessa, TX St. Elizabeth Ann Seton.
Maniola, Rev. Msgr. Francis N. '38 (CHI) Chicago, IL St. Symphorosa and Seven Sons Retired.
Manion, Thomas F. '57 (PIT)[M] Pittsburgh, PA Cardinal Dearden Center Retired.
Maniscalco, Rev. Msgr. Francis J. '71 (RVC) West Hempstead, NY St. Thomas, the Apostle.
Maniscalco, Paul *s.d.b.* '44 (SFR) San Francisco, CA SS. Peter and Paul Retired.
Manista, Clemens D. '74 (WIL) National Conference for Community and Justice; Governor Bacon Health Center; Delaware City, DE St. Paul; Wilmington, DE Wilmington Hospital.
Maniyangat, Jose '75 (STA) Legion of Mary; Orange Park, FL St. Catherine's.
Manjadi, George '67 (WH) Camden, WV St. Boniface.
Manjakunnel, Jose '98 (CAM) Berlin, NJ Saint Simon Stock Parish, Berlin, N.J.
Manjaly, Jose Luis *m.s.* '05 (ATL) Smyrna, GA St. Thomas the Apostle.
Mank, Rev. Msgr. Virgil W. '65 (SFD) Retired.
Mankel, Rev. Msgr. Francis Xavier '61 (KNX)[K] Knoxville, TN Diocesan Council of Catholic Women; [K] Knoxville, TN Ladies of Charity; Presbyteral Council; Diocesan Consultors; Diocesan Finance Council; Diocesan Council of Catholic Women; Knoxville, TN Holy Ghost; Vicars General.
Mankena, Rajesh K. '00 (OKL) Enid, OK St. Francis Xavier.
Manko, Andriy *c.ss.r.* '95 (PHU) Newark, NJ St. John the Baptist.
Mankowski, Maciej '01 (Y) Alliance, OH St. Joseph; Sebring, OH St. Ann.
Mankowski, Paul V. *s.j.* '87 (CHI)[N] Chicago, IL Woodlawn Jesuit Community.
Manley, Bernard A. '87 (CHL) Retired.
Manly, Rev. Msgr. Alexander F. '57 (RVC) Kings Park, NY St. Joseph's Retired.
Man Minh Tran, Matthias M. *c.m.c.* '63 (SPC)[F] Carthage, MO Congregation of the Mother Coredemptrix, United States Assumption Province.
Mann, Christopher M. *c.f.r.* '03 (CAM) Cape May Court House, NJ The Church of Our Lady of the Angels, Cape May Court House, N.J.
Mann, Frank '79 (BRK) College Point, NY St. Fidelis.
Mann, Gordon '92 (EVN) Washington, IN Our Lady of Hope.
Mann, Lawrence *s.m.* '45 (SJ)[M] Cupertino, CA The Marianist Center.
Mann, Quentin A. '06 (GB)[N] Oshkosh, WI University of Wisconsin Oshkosh, Newman Center; Special Assignment; [O] Appleton, WI Catholic Youth Expeditions, Inc.; Vocations; Appleton, WI St. Pius X.
Mann, Raymond *o.f.m.* '59 (BO)[Z] Boston, MA St. Anthony Shrine.
Mann, Robert G. '59 (PEO) Retired.
Manna, David '06 (HRT) Leave of Absence.
Manna, Louis '73 (IND) Salem, IN St. Patrick Catholic Church, Salem, Inc.; Scottsburg, IN Church of the American Martyrs, Scottsburg, Inc.
Mannaparambil, Augustine *m.s.f.s.* '04 (TYL)[C] Whitehouse, TX The Missionaries of St. Francis de Sales.
Mannara, Frederick R. '63 (SY) Syracuse, NY Most Holy Rosary.
Mannebach, Thomas M. '99 (CIN) New Bremen, OH Holy Redeemer; Presbyteral Council; Vicarri Foranei (Deans); Consultors.
Mannhardt, Daniel C. '57 (DAV) Retired.
Manning, Brian F. '74 (BO) Franklin, MA St. Mary; Members.
Manning, C. Robert '97 (COS) Colorado Springs, CO St. Gabriel the Archangel.
Manning, Charles T. '75 (ROC) Absent on Leave.
Manning, Francis J. '51 (SPR) Priests' Retirement Program; Retired Priests' Service Retired.

Manning, J. Patrick '78 (Y)[B] North Canton, OH Walsh University.
Manning, James J. '75 (CIN) Franklin, OH St. Mary.
Manning, James *s.m.m.* '58 (RVC)[N] Bay Shore, NY Montfort Missionaries.
Manning, John E. '72 (CLV) Cleveland, OH St. Vincent de Paul; Associate Judges.
Manning, Michael *s.v.d.* '69 (SB)[N] San Bernardino, CA Wordnet, Inc.
Manning, Michael '97 (TR) Rumson, NJ Holy Cross.
Manning, Paul R. '59 (NEW) Retired.
Manning, Paul S. '85 (PAT) Clifton, NJ St. Philip the Apostle; School Division; Education.
Manning, Robert A. '83 (E) Stoneboro, PA St. Columbkille.
Manning, Robert C. '97 (STL) Retired.
Mannion, J. Patrick '55 (WCH) Retired.
Mannion, James P. '81 (RVC) Setauket, NY St. James; Procurator & Advocates.
Mannion, John H. '68 (IND)[G] Beech Grove, IN Franciscan St. Francis Health; On Duty Outside the Diocese.
Mannion, Rev. Msgr. M. Francis '73 (SLC) Salt Lake City, UT Saint Vincent de Paul LLC 250.
Mannion, Mark (POD) Oak Park.
Mannion, Mark '95 (CHI)[V] Oak Park, IL Oak Park Study Center.
Mannion, Rev. Msgr. Martin J. '62 (CAM) Retired.
Mannion, Martin K. '66 (STL) Retired.
Mannion, Rev. Msgr. Michael T. '71 (CAM) Office of Community Relations; Pennsauken, NJ Mary, Queen of All Saints, Pennsauken, N.J.
Mannion, Patrick John '66 (SAT) On Duty Outside the Archdiocese Retired.
Mannion, Thomas Ignatius '65 (HBG) Catawissa, PA Our Lady of Mercy.
Mannion, William D. '63 (CHI) Rosemont, IL Our Lady of Hope Retired.
Manno, John D. '01 (SY) Syracuse, NY St. James; Presbyteral Council; Finance Committee.
Manno, John K. '68 (SCR) Montoursville, PA Our Lady of Lourdes.
Mannoorvadakkethil, Mathai (MCE) Landover Hills, MD St. Mary's Malankara Catholic Church; Promoter of Justice; Family Apostolate Director; Elected Members; Priests – Heads of Apostolates.
Manohar, John Selva (LC) Sparta, WI St. Patrick; Sparta, WI St. John the Baptist.
Manolev, Kiril '01 (STF) Colchester, CT St. Mary Dormition; Glastonbury, CT St. John The Baptist.
Manos, James M. '96 (NEW) Presbyteral Council; Fairfield, NJ St. Thomas More.
Manrique, Ramon S. '04 (NY) Bronx, NY St. Rita of Cascia Shrine Church.
Manrique, Rev. Msgr. Wilfredo S. '88 (SJ) San Jose, CA St. Christopher; College of Consultors; Judges.
Manriquez, Raymundo '00 (LUB) Plainview, TX Our Lady of Guadalupe; Vicars Forane; Presbyteral Council.
Mans, Leo J. '53 (ROC) Retired.
Mansell, Nicholas '84 (SAV) Kathleen, GA St. Patrick.
Mansfield, John L. '53 (BO) Senior Priests. Retired.
Mansfield, Scott '00 (SFE) Rio Rancho, NM St. Thomas Aquinas.
Manship, D. Joseph '76 (PRT) St. Mary's Regional Medical Center; [G] Lewiston, ME St. Marguerite d'Youville Pavilion; [H] Lewiston, ME St. Mary's Regional Medical Center.
Manship, James C. '98 (HRT) New Haven, CT St. Rose of Lima.
Mansini, Guy *o.s.b.* '77 (IND) Bristow, IN St. Isidore the Farmer Catholic Church, Bristow, Inc.; [A] Saint Meinrad, IN Saint Meinrad School of Theology; [K] Saint Meinrad, IN St. Meinrad Archabbey.
Manso, Bobby '00 (SPC) Charleston, MO Southeast Correctional Center.
Manso, Robert F. '00 (SPC) Cape Girardeau, MO St. Vincent de Paul.
Manson, Brendan '06 (ORG) Garden Grove, CA St. Columban.
Manson, Sean '99 (NEW) Woodcliff Lake, NJ Our Lady Mother of the Church.
Mansoor, Awraha '00 (SPA) Santa Ana, CA St. George Chaldean Catholic Church; [C] Perris, CA St. George Monastery/Retreat Center; Perris, CA St. Hormizdah Mission.
Mansoor, Michael '98 (SPA) El Cajon, CA St. Michael Chaldean Catholic Church.
Manternach, Carl J. '55 (DUB) Retired.
Manternach, Neil J. '85 (DUB) Personnel Advisory Board; [F] Cedar Rapids, IA Regis Middle School; Hiawatha, IA St. Elizabeth Ann Seton Parish; Building Commission; Church Design/Renovation Commission; Seminary Admissions and Advisory Board.
Mantia, Armand '85 (NEW) Union, NJ Holy Spirit.
Mantovani, Firmo *c.s.* '73 (SJ) San Jose, CA Holy Cross.
Manuel, Gerdenio S. *s.j.* '79 (SFR)[N] San Francisco, CA Loyola House Jesuit Community.
Manuel, Herman *s.v.d.* '04 (SD) Pala, CA Mission San Antonio de Pala Catholic Parish.
Manuel, Jose '00 (NEW) Ridgefield, NJ St. Matthew's.
Manuel, Lukose *o.s.h.* '02 (GAL) Houston, TX Notre Dame; [O] Missouri City, TX The Society of the Oblates of Sacred Heart.
Manuel, Vincent '81 (MO) Army Chaplains.
Manuele, Christopher '06 (NTN) Rochester, NY St. Nicholas; Presbyteral Council.
Manuppella, Anthony J. '76 (CAM) Merchantville, NJ St. Peter's Catholic Church, Merchantville, N.J.; Appointed Members; Members.
Manvelpillai, David '89 (NY) Bronx, NY St. Margaret of Cortona.
Manville, Alexander *o.f.m.* '53 (LA)[V] Malibu, CA Serra Retreat Retired.
Many, Sebastian (BRK) Long Island City, NY Queen of Angels.
Manyama, Augustine *a.j.* '02 (P)[J] Portland, OR Providence Health & Services–Oregon.
Manz, Michael J. '79 (POD) Houston; [N] Houston, TX Opus Dei; San Antonio.
Manz, Michael (VIC)[C] Schulenburg, TX Opus Dei.
Manzano, Eurel '11 (GAL) Houston, TX Prince of Peace.
Manzano, Mark Francis *o.p.* '11 (FgM) Oakland, CA Province of the Holy Name (Western Dominican Province).
Manzo, Louis A. *c.s.c.* '65 (FTW)[H] Notre Dame Congregation of Holy Cross, United States Province of Priests & Brothers.
Mapara, Ildefonce *o.s.b.* '00 (BAK) Klamath Falls, OR St. Pius X.
Maples, Frederic A. *s.j.* '72 (BO)[U] Boston The Society of Jesus of New England–Provincial Offices.
Mappilaparambil, Joshy Abraham *o.ss.t.* '09 (BAL)[Q] In Residence – Holy Trinity Monastery Baltimore.
Marabe, Jose '70 (NY) New York, NY Cathedral of St. Patrick; Defenders of the Bond.
Marable, Gerard C. '88 (CAM) Continuing Education & Spiritual Formation of Priests (CESF); Camden, NJ St. Josephine Bakhita Parish, Camden, N.J.
Maraczewski, Edward S. '45 (CHI) Waukegan, IL St. Anastasia Retired.
Maramattam, Jose J. '80 (MAR) Gladstone, MI Holy Family.
Maramot, Faustino '74 (MEM) Federal Correctional Institute at Memphis.
Marandu, Nicolaus '82 (P) Portland, OR Immaculate Heart of Mary.
Marani, Philip *o.carm.* '65 (NY) Tarrytown, NY Transfiguration.
Marankulam, Mathew M. '78 (SAC) Vacaville, CA St. Joseph; Vicars Forane.
Marano, Fred '91 (BRK)[B] Douglaston, NY Cathedral Seminary Residence of the Immaculate Conception; [B] Elmhurst, NY Cathedral Preparatory Seminary of the Immaculate Conception.
Marano, Zaya (EST) Chicago, IL St. Ephrem's Church.
Maranowski, Michael J. '87 (PIT) Coraopolis, PA St. Malachy.
Maranto, Samuel C. *c.ss.r.* '72 (BR)[H] Baton Rouge, LA St. Gerard Residence; [L] Baton Rouge, LA Redemptorist Fathers of Baton Rouge, Inc.; Baton Rouge, LA St. Gerard Majella.
Marat, Wojciech A. '88 (CHI) Judges; Chicago, IL St. Thecla; Advocates.
Maravi, Raul *o.carm.* '97 (JOL)[L] Darien Carmelite Provincial Office.
Maraya, Felipe '62 (ELP) Absent on Leave.
Marbach, Lawrence J. '52 (SFS) Federal Prison Camp Retired.
Marbury, Cabell B. '64 (ALB) Albany, NY St. Francis of Assisi Parish Retired.
Marcaccio, Rev. Msgr. Anthony J. '91 (CHL) Greensboro, NC St. Pius the Tenth; Vice Chancellor; Diocesan Consultors.
Marcaida, Epifanio '83 (NY) Rye, NY Resurrection.
Marca Mansilla, Alejandro Jesus *o.c.d.* '94 (CHI) Calumet City, IL St. Victor.
Marcantonio, Clement '59 (PBL) Retired.
Marcantuono, Anthony L. '10 (NEW) Absent on Leave.
Marceau, Emmett L. '67 (SAG) Retired.
Marceau, Timothy R. *o.s.b.* '52 (JOL)[L] Lisle, IL St. Procopius Abbey.
Marcell, Robert G. '56 (BR) Retired.
Marcelli, Michael '11 (Y) Boardman, OH St. Charles Borromeo.
Marcello, Albert P. '09 (PRO) Cranston, RI St. Paul.
Marcello, Joseph A. '03 (BGP) Secretary to the Bishop; Assistant Vocation Directors; Priest Vocation Advisory Board; Presbyteral Council.
Marcellus, Gordon E. *o.s.a.* '63 (PH)[Y] Villanova, PA St. Thomas Monastery.
Marcelo, Florante E. '96 (CHY) Jackson, WY Our Lady of the Mountains.
Marcelo, Jeronimo '92 (SAC) Sacramento, CA St. Charles Borromeo.
Marcelo, Jose M. '79 (MET) Bound Brook, NJ St. Joseph.
March, Nathan D. '07 (PRT) Catholic Scouting; Lewiston, ME Prince of Peace Parish; [M] Lewiston, ME Bates College.
March, Nicholas B. '04 (DUB) Ex–Officio; [F] Protivin, IA Trinity Catholic School; Protivin, IA St. John Nepomucene; Lawler, IA Our Lady of Mt. Carmel; Protivin, IA Assumption of the B.V.M.; Protivin, IA Holy Trinity; St. Lucas, IA St. Luke; Waucoma, IA St. Mary.
March, Ralph *o.cist.* '45 (DAL)[B] University of Dallas; [J] Irving, TX Cistercian Abbey of Our Lady of Dallas.
Marcham, David S. '05 (BO) On Duty Outside the Archdiocese.
Marcham, David S. '05 (FR) Taunton, MA St. Mary's.
Marchand, Gerald A. '54 (NEW) Retired.
Marchand, Robert A. '52 (MAN) Retired.
Marchesani, Gino *f.d.p.* '56 (BO)[S] East Boston, MA Don Orione Nursing Home.
Marchese, Joseph P. '69 (SPR) On Duty Outside the Diocese.
Marchese, Rev. Msgr. Richard E. '70 (BRK) Released from Diocesan Assignment.
Marchessault, Edward T. *c.s.sp.* '64 (FgM) Bethel Park, PA CONGREGATION OF THE HOLY SPIRIT.
Marchetti, Michael H. '82 (SCR) Unassigned or Leave of Absence.
Marchetto, Ezio '82 (NY)[DD] Staten Island, NY Scalabrinian Missionaries.
Marchewka, Jacek '00 (NEW) Upper Saddle River, NJ Church of the Presentation.
Marchionda, James *o.p.* '73 (CHI)[N] Oak Park, IL Dominican Community of St. Martin de Porres.
Marchitell, Rev. Msgr. Anthony '76 (NY) Bronx, NY Our Lady of the Assumption.
Marchlewski, Michael A. *s.j.* '67 (STL)[F] St. Louis, MO St. Louis University High School, George H. Backer Memorial; [O] Saint Louis, MO St. Louis University High School Jesuit Community.
Marchwiany, Robert P. '03 (CHI) River Forest, IL St. Luke.
Marciano, Robert L. '83 (PRO) Mapleville, RI Our Lady of Good Help; [R] Smithfield, RI Bryant University.
Marcil, Michel *s.j.* '74 (NEW)[L] Jersey City, NJ Jesuits of Saint Peter's College, Inc.; Chinese Apostolate; [Q] South Orange, NJ U.S. Catholic China Bureau; [B] Jersey City, NJ Jesuit Center.
Marcil, Michel *s.j.* '74 (OAK)[L] Oakland, CA Jesuit Fathers and Brothers.
Marciniak, Bartlomiej *o.s.p.p.e.* '93 (PH)[Y].
Marciniak, Rev. Canon Felix R. '79 (NEW) Wallington, NJ Most Sacred Heart of Jesus.
Marciniak, John '56 (NOR) Retired.
Marciniak, Stanislaw P. '86 (SAT) Karnes City, TX St. Cornelius.
Marciniak, Thomas R. *s.j.* '76 (NY)[DD] Loyola Hall, Jesuit Community.
Marco, Alfredo '60 (LKC) Retired.
Marco, Michael J. *s.j.* '96 (WDC)[E] North Bethesda, MD Georgetown Preparatory School.
Marcoe, Timothy D. '07 (HBG) Appointed; [I] Bloomsburg, PA Bloomsburg University of Pennsylvania; Benton, PA Christ the King.
Marcone, Eugene F. '64 (NEW) Retired.
Marconi, John E. '87 (LR) Presbyteral Council; Conway, AR St. Joseph; [I] Conway, AR University of Central Arkansas & Hendrix College Catholic Campus Ministry; Clergy Personnel Advisory Board (Diocesan); Diocesan Consultors.
Marconi, Joseph Patrick '01 (LR) Fayetteville, AR St. Thomas Aquinas University Parish; [I] Fayetteville, AR University of Arkansas, St. Thomas Aquinas University Parish.
Marconi, Paul M. *c.r.s.p.* '58 (ALN)[K] Bethlehem, PA The Barnabite Fathers Barnabite Spiritual Center.
Marconi, Theodore B. '84 (E) Erie, PA Our Lady of Peace.
Marcotte, David P. *s.j.* '92 (NY)[DD] Cardinal Spellman Hall, Jesuit Community.
Marcotte, Joseph A. '69 (WOR) Webster, MA St. Louis.
Marcouiller, Douglas W. *s.j.* '86 (FgM)[O] St. Louis, MO The Jesuits of the Missouri Province; St. Louis, MO Society of Jesus.
Marcouiller, Douglas W. *s.j.* '86 (STL) Saint Louis, MO; [O] St. Louis, MO Sacred Heart Jesuit Community.
Marcoux, A. Stephen '93 (MAN) Windham, NH St. Matthew.
Marcoux, Joseph W. '01 (ROC) Censores Librorum; Ithaca, NY St. Catherine of Siena.
Marcucci, John A. '68 (PIT) Glenshaw, PA St. Mary of the Assumption.
Marcy, Bede *o.s.b.* '09 (BIR)[E] Cullman, AL St. Bernard Abbey.
Marczewski, Robert '95 (PH) On Duty Outside the Archdiocese.
Marczewski, Robert (DET)[A] Orchard Lake, MI SS. Cyril and Methodius Seminary.
Marczewski, Rev. Msgr. Ronald J. '74 (NEW) Bayonne, NJ Mt. Carmel.
Marczuk, Rev. Msgr. Scott L. '81 (LR) Bentonville, AR St. Stephen; Diocesan Consultors; Clergy Personnel Advisory Board (Diocesan).
Marczuk, Rev. Msgr. Scott L. (SPP) Judges.
Mardian, Pius '44 (SFS) Retired.
Marecki, Ronald '83 (SP) Homosassa, FL St. Thomas the Apostle.

Marek, Dean V. '65 (WIN) Retired.
Marek, Dean V. '65 (MIL) Retired.
Marek, Raymond John *o.m.i.* '89 (SAT)[L] San Antonio, TX De Mazenod House; Councilors.
Marek, Raymond John *o.m.i.* '89 (WDC)[O] Washington, DC Provincial Offices of the United States Province of the Missionary Oblates of Mary Immaculate; [O] Washington, DC Oblate Community.
Mares, Philip W. *m.m.* '86 (FgM) Maryknoll, NY MARYKNOLL.
Maresca, Rev. Msgr. Ralph J. '78 (BRK) Astoria, NY St. Francis of Assisi.
Maresh, Mark '94 (GI) Ord, NE Our Lady of Perpetual Help.
Marflak, Albert *o.s.b.* '75 (CLV)[N] Cleveland, OH; Cleveland, OH.
Marfori, Antonio '78 (SCL) Special Assignment.
Margallo, Roy '00 (MRY) Salinas, CA Sacred Heart.
Margarito, Luis A. Bonilla '00 (ALN) Unassigned.
Margason, Rev. Msgr. James E. '71 (BEL) Lebanon, IL St. Joseph; Judges; Shiloh, IL Corpus Christi.
Margevicius, Thomas '99 (STP)[A] Saint Paul, MN The Saint Paul Seminary; [C] St. Paul, MN University of St. Thomas; Minneapolis, MN Our Lady of Mount Carmel.
Marggraf, Brian *ss.cc.* '55 (FR)[F] Fairhaven, MA Damien Residence Retired.
Margherio, Ronald L. *o.s.b.* '78 (PEO)[A] Peru, IL St. Bede Abbey; [C] Peru, IL St. Bede Academy.
Marginean, Ovidiu Ioan '06 (ROM) Chancellor and Moderator of the Curia; Finance Council; Canton, OH St. George Cathedral.
Marhafer, Maury *o.f.m.conv.* '54 (FgM) Rensselaer, NY Province of the Immaculate Conception.
Maria, Pio *c.f.r.* '07 (FWT)[H] Fort Worth, TX Community of Franciscan Friars of the Renewal Sacred Heart of Jesus Friary.
Mariani, Paul P. *s.j.* '02 (SJ)[B] Santa Clara, CA Jesuit Community.
Mariano, Remigio "Miguel" '94 (TUC) Tucson, AZ Saint Joseph Roman Catholic Parish – Tucson; Diocesan Liturgical Coordinators; Office of Worship.
Mariasoosai, Benjamin '84 (NY) Bronx, NY St. Barnabas.
Mariasoosai, Gnanapragasam '81 (CHL) High Point, NC Christ the King.
Mariasoosai, Lawrence *o.m.i.* '97 (BEL) Walsh, IL St. Pius V; Sparta, IL Our Lady of Lourdes.
Marick, Thomas D. '97 (STN) Retired.
Marickovic, Thomas C. '81 (HBG) Spring Grove, PA Sacred Heart.
Marien, Roy C. '85 (PT) Panama City, FL St. John the Evangelist.
Marien, Roy C. '85 (PT) Seminarian Candidate Review Board.
Marier, Edward '88 (SPK) Newport, WA Our Lady of Sorrows; Newport, WA St. Anthony; Newport, WA St. Jude.
Marigliano, Michael *o.f.m.cap.* '84 (NY) Definitors:; New York, NY Our Lady of Sorrows; [DD] White Plains, NY St. Conrad Friary.
Marilag, Nelson '87 (ANC) Dillingham, AK Holy Rosary.
Marin, John L. '85 (MET) On Duty Outside the Diocese.
Marin, Jose G. (TYL) Teague, TX St. Mary; Teague, TX Boyd Unit, Texas Department of Correction.
Marin, Miguel '78 (ELP) Absent on Leave.
Marin, Moises '95 (CHI) Other Assignments.
Marin, Rev. Msgr. Tomas M. '89 (MIA) Miami, FL St. Timothy; Judges; Catholic Health Services, Inc.; Archdiocese of Miami Health Plan Trust; Catholic Physicians' and Dentists' Guild; Catholic Fire Service Ministry; [N] Miami Shores, FL Bahamas Mission of Florida, Inc.; Members; Pension.
Marin–Cardona, Jaime '10 (BGP) Norwalk, CT St. Joseph.
Marin–Leon, Rafael '78 (LA) Santa Barbara, CA Our Lady of Guadalupe; Deanery 2; Members.
Marinacci, Rev. Msgr. Nicolas '38 (NY) Retired.
Marinak, Andrew P. '56 (HBG) Retired.
Marincioni, Raniero A. '90 (MET) On Duty Outside the Diocese.
Marine, Rev. Msgr. John C. '76 (PH) Holland, PA St. Bede the Venerable.
Marini, Francis J. '95 (SAM) Scranton, PA St. Ann; Judicial Vicar; Presbyteral Council; College of Consultors; Board of Pastors.
Marini, Francis J. '95 (SCR) Promoter of Justice.
Marini, Francis J. '95 (ROM) Judicial Vicar.
Marini, Joseph J. '52 (SFR) Retired.
Marini, Michael '72 (MRY) Advocates; Presbyteral Council Retired.
Marino, Christopher '93 (MIA) Miami, FL St. Michael the Archangel; Deans and Deaneries; Italian; Catholic Educators' Guild; East Dade Deanery.
Marino, John J. *o.f.m.* '88 (SP)[N] St. Petersburg, FL St. Anthony Friary; Clearwater, FL St. Catherine of Siena.
Marino, Jose Humberto Lopez '98 (SJN) Guaynabo, PR Nuestra Senora de la Paz.
Marino, Rev. Msgr. Joseph T. '75 (PH) Strafford, PA Our Lady of the Assumption.
Marino, Robert '08 (BUF) Franklinville, NY St. Philomena.
Marino, Rev. Msgr. Ronald T. '73 (BRK) Brooklyn, NY St. Rosalia–Regina Pacis; Vicar for Migrant and Ethnic Apostolates; Assignment Board.
Marinucci, Steven J. '74 (PH) Philadelphia, PA St. Matthew.
Maristany, Edward G. '80 (CHI)[V] Chicago, IL Prelature of the Holy Cross and Opus Dei; Chicago.
Maristela, Victor '87 (SD) Jamul, CA Saint Pius X Catholic Parish Jamul.
Mark, John F. (STV)[A] St. Croix, VI St. Joseph High School.
Mark, John K. '01 (STV) Kingshill, VI Church of St. Joseph; [B] St. Croix, VI Hispanic Ministry; Diocesan Consultors; Hispanic Ministry.
Mark, Urey P. *s.v.d.* '07 (STL) St. Louis, MO St. Nicholas.
Markalonis, Joseph *t.o.r.* '66 (PIT)[M] Pittsburgh, PA Franciscan Friars, T.O.R.
Markantonis, Steven '10 (NY) Bronx, NY St. Philip Neri.
Markell, John W. '84 (PIT) Retired.
Markellos, Christopher M. '06 (CAM) Williamstown, NJ Our Lady of Peace Parish, Monroe Township, N.J.
Markelz, Carl J. *o.carm.* '91 (CHI)[D] Chicago, IL; [N] Chicago Carmelite Priory of St. Cyril; Chicago, IL St. Barnabas.
Markelz, Carl *o.carm.* '91 (JOL)[L] Darien, IL Carmelite Provincial Office; Darien, IL Provincial Headquarters, Carmelite Provincial Office; [O] Darien, IL Provincial Office of Lay Carmelites and Scapular Center.
Markert, Leo '62 (ALB) Retired.
Markewych, Rev. Archpriest Uriy '65 (PHU) Retired.
Markey, Earle L. *s.j.* '63 (WOR)[N] Worcester, MA Jesuits of the Holy Cross, Inc.
Markey, Greg J. '99 (BGP) Norwalk, CT St. Mary.
Markey, John J. *o.p.* '93 (SAT)[L] San Antonio, TX Dominican Priory of San Juan Macias.
Markey, John *o.m.i.* '93 (SAT)[C] Oblate School of Theology.
Markham, Rev. Msgr. James J. '51 (MAN) Manchester, NH Parish of the Transfiguration Retired.
Markham, John C. '03 (SAV) Special Assignment; Savannah, GA St. Frances Xavier Cabrini.
Markiewicz, Stanley T. *o.s.b.* '61 (GBG)[H] Latrobe, PA Saint Vincent Archabbey.
Markley, Edward P. *o.s.b.* '66 (BIR) Florence, AL St. Michael; [E] Cullman, AL St. Bernard Abbey.
Markman, Christopher J. '11 (FAR) Graduate Studies.
Marko, Andrew '98 (SJP) Presbyters Retired.
Markovic, Viktor '10 (NEW) Ridgefield Park, NJ St. Francis of Assisi.
Marks, Kevin E. '04 (PBR) Aliquippa, PA St. George the Great Martyr; Ambridge, PA St. Mary's; Vocations; Elected Deanery Representatives.
Marks, Thomas C. '79 (LR) Blytheville, AR Immaculate Conception; Osceola, AR St. Matthew; [K] Blytheville, AR Immaculate Conception Trust Fund; Marked Tree, AR St. Norbert.
Marks, William G. '92 (IND) Indianapolis, IN St. Simon the Apostle Catholic Church, Indianapolis, Inc.
Markus, Anthony L. '80 (CHI) Stickney, IL St. Pius X.
Markwell, Benjamin *o.f.m.cap.* '66 (DET) Detroit, MI Province of St. Joseph; [K] Detroit St. Bonaventure Friary.
Markwell, George *m.afr.* '65 (WDC)[L] Silver Spring, MD Holy Cross Hospital of Silver Spring, Inc.; [O] Washington, DC Missionaries of Africa; Washington, DC; Washington, DC MISSIONARIES OF AFRICA.
Marley, John *s.s.c.* '50 (PRO)[O] Bristol, RI St. Columban's Retirement House Retired.
Marley, John *s.s.c.* '50 (OM)[J] St. Columbans Missionary Society of St. Columban.
Marneni, Ignatius '69 (PH) On Special or Other Archdiocesan Assignment; Philadelphia, PA St. Jerome.
Marneni, Julian '67 (WH) Wayne, WV Nativity of Our Lord.
Marneni, Ravi Thanaiah '03 (DET) Detroit, MI St. Hedwig; [K] Detroit, MI P.I.M.E. Missionaries; Detroit, MI St. Francis D'Assisi.
Marney, Matthew D. '07 (WCH) Ongoing Formation of the Clergy Committee; Wichita, KS Christ the King.
Maroney, Frank '92 (DEN) Longmont, CO St. Francis of Assisi; College of Consultors.
Maroney, Maurice J. '67 (HRT) Milford, CT St. Gabriel.
Maroon, Donald M. '67 (COL) Wellston, OH SS. Peter and Paul.
Maroor, Joseph '63 (MIA) Lighthouse Point, FL St. Paul the Apostle.
Marot, Roger L. '50 (PRO) Woonsocket, RI Precious Blood Retired.
Marotta, Michael *c.r.m.* '87 (NEW) Lodi, NJ St. Joseph's.
Marotta, Robert G. '63 (NEW) Retired.
Maroun, George F. '74 (OG) Carthage, NY St. James Minor; Copenhagen, NY St. Mary.
Maroun, Rev. Msgr. Sharbel '89 (OLL) Minneapolis, MN St. Maron Maronite Catholic Church; College of Consultors; Office of Priestly Vocations; Presbyteral Council; Protopresbyters; Personnel Board.
Marquard, Elmer E. '66 (CLV) Retired.
Marquardt, Donald '51 (GB) Retired.
Marquart, Ernest J. '70 (SPC) Mountain View, MO St. John Vianney; Region V.
Marques, Anthony E. '06 (RIC) Danville, VA Sacred Heart.
Marques, Eduardo (BO) Brazilian.
Marques, Jesus *sch.p.* '64 (SJN) San Juan, PR Santisimo Salvador; [B] San Juan, PR Colegio Calasanz.
Marques, Jose E. (BO) Allston, MA St. Anthony of Padua.
Marquez, Esteban '95 (LA) On Sick Leave.
Marquez, Fabian '04 (ELP) Pecos, TX St. Catherine; Pecos, TX Santa Rosa de Lima.
Marquez, Fausto '97 (ATL) Atlanta, GA Holy Cross.
Marquez, Gregory '03 (ORG)[G] Fullerton, CA St. Jude Medical Center; Anaheim, CA St. Boniface.
Marquez, Humberto '05 (DEN) Brighton, CO St. Augustine.
Marquez, Jose E. '99 (NEW) Union City, NJ St. Anthony of Padua.
Marquez, Raul '10 (P) Stayton, OR Immaculate Conception.
Marquez, Raymond '10 (LA) Santa Clarita, CA Our Lady of Perpetual Help.
Marquez–Munoz, Salvador '03 (LR) Siloam Springs, AR St. Mary.
Marquis, Joseph '06 (PRM) Priest's Pension Board; Livonia, MI Sacred Heart.
Marquis, Paul R. '86 (PRT) Portland, ME Maine Medical Center; Portland, ME St. Louis.
Marquis, William Paul *o.p.* '83 (NY) New York, NY; [HH] New York, NY St. Thomas Aquinas Foundation; [DD] New York, NY St. Vincent Ferrer Priory.
Marquis, William '03 (CC) Corpus Christi, TX Saint Helena of the True Cross of Jesus.
Marr, Thomas P. '70 (MAD) Deaneries Retired.
Marra, James *s.d.b.* '83 (NEW)[C] Ramsey, NJ Don Bosco Preparatory High School; [L] Ramsey, NJ Don Bosco Prep Salesian Residence.
Marreddy, Allam '79 (CHR) Abbeville, SC Sacred Heart.
Marrell, Dennis P. '78 (LA) Pasadena, CA St. Philip the Apostle; Los Angeles, CA St. Basil's.
Marren, Rev. Msgr. Hugh M. '76 (ATL) Dunwoody, GA All Saints.
Marren, Martin T. '84 (CHI) Country Club Hills, IL St. Emeric.
Marrero, Adan *s.d.b.* '97 (SJN)[C] Catano, PR Prenoviciado Salesiano.
Marrero, Adan (ARE) Orocovis, PR San Juan Bautista.
Marrero, Jose A. (FAJ) Humacao, PR Maria Reina de la Paz.
Marrin, Joseph *c.ss.r.* (BRK) Legion of Mary.
Marrion, Malachy *o.c.s.o.* '54 (ARL)[H] Berryville, VA Cistercian Abbey of Our Lady of the Holy Cross.
Marro, Nicholas A. *c.s.* '63 (CHI) Chicago, IL Santa Lucia–Santa Maria Incoronata.
Marro, Simeon D. *o.carm.* '55 (GBG)[H] Bolivar, PA Mount Carmel Hermitage; Bolivar, PA.
Marrodan, Francisco J. *c.m.* (SJN)[E] Hato Rey, PR Hospital Auxilio Mutuo; [E] San Juan, PR Centro Medico de P.R.
Marron, Leonard J. *m.m.* '57 (FgM) Maryknoll, NY MARYKNOLL.
Marron, Rev. Msgr. Patrick L. '67 (SAT) Retired.
Marrone, Michael V. '07 (PH) Philadelphia, PA St. John the Baptist.
Marrone, Robert J. '73 (CLV) Absent on Leave.
Marroquin, Luis '86 (WDC) Wheaton, MD St. Catherine Laboure.
Marrow, Stanley B. *s.j.* '61 (BO)[U] Weston, MA Campion Health Center, Inc.
Marrufo, Ramon '76 (SD) Fallbrook, CA Saint Peter the Apostle Catholic Parish.
Marsal, Armando *d.c.j.m.* '93 (DEN) Aurora, CO St. Pius X; [N] Littleton, CO Disciples of the Hearts of Jesus and Mary; Littleton, CO St. Mary.
Marse, John J. '81 (NO) Metairie, LA East Jefferson General Hospital; Norco, LA Sacred Heart of Jesus.
Marsh, Ivan *o.carm.* (TUC) Tucson, AZ Saint Cyril of Alexandria Roman Catholic Parish – Tucson.
Marshack, Matthew (NEW)[L] Ramsey, NJ Don Bosco Prep Salesian Residence.
Marshall, Anthony J. *s.s.s.* '11 (CLV)[N] Cleveland Congregation of the Blessed Sacrament Provincial House.
Marshall, Anthony *s.s.s.* '11 (CHI) Chicago, IL Blessed Sacrament.
Marshall, Eugene C. *o.s.b.* '50 (OKL)[I] Shawnee, OK St. Gregory's Abbey.
Marshall, James C. '59 (STL) Retired.
Marshall, James '04 (SFE) Abiquiu, NM St. Thomas Apostle; El Rito, NM San Juan Nepomuceno.
Marshall, James *s.j.* '03 (SAT) San Antonio, TX Our Lady of Guadalupe.
Marshall, Joseph Mary *s.m.* '93 (SAT)[L] San Antonio, TX Casa San Juan Marianist Community; [S] San

Antonio, TX Brothers of the Beloved Disciple; San Antonio, TX St. Mary Magdalen.
Marshall, Patrick M. '79 (CHI)[U] Chicago, IL University of Illinois at Chicago – John Paul II Newman Center.
Marshall, Paul *s.m.* '76 (STL) Councilors:; [O] St. Louis, MO Marianists, Province of the United States (Society of Mary); [O] Saint Louis, MO Salve Marianist Community.
Marshall, Peter A. '09 (IND) Indianapolis, IN St. Pius X Catholic Church, Indianapolis, Inc.
Marshall, Robert A. '61 (STL) Retired.
Marshall, Robert W. '00 (MEM) Memphis, TN Church of the Ascension; Clergy Personnel Board; Presbyteral Council; College of Consultors.
Marshall, Thomas R. *c.s.p.* '59 (BRK)[R] Paulist Priests at Paulist Foundations Outside the U.S.
Marshall, William '63 (OAK) Retired.
Marsicek, Robert *s.d.s.* '68 (MIL)[P] Milwaukee Salvatorian Provincial Offices; Wauwatosa, WI St. Pius X; Milwaukee, WI Mother of Good Counsel; Consultors.
Marsick, James J. '72 (CLV) Cuyahoga Falls, OH St. Joseph; Cuyahoga Falls, OH General Hospital.
Marstall, David '04 (WCH) Wichita, KS St. Anne.
Marszal, Theodore '68 (CLV) Cleveland, OH Cathedral of St. John the Evangelist; [X] Cleveland, OH St. John Cathedral Endowment Trust; Administrative Assistant to the Bishop.
Marszalek, Paul B. '52 (CHI) Chicago, IL St. Jane de Chantal Retired.
Marta, Rev. Msgr. Raul '72 (FRS) Tulare, CA St. Aloysius.
Marteka, Anthony T. '61 (WOR) Retired.
Martel, C. James '70 (PRT) Retired.
Martel, Christopher M. '09 (MAN) Newmarket, NH St. Mary; Exeter, NH St. Michael.
Martel, Leo E. '63 (BO) Senior Priests. Retired.
Martel, Luc *a.a.* '73 (BO)[U] Boston Assumptionist Center.
Martel, Marcel I. '79 (MAN) Littleton, NH St. Rose of Lima.
Martell, James J. '88 (MEM) Memphis, TN Holy Rosary; College of Consultors; Presbyteral Council.
Martelli, Jose M. *c.s.c.* '73 (FTW)[H] Notre Dame Congregation of Holy Cross, United States Province of Priests & Brothers.
Martello, Ernest *o.s.c.* '70 (SCL)[I] Onamia, MN Crosier Priory.
Martello, Lawrence N. '74 (CLV) Amherst, OH St. Joseph; Associate Judges; South Amherst, OH Nativity of Blessed Virgin Mary.
Martens, L. Gene *s.j.* '63 (STL)[O] St. Louis, MO Jesuit Community Corporation at Saint Louis University – Jesuit Hall.
Martensen, Carsten P. *s.j.* '77 (SY)[Q] Syracuse, NY Jesuits at LeMoyne, Inc.
Martensen, Carsten *s.j.* '77 (ROC)[N] Ithaca, NY The Catholic Community of Ithaca College.
Marthaler, Andrew '90 (SCL) Retired.
Marthaler, Berard L. *o.f.m.conv.* '52 (WDC) Washington, DC St. Anthony; [B] Silver Spring, MD St. Bonaventure Friary; [C] Catholic University of America, The Retired.
Marti, Antonio *o.f.m.cap.* '96 (LA)[F] La Canada Flintridge, CA St. Francis High School of La Canada–Flintridge; Definitors.
Marti, Ramon *sch.p.* '55 (LA) Monrovia, CA Annunciation.
Marti, Thomas J. *m.m.* '65 (NY)[DD].
Martignetti, Richard *o.f.m.* '97 (NY)[DD] New York Franciscan Province of the Immaculate Conception.
Martignetti, Richard *o.f.m.* '97 (STU)[A] Steubenville, OH Franciscan University of Steubenville; [H] Steubenville, OH Holy Spirit Friary.
Martignon, John E. '84 (MAR) Houghton, MI St. Ignatius Loyola; Houghton, MI Holy Family; Vicars Forane.
Martin, Rev. Msgr. Andrew E. '67 (CAM) Retired.
Martin, Anselm *o.f.m.cap.* '45 (PH) Philadelphia, PA St. John the Evangelist.
Martin, Benjamin '75 (DOD) Marienthal, KS St. Anthony of Padua Catholic Church of Leoti, Kansas; Marienthal, KS St. Mary Catholic Church of Marienthal, Kansas; Tribune, KS St. Joseph the Worker Catholic Church of Tribune, Kansas.
Martin, Benjamin *s.o.l.t.* '06 (CC)[G] Robstown, TX Society of Our Lady of the Most Holy Trinity.
Martin, C. Lou '76 (BAL) Baltimore, MD St. Clare.
Martin, Christopher M. '06 (STL) Office of Vocations; [V] St. Louis, MO Archdiocesan Stewardship Education Committee; Brentwood, MO St. Mary Magdalen.
Martin, Clifford '76 (SFR) Burlingame, CA St. Catherine of Siena.
Martin, Cristobal *m.id.* '96 (NY) Bronx, NY Santa Maria; [DD] Bronx, NY Idente Missionaries – Santa Maria Residence.
Martin, Cristobal *id.m.* '96 (BRK)[D] Brooklyn, NY Campus Ministers and Ministry Centers.
Martin, David L. '73 (ARL) McLean, VA St. Luke.
Martin, David '76 (EVN) Evansville, IN St. John the Evangelist.
Martin, Dennis A. '75 (E) Erie, PA St. Vincent's Health Center; [H] Erie, PA Saint Vincent Health Center.
Martin, Dennis C. '67 (DAV) West Branch, IA St. Bernadette; West Liberty, IA St. Joseph's.
Martin, Donald *s.j.* '82 (NO)[A] New Orleans, LA Notre Dame Seminary Graduate School of Theology.
Martin, Edward '77 (MO) Military Chaplains; Army Chaplains.
Martin, Elijah *o.c.d.* '01 (MIL)[P] Milwaukee Provincial Offices – Discalced Carmelites.
Martin, Rev. Msgr. Emilio '52 (MIA) Retired.
Martin, Francis R. '56 (WDC) Special Ministries Retired.
Martin, Gerald R. '89 (BR) Board Members.
Martin, Gerard R. '73 (BR) Baton Rouge, LA St. Patrick; Defenders of the Bond.
Martin, Gilmer '74 (NO) Lacombe, LA St. John of the Cross.
Martin, Harry '66 (SAT) Retired.
Martin, Hilary *o.p.* '55 (OAK)[L] Oakland, CA Order of Preachers (Province of the Most Holy Name of Jesus – Western Dominican Province); [L] Oakland Order of Preachers (Province of the Most Holy Name of Jesus – Western Dominican Province); [A] Berkeley, CA Dominican School of Philosophy and Theology.
Martin, J. Dennis *c.m.* '62 (STL)[O] Perryville, MO Congregation of the Mission.
Martin, James J. *s.j.* '99 (BO)[U] Boston The Society of Jesus of New England–Provincial Offices.
Martin, James J. *s.j.* '99 (NY)[DD] New York, NY "America;" Residence and publication office of the America Press.
Martin, James J. '63 (PH) Retired.
Martin, James *c.s.c.* '93 (AUS) Austin, TX St. Ignatius Martyr.
Martin, Jeffrey D. '05 (LFT) Lafayette, IN St. Boniface.
Martin, Joel W. *o.s.b.* '91 (BIR)[B] Cullman, AL St. Bernard Preparatory School; [E] Cullman, AL St. Bernard Abbey.
Martin, Rev. Msgr. John J. '72 (ALN) Bethlehem, PA Assumption B.V.M.
Martin, John J. '65 (SR) Retired.
Martin, John M. *s.j.* '84 (PHX)[F] Phoenix, AZ Society of Jesus; Phoenix, AZ St. Francis Xavier Roman Catholic Parish.
Martin, Rev. Msgr. John P. '61 (RVC) Retired.
Martin, John P. *m.m.* '66 (FgM) Maryknoll, NY MARYKNOLL.
Martin, John Randall '89 (TYL) On Duty Outside the Diocese.
Martin, John '65 (NEW) Elizabeth, NJ St. Mary of the Assumption.
Martin, Rev. Msgr. Joseph A. '67 (NY) Fishkill, NY Church of St. Mary, Mother of the Church.
Martin, Joseph I. '56 (BO) Senior Priests. Retired.
Martin, Rev. Msgr. Kelly Ireland '47 (NEW) Retired.
Martin, Kevin J. '03 (PRT) Augusta, ME St. Michael Parish.
Martin, Larok '80 (OKL)[K] Tonkawa, OK Northern Oklahoma College.
Martin, Leon J. *s.a.c.* '75 (MIL)[Y] Milwaukee, WI Pallottine Fathers and Brothers, Inc., Disability Trust; [Y] Milwaukee, WI Pallottine Fathers and Brothers, Inc., Educational and Apostolic Ministry Trust; Milwaukee, WI; [P] Milwaukee, WI Pallotti House.
Martin, Leonard A. *s.j.* '73 (SCR)[B] Scranton, PA The University of Scranton.
Martin, Leonard A. *s.j.* '73 (WDC)[E] North Bethesda, MD Georgetown Preparatory School.
Martin, Leonard A. *s.j.* '73 (PSC) Scranton, PA St. Mary's; Olean, NY St. Mary's.
Martin, Malcolm *s.a.* '62 (BO)[N] Brockton, MA Chapel of Our Savior–Catholic Pastoral and Information Center; [U] Brockton, MA Chapel of Our Savior; [Z] Brockton, MA Chapel of Our Saviour Retired.
Martin, Malcolm *s.a.* '62 (NY)[DD] Brockton, MA Chapel of Our Savior.
Martin, Michael J. *c.s.p.* '77 (PMB)[H] Vero Beach, FL Paulist Fathers Residence.
Martin, Michael *o.f.m.conv.* '89 (R)[I] Durham, NC Newman Catholic Student Center Duke University; [F] Pittsboro, NC Our Lady of Guadalupe Friary.
Martin, Normand J. *s.m.* '59 (BO)[U] Boston, MA Marist Fathers Lourdes Residence; [Z] Boston, MA Marist Fathers Residence.
Martin, Oscar '01 (NEW) On Duty Outside the Archdiocese.
Martin, Patrick A. '78 (NOR) On Duty Outside the Diocese.
Martin, Patrick '78 (NY) New York, NY Our Lady of Guadalupe at St. Bernard's.
Martin, Rev. Msgr. Ralph L. '65 (WIL) Retired.
Martin, Raymond D. '94 (BAL) Priests Sick or Absent.
Martin, Reginald *o.p.* '74 (OAK)[L] Oakland, CA Order of Preachers (Province of the Most Holy Name of Jesus – Western Dominican Province).
Martin, Richard B. '66 (ARL) Burke, VA Church of the Nativity.
Martin, Richard J. '63 (CHI) Retired.
Martin, Robert A. '83 (BUF)[N] Buffalo, NY Sheehan Residence for Priests Retired.
Martin, Robert *c.ss.r.* '50 (FgM) Denver, CO Denver Province.
Martin, Roosevelt '88 (GAL) Retired.
Martin, Samuel A. '99 (LC) Marshfield, WI St. John the Baptist; Marshfield, WI Christ the King; Office of Ecumenism; Appointed Members.
Martin, Sean '81 (DAL) On Duty Outside the Diocese.
Martin, Seán '79 (STL)[B] St. Louis, MO Aquinas Institute of Theology.
Martin, Rev. Msgr. Stephen E. '98 (MOB) Mobile, AL Cathedral of the Immaculate Conception; Mobile, AL St. Joseph; Vicar General and Moderator of the Curia; Archdiocesan Consultors; Catholic Housing of Mobile, Inc.; Censor Librorum; Liturgical Commission; Officers.
Martin, Ted '11 (KAL) Kalamazoo, MI St. Augustine Cathedral.
Martin, Rev. Msgr. Thomas A. '79 (KAL) Kalamazoo, MI St. Augustine Cathedral; Judicial Vicar; Diocesan Consultors; Delegate for Ecumenical and Interreligious Concerns; Presbyteral Council Members; Presbyteral Council Members; Vicar for Canonical Concerns.
Martin, Thomas P. *s.j.* '66 (BAL)[Q] Baltimore, MD Colombiere Jesuit Community.
Martin, Thomas P. *s.j.* '66 (PH)[Y] Loyola Center and Manresa Hall.
Martin, Thomas '70 (OAK) Oakland, CA St. Jarlath.
Martin, Thomas *o.c.d.* '61 (MIL)[P] Milwaukee Provincial Offices – Discalced Carmelites.
Martin, Victor T. '80 (BGP) Fairfield, CT St. Thomas Aquinas.
Martin, William F. '63 (NY) On Duty Outside the Archdiocese.
Martin, William F. '78 (STP) Richfield, MN St. Richard.
Martin, William J. '71 (L) Retired.
Martin–Calama, Florian '95 (DEN)[A] Denver, CO Redemptoris Mater House of Formation; The Redemptoris Mater House of Formation.
Martina, Joseph A. '89 (SHP) Many, LA St. John the Baptist; Priests' Retirement Board.
Martine, Michael T. '97 (NY) Staten Island, NY St. Joseph; [A] Yonkers, NY St. Joseph's Seminary; Judicial Vicar.
Martine, Michael T. '97 (ALB) Interdiocesan Tribunal for the Province of NY Archdiocese.
Martineau, Albert P. *o.m.i.* '59 (BO)[X] Tewksbury, MA Immaculate Heart of Mary Residence.
Martinek, John '73 (FBK) Delta Junction, AK Our Lady of Sorrows Catholic Church Delta Junction; Presbyteral Council; Consultors.
Martinez, Abelardo Huanca *o.f.m.conv.* '99 (ATL) Jonesboro, GA St. Philip Benizi.
Martinez, Adam '85 (AUS) Killeen, TX St. Joseph.
Martinez, Alex (WDC) Cheverly, MD St. Ambrose.
Martinez, Alfredo (CGS) Retired.
Martinez, Andrew *o.f.m.conv.* '09 (FTW) Angola; LaGrange, IN St. Joseph; LaGrange; Angola, IN St. Anthony.
Martinez, Antonio *o.a.r.* '48 (LSC)[B] Mesilla, NM Augustinian Recollect Fathers.
Martinez, Antonio *s.j.* (GAL)[E] Houston, TX Jesuit Cristo Rey High School of Houston, Inc.
Martinez, Carlos '10 (LEX) Somerset, KY St. Mildred.
Martinez, Carlos (GRY) East Chicago, IN Our Lady of Guadalupe.
Martinez, Charlie *o.f.m.* '80 (LSC) Vicars; Roswell, NM St. Peter; Presbyteral Council.
Martinez, Daniel M. '04 (LA) Maywood, CA St. Rose of Lima.
Martinez, Danilo '03 (SJN) Resident Chaplains; San Juan, PR Santa Cecilia.
Martinez, Efrain '04 (FRS) Selma, CA St. Joseph.
Martinez, Ernest R. *s.j.* '62 (FgM) Los Gatos, CA Society of Jesus.
Martinez, Eusebio '03 (BWN) Edinburg, TX Holy Family.
Martinez, Felipe Antonio '96 (TUC) Administrative Leave of Absence.
Martinez, Francisco Xavier *s.t.l.* '89 (CC) On Special Assignment.
Martinez, Frank '90 (CC)[D] Corpus Christi, TX CHRISTUS Spohn Hospital Corpus Christi – Shoreline.
Martinez, Gilbert S. *c.s.p.* '95 (NY) New York, NY St. Paul the Apostle; [DD] New York, NY Paulist Fathers' Motherhouse.
Martinez, Ignacio '93 (MRY) Salinas, CA Sacred Heart.
Martinez, Ivan '08 (ARE) Director of Youth.
Martinez, James E. *o.s.a.* '57 (PH)[Y] Villanova, PA St. Augustine Friary.
Martinez, Jery Rivera '00 (PCE) Ensenada, PR Sacred Heart.
Martinez, Jesus E. '02 (WOR) Holy Spirit.
Martinez, Jesus Eduardo '07 (LA) Los Angeles, CA St. Columbkille.
Martinez, Joaquin *s.j.* (TOL)[C] Toledo, OH St. John's Jesuit High School.
Martinez, John J. *s.j.* '62 (ALN)[A] Wernersville, PA Jesuit Center–Jesuit Community.
Martinez, Jorge Bravo *c.s.* '04 (CHI) Melrose Park, IL

St. Charles Borromeo.

Martinez, Jose Jesus '11 (LA) South El Monte, CA Epiphany.

Martinez, Jose Luis *o.a.r.* '64 (NY)[FF] Bronx, NY St. Joseph's Center; [HH] Bronx, NY St. Joseph's Center.

Martinez, Jose Luis *o.a.r.* '64 (ORG) Santa Ana, CA Our Lady of the Pillar.

Martinez, Jose Rogelio '05 (LSC) La Mesa, NM San Jose; Diocesan Tribunal; Judges; Judicial Vicar; Diocesan Consultors; Presbyteral Council.

Martinez, Jose Vicente *c.m.f.* (SJN) Spiritual Directors.

Martinez, Jose '69 (NY) Bronx, NY St. Roch.

Martinez, Joyle '91 (SAC) Red Bluff, CA Sacred Heart; Vicars Forane.

Martinez, Juan *s.d.b.* (ARE) Orocovis, PR San Juan Bautista.

Martinez, Juan *m.n.m.* '82 (ELP) San Elizario, TX San Elceario.

Martinez, Rev. Msgr. Leo '63 (SAT) Retired.

Martinez, Leonel *o.s.a.* '74 (LAR) Laredo, TX St. Vincent de Paul.

Martinez, Rev. Msgr. Leonel '63 (SAT)[K] San Antonio, TX Padua Place.

Martinez, Manuel '66 (SAT) On Duty Outside the Archdiocese.

Martinez, Rev. Msgr. Marcos '59 (CC) Corpus Christi, TX Our Lady of Pilar; Presbyteral Council.

Martinez, Margarito Severino *c.m.* '00 (LA) Los Angeles, CA Our Lady of the Rosary of Talpa.

Martinez, Mario Castro *o.f.m.conv.* (AUS) Austin, TX Cristo Rey.

Martinez, Mark (LA) Los Angeles, CA St. Camillus Center for Spiritual Care; Los Angeles, CA Norris Cancer and USC University Hospital.

Martinez, Martin S. '93 (TUC) Nogales, AZ Sacred Heart of Jesus Roman Catholic Parish – Nogales.

Martinez, Matthias *o.s.b.* '08 (GBG)[H] Latrobe, PA Saint Vincent Archabbey.

Martinez, Michael '89 (TUC) Tucson, AZ Christ the King Chapel; Air National Guard Chaplains; On Duty Outside the Diocese.

Martinez, Miguel Angel '01 (CHI)[W] Des Plaines, IL Maryville–Our Lady of Guadalupe Chapel.

Martinez, Omar *o.p.* '00 (SB) Cathedral City, CA St. Louis.

Martinez, Oscar Ramirez '97 (LAR) Asherton, TX Immaculate Conception.

Martinez, Oscar '06 (SLC) Salt Lake City, UT Our Lady of Guadalupe LLC 208; Team.

Martinez, Pablo A. '09 (NEW) Plainfield, NJ St. Mary.

Martinez, Peter G. '04 (CC) Corpus Christi, TX St. Paul the Apostle; Presbyteral Council.

Martinez, Roberto *o.f.m.cap.* '92 (SJN)[C] San Juan, PR Fraternidad San Antonio; San Juan, PR San Antonio; Rio Piedras, PR; [H] San Juan, PR The Capuchin Formation Trust of Puerto Rico.

Martinez, Roy F. *o.f.m.cap.* '85 (ARE) Arecibo, PR Santisimo Sacramento; Arecibo, PR Church of Santa Cecilia.

Martinez, Timothy A. '90 (SFE) Albuquerque, NM Shrine of St. Bernadette; Presbyteral Council of the Archdiocese of Santa Fe.

Martinez, Vidal M. *o.s.m.* '75 (CHI)[N] Chicago, IL Order of Friar Servants of Mary (Servites) United States of America Province, Inc.; Chicago, IL Our Lady of Sorrows, Basilica of; [N] Chicago, IL Servite Secular Order; Chicago, IL; [N] Chicago, IL Monastery of Our Lady of Sorrows.

Martinez, Vidal '70 (SFE) Retired.

Martinez, Virgilio '65 (SJN) Bayamon, PR Santa Rosa de Lima.

Martinez, Zacharis '04 (ARL) Woodstock, VA St. John Bosco.

Martinez–Irigoyen, Jesus M. '67 (GAL) South Houston, TX Our Lady of Grace.

Martinez Adorno, Ivan '08 (ARE) Arecibo, PR Our Lady of Hope.

Martinez Adorno, P. Ivan (PCE)[B] The Pontifical Catholic University of Puerto Rico.

Martinez de Espronceda, Jesus *o.a.r.* '62 (LSC) Las Cruces, NM Santa Rosa de Lima; [B] Mesilla, NM Augustinian Recollect Fathers.

Martínez Galvez, Mariano *o.m.i.* '86 (SJN) San Juan, PR Maria Reina del Mundo.

Martinez Medina, P. Omar '00 (PCE) Ponce, PR San Jose Obrero.

Martinez Solis, Jesus E. '07 (CHI) Other Assignments.

Martinez Tobon, Jose Dario '87 (SJN) Toa Baja, PR Ntra. Sra. de la Candelaria.

Martinez y Alire, Rev. Msgr. Jerome '76 (SFE) Santa Fe, NM The Cathedral Basilica of St. Francis of Assisi; Santa Fe, NM Cristo Rey; Vicars Forane (Deans); Promoter of Justice; Presbyteral Council of the Archdiocese of Santa Fe.

Martini, Rev. Msgr. Richard '80 (LA) Santa Clarita, CA Our Lady of Perpetual Help; Chairman; San Fernando Region; Members.

Martino, José D. Rodriguez (PCE)[B] The Pontifical Catholic University of Puerto Rico.

Martinosky, Joseph A. '57 (STU) Retired.

Martin Pinillos, Ricardo '03 (MIL) Study Leave.

Martins, Celso *c.ss.r.* (NEW) Newark, NJ St. James.

Martins, Jose Brito '00 (BGP) Danbury, CT Immaculate Heart of Mary.

Martins, Orlando '05 (CHI) Oak Lawn, IL St. Linus.

Martinson, George G. *s.j.* '73 (FgM) Los Gatos, CA Society of Jesus.

Martinson, Keith Barry *s.j.* '75 (FgM) Los Gatos, CA Society of Jesus.

Martinson, Timothy James '10 (CHY) Gillette, WY St. Matthew's.

Martiny, Leon Martin A. *o.p.* '98 (FgM) New York, NY Province of St. Joseph (Eastern).

Martis, Douglas A. '89 (CHI)[A] Mundelein, IL The Liturgical Institute; [A] Mundelein, IL University of St. Mary of the Lake/Mundelein Seminary.

Martis, Douglas '89 (JOL) On Duty Outside the Diocese.

Martis, Samuel '83 (BGP)[M] Norwalk, CT Notre Dame Convalescent Home.

Martlock, Loville N. '63 (BUF) Retired.

Martocchio, Rev. Msgr. Peter T. '57 (BO) Weymouth, MA St. Jerome; Senior Priests. Retired.

Marton, Bernard *o.cist.* '67 (DAL)[J] Irving, TX Cistercian Abbey of Our Lady of Dallas; Irving, TX.

Martorano, Nicholas *o.s.a.* '77 (PH) Philadelphia, PA St. Nicholas of Tolentine; [Y] Philadelphia, PA Augustinian Community (O.S.A.).

Martos, Rafael E. '96 (SP) Cursillo, Spanish; Plant City, FL St. Clement.

Martyniuk, Pawlo '92 (STF) Hartford, CT St. Michael.

Marucci, Rev. Msgr. Louis A. '87 (CAM) Gibbsboro, NJ St. Andrew the Apostle's R.C. Church, Gibbsboro, N.J.; Haddonfield, NJ St. Joseph the Worker Parish, Haddon Township, N.J.

Marullo, Lawrence E. '75 (OG) Constableville, NY St. Mary; Port Leyden, NY St. Martin; Constableville, NY St. Mary's Nativity.

Marus, Andrew G. '71 (BGP) Stratford, CT Holy Name of Jesus.

Marusceac, Vladimir '88 (STF) Cohoes, NY SS. Peter and Paul; Albany.

Marut, Thomas '74 (STU) Martins Ferry, OH St. Mary.

Maruthukunnel Thomas, James *c.m.i.* '77 (SAL) Park, KS St. Agnes Parish; Park, KS Sacred Heart Parish; Grinnell, KS Immaculate Conception of the Blessed Virigin Mary Parish.

Marva, Robert *o.f.m.cap.* '97 (CLV) Cleveland, OH St. Agnes – Our Lady of Fatima; [N] Cleveland, OH St. Paul Friary; [N] Cleveland, OH St. Agnes–Our Lady of Fatima.

Marx, Louis N. '66 (SB) Guasti, CA San Secondo d'Asti.

Marx, Paul *o.m.i.* '65 (FgM) Washington, DC AMERICAN OBLATE MISSIONS.

Marx, Robert '88 (SJ) On Leave of Absence.

Maryanski, Fabian J. '71 (BUF) Vicars; Sloan, NY St. Andrew; Finance Council.

Maryland, Joseph A. '40 (E) Retired.

Marzan, Eddie Rivera '91 (SJN) San Juan, PR San Luis Gonzaga; [E] San Juan, PR Centro Medico de P.R.

Marzetti, Raul Lopez '85 (PHX) Phoenix, AZ SS. Simon and Jude Roman Catholic Cathedral.

Marzocchi, Mario *s.s.s.* '84 (SAT) San Antonio, TX St. Joseph.

Marzynski, Janusz '04 (DET) Detroit, MI St. John Hospital; Memphis, MI Holy Family.

Masabakhwa, Raphael '95 (DM) Neola, IA St. Patrick; Neola, IA St. Columbanus.

Masad, Frederick F. '60 (CHR) Retired.

Masakowski, Edward M. '57 (SCR) Retired.

Mascardo, Editho '83 (STO) Sonora, CA St. Patrick Church of Sonora (Pastor of).

Mascarella, Patrick J. '66 (BR) Retired.

Mascari, Michael A. *o.p.* '87 (STL)[O] St. Louis, MO Dominican Studentate.

Mascari, Michael A. *o.p.* '87 (CHI)[N] Chicago Dominicans (Provincial Office).

Masciocchi, Robert *c.s.s.* '54 (BO)[U] Waltham, MA Stigmatine Fathers & Brothers Provincial House; [W] Waltham, MA Espousal Retreat House and Conference Center.

Mascioli, Joseph M. '57 (WH) Retired.

Mascolino, Charles E. '54 (STU) College of Consultors Retired.

Mascorro, Miguel *sch.p.* '96 (LA) Los Angeles, CA St. Lucy; Los Angeles, CA Santa Teresita.

Masello, David W. '78 (PRO) Warren, RI St. Alexander; Defenders of the Bond.

Mash, Wesley M. '90 (PBR) Tarentum, PA Sts. Peter and Paul.

Masiello, John *s.d.b.* '58 (SP)[P] Tampa, FL Mary Help of Christians Center.

Masiello, Rev. Msgr. Joseph P. '69 (NEW) Westfield, NJ Holy Trinity; Members.

Masinde, Steven '00 (NY) Bronx, NY SS. Philip and James.

Maslach, Paul *o.f.m.* '62 (MIL) Milwaukee, WI Sacred Heart; Chicago, IL.

Maslach, Paul *o.f.m.* '62 (CHI)[N] Chicago, IL Croatian Franciscan Custody of the Holy Family.

Maslak, Gregory '72 (PHU) Bristol, PA St. Mary's.

Maslanka, Piotr J. '04 (NEW) Elizabeth, NJ St. Hedwig's.

Maslar, George *o.f.m.conv.* (BGP) Bridgeport, CT Bridgeport Health Care.

Maslejak, Andrzej *s.ch.* '79 (CHI) Chicago, IL Holy Trinity Mission.

Maslowski, Krzysztof K. '88 (NEW) Roselle, NJ Church of St. Joseph the Carpenter.

Maslowski, Stanley J. '63 (STP) Retired.

Maslowsky, Michael '86 (P)[K] Portland, OR St. Anthony Village (activity of St. Anthony Village Enterprise); [K] Portland, OR Assumption Village (activity of St. Anthony Village Enterprise).

Maslowsky, Michael '87 (P) Special Assignment.

Masluk, Alexander '79 (PH) Philadelphia, PA Saint Martha.

Masnicki, Marek '92 (NOR) Colchester, CT St. Andrew; Lebanon, CT St. Francis of Assisi.

Maso, Dario *s.x.* '82 (PAT)[N] Wayne Xaverian Missionary Fathers; Wayne, NJ XAVERIAN MISSIONARY FATHERS.

Mason, Brian G. '93 (MIL)[H] Milwaukee, WI All Saints Catholic East School System, Inc.; Milwaukee, WI Old St. Mary; Milwaukee, WI Three Holy Women Catholic Parish; Milwaukee, WI Our Lady of Divine Providence; Milwaukee, WI SS. Peter and Paul; Archdiocesan Council of Priests.

Mason, Carl '64 (NY) Manhattan, NY Hospital for Special Surgery.

Mason, Charlon O. '79 (GR) Pewamo, MI St. Joseph's.

Mason, Dennis *o.f.m.conv.* '78 (BGP) Danbury, CT Sacred Heart of Jesus; Presbyteral Council.

Mason, Edward J. '87 (BRK) Our Lady of Mercy; Brooklyn, NY Our Lady of the Presentation–Our Lady of Loreto.

Mason, James E. '01 (SFS) Sioux Falls, SD St. Lambert; Vice Chancellors; Diocesan Consultors; Presbyteral Council.

Mason, Louis C. *o.p.* '64 (NY) Manhattan, NY Memorial Sloan Kettering Cancer Center; [DD] New York, NY St. Catherine of Siena Priory; New York, NY St. Catherine of Siena; Manhattan, NY New York Presbyterian Hospital.

Mason, Mark E. '75 (OKL) Union City, OK St. Joseph's; El Reno, OK Sacred Heart.

Mason, Matthew J. '09 (MAN) Laconia, NH St. Andre Bessette.

Mason, Robert E. '56 (RVC) Massapequa Park, NY Our Lady of Lourdes Retired.

Mason, William *o.m.i.* '71 (MIA) Miami, FL Christ the King.

Mass, Ronald J. '70 (CHI) Palos Heights, IL Incarnation.

Massa, James '86 (BRK) Brooklyn, NY St. Patrick.

Massa, Mark S. *s.j.* '80 (BO)[C] The School of Theology and Ministry; [U] Newton, MA The Jesuit Community at Boston College.

Massad, Tony '10 (OLL) Cleveland, OH St. Maron Maronite Catholic Church; Office of Priestly Vocations.

Massar, Richard A. '69 (BUF)[N] Lackawanna, NY Bishop Head Residence Retired.

Massarella, Francis A. '46 (CIN) Priests Commended to a Life of Prayer and Penance Retired.

Massari, John Charles *c.s.* (NY) New York, NY Our Lady of Pompeii.

Massaro, Michael A. *c.s.c.* '81 (FTW)[H] Notre Dame Congregation of Holy Cross, United States Province of Priests & Brothers.

Massaro, Michael *c.s.c.* '81 (PMB) Vero Beach, FL Holy Cross.

Massaro, Thomas *s.j.* '93 (BO)[U] Brighton, MA Francis Xavier House.

Massart, James P. '66 (GB) Ecumenical Liaison Retired.

Massawe, Andrew *c.s.c.* '03 (FTW)[H] Notre Dame Congregation of Holy Cross, United States Province of Priests & Brothers.

Massawe, Aristides *c.s.c.* '02 (FTW)[H] Notre Dame Congregation of Holy Cross, United States Province of Priests & Brothers.

Massett, Rev. Msgr. Robert D. '66 (NO) Metairie, LA St. Mary Magdalen; Council of Catholic School Cooperative Clubs; Serra Club of East Jefferson.

Massetti, Philip V. *o.s.j.* '76 (SCR) Pittston, PA; Exeter, PA Saint Barbara Parish.

Massetti, Philip *o.s.j.* '76 (SCR)[L] Pittston, PA Our Lady of Sorrows Province of the Oblates of St. Joseph.

Massey, Robert E. '66 (MIL) West Allis, WI Holy Assumption Retired.

Massi, Anthony '84 (MIA) Retired.

Massicotte, Bernard *o.s.b.cam.* '57 (MRY)[F] Big Sur, CA New Camaldoli Hermitage.

Massie, Rev. Msgr. Guy A. '83 (BRK) Brooklyn, NY St. Andrew the Apostle; Ecumenical and Interreligious Affairs, Diocesan Commission for; Committee for Catholic–Jewish Relations; Catholic Muslim Dialogue.

Massillon, Nazaire '00 (ORL) Kissimmee, FL St. Catherine of Siena.

Massimino, Jerome *o.f.m.* '77 (SP)[J] St. Petersburg, FL St. Anthony's Hospital, Inc.; [N] St. Petersburg, FL St. Anthony Friary.
Massingale, Bryan N. '83 (MIL) Special Assignment.
Masson, Paul R. *m.m.* '72 (NY) Maryknoll, NY; Maryknoll, NY; [DD] Maryknoll Maryknoll Fathers and Brothers.
Massoth, Rt. Rev. Charles *o.s.b.* '51 (OKL)[I] Shawnee, OK St. Gregory's Abbey; Shawnee, OK Retired.
Massucci, Joseph D. '70 (STU)[D] Dayton, OH The University of Dayton; On Duty Outside the Diocese.
Mastalir, Peter '92 (GB) Absent on Leave, Sick or Disabled.
Masters, Burke '02 (JOL) Vocations; [O] Joliet, IL John Paul II House; Secretary.
Masters, Gerard G. '66 (HRT) Milford, CT Christ the Redeemer.
Masterson, Thomas D. *s.j.* '64 (PH)[Y] Loyola Center and Manresa Hall.
Mastey, Gregory '95 (SCL) Vocations.
Mastin, Mark *s.c.j.* '07 (MIL)[P] Hales Corners Priests of the Sacred Heart.
Mastin, Mark *s.c.j.* '07 (MO) Army Chaplains.
Mastrangelo, David F. *s.j.* '87 (DET)[E] Detroit, MI Loyola High School; [E] Detroit, MI Loyola Work Experience Program, Inc.
Mastrangelo, Mario *o.f.m.cap.* '58 (PCE) Ponce, PR Santa Teresita; [B] The Pontifical Catholic University of Puerto Rico; [E] Ponce, PR Fraternidad Santa Teresita, Frailes Capuchinos; Episcopal Vicar for Religious; Pittsburgh, PA Province of St. Augustine.
Mastrangelo, Nicholas '64 (PIT) Munhall, PA St. Rita; Munhall, PA St. Therese of Lisieux; West Mifflin, PA Resurrection.
Mastria, Angelo *o.carm.* '58 (TUC)[A] Tucson, AZ Salpointe Catholic High School; [C] Tucson, AZ Chaplaincy–Pastoral Ministry to Non–Denominational Nursing Homes; [E] Tucson, AZ Carmelite Priory.
Mastrian, Mark J. '87 (E) Grampian, PA St. Bonaventure; Curwensville, PA St. Timothy.
Mastrobuono, Peter *s.c.j.* '66 (GAL) Houston, TX Our Lady of Guadalupe.
Mastroeni, Anthony J. '72 (PAT)[Q] Paterson, NJ Cor Jesu Mission Fund Inc; Theological Commission; Unassigned.
Mastrogiacomo, Richard J. '11 (RVC) Academic Leave.
Mastrolia, Arthur '87 (NY) Congers, NY St. Paul.
Maszczyk, Zenon *o.f.m.cap.* '00 (HBG) York, PA St. Joseph.
Mata, Luke J. '06 (POD) Los Angeles; Vicar for California.
Mata, Luke '06 (LA)[W] Los Angeles, CA Prelature of the Holy Cross and Opus Dei.
Mata, Octavio '05 (LA) Los Angeles, CA Immaculate Conception.
Mata, Theodoro '98 (VEN) Sarasota, FL St. Jude.
Matarazzo, Rev. Msgr. Francis '67 (PAT) Clifton, NJ St. Brendan Retired.
Matas, Rev. Msgr. Juan '65 (LA) Montebello, CA Our Lady of the Miraculous Medal; Cursillo Movement Retired.
Matejek, John M. '03 (ATL) Kennesaw, GA St. Catherine of Siena.
Mateljan, Roy A. '67 (MIL) Retired.
Mateo, Arturo P. *m.s.c.* '76 (SB) Riverside, CA St. Catherine of Alexandria.
Mateo, Mateo *ss.cc.* '47 (SJN) Guaynabo, PR Sagrados Corazones.
Mateo, Miguel *s.f.* (BAL) Frederick, MD St. John the Evangelist.
Mateos, Tomas '45 (BWN) Retired.
Mateos, Tomas '45 (BWN)[K] Mission, TX Fraternity of Our Lady of Guadalupe Secular Franciscan Order.
Matera, Frank J. '68 (WDC) On Duty Outside the Archdiocese; [C] Catholic University of America, The.
Matera, Philip T. '51 (TR) Retired.
Materu, Paul *a.l.c.p.* '98 (P) Tigard, OR St. Anthony.
Mateus, Norberto '81 (ATL) Without Archdiocesan Assignment or Faculties; On Leave of Absence.
Mateus–Ariza, Hector '09 (BAL) Forest Hill, MD St. Ignatius.
Mathabela, Sipho (B) Orofino, ID St. Theresa's.
Mathai, Joseph Kappilumakkal *c.m.i.* '86 (SPC) Poplar Bluff, MO Sacred Heart; Doniphan, MO St. Benedict.
Mathai, Mani *c.m.i.* '80 (TYL) Winnsboro, TX Clyde Johnston Unit, Texas Department of Corrections.
Mathaner, John P. '93 (E) Oil City, PA Our Lady Help of Christians.
Matheny, William K. '96 (WH) Wheeling, WV St. Michael.
Mathers, Rev. Msgr. Douglas J. '85 (NY) Vice–Chancellors; Conciliation and Arbitration, Office of; New York, NY St. John the Evangelist.
Mathesius, William P. '76 (WIL) Retired.
Matheu, Santiago '75 (MIA) Cursillos de Cristiandad (Spanish).
Mathew, Abraham P. '97 (BRK) Jamaica, NY St. Nicholas of Tolentine.
Mathew, Antony *t.o.r.* '96 (FWT) Fort Worth, TX St. Thomas.
Mathew, Biju *c.f.i.c.* '98 (STP) St. Paul, MN St. Mary; [J] St. Paul, MN Congregation of the Sons of the Immaculate Conception.
Mathew, Charles *o.f.m.* '74 (NSH) Clarksville, TN Immaculate Conception.
Mathew, James '97 (SYM) Cortlandt Manor, NY Syro–Malabar Knanaya Catholic Mission of Westchester, NY; Cortlandt Manor, NY Syro–Malabar Knanaya Catholic Mission of Rockland, NY; Cortlandt Manor, NY Syro–Malabar Knanaya Catholic Mission Connecticut.
Mathew, Jose '10 (SYM) Missouri City, TX St. Mary's Syro–Malabar Knanaya Catholic Church of Houston.
Mathew, Joshy *c.m.i.* '05 (SAC) Roseville, CA St. Rose of Lima.
Mathew, Pius T. '90 (AUS) Smithville, TX St. Paul Catholic Church.
Mathew, Sunny *o.carm.* '99 (NY) New York, NY St. Teresa; New York, NY St. John the Martyr.
Mathew, Sunny (MCE) New Rochelle, NY St. Mary's Malankara Catholic Church; Vice Chancellor; Judicial Vicar; Ex Officio Members; Ex Officio Members.
Mathew, T. Shane '05 (E)[C] Erie, PA Villa Maria Academy.
Mathews, James D. '62 (SY) Syracuse, NY St. Lucy.
Mathews, Michael C. *c.s.c.* '99 (FTW) South Bend, IN Holy Cross; Provincial Councilors:; [H] Notre Dame Congregation of Holy Cross, United States Province of Priests & Brothers; [H] Notre Dame, IN Congregation of Holy Cross, United States Province of Priests & Brothers.
Mathews, Ron '75 (AMA)[G] Prayer Town, TX Disciples of the Lord Jesus Christ.
Mathews, Ronald J. '75 (ALX) On Duty Outside the Diocese.
Mathewson, Dean '73 (COL) Columbus, OH St. Thomas the Apostle.
Mathewson, Robert B. *s.j.* '62 (SJ)[D] San Jose, CA Bellarmine College Preparatory.
Mathias, Arulanasu (CC) Corpus Christi, TX Holy Cross.
Mathias, Edwin J. '67 (TR) Browns Mills, NJ St. Ann.
Mathias, Gregory A. '91 (FR) North Dartmouth, MA St. Julie Billiart; [B] North Dartmouth, MA Bishop Stang High School; Diocesan Consultors; Family Ministry.
Mathie, D. Edward *s.j.* '68 (MIL)[X] Milwaukee, WI Marquette University/Campus Ministry; [C] Marquette University; [P] Milwaukee, WI Jesuit Community at Marquette University.
Mathieu, Rev. Msgr. Rene T. '77 (PRT) Diocesan Consultors; Saco, ME Good Shepherd Parish.
Mathieu, Robert E. '76 (GLP) Aztec, NM St. Joseph; Bloomfield, NM St. Rose of Lima; Bloomfield, NM St. Mary; Aztec, NM Holy Trinity; Cursillos.
Mathis, Christian '00 (KNX) Lenoir City, TN St. Thomas the Apostle; Presbyteral Council.
Mathis, George *g.h.m.* '55 (CIN)[N] Cincinnati Headquarters of Glenmary Home Missioners Retired.
Mathis, R. Paul '72 (SY) Cleveland, NY St. Mary of the Assumption.
Mathur, Keith A. '09 (ALN) Allentown, PA St. Thomas More.
Mathy, H. Francis *s.j.* '58 (FgM) Milwaukee, WI Society of Jesus.
Matiz, Jose Aurelio Ortiz '03 (MRY) Castroville, CA Our Lady of Refuge.
Matocha, Rev. Msgr. John L. '47 (SAT) Retired.
Matonti, Charles J. '60 (BRK) Brooklyn, NY St. Columba Retired.
Matos, Angel R. '97 (WOR) Worcester, MA St. Paul Cathedral; Diocesan Hispanic Apostolate; St. Paul.
Matro, Justin M. *o.s.b.* '89 (GBG)[A] Latrobe, PA St. Vincent Seminary; [H] Latrobe, PA Saint Vincent Archabbey.
Matsongani, Malumba '06 (WOR)[N] Worcester, MA Assumptionists of Assumption College.
Matt, Erwin H. '56 (MIL) Retired.
Matt, J. Wilson '45 (LAF) Retired.
Matt, Joseph H. '74 (KC) Independence, MO St. Joseph the Worker.
Matta, Pablo '90 (ELP) El Paso, TX San Judas Tadeo; Canutillo, TX St. Patrick; Presbyteral Council; [J] El Paso, TX Cursillos de Cristianidad.
Mattaliano, James R. *s.j.* '90 (BO)[W] Weston, MA Campion Renewal Center; [U] Weston, MA Campion Jesuit Community.
Mattappillil, Jacob '84 (NY) Highland Mills, NY St. Patrick.
Mattar, Ghassan *m.l.m.* '96 (OLL) San Antonio, TX St. George Maronite Catholic Church; [A] Houston, TX The Congregation of Maronite Lebanese Missionaries; Presbyteral Council.
Mattas, Louis '60 (SAL) Retired.
Mattathilanickal, Cyriac *m.s.* '99 (FR)[F] Attleboro, MA La Salette Shrine; [H] Attleboro, MA La Salette Retreat Center.
Mattathilanickal, George (NOR) New London, CT St. Joseph.
Mattern, Joseph A. '59 (GB) Redgranite, WI Sacred Heart of Jesus; Redgranite, WI St. Mark Retired.
Matteucig, Giuseppe *s.x.* '84 (BO)[U] Holliston, MA Xaverian Missionaries.
Mattey, Joseph J. '65 (SCR)[M] Dunmore, PA Villa St. Joseph Retired.
Matthew, Abraham '97 (BRK) Catholic Hindu/Buddhist Dialogue.
Matthew, Armand *o.m.i.* '49 (BWN) Brownsville, TX Immaculate Conception Cathedral.
Matthews, Andre '84 (ROM) College of Consultors; Vicar for Clergy; Unassigned.
Matthews, James V. '74 (OAK) Oakland, CA St. Benedict; Deanery #4; Presbyteral Council.
Matthews, Jay '74 (OAK) Priest Representatives – Alameda County.
Matthews, Jerome F. *c.s.c.* (FTW)[H] Notre Dame Congregation of Holy Cross, United States Province of Priests & Brothers.
Matthews, Michael C. *c.s.c.* '99 (FTW) South Bend, IN St. Stanislaus.
Matthys, Donald R. *s.j.* '68 (MIL)[P] Milwaukee, WI Jesuit Community at Marquette University.
Matti, Wisam '97 (EST) Southfield, MI Our Lady of Chaldeans Cathedral, Mother of God Chaldean Parish; Eparchial College of Consultors.
Mattice, George F. '64 (SY) Retired.
Mattimoe, Edward J. *s.j.* '65 (DET)[K] Clarkston, MI Colombiere Center.
Mattimore, John J. *s.j.* '88 (BUF) Buffalo, NY St. Michael; U.S. Department of Immigration & Naturalization Federal Detention Center; Council of Priests.
Mattina, Louis A. '95 (MO) Air Force Reserve Chaplains; Piscataway, NJ Our Lady of Fatima.
Mattingly, Basil *o.s.b.* '46 (SD)[J] Oceanside, CA Prince of Peace Abbey.
Mattingly, John F. *s.s.* '48 (BAL)[M] Baltimore, MD St. Charles Villa; [Q] Baltimore Society of St. Sulpice, Province of the United States Retired.
Mattingly, Lawrence *o.f.m.conv.* '64 (SAT)[B] San Antonio, TX San Damiano Friary, Prenovitiate House of Formation; [L] San Antonio, TX San Damiano Friary; San Antonio, TX Christ the King.
Mattingly, Robert B. '68 (VEN) Retired.
Mattingly, Thomas E. '97 (RIC) Harrisonburg, VA Blessed Sacrament.
Mattison, Thomas V. '73 (BUR) Judges; Manchester Center, VT Christ Our Savior Parish; Elected Members; Deans; Ecumenical Commission.
Mattler, Albert A. '56 (STL) Retired.
Mattox, Randall T. '01 (ATL) Ellijay, GA Good Samaritan Catholic Church; Advocates; Deans.
Mattscheck, John J. '53 (CIN) Retired.
Mattson, Steven M. '05 (LAN) Department of Education and Catechesis; Superintendent of Schools; Swartz Creek, MI St. Mary.
Mattulke, Arthur E. '97 (BUF) Vicars; Oakfield, NY St. Padre Pio.
Matty, Richard A. '83 (ELP) El Paso, TX St. Patrick Cathedral; Diocesan Review Board; St. Peter; Priests' Personnel Advisory Committee; Ex Officio Members.
Matula, Lawrence '62 (VIC) El Campo, TX St. Robert Bellarmine.
Matulewicz, Ronald G. '59 (ALB) Johnstown, NY Holy Trinity Parish Retired.
Matunog, Reynaldo B. '91 (LA) Defenders of the Bond; Los Angeles, CA Sacred Heart; Adjutant Judicial Vicar; Judges.
Maturi, Gregory *o.p.* '94 (Y) Youngstown, OH St. Dominic; Presbyteral Council.
Matus, Thomas *o.s.b.cam.* '70 (OAK)[L] Berkeley, CA Incarnation Monastery, Camaldolese Benedictines.
Matus, Thomas *o.s.b.conv.* '70 (MRY)[F] Big Sur New Camaldoli Hermitage.
Matus, Walter J. '70 (AUS) Burlington, TX St. Joseph; Burlington, TX SS. Cyril and Methodius Catholic Church – Marak, Texas.
Matusak, Rev. Msgr. Michael W. '75 (GBG) Uniontown, PA St. Therese, the Little Flower of Jesus; Deaneries; College of Consultors; Bishop's Priests Council; College of Deans.
Matusiak, Waldemar *s.ch.* '95 (GAL) Houston, TX Our Lady of Czestochowa.
Matusz, Michael A. '89 (CLV) Garfield Heights, OH SS. Peter and Paul.
Matuszak, Edward S. (E) Retired.
Matuszak, Edward S. '55 (LFT) Retired.
Matuszak, Jerzy '91 (CHI) Chicago, IL St. Wenceslaus.
Matuszak, Walter L. '58 (BUF)[N] Depew, NY Msgr. Conniff Residence Retired.
Matveenko, Michael J. '82 (CAM) Sicklerville, NJ The Church of St. Charles Borromeo, Washington Township, N.J.
Maty, Robert J. '57 (BGP) Retired.
Matya, Robert A. '95 (LIN) Lincoln, NE St. Thomas Aquinas; [I] Lincoln, NE University of Nebraska, Newman Club; Diocesan Consultors; Presbyteral Council; Bishop's Lay Committee for Vocations; Newman Center University of Nebraska; Serra Club; Vocations.
Matysik, Robert B. '84 (CAM) Atlantic City, NJ Church of St. Nicholas, Atlantic City, N.J.
Matz, David *c.pp.s.* '95 (OAK)[L] Berkeley, CA Society of the Precious Blood (Kansas City Province).

Matz, Joseph A. '64 (SCR) Retired.
Matz, Leo '61 (MRY) Retired.
Matz, Rev. Msgr. Michael J. '84 (PH) Flourtown, PA St. Genevieve.
Matzek, William J. '63 (LC) River Falls, WI Nativity of the Blessed Virgin Mary.
Matzinger, Robert J. *c.s.b.* '57 (GAL) Houston, TX St. Clare of Assisi.
Matzko, David G. *s.j.* '79 (RC) Rapid City, SD St. Isaac Jogues; [C] Howes, SD Kino Jesuit Community; Deaneries.
Mau, Nguyen Duc *c.ss.r.* '70 (LA)[P] Baldwin Park Vietnamese Redemptorist Mission.
Mauch, Ted J. '10 (GRY) Adjutant Defender of the Bond; [L] Valparaiso, IN Newman Apostolate–Valparaiso University; Schererville, IN St. Michael; Bishop's Council of Priests.
Mauck, George A. '77 (BEL) Carlyle, IL St. Mary; Carlyle, IL St. Teresa of Avila; Centralia, IL Centralia Correctional Center.
Mauel, James E. *s.j.* '57 (MIL)[P] Wauwatosa, WI Jesuit Community at St. Camillus.
Mauer, Elmar *o.m.i* '64 (BEL)[F] Belleville, IL Missionary Oblates of Mary Immaculate – St. Henry's Oblate Residence; Fayetteville, IL St. Pancratius.
Maughan, Richard N. '72 (NO) New Orleans, LA St. James Major.
Mauk, Dismas *s.v.d.* '03 (LAF) Franklin, LA St. Peter the Apostle; Jeanerette, LA Our Lady of the Rosary.
Mauman, Adam '10 (LFT) Carmel, IN Our Lady of Mount Carmel.
Maung, Chrysostom Ah '74 (WCH) Columbus, KS St. Joseph; Columbus, KS St. Rose; Columbus, KS St. Patrick; Columbus, KS St. Bridget's.
Maung, John S. '63 (IND) Retired.
Mauntel, Robert J. '49 (CIN) Retired.
Maurer, Carl R. '01 (SAT) San Antonio, TX El Carmen Catholic Church; [S] San Antonio, TX Ladies of Charity of El Carmen.
Maurer, Daniel J. '97 (PIT) Pittsburgh, PA SS. Simon and Jude.
Maurer, Jacob M. '09 (SEA) Tacoma, WA St. Joseph; Tacoma, WA Holy Rosary.
Maurer, Jeffrey E. '05 (NY) Washingtonville, NY St. Mary.
Maurer, Russell J. '60 (PIT) Retired.
Mauricci, Bruno '90 (LAV) Henderson, NV St. Peter the Apostle.
Maurice, Francis '98 (NY) New Rochelle, NY Holy Name of Jesus.
Mauriello, Rev. Canon Matthew '88 (BGP) Greenwich, CT St. Roch.
Mauritzen, Joseph H. '96 (FR) Woods Hole, MA St. Joseph's; Falmouth Hospital.
Maurizio, Joseph D. '87 (ALT) Central City, PA Our Lady Queen of Angels.
Maus, Christopher P. '93 (DET) Clarkston, MI St. Daniel.
Maus, Le Roy '66 (SCL) Retired.
Mauthe, Richard '58 (GB) Retired.
Mawhinney, John J. *s.j.* '65 (PH)[Y] Loyola Center and Manresa Hall.
Mawn, Francis X. '85 (BO) Lawrence, MA Corpus Christi.
Maxa, Edward J. '59 (CHI) Chicago, IL Immaculate Conception Retired.
Maxfield, Dale A. '10 (BEL) Waterloo, IL SS. Peter and Paul; Waterloo, IL Immaculate Conception.
Maxfield, Leo *m.s.* '55 (MAN)[K] Enfield, NH Shrine of Our Lady of La Salette; [N] Enfield, NH Shrine of Our Lady of La Salette Retired.
Maxim, Craig '91 (KCK) Shawnee, KS Sacred Heart.
Maximino, Diego *m.i.c.* '94 (SPR)[G] Stockbridge, MA Congregation of Marian Fathers of The Immaculate Conception of the Most Blessed Virgin Mary.
Maxwell, Daniel J. '09 (BAK) Hermiston, OR Our Lady of Angels.
Maxwell, Finbar *s.s.c.* '88 (OM)[J] St. Columbans Missionary Society of St. Columban.
Maxwell, Palmer '88 (SAT) On Sabbatical.
May, Anthony C. '75 (SD) San Diego, CA Saint Mary Magdalene Catholic Parish Retired.
May, Brian T. '10 (B) Moscow, ID St. Mary's.
May, Darrin M. '99 (WCH) Fort Scott, KS Mary Queen of Angels.
May, Douglas E. *m.m.* '86 (FgM) Maryknoll, NY MARYKNOLL.
May, Gregory *c.ss.r.* '88 (TUC)[G] Tucson, AZ Redemptorist Society of Arizona Redemptorist Renewal Center.
May, Herbert J. '75 (LAF) Judges; Assessors.
May, Rev. Archimandrite Herbert J. '75 (LKC) Welsh, LA Our Lady of Seven Dolors; Diocesan Consultors; Promoter of Justice.
May, Herbert (NTN) Judges.
May, James '98 (STA) Retired.
May, Michael K. *s.j.* '93 (STL)[C] Saint Louis University; [O] St. Louis, MO Jesuit Community Corporation at Saint Louis University – Jesuit Hall.
May, Raymond '93 (KCK) Emporia, KS St. Catherine; [L] Emporia, KS.
May, Ronald P. '86 (HRT) Commission for Priests' Retreats; Appointed; Southington, CT St. Dominic.
May, Thomas P. '83 (CHI) Riverside, IL St. Mary.
Mayall, Rev. Msgr. Daniel G. '77 (CHI) Chicago, IL Holy Name Cathedral.
Maybrier, Michael J. '86 (WCH) Mulvane, KS St. Michael the Archangel.
Maydya, Gregory (SJP) Alternates.
Mayefske, Thomas J. '62 (SFE) Retired.
Mayefske, Thomas '62 (SFE) Presbyteral Council of the Archdiocese of Santa Fe Retired.
Mayer, Cory A. '09 (VEN) Vocations/Seminarian Formation; Venice, FL Epiphany Cathedral.
Mayer, David *s.v.d.* '66 (FgM) Techny, IL.
Mayer, Douglas J. '86 (GRY) Valparaiso, IN St. Elizabeth Seton; Bishop's Council of Priests; Priests' Personnel Board.
Mayer, Gary A. '09 (DUB) Dubuque, IA Church of the Resurrection.
Mayer, James W. *o.de.m.* '93 (PH) Philadelphia, PA Our Lady of Lourdes.
Mayer, John L. '64 (STL) St. Louis, MO St. John the Baptist Retired.
Mayer, Jules Anthony '64 (LA) Retired.
Mayer, Michael A. '98 (ROC) Rochester, NY St. Pius Tenth.
Mayer, Rev. Msgr. Richard G. '61 (E) Erie, PA Blessed Sacrament Retired.
Mayer, Robert *o.m.i.* '67 (FgM) Washington, DC AMERICAN OBLATE MISSIONS.
Mayer, Walter W. '59 (OAK) Livermore, CA St. Michael Retired.
Mayer, William C. *c.s.v.* '56 (CHI)[N] Arlington Heights, IL Viatorian Province Center–Clerics of St. Viator.
Mayers, Gregory *c.ss.r.* '70 (TUC)[G] Tucson, AZ Redemptorist Society of Arizona Redemptorist Renewal Center.
Mayfield, Olin '96 (LA) Santa Clarita, CA St. Clare.
Mayfield, Phillip *p.i.m.e.* '78 (LAN)[N] Ypsilanti, MI Holy Trinity Student Parish; Ypsilanti, MI Holy Trinity Student Parish.
Mayhew, John A. *c.j.* '65 (LA) Santa Maria, CA St. Louis de Montfort; [B] Santa Maria, CA St. Joseph Seminary (Josephite Fathers' Novitiate).
Maynard, Jack G. '78 (COL) Dresden, OH St. Ann's.
Maynard, Joseph V. *m.m.* '48 (NY)[DD] Retired.
Maynard, Lewis H. '69 (BRK) Brooklyn, NY St. Agatha's Retired.
Maynard, Richard C. '56 (PRO) Retired.
Mayne, Kenneth '94 (LAF) Abbeville, LA St. Theresa of the Child Jesus.
Maynigo–Arenas, Joseph Victor '70 (NY) Staten Island, NY St. Patrick.
Mayo, James '76 (P) Portland, OR Church of St. Michael the Archangel; Area Vicars; Judges; Liturgical Commission.
Mayo, John W. '09 (STL) Washington, MO St. Francis Borgia.
Mayo, Rev. Msgr. Joseph M. '73 (SLC) College of Consultors; Salt Lake City, UT Cathedral of the Madeleine LLC 202; Ecumenical Commission; Defenders of the Bond; Board of Directors; Priests' Personnel Board.
Mayo, Rev. Msgr. Reid C. '63 (BUR) Canon 1742 Panel of Pastors; Diocesan Consultors; Diocesan Administrative Board Retired.
Mayor, Paul '94 (LA) Hospital Chaplains.
Mayorga, J. Guadalupe '01 (AMA) Perryton, TX Immaculate Conception.
Mayorga, Lupe '02 (AMA) Presbyteral Council.
Mayorga, Victor '95 (AUS) San Marcos, TX St. John the Evangelist.
Mayorga–Fonseca, Joaquin '89 (SJN) Rio Piedras; San Juan, PR Sagrada Familia.
Mayotte, Allan J. '60 (MAR) Retired.
Mayovsky, David L. '97 (SEA) Poulsbo, WA St. Olaf.
Mayovsky, Frederick P. *s.j.* '75 (SEA)[C] Tacoma, WA Bellarmine Preparatory School; [C] Tacoma, WA Bellarmine Preparatory School.
Mayovsky, Gerald L. '59 (SEA) Seattle, WA Our Lady of Lourdes; Tukwila, WA St. Thomas.
Mayta, Robert A. '95 (LIN) Priests' Continuing Education Committee.
Mayworm, James A. '66 (DET) Retired.
Mayzik, James J. *s.j.* '85 (BGP)[B] Fairfield, CT Fairfield University; [O] Fairfield, CT The Fairfield Jesuit Community–Fairfield University.
Mazanec, James F. '81 (CLV) Parma, OH St. Columbkille.
Mazanowski, Zygmunt *t.o.r.* '11 (ARL) Herndon, VA St. Joseph.
Mazarati, Jean Baptiste *s.j.* '01 (WDC)[O] Washington, DC The Jesuit Community at Georgetown University.
Mazariegos, Edgar '80 (PMB) Palm Beach Gardens, FL Cathedral of St. Ignatius Loyola.
Mazich, Edward M. *o.s.b.* '01 (GBG)[H] Latrobe, PA Saint Vincent Archabbey.
Mazon, Diego *o.f.m.* '60 (SFE)[H] Albuquerque, NM The Province of Our Lady of Guadalupe.
Mazouch, Charles '73 (DOD) Claflin, KS Immaculate Conception Catholic Church of Claflin, Kansas; Ellinwood, KS St. Joseph Catholic Church of Ellinwood, Kansas; Claflin, KS Holy Family Catholic Church of Odin, Kansas; Deans; [F] Dodge City, KS The Diocese of Dodge City Priest Retirement Fund, Inc.; [C] Ellinwood, KS St. Joseph School Education Endowment Fund.
Mazuchowski, Rev. Msgr. Hyacinth '63 (BEL) Retired.
Mazuelos, P. Paulino '54 (MGZ) Mayaguez, PR Cathedral of Our Lady of Purification.
Mazur, Francis X. '76 (BUF) Ecumenism; Defenders of the Bond; Erie County Medical Center.
Mazur, Jacek P. '04 (BUF) Niagara Falls, NY St. Mary of the Cataract; Niagara Falls, NY Divine Mercy; Council of Priests.
Mazur, Jacek '01 (VEN) Port Charlotte, FL San Antonio.
Mazur, Kenneth *p.i.m.e.* '82 (DET)[K] Detroit, MI P.I.M.E. Missionaries; Detroit, MI St. Francis D'Assisi; Detroit, MI St. Hedwig; Detroit, MI Pontifical Institute for Foreign Missions, P.I.M.E., Inc.
Mazur, Rev. Msgr. Robert C. '76 (ALT) Liturgy; Altoona, PA Cathedral of the Blessed Sacrament; Parish Life Office; Diocesan Contact for Parish Pastoral Councils; Stewardship.
Mazur, Timothy P. '95 (DET) Shelby Twp., MI St. John Vianney Church.
Mazurek, James K. '73 (PIT) Natrona Heights, PA Our Lady of the Most Blessed Sacrament; Natrona Heights, PA St. Joseph.
Mazurkiewicz, Rev. Msgr. Harry '51 (AUS) Retired.
Mazurowski, Rafal '05 (STA) Jacksonville, FL Assumption.
Mazuryk, Ivan '94 (STF) Auburn, NY SS. Peter and Paul.
Mazza, Rev. Msgr. Louis J. '53 (NY) Sleepy Hollow, NY Immaculate Conception.
Mazza, Mark G. '80 (SFR) Pacifica, CA St. Peter.
Mazza, Victor J. '70 (PAT) Retired.
Mazzarella, Cadmus D. '85 (CAM) Williamstown, NJ Our Lady of Peace Parish, Monroe Township, N.J.
Mazzarella, Frederick *o.f.m.* '61 (NY)[DD] New York Franciscan Province of the Immaculate Conception.
Mazzei, John C. '92 (PRT) Skowhegan, ME Christ the King Parish.
Mazzola, Robert E. '63 (IND) Retired.
Mazzone, James S. '99 (WOR) Diocesan Scouts; Vocation Office.
Mazzone, Joseph M. (BO) Hull, MA St. Mary of the Assumption.
Mazzuchelli, Matthew C. *o.s.b.* '58 (PEO)[A] Peru, IL St. Bede Abbey.
Mbaegbu, Anthony '92 (BAK) Lakeview, OR St. Patrick.
Mbaegbu, Theo (PIT) Pittsburgh, PA St. Mary of Mercy.
Mbagwa, Paschal '00 (TLS) Sand Springs, OK St. Patrick's.
Mbagwu, Brendan O. '95 (LFT) Carmel, IN St. Elizabeth Ann Seton.
Mbalo, Firmin Mola *c.m.* '93 (CHI)[N] Chicago DePaul Vincentian Residence.
Mbanefo, Anthony *m.s.p.* '92 (SAV) Eastman, GA St. Mark; McRae, GA Holy Redeemer.
Mbanu, Celestine '78 (SB) Moreno Valley, CA Riverside County Regional Medical Center.
Mbazuigwe, Patrick '93 (LA) San Gabriel, CA St. Anthony.
Mbidoaka, Eusebius '94 (IND) Indianapolis, IN St. Rita Catholic Church, Indianapolis, Inc.
Mbinda, Rev. Msgr. John Mutiso '68 (HON) Mililani Town, HI St. John Apostle and Evangelist; Censor Liborum.
Mbiti, Jacob Mugo *o.c.d.* '08 (MIL)[P] Milwaukee Provincial Offices – Discalced Carmelites.
Mblarawa, Polycarp P. '99 (GLD) Gaylord, MI St. Mary Cathedral; Elmira, MI St. Thomas Aquinas; Grayling, MI St. Mary; Gaylord, MI Holy Redeemer.
Mbogo, Nicholas Mukama '05 (NOR) North Grosvenordale, CT St. Joseph.
Mbonu, Michael '95 (BEL) Fairfield, IL St. Edward; Mount Carmel, IL St. Sebastian.
McAfee, Franklyn M. '71 (ARL) McLean, VA St. John the Beloved.
McAlear, Richard *o.m.i.* '70 (BO)[X] Tewksbury, MA Immaculate Heart of Mary Residence.
McAleenan, Aidan '05 (OAK) Oakland, CA St. Columba.
McAleer, Robert T. '71 (DAV) Bettendorf, IA St. John Vianney; Judges.
McAlister, Richard A. *o.p.* '61 (PRO)[O] Providence St. Thomas Aquinas Priory at Providence College.
McAllister, Alex '86 (SR) On Leave.
McAllister, Donald '71 (PRT) Retired.
McAllister, Donald '71 (MAN)[J] Dover, NH St. Ann Rehabilitation and Nursing Center Retired.
McAloon, Francis X. *s.j.* '92 (OAK)[A] Berkeley, CA Jesuit School of Theology of Santa Clara University (Berkeley, California Campus).
McAloon, Francis X. *s.j.* '92 (SJ)[B] Santa Clara, CA Jesuit Community; [M] Santa Clara, CA Casa San Inigo, Jesuit Residence.
McAlpin, Andrew M. *o.p.* '09 (CHI) River Forest, IL St. Vincent Ferrer.

McAlpin, James C. '64 (SC) Retired.
McAlpine, Harry D. '87 (SC) Retired.
McAndrew, John P. '86 (ORG) Inactive Leave Retired.
McAndrew, Joseph P. '85 (NY) Retired.
McAndrew, Michael *c.ss.r.* '73 (LA)[P] In Res; Whittier, CA St. Mary of the Assumption.
McAndrew, Michael *c.ss.r.* '73 (FRS) Multicultural and Campesino Ministry (Spanish).
McAndrew, Thomas F. '61 (DUB) Retired.
McAndrews, Rev. Msgr. Donald A. '54 (SCR)[M] Dunmore, PA Villa St. Joseph; Presbyteral Council Retired.
McAndrews, James F. *s.j.* '62 (PH) Philadelphia, PA Old St. Joseph's Retired.
McAndrews, Richard J. '67 (PH) Quakertown, PA St. Isidore.
McAnerney, Brendan *o.p.* '88 (OAK)[L] Oakland, CA Order of Preachers (Province of the Most Holy Name of Jesus – Western Dominican Province); [A] Berkeley, CA Dominican School of Philosophy and Theology.
McAnerney, Brendan *o.p.* (NTN) Sacramento, CA St. George.
McAniff, Bernard F. *s.j.* '03 (CLV)[B] University Heights, OH John Carroll Jesuit Community.
McArdle, John F. '51 (MAR) Retired.
McArdle, Kevin *o.c.d.* '43 (TUC)[E] Tucson, AZ Discalced Carmelite Friars of St. Margaret Mary's.
McAree, Rev. Msgr. Francis J. '75 (NY) Harrison, NY St. Gregory the Great; Censors Librorum; Canon 1742 Panel of Pastors.
McArthur, Rev. Msgr. John B. '74 (MEM) Memphis, TN St. Louis; [I] Memphis, TN Serra Club of Memphis; College of Consultors; Clergy Personnel Board; Presbyteral Council.
McArtney, Robert J. '60 (BUF) Retired.
McAtee, John F. *o.s.a.* '66 (FgM) Villanova, PA Province of St. Thomas of Villanova (Eastern).
McAteer, James *i.c.* '64 (SP) Spring Hill, FL St. Theresa.
McAteer, Rev. Msgr. Kenneth P. '73 (PH) Bensalem, PA Saint Ephrem; Approved Advocates.
McAteer, Patrick J. *s.j.* '73 (CHI) Chicago, IL St. Ignatius; [C] Chicago, IL Jesuit Community at Loyola University Chicago.
McAughan, Andrew *o.c.s.o.* '92 (L)[L] Trappist, KY Abbey of Our Lady of Gethsemani, of the Order of Cistercians of the Strict Observance.
McAuley, Edward J. '06 (BGP) Bethel, CT St. Mary.
McAuley, James D. *m.m.* '80 (FgM) Maryknoll, NY MARYKNOLL.
McAuley, John J. *m.m.* '81 (FgM) Maryknoll, NY MARYKNOLL.
McAuliff, R. Richard *s.j.* '92 (FgM) New York, NY Society of Jesus.
McAuliff, Richard *s.j.* (CI)[B] Chuuk, FM Xavier High School.
McAuliffe, Dennis '73 (RIC) Charlottesville, VA Church of the Holy Comforter; Scottsville, VA St. George.
McAvoy, Rev. Msgr. C. John '63 (OG) Retired.
McBeth, Jeffrey R. '06 (TOL) Toledo, OH Good Shepherd; Toledo, OH St. Thomas Aquinas; Blessed Kateri Tekakwitha Deanery; Youth, Young Adult and Campus Ministry.
McBrady, Lawrence P. '71 (CHI) Glenview, IL Our Lady of Perpetual Help.
McBrearity, Gerald D. *s.s.* '73 (BAL)[Q] Baltimore, MD Society of St. Sulpice, Province of the United States; Baltimore, MD.
McBrearity, Gerald D. *s.s.* '73 (WDC)[A] Washington, DC Theological College of the Catholic University of America.
McBrearty, John J. *s.s.j.* '68 (BLX) Gulfport, MS St. Therese.
McBriar, David J. *o.f.m.* '64 (R) Raleigh, NC St. Francis of Assisi.
McBride, Alfred A. *o.praem.* '53 (GB)[J] De Pere, WI St. Joseph Priory.
McBride, Brendan '75 (SFR) San Francisco, CA St. Philip the Apostle; Irish Ministry.
McBride, Daniel '51 (CLV) Administrative Leave Retired.
McBride, Daniel '95 (PHX) Chandler, AZ St. Mary Roman Catholic Parish; Deans.
McBride, Eugene J. *o.s.f.s.* '89 (WIL)[J] Childs, MD Retirement and Assisted Care Facility Retired.
McBride, Henry J. '61 (CAM) Retired.
McBride, Rev. Msgr. James P. '56 (PH) Tresckow, PA Retired.
McBride, John F. '62 (PH) Glenside, PA St. Luke the Evangelist.
McBride, John P. *s.j.* (SPK)[J] Spokane, WA Regis Community.
McBride, Larry '87 (OWN) Henderson, KY Holy Name of Jesus; Pastoral Office for Worship; Diocesan Liturgical Committee; Priest Personnel Committee.
McBride, Rev. Msgr. Peter A. '60 (PAT)[Q] Chester, NJ Nazareth Village Retired.
McBride, Robert G. '72 (NEW) Union County Southeast Deanery 24; Metropolitan Judicial Vicar; Archdiocesan Judges; Linden, NJ St. John the Apostle; Metropolitan Tribunal.
McBrien, Kevin F. '86 (BRK) Rosedale, NY St. Clare.
McBrien, Kevin *o.carm.* (CHI) Chicago, IL St. Thomas Apostle.
McBrien, Richard P. '62 (FTW)[B] University of Notre Dame Du Lac.
McBrien, Richard P. '62 (HRT) On Duty Outside the Archdiocese.
McBurney, James D. *o.s.a.* '84 (PH) Philadelphia, PA St. Augustine.
McCabe, Charles J. '92 (MOB) Montgomery, AL St. Peter.
McCabe, Edward D. '68 (MO) West Bridgewater, MA St. Ann; Army Reserve Chaplains.
McCabe, James F. *c.s.p.* '57 (BRK)[R] Paulist Priests at Paulist Foundations Outside the U.S.
McCabe, James T. '71 (PH) Philadelphia, PA St. Cecilia.
McCabe, James *c.pp.s.* '58 (CIN)[N] Carthagena, OH St. Charles Retired.
McCabe, John H. '55 (RVC)[N] Amityville, NY St. Pius X Residence Retired.
McCabe, Joseph V. *m.m.* '77 (NY)[DD] Maryknoll Maryknoll Fathers and Brothers.
McCabe, Joseph *m.m.* '77 (RVC) Hicksville, NY St. Ignatius Loyola; Mission Office.
McCabe, Kenneth *ss.cc.* '65 (LA)[P] La Verne, CA Congregation of the Sacred Hearts of Jesus and Mary.
McCabe, Kevin P. '03 (PH) Malvern, PA St. Patrick; [D] Downingtown, PA Bishop Shanahan High School.
McCabe, Louis J. *s.j.* '71 (STL)[O] St. Louis, MO Sacred Heart Jesuit Community; [O] St. Louis, MO The Jesuits of the Missouri Province.
McCabe, Michael G. '89 (LIN) Nebraska City, NE St. Mary's; [C] Nebraska City, NE Lourdes Central Catholic Schools; [L] Nebraska City, NE Lourdes Central High School Endowment Fund; Members.
McCabe, Patrick A. '61 (CAM) Retired.
McCabe, Peter '70 (AUS) Retired.
McCabe, Ramon J. *m.m.* '56 (FgM) Maryknoll, NY MARYKNOLL.
McCabe, Rev. Msgr. Robert J. '64 (NY) Haverstraw, NY St. Mary of the Assumption.
McCabe, Robert J. '95 (DET) Southgate, MI St. Pius X.
McCabe, Thomas E. '92 (STP) Lonsdale, MN Immaculate Conception; [F] Webster, MN Holy Cross Catholic School.
McCabe, Rev. Msgr. Vincent '46 (LA) Retired.
McCafferty, David L. '64 (CLV) Wickliffe, OH Our Lady of Mount Carmel; Akron, OH St. Vincent Retired.
McCafferty, James B. *s.m.* '70 (WH) Paden City, WV Mater Dolorosa; Sistersville, WV Holy Rosary.
McCafferty, Michael F. '67 (CHR) Gaffney, SC Sacred Heart; Union, SC St. Augustine.
McCafferty, Richard B. *s.j.* '62 (BO)[U] Boston The Society of Jesus of New England–Provincial Offices.
McCafferty, Richard *s.j.* '62 (OAK) Livermore, CA St. Charles Borromeo Retired.
McCaffery, Sean '11 (KC) Kansas City, MO St. Peter's.
McCaffrey, Daniel '58 (OKL) Special Assignment; Catholic Physicians Guild.
McCaffrey, Edmund M. '59 (CHR) Retired.
McCaffrey, Rev. Msgr. John A. '76 (AUS) Bryan, TX St. Joseph; [M] Bryan, TX St. Joseph Memorial Endowment Fund; [M] St. Joseph's School Memorial Endowment Fund; Finance Council; Presbyteral Council; College of Consultors.
McCaffrey, Joseph C. '99 (PH)[D] Philadelphia, PA Little Flower Catholic High School for Girls; Upper Darby, PA St. Laurence.
McCaffrey, Joseph P. '77 (ROC) Wolcott, NY Catholic Community of the Blessed Trinity of Wolcott, NY.
McCaffrey, Joseph R. '87 (PIT) Sewickley, PA Saints John and Paul.
McCaffrey, Kevin '02 (Y) Andover, OH Our Lady of Victory; Andover, OH St. Patrick.
McCaffrey, Kilian '07 (PHX) Phoenix, AZ St. Vincent de Paul Roman Catholic Parish.
McCaffrey, Rev. Msgr. William J. '72 (PRO) Rumford, RI St. Margaret.
McCahill, Rev. Msgr. Patrick P. '68 (NY) New York, NY St. Elizabeth of Hungary; [O] New York, NY New York Catholic Deaf Center; Deaf, Catholic Center for; [M] Deaf Apostolate.
McCahill, Robert T. *m.m.* '64 (FgM) Maryknoll, NY MARYKNOLL.
McCahon, Rev. Msgr. Joseph F. '75 (SP) Retired.
McCain, William H. '86 (SFR) Novato, CA Our Lady of Loretto.
McCall, Edward (BGP) On Duty Outside the Diocese.
McCall, Stephen P. '79 (SD) San Diego, CA Saint Mary Magdalene Catholic Parish.
McCallister, Richard '91 (SEA) Puyallup, WA All Saints.
McCallum, David C. *s.j.* '00 (SY)[Q] Syracuse, NY Jesuits at LeMoyne, Inc.
McCallum, Dougald '97 (HEL) Choteau, MT St. Joseph; Fairfield, MT St. John the Evangelist.
McCallum, Gregory P. '97 (GLD) Alpena, MI St. Anne; Alpena, MI St. Bernard; Alpena, MI St. John the Baptist; Alpena, MI St. Mary; Herron, MI St. Rose of Lima.
McCallum, Paul F. '62 (AUS) Presbyteral Council Retired.
McCambridge, Jared *f.s.s.p.* '08 (LIN)[L] Lincoln, NE St. Francis of Assisi Church; Presbyteral Council; 1962 Mass Apostolate.
McCandless, Michael P. '08 (CLV) Vocations Office.
McCandless, William T. *o.s.f.s.* '94 (WIL)[J] Wilmington Wilmington–Philadelphia Province of the Oblates of St. Francis de Sales.
McCandless, William T. *o.s.f.s.* '94 (MO) Navy Reserve Chaplains.
McCann, Arthur L. '62 (DM) Retired.
McCann, Charles '69 (WDC) Retired.
McCann, James M. *s.j.* '79 (CHI)[N] Chicago Chicago Province of the Society of Jesus–Provincial Office.
McCann, Rev. Msgr. John B. '85 (ALN) Douglassville, PA Immaculate Conception.
McCann, John H. *s.m.m.* '55 (HRT) Bantam, CT Our Lady of Grace.
McCann, Rev. Msgr. John J. '65 (RVC) Manhasset, NY St. Mary's; North Hempstead Deanery.
McCann, Luke W. '79 (NY) Kingston, NY St. Colman Retired.
McCann, Robert J. '81 (OAK) Diocesan Review Board.
McCann, Robert J. '81 (OAK) Oakland, CA St. Theresa of the Infant Jesus (The Little Flower); Judges; Censor; [A] Berkeley, CA Franciscan School of Theology; Adjutant Judicial Vicars.
McCann, Thomas M. '98 (NO) Destrehan, LA St. Charles Borromeo.
McCann, Thomas W. '68 (CLV) Cuyahoga Falls, OH Immaculate Heart of Mary; Associate Judges Retired.
McCann, Thomas *c.p.* '64 (BAL) Baltimore, MD St. Joseph Passionist Monastery Parish; [Q] Baltimore, MD St. Joseph's Passionist Community.
McCann, William '94 (LSC) Las Cruces, NM Cathedral of the Immaculate Heart of Mary.
McCann, William '94 (LSC) Presbyteral Council; Clergy Personnel Board; Priests Retirement Fund Committee; Finance Council; Diocesan Consultors.
McCarren, Rev. Msgr. Gerard H. '91 (NEW)[A] South Orange, NJ Immaculate Conception Seminary School of Theology; [A] South Orange, NJ Immaculate Conception Seminary School of Theology; [B] Seton Hall University; Archdiocesan Liturgical Commission; Censores Librorum.
McCarren, Paul J. *s.j.* '74 (WDC)[C] Washington, DC Georgetown University.
McCarren, Rev. Msgr. Stephen A. '55 (GBG) Retired.
McCarron, Gerard J. '70 (TR)[N] Trenton, NJ Villa Vianney Retired.
McCarron, Rev. Msgr. Michael D. '77 (RIC) Williamsburg, VA St. Bede.
McCarthy, Anthony T. '71 (MIL) North Lake, WI Blessed Teresa of Calcutta.
McCarthy, Brian P. '75 (NY) Bronx, NY St. Margaret of Cortona; Inter–Parish Financing, Commission for.
McCarthy, C. Ryan '01 (IND) Brookville, IN St. Michael the Archangel Catholic Church, Brookville, Inc.; Brookville, IN Holy Guardian Angels Catholic Church, Cedar Grove, Inc.
McCarthy, Carl '95 (OWN) Owensboro, KY SS. Joseph and Paul; Diocesan Liturgical Committee.
McCarthy, Charles A. *c.s.sp.* '51 (PEO) Streator, IL Annunciation of Blessed Virgin Mary; Tonica, IL SS. Peter and Paul's.
McCarthy, Charles *o.f.m.conv.* (STP) Richfield, MN The Church of the Assumption/La Iglesia de La Asuncion; [J] Bloomington, MN St. Bonaventure Friary.
McCarthy, Daniel P. '67 (CHI) Chicago, IL St. Tarcissus.
McCarthy, Daniel *o.s.b.* '91 (KCK)[I] Atchison, KS St. Benedict's Abbey.
McCarthy, David J. '60 (CLV) Doylestown, OH SS. Peter and Paul; Cuyahoga Falls, OH St. Joseph Retired.
McCarthy, Donal *ss.cc.* '65 (LA)[P] La Verne, CA Congregation of the Sacred Hearts of Jesus and Mary.
McCarthy, Donald G. '54 (CIN) Imprimatur Censors; Cincinnati, OH St. Ignatius of Loyola Retired.
McCarthy, Donald '59 (SAL) Retired.
McCarthy, Edward '71 (ORL) Sanford, FL All Souls Retired.
McCarthy, Emmanuel Charles '81 (NTN) Priests Serving Outside the Eparchy.
McCarthy, Eugene '60 (VEN) Retired.
McCarthy, George B. '56 (PRO) Newport, RI St. Mary.
McCarthy, Gerald A. '57 (FAR) Apostolate for Native Americans Retired.
McCarthy, J. Joseph '66 (FgM) Boston, MA St. James the Apostle, Inc.
McCarthy, James H. '55 (CHI) Special Religious Education (SPRED) Retired.
McCarthy, James J. '63 (BO) Braintree, MA St. Thomas More.
McCarthy, Rev. Msgr. Jeremiah H. '72 (ARL) Alexandria, VA St. Rita.

McCarthy, Jeremiah J. '66 (BO) Society of St. James the Apostle.
McCarthy, Jeremiah J. '72 (TUC) On Duty Outside the Diocese.
McCarthy, Jeremiah J. '78 (SAV) Savannah, GA Most Blessed Sacrament; Officialis; Tribunal Judges; College of Consultors.
McCarthy, Jeremiah *m.s.c.* '50 (SAT)[L] San Antonio, TX Missionaries of the Sacred Heart.
McCarthy, John D. '08 (RVC) Serving Outside the Diocese.
McCarthy, Rev. Msgr. John F. '55 (HEL) On Duty Outside the Diocese.
McCarthy, Rev. Msgr. John F. '55 (LC)[M] Eastman, WI Marian Academy of the Oblates of Holy Tradition.
McCarthy, Rev. Msgr. John F. '55 (STL) St. Louis, MO St. Mary of Victories; [U] Saint Louis, MO Oblates of Wisdom Study Center.
McCarthy, Rev. Msgr. John J. '84 (HRT) Hartford, CT Cathedral of St. Joseph; Chancellor; Promoter of Justice; College of Consultors; Special and other Archdiocesan Assignment; Ex Officio Members.
McCarthy, John J. *m.s.* '69 (HRT)[L] Hartford, CT Missionaries of LaSalette.
McCarthy, John L. *s.j.* '62 (STL)[O] St. Louis, MO Jesuit Community Corporation at Saint Louis University – Jesuit Hall.
McCarthy, Rev. Msgr. John M. '54 (NY) Staten Island, NY St. Patrick.
McCarthy, John M. (BO) Dorchester, MA St. Brendan.
McCarthy, John *c.ss.r.* '62 (FgM) Denver, CO Denver Province.
McCarthy, John '05 (NY) Staten Island, NY St. Ann.
McCarthy, Joseph F. '48 (SFD) Burlington, VT Retired.
McCarthy, Joseph S. '96 (BO) Pembroke, MA St. Thecla Retired.
McCarthy, Joseph '48 (BUR) Retired.
McCarthy, Joseph *o.carm.* '60 (VEN)[I] Venice, FL Our Lady of Perpetual Help Retreat and Spirituality Center.
McCarthy, Kevin P. '89 (GRY)[L] Valparaiso, IN Newman Apostolate–Valparaiso University; Campus Ministry.
McCarthy, Rev. Msgr. Leo F. '59 (BUF) Tonawanda, NY Blessed Sacrament Retired.
McCarthy, Matthew *f.s.sp.* '11 (ATL) Mableton, GA St. Francis de Sales.
McCarthy, Michael C. *s.j.* '96 (SJ)[B] Santa Clara, CA Jesuit Community.
McCarthy, Patrick J. '08 (NY) Staten Island, NY Our Lady, Queen of Peace.
McCarthy, Patrick R. *m.s.* '78 (HRT)[L] Hartford, CT Missionaries of LaSalette.
McCarthy, Paul J. *s.j.* '57 (SLC) Sandy, UT Saint Thomas More Catholic Church LLC 248.
McCarthy, Paul '84 (FTW) South Bend Serra Club; New Carlisle, IN St. Stanislaus Kostka.
McCarthy, Raymond P. *c.ss.r.* '47 (NY)[DD] New York, NY Redemptorist Priests and Brothers, C.Ss.R.
McCarthy, Rev. Msgr. Robert J. '46 (OG) Retired.
McCarthy, Rev. Msgr. Robert '58 (STL) Retired.
McCarthy, Scott '74 (MRY) Special Assignment.
McCarthy, Sean M. '91 (BO) Health Leave.
McCarthy, Stephen '10 (PH) Philadelphia, PA St. William.
McCarthy, Terrence A. '74 (CHI) Retired.
McCarthy, Rev. Msgr. Thomas A. '59 (NEW) Retired.
McCarthy, Thomas H. '07 (CIN) Trenton, OH Holy Name.
McCarthy, Thomas J. '61 (Y) Judges; Warren, OH Blessed Sacrament.
McCarthy, Thomas J. '80 (BUF) Retired.
McCarthy, Thomas R. *o.s.a.* '94 (CHI)[D] Chicago, IL St. Rita of Cascia High School; [N] Chicago, IL St. Rita Monastery; Olympia Fields, IL; [N] Chicago, IL The Augustinians–Provincialate; Chicago, IL St. Cajetan.
McCarthy, Thomas *s.j.* '62 (P) Sherwood, OR St. Francis.
McCarthy, Thomas '53 (RVC) Retired.
McCarthy, Thomas '61 (Y) Presbyteral Council.
McCarthy, Vincent *s.s.c.* '64 (OM)[J] St. Columbans Missionary Society of St. Columban Retired.
McCarthy, Warren J. '52 (CHI) Retired.
McCarthy, William A. '03 (SC) Remsen, IA St. Catherine's; Remsen, IA St. Mary's.
McCarthy, William E. *m.m.* '58 (NY)[DD] Retired.
McCarthy, William E. *m.m.* '58 (RVC) Retired.
McCarthy, William *m.s.a.* '59 (NOR)[G] Cromwell, CT Society of the Missionaries of the Holy Apostles.
McCarthy, Rev. Msgr. William '63 (PAT) Retired.
McCartney, James J. *o.s.a.* '70 (PH)[C] Villanova University; [Y] Rosemont, PA Saxony Hall.
McCartney, James '84 (LUB) Littlefield, TX Sacred Heart; Priests' Pension Board.
McCartney, John J. '99 (RVC) Floral Park, NY Our Lady of Victory.
McCarty, Bruce '89 (OWN) Owensboro, KY Precious Blood; Curdsville, KY St. Elizabeth; Consultors; Priest Personnel Committee; Priests' Council.
McCarty, Joshua A. '09 (OWN) Bowling Green, KY St. Joseph.
McCarty, Lawrence L. '63 (SC) Retired.
McCarty, Paul T. *s.j.* '67 (BO)[U] Weston, MA Campion Health Center, Inc.
McCarty, Robert E. *s.j.* '67 (NEW)[B] Jersey City, NJ Jesuit Center; [L] Jersey City, NJ Jesuits of Saint Peter's College, Inc.
McCartyy, Terrance A. '74 (CHI) Highland Park, IL Immaculate Conception.
McCaslin, John O. '55 (OM) Retired.
McCaslin, John P. '02 (IND) Indianapolis Fire Department; Indianapolis, IN St. Anthony Catholic Church, Indianapolis, Inc.; Indianapolis, IN Holy Trinity Church, Indianapolis, Inc.; Priests' Personnel Board.
McCaslin, John T. *s.j.* '66 (ALN)[A] Wernersville, PA Jesuit Center–Jesuit Community.
McCaslin, R. Patrick '61 (OM) Omaha, NE St. John Vianney.
McCaslin, Richard *s.j.* '65 (MIL)[P] Wauwatosa, WI Jesuit Community at St. Camillus.
McCauley, David '63 (STP) Retired.
McCauley, James A. '56 (WIN) Retired.
McCauley, James P. *s.j.* '56 (SJ)[M] Los Gatos, CA Sacred Heart Jesuit Center.
McCauley, James R. *c.s.p.* '74 (P)[Q] Portland, OR Paulist Fathers Catholic Center for Evangelization; Portland, OR St. Philip Neri.
McCaulley, Barbara (DUB)[H] Mason City, IA Mercy Medical Center–North Iowa.
McCaulley, Cornelius W. '66 (PIT) Pittsburgh, PA Epiphany Retired.
McCawley, Scott M. '93 (JOL) Elmhurst, IL Immaculate Conception.
McChesney, Robert W. *s.j.* '81 (OAK)[L] Berkeley, CA Jesuit Fathers and Brothers; [A] Berkeley, CA Jesuit School of Theology of Santa Clara University (Berkeley, California Campus).
McClain, J. Thomas *s.j.* '77 (DET)[K] Detroit Detroit Province of the Society of Jesus–Provincial Office.
McClain, Matthew R. '02 (PIT) Glenshaw, PA St. Bonaventure; Priest Council.
McClanahan, Robert P. '84 (PT) Military Chaplains; Navy Chaplains.
McClane, Michael T. '06 (TR) Princeton, NJ St. Paul; Defenders of the Bond; Vice Chancellors.
McClean, Rev. Msgr. John R. '57 (DUB) Pontifical Missions/Mission Awareness; Directors Retired.
McClellan, Keith J. '79 (GRY) Michigan City, IN Notre Dame.
McClellan, Keith '79 (GRY) Bishop's Council of Priests.
McClellan, Robert J. '81 (RCK) South Beloit, IL St. Peter.
McClintock, James '86 (BEA) Beaumont, TX St. Martin de Porres Mission; Beaumont, TX St. Mary.
McClory, Bernard J. '53 (COL) Retired.
McClory, Rev. Msgr. Robert J. '99 (DET)[Q] Detroit, MI Catholic Community Services of the Archdiocese of Detroit, Inc.; Moderator of the Curia; Archdiocesan Theological Commission; Detroit, MI Presentation/Our Lady of Victory.
McClory, Rev. Msgr. Robert '99 (DET) Presbyteral Council.
McCloskey, C. John '81 (CHI) Chicago; [V] Chicago, IL Midtown Residence.
McCloskey, Francis G. '63 (ALB) Retired.
McCloskey, Gary N. *o.s.a.* '77 (PH)[Y] Villanova, PA St. Thomas Monastery; Counselors.
McCloskey, Rev. Msgr. James A. '46 (SY) Fayetteville, NY Immaculate Conception; Promoters of Justice Retired.
McCloskey, James P. *c.s.sp.* (PIT)[B] Pittsburgh, PA Duquesne University of the Holy Spirit.
McCloskey, John *o.f.m.cap.* '98 (HBG) Dallastown, PA St. Joseph; York, PA St. Joseph.
McCloskey, Joseph M. *s.j.* '63 (WDC)[O] Washington, DC The Jesuit Community of St. Aloysius Gonzaga.
McCloskey, Joseph W. '61 (PH) Retired.
McCloskey, Lester '64 (SEA) Retired.
McCloskey, Patrick *o.f.m.* '75 (CIN)[N] Cincinnati, OH St. Clare Friary; Councillors.
McCloskey, Terrence *c.ss.r.* '66 (NO) New Orleans, LA St. Alphonsus; New Orleans, LA St. Mary's Assumption.
McClosky, Rev. Msgr. Adam S. '67 (GAL) Houston, TX All Saints.
McClure, Jack H. *c.pp.s.* '76 (DUB) Osage, IA Sacred Heart; Osage, IA Church of the Visitation.
McClure, Jason Wayne '03 (OWN) Murray, KY St. Leo; [I] Murray, KY Murray State University Newman House; Priest Personnel Committee; Deans; Priests' Council.
McCluskey, James F. '68 (OM) Laurel, NE St. Mary; [M] Laurel, NE St. Anne Church of Dixon Cemetery Endowment Trust Fund.
McCluskey, Thomas *c.ss.r.* '08 (PH) Philadelphia, PA Visitation B.V.M.
McCluskey, Tom *c.ss.r.* '08 (NY) New York, NY Most Holy Redeemer.
McColligan, Raymond '43 (PIT) Retired.
McCollum, Paul '98 (RNO) Gardnerville, NV St. Gall; Diocesan Board of Consultors; Presbyteral Council.
McComiskey, Joseph C. '70 (RVC) Retired.
McConnell, James J. *s.m.a.* '72 (NEW)[L] Tenafly, NJ Society of African Missions, Provincialate, S.M.A. Fathers.
McConnell, James J. '54 (TR)[N] Trenton, NJ Villa Vianney Retired.
McConnell, John M. *s.j.* '55 (NY)[DD] New York, NY Murray–Weigel Hall.
McConnell, William J. '53 (BO) Senior Priests. Retired.
McConvey, Michael '79 (GLP) On Leave of Absence.
McConville, William E. *o.f.m.* '73 (R) Raleigh, NC St. Francis of Assisi.
McConway, Sean J. *o.p.* '87 (NY) Pleasantville, NY Holy Innocents.
McCoog, Thomas M. *s.j.* '79 (NY)[DD] Cardinal Spellman Hall, Jesuit Community.
McCool, Naos *c.s.sp.* (PIT)[B] Pittsburgh, PA Duquesne University of the Holy Spirit.
McCool, Patrick *o.s.b.* '63 (OKL)[I] Shawnee, OK St. Gregory's Abbey.
McCord, Kent G. '81 (MO) On Duty Outside the Diocese; DEPARTMENT OF VETERANS AFFAIRS HOSPITALS AND CHAPLAINS.
McCorkell, Patrick M. *s.j.* '74 (STP)[M] Lake Elmo, MN Jesuit Retreat House.
McCorkle, Rev. Msgr. Louis W. '53 (JC) Retired.
McCormac, Rev. Msgr. Michael P. '80 (PH) Fairless Hills, PA St. Frances Cabrini.
McCormack, John '61 (KC)[I] Kansas City, MO Jeanne Jugan Center Retired.
McCormack, Michael J. *o.p.* '87 (WDC)[B] Washington, DC Dominican House of Studies.
McCormack, Rev. Msgr. Robert '47 (NY) Retired.
McCormick, Brian '66 (TR)[U] Trenton, NJ Martin House; Martin House.
McCormick, Daniel J. '57 (ATL) Dunwoody, GA All Saints; Defenders of the Bond; Promoter of Justice; Decatur, GA Atlanta Veterans Administration Hospital.
McCormick, Frank '68 (HEL) Retired.
McCormick, Gregory *s.p.* '49 (SFE) Jemez Springs, NM Our Lady of the Assumption; [H] Jemez Springs, NM Our Lady of Lourdes.
McCormick, Howard W. '57 (SPR) Diocesan Consultors Retired.
McCormick, James D. '62 (SC)[F] Auburn, IA Opus Spiritus Sancti; Auburn, IA Opus Spiritus Sancti Retired.
McCormick, James '82 (E) Erie, PA St. James; [C] Erie, PA Cathedral Preparatory School.
McCormick, Jeffrey '96 (MIA) Pembroke Pines, FL St. Maximilian Kolbe.
McCormick, Jerry '73 (MRY) Catholic Charities Board Retired.
McCormick, John J. '56 (BO) Billerica, MA St. Theresa of Lisieux; Senior Priests. Retired.
McCormick, John M. '75 (ORL) Orlando, FL St. James Cathedral; Ethnic Ministries; Propagation of the Faith.
McCormick, John '99 (SR) Unassigned.
McCormick, Joseph *o.s.a.* (KAL) Edwardsburg, MI Our Lady of the Lake; Presbyteral Council Members; Presbyteral Council Members; Vicars Forane.
McCormick, Justin J. *c.s.p.* '61 (BRK)[R] On Special Assignment in the U.S.
McCormick, Kieran J. '64 (SFR) Retired.
McCormick, Louis M. *o.f.m.* '65 (BUF)[P] West Clarksville, NY Mount Irenaeus, Franciscan Mountain Retreat & Holy Peace Friary; [Q] St. Bonaventure, NY St. Bonaventure University.
McCormick, Mark '91 (RC) Fort Pierre, SD St. John; Diocesan Consultors.
McCormick, Rev. Msgr. Maurice M. '58 (SFR) San Francisco, CA St. Cecilia Retired.
McCormick, Michael S. '85 (SCR) Canton, PA St. Michael.
McCormick, Myron *o.f.m.* '52 (BO)[Z] Boston, MA St. Anthony Shrine.
McCormick, Patrick G. '96 (PH) Philadelphia, PA St. Timothy.
McCormick, Patrick J. '68 (ATL) Military Chaplains.
McCormick, Rev. Msgr. Patrick Joseph '75 (FRS) Merced, CA Our Lady of Mercy/St. Patrick's; Defenders of the Bond; Diocesan Consultors; Master of Ceremonies; Personnel Board; Planada, CA Sacred Heart.
McCormick, Rev. Msgr. Patrick '75 (FRS) Vicars Forane.
McCormick, Paul *o.cist.* '97 (DAL)[J] Irving, TX Cistercian Abbey of Our Lady of Dallas.
McCormick, Peter M. *c.s.c.* '07 (FTW)[B] University of Notre Dame Du Lac; [A] Notre Dame, IN; [H] Notre Dame Congregation of Holy Cross, United States Province of Priests & Brothers; [H] Notre Dame, IN Holy Cross Community, Corby Hall, University of Notre Dame.
McCormick, Robert F. (BGP)[S] Darien, CT Convent of St. Birgitta.
McCormick, Thomas '59 (DEN) Aurora, CO St. Therese; [N] Aurora, CO Maryknoll Fathers and Brothers Retired.

McCorry, Rev. Msgr. Edward J. '56 (NY) Retired.
McCorry, Patrick G. '01 (NOR) Retired.
McCotter, Daniel E. *c.s.p.* '81 (SFR) San Francisco, CA Holy Family Chinese Mission; San Francisco, CA Old St. Mary's Cathedral.
McCouch, Richard S. *s.j.* '93 (WDC)[E] North Bethesda, MD Georgetown Preparatory School; Towson, MD.
McCouch, Richard S. *s.j.* '93 (BAL)[Q] Towson, MD Maryland Province of the Society of Jesus.
McCouch, Richard S. *s.j.* '93 (PH)[Y] Philadelphia, PA Jesuit Community, Arrupe House.
McCourt, Gerald P. *s.j.* '72 (SAC)[H] Carmichael, CA Sacramento Jesuit Community; Sacramento, CA St. Ignatius of Loyola.
McCown, Robert M. *sj* '63 (NO)[R] New Orleans, LA Ignatius Residence Retired.
McCoy, Alfred E. '54 (SC) Retired.
McCoy, Charles F. *c.s.c.* '09 (FTW)[H] Notre Dame Congregation of Holy Cross, United States Province of Priests & Brothers.
McCoy, Charles *c.s.c.* '09 (P)[B] University of Portland; [L] Portland, OR Holy Cross Fathers & Brothers, C.S.C. – University of Portland.
McCoy, Daniel P. '03 (BO) Saugus, MA Blessed Sacrament; Saugus, MA St. Margaret.
McCoy, Floyd '83 (SJN) On Duty Outside the Archdiocese.
McCoy, James B. '63 (PH)[BB] Chalfont, PA Delaware Valley College of Science and Agriculture.
McCoy, Rev. Msgr. James P. '63 (PH) Chalfont, PA St. Jude.
McCoy, John J. '93 (STU) Amsterdam, OH St. Joseph; Richmond, OH St. John Fisher; [M] Richmond, OH Boy Scouts; College of Consultors.
McCoy, Rev. Msgr. Kevin C. '81 (SC)[G] Fort Dodge, IA Saint Edmond Catholic Schools Foundation; [G] Fort Dodge, IA Holy Trinity Parish Cemetery Improvement Society; Fort Dodge, IA Holy Trinity Parish of Webster County; [G] Fort Dodge, IA Holy Trinity Parish Foundation of Webster County; Presbyteral Council; Deans; Priests' Personnel Board.
McCoy, Perry *o.s.m.* '93 (ORG)[I] Anaheim, CA Servite Fathers and Brothers.
McCoy, Ryan M. '11 (BLX) Biloxi, MS Our Lady of Fatima.
McCracken, John E. '79 (GLD) Manistee, MI Guardian Angels; Manistee, MI St. Joseph; Manistee, MI St. Mary of Mt. Carmel Shrine; Members of the College of Consultors; Vicar for Clergy; Elected Members.
McCracken, Rev. Msgr. John T. '44 (OAK) Danville, CA St. Isidore Retired.
McCracken, Kevin *c.m.* '82 (LA)[A] Camarillo, CA St. John's Seminary; Appointed Membership.
McCrane, Gerard T. *m.m.* '59 (NY)[DD] Maryknoll Maryknoll Fathers and Brothers Retired.
McCrann, Peter J. *s.m.m.* '58 (RVC) Bay Shore, NY Southside Hospital; [N] Bay Shore, NY Montfort Missionaries.
McCrate, D. Stephen '89 (BEA) Diocesan College of Consultors; Port Arthur, TX St. Joseph.
McCray, Trinette '81 (MIL)[C] Milwaukee, WI Cardinal Stritch University.
McCreanor, James '78 (MIA) Homestead, FL Sacred Heart.
McCreary, Glenn E. '95 (SCR) Regional Episcopal Vicars; Muncy, PA Resurrection; Muncy, PA Muncy Prison; Ex Officio.
McCreary, Robert E. *o.f.m.cap.* '64 (PIT)[M] Beaver, PA St. Fidelis Friary; Pittsburgh International Airport; Beaver County, PA Heritage Valley Beaver.
McCreary, Robert L. *o.f.m.cap.* '59 (WDC)[B] Washington, DC St. Francis Friary–Capuchin College.
McCreedy, Harry E. '72 (PH) Norristown, PA St. Paul.
McCreedy, Justin D. *o.s.b.* '70 (SEA)[M] Lacey, WA St. Martin's Abbey; Puyallup, WA All Saints; [H] Tacoma, WA Catholic Pastoral Care–Hospital Tacoma Ministry.
McCreesh, Thomas P. *o.p.* '72 (PRO)[O] Providence St. Thomas Aquinas Priory at Providence College.
McCreight, James H. '68 (CLV) Cleveland, OH St. Michael the Archangel; [V] Cleveland, OH St. Michael.
McCrone, John M. '82 (NEW) Mountainside, NJ Church of Our Lady of Lourdes; Union Northwest Deanery 22; Archdiocesan Stewardship Advisory Committee.
McCue, Michael J. *o.s.f.s.* '90 (CAM) Rutgers University; [Q] Camden, NJ Rutgers University; Camden, NJ The Parish of the Cathedral of the Immaculate Conception, Camden, N.J.
McCue, Richard T. '58 (CHL) Retired.
McCue, Scott E. '01 (R) Chapel Hill, NC St. Thomas More.
McCulken, Rev. Msgr. Michael T. '76 (PH)[CC] Downingtown, PA Catholic Clinical Consultants; Bala Cynwyd, PA St. Matthias; Deans; Deans; Pastors Review Board; College of Consultors.
McCulloch, Lawrence F. *m.m.* '70 (NY)[DD] Maryknoll Maryknoll Fathers and Brothers Retired.
McCullough, Hugh J. '79 (FR) Provincetown, MA St. Peter the Apostle; Wellfleet, MA Our Lady of Lourdes.
McCullough, Rev. Msgr. J. Edward '67 (GBG) Dunbar, PA St. Aloysius; Catholic Relief Services Representative; Missions; Apostleship of Prayer; Holy Childhood Association; Priests' Eucharistic League; Board of Trustees.
McCullough, Michael P. '73 (LA) Los Angeles, CA Transfiguration; L.A. Police Dept.
McCumber, Rev. Msgr. William W. '83 (STL) St. Louis, MO St. Luke the Evangelist; Archdiocesan Office of Worship.
McCurdy, William J. *s.j.* '61 (BUF)[N] Buffalo, NY Canisius Jesuit Community Inc.; [D] Buffalo, NY Canisius High School.
McCurry, James *o.f.m.conv.* '77 (FgM) Ellicott City, MD Province of Saint Anthony of Padua; Ellicott City, MD; [Q] Ellicott City Order of Friars Minor Conventual.
McDade, Pedro *s.j.* '11 (BO)[U] Brighton, MA Edmund Campion House.
McDade, Robert *m.ss.cc.* '76 (CAM)[L] Linwood, NJ Villa Pieta. Missionaries of the Sacred Hearts of Jesus & Mary; Linwood, NJ.
McDade, Rev. Msgr. Thomas J. '74 (PAT)[B] Morristown, NJ College of Saint Elizabeth; Mountainside, NJ Church of Our Lady of Lourdes.
McDaid, Henry '63 (BIR) Birmingham (Hoover), AL Prince of Peace Retired.
McDaid, Rev. Msgr. J. Anthony '75 (DEN) On Duty Outside the Archdiocese.
McDaid, Patrick *s.m.* '08 (SAT)[F] San Antonio, TX Central Catholic High School; [L] San Antonio, TX Woodlawn Marianist Community.
McDaniel, George W. '70 (DAV) Davenport, IA Holy Family; [A] St. Ambrose University; Chancellor; Judges; Diocesan Corporate Board; Finance Council; Priests' Aid Society; Propagation of the Faith; Notaries; Archivist.
McDaniel, Isaac '82 (L)[A] Bellarmine University.
McDaniel, John W. *s.j.* '71 (PH)[Y] Loyola Center and Manresa Hall.
McDaniel, Ray '07 (FWT) Lindsay, TX St. Peter; Diocesan Pastoral Finance Committee.
McDarby, J. Patrick *o.s.b.* '53 (SCL)[I] Collegeville, MN St. John's Abbey, of the Order of St. Benedict.
McDermott, Brian O. *s.j.* '68 (BAL)[B] Jesuit Community of Loyola University, Inc.; [Q] Baltimore, MD Jesuit Community of Loyola University, Inc.
McDermott, Charles B. '73 (NEW) Union, NJ St. Michael's.
McDermott, Charles B. '63 (PRO) Retired.
McDermott, Christopher H. *c.s.sp.* '81 (PH)[Y] Bensalem, PA Congregation of the Holy Spirit; [F] Bensalem, PA Holy Ghost Preparatory School.
McDermott, H. Thomas *c.s.c.* '79 (FgM) New Rochelle, NY Eastern Brothers Province.
McDermott, J. Patrick '67 (SEA) Lacey, WA Sacred Heart of Jesus.
McDermott, James *s.j.* '03 (LA)[C] Los Angeles, CA Jesuit Community.
McDermott, John J. '86 (DUB) On Leave of Absence (Not Authorized for Priestly Ministry).
McDermott, Rev. Msgr. John J. '89 (BUR) Ex Officio Members; Members Ex Officio; Vicars General; Chancery Office; Office of Diocesan Pastoral Planning; Promoter of Justice; Diocesan Administrative Board; Diocesan Archives; The Review Board; Victim's Advocacy Board; [G] Burlington, VT University of Vermont–The Catholic Center at UVM; Defenders of the Bond; Diocesan Consultors; Institute for Catholic Enrichment and Lay Apostolate Formation.
McDermott, Joseph M. '95 (PH) Primos, PA St. Eugene.
McDermott, Joseph P. '62 (BO) Stoughton, MA Immaculate Conception.
McDermott, Joseph *s.v.d.* '52 (DUB)[B] Epworth, IA Divine Word College.
McDermott, Martin F. *s.j.* '64 (FgM) Watertown, MA Society of Jesus.
McDermott, Michael A. '66 (PIT) Retired.
McDermott, Michael F. '79 (GI) Grand Island, NE Resurrection; Vicar–Judicial; Judges; Diocesan Consultors; Priests' Advisory Board (Presbyteral Council); Community Mental Health.
McDermott, Michael J. '75 (WIL) Unassigned or Leave of Absence.
McDermott, Michael J. '65 (SEA) Tacoma, WA St. Charles Borromeo; College of Consultors; Presbyteral Council.
McDermott, Neal W. *o.p.* '61 (NO) Archdiocesan Consultors; Rosary Congress Committee; New Orleans, LA St. Anthony of Padua; Special Projects for the Archbishop and Vicar General.
McDermott, Patrick M. '64 (BLX) Retired.
McDermott, Robert B. '90 (PH)[A] Wynnewood, PA Theological Seminary of St. Charles Borromeo, Overbrook.
McDermott, Robert J. '81 (STA) Gainesville, FL St. Patrick Church.
McDermott, Rev. Msgr. Robert T. '69 (CAM) Camden, NJ St. Joseph Catholic Church, East Camden, N.J. (Pro–Cathedral); Vicars General; Members; Ex Officio Members; Ex Officio Members; Ex Officio Members.
McDermott, Robert T. '81 (MIL) On Duty Outside the Archdiocese.
McDermott, Robert T. '81 (STL) St. Louis, MO St. Roch.
McDermott, Robert '83 (STA) Special Assignment.
McDermott, Stephen C. '03 (MO) Military Chaplains; Army Reserve Chaplains.
McDermott, Thomas J. '97 (DUB) Seminary Admissions and Advisory Board; Waterloo, IA Blessed Sacrament; Personnel Advisory Board; Directors.
McDermott, Thomas *o.p.* '83 (CHI)[N] Chicago Dominicans (Provincial Office).
McDermott, Thomas *o.p.* '83 (STL)[O] Saint Louis, MO St. Dominic Priory.
McDermott, William '98 (FAR) Langdon, ND St. Alphonsus Church of Langdon; Langdon, ND St. Michael's; Langdon, ND St. Edward.
McDevitt, Edward P. *c.o.* '71 (CHR)[E] Rock Hill, SC Oratory of St. Philip Neri, Congregation of the Oratory of Pontifical Rite.
McDevitt, James A. '90 (BGP) Greenwich, CT St. Agnes; On Duty Outside the Diocese.
McDevitt, James '90 (NY) Otisville, NY Federal Correctional Institution.
McDevitt, Michael V. '71 (SPC) Springfield, MO Cathedral of St. Agnes; Aurora, MO Holy Trinity; Region IV; Priests' Eucharistic League Confraternity of The Most Blessed Sacrament; Region IV; Advocates for the Respondent.
McDevitt, Michael '71 (SPC) Aurora, MO Sacred Heart.
McDevitt, Robert *s.j.* '60 (SJ)[M] Los Gatos, CA Sacred Heart Jesuit Center.
McDonagh, Donat Michael '74 (SP) On Duty Outside the Diocese.
McDonagh, John P. '82 (SPR) On Duty Outside the Diocese.
McDonagh, John P. '81 (NY) Yonkers, NY St. Ann.
McDonagh, John '82 (NY)[GG] New York, NY Fordham Lincoln Center.
McDonald, A. John '56 (BR) Retired.
McDonald, Alan Paul '11 (DAL) Dallas, TX St. Patrick.
McDonald, Allan J. '80 (SAV) Macon, GA St. Joseph.
McDonald, Bernard J. '59 (NY) Retired.
McDonald, C. Alexander '91 (CHR) Columbia, SC St. John Neumann; Deans; Personnel Committee; Administrator for Ecumenical & Interreligious Affairs; Presbyteral Council; College of Consultors.
McDonald, Charles J. '65 (LEX) Retired.
McDonald, Charles '71 (BRK) Brooklyn, NY Our Lady of Perpetual Help Basilica.
McDonald, Daniel C. *s.j.* '81 (MIL)[P] Milwaukee Jesuit Provincial Office, Wisconsin Province.
McDonald, Elmer J. '49 (ROC) Retired.
McDonald, Finian *o.s.b.* '62 (SCL)[I] Collegeville, MN St. John's Abbey, of the Order of St. Benedict.
McDonald, Francis B. '60 (JOL) Roselle, IL St. Walter Retired.
McDonald, G. Malcolm '85 (PIT) Allegheny County, PA Allegheny County Jail.
McDonald, James E. *c.s.c.* '84 (FTW)[B] University of Notre Dame Du Lac; [B] University of Notre Dame Du Lac; Provincial Councilors:; [H] Notre Dame Congregation of Holy Cross, United States Province of Priests & Brothers; [H] Notre Dame, IN Holy Cross Community, Corby Hall, University of Notre Dame; [H] Notre Dame, IN Congregation of Holy Cross, United States Province of Priests & Brothers.
McDonald, Rev. Msgr. James M. '67 (RVC) Williston Park, NY St. Aidan's Church; Procurator & Advocates; Apostleship of Prayer; Nocturnal Adoration Society; Legion of Mary.
McDonald, James *c.ss.r.* '90 (TR)[R] Long Branch, NJ San Alfonso Retreat House.
McDonald, John G. '07 (BIR)[A] Birmingham, AL John Carroll Catholic High School; Birmingham, AL St. Francis Xavier.
McDonald, John J. *s.j.* '57 (NY)[DD] New York, NY Murray–Weigel Hall.
McDonald, Joseph F. '87 (B) College of Consultors; Deans; Promoters of Justice.
McDonald, Joseph F. '87 (B) Hailey, ID St. Charles Borromeo; Sun Valley, ID Our Lady of the Snows.
McDonald, Kenneth '57 (LAN) Retired.
McDonald, Malcolm '85 (PIT)[M] Pittsburgh, PA St. John Vianney Manor.
McDonald, Mark *m.s.c.* '68 (FgM) Aurora, IL MISSIONARIES OF THE SACRED HEART.
McDonald, Martin '62 (MRY) Retired.
McDonald, Michael D. '85 (GI) Kearney, NE Prince of Peace; Propagation of the Faith.
McDonald, Paul F. '51 (DUB) Retired.
McDonald, Perry *o.f.m.cap.* (MIL) Milwaukee, WI St. Francis of Assisi.
McDonald, Peter '59 (SFR) In. Res. Retired.
McDonald, Richard J. '99 (KCK) Basehor, KS Holy Angels.
McDonald, Thomas F. '52 (NY)[DD] Bronx, NY John Cardinal O'Connor Residence; Yonkers Fire Department Retired.
McDonald, Vincent *o.carm.* '47 (NY)[DD] Middletown, NY St. Albert's Priory.
McDonald, William '89 (STO) Absent on Leave.

McDonell, Clint W. '08 (DET) Graduate Studies.
McDonnell, Anthony '70 (LA) On Sick Leave.
McDonnell, David '72 (PAT) Priestly Life Committee; Sparta, NJ Our Lady of the Lake; Presbyteral Council; College of Consultors.
McDonnell, Donald C. '47 (SFR) Retired.
McDonnell, Francis E. '51 (RCK) Pro Synodal Judges; Censores Librorum Retired.
McDonnell, John H. '56 (WH) Retired.
McDonnell, John J. '73 (CHI) Chicago, IL St. Mary, Star of the Sea.
McDonnell, Joseph F. '55 (CHI) Western Springs, IL St. John of the Cross Retired.
McDonnell, Rev. Msgr. Joseph '67 (DM) Urbandale, IA St. Pius X.
McDonnell, Joseph '04 (STA) Chiefland, FL St. John the Evangelist.
McDonnell, Kilian *o.s.b.* '51 (SCL)[I] Collegeville, MN St. John's Abbey, of the Order of St. Benedict.
McDonnell, Lawrence V. *c.s.p.* '53 (NY)[DD] New York, NY Paulist Fathers' Motherhouse Retired.
McDonnell, Rev. Msgr. Martin '68 (PAT) Andover, NJ Good Shepherd.
McDonnell, Michael *o.f.m.* '65 (NY) New York, NY Holy Name of Jesus.
McDonnell, Rev. Msgr. P. William '64 (RCK) Freeport, IL St. Thomas Aquinas; Deans; Diocesan Consultors.
McDonnell, Patrick J. '73 (TR) Hightstown, NJ St. Anthony of Padua.
McDonnell, Paul A. *o.s.j.* '91 (SCR) Blue Army of Our Lady of Fatima; Councilors:; [A] Pittston, PA St. Joseph's Oblate Seminary.
McDonnell, Paul A. *o.s.j.* '91 (SCR)[L] Pittston, PA Our Lady of Sorrows Province of the Oblates of St. Joseph.
McDonnell, Sean '88 (PAT) Whippany, NJ Our Lady of Mercy.
McDonnell, Thomas P. *m.m.* '65 (NY)[DD] Maryknoll Maryknoll Fathers and Brothers; [DD] Maryknoll, NY Maryknoll Fathers and Brothers Charitable Trust Retired.
McDonnell, Thomas P. *s.j.* '68 (CHL) Charlotte, NC St. Peter; [J] Mooresville, NC Jesuit Community.
McDonough, James A. *o.p.* '62 (AUS)[G] Austin, TX Dominican Friars of Austin.
McDonough, James A. *s.j.* '61 (NY)[DD] New York, NY Murray–Weigel Hall.
McDonough, James P. '84 (PIT) Judges.
McDonough, Rev. Msgr. James T. '57 (PH) Strafford, PA Our Lady of the Assumption; Pontifical Mission Society of St. Peter Apostle; Pontifical Missionary Union; Pontifical Mission Society for the Propagation of the Faith Retired.
McDonough, Rev. Msgr. John P. '52 (BO) Senior Priests. Retired.
McDonough, John P. '95 (WH) New Martinsville, WV St. Vincent de Paul.
McDonough, John T. '50 (CLV) Akron, OH St. Sebastian; Hinckley, OH Our Lady of Grace; Presbyteral Council Retired.
McDonough, John T. '00 (PHX) Fountain Hills, AZ Ascension Roman Catholic Parish.
McDonough, Joseph '69 (BAL) Glen Burnie, MD Holy Trinity.
McDonough, Kevin M. '80 (STP) St. Paul, MN St. Peter Claver; Minneapolis, MN Church of the Incarnation; [S] Minneapolis, MN Sagrado Corazon de Jesus; Commission for Black Catholics; Office for Safe Environment.
McDonough, Patrick M. '68 (WH) St. Albans, WV St. Francis of Assisi.
McDonough, Roger F. '76 (BGP) Fairfield, CT St. Thomas Aquinas.
McDonough, Thomas R. '89 (STP) Retired.
McDonough, Vincent *s.j.* '62 (ROC)[B] Rochester, NY McQuaid Jesuit High School.
McDougal, H. Jon '79 (LR) Fort Smith, AR St. Boniface.
McDougall, James G. '75 (LAN) Ann Arbor, MI St. Francis of Assisi.
McDougall, Russell K. *c.s.c.* '91 (FgM)[H] Notre Dame Congregation of Holy Cross, United States Province of Priests & Brothers; New Rochelle, NY Eastern Brothers Province; [H] Notre Dame Congregation of Holy Cross, United States Province of Priests & Brothers.
McDowell, John W. *o.f.m.* '77 (CHR) Clemson, SC St. Andrew.
McDowell, Leo G. '94 (MO) Air Force Reserve Chaplains.
McDowell, Leo G. '94 (GF) Fort Benton, MT Immaculate Conception; Catholic Committee on Scouting; Finance Council; Director of Vocations and Recruitment.
McDowell, Patrick D. '68 (SCR) Weston, PA Sacred Heart.
McDuffie, Paul A. '95 (BR) Defenders of the Bond; Baton Rouge, LA Sacred Heart of Jesus.
McEachin, Donald J. *c.s.sp.* '81 (FgM) Bethel Park, PA CONGREGATION OF THE HOLY SPIRIT.
McElduff, Edward W. '53 (ALN) Retired.
McEleney, Robert J. '58 (RIC) Retired.
McElheron, J. Daniel '01 (HRT) Enfield, CT St. Martha.
McElligott, Thomas J. '69 (OAK)[B] St. Mary's College; [O] Moraga, CA St. Mary's College Mission and Ministry Center; On Duty Outside the Archdiocese.
McElroy, Charles J. '64 (PH) Schwenksville, PA St. Mary.
McElroy, Damian J. '88 (TR) Moorestown, NJ Our Lady of Good Counsel; Vicars Forane (Deans); College of Consultors; Censores Librorum.
McElroy, David R. *o.praem.* '02 (GB)[B] St. Norbert College; [J] De Pere, WI St. Norbert Abbey.
McElroy, John J. '45 (PRO) Pawtucket, RI St. Teresa of the Child Jesus Retired.
McElroy, John W. '56 (BO) Senior Priests. Retired.
McElroy, Thomas *ss.cc.* '67 (FR) Fairhaven, MA St. Joseph's; [F] Fairhaven, MA Sacred Hearts Provincial House; Fairhaven, MA.
McElwee, Robert W. '83 (WCH) Retired.
McEnery, James G. '53 (MAD) Retired.
McEnhill, Gerald A. '72 (DET) Orchard Lake, MI Our Lady of Refuge; College of Consultors; Presbyteral Council.
McEnhill, John *s.m.* '56 (SJ)[M] Cupertino, CA The Bordeaux House.
McEnnis, Thomas '45 (SEA) Retired.
McEntee, John B. '61 (STL) Retired.
McEvilly, John W. '64 (BEL) Belleville, IL Our Lady Queen of Peace; Belleville, IL Chapel of St. John Children's Home; [C] Belleville, IL Chancery Office; [J] Belleville, IL D & L Fund, NFP; [J] Belleville, IL Property & Liability Insurance Fund, NFP; [J] Belleville, IL Ministry Formation Fund, NFP; Vicar General; Moderator of the Curia; Diocesan Consultors; Diocesan Finance Council.
McEvoy, David *o.carm.* '88 (KCK) Leavenworth, KS Immaculate Conception–St. Joseph.
McEvoy, John '76 (SP) Ruskin, FL St. Anne; Vicars Forane; Diocesan Council of Catholic Women; Central Council of St. Petersburg Diocese.
McEvoy, William '87 (KCK)[A] Leavenworth, KS University of Saint Mary; Lansing, KS St. Francis de Sales.
McEwan, Kevin D. '02 (OG) Ticonderoga, NY Sacred Heart Church; Ticonderoga, NY St. Mary.
McFadden, Brian F. '88 (NEW) Medical Leave.
McFadden, Frank '83 (BAL) Priests Sick or Absent.
McFadden, J. Michael '74 (HBG) New Cumberland, PA St. Theresa of the Infant Jesus.
McFadden, John R. '62 (PH) Retired.
McFadden, Rev. Msgr. Leo E. '53 (RNO) Retired.
McFadden, Michael '61 (SAC) Vacaville, CA St. Mary.
McFadden, Michael *o.s.a.* '67 (SD) San Diego, CA Saint Patrick Catholic Parish San Diego; [J] San Diego, CA Austin House.
McFadden, Richard K. '05 (PH) Bensalem, PA St. Charles Borromeo.
McFadden, William C. *s.j.* '59 (WDC)[O] Washington, DC The Jesuit Community at Georgetown University.
McFadin, Marcus '92 (ELP) Office of Worship; El Paso, TX St. Stephen, Deacon and Martyr; Diocesan Master of Ceremonies; Diocesan Building Committee.
McFalls, Dean '95 (STO) Deans; Stockton, CA St. Mary of the Assumption Church (Pastor of).
McFarland, Michael C. *s.j.* '84 (WOR)[A] Worcester, MA College of the Holy Cross, Inc.; [N] Worcester, MA Jesuits of the Holy Cross, Inc.
McFarland, Timothy D. *c.pp.s.* '83 (LFT)[A] Rensselaer, IN Saint Joseph's College.
McFarlane, William M. '05 (CHI) Lansing, IL St. Ann.
McGaffin, Joseph P. '96 (PHX) Sun City, AZ St. Elizabeth Seton Roman Catholic Parish.
McGahagan, James E. '68 (SCR) Wilkes–Barre, PA St. Andrew Parish.
McGahee, Thomas *s.d.b.* '77 (NO)[D] Marrero, LA Archbishop Shaw High School.
McGahren, Joseph J. *m.m.* '51 (NY)[DD] Maryknoll Maryknoll Fathers and Brothers Retired.
McGann, Diarmuid F. '64 (RVC) Blue Point, NY Our Lady of the Snow Retired.
McGann, Rev. Msgr. Francis J. '49 (BO) Needham, MA St. Joseph; Senior Priests.; Presbyteral Council Retired.
McGann, L. Philip '71 (WIL) Retired.
McGann, Thomas A. *c.m.f.* '76 (SPC)[J] Springfield, MO Catholic Campus Ministry O'Reilly Catholic Student Center, Missouri State University, Drury University, Ozarks Technical Community College; Campus Ministries; [F] Springfield, MO Claretians Missionaries' Residence–Villa Claret; Presbyteral Council.
McGarril, Colman J. *t.o.r.* '54 (ALT)[G] Loretto, PA St. Francis Friary at Mount Assisi.
McGarrity, Patrick *c.ss.r.* '61 (HBG)[G] Ephrata, PA St. Clement's Mission House.
McGarry, Rev. Msgr. James J. '70 (SCR) Clarks Summit, PA Our Lady of the Snows; Keystone College; Presbyteral Council.
McGarry, John P. *s.j.* '93 (SJ)[B] Santa Clara, CA Jesuit Community.
McGarry, Michael B. *c.s.p.* (BRK)[R] Jamaica Estates, NY Paulist Fathers – Generalate.
McGarry, Peter *o.carm.* '69 (CHI)[D] Chicago, IL; [N] Chicago Carmelite Priory of St. Cyril; Chicago, IL St. Cajetan.
McGarry, William C. '59 (BUF) Retired.
McGarry, William J. *s.j.* '58 (FgM) New York, NY Society of Jesus.
McGarty, Rev. Msgr. Bernard O. '49 (LC) Retired.
McGaugh, Philip E. '78 (BO) Needham, MA St. Bartholomew.
Mc Gavock, Sabrina '03 (SP)[J] Tampa, FL St. Joseph's Hospital, Inc.
McGee, Rev. Msgr. H. Desmond '71 (E) Clearfield, PA St. Francis; Deans; Priest Personnel Board; College of Consultors; Presbyteral Council.
McGee, James J. '85 (OAK) Walnut Creek, CA St. John Vianney; Diocesan Review Board.
McGee, John E. *o.s.f.s.* '82 (R) Wilmington, NC Immaculate Conception.
McGee, Michael J. '77 (BRK) Brooklyn, NY Good Shepherd.
McGee, Richard *c.r.* '74 (SB)[I] Apple Valley, CA Congregation of the Resurrection, CR Retired.
McGee, Thomas J. *o.s.f.s.* '71 (CAM) Cape May, NJ The Church of Our Lady Star of the Sea, Cape May.
McGee, Rev. Msgr. Timothy H. '87 (CR) Deans; Diocesan Consultors; Detroit Lakes, MN Holy Rosary; Members; Finance Council.
McGeean, John T. '86 (JOL) Manhattan, IL St. Joseph.
McGeough, Jude P. '58 (PRO) Retired.
McGeough, Martin *c.m.* (RVC) Procurator & Advocates.
McGeown, Rev. Msgr. Joseph P. '65 (PH) Philadelphia, PA Immaculate Heart of Mary.
McGeown, William F. '70 (PH) Feasterville, PA Assumption B.V.M.
McGerity, Francis X. '84 (CC) On Duty Outside the Diocese.
McGettigan, Neil J. *o.s.a.* '53 (PH)[C] Villanova University; [Y] Villanova, PA St. Thomas Monastery Retired.
McGettrick, Rev. Msgr. Tom '56 (CC) Deans; College of Consultors; Presbyteral Council; Corpus Christi, TX Saint Andrew By the Sea Parish.
McGhee, James (FWT) Keller, TX St. Elizabeth Ann Seton.
McGhee, Jim '95 (AMA) Retired.
McGhee, Rev. Msgr. William P. '82 (BEL) Belleville, IL St. Mary; Co Directors; Diocesan Consultors.
McGillicuddy, Patrick *c.ss.r.* '79 (FgM) Baltimore Province.
McGillicuddy, Sean J. *c.ss.r.* '86 (NY) New York, NY Most Holy Redeemer.
McGing, Thomas '71 (JKS) Clinton, MS Holy Savior; [H] Clinton, MS Mississippi College Newman Center; Defenders of the Bond; Association of Priests; Personnel Board.
McGing, Thomas '71 (BLX) Association of Priests (Diocese of Biloxi and Jackson).
McGinley, Bernard P. '61 (HBG) Harrisburg, PA St. Catherine Laboure Retired.
McGinley, Jeremiah V. *o.f.m.* '55 (PAT)[N] Butler, NJ St. Anthony Friary.
McGinley, John F. *o.s.f.s.* '68 (WIL) Wilmington, DE St. Anthony of Padua.
McGinn, Anthony F. *s.j.* '79 (STL)[O] St. Louis, MO Jesuit Community Corporation at Saint Louis University – Jesuit Hall.
McGinn, Daniel *s.s.c.* '53 (PRO)[O] Bristol, RI St. Columban's Retirement House Retired.
McGinn, Daniel *s.s.c.* '53 (OM)[J] St. Columbans Missionary Society of St. Columban.
McGinn, Finian *o.f.m.* '60 (OAK)[L] Berkeley, CA Franciscan Friars (Province of St. Barbara).
McGinness, Matthew C. '89 (WCH) Wichita, KS St. Thomas Aquinas; Vicar for Clergy; Apostleship of Prayer; Presbyteral Council/College of Consultors.
McGinnis, Albin C. '77 (PIT) Pittsburgh, PA St. John Neumann.
McGinnis, Charles E. '06 (WH) Glenville, WV Good Shepherd.
McGinnis, J. Donald *m.m.* '53 (FgM) Maryknoll, NY MARYKNOLL.
McGinnis, Jack P. '63 (GAL) On Duty Outside the Archdiocese.
McGinnis, Jay W. '76 (BUF) Kenmore, NY St. Paul.
McGinnis, John Arthur '04 (FAR) Conshohocken, PA St. Mary Retired.
McGinnis, John P. (GAL) Retired.
McGinnity, John C. '75 (WH) Retired.
McGinnity, John '75 (RIC) Hot Springs, VA The Shrine of the Sacred Heart Retired.
McGinnity, P. J. '91 (KNX) Madisonville, TN St. Joseph the Worker.
McGinnity, Robert F. '55 (CHI) Palos Hills, IL Sacred Heart Retired.
McGivern, Gregory '85 (SFR)[E] San Francisco, CA Mercy High School (Girls).
McGivern, John W. '91 (CHI) Oak Park, IL St. Edmund.
McGivney, Thomas '90 (JOL) Lockport, IL St. Joseph.
McGlinchey, James J. '56 (TLS) Retired.

McGlinn, Rev. Msgr. Charles '67 (KCK) Leawood, KS Curé of Ars; Archdiocesan Consultors.
McGlinn, Robert J. '55 (CHI) Milwaukee, WI Retired.
McGloin, James P. *s.j.* '74 (FgM) Portland, OR Society of Jesus.
McGlone, Gerald J. *s.j.* '87 (PH) Philadelphia, PA Old St. Joseph's.
McGlone, Gerard M. '84 (SCR) Jessup, PA Queen of Angels Parish.
McGlothlin, Eugene J. *o.s.b.* '60 (SCL)[I] Collegeville, MN St. John's Abbey, of the Order of St. Benedict.
McGlynn, Rev. Msgr. Daniel J. '82 (WIL) Dover, DE Holy Cross.
McGlynn, Thomas E. '84 (FR) Centerville, MA Our Lady of Victory.
McGoldrick, James F. (BRK) Brooklyn, NY St. Francis of Assisi–St. Blaise.
McGoldrick, Kevin B. '03 (PH) Philadelphia, PA Holy Name of Jesus.
McGonagle, Douglas '00 (SPR) Easthampton, MA Our Lady of the Valley.
McGonegal, James R. '71 (CLV) Cleveland, OH St. Ignatius of Antioch.
McGonigle, Thomas *o.p.* '68 (CHI)[N] Chicago, IL St. Pius V Priory.
McGough, Rev. Msgr. James P. '57 (BLX) Pro–Synodal Judge Retired.
McGough, Rev. Msgr. Stephen D. '68 (SCR) Williamsport, PA St. Lawrence; Williamsport, PA St. Boniface.
McGough, Timothy *o.c.d.* '49 (MIL)[P] Milwaukee Provincial Offices – Discalced Carmelites Retired.
McGough, William J. '57 (NO) Retired.
McGourn, Francis T. *m.m.* '64 (NY)[DD] Maryknoll Maryknoll Fathers and Brothers Retired.
McGourn, Francis T. *m.m.* '64 (NY)[DD] New York, NY Maryknoll House.
McGovern, Brian J. '69 (SEA) Retired.
McGovern, Edward J. '51 (PRO)[O] Providence, RI St. John Vianney Residence; Assessor and Auditor; College of Consultors; Council Members Retired.
McGovern, Edward J. *m.m.* '04 (FgM) Maryknoll, NY; Maryknoll, NY; [DD] Maryknoll Maryknoll Fathers and Brothers.
McGovern, Eugene F. '29 (BRK) Retired.
McGovern, Eugene '56 (BRK)[R] Douglaston, NY Bishop Mugavero Residence Retired.
McGovern, Gerald T. '57 (BEL)[F] Belleville, IL Missionary Oblates of Mary Immaculate – St. Henry's Oblate Residence.
McGovern, Rev. Msgr. James J. '58 (TR) Retired.
McGovern, Rev. Msgr. James O. '67 (BAL) Priest Personnel Board Retired.
McGovern, John P. '65 (NEW) Cranford, NJ St. Michael's Retired.
McGovern, Rev. Msgr. Lawrence '67 (STO) Stockton, CA Presentation Church (Pastor of); Personnel Board.
McGovern, Mark J. '67 (DUB) Retired.
McGovern, Michael G. '94 (CHI) Lake Forest, IL St. Mary; College of Consultors; Deans.
McGovern, Robert C. *m.afr.* '63 (FgM) Washington, DC MISSIONARIES OF AFRICA; Washington, DC; [O] Washington, DC Missionaries of Africa Retired.
McGovern, Thomas A. '58 (CLV) Akron, OH St. Matthew Retired.
McGovern, Rev. Msgr. Thomas '46 (LA) Retired.
McGovern, Walter J. '64 (BAL) Randallstown, MD Holy Family Retired.
McGowan, Rev. Msgr. Anthony '41 (ORG) Retired.
McGowan, Denis *c.p.* '55 (FgM).
McGowan, Dennis M. *o.s.a.* '83 (PH) Bryn Mawr, PA Our Mother of Good Counsel; [Y] Bryn Mawr, PA Augustinians Friars (O.S.A.).
McGowan, Frederick R. '49 (BO) Senior Priests. Retired.
McGowan, James J. '62 (BO) Senior Priests. Retired.
McGowan, James '02 (SFE) Portales, NM St. Helen; [K] Portales, NM University Catholic Center – St. Thomas More Chapel; PORTALES: St. Thomas Moore Newman Center.
McGowan, Jeffrey A. '89 (STA) Gainesville, FL Queen of Peace.
McGowan, John *c.ss.r.* '62 (TR)[R] Long Branch, NJ San Alfonso Retreat House.
McGowan, Joseph F. *o.carm.* '62 (NEW) Cresskill, NJ St. Therese of Lisieux.
McGowan, Joseph O. *s.j.* '74 (SEA)[C] Tacoma, WA Bellarmine Preparatory School.
McGowan, Richard A. *s.j.* '83 (BO)[U] Newton, MA The Jesuit Community at Boston College.
McGowan, Richard W. *s.j.* '60 (SFE) Albuquerque, NM Immaculate Conception.
McGowan, Rev. Msgr. Seamus '57 (CC) Retired.
McGowan, Timothy '79 (LA) Montrose, CA Holy Redeemer.
McGrade, Kevin M. '85 (BO) Permanent Disability.; Air Force Reserve Chaplains.
McGrail, Charles A. '80 (NOR) Retired.
McGrann, John '67 (P) Retired.
McGrath, Andre *o.f.m.* '67 (SHP) Shreveport, LA Our Lady of the Blessed Sacrament.
McGrath, Brian F. '92 (SPR) Westfield, MA St. Mary's; Bishop's Commission for Clergy; Diocesan Consultors; Deans.
McGrath, Rev. Msgr. Conor '74 (SAT) San Antonio, TX St. Elizabeth Ann Seton.
McGrath, Edward F. '80 (WIN) Owatonna, MN St. Joseph's.
McGrath, Felix P. *o.f.m.* '61 (NY) New York, NY St. Francis of Assisi.
McGrath, Rev. Msgr. Frank C. '70 (BGP) Darien, CT St. John.
McGrath, James *c.s.c.* (FTW)[H] Holy Cross House.
McGrath, Rev. Msgr. Jeremiah J. '80 (BEA) Ecumenical Interreligious Affairs Officer; Diaconate, Permanent Diaconate; Beaumont, TX St. Anthony Cathedral Basilica.
McGrath, John A. '66 (CIN)[D] Dayton, OH The University of Dayton; [N] Dayton, OH Marianist Community.
McGrath, John F. '44 (CHI) Chicago, IL St. Thomas More Retired.
McGrath, Rev. Msgr. John R. '82 (BLX) Biloxi, MS Cathedral of the Nativity of the Blessed Virgin Mary; Personnel Board; Tribunal Judges; Special Delegate for Matrimonial Dispensations; Judicial Vicar; Deans; College of Consultors; Catholic Housing Board; Presbyteral Council.
McGrath, John '59 (MIA) Retired.
McGrath, John *o.m.i.* '53 (SAT)[K] San Antonio, TX Oblate Madonna Residence.
McGrath, Jordan A. *o.p.* '59 (CHI)[N] River Forest, IL St. Thomas Aquinas Priory.
McGrath, Joseph '85 (LKC) On Medical Leave.
McGrath, Kevin Anthony *o.p.* '96 (L) Springfield, KY St. Rose.
McGrath, Kevin D. *o.s.b.* '74 (BIR)[E] Cullman, AL St. Bernard Abbey; Cullman, AL.
McGrath, Lancelot '85 (MET) North Plainfield, NJ St. Luke.
McGrath, Rev. Msgr. Laurence W. '57 (BO) Senior Priests. Retired.
McGrath, Noel '80 (PMB) Stuart, FL St. Joseph.
McGrath, Patrick E. *s.j.* '06 (CHI)[D] Wilmette, IL Loyola Academy; [W] Wilmette, IL Loyola Recreational Facility Corp.; [E] Chicago, IL Chicago Jesuit Academy.
McGrath, Peter (TYL) Hallsville, TX Our Lady of Grace.
McGrath, Richard J. *o.s.a.* '73 (JOL)[C] New Lenox, IL Providence Catholic High School; [L] New Lenox, IL Augustinian Friary.
McGrath, Robert '67 (DET) Farmington Hills, MI St. Alexander.
McGrath, Rev. Msgr. Roger E. '71 (CAM)[F] Camden, NJ The Frank J. and Rosina W. Suttill Catholic Foundation; [F] Camden, NJ Francis, Elizabeth and Edward Roger Welsh Scholarship Trust; Vicars General; Members; Ex Officio Members; Ex Officio Members; Office of Vocations; Ex Officio Members; Vocation Advisory Board; Officers; [F] Camden, NJ The Sharkey Family Charitable Trust; Haddonfield, NJ Church of Christ the King, Haddonfield, N.J.
McGrath, Sean J. '91 (DEN) Littleton, CO St. Frances Cabrini.
McGrath, Thomas B. *s.j.* '64 (AGN) Agana, GU Dulce Nombre de Maria Cathedral – Basilica; New York, NY Society of Jesus; [F] Tamuning, GU Society of Jesus Micronesia.
McGrath, Thomas E. '77 (JC) Retired.
McGrath, Thomas J. '59 (SY) Retired.
McGrath, Thomas (PAT) Special Assignment; Adoption and Counseling Services.
McGrath, Thomas (SY)[S] Skaneateles, NY Stella Maris Retreat & Renewal Center Retired.
McGrath, William J. *s.j.* '59 (PH)[Y] Loyola Center and Manresa Hall.
McGrath, William '00 (ROC)[O] Rochester, NY Catholic Committee on Scouting; Rochester, NY Roman Catholic Parish of St. Francis Xavier Cabrini.
McGratty, John J. '71 (RVC) Retired.
McGraw, Howard *o.s.a.* '62 (PH)[Y] Philadelphia, PA Augustinian Community (O.S.A.).
McGraw, Rev. Msgr. John T. '56 (SY) Retired.
McGraw, Rev. Msgr. Michael D. *m.ss.a.* '75 (PMB) Boca Raton, FL St. Joan of Arc.
McGraw, Rene *o.s.b.* '62 (SCL)[I] Collegeville, MN St. John's Abbey, of the Order of St. Benedict.
McGraw, Robert H. '76 (LAN) Fowlerville, MI St. Agnes; Regional Vicars.
McGraw, Sean D. *c.s.c.* '01 (FTW)[H] Notre Dame Congregation of Holy Cross, United States Province of Priests & Brothers; [B] University of Notre Dame Du Lac; [H] Notre Dame, IN Holy Cross Community, Corby Hall, University of Notre Dame.
McGraw, Stephen F. '01 (ARL) Dale City, VA Holy Family.
McGraw, W. Howard *o.s.a.* '62 (PH) Philadelphia, PA St. Nicholas of Tolentine.
McGray, James '67 (SD) Retired.
McGread, Rev. Msgr. Thomas '53 (WCH) Retired.
McGready, Rev. Msgr. Oliver W. '62 (WDC) Waldorf, MD St. Peter Retired.
McGreevy, John G. *o.p.* '64 (DEN) Denver, CO St. Dominic; [N] Denver, CO Dominican Friars.
McGreevy, Thomas More J. *o.p.* '64 (P)[L] Portland, OR Holy Rosary Priory; Portland, OR Holy Rosary Parish & Dominican Priory Retired.
McGregor, Mark D. *s.j.* '96 (MO) Air Force Chaplains.
McGroarty, Rev. Msgr. Charles E. '62 (PH) Philadelphia, PA St. Matthew.
McGroarty, Hugh H. '45 (SCR) Pittston, PA St. John the Evangelist.
McGrogan, James P. '64 (GRY) Cursillos in Christianity; Chesterton, IN St. Patrick Retired.
McGuffey, James W. '95 (MET) Carteret, NJ St. Joseph.
McGuigan, David *s.m.* '01 (CIN)[R] Dayton, OH University of Dayton Campus Ministry; [D] Dayton, OH The University of Dayton; [N] Dayton, OH Marianist Community.
McGuigan, Hugh J. *o.s.f.s.* '97 (VEN) Presbyteral Council; Fort Myers, FL Our Lady of Light.
McGuigan, Patrick *o.carm.* '79 (NY) Middletown, NY Our Lady of Mt. Carmel; [DD] Middletown, NY Carmelite Friars (North American Province of St. Elias).
McGuill, Martin F. '64 (MO) Air Force Reserve Chaplains.
McGuill, Martin '64 (ARL) Retired.
McGuine, Peter M. '90 (MO) Air Force Reserve Chaplains.
McGuine, Peter '90 (SD) Spring Valley, CA Santa Sophia Catholic Parish; Clergy Personnel Board.
McGuiness, Edward J. '61 (SB) Retired.
McGuinn, James T. '88 (PH) Philadelphia, PA St. Agatha–St. James; [BB] Philadelphia, PA Drexel University; [BB] Philadelphia, PA University of Pennsylvania; On Special or Other Archdiocesan Assignment.
McGuinness, David '77 (ATL) Athens, GA St. Joseph; Deans.
McGuinness, Fergal '86 (SR) Adjutant Judicial Vicar; Diocesan Judges; Santa Rosa, CA Cathedral of St. Eugene.
McGuinness, J. Roger '65 (OG) West Chazy, NY St. Joseph.
McGuire, Anthony E. '65 (SFR) San Mateo, CA St. Matthew; Deans.
McGuire, Rev. Msgr. Anthony W. '57 (PH) Retired.
McGuire, Bonaventure M. *f.i.* '99 (NOR)[G] Griswold, CT Marian Friary of Our Lady of Guadalupe.
McGuire, Brendan P. (SJ) San Jose, CA Pastor of Our Lady of Refuge.
McGuire, Brendan '00 (SJ) San Jose, CA Holy Spirit; Notre Dame Club of San Jose/Silicon Valley; College of Consultors; Council of Priests; Vicar General, Office for Special Projects; Special Assignment; Bishop's Cabinet.
McGuire, David V. '88 (RIC) Military Chaplains; Air Force Chaplains.
McGuire, Frederick J. '81 (CIN) On Duty Outside the Archdiocese.
McGuire, J. Frederick '81 (SP) St. Petersburg, FL Blessed Trinity.
McGuire, James D. *o.a.r.* '54 (LA) Montebello, CA St. Benedict.
McGuire, Rev. Msgr. John A. '50 (RVC) Sound Beach, NY St. Louis de Montfort Retired.
McGuire, John F. '76 (P) Coquille, OR Holy Name.
McGuire, John Patrick *o.p.* '73 (NY) New York, NY St. Joseph.
McGuire, John *o.p.* '79 (NY)[GG] New York, NY New York University; [GG] New York, NY Pace University.
McGuire, Joseph E. '65 (DUB) Retired.
McGuire, Ken *c.s.p.* '68 (ALB)[L] Lake George, NY St. Mary of the Lake.
McGuire, Kenneth H. *c.s.p.* '68 (BRK)[R] Retired Retired.
McGuire, Paul J. *s.c.j.* '68 (MIL)[P] Franklin, WI St. Francis Residence; [Y] Hales Corners, WI Congregation of the Priests of the Sacred Heart Support and Maintenance Trust; [P] Franklin, WI Dehon Study Center.
McGuire, Richard G. *o.c.s.o.* '57 (CHR)[E] Moncks Corner, SC Mepkin Abbey.
McGuire, Rev. Msgr. Richard J. '60 (E) Retired.
McGuire, Richard '67 (SCL) Greenwald, MN St. Michael's Retired.
McGuire, Richard *o.s.c.* '73 (PHX)[F] Phoenix, AZ Crosier Community of Phoenix (Canons Regular of the Order of the Holy Cross); Chandler, AZ St. Andrew the Apostle Roman Catholic Parish; Provincial Councilors.
McGuire, Robert *s.j.* '58 (ALB)[N] Fultonville, NY Shrine of Our Lady of Martyrs; Apostleship of Prayer.
McGuire, Thaddeus '99 (PHX) Scottsdale, AZ St. Daniel the Prophet Roman Catholic Parish; Members.
McGuire, Thomas D. '81 (LIN) Indianola, NE St. Catherine's; Diocesan Area CCD Directors; Diocesan Council of Catholic Women; Advocates.
McGuire, Timothy P. '84 (STU) Cadiz, OH St. Teresa; Cadiz, OH Sacred Heart; Cadiz, OH St. Matthias

Mission; Presbyteral Council; Woman's Club; College of Consultors.
McGuire, William A. *o.s.a.* '65 (PH)[Y] Villanova, PA St. Thomas Monastery.
McGuirk, Alan B. *m.s.* '56 (HRT)[L] Hartford, CT Missionaries of LaSalette.
McGuirk, John J. '70 (SC) Sac City, IA Sacred Heart; Sac City, IA St. Mary's; Sac City, IA St. Joseph's; Presbyteral Council.
McGuirk, William C. '82 (GBG) Republic, PA Madonna of Czestochowa; Republic, PA Holy Rosary.
McGuirl, Rev. Msgr. John A. '72 (BRK) Forest Hills, NY Our Lady of Mercy.
McGurk, Patrick C. '58 (HEL) Associate Judges Retired.
McGurn, Richard H. *s.j.* '75 (CHI)[D] Wilmette, IL Loyola Academy; [E] Chicago, IL Chicago Jesuit Academy.
McHale, John F. '04 (SCR) White Haven, PA St. Patrick.
McHenry, Raymond '00 (DM) Indianola, IA St. Thomas Aquinas; Continuing Education for Clergy; St. Marys, IA Immaculate Conception.
McHenry, Rev. Msgr. Stephen P. '73 (PH) Ambler, PA St. Anthony of Padua; Deans; Deans.
McHenry, V. F. *o.p.* '49 (WDC) Washington, DC St. Dominic Church & Priory.
McHugh, Adrian '92 (RVC) Rockville Centre, NY St. Agnes Cathedral.
McHugh, Alphonsus *ss.cc.* '69 (BWN) Harlingen, TX Queen of Peace.
McHugh, Brian J. '88 (BO) Somerville, MA St. Ann; Somerville, MA St. Catherine of Genoa.
McHugh, Conall *o.f.m.conv.* '56 (TR) Seaside Park, NJ St. Catharine of Siena.
McHugh, Connell A. '72 (SCR) Conyngham, PA St. John Bosco; Drums, PA Church of the Good Shepherd.
McHugh, Dennis (PAT) Retired.
McHugh, Donald '57 (P) Retired.
McHugh, Francis '97 (SAT) San Antonio, TX St. Pius X.
McHugh, James L. '60 (COV) Retired.
McHugh, James *o.s.f.s.* '77 (LAN)[M] Brooklyn, MI Lake Vineyard Camps, Inc., (De Sales Center); [J] Brooklyn, MI Thorrez Vocational Trust, Ltd.
McHugh, Jerome *o.f.m.cap.* '60 (NY)[DD] White Plains, NY St. Conrad Friary; [DD] White Plains, NY Capuchin Friars International, Inc.; [DD] White Plains, NY St. Francis of Assisi Foundation; [DD] White Plains, NY Capuchin Friars of North America.
Mc Hugh, John F. *o.m.i.* '73 (BO)[X] Tewksbury, MA Immaculate Heart of Mary Residence.
McHugh, John P. '91 (HRT) Collinsville, CT St. Patrick.
McHugh, John W. '76 (HRT) Avon, CT St. Ann's.
McHugh, John *s.o.l.t.* '52 (SFE) Mora, NM St. Gertrude.
McHugh, John *o.f.m.cap.* '69 (PRT)[M] Standish, ME Saint Joseph's College; Yarmouth, ME Parish of the Holy Eucharist.
McHugh, Joseph B. *s.j.* '58 (BO)[U] Weston, MA Campion Health Center, Inc.
McHugh, Joseph F. *s.j.* (FgM) Watertown, MA Society of Jesus.
McHugh, Joseph *s.j.* '83 (BO)[W] Gloucester, MA Eastern Point Retreat House.
McHugh, Rev. Msgr. Kieran A. '70 (PAT)[Q] Sparta, NJ Pope John XXIII High School Special Project Foundation, Inc; [C] Sparta, NJ Pope John XXIII High School; [Q] Sparta, NJ The Catholic Academy of Sussex County, Inc.
McHugh, Michael J. '80 (BRK) Woodside, NY St. Sebastian.
McHugh, Paul F. '53 (MAN) Retired.
McHugh, Rev. Msgr. Peter J. '65 (PAT)[Q] Chester, NJ Nazareth Village Retired.
McIlhenny, Bernard R. *s.j.* '56 (SCR)[B] Scranton, PA The University of Scranton.
McIlhone, James P. '74 (CHI) Chicago, IL St. Edward.
McIlvane, Donald W. '52 (PIT) Retired.
McInerney, Blaise *o.carm.* '54 (JOL)[L] Darien Carmelite Provincial Office.
McInerney, Henry '77 (BLX) Ocean Springs, MS St. Alphonsus.
McInerney, Kieran *o.s.b.* '52 (FgM) Atchison, KS St. Benedict's Abbey.
McInerny, Kieran *o.s.b.* '52 (KCK)[I] Atchison, KS St. Benedict's Abbey.
McInerny, Rev. Msgr. Lawrence B. '79 (CHR) Sullivan's Island, SC Stella Maris; Presbyteral Council.
McInerny, Rev. Msgr. Paul B. '72 (BO) On Duty Outside the Archdiocese.
McInnis, Francis L. '56 (GF) Retired.
McInnis, Francis '57 (GF)[B] Great Falls, MT Great Falls Central Catholic High School.
McInnis, Gary '98 (LAN) Egeler Correctional Facility.
McInnis, Gary '74 (LAN) Retired.
McInnis, George L. *c.p.m.* '07 (OWN)[F] Auburn, KY Fathers of Mercy.
McInnis, Thomas J. '57 (LC) Retired.
McIntire, William J. *m.m.* '67 (FgM) Maryknoll, NY MARYKNOLL.
McIntosh, Martin *s.j.* (TUC)[I] Nogales, AZ Kino Border Initiative.
McIntosh, Robert K. *s.j.* '72 (FgM) Milwaukee, WI Society of Jesus.
McIntosh, Thomas *c.ss.r.* '66 (FgM) Denver, CO Denver Province.
McIntyre, Garrett K. '11 (LAF) Ville Platte, LA Sacred Heart of Jesus; Ville Platte, LA St. Joseph.
McIntyre, Gerald J. *s.j.* '74 (PAT)[J] Morristown, NJ Loyola House of Retreats.
McIntyre, Gerald J. *s.j.* '74 (NY)[DD] Loyola Hall, Jesuit Community.
McIntyre, James *o.f.m.cap.* '53 (NY)[DD] Yonkers, NY St. Clare Friary.
McIntyre, John P. *s.j.* '63 (BO)[U] Weston, MA Campion Health Center, Inc.
McIntyre, Justin '81 (SR) Retired.
McIntyre, Patrick '60 (FgM) Boston, MA St. James the Apostle, Inc.
McIntyre, Thomas J. *c.m.* '50 (LA)[V] Montebello, CA DePaul Evangelization Center Retired.
McIntyre, Rev. Msgr. Thomas J. '66 (CAM) Retired.
McIntyre, William *o.f.m.* '95 (R) Durham, NC Immaculate Conception.
McKale, Harold B. '10 (PH) Holland, PA St. Bede the Venerable.
McKamy, Eldon J. '63 (OM) Retired.
McKane, Wm. Paul *o.s.b.* '88 (GF) Belt, MT St. Mark the Evangelist.
McKarns, James E. '62 (Y) North Canton, OH St. Paul Retired.
McKay, Alistair (ORL) New Smyrna Beach, FL Sacred Heart.
McKay, Douglas M. '82 (PH)[W] Philadelphia, PA Holy Family Home; On Special or Other Archdiocesan Assignment.
McKay, Rev. Msgr. James P. '56 (SFR) Retired.
McKay, James R. *s.m.* '44 (CIN)[N] Dayton, OH Mercy Siena Gardens.
McKay, John F. '73 (WDC) Hospital & Nursing Home Ministries; Bethesda, MD St. Jane Frances de Chantal.
McKay, Robert '70 (SJ)[H] San Jose, CA O'Connor Hospital.
McKeaney, James J. '69 (PH) Bryn Mawr, PA St. John Neumann.
McKearney, James L. *s.s.* '97 (HRT) On Duty Outside the Archdiocese.
McKearney, James L. *s.s.* '97 (BAL)[Q] Baltimore Society of St. Sulpice, Province of the United States.
McKearney, James L. *s.s.* '97 (SFR)[A] Menlo Park, CA St. Patrick Seminary and University; [A] Menlo Park, CA St. Patrick Seminary and University.
McKee, Francis X. '66 (PH) Philadelphia, PA Holy Family.
McKee, Henry J. '72 (PH) Havertown, PA Sacred Heart.
McKee, Jay R. '02 (WIL) Perryville, MD Church of the Good Shepherd.
Mckee, Shane *s.o.l.t.* '07 (FAR) Belcourt, ND St. Ann; Belcourt, ND St. Ann.
McKee, William '83 (SEA) Federal Way, WA St. Vincent De Paul.
McKeefry, Brendan '67 (SAC) Carmichael, CA Our Lady of the Assumption.
McKeever, Henry *c.ss.r.* '48 (STL)[O] Liguori, MO St. Clement Health Care Center Retired.
McKeever, Martin *c.ss.r.* '87 (STL)[O] Liguori, MO Alphonsian Foundation.
McKelvey, James P. '93 (PH)[T] Immaculata, PA Camilla Hall Nursing Home; On Special or Other Archdiocesan Assignment.
McKenna, Brian *o.f.m.cap.* '66 (SFR) Burlingame, CA Our Lady of Angels.
McKenna, Colin J. '99 (BGP) Georgetown, CT Sacred Heart.
McKenna, Edward J. '65 (CHI) Retired.
McKenna, Rev. Msgr. Enda '64 (SAT) Fredericksburg, TX St. Mary's.
McKenna, Eugene J. '63 (PRO) Retired.
McKenna, F. Charles '60 (ALN)[J] Bethlehem, PA Holy Family Villa Retired.
McKenna, Frank W. '94 (NOR) Retired.
McKenna, George P. '44 (CHI) Oak Lawn, IL St. Catherine of Alexandria Retired.
McKenna, James George '61 (DAL) Dallas, TX Holy Cross Retired.
McKenna, James *s.d.b.* '80 (NO)[D] Marrero, LA Archbishop Shaw High School; [H] Marrero, LA Archbishop Shaw Junior High School.
McKenna, James *s.d.b.* '80 (NY)[FF] Stony Point, NY Don Bosco Retreat Center and Marian Shrine.
McKenna, Jerome *c.p.* '58 (ATL) Atlanta, GA St. Paul of the Cross.
McKenna, John H. *c.m.* '64 (BRK)[R] Jamaica, NY St. Vincent's House.
McKenna, John J. '47 (NY) Sloatsburg, NY St. Joan of Arc Retired.
McKenna, John L. '88 (PIT) Pittsburgh, PA Epiphany; Pittsburgh, PA St. Mary of Mercy.
McKenna, John '77 (BRK) Brooklyn, NY Our Lady of Perpetual Help Basilica.
McKenna, Joseph J. *o.s.f.s.* '57 (WIL) Wilmington, DE St. Francis Hospital; [I] Wilmington, DE St. Francis Hospital, Inc.; [J] Wilmington, DE DeSales House.
McKenna, Joseph R. '57 (PRT) Portland, ME St. Joseph's Manor Retired.
McKenna, Kenneth N. *o.s.f.s.* '85 (TOL)[H] Toledo, OH Provincial Residence; [H] Toledo Oblates of St. Francis de Sales.
McKenna, Kevin E. '77 (ROC) Rochester, NY Sacred Heart Cathedral; Priest Consultors; Judges.
McKenna, Peter '57 (SAT) Retired.
McKenna, Philip A. '62 (MOB) Montgomery, AL Church of the Holy Spirit; Sacramental Ministers.
McKenna, Timothy J. '79 (MO) Air National Guard Chaplains.
McKenna, Timothy '79 (SEA) Auburn, WA Holy Family.
McKenna, William A. *s.j.* '68 (NEW)[B] Jersey City, NJ Jesuit Center; [L] Jersey City, NJ Jesuits of Saint Peter's College, Inc.
McKenzie, John J. *o.s.a.* '65 (PH) Conshohocken, PA SS. Cosmas and Damian; [Y] Rosemont, PA Saxony Hall.
McKenzie, John '85 (CC) Refugio, TX St. James the Apostle.
McKenzie, Mark D. *s.j.* '69 (STL) St. Louis, MO St. Matthew, Apostle; [O] St. Louis, MO St. Matthew Jesuit Community.
McKenzie, William L. '82 (KNX) Alcoa, TN Our Lady of Fatima; Diocesan Finance Council.
McKeon, Gerard R. *s.j.* '86 (BO)[AA] Salem, MA Salem State College, Catholic Campus Ministry; Salem State College; [D] Boston, MA Boston College High School.
McKeon, John Aedan *o.p.* '56 (NY)[DD] New York St. Vincent Ferrer Priory.
McKeon, Michael C. '65 (SAC) Roseville, CA St. Rose of Lima Retired.
McKeon, Raymond T. '63 (NEW) Jersey City, NJ St. Paul's Retired.
McKeon, Robert F. '90 (NY) Brewster, NY St. Lawrence O'Toole; Canon 1742 Panel of Pastors.
McKeon, Robert '59 (LAN) Gaines, MI St. Joseph Retired.
McKeough, Brendan J. *o.praem.* '53 (GB)[J] De Pere, WI St. Joseph Priory.
McKercher, Mark J. '97 (OM) Omaha, NE St. Cecilia Cathedral.
McKernan, Leo J. '83 (SCR) West Wyoming, PA Saint Monica Parish.
McKernan, Louis F. *c.s.p.* '54 (BRK)[R] Retired Retired.
McKernan, Louis *c.s.p.* '54 (WDC)[B] Washington, DC St. Paul's College.
McKevitt, Gerald L. *s.j.* '75 (SJ)[B] Santa Clara, CA Jesuit Community.
McKiernan, Rev. Msgr. J. Michael '91 (ORG) Council of Priests; Consultors; Liturgical Commission; Building and Renovation Committee of the Liturgical Commission; Santa Ana, CA Christ Our Savior Cathedral; Council of Priests.
McKiernan, Joseph W. '51 (WOR) Retired.
McKiernan, Vincent W. *c.s.p.* '57 (COL)[I] Columbus, OH Campus Ministry.
McKillin, David *o.s.b.* '76 (LR)[H] Fort Smith, AR St. Scholastica Monastery–Motherhouse.
McKinley, Joseph *s.s.j.* '85 (NO)[R] New Orleans, LA The Josephite Faculty House of St. Augustine High School.
McKinley, Michael J. '85 (LFT) Union City, IN St. Mary; Union City, IN St. Joseph.
McKinley, Stephen *o.f.m.conv.* '94 (CHI)[N] Libertyville, IL Marytown, Our Lady of Fatima Friary.
McKinney, Floyd E. '80 (DOD) Presbyteral Council; Pratt, KS Sacred Heart Catholic Church of Pratt, Kansas; St. John, KS St. John the Apostle Catholic Church of St. John, Kansas; On Duty Outside the Diocese.
McKinney, Michael A. '93 (LFT) Logansport, IN All Saints; Diocesan Consultors; Members.
McKinney, Ronald H. *s.j.* '83 (SCR)[B] Scranton, PA The University of Scranton.
McKinney, Thomas A. '61 (GR) Retired.
McKinnon, Eymard '54 (NY)[DD] Yonkers, NY St. Clare Friary.
McKitrick, James V. '58 (RCK) Retired.
McKnight, Albert *c.s.sp.* '52 (SB)[I] Hemet, CA Congregation of the Holy Spirit Retired.
McKnight, James '59 (SAC) Retired.
McKnight, Kevin F. '94 (PIT)[M] Pittsburgh, PA St. John Vianney Manor.
McKnight, W. Shawn '94 (WCH) On Duty Outside the Diocese; Staff.
McKone, John '08 (FWT) Vernon, TX St. Joseph; Vernon, TX St. Mary; Vernon, TX Holy Family; Deans; Mission Council.
McKusky, Kristoffer '05 (DUL) International Falls, MN St. Thomas Aquinas; International Falls, MN St. Columban.
McLachlan, Frederick E. *s.s.e.* '64 (BUR) Putney, VT Our Lady of Mercy.
McLafferty, Joseph M. '00 (NY) Staten Island, NY St. Christopher.

McLain, John J. *s.j.* '98 (P)[L] Portland Jesuit Provincial Office (Society of Jesus, Oregon Prov.).
McLain, Michael D. '08 (SUP) Merrill, WI St. Francis Xavier.
McLaughlin, Anthony K.W. '97 (TYL) Tyler, TX Cathedral of the Immaculate Conception; Judicial Vicar.
McLaughlin, Anthony '97 (TYL) Judges.
McLaughlin, Daniel F. *m.m.* '61 (FgM) Maryknoll, NY MARYKNOLL.
McLaughlin, Daniel *o.s.a.* '83 (PH) Philadelphia, PA St. Rita of Cascia.
McLaughlin, Daniel *s.t.* '63 (WDC)[O] Adelphi, MD Father Judge Missionary Cenacle.
McLaughlin, David S. '96 (NEW) Hackensack, NJ Holy Trinity.
McLaughlin, Don E. '81 (JOL) Wheaton, IL St. Michael.
McLaughlin, Donald E. '67 (NEW) Retired.
McLaughlin, Edward J. '52 (BO) Senior Priests. Retired.
McLaughlin, Edward '59 (CHI) Palos Heights, IL Incarnation; Orland Park, IL St. Michael Retired.
McLaughlin, Farrell E. '71 (PRO) Cranston, RI St. Ann.
McLaughlin, Gerald L. *s.j.* '59 (FgM) Watertown, MA Society of Jesus.
McLaughlin, Gregory '85 (AUS) Salado, TX St. Stephen.
McLaughlin, James J. '70 (PH) Retired.
McLaughlin, James W. '96 (MET) Retired.
McLaughlin, James '73 (SB) College of Consultors; La Quinta, CA St. Francis of Assisi.
McLaughlin, John R. '95 (BO) East Boston, MA Sacred Heart.
McLaughlin, John '61 (SEA) Retired.
McLaughlin, John '66 (MIA) Retired Priests' Committee Retired.
McLaughlin, Joseph J. '66 (PH) Richboro, PA St. Vincent de Paul.
McLaughlin, Joseph J. *s.m.* '72 (FgM) Boston, MA U.S. Mission Promoter; Atlanta, GA; Boston, MA Our Lady of Victories.
McLaughlin, Joseph M. *s.s.e.* '70 (BUR)[E] Colchester, VT Society of St. Edmund; [A] Colchester, VT St. Michael's College.
McLaughlin, Joseph P. *o.praem.* '70 (PH)[Y] Paoli, PA Daylesford Abbey.
McLaughlin, Joseph P. *o.praem.* '70 (WIL)[B] Claymont, DE Archmere Academy.
McLaughlin, Michael R. '82 (DM) Dexter, IA Des Moines City Chaplaincy Program; [J] West Des Moines, IA City Hospital Chaplaincy Service; On Special Assignment.
McLaughlin, Patrick A. '03 (OM) Dodge, NE St. Wenceslaus.
McLaughlin, Patrick J. '61 (BO) Medford, MA St. Joseph; Presbyteral Council.
McLaughlin, Patrick J. '74 (SCR) Scranton, PA Immaculate Conception; Presbyteral Council.
McLaughlin, Paul F. '71 (VEN) Bradenton, FL St. Joseph; Presbyteral Council; College of Consultors.
McLaughlin, Peter A. '78 (CAM) On Duty Outside the Diocese; Pensacola, FL St. Michael.
McLaughlin, Peter '78 (PT) Apostleship of the Sea, Office of the.
McLaughlin, Richard C. '74 (PRT) Members; Auburn, ME Immaculate Heart of Mary Parish; Norway, ME Blessed Teresa of Calcutta Parish.
McLaughlin, Richard P. '68 (BO) Senior Priests. Retired.
McLaughlin, Robert P. '11 (NEW) Cedar Grove, NJ St. Catherine of Siena.
McLaughlin, Rev. Msgr. Thomas C. '56 (VIC) Victoria, TX Retired.
McLaughlin, Thomas D. '76 (SCR) Stroudsburg, PA St. Luke; Diocesan Finance Council; Deans; Presbyteral Council.
McLaughlin, Thomas R. '81 (NEW) Medical Leave.
McLaughlin, William A. '92 (BRK) College Point, NY St. Fidelis.
McLaughlin, William H. '68 (BO) Newburyport, MA Immaculate Conception.
McLaughlin, Rev. Msgr. William '58 (ORG) Retired.
McLaverty, Albert J. '00 (CAM) On Leave of Absence.
McLean, Barry L. '90 (SAN) Diocesan Consultors; Board of Directors; Presbyteral Council; Continuing Education of the Clergy; Vocations.
McLean, Edward J. '52 (HRT) Glastonbury, CT St. Paul Retired.
McLean, George F. *o.m.i.* '55 (WDC)[X] Washington, DC Council for Research in Values and Philosophy; Washington, DC The National Center for Urban Ethnic Affairs (1971).
McLean, George *o.m.i.* (BO)[X] Tewksbury, MA Immaculate Heart of Mary Residence.
McLean, William '69 (LA) Chatsworth, CA St. John Eudes.
McLearen, Daniel J. '92 (HRT) New Haven, CT St. Francis; New Haven Vicariate.
McLellan, Daniel *o.f.m.* '76 (R) Durham, NC Immaculate Conception.
McLellan, James R. '70 (FR) Retired.
McLellan, Michael F. '76 (BO) Canton, MA St. John the Evangelist.
McLelland, James R. '00 (SHP) Vivian, LA St. Clement; [B] Shreveport, LA CHRISTUS Health Northern Louisiana; [B] Shreveport, LA CHRISTUS Schumpert Highland; Priests' Retirement Board.
McLeod, Frederick G. *s.j.* '62 (BO)[U] Boston The Society of Jesus of New England–Provincial Offices.
McLeod, Frederick G. *s.j.* '62 (STL)[O] St. Louis, MO Jesuit Community Corporation at Saint Louis University – Jesuit Hall.
McLinden, James E. *s.s.j.* '71 (BAL) Baltimore, MD St. Francis Xavier.
McLinden, James E. *s.s.j.* '62 (WDC)[B] Washington, DC Josephite Pastoral Center.
McLoone, Rev. Msgr. Joseph C. '88 (PH) Chester, PA Saint Katharine Drexel; Downingtown, PA St. Joseph; [BB] Chester, PA Widener University.
McLoud, Steven J. '94 (SC) Sioux City, IA Nativity of Our Lord Jesus Christ.
McLoughlin, Brendan '70 (PAT) On Duty Outside the Diocese.
McLoughlin, Rev. Msgr. James W. '65 (RCK) Deans Retired.
McLoughlin, John T. '73 (NY) Mount Vernon, NY St. Ursula.
McLoughlin, John *c.ss.r.* '92 (HBG) Ephrata, PA Mother of Perpetual Help; [G] Ephrata, PA St. Clement's Mission House.
McLoughlin, Luke '66 (STA) Catholic Women, Council of.
McLoughlin, Michael P. '81 (NY) Warwick, NY St. Stephen.
McLoughlin, Nicholas '66 (VEN) Avon Park, FL Our Lady of Grace.
McLoughlin, Paul J. '71 (SPC) Cassville, MO St. Edward; Monett, MO St. Lawrence; Monett, MO SS. Peter and Paul; Region II; Diocesan Consultors.
McLucas, James (NY) On Leave of Absence.
McMackin, Thomas P. '63 (ORL) Retired.
McMahon, Albert *o.f.m.* '60 (ALB)[A] Catskill, NY St. Anthony Friary.
McMahon, Bartholomew *o.f.m.* '62 (FgM) New York, NY Holy Name Province.
McMahon, Brian F. '80 (BO) Dorchester, MA St. Brendan.
McMahon, Charles E. *s.s.j.* '58 (BLX) Pascagoula, MS St. Peter the Apostle; College of Consultors.
McMahon, Craig *o.m.v.* '90 (BO)[U] Milton, MA Oblate Residence (St. Joseph House).
McMahon, Edward J. *s.j.* '60 (NY)[DD] New York, NY Xavier Jesuit Community.
McMahon, Francis X. *s.s.e.* '54 (BUR) Putney, VT Our Lady of Mercy Retired.
McMahon, Gerard J. '59 (ROC) Retired.
McMahon, Rev. Msgr. John J. '48 (PHX)[G] Phoenix, AZ Mount Claret Roman Catholic Retreat Center Retired.
McMahon, Rev. Msgr. John '66 (PMB) Elected Members Retired.
McMahon, Joseph R. '71 (WIL) Wilmington, DE St. Mary·Magdalen; Apostleship of Prayer.
McMahon, Joseph S. '68 (P) Lake Oswego, OR Our Lady of the Lake; Liturgical Commission.
McMahon, Joseph V. '84 (NSH) Nashville, TN Christ the King.
McMahon, Joseph '84 (NSH) Presbyteral Council.
McMahon, Rev. Msgr. Kevin T. '75 (WIL) On Duty Outside the Diocese.
McMahon, Rev. Msgr. Kevin T. '75 (COL)[A] Columbus, OH Pontifical College Josephinum.
McMahon, Kieran M. '65 (SAC) Sacramento, CA Cathedral of the Blessed Sacrament.
McMahon, Michael F. '88 (CHI) Antioch, IL St. Peter.
McMahon, Michael J. '04 (PRO) Providence, RI St. Augustine.
McMahon, Patrick *o.carm.* '76 (WDC)[B] Washington, DC Whitefriars Hall; [B] The Carmelitana Library.
McMahon, Timothy M. *s.j.* '87 (DEN)[D] Denver, CO Arrupe Jesuit High School; [N] Denver, CO Regis Jesuit Community (The Jesuits at Regis University).
McMahon, Walter M. '73 (SJ) San Jose, CA Church of the Transfiguration.
McManaman, Kevin (MIL) Shorewood, WI St. Robert; Whitefish Bay, WI Holy Family.
McManamon, James *o.f.m.* '49 (CLV)[N] Brooklyn, OH St. Anthony of Padua Friary.
McManamon, John M. *s.j.* '80 (DET)[K] Detroit Detroit Province of the Society of Jesus–Provincial Office.
McManamon, John M. *s.j.* '80 (CHI)[C] Chicago, IL Jesuit Community at Loyola University Chicago.
McManus, Dennis Douglas '05 (MOB) On Leave from the Archdiocese.
McManus, Dominic J. *o.p.* '11 (CHI)[N] Chicago Dominicans (Provincial Office).
McManus, Eamon '54 (WDC) Retired.
McManus, Francis J. *s.j.* '73 (BO)[U] Weston, MA Campion Jesuit Community.
McManus, Rev. Msgr. Gerald D. '79 (PH) Military Chaplains; Air Force Chaplains.
McManus, Rev. Msgr. Hugh F. '61 (NY) Scarsdale, NY Our Lady of Fatima.
McManus, Michael K. '85 (FR) Raynham Center, MA St. Ann; Chancellor; Diocesan Consultors; Members.
McManus, Rev. Msgr. Michael '48 (SAT)[K] San Antonio, TX Casa De Padres Retired.
McManus, Paul C. '65 (DUB) Retired.
McManus, Paul G. '87 (BO) Peabody, MA St. John the Baptist; Salem, MA Immaculate Conception.
McManus, Rev. Msgr. Paul J. '42 (BO) Senior Priests. Retired.
McManus, Richard *o.f.m.* '82 (LA)[P] Santa Barbara, CA Franciscan Friary, Order of Friars Minor (Old Mission).
McManus, Rev. Msgr. Robert T. '52 (PH) Retired.
McMaster, Brian '01 (AUS) Vocations.
McMenamy, Alvin *s.m.* '53 (STL)[O] St. Louis, MO Maryland Avenue Marianist Community.
McMichael, Steven J. *o.f.m.cap.* '03 (STP)[C] St. Paul, MN University of St. Thomas.
McMichael, Steven *o.f.m.conv.* '02 (STP)[M] Prior Lake, MN Franciscan Retreats; [J] Prior Lake, MN St. Joseph Cupertino Friary.
McMichael, Thomas '09 (SEA) Burlington, WA St. Charles; La Conner, WA Sacred Heart; Sedro Woolley, WA Immaculate Heart of Mary; Mount Vernon, WA Immaculate Conception.
McMillan, Cliff J. '90 (DEN) Glenwood Springs, CO St. Stephen.
McMillan, John F. *c.p.* '56 (PIT)[M] Pittsburgh, PA St. Paul of the Cross Monastery.
McMillan, Robert G. *s.j.* '62 (BO)[U] Boston, MA Loyola House; Members.
McMillen, Michael *s.c.j.* '67 (MIL)[P] Hales Corners Priests of the Sacred Heart.
McMillin, Charles '02 (LKC) Jennings, LA Our Lady Help of Christians.
McMorrow, Matthew '05 (RCK) Special Assignment; Scouts; [B] Rockford, IL Boylan Central Catholic High School.
McMullan, John '61 (SEA) Retired.
McMullen, Francis R. '51 (RVC) Retired.
McMullen, John *o.s.b.* '66 (SFS) Wilmot, SD St. Mary; [F] Marvin, SD Blue Cloud Abbey; [I] Marvin, SD Blue Cloud Abbey Retirement Trust; [I] Marvin, SD Asociacion Benedictina de Coban Resurrection Priory.
McMullen, Patrick M. '06 (CIN) Cincinnati, OH Our Lady of the Visitation.
McMullen, Roger '67 (SHP) Retired.
McMullin, Daniel T. '81 (ROC)[N] Ithaca, NY The Cornell Catholic Community, Inc. (Ithaca); Ithaca, NY Cornell University.
McMurry, John E. *s.s.* '56 (BAL)[Q] Baltimore Society of St. Sulpice, Province of the United States; [M] Baltimore, MD St. Charles Villa Retired.
McMurry, John E. *s.s.* '56 (NSH) Retired.
McMurry, Vincent deP. *s.s.* '49 (BAL)[M] Baltimore, MD St. Charles Villa; [Q] Baltimore Society of St. Sulpice, Province of the United States Retired.
McMurry, Vincent deP. *s.s.* '49 (NSH) Retired.
McNair, Andrew *l.c.* '97 (PRO) Black Catholic Ministry; West Warwick, RI SS. John and James Parish.
McNalis, John P. '76 (CHI) Other Assignments.
McNally, Dennis E. *s.j.* '74 (PH)[C] Jesuit Fathers; [Y] Loyola Center and Manresa Hall.
McNally, Edward F. '95 (SY) Absent on Leave.
McNally, Joseph J. '58 (IND) Retired.
McNally, Lawrence R. '77 (CHI) Oak Park, IL Ascension.
McNally, Michael J. '73 (PMB) Fort Pierce, FL St. Mark the Evangelist.
McNally, Michael R. '59 (SB) Retired.
McNally, Nathan *o.f.m.* '57 (STL)[O] St. Louis, MO Franciscan Friary of St. Anthony of Padua.
McNally, Richard *ss.cc.* '75 (FR)[F] Fairhaven National Center of the Enthronement.
McNally, Stephen '86 (RIC) Fincastle, VA Church of the Transfiguration; New Castle, VA Saint John the Evangelist Mission; Clifton Forge, VA St. Joseph.
McNally, Theodore A. *o.f.m.* '55 (PAT)[N] Ringwood, NJ Holy Name Friary, Inc.
McNally, Thomas *c.s.c.* '59 (FTW)[H] Notre Dame Congregation of Holy Cross, United States Province of Priests & Brothers.
McNally, Vincent M. *s.j.* '48 (NY)[DD] New York, NY Murray–Weigel Hall.
McNamara, Anthony *o.carm.* '69 (JOL)[L] Darien Carmelite Provincial Office.
McNamara, Rev. Msgr. Brian J. '84 (RVC) Priests' Retirement Board; Secretary for Ministerial Personnel; Clergy Personnel; Priests' Personnel Assignment Board; Priests' Personnel Policy Board; Garden City, NY St. Joseph's.
McNamara, Brian J. '84 (MO) Air Force Reserve Chaplains.
McNamara, Daniel J. *s.j.* '80 (FgM) New York, NY Society of Jesus.
McNamara, Dennis L. *s.j.* '76 (WDC)[O] Washington, DC The Jesuit Community at Georgetown University.
McNamara, Donald P. '61 (PH) Retired.
McNamara, Rev. Msgr. Eugene P. '53 (BO) Senior Priests. Retired.
McNamara, Rev. Msgr. James M. '71 (RVC) Nesconset,

NY Church of the Holy Cross.
McNamara, Rev. Msgr. John P. '56 (CHI) Palatine, IL St. Theresa Retired.
McNamara, Michael J. '80 (BO) Hanson, MA St. Joseph the Worker.
McNamara, Rev. Msgr. Patrick V. '60 (NY) New Rochelle, NY St. Gabriel.
McNamara, Philip D. '56 (WOR) Retired.
McNamara, Philip *s.a.c.* '58 (FWT) Stephenville, TX St. Brendan; Stephenville, TX Our Lady of Guadalupe; Stephenville, TX Sacred Heart.
McNamara, Robert J. '69 (LA) Woodland Hills, CA St. Bernardine of Siena.
McNamara, Rev. Msgr. Stephen E. '67 (VEN) Fort Myers, FL Church Of The Resurrection Of Our Lord; Vicar General; College of Consultors; Deans; Priest Personnel Board; Priest Personnel Board; Presbyteral Council; Pastor's Peer Review Committee.
McNamara, Thomas J. '82 (SAG) Saginaw, MI Cathedral of Mary the Assumption; Vicar General; Diocesan College of Consultors.
McNamara, Thomas *o.f.m.cap.* '07 (NY) New York, NY Our Lady of Sorrows.
McNamara, William '65 (SAT) Elmendorf, TX St. Anthony; Archdiocesan Council of Catholic Women.
McNamee, Rev. Msgr. Charles W. '50 (RCK) Censores Librorum Retired.
McNamee, Francis G. '95 (ATL) Vicars for Clergy; Priest Personnel; College of Consultors; Atlanta, GA Cathedral of Christ the King.
McNamee, James P. '73 (LC) Adams, WI St. Joseph; Adams, WI St. Ann.
McNamee, John P. '59 (PH) Retired.
McNamee, Patrick '70 (P) Beaverton, OR St. Cecilia; Area Vicars; Building Commission.
McNea, Mark C. '89 (WIN) Rochester, MN St. Francis of Assisi; Diocesan Consultors.
McNeeley, Maurice '58 (HON) Retired.
McNeeley, William J. '07 (KNX) Alcoa, TN Our Lady of Fatima.
McNeely, Matthew *f.s.s.p.* '07 (SAC) "Ecclesia Dei" Community (Latin Mass); Sacramento, CA St. Stephen the First Martyr Parish.
McNeese, Robert J. '98 (SPK) Spokane, WA St. Augustine.
McNeil, Aubrey *o.f.m.* '85 (CHR) Anderson, SC St. Mary of the Angels.
McNeil, Dennis '75 (CLV) Brunswick, OH St. Ambrose.
McNeil, Joel '87 (DM) On Special Assignment; Des Moines, IA St. Catherine of Siena Catholic Student Center; [I] Des Moines, IA St. Catherine of Siena Catholic Student Center; On Duty Outside the Diocese.
McNeil, Joel (DM) Campus Ministry.
McNeil, John R. '61 (BO) On Duty Outside the Archdiocese. Retired.
McNeil, Lawrence J. '73 (HBG) Hanover, PA Basilica of the Sacred Heart of Jesus; Presbyteral Council; Consultors, College.
McNeil, Lawrence J. '73 (BAL)[A] Emmitsburg, MD Mount St. Mary's Seminary.
McNeill, Donald *c.s.c.* '65 (FTW)[H] Notre Dame Congregation of Holy Cross, United States Province of Priests & Brothers; [B] University of Notre Dame Du Lac; [H] Notre Dame, IN Holy Cross Community, Corby Hall, University of Notre Dame.
McNeill, Neil (LAF) Mermentau, LA St. John the Evangelist.
McNeilly, Dennis P. *s.j.* '85 (OM)[J] Omaha, NE Jesuit Community at Creighton University.
McNelis, Paul D. *s.j.* '77 (NY)[DD] Cardinal Spellman Hall, Jesuit Community.
McNellis, Paul *s.j.* '87 (BO)[U] Newton, MA The Jesuit Community at Boston College.
McNew, Dwayne A. '95 (COL) Portsmouth, OH Holy Redeemer.
McNulty, Edward P. '93 (SD) San Diego, CA Saint Agnes Catholic Parish; Adjutant Judicial Vicar; Clergy Personnel Board; Presbyteral Council.
McNulty, Francis J. '52 (NEW)[L] Caldwell, NJ The Rev. Msgr. James F. Kelley Residence for Retired Priests Retired.
McNulty, Gerard J. '67 (LA) Retired.
McNulty, James '03 (DET) Livonia, MI St. Edith.
McNulty, John P. '73 (CLV) Cleveland Heights, OH Communion of Saints Parish.
McNulty, John T. '74 (PRO) Newport, RI St. Augustin.
McNulty, Joseph D. '69 (CLV) Cleveland, OH St. Augustine; Office of Ministry for Persons with Disabilities.
McNulty, Martin J. '03 (BO) Permanent Disability.
McNulty, Michael T. *s.j.* '73 (WDC)[O] Washington, DC The Jesuit Community of St. Aloysius Gonzaga.
McNulty, Patrick J. '60 (FTW) Retired.
McNulty, Rev. Msgr. Patrick '53 (LA) Los Angeles, CA St. Bernard Retired.
McNulty, Robert E. '56 (NOR) Retired.
McNulty, William J. '61 (CHI) Lake Forest, IL St. Patrick Retired.
McNulty, William J. '64 (NOR) Retired.
McPadden, Charles J. *m.m.* '69 (NY)[DD] Maryknoll Maryknoll Fathers and Brothers Retired.
McPartlan, Rev. Msgr. Paul '84 (WDC)[C] Catholic University of America, The.
McPartland, Guy *o.carm.* '55 (NEW) Teaneck, NJ Carmelite Chapel of St. Therese.
McPartland, Guy *o.carm.* '55 (JOL)[L] Darien Carmelite Provincial Office.
McPartland, Patrick '08 (TR) Toms River, NJ St. Joseph.
McPartland, Paul G. '57 (BO) Senior Priests. Retired.
McPhail, J. Stuart *o.p.* '69 (PRO)[O] Providence St. Thomas Aquinas Priory at Providence College.
McPhee, Rev. Msgr. Marvin '65 (SFS) Retired.
McPhillips, James G. '83 (CLV) Newbury, OH St. Helen; Chardon, OH Geauga Community Hospital.
McProud, Bryce '11 (P) Eugene, OR St. Mary.
McQuade, Brian '94 (RVC) Commack, NY Christ the King.
McQuade, Donald P. *m.m.* '65 (SJ)[M] Los Altos, CA Maryknoll.
McQuade, James F. *c.s.p.* '56 (NY)[DD] New York, NY Paulist Fathers' Motherhouse; Roosevelt Site.
McQuade, Richard E. '57 (BO) Senior Priests. Retired.
McQuaid, Thomas W. '79 (CHI) Other Assignments.
McQuaide, Joseph F. '11 (WIL) Dover, DE Holy Cross.
McQuesten, Mark A. '87 (MAR) Bark River, MI St. Elizabeth Ann Seton; Executive Board.
McQuillan, Cornelius T. *c.ss.p.* '75 (SJN)[F] Dorado, PR Santuario del Espiritu Santo.
McQuillen, Paul *s.s.e.* '77 (MOB) Montgomery, AL St. Jude Parish; [J] Montgomery, AL City of St. Jude, Inc., The; [G] Selma, AL Edmundite Fathers.
McQuillen, Thomas J. '96 (TOL) Mansfield, OH St. Peter.
McQuinn, Peter B. '91 (CHI) Arlington Heights, IL Our Lady of the Wayside.
McQuone, Kevin '10 (PT) Panama City, FL St. Dominic.
McRae, Rev. Msgr. Cornelius M. '61 (BO) Trustees.
McReynolds, Eugene *o.s.b.* '70 (OM) Boys Town, NE Immaculate Conception B.V.M.; [J] Elkhorn, NE Mount Michael Benedictine Abbey.
McShane, John A. '57 (BRK)[R] Douglaston, NY Bishop Mugavero Residence Retired.
McShane, John '74 (LAV) Caliente, NV Holy Child; Amargosa Valley, NV Christ of the Desert Catholic Church.
McShane, Joseph M. *s.j.* '77 (NY)[C] Bronx, NY Fordham University; [DD] Cardinal Spellman Hall, Jesuit Community.
McShane, Thomas S. *s.j.* '60 (OM)[J] Omaha, NE Jesuit Community at Creighton University.
McSherry, John G. *s.j.* '72 (NY)[DD] New York, NY Jesuit Community of the Immaculate Conception.
McSherry, John *s.v.d.* '61 (CHI)[N] Techny, IL Divine Word Residence.
McSherry, John *s.v.d.* '61 (TR)[N] Bordentown, NJ Society of the Divine Word.
McSherry, Patrick *o.f.m.cap.* '78 (DET)[K] Detroit, MI Provincialate; [K] Detroit St. Bonaventure Friary.
McSherry, Thomas '71 (OKL) Oklahoma City, OK St. Patrick.
McSorley, Aidan *o.s.b.* '69 (KC)[A] Conception, MO Conception Seminary College; [J] Conception, MO Conception Abbey.
McSorley, Gerald Hugh '64 (LA) Los Angeles, CA St. Bernard Retired.
McSorley, Matthew T. *o.s.b.* '49 (CHL)[J] Belmont, NC Belmont Abbey.
McSpiritt, John *s.t.* '59 (WDC)[O] Adelphi, MD Father Judge Missionary Cenacle.
McStravog, Patrick B. '89 (CAM)[C] Richland, NJ St. Augustine Preparatory School.
McSweeney, Brian T. '88 (NY) Cold Spring, NY Our Lady of Loretto.
McSweeney, James '74 (SR) Middletown, CA St. Joseph.
McSweeney, Jeremiah F. '72 (WH) Wheeling, WV St. Michael.
McSweeney, Rev. Msgr. John J. '74 (CHL) Charlotte, NC St. Matthew.
McSweeney, Rev. Msgr. John R. '61 (BUR) Judges Retired.
McSweeney, Joseph *s.s.c.* '58 (PRO)[O] Bristol, RI St. Columban's Retirement House.
McSweeney, Joseph *s.s.c.* '58 (OM)[J] St. Columbans Missionary Society of St. Columban.
McSweeney, Liam P. '63 (SAC) Fair Oaks, CA St. Mel.
McSweeney, Rev. Msgr. Thomas J. '71 (E) Erie, PA Holy Trinity.
McSweeney, William *o.m.i.* '52 (BO)[X] Tewksbury, MA Immaculate Heart of Mary Residence.
McSweeny, Joseph *s.s.c.* '90 (FgM)[J] St. Columbans Missionary Society of St. Columban; St Columbans, NE House of Post–Graduate Studies.
McSwiggan, Rev. Msgr. Thomas '67 (SAT) Retired.
McTaggart, Rev. Msgr. Edward P. '55 (SFR) San Mateo, CA St. Gregory; Serra Club of San Francisco (Golden Gate); [S] San Francisco, CA Archdiocesan Council of Catholic Women Retired.
McTavey, Lawrence '55 (ALB) Retired.
McTeigue, Robert J. *s.j.* '97 (BAL)[Q] Towson Maryland Province of the Society of Jesus.
McTighe, Edward P. *s.j.* '61 (P)[D].
McTigue, Norman P. '70 (BUF) Retired.
McVean, John J. *o.f.m.* '67 (NY) New York, NY St. Francis of Assisi.
McVeigh, James E. '73 (PH) Retired.
McVeigh, John J. '58 (LAV) Retired.
McWeeney, Brian E. '73 (NY) Mount Vernon, NY SS. Peter and Paul.
McWhorter, Michael L. '92 (ATL) Fayetteville, GA St. Gabriel.
Mead, Gary M. '97 (NY) New York, NY Holy Trinity.
Mead, James Herbert *s.j.* '62 (NO)[R] New Orleans, LA Ignatius Residence Retired.
Mead, Leland C. '68 (NU) Retired.
Meade, Denis *o.s.b.* '55 (FgM)[I] Atchison, KS St. Benedict's Abbey; [A] Atchison, KS Benedictine College; Atchison, KS St. Benedict's Abbey; Judges.
Meade, James W. '81 (CIN) Cincinnati, OH Corpus Christi.
Meade, James W. '86 (GRY) Chesterton, IN St. Patrick.
Meade, Maurice P. '48 (BO) Senior Priests. Retired.
Meade, Pachomius *o.s.b.* '09 (KC)[A] Conception, MO Conception Seminary College.
Meagher, Rt. Rev. Cletus *o.s.b.* '71 (BIR)[I] Cullman, AL St. Bernard Preparatory School Educational Foundation; [I] Cullman, AL St. Bernard Abbey Foundation.
Meagher, Rev. Msgr. Frank J. '60 (COL) College of Consultors Retired.
Meagher, Joseph A. '92 (NEW) Respect Life Office; Jersey City, NJ St. John the Baptist.
Meagher, Rev. Msgr. Michael T. '65 (SY) Binghamton, NY Saints John & Andrew; Priests' Personnel Committee.
Meagher, Thomas L. '64 (DET) White Lake, MI St. Patrick.
Mealey, Mark S. *o.s.f.s.* '79 (ARL) Vienna, VA Our Lady of Good Counsel; [L] Arlington, VA Rooted in Faith–Forward in Hope, Inc.; Vicar General for Administration and Moderator of the Curia; Diocesan Judges; Diocesan Consultors; Provincial Councilors:; Judicial Vicar; [L] Arlington, VA Arlington Diocesan Investment and Loan Corp.; [L] Arlington, VA The Foundation for the Catholic Diocese of Arlington, Inc.
Meaney, Brendan J. '65 (CAM) Retired.
Meaney, Patrick '87 (CC)[G] Hebbronville, TX Catholic Solitudes.
Means, David A. '81 (STL) On Duty Outside the Archdiocese.
Means, David A. '81 (JC) Chamois, MO Most Pure Heart of Mary; Chamois, MO Assumption.
Meany, John J. *o.p.* '87 (CHI)[N] Chicago, IL St. Pius V Priory.
Meany, John J. *o.p.* '87 (IND) Bloomington, IN St. Paul Catholic Center, Bloomington, Inc.
Meany, Michael G. '80 (CHI) Niles, IL St. John Brebeuf.
Meany, Neill R. *s.j.* '54 (YAK) Diocesan Catholic Committee on Scouting.
Meany, Neill R. *s.j.* '54 (SPK)[J] Spokane, WA Regis Community.
Meares, Clyde Timberlake '02 (R) Rocky Mount, NC Our Lady of Perpetual Help.
Measer, Donald L. '63 (BUF) Tonawanda, NY St. Amelia Retired.
Mecca, Gregg D. '96 (BGP) Danbury, CT St. Peter.
Meccia, Francis S. *m.m.* '66 (NY)[DD].
Mech, John J. '95 (DET) Troy, MI St. Anastasia.
Mecir, Joseph S. '80 (CLV) Hinckley, OH Our Lady of Grace.
Meconi, David V. *s.j.* '03 (STL)[C] Saint Louis University; [O] St. Louis, MO Jesuit Community Corporation at Saint Louis University – Jesuit Hall.
Mecwel, Pawel J. '90 (MAR) St. Ignace, MI Immaculate Conception; St. Ignace, MI St. Ignatius Loyola.
Medairos, Anthony J. '73 (BO) Carver, MA Our Lady of Lourdes.
Medas, Michael B. '88 (BO)[CC] Braintree, MA KOLBE Association, Inc.; Clergy Personnel; [A] Brighton, MA St. John Seminary; Air Force Reserve Chaplains; Milton, MA St. Elizabeth.
Medeiros, Antonio F. '93 (BO)[B] Chestnut Hill, MA Redemptoris Mater Archdiocesan Missionary Seminary.
Medeiros, Antonio S. '54 (BO) Senior Priests. Retired.
Medeiros, Arnold R. '75 (FR) North Falmouth, MA St. Elizabeth Seton; Pocasset, MA St. John the Evangelist.
Medeiros, Benjamin *t.o.r.* '77 (ALT)[G] Loretto, PA St. Francis Friary at Mount Assisi.
Medeiros, Leonel S. '04 (BGP) Priest Vocation Advisory Board; Assistant Vocation Directors; Presbyteral Council; Members of the Clergy Personnel Committee.
Medeiros, Paul *o.m.i.* '64 (FgM) Washington, DC AMERICAN OBLATE MISSIONS.
Mediana, Gil '81 (DAL) Mesquite, TX Divine Mercy of Our Lord.
Medina, David '02 (TLS) Tulsa, OK St. Francis Xavier Church and Diocesan Marian Shrine & Expiatory

Temple of Our Lady of Guadalupe; Seminary Board.
Medina, Eduardo '04 (PMB) Port St. Lucie, FL Holy Family.
Medina, Efrain '01 (MRY) Gonzales, CA St. Theodore; Clergy Personnel Board.
Medina, Fabio E. '83 (SFR) Menlo Park, CA St. Anthony.
Medina, Rev. Msgr. Francisco '89 (SJN) Istepa.
Medina, George A. '87 (TR) Trenton, NJ St. Joseph; Censores Librorum.
Medina, George '87 (PCE) On Duty Outside the Diocese.
Medina, Gilbert '07 (ORL) Eustis, FL St. Mary of the Lakes.
Medina, Hector '84 (FWT) Arlington, TX St. Matthew; Consultors.
Medina, Ignazio C. '78 (JC) Bonnots Mill, MO Our Lady Help of Christians; Linn, MO St. George; VIII. Westphalia.
Medina, Israel *m.n.m.* (ARE) Camuy, PR Our Lady of the Miraculous Medal.
Medina, Jesus S. '10 (MIA) Miami, FL St. John Neumann.
Medina, Joel *s.j.* '11 (CHI)[D] Chicago, IL St. Ignatius Jesuit Community.
Medina, Jose Antonio '82 (SJ) Sunnyvale, CA St. Martin.
Medina, Jose de Jesus '06 (CHI) Chicago, IL St. Bede the Venerable.
Medina, Jose *f.s.c.b.* '00 (BO) Lexington, MA; [U] Lexington, MA Priestly Fraternity of the Missionaries of St. Charles Borromeo, Inc.; [D] Boston, MA Cristo Rey Boston High School, Inc.
Medina, Juan B. '69 (CGS) Caguas, PR San Pablo Apostol.
Medina, Julian '73 (SAC) Sacramento, CA St. Peter; Sacramento, CA All Hallows.
Medina, Leonardo '07 (TLS) Hispanic Ministry; Special Assignment.
Medina, Mauricio '64 (B) Cursillo Movement Retired.
Medina, Rolando '71 (MIA) Retired.
Medina–Algaba, Felix P. '04 (DEN) Denver, CO St. James.
Medina–Cruz, Jamie '99 (ALX) Cottonport, LA St. Mary Assumption.
Medio, Joseph Paul *f.p.o.* '99 (BO)[U] Lawrence, MA Franciscans of Primitive Observance; On Duty Outside the Archdiocese.
Medipalli, Kiran Kumar (STA) Jacksonville, FL Sacred Heart.
Medley, Rev. Msgr. Robert W. '90 (MET) Plainsboro, NJ Queenship of Mary; Office of Worship and Episcopal Ceremonies; Liturgical Advisor.
Medlin, Douglas S. '02 (ATL) Retired.
Medlock, Scott '96 (ANC) Anchorage, AK St. Patrick; Diocesan Consultors.
Medow, David '01 (JOL) Plainfield, IL St. Mary Immaculate.
Medrano, Adolfo *o.carm.* '08 (JOL)[L] Darien Carmelite Provincial Office.
Medrano, Marcus '86 (DEN) Retired.
Medrek, Tomasz '04 (ARL) Alexandria, VA St. Lawrence.
Medve, Kenneth A. '97 (ALN)[C] Tamaqua, PA Marian Catholic High School; Elected Members; Lansford, PA St. Katharine Drexel Parish.
Medwid, John M. '90 (ALB) Amsterdam, NY St. Mary.
Mee, Michael (Brian) *o.s.b.* '78 (SPK) Spokane, WA St. Peter.
Mee, Michael *o.s.b.* '78 (P)[L] St. Benedict, OR Mt. Angel Abbey.
Meehan, Barry M. '78 (PRO) Warwick, RI St. Timothy.
Meehan, Gabriel '59 (CHL) Retired.
Meehan, Gery G. *o.praem.* '60 (GB)[J] De Pere, WI St. Joseph Priory.
Meehan, James N. *s.j.* '59 (SPK)[B] Spokane, WA Gonzaga University.
Meehan, James T. *s.j.* '63 (FgM) New York, NY Society of Jesus.
Meehan, Joseph J. '61 (PH) Springfield, PA St. Francis of Assisi Retired.
Meehan, Joseph '66 (STA) Retired.
Meehan, Kenneth E. *s.j.* '71 (WDC)[O] Washington, DC The Jesuit Community of St. Aloysius Gonzaga; [E] Washington, DC Gonzaga College High School.
Meehan, Peter '68 (NY) New York, NY Our Lady of the Rosary.
Meehan, T. J. '72 (ATL) Atlanta, GA The Basilica of the Sacred Heart of Jesus.
Meehan, Terence A. '67 (CIN) Retired.
Meehan, Thomas J. *o.s.a.* '80 (PH)[F] Malvern, PA Malvern Preparatory School for Boys; [Y] Malvern, PA Augustinian Friars (O.S.A.).
Meehan, Timothy A. '59 (HRT) North Haven, CT St. Therese; North Haven, CT St. Frances Cabrini.
Meeks, Delphyn J. '83 (BEA) Buna, TX St. Francis of Assisi Mission; Mauriceville, TX St. Maurice.
Meenihan, Regis J. '92 (E) Retired.
Meeuwsen, Jeffrey '07 (P) Forest Grove, OR St. Anthony; North Plains, OR St. Edward; [P] Forest Grove, OR Pacific University (Forest Grove).
Megge, Paul '98 (GLD) Cheboygan, MI St. Mary–St. Charles; Pellston, MI St. Clement; Pellston, MI Sacred Heart.
Mehan, Joseph A. '96 (DAL) Garland, TX St. Michael the Archangel; Procurator–Advocates.
Mehm, Richard J. '77 (BO) Malden, MA Immaculate Conception.
Mehrkens, Rev. Msgr. William '50 (CR) Diocesan Board of Conciliation and Arbitration Retired.
Meidl, Gerald S. '74 (NU) Hutchinson, MN Church of St. Anastasia; Stewart, MN Church of St. Boniface.
Meier, Rev. Msgr. Allen J. '51 (COV) Retired.
Meier, Denis E. '63 (MO) DEPARTMENT OF VETERANS AFFAIRS HOSPITALS AND CHAPLAINS.
Meier, Denis '63 (SFS) Retired.
Meier, Emeric *o.f.m.* '68 (BO)[Z] Boston, MA St. Anthony Shrine.
Meier, Gary M. '98 (STL) Deaneries/Deans; Saint Louis, MO Sts. Teresa and Bridget.
Meier, Gerald A. '66 (STL) Affton, MO St. Dominic Savio.
Meier, John P. (FTW)[B] University of Notre Dame Du Lac.
Meier, Rev. Msgr. John P. '67 (NY) On Duty Outside the Archdiocese.
Meier, Laverne G. '58 (MAD)[F] Madison, WI Bishop O'Connor Catholic Pastoral Center Retired.
Meier, Timothy *s.j.* '91 (MO) Army National Guard Chaplains.
Meiklejohn, Norman *a.a.* '54 (WOR)[N] Worcester, MA Assumptionists (Augustinians of the Assumption).
Meiman, Louis J. '87 (L) Louisville, KY St. Francis of Assisi; Ex Officio.
Meinen, Dennis W. '87 (SC)[D] Sioux City, IA Holy Spirit Retirement Home; [C] Sioux City, IA Mercy Medical Center – Sioux City Retired.
Meiners, Andrew *c.ss.r.* '70 (STL)[O] Liguori, MO Liguori Mission House/Redemptorists.
Meinholz, John '77 (MAD) Bloomington, WI St. Mary; Cassville, WI St. Charles Borromeo; Cassville, WI St. Mary Help of Christians; Bloomington, WI St. John; Diocesan Consultors.
Meirose, Harold R. *s.j.* '62 (DET)[K] Clarkston, MI Colombiere Center.
Meis, Anthony '72 (JOL) Retired.
Meis, Peter *o.f.m.cap.* '67 (FgM) Denver, CO Province of Mid–America.
Meisel, Rev. Msgr. Charles F. '50 (BAL) Retired.
Meisel, Gerald A. '61 (LA) Long Beach, CA St. Matthew Retired.
Meismer, Paul J. '69 (PEO) Retired.
Meissner, Robert J. '69 (SAG) Bay City, MI St. Vincent de Paul; Diocese of Saginaw Priests' Retirement Association.
Meitl, Roger K. '59 (SAL) St. Francis, KS St. Joseph Parish; St. Francis, KS St. Francis of Assisi Parish.
Mejia, Gustavo '68 (LA) Los Angeles, CA Resurrection.
Mejia, Jose '91 (LA) Lynwood, CA St. Philip Neri.
Mejia, Manuel J. *m.m.* '63 (SFR) Holy Childhood Association Coordinator.
Mejia, Manuel J. *m.m.* '63 (NY)[DD] Retired.
Mejia, Miguel '00 (SPK) Cheney, WA St. Rose of Lima; Detention Ministry.
Mekkat, Benny *c.f.i.c.* (STP) St. Paul, MN St. Mary.
Melaba, Daniel Ter '91 (SAV) Macon, GA St. Peter Claver.
Meladath, Mathew '99 (SYM) Berkley, MI St. Mary's Syro–Malabar Knanaya Catholic Church of Detroit.
Melancon, Andre '11 (HT) Houma, LA Cathedral of St. Francis De Sales.
Melancon, Bill '93 (LAF) Erath, LA Our Lady of Lourdes.
Melancon, J. Aaron '97 (LAF) Milton, LA St. Joseph.
Melancon, Rev. Msgr. Louis '63 (LKC) Retired.
Melancon, Mark '04 (LAF) Mamou, LA St. Ann.
Melancon, Thomas J. *s.j.* '74 (STL)[O] St. Louis, MO Jesuit Community Corporation at Saint Louis University – Jesuit Hall.
Melaniuk, J. Maciej '86 (MET) South Plainfield, NJ Our Lady of Czestochowa.
Melcher, Michael '92 (LUB) Anson, TX St. Michael; Vicars Forane; Priests' Pension Board; Presbyteral Council.
Melchior, Carl J. '09 (SP) Clearwater, FL St. Catherine of Siena; Elected Parochial Vicars; Vocations Office.
Melchior, Frank '59 (GB) Retired.
Melchior, Gerald P. '90 (OM) Omaha, NE St. Bernard; Deans; Deans.
Melchior, Thomas '65 (KCK) Retired.
Mele, Carmen *o.p.* '80 (FWT) Pope John Paul II Institute for Lay Ministry; Fort Worth, TX St. George.
Mele, Joseph M. '73 (PIT)[A] Pittsburgh, PA Saint Paul Seminary; Post–Ordination Formation, Department for; Pre–Ordination Formation, Department for; St. Paul Seminary; Priest Council; Clergy Personnel Board.
Meledom, Joseph '68 (FWT) Burkburnett, TX St. Jude Thaddeus.
Melendez, Daniel J. '02 (CAM) On Leave of Absence.
Melendez, Elberto '04 (RNO) Battle Mountain, NV St. John Bosco.
Melendez, Emlio '91 (BRK) Brooklyn, NY St. Brigid.
Melendez, Fernando '93 (R) Red Springs, NC St. Andrew.
Melendez, Hector '80 (PAT) Clifton, NJ SS. Cyril and Methodius.
Melepuram, John P. '78 (PH) Abington, PA Our Lady Help of Christians; Indian Apostolate–Knanayan Comm. Syro–Malabar Rite.
Melepuram, John '78 (SYM) Philadelphia, PA St. Thomas Syro–Malabar Catholic Church (Philadelphia).
Melevage, Rev. Msgr. F. J. '42 (GRY) Retired.
Melfi, F. Patrick '06 (BUF) Council of Priests; Limestone, NY St. Patrick; Salamanca, NY Our Lady of Peace.
Meliams–Figueredo, Esteban '03 (SJN) San Juan, PR Resurreccion del Senor.
Melillo, William J. '66 (NEW)[C] West Orange, NJ Seton Hall Preparatory School Retired.
Melito, Ignatius M. *c.m.* '51 (STL)[O] St. Louis, MO Lazarist Residence.
Melka, John *o.c.d.* '64 (P)[Q] Mount Angel, OR Carmelite House of Studies.
Melle, James J. '72 (PH) Retired.
Melley, James J. '77 (MIA) Retired.
Mellitt, John *o.f.m.cap.* '75 (RVC) East Patchogue, NY St. Joseph the Worker.
Mello, Jay '07 (FR) Vocations; Falmouth, MA St. Patrick's.
Mello, Matthew '87 (ORL) Lakeland, FL Church of the Resurrection.
Melloh, John A. *s.m.* '61 (STL)[O] St. Louis Marianists, Province of the United States (Society of Mary).
Mellone, Rev. Msgr. Michael J. '76 (WDC) Washington, DC St. Thomas Apostle.
Mellone, Vincent P. '65 (BO) Woburn, MA St. Barbara; Presbyteral Council.
Melmer, John H. '91 (ARL) Manassas, VA All Saints.
Melnic, Rev. Msgr. James T. '78 (PHU) McAdoo, PA St. Michael's; McAdoo, PA St. Mary's; [D] Philadelphia, PA Ascension Manor, Inc.; Board Members.
Melnick, James P. '09 (LR) Conway, AR St. Joseph.
Melnick, John E. '86 (SCR) On Duty Outside the Diocese.
Melnick, John P. '00 (HRT) Enfield, CT St. Bernard.
Melnick, John *s.s.a.* '86 (KCK) Kansas City, KS St. Mary–St. Anthony.
Melnick, John *s.s.a.* '86 (KCK)[K] Kansas City, KS Society of St. Augustine – Public Association of the Faithful.
Melnick, Robert *o.f.m.conv.* (RCK) Rockford, IL St. Anthony of Padua.
Melnick, William D. '75 (WIL) Unassigned or Leave of Absence.
Melnicki, Claudio '10 (SJP) Parma, OH St. Josaphat Cathedral.
Melo, Fidel C. '96 (CHL) Greensboro, NC Our Lady of Grace; [O] Charlotte, NC Diocesan Hispanic Ministry; Hispanic Ministry.
Melo, Nicholas P. '83 (HRT) Southington, CT St. Thomas.
Melocoton, Carlos L. '09 (WH) Charleston, WV Basilica of the Co–Cathedral of the Sacred Heart.
Melody, William P. *c.s.c.* '59 (FTW)[H] Holy Cross House.
Melone, Rt. Rev. Archimandrite Mark E. '78 (NTN) Lawrence, MA St. Joseph.
Melton, Thomas K. '59 (TLS) Retired.
Meluskey, Andre J. '59 (HBG) Carlisle, PA Saint Patrick Retired.
Melvin, Thomas P. '01 (WIN) Rollingstone, MN St. Mary's; Rollingstone, MN Holy Trinity; [A] Winona, MN Immaculate Heart of Mary Seminary; Vocations; Vicar for Clergy; Diocese of Winona Incardination Board; Rollingstone, MN St. Paul's; Elected Deanery Representatives; Priest Assignments Committee; Vicar for Clergy; Vicar for Clergy.
Memenas, Vytas '57 (JOL) Shorewood, IL Holy Family Retired.
Mena, Abel '02 (SR) Crescent City, CA St. Joseph; Diocesan Judges.
Mena, Antonio '81 (ELP) Fabens, TX Our Lady of Guadalupe; Presbyteral Council.
Mena, Jesus Maria *o.a.r.* '86 (ELP) El Paso, TX Guardian Angel.
Mena, Jose '92 (NY) Bronx, NY St. Joan of Arc.
Mena–Mena, Sergio '10 (CHI) Cicero, IL St. Frances of Rome; Cicero, IL Our Lady of Charity.
Menapace, James L. '63 (MAR) Retired.
Menard, Clarence *o.m.i.* '59 (SAT)[K] San Antonio, TX Oblate Madonna Residence.
Menard, Gerard E. *s.j.* '99 (DEN)[N] Denver, CO Regis Jesuit Community (The Jesuits at Regis University).
Menard, Gilbert B. '55 (OG) Judges Retired.
Menasco, Edward T. '90 (OKL) Norman, OK St. Joseph's; Special Assignment; Priests' Retirement Trust Fund; Region I–B; Advocates.
Menchaca, Gerardo '95 (SJ) San Jose, CA Cathedral Basilica of St. Joseph.
Mencias, Jaime '90 (ANC) Palmer, AK St. Michael.
Mende, Dennis W. '83 (BUF) Jamestown, NY Holy

Apostles; [G] Jamestown, NY Catholic Academy of the Holy Family.
Mendem, Marianand '93 (KCK) Burlington, KS St. Francis Xavier; Burlington, KS St. Patrick; Burlington, KS St. Joseph; Burlington, KS St. Teresa.
Mendes, Joseph *m.s.f.s.* '63 (ATL) Lawrenceville, GA St. Marguerite D'Youville; Snellville, GA; [F] Snellville, GA The Missionaries of St. Francis De Sales.
Mendes, Joseph *m.s.f.s.* '63 (TYL)[C] Whitehouse, TX The Missionaries of St. Francis de Sales.
Mendes, Rony '06 (BRK) Brooklyn, NY Our Lady of Refuge.
Mendez, Angel Mendez '90 (MGZ) Moca, PR Our Lady of Monserrate.
Mendez, Angel (SJN) Clergy Social Security (Prevision Social del Clero).
Mendez, David Perez '87 (MGZ) Maricao, PR St. John the Baptist.
Mendez, Fernando *c.o.r.c.* (FWT) Fort Worth, TX Immaculate Heart of Mary.
Mendez, Francisco '60 (ARL) Retired.
Mendez, Jaime Alejandro Olayo *s.j.* '11 (BO)[U] Brighton, MA Miguel Pro House.
Mendez, Jose C. *c.o.r.c.* '07 (SB) Barstow, CA St. Joseph; Barstow, CA St. Philip Neri.
Mendez, Juan '73 (SFE) Albuquerque, NM Nativity of the Blessed Virgin Mary.
Mendez, Luis A. *s.e.m.v.* '95 (ARE) Arecibo, PR Our Lady of Guadalupe.
Mendez, Oscar A. *o.f.m.* '89 (OAK) Oakland, CA St. Elizabeth; [L] Oakland, CA Franciscan Friars (Province of St. Barbara).
Mendez, Oscar *s.j.* '64 (MIA)[H] Miami, FL Villa Javier Retired.
Mendez, P. Carlos F. '09 (MGZ) Aguadilla, PR St. Charles Borromeo.
Mendez, Rafael '93 (MGZ) San German, PR San German de Auxerre.
Mendez, Winston R. '03 (PCE) Ponce, PR Good Shepherd Parish.
Mendez–Cobos, Manuel (MAD) Madison, WI Good Shepherd Parish.
Mendez–Hernandez, Rafael '94 (SJN) Guaynabo, PR Maria Madre de la Misericordia.
Mendez Izquierdo, Jose Carmen '02 (CHI) Maywood, IL St. Eulalia; Presbyteral Council.
Mendicoa, John M. (BO) Roslindale, MA Sacred Heart.
Mendis, Linus (BO) Lynnfield, MA Our Lady of the Assumption.
Mendl, Michael *s.d.b.* '78 (NY)[DD] New Rochelle, NY Salesian Provincial House.
Mendonca, John '79 (BRK) Rego Park, NY Our Lady of the Angelus.
Mendonca, Johnny '91 (RVC) Franklin Square, NY St. Catherine of Sienna.
Mendonca, Robert '00 (OAK) Livermore, CA St. Michael; Deanery #14.
Mendonca, Walter *s.v.d.* '76 (FgM) Techny, IL.
Mendoza, Andres '95 (LUB) Lubbock, TX Our Lady of Guadalupe; Priests Personnel Board; Vicars Forane.
Mendoza, Anthony Maria *o.s.b.* '95 (SAT) San Antonio, TX Santo Nino de Cebu.
Mendoza, Diodoro '11 (HPM) Phoenix, AZ St. Stephen Cathedral.
Mendoza, Eduardo W. *p.e.s.* '99 (SAC) Dixon, CA St. Peter.
Mendoza, Francis '04 (LA) Los Angeles, CA Nativity; Los Angeles, CA St. Columbkille; Members.
Mendoza, Francisco *s.s.s.* '83 (CLV)[N] Cleveland, OH Congregation of the Blessed Sacrament.
Mendoza, Gerald *o.p.* '09 (AUS)[G] Austin, TX Dominican Friars of Austin.
Mendoza, Gerardo '88 (SB) Fontana, CA St. George.
Mendoza, Jose Eduardo '84 (SFR) San Francisco, CA Visitacion, Church of the.
Mendoza, Jose '99 (OM) Omaha, NE Our Lady of Guadalupe – St. Agnes Parish.
Mendoza, Oscar Juan '99 (TLS) Tulsa, OK St. Francis Xavier Church and Diocesan Marian Shrine & Expiatory Temple of Our Lady of Guadalupe; Hispanic Ministry.
Mendoza, Paul Christian '10 (OAK) San Ramon, CA St. Joan of Arc.
Mendoza, R. Anthony '99 (LAR) La Pryor, TX St. Joseph; Vicar General; College of Consultors; Office of Respect Life; Priests Personnel Board; Ex Officio Members.
Mendyuk, Jaroslav '93 (STN).
Mendyuk, Yaroslav '93 (STN) Munster, IN St. Josaphat; Presbyteral Council.
Menegatto, Gaetano *c.s.j.* '42 (CLV)[N] Avon, OH Congregation of St. Joseph.
Menegay, David C. '88 (PIT) Absent on Sick Leave; Louisville, OH St. Louis.
Menegay, Greg '98 (PHX) Gilbert, AZ St. Mary Magdalene Roman Catholic Parish; Presbyteral Council; Priests' Assurance Association.
Menei, Francis T. '67 (PH) On Duty Outside the Archdiocese.
Menei, Francis '67 (HBG) Manheim, PA St. Richard.
Menendez, Adolph J. *s.x.* '68 (BO)[U] Holliston, MA Xaverian Missionaries.
Menendez, Jose L. '77 (MIA) Miami, FL Corpus Christi.
Meneses, Isaque '10 (FRS) Lemoore, CA St. Peter Prince of Apostles.
Meneses, Miguel '61 (ELP) Retired.
Menezes, Mark '59 (JOL) Monee, IL St. Boniface.
Menezes, Wade *c.p.m.* '00 (OWN)[F] Auburn, KY Fathers of Mercy.
Meng, David P. '89 (ARL) Lake Ridge, VA St. Elizabeth Ann Seton; Diocesan Consultors.
Mengel, Mark M. *s.s.c.* '71 (SPR) Springfield, MA Holy Name; Presbyteral Council.
Mengel, Mark *s.s.c.* '71 (OM)[J] St. Columbans Missionary Society of St. Columban.
Menghini, Peter D. '80 (SCR)[K] Elmhurst Twp., PA St. Mary's Villa Nursing Home; [K] Moscow, PA St. Mary's Villa Residence; Roaring Brook Twp., PA St. Eulalia.
Mengon, Albert *s.d.b.* '66 (MRY) St. Francis Central Coast Catholic High School, Inc.; [C] Watsonville, CA St. Francis Youth Center; [F] Watsonville, CA Saint Francis Salesian Community; Watsonville, CA Our Lady Help of Christians.
Menig, Walter J. *c.m.* '47 (PH)[Y].
Menihane, Daniel J. '57 (PH)[Y] Villanova, PA St. Thomas Monastery.
Meninger, William *o.c.s.o.* '58 (DEN)[N] Snowmass, CO St. Benedict's Monastery.
Menjivar, Evelio '04 (WDC) Washington, DC St. Matthew Cathedral.
Menke, Andrew V. '99 (LIN) On Duty Outside the Diocese.
Menke, George R. *s.j.* '75 (IND)[D] Indianapolis, IN Brebeuf Jesuit Preparatory School, Inc.
Menke, Paul F. '66 (LA) Retired.
Menker, Joseph *o.m.i.* '53 (BEL)[F] Belleville, IL Shrine of Our Lady of the Snows.
Menkhus, James *o.f.m.cap.* '73 (PIT) Freedom, PA St. Felix; Rochester, PA St. Cecilia; [M] Beaver, PA St. Fidelis Friary.
Menna, Rev. Msgr. Francis A. '64 (PH) Darby, PA Retired.
Menna, Michael J. '99 (PRO) Providence, RI St. Ann.
Menner, Michael L. '93 (PEO) Penfield, IL St. Lawrence's; [O] Moline, IL The Order of the Legion of Little Souls of the Merciful Heart of Jesus.
Menner, Robert J. '68 (STL) On Duty Outside the Archdiocese.
Menniti, Daniel J. '53 (HBG) Carlisle, PA Saint Patrick Retired.
Mens, Theodore J. '67 (GRY) Griffith, IN St. Ann; Griffith, IN St. Mary; Pro–Life Activities; Bishop's Council of Priests.
Mensah, Emmanuel T. (BAL) Baltimore, MD St. Ursula.
Mensah, Gabriel Justus '90 (VIC) On Duty Outside the Diocese; Navy Chaplains; Victoria, TX Our Lady of Sorrows.
Mensah, Isaac Ebo (BO) Bedford, MA St. Michael.
Mensah, John M. '86 (NY) Staten Island, NY Holy Family.
Mensah, Tony Kyere '83 (MO) DEPARTMENT OF VETERANS AFFAIRS HOSPITALS AND CHAPLAINS.
Mensinger, Gary J. '98 (PSC) Old Forge, PA St. Nicholas; Retirement Plan Board; Notaries; Presbyteral Council.
Menty, Ronald '69 (ALB) Albany, NY All Saints Catholic Church; Priestly Life and Ministry Council; Members; Priests Placement Committee; Priests Retirement Board/Priests Retirement Plan Board.
Menuba, Elias '74 (HRT)[H] Hartford, CT Saint Francis Hospital and Medical Center.
Meny, Hilary G. '40 (IND) Retired.
Menzel, William G. '67 (LC) Retired.
Meogrossi, Romuald *o.f.m.conv.* (BAL) Baltimore, MD St. Casimir.
Meogrossi, Romuald *o.f.m.conv.* '68 (WDC)[C] Catholic University of America, The.
Mera–Vallejos, Jose E. '09 (HBG) Lancaster, PA Iglesia Catolica San Juan Bautista.
Mercado, Edwin A. '86 (ARE) Arecibo, PR Santa Ana.
Mercado, Floyd '03 (FAJ) Humacao, PR Concathedral Dulce Nombre de Jesus.
Mercado, Heriberto '06 (LUB) Morton, TX St. Ann.
Mercado, Jose A. '06 (HRT) Office for Hispanic Evangelization; Hartford, CT St. Augustine; [S] Bloomfield, CT Office for Hispanic Evangelization; Special and other Archdiocesan Assignment.
Mercado, Marco A. '98 (CHI) Chicago, IL St. Gall; Consejo Pastoral Arquidiocesano Hispano – Americano; Ethnic Offices.
Mercado, Miguel '83 (ARE) Arecibo, PR Nuestra Senora del Carmen.
Mercado, Rev. Msgr. Thaddeus F. '67 (HON) Pearl City, HI Our Lady of Good Counsel; [C] Honolulu, HI St. Francis Healthcare System of Hawaii.
Merced, Miguel A. '00 (CGS) Diocesan Tribunal of Caguas; Punta Santiago, PR Nuestra Senora del Carmen.
Merced, Roberto *o.p.* '06 (BR) Hammond, LA Holy Ghost; Tickfaw, LA Our Lady of Pompeii.
Merced Reyes, Miguel A. '00 (FAJ) Sec. Chancellor.
Mercer, David '87 (SJ) San Jose, CA St. Christopher.
Mercer, Robert *s.a.* '82 (NY)[DD] Garrison Franciscan Friars of the Atonement, Minister General Office.
Mercieca, Cyprian J. *t.o.r.* '61 (ALT)[G] Hollidaysburg, PA St. Bernardine Monastery Retired.
Mercier, Rev. Msgr. Joseph '55 (BLX) Retired.
Mercier, Ronald A. *s.j.* '87 (BO)[U] Boston The Society of Jesus of New England–Provincial Offices.
Mercier, Ronald A. *s.j.* '87 (STL)[O] St. Louis, MO Bellarmine House of Studies; [C] Saint Louis University.
Mercieri, Dennis J. '05 (NOR) Rockville, CT St. Bernard.
Mercure, Jerome '79 (BUR) Canon 1742 Panel of Pastors; Waterbury, VT St. Andrew; State Hospital; Vermont Cursillo.
Mercurio, Gregory (BO) Lynn, MA Holy Family.
Merdian, Rev. Msgr. Mark J. '93 (PEO) Champaign, IL St. Matthew.
Merdinger, Philip E. '64 (BO)[A] Brighton, MA St. John Seminary.
Meredith, John R. '80 (OWN) Owensboro, KY Blessed Mother; [J] Owensboro, KY Gideon Productions, Inc.; Television and Radio Broadcast Communications.
Meredith, Richard '78 (OWN) Judges; Ongoing Formation of Priests; Hopkinsville, KY SS. Peter and Paul.
Mergenhagen, John J. '54 (BUF) Retired.
Mericantante, John J. '75 (PMB) Pahokee, FL St. Mary.
Merino, Rev. Msgr. Baudilio '48 (SJN) Rio Piedras, PR Nuestra Senora de la Providencia; Police Chaplains.
Merino, Santiago James '46 (LA) Retired.
Merino Merino, Rev. Msgr. Baudilio '48 (SJN) Catholic Charismatic Renewal.
Meriwether, Stephen A. '83 (SFR) Defenders of the Bond; San Francisco, CA Most Holy Redeemer.
Merkatoris, Ralph '58 (GB) Retired.
Merkel, Thomas *s.j.* (OM)[C] Omaha, NE Creighton Preparatory School.
Merkelis, John D. *o.s.a.* '85 (CHI)[N] Chicago, IL The Augustinians–Provincialate.
Merkelis, John D. *o.s.a.* '85 (JOL)[C] New Lenox, IL Providence Catholic High School; [L] New Lenox, IL Augustinian Friary.
Merkle, Charles W. '88 (ARL) Annandale, VA St. Ambrose.
Merkovsky, Paul W. '90 (PIT) McMurray, PA St. Benedict the Abbot.
Merkt, Joseph T. '66 (L) Louisville, KY St. Francis of Assisi Retired.
Merkt, Michael F. '81 (MIL) Menomonee Falls, WI St. Mary.
Merlino, Darrin *c.m.f.* '00 (LA)[V] Los Angeles, CA Tepeyac House.
Merman, Rev. Msgr. Raymond F. '60 (ALN)[J] Bethlehem, PA Holy Family Villa Retired.
Merold, James E. '71 (CHI) Chicago, IL St. Gabriel Retired.
Merrick, Andrew '08 (BR) Belle Rose, LA St. Jules; Paincourtville, LA St. Elizabeth.
Merrill, Thomas *o.f.m.conv.* '79 (STP) Shakopee, MN St. Mark; Shakopee, MN Church of St. Mary; Shakopee, MN St. Mary of the Purification; [J] Prior Lake, MN St. Joseph Cupertino Friary; [M] Prior Lake, MN Franciscan Retreats.
Merris, Christopher '82 (MO) Military Chaplains; Navy Chaplains.
Merry, Paul F. '71 (BGP) Danbury, CT St. Peter.
Mersinger, Norbert A. '55 (STL) Retired.
Merta, Lawrence '02 (SFE) Moriarty, NM Estancia Valley Catholic Parish.
Mertens, Michael G. '45 (LC)[H] La Crosse, WI Holy Cross (Seminary) Diocesan Center Retired.
Mertensotto, Leon J. *c.s.c.* '56 (FTW)[B] University of Notre Dame Du Lac; [H] Notre Dame, IN Holy Cross Community, Corby Hall, University of Notre Dame.
Mertes, Mark '87 (KCK) Kansas City, KS Blessed Sacrament; Kansas City, KS Christ the King; Kansas City, KS Our Lady and St. Rose.
Mertes, Robert *s.v.d.* '78 (WDC)[O] Washington, DC Society of the Divine Word/Divine Word House.
Merwald, Melvin J. '71 (OM) Retired.
Merz, Albert *o.f.m.* '66 (NSH)[H] Nashville, TN Franciscan Friars.
Merz, Daniel J. '98 (JC) Liturgical Commission; On Duty Outside the Diocese.
Merz, Eugene F. *s.j.* '61 (MIL)[P] Milwaukee, WI Arrupe House Jesuit Community.
Merzweiler, David W. '77 (Y) North Jackson, OH Our Lady of the Lakes Parish, St. Catherine Church; North Jackson, OH Our Lady of the Lakes Parish, St. James Church.
Mesa, Jose A. *s.j.* '92 (CHI)[C] Chicago, IL Jesuit Community at Loyola University Chicago.
Mesa, Jose L. *s.j.* '77 (STA) Gainesville, FL St. Augustine.
Mesa, Luis (STL) On Duty Outside the Archdiocese.
Mesa, Ruel Z. '08 (SAC) Vacaville, CA St. Mary.
Mescall, Rev. Msgr. John '52 (NY) New Rochelle, NY Holy Family Retired.

Mescall, Thomas J. '04 (CHI) Chicago, IL St. Adrian; Chicago, IL Nativity of the Blessed Virgin Mary.
Mescher, Michael J. '83 (DUB) Tama, IA St. Patrick; Tama, IA St. Joseph; Belle Plaine, IA St. Michael; Deans; Directors.
Mesh, Moises L. *c.s.v.* '11 (CHI)[N] Arlington Heights Viatorian Province Center–Clerics of St. Viator.
Mesi, Vincent *o.f.m.* '72 (PHX) Phoenix, AZ St. Mary's Roman Catholic Basilica; Phoenix, AZ Banner Good Samaritan Medical Center.
Meskell, David B. '55 (BO) Senior Priests. Retired.
Meskill, Thomas A. '60 (LA) Retired.
Mesley, Jerome T. '73 (GLP) Retired.
Mesmer, William A. '68 (SY) Sherrill, NY St. Helena; Vernon, NY Holy Family.
Messaro, Michael A. *m.ss.cc.* '68 (HBG) Fairfield, PA St. Rita; Fairfield, PA Immaculate Conception of the Blessed Virgin Mary.
Messer, Joseph V. '61 (BAL) Retired.
Messer, Paul A. *s.j.* '67 (BO)[U] Weston, MA Campion Health Center, Inc.
Messer, Terrence *c.f.r.* '94 (NY)[DD] Bronx, NY Our Lady of the Angels Friary.
Messick, Severin *o.s.b.* '82 (IND) Greenfield, IN St. Michael Catholic Church, Greenfield, Inc.; [K] Saint Meinrad St. Meinrad Archabbey.
Messier, Gerard *a.a.* '58 (BO)[U] Brighton, MA Assumption Guild.
Messier, Gerard *a.a.* (NY) New York, NY St. Vincent de Paul.
Messina, Angelo '68 (ALX) Retired.
Messina, D. Andrew '09 (PRO) North Kingstown, RI St. Francis De Sales.
Messina, John '96 (BAL) Priests Sick or Absent.
Messina, Joseph '72 (CAM) Retired.
Messina, Richard C. '65 (BO) Winchester, MA St. Mary.
Messina, Samuel '65 (JKS) Batesville, MS St. Mary; Priests' Council.
Messina, Victor G. '74 (BR) Retired.
Messingue, Jean *s.j.* '11 (BO)[U] Newton, MA The Jesuit Community at Boston College.
Messler, Charles *c.r.* '11 (SB)[I] Apple Valley, CA Congregation of the Resurrection, CR.
Messner, Michael E. '98 (HBG) Lancaster, PA Sacred Heart of Jesus; [I] Lancaster, PA Franklin and Marshall College, Lancaster.
Messner, Thomas *o.f.m.* '67 (LA)[P] Santa Barbara, CA Franciscan Friary, Order of Friars Minor (Old Mission).
Mestas, Leonard J. '81 (MO) On Assignment Outside the Diocese; DEPARTMENT OF VETERANS AFFAIRS HOSPITALS AND CHAPLAINS.
Mestos, Leonard '81 (SB) Loma Linda, CA Jerry L. Pettis Memorial Veterans Hospital.
Mestriparampil, Thomas '89 (NY) East Elmhurst, NY George M. Motchan Detention Center; East Elmhurst, NY Otis Bantum Correctional Center; New York, NY St. Charles Borromeo.
Mesure, Rev. Msgr. Gerard C. '84 (PH) On Special or Other Archdiocesan Assignment; Conshohocken, PA St. Mary; West Conshohocken, PA St. Gertrude; The Chancery; Defenders of the Bond; Promoters of Justice; College of Consultors.
Mesure, Rev. Msgr. Gerard C. '84 (PH) Consultant.
Meszaros, James J. '69 (BRK) Bayside, NY St. Josaphat Retired.
Metcalf, Andrew '86 (SR) Santa Rosa, CA St. Rose of Lima.
Method, Fredrick '66 (DUL) Diocesan Deans; Buhl, MN Our Lady of the Sacred Heart; Chisholm, MN St. Joseph; College of Consultors.
Metrejean, Rev. Msgr. Paul '63 (LAF) Retired.
Metro, LeRoy '63 (SAL) Retired.
Metts, Ralph E. *s.j.* '73 (WDC)[O] Washington, DC The Jesuit Community at Georgetown University.
Metz, Bradley J. *c.s.c.* '02 (FTW)[B] University of Notre Dame Du Lac; [H] Notre Dame Congregation of Holy Cross, United States Province of Priests & Brothers; [H] Notre Dame, IN Holy Cross Community, Corby Hall, University of Notre Dame; [A] Notre Dame, IN Moreau Seminary; [A] Notre Dame, IN Moreau Seminary.
Metz, David '97 (SAL) Hanover, KS Sacred Heart Parish; Hanover, KS St. John the Baptist Parish; Washington, KS Saints Peter and Paul Parish; Washington, KS St. Augustine Parish.
Metz, Ken (ORL) Sanford, FL All Souls.
Metz, Kenneth J. '65 (MIL) Retired.
Metzbower, Francis X. *s.j.* '63 (BAL)[Q] Baltimore, MD Colombiere Jesuit Community.
Metzdorf, William C. '73 (WDC) Retired.
Metzger, Andrew *o.s.b.* '56 (SP)[N] Saint Leo, FL St. Leo Abbey.
Metzger, Christopher P. *c.f.r.* '06 (NY)[DD] Yonkers, NY St. Leopold's Friary.
Metzger, Rev. Msgr. Dennis M. '74 (TOL) Sylvania, OH St. Joseph; St. Luke Deanery; Members.
Metzger, Edwin '55 (ROC) Rochester, NY Our Mother of Sorrows Retired.
Metzger, John L. '67 (COL) Retired.
Metzger, Joseph H. '91 (RIC) Norfolk, VA Blessed Sacrament; Presbyteral Council.
Metzger, Rev. Msgr. Paul E. '43 (STU) Retired.
Metzger, Richard L. '67 (COL) Groveport, OH St. Mary.
Metzger, Rev. Msgr. Robert E. '60 (COL) Retired.
Metzger, Rev. Msgr. Sam S. '59 (TYL) Retired.
Metzger, Stephen A. '70 (COL) Utica, OH Church of the Nativity.
Metzger, Thomas H. '82 (LFT) Noblesville, IN Our Lady of Grace.
Metzger, William A. '78 (COL) Columbus, OH St. John the Baptist; Columbus, OH Sacred Heart; Diocesan Judges.
Metzger, William J. *o.s.f.s.* '71 (ARL) Vienna, VA Our Lady of Good Counsel.
Metzger, William J. '62 (COL) Retired.
Metzinger, John R. '82 (OKL) Edmond, OK St. John the Baptist; Council of Priests Archdiocesan; Consultors Archdiocesan.
Metzinger, John '82 (OKL)[K] Edmond, OK University of Central Oklahoma.
Metzler, Warren W. '64 (PIT) Pittsburgh, PA St. James.
Metzler, William R. '72 (HRT) Simsbury, CT St. Mary.
Meulemans, Carl P. *m.m.* '60 (NY)[DD] Maryknoll Maryknoll Fathers and Brothers Retired.
Meulemans, Dennis T. '61 (SUP) Board of Directors Retired.
Meulemans, Rev. Msgr. Edward G. '60 (SUP) Retired.
Meulemans, Thomas O. *o.praem.* '59 (PH)[Y] Paoli, PA Daylesford Abbey.
Meuret, Donald L. '84 (LC) Consultors; Thorp, WI St. Bernard–St. Hedwig Parish; Appointed Members.
Mevissen, Richard *c.ss.r.* '66 (MIL)[S] Oconomowoc, WI The Redemptorist Retreat Center.
Meyer, Albert *o.s.b.* '56 (MRY)[F] San Luis Obispo, CA Men's Residence.
Meyer, Arthur D. '61 (PEO) Lacon, IL Immaculate Conception Retired.
Meyer, Benedict *o.s.b.* '54 (IND)[K] Saint Meinrad, IN St. Meinrad Archabbey.
Meyer, Bernard A. '59 (SFD) Retired.
Meyer, Rev. Msgr. Charles R. '45 (CHI)[A] Mundelein, IL University of St. Mary of the Lake/Mundelein Seminary Retired.
Meyer, Daniel J. '82 (CIN) Dayton, OH Holy Angels; [U] Dayton, OH Catholic Alumni Club (Dayton Chapter).
Meyer, Dennis J. *m.s.* '70 (STL)[O] St. Louis, MO Missionaries of LaSalette, Province of Mary, Mother of the Americas; [O] St. Louis, MO La Salette Novitiate.
Meyer, Earl *o.f.m.cap.* '60 (SAL)[D] Hays, KS St. Joseph's Friary; Victoria, KS St. Fidelis Parish; [F] Victoria, KS Capuchin Center for Spiritual Life.
Meyer, Emmett F. '64 (OM) Retired.
Meyer, Eric *c.p.* '66 (CHI) Chicago, IL Immaculate Conception; [N] Chicago, IL Passionist Community–Immaculate Conception Community.
Meyer, Frederick A. '65 (STL) St. Charles, MO St. Peter.
Meyer, Frederick C. '56 (STP) Retired.
Meyer, Gerald J. '96 (PEO) Retired.
Meyer, Rev. Msgr. Gilbert '42 (FRS) Retired.
Meyer, Harold K. *o.c.s.o.* '62 (SAC)[A] Vina, CA Abbey of New Clairvaux, Trappist Seminary; [H] Vina, CA Abbey of New Clairvaux, Trappist.
Meyer, Harry J. '64 (CIN) Retired.
Meyer, James A. '94 (FAR) Diocesan College of Consultors.
Meyer, James '94 (FAR) West Fargo, ND Holy Cross Church of West Fargo; Deanery 2.
Meyer, James '60 (DET) Retired.
Meyer, John A. '82 (IND) Greensburg, IN St. Mary Catholic Church, Greensburg, Inc.
Meyer, John A. '82 (IND) Deaneries and Deans.
Meyer, John D. '08 (STP) St. Paul, MN Cathedral of Saint Paul.
Meyer, John R. '89 (POD) Los Angeles.
Meyer, John R. '89 (LA)[W] Los Angeles, CA Prelature of the Holy Cross and Opus Dei.
Meyer, Jonathan P. '03 (IND) North Vernon, IN St. Mary Catholic Church, North Vernon, Inc.; North Vernon, IN St. Ann Catholic Church, Jennings County, Inc.; North Vernon, IN St. Joseph Catholic Church, Jennings County, Inc.
Meyer, Leo A. '65 (NO) Liaisons Retired.
Meyer, Luke D. '06 (FAR) Special Assignment; [I] Fargo, ND Catholic Chaplains Association; Chancellor and Secretary to the Bishop; Archivist; Notaries; Corporate Board; Diocesan Finance Council; Office of Worship and Sacraments; Holy Childhood Association; Propagation of the Faith; Liaison with Charismatic Movement.
Meyer, Nick '52 (SFD)[K] Sherman, IL Blessed Giles Friary.
Meyer, Robert G. '74 (WIN) Diocesan Consultors Retired.
Meyer, Robert J. '64 (PIT) Bridgeville, PA Holy Child; [M] Pittsburgh, PA St. John Vianney Manor.
Meyer, Rev. Msgr. Robert S. '88 (NEW) Hoboken, NJ Ss. Peter and Paul Church; Defenders of the Bond.
Meyer, Ronald *o.m.i.* '71 (NOR)[I] Willimantic, CT Immaculata Retreat House; [G] Willimantic, CT Missionary Oblates of Mary Immaculate.
Meyer, Stephen L. '79 (DUB)[O] Webster City, IA St. Thomas Aquinas Foundation; Webster City, IA St. Thomas Aquinas; Williams, IA St. Mary.
Meyer, Steven J. '90 (FAR) Wimbledon, ND St. Mary's Church of Dazey; Wimbledon, ND St. John's Church of Kensal; Wimbledon, ND St. Boniface Church of Wimbledon.
Meyer, Thomas C. '98 (SFD) Jacksonville, IL Our Saviour; [M] Jacksonville, IL Illinois College Newman Catholic Community; [M] Jacksonville, IL MacMurray College Newman Catholic Community; Comite Diocesano de Ministerio Hispano – Diocesan Committee for Hispanic Ministry; Board of Catholic Education; Priests' Personnel Board.
Meyer, Thomas E. '70 (CIN) Dayton, OH St. Albert the Great.
Meyer, Thomas *o.m.i.* '70 (BEL)[F] Belleville, IL Missionary Oblates of Mary Immaculate – St. Henry's Oblate Residence.
Meyer, William J. *s.m.* '79 (STL) Councilors:; [O] St. Louis, MO Marianists, Province of the United States (Society of Mary); [O] Saint Louis, MO Salve Marianist Community.
Meyer, William O. '49 (DAV) Davenport, IA Our Lady of Victory Retired.
Meyers, James P. '70 (WDC) Rockville, MD St. Raphael.
Meyers, John F. '83 (PH) Philadelphia, PA St. Martin of Tours.
Meyers, Rev. Msgr. John F. '56 (DAL) Dallas, TX St. Monica Retired.
Meyers, Rev. Msgr. Michael M. '77 (LA) Redondo Beach, CA St. James.
Meyers, Nathaniel Rene Francis '10 (STP) St. Michael, MN St. Michael.
Meyers, Robert V. '87 (MET) Laurence Harbor, NJ St. Lawrence.
Meyr, Herbert J. '60 (CHI) Melrose Park, IL Sacred Heart Retired.
Meysenburg, James J. '89 (LIN) Lincoln, NE Cathedral of the Risen Christ; [C] Lincoln, NE Pius X Catholic High School; [L] Lincoln, NE Pius X Foundation and Pius X Endowment Fund.
Meystrik, Gregory C. '90 (JC) Jefferson City, MO St. Margaret of Antioch; Jefferson City, MO St. Stanislaus; III. Jefferson City; Finance Committee; Chair Couple; Board of Trustees.
Meza, Rev. Msgr. Arturo '88 (AMA) Neocatechumenite.
Meza, Fernando '95 (SAC) Lincoln, CA St. Joseph.
Meznar, Joseph A. '58 (DEN) Retired.
Mezquida, Ramon '58 (PCE) On Duty Outside the Diocese.
Mezydlo, James A. '77 (CHI) Chicago, IL St. Florian.
Mfodwo, Francis (NY) Poughkeepsie, NY Our Lady of Mt. Carmel.
Mgaya, Bruno (B) Boise, ID St. Mark's.
Mgbeajuo, Donatus C. *m.s.p.* '97 (SAV) Columbus, GA St. Benedict the Moor.
Mgimba, Thadeo E. '08 (CHI) Harvey, IL Ascension–St. Susanna; Markham, IL St. Gerard Majella.
Mhagama, Laurent '08 (CHI) Midlothian, IL St. Christopher.
Mhanna, Andre '01 (OLL) Special Assignment.
Miah, Gabriel '77 (RVC) Mineola, NY Corpus Christi; Elmont, NY St. Boniface.
Miarecki, Marek '01 (PAT) Passaic, NJ Holy Rosary.
Micallef, Rene Mario *s.j.* '08 (BO)[U] Brighton, MA Miguel Pro House.
Micarelli, Edmond C. '59 (PRO) Retired.
Micca, Louis F. *s.a.c.* '66 (BAL) Baltimore, MD St. Jude Shrine.
Micciulla, Angelo J. '05 (NY) Suffern, NY Sacred Heart.
Micek, Sylvester '51 (SFD)[K] Sherman, IL Blessed Giles Friary.
Miceli, John P. '94 (CLV) Cleveland, OH St. Mark.
Miceli, Michael A. '97 (BR) Vacherie, LA Our Lady of Peace.
Miceli, Paul E. '72 (BO)[A] Weston, MA Blessed John XXIII National Seminary.
Miceli, Ross R. '10 (E) Ridgway, PA St. Leo the Great; [F] St. Marys, PA Elk County Catholic High School.
Miceli, Vincent F. '91 (BRK) Brooklyn, NY St. Fortunata.
Mich, Kenneth A. '70 (MIL) Menomonee Falls, WI Good Shepherd.
Michael, Babu '89 (RVC) Holbrook, NY Good Shepherd.
Michael, Rev. Msgr. Chester P. '42 (RIC) Retired.
Michael, David C. '86 (BO) Needham, MA St. Joseph; Vicariate III; Jewish Relations.
Michael, David F. (SAM) On Duty Outside the Diocese.
Michael, David '96 (CHR) Cheraw, SC St. Peter.
Michael, George *v.c.* '95 (SCL) Dent, MN Sacred Heart; Perham, MN St. Lawrence; [I] Saint Cloud, MN St. Joseph Province of the Vincentian Congregation.
Michael, Gnanadhas George '78 (NY) Wappingers Falls, NY St. Mary.
Michael, Rev. Msgr. Kenneth '65 (OLL) Retired.
Michael, Lawrence P. '75 (SAM) Torrington, CT St. Maron.
Michael, Peter *s.v.d.* '40 (FgM) Techny, IL.

Michael, Tukura *o.p.* '02 (WDC) Washington, DC Children's Medical Center.
Michaels, Dana P. '82 (OAK) Alameda, CA St. Barnabas.
Michaels, Patrick T. '82 (SFR) Mill Valley, CA Our Lady of Mt. Carmel.
Michaelson, Sean D. *s.j.* '06 (SFR)[N] San Francisco, CA Loyola House Jesuit Community.
Michalak, Jan *o.s.p.p.e.* '81 (PH)[Y].
Michalak, Jaromir '91 (CAM) Clayton, NJ Parish of St. Michael the Archangel, Franklinville, N.J.
Michalchuk, Jack H. '01 (ALX) Bunkie, LA St. Anthony of Padua.
Michalcka, John J. '59 (OKL) Retired.
Michalczak, John T. '70 (NEW) Teaneck, NJ Holy Name Hospital; [F] School of Nursing.
Michalek, Rev. Msgr. George C. '78 (LAN) Lansing, MI St. Mary Cathedral; Bishop's Office; Diocesan Archivist; Judicial Vicar; Tribunal Judges.
Michalek, Stanislaw *s.ch.* '88 (SEA) Seattle, WA St. Margaret of Scotland; Polish Speaking, Ministry to.
Michalenko, Alexei '68 (HPM) On Special Assignment.
Michalenko, Seraphim *m.i.c.* '56 (SPR)[G] John Paul II Institute of Divine Mercy; [G] Stockbridge, MA Congregation of Marian Fathers of The Immaculate Conception of the Most Blessed Virgin Mary.
Michaletz, James E. *c.s.v.* '60 (JOL) Bourbonnais, IL Maternity of the Blessed Virgin Mary.
Michaletz, James E. *c.s.v.* '60 (CHI)[N] Arlington Heights, IL Viatorian Province Center–Clerics of St. Viator.
Michalik, Gary '80 (DET) Livonia, MI St. Colette.
Michalisin, Gregory J. '92 (PBR) Windber, PA St. Mary (Dormition) Church; Notaries; Elected Deanery Representatives; Windber, PA SS. Peter and Paul.
Michalowski, John W. *s.j.* '81 (BO)[U] Boston The Society of Jesus of New England–Provincial Offices.
Michalowski, John W. *s.j.* '81 (MAN) Salem, NH Saints Mary and Joseph.
Michalowski, Marcin '11 (PAT) Rockaway, NJ St. Cecilia's; Rockaway, NJ Sacred Heart.
Michalski, Edward '80 (WOR) Leominster, MA St. Cecilia.
Michalski, James L. *s.j.* '72 (OM)[J] Omaha, NE Jesuit Community at Creighton University.
Michalski, Jan (STP) Minneapolis, MN Holy Cross.
Michalski, Melvin E. '70 (MIL)[B] Hales Corners, WI Sacred Heart School of Theology Retired.
Michalski, Michael F. '76 (MIL) Milwaukee, WI SS. Peter and Paul; Milwaukee, WI Old St. Mary; Milwaukee, WI Our Lady of Divine Providence; Milwaukee, WI Three Holy Women Catholic Parish.
Michalski, Simon Felix *o.p.* '08 (JC)[D] Columbia, MO St. Thomas More Newman Center; Columbia, MO St. Thomas More Newman Center, University of Missouri.
Michatek, William C. '66 (ROC) Retired.
Michaud, Gregory A. '09 (LC) Custer, WI Sacred Heart; Rosholt, WI St. Adalbert; Stevens Point, WI St. Mary; [C] Wausau, WI Newman Catholic High School.
Michaud, James L. '77 (PRT) Special or Other Diocesan Assignment.
Michel, Delix *s.s.l.* '88 (SFD) Alton, IL Ss. Peter and Paul; Black Catholic Advisory Board; Vandalia, IL Vandalia Correctional Center.
Michel, Engelbert G. '66 (PH)[CC] Philadelphia, PA Catholic Kolping Society; Philadelphia, PA St. Christopher.
Michel, Eugene *o.f.m.* '64 (STP) St. Paul, MN Sacred Heart; [J] St. Paul, MN Sacred Heart Friary.
Michel, Gabriel (BO) Haitian.
Michele, Robert P. *c.s.p.* '55 (AUS) Austin, TX St. Austin.
Michelini, Edward L. '05 (SCR) Dalton, PA Our Lady of the Abingtons; Nicholson, PA St. Patrick.
Michelini, Michael S. '71 (CHI) Chicago, IL St. Adalbert.
Michell, Timothy *o.c.s.o.* '65 (P)[L] Lafayette, OR The Cistercian (Trappist) Abbey of Our Lady of Guadalupe.
Michels, Andrew J. '85 (NU) Boy Scouts; Sleepy Eye, MN St. Mary; Priests' Council.
Michelson, Chris '80 (KNX) Deans of the Diocese; Presbyteral Council; Diocesan Finance Council; Ministries of the Smoky Mtn. Deanery; Knoxville, TN St. Albert the Great Church; [B] Knoxville, TN Saint Joseph School of Knoxville.
Michiels, Kenneth J. '91 (ALX) Appointed Members; Leesville, LA St. Michael; College of Consultors; Vocations and Seminarians.
Michiels, Philip F. '69 (SHP) Shreveport, LA St. Elizabeth Ann Seton; Shreveport, LA Overton Brooks Veteran's Administration Medical Center; Defenders of the Bond; Presbyteral Council; Diocesan Liturgy Commission; College of Consultors; DEPARTMENT OF VETERANS AFFAIRS HOSPITALS AND CHAPLAINS.
Michini, F. Joseph *s.j.* '80 (BAL)[D] Baltimore, MD Loyola Blakefield; [Q] Baltimore, MD Jesuit Community of Loyola University, Inc.
Michka, Aaron J. *c.s.c.* '09 (FTW)[H] Notre Dame Congregation of Holy Cross, United States Province of Priests & Brothers.
Michler, James R. '75 (STL) On Duty Outside the Archdiocese.
Michlik, Valerian '00 (SJP) Pittsburgh, PA St. George; Liturgical Commission; League of Ukrainian Catholics; Personnel Board; Vice Chancellor; Alternates; Presbyteral Council; Presbyters.
Michniewicz, Martin E. '86 (CHI) Palos Heights, IL St. Alexander.
Michota, Peter '85 (NEW) Absent on Leave.
Mick, Lawrence E. '72 (CIN) Retired.
Mick, Lawrence J. '49 (CIN) Cincinnati, OH St. Antoninus Retired.
Micka, A. *m.i.c.* '49 (JOL) Retired.
Mickey, Richard L. '88 (MEM)[F] Cordova, TN Villa Vianney Senior Priests Residence; Archives; Villa Vianney Priests Retirement Residence.
Mickiewicz, David '84 (ALB) Ecumenical and Interreligious Affairs of the Roman Catholic Diocese of Albany, Commission for; Members.
Mickiewicz, J. William '62 (MET) Califon, NJ St. John Neumann; Episcopal Vicars.
Mickler, Jeffrey *s.s.p.* '74 (Y)[A] Canfield, OH Society of St. Paul.
Mickus, James J. '72 (OKL) Chandler, OK Our Lady of Sorrows.
Miclot, Brian *ph.d.* '74 (DAV)[A] St. Ambrose University.
Midor, Adam '91 (TR) Roebling, NJ The Church of Saints Francis and Clare, Florence Township, N.J.
Midura, Rev. Msgr. Francis S. '70 (RVC) Hauppauge, NY St. Thomas More; Judges for Interdiocesan Tribunal; Presbyteral Council.
Midzak, Rt. Rev. Mitred Archpriest Ihor '90 (STF) Personnel Board; Stamford, CT St. Vladimir Cathedral; Vicar General; Diocesan Consultors; Presbyteral Council; Administrative Council; Directors; Chaplain to the Ukrainian American Youth Association.
Mieczkowski, Rev. Msgr. Chester J. '45 (BAL) Retired.
Miekina, Stanley *c.m.* '59 (HRT) New Haven, CT St. Stanislaus.
Miele, Joseph J. '56 (TR) Manasquan, NJ St. Denis Retired.
Mieliwocki, Richard J. '72 (NEW) Absent on Leave.
Mien, Francis '65 (SEA) Retired.
Mierenfeld, Lawrence E. '73 (CIN) Centerville, OH Incarnation; Vicarri Foranei (Deans).
Mierzwa, Ronald B. '76 (BUF) Ellicottville, NY Holy Name of Mary.
Mieszala, Raphael *b.g.s.* '05 (MIA)[F] Brothers of the Good Shepherd of Florida, Inc.
Mifsud, Carmelo '59 (OAK) Retired.
Migliore, Angelus *t.o.r.* '64 (SP) Cursillo, English; Tampa, FL St. Patrick.
Migone, Pablo '09 (SAV) Warner Robins, GA Sacred Heart.
Miguel, Eutiquiano *o.f.m.cap.* '51 (NO) New Orleans, LA St. Theresa of Avila; New Orleans, LA University Hospital.
Miguélez, Rev. Msgr. Valeriano '66 (SJN) San Juan, PR Espiritu Santo; [E] San Juan, PR Hospital Pavia; Police Chaplains; [E] San Juan, PR Centro Medico de P.R.; [B] San Juan, PR Colegio Espiritu Santo.
Miguez, Raul G. '99 (NY) Bronx, NY Blessed Sacrament.
Mihalak, James J. '76 (ALN) Retired.
Mihalco, John J. '83 (PBR) Sykesville, PA Holy Trinity; Protopresbyters; Defender of the Bond; Promoter of Justice; Elected Deanery Representatives; Du Bois, PA Nativity of the Mother of God.
Mihalic, Peter M. '76 (CLV) Fairport Harbor, OH St. Anthony of Padua.
Mihalik, Rev. Msgr. Alexis E. '64 (PBR) Retired.
Mihan, Rev. Msgr. John A. '59 (LA) Retired.
Mihayli, Gilbert *o.praem.* '43 (GB)[J] De Pere, WI St. Norbert Abbey.
Mijas, Paul J. '85 (RVC) Kings Park, NY St. Joseph's.
Mikalajunas, John E. '69 (SY) Utica, NY Holy Trinity.
Mikalofsky, Hilarion A. '75 (MIL) On Duty Outside the Archdiocese.
Mikalonis, Estanislao '05 (SJ) Milpitas, CA St. Elizabeth.
Mikes, Pavel '90 (FAR) On Duty Outside the Diocese.
Mikesch, Rev. Msgr. Gregory R. '75 (STL) Wildwood, MO St. Alban Roe; [V] St. Louis, MO Archdiocesan Stewardship Education Committee.
Mikhael, Elie Hares '95 (SAM) Miami, FL Our Lady of Lebanon; Young Adult Ministry.
Mikkelson, Scott '82 (AUS) Retired.
Mikobi, Alidor *c.j.* '02 (LA) Santa Maria, CA St. Louis de Montfort.
Mikolaitis, Vito E. '43 (CHI) Chicago, IL Holy Cross/ Immaculate Heart of Mary Retired.
Mikolajczyk, Bruno '88 (CC) Retired.
Mikolajczyk, Edward M. '73 (CHI) Evergreen Park, IL Queen of Martyrs; College of Consultors.
Mikonis, Gerald S. '74 (PIT) Charleroi, PA Mary Mother of the Church.
Miksch, Joseph A. '66 (OM) Columbus, NE St. Isidore.
Mikstay, Michael '81 (Y) Military Chaplains; Navy Chaplains.
Mikulanis, Rev. Msgr. Dennis '77 (SD) Vicars Forane; San Diego, CA San Rafael Catholic Parish; Cemetery Committee; Ecumenical and Interreligious Affairs.
Mikulcik, Kenneth '98 (OWN) Non–Parochial Assignments; Scouting Activities.
Mikulik, Kenneth E. '52 (GAL) Retired.
Mikulski, Marcin *o.s.p.p.e.* (NOR) Rockville, CT St. Joseph.
Mikus, Elemir '57 (DET) Retired.
Milanese, John M. '74 (BUR)[G] Randolph, VT Vermont Technical College; Randolph, VT Our Lady of the Angels.
Milani, Rev. Msgr. Joseph J. '50 (SJ) Cupertino, CA St. Joseph of Cupertino; Diocesan Clergy Personnel Board; [O] Cupertino, CA St. Joseph Cupertino Retirement Residence Retired.
Milano, Cleo J. '83 (BR) Plaquemine, LA St. John the Evangelist.
Milanowski, Paul '65 (GR) East Grand Rapids, MI St. Stephen Catholic Church.
Milbauer, Robert L. '66 (LA) Granada Hills, CA St. John Baptist de la Salle; Deanery 5.
Milby, Lawrence M. '65 (BUF) Retired.
Milek, Richard '83 (CHI) Chicago, IL St. Francis Borgia.
Miles, C. Thomas '99 (CHR) Promoter of Justice; Defenders of the Bond.
Miles, Cassian A. *o.f.m.* '61 (PAT)[N] Butler, NJ St. Anthony Friary.
Miles, James '78 (BAL) Baltimore, MD Little Flower, Shrine of.
Miles, James '78 (LKC) On Leave.
Miles, John *c.r.* '51 (L)[L] Louisville, KY Villa Pacis, Resurrectionist Retirement Home; Louisville, KY St. Margaret Mary; Louisville, KY.
Miles, Richard M. '84 (NO) Kenner, LA Our Lady of Perpetual Help.
Miles, Thomas '99 (CHR) Graduate Studies.
Milewski, Casimir '69 (TR) Retired.
Milewski, Douglas J. '89 (NEW)[A] South Orange, NJ Immaculate Conception Seminary School of Theology; [A] South Orange, NJ Immaculate Conception Seminary School of Theology.
Milewski, John A. '93 (MO) Presbyteral Council.
Milewski, John A. '93 (MO) DEPARTMENT OF VETERANS AFFAIRS HOSPITALS AND CHAPLAINS.
Milewski, Richard R. '83 (TR)[N] Trenton, NJ Villa Vianney.
Milewski, Rev. Msgr. Stanley E. '55 (DET) Priests Conference for Polish Affairs of the Archdiocese of Detroit Retired.
Miley, Eamon '73 (MOB) Special Assignment; Whistler, AL St. Bridget.
Milich, Nicholas '01 (YAK) On Duty Outside the Diocese.
Milienewicz, Rt. Rev. Frank J. '76 (NTN) Birmingham, AL St. George; Protopresbyters; College of Eparchial Consultors; Presbyteral Council.
Militante, Henry A. '84 (TR) Capital Health System: Mercer Campus & Fluid Campus; Trenton, NJ Blessed Sacrament–Our Lady of the Divine Shepherd Parish.
Millan, Jose Luis '00 (SPK) Pullman, WA Sacred Heart; Defenders of the Bond.
Millane, Rev. Msgr. Thomas J. '63 (TUC) Directors; Vicar for Retired Priests Retired.
Millard, Glen Michael '06 (BIS) Stanley, ND Queen of the Most Holy Rosary.
Millard, Mike '06 (BIS) Stanley, ND St. Ann.
Millbourn, Richard L. *s.j.* '01 (CHI)[E] Chicago, IL Chicago Jesuit Academy.
Millbourn, Richard *s.j.* '01 (CIN)[N] Cincinnati, OH Jesuit Community at St. Xavier High School.
Millea, Thomas V. (CHI) Retired.
Millea, Rev. Msgr. William V. '80 (BGP) On Duty Outside the Diocese.
Miller, Abraham '79 (STN) Seattle, WA Our Lady of Zarvanytsya.
Miller, Arnie (B) Boise, ID St. Mary's.
Miller, Bert '91 (FAR) West Fargo, ND Blessed Sacrament Church of West Fargo.
Miller, Bertin *o.f.m.* '64 (STL)[S] Dittmer, MO Il Ritiro–The Little Retreat.
Miller, Brendan *o.s.b.* '83 (LR)[A] Subiaco, AR Subiaco Abbey.
Miller, Brian M. '10 (ALN) Allentown, PA Cathedral of St. Catharine of Siena; Advocates.
Miller, Bruce '77 (ALX) Episcopal Vicar for Administration; Judges; Pineville, LA Sacred Heart; Appointed Members.
Miller, Byron J. *c.ss.r.* '90 (NO) New Orleans, LA St. Alphonsus; New Orleans, LA National Shrine of Blessed Francis Xavier Seelos; New Orleans, LA Blessed Seelos Center.
Miller, C. Anthony '80 (HBG) Lykens, PA Our Lady Help of Christians; Williamstown, PA Sacred Heart of Jesus.

Miller, Casper J. *s.j.* '64 (FgM) Chicago, IL Society of Jesus.
Miller, Charles E. '91 (SB) Idyllwild, CA Queen of Angels.
Miller, Charles J. *o.f.m.* '72 (NEW) Bloomfield, NJ Church of St. Thomas the Apostle.
Miller, Charles J. *o.f.m.* '66 (ARL) Triangle, VA St. Francis of Assisi.
Miller, Charles '72 (NEW) Members.
Miller, Christopher J. '08 (LIN) Lincoln, NE St. Peter; Advocates.
Miller, Christopher T. '93 (LFT) Frankfort, IN St. Mary; Vicar for Hispanic Ministry in White County; Special Assignment.
Miller, Cletus *o.s.b.* '44 (SFS)[F] Marvin, SD Blue Cloud Abbey; Marvin, SD Blue Cloud Abbey.
Miller, David L. '81 (SPC) Lebanon, MO St. Francis De Sales; Apostolate to the Deaf; Buffalo, MO St. William.
Miller, David P. '10 (CHL) Huntersville, NC St. Mark.
Miller, Dennis W. '02 (DUB) Deanery Representatives; Priests' Council; Britt, IA St. Patrick; Forest City, IA St. Patrick; Garner, IA St. Wenceslaus; Forest City, IA St. James; Garner, IA St. Boniface; Forest City, IA St. Patrick.
Miller, Donald A. *o.f.m.* '72 (CIN)[N] Cincinnati, OH Brother Juniper Friary.
Miller, Rev. Msgr. Edward M. '71 (BAL) Baltimore, MD St. Bernardine; Advocates; Priest Personnel Board.
Miller, Francis *o.c.d.* '49 (WDC)[B] Washington, DC Discalced Carmelite Friars Retired.
Miller, Rev. Msgr. Frank '54 (AUS) Retired.
Miller, Franklin '89 (FAR) Harvey, ND St. Cecilia's Church of Harvey; Selz, ND St. Anthony; Deanery 6.
Miller, Frederick L. '72 (NEW) On Duty Outside the Archdiocese.
Miller, Frederick L. '72 (BAL)[A] Emmitsburg, MD Mount St. Mary's Seminary.
Miller, Gary M. '72 (CHI) Evergreen Park, IL St. Bernadette.
Miller, George P. '78 (TOL) Judges.
Miller, Rev. Msgr. George P. '78 (DET) Judges; Clinton Township, MI St. Ronald.
Miller, Gregory *o.s.b.* '73 (SCL)[I] Collegeville, MN St. John's Abbey, of the Order of St. Benedict.
Miller, Jake '01 (FAR) Rolla, ND Immaculate Heart of Mary Church of Rock Lake; Rolla, ND St. Joachim's Church of Rolla.
Miller, James H. '68 (LC) Cashton, WI St. Augustine of Hippo Retired.
Miller, James H. *c.s.c.* (FTW)[H] Notre Dame Congregation of Holy Cross, United States Province of Priests & Brothers.
Miller, James L. '76 (DUB) Permanent Diaconate Formation Board; Marshalltown, IA St. Mary; Vicar for Hispanic Ministry; Deanery Representatives; [F] Marshalltown, IA Marshalltown Area Catholic Schools; Vicar for Hispanic Ministry; On Special or Other Archdiocesan Assignment.
Miller, James Norman '59 (NSH) Nashville, TN St. Mary of the Seven Sorrows; DEPARTMENT OF VETERANS AFFAIRS HOSPITALS AND CHAPLAINS.
Miller, James *c.pp.s.* '54 (CIN)[N] Carthagena, OH St. Charles Retired.
Miller, James '68 (FWT)[G] Crowley, TX St. Francis Village, Inc. Retired.
Miller, James *o.m.i.* '57 (SAT)[K] San Antonio, TX Oblate Madonna Residence.
Miller, John A. '08 (TOL) Bucyrus, OH Holy Trinity; Galion, OH St. Joseph.
Miller, John C. '95 (BRK) On Leave/Unassigned.
Miller, Rev. Msgr. John J. '64 (PH) Philadelphia, PA St. Michael; Philadelphia, PA Saint Martha.
Miller, John L. '09 (E) Erie, PA St. Peter Cathedral; [C] Erie, PA Cathedral Preparatory School.
Miller, John P. '78 (HEL) Columbia Falls, MT St. Richard; Deaneries.
Miller, John P. '82 (WCH) Cunningham, KS Sacred Heart; Nashville, KS St. Leo the Great; Zenda, KS St. Peter's; Zenda, KS St. John.
Miller, Joseph A. '89 (BRK) On Leave/Unassigned.
Miller, Joseph C. '49 (OWN) Retired.
Miller, Joseph K. '57 (SAG) Pinconning, MI St. Mary; Pinconning, MI St. Michael.
Miller, Joseph *c.pp.s.* '77 (KC) Warrensburg, MO Sacred Heart; Presbyteral Council.
Miller, Joseph *s.v.d.* '68 (SD) Missions; Propagation of the Faith; San Diego, CA Saint Catherine Laboure Catholic Parish.
Miller, Joshua '10 (JOL) Naperville, IL Sts. Peter and Paul.
Miller, Rev. Msgr. Kenneth E. '77 (Y) Youngstown, OH Immaculate Heart of Mary.
Miller, Rev. Msgr. Lawrence J. '69 (NEW) Bayonne, NJ St. Mary Star of the Sea; Serra Club of Hudson County; Archdiocesan Stewardship Advisory Committee.
Miller, Leo *o.m.i.* '52 (BEL)[F] Belleville, IL Shrine of Our Lady of the Snows Retired.
Miller, Loran *o.f.m.cap.* '64 (MAD)[I] Madison, WI San Damiano Friary Retired.
Miller, Mardean E. '94 (PH) Philadelphia, PA St. Cecilia.
Miller, Mark O. '05 (PEO) Nauvoo, IL SS. Peter and Paul; Warsaw, IL Sacred Heart.
Miller, Mark *c.pp.s* '71 (JC) Sedalia, MO St. Patrick; Sedalia, MO Sacred Heart.
Miller, Martin J. '02 (PIT)[L] Pittsburgh, PA Prelature of the Holy Cross and Opus Dei.
Miller, Martin John (POD) Pittsburgh.
Miller, Martin Joseph '94 (TR)[S] Princeton, NJ Opus Dei; Princeton.
Miller, Meinrad *o.s.b.* '94 (KCK)[A] Atchison, KS Benedictine College; [I] Atchison, KS St. Benedict's Abbey; Atchison, KS.
Miller, Michael I. *m.s.c.* '85 (RCK) Aurora, IL St. Therese of Jesus; [G] Aurora, IL Missionaries of the Sacred Heart Community.
Miller, Michael J. '72 (MRY) Special Assignment.
Miller, Michael J. '96 (STP) Stillwater, MN St. Mary; Stillwater, MN St. Michael; [F] Stillwater, MN St. Croix Catholic School.
Miller, Michael J. '72 (SFR)[A] Menlo Park, CA St. Patrick Seminary and University.
Miller, Paul A. *c.ss.r.* '62 (ROC)[M] Canandaigua, NY Notre Dame Retreat House.
Miller, Paul D. '44 (FTW) Retired.
Miller, Philip '77 (Y) Conneaut, OH Saint Mary/Saint Frances Cabrini.
Miller, Robert J. '80 (PIT) Pittsburgh, PA Our Lady of Loreto; Pittsburgh, PA St. Pius X.
Miller, Robert J. '76 (CHI) Chicago, IL St. Dorothy.
Miller, Robert L. '70 (SB) College of Consultors Retired.
Miller, Robert M. '92 (PIT) Clergy Personnel Board; McMurray, PA St. Benedict the Abbot.
Miller, Robert M. '02 (Y) Ravenna, OH Immaculate Conception.
Miller, Theodore J. '75 (TOL) Gibsonburg, OH St. Michael Church; Helena, OH St. Mary.
Miller, Thomas C. '93 (STL) St. Louis, MO Epiphany of Our Lord.
Miller, Rev. Msgr. Thomas G. '71 (RIC) Roanoke, VA St. Andrew.
Miller, Thomas M. *c.s.b.* '45 (ROC)[K] Rochester, NY Basilian Residence.
Miller, Thomas R. '77 (PIT) Pittsburgh, PA St. Joseph.
Miller, Tyler '07 (SFD) Absent on Leave.
Miller, Vincent '98 (CR) Vocations.
Miller, Whitney '80 (LKC)[C] Moss Bluff, LA St. Charles Center; Counseling; St. Charles Retreat Center; Presbyteral Council.
Miller, William C. '83 (E) Lucinda, PA St. Joseph.
Miller, William T. *s.j.* '55 (DEN)[N] Denver, CO Xavier Jesuit Center.
Miller, William T. *i.c.* '84 (PEO) Abingdon, IL Sacred Heart; Galesburg, IL Corpus Christi; Galesburg, IL St. Patrick's; [A] Peoria, IL Rosminian House; Diocesan College of Consultors; Peoria, IL.
Miller, William T. *s.j.* '72 (BAL)[Q] Baltimore, MD Jesuit Community of Loyola University, Inc.
Miller, William '61 (L) Retired.
Miller, William '91 (LKC) Lake Charles, LA St. Margaret.
Miller, William *s.j.* '55 (BAL)[A] Baltimore, MD St. Mary's Seminary and University.
Millerd, William H. *s.j.* '68 (BAL)[Q] Baltimore, MD Colombiere Jesuit Community.
Millican, Ronald C. '81 (P) Portland, OR Our Lady of Sorrows; Personnel Board.
Milligan, Ronald '72 (DET) Sterling Heights, MI St. Ephrem.
Milliken, Damian J. *o.s.b.* '58 (PAT)[N] Newton St. Paul's Abbey.
Milliken, Damian *o.s.b.* '58 (FgM) Newton, NJ St. Paul's Abbey.
Milliken, David W. '77 (NEW) New Milford, NJ Ascension; Central Bergen Region Deanery 3.
Milling, Robert T. '04 (BO) Plymouth, MA St. Peter.
Millis, Karl '99 (CHY) St. Joseph's Society for Priests (Clergy Mutual Benefit Society); Saratoga, WY St. Ann's; Rawlins, WY Wyoming State Penitentiary.
Millisor, Daniel J. '86 (COL) Grove City, OH Our Lady of Perpetual Help; Diocesan Judges.
Millott, Thirburse F. '75 (WOR) West Boylston, MA Our Lady of Good Counsel.
Mills, Alexander M. '90 (TUC) Tubac, AZ Saint Ann's Roman Catholic Parish and Missions – Tubac; Vicars Forane; All Vicars Forane; Council of Priests.
Mills, Elias Mary *f.i.* (IND)[K] Bloomington, IN Marian Friary of Our Lady Coredemptrix, Franciscans of the Immaculate.
Mills, Joseph M. '53 (OWN) Defender of the Bond; Age Group Six Representative; Priests' Council Retired.
Milon, Augustin *o.f.m.* '70 (CHI)[I] Chicago, IL Port Ministries.
Milosz, Bogdan '80 (DET) Hamtramck, MI Our Lady Queen of Apostles.
Milota, Thomas '92 (JOL) Naperville, IL Sts. Peter and Paul.
Milsted, Gordon N. '63 (MOB) Atmore, AL St. Robert Bellarmine; Bay Minette, AL St. Agatha Church.
Milton, Hilary *o.carm.* '63 (NEW) Englewood, NJ St. Cecilia's.
Milton, John W. *c.s.v.* '57 (CHI)[N] Arlington Heights, IL Viatorian Province Center–Clerics of St. Viator.
Milton, Kevin *c.ss.r.* '67 (BAL) Annapolis, MD St. Mary.
Milunski, Brad '93 (SY) Syracuse, NY Assumption B.V.M.; Presbyteral Council.
Mimnaugh, Stephen D. *o.f.m.* '09 (NY) New York, NY St. Francis of Assisi.
Mina, John L. '89 (PBR) Clairton, PA Ascension of Our Lord; Archives.
Minch, Richard '69 (SAV) Retired.
Minchak, Paul L. *o.f.m.cap.* '69 (HON) Waipahu, HI Resurrection of the Lord.
Mindling, J. Daniel *o.f.m.cap.* '80 (BAL)[A] Emmitsburg, MD Mount St. Mary's Seminary; Consultants.
Mindling, J. Daniel *o.f.m.cap.* '80 (WDC)[B] Washington, DC St. Francis Friary–Capuchin College; Consultants.
Mindling, Joseph *o.f.m.cap.* '66 (WDC)[B] Washington, DC St. Francis Friary–Capuchin College.
Minelli, Peter A. '63 (MAR) Retired.
Mingollo, Rodrigo '02 (RIC) Onley, VA St. Peter the Apostle.
Minh, Vu Duc '80 (TLS) On Duty Outside the Diocese.
Minh Nguyen, Andrew Tu '69 (BUF) Buffalo, NY Coronation of the Blessed Virgin Mary.
Minhoto, Rev. Msgr. Walter F. '64 (FRS) Retired.
Minh Vu, Joseph P. '80 (COS) Colorado Springs, CO The Vietnamese Holy Martyrs Parish.
Minichello, Arthur G. '73 (BRK) Brooklyn, NY SS. Simon and Jude.
Minifie, Michael J. *c.c.* '05 (GAL) Houston, TX Queen of Peace; [S] Houston, TX Catholic Charismatic Center.
Minigan, William J. '86 (BO) Malden, MA St. Joseph.
Miniscalco, Donald *c.ss.r.* '68 (PH) Philadelphia, PA St. Peter the Apostle.
Minj, Sylvester *i.m.s.* '97 (BR) Grosse Tete, LA St. Joseph; Livonia, LA St. Frances Xavier Cabrini; Grosse Tete, LA Immaculate Heart of Mary.
Minja, Alfons *c.pp.s.* (TOL) Ottawa, OH SS. Peter and Paul.
Minja, Alfons *c.pp.s.* '98 (CIN)[N] Dayton, OH Provincial Office of the Cincinnati Province of the Society of the Precious Blood.
Mink, John J. '85 (WIL) New Castle, DE Our Lady of Fatima; Priests' Personnel Committee; New Castle, DE; Air National Guard Chaplains; Priest Personnel Committee; Coordinator of Institutional Chaplains.
Minkel, William *o.f.m.* '05 (OAK)[L] Oakland Franciscan Friars of California, (Province of St. Barbara).
Minkler, Jeffrey R. '05 (SPR) Absent on Leave.
Minner, Ronald J. '01 (ALN) McAdoo, PA All Saints Parish.
Minnich, John F. '51 (GRY) Retired.
Minnihan, Paul D. '93 (OAK) Oakland, CA St. Paschal Baylon; Diocesan Worship; Design Review Board; Episcopal Liturgist.
Minniti, Anthony L. '70 (CAM) Retired.
Minniti, David V. '72 (CAM) Merchantville, NJ St. Peter's Catholic Church, Merchantville, N.J. Retired.
Minogue, Michael J. '81 (PHX) Retired.
Minson, Bartholomew *o.f.m.cap.* '61 (ROC) Ovid, NY St. Francis Solanus; Ovid, NY Holy Cross; [K] Interlaken, NY St. Fidelis Friary.
Minsterman, Joseph '61 (GBG) Retired.
Mintes, Wilson '06 (MGZ) Moca, PR Our Lady of Monserrate.
Mintjal, Frank '59 (Y) Retired.
Minturn, Joseph '57 (RVC) Retired.
Minuth, Joseph *o.p.* '11 (LFT) West Lafayette, IN St. Thomas Aquinas; [H] West Lafayette, IN St. Thomas Aquinas Parish and Foundation for Catholic Students Attending Purdue University.
Minzaki, Franklin *c.j.* '10 (LA)[B] Santa Maria, CA St. Joseph Seminary (Josephite Fathers' Novitiate); Santa Maria, CA St. Louis de Montfort.
Mioduszewski, Marcin A. '07 (PRO) Woonsocket, RI St. Stanislaus; Woonsocket, RI St. Joseph.
Miola, Luigi C. '77 (CLV) Maple Heights, OH St. Martin of Tours.
Miotke, Carmel F. *o.f.m.* '60 (BO)[X] Boston, MA Saint Anthony Residence Retired.
Miqueli, Peter A. '91 (NY) Roosevelt Island, NY St. Frances Cabrini.
Miquilena, Iden Jose Bello '05 (LAR) Casa Guadalupe House of Discernment; Vice Chancellor; College of Consultors; Ex Officio Members.
Mira Alvarez, Victor Hugo *ss.cc.* (SJN) Guaynabo, PR Sagrados Corazones; Guaynabo, PR Corazon de Jesus.
Mirabelli, Daniel J. *c.s.v.* '60 (PEO)[B] Rock Island, IL Alleman High School.
Mirabelli, Daniel J. *c.s.v.* '60 (CHI)[N] Arlington Heights Viatorian Province Center–Clerics of St. Viator.
Miracky, James J. *s.j.* '88 (BAL)[B] Timonium, MD Loyola Graduate Center–Timonium Campus; [Q] Baltimore, MD Jesuit Community of Loyola University, Inc.
Miralbes–Drago, Julio E. '72 (MIL) Retired.
Miramontes, Francisco '91 (SJ) Alviso, CA Our Lady,

Star of the Sea; Deans.
Miramontes, Jorge A. '11 (MAD) Watertown, WI St. Henry.
Miranda, Dario R. '82 (LA) Maywood, CA St. Rose of Lima.
Miranda, Rev. Msgr. Lorenzo '91 (LA) North Hollywood, CA St. Charles Borromeo; Vicar for Clergy; Clergy, Vicar for; Ex Officio.
Miranda, Luis *o.carm.* '84 (SJN) Carmelite Third Order.
Miranda, Luke '55 (FWT) Retired.
Miranda, Victor Hugo *s.j.* '11 (BO)[U] Brighton, MA Francis Xavier House.
Miranne, Paul *o.s.b.* '47 (NO)[R] St. Benedict, LA St. Joseph Abbey.
Mirchuk, Rev. Archpriest Mitrat Roman '76 (PHU) Whippany, NJ St. John the Baptist; Whippany, NJ St. Paul.
Miriani, Gerald C. '62 (BEL) Retired.
Miriani, Gerry '62 (TUC) Tucson, AZ Saint Pius X Roman Catholic Parish – Tucson Retired.
Miriyala, Balachandra '02 (KCK) Corning, KS St. Patrick; Onaga, KS St. Vincent de Paul.
Mirro, Joseph A. '76 (RVC) Westhampton Beach, NY Immaculate Conception; Procurator & Advocates; Peconic Deanery.
Mirsberger, Richard E. '66 (MIL) Retired.
Mirto, Gregorio L. '65 (DEN) Fort Lupton, CO St. William.
Misakabo, Faustin *o.praem.* '80 (JKS) Port Gibson, MS St. Joseph.
Misbrener, David M. '95 (Y) Rootstown, OH St. Peter of the Fields; Presbyteral Council.
Miscamble, Wilson D. *c.s.c.* '88 (FTW)[A] Notre Dame, IN Moreau Seminary; [B] University of Notre Dame Du Lac; [H] Notre Dame, IN Holy Cross Community, Corby Hall, University of Notre Dame.
Mischke, Bernard *o.s.c.* '51 (SCL)[I] Onamia Crosier Priory.
Mischke, Gerald '64 (SCL) Diocesan Priests Pension Plan Trustees; St. Cloud, MN St. Mary's Cathedral of St. Cloud Retired.
Mischkowiuski, Henry B. '65 (LR) Barling, AR Sacred Heart of Mary; Fort Smith, AR SS. Sabina & Mary Church.
Mischler, Thomas E. '81 (GRY) Crown Point, IN Holy Spirit.
Misenko, John A. '78 (CLV) Avon, OH Holy Trinity.
Mish, Roy L. '60 (LC) Retired.
Misiewicz, Chester J. '73 (WOR) Worcester, MA Blessed Sacrament.
Misiolek, Frederick '65 (DET) Retired.
Miskella, Richard '65 (LA) Retired.
Misko, James '07 (AUS) Belton, TX Christ the King; Presbyteral Council; College of Consultors.
Misko, Lukasz *o.p.* '07 (ANC) Anchorage, AK Holy Family Cathedral.
Miskvewicz, Paul *o.f.m.conv.* '76 (BAL)[Q] Ellicott City Order of Friars Minor Conventual.
Missimi, Rev. Msgr. Anthony N. '62 (COL) Retired.
Missinne, William *c.i.c.m.* '54 (FgM) Arlington, VA MISSIONHURST.
Missler, John C. '78 (TOL) Port Clinton, OH Immaculate Conception; Our Lady of the Lake Deanery.
Mistor, Todd C. '04 (DET) Absent on Leave.
Misurda, Matthew '77 (ALT) Portage, PA Our Lady of the Sacred Heart.
Mitas, Rev. Msgr. Matthew M. '79 (STL) Union, MO Immaculate Conception; Deaneries/Deans.
Mitchell, Charles I. '84 (ORL) Altamonte Springs, FL St. Mary Magdalen.
Mitchell, Darell J. '98 (YAK) Calvary Cemetery; Special Assignment.
Mitchell, Douglas J. '01 (SFE) Presbyteral Council of the Archdiocese of Santa Fe; Los Lunas, NM San Clemente; Vicars Forane (Deans).
Mitchell, Edward J. '54 (DET) Retired.
Mitchell, Rt. Rev. Eugene *b.s.o.* '92 (NTN) Miami, FL St. Jude; Methuen, MA Basilian Salvatorian Order; Methuen, MA.
Mitchell, George J. '64 (RVC) Retired.
Mitchell, Rev. Msgr. John J. '63 (RCK) Diocesan Consultors Retired.
Mitchell, John J. '96 (STP) Columbia Heights, MN Immaculate Conception.
Mitchell, John T. *s.j.* '72 (OAK)[L] Berkeley, CA Jesuit Fathers and Brothers.
Mitchell, Joseph P. '79 (SEA) Vancouver, WA Holy Redeemer.
Mitchell, Joseph *c.p.* '81 (L)[L] Louisville, KY Sacred Heart Retreat.
Mitchell, Joseph *c.p.* '81 (L) Louisville, KY St. Agnes.
Mitchell, Mark E. '76 (GR) Retired.
Mitchell, Rev. Msgr. Michael J. '65 (SJ) Retired.
Mitchell, Michael J. '05 (NO)[J] New Orleans, LA Holy Cross School; Metairie, LA Our Lady of Divine Providence.
Mitchell, Peter G. '51 (HRT) Retired.
Mitchell, Peter M. '99 (LIN) Nebraska City, NE St. Mary's.
Mitchell, Peter '78 (ORL) Retired.
Mitchell, Robert J. '85 (PAT) College of Deans; Deans; Chatham, NJ St. Patrick's.
Mitchell, Robert W. '73 (ORL) Haines City, FL St. Ann.
Mitchell, Royce J. '74 (NO) Retired.
Mitchell, Rev. Msgr. Salvatore P. '42 (E) Retired.
Mitchell, Thomas R. '79 (HRT) Consultors – Canon 1742; New Britain, CT St. Ann; New Britain, CT St. Mary's.
Mitchell, Walter A. '61 (BRK) Retired.
Mitchell, Walter '91 (MIA) Retired.
Mitchko, James '77 (PSC) Leave of Absence.
Mitek, Jozef '84 (LA) Carson, CA St. Philomena.
Mitera, Andrzej (STA) Live Oak, FL St. Francis Xavier.
Miti, Peter '07 (HON) Honolulu, HI St. Philomena.
Mitka, John J. '66 (BUF)[N] Depew, NY Msgr. Conniff Residence Retired.
Mitolo, Frank '68 (PIT) Pittsburgh, PA Resurrection.
Mitrano, Joseph Charles *c.s.b.* '69 (GAL)[O] Houston, TX Dillon House Retired.
Mittempergher, Giancarlo *c.s.s.* '66 (SAC) Special Assignment; Sacramento, CA St. Elizabeth; West Sacramento, CA Holy Cross.
Mitten, Stephen F. *s.j.* '95 (CHI)[C] Chicago, IL Jesuit Community at Loyola University Chicago.
Mitulski, James M. '72 (STL) Deaneries/Deans; Florissant, MO St. Norbert.
Mitzel, Daniel C. '81 (HBG) Lancaster, PA St. Anthony of Padua; Appointed.
Mitzi, John (ORL) Retired.
Miyares, Carlos '81 (MIA) Retired.
Mizeur, Thomas R. '73 (PEO) Henry, IL St. Joseph's; Henry, IL St. Mary's; Lacon, IL Immaculate Conception; Air National Guard Chaplains.
Mizicko, Carroll *o.f.m.* '68 (BEL)[F] East Saint Louis, IL St. Benedict the Black Friary; East Saint Louis, IL St. Augustine of Hippo.
Mizzi–Gili, Anthony '09 (NY) Bronx, NY Our Lady of the Assumption.
Mlakic, Tomislav (NY) Crestwood, NY Church of the Annunciation.
Mlay, Mark *a.l.c.p.* '84 (PMB) Fort Pierce, FL St. Anastasia.
Mlsna, Todd A. '98 (LC) La Crosse, WI St. Joseph the Workman Cathedral; [D] La Crosse, WI Mayo Clinic Health System – Franciscan Healthcare, La Crosse Campus Medical Center; [N] La Crosse, WI Mayo Clinic Health System – Franciscan Medical Center, Inc.
Mmegbuadimma, Maurice '01 (BRK) Ozone Park, NY St. Elizabeth.
Mnubi, Charles L. '08 (MIL)[P] Milwaukee, WI Jesuit Community at Marquette University.
Moan, Francis X. *s.j.* '57 (BAL)[Q] Baltimore, MD Colombiere Jesuit Community.
Mocarski, Janusz '09 (RVC) East Islip, NY St. Mary's.
Moccia, Bonaventure *c.p.* '52 (BRK)[R] Jamaica, NY Immaculate Conception Monastery.
Mocio, Stephen J. '76 (DAL) Denison, TX St. Patrick.
Mock, Robert M. '84 (BUF) West Seneca, NY Fourteen Holy Helpers; [C] Buffalo, NY Trocaire College.
Mock, Timothy *c.m.m.* '52 (DET)[K] Vocation Office.
Mockaitis, Timothy '78 (P) Salem, OR Queen of Peace; Life, Justice and Peace.
Mockel, George E. '75 (OAK) Ex Officio; Moderator of the Curia and Vicar General; Consultors; Diocesan Finance Council; Pontifical Association of the Holy Childhood; Propagation of the Faith; St. Peter the Apostle Society; Ex Officio; John Paul II High School, a California nonprofit religious corporation; Ex Officio; Ex Officio; Officers; Officers; Alameda, CA St. Philip Neri–St. Albert the Great.
Mockevicius, Dominic F. '48 (ROC) Rochester, NY St. George Retired.
Mockler, Patrick J. '79 (MO) Air Force Reserve Chaplains; Presbyteral Council.
Mockler, Patrick J. '79 (BLX) Trustees; Biloxi, MS Our Lady of Fatima; Advocates.
Mockler, Patrick '79 (JKS) Trustees.
Mockler, Peter F. '73 (BLX) Gulfport, MS St. Ann; Deans; College of Consultors; Finance Council; Presbyteral Council.
Moczko, Michael A. '10 (CHI) Oak Lawn, IL St. Gerald.
Moczulski, David *o.f.m.* '93 (PIT) Allegheny County, PA West Penn Allegheny Health System–Allegheny General; [M] Pittsburgh, PA Holy Family Friary; Pittsburgh, PA.
Moczydlowski, Rev. Msgr. Chester M. '73 (CHR) Mount Pleasant, SC St. Benedict; Presbyteral Council.
Moczydlowski, Stanley M. '02 (ALN) Bethlehem, PA Incarnation of Our Lord Parish; Advocates.
Modde, Bradley E. '97 (STL) St. Louis, MO Immaculate Heart of Mary.
Mode, Daniel L. '92 (ARL) On Duty Outside the Diocese; Military Chaplains; Navy Chaplains.
Mode, Daniel (NOR) New London, CT U.S. Coast Guard Memorial Chapel.
Modebei, Sylvester '03 (PHX) Surprise, AZ St. Clare of Assisi Roman Catholic Parish.
Modino, Roman '89 (TR) Freehold, NJ St. Rose of Lima.
Modrys, Walter J. *s.j.* '78 (NY)[DD] New York, NY Society of Jesus, New York Province; [DD] New York, NY "America;" Residence and publication office of the America Press.
Modugno, Rev. Msgr. Thomas A. '66 (NY) New York, NY St. Monica; Manhattan (East).
Moeder, August L. '53 (SAL) Retired.
Moeder, John '57 (SAL) Retired.
Moeggenberg, Raymond '56 (SAG) Retired.
Moeglein, James *o.s.c.* '70 (SCL)[I] Onamia, MN Crosier Priory.
Moellenberndt, Rev. Msgr. Duane R. '76 (MAD) Sun Prairie, WI Sacred Hearts of Jesus and Mary; Building Commission; Council of Catholic Women.
Moeller, Rev. Msgr. George B. '62 (BAL) Retired.
Moen, Brian '03 (FAR) St. Michael, ND St. Michael's Church of St. Michael; St. Michael, ND St. Michael's Church of St. Michael.
Moenkedick, Leo '86 (SCL) Foley, MN St. Elizabeth of Hungary; Gilman, MN SS. Peter and Paul; Foley, MN St. Joseph's; Air National Guard Chaplains.
Moerman, Stephen A. '94 (PH) Wayne, PA St. Isaac Jogues.
Moeslein, Rev. Msgr. Francis R. '58 (R) Morehead City, NC St. Egbert; Apostleship of the Sea Retired.
Mofan, Feliciano '79 (SFR) San Rafael, CA St. Isabella.
Moffatt, Charles *s.s.j.* (LAF) Breaux Bridge, LA St. Francis of Assisi.
Moga, Michael D. *s.j.* '64 (FgM) New York, NY Society of Jesus.
Mohammed, Nigel R. '03 (NEW) Jersey City, NJ St. Anne's.
Mohan, Bernard N. '61 (NEW) Archdiocesan Judges Retired.
Mohan, Brian Quinn '05 (COS) Littleton, CO Pax Christi Catholic Church; Presbyteral Council.
Mohan, Oliver *o.m.i.* '48 (PHX) Mesa, AZ St. Timothy Roman Catholic Parish Retired.
Mohl, Andrew S. '84 (BAL) Randallstown, MD Holy Family.
Mohnickey, Ronald J. *t.o.r.* '71 (STU)[A] Steubenville, OH Franciscan University of Steubenville; [H] Steubenville, OH Holy Spirit Friary.
Mohr, J. Patrick *s.j.* '75 (SCR)[B] Scranton, PA The University of Scranton.
Mohr, Richard G. '67 (BEL) Retired.
Mohr, Thomas H. '58 (DAV) Retired.
Mohrman, J. Gregory *o.s.b.* '86 (STL)[F] Creve Coeur, MO St. Louis Priory School; [O] St. Louis, MO The Abbey of St. Mary and St. Louis.
Moineau, John A. '87 (GBG) Irwin, PA Immaculate Conception; College of Consultors; Bishop's Priests Council.
Moisant, William C. '01 (P) Tualatin, OR Resurrection Catholic Church; Area Vicars.
Moisin, Michael '88 (ROM) Brookline, MA Romanian Catholic Mission of Boston; Finance Council; College of Consultors; Office to Aid the Church in Romania.
Moka, Willy Mubelo *s.j.* '07 (BO)[U] Newton, MA The Jesuit Community at Boston College.
Mokarzel, Galeb *o.m.i.* '57 (SAT)[K] San Antonio, TX Oblate Madonna Residence.
Mokluk, John M. *o.s.f.s.* '70 (WIL)[B] Wilmington, DE Salesianum School.
Mol, Joseph C. '77 (CHI) Delegate of the Archbishop for Privilege Cases; Advocates.
Molano, Ernesto '56 (MIA) Retired.
Molano, Isaiah *o.p.* '10 (SJ) Stanford, CA Catholic Community at Stanford.
Molenda, Bogdan *s.ch.* '84 (CHI) Chicago, IL Holy Trinity Mission.
Moleski, Martin X. *s.j.* '81 (BUF)[N] Buffalo, NY Canisius Jesuit Community Inc.
Molewski, Andrew '82 (WIL) Wilmington, DE St. Hedwig.
Molewski, Pawel '86 (NEW) Harrison, NJ Our Lady of Czestochowa.
Moley, Kevin J. *c.ss.r.* '70 (BRK)[R] Brooklyn, NY Redemptorist Fathers of New York, Inc.–Baltimore Province; Brooklyn, NY.
Molgano, James '03 (PMB) Jensen Beach, FL St. Martin de Porres.
Molina, Alfredo Valdez '02 (PHX) Chandler, AZ St. Mary Roman Catholic Parish.
Molina, Angel '94 (CGS) Caguas, PR San Juan Apostol y Evangelista; Sec. Chancellor; Priests Senate.
Molina, Arturo '83 (LEX) Special Assignment.
Molina, Benjamin '82 (DAL) Dallas, TX St. Elizabeth of Hungary.
Molina, Joe '95 (ELP) El Paso, TX Most Holy Trinity; St. John; Ex Officio Members; Priests' Personnel Advisory Committee.
Molina, Jonathan B. '04 (SAC) Redding, CA Our Lady of Mercy; Priests' Personnel Board, Diocesan; Presbyteral Council.
Molina, Juan Francisco '90 (TOL) Toledo, OH SS. Peter and Paul; Toledo, OH St. Stephen.
Molina, Juan *o.ss.t.* '99 (BAL)[Q] Archdiocese of Washington, DC.
Molina, Milhton Scarpetta '01 (SEA) Bellevue, WA St. Louise.
Molina, Rolando *c.m.* '07 (FgM) Philadelphia, PA Eastern Province.

Molina, Seraphim *s.t.* '97 (TUC) Tucson, AZ Blessed Kateri Tekakwitha Roman Catholic Missions Parish – Tucson; [I] South Tucson, AZ Blessed Kateri Tekakwitha Parish Center.
Molina–Juarez, Jaime *m.n.m.* '88 (ATL) Smyrna, GA St. Thomas the Apostle.
Molina–Ramirez, Bolivar G. '06 (CHI) Brookfield, IL St. Barbara.
Molina–Restrepo, Fernando '99 (ATL) Douglasville, GA St. Theresa of the Child Jesus.
Molinari, Todd '95 (P) Salem, OR St. Joseph; [P] Salem, OR Willamette University (Salem); College of Consultors.
Molinaro, Kenneth M. *c.s.c.* '76 (FTW)[H] Notre Dame, IN Congregation of Holy Cross, United States Province of Priests & Brothers; South Bend, IN; Austin, TX.
Molini, Thomas M. '85 (STL) Kirkwood, MO St. Gerard Majella.
Molitor, Donald F. '63 (STL) Retired.
Molka, Victor J. '78 (PIT) New Castle, PA Mary, Mother of Hope; New Castle, PA St. Joseph the Worker.
Moll, Daniel J. '07 (MAR) On Duty Outside the Diocese.
Moll, Walter J. '85 (ALT) Priests' Retirement Plan; Portage, PA St. Joseph's.
Mollenhauer, Arthur '97 (BGP) Stamford, CT Saint Benedict – Our Lady of Montserrat; Stamford, CT St. Mary.
Molling, Mark '80 (MIL) Genesee Depot, WI St. Paul.
Mollner, Jeffrey J. '08 (OM) Omaha, NE St. Stephen the Martyr; Age Groups.
Molloy, John (FgM) Boston, MA St. James the Apostle, Inc.
Molloy, Joseph '83 (SFD) Decatur, IL Holy Family; Priests' Personnel Board.
Molloy, Kevin '72 (SP) Tarpon Springs, FL St. Ignatius of Antioch.
Molloy, Rev. Msgr. Thomas E. '70 (RVC) Brentwood, NY St. Luke; Judges for Interdiocesan Tribunal Retired.
Molnar, Jeffrey T. '03 (PIT) Pittsburgh, PA St. Athanasius.
Molnar, Michael '76 (DET) Grosse Ile, MI Sacred Heart.
Molokie, Jerome M. *o.praem.* '95 (ORG)[D] Silverado, CA St. Michael's Preparatory School; [I] Silverado, CA Norbertine Fathers of Orange Inc.
Moloney, Daniel P. '10 (BO) Brighton, MA St. Columbkille.
Moloney, Rev. Msgr. James A. '56 (DET) Dearborn Heights, MI St. Anselm; College of Consultors; Propagation of the Faith (Missions).
Moloney, John C. '91 (PH) Springfield, PA St. Kevin.
Moloney, John Jesus *c.s.j.* '95 (LAR)[D] Laredo, TX St. John Priory, F.J.; Ex Officio Members; [F] Laredo, TX Holy Spirit Retreat and Conference Center.
Moloney, John '72 (LA) Norwalk, CA St. John of God.
Moloney, Patrick W. '77 (NTN) Retired.
Moloney, Rev. Msgr. Stephan J. '82 (COL) Columbus, OH Immaculate Conception; Vicar General; College of Consultors; Parochial Examiners; Presbyteral Council; Promoter of Justice; Diocesan Board of Review for the Protection of Children; Diocesan Finance Council; Victim Assistance Coordinator; Bishop's Council.
Molter, Richard J. '64 (MIL) Retired.
Molumby, Edward J. *s.t.* '61 (SB) Rancho Cucamonga, CA Sacred Heart.
Molyn, John A. '81 (ALB) Valatie, NY St. John the Baptist; Deans.
Molyneux, John *c.m.f.* '97 (CHI)[N] Chicago, IL Claretian Missionaries, St. Jude League, Inc.
Molyneux, John *c.m.f.* '98 (ATL) Stone Mountain, GA Corpus Christi.
Monaco, David *c.p.* '90 (COL)[A] Columbus, OH Pontifical College Josephinum; [A] Columbus, OH Pontifical College Josephinum.
Monaco, Harry *o.f.m.* '09 (WDC)[B] Silver Spring, MD Holy Name College.
Monaco, James M. '85 (BUF) Buffalo, NY St. Katharine Drexel.
Monaghan, Rev. Msgr. Charles J. '41 (PH) Retired.
Monaghan, George P. '80 (DAL) Rockwall, TX Our Lady of the Lake.
Monaghan, J. Fergus '72 (SPC) Springfield, MO Holy Trinity.
Monaghan, John T. '63 (NY)[E] Bronx, NY Cardinal Spellman High School.
Monaghan, Justin D. '66 (SPC) Joplin, MO St. Mary; Region I.
Monaghan, Robert T. '62 (STP) Retired.
Monaghan, Thomas J. '70 (MAD) Reedsburg, WI Sacred Heart.
Monagle, Robert J. '91 (BO) Air Force Chaplains; Military & VA Chaplains.
Monahan, John C. *s.j.* '99 (BO)[U] Boston The Society of Jesus of New England–Provincial Offices.
Monahan, John C. *s.j.* '99 (MO) Navy Chaplains.
Monahan, Joseph E. '77 (DEN) Golden, CO St. Joseph.
Monahan, Joseph R. '62 (STL) Retired.
Monahan, Joseph *t.o.r.* '90 (WIL)[I] Wilmington, DE St. Francis Hospital, Inc.
Monahan, Kieran *o.f.m.* '65 (BO)[U] Boston, MA St. Christopher Friary.
Monahan, Paul '60 (DM) Diocesan Consultors Retired.
Monahan, Shawn *o.m.v.* '02 (SFD) Alton, IL St. Mary's.
Monahan, Rev. Msgr. Thomas J. '58 (RCK) Experts; Priests' Eucharistic League Retired.
Monahan, William J. '07 (PH) Philadelphia, PA St. Katherine of Siena.
Monan, J. Donald *s.j.* '55 (BO)[U] Newton, MA The Jesuit Community at Boston College.
Monastere, Bony '07 (BRK) Brooklyn, NY Holy Innocents.
Moncada, Fabio '81 (FAJ) Canovanas, PR Nuestra Senora del Pilar.
Moncada Laguado, Cayetano (NEW) Newark, NJ St. Francis Xavier.
Moncher, Raymond F. '58 (MAR) Marenisco, MI St. Catherine Retired.
Mondello, Rev. Msgr. Donald J. '60 (GBG) Diocesan Council of Catholic Women.
Mondiek, Stephen J. '03 (CIN) Hamilton, OH St. Ann; Hamilton, OH St. Joseph.
Mondik, Michael '73 (PSC) Rahway, NJ St. Thomas the Apostle; Syncellus; Eparchial College of Consultors; Building and Properties Commission; Eparchial Liturgy and Art Commission; Presbyteral Council; Evangelization.
Mondji, Jean–Marie Amevi '08 (BEL) Radom, IL St. Michael; Scheller, IL St. Barbara.
Mondji, Jean–Marie '09 (PBL) On Duty Outside the Diocese.
Mondor, Christian *o.f.m.* '51 (ORG) Huntington Beach, CA SS. Simon and Jude; Ecumenical and Interreligious Affairs.
Mondragon, Antonio '63 (SFE) Retired.
Mondragon, Ezequiel '62 (DET) Absent on Leave.
Mondzelewski, Dominic *o.s.b.* '69 (CLV)[N] Cleveland, OH.
Moneck, George J. '89 (PIT) California, PA St. Thomas Aquinas; Roscoe, PA St. Joseph; [P] California, PA California University (California).
Mones, Benjamin '58 (ELP) El Paso, TX Cristo Rey Church; [J] El Paso, TX Blue Army.
Monestero, John '75 (ORG) Anaheim, CA St. Justin Martyr; Absent on Sick Leave; Ecumenical and Interreligious Affairs.
Monestime, Perard C. *s.j.* '85 (FgM) Watertown, MA Society of Jesus.
Monet, Zachary *o.carm.* '60 (JOL)[L] Darien Carmelite Provincial Office.
Monette, Michael R. '99 (MAN) Keene, NH Mary, Queen of Peace Parish; Keene, NH Parish of the Holy Spirit.
Monevne, Nnamdi *o.m.v.* '09 (BO)[B] Boston, MA Oblate Provincialate.
Moneypenny, John W. '98 (ORG) Santa Ana, CA St. Joseph; Council of Priests; Clergy Personnel Board.
Monforton, Rev. Msgr. Jeffrey M. '94 (DET)[A] Detroit, MI Sacred Heart Major Seminary, Inc.
Mongelluzzo, Rev. Msgr. James A. '74 (WOR) On Duty Outside the Diocese.
Mongeon, Peter M. '83 (NO) On Medical Leave of Absence.
Mongeon, Peter M. '83 (PRO) Retired.
Mongiello, Anthony P. '80 (ALN) Bethlehem, PA St. Anne; Serra Club of Bethlehem.
Mongiello, Robert '87 (VEN) Retired.
Mongrain, Dennis '77 (LA) Diamond Bar, CA St. Denis.
Monico, Gilberto '02 (LA) Long Beach, CA Holy Innocents.
Moniuk, Evhan '92 (PHU) Palmerton, PA St. Vladimir's.
Moniz, Joseph V. '64 (LA) Pasadena, CA St. Philip the Apostle.
Monnig, Matthew S. *s.j.* '07 (BO)[U] Boston The Society of Jesus of New England–Provincial Offices.
Monnig, Matthew S. *s.j.* '07 (R)[F] Raleigh Jesuit Community.
Monnin, Robert J. '55 (CIN) Retired.
Monogue, Michael G. '85 (STP) United Hospitals, Inc.; Children's Hospital.
Monohan, Duncan W. '77 (SD) Winterhaven, CA Saint Thomas Indian Mission Catholic Parish.
Monostori, Benedict *o.cist.* '44 (DAL)[J] Irving, TX Cistercian Abbey of Our Lady of Dallas.
Monreal, Jesus *o.carm.* '69 (ARE) Morovis, PR Nuestra Senora del Carmen; Priest's Senate (Consejo Presbiteral).
Monreal, Melchisedech '95 (SD) Poway, CA Saint Michael Catholic Parish Poway.
Monroe, Charles F. '75 (WOR) Worcester, MA Our Lady of the Angels.
Monroe, Edward F. *c.ss.r.* '61 (MIL)[S] Oconomowoc, WI The Redemptorist Retreat Center.
Monsalve, Carlos *o.c.d.* '88 (CHI)[A] Mundelein, IL Instituto De Liderazgo Pastoral (Hispanic Programs for Lay Ministry and Permanent Diaconate).
Monsalve, German Barona *m.s.c.* '86 (FgM) Aurora, IL MISSIONARIES OF THE SACRED HEART.
Monshau, Michael J. *o.p.* '88 (CHI)[N] Chicago Dominicans (Provincial Office).
Monsour, Raymond G. '63 (STP) Retired.
Montag, John F. '93 (MIL)[P] Milwaukee Jesuit Provincial Office, Wisconsin Province.
Montague, George T. *s.m.* '58 (SAT)[C] San Antonio, TX St. Mary's University of San Antonio, Texas; [L] San Antonio, TX Casa San Juan Marianist Community; [S] San Antonio, TX Brothers of the Beloved Disciple; San Antonio, TX St. Mary Magdalen.
Montague, Hugh *s.o.cist.* '82 (ALN)[K] New Ringgold, PA Cistercian Monastery.
Montalbano, Francis *o.m.i.* '47 (SAT)[K] San Antonio, TX Oblate Madonna Residence.
Montalbano, Joseph E. '55 (ALX) Retired.
Montana, Angel '92 (CC) Corpus Christi, TX St. Joseph.
Montana, Edwin '11 (WOR) Fitchburg, MA St. Anthony of Padua; Sacred Heart of Jesus.
Montanaro, Guido G. '69 (BGP) Fairfield, CT Holy Family.
Montanaro, James *o.m.v.* '83 (BO)[U] Milton, MA Oblate Residence (St. Joseph House).
Montanez, Edwin '98 (RIC) Charlottesville, VA Church of the Incarnation.
Montanez, Eliecer *m.c.m.* '07 (BR) Hispanic Apostolate; Baton Rouge, LA Christ the King.
Montanez, Gustavo *o.p.* '08 (SAT)[L] San Antonio, TX Dominican Priory of San Juan Macias.
Montanez, Melvin '06 (CGS) Las Piedras, PR Inmaculada Concepcion; Priests Senate; Liturgical Consultor; Master of Ceremonies.
Montanez Lopez, Jose R. *c.p.* '95 (SJN) Carolina, PR Santa Gema Galgani.
Montano, Angel '92 (CC) Defenders of the Bond.
Montavon, Thomas G. '61 (CLV) Brunswick, OH St. Colette; Garfield Heights, OH St. Monica Retired.
Montecalvo, Rev. Msgr. Carlo F. '73 (PRO) Johnston, RI Our Lady of Grace.
Monteiro, Alfredo '73 (NY) Mount Vernon, NY St. Mary.
Monteiro, Ralph J. *o.s.a.* '66 (PH)[Y] Villanova, PA St. Thomas Monastery.
Montejano, John '94 (LA) Graduate Studies.
Montekio, Bruno *l.c.* '01 (DAL)[D] Irving, TX The Highlands School; [J] Irving, TX Legionaries of Christ.
Montelaro, Thomas '75 (LAF) Retired.
Monteleone, Jacob '75 (SP) Clearwater, FL Light of Christ.
Montella, Alban V. *o.f.m.* '55 (NY)[DD] New York, NY Padua Friary Retired.
Montemayor, Ted *s.d.b.* '83 (LA) Bellflower, CA St. Dominic Savio; [V] Rosemead, CA St. Joseph's Salesian Youth Renewal Center.
Montenegro, Blas *o.a.r.* '49 (NEW) Union City, NJ St. Augustine's.
Montenegro–Calero, Manuel '01 (AUS) Austin, TX St. Louis.
Montero, Alvaro *d.c.j.m.* '04 (DEN) Littleton, CO St. Mary; [N] Littleton, CO Disciples of the Hearts of Jesus and Mary.
Montero, Eduardo G. '83 (PH) Assistant Judicial Vicars; Wynnewood, PA Presentation B.V.M.
Montero, Hugo L. '92 (STP)[C] St. Paul, MN University of St. Thomas.
Montero, Romulo (NY) New York, NY Our Lady of Pompeii.
Montes, Francisco J. '03 (MRY) Pajaro, CA Our Lady of the Assumption.
Montes, Jesse *s.d.b.* '79 (OAK) Berkeley, CA St. Ambrose.
Montes, Jose Felipe *c.s.v.* '01 (CHI)[N] Arlington Heights Viatorian Province Center–Clerics of St. Viator.
Montes–Colon, Flavio '05 (MIA) Coral Springs, FL St. Andrew.
Montesanti, Steven G. '99 (MAN) Hampstead, NH St. Anne; Lay Ministry Formation Commission.
Montesi, Eugene *s.x.* '62 (PAT)[N] Wayne Xaverian Missionary Fathers; Wayne, NJ XAVERIAN MISSIONARY FATHERS.
Montesino, Efraín '85 (ARE) Arecibo, PR San Juan Bosco.
Montez, Paul *o.s.b.* (B)[C] Jerome, ID Monastery of the Ascension.
Montgomery, Joseph T. '58 (HRT) Retired.
Montgomery, William L. '79 (WDC) Washington, DC Assumption.
Monti, Dominic *o.f.m.* '71 (NY)[DD] New York, NY Franciscan Friars, Holy Name Province; New York, NY St. Francis of Assisi.
Monti, Robert M. '61 (LC) Retired.
Monti, Robert '61 (MIA)[G] Fort Lauderdale, FL Holy Cross Hospital.
Monticello, Rev. Msgr. Robert V. '51 (DET) Presbyteral Council Retired.
Montiel, Jose '57 (FRS) Retired.
Montminy, Marc R. '77 (MAN) Newmarket, NH St. Mary; Exeter, NH St. Michael.
Montminy, Paul D. '78 (MAN) Manchester, NH St. Catherine of Siena.
Montondon, Rev. Msgr. Walter '57 (BEA) Retired.
Montoro Sasia, Roberto H. (SLC) West Valley City, UT Saints Peter and Paul LLC 243.
Montoya, Armando Rodrigaez '01 (CAM) Egg Harbor

City, NJ St. Nicholas' Church, Egg Harbor City.
Montoya, Francisco '00 (SAL) On Duty Outside the Diocese.
Montoya, Jose '86 (BGP) Danbury, CT Our Lady of Guadalupe.
Montoya, Juan Camilo '10 (LSC) Absent On Leave.
Montoya, Michael *m.j.* '94 (LA) Washington, DC United States Catholic Mission Association; [P] Los Angeles, CA Missionaries of Jesus, Inc.
Montoya, Rev. Msgr. Paul M. '73 (LA) Moderator.
Montoya, Pedro N. '93 (ARE) Camuy, PR St. Joseph.
Monturo, Christopher W. '03 (NY) West Harrison, NY St. Anthony of Padua.
Montz, Jeffrey A. '08 (NO) Kenner, LA Divine Mercy.
Monzillo, Oneil '53 (NO) Retired.
Monzon–Balagat, Arturo J. '75 (SB) On Leave of Absence.
Moodie, Michael *s.j.* '79 (SJ)[D] San Jose, CA Bellarmine College Preparatory.
Moody, Kenneth J. *m.m.* '70 (FgM) Maryknoll, NY MARYKNOLL.
Moody, Quentin E. '85 (NO) New Orleans, LA St. Augustine.
Moody, William J. '70 (BAL) Retired.
Moon, Michael E. '02 (MAD) Belleville, WI St. Francis of Assisi.
Moon, Michael (NY) Staten Island, NY Blessed Sacrament.
Mooney, Dennis M. '77 (PH) Bristol, PA St. Mark.
Mooney, Rev. Msgr. Michael P. '63 (PT) Pensacola, FL Nativity of Our Lord; Priests' Pension Plan, Board for.
Mooney, Richard T. '79 (RIC) Lynchburg, VA St. Thomas More.
Mooney, William C. '68 (STA) St. Augustine, FL Corpus Christi.
Mooney, William J. '68 (PAT) Florham Park, NJ Holy Family.
Mooney, William '55 (SD) Retired.
Moonnanappallil, Joseph '92 (HRT) Manchester, CT Assumption; Manchester, CT St. James.
Moons, Joseph *c.p.* '77 (GAL)[O] Houston, TX Congregation of the Passion, Holy Name Passionist Community and Retreat Center; [Q] Houston, TX Holy Name Retreat Center; Consultors.
Moons, Joseph *c.p.* '76 (CHI)[N] Chicago, IL Passionist Provincial Office.
Mooradd, Paul '84 (SAM) Worcester, MA Our Lady of Mercy.
Moorby, William A. '82 (ROC) Owego, NY St. Patrick; Owego, NY Blessed Trinity.
Moore, Andrew '97 (BEA) Director of Seminarians; Kountze, TX Holy Spirit Mission; Lumberton, TX Infant Jesus.
Moore, Anthony F. *o.f.m.* '51 (NY) Yulan, NY St. Anthony of Padua.
Moore, Augustine J. '60 (SFE) Retired.
Moore, Rev. Msgr. Brian R. '83 (DOD) College of Consultors; Priest Continuing Formation Commission; [F] Dodge City, KS The Diocese of Dodge City Priest Retirement Fund, Inc. Retired.
Moore, Christian *o.f.m.conv.* '65 (L) Louisville, KY Incarnation; [L] Louisville, KY St. Francis of Assisi Friary.
Moore, Christopher P. '77 (BAL) Hagerstown, MD St. Ann; Hagerstown, MD St. Joseph; Priest Personnel Board.
Moore, Daniel F. *s.s.* '84 (BAL)[Q] Baltimore Society of St. Sulpice, Province of the United States.
Moore, Daniel F. *s.s.* '84 (WDC)[A] Washington, DC Theological College of the Catholic University of America.
Moore, Daniel *s.e.m.v.* (STP) St. Paul, MN St. Francis De Sales.
Moore, Donald J. *s.j.* '60 (NY)[DD] Loyola Hall, Jesuit Community.
Moore, Rev. Msgr. Edmund J. '59 (SHP) Monroe, LA Jesus the Good Shepherd Retired.
Moore, Edward F. *m.m.* '58 (NY)[DD] Maryknoll Maryknoll Fathers and Brothers Retired.
Moore, Frederick Thomas '75 (STA) Retired.
Moore, George B. '66 (PH) Philadelphia, PA St. Benedict.
Moore, Gregory J. *o.p.* '55 (CHI)[N] Chicago, IL St. Pius V Priory.
Moore, James J. *o.p.* '08 (TUC)[H] Tucson, AZ University of Arizona.
Moore, Rev. Msgr. James R. '67 (NY) Croton Falls, NY St. Joseph.
Moore, James T. '84 (GAL) Retired.
Moore, James W. *s.j.* '59 (PH)[Y] Loyola Center and Manresa Hall.
Moore, James '74 (SB) Retired.
Moore, James '88 (SFE) Retired.
Moore, James *o.p.* '08 (WDC)[B] Washington, DC Dominican House of Studies.
Moore, Jeffery Wade '10 (SAT) San Antonio, TX Our Lady of the Atonement Catholic Church.
Moore, John Charles '78 (BAL) Middletown, MD Holy Family Catholic Community Retired.
Moore, Rev. Msgr. John F. '60 (FR) Retired.
Moore, Jon H. '81 (WIN) Austin, MN Queens of Angels Hermitage; [A] Winona, MN Immaculate Heart of Mary Seminary; [H] Austin, MN Annunciation Hermitage, Carmelites of St. Joseph.
Moore, Lawrence *s.j.* '77 (NO)[C] New Orleans, LA Loyola University New Orleans.
Moore, Mark J. '03 (STU) Assistant Directors.
Moore, Mark '03 (STU) Campus Ministry; Athens, OH Christ the King University Parish; Athens, OH St. Paul's.
Moore, Michael '97 (FRS) Hanford, CA St. Brigid; Cliffside Park, NJ St. Patrick's Missionary Society.
Moore, Michael *s.p.s.* '84 (SJ) Saratoga, CA; [M] Saratoga, CA St. Patrick's Missionary Society.
Moore, Michael *o.s.f.s.* '68 (FgM) Wilmington, DE OBLATES OF ST. FRANCIS DE SALES MISSIONS.
Moore, Neil '60 (P) Retired.
Moore, Patrick *o.s.b.* '66 (BIS) New England, ND St. Elizabeth; New England, ND St. Mary; Richardton, ND; [A] Richardton, ND Assumption Abbey.
Moore, Raymond H. '81 (WDC) Washington, DC St. Thomas More; Deans; Priest Council.
Moore, Robert O. *o.c.s.o.* '49 (ROC)[K] Piffard, NY Abbey of the Genesee.
Moore, Steven C. '76 (ANC) Office of Finance.
Moore, Steven C. '76 (ANC) Diocesan Consultors; Chief Operating Officer and Chief Finance Officer.
Moore, Rev. Msgr. Terence M. '67 (SLC) Board of Directors; College of Consultors; Draper, UT Saint John the Baptist LLC 252; Presbyteral Council.
Moore, Thomas *o.s.f.s.* '66 (FgM) Wilmington, DE OBLATES OF ST. FRANCIS DE SALES MISSIONS.
Moore, Ward P. '72 (NEW) Fairfield, NJ St. Thomas More; Serra Club of North Essex; Union, NJ St. Michael's Retired.
Moore, Wilbur E. '57 (OKL) Retired.
Moore, Rev. Msgr. William C. '68 (STO) Stockton, CA St. Bernadette Church (Pastor of); Air Force Reserve Chaplains.
Moore, William C. *ss.cc.* '75 (LA)[P] La Verne, CA Congregation of the Sacred Hearts of Jesus and Mary.
Moore, William F. '69 (CAM) Pennsauken, NJ Mary, Queen of All Saints, Pennsauken, N.J.; Continuing Education & Spiritual Formation of Priests (CESF); Vocation Advisory Board.
Moore, Rev. Msgr. William '68 (STO) Diocesan Building Committee.
Moorman, Dennis *m.m.* '98 (FgM) Maryknoll, NY MARYKNOLL.
Moorman, William J. *o.ss.t.* '79 (BAL)[N] Baltimore, MD Trinitarian Counseling Services, Inc.; [Q] Archdiocese of Baltimore, MD – Assigned Elsewhere.
Moorman, William J. *o.ss.t.* '79 (VIC) On Special or Other Diocesan Assignment; Victoria, TX Our Lady of Sorrows.
Moorse, Dunstan *o.s.b.* '78 (SCL)[I] Collegeville, MN St. John's Abbey, of the Order of St. Benedict.
Moortgat, Luke *c.i.c.m.* '65 (FgM) Arlington, VA MISSIONHURST.
Moothasseril, Mathew '83 (SP) Tarpon Springs, FL St. Ignatius of Antioch.
Mooya, Cletus '07 (HON) Mililani Town, HI St. John Apostle and Evangelist.
Mora, Guillermo '96 (NEW) Ridgefield Park, NJ St. Francis of Assisi.
Mora, Ismael '02 (SR) Eureka, CA Sacred Heart.
Mora, Juan R. '92 (ARE) Barceloneta, PR Our Lady of Victory.
Mora, Pedro M. *c.s.b.* '04 (GAL)[O] Sugar Land Basilian Mission Center.
Mora, Sergio '94 (OAK) Pittsburg, CA St. Peter, Martyr of Verona.
Mora, Tito Abdenago Medina *m.s.c.* '92 (FgM) Aurora, IL MISSIONARIES OF THE SACRED HEART.
Morabito, Vincent R. '87 (PH) Secane, PA Our Lady of Fatima.
Moraga, Cecilio '84 (SD) Julian, CA Saint Elizabeth of Hungary Catholic Parish; Santa Ysabel, CA Santa Ysabel Indian Mission Catholic Parish.
Moral, Alejandro *o.c.d.* '60 (CGS)[A] Caguas, PR Colegio San Jose Superior; Caguas, PR San Jose.
Morales, Anibal '93 (MIA) Miami, FL Corpus Christi.
Morales, Carlos R. *o.s.a.* (SJN) Santa Monica.
Morales, Dan '90 (VIC) Victoria, TX St. Mary's; Defenders of the Bond; Campaign For Human Development and Catholic Relief Services; Vocations Director; Director of Seminarians.
Morales, Eduardo D. '96 (SAT) San Antonio, TX St. Peter Prince of the Apostles; In Metropolitan Area; Archdiocesan Presbyteral Council; Priests Personnel Board.
Morales, Rev. Msgr. Elias S. '91 (PCE)[A] Ponce, PR Diocesan Seminary Regina Cleri; Judicial Vicar; Diocesan Consultors; Vocations.
Morales, Fabio Mavin *c.ss.r.* (BAL) Annapolis, MD St. Mary.
Morales, Geovany *c.m.* '01 (FgM) Philadelphia, PA Eastern Province.
Morales, Gonzalo '85 (FWT) Granbury, TX St. Frances Cabrini.
Morales, Harry Flores *s.m.m.* '09 (BRK)[R] Ozone Park Montfort Missionaries Provincialate (Missionaries of the Company of Mary).
Morales, Hugo '06 (CHI) Cicero, IL Mary, Queen of Heaven.
Morales, Ignacio Jimenez '11 (BLX) Laurel, MS Immaculate Conception.
Morales, Ignacio '09 (ATL) Cumming, GA Good Shepherd; Dahlonega, GA St. Luke.
Morales, Rev. Msgr. John F. '60 (GRY) Retired.
Morales, Jose A. '10 (ELP) El Paso, TX St. Mark.
Morales, Jose L. '04 (WIN) Worthington, MN St. Mary's.
Morales, Juan P. '11 (NEW) Jersey City, NJ St. Paul's.
Morales, Leocadio '89 (FRS) Planada, CA Sacred Heart; Merced, CA Our Lady of Mercy/St. Patrick's.
Morales, Raul (CGS) Caguas, PR Nuestra Senora del Perpetuo Socorro; Priests Senate.
Morales, Raymond D. '81 (LA) Long Beach, CA Our Lady of Refuge.
Morales, Ricardo Hernandez '98 (SJN) Spiritual Directors; Guaynabo, PR San Jose.
Morales, Robert P. '66 (BRK) Richmond Hill, NY Our Lady of the Cenacle.
Morales, Roberto *sch.p.* '96 (LA) Los Angeles, CA Our Lady Help of Christians (Maria Auxiliadora).
Morales, Romain G. *c.m.* '73 (STL)[O] St. Louis, MO Vincentian Residence.
Morales, Ruben '04 (OAK) Presbyteral Council.
Morales, Salomon J. '68 (ARE) Retired.
Morales–Martinez, Armando '05 (CHI) Chicago, IL Immaculate Conception.
Morales–Morfin, Ruben '04 (OAK) Walnut Creek, CA St. Mary.
Morales Cruz, Oscar *o.p.* (SJN) Bayamon, PR Catalina de Siena.
Morales Figueroa, Angel L. '83 (SJN) San Juan, PR Nuestra Senora de Lourdes.
Moralez Feliu, Francisco '89 (SJN) Carolina, PR Epifania Del Senor.
Moran, Charles '67 (STU) Chesapeake, OH St. Ann.
Moran, Edward J. '62 (WOR) Retired.
Moran, Edward M. '76 (HRT) West Hartford, CT St. Thomas the Apostle.
Moran, Edward '89 (RIC) Retired.
Moran, Edwin *c.p.* '61 (PIT)[M] Pittsburgh, PA St. Paul of the Cross Monastery.
Moran, Gerard K. '71 (OAK) Danville, CA St. Isidore.
Moran, Rev. Msgr. J. Thomas '57 (BUF) Finance Council; Youngstown, NY St. Bernard's.
Moran, James E. '59 (NU) Retired.
Moran, James F. '71 (BO) Permanent Disability.
Moran, James M. '74 (HRT) Wethersfield, CT Incarnation.
Moran, James M. '03 (NEW) Westfield, NJ Holy Trinity.
Moran, Rev. Msgr. James P. '72 (MET) South Bound Brook, NJ Our Lady of Mercy.
Moran, James *c.o.* '89 (CHR)[E] Rock Hill, SC Oratory of St. Philip Neri, Congregation of the Oratory of Pontifical Rite.
Moran, John J. *m.m.* '66 (NY)[DD] Maryknoll Maryknoll Fathers and Brothers.
Moran, John P. *s.s.c.* '50 (FgM) St Columbans, NE House of Post–Graduate Studies.
Moran, John *s.s.c.* '50 (PRO)[O] Bristol, RI St. Columban's Retirement House Retired.
Moran, John *s.s.c.* '82 (OM)[J] St. Columbans Missionary Society of St. Columban.
Moran, Joseph P. '71 (HEL) Health Leave.
Moran, Kevin '65 (SEA) Retired.
Moran, Rev. Msgr. Lawrence J. '52 (IND) Retired.
Moran, Martin O. '88 (HBG) On Duty Outside the Diocese.
Moran, Martin O. '88 (CIN) Cincinnati, OH Holy Cross–Immaculata; Cincinnati, OH Old St. Mary.
Moran, Michael F. '82 (MIL) Menomonee Falls, WI St. James.
Moran, Michael J. '58 (NEW) Retired.
Moran, Michael P. *s.m.a.* '81 (FgM)[L] Tenafly, NJ Society of African Missions, Provincialate, S.M.A. Fathers; Tenafly, NJ SOCIETY OF AFRICAN MISSIONS; Tenafly, NJ; Tenafly, NJ Society of African Missions.
Moran, Rev. Archpriest Michael '63 (HPM) Retired.
Moran, Owen B. '91 (PAT) East Hanover, NJ St. Rose of Lima.
Moran, Patrick '58 (DUL) Retired.
Moran, Pedro Lopez *c.m.f.* '52 (SJN) Bayamon, PR Santa Maria.
Moran, Rev. Msgr. Peter C. '65 (LA) Northridge, CA Our Lady of Lourdes Retired.
Moran, Richard S. '61 (BO) Senior Priests. Retired.
Moran, Robert B. '64 (SJ) Mountain View, CA St. Joseph.
Moran, Robert E. '69 (LFT) Portland, IN Immaculate Conception; Deans; Members.
Moran, Stephen P. '92 (CLV) Wooster, OH St. Mary of the Immaculate Conception; Rittman, OH St. Anne; [V] Wooster, OH St. Mary of the Immaculate Conception.
Moran, Terence J. '90 (BO) Chelsea, MA St. Rose of

Lima; Vicariate IV.
Moran, Thomas A. '71 (CHI) Northbrook, IL Our Lady of the Brook.
Moran, Thomas D. '88 (SFR) San Carlos, CA St. Charles Retired.
Moran, Thomas *c.m.f.* '55 (CHI) Chicago, IL Our Lady of Guadalupe; [N] Oak Park Claretian Missionaries USA Eastern Province.
Moran, Rev. Msgr. Timothy J. '76 (BO) Medway, MA St. Joseph.
Moran, Timothy '06 (ATL)[F] Alpharetta, GA Norcross Pastoral Center, Inc.
Morand, Robert '57 (DET) Detroit, MI Our Lady of the Rosary.
Moras, Leo '89 (MO) Army Chaplains.
Moratelli, Ronald J. '69 (HBG) Quarryville, PA St. Catherine of Siena.
Moravitz, Ryan John '08 (DUL) Crosslake, MN Immaculate Heart; Emily, MN St. Emily.
Morawski, Stefan *o.f.m.conv.* '68 (BGP) Bridgeport, CT St. Michael The Archangel.
Morbito, Angelo L. '56 (SY)[Q] Syracuse, NY Tommy Coyne Residence Dillon Hall Retired.
Morciniec, Peter J. '70 (SPC) Pierce City, MO St. Mary; Pierce City, MO St. Agnes.
Morcone, Nicholas J. *o.s.b.* '69 (BO)[U] Hingham, MA Glastonbury Abbey.
Moreau, Maurice *o.f.m.cap.* '98 (NY) Yonkers, NY Sacred Heart.
Moreau, Paul *l.c.* '02 (ATL)[C] Atlanta, GA Donnellan School Inc.; Woodstock, GA St. Michael the Archangel.
Moreau, Randall '87 (LAF) Church Point, LA Our Lady of the Sacred Heart; Absent on Sick Leave.
Moreau, Raymond J. '85 (OG) Chazy, NY Sacred Heart; Defenders of the Bond; Committee on Assignments.
Moreira, Adelson S. *o.ss.t.* '03 (BAL)[Q] Diocese of Victoria, TX.
Moreira, Adelson *o.s.s.t.* '03 (MIA) Miami, FL Our Lady of the Holy Rosary – St. Richard Church.
Moreira, Nelson A. *s.s.j.* '72 (BAL)[Q] Baltimore, MD St. Joseph Society of the Sacred Heart House of Central Administration; [U] Baltimore, MD Friends of Ijebu–Ode Diocese, Inc.
Morel, John J. '55 (NEW)[L] Rutherford, NJ St. John Vianney Residence for Priests Retired.
Morel, John *c.i.c.m.* '39 (ARL)[H] Arlington, VA Missionhurst, C.I.C.M.–Central House and Provincialate.
Moreland, J. Gordon *s.j.* '64 (ORG) Special Assignment; [L] Orange, CA House of Prayer for Priests.
Morell, Fernando '87 (ARE) Hatillo, PR Our Lady of Mt. Carmel; Priest's Senate (Consejo Presbiteral).
Morell, J. William *o.m.i.* '70 (WDC)[O] Washington, DC Oblate Community.
Morelle, Edmund J. '53 (SY) Retired.
Morelli, Attilio '98 (NEW) On Duty Outside the Archdiocese.
Morelli, Attilio '98 (PEO) Creve Coeur, IL Sacre Coeur.
Morelli, Gary '74 (SEA) Retired.
Morelli, Gary '81 (DET) Wyandotte, MI Henry Ford Wyandotte Hospital; Inkster, MI Holy Family Parish.
Morello, Carl '83 (CHI) Oak Park, IL St. Giles; College of Consultors.
Morello, Peter '78 (GLP) Retired.
Morello, Sam Anthony *o.c.d.* '62 (LR)[A] Little Rock, AR Marylake – Carmelite Novitiate.
Morelock, George L. '65 (SFD) Retired.
Morelos, Gustavo *s.d.w.* '59 (ORL) Retired.
Morena–Urzua, Moises '10 (KNX) Chattanooga, TN St. Jude.
Morency, Raymond P. '87 (PRT) Caribou, ME Parish of the Precious Blood.
Moreno, Antonio O. (MOB) Retired.
Moreno, Dario E. *m.s.c.* '04 (CHI) Chicago, IL St. Joseph.
Moreno, Dario *m.s.c.* '03 (RCK)[G].
Moreno, David *s.d.b.* '79 (NEW)[L] Orange, NJ The Salesian Community.
Moreno, Gonzalo *o.f.m.* '08 (SFE) Councilors:; [H] Albuquerque, NM The Province of Our Lady of Guadalupe.
Moreno, Hector C. '05 (LC) Necedah, WI St. Francis of Assisi.
Moreno, James S. '76 (DEN) Denver, CO Holy Family; Judicial Vicar; Metropolitan Judges.
Moreno, Jorge '63 (SD) Brawley, CA Our Lady of Perpetual Help Catholic Parish Brawley.
Moreno, Jose Alfredo '87 (SD) El Centro, CA Our Lady of Guadalupe Catholic Parish El Centro.
Moreno, Jose Luis *s.j.* '89 (MIL) Milwaukee, WI Our Lady of Guadalupe Parish; Milwaukee, WI St. Patrick.
Moreno, Jose *s.j.* '89 (MIL)[P] Milwaukee, WI Jesuit Community at Marquette University.
Moreno, Joseph F. '86 (BUF) Buffalo, NY St. Lawrence; Cattaraugus, NY St. Mary.
Moreno, Juan '60 (LSC) Las Cruces, NM St. Genevieve.
Moreno, Luis Carlos '09 (PAT) Hawthorne, NJ St. Anthony's.
Moreno, Martin '03 (DAL) Waxahachie, TX St. Joseph.
Moreno, Robert '93 (STF) Lancaster, NY St. Basil; Alden, NY Erie County Home; Alden, NY Erie County Correctional Facility.
Moreshead, Harold D. '55 (PRT) Portland, ME Our Lady of Hope Parish Retired.
Moreton, Rev. Msgr. John '64 (FRS) Fresno, CA Our Lady of Victory; Advocates; Personnel Board.
Moretta, Rev. Msgr. John T. '68 (LA) Los Angeles, CA Resurrection; Deanery 9; San Gabriel Region.
Morette, Thomas '05 (ALB) Presbyteral Council.
Moretti, Mark E. '95 (ARL) Warrenton, VA St. John the Evangelist.
Morey, Daniel B. *o.f.m.* '73 (NY)[DD] New York, NY Padua Friary.
Morey, Joshua *o.s.b.* '09 (TLS)[G] Hulbert, OK Our Lady of the Annunciation of Clear Creek Monastery.
Morey, Robert E. '96 (BAL) On Duty Outside the Archdiocese.
Morey, Robert E. '96 (CHR) Florence, SC St. Anthony.
Morfin, John N. '67 (GAL) Retired.
Morgan, Brendan P. '64 (NO) Retired.
Morgan, Charles J. '79 (ALX) Plaucheville, LA Mater Dolorosa.
Morgan, D. Terrence '76 (STA) St. Augustine, FL St. Anastasia; Presbyteral Council.
Morgan, Drew P. *c.o.* '85 (PIT)[M] Pittsburgh, PA Congregation of the Oratory of St. Philip Neri; Pittsburgh, PA.
Morgan, Edward *c.ss.r.* '64 (KC) Kansas City, MO Our Lady of Perpetual Help; [J] Kansas City, MO Redemptorists Fathers of Kansas City, Missouri.
Morgan, Guy *o.f.m.* '54 (PAT)[N] Butler, NJ St. Anthony Friary.
Morgan, James P. '01 (SFS) Sioux Falls, SD Holy Spirit; [I] Sioux Falls, SD Holy Spirit School Permanent Trust.
Morgan, Jerome L. '62 (SAL) Diocesan Finance Officer; Diocesan Finance Council; College of Consultors; Art and Architecture Commission; Ex Officio; Consultors; [H] Salina, KS St. Joseph Annex, Inc.
Morgan, Rev. Msgr. John W. '58 (B) Retired.
Morgan, John (B) Judges.
Morgan, Joseph A. '81 (OG) Defenders of the Bond; Diocesan Consultors; Ogdensburg, NY St. Mary's Cathedral.
Morgan, Julian *c.p.* '53 (BRK)[R] Jamaica, NY Immaculate Conception Monastery Retired.
Morgan, Martin J. '70 (TLS) Retired.
Morgan, Michael P. '01 (STA) Chancellor; Diocesan Consultors; Presbyteral Council; Building Commission; Ecumenism and Interfaith; Associate Judges; Jacksonville, FL Sacred Heart.
Morgan, Rev. Msgr. Thomas J. '65 (CAM) Cherry Hill, NJ St. Mary's R.C. Church, Delaware Township, N.J.; Cherry Hill, NJ The Church of St. Thomas More, Cherry Hill, New Jersey; Deanery Representatives; Vocation Advisory Board; Members.
Morgan, Thomas '84 (SP)[L] Tampa, FL St. Lawrence Housing, Inc.; Tampa, FL St. Lawrence; [L] Tampa, FL St. Lawrence Housing II, Inc.
Morgan, W. Donald '07 (SJ) Cupertino, CA St. Joseph of Cupertino.
Morgan, William P. '57 (BUR) Retired.
Morgera, Michael A. '85 (MEM) Paris, TN Holy Cross; [I] Memphis, TN Society of St. Vincent DePaul.
Morgewicz, Robert A. '09 (HRT) Hamden, CT St. Ann; New Haven, CT St. John the Baptist.
Morgia, Robustiano D. '76 (NO) Filipino Catholic Ministry; New Orleans, LA St. Maria Goretti.
Morhous, Robert *o.c.s.o.* '59 (WOR)[N] Spencer, MA St. Joseph's Abbey.
Moriarity, Daniel J. '64 (PH) Philadelphia, PA Nativity of the Blessed Virgin Mary Retired.
Moriarity, Robert T. '92 (SLC) Presbyteral Council.
Moriarity, William J. '66 (CHI) Chicago, IL Holy Name Cathedral; Streamwood, IL St. John the Evangelist.
Moriarty, Edward *c.ss.r.* '42 (FgM) Baltimore Province.
Moriarty, James F. '51 (CHI) Evanston, IL St. Joan of Arc Retired.
Moriarty, John J. '62 (JOL) Retired.
Moriarty, John '91 (LEX) Lexington, KY St. Elizabeth Ann Seton; College of Consultors; Fayette.
Moriarty, Joseph B. '93 (IND) French Lick, IN Our Lady of the Springs Catholic Church, French Lick, Inc.; French Lick, IN Our Lord Jesus Christ the King Catholic Church, Paoli, Inc.; [A] Saint Meinrad, IN Saint Meinrad School of Theology.
Moriarty, Mark D. '99 (STP) Rogers, MN The Catholic Church of Mary Queen of Peace.
Moriarty, Robert T. '92 (SLC) Kearns, UT Saint Francis Xavier LLC 222; Team.
Moriarty, Thomas '92 (RVC) Inwood, NY Our Lady of Good Counsel; Hewlett, NY St. Joseph's.
Moriarty, Timothy J. '03 (HEL) Anaconda, MT Anaconda Catholic Community.
Morin, Benjamin R. *s.j.* '56 (DET)[K] Clarkston, MI Colombiere Center.
Morin, Eddy '99 (PRT) Special or Other Diocesan Assignment.
Morin, Francis P. '73 (PRT) Augusta, ME St. Michael Parish.
Morin, George E. '70 (BO) Merrimac, MA Holy Redeemer.
Morin, John *o.m.i.* '51 (NO) New Orleans, LA Our Lady of Guadalupe /International Shrine of St. Jude.
Morin, Joseph J. *c.ss.r.* '64 (CHI)[N] Chicago, IL The Redemptorist Fathers of Chicago; Chicago, IL St. Michael in Old Town.
Morin, Maurice N. '64 (PRT) Lewiston, ME Prince of Peace Parish Retired.
Morin, Michael J. '88 (LIN) Lincoln, NE Sacred Heart; Presbyteral Council; Apostleship of Prayer; Advocates.
Morin, Robert *o.m.i.* '69 (STP)[J] St. Paul, MN Oblate Residence.
Morin, Timothy '77 (STP) Special Assignment.
Moris, Daniel Lee '10 (SFS) Sioux Falls, SD St. Michael.
Morisette, Alfred *s.j.* '61 (SPK)[B] Spokane, WA Gonzaga University.
Morisette, Richard P. '61 (SY) Retired.
Morlan, Lawrence A. '95 (PEO) On Leave of Absence.
Morley, Craig '01 (SP) Brooksville, FL St. Anthony the Abbot; Appointed Members; College of Consultors.
Morley, Ed *o.c.s.o.* '83 (ATL)[F] Conyers, GA The Monastery of the Holy Spirit.
Morley, John F. '62 (NEW)[B] Seton Hall University; [B] Seton Hall University Retired.
Morley, John J. '04 (MET) Perth Amboy, NJ Holy Spirit; Perth Amboy, NJ Raritan Bay Medical Center.
Morley, John M. '61 (NEW) Retired.
Morlino, Rt. Rev. Paschal A. *o.s.b.* '66 (BAL) Baltimore, MD St. Benedict.
Morlino, Paschal A. *o.s.b.* '66 (GBG)[H] Latrobe, PA Saint Vincent Archabbey.
Morman, David G. '89 (BIS) Bowman, ND St. Charles; [I] Sentinel Butte, ND Home On The Range Foundation; Bowman, ND St. Mary; Bowman, ND St. Mel; Priests' Benefit Association.
Morman, James V. *t.o.r.* '92 (ALT)[G] Loretto, PA St. Francis Friary at Mount Assisi.
Morman, Ken '73 (CIN)[B] Cincinnati, OH Mount St. Mary's Seminary of the West.
Morman, Kenneth G. '73 (TOL) On Duty Outside the Diocese.
Mormando, Nicholas A. *o.f.m.cap.* '01 (NEW)[L] Union City, NJ Capuchin Friars – Province of the Sacred Stigmata of St. Francis.
Moroney, Rev. Msgr. James P. '80 (BO)[A] Brighton, MA St. John Seminary.
Moroney, Rev. Msgr. James P. '80 (WOR) On Duty Outside the Diocese.
Moroney, Martin J. '67 (SAC) Retired.
Moroney, Michael J. '71 (BR) Judges; Ecumenical Affairs; Presbyteral Council; Greenwell Springs, LA St. Alphonsus Liguori.
Moroney, William *m.afr.* '61 (FgM) Washington, DC MISSIONARIES OF AFRICA.
Moronta, Andris Alexis *i.v.e.* '02 (PH) Philadelphia, PA Ascension of Our Lord; Philadelphia, PA St. Hugh of Cluny.
Morosini, Louis *s.m.* '56 (FgM) THE SOCIETY OF MARY.
Morozowich, Mark '91 (SJP) On Assignment Outside the Diocese; Administrative Council; Liturgical Commission; Vocations; [C] Catholic University of America, The; Presbyters.
Morras, Ignacio '49 (MIA) Retired.
Morras, Rev. Msgr. Xavier '50 (MIA) Retired Priests' Committee Retired.
Morreale, Matthew *o.f.m.* '85 (NY) Bronx, NY Our Lady of Pity.
Morreale, Matthew *o.f.m.* (HRT) New Milford, CT St. Francis Xavier.
Morrette, Thomas '05 (ALB) Members; Diocesan Board of Consultors; Johnstown, NY Holy Trinity Parish.
Morrier, David *t.o.r.* '97 (STU)[A] Steubenville, OH Franciscan University of Steubenville; [H] Steubenville, OH Holy Spirit Friary; Councilors.
Morrill, Bruce T. *s.j.* '92 (BO)[U] Boston The Society of Jesus of New England–Provincial Offices.
Morris, Alan E. '92 (PIT) Harwick, PA Our Lady of Victory.
Morris, Alexis P. *o.f.m.* '56 (SP)[N] St. Petersburg, FL St. Anthony Friary Retired.
Morris, Anthony W. *c.ss.r.* '94 (RIC) Blackstone, VA Immaculate Heart of Mary; Farmville, VA Church of the Nativity; Farmville, VA St. Theresa; Meherrin, VA Sacred Heart.
Morris, Rev. Msgr. C. Eugene '96 (STL) Special Assignment.
Morris, Charles M. '83 (DET) Detroit, MI St. Christopher.
Morris, Rev. Msgr. Eugene C. '96 (COL)[A] Columbus, OH Pontifical College Josephinum; [A] Columbus, OH Pontifical College Josephinum.
Morris, George O. *s.j.* '68 (SPK)[B] Spokane, WA Gonzaga University.
Morris, Gerald R. '70 (MIA) Marathon, FL San Pablo; Deans and Deaneries; Monroe Deanery.
Morris, James H. '66 (SFR) Retired.
Morris, James '93 (STF) Salem, MA St. John the

Baptist; Educational Institutions.
Morris, James (KAL) St. Joseph, MI St. Joseph.
Morris, John J. '60 (NEW) Retired.
Morris, John J. *s.j.* '62 (P)[L] Portland, OR Colombiere Community.
Morris, John S. '62 (BO) Senior Priests. Retired.
Morris, John *o.p.* '66 (OAK)[B] St. Mary's College; [L] Oakland, CA Order of Preachers (Province of the Most Holy Name of Jesus – Western Dominican Province).
Morris, Jonathan (NY) New York, NY Basilica of St. Patrick's Old Cathedral.
Morris, Joseph E. '96 (ATL)[I] Kennesaw, GA Kennesaw State University; Special or Other Archdiocesan Assignment.
Morris, Joseph *s.j.* '59 (LA) Santa Barbara, CA Our Lady of Sorrows.
Morris, Kenan *o.f.m.* '50 (PAT)[N] Ringwood, NJ Holy Name Friary, Inc.
Morris, Kevin '97 (IND) Plainfield, IN St. Susanna Catholic Church, Plainfield, Inc.
Morris, Loyd '95 (DAL) Retired.
Morris, Michael E. *s.p.s.* '76 (NEW)[L] Cliffside Park, NJ St. Patrick's Missionary Society; Saratoga, CA; Cliffside Park, NJ St. Patrick's Missionary Society.
Morris, Michael J. '05 (SP) On Duty Outside the Diocese; Air Force Chaplains.
Morris, Michael T. *o.p.* '77 (OAK)[A] Berkeley, CA Dominican School of Philosophy and Theology; [L] Oakland, CA Order of Preachers (Province of Holy Name of Jesus – Western Dominican Province).
Morris, Michael '89 (NY) Archives.
Morris, Michael *o.p.* '77 (OAK)[L] Oakland, CA Order of Preachers (Province of the Most Holy Name of Jesus – Western Dominican Province).
Morris, Rev. Msgr. Philip D. '62 (NEW) Hillsdale, NJ St. John the Baptist; Short Hills, NJ St. Rose of Lima Retired.
Morris, Robert A. *o.p.* '50 (PRO)[O] Providence St. Thomas Aquinas Priory at Providence College.
Morris, Robert F. '66 (PT) Destin, FL Corpus Christi; Catholic Daughters of the Americas.
Morris, Rev. Msgr. Robert F. '91 (SP) Moderator of the Curia; Executive Committee; Vicar General; College of Consultors; Personnel Board; Ex Officio; Saint Petersburg, FL Cathedral of St. Jude the Apostle; Secretary of Christian Formation; Department of Christian Formation.
Morris, Robert J. '04 (NY) White Plains, NY St. Bernard; [HH] White Plains, NY The Little Disciple Learning Center, Inc.
Morris, Rev. Msgr. Robert '91 (SP)[H] Spring Hill, FL Father William F. Balfe Memorial Library; Clearwater, FL St. Catherine of Siena.
Morris, Stephen '79 (RVC) Seaford, NY Maria Regina.
Morris, Thomas A. *o.ss.t.* '81 (PH) Bristol, PA St. Ann.
Morris, Thomas A. *o.ss.t.* '81 (BAL)[Q] Archdiocese of Philadelphia, PA.
Morris, Wayne E. '01 (STU) Caldwell, OH Corpus Christi; Caldwell, OH St. Stephen; Priests Personnel Board.
Morris, Wayne '01 (STU) Caldwell, OH St. Michael; Caldwell, OH Immaculate Conception.
Morris, William T. '69 (MET)[B] Watchung, NJ Mount St. Mary Academy.
Morris, William T. '69 (NEW)[M] Englewood Cliffs, NJ St. Michael Villa.
Morrisey, Paul F. *o.s.a.* '67 (PH) Philadelphia, PA St. Augustine.
Morrison, Craig *o.carm.* '87 (WDC)[B] Washington, DC Whitefriars Hall.
Morrison, Rev. Msgr. David J. '54 (ALN) Bethlehem, PA Our Lady of Perpetual Help; Judges Retired.
Morrison, Douglas A. '56 (HRT) Retired.
Morrison, Jack '92 (SAM) Ministries (Permanent Deacons and Subdeacons); [E] New Bedford, MA Cedar Holdings, Inc.
Morrison, James J. '74 (PRT) Retired.
Morrison, James N. '10 (MOB) Auburn, AL St. Michael.
Morrison, John A. '92 (SAM) New Bedford, MA Our Lady of Purgatory.
Morrison, Larry '79 (RNO) Reno, NV St. Rose of Lima.
Morrison, Michael G. *s.j.* '68 (MIL)[P] Wauwatosa, WI Jesuit Community at St. Camillus.
Morrison, Thomas A. *o.p.* '55 (CHI)[N] Chicago, IL St. Pius V Priory.
Morrison, Thomas F. '76 (CHR) Absent On Leave.
Morrissette, Dominic '45 (JOL) Retired.
Morrissey, Daniel W. *o.p.* '62 (CHI)[N] Chicago Dominicans (Provincial Office).
Morrissey, J. Michael '78 (P) Veneta, OR St. Catherine of Siena.
Morrissey, John '63 (PMB) Fellsmere, FL Our Lady of Guadalupe Mission; Sebastian, FL St. Sebastian.
Morrissey, Joseph G. '77 (WIL)[B] Wilmington, DE Salesianum School.
Morrissey, Michael E. '86 (RCK) Dixon, IL St. Anne.
Morrissey, Rev. Msgr. Michael J. '65 (DAV) Adjutant Judicial Vicar; Judges; Diocesan Consultors; [J] Davenport, IA St. Vincent Center Retired.
Morrissey, Paul F. *s.m.* '75 (STP) St. Paul, MN St. Louis King of France.
Morrissey, Rev. Msgr. Robert O. '83 (RVC) Secretary to the Bishop; Vice Chancellor; Censors of Books; Judges for Interdiocesan Tribunal; Presbyteral Council; Secretary to the Bishop; College of Consultors.
Morrissey, Robert '76 (BGP) Leave of Absence.
Morrissy, Dennis M. '06 (RCK) Maple Park, IL St. Mary.
Morrone, Louis *o.p.* '92 (CHI)[N] Chicago, IL St. Pius V Priory; [N] Chicago Dominicans (Provincial Office); [W] Chicago, IL St. Thomas Aquinas Foundation; [W] Chicago, IL The Bolivian Trust of the Dominicans.
Morrow, Brian '80 (DEN) Graduate Studies.
Morrow, Dennis W. '75 (GR) Grand Rapids, MI SS. Peter and Paul; On Special Assignment; Archivist.
Morrow, Michael D. (NY) Yonkers, NY St. Eugene.
Morrow, Michael J. '86 (MO) Air Force Reserve Chaplains.
Morrow, Richard B. '55 (ATL) Atlanta, GA Cathedral of Christ the King; Judges; Vicars for Clergy Retired.
Morrow, Thomas G. '82 (WDC) Wheaton, MD St. Catherine Laboure.
Morse, Frederick '95 (PRT) Brunswick, ME All Saints Parish.
Morse, James H. '67 (FR) Retired.
Morse, John J. *s.j.* '61 (SPK)[J] Spokane, WA Regis Community.
Morse, Jonathan K. '88 (MO) Army Reserve Chaplains.
Morse, Michael '84 (STA) Absent or Sick Leave.
Morse, Richard E. *o.s.f.s.* '69 (TOL)[H] Toledo, OH.
Morse, Richard *o.s.f.s.* '69 (STO) Deans.
Mort, Ernest C. *c.s.p.* '59 (BRK)[R] Retired Retired.
Mortell, Anthony *s.s.c.* '60 (LA)[P] Los Angeles, CA Columban Fathers, Procure House.
Mortell, Anthony *s.s.c.* '60 (OM)[J] St. Columbans, NE Missionary Society of St. Columban.
Mortimer, Rev. Msgr. James E. '52 (PH) Retired.
Morton, Jake *s.j.* '75 (SPK) Inchelium, WA St. Michael's Mission; Nespelem, WA Sacred Heart Mission; Keller, WA St. Rose of Lima; Omak, WA St. Joseph.
Morton, Vincent '86 (SP) Retired.
Morton, William *s.s.c.* '60 (OM)[J] St. Columbans Missionary Society of St. Columban; St Columbans, NE; St Columbans, NE House of Post–Graduate Studies.
Morugui, Bhaskar (SAN) Abilene, TX St. Francis of Assisi.
Mosan–Rosero, Norman H. '05 (CHI) Chicago, IL St. Genevieve.
Mosbrucker, Jacob A. '66 (P) Retired.
Moscaritolo, Mario '64 (KC) Retired.
Moscinski, Fidelis *c.f.r.* '01 (NY)[DD] Bronx, NY Our Lady of the Angels Friary.
Mose, Stephen Nyakundi *o.c.d.* '11 (MIL)[P] Milwaukee Provincial Offices – Discalced Carmelites.
Mosele, Victor *s.x.* '60 (MIL)[B] Franklin, WI Xaverian Missionary Fathers College Seminary.
Moser, Albert *c.s.p.* '60 (OAK) Berkeley, CA Holy Spirit Parish/Newman Hall.
Moser, Claudio *o.f.m.* '63 (NY)[DD] St. Peter Friary.
Moser, John A. '86 (DUB) Lansing, IA St. Joseph; Lansing, IA Immaculate Conception; Lansing, IA Immaculate Conception; Lansing, IA St. Ann–St. Joseph.
Moser, Thomas W. '94 (KNX) Cleveland, TN St. Therese of Lisieux.
Moses, Patrick '03 (ORG) Cypress, CA St. Irenaeus.
Mosey, Douglas L. *c.s.b.* '74 (NOR)[A] Cromwell, CT Holy Apostles College and Seminary; [L] Cromwell, CT Basilian Fathers of Connecticut, Inc.
Mosha, Benedict Ndeyekiyo *a.l.c.p.* '89 (PMB) Tequesta, FL St. Jude.
Mosher, Robert *s.s.c.* '82 (FgM)[J] St. Columbans Missionary Society of St. Columban; St Columbans, NE House of Post–Graduate Studies.
Mosher, Thomas L. '81 (BUR) Woodstock, VT Our Lady of the Snows; Deans; Elected Members.
Mosimann, John P. '97 (ARL) Leesburg, VA St. John the Apostle; Defenders of the Bond.
Moskal, Joseph E. '65 (SY) Utica, NY Holy Trinity.
Mosko, Rt. Rev. Mitred Msgr. Leon '56 (STF) Retired.
Moskus, John T. '63 (HRT) Retired.
Mosley, Charles A. '85 (GRY) Hammond, IN Our Lady of Perpetual Help; Bishop's Council of Priests.
Mosley, Daniel E. '77 (STL) Warson Woods, MO Ste. Genevieve Du Bois.
Mosley, Rev. Msgr. Godfrey T. '79 (WDC) Washington, DC St. Ann; Adjutant Judicial Vicar.
Moslosky, Robert W. *c.s.b.* '74 (DET)[E] Novi, MI Catholic Central High School.
Moss, Brendan *o.s.b.* '01 (IND)[K] Saint Meinrad, IN St. Meinrad Archabbey; [A] Saint Meinrad, IN Saint Meinrad School of Theology.
Moss, Darius G. C. '97 (HBG) Millersburg, PA Queen of Peace.
Moss, James (PAT) Paterson, NJ Preakness Hospital; Budd Lake, NJ St. Jude.
Moss, James '82 (STA) Absent or Sick Leave.
Moss, Raymond B. '86 (CHY) Cheyenne, WY St. Joseph's.
Moss, Robert D. '69 (BUF) Absent on Leave.
Moss, Robert H. *c.s.c.* '74 (FTW)[A] Notre Dame, IN Moreau Seminary.
Mossa, Mark S. *s.j.* '08 (NY)[DD] Cardinal Spellman Hall, Jesuit Community.
Mossett, Robert C. *o.s.f.s.* '65 (DET) Monroe, MI St. Anne.
Mossholder, Francis D. '88 (LAN) Charlotte, MI St. Mary; Bellevue, MI St. Ann.
Mossi, John P. *s.j.* '73 (SJ)[O] Los Gatos, CA Jesuit Seminary Association; [B] Santa Clara, CA Jesuit Community.
Mostardi, Joseph S. *o.s.a.* '75 (PH)[C] Villanova University; [Y] Villanova, PA Provincial Offices of the Order of St. Augustine, Province of St. Thomas of Villanova; [Y] Villanova, PA Fray de Leon Community; Counselors.
Mostardi, Joseph S. *o.s.a.* '75 (CAM)[L] Ocean City, NJ Augustinian Friars.
Moster, Humbert *o.f.m.* '57 (CIN)[C] Cincinnati, OH St. Anthony Shrine, Franciscan Postulancy.
Moster, Humbert *o.f.m.* '57 (IND) Brookville, IN St. Peter Catholic Church, Franklin County, Inc.
Moster, James E. *o.f.m. cap.* '76 (COS)[H] Colorado Springs, CO Catholic Center at the Citadel; [E] Colorado Springs, CO Solanus Casey Friary.
Moster, James *o.f.m.cap.* '76 (MO) DEPARTMENT OF VETERANS AFFAIRS HOSPITALS AND CHAPLAINS.
Moszur, Edward J. '71 (GRY) Highland, IN Our Lady of Grace; Priests' Personnel Board; Bishop's Council of Priests.
Motl, James R. *o.p.* '62 (CHI)[N] Chicago, IL St. Pius V Priory.
Motsay, Joseph R. '78 (SCR) Retired.
Motsay, Russell E. '72 (SCR) Carbondale, PA Our Lady of Mt. Carmel.
Mott, Allen P. '03 (MAR) Chassell, MI St. Anne; Houghton, MI St. Albert the Great University Parish; [G] Houghton, MI St. Albert the Great, University Parish.
Mott, James A. *o.s.a.* '65 (LA) Los Angeles, CA Our Mother of Good Counsel.
Motta, Anthony '63 (ALB) Haines Falls, NY Sacred Heart–Immaculate Conception Church.
Motta, Jairo '83 (CC) Corpus Christi, TX Sacred Heart.
Motta, Rev. Msgr. Michael J. '72 (HRT) West Hartford, CT St. Mark the Evangelist; Special and other Archdiocesan Assignment; Office of Religious Education; Evangelization.
Mottau, Robert S. '58 (BO) Senior Priests. Retired.
Mottet, Rev. Msgr. Marvin A. '56 (DAV)[J] Davenport, IA St. Vincent Center Retired.
Motyka, Matthew J. *s.j.* '10 (SFR)[N] San Francisco, CA Loyola House Jesuit Community.
Mouannes, Nabil '84 (OLL) El Cajon, CA St. Ephrem Maronite Catholic Church; Pro–Life & Family Life Office.
Mouannes, Tanios '05 (SAM) Brockton, MA St. Theresa.
Mouawad, Paul '69 (SAM) Newtown Square, PA St. Sharbel.
Mouch, Rev. Msgr. Frank M. '58 (VEN) Retired.
Moudry, Paul '87 (STP) Golden Valley, MN St. Margaret Mary.
Moudry, Rev. Msgr. Richard P. '50 (STP) Retired.
Mould, Christopher J. '88 (ARL) Alexandria, VA St. Lawrence.
Moulder, John P. '90 (CHI) Chicago, IL St. Gregory, the Great.
Mount, Maurus B. *o.s.b.* '06 (GBG)[H] Latrobe Saint Vincent Archabbey; [H] Latrobe, PA Saint Vincent Archabbey.
Mountain, Edward C. '47 (WIN) Retired.
Mountain, Rev. Msgr. Joseph W. '52 (WIN) Retired.
Mounteer, Louis A. *s.j.* '56 (NY)[DD] New York, NY Murray–Weigel Hall.
Moussier, Howard R. *o.s.b.* '65 (BIR)[E] Cullman, AL St. Bernard Abbey.
Moutenot, Charles *s.j.* '84 (PAT)[J] Morristown, NJ Loyola House of Retreats.
Mouthevil, Ambrose (PIT) Allegheny County, PA Kane Regional Center – Ross.
Mouton, Rev. Msgr. Richard von Phul '55 (LAF) Diocesan Consultors; Holy Childhood; Pontifical Mission Societies; Lafayette, LA Cathedral of St. John the Evangelist; Instructors Retired.
Mouton, Thomas Jason '92 (LAF) Youngsville, LA St. Anne.
Mower, Scott M. '97 (PRT) Ellsworth, ME St. Joseph; Ellsworth, ME Stella Maris Parish.
Mowrer, Patrick '97 (PHX) Flagstaff, AZ San Francisco de Asis Roman Catholic Parish; Grand Canyon, AZ El Cristo Rey Roman Catholic Parish; Deans.
Moy, Francis J. *s.j.* '69 (BO)[U] Boston The Society of Jesus of New England–Provincial Offices.
Moy, Francis J. *s.j.* '69 (FR) South Dartmouth, MA St. Mary's.
Moyer, Joseph *c.s.c.* '94 (P)[B] University of Portland; [L] Portland, OR Holy Cross Fathers & Brothers, C.S.C. – University of Portland.
Moyer, Rev. Msgr. Richard W. '64 (PHX) Retired.
Moyher, Francis *t.o.r.* '63 (ALT)[G] Loretto, PA St.

Francis Friary at Mount Assisi.
Moylan, Thomas *l.c.* '69 (MAD)[F] Edgerton, WI Koshkonong Pastoral Center; [I] Edgerton, WI Oaklawn Incorporated.
MoyLan, Thomas *l.c.* '69 (SAC) Sacramento, CA Our Lady of Guadalupe Shrine.
Moyna, John L. '73 (ALB) Coxsackie, NY St. Mary; Coxsackie Correctional Facility; Advocates; Deans.
Moynahan, Michael E. *s.j.* '73 (SAC) Sacramento, CA St. Ignatius of Loyola; [H] Carmichael, CA Sacramento Jesuit Community.
Moynihan, Jeremiah P. '74 (ROC) Elmira, NY St. Mary Retired.
Moynihan, John C. *m.m.* '67 (FgM) Maryknoll, NY MARYKNOLL.
Moynihan, Noel *c.ss.p.* '77 (BRK) Woodside, NY Blessed Virgin Mary, Help of Christians.
Moynihan, T. Joseph '57 (BO) Senior Priests. Retired.
Moys, Rev. Msgr. Gregory '64 (P) St. Paul, OR St. Paul; Defenders of the Bond.
Mozdyniewicz, Piotr '94 (DEN) Arvada, CO Shrine of St. Anne.
Mozer, Joseph F. '97 (BO) Tribunal Court; Canonical Affairs Committee; Dedham, MA St. Mary.
Mpagi, Anthony '06 (WOR) African Ministry.
Mpanda, Apo T. '88 (DAV) Davenport, IA St. Anthony's; Blue Grass, IA St. Andrew.
Mpeka, Rogatus '82 (TR) Yardville, NJ St. Vincent de Paul.
Mpuya, Claudius '93 (SP) Largo, FL St. Patrick.
Mraz, Rev. Msgr. John S. '75 (ALN) Emmaus, PA St. Ann; Office of Ecumenical and Interreligious Dialogue.
Mraz, Louis R. *o.s.c.* '59 (PHX)[F] Phoenix, AZ Crosier Community of Phoenix (Canons Regular of the Order of the Holy Cross) Retired.
Mraz, Robert J. '74 (NU) Tracy, MN St. Mary; Walnut Grove, MN St. Paul; Priests' Council.
Mrnarevic, Daniel '84 (FAR) Grand Forks, ND St. Mary.
Mroczkowski, Joseph A. '45 (LIN) Retired.
Mroczkowski, Rev. Msgr. Joseph L. '42 (CHI) Chicago, IL St. Turibius Retired.
Mroczynski, Edward *s.ch.* '57 (SJ) San Jose, CA St. Brother Albert Chmielowski Polish Catholic Pastoral Mission.
Mrosso, Dennis '82 (CLV)[I] Garfield Heights, OH Marymount Hospital, Inc.
Mrowka, Chester R. *c.m.* '59 (HRT)[L] Manchester, CT DePaul Provincial Residence.
Mroz, Richard J. '92 (NEW) Closter, NJ St. Mary.
Mroziewski, Witold '91 (BRK) Brooklyn, NY Our Lady of Czestochowa–St. Casimir; [Q] Polish Apostolate; Attorneys and Counselors at Canon Law; Defenders of the Marriage Bond; Promoters of Justice.
Msaki, Beda *a.l.c.p.* '98 (SLC) Vernal, UT Saint James the Greater LLC 227.
Msoka, Gabriel *a.j.* (PEO) Lewistown, IL St. Mary's.
Msongore, Josaphat *c.s.sp.* '63 (FgM) Bethel Park, PA CONGREGATION OF THE HOLY SPIRIT.
Mtenga Ngayaku, Dominic J. '92 (CAM) Collingswood, NJ Blessed Teresa of Calcutta Parish, Collingswood, N.J.
Mubenga, Alex–Louis *c.j.* '89 (LA)[B] Santa Maria, CA St. Joseph Seminary (Josephite Fathers' Novitiate).
Muc, John *o.cist.* '90 (CHI)[N] Willow Springs, IL Cistercian Fathers, Our Lady Mother of the Church Polish Mission; Argo, IL Our Lady, Mother of the Church Polish Mission.
Mucci, Flavian *o.f.m.* '63 (FgM) New York, NY Franciscan Province of the Immaculate Conception.
Mucci, Robert V. '09 (BRK) Brooklyn, NY St. Mary Mother of Jesus; Vice Chancellors; Diocesan Judges; Attorneys and Counselors at Canon Law.
Muccilli, Sebastian '57 (MET) Retired.
Muccino, Keith F. *s.j.* '96 (CHI)[C] Chicago, IL Jesuit Community at Loyola University Chicago.
Mucha, Jan '54 (DEN) Retired.
Mucha, Jan '83 (CHI) Chicago, IL St. Ladislaus.
Mucha, John '81 (STU) Bridgeport, OH St. Anthony of Padua; Bridgeport, OH St. Joseph; Priests Personnel Board.
Mucha, Jozef '01 (SY) Pulaski, NY Christ Our Light.
Muckenhaupt, Gregory F. *s.j.* '88 (CI) Pohnpei, FM Sacred Heart; [C] Kolonia, Pohnpei, FM Jesuit House.
Muckenhaupt, Gregory F. *s.j.* '88 (FgM) New York, NY Society of Jesus.
Mucowski, Richard J. *o.f.m.* '71 (NEW) Wood Ridge, NJ Our Lady of the Assumption.
Mucowski, Richard *o.f.m.* (PAT) Consulting Psychologists and Experts.
Mucowski, Richard *o.f.m.* '71 (MET) Psychological Consultants.
Muda, Adam '09 (PAT) Hewitt, NJ Our Lady Queen of Peace.
Mudakodiyil, Jose Thomas '02 (BAK) La Pine, OR Holy Redeemer.
Mudavankunnel, Jose *m.s.f.s.* '81 (TYL)[C] Whitehouse, TX The Missionaries of St. Francis de Sales.
Mudavankunnel, Joseph *m.s.f.s.* (MOB) Lillian, AL St. Joseph.
Mudd, David A. '80 (WDC) Navy Chaplains Retired.
Mudd, Earl '60 (BEA) Retired.
Mudd, Gerald R. *o.f.m.* '66 (ALB)[B] Siena College; [R] Albany, NY St. Francis Chapel.
Mudd, James T. '64 (L) Louisville, KY St. Gabriel the Archangel Retired.
Mudd, Joachim Mary *f.i.* (IND)[K] Bloomington, IN Marian Friary of Our Lady Coredemptrix, Franciscans of the Immaculate.
Mudd, John '69 (WDC) Special Ministries; [D] Washington, DC Archbishop Carroll High School.
Mudrak, Lloyd '62 (DUL) Boy Scouts Retired.
Mudry, Lubomyr '51 (STF) Retired.
Mueggenborg, Rev. Msgr. Daniel H. '89 (TLS) Diocesan Consultors; Clergy Education; Staff; Diocesan Senators.
Mueggenborg, Rev. Msgr. Daniel M. '89 (TLS) Tulsa, OK Christ the King.
Mueller, Donald R. '61 (TOL) Retired.
Mueller, Eric '09 (TOL) Norwalk, OH St. Paul.
Mueller, Eugene J. '56 (CIN) Retired.
Mueller, Eugene *s.t.* '55 (WDC)[O] Adelphi, MD Father Judge Missionary Cenacle.
Mueller, Glenn R. *s.j.* '73 (KC) Kansas City, MO Guardian Angels; [J] Kansas City, MO Rockhurst Jesuit Community.
Mueller, James *o.carm.* '69 (JOL)[L] Darien Carmelite Provincial Office.
Mueller, James *s.m.* '53 (LA)[F] Marianist Community.
Mueller, Jerome D. *o.f.m.* '73 (SFE) Albuquerque, NM St. Charles Borromeo.
Mueller, John J. '59 (CLV) Wooster, OH St. Mary of the Immaculate Conception Retired.
Mueller, John J. *s.j.* '75 (STL)[C] Saint Louis University; [O] St. Louis, MO Jesuit Community Corporation at Saint Louis University – Jesuit Hall.
Mueller, Joseph G. *s.j.* '93 (MIL)[P] Milwaukee, WI Jesuit Community at Marquette University.
Mueller, Kevin A. '92 (BAL) Baltimore, MD Our Lady, Queen of Peace.
Mueller, Matthias R. *o.p.* '49 (CHI)[N] Chicago, IL Dominican Community; Chicago, IL St. Pius V.
Mueller, Michael '85 (MO) On Duty Outside the Diocese; Navy Chaplains.
Mueller, Noel *o.s.b.* '68 (IND)[K] Saint Meinrad, IN St. Meinrad Archabbey.
Mueller, Paul R. *s.j.* '93 (CHI)[N] Chicago Chicago Province of the Society of Jesus–Provincial Office.
Mueller, Richard J. '63 (CHI) Northbrook, IL St. Norbert Retired.
Mueller, Richard J. '66 (PIT) Retired.
Mueller, Robert F. '46 (MIL) Retired.
Mueller, Roman *s.d.s.* '74 (SAC) Orangevale, CA Divine Savior.
Muench, Rev. Msgr. R. Francis '81 (RIC) Regional Vicars; Judicial Vicar.
Muenchrath, David '04 (DM)[J] Panora, IA St. Thomas More Center; Vocations.
Muenks, Nicholas J. '06 (STL) St. Louis, MO St. Francis of Assisi.
Mugabe, Pascal *c.s.c.* '05 (FTW)[H] Notre Dame Congregation of Holy Cross, United States Province of Priests & Brothers.
Mugabowakigeri, Bernardin '96 (SAC) Alturas, CA Sacred Heart.
Mugan, William L. *s.j.* '55 (MIL)[P] Wauwatosa, WI Jesuit Community at St. Camillus.
Muganyizi, George *c.s.c.* '98 (FTW)[H] Notre Dame Congregation of Holy Cross, United States Province of Priests & Brothers.
Mugasha, Chrisanth *a.j.* '99 (NY) Manhattan, NY New York University Medical Center; New York, NY St. Cecilia.
Mugavero, Anthony P. '81 (ROC) Rochester, NY Holy Apostles.
Mugerwa, Paschal (BO) Dorchester, MA St. Mark.
Muggli, Boniface *o.s.b.* '90 (BIS) Richardton, ND St. Mary; [A] Richardton, ND Assumption Abbey; Richardton, ND St. Thomas; Richardton, ND St. Stephen.
Muggli, Odo *o.s.b.* '66 (BIS)[A] Richardton, ND Assumption Abbey; [I] Richardton, ND Sacred Heart Mission.
Muguerza, Octavio A. '92 (SAT) San Antonio, TX St. John Neumann.
Muha, Joseph '60 (B) Priest Retirement Committee Retired.
Muha, Peter J. '88 (GRY) Merrillville, IN Our Lady of Consolation.
Muhich, Peter '89 (DUL) Duluth, MN Cathedral of Our Lady of the Rosary; Mission Outreach and Propagation of the Faith.
Muhlbaier, Howard E. '65 (CAM) Gibbsboro, NJ St. Andrew the Apostle's R.C. Church, Gibbsboro, N.J.
Muhlen, Micah *o.f.m.* '91 (PHX) Advocates; Phoenix, AZ St. Mary's Roman Catholic Basilica.
Muhlenkamp, Robert K. '10 (CIN)[E] Hamilton, OH Stephen T. Badin High School; Liberty Township, OH St. Maximilian Kolbe.
Muhm, William M. '95 (MO) Military Chaplains; Navy Chaplains; Presbyteral Council.
Muhr, Rev. Msgr. Michael '83 (PMB)[A] Boynton Beach, FL St. Vincent de Paul Regional Seminary.
Muhr, Michael '83 (SP) On Duty Outside the Diocese.
Muir, Edmund D. '49 (DET) Retired.
Muir, Gavin W. '65 (PH) Riegelsville, PA St. Lawrence.
Muir, John '07 (PHX) Worship and Liturgy, Office of; [H] Tempe, AZ Arizona State University; Tempe, AZ All Saints Roman Catholic Newman Center.
Mujule, Christopher Michael '78 (BEL) Metropolis, IL St. Rose of Lima.
Mujuni, John Bosco (CHI) Chicago, IL St. Felicitas.
Mukalel, Joseph V. '58 (NEW) Retired.
Mukamba, Benoit *c.s.sp.* '92 (LR) Brinkley, AR St. John the Baptist; Forrest City, AR St. Francis of Assisi; Helena, AR St. Mary; Marianna, AR St. Andrew; Helena, AR St. Mary of the Lake Church.
Mukasa, Edoth *s.j.* '05 (FTW)[K] South Bend, IN Jesuit Community.
Mukasa, Edoth *s.j.* '05 (CHI)[N] Chicago Chicago Province of the Society of Jesus–Provincial Office.
Mukeya, Felix Kalila *o.c.d.* '01 (MIL)[P] Milwaukee Provincial Offices – Discalced Carmelites.
Mukkoot, Saji G. (MCE) New Baltimore, MI St. Joseph's Malankara Catholic Church; Vocation Promotion Director; Elected Members; Priests – Heads of Apostolates; Council for the Promotion of Culture and Heritage.
Mukkoot, Saji George '92 (CHI) Evanston, IL Divine Liturgy–Ascension Church; [J] Chicago, IL Resurrection Medical Center.
Mukkoot, Saji George '92 (DET) New Baltimore, MI St. Mary Queen of Creation.
Mukuka, George S. '11 (HRT) Naugatuck, CT St. Francis of Assisi.
Mukundi, Samson Ngatia '03 (CHI) Grayslake, IL St. Gilbert.
Mulakaleti, Yesuratnam '04 (SAN) Midland, TX St. Ann's.
Mulangattil, Joseph *m.c.b.s.* '74 (MIL)[P] Kenosha, WI Missionary Congregation of the Blessed Sacrament, Inc., Zion Province.
Mulanjanani, Thomas *c.sr.r.* (TOL) Toledo, OH St. Joseph.
Mularczyk, Mariusz (PIT) Aliquippa, PA St. Frances Cabrini.
Mulavanal, Thomas '90 (SYM) South Gate, CA St. Pius X Syro–Malabar Knanaya Catholic Mission of Los Angeles; Eparchial Consultors; Las Vegas, NV St. Stephen's Syro–Malabar Knanaya Catholic Mission, Las Vegas.
Mulcahey, Andrew T. '96 (RCK) Rockford, IL Holy Family.
Mulcahy, Brian Martin *o.p.* '90 (NY)[DD] New York, NY St. Vincent Ferrer Priory.
Mulcahy, Brian *o.p.* '90 (NY)[HH] New York, NY St. Thomas Aquinas Foundation.
Mulcahy, Daniel R. '79 (WOR) Millville, MA St. Augustine.
Mulcahy, Rev. Msgr. Donal '51 (LA) Ventura, CA Our Lady of the Assumption Retired.
Mulcahy, Gerald F. '62 (CHI) Hickory Hills, IL St. Patricia Retired.
Mulcahy, John M. *c.s.c.* '65 (FTW)[H] Notre Dame Congregation of Holy Cross, United States Province of Priests & Brothers.
Mulcahy, John P. '05 (WH) Wheeling, WV St. Vincent de Paul.
Mulcahy, Louis *o.s.b.* '89 (IND)[K] Saint Meinrad, IN St. Meinrad Archabbey.
Mulcahy, Matthew Bernard *o.p.* '03 (WDC)[B] Washington, DC Dominican House of Studies.
Mulcahy, Patrick J. '95 (SD) Bonita, CA Corpus Christi Catholic Parish.
Mulcahy, Patrick M. '06 (JOL) Clarendon Hills, IL Notre Dame.
Mulcahy, Sean '62 (MIA) Retired.
Mulcair, William W. *m.s.* '65 (HRT)[L] Hartford, CT Missionaries of LaSalette.
Mulcrone, Joseph A. '71 (CHI) Chicago, IL St. Francis Borgia; [W] Chicago, IL Catholic Office of the Deaf; Catholic Office of the Deaf.
Mulcrone, Thomas A. '77 (CHI)[L] Chicago, IL St. Mary of Providence; Fire Department Chaplain.
Mulderry, Anthony '67 (MIA) Pompano Beach, FL St. Gabriel; Chaplain—Broward County – Serra Club.
Muldoon, Rev. Msgr. Brendan '64 (SP) Indian Rocks Beach, FL St. Jerome; [F] Largo, FL St. Jerome Early Childhood Center.
Muldoon, P. Christopher '71 (PAT) Lake Hopatcong, NJ Our Lady Star of the Sea; Deans.
Muldowney, Thomas M. '03 (SCR) Episcopal Vicar for Clergy; Priests' Purgatorial Society; Scranton, PA St. Peter's Cathedral; Ex Officio.
Mulewski, Patrick M. '79 (NEW) Old Tappan, NJ St. Pius X.
Mulgrew, John E. '56 (PH) Media, PA St. Mary Magdalen Retired.
Mulhall, Michael *o.carm.* (CHI) Chicago, IL St. Thomas Apostle.
Mulhall, Michael *o.carm.* '67 (JOL)[L] Darien Carmelite Provincial Office.

Mulhauser, Daniel J. *s.j.* '60 (SY) Presbyteral Council; [Q] Syracuse, NY Jesuits at LeMoyne, Inc.
Mulhearn, Michael *c.m.* '68 (KC)[J] Independence, MO Vincentian Parish Mission Center.
Mulhern, Kevin P. '76 (SCR) Hanover Township, PA Exaltation of the Holy Cross; Wilkes–Barre, PA St. Robert Bellarmine Parish.
Mulholland, David T. '02 (SEA) Special Assignment; Presbyteral Council; Vicar for Clergy, Office of; Seattle, WA Our Lady of Fatima.
Muli, Killian '01 (CHY) Pine Bluffs, WY St. Paul's.
Mulka, Arthur C. '51 (GLD) Retired.
Mulka, Raymond C. '49 (GLD) Retired.
Mulkerin, Terrence J. '61 (BRK) Mission Office; Brooklyn, NY Holy Name; [V] Brooklyn, NY Society of the Immaculate Conception of Brooklyn Retired.
Mulkern, Daniel J. *t.o.r.* '66 (ALT)[G] Loretto, PA St. Francis Friary at Mount Assisi.
Mulkern, Stephen M. '49 (PRT) Retired.
Mull, Thomas P. '76 (ROC) Canadaigua, NY St. Mary; [O] Rochester, NY Apostleship of Prayer; East Bloomfield, NY St. Bridget.
Mullady, Brian T.B. *o.p.* '72 (P)[L] Portland, OR Holy Rosary Priory; Portland, OR Holy Rosary Parish & Dominican Priory.
Mullakara, Tijo Joy '06 (PH) Philadelphia, PA St. Josaphat.
Mullakkara, Joseph *m.s.f.s.* '75 (ATL)[E] Atlanta, GA Our Lady of Perpetual Help Home; Johns Creek, GA St. Benedict; [F] Snellville, GA The Missionaries of St. Francis De Sales.
Mullakkara, Joseph *m.s.f.s.* '75 (TYL)[C] Whitehouse, TX The Missionaries of St. Francis de Sales.
Mullally, Thomas A. *s.v.d.* '70 (JKS) Greenville, MS Sacred Heart; Shaw, MS St. Francis of Assisi.
Mullan, Glen F. '94 (CC) Corpus Christi, TX Christ the King.
Mullan, Patrick '67 (PAT)[Q] Chester, NJ Nazareth Village Retired.
Mullan, Rev. Msgr. Raymund A. '62 (FWT) Graham, TX St. Mary; Graham, TX St. Theresa of the Infant Jesus; Deans.
Mullan, William F. *m.m.* '62 (FgM) Maryknoll, NY MARYKNOLL.
Mullane, Bernard J. '56 (RCK) Retired.
Mullane, Thomas '68 (MIA) Big Pine Key, FL St. Peter.
Mullaney, Aidan '52 (ALT)[G] Loretto, PA St. Francis Friary at Mount Assisi.
Mullaney, Cornelius J. '71 (BO) Lynn, MA St. Pius Fifth.
Mullaney, Gregory C. '90 (NOR)[K] Storrs, CT University of Connecticut; Chaplains; Storrs, CT St. Thomas Aquinas.
Mullaney, Lawrence J. '88 (RIC) Elkton, VA Holy Infant; Quinque, VA Shepherd of the Hills.
Mullaney, Leonard M. '62 (FR) Retired.
Mullaney, Mark '03 (ARL) Clifton, VA St. Andrew the Apostle; Notaries.
Mullarkey, John T. '64 (GB) Clintonville, WI St. Mary; Clintonville, WI St. Rose Retired.
Mullarkey, Rev. Msgr. Patrick J. '64 (SD) San Diego, CA Saint Catherine Laboure Catholic Parish.
Mullelly, Thomas J. '80 (TR) Episcopal Council; [T] Princeton, NJ Campus Ministry for the Diocese of Trenton; Vicar; Ministry of Clergy Personnel.
Mullen, Rev. Msgr. Austin '65 (SP) Retired.
Mullen, Bernard *c.pp.s.* '48 (CIN)[N] Carthagena, OH St. Charles Retired.
Mullen, Charles *c.pp.s.* '64 (CIN)[N] Carthagena, OH St. Charles Retired.
Mullen, David J. '82 (BO) Bellingham, MA St. Brendan.
Mullen, Dennis M. '70 (SUP) Frederic, WI St. Dominic; Frederic, WI Immaculate Conception; Board of Directors.
Mullen, Godfrey *o.s.b.* '94 (IND)[A] Saint Meinrad, IN Saint Meinrad School of Theology; [K] Saint Meinrad, IN St. Meinrad Archabbey.
Mullen, Kevin *o.f.m.* '80 (ALB)[B] Loudonville, NY Siena College; [B] Siena College.
Mullen, Rev. Msgr. Michael '62 (KCK) Kansas City, KS St. Patrick's; Co Directors Seminarians; Archdiocesan Consultors.
Mullen, Michael '75 (VEN) Bradenton Beach, FL St. Bernard.
Mullen, Owen J. '64 (WIL) Retired.
Mullen, Owen '64 (SD)[B] University of San Diego.
Mullen, Patrick '85 (LA) Camarillo, CA Blessed Junipero Serra.
Mullen, Paul M. '73 (SCR) Milford, PA St. Vincent de Paul.
Mullen, Richard *o.s.a.* '81 (MIA) Office of Ecumenical and Inter–Faith Relations; Hollywood, FL Little Flower.
Mullen, Richard '55 (PEO) Retired.
Mullen, Thomas G. '56 (LKC) Retired.
Mullen, Thomas J. *ss.cc.* '75 (LA)[P] La Verne, CA Congregation of the Sacred Hearts of Jesus and Mary.
Mullen, Thomas *ss.cc* '75 (SB) Chino Hills, CA St. Paul the Apostle.
Mullen, Tom *ss.cc.* '75 (SB)[I] Chino Hills, CA Congregation of the Sacred Hearts of Jesus & Mary, SS.CC.
Muller, Anthony J. '68 (CIN) Cincinnati, OH St. Ann Retired.
Muller, James B. *o.p.* '59 (L) Louisville, KY St. Louis Bertrand; [L] Louisville, KY St. Louis Bertrand Priory.
Muller, Joseph T. *m.s.c.* '58 (ALN)[A] Center Valley, PA Sacred Heart Villa, Missionaries of the Sacred Heart.
Muller, Kennard '66 (BAL) Forest Hill, MD St. Ignatius Retired.
Muller, Rev. Msgr. Martin M. '57 (BIR) Birmingham, AL Our Lady of Sorrows; Diocesan College of Consultors; Priests'/Presbyteral Council; Diocesan College of Vicars.
Muller, Myles '48 (BAL) Retired.
Muller, Stephen *o.c.s.o.* '06 (ROC)[K] Piffard, NY Abbey of the Genesee.
Muller, William H. *s.j.* '73 (LA)[D] Los Angeles, CA Verbum Dei High School; [F] In Res.
Mullet, John '56 (SAG) Outside the Diocese.
Mullet, John '91 (SP)[J] St. Petersburg, FL St. Anthony's Hospital, Inc.
Mullett, Rev. Msgr. Gene W. '76 (STU) Tiltonsville, OH St. Joseph; Tiltonsville, OH St. Lucy's; Judges.
Mulligan, Bede J.K. *o.carm.* '58 (GBG)[H] Bolivar, PA Mount Carmel Hermitage; Bolivar, PA.
Mulligan, Bertram *o.f.m.cap.* '49 (SFR)[N] Burlingame, CA Capuchin Provincial House Retired.
Mulligan, Rev. Msgr. Edward '56 (SP) Clearwater, FL St. Brendan Retired.
Mulligan, George B. *c.s.c.* '82 (ORL)[F] Cocoa Beach, FL Congregation of Holy Cross, United States Province.
Mulligan, George B. *c.s.c.* '82 (FTW)[H] Notre Dame Congregation of Holy Cross, United States Province of Priests & Brothers.
Mulligan, Rev. Msgr. James J. '61 (ALN) Censor of Books; Priestly Life and Ministry Office; Diocesan Medical Ethicist; Northampton, PA Queenship of Mary Parish.
Mulligan, James J. '66 (PH) Doylestown, PA Our Lady of Mount Carmel.
Mulligan, James *s.o.l.t.* (PAT)[J] Branchville, NJ Sanctuary of Mary–Our Lady of the Holy Spirit.
Mulligan, John M. '64 (ROC) Rochester, NY; Vicars General; Judges; Priest Consultors; Rochester, NY Sacred Heart Cathedral Retired.
Mulligan, Rev. Msgr. John T. '64 (NY) Piermont, NY St. John the Baptist.
Mulligan, Joseph E. *s.j.* '73 (FgM)[K] Detroit Detroit Province of the Society of Jesus–Provincial Office; Chicago, IL Society of Jesus.
Mulligan, Joseph V. '75 (CHL) On Duty Outside the Diocese.
Mulligan, Paul F. '57 (BO) Senior Priests. Retired.
Mulligan, Robert G. *o.s.f.s.* '85 (PH)[Y] Philadelphia, PA Father Louis Brisson Residence.
Mulligan, William L. *s.j.* '65 (BO)[CC] Cambridge, MA The Youville House, Inc.
Mullin, Douglas *o.s.b.* '07 (SCL)[B] Saint John's University; [I] Collegeville, MN St. John's Abbey, of the Order of St. Benedict.
Mullin, Edward J. *c.m.* '54 (STL)[O] Perryville, MO Congregation of the Mission.
Mullin, Hugh J. '46 (KC) Retired.
Mullin, John A. *s.j.* '75 (NEW)[B] Jersey City, NJ Jesuit Center; [L] Jersey City, NJ Jesuits of Saint Peter's College, Inc.
Mullin, John A. *s.j.* '75 (NEW)[C] Jersey City, NJ Jesuit Community; [L] Jersey City, NJ Jesuit Community of St. Peter's Prep, Inc.
Mullin, Patrick J. *c.m.* '75 (LA)[P] Santa Barbara, CA St. Mary's Evangelization Center; [V] Santa Barbara, CA St. Mary's Seminary Center.
Mullin, Rev. Msgr. Thomas M. '75 (PH) Uwchlan, PA Saint Elizabeth.
Mullins, Kevin C. *o.s.a.* '90 (MIL) Racine, WI St. Rita.
Mullins, Kevin *s.s.c.* '78 (OM)[J] St. Columbans Missionary Society of St. Columban; Council.
Mullins, Michael E. '05 (ALN) Whitehall, PA St. Elizabeth; Advocates.
Mullins, Rev. Msgr. Raymond '52 (PT) Pensacola, FL Nativity of Our Lord Retired.
Mullins, Richard A. '95 (ARL) Alexandria, VA St. Louis.
Mullonkal, George '71 (SJP) Rossford, OH St. Michael; Presbyters.
Mullowney, Edward J. *s.s.j.* '55 (BAL)[Q] Baltimore, MD St. Joseph's Manor.
Mullowney, Thomas E. '55 (GI) Retired.
Mulloy, James *s.d.b.* '85 (NY)[E] New Rochelle, NY Salesian High School.
Mulloy, James *s.d.b.* (NEW)[L] Orange, NJ The Salesian Community.
Mulloy, John F. '70 (BO) Malden, MA St. Joseph.
Mulloy, Michel '79 (RC) Rapid City, SD Cathedral of Our Lady of Perpetual Help; Diocesan Consultors.
Mulqueen, John D. '62 (Y) Retired.
Mulqueen, Rev. Msgr. Joseph C. '57 (BRK) Defenders of the Marriage Bond; Long Island City, NY St. Mary; Attorneys and Counselors at Canon Law Retired.
Mulqueen, Martin B. '74 (PMB) Palm City, FL Holy Redeemer.
Mulranen, Francis J. '82 (PH) Coatesville, PA St. Cecilia.
Mulrenan, Alexius J. *o.f.m.* '60 (SP)[N] St. Petersburg, FL St. Anthony Friary Retired.
Mulroney, Joseph G. '93 (R) Promoter of Justice; Absent on Leave.
Mulrooney, Conan P. *o.praem.* '67 (GB)[J] De Pere, WI St. Norbert Abbey.
Mulroy, Timothy *s.s.c.* '95 (CHI)[N] Chicago, IL Columban Fathers Theologate.
Mulroy, Timothy *s.s.c.* '95 (OM)[J] St. Columbans Missionary Society of St. Columban.
Mulvanerty, Rev. Msgr. Thomas F. '79 (RVC)[N] Amityville, NY St. Pius X Residence; Ministry to Senior Priests; Priests' Retirement Board; [N] Amityville, NY St. Pius X Residence; Priests' Personnel Policy Board.
Mulvaney, Frank '08 (NY) Bronx, NY Immaculate Conception.
Mulvanity, Francis C. '51 (CLV) Retired.
Mulvany, Michael '88 (KCK) Lawrence, KS Corpus Christi.
Mulvehill, John R. '57 (BO) Cohasset, MA St. Anthony of Padua.
Mulvehill, Louis J. '53 (ALT) Retired.
Mulvey, Gerard *o.f.m.cap.* '91 (NY) New York, NY St. John the Baptist.
Mulvihill, David J. '72 (CHI) Zion–Beach Park, IL Our Lady of Humility Retired.
Mulvihill, John E. '64 (CHI) Highwood, IL St. James.
Mulvihill, Martin J. '83 (STL) Pacific, MO St. Bridget Church.
Muma, Sama F. '08 (DET) Temperance, MI Our Lady of Mt. Carmel.
Mumba, David *s.o.l.t.* '09 (FAR) Belcourt, ND St. Ann.
Mumper, Edward '63 (JOL) Retired.
Mundackal, Sebastian *o.s.b.* '91 (STL) High Ridge, MO St. Anthony of Padua.
Mundadan, Joe '84 (BEA)[B] Port Arthur, TX CHRISTUS Health Southeast Texas – CHRISTUS Hospital – St. Mary.
Mundakal, Joseph *c.m.i.* '83 (NSH) Lawrenceburg, TN Sacred Heart.
Mundanmani, Paulson '91 (OAK) Walnut Creek, CA St. Mary; Consultors.
Munday–Kukana, Raphael '07 (BRK) Forest Hills, NY Our Lady of Mercy.
Mundwiller, Edmund *o.f.m.* '81 (STL)[O] St. Louis, MO Franciscan Friary of St. Anthony of Padua.
Mung'amo, Casmir '11 (NY) Warwick, NY St. Stephen.
Mungovan, Reed *s.d.s.* '09 (MIL)[P] St. Francis, WI St. Joseph's Salvatorian Community (Novitiate).
Mungujakisa, Alfred '94 (CAM) Brigantine, NJ St. Thomas' Catholic Church, Brigantine, N.J.
Munishi, Honest *c.s.sp.* '00 (LR) Brinkley, AR St. John the Baptist; Forrest City, AR St. Francis of Assisi; Helena, AR St. Mary; Helena, AR St. Mary of the Lake Church; Marianna, AR St. Andrew.
Muniz, Alberto '77 (PCE) Salinas, PR Our Lady of Monserrat.
Muniz, Orlando Rosas '97 (MGZ) Mayaguez, PR Santa Teresita.
Muniz, William '94 (MIA)[G] Fort Lauderdale, FL Holy Cross Hospital.
Munjanath, Mathews Kurian '92 (SYM) Phoenix, AZ Holy Family Syro–Malabar Catholic Mission (Phoenix).
Munjanath, Mathews '92 (PHX) Phoenix, AZ Maricopa County Medical Center.
Munkelt, Richard A. '01 (SCR) On Duty Outside the Diocese.
Munley, J. Thomas '93 (LAN) On Leave of Absence.
Munoz, Arcadio B. '76 (NEW) Bergenfield, NJ St. John the Evangelist.
Munoz, David *o.m.i.* '10 (LAR) Laredo, TX Our Lady of Guadalupe.
Munoz, Eduard (TR) Hightstown, NJ St. Anthony of Padua.
Munoz, Elbano *c.o.* '05 (CHR) Rock Hill, SC St. Anne; [E] Rock Hill, SC Oratory of St. Philip Neri, Congregation of the Oratory of Pontifical Rite.
Munoz, Eusiquio–Arranz '64 (WOR) Retired.
Munoz, Francisco Ortega '05 (CHI) Chicago, IL St. Nicholas of Tolentine.
Munoz, Jacobo *l.c.* (NY)[HH] Thornwood, NY Alpha Omega Family Center, Inc.
Munoz, Javier (ATL) Marietta, GA St. Joseph.
Munoz, Jesus M. '01 (ARE) On Duty Outside the Diocese.
Munoz, Jose '96 (ORL) Orlando, FL St. Isaac Jogues.
Munoz, Juan Francisco *s.d.b.* '73 (LA) Los Angeles, CA St. Mary; [P] Los Angeles, CA Dominic Savio Salesian Residence.
Munoz, Manuel '98 (ELP) Absent on Leave.
Munoz, Martin *m.d.m.* '10 (PHX) Phoenix, AZ St. Edward Confessor Roman Catholic Parish; Tempe, AZ Holy Family Roman Catholic Parish; Tempe, AZ St. Martin de Porres Roman Catholic Parish.

Munoz, Mauro *o.f.m.* '91 (ELP) El Paso, TX Our Lady of Guadalupe.
Munoz, Octavio '04 (CHI) Casa Jesus; Chicago, IL Seminary Formation House–Casa Jesus.
Munoz, Oscar '97 (NY) Bronx, NY St. Margaret Mary.
Munoz, Rafael '60 (PCE) On Duty Outside the Diocese.
Munoz, Ruben D. '05 (GLD) Onekama, MI St. Raphael; Onekama, MI St. Joseph.
Munoz, Tomas G. '85 (TUC) Somerton, AZ Immaculate Heart of Mary Roman Catholic Parish – Somerton.
Munoz, Wellington Manuel '10 (NEW) Elizabeth, NJ Immaculate Heart of Mary and Saint Patrick.
Munoz–Capetillo, Octavio '04 (CHI) Other Assignments.
Munoz–Lasalle, Jesus M. '01 (MO) Army Reserve Chaplains.
Munoz–Sanchez, Ariel *o.r.c.* '97 (STO) Ceres, CA St. Jude Church (Pastor of).
Munro, Donald '87 (PMB) Wellington, FL St. Rita.
Munroe, Rev. Msgr. Henry T. '53 (FR) Retired.
Munsch, Nathan J. *o.s.b.* '91 (GBG)[H] Latrobe, PA Saint Vincent Archabbey.
Munsch, Nathan *o.s.b.* (ALT) Salisbury, PA St. Michael's.
Munshower, William G. '58 (IND)[J] Indianapolis, IN Our Lady of Fatima Retreat House, Inc.; [D] Indianapolis, IN Cathedral High School (Cathedral Trustees, Inc.); Indianapolis, IN St. Andrew the Apostle Catholic Church, Indianapolis, Inc. Retired.
Muntone, Rev. Msgr. Anthony D. *s.t.l.* '64 (ALN) Whitehall, PA St. Elizabeth.
Munung, Osward *a.j.* (SAG)[D] Saginaw, MI St. Mary's of Michigan Medical Center.
Munyaneza, Elias *a.j.* '91 (ALN) Easton, PA Our Lady of Mercy Parish.
Munz, Theodore G. *s.j.* '83 (CHI) Chicago, IL; Detroit, MI; [N] Evanston, IL Canisius House.
Munz, Theodore G. *s.j.* '83 (DET)[K] Chicago, IL Detroit Province of the Society of Jesus–Provincial Office.
Munz, Theodore G. *s.j.* '83 (CHI)[N] Chicago, IL Chicago Province of the Society of Jesus–Provincial Office.
Munz, Theodore G. *s.j.* '83 (MIL)[P] Milwaukee, WI Jesuit Provincial Office, Wisconsin Province; [Y] Milwaukee, WI The Jesuit Partnership.
Munzing, Joel *o.f.m.* '47 (PAT)[N] Ringwood, NJ Holy Name Friary, Inc.
Muodiaju, Samuel *c.s.sp.* '85 (MIA) Miami Gardens, FL St. Monica.
Muoneke, Romanus O. '74 (GAL) Houston, TX St. Peter Claver.
Muorah, Charles '91 (TR) Medford, NJ St. Mary of the Lakes; Marlton, NJ St. Isaac Jogues.
Mupparathara, Abraham J. *m.c.b.s.* '94 (MAR) Calumet, MI Our Lady of Peace; Calumet, MI Sacred Heart; Calumet, MI St. Paul the Apostle.
Mur, Rev. Msgr. Rogelio *o.carm.* '56 (MGZ) For Pastoral; Diocesan Consultors; Diocesan Board of Administration; Parish Priests Consultors; Development and Planification.
Murasso, Jeremiah N. '79 (HRT) South Windsor, CT St. Francis of Assisi.
Murawka, Slawomir *s.ch.* '94 (DET) Sterling Heights, MI Our Lady of Czestochowa.
Murcko, Rev. Msgr. Charles S. '52 (E)[L] Hermitage, PA John XXIII Home Retired.
Murd, Francis A. '76 (TOL)[I] Tiffin, OH St. Francis Convent.
Murdock, Paul J. '75 (NOR) Windham, CT Sagrado Corazon de Jesus; Auditor/Assessors; Iglesia del Sagrado Corazon de Jesus; Liturgical Commission; Windham.
Murhammer, Francis J. '88 (PIT) Pittsburgh, PA St. Margaret.
Murhula, Kafarhire *s.j.* '06 (CHI)[C] Chicago, IL Jesuit Community at Loyola University Chicago.
Murillo, Jose Mario '05 (PBL) Pueblo, CO St. Joseph; Avondale, CO Sacred Heart; Pueblo, CO St. Therese.
Murin, Frantisek '04 (HPM) Sacramento, CA St. Philip the Apostle.
Murnane, Patrick J. '60 (MIA) Hollywood, FL Nativity.
Murnane, Theodore *s.v.d.* '59 (FgM) Techny, IL.
Murnane, Thomas M. *o.s.a.* '65 (PH)[Y] Villanova, PA St. Thomas Monastery.
Murnane, Thomas *o.s.a.* '61 (PH)[C] Villanova University.
Muro, Jose Luis '01 (SD) Chula Vista, CA Our Lady of Guadalupe Catholic Parish Chula Vista.
Muro, Rev. Msgr. Victor S. '66 (CAM)[N] Vineland, NJ Pope John Paul II Retreat Center; Vicar for Hispanics; Vineland, NJ Divine Mercy, Vineland, N.J.
Murphy, Rev. Msgr. A. Robert '74 (KC) Administrative Committee; Special Assignment; Vicar General; Consultors; Permanent Diaconate.
Murphy, Arthur J. '55 (HRT) West Hartford, CT St. Thomas the Apostle Retired.
Murphy, Rt. Rev. Austin *o.s.b.* '04 (JOL)[A] Lisle, IL Benedictine University; [L] Lisle, IL St. Procopius Abbey; [C] Lisle, IL Benet Academy.
Murphy, Austin '03 (BAL)[U] Baltimore, MD Serra Club; [A] Baltimore, MD St. Mary's Seminary and University.
Murphy, Bartholomew J. *s.j.* '72 (P)[L] Portland Jesuit Provincial Office (Society of Jesus, Oregon Prov.); Portland, OR Society of Jesus.
Murphy, Bernard Marie *c.f.r.* '98 (NY)[DD] Bronx, NY Saint Lawrence Friary.
Murphy, Bernard Marie *c.f.r.* (PAT)[N] Paterson, NJ Saint Michael's Friary.
Murphy, Brendan *o.p.* '00 (PRO)[B] Providence, RI Providence College.
Murphy, Brendan *s.v.d.* '73 (GAL) Houston, TX Holy Name.
Murphy, Rev. Msgr. Charles M. '61 (PRT) Diaconate Retired.
Murphy, Charles R. '91 (OKL) Personnel Committee; Oklahoma City, OK St. Francis of Assisi.
Murphy, Charles R. '91 (OKL) Scouting.
Murphy, Christopher D. '96 (ARL) Washington, VA St. Peter; Doral, FL San Francisco de Asis, Banica; Doral, FL San Jose, Pedro Santana; On Duty Outside the Diocese.
Murphy, Rev. Msgr. D. Declan '49 (MRY) Retired.
Murphy, Daniel J. '56 (DET) Retired.
Murphy, Daniel S. '70 (BRK) Brooklyn, NY St. Saviour.
Murphy, Daniel T. '62 (MIL) Retired.
Murphy, Daniel W. '73 (PAT) Randolph, NJ St. Matthew the Apostle.
Murphy, David Brendan *o.p.* '00 (PRO)[O] Providence St. Thomas Aquinas Priory at Providence College.
Murphy, David F. '87 (WIL) New Castle, DE; Army National Guard Chaplains; Wilmington, DE St. Joseph on the Brandywine.
Murphy, David M. '53 (ROC) Retired.
Murphy, Dennis '75 (ALB) Fort Plain, NY Parish of Our Lady of Hope.
Murphy, Dennis '74 (RIC) Unassigned.
Murphy, Denny *s.c.a.* (DET)[K] Wyandotte, MI Pallottine Missionary Center (Irish Province).
Murphy, Dominic Savio Mary *f.i.* '05 (NOR)[G] Griswold, CT Marian Friary of Our Lady of Guadalupe.
Murphy, Edward A. '98 (FR) Morton Hospital; Diocesan Liaison with Charismatic Groups; Taunton, MA St. Jude the Apostle.
Murphy, Edward F. *c.m.* '79 (STL) St. Louis, MO St. Vincent de Paul; [L] St. Louis, MO Guardian Angel Settlement Association; [O] St. Louis, MO Vincentian Residence.
Murphy, Edward J. *s.j.* '68 (NY)[DD] New York, NY Murray–Weigel Hall.
Murphy, Edward W. '92 (STA) Scouts; Jacksonville, FL Immaculate Conception.
Murphy, Emmet *o.f.m.* '86 (R) Raleigh, NC St. Francis of Assisi.
Murphy, Eoin '64 (LAN) St. Johns, MI St. Joseph.
Murphy, Eugene A. '10 (SUP) Hudson, WI St. Patrick.
Murphy, Rev. Msgr. Eugene F. '52 (RVC)[N] Amityville, NY St. Pius X Residence Retired.
Murphy, Rev. Msgr. Francis C. '46 (MOB) Mobile, AL St. Dominic Parish, Mobile Retired.
Murphy, Francis J. *c.s.c.* '86 (FTW)[H] Notre Dame Congregation of Holy Cross, United States Province of Priests & Brothers; Provincial Councilors:; [H] Notre Dame, IN Congregation of Holy Cross, United States Province of Priests & Brothers.
Murphy, Francis J. '66 (GLD) Cadillac, MI St. Ann; Cadillac, MI St. Edward; Lake City, MI St. Stephen; Lake City, MI St. Theresa; Vicar General; Finance Council, Diocesan.
Murphy, Francis J. '51 (LIN) Retired.
Murphy, Francis J. *s.j.* '56 (STL)[O] St. Louis, MO Jesuit Community Corporation at Saint Louis University – Jesuit Hall.
Murphy, Rev. Msgr. Francis '46 (MOB) Retired.
Murphy, Francis *c.s.c.* '86 (P)[B] University of Portland; [L] Portland, OR Holy Cross Fathers & Brothers, C.S.C. – University of Portland.
Murphy, Rev. Msgr. Frederick J. '57 (BO) Senior Priests.; Danvers, MA St. Mary of the Annunciation Retired.
Murphy, G. Ronald *s.j.* '69 (WDC)[O] Washington, DC The Jesuit Community at Georgetown University.
Murphy, G. Ronald *s.j.* '69 (NY)[DD] Cardinal Spellman Hall, Jesuit Community.
Murphy, George E. '66 (BLX) Gulfport, MS St. Joseph Catholic Church.
Murphy, George R. *s.j.* '71 (OAK)[A] Berkeley, CA Jesuit School of Theology of Santa Clara University (Berkeley, California Campus); [L] Berkeley, CA Jesuit Fathers and Brothers; [A] Berkeley, CA Jesuit School of Theology of Santa Clara University (Berkeley, California Campus).
Murphy, Rt. Rev. Archimandrite Gerasimos '67 (NTN) Judicial Vicar.
Murphy, H. Joseph '61 (BO) Senior Priests. Retired.
Murphy, Harold B. '68 (CHI) Chicago, IL St. Margaret Mary; Chicago, IL St. Timothy Retired.
Murphy, Hugh P. '71 (PAT) Mount Arlington, NJ Our Lady of the Lake.
Murphy, J. Patrick *c.m.* '76 (CHI)[N] Chicago, IL Vincentian Community, Congregation of the Mission, Western Province.
Murphy, J. Wayne '65 (L) Defenders of the Bond Retired.
Murphy, James E. '55 (GI) Retired.
Murphy, James F. '70 (PIT) Butler, PA St. Fidelis of Sigmaringen.
Murphy, James F. '01 (GAL)[E] Houston, TX St. Thomas High School.
Murphy, James F. *c.s.c.* '58 (FTW)[H] Notre Dame Congregation of Holy Cross, United States Province of Priests & Brothers.
Murphy, James G. *s.j.* '64 (CHI)[C] Chicago, IL Jesuit Community at Loyola University Chicago.
Murphy, James H. '81 (MAD) Briggsville, WI St. Mary Help of Christians; Portage, WI St. Mary of the Immaculate Conception.
Murphy, James J. '54 (WH) Retired.
Murphy, James P. '65 (CHI) Glenview, IL St. Catherine Laboure Retired.
Murphy, Rev. Msgr. James T. '68 (SAC) Presbyteral Council; Moderator of the Curia; Vicar General; Interim Vicar Episcopal for Clergy; Interim Director Permanent Diaconate; College of Consultors; Ex Officio; Ongoing Education of Clergy; Permanent Diaconate Office; Priests' Personnel Board, Diocesan; Presbyteral Council; [N] Sacramento, CA PAX Ministerio Foundation Trust Fund; Sacramento, CA Cathedral of the Blessed Sacrament.
Murphy, James W. '48 (MEM) Retired.
Murphy, James Wayne '65 (L) Retired.
Murphy, James '78 (JOL) Bloomingdale, IL St. Isidore.
Murphy, James '70 (MIA) Retired.
Murphy, James *c.s.c.* '58 (ORL)[F] Cocoa Beach, FL Congregation of Holy Cross, United States Province Retired.
Murphy, James *c.m.* '85 (CHI)[N] Chicago, IL Vincentian Community, Congregation of the Mission, Western Province.
Murphy, Rev. Msgr. Jeremiah '63 (LA) West Hollywood, CA St. Victor.
Murphy, John C. '65 (SP) Dade City, FL Sacred Heart.
Murphy, John D. *s.j.* '77 (LA)[C] Los Angeles, CA Jesuit Community.
Murphy, John F. '59 (CLV)[A] Wickliffe, OH Borromeo Seminary Retired.
Murphy, John J. '68 (DEN) On Duty Outside the Archdiocese.
Murphy, John J. '68 (E) Erie, PA Hamot Medical Center.
Murphy, Rev. Msgr. John P. '64 (ALN) Allentown, PA St. Thomas More; Elected Members; College of Consultors; Operation Rice Bowl; Legatus.
Murphy, John P. *s.j.* '69 (CIN) Cincinnati, OH St. Francis Xavier.
Murphy, Rev. Msgr. John R. '73 (OG) Norfolk, NY Visitation of the B.V.M.; Norfolk, NY St. Raymond; Episcopal Vicar for Pastoral Services and Moderator of the Curia; Advocates; Committee on Assignments.
Murphy, John T. *o.p.* '54 (WDC) Washington, DC St. Dominic Church & Priory.
Murphy, John V. *s.j.* '52 (P)[L] Portland, OR Colombiere Community.
Murphy, John *f.m.s.i.* '72 (BO)[B] Framingham, MA Sylva Maria; Framingham, MA.
Murphy, John (ATL) Peachtree City, GA Holy Trinity.
Murphy, Joseph A. *s.j.* '73 (COL)[A] Columbus, OH Pontifical College Josephinum.
Murphy, Joseph E. '61 (PAT)[Q] Chester, NJ Nazareth Village Retired.
Murphy, Joseph H. '61 (NEW) Retired.
Murphy, Rev. Msgr. Joseph P. '54 (NY)[HH] Staten Island, NY Emmaus Ministries, Ltd.
Murphy, Joseph T. '47 (PH) Retired.
Murphy, Jude *o.f.m.* (BO)[X] Boston, MA Saint Anthony Residence.
Murphy, Kenneth R. '86 (MET) Sayreville, NJ St. Stanislaus Kostka.
Murphy, Kevin F. '81 (NEW) Scotch Plains, NJ St. Bartholomew; [D] Clark, NJ Mother Seton (Girls) Regional High School.
Murphy, Kevin J. *o.s.b.* '62 (MIL)[P] Benet Lake, WI St. Benedict's Abbey.
Murphy, Kevin P. '68 (ROC) Retired.
Murphy, Laurence T. *m.m.* '54 (NY)[DD] Maryknoll Maryknoll Fathers and Brothers Retired.
Murphy, Lawrence *c.ss.r.* (HBG)[G] Ephrata, PA St. Clement's Mission House.
Murphy, Louis *s.t.* '60 (WDC)[O] Adelphi, MD Father Judge Missionary Cenacle.
Murphy, Mark W. '11 (BO) Milton, MA St. Agatha.
Murphy, Michael A. '92 (BAL) Special Assignment; Severn, MD St. Bernadette.
Murphy, Rev. Msgr. Michael D. '66 (LAN) College of Consultors Retired.
Murphy, Michael D. '77 (PH) Drexel Hill, PA St. Dorothy.
Murphy, Michael F. '83 (SD) Coronado, CA Sacred Heart Catholic Parish Coronado.
Murphy, Michael G. '87 (STL) House Springs, MO Our Lady, Queen of Peace.
Murphy, Michael P. '89 (JC) Diocesan Consultors; [D]

Rolla, MO Catholic Newman Center, Missouri University of Science and Technology; Senators; Rolla, MO St. Patrick.
Murphy, Michael '83 (SD) Priests; Presbyteral Council.
Murphy, Myles P. '90 (NY) New York, NY St. Agnes; New York, NY St. Michael.
Murphy, Owen *s.a.* '52 (NY)[DD] Garrison, NY Franciscan Friars of the Atonement Retired.
Murphy, Owen *s.a.* '52 (PAT)[N] Ringwood, NJ Holy Name Friary, Inc.
Murphy, Patrick E. '85 (MO) On Duty Outside the Diocese; DEPARTMENT OF VETERANS AFFAIRS HOSPITALS AND CHAPLAINS.
Murphy, Patrick F. '67 (LIN) Manley, NE St. Patrick's.
Murphy, Patrick J. '97 (SD) Clergy Personnel Board; San Diego, CA Our Lady of Mt. Carmel Catholic Parish San Diego.
Murphy, Patrick L. *s.j.* '67 (MIL)[P] Milwaukee Jesuit Provincial Office, Wisconsin Province.
Murphy, Patrick *c.s.* '80 (KCK) Hispanic Ministry.
Murphy, Patrick *c.s.* (KC) Kansas City, MO Holy Rosary.
Murphy, Patrick '04 (JOL) Naperville, IL Edward Hospital; Elmhurst, IL Elmhurst Memorial Hospital; Naperville, IL St. Elizabeth Seton.
Murphy, Patrick *l.c.* '97 (CHI)[N] Hillside, IL Legion of Christ.
Murphy, Paul G. '94 (BGP) Darien, CT St. Thomas More; Presbyteral Council; Parochial Examiners.
Murphy, Paul P. '78 (MRY) Pacific Grove, CA St. Angela Merici Church; Vicar for Clergy; Diocesan Consultors; Clergy Life & Ministry; Clergy Life and Ministry Board; Clergy Personnel Board; Presbyteral Council; Diocesan Consultors.
Murphy, Peter P. '68 (PIT) Wexford, PA St. Alphonsus.
Murphy, Richard D. '96 (BGP) Stratford, CT Our Lady of Peace; Priest Vocation Advisory Board.
Murphy, Rev. Msgr. Richard J. '73 (BAL) Frederick, MD St. John the Evangelist.
Murphy, Richard M. '65 (ROC)[N] Auburn, NY New York Chiropractic College; Auburn, NY St. Francis of Assisi; Auburn, NY St. Hyacinth Retired.
Murphy, Richard '65 (PMB) Vero Beach, FL Holy Cross; [K] Diocesan Property & Liability Insurance Committee; Consultors; Building, Construction, Real Estate Office; Real Estate; Ex Officio.
Murphy, Richard '80 (Y) Mineral Ridge, OH St. Mary; [C] Youngstown, OH Ursuline High School; Presbyteral Council.
Murphy, Richard '57 (PMB) Retired.
Murphy, Rev. Msgr. Robert '74 (KC) Pleasant Hill, MO St. Bridget.
Murphy, Robert '93 (VEN) Fort Myers Beach, FL Ascension.
Murphy, Ronan B. '00 (CAM) On Duty Outside the Diocese.
Murphy, Rory E. '88 (SFR)[J] Daly City, CA Seton Medical Center; Seton Hospital; San Francisco, CA St. Philip the Apostle.
Murphy, T. Austin '03 (BAL) Towson, MD Church of the Immaculate Conception; Vocation Office; Special Assignment.
Murphy, Theodore *s.m.m.* '58 (RVC)[N] Bay Shore, NY Montfort Missionaries Retired.
Murphy, Thomas E. *o.s.f.s.* '76 (ARL) Reston, VA St. John Neumann.
Murphy, Thomas J. '85 (IND) Retired.
Murphy, Thomas J. '87 (SAV) Hinesville, GA St. Stephen, First Martyr.
Murphy, Thomas K. *o.f.m.* '58 (SP)[N] St. Petersburg, FL St. Anthony Friary.
Murphy, Thomas M. '79 (PRT) Wells, ME Holy Spirit Parish.
Murphy, Thomas P. *s.j.* '57 (NY)[DD] New York, NY Murray–Weigel Hall.
Murphy, Thomas P. *c.s.p.* '62 (BRK)[R] Paulist Priests at Paulist Foundations Outside the U.S.
Murphy, Thomas R. E. *s.j.* '99 (BO)[U] Boston The Society of Jesus of New England–Provincial Offices.
Murphy, Thomas R.E. *s.j.* '99 (SEA)[A] Seattle, WA Seattle University; [M] Seattle, WA Arrupe Jesuit Community at Seattle University.
Murphy, Thomas *o.f.m.cap.* '71 (NY) Yonkers, NY Sacred Heart; Yonkers, NY St. Joseph's Medical Center; [W] Yonkers, NY St. Joseph's Medical Center.
Murphy, Rev. Msgr. Thomas '66 (SAT) Defenders of the Bond; San Antonio, TX; [K] San Antonio, TX Casa De Padres; College of Consultors Retired.
Murphy, Thomas (IND)[I] Beech Grove, IN St. Paul Hermitage.
Murphy, Rev. Msgr. Tim '43 (P) Portland, OR St. John Fisher.
Murphy, Timothy J. '63 (BO) Salem, MA Immaculate Conception.
Murphy, Timothy J. '74 (SPR) Hampden, MA St. Mary's.
Murphy, Timothy '67 (P)[C] Portland, OR Central Catholic High School.
Murphy, Timothy '60 (VEN) Retired.
Murphy, Timothy '93 (JKS) Pontotoc, MS St. Christopher.
Murphy, Tommy *s.s.c.* (FgM).
Murphy, Ultan P. '53 (DOD) Olmitz, KS St. Ann Catholic Church of Olmitz, Kansas.
Murphy, Venard *o.f.m.* '61 (SP)[N] St. Petersburg, FL St. Anthony Friary Retired.
Murphy, Rev. Msgr. Walter C. '58 (BRK)[R] Douglaston, NY Bishop Mugavero Residence; Courage Ministry; Accountant Retired.
Murphy, William F. '56 (PRO)[O] Providence St. John Vianney Residence Retired.
Murphy, William J. '96 (SUP) Board of Directors Retired.
Murphy, William J. '57 (DET) Retired.
Murphy, William P. '86 (SPR) Great Barrington, MA St. Peter's; Housatonic, MA Blessed Teresa of Calcutta Parish.
Murphy, William S. '90 (PH) West Grove, PA Assumption B.V.M.
Murphy, William *c.p.* '73 (BAL) Baltimore, MD St. Joseph Passionist Monastery Parish; [Q] Baltimore, MD St. Joseph's Passionist Community.
Murphy, William *s.j.* '08 (CLV)[D] Cleveland, OH St. Ignatius High School.
Murphy–O'Connor, James (FTW)[B] University of Notre Dame Du Lac.
Murray, Brendan J. '68 (PAT) Dover, NJ Sacred Heart; Dover, NJ Our Lady Queen of the Most Holy Rosary.
Murray, Charles A. *m.m.* '51 (SJ)[M] Los Altos, CA Maryknoll.
Murray, Cornelius J. '63 (CLV) North Olmsted, OH St. Brendan Retired.
Murray, Rev. Msgr. Daniel A. '64 (PH) North Wales, PA St. Rose of Lima.
Murray, Donald J. '61 (MAD) Retired.
Murray, Donnon P. *o.f.m.* '56 (FgM) New York, NY Holy Name Province.
Murray, Edward K. '62 (SFR) St. Mary's Medical Center; [J] San Francisco, CA St. Mary's Medical Center; San Francisco, CA St. Stephen.
Murray, Eugene M. *m.m.* '58 (FgM) Maryknoll, NY MARYKNOLL.
Murray, Eugene '65 (SC) Retired.
Murray, Francis J. '51 (LAN) Retired.
Murray, Francis K. '53 (SFR) Retired.
Murray, Frank J. '81 (PRT) Ex Officio Members; Seminarians; Brunswick, ME All Saints Parish.
Murray, Frank '81 (PRT) Pastoral Associates; [M] Brunswick, ME Bowdoin College.
Murray, George B. *s.j.* '65 (BO)[U] Weston, MA Campion Jesuit Community.
Murray, Gerald E. '84 (NY) New York, NY St. Vincent de Paul; Legion of Mary.
Murray, Rev. Msgr. Ignatius L. '57 (PH) Norristown, PA Visitation B.V.M. Retired.
Murray, James B. '57 (NSH) Retired.
Murray, Rev. Msgr. James H. '56 (PAT) Retired.
Murray, James M. *o.s.b.* '93 (PEO)[A] Peru, IL St. Bede Abbey.
Murray, James Stephen *o.p.* '50 (L) Springfield, KY St. Rose.
Murray, John A. '62 (BO) Senior Priests. Retired.
Murray, John C. *c.s.b.* '57 (ROC)[K] Rochester, NY Basilian Residence.
Murray, John D. '62 (LA) Burbank, CA St. Francis Xavier Retired.
Murray, John E. '63 (HEL) Retired.
Murray, John F. *c.ss.r.* '73 (TR)[R] Long Branch, NJ San Alfonso Retreat House.
Murray, John F. *c.ss.r.* '94 (ORL) New Smyrna Beach, FL Sacred Heart.
Murray, John Francis *s.m.a.* '57 (NEW)[L] Tenafly, NJ Society of African Missions, Provincialate, S.M.A. Fathers.
Murray, John M. '98 (FR) Attleboro, MA St. Joseph's; Attleboro, MA Holy Ghost; Attleboro.
Murray, John P. '54 (RVC) Retired.
Murray, John S. '69 (ORL) New Smyrna Beach, FL Our Lady Star of the Sea.
Murray, John W. '68 (CHI) Retired.
Murray, John *c.s.b.* '67 (ROC)[O] Rochester, NY Marriage Encounter Apostolate.
Murray, John '60 (CHY) Retired.
Murray, Rev. Msgr. Joseph W. '61 (PH) King of Prussia, PA Mother of Divine Providence; By Election Retired.
Murray, Kevin P. '77 (PH) Rydal, PA St. Hilary of Poitiers.
Murray, Leo A. *s.j.* '62 (WDC) Washington, DC Holy Trinity.
Murray, Maurice M. *s.j.* '66 (FgM) St. Louis, MO Society of Jesus.
Murray, Rev. Msgr. Michael J. '76 (WDC) Special Ministries.
Murray, Michael S. *o.s.f.s.* '86 (WIL)[J] Childs, MD Retirement and Assisted Care Facility; [M] Wilmington, DE De Sales Spirituality Services.
Murray, Paul G. '09 (PRT) Dexter, ME St. Agnes; Dexter, ME Our Lady of the Snows Parish.
Murray, Peter J. *s.j.* '72 (ALB)[N] Fultonville, NY Shrine of Our Lady of Martyrs; Special Assignment; Members.
Murray, Peter J. *s.j.* '72 (BUF) Buffalo, NY St. Michael.
Murray, Rev. Msgr. Richard Hayes '43 (LA) Woodland Hills, CA St. Bernardine of Siena Retired.
Murray, Robert J. *o.s.a.* '83 (PH)[C] Villanova University; [Y] Villanova, PA St. Thomas Monastery.
Murray, Robert W. '88 (BO) Haverhill, MA St. James; Haverhill, MA St. John the Baptist.
Murray, Russel T. *o.f.m.* '98 (WDC)[O] Silver Spring, MD Gemelli House.
Murray, Russell T. '98 (ALB)[B] Siena College.
Murray, Rev. Msgr. Sean '52 (SD) San Diego, CA Saint Brigid Catholic Parish Retired.
Murray, Stan '69 (ORL) Deans; Ex Officio Members.
Murray, Steven J. '00 (PBL) Gunnison, CO Queen of All Saints; Gunnison, CO St. Peter.
Murray, Steven M. '88 (OG) Watertown, NY Holy Family.
Murray, Rev. Msgr. Thomas A. '68 (PH) Norristown, PA Visitation B.V.M.
Murray, Thomas F. '57 (BO) Senior Priests. Retired.
Murray, Thomas P. '81 (RVC) Greenport, NY St. Agnes.
Murray, Thomas (RVC) Shelter Island Heights, NY Our Lady of the Isle.
Murray, Trevor '01 (BEL) Royalton, IL St. Aloysius/Sacred Heart.
Murray, Rev. Msgr. William C. '55 (CC) Robstown, TX St. Anthony.
Murray, Rev. Msgr. William F. '45 (PRO) Retired.
Murray, William F. '54 (MIL) Retired.
Murrin, Donald *s.v.d.* '60 (BLX) Bay St. Louis, MS St. Rose De Lima.
Murrin, Raymond J. '57 (BIR) Retired.
Murrin, Robert '99 (MRY) Boulder Creek, CA St. Michael.
Murrman, Jonathan J. *o.s.b.* '65 (GBG)[H] Latrobe, PA Saint Vincent Archabbey.
Murrman, Warren D. *o.s.b.* '65 (GBG)[H] Latrobe, PA Saint Vincent Archabbey.
Murry, Trevor K. '01 (BEL) Diocesan Consultors; West Frankfort, IL St. John the Baptist; Co Directors.
Murtagh, Henry Paul *ss.cc.* '67 (LA)[P] La Verne, CA Congregation of the Sacred Hearts of Jesus and Mary.
Murtagh, James '66 (PMB) West Palm Beach, FL St. Ann Retired.
Murtagh, John J. '69 (YAK) Moxee, WA Holy Rosary.
Murtagh, Paul *ss.cc.* '67 (LSC) Artesia, NM Our Lady of Grace; Artesia, NM St. Anthony.
Murtaugh, Lewis C. *s.j.* '69 (CHI)[N] Chicago Chicago Province of the Society of Jesus–Provincial Office.
Murtaugh, Lewis Charles *s.j.* (FgM) Chicago, IL Society of Jesus.
Murtaugh, William A. '72 (STP) Deanery 15; Eden Prairie, MN Pax Christi.
Murtha, Chester '93 (SFS) Miller, SD St. Ann; Presbyteral Council.
Muruli, Martin R. '98 (SFR) St. Anne's Home; [K] San Francisco, CA Home for the Aged of the Little Sisters of the Poor.
Muscalino, Daniel C. '78 (SY) Special Assignment; Marcellus, NY St. Francis Xavier.
Musco, Joseph '06 (SP) Safety Harbor, FL Espiritu Santo; Elected Parochial Vicars.
Muscolino, Frank J. '68 (BIR) Retired.
Mushalla, Walter '98 (SAT) Somerset, TX Retired.
Mushi, Peter *a.j.* '87 (NY) New York, NY St. Cecilia.
Mushinsky, John E. (PAT) Retired.
Musial, George '67 (CHI)[N] Chicago, IL St. Peter's Friary.
Musico, Edwin '85 (STO) Stockton, CA St. George Church (Pastor of).
Musinguzi, John Bosco '00 (LA) Glendale, CA Holy Family.
Musiol, Josef *s.d.s.* '72 (SAT)[L] Falls City, TX Salvatorian Fathers Community of Texas.
Musiol, Jozef *s.d.s.* '72 (AUS) Chappell Hill, TX St. Stanislaus; Adjutant Judicial Vicar.
Musselman, Randall '09 (MIA) Hollywood, FL Nativity.
Mussett, Peter '06 (DEN) Boulder, CO St. Thomas Aquinas University Parish.
Musso, David D. *s.m.* '98 (ATL)[C] Atlanta, GA Marist School.
Mustaciuolo, Rev. Msgr. Gregory '90 (NY) New York, NY; Chancellor and Moderator of the Curia; Archdiocesan Consultors.
Musuande, Salvatore *a.a.* '00 (WOR) Fiskdale, MA St. Anne's and St. Patrick's.
Musula, Charles E. '07 (CHI) Park Ridge, IL St. Paul of the Cross.
Musumbu, Gilbert Malu '88 (TUC) Douglas, AZ Immaculate Conception Roman Catholic Parish – Douglas; Douglas, AZ Saint Luke Roman Catholic Church – Douglas; Pirtleville, AZ Saint Bernard Roman Catholic Church – Pirtleville; [H] Douglas, AZ Cochise Community College.
Musuubire, Gerald F. '06 (RIC) Columbia, VA St. Joseph's/Shrine of St. Katharine Drexel; Palmyra, VA Ss. Peter & Paul.
Muszkiewicz, Joseph '08 (GLD) Roscommon, MI St. Michael; Prudenville, MI Our Lady of the Lake; Higgins Lake, MI St. Hubert; Higgins Lake, MI St. James; Elected Members.

Muteru, Gabriel '87 (RVC)[B] Rockville Centre, NY Molloy College; Roosevelt, NY Queen of the Most Holy Rosary.
Muth, Joseph L. '74 (BAL) Baltimore, MD Blessed Sacrament Church; Baltimore, MD St. Matthew; [T] Baltimore, MD St. Matthew's Parish Endowment Trust.
Muth, Stephen '82 (PRM) Whiting, IN Assumption of the Blessed Virgin.
Mutholathu, Abraham '80 (SYM) Eparchial Consultors; Morton Grove, IL St. Mary's Syro–Malabar Knanaya Catholic Church (Morton Grove).
Muthu, Anthony *h.g.n.* '03 (LEX) Williamsburg, KY Our Lady of Perpetual Help; [L] Barbourville, KY St. Gregory Church–Union College; Barbourville, KY St. Gregory.
Muthu, Antony Savari '90 (CAM)[H] Newfield, NJ The Mater Dei Nursing Home, Newfield, New Jersey; Mullica Hill, NJ Catholic Community of the Holy Spirit, Mullica Hill, N.J.
Muthukatti, Thomas '66 (BRK) South Richmond Hill, NY St. Benedict Joseph Labre Retired.
Muthuplackal, Joseph *o.ss.t.* '04 (BAL)[Q] Assigned in India.
Mutsko, Frank J. '00 (ORL) Lady Lake, FL Retired.
Muwanga, Godfrey '84 (RC) Bonesteel, SD Immaculate Conception; Fairfax, SD St. Anthony's; Gregory, SD St. Joseph; Burke, SD Sacred Heart.
Muweesi, John Vianney *s.d.s.* '86 (MIL)[P] Milwaukee Salvatorian Provincial Offices.
Muwonge, Charles '93 (LAN)[D] Plymouth, MI Spiritus Sanctus Academy.
Muwonge, Expedito '89 (L) Norton Hospitals.
Mux, Juan Francisco Peren *o.s.b.* '07 (RCK)[G] Aurora, IL Marmion Abbey.
Muzas, Brian Keenan '03 (NEW)[B] Seton Hall University.
Muzdakis, John J. *o.s.f.s.* '65 (WIL)[J] Childs, MD Retirement and Assisted Care Facility Retired.
Muzzey, Charles H. '65 (WDC) Retired.
Muzzin, Victor *f.d.p.* '72 (NY) New York, NY St. Francis de Sales.
Mvondo, Laurent '81 (SAN) Crane, TX Good Shepherd; McCamey, TX Sacred Heart.
Mwageni, Honoratus C. (CHI) Chicago, IL St. Helena of tghe Cross.
Mwampela, Ayub '00 (BGP) Greenwich, CT Greenwich Hospital; Stamford, CT St. Maurice.
Mwampela, Ayub '00 (NY) Manhattan, NY Terence Cardinal Cooke Health Care Center.
Mwanamwambwa, Victor *s.s.* '05 (BAL)[Q] Baltimore, MD St. Mary's Seminary & University.
Mwanza, Eugene H. '04 (BAL)[Q] Baltimore, MD St. Mary's Seminary & University.
Mwaura, Peter James '03 (CHY) Pinedale, WY Our Lady of Peace.
Myers, Christopher P. *s.o.l.t.* '90 (MO) Air National Guard Chaplains; DEPARTMENT OF VETERANS AFFAIRS HOSPITALS AND CHAPLAINS.
Myers, Edward T. *o.p.* '65 (PRO)[O] Providence St. Thomas Aquinas Priory at Providence College.
Myers, Gabriel *o.s.b.* '99 (WDC)[O] Washington, DC St. Anselm's Abbey.
Myers, Gerald L. '94 (TUC) Nogales, AZ Sacred Heart of Jesus Roman Catholic Parish – Nogales.
Myers, Gerald '94 (FAR) Retired.
Myers, J. Edward '55 (NEW) Retired.
Myers, James E. '80 (PEO) On Duty Outside the Diocese.
Myers, James E. *s.s.* '80 (SFR)[A] Menlo Park, CA Vatican II Institute for Clergy Formation.
Myers, James E. *s.s.* '80 (BAL)[Q] Baltimore Society of St. Sulpice, Province of the United States.
Myers, Jeremy '84 (DAL) Sherman, TX St. Francis of Assisi (Quasi Parish); Sherman, TX St. Mary.
Myers, Rev. Msgr. William R. '69 (STU) Retired.
Myers, William '88 (SFR) Absent on Leave.
Myers, William '88 (STO) On Duty Outside the Diocese.
Myett, Robert D. *o.p.* '60 (PRO)[O] Providence St. Thomas Aquinas Priory at Providence College.
Myhalyk, Richard *s.s.e.* '71 (MOB)[G] Selma, AL Edmundite Fathers; [J] Selma, AL Edmundite Guild.
Mykyta, Myron '97 (LA) Los Angeles, CA Nativity of Blessed Virgin Mary.
Mykyta, Myron '97 (STN) Hollywood, CA Nativity of B.V.M.; Presbyteral Council.
Myladil, Thomas *o.c.d.* '76 (MET) Bridgewater, NJ Holy Trinity.
Myladiyil, Sebastian *s.v.d.* '68 (BEA) Liberty, TX Immaculate Conception.
Myler, John T. '82 (BEL) Belleville, IL Cathedral of St. Peter; [J] Belleville, IL World Apostolate of Fatima, The Blue Army, U.S.A.; Formation of Priests; Advocate; Diocesan Consultors; Diocesan Deans; Holy Childhood Association; Propagation of the Faith.
Myles, John J. '64 (SAC) Williams, CA Sacred Heart Retired.
Mylet, James J. *m.m.* '75 (FgM) Maryknoll, NY MARYKNOLL.
Myronyuk, Myron (PHU) Philadelphia, PA Immaculate Conception of Blessed Virgin Mary, Cathedral.
Myshchuk, Mikhail '94 (STF) Troy, NY Protection of B.V.M.; Watervliet, NY St. Nicholas.
Myslinski, Rev. Msgr. John F. '80 (WDC) Retired.
Mysliwiec, Haldane '70 (CHI)[J] Des Plaines, IL Holy Family Medical Center.
Mysliwiec, Jan J. *s.d.s.* '62 (NEW)[L] Verona, NJ The Salvatorian Fathers.
Myszka, Rev. Msgr. Daniel J. '58 (BUF) Retired.
MyViet Tran, (Timothy M.) *c.m.c.* '11 (SPC)[F] Carthage, MO Congregation of the Mother Coredemptrix, United States Assumption Province.

N

N'go, Anthony Chinh '94 (L) Louisville, KY St. John Vianney.
N'Guessan, Sess Julien *s.j.* '97 (OAK)[L] Berkeley, CA Jesuit Fathers and Brothers.
N'Zilamba, Norbert *o.praem.* '87 (JKS)[E] Raymond, MS Priory of St. Moses the Black.
Naa, Anayo *c.ss.r.* '03 (PH) Philadelphia, PA St. Athanasius.
Naas, Stephen '78 (KAL) Marshall, MI St. Mary.
Nabbefeld, Grant '95 (SJ) On Leave of Absence.
Nabozny, Peter '54 (ALB) Retired.
Nacarino, Raymond L. '85 (MET) New Brunswick, NJ Our Lady of Mt. Carmel; [M] Stewartsville, NJ Society of Jesus Christ the Priest.
Naccarato, Frank '79 (NY) Staten Island, NY Arthur Kill Correctional Facility.
Nacciarone, Ugo R. *s.j.* '64 (NY)[DD] New York, NY St. Ignatius Loyola Residence; New York, NY St. Ignatius Loyola.
Nace, Rev. Msgr. Arthur J. '57 (PH) Retired.
Nacius, Michael A. '89 (CHI) Flossmoor, IL Infant Jesus of Prague; Deans.
Nacke, Xavier *o.s.b.* '63 (KC)[A] Conception, MO Conception Seminary College; [J] Priests Elsewhere.
Nacorda, Cirilo A. '92 (CLV) Cleveland Clinic Foundation; Cleveland, OH St. Vitus.
Nadackal, Zacharias *c.m.i.* '64 (NY) Rye, NY Resurrection.
Naddeo, Henry M. '56 (NEW) Retired.
Nadeau, James L. '88 (PRT) Fort Kent, ME St. John Vianney Parish.
Nadeau, Lance P. *m.m.* '90 (FgM) Maryknoll, NY MARYKNOLL.
Nadeau, Real J. '62 (PRT) Retired.
Nadeau, Richard A. '80 (PRT) Retired.
Nadeau, Roland P. '00 (PRT) Bangor, ME St. Joseph's Hospital; [H] Bangor, ME Pastoral Care Dept.; Bangor, ME Saint Paul the Apostle Parish.
Nadeau, Roland *m.s.* '69 (ORL) Orlando, FL Blessed Trinity.
Nadeau, Thomas D. '05 (BUR) Swanton, VT Nativity of the Blessed Virgin Mary–St. Louis.
Nadeau, Timothy J. '91 (PRT) Bangor, ME Saint Paul the Apostle Parish; Diocesan Priests' Benefit Plan – Trustees.
Nadeau, William '68 (RNO) Incline Village, NV St. Francis of Assisi; Life, Peace & Justice Commission.
Nadicksbernd, Elmer *s.v.d.* '64 (COV)[N] Melbourne, KY St. Anne Convent Retired.
Nadine, Jerome E. '58 (BRK) Retired.
Nadolny, Edmund S. '59 (HRT) East Berlin, CT Sacred Heart.
Nadolny, Paul *s.v.d.* '89 (FgM) Techny, IL.
Nadolny, Stanley J. '68 (TUC) Apache Junction, AZ Saint George Roman Catholic Parish – Apache Junction.
Nadolski, Kevin M. *o.s.f.s.* '97 (WIL)[J] Wilmington, DE Wilmington–Philadelphia Province of the Oblates of St. Francis de Sales.
Nadres, Sergio O. '91 (NEW) Hillside, NJ Christ the King.
Naduviledathu, Thomas *s.d.v.* '08 (BUR) Derby Line, VT St. Edward; Newport, VT St. Mary Star of the Sea.
Naduvilekoot, Augustine '71 (NOR) Versailles, CT St. Joseph.
Naduvilekoot, Joseph J. '78 (SYM) East Hartford, CT St. Thomas Syro–Malabar Catholic Mission of Hartford.
Naduvilekoot, Joseph (HRT) West Hartford, CT St. Helena; East Hartford, CT St. Mary.
Naedele, Rev. Msgr. William B. '49 (NEW) Office of Catholic Cemeteries Retired.
Naegele, Gary P. '79 (WH) Wheeling, WV St. Vincent de Paul.
Naegele, Zacchaeus Maria *o.s.b.cam.* '98 (MRY)[F] Big Sur, CA New Camaldoli Hermitage.
Naessens, Philip *o.f.m.cap.* '86 (DET)[K] Detroit St. Bonaventure Friary.
Naffate, Lenin '00 (SAT) Priests Personnel Board; In Metropolitan Area; Archdiocesan Presbyteral Council; San Antonio, TX St. Joseph.
Nagai, Rev. Msgr. Alan A. '58 (HON) Retired.
Nagel, Kurt '97 (SEA) Kirkland, WA Holy Family; College of Consultors; Presbyteral Council.
Nagel, Rick '07 (IND) Indianapolis, IN St. John the Evangelist Catholic Church, Indianapolis, Inc.; Young Adult and College Campus Ministry.
Nagengast, Maynard G. *o.s.b.* '62 (NEW)[L] Newark, NJ Newark Abbey.
Nagle, Austin *ss.cc.* '54 (FR)[F] Fairhaven, MA Damien Residence.
Nagle, Edmund W. *s.j.* '63 (PAT)[J] Morristown, NJ Loyola House of Retreats.
Nagle, Edmund W. *s.j.* '63 (BUF) Buffalo, NY St. Michael.
Nagle, Gerald J. *m.m.* '57 (NY)[DD] Maryknoll Maryknoll Fathers and Brothers Retired.
Nagle, Rev. Msgr. Joseph P. '71 (BRK) Brooklyn, NY St. Patrick; Diocesan Insurance Committee.
Nagle, Michael R. '72 (FR) Vineyard Haven, MA Good Shepherd.
Nagle, Walter M. '99 (NOR) East Hampton, CT St. Patrick; Diocesan Pastoral Council; Continuing Education and Formation Commission for the Clergy.
Nagle, Rev. Msgr. William A. '49 (BGP)[O] Stamford, CT The Catherine Dennis Keefe Queen of the Clergy Retired Priests' Residence Retired.
Naglich, Robert *s.c.j.* '91 (MIL) Franklin, WI St. Martin of Tours; [P] Franklin, WI St. Joseph's at Monastery Lake.
Naguit, Glenn A. '05 (OAK) Concord, CA St. Francis of Assisi.
Nahal, John '93 (OLL) Millbrae, CA Our Lady of Lebanon Maronite Catholic Church.
Nahas, Joseph '06 (NY) Unassigned; New York, NY St. Stephen and Our Lady of the Scapular.
Nahas, Joseph (NTN) Cliffside Park, NJ St. Demetrius.
Nahman, Richard *o.s.a.* '65 (NY) Bronx, NY St. Nicholas of Tolentine.
Nahoe, Francisco *o.f.m.conv.* '94 (RNO) Reno, NV St. Thomas Aquinas Cathedral.
Naickamparambil, Varghese '72 (SYM) Eparchial Consultors.
Naickamparampil, Varghese '72 (SYM) Framingham, MA St. Thomas the Apostle Syro–Malabar Catholic Church (Boston).
Naill, Joseph P. '97 (RCK) Divine Worship, Office for; Liturgical Commission, Diocesan; Oregon, IL St. Mary; Special Assignment.
Nairki, Modi Abil *m.c.c.j.* '71 (LA) Los Angeles, CA Holy Cross.
Nairki Modi, Abil *m.c.c.j.* '71 (CHI)[N] La Grange Park, IL Comboni Missionaries.
Nairn, Thomas *o.f.m.* '75 (STL)[O] St. Louis, MO Franciscan Friary of St. Anthony of Padua.
Najera, Arthur '09 (SAC) Carmichael, CA St. John the Evangelist.
Najim, Michael J. '01 (PRO)[A] Providence, RI Seminary of Our Lady of Providence; [E] Providence, RI La Salle Academy; Vocations.
Najjar, Samuel A. '84 (SAM) Fayetteville, NC St. Michael the Archangel; Protopresbyters (Deans); Presbyteral Council; Office of Ecumenism and Interreligious Dialogue.
Najmowski, James T. *m.m.* '76 (FgM) Maryknoll, NY MARYKNOLL.
Nakagawa, Francis *s.m.* '57 (HON)[D] Honolulu, HI.
Nakagawa, Francis *s.m.* '57 (STL)[O] St. Louis Marianists, Province of the United States (Society of Mary).
Nakowicz, Stanley T. '67 (PRO) East Providence, RI Our Lady of Loreto; Council Members.
Nakvasil, Richard '05 (DEN) Westminster, CO Holy Trinity.
Nakwah, Joseph C. '90 (LC) Coon Valley, WI St. Mary; La Crosse, WI St. Joseph; Rockland, WI St. Peter.
Nale, Joseph C. '03 (ALT) McConnellsburg, PA St. Stephen's; Orbisonia, PA St. Mary's.
Nalepa, Rev. Msgr. Damien G. '70 (BAL) Baltimore, MD St. Gregory the Great; Baltimore, MD Baltimore City Detention Center – Men.
Nalepa, Richard A. *c.p.* '70 (BRK)[R] Jamaica, NY Immaculate Conception Monastery.
Nall, Brent C. '93 (SAC) Sacramento, CA St. Charles Borromeo.
Nall, James M. '87 (BEL) New Athens, IL St. Agatha; Judicial Vicar; Judges.
Nallen, James F. '66 (CHI) Chicago, IL St. Columba.
Nalley, Robert W. '75 (GLD) Elected Members; Tribunal Diocesan Retired.
Nally, Joseph M. '72 (WOR) Diocesan College of Consultors; Minister to Priests.
Nalty, Rev. Msgr. Christopher '99 (NO) New Orleans, LA Good Shepherd.
Nalugon, Nilo '94 (SAN) Ozona, TX Our Lady of Perpetual Help.
Nalysnyk, Bohdan '95 (STN) Chicago, IL St. Nicholas Ukrainian Catholic Cathedral.
Nalysnyk, Jaroslaw '90 (STF) Jamaica Plain, MA Christ the King; Boston.
Nam, Francis de Sales Vu Khac (SAC)[H] Walnut Grove, CA Monastery of Chau Son Sacramento.
Nam, Heebong '97 (BRK) Brooklyn, NY Holy Spirit; [Q] Korean Apostolate.
Nam, Simon '76 (NY) Bronx, NY St John Nam.
Nambatac, Alner U. '96 (MO) Army National Guard Chaplains.
Nambatac, Alner '96 (SFR) San Rafael, CA St. Isabella.

Nambusseril, Thankachan (John) *c.m.i.* '93 (HT) Montegut, LA Sacred Heart; Priests Council.
Namiotka, Edward F. '87 (CAM) Deanery Representatives; Somers Point, NJ St. Joseph's Church, Somers Point, N.J.; Consultants.
Namo, Warlito F. '91 (SFR) Ross, CA St. Anselm.
Namocatcat, Felix S. '62 (SFR) Retired.
Nangachiveettil, George Joseph '83 (IND) Oldenburg, IN St. John The Evangelist Catholic Church, Enochsburg, Inc.; Oldenburg, IN St. Anne Catholic Church, Hamburg, Inc.; Greensburg, IN St. Maurice Catholic Church, St. Maurice, Inc.
Nangle, Joseph J. *o.f.m.* '58 (NY)[DD] New York Franciscan Friars, Holy Name Province; Provincial Councilors.
Nangle, Thomas R. '70 (CHI) Other Assignments; Police Department Chaplain.
Nano, Efren '87 (TYL) Mineola, TX St. Peter the Apostle; Presbyteral Council.
Nanz, John D. '71 (PIT) Washington County, PA West Penn Allegheny Health System–Canonsburg Hospital; Canonsburg, PA St. Patrick; Washington County, PA Beverly South Hills; Washington County, PA Canon House; Washington County, PA Charles House Home for the Aged; Washington County, PA Greenery Nursing Home; Washington County, PA Horizon Senior Care; Washington County, PA Rest Haven Personal Care Home.
Napier, Robert L. '90 (STA) Interlachen, FL St. John.
Napieralski, Maciej '83 (MO) Army Chaplains.
Naples, Timothy '09 (BUR) Barton, VT Most Holy Trinity.
Napoli, Carol *t.o.r.* (PIT)[M] Pittsburgh, PA Franciscan Friars, T.O.R.
Napoli, Peter *o.f.m.cap.* '73 (NY) Bronx, NY Immaculate Conception; [DD] New York, NY Immaculate Conception Friary.
Napolitano, Joseph V. '76 (HRT) Ansonia, CT Holy Rosary; Ansonia, CT St. Anthony.
Napora, Jacek J. '06 (NEW) Bayonne, NJ St. Vincent de Paul.
Nappo, Michael *o.f.m.* '91 (NY)[FF] Wappingers Falls, NY Mt. Alvernia Retreat House.
Naquin, Roch R. '32 (HT) Cursillo.
Naquin, Roch '62 (HT) Retired.
Naranjo, Francisco '95 (STO) Lathrop, CA Our Lady of Guadalupe Church (Pastor of).
Narciso, Richard A. '07 (PRO) East Providence, RI St. Francis Xavier.
Nardoianni, Antonio *o.f.m./i.c.* '74 (BO) Boston, MA St. Leonard of Port Maurice.
Nardoianni, Antonio *o.f.m.* (BO) Italian.
Nardone, Amedeo *o.f.m.* '68 (NY)[DD] New York Franciscan Province of the Immaculate Conception.
Narez, Juan '93 (ELP) Absent on Leave.
Narichetti, Jesuprathap '92 (CHR) Folly Beach, SC Our Lady of Good Counsel.
Narimattam, Joseph T. '66 (WIL) Retired.
Narithookil, James *c.m.i.* '72 (SAC) Sacramento, CA St. Mary.
Narivelil, Victor Z. *c.m.i.* '64 (STA) Jacksonville, FL Sacred Heart.
Narla, L. Dhanraj '95 (LR) Little Rock, AR Our Lady of the Holy Souls.
Narog, Joseph L. *o.s.a.* '05 (PH) Rosemont, PA St. Thomas of Villanova Parish; [C] Villanova, PA Villanova University.
Nartey, Emmanuel '96 (BRK) Whitestone, NY Holy Trinity.
Nartker, Michael F. *s.m.* '96 (STL)[O] St. Louis Marianists, Province of the United States (Society of Mary).
Nasar, Ayub '85 (GR)[G] Grand Rapids, MI Saint Mary's Health Care.
Nascimento, Daniel '98 (SFR) San Francisco, CA St. Brendan.
Naseman, Alfred *c.pp.s.* '67 (CIN)[N] Carthagena, OH St. Charles.
Nash, Dom Stephen *can.reg.* (RVC) Glen Cove, NY St. Patrick's.
Nash, Francis J. *s.j.* '69 (BAL)[Q] Baltimore, MD Jesuit Community of Loyola University, Inc.; [B] Jesuit Community of Loyola University, Inc.
Nash, James R. '89 (SCR) Nanticoke, PA Saint Faustina Kowalska Parish; Nanticoke, PA St. Mary of Czestochowa; Priests' Retirement Advisory Board.
Nash, James '94 (WIL) Newark, DE Holy Family.
Nash, Robert C. '48 (WH) Retired.
Nash, Robert (RIC) Retired.
Nasini, Gino *s.x.* '65 (FgM)[N] Wayne Xaverian Missionary Fathers; Wayne, NJ XAVERIAN MISSIONARY FATHERS.
Naskar, Lawrence '98 (NY) Port Chester, NY Our Lady of Mercy.
Nasr, Kamil '05 (NTN) Leave of Absence.
Nasr, Toufic M. '97 (OLL) Fairlawn, OH Our Lady of the Cedars of Mt. Lebanon Maronite Catholic Church.
Nasri, Rev. Msgr. Youssef Bochra '85 (BRK) Brooklyn, NY St. Michael; Brooklyn, NY Resurrection Catholic Coptic Chapel.
Nassal, Joseph *c.pp.s.* '82 (KC)[A] Liberty, MO Society of the Precious Blood Provincial Offices; [J] Liberty, MO Society of the Precious Blood Provincial Office; [N] Liberty, MO St. Gaspar Society.
Nassaney, Daniel *o.m.i.* '74 (BO)[X] Tewksbury, MA Immaculate Heart of Mary Residence.
Nasser, Joseph M. *s.j.* '75 (TYL) Hemphill, TX St. Pius I.
Nassetta, Peter W. *y.a.* '89 (ARL)[K] Fairfax, VA George Mason University, Catholic Campus Ministry; [K] Fairfax, VA St. Robert Bellarmine Chapel; Campus Ministry; [L] McLean, VA Youth Apostles Institute, An Association of Christian Faithful.
Nassr, Martin B. '67 (TOL) Sandusky, OH SS. Peter and Paul.
Nasta, Thomas A. '82 (PH) Stowe, PA St. Gabriel of the Sorrowful Mother.
Natad, Diosmar '04 (ATL)[I] Atlanta, GA Emory University, Agnes Scott College; Special or Other Archdiocesan Assignment.
Natale, Samuel '79 (RIC) Retired.
Natalizia, Louis T. '80 (PRO) North Providence, RI Presentation of the Blessed Virgin Mary.
Nathan, Aro '83 (NEW) Montclair, NJ Immaculate Conception.
Nathan, Matthew '09 (JOL) West Chicago, IL St. Mary.
Nathan, Sahayanathan (LC) Wisconsin Rapids, WI Our Lady, Queen of Heaven.
Nathe, Thomas '04 (SEA) Port Angeles, WA Queen of Angels; Sequim, WA St. Joseph.
Nations, David G. *c.m.* '97 (STL)[O] St. Louis, MO Vincentian Residence.
Nations, David *c.m.* '97 (NO) Marrero, LA Immaculate Conception.
Natsuhara, Bruce K. '78 (OKL) Oklahoma City, OK St. Joseph; Consultors Archdiocesan; Council of Priests Archdiocesan.
Nattunilam, Dominic *c.m.i.* '86 (MET)[J] Flemington, NJ The Carmel of Mary Immaculate and St. Mary Magdalen.
Nau, Dale '78 (DUL) Duluth, MN St. Raphael; Chancellor; Defender of the Bond; Department of Continuing Formation of Clergy; Safe Environment; Diocesan Corporate Board.
Nau, Thomas R. '78 (STU) Steubenville, OH Holy Name Cathedral; Steubenville, OH Triumph of the Cross.
Naucke, Alfred E. *s.j.* '65 (SJ)[B] Santa Clara, CA Jesuit Community; [M] Los Gatos, CA California Province of the Society of Jesus, Jesuit Provincial Office; Los Gatos, CA.
Naughton, James J. *s.d.b.* '67 (BIR) Leeds, AL St. Theresa's.
Naughton, Rev. Msgr. John Thomas '49 (LA) Retired.
Naughton, Michael *o.s.b.* '66 (SCL) Albany, MN Seven Dolors; Albany, MN St. Anthony's; [I] Collegeville, MN St. John's Abbey, of the Order of St. Benedict.
Naughton, Patrick J. '91 (COL) On Duty Outside the Diocese.
Naughton, Patrick J. '91 (MIA) Plantation, FL St. Gregory.
Naughton, Thomas J. '61 (BO) Senior Priests. Retired.
Naughton, Rev. Msgr. William M. '72 (PAT) Unassigned.
Naugle, John F. '09 (PIT) Pittsburgh, PA St. Louise de Marillac.
Naumann, Paul S. *s.j.* '63 (SY)[Q] Syracuse, NY Jesuits at LeMoyne, Inc.
Naumes, Matthew '63 (SEA) Retired.
Naus, John E. *s.j.* '55 (MIL)[P] Wauwatosa, WI Jesuit Community at St. Camillus.
Naval, Thomas Paul K. *a.m.* '89 (ORG) Anaheim, CA St. Justin Martyr.
Navalo, Hector M. *c.m.f.* '03 (CHI)[N] Oak Park Claretian Missionaries USA Eastern Province; Chicago, IL Holy Cross/Immaculate Heart of Mary.
Navaratne, Louis–Marie *o.s.b.* '76 (PAT)[N] Clifton, NJ Holy Face of Jesus Monastery.
Navarra, Peter '81 (SD) Lemon Grove, CA Saint John of the Cross Catholic Parish.
Navarrete, Jesus '87 (MO) Air Force Chaplains.
Navarro, Allen '09 (SJ) Sunnyvale, CA Church of The Resurrection.
Navarro, Edison *c.r.l.* '04 (ARE) Corozal, PR Christ the King.
Navarro, George A. *s.j.s.* '09 (MAD) Sauk City, WI St. Norbert; Sauk City, WI Divine Mercy Parish; Mazomanie, WI Holy Cross Parish.
Navarro, Juan B. (ORG) Garden Grove, CA St. Callistus.
Navarro, Marcelo Javier *i.v.e.* '94 (SJ) San Jose, CA St. Leo the Great; Deans.
Navarro, Nicolas *s.d.b.* '69 (SJN) San Juan, PR Maria Auxiliadora; [B] San Juan, PR Colegio San Juan Bosco.
Navarro, Rev. Msgr. Pablo A. '78 (MIA) Miami, FL St. John Neumann; Consultors; Incardinated Priests.
Navarro, Rev. Msgr. Pablo '78 (MIA) Deans and Deaneries.
Navarro, Pedro '63 (NEW) Retired.
Navas, Marvin A. *c.m.* '10 (PH) Philadelphia, PA St. Francis of Assisi.
Nave, Arthur '08 (PHX) Tempe, AZ Church of the Resurrection Roman Catholic Parish.
Nave, Rev. Msgr. Francis A. '92 (ALN) Bath, PA Sacred Heart of Jesus.
Navin, Timothy M. '79 (VEN) Marco Island, FL San Marco.
Navins, Robert J. '50 (NY) Staten Island, NY Sacred Heart Retired.
Navone, John *s.j.* (SPK)[B] Spokane, WA Gonzaga University.
Navoy, Ronald W. '71 (CHI) Mt. Prospect, IL St. Emily.
Nawalaniec, Mariusz J. '93 (CHI) Chicago, IL St. Symphorosa and Seven Sons.
Nawarskas, Rev. Msgr. Frederick '67 (SAN) Abilene, TX Holy Family; Priests' Personnel Board; Diocesan Consultors; Presbyteral Council; Deans; Pastor Review Board.
Nawrocki, Norman D. '82 (DET) Troy, MI St. Elizabeth Ann Seton; Defenders of Bond.
Nawrocki, Robert W. '61 (MIL) Retired.
Nawrocki, Zdzislaw *s.ch.* (BAL) Baltimore, MD Holy Rosary.
Nayak, Alexis *ss.cc.* '00 (FR)[F] Fairhaven National Center of the Enthronement.
Nayak, Christudas '68 (ALX)[B] Alexandria, LA Christus Health Central Louisiana; Alexandria, LA Our Lady of Prompt Succor; Alexandria, LA Christus St. Frances Cabrini Hospital.
Nayak, Prodeep Chandra (NOR) New London, CT St. Joseph.
Nayak, Subal *ss.cc.* (FR)[F] Fairhaven National Center of the Enthronement.
Nayak, Sudhir Cristo Das *ss.cc.* '06 (FR)[F] Fairhaven National Center of the Enthronement.
Nayak, Sudhir *ss.cc.* '03 (FR)[F] Fairhaven National Center of the Enthronement.
Naylor, David W. '00 (L) Louisville, KY St. Ignatius.
Naylor, Ronald J. '60 (RIC) Retired.
Nazareth, Andrew L. '87 (FTW) Garrett, IN St. Joseph.
Nazimek, David '93 (GBG) Monessen, PA The Epiphany of Our Lord.
Nazzani, Ermete *c.s.* '61 (LA)[O] Sun Valley, CA Villa Scalabrini.
Nazzaro, Alfonse *l.c.* '03 (DAL) Dallas, TX St. Monica.
Nazzaro, John *s.d.b.* '83 (BO)[M] Boston, MA Orient Heights Unit; Salesian Boys and Girls Club.
Ndagizimana, Isidore '85 (AUS) Austin, TX St. Albert The Great.
Ndeanaefo, Aloysius Okey '05 (SFD) Robinson, IL Our Lady of Lourdes; Robinson, IL St. Elizabeth.
Ndebilie, Valentine '05 (TLS) Poteau, OK Immaculate Conception.
Ndugbu, Jude (AUS) Austin, TX Seton/Brackenridge Hospital.
Ndugbu, Polycarp '73 (SAC) Represa, CA.
Nduka, Pascal E. '96 (IND) Morris, IN St. Anthony of Padua Catholic Church, Morris, Inc.
Nduke, Emmanuel Lugard '99 (TLS) Stillwater, OK St. John the Evangelist Parish and Newman Center.
Ndulaka, Matthias '78 (NY) Woodbourne, NY Woodbourne Correctional Facility; Wurtsboro, NY St. Joseph.
Ndyomugaloe, Balthazar '87 (CHI) Chicago, IL St. Basil/Visitation.
Neal, Mark '06 (DM) Des Moines, IA St. Theresa of the Child Jesus.
Nealon, Rev. Msgr. Joseph A. '61 (STU) Retired.
Neary, Mark '83 (SJ) Absent on Sick Leave.
Neault, Armand R. '52 (PRT) Retired.
Nebelung, Edwardo '84 (BAK) Boardman, OR Our Lady of Guadalupe.
Nedder, Edward T. '87 (SAM) Lincoln, RI St. George.
Nedeff, George *s.o.l.t.* '07 (CC) Robstown, TX St. Anthony; [G] Robstown, TX Society of Our Lady of the Most Holy Trinity.
Nediakala, Kuriakose *m.c.b.s.* '78 (DUL) Cass Lake, MN St. Charles.
Nedumankuzhiyil, Joseph '99 (RVC) Hempstead, NY St. John Chrysostom Malankara Mission.
Nedumankuzhiyil, Joseph (MCE) Garland, TX St. Mary's Malankara Catholic Church; Ecumenism and MCA Director; Presbyteral Council; Priests – Heads of Apostolates.
Nedumankuzhiyil, Joseph (DAL) Mesquite, TX St. Mary Malankara.
Nedumaruthumchalil, George K. '78 (NY) New Rochelle, NY Holy Family.
Nedumcheril, John '90 (DET) Richmond, MI St. Augustine.
Nedungadan, Johnson *c.m.* '91 (BRK) Bellerose, NY St. Gregory the Great.
Neduvelichalumkal, Kurian '91 (SYM) Milpitas, CA St. Thomas Syro–Malabar Catholic Church of San Francisco.
Nee, Eugene O. '64 (SAT) Military Chaplains.
Nee, Robert E. '71 (BO) Cambridge, MA St. John the Evangelist; Senior Priests. Retired.
Nee, Thomas M. '39 (PIT) Retired.
Needles, Brian X. '06 (NEW) Livingston, NJ St. Philomena.
Neeley, Peter *s.j.* (TUC)[I] Nogales, AZ Kino Border Initiative.

Neely, Bradley '03 (B) Grangeville, ID SS. Peter and Paul; Priest Personnel Commission.
Neely, Bradley '03 (B) Moscow, ID St. Mary's.
Neely, Harry M. *o.s.a.* '53 (SD)[J] San Diego, CA Augustinian Community.
Neenan, Benedict *o.s.b.* '88 (KC)[A] Conception, MO Conception Seminary College; [J] Conception, MO Conception Abbey.
Neenan, William B. *s.j.* '61 (BO)[U] Newton, MA The Jesuit Community at Boston College.
Neff, Eugene J. '71 (BEL) Lebanon, IL St. Joseph; Hospitals; Sick and Aged (Ministry); New Baden, IL St. George.
Neff, John '86 (E) Youngsville, PA St. Luke.
Neff, Rev. Msgr. John '52 (SP) Retired.
Neff, Steven V. '05 (PIT) Butler, PA St. Paul; Butler, PA St. Wendelin.
Negley, Phil "Skip" M. *m.s.* '73 (GAL) Friendswood, TX Mary, Queen.
Negparanon, Nixon '05 (RIC) Norfolk, VA St. Pius X; South Hill, VA Good Shepherd.
Negrete, Wayne *s.j.* '91 (LA) Los Angeles, CA Blessed Sacrament; [P] Los Angeles, CA Colombiere House.
Negro, Fernando *sch.p.* '81 (NY) Washington, DC; Coto Laurel, PR; New York, NY Annunciation; [DD] New York, NY Calasanzian Fathers (Piarists).
Negron, Juan Luis '89 (CGS) Priests Senate.
Negron, Juan Luis '89 (SJN)[C] Rio Piedras, PR Seminario Mayor Regional San Juan Bautista; San Juan Bautista Regional Seminary.
Negron, Ramon Hiram *o.f.m.cap.* '93 (SJN) San Juan, PR San Antonio; Vicar for Youth; Youth Ministries; Consejo Arquidiocesano De Pastoral Juvenil.
Nehrig, Robert V. *m.m.* '54 (FgM) Maryknoll, NY MARYKNOLL.
Neidhart, William *c.s.c.* (FTW)[H] Notre Dame Congregation of Holy Cross, United States Province of Priests & Brothers.
Neiheisel, Stanley H. '60 (CIN) Cincinnati, OH St. Stephen Retired.
Neilson, James P. *o.praem.* '93 (GB)[B] St. Norbert College; [J] De Pere, WI St. Norbert Abbey.
Neilson, Kieran A. *o.s.b.* '60 (CHL)[J] Belmont, NC Belmont Abbey.
Neilson, Richard J. '83 (NY) Retired.
Neiman, John '86 (LA) Camarillo, CA St. Mary Magdalen.
Neis, William P. '67 (LC) Leave of Absence.
Neitzke, Ron P. '89 (MO) Navy Reserve Chaplains; Joliet, IL St. Mary Nativity; Joliet, IL Holy Cross.
Neitzke, Thomas W. *s.j.* '10 (OM) Omaha, NE St. Thomas More; [E] Omaha, NE Jesuit Academy; [J] Omaha, NE Jesuit Community at Creighton University.
Nekic, Simon J. '43 (CLV) Retired.
Nekoliczak, Ted A. '59 (GI) Retired.
Nelan, Rev. Msgr. Kevin J. '77 (NY) Manhattan (South); Apostleship of the Sea.
Nelan, Rev. Msgr. Kevin '77 (NY) New York, NY Immaculate Conception.
Nellikunnell, James *c.m.i.* '79 (ALX) Winnsboro, LA St. Mary.
Nellis, Thomas F. '66 (ROC) Retired.
Nellisary, Joy (BIR) Birmingham, AL St. Peter the Apostle.
Nellissery, Johnson '97 (MIL)[T] Waukesha, WI Schoenstatt Fathers.
Nelson, Andrew L. '57 (MIL) Retired.
Nelson, Brian D. '03 (WCH) South Hutchinson, KS Our Lady of Guadalupe; [B] Hutchinson, KS Trinity Catholic High School; Presbyteral Council/College of Consultors.
Nelson, Caye A. '88 (BR) Baton Rouge, LA St. Jude the Apostle.
Nelson, Charles T. '87 (SFD) Retired.
Nelson, Daniel C. *o.f.m.* '77 (ALB)[B] Siena College.
Nelson, Dennis (Dan) '08 (STA) Orange Park, FL St. Catherine's.
Nelson, Rev. Msgr. Francis J. '66 (SAV) Savannah, GA St. Frances Xavier Cabrini; Tribunal Judges; College of Consultors.
Nelson, Francis M. '88 (RVC) Brentwood, NY St. Anne's; Priests' Personnel Assignment Board.
Nelson, Francis *c.ss.r.* '64 (ORL) New Smyrna Beach, FL Sacred Heart.
Nelson, Rev. Msgr. Glenn L. '93 (RCK) DeKalb, IL Christ the Teacher, University Parish of Northern Illinois University; Special Assignment; [L] DeKalb, IL Newman Foundation for Catholic Students of Northern Illinois University; Vicars General; Moderator of the Curia; Deans; Catholic Office of the Deaf; Newman–Campus Ministry; Pro Synodal Judges.
Nelson, Greg '97 (PEO) Danville, IL St. Paul's; Clergymen's Aid, Inc.
Nelson, Kevin '00 (PMB) Assessors; Advocates; Lantana, FL Holy Spirit.
Nelson, Linden (LC)[D] Spiritual Services Dept.
Nelson, Martin Lester '97 (BEA) Diocesan Judges; Catholic Women, Council of; Sour Lake, TX Our Lady of Victory; Presbyteral Council.
Nelson, Patrick *s.d.s.* '09 (BIR) Huntsville, AL St. Joseph's.
Nelson, Patrick *s.d.s.* '09 (GB) St. Nazianz, WI St. Gregory; Kiel, WI Holy Trinity.
Nelson, Paul E. '61 (WIN) Rochester, MN St. Pius X; Priests' Pension Board.
Nelson, Robert W. '77 (LC) Pittsville, WI St. Joachim; Pittsville, WI Holy Rosary; Vesper, WI St. James.
Nelson, Ronald '07 (P) Gervais, OR Sacred Heart–St. Louis.
Nelson, Thomas J. *c.m.* '75 (DEN)[N] Denver, CO Congregation of the Mission Western Province: De Paul House.
Nelson, Thomas W. *o.praem.* '81 (ORG)[A] Silverado, CA St. Michael's Norbertine Postulancy, Novitiate and Juniorate; [I] Silverado, CA Norbertine Fathers of Orange Inc.
Nelson, Thomas *o.praem.* '81 (CHI)[T] Libertyville, IL Institute on Religious Life.
Nelson, Timothy '00 (LAN) Priests' Assignment Commission; Jackson, MI St. Mary Star of the Sea.
Nemchausky, Matthew '09 (CHI) Evergreen Park, IL Most Holy Redeemer.
Nemec, Rev. Msgr. Joseph J. '84 (LIN) Lincoln, NE St. Teresa's; [G] Lincoln, NE Adoration Convent and Church of Christ the King; Commission for Sacred Liturgy and Sacred Music; Diocesan Director of Liturgy; Evangelization Committee.
Nemecek, Cyril '60 (CHI) Retired.
Nemecek, M. Cyril '60 (CHI) North Riverside, IL Mater Christi.
Nemeck, Francis Kelly *o.m.i.* '61 (SAT)[C] Oblate School of Theology.
Nemeck, Francis Kelly *o.m.i.* '61 (CC)[F] Sarita, TX Lebh Shomea House of Prayer.
Nemer, Lawrence *s.v.d.* '60 (FgM) Techny, IL.
Nemergut, Robert S. '77 (EVN) Special Assignment.
Nemeth, Edward M. *s.j.* '65 (DET)[K] Clarkston, MI Colombiere Center.
Nemeth, Maurus B. *o.s.b.* '72 (SFR)[N] Portola Valley, CA Woodside Priory.
Nemmers, Francis J. '57 (SC) Retired.
Nemmers, Mark R. '66 (DUB) Judges Retired.
Neneman, John '00 (ORG) Special Assignment; Vocations Office.
Nenneau, Thomas D. '81 (LAN) Mount Morris, MI St. Mary.
Nentwick, John '65 (Y) Retired.
Nepil, John '11 (DEN) Boulder, CO St. Thomas Aquinas University Parish; [R] Denver, CO Companions of Christ.
Nerbun, David '11 (CHR) Bluffton, SC St. Gregory the Great.
Nereparampil, Paul *c.m.i.* '85 (SFS) Highmore, SD St. Mary.
Nerino, Joseph C. *m.m.* '46 (SJ)[M] Los Altos, CA Maryknoll.
Nerio, Jose Luis *o.f.m.* '11 (P)[L] Portland, OR Ascension Friary.
Nerio, Jose Luis *o.f.m.* (P) Portland, OR Ascension.
Nero, James *o.f.m.* '71 (MIA)[G] Fort Lauderdale, FL Holy Cross Hospital.
Neroda, Edward J. '57 (Y) Youngstown, OH St. Stanislaus Kostka.
Nesbit, Jason P. *c.s.v.* '11 (CHI)[N] Arlington Heights Viatorian Province Center–Clerics of St. Viator.
Nesbit, Jason *c.s.v.* '11 (JOL) Bourbonnais, IL Maternity of the Blessed Virgin Mary.
Nesbit, Walter G. *s.j.* '59 (STL)[O] St. Louis, MO Jesuit Community Corporation at Saint Louis University – Jesuit Hall.
Nesbitt, John B. '62 (SD) Retired.
Neske, Mark I. '83 (MOB) Mobile, AL Holy Family; Archdiocesan Consultors.
Nesrsta, Steven '95 (AUS) Fayetteville, TX St. John the Baptist; Fayetteville, TX St. Mary Catholic Church.
Ness, Bernardine *o.s.b.* '64 (SFS)[F] Marvin, SD Blue Cloud Abbey; Marvin, SD Blue Cloud Abbey.
Nessel, William *o.s.f.s.* '56 (PH)[Y] Philadelphia, PA Father Louis Brisson Residence Retired.
Nesti, Donald S. *c.s.sp.* '63 (GAL)[C] Houston, TX University of St. Thomas; [S] Houston, TX The Society of the Holy Spirit; Houston, TX St. Theresa.
Nestler, W. David *o.f.m.cap.* '89 (PIT) Pittsburgh, PA; [M] Allison Park, PA St. Conrad Friary.
Nestler, W. David *o.f.m.cap.* '89 (FgM) Pittsburgh, PA Province of St. Augustine.
Nestor, Rev. Msgr. Michael '65 (SJP) Presbyters Retired.
Nestor, Robert P. '70 (NEW)[B] Seton Hall University Retired.
Nestor, Thomas F. '81 (BO) Vicariate III; Winchester, MA St. Eulalia.
Nesvadba, Rev. Msgr. Reginald R. '66 (GAL) Pearland, TX St. Helen.
Netta, John G. '57 (NEW) Retired.
Nettekoven, Joseph M. '75 (ORG) Anaheim, CA San Antonio de Padua Del Cañon Church; Judges; Apostleship of Prayer.
Nettem, Joseph '99 (OKL) Duncan, OK Assumption.
Neu, Rev. Msgr. Leon M. '52 (BUF)[N] Lackawanna, NY Bishop Head Residence Retired.
Neubert, Germar *o.s.b.* '65 (OM)[M] Schuyler, NE St. Benedict Center Endowment Fund.
Neuhaus, Rev. Msgr. William B. '83 (COV) Covington, KY Cathedral, Basilica of the Assumption; Diocesan Consultors; Deans; Ministry Development Program for Deacons; Permanent Diaconate Formation; Promoter of Justice.
Neuizil, Lowell Greg '67 (MO) DEPARTMENT OF VETERANS AFFAIRS HOSPITALS AND CHAPLAINS.
Neuman, James L. '71 (SFD) Hillsboro, IL St. Agnes; Litchfield, IL Holy Family; Litchfield Deanery; Diocesan Finance Council; Priests' Personnel Board.
Neuman, Matthias *o.s.b.* '67 (IND)[K] Saint Meinrad St. Meinrad Archabbey; [L] Beech Grove, IN.
Neuman, Peter *i.c.m.* '80 (BR)[H] Baton Rouge, LA Incarnatio Consecratio Missio.
Neumann, Aloysius J. '60 (RCK) Retired.
Neumann, Don A. '72 (GAL)[S] Houston, TX The Catholic Chaplain Corps; Houston, TX St. Thomas More.
Neumann, Paul *s.m.* '59 (SAT)[L] San Antonio, TX Marianist Residence.
Neumann, Richard J. '65 (HRT) Windsor, CT St. Gabriel.
Neumann, William J. '75 (ORL) Casselberry, FL St. Augustine.
Neumeier, Larry S. '95 (LA) Encino, CA St. Cyril.
Neurohr, Gilbert N. '54 (MAR) Retired.
Neusch, Tony '04 (AMA) Shamrock, TX Our Mother of Mercy; Vocation Development Team; Advocates.
Neuser, John '62 (GB) Retired.
Neuzil, Gregory '67 (KNX) Retired.
Neuzil, Lowell G. '67 (CLV) Cleveland, OH Cleveland V.A.
Nevels, Thomas A. '99 (CIN) Miamisburg, OH Our Lady of Good Hope.
Neville, Joseph B. *s.j.* '60 (SY)[Q] Syracuse, NY Jesuits at LeMoyne, Inc.
Neville, Thomas '52 (RCK) Retired.
Nevin, Rev. Msgr. Emmet R. '77 (NY) Blauvelt, NY St. Catharine.
Nevins, Donald J. '75 (CHI) Chicago, IL St. Agnes of Bohemia; Chicago, IL Good Shepherd; Deans.
Nevins, Eugene J. *s.j.* '80 (CHI) Chicago, IL John H. Stroger, Jr. Hospital of Cook County; [D] Chicago, IL St. Ignatius Jesuit Community.
Nevins, John J. '57 (PH) Retired.
Nevins, Troy '96 (GR) Grand Rapids, MI Immaculate Heart of Mary.
Nevlud, Gregory J. '82 (SAT) Seguin, TX St. James.
New, Gary *s.d.s.* '91 (BIR) Huntsville, AL St. Joseph's; [H] Huntsville, AL Campus Ministry – University of Alabama in Huntsville.
Newbold, Ronan *c.p.* '69 (CHI) Chicago, IL Immaculate Conception; [N] Chicago, IL Passionist Community–Immaculate Conception Community.
Newburn, Charles *sch.p.* '79 (MIA)[D] Fort Lauderdale, FL Cardinal Gibbons High School.
Newbury, Robert G. '07 (COS) Stratton, CO St. Charles Borromeo.
Newbury, Robert '07 (COS) Burlington, CO St. Catherine of Siena; College of Consultors.
Newell, John J. '58 (BRK) Retired.
Newland, Rev. Msgr. Ronald A. '67 (NEW) Military Chaplains Retired.
Newland, Rev. Msgr. Ronald '67 (BRK) Rockaway Point, NY Blessed Trinity Roman Catholic Church.
Newman, Brian *o.f.m.cap.* '61 (FgM) Pittsburgh, PA Province of St. Augustine.
Newman, Jay Scott '93 (CHR) Greenville, SC St. Mary; [H] Greenville, SC Furman University Campus Ministry; Deans; Presbyteral Council; College of Consultors; Personnel Committee.
Newman, Louis I. '58 (RVC) Retired.
Newman, Mark L. *c.j.* '60 (LA) Santa Maria, CA St. Louis de Montfort; [B] Santa Maria, CA St. Joseph Seminary (Josephite Fathers' Novitiate).
Newman, Michael T. '67 (MIL) Kenosha, WI St. Mary; Judges for Second Instance.
Newman, Michael *s.d.s.* '67 (MIL)[P] Milwaukee Salvatorian Provincial Offices Retired.
Newman, Rev. Msgr. Nelson A. '54 (OM) Central City, NE St. Michael.
Newns, John J. '74 (PH) Phoenixville, PA St. Ann.
Newton, David J. '88 (LFT) Dunkirk, IN St. Mary; Hartford City, IN St. John the Evangelist; Associate Judges.
Newton, Joseph L. '08 (IND) Graduate Studies.
Newton, Stephen P. *c.s.c.* '89 (FTW)[H] Notre Dame Congregation of Holy Cross, United States Province of Priests & Brothers.
Newton, Stephen P. *c.s.c.* '89 (P) Portland, OR St. Andre Bessette Church.
Newton, Thomas A. '88 (CAM) Appointed Members; Cherry Hill, NJ The Catholic Community of Christ Our Light, Cherry Hill, N.J.; Consultant for Clergy Health and Wellness; Ex Officio Members; Members.

Neylon, Bruce M. '75 (FR) Fall River, MA St. Stanislaus; Procurator–Advocates; Diocesan Guild for the Blind.
Neyra, Hugo R. '84 (LA) Winnetka, CA St. Joseph the Worker.
Neyrey, Jerome H. *s.j.* '70 (LAF)[J] Grand Coteau, LA Our Lady of the Oaks Retreat House.
Ng, Andrew *s.d.b.* '97 (OAK)[L] Berkeley Salesians of Don Bosco.
Ng, Francis '09 (ORG) Anaheim, CA St. Justin Martyr.
Ng, Thomas '61 (OAK) Oakland, CA St. Leo the Great Retired.
Ngageno, Robert '97 (CAM) Carney's Point, NJ Saint Gabriel the Archangel Parish, Carneys Point, N.J.
Ngan, Joseph M. Vu Kim *c.m.c.* '04 (DEN) Wheat Ridge, CO Queen of Vietnamese Martyrs.
Nganga, Daniel '02 (SD) San Diego, CA Saint Therese Catholic Parish.
Nganzi, Bernardine '88 (BEL) Lawrenceville, IL Immaculate Conception; Lawrenceville, IL St. Lawrence; Lawrenceville, IL St. Francis Xavier.
Nghia, Ho Anh *c.ss.r.* '10 (LA)[P] Baldwin Park, CA Vietnamese Redemptorist Mission.
Nghiem, Peter '72 (GR) Wyoming, MI Our Lady of LaVang; On Special Assignment; Vietnamese Ministry.
Ngidjoi, Joseph *p.i.m.e.* '09 (LAN)[N] Ypsilanti, MI Holy Trinity Student Parish; Ypsilanti, MI Holy Trinity Student Parish.
Ngo, Anthony '94 (RIC) Retired.
Ngo, Chi V. *s.j.* '00 (SJ)[M] Los Gatos, CA California Province of the Society of Jesus, Jesuit Provincial Office; [M] Santa Clara, CA Casa San Inigo, Jesuit Residence; [B] Santa Clara, CA Jesuit Community.
Ngo, Chu *s.j.* '07 (SJ) San Jose, CA Most Holy Trinity.
Ngo, Francis Huan Ton '89 (GAL) Houston, TX St. Gregory the Great.
Ngo, Lan *s.j.* '04 (WDC)[O] Washington, DC The Jesuit Community at Georgetown University.
Ngo, Peter T.C. '93 (LA) Los Angeles, CA Our Lady of Guadalupe; Cursillo Movement.
Ngo, Tammylee *o.f.m.conv.* '11 (OAK) San Pablo, CA St. Paul.
Ngo, Thich *o.p.* '05 (ARL) Arlington, VA Holy Martyrs of Vietnam.
Ngo, Tich Van *o.p.* '05 (PHX) Phoenix, AZ Vietnamese Martyrs Parish Roman Catholic Parish.
Ngoc Lien, Joseph To *c.m.c.* '62 (SPC)[F] Carthage, MO Congregation of the Mother Coredemptrix, United States Assumption Province.
Nguyen, (Dominic M.) Hoan Dinh *c.m.c.* '09 (SPC)[F] Carthage, MO Congregation of the Mother Coredemptrix, United States Assumption Province.
Nguyen, Andrew C. '11 (SJ) San Jose, CA St. Christopher.
Nguyen, Andrew M. Tuan Van '11 (FWT) Arlington, TX Church of the Vietnamese Martyrs.
Nguyen, Andrew V. '09 (SJ) San Jose, CA St. Patrick; Council of Priests.
Nguyen, Andrew *o.s.b.* '07 (SFE)[H] Abiquiu, NM Monastery of Christ in the Desert.
Nguyen, Anh Tuan '98 (ORG) Administrative Leave.
Nguyen, Anh–Tuan Dominic '07 (LA) Pomona, CA St. Joseph.
Nguyen, Anthony G. '66 (BO) Presbyteral Council.
Nguyen, Anthony Phuc *c.ss.r.* '92 (LA)[P] In Res; Whittier, CA St. Mary of the Assumption.
Nguyen, Anthony Quyen *c.m.f.* '07 (LA) San Gabriel, CA San Gabriel Mission.
Nguyen, Anthony Tin '06 (HT) Morgan City, LA Thanh Gia.
Nguyen, Anthony *c.ss.r.* '92 (OAK)[L] Berkeley, CA Redemptorist Fathers (Denver Province).
Nguyen, Anthony '00 (SJ) Los Altos, CA St. Simon.
Nguyen, Bao Huy '10 (LA) Lomita, CA St. Margaret Mary Alacoque.
Nguyen, Benjamin N. '05 (WCH) Coffeyville, KS Holy Name; Ongoing Formation of the Clergy Committee.
Nguyen, Bich N. '03 (OAK) Oakland, CA St. Lawrence O'Toole–St. Cyril of Jerusalem; Presbyteral Council; Judges.
Nguyen, Bieu Van '00 (MOB) Bayou LaBatre, AL St. Margaret; Coden, AL St. Michael the Archangel.
Nguyen, Binh T. '01 (ORG) Director of Clergy Personnel; Secretary to the Bishop; Staff; Liturgical Commission; Special Assignment; Council of Priests; Clergy Personnel Board.
Nguyen, Binh Thanh *s.v.d.* '02 (WDC)[O] Washington, DC Society of the Divine Word/Divine Word House.
Nguyen, Binh Van *c.m.* '82 (LA)[P] Montebello, CA DePaul Evangelization Center; [V] Montebello, CA DePaul Evangelization Center.
Nguyen, Binh *o.f.m.* '09 (WDC)[B] Silver Spring, MD Holy Name College.
Nguyen, Chanh (LAF) Krotz Springs, LA St. Anthony of Padua.
Nguyen, Charles '89 (SAC) Absent on Leave.
Nguyen, Chau J. '89 (ORL) Vietnamese Ministry; Orlando, FL St. Philip Phan Van Minh Catholic Church.
Nguyen, Chien '97 (ORL) Orlando, FL St. Philip Phan Van Minh Catholic Church.
Nguyen, Chinh '94 (SR)[J] Penngrove, CA Newman Hall, Sonoma State University, Intercollegiate Catholic Ministries.
Nguyen, Christopher T. *s.j.* '01 (LA)[P] Culver City, CA Ignatius House, The Novitiate of the California Province, Society of Jesus.
Nguyen, Christopher *s.j.* '01 (SJ)[D] San Jose, CA Bellarmine College Preparatory; Council of Religious.
Nguyen, Cuong (Paul) Hung *s.v.d.* '00 (DUB)[B] Epworth, IA Divine Word College.
Nguyen, Cuong H. *m.m.* '98 (FgM) Maryknoll, NY MARYKNOLL.
Nguyen, Dam D. '93 (PIT) Pittsburgh, PA Sacred Heart; Chaplain to Vietnamese Catholic Community.
Nguyen, Daokim '93 (GAL) New Waverly, TX St. Joseph.
Nguyen, Doanh "John" *s.j.* '01 (SJ) San Jose, CA Most Holy Trinity.
Nguyen, Dominic Hanh *o.s.b.* (DAL)[J] Kerens, TX Benedictine Monastery of Thien Tam.
Nguyen, Dominic Huyen Duc '64 (NO) New Orleans, LA Our Lady of La Vang.
Nguyen, Dominic M. Trung *c.m.c.* (FWT) Arlington, TX Church of the Vietnamese Martyrs.
Nguyen, Dominic Trung *c.ss.r.* '03 (VIC) Palacios, TX St. Anthony's; Palacios, TX Vietnamese Apostolate.
Nguyen, Dominic *s.v.d.* (STL) St. Louis, MO Resurrection of Our Lord.
Nguyen, Dominic *c.ss.r.* '03 (VIC) Vietnamese Apostolate.
Nguyen, Dovan '93 (TLS) Tulsa, OK St. Joseph Church.
Nguyen, Duc Cong '06 (SEA) Yelm, WA St. Columban.
Nguyen, Duc '09 (KC) Chillicothe, MO St. Joseph's.
Nguyen, Dung '02 (ATL) Milledgeville, GA Sacred Heart of Jesus.
Nguyen, Duong *s.v.d.* '05 (SD) San Diego, CA Our Lady of the Sacred Heart Catholic Parish.
Nguyen, Duy *s.c.j.* '11 (JKS)[E] Nesbit, MS St. Michael Community House; Robinsonville, MS Good Shepherd Catholic Church.
Nguyen, Francis Khoi '90 (DOD) Elkhart, KS St. Joan of Arc Catholic Church of Elkhart, Kansas; Hugoton, KS St. Helen Catholic Church of Hugoton, Kansas.
Nguyen, Francis (WDC) Washington, DC Shrine of the Sacred Heart.
Nguyen, Gan *c.ss.r.* (LSC) On Leave for Military.
Nguyen, Greg Viet *i.c.m.* '98 (GAL) Houston, TX St. Justin Martyr.
Nguyen, Hien Minh '85 (SJ) Special Assignment.
Nguyen, Hien Paul '00 (WCH) Marion, KS Holy Family.
Nguyen, Hieu Trong *s.v.d.* '06 (SB) San Bernardino, CA Our Lady of the Rosary Cathedral.
Nguyen, Hieu '69 (SC) Sioux City, IA Cathedral of the Epiphany.
Nguyen, Hilary M. Khanh Hia *c.m.c.* '94 (LIN) Lincoln, NE Immaculate Heart of Mary.
Nguyen, Hoa Van '76 (HBG) Vietnamese Ministry.
Nguyen, Hoa '98 (FWT) Wichita Falls, TX Sacred Heart; Consultors.
Nguyen, Hoai Thanh '06 (NO) La Place, LA St. Joan of Arc.
Nguyen, Hoang D. '05 (STP) St. Paul, MN St. Columba.
Nguyen, Hoang H. '04 (CHI) Military Chaplains.
Nguyen, Hoang Peter '04 (MO) Air Force Chaplains.
Nguyen, Huan Tien '66 (CIN) Retired.
Nguyen, Hung Joseph '94 (STO) Lodi, CA St. Anne Church (Pastor of).
Nguyen, Hung Van *s.o.l.t.* '02 (MO) Air Force Reserve Chaplains.
Nguyen, Hung Viet *i.c.m.* '69 (BR)[H] Baton Rouge, LA Incarnatio Consecratio Missio; [L] Baton Rouge, LA St. Michael's Home.
Nguyen, Hung '94 (SEA) Friday Harbor, WA St. Francis.
Nguyen, Hung *o.f.m.cap.* '99 (LA)[F] La Canada Flintridge, CA St. Francis High School of La Canada–Flintridge.
Nguyen, Huy H. '09 (BO) Dorchester, MA St. Ambrose; Dorchester, MA Holy Family; Dorchester, MA St. Peter; Dorchester, MA Blessed Mother Teresa of Calcutta.
Nguyen, Huy '95 (LA) Norwalk, CA St. Linus.
Nguyen, Hy K. *s.s.* '97 (BAL)[Q] Baltimore Society of St. Sulpice, Province of the United States; [A] Baltimore, MD St. Mary's Seminary and University.
Nguyen, Hy *s.s.* '97 (OAK) On Duty Outside the Diocese.
Nguyen, J. Christopher C. '08 (GAL) Pasadena, TX St. Pius the Fifth.
Nguyen, J. B. Duc Minh *o.p.* '09 (GAL) Houston, TX Our Lady of Lourdes.
Nguyen, James Bam '01 (LAF) Melville, LA St. John the Evangelist.
Nguyen, Rev. Msgr. Joe Van Anh '68 (AUS) Austin, TX Holy Vietnamese Martyrs Catholic Church – Austin, Texas.
Nguyen, John C. '99 (PH)[D] Warminster, PA Archbishop Wood Catholic High School; Horsham, PA St. Catherine of Siena.
Nguyen, John Hoa '72 (LA) Arcadia, CA Holy Angels.
Nguyen, John Hung Manh '00 (GAL) Houston, TX Vietnamese Martyrs.
Nguyen, John Luat *o.f.m.* '94 (SFR) San Francisco, CA St. Boniface.
Nguyen, John Tran *o.f.m.* '06 (OAK)[L] Oakland, CA Franciscan Friars of California, (Province of St. Barbara).
Nguyen, John Tung '07 (WDC) Rockville, MD Shrine of St. Jude.
Nguyen, John Baptist Vuong Duc *o.p.* '00 (ARL) Arlington, VA Holy Martyrs of Vietnam.
Nguyen, Joseph C. '78 (ORG) Stanton, CA St. Polycarp.
Nguyen, Joseph Chau *s.v.d.* '08 (DUB)[B] Epworth, IA Divine Word College.
Nguyen, Joseph Chinh (BO) Dorchester, MA St. Ambrose.
Nguyen, Joseph D. '08 (ORG) Newport Beach, CA Our Lady Queen of Angels.
Nguyen, Joseph H. *s.j.* '07 (OAK)[L] Berkeley, CA Jesuit Fathers and Brothers.
Nguyen, Joseph Hau Duc '69 (P) Retired.
Nguyen, Joseph Huyen '95 (SAC) Judges.
Nguyen, Joseph Kim Dang '93 (LA) Alhambra, CA All Souls.
Nguyen, Joseph Lam *c.s.sp.* '06 (GAL)[R] Houston, TX Satellite Office; [R] Houston, TX Catholic Newman Association at the University of Houston Central Campus.
Nguyen, Joseph Liem '99 (ATL) Blairsville, GA St. Francis of Assisi.
Nguyen, Joseph Long Kim '02 (ORG) Garden Grove, CA St. Callistus.
Nguyen, Joseph Luan '90 (ORG) Santa Ana, CA Our Lady of La Vang.
Nguyen, Joseph Luu '66 (HT) Retired.
Nguyen, Joseph Luu *s.d.d.* '66 (NO) Retired.
Nguyen, Joseph Minh *s.d.d.* '10 (HT) Thibodaux, LA St. Joseph Co–Cathedral.
Nguyen, Joseph Minh Tri '61 (NEW) Vietnamese Apostolate; Jersey City, NJ Parish of the Resurrection.
Nguyen, Joseph Minh Vu *s.v.d.* '96 (FgM) Techny, IL.
Nguyen, Joseph Phien '92 (RIC) Norfolk, VA Our Lady of Vietnam Chapel; Norfolk, VA Our Lady of Lavang.
Nguyen, Joseph Phiet The '73 (GAL) Danbury, TX St. Anthony de Padua.
Nguyen, Joseph Q. *c.s.sp.* '10 (FgM) Bethel Park, PA CONGREGATION OF THE HOLY SPIRIT.
Nguyen, Joseph Quan '05 (LA) Claremont, CA Our Lady of the Assumption; Cardinal McIntyre Fund for Charity Board of Directors.
Nguyen, Joseph Son '89 (ORG) Orange, CA UCI Medical Center.
Nguyen, Joseph T. '10 (DAV) Clinton, IA Jesus Christ, Prince of Peace.
Nguyen, Joseph T. '11 (CC) Corpus Christi, TX St. Pius X.
Nguyen, Joseph Tan Doan *o.f.m.* '86 (FgM) U.S. Religious Serving Elsewhere.
Nguyen, Joseph Thai '95 (CHI) Other Assignments.
Nguyen, Joseph Thieu '04 (OAK) Berkeley, CA St. Joseph The Worker.
Nguyen, Joseph Trong '69 (LAV) Retired.
Nguyen, Joseph Tuoc *s.j.* '89 (DEN) Denver, CO St. Ignatius Loyola; [N] Denver, CO Society of Jesus – St. Ignatius Loyola Jesuit Community.
Nguyen, Joseph '73 (FRS) Fresno, CA Our Lady of Lavang.
Nguyen, Joseph *o.s.b.* '03 (P)[L] St. Benedict, OR Mt. Angel Abbey.
Nguyen, Joseph *o.p.* '93 (PHX) Phoenix, AZ Vietnamese Martyrs Parish Roman Catholic Parish.
Nguyen, Joseph *s.j.* (SEA)[M] Seattle, WA Jesuit House, Seattle.
Nguyen, Joseph '05 (OAK) Oakland, CA Cathedral Parish of Christ the Light.
Nguyen, Khanh D. '06 (SEA) Ferndale, WA St. Joseph; Presbyteral Council; Deans.
Nguyen, Khanh Pham '97 (HON) Honolulu, HI St. Stephen Catholic Parish.
Nguyen, Khiem '11 (FWT) Bedford, TX St. Michael.
Nguyen, Khiet T. '96 (TLS) Judges; Okmulgee, OK St. Anthony's.
Nguyen, Khoa Quang *s.v.d.* '08 (WDC)[O] Washington, DC Society of the Divine Word/Divine Word House.
Nguyen, Khoa *s.v.d.* '08 (DUB)[B] Epworth, IA Divine Word College.
Nguyen, Kim Son '87 (SAV) Savannah, GA Sts. Peter and Paul.
Nguyen, Lam (STA) Jacksonville, FL Blessed Trinity.
Nguyen, Lawrence M. *c.m.c.* '09 (SPC)[F] Carthage, MO Congregation of the Mother Coredemptrix, United States Assumption Province.
Nguyen, Lich Van '84 (NO) Harvey, LA St. Martha.
Nguyen, Liem *o.s.b.* '94 (P)[A] St. Benedict, OR Mount Angel Seminary.
Nguyen, Linh N. '06 (CIN) On Duty Outside the Archdiocese.
Nguyen, Linh N. '06 (GAL) Houston, TX St. John Neumann.

Nguyen, Linh T. (BO) Randolph, MA St. Bernadette.
Nguyen, Linh Tien '04 (SFR) South San Francisco, CA St. Veronica.
Nguyen, Linh '97 (LEX) Georgetown, KY SS. Francis & John Catholic Church.
Nguyen, Long Phi *s.v.d.* '07 (FgM) Techny, IL.
Nguyen, Long '08 (LA) Lynwood, CA St. Emydius.
Nguyen, Long *s.v.d.* '08 (SB)[I] Riverside, CA Divine Word Seminary.
Nguyen, Luan D. '08 (P) Brookings, OR Star of the Sea.
Nguyen, Luke Hungdung '02 (NO) Metairie, LA St. Ann Church and Shrine.
Nguyen, Martin Lam *c.s.c.* '89 (FTW)[B] University of Notre Dame Du Lac; [H] Notre Dame, IN Holy Cross Community, Corby Hall, University of Notre Dame.
Nguyen, Martin Thanh *i.c.m.* '97 (BR)[H] Baton Rouge, LA Incarnatio Consecratio Missio.
Nguyen, Martin '05 (ORG) Brea, CA St. Angela Merici.
Nguyen, Martino Ba Thong '04 (SAV) Americus, GA St. Mary.
Nguyen, Matthias Huy Chuong *c.m.c.* '81 (SB) Special or Other Diocesan Assignment.
Nguyen, Michael Manh *c.m.* '95 (CHL) Greensboro, NC St. Mary; Consultors.
Nguyen, Michael Nam Hoang '93 (NO) Terrytown, LA Christ the King.
Nguyen, Michael Quang *s.v.d.* '02 (FgM) Techny, IL.
Nguyen, Michael Tung '03 (ORG) Irvine, CA St. John Neumann.
Nguyen, Michael Joseph Vinh Ngoc '90 (NO) Liaisons for the Vietnamese Community.
Nguyen, Minh '08 (SB) Colton, CA Immaculate Conception; Colton, CA San Salvador.
Nguyen, Nghiem Van '89 (NO) New Orleans, LA Mary, Queen of Vietnam; New Orleans, LA Chapel of the Vietnamese Martyrs; Liaisons for the Vietnamese Community.
Nguyen, Nguyen Van '02 (NO) New Orleans, LA Chapel of the Vietnamese Martyrs.
Nguyen, Nguyen Van '02 (NO) New Orleans, LA Mary, Queen of Vietnam.
Nguyen, Nhuan D. *m.m.* '93 (FgM) Maryknoll, NY MARYKNOLL.
Nguyen, Nick Hien *s.v.d.* '00 (DUB)[B] Epworth, IA Divine Word College.
Nguyen, Nicolas T. '11 (ORG) Anaheim, CA St. Boniface.
Nguyen, Odon *o.s.b.* '65 (SFE)[H] Abiquiu, NM Monastery of Christ in the Desert.
Nguyen, Paul Chung '00 (PMB) Palm Beach Gardens, FL Cathedral of St. Ignatius Loyola.
Nguyen, Paul Chuong *s.d.b.* '88 (SP)[P] Tampa, FL Mary Help of Christians Center.
Nguyen, Paul Cuong Hung *s.v.d.* (DM) West Des Moines, IA Sacred Heart.
Nguyen, Paul Dean '07 (WDC) Bethesda, MD St. Jane Frances de Chantal.
Nguyen, Paul Van Tung '79 (NO) Covington, LA St. Peter.
Nguyen, Paul '06 (DAL) Dallas, TX All Saints.
Nguyen, Peter Duc Hung '97 (SC) Wesley, IA St. Benedict's; Wesley, IA St. Joseph's.
Nguyen, Peter H. (BRK)[Q] Vietnamese Apostolate.
Nguyen, Peter Hung *s.o.l.t.* '00 (SFE) La Joya, NM Our Lady of Sorrows.
Nguyen, Peter P. *s.j.* '08 (CHI)[N] Chicago Chicago Province of the Society of Jesus–Provincial Office.
Nguyen, Rev. Msgr. Peter Quang '90 (DEN) Denver, CO Our Lady of Lourdes; Deaneries.
Nguyen, Peter Sam Cao *s.v.d.* '86 (FgM) Techny, IL.
Nguyen, Peter *c.s.j.b.* '03 (BRK) Long Island City, NY Our Lady of Mount Carmel.
Nguyen, Phi '06 (CHI) Oak Forest, IL St. Damian.
Nguyen, Phien T. '92 (CHI) Other Assignments.
Nguyen, Phillip D. '87 (GR) Personal Leave.
Nguyen, Phong Cao *s.v.d.* '06 (FgM) Techny, IL.
Nguyen, Phuong J. '11 (GAL) Houston, TX St. Rose of Lima.
Nguyen, Polycarp *c.m.c.* '91 (FWT) Arlington, TX Church of the Vietnamese Martyrs.
Nguyen, Qui–Thac '04 (SEA)[P] Bellingham, WA Western Washington University (Bellingham); Bellingham, WA Sacred Heart.
Nguyen, Quoc *o.f.m.cap.* '02 (SFR)[B] San Francisco, CA Capuchin Franciscan Order San Buenaventura Friary.
Nguyen, Raphael Xuan '96 (ORG) Santa Ana, CA St. Barbara Catholic Church.
Nguyen, Scott C. '97 (SB) San Bernardino, CA Our Lady of Hope Catholic Community, Inc.
Nguyen, Scott C. '97 (WCH) On Duty Outside the Diocese.
Nguyen, Simon T. *c.s.sp.* '10 (FgM) Bethel Park, PA CONGREGATION OF THE HOLY SPIRIT.
Nguyen, Son Anh '03 (WOR) Worcester, MA Our Lady of Vilna.
Nguyen, Son *s.v.d.* '03 (MO) Air Force Chaplains.
Nguyen, Stephen Kha *s.v.d.* '06 (DUB)[B] Epworth, IA Divine Word College.
Nguyen, Steve '99 (HON) Honolulu, HI Blessed Sacrament; Judge.
Nguyen, Sy '91 (ORG) Yorba Linda, CA St. Martin de Porres; Promoter of Justice; Cursillo Movement; Council of Priests; Consultors.
Nguyen, Tai '10 (SLC) St. George, UT St. George LLC 223.
Nguyen, Tam N. '82 (TLS) Diocesan Consultors; Priests' Personnel Committee.
Nguyen, Tam '82 (TLS) Special Assignment.
Nguyen, Tam (OKL) Adjutant Judicial Vicars.
Nguyen, Tan Viet *i.c.m.* '01 (BR) Baton Rouge, LA Sts. Anthony of Padua and Le Van Phung; Vietnamese Apostolate.
Nguyen, Tan Viet *sv.d.* (GAL) Houston, TX St. Mary of the Purification.
Nguyen, Tan Viet *s.v.d.* '03 (MEM)[F] Memphis, TN Society of the Divine Word (Chicago Province).
Nguyen, Tan '09 (SJ) San Jose, CA St. Patrick.
Nguyen, Te Van '86 (SFR) San Francisco, CA St. Brendan; Vietnamese Catholic Ministry; Laguna Honda Home.
Nguyen, Thai Hung '09 (SAG) Alma, MI St. Mary; St. Louis, MI St. Joseph.
Nguyen, Thanh N. '94 (R) Durham, NC St. Matthew.
Nguyen, Thanh T. '91 (STA) Jacksonville, FL Christ the King; Diocesan Consultors; Presbyteral Council.
Nguyen, Thanh Van '00 (OKL) Oklahoma City, OK Cathedral of Our Lady of Perpetual Help.
Nguyen, Thanh *l.c.* '00 (MAN)[A] Center Harbor, NH Immaculate Conception Apostolic School.
Nguyen, Thanh '67 (PRT) Retired.
Nguyen, Thao N. *s.j.* '08 (SJ)[B] Santa Clara, CA Jesuit Community.
Nguyen, That Son '90 (SJ) San Jose, CA St. Francis of Assisi.
Nguyen, That Son Ngoc '90 (WH) War, WV Christ the King; Absent on Leave.
Nguyen, Thien Van '89 (WIN) Madelia, MN St. Mary; St. James, MN St. James; Madelia, MN St. Katherine.
Nguyen, Thien '01 (WOR) Leominster, MA St. Leo.
Nguyen, Thien '01 (MAN) Vietnamese Apostolate.
Nguyen, Thinh *s.d.b.* '99 (LA) Bellflower, CA St. Dominic Savio.
Nguyen, Thomas Thanh '69 (LAF) Franklin, LA St. Helena.
Nguyen, Thu Ngoc '93 (GAL) Houston, TX Co–Cathedral of the Sacred Heart; Archdiocesan Judges; Priests Personnel Committee.
Nguyen, Thu '92 (FWT) Fort Worth, TX St. George.
Nguyen, Thuong Hoai '91 (OAK) El Cerrito, CA St. John the Baptist.
Nguyen, Thuy Quang '98 (GAL) Sealy, TX St. Mary; Wallis, TX Guardian Angel.
Nguyen, Tien Duc (ORG) Retired.
Nguyen, Tien–Tri '96 (SFE) Santa Fe, NM Our Lady of Guadalupe.
Nguyen, Timothy '08 (ORG) Orange, CA Cathedral of the Holy Family.
Nguyen, Tinh Van '98 (BO) Dorchester, MA St. Ambrose.
Nguyen, Tinh *s.v.d.* '10 (LA) Los Angeles, CA Our Lady of Lourdes.
Nguyen, Toan X. '96 (SFR) Sabbatical.
Nguyen, Tong Ba '09 (SB) Upland, CA St. Joseph.
Nguyen, Tran *o.f.m.* (SAC) Sacramento, CA St. Francis of Assisi.
Nguyen, Trong Joseph *s.v.d.* '91 (SB) Beaumont, CA Blessed Kateri Tekakwitha Catholic Community, Inc.; Elected At–Large Members.
Nguyen, Truc Q. '00 (LA) Defenders of the Bond; Los Angeles, CA Cathedral Chapel.
Nguyen, Trung V. '94 (GAL)[A] Houston, TX St. Mary's Seminary; Archdiocesan Judges.
Nguyen, Truyen '03 (SJ) Los Gatos, CA St. Mary of the Immaculate Conception.
Nguyen, Tu T. '07 (SAT) San Antonio, TX St. Lawrence.
Nguyen, Tuan Van '86 (JOL) Villa Park, IL St. Alexander.
Nguyen, Tuan '92 (SEA) Tacoma, WA St. Ann; Tacoma, WA St. John of the Woods; Tacoma, WA Sacred Heart; College of Consultors; Presbyteral Council; Samoan, Ministry to.
Nguyen, Tuan *s.d.b.* '88 (STO) Stockton, CA St. Luke Church of Stockton (Pastor of); Members Appointed.
Nguyen, Tuan *c.ss.r.* (STP)[J] Brooklyn Center, MN Redemptorist Fathers of Hennepin County; Brooklyn Center, MN St. Alphonsus.
Nguyen, Tuan '95 (ORG) Garden Grove, CA St. Columban.
Nguyen, Tuyen '87 (ORG) Garden Grove, CA St. Callistus.
Nguyen, Ty Van '85 (HT) Bourg, LA St. Ann.
Nguyen, Van T. '79 (MO) Navy Reserve Chaplains.
Nguyen, Vandennis '90 (YAK) Richland, WA Christ the King.
Nguyen, vanThanh *s.v.d.* '97 (CHI)[N] Chicago, IL Divine Word Theologate; [B] Chicago, IL Catholic Theological Union.
Nguyen, Vien The '89 (NO) Judges; [A] New Orleans, LA Notre Dame Seminary Graduate School of Theology; Adjutant Judicial Vicars; Canonical Consultant to the Archbishop.
Nguyen, Vien *s.c.j.* '04 (GAL) Houston, TX Our Lady of Guadalupe.
Nguyen, Vincent Kien '89 (HON) Vietnamese Catholic Community.
Nguyen, Vincent Liem *o.s.b.* '94 (P)[L] St. Benedict, OR Mt. Angel Abbey.
Nguyen, Vincent Van Dao '05 (SPK) Valley, WA St. Mary of the Rosary; Valley, WA Sacred Heart; Valley, WA Holy Ghost.
Nguyen, Vincent Vuong Quoc '99 (GAL) Houston, TX St. Clare of Assisi.
Nguyen, Vinh Daniel *s.v.d.* '07 (FgM) Techny, IL.
Nguyen, Vinh Quang '86 (NEW) Bayonne, NJ St. Vincent de Paul.
Nguyen, Vinh Quang '86 (NEW) Englewood, NJ Englewood Hospital & Medical Center.
Nguyen–Thanh–Long, Peter '65 (WDC) Silver Spring, MD Our Lady of Vietnam.
Nguyen Hong An, Andrew M. *c.m.c.* '87 (SPC)[F] Carthage, MO Congregation of the Mother Coredemptrix, United States Assumption Province.
Nguyen Van Quy, Peter *o.f.m.* '71 (NY)[DD] New York Franciscan Province of the Immaculate Conception.
Ngwila, Filbert '11 (CHI) Western Springs, IL St. John of the Cross.
Ngwili, Daniel Mutuku *o.c.d.* '10 (MIL)[P] Milwaukee Provincial Offices – Discalced Carmelites.
Ngyen, Joseph Liep Van '63 (CC) Retired.
Nhien, Louis M. Vu Minh *c.m.c.* '92 (SPC)[A] Carthage, MO Congregation of the Mother Co–Redemptrix; [F] Carthage, MO Congregation of the Mother Coredemptrix, United States Assumption Province.
Niblick, Charles W. '74 (GRY) Dyer, IN St. Maria Goretti.
Nicastro, Thomas D. '90 (NEW) Nutley, NJ St. Mary's.
Niccolls, Edward D. '74 (WOR) Auburn, MA St. Joseph's; Clergy Benefit Plan.
Nicgorski, David *o.m.v.* '91 (BO)[B] Boston, MA Oblate Provincialate; [U] Milton, MA Oblate Residence (St. Joseph House); Boston, MA.
Nicholas, D'Cruz *s.m.* '03 (CIN)[N] Dayton, OH Marianist Community, Novitiate.
Nicholas, Gerald *o.s.a.* '66 (JOL)[C] New Lenox, IL Providence Catholic High School; [L] New Lenox, IL Augustinian Friary.
Nicholas, William C. '01 (SFR) San Francisco, CA Mission Dolores Basilica.
Nicholl, Rev. Msgr. Rex '67 (AMA) Diocesan Council of Catholic Women; Cursillo Movement; Amarillo, TX St. Martin De Porres Mission; College of Consultors.
Nicholls, Trevor '90 (NY)[E] Bronx, NY Cardinal Spellman High School.
Nichols, Aquinas *o.s.b.* '80 (DM) Des Moines, IA Basilica of Saint John.
Nichols, Harry E. '73 (PIT) Pittsburgh, PA St. Patrick–St. Stanislaus Kostka.
Nichols, Henry P. '70 (BO) Pastoral Care; Senior Priests. Retired.
Nichols, Irby C. '01 (SFE) Albuquerque, NM St. Anne.
Nichols, John J. '62 (BO) Senior Priests. Retired.
Nichols, Joseph E. '62 (NOR) Norwich, CT St. Patrick Cathedral Retired.
Nichols, Louis J. '60 (SR) Mendocino, CA St. Anthony; On Duty Outside the Diocese.
Nichols, Roderick '89 (LSC) Silver City, NM St. Vincent de Paul.
Nichols, Rev. Msgr. Timothy E. '73 (LA) Hacienda Heights, CA St. John Vianney.
Nickel, Leander '47 (GB) Retired.
Nickels, Lawrence M. *o.f.m.* '86 (BEL) Carlyle, IL St. Felicitas; Carlyle, IL St. Teresa of Avila.
Nickels, Lawrence M. *o.f.m.* (STL)[V] St. Louis, MO The Franciscan Connection.
Nickerson, Oliver E. *s.j.* '54 (FgM) Watertown, MA Society of Jesus.
Nickle, Fred *o.f.m.cap.* '65 (NY)[DD] Beacon, NY St. Joachim Friary; [P] Garrison, NY Capuchin Youth and Family Ministries.
Nicknair, Harold W. '61 (PRT) Retired.
Nicknair, Rev. Msgr. Leopold G. '58 (PRT) Retired.
Nickol, Eugene '73 (BAL) Priest Personnel Board.
Nickol, G. Eugene '73 (BAL) Millersville, MD Our Lady of the Fields.
Nicks, Matthew '08 (SPK) Brewster, WA Sacred Heart; Twisp, WA St. Genevieve.
Nicola, John J. '55 (CHI) Retired.
Nicolas, Jeffrey S. '93 (L) Louisville, KY Cathedral of the Assumption; Priest Personnel Commission.
Nicolau, Rev. Msgr. Juan '60 (BWN) McAllen, TX Our Lady of Perpetual Help; Board Members.
Nicoletti, Maurizio *o.cist.* '65 (TR) Mount Laurel, NJ St. John Neumann; [N] Mount Laurel, NJ Cistercian Monastery of Our Lady of Fatima; Mount Laurel, NJ.
Nicolicchia, J. Andrew *o.p.* '65 (WDC) Washington, DC St. Dominic Church & Priory.
Nicoll, Leo A. *s.j.* '61 (NO)[C] New Orleans, LA Loyola University New Orleans.
Nicolo, Rev. Msgr. Joseph J. '74 (PH) Blue Bell, PA St. Helena; Deans; Approved Advocates; Deans; [BB] Center Square, PA Montgomery County Community College.

Nicolosi, Mark Ronald *o.s.b.* '67 (BUR)[E] Weston, VT Priory of Benedictine Monks.
Nicosia, Peter *o.f.m.cap.* '59 (SP) Tampa, FL Most Holy Redeemer.
Nieberding, Rick *c.pp.s.* '80 (CIN) Minster, OH St. Joseph; Minster, OH St. Augustine.
Nieberding, Robert '56 (LEX) Retired.
Nieblas, James *s.d.b.* '86 (LA)[P] Los Angeles, CA Dominic Savio Salesian Residence.
Niebrzydowski, Rev. Msgr. Walter J. '59 (NY) New York, NY Epiphany; New York, NY St. Stephen and Our Lady of the Scapular Retired.
Nieckarz, James P. *m.m.* '66 (NY)[DD] Retired.
Niedergeses, Bernard '50 (NSH) Retired.
Niedermier, Jerome G. '52 (TOL) Retired.
Niehaus, Charles W. *s.j.* '74 (LEX) Lexington, KY St. Paul.
Niehaus, Francis H. '55 (CIN) Retired.
Niehaus, Jonathan J. '94 (MIL)[T] Waukesha, WI Schoenstatt Fathers.
Niehaus, Mark J. '03 (MIL)[T] Waukesha, WI Schoenstatt Fathers.
Niehaus, Thomas M. '08 (WIN) Wells, MN Our Lady of Mount Carmel; Wells, MN St. John the Baptist; Wells, MN St. Casimir's; Defenders of the Bond.
Niehoff, Edmund A. (Larry) '64 (SHP) Mansfield, LA St. Joseph.
Niehoff, Kevin W. *o.p.* '93 (SFE) Albuquerque, NM St. Thomas Aquinas University Parish; Adjutant Judicial Vicar; Presbyteral Council of the Archdiocese of Santa Fe; [K] Albuquerque, NM St. Thomas Aquinas (Newman Center) University Parish.
Niehoff, Robert J. *s.j.* '82 (CLV)[B] University Heights, OH John Carroll University; [B] University Heights, OH John Carroll Jesuit Community.
Niekamp, Philip E. '05 (JC) Freeburg, MO Holy Family; Rich Fountain, MO Sacred Heart; Appointed Members; Diocesan Consultors.
Nieli, Bruce *c.s.p.* '73 (MEM) Memphis, TN St. Patrick's.
Nielsen, Eric H. '95 (MAD) Madison, WI St. Paul University Parish; [I] Madison, WI St. Paul University Catholic Foundation, Inc.
Nielsen, Kenneth M. '80 (BUF) On Duty Outside the Diocese.
Nielsen, Philip W. *o.f.m.* '48 (PAT)[N] Ringwood, NJ Holy Name Friary, Inc.
Nielson, Kenneth (Karl) '99 (AUS) Chaplains of the Military.
Nielson, Kenneth W. '99 (MO) Army Chaplains.
Nielson, Thomas A. '59 (NY) Retired.
Niemann, Paul J. '80 (STL) St. Ann, MO Holy Trinity.
Niemann, Paul '80 (PRM) St. Louis, MO St. Louis Mission.
Niemczyk, Stefan J. '87 (SPR) Deans; Presbyteral Council; Three Rivers, MA Divine Mercy Parish.
Niemeier, Dennis A. '73 (CIN) Retired.
Niemiec, Antoninus *o.p.* '01 (NY)[DD] New York, NY St. Vincent Ferrer Priory.
Niemiec, C. Antoninus *o.p.* '01 (Y) Youngstown, OH St. Dominic.
Niemira, Thomas '65 (JKS) Retired.
Niemira, Thomas '65 (AUS) Retired.
Nienaber, Paul J. *s.j.* '99 (CHI)[N] Chicago Chicago Province of the Society of Jesus–Provincial Office.
Nienaber, Paul J. *s.j.* '99 (WIN) Additional Diocesan Assignments.
Nienaber, Rev. Msgr. Robert H. '63 (OM) Retired.
Nienhaus, Gerald T. '62 (STL) Retired.
Nienhaus, Ivan R. '89 (DUB) Cedar Rapids, IA St. Patrick.
Niese, Larry '95 (ATL) Woodstock, GA St. Michael the Archangel.
Nieset, Frank E. '56 (TOL) Retired.
Niespolo, Aelred *o.s.b.* '05 (LA)[P] Valyermo, CA St. Andrew's Abbey; [A] Camarillo, CA St. John's Seminary.
Niessen, John A. *s.v.d.* '45 (SB)[I] Riverside, CA Divine Word Seminary.
Nietfeld, Fred J. '46 (TOL) Retired.
Nieto, Gustavo Javier *i.v.e.* (NY) Bronx, NY St. Jerome's; [DD] New York, NY Institute of the Incarnate Word, Inc.; New York, NY.
Nieto–Ruiz, Jesus '94 (OAK) Oakland, CA St. Anthony; Oakland, CA Mary Help of Christians Church; Deanery #3.
Nieva, Constantino S. '63 (RVC) Retired.
Nieva, Javier *d.c.j.m.* '00 (DEN) Littleton, CO St. Mary; [N] Littleton, CO Disciples of the Hearts of Jesus and Mary.
Nieves, Angel Valle '08 (MGZ) Aguadilla, PR St. Charles Borromeo.
Nieves, Carlos '86 (PCE) On Duty Outside the Diocese.
Nieves, Encarnación '83 (CGS) Hospitals; Caguas, PR Maria Madre de la Iglesia; Hospital Interamericano de Medicina Avanzada (HIMA); San Juan Bautista Hospital.
Nieves, Pablo *s.x.* '99 (PAT)[N] Wayne Xaverian Missionary Fathers; Wayne, NJ XAVERIAN MISSIONARY FATHERS.
Niewczas, Taddeus '52 (RVC) Retired.
Niewiadomski, Arthur J. '94 (TOL) Edgerton, OH St. Mary; Hicksville, OH St. Michael; Procurator–Advocate for Respondents; Associate Judges.
Niggel, Clement '03 (SFE) Taos, NM Nuestra Senora De Guadalupe; Presbyteral Council of the Archdiocese of Santa Fe.
Nigli, Francis A. '97 (OM) O'Neill, NE St. Patrick.
Nigro, Armand *s.j.* '56 (SPK)[B] Spokane, WA Gonzaga University.
Nijem, Rev. Msgr. Fred J. '68 (SAV) Warner Robins, GA Sacred Heart; Macon Deanery.
Niklas, Gerald R. '59 (CIN) Retired.
Nikodem, Ronald J. *s.m.* '94 (WH) Buckhannon, WV Holy Rosary; [O] Buckhannon, WV West Virginia Wesleyan College Newman Center.
Nikolic, Dennis A. '02 (NY) Middletown, NY St. Joseph.
Nilema, Nicholas *a.l.c.p./o.s.s.* '88 (P) Seaside, OR Our Lady of Victory.
Nilema, Nicholas (FTW) Columbia City, IN St. Paul of the Cross.
Nilles, Rev. Msgr. Allan F. '49 (FAR) Retired.
Nilles, Roger G. '59 (MAD) Retired.
Nilsson, Richard A. '71 (RVC)[N] Amityville, NY St. Pius X Residence.
Nimerichter, Dean '92 (DM) Lacona, IA Holy Trinity Church of Southeast Warren County.
Nimocks, Michael '96 (COL) Marion, OH St. Mary.
Nimu, Lusius *ss.cc.* '03 (HON) Honolulu, HI St. Augustine by the Sea.
Nin, Felino Reyes '89 (NY) New York, NY Incarnation.
Ninemire, Kerry '75 (SAL) Salina, KS St. Mary Queen of the Universe Parish; College of Consultors; Priests' Continuing Formation Committee; Personnel Board.
Nino, Anibal Loarte *c.s.c.* '04 (FTW)[H] Notre Dame Congregation of Holy Cross, United States Province of Priests & Brothers.
Nirappel, James '90 (SYM) Hagerstown, MD Syro–Malabar Catholic Mission of Baltimore.
Nirappel, James (BAL) Hagerstown, MD St. Mary.
Nirappel, Joshy T. *c.m.f.* '95 (MET) Perth Amboy, NJ Our Lady of Fatima.
Nirschl, Nicholas E. *o.praem.* '56 (SFE)[H] Albuquerque, NM Santa Maria de la Vid Priory.
Nisari, Joseph '68 (AUS) Granger, TX SS. Cyril and Methodius; [M] Sts. Cyril & Methodius School Endowment.
Nischan, James R. '83 (PCE) On Duty Outside the Diocese.
Nishimura, Bryce T. *m.m.* '56 (FgM) Maryknoll, NY MARYKNOLL.
Nishimuta, James K. *m.m.* '54 (NY)[DD] Retired.
Niskanen, Stephen *c.m.f.* '90 (LA) San Gabriel, CA San Gabriel Mission.
Nitz, Eliot *s.d.s.* '68 (WDC)[B] Silver Spring, MD Salvatorian Community.
Niven, Timothy L. '98 (ROC) Victor, NY St. Patrick.
Nix, Albert P. '73 (PAT) Retired.
Nix, Julian *o.s.b.* '87 (BIS)[A] Richardton, ND Assumption Abbey.
Nixon, George K. '11 (PRO) Graduate Studies.
Nixon, Jean–Francois '10 (BRK) Brooklyn, NY Holy Cross.
Nixon, Joseph J. '85 (RVC) North Merrick, NY Sacred Heart.
Nixon, Michael J. '10 (PT) Pensacola; Pensacola, FL St. Paul.
Niziolek, Terry *m.s.* '48 (ORL) Orlando, FL Good Shepherd.
Njau, Francis *a.j.* '98 (P)[J] Portland, OR Providence Health & Services–Oregon.
Njau, Patrick K. '00 (MAN) Elliott Hospital; Manchester, NH St. Anthony of Padua.
Njenga, Martin (NY) Hawthorne, NY Holy Rosary.
Njoku, Francis '97 (SAN) Brownwood, TX St. Mary's.
Njoku, Hippolytus *s.m.m.m.* '95 (CHI) Chicago, IL St. Bartholomew.
Njoku, Innocent E. *c.s.sp* '85 (MO) DEPARTMENT OF VETERANS AFFAIRS HOSPITALS AND CHAPLAINS.
Njoku, Titus C. '04 (NEW) Jersey City, NJ St. Anne's.
Njus, Jeffrey '03 (LAN) Hillsdale, MI St. Anthony.
Njuu, Augustine R. *a.j.* '83 (SPC) St. John's Regional Health Center; [D] Springfield, MO Mercy Hospital Springfield.
Nkachukwu, Michael C. '80 (DET) Presbyteral Council; Detroit, MI Good Shepherd; Archdiocesan Vicars.
Nkadimeng, Thabang *o.m.i.* '11 (WDC)[O] Washington, DC Oblate Community.
Nkansah, Samuel Oppong *c.s.sp.* '09 (OAK)[L] Berkeley Salesians of Don Bosco.
Nketiah, Andrew (NY) Millbrook, NY St. Joseph.
Nkuanga, Anselme Malonda *c.i.c.m.* '92 (FgM) Arlington, VA MISSIONHURST; Arlington, VA.
Nkuanga, Anselme Malonda *c.i.c.m.* '92 (ARL)[H] Arlington, VA Missionhurst, C.I.C.M.–Central House and Provincialate.
Nkumbi, Paul '96 (SFE) Roy, NM Holy Family–St. Joseph; Wagon Mound, NM Santa Clara.
Nkwasibwe, L. Frederick *a.j.* '99 (HBG) York, PA Immaculate Conception of the Blessed Virgin Mary; York, PA York Hospital.
Nnabugo, Theodore '00 (BAK) Hermiston, OR Our Lady of Angels.
Nnabuife, Charles Chika '05 (BAK) Council of Priests and Diocesan Consultors; The Dalles, OR St. Peter; Board of Education.
Nnadozie, Edmund C. *m.s.p.* '97 (GAL) Houston, TX St. Francis of Assisi.
Nnajiofor, Polycarp '91 (RVC) Mineola, NY Corpus Christi; Mineola, NY Winthrop Hospital.
Nnamezie, Tema Godwin '98 (PBL)[C] Canon City, CO Centura Health–St. Thomas More Hospital.
Nnaso, Sylvester A. '02 (RCK) Hampshire, IL St. Charles Borromeo.
Nnaukwu, Alex C. '93 (NEW) Hackensack, NJ Hackensack University Medical Center.
Nnorom, Columba A. '74 (RIC) Ebony, VA St. Richard; Ebony, VA St. Peter The Apostle.
Noah, Timothy T. '47 (CR) Retired.
Nobbe, Scott E. '06 (IND) Guilford, IN St. Paul Catholic Church, New Alsace, Inc.; Guilford, IN St. Martin Catholic Church, Yorkville, Inc.; Guilford, IN St. John the Baptist Catholic Church, Dover, Inc.; West Harrison, IN St. Joseph Catholic Church, St. Leon, Inc.
Nobile, Angelo '53 (MEM) Retired.
Nobiletti, Raymond J. *m.m.* '69 (NY) New York, NY Transfiguration.
Noble, Jeffery J. '86 (E) Hermitage, PA Church of Notre Dame; Deans.
Noble, Paul A. '81 (COL) Diocesan Judges; Office of Vocations; Diocesan Board of Review for the Protection of Children; Columbus, OH St. Joseph Cathedral.
Noble, Wayne E. '94 (LA) Pomona, CA St. Madeleine.
Nobrega, Kenneth '08 (OAK) Vocations; Exorcist.
Nocchi, Martin S. '04 (BAL) Hagerstown, MD St. Ann.
Nocero, Pascal Francis '48 (LA) Retired.
Noche, Joselito M. '07 (TR) Middletown, NJ St. Mary.
Nochelski, Paul W. *s.j.* '71 (BUF)[N] Buffalo, NY Canisius Jesuit Community Inc.
Nock, James J. '64 (HRT) East Hartford, CT Blessed Sacrament; East Hartford, CT Our Lady of Peace.
Nockunas, Anthony *m.i.c.* (SPR)[G] Stockbridge, MA Congregation of Marian Fathers of The Immaculate Conception of the Most Blessed Virgin Mary.
Noda, Jorge '84 (MIA) Miami, FL St. John Bosco.
Noe, John P. '74 (LEX) Ashland, KY Holy Family; [D] Ashland, KY Our Lady of Bellefonte Hospital, Inc.; College of Consultors; Big Sandy/Licking.
Noel, Brian W. '10 (PIT) Pittsburgh, PA St. Bernard.
Noel, Guyma '97 (ATL) Lithonia, GA Christ Our Hope.
Noel, Marc A. '98 (ALX) Moreauville, LA Sacred Heart.
Noelker, Timothy J. '10 (STL) Valley Park, MO Sacred Heart.
Noesen, Rev. Msgr. Gerald '50 (CR) Retired.
Noesen, Rev. Msgr. Jerry '55 (CR) Diocesan Consultors; Priests' Council; Priests Retirement Board of Trustees.
Noesen, Robert '93 (JOL) Coal City, IL Assumption of the Blessed Virgin Mary.
Noesen, Thomas *o.p.* '76 (SFE) Albuquerque, NM San Felipe de Neri; Albuquerque, NM St. Thomas Aquinas University Parish.
Noesen, Tom *o.p.* '76 (SFE)[K] Albuquerque, NM St. Thomas Aquinas (Newman Center) University Parish.
Nofi, Michael *m.s.a.* '74 (NOR)[G] Cromwell Society of the Missionaries of the Holy Apostles.
Noga, Edward P. '76 (Y) Youngstown, OH St. Patrick.
Noga, Gregory J. '79 (PSC) Trenton, NJ St. Mary; Central New Jersey Protopresbyterate; Office for Eastern Christian Formation (formerly: Office of Religious Education); Notaries.
Noga, Henry *s.v.d.* '96 (ORG)[H] Yorba Linda, CA Pope John Paul II Polish Center.
Noga, John T. '99 (CHI) Chicago, IL St. Daniel the Prophet; Presbyteral Council.
Nogaro, Paul M. '71 (BUF) Grand Island, NY St. Stephen.
Nogosek, Robert J. *c.s.c.* '56 (FTW)[H] Holy Cross House.
Noguera, Dagoberto '83 (BRK) Brooklyn, NY St. Anthony of Padua–St. Alphonsus.
Noguera, Ronald '81 (MIA) Retired.
Nohs, Joseph E. '93 (RVC) New Hyde Park, NY Holy Spirit.
Noiseux, Donald A. '84 (SPR) On Sabbatical.
Nolan, Brian J. '91 (MET) Watchung, NJ St. Mary–Stony Hill; Deans.
Nolan, Brian P. '01 (BAL)[B] Emmitsburg, MD Mount Saint Mary's University; Special Assignment; [S] Emmitsburg, MD Mount St. Mary's University.
Nolan, Colman J. *s.t.* '56 (B) Post Falls, ID St. George's.
Nolan, Daniel T. *c.s.v.* '83 (CHI)[N] Arlington Heights Viatorian Province Center–Clerics of St. Viator.
Nolan, David E. '95 (NY) New York, NY St. Joseph of the Holy Family; Beacon, NY St. John the Evangelist.
Nolan, Emmet J. *c.m.* '92 (BRK)[R] Brooklyn, NY St. John the Baptist Rectory; Brooklyn, NY St. John the Baptist.
Nolan, Eugene A. *s.j.* '71 (WDC)[O] Washington, DC

The Jesuit Community at Georgetown University.
Nolan, James L. *o.s.a.* '46 (PH)[Y] Villanova, PA St. Thomas Monastery.
Nolan, Jerome M. '74 (TR) Bradley Beach, NJ Ascension.
Nolan, John '77 (SFD) Chatham, IL St. Joseph the Worker; Springfield Deanery.
Nolan, Joseph A. '60 (ORL) Melbourne Beach, FL Immaculate Conception.
Nolan, Joseph J. *m.s.* '48 (HRT)[L] Hartford, CT Missionaries of LaSalette.
Nolan, Joseph M. '47 (BRK) Cambria Heights, NY Sacred Heart Retired.
Nolan, Joseph T. '53 (WCH) Retired.
Nolan, Justin *o.s.b.* '55 (GBG)[H] Latrobe, PA Saint Vincent Archabbey.
Nolan, Kevin L. '90 (LA) Culver City, CA St. Augustine; Army Reserve Chaplains.
Nolan, Kieran *o.s.b.* '59 (SCL)[I] Collegeville St. John's Abbey, of the Order of St. Benedict; Collegeville, MN St. John's Abbey.
Nolan, Michael E. '84 (WCH) Goddard, KS Holy Spirit; Adjutant Judicial Vicar; Judges; Ongoing Formation of the Clergy Committee; Building Commission; Worship Office.
Nolan, Michael F. '87 (KNX) Diocesan Consultors; Kingsport, TN St. Dominic; Presbyteral Council.
Nolan, Michael L. (BO) Waltham, MA St. Mary.
Nolan, Michael '00 (BO)[AA] Bridgewater, MA Bridgewater State College Catholic Center.
Nolan, Niall '80 (GAL) Houston, TX St. Catherine of Siena.
Nolan, Paul J. '57 (NEW) South Kearny, NJ Hudson County Correctional Center; Newark, NJ Delaney Hall Assessment Center; Newark, NJ Essex County Correctional Facility Retired.
Nolan, Peter P. *c.s.sp.* '59 (BO) Hyde Park, MA Most Precious Blood; Milton, MA St. Pius Tenth.
Nolan, Robert *s.a.c.* '70 (CAM)[C] Pennsauken, NJ Bishop Eustace Prep School.
Nolan, Rev. Msgr. Terence '66 (SAT)[K] San Antonio, TX Casa De Padres; Chancellor; College of Consultors; Archdiocesan Presbyteral Council; Judicial Vicar; Judges; Catholic Lawyers Guild.
Nolan, Timothy F. '67 (STP) Retired.
Nolan, Timothy M. '02 (WIL) Wilmington, DE Corpus Christi; Associate Directors.
Nolan, Rev. Msgr. Timothy '92 (PEO) Pekin, IL St. Joseph's; Vicariates and Vicars; Permanent Diaconate, Office of.
Nolan, Rev. Msgr. Walter E. '69 (TR) Tribunal Judges Retired.
Nolan, William A. '85 (MAD) Retired.
Nolette, Mark P. '87 (PRT) Special or Other Diocesan Assignment.
Nolker, Thomas C. '72 (CIN) Cincinnati, OH St. James the Greater; Judges.
Noll, Daniel J. '76 (LEX) Lexington, KY Mary, Queen of the Holy Rosary; College of Consultors; Priests' Personnel.
Nollette, Louis A. '75 (GI) Ongoing Formation for Clergy and Liturgy; Alliance, NE Holy Rosary; Diocesan Consultors.
Nollette, Neal P. '80 (GI) Chappell, NE St. Joseph's; Priests' Advisory Board (Presbyteral Council); Rural Life Conference.
Nolte, Walter L. '03 (OM) Creighton, NE St. Ludger; Deans; Officers; Deans.
Nombre, Ronnie (NEW) Elizabeth, NJ St. Genevieve's.
Nomellini, Paul J. '77 (MAR) Retired.
Nondorf, Aloysius J. '57 (GRY) Retired.
Nondorf, Timothy '99 (SAC) Presbyteral Council; Vice Chancellor and Secretary to the Bishop; Priests' Personnel Board, Diocesan.
Nonis, Pattinikuttige Kingsley '93 (BEL) Newman Catholic Student Center; Carterville, IL Church of the Holy Spirit.
Nontol, Lucio M. *t.o.r.* '06 (NEW) Newark, NJ Immaculate Heart of Mary; [M] Newark, NJ Missionary Sisters of the Most Blessed Sacrament and Mary Immaculate.
Noon, Rev. Msgr. Robert L. '51 (COL) Retired.
Noonan, Bradford '99 (COS) Castle Rock, CO St. Francis of Assisi; Northern Deanery; Vicars Forane.
Noonan, Guy '76 (STA) St. Augustine, FL Our Lady of Good Counsel; Building Commission.
Noonan, James P. *m.m.* '60 (NY)[DD] Retired.
Noonan, Joseph T. '95 (CHI) Oak Forest, IL St. Damian.
Noonan, Mark J. '07 (BUF) Holley, NY St. Mary; Holley, NY St. Mark.
Noonan, Mark L. '59 (BO) Senior Priests. Retired.
Noonan, Patrick '63 (JKS) Retired.
Noonan, Robert C. '64 (HEL) Defenders of the Bond Retired.
Noonan, Robert (GF)[J] Great Falls, MT Retrouvaille of Montana.
Noonan, Rev. Msgr. Thomas F. '45 (BRK) Teachers Retired.
Noone, Charles J. '67 (PH) Oreland, PA Holy Martyrs Retired.
Noone, David E. '66 (ALB) Loudonville, NY Christ Our Light Roman Catholic Church.
Noone, John T. '67 (BLX) Kiln, MS Annunciation.
Noone, Rev. Msgr. Kevin B. '70 (BRK) Brooklyn, NY Our Lady of Angels; Presbyteral Council.
Nooney, P. Joseph '52 (SC) Retired.
Noradounghian, Antoine '96 (OLN) Brooklyn, NY St. Ann's Armenian Catholic Cathedral.
Norbeck, Ernest '84 (JOL) Downers Grove, IL St. Mary of Gostyn; Presbyteral Council.
Norcavage, Albert R. '50 (ALT) Absent on Leave.
Nord, Aaron P. '07 (STL) Special Assignment.
Nord, Paul *o.s.b.* '07 (IND)[K] Saint Meinrad St. Meinrad Archabbey; [A] Saint Meinrad, IN Saint Meinrad School of Theology.
Nordeman, John J. '01 (PH)[BB] West Chester, PA West Chester University; On Special or Other Archdiocesan Assignment; West Chester, PA St. Maximilian Kolbe.
Norden, Emmett M. '62 (MAR)[C] Escanaba, MI O.S.F. St. Francis Hospital Retired.
Nordenbrock, William *c.pp.s.* '83 (CHI)[W] Chicago, IL Precious Blood Ministry of Reconciliation.
Nordenbrock, William *c.pp.s.* '83 (CIN)[N] Dayton Provincial Office of the Cincinnati Province of the Society of the Precious Blood.
Norder, John R. '66 (MAD)[F] Madison, WI Bishop O'Connor Catholic Pastoral Center Retired.
Nordick, Jack (John) A. '90 (NU) Cottonwood, MN St. Mary; Marshall, MN St. Clotilde.
Nordmeyer, Emeric *o.f.m.* '56 (SFE) Albuquerque, NM Queen of Angels Native American Center and Archdiocesan Shrine to Kateri Tekakwitha; [H] Albuquerque, NM The Province of Our Lady of Guadalupe.
Nordquist, Theodore A. '80 (GRY) Lowell, IN St. Edward; Girl Scout Liaison.
Noreika, Michael *s.s.s.* '70 (CLV)[N] Cleveland, OH Congregation of the Blessed Sacrament.
Norena, Nicholas '94 (MET) Perth Amboy, NJ La Asuncion.
Norfolk, Jeffrey Thomas '09 (SFS) Sioux Falls, SD St. Mary.
Norick, Daniel J. '97 (DEN) Carbondale, CO St. Mary.
Noriega, Arnoldo '75 (TUC) Leave of Absence.
Noriega, Manuel Segundo (R) Edenton, NC St. Anne.
Norkett, Michael P. '68 (OAK) Retired.
Norman, Charles J. *o.s.f.s.* '65 (PH)[Y] Wyndmoor, PA Villa de Sales Oblate Residence.
Norman, Gary '94 (YAK) Waterville, WA St. Joseph's.
Norman, John (SLC) Magna, UT Our Lady of Lourdes LLC 209.
Norman, Reginald D. '09 (BGP) African Americans, Apostolate of; Bridgeport, CT Blessed Sacrament; Presbyteral Council.
Noronha, Konrad *s.j.* '06 (BAL)[Q] Baltimore, MD Jesuit Community of Loyola University, Inc.
Norris, David J. '74 (FRS) On Special Assignment; [A] Fresno, CA San Joaquin Memorial High School; Fresno, CA St. Paul Newman Center.
Norris, Patrick F. *o.p.* '89 (MAD) Madison, WI Blessed Sacrament; Chicago, IL.
Norris, Patrick *o.p.* '89 (CHI)[N] Chicago Dominicans (Provincial Office).
Norris, Robert J. '80 (NY) Elmsford, NY Our Lady of Mt. Carmel.
Norris, Thomas P. *o.s.f.s.* '73 (R) Goldsboro, NC St. Mary.
Norris, Timothy L. '94 (STP) On Duty Outside the Archdiocese.
Norris, Walter A. '73 (CAM) Auditors; Continuing Education & Spiritual Formation of Priests (CESF); Haddonfield, NJ St. Joseph the Worker Parish, Haddon Township, N.J.
Norsworthy, Richard '85 (SHP) Priests' Retirement Board; Bastrop, LA St. Joseph.
Northrop, James '97 (SEA) Bothell, WA St. Brendan.
Northrop, John B. *m.m.* '98 (FgM) Maryknoll, NY MARYKNOLL.
Norton, Robert A. '72 (PIT) Pittsburgh, PA St. Athanasius.
Norton, Robert J. *o.f.m.* (PAT) Lincoln Park, NJ St. Joseph's; Pompton Plains, NJ Chilton Memorial Hospital.
Norton, Stephen P. '01 (NY) Bronx, NY St. Benedict.
Norton, Thomas '63 (NEW) Retired.
Nortz, Alfred E. '55 (SY)[Q] Syracuse, NY Tommy Coyne Residence Dillon Hall Retired.
Nortz, Robert *m.m.a.* '07 (SAM)[B] Petersham, MA Maronite Monks of Adoration Most Holy Trinity Monastery.
Norvel, William L. *s.s.j.* '65 (BAL)[T] Baltimore, MD St. Joseph Manor Foundation, Inc.; [T] Baltimore, MD The Josephite Seminarian Education Trust; [T] Baltimore, MD The Josephite Retirement and Disability Benefits Trusts.
Nosbush, Peter C. '70 (NU) North Mankato, MN Holy Rosary.
Nosser, Rev. Msgr. Charles J. '53 (RVC) Floral Park, NY Our Lady of Victory Retired.
Nosser, Rev. Msgr. John C. '64 (RVC) Ocean Beach, NY Our Lady of the Magnificat; Judges for Interdiocesan Tribunal Retired.
Notabartolo, Charles E. '77 (PMB)[K] Diocesan Pension Plan Trust; Vicar General; Moderator of Curia; Consultors; [K] Diocese of Palm Beach Health Plan Trust; Ex Officio; Tequesta, FL St. Jude.
Notaro, Carlo *m.i.* '88 (MIL)[P] Milwaukee, WI St. Camillus Delegate House.
Notarpole, Joseph '49 (STA) Retired.
Notebaart, James C. '71 (STP) Retired.
Nott, David L. '93 (RIC) Tribunal Staff; Ladysmith, VA St. Mary of the Annunciation.
Notter, Richard E. '63 (TOL) Retired.
Nourie, Paul *o.m.i.* '64 (SD) Chula Vista, CA Most Precious Blood Catholic Parish.
Nouza, Frank M. *o.p.* '58 (CHI)[N] Chicago Dominicans (Provincial Office).
Nouza, Frank '58 (SD)[O] Valley Center, CA San Diego North County Magnificat – Our Lady of Guadalupe Chapter.
Novack, Kevin '81 (PBL) Canon City, CO St. Michael; Elected.
Novajosky, Michael P. '10 (BGP) Monroe, CT St. Jude.
Novak, David A. '79 (CLV) Euclid, OH SS. Robert & William.
Novak, David A. '77 (STL) Retired.
Novak, Francis A. *c.ss.r.* '49 (STL)[O] Liguori, MO St. Clement Health Care Center; Liguori, MO National Catholic Conference for Total Stewardship (NCCTS) Retired.
Novak, Henry J. *c.ss.r.* '50 (STL)[O] Liguori, MO St. Clement Health Care Center.
Novak, Norbert *o.s.b.* '64 (B)[C] Jerome, ID Monastery of the Ascension.
Novak, Paul E. *o.s.m.* '90 (CHI)[D] Chicago, IL Institute Campus for Young Men; [D] Chicago, IL Lourdes Hall Campus for Young Women.
Novak, Robert J. '42 (CHI) Retired.
Novak, Thomas *s.d.s.* '59 (MIL)[P] Milwaukee, WI Salvatorians – Jordan Hall Retired.
Novak, Vincent M. *s.j.* '55 (NY)[DD] Loyola Hall, Jesuit Community.
Novak, William L. '97 (OKL) Yukon, OK St. John Nepomuk; Region II–A; Vocations and Seminarians.
Novakowski, James E. '95 (GI) Personnel Board; Diocesan Consultors; North Platte, NE Holy Spirit.
Novell, Ramon *sch.p.* '66 (LA) Los Angeles, CA St. Lucy; Los Angeles, CA Santa Teresita.
Novelly, Duane R. '79 (DET) Detroit, MI St. Matthew.
Novick, Michael '01 (CHI) Matteson, IL St. Lawrence O'Toole.
Novielli, John Joseph *o.praem.* '74 (PH)[B] Paoli, PA Daylesford Abbey; [Y] Paoli, PA Daylesford Abbey; Paoli, PA.
Noviello, Harold J. '09 (RVC) Bay Shore, NY St. Patrick's.
Novoa, Jose Marino *c.m.f.* '79 (CHI) Chicago, IL Holy Cross/Immaculate Heart of Mary; [N] Oak Park Claretian Missionaries USA Eastern Province.
Novokowsky, Robert *f.s.s.p.* '00 (RIC) Richmond, VA St. Joseph.
Novotny, James F. '64 (OM) Lindsay, NE Holy Family.
Novotny, Jerome *o.m.i.* '68 (FgM) Washington, DC AMERICAN OBLATE MISSIONS.
Novotny, Richard '81 (MO) On Duty Outside the Diocese; Air Force Chaplains.
Novotny, Robert J. '50 (MIL) Retired.
Nowacki, Jaroslaw '02 (RIC) Portsmouth, VA St. Paul; Portsmouth, VA Church of the Resurrection; Portsmouth, VA Church of the Holy Angels; Chesapeake, VA St. Mary.
Nowacki, Jerome A. '93 (MAR) Retired.
Nowacki, Piotr *s.chr.* '95 (ATL) Lawrenceville, GA St. Marguerite D'Youville.
Nowak, Bernard U. '74 (BUF) Orchard Park, NY Nativity of Our Lord.
Nowak, Christopher '97 (RVC) Central Islip, NY St. John of God; Procurator & Advocates.
Nowak, David G. '85 (GRY) East Chicago, IN St. Patrick; East Chicago, IN St. Patrick.
Nowak, Edward C. *c.s.p.* '89 (AUS) Austin, TX St. Austin; [L] Austin, TX University Catholic Center; Presbyteral Council.
Nowak, Eugene J. '70 (CHI) Grayslake, IL St. Gilbert.
Nowak, Jacek *s.ch.* '94 (CHI) Palatine, IL St. Theresa.
Nowak, James '67 (JOL)[K] Naperville, IL St. John Vianney Villa Retired.
Nowak, John H. *c.r.* '71 (CHI)[M] Chicago, IL Franciscan Communities; Chicago, IL St. Wenceslaus.
Nowak, Krzysztof '05 (DET) Waterford, MI Our Lady of the Lakes.
Nowak, Lukasz *o.c.d.* '08 (GRY)[H] Munster, IN Discalced Carmelite Fathers Monastery.
Nowak, Mark A. '75 (E) Mc Kean, PA St. Francis Xavier; [G] Fairview, PA Camp Notre Dame; Permanent Diaconate Program.
Nowak, Randolph *o.f.m.cap.* '52 (FgM)[F] Agana Heights, GU St. Fidelis Friary; White Plains, NY The Province of St. Mary of the Capuchin Order.
Nowakowski, Edward S. '48 (GB) Retired.
Nowakowski, Jerome F. '63 (TOL) Toledo, OH Good

Shepherd; Ministry To Catholic Charismatic Renewal (MCCR) Retired.
Nowakowski, Rudolph *o.m.i.* '60 (SFD)[A] Godfrey, IL Immaculate Heart of Mary Novitiate.
Nowel, Mark D. *o.p.* '86 (PRO)[O] Providence St. Thomas Aquinas Priory at Providence College.
Nowel, Mark S. *o.p.* '86 (PRO)[B] Providence, RI Providence College.
Nowicki, Andrzej '09 (CHI) Niles, IL St. John Brebeuf.
Nowicki, Gary D. '96 (MIL) Awaiting Assignment.
Nowicki, Marcin '11 (WOR) Shrewsbury, MA St. Mary's.
Nowinski, Claudius S. *m.s.* '65 (HRT)[L] Hartford, CT Missionaries of LaSalette.
Nowinski, Claudius *m.s.* (BO) Pastoral Care.
Nowinski, Dennis J. '73 (DET) Roseville, MI St. Angela.
Nowlan, John T. '66 (DET) Oak Park, MI Our Lady of Fatima Retired.
Noyola, Miguel A. *s.o.l.t.* '07 (CC) Robstown, TX St. Anthony; [G] Robstown, TX Society of Our Lady of the Most Holy Trinity.
Nsionu, Patrick '85 (NEW) Newark, NJ The Parish of the Transfiguration.
Nsubuga, Lutakome '10 (SPK) Pasco, WA St. Patrick.
Ntahondi, Remigius Bukuru '89 (BUR) Rutland, VT Immaculate Heart of Mary.
Ntaiyia, Symon Peter '80 (ROC) Ontario, NY St. Maximilian Kolbe.
Ntibeshya, Jean De Dieu *o.p. miss.* '04 (SFD)[K] Madison, IL Dominican Missionaries for the Deaf Apostolate.
Ntsiful–Amissah, Dominic Kofi '79 (MO) DEPARTMENT OF VETERANS AFFAIRS HOSPITALS AND CHAPLAINS.
Ntsiful–Amissah, Kofi '79 (ALB) Black Catholic Apostolate of the Diocese of Albany.
Nuanez, Anthony '79 (LA) On Sick Leave.
Nuelle, John *m.s.* '64 (STL)[O] LaSalette Spirituality Center Retired.
Nugent, Anthony A. '72 (JOL) Bradley, IL St. Joseph.
Nugent, C. Robert *s.d.s.* '65 (HBG) New Freedom, PA St. John the Baptist.
Nugent, Rev. Msgr. Irvine '54 (PMB) Vero Beach, FL St. Helen Retired.
Nugent, Rev. Msgr. James B. '56 (STU) Retired.
Nugent, James J. *c.ss.r.* '50 (STL)[O] Liguori, MO St. Clement Health Care Center Retired.
Nugent, Rev. Msgr. Joseph A. '71 (BRK) Brooklyn, NY St. Vincent Ferrer.
Nugent, Kevin *s.t.* '51 (WDC)[O] Adelphi, MD Father Judge Missionary Cenacle.
Nugent, Rev. Msgr. Peter D. '62 (LA) Retired.
Nugent, Robert *s.d.s.* '65 (WDC)[B] Silver Spring, MD Salvatorian Community.
Nunan, Jeremiah '63 (ALB) Cairo, NY Sacred Heart.
Nundwe, Saviour '08 (SPC) Ozark, MO St. Joseph the Worker; [B] Springfield, MO Springfield Catholic High School.
Nunes, Brian '08 (LA) San Pedro, CA Mary, Star of the Sea; Appointed Membership.
Nunes, James *m.s.* '91 (BRK) Jamaica Hospital – Trump Pavilion.
Nunez, Albert Gayle '64 (LAF) Washington, LA Immaculate Conception; Washington, LA Holy Trinity; Diocesan Consultors.
Nunez, Baltazar '88 (CGS) Barranquitas, PR Church of St. Anthony of Padua.
Nuñez, Rev. Msgr. Edward H. '76 (PBL) Deans; College of Consultors; Elected.
Nunez, Rev. Msgr. Edward H. '76 (PBL) Pueblo, CO Shrine of St. Therese.
Nunez, Felix '99 (CGS)[F] Caguas, PR Diocesan Tribunal of Caguas; Diocesan Tribunal of Caguas; Priests Senate; Aguas Buenas, PR Espiritu Santo.
Nunez–Carrion, Phillip '88 (SJN) Guaynabo, PR Maria Madre de Mi Senor; Vicar of Family Affairs.
Nunning, David H. '69 (EVN) Evansville, IN Sacred Heart; Evansville, IN St. Agnes; Deans.
Nuno, Rafael '69 (ARE) Utuado, PR San Pedro y San Pablo.
Nurnberger, Lothar *s.j.* '44 (DET)[K] Clarkston, MI Colombiere Center.
Nurre, Henry V. *o.s.b.* '56 (MIL)[P] Benet Lake, WI St. Benedict's Abbey; Benet Lake, WI.
Nusbaum, Daniel C. '61 (ALB) Retired.
Nuss, David W. '93 (TOL) Sandusky, OH St. Mary.
Nuss, Francis B. '61 (RVC)[N] Amityville, NY St. Pius X Residence Retired.
Nuthulapati, Jaya Babu *c.pp.s.* '06 (OAK) Newark, CA St. Edward.
Nuthulapati, JayaBabu *c.pp.s.* '06 (CIN)[N] Dayton, OH Provincial Office of the Cincinnati Province of the Society of the Precious Blood.
Nutt, Maurice J. *c.ss.r.* '89 (CHI)[N] Chicago, IL The Redemptorist Fathers of Chicago; Chicago, IL St. Michael in Old Town.
Nutter, Charles W. '06 (BLX) Gautier, MS St. Mary; Tribunal Judges.
Nutter, Nicholas John '89 (BR) Baton Rouge, LA St. Louis, King of France; Propagation of the Faith and Association of Holy Childhood; Presbyteral Council.
Nuzzi, Ronald J. (FTW)[B] University of Notre Dame Du Lac.
Nuzzi, Ronald '84 (Y) On Duty Outside the Diocese.
Nwabichie, Remigius '89 (BGP) Bridgeport, CT Bridgeport Hospital.
Nwabueze, Lawrence *o.p.* '04 (WDC) Washington, DC National Rehabilitation Hospital; Washington, DC Washington Hospital Center; [X] Mount Rainier, MD Dominican Fathers & Brothers Inc. Province of Nigeria.
Nwabugwu, Edwin Okey '90 (BRK) Brooklyn, NY Resurrection.
Nwachukwu, Benedict C. '95 (SB) Colton, CA Immaculate Conception; Colton, CA San Salvador; Appointed Members.
Nwachukwu, Jude *s.m.m.m.* '06 (BAK) Board of Education; Ontario, OR Blessed Sacrament.
Nwachukwu, Oliver '82 (BEL) Tamaroa, IL Immaculate Conception; Dubois, IL St. Charles Borromeo.
Nwachukwu, Peter C. '86 (TUC) Ajo, AZ Immaculate Conception Roman Catholic Church – Ajo.
Nwachukwu, Raymond '87 (BWN) Progreso, TX Holy Spirit.
Nwachukwu, Thomas Kizito '82 (CC) On Special Assignment; [D] Corpus Christi, TX CHRISTUS Spohn Hospital Corpus Christi – Memorial.
Nwadimkoa, Peter Onyibuchi '98 (BRK) Long Island City, NY Most Precious Blood.
Nwagbara, Anselm '96 (BO) Roxbury, MA St. Katharine Drexel; [O] Brighton, MA Caritas St. Elizabeth's Medical Center of Boston, Inc.; Nigerian; Peabody, MA St. John the Baptist; Peabody, MA St. Thomas the Apostle.
Nwagbaraocha, John *d.s.* '80 (BUR) Burlington, VT Fletcher Allen Health Care.
Nwagwu, Nicholas '98 (NY) Yonkers, NY St. John's Riverside Hospital.
Nwambu, Paul (PAT) Denville, NJ St. Clare Hospital; [K] Denville, NJ Saint Clare's Hospital, Inc.
Nwanekezie, Peter (KCK) Topeka, KS Mater Dei.
Nwankwo, Fidelis *c.s.sp.* '94 (MIA) Miami, FL Holy Redeemer; Special Assignment.
Nwankwor, Ruben C. '93 (GAL) Houston, TX St. Bernadette Soubirous.
Nwanonenyi, Benjamin '97 (PH) Philadelphia, PA St. Agatha–St. James.
Nwaogu, Sylvester N. '64 (TUC) Tombstone, AZ Sacred Heart of Jesus Roman Catholic Parish – Tombstone.
Nwaogwugwu, Cletus '92 (RVC) West Islip, NY Good Samaritan Hospital Medical Center.
Nwaorgu, Rev. Msgr. Anselm I. '92 (NEW) Newark, NJ Blessed Sacrament–St. Charles Borromeo; Nigerian IBO Catholic Community.
Nwaru, Romanus N. '95 (MIL) Milwaukee, WI St. Paul; [H] Milwaukee, WI St. Thomas Aquinas Academy; Archdiocesan Council of Priests.
Nwauzor, Pius '02 (PBL) Paonia, CO Sacred Heart.
Nwauzor, Reginald '80 (B) Pocatello, ID Holy Spirit Catholic Community.
Nwgnkwocha, Ignatius C. (GAL) Houston, TX Christ the Redeemer.
Nwobi, Paul F. '88 (NY) Bronx, NY Montefiore Medical Center.
Nwobi, Paul '88 (RVC) West Islip, NY Good Samaritan Hospital Medical Center.
Nwoga, Laserian '95 (CAM) On Duty Outside the Diocese; Air Force Chaplains.
Nwohu, Rev. Msgr. Ambrose O. '66 (TUC) Oracle, AZ St. Helen.
Nwokocha, Rowland '97 (LA) Lomita, CA St. Margaret Mary Alacoque.
Nwokorie, Fabian '90 (BAK) Dufur, OR St. Alphonsus; Wasco, OR St. Mary.
Nwokoye, Patrick I. '02 (SPC)[J] Cape Girardeau, MO Catholic Campus Ministry Southeast Missouri State University, Newman Center; Campus Ministries; Catholic Scouting; Vocations–Seminarians.
Nwokoye, Peter '99 (SAG) Ruth, MI St. Mary; Palms, MI St. Patrick; Ruth, MI SS. Peter and Paul.
Nwosu, Abuchi '08 (PAT) Long Valley, NJ Our Lady of the Mountain; Long Valley, NJ St. Mark the Evangelist.
Nwosu, Benjamin '01 (JC) Iberia, MO St. Anthony; St. Elizabeth, MO St. Lawrence.
Nwosu, Malachy '93 (ROC) Freeville, NY Holy Cross; Groton, NY St. Anthony; Lansing, NY All Saints.
Nwudah, Anthony '90 (AUS) Austin, TX Seton/Brackenridge Hospital; Diocesan Tribunal Judges; Austin, TX Sacred Heart.
Nyache, Collins Kisaka '11 (CHI) Winnetka, IL Sacred Heart.
Nyaga, Patrick Gitonga '02 (SAC) Fairfield, CA Our Lady of Mount Carmel,.
Nyaki, Casimir Lawrence (PIT)[B] Pittsburgh, PA Duquesne University of the Holy Spirit.
Nyamai Munini, Dominic '97 (ROC) Canadaigua, NY St. Mary; East Bloomfield, NY St. Bridget.
Nyambe, Shoba '03 (BAL)[Q] Baltimore, MD St. Mary's Seminary & University.
Nyambo, Callist N. '69 (SP) Clearwater, FL All Saints.
Nyanguf, Frederick O. *a.j.* '98 (NY) Bellevue Hospital.
Nyardy, Jeffrey S. *o.s.b.* '90 (SAV)[B] Savannah, GA Benedictine Military School.
Nyardy, Jeffrey *o.s.b.* '90 (GBG)[I] Greensburg, PA Benedictine Nuns; [J] Greensburg, PA St. Emma Retreat House; [H] Latrobe, PA Saint Vincent Archabbey.
Nycz, Matt Mieczyslaw '94 (BUF) Dunkirk, NY Blessed Mary Angela Parish.
Nydegger, Thomas P. '92 (NEW)[B] Serra Club of the Oranges; [B] Seton Hall University.
Nygaard, Robert C. '64 (STP)[Q] Roseville, MN Catholic Youth Camps, Inc. Retired.
Nyimi, Roger Malonda (R) Garner, NC St. Mary, Mother of the Church.
Nyl, Steven *c.ss.r.* (STP) Brooklyn Center, MN St. Alphonsus; [J] Brooklyn Center, MN Redemptorist Fathers of Hennepin County.
Nyman, Vincent R. '99 (STL) Luebbering, MO St. Francis of Assisi.
Nyquist, Raymond J. '54 (GF) Roundup, MT St. Benedict Retired.
Nys, Loren *s.d.s.* '67 (GB) Kiel, WI SS. Peter and Paul.
Nzeabalu, Cosmas '01 (BRK) Springfield Gardens, NY St. Mary Magdalene.
Nzegwu, Anthony '99 (BRK)[Q] Nigerian Apostolate; Jamaica, NY St. Nicholas of Tolentine.
Nzegwu, Anthony '99 (NY) Bronx, NY Calvary Hospital.
Nzeh, Godwin O. *c.m.f.* (LAF) Port Barre, LA St. Mary.
Nzekwe, Aloysius *m.s.p.* '04 (GAL) Houston, TX St. Peter the Apostle.
Nzomo, Boniface '86 (SR) Petaluma, CA St. James.

O

O'Bell, John C. '91 (SCR) Carbondale, PA St. Rose of Lima.
O'Blaney, James *c.ss.r.* '58 (HBG) Lititz, PA St. James; [G] Ephrata, PA St. Clement's Mission House.
O'Brien, Anthony '68 (MIA) Tamarac, FL St. Malachy.
O'Brien, Rev. Msgr. Bartholomew J. '65 (PH) Retired.
O'Brien, Brian D. '07 (TLS)[A] Tulsa, OK Bishop Kelley High School; [J] Tulsa, OK Bishop Kelley High School Endowment Trust; Diocesan Senators; Diocesan Consultors; Special Assignment.
O'Brien, Charles *o.p.* '54 (WDC) Washington, DC St. Dominic Church & Priory.
O'Brien, Cornelius '55 (ARL) Retired.
O'Brien, Daniel A. *s.j.* '93 (RVC) Oceanside, NY St. Anthony.
O'Brien, Daniel J. *s.j.* '59 (NY)[DD] Cardinal Spellman Hall, Jesuit Community.
O'Brien, Daniel P. '85 (HBG) Orrtanna, PA St. Ignatius Loyola.
O'Brien, David W. *c.s.p.* '56 (COL)[I] Columbus, OH Campus Ministry Retired.
O'Brien, David *o.m.i.* '59 (FgM) Washington, DC AMERICAN OBLATE MISSIONS.
O'Brien, Dennis J. '81 (FgM) Boston, MA St. James the Apostle, Inc.; On Duty Outside the Diocese.
O'Brien, Donald J. '61 (GI) Cozad, NE Christ the King.
O'Brien, Edmund M. '57 (HRT) Enfield, CT St. Adalbert's Retired.
O'Brien, Elias *o.carm.* (CHI) Chicago, IL St. Thomas Apostle.
O'Brien, Francis P. '85 (BO) Marlborough, MA St. Matthias.
O'Brien, Frederick W. '50 (BO) Senior Priests. Retired.
O'Brien, George '58 (LA) Beverly Hills, CA Good Shepherd.
O'Brien, Gerard C. *s.j.* '59 (BO)[U] Newton, MA The Jesuit Community at Boston College.
O'Brien, Gerard '95 (LA) Pasadena, CA Assumption of the Blessed Virgin Mary.
O'Brien, Howard E. *m.m.* '55 (NY)[DD] Retired.
O'Brien, James A. *s.j.* '60 (WH) Towson, MD; [A] Wheeling, WV Wheeling Jesuit University.
O'Brien, James C. *s.j.* '61 (BO)[U] Weston, MA Campion Health Center, Inc.
O'Brien, James E. '60 (Y) Boardman, OH St. Luke Retired.
O'Brien, James J. *m.a.* '60 (CHI) Chicago, IL St. Monica; Chicago, IL St. Eugene Retired.
O'Brien, James R. '66 (HBG) Chambersburg, PA Corpus Christi.
O'Brien, James T. '70 (SY) Liverpool, NY Pope John XXIII RC Church; Western Area Vicars; Board of Diocesan Consultors; Priests' Personnel Committee; Presbyteral Council.
O'Brien, John E. '87 (BAL) Priests Sick or Absent.
O'Brien, Rev. Msgr. John F. '61 (PH) Retired.
O'Brien, Rev. Msgr. John H. '62 (BRK) Retired.
O'Brien, John J. *m.m.* '52 (NY)[DD] Retired.
O'Brien, John J. '07 (STL) Special Assignment.
O'Brien, John M. *o.c.s.o.* '81 (ATL)[F] Conyers, GA The Monastery of the Holy Spirit.
O'Brien, John P. '49 (SPK) Retired.
O'Brien, John W. '67 (BO) Quincy, MA Sacred Heart.
O'Brien, John W. '82 (PRO) Middletown, RI St. Lucy; [T] Middletown, RI Charismatic Renewal.
O'Brien, John '55 (GB) Retired.
O'Brien, Rev. Msgr. John '62 (BRK) Jamaica, NY

Presentation of the Blessed Virgin Mary.
O'Brien, John '96 (ALX) Natchitoches, LA St. Anthony of Padua.
O'Brien, Jon J. *s.j.* '63 (WDC)[C] Catholic University of America, The; [O] Washington, DC The Jesuit Community at Georgetown University Retired.
O'Brien, Joseph E. '51 (PH) Philadelphia, PA St. Leo Retired.
O'Brien, Joseph L. '55 (TOL)[G] Oregon, OH Sacred Heart Home Retired.
O'Brien, Joseph P. *o.carm.* '63 (NEW) Cresskill, NJ St. Therese of Lisieux.
O'Brien, Joseph '91 (ALB) East Greenbush, NY Holy Spirit; Advocates.
O'Brien, Joseph '57 (CHI) Chicago, IL St. Clement Retired.
O'Brien, Joseph *o.p.* '78 (LAV)[F] Henderson, NV Saint Therese Center; [C] Las Vegas, NV Dominican Rectory, Fra Angelico House.
O'Brien, Rev. Msgr. Joseph '57 (DUB) Retired.
O'Brien, Kevin F. *s.j.* '06 (WDC)[O] Washington, DC The Jesuit Community at Georgetown University.
O'Brien, Kevin J. '81 (OG) Brownville, NY Roman Catholic Community of Brownville and Dexter; Brownville, NY St. Andrew; Diocesan Consultors.
O'Brien, Kevin J. '79 (RIC) Chesapeake, VA St. Therese of Lisieux; Judges.
O'Brien, Rev. Msgr. Kevin P. '73 (NY) Bronx, NY St. Philip Neri; Canon 1742 Panel of Pastors.
O'Brien, Leo P. '56 (ALB) Albany, NY St. Francis of Assisi Parish Retired.
O'Brien, Maurice '68 (SAC) Willows, CA St. Monica.
O'Brien, Michael T. '79 (SP) Seminole, FL St. Justin Martyr; Vicars Forane.
O'Brien, Michael '72 (JKS) Notaries; Personnel Board; Jackson, MS St. Richard of Chichester; Institute for the Blind, Institute for the Deaf and Speech Impaired; Priests' Council; Diocesan Consultors.
O'Brien, Michael *m.s.c.* '69 (SAT)[L] San Antonio, TX Missionaries of the Sacred Heart.
O'Brien, Michael '05 (LAN) Owosso, MI St. Paul.
O'Brien, Nicholas J. '83 (ORL) Lakeland, FL St. Anthony Catholic Church.
O'Brien, Patrick J. '64 (PIT) Retired.
O'Brien, Patrick '74 (HT) Retired.
O'Brien, Patrick '69 (SAV) Retired.
O'Brien, Patrick '46 (SEA) Retired.
O'Brien, Patrick *c.ss.r.* '64 (OAK)[N] Oakland, CA Holy Redeemer Center; [Q] Oakland, CA Redemptorist Vice Province Initiative; [L] Oakland, CA Redemptorist Fathers (Denver Province).
O'Brien, Paul A. *m.m.* '59 (NY)[DD] Maryknoll Maryknoll Fathers and Brothers Retired.
O'Brien, Paul B. '91 (BO) Lawrence, MA St. Patrick; Trustees.
O'Brien, Paulinus *o.c.s.o.* '77 (WOR)[N] Spencer, MA St. Joseph's Abbey.
O'Brien, Peter *s.j.* '71 (NEW)[L] Jersey City, NJ Jesuits of Saint Peter's College, Inc.; [B] Jersey City, NJ Jesuit Center.
O'Brien, Peter '05 (P) Board Members; Lebanon, OR St. Edward; Scio, OR St. Bernard.
O'Brien, Raymond C. '75 (WDC) Special Ministries; [C] Catholic University of America, The.
O'Brien, Richard M. '92 (BO) Methuen, MA St. Monica.
O'Brien, Richard (BO)[O] Methuen, MA Caritas Holy Family Hospital, Inc.
O'Brien, Roger '61 (SEA) Retired.
O'Brien, Scott *o.p.* '92 (MIA) Barry University.
O'Brien, Scott *o.p.* '86 (DAL)[J] Irving, TX Dominican Priory of St. Albert the Great and Novitiate.
O'Brien, Seamus (MRY) Scotts Valley, CA San Agustin.
O'Brien, Sean P. '93 (SY) Boonville, NY St. Joseph; Forestport, NY St. Patrick.
O'Brien, Sean Patrick '93 (MO) Navy Reserve Chaplains.
O'Brien, Sean *o.f.m.* '98 (SP) Tampa, FL Sacred Heart.
O'Brien, Steven G. '86 (DUB) On Leave of Absence (Not Authorized for Priestly Ministry).
O'Brien, Thomas F. '56 (WOR) Retired.
O'Brien, Thomas F. '83 (STP) Minneapolis, MN Visitation.
O'Brien, Thomas J. *m.m.* '74 (FgM) Maryknoll, NY MARYKNOLL.
O'Brien, Thomas *o.m.i.* '55 (FgM) Washington, DC AMERICAN OBLATE MISSIONS.
O'Brien, Timothy A. '94 (HRT) Harwinton, CT Immaculate Heart of Mary; New Hartford, CT Immaculate Conception; Special and other Archdiocesan Assignment.
O'Brien, Timothy J. '69 (MIL) Special Assignment.
O'Brien, Vincent M. *s.j.* '59 (PH)[Y] Loyola Center and Manresa Hall.
O'Brien, Walter '37 (NY)[DD] Yonkers, NY St. Clare Friary.
O'Brien, Rev. Msgr. William B. '51 (NY) Scarsdale, NY St. Pius X Retired.
O'Brien, William D. '50 (DUB) Retired.
O'Brien, William G. '51 (WOR) Retired.
O'Brien, William J. '78 (BAL) Havre de Grace, MD St. Patrick's.
O'Brien, William J. '80 (E) Girard, PA St. John the Evangelist.
O'Brien, William J. *c.m.* '67 (PH)[Y] Philadelphia Congregation of the Mission.
O'Brien, William P. *s.j.* '02 (STL)[O] St. Louis, MO Sacred Heart Jesuit Community; [C] Saint Louis University.
O'Brien, William S. '69 (RIC) Retired.
O'Brien, William '90 (GB) Luxemburg, WI St. Thomas the Apostle; New Franken, WI St. Kilian; New Franken, WI St. Joseph.
O'Brien, William '61 (NEW) Retired.
O'Brien, William '88 (HPM) Spokane Valley, WA SS. Cyril & Methodius.
O'Bryan, Michael '06 (NSH) Lebanon, TN St. Frances Cabrini; Deans.
O'Byrne, John '61 (LA) Torrance, CA St. Catherine Laboure.
O'Byrne, Patrick J. '60 (LIN) Retired.
O'Callaghan, Rev. Msgr. Eugene '55 (SAT) Retired.
O'Callaghan, John J. *s.j.* '62 (CHI)[C] Chicago, IL Jesuit Community at Loyola University Chicago; [J] Maywood, IL Loyola University Medical Center.
O'Callaghan, Patrick '55 (SAT) Retired.
O'Callaghan, Thomas '54 (SEA) Retired.
O'Callaghan, Tiernan *o.carm.* '56 (PHX)[F] Phoenix, AZ Carmelite Community Retired.
O'Carroll, Eugene '62 (PHX) Retired.
O'Carroll, Patrick J. '54 (ORL) Retired.
O'Cinnsealaigh, Benedict '93 (CIN)[A] Cincinnati, OH The Athenaeum of Ohio; [B] Cincinnati, OH Mount St. Mary's Seminary of the West; [B] Cincinnati, OH Mount St. Mary's Seminary of the West.
O'Connell, Brendan M. *m.m.* '63 (FgM) Maryknoll, NY MARYKNOLL.
O'Connell, Cuthbert R. '86 (BLX) Waveland, MS St. Clare; College of Consultors; Priests' Continuing Education and Retreat Programs.
O'Connell, Damian *s.j.* '75 (NY)[DD] New York, NY "America;" Residence and publication office of the America Press.
O'Connell, Daniel C. '83 (BO) Boston, MA St. Joseph.
O'Connell, Daniel C. *s.j.* '58 (STL)[O] St. Louis, MO Ignatius House.
O'Connell, Daniel P. '71 (SAV)[G] Valdosta, GA St. Francis Center; Valdosta, GA St. John the Evangelist.
O'Connell, Daniel (BO) Spiritual Life.
O'Connell, Rev. Msgr. David G. '79 (LA) Los Angeles, CA St. Michael; Deanery 16; Archdiocesan Finance Council Members 2011–2012.
O'Connell, James R. *o.f.m.* '83 (NY) New York, NY St. Francis of Assisi.
O'Connell, John R. '73 (NEW) Westwood, NJ St. Andrew's.
O'Connell, Joseph A. '51 (SFR)[K] San Rafael, CA Nazareth House of San Rafael, Inc. Retired.
O'Connell, Kevin G. *s.j.* '69 (FgM) Watertown, MA Society of Jesus.
O'Connell, Mark A. '79 (NEW) Belleville, NJ St. Peter's Retired.
O'Connell, Mark '90 (BO) Judicial Vicar of the Archdiocese; Canonical Affairs Committee; Braintree, MA St. Francis of Assisi; Tribunal Court.
O'Connell, Marvin R. '56 (STP) On Duty Outside the Archdiocese Retired.
O'Connell, Rev. Msgr. Maurice V. '72 (WDC) Washington, DC Blessed Sacrament, Shrine of the Most; Ridge, MD St. Michael Retired.
O'Connell, Michael W. '83 (CHI) Orland Park, IL Our Lady of the Woods.
O'Connell, Michael '67 (STP) Minneapolis, MN Ascension; Minneapolis, MN St. Philip.
O'Connell, Neil J. *o.f.m.* '64 (NY)[GG] Bronx, NY Herbert H. Lehman College; [GG] New York, NY Borough of Manhattan; New York, NY St. Joseph of the Holy Family.
O'Connell, Paul A. '03 (SAV) Waycross, GA St. Joseph's.
O'Connell, Paul T. '60 (WOR) Associate Judicial Vicar; Judges; Shrewsbury, MA St. Anne.
O'Connell, Richard C. '51 (ROC) Retired.
O'Connell, Sean T. '09 (MIL) Brookfield, WI St. Dominic.
O'Connell, Terrence E. *o.m.i.* '78 (BO)[Z] Lowell, MA Andre Garin Residence.
O'Connell, Terry J. '92 (MO) Navy Reserve Chaplains.
O'Connell, Terry '92 (P) Grand Ronde, OR St. Michael; McMinnville, OR St. James; Sheridan, OR Good Shepherd.
O'Connell, Thomas P. '63 (KNX) Retired.
O'Connell, Thomas P. '63 (PBR) Knoxville, TN Holy Resurrection Mission.
O'Connell, Rev. Msgr. Timothy P. '63 (LA) Chairman and Coordinator of Activities; Respect Life Office; Hospital Chaplains Retired.
O'Connell, Walter T. *o.p.* '58 (CHI)[N] Chicago, IL St. Pius V Priory.
O'Connell, William A. '55 (SFR) Retired.
O'Connell, Rev. Msgr. William '57 (RC) Retired.
O'Connell, William '66 (VEN) Retired.
O'Connell, William *s.m.* '56 (SJ)[M] Cupertino, CA The Marianist Center.
O'Conner, Rev. Msgr. Gerard P. '00 (FR) Acushnet, MA St. Francis Xavier's.
O'Conner, James T. '54 (CHI) Lyons, IL St. Hugh.
O'Conner, Joseph '05 (SY) Syracuse, NY Blessed Sacrament.
O'Connor, Rev. Msgr. Albert G. '67 (SAC) Sacramento, CA Holy Spirit Retired.
O'Connor, Albert '67 (SAC) College of Consultors; Priests' Personnel Board, Diocesan Retired.
O'Connor, Andrew M. '87 (NY) Bronx, NY Holy Family.
O'Connor, Andrew '87 (STL) Special Assignment; [N] St. Louis, MO Nazareth Living Center.
O'Connor, Bernard F. *o.s.f.s.* '73 (ALN)[B] Center Valley, PA DeSales University; [K] Center Valley, PA Oblates of St. Francis de Sales.
O'Connor, Bernard *c.m.f.* '50 (LA)[V] Rancho Dominguez, CA Dominguez Seminary Inc.
O'Connor, Charles J. *o.f.m.* '73 (PRO)[O] Providence, RI St. Francis Friary; Providence, RI St. Mary.
O'Connor, Charles T. '83 (MET) Bound Brook, NJ St. Joseph.
O'Connor, Christopher K. '98 (BO)[A] Brighton, MA St. John Seminary.
O'Connor, Christopher M. '99 (BRK) Jamaica, NY Presentation of the Blessed Virgin Mary; Diocesan Consultors.
O'Connor, Christopher *l.c.* '06 (HRT)[B] Cheshire, CT Novitiate of the Legion of Christ.
O'Connor, Daniel P. '90 (ALX) College of Consultors; Elected Members; Deans; Alexandria, LA Our Lady of Prompt Succor; Diaconate Program.
O'Connor, Daniel *m.h.m.* '00 (OAK) Pleasant Hill, CA Christ the King.
O'Connor, David H. '86 (DUB) Cedar Rapids, IA All Saints; Permanent Diaconate Formation Board.
O'Connor, David '64 (JKS) Continuing Formation Committee; Natchez, MS Assumption of the B.V.M.; Natchez, MS St. Mary Basilica; Priests' Council.
O'Connor, Dennis '98 (SD) Retired.
O'Connor, Rev. Msgr. Desmond '80 (NY) LaGrangeville, NY Blessed Kateri Tekakwitha.
O'Connor, Desmond *s.p.s.* '50 (PAT) Mount Arlington, NJ Our Lady of the Lake.
O'Connor, Dominic E. (SCR) On Duty Outside the Diocese.
O'Connor, Donald *s.v.d.* '64 (SB)[I] Riverside, CA Divine Word Seminary.
O'Connor, Edward D. *c.s.c.* '48 (FTW)[B] University of Notre Dame Du Lac; [H] Notre Dame, IN Holy Cross Community, Corby Hall, University of Notre Dame.
O'Connor, Rev. Msgr. Edward J. '81 (ALN) Pottsville, PA St. Patrick; Vicars Forane.
O'Connor, Edward '60 (ATL) Retired.
O'Connor, Rev. Msgr. Eugene '54 (BIR) Birmingham, AL St. Barnabas Retired.
O'Connor, Francis '62 (ALB) Albany, NY Shrine of Our Lady of the America's.
O'Connor, Frank '62 (ALB) Retired.
O'Connor, Rev. Msgr. Fred P. '52 (GAL) Crosby, TX Sacred Heart Retired.
O'Connor, Gerald P. *m.m.* '69 (FgM) Maryknoll, NY MARYKNOLL.
O'Connor, Gerald V. *s.j.* '76 (WDC)[O] Washington, DC The Jesuit Community of St. Aloysius Gonzaga; [E] Washington, DC Gonzaga College High School.
O'Connor, Glenn L. '80 (IND) Indianapolis, IN St. Ann Catholic Church, Indianapolis, Inc.; Indianapolis, IN St. Joseph Catholic Church, Indianapolis, Inc.; Indianapolis International Airport.
O'Connor, James C. '71 (BUF) Getzville, NY St. Pius X.
O'Connor, James E. *o.c.s.o.* '57 (DUB)[K] Peosta, IA New Melleray Abbey, Order of Cistercians of the Strict Observance.
O'Connor, James E. '84 (WH) Grafton, WV St. Augustine.
O'Connor, James J. '54 (CIN) Retired.
O'Connor, James M. '52 (LIN) Retired.
O'Connor, James T. '54 (CHI) La Grange, IL St. Francis Xavier Retired.
O'Connor, Rev. Msgr. James T. '66 (NY) Millbrook, NY St. Joseph.
O'Connor, Rev. Msgr. James '70 (LUB) Priests' Pension Board; Priests Personnel Board; Vicar of Retired Priests.
O'Connor, James '82 (WH) Philippi, WV St. Elizabeth Parish; [O] Philippi, WV Alderson–Broaddus College Newman Center.
O'Connor, Rev. Msgr. James '70 (LUB) Lubbock, TX St. Patrick.
O'Connor, Javier *d.c.j.m.* '91 (DEN)[N] Littleton, CO Disciples of the Hearts of Jesus and Mary.
O'Connor, Rev. Msgr. Jay F. '74 (BAL) Baltimore, MD St. Michael; Special Assignment; Office of Diaconate.
O'Connor, Rev. Msgr. John F. '73 (R) Raleigh, NC St. Luke the Evangelist.
O'Connor, John F. *o.f.m.* '73 (NY) New York, NY St. Francis of Assisi; [DD] New York, NY Franciscan Friars, Holy Name Province; [HH] New York, NY Shrine of St. Jude, Inc.; [HH] New York, NY Franciscans of Holy Name Province Benevolence

Trust, Inc.; [HH] New York, NY Foundation of the Order of Friars Minor of the Province of the Most Holy Name; [HH] New York, NY Franciscans of Holy Name Province Education and Formation Trust; [HH] New York, NY The Fratecelli Corporation; [HH] New York, NY Franciscans of Holy Name Province Sick, Aged and Retired Trust.
O'Connor, John H. (PAT) Retired.
O'Connor, John J. '93 (BRK) Queens Village, NY Incarnation; Diocesan Liturgy Office.
O'Connor, John J. '58 (DUB)[F] New Vienna, IA Archbishop Hennessy Catholic School; New Vienna, IA St. Boniface; Dyersville, IA SS. Peter and Paul.
O'Connor, Rev. Msgr. John J. '60 (SFR) Retired.
O'Connor, John L. '63 (ROC) Retired.
O'Connor, Rev. Msgr. John Philip '61 (NEW) Scotch Plains, NJ St. Bartholomew Retired.
O'Connor, Joseph X. *o.s.a.* '53 (PH)[Y] Villanova, PA St. Thomas Monastery.
O'Connor, Joseph '05 (SY) Vocation Promotion.
O'Connor, Kent '03 (KCK) Kansas City, KS Our Lady of Unity.
O'Connor, Mark *s.a.* '84 (NY)[DD] Garrison, NY Franciscan Friars of the Atonement.
O'Connor, Matthew J. '56 (SPR) Retired.
O'Connor, Matthew '71 (MOB) Daphne, AL Christ the King Parish, Daphne.
O'Connor, Maurice J. '53 (BO) Senior Priests. Retired.
O'Connor, Michael G. '56 (KC) Kansas City, MO St. Thomas More.
O'Connor, Michael J. '72 (TR) Lakewood, NJ St. Mary of the Lake.
O'Connor, Michael J. '85 (AUS) St. John Vianney.
O'Connor, Michael J. *o.s.a.* '71 (CHI)[N] Matteson, IL Austin Friary.
O'Connor, Michael P. '05 (BLX) Pass Christian, MS Sacred Heart; Cursillo and Retreats; Presbyteral Council; CIVIL AIR PATROL; College of Consultors.
O'Connor, Michael '85 (AUS) Georgetown/Round Rock.
O'Connor, Neil D. '69 (CLV) Parma, OH St. Columbkille.
O'Connor, Noel *s.c.a.* '78 (DET)[K] Wyandotte, MI Society of the Catholic Apostolate (Pallottine Fathers); [K] Wyandotte, MI Pallottine Missionary Center (Irish Province).
O'Connor, Patrick C. '78 (SAG) Midland, MI St. Brigid.
O'Connor, Patrick J. '64 (GBG) Retired.
O'Connor, Patrick T. *o.s.f.s.* '97 (VEN) Fort Myers, FL Jesus the Worker Mission (Jesus Obrero); Fort Myers, FL San Jose Mission.
O'Connor, Patrick *m.s.c.* '52 (SAT)[L] San Antonio, TX Missionaries of the Sacred Heart.
O'Connor, Paul F. *o.s.b.* '70 (NY) Bronx, NY Veterans Administration Hospital; James F. Peters Medical Center.
O'Connor, Paul F. *c.s.b.* '70 (ROC)[K] Rochester Basilian Residence.
O'Connor, Rev. Msgr. Paul '45 (CAM) Retired.
O'Connor, Paul *s.j.* '00 (CIN)[N] Cincinnati, OH Jesuit Community at St. Xavier High School.
O'Connor, Pio *o.f.m.* '94 (SFE)[H] Albuquerque, NM The Province of Our Lady of Guadalupe.
O'Connor, Pio *o.f.m.* (GLP) Tohatchi, NM St. Mary Church.
O'Connor, Raymond E. *c.m.f.* '64 (CHI)[N] Oak Park, IL Claretian Missionaries USA Eastern Province; Chicago, IL St. Ferdinand.
O'Connor, Rev. Msgr. Robert B. '56 (NY) New York, NY Blessed Sacrament.
O'Connor, Robert D. '55 (PEO) Retired.
O'Connor, Robert F. *s.j.* '79 (OM)[J] Omaha, NE Jesuit Community at Creighton University; Religious Orders.
O'Connor, Rev. Msgr. Robert W. '48 (PEO) Retired.
O'Connor, Shaun '82 (SPR) Hadley, MA Most Holy Redeemer.
O'Connor, Terrence P. '01 (PIT)[A] Pittsburgh, PA Saint Paul Seminary; St. Paul Seminary; Continuing Education of Clergy, Office for; Clergy Personnel Board.
O'Connor, Thomas J. '93 (BO)[U] Hingham, MA Glastonbury Abbey.
O'Connor, Thomas V. *s.j.* '60 (NY)[DD] Loyola Hall, Jesuit Community.
O'Connor, Timothy J. '75 (CLV) Avon Lake, OH St. Joseph.
O'Connor, Timothy *c.s.c.* '91 (FTW)[H] Holy Cross House; Notre Dame, IN Sacred Heart.
O'Connor, Vincent M. '48 (SPR) Haydenville, MA Our Lady of the Hills Retired.
O'Connor, William J. '58 (BO) Senior Priests. Retired.
O'Connor, William *c.s.c.* '49 (FTW)[H] Holy Cross House.
O'Dea, Loren F. '93 (DET) Retired.
O'Dea, Thomas '58 (PHX) Retired.
O'Dell, Kevin '00 (SFS) Tea, SD St. Nicholas.
O'Dell, W. Paul '93 (SFR) South San Francisco, CA All Souls.
O'Doherty, Rev. Msgr. Jude '65 (MIA) Miami, FL Epiphany; Members; Pension.
O'Doherty, Liam Tomas *o.s.a.* '76 (NY) Staten Island, NY Our Lady of Good Counsel.
O'Doherty, Patrick J. '70 (ORL) Ocala, FL Queen of Peace.
O'Donnell, Brian J. '09 (BUR) St. Albans, VT Immaculate Conception.
O'Donnell, Brian P. *s.j.* '86 (WH) Catholic Conference of West Virginia; [A] Wheeling, WV Wheeling Jesuit University; Executive Secretary.
O'Donnell, Dennis J.W. '74 (PH) On Special or Other Archdiocesan Assignment; Philadelphia, PA St. Christopher; [Z] Huntingdon Valley, PA Sisters of the Holy Redeemer Provincialate.
O'Donnell, Dennis '83 (GR) Free Soil, MI St. John Cantius; Irons, MI St. Bernard's.
O'Donnell, Edmond "Ned" '64 (SB) Retired.
O'Donnell, Edmond "Ned" G. '64 (SB) Patton, CA Patton State Hospital.
O'Donnell, Rev. Msgr. Edward D. '54 (NY) Rye, NY Resurrection Retired.
O'Donnell, Edward T. *s.j.* '74 (PH) Philadelphia, PA Old St. Joseph's.
O'Donnell, Eugene P. '73 (SJ) San Jose, CA St. Francis of Assisi; Deans.
O'Donnell, Frank T. *m.m.* '55 (NY)[DD] Retired.
O'Donnell, Gabriel *o.p.* '70 (WDC)[B] Washington, DC Dominican House of Studies.
O'Donnell, Harold F.X. *s.j.* '64 (NY)[DD] New York, NY Murray–Weigel Hall.
O'Donnell, Rev. Msgr. Hugh A. '54 (NEW) Retired.
O'Donnell, Hugh '58 (SFR)[K] San Rafael, CA Nazareth House of San Rafael, Inc. Retired.
O'Donnell, James A. *s.j.* '61 (FgM) New York, NY Society of Jesus.
O'Donnell, James P. '56 (CLV) Cuyahoga County Detention Home; Northeast Pre Release Center; [R] Cleveland, OH Community of Little Brothers and Sisters of the Eucharist, Inc.; Central City Ministry with Poor.
O'Donnell, James *o.s.b.* '42 (PAT)[N] Morristown, NJ St. Mary's Abbey.
O'Donnell, John F. '63 (BO) Senior Priests. Retired.
O'Donnell, Rev. Msgr. John F. '54 (LR)[G] Little Rock, AR St. John Manor; Assistant Directors Retired.
O'Donnell, John *o.s.b.* '98 (BIR) Cullman, AL Sacred Heart; On Special or Other Diocesan Assignment; [E] Cullman, AL St. Bernard Abbey.
O'Donnell, John '72 (DUL) Virginia, MN Sacred Heart; Virginia, MN Holy Spirit; Virginia, MN Sacred Heart; Diocesan Deans; College of Consultors.
O'Donnell, Joseph F. *c.s.c.* '60 (PHX)[F] Phoenix, AZ Holy Cross Congregation/Casa Santa Cruz Retired.
O'Donnell, Joseph P. '76 (CLV) Uniontown, OH Queen of Heaven.
O'Donnell, Joseph *c.s.c.* (FTW)[H] Notre Dame Congregation of Holy Cross, United States Province of Priests & Brothers.
O'Donnell, Mark D. '85 (NOR) Diocesan Commission for Ecumenical and Interreligious Affairs; Niantic, CT St. Agnes; Advisory Board; Continuing Education and Formation Commission for the Clergy; Corrigan–Radgowski Correctional Institution.
O'Donnell, Paul J. '02 (PH)[D] Springfield, PA Cardinal O'Hara High School; Havertown, PA Sacred Heart.
O'Donnell, Paul L. '93 (LA) Los Angeles, CA Assumption; Los Angeles, CA San Antonio de Padua.
O'Donnell, Rev. Msgr. Peter C. '58 (NY)[DD] Bronx, NY John Cardinal O'Connor Residence Retired.
O'Donnell, Peter '10 (SAL)[A] Salina, KS Sacred Heart Junior–Senior High School; Salina, KS St. Mary Queen of the Universe Parish.
O'Donnell, Philip '58 (LAV) Retired.
O'Donnell, Ralph B. '97 (KC)[A] Conception, MO Conception Seminary College.
O'Donnell, Raymond G. '72 (SD) La Jolla, CA All Hallows Catholic Parish; Presbyteral Council.
O'Donnell, Richard C. '05 (BUR) Elected Members; Deans; Brattleboro, VT St. Michael.
O'Donnell, Rev. Msgr. Richard J. '35 (CHI) Retired.
O'Donnell, Richard *m.i.* '64 (MIL)[Y] Wauwatosa, WI St. Camillus Health System, Inc.; [Y] Milwaukee, WI St. Camillus Communities, Inc. – House I; [Y] Wauwatosa, WI St. Camillus Ministries, Inc.; [P] Milwaukee, WI St. Camillus Delegate House; [N] Wauwatosa, WI St. Camillus Health Center, Inc.; [Y] Wauwatosa, WI San Camillo, Inc.; Milwaukee, WI; [Y] Wauwatosa, WI Order of St. Camillus Foundation, Inc.
O'Donnell, Rev. Msgr. Richard '35 (CHI) Chicago, IL Blessed Sacrament.
O'Donnell, Robert A. *c.s.p.* '51 (NY)[DD] New York, NY Paulist Fathers' Motherhouse Retired.
O'Donnell, Robert J. '74 (STP) Minneapolis, MN St. Lawrence; [J] Minneapolis, MN Paulist Fathers; [R] Minneapolis, MN Newman Center at St. Lawrence.
O'Donnell, Simon *o.s.b.* '68 (LA)[P] Valyermo, CA St. Andrew's Abbey.
O'Donnell, Terrence *s.d.b.* '70 (NY)[DD] New Rochelle, NY Salesian Provincial House.
O'Donnell, Thomas M. '61 (HEL) East Helena, MT SS. Cyril and Methodius.
O'Donnell, Thomas M. '60 (PIT) Pittsburgh, PA St. Mary of Mercy; Judges; Pittsburgh, PA Retired.
O'Donnell, Thomas M. '61 (HEL) Presbyteral Council; Diocesan Consultors.
O'Donnell, Thomas V. '67 (CLV) Garfield Heights, OH St. Therese Retired.
O'Donnell, Walter *s.t.* '55 (WDC)[O] Adelphi, MD Father Judge Missionary Cenacle.
O'Donnell, William J. '52 (ALN) Retired.
O'Donnell, William J. '66 (NO) Defenders of the Bond Retired.
O'Donnell, Rev. Msgr. William J. J. '52 (PH) Retired.
O'Donnell, William *c.pp.s.* '77 (CIN) Dayton, OH Precious Blood; Presbyteral Council; Dayton, OH St. Rita.
O'Donnell, William *o.m.i.* '77 (STP) St. Paul, MN St. Patrick; St. Paul, MN St. Casimir.
O'Donoghue, Brendan W. '50 (WOR) Retired.
O'Donoghue, Rev. Msgr. James P. '43 (SD) Retired.
O'Donoghue, John '64 (SAT) San Antonio, TX Blessed Sacrament.
O'Donoghue, Kevin J. '58 (BRK)[R] Douglaston, NY Bishop Mugavero Residence Retired.
O'Donoghue, Neil Xavier '00 (NEW)[A] Kearny, NJ Redemptoris Mater Archdiocesan Missionary Seminary; Members.
O'Donoghue, Patrick '61 (BIR) Retired.
O'Donohue, John M. '00 (ARL) Kilmarnock, VA St. Francis de Sales.
O'Donohue, Neville *s.m.* '02 (BAL) Eldersburg, MD St. Joseph; [T] Sykesville, MD St. Joseph Catholic Community Endowment Trust.
O'Donovan, Rev. Msgr. Dennis '69 (P)[Q] Portland, OR Oregon Catholic Conference; Vicar General and Moderator of the Curia; Pastoral Services; College of Consultors; Ex Officio; Building Commission; Finance Council; Oregon Catholic Conference; Pastoral Services; Secretary–Treasurer; Cemeteries.
O'Donovan, Donal '50 (WH) Retired.
O'Donovan, Leo J. *s.j.* '66 (NY)[DD] New York, NY "America;" Residence and publication office of the America Press.
O'Donovan, Martin E. '78 (CHI) Winnetka, IL SS. Faith, Hope and Charity; Members.
O'Donovan, Patrick G. '72 (PAT) New Vernon, NJ Christ the King.
O'Donovan, Thomas P. '70 (CC) Retired.
O'Donovan, Rev. Msgr. Timothy John '49 (B) Retired.
O'Dougherty, Gerard *s.v.d.* '74 (SB)[I] Riverside, CA Divine Word Seminary.
O'Dowd, Bernard J. *o.s.a.* '58 (PH)[Y] Villanova, PA St. Thomas Monastery.
O'Dowd, Francis '01 (TYL) Lufkin, TX St. Patrick; Tyler Catholic Committee on Scouting.
O'Driscoll, James (BO) Rockland, MA Holy Family.
O'Dwyer, Dominick '66 (MIA) Tamarac, FL St. Malachy.
O'Dwyer, James '65 (STO) Diamond Springs, CA Retired.
O'Dwyer, Michael *s.a.c.* '61 (LUB) Retired.
O'Dwyer, Thomas '70 (MIA) Hollywood, FL Little Flower; Consultors; Deans and Deaneries; Ministry of Persons; Archdiocesan Vocations Review Board; South Broward Deanery.
O'Farrell, John V. '02 (RVC) Floral Park, NY Our Lady of Victory.
O'Flaherty, Edward M. *s.j.* '65 (BO)[U] Newton, MA The Jesuit Community at Boston College.
O'Flaherty, Michael '75 (PMB) Boca Raton, FL St. John the Evangelist.
O'Flanagan, Thomas P. '95 (PMB) Released from Diocesan Assignment; Navy Chaplains.
O'Flynn, John '61 (PBL) Retired.
O'Flynn, Seamus '59 (STA) Retired.
O'Friel, Rev. Msgr. John '45 (FRS) Retired.
O'Gara, James R. *c.s.p.* '61 (BRK)[R] Retired Retired.
O'Gara, Stephen R. '71 (STP) St. Paul, MN Assumption.
O'Gorman, Rev. Msgr. Charles Francis '49 (LA) Oxnard, CA Santa Clara Retired.
O'Gorman, Eamon T. '67 (ORG) Laguna Beach, CA St. Catherine of Siena.
O'Gorman, Rev. Msgr. Michael B. '64 (SAT) San Antonio, TX St. Gregory's.
O'Gorman, Thomas H. *s.j.* '63 (FgM) New York, NY Society of Jesus.
O'Grady, Dennis R. '61 (CLV) Cleveland, OH St. Michael the Archangel Retired.
O'Grady, Frank (PAT) Military Chaplains.
O'Grady, J. Frank '69 (MO) Army Chaplains.
O'Grady, James F. '58 (LA) Los Angeles, CA Visitation Retired.
O'Grady, James Francis '54 (LA) Retired.
O'Grady, John F. '66 (ALB) Retired.
O'Grady, Rev. Msgr. Michael '58 (PHX) Retired.
O'Grady, Peter '63 (NO) Retired.
O'Grady, Robert A. '72 (HRT) Windsor Locks, CT St. Mary; Windsor Locks, CT St. Robert Bellarmine; Hartford, CT Hartford Correctional Institution; Special and other Archdiocesan Assignment; Hartford Vicariate.
O'Grady, Robert M. '78 (BO) Boston Catholic Directory; Arlington, MA St. Camillus.

O'Guinn, Jon '93 (BEL) Leave of Absence.
O'Hagan, Patrick J. *ss.cc.* '48 (SB)[I] Chino Hills, CA Congregation of the Sacred Hearts of Jesus & Mary, SS.CC.; Office of the Vicar for Priests.
O'Hagan, Patrick J. *ss.cc.* '65 (LA)[P] La Verne, CA Congregation of the Sacred Hearts of Jesus and Mary.
O'Hala, Steven '88 (MIA) Pompano Beach, FL St. Elizabeth of Hungary Catholic Church.
O'Hallaran, John E. *s.s.j.* '85 (NO) New Orleans, LA St. David.
O'Hallaran, John *s.s.j.* '85 (LAF) Lebeau, LA Immaculate Conception.
O'Halloran, Edward P. '78 (NY) Yonkers, NY; Yonkers, NY St. Denis.
O'Hanlon, Michael A. '57 (GF) Retired.
O'Hara, Charles R. '70 (PH) Spring City, PA St. Joseph.
O'Hara, Daniel J. '87 (MO) Air Force Reserve Chaplains; Liverpool, NY Immaculate Heart of Mary; Liverpool, NY St. Joseph the Worker.
O'Hara, Edward '60 (SAC) Retired.
O'Hara, Eugene *o.f.m.cap.* '61 (ROC)[K] Interlaken, NY St. Fidelis Friary.
O'Hara, Francis A. '56 (BO) Senior Priests. Retired.
O'Hara, Francis W. '59 (PRO) Retired.
O'Hara, James T. '66 (E) Legion of Mary; Erie, PA Our Mother of Sorrows.
O'Hara, John J. '84 (NY) Staten Island, NY St. Teresa.
O'Hara, John T. '80 (ARL) Dale City, VA Holy Family.
O'Hara, John '79 (PRT) Bar Harbor, ME Parish of the Transfiguration.
O'Hara, Joseph M. '01 (LC) Dodge, WI Most Sacred Heart.
O'Hara, Michael D. '60 (BUF) Retired.
O'Hara, Michael *o.m.i.* '76 (NY) New York, NY Metropolitan Correctional Center.
O'Hara, Thomas J. *c.s.c.* '78 (SCR)[B] Holy Cross Community; Prov. Councilors.
O'Hara, Thomas J. *c.s.c.* '78 (FTW)[H] Notre Dame Congregation of Holy Cross, United States Province of Priests & Brothers.
O'Hare, Daniel G. *s.j.* '79 (NY)[DD] New York, NY St. Ignatius Loyola Residence.
O'Hare, Daniel M. '65 (NY) Maybrook, NY Church of the Assumption; Montgomery, NY Holy Name of Mary.
O'Hare, Donal J. '54 (WCH) Retired.
O'Hare, John B. '53 (PMB) Vero Beach, FL Holy Cross Retired.
O'Hare, Joseph A. *s.j.* '61 (NY)[DD] New York, NY "America;" Residence and publication office of the America Press.
O'Hare, Keith M. '97 (ARL) Doral, FL San Francisco de Asis, Banica; Doral, FL San Jose, Pedro Santana.
O'Hare, Robert V. *s.j.* '95 (NEW)[C] Jersey City, NJ Jesuit Community; [L] Jersey City, NJ Jesuit Community of St. Peter's Prep, Inc.; [B] Jersey City, NJ Jesuit Center; [L] Jersey City, NJ Jesuits of Saint Peter's College, Inc.
O'Hearn, Michael J. '95 (FR)[F] Fall River, MA Priests' Hostel.
O'Hern, Mark '02 (E) Deans; Meadville, PA St. Brigid; Presbyteral Council.
O'Hotto, Kenneth L. '80 (STP) Waverly, MN St. Mary.
O'Kane, James D. '65 (GI) Retired.
O'Kane, John J. '08 (MET) Flemington, NJ St. Magdalen de Pazzi.
O'Kane, John '04 (ALB) Presbyteral Council; Diocesan Board of Consultors; Chestertown, NY Parish of St. Isaac Jogues; North Creek, NY St. James.
O'Kane, Patrick J. '77 (SC) Onawa, IA St. Joseph's; Onawa, IA St. John.
O'Keefe, Daniel Paul *o.s.b.* '93 (GBG) Latrobe, PA St. Vincent Basilica; [H] Latrobe, PA Saint Vincent Archabbey.
O'Keefe, J. Kevin '95 (ARL) Woodbridge, VA Our Lady of Angels.
O'Keefe, Rev. Msgr. John J. '72 (NY) Pearl River, NY St. Margaret of Antioch.
O'Keefe, John J. '68 (DET) Westland, MI St. Theodore of Canterbury.
O'Keefe, Joseph L. '75 (BUR) Veterans Administration Hospital.
O'Keefe, Joseph M. *s.j.* '86 (BO)[U] Newton, MA The Jesuit Community at Boston College.
O'Keefe, Lawrence J. '70 (GLP) Gallup, NM Cathedral of the Sacred Heart; Crownpoint, NM St. Paul; Adjutant Judicial Vicar; Judges; Presbyteral Council; Diocesan Consultors.
O'Keefe, Mark *o.s.b.* '83 (IND)[K] Saint Meinrad St. Meinrad Archabbey; [A] Saint Meinrad, IN Saint Meinrad School of Theology.
O'Keefe, Mark *o.s.b.* '83 (EVN) Huntingburg, IN Visitation of the Blessed Virgin Mary; Diocesan Council of Priests.
O'Keefe, Michael *o.carm.* '75 (JOL) Darien, IL Our Lady of Mount Carmel.
O'Keefe, Patrick T. '96 (BUF)[Q] Buffalo, NY D'Youville College; [C] Buffalo, NY D'Youville College; Oakfield, NY St. Padre Pio.
O'Keefe, Vincent T. *s.j.* '50 (NY)[DD] New York, NY Murray–Weigel Hall.
O'Keefe, William F. '60 (HRT)[A] In Res. at the Archbishop Daniel A. Cronin Retirement Residence at St. Thomas Seminary Retired.
O'Keefe, Rev. Msgr. William Joseph '59 (LA) Retired.
O'Keeffe, Dennis J. '84 (LFT) Zionsville, IN St. Alphonsus.
O'Keeffe, Donal *l.c.* '81 (WDC)[O] Potomac, MD Legionaries of Christ.
O'Keeffe, Jeremiah E. '66 (LA) Northridge, CA Our Lady of Lourdes.
O'Keeffe, Joseph '75 (ALB) DEPARTMENT OF VETERANS AFFAIRS HOSPITALS AND CHAPLAINS; On Duty Outside the Diocese; Military Chaplains.
O'Keeffe, Michael '68 (ORL) Ocala, FL Blessed Trinity.
O'Keeffe, Michael '68 (SAV) Retired.
O'Keeffe, Rev. Msgr. Richard W. '59 (TUC) Special Assignment; Council of Priests; Episcopal Vicar; Episcopal Vicar Retired.
O'Keeffe, Rev. Msgr. William J. '59 (LA) Long Beach, CA Our Lady of Refuge.
O'Kelly, P. Colm '64 (SAC) Retired.
O'Kennedy, Philip N. '71 (BIR) Madison, AL St. John the Baptist; [I] Madison, AL St. John's Educational Foundation.
O'Kielty, James P. '54 (PAT) Retired.
O'Kielty, James P. '54 (PAT)[Q] Chester, NJ Nazareth Village.
O'Konsky, Stanley J. *s.j.* '72 (NY)[E] Bronx, NY Fordham Preparatory School; [DD] Jesuit Community, Kohlmann Hall.
O'Kruta, Francis A. '94 (WH) Wheeling, WV St. Alphonsus.
O'Laughlin, Rev. Msgr. Patrick J. '67 (STL) Wentzville, MO St. Patrick.
O'Leary, Barry P. '07 (PIT) Pittsburgh, PA St. Paul Cathedral; SCI Pittsburgh.
O'Leary, Cornelius F. '56 (WOR) Retired.
O'Leary, Rev. Msgr. Cornelius P. '48 (CAM) Retired.
O'Leary, Daniel *o.m.i.* (BO)[X] Tewksbury, MA Immaculate Heart of Mary Residence.
O'Leary, David M. '85 (BO) Medford, MA St. Clement.
O'Leary, Hilary *o.s.b.* '68 (PAT)[N] Morristown, NJ St. Mary's Abbey.
O'Leary, James E. '68 (BO) Arlington, MA St. Camillus.
O'Leary, James J. *s.j.* '65 (MIL)[P] Milwaukee, WI Jesuit Community at Marquette University.
O'Leary, James J. '56 (DET) Retired.
O'Leary, James M. *s.j.* '91 (CHI)[N] Chicago Chicago Province of the Society of Jesus–Provincial Office.
O'Leary, James M. *s.j.* (STL)[O] St. Louis, MO Jesuit Community Corporation at Saint Louis University – Jesuit Hall.
O'Leary, James S. '61 (KAL) Parchment, MI St. Ambrose.
O'Leary, John A. '78 (CAM) Cape May Court House, NJ The Church of Our Lady of the Angels, Cape May Court House, N.J.
O'Leary, John P. '54 (BIS)[G] Bismarck, ND Emmaus Place Retired.
O'Leary, John '67 (MIA) On Duty Outside the Archdiocese; Boston, MA St. James the Apostle, Inc.
O'Leary, John *s.j.* '60 (SEA)[M] Seattle, WA Jesuit House, Seattle.
O'Leary, John '67 (BRK) The Brooklyn Hospital.
O'Leary, Kevin J. '95 (BO) Boston, MA Cathedral of the Holy Cross; Boston, MA St. James the Greater; Vicariate III.
O'Leary, Lawrence J. '56 (RVC) West Brentwood, NY Pilgrim Psychiatric Center Retired.
O'Leary, Rev. Msgr. Lawrence '53 (LA) Los Angeles, CA St. Martin of Tours Retired.
O'Leary, Malcolm *s.v.d.* '61 (JKS) Vicksburg, MS St. Mary.
O'Leary, Mark *o.p.* '85 (OAK)[L] Oakland, CA Order of Preachers (Province of the Most Holy Name of Jesus – Western Dominican Province).
O'Leary, Matthew L. '03 (SEA) Presbyteral Council; Deans; Puyallup, WA Holy Disciples.
O'Leary, Niall Finbarr '60 (LA) South Pasadena, CA Holy Family Retired.
O'Leary, Patrick B. *s.j.* '61 (SEA)[A] Seattle, WA Seattle University; [M] Seattle, WA Arrupe Jesuit Community at Seattle University.
O'Leary, Peter P. '01 (BUR) Colchester, VT Our Lady of Grace.
O'Leary, Raymond J. '62 (ORL) Retired.
O'Leary, Richard T. *o.s.a.* (BO) Andover, MA St. Augustine.
O'Leary, Robert A. '53 (NEW) Retired.
O'Leary, Sean '61 (SAC) Retired.
O'Leary, Rev. Msgr. Thomas M. '57 (NEW) Hillsdale, NJ St. John the Baptist Retired.
O'Leary, Rev. Msgr. Timothy F. (BO) Boston, MA St. Stephen.
O'Leary, Rev. Msgr. Todd '58 (TUC) Tucson, AZ Saint Thomas the Apostle Roman Catholic Parish – Tucson Retired.
O'Leary, William F. *s.j.* '62 (MIL)[P] Wauwatosa, WI Jesuit Community at St. Camillus.
O'Loghlen, Martin P. *ss.cc.* '61 (LA)[P] La Verne, CA Congregation of the Sacred Hearts of Jesus and Mary.
O'Loughlin, Francis A. '80 (PRO) Newport, RI Jesus Saviour; Newport Hospital; Council Members.
O'Loughlin, Frank '65 (PMB) Retired.
O'Loughlin, Michael '05 (HPM) Denver, CO Holy Protection of the Mother of God; Vocations Office.
O'Loughlin, Padhraic *s.s.c.* '57 (FgM) St Columbans, NE House of Post–Graduate Studies.
O'Loughlin, Patrick J. '99 (MIL) Oak Creek, WI St. Matthew.
O'Mahony, Maurice K. '67 (LA) Santa Barbara, CA Our Lady of Mount Carmel Retired.
O'Malley, Rev. Msgr. James E. '46 (SFR)[K] San Rafael, CA Nazareth House of San Rafael, Inc. Retired.
O'Malley, James F. '56 (CHI) Highwood, IL St. James Retired.
O'Malley, John J. *o.p.* '59 (CHI) River Forest, IL St. Vincent Ferrer.
O'Malley, John J. '65 (PIT) Retired.
O'Malley, John L. *s.j.* '63 (FgM) Chicago, IL Society of Jesus.
O'Malley, John W. *s.j.* '57 (WDC)[O] Washington, DC The Jesuit Community at Georgetown University.
O'Malley, Kenneth *c.p.* '64 (CHI)[N] Chicago, IL Passionist Archives.
O'Malley, Kenneth *c.p.* '64 (GAL)[O] Houston, TX Congregation of the Passion, Holy Name Passionist Community and Retreat Center.
O'Malley, Leonard F. '74 (BO) Appointed; Cambridge, MA St. Peter.
O'Malley, Mark Francis '95 (NEW)[A] South Orange, NJ Immaculate Conception Seminary School of Theology; Censores Librorum.
O'Malley, Mark '95 (NEW)[B] Seton Hall University.
O'Malley, Patrick J. '57 (CHI)[A] Mundelein, IL University of St. Mary of the Lake/Mundelein Seminary; Elmwood Park, IL St. Celestine Retired.
O'Malley, Paul *s.s.c.* '57 (OM)[J] St. Columbans Missionary Society of St. Columban Retired.
O'Malley, Paul *s.s.c.* '57 (PRO)[O] Bristol, RI St. Columban's Retirement House.
O'Malley, Terence *s.c.j.* '60 (OAK) Castro Valley, CA Transfiguration.
O'Malley, Thomas J. '66 (SCR) Ashley, PA St. Leo's.
O'Malley, Timothy J. '97 (CHI) Round Lake, IL St. Joseph.
O'Malley, Vincent J. *c.m.* '73 (PH)[Y].
O'Malley, Vincent J. *c.m.* '73 (GR)[J] Spring Lake, MI St. Lazare Retreat House.
O'Malley, William J. *s.j.* '63 (NY)[E] Bronx, NY Fordham Preparatory School.
O'Malley, William J. *s.j.* '51 (NY)[DD] Jesuit Community, Kohlmann Hall.
O'Malley, William *o.carm.* '65 (NEW) Teaneck, NJ St. Anastasia's.
O'Mannion, Sean '08 (SPR) Northampton, MA Saint Elizabeth Ann Seton.
O'Mara, Dennis Timothy '04 (WOR) Blackstone, MA St. Paul.
O'Mara, Dennis *s.s.c.* '61 (OM)[J] St. Columbans Missionary Society of St. Columban.
O'Mara, Michael E. '88 (IND) Indianapolis, IN Saint Mary of the Immaculate Conception Catholic Church, Indianapolis, Inc.
O'Mara, William T. '58 (CHI) Orland Hills, IL St. Elizabeth Seton; Chicago Heights, IL St. Agnes Retired.
O'Meara, Gerard J. '56 (BO) Senior Priests. Retired.
O'Meara, Gerard '56 (FgM) Boston, MA St. James the Apostle, Inc.
O'Meara, Gregory J. *s.j.* '02 (MIL)[P] Milwaukee, WI Jesuit Community at Marquette University.
O'Meara, Joseph P. '53 (NY) New York, NY Retired.
O'Meara, Joseph '67 (BAL) Retired.
O'Meara, Joseph '52 (NY) New York, NY Our Lady of Guadalupe at St. Bernard's.
O'Meara, Noel P. *c.s.sp.* '65 (BRK)[R] Long Island City, NY Holy Ghost Fathers of Ireland; [V] Long Island City, NY World Compassion Link; Councilors.
O'Meara, Thomas F. *o.p.* '62 (CHI)[N] River Forest, IL St. Thomas Aquinas Priory.
O'Melia, Edward A. '77 (DAV) Davenport, IA St. Mary's.
O'Mullane, Daniel '10 (PAT) Rockaway, NJ St. Cecilia's; Rockaway, NJ Sacred Heart.
O'Neal, James E. '80 (MO) On Duty Outside the Diocese; Army Chaplains.
O'Neal, Norman B. *s.j.* '59 (NO)[E] New Orleans, LA Jesuit High School.
O'Neal, Patrick '90 (PEO) Peoria, IL St. Philomena.
O'Neal, Shawn '00 (CHL) Bryson City, NC St. Joseph.
O'Neil, Edward '63 (NY) Mamaroneck, NY St. Vito.
O'Neil, Flann *o.f.m.* '52 (GLP) Ganado, AZ All Saints; St. Michaels, AZ St. Michael.
O'Neil, James W. *s.j.* '57 (BO)[D] Boston, MA Boston College High School.
O'Neil, James '85 (GF) Personnel Board.
O'Neil, Jim '85 (GF) Sidney, MT St. Matthew.
O'Neil, Joseph *m.s.* '93 (ORL) Orlando, FL Good Shepherd.
O'Neil, Kevin *c.ss.r.* '81 (WDC)[O] Washington, DC Holy

Redeemer College.
O'Neil, Michael '59 (SEA) Retired.
O'Neil, Rev. Msgr. Philip E. '54 (RCK) Rockford, IL St. Bernadette Retired.
O'Neil, Robert J. *m.h.m.* '65 (NY) New York, NY St. Mary; [DD] Hartsdale, NY Mill Hill Fathers Residence.
O'Neil, Thomas D. '69 (PIT) Washington, PA St. Hilary.
O'Neill, Anthony '11 (STP) Eagan, MN St. John Neumann; [E] Mendota Heights, MN Convent of the Visitation School.
O'Neill, Blane *o.f.m.* '51 (SHP) Ruston, LA St. Thomas Aquinas.
O'Neill, Brian E. '68 (CAM) Retired.
O'Neill, Daniel J. '76 (ALT) Southern Deanery; Somerset, PA St. Peter's.
O'Neill, Daniel *o.carm.* '69 (NEW) Teaneck, NJ St. Anastasia's.
O'Neill, Dennis B. '73 (CHI) Morton Grove, IL St. Martha.
O'Neill, Rev. Msgr. Edward M. '71 (MET) Colonia, NJ St. John Vianney; Diocesan Council of Catholic Women.
O'Neill, Rev. Msgr. Felix M. '55 (CAM) Retired.
O'Neill, George F. '97 (BGP) Brookfield, CT St. Joseph.
O'Neill, Hugh '77 (GLP) Retired.
O'Neill, James M. *c.s.b.* '86 (DET)[E] Novi, MI Catholic Central High School.
O'Neill, James '57 (ALB) Retired.
O'Neill, Rev. Msgr. James '54 (CHY) Casper, WY Saint Patrick's; Diocesan Pastoral Council Retired.
O'Neill, James '07 (TR) Moorestown, NJ Our Lady of Good Counsel.
O'Neill, James '85 (GF) Diocesan Consultors; Priests' Council.
O'Neill, Jeremiah '59 (LA) Alhambra, CA St. Thomas More Retired.
O'Neill, John D. *s.j.* '60 (DET)[K] Clarkston, MI Colombiere Center.
O'Neill, John J. *m.s.* '62 (NOR) Danielson, CT St. James; Brooklyn, CT Our Lady of La Salette.
O'Neill, John J. '67 (MO) Navy Reserve Chaplains Retired.
O'Neill, John (NSH)[A] Nashville, TN Aquinas College; [L] Nashville, TN Dominican Campus.
O'Neill, John *i.v.dei.* '00 (BRK) Woodside, NY Corpus Christi.
O'Neill, John *o.s.f.s.* '73 (ALN)[B] Center Valley, PA DeSales University; [K] Center Valley, PA Oblates of St. Francis de Sales.
O'Neill, John '00 (NY)[A] Yonkers, NY St. Joseph's Seminary.
O'Neill, Joseph P. '98 (DAL) Coppell, TX Dallas/Fort Worth Airport Catholic Chaplain.
O'Neill, Keith *o.f.m.conv.* '66 (SAV) Jesup, GA St. Joseph.
O'Neill, Rev. Msgr. Kevin S. '77 (HEL) Helena, MT Cathedral of St. Helena; Presbyteral Council; Vicar General; Diocesan Consultors; Diocesan Finance Council; Deaneries; Personnel Board.
O'Neill, Rev. Msgr. Kevin T. '61 (BUF)[G] Cheektowaga, NY Mary Queen of Angels Catholic School; [N] Lackawanna, NY Bishop Head Residence Retired.
O'Neill, Michael F. '76 (NO) Retired.
O'Neill, Michael *i.c.* '70 (SP) Seffner, FL St. Francis of Assisi.
O'Neill, Patrick G. '53 (SEA) Retired.
O'Neill, Patrick H. '67 (MIA) Office of Ecumenical and Inter–Faith Relations.
O'Neill, Patrick J. '90 (CHI) Palos Heights, IL St. Alexander.
O'Neill, Rev. Msgr. Patrick J. '45 (SD) La Mesa, CA Saint Martin of Tours Catholic Parish Retired.
O'Neill, Patrick '67 (MIA) Retired.
O'Neill, Raymond F. '66 (SP) Spring Hill, FL Saint Joan of Arc.
O'Neill, Richard V. '54 (SY) Marcy, NY Central New York Psychiatric Center Retired.
O'Neill, Robert '95 (STO) On Duty Outside the Diocese.
O'Neill, Seamus '74 (NY)[HH] New York, NY St. Patrick's International Inc.
O'Neill, Sean F. '03 (PH) Philadelphia, PA Incarnation of Our Lord.
O'Neill, Thomas D. '68 (PRO) West Warwick, RI St. Mary.
O'Neill, Thomas H. *s.j.* '90 (SFR)[E] San Francisco, CA St. Ignatius College Preparatory (Coed); [N] San Francisco, CA Jesuit Community at St. Ignatius College Preparatory.
O'Neill, Thomas '62 (FRS) Frazier Park, CA Our Lady of the Snows Mission.
O'Neill, Timothy H. '67 (Y) Hubbard, OH St. Patrick.
O'Neill, William J. '65 (PRO) Jamestown, RI St. Mark.
O'Neill, Rev. Msgr. William O. '67 (SAV) Savannah, GA Cathedral of St. John the Baptist; Vicars General.
O'Neill, William P. '61 (CLV) Hinckley, OH Our Lady of Grace; Judges in Second Instance Retired.
O'Neill, William R. *s.j.* '81 (OAK)[A] Berkeley, CA Jesuit School of Theology of Santa Clara University (Berkeley, California Campus); [L] Berkeley, CA Jesuit Fathers and Brothers.
O'Nyamwaro, Richard *a.j.* (CHI)[J] Chicago, IL Saint Joseph Hospital.
O'Rafferty, Patrick '51 (SAC) Retired.
O'Regan, Hugh H. '57 (BO) Senior Priests. Retired.
O'Reilly, Aidan '60 (SAC) Retired.
O'Reilly, Andrew *c.pp.s.* '73 (CIN)[N] Dayton, OH Provincial Office of the Cincinnati Province of the Society of the Precious Blood.
O'Reilly, Bernard M. '69 (PRO) Harrisville, RI St. Patrick.
O'Reilly, Daniel '03 (NY)[D] Yonkers, NY University Apostolate –Campus Ministry; [GG] Yonkers, NY University Apostolate; [GG] New York, NY Columbia University; New York, NY Notre Dame.
O'Reilly, Desmond T. '90 (SAC) El Dorado Hills, CA Holy Trinity.
O'Reilly, Edward M. '68 (NY) Military Chaplains Retired.
O'Reilly, Gabriel '67 (MIA) Davie, FL Saint David; Members.
O'Reilly, Gerald K. '85 (CHI) Mundelein, IL Santa Maria Del Popolo.
O'Reilly, James E. *s.j.* '57 (DET) Detroit, MI St. Peter Claver; [E] Detroit, MI Loyola High School.
O'Reilly, Joseph F. '56 (WH) Retired.
O'Reilly, Joseph '49 (SFD) Retired.
O'Reilly, Kevin P. '84 (WDC) Barnesville, MD St. Mary Church and Shrine of Our Lady of Fatima.
O'Reilly, Kevin '96 (NY)[A] Yonkers, NY St. Joseph's Seminary.
O'Reilly, Michael '96 (SAC) Roseville, CA St. Rose of Lima.
O'Reilly, Patrick J. '65 (OG) Retired.
O'Reilly, Rev. Msgr. Peter A. '61 (LA) Claremont, CA Our Lady of the Assumption Retired.
O'Reilly, Vincent P. '62 (SAC) Vacaville, CA St. Joseph.
O'Riley, Dennis H. '59 (PEO) Retired.
O'Riordan, James '64 (JKS) Retired.
O'Riordan, Jeremiah '67 (PAT)[Q] Chester, NJ Nazareth Village Retired.
O'Riordan, William '85 (NO) Belle Chasse, LA Our Lady of Perpetual Help; Deans.
O'Rorke, Rev. Msgr. James H. '61 (PAT) Presbyteral Council; College of Consultors Retired.
O'Rourke, Bryan A. '66 (STP) Retired.
O'Rourke, Charles *s.s.c.* '57 (OM)[J] St. Columbans, NE Missionary Society of St. Columban.
O'Rourke, Daniel '88 (GF) Lewistown, MT St. Leo; [J] Lewistown, MT St. Leo's Catholic Education Trust.
O'Rourke, David K. *o.p.* '62 (OAK)[L] Oakland, CA Order of Preachers (Province of Holy Name of Jesus – Western Dominican Province); Defenders of the Bond; Point Richmond, CA Our Lady of Mercy.
O'Rourke, Dennis '80 (PHX) Scouting, Catholic Committee on; Cave Creek, AZ St. Gabriel Roman Catholic Parish; Deans.
O'Rourke, Francis J. *c.ss.r.* '62 (NY)[DD] New York, NY Redemptorist Priests and Brothers, C.Ss.R.
O'Rourke, Francis J. '75 (CHL) Charlotte, NC St. Gabriel Retired.
O'Rourke, John F. *o.s.a.* '61 (VEN) Cape Coral, FL Saint Katharine Drexel.
O'Rourke, Kevin *o.p.* '54 (CHI) River Forest, IL St. Vincent Ferrer.
O'Rourke, Matthew J. *s.s.j.* '47 (BAL)[Q] Baltimore, MD St. Joseph's Manor.
O'Rourke, Michael J. *o.p.* '96 (NO)[E] New Orleans, LA Mount Carmel Academy.
O'Rourke, Michael *o.p.* '96 (NO) New Orleans, LA St. Dominic.
O'Rourke, P. Gerard '50 (SFR) Retired.
O'Rourke, Peter J. '99 (SCR) West Hazleton, PA Holy Name of Jesus Parish.
O'Rourke, Peter '64 (RVC) Stony Brook, NY L.I. State Veterans' Home.
O'Rourke, Richard *m.s.c.* '65 (AUS) Harker Heights, TX St. Paul Chong Hasang; Killeen/Temple.
O'Rourke, Robert *s.s.c.* '58 (PRO)[O] Bristol, RI St. Columban's Retirement House Retired.
O'Rourke, Robert *s.s.c.* '58 (OM)[J] St. Columbans Missionary Society of St. Columban Retired.
O'Rourke, Thomas J. '64 (HRT) Hamden, CT Ascension.
O'Rourke, William D. '58 (RVC) Franklin Square, NY St. Catherine of Sienna Retired.
O'Ryan, Colm '55 (LA) Beverly Hills, CA Good Shepherd Retired.
O'Shaughnessy, Denis (STA) Jacksonville, FL Mary Queen of Heaven.
O'Shaughnessy, Gerard *s.s.c.* '60 (SB) Fontana, CA St. Mary.
O'Shaughnessy, Gerard *s.s.c.* '60 (OM)[J] St. Columbans Missionary Society of St. Columban.
O'Shaughnessy, James J. '68 (NY)[E] Bronx, NY Cardinal Spellman High School.
O'Shaughnessy, Rev. Msgr. Michael A. '50 (VIC) Retired.
O'Shaughnessy, Patrick '68 (BLX) Retired.
O'Shea, Daniel *s.a.* '64 (BO)[N] Brockton, MA Chapel of Our Savior–Catholic Pastoral and Information Center; [U] Brockton, MA Chapel of Our Savior; [Z] Brockton, MA Chapel of Our Saviour.
O'Shea, Daniel *s.a.* '64 (NY)[DD] Brockton, MA Chapel of Our Savior.
O'Shea, David T. '61 (PT) Retired.
O'Shea, Gerard '66 (NY) Retired.
O'Shea, Howard *o.f.m.* '58 (NY)[DD] New York Franciscan Friars, Holy Name Province.
O'Shea, James B. '65 (WOR) Worcester, MA Our Lady of Lourdes; Deans; Presbyteral Council.
O'Shea, James D. '64 (SFD) Retired.
O'Shea, James *c.p.* '89 (FgM) New Rochelle, NY St. Paul of the Cross Province; New Rochelle, NY.
O'Shea, James *c.p.* '89 (NY)[DD] Pelham Manor, NY St. Vincent's Residence.
O'Shea, Jeremiah T. '64 (PIT) Bethel Park, PA St. Valentine; Priest Council.
O'Shea, John G. '60 (YAK) Kennewick, WA Holy Spirit.
O'Shea, John J. '50 (WCH) Retired.
O'Shea, John L. '81 (PIT) Pittsburgh, PA St. Sebastian.
O'Shea, Rev. Msgr. Lawrence '56 (DUL) Retired.
O'Shea, Michael James *o.f.m.* '54 (SFR) Burlingame, CA Our Lady of Angels.
O'Shea, Michael '52 (LA) Retired.
O'Shea, Patrick '61 (LA) On Duty Outside the Archdiocese.
O'Shea, Patrick *m.s.c.* '73 (SAT)[L] San Antonio, TX Missionaries of the Sacred Heart.
O'Shea, Philip *o.f.m.* '75 (BO)[Z] Boston, MA St. Anthony Shrine.
O'Shea, William D. '62 (PMB) North Palm Beach, FL St. Clare.
O'Shea, William J. '63 (JOL) Retired.
O'Sullivan, Brendan *s.s.c.* '70 (FgM) St Columbans, NE House of Post–Graduate Studies.
O'Sullivan, Brendan *s.s.c.* '70 (LA)[P] Los Angeles, CA Columban Fathers, Procure House.
O'Sullivan, Brendan *s.s.c.* '70 (OM)[J] St. Columbans Missionary Society of St. Columban.
O'Sullivan, Carrol '51 (LA) Santa Barbara, CA Our Lady of Mount Carmel Retired.
O'Sullivan, Cyril J. '80 (SFR) Lagunitas, CA St. Cecilia; Deans.
O'Sullivan, Daniel A. '63 (LA) Ventura, CA Sacred Heart Retired.
O'Sullivan, Daniel '60 (DET) Retired.
O'Sullivan, Daniel '70 (FgM) Boston, MA St. James the Apostle, Inc.
O'Sullivan, Denis A. '72 (SR) Santa Rosa, CA St. Rose of Lima.
O'Sullivan, Rev. Msgr. Francis G. '47 (BO) Peabody, MA St. John the Baptist; Senior Priests. Retired.
O'Sullivan, Rev. Msgr. Jeremiah '58 (SD) Coronado, CA Sacred Heart Catholic Parish Coronado Retired.
O'Sullivan, Rev. Msgr. John V. '68 (PT) Woodville, FL St. Stephen the Protomartyr.
O'Sullivan, Rev. Msgr. John V. '68 (PT) Tallahassee, FL Blessed Sacrament; Orders & Ministries, Commission for; Priests' Pension Plan, Board for.
O'Sullivan, John '50 (B) Retired.
O'Sullivan, Michael J. '55 (WDC) Retired.
O'Sullivan, Peter '83 (KCK) Topeka, KS Christ the King.
O'Sullivan, Raymond S. '68 (BO) Society of St. James the Apostle.; Boston, MA St. James the Apostle, Inc.
O'Sullivan, Sean A. *s.j.* '99 (CHI) Chicago, IL St. Procopius; [N] Chicago, IL Miguel Pro Jesuit Community.
O'Sullivan, Sean '64 (MIA) Retired.
O'Sullivan, Rev. Msgr. T. Brendan '56 (SAC) Members; Sacramento, CA St. Anthony Retired.
O'Sullivan, Thomas Carrol '51 (LA) Retired.
O'Sullivan, Timothy F. '94 (PH) Levittown, PA Immaculate Conception B.V.M.
O'Sullivan, Tracy *o.carm.* '62 (LA) Los Angeles, CA St. Raphael.
O'Toole, Brian P. '86 (WOR) Diocesan College of Consultors; Gardner, MA Our Lady of the Holy Rosary; Gardner, MA Sacred Heart of Jesus.
O'Toole, James '64 (FWT) Retired.
O'Toole, John M. '67 (PIT) Retired.
O'Toole, Lawrence J. *s.j.* '58 (BO)[U] Weston, MA Campion Health Center, Inc.
O'Toole, Matthew L. '95 (STL) St. Louis, MO St. Margaret of Scotland; [F] St. Louis, MO Christian Brothers College High School (C.B.C.).
O'Toole, Rev. Msgr. Patrick F. '60 (BRK) Retired.
O'Toole, Robert F. *s.j.* '67 (NY)[DD] New York, NY "America;" Residence and publication office of the America Press; [HH] New York, NY Gregorian University Foundation, The.
O'Toole, Timothy '89 (PMB) Released from Diocesan Assignment.
O'Toole, William F. '96 (GRY) Hammond, IN St. Casimir; Bishop's Council of Priests; Priests' Personnel Board.
O'Toole, Rev. Msgr. William P. '61 (LA) Alhambra, CA All Souls Retired.
Oajaca–Lopez, Gonzalo '08 (RVC) Brentwood, NY St. Anne's; Presbyteral Council.
Oakes, Edward T. *s.j.* '79 (CHI)[A] Mundelein, IL

University of St. Mary of the Lake/Mundelein Seminary.
Oakes, R. Eathan '03 (BEA) Port Arthur, TX St. James.
Oakham, Ronald A. *o.carm.* '77 (TUC) Council of Priests; Vicars Forane; All Vicars Forane; Tucson, AZ Saint Cyril of Alexandria Roman Catholic Parish – Tucson.
Oakland, Matthew T. '10 (SEA) Camas, WA St. Thomas Aquinas.
Oakshott, Ward B. '77 (SEA) Lynnwood, WA St. Thomas More Retired.
Oates, Eugene M. *c.ss.r.* '44 (STL)[O] Liguori, MO St. Clement Health Care Center Retired.
Oates, Thomas F. '63 (BO) Society of St. James the Apostle.
Oates, Thomas '63 (FgM) Boston, MA St. James the Apostle, Inc.
Obando, Gustavo '87 (BWN) Weslaco, TX San Martin de Porres.
Obasi, Augustine I. '97 (SB) Ontario, CA St. Elizabeth Ann Seton.
Obasi, John (PIT) Allegheny County, PA UPMC University of Pittsburgh Medical Center.
Obatama, Raphael '87 (BIR) Bessemer, AL St. Francis of Assisi.
Obayashi, Hal N. '02 (BO) Natick, MA St. Patrick.
Obaza, Theodore L. '61 (SCR) Retired.
Obele, Oliver O. *m.s.p.* '95 (GAL) Houston, TX St. Anne de Beaupre.
Obeng, Simon '89 (STV) On Duty Outside the Diocese.
Obeng, Simon (OG) U.S. Army Headquarters.
Obeng–Kyeremeh, Simon '89 (MO) Army Chaplains.
Ober, Lawrence M. *s.j.* '77 (CLV)[D] Cleveland, OH St. Ignatius High School.
Oberch, Rev. Msgr. Rick J. '85 (PEO) Defender of the Bond; [L] East Peoria, IL Mt. Alverno Novitiate; Promoter of Justice.
Oberg, Paul *s.s.j.* '85 (BIR) Birmingham, AL Our Lady of Fatima; [I] Birmingham, AL The Fatima Educational Foundation.
Oberle, Gerard *c.ss.r.* '55 (NEW) Newark, NJ St. James.
Oberle, James P. *s.s.* '87 (WDC) On Duty Outside the Archdiocese.
Oberle, James P. *s.s.* '87 (BAL)[Q] Baltimore Society of St. Sulpice, Province of the United States.
Oberle, James P. *s.s.* '87 (DAL)[A] Irving, TX Holy Trinity Seminary.
Obermeyer, Robert A. '61 (CIN) Judges Retired.
Obermiller, Edwin H. *c.s.c.* '96 (FTW) South Bend, IN; [B] University of Notre Dame Du Lac; [H] Notre Dame, IN Holy Cross Community, Corby Hall, University of Notre Dame; [H] Notre Dame, IN Congregation of Holy Cross, United States Province of Priests & Brothers.
Obero, Eduardo '93 (SJ) Ongoing Formation of Clergy.
Obersinner, Joseph L. *s.j.* '57 (SPK)[J] Spokane, WA Regis Community.
Oberstar, Richard G. *m.s.f.* (DUL) Brainerd, MN St. Mathias Retired.
Obersteiner, Ernest '77 (GLP) On Leave of Absence.
Oberto, Rev. Msgr. Peter '78 (MAR) Negaunee, MI St. Paul; [B] Negaunee, MI Negaunee St. Paul Endowment Fund; Judicial Vicar; Diocesan Judge.
Oberts, David P. '69 (SUP) Rice Lake, WI St. John Evangelist; Rice Lake, WI Our Lady of Lourdes; Rice Lake, WI Holy Trinity.
Obiatuegwu, Thomas '95 (MO) Army Chaplains.
Obidiegwu, Celestine '04 (TLS) Langley, OK St. Frances of Rome; Pryor, OK St. Mark's.
Obiechina, Jude M. *c.m.f.* '83 (LAF) Opelousas, LA St. Joseph.
Obiekezie, Matthew U. '85 (BRK) Astoria, NY St. Francis of Assisi.
Obiekwe, Kenneth '93 (ALX) Cloutierville, LA St. John the Baptist.
Obijekwu, Francis *s.m.m.m.* '06 (BAK) Enterprise, OR St. Katherine's.
Obikwelu, Uche '09 (AUS) College Station, TX St. Thomas Aquinas.
Obin, Arthur *o.m.i.* '64 (PMB) Riviera Beach, FL St. Francis of Assisi.
Obin, Gilbert *c.i.c.m.* '67 (SAT) San Antonio, TX St. Martin de Porres.
Obinwa, Charles '95 (TOL)[F] Lima, OH St. Rita's Medical Center; Delphos, OH St. John the Evangelist.
Obisike, Bonaventure '01 (SPK) Special Ministry.
Obiudu, Alfred U. '05 (WH) Salem, WV Sacred Heart; Clarksburg, WV St. James the Apostle.
Oblinger, Joseph B. '46 (HEL) West Yellowstone, MT Our Lady of the Pines Retired.
Obloj, Stanislaw '93 (DET) Plymouth, MI Our Lady of Good Counsel.
Obloy, Leonard G. '77 (CLV) Released from Diocesan Assignment.
Obol, Robert (TOL)[F] Toledo, OH Mercy Hospital St. Anne; [F] Oregon, OH Mercy Hospital St. Charles.
Oborny, Paul J. '63 (WCH) Harvest House; [K] Wichita, KS Marriage Encounter Retired.
Oborny, Rudolf F. '71 (LIN) Hebron, NE Sacred Heart; Diocesan Area CCD Directors; Deaneries and Deans.
Obregon, Miguel *o.f.m.* (OAK)[L] Oakland Franciscan Friars of California, (Province of St. Barbara).
Obregon–Vallejos, Miguel '81 (GAL) Sugar Land, TX St. Theresa.
Obrimski, Paul '70 (PH) Philadelphia, PA Immaculate Heart of Mary.
Obu–Mends, Francis JoJo '92 (BRK) Rockaway Point, NY Blessed Trinity Roman Catholic Church.
Obwaka, Sylvestre L. '10 (GLD) Manistee, MI St. Joseph; Manistee, MI Guardian Angels; Manistee, MI St. Mary of Mt. Carmel Shrine.
Obwona, Martin Larok *f.c.* '80 (OKL) Blackwell, OK St. Joseph's; Tonkawa, OK St. Joseph's.
Ocampo, Alfredo *c.p.* '11 (GAL)[O] Houston, TX Congregation of the Passion, Holy Name Passionist Community and Retreat Center.
Ocampo, Arturo M. *o.f.m.* '85 (IND) Indianapolis, IN Sacred Heart of Jesus Catholic Church, Indianapolis, Inc.; Indianapolis, IN St. Patrick Catholic Church, Indianapolis, Inc.
Ocampo, P. Ramón Conde *o.de.m.* '59 (PCE) Ponce, PR Santuario San Judas Tadeo.
Ocariz, Rev. Msgr. Fernando '71 (POD) Vicar General.
Ocasio, Edgardo Acosta '83 (MGZ) Sabana Grande, PR Church of San Isidro; Communications Media; Cursillos de Cristiandad.
Occeno, Adolfo (NY) Fishkill, NY Church of St. Mary, Mother of the Church.
Occhiuto, Joseph L. '79 (MRY) Santa Cruz, CA Holy Cross; Administrative Committee Priests' Pension Plan.
Ochalek, Arkadiusz '99 (MO) Army Reserve Chaplains; Military Chaplains.
Ochasi, Aloysius '01 (PH) Roslyn, PA St. John of the Cross; [Z] Huntingdon Valley, PA Sisters of the Holy Redeemer Provincialate.
Ochej, Tomasz '00 (VEN) Absent on Leave.
Ochetti, Jerome '02 (SB) Upland, CA St. Joseph; Elected Members.
Ochiabuto, Isidore '01 (SAN) Big Lake, TX St. Margaret of Cortona.
Ochieze, Oliver '88 (LR) Fairfield Bay, AR St. Francis Assisi; Clinton, AR St. Jude Church.
Ochoa, Anthony B. '10 (STL) St. Ann, MO Holy Trinity.
Ochoa, Carlos '09 (WIL) Dover, DE Holy Cross.
Ochoa, David '72 (LA) Huntington Park, CA St. Matthias.
Ochoa, Einer '85 (SAT) Cursillos of Christianity of the Archdiocese of San Antonio Retired.
Ochoa, Guillermo J. '11 (WOR) Milford, MA St. Mary of the Assumption; St. Mary.
Ochoa, Jorge Arturo *s.j.* '06 (OAK)[L] Berkeley, CA Jesuit Fathers and Brothers.
Ochoa, Jorge *m.c.c.j.* (CIN)[U] Cincinnati, OH Hispanic Ministry at St. Charles Borromeo, Archdiocese of Cincinnati.
Ochoa, Jorge *m.c.c.j.* '96 (LA) Los Angeles, CA St. Cecilia.
Ochoa, Rafael '78 (LA) Los Angeles, CA Immaculate Conception.
Ochoa, Steven *o.s.a.* '83 (LA) Ojai, CA St. Thomas Aquinas.
Ochoa–Lugo, Adrian *o.de.m.* '97 (SB) Riverside, CA St. Anthony of Padua.
Ochs, Bryan A. '11 (SEA) Renton, WA St. Anthony.
Ochs, Daniel L. '76 (COL) Columbus, OH St. Agatha.
Ochs, Robert J. *s.j.* '61 (CHI)[N] Chicago Chicago Province of the Society of Jesus–Provincial Office.
Ochs, Robert J. *s.j.* '61 (OAK)[L] Berkeley, CA Jesuit Fathers and Brothers.
Ochu, Austin Charles *s.m.a.* '92 (WDC)[O] Takoma Park, MD House of Studies.
Ochu, Austin Charles *s.m.a.* '92 (MO) DEPARTMENT OF VETERANS AFFAIRS HOSPITALS AND CHAPLAINS.
Ocilka, John A. '94 (CLV) Absent on Sick Leave.
Ocran, David '03 (LA) Los Angeles, CA St. Malachy.
Ocun, Godfred *a.j.* '96 (P)[J] Portland, OR Providence Health & Services–Oregon; [M] Beaverton, OR Sisters of St. Mary of Oregon.
Odbert, Jerome K. *s.j.* '69 (DET)[E] Detroit, MI University of Detroit Jesuit High School and Academy.
Oddo, Peter A. '61 (NEW) Retired.
Odemokpa, Paschal '79 (MO) DEPARTMENT OF VETERANS AFFAIRS HOSPITALS AND CHAPLAINS.
Odenbrett, Stephen *o.s.b.* '46 (MRY)[F] San Luis Obispo, CA Men's Residence.
Odermann, Valerian *o.s.b.* '73 (BIS)[A] Richardton, ND Assumption Abbey; [B] Bismarck, ND University of Mary; President's Council.
Odero, John (SCL) Freeport, MN St. Francis of Assisi; Bowlus, MN St. Stanislaus Kostka; Upsala, MN St. Edward's; Upsala, MN St. Mary.
Odey, Thomas E. (TOL) Retired.
Odeyemi, John (PIT) Pittsburgh, PA Epiphany.
Odien, Terry M. '73 (CAM) Ex Officio Members; Vicar for Clergy; Ex Officio Members; Advanced Studies for Priests; Ex Officio Members; Members; Cherry Hill, NJ The Catholic Community of Christ Our Light, Cherry Hill, N.J.
Odikanoro, Vincent '83 (NY)[W] Port Jervis, NY Bon Secours Community Hospital; Port Jervis, NY Bon Secours Community Hospital.
Odimmeywua, Augustine '90 (NEW) Elizabeth, NJ Union County Jail; Newark, NJ The Parish of the Transfiguration.
Odiong, Anthony '93 (AUS) West, TX St. Mary, Church of the Assumption; [L] Waco, TX St. Peter Catholic Student Center at Baylor University; Presbyteral Council.
Odoh, Malachy E. '01 (NEW) Nutley, NJ Our Lady of Mount Carmel.
Odor, Luke U. '83 (MO) DEPARTMENT OF VETERANS AFFAIRS HOSPITALS AND CHAPLAINS.
Odor, Luke U. (BO) Stow, MA St. Isidore.
Odorizzi, Thomas A. *c.o.* '92 (MET) New Brunswick, NJ St. Peter the Apostle; [I] New Brunswick, NJ The New Brunswick Congregation of the Oratory of St. Philip Neri; New Brunswick, NJ.
Odozor, Paulinus I. *c.s.sp.* (FTW)[B] University of Notre Dame Du Lac.
Odriozola, Antonio *s.s.s.* (CGS) Caguas, PR Santisimo Sacramento.
Oduro, Charles Akoto '89 (BRK) Brooklyn, NY St. Catherine of Genoa; [Q] Ghanaian Apostolate.
Oehmler, Gary W. '83 (PIT) McDonald, PA St. Alphonsus; Oakdale, PA St. Patrick.
Oelrich, Anthony '92 (SCL) St. Cloud, MN St. Mary's Cathedral of St. Cloud; St. Cloud, MN St. Augustine; [L] St. Cloud, MN Newman Center, Inc.; Campus Ministry; Continuing Formation of Priests; St. Cloud, MN Christ Church.
Oen, Edward J. *c.pp.s.* '64 (KCK) Baileyville, KS Sacred Heart; St. Benedict, KS St. Mary.
Oenbrink, Michael J. '99 (CHR) Hilton Head Island, SC St. Francis By the Sea.
Oesterle, John G. '67 (PIT) Allegheny County, PA Mercy Health System of Pittsburgh–Pittsburgh Mercy Hospital.
Oestreich, Brian W. '93 (NU) Appleton, MN St. John; Madison, MN St. Michael; Prairie Correctional Facility; Committee on Parishes.
Ofalsa, Rheo C. '11 (OM) Graduate Studies.
Offeh, Joseph Mary '91 (SY) Binghamton, NY St. Mary of the Assumption.
Offerman, Paul '57 (SFS) Bridgewater, SD St. Stephen.
Offor, Celsius '95 (LKC) Jennings, LA Our Lady of Perpetual Help; Welsh, LA St. Joseph; Presbyteral Council.
Offor, John '02 (OAK) Fremont, CA Holy Spirit.
Offor, Oliver (NY) Pelham Manor, NY Our Lady of Perpetual Help.
Offutt, Rev. Msgr. Bradley S. '86 (KC) Chancellor; Consultors; Building Commission; Special Assignment; Kansas City, MO Cathedral of Immaculate Conception.
Offutt, J. James '62 (JC) Centralia, MO Holy Spirit; Judges.
Ofoegbu, Jerome '80 (NY) Bronx, NY St. Helena.
Oforchukwu, Joachim *c.s.sp.* '90 (CAM) New Jersey State Psychiatric Hospital; Hammonton, NJ Saint Mary of Mount Carmel Parish, Hammonton, N.J.
Ofori–Domah, John '81 (LC) Camp Douglas, WI St. James; Camp Douglas, WI St. Michael.
Oganda, Joseph '10 (BEL) Belleville, IL Cathedral of St. Peter.
Ogbemure, Raymond '74 (OAK) Richmond, CA St. Cornelius.
Ogbonna, Christian Iheanyichukwu '79 (ALX) Winnfield, LA Our Lady of Lourdes.
Ogbonna, Joseph '02 (SAN) Eden, TX St. Charles.
Ogbonna, Leonard '93 (BEA)[B] Beaumont, TX CHRISTUS Health Southeast Texas – CHRISTUS Hospital – St. Elizabeth.
Ogbonna, Stanislaus *c.s.sp.* '73 (NY) Monticello, NY St. Peter; Fallsburg, NY Sullivan Correctional Facility.
Ogbuji, Udochukwu Vincent '97 (LR)[H] Jonesboro, AR Holy Angels Convent–Motherhouse.
Ogden, Louis P. '85 (HBG) Middletown, PA Seven Sorrows of the Blessed Virgin Mary; Presbyteral Council; Consultors, College.
Oge, Raymond J. '67 (STL) Retired.
Ogg, Thomas '68 (CHY) St. Joseph's Society for Priests (Clergy Mutual Benefit Society) Retired.
Oggioni, Paul *sd.c* '70 (PH)[L] Springfield, PA Divine Providence Village; [B] Springfield, PA Servants of Charity Sd.C.
Ogle, Rev. Msgr. Sean G. '77 (BRK) Long Island City, NY Our Lady of Mount Carmel; Diocesan Finance Council.
Ogonwa, Stephen '01 (ORL) Ormond Beach, FL Prince of Peace.
Ogorevc, Metod *o.f.m.* '92 (CHI) Lemont, IL Slovenian Catholic Mission; [N] Lemont, IL The Slovene Franciscan Fathers, Order of Friars Minor, Commissariat of the Holy Cross.
Ogorzaly, Adam '85 (ROC) Rochester, NY St. Stanislaus.
Ogrodowski, Rev. Msgr. William M. '75 (PIT) Defenders of the Bond.
Oguagua, Thomas E. *s.j.* '05 (CHI)[C] Chicago, IL

Jesuit Community at Loyola University Chicago.
Oguamana, Mark E. '83 (WIL) Veterans Admin.
Ogumere, Augustine *c.s.sp.* '82 (PHX) Sun City, AZ St. Clement of Rome Roman Catholic Parish.
Ogumoro, Isidro T. '89 (CHK) Tinian, MP San Jose; [A] Tinian, MP St. Joseph Catholic School; Presbyteral Council; St. Joseph Catholic School (Tinian).
Ogurchock, John J. *m.m.* '54 (FgM) Maryknoll, NY MARYKNOLL.
Oh, Paul Saewan '83 (OM) Omaha, NE St. Andrew Kim Taegon Catholic Community.
Ohajunwa, Martin E. '00 (BEL) Flora, IL St. Stephen.
Ohanete, Michael '96 (LA) Lancaster, CA Sacred Heart.
Ohankwere, Desmond C. *m.s.p.* '92 (GAL) Houston, TX St. Nicholas.
Ohlig, John '95 (AMA) Amarillo, TX St. Joseph's.
Ohlinger, Vincent *s.v.d.* '68 (MIL)[P] East Troy, WI Divine Word Missionaries.
Ohm, Edward U. '92 (MO) On Duty Outside the Diocese; Army Chaplains.
Ohmann, Daniel F. *m.m.* '55 (FgM) Maryknoll, NY MARYKNOLL.
Ohner, John M. *o.s.a.* '74 (JOL) Homer Glen, IL Our Mother of Good Counsel.
Ohno, Ignatius F. *s.j.* '92 (SEA)[A] Seattle, WA Seattle University; [M] Seattle, WA Arrupe Jesuit Community at Seattle University.
Ohuche, Evaristus C. '02 (NY) Bronx, NY Blessed Sacrament.
Oiland, Kevin '09 (SPK) Colville, WA Immaculate Conception; Ione, WA St. Bernard; Colville, WA Sacred Heart of Jesus; Metaline Falls, WA St. Joseph; Colville, WA Pure Heart of Mary.
Ojeda, Uriel '07 (SAC) Redding, CA Our Lady of Mercy.
Oji, Joseph Kalu *c.s.sp.* '95 (R) Cary, NC St. Michael the Archangel.
Ojibway, V. Paul *s.a.* '78 (WDC)[B] Washington, DC Atonement Seminary–Franciscan Friars of the Atonement.
Ojibway, V. Paul *s.a.* '78 (NY)[DD] Garrison, NY Franciscan Friars of the Atonement, Minister General Office; [DD] Garrison Graymoor Ecumenical and Interreligious Institute; General Council.
Okafor, Bernard '85 (CHI) Chicago, IL St. John de la Salle.
Okafor, Gabriel '99 (DEN)[H] Denver, CO Saint Joseph Hospital.
Okafor, Gregory '88 (TUC) Tucson, AZ Saint Pius X Roman Catholic Parish – Tucson.
Okafor, Jerome '83 (FAR) Lamoure, ND Assumption of Mary; La Moure, ND Holy Rosary Church of La Moure; Lamoure, ND St. Raphael's Church of Verona.
Okafor, Jude '96 (FAR) Walhalla, ND St. Boniface Church of Walhalla; Walhalla, ND Sts. Nereus & Achilleus Church of Neche.
Okafor, Patrick Chudi '92 (RVC) Stony Brook, NY Stony Brook University Hospital.
Okafor, Patrick '96 (RVC) Stony Brook, NY Stony Brook University Hospital.
Okafor, Samuel '99 (LA) Los Angeles, CA St. Jerome.
Okagbue, Bartholomew '88 (GR)[G] Muskegon, MI Mercy Health Partners.
Okeahialam, George *m.s.p.* '02 (BEA) Liberty, TX Our Mother of Mercy; Raywood, TX Sacred Heart.
Okeahialam, Uju Patrick *c.s.sp.* '94 (PBL) Appointed; Pueblo, CO St. Francis Xavier.
Okechukwu, Michael K. *s.s.j.* '11 (WDC) Washington, DC Our Lady of Perpetual Help.
Okeiyi, Athanasius N. '91 (LR)[K] Pocahontas, AR St. Paul the Apostle Catholic Church – Capital Improvement Trust Fund; Corning, AR St. Joseph the Worker Church; Pocahontas, AR St. Paul the Apostle; Pocahontas, AR St. John the Baptist.
Okeiyi, Emmanuel '03 (RVC) Roslyn, NY St. Francis Hospital.
Okeke, Anselm '98 (RVC) Smithtown, NY St. Catherine of Siena Hospital.
Okeke, Charles '11 (ATL) Johns Creek, GA St. Benedict.
Okeke, Christopher '91 (LR) Mountain View, AR St. Mary Church; Mountain Home, AR St. Peter the Fisherman.
Okeke, Gerald '01 (IND) Richmond, IN Holy Family Catholic Church, Richmond, Inc.; Richmond, IN St. Andrew Catholic Church, Richmond, Inc.; Richmond, IN St. Mary Catholic Church, Richmond, Inc.
Okeke, Kizito '95 (ATL) Douglasville, GA St. Theresa of the Child Jesus.
Okeke, Stephen '96 (NY) Manhattan, NY New York University Medical Center; New York, NY St. Stephen and Our Lady of the Scapular.
Okenedo, Marcelinus *s.m.m.m.* '04 (FRS) Kerman, CA St. Patrick; Tranquillity, CA St. Paul.
Okere, Bartholomew N. '90 (LR) North Little Rock, AR St. Augustine.
Okere, Michael C. '91 (CHR) Columbia, SC Saint Martin de Porres; Presbyteral Council.
Okere, Remigius C. *c.s.sp.* '94 (DM) Granger, IA Assumption of the Blessed Virgin Mary.
Okhuoya, Kizito '96 (OM) Omaha, NE St. Wenceslaus.
Okiria, Richard P. '86 (HRT) Waterbury, CT St. Joseph; Waterbury, CT St. Patrick.
Okochi, Augustine '93 (RVC) Valley Stream, NY Franklin Medical Center Hospital.
Okochi, Chux '88 (RVC) Malverne, NY Our Lady of Lourdes; Serving Outside the Diocese.
Okochi, Chux '88 (NY) Bronx, NY Calvary Hospital; [X] Bronx, NY Calvary Hospital.
Okogba, Joseph '80 (FAR) Drayton, ND St. Edward's Church of Drayton; Pembina, ND Assumption Church of Pembina.
Okokon, Bernard '85 (CHR) Clemson, SC St. Andrew.
Okoli, Christopher '92 (RVC) Bay Shore, NY Southside Hospital; Islip Terrace, NY St. Peter the Apostle.
Okoli, Eugene '93 (DAL) Allen, TX St. Jude.
Okoli, Francis '00 (NY) Manhattan, NY Beth Israel Medical Center; Bellevue Hospital, Chapel of Our Lady Helper of the Sick; New York, NY Epiphany.
Okoli, Gerald C. '10 (GLD) Alpena, MI St. Anne; Alpena, MI St. Bernard; Alpena, MI St. John the Baptist.
Okoli, Jovita '96 (DET) Judges; Detroit, MI St. Jude.
Okon, Alan J. '98 (PH) Norristown, PA Holy Saviour; [D] Royersford, PA Pope John Paul II High School.
Okonkwo, Barthlomew I. '98 (BRK) Long Island Jewish Hospital.
Okonkwo, Bartholomew (BRK) Floral Park, NY Our Lady of the Snows.
Okonkwo, Ben '84 (IND)[G] Indianapolis, IN St. Vincent Hospital and Health Care Center, Inc.
Okonkwo, Ignatius '98 (BEL) Eldorado, IL St. Mary; Elizabethtown, IL St. Joseph; Harrisburg, IL St. Mary.
Okonkwo, Jovita '97 (TLS) Sapulpa, OK Sacred Heart.
Okonkwo, Patrick E. '04 (NU) Silver Lake, MN Church of the Holy Family; Winsted, MN Holy Trinity.
Okonski, Joseph F. '90 (PH) Philadelphia, PA St. Athanasius.
Okore, Innocent '93 (LR) Arkadelphia, AR St. Mary; Malvern, AR St. John the Baptist.
Okorie, Ferdinand *c.m.f.* '09 (CHI) Chicago, IL Our Lady of Guadalupe; [N] Oak Park Claretian Missionaries USA Eastern Province.
Okorie, Onyema '99 (MO) Air Force Chaplains; On Duty Outside the Diocese.
Okoro, Alexander A. '86 (COV) Veterans Hospital.
Okoro, Bonaventure '02 (RCK) Lee, IL St. James.
Okoro, Damasus *c.s.sp.* '01 (PBL) Holly, CO St. Frances of Rome; Lamar, CO St. Francis De Sales–Our Lady of Guadalupe; Springfield, CO Our Lady of the Annunciation.
Okoro, George (STO) Stockton, CA Presentation Church (Pastor of).
Okoro, John '95 (OWN) Calhoun, KY St. Sebastian; Calhoun, KY St. Charles Borromeo.
Okoro, Martin *c.m.f.* '97 (NEW) Hoboken, NJ Our Lady of Grace and Saint Joseph Parish.
Okoroafor, Augustine (HRT) Meriden, CT St. Mary; Meriden, CT St. Joseph.
Okorobia, Gregory (MOB) Enterprise, AL St. John.
Okorochukwu, Pius (OKL) Judges.
Okoroh, Patrick (GRY)[D] Crown Point, IN Franciscan St. Anthony Health – Crown Point.
Okoroji, Ignatius *s.d.v.* '04 (PAT)[N] Florham Park, NJ Father Justin Vocationary; Florham Park, NJ.
Okorougo, Charles '87 (LKC)[B] Lake Charles, LA CHRISTUS Health Southwestern Louisiana.
Okot, William *a.j.* '99 (PIT) Pittsburgh, PA St. Bede.
Okoth, Crispin '90 (SEA) Seattle, WA St. John the Evangelist.
Okoth, George '89 (MO) Army Chaplains.
Okoye, Charles '92 (NEW) Hackensack, NJ Hackensack University Medical Center.
Okoye, James C. *c.s.sp.* '70 (CHI) Chicago, IL St. Mary Magdalene; [B] Chicago, IL Catholic Theological Union.
Okpala, Paulinus '01 (ROC) Hornell, NY Our Lady of the Valley.
Okpalauwaekwe, Emmanuel '91 (NY) Manhattan, NY Harlem Hospital; [E] Bronx, NY Cardinal Hayes High School.
Okpara, Benson Claret '91 (Y) Canton, OH St. Mary/St. Benedict Parish.
Okpara, Theophilus '96 (LR) Lake Village, AR Holy Spirit Church; Lake Village, AR Our Lady of the Lake; Crossett, AR Holy Cross.
Okpe, Balonwu Augustine (COL) Delaware, OH St. Mary.
Okpechi, Chukwubikem *o.p.* '76 (HBG) Hershey, PA St. Joan of Arc; Hershey, PA Milton J. Hershey Medical Center.
Okpogba, Desmond '89 (TLS) Sallisaw, OK St. Francis Xavier.
Okumu, Richard U. '81 (DAV) Camanche, IA Church of the Visitation.
Okumu, Stephen '86 (SEA) Seattle, WA St. Therese.
Okure, Aniedi *o.p.* '80 (WDC)[X] Washington, DC Africa Faith & Justice Network.
Okwara, Marcel E. *c.ss.r.* '07 (BR) Baton Rouge, LA St. Gerard Majella.
Okwaraocha, Emmanuel (AUS) Austin, TX St. Theresa.
Okwir, Martin '90 (BO) Charlestown, MA St. Francis de Sales; [S] Cambridge, MA Youville Hospital & Rehabilitation Center, Inc.
Okwumuo, Patrick '00 (BEL) Belleville, IL St. Augustine of Canterbury.
Okwuzu, Augustine *s.m.m.m.* (CLV) Cleveland, OH Our Lady of Peace.
Olaleye, Patrick (DAL) Coppell, TX St. Ann.
Olbrys, Mariusz '07 (BGP) Leave of Absence.
Olczak, Joseph M. *o.s.p.p.e.* '65 (PH)[Y].
Oldani, Louis J. *s.j.* '64 (KC)[J] Kansas City, MO Rockhurst Jesuit Community.
Oldenski, Kenneth E. '66 (PIT) Retired.
Oldershaw, Robert H. '62 (CHI) Evanston, IL St. Nicholas Retired.
Oldfield, Albert E. '59 (SCR) Retired.
Oldfield, John *o.a.r.* '63 (NY)[B] Suffern, NY Tagaste Monastery.
Oldham, David A. '03 (LIN) Rulo, NE Immaculate Conception; [C] Falls City, NE Sacred Heart School; Advocates.
Olds, Daryl *c.m.f.* '92 (PHX) Prescott, AZ Sacred Heart Roman Catholic Parish; Temple City, CA.
Olds, Steven '88 (ORL) On Duty Outside the Diocese; [A] Boynton Beach, FL St. Vincent de Paul Regional Seminary; Censor of Books.
Olea, Mario Roberto *s.v.d.* '87 (OAK) Hayward, CA St. Joachim.
Olek, Ralph F. *s.m.* '74 (ATL)[C] Atlanta, GA Marist School.
Oleksiak, Donald P. '89 (CLV) College of Consultors; Clergy Personnel Board; Garfield Heights, OH SS. Peter and Paul; Presbyteral Council.
Oleksy, Kazimierz *s.d.s.* '92 (SAT) Jourdanton, TX St. Matthew's; [L] Falls City, TX Salvatorian Fathers Community of Texas.
Oleksy, Stanislaw *s.d.s.* '82 (SAT) Bandera, TX St. Stanislaus; [L] Falls City, TX Salvatorian Fathers Community of Texas.
Oleksy, Wojciech Jan '11 (CHI) Palatine, IL St. Thomas of Villanova.
Olendzki, Rev. Msgr. Joaquim J. '58 (NY) Red Hook, NY St. Christopher; Tivoli, NY St. Sylvia.
Olenick, John *c.ss.r.* '03 (PH) Philadelphia, PA Visitation B.V.M.
Olenowski, Mark '85 (PAT) Montville, NJ St. Pius X; Priestly Life Committee.
Olesik, William J. '72 (NOR) Pontifical Association of the Holy Childhood; Pontifical Society for the Propagation of the Faith; Tolland, CT St. Matthew.
Oleszczuk, Adam *s.v.d.* '98 (CHI)[N] Techny, IL Society of the Divine Word, Provincial Headquarters–Chicago Prov.
Olges, H. Anthony '70 (L) Louisville, KY St. Elizabeth of Hungary; Louisville, KY Holy Family; Louisville, KY St. Therese; Priest Personnel Commission.
Olguin, Jacinto '74 (LAR) Ex Officio Members; Laredo, TX St. Patrick.
Olguin, Luis '92 (SY) Utica, NY St. John; Utica, NY St. Mary of Mt. Carmel/Blessed Sacrament; Rome, NY Walsh Regional Medical Unit; Special Assignment.
Oligschlaeger, P. Gregory '93 (JC) Martinsburg, MO St. Joseph; Martinsburg, MO Church of the Resurrection; Appointed Members; Jonesburg, MO St. Patrick; Montgomery City, MO Immaculate Conception; Judges; Diocesan Consultors; Priestly and Religious Vocations Committee.
Olikkara, Joseph *m.s.t.* '87 (CC)[D] Corpus Christi, TX CHRISTUS Spohn Hospital Corpus Christi – Shoreline; Corpus Christi, TX Our Lady of Perpetual Help.
Olinger, Gerry *c.s.c.* '10 (P)[B] University of Portland; [L] Portland, OR Holy Cross Fathers & Brothers, C.S.C. – University of Portland.
Olisaemeka, Justin '01 (BEL) Centralia, IL St. Mary; Sandoval, IL St. Lawrence.
Olivares, Jesus *c.s.* '97 (KCK) Hispanic Ministry.
Olivares, Jesus *c.s.* (KC) Kansas City, MO Holy Rosary.
Olivares, Romeo D. *c.i.c.m.* '74 (SAT) Lytle, TX St. Andrew.
Olivas, Abel *o.f.m.* (GLP) St. Michaels, AZ St. Michael.
Olivas, J. Alfredo '81 (ELP) Absent on Leave.
Olive, Alphonsus *c.ss.r.* '86 (BAL) Annapolis, MD St. Mary.
Olive, Rodney J. *c.ss.r.* '86 (FgM) Brooklyn, NY AMERICAN REDEMPTORIST FATHERS.
Oliveira, Gastao A. '72 (FR) Fall River, MA Santo Christo.
Oliveira, Joel D. '54 (PRO) Retired.
Oliveira, John J. '77 (FR) New Bedford, MA Our Lady of Mt. Carmel; New Bedford, MA St. John the Baptist; Diocesan Consultors; Director of Portuguese Ministry.
Oliveira, Rev. Msgr. John J. '66 (FR) New Bedford, MA St. Mary's; Holy Childhood Association, The; Missionary Cooperative Plan; Permanent Diaconate Program; Propagation of the Faith.
Oliveira, Manoel J. '04 (NEW) Newark, NJ St. Benedict's.
Oliveira, Robert A. '77 (FR) New Bedford, MA Holy Name of the Sacred Heart of Jesus.

Oliveira, Vitor '73 (SPR) Ludlow, MA Our Lady of Fatima.
Olivencia, Ramon '97 (ARE) Seminary Board and Vocation Program.
Oliver, Harry T. *s.j.* (PHX)[B] Phoenix, AZ Brophy College Preparatory.
Oliver, James M. '88 (PH) On Special or Other Archdiocesan Assignment; Philadelphia, PA St. Philip Neri; The Chancery; Defenders of the Bond; Office for Clergy; Promoters of Justice.
Oliver, John '82 (STA) Absent or Sick Leave.
Oliver, Marc K. '89 (NY)[GG] Kingston, NY Culinary Institute of America; [GG] Kingston, NY Dutchess Community College; Kingston, NY St. Peter; Hyde Park, NY Hyde Park, P.J. Kenedy Memorial Chapel of Our Lady of the Way.
Oliver, Robert J. *b.h.* (BO) Assistant to the Moderator of the Curia for Canonical Affairs.
Oliver, Robert W. '00 (BO) Associates; [A] Brighton, MA St. John Seminary.
Oliver, William A. '77 (GAL) Houston, TX St. Thomas More; [S] Houston, TX The St. Thomas More Parish School Endowment Foundation.
Olivera, Carlos Alberto '84 (SJ) Chinese Catholic Community; Santa Clara, CA Chinese Catholic Community; Santa Clara, CA St. Clare.
Oliveras, Evaristo *c.m.* '88 (SJN) San Juan, PR San Vicente de Paul; Santurce, PR Hospital Pavia–Santurce; [B] San Juan, PR Colegio San Vicente de Paul.
Oliveras, Jose '95 (ARE) Morovis, PR Nuestra Senora del Carmen.
Olivere, Michael S. '94 (PH) Philadelphia, PA Divine Mercy Parish.
Oliveri, Armand *s.d.b.* '50 (SFR) San Francisco, CA SS. Peter and Paul.
Oliveri, Richard H. '66 (PAT) Retired.
Oliverio, Rev. Msgr. Francis E. '56 (NY) Retired.
Olivero, Michael A. '74 (CHI) Mt. Prospect, IL St. Cecilia.
Olivier, Harry T. *s.j.* '57 (PHX)[F] Phoenix, AZ Society of Jesus.
Olivier, John H. *s.s.* '47 (BAL)[M] Baltimore, MD St. Charles Villa; [Q] Baltimore Society of St. Sulpice, Province of the United States Retired.
Olivier, John H. *s.s.* '47 (MAR) Retired.
Olivieri, Humbert '77 (MAN) Retired.
Olivieri, Joel D. '54 (BO) Senior Priests. Retired.
Ollendick, William *o.f.m.* '01 (DET) Southfield, MI Church of the Transfiguration.
Ollison, Vernetta (P)[J] Portland, OR Providence Health & Services–Oregon.
Olmer, Vernon *o.f.m.* '62 (SFD) Montrose, IL St. Rose of Lima; Teutopolis, IL St. Francis of Assisi; [K] Teutopolis, IL St. Francis Assisi Friary.
Olmo, Luis S. *o.f.m.* '85 (SJN) Carolina, PR Santa Clara de Asis.
Olmstead, Daryl '75 (SAL) Hays, KS St. Nicholas of Myra Parish; Munjor, KS St. Francis of Assisi Parish.
Olnhausen, James Robert '70 (AUS) Giddings, TX St. Margaret; Giddings, TX St. Mary; State School.
Olnhausen, James '70 (AUS) Brenham/La Grange.
Olnhausen, James '70 (AUS) Presbyteral Council; College of Consultors.
Olobo, Leonard *c.s.c.* '04 (FgM) Notre Dame, IN HOLY CROSS MISSION CENTER; [H] Notre Dame Congregation of Holy Cross, United States Province of Priests & Brothers; [B] University of Notre Dame Du Lac; [H] Notre Dame, IN Holy Cross Community, Corby Hall, University of Notre Dame.
Olona, Rev. Msgr. Richard '70 (SFE) Albuquerque, NM Risen Savior Catholic Community; Ecumenical Commission and Interreligious Affairs; College of Consultors.
Olowin, Rev. Msgr. Jan C. '68 (E) Emlenton, PA St. Michael; [Q] Emlenton, PA Clarion University of Pennsylvania.
Oloyede, Samuel '00 (CHR) Summerton, SC St. Mary; Santee, SC St. Ann.
Ols, James R. '75 (CLV) Elyria Township, OH St. Vincent de Paul.
Olsavsky, John R. '62 (CLV) Judges in Second Instance; Presbyteral Council; Chagrin Falls, OH St. Joan of Arc Retired.
Olsavsky, John R. (Y) Judges.
Olsem, Andrew D. '67 (WIN) Retired.
Olsen, Arthur J. '99 (CHI) Chicago, IL St. Hilary.
Olsen, Brian A. '04 (RCK) Loves Park, IL St. Bridget.
Olsen, Charles R. *s.j.* '68 (SAC)[C] Sacramento, CA Jesuit High School; [H] Carmichael, CA Sacramento Jesuit Community.
Olsen, Eric F. '09 (STL) Florissant, MO St. Norbert.
Olsen, Eric S. '02 (OM) Wynot, NE Holy Family Parish of Cedar County; Deans; Deans.
Olsen, Kenneth '73 (P)[J] Eugene, OR Sacred Heart Medical Center; Springfield, OR St. Michael Catholic Church.
Olson, David P. '98 (LC) La Crosse, WI Blessed Sacrament; Appointed Members.
Olson, Eric E. '84 (MAR) Escanaba, MI St. Joseph & St. Patrick.
Olson, Hans M. '83 (SEA) Everett, WA St. Mary Magdalen; Presbyteral Council; College of Consultors.
Olson, James P. '88 (PH) East Lansdowne, PA St. Cyril of Alexandria; [A] Wynnewood, PA Theological Seminary of St. Charles Borromeo, Overbrook; [D] Drexel Hill, PA Monsignor Bonner and Archbishop Prendergast Catholic High School.
Olson, John E. '07 (WIL) Easton, MD SS. Peter and Paul.
Olson, Michael F. '94 (FWT) On Duty Outside the Diocese.
Olson, Rev. Msgr. Michael F. '94 (DAL)[A] Irving, TX Holy Trinity Seminary.
Olson, Michael P. '94 (GR) Retired.
Olson, Rev. Msgr. Michael '94 (FWT) Consultors.
Olson, Randy G. '90 (LC) Leave of Absence.
Olson, Ronald *o.f.m.conv.* '58 (SUP) Superior, WI Holy Assumption of the B.V.M.; Superior, WI St. William; Pastoral Consultors.
Olson, Theodore '72 (ORG) Buena Park, CA St. Pius V; Council of Priests; Judges; Consultors.
Olson, Thomas '73 (SCL) Kimball, MN Church of Saint Anne; Watkins, MN St. Nicholas; Defensor Vinculi; Diocesan Priests Pension Plan Trustees.
Olsovsky, George J. '56 (GAL) Retired.
Olszamowski, Leon M. *s.m.* '76 (DET)[D] Pontiac, MI Notre Dame Preparatory School and Marist Academy; Atlanta, GA; Boston, MA.
Olszewski, Clarence A. '57 (HBG) Retired.
Olszewski, Daniel D. '51 (SCR) Retired.
Olszewski, Gregory J. '06 (CLV) Brookpark, OH Mary Queen of the Apostles Parish.
Olszewski, John S. '47 (NEW) Retired.
Olszewski, Laurence M. *c.s.c.* '64 (FTW)[H] Notre Dame Congregation of Holy Cross, United States Province of Priests & Brothers.
Olszewski, Laurence *c.s.c.* '64 (ORL)[F] Cocoa Beach, FL Congregation of Holy Cross, United States Province.
Olszewski, Michael '03 (SAC) Vallejo, CA St. Catherine of Siena.
Olszewski, Paul A. '93 (CAM) Millville, NJ The Parish of All Saints, Millville, N.J.
Olszewski, Ronald W. E. *o.s.f.s.* '74 (TOL)[C] Toledo, OH St. Francis de Sales High School; [H] Toledo, OH; [H] St. Francis de Sale High School Endowment Fund, Inc.; Toledo, OH.
Olszyk, Thomas P. '71 (MIL) On Duty Outside the Archdiocese.
Olszyk, Rev. Msgr. Thomas P. '71 (MO) Judicial Vicar; Presbyteral Council.
Olugbami, Godwin (JOL) Frankfort, IL St. Anthony.
Olzacki, Bogdan *o.s.p.p.e.* '01 (CHI) Harwood Heights–Norridge, IL St. Rosalie.
Olzacki, Tadeuz (ORL) Summerfield, FL St. Mark the Evangelist.
Omalanga, Jules Omba '93 (STP) North Memorial Hospital; [S] St. Paul, MN Francophone African Chaplaincy.
Omana, Max B. '79 (MO) Air Force Chaplains.
Ombao, Manny '70 (AGN) Agana, GU San Juan Bautista.
Omeaku, Fidelis C. '08 (LA) Palmdale, CA St. Mary.
OMearain, Rev. Msgr. Ciaran P. '60 (CAM) Retired.
Omenihu, Anthony '96 (NY) Washingtonville, NY St. Mary; Judges.
Omernick, Kenneth E. '74 (MIL) Hartland, WI St. Charles.
Omogo, Peter O. '04 (GR) Fremont, MI All Saints; White Cloud, MI St. Joseph's.
Omollo, Peter Otieno *s.j.* '05 (CHI)[C] Chicago, IL Jesuit Community at Loyola University Chicago.
Omolo, Gilbert Otieno *c.p.* '07 (BRK)[R] Jamaica, NY Immaculate Conception Monastery.
Omotu, Charles '94 (RVC) Bellmore, NY St. Barnabas the Apostle.
Omwando, George O. '07 (CHI) Chicago Ridge, IL Our Lady of the Ridge.
Onate–Melendez, Refugio (ATL) Norcross, GA Saint Patrick.
Onderko, John M. '62 (PEO) Retired.
Ondo, Michael A. '54 (LFT) Retired.
Ondreyka, Richard J. *m.s.* '54 (CLV) Retired.
Onegiu, Benedict '93 (PHX) Cave Creek, AZ St. Gabriel Roman Catholic Parish.
Oneko, Chrispin Q. B. '90 (OWN) Hawesville, KY Immaculate Conception; Lewisport, KY St. Columba.
Oneyeabor, Ukachukwu '86 (TUC)[D] Tucson, AZ Carondelet St. Mary's Hospital.
Ong, Antonio '92 (CHI)[M] Wheeling, IL Addolorata Villa.
Ong, Tony '83 (DET) Royal Oak, MI St. Dennis.
Ongaro, Mario *m.c.c.j.* '51 (CIN)[N] Cincinnati, OH Comboni Missionaries (Verona Fathers)–Comboni Mission Center Retired.
Oni, Andrew (NY) Elmsford, NY Our Lady of Mt. Carmel.
Onida, George *s.m.* '86 (BAL)[T] Sykesville, MD St. Joseph Catholic Community Endowment Trust; Eldersburg, MD St. Joseph.
Oniwe, Bernard *o.p.* '00 (CHR) Columbia, SC Saint Martin de Porres.
Onogbosele, Jude E. '03 (BAK) Judicial Vicar and Chief Judge; Sisters, OR St. Edward the Martyr.
Onsongo, Raymond Achuka *o.c.d.* '09 (MIL)[P] Milwaukee Provincial Offices – Discalced Carmelites.
Ontiveros, Omar '06 (SLC) West Valley City, UT Saints Peter and Paul LLC 243.
Onubogu, Charles '88 (SFR) In Res.
Onubugo, Charles '88 (SFR) Igbo Nigerian Ministry.
Onuegbe, Paul '95 (LAF) Loreauville, LA Our Lady of Victory.
Onumaegbu, Ted '02 (NY) Irvington–on–the–Hudson, NY Immaculate Conception.
Onunkwo, Vincent '92 (BUR) Bradford, VT Our Lady of Perpetual Help.
Onunwa, Paschal U. '74 (PH) Doylestown, PA Our Lady of Mount Carmel.
Onuoha, Christopher N. '06 (OM) Omaha, NE Christ the King.
Onuoha, Gerald U. '93 (MO) Army Reserve Chaplains.
Onuoha, Silas '91 (CC)[D] Corpus Christi, TX CHRISTUS Spohn Hospital Corpus Christi – Memorial; On Special Assignment.
Onuora, Felix A. *c.s.sp.* '79 (DM) Dunlap, IA St. Patrick; Dunlap, IA Holy Family; Dunlap, IA Sacred Heart.
Onushco, William J. '76 (ALN) Unassigned.
Onuwmere, Leonard *j.p.* '90 (MO) DEPARTMENT OF VETERANS AFFAIRS HOSPITALS AND CHAPLAINS.
Onwere, Chukwudi Callistus, O. '82 (STA) Jacksonville, FL Church of the Crucifixion; Jacksonville, FL St. Pius the Fifth.
Onwubiko, Augustus (NY) Bronx, NY St. Mary Star of the Sea.
Onwuegbule, Stanley I. '93 (SB) Loma Linda, CA Loma Linda University Medical Center.
Onwuegbuzie, Mike O. '86 (IND)[G] Beech Grove, IN Franciscan St. Francis Health.
Onwugbenu, Paschal '03 (RVC) Long Beach, NY St. Mary of the Isle.
Onwughalu, Jerome *c.s.sp.* (CHI)[J] Chicago, IL Resurrection Medical Center.
Onwumelu Onyema, Benjamin '94 (GLP) Shiprock, NM Christ the King; Waterflow, NM Sacred Heart.
Onyango, Anthony O. '11 (BEL) Fairview Heights, IL Holy Trinity Catholic Church; Caseyville, IL St. Stephen.
Onyeabor, Ukachukwu '86 (PH) Philadelphia, PA Veterans Administration Medical Center; Lansdowne, PA St. Philomena.
Onyeachonam, Sylvester '00 (COL) Columbus, OH Christ the King; Children's Hospital.
Onyegbule, Cletus S. '02 (ALN) Sinking Spring, PA St. Ignatius Loyola.
Onyejegbu, Cyriacus N. '03 (MO) Air Force Chaplains.
Onyekuru, Kingsley *c.ss.r.* '01 (DEN)[N] Denver The Redemptorists/Denver Province.
Onyekuru, Michael U. '00 (ATL) Archdiocesan Judges; Adjutant Judicial Vicars.
Onyekwere, Godfrey C. '03 (GR) Grand Rapids, MI St. Mary Magdalen; Presbyteral Council; College of Consultors; Inclusion/Diversity Initiatives; Black Catholic Ministry; On Special Assignment.
Onyekwere, Michael *s.d.v.* '95 (MET) Robert Wood Johnson University Hospital; Highland Park, NJ Transfiguration of the Lord Parish.
Onyemaobi, Nnaemeka A. '09 (NEW) Bloomfield, NJ Church of St. Thomas the Apostle.
Onyenagubo, Innocent (SY) Syracuse, NY Upstate University Hospital.
Onyenobi, Christopher '83 (LA)[J] Torrance, CA Providence Little Company of Mary Medical Center Torrance; [J] San Pedro, CA Providence Little Company of Mary Medical Center San Pedro; Hospital Chaplains; Hospital Chaplains; Santa Monica, CA St. Anne.
Onyeocha, Chinemere '08 (ALT) State College, PA Our Lady of Victory.
Onyia, Joseph Bernardine '95 (NY) Bronx, NY St. Augustine; Bronx, NY Bronx–Lebanon Hospital Center.
Onyutha, Alfred '90 (CAM) Woodbury, NJ Holy Angels Parish, Woodbury, N.J.
Oonnoonny, George '91 (NY) Yonkers, NY Most Holy Trinity; Judges.
Opalalic, Agustin '77 (SD) San Diego, CA Blessed Sacrament Catholic Parish.
Opalda, Jose (BAL) Millersville, MD Our Lady of the Fields.
Opara, Christopher '92 (MO) Army Chaplains.
Opara, Isaac '88 (MO) Army Chaplains.
Opara, Peter Ben '88 (DET)[H] Livonia, MI St. Mary Mercy Hospital.
Opara, Peter C. *m.i.* '04 (MIL)[Y] Milwaukee, WI St. Camillus Communities, Inc. – House I.
Opara, Vitalis N. '88 (BRK) Brooklyn, NY Holy Family.
Oparaekwe, Godfrey '83 (TUC) Bisbee, AZ Saint Patrick Roman Catholic Parish – Bisbee.
Opeil, Cyril *s.j.* '94 (BO)[U] Newton, MA The Jesuit Community at Boston College.

Opem, Anthony '68 (SFS) Retired.
Opendi, Richard *o.c.d.* '08 (MIL)[P] Milwaukee Provincial Offices – Discalced Carmelites.
Ophals, Donald J. '61 (ALB) Retired.
Opira, Simon Peter '93 (STV) Kingshill, VI Church St. Ann.
Opoka, Lloyd E. '68 (KC) Kansas City, MO St. Matthew Apostle.
Opondo–Owora, Charles '93 (SY) Endicott, NY St. Joseph.
Oppenheim, Frank M. *s.j.* '55 (DET)[K] Clarkston, MI Colombiere Center.
Oppong, Charles '96 (RVC) Port Jefferson, NY St. Charles Hospital, Port Jefferson, New York.
Opris, Gheorghe '71 (ROM) Dearborn, MI St. Mary.
Oracion, Samuel B. '82 (LUB) Ralls, TX St. Michael.
Orama, Ramon (PAT) Paterson, NJ Our Lady of Lourdes; Paterson, NJ Blessed Sacrament.
Orama, Raymond '08 (PAT) English Cursillos.
Oranefo, Francis '94 (RVC) Rockville Centre, NY Mercy Medical Center.
Oranefo, Francis (PIT) Pittsburgh, PA St. Mary of Mercy.
Oranyelli, Christopher *o.p.* '00 (CHR) Summerville, SC St. John the Beloved.
Orapankal, Abraham '83 (MET) East Brunswick, NJ St. Bartholomew.
Oravec, Christian R. *t.o.r.* '64 (FgM)[G] Loretto, PA St. Francis Friary at Mount Assisi; Loretto, PA THIRD ORDER REGULAR MISSIONS.
Oravetz, Robert F. '97 (PBR) Lyndora, PA St. John the Baptist; Archives; Evangelization, Mission Activity and Ecumenism.
Orbanek, Rev. Msgr. Gerald L. '66 (E) Pleasant Ridge Manor East Retired.
Orchik, Michael J. '73 (BAL) Baltimore, MD Little Flower, Shrine of.
Orci, Ernesto '09 (SJ) Santa Clara, CA St. Lawrence, the Martyr; Council of Priests.
Ordax, Rev. Msgr. Emiliano '48 (MIA) Retired.
Ordiales Reniva, Cary '09 (P) Woodburn, OR St. Luke.
Ordonez, Jose Naul '99 (CC) Kingsville, TX St. Martin.
Ordonez, Mario Ricky '08 (TUC) Council of Priests.
Ordonez, Mario (Ricky) V. '08 (TUC) Tucson, AZ Saint Joseph Roman Catholic Parish – Tucson; Vocations.
Orellana, Jose A. *i.v.e.* '03 (BRK) Brooklyn, NY Mary Mother of the Church.
Orellana, Roberto '01 (ATL) Covington, GA St. Augustine of Hippo.
Orengo, Rev. Msgr. Juan Rodriguez '79 (PCE) Ponce, PR Christ the King; Episcopal Vicar for Pastoral Coordination; Parish Priests Consultors; Children of Mary; Ecumenism; Legion of Mary; [B] The Pontifical Catholic University of Puerto Rico; [H] Ponce, PR Fundacion Surinach; Propagation of the Faith.
Oreshoski, Gary '88 (RC) Presho, SD St. Martin; Presho, SD Christ the King; Deaneries.
Orf, Rev. Msgr. Raymond V. '55 (SPC) Springfield, MO Immaculate Conception; Priests' Mutual Benefit Society Retired.
Organ, Patrick C. '71 (VEN) North Port, FL San Pedro.
Ori, Kevin (MIL)[K] Milwaukee, WI Wheaton Franciscan Healthcare – St. Francis, Inc.
Oria, Enrique *o.carm.* '58 (ARE) Morovis, PR Nuestra Senora del Carmen.
Orians, Thomas A. *s.a.* '92 (NEW) Newark, NJ St. John's.
Orians, Thomas *s.a.* '92 (NY)[DD] Garrison, NY Franciscan Friars of the Atonement.
Orimaco, Domingo '72 (SFR) Daly City, CA Our Lady of Mercy.
Oriole, Philip M. '70 (E) Albion, PA St. Lawrence.
Orique, David T. *o.p.* '01 (PRO)[O] Providence St. Thomas Aquinas Priory at Providence College.
Orjianioke, Martin M. '95 (MEM) Memphis, TN Holy Names of Jesus and Mary; African Catholic Ministry.
Orlandi, Joseph J. '73 (PAT) Budd Lake, NJ St. Jude.
Orlandi, Nazareno '61 (NEW) Lyndhurst, NJ Our Lady of Mount Carmel.
Orlando, Vincent A. *s.j.* '74 (NO)[R] New Orleans, LA Ignatius Residence.
Orlik, Dale A. '67 (SAG) Bay City, MI St. Boniface; Bay City, MI St. Joseph.
Orlinski, Richard A. '73 (GRY) Hammond, IN St. John Bosco; Hammond, IN St. Joseph; Deans; Priests' Personnel Board; Bishop's Council of Priests; Consultors.
Orloski, Joseph F. '94 (SCR) Retired.
Orloski, Raymond J. '62 (HBG) Retired.
Orlosky, Anselm '53 (PBR)[C] Butler, PA Holy Trinity Monastery.
Orlowski, Robert J. '97 (BUF) Corfu, NY St. Maximilian Kolbe Parish.
Orlowski, Rev. Msgr. Walter C. '79 (BGP) Norwalk, CT St. Matthew; Diocesan Consultors; Parochial Examiners; Presbyteral Council.
Orlowsky, Michael T. '93 (ARL) Madison, VA Our Lady of the Blue Ridge.
Ormechea, John B. *c.p.* '65 (FgM).
Ormechea, John B. *c.p.* '65 (CHI)[N] Chicago Passionist Provincial Office.
Ormond, Henry *o.carm.* '77 (JOL)[L] Darien Carmelite Provincial Office.
Ormond, Henry *o.carm.* '77 (OAK)[A] Berkeley, CA Dominican School of Philosophy and Theology.
Orndorff, Christopher M. '97 (TUC) Yuma, AZ Saint Francis of Assisi Roman Catholic Parish – Yuma.
Orndorff, Jared P. '08 (CLV) Mentor, OH St. John Vianney.
Ornowski, Gerald *m.i.c.* '62 (FBK) Presbyteral Council; Office of Urban Permanent Diaconate; Consultors; [C] Fairbanks, AK Kobuk Center.
Oroffa, Francis *m.s.p.* '91 (DOD) Hoisington, KS St. John the Evangelist Catholic Church of Hoisington, Kansas.
Orosa, Augustin *m.i.* '94 (MIL)[N] Wauwatosa, WI St. Camillus Health Center, Inc.; [Y] Wauwatosa, WI St. Camillus Communities, Inc. – House II.
Orosco, James P. '81 (DAL) Terrell, TX St. John; Terrell, TX State Hospital.
Orozco, Argemiro '92 (YAK) East Wenatchee, WA Holy Apostles; Diocesan Consultors; Presbyteral Council Executive Committee; [F] East Wenatchee, WA Holy Apostles Parish.
Orozco, Avelino '04 (ORG) Orange, CA La Purisima.
Orozco, Edicson '99 (BGP)[U] St. Charles Outreach Program; Bridgeport, CT St. Charles Borromeo; Priest Vocation Advisory Board.
Orozco, Isaac '07 (FWT) Diocesan Pastoral Council; Priest Secretary to the Bishop; Fort Worth, TX St. Patrick Cathedral.
Orozco, Ramon '96 (LA) Los Angeles, CA Presentation of Mary Parish.
Orpilla, Julito R. '06 (SAC) Nevada City, CA St. Canice; Grass Valley, CA St. Patrick.
Orr, James R. '79 (PIT) Pittsburgh, PA St. Albert the Great.
Orr, John Arthur '01 (KNX) Knoxville, TN Holy Ghost.
Orr, Joseph T. '82 (ALT) Scouting; [I] Lock Haven, PA Lock Haven University (Lock Haven); Lock Haven, PA St. Agnes.
Orr, Sherman A. '91 (WCH) Wichita, KS St. Elizabeth Ann Seton.
Orr, Rev. Msgr. Stephen L. '74 (DM) Ankeny, IA Our Lady's Immaculate Heart; Judges.
Orrabazo, Rosendo *c.m.f.* '78 (LA)[V] Temple City, CA Claretian Missionaries – Western Province, Inc.
Orrigo, Mario J. '96 (BO) Stoneham, MA St. Patrick.
Orsborn, Bruce J. '81 (SD)[N] San Diego, CA Newman Center – SDSU; College of Consultors; Presbyteral Council; Vicars Forane; San Diego, CA Blessed Sacrament Catholic Parish; San Diego, CA Saint Therese Catholic Parish.
Orsi, Michael P. '76 (CAM) On Duty Outside the Diocese.
Orsini, James '74 (HON) Diocesan Pastoral Council; Kihei, HI St. Theresa Retired.
Orsini Baez, Jayson '10 (PCE) Ponce, PR Cathedral of Our Lady of Guadalupe.
Orsino, Jerry '66 (BEL)[F] Belleville, IL Missionary Oblates of Mary Immaculate – St. Henry's Oblate Residence.
Orso, Clair *c.s.* '91 (DAL) Irving, TX St. Luke.
Orsolits, Norbert F. '65 (BUF) Retired.
Orsulak, Rev. Msgr. Thomas J. '90 (ALN) Reading, PA St. Peter the Apostle.
Orsy, Ladislas *s.j.* '51 (WDC)[O] Washington, DC The Jesuit Community at Georgetown University.
Orszulak, Henry A. '67 (BUF) Judges; Lackawanna, NY St. Anthony.
Ortega, Carlos '99 (SR) Healdsburg, CA St. John the Baptist; Renovacion Carismatica Catolica.
Ortega, Christopher '11 (SAV) Savannah, GA Cathedral of St. John the Baptist.
Ortega, Eduardo '95 (BWN) Mercedes, TX Sacred Heart Church.
Ortega, Efren '72 (DAL) Retired.
Ortega, Fernando '08 (STP) White Bear Lake, MN St. Pius X; Appointees.
Ortega, Jose F. *l.c.* '01 (PRO)[T] Wakefield, RI Overbrook, Incorporated; [T] Wakefield, RI Ocean Pastoral Center, Inc.; [T] Greenville, RI Vocation Action Circle, Inc.; [T] Greenville, RI LC Pastoral Services, Inc.
Ortega, Jose F. *l.c.* (ATL)[K] Alpharetta, GA LCNA Atlanta, Incorporated; [K] Alpharetta, GA Youth for the Third Millennium, Inc.
Ortega, Jose F. *l.c.* '01 (CHI)[E] Lemont, IL Everest Academy of Lemont, Inc.
Ortega, Jose Felix *l.c.* '01 (LA)[BB] Thornwood, NY Territorial Administrative Office.
Ortega, Jose Felix *l.c.* '01 (HRT)[U] Cheshire, CT Racebrook, Inc.; [U] Cheshire, CT Rossotto, Inc.; [U] Cheshire, CT Horizons Institute, Inc.; [U] Cheshire, CT The Legion of Christ, Incorporated; [U] Cheshire, CT Logos, Inc.; [U] Cheshire, CT LUX ET VITA, INC.; [C] Cheshire, CT Legion of Christ College, Inc.
Ortega, Jose Felix *l.c.* '01 (NY)[U] Thornwood, NY Catholic World Mission, Inc.; [BB] Thornwood, NY Mission Network Activities USA, Inc.; [HH] Thornwood, NY Legion of Christ, Incorporated; [HH] Thornwood, NY Familia USA, Inc.; [HH] Thornwood, NY Catholic Net, Inc.; [HH] Thornwood, NY Mission Network Programs USA, Inc.; [HH] Thornwood, NY Helping Hands Medical Missions, Inc.; [HH] Thornwood, NY Youth and Family Encounter, Inc.; [HH] Mt. Kisco, NY Regina Apostolorum, Inc.; [HH] Thornwood, NY Consolidated Catholic Administrative Services, Inc.; [HH] Rye, NY Pastoral Support Services, Inc.; [HH] Rye, NY Legion of Christ North America, Inc.; [HH] Thornwood, NY Nueva Primavera Inc.; [HH] Thornwood, NY Legion of Christ and Consecrated Regnum Christi Members Assistance Foundation; [HH] Thornwood, NY Arke, Inc.
Ortega, Jose Felix *l.c.* (STL)[V] Chesterfield, MO Gateway Academy Incorporated; [V] Chesterfield, MO Gateway Educational Foundation, Inc.
Ortega, Jose Felix *l.c.* '01 (WDC)[X] Bethesda, MD Woodmont Educational Foundation, Inc.; [X] Bethesda, MD Mission Network Young Mens Program USA, Inc.
Ortega, Jose Felix *l.c.* '01 (MAD)[I] Edgerton, WI Oaklawn Incorporated; [F] Edgerton, WI Koshkonong Pastoral Center.
Ortega, Jose Felix *l.c.* '01 (DET)[T] Bloomfield Hills, MI Opdyke, Inc.
Ortega, Jose Felix *l.c.* '01 (MAN)[K] Center Harbor, NH L.C. Center Harbor, Inc.
Ortega, Jose Felix *l.c.* '01 (SAT)[G] San Antonio, TX Rolling Hills Academy, Inc.; [S] San Antonio, TX San Antonio Rolling Hills, Inc.
Ortega, Jose Felix *l.c.* '01 (ATL)[K] Atlanta, GA National Consultants for Education, Inc.; [F] Alpharetta, GA Norcross Pastoral Center, Inc.
Ortega, Jose *m.sp.s.* '66 (P) Hillsboro, OR St. Matthew; [L] Hillsboro, OR Missionaries of the Holy Spirit, M.Sp.S.
Ortega, Leo '08 (LA) Los Angeles, CA St. Thomas the Apostle.
Ortega, Marco Antonio '95 (NY) New York, NY Our Lady Queen of Martyrs.
Ortega, Miguel Angel '09 (BWN) La Joya, TX Our Lady, Queen of Angels.
Ortega, Oliver '04 (LA) North Hollywood, CA St. Patrick.
Ortega, Ovidio '83 (SJN) Courage Puerto Rico.
Ortega, Ricardo '11 (PAT) Little Falls, NJ Our Lady of the Holy Angels.
Ortega, Santos L. '96 (SB) Hesperia, CA Holy Family; High Desert; Appointed Members.
Ortega–Ruiz, Agustin '93 (JOL) Bensenville, IL St. Alexis.
Ortega Lemus, Ovidio '83 (SJN) San Juan, PR Sagrado Corazon de Jesus.
Ortega y Ortiz, Adam Lee '92 (SFE) Santa Fe, NM Santa Maria de la Paz Catholic Community; College of Consultors.
Ortez, Sofonias '96 (VEN) Secretariado Hispano de Cursillos; Arcadia, FL St. Paul.
Orth, Anthony F. '75 (PH) Essington, PA St. Margaret Mary Alacoque.
Orthel, Joseph A. '89 (SPC) Special Assignment.
Orthel, Joseph A. '89 (TLS) Wagoner, OK Holy Cross.
Orthmann, James *o.c.s.o.* '94 (ARL)[H] Berryville, VA Cistercian Abbey of Our Lady of the Holy Cross.
Ortigas, Jose Ignacio A. '09 (BGP) Newtown, CT St. Rose of Lima.
Ortiz, Alex *c.ss.r.* '76 (NY)[DD] New York, NY Redemptorist Priests and Brothers, C.Ss.R.
Ortiz, Angel '87 (MGZ) Cabo Rojo, PR St. Michael.
Ortiz, Antonio '78 (SAT)[A] San Antonio, TX Assumption Seminary.
Ortiz, Arnold *o.s.j.* '72 (SAC)[A] Loomis, CA Mount St. Joseph Novitiate and Seminary; Councilors:; Granite Bay, CA St. Joseph Marello; Vicars Forane.
Ortiz, Edsil *o.f.m.* '88 (SJ) Santa Clara, CA St. Justin.
Ortiz, Emerito Gomez *o.f.m.* '82 (FAJ) Palmer, PR Cristo Rey.
Ortiz, Emerito '96 (WOR) St. Francis; Fitchburg, MA St. Francis of Assisi.
Ortiz, J.C. '91 (PHX) West Sedona, AZ St. John Vianney Roman Catholic Parish.
Ortiz, Jorge '04 (BRK) Brooklyn, NY St. Joseph.
Ortiz, Jose A. '66 (LA) South El Monte, CA Epiphany.
Ortiz, Jose Juan *c.o.* '05 (BWN) Pharr, TX St. Jude Thaddeus; Pharr, TX Oratory Academy of St. Philip Neri; [B] Pharr, TX Oratory Athenaeum for University Preparation; [C] Pharr, TX Oratory Academy of St. Philip Neri; [F] Pharr, TX Pharr Oratory of St. Philip Neri of Pontifical Right; Pharr, TX Oratory – Athenaeum for University Preparation.
Ortiz, Jose '00 (CC) Gregory, TX Immaculate Conception.
Ortiz, Leo W. '00 (SFE) Santa Fe, NM St. Anne's.
Ortiz, Marco Antonio '00 (LA) Los Angeles, CA Divine Saviour; Los Angeles, CA St. Ann.
Ortiz, Maximo J. *o.s.a.* '74 (WDC) Washington, DC St. Elizabeth's Hospital (Government Operated).
Ortiz, Maximo J. *o.s.a.* '74 (MIA)[H] Miami Gardens, FL Casa San Lorenzo.
Ortiz, Michael '56 (SD) Retired.
Ortiz, Miguel Angel *o.f.m.cap.* '86 (SFR)[N] Burlingame, CA Capuchin Provincial House; Definitors.

Ortiz, Roberto '09 (NEW) Wyckoff, NJ St. Elizabeth.
Ortiz, Rodrigo *o.f.m.* '73 (OAK)[L] Oakland Franciscan Friars of California, (Province of St. Barbara).
Ortiz, Victor G. '86 (CGS) Caguas, PR El Salvador.
Ortiz, Victor (SJN)[A] Bayamon Central University.
Ortiz–Garay, Jorge '04 (NEW) On Duty Outside the Archdiocese.
Ortiz–Mangual, Julio '02 (SJN) Carolina, PR San Juan de Dios.
Ortiz–Montelongo, Ruben '07 (WCH) Arkansas City, KS Sacred Heart.
Ortiz–Santiago, Eduardo '11 (STV) Charlotte Amalie, VI Our Lady of Perpetual Help.
Ortiz Dominichi, Arnaldo '10 (PCE) Ponce, PR Christ the King.
Ortiz Gonzalez, Jose A. '85 (SJN) Toa Alta, PR Nuestra Senora de la Medalla Milagrosa.
Ortman, John '82 (DET) Dryden, MI St. Cornelius; Allenton, MI St. John the Evangelist; Capac, MI St. Nicholas.
Ortmeier, Paul R. '72 (OM) Lyons, NE Holy Cross; Lyons, NE St. Joseph.
Oruko, William Dickson *a.j.* '99 (KNX) Athens, TN St. Mary.
Orum, Vincent *a.j.* '92 (CAM) Continuing Education & Spiritual Formation of Priests (CESF).
Orum, Vincent *a.j.* '94 (CAM) Sicklerville, NJ The Church of St. Charles Borromeo, Washington Township, N.J.
Orzech, Eric '93 (CLV) Lorain, OH St. Peter.
Orzech, Eric '93 (SAT)[S] San Antonio, TX Polish American Priest Association (P.A.P.A.).
Orzechowski, Jacek *o.f.m.* '02 (WDC) Silver Spring, MD St. Camillus.
Orzechowski, Walter B. '49 (MIL) Retired.
Orzel, David J. '79 (SY) Utica, NY St. Peter.
Osbahr, Theodore W. '67 (NEW) Retired.
Osborn, Douglas '68 (LAN) Retired.
Osborn, Rev. Msgr. Michael A. '92 (KAL) Special Assignment.
Osborn, Rev. Msgr. Michael A. '92 (COL)[A] Columbus, OH Pontifical College Josephinum.
Osborn, William '66 (SFS) Retired.
Osborne, Rev. Msgr. Michael A. '92 (COL)[A] Columbus, OH Pontifical College Josephinum.
Osborne, Paul J. *o.f.m.* '64 (FgM) New York, NY Holy Name Province.
Osborne, Robert E. '54 (L) Defenders of the Bond Retired.
Osborne, Robert *s.m.* '66 (STL)[O] St. Louis, MO Maryland Avenue Marianist Community.
Osborne, Stanley J. '59 (L) Elizabethtown, KY St. James Retired.
Osburg, Frank C. '60 (LEX) College of Consultors; Priests' Retirement Committee Retired.
Osburg, Gregory E. '77 (COV) Wilder, KY St. John the Baptist; Defenders of the Bond.
Oschwald, Daniel D. '98 (R) Raleigh, NC Cathedral of the Sacred Heart; Council of Priests.
Osebold, Richard A. '60 (DET) Redford, MI St. John Bosco.
Oseguera, Melvin '94 (NEW) Fairview, NJ St. John the Baptist.
Osei, Francis (FWT) Tribunal.
Osei–Fosu, Paul (NY) Pearl River, NY St. Margaret of Antioch.
Osei–Nyarko, Rev. Msgr. Francis (SY) Syracuse, NY Holy Family.
Osendorf, James *c.m.* '80 (LA)[P] Montebello, CA DePaul Evangelization Center; [V] Montebello, CA DePaul Evangelization Center.
Oser, Donald J. '53 (Y) North Canton, OH St. Paul Retired.
Oser, Ronald E. '92 (ORL) Retired.
Osiander, Alfons M. '73 (BUF)[A] East Aurora, NY Christ the King Seminary; Sardinia, NY St. Jude.
Osias, Jean Max '94 (NEW) East Orange, NJ Holy Spirit–Our Lady Help of Christians.
Osinski, Ronald V. '72 (MO) Air Force Reserve Chaplains; Altoona, PA St. Mark's.
Osom, John *m.s.p.* '85 (BR) Napoleonville, LA St. Benedict the Moor.
Osorio, Abel *c.m.* (CHL) Charlotte, NC Our Lady of Guadalupe Church.
Osorio, Celimo '87 (ELP) San Elizario, TX San Felipe de Jesus.
Osorio, Francisco J. '86 (PMB) Spanish.
Osorio, Francisco '86 (PMB) Indiantown, FL Holy Cross; Defender of the Bond.
Osorio, German '10 (B) Nampa, ID St. Paul's.
Osorio, Louis '58 (CHL) On Duty Outside the Diocese.
Osorio, Luis '00 (ORL) Rockledge, FL St. Mary's.
Osorio, Rudolfo B. '55 (NEW) Retired.
Osorio Mourino, Jose B. (SJN) San Juan, PR Ntra. Sra. de Fatima.
Osorio Mourino, Jose Benito *o.de.m.* '62 (SJN) San Juan, PR Nuestra Senora de la Merced.
Osorio Osorio, P. Jose Fernando *o.p.* (PCE) Yauco, PR Holy Rosary.
Osowski, Chester J. '49 (LC) Retired.
Ospina, Diego '05 (RCK) Belvidere, IL St. James.
Ospina–Briceno, Walter '02 (R) Absent on Leave.
Ossa, Diego (SP) Tampa, FL Incarnation.
Ossa, Pedro N. '63 (BRK) Retired.
Ossino, Angelo '57 (DEN) Retired.
Ossola, Rev. Msgr. John R. '64 (SFD) Springfield, IL Little Flower; Commission for the Care of Infirm and Retired Priests; Priests' Personnel Board; Presbyteral Council.
Ostaszewski, Andrzej '84 (NEW) Newark, NJ St. Casimir's; Polish Apostolate.
Ostdick, Rupert *o.s.b.* '48 (IND)[K] Saint Meinrad, IN St. Meinrad Archabbey.
Ostdiek, Gilbert *o.f.m.* '60 (CHI)[B] Chicago, IL Catholic Theological Union; [N] Chicago, IL Holy Spirit Friary, Order of Friars Minor.
Ostdiek, John Leonard *o.f.m.* '49 (SFD)[K] Quincy, IL Holy Cross Friary Retired.
Ostendorf, Mark '81 (SCL) St. Cloud, MN St. Wendelin's; Rockville, MN Mary of the Immaculate Conception; Kimball, MN Holy Cross.
Osterhage, Louis *c.pp.s.* '58 (CIN)[N] Carthagena, OH St. Charles Retired.
Osterhaus, Mark '85 (DUB)[E] New Hampton, IA St. John School of Religion; New Hampton, IA Holy Family; New Hampton, IA Immaculate Conception; New Hampton, IA St. Boniface.
Osterle, Paul *s.j.* '59 (NO) New Orleans, LA Immaculate Conception.
Osterman, Gerald J. '67 (BO) Everett, MA Immaculate Conception; Roxbury, MA St. Katharine Drexel.
Osterman, Richard '69 (GF) Retired.
Ostini, Anthony H. *s.j.* '72 (LAF)[J] Grand Coteau, LA Jesuit Spirituality Center (St. Charles College).
Ostler, David M. '87 (PHX) Sun City West, AZ Our Lady of Lourdes Roman Catholic Parish.
Ostrander, Gary L. '71 (OM) Omaha, NE St. Patrick (Elkhorn); Officers; Age Groups.
Ostrowski, David T. '89 (STP) Minnetonka, MN Immaculate Heart of Mary.
Ostrowski, Eugene S. '77 (WH) Wheeling, WV Corpus Christi; Vicars Forane.
Ostrowski, John T. '98 (CLV) Casa Parroquial San Pedro Teotepeque.
Ostrowski, Joseph C. '52 (SCR) Retired.
Ostrowski, Theodore L. '81 (CHI) Chicago, IL St. Denis.
Ostrowski, Walter *s.v.d.* '65 (PIT)[M] Pittsburgh, PA Society of The Divine Word.
Osuagwa, Peter Chici (BRK) Elmhurst, NY Ascension.
Osuch, Michal *c.r.* '80 (CHI) Chicago, IL St. Hyacinth Basilica; Deans.
Osudibia, Kizito '93 (COS) Bailey, CO St. Mary of the Rockies.
Osuegbu, Cyprian '03 (RVC) East Meadow, NY Nassau University Medical Center; Levittown, NY St. Bernard.
Osuji, Cletus (P)[J] Roseburg, OR Mercy Medical Center, Inc.
Osuji, Ngozi (HBG) Lewisburg, PA U.S. Penitentiary.
Osuji, Peter I. (PIT)[B] Pittsburgh, PA Duquesne University of the Holy Spirit.
Osuji, Urban *c.m.* '86 (BEL) Diocesan Consultors; Valmeyer, IL Seven Dolors of the B.V.M.
Osuna, E. Donald '63 (OAK) Retired.
Osunkwo, Jude T. (BO) Roxbury, MA St. Katharine Drexel.
Oswald, John '61 (LR)[G] Little Rock, AR St. John Manor Retired.
Oswald, Leo P. '78 (PH) Willow Grove, PA St. David.
Oswald, Norman R. '72 (MIL) Wood, WI Veterans Administration Medical Center; Special Assignment; DEPARTMENT OF VETERANS AFFAIRS HOSPITALS AND CHAPLAINS.
Oswald, Randall J. '97 (CHY) Jackson, WY Our Lady of the Mountains; Advocates.
Oswald, Rev. Msgr. Richard S. '65 (LR) Office of Divine Worship; Presbyteral Council; Little Rock, AR St. Edward.
Oswald, Robert '02 (GF) Miles City, MT Sacred Heart; Personnel Board; Diocesan Consultors; Vicars Forane; Priests' Council.
Oswalt, M. Price '96 (OKL) Prague, OK St. Wenceslaus, National Shrine of the Infant Jesus of Prague.
Otanga, Thomas Ochieng *o.c.d.* '03 (WDC)[B] Washington, DC Discalced Carmelite Friars.
Otanwa, John Paul A. '05 (SFR) San Francisco, CA St. Finn Barr.
Otellini, Rev. Msgr. Steven D. '78 (SFR) Menlo Park, CA The Church of the Nativity; Knights of Malta; Deans.
Otero, Rev. Msgr. Henry '62 (WDC) Retired.
Otero, Lino O. *l.c.* '01 (SAC) Sacramento, CA Our Lady of Guadalupe Shrine; Vicars Forane; Presbyteral Council.
Otillio, Peter *o.p.* '57 (FgM)[N] Chicago Dominicans (Provincial Office); Chicago, IL Province of St. Albert the Great (Central).
Otor, Patrick A. '92 (SAV) Waynesboro, GA Sacred Heart.
Otsiwah, Charles E. '85 (VIC) Victoria, TX Our Lady of Victory Cathedral.
Ott, Rev. Msgr. Alfred R. '60 (ALN)[J] Bethlehem, PA Holy Family Villa Retired.
Ott, Jeffery *o.p.* '01 (ATL) Atlanta, GA Our Lady of Lourdes; Council of Priests; Board of Directors:; [F] Atlanta, GA Augustine House, Dominicans Friars of Atlanta.
Ott, Richard W. *s.j.* '72 (OM)[J] Omaha, NE Jesuit Community at Creighton University.
Ott, Vincent *o.m.i.* '56 (BEL)[F] Belleville, IL Shrine of Our Lady of the Snows.
Ottagon, Anthoni *h.g.n.* '03 (OWN) Calvert City, KY St. Pius Tenth; Grand Rivers, KY St. Anthony of Padua.
Otten, Lammert B. *s.j.* '65 (FgM) St. Louis, MO Society of Jesus.
Otting, Loras C. '62 (DUB) Retired.
Otting, Paul J. '66 (DUB) Retired.
Ottman, Timothy *o.s.b.* '78 (HON)[D] Waialua, HI Benedictine Monastery of Hawaii/Retreat Center.
Otto, David C. '77 (KAL) Niles, MI St. Mary of the Imm. Conception Church.
Otto, James C. '97 (PH) Philadelphia, PA Maternity B.V.M.
Otto, Leo '56 (SCL) Retired.
Ottonello, Pedro *o.a.d.* '47 (SJ) Santa Clara, CA Oratory of Our Mother of Perpetual Help.
Otuibe, Chris Angelo *o.p.* '78 (ELP) El Paso, TX Our Lady of the Light.
Otusafo, Joshua *c.s.sp.* '04 (CIN) Dayton, OH Corpus Christi; Dayton, OH Our Lady of Mercy; Dayton, OH Queen of Martyrs.
Otuwurunne, Onyedika Michael '96 (NEW) Hackensack, NJ Bergen County Correctional Facility; Dumont, NJ St. Mary's.
Oubre, Carroll L. '91 (ARL) Arlington, VA St. Agnes.
Oubre, Sinclair '86 (BEA) Southern Vicariate; Diocesan Judges; Apostleship of the Sea; Diaconate Formation; Port Arthur, TX St. John; [H] Port Arthur, TX Apostleship of the Sea of the United States of America (AOSUSA); Port Arthur, TX Apostleship of the Sea of the United States of America (AOSUSA).
Oudenhoven, Timothy L. '10 (LC) Independence, WI SS. Peter and Paul.
Ouderkirk, Lloyd Paul '59 (DUB) Retired.
Ouedraogo, Evariste '94 (NY) New York, NY Holy Name of Jesus.
Ouellette, Anthony '06 (KCK) Council for Catholic Charismatic Renewal; Osage City, KS St. Patrick; Osage City, KS St. Patrick.
Ouellette, Donald C. '90 (WOR) Worcester, MA St. Peter; Millbury, MA St. Brigid.
Ouellette, John C. '95 (CC) Deans; Premont, TX St. Theresa of the Infant Jesus; Presbyteral Council.
Ouellette, Kent R. '05 (PRT) Dexter, ME Our Lady of the Snows Parish; Dexter, ME St. Agnes.
Ouellette, Louis M. *m.s.* '61 (HRT)[L] Hartford, CT Missionaries of LaSalette.
Ouellette, Paul *o.m.i.* '67 (BO) Lowell, MA St. Patrick.
Ouellette, Richard R. '75 (PRT) Retired.
Ouellette, Richard T. *m.m.* '63 (NY)[DD] Retired.
Ouellette, Richard *m.m.* '63 (LA)[P] Monrovia, CA Retired.
Ouillette, Arthur A. '55 (WOR) Retired.
Oulds, John V. '68 (PH) Coatesville, PA St. Joseph; Coatesville, PA St. Stanislaus Kostka.
Ouletta, James F. '60 (CHI) Retired.
Oulvey, William T. *s.j.* '85 (KC)[J] Kansas City, MO Rockhurst Jesuit Community; [B] Kansas City, MO Rockhurst University.
Ouper, John J. '84 (JOL) Glen Ellyn, IL St. James the Apostle.
Ours, Donald J. *c.m.* '94 (DAL)[J] Dallas, TX Congregation of the Mission, Western Province; Dallas, TX Holy Trinity.
Ours, Robert A. '80 (SY) Special Assignment; Endicott, NY St. Joseph.
Ouseph, Kuriakose '87 (CC) Corpus Christi, TX Christ the King.
Ovalle, Thomas *o.m.i.* '77 (WDC)[O] Washington, DC Provincial Offices of the United States Province of the Missionary Oblates of Mary Immaculate.
Ovalle, Thomas *o.m.i.* '77 (BEL)[F] Belleville, IL Shrine of Our Lady of the Snows.
Ovando, Sergio '93 (SJ) On Duty Outside the Diocese; Special Assignment.
Overbaugh, Rev. Msgr. Hugh A. '61 (HBG) Retired.
Overbeck, Kenneth C. '97 (BO) Manomet, MA St. Bonaventure.
Overbeck, T. Jerome *s.j.* '74 (CHI)[C] Chicago, IL Jesuit Community at Loyola University Chicago.
Overend, James *c.m.f.* '77 (LA)[V] Rancho Dominguez, CA Dominguez Seminary Inc.
Overman, Rev. Msgr. Robert F. '45 (STL) Retired.
Overmyer, John '97 (FTW)[F] Fort Wayne, IN Saint Anne Home & Retirement Community.
Overton, Troy '89 (L) New Haven, KY Immaculate Conception; New Haven, KY St. Catherine.
Oviedo, Francisco *o.a.r.* '69 (LSC) Las Cruces, NM Our Lady of Health; [B] Mesilla, NM Augustinian Recollect Fathers.
Ovienloba, Andrew '95 (NY) Bronx, NY St. Ann.
Ovsak, William '99 (FAR) Retired.

Owen, Michael J. '09 (CHI) Chicago, IL St. Mary of the Woods.
Owen, Phillip T. '11 (CHI) Chicago, IL St. Cajetan.
Owens, Bernard C. *c.s.b.* '67 (GAL)[O] Sugar Land Basilian Mission Center.
Owens, Bernard J. *s.j.* '72 (DET)[P] Bloomfield Hills, MI Manresa Jesuit Retreat House.
Owens, Brian S. '95 (WH) Absent on Leave.
Owens, Douglas '11 (KNX) Knoxville, TN St. John Neumann.
Owens, J. Edward *o.ss.t.* '80 (BAL) Baltimore, MD; [Q] In Residence – Holy Trinity Monastery Baltimore.
Owens, Joseph V. *s.j.* '71 (BO)[U] Weston, MA Campion Jesuit Community.
Owens, Leroy E. '64 (BO) Medfield, MA St. Edward the Confessor.
Owens, Michael J. '84 (HON)[G] Kaneohe, HI Saint Stephen Diocesan Center.
Owens, Rev. Msgr. Thomas J. '74 (PH) Maple Glen, PA St. Alphonsus.
Owera, Ramon *c.f.i.c.* (COL) Columbus, OH Holy Cross; Council for Religious.
Owuamanam, Remigius *s.m.m.m.* '95 (ALX) Alexandria, LA St. James Memorial; Alexandria, LA St. Juliana.
Owusa–Mensah, Sebastian '01 (RVC) East Meadow, NY Nassau University Medical Center; Hicksville, NY Holy Family.
Owusu–Boateng, Johnson '85 (VIC) Vanderbilt, TX St. John Bosco; Procurator Advocate.
Oxley, Walter R. '03 (TOL) On Duty Outside the Diocese.
Oxley, Walter R. '03 (COL)[A] Columbus, OH Pontifical College Josephinum; [A] Columbus, OH Pontifical College Josephinum.
Oyafemi, Clement O. '94 (CHI) Chicago, IL St. Basil/ Visitation.
Oyarzo, Luis A. *s.d.b.* '98 (MRY) Watsonville, CA Our Lady Help of Christians.
Oye, Paul *o.p.* '94 (LAV) Ely, NV Sacred Heart.
Oyo, Charles *c.s.c.* '01 (FTW) South Bend, IN St. Jude Church; South Bend, IN Sacred Heart of Jesus (Lakeville).
Ozele, Anthony M. '92 (BRK) Brooklyn, NY Good Shepherd.
Ozella, John '07 (PBL) Pueblo, CO St. Pius X.
Ozimek, Adam Z. '94 (ATL) Atlanta, GA St. Jude.
Ozimek, Anthony J. *o.s.b.* '68 (CLV)[N] Billings, MT.
Ozimek, Anthony J. *o.s.b.* '68 (GF) Colstrip, MT St. Margaret Mary.
Ozminkowski, Clyde *o.carm.* '54 (JOL)[L] Darien Carmelite Provincial Office.
Ozoa, Jaime Sullan '90 (GBG) Harrison City, PA St. Barbara.
Ozoagu, Uche Cosmas '78 (WDC) Silver Spring, MD St. John the Baptist.
Ozug, John C. '77 (FR) New Bedford, MA Our Lady of Fatima.

P

Paala, Jonathan '75 (SFR) Foster City, CA St. Luke.
Pabin, Chester J. '92 (STU) Caldwell, OH Corpus Christi; Caldwell, OH St. Stephen; Caldwell, OH St. Michael; Caldwell, OH Immaculate Conception.
Pable, Martin *o.f.m.cap.* '58 (MIL)[P] Milwaukee, WI St. Conrad Friary; Minister to Priests.
Pablo, Calixto A. '83 (SFR) San Francisco, CA St. Patrick.
Pabst, Peter *s.j.* '86 (SJ)[E] San Jose, CA Sacred Heart Nativity School; [M] Santa Clara, CA Casa San Inigo, Jesuit Residence; [B] Santa Clara, CA Jesuit Community.
Pacciana, Marco '11 (NEW) Newark, NJ Immaculate Conception; Newark, NJ Our Lady of Good Counsel.
Pace, Paul J. '66 (HRT) Waterbury, CT St. Francis Xavier; Waterbury Vicariate.
Pace, Woodrow H. '95 (LC) Independence, WI SS. Peter and Paul; Deans; Personnel Council; Whitehall, WI St. John the Apostle.
Pachana, Robert A. '98 (NEW) Bayonne, NJ Mt. Carmel.
Pacheco, Rev. Msgr. Agostinho S. '60 (BWN) Edinburg, TX Doctor's Hospital at Renaissance Retired.
Pacheco, Alexandre '68 (STO) Diamond Springs, CA Retired.
Pacheco, John '09 (FWT) Wichita Falls, TX Our Lady of Guadalupe; Presbyteral Council.
Pacheco, Lionel '96 (ORL) Saint Cloud, FL St. Thomas Aquinas.
Pacheco, Mario '76 (LA) Sherman Oaks, CA St. Francis de Sales.
Pacheco, Norbert A. *m.m.* '79 (FgM) Maryknoll, NY MARYKNOLL.
Pacheco, Saul '10 (ELP) Advocates.
Pacheco–Sanchez, Luis (MIL) Milwaukee, WI St. Rafael the Archangel; Milwaukee, WI St. Adalbert; Archdiocesan Council of Priests.
Pachence, Ron '74 (SD)[B] University of San Diego Retired.
Pachence, Ronald A. '74 (SAV) On Duty Outside the Diocese.
Pachla, Stanley L. '83 (DET) Eastpointe, MI St. Veronica.
Pacholczyk, Tadeusz '99 (PH)[CC] Philadelphia, PA National Catholic Bioethics Center.
Pacholczyk, Tadeusz '99 (PH) Havertown, PA Annunciation B.V.M.
Pacholczyk, Tadeusz '99 (FR) On Duty Outside the Diocese.
Pacholec, Daniel S. '96 (SPR) Westfield, MA Our Lady of the Blessed Sacrament.
Pacini, Peter *c.s.c.* '00 (FTW) South Bend; South Bend, IN St. Casimir; South Bend, IN St. Adalbert; [H] Notre Dame Congregation of Holy Cross, United States Province of Priests & Brothers.
Pacitti, Gary T. '89 (PH) Kimberton, PA St. Basil the Great.
Packard, Walter E. '71 (E) Titusville, PA St. Titus; Titusville, PA St. Walburga; Presbyteral Council.
Packuvettithara, George '94 (MIA) Davie, FL Saint David.
Pacocha, Edwin D. '62 (CHI) Chicago, IL St. Cornelius Retired.
Pacquing, Joseph '83 (LSC) Roswell, NM Assumption of the Blessed Virgin Mary.
Pacudan, Roland '83 (HON) On Leave of Absence.
Paculan, Wilson A. '07 (NEW) Union, NJ St. Michael's.
Pacwa, Mitchell C. *s.j.* '76 (CHI)[N] Chicago Chicago Province of the Society of Jesus–Provincial Office.
Paczesny, John R. '61 (MIL) Whitefish Bay, WI St. Monica; [K] Milwaukee, WI Columbia St. Mary's Hospital Ozaukee, Inc. Retired.
Paczkowski, Vincent *s.d.b.* '86 (NY) Port Chester, NY Corpus Christi.
Padamattummal, Bosco '92 (LAN) Catholic Deaf Ministry; Ann Arbor, MI St. Francis of Assisi.
Padavick, William B. '63 (CLV) Oberlin, OH Sacred Heart Retired.
Padazinski, Rev. Msgr. C. Michael '88 (SFR) Judicial Vicar and Director; Archbishop's Cabinet; On Special Assignment; College of Consultors; Chancellor; San Francisco, CA Cathedral of St. Mary (Assumption).
Padazinski, Rev. Msgr. C. Michael '88 (SFR) Judges.
Padazinski, Michael C. '88 (MO) Air Force Reserve Chaplains.
Padberg, John W. *s.j.* '57 (STL)[O] St. Louis, MO Jesuit Community Corporation at Saint Louis University – Jesuit Hall; [V] St. Louis, MO Institute of Jesuit Sources.
Paddack, Rev. Msgr. John N. '84 (NY) New York, NY Notre Dame.
Paddock, Rev. Msgr. John '84 (NY)[GG] New York, NY Columbia University.
Padelli, Emilio P. '62 (HRT) Retired.
Paderon, Gerardo B. '94 (MET) Metuchen, NJ Cathedral of St. Francis of Assisi.
Padget, Leo L. '01 (SFE) Albuquerque, NM Santuario San Martin de Porres.
Padgett, Gary T. '99 (L) Louisville, KY Ascension of Our Lord; Archdiocesan Examiners.
Padilla, Aquino '60 (SFR) San Francisco, CA Church of the Epiphany Retired.
Padilla, Glibert '55 (TUC) Retired.
Padilla, Jose D. *o.p.* '04 (NO)[R] New Orleans Dominican Friars, Southern Dominican Province of St. Martin de Porres; Metairie, LA St. Martin de Porres Province (Southern Dominican Province).
Padilla, Jose Manuel '03 (TUC) Pearce, AZ Saint Jude Thaddeus Roman Catholic Parish – Pearce Sunsites.
Padilla, Luis Alfonso '04 (SJN) Guaynabo, PR Sagrados Corazones.
Padilla, Manuel G. '99 (CHI) Chicago, IL Our Lady of Lourdes.
Padilla, Norberto *c.m.f.* '90 (SJN) Bayamon, PR San Antonio Maria Claret.
Padilla, Rafael '89 (VEN) Presbyteral Council; Promoter of Justice; Judges; Hispanic, Migrant and Spanish Speaking Apostolates; Port Charlotte, FL St. Maximilian Kolbe; College of Consultors.
Padilla, Rafael '03 (AUS) Associate Directors.
Padilla, Roberto '10 (TR) Trenton, NJ Our Lady of the Angels Parish; Bayville, NJ St. Barnabas.
Padilla Cruz, Luis Oscar *o.f.m.cap* (MGZ) Aguada, PR Santuario Protomartires de la Concepcion.
Padinjarepeedika, Joseph L.F. *c.m.i.* '72 (LAF) St. Martinville, LA St. Elizabeth.
Padit, Jose Pelagio A. '96 (SFR) San Francisco, CA St. John the Evangelist.
Pado, Thomas '75 (ORG) Irvine, CA St. Elizabeth Ann Seton.
Padovani, Martin *s.v.d.* '60 (TR)[N] Bordentown, NJ Society of the Divine Word.
Padrez, Mark C. *o.p.* '95 (FgM)[L] Oakland, CA Order of Preachers (Province of Holy Name of Jesus – Western Dominican Province); [Q] Oakland, CA Dominican Community Support Charitable Trust; [L] Oakland, CA Order of Preachers (Province of the Most Holy Name of Jesus – Western Dominican Province); Oakland, CA Province of the Holy Name (Western Dominican Province).
Padrez, Mark *o.p.* (NY)[HH] New York, NY St. Thomas Aquinas Foundation.
Padrnos, David *s.s.c.* '71 (FgM) St Columbans, NE House of Post–Graduate Studies.
Padula, Armand *o.f.m.* '56 (NY)[FF] Wappingers Falls, NY Mt. Alvernia Retreat House.
Paez, Abelardo Mojica (SJN) Bayamon, PR Nuestra Sra. del Rosario.
Paffel, Gregory '01 (SCL) Fergus Falls, MN Our Lady of Victory; Presbyteral Council.
Pagan, Jose R. Linares (PCE)[B] The Pontifical Catholic University of Puerto Rico.
Pagan, Miguel '04 (WOR) Chaplain; Clinton, MA St. John the Guardian of Our Lady; St. John.
Pagano, Nicholas A. '06 (LEX) Lexington, KY Pax Christi Catholic Church.
Pagano, Nick A. '06 (LEX) Ecumenical Liaison.
Pagano, Peter E. '52 (SPR) Retired.
Page, Anthony J. '69 (LA) La Mirada, CA Beatitudes of Our Lord.
Page, Bryan E. '06 (NEW) Newark, NJ Essex County Juvenile Detention Center; [O] Newark, NJ The Newman Catholic Center at University Heights (Rutgers/Newark/NJIT); Elected Members.
Page, Rev. Msgr. David '58 (ORL) Indialantic, FL Holy Name of Jesus; Representative – Retired Priests; Indialantic, FL Holy Name of Jesus Retired.
Page, Hugh R. '80 (FTW)[B] University of Notre Dame Du Lac.
Page, Joselito '05 (SJ) Campbell, CA St. Lucy.
Page, Leon J. '56 (DET) Retired.
Page, Stephen C. '87 (DAV) Fairfield, IA St. Mary's.
Page, Thomas P. '79 (GR) Grand Rapids, MI St. Jude; On Special Assignment; Associate Vicar for Priests; Associate Vicar for Clergy.
Pagel, John M. '80 (CHL) On Duty Outside the Diocese.
Pagidela, Chinnapureddy '02 (SAN) Wall, TX St. Ambrose.
Pagliara, Alfonso D. *o.f.m.cap.* '81 (SP) Tampa, FL Most Holy Redeemer.
Pagliari, Robert M. '75 (BRK)[R] Brooklyn, NY Redemptorist Fathers of New York, Inc.–Baltimore Province.
Pagnotta, James V. '69 (NEW) Jersey City, NJ St. Joseph.
Pagones, Peter '68 (ALB) Schenectady, NY St. Paul the Apostle; Presbyteral Council; Deans; Diocesan Board of Consultors.
Paguaga, Juan Carlos '00 (MIA) Miami, FL St. John Bosco; Archdiocesan Vocations Review Board; Consultors; Age Group I.
Pahamtang, Leonardo '77 (LUB) Muleshoe, TX Immaculate Conception; Priests' Pension Board.
Pahl, John E. '10 (HRT) Enfield, CT Holy Family.
Pahler, Robert E. '57 (CLV) Cuyahoga Falls, OH Immaculate Heart of Mary; Uniontown, OH Queen of Heaven Retired.
Paider, Paul J. '92 (GB) Menasha, WI St. John; Menasha, WI St. Mary.
Paillacho, Jose J. '87 (MOB) Montgomery, AL St. Bede the Venerable Catholic Church; Sacramental Ministers.
Pais, Rohwin *o.f.m.* '89 (NY)[DD] New York Franciscan Province of the Immaculate Conception.
Paisley, James J. '85 (SCR) Shavertown, PA St. Therese; Deans.
Paisley, John C. '62 (DUB) Retired.
Paiva, Antonio M. '49 (PRO) Providence, RI Our Lady of the Rosary Retired.
Paiz, William *c.m.f.* '79 (SPC)[F] Springfield, MO Claretians Missionaries' Residence–Villa Claret; Aurora, MO Holy Trinity; Aurora, MO Sacred Heart.
Pajarillo, Cesar C. '03 (MO) Aurora, IL St. Rita of Cascia; Army Chaplains.
Pajerski, Daniel *l.c.* '04 (DET)[T] Bloomfield Hills, MI Logos, Inc. (Michigan); [T] Clarkston, MI Clarkston Pastoral Center, Inc.
Pajk, Thomas J. '87 (CLV) North Royalton, OH St. Albert the Great.
Pajor, Robert M. '07 (CHI) Chicago, IL St. Ferdinand.
Pak, Ki–Jun Lawrence '88 (LA) Los Angeles, CA St. Basil's.
Pak, Sang–Hun *s.j.* '01 (MIL)[P] Milwaukee, WI Arrupe House Jesuit Community.
Pakosta, Francis J. '52 (SUP) Retired.
Pakula, Michael G. '73 (PEO) Geneseo, IL St. Malachy's.
Pala, Manuel Soler *m.ss.cc.* '70 (SJN)[A] Bayamon Central University.
Palacino, Joseph '82 (BGP) Norwalk, CT St. Jerome Retired.
Palacio, Jorge M. *o.s.m.* '79 (ELP) El Paso, TX St. Ignatius of Loyola.
Palacios, Antonio *o.a.r.* '71 (NY) Bronx, NY St. Anselm.
Palacios, Benjamin *d.v.m.* (NY) Bronx, NY St. Anthony of Padua.
Palacios, Joseph M. '87 (LA) In Transition.
Palackal, Joseph *c.m.i.* '79 (BRK) Maspeth, NY St. Stanislaus Kostka.
Palackaparampil, Augustine '77 (SYM) Santa Ana, CA St. Thomas Apostle Syro–Malabar Catholic Church (Santa Ana).
Palacpac, Luello N. '86 (SFR) South San Francisco, CA St. Augustine.

Paladino, John J. '91 (NEW) Scotch Plains, NJ St. Bartholomew; Union County Southwest Deanery 26; Presbyteral Council.
Palafox, Lorenzo J. *s.j.* '67 (SJ)[M] Los Gatos, CA Sacred Heart Jesuit Center.
Palakudy, James *s.a.c.* '78 (MIL)[P] Milwaukee, WI Pallotti House.
Palakudy, James *s.a.c.* '78 (SFD) Petersburg, IL St. Peter.
Palanca, Mario S. '83 (AGN) Tamuning, GU St. Anthony and St. Victor.
Palang, Mansueto P. '77 (BR) Retired.
Palang, Mansueto P. '77 (ATL) McDonough, GA St. James the Apostle.
Palanthara, Jose '70 (ALX) Moreauville, LA Our Lady of Sorrows.
Palardy, William B. '85 (BO)[A] Weston, MA Blessed John XXIII National Seminary.
Palas, Sean '10 (BEL) Belleville, IL St. Teresa of the Child Jesus; [A] Belleville, IL Althoff Catholic High School; Belleville, IL St. Luke.
Palasits, John A. '58 (NEW) Retired.
Palathara, Jose *c.m.i.* '70 (ALX) Mansura, LA Our Lady of Prompt Succor.
Palathingal, Joseph '90 (SFR) Daly City, CA Our Lady of Mercy; Seton Hospital; [J] Daly City, CA Seton Medical Center.
Palatty, Sibi Antony *o.ss.t.* '10 (BAL)[Q] Assigned in India.
Palatucci, John F. '04 (MO) DEPARTMENT OF VETERANS AFFAIRS HOSPITALS AND CHAPLAINS; Congers, NY St. Paul.
Palazzo, Michael L. '87 (NY) Hyde Park, NY Regina Coeli.
Palazzolo, Anthony P. '93 (STA) Special Assignment.
Palcheck, Gerald F. '67 (SD) Descanso, CA Our Lady of Light Catholic Parish.
Palcisko, Raymond '58 (CR) Retired.
Palecko, Roman Dominic *c.o.* '98 (NY) Tappan, NY Our Lady of the Sacred Heart.
Palermo, Frank C. '55 (SPC) Springfield, MO Holy Trinity; St. Francis de Sales Association Retired.
Palermo, Jason P. '07 (BR) French Settlement, LA St. Joseph; Maurepas, LA St. Stephen the Martyr; Presbyteral Council.
Palermo, Joseph S. '94 (NO)[A] New Orleans, LA Notre Dame Seminary Graduate School of Theology; St. Thomas More Catholic Lawyers Association; Archdiocesan Consultors.
Palica, Jacek *o.c.d.* '96 (GRY)[H] Munster, IN Discalced Carmelite Fathers Monastery.
Palick, George '58 (PIT) Butler, PA St. Fidelis of Sigmaringen.
Paligutan, Alvin *o.s.a.* '07 (SD)[C] San Diego, CA St. Augustine High School; [J] San Diego, CA Augustinian Community.
Palis, Theo '45 (OAK) Retired.
Palisada, Arthur *s.s.p.* '68 (NY)[B] Staten Island, NY Society of St. Paul.
Palisada, Arthur *s.s.p.* (DET)[K] Dearborn, MI Society of St. Paul.
Paliwoda, Rev. Canon Steven '94 (SJP) Lorain, OH St. John the Baptist; Chancellor; Consultors; Eparchial Corporation; Western Protopresbytery; Presbyteral Council; Personnel Board; St. Josaphat Sacerdotal Society; Presbyters.
Paliyathara, George *o.s.j.* '08 (FRS) Madera, CA St. Joachim.
Palka, Bernard R. *s.a.* (ARL) Sterling, VA Christ the Redeemer.
Palka, Bernard *s.a.* '72 (NY)[DD] Garrison, NY St. Christopher's Inn; [DD] Garrison Franciscan Friars of the Atonement, Minister General Office.
Palka, Bogdan *s.d.s.* '92 (WDC)[B] Silver Spring, MD Salvatorian Community.
Palka, Edwin '96 (SP) San Antonio, FL St. Anthony of Padua.
Palko, John A. '54 (PIT) Retired.
Palko, Raymond (STF) Buffalo, NY St. Nicholas; Niagara Falls, NY Protection of B.V.M.
Palko, Thomas J. *o.s.f.s.* '59 (WIL)[J] Wilmington Wilmington–Philadelphia Province of the Oblates of St. Francis de Sales.
Palkowski, Jan '76 (PH) Clifton Heights, PA Sacred Heart.
Palkowski, Matthew *o.f.m.cap.* '05 (HBG) Harrisburg, PA Polyclinic Medical Clinic; Community General Osteopathic Hospital; Harrisburg, PA Pinnacle Health System; Harrisburg, PA St. Francis of Assisi.
Palkudy, James *s.a.c.* '78 (SFD) Petersburg, IL Holy Family.
Palladino, Rev. Msgr. Alfonso G. '43 (BO) Senior Priests. Retired.
Palladino, Robert J. '58 (P) Retired.
Palladino, William C. '06 (BO) Westwood, MA St. Margaret Mary.
Pallardy, James G. '87 (PEO) Kewanee, IL St. Francis of Assisi; Kewanee, IL St. Mary's Catholic Church; Vicariates and Vicars; Finance Council (Canon 492).
Palliparambil, Jose Simon '62 (RVC) Plainview, NY North Shore Hospital at Plainview; [N] Amityville, NY St. Pius X Residence Retired.
Pallipparambil, Binochan *o.s.b.silv.* '02 (ALX) Glenmora, LA St. Louis.
Pallipurath, Jose *o.s.b.silv.* '01 (ALX) Marksville, LA St. Genevieve.
Pallo, Joseph L. '61 (LR) Retired.
Palluck, M. Charles '66 (SEA) Retired.
Palma, Raul *sch.p.* '58 (LA)[P] Los Angeles, CA Piarist Fathers.
Palmer, Frank S. '62 (DM) Retired.
Palmer, Herbert *o.s.b.* '39 (SD)[J] Oceanside, CA Prince of Peace Abbey.
Palmer, John M. *c.s.v.* '71 (CHI)[N] Arlington Heights Viatorian Province Center–Clerics of St. Viator.
Palmer, John *c.s.v.* '71 (JOL)[A] Lisle, IL Benedictine University.
Palmer, Michael C. '63 (BGP) Wilton, CT Our Lady of Fatima.
Palmer, Richard *o.s.a.* '87 (FgM) Olympia Fields, IL Province of Our Mother of Good Counsel (Midwestern).
Palmer, Rev. Msgr. Thomas '58 (SAT)[K] San Antonio, TX Padua Place Retired.
Palmer, William '03 (TYL) Malakoff, TX Mary, Queen of Heaven Church.
Palmese, Anthony '76 (ORL) Retired.
Palmieri, Armando M. *s.d.v.* '98 (NEW) Palisades Park, NJ St. Nicholas.
Palmieri, Frank *c.r.m.* '62 (CHR) Spartanburg, SC Jesus Our Risen Savior.
Palmieri, Louis R. '93 (BO) Amesbury, MA Star of the Sea; Amesbury, MA Holy Family.
Palmieri, Luigi '67 (ALN)[J] Bethlehem, PA Holy Family Villa Retired.
Palmigiano, James '88 (WOR)[N] Spencer, MA St. Joseph's Abbey.
Palmiotto, Paul C. '82 (BRK) Ozone Park, NY Nativity of the Blessed Virgin Mary; Ozone Park, NY St. Stanislaus Bishop and Martyr.
Palmisano, Joseph R. *s.j.* '08 (BO)[U] Boston The Society of Jesus of New England–Provincial Offices.
Palmisano, Peter J. '93 (NEW) Garfield, NJ Our Lady of Mt. Virgin; Our Lady of Fatima First Saturday Family.
Palmitessa, Paul '56 (SD) Retired.
Palo, Anthony *o.carm.* '64 (NEW) Englewood, NJ St. Cecilia's.
Paloma, Victor E. '70 (NEW) Jersey City, NJ Our Lady of Victories.
Palomanes–Vega, Jesus *s.t.* '92 (FAJ) Canovanas, PR Resurreccion del Señor.
Palomera, Ramon '99 (LA) On Administrative Leave.
Palomino, Esviardo '49 (NY) New York, NY St. Lucy Retired.
Palomino, Humberto *p.e.s.* (STP) St. Paul, MN St. Mark.
Palomino, Ignacio '85 (HBG) Chambersburg, PA Corpus Christi.
Palomo, Benigno *o.s.a.* '66 (SJN) Bayamon, PR Santa Rita de Casia.
Palos, Anthony *o.a.r.* '60 (ORG) Santa Ana, CA Our Lady of the Pillar; [I] Santa Ana, CA Our Lady of the Pillar.
Paloso, Nicasio G. '75 (SFR) San Francisco, CA Holy Name of Jesus.
Palparayil, George '67 (NY) MID Hudson Psychiatric Center.
Palsa, Steven M. '79 (PIT) Pittsburgh, PA St. Paul Cathedral.
Paluch, Krzysztof '05 (CHI) Chicago, IL St. Juliana.
Paluck, Casimir S. '61 (BIS) Retired.
Palumbo, Eugene *s.d.b.* '51 (NEW)[L] Ramsey, NJ Don Bosco Prep Salesian Residence; [C] Ramsey, NJ Don Bosco Preparatory High School.
Palumbos, Edward L. '72 (ROC) Fairport, NY Assumption of the Blessed Virgin Mary; Department of Priest Personnel; Priests' Personnel Board; Pension Committee (Lay and Priests); Priest Consultors.
Palys, Daniel J. '69 (BUF) Elma, NY St. Gabriel.
Pambello, Louis M. '81 (NEW) Montclair, NJ Immaculate Conception.
Pambello, Louis '81 (NEW) Medical Leave.
Pamintuan, Edison *m.s.* '02 (HON) Kalaheo, HI Holy Cross.
Pamment, Duaine H. '64 (LAN) Laingsburg, MI St. Isidore.
Pamplaniyil, Mathew V. '76 (FAR) Munich, ND St. Mary; Munich, ND Assumption Church of Starkweather.
Pamula, Robert '87 (MO) Army Reserve Chaplains.
Panackachira, Mathew Joseph *m.c.b.s.* '95 (MEM) Memphis, TN Church of the Holy Spirit.
Panackal, James *c.m.i.* '84 (NSH)[I] Nashville, TN Mercy Convent; Nashville, TN Holy Rosary; [K] Liberty, TN Carmel Center of Spirituality.
Panackal, Philip '89 (CC) Deans; College of Consultors; Personnel Board – Priests; Presbyteral Council; Refugio, TX Our Lady of Refuge.
Panagia, Sal J. '73 (PAT) Paterson, NJ Our Lady of Pompei Retired.
Panagoplos, Christopher *t.o.r.* '76 (ALT) Altoona, PA Altoona Hospital Campus; [G] Hollidaysburg, PA St. Joseph Friary.
Panakal, Alex *o.c.d.* '75 (ORL) Ocala, FL Queen of Peace.
Panakal, Thomson '60 (JOL) Lockport, IL St. Dennis.
Panaligan, Vicente '77 (LAV) Las Vegas, NV Our Lady of Las Vegas; Hospital Apostolate.
Panares, Auxentius '62 (WDC) Retired.
Panaretos, Paul D. *s.j.* '84 (CLV)[B] University Heights, OH John Carroll Jesuit Community.
Panaretos, Paul D. *s.j.* (E) Fairview, PA Holy Cross.
Panchot, Daniel A. *c.s.c.* '65 (FgM) New Rochelle, NY Eastern Brothers Province.
Panchot, Daniel *c.s.c.* (FTW)[H] Notre Dame Congregation of Holy Cross, United States Province of Priests & Brothers.
Panchuk, Myron '82 (STN) On Leave.
Pancorbo, Rev. Msgr. Marcos A. '58 (PCE) Ponce, PR Cathedral of Our Lady of Guadalupe; Diocesan Consultors; Diocesan Board of Administration; Parish Priests Consultors.
Pancorbo, Rev. Msgr. Marcos '58 (PCE) Police Chaplains.
Panczuk, Bernard J. *o.s.b.m.* '63 (STF) New York, NY St. George; Missionaries, Diocesan.
Pandarathikudiyil, Sebastian *v.c.* '88 (NY) Bronx, NY Holy Rosary.
Pandzic, Stjepan *o.f.m.* '75 (STL) St. Louis, MO St. Joseph.
Pane, Andrew M. '87 (NY)[DD] Bronx, NY Retired.
Panek, Andrzej K. (LC) Junction City, WI St. Michael; Milladore, WI St. Wenceslaus; Stevens Point, WI St. Bartholomew.
Panek, Edward B. '91 (CHI) Mt. Prospect, IL St. Thomas Becket; Deans.
Panek, Robert M. '70 (NY) Gardiner, NY St. Charles Borromeo; Archdiocesan Consultors.
Panes, Romeo *o.s.j.* '86 (NEW) Ridgefield, NJ St. Matthew's.
Pangilinan, Alfie A. '11 (NEW) Jersey City, NJ St. Paul of the Cross.
Pangratz, Clement *o.s.b.* '47 (SEA)[M] Lacey, WA St. Martin's Abbey; Lacey, WA.
Paniagua, Edwin *o.f.m.* '00 (NY)[DD] New York Franciscan Province of the Immaculate Conception; [DD] New York Franciscan Province of the Immaculate Conception.
Paniagua, Jaime *l.c.* '08 (WDC)[O] Potomac, MD Legionaries of Christ.
Paniagua, Jose L. '62 (MIA) Hialeah, FL St. Benedict.
Paninski, John *m.s.* '61 (PEO) Georgetown, IL St. Isaac Jogues; [K] Georgetown, IL La Salette Missionaries.
Pankanin, Krzysztof '02 (CHI) Chicago, IL St. James.
Panke, Rev. Msgr. Robert J. '96 (WDC) Pastoral Center Special Ministries; Continuing Education for Clergy; Blessed John Paul II Seminary; [A] Washington, DC Blessed John Paul II Seminary.
Pankiewicz, James '10 (PEO) Pekin, IL St. Joseph's.
Pankiraj, Theesmas '90 (NEW) Saddle Brook, NJ St. Philip the Apostle.
Pankratz, Richard L. *s.s.c.* '74 (FgM) St Columbans, NE House of Post–Graduate Studies; [O] Bristol, RI St. Columban's Retirement House.
Panlasigui, Renato *r.c.j.* '88 (FRS) Sanger, CA St. Mary; Sanger, CA St. Katherine.
Panlilio, Christopher '91 (NEW) Jersey City, NJ Our Lady of Victories.
Panos, Rev. Msgr. Patrick G. '68 (PAT) Ringwood, NJ St. Catherine of Bologna; Deans; [Q] Ringwood, NJ NCPC, Inc.
Panossian, Antoine '66 (OLN) Los Angeles, CA Our Lady Queen of Martyrs.
Panossian, Antoine *p.i.a.* '66 (LA) Los Angeles, CA Our Lady Queen of Martyrs.
Panqueva, Alvaro '98 (DEN) Denver, CO St. Anthony of Padua.
Panthalanickal, Abraham M. '88 (NSH) Joelton, TN St. Lawrence.
Panthananickal, George *c.m.i.* (CHI) Evergreen Park, IL Queen of Martyrs.
Pantle, G. Donald *s.j.* '60 (SCR)[B] Scranton, PA The University of Scranton.
Pantoja, Lucas '05 (MRY) Clergy Life and Ministry Board; Los Osos, CA St. Elizabeth Ann Seton; Vocations Board.
Pantuso, John *s.d.s.* '67 (NSH) Sparta, TN St. Andrew.
Pantyra, Anthony '78 (RCK) Rockford, IL St. Edward.
Panula, Arne A. '73 (POD) Washington.
Panula, Arne A. '73 (WDC)[V] Washington, DC Prelature of the Holy Cross and Opus Dei; [T] Washington, DC Catholic Information Center.
Panuska, Joseph A. *s.j.* '60 (BAL)[Q] Baltimore, MD Colombiere Jesuit Community.
Panza, Rev. Msgr. Paul D. '54 (ALT) Retired.
Panza, Paulo Sergio *o.s.b.* '03 (GBG)[H] Latrobe Saint Vincent Archabbey; [H] Latrobe, PA Saint Vincent Archabbey.
Panzer, Joel '94 (LIN) Army Chaplains; On Duty Outside the Diocese.
Paolicelli, Lawrence '84 (NY) Highland, NY St. Augustine.

Paolino, Stephen H. '07 (PH)[D] Philadelphia, PA John W. Hallahan Catholic Girls High School; Philadelphia, PA Mother of Divine Grace.
Paolozzi, Joseph L. '61 (MEM) Retired.
Paonessa, Ralph *o.f.m.* '63 (NY)[DD] New York Franciscan Province of the Immaculate Conception.
Papa, Charles E. '67 (RVC) Sound Beach, NY St. Louis de Montfort.
Papa, Christopher J. '89 (PH) Glenolden, PA St. George.
Papa, Dominic *c.p.* '60 (BRK)[R] Jamaica, NY Immaculate Conception Monastery.
Papaiah, Joseph '93 (AMA) Sunray, TX Christ the King.
Papaj, Joseph J. *s.j.* '70 (NEW)[B] Jersey City, NJ Jesuit Center; [L] Jersey City, NJ Jesuits of Saint Peter's College, Inc.
Papalia, Pasquale A. '74 (TR) Whiting, NJ St. Elizabeth Ann Seton.
Papania, Bernard J. (BLX) Biloxi, MS Cathedral of the Nativity of the Blessed Virgin Mary.
Pape, William H. '70 (ALB) Albany, NY Cathedral of the Immaculate Conception; [R] Albany, NY The Cathedral Restoration Corp.
Papen, Gerald T. *c.s.c.* '63 (FTW)[H] Notre Dame Congregation of Holy Cross, United States Province of Priests & Brothers; New Rochelle, NY Eastern Brothers Province.
Papera, Rev. Msgr. Lewis V. '67 (NEW) Members.
Papera, Rev. Msgr. Lewis V. '67 (NEW) Hasbrouck Heights, NJ Corpus Christi; South Bergen Region Deanery 7; Presbyteral Council.
Paperini, J. Richard '77 (P)[A] St. Benedict, OR Mount Angel Seminary.
Papes, Joseph M. '01 (PMB) Elected Members; Lake Worth, FL Sacred Heart.
Papes, Rudy *c.ss.r.* '65 (STL)[O] Liguori, MO Liguori Mission House/Redemptorists.
Papesh, Michael L. '83 (PBL) College of Consultors; Diocesan Pastoral Council; Ex Officio; Moderator of the Curia; Vice Chancellor; Moderator of the Curia.
Papineau, Andre *s.d.s.* '65 (MIL)[P] Greendale, WI; [B] Hales Corners, WI Sacred Heart School of Theology.
Papineau, Daniel R. '98 (SPR) On Duty Outside the Diocese.
Papineau, Daniel '98 (CHR) Simpsonville, SC St. Mary Magdalene.
Papp, Edward E. '60 (OG) Ogdensburg, NY St. Mary's Cathedral Retired.
Pappu, Rev. Msgr. Xavier '81 (TYL) Texarkana, TX Sacred Heart; Texarkana, TX Federal Corrections Institution; College of Consultors; Diocesan Finance Council; Diocesan Building Board; Priests' Pension Board; Priests' Personnel Board; Presbyteral Council; Northern Vicariate.
Paqueo, Teresito P. *m.s.c.* (LUB) Rotan, TX St. Joseph.
Paquet, Fernand *m.m.* '56 (NY)[DD] Maryknoll Maryknoll Fathers and Brothers Retired.
Paquet, Hubert J. '55 (PRT) Retired.
Paquet, Joseph A. *s.j.* '59 (BO)[U] Weston, MA Campion Health Center, Inc.
Paquette, Francis '57 (DUL) Silver Bay, MN St. Mary Retired.
Paquette, Joseph '78 (PRO) Pawtucket, RI St. Teresa of the Child Jesus.
Paquette, Neil *o.c.s.o.* '94 (DUB)[K] Peosta, IA New Melleray Abbey, Order of Cistercians of the Strict Observance; Peosta, IA.
Parackal, George '67 (OKL) Oklahoma City, OK St. Joseph; Special Assignment; [E] Oklahoma City, OK St. Anthony Hospital.
Paraday, Mark *o.p.* '83 (CHI) Chicago, IL St. Pius V.
Paraday, Mark *o.p.* '88 (CHI)[N] Chicago, IL St. Pius V Priory.
Paradis, Donald *m.s.* '58 (FR)[F] Attleboro, MA La Salette Shrine Retired.
Paradis, James D. *o.s.a.* '91 (PH) Philadelphia, PA St. Augustine; [C] Villanova, PA Villanova University.
Paradis, Steve '10 (TYL) Mount Pleasant, TX St. Michael.
Paradis, Rev. Msgr. Wilfrid H. '49 (MAN) Retired.
Paragas, Rudsend *s.s.s.* '05 (CHI) Chicago, IL Blessed Sacrament.
Paraguya, Felipe '68 (SAC) Sacramento, CA St. Paul.
Paraiso, Oscar (RIC) Hampton, VA St. Joseph.
Parakkal, Baiju *o.ss.t.* '05 (BAL)[Q] Assigned in India.
Paramo, Raymond *c.s.b.* '66 (DET)[E] Novi, MI Catholic Central High School.
Parampakattil, Jacob Christy '90 (SYM) Stafford, TX St. Joseph Syro–Malabar Catholic Church (Houston); Stafford, TX St. Joseph Syro–Malabar Catholic Church.
Parampath, Joseph K. '53 (BGP)[O] Stamford, CT The Catherine Dennis Keefe Queen of the Clergy Retired Priests' Residence Retired.
Parampil, Jojo George Padinjare Pariyathu *o.ss.t.* '11 (BAL)[Q] In Residence – Holy Trinity Monastery Baltimore.
Parangan, Maynard V. '06 (GAL) Highlands, TX St. Jude Thaddeus.
Paraniuk, Michael A. '81 (CIN) Hillsboro, OH St. Mary; Greenfield, OH St. Benignus.
Parappally, Rev. Msgr. James '59 (MIA) Retired.
Parathanal, Jose '90 (LA) South Pasadena, CA Holy Family.
Paratore, Matthew R. '09 (MET) Canonical Staff; Middlesex, NJ Our Lady of Mount Virgin.
Parayno, Martin *o.s.b.* '94 (SAT) San Antonio, TX Santo Nino de Cebu.
Parchem, Peter *o.f.m.conv.* '51 (MRY) Pismo Beach, CA St. Paul the Apostle.
Parcon, Jose Maria M. '89 (NEW) Jersey City, NJ Parish of the Resurrection.
Pardee, Charles D. '84 (JC) Saint James, MO St. Anthony; Saint James, MO Immaculate Conception.
Pardue, John '88 (ALX) Woodworth, LA Congregation of Mary, Mother of Jesus Roman Catholic Church, Woodworth, Louisiana.
Pare, Arthur H. *s.j.* '60 (BO)[U] Boston The Society of Jesus of New England–Provincial Offices; [U] Weston, MA Campion Health Center, Inc.
Pare, Paul M. '53 (PRT) Lewiston, ME Prince of Peace Parish Retired.
Pare, Paul *o.f.m.* '00 (SUP) Ashland, WI St. Mary; North Central Deanery; Ashland, WI Our Lady of the Lake Catholic Community.
Pare, Robert '79 (SAG) Caseville, MI St. Roch; Kinde, MI St. Felix; Territorial Vicars.
Paredes, Edmundo B. '85 (DAL) Dallas, TX St. Cecilia; Personnel Board; At Large Members.
Paredes, Gabriel '91 (SFE) Defenders of the Bond; Albuquerque, NM San Jose; Albuquerque, NM St. Francis Xavier; Vicars Forane (Deans); Presbyteral Council of the Archdiocese of Santa Fe.
Paredes, Gregorio '68 (MGZ) San Sebastian, PR San Sebastian Martir.
Paredes, Hernan *s.j.* '95 (NY)[DD] New York, NY St. Ignatius Loyola Residence.
Paredes, Jorge '95 (ARE) Vega–Baja, PR Holy Rosary.
Paredes Monjaras, Antonio Francisco *s.s.p.* (LA)[P] Los Angeles, CA The Society of St. Paul.
Parekkat, Winson '68 (BRK) Brooklyn, NY St. Bernard of Clairvaux.
Parekkat, Winson *c.m.i.* '72 (L) Louisville, KY St. Luke; Louisville, KY St. Rita.
Parekkatt, Joseph '74 (OAK) Walnut Creek, CA St. Anne.
Parel, Joseph '67 (HRT) Northford, CT St. Monica.
Parent, Basil R. '86 (NTN) Priests Serving Outside the Eparchy.
Parent, Rev. Msgr. J. Wilfrid '91 (WDC) Waldorf, MD St. Peter; Deans.
Parent, Lawrence *o.f.m.* '98 (HRT) New Milford, CT St. Francis Xavier.
Parent, Norman E. *o.m.i.* (BO)[Z] Lowell, MA Andre Garin Residence; Lowell, MA Holy Family.
Parent, Philip E. *s.m.* '81 (BO) Boston, MA Our Lady of Victories.
Parent, Rene L. *m.s.* '76 (SPR) Westfield, MA Holy Trinity.
Parent, Robert '86 (PRT) Latin Mass.
Parent, Royal J. '56 (PRT) Retired.
Parente, Lino S. *o.cist.* '65 (TR) Mount Laurel, NJ St. John Neumann; [N] Mount Laurel, NJ Cistercian Monastery of Our Lady of Fatima; Mount Laurel, NJ.
Parenti, Thomas M. '74 (SFR) Sausalito, CA St. Mary Star of the Sea; Navy Reserve Chaplains.
Paretsky, Albert *o.p.* '81 (OAK) Berkeley, CA St. Mary Magdalen; [A] Berkeley, CA Dominican School of Philosophy and Theology.
Paretsky, J. Albert *o.p.* '81 (NY)[DD] New York St. Vincent Ferrer Priory.
Parfienczyk, Rev. Msgr. Stanislaw (BO) Salem, MA St. John the Baptist.
Parham, William J. '76 (MEM) Collierville, TN Church of the Incarnation.
Paril, Rico '98 (MET) Martinsville, NJ Blessed Sacrament.
Parillo, Emery *o.f.m.* '51 (NY)[DD] New York Franciscan Province of the Immaculate Conception.
Parillo, Emery *o.f.m.* '55 (BO)[U] Boston, MA St. Christopher Friary Retired.
Paris, Basil '98 (STN)[A] Eagle Harbor, MI Holy Transfiguration Skete.
Paris, Benedetto J. '95 (MAR) Marquette, MI St. Louis the King (Harvey); Apostleship of the Sea; Chancellor; Administrator and Notary; Vicars Forane; Bishop Baraga Association Inc.; Cemeteries; Knights of Columbus; Promoter of Justice.
Paris, Benedetto J. (GLD) Defender of the Bond.
Paris, John U. '50 (BO)[D] Needham, MA St. Sebastian's School, Inc.
Paris, John *s.j.* '69 (BO)[U] Newton, MA The Jesuit Community at Boston College.
Paris, Michael '11 (WDC) Rockville, MD St. Patrick.
Parise, Michael '79 (BO) Absent on Leave.
Parisi, Frank J. '85 (RVC) Malverne, NY Our Lady of Lourdes.
Parisi, Joseph L. '74 (STL) Overland, MO St. Jude.
Parisi, Michael R. '28 (BRK) Retired.
Parisi, Michael '55 (BRK) Flushing, NY St. Kevin Retired.
Parisi, Michael '82 (MO) Military Chaplains; Navy Chaplains; Presbyteral Council.
Parizek, Rev. Msgr. James F. '72 (DAV) Davenport, IA Our Lady of Victory; [M] Davenport, IA Quad Cities Catholic Deaf Ministry; Deans; Promoters of Justice.
Park, Adam Y. '05 (WDC) Secretary to the Archbishop; Pastoral Center Special Ministries.
Park, Andrew J. '09 (NEW) Bloomfield, NJ Sacred Heart.
Park, Rev. Msgr. Augustin C. '61 (NEW) Maplewood, NJ St. Andrew Kim; [Q] Orange, NJ Mee Joo Catholic Inc.; Our Lady Mother of God Curia (Korean); Our Lady, Gate of Heaven Curia (Korean) Retired.
Park, Augustine '93 (FWT) Hurst, TX Korean Martyrs.
Park, Austin N. *s.j.* '55 (NO)[R] New Orleans, LA Ignatius Residence Retired.
Park, Hongshik Don Bosco '01 (NEW) Saddle Brook, NJ Church of Korean Martyrs.
Park, John Sung Woo '93 (PH) Philadelphia, PA Holy Angels; Korean Apostolate.
Park, Robert G. '57 (WH) Wheeling, WV St. Joseph's Cathedral; Behavioral Counseling and Ministry.
Park, Shin–Hwa '89 (LA) Hospital Chaplains.
Park, Thomas R. '65 (SEA) Federal Way, WA St. Vincent De Paul.
Parke, Frederick R. '75 (STA) Jacksonville, FL Assumption.
Parke, James E. '65 (RIC) Virginia Beach, VA Church of the Holy Apostles.
Parker, Adam J. '00 (BAL) Special Assignment.
Parker, Adam '94 (BAL) Baltimore, MD Basilica of the National Shrine of the Assumption of the Blessed Virgin Mary.
Parker, Carroll *o.m.i.* '61 (FgM) Washington, DC AMERICAN OBLATE MISSIONS.
Parker, Charles '71 (PHX) Retired.
Parker, Frank J. *s.j.* '73 (BO)[U] Newton, MA The Jesuit Community at Boston College.
Parker, Glenn D. *c.ss.r.* '85 (ORL)[F] New Smyrna Beach, FL Redemptorist Fathers of the Vice Province of Richmond; [F] New Smyrna Beach, FL St. Alphonsus Villa–Redemptorist Fathers and Brothers; Consultors.
Parker, James W. '03 (RCK) East Dubuque, IL St. Mary; East Dubuque, IL Nativity of the Blessed Virgin Mary.
Parker, James '82 (CHR) Retired.
Parker, John W. '70 (CHI) Chicago, IL All Saints–St. Anthony.
Parker, Kenneth '65 (R) Retired.
Parker, Larry '84 (WCH) Oswego, KS Mother of God.
Parker, Michael J. '83 (BUF) Kenmore, NY St. John the Baptist.
Parker, Nicholas '08 (SAL) Atwood, KS Sacred Heart Parish; Atwood, KS St. John Nepomucene Parish; Atwood, KS Assumption of Mary Parish; Priests' Continuing Formation Committee.
Parker, Theodore K. '72 (DET) Detroit, MI St. Cecilia; Detroit, MI St. Leo; College of Consultors.
Parker, William C. '64 (TOL) Judges Retired.
Parker, William *c.ss.r.* '73 (STL)[O] Liguori, MO Liguori Mission House/Redemptorists.
Parkerson, Paul M. '98 (R) Dunn, NC Sacred Heart.
Parkes, Gregory '99 (ORL) Ex Officio Members.
Parkes, Gregory '99 (ORL) Vicar General and Chancellor for Canonical Affairs; Defenders of the Bond; Celebration, FL Corpus Christi.
Parkes, Joseph P. *s.j.* '76 (NY)[E] New York, NY Cristo Rey New York High School, Inc.; [DD] New York, NY "America;" Residence and publication office of the America Press; [E] New York, NY Cristo Rey New York High School, Inc.
Parkes, Stephen D. '98 (ORL) Longwood, FL Annunciation; Deans; Ex Officio Members.
Parkos, John F. '64 (STP) Retired.
Parks, John '10 (PHX) Mesa, AZ St. Timothy Roman Catholic Parish.
Parks, John '10 (PHX)[A] Scottsdale, AZ Notre Dame Preparatory Roman Catholic High School.
Parks, Rev. Msgr. Richard E. '59 (BAL) Baltimore, MD Sacred Heart of Mary Retired.
Parks, Richard L. *c.p.* '70 (SAC)[H] Citrus Heights, CA Christ the King Passionist Retreat Center; Presbyteral Council.
Parlante, Rev. Msgr. Gregory J. '82 (PH) Chadds Ford, PA St. Cornelius; Permanent Diaconate Department; On Special or Other Archdiocesan Assignment.
Parle, Richard '56 (SEA) Retired.
Parlet, Stephen J. '97 (COS) Buena Vista, CO St. Rose of Lima; Western Deanery; Presbyteral Council; Vicars Forane.
Parlette, Thomas L. '89 (DAV) Davenport, IA St. Alphonsus; Buffalo, IA St. Peter's.
Parnassas, Rev. Msgr. George John '53 (LA) West Hollywood, CA St. Victor Retired.
Parnell, Dennis R. *s.j.* '93 (SJ)[M] Los Gatos, CA California Province of the Society of Jesus, Jesuit Provincial Office; [B] Santa Clara, CA Jesuit Community.
Paron, William J. '69 (STP) Retired.

Parqualetto, Vicente *s.t.* '70 (FAJ) Vicar General.
Parr, Charles J. '73 (PAT) Theological Commission; Wayne, NJ Holy Cross; Ecumenical Officer; Pompton Plains, NJ Our Lady of Good Counsel Retired.
Parr, John L. '78 (LC) Holmen, WI St. Elizabeth Ann Seton.
Parra, Andres '05 (SJ) San Jose, CA Sacred Heart of Jesus.
Parra, Pedro *c.s.c.* '99 (FTW)[H] Notre Dame Congregation of Holy Cross, United States Province of Priests & Brothers.
Parrinello, Frank P. '00 (OM) On Duty Outside the Archdiocese.
Parrinello, Frank *f.s.s.p.* '99 (HBG) Mater Dei Community.
Parrish, Bryan K. '88 (BO) Trustees; Quincy, MA Sacred Heart.
Parrish, Bryan K. '88 (BO) Assistant to the Moderator of the Curia.
Parrish, Bryon (BO)[CC] Braintree, MA Caritas Christi Retirement Plan and Trust.
Parrish, Daniel J. *c.s.c.* (FTW)[H] Notre Dame Congregation of Holy Cross, United States Province of Priests & Brothers.
Parrish, L. Jerome '04 (CHI) Other Assignments.
Parrott, Gregory '09 (WIN)[C] Austin, MN Pacelli Catholic Middle/Senior High School; Austin, MN Queen of Angels; Austin, MN Our Lady of Loretto.
Parrotta, Michael '01 (FAR) Wellington, FL St. Rita Retired.
Parry, Rev. Msgr. Charles J. '81 (WDC) Bowie, MD Sacred Heart; Deans.
Parry, Denis '94 (FgM) Boston, MA St. James the Apostle, Inc.
Parsch, David L. '80 (SAG) Saginaw, MI Holy Spirit.
Parson, Donald J. '90 (BAL) Oakland, MD St. Peter the Apostle; Advocates.
Parsons, LaSalle *o.f.m.cap.* '57 (FgM) White Plains, NY The Province of St. Mary of the Capuchin Order.
Parsons, Vincent L. '01 (GI) Scottsbluff, NE St. Agnes; Priests' Advisory Board (Presbyteral Council).
Partain, Chad A. '03 (ALX) Archivist; College of Consultors; Elected Members; Mansura, LA St. Paul the Apostle; Chancellor.
Partee, Chrysostom *o.f.m.* '50 (SFE)[H] Albuquerque, NM The Province of Our Lady of Guadalupe.
Partida, Rafael A. '86 (SB) Fontana, CA Blessed John XXIII Catholic Community, Inc.; Elected Members.
Partida, Rafael '86 (SB) Elected Members.
Partika, Richard '51 (DUL) Retired.
Partin, Lamar *c.ss.r.* '11 (GR)[L] Grand Rapids, MI The Society of the Redemptorists of the City of Grand Rapids; Grand Rapids, MI St. Alphonsus.
Partridge, Bede *o.s.b.* '58 (P)[L] St. Benedict, OR Mt. Angel Abbey.
Partridge, Francis C. '60 (GLD) Retired.
Partusch, Frank A. '72 (OM) Omaha, NE St. Bridget; Omaha, NE St. Rose.
Parzymies, Joseph K. '78 (HRT) Retired.
Parzynski, Tomasz P. '10 (SPR) Springfield, MA Our Lady of the Sacred Heart.
Pasadilla, Nicolas O. '72 (GAL) Magnolia, TX St. Matthias the Apostle.
Pasala, Balaswamy (CC) Beeville, TX St. James.
Pasala, Lourdu '80 (GRY) Hobart, IN Assumption of the Blessed Virgin Mary; Judges.
Pasalic, Nikola *o.f.m.* (NY) New York, NY SS. Cyril and Methodius – St. Raphael.
Pascazi, Louis F. '80 (PIT) Ellwood City, PA Holy Redeemer Parish.
Pasche, Fred *o.f.m.conv.* '64 (FTW) Angola, IN St. Anthony.
Pasciak, Marcel J. '74 (CHI) Hickory Hills, IL St. Patricia.
Pasciuto, Joseph C. '91 (BRK) Retired.
Pascoe, Louis B. *s.j.* '64 (NY)[DD] Loyola Hall, Jesuit Community.
Pascual, Antonio S. '60 (RVC) Wantagh, NY St. Frances de Chantal Retired.
Pascual, Celestino V. (BO) Filipino.
Pascual, Lope D. '82 (MET)[M] Stewartsville, NJ Society of Jesus Christ the Priest.
Pascual, Manuel '46 (FRS) Retired.
Pascucci, Philip *s.d.b.* '51 (NEW)[C] Ramsey, NJ Don Bosco Preparatory High School; [L] Ramsey, NJ Don Bosco Prep Salesian Residence Retired.
Pashley, Rev. Msgr. Wilfred J. '63 (PH) Philadelphia, PA St. Barbara; Philadelphia, PA St. Rose of Lima.
Pasieczny, Roman '80 (DET) Warren, MI St. Martin de Porres; Presbyteral Council.
Pasik, Mark A. '76 (SY) Utica, NY St. Mark.
Paskey, Robert V. *s.j.* '66 (PRT) Portland, ME Our Lady of Hope Parish; Portland, ME Mercy Hospital.
Paskowicz, Marian '54 (ALN) Retired.
Pasley, Robert C. '82 (CAM)[O] Berlin, NJ Mater Ecclesiae Mission.
Pasqualetto, Vicente *s.t.* '70 (FAJ) Luquillo, PR San Jose.
Pasqualetto, Vicente *s.t.* '70 (SJN) Apostolado Del Cenaculo Misionero.
Pasquinelli, Rev. Msgr. Frederick A. '52 (STU) Retired.
Pasquini, John J. '98 (PMB) Vero Beach, FL St. John of the Cross.
Passalacqua, Robert '83 (SJ) Retired.
Passamonti, Paul G. '95 (WDC) Military Chaplains; Army Chaplains.
Passant, Paul A. '98 (NEW) On Duty Outside the Archdiocese.
Passant, Paul '98 (PHX) Tolleson, AZ Blessed Sacrament Roman Catholic Parish.
Passauer, Gregory P. '86 (E) Crown, PA St. Mary.
Passenant, Francis J. (BRK) Forest Hills, NY Our Lady Queen of Martyrs.
Passeri, Richard *o.f.m.* '47 (BO)[U] Boston, MA St. Christopher Friary Retired.
Passero, Ernest F. *s.j.* '70 (BO)[U] Weston, MA Campion Health Center, Inc.
Passos, Preston P. '08 (LA) North Hollywood, CA St. Charles Borromeo.
Pastick, Joseph A. '49 (CHI) Retired.
Pastirik, Joachim *o.s.b.* '69 (CLV)[N] Cleveland, OH.
Pastizzo, Michael H. *s.j.* '70 (BUF)[N] Buffalo, NY Canisius Jesuit Community Inc.
Pastores, Jerome '86 (OG)[I] Hogansburg, NY St. Regis Mission.
Pastorius, Thomas M. '03 (STL) St. Louis, MO St. Mark.
Pastors, Jerome P. '98 (GB) Kaukauna, WI St. Katharine Drexel.
Pastro, Vincent '78 (SEA) Kent, WA Holy Spirit Parish.
Pasupalety, Sebastian '81 (CC) Corpus Christi, TX Our Lady of Mount Carmel.
Paszko, John M. '74 (MIA) Coral Springs, FL St. Elizabeth Ann Seton.
Patalano, Anthony *o.p.* '86 (ANC) Anchorage, AK Holy Family Cathedral.
Patalinghug, Leo E. '99 (BAL) Special Assignment; [A] Emmitsburg, MD Mount St. Mary's Seminary.
Patalino, Anthony *o.p.* '76 (ANC) Diocesan Consultors.
Patau, Siaosi E. '04 (DET) Armada, MI St. Mary Mystical Rose.
Patella, Michael *o.s.b.* '90 (SCL)[A] Collegeville, MN St. John's School of Theology and Seminary; [I] Collegeville, MN St. John's Abbey, of the Order of St. Benedict.
Pateno, Pelagio Calambia *s.v.d.* (TR) Lakewood, NJ St. Anthony Claret.
Pater, Aurel '90 (ROM) Aurora, IL St. Michael; Finance Council; College of Consultors; Aurora Deanery.
Pater, Daniel R. '79 (CIN) Priests On Administrative Leave.
Pater, Giles H. '58 (CIN) Retired.
Paternoster, Alejandro '94 (LFT) Alexandria, IN St. Mary; Elwood, IN St. Joseph; Wheatfield, IN Sorrowful Mother.
Patete, Michael A. '62 (NEW) Retired.
Pathe, Eugene '56 (PT) Charismatic Renewal, Diocesan Commission for.
Pathirana, Angelo Sujeewa *s.j.* '05 (NY)[DD] Loyola Hall, Jesuit Community.
Pathiyamoola, Paul '70 (SFS) Canton, SD St. Dominic.
Pathiyamoola Ouseph, Jolly '02 (GF) Wolf Point, MT Immaculate Conception; Special Assignment.
Pathiyil, Joseph '88 (HON) Lahaina, HI Maria Lanakila.
Pathmarajah, T. Pius '72 (ROC) Judges; Rochester, NY St. John the Evangelist.
Patillo, Rev. Msgr. Bennie J. '67 (BEA) Diocesan College of Consultors; Clergy Personnel Board; Diocesan Judges; Port Neches, TX St. Elizabeth; Presbyteral Council.
Patin, Lawrence *c.ss.r.* '63 (FgM) Denver, CO Denver Province.
Patin, Paul B. *s.j.* '73 (LAF)[J] Grand Coteau, LA Our Lady of the Oaks Retreat House.
Patino, Carlos (FR) West Harwich, MA Holy Trinity.
Patino, Ruben M. *c.s.p.* '79 (AUS) Horseshoe Bay, TX St. Paul the Apostle.
Patino Montoya, Fredy '10 (NY) Haverstraw, NY St. Peter.
Patino Villa, Carlos Alberto '00 (FR) Cape Cod; Nantucket.
Patnode, Rev. Msgr. Michael '72 (CR) Diaconate Office; Georgetown, MN St. John; Moorhead, MN St. Francis de Sales.
Patnode, Ronald J. '61 (YAK) Clergy Personnel Board; Yakima, WA Holy Family Retired.
Patout, Rivers '67 (GAL) Houston, TX St. Alphonsus; Apostleship of the Sea (Port Ministry); Area Representatives.
Patricius, J. M. '57 (NEW) Retired.
Patrick, Rev. Msgr. John E. '67 (MAR) Retired.
Patrick, Michael '83 (P) Bandon, OR Holy Trinity; Judges; Board Members.
Patrick, Richard Martin *o.p.* '65 (GAL)[O] Houston, TX Dominican Friars, St. Mark Priory, Inc.
Patrick, William J. '58 (CLV) Released from Diocesan Assignment Retired.
Patriquin, Garry D. '84 (PIT) Absent on Sick Leave.
Patrizio, Anthony '66 (CAM) Mays Landing, NJ St. Vincent de Paul Parish, Mays Landing, N.J.
Patron, Charles A. '62 (SB) Riverside, CA Our Lady of Perpetual Help.
Patrylak, Frank '62 (PHU) Retired.
Patte, Steven W. '69 (CHI) Other Assignments.
Pattee, Daniel *t.o.r* '87 (STU)[A] Steubenville, OH Franciscan University of Steubenville; [H] Steubenville, OH Holy Spirit Friary.
Patten, Patrick A. *c.s.sp.* '78 (FgM) Bethel Park, PA CONGREGATION OF THE HOLY SPIRIT.
Patterson, Alfred *o.s.b.* '90 (ALT) Summerhill, PA St. John.
Patterson, Alfred *o.s.b.* '90 (GBG)[H] Latrobe, PA Saint Vincent Archabbey.
Patterson, Bruce '86 (ORG) Mission Viejo, CA St. Kilian; Sexual Misconduct and Oversight Review Board (SMORB); Council of Priests.
Patterson, Bryan D. '99 (BRK) Cambria Heights, NY Sacred Heart; Censors of Books.
Patterson, Frank '67 (SAV) Columbus, GA Holy Family.
Patterson, James *c.ss.r.* '50 (STL)[O] Liguori, MO St. Clement Health Care Center Retired.
Patterson, John H. *s.o.l.t.* '02 (CC)[G] Robstown, TX Society of Our Lady of the Most Holy Trinity.
Patterson, Patrick *c.pp.s.* '65 (COL) Columbus, OH St. James–the–Less.
Patterson, Ralph '03 (OWN) Absent on Leave.
Patterson, Randall P. '70 (ALB) Troy, NY Our Lady of Victory; Deans; Architecture and Building Commission; Troy, NY Our Lady of Victory Education Center.
Patterson, Stephen *s.j.* '08 (OAK)[L] Berkeley, CA Jesuit Fathers and Brothers.
Patterson, Terrence R. '66 (OG) Retired.
Patti, Angelo J. '82 (ALT) Presbyteral Council; Johnstown, PA St. Andrew.
Patti, Steven R. *o.f.m.* '01 (PRO) Providence, RI St. Mary; [O] Providence, RI St. Francis Friary.
Pattison, Rev. Msgr. W. Francis '58 (SD) Retired.
Patton, James J. '65 (CLV) Perry, OH St. Cyprian Retired.
Patton, Mel *o.s.b.* '56 (IND)[K] Saint Meinrad St. Meinrad Archabbey.
Patullo, Michael '02 (DUL) On Duty Outside the Diocese.
Paul, Benedict '84 (NY) Bronx, NY St. Michael.
Paul, David *s.m.* '70 (STL)[O] St. Louis Marianists, Province of the United States (Society of Mary).
Paul, Dennis '93 (JOL) Bloomingdale, IL St. Isidore.
Paul, Gregory *c.p.* '58 (HRT)[L] West Hartford Holy Family Monastery/Retreat; [P] West Hartford, CT Holy Family Passionist Retreat Center.
Paul, Jeyamani '92 (P) Coos Bay, OR St. Monica.
Paul, John F. *s.j.* '92 (NO) Gretna, LA Jefferson Parish Correctional Center; [R] New Orleans, LA Ignatius Residence.
Paul, John J. *m.s.c.* '58 (ALN) Diocesan Tribunal; [A] Center Valley, PA Sacred Heart Villa, Missionaries of the Sacred Heart.
Paul, John M. *s.j.* '80 (MIL)[P] Milwaukee, WI Jesuit Provincial Office, Wisconsin Province; Milwaukee, WI; [P] Milwaukee, WI Arrupe House Jesuit Community.
Paul, John P. '72 (PH) Philadelphia, PA Our Lady of Calvary.
Paul, Kasiano '02 (CI) Our Lady of Mercy.
Paul, Pinto *c.s.c.* '99 (FR)[A] North Easton, MA Holy Cross Fathers Religious; [A] North Easton, MA Stonehill College.
Paul, Raphael '87 (SFD) Brighton, IL St. Alphonsus; Brighton, IL St. John the Evangelist.
Paul, Raymond L. '62 (Y) Massillon, OH St. Joseph; Defenders of the Bond.
Paul, Thomas Elmus '07 (ALX) Natchitoches, LA St. Anthony of Padua.
Paul, Thomas '77 (JOL) Elmhurst, IL Immaculate Conception.
Paulin, Jeremy *o.m.v.* '06 (BO)[B] Boston, MA Our Lady of Grace Seminary.
Paulino, Felino '77 (SEA) Seattle, WA St. Edward; Seattle, WA St. George; Seattle, WA St. Paul; Seattle, WA St. Mary.
Paulino, P. Samuel Fernandez *o.c.d.* (CGS)[A] Caguas, PR Colegio San Jose Elemental.
Paulish, W. Jeffrey '88 (MO) DEPARTMENT OF VETERANS AFFAIRS HOSPITALS AND CHAPLAINS; Unassigned or Leave of Absence.
Paulissen, Richard E. *m.m.* '63 (GAL)[O] Houston Maryknoll Fathers and Brothers.
Paulissen, Richard E. *m.m.* '63 (NY)[DD] Retired.
Paulli, Kenneth *o.f.m.* '90 (ALB)[B] Loudonville, NY Siena College; [B] Siena College.
Paulos, George Maliekal '01 (SYM) Seffner, FL St. Joseph Syro–Malabar Catholic Church (Tampa).
Paulose, Antony *c.m.i.* '97 (BEA) Beaumont, TX Our Lady of the Assumption.
Paulose, Wilson Kidangan '80 (CAM) Lindenwold, NJ Our Lady of Guadalupe Parish, Lindenwold, N.J.
Paulsen, Harold P. '78 (TYL) Palestine, TX Powledge Unit, Texas Department of Criminal Justice.
Paulsen, Timothy W. *o.m.i.* '97 (BWN) Brownsville, TX St. Eugene De Mazenod.
Paulson, Brian G. *s.j.* '92 (CHI)[C] Chicago, IL Jesuit Community at Loyola University Chicago.
Paulson, Harold P. '78 (TYL) Tennessee Colony, TX

Coffield Unit, Texas Department of Hodge Unit and Skyview Unit, Texas Department of Criminal Justice; Tennessee Colony, TX Gurney Unit; Tennessee Colony, TX Michael Unit Retired.
Paulson, Jerome E. '76 (NU) College of Consultors; Priests' Council; Spicer, MN Our Lady of the Lakes.
Paur, Roman *o.s.b.* '66 (SCL)[I] Collegeville St. John's Abbey, of the Order of St. Benedict.
Paurazas, Peter P. '55 (CHI) Chicago, IL St. Rene Goupil Retired.
Pausche, Frederick F. '78 (CLV) Concord Twp., OH St. Gabriel.
Pauselli, Francis L. '75 (SCR) Scranton, PA Divine Mercy.
Pautler, Mark '74 (SPK) Spokane, WA Sacred Heart; Chancellor; Judicial Vicar.
Pavamkott, George *o.praem.* '92 (SFE) Isleta, NM St. Augustine; [H] Albuquerque, NM Santa Maria de la Vid Priory.
Pavela, Wayne (OM) Humphrey, NE St. Francis.
Pavelis, Harold '51 (SCL) Retired.
Pavia, Nicholas S. '00 (BGP) Vicariate IV (East Bridgeport, Stratford, Trumbull, Monroe, Shelton); Shelton, CT St. Joseph.
Pavich, Philip *o.f.m.* '57 (CHI)[N] Chicago, IL St. Anthony's Friary.
Pavich, Philip *o.f.m.* '57 (DET) Troy, MI St. Lucy.
Pavignano, Steven J. *o.f.m.* '78 (BUF)[N] Buffalo, NY St. Patrick Friary; Buffalo, NY St. Clare.
Pavignano, Steven *o.f.m.* '78 (NY) New York, NY All Saints; [DD] New York, NY All Saints Friary.
Pavis, Rev. Msgr. Victor S. '43 (NY)[DD] Bronx, NY Retired.
Pavlak, Andrew J. '00 (SFE) Socorro, NM San Miguel.
Pavlakovich, Michael '87 (DEN) Littleton, CO Light of the World Parish; Deaneries.
Pavlicek, Edward A. '83 (SAT) Schertz, TX Church of the Good Shepherd.
Pavlicek, Rev. Msgr. Louis '71 (AUS) Associate Directors; Presbyteral Council Retired.
Pavlick, Raymond A. '71 (NY) Castle Point, NY V.A. Hudson Valley Healthcare.
Pavlick, Raymond A. '71 (MO) On Duty Outside the Diocese; DEPARTMENT OF VETERANS AFFAIRS HOSPITALS AND CHAPLAINS.
Pavlik, David P. '78 (CHI) Chicago, IL Saint Ita.
Pavlik, John *o.f.m.cap.* (WDC) Washington, DC Shrine of the Sacred Heart.
Pavlik, Mark L. '03 (STP) Minneapolis, MN St. Olaf.
Pavlik, Paul R. *t.o.r.* '59 (FgM) Loretto, PA THIRD ORDER REGULAR MISSIONS.
Pavlock, Martin L. '66 (BUF) Retired.
Pavlovsky, Wencil C. '91 (GAL) Houston, TX St. Paul.
Pavone, Frank '88 (AMA)[G] Prayer Town, TX Disciples of the Lord Jesus Christ.
Pavur, Claude N. *s.j.* '84 (STL)[C] Saint Louis University; [O] St. Louis, MO Jesuit Community Corporation at Saint Louis University – Jesuit Hall.
Pawelec, Henryk '04 (MIA) Tavernier, FL San Pedro; Spiritual Moderators.
Pawelko, Michael '10 (PH) Southampton, PA Our Lady of Good Counsel.
Pawell, Robert '66 (CHI)[N] Chicago, IL Holy Evangelists Friary.
Pawlaczyk, Miroslaw '92 (NY) Mahopac, NY St. John the Evangelist.
Pawlicki, James *s.v.d.* '73 (BLX)[D] Bay St. Louis, MS St. Augustine's Residence; [D] Bay St. Louis, MS Southern Province of St. Augustine – Provincial Offices; [D] Bay St. Louis, MS Media Production Center "In A Word"; Bay Saint Louis, MS Southern Province; Bay Saint Louis, MS.
Pawlik, Walter M. *s.d.s.* '58 (GRY)[H] Merrillville, IN Salvatorian Fathers (Society of the Divine Savior).
Pawlikowski, John M. *o.s.m.* '67 (CHI) Chicago, IL Assumption of the Blessed Virgin Mary; [B] Chicago, IL Catholic Theological Union; [N] Chicago, IL Assumption Priory.
Pawlikowski, Matthew '97 (MO) Military Chaplains; Army Chaplains.
Pawloski, Gregory P. '74 (LIN) Auburn, NE St. Joseph's.
Pawlowski, Joseph M. '73 (GRY) Valparaiso, IN St. Paul; Bishop's Council of Priests; Vicar General; Deans; Consultors; Priests' Personnel Board; Finance Council.
Pawlowski, Maciej J. *s.m.* (BRK) Brooklyn, NY St. Francis of Assisi–St. Blaise.
Pawlus, Piotr '10 (SPR) Easthampton, MA Our Lady of the Valley.
Pawson, Rev. Msgr. Robert J. '66 (BRK) Queens Village, NY Our Lady of Lourdes; Diocesan Finance Council.
Pax, Ulric *o.f.m.* '59 (SFE)[H] Albuquerque, NM The Province of Our Lady of Guadalupe.
Paxton, Philip *c.p.* '95 (DET)[P] Detroit, MI St. Paul of the Cross Passionist Retreat; [K] Detroit, MI St. Paul of the Cross Community, Congregation of the Passion.
Payea, Gerald *o.carm.* '70 (FgM) Darien, IL Provincial Headquarters, Carmelite Provincial Office.
Payea, Gerald *o.carm.* '70 (JOL)[L] Darien Carmelite Provincial Office.
Payer, Emil S. '71 (GBG)[G] Greensburg, PA Neumann House.
Payne, Charles E. *o.f.m.* (CHI)[N] Chicago, IL Holy Spirit Friary, Order of Friars Minor.
Payne, Gary '85 (OWN) Absent on Leave.
Payne, Jeremiah L. '07 (PMB)[A] Boynton Beach, FL St. Vincent de Paul Regional Seminary; On Duty Outside the Diocese.
Payne, John J. '01 (NO) Judges.
Payne, John Michael *o.c.d.* (DAL) Dallas, TX St. Mary of Carmel.
Payne, Mark '94 (MIL) Milwaukee, WI St. Veronica.
Payne, Nathaniel '10 (CHI)[A] Mundelein, IL University of St. Mary of the Lake/Mundelein Seminary; Mundelein, IL St. Mary of the Annunciation.
Payne, Stephen J. '71 (GAL) Huntsville, TX St. Thomas the Apostle; Northern Vicariate.
Payne, Steven *o.c.d.* '82 (MIL)[P] Milwaukee Provincial Offices – Discalced Carmelites.
Payo, Reuben '84 (DEN) Wheat Ridge, CO Sts. Peter and Paul.
Paysse, Wayne C. '87 (NO) On Duty Outside the Archdiocese; Board of Directors:; Board of Directors:; Board of Directors; Consultants.
Pazdan, Benedykt M. '06 (CHI) Arlington Heights, IL St. Edna.
Paz en la Casa, Vincente '66 (PBL) Florence, CO St. Benedict.
Pazhayakari, Philip *c.m.i.* '62 (SHP) Rayville, LA Sacred Heart.
Pazhayapurackal, Emmanuel J. *c.m.i.* '75 (STA) Gainesville, FL Holy Faith.
Pazhayaveetil, Binu Joseph *o.praem* '04 (SFE) Albuquerque, NM Our Lady of Most Holy Rosary; [H] Albuquerque, NM Santa Maria de la Vid Priory.
Pazheparambil, Thomas J. '00 (BLX) Pass Christian, MS Holy Family Parish.
Pazheveettil, Jose *m.s.t.* '97 (DAL) McKinney, TX St. Gabriel the Archangel.
Pazhoor, Mathew (NY) Mamaroneck, NY Most Holy Trinity.
Pazhukkathara, Shaji Joseph '02 (SUP) Ladysmith, WI St. Mary; Ladysmith, WI St. Francis of Assisi; Ladysmith, WI St. Mary of Czestochowa; Ladysmith, WI Our Lady of Sorrows; Ladysmith, WI St. Anthony de Padua; Ladysmith, WI SS. Peter and Paul.
Peach, Patrick Peter *o.carm.* '06 (STP) Lake Elmo, MN; [J] Lake Elmo, MN Carmelite Hermitage of the Blessed Virgin Mary.
Peach, Peter of Jesus *o.carm.* '06 (BAL) Priests Sick or Absent.
Peacha, Thomas James '59 (LA) Los Angeles, CA Holy Trinity Retired.
Peacher, Ignatius *o.cist.* '11 (DAL)[J] Irving, TX Cistercian Abbey of Our Lady of Dallas.
Peacock, Mark E. '07 (GR) Ada, MI St. Patrick's.
Peacock, Thomas E. *s.j.* '63 (BAL)[Q] Baltimore, MD Colombiere Jesuit Community.
Peak, James '07 (SPK) On Duty Outside the Diocese; Army Chaplains.
Pearce, Donald *s.j.* '59 (NO)[R] New Orleans, LA Ignatius Residence Retired.
Pearce, Joseph Francis *c.o.* '99 (CHR)[E] Rock Hill, SC Oratory of St. Philip Neri, Congregation of the Oratory of Pontifical Rite; Fort Mill, SC St. Philip Neri.
Pearsall, William T. '53 (BO) Senior Priests. Retired.
Pearson, Everett '91 (WDC) Forestville, MD Mt. Calvary.
Pearson, John A. '66 (NU) Committee for Continuing Education of Clergy; Darwin, MN St. John; Litchfield, MN St. Gertrude.
Pearson, John H. *c.s.c.* '73 (FTW)[A] Notre Dame, IN Moreau Seminary.
Pearson, Rev. Msgr. Robert A. '65 (SPK) Spokane, WA Retired.
Pearson, Robert A. '78 (TR) Retired.
Pease, Raymond A. *s.j.* '68 (FgM) St. Louis, MO Society of Jesus.
Peatee, Gregory L. '92 (TOL) Toledo, OH St. Charles Borromeo; Toledo, OH St. Hyacinth; College of Consultors.
Pecaric, Alfred F. '82 (BGP) Defenders of the Bond; Fairfield, CT Holy Cross.
Pecchie, Paul '95 (SP) Largo, FL St. Patrick; Elected Pastors.
Pecci, Ronald J. *o.f.m.* '83 (WIL) Wilmington, DE St. Paul's.
Pecevich, Conrad S. '77 (WOR) Southborough, MA St. Anne.
Pecharroman, Ovidio '65 (WDC) Washington, DC Diocesan Laborer Priests; [B] Washington, DC Diocesan Laborer Priests, House of Studies.
Pechillo, Arthur C. '01 (PRT) Retired.
Pecht, Gerard J. *c.ss.r.* '50 (STL)[O] Liguori, MO St. Clement Health Care Center Retired.
Peck, David A. '94 (RCK) Rockford, IL St. Rita; [B] Elgin, IL St. Edward Central Catholic High School; Special Assignment.
Peck, John J. *o.s.b.* '89 (HBG) Annville, PA St. Paul the Apostle; [I] Annville, PA Lebanon Valley College.
Peck, John W. *s.j.* (BAL)[B] Jesuit Community of Loyola University, Inc.; [Q] Baltimore, MD Jesuit Community of Loyola University, Inc.
Peck, John *o.s.b.* '89 (GBG)[H] Latrobe, PA Saint Vincent Archabbey.
Peck, Michael R. '11 (PIT) Ambridge, PA Good Samaritan; Baden, PA St. John the Baptist.
Pecklers, Keith F. *s.j.* '91 (NY)[DD] New York Jesuit Provincial's Office.
Peckman, R. William '97 (JC) Bowling Green, MO St. Clement; II. Hannibal; Ministry to Priests; Priestly and Religious Vocations Committee.
Pecoraro, Robert J. *s.j.* '10 (BUF)[N] Buffalo, NY Canisius Jesuit Community Inc.; [D] Buffalo, NY Canisius High School.
Pecotte, Robert '04 (FAR) Cavalier, ND St. Brigid of Ireland Church of Cavalier; Cavalier, ND St. Patrick's Church of Crystal.
Peddicord, Richard A. *o.p.* '86 (STL)[B] St. Louis, MO Aquinas Institute of Theology; [O] St. Louis, MO Dominican Community of St. Louis.
Pedersen, Bryan J. B. '03 (STP) Robbinsdale, MN Sacred Heart.
Pedersen, Gregg '11 (DEN) Foxfield, CO Our Lady of Loreto.
Pedi, Mario *o.s.b.* '57 (RCK)[G] Aurora, IL Marmion Abbey; [C] Aurora, IL Marmion Academy.
Pedigo, Jon '91 (SJ) San Jose, CA St. Julie Billiart.
Pednekar, Joseph Charles *m.s.f.s.* '62 (TYL)[C] Whitehouse, TX The Missionaries of St. Francis de Sales.
Pednekar, Joseph (CLV) North Olmsted, OH St. Brendan.
Pedone, Rev. Msgr. F. Stephen '78 (WOR) Judicial Vicar and Vicar for Canonical Affairs; Judges; Diocesan College of Consultors; Presbyteral Council; West Boylston, MA Our Lady of Good Counsel.
Pedrano, Stephanos *o.s.b.* '91 (SD)[J] Oceanside, CA Prince of Peace Abbey.
Pedrera, Gerald '11 (OAK) San Leandro, CA St. Leander.
Pedretti, Raymond J. '56 (LC) Retired.
Pedretti, Robert F. '64 (LC) Retired.
Pedrizetti, Raymond *o.s.b.* '58 (SCL)[I] Collegeville, MN St. John's Abbey, of the Order of St. Benedict.
Pedroso, Rafael '64 (MIA) Retired.
Pedroza, Peter *c.m.f.* (ATL) Stone Mountain, GA Corpus Christi.
Pedroza, Salvador '81 (LAR) Laredo, TX San Martin de Porres; Laredo, TX Santa Teresita Mission.
Peduti, Douglas *s.j.* '96 (BGP)[O] Fairfield, CT The Fairfield Jesuit Community–Fairfield University; [B] Fairfield, CT Fairfield University.
Pedzich, Henry J. '72 (SY) Syracuse, NY St. Michael & St. Peter.
Pedzik, Vitalis B. '61 (RVC) Retired.
Peek, Kevin T. '98 (ATL)[I] Atlanta, GA Georgia Institute of Technology; Special or Other Archdiocesan Assignment; Army Chaplains.
Peelo, Adrian *o.f.m.* '83 (SD) Oceanside, CA Mission San Luis Rey Catholic Parish.
Peeters, John N. *c.s.v.* '83 (CHI)[N] Arlington Heights Viatorian Province Center–Clerics of St. Viator.
Peeters, John N. *c.s.v.* '83 (JOL) Kankakee, IL St. Patrick.
Peffley, Francis J. '90 (ARL) Leesburg, VA St. John the Apostle.
Pegnam, William '67 (SJ) San Jose, CA Santa Teresa Retired.
Pehl, Jeffery '95 (SAT) Department of Assumption–St. John's Seminary; [A] San Antonio, TX Assumption Seminary.
Pehrsson, Alfred R. *c.m.* '58 (PH)[Y].
Peiffer, James E. '67 (TOL) Ecumenical and Interreligious Affairs Retired.
Peil, L. William '49 (GRY) Retired.
Peil, William '49 (FTW) Retired.
Peinado, Louis A. *s.j.* '60 (SJ)[M] Los Gatos, CA Sacred Heart Jesuit Center.
Peinemann, Michael E. '05 (SAT)[A] San Antonio, TX Assumption Seminary.
Peinemann, Michael E. '05 (SAT) Harper, TX St. Anthony's.
Peirano, Daniel '04 (TR) Long Branch, NJ The Church of Christ the King, Long Branch, N.J.
Peiris, Richard '62 (OAK) Retired.
Peixotto, Joseph *c.s.c.* '61 (FgM) New Rochelle, NY Eastern Brothers Province.
Pekar, Athanasius B. *o.s.b.m.* '46 (RVC)[N] Glen Cove, NY St. Josaphat's Monastery, Novitiate and Retreat House.
Pekar, Rev. Msgr. Joseph W. '57 (BGP) Bridgeport, CT SS. Cyril and Methodius.
Pekarske, Daniel *s.d.s.* '90 (MIL)[P] Milwaukee Salvatorian Provincial Offices; [B] Hales Corners, WI Sacred Heart School of Theology.
Peklo, Edward *s.v.d.* '69 (MIL)[P] East Troy, WI Divine Word Missionaries.
Pekola, David J. '86 (MET) Hackettstown, NJ Assumption of the Blessed Virgin Mary.
Pelaez, Oskar '94 (STO) Absent on Leave.

Pelak, Anthony M. '03 (GR) North Muskegon, MI Prince of Peace.
Pelc, Timothy R. '74 (DET) Grosse Pointe Park, MI St. Ambrose.
Pelczar, Edward A. '62 (PH) On Special or Other Archdiocesan Assignment; Philadelphia, PA St. Helena.
Pelczarski, Wojciech *s.d.s.* (NOR) Bolton, CT St. Maurice.
Peles, David S. '84 (ALT) Johnstown, PA St. Benedict's.
Pellegrini, Frederick J. *s.j.* '84 (NY) New York, NY St. Aloysius; [DD] New York, NY St. Ignatius Loyola Residence.
Pellegrino, Joseph A. '77 (SP) Tarpon Springs, FL St. Ignatius of Antioch; [F] Tarpon Springs, FL St. Ignatius Early Childhood Center; Diocesan Finance Council; Elected Pastors; Personnel Board.
Pellerin, Keith '98 (LKC) Lake Charles, LA St. Martin dePorres.
Pelletier, Emile "Bud" '94 (PHX) Priestly Life and Ministry Board.
Pelletier, Emile '94 (PHX) Phoenix, AZ St. Gregory Roman Catholic Parish.
Pelletier, Gerard E. *s.m.* '60 (WDC)[O] Washington, DC Marist Center.
Pelletier, Norman B. *s.s.s.* '69 (CLV)[N] Highland Heights, OH Congregation of the Blessed Sacrament Provincial House; [N] Cleveland, OH Congregation of the Blessed Sacrament; Cleveland, OH.
Pelletier, Walter R. *s.j.* '60 (BGP)[O] Fairfield, CT The Fairfield Jesuit Community–Fairfield University Retired.
Pellini, Robert R. *m.m.* '59 (FgM) Maryknoll, NY MARYKNOLL.
Pellissier, Francois *g.h.m.* '81 (LR) Danville, AR Saint Andrew Church; Waldron, AR St. Jude Thaddeus Church.
Peloso, John P. '96 (MIA) Pembroke Pines, FL St. Edward.
Pelotte, Dana *s.s.s.* '99 (GAL) Houston, TX Corpus Christi.
Pelous, Donald '77 (LAF) Retired.
Pelrine, Edward '01 (CHI) Elk Grove Village, IL Queen of the Rosary.
Pelster, Christopher *f.s.s.p.* '11 (OKL) Edmond, OK St. Damien of Molokai Chapel.
Pelton, Robert S. *c.s.c.* '49 (FTW)[B] University of Notre Dame Du Lac; [H] Notre Dame, IN Holy Cross Community, Corby Hall, University of Notre Dame.
Pelton, Thomas '66 (CHI) Chicago, IL Maternity of the Blessed Virgin Mary.
Peltz, Carl F. '77 (KAL) Buchanan, MI St. Anthony.
Peltzer, Michael '80 (WCH) Harper, KS St. Joan of Arc.
Peluse, Dominic *s.c.j.* '74 (MIL)[P] Franklin, WI St. Francis Residence.
Peluso, Frank *o.a.r.* '61 (NY) St. Joseph's Cursillo Center.
Pelzel, Bradley C. '02 (SC) Diocesan Consultors; Vocations; Sioux City, IA St. Joseph; Presbyteral Council; [A] Sioux City, IA Briar Cliff University.
Pemberton, James '05 (FWT) Fort Worth, TX St. Bartholomew.
Pemberton, Joseph '77 (FWT) Fort Worth, TX St. Patrick Cathedral.
Pena, Cesar E. '08 (MIA) Miami, FL Epiphany.
Pena, Giovanni de Jesus '10 (MIA) Miami, FL St. Michael the Archangel.
Pena, Richard '92 (SAT) San Antonio, TX St. Gabriel.
Pena, Roberto *o.m.i.* '55 (SAT)[K] San Antonio, TX Oblate Madonna Residence.
Pena–Moredo, Rev. Msgr. Wilfredo '74 (SJN) San Juan, PR Santa Bernardita Soubirous.
Penafiel, Fausto '83 (PHX) Phoenix, AZ St. Mark Roman Catholic Parish; Phoenix, AZ St. Philip the Deacon Mission, A Quasi–Parish; Priestly Life and Ministry Board.
Penalba, Vincent '69 (CGS) Caguas, PR Inmaculado Corazon de Maria.
Penalosa, Luis M. '99 (SR) Santa Rosa, CA Holy Spirit; Santa Rosa, CA Star of the Valley.
Penaloza, Jorge A. '60 (LA) Pico Rivera, CA St. Francis Xavier Retired.
Penascoza, Demitro '86 (CHY) Riverton, WY St. Margaret's; Diocesan Schools Advisory Group.
Penchi, Edward J. '56 (LC) Retired.
Pendergast, Richard J. *s.j.* '63 (NY)[DD] New York, NY Murray–Weigel Hall.
Penderghest, William T. *ss.cc.* '67 (BWN) Harlingen Deanery; Board Members; Harlingen, TX Queen of Peace.
Pendergraft, Gregory *f.s.s.p.* '05 (SCR)[L] Elmhurst Twp., PA Priestly Fraternity of St. Peter (F.S.S.P.), North American District Headquarters; Elmhurst Twp., PA.
Pendergraft, Michael '81 (STA) Lake City, FL Epiphany; Deans; Rural Life Director; Diocesan Consultors.
Pendleton, Arthur J. *o.s.b.* '64 (CHL)[J] Belmont, NC Belmont Abbey.
Pendolphi, Richard J. '76 (COL) Worthington, OH St. Michael.
Pendrick, Thomas E. '03 (NEW)[D] Paramus, NJ Paramus Catholic High School; Ridgewood, NJ Our Lady of Mount Carmel.
Pendzick, John S. '97 (ALN) Allentown, PA Our Lady Help of Christians.
Penez, Francisco '00 (AMA) Vicars Forane.
Peng, John B. '55 (CHI) Retired.
Penhallurick, Robert '96 (COL) Newark, OH St. Francis de Sales; [C] Newark, OH Newark Catholic High School.
Penisten, Edmund J. '02 (JUN) Yakutat, AK St. Ann.
Penisten, Edmund J. '02 (JUN) Diocesan Consultors.
Penkala, Rev. Msgr. Edmund S. '45 (SCR)[M] Dunmore, PA Villa St. Joseph Retired.
Penko, Francis '60 (SD) Retired.
Penn, Churchill '96 (BGP) Bridgeport, CT St. Ambrose.
Penn, Michael W. '03 (JC) Monroe City, MO St. Stephen; Monroe City, MO Holy Rosary; To The Bishop; Palmyra, MO St. Joseph.
Penna, Rev. Msgr. Joseph P. '67 (NY) Pearl River, NY St. Aedan.
Penna, Michael Della *o.f.m.* '99 (FgM) New York, NY Franciscan Province of the Immaculate Conception; Definitors.
Penna, Tony (BO) Boston College.
Pennett, Frederick J. '71 (MAN) Londonderry, NH St. Mark the Evangelist; Vicars Forane; Presbyteral Council.
Pennings, Gary '01 (KCK) Vicars General; Department of Parish Ministries; Ex Officio; Archdiocesan Consultors; Archdiocesan Council on Finances; Archdiocesan Administrative Team; Kansas City, KS St. Patrick's.
Pennington, John F. *s.j.* '70 (DET)[K] Clarkston, MI Colombiere Center.
Pennington, Rev. Msgr. John R. '79 (WDC) Silver Spring, MD St. John the Evangelist.
Pennington, Matthew '88 (MRY) Capitola, CA St. Joseph; Vicars Forane; Presbyteral Council; Diocesan Consultors; Diocesan Consultors.
Pennock, Michael '95 (JOL) Gilman, IL Immaculate Conception; Gilman, IL St. Peter.
Penonzek, Edward M. *o.s.m.* '58 (ORG)[I] Anaheim, CA Servite Fathers and Brothers.
Penta, Leo J. '78 (BRK) Released from Diocesan Assignment.
Pentareddy, John Paul Reddy '94 (CHR) Hilton Head Island, SC St. Francis By the Sea.
Pentecost, Denver B. '69 (NO) Marrero, LA Wynhoven Health Care Center.
Pentello, Richard J. '79 (Y) Kent, OH St. Patrick's.
Pentony, Liam '55 (JKS) Retired.
Pepe, Robert F. '50 (WCH) Retired.
Pepez, Ricardo A. '02 (BRK) Long Island City, NY Queen of Angels.
Pepin, Darryl J. '78 (MAR) Ironwood, MI Our Lady of Peace; [B] Ironwood, MI Our Lady of Peace School Educational Fund.
Pepin, Normand A. *s.j.* '63 (BO)[U] Weston, MA Campion Health Center, Inc.
Peplowski, Sigmund A. '75 (PAT) Rockaway, NJ Sacred Heart; Rockaway, NJ St. Cecilia's.
Peplowski, Sigmund (PAT) Vocations Board.
Pepowski, Bert *o.f.m.* '61 (GRY)[H] Cedar Lake, IN Our Lady of Lourdes Friary.
Peppard, Patrick F. *s.j.* '73 (DET)[E] Detroit, MI University of Detroit Jesuit High School and Academy.
Pepper, J. David '58 (DUB) Retired.
Pera, Sylvano *o.f.m.* '52 (SFD)[K] Teutopolis, IL St. Francis Assisi Friary; Teutopolis, IL St. Francis of Assisi.
Perales, Jorge '78 (SAM) Greenacres, FL Mary Mother of the Light Maronite Mission.
Perales, Jorge '78 (MIA) On Leave.
Perata, Stephen '58 (SJ) San Jose, CA St. Victor; Priests' Retirement Board Retired.
Percell, Lawrence J. '03 (SJ) Ongoing Formation of Clergy.
Percell, Lawrence P. '03 (SJ) Los Altos, CA St. Nicholas.
Perdue, John *m.ss.cc.* '90 (CAM) Linwood, NJ; [L] Linwood, NJ Villa Pieta. Missionaries of the Sacred Hearts of Jesus & Mary.
Perea, Donald '98 (SEA) First Hills Hospital.
Perea, Michael U. *o.praem.* '90 (LA) Wilmington, CA SS. Peter and Paul.
Pereda, Rev. Msgr. James F. '81 (RVC) Judicial Vicar; Catholic Lawyer's Guild.
Pereda, Rev. Msgr. James *c.r.c.* '81 (BRK)[S] Queens Village, NY St. Ann's Novitiate, Little Sisters of the Poor.
Perehubka, Jozef '84 (HEL) Libby, MT St. Joseph.
Pereida, Alex '08 (SAT) Vocation Office; [Q] San Antonio, TX National Foundation for Mexican–American Vocations; [A] San Antonio, TX Assumption Seminary.
Pereira, Anand *s.j.* '00 (OM)[J] Omaha, NE Jesuit Community at Creighton University.
Pereira, Anthony '82 (SJ) On Leave of Absence.
Pereira, Cyril F. '54 (ALB) Retired.
Pereira, Joseph '74 (HT) Galliano, LA St. Joseph.
Pereira, Junil *i.m.s.* (BGP) Norwalk, CT St. Thomas the Apostle.
Pereira, Luciano J. '54 (FR) Retired.
Pereira, Manuel C. *m.s.* '95 (FR)[F] Attleboro, MA La Salette Communications Office; [F] Attleboro, MA La Salette Shrine.
Pereira, Robert J. '62 (STO) Diamond Springs, CA Retired.
Perelli, Robert J. *c.j.m.* '76 (BUF)[N] Buffalo, NY The Eudists – Congregation of Jesus and Mary.
Pereppadan, Jose *c.m.i.* '79 (COV) Fort Mitchell, KY Blessed Sacrament.
Perera, Denzil M. '58 (NO) Retired.
Perera, George '92 (NY) Staten Island, NY Our Lady Star of the Sea.
Perera, J. Bosco '69 (FTW) Geneva, IN St. Mary of the Presentation.
Peres, Mark *c.pp.s.* '85 (CIN)[N] Dayton Provincial Office of the Cincinnati Province of the Society of the Precious Blood.
Peretti, Peter L. '73 (GBG) New Salem, PA St. Thomas; New Salem, PA St. Procopius.
Perez, Alex '10 (NY) Bronx, NY St. Thomas Aquinas.
Perez, Angel A. '02 (P) Woodburn, OR St. Luke.
Perez, Angel Antonio *c.p.* '87 (MGZ) San Sebastian, PR San Sebastian Martir.
Perez, Angel '02 (P) Area Vicars.
Perez, Angel '05 (DEN) Graduate Studies.
Perez, Antonio (AUS) Martindale, TX Immaculate Heart of Mary; Uhland, TX St. Michael.
Perez, Armando S. '02 (SEA) Vancouver, WA St. John the Evangelist; Deans; Presbyteral Council.
Perez, Armando '62 (MIA) Retired.
Perez, Aurelio H. '86 (MIL) Wind Lake, WI St. Clare.
Perez, Carlos '92 (B) Bonners Ferry, ID St. Ann's.
Perez, David Guzman *m.x.y.* '88 (NY)[DD] Bronx, NY Yarumal Mission Society, Inc.
Perez, David Guzman *m.x.y.* '88 (NY) Bronx, NY Our Saviour.
Perez, Eduardo '95 (STO) Stockton, CA St. Gertrude Church (Pastor of).
Perez, Edwin E. '01 (ARL)[D] Alexandria, VA Bishop Ireton High School; Alexandria, VA St. Rita.
Perez, Eleazar (LSC) Presbyteral Council.
Perez, Francisco '00 (AMA) Advocates; Ex Officio; Chancellor; Vocation Development Team; Pampa, TX St. Vincent de Paul; Priests' Pension Plan Retirement Committee; College of Consultors.
Perez, Gabino *o.a.r.* '51 (ORG) Santa Ana, CA Our Lady of the Pillar.
Perez, Hector A. '07 (MIA) Miami, FL St. James.
Perez, Hector R.G. '81 (PT) Pensacola, FL St. Stephen; Legion of Mary.
Perez, Horacio *s.x.* '03 (PAT)[N] Wayne Xaverian Missionary Fathers; Wayne, NJ XAVERIAN MISSIONARY FATHERS.
Perez, Isidro '81 (MIA) Miami Springs, FL Blessed Trinity.
Perez, J. Santos *o.f.m.* '85 (ELP) El Paso, TX Our Lady of Guadalupe.
Perez, Jaime *o.f.m.cap.* (SJN)[H] San Juan, PR The Viceprovince of Saint John the Baptist, Puerto Rico, of the Order Friars Minor Capuchin.
Perez, Javier H. '93 (TUC) Yuma, AZ Immaculate Conception Roman Catholic Parish & Guadalupe Mission – Yuma; Vicars Forane; All Vicars Forane; Council of Priests.
Perez, Jesse L. '74 (PBL) On Duty Outside the Diocese Retired.
Perez, Jesse (COS) Leadville, CO Holy Family Parish.
Perez, John Jairo '03 (BGP) Stamford, CT St. Mary; Stamford, CT Saint Benedict – Our Lady of Montserrat.
Perez, John '96 (L) Shelbyville, KY Annunciation of the Blessed Virgin Mary.
Perez, Jose '99 (BRK) On Leave/Unassigned.
Perez, Jose '64 (COL) Columbus, OH Santa Cruz Parish.
Perez, Joseph '69 (GAL) On Duty Outside the Archdiocese.
Perez, Juan Antonio *o.ss.t.* '88 (LAV) Las Vegas, NV Prince of Peace.
Perez, Juan Rommel *o.f.m.* '11 (JOL) Joliet, IL St. John the Baptist.
Perez, Juan '98 (SAC) Marysville, CA St. Joseph.
Perez, Lazaro '89 (MET)[G] New Brunswick, NJ Saint Peter's University Hospital; Spotswood, NJ Immaculate Conception.
Perez, Leon '60 (ARE) Retired.
Perez, Leopoldo G. *o.m.i.* '84 (SAT)[C] Oblate School of Theology; [R] San Antonio, TX Oblate Lourdes Grotto Shrine of the Southwest, Tepeyac de San Antonio.
Perez, Luis A. '95 (MIA) Miami, FL Our Lady of the Holy Rosary – St. Richard Church.
Perez, Rev. Msgr. Manuel Garcia '75 (SJN) San Juan, PR San Luis Rey; Clergy Social Security (Prevision Social del Clero).
Perez, Manuel '05 (KNX) Johnson City, TN St. Mary.
Perez, Modesto Lewis '84 (LA) Altadena, CA St. Elizabeth of Hungary; Cursillo Movement.

Perez, Rev. Msgr. Nelson J. '89 (PH) West Chester, PA St. Agnes.
Perez, Orlando Lugo '10 (ARE) Camuy, PR St. Joseph.
Perez, Oscar A. '03 (OM) South Sioux City, NE St. Michael.
Perez, Osualdo *c.s.sp.* '88 (ARE) Orocovis, PR Our Lady of Fatima.
Perez, Ovidio '00 (ARE) Corozal, PR Holy Family; Priest's Senate (Consejo Presbiteral).
Perez, Rev. Msgr. Pedro Luis '52 (MIA) Retired.
Pérez, Perfecto '56 (MGZ) Aguadilla, PR La Milagrosa.
Perez, Rafael *o.s.b.* '79 (FAJ)[B] Humacao, PR San Antonio Abad Abbey of the Order of St. Benedict.
Perez, Raymond L. *o.praem.* '88 (LA) Wilmington, CA SS. Peter and Paul.
Perez, Rene '03 (LUB) Lubbock, TX San Ramon; St. Francis of Assisi Mission.
Perez, Restituto *o.p.* '60 (MIA) Miami, FL St. Dominic; [H] Miami, FL Dominican Fathers of Miami, Inc.
Perez, Robert R. '86 (CHI) Chicago, IL St. Michael the Archangel.
Perez, Ronald P. '08 (NY) Staten Island, NY St. Charles.
Perez, Salvador '61 (FWT) Retired.
Perez, Samuel F. '01 (NU) Henderson, MN St. John–Assumption; Henderson, MN St. Joseph; Henderson, MN St. Thomas (Oratory).
Perez, Samuel '03 (TLS) Tulsa, OK St. Thomas More; Diocesan Consultors; Defender of the Bond; Promoter of Justice; Hispanic Ministry.
Perez, Victor '75 (P) Salem, OR Oregon State Correctional Institution; Salem, OR Santiam Correctional Institution; Salem, OR Mill Creek Correctional Facility; Salem, OR Oregon State Penitentiary.
Perez, Victor '11 (GAL) Houston, TX St. Cecilia.
Perez, Viktor *o.f.m.conv.* '89 (FRS) Coalinga, CA St. Paul The Apostle; Arroyo Grande, CA.
Perez, William A. *o.s.a.* '62 (TLS)[B] Tulsa, OK Cascia Hall Preparatory School.
Perez–Barrera, Jesus Alejandro '02 (TUC) Douglas, AZ Immaculate Conception Roman Catholic Parish – Douglas; Douglas, AZ Saint Luke Roman Catholic Church – Douglas; Pirtleville, AZ Saint Bernard Roman Catholic Church – Pirtleville.
Perez–Cobo, Raul '06 (CR) Kelliher, MN St. Patrick; Priests' Council.
Perez–Diaz, German '97 (KAL) White Pigeon, MI St. Joseph; Sturgis, MI Holy Angels; Vicars Forane.
Perez–Lerena, Francisco *s.j.* '58 (MIA)[E] Miami, FL Belen Jesuit Preparatory School; [H] Miami, FL Villa Javier.
Perez–Martinez, Jose Ramon '80 (SAT) San Antonio, TX Cathedral of San Fernando.
Perez–Martinez, Jose Ramon '80 (SAT)[A] San Antonio, TX Assumption Seminary.
Perez–Ojeda, Juan Antonio *o.ss.t.* '88 (BAL)[Q] Diocese of Victoria, TX.
Perez–Rodriguez, Arturo '72 (CHI) Jail Ministry/Kolbe House; [W] Chicago, IL Kolbe House; Kolbe House.
Perez Cruz, Benjamin Antonio (SJN) Carolina, PR Inmaculada Concepcion; Carolina, PR Ntra. Sra. Reina de Los Angeles.
Perez Gonzalez, Osvaldo *c.s.sp.* (SJN)[C] Bayamon, PR Seminario Misionero del Espiritu Santo.
Perez Lopez, P. Nicolas '03 (PCE) Jayuya, PR Our Lady of Monserrate.
Perez Torres, Ernesto '11 (ARE) Arecibo, PR Church of Sagrado Corazon de Jesus.
Perez Vazquez, Juan De La Cruz '96 (SJN) Military Services.
Perfetto, Richard A. '66 (DET) Retired.
Pergjini, Nikolin '99 (NY) Bronx, NY St. Lucy.
Perham, Arnold E. *c.s.v.* '56 (CHI)[N] Arlington Heights, IL Viatorian Province Center–Clerics of St. Viator; [D] Arlington Heights, IL St. Viator High School.
Peri, Asuramonil F. '79 (NY) Sleepy Hollow, NY St. Teresa of Avila.
Peri, Paul '71 (P)[A] St. Benedict, OR Mount Angel Seminary.
Periannan, Selvaraj *m.s.f.x.* '88 (BIS) Kenmare, ND St. Anthony; Kenmare, ND St. Joseph (Bowbells); Kenmare, ND St. Agnes.
Pericone, Nicholas P. '96 (NO) Metairie, LA St. Mary Magdalen; Defenders of the Bond; Metairie, LA St. Mary Magdalen.
Periello, Robert (WH)[O] Fairmont, WV Fairmont State University Newman Center.
Peries, Angelito '74 (SR) Windsor, CA Our Lady of Guadalupe; Deans; Board of Consultors; Priests' Council; Clergy Personnel Committee.
Perikala, Alfhones '02 (SCR) Susquehanna, PA St. John the Evangelist; Great Bend, PA St. Lawrence; Susquehanna, PA St. Martin of Tours.
Perin, Glen W. '53 (CIN) Retired.
Perini, Rev. Msgr. Armando J. '56 (MET) Retired.
Perino, John M. '79 (NO) Luling, LA Holy Family.
Perissinotto, Rodrigo *o.s.b.* '04 (KCK)[I] Atchison, KS St. Benedict's Abbey.
Perkin, David R. '78 (NSH) Nashville, TN St. Patrick; On Special Assignment; Vicars General; Moderator of the Curia and Vicar General; Adjutant Judicial Vicar; Judges; Presbyteral Council; Diocesan Finance Board; Clergy Personnel Board; Priest Benefit Foundation.
Perkins, Charles '78 (HT) Catholic Daughters of the Americas; Houma, LA St. Bernadette.
Perkins, Dennis M. '95 (NOR) Pawcatuck, CT St. Michael; College of Consultors; Members; Vicar for Clergy; Bishop's Liaison with Retired Clergy; Continuing Education and Formation Commission for the Clergy; Priests' Retirement Plan Board; Diocesan Panel of Pastors, Canon 1742; Advisory Ministry Evaluation Committee.
Perkins, Joseph F. '68 (WDC) Garrett Park, MD Holy Cross.
Perkins, Rev. Msgr. Robert M. '71 (RIC) Hampton, VA Immaculate Conception.
Perkinton, Rev. Msgr. John J '85 (LIN)[F] Waverly, NE Our Lady of Good Counsel Retreat House; [H] Lincoln, NE Villa Marie School and Home for the Educable Mentally Handicapped; Diocesan Consultors; Presbyteral Council; Building Commission; Priests' Continuing Education Committee; Schools; Diocesan Housing Ministries, Inc.; [L] Lincoln, NE Blessed John XXIII Diocesan Center.
Perkl, James M. '84 (STP) Hastings, MN St. Elizabeth Ann Seton; College of Consultors.
Perko, Richard '04 (STA) Callahan, FL Our Lady of Consolation.
Perkovic, Anton '46 (NO) Retired.
Perkovich, Frank '54 (DUL) Retired.
Perl, Richard D. *s.j.* '78 (FgM) St. Louis, MO Society of Jesus.
Perlinski, Daniel A. '57 (TLS) Retired.
Perluzzi, James *o.f.m.* '65 (CHI)[N] Chicago, IL St. Peter's Friary.
Permuy, Francisco J. *s.j.* '06 (MIA) Miami, FL Gesu.
Pernia, Rev. Msgr. John R. '58 (SFR) Retired.
Perozich, Richard L. '92 (SD) Escondido, CA Saint Mary Catholic Parish Escondido; Presbyteral Council.
Perrault, Joseph E. '75 (CAM) Diocesan Finance Council.
Perreault, Joseph A. '75 (CAM) Sea Isle City, NJ St. Joseph's Catholic Church, Sea Isle City, N.J.
Perrera, Leo (NY) Yonkers, NY St. Eugene.
Perretta, Andrew T. '75 (PAT) Clifton, NJ Sacred Heart.
Perri, Dean Patrick '02 (PRO) Providence, RI St. Casimir; Judges; Providence, RI St. Joseph; Assistant Chancellor.
Perri, Rogerio Silva '01 (BGP) Bridgeport, CT St. Charles Borromeo.
Perricone, Charles A. '74 (PAT) Sussex, NJ St. Monica.
Perriello, Robert A. '76 (WH) Fairmont, WV St. Peter the Fisherman Catholic Church.
Perrier, Monroe *c.ss.r.* '58 (SAT) San Antonio, TX St. Gerard Majella; [L] San Antonio, TX Redemptorists of Texas–San Antonio #1.
Perrin, Thomas *s.d.s.* '97 (MIL) Whitewater, WI St. Patrick; [P] Milwaukee Salvatorian Provincial Offices.
Perron, Gary *a.a.* '66 (BO)[U] Boston Assumptionist Center.
Perron, Gregory (JOL)[L] Lisle, IL St. Procopius Abbey.
Perron, Richard J. '46 (BO) Senior Priests. Retired.
Perron, Robert P. '81 (PRO) Pawtucket, RI Holy Family Parish, Pawtucket; Finance Council.
Perrone, Eduard '78 (DET) Detroit, MI Assumption Grotto.
Perrone, Vito J. '01 (SFR)[S] South San Francisco, CA The Contemplatives of Saint Joseph.
Perrotta, Jonathan P. '11 (LAN) Grand Blanc, MI Holy Family.
Perry, Carmen J. '77 (SCR) Stroudsburg, PA St. Luke.
Perry, David A. '01 (E) Frenchville, PA St. Mary of the Assumption.
Perry, Francis J. '50 (DUB) Retired.
Perry, Francis '98 (R) Retired.
Perry, Rev. Msgr. John A. '63 (FR) Falmouth, MA St. Patrick's; Diocesan Consultors; Members; Diocesan Pastoral Council; Vicar General.
Perry, John J. '83 (FR) Auditors; Diocesan Director of Cemeteries; Taunton, MA St. Jude the Apostle.
Perry, Lee '75 (HPM) Olympia, WA St. George Byzantine Catholic Church; Pro–Life Coordinator.
Perry, Michael A. '71 (BRK) Brooklyn, NY Our Lady of Refuge.
Perry, Michael E. *o.de.m.* '85 (SP)[N] St. Petersburg, FL St. Peter Nolasco Residence.
Perry, Michael *o.f.m.* '84 (STL)[O] St. Louis Franciscan Friary of St. Anthony of Padua.
Perry, Paul E. '67 (SFR) Greenbrae, CA St. Sebastian.
Perry, Richard *s.j.* '70 (HEL) Missoula, MT St. Francis Xavier.
Perry, Ronald V. *s.j.* '76 (BO)[D] Boston, MA Boston College High School.
Pers, Thomas J. '04 (RVC) Patchogue, NY St. Francis de Sales.
Persha, Gerald J. *m.m.* '70 (NY)[DD] Retired.
Pershe, Joseph N. *s.j.* '66 (MIL)[P] Wauwatosa, WI Jesuit Community at St. Camillus.
Persia, William R. *c.s.c.* '62 (FTW)[H] Notre Dame Congregation of Holy Cross, United States Province of Priests & Brothers.
Persia, William *c.s.c.* '62 (SP) Dade City, FL St. Rita.
Persich, Roy A. *c.m.* '60 (LA)[P] Santa Barbara, CA St. Mary's Evangelization Center; [V] Santa Barbara, CA St. Mary's Seminary Center Retired.
Persico, Rev. Msgr. Lawrence T. '77 (GBG) New Alexandria, PA St. James; College of Consultors; Vicar General/Chancellor; Defender of Bond; Bishop's Priests Council; Finance Council; Members of the Corporation; Board of Members of the Corporation; Greensburg Catholic Accent and Communications, Inc.; Bishop's Delegate; Vice President; St. Luke Society for Health Care Professionals.
Persico, Philip T. '99 (NY) Valhalla, NY Holy Name of Jesus.
Persing, Charles L. '88 (HBG) New Oxford, PA Immaculate Conception of the Blessed Virgin Mary.
Persinger, Patrick '87 (FRS) Retired.
Perucho, Michael '11 (LA) Glendale, CA Holy Family.
Perumbillikunnel, Mathew (MCE) Evanston, IL St. Mary's Malankara Catholic Church; Priests – Heads of Apostolates.
Perumbillikunnel, Mathew (MCE) Faith Formation (Catechism) Director; Elected Members.
Perumpally, Mathew '73 (NSH) Dickson, TN St. Christopher.
Perunilam, Dominic '85 (MET) Belvidere, NJ St. Patrick.
Perunilam, Thomas V. '64 (MET) Retired.
Perupayikkad, Thomas Babu '99 (RNO) Reno, NV St. Michael's.
Pesarchick, Robert A. '91 (PH)[A] Wynnewood, PA Theological Seminary of St. Charles Borromeo, Overbrook; Censores Librorum.
Pesaresi, Thomas E. *m.m.* '85 (NY)[DD] Maryknoll Maryknoll Fathers and Brothers.
Pesaresi, Thomas *m.m.* '85 (MO) DEPARTMENT OF VETERANS AFFAIRS HOSPITALS AND CHAPLAINS.
Pescatello, Joseph A. '89 (PRO) North Providence, RI Mary, Mother of Mankind.
Pescatore, Terence *o.f.m.conv.* '62 (TR) Seaside Park, NJ St. Catharine of Siena.
Pesce, John Baptist *c.p.* '51 (HRT)[L] West Hartford Holy Family Monastery/Retreat; [P] West Hartford, CT Holy Family Passionist Retreat Center.
Pesch, Elroy *o.f.m.cap.* '63 (MIL)[P] Mount Calvary, WI St. Lawrence Friary Retired.
Peschel, Roland A. '60 (OM) Retired.
Peschiera, Rev. Msgr. Bruno '54 (SFR) Italian Ministry.
Pesci, Thomas A. *s.j.* '79 (BAL)[D] Baltimore, MD Loyola Blakefield; [Q] Baltimore, MD Jesuit Community of Loyola University, Inc.
Pesek, Anthony '65 (SAT) New Braunfels, TX SS. Peter and Paul.
Pesek, Fred '89 (CHI) Wadsworth, IL St. Patrick.
Peshu, Kombo L. '01 (CHI) Bellwood, IL St. Simeon; [W] Chicago, IL Mughamba Scholarship Foundation.
Pesola, Joseph G. '97 (IND) Fortville, IN St. Thomas The Apostle, Fortville, Inc.
Pesola, Joseph '97 (LFT) Pendleton, IN Indiana State Reformatory, St. Christopher Chapel; Pendleton, IN Correctional Industrial Complex Ecumenical Chapel.
Pesongco, Rudy '82 (RVC) Garden City, NY St. Anne.
Pestano, Leonardo '94 (SEA) Federal Way, WA St. Theresa.
Pestin, Arturo P. *o.p.* '83 (SAN) Odessa, TX Holy Redeemer.
Pestun, Aloysius J. *s.d.b.* '59 (SFR) San Francisco, CA Corpus Christi.
Petcavage, Paschal *o.s.b.* '81 (CLV)[N] Cleveland, OH.
Pete, Joseph P. '76 (WIN) Rushford, MN St. Peter's; Rushford, MN St. Joseph's; Deposit and Loan Board; Rushford, MN St. Mary's; Elected Deanery Representatives.
Petekiewicz, Robert P. '91 (LAV) Unassigned.
Petelo, Fila Filipo *m.f.* '01 (SPP) Pago Pago, AS Our Lady of Fatima.
Peter, Abednecco Wambua *o.c.d.* '09 (MIL)[P] Milwaukee Provincial Offices – Discalced Carmelites.
Peter, Arul Rajan '84 (NOR) Canterbury, CT St. Augustine; Plainfield, CT St. John the Apostle.
Peter, David J. '66 (BUF) Retired.
Peter, Martin A. '67 (IND) Retired.
Peter, Patrick N. '75 (BEL) Breese, IL St. Dominic.
Peter, Valentine J. '59 (OM) Boys Town, NE Immaculate Conception B.V.M.
Petering, Michael '99 (VIC) Edna, TX St. Agnes; Presbyteral Council; Council of Catholic Women (DCCW).
Peterka, Dale C. '68 (CIN) Cincinnati, OH St. John the Evangelist; On Special and Archdiocesan Assignment.
Peterka, Sylvester *c.m.* '76 (BAL) Baltimore, MD St. Cecilia; Baltimore, MD Immaculate Conception.
Peterman, Thomas J. '57 (WIL) Wilmington, DE St. Catherine of Siena Retired.
Petermeier, Virgil *o.s.c.* '77 (SCL)[I] Onamia, MN Crosier Priory.
Peters, Aaron *o.s.b.* '77 (KCK)[I] Atchison, KS St. Benedict's Abbey.

Peters, David L. '58 (SFD) Ex Officios; Vicar for Clergy.
Peters, David '58 (SFD) Retired.
Peters, Eric '80 (SP) Citrus Springs, FL St. Elizabeth Ann Seton.
Peters, John B. *c.i.c.m.* '53 (ARL)[H] Arlington, VA Missionhurst, C.I.C.M.–Central House and Provincialate.
Peters, John C. '74 (VIC) Hallettsville, TX Sacred Heart; Hallettsville, TX St. Mary; Hallettsville, TX St. John the Baptist; Vicar General; Diocesan Consultors; Presbyteral Council; Priests' Personnel Board.
Peters, Rev. Msgr. John '60 (ELP) Priests' Retirement and Disability Plan Retired.
Peters, Jude *o.c.d.* '89 (MIL)[P] Hubertus, WI Discalced Carmelite Monastery – Holy Hill Basilica of the National Shrine of Mary, Help of Christians, Holy Hill.
Peters, Julian *o.s.b.* '88 (IND)[K] Saint Meinrad, IN St. Meinrad Archabbey; [A] Saint Meinrad, IN Saint Meinrad School of Theology.
Peters, Kenan *c.p.* '60 (BRK)[R] Jamaica, NY Immaculate Conception Monastery.
Peters, Kevin '90 (Y) Youngstown, OH St. Angela Merici Parish; Presbyteral Council.
Peters, Michael G. '88 (DM) Guthrie Center, IA St. Patrick; Guthrie Center, IA St. Mary; Guthrie Center, IA St. Cecilia.
Peters, Paul R. '62 (DUB) Strawberry Point, IA St. Mary; Volga, IA Sacred Heart; Elkader, IA St. Joseph; Deans.
Peters, Stephen '67 (ELP) Adjutant Vicars; Judges; [A] El Paso, TX St. Charles Seminary.
Peters, Timothy J. '03 (ORG) San Juan Capistrano, CA Mission Basilica – San Juan Capistrano.
Petersen, Rev. Msgr. E. James '59 (FRS) Diocesan Consultors; Diocesan Newspaper; On Special Assignment; Vice Chancellor Retired.
Petersen, Michael C. '92 (MIL) Fond du Lac, WI Sons of Zebedee: Saints James and John.
Petersen, Todd J. '99 (NU) Lucan, MN Our Lady of Victory; Wabasso, MN St. Mary; Wabasso, MN St. Anne; Wabasso, MN St. Mathias; Priest Personnel Board; Vocations Team; On Special or Other Diocesan Assignment.
Petersen, Vincent *o.f.m.conv.* '85 (LSC) Mesilla Park, NM Shrine and Parish of Our Lady of Guadalupe.
Peterson, Bradley L. *o.carm.* '92 (PHX) Phoenix, AZ St. Agnes Roman Catholic Parish.
Peterson, Bruce '57 (STP) Bellechester, MN St. Mary; Goodhue, MN St. Columbkill; Goodhue, MN The Church of the Holy Trinity.
Peterson, C. Vincent '74 (SEA) Retired.
Peterson, Casimir M. '47 (BAL)[U] Baltimore, MD Reparation Society of the Immaculate Heart of Mary, Inc. Retired.
Peterson, Charles J. *s.j.* '69 (FBK) Bethel, AK Immaculate Conception Catholic Church Bethel; Presbyteral Council; [E] Bethel, AK Brother Joe Prince Jesuit Community; Consultors.
Peterson, Dennis M. '06 (MRY) King City, CA St. John the Baptist.
Peterson, Eric '89 (MEM) Memphis, TN St. Mary Church.
Peterson, Frederick *o.s.b.* '95 (RCK)[G] Aurora, IL Marmion Abbey.
Peterson, Frederick *o.s.b.* '95 (ROM) Aurora, IL St. George.
Peterson, Gerald *g.h.m.* '56 (CIN)[N] Cincinnati Headquarters of Glenmary Home Missioners Retired.
Peterson, Harry *s.d.b.* '61 (FgM) New Rochelle, NY SALESIANS OF DON BOSCO.
Peterson, Rev. Msgr. James W. '47 (E)[M] Erie, PA Maria House Projects Retired.
Peterson, Jay H. '78 (GF) Finance Council; Great Falls, MT Corpus Christi; Moderator of the Curia; Newspaper; Pastoral Outreach; Vicar General; Priests' Council; Director of Seminarian Formation; Office of Ministry Formation.
Peterson, Jay H. '78 (GF) Diocesan Pastoral Council; Worship Commission.
Peterson, John P. *y.a.* '89 (ARL)[K] Arlington, VA Marymount University; [L] McLean, VA Youth Apostles Institute, An Association of Christian Faithful; [A] Arlington, VA Marymount University.
Peterson, John S. *o.p.* '62 (PRO)[O] Providence St. Thomas Aquinas Priory at Providence College.
Peterson, Joseph L. '75 (WH) Parkersburg, WV St. Margaret Mary; Diocesan Consultors; Vicars Forane.
Peterson, Louis P. '74 (BEL) Retired.
Peterson, Maurice F. '87 (YAK) Retired.
Peterson, Michael *o.s.b.* '06 (SFS)[F] Marvin, SD Blue Cloud Abbey.
Peterson, Michael '11 (KCK) Overland Park, KS St. Michael the Archangel.
Peterson, Paul *s.j.* '61 (IND)[D] Indianapolis, IN Brebeuf Jesuit Preparatory School, Inc.
Peterson, Steven J. '73 (RVC) Port Washington, NY Our Lady of Fatima.
Peterson, Steven J. '94 (WIN) Spring Valley, MN St. Finbarr's; Spring Valley, MN St. Patrick's; Spring Valley, MN St. Ignatius; Deans; Priests' Pension Board.
Peterson, Steven *o.s.j.* '04 (SAC)[A] Loomis, CA Mount St. Joseph Novitiate and Seminary.
Peterson, William F. '59 (RCK) Retired.
Peterson, William *g.h.m.* '59 (SAV) Retired.
Peterson, William *c.ss.r.* '67 (SEA)[M] Seattle, WA The Redemptionist Society of Washington; Seattle, WA Sacred Heart of Jesus.
Peterson, Zachary D. '11 (NU) Hutchinson, MN Church of St. Anastasia.
Petilla, Antonio G. '61 (SFR) San Francisco, CA St. John the Evangelist Retired.
Petilla, Rev. Msgr. Cesar '77 (SP) Plant City, FL St. Clement.
Petinge, Roland *o.f.m.* '61 (BO)[U] Andover St. Francis Friary; [U] Boston, MA St. Christopher Friary Retired.
Petit, Leo *m.s.c.* '50 (ALN)[A] Center Valley, PA Sacred Heart Villa, Missionaries of the Sacred Heart.
Petit–Homme, Fracilus *s.m.m.* '70 (ORL) Winter Haven, FL St. Joseph's.
Petkash, Donald J. *s.j.* '71 (CLV)[D] Cuyahoga Falls, OH Walsh Jesuit High School.
Petosa, Joseph '55 (SEA) Retired.
Petraitis, David *o.s.a.* '79 (CHI)[J] Chicago, IL St. Anthony Hospital; [N] Chicago, IL St. John Stone Friary.
Petraitis, Joseph *m.i.c.* (SPR)[G] On Duty Outside of the USA.
Petrarulo, John D. '53 (PIT)[M] Pittsburgh, PA St. John Vianney Manor Retired.
Petras, David M. '67 (PBR)[A] Pittsburgh, PA Byzantine Catholic Seminary of SS. Cyril and Methodius.
Petras, Rev. Archpriest David '67 (PRM) On Duty Outside the Diocese; Eparchial Consultors; Eparchial Censor; Sacred Liturgy; Building Commission; Cantors' Institute Faculty; Seminary Education Formation Board; Office of Ecumenical Activity Retired.
Petrasic, Martin J. '43 (OM) Retired.
Petrauskas, John *m.i.c.* '43 (NOR)[C] Thompson, CT Congregation of Marians of the Immaculate Conception; [G] Thompson, CT Marian Fathers.
Petri, Gregg *o.f.m.* (PEO) Bloomington, IL St. Mary's.
Petri, Jacob *o.p.* '09 (PRO)[O] Providence St. Thomas Aquinas Priory at Providence College.
Petrich, John C. '83 (DUL) Duluth, MN St. Mary Star of the Sea; St. Luke's Hospital; Northeast Regional Correctional Institution; Duluth, MN Our Lady of Mercy.
Petrie, Michael J. '87 (MIL) Horicon, WI Sacred Heart; Archdiocesan Council of Priests.
Petrie, Roderic *o.f.m.* '59 (SP)[N] St. Petersburg, FL St. Anthony Friary.
Petrie, William F. *ss.cc.* '69 (FR)[F] Fairhaven, MA Sacred Hearts Provincial House.
Petrikovic, John *o.f.m.cap.* '81 (WH)[L] Wheeling, WV Capuchin Hermitage of St. Joseph.
Petrillo, Rev. Msgr. Joseph A. '77 (NEW) West Orange, NJ Our Lady of Lourdes; Priest Personnel Policy Board; Office of Clergy Personnel; Elected Members.
Petrillo, Rev. Msgr. Thomas F. '83 (NY) Larchmont, NY SS. John and Paul.
Petrillo, Thomas J. '59 (NEW) Retired.
Petrillo, Thomas '59 (TR) Jackson, NJ Church of St. Monica.
Petrimoulx, Leo *o.f.m.cap.* '66 (MAD)[D] Madison, WI St. Mary's Hospital; [I] Madison, WI San Damiano Friary Retired.
Petringa, Gerard (BO) Belmont, MA St. Luke; Presbyteral Council.
Petrino, Juan Daniel '84 (ORL) Orlando, FL St. John Vianney.
Petriv, Vasyl '92 (SJP) Parma, OH St. Josaphat Cathedral; Presbyters.
Petriv, Volodymyr '89 (STN) Dearborn Heights, MI Our Lady of Perpetual Help; Detroit; Presbyteral Council.
Petro, Rev. Archpriest John G. '68 (PBR) Beaver, PA Saint Nicholas Chapel; [A] Pittsburgh, PA Byzantine Catholic Seminary of SS. Cyril and Methodius; Diaconate Program.
Petro, Thomas J. '00 (SCR) Towanda, PA SS. Peter and Paul; Judges.
Petro, William '70 (WH) Absent on Sick Leave.
Petrocelli, John N. '71 (PRO) Absent on Leave.
Petron, David Jeffrey '06 (SCL) Carlos, MN St. Nicholas; Osakis, MN Immaculate Conception.
Petron, William G. '57 (DET) Retired.
Petronek, Rev. Msgr. Thomas C. '65 (STU) Retired.
Petronio, Rolando C. '77 (STO) Angels Camp, CA St. Patrick Church of Angels Camp (Pastor of).
Petroske, Peter '84 (DET) Dearborn, MI Sacred Heart.
Petroski, Michael A. '00 (LAN) Leslie, MI SS. Cornelius and Cyprian.
Petrosky, Arnold *t.o.r.* '57 (ALT)[G] Loretto, PA St. Francis Friary at Mount Assisi.
Petrovsky, Felix *o.f.m.cap.* '55 (SAL) Hays, KS St. Joseph Parish.
Petrovsky, James F. '68 (GBG) Smock, PA St. Hedwig.
Petroy, Dominic J. *o.s.b.* '87 (GBG) Latrobe, PA Excela Health – Latrobe Area Hospital; [H] Latrobe, PA Saint Vincent Archabbey.
Petru, Augustine *o.m.i.* '53 (FgM) Washington, DC AMERICAN OBLATE MISSIONS.
Petru, Rev. Msgr. Stanley J. '48 (VIC) Retired.
Petru, Rev. Msgr. Stanley '48 (SAT)[K] San Antonio, TX Oblate Madonna Residence.
Petrucci, Peter J. *m.m.* '49 (NY)[DD] Retired.
Petrucci, Raymond K. '73 (BGP) Danbury, CT St. Joseph; Danbury, CT Danbury Hospital.
Petruha, Louis *o.f.m.cap.* '65 (HBG) York, PA St. Joseph.
Petruska, Christopher '59 (PSC) Retired.
Petruska, Gregory '53 (PBR) Retired.
Petruska, William M. '73 (SCR) Military Chaplains.
Petruska, William M. '73 (SD) Presbyteral Council.
Petry, Thomas G. '78 (COL) Columbus, OH Saint Anthony.
Petryshak, Roman '02 (PHU) Plymouth, PA SS. Peter and Paul; Nanticoke, PA Transfiguration of Our Lord.
Petsch, Rev. Msgr. Joseph '50 (SAT)[K] San Antonio, TX Casa De Padres Retired.
Petsche, Daniel *o.s.b.* '67 (KC)[A] Conception, MO Conception Seminary College; Conception, MO.
Petta, Gerard *m.s.a.* '84 (NOR)[G] Cromwell Society of the Missionaries of the Holy Apostles.
Petta, Philip '11 (FWT) Arlington, TX St. Matthew.
Pettei, Thomas G. '86 (BRK) Jamaica, NY St. Nicholas of Tolentine.
Petter, Rev. Msgr. Henry V. '76 (DAL) Appointed Members; Pastors Consultors; Coppell, TX St. Ann; Personnel Board; College of Consultors.
Pettingill, David M. '62 (SFR) San Francisco, CA St. Emydius Retired.
Pettit, Edward G. '51 (PBL) Retired.
Pettit, Joseph H. '56 (HRT) Retired.
Pettke, Lawrence A. '81 (DET) Clinton Township, MI St. Louis.
Peyton, Mark J. '77 (CLV) Parma, OH St. Francis de Sales.
Peyton, Thomas A. *m.m.* '58 (FgM) Maryknoll, NY MARYKNOLL.
Peyton, Thomas J. '74 (SAV) Tybee Island, GA St. Michael.
Pezzi, John Paul *m.c.c.j.* '68 (CHI)[N] La Grange Park, IL Comboni Missionaries.
Pezzulo, Angelo B. '62 (BRK) Ozone Park, NY Nativity of the Blessed Virgin Mary; Ozone Park, NY St. Stanislaus Bishop and Martyr Retired.
Pezzulo, Neil *g.h.m.* '99 (CIN)[N] Fairfield, OH.
Pfab, Cletus H. *s.j.* '69 (DET)[K] Clarkston, MI Colombiere Center.
Pfaff, Aaron J. '96 (IND) Shelbyville, IN St. Joseph Catholic Church, Shelbyville, Inc.
Pfalzer, Miles *o.f.m.* '47 (ALN)[K] Easton, PA St. Francis Friary.
Pfander, Timothy '04 (BIR)[G] Hamilton, AL Christian Center of Concern; [G] Sulligent, AL Christian Center of Concern; Guntersville, AL St. William; [G] Winfield, AL Christian Center of Concern.
Pfannenstiel, Donald F. '75 (SAL) WaKeeney, KS Christ the King Parish; Board of Trustees; Personnel Board.
Pfannenstiel, John *o.f.m.cap.* '82 (FgM)[Q] Pittsburgh, PA The Capuchin Franciscan Volunteer Corps, Inc.; Pittsburgh, PA Province of St. Augustine; Pittsburgh, PA; [M] Pittsburgh, PA St. Augustine Friary.
Pfannenstiel, Richard '93 (NEW) South Orange, NJ Our Lady of Sorrows.
Pfau, Bernard '65 (FAR) New Rockford, ND Sts. Peter & Paul Church of McHenry; New Rockford, ND St. John's Church of New Rockford.
Pfeffer, Rev. Msgr. Edward B. '56 (DM) Judges Retired.
Pfeifer, Francis *o.m.i.* '59 (SAT)[K] San Antonio, TX Oblate Madonna Residence.
Pfeifer, Frederick A. '93 (NEW) East Orange, NJ Saint Joseph Parish.
Pfeifer, James E. *o.m.i.* '51 (BWN) Mission, TX Our Lady of Guadalupe.
Pfeifer, John M. '65 (BIS) Watford City, ND Epiphany; Watford City, ND Our Lady of Consolation.
Pfeifer, John M. '07 (CLV) Northfield, OH St. Barnabas.
Pfeifer, Neil J. '11 (FAR) Grand Forks, ND St. Michael's Church of Grand Forks.
Pfeiffer, David L. *m.m.* '66 (NY)[DD] Maryknoll Maryknoll Fathers and Brothers.
Pfeiffer, Rev. Msgr. Joseph C. '58 (BRK) Howard Beach, NY St. Helen Retired.
Pfeiffer, Mark S. '82 (LIN) Grant, NE Mother of Sorrows; Wallace, NE St. Mary's; Presbyteral Council.
Pfeiffer, Matthew E. '09 (CLV) Akron, OH St. Sebastian.
Pfeiffer, Robert F. '61 (CLV) Medina, OH Holy Martyrs; Judges in Second Instance Retired.
Pfeiffer, Robert F. (Y) Judges.
Pfister, John F. '66 (FTW) Huntington, IN St. Mary; Presbyteral Council.
Pfleger, Michael L. '75 (CHI) Chicago, IL St. Sabina.
Pfleger, Phillip C. '79 (TR) College of Consultors; Marlton, NJ St. Isaac Jogues.

Pflomm, Rev. Msgr. Peter J. '70 (RVC) Seaford, NY Maria Regina; Seaford Deanery; Priests' Personnel Assignment Board.
Pflumm, Robert '60 (KCK) Retired.
Pfnausch, Edward G. '68 (HRT) Retired.
Pfotenhauer, Frederick W. '57 (FTW)[B] University of Notre Dame Du Lac.
Pfundstein, George A. '63 (BRK) Flushing, NY St. Ann Retired.
Phalan, James H. *c.s.c.* '92 (FR)[A] North Easton, MA Holy Cross Fathers Religious; [L] North Easton, MA Holy Cross Family Ministries.
Phalan, James H. *c.s.c.* '92 (FTW)[H] Notre Dame Congregation of Holy Cross, United States Province of Priests & Brothers.
Phalen, John L. '59 (DET) Retired.
Phalen, John P. *c.s.c.* '74 (ALB)[R] North Easton, MA Crusade for Family Prayer, Inc.
Phalen, John P. *c.s.c.* (FR)[L] North Easton, MA Holy Cross Family Ministries; Prov. Councilors:; Taunton, MA St. Mary's.
Phalen, John P. *c.s.c.* '74 (FTW)[H] Notre Dame Congregation of Holy Cross, United States Province of Priests & Brothers.
Pham, Andrew Thu *s.v.d.* (FTW) Fort Wayne.
Pham, Ansgar *s.d.d.* '07 (DAL) Grand Prairie, TX St. Joseph Vietnamese Parish.
Pham, Bartholomew Dat H. *s.d.d.* '03 (P) Portland, OR Our Lady of Lavang.
Pham, Bernardo Son *s.d.d.* '63 (NO) Retired.
Pham, Charles *c.m.c.* '05 (SAC) Sacramento, CA Vietnamese Martyrs Parish.
Pham, Chau '95 (CIN)[U] Cincinnati, OH Vietnamese Catholic Community of Our Lady of Lavang.
Pham, Christopher Tuan '07 (ORG) Los Alamitos, CA St. Hedwig.
Pham, Cuong M. '01 (BRK) Graduate Studies.
Pham, Doan The '98 (LA) El Monte, CA Nativity.
Pham, Dominic Phuc *c.ss.r.* '05 (TUC) Tucson, AZ Our Lady of LaVang Roman Catholic Parish – Tucson.
Pham, Dominic Savio *s.v.d.* '11 (STL) St. Louis, MO Resurrection of Our Lord.
Pham, Dominic Thao '98 (ALN)[P] Bath, PA Blue Army of Our Lady of Fatima; Emmaus, PA St. Ann; Blue Army of Our Lady of Fatima.
Pham, Dominic *l.c.* '04 (ATL)[K] Alpharetta, GA Home and Family, Inc.; [C] Cumming, GA Pinecrest Academy, Inc.; [F] Alpharetta, GA Legionaries of Christ, Incorporated.
Pham, Dominic *c.ss.r.* '05 (LA)[P] Baldwin Park Vietnamese Redemptorist Mission.
Pham, Francis Han *c.ss.r.* '93 (SAT) San Antonio, TX St. Gerard Majella; San Antonio, TX Vietnamese Martyrs Catholic Center; [L] San Antonio, TX Redemptorists of Texas–San Antonio #1.
Pham, Hanh *s.j.* '08 (DEN)[N] Denver, CO Regis Jesuit Community (The Jesuits at Regis University).
Pham, Hien Xuan *s.v.d.* '99 (MEM)[F] Memphis, TN Society of the Divine Word (Chicago Province).
Pham, Hung Q. '89 (WCH) Wichita, KS St. Anthony.
Pham, Hung *s.j.* '06 (FgM) St. Louis, MO Society of Jesus.
Pham, James Chau *c.ss.r.* '96 (BLX) Biloxi, MS Church of the Vietnamese Martyrs; Vietnamese Apostolate.
Pham, Rev. Msgr. James Ninh Van '67 (P) Retired.
Pham, Joseph Hung '70 (SFR) Retired.
Pham, Joseph Luong T. '98 (CAM) Atlantic City, NJ Our Lady, Star of the Sea, Atlantic City, N.J.; Vocation Advisory Board; Consultants.
Pham, Joseph–Cuong M. (CAM) Runnemede, NJ Holy Child Parish, Runnemede, N.J.
Pham, Josephtan '70 (BRK) Long Island City, NY Our Lady of Mount Carmel.
Pham, Khoi '94 (STO) Modesto, CA Our Lady of Fatima Church (Pastor of).
Pham, Le–Minh '93 (AUS) Cedar Park, TX St. Margaret Mary.
Pham, Linh *s.v.d.* '09 (DUB)[B] Epworth, IA Divine Word College.
Pham, M. Anthony Hanh Si *o.cist.* '04 (SB)[I] Lucerne Valley, CA The Cistercian Congregation of the Holy Family, St. Joseph Monastery.
Pham, Marty '04 (GAL) Lake Jackson, TX St. Michael.
Pham, Michael '99 (SD) San Diego, CA Holy Family Catholic Parish; Clergy Personnel Board.
Pham, Michael *o.s.b.* '10 (SD)[J] Oceanside, CA Prince of Peace Abbey.
Pham, Minh J. *c.m.* '91 (DAL)[J] Dallas, TX Congregation of the Mission, Western Province.
Pham, Peter Huong *o.p.* '85 (RIC) Richmond, VA Church of the Vietnamese Martyrs; Lay Fraternity of St. Dominic.
Pham, Peter Nghi Duc *s.o.l.t.* '99 (CC) Rockport, TX St. Peter's Parish.
Pham, Peter T. '98 (CHL) Charlotte, NC St. John Neumann.
Pham, Peter *s.o.l.t.* '99 (CC)[G] Robstown, TX Society of Our Lady of the Most Holy Trinity.
Pham, Quyet A. '04 (ALN) Reading, PA St. Paul.
Pham, Tan *s.j.* (ATL) Holy Vietnamese Martyrs.
Pham, Thang John '07 (BLX) Vancleave, MS Holy Spirit Catholic Church.
Pham, Thang M. '10 (ATL) Roswell, GA St. Peter Chanel.
Pham, Thanh Q. '07 (CAM) Mantua, NJ R.C. Church of the Incarnation, Township of Mantua, New Jersey.
Pham, The Joseph *c.ss.r.* '98 (STL) St. Louis, MO St. Alphonsus Liguori.
Pham, Thi *s.v.d.* '02 (FgM) Techny, IL.
Pham, Thi *s.c.j.* '07 (MIL) Franklin, WI St. Martin of Tours; [P] Franklin, WI St. Joseph's at Monastery Lake.
Pham, Thinh Duc '02 (LA) Graduate Studies.
Pham, Thomas *c.ss.r.* '09 (STP) Brooklyn Center, MN St. Alphonsus; [J] Brooklyn Center, MN Redemptorist Fathers of Hennepin County.
Pham, Thu *s.v.d.* '03 (FTW) Fort Wayne, IN St. Patrick.
Pham, Thuy (RIC) Retired.
Pham, Tin Cosmas Kim '95 (GAL) Brazoria, TX St. Joseph on the Brazos.
Pham, Tri '04 (PMB) Vero Beach, FL St. Helen.
Pham, Tu Van *s.j.* '06 (BO)[U] Brighton, MA Isaac Jogues House.
Pham, Tuan Anh '99 (NO) Gretna, LA St. Cletus.
Pham, Tuan Anh *c.ss.r.* (CHI)[N] Chicago, IL Redemptorist Theology Residence.
Pham, Rev. Msgr. Tuan Joseph '94 (ORG) Fountain Valley, CA Holy Spirit; Adjutant Judicial Vicars; Building and Renovation Committee of the Liturgical Commission.
Pham, Tuan Ngoc '88 (ORG) Westminster, CA Blessed Sacrament.
Pham, Tuan Ngoc *o.m.i.* (BO) Lowell, MA St. Patrick.
Pham, Vincent Hung '97 (ORG) Orange, CA La Purisima.
Pham, Vincent Huu (MOB)[I] Monroeville, AL Alabama Southern Community College Newman Center.
Pham Van Lan, Augustine '63 (CLV) Cleveland, OH St. Boniface; Translators.
Pham Van Tue, Joseph '73 (NO) Marrero, LA St. Agnes Le Thi Thanh.
Phan, An Duy '06 (OM) Omaha, NE St. Leo.
Phan, Anthony Lam '62 (OAK) Retired.
Phan, Anton Ba '01 (NO) Ama, LA St. Mark; Luling, LA St. Anthony of Padua.
Phan, Cho Dink Peter '72 (DAL) On Duty Outside the Diocese.
Phan, David Q. *o.f.m.* (CHR) Vicar for Vietnamese Ministry; Greenville, SC Our Lady of the Rosary; Greenville, SC St. Anthony of Padua.
Phan, David *o.f.m.* '10 (NY)[DD] New York Franciscan Friars, Holy Name Province.
Phan, Dominic T.H. '09 (LIN) Advocates; Lincoln, NE Sacred Heart.
Phan, Dominic '70 (BLX) Retired.
Phan, John '05 (JOL) Gibson City, IL Our Lady of Lourdes; Air Force Reserve Chaplains.
Phan, Joseph Duong '93 (OAK) Apostleship of the Sea; San Leandro, CA Assumption of the Blessed Virgin Mary.
Phan, Joseph Loc D. '02 (GAL) The Woodlands, TX Sts. Simon and Jude.
Phan, Joseph Son Thanh '03 (GAL) Damon, TX Sts. Cyril and Methodius; Needville, TX St. Michael.
Phan, Khoi '09 (ORG) Buena Park, CA St. Pius V.
Phan, Long N. '09 (OKL) Oklahoma City, OK St. Charles Borromeo.
Phan, Ngoan V. '07 (SFR) San Rafael, CA St. Raphael; Serra Club of Marin.
Phan, Nguyen Van *c.ss.r.* '93 (LA)[P] Baldwin Park, CA Vietnamese Redemptorist Mission.
Phan, Paul Cuong '99 (SJ) San Jose, CA St. Victor.
Phan, Peter Luc '90 (SJ) San Jose, CA St. Julie Billiart.
Phan, Peter '10 (SB) Perris, CA St. James.
Phan, Philip S. '85 (NY) New York, NY Guardian Angel.
Phan, Phu T. '92 (AMA) Ex Officio; Vicar General; Judicial Vicar; Ex Officio; College of Consultors; Canyon, TX St. Ann's.
Phan, Vincent Huu '95 (MOB) Monroeville, AL St. Joseph; Monroeville, AL Annunciation.
Phan Bao Luyen, Francis Xavier (SAC)[H] Walnut Grove, CA Monastery of Chau Son Sacramento.
Phat, Rev. Msgr. Peter Tran Van '67 (NY) Otisville, NY Holy Name.
Phelan, Cornelius Noel '59 (LA) Los Angeles, CA St. Basil's Retired.
Phelan, Edward '63 (SFR) San Francisco, CA St. Patrick Retired.
Phelan, Matthew H. *o.de.m* '02 (PH)[Y] Philadelphia, PA Monastery of Our Lady of Mercy.
Phelan, Thomas E. '76 (BEA) Diocesan College of Consultors; Orange, TX St. Francis of Assisi.
Phelan, Thomas '53 (SEA) Retired.
Phelps, Anthony '08 (LUB) Lubbock, TX Our Lady of Grace.
Phelps, John *c.ss.r.* '68 (CHI)[N] Chicago, IL The Redemptorist Fathers of Chicago; Chicago, IL St. Michael in Old Town.
Phelps, Lawrence J. *o.s.b.* '63 (NO)[R] St. Benedict, LA St. Joseph Abbey.
Philbin, Patrick B. *s.m.* '72 (ORG)[L] Orange, CA House of Prayer for Priests Retired.
Philbin, Patrick *s.m.* '52 (STL)[O] St. Louis Marianists, Province of the United States (Society of Mary).
Philen, Michael *c.m.f.* '99 (LA)[V] Rancho Dominguez, CA Dominguez Seminary Inc.
Philibert, Paul *o.p.* '63 (NO)[R] Metairie, LA Dominican Friars, Southern Dominican Province of St. Martin de Porres.
Philibert, Paul *o.p.* (TYL)[D] Lufkin, TX Monastery of the Infant Jesus.
Philip, Thomas M. '98 (LA)[J] Lynwood, CA St. Francis Medical Center.
Philip, Thomas '90 (LA) Hospital Chaplains.
Philiposki, Richard *s.ch.* '79 (BAL) Baltimore, MD Holy Rosary.
Philiposki, Richard *s.ch.* (LAV) Las Vegas, NV St. Anthony of Padua.
Philippe, Jean–Rony '99 (BGP) Haitian American Catholic Center of Greater Stamford; [W] Stamford, CT Haitian American Catholic Center.
Philips, Ligory Johnson '91 (SYM) West Hempstead, NY St. Mary Syro–Malabar Catholic Church (West Hempstead).
Philipsen, Todd K. '89 (GI) Grand Island, NE Blessed Sacrament.
Philius, Vilaire '09 (ORL) Winter Park, FL St. Margaret Mary.
Phillip, Alan *c.p.* '67 (LA)[P] Sierra Madre, CA Passionist Residence.
Phillippino, Michael L. '79 (NOR) Middletown, CT St. John; Members; Seminarian Advisory Board; Deans.
Phillips, Ambrose K. *t.o.r.* '71 (WDC)[O] Washington, DC St. Louis Friary; Councilors.
Phillips, Benet C. *o.s.b.* '92 (MAN)[K] Manchester, NH St. Anselm Abbey; Presbyteral Council.
Phillips, C. Frank *c.r.* '77 (CHI) Chicago, IL St. John Cantius; [P] Chicago, IL Canons Regular of Saint John Cantius.
Phillips, Christopher G. '83 (SAT) San Antonio, TX Our Lady of the Atonement Catholic Church.
Phillips, Clyde *m.m.* '78 (FgM) Maryknoll, NY MARYKNOLL.
Phillips, Edward J. *m.m.* '74 (FgM) Maryknoll, NY MARYKNOLL.
Phillips, Gene D. *s.j.* '65 (CHI)[N] Evanston, IL Canisius House.
Phillips, Glenn '66 (CHI)[N] Chicago, IL St. Peter's Friary.
Phillips, Gregory *o.s.b.* '01 (WOR)[N] Petersham, MA St. Mary's Monastery.
Phillips, John M. '87 (STA) Gainesville, FL Holy Faith; Priests' Spirituality Committee.
Phillips, John '55 (ROC) Retired.
Phillips, Joseph H. '68 (SY) Truxton, NY St. Patrick; Special Assignment; [L] Syracuse, NY Family Life Education; Management Team; Family Life Education; Propagation of the Faith.
Phillips, Kenneth G. '91 (BIS) Mandan, ND Christ the King; Priests' Benefit Association.
Phillips, Louis J. '81 (PRT) Portland, ME Cathedral of the Immaculate Conception; Portland, ME St. Louis; Portland, ME St. Peter's; Portland, ME St. Christopher's; Members; Portland, ME Sacred Heart/St. Dominic.
Phillips, Rev. Msgr. Michael J. '60 (BRK) Brooklyn, NY St. Anselm Retired.
Phillips, Michael T. '69 (DAV) Iowa City, IA St. Wenceslaus; Priests Eucharistic League.
Phillips, Randall '83 (DET) Sterling Heights, MI St. Blase.
Phillips, Randy '97 (SFS) Ipswich, SD Holy Cross.
Phillips, Rene F. *o.f.m.* '56 (NY)[DD] New York Franciscan Friars, Holy Name Province.
Phillips, Robert L. *s.j.* '59 (BAL)[Q] Baltimore, MD Jesuit Community of Loyola University, Inc.
Phillips, Robert *s.j.* '72 (BAL)[K] Towson, MD St. Joseph Medical Center, Inc.
Phillips, Rev. Msgr. Thomas L. '71 (BAL) Baltimore, MD St. Gabriel.
Phillipson, David '03 (SFE) On Duty Outside the Archdiocese.
Philominsamy, Michaelraj '91 (SR) Fort Bragg, CA Our Lady of Good Counsel; Clergy Personnel Committee; Parish Priest Consultors; Clergy Formation.
Phinn, Paul A. '57 (BO) Senior Priests. Retired.
Phipps, Charles T. *s.j.* '59 (SJ)[B] Santa Clara, CA Jesuit Community.
Phipps, Ricardo M. '02 (JKS) New Albany, MS St. Francis of Assisi.
Phiri, Joseph *o.m.i.* '98 (WDC)[O] Washington, DC Oblate Community.
Phiri, Mabvuto Felix (BO) Haverhill, MA St. James.
Pho, Luan *o.p.* '08 (ARL) Arlington, VA Holy Martyrs of Vietnam.
Phongo, Jean–Marie Mvumbi *c.i.c.m.* '03 (SAT) San Antonio, TX Divine Providence.
Phuc, Tran Dinh *c.ss.r.* '56 (LA)[P] Baldwin Park Vietnamese Redemptorist Mission.
Phung, Chi Peter '90 (TLS) Henryetta, OK St. Michael; Henryetta, OK St. Stephen's.
Phung, Joseph P. V. '00 (DAV) Mount Pleasant, IA St. Alphonsus.
Phung, Le Quang *c.ss.r.* '69 (LA)[P] Baldwin Park

Vietnamese Redemptorist Mission.
Phung, Vincent '96 (DEN) Graduate Studies.
Phuoc Hoa, Dang *c.ss.r.* '03 (LA)[P] Baldwin Park Vietnamese Redemptorist Mission.
Phuong, Rev. Msgr. Francis '66 (ATL) Vicars for Clergy.
Piacentini, David A. '71 (PRO) Ashaway, RI Our Lady of Victory; Bradford, RI St. Vincent de Paul.
Piansay, Victor '64 (FRS) Riverdale, CA St. Ann.
Piasecki, Adam *c.r.* (CHI) Chicago, IL St. Hyacinth Basilica.
Piasecki, Timothy '73 (RCK) Aurora, IL St. Mary.
Piasta, Krystian J. *o.f.m.* '95 (BRK) Jamaica, NY St. Joseph; Jamaica, NY Our Lady of the Skies Chapel.
Piatt, Charles E. *s.t.* '03 (WDC)[O] Riverdale, MD Holy Spirit Missionary Cenacle.
Piazza, Rev. Msgr. Benjamin A. '49 (NEW) Caldwell, NJ St. Aloysius Retired.
Picard, Daniel '79 (LAF) Port Barre, LA Sacred Heart of Jesus.
Picard, Rev. Msgr. Michael C. '66 (PH) Newtown, PA St. Andrew; [BB] Newtown, PA Bucks County Community College.
Picard, Raymond '65 (PRT) Retired.
Picardi, Aubert Marie *o.f.m.* '62 (BO)[U] Boston, MA St. Christopher Friary.
Picardi, John M. '83 (BO) Unassigned.
Picarella, Dale '84 (BAL) Linthicum Heights, MD St. Philip Neri.
Picariello, Anthony R. *s.j.* '80 (BO)[U] Weston, MA Campion Health Center, Inc.
Picazo, Luis *s.f.* '72 (WDC)[B] Silver Spring, MD Holy Family Seminary; Silver Spring, MD.
Picciano, Rev. Msgr. Daniel A. '71 (RVC) Lake Ronkonkoma, NY St. Elizabeth Ann Seton.
Piccinino, Corey V. '86 (BGP) Bethel, CT St. Mary; Vicariate V (Bethel, Brookfield, Danbury, Georgetown, Newtown, New Fairfield, Redding, Ridgefield, Sherman); Members of the Clergy Personnel Committee.
Piccola, Michael J. '78 (SCR) Hazleton, PA SS. Cyril & Methodius, Hazleton; Hazleton, PA St. Stanislaus; Deans.
Piccoli, Gino L. *o.f.m.* '65 (TUC) San Carlos, AZ San Carlos Apache Roman Catholic Community – San Carlos.
Piccolomini, Rev. Msgr. Rocco M. '85 (WOR) Diocesan College of Consultors; Worcester State Hospital; Worcester, MA Our Lady of Mt. Carmel and St. Ann.
Pichalakkattu, Binoy Jacob *s.j.* '07 (OAK)[L] Berkeley, CA Jesuit Fathers and Brothers.
Pichard, Rev. Msgr. Lawrence '73 (DAL) Pastors Consultors; Frisco, TX St. Francis of Assisi.
Piche, Donald J. '77 (STP) Maple Grove, MN St. Joseph the Worker.
Picinic, John P. *s.a.c.* '05 (CAM) Mullica Hill, NJ Catholic Community of the Holy Spirit, Mullica Hill, N.J.
Pick, Anthony '67 (SC) Retired.
Pick, Edward '60 (VEN) Retired.
Pickard, William B. '76 (SCR) Scranton, PA Saint John Neumann, Scranton; [I] Scranton, PA St. Joseph's Center.
Pickard, Rev. Msgr. William M. '54 (GAL) Defenders of the Bond Retired.
Pickarts, Bernard J. '55 (MAD) Retired.
Pickens, David '09 (PAT) Little Falls, NJ Our Lady of the Holy Angels.
Picket, James '61 (SFR) San Francisco, CA Most Holy Redeemer Retired.
Pickett, James B. '61 (OAK) Retired.
Pico, Fernando *s.j.* '71 (SJN)[H] Hato Rey, PR Jesuit Community – Casa Claver.
Picollo, Christopher P. '11 (TR) Red Bank, NJ St. James.
Picone, Alfonso '00 (NEW) On Duty Outside the Archdiocese.
Picone, Alfonso '00 (BGP) Bridgeport, CT St. Raphael.
Picos, Oscar M. '06 (SLC) St. George, UT St. George LLC 223.
Picton, James D. '75 (SEA) Bellevue, WA St. Madeleine Sophie; Presbyteral Council; Deans.
Picton, Thomas D. *c.ss.r.* '71 (TUC)[G] Cortaro, AZ Redemptorist Society of Arizona Desert House of Prayer.
Pidel, Aaron '11 (MIA) Miami, FL Gesu.
Piderit, John J. *s.j.* '71 (CHI)[W] Chicago, IL The Catholic Education Institute.
Piderit, John J. *s.j.* '71 (NY) Bronx, NY St. Anthony.
Pidgeon, John '87 (PH) Philadelphia, PA Epiphany of Our Lord.
Pieber, Carl L. *c.m.* '80 (PH)[CC] Philadelphia, PA The Central Association of the Miraculous Medal; Philadelphia, PA Immaculate Conception; [B] Philadelphia, PA St. Vincent's Seminary.
Piechocki, Rev. Msgr. Bruce '84 (FTW) Mishawaka, IN St. Monica; Presbyteral Council; Pro–Synodal Judges; Consultors; Appeal Court Judges; Defenders of the Bond.
Piechocki, Raymond S. '47 (ALB) Retired.
Piechota, Rev. Msgr. Lech '89 (SFR) On Duty Outside the Archdiocese.
Pieczara, Stanislaw *s.d.s* '76 (SAT)[R] San Antonio, TX Our Lady of Czestochowa; [M] San Antonio, TX Seraphic Sisters of Our Lady of Sorrows Convent.
Piedra, Ruskin *c.ss.r.* '60 (BRK) Brooklyn, NY Our Lady of Perpetual Help Basilica.
Piedrahita, Jose Gabriel '86 (NY) New York, NY St. Benedict the Moor; New York, NY Sacred Heart of Jesus.
Piekarczyk, Marian A. *s.d.s.* '80 (MO) DEPARTMENT OF VETERANS AFFAIRS HOSPITALS AND CHAPLAINS; Army Reserve Chaplains.
Piekarczyk, Marian *s.d.s.* '80 (SAT) San Antonio, TX Our Lady of Sorrows; San Antonio, TX Methodist Hospital; [L] Falls City, TX Salvatorian Fathers Community of Texas.
Piekarski, Joseph J. '86 (WIL) Elkton, MD Immaculate Conception; Associate Directors.
Pienkos, Zbigniew *c.ss.r.* '91 (CHI) Cicero, IL St. Mary of Czestochowa.
Pienkowski, Marek *o.p.* '80 (NY)[GG] New York, NY Columbia University.
Pienta, Robert J. '99 (LAN) Priests' Assignment Commission; Jackson, MI St. John the Evangelist.
Pientek, Placid *o.s.b.* '44 (CLV)[N] Cleveland, OH.
Pieper, Rev. Msgr. James E. '57 (STL) St. Louis, MO St. Clement.
Pieper, Theodore X. '62 (STL) Cadet, MO St. Joachim; Cadet, MO St. Joseph.
Piepmeyer, Ronald J. '97 (CIN) Morrow, OH St. Philip the Apostle.
Pierce, Bradley *m.s.a.* '83 (NOR)[A] Cromwell, CT Holy Apostles College and Seminary; [G] Cromwell, CT Society of the Missionaries of the Holy Apostles.
Pierce, Brian J. *o.p.* '83 (FgM) Metairie, LA St. Martin de Porres Province (Southern Dominican Province).
Pierce, Douglas Arthur Louis–Marie '10 (STP) Shoreview, MN St. Odilia.
Pierce, Edward J. '72 (SFS) Retired.
Pierce, James L. *s.j.* '77 (NY)[DD] New York, NY Xavier Jesuit Community.
Pierce, John J. *o.f.m.* '63 (PAT)[N] Butler, NJ St. Anthony Friary.
Pierce, Joseph B. '92 (WDC) Cheverly, MD St. Ambrose.
Pierce, Larry E. '58 (SAL) Retired.
Pierce, Mark R. '81 (LC) Chippewa Falls, WI Notre Dame.
Pierce, William M. '71 (CAM) Retired.
Pierceall, Patrick L. '69 (JC) Retired.
Pierini, Raymond G. *m.m.* '87 (NY)[DD] Bronx, NY Calvary Hospital.
Pierino, Vicente '64 (SJN) On Duty Outside the Archdiocese.
Pierjok, Peter Augustine H. *o.s.b.* '88 (GBG) Whitney, PA St. Cecilia; Whitney, PA Sacred Heart; [H] Latrobe, PA Saint Vincent Archabbey.
Pieroni, Edward L. '85 (PRO) Providence, RI St. Raymond; Providence, RI Miriam Hospital.
Pierre, Darren Michael *o.p.* '04 (NY)[DD] New York, NY St. Vincent Ferrer Priory; [HH] New York, NY The Lay Fraternity of St. Dominic, Inc.
Pierre, Jaccius Jean '01 (NY) White Plains, NY St. John the Evangelist.
Pierre, Jean Y. '85 (BRK) Far Rockaway, NY St. Mary Star of the Sea and St. Gertrude.
Pierre, Rev. Msgr. Jean '88 (MIA) Miami, FL St. James; Ministry to Cultural Groups (Non–Hispanic Ethnicities); Haitians; Native Americans; Archdiocesan Vocations Review Board.
Pierre, Kenneth J. '63 (STP) Retired.
Pierre, Lucien '77 (MIA)[A] Miami, FL St. John Vianney College Seminary.
Pierre, Roger P. '63 (STP) Retired.
Pierre, Yvon '85 (BRK)[V] Brooklyn, NY National Center of the Haitian Apostolate.
Pierre–Jules, Oswald P. *s.s.j.* '06 (NO) New Orleans, LA St. David.
Pierre–Louis, Andre Dumarsais '01 (PMB)[B] West Palm Beach, FL Cardinal Newman High School, Inc.; West Palm Beach, FL St. Ann.
Pierro, Sebastian C. '82 (BUF) Hamburg, NY SS. Peter and Paul.
Pierson, Robert *o.s.b.* '84 (SCL)[I] Collegeville, MN St. John's Abbey, of the Order of St. Benedict.
Pierzchala, Ireneusz '08 (NEW) Linden, NJ St. Theresa of the Child Jesus.
Pietramale, John L. '92 (OM) Omaha, NE St. Adalbert; Omaha, NE Our Lady of Lourdes; Age Groups.
Pietras, Robert E. '62 (JOL)[K] Naperville, IL St. John Vianney Villa Retired.
Pietraszko, Andrzej '03 (MIA) Miami, FL Our Lady of Lourdes.
Pietropinto, Joseph P. '70 (NEW) Secaucus, NJ Immaculate Conception.
Pietrowski, Stephen J. '92 (RVC) Bay Shore, NY St. Patrick's.
Pietrucha, Edward S. *c.s.p.* '57 (TUC) Tucson, AZ Saint Cyril of Alexandria Roman Catholic Parish – Tucson Retired.
Pietrzak, Bernard J. '81 (CHI) Barrington, IL St. Anne.
Pietrzyk, Paul J. *o.de.m.* '02 (CLV) Cleveland, OH St. Rocco; Lutheran Medical Center.
Pifher, Cletus *o.f.m.conv.* '64 (SAV) Brunswick, GA St. Francis Xavier.
Pifher, William A. '94 (TOL) Monroeville, OH St. Joseph; Monroeville, OH St. Alphonsus Liguori.
Piga, Stephen M. '02 (TR) Freehold, NJ St. Rose of Lima.
Pigan, Janusz '11 (NEW) Kearny, NJ St. Cecilia's.
Piggford, George *c.s.c.* '05 (FR)[A] North Easton, MA Holy Cross Fathers Religious; [A] North Easton, MA Stonehill College.
Piggford, George *c.s.c.* '05 (FTW)[H] Notre Dame Congregation of Holy Cross, United States Province of Priests & Brothers.
Pighini, Richard J. *c.s.v.* '85 (CHI)[N] Arlington Heights Viatorian Province Center–Clerics of St. Viator.
Pighini, Richard *c.s.v.* '85 (JOL) Bourbonnais, IL Maternity of the Blessed Virgin Mary.
Pignato, David A. '01 (FR) On Duty Outside the Diocese.
Pignato, Salvatore A. '68 (PSC) Orlando, FL St. Nicholas of Myra; Vocations; Retirement Plan Board.
Pigott, Edward L. *s.j.* '68 (CIN)[F] Cincinnati, OH St. Xavier High School; [N] Cincinnati, OH Jesuit Community at St. Xavier High School.
Piku, Karl *f.s.s.p.* '92 (IND) Brookville, IN SS. Philomena and Cecilia Catholic Church, Brookville, Inc.
Pikulinski, Jerzy '01 (NEW) Wallington, NJ Most Sacred Heart of Jesus.
Pilaczynski, John E. *o.m.i.* '58 (STP)[J] St. Paul, MN Oblate Residence.
Pilarski, Bernard '56 (DET) Wayne, MI Oakwood Annapolis Hospital; Garden City, MI Garden City Hospital.
Pilarski, Chester J. '50 (SAG) Retired.
Pilarski, Peter R. '59 (PIT) Plum, PA St. Januarius Retired.
Pilarz, Scott R. *s.j.* '92 (MIL)[C] Marquette University; [P] Milwaukee, WI Jesuit Community at Marquette University.
Pilat, Edmund S. '56 (SY) Retired.
Pilato, Rev. Msgr. Sabato "Sal" A. '92 (LA) Superintendent Secondary Schools; Members; Inglewood, CA St. John Chrysostom; Commission Members.
Pilcher, Gregory *o.s.b.* '78 (LR) El Dorado, AR Holy Redeemer.
Pilcher, John '99 (KCK) Wamego, KS Holy Family; Wamego, KS St. Joseph; Paxico, KS Sacred Heart; Wamego, KS St. Bernard.
Pileggi, Anthony J. '81 (KC) Kansas City, MO Our Lady of Sorrows.
Pileggi, Francis J. *o.s.f.s.* '61 (WIL)[B] Wilmington, DE Salesianum School.
Piletic, William R. *c.m.* '77 (LA)[P] Los Angeles, CA Amat Residence 1.
Pilger, G. Richard *i.c.* '79 (SP) Seminole, FL Blessed Sacrament.
Pilgram, Paul C. *s.j.* '70 (STL)[O] St. Louis, MO Ignatius House.
Pilipie, John P. '82 (PAT) Ogdensburg, NJ St. Thomas of Aquin; Deans.
Pilla, P. Carl '54 (SY) Retired.
Pilla, Raju '91 (PH) Penndel, PA Our Lady of Grace.
Pillai, Joseph '93 (CHI) Chicago, IL St. Benedict.
Pillari, Moses de Jesus '07 (SAT) Special Assignment.
Pilola, Joseph '87 (HT) Thibodaux, LA St. Thomas Aquinas; Campus Ministry.
Pilon, Rev. Msgr. Daniel J. '76 (FAR) Enderlin, ND St. Patrick's Church of Enderlin; Enderlin, ND Holy Trinity Church of Fingal; Enderlin, ND Our Lady of the Scapular Church of Sheldon; Defensor Vinculi.
Pilon, James F. '67 (HRT) Retired.
Pilon, Jean–Pierre G. '02 (SCR) On Duty Outside the Diocese.
Pilon, Mark A. '75 (ARL) Springfield, VA St. Raymond of Penafort.
Pilon, Peter A. '00 (PEO) Wapella, IL St. Patrick Church; [B] Bloomington, IL Central Catholic High School.
Pilsner, Joseph E. *c.s.b.* '91 (GAL)[O] Houston, TX Residence of the Basilian Fathers of the University of St. Thomas; [C] Houston, TX University of St. Thomas.
Pilsner, Peter R. '89 (NY)[E] Bronx, NY Cardinal Spellman High School.
Pilus, Jaroslaw '98 (DET) Detroit, MI SS. Peter and Paul; Detroit, MI St. Suzanne/Our Lady Gate of Heaven.
Pimentel, Jose W. *o.p.* '90 (MO) Navy Reserve Chaplains.
Pina, Jorge Luis Rodriguez *c.o.r.c.* '08 (SB) San Bernardino, CA Our Lady of Guadalupe; [I] Corona, CA Confraternity of Operarios Del Reino De Cristo, C.O.R.C.
Pina, Martin '93 (LUB) Lubbock, TX St. Joseph's.
Pina, Salomon Covarrubias '91 (YAK) Defenders of the Bond.
Pinapati, Lucas Raj '98 (OKL) Harrah, OK St. Teresa of Avila.
Pinarkayil, Saji Kurian '99 (SYM) Maywood, IL Sacred Heart Syro–Malabar Knanaya Catholic Church (Maywood).

Pincelli, Thomas L. '84 (BWN) Brownsville, TX Our Lady of Good Counsel.
Pinchock, Joseph '72 (ORL) Port Orange, FL Our Lady of Hope Retired.
Pinciaro, Albert G. '84 (BGP) Stamford, CT St. Maurice.
Pincince, Gerald P. '65 (PRO) Retired.
Pinczewski, Phillip A. '87 (E) Kane, PA St. Callistus; Deans; Eastern Vicariate.
Pineda, Jose Humberto '06 (LA) Reseda, CA St. Catherine of Siena; Van Nuys, CA St. Bridget of Sweden.
Pineda, Juan G. '90 (GAL) Navasota, TX Christ Our Light; Hempstead, TX St. Katherine Drexel.
Pineda, Vincent '05 (SJ) Cupertino, CA St. Joseph of Cupertino.
Pinette, Stuart H. '95 (HRT) Rocky Hill, CT St. Elizabeth Seton.
Ping, Dong *f.l.* '99 (CHI) Chicago, IL St. Therese Catholic Chinese Church.
Pinillos, Ricardo Martin '03 (ARL) Alexandria, VA Good Shepherd.
Pinizzotto, Anthony J. *o.s.f.s.* '78 (ARL) Chantilly, VA St. Timothy.
Pinkerton, Samuel J. '95 (WCH) Garden Plain, KS Immaculate Conception; Garden Plain, KS St. Anthony.
Pinkston, Robert *c.s.p.* '69 (NY)[DD] New York, NY Paulist Fathers' Motherhouse Retired.
Pinne, Chris D. *s.j.* '81 (STL)[C] Saint Louis University.
Pinne, Christopher P. *s.j.* '87 (STL)[O] St. Louis, MO Jesuit Community Corporation at Saint Louis University – Jesuit Hall.
Pino, Justin P. '07 (E) Oil City, PA St. Joseph; Oil City, PA Assumption of the Blessed Virgin Mary; Diocesan Archivist.
Pins, Herbert J. '71 (HEL) Dillon, MT St. Rose of Lima; Warm Springs State Hospital; [G] Dillon, MT University of Montana – Western.
Pins, Rev. Msgr. Joseph D. '70 (STL) St. Louis, MO Cathedral Basilica of Saint Louis; Archdiocesan Newspaper "The St. Louis Review".
Pins, Joseph (DM) Creston, IA Holy Spirit; Creston, IA St. Edward; Diocesan Consultors.
Pintabone, Rev. Canon John A. '79 (NY) Unassigned.
Pintacura, Michael '93 (STO) On Duty Outside the Diocese.
Pinti, Domenico C. '85 (TUC) Diocesan Consultors; Apache Junction, AZ Saint George Roman Catholic Parish – Apache Junction; Council of Priests; Vicars Forane; Directors; All Vicars Forane.
Pinto, Agnelo '71 (BRK) Brooklyn, NY St. Augustine.
Pinto, Alex '69 (NEW) Co Presidents.
Pinto, Danny '63 (FTW) Churubusco, IN St. John Bosco; Churubusco, IN Immaculate Conception.
Pinto, Edgaro '80 (SJN) Bayamon, PR Nuestra Senora de la Milagrosa.
Pinto, Franco *s.d.b.* '97 (NEW)[L] Ramsey, NJ Don Bosco Prep Salesian Residence.
Pinto, Franco *s.d.b.* '92 (NY)[FF] Stony Point, NY Don Bosco Retreat Center and Marian Shrine.
Pinto, P. Francis *s.d.b.* '97 (NEW)[Q] Offices of Vocation and Youth Ministry.
Pintye, Louis M. *o.f.m.* '90 (BGP) Fairfield, CT St. Emery.
Pintye, Louis M. *o.f.m.* '90 (HRT) Winsted, CT St. Joseph.
Pinyan, Charles '92 (NEW) Allendale, NJ Guardian Angel; Members; Elected Members; Archdiocesan Stewardship Advisory Committee.
Pinzon, Alvaro '91 (MIA) Miami, FL St. Mary's Cathedral; Defenders of the Bond; Judges; Confraternity of Our Lady of Chiquinquira.
Pinzon, Cesar Augusto Torres *i.m.e.y.* (CHR) Beaufort, SC St. Peter.
Pinzon, Eduardo *s.j.* '60 (CHI) Chicago, IL St. Bartholomew Retired.
Piontkowski, Richard L. '82 (GI) Adjutant Vicars–Judicial; Judges; Diocesan Consultors; Grand Island, NE Cathedral of the Nativity of the Blessed Virgin Mary; Army Reserve Chaplains.
Piorkowski, Robert '76 (STN) Madison, IL St. Mary's.
Piorkowski, Rev. Msgr. Stanley W. '51 (SCR)[M] Dunmore, PA Villa St. Joseph Retired.
Piotrowski, Adrian *o.s.c.* '64 (SCL)[I] Onamia Crosier Priory.
Piotrowski, Leonard '93 (SP) Tampa, FL St. Paul; [F] Tampa, FL St. Paul Child Enrichment; Secretary for Priest Personnel; Personnel Board; Ex Officio; Executive Committee.
Piovan, Benjamin '64 (NO) Retired.
Piovan, Benjamin '64 (BLX) Latin American Apostolate.
Piovan, Benjamin '64 (JKS)[I].
Pipa, Krzysztof B. *s.v.d.* '98 (CHI) Wheeling, IL St. Joseph the Worker.
Pipp, Thomas J. *s.j.* '92 (STP)[B] St. Paul, MN Jesuit Novitiate.
Pipta, Robert M. '94 (HPM) Vocations Office; San Diego, CA Holy Angels; College of Consultors; Personnel Board.
Piquado, Thomas G. *s.j.* '72 (SAC) Sacramento, CA St. Ignatius of Loyola; [H] Carmichael, CA Sacramento Jesuit Community.
Pira, Reginald Paul S. '98 (HON) Lanai City, HI Sacred Hearts of Jesus and Mary Parish.
Piraro, Don '67 (LKC)[C] Moss Bluff, LA St. Charles Center; Diocesan Consultors.
Pires, Francisco '84 (SLC) Board of Directors; Hyde Park, UT Saint Thomas Aquinas LLC 247; College of Consultors.
Piro, Francis '54 (PH) Philadelphia, PA St. Philip Neri Retired.
Piro, Frank R. '62 (SFR) Retired.
Piro, Gerald J. '79 (BRK) On Leave/Unassigned.
Pirrera, Aaron *o.s.b.* '85 (LR) Altus, AR St. Mary; Subiaco, AR St. Benedict.
Pirrone, Roberto '88 (LA) Inglewood, CA St. John Chrysostom.
Pisaneschi, Joseph J. '01 (SCR) Swoyersville, PA Holy Name/St. Mary's; Swoyersville, PA Holy Trinity.
Pisano, Joseph Daniel '07 (WH) Wellsburg, WV St. John The Evangelist.
Pisano, Mario *o.m.* '68 (LA)[P] Los Angeles, CA Minim Fathers; Los Angeles, CA All Saints; Los Angeles, CA.
Pisano, Stephen *s.j.* '75 (FgM) Los Gatos, CA Society of Jesus.
Pisarcik, John G. (PAT) Retired.
Pisciotta, Justin M. *o.s.m.* '64 (ORG) Fullerton, CA St. Philip Benizi.
Piscitello, Primo P. *o.f.m.* '60 (NY)[DD] New York, NY Franciscan Province of the Immaculate Conception; [HH] Mount Vernon, NY Franciscan Mission Associates; [HH] Mount Vernon, NY St. Dymphna Devotion; New York, NY.
Pisegna, Cedric *c.p.* '91 (GAL)[O] Houston, TX Congregation of the Passion, Holy Name Passionist Community and Retreat Center.
Piselli, Costanzo J. '69 (PRT) Retired.
Pish, Robert H. '05 (STP)[C] St. Paul, MN University of St. Thomas; [A] Saint Paul, MN The Saint Paul Seminary.
Piskura, Joseph '54 (CLV) Retired.
Piso, Rafael *s.t.* (PAT)[N] Stirling, NJ Shrine of St. Joseph.
Piso, Volodymyr '73 (STF) Kerhonkson, NY Holy Trinity.
Pisors, John A. *c.s.v.* '66 (CHI)[N] Arlington Heights Viatorian Province Center–Clerics of St. Viator.
Pisso, Raphael *s.t.* (PAT) Migrant Ministry.
Pistacchio, Gene *o.f.m.* '89 (BO)[Z] Boston, MA St. Anthony Shrine.
Pistacchio, Gene *o.f.m.* '89 (WDC)[W] Washington, DC Missionaries of the Kingship of Christ.
Pistone, Benardo '73 (HBG) Gettysburg, PA St. Francis Xavier's.
Pisut, Christopher '02 (DM) Chariton, IA Sacred Heart; Leon, IA St. Brendan; Judicial Vicar; Judges; Chariton, IA St. Francis.
Piszker, James '91 (E)[B] Erie, PA Mercyhurst College; [Q] Erie, PA Mercyhurst College.
Pitcavage, William *s.c.j.* '76 (MIL)[P] Franklin, WI Sacred Heart at Monastery Lake.
Pitre, Eric J. '81 (GAL) Sealy, TX Immaculate Conception; Archdiocesan Judges; Western Vicariate; Area Representatives.
Pitstick, Martin John '08 (COV) California, KY Sts. Peter and Paul; [B] Alexandria, KY Bishop Brossart High School.
Pitstick, Rory K. '94 (MO) Air National Guard Chaplains.
Pitstick, Rory '94 (SPK) On Duty Outside the Diocese.
Pitstick, Rory '94 (P)[A] St. Benedict, OR Mount Angel Seminary.
Pitt, Rev. Msgr. William L. '61 (RIC) Retired.
Pittard, Wayne M. '83 (GF) Big Timber, MT St. Joseph; Livingston, MT St. Mary; Clerical Benefit Association.
Pittman, Robert S. *s.s.s.* '58 (WDC)[X] Waldorf, MD Black Leadership and Christ's Kingdom Society.
Pitts, Joseph *o.m.i.* '59 (BEL)[F] Belleville, IL Shrine of Our Lady of the Snows.
Pitts, William L. '70 (R) Edenton, NC St. Anne.
Pitula, Roman '98 (PHU) Presbyteral Council; Hillsborough, NJ St. Michael's; New Brunswick, NJ Nativity of B.V.M.
Pitzer, John M. *o.p.* '99 (NO)[R] Metairie, LA Southern Dominican Foundation; [U] Metairie, LA Southern Dominican Foundation; [R] Metairie, LA Dominican Friars, Southern Dominican Province of St. Martin de Porres; New Orleans, LA St. Anthony of Padua.
Pivarnik, R. Gabriel *o.p.* '97 (PRO)[O] Providence St. Thomas Aquinas Priory at Providence College.
Pivonka, David *t.o.r.* '96 (WDC)[O] Washington, DC St. Louis Friary.
Pivonka, Rev. Msgr. Leonard '77 (CC) Deans; College of Consultors; Presbyteral Council; Judges; Alice, TX St. Elizabeth of Hungary.
Piwowar, Stanley J. '51 (MAN) Retired.
Pizmoht, Louis A. '66 (CLV) Retired.
Pizzamiglio, Rev. Msgr. Ernest E. '66 (PEO) Galesburg, IL Immaculate Heart of Mary; Vicariates and Vicars.
Pizzarelli, Francis *s.m.m.* '79 (RVC) Port Jefferson, NY Most Precious Blood; [N] Bay Shore, NY Montfort Missionaries; Presbyteral Council.
Pizzo, Anthony B. *o.s.a.* '84 (CHI) Chicago, IL St. Rita of Cascia; Deans.
Pizzo, Philip J. '77 (BRK) South Richmond Hill, NY St. Benedict Joseph Labre.
Pizzuto, Alfred '55 (NY)[DD] Bronx, NY John Cardinal O'Connor Residence Retired.
Placa, Rev. Msgr. Alan J. '70 (RVC) Great Neck, NY St. Aloysius Retired.
Place, Michael D. '70 (CHI) Members.
Placette, David D. '04 (BEA) Nederland, TX St. Charles Borromeo.
Plagens, Rev. Msgr. James A. '65 (SAN) Promoter Justitiae; Midland, TX St. Ann's.
Plaisted, Eugene D. *o.s.c.* '61 (SCL)[I] Onamia, MN Crosier Priory.
Plakut, Peter *o.c.s.o.* '58 (P)[L] Lafayette, OR The Cistercian (Trappist) Abbey of Our Lady of Guadalupe.
Plammoottil, Sunny Joseph *o.s.h.* '93 (GAL)[O] Missouri City, TX The Society of the Oblates of Sacred Heart; Missouri City, TX Holy Family.
Plamondon, Donald J. '72 (DUB) Independence, IA St. Patrick; Independence, IA St. John the Evangelist; Defenders of the Bond.
Planas, Salvador '54 (MIA) Retired.
Plancher, Christian E. *s.m.m.* '98 (MIA) Homestead, FL Sacred Heart.
Planea, John '82 (NO) On Duty Outside the Archdiocese.
Plank, Stephen J. *o.s.b.* '94 (OM)[C] Elkhorn, NE Mount Michael Benedictine School; [J] Elkhorn, NE Mount Michael Benedictine Abbey.
Planning, Stephen W. *s.j.* '99 (WDC)[E] Washington, DC Gonzaga College High School; [O] Washington, DC The Jesuit Community of St. Aloysius Gonzaga.
Plans, John F. *s.f.* '67 (WDC) Silver Spring, MD Christ the King.
Plans, John *s.f.* '67 (SFE) Santa Cruz, NM Holy Cross.
Plant, Christopher M. '08 (GAL) Houston, TX Resurrection.
Plante, Rev. Msgr. Jacques L. '82 (PRO) Evangelization & Pastoral Planning.
Plante, Paul A. '71 (PRT) Oquossoc, ME Our Lady of the Lakes; Vicar for Priests; Ex Officio Members; Diocesan Consultors; Ministry to Priests; Diocesan Priests' Benefit Plan – Trustees.
Plante, Pierre J. '78 (PRO) Warwick, RI St. Francis of Assisi.
Plante, Roger J. *m.s.* '61 (MAN)[K] Enfield, NH Shrine of Our Lady of La Salette; [N] Enfield, NH Shrine of Our Lady of La Salette.
Planty, Donald J. '93 (ARL)[A] Front Royal, VA Christendom College; Defenders of the Bond.
Plasker, Alexander *o.s.b.* '62 (P)[L] St. Benedict, OR Mt. Angel Abbey.
Plasse, Eugene J. '72 (SPR) Palmer, MA St. Thomas the Apostle.
Plaster, George F. '80 (IND) Indianapolis, IN St. Mark the Evangelist Catholic Church, Indianapolis, Inc.
Plata, Gregory *o.f.m.* '85 (JKS) Greenwood, MS Immaculate Heart of Mary; Greenwood, MS St. Francis of Assisi; Lexington, MS St. Thomas; Winona, MS Sacred Heart; [H] Lexington, MS Holmes Community College Newman Center; Provincial Councilors:; Priests' Council.
Plate, Brian G. '96 (NEW) Summit, NJ St. Teresa's.
Plateaux, Jean Frederic *c.s.j.* '99 (LAR)[D] Laredo, TX St. John Priory, F.J.
Plathanam, Ignatius J. *c.m.i.* '72 (STA) Palatka, FL St. Monica.
Plathe, Anthony H. '63 (NU) Retired.
Plathottam, Thomas *c.s.t.* '74 (NOR) Ellington, CT St. Luke.
Plathottam, Thomas *c.s.t.* '74 (HRT) Enfield, CT Carl Robinson Correctional Institution; Enfield, CT Enfield Correctional Institute.
Platt, Philip Wallace *c.s.b.* '50 (GAL)[O] Sugar Land Basilian Mission Center.
Platt, Stewart '51 (Y) Retired.
Platt, William (HRT)[H] Waterbury, CT Saint Mary's Hospital.
Plaushin, Mark *o.s.f.s.* '89 (MO) Army Reserve Chaplains.
Plaushin, Mark *o.s.f.s.* '89 (ALN)[B] Center Valley, PA DeSales University; [K] Center Valley, PA Oblates of St. Francis de Sales.
Plavac, Timothy J. '86 (CLV) Mentor, OH St. Bede the Venerable.
Plavcan, Jon J. '94 (GRY) Gary, IN Cathedral of Holy Angels; Gary, IN Holy Rosary; Deans; Administrative Assistant to the Bishop; Bishop's Council of Priests; Consultors; Priests' Personnel Board.
Plawecki, Joseph A. '83 (DET) Richmond, MI St. Augustine.
Plazewski, Leonard '91 (SP) Elected Parochial Vicars; Executive Committee.
Pleban, Alexander L. '57 (GBG)[G] Greensburg, PA

Neumann House Retired.
Pleban, Leo '60 (Y) Retired.
Pleho, Anthony J. '79 (NY)[Z] New York, NY Kateri Residence.
Pleier, David J. '75 (GB) Green Bay, WI St. Bernard; Green Bay, WI St. Philip the Apostle.
Pleiman, Kenneth F. *c.pp.s.* '70 (CIN)[T] Dayton, OH Community Support Charitable Trust.
Pleiman, Kenneth *c.pp.s.* '70 (CIN) Dayton, OH Emmanuel; Dayton, OH Holy Trinity; Dayton, OH St. Joseph.
Pleiness, Gregg A. '81 (LAN) Howell, MI St. Augustine.
Plesa, Andrew J. '56 (RCK) Elgin, IL St. Thomas More Retired.
Pleskac, Rev. Msgr. Myron J. '60 (LIN)[G] Lincoln, NE School Sisters of Christ the King, Villa Regina Motherhouse & Novitiate; Lincoln, NE St. Luke's Czech Catholic Shrine; Evangelization Committee Retired.
Pleus, Adrian C.H. '99 (ATL) Dallas, GA St. Vincent de Paul.
Pleva, Gerald *s.m.* '77 (SAT)[L] San Antonio, TX Marianist Residence.
Pleva, Gerald *s.m.* '77 (HON) Wailuku, HI St. Anthony of Padua.
Plewka, Rev. Msgr. Mark A. '76 (PBL) Chancellor; Judicial Vicar; Judge; Tribunal; College of Consultors; Ex Officio.
Pliego, Jairo Sandoval (AUS) Georgetown, TX St. Helen.
Plishka, Andrew '06 (STN) St. Louis, MO Assumption B.V.M.
Plishka, Andrew '96 (STN) Palatine, IL Immaculate Conception.
Plishka, Richard '08 (PRM) Office of Evangelization and Missionary Activity; Cleveland, OH St. Nicholas; Notaries; Priest Secretary to the Bishop; Young Adults; Byzantine Catholic Cultural Center.
Plo, Rev. Msgr. John '61 (NY) Retired.
Ploch, Jacek '08 (PRO) Westerly, RI Immaculate Conception.
Ploch, Robert '92 (SAT) Devine, TX St. Joseph's.
Ploch, Timothy *s.d.b.* '76 (MRY) St. Francis Central Coast Catholic High School, Inc.; San Francisco, CA.
Ploch, Timothy *s.d.b.* '76 (SFR)[N] San Francisco, CA Salesian Provincial Residence.
Plocharczyk, Rev. Msgr. Daniel J. '74 (HRT) Hartford Vicariate; New Britain, CT Sacred Heart of Jesus.
Plocke, Donald J. *s.j.* '64 (BO)[U] Weston, MA Campion Health Center, Inc.
Plominski, Walter J. '68 (ROC) Rochester, NY Unity Health System; Rochester, NY St. Theodore.
Ploof, Gerald '75 (LAN) Retired.
Ploplis, Theodore '77 (CHI)[J] Chicago, IL Saint Joseph Hospital.
Plotkowski, Jerome '65 (SFE) Albuquerque, NM Risen Savior Catholic Community.
Plotkowski, John S. '74 (CHI) Des Plaines, IL St. Zachary.
Ploude, Thomas E. '64 (CAM) Retired.
Plough, James H. '58 (PBL) Retired.
Plourde, James S. '82 (PRT) Calais, ME Blessed Kateri Tekakwitha Parish.
Plow, Gregory *t.o.r.* '08 (STU)[A] Steubenville, OH Franciscan University of Steubenville; [H] Steubenville, OH Holy Spirit Friary.
Pluciennik, Marcin P. '09 (HRT) Manchester, CT St. Bartholomew; Manchester, CT St. Bridget; [D] Manchester, CT East Catholic High School.
Plunkett, Craig '06 (FRS) Clovis, CA Our Lady of Perpetual Help.
Plunkett, Rev. Msgr. Joseph P. '60 (NEW) Harrison, NJ Our Lady of Czestochowa Retired.
Pluth, Paul R. '96 (SEA) Judges; Adjunct Judicial Vicar; Special Assignment.
Plutz, Stanley *s.v.d.* '53 (BLX)[D] Bay St. Louis, MS St. Augustine's Residence.
Po, Fernando R. '84 (NEW) Retired.
Poandl, Robert '68 (SAV) Claxton, GA St. Christopher.
Pobalao, Florecito *o.f.m.* (GLP) St. Michaels, AZ St. Michael.
Poblocki, Richard M. I. '83 (BUF) Apostleship of Prayer; Cheektowaga, NY St. Josaphat.
Pocernich, Eugene '74 (MIL) On Duty Outside the Archdiocese.
Pocetto, Alexander T. *o.s.f.s.* '55 (ALN)[B] Center Valley, PA DeSales University; [K] Center Valley, PA Oblates of St. Francis de Sales.
Poche, Daniel M. '78 (HT) Defender of the Bond; College of Consultors.
Poche, Daniel M. '78 (HT) Morgan City, LA Holy Cross.
Poche, Louis *s.j.* '55 (NO)[R] New Orleans, LA Ignatius Residence Retired.
Pochetti, Angelo (NEW) West New York, NJ Holy Redeemer.
Poczworowski, Luke *o.f.m.conv.* '64 (PEO) Wenona, IL St. John the Baptist's; Minonk, IL St. Patrick's; Wenona, IL St. Mary's.
Podeszwik, Wladyslaw (CHI) Chicago, IL St. Constance Retired.
Podhajsky, Christopher R. '01 (DUB) Cedar Rapids, IA Immaculate Conception; Cedar Rapids, IA St. Wenceslaus.
Podhajsky, Michael J. '03 (DUB) Peosta, IA Holy Family; Judges.
Podlesny, James F. *o.s.b.* '80 (HBG) Palmyra, PA Church of the Holy Spirit.
Podlesny, James *o.s.b.* '80 (GBG)[H] Latrobe, PA Saint Vincent Archabbey.
Podraza, Timothy '97 (OM) Butte, NE Sacred Heart Parish of Boyd County.
Podsiadlo, Grzegorz *s.d.s.* '01 (NEW) Bayonne, NJ Mt. Carmel.
Podsiadlo, Jack *s.j.* '72 (BRK)[J] Brooklyn, NY Brooklyn Jesuit Prep.
Podsiedlik, Slawomir S. *o.c.d.* '02 (STA) Bunnell, FL St. Mary; [H] Bunnell, FL Discalced Carmelite Fathers of Florida.
Podvin, Albert J. '62 (SFE) Retired.
Podwysocki, Grzegorz '08 (JOL) Romeoville, IL St. Andrew the Apostle.
Podymniak, Miroslaw *o.f.m.conv.* (PAT) Clifton, NJ St. John Kanty.
Podziadlo, John J. (BRK) Brooklyn, NY St. Ignatius.
Poecking, David G. '96 (PIT) Carnegie, PA St. Elizabeth Ann Seton.
Poecking, Kevin G. '04 (PIT)[Q] Pittsburgh, PA Christ Child Society of Pittsburgh; Slippery Rock, PA St. Peter; [P] Slippery Rock, PA Slippery Rock University, Newman Center (Slippery Rock).
Poehlmann, Edward J. '67 (DEN) Denver, CO Presentation of Our Lady.
Poerio, John '59 (LKC) Advocates Retired.
Poettgen, Edward '80 (ORG) Santa Ana, CA Immaculate Heart of Mary; Consultors; Council of Priests; Land Advisory Board.
Poetzel, Richard K. *c.ss.r.* '63 (BAL) Baltimore, MD Our Lady of Fatima.
Poff, Edward '58 (JOL) Retired.
Poff, Pius *o.f.m.conv.* '61 (IND) Floyds Knobs, IN St. Mary of the Annunciation Catholic Church, Navilleton, Inc.
Pogatchnik, Scott '10 (SCL) Personnel Committee; St. Cloud, MN St. Mary's Cathedral of St. Cloud; St. Cloud, MN St. Augustine; St. Cloud, MN Christ Church.
Poggemeyer, Joseph T. '97 (TOL) Toledo, OH St. Joseph; Toledo, OH SS. Adalbert & Hedwig.
Pogorelc, Anthony J. *s.s.* '88 (SAT) On Duty Outside the Archdiocese.
Pogorelc, Anthony J. *s.s.* '88 (WDC)[A] Washington, DC Theological College of the Catholic University of America; [C] Catholic University of America, The.
Pogorelc, Anthony J. *s.s.* '88 (BAL)[Q] Baltimore Society of St. Sulpice, Province of the United States.
Pogorzelski, Andrzej '77 (HRT) Hartford, CT SS. Cyril and Methodius.
Pogue, Sean V. '11 (LFT) Carmel, IN St. Elizabeth Ann Seton.
Pohl, Rev. Msgr. Daniel J. '53 (LIN)[E] Lincoln, NE Bonacum House Retired.
Pohl, Jerome H. '67 (PH) Retired.
Pohl, Leon H. '56 (KAL) Retired.
Pohl, Stephen A. '85 (L) Louisville, KY St. Margaret Mary.
Pohlman, Stephen J. '84 (SFD) Godfrey, IL St. Michael; Godfrey, IL St. Ambrose.
Pohlmeier, Erik '98 (LR) Little Rock, AR Our Lady of the Holy Souls; Assistant Directors; Presbyteral Council; Clergy Personnel Advisory Board (Diocesan).
Pohlmeier, Loren G. '82 (GI) Ogallala, NE St. Luke's Retired.
Pohorlak, Joseph '61 (PRM) Retired.
Pohto, J. Thomas *o.s.a.* '67 (PH)[Y] Villanova, PA St. Thomas Monastery.
Pointek, Rev. Msgr. Francis J. '40 (FRS) Retired.
Poirier, David *s.a.* '77 (NY)[DD] Garrison Franciscan Friars of the Atonement, Minister General Office.
Poirier, Ralph J. *c.s.sp.* '63 (PIT)[O] Bethel Park, PA The Spiritan Center.
Poirier, Robert L. *s.j.* '77 (STL)[O] St. Louis, MO Leo Brown Jesuit Community; [C] Saint Louis University.
Poirier, Vincent J. '85 (BO) Senior Priests. Retired.
Poirot, Jeff '01 (FWT) Fort Worth, TX Holy Family; Diocesan Pastoral Finance Committee.
Poissant, Rev. Msgr. Leeward J. '63 (OG) Keeseville, NY St. John the Baptist (The Roman Catholic Community of Keeseville); Deans.
Poisson, Thomas L. '78 (MAR) Retired.
Poitras, Robert A. '05 (BO) Georgetown, MA St. Mary.
Pokorsky, Jerry '90 (ARL) Annandale, VA St. Michael.
Pokrzewinski, Justus M. *o.p.* '60 (CHI)[N] Chicago Dominicans (Provincial Office).
Pokrzewinski, Justus *o.p.* '60 (FgM) Chicago, IL Province of St. Albert the Great (Central).
Pokusa, Rev. Msgr. Joseph W. '70 (CAM) On Duty Outside the Diocese.
Polak, Michael J. '58 (PIT)[M] Pittsburgh, PA St. John Vianney Manor Retired.
Polanco, Dennis *s.a.* '74 (WDC)[B] Washington, DC Atonement Seminary–Franciscan Friars of the Atonement.
Polando, Rev. Msgr. Peter M. '80 (Y) Finance Council; Youngstown, OH SS. Cyril and Methodius; Youngstown, OH St. Matthias; Adjutant Judicial Vicar; Youngstown, OH Holy Name of Jesus; [P] Youngstown, OH Conference of Slovak Clergy.
Polanki, Joseph K. '01 (SCR) Wilkes–Barre, PA St. Robert Bellarmine Parish; Hanover Township, PA Exaltation of the Holy Cross.
Polansky, Lawrence E. '09 (CAM) Continuing Education & Spiritual Formation of Priests (CESF).
Polasek, Jeffrey S. '91 (TLS) Tahlequah, OK St. Brigid; [I] Tahlequah, OK Northeastern State University Catholic Student Organization.
Polczyk, Stanislaus '82 (TR) Leave of Absence; [N] Trenton, NJ St. Lawrence Rehabilitation Center.
Polczynski, Alan N. '07 (GBG) Greensburg, PA Blessed Sacrament Cathedral.
Polednak, John V. '76 (SCR) Kingston, PA St. Ignatius Loyola, Kingston; Regional Episcopal Vicars; Ex Officio; Ex Officio.
Polek, David *c.ss.r.* '62 (STL) St. Louis, MO St. Alphonsus Liguori; [O] St. Louis, MO Redemptorist Fathers.
Polek, Ryszard (WOR) Worcester, MA Our Lady of Czestochowa.
Polenz, Gordon '82 (ALB) Sidney, NY Sacred Heart; Deans.
Polgar, Capistran L. *o.f.m.* '67 (MET) New Brunswick, NJ St. Ladislaus.
Poliafico, David A. '95 (COL) Deanery 7: Marion; Marysville, OH Our Lady of Lourdes; Parochial Examiners; Presbyteral Council.
Polich, David J. '76 (DM) Perry, IA St. Patrick; Defenders of the Bond.
Policicchio, Luke E. *o.s.b.* '88 (GBG)[H] Latrobe, PA Saint Vincent Archabbey.
Polidano, Carmel F. '81 (CAM) Bellmawr, NJ Parish of Saint Rita, Bellmawr, N.J.
Polifka, Charles *o.f.m.cap.* '71 (DEN) Denver, CO; [N] Denver, CO St. Francis of Assisi Friary; [N] Denver, CO Capuchin Province of Mid–America, Inc.
Polifka, Charles *o.f.m.cap.* '71 (FgM) Denver, CO Province of Mid–America.
Polinek, Michael C. '10 (E) Warren, PA St. Joseph.
Polito, Martin F. '76 (CLV) Cleveland, OH Holy Redeemer; Presbyteral Council; Presbyteral Conveners.
Polito, Victor V.J. '54 (MAN) Retired.
Polizzi, Rev. Msgr. Salvatore E. '56 (STL) St. Louis, MO St. Roch; Archdiocesan Office of Urban and Community Affairs; Washington, DC The National Center for Urban Ethnic Affairs (1971).
Poljicak, Vlatko '65 (LA) Retired.
Polk, Page E. *o.f.m.* '86 (GAL)[S] Houston, TX The Catholic Chaplain Corps; Catholic Chaplain Corps (Hospital Chaplains); Chaplains.
Polk, Page *o.f.m.* '86 (CIN)[N] Cincinnati, OH St. Francis Seraph Friary.
Poll, Jeffrey A. '05 (LAN) Durand, MI St. Mary; College of Consultors; Presbyteral Council.
Pollard, Christopher J. '98 (ARL) On Duty Outside the Diocese.
Pollard, John L. '83 (STA) Absent or Sick Leave.
Pollard, Rev. Msgr. John '74 (CHI) Chicago, IL Queen of All Saints Basilica.
Pollard, Marcus A. '90 (ARL) Alexandria, VA Queen of Apostles.
Pollard, Rev. Msgr. Patrick J. '72 (CHI) Chicago, IL Notre Dame de Chicago; Hillside, IL Central Office; College of Consultors; Catholic Cemeteries; Cincinnati, OH The National Association of Church Personnel Administrators (NACPA).
Pollard, Roy F. '66 (WIL) Retired.
Pollard, Thomas W. '66 (WDC) Retired.
Pollie, A. Frank '67 (DET) Retired.
Pollis, Robert G. '57 (BO) Senior Priests. Retired.
Pollock, Jonah *o.p.* (HRT) New Haven, CT St. Mary's.
Pollock, Paul E. *s.j.* '73 (FgM) Los Gatos, CA Society of Jesus.
Polmounter, Richard J. '78 (SCR) Tunkhannock, PA St. Mary of the Lake; Tunkhannock, PA Nativity of Blessed Virgin Mary; Diocesan Finance Council; Diocesan Consultors; Presbyteral Council.
Polo, Antonio *s.d.b.* '56 (SJN) San Juan, PR Maria Auxiliadora.
Poloche, Pedro '98 (ATL) Special or Other Archdiocesan Assignment; Judicial Vicar; Judicial Vicar; College of Consultors; Vicars for Clergy; Auditors.
Polosky, Michael '91 (SJP) Ambridge, PA Ss. Peter and Paul; Consultors; Youth Ministries; Presbyteral Council; Personnel Board; Presbyters.
Poloway, Rev. Msgr. Mitred Michael '54 (SJP) Presbyters Retired.
Polselli, Leo *c.s.c.* '70 (FR)[A] North Easton, MA Holy Cross Fathers Religious.
Polselli, Leo *c.s.c.* '70 (FTW)[H] Notre Dame Congregation of Holy Cross, United States Province of Priests & Brothers.
Polson, Mikel Anthony '02 (LAF) Iota, LA St. Joseph.

Poltorak, Stanley '82 (SAC) Rocklin, CA SS. Peter and Paul.
Poltorek, George *s.a.c.* '90 (BRK) Ridgewood, NY St. Aloysius.
Poluikis, John A. *c.s.b.* '51 (ROC)[K] Rochester, NY Basilian Residence.
Polyak, Anthony V. *m.m.* '62 (FgM) Maryknoll, NY MARYKNOLL.
Polyak, John V. '69 (MET) North Brunswick, NJ Our Lady of Peace.
Polycarpe, Pierre G. '99 (RCK) Special Assignment; Rockford, IL St. Bernadette.
Pomerleau, Claude *c.s.c.* '65 (P)[B] University of Portland; [L] Portland, OR Holy Cross Fathers & Brothers, C.S.C. – University of Portland.
Pomerleau, Claude *c.s.c.* (FTW)[H] Notre Dame Congregation of Holy Cross, United States Province of Priests & Brothers.
Pomerleau, William A. '79 (SPR) Springfield, MA Our Lady of the Sacred Heart; Diocesan Commission for Ecumenism.
Pomeroy, Thomas '93 (GB) Kaukauna, WI Holy Cross.
Pomilio, Matthew J. '62 (BRK) Retired.
Pommier, Richard *o.m.i.* '66 (FgM) Washington, DC AMERICAN OBLATE MISSIONS.
Pompei, Francis *o.f.m.* '74 (BUF)[S] Buffalo, NY Franciscan Mystery Players, Inc.; [N] Buffalo, NY St. Patrick Friary.
Pompei, Frederick A. '66 (SY) Syracuse, NY Our Lady of Pompei/St. Peter; Special Assignment.
Pomposello, Peter A. '04 (NY) Bronx, NY Holy Cross.
Ponce, Demetrio '88 (ELP) Absent on Leave.
Ponce, James '01 (COS) On Duty Outside Diocese.
Ponce, Jose Antonio *o.m.i.* '09 (LA) San Fernando, CA Santa Rosa.
Ponce, Juan Manuel '00 (SAC) Chico, CA St. John the Baptist.
Poncelet, Frank '87 (SCL) Retired.
Poncini, John '05 (SJ) Diocesan Clergy Personnel Board; Vocation Office; Special Assignment; Ongoing Formation of Clergy.
Poncini, Laurence *o.c.d.* '04 (TUC) Tucson, AZ Saint Margaret Mary Alacoque Roman Catholic Parish – Tucson.
Pondo, Stanley '98 (IND) Vicariate Judicial Metropolitan Tribunal.
Ponessa, Joseph '74 (GF) Circle, MT St. Francis Xavier; Glendive, MT Sacred Heart.
Ponnapati, Lourdu Reddy '97 (OKL) Medford, OK St. Mary's.
Ponnet, Christopher D. '83 (LA) Los Angeles, CA St. Camillus Center for Spiritual Care; Los Angeles, CA Norris Cancer and USC University Hospital; Co Chair; AIDS/HIV Ministry; Hospital Chaplains.
Ponnet, Christopher Dennis '83 (LA) LAC + USC Medical Center.
Pons, Miguel '53 (SJN) Trujillo Alto, PR San Judas Tadeo.
Pons, Ramon '88 (SR) Fortuna, CA St. Joseph.
Pontarelli, Michael M. *o.s.m.* '82 (CHI) Chicago, IL; [N] San Juan Capistrano, CA Servite Vocation Team Coordinator; [N] Chicago, IL Order of Friar Servants of Mary (Servites) United States of America Province, Inc.
Pontarelli, Michael M. *o.s.m.* '82 (ORG) San Juan Capistrano, CA Mission Basilica – San Juan Capistrano.
Pontes, Scott J. '04 (PRO) Bristol, RI St. Elizabeth.
Ponticello, Robert D. '81 (MEM) Union City, TN Immaculate Conception; Defenders of the Bond; Promoter of Justice.
Pontzer, Stephen '07 (SAV) Albany, GA St. Teresa.
Ponzini, Thomas V. '96 (GAL) Texas City, TX St. Mary.
Pookkattu, George *c.m.i.* '72 (ALX) Vidalia, LA Our Lady of Lourdes.
Pool, Jefferson *s.v.d.* '92 (TR)[N] Bordentown, NJ Society of the Divine Word.
Poole, Michael P. '98 (HEL) Bonner, MT St. Ann.
Poole, Richard '94 (MO) On Duty Outside the Diocese; Air Force Chaplains.
Poole, Stafford *c.m.* '56 (LA)[P] Los Angeles, CA Amat Residence II Retired.
Poole, Steven F. '96 (BEL) Okawville, IL St. Barbara.
Poole, William G. '63 (LEX) Retired.
Pooler, Alfred *c.p.* '60 (LA)[V] Sierra Madre, CA Mater Dolorosa Passionist Retreat Center, Inc.
Pooler, Alfred *c.p.* '60 (L)[L] Louisville, KY Sacred Heart Retreat.
Poon, Stanislaus '62 (OAK) Retired.
Poonely, George *o.s.b.* (LUB) Shallowater, TX St. Philip Benizi.
Poore, Charles '89 (Y) Jefferson, OH St. Joseph Calasanctius; Kingsville, OH St. Andrew Bobola.
Poorman, Mark *c.s.c.* '82 (P)[B] University of Portland; [B] University of Portland; [L] Portland, OR Holy Cross Fathers & Brothers, C.S.C. – University of Portland.
Poorten, William P. *s.j.* '63 (PAT)[J] Morristown, NJ Loyola House of Retreats.
Poorten, William P. *s.j.* '63 (BUF) Buffalo, NY St. Michael.
Poovakulam, Antony P. '63 (TR) Retired.
Poovathinal, Emmanuel *c.m.i.* '03 (NY) Dobbs Ferry, NY Sacred Heart.
Pop, Carlos Antonio *o.s.b.* '99 (SFS)[F] Marvin, SD Blue Cloud Abbey.
Popadick, Rev. Msgr. Peter J. '70 (BUF) Cheektowaga, NY St. Aloysius Gonzaga.
Pope, Rev. Msgr. Charles E. '89 (WDC) Washington, DC Holy Comforter—St. Cyprian; [X] Silver Spring, MD Archdiocese of Washington Division, The Blue Army; Deans.
Pope, George F. *c.s.c.* '58 (FgM) New Rochelle, NY Eastern Brothers Province.
Pope, Nicholas F. *s.j.* '72 (MIL)[P] Milwaukee, WI Jesuit Community at Marquette University.
Popelka, Joseph '92 (SAL) Manhattan, KS Seven Dolors of the Blessed Virgin Mary Parish; Manhattan, KS St. Patrick Parish.
Popivchak, Rev. Msgr. Ronald P. '67 (PHU) Bridgeport, PA SS. Peter and Paul; Protopresbyters (Deans); Censor.
Popochock, James L. '68 (GBG) Farmington, PA St. Joan of Arc.
Popov, Pavlo '09 (STN) The Colony, TX St. Sophia Ukrainian Catholic Church.
Popovich, Peter '85 (NY) Hartsdale, NY Church of Our Lady of Shkodra.
Popovich, Stephen E. '81 (Y) New Middletown, OH St. Paul the Apostle.
Popovici, Olvian '98 (STF) Lindenhurst, NY Holy Family; Apostleship of Prayer.
Popp, Kenneth '83 (SCL) Breckenridge, MN St. Mary of the Presentation; Kent, MN St. Thomas; [G] Breckenridge, MN St. Francis Medical Center; [H] Breckenridge, MN St. Francis Home.
Popravak, Christopher *o.f.m.cap.* '74 (DEN) Denver, CO; [N] Denver, CO San Damiano Friary.
Popson, Michael G. '87 (PSC) Harrisburg, PA St. Ann.
Popyk, Volodymyr '97 (PHU) Presbyteral Council; Trenton, NJ St. Josaphat's; Department of Religious Education.
Porada, Casey '89 (LIN) Lincoln, NE Blessed Sacrament; Health Care Facilities.
Pork, Jacobus Seokroul '03 (STA) Jacksonville, FL St. Francis Choe Chapel.
Porpiglia, Joseph D. '86 (MO) Navy Reserve Chaplains; Eggertsville, NY St. Benedict.
Porpora, Robert D. '90 (NY) Middletown, NY Holy Cross; Otisville, NY Federal Correctional Institution.
Porras, Adrian '01 (CHL) Arden, NC St. Barnabas.
Port, Dennis R. '74 (STL) St. Louis, MO St. Matthias.
Portalatin, Antonio '91 (ARE) Hatillo, PR Perpetual Help.
Portalatin Rodriguez, Antonio (PCE)[B] The Pontifical Catholic University of Puerto Rico.
Portasik, Richard *o.f.m.* '52 (PIT)[M] Pittsburgh, PA Holy Family Friary Retired.
Portelli, Joseph Marcel '11 (SAG) Bannister, MI St. Cyril; Chesaning, MI Our Lady of Perpetual Help; Oakley, MI St. Michael.
Porter, Charles Daniel *c.s.b.* '75 (GAL)[O] Sugar Land Basilian Mission Center.
Porter, Jack W. '75 (IND) On Special or Other Archdiocesan Assignment; Archdiocesan Historian Retired.
Porter, John E. '56 (CIN) Retired.
Porter, Rev. Msgr. John F. '57 (GR) Retired.
Porter, Rev. Msgr. John F. '57 (GLD) Frankfort, MI St. Ann Retired.
Porter, Lawrence B. '74 (NEW)[A] South Orange, NJ Immaculate Conception Seminary School of Theology; [A] South Orange, NJ Immaculate Conception Seminary School of Theology; [B] Seton Hall University; Censores Librorum.
Porter, Robert G. '81 (HEL) Deer Lodge, MT Immaculate Conception; Montana State Prison.
Porter, Robert N. '64 (SFD) Retired.
Porter, Rocco S. '97 (DEN) Fort Collins, CO Blessed John XXIII.
Porter, Rocco '00 (DEN)[S] Fort Collins, CO West African Development Support Organization.
Porter, Stephen C. '81 (SB) Rialto, CA St. Catherine of Siena.
Porter, William J. '75 (WIL) Pocomoke City, MD Holy Name of Jesus.
Porter, William '80 (KCK) Overland Park, KS St. Michael the Archangel; Archdiocesan Consultors; Priests' Council.
Porterfield, David J. *c.s.c.* '79 (FTW)[H] Holy Cross House Retired.
Porterfield, Mark A. '94 (JC) St. Thomas, MO St. Cecilia; St. Thomas, MO St. Thomas the Apostle; Promoter of Justice; Judges.
Portes, Oscar Jimenez *o.s.a.* (SJN) San Juan, PR Ntra. Sra. de la Monserrate.
Portland, Paul *s.d.s.* '76 (MIL)[P] Milwaukee Salvatorian Provincial Offices.
Portman, Rev. Msgr. John R. '56 (SD) Retired.
Portzer, Joseph *f.s.s.p.* '99 (OKL) Edmond, OK St. Damien of Molokai Chapel.
Posadas, J. Antonio *o.f.m.* '95 (SAT) San Antonio, TX San Jose y San Miguel.
Posch, Christopher J. *o.f.m.* '95 (WIL) Wilmington, DE St. Paul's; Wilmington Office.
Poschen, Rev. Msgr. Ed '53 (FRS) Retired.
Poser, Gregory *o.s.c.* '75 (SCL)[I] Onamia, MN Crosier Priory; Hillman, MN St. Rita's; Onamia, MN The Church of the Holy Cross of Onamia; Onamia, MN St. Therese; Wahkon, MN Sacred Heart.
Posey, Patrick L. '91 (ARL) Falls Church, VA St. James; Pontifical Mission Societies and Propagation of the Faith.
Posey, Thaddeus J. *o.f.m.cap.* '71 (SAL)[D] Victoria, KS St. Fidelis Friary Retired.
Posiewala, John *s.a.c.* '76 (BUF)[N] North Tonawanda, NY Society of the Catholic Apostolate; North Tonawanda, NY.
Posluszny, Francis '62 (BGP) On Duty Outside the Diocese.
Post, Joseph S. '07 (STL) St. Charles, MO St. Joseph.
Post, Robert J. '82 (BGP) Darien, CT St. Thomas More.
Postell, Philip S. *s.j.* '70 (PHX)[B] Phoenix, AZ Brophy College Preparatory; [F] Phoenix, AZ Society of Jesus.
Poster, James M. '03 (MAD) Baraboo, WI St. Joseph; Elected.
Poston, J. Collin '03 (BAL) Hagerstown, MD St. Mary.
Poszwa, Stanislaw *s.ch.* '83 (DAL) Dallas, TX St. Peter.
Potaczek, John A. '99 (LC) Bloomer, WI St. Paul; Bloomer, WI St. John the Baptist; Consultors; Ex Officio.
Poth, Thomas D. *s.m.m.* '83 (BRK)[R] Ozone Park Montfort Missionaries Provincialate (Missionaries of the Company of Mary).
Pothier, Glen J. '95 (PMB) Adjutant Judicial Vicar; Judges; Elected Members.
Pothireddy, Marreddy '94 (WIN) Lewiston, MN St. Anthony's; Lewiston, MN St. Rose of Lima; Lewiston, MN Immaculate Conception; Appointed Members.
Pothireddy, Swaminatha R. '93 (WIN) New Richland, MN St. Aidan; New Richland, MN St. Mary; New Richland, MN All Saints.
Pottamplackal, Ephrem *m.c.b.s.* '74 (NY) Bronx, NY Montefiore Medical Center.
Pottemmel, Joseph *m.s.f.s.* '76 (TYL)[C] Whitehouse, TX The Missionaries of St. Francis de Sales.
Pottenparambil, Joseph '90 (MIL)[P] Kenosha, WI Missionary Congregation of the Blessed Sacrament, Inc., Zion Province.
Potter, Gerald '54 (FAR) Retired.
Potter, Harold G. '09 (KAL) Battle Creek, MI St. Philip.
Potter, Rev. Msgr. Joseph D. '54 (BGP) On Duty Outside the Diocese Retired.
Potthast, Richard L. *c.s.c.* '67 (FTW) New Rochelle, NY Eastern Brothers Province; [H] Notre Dame Congregation of Holy Cross, United States Province of Priests & Brothers.
Potthoff, Donald William '49 (LA) Diamond Bar, CA St. Denis Retired.
Potthoff, Rev. Msgr. Fred E. '44 (LFT) Associate Judges Retired.
Pottokaran, Jose *c.m.i.* '67 (GRY)[D] Michigan City, IN Franciscan St. Anthony Health – Michigan City.
Pottorff, Lisle J. '49 (DOD) Retired.
Potts, Donald G. '60 (KAL) Cassopolis, MI St. Ann; Presbyteral Council Members; Presbyteral Council Members.
Potts, Richard M. *c.ss.r.* '91 (STL)[O] St. Louis, MO Redemptorist Fathers.
Potts, Robert J. '64 (ALN) Fountain Hill, PA St. Ursula.
Potts, Ronald A. '89 (WDC) Washington, DC Blessed Sacrament, Shrine of the Most; Priest Council; Archdiocesan Chaplain – Catholic Committee on Girl Scouts.
Potts, Thomas *s.v.d.* '61 (BLX)[D] Bay St. Louis, MS St. Augustine's Residence; [D] Bay St. Louis, MS Province Development Office.
Potts, Thomas *s.v.d.* '61 (JKS)[F] Chatawa, MS St. Mary of the Pines; [G] Chatawa, MS St. Mary of the Pines.
Potvin, Leo F. '64 (ALB) Retired.
Potvin, Raymond J. '80 (MAN) Penacook, NH Immaculate Conception; Public Policy Commission.
Poulang Mot, Rigobert '01 (BWN) Rio Hondo, TX St. Helen.
Poulin, Arthur *o.s.b.cam.* '81 (MRY)[F] Big Sur New Camaldoli Hermitage.
Poulin, Arthur *o.s.b.cam.* '81 (OAK)[L] Berkeley, CA Incarnation Monastery, Camaldolese Benedictines.
Poulin, Calvin H. *s.j.* '62 (FgM) New York, NY Society of Jesus.
Pouliot, Eugene A. '70 (STP) Retired.
Pouliot, Francis A. '58 (STP) St. Paul, MN Maternity of the Blessed Virgin Retired.
Pouliot, Francois *o.p.* '93 (GAL) Houston, TX Holy Rosary.
Poulose, Skariya Azhikannikkal (SYM)[B] Glenview, IL Missionary Society of St. Thomas the Apostle, M.S.T.
Poulose, Skariya *m.s.t.* '86 (CHI)[J] Chicago, IL Saints Mary and Elizabeth Medical Center.
Poulsen, James N. '68 (SD) La Mesa, CA Saint Martin of Tours Catholic Parish; Vicars Forane; Clergy Personnel Board.

Poulsen, Thomas R. *o.p.* '67 (IND)[O] Bloomington, IN Indiana University, Bloomington.
Poulson, David L. '79 (E) World Apostolate of Fatima (Blue Army); Cambridge Springs, PA St. Anthony.
Poumade, James M. '01 (ARL) McLean, VA St. John the Beloved.
Poupore, J. Gareth *c.s.b.* '53 (ROC)[K] Rochester Basilian Residence.
Poupore, Norman E. '50 (OG) Retired.
Poussard, Bertrand R. '67 (PRT) Retired.
Pousson, Donald '66 (LAF) Breaux Bridge, LA St. Bernard.
Poveromo, Robert J. '72 (NY) New York, NY St. Vincent de Paul; [E] New York, NY Cathedral High School; Staten Island, NY Our Lady Star of the Sea.
Powell, Daniel F.X. '92 (HBG) Harrisburg, PA St. Margaret Mary Alacoque.
Powell, Edward F. '54 (SUP) Retired.
Powell, Rev. Msgr. Eric S. '90 (PEO) Normal, IL Epiphany.
Powell, Leon A. '71 (LC) Special Assignment; [H] La Crosse, WI Holy Cross (Seminary) Diocesan Center; Vice–Chancellor; Ecclesiastical Notaries.
Powell, Marc L. '03 (SEA) Vashon, WA St. John Vianney.
Powell, Matthew D. *o.p.* '75 (PRO)[O] Providence St. Thomas Aquinas Priory at Providence College.
Powell, Michael '89 (JOL) Watseka, IL St. Edmund; Deans.
Powell, Michael *o.m.i.* (BO) Tewksbury, MA St. William.
Powell, Paul '48 (OWN) Retired.
Powell, Philip Neri *o.p.* (NO)[R] New Orleans Dominican Friars, Southern Dominican Province of St. Martin de Porres.
Powell, Philip *o.p.* '05 (FgM) Metairie, LA St. Martin de Porres Province (Southern Dominican Province).
Powell, Robert J. '76 (FR) Orleans, MA St. Joan of Arc.
Powell, Rev. Msgr. Robert J. '74 (PH) Jamison, PA St. Cyril of Jerusalem; Defenders of the Bond.
Power, David N. *o.m.i., s.t.d.* '56 (WDC)[O] Washington, DC Oblate Community.
Power, Eugene J. *s.j.* '51 (PH)[Y] Loyola Center and Manresa Hall.
Power, Frank *s.v.d.* '73 (FgM) Techny, IL.
Power, Gerard *o.carm.* '99 (JOL)[L] Darien Carmelite Provincial Office.
Power, J. Timothy '66 (STP) Retired.
Power, Patrick *c.ss.r.* '66 (KC) Kansas City, MO Our Lady of Perpetual Help; [J] Kansas City, MO Redemptorists Fathers of Kansas City, Missouri.
Powers, Aloysius '48 (OWN) Retired.
Powers, Rev. Msgr. Bernard '52 (OWN) Daughters of Isabella Retired.
Powers, Bruce J. '73 (RVC) Manorville, NY Sts. Peter & Paul; Chaplains of the Suffolk County Police Department.
Powers, Daniel *s.j.* '68 (HEL) Heart Butte, MT St. Anne (Blackfeet Reservation).
Powers, Glenn E. '87 (MIL) Sheboygan, WI SS. Cyril and Methodius; Sheboygan, WI Immaculate Conception.
Powers, Isaias *c.p.* '61 (BRK)[R] Jamaica, NY Immaculate Conception Monastery Retired.
Powers, James P. '90 (SUP) Rice Lake, WI St. Joseph; Vicar General; Adjutant Judicial Vicar; Ex Officio Members; Presbyteral Council & Diocesan Consultors; Board of Directors.
Powers, John J. '51 (CHI) South Holland, IL St. Jude the Apostle Retired.
Powers, John *c.p.* '77 (BRK)[R] Jamaica, NY Immaculate Conception Monastery.
Powers, Joseph '79 (KC) St. Joseph, MO Co–Catherdral of St. Joseph; Special Assignment; Vicar for Clergy.
Powers, Richard E. '56 (Y)[I] Canton, OH House of Loreto Retired.
Powers, Rev. Msgr. Richard T. '63 (PH) Philadelphia, PA Epiphany of Our Lord Retired.
Powers, Richard '59 (OWN) Retired.
Powers, Robert M. '92 (BRK) Brooklyn, NY Saint Paul and Saint Agnes Roman Catholic Church.
Powers, Thomas F. '66 (BO) Wellesley, MA St. John the Evangelist.
Powers, Thomas J. (BO) Lynnfield, MA St. Maria Goretti.
Powers, Thomas M. '62 (ALB) Retired.
Powers, Thomas M. '49 (CHI) River Grove, IL St. Cyprian Retired.
Powers, Thomas '97 (BGP) On Duty Outside the Diocese.
Powers, Troy David '87 (SAC) Sacramento, CA Our Lady of Lourdes.
Powers, William V. '58 (PBL) Retired.
Powhida, Robert '78 (ALB) Schenectady, NY St. Madeleine Sophie; Schenectady, NY St. Gabriel the Archangel.
Powis, Rev. Msgr. John J. '59 (BRK) Retired.
Pozen, Matthew '01 (JOL) Leave of Absence.
Pozza, Aldo *m.c.c.j.* '66 (LA) Los Angeles, CA St. Cecilia.
Prabell, Paul '72 (LEX) Defenders of the Bond; Promoter of Justice; [L] Morehead, KY Catholic Student Center–Morehead State University; Morehead, KY Church of Jesus Our Savior.
Prachar, Andrew M. '90 (NEW) Berkeley Heights, NJ Church of the Little Flower.
Pracz, Thaddeus '66 (PEO) Danville, IL Holy Family; Diocesan College of Consultors; Vicariates and Vicars.
Prada, John J. '09 (NEW) Secaucus, NJ Immaculate Conception.
Prada, Mario '07 (CR) Hispanic Ministry.
Prado, A. Benito '04 (NEW) Hoboken, NJ Ss. Peter and Paul Church.
Prado, Amilcar B. (NEW)[O] Hoboken, NJ Catholic Campus Ministry at Stevens Institute of Technology.
Prado, Giopre '09 (OAK) Hayward, CA St. Clement.
Prado, Rodolfo '04 (LA) North Hills, CA Our Lady of Peace.
Prado, Teodoro Tim Y. '77 (GAL)[S] Houston, TX The Catholic Chaplain Corps.
Prado, Victor M. '01 (MRY) Pajaro, CA Our Lady of the Assumption.
Pragasam, John Peter '05 (STO) Riverbank, CA St. Frances of Rome Church (Pastor of).
Prager, John P. *c.m.* '82 (FgM) Philadelphia, PA Eastern Province.
Prakash, Gnana '80 (NY) Bronx, NY Our Lady of the Assumption.
Prakash, Madineni '92 (OKL) Elgin, OK St. Ann.
Prakuzhy, Zacharias *c.m.i.* '68 (SHP).
Prall, Arthur J. *m.m.* '52 (NY)[DD] Retired.
Pranaitis, Mark S. *c.m.* '93 (STL)[O] Earth City, MO Congregation of the Mission Western Province (Vincentians).
Pranzo, Joseph F. *c.s.* '71 (MIA) Margate, FL St. Vincent; Brazilian and Portuguese Apostolate.
Prasad, Ananda *m.s.f.s.* '96 (TYL)[C] Whitehouse, TX The Missionaries of St. Francis de Sales.
Praski, Jacek *c.r.* '91 (CHI) Chicago, IL St. Wenceslaus.
Prasser, Jeffery A. '89 (MIL) West Allis, WI Immaculate Heart of Mary; West Allis, WI Mary, Queen of Heaven; West Allis, WI St. Aloysius Gonzaga.
Prat, Camille J. *s.j.* '62 (SJ)[M] Los Gatos, CA Sacred Heart Jesuit Center.
Pratico, Rev. Msgr. Patrick J. '79 (SCR) Dickson City, PA Visitation of the Blessed Virgin Mary; Judges; Judges.
Pratscher, Matthew '08 (JOL) Bolingbrook, IL St. Dominic.
Pratt, Dean '97 (DAL) On Leave of Absence Retired.
Pratt, Edward '08 (CIN) Monroe, OH Our Lady of Sorrows.
Pratt, James F.X. *s.j.* '86 (BO)[U] Boston The Society of Jesus of New England–Provincial Offices.
Pratt, Lawrence E. '62 (BO) Presbyteral Council; Senior Priests. Retired.
Pratt, Michael '11 (TLS) On Duty Outside the Diocese.
Pratt, Oscar J. '96 (BO) West Roxbury, MA Holy Name.
Pravetz, Matthew A. *o.f.m.* '79 (NY) New York, NY Holy Name of Jesus.
Prechtl, Ronald G. '80 (WH) Harrisville, WV Christ Our Hope; St. Marys, WV St. John.
Preciado, Fernando '10 (FWT) Bedford, TX St. Michael; Wichita Falls, TX Sacred Heart.
Preciado, Guillermo '02 (FRS) Firebaugh, CA St. Joseph.
Preciado, Rudolph J. '69 (ORG) Anaheim, CA St. Anthony Claret.
Precourt, Peter *a.a.* '76 (WOR) Fiskdale, MA St. Anne's and St. Patrick's.
Predelus, Dessier (NY) Spring Valley, NY St. Joseph.
Pregana, Craig A. '89 (FR) Special Assignment.
Prehn, James S. *s.j.* '99 (DET) Chicago, IL; [K] Chicago, IL Detroit Province of the Society of Jesus–Provincial Office; Detroit, MI.
Prehn, James S. *s.j.* '99 (CHI)[N] Chicago, IL Chicago Province of the Society of Jesus–Provincial Office; [D] Wilmette, IL Loyola Academy; Milwaukee, WI; [N] Evanston, IL Canisius House.
Prehn, James S. *s.j.* '99 (MIL)[P] Milwaukee, WI Jesuit Provincial Office, Wisconsin Province.
Preisinger, Robert F. '63 (OM)[H] Omaha, NE New Cassel Retirement Center Retired.
Prendergast, Edmond '73 (MIA) Davie, FL St. Bonaventure.
Prendergast, Fergus J. '94 (MOB) On Leave from the Archdiocese.
Prendergast, Rev. Msgr. John J. '76 (PEO) Washington, IL St. Patrick's; Diocesan College of Consultors.
Prendergast, Joseph *c.s.sp.* '54 (SJ) Santa Clara, CA St. Justin Retired.
Prendergast, Noel '58 (JKS) Retired.
Prendergast, Richard J. '79 (CHI) Chicago, IL St. Josaphat.
Prendergast, Robert E. '50 (PEO) Retired.
Prendergast, Rev. Msgr. Thomas '56 (SD) Retired.
Prendiville, Edmond P. '63 (PRO) On Duty Outside the Diocese.
Prendiville, Eugene V. '58 (BEL)[F] Belleville, IL Missionary Oblates of Mary Immaculate – St. Henry's Oblate Residence.
Prendiville, Kerry '84 (RC) Lead, SD St. Ambrose; Lead, SD St. Patrick's; [E] McLaughlin, SD Priest Retirement and Aid Association/Pension Plan Board.
Prendiville, Thomas *s.d.b.* '56 (SFR)[N] San Francisco, CA Salesian Provincial Residence.
Preneta, Henry S. '67 (GBG)[G] Greensburg, PA Neumann House Retired.
Prengaman, Leo P. *s.j.* '93 (LA) Los Angeles, CA Blessed Sacrament.
Prensa, Pedro Velez '04 (PHX) Tolleson, AZ Blessed Sacrament Roman Catholic Parish.
Prentice, Theodore R. '04 (P) Molalla, OR St. James.
Presenti, Richard *s.d.b.* '68 (SFR)[N] San Francisco, CA Salesian Provincial Residence.
Preske, Venantius '52 (LR) Retired.
Preskenis, James T. *c.s.c.* '75 (FR)[F] North Dartmouth, MA Holy Cross Residence; [F] North Dartmouth, MA St. Joseph's Hall.
Preskenis, James T. *c.s.c.* '75 (FTW)[H] Notre Dame Congregation of Holy Cross, United States Province of Priests & Brothers.
Presley, Joseph *i.c.* '01 (PEO) Galesburg, IL Corpus Christi; Abingdon, IL Sacred Heart; Galesburg, IL St. Patrick's.
Presmanes, Jorge L. *o.p.* '91 (MIA)[H] Miami, FL Dominican Fathers of Miami, Inc.; [C] Miami, FL Barry University.
Presta, James '86 (CHI)[A] Mundelein, IL University of St. Mary of the Lake/Mundelein Seminary; [A] Mundelein, IL University of St. Mary of the Lake/ Mundelein Seminary.
Preston, Laurence *m.s.a.* '94 (NOR)[G] Cromwell Society of the Missionaries of the Holy Apostles.
Presutti, Robert *l.c.* (ATL)[F] Alpharetta, GA Legionaries of Christ, Incorporated.
Pretto, Franklin D. '72 (SFE) Santa Fe, NM San Isidro.
Preugaman, Leo P. *s.j.* '93 (LA)[P] Los Angeles, CA Colombiere House.
Preuss, David *o.f.m.cap.* '79 (MIL)[P] Milwaukee, WI St. Conrad Friary; Milwaukee, WI St. Martin de Porres.
Preuss, Richard *c.m.* '73 (FgM) Earth City, MO Western Province.
Previtali, Joseph F. '09 (SFR) San Francisco, CA St. Gabriel.
Previte, Joseph '07 (CLV) Cleveland, OH Holy Rosary; Retirement Board.
Prevost, Robert F. *o.s.a.* '82 (CHI)[N] Chicago, IL The Augustinians–Provincialate.
Prevosto, Paul '96 (NEW) Hackensack, NJ Holy Trinity.
Prez, Daniel J. '74 (E) Cambridge Springs Correction Institution; Pleasant Ridge Manor West; Erie, PA St. Patrick.
Pribek, James M. *s.j.* '99 (BUF)[N] Buffalo, NY Canisius Jesuit Community Inc.
Pribonic, Phillip '67 (PIT) South Park, PA St. Joan of Arc.
Pribula, Duane '70 (CR) Nevis, MN Our Lady of the Pines; Nevis, MN St. Theodore of Tarsus – Laporte; Priests' Council.
Pribyl, Ross *s.j.* '99 (CHI)[D] Chicago, IL St. Ignatius College Prep; [D] Chicago, IL St. Ignatius Jesuit Community.
Pricco, Rev. Msgr. Richard A. '62 (PEO) Macomb, IL St. Paul's; Vicariates and Vicars.
Price, Bede *o.s.b.* '96 (STL)[O] St. Louis, MO The Abbey of St. Mary and St. Louis; [F] Creve Coeur, MO St. Louis Priory School; Creve Coeur, MO Saint Gregory the Great and Saint Augustine of Canterbury Oratory.
Price, David Ramsey '10 (COS) Colorado Springs, CO Saint Paul.
Price, James *c.p.* '94 (SCR)[Q] Scranton, PA St. Ann's Foundation; [L] Scranton, PA Saint Ann's Passionist Monastery.
Price, John R. '66 (CHI) Retired.
Price, Rothell '88 (SHP) Vicar General and Moderator of the Curia; Adjutant Judicial Vicar; Judges; Corporate Council; Finance Council; Black Catholic Commission; Campaign for Human Development; Catholic Relief Services; Church Vocations Board & Vocations Office; Mission Director; Propagation of the Faith; Ex Officio Members; College of Consultors.
Priebe, Rev. Msgr. Norman F. '67 (LA) Los Angeles, CA St. Jerome; Deanery 13.
Priest, Rev. Msgr. Gerald A. '68 (TYL) College of Consultors; Priests' Pension Board Retired.
Priestly, Joseph *s.m.* '55 (HON)[D] Honolulu, HI Marianist Hall Community.
Prieto, Frank '64 (SFE) Retired.
Prietto, Mario J. *s.j.* '73 (SFR)[N] San Francisco, CA Loyola House Jesuit Community.
Prill, Mark P. '08 (DET) Canton, MI Saint John Neumann.
Primavera, Mauro '09 (NEW) Nutley, NJ Holy Family.
Primich, John '95 (MET) Hunterdon Medical Center; Whitehouse Station, NJ Our Lady of Lourdes.
Primor, Salvino '99 (LAF) Centerville, LA St. Joseph.
Prince, Joseph A. '71 (BGP) Ridgefield, CT St. Elizabeth Seton; Priest Vocation Advisory Board.
Prince, Leo R. '86 (NY) Staten Island, NY St. Roch.
Prince, Michael J. '98 (DET) Absent on Leave.

Prince, Philip Aju *h.g.n.* (FWT) Gainesville, TX St. Mary.
Principe, Francis J. '53 (NY)[E] Bronx, NY Cardinal Spellman High School.
Prinelli, John '78 (RIC) Christiansburg, VA Holy Spirit Catholic Church; Pearisburg, VA Holy Family.
Pringle, John R. '72 (MET) Bridgewater, NJ Holy Trinity.
Printy, Michael G. '57 (OM) Retired.
Prior, Felix *o.carm.* '58 (BO)[Z] Peabody, MA St. Theresa Carmelite Chapel; [U] Peabody, MA Our Lady of the Scapular Priory.
Prior, James G. *c.m.* '53 (ALN) Roseto, PA Our Lady of Mt. Carmel.
Prior, Rev. Msgr. Joseph G. '90 (PH) Morrisville, PA St. John the Evangelist; Censores Librorum.
Prior, Richard '01 (SY) Syracuse, NY Holy Family.
Prior, Robert J. *c.m.* '94 (BAL) Emmitsburg, MD St. Joseph; [Q] Emmitsburg, MD Vincentian House.
Prior, Thomas W. *c.m.* '59 (ALN) Roseto, PA Our Lady of Mt. Carmel.
Priore, John Del *s.j.p.* '08 (MAD)[I] Platteville, WI St. Augustine Newman Center.
Priscaro, Jerry S. '93 (E) Erie, PA Our Mother of Sorrows; Soldiers and Sailors Home.
Prisco, Dennis '95 (LUB) Lubbock, TX St. Theresa's.
Prist, Rev. Msgr. Wayne '67 (CHI) Chicago, IL Queen of All Saints Basilica Retired.
Pritt, Phillip P. '62 (CLV) Rittman, OH St. Anne; Administrative Leave Retired.
Prive, Francis R. '69 (BUR) Morrisville, VT Parish of the Holy Name of Jesus.
Privett, John *s.j.* '72 (SJ)[M] Los Gatos, CA Sacred Heart Jesuit Center.
Privett, Stephen A. *s.j.* '72 (SFR)[C] San Francisco, CA University of San Francisco; [N] San Francisco, CA Loyola House Jesuit Community.
Probst, R. Dean '81 (SFD) Rochester, IL St. Jude; Office for Tribunal Services.
Procaccini, David C. '93 (PRO) Providence, RI Holy Cross.
Procella, Rev. Msgr. Paul '87 (GAL) Retired.
Prochaska, John '93 (OAK) Fremont, CA Our Lady of Guadalupe; Deanery #15; Priest Representative; Pastoral Leadership Placement Board (PLPB).
Prochnow, Josef *o.f.m.* '63 (OAK)[N] Danville, CA San Damiano Retreat.
Procopio, Clement *o.f.m.* '44 (NY)[DD] New York Franciscan Province of the Immaculate Conception.
Proctor, John '72 (SD) Presbyteral Council.
Procyk, Marijan '80 (STF) Buffalo, NY St. Nicholas; Buffalo; League of Ukrainian Catholics.
Prodanets, Mykhaylo '01 (PSC) Kingston, PA St. Mary's.
Prodehl, Richard B. '66 (JOL) Retired.
Proehl, Douglas '74 (CLV) Absent on Leave.
Profeta, Salvatore '50 (PMB) Retired.
Proffitt, James (BAL) Severna Park, MD St. John the Evangelist; Senior Priests' Retirement Board.
Profota, James H. '75 (DET) Retired.
Prokes, Francis A. *s.j.* '57 (OM)[J] Omaha, NE Jesuit Community at Creighton University.
Promesso, William J. '89 (DET) Riverview, MI St. Cyprian.
Pronesti, Salvatore J. '67 (PH) Bridgeport, PA Our Lady of Mt. Carmel.
Proppe, John *o.f.m.cap.* '47 (NY)[DD] Yonkers, NY St. Clare Friary.
Propst, Sergius *o.p.* '73 (OAK)[L] Oakland, CA Order of Preachers (Province of the Most Holy Name of Jesus – Western Dominican Province); [A] Berkeley, CA Dominican School of Philosophy and Theology.
Prosperi, Paolo *f.s.c.b.* '03 (WDC) Lexington, MA; [O] Bethesda, MD Priestly Fraternity of the Missionaries of St. Charles Borromeo, Inc.
Prosperi, Paolo *f.s.c.b.* '03 (BO)[U] Bethesda, MD House of Washington DC.
Prospero, William *s.j.* '98 (SAG) Mount Pleasant, MI St. Mary University Parish.
Prost, Charles E. *c.m.* '78 (STL)[O] Perryville, MO Congregation of the Mission.
Protack, Thomas J. '96 (WIL) Unassigned or Leave of Absence.
Protano, Joseph '63 (PRO) Block Island, RI St. Andrew.
Proterra, Michael *s.j.* '71 (R) Raleigh, NC St. Raphael the Archangel; [F] Raleigh Jesuit Community.
Protopapas, George *o.m.i.* '43 (SAT)[K] San Antonio, TX Oblate Madonna Residence.
Proulx, Arthur '70 (SP) Brandon, FL Church of the Nativity; College of Consultors; Appointed Members.
Prout, Thomas S. *s.j.* '92 (NY)[DD] New York, NY Murray–Weigel Hall.
Provanzano, Thomas *s.d.b.* (NY)[E] New Rochelle, NY Salesian High School.
Provenza, Rev. Msgr. Earl V. '64 (SHP) Shreveport, LA Holy Trinity; Vicars Forane; College of Consultors; Ex Officio Members.
Provenza, John F. '90 (LA) San Pedro, CA Mary, Star of the Sea.
Provinsal, Thomas G. *s.j.* '75 (FBK)[E] Bethel, AK Brother Joe Prince Jesuit Community.
Provinzano, Rocco '66 (NEW) Retired.
Provost, John T. '73 (ALB) Priestly Life and Ministry Council.
Provost, John T. '73 (ALB) Priests Retirement Board/ Priests Retirement Plan Board; Averill Park, NY St. Henry; Nassau, NY St. Mary.
Proxell, Leo J. '77 (HEL) Bozeman, MT Holy Rosary; Presbyteral Council; Diocesan Consultors; Deaneries.
Prucha, Francis Paul *s.j.* '57 (MIL)[P] Wauwatosa, WI Jesuit Community at St. Camillus.
Pruett, Bill H. '79 (OKL) Defenders of the Bond; Oklahoma City, OK St. James The Greater.
Prunty, Brian J. *o.praem.* '65 (GB)[J] De Pere, WI St. Joseph Priory.
Prus, Edward J. '61 (DET) Retired.
Prus, Rev. Msgr. Eugene '64 (MET) Martinsville, NJ Blessed Sacrament.
Prusaitis, John P. '78 (BO) Maynard, MA St. Bridget.
Prusakowski, Gerald A. *o.f.m.* '65 (GB) Suamico, WI St. Pius; Suamico, WI St. Benedict; [J] Wausaukee, WI Villa Alverna; Sobieski, WI St. Maximilian Kolbe.
Pruss, Rodney Lee A. '69 (GI) Retired.
Prusynski, Chester *c.s.c.* (FTW)[H] Notre Dame Congregation of Holy Cross, United States Province of Priests & Brothers.
Pruszynski, Konstanty J. '83 (PH) Philadelphia, PA St. John Cantius.
Pruys, George L. '75 (STN) Wilton, ND SS. Peter and Paul.
Pryor, G. Robert '55 (CR) Retired.
Przepiora, Mieczyslaw "Mitchell" '90 (AMA) Defenders of the Bond; Propagation of the Faith; Panhandle, TX St. Theresa; White Deer, TX Sacred Heart.
Przybilla, Troy D. '05 (STP) Archdiocesan Vocation Office.
Przybocki, Rev. Msgr. Bernard A. '58 (ALT) Retired.
Przybyla, Kenneth E. '77 (COS) Colorado Springs, CO St. Francis of Assisi; College of Consultors.
Przybyla, Philip J. '70 (PIT) Verona, PA St. Joseph.
Przybylski, Donald L. '74 (LC) Mosinee, WI St. Paul.
Przybysz, Joseph J. '75 (TOL) Fort Jennings, OH St. Joseph.
Przybysz, Mark C. '90 (GR) Grand Rapids, MI St. Anthony of Padua; On Special Assignment; Continuing Education for Clergy.
Przygocki, Edward *m.s.a.* '81 (NOR)[G] Cromwell Society of the Missionaries of the Holy Apostles.
Przystasz, Wojciech '98 (LAR) Laredo, TX Blessed Sacrament.
Przywara, Artur '10 (CHR) Orangeburg, SC St. Andrew; Orangeburg, SC Holy Trinity.
Przywara, Gerald A. '67 (RIC) Retired.
Ptacek, John P. '55 (DUB) Retired.
Ptak, Slawomir '03 (BEL) Dahlgren, IL St. John Nepomucene; Mc Leansboro, IL St. Clement; Mc Leansboro, IL St. John the Baptist.
Ptak, Walter J. '87 (DET) Wyandotte, MI St. Stanislaus Kostka; Wyandotte, MI Our Lady of Mt. Carmel.
Ptaszynski, Thomas E. '73 (HRT) Granby, CT St. Therese.
Pu, Matthew '53 (B) Retired.
Pua'auli, Kelemete '01 (SPP) Pago Pago, AS Co–Cathedral of St. Joseph the Worker; Faculty Members; Auditors; Diocesan Consultors.
Pucar, August '63 (BEA) Retired.
Pucci, Alfred '54 (NY) Retired.
Pucciarelli, George W. '74 (BO) On Duty Outside the Archdiocese.
Puccinelli, Alfred *s.m.* '66 (FgM) THE SOCIETY OF MARY.
Puchalski, Andrzej '75 (PAT) Passaic, NJ St. Joseph's.
Puchner, Augustine R. *o.praem.* '97 (ORG)[I] Silverado, CA Norbertine Fathers of Orange Inc.; Costa Mesa, CA St. John the Baptist.
Pucke, Michael U. '73 (CIN) Hamilton, OH St. Julie Billiart.
Pudhota, John Bosco '86 (MAD) Shullsburg, WI St. Peter; Shullsburg, WI Our Lady of Hope; Shullsburg, WI St. Matthew.
Pudichery, Joseph P. '62 (PIT) Chicora, PA Mater Dolorosa; Chicora, PA St. Joseph.
Pudota, Joseph B. (SCR) Hawley, PA Blessed Virgin Mary, Queen of Peace.
Pudota, Joseph Sundar Raju '82 (OKL) Altus, OK Prince of Peace.
Pudota, Shouraiah '79 (SFR) Tomales, CA Church of the Assumption.
Pudota, Thomas (GLP) Aztec, NM St. Joseph; Aztec, NM Holy Trinity.
Puente, Benjamin '07 (STO) Stockton, CA Cathedral of the Annunciation (Pastor of).
Puente, Jose Francisco '00 (SAT) San Antonio, TX St. Joan of Arc.
Puentes, Jesus '86 (CHI) Chicago, IL St. Philomena.
Puerta, Jorge I. '60 (MIA) Parkland, FL Mary Help of Christians Church.
Puetz, Richard W. '45 (LFT) Retired.
Puga, Edgardo Espinoza '92 (LA) Hawthorne, CA St. Joseph.
Puga, Gerardo *c.c.r.* '94 (DEN) Denver, CO Church of the Ascension.
Puga, Manuel '97 (STA) Jacksonville, FL St. Paul's.
Pugat, Gaudencio G. *s.v.d.* '85 (RIC) Virginia Beach, VA Holy Family.
Pugh, James L. '67 (MEM) Memphis, TN St. Paul The Apostle.
Pugliese, Francis A. '68 (NY) Military Chaplains.
Pugliese, Rev. Msgr. Frank A. '68 (MO) Vicar General & Moderator of the Curia; Presbyteral Council.
Puglisi, James F. *s.a.* '73 (NY)[DD] Garrison, NY Franciscan Friars of the Atonement, Minister General Office; [DD] Garrison Franciscan Friars of the Atonement, Minister General Office; General Council.
Puhak, Rev. Msgr. Nicholas I. '57 (PSC) Freeland, PA St. Mary's Retired.
Puhlman, Robert W. '84 (LAV) Overton, NV St. John the Evangelist; Priests' Pension Board; Mesquite, NV La Virgen de Guadalupe; Presbyteral Council for the Diocese of Las Vegas.
Puigbo, Juan (ARL) Manassas, VA All Saints.
Puisis, Leonard '52 (MIA) Retired.
Pujante, P. Jesus Monreal *o.carm.* '69 (ARE) Diocesan Consultors.
Pujdak, Steve *s.c.j.* '69 (SP)[N] Pinellas Park, FL Priests of the Sacred Heart.
Pujos, Nathanael '04 (DEN)[R] Denver, CO The Catholic Community of the Beatitudes; Denver, CO St. Catherine of Siena.
Pulaski, Joseph S. *m.m.* '47 (NY)[DD] Retired.
Puleo, Augustus C. '05 (PH) Norristown, PA St. Patrick.
Puleo, Derek J. '10 (PRO) Coventry, RI SS. John and Paul.
Puleo, Rev. Msgr. Edward C. '88 (MET) College of Consultors; Department of Clergy and Religious Personnel; Office for Priest Personnel; Peapack, NJ St. Elizabeth – St. Brigid.
Pulice, John J. '66 (MIL) Milwaukee, WI St. Roman Retired.
Pulickal, Sony G. '83 (OG) Speculator, NY St. James Major; Speculator, NY St. Ann's; Deans.
Pulickaparambil, Alex '05 (GF) Circle, MT St. Francis Xavier; Special Assignment; Glendive, MT Sacred Heart.
Pulido, Felipe '02 (YAK) Yakima, WA St. Joseph Parish; Diocesan Consultors; Vocations.
Pulido, Luis '96 (NY) New York, NY St. Gregory.
Puling, Tarsisius *s.v.d.* '04 (JKS) Indianola, MS St. Benedict the Moor; Indianola, MS Immaculate Conception.
Puliyanampattayil, Tomy Joseph *m.s.f.s.* '94 (SYM) Madison, TN Blessed Mother Theresa Syro–Malabar Mission Nashville, TN.
Puliynampattayil, Tomy *m.s.f.s.* '94 (TYL)[C] Whitehouse, TX The Missionaries of St. Francis de Sales.
Pullambrayil, George '93 (FWT) Denton, TX St. Mark.
Pullikattil, Joseph '00 (HRT)[H] Waterbury, CT Saint Mary's Hospital.
Pullis, Stephen '11 (DET) Lake Orion, MI St. Joseph.
Pullukattu, Anthony *o.ss.t.* '04 (BAL)[Q] Assigned in India.
Pulparayil, George '67 (NY) Monroe, NY Sacred Heart Church.
Pulskamp, Rev. Msgr. James E. '67 (SR) Vicar General; Chancellor; Director of Clergy Personnel; Notaries; Board of Consultors; Priests' Council; Finance Committee; Diocesan Building Committee; Review Board; Archivist; Clergy Personnel Committee; Custodian of Records; Santa Rosa, CA Cathedral of St. Eugene.
Pulugujju, Mariyanandam '92 (OKL) Oklahoma City, OK Church of the Epiphany of the Lord.
Puma, Rev. Msgr. Vincent E. (PAT) Retired.
Punakkattu, Sojan '00 (SP) Lutz, FL St. Timothy.
Punch, Nicholas W. *o.p.* '66 (SUP)[H] Webster, WI Thomas More Center for Preaching and Prayer, Inc.
Punchayil, Mathew '72 (SYM) Darnestown, MD Syro–Malabar Catholic Mission of Greater Washington; Darnestown, MD Our Lady of the Visitation; Darnestown, MD St. Jude Syro–Malabar Catholic Mission of Northern Virginia.
Punderson, Rev. Msgr. Joseph R. '76 (TR) On Duty Outside the Diocese.
Pung, Karl L. '97 (LAN) Brighton, MI St. Patrick; Priests' Assignment Commission; Priestly Life and Ministry.
Punnackal, Antony *c.m.i.* '92 (KNX) Crossville, TN St. Alphonsus.
Punnakunnel, John '79 (BGP) Retired.
Punnakuzhiyil, Sunny Joseph *m.s.f.s.* (TYL)[C] Whitehouse, TX The Missionaries of St. Francis de Sales.
Punnoose, Siby '98 (SC) Fonda, IA Our Lady of Good Counsel; Fonda, IA St. Columbkille's.
Punnour, Samuel (TOL) Toledo, OH Blessed Sacrament.
Puntal, Peter '82 (ORL) Deans; Winter Haven, FL St. Joseph's; Ex Officio Members.
Puntel, Adam D. '11 (CIN) Cincinnati, OH Immaculate Heart of Mary.
Punti, George '55 (RVC) Elmont, NY St. Boniface Retired.
Puntino, John *s.d.b.* '78 (NY)[FF] Stony Point, NY

Marian Shrine.
Puntrello, Philip *r.c.j.* '63 (FRS) Sanger, CA St. Katherine; Sanger, CA St. Mary; Sanger, CA.
Punzalan, Manolo '92 (NEW) Maplewood, NJ St. Joseph's.
Puodziunas, John *o.f.m.* '87 (MIL)[P] Provincial Offices of the Franciscan Friars, Assumption BVM Province, Inc.
Puopolo, Rocco N. *s.x.* '77 (BO)[U] Holliston, MA Xaverian Missionaries.
Pupius, George '63 (OKL) Oklahoma City, OK Immaculate Conception.
Pupsys, Adam '52 (NOR) Retired.
Puraidam, George *m.s.f.s.* '75 (TYL) Snellville, GA; [C] Whitehouse, TX The Missionaries of St. Francis de Sales.
Purawan, Lucito T. '96 (NY) Staten Island, NY St. John Neumann.
Purcaro, Arthur P. *o.s.a.* '75 (FgM) Villanova, PA Province of St. Thomas of Villanova (Eastern).
Purcell, Henry K. '11 (STL) Manchester, MO St. Joseph.
Purcell, Rev. Msgr. Lawrence M. '65 (SD) Rancho Santa Fe, CA Church of the Nativity Catholic Parish; Vicars Forane.
Purcell, Mark *o.s.b.* '05 (RIC)[K] Richmond, VA Mary Mother of the Church Abbey.
Purcell, Mark (STU) Ironton, OH St. Joseph; Ironton, OH St. Lawrence.
Purcell, Rev. Msgr. Paul J. '54 (SCR) Retired.
Purcell, Robert '74 (ALB) Retired.
Purdy, David *s.d.b.* '70 (MRY) Watsonville, CA Our Lady Help of Christians; [B] Watsonville, CA St. Francis Central Coast Catholic High School; [F] Watsonville, CA Saint Francis Salesian Community.
Purfield, James R. '54 (DEN) Denver, CO All Saints.
Purpura, Peter J. '07 (BRK) Vice Officiale–Associate Judicial Vicar; Middle Village, NY Our Lady of Hope; Vice Chancellors; Attorneys and Counselors at Canon Law.
Purta, Jerome J. *o.s.b.* '61 (GBG)[H] Latrobe, PA Saint Vincent Archabbey.
Purtell, John J. '68 (DUB) Retired.
Purtell, Thomas J. '61 (CHI) Chicago, IL St. John Fisher; Chicago, IL St. Christina Retired.
Purvey, John J. '84 (BAL) Retired.
Puryear, Stan '95 (OWN) On Duty Outside the Diocese.
Pusak, Ronald '61 (MIA) Defenders of the Bond Retired.
Pusateri, Christian *o.s.b.* '55 (RCK)[G] Aurora, IL Marmion Abbey.
Pusateri, Joseph M. *s.m.* '66 (WDC)[O] Washington, DC Marist Center Retired.
Pusateri, Samuel D. *o.s.b.* '79 (PEO)[A] Peru, IL St. Bede Abbey.
Pushpanathan, Zacarias '81 (HRT) Hartford, CT St. Anne–Immaculate Conception.
Pushpanathan, Zacarias (NOR) Osborn Correctional Institution.
Putano, John P. '70 (SY) Binghamton, NY St. Patrick; Binghamton, NY St. Thomas Aquinas; Southern Area Vicar; Presbyteral Council; Board of Diocesan Consultors.
Putenparambil, James '80 (CC) Mathis, TX Sacred Heart.
Putera, Vasyl '96 (PHU) Jersey City, NJ SS. Peter and Paul.
Putharayil, Benny D. '94 (BIS) Tioga, ND St. Thomas; Tioga, ND St. Michael; Tioga, ND St. James.
Puthenkulathil, Joseph '76 (SFS) Tabor, SD St. Wenceslaus.
Puthenpeedika, George '79 (LAN) Flint, MI Holy Rosary.
Puthenpurackal, Binoj Mathew *o.ss.t.* '08 (BAL)[Q] Assigned in India.
Puthenpurakal, Bitaju *o.ss.t.* '01 (BAL)[Q] Assigned in India.
Puthenveettil, Pradeep *o.ss.t.* '05 (BAL)[Q] Assigned in India.
Puthiaparampil, Abraham *m.s.f.s.* '98 (ATL)[F] Snellville, GA The Missionaries of St. Francis De Sales.
Puthiyaparampil, Johnny *m.s.f.s.* '98 (TYL) Snellville, GA; [C] Whitehouse, TX The Missionaries of St. Francis de Sales.
Puthoff, Chad *s.d.s.* '71 (NSH) Cookeville, TN St. Thomas Aquinas.
Puthota, Charles I. '89 (SFR) Deans.
Puthota, Charles '89 (SFR) South San Francisco, CA St. Veronica.
Puthumayil, Chacko '71 (GAL) La Marque, TX Queen of Peace.
Puthuparambil, Jacob P. *o.s.b.* (LUB) Petersburg, TX St. Isidore.
Puthuppally, Joseph '66 (SHP) Monroe, LA St. Matthew; College of Consultors.
Puthusseril, George '79 (MIA) Coral Springs, FL St. Andrew; Judicial Vicar; Consultors; Northwest Broward Deanery.
Puthusseril, Thomas Joseph *o.s.h.* '78 (GAL) Houston, TX St. Luke the Evangelist; [O] Missouri City, TX The Society of the Oblates of Sacred Heart.
Puthusseril, Tom *m.s.* '03 (FR)[H] Attleboro, MA La Salette Retreat Center; [F] Attleboro, MA La Salette Shrine.
Puthussery, JoJo *m.f.* '02 (OAK) Alameda, CA St. Philip Neri–St. Albert the Great.
Puthussery, Jojo *m.f.* '02 (SR) Sonoma, CA St. Leo.
Puthussery, Sibi Rocky *o.ss.t.* '09 (BAL)[Q] Assigned in India.
Putich, Michael J. *o.f.m.* '68 (BUF) Boy Scouts; Veterans Hospital.
Putich, Michael J. *o.f.m.* '68 (MO) DEPARTMENT OF VETERANS AFFAIRS HOSPITALS AND CHAPLAINS.
Putka, John *s.m.* '69 (CIN)[N] Dayton, OH Marianist Community.
Putnam, John T. '92 (CHL) Salisbury, NC Sacred Heart; Judicial Vicar; Diocesan Consultors.
Putnam, Richard *s.d.b.* '89 (BO)[M] Salesian Staff.
Putrimas, Rev. Msgr. Edmond '85 (LIT) Lithuanian R. Catholic Religious Aid, Inc.
Putrimas, Rev. Msgr. Edmond '85 (LIT).
Putten, Angelo Van der *f.s.s.p.* '96 (TLS) Tulsa, OK Parish of Saint Peter.
Putthoff, Jeffrey P. *s.j.* '98 (PH)[Y] Philadelphia, PA Jesuit Community, Arrupe House.
Putthoff, Jeffrey *s.j.* '98 (CAM)[T] Camden, NJ Hopeworks N Camden, Inc.; Hopeworks 'N Camden.
Putz, Kenneth '73 (PH) West Grove, PA Assumption B.V.M.
Putzer, John D. '10 (MAD) Sun Prairie, WI Sacred Hearts of Jesus and Mary.
Puzio, Thomas '70 (DET) Detroit, MI Our Lady Queen of Heaven; Detroit, MI St. Raymond–Our Lady of Good Counsel.
Puznakoski, Gilbert Z. '75 (PIT) Allegheny County, PA West Penn Allegheny Health System–Allegheny General; Allegheny County, PA Kane Regional Center – Scott.
Pyka, Frank *c.m.f.* '46 (LA)[V] Rancho Dominguez, CA Dominguez Seminary Inc. Retired.
Pyo, Edward J. '85 (PBR) Retired.

Q

Quach, Binh T. *c.s.sp.* '91 (FgM) Bethel Park, PA CONGREGATION OF THE HOLY SPIRIT.
Quade, Alvin '54 (SCL) Retired.
Quadrini, Angelo '65 (EVN)[D] Jasper, IN Providence Home, Nursing Home for the Needy.
Quaine, Michael W. '85 (DET) Sterling Heights, MI St. Michael.
Quainoo, Clement '82 (VIC) El Campo, TX St. Andrew.
Qualizza, Franco *s.x.* '71 (FgM)[N] Wayne Xaverian Missionary Fathers; Wayne, NJ XAVERIAN MISSIONARY FATHERS.
Quang, John '70 (SAV) Military Chaplains.
Quang Chau, Peter Do '73 (NSH) Ashland City, TN St. Martha.
Quang Le, Peter '79 (LR) Barling, AR Sacred Heart of Mary.
Quang Van Do, Michael M. *c.m.c.* '93 (SPC) Seneca, MO St. Mary.
Quant, Roberto A. '91 (OKL) Oklahoma City, OK Sacred Heart; Judicial Vicar.
Quante, Paul E. *o.s.a.* '84 (OAK) Castro Valley, CA Our Lady of Grace.
Quanz, Paul E. *c.s.b.* '84 (GRY)[B] Merrillville, IN Andrean High School; [H] Merrillville, IN Basilian Fathers Residence.
Quarato, Robert A. '91 (NY) Bronx, NY Holy Rosary.
Quarshie, Felix '92 (BRK) Brooklyn, NY Holy Name.
Quartier, Rev. Msgr. Neal E. '76 (SY) Syracuse, NY The Cathedral of the Immaculate Conception; Special Assignment; Personal Resource Center.
Que, Dinh Ngoc *c.ss.r.* '56 (LA)[P] Baldwin Park Vietnamese Redemptorist Mission.
Quealy, Philip J. '83 (NY) White Plains, NY Our Lady of Sorrows.
Quebedeaux, Carl J. *c.m.f.* '82 (CHI) Chicago, IL Our Lady of Guadalupe; Deans; Oak Park, IL; [N] Oak Park Claretian Missionaries USA Eastern Province.
Queen, James T. (ORL) Ormond Beach, FL St. Brendan Retired.
Quejadas, Mario S. '00 (JOL) Kankakee, IL St. Martin of Tours.
Quera, Jose Maria '10 (DEN) Loveland, CO St. John the Evangelist.
Querin, Michele *c.m.v.* (ARE) Sabana Hoyos, PR Nuestra Senora de Fatima.
Quetchenbach, Raymond *s.v.d.* '57 (CHI)[N] Techny, IL Divine Word Residence.
Quevedo, Alfredo S. *s.j.* '56 (NY)[DD] New York, NY Murray–Weigel Hall.
Quezada, Francisco J. '88 (COS) Colorado Springs, CO St. Mary Cathedral; Hispanic Ministry; Vicar for Hispanic Ministry; College of Consultors.
Quezada, Joel *m.sp.s.* '05 (P)[A] Mount Angel, OR Felix Rougier House of Studies; [A] St. Benedict, OR Mount Angel Seminary; [L] Mount Angel, OR Missionaries of the Holy Spirit, M.Sp.S.
Quezada, Sixto '83 (NY) New York, NY Ascension; Bronx, NY Christ the King.
Qui, Vincent '68 (NO) Retired.
Quic, Cristobal Coche *o.s.b.* '92 (RCK)[G] Aurora, IL Marmion Abbey.
Quiceno, Jose Francisco (SJN) Bayamon, PR Nuestra Senora del Rosario.
Quickley, George W. *s.j.* '80 (NY)[DD] Cardinal Spellman Hall, Jesuit Community.
Quigley, Brian *m.c.c.j.* '77 (CIN)[N] Cincinnati, OH Comboni Missionaries (Verona Fathers)–Comboni Mission Center; [U] Cincinnati, OH The Comboni Missionaries Auxiliary, Inc.; Cincinnati, OH U.S. Headquarters, Comboni Mission Center; Cincinnati, OH; Cincinnati, OH Comboni Missionaries of the Heart of Jesus, Inc. (Verona Fathers).
Quigley, Brian *m.c.c.j.* '77 (CHI)[W] Chicago, IL The Peace Corner, Incorporated.
Quigley, James Ferrer *o.p.* '65 (PRO)[O] Providence St. Thomas Aquinas Priory at Providence College.
Quigley, John *o.f.m.* '72 (CIN)[U] Cincinnati, OH Franciscans Network; [N] Cincinnati, OH Pleasant Street Friary.
Quigley, Joseph P. '60 (BRK) Brooklyn, NY St. Mark; Coney Island Hospital Retired.
Quigley, William G. *c.i.c.m.* (R)[I] Greenville, NC Newman Catholic Student Center of East Carolina University.
Quijano, Anthony '92 (RNO) Diocesan Board of Consultors; Presbyteral Council.
Quijano, Antonio '92 (RNO) Fallon, NV St. Patrick.
Quijano, Carlos *s.j.* '98 (BRK) Brooklyn, NY St. Ignatius.
Quijano, Jose Juan '73 (PMB)[A] Boynton Beach, FL St. Vincent de Paul Regional Seminary.
Quijano, Jose Juan '73 (MIA) On Duty Outside the Archdiocese.
Quilcate, Jose '99 (RVC) Hicksville, NY St. Ignatius Loyola.
Quill, J. Michael '82 (WDC) Beltsville, MD St. Joseph.
Quill, James E. '53 (COV) Fort Wright, KY St. Agnes; [I] Edgewood, KY St. Elizabeth Edgewood; Censor Librorum Retired.
Quill, John A. '74 (NEW) Paramus, NJ Bergen Regional Medical Center; Lyndhurst, NJ St. Michael's.
Quillen, Andrew M. '91 (BO)[U] Hingham, MA Glastonbury Abbey.
Quilligan, Michael '71 (MIA) West Hollywood, FL Annunciation.
Quimno, Matias M. '10 (E)[L] Du Bois, PA Christ the King Manor, Inc.; Du Bois, PA St. Catherine; Du Bois, PA Du Bois Regional Hospital.
Quindlen, Joseph J. '73 (PH) Plymouth Meeting, PA Epiphany of Our Lord.
Quinlan, Edward J. '78 (HBG) Harrisburg, PA Holy Name of Jesus; [J] Harrisburg, PA The Neumann Scholarship Foundation; Secretary for Education.
Quinlan, Jack '97 (DET) Absent on Leave.
Quinlan, James V. '76 (CHI) Other Assignments.
Quinlan, Joseph M. '52 (NEW) Serra Club of Bergen County; Lincroft, NJ St. Leo the Great Retired.
Quinlan, Thomas J. '58 (RIC) Virginia Beach, VA Retired.
Quinlan, William M. '99 (BGP) Judges; Stamford, CT St. Leo.
Quinlivan, Anthony F. *c.ss.r.* '71 (ORL) Cocoa, FL Blessed Sacrament.
Quinlivan, Frank J. *c.s.c.* '70 (FgM) New Rochelle, NY Eastern Brothers Province.
Quinlivan, Thomas J. '72 (BUF) Vicars; West Seneca, NY Queen of Heaven.
Quinlivan, William J. '95 (BUF) Tonawanda, NY Blessed Sacrament.
Quinn, Bernard J. *c.m.* (FgM) Earth City, MO Western Province.
Quinn, Brendan '74 (NEW) Elizabeth, NJ Immaculate Conception; Elizabeth, NJ Trinitas Regional Medical Center.
Quinn, Brian P. '10 (PAT) Boy Scouting; Clifton, NJ St. Philip the Apostle.
Quinn, Bruce *o.f.m.cap.* '57 (NOR) Middletown, CT St. Pius X Retired.
Quinn, Charles J. '61 (WIN) Elected Senior Member Retired.
Quinn, Charles P. '66 (PRO) Retired.
Quinn, Desmond *s.s.c.* '54 (FgM) St Columbans, NE House of Post–Graduate Studies.
Quinn, Edward J. *m.m.* '47 (SJ)[M] Los Altos, CA Maryknoll.
Quinn, Edward *s.s.c.* '55 (FgM)[J] St. Columbans, NE Missionary Society of St. Columban; St Columbans, NE House of Post–Graduate Studies.
Quinn, J. Patrick *t.o.r.* '84 (ALT)[G] Hollidaysburg, PA St. Bernardine Monastery.
Quinn, James A. '67 (MIA) Hallandale Beach, FL St. Matthew; Catholic Fire Service Ministry.
Quinn, James F. '58 (SY) Retired.
Quinn, John F. '71 (NY) Armonk, NY St. Patrick.
Quinn, John L. '62 (NY) On Duty Outside the Archdiocese.
Quinn, John M. '57 (SY) New Hartford, NY St. Thomas.
Quinn, Rev. Msgr. John P. '68 (MAN) Bedford, NH St. Elizabeth Seton; Vicars Forane; Presbyteral Council;

College of Consultors; Priest Personnel Board.
Quinn, John T. '67 (SD) Retired.
Quinn, John *s.j.* '92 (LA)[F] Los Angeles, CA Loyola High School of Los Angeles.
Quinn, Rev. Msgr. Joseph G. '85 (SCR) On Duty Outside the Diocese.
Quinn, Rev. Msgr. Joseph G. '85 (SAM) Defender of the Bond.
Quinn, Rev. Msgr. Joseph '45 (NY)[C] Bronx, NY Fordham University.
Quinn, Kenneth B. (BO) Hingham, MA Resurrection of Our Lord and Savior Jesus Christ.
Quinn, Kevin P. *s.j.* '85 (SCR)[B] Scranton, PA The University of Scranton.
Quinn, Lawrence J. '71 (NY) Mount Vernon, NY Our Lady of Mount Carmel.
Quinn, Liam T. '83 (MIA) Sunrise, FL All Saints.
Quinn, Michael F. '70 (JC) Hannibal, MO Holy Family; Judges; Coordinators; Ministry to Priests.
Quinn, Michael F. '09 (SFR) San Francisco, CA St. Brendan; [S] San Francisco, CA Italian Catholic Federation.
Quinn, Michael P. *c.ss.r.* '72 (STL)[O] Liguori, MO St. Clement Health Care Center.
Quinn, Patrick T. *s.j.* '88 (STL)[C] Saint Louis University.
Quinn, Peter F. '72 (BO) Westford, MA St. Catherine of Alexandria; Presbyteral Council.
Quinn, Peter N. '75 (PH) Upper Darby, PA St. Alice.
Quinn, Peter '50 (ORL) Retired.
Quinn, Richard J. *m.m.* '54 (FgM) Maryknoll, NY MARYKNOLL.
Quinn, Richard *c.ss.r* '62 (KC)[J] Kansas City, MO Redemptorists Fathers of Kansas City, Missouri; Kansas City, MO Our Lady of Perpetual Help.
Quinn, Robert C. '61 (ALN) Mohnton, PA St. Benedict's Retired.
Quinn, Robert F. *c.s.p.* '53 (BRK)[R] Retired Retired.
Quinn, Terence *o.p.* '55 (CIN) Cincinnati, OH St. Gertrude; [N] Cincinnati, OH St. Gertrude Priory.
Quinn, Thomas J. *s.j.* '68 (PBL) Retired.
Quinn, Thomas Patrick '05 (NEW) Ridgewood, NJ Our Lady of Mount Carmel.
Quinn, Thomas '62 (SEA) Retired.
Quinn, Walter J. *o.s.a.* '61 (PH)[Y] Villanova, PA St. Thomas Monastery.
Quinn, William P. '55 (SFR) Retired.
Quinn, Rev. Msgr. William '62 (CAM) Members; Avalon, NJ St. Brendan the Navigator Parish, Avalon, N.J. Retired.
Quinnan, Michael F. '86 (SCR) Brodheadsville, PA Our Lady Queen of Peace.
Quinones, Francisco Javier '82 (SJN)[B] San Juan, PR Academia Sagrado Corazon.
Quinones, Leoncio '46 (PCE) On Duty Outside the Diocese.
Quinones, Luis '97 (ARL) Alexandria, VA Good Shepherd.
Quinones–Rivera, Leoncio '46 (SJN) Retired.
Quinones Diaz, Francisco J. '82 (SJN) Bayamon, PR Santo Domingo De Guzman.
Quint, Dennis J. '96 (DUB)[D] Dyersville, IA Beckman High School; Earlville, IA St. Joseph; Personnel Advisory Board; Worship Commission; Dyersville, IA Basilica of St. Francis Xavier; Worthington, IA St. Paul.
Quintal, Gerald '65 (P) Retired.
Quintana, Jose '96 (GR) Grand Rapids, MI Shrine of St. Francis Xavier and Our Lady of Guadalupe; On Special Assignment.
Quintana–Puente, Rev. Msgr. Carlos '02 (SJN) Santurce, PR Ntra. Sra. del Perpetuo Socorro.
Quinter, Paul S. '82 (PH) Philadelphia, PA Maternity B.V.M.
Quintero, Carlos '84 (ATL) Johns Creek, GA St. Benedict.
Quintero, Gilberto '88 (SP) Clearwater, FL St. Cecelia; Incardination Committee.
Quintero, Gustavo V. '80 (STO) Stockton, CA St. Linus Church (Pastor of).
Quintero, Haider '11 (AMA) Hereford, TX St. Anthony's.
Quintero, John Fredy '02 (HON) Honolulu, HI St. John the Baptist.
Quintero, Manuel '81 (LAV) Las Vegas, NV St. Francis de Sales; Priests' Pension Board.
Quintero–Angueira, Jose Francisco '89 (SJN) Vicar for Priests.
Quinteros, Ruben '10 (LR) Cursillo Movement; Springdale, AR St. Raphael.
Quinto, Armand *s.d.b.* '75 (NEW) Orange, NJ Our Lady of the Valley.
Quinto, Jupeter *r.c.j.* '99 (FRS) Sanger, CA St. Mary; Sanger, CA St. Katherine.
Quiogue, Roy *c.i.c.m.* '82 (SAT) San Antonio, TX Santa Rosa Hospital System; [H] San Antonio, TX Christus Santa Rosa Health Care Corporation; San Antonio, TX Sacred Heart.
Quiray, Danilo '90 (CAM) Turnersville, NJ The Church of Saints Peter and Paul, Washington Township, N.J.
Quirk, Rev. Msgr. Kevin M. '93 (WH) Wheeling, WV St. Joseph's Cathedral; Assistant to the Bishop; Judicial Vicar; Apostleship of Prayer; Censor Librorum.
Quirk, Richard J. '78 (STL) St. Louis, MO Basilica of St. Louis, King of France.
Quiroz, Jesus Salvador '96 (OAK) Pittsburg, CA St. Peter, Martyr of Verona.
Quitalig, Angel N. '98 (SFR) On Special Assignment; South San Francisco, CA Mater Dolorosa; Judges.
Quitugua, Rev. Msgr. David C. '84 (AGN) Moderator of the Curia and Vicar General; Archdiocesan College of Consultors; Archdiocesan Presbyteral Council; Judicial Vicar; Pontifical Holy Childhood Association & Pontifical Society for the Propagation of the Faith; Legion of Mary; Judicial Vicar.
Quitugua, Rev. Msgr. David I.A. '64 (AGN) Agana, GU San Juan Bautista; Archdiocesan Presbyteral Council.
Quyet, Anthony '83 (JKS) Office of Vocations; Jackson, MS Christ the King; Jackson, MS St. Mary.

R

R., Eduardo Lopez '03 (TUC) Nogales, AZ Sacred Heart of Jesus Roman Catholic Parish – Nogales.
Raab, John *c.m.f.* '76 (LA)[V] Los Angeles, CA Tepeyac House.
Raab, Ronald P. *c.s.c.* '83 (P) Portland, OR St. Andre Bessette Church.
Raab, Ronald *c.s.c.* (FTW)[H] Notre Dame Congregation of Holy Cross, United States Province of Priests & Brothers.
Raaser, Eric P. '85 (NY) Tuckahoe, NY Immaculate Conception; Tuckahoe, NY Assumption.
Raaz, Paul A. '70 (SAT) Gonzales, TX St. James; Gonzales, TX Sacred Heart.
Rabalais, Rusty P. '97 (ALX) Marksville, LA St. Joseph's.
Rabbat, Rt. Rev. Archimandrite Robert '94 (NTN) Presbyteral Council.
Rabe, David L. '83 (NO) Luling, LA St. Anthony of Padua; Ama, LA St. Mark.
Rabenecker, David *o.s.b.* '91 (LEX) Lexington, KY Federal Medical Center.
Rabenecker, David *o.s.b.* '91 (IND)[K] Saint Meinrad St. Meinrad Archabbey.
Rabiy, Andriy '01 (PHU) College of Archeparchial Consultors; Presbyteral Council; Archeparchial Seminary Advisory and Admissions Board; Victim Assistance Coordinator; Reading, PA Nativity of Blessed Virgin Mary; Archdiocesan Bulletin; Auditor; Vice Chancellor.
Rable, Cyril J. '56 (SCR) Retired.
Rable, Cyril J. '56 (SCR)[M] Dunmore, PA Villa St. Joseph.
Racco, Philip '77 (CLV) Westlake, OH St. Bernadette.
Rached, José J. *c.ss.r.* '70 (PCE) Guayama, PR St. Anthony of Padua.
Rachford, Nicholas '71 (PRM) Boy Scout Chaplain; Lorain, OH St. Nicholas; Presbyteral Council; Eparchial Consultors; Vicar Judicialis; Cantors' Institute Faculty.
Rachunek, Henry C. '62 (VIC) Retired.
Racine, Michael S. '95 (FR) Assonet, MA St. Bernard's.
Racivitch, Herve P. *s.j.* '62 (NO)[R] New Orleans, LA Ignatius Residence Retired.
Racki, Rev. Msgr. Leonard E. '62 (PBL) Pueblo, CO Sacred Heart Cathedral; Clergy Assembly Retired.
Raczka, Rt. Rev. Archimandrite Philip '80 (NTN) West Roxbury, MA Annunciation Cathedral; West Roxbury, MA Seminary of St. Gregory the Theologian; Protosyncellus; College of Eparchial Consultors; Presbyteral Council; Diocese of Newton for the Melkites in the USA, Inc., a Massachusetts Corporation; Vocations Office.
Raczynski, Paul L. '72 (MIL) Sturtevant, WI St. Sebastian; Kenosha, WI St. Anthony.
Raczynski, Theodore T. '56 (HRT) Suffield, CT Sacred Heart Retired.
Radaich, Thomas '70 (DUL) Duluth, MN St. Michael; Diocesan Deans.
Radano, Rev. Msgr. John A. '65 (NEW)[B] Seton Hall University.
Radano, Rev. Msgr. John A. '65 (NY)[A] Yonkers, NY St. Joseph's Seminary.
Radde, James M. *s.j.* '72 (MIL)[P] Milwaukee Jesuit Provincial Office, Wisconsin Province.
Radecki, Dane J. *o.praem.* '77 (GB) Green Bay, WI St. Agnes.
Radecki, Dane *o.praem.* '77 (GB) Vicariate.
Radek, James '89 (JOL) Lombard, IL Sacred Heart.
Rademacher, Germain P. '58 (NU) Retired.
Rademacher, John R. '70 (GI) Retired.
Rademacher, Robert *g.h.m.* '55 (CIN)[N] Cincinnati Headquarters of Glenmary Home Missioners Retired.
Rademacher, Robert (RIC) Retired.
Rader, John '91 (SFS) Parkston, SD Sacred Heart.
Rader, Matthew R. '10 (TOL) Fostoria, OH St. Wendelin.
Radermacher, Michael '06 (SEA) Vancouver, WA Our Lady of Lourdes.
Radetski, John J. '77 (MIL) West Bend, WI Immaculate Conception.
Radetski, Paul J. '82 (GB) Absent on Leave, Sick or Disabled.
Radice, Lawrence D. *m.m.* '85 (FgM) Maryknoll, NY MARYKNOLL.
Radke, Barnabas '08 (AMA) Vega, TX Immaculate Conception.
Radloff, James A. '93 (BAK) Council of Priests and Diocesan Consultors; Director of Youth Ministry; Vocation Promoter; Sisters, OR St. Edward the Martyr.
Radloff, Thomas H. *s.j.* '61 (TOL) Associate Vicar for Priests.
Radocha, Rev. Msgr. Stephen J. '77 (ALN) Easton, PA St. Jane Frances de Chantal; Vicars Forane; College of Consultors.
Radomski, Joseph A. '62 (TR)[N] Trenton, NJ Villa Vianney Retired.
Radosevich, Eugene A. '90 (PEO) Eureka, IL St. Luke.
Radosevich, George '68 (SFD) Livingston, IL Sacred Heart; Staunton, IL St. Michael the Archangel.
Radowicz, Michael R. '05 (MAD) Waterloo, WI St. Mary of the Nativity; Waterloo, WI St. Joseph; Advocate/Procurator (cc.1481–1490).
Radtke, Fred *o.f.m.* '67 (JOL) Joliet, IL St. John the Baptist; [L] Joliet, IL St. John the Baptist Friary.
Radvansky, Joseph R. '65 (TOL) Retired.
Radwan, John Z. '05 (NEW) Saddle Brook, NJ St. Philip the Apostle.
Raef, Scott '94 (AMA) Ex Officio; Vicars Forane; Vocation Development Team; Dalhart, TX St. Anthony of Padua.
Raeke, Joseph K. '80 (BO)[CC] Braintree, MA Caritas Christi Retirement Plan and Trust; Vicariate III; Brockton, MA St. Edith Stein; Brockton, MA Christ the King; Health Benefit Trust, Insurance and Pension Trusts, Caritas Christi Retirement Plan; Brockton, MA Our Lady of Lourdes.
Raether, Philip '04 (SEA) Oak Harbor, WA St. Augustine.
Rafacz, Joseph J. '56 (LC) Retired.
Rafaj, Elias L. '99 (PBR) Houston, TX St. John Chrysostom; Protopresbyters; Office of Religious Education.
Raffel, Godfrey '53 (FRS) Retired.
Rafferty, Brian M. '62 (BAL) Pasadena, MD Our Lady of the Chesapeake.
Rafferty, Brian M. '94 (RIC) Chesapeake, VA St. Stephen, Martyr.
Rafferty, Gerard F. *s.s.l.* '79 (NY) West Nyack, NY St. Francis of Assisi; [A] Yonkers, NY St. Joseph's Seminary.
Rafferty, James A. '94 (SCR) Vocations; Scranton, PA St. Paul's.
Rafferty, James F. '63 (BO) Hingham, MA St. Paul.
Rafferty, James R. '01 (DET) Rockwood, MI St. Mary; Gibraltar, MI St. Victor.
Rafferty, James '72 (SD) La Jolla, CA Mary, Star of the Sea Catholic Parish.
Rafferty, John Michael *o.a.r.* '03 (LA) Oxnard, CA Mary Star of the Sea; [P] Oxnard, CA Order of Augustinian Recollects (O.A.R.), St. Augustine Priory.
Rafferty, Lawrence B. '67 (RVC) Woodbury, NY Holy Name of Jesus.
Rafferty, Michael J. '57 (SCR)[M] Dunmore, PA Villa St. Joseph Retired.
Rafferty, Raymond J. '54 (PRO) Retired.
Rafferty, Raymond M. '66 (NY) New York, NY Corpus Christi.
Rafferty, Thomas F. '83 (GAL) The Woodlands, TX St. Anthony of Padua.
Rafferty, Thomas S. '05 (BO) Nahant, MA St. Thomas Aquinas; Swampscott, MA St. John the Evangelist.
Raffo, Cesar '85 (LA) Los Angeles, CA St. Frances Xavier Cabrini.
Raffo, Frank M. '98 (R) Tarboro, NC St. Catherine of Siena.
Raftery, Paul *o.p.* '84 (LA)[C] Santa Paula, CA Thomas Aquinas College.
Raftis, Sean '06 (SPK) Spokane, WA Assumption of the Blessed Virgin Mary.
Ragan, Gerald '79 (SAV) Augusta, GA St. Mary on the Hill; Augusta Deanery; College of Consultors.
Ragan, James A. '98 (PBR) Charleroi, PA Holy Ghost.
Ragis, Gerald '63 (BUR) Retired.
Ragni, Richard R. '66 (PIT)[M] Pittsburgh, PA Cardinal Dearden Center Retired.
Ragnoni, James V. '60 (CLV) Akron, OH St. Anthony of Padua.
Ragsag, Glendino (NY) Staten Island, NY St. Peter.
Ragsdale, Rev. Msgr. Patrick J. '72 (SAT) In Metropolitan Area; San Antonio, TX Shrine of St. Padre Pio of Pietrelcina; Archdiocesan Presbyteral Council; Permanent Diaconate Program; Priests Personnel Board.
Ragsdale, Rev. Msgr. Patrick '72 (SAT)[A] San Antonio, TX Diaconate Program.
Ragusa, Salvatore *s.d.s.* '88 (OAK)[O] Moraga, CA St. Mary's College Mission and Ministry Center; [B] St. Mary's College.
Raharjo, Johanes Teguh *c.i.c.m.* '06 (R) Louisburg, NC

Our Lady of the Rosary.
Rahilly, Rev. Msgr. Paul '81 (RVC) Cedarhurst, NY St. Joachim; College of Consultors; Presbyteral Council.
Rahoy, Nicholas P. '77 (CI) Chuuk, FM Immaculate Heart of Mary Cathedral; [C] Tunnuk, Chuuk, FM Vicariate Residence; Diocesan Consultors; Chuuk; Defenders of the Bond.
Rai, Kevin '74 (AUS) Austin, TX San Jose.
Raia, Jonathan D. '09 (AUS) Associate Directors; Round Rock, TX St. William.
Raible, Daniel *c.pp.s.* '43 (CIN)[N] Carthagena, OH St. Charles Retired.
Raica, Rev. Msgr. Steven J. '78 (LAN) Bishop's Office; Lansing, MI St. Mary Cathedral; Tribunal Judges; College of Consultors.
Raiche, Brian '95 (ALB) Leave of Absence.
Raila, Donald *o.s.b.* '83 (GBG)[H] Latrobe, PA Saint Vincent Archabbey.
Raimer, Chester J. '74 (GBG) Blairsville, PA SS. Simon and Jude; Torrance, PA Torrance State Hospital.
Raimondi, Michele A. '50 (SFR) Retired.
Rainaldo, John H. *s.j.* '64 (MIL)[P] Wauwatosa, WI Jesuit Community at St. Camillus.
Rainforth, Thomas G. '73 (PAT)[K] Paterson, NJ St. Joseph's Hospital and Medical Center; Wayne, NJ St. Joseph's Wayne Hospital; Paterson, NJ St. Joseph Hospital.
Rainone, John J. '70 (PRO)[K] Providence, RI St. Joseph Health Services of Rhode Island; [K] North Providence, RI St. Joseph Health Services of Rhode Island – Our Lady of Fatima Hospital; [O] Providence St. John Vianney Residence.
Rainville, Marcel R. *s.s.e.* '71 (BUR)[E] South Burlington, VT Edmundite House of Formation.
Rainwater, Randall '96 (STO) Stockton, CA DeWitt Nelson Training Center.
Raj, Babu Arul Raj Jesu (MOB) Fairhope, AL St. Lawrence.
Raj, Percy Joseph '74 (NY) Staten Island, NY Staten Island University Hospital South; Staten Island University Hospital North.
Raj, Peter '05 (LC) Auburndale, WI Nativity of the Blessed Virgin Mary; Milladore, WI St. Kilian; Hewitt, WI St. Michael.
Raja, Joseph Anthony *ss.cc.* '06 (FR)[F] Fairhaven National Center of the Enthronement.
Raja, Tiburtis Antony '96 (HBG) New Cumberland, PA St. Theresa of the Infant Jesus.
Rajaian, Suresh *s.a.c.* '00 (DET) Redford, MI St. Valentine.
Rajamanickam, Masilamani '95 (AUS) Austin, TX St. Catherine of Siena.
Rajanayagam, Thomas M. '66 (STO) Diamond Springs, CA Retired.
Rajappa, Dominic Savio '92 (FRS) Fresno, CA St. Alphonsus; Community Regional Medical Center; Fresno, CA Veterans Administration Medical Center.
Rajareegam, Paul (CC) Sinton, TX Sacred Heart.
Rajayan, Antony William '96 (WIL) Wilmington, DE Wilmington Hospital; Newark, DE Holy Family.
Raj Cruz, Soosai '05 (BUR) Milton, VT St. Ann; Fairfax, VT St. Luke.
Rajendran, Xavier Bruce '82 (WIL) Wilmington, DE St. Thomas the Apostle; Wilmington, DE St. Francis Hospital; [I] Wilmington, DE St. Francis Hospital, Inc.
Raji, Arokiadoss '10 (NEW) East Rutherford, NJ St. Joseph's.
Raj Samala, Arokia '02 (AMA) Clarendon, TX St. Mary's; Groom, TX Immaculate Heart of Mary.
Rajski, Daniel '11 (BRK) Rockaway Beach, NY St. Rose of Lima.
Raju, Madanu Sleeva (SUP) Stetsonville, WI Sacred Heart of Jesus.
Rakoczy, Richard S. '59 (DET) Retired.
Rakoczy, Walter J. '78 (GRY) Michigan City, IN St. Mary of the Immaculate Conception; Michigan City, IN Sacred Heart Mission.
Rakotovoavy, Francois *m.s.f.* '00 (SAT) Seguin, TX Our Lady of Guadalupe.
Rakowicz, William J. *s.j.* '80 (CI) Judical Vicar.
Rakowicz, William J. *s.j.* '80 (PAT)[J] Morristown, NJ Loyola House of Retreats.
Rakowski, Helmut *o.f.m.cap.* (FgM) AMERICAN CAPUCHIN MISSIONS.
Ralko, Martin J. '84 (COL) Zanesville, OH St. Nicholas; [C] Zanesville, OH Bishop Rosecrans High School; [K] Zanesville, OH St. Nicholas Foundation.
Ralph, Francis *o.p.* '72 (L)[M] St. Catharine, KY Sansbury Care Center, Inc.; Springfield, KY St. Rose.
Ralph, John '55 (WH) Retired.
Ralph, Sean P. '09 (CLV) Olmsted Falls, OH St. Mary of the Falls.
Ralph, Rev. Msgr. Thomas J. '56 (DUB) Retired.
Ralston, Timothy W. '10 (CIN) Dayton, OH St. Charles Borromeo.
Rama, Sebastian *m.s.f.s.* '90 (GAL) Deer Park, TX St. Hyacinth.
Ramacciotti, Gabriel M. *o.s.m.* '51 (DEN) Denver, CO Our Lady of Mount Carmel.
Ramacciotti, Rev. Msgr. James J. '85 (STL) Lemay, MO St. Martin of Tours; [A] St. Louis, MO Kenrick School of Theology.
Ramaeker, Victor '61 (SC) Whittemore, IA St. Joseph's; Whittemore, IA St. Michael's.
Ramaekers, Timothy '82 (ORG) Placentia, CA St. Joseph.
Ramat, Martin J. '07 (SAC) Vallejo, CA St. Vincent Ferrer.
Ramatowski, Edward F. '03 (STL) Air National Guard Chaplains; Military Chaplains.
Ramelow, Anselm *o.p.* '03 (OAK)[A] Berkeley, CA Dominican School of Philosophy and Theology.
Ramelow, Anselm *o.p.* '03 (SFR)[N] San Francisco, CA St. Dominic Priory; San Francisco, CA St. Dominic.
Ramen, Paul F. '60 (NOR) Retired.
Ramenaden, Bernard *o.s.b.* '75 (FTW) Rome City, IN St. Gaspar del Bufalo.
Ramer, Rev. Msgr. James K. '86 (PEO) Mahomet, IL Our Lady of the Lake.
Ramirez, Allen *o.f.m.conv.* '72 (LA) Hermosa Beach, CA Our Lady of Guadalupe.
Ramirez, Carlos Reyes *c.s.* '05 (WDC) Riverdale, MD Our Lady of Fatima Parish.
Ramirez, Cesar Rebolledo '97 (CAM) International Priests Representatives.
Ramirez, Charles J. '87 (LA) Claremont, CA Our Lady of the Assumption.
Ramirez, Cornelio C. *s.a.c.* '67 (LUB) Retired.
Ramirez, David '01 (NSH) Hispanic Ministry; Presbyteral Council.
Ramirez, Edinson E. '10 (NEW) Jersey City, NJ St. John the Baptist.
Ramirez, Enrique Espinosa *m.sp.s.* '79 (LA) Huntington Park, CA St. Martha.
Ramirez, Fernando '78 (SD) Escondido, CA Church of St. Timothy Catholic Parish.
Ramireker, Francisco Javier *c.m.* (PCE) Ponce, PR San Vicente–Cantera.
Ramirez, Francisco X. '79 (LA) Los Angeles, CA St. Patrick; Los Angeles, CA St. Stephen of Hungary.
Ramirez, Francisco *o.f.m.cap.* '04 (DEN) Denver, CO Annunciation; [N] Denver, CO San Antonio Friary.
Ramirez, Gerardo (PCE) Pastoral Carcelaria.
Ramirez, Hernando J. *s.j.* '75 (LAF)[J] Grand Coteau, LA Jesuit Spirituality Center (St. Charles College).
Ramirez, Ivan D. '03 (HRT) East Hartford, CT St. Isaac Jogues; East Hartford, CT St. Mary; East Hartford, CT St. Rose.
Ramirez, J. Jesus '86 (YAK) Royal City, WA St. Michael the Archangel.
Ramirez, Jairo H. '88 (STO) Turlock, CA Sacred Heart Church of Turlock (Pastor of).
Ramirez, Jorge '06 (B) On Duty Outside the Diocese.
Ramirez, Jorge '06 (KC) St. Joseph, MO St. Patrick.
Ramirez, Jose Alfredo *o.f.m.* '99 (ELP)[B] El Paso, TX St. Anthony's School of Theology.
Ramirez, Jose de Jesus '86 (YAK) Spanish.
Ramirez, Jose Nieves '79 (ELP) Absent on Leave.
Ramirez, Jose T. '10 (B) Boise, ID Cathedral of St. John the Evangelist.
Ramirez, Jose *s.m.* '69 (STL)[O] Eureka, MO Marycliff Marianist Community; [O] St. Louis, MO Marianist Community; [S] Eureka, MO Marianist Retreat & Conference Center.
Ramirez, Juan Carlos '07 (LSC) Presbyteral Council; Hobbs, NM St. Helena.
Ramirez, Luis A. '94 (LR) North Little Rock, AR St. Anne.
Ramirez, Mario V. *m.s.c.* '83 (SB) Adelanto, CA Christ the Good Shepherd.
Ramirez, Mario *s.t.b.* '05 (DEN) Denver, CO St. Joseph.
Ramirez, Oran de Jesus '67 (PCE) Jayuya, PR Our Lady of Monserrate.
Ramirez, Rev. Msgr. Pedro '74 (SPK) Members Retired.
Ramirez, Rafael M. *s.s.* '94 (BAL)[A] Baltimore, MD St. Mary's Seminary and University; [Q] Baltimore, MD St. Mary's Seminary & University.
Ramirez, Renelmo '85 (TYL) Palestine, TX Sacred Heart; Palestine, TX Powledge Unit, Texas Department of Criminal Justice.
Ramirez, Roland B. '08 (SAC) Jackson, CA St. Patrick's; Jackson, CA Immaculate Conception; Ione, CA Sacred Heart of Jesus.
Ramirez, Salvador '04 (BWN) Edinburg, TX St. Joseph the Worker.
Ramirez, Thielo '09 (PHX) Phoenix, AZ St. Catherine of Siena Roman Catholic Parish.
Ramirez, Tulio E. *m.x.y.* '90 (NY)[DD] Bronx, NY Yarumal Mission Society, Inc.; Bronx, NY Our Saviour.
Ramirez, Ybain F. '96 (ORL) Casselberry, FL St. Augustine; Appointed Members.
Ramirez–Alejos, Rev. Msgr. Pedro '74 (SPK) Spokane, WA St. Thomas More.
Ramirez–Portugal, Daniel '91 (LAR) Laredo, TX St. John Neumann.
Ramirez–Ruiz, Armando '89 (CHI) Round Lake, IL St. Joseph.
Ramirez Jonelez, Jorge Alberto (SJN) San Juan, PR Nuestra Senora del Pilar.
Ramirez Torres, Gerardo '91 (PCE) Orocovis, PR Our Lady Mother of Divine Providence; Cursillos de Cristiandad.
Ramiriz, Cesar A. Rebolledo *o.f.m.* '97 (CAM) Millville, NJ The Parish of All Saints, Millville, N.J.
Ramler, Michael J. '74 (LEX) Priests' Retirement Committee; Somerset, KY St. Mildred; Mountain West.
Ramon, Edilberto '04 (CHI) Chicago, IL St. Francis de Sales.
Ramon, Gustavo J. '92 (LA) Los Angeles, CA Assumption; Los Angeles, CA San Antonio de Padua; Cardinal McIntyre Fund for Charity Board of Directors.
Ramon, Rodolfo '99 (ORL) Kissimmee, FL Holy Redeemer.
Ramon, Valentin '64 (PHX) Prescott, AZ Sacred Heart Roman Catholic Parish.
Ramon–Landry, Kenneth '87 (BLX) Hattiesburg, MS Sacred Heart; Hattiesburg, MS Holy Rosary.
Ramos, A.W. '94 (SFS) South Dakota State Penitentiary & Minnehaha County Correctional Centers.
Ramos, Alex L. '94 (BRK) Woodside, NY Corpus Christi.
Ramos, Andres '88 (SD) Ramona, CA Immaculate Heart of Mary Catholic Parish.
Ramos, Angel Roman '90 (MGZ) Rincon, PR St. Rose of Lima.
Ramos, Cipriano '52 (SAC) Retired.
Ramos, Julio *m.g.* '01 (LA) Los Angeles, CA St. Paul.
Ramos, June N. '10 (SFE) Albuquerque, NM Annunciation.
Ramos, Justin S. *o.praem.* '95 (ORG)[D] Silverado, CA St. Michael's Preparatory School; [I] Silverado, CA Norbertine Fathers of Orange Inc.
Ramos, Marcos *o.p.* '01 (FgM) Metairie, LA St. Martin de Porres Province (Southern Dominican Province).
Ramos, Marcos *o.p.* '01 (NO)[R] New Orleans Dominican Friars, Southern Dominican Province of St. Martin de Porres.
Ramos, Orlando *o.c.d.* '93 (PCE) Ponce, PR San José.
Ramos, Ponciano *s.v.d.* '45 (SB)[I] Riverside, CA Divine Word Seminary.
Ramos, Rafael A. '10 (ARE) Arecibo, PR Church of San Martin de Porres.
Ramos, Sergio '99 (ORG) Santa Ana, CA St. Barbara Catholic Church.
Ramos, Victor Raul '84 (LA) Los Angeles, CA Mother of Sorrows; Los Angeles, CA St. Malachy.
Ramos, Victoriano '54 (SJN) Union Eucaristica Reparadora (UNER) Retired.
Ramos Cintron, Israel '08 (CGS) Aibonito, PR Church of St. Joseph.
Ramoso, Rene R. '89 (SFR) South San Francisco, CA St. Augustine; Deans.
Ramsak, Finbar *o.s.b* '11 (CLV)[D] Cleveland, OH Benedictine High School.
Ramsey, James Boniface '73 (NY) New York, NY St. Joseph; [HH] New York, NY Patrons of the Arts in Vatican Museums.
Ramsey, James '84 (GAL) Houston, TX Our Lady of Walsingham.
Ramsey, John David '10 (RIC) Williamsburg, VA St. Bede.
Ramson, Ronald *c.m.* '59 (DAL)[A] Irving, TX Holy Trinity Seminary; [J] Dallas, TX Congregation of the Mission, Western Province.
Ranada, Arnel '98 (NY) Staten Island, NY St. Joseph, St. Thomas.
Ranalletti, Richard A. *c.s.b.* '73 (DET)[E] Novi, MI Catholic Central High School.
Ranallo, Albert A. '07 (PRO) Providence, RI Blessed Sacrament; Providence, RI Rhode Island Hospital.
Rances, Ronan '07 (OAK) Concord, CA St. Bonaventure.
Randall, Rev. Msgr. Edward '64 (GAL) Retired.
Randall, Jude D. *o.s.b.* '60 (JOL)[C] Lisle, IL Benet Academy; [L] Lisle, IL St. Procopius Abbey; Lisle, IL.
Randall, Rev. Msgr. Kevin S. '92 (NOR) On Duty Outside the Diocese; Air Force Reserve Chaplains.
Randall, Robert J. '51 (PRO) Retired.
Randazzo, Anthony J. '86 (NEW) North Caldwell, NJ Notre Dame; West Essex Deanery 15.
Randone, Michael C. '95 (BO) Unassigned.
Randrianary, Jacques *s.j.* '09 (LA)[C] Los Angeles, CA Jesuit Community.
Ranek, Jerome '91 (SFS) Alexandria, SD St. Mary of Mercy; Propagation of the Faith; Presbyteral Council.
Raneri, Carmine B. '55 (HRT) Waterbury, CT Blessed Sacrament Retired.
Raney, Richard E. '38 (PEO) Retired.
Rangel, Carlos '98 (TYL) Marshall, TX St. Joseph; Tatum, TX San Pedro the Fisherman.
Rangel, Marco '10 (DAL) Plano, TX St. Mark the Evangelist.
Rangel, Maximino J. *o.f.m.* '95 (ELP)[B] El Paso, TX St. Anthony's School of Theology; El Paso, TX St. Francis of Assisi Mission.
Ranges, Charles H. *s.s.e.* '72 (BUR) Essex Junction, VT Holy Family–St. Lawrence.
Ranieri, John J. '82 (NEW)[B] Seton Hall University.
Ranieri, Rev. Msgr. Joseph A. '57 (WDC) Pastoral

Center Special Ministries; Pastoral Care of Priests; Archdiocesan Building Commission.
Ranin, Geraldo J. '06 (SAC) Westwood, CA Our Lady of the Snows; Quincy, CA St. John.
Ranjo, Carlito '96 (HON) Pahoa, HI Sacred Heart.
Rank, Robert F. '68 (GB) Neopit, WI St. Anthony; Gresham, WI St. Francis Solanus; Keshena, WI St. Michael.
Rank, Ronald G. '58 (MAD) Retired.
Rankin, Joseph M. '79 (L) Louisville, KY St. Luke; Louisville, KY St. Rita; College of Consultors; Ex Officio.
Rankin, Robert '80 (HPM) Tucson, AZ St. Melany; Youth.
Ranly, Ernest W. *c.pp.s.* '56 (CIN)[N] Carthagena, OH St. Charles Retired.
Rannazzisi, Gregory '09 (RVC) Westbury, NY St. Brigid.
Ranoa, Bernardo '84 (SD)[O] San Diego, CA Christ Child Society; San Diego, CA Saint Michael Catholic Parish San Diego.
Ranola, Hildritho '04 (SPP) Auditors.
Ransom, Donald B. '64 (NEW) Retired.
Ranzino, Thomas C. '78 (BR) Baton Rouge, LA St. Jean Vianney; Chancellor; Diocesan Corporation (The Roman Catholic Church of the Diocese of Baton Rouge); Worship, Office of; [A] St. Benedict, LA St. Joseph Seminary College.
Ranzino, Tom '78 (NO) Washington, DC Federation of Diocesan Liturgical Commissions; [A] St. Benedict, LA St. Joseph Seminary College.
Rapaglia, Eric '00 (NY) Bronx, NY Our Lady of Mt. Carmel.
Raphael, John J. *s.s.j.* '95 (NO)[U] New Orleans, LA Pierre Toussaint Foundation of New Orleans, Inc.; [R] New Orleans, LA The Josephite Faculty House of St. Augustine High School.
Raphael, John *s.s.j.* '95 (WDC)[U] Washington, DC Howard Univ. Newman Center.
Raphael, Mark S. '98 (NO)[A] New Orleans, LA Notre Dame Seminary Graduate School of Theology; Continuing Formation for Priests; Metairie, LA St. Edward the Confessor.
Rapisarda, John '08 (BAL) Baltimore, MD Our Lady of Mount Carmel.
Rapisarda, P. Gregory '10 (BAL) Clarksville, MD St. Louis.
Rapose, Mario D. '00 (OM) Blair, NE St. Francis Borgia; Fort Calhoun, NE St. John the Baptist.
Raposo, John A. '77 (FR)[E] Fall River, MA Catholic Memorial Home Inc.; Fall River, MA Holy Name.
Raposo, Peter '98 (CHI) Skokie, IL St. Peter.
Rapozo, Anthon W. '11 (HON) Lihue, HI Immaculate Conception.
Rapp, Bernard A. '77 (SD) Retired.
Rapp, Michael '10 (DEN) Craig, CO Saint Michael.
Rappold, Norbert F. '99 (LR) Mena, AR St. Agnes; Mount Ida, AR All Saints Church; Glenwood, AR Our Lady of Guadalupe Church.
Rapposelli, Stephen J. '98 (CAM) Blackwood, NJ Our Lady of Hope Parish, Blackwood, N.J.
Raptosh, R. Joseph '87 (PBR) Monroeville, PA Church of the Resurrection; Elected Deanery Representatives; [A] Pittsburgh, PA Byzantine Catholic Seminary of SS. Cyril and Methodius.
Raquepo, Mario '79 (HON) Honolulu, HI St. John the Baptist; [C] Honolulu, HI St. Francis Healthcare System of Hawaii.
Rareshide, Rev. Msgr. Lanaux J. '61 (NO) Slidell, LA St. Margaret Mary; Liaisons.
Rasby, Rev. Msgr. James W. '52 (DEN) Retired.
Rasch, Richard S. *o.de.m.* '84 (CLV) Cleveland, OH Our Lady of Mount Carmel; [N] Cleveland, OH Mercedarians.
Rascher, Joseph C. '81 (BEL) Trenton, IL St. Mary.
Raschko, Michael '75 (SEA) Special Assignment; Censor Librorum; Theological Resources.
Rashford, John *s.j.* '71 (SEA)[M] Seattle, WA Jesuit House, Seattle.
Rashford, Nicholas J. *s.j.* '71 (PH)[C] Jesuit Fathers; [Y] Loyola Center and Manresa Hall.
Rasing, Linus E. '53 (DUB) Retired.
Rask, Phillip J. '72 (STP) Shoreview, MN St. Odilia.
Rasky, Joseph G. *s.m.* '65 (SAT)[L] San Antonio, TX Central Catholic Marianist Community; Movimiento de Apostolado Familiar & Marriage Encounter (Rural).
Rasmussen, John '69 (SFS) Retired.
Rasner, David L. '82 (LFT) Attica, IN St. Francis Xavier; Covington, IN St. Joseph; Presiding Judge; Censor Librorum; Associate Judges.
Raso, Anthony F. '75 (BRK) Brooklyn, NY St. Sylvester.
Rasquinha, G. Ignatius '65 (SB) Retired.
Rassley, George *c.ss.r.* '53 (STL)[O] Liguori, MO St. Clement Health Care Center Retired.
Rassmussen, Terrence '79 (STP) New Hope, MN St. Joseph.
Rastrelli, Thomas P. '02 (DUB) On Leave of Absence (Not Authorized for Priestly Ministry).
Rasura, Jamie J. *s.j.* '56 (SJ)[M] Los Gatos, CA Sacred Heart Jesuit Center.
Rata, Jovito '07 (SAC) Fairfield, CA Holy Spirit.
Rataj, Stanley G. '79 (CHI) Chicago, IL Our Lady of the Snows.
Ratajczak, Justin A. *o.f.m.conv.* '77 (ALT) Boswell, PA All Saints.
Ratajczak, Michael '75 (SD) Oceanside, CA Saint Thomas More Catholic Parish; Presbyteral Council.
Ratazak, Bernard A. '76 (RCK) Retired.
Ratchford, Robert J. *s.j.* '61 (NO)[R] New Orleans, LA Ignatius Residence Retired.
Raterman, Herbert J. *s.j.* '55 (CIN)[U] Cincinnati, OH Living Monuments of Reparation.
Raterman, Herbert J. *s.j.* '55 (DET)[K] Clarkston, MI Colombiere Center.
Ratermann, Rev. Msgr. David A. '51 (STL) Retired.
Ratermann, Jerome B. '57 (BEL) Retired.
Rath, Martin *o.s.b.* '83 (SCL)[I] Collegeville, MN St. John's Abbey, of the Order of St. Benedict.
Rath, Richard J. '88 (STL) St. Louis, MO St. John the Baptist.
Rath, Thomas V. '49 (CLV) Retired.
Rathfon, John R. '54 (CLV) Cuyahoga Falls, OH Immaculate Heart of Mary Retired.
Rathgeb, Rev. Msgr. William R. '67 (GBG) Judicial Vicar; Greensburg, PA St. Paul.
Rathinam, Bala '74 (RVC) Seaford, NY St. William the Abbot.
Rathschmidt, John *o.f.m.cap.* '69 (BO)[U] Jamaica Plain, MA St. Francis of Assisi Friary.
Rathschmidt, John *o.f.m.cap.* '69 (NOR) Middletown, CT St. Pius X.
Ratigan, Patrick A. '83 (OG) Adams, NY St. Cecilia.
Rativa, Jorge *o.p.* '10 (LUB) Lubbock, TX St. Elizabeth University Parish.
Ratterman, Kevin J. '94 (OKL)[H] Ponca City, OK St. Mary's Housing Foundation; Region VIII; Ponca City, OK Church of St. Mary.
Ratzmann, George '87 (VEN) Naples, FL St. William; Presbyteral Council.
Rau, Peter J. '85 (ATL) Roswell, GA St. Peter Chanel; Deans; College of Consultors.
Rauch, David E. '70 (STL) St. Louis, MO Our Lady of Providence.
Rauch, Edward L. *o.s.f.s.* '64 (PH) Philadelphia, PA Our Lady of Ransom Retired.
Rauch, Laszlo F. '49 (TR)[N] Trenton, NJ St. Lawrence Rehabilitation Center Retired.
Raudabaugh, Joseph R. '62 (CIN) Retired.
Raudes, Santiago '02 (SAC) Sacramento, CA St. Robert.
Raulli, Enrico *s.j.* '65 (NEW)[C] Jersey City, NJ Jesuit Community.
Raulli, Enrico *s.j.* '65 (NY)[DD] New York, NY Jesuit Community of the Immaculate Conception.
Raun, Rev. Msgr. Douglas A. '82 (SFE) Rio Rancho, NM St. Thomas Aquinas; Vicars Forane (Deans); Presbyteral Council of the Archdiocese of Santa Fe.
Rausch, Clyde *o.m.i.* '68 (FgM) Washington, DC AMERICAN OBLATE MISSIONS.
Rausch, Dale J. '68 (DUB) West Union, IA Holy Name; Clermont, IA St. Peter; Fayette, IA St. Francis of Assisi; Sumner, IA Immaculate Conception.
Rausch, Dennis '80 (MIA) Retired.
Rausch, John W. '47 (MIL) Retired.
Rausch, John *o.f.m.* '76 (STL)[O] St. Louis, MO Franciscan Friary of St. Anthony of Padua.
Rausch, John *g.h.m.* '72 (LEX)[M] Martin, KY The Catholic Committee of Appalachia.
Rausch, Leon S. *s.j.* '59 (MIL)[P] Wauwatosa, WI Jesuit Community at St. Camillus.
Rausch, Thomas P. *s.j.* '72 (LA)[C] Los Angeles, CA Jesuit Community; Co Chairmen.
Rauscher, Rev. Msgr. Joseph G. '67 (SCR) Wilkes–Barre, PA St. Nicholas.
Rauscher, Rev. Msgr. Martin F. '60 (PAT) Retired.
Rauscher, Russell G. '75 (CLV) Mentor, OH St. John Vianney.
Rausehuber, Anthony G. *s.j.* '05 (BR)[J] Convent, LA Manresa House of Retreats.
Rausseo Gomez, Jose Gregorio '07 (SLC) Orem, UT St. Francis of Assisi LLC 221.
Rautenberg, Joseph F. '73 (IND) Cambridge City, IN St. Elizabeth of Hungary Catholic Church, Cambridge City, Inc.; Knightstown, IN St. Rose of Lima Catholic Church, Knightstown, Inc.; New Castle, IN St. Anne Catholic Church, New Castle, Inc.; Vicariate for Advocacy to Priests.
Rauth, Philip J. '59 (LIN) Retired.
Raux, Redmond P. '82 (MO) Military & VA Chaplains.; Air Force Chaplains; Presbyteral Council.
Rauzi, Mario *c.s.* '45 (CIN) Cincinnati, OH Sacred Heart.
Ravenkamp, Michael W. *s.j.* '96 (LA) Santa Barbara, CA Our Lady of Sorrows.
Ravey, Donald J. '61 (BUR) Elected Members Retired.
Ravi, Joseph '97 (AMA) Pampa, TX St. Vincent de Paul.
Ravizza, Mark A. *s.j.* '99 (SJ)[B] Santa Clara, CA Jesuit Community.
Rawa, Jerome D. *s.m.* '55 (WH) Richwood, WV Holy Family.
Rawden, Rev. Msgr. John A. '55 (LA) Retired.
Ray, Daniel *l.c.* '06 (DAL)[D] Irving, TX The Highlands School; [J] Irving, TX Legionaries of Christ.
Ray, Robert E. '69 (L) Fairdale, KY Blessed Teresa of Calcutta; Ex Officio.
Rayar, Thomas '93 (STP) Northfield, MN Annunciation.
Rayder, Peter J. '02 (BRK) Brooklyn, NY Our Lady Help of Christians.
Rayen, Germanus *o.f.m.cap.* '72 (AUS) Austin, TX St. Mary Cathedral.
Rayer, Daniel J. '99 (LIN) Chancellor; Judge; Diocesan Consultors; Catholic Relief Services; Liturgical Ministries; Permanent Deacon Continuing Education Committee; Diocesan Housing Ministries, Inc.; Presbyteral Council; Priests' Continuing Education Committee; [J] Lincoln, NE Mass Stipends.
Rayes, Emanuel '54 (EST) Retired.
Raymond, David R. '89 (SPR) Cheshire, MA St. Mary of the Assumption.
Raymond, David R. '03 (PRT) Houlton, ME St. Mary of the Visitation; Houlton, ME St. Agnes.
Raymond, Wilfred J. *c.s.c.* '71 (FTW)[H] Notre Dame Congregation of Holy Cross, United States Province of Priests & Brothers.
Raymond, Wilfred *c.s.c.* '71 (FR)[L] North Easton, MA Holy Cross Family Ministries.
Raymond, Willie *c.s.c.* '71 (LA) Santa Monica, CA St. Monica.
Rayson, Robert '99 (PEO) Dalzell, IL St. Thomas More.
Rayson, Robert '99 (PEO) La Salle, IL Shrine of Queen of the Holy Rosary; La Salle, IL St. Hyacinth's; La Salle, IL Resurrection; La Salle, IL St. Patrick's.
Razo, Manuel Alfredo '11 (BWN) San Juan, TX Basilica of Our Lady of San Juan del Valle–National Shrine.
Razo Meza, Gonzalo E. '09 (SAT) Selma, TX Our Lady of Perpetual Help.
Razumov, Victor (PAT)[K] Denville, NJ Saint Clare's Hospital, Inc.
Re, Angelo '60 (SJ) Retired.
Read, Ignacio *o.c.d.* '56 (MIL)[P] Milwaukee Provincial Offices – Discalced Carmelites.
Reade, John M. '09 (COL)[C] Lancaster, OH William V. Fisher Catholic High School; Bremen, OH St. Mary; Lancaster, OH St. Bernadette.
Reader, Daniel B. '11 (ORG) Cypress, CA St. Irenaeus.
Reading, Edward '72 (PAT) On Duty Outside the Diocese.
Ready, Frank J. '59 (ARL) Vicar for Religious; Diocesan Consultors; Diaconal Formation Program; Vicar General for Pastoral Services; Arlington, VA St. Agnes.
Reagan, Robert '04 (PRT) Retired.
Real, Fernando *m.id.* '81 (NY)[DD] Bronx, NY Idente Missionaries – Santa Maria Residence.
Reale, Frank *s.j.* '81 (STL)[C] Saint Louis University; [O] St. Louis, MO Bellarmine House of Studies; [O] St. Louis, MO Sacred Heart Jesuit Community.
Realmuto, George *m.s.a.* '87 (NOR)[G] Cromwell, CT Society of the Missionaries of the Holy Apostles.
Reamer, Mark G. *o.f.m.* '91 (MO) Navy Reserve Chaplains.
Reamer, Mark G. *o.f.m.* '91 (R) Council of Priests; Raleigh, NC St. Francis of Assisi; Deans.
Reamer, William G. '87 (OG) Plattsburgh, NY Our Lady of Victory; Plattsburgh, NY Champlain Valley Physicians Hospital Medical Center; Advocates.
Reardon, Daniel '97 (KC) On Duty Outside the Diocese.
Reardon, Dennis A. '72 (PRO) Woonsocket, RI All Saints Parish.
Reardon, Francis '78 (PMB) Boca Raton, FL Our Lady of Lourdes.
Reardon, John D. '73 (PH) Defenders of the Bond.
Reardon, John F. '76 (BO) Canton, MA St. John the Evangelist.
Reardon, John F. '50 (NY) Staten Island, NY St. Rita; [DD] Bronx, NY John Cardinal O'Connor Residence Retired.
Reardon, Joseph D. '97 (MO) Navy Chaplains.
Reardon, Michael '74 (LA) Whittier, CA St. Bruno.
Reardon, Michael *s.d.v.* '99 (BUR) Elected Members; Derby Line, VT St. Edward; Newport, VT St. Mary Star of the Sea.
Reardon, Patrick *o.p.* '60 (DEN) Denver, CO St. Dominic; [N] Denver, CO Dominican Friars.
Reardon, Robert J. '59 (PIT)[M] Pittsburgh, PA St. John Vianney Manor; Pittsburgh, PA Retired.
Reasoner, Mark J. '98 (DUB) Directors; [F] Cedar Rapids, IA LaSalle Middle School; Cedar Rapids, IA St. Jude; Priests' Council; [F] Cedar Rapids, IA Holy Family Consolidated School.
Reaume, Michael R. *s.m.* '69 (STL)[O] St. Louis Marianists, Province of the United States (Society of Mary).
Reaves, Phillip A. '94 (LR) Batesville, AR St. Mary; Batesville, AR St. Cecilia; Weiner, AR St. Anthony.
Rebacz, Jerzy (LC) Stevens Point, WI St. Joseph; Stevens Point, WI St. Stephen.
Rebamontan, Marito F. '70 (ORG) Laguna Beach, CA St. Catherine of Siena.
Rebanal, Rev. Msgr. Jeremias R. '55 (NEW) Elizabeth, NJ St. Mary of the Assumption Retired.
Rebaque, Jose *s.a.c.* '70 (BGP) Bridgeport, CT St. Peter.
Rebatzki, George M. '64 (MIL) Retired.
Rebeck, Rev. Msgr. Eugene M. '65 (TR) Episcopal

Council; Holmdel, NJ St. Catharine; Monmouth County; Tribunal Judges.
Rebel, John W. '65 (PIT) Lawrence County, PA Youth Development Center Retired.
Rebel, Patrick M. '85 (SP) Largo, FL St. Matthew.
Rebello, Hendrico '06 (DET) Livonia, MI St. Michael.
Rebello, Valentine D. '89 (RVC) Bellmore, NY St. Barnabas the Apostle.
Rebeta, James L. *c.s.c.* '73 (FTW)[H] Notre Dame Congregation of Holy Cross, United States Province of Priests & Brothers.
Rebeyro, Lloyd '70 (ALB) Retired.
Rebman, Rev. Msgr. Joseph F. '60 (WIL) Wilmington, DE St. Joseph on the Brandywine; Vicar General for Pastoral Services; Secretary, Pastoral Services Department; Catholic Cemeteries; Ecumenical Liaison; Marian Devotions; College of Consultors; Catholic Cemeteries, Inc.; Catholic Diocese of Wilmington, Inc.; Black & Native American Missions.
Rebol, Anthony '56 (CLV) Administrative Leave.
Reboli, John P. *s.j.* '70 (WOR)[N] Worcester, MA Jesuits of the Holy Cross, Inc.
Rebong, Rev. Msgr. Nestor D. '86 (LA) West Covina, CA St. Christopher; Deanery 11; Cursillo Movement; Archdiocesan Finance Council Members 2011–2012.
Rebosura, Sabino B. '87 (HT) Raceland, LA Community of St. Anthony; Raceland, LA St. Hilary of Poitiers.
Rebuldela, Alfred '72 (HON) Captain Cook, HI St. Benedict.
Reburiano, V. Mark '05 (SFR) San Rafael, CA St. Isabella.
Recaido, Florentino E. '02 (CHK) Presbyteral Council; Adult Leaders; Saipan, MP Cathedral of Our Lady of Mt. Carmel.
Recchuti, William A. *o.s.a* '61 (PH) Philadelphia, PA St. Rita of Cascia.
Receconi, Edward R. *o.s.b.* '79 (SEA)[M] Lacey, WA St. Martin's Abbey.
Recera, Manuel '85 (MRY) Campus Ministry Department.
Rechenburg, Basil *o.s.b.* '68 (WOR)[N] Still River, MA Benedictine Monks, St. Benedict Abbey.
Recio, Dennis C. *s.j.* '04 (SFR)[N] San Francisco, CA Loyola House Jesuit Community.
Reck, Donald W. *s.j.* '65 (STL)[O] St. Louis, MO Jesuit Community Corporation at Saint Louis University – Jesuit Hall Retired.
Recker, Anthony L. '09 (TOL) Toledo, OH St. Joan of Arc.
Recker, Odo *o.s.b.* '78 (P)[L] St. Benedict, OR Mt. Angel Abbey; Saint Benedict, OR.
Recker, Philip F. '59 (DUB) Retired.
Recker, Ralph *o.s.b.* '09 (P)[A] St. Benedict, OR Mount Angel Seminary; [A] St. Benedict, OR Mount Angel Seminary; [L] St. Benedict, OR Mt. Angel Abbey.
Reckinger, Robert A. '51 (DET) Retired.
Reckker, Stephen C. '63 (DET) Romeo, MI St. Clement of Rome.
Reczek, Felix *o.f.m.* '44 (MIL)[P] Burlington, WI Queen of Peace Friary.
Reczek, Paul *o.f.m.* '72 (MIL)[P] Provincial Offices of the Franciscan Friars, Assumption BVM Province, Inc.
Red, Armando V. '03 (SEA) Centralia, WA St. Mary; Pe Ell, WA St. Joseph; Toledo, WA St. Francis Xavier; Winlock, WA Sacred Heart; Chehalis, WA St. Joseph.
Redcay, Christopher '89 (PH) Malvern, PA St. Patrick.
Redden, Michael J. '72 (ATL) Retired.
Reddick, E. Peter '72 (SY) Syracuse, NY Blessed Sacrament.
Reddy, Louis Maram '89 (NY) White Plains, NY St. Bernard.
Reddy, Reginald J. *o.f.m.* '61 (ALB)[B] Siena College; [R] Albany, NY St. Francis Chapel.
Redfern, Damian Joseph '06 (LC) Altoona, WI St. Mary.
Reding, Michael A. '97 (STP) Wayzata, MN St. Bartholomew.
Redington, James D. *s.j.* '78 (PH)[C] Jesuit Fathers; [Y] Philadelphia, PA St. Alphonsus House; Towson, MD.
Redlon, Reginald *o.f.m.* '49 (PAT)[N] Ringwood, NJ Holy Name Friary, Inc.
Redmond, Arthur S. '55 (LC) Stratford, WI St. Andrew Retired.
Redmond, Daniel P. '96 (CLV) Chardon, OH St. Mary.
Redmond, Donald *o.s.b* '57 (KCK)[I] Atchison, KS St. Benedict's Abbey Retired.
Redmond, Paul V. '54 (ALB) Retired.
Redmond, Paul V. '54 (BAL)[B] Emmitsburg, MD Mount Saint Mary's University Retired.
Redolad, Esteban '96 (MIL) Racine, WI Cristo Rey; Racine, WI St. Patrick.
Redondo, Carmelito '82 (HON) Mountain View, HI St. Theresa.
Redstone, James '90 (NEW) Retired.
Redulla, Arsenio C. '74 (LUB) Plainview, TX Sacred Heart; Presbyteral Council; Priests Personnel Board; Vicar General Finance.
Redulla, Flordito *s.v.d.* '83 (FRS) Fresno, CA Shrine of St. Therese.
Redwanski, Dale H. *o.s.c.* '71 (DET) Retired.
Reece, Richard T. *o.s.f.s.* '65 (PH)[Y] Wyndmoor, PA Villa de Sales Oblate Residence.
Reece, Robert G. *o.s.f.s.* '65 (PH)[Y] Wyndmoor, PA Villa de Sales Oblate Residence.
Reed, Albert *c.pp.s.* '54 (CIN)[N] Carthagena, OH St. Charles Retired.
Reed, Daniel J. '84 (CLV)[V] Akron, OH Parishes with Ministry to Spanish Speaking: St. Bernard – St. Mary; Akron, OH St. Bernard – St. Mary Parish.
Reed, David '05 (FRS) Kerman, CA St. Patrick; Tranquillity, CA St. Paul.
Reed, Douglas '71 (R) Cary, NC St. Michael the Archangel.
Reed, Frowin *o.s.b.* '07 (KC)[A] Conception, MO Conception Seminary College.
Reed, Rev. Msgr. Michael V. '84 (PT) Pensacola, FL Cathedral of the Sacred Heart; Pensacola, FL St. Anthony of Padua; Chancellor; Promoter of Justice; Administrative Council; Building & Renovation, Diocesan Commission for; Finance, Diocesan Commission for; Holy Name Society; Orders & Ministries, Commission for; Moderator of the Curia; Priests' Pension Plan, Board for; College of Consultors.
Reed, Robert P. '85 (BO) Radio; Boston, MA St. Joseph; Catholic Television.
Reed, William C. '74 (NEW) Retired.
Reedy, Gerard *s.j.* '70 (NY)[DD] Cardinal Spellman Hall, Jesuit Community.
Reen, Jeremiah *s.d.b.* '71 (SP)[P] Tampa, FL Mary Help of Christians Center.
Reese, Benjamin '91 (MIL) On Duty Outside the Diocese; Kenosha, WI Our Lady of Mount Carmel.
Reese, Charles T. '49 (CHL) Retired.
Reese, David '08 (RCK) Elgin, IL St. Mary.
Reese, Edward *s.j.* '73 (PHX)[B] Phoenix, AZ Brophy College Preparatory; [F] Phoenix, AZ Society of Jesus.
Reese, Francis X. *s.j.* '60 (CHL)[J] Mooresville, NC Jesuit Community.
Reese, Matthew A. '02 (ALT)[I] Johnstown, PA University of Pittsburgh at Johnstown; Johnstown, PA St. Patrick's.
Reese, Robert P. '89 (ALT) South Fork, PA Most Holy Trinity; Wilmore, PA St. Bartholomew's.
Reese, Thomas J. *s.j.* '74 (WDC)[O] Washington, DC Woodstock Jesuit Community; [X] Washington, DC Woodstock Theological Center; [O] Washington, DC The Jesuit Community at Georgetown University.
Reesman, Nathan D. '06 (MIL) West Bend, WI St. Frances Cabrini.
Reeson, David G. '80 (OM) Omaha, NE Our Lady of Lourdes.
Reeves, Harold Smith '06 (WDC) Absent On Leave.
Reeves, Joseph '76 (BAK) Retired.
Reeves, Marc *s.j.* '05 (LA)[C] Los Angeles, CA Jesuit Community.
Reeves, Mark Thomas '02 (MIA) Judges Retired.
Reeves, Thomas R. *o.c.d.* (TUC) Tucson, AZ Santa Cruz Roman Catholic Parish – Tucson.
Refermat, Thomas '94 (CHI) Northlake, IL St. John Vianney, Cure of Ars.
Refosco, Fabio *c.o.* '04 (CHR)[E] Rock Hill, SC Oratory of St. Philip Neri, Congregation of the Oratory of Pontifical Rite; Catholic Women, Council of; Rock Hill, SC St. Anne.
Regalado, Luis *o.s.b.* '84 (SFE)[H] Abiquiu, NM Monastery of Christ in the Desert.
Regales, Oriol '01 (MIL) Delavan, WI St. Andrew; Elkhorn, WI St. Patrick.
Regan, Rev. Msgr. Charles W. '58 (WCH) Retired.
Regan, Columkille '49 (NY)[DD] Bronx, NY Passionist Residence.
Regan, Columkille *c.p.* (HRT)[L] West Hartford Holy Family Monastery/Retreat.
Regan, David Matthew '10 (RVC) Smithtown, NY St. Patrick.
Regan, Desmond '46 (BIR) Retired.
Regan, Gerald T. *s.j.* '64 (MIL)[P] Wauwatosa, WI Jesuit Community at St. Camillus.
Regan, James J. *s.j.* '67 (FgM) Chicago, IL Society of Jesus.
Regan, Rev. Msgr. John D. '53 (HRT)[A] In Res. at the Archbishop Daniel A. Cronin Retirement Residence at St. Thomas Seminary; Appointed Members Retired.
Regan, Rev. Msgr. John J. '53 (FR) Retired.
Regan, John '89 (JOL) Leave of Absence.
Regan, Kevin '08 (WDC) Washington, DC St. Matthew Cathedral.
Regan, Michael J. '62 (BO) Senior Priests. Retired.
Regan, Richard J. *s.j.* '63 (NY)[DD] Loyola Hall, Jesuit Community.
Regan, Richard J. '85 (SAN) Retired.
Regan, Robert F. *s.j.* '59 (BO)[U] Boston The Society of Jesus of New England–Provincial Offices.
Regan, Robert F. *s.j.* '59 (PRT) Portland, ME Our Lady of Hope Parish.
Regan, Terrence P. '68 (GF) Great Falls, MT Retired.
Regan, Thomas J. *s.j.* '87 (BO)[U] Boston The Society of Jesus of New England–Provincial Offices.
Regan, Thomas J. *s.j.* '87 (CHI)[C] Chicago, IL Jesuit Community at Loyola University Chicago.
Regan, Thomas *s.j.* (CHI)[A] Chicago, IL St. Joseph College Seminary.
Regan, Timothy J. '91 (DAV) Davenport, IA St. Paul the Apostle.
Regan, William P. '56 (SY)[Q] Syracuse, NY Tommy Coyne Residence Dillon Hall Retired.
Regaspi, Roy B. '11 (NEW) New Milford, NJ St. Joseph's.
Reger, George L. '69 (BUF) Buffalo, NY Blessed Trinity.
Reginato, Julian '64 (GR) Retired.
Regoli, Rev. Msgr. John A. '61 (GBG)[G] Greensburg, PA Neumann House Retired.
Regotti, Benjamin R. *o.f.m.cap.* '79 (PH) Philadelphia, PA St. John the Evangelist; Philadelphia Federal Detention Center.
Regula, Gary R. '00 (PHX) Phoenix, AZ St. Benedict Roman Catholic Parish; Presbyteral Council.
Regula, Ronald R. '57 (NEW) Retired.
Regynski, Larry '95 (SFS) Mitchell, SD Holy Family.
Rehkemper, Rev. Msgr. Robert C. '49 (DAL) Retired.
Rehrauer, Matthew J. '92 (SPC) Houston, MO St. Mark; South Central Correctional Center.
Rehrauer, Stephen *c.ss.r.* '80 (CHI)[N] Chicago Redemptorist Theology Residence.
Rehrauer, Stephen *c.ss.r.* '80 (DEN)[N] Denver The Redemptorists/Denver Province.
Reich, John C. '84 (WH) Mullens, WV St. John the Evangelist.
Reich, Paul A. *s.m.* '57 (BAL) Eldersburg, MD St. Joseph; [T] Sykesville, MD St. Joseph Catholic Community Endowment Trust.
Reichel, Bill *o.f.m.* '61 (CIN)[N] Cincinnati, OH St. John the Baptist Friary.
Reichenbacher, Charles *o.s.b.* '67 (RCK)[G] Aurora, IL Marmion Abbey.
Reicher, A. Paul '62 (CHI) Chicago, IL St. John Berchmans; Chicago, IL Notre Dame de Chicago Retired.
Reichert, J. Lawrence '71 (COL) Johnstown, OH Church of the Ascension.
Reichert, Rev. Msgr. James J. '71 (ALN) Martins Creek, PA St. Rocco; College of Consultors.
Reichert, James *o.s.b.* '59 (SCL)[I] Collegeville, MN St. John's Abbey, of the Order of St. Benedict.
Reichert, Kenneth *o.s.b.* '59 (KC)[J] Conception, MO Conception Abbey.
Reichlen, Gregory A. '08 (SCR) On Duty Outside the Diocese.
Reichling, David *o.f.m.cap.* '67 (GF) Billings, MT St. Bernard.
Reichmann, James B. *s.j.* '53 (SEA)[A] Seattle, WA Seattle University; [M] Seattle, WA Arrupe Jesuit Community at Seattle University.
Reicks, Allan A. '76 (SC) Sheldon, IA St. Patrick's.
Reid, Adam R. '05 (WOR) Webster, MA Sacred Heart of Jesus.
Reid, Gerard E. '77 (BO) Woburn, MA St. Barbara.
Reid, Henry W. '06 (RVC) Selden, NY St. Margaret of Scotland.
Reid, Malcolm '57 (CHY) Retired.
Reid, Rev. Msgr. Michael J. '78 (BRK)[V] Brooklyn, NY Compostela Fund of the Roman Catholic Diocese of Brooklyn; Diocesan Budget Committee; Catholic Cemetery Guild; Diocesan Finance Council; Secretariat for Financial Administration/Econome; Diocesan Consultors; Assignment Board.
Reid, Michael P. '00 (HBG) Deans.
Reid, Michael P. '00 (HBG) Lebanon, PA Assumption of the Blessed Virgin Mary.
Reid, Nicholas J. '11 (JC) To The Bishop; Jefferson City, MO St. Joseph Cathedral.
Reid, R. Michael '69 (RVC) Uniondale, NY Holly Patterson Geriatric Center Retired.
Reid, R. Michael '67 (RVC) Hicksville, NY Holy Family.
Reid, Timothy S. '04 (CHL) Charlotte, NC St. Ann.
Reidman, Joseph G. '56 (IND) Retired.
Reidy, James E. '56 (STP) Retired.
Reidy, Richard F. '94 (WOR) North Oxford, MA St. Ann; Defenders of the Bond.
Reidy, Robert J. '75 (CLV) Cleveland, OH Sagrada Familia; [V] Cleveland, OH Hispanic Parishes: Iglesia La Sagrada Familia.
Reidy, Rev. Msgr. Robert '62 (Y) Retired.
Reidy, Rev. Msgr. Thomas E. '67 (SPC) Springfield, MO St. Elizabeth Ann Seton; Vicar General; Chancellor; Catholic Foundation Of The Diocese Of Springfield–Cape Girardeau; Vicar For The Religious; Catholic Relief Services; Cemeteries; National Shrine Of The Immaculate Conception; Priests' Mutual Benefit Society; Diocesan Consultors; Appointed Member; Nixa, MO St. Francis of Assisi; Judges; Auditor.
Reif, Bryan T. '01 (CIN) Priests On Personal Leave.
Reif, John '65 (ROC) Rochester, NY Holy Cross Retired.
Reifel, Mark *t.o.r.* '55 (ALT) Windber, PA St. Anthony of Padua.
Reifenberg, Philip D. '79 (MIL) Cudahy, WI Nativity of the Lord Parish; Judges for Second Instance; Promoter of Justice.
Reiff, Dale E. '67 (SC) Retired.
Reiff, Dennis E. '81 (NEW) Nutley, NJ Our Lady of Mount Carmel.

Reigle, Gordon P. '05 (LAN)[B] Lansing, MI Lansing Catholic Central High School.
Reiker, John H. '78 (STL) St. Charles, MO St. Charles Borromeo.
Reiker, Robert J. '73 (STL) Webster Groves, MO Mary, Queen of Peace.
Reiley, Robert J. *m.m.* '59 (NY)[DD] Maryknoll Maryknoll Fathers and Brothers Retired.
Reilley, Patrick R. '10 (WCH) Wichita, KS Cathedral of the Immaculate Conception.
Reilly, A. Leo *c.s.b.* '62 (DET) Detroit, MI Ste. Anne de Detroit.
Reilly, Bernard '73 (LAN) Lansing, MI St. Mary Cathedral; College of Consultors; Presbyteral Council; Priests' Assignment Commission.
Reilly, Cristobal *s.t.* '55 (PCE) Coamo, PR St. Blase.
Reilly, David F. '75 (CIN) Priests On Administrative Leave.
Reilly, Denis *o.p.* '70 (SLC) Midvale, UT Saint Therese of the Child Jesus LLC 246.
Reilly, Donald F. *o.s.a.* '74 (CAM)[C] Richland, NJ St. Augustine Preparatory School.
Reilly, Rev. Msgr. Edward W. '54 (STL) Retired.
Reilly, Francis E. '80 (SPR) Longmeadow, MA St. Mary's.
Reilly, George M. '60 (NEW) Garfield, NJ Our Lady of Mt. Virgin; New Milford, NJ St. Joseph's Retired.
Reilly, James F. '68 (NEW) Palisades Park, NJ St. Michael's.
Reilly, James J. '68 (NEW)[L] Rutherford, NJ St. John Vianney Residence for Priests.
Reilly, James '68 (NEW) Retired.
Reilly, John E. *s.j.* '59 (DET)[K] Clarkston, MI Colombiere Center.
Reilly, Rev. Msgr. Joseph R. '91 (NEW)[A] South Orange, NJ Seton Hall University College Seminary; [B] Seton Hall University; Censores Librorum.
Reilly, Kevin M. '03 (NOR) Mystic, CT St. Patrick; [B] Uncasville, CT Saint Bernard School; Seminarian Advisory Board; Members.
Reilly, Lawrence T. '64 (YAK) Vicar for Priests; Clergy Personnel Board; Cle Elum, WA St. John the Baptist; Cle Elum, WA Immaculate Conception; Diocesan Consultors.
Reilly, Liam '00 (FgM) Boston, MA St. James the Apostle, Inc.
Reilly, Mark R. '97 (OG) Saranac Lake, NY St. Paul; Lake Clear, NY St. John in the Wilderness; Saranac Lake, NY St. Bernard; Campus Ministry; Navy Reserve Chaplains.
Reilly, Michael J. '01 (PH) Collingdale, PA St. Joseph.
Reilly, Michael P. '92 (NY)[E] Staten Island, NY St. Joseph by the Sea, High School; [S] Staten Island, NY Mission of the Immaculate Virgin.
Reilly, Rev. Msgr. Patrick '58 (LA) Burbank, CA St. Robert Bellarmine Retired.
Reilly, Rev. Msgr. Philip J. '60 (BRK)[S] Brooklyn, NY Monastery of the Sisters Adorers of the Precious Blood Retired.
Reilly, Rembert F. *o.s.b.* '59 (PAT)[N] Morristown, NJ St. Mary's Abbey.
Reilly, Robert E. '58 (L) Retired.
Reilly, Rev. Msgr. Robert J. '45 (E) Retired.
Reilly, Terence *o.p.* '59 (OAK)[L] Oakland, CA Order of Preachers (Province of Holy Name of Jesus – Western Dominican Province).
Reilly, Thomas A. *m.s.* '72 (ATL) Marietta, GA St. Ann.
Reilly, Thomas J. '00 (BO) North Reading, MA St. Theresa of Lisieux.
Reilly, Thomas J. '67 (BO) Senior Priests. Retired.
Reilly, Thomas J. *s.j.* '95 (SJ)[M] Los Gatos, CA Sacred Heart Jesuit Center.
Reilly, Thomas W. *m.afr.* '78 (WDC)[O] Washington, DC Missionaries of Africa Retired.
Reilly, Thomas *m.afr.* '78 (FgM) Washington, DC; Washington, DC MISSIONARIES OF AFRICA.
Reilly, Timothy D. '03 (PRO) Providence, RI St. Maron; [T] Providence, RI Miscellaneous Listings for the Diocese of Providence; Chancellor; Advocate; [A] Providence, RI Seminary of Our Lady of Providence; Seminary of Our Lady of Providence.
Reilly, Rev. Msgr. William J. '65 (NEW) Garfield, NJ Holy Name; Southwest Bergen Region Deanery 4; Multicultural Affairs.
Reilman, Thomas J. '61 (DAV) Retired.
Reily, Dennis *o.p.* (SLC) West Valley City, UT Saints Peter and Paul LLC 243.
Reim, Daniel T. *s.j.* '95 (LAN) Ann Arbor, MI St. Mary Student Parish; [J] Ann Arbor, MI Detroit Province of the Society of Jesus – Jesuit Residence.
Reimer, Edward J. '67 (SY) Chittenango, NY St. Patrick; Jamesville, NY Jamesville Penitentiary.
Reina, Nicholas J. *s.d.b.* '78 (OAK)[E] Richmond, CA Salesian High School.
Reina, Richard A. '70 (BUF) Council of Priests; [A] East Aurora, NY Christ the King Seminary; [A] East Aurora, NY Christ the King Seminary.
Reinbold, Charles '56 (NEW) Retired.
Reinders, David H. '97 (TUC) Tucson, AZ U.S. Veterans Hospital; DEPARTMENT OF VETERANS AFFAIRS HOSPITALS AND CHAPLAINS.
Reinersman, Gerald L. '79 (COV) Cold Spring, KY St. Joseph; Deans; Continuing Education of Priests; Diocesan Consultors.
Reinert, Duane F. *o.f.m.cap.* '76 (KCK) Haskell Institute; [I] Lawrence, KS St. Conrad Friary; [L] Lawrence, KS Haskell Catholic Campus Center.
Reinert, Duane F. *o.f.m.cap.* '76 (KC)[A] Conception, MO Conception Seminary College.
Reinert, Rev. Msgr. James M. '83 (LIN) York, NE St. Joseph's; Presbyteral Council; Lincoln, NE Nebraska Penal Complex.
Reinhard, William *o.m.i.* '61 (FgM) Washington, DC AMERICAN OBLATE MISSIONS.
Reinhardt, Leo J. '78 (ROC) Ithaca, NY Immaculate Conception.
Reinhardt, Mark S. '96 (PRT) Camden, ME Saint Brendan the Navigator Parish.
Reinhardt, Michael Accinni '01 (PHX) Flagstaff, AZ San Francisco de Asis Roman Catholic Parish.
Reinhart, Blaise R. *o.f.m.* '55 (ALB)[B] Siena College.
Reinhart, David A. '98 (MO) Military Chaplains; Air Force Chaplains.
Reinhart, David (RC) Ellsworth AFB.
Reinhart, James M. '10 (L) Campbellsville, KY Our Lady of Perpetual Help; Campbellsville, KY Our Lady of the Hills.
Reinhart, Kenneth *o.f.m.cap.* '68 (DET)[P] Washington, MI Capuchin Retreat.
Reinhart, Robert J. '61 (TOL) Retired.
Reinhart, Robert *c.pp.s.* '53 (CIN)[N] Carthagena, OH St. Charles Retired.
Reinig, Joseph N. '98 (BAK) Council of Priests and Diocesan Consultors; Central; Director of Catholic Hospitals; Vicar General; Building Committee.
Reinke, Francis P. '57 (GB) Retired.
Reinke, Robert J. '57 (COV) Covington, KY St. Augustine Retired.
Reinke, Robert J. '49 (COV) Retired.
Reinkemeyer, John C. '51 (WCH) Garden Plain, KS Immaculate Conception.
Reinkemeyer, John '57 (WCH) Retired.
Reis, Daniel O. '75 (FR) New Bedford, MA Our Lady of the Immaculate Conception.
Reis, Justin J. '69 (COL) Columbus, OH St. Peter.
Reis, Lancelot '67 (PAT) Haskell, NJ St. Francis of Assisi.
Reis, Michael J. '67 (COL) Heath, OH St. Leonard.
Reis, Timothy P. '86 (FR) Taunton, MA Saint Andrew the Apostle Parish; Taunton Deanery.
Reischl, Fred P. '55 (DM) Retired.
Reischman, Virgil '69 (STU) Marietta, OH St. John the Baptist.
Reiser, Richard J. '80 (OM) Omaha, NE St. James.
Reiser, Robert E. *s.j.* '97 (NEW)[C] Jersey City, NJ St. Peter's Preparatory School; [C] Jersey City, NJ Jesuit Community.
Reiser, William E. *s.j.* '72 (WOR)[N] Worcester, MA Jesuits of the Holy Cross, Inc.; Our Lady of Providence.
Reisert, Gregory *o.f.m.cap.* '64 (SP)[N] Seminole, FL Capuchin Franciscan Residence.
Reising, Christopher (DM) Des Moines, IA Our Lady of the Americas.
Reisinger, Walter J. *c.m.* '55 (JC) Dixon, MO St. Cornelius; Dixon, MO St. Theresa.
Reiss, John E. '69 (Y) Retired.
Reissmann, Richard A. '63 (WIL) Retired.
Reist, Thomas *o.f.m.conv.* '79 (BAL)[Q] Ellicott City Order of Friars Minor Conventual.
Reisteter, William *o.f.m.* '71 (ALN)[K] Easton, PA St. Francis Friary.
Reites, James W. *s.j.* '71 (SJ)[B] Santa Clara, CA Jesuit Community.
Reith, David H. '76 (MIL) Brookfield, WI St. Dominic; Archdiocesan Council of Priests; Archdiocesan Pastoral Council.
Reitmeyer, Larry '89 (LSC) Retired.
Reitter, Frank '84 (ANC) Glennallen, AK Holy Family; Valdez, AK St. Francis Xavier.
Reitz, Andrew J. *o.f.m.* '71 (NY) New York, NY St. Francis of Assisi; [DD] New York, NY Saint Francis Monastery, Inc.; [HH] New York, NY St. Francis Monastery Breadline for the Poor, Inc.
Reitz, Glenn (STL)[J] Bridgeton, MO SSM De Paul Health Center Foundation.
Reitz, Joseph A. '53 (GLD) Retired.
Reitz, Louis M. *s.s.* '55 (BAL)[Q] Baltimore Society of St. Sulpice, Province of the United States Retired.
Reitz, William J. '47 (GR) Retired.
Rejsek, Rev. Msgr. J. Brian '86 (PEO) Judges; Marseilles, IL St. Joseph's; Marseilles, IL St. Patrick's.
Rekasi, Joseph S. *o.praem.* '46 (GB)[J] De Pere, WI St. Joseph Priory; [O] De Pere, WI Canons Regular of Magnovarad, Ltd.
Reker, Timothy T. '82 (WIN) Albert Lea, MN St. Theodore; Albert Lea, MN St. James; [J] Albert Lea, MN St. Theodore Catholic School Endowment; Censors of Books and Periodicals; Commission on Sacred Liturgy.
Reker, Timothy '82 (WIN)[C] Albert Lea, MN St. Theodore School.
Rekofke, Robert F. *s.j.* '59 (SPK)[J] Spokane, WA Regis Community Retired.
Relihan, Thomas '47 (SAC) Ione, CA Sacred Heart of Jesus Retired.
Reller, Gary W. '71 (HEL) Missoula, MT St. Anthony; Episcopal Vicar for Clergy; Defenders of the Bond; Personnel Board.
Remick, Todd M. '06 (BUF) Council of Priests; Chautauqua Catholic Community, Chautauqua Institution; Bemus Point, NY St. Mary of Lourdes.
Remillard, Andre N. '70 (WOR) Jefferson, MA St. Mary.
Remington, Leo '65 (P) Retired.
Remke, Raymond J. '88 (BIR) Decatur, AL Annunciation of the Lord; Propagation of the Faith and Holy Childhood; Diocesan College of Consultors; Diocesan College of Vicars.
Remm, George F. '60 (PEO) Retired.
Remmel, William *s.d.s.* '67 (TUC) Tucson, AZ Most Holy Trinity Roman Catholic Parish – Tucson.
Remmerswaal, James H. *o.s.c.* '65 (SCL) Foreston, MN St. Louis Bertrand; Milaca, MN St. Mary's; [I] Onamia, MN Crosier Priory.
Remmes, Richard R. '62 (SC) Retired.
Rempe, Melvin '65 (LIN) York, NE St. Joseph's.
Remski, Howard *r.s.s.p.* '00 (ORL) Retired.
Remski, Howard *f.s.s.p.* '00 (VEN) Sarasota, FL Christ the King.
Remuzgo, Jorge *o.carm.* '83 (JOL)[L] Darien Carmelite Provincial Office.
Remy, David P. '67 (DUB) Retired.
Remy, Dickens *c.i.c.m.* '02 (SD) San Marcos, CA Saint Mark Catholic Parish.
Renard, Eugene C. *s.j.* '60 (STL)[S] St. Louis, MO Retreat House; [O] St. Louis, MO.
Renard, John F. '65 (NEW) Retired.
Renard, Peter J. *o. praem.* '68 (GB)[J] De Pere, WI St. Joseph Priory.
Render, Patrick W. *c.s.v.* '68 (LAV) Henderson, NV St. Thomas More; Presbyteral Council for the Diocese of Las Vegas.
Render, Patrick W. *c.s.v.* '68 (CHI)[N] Arlington Heights Viatorian Province Center–Clerics of St. Viator.
Rendon, Luis A. '73 (PAT) Paterson, NJ St. Agnes; Passaic County Jail.
Rendon, Mathias *o.f.m.* (OG) U.S. Army Headquarters.
Rendon, Matthias *o.f.m.* '92 (FgM) Army Chaplains; Washington, DC COMMISSARIAT OF THE HOLY LAND.
Rendon, Rev. Msgr. Nicolas '76 (LUB) Slaton, TX St. Joseph's; Presbyteral Council; Director of Scouting.
Rendon, Samuel '92 (LA) On Sick Leave.
Renehan, Rev. Msgr. Edmond M. '58 (LA) Santa Clarita, CA St. Clare Retired.
Renfroe, Frank *s.j.* '73 (ELP) El Paso, TX Sacred Heart.
Renggli, John J. '68 (SEA) Tacoma, WA Holy Cross.
Rengifo, Jesus Orlando '85 (NEW) West New York, NJ St. Joseph of the Palisades.
Renic, Stipe *o.f.m.* (NY) New York, NY SS. Cyril and Methodius – St. Raphael.
Renken, Rev. Msgr. John '79 (SFD) On Duty Outside the Diocese.
Renna, Anton J. *s.j.* '65 (SJ)[M] Los Gatos, CA Sacred Heart Jesuit Center.
Renner, Christopher A. '91 (DEN) Evergreen, CO Christ the King.
Renner, Frank G. '81 (EVN) Sullivan, IN St. Mary; Sullivan, IN St. Joan of Arc.
Renner, Louis *s.j.* '57 (SPK)[B] Spokane, WA Gonzaga University.
Renner, Ralph C. *s.j.* '70 (STL)[O] St. Louis, MO Jesuit Community Corporation at Saint Louis University – Jesuit Hall.
Renninger, Michael A. '93 (RIC) Richmond, VA St. Mary.
Rensing, William F. '55 (BEL) Retired.
Renteria, Javier *sch.p.* '83 (PH)[F] Devon, PA Devon Preparatory School; [Y] Devon Piarist Fathers (Order of the Pious Schools).
Rentner, Randall C. *c.s.c.* '90 (FTW)[H] Notre Dame Congregation of Holy Cross, United States Province of Priests & Brothers.
Rentner, Randall C. *c.s.c.* '90 (P)[B] University of Portland; [L] Portland, OR Holy Cross Fathers & Brothers, C.S.C. – University of Portland.
Rento, Richard G. '58 (PAT) Retired.
Renz, Christopher J. *o.p.* '97 (OAK) Berkeley, CA St. Mary Magdalen; [A] Berkeley, CA Dominican School of Philosophy and Theology.
Renz, Timothy J. '11 (MAD) Baraboo, WI St. Joseph.
Repenshek, Jerome V. '63 (MIL) Retired.
Repko, Cyril *o.f.m.cap.* '62 (FgM) Pittsburgh, PA Province of St. Augustine.
Repko, Joseph '95 (PRM) Bedford, OH St. Eugene; Solon, OH St. John the Baptist; Eparchial Pastoral Council; DEPARTMENT OF VETERANS AFFAIRS HOSPITALS AND CHAPLAINS.
Replogle, John F. *s.j.* '64 (NY)[DD] New York, NY Xavier Jesuit Community.
Repole, Charles *o.f.m.cap.* '43 (BRK) Legion of Mary; [O] Queens Village, NY Queen of Peace Residence Retired.

Reschick, Joseph W. '77 (PIT) Pittsburgh, PA St. Rosalia.
Resconich, Emil *t.o.r.* '54 (ALT)[G] Loretto, PA St. Francis Friary at Mount Assisi.
Resen, William Patrick '07 (KNX) Copperhill, TN St. Catherine Laboure; Madisonville, TN St. Joseph the Worker.
Reskey, George A. '73 (MOB) Retired.
Resko, Blane L. *o.s.b.* '57 (GBG)[H] Latrobe, PA Saint Vincent Archabbey.
Resma, Luis V. '62 (SAC) Vallejo, CA St. Vincent Ferrer.
Resop, Michael A. '79 (MAD) Plain, WI St. Luke; Spring Green, WI St. John the Evangelist; Elected.
Ressler, Clint C. '93 (GAL) Houston, TX St. Rose of Lima; Western Vicariate.
Ressler, Mark A. '76 (DUB) Dubuque, IA St. Joseph the Worker.
Ressler, Rev. Msgr. Wayne A. '64 (DUB) Retired.
Restivo, Maurice L. '86 (GAL) Angleton, TX Most Holy Trinity; Southern Vicariate.
Restrepo, Francisco '88 (DET) Sterling Heights, MI St. Matthias.
Restrepo, George A. *s.j.* '65 (BUF)[N] Buffalo, NY Canisius Jesuit Community Inc.
Restrepo, Jaime Perez (R) Cary, NC St. Michael the Archangel.
Restrepo, Jairo '92 (B) Defenders of the Bond; Idaho Falls, ID Blessed John Paul II Parish; Judges.
Restrepo, John G. *o.p.* '04 (NO) New Orleans, LA St. Anthony of Padua.
Restrepo, Martin '86 (R) Kenansville, NC Maria, Reina De Las Americas.
Restrepo, Ruben D. *c.m.* '97 (LA) Los Angeles, CA St. Vincent De Paul.
Restrick, Jacob *o.p.* '89 (NY) Hawthorne, NY Rosary Hill Home; [DD] New York St. Vincent Ferrer Priory.
Reszel, Marc W. '88 (CHI) Buffalo Grove, IL St. Mary.
Retar, John '03 (CLV) Lorain, OH St. Frances Xavier Cabrini Parish.
Reteneller, Charles E. '60 (L) Retired.
Rethinger, Omer '53 (TOL) Retired.
Retnazihamoni, Joy Antony '98 (ALX) Pineville, LA Sts. Francis and Anne Catholic Church.
Retortillo, Benito *o.p.* '62 (CC) San Diego, TX St. Francis de Paula; [G] San Diego, TX Vicariate of Holy Rosary; San Diego, TX.
Rettger, Thaddeus E. *o.s.b.* '74 (ALT) Hastings, PA St. Bernard.
Rettger, Thaddeus E. *o.s.b.* '74 (GBG)[H] Latrobe, PA Saint Vincent Archabbey.
Rettig, Donald R. '71 (CIN) Cincinnati, OH St. Vincent de Paul; [E] Cincinnati, OH Elder High School.
Rettig, Kevin E. '84 (LA) Winnetka, CA St. Joseph the Worker.
Retzel, Joseph R. *s.j.* '60 (GF) Hays, MT St. Paul's Indian Mission.
Retzner, James P. *o.s.a.* '95 (LA) Los Angeles, CA Our Mother of Good Counsel.
Reuse, Patrick *s.j.* '73 (SLC) Brigham City, UT Saint Henry LLC 225.
Reutemann, John F. '10 (WDC) La Plata, MD Sacred Heart.
Reuter, Arnold F. '52 (LC)[H] La Crosse, WI Holy Cross (Seminary) Diocesan Center Retired.
Reuter, Christian *o.f.m.* '66 (BEL) Oakdale, IL St. Anthony; [F] East Saint Louis, IL St. Benedict the Black Friary; Vienna, IL Shawnee Correctional Center; Vienna Correctional Center; St. Libory, IL St. Liborius.
Reuter, James B. *s.j.* '46 (FgM) New York, NY Society of Jesus.
Reuter, John F. '67 (GB) On Duty Outside the Diocese.
Reuter, Lloyd E. '57 (DUB) Retired.
Reuther, John N. *i.m.c.* '73 (BUF)[N] Williamsville, NY Consolata Fathers.
Reutter, James G. '04 (CIN) Cincinnati, OH Our Lady of Victory.
Revent, Michael (KAL) Benton Harbor, MI Ss. John & Bernard.
Revilla, Francisco '54 (STA) Retired.
Revilla, Isaias *o.s.a.* '60 (MGZ) Aguada, PR St. Francis of Assisi; Censor Librorum.
Revuelto, Manuel '59 (NEW) Retired.
Rewak, William J. *s.j.* '64 (SJ)[B] Santa Clara, CA Jesuit Community.
Rewtiuk, Rev. Msgr. Mitred Michael '69 (SJP) On Leave; Presbyters Retired.
Rey, Francisco J. Arizcuren '93 (SJN)[F] Santurce, PR Casa de Ninos Manuel Fernandez Juncos.
Reyaan, Amandus *m.s.c.* '82 (MI) Majuro, MH Sacred Heart of Jesus; Prefecture Consultors.
Reyburn, Calvin (GB)[G] Appleton, WI St. Elizabeth Hospital, Inc.
Reycraft, Robert J. '75 (DEN) Englewood, CO St. Louis King of France.
Reyes, Andres J. '70 (NEW) Jersey City, NJ St. Paul of the Cross; Jersey City North Region Deanery 10.
Reyes, Carlos A. *o.f.m.cap.* '06 (FgM) Pittsburgh, PA Province of St. Augustine.
Reyes, Carlos *o.f.m.cap.* '06 (ARE) Utuado, PR San Miquel.
Reyes, Eider '05 (PAT) Paterson, NJ St. Anthony's; Presbyteral Council; College of Consultors.
Reyes, Emilio S. *s.v.d.* '85 (SFR) San Francisco, CA St. Kevin.
Reyes, Felix A. *c.r.l.* (ARE) Corozal, PR La Milagrosa.
Reyes, Gaylord '02 (LA) Bellflower, CA St. Bernard.
Reyes, Jaime *o.s.b.* '64 (FAJ)[B] Humacao, PR San Antonio Abad Abbey of the Order of St. Benedict.
Reyes, Javier *o.f.m.* '98 (SJ) San Jose, CA Our Lady of Guadalupe.
Reyes, Jesse T. '07 (CHK) Saipan, MP San Jose Parish; Presbyteral Council; Legion of Mary at San Jose Parish/Rainan i Gef Santos Na Lisayo; Commission on Vocation Team; Prison Chaplaincy; Police and Fire Departments Chaplaincy; Director of Vocations; Confraternity of Christian Mothers; Divine Mercy.
Reyes, Jesus *c.s.* '93 (CHI) Chicago, IL Santa Maria Addolorata; [N] Chicago, IL Scalabrini House of Theology.
Reyes, Jorge A. *o.s.a.* '96 (BO) Secular Augustinians.
Reyes, Juan Alberto Torres '96 (PCE) Santa Isabel, PR St. James.
Reyes, Rev. Msgr. Lonnie C. '69 (AUS) Retired.
Reyes, Marco D. '85 (LA) Lynwood, CA St. Emydius.
Reyes, Noel Beltran '05 (CHI) Des Plaines, IL St. Stephen Protomartyr.
Reyes, Raul *o.c.d.* '69 (OKL) Oklahoma City, OK Our Lady of Mount Carmel and St. Therese Little Flower.
Reyes, Raymund M. '88 (SFR) San Francisco, CA St. Anne; [S] Tiburon, CA Catholic Charismatic Movement; Deans; College of Consultors.
Reyes, Victor J. '94 (ATL) Canton, GA Our Lady of LaSalette; Advocates.
Reyes–Garced, Wilberto *l.d.* '93 (NY)[HH] New York, NY Lumen Dei.
Reyes–Garcia, Jose *o.de.m.* (SJN) San Juan, PR Ntra. Sra. de Fatima.
Reyes–Ramirez, Carlos *c.s.* '05 (VEN) Immokalee, FL Our Lady of Guadalupe.
Reyes Lebrón, Pedro Luis '90 (SJN) Bayamon, PR Sagrada Familia; Diocesan Consultors; Adjunct Vicars.
Reyesmedina, Carlos '87 (DET) Retired.
Reyes Pichardo, Elky '09 (NEW) Newark, NJ St. Aloysius.
Reyling, Mark D. '98 (BEL) Freeburg, IL St. Joseph.
Reymann, James J. '58 (CLV) Wellington, OH St. Patrick.
Reyna, Alan '83 (WIL) Newark, DE St. John the Baptist–Holy Angels.
Reyna, Cecilio C. '94 (LAN) Flint, MI Our Lady of Guadalupe.
Reyna, Marcos '86 (LSC) Truth or Consequences, NM Our Lady of Perpetual Help; Diocesan Consultors; Clergy Personnel Board; Priestly Life and Ministry Committee.
Reynalte, Fabian '87 (SB) Murrieta, CA St. Martha.
Reynebeau, Thomas J. '87 (GB) Two Rivers, WI St. Peter the Fisherman; Vicariate.
Reynierse, Peter '95 (WDC) Retired.
Reynolds, Brad R. *s.j.* '77 (P)[L] Portland, OR Colombiere Community.
Reynolds, Daniel '53 (P) Retired.
Reynolds, Fred G. *s.j.* '78 (NO)[R] New Orleans, LA Ignatius Residence Retired.
Reynolds, George J.D. *o.p.* '59 (SFE)[K] Albuquerque, NM St. Thomas Aquinas (Newman Center) University Parish.
Reynolds, George '97 (LA) Long Beach, CA St. Barnabas.
Reynolds, J. Patrick '80 (OWN) Paducah, KY St. Thomas More; Vicar General; Diocesan Finance Council; Priest Personnel Committee; LaCenter, KY St. Mary; Priests' Council.
Reynolds, Rev. Msgr. James B. '50 (MIA) Retired.
Reynolds, James J. '84 (BRK)[R] Douglaston, NY Bishop Mugavero Residence; On Leave/Unassigned.
Reynolds, Jeffrie S. '90 (BIR) On Duty Outside the Diocese Retired.
Reynolds, John C. '90 (KCK) On Sabbatical.
Reynolds, John R. '83 (STA) Bunnell, FL St. Stephen; Palm Coast, FL St. Elizabeth Ann Seton; Presbyteral Council.
Reynolds, Kirk R. *s.j.* '79 (PAT)[J] Morristown, NJ Loyola House of Retreats.
Reynolds, Paul F. '65 (PRO)[L] Pawtucket, RI Jeanne Jugan Residence Retired.
Reynolds, Rubin R. '79 (BR) Gonzales, LA St. Mark.
Reynolds, Stephen B. '89 (GAL) Sugar Land, TX St. Theresa; Western Vicariate.
Reynolds, Thomas P. *s.s.c.* '61 (FgM) St Columbans, NE U.S. Foundation & Administration.
Reynolds, Thomas *s.s.c.* '61 (OM)[J] St. Columbans Missionary Society of St. Columban.
Reynolds, William E. '81 (DAV) Newton, IA Sacred Heart; Defenders of the Bond; Colfax, IA Immaculate Conception.
Reynolds., George J.D. *o.p.* '59 (SFE) Albuquerque, NM St. Thomas Aquinas University Parish.
Reynoso, Ernesto '07 (PHX) Members; Tempe, AZ Our Lady of Mt. Carmel Roman Catholic Parish; Adjutant Judicial Vicar.
Reynoso, Marco Antonio '11 (BWN) Rio Grande City, TX Immaculate Conception.
Reynoso, Oscar '05 (SB) Redlands, CA The Holy Name of Jesus Catholic Community, Inc.
Rezac, Keith D. '87 (OM) Pierce, NE St. Joseph; Plainview, NE St. Paul.
Rezac, Robert *i.m.c.* '77 (MET)[I] Somerset, NJ Consolata Society for Foreign Missions; Somerset, NJ; Somerset, NJ Consolata Missionaries.
Rezula, Leon J. '69 (CHI) Elk Grove Village, IL St. Julian Eymard.
Rhinehart, R. William *c.m.* (STL) Perryville, MO Christ the Savior; Perryville, MO Our Lady of Victory.
Rhodes, Rev. Msgr. David W. '65 (Y) Youngstown, OH St. Christine; Judges; College of Consultors.
Rhomberg, Thomas W. '53 (DUB) Retired.
Rhyner, Robert E. '59 (GB) Retired.
Riani, Rev. Msgr. Peter R. '55 (OG) Elizabethtown, NY St. Elizabeth; Elizabethtown, NY St. Philip Neri; Promoter of Justice; Deans.
Riano, Camilo *c.m.f.* '47 (SJN) Bayamon, PR San Jose.
Riascos, Eduard *m.s.c.* '10 (FgM) Aurora, IL MISSIONARIES OF THE SACRED HEART.
Ribaudo, Rev. Msgr. Charles A. '67 (RVC) Retired.
Ribbens, William H. *o.praem.* '62 (GB)[J] De Pere, WI St. Norbert Abbey.
Ribble, Rev. Msgr. James M. '57 (SPK) Retired.
Ribeiro, George *s.a.* '67 (NY)[DD] Garrison, NY Franciscan Friars of the Atonement.
Ribits, Thomas A. *o.s.f.s.* '82 (TOL)[H] Toledo Oblates of St. Francis de Sales.
Ribits, Thomas *o.s.f.s.* '82 (BUF)[S] Buffalo, NY Salesian Studios.
Ricafort, Jovencio D. '82 (SD) Chula Vista, CA Mater Dei Catholic Parish.
Ricard, David F. '69 (PRO) Warwick, RI St. Gregory the Great; Kent County Memorial Hospital.
Ricard, Richard J. '98 (NOR) Rockville, CT St. Bernard; Bishop's Delegate for Safe Environments; Safe Environments, Office of; Diocesan Panel of Pastors, Canon 1742; Seminarian Advisory Board; Presbyteral Council.
Ricard, Rodney Anthony '95 (NO) New Orleans, LA Our Lady Star of The Sea.
Ricarte, Antonio L. '98 (NEW) Haworth, NJ Sacred Heart; [C] Oradell, NJ Bergen Catholic.
Ricarte, Basilio Roldan '59 (PCE) Ponce, PR La Milagrosa.
Ricbe, Todd '80 (IND)[C] Richmond, IN Seton Catholic High School.
Ricca, Francis '05 (MAR) Newberry, MI St. Gregory.
Riccardi, Salvatore *c.p.* '62 (BRK)[R] Jamaica, NY Immaculate Conception Monastery.
Riccardi, Salvatore *c.p.* (NY) Crestwood, NY Church of the Annunciation.
Riccardo, John '96 (DET) Plymouth, MI Our Lady of Good Counsel.
Riccardo, Rev. Msgr. Joseph J. '75 (E) Punxsutawney, PA St. Joseph, Husband of Mary; Punxsutawney, PA SS. Cosmas and Damian; Punxsutawney, PA St. Anthony of Padua; Deans.
Ricchini, Joseph *o.f.m.* '64 (CIN)[C] Cincinnati, OH St. Anthony Shrine, Franciscan Postulancy.
Ricci, Alfred V. '80 (PRO) Warwick, RI St. Gregory the Great.
Ricci, Andrew P. '97 (SUP) Superior, WI Cathedral of Christ the King; Board of Directors.
Ricci, Daniel A. *c.m.* '74 (STL)[O] St. Louis, MO Vincentian Residence.
Ricci, Rev. Msgr. Philip C. '65 (PH) Retired.
Ricciardelli, Albert '84 (TR) Brick, NJ Visitation.
Ricciardi, August A. '83 (SCR) Matamoras, PA St. Joseph; Deans; Catholic Charismatic Renewal.
Ricciardi, Robert P. '79 (HRT) Cheshire, CT St. Bridget.
Riccio, Antonio *o.f.m.* '70 (NY)[DD] New York Franciscan Province of the Immaculate Conception.
Riccio, Fred A. '77 (OAK) Alameda, CA St. Joseph Basilica; Pastoral Leadership Placement Board (PLPB); Design Review Board.
Riccio, Fred '77 (OAK) Deanery #5.
Riccio, Salvatore M. '66 (PH) Strafford, PA Our Lady of the Assumption.
Rice, Anthony *s.j.c.* '08 (CHI) Volo, IL St. Peter; [P] Chicago, IL Canons Regular of Saint John Cantius.
Rice, G. Nicholas '67 (L)[P] Louisville, KY Mass of the Air Retired.
Rice, Gregory P. *m.h.m.* '72 (NY)[DD] Hartsdale, NY Mill Hill Fathers Residence.
Rice, John '03 (WH) Montgomery, WV Immaculate Conception.
Rice, Joseph P. '77 (NEW)[L] Rutherford, NJ St. John Vianney Residence for Priests Retired.
Rice, Lawrence A. *c.s.p.* (BRK)[R] Jamaica Estates, NY Paulist Fathers – Generalate.
Rice, Michael D. '64 (KC) Retired.
Rice, Morgan *c.s.b.* '09 (ROC) Rochester, NY Kateri Tekakwitha Roman Catholic Parish.
Rice, Patrick '74 (PAT) Sparta, NJ Blessed Kateri Tekakwitha; Justice and Peace Commission; Presbyteral Council; College of Consultors.

Rice, Richard P. '60 (PRT) Charismatic Renewal Retired.
Rice, Robert A. *s.j.* '53 (FgM) New York, NY Society of Jesus.
Rice, Rev. Msgr. Thomas G. '77 (DET) Warren, MI St. Louise; Office of Digital Media.
Rice, William A. '63 (E) Retired.
Rich, John A. *m.m.* '58 (NY)[DD] Retired.
Rich, John A. *m.m.* (MO) DEPARTMENT OF VETERANS AFFAIRS HOSPITALS AND CHAPLAINS.
Rich, Joseph '74 (SJ) On Duty Outside the Diocese.
Richard, Edward J. *m.s.* '91 (LKC) Sulphur, LA Our Lady of Prompt Succor.
Richard, Edward '41 (TLS) Retired.
Richard, Joseph E. '58 (SFR) Retired.
Richard, Louis J. '81 (LAF) Broussard, LA Sacred Heart of Jesus.
Richard, Normand P. '72 (PRT) Portland, ME Our Lady of Hope Parish; Resource Center; Special or Other Diocesan Assignment.
Richard, Raymond *o.f.m.cap.* '72 (FgM) White Plains, NY The Province of St. Mary of the Capuchin Order.
Richard, Rusty P. '97 (LAF) St. Martinville, LA St. Martin of Tours.
Richard, Theodule J. *m.s.* '51 (HRT)[L] Hartford, CT Missionaries of LaSalette.
Richards, Damian '92 (SAL) Osborne, KS St. Aloysius Gonzaga Parish; Tipton, KS St. Boniface Parish; Salina Diocesan Council of Catholic Women (S.D-.CC.W.); Tipton, KS Saints Peter and Paul Parish; Osborne, KS St. Mary Parish; Cursillo.
Richards, David I. '10 (BUF) Williamsville, NY St. Gregory the Great.
Richards, George J. '95 (NOR) Willimantic, CT St. Joseph; Associate Judicial Vicar; Judges; Notaries.
Richards, Joseph '90 (CR) Fertile, MN St. Joseph; Mentor, MN St. Lawrence.
Richards, Lawrence R. '89 (E) Erie, PA St. Joseph; Bread of Life Community.
Richards, Mark R. '93 (SAC)[M] Sacramento, CA Catholic Committee on Scouting; Judicial Vicar; Presbyteral Council; Due Process; Members; Scouting, Diocesan Catholic Committee on; College of Consultors; Sacramento, CA Cathedral of the Blessed Sacrament.
Richards, Paul *o.s.b.* (SCL)[I] Collegeville, MN St. John's Abbey, of the Order of St. Benedict.
Richards, Peter M. '98 (STP) St. Michael, MN St. Michael; Deanery 11.
Richards, Ronald '04 (DET) Canton, MI Saint John Neumann; Marriage Permissions/Dispensations; Defenders of Bond.
Richardson, David P. '03 (PEO) Peoria, IL St. Philomena; Assistant Directors.
Richardson, Donald '57 (GLP) Priests' Retirement Board Retired.
Richardson, Francis X. '93 (ATL) Cumming, GA Good Shepherd.
Richardson, James E. '65 (WIL) Retired.
Richardson, James W. *s.c.* '92 (HRT) Wallingford, CT Holy Trinity.
Richardson, James '06 (KAL)[A] Kalamazoo, MI Msgr. Hackett Catholic Central High School.
Richardson, John L. '54 (R) Retired.
Richardson, John T. *c.m.* '49 (CHI)[C] Chicago, IL De Paul University; [N] Chicago, IL DePaul Vincentian Residence.
Richardson, M. Paul '91 (ARL) Retired.
Richardson, Paul *s.s.c.* '54 (FgM)[J] St. Columbans Missionary Society of St. Columban; St Columbans, NE House of Post–Graduate Studies.
Richardson, Paul *s.s.c.* '54 (PRO)[O] Bristol, RI St. Columban's Retirement House Retired.
Richardson, Robert C. '71 (WDC) Retired.
Richardson, Stephen S. '03 (BAL) Priests Sick or Absent.
Richardson, William J. *s.j.* '53 (BO)[U] Newton, MA The Jesuit Community at Boston College.
Richardson, Rev. Msgr. William M. '72 (HBG) Lewisburg, PA Sacred Heart of Jesus; Deans.
Richardson, William *s.f.o.* (WDC)[X] Washington, DC Catholic Historical Society of Washington.
Richardt, J. Lawrence '62 (IND) Retired.
Richart, Paul F. '61 (IND) Sellersburg, IN St. Paul Catholic Church, Sellersburg, Inc.
Richel, Michael C. '87 (MAD) Deaneries; Montello, WI St. John the Baptist; Montello, WI Good Shepherd.
Richetta, John J. '55 (MIL) Retired.
Richey, Rev. Msgr. Terrence '64 (LA) Los Angeles, CA St. Basil's; Alcohol and Substance Abuse; Alcohol and Substance Abuse Ministry Retired.
Richling, Theodore L. '71 (OM) Retired.
Richmeier, Garry *c.pp.s.* '83 (KC)[A] Kansas City, MO Gaspar Mission House; Kansas City, MO St. James.
Richmond, Troy A. '03 (DAV) Washington, IA St. James.
Richstatter, Thomas *o.f.m.* '66 (IND)[A] Saint Meinrad, IN Saint Meinrad School of Theology.
Richter, Anthony Charles '03 (DET) Lincoln Park, MI Christ the Good Shepherd.
Richter, David T. '86 (SHP) Monroe, LA Jesus the Good Shepherd; Judges; Church Vocations; Church Vocations Board & Vocations Office; College of Consultors.
Richter, David '00 (BIS) Hazelton, ND St. Paul; Linton, ND St. Anthony; Associate Judges; Linton, ND St. Katherine; Priests' Benefit Association.
Richter, Helmut W. '94 (OAK) Pittsburg, CA Good Shepherd.
Richter, Rev. Msgr. John A. '64 (NU) New Ulm, MN Cathedral of The Holy Trinity; New Ulm, MN St. John the Baptist; Priest Personnel Board; [A] New Ulm, MN New Ulm Area Catholic Schools.
Richter, Kevin M. '88 (SC) Le Mars, IA St. Joseph's; [B] Le Mars, IA Gehlen Catholic School.
Richter, Robert J. '67 (MIL) Personal Leave.
Richter, Robert J. '67 (ARL) Arlington, VA Our Lady, Queen of Peace.
Richter, Thomas J. '96 (BIS) Office of Vocations; Vicar for Deacons; Priests' Personnel Board.
Richtsteig, Erik J. '94 (MO) Air Force Reserve Chaplains; Ogden, UT Saint James the Just LLC 226.
Rickels, Raymond *o.f.m.* (STP)[J] St. Paul, MN Sacred Heart Friary.
Ricker, John Michael '55 (TOL) Retired.
Rickert, John *f.s.s.p.* '10 (LEX) Regina Pacis Community.
Rickert, William '45 (GB) Retired.
Rickey, James E. '69 (PEO) Dwight, IL St. Patrick's; Dwight, IL Dwight Correctional Center.
Rickle, William C. *s.j.* '79 (BAL)[Q] Towson, MD Maryland Province of the Society of Jesus; [Q] Baltimore, MD Colombiere Jesuit Community.
Rickles, Gary A. '96 (GAL) La Porte, TX St. Mary.
Ricks, Paul '78 (SAC) Retired.
Rico, Dairo Antonio '03 (ATL) Peachtree City, GA Holy Trinity.
Rico, Jose Luis '01 (FRS) Parlier, CA Our Lady of Sorrows.
Ridgeway, Kenneth *s.m.* '69 (BUR) White River Junction, VT St. Anthony.
Ridgley, Lawrence P. '02 (BUR) Alburgh, VT St. Amadeus; South Hero, VT St. Rose of Lima.
Ridgway, John *s.j.* '82 (P)[L] Portland, OR Colombiere Community; Portland, OR St. Ignatius.
Ridick, George J. '73 (WOR) Advocates; Worcester, MA Sacred Heart of Jesus–St. Catherine of Sweden.
Riding, Raymond *s.t.* '75 (FgM) Silver Spring, MD MISSIONARY SERVANTS OF THE MOST HOLY TRINITY.
Ridore, Danis '67 (PMB) Legion of Mary, Palm Beach Curia; Delray Beach, FL St. Vincent Ferrer.
Riebe, Bruce '85 (PRM) Brecksville, OH St. Joseph; Office of Youth Ministry.
Riebe, Todd M. '80 (IND) Richmond, IN Holy Family Catholic Church, Richmond, Inc.; Richmond, IN St. Andrew Catholic Church, Richmond, Inc.; Richmond, IN St. Mary Catholic Church, Richmond, Inc.; Richmond State Hospital; [O] Richmond, IN Earlham College.
Riebe–Estrella, Gary L. *s.v.d.* '71 (CHI)[N] Chicago, IL Edward McGuinn, S.V.D. Residence.
Riedel, Richard R. *c.pp.s.* '52 (CIN)[N] Carthagena, OH St. Charles Retired.
Riedemann, Kenneth '64 (SCL) Retired.
Rieder, Donald '55 (SCL) Retired.
Rieder, Michael J. '94 (RVC) Montauk, NY St. Therese of Lisieux; Presbyteral Council.
Rieder, Ronald *o.f.m.cap.* '63 (FTW) Huntington, IN SS. Peter and Paul.
Riedlinger, Matthew L. '10 (TR) Jackson, NJ St. Aloysius.
Riedman, Boniface *s.a.* '45 (PAT)[N] Ringwood, NJ Holy Name Friary, Inc.
Riedman, John '62 (SFS) Retired.
Riedman, Rev. Msgr. Joseph G. '56 (IND) Retired.
Riedmann, Boniface *s.a.* '45 (NY)[DD] Garrison Graymoor Ecumenical and Interreligious Institute Retired.
Rieger, Alan J. *o.c.d.* '61 (MIL)[P] Milwaukee Provincial Offices – Discalced Carmelites.
Riegger, Patrick M. '01 (RVC) Port Jefferson, NY Infant Jesus.
Riegler, Frederick J. '67 (PH) Quakertown, PA St. Isidore.
Riehl, Christopher '09 (KNX) Oak Ridge, TN St. Mary.
Riel, Robert H. '80 (SPR) Springfield, MA Holy Cross Retired.
Rieman, Richard W. '58 (POD)[T] Newton, MA Prelature of the Holy Cross and Opus Dei; Chestnut Hill.
Riemer, Lawrence H. '95 (DAL) On Duty Outside the Diocese.
Riemer, Robert *s.v.d.* '60 (FgM) Techny, IL.
Rien, Robert K. '74 (OAK) Antioch, CA St. Ignatius of Antioch; Pastoral Leadership Placement Board (PLPB).
Riendeau, Alfred A. '98 (BGP) Sherman, CT Holy Trinity.
Riendeau, Richard A. '57 (SPR) Holyoke, MA Blessed Sacrament Retired.
Ries, Carl A. '70 (DUB) Nashua, IA St. Michael; Charles City, IA Immaculate Conception; Deans.
Ries, Donald C. '59 (SC) Churdan, IA St. Columbkille; Grand Junction, IA St. Brigid's; Jefferson, IA St. Joseph's; Churdan, IA St. Paul's.
Ries, James C. '93 (ORG) Fullerton, CA St. Mary's; Council of Priests.
Ries, Richard S. '63 (SC) Manson, IA St. Thomas; Manson, IA St. Mary's; Rockwell City, IA St. Francis of Assisi; Calhoun County State Reformatory, Minimum Security for Men Retired.
Riesenberg, John J. '60 (COV) Edgewood, KY St. Pius X; [J] Villa Hills, KY Madonna Manor Retired.
Rietti, John '57 (JKS) Retired.
Riffle, David '67 (B) Retired.
Riffle, Donald J. '62 (B) Retired.
Riffle, Henry J. '70 (SP) Hudson, FL St. Michael the Archangel.
Riffle, Patrick J. '08 (WDC) Washington, DC St. Peter.
Riffle, Rev. Msgr. Raymond E. '79 (GBG) Greensburg, PA Blessed Sacrament Cathedral; Catholic Charities of the Diocese of Greensburg, PA, Inc.; Catholic Charities; Victim Assistance Coordinators; Diocese of Greensburg – Managing Directors.
Rigali, Joseph *o.f.m.* '58 (CIN)[N] Cincinnati St. Francis Seraph Friary.
Rigali, Norbert J. *s.j.* '59 (SJ)[M] Los Gatos, CA Sacred Heart Jesuit Center.
Rigatuso, Leo A. '94 (OM) Howells, NE Holy Trinity; Howells, NE SS. Peter and Paul; Howells, NE St. John Nepomucene; [D] Howells, NE Howells Community Catholic School; Deans; Deans.
Rigdon, Vincent J. '77 (WDC) Poolesville, MD Our Lady of the Presentation.
Rigdon, Vincent '97 (MO) Defenders of the Bond.
Rigert, James *c.s.c.* (FTW)[H] Notre Dame Congregation of Holy Cross, United States Province of Priests & Brothers.
Rigert, James *c.s.c.* '66 (P)[L] Portland, OR Holy Cross Fathers & Brothers, C.S.C. – University of Portland[B] Retired.
Rightor, Harold W. '02 (IND) Seelyville, IN Holy Rosary Catholic Church, Seelyville, Inc.; Brazil, IN Annunciation Catholic Church, Brazil, Inc.
Rigney, Rev. Msgr. Dennis A. '66 (ALN) Retired.
Rigoli, Anthony *o.m.i.* '72 (NO) International Shrine of St. Jude; New Orleans, LA Our Lady of Guadalupe /International Shrine of St. Jude; New Orleans, LA Shrine of St. Jude Thaddeus.
Rigonan, Antonio R. '88 (MO) Air Force Chaplains.
Riha, Francis A. *m.m.* '68 (FgM) Maryknoll, NY MARYKNOLL.
Rihn, Rev. Msgr. Roy '42 (SAT)[K] San Antonio, TX Casa De Padres Retired.
Riley, Andrew '10 (CHR) North Charleston, SC St. Thomas The Apostle.
Riley, Daniel J. '84 (BO) Vicariate II; Weymouth, MA Sacred Heart.
Riley, Daniel P. *o.f.m.* '71 (BUF)[P] West Clarksville, NY Mount Irenaeus, Franciscan Mountain Retreat & Holy Peace Friary; [Q] St. Bonaventure, NY St. Bonaventure University.
Riley, David J. '64 (BGP) Stamford, CT St. Cecilia.
Riley, Dennis S. '79 (CHI) Other Assignments.
Riley, Edward H. *o.p.* '60 (FgM)[N] Chicago Dominicans (Provincial Office); Chicago, IL Province of St. Albert the Great (Central).
Riley, Eric D. '98 (OWN) Beaver Dam, KY Holy Redeemer; Mayfield, KY St. Joseph; Teens Encounter Christ; Deans; Priest Personnel Committee; Priests' Council.
Riley, Finian A. *o.f.m.* '54 (PAT)[N] Ringwood, NJ Holy Name Friary, Inc.
Riley, George F. *o.s.a.* '62 (PH)[C] Villanova University; [Y] Villanova, PA St. Thomas Monastery.
Riley, James F. *s.j.* '74 (DET)[K] Chicago, IL Detroit Province of the Society of Jesus–Provincial Office.
Riley, James F. '74 (CHI)[D] Chicago, IL St. Ignatius Jesuit Community.
Riley, James H. '58 (BO) Senior Priests. Retired.
Riley, John A. '03 (KCK) Chancellor; Archdiocesan Council on Finances; Archdiocesan Consultors.
Riley, John F. '55 (STP) Retired.
Riley, John J. '91 (ARL) On Duty Outside the Diocese.
Riley, John P. *c.s.c.* '94 (FTW) South Bend, IN St. Joseph.
Riley, John '03 (KCK) Archdiocesan Administrative Team; Ex Officio; Safe Envrionment Coordinator.
Riley, John '06 (KCK) Shawnee, KS Sacred Heart.
Riley, Kenneth A. '92 (KC) Kansas City, MO St. Charles Borromeo.
Riley, Leo P. '82 (VEN) Punta Gorda, FL Sacred Heart.
Riley, Mark J. (BO) Wellesley, MA St. Paul.
Riley, Mark R. '95 (CLV) Painesville, OH St. Mary.
Riley, Miles O'Brien '63 (SFR) Retired.
Riley, Patric '81 (KCK) Eudora, KS Holy Family; Regional Pastoral Leaders.
Riley, Walter J. '06 (WOR) Worcester, MA Immaculate Conception; Deans; Presbyteral Council.
Rimelspach, Jeffrey J. '85 (COL) Columbus, OH St. Margaret of Cortona.
Rimes, Robert B. *s.j.* '55 (MOB)[A] Mobile, AL Spring Hill College; Vicars for Religious.
Rimmele, Leo R. *o.s.b.* '55 (MO) DEPARTMENT OF

VETERANS AFFAIRS HOSPITALS AND CHAPLAINS.
Rimmele, Leo R. *o.s.b.* '55 (SEA) Veterans Admin. Medical Center.
Rimmele, Leo *o.s.b.* '55 (P)[L] St. Benedict, OR Mt. Angel Abbey.
Rimselis, Victor *m.i.c.* '43 (NOR)[G] Bros. & Priests Elsewhere.
Rimshaw, Joseph J. *s.s.j.* '48 (BAL)[Q] Baltimore, MD St. Joseph Society of the Sacred Heart House of Central Administration Retired.
Rimshaw, Joseph J. *s.s.j.* '48 (ORL) Melbourne, FL Our Lady of Lourdes Retired.
Rinaldi, Francis *o.s.f.s.* '69 (WIL) Wilmington, DE St. Anthony of Padua.
Rinaldo, Joseph *s.c.* '67 (LAN)[E] Chelsea, MI St. Louis Center for Exceptional Children & Adults; [R] Grass Lake, MI The Pious Union of St. Joseph.
Rindos, Paul T. '59 (HBG) Harrisburg, PA Retired.
Riney, C. Phillip '48 (OWN) Board Members.
Riney, Jerry '75 (OWN) Bowling Green, KY Holy Spirit; Consultors; Priests' Council.
Riney, Maury D. '77 (OWN) Owensboro, KY St. Martin; [E] Owensboro, KY Carmel Home; Non–Parochial Assignments.
Riney, Philip C. '48 (OWN) Retired.
Ring, Daniel J. '68 (TOL) Marblehead, OH St. Joseph.
Ring, John K. '61 (SFR) Retired.
Ring, Joseph G. '88 (SFD) Riverton, IL St. James; Corporate Board Directors; Ex Officios; Vicar for Clergy; Priests' Personnel Board; Illiopolis, IL Resurrection Parish; Bishop's Cabinet; Ex Officio.
Ring, Paul L. '95 (BO) Pepperell, MA Our Lady of Grace.
Ring, Robert P. '82 (ROC) Pittsford, NY St. Louis.
Ring, Vincent D. '64 (SFR) San Bruno, CA St. Robert Retired.
Ringenback, Gerard A. '72 (RVC) Levittown, NY St. Bernard; Hicksville Deanery; Catholic Youth Organization of Nassau and Suffolk.
Ringenberger, Harry '69 (MIA) Fort Lauderdale, FL St. Pius X.
Ringley, F. John '01 (BGP)[C] Bridgeport, CT Kolbe–Cathedral High School.
Rini, John '67 (ELP)[A] Conception, MO Conception Seminary College Retired.
Rink, George '57 (SEA) Retired.
Rink, Louis W. *c.s.c.* '58 (FTW)[H] Holy Cross House Retired.
Rinn, Richard A. *c.s.v.* '81 (LAV) Las Vegas, NV St. Viator.
Rinn, Richard A. *c.s.v.* '81 (CHI)[N] Arlington Heights Viatorian Province Center–Clerics of St. Viator.
Rinzel, Jerome A. '64 (MIL) Retired.
Riomalos, Mark Aaron *a.m.* (NY) Scarsdale, NY St. Pius X.
Riordan, Rev. Msgr. Brendan P. '70 (RVC) Great Neck, NY St. Aloysius; College of Consultors; Presbyteral Council.
Riordan, John B. *o.f.m.cap.* '71 (NY) New York, NY St. John the Baptist.
Riordan, Patrick M. '90 (PEO) Princeville, IL St. Mary of the Woods; Clergymen's Aid, Inc.
Rios, Francisco Alanis '01 (SFE)[H] Abiquiu, NM Monastery of Christ in the Desert.
Rios, Francisco '91 (SJ) Diocesan Clergy Personnel Board.
Rios, Guadalupe '09 (FRS) Los Banos, CA St. Joseph.
Rios, Juan Carlos '93 (MIA)[A] Miami, FL St. John Vianney College Seminary.
Rios, Manuel D. '86 (NEW) Union City, NJ Saint Rocco/Saint Brigid.
Rios, Matthew *o.s.b.* '05 (LA)[P] Valyermo, CA St. Andrew's Abbey.
Rios, Matthew *o.s.b.cam.* '05 (OAK)[L] Berkeley, CA Incarnation Monastery, Camaldolese Benedictines.
Rios, Ruben *i.v.e.* '06 (CHI) Chicago, IL St. Francis of Assisi.
Rios, Secundino *c.m.* '01 (FgM) Philadelphia, PA Eastern Province.
Rios, Teodoro A. *c.m.* '76 (FgM) Philadelphia, PA Eastern Province.
Rios Matos, P. Angel L. (PCE)[B] The Pontifical Catholic University of Puerto Rico.
Rios Matos, P. Angel Luis '85 (MGZ) Mayaguez, PR Sacred Heart.
Rioux, J. Robert *c.s.c.* '56 (FR)[F] North Dartmouth, MA St. Joseph's Hall; [F] North Dartmouth, MA Holy Cross Residence Retired.
Rioux, J. Robert *c.s.c.* '56 (FTW)[H] Notre Dame Congregation of Holy Cross, United States Province of Priests & Brothers.
Rioux, Ray '94 (SR) Guerneville, CA St. Elizabeth.
Ripko, DePaul *o.f.m.cap.* '53 (PIT)[M] Butler, PA St. Mary's Friary.
Ripp, Anthony *m.s.c.* '68 (PH) Ottsville, PA St. John the Baptist.
Ripperger, Chad *f.s.s.p.* '97 (TLS) Special Assignment.
Ripperger, Harold A. '58 (IND) Retired.
Ripperger, Mark *o.cist.* '93 (DAL)[J] Irving, TX Cistercian Abbey of Our Lady of Dallas.
Ripperger, William '55 (IND) Retired.
Rippinger, Joel *o.s.b.* '74 (RCK)[G] Aurora, IL Marmion Abbey.
Rippy, Robert J. '84 (ARL) Arlington, VA Cathedral of St. Thomas More; Deans; Diocesan Consultors.
Riquelme, Alvaro A. *c.ss.r.* '97 (CHL) Kannapolis, NC St. Joseph Church.
Risacher, James E. '52 (TOL) Retired.
Risacher, James (BAL) Baltimore, MD Immaculate Heart of Mary.
Risley, John C. *o.p.* '65 (MAD)[G] Sinsinawa, WI Dominican Motherhouse.
Ristic, Damjan '07 (BO)[U] Brighton, MA Francis Xavier House.
Ristuccia, Leon C. *o.f.m.* '45 (PAT)[N] Butler, NJ St. Anthony Friary.
Rita, Thomas L. '70 (FR) Judges; Seekonk, MA Our Lady Queen of Martyrs.
Ritari, Raymond J. '83 (PHX) Phoenix, AZ St. Matthew Roman Catholic Parish.
Ritchey, Timothy M. '85 (B) Post Falls, ID St. George's; College of Consultors; Priest Personnel Commission; Priest Retirement Committee; St. Maries, ID St. Mary Immaculate.
Ritchie, David L. '01 (TOL) Genoa, OH Our Lady of Lourdes; Oak Harbor, OH St. Boniface; St. Philomena Deanery.
Ritchie, Rev. Msgr. Gerald T. '68 (E) Harborcreek, PA Our Lady of Mercy.
Ritchie, Rev. Msgr. Robert '71 (NY)[Q] New York, NY Society of St. Vincent De Paul, Archdiocesan Central Council of New York; New York, NY Cathedral of St. Patrick.
Riter, Dennis G. '71 (BUF) Vicars; Dunkirk, NY St. Elizabeth Ann Seton.
Ritt, Paul E. '81 (BO) Chelmsford, MA St. John the Evangelist; Vicariate I; Presbyteral Council.
Ritter, Charles F. '67 (TOL) Sylvania, OH St. Joseph.
Ritter, Eric '03 (SAT) San Antonio, TX St. Dominic.
Ritter, Patrick '74 (SEA) Bellevue, WA Sacred Heart.
Ritz, Eugene P. '09 (ALN) Reading, PA St. Catharine of Siena.
Ritz, Robert G. *c.s.b.* '51 (GAL)[O] Houston, TX Dillon House Retired.
Ritzert, William J. '64 (PIT) VA Medical Center Butler Retired.
Ritzman, Joseph M. *s.j.* (BAL)[Q] Baltimore, MD Colombiere Jesuit Community.
Riva, Gerald '68 (JOL) Woodridge, IL St. Scholastica.
Riva, Paul *c.r.s.* '96 (MAN)[H] Allenstown, NH Pine Haven Boys Center.
Rivard, Robert *f.m.s.i.* '77 (BO) Norfolk, MA St. Jude; [B] Framingham, MA Sylva Maria.
Rivard, Rev. Msgr. Roland J. '56 (BUR) Retired.
Rivas, David '85 (ARE) Lares, PR St. Judas Tadeos; Priest's Senate (Consejo Presbiteral).
Rivas, Jose '89 (NY) Bronx, NY St. Athanasius.
Rivas, Juan *l.c.* '82 (LA)[BB] El Monte, CA Hombre Nuevo.
Rivas, Manuel de Jesus '92 (ATL) Kennesaw, GA St. Catherine of Siena.
Rivas, Rigoberto Caloca *o.f.m.* '82 (OAK)[Q] Board of Directors.
Rivas, Silvestre Rodriguez *o.f.m.* '48 (LAR) Hebbronville, TX Our Lady of Guadalupe.
Rivera, Adalin '77 (PCE)[B] The Pontifical Catholic University of Puerto Rico; Censores Librorum.
Rivera, Adrian Alicea '90 (FAJ) Ceiba, PR San Antonio de Padua.
Rivera, Anastacio S. *s.j.* '74 (SJ)[M] Los Gatos, CA Sacred Heart Jesuit Center.
Rivera, Anastacio *s.j.* '74 (LA) Los Angeles, CA Blessed Sacrament; [P] Los Angeles, CA Colombiere House.
Rivera, Andres *s.d.b.* '74 (SJN) San Juan, PR Maria Auxiliadora.
Rivera, David '10 (CAM) Merchantville, NJ St. Peter's Catholic Church, Merchantville, N.J.
Rivera, Diego *o.f.m.* '72 (AMA) Amarillo, TX St. Laurence Church.
Rivera, Guadalupe '49 (SFE) Retired.
Rivera, Rev. Msgr. Hector E. '82 (MGZ) For Diocesan Administration.
Rivera, Israel '04 (HRT) Bristol, CT St. Joseph.
Rivera, Isreal '04 (HRT)[D] Bristol, CT St. Paul Catholic High School.
Rivera, Jaime '07 (ATL) Atlanta, GA Cathedral of Christ the King.
Rivera, Jorge L. *o.carm.* '96 (ARE) Ciales, PR Holy Rosary.
Rivera, Juan Carlos (TYL) Tyler, TX Cathedral of the Immaculate Conception; Texarkana, TX Sacred Heart.
Rivera, Luis J. '06 (ARE) Vega–Baja, PR Our Lady of Lourdes.
Rivera, Luis J. (ARE) Priest's Senate (Consejo Presbiteral).
Rivera, Luis M. Miranda *o.carm.* '83 (SJN) San Juan, PR Santa Teresita Del Nino Jesus.
Rivera, Luis R. '84 (MIA) Fort Lauderdale, FL St. Pius X; Knights of Columbus (English and Spanish).
Rivera, Luis '83 (CGS) Cidra, PR Nuestra Senora de Fatima; Priests Senate.
Rivera, Miguel '83 (ARE) Corozal, PR Our Lady of the Seven Sorrows.
Rivera, Miguel *s.d.b.* '86 (SJN) San Juan, PR San Juan Bosco.
Rivera, Nelson '11 (WOR) Southbridge, MA Blessed John Paul II.
Rivera, Oscar '79 (CGS) Comerio, PR Santo Cristo de la Salud.
Rivera, Oscar '79 (CGS) Diocesan Consultors; Priests Senate.
Rivera, Pedro '06 (SD) San Diego, CA Saint Jude Shrine of the West Catholic Parish.
Rivera, Raimundo '11 (PAT) Parsippany, NJ St. Peter the Apostle.
Rivera, Ralph *s.j.* '07 (NY)[E] New York, NY Xavier High School; [DD] New York, NY Xavier Jesuit Community.
Rivera, Raymond L. '86 (PCE) Guayanilla, PR Immaculate Conception.
Rivera, Rolando (SAT) San Antonio, TX Cathedral of San Fernando; Somerset, TX St. Mary's.
Rivera, Walter Espinoza '99 (MRY) On Leave.
Rivera–Marzan, Eddie '90 (SJN)[E] San Juan, PR VA Medical Center.
Rivera–Soto, Orlando '90 (PCE) Juana Diaz, PR Santa Teresita del Nino Jesus.
Rivera–Vigo, Milton Agustin '05 (SJN) Toa Baja, PR Espiritu Santo; Diocesan Consultors.
Rivera Maldonado, Jose A. '84 (FAJ) Canovanas, PR Santa Maria Madre de Dios.
Rivera Medina, Juan Carlos '10 (PCE) Coamo, PR St. Blase.
Rivera Perez, Marco Antonio '06 (SJN) San Juan, PR San Francisco Javier; Diocesan Consultors.
Rivera Rivera, Felix '91 (FAJ) Loiza, PR San Patricio.
Rivero, Andres *o.f.m.* '75 (SD) Hispanic; [J] Oceanside, CA Old Mission San Luis Rey.
Rivero, Eduardo *o.carm.* '02 (JOL)[L] Darien Carmelite Provincial Office.
Rivero, Jordi '82 (MIA) On Leave.
Rivero, Rev. Msgr. Juan '72 (FWT) Glen Rose, TX St. Rose of Lima; Granbury, TX St. Frances Cabrini; Deans; Priests' Personnel Board; Priests' Pension Plan Trustees; Clergy Personnel Services; Priests' Care Fund; Continuing Pastoral Formation; Vicar for Priests; Consultors; Presbyteral Council.
Rivero, Julio *t.o.r.* (SP) St. Petersburg, FL St. Mary Our Lady of Grace.
Rivero, Leonides '78 (ELP) Priests' Retirement and Disability Plan; El Paso, TX San Antonio.
Rivero, Luis Ardiel '10 (MIA) Key Biscayne, FL St. Agnes.
Riveroll, Jesus R. *s.j.* '88 (FgM) St. Louis, MO Society of Jesus.
Riveros, Wilfredo '97 (CGS) Cayey, PR Nuestra Senora de la Merced.
Rivituso, Rev. Msgr. Mark S. '88 (STL) St. Louis, MO Cure' of Ars; Vicars General.
Rizk, Antoine *b.s.o.* '96 (NTN) Brooklyn, NY Church of the Virgin Mary; Methuen, MA; Presbyteral Council.
Rizo, Sergio '89 (FWT) Cleburne, TX St. Joseph.
Rizzo, David R. '99 (ALT) Tribunal; Altoona, PA Our Lady of Lourdes.
Rizzo, Giovanni '00 (NEW) On Duty Outside the Archdiocese.
Rizzo, Mark '68 (ELP) Retired.
Rizzo, Matteo '73 (BRK) Brooklyn, NY St. Francis of Paola; On Leave/Unassigned; Douglaston, NY St. Anastasia.
Rizzo, Robert C. '74 (CHI) Hoffman Estates, IL St. Hubert.
Rizzuto, Mariano J. *s.m.* '59 (WDC)[O] Washington, DC Marist Center Retired.
Ro, Matheus B. *s.v.d.* '07 (WH) Gassaway, WV St. Thomas; Maysel, WV Risen Lord; Webster Springs, WV St. Anne's.
Roa, Daniel '08 (SAG) Saginaw, MI St. Andrew; Saginaw, MI St. Helen; Saginaw, MI Holy Family.
Roach, Daniel *o.p.* '56 (FgM) Chicago, IL Province of St. Albert the Great (Central).
Roach, Francis J. '56 (STP) Retired.
Roach, Francis J. '73 (WOR) Worcester, MA Our Lady of Lourdes; University of Mass Medical Center.
Roach, Joseph W. '48 (SAG) Retired.
Roach, Michael J. '71 (BAL) Manchester, MD St. Bartholomew; [A] Emmitsburg, MD Mount St. Mary's Seminary.
Roach, Michael '81 (KC) Liberty, MO St. James.
Roach, Michael '81 (KC) Kansas City, MO St. Therese Parish.
Roach, Thomas *s.j.* '69 (SCR)[B] Scranton, PA The University of Scranton.
Roache, James P. '59 (CHI) Retired.
Roark, John D. '56 (SY) Retired.
Roark, Michael B. '70 (WIL) Marydel, MD Immaculate Conception; Deans.
Robak, Anthony G. '74 (NEW) North Bergen, NJ Sacred Heart.
Robb, Dennis E. '74 (SEA) Aberdeen, WA St. Mary; Aberdeen, WA SS. Peter and Paul; Aberdeen, WA Our Lady of Good Help; Aberdeen, WA St. Jerome.

Robb, Kevin D. *o.p.* '77 (PRO)[O] Providence St. Thomas Aquinas Priory at Providence College.
Robbins, Anthony '10 (LR) Warren, AR St. Luke Church; Camden, AR St. Louis; Magnolia, AR Immaculate Heart of Mary; [I] Magnolia, AR Southern Arkansas University Catholic Campus Ministry.
Robbins, John W. '01 (BAL) Priests Sick or Absent.
Robbins, Robert J. '74 (NY) New York, NY Holy Family; Office of Ecumenical and Interreligious Affairs.
Robbins, Rev. Msgr. Roger P. '63 (SAT) Schertz, TX Church of the Good Shepherd.
Robbins, Thomas P. '74 (COV)[B] Covington, KY Holy Cross High School; Air Force Reserve Chaplains; Edgewood, KY St. Pius X.
Robel, Stanley *o.f.m.cap.* (PAT) Passaic, NJ St. Mary Hospital.
Roberge, Francis A. '78 (WOR) Baldwinville, MA St. Vincent De Paul.
Roberge, Richard A. '85 (MAN) Vicars Forane; N.H. Prison for Men; Priest Personnel Board; Concord, NH Christ the King Parish.
Roberson, Henry '71 (OKL) Retired.
Roberson, Michael '74 (NO) New Orleans, LA Holy Name of Mary (Algiers).
Roberson, Ronald G. *c.s.p.* '77 (WDC)[B] Washington, DC St. Paul's College; Staff.
Roberson, Shawn *t.o.r.* '02 (ALT)[I] Loretto, PA St. Francis University (Loretto); [G] Loretto, PA St. Francis Friary at Mount Assisi; [G] Loretto, PA St. Bonaventure Friary; [A] Loretto, PA St. Francis University.
Robert, Darin T. '71 (LAN) Retired.
Robert, John (LC) Prescott, WI St. Joseph.
Robert, Rene '89 (STA) Fleming Island, FL Sacred Heart.
Roberts, Allan '80 (LA) Los Angeles, CA St. Bernadette.
Roberts, Anthony P. *s.j.* '56 (PH)[Y] Loyola Center and Manresa Hall.
Roberts, Benjamin A. '09 (CHL) Salisbury, NC Sacred Heart.
Roberts, Christopher George '07 (LFT) Zionsville, IN St. Alphonsus.
Roberts, Don J. '78 (SFD) Hardin, IL St. Francis of Assisi; Brussels, IL Blessed Trinity.
Roberts, Edward Arthur *c.s.b.* '55 (GAL)[O] Houston, TX Dillon House Retired.
Roberts, Edward *s.s.c.* '60 (OM)[J] St. Columbans Missionary Society of St. Columban.
Roberts, Eugene J. '75 (TR) Marlboro, NJ St. Gabriel.
Roberts, G. Richard '91 (LC) La Crosse, WI Holy Trinity.
Roberts, Guy R. '98 (IND) Indianapolis, IN St. Joan of Arc Catholic Church, Indianapolis, Inc.; Deaneries and Deans.
Roberts, Joseph '02 (ORL) Retired.
Roberts, Marshall M. '96 (SCR) Unassigned or Leave of Absence.
Roberts, Nathanael *o.s.b.* '03 (RCK)[G] Aurora, IL Marmion Abbey.
Roberts, Ralph *s.s.s.* '75 (CLV)[N] Cleveland Congregation of the Blessed Sacrament Provincial House.
Roberts, Stephen '07 (LEX) Vocations; [L] Lexington, KY The Newman Center Holy Spirit Parish University of Kentucky; Lexington, KY The Newman Center, Holy Spirit.
Roberts, Thomas C. '84 (NEW) Newark, NJ Northern State Prison; Bayonne, NJ Our Lady of the Assumption.
Robertson, Curtis L. '10 (WCH) Wichita, KS St. Francis of Assisi.
Robertson, Douglas C. '96 (LC) La Crosse, WI Mary, Mother of the Church.
Robertson, Eugene G. '78 (STL) Marthasville, MO St. Vincent de Paul.
Robertson, James E. '77 (GAL)[A] Houston, TX St. Mary's Seminary.
Robertson, John W. '71 (HEL) Helmville, MT St. Thomas; Special Assignments; Episcopal Vicar for Canonical Services; Chancellor; Diocesan Tribunal; Judicial Vicar; Office of Due Process; Permanent Deacons; Program of Formation for the Permanent Diaconate; Diocesan Finance Council.
Robertson, John W. '71 (GF) Promoter of Justice.
Robertson, John '71 (HEL) Propagation of the Faith.
Robertson, Luke *t.o.r.* '99 (FWT) Fort Worth, TX St. Andrew.
Robertson, Thomas M. '65 (STL) St. Louis, MO St. George.
Robeson, Robert J. '03 (IND)[B] Indianapolis, IN Marian University; Bishop Simon Brute College Seminary; [A] Indianapolis, IN Bishop Simon Bruté College Seminary; Indianapolis, IN St. Anthony Catholic Church, Indianapolis, Inc.
Robeson, Steven P. '84 (STL) Imperial, MO St. John.
Robichaud, Paul G. *c.s.p.* '75 (MO) Navy Reserve Chaplains.
Robichaud, Paul G. *c.s.p.* '75 (WDC)[B] Washington, DC St. Paul's College.
Robichaux, Rev. Msgr. Robie E. '76 (LAF) Lafayette, LA St. Leo the Great; Judicial Vicar; Clergy Personnel Advisory Board.
Robicheaux, David J. '98 (NO) New Orleans, LA Our Lady of The Rosary; Deans.
Robideau, Jeffrey '97 (LAN)[Q] Lansing, MI Blessed John XXIII Community.
Robillard, Joseph '84 (ORG) Anaheim, CA St. Justin Martyr; Council of Priests.
Robin, Richard A. *s.j.* '67 (LA)[C] Los Angeles, CA Jesuit Community.
Robine, Paul M. '59 (ALT) Retired.
Robins, Dean L. '87 (NO) Covington, LA Most Holy Trinity.
Robinson, Charles *o.f.m.cap.* '70 (GF) Crow Agency, MT St. Dennis.
Robinson, Christopher S. *c.m.* '89 (CHI) Chicago, IL St. Vincent de Paul; [N] Chicago, IL Vincentian Community, Congregation of the Mission, Western Province.
Robinson, David C. *s.j.* '92 (ORG)[H] Yorba Linda, CA Pope John Paul II Polish Center; [H] Orange, CA Loyola Institute for Spirituality; [I] Anaheim, CA Manresa Jesuit Residence.
Robinson, David J. *s.j.* '90 (PHX)[F] Phoenix, AZ Society of Jesus; Phoenix, AZ St. Francis Xavier Roman Catholic Parish.
Robinson, Denis *o.s.b.* '93 (IND)[K] Saint Meinrad, IN St. Meinrad Archabbey; [A] Saint Meinrad, IN Saint Meinrad School of Theology.
Robinson, Donald A. '80 (OG) Watertown, NY St. Anthony; Watertown, NY St. Patrick.
Robinson, Edmund J. *s.j.* '55 (SPK)[J] Spokane, WA Regis Community Retired.
Robinson, Edward M. *o.p.* '41 (DAL)[J] Irving, TX Dominican Priory of St. Albert the Great and Novitiate.
Robinson, Edwin F.D. *o.f.m.* '68 (NY) Dobbs Ferry, NY St. Cabrini Nursing Home; [Z] Dobbs Ferry, NY Cabrini of Westchester.
Robinson, Edwin F.D. *o.f.m.* '68 (PAT)[N] Butler, NJ St. Anthony Friary.
Robinson, Gerald *s.j.* '77 (SJ) San Jose, CA Most Holy Trinity.
Robinson, Jack Clark *o.f.m.* '86 (LA)[P] Santa Barbara, CA Franciscan Friary, Order of Friars Minor (Old Mission).
Robinson, Jack Clark *o.f.m.* '86 (SAT)[B] San Antonio, TX San Antonio de Padua Friary.
Robinson, Rev. Msgr. James P. *s.s.e.* '57 (DET) Detroit, MI Cathedral, Church of the Most Blessed Sacrament.
Robinson, Jerome '75 (MOB) On Leave from the Archdiocese.
Robinson, John C. '54 (MOB) Retired.
Robinson, John '54 (BIR) Birmingham, AL St. Peter the Apostle.
Robinson, Joseph A. '64 (CIN) Cincinnati, OH St. Boniface; Vicarri Foranei (Deans).
Robinson, Joseph P. '68 (BO) Burlington, MA St. Margaret.
Robinson, Ken '92 (FWT) Deans; Muenster, TX Sacred Heart.
Robinson, Lawrence F. *s.j.* '65 (P)[D].
Robinson, Michael '96 (SD) San Diego, CA Good Shepherd Catholic Parish.
Robinson, Monte E. '75 (MAD) Belmont, WI St. Philomena; Belmont, WI St. Michael; Belmont, WI Immaculate Conception.
Robinson, Patrick '91 (PHX) Scottsdale, AZ Blessed Sacrament Roman Catholic Parish.
Robinson, Paul F. *o.carm.* '67 (FR) Judicial Vicar; Judges.
Robinson, Paul *o.carm.* '67 (JOL)[L] Darien Carmelite Provincial Office.
Robinson, Perry L. *s.j.* '72 (OM)[J] Omaha, NE Jesuit Community at Creighton University.
Robinson, Ralph C. '03 (CHR) Absent On Leave.
Robinson, Richard J. '63 (MIL) Big Bend, WI St. Joseph.
Robinson, Robert M. '69 (BRK) Queens Village, NY SS. Joachim and Anne.
Robinson, Tyrone '79 (DET) Detroit, MI St. Luke; Detroit, MI St. Mary's of Redford.
Robinson, William *o.f.m.conv.* '74 (CHL) Winston-Salem, NC Our Lady of Mercy.
Robisch, David C. '62 (CIN) Retired.
Robitaille, Jean-Claude *m.afr.* '73 (WDC) Washington, DC; Washington, DC MISSIONARIES OF AFRICA; [O] Washington, DC Missionaries of Africa.
Robitaille, Raymond '47 (LAF) Retired.
Robledo, Jaime E. '90 (BAL)[Q] Baltimore, MD St. Mary's Seminary & University.
Robledo, Jaime E. '90 (SFR)[A] Menlo Park, CA St. Patrick Seminary and University.
Robles, Antonio *s.d.b.* (CGS)[C] Aibonito, PR Casa Salesiana de Retiros.
Robles, Ariel (TR) Red Bank, NJ St. James.
Robles, Daniel '01 (SPC) Springfield, MO Sacred Heart; Presbyteral Council.
Robles, Juan Pablo '07 (BWN) On Leave.
Robles, Vidal '98 (ELP) Promoter of Justice; Defenders of the Bond; La Tuna Federal.
Robles-Sanchez, Jose A. '95 (ALX) Liturgy Commission; Alexandria, LA St. Frances Xavier Cabrini.
Robotnik, Lawrence R. '57 (COV)[N] Erlanger, KY Monastery of the Sacred Passion Retired.
Robu, Emil '98 (MRY) Carmel Valley, CA Our Lady of Mt. Carmel.
Roby, Brian '96 (OWN) Paducah, KY St. Francis de Sales; Paducah, KY Rosary Chapel; Paducah, KY Mt. Carmel Interparochial Cemetery.
Roby, Bruce '09 (BGP) Stratford, CT St. James.
Roca, Albert L. '77 (MET) Retired.
Roca, Casimiro *s.f.* '43 (SFE) Chimayo, NM Holy Family.
Rocca, Peter D. *c.s.c.* '74 (FTW)[A] Notre Dame, IN Moreau Seminary; [A] Notre Dame, IN Moreau Seminary; [B] University of Notre Dame Du Lac; Liturgical Commission; [H] Notre Dame, IN Holy Cross Community, Corby Hall, University of Notre Dame.
Rocchi, Frank J. '82 (NEW) Irvington, NJ Good Shepherd.
Rocco, Daniel M. '90 (CAM) Pennsauken, NJ St. Stephen's R.C. Church, Pennsauken Township, N.J.
Rocco, Rev. Msgr. Remigio G. '66 (PAT) Retired.
Rocha, Antonio Nuno '06 (NEW) Newark, NJ Our Lady of Fatima.
Rocha, Constantino '95 (FTW) Warsaw, IN Our Lady of Guadalupe; Warsaw.
Rocha, Rev. Msgr. Ivo D. '66 (STO) Tracy, CA St. Bernard Church (Pastor of); Members at Large.
Rocha, Jose F. '04 (PRO) Pawtucket, RI St. Anthony.
Rocha, Michael '88 (LA) Venice, CA St. Mark.
Rocha, Richard '02 (KC) Kansas City, MO St. John Francis Regis; Vocation Office; Special Assignment.
Rocha, Ruben '98 (LA) Wilmington, CA Holy Family.
Rocha, Victor J. '53 (PIT) Pittsburgh, PA Resurrection Retired.
Roche, Amalraj '98 (BIS) New Salem, ND St. Pius V; Center, ND St. Martin; New Salem, ND St. Mary, Queen of Peace.
Roche, David '58 (PEO) Retired.
Roche, John F. *s.s.c.* '56 (PRO)[O] Bristol, RI St. Columban's Retirement House Retired.
Roche, John J. *s.d.b.* '86 (OAK)[A] Berkeley, CA Dominican School of Philosophy and Theology.
Roche, John *ss.cc.* '82 (LA)[P] La Verne, CA Congregation of the Sacred Hearts of Jesus and Mary.
Roche, John *c.ss.r.* '63 (FgM) Baltimore Province.
Roche, John *s.d.b.* '86 (OAK)[L] Berkeley Salesians of Don Bosco.
Roche, John *s.s.c.* '56 (OM)[J] St. Columbans Missionary Society of St. Columban.
Roche, Joseph L. *s.j.* '58 (FgM) New York, NY Society of Jesus.
Roche, Matthew F. *s.j.* '81 (NY)[FF] Staten Island, NY Mount Manresa Jesuit Retreat House; Staten Island, NY Our Lady of Mt. Carmel-St. Benedicta.
Roche, Michael J. '11 (PIT) Pittsburgh, PA St. Paul Cathedral.
Roche, Randall *s.j.* '68 (LA)[C] Los Angeles, CA Jesuit Community.
Roche, Robert J. *o.s.b.* '62 (GBG)[H] Latrobe, PA Saint Vincent Archabbey.
Roche, Ron '61 (PBL) Retired.
Roche, Rev. Msgr. William H. '50 (BO) Senior Priests.; [CC] Boston, MA Sancta Maria House, Inc. Retired.
Roche Alfred, Antony '95 (NY) New York, NY Immaculate Conception.
Rochford, John J. '47 (CHI) Country Club Hills, IL St. Emeric Retired.
Rochford, Jude *o.f.m.conv.* '55 (STP)[J] Prior Lake, MN St. Joseph Cupertino Friary.
Rochford, Thomas M. *s.j.* '76 (STL)[O] St. Louis, MO Leo Brown Jesuit Community; [O] St. Louis, MO The Jesuits of the Missouri Province; Saint Louis, MO.
Rochon, Robert A. '74 (PRO) Johnston, RI St. Brigid.
Rock, Larry G. '00 (BAL) Priests Sick or Absent.
Rock, Martin I. *s.j.* '59 (SJ)[M] Los Gatos, CA Sacred Heart Jesuit Center.
Rock, Michael R. *o.de.m.* '86 (BUF) Council of Priests; [N] Le Roy, NY Order of the BVM of Mercy/ Mercedarian Friars; Le Roy, NY Our Lady of Mercy; [N] Le Roy, NY St. Raymond Nonnatus Novitiate; Bergen, NY St. Brigid.
Rock, Richard J. *c.m.* '73 (PH) Philadelphia, PA St. Vincent de Paul.
Rock, Rev. Msgr. Russell L. '62 (CAM) Retired.
Rock, Stephen B. '74 (BO) Reading, MA St. Agnes.
Rock, William J. *o.p.* '58 (Y) Youngstown, OH St. Dominic.
Rocker, Stephen '79 (OG) Gouverneur, NY Sacred Heart; Gouverneur, NY St. James.
Rockers, Alfred '62 (KCK) Leawood, KS Church of the Nativity Retired.
Rocks, Jason T. '02 (CAM) Glassboro, NJ Mary, Mother of Mercy Parish, Glassboro, N.J.
Rocus, John George '01 (LAN) Brighton, MI Holy Spirit; W. J. Maxey Boys Training School.
Rodak, Joseph *c.pp.s.* '62 (CIN)[N] Dayton Provincial Office of the Cincinnati Province of the Society of the Precious Blood.
Rodak, Michael '07 (PAT) Presbyteral Council; College of Consultors; Hewitt, NJ Our Lady Queen of Peace.

Rodas, Mauro G. '65 (IND) Greenwood, IN Our Lady Of The Greenwood Catholic Church, Inc. Retired.
Rodell, Jeremiah J. '47 (CHI) Retired.
Roden, Raymond '81 (BRK) Special Assistant to Vicar for Clergy; Long Island City, NY Our Lady of Mount Carmel.
Roden–Lucero, Edward Paul '82 (ELP) El Paso, TX San Juan Diego Parish; Presbyteral Council.
Roden–Lucero, Edward '82 (SAT) Defenders of the Bond.
Rodenfels, Jerome P. '74 (COL) New Albany, OH Church of the Resurrection.
Roder, Terry A. '88 (SC) Anthon, IA St. Joseph's; Danbury, IA St. Mary's; Board of Education.
Rodes, Kenneth *s.d.b.* (NO) Harvey, LA St. Rosalie.
Rodgers, Rev. Msgr. Arthur E. '65 (PH) Philadelphia, PA Cathedral Basilica of SS. Peter and Paul; Office of the Moderator of the Curia.
Rodgers, Hilary R. '04 (WIL) Ridgely, MD St. Benedict.
Rodgers, Philip F. '81 (ALN) Mohnton, PA St. Benedict's.
Rodgers, Rev. Msgr. William J. '49 (BRK)[O] Queens Village, NY Queen of Peace Residence Retired.
Rodia, James C. *o.praem.* '72 (PH)[Y] Paoli, PA Daylesford Abbey; Philadelphia, PA St. Monica.
Rodighiero, Dominic *c.s.* '61 (WDC)[M] Mitchellville, MD Villa Rosa Nursing Home, Inc.
Rodighiero, Dominic *c.s.* (BO) Everett, MA St. Anthony of Padua.
Rodillas, Raynato *s.v.d.* '97 (SLC) Bountiful, UT Saint Olaf LLC 239.
Rodis, James '60 (STL) Retired.
Rodlach, Alexander *s.v.d.* '90 (CHI)[N] Techny, IL Divine Word Residence.
Rodney, John *s.v.d.* '60 (CHI)[N] Techny, IL Divine Word Residence.
Rodoni, Rick '91 (SJ) Los Gatos, CA St. Mary of the Immaculate Conception; [D] San Jose, CA Presentation High School; College of Consultors.
Rodrgiez, Manuel *c.ss.r.* '71 (PCE) Guayama, PR St. Anthony of Padua.
Rodrigalvarez, Jose Antonio *o.a.r.* (NY) Bronx, NY St. Anselm.
Rodrigo, Niranjan '99 (NY) Bronx, NY St. Theresa of the Infant Jesus; Sloatsburg, NY St. Joan of Arc.
Rodrigo, Stephen *s.j.* '75 (KAL) Byron Center, MI St. Mary's Visitation.
Rodrigue, Josh (NO)[A] St. Benedict, LA St. Joseph Seminary College.
Rodrigue, Joshua John '02 (HT) Houma, LA St. Anthony of Padua; Vocations; Serra Club of Thibodaux.
Rodrigue, Joshua (HT) Priests Council.
Rodrigue, Raymond E. '97 (NEW) Midland Park, NJ Nativity.
Rodrigues, Amancio J. '66 (P) Lincoln City, OR St. Augustine.
Rodrigues, Carlos R. '95 (BGP) Stamford, CT Sacred Heart; [W] Stamford, CT St. Camillus Health Center.
Rodrigues, Charles *s.j.* '08 (STP)[B] St. Paul, MN Jesuit Novitiate.
Rodrigues, Ignatius H. '66 (SB) Patton, CA Patton State Hospital Retired.
Rodrigues, Jeremy J. '08 (PRO) Greenville, RI St. Philip.
Rodrigues, Joseph *s.d.s.* '93 (MIL)[P] St. Francis, WI St. Joseph's Salvatorian Community (Novitiate).
Rodrigues, Marlon *o.c.d.* '96 (DEN) Centennial, CO St. Thomas More.
Rodrigues, Sabbas '61 (RVC) Hampton Bays, NY St. Rosalie's.
Rodrigues, Tommy '69 (TOL) Deshler, OH Immaculate Conception; North Baltimore, OH Holy Family.
Rodrigues, Urbano '94 (NY) Bronx, NY Our Lady of Angels.
Rodrigues, Wenceslaus '91 (NY) Hartsdale, NY Sacred Heart.
Rodrigues, William M. '00 (FR) New Bedford, MA Our Lady of Mt. Carmel; New Bedford, MA St. John the Baptist.
Rodriguez, Agustin *m.sp.s.* '06 (LA) Oxnard, CA Our Lady of Guadalupe Parish.
Rodriguez, Alberto A. '81 (GAL) Houston, TX St. Joseph.
Rodriguez, Alberto *o.p.* '71 (MIA) Miami, FL St. Dominic; [H] Miami, FL Dominican Fathers of Miami, Inc.
Rodriguez, Alberto *o.ss.t.* '87 (BAL)[Q] In Residence – Holy Trinity Monastery Baltimore.
Rodriguez, Alberto *d.ss.t.* '87 (MIA) Pembroke Pines, FL St. Maximilian Kolbe.
Rodriguez, Alejandro J. '08 (MIA) Miami, FL St. Catherine of Siena; South Dade Deanery.
Rodriguez, Alejandro *s.d.b.* '03 (OAK)[L] Berkeley Salesians of Don Bosco.
Rodriguez, Allen D. *s.t.* '07 (SB) Special or Other Diocesan Assignment; Coachella, CA Our Lady of Soledad.
Rodriguez, Ambiorix '97 (NY) Bronx, NY Our Lady of Mercy.
Rodriguez, Antonio L. '49 (BUF) Retired.
Rodriguez, Antonio Salvador '68 (DAL) Dallas, TX St. Cecilia.
Rodriguez, Antonio '63 (LA) Long Beach, CA St. Lucy.
Rodriguez, Antonio '93 (PAT) Passaic, NJ Holy Trinity; Deans; Presbyteral Council; College of Consultors.
Rodriguez, Armando Flores (FWT) Fort Worth, TX St. George.
Rodriguez, Armando J. '55 (GAL)[L] Houston, TX Pope John Paul XXIII Priests' Residence Retired.
Rodriguez, Arthur '10 (AMA) Dimmitt, TX Immaculate Conception.
Rodriguez, Arturo Perez '72 (CHI) Chicago, IL Assumption.
Rodriguez, Astor *c.m.* '93 (BRK) Brooklyn, NY St. John the Baptist; [R] Jamaica, NY Reverend John B. Murray, CM, House.
Rodriguez, Rev. Msgr. Benigno Antonio '66 (LA) Retired.
Rodriguez, Bernardo C. '80 (BGP) Bridgeport, CT St. Patrick Church; Bridgeport, CT Bridgeport Community Correctional Facility.
Rodriguez, Carlos L. *c.p.* '99 (ARE) Lares, PR St. Joseph.
Rodriguez, Carlos *o.c.s.o.* '70 (L)[L] Trappist, KY Abbey of Our Lady of Gethsemani, of the Order of Cistercians of the Strict Observance.
Rodriguez, Carlos '87 (NY) Bronx, NY St. John Chrysostom.
Rodriguez, Carlos '10 (CHI) Orland Park, IL St. Michael.
Rodriguez, David *o.f.m.* '89 (CHI)[D] Chicago, IL Hales Franciscan High School, Inc.; [N] Chicago, IL Holy Spirit Friary, Order of Friars Minor.
Rodriguez, Delfin '86 (ARE) Corozal, PR Holy Family.
Rodriguez, Domingo *s.t.* '67 (WDC) Silver Spring, MD; [O] Riverdale, MD Holy Spirit Missionary Cenacle.
Rodriguez, Edgar '03 (CHI) La Grange, IL St. Cletus.
Rodriguez, Edmundo *s.j.* '66 (FWT)[J] Lake Dallas, TX Montserrat Foundation, Inc.; [J] Lake Dallas, TX Montserrat Jesuit Retreat House.
Rodriguez, Eduardo *o.c.s.o.* '69 (ATL)[F] Conyers, GA The Monastery of the Holy Spirit.
Rodriguez, Edvin '07 (SAT) San Antonio, TX Cathedral of San Fernando.
Rodriguez, Eleazar Perez '88 (LSC) Sunland Park, NM St. Martin de Porres.
Rodriguez, Emilio *o.carm.* '05 (JOL)[L] Darien Carmelite Provincial Office.
Rodriguez, Epifanio *o.p.* '54 (CC) San Diego, TX St. Francis de Paula; San Diego, TX; [G] San Diego, TX Vicariate of Holy Rosary.
Rodriguez, Ernesto '11 (Y) Ashtabula, OH Our Lady of Peace Parish.
Rodriguez, Fabian *s.j.* '66 (FAJ) Canovanas, PR Sagrado Corazon de Jesus.
Rodriguez, Feliciano '85 (CGS) Pastoral Vicar.
Rodriguez, Felix M. '97 (YAK) On Duty Outside the Diocese.
Rodriguez, Fidel (ORL) Winter Park, FL Saints Peter and Paul.
Rodriguez, Florencio *t.o.r.* '80 (AUS) Austin, TX Our Lady of Guadalupe.
Rodriguez, Francis *o.c.s.o.* '55 (WOR)[N] Spencer, MA St. Joseph's Abbey.
Rodriguez, Francisco J. '10 (NEW) Harrison, NJ Holy Cross; East Newark, NJ St. Anthony's.
Rodriguez, Franklin '64 (CGS) San Lorenzo, PR Sagrado Corazon de Jesus y 12 Apostoles.
Rodriguez, Gilbert '74 (SAN) Midland, TX St. Stephen's.
Rodriguez, Guillermo '69 (LA) Long Beach, CA St. Matthew.
Rodriguez, Guillermo '56 (SFR) Retired.
Rodriguez, Gustavo Ortega *o.f.m.* '07 (LAR) Laredo, TX Nuestra Senora del Rosario.
Rodriguez, Gustavo Ortega *o.f.m.* '07 (LAR) Laredo, TX Sagrado Corazon de Jesus Mission.
Rodriguez, Henry '86 (SD) Unassigned.
Rodriguez, Heriberto '09 (OWN) Elkton, KY St. Susan; Guthrie, KY Sts. Mary & James.
Rodriguez, Hernan Quevedo '97 (ATL) Hapeville, GA St. John the Evangelist.
Rodriguez, Israel J. '09 (BO) Lawrence, MA St. Patrick.
Rodriguez, James '08 (BRK)[G] Astoria, NY St. John Preparatory School; Long Island City, NY Most Precious Blood.
Rodriguez, Jesus A. '93 (ARE) Vega–Baja, PR Our Lady of Carmen–Playa.
Rodriguez, Joaquin '72 (MIA) Leisure City, FL St. Martin de Porres Catholic Church.
Rodriguez, Rev. Msgr. John F. '59 (SFR) Our Lady of the Wayside; Menlo Park, CA St. Denis Retired.
Rodriguez, Jorge I. '86 (PAT) Paterson, NJ St. Mary's.
Rodriguez, Jorge L. '01 (MIA) Fort Lauderdale, FL Our Lady Queen of Martyrs.
Rodriguez, Jorge '87 (DEN)[A] Denver, CO Saint John Vianney Theological Seminary.
Rodriguez, Rev. Msgr. Jose A. '64 (SFR) Portola Valley, CA Our Lady of the Wayside; Our Lady of the Wayside; Menlo Park, CA St. Denis Retired.
Rodriguez, Jose A. '95 (WOR) Worcester, MA St. Joan of Arc; Director of Priest Personnel; Priests' Personnel Board; Director of Priest Personnel; St. Joan of Arc.
Rodriguez, Jose Alberto '05 (AGN) San Vicente Ferrer Parish; Barrigada, GU San Vicente Ferrer.
Rodriguez, Jose Diego '81 (PCE) Coamo, PR St. Blase; Parish Priests Consultors.
Rodriguez, Jose Alberto '05 (AGN) Archdiocesan College of Consultors; Archdiocesan Presbyteral Council.
Rodriguez, L. Antonio '49 (BUF)[N] Lackawanna, NY Bishop Head Residence Retired.
Rodriguez, Lawrence '52 (LA) Retired.
Rodriguez, Luis F. '01 (NO) Metairie, LA St. Clement of Rome.
Rodriguez, Luis R. '93 (HBG) Mount Joy, PA Mary, Mother of the Church.
Rodriguez, Luis *s.j.* '65 (MIL)[P] Milwaukee, WI Jesuit Community at Marquette University.
Rodriguez, Luis *s.d.b.* (SJN) Catano, PR San Francisco de Sales.
Rodriguez, Luis *s.j.* '65 (RC)[C] Howes, SD Kino Jesuit Community; St. Francis, SD St. Charles Borromeo.
Rodriguez, Manuel de Jesus '04 (BRK) Brooklyn, NY SS. Peter and Paul.
Rodriguez, Manuel (BRK) Brooklyn, NY St. Michael.
Rodriguez, Mario *m.sp.s.* '00 (LA) Huntington Park, CA St. Martha.
Rodriguez, Martin S. *c.o.r.c.* '92 (SB)[I] Corona, CA Confraternity of Operarios Del Reino De Cristo, C.O.R.C.; Riverside, CA Sacred Heart.
Rodriguez, Matias '66 (TYL) Kilgore, TX Christ the King.
Rodriguez, Michael '96 (ELP) Presidio, TX Santa Teresa de Jesus.
Rodriguez, Nestor '93 (PMB) Elected Members; Damas Catolicas en Acion; West Palm Beach, FL St. Ann.
Rodriguez, Rev. Msgr. Pablo M. '61 (RVC) Hempstead, NY Our Lady of Loretto.
Rodriguez, Pablo Ponce '02 (AGN)[A] Yona, GU Redemptoris Mater Archdiocesan Missionary Seminary.
Rodriguez, Prudencio *c.m.* '65 (LA) Los Angeles, CA St. Vincent De Paul.
Rodriguez, Rafael G. '04 (MIL)[A] St. Francis, WI Saint Francis de Sales Seminary; Special Assignment; Archdiocesan Council of Priests.
Rodríguez, Rafael *s.j.* '84 (SJN)[A] Sacred Heart University; [D] San Juan, PR Centro Universitario Catolico; [H] San Juan, PR; UPR Catholic Student Center.
Rodriguez, Rafael (ARE) Caonillas–Utuado, PR Nuestra Senora del Monte Carmelo.
Rodriguez, Ray '94 (CHY) Worland, WY St. Mary Magdalen; Presbyteral Council.
Rodriguez, Raymond P. '94 (CHY) Greybull, WY Sacred Heart.
Rodriguez, Reyes G. '67 (SLC) Retired.
Rodriguez, Robert A. '08 (TUC) Douglas, AZ Immaculate Conception Roman Catholic Parish – Douglas; Douglas, AZ Saint Luke Roman Catholic Church – Douglas; Pirtleville, AZ Saint Bernard Roman Catholic Church – Pirtleville.
Rodriguez, Robert '53 (MIL) Retired.
Rodriguez, Roberto *m.m.* '95 (FgM) Maryknoll, NY MARYKNOLL.
Rodriguez, Santos '70 (SFR) San Rafael, CA St. Raphael.
Rodriguez, Tobias '02 (NEW)[A] Kearny, NJ Redemptoris Mater Archdiocesan Missionary Seminary.
Rodriguez, Val Gabriel '98 (AGN) Tamuning, GU St. Anthony and St. Victor.
Rodriguez, Victor Rojas '85 (ARE) Movimiento Familiar Cristiano (CFM).
Rodriguez, William H. '02 (R) Roxboro, NC Sts. Mary and Edward.
Rodriguez, William '79 (LA) Los Angeles, CA St. Thomas the Apostle.
Rodríguez, Wilson Montes '06 (MGZ) Vocations.
Rodriguez–Delgado, Emerson *o.f.m.* '07 (NY)[DD] New York Franciscan Friars, Holy Name Province.
Rodriguez–Fuentes, Rafael '07 (LIN) Advocates; Seward, NE St. Vincent de Paul.
Rodriguez–Hernandez, Edwin '95 (ALX) Hessmer, LA St. Alphonsus.
Rodriguez–Jimenes, Rev. Msgr. Leonardo J. '90 (SJN) Moderator; Subcommission for Ministries; for Administration of Temporalities; Commission for Sacred Liturgy and Popular Piety; Vicar General; Diocesan Consultors; Subcommission for Sacred Art; Guaynabo, PR Maria Madre de la Misericordia.
Rodriguez–Leon, Mario '91 (SJN)[A] Bayamon Central University.
Rodriguez–Otero, Rev. Msgr. Efrain '74 (SJN) Carolina, PR San Fernando; Vicar of Cultural Affairs; Diocesan Consultors.
Rodriguez Ochoa, Leonardo '91 (FAJ) Naguabo, PR Nuestra Senora del Rosario.
Rodriguez Orengo, Rev. Msgr. Juan '79 (PCE) Diocesan Consultors; Master of Ceremonies to the Bishop; Cofradia Ntra. Sra. de la Dolorosa.
Rodriguez Reyes, Jose Angel (SJN) Dorado, PR San Antonio de Padua.
Rodriques, Carlos '95 (BGP) Greenwich, CT St. Roch.
Rodriquez, Feliciano '85 (CGS) Priests Senate; Pastoral

Social; Juncos, PR Inmaculada Concepcion.
Rodriquez, Felix (TUC) Casa Grande, AZ Saint Anthony of Padua Roman Catholic Parish – Casa Grande.
Roebert, Michael '66 (LA) Long Beach, CA St. Lucy.
Roebuck, John H. '76 (PH) Glen Mills, PA St. Thomas the Apostle.
Roedel, Richard P. '59 (STP) Retired.
Roedig, Robert L. '53 (STL) Retired.
Roehrich, David '84 (SFS) Jefferson, SD St. Peter.
Roehrig, Matthew *s.s.p.* '84 (NY)[B] Staten Island, NY Society of St. Paul.
Roemer, Richard *c.f.r.* '98 (NY) Bronx, NY; [HH] Bronx, NY St. Anthony Shelter for Renewal.
Roemmele, Michael P. '11 (TOL)[B] Tiffin, OH Calvert High School; Sycamore, OH St. Pius X; Tiffin, OH St. Mary.
Roensch, Frederick J. '55 (MIL) Retired.
Roensch, Rev. Msgr. Roger '57 (WDC) On Duty Outside the Archdiocese.
Roesch, David H. '67 (MO) Bellwood, PA St. Joseph's; Altoona, PA Veterans Medical Center; DEPARTMENT OF VETERANS AFFAIRS HOSPITALS AND CHAPLAINS.
Roesch, Joseph *m.i.c.* (SPR)[G] On Duty Outside of the USA.
Roesch, Karl J. *o.s.b.* '60 (CHR) Hartsville, SC St. Mary the Virgin Mother; [H] Hartsville, SC Coker College; Deans; College of Consultors; Personnel Committee.
Roesch, Karl J. *o.s.b.* '60 (PAT)[N] Morristown St. Mary's Abbey.
Roesch, Karl *o.s.b.* '60 (CHR) Presbyteral Council.
Roeseler, Brian '11 (COS) Colorado Springs, CO Divine Redeemer.
Roeten, Rev. Msgr. Winus '48 (NO) Retired.
Roetzel, Robert E. *c.s.c.* '87 (FTW)[H] Notre Dame Congregation of Holy Cross, United States Province of Priests & Brothers.
Roetzer, James M. '98 (MAR) Garden, MI St. John the Baptist; Garden, MI St. Andrew; Advocates; Garden, MI St. Mary Magdalene.
Rog, Francis *c.r.* '55 (CHI) Chicago, IL St. Hyacinth Basilica.
Rog, Stanislaw (HEL) Conrad, MT St. Michael; Dutton, MT St. William.
Rog, Theodore C. '64 (BUF)[N] Lackawanna, NY Bishop Head Residence Retired.
Rogaczewski, Dan '00 (ATL)[B] Atlanta, GA St. Pius X Catholic High School.
Rogala, Gerald E. '66 (CHI) Chicago, IL St. Thecla Retired.
Rogalla, William G. '93 (LAF) Morgan City, LA St. Bernadette.
Rogan, Brian '56 (SB) Retired.
Rogawski, Ralph *o.p.* '59 (AUS)[G] Austin, TX Dominican Friars of Austin.
Roger, Richard G. '64 (WOR) Worcester, MA Holy Family Parish.
Rogers, Christopher B. '01 (PH) On Special or Other Archdiocesan Assignment.
Rogers, Daniel J. '53 (DUB) Retired.
Rogers, James '39 (EVN) Retired.
Rogers, James '39 (IND)[I] Beech Grove, IN St. Paul Hermitage.
Rogers, Jerry '76 (CR) Red Lake, MN St. Mary's Mission Church; Diocesan Consultors.
Rogers, Joel C. *c.p.m.* '00 (L) Albany, KY Emmanuel Catholic; Glasgow, KY St. Helen.
Rogers, Joseph E. '07 (WDC) Olney, MD St. Peter.
Rogers, Joseph '54 (DAV)[I] Davenport, IA Kahl Home for the Aged and Infirm Retired.
Rogers, Patrick D. *s.j.* '02 (WDC)[C] Washington, DC Georgetown University; [O] Washington, DC The Jesuit Community at Georgetown University.
Rogers, Patrick W. '82 (MO) Columbus, OH St. Philip The Apostle; Air National Guard Chaplains.
Rogers, Paul E. '77 (RVC) Leave of Absence.
Rogers, Peter S. *s.j.* '74 (NO)[C] New Orleans, LA Loyola University New Orleans; [R] New Orleans, LA Loyola Jesuit Community.
Rogers, Peter *o.p.* '02 (LA) Los Angeles, CA St. Dominic.
Rogers, Philip E. '80 (Y) Boardman, OH St. Charles Borromeo.
Rogers, Robert C. '92 (HT) Lockport, LA Holy Savior; Priests Council; South Lafourche Deanery.
Rogers, Roy (GB)[G] Appleton, WI St. Elizabeth Hospital, Inc.
Rogers, Sean '04 (SR) Petaluma, CA St. Vincent de Paul; Priests' Council.
Rogers, Steven C. '06 (KC) Raytown, MO Our Lady of Lourdes.
Rogers, Vincent M. '93 (KC) Gladstone, MO St. Andrew the Apostle; Deans.
Rogers, Vincent *o.s.c.o.* '10 (WOR)[N] Spencer, MA St. Joseph's Abbey.
Rogerson, David '77 (SEA) Redmond, WA St. Jude; Duvall, WA Holy Innocents.
Roggenbuck, Robert '03 (LAN) Ypsilanti, MI St. John.
Rogina, Walter '85 (SR) Healdsburg, CA St. John the Baptist.
Rogliano, Joseph S. '85 (BUF) Buffalo, NY St. Mark; Buffalo, NY St. Rose of Lima.
Rogmans, Gerard *c.i.c.m.* '55 (FgM) Arlington, VA MISSIONHURST.
Roh, Raymond V. *o.s.b.* '59 (MRY)[F] San Luis Obispo, CA Men's Residence.
Roh, Rev. Msgr. Robert A. '65 (LIN) Falls City, NE SS. Peter and Paul; [C] Falls City, NE Sacred Heart School; [L] Falls City, NE Sacred Heart High School Endowment Fund; Presbyteral Council; Deaneries and Deans.
Rohan, John P. '72 (HRT) East Hartford, CT St. Isaac Jogues; East Hartford, CT St. Mary; East Hartford, CT St. Rose.
Rohen, Patrick J. '96 (TOL) Retired.
Rohleder, Earl '63 (EVN) Santa Fe, NM Santa Maria de la Paz Catholic Community Retired.
Rohlfing, Cory J. '01 (STP) Mahtomedi, MN St. Jude of the Lake.
Rohlfs, Rev. Msgr. Steven P. '76 (PEO) On Duty Outside the Diocese.
Rohlfs, Rev. Msgr. Steven P. '76 (BAL)[B] Emmitsburg, MD Mount Saint Mary's University; [A] Emmitsburg, MD Mount St. Mary's Seminary.
Rohling, Rev. Msgr. Paul L. '75 (BIR) Birmingham, AL Our Lady of the Valley; [I] Birmingham, AL Catholic Housing of Birmingham, Inc.; Diocesan College of Vicars; Judges; Priests'/Presbyteral Council; Diocesan College of Consultors.
Rohlman, Seraphim Ralph (BGP) Bridgeport, CT Our Lady of Good Counsel.
Rohloff, Ivan (FgM) Mount Saint Francis, IN Province of Our Lady of Consolation.
Rohr, Jerome M. '94 (DEN) Denver, CO St. Rose of Lima; Deaneries.
Rohr, Richard *o.f.m.* '70 (SFE) Albuquerque, NM Holy Family; [L] Albuquerque, NM Center for Action and Contemplation; [H] Albuquerque, NM The Province of Our Lady of Guadalupe.
Rohrer, Richard '94 (PSC) Cary, NC SS. Cyril & Methodius Byzantine Catholic.
Rohrich, Robert R. *c.m.* '61 (CHI)[N] Chicago DePaul Vincentian Residence.
Rohrkemper, Charles '43 (CIN)[N] Carthagena, OH St. Charles Retired.
Roia, Martino *s.x.* '82 (FgM)[N] Wayne Xaverian Missionary Fathers; Wayne, NJ XAVERIAN MISSIONARY FATHERS.
Roig, Vicente Perez '58 (PCE) Coamo, PR St. Blase.
Roig Lorenzo, Ricardo Augusto '97 (SJN) Judicial Vicar; Guaynabo, PR Maria Madre de la Misericordia; Diocesan Consultors.
Rojas, Arthur F. '06 (NY) Yonkers, NY St. Joseph Parish.
Rojas, Benito *m.s.p.* '03 (LA) Los Angeles, CA Our Lady of Solitude.
Rojas, Carlos '06 (SP) Elected Parochial Vicars; Brandon, FL Church of the Nativity.
Rojas, Francisco '85 (MIL)[T] Waukesha, WI Schoenstatt Fathers.
Rojas, Hugo Marcelo '97 (SJ) Gilroy, CA St. Mary.
Rojas, Joaquín J. *m.n.m.* '02 (ARE) Quebradillas, PR Our Lady of Monserrate.
Rojas, Juan Carlos *c.s.b.* '06 (GAL)[O] Sugar Land Basilian Mission Center.
Rojas, Loreto Bong '00 (SAC) Davis, CA St. James; Vicars Forane.
Rojas, Louis E. *s.a.c.* (NSH) Columbia, TN St. Catherine.
Rojas, Melquiades '91 (ARE) Manati, PR Our Savior; Diocesan Consultors.
Rojas, Oscar Borda '99 (CHR) Greer, SC Blessed Trinity; Spartanburg, SC Jesus Our Risen Savior.
Rojas, Roberto P. *c.s.b.* '98 (GAL)[O] Sugar Land Basilian Mission Center.
Rojas, Roberto '96 (SJ) On Leave of Absence.
Rojas, Tito Nels '68 (ORL) Retired.
Rojas, Victor '85 (ARE) Barceloneta, PR Church of Our Lady of Mt. Carmel; Diocesan Consultors; Priest's Senate (Consejo Presbiteral); Pastoral Vocational Program; Seminary Board and Vocation Program.
Rojas Hidalgo, Jaime '86 (PCE) Patillas, PR Inmaculado Corazon de Maria.
Rojas Paniagua, Oscar E. *c.ss.r* '87 (CHL) Concord, NC St. James.
Rokosz, Charles W. '70 (SCR) Duryea, PA Nativity of Our Lord Parish; Duryea, PA Sacred Heart of Jesus.
Roland, Glynn (Bud) '99 (AUS) Austin, TX St. John Neumann; Associate Directors; Austin South.
Roldan, Joseph L. '02 (TR) Trenton, NJ St. Mary Cathedral; Mount Holly, NJ Christ the Redeemer.
Roldan, Jovito B. '98 (STO) Judicial Vicar; Tracy, CA St. Bernard Church (Pastor of).
Roldan, Juan '56 (SJN) On Duty Outside the Archdiocese.
Roleau, Francis (NOR) Chaplain and Director of Twinning in Haiti.
Roleke, H. James *s.j.* '62 (BUF) Buffalo, NY St. Michael.
Rolewicz, Richard S. *m.m.* '65 (FgM) Maryknoll, NY MARYKNOLL.
Rolf, Rev. Msgr. John J. '57 (LEX) Retired.
Rolfes, Robert '77 (SCL) Personnel Committee; St. Cloud, MN St. Mary Help of Christians; Vicar General; Judges; Notaries; Diocesan Corporate Board; Diocesan Finance Council; Presbyteral Council; Clerical Aid Association; Diocesan Priests Pension Plan Trustees; Director of Retired Priests; Legion of Decency; Defensor Vinculi; Diocesan Planning Council; Diocesan Consultors.
Rolfs, Richard W. *s.j.* '61 (LA)[C] Los Angeles, CA Jesuit Community.
Rolheiser, Ronald *o.m.i.* '72 (SAT)[C] San Antonio, TX Oblate School of Theology; [C] San Antonio, TX The United Colleges of San Antonio; [L] San Antonio, TX.
Roll, Bertin *o.f.m.cap.* '42 (PIT)[M] Pittsburgh, PA St. Augustine Friary Retired.
Roll, Robert J. '77 (CHI) Chicago, IL St. Bride.
Rolland, Daniel *o.p.* '93 (P) Eugene, OR St. Thomas More Church; [P] Eugene, OR University of Oregon (Eugene).
Rolland, Michael *o.p.* '93 (FgM) Oakland, CA Province of the Holy Name (Western Dominican Province).
Roller, John W. '60 (CHI) Mt. Prospect, IL St. Emily Retired.
Rolling, Brendan *o.s.b.* '00 (KCK)[A] Atchison, KS Benedictine College; [I] Atchison, KS St. Benedict's Abbey.
Rolling, Matthew M. '10 (LIN) Nebraska City, NE St. Mary's; Advocates; Apostolate to the Spanish Speaking.
Rolon, Alfredo '02 (MIA) Coral Gables, FL Little Flower.
Rolon Torres, Julio A. '93 (PCE)[A] Ponce, PR Diocesan Seminary Regina Cleri; [B] The Pontifical Catholic University of Puerto Rico.
Rolph, Edward *s.p.* '70 (STL)[O] Saint Louis, MO Servants of the Paraclete.
Rolwing, Rev. Msgr. Richard C. '53 (SPC) Retired.
Rom, Gregory A. '75 (CHI) Chicago, IL St. Felicitas.
Roman, Carlos '89 (PCE) On Duty Outside the Diocese.
Roman, Charles '70 (HEL) Retired.
Roman, Darrell '93 (DET) Detroit, MI St. Josaphat; Detroit, MI St. Joseph; Detroit, MI Sweetest Heart of Mary.
Roman, Jorge A. '81 (STO) Tracy, CA St. Bernard Church (Pastor of).
Roman, Jose Antonio Landrau '90 (SJN) San Juan, PR San Francisco de Monte Alvernia.
Roman, Julio '73 (LA) Retired.
Roman, Manuel R. '56 (BAL) Retired.
Roman, Paul *f.s.s.p.* '99 (BWN) Weslaco, TX San Martin de Porres.
Roman, Pedro *o.p.* '84 (VEN) Naples, FL St. Peter the Apostle.
Roman, Stephen '57 (SEA) Aberdeen, WA St. Jerome Retired.
Roman, Thomas J. '10 (BUF) Wellsville, NY Immaculate Conception.
Roman, Victor '84 (DET) Newport, MI St. Charles Borromeo.
Romanek, Janusz '07 (MAR) Goetzville, MI Sacred Heart; Goetzville, MI St. Stanislaus Kostka.
Romanello, Carmelo '06 (MIA) Navy Chaplains; On Leave.
Romano, Blase *t.o.r.* '89 (ORL) Mount Dora, FL St. Patrick's.
Romano, Charles '79 (RVC) East Rockaway, NY St. Raymond's.
Romano, Eugene C. '57 (PAT)[Q] Paterson, NJ Cor Jesu Mission Fund Inc; [J] Chester, NJ Hermits of Bethlehem in the Heart of Jesus.
Romano, Harry A. '57 (PH) Retired.
Romano, Joseph E. '90 (BUR) Retired.
Romano, Joseph L. '63 (DET) Retired.
Romano, Michael M. '07 (CAM)[A] Haddonfield, NJ Paul VI High School, Haddon Township, N.J.; Office of Vocations; Continuing Education & Spiritual Formation of Priests (CESF); Cherry Hill, NJ St. Mary's R.C. Church, Delaware Township, N.J.
Romano, Philip *o.f.m.cap.* '94 (NY)[DD] Yonkers, NY St. Clare Friary.
Romano, Robert J. '77 (BRK) Police Department.
Romano, Rev. Msgr. Robert '78 (BRK) Brooklyn, NY Our Lady of Guadalupe.
Romanoski, Joseph V. '86 (MET) South Amboy, NJ Sacred Heart.
Romanowski, Brian J. '03 (NOR) Oakdale, CT Our Lady of the Lakes; On Duty Outside the Diocese; Members; Auditor/Assessors.
Romanowski, Jerome C. '64 (CAM) Retired.
Romanowski, Slawomir *c.ss.r.* '99 (MET) Manville, NJ Christ the King.
Romans, Jeffrey V. '03 (HRT) Assistant Chancellor; Special and other Archdiocesan Assignment; Secretary to the Archbishop.
Romanski, Aloysius *o.f.m.conv.* '57 (CHI)[L] Lake Zurich, IL Mt. St. Joseph Home.
Romanski, Edward '75 (CHI) Harvey, IL St. John the Baptist.
Romanski, Gregory A. '77 (AUS) Retired.
Romanyuk, Ruslan '09 (PHU) Cherry Hill, NJ St. Michael's; Cherry Hill, NJ SS. Peter and Paul.

Romea, Jonas '82 (SFE) Albuquerque, NM Queen of Heaven.
Romeo, Peter '72 (RPM) Promoter of Justice.
Romeo, Peter '72 (RNO) Judges.
Romeo, Robert A. '87 (RVC) Sea Cliff, NY St. Boniface Martyr; Procurator & Advocates.
Romeo, Robert '87 (RVC) Oyster Bay Deanery.
Romerde, Manuel R. '08 (NEW) On Duty Outside the Archdiocese.
Romero, Alejandro *c.s.b.* '00 (GAL)[O] Sugar Land Basilian Mission Center.
Romero, Anthony E. '05 (SFE) Retired.
Romero, David H. *s.j.* '91 (NO)[R] New Orleans Jesuit Provincial Office.
Romero, Domingo *o.f.m.cap.* '00 (FWT) Fort Worth, TX Our Lady of Guadalupe; Mission Council.
Romero, Donald '91 (DEN) Air Force Chaplains; On Duty Outside the Archdiocese.
Romero, Elmer '03 (CHI) Chicago, IL St. Mark.
Romero, Gilbert Claude '61 (LA) Retired.
Romero, Rev. Msgr. J. Robert '75 (LAF) Eunice, LA St. Anthony of Padua; Eunice, LA Annunciation of the B.V.M.
Romero, Jose *o.s.a.* '77 (GAL) Pasadena, TX St. Juan Diego.
Romero, Joseph J. '69 (BEA) Retired.
Romero, Juan R. '64 (LA) Retired.
Romero, M. Ross *s.j.* '05 (OM)[J] Omaha, NE Jesuit Community at Creighton University.
Romero, Marion P. '90 (LAF) Ville Platte, LA Our Lady Queen of All Saints.
Romero, Marion '90 (LAF) Absent on Sick Leave.
Romero, P. Jesus *sch.p.* '03 (PCE)[C] Coto Laurel, PR Colegio Ponceno.
Romero, Ruben '91 (LSC) Hobbs, NM Our Lady of Guadalupe.
Romero–Rios, Adolfo '88 (NY) Bronx, NY St. Pius V.
Romfh, Paul *o.s.b.* '63 (SP)[N] Saint Leo, FL St. Leo Abbey.
Romito, Rev. Msgr. Donald '74 (ORG) Irvine, CA St. John Neumann; Clergy Personnel Board.
Romke, Keith D. '11 (RCK) Batavia, IL Holy Cross.
Romo, Antonio *s.v.d.* '05 (MEM) Memphis, TN St. Joseph's; Memphis, TN Sacred Heart Church.
Romo, Jose Valdez *m.s.c.* '95 (LA) Los Angeles, CA San Miguel.
Romo, Sergio '93 (CHI) Chicago, IL St. Andrew.
Romo–Romo, Antonio *s.v.d.* '05 (MEM)[F] Memphis, TN Society of the Divine Word (Chicago Province).
Romuals, Vincent *s.r.c.* '91 (AUS) Killeen, TX St. Joseph.
Romza, Rev. Msgr. Victor G. '54 (PBR) Campbell, OH St. Michael.
Ronaghan, John J. '80 (BO) Quincy, MA St. Ann; Presbyteral Council.
Ronald, Rev. Msgr. Roy K. '60 (BUF) Retired.
Ronan, Gerald C. '74 (PH) Hatboro, PA St. John Bosco.
Ronan, Rev. Msgr. Hugh F. '61 (TR)[N] Trenton, NJ Villa Vianney Retired.
Ronan, James J. '82 (BO) Charlestown, MA St. Mary – St. Catherine of Siena.
Roncancio, Luis Alphonse '95 (TYL) Nacogdoches, TX Our Lady of Guadalupe.
Roncase, Robert A. '82 (PH) Pennsburg, PA St. Philip Neri.
Ronchi, Vincenzo *c.s.* '91 (PMB) Delray Beach, FL Our Lady Queen of Peace.
Rondeau, Lawrence J. '58 (BO) Salem, MA St. James; Senior Priests. Retired.
Roney, George '78 (LUB) Stamford, TX St. Ann; Priests' Pension Board.
Ronik, Rev. Msgr. Michael '57 (Y) Retired.
Ronquest, Rev. Msgr. John T. '45 (STL) Retired.
Roock, John D. '59 (SY)[Q] Syracuse, NY Tommy Coyne Residence Dillon Hall Retired.
Roodbeen, Henry W. '75 (DET) Retired.
Roof, Francis M. '72 (MO) DEPARTMENT OF VETERANS AFFAIRS HOSPITALS AND CHAPLAINS.
Roof, Frank '72 (OWN) On Duty Outside the Diocese.
Rookey, Peter M. *o.s.m.* '41 (CHI)[N] Berwyn, IL St. Bonfilius Priory.
Rooks, Charles W. '52 (COV) Retired.
Rooney, Aidan R. *c.m.* '84 (FgM) Philadelphia, PA Eastern Province.
Rooney, Aidan R. *c.m.* '84 (PH)[Y].
Rooney, Donald J. '94 (ARL) Fredericksburg, VA St. Mary of the Immaculate Conception; Ecumenical and Interreligious Affairs Commission; Fredericksburg, VA Catholic Association of Diocesan Ecumenical and Interreligious Officers (CADEIO).
Rooney, Edward K. '62 (STA) Diocesan Schools and Social Action Appeal Retired.
Rooney, Edward '62 (STA) Presbyteral Council.
Rooney, Francis V. *s.j.* '60 (NY)[DD] New York, NY Murray–Weigel Hall.
Rooney, John C. '89 (LIN) Shelby, NE Sacred Heart; Building Commission; Deaneries and Deans; Commission on Alcohol and Drug Abuse.
Rooney, John J. '62 (ALB) Retired.
Rooney, John '01 (GAL) Missouri City, TX St. Angela Merici.
Rooney, Jordon *o.carm.* '54 (JOL)[L] Darien Carmelite Provincial Office.
Rooney, Joseph S. *s.j.* '66 (SLC) Payson, UT Saint Patrick LLC 257; Payson, UT San Andres LLC 212.
Rooney, Kevin E. '62 (BUR) Northfield, VT St. John the Evangelist.
Rooney, Martin *m.s.a.* '93 (NOR)[G] Cromwell Society of the Missionaries of the Holy Apostles.
Rooney, Martin '93 (PAT) Paterson, NJ St. Joseph Hospital; [K] Paterson, NJ St. Joseph's Hospital and Medical Center; Office of Health Care Ministry.
Rooney, Robert B. '63 (GI) Retired.
Rooney, Ryan '11 (SPR) Westfield, MA St. Mary's.
Rooney, Sean *s.d.b.* '66 (NY)[DD] New Rochelle, NY Salesian Provincial House.
Rooney, Stephen '85 (DET) Temperance, MI Our Lady of Mt. Carmel.
Rooney, William J. *o.f.m.* '81 (CLV)[N] Brooklyn, OH St. Anthony of Padua Friary; Lakewood, OH Transfiguration.
Roos, Rev. Msgr. H. Jules '56 (PIT) On Duty Outside the Diocese.
Roos, John R. '55 (ALB) Cherry Valley, NY St. Thomas the Apostle; Censor Librorum Retired.
Roos, Rev. Msgr. Jules '56 (FgM) Boston, MA St. James the Apostle, Inc.
Roos, Lee R. '90 (ARL) Arlington, VA St. Agnes; Adjutant Judicial Vicar; Diocesan Judges.
Roos, Richard H. *s.j.* '74 (BO)[U] Brighton, MA Miguel Pro House.
Roost, Joseph F. '89 (DAV) Marengo, IA St. Patrick's; North English, IA St. Joseph's; Williamsburg, IA St. Mary's.
Root, Rev. Msgr. James A. '84 (SAM) Brooklyn, NY Cathedral of Our Lady of Lebanon; Presbyteral Council; Protopresbyters (Deans).
Root, Richard '90 (SPK) Clarkston, WA Holy Family.
Ropel, Mark *s.o.l.t.* '02 (FAR) Belcourt, ND St. Ann; Belcourt, ND St. Anthony; Belcourt, ND St. Ann.
Roppolo, Rev. Msgr. Ignatius M. '54 (NO) Retired.
Roque, Alejandro *o.m.i.* '88 (MIA) Miramar, FL St. Stephen; Religious Priests.
Roque, Reynaldo '86 (SD) Imperial, CA Saint Anthony of Padua Catholic Parish Imperial.
Roque–Torres, Sigifredo Martin '02 (LA) Bell Gardens, CA St. Gertrude.
Ros, Manuel '60 (BRK) Corona, NY Our Lady of Sorrows Retired.
Rosa, Rev. Msgr. Joseph R. '76 (BRK) Legion of Mary Retired.
Rosa, Rev. Msgr. Joseph '76 (BRK) Brooklyn, NY Most Precious Blood.
Rosa, Michak '05 (CHI) Chicago, IL St. Ferdinand.
Rosa, Salvatore J. '68 (HRT)[A] In Res. at the Archbishop Daniel A. Cronin Retirement Residence at St. Thomas Seminary Retired.
Rosado, Adaly '11 (NY) Goshen, NY St. John the Evangelist.
Rosado Sosa, Amilcar Matias '91 (E) Erie, PA St. Stephen; Hispanic Apostolate.
Rosaforte, Rev. Msgr. Anthony S. '70 (NOR) Norwich, CT St. Patrick Cathedral; College of Consultors; Members; Diocesan Panel of Pastors, Canon 1742.
Rosal, Rey '88 (CHK) Saipan, MP San Vicente Parish; Presbyteral Council; Children of God the Father, Inc.
Rosales, Deo G. '82 (POD) New York.
Rosales, Deogracias '82 (NY)[II] New York, NY Prelature of the Holy Cross and Opus Dei.
Rosales, Freddi A. '92 (BRK) Flushing, NY St. Michael.
Rosales, Fredy B. '03 (LA) Pacoima, CA Guardian Angel.
Rosales, Samuel *s.j.* '73 (ELP) El Paso, TX Sacred Heart.
Rosalinas, Rogel *s.o.l.t.* '94 (CC)[G] Robstown, TX Society of Our Lady of the Most Holy Trinity.
Rosario, Angel Cuevas '90 (SJN) Carolina, PR Ntra. Sra. Reina de la Paz.
Rosario, Jacinto *o.c.d.* '91 (PCE) Ponce, PR San Jose.
Rosario, William D. '90 (OAK) Presbyteral Council.
Rosario, William '90 (OAK) Dublin, CA St. Raymond.
Rosas, Orlando '97 (MGZ) Vocations; Catholic Social Services.
Rosato, Philip J. *s.j.* '71 (WDC)[E] North Bethesda, MD Georgetown Preparatory School.
Rosca, Paschal *o.de.m.* '63 (CLV) Cleveland, OH St. Rocco.
Roscioli, Dominic J. '74 (MIL) Retired.
Rose, Alphonse G. '56 (BAL) Retired.
Rose, Rev. Msgr. Donald '53 (GB) Retired.
Rose, Frank '90 (NEW) Plainfield, NJ The Parish of St. Bernard and St. Stanislaus; Archdiocesan Judges.
Rose, Geoff *o.s.f.s.* '02 (LAN)[B] Jackson, MI Lumen Christi Catholic High School; Toledo, OH.
Rose, James '57 (FTW) U.S. Veteran's Hospital Retired.
Rose, John (WDC) Beltsville, MD St. Joseph.
Rose, Justin '95 (NTN) San Bernardino, CA St. Philip; MAYA (Melkite Assoc. of Young Adults).
Rose, Michael F. '81 (WOR) Shrewsbury, MA St. Mary's; Deans; Presbyteral Council.
Rose, William J. '96 (TOL) Toledo, OH Christ the King.
Rosebrough, Robert T. '69 (STL) Ferguson, MO Blessed Teresa of Calcutta.
Roselada, Eulogio *o.f.m.* '93 (CHI)[N] Chicago, IL Holy Evangelists Friary; [J] Evanston, IL Saint Francis Hospital.
Roselli, Marc J. *s.j.* '85 (FgM) New York, NY Society of Jesus.
Rosemeyer, John C. '58 (CHI) Westchester, IL Divine Providence Retired.
Rosemeyer, Paul F. '52 (CHI) Palatine, IL St. Theresa; Des Plaines, IL St. Mary Retired.
Rosen, Cyprian *o.f.m.cap.* '62 (WIL)[J] Wilmington, DE Capuchin Franciscan Friars, St. Francis Renewal Center; [M] Wilmington, DE St. Francis Renewal Center; Defenders of the Bond.
Rosenau, Alan '88 (LR)[D] Hot Springs National Park, AR St. Joseph's Mercy Health Center; Hot Springs National Park, AR St. John the Baptist.
Rosenbaum, Mark '07 (JOL) Plainfield, IL St. Mary Immaculate.
Rosenbaum, William E. '76 (ALT) Johnstown, PA St. Clement's.
Rosenberg, David B. '11 (LAN) Saline, MI St. Andrew the Apostle.
Rosensweig, Rev. Msgr. Walter F. '53 (TUC) Retired.
Rosette, Fabian Maria *o.carm.* '80 (SAN)[A] Christoval, TX Hermits of the Blessed Virgin Mary of Mount Carmel.
Rosevear, Anthony R. *o.p.* '78 (SFR) San Francisco, CA St. Dominic; [N] San Francisco, CA St. Dominic Priory.
Rosevear, Anthony *o.p.* '78 (OAK)[L] Oakland, CA Order of Preachers (Province of the Most Holy Name of Jesus – Western Dominican Province).
Rosie, Rev. Msgr. Joseph N. '90 (TR) Princeton, NJ St. Paul.
Rosimo, Cosmenio '91 (HON) Ewa Beach, HI Our Lady of Perpetual Help.
Rosing, Paul J. '73 (CLV) Stow, OH Holy Family; Presbyteral Council; Associate Judges.
Rosing, Robert C. '53 (COV)[N] Park Hills, KY Provincial House of the Sisters of Notre Dame; [I] Edgewood, KY St. Elizabeth Edgewood Retired.
Rosinski, Bernard *s.c.j.* '59 (SFS) Lower Brule, SD Immaculate Conception; Fort Thompson, SD St. Joseph Retired.
Rosinski, Edward B. '63 (CAM) Retired.
Rosinski, Richard A. '91 (RCK) Saint Charles, IL St. John Neumann.
Rosko, Ladislaus '52 (CLV) Retired.
Roslak, Thomas (NY) Staten Island, NY St. Clare.
Roslovich, Peter J. *s.j.* '63 (NY)[DD] New York, NY Murray–Weigel Hall.
Rosolen, Emil '86 (AMA) On Duty Outside the Diocese.
Rosolowski, Romulus *o.f.m.conv.* '74 (BUF) Lackawanna, NY Our Lady of Victory National Shrine; [N] Athol Springs, NY St. Maximilian Kolbe Friary.
Rosonke, Steven J. '82 (DUB) Dubuque, IA St. Anthony.
Rosonke, Vince G. '75 (DM) Waukee, IA St. Boniface.
Rospond, Paul *c.s.p.* '81 (LA) Los Angeles, CA St. Paul the Apostle.
Ross, Daniel J. *s.j.* '66 (FgM) Los Gatos, CA Society of Jesus.
Ross, David M. '75 (TOL) Promoter of Justice; Judges; Lima, OH St. John the Evangelist; Lima, OH St. Rose of Lima; College of Consultors.
Ross, David M. '75 (TOL) Blessed Junipero Serra Deanery.
Ross, Gregory *o.c.d.* '95 (SAT)[L] San Antonio, TX Discalced Carmelite Fathers of San Antonio; San Antonio, TX Basilica of the National Shrine of the Little Flower, Our Lady of Mt. Carmel and St. Therese Parish.
Ross, Joseph R. '69 (OKL) Personnel Committee; Ministry to Priests Program; Lawton, OK Blessed Sacrament; Special Assignment.
Ross, Joseph *m.s.* '55 (MAN)[K] Enfield, NH Shrine of Our Lady of La Salette; [N] Enfield, NH Shrine of Our Lady of La Salette Retired.
Ross, Justin *o.f.m.conv.* '08 (BUF)[D] Athol Springs, NY St. Francis High School; [N] Athol Springs, NY St. Francis of Assisi Friary.
Ross, Kenneth '92 (ORL) Retired.
Ross, Mark J. '88 (SAV) Savannah, GA St. James.
Ross, Richard '67 (JOL) Joliet, IL St. Bernard; Joliet, IL Dept. of Corrections.
Ross, Richard *s.j.* '10 (BO)[U] Newton, MA The Jesuit Community at Boston College.
Ross, Robert *s.j.* (GLP) Tohatchi, NM St. Mary Church.
Ross, Theodore *s.j.* '67 (CIN)[B] Cincinnati, OH Mount St. Mary's Seminary of the West.
Ross, William B. '54 (OKL) Health Panel, Archdiocesan; Oklahoma City, OK St. Eugene's Retired.
Rossa, Peter '03 (PHX) Scottsdale, AZ St. Bernadette Roman Catholic Parish; Priestly Life and Ministry Board.
Rosse, Jack '54 (ROC) Rochester, NY Kateri Tekakwitha Roman Catholic Parish.
Rosse, John '54 (ROC) Retired.
Rossell, Richard *o.f.m.conv.* '61 (TR) Seaside Heights, NJ Our Lady of Perpetual Help.
Rossello, Nicholas A. '60 (BUF) Retired.

Rossetti, Rev. Msgr. Stephen J. '84 (WDC)[C] Catholic University of America, The.
Rossetti, Rev. Msgr. Stephen '84 (SY) On Duty Outside the Diocese.
Rossey, Stephen J. *o.praem.* '59 (GB)[J] De Pere, WI St. Norbert Abbey.
Rossi, Anthony T. '09 (PH) Philadelphia, PA St. Jerome.
Rossi, Attilio *s.v.d.* '89 (WDC)[O] Washington, DC Society of the Divine Word/Divine Word House.
Rossi, Desmond '92 (ALB) Leave of Absence.
Rossi, Domenic A. *o.praem.* '74 (PH)[Y] Paoli, PA Daylesford Abbey.
Rossi, Rev. Msgr. Frank H. '83 (GAL) Houston, TX St. Michael; Ex Officio Members; College of Consultors; Priests Personnel Committee; Vicars General.
Rossi, Innocenti (PRM) Bay City, MI Saint George; Omer, MI St. John.
Rossi, John A. '09 (CAM) Sicklerville, NJ The Church of St. Charles Borromeo, Washington Township, N.J.; Continuing Education & Spiritual Formation of Priests (CESF).
Rossi, Joseph M. '84 (BO) Lynn, MA St. Pius Fifth.
Rossi, Joseph S. *s.j.* '80 (BAL)[B] Timonium, MD Loyola Graduate Center–Timonium Campus; [Q] Baltimore, MD Jesuit Community of Loyola University, Inc.; [B] Jesuit Community of Loyola University, Inc.
Rossi, Lucas '09 (CHL) Winston–Salem, NC St. Leo the Great.
Rossi, Pat F. '82 (NY) Bronx, NY St. Michael.
Rossi, Paul J. '74 (SFR) Redwood City, CA St. Pius.
Rossi, Philip J. *s.j.* '71 (MIL)[P] Milwaukee, WI Arrupe House Jesuit Community; [C] Marquette University.
Rossi, Raymond R. '58 (LR) Retired.
Rossi, Robert J. *o.s.c.* '70 (PHX)[F] Phoenix, AZ Crosier Community of Phoenix (Canons Regular of the Order of the Holy Cross).
Rossi, Ronald J. *o.praem.* '70 (PH)[B] Paoli, PA Daylesford Abbey; [Y] Paoli, PA Daylesford Abbey; Paoli, PA.
Rossi, Thomas J. *o.praem.* '73 (PH)[Y] Paoli, PA Daylesford Abbey.
Rossi, Thomas P. (BO) Lowell, MA St. Michael.
Rossi, Rev. Msgr. Walter R. '87 (WDC) On Duty Outside the Diocese; [S] Washington, DC Basilica of the National Shrine of the Immaculate Conception.
Rossi, Rev. Msgr. Walter R. '87 (WDC)[C] Catholic University of America, The.
Rossier, Francois *s.m.* (CIN)[D] The Marian Library/ International Marian Research Institute (IMRI); [D] Dayton, OH The University of Dayton; [N] Dayton, OH Marianist Community.
Rossman, Christopher '07 (KCK) Holton, KS St. Francis Xavier; Holton, KS St. Dominic.
Rossman, Richard '71 (P) Eugene, OR St. Mark; Eugene, OR St. Peter; Area Vicars.
Rosso, Mario A. *s.d.b.* '49 (SFR) San Francisco, CA SS. Peter and Paul.
Rosso, Norbert T. *c.s.sp.* '54 (PIT)[O] Bethel Park, PA The Spiritan Center.
Rosson, John P. '75 (ALB) Cooperstown, NY St. Mary.
Rossotti, Pietro *f.s.c.b.* '09 (WDC) Lexington, MA; [O] Bethesda, MD Priestly Fraternity of the Missionaries of St. Charles Borromeo, Inc.
Rossotti, Pietro *f.s.c.b.* '09 (BO)[U] Bethesda, MD House of Washington DC.
Rosswog, Kenneth *o.f.m.* '57 (SFD) Montrose, IL St. Rose of Lima; Teutopolis, IL St. Francis of Assisi; [K] Teutopolis, IL St. Francis Assisi Friary.
Rost, Rev. Msgr. George W. '51 (HBG) Retired.
Rost, Louis B. *m.m.* '55 (FgM) Maryknoll, NY MARYKNOLL.
Rost, Robert '74 (KC) Hamilton, MO Sacred Heart; Gallatin, MO Mary Immaculate.
Rostro, Lino Rico '78 (ARL) Arlington, VA St. Ann.
Roszko, Edward J. *o.s.f.s.* '70 (WIL)[B] Wilmington, DE Salesianum School.
Roszkowski, Donald F. '97 (PEO) Metamora, IL St. Mary's.
Roten, Johann B.G. *s.m.* '69 (CIN)[D] Dayton, OH The University of Dayton; [N] Dayton, OH Marianist Community.
Rotert, Matthew '94 (KC) Independence, MO St. Mary's.
Rotert, Norman '57 (KC) Retired.
Roth, Donald *c.ss.r.* '75 (FgM) Baltimore Province.
Roth, James J. '46 (WCH) Retired.
Roth, James *m.m.* '54 (SJ)[M] Los Altos, CA Maryknoll.
Roth, Timothy *m.i.c.* '74 (NOR)[C] Thompson, CT Marianapolis Preparatory School; [G] Thompson, CT Marian Fathers; Provincial Councilors.
Roth, Timothy *m.i.c.* '74 (SPR)[G] Provincial Office.
Rothan, Michael W. '04 (HBG) Hershey, PA St. Joan of Arc; [A] Lebanon, PA Lebanon Catholic School.
Rothe, James A. '56 (LA) Retired.
Rother, Michael '07 (VIC) Victoria, TX Our Lady of Victory Cathedral; Procurator Advocate.
Rothermel, Paul L. '94 (ALN) Holy Name Societies; Serra Club of Reading; Tremont, PA Most Blessed Trinity Parish.
Rothfuchs, Gregory '95 (JOL) Joliet, IL St. Paul the Apostle.
Rothrauff, Noel H. *o.s.b.* '54 (GBG)[H] Latrobe, PA Saint Vincent Archabbey; Latrobe, PA St. Vincent Archabbey.
Rothrock, Theodore D. '83 (LFT) Carmel, IN St. Elizabeth Ann Seton; Deans; Diocesan Consultors; Building Commission; Presbyteral Council; Members.
Rothschild, Paul J. '84 (STL)[A] St. Louis, MO Kenrick School of Theology.
Rothwell, Joseph T. '52 (BO) Senior Priests. Retired.
Rotok, Siprianus Ola *s.v.d.* '95 (GAL) Houston, TX Holy Name.
Rotola, Albert C. *s.j.* '68 (STL)[O] St. Louis, MO Jesuit Community Corporation at Saint Louis University – Jesuit Hall; [C] Saint Louis University.
Rotondi, Paul *o.f.m.* (NY)[DD] New York, NY Padua Friary Retired.
Rott, Bernard E. '79 (MAD) Dickeyville, WI Holy Ghost; Kieler, WI Immaculate Conception.
Rott, Jeffrey M. '09 (PH) West Chester, PA SS. Simon and Jude.
Rottgers, Robert A. '09 (COV)[B] Newport, KY Newport Central Catholic High School; Melbourne, KY St. Philip.
Rottman, Gary '03 (TYL) Crockett, TX St. Francis of the Tejas; Crockett, TX Crockett State School.
Rottman, Nicholas E. C. '11 (COV)[B] Erlanger, KY St. Henry District High School; Erlanger, KY Mary, Queen of Heaven.
Rotunno, Floyd '70 (NEW) Mahwah, NJ Immaculate Heart of Mary.
Rotunno, Philip J. '66 (NEW) Charismatic Renewal; West New York, NJ Our Lady of Libera Retired.
Rouch, Nicholas J. '89 (E)[A] Erie, PA St. Mark's Seminary; [N] Erie, PA Holy Family Monastery; Administrative Cabinet; Pennsylvania Catholic Conference; The Bishop's Theological Advisory Committee; Vicar for Catholic Education; St. Mark Seminary; Presbyteral Council.
Rouech, Chris W. '96 (GR) Grandville, MI St. Pius X; Worship; On Special Assignment.
Rougeau, Marc *s.d.b.* '77 (LA) Los Angeles, CA St. Mary; [V] Rosemead, CA St. Joseph's Salesian Youth Renewal Center; [P] Los Angeles, CA Dominic Savio Salesian Residence.
Rouleau, Francis C. '00 (NOR) On Duty Outside the Diocese; Diocesan Commission for Ecumenical and Interreligious Affairs.
Rourke, John '63 (VEN) Retired.
Rourke, Paul K. *s.j.* '10 (BAL)[Q] Towson Maryland Province of the Society of Jesus.
Rouse, C. Paul '67 (BO) Senior Priests.; South Boston, MA St. Brigid Retired.
Rouse, Silvan *c.p.* '49 (ALT)[K] Bedford, PA St. Mary's House of Solitude.
Rouse, Warren *o.f.m.* '57 (LA)[V] Malibu, CA Serra Retreat.
Rousseau, Julian *s.s.s.* '50 (CLV)[N] Richfield, OH Regina Health Center.
Rousseau, Peter A. '49 (BUR) Retired.
Rousseau, Richard W. *s.j.* '54 (BO)[U] Weston, MA Campion Health Center, Inc.
Rousseau, Robert J. '67 (HRT) North Branford, CT St. Augustine; Pro–Life Activities; Special and other Archdiocesan Assignment.
Rousseau, Rev. Msgr. Stanley B. '56 (BGP)[O] Stamford, CT The Catherine Dennis Keefe Queen of the Clergy Retired Priests' Residence Retired.
Rousseau, Rev. Msgr. Stanlislaus B. '56 (BGP) Retired.
Rousseau, William C. '95 (SPR) Chicopee, MA St. Anne's.
Routhier, Rev. Msgr. Peter A. '77 (BUR) Burlington, VT Cathedral of the Immaculate Conception; Members Ex Officio; Vicars General; Advocate; Ex Officio Members; Liturgical Commission; Diocesan Administrative Board; Diocesan Consultors; Ecumenical Commission; Ex Officio/Consultant; Victim's Advocacy Board; Burlington, VT St. Joseph's Co–Cathedral.
Roux, Christopher A. '01 (CHL) Special Assignment; Charlotte, NC St. Patrick Cathedral; Diocesan Consultors.
Roux, G. Albert '66 (PRT) Retired.
Roux, Philippe D. '73 (SPR) South Deerfield, MA Holy Family Parish.
Roux, Randy P. '79 (NO) New Orleans, LA Children's Hospital.
Roverse, Michael E. '84 (SAV) Grovetown, GA St. Teresa of Avila.
Rowan, Rev. Msgr. John J. '61 (RVC) Wantagh, NY St. Frances de Chantal Retired.
Rowan, John M. '89 (BO) Framingham, MA St. George.
Rowan, Mark P. '91 (RVC) Serving Outside the Diocese; Air Force Chaplains.
Rowan, Stephen C. '70 (SEA) On Duty Outside the Archdiocese.
Rowan, Stephen C. (P)[B] College of Arts and Sciences.
Rowe, Charles '99 (KC) Weston, MO Holy Trinity; Presbyteral Council; Deans; Weston, MO Twelve Apostles Parish.
Rowe, Donald F. *s.j.* '72 (CHI)[C] Chicago, IL Jesuit Community at Loyola University Chicago.
Rowe, William J. '64 (BEL) Mount Carmel, IL St. Mary.
Rowgh, Matthew T. '75 (MO) DEPARTMENT OF VETERANS AFFAIRS HOSPITALS AND CHAPLAINS.
Rowgh, T. Matthew '75 (WH) Shepherdstown, WV St. Agnes.
Rowland, Anthony T. '11 (LFT) Kokomo, IN St. Joan of Arc; Kokomo, IN St. Patrick.
Rowland, Rev. Msgr. Charles H. '70 (CHR) Johns Island, SC Church of the Holy Spirit; Office of Tribunal; College of Consultors; Presbyteral Council; Curia.
Rowland, Edward P. '53 (JOL)[K] Naperville, IL St. John Vianney Villa Retired.
Rowland, James '09 (TYL) Nacogdoches, TX Sacred Heart; San Augustine, TX St. Augustin Mission.
Rowland, Thomas '49 (ELP) On Duty Outside of Diocese.
Rowland, William F. *c.j.m.* '70 (SD) Carlsbad, CA Saint Patrick Catholic Parish Carlsbad.
Rowland, William F. *s.m.* '79 (ATL)[C] Atlanta, GA Marist School.
Rowntree, Stephen C. *s.j.* '75 (NO)[C] New Orleans, LA Loyola University New Orleans.
Rowsome, Rev. Msgr. Morgan J. '70 (CC) Deans; College of Consultors; Presbyteral Council; Corpus Christi, TX St. Peter Prince of Apostles; Finance Council.
Roxas, Rodolfo P. (SAV) Retired.
Roy, Rev. Msgr. Allen J. '58 (NO) Retired.
Roy, Donald J. '70 (BUR) Retired.
Roy, Duane *o.s.b.* '67 (FgM)[I] Atchison, KS St. Benedict's Abbey; Atchison, KS St. Benedict's Abbey.
Roy, Rev. Msgr. F. Gilles '57 (WOR) Retired.
Roy, George *o.m.i.* '73 (MIA) Miramar, FL St. Stephen.
Roy, James R. *m.m.* '61 (NY)[DD] Retired.
Roy, James '61 (ALX) Retired.
Roy, Maurice J. '73 (BUR) Deans; St. Albans, VT Holy Angels; Canon 1742 Panel of Pastors; Elected Members.
Roy, Michael J. '75 (WOR) Oxford, MA St. Roch.
Roy, Richard M. '75 (FR) Attleboro, MA St. John the Evangelist.
Roy, Richard Paul *m.afr.* '71 (SP)[N] St. Petersburg, FL Missionaries of Africa Retired.
Roy, Richard *m.afr.* '71 (FgM) Washington, DC; Washington, DC MISSIONARIES OF AFRICA; Washington, DC MISSIONARIES OF AFRICA Retired.
Roy, Robert P. '94 (HRT) East Hartford, CT St. Mary; East Hartford, CT St. Rose; East Hartford, CT St. Isaac Jogues; Appointed.
Royal, Rev. Msgr. Kevin T. '85 (BGP) Episcopal Vicar for Clergy; Office for Clergy and Religious; Office for the Continuing Education of Clergy; Members of the Clergy Personnel Committee; Presbyteral Council; Priest Vocation Advisory Board.
Royce, Thomas *s.j.* '56 (P) Portland, OR St. Ignatius; [L] Portland, OR Colombiere Community.
Royer, Francis *s.s.c.* '57 (OM)[J] St. Columbans Missionary Society of St. Columban Retired.
Royer, Rev. Msgr. Ronald Edmund '58 (LA) Retired.
Royer, Rev. Msgr. Ronald '58 (FRS) Porterville, CA St. Anne Retired.
Royer, Thomas J. '60 (PEO) Retired.
Royer, Yvon J. '90 (BUR) Deans; Daughters of Isabella; Bristol, VT St. Ambrose; Vergennes, VT St. Peter; Canon 1742 Panel of Pastors.
Royik, Ihor '92 (PHU) Melrose Park, PA Annunciation of the B.V.M.; The Way – Online Newspaper.
Roza, Andrew J. '07 (OM)[B] Columbus, NE Scotus Central Catholic High School; Columbus, NE St. Bonaventure.
Rozansky, Joseph G. *o.f.m.* (NY)[DD] New York Franciscan Friars, Holy Name Province.
Rozario, Christal '00 (PH)[S] Darby, PA Mercy Fitzgerald Hospital.
Rozborski, Grzegorz '05 (DET) South Lyon, MI St. Joseph.
Rozek, Piotr '88 (RVC) Copiague, NY Our Lady of the Assumption; Floral Park, NY St. Hedwig's.
Rozembajgier, John M. '04 (MET) On Duty Outside the Diocese.
Rozembajgier, John M. '04 (COL)[A] Columbus, OH Pontifical College Josephinum; [A] Columbus, OH Pontifical College Josephinum.
Rozic, Peter *s.j.* '07 (WDC)[O] Washington, DC The Jesuit Community at Georgetown University.
Rozman, Thomas J. '86 (HBG) Harrisburg, PA Cathedral Parish of St. Patrick.
Rozmarynowycz, Mychail '95 (PRM) Sterling Heights, MI St. Basil.
Rozniak, Rev. Msgr. Ronald J. '71 (NEW) Ridgewood, NJ Our Lady of Mount Carmel; Members; Administration; Members; Presbyteral Council; [Q] Ridgewood, NJ Trinity Management & Technology Corp.; Episcopal Vicar for Healthcare and Social Concerns.
Rozum, George A. *c.s.c.* '68 (FTW)[B] University of Notre Dame Du Lac; [H] Notre Dame, IN Holy Cross Community, Corby Hall, University of Notre Dame.
Rozycki, Rev. Msgr. Isidore '68 (AUS) West, TX St. Martin; West, TX St. Joseph.

Ruan, Joseph Guo Zhang (NY) New York, NY St. Teresa.
Ruane, Dennis *s.s.s.* '59 (CLV)[N] Cleveland Congregation of the Blessed Sacrament Provincial House.
Ruane, Dennis '59 (SLC) Copperton, UT Immaculate Conception LLC 206.
Ruane, Edward *o.p.* '69 (CHI)[N] Chicago Dominicans (Provincial Office).
Ruane, George '73 (NEW) Edgewater, NJ Holy Rosary.
Ruane, Gerald P. '60 (NEW) Retired.
Ruane, John P. *s.j.* '49 (NEW)[B] Jersey City, NJ Jesuit Center; [L] Jersey City, NJ Jesuits of Saint Peter's College, Inc.
Ruane, Martin '63 (JKS) Grenada, MS St. Peter.
Ruane, Michael J. '69 (BAL) Mount Airy, MD St. Michael.
Ruani, Pablo '92 (BRK) Brooklyn, NY St. Michael – Saint Malachy.
Ruba, Rev. Msgr. Nicholas J. '51 (SC) Retired.
Rubadue, Paul E. *o.s.b.* '86 (GBG)[H] Latrobe, PA Saint Vincent Archabbey.
Rubaj, Leon B. '60 (SAT) San Antonio, TX; [K] San Antonio, TX Casa De Padres Retired.
Rubbelke, Ronald J. '64 (STL) O'Fallon, MO Assumption.
Rubey, Charles T. '66 (CHI)[G] Administration:; [G] Administration:; Office for Persons with Disabilities; Office for Persons with Disabilities; Associate Administrators Retired.
Rubey, Charles (CHI)[G] Chicago, IL LOSS (Loving Outreach to Survivors of Suicide).
Rubiano, Cesar A. '96 (TR) On Duty Outside the Diocese.
Rubiano, Luis Eduardo *o.f.m.cap.* '81 (NY)[DD] White Plains, NY Capuchin Friars International, Inc.
Rubino, Rev. Msgr. David A. '73 (E)[B] Erie, PA Mercyhurst College.
Rubino, Vincent *o.f.m.conv.* '00 (PMB) Port St. Lucie, FL St. Lucie.
Rubio, Jose Antonio '80 (SJ) Special Assignment; Ecumenical and Interreligious Affairs.
Rubio, Jose Antonio '80 (SFR)[A] Menlo Park, CA St. Patrick Seminary and University.
Rubio, Juan *o.f.m.* '03 (AMA) Amarillo, TX St. Laurence Church.
Rubio, Santiago '80 (NY) New York, NY Our Lady of Guadalupe at St. Bernard's; Bronx, NY Sacred Heart.
Rubio–Boitel, Fernando '75 (SFE) Retired.
Ruby, David C. '91 (GB) Egg Harbor, WI Stella Maris.
Rucando, Anthony M. '70 (BRK) Howard Beach, NY Our Lady of Grace.
Ruchgy, Rev. Canon Wayne J. '66 (STN) Dearborn, MI St. Michael's; Protosyncellus; Diocesan Consultors; Personnel Board; Presbyteral Council.
Ruchinski, David '07 (STA) Vocations; Gainesville, FL St. Augustine.
Rucker, Lawrence *s.c.j.* '66 (MIL)[P] Franklin, WI Sacred Heart at Monastery Lake; [P] Franklin Sacred Heart at Monastery Lake.
Rudcki, Stanley R. '53 (CHI) Retired.
Rudd, Thad B. '91 (ATL) Retired.
Rudden, Matthew T. '59 (RCK) Retired.
Ruddy, Paul *o.s.f.s.* '64 (LAN) Tecumseh, MI St. Dominic Oratory.
Rude, James *s.j.* '64 (FRS) Co Editors.
Rudecki, Marek *s.a.c.* '83 (BRK) Ridgewood, NY St. Aloysius.
Rudjak, Joseph '00 (Y) Youngstown, OH Holy Apostles Parish.
Rudnick, Kenneth *s.j.* '91 (LA)[C] Los Angeles, CA Jesuit Community; [AA] Los Angeles, CA Loyola Law School.
Rudnicki, Zbigniew A. '90 (PMB) Royal Palm Beach, FL Our Lady Queen of Peace Catholic Cemetery, Inc.; Royal Palm Beach, FL Our Lady Queen of the Apostles; Cemetery: Our Lady Queen of Peace.
Rudnik, John J. '61 (CHI) Chicago, IL Transfiguration of Our Lord Retired.
Rudnik, Tadeusz '55 (SY) Syracuse, NY Transfiguration.
Rudolf, Rosendo '07 (CI) Chancellor; Finance Committee; [C] Tunnuk, Chuuk, FM Vicariate Residence.
Rudolph, Michael L. '05 (STP) West St. Paul, MN St. Michael.
Rudolph, Patrick '88 (ORG) Orange, CA St. Norbert.
Rudolph, Thomas J. '61 (LC) Retired.
Rudolphi, Stephen A. '79 (BEL) Carmi, IL St. Polycarp (German); Carmi, IL St. Patrick.
Rudolphi, Timothy C. '89 (STP) Edina, MN St. Patrick.
Rudy, Noel '53 (SAG) Harrison, MI St. Athanasius Retired.
Rudy, Richard E. '76 (PH) Bensalem, PA Saint Ephrem.
Rudzewicz, Jan '83 (OAK) San Leandro, CA Our Lady of Good Counsel.
Ruede, Ernest J. '66 (R) Jacksonville, NC Shrine of the Infant of Prague, Church of the Holy Spirit; Diocesan Consultors; Council of Priests.
Ruedisueli, Robert A. '69 (DET) Retired.
Ruef, Rev. Msgr. James L.T. '78 (COL) Judicial Vicar; Presiding Judge in Second Instance Retired.
Rueger, William J. '75 (BRK) Brooklyn, NY St. Francis Xavier.
Ruekert, Thomas E. *s.d.b.* '73 (NY) Port Chester, NY Corpus Christi.
Ruelle, Gerald *o.s.b.* '50 (BIS)[A] Richardton, ND Assumption Abbey Retired.
Ruelle, William A. '11 (BIS) Mandan, ND Spirit of Life.
Ruessmann, John J. *m.m.* '79 (NY)[DD].
Ruetz, Edward J. '62 (FTW) Retired.
Ruff, Anthony *o.s.b.* '93 (SCL)[I] Collegeville, MN St. John's Abbey, of the Order of St. Benedict.
Ruff, Charles R. '46 (STL) Retired.
Ruff, Daniel M. *s.j.* '86 (PH) Philadelphia, PA Old St. Joseph's.
Ruff, Frank *g.h.m.* '63 (OWN) Elkton, KY St. Susan; Guthrie, KY Sts. Mary & James; Deans; Priests' Council.
Ruff, Frank *g.h.m.* '63 (CIN)[N] Cincinnati Headquarters of Glenmary Home Missioners Retired.
Ruffalo, Michael R. '08 (PIT) Washington, PA Immaculate Conception; [P] Washington, PA Washington and Jefferson College (Washington).
Ruffing, Joseph R. '55 (LFT) Retired.
Ruffing, Norman '63 (OAK) Retired.
Ruffo, John L. *o.f.m.conv.* (TR) Seaside Park, NJ St. Catharine of Siena.
Ruffolo, George *c.m.f.* '59 (CHI) Chicago, IL Holy Cross/Immaculate Heart of Mary.
Rufo, Henry '01 (P) Rainier, OR Nativity B.V.M.
Rufo, Nicholas (CIN)[N] Dayton, OH Mercy Siena Support Community.
Ruge, Paul '97 (FAR) Retired.
Rugen, Patrick J. '76 (CHI) Waukegan, IL St. Dismas; Deans.
Ruggere, Peter L. *m.m.* '68 (NY)[DD] Maryknoll Maryknoll Fathers and Brothers Retired.
Ruggeri, Joseph A. '65 (BO) Senior Priests. Retired.
Ruggeri, Salvatore M. '99 (CLV) Richmond Heights Hospital; Euclid, OH St. John of the Cross.
Ruggieri, James T. '95 (PRO) Providence, RI St. Patrick.
Ruggieri, Joseph '95 (Y) Campbell, OH St. John the Baptist; Campbell, OH St. Joseph the Provider; Campbell, OH St. Lucy; Campbell, OH St. Rose of Lima.
Ruggieri, Pasquale *f.d.p.* '52 (NY) New York, NY St. Ann.
Ruggiero, Philip '81 (TR) Matawan, NJ St. Clement.
Ruggiero, Russell '10 (VEN) Bradenton, FL SS. Peter and Paul the Apostles.
Ruggles, Christopher V. '79 (TYL) Judges; On Duty Outside the Diocese.
Ruggles, Christopher V. '79 (BRK) Brooklyn, NY St. Finbar.
Ruhl, William J. *o.s.f.s.* '62 (ARL) Vienna, VA Our Lady of Good Counsel; Diocesan Judges Retired.
Ruhlin, James '02 (SP) Gulfport, FL Most Holy Name of Jesus.
Ruhnke, Robert A. *c.ss.r.* '66 (SAT)[L] San Antonio, TX Redemptorists of Texas–San Antonio #1.
Ruisanchez, Jose P. '86 (BO)[T] Newton, MA Prelature of the Holy Cross and Opus Dei; Chestnut Hill.
Ruiz, Albert Capello '73 (AUS) Austin, TX Nuestra Senora De Dolores.
Ruiz, Antonio A. '71 (TUC) Retired.
Ruiz, Dominic *o.s.b.* '83 (SCL)[I] Collegeville, MN St. John's Abbey, of the Order of St. Benedict.
Ruiz, Eddie '99 (SD) Brawley, CA Sacred Heart Catholic Parish Brawley; Vicars Forane; Brawley, CA Saint Margaret Mary Catholic Parish; Presbyteral Council.
Ruiz, Edgar '01 (PAT) Passaic, NJ Assumption of the Blessed Virgin Mary; Passaic, NJ St. Nicholas.
Ruiz, Enrique '56 (SAT) On Leave.
Ruiz, Faustino *s.j.p.* '91 (MAD) Platteville, WI St. Mary; Platteville, WI St. Augustine University Parish; [I] Platteville, WI St. Augustine Newman Center.
Ruiz, Gabriel *c.m.f.* '89 (FRS) Fresno, CA St. Anthony Claret.
Ruiz, Giovanni (CGS) San Lorenzo, PR Sagrado Corazon de Jesus y 12 Apostoles; Priests Senate.
Ruiz, Jean–Pierre '82 (BRK) Released from Diocesan Assignment; Queens Village, NY SS. Joachim and Anne.
Ruiz, John Martin *o.p.* '08 (WDC)[B] Washington, DC Dominican House of Studies.
Ruiz, John '55 (HT) Retired.
Ruiz, Jose Domingo '89 (STO) Stockton, CA St. Linus Church (Pastor of); Spanish.
Ruiz, Joseph B. '66 (CHI) Oak Park, IL St. Edmund Retired.
Ruiz, Juan Antonio *c.m.* '65 (DAL) Dallas, TX Holy Trinity; [J] Dallas, TX Congregation of the Mission, Western Province.
Ruiz, Juan '98 (BRK) Corona, NY Our Lady of Sorrows.
Ruiz, Lorenzo '63 (SJN) San Juan, PR San Juan Bosco.
Ruiz, Luis M. '85 (FAJ) Culebra, PR Nuestra Senora del Carmen.
Ruiz, Luis '68 (SAT) San Antonio, TX St. Stephen.
Ruiz, Miguel A. *s.v.d.* '95 (SB) Riverside, CA Queen of Angels.
Ruiz, Orlando '05 (BRK) Brooklyn, NY Our Lady of Peace.
Ruiz, Raul Gomez *s.d.s.* '87 (MIL)[P] Franklin, WI Salvatorian Formation House; [B] Hales Corners, WI Sacred Heart School of Theology.
Ruiz, Rick '92 (ELP) Absent on Leave.
Ruiz, Rudy '79 (MRY) Vicars Forane; Hollister, CA Sacred Heart/St. Benedict Catholic Community; Presbyteral Council.
Ruiz, Ryan '05 (CIN) On Special and Archdiocesan Assignment.
Ruiz–Marentes, Jose–Hugo *o.f.m.* '96 (CHR) Bluffton, SC St. Gregory the Great.
Ruiz–Santos, Carlos '03 (SAL) Salina, KS Sacred Heart Cathedral Parish; Catholic Charities Board; Office of Hispanic Ministry.
Rukavina, Steven '87 (B) Boise, ID St. Mark's.
Rukstalis, Simeon *o.f.m.conv.* '64 (SY) Binghamton, NY SS. Cyril and Method; Binghamton, NY Holy Trinity.
Rukuratwa, Avitus L. '06 (CHI) Chicago, IL St. John de la Salle.
Rule, Philip C. *s.j.* '62 (WOR)[N] Worcester, MA Jesuits of the Holy Cross, Inc.
Rule, Philip C. *s.j.* '62 (BO)[U] Weston, MA Campion Health Center, Inc.
Rule, Steven R. '75 (RIC) Sabbatical.
Rumble, Clarence F. '86 (SY) Endwell, NY Church of the Holy Family.
Runde, David H. '57 (MAD)[F] Madison, WI Bishop O'Connor Catholic Pastoral Center Retired.
Runde, Luis *o.f.m.* '65 (FWT)[H] Crowley, TX St. Maximilian Kolbe Friary.
Runde, Raymond E. '56 (MAD) Retired.
Rundzio, Mark A. '81 (MAN) Retired.
Runkle, Roy '10 (BIR) Madison, AL St. John the Baptist.
Runnion, David A. '06 (CHR) Chester, SC St. Joseph; Lancaster, SC St. Catherine.
Runyon, Jacob '09 (FTW) Vocation Office; South Bend, IN St. Matthew Cathedral.
Ruoff, Lou '84 (RIC) Colonial Heights, VA St. Ann.
Rupert, Rev. Msgr. Dale R. '77 (SCR) Jermyn, PA Sacred Hearts of Jesus & Mary, Jermyn; Diocesan Office for Parish Life.
Rupp, Daniel J. '98 (BUR) Deans; Burlington, VT Christ the King–St. Anthony; Elected Members; Canon 1742 Panel of Pastors; Diocesan Consultors.
Rupp, Daniel N. '66 (MAR) Retired.
Rupp, Edward F. '60 (CLV) Life of Prayer and Penance.
Rupp, William '10 (PBR) Hawk Run, PA St. John the Baptist; State College, PA State College PA Byzantine Catholic Community; Hawk Run, PA Dormition of the Mother of God.
Ruppenkamp, Raymond '50 (DAV) Retired.
Ruppert, Alan E. '78 (BEL) Leave of Absence.
Ruppert, David '05 (FTW) South Bend, IN St. Anthony de Padua; Presbyteral Council.
Ruppert, Donald R. '78 (VIC) East Bernard, TX Holy Cross; Diocesan Finance Board; Presbyteral Council.
Rurangirwa, Romain (BO) Carlisle, MA St. Irene.
Rusay, Leonard F.A. '85 (MET) Whitehouse Station, NJ Our Lady of Lourdes; Deans.
Rusch, Donald '61 (LAN) Retired.
Ruschman, Albert E. '53 (COV) Fort Thomas, KY St. Thomas Retired.
Rusconi, Rev. Msgr. Richard A. '72 (PAT) Clifton, NJ St. Andrew the Apostle.
Ruse, Fred R. '76 (ORL) On Duty Outside the Diocese.
Rush, Ernest G. '02 (NEW) Nutley, NJ St. Mary's.
Rush, Gerald *o.f.m.* '89 (LIN) Lincoln, NE St. Teresa's.
Rush, Rev. Msgr. J. Kenneth '71 (RIC) Lynchburg, VA Holy Cross; Regional Vicars; Judges.
Rush, James C. '68 (HRT) Retired.
Rush, James P. '72 (CAM) Margate City, NJ Holy Trinity Parish, Margate, N.J.
Rush, Joseph E. '64 (CAM) Retired.
Rush, Michael P. '73 (CAM) Ocean City, NJ Saint Damien Parish, Ocean City, N.J.
Rush, Patrick J. '69 (KC) Kansas City, MO Visitation of the Blessed Virgin Mary.
Rush, Thomas *o.m.i.* '73 (FgM) Washington, DC AMERICAN OBLATE MISSIONS.
Rush, Rev. Msgr. Vincent '72 (RVC) West Babylon, NY Our Lady of Grace.
Rushford, William A. '55 (BIS)[G] Bismarck, ND Emmaus Place Retired.
Rushofsky, John R. '79 (PIT) Pittsburgh, PA St. Sebastian.
Rusin, Joseph C. '46 (SCR) Dickson City, PA Visitation of the Blessed Virgin Mary Retired.
Rusin, Krzysztof '07 (MEM) Memphis, TN Cathedral of the Immaculate Conception.
Rusk, Richard M. '90 (MET) Belvidere, NJ St. Patrick; Oxford, NJ St. Rose of Lima; [M] Oxford, NJ The Anawim Community; Episcopal Vicars.
Rusk, Richard M. '90 (ROC)[O] Corning, NY Anawim Community Center.
Rusk, Ron L. '68 (SB) Palm Springs, CA St. Theresa.
Ruskamp, Robert L. '85 (ARL) Alexandria, VA St. Mary's.

Ruskoski, William Paul '74 (LAF) Rayne, LA St. Joseph.
Ruskowski, Clifford F. '62 (DET) Retired.
Rusnak, Anton *o.c.s.o.* '03 (L)[L] Trappist, KY Abbey of Our Lady of Gethsemani, of the Order of Cistercians of the Strict Observance.
Rusnak, Melvin E. '70 (Y) Geneva, OH Assumption B.V.M.
Rusnak, Tadeusz *s.ch.* '85 (SFR) Polish, Croatian, Slovenian Mission.
Rusnak, Tadeusz *s.ch.* '87 (SFR) San Francisco, CA Nativity.
Russeau, Kevin *c.s.c.* '01 (COS)[E] Cascade, CO Holy Cross Novitiate.
Russell, Alfred J. '66 (KAL) Retired.
Russell, Benjamin Joseph *o.p.* '60 (LFT)[I] West Lafayette, IN Dominicans, Community of St. Thomas Aquinas, Inc.
Russell, David P. '81 (WDC) North Beach, MD St. Anthony.
Russell, David '64 (MIA) Incardinated Retired Priests Retired.
Russell, Dean E. '00 (RCK) Rockford, IL St. James.
Russell, Edward K. '83 (NY) New York, NY Our Lady of Esperanza; New York, NY St. Rose of Lima; Canon 1742 Panel of Pastors.
Russell, James A. *s.m.* '64 (CIN)[N] Huntsville, OH St. George Chapel of Marianist Community.
Russell, James D. '60 (WIN) Retired.
Russell, John F. *o.carm.* '60 (NEW) Tenafly, NJ Our Lady of Mount Carmel.
Russell, Kenneth '58 (OAK) Retired.
Russell, Nock W. '08 (AUS) Washington, TX Blessed Virgin Mary; Somerville, TX St. Ann.
Russell, Rev. Msgr. Paul F. '87 (BO) On Duty Outside the Archdiocese.
Russell, Raymond R. '56 (BUF) Retired.
Russell, Richard R. '61 (HRT)[A] In Res. at the Archbishop Daniel A. Cronin Retirement Residence at St. Thomas Seminary Retired.
Russell, Samuel *o.s.b.* '94 (KC)[A] Conception, MO Conception Seminary College; [J] Conception, MO Conception Abbey.
Russell, Stanley J. '61 (WIL) Wilmington, DE St. Helena; Deans.
Russell, Wade '10 (AUS) Austin, TX St. Thomas More.
Russell, William C. *s.j.* '65 (BO)[U] Newton, MA The Jesuit Community at Boston College.
Russi, Fred '67 (LKC) Diocesan Consultors; Presbyteral Council Retired.
Russick, Matthew '09 (ALT)[G] Loretto, PA St. Francis Friary at Mount Assisi.
Russick, Matthew *t.o.r.* (ALT)[A] Loretto, PA St. Francis University; [I] Loretto, PA St. Francis University (Loretto).
Russo, Anthony J. '00 (BR) Retired.
Russo, Anthony J. (MIL) New Munster, WI St. Alphonsus; Twin Lakes, WI St. John the Evangelist.
Russo, Anthony P. *s.c.j.* '66 (MIL)[P] Franklin, WI Sacred Heart at Monastery Lake.
Russo, Anthony S. '00 (GR) Rockford, MI Our Lady of Consolation.
Russo, Anthony T. *c.ss.r.* '65 (PH) Deaf Apostolate; Philadelphia, PA Visitation B.V.M.
Russo, Anthony (NO)[A] St. Benedict, LA St. Joseph Seminary College.
Russo, Caesar '74 (STA) Defenders of the Bond.
Russo, Rev. Msgr. Charles J. (PAT) Retired.
Russo, Rt. Rev. Economos Roman V. '77 (NY) New York, NY St. Michael Chapel.
Russo, Francis X. *o.f.m.cap.* '59 (WDC) Washington, DC Shrine of the Sacred Heart; [B] Washington, DC St. Francis Friary–Capuchin College.
Russo, Frank '81 (LA) On Sick Leave.
Russo, Michael A. '71 (NEW) On Duty Outside the Archdiocese; [B] St. Mary's College.
Russo, Michael '89 (LAF) Lafayette, LA Our Lady of Fatima.
Russo, Peter '76 (ALB) Scotia, NY St. Joseph Church.
Russo, Reginald *o.f.m.cap.* '67 (PIT) Pittsburgh, PA Our Lady of the Angels; [N] Pittsburgh, PA Sisters of Charity of Nazareth.
Russo, Ricardo *o.f.m.* '74 (MO) Army National Guard Chaplains.
Russo, Ricardo *o.f.m.* '74 (SFE)[I] Santa Fe, NM Discalced Carmelite Monastery.
Russo, Richard M. '82 (RCK) Marengo, IL Sacred Heart.
Russo, Robert T. '61 (HRT)[A] In Res. at the Archbishop Daniel A. Cronin Retirement Residence at St. Thomas Seminary Retired.
Russo, Rt. Rev. Roman V. (BRK)[Q] Russian Apostolate.
Russo, Rt. Rev. Romanos V. '77 (NTN) Priests Serving Outside the Eparchy.
Rust, Adam M. '09 (MEM) Memphis, TN St. Louis; Bartlett, TN Church of The Nativity.
Ruston, Robert L. '76 (ALT) Johnstown, PA SS. Gregory & Barnabas.
Ruszel, Henry A. *c.r.* '54 (SB)[I] Apple Valley, CA Congregation of the Resurrection, CR; Apple Valley, CA Our Lady of the Desert Retired.
Ruteaga, Rogelio Martinez *o.f.m.* '03 (JOL)[L] Joliet, IL St. John the Baptist Friary.
Ruth, John C. '85 (SCR) Hispanic Ministry Outreach; Scranton, PA Saint John Neumann, Scranton.
Ruth, Robert F. '60 (RIC) Retired.
Ruthenberg, Gari *o.m.i.* '95 (STP)[M] Buffalo, MN Christ the King Retreat Center.
Ruther, William E. '90 (LA) Carson, CA St. Philomena.
Rutherford, Donald I. '81 (ALB) Military Chaplains.
Rutherford, Rev. Msgr. Donald L. '81 (MO) Presbyteral Council; Army Chaplains.
Rutherford, H. *c.s.c.* (FTW)[H] Notre Dame Congregation of Holy Cross, United States Province of Priests & Brothers.
Rutherford, Mark J. '09 (LAN) Brighton, MI St. Patrick.
Rutherford, Richard *c.s.c.* '64 (P)[B] University of Portland; [L] Portland, OR Holy Cross Fathers & Brothers, C.S.C. – University of Portland; Liturgical Commission.
Rutkowski, George A. '60 (DET) Retired.
Rutkowski, N. James '77 (SAT)[O] San Antonio, TX Catholic Counseling and Consultation Center; San Antonio, TX Purisima Concepcion; San Antonio, TX Purisima Concepcion; San Antonio, TX St. Ann.
Rutkowski, Ronald J. '69 (GBG) Retired.
Rutkowski, Theodore A. '63 (PIT) Retired.
Rutkowski, William J. '87 (SAG) Clare, MI St. Cecilia; Diocesan College of Consultors; Coleman, MI St. Philip Neri.
Rutledge, Robert *o.s.f.s.* '89 (ALN)[B] Center Valley, PA DeSales University; [K] Center Valley, PA Oblates of St. Francis de Sales.
Rutledge, William G. '53 (PIT) Retired.
Rutledge, William M. *o.s.f.s.* '89 (ARL) Reston, VA St. John Neumann.
Rutler, George W. '81 (NY) New York, NY Our Saviour; [HH] New York, NY Guild of Catholic Lawyers, The.
Rutowski, William J. '87 (SAG) Rosebush, MI St. Henry/ St. Charles.
Rutten, Erich '05 (STP)[C] St. Paul, MN University of St. Thomas; Ecumenical and Interreligious Affairs; Fredericksburg, VA Catholic Association of Diocesan Ecumenical and Interreligious Officers (CADEIO).
Rutten, Paul A. '02 (SFS) Vocations.
Rutten, Paul J. '58 (LIN)[E] Lincoln, NE Bonacum House Retired.
Ruttle, Paul *c.p.* (FgM) New Rochelle, NY St. Paul of the Cross Province.
Rutz, Rev. Msgr. Gilbert J. '66 (COV) Retired.
Rutz, Rev. Msgr. Gilbert J. '66 (PHX)[G] Phoenix, AZ Mount Claret Roman Catholic Retreat Center Retired.
Ruvalcaba, Victor J. '96 (LA) Los Angeles, CA Holy Spirit; Los Angeles, CA St. Mary Magdalen.
Ruvo, Rev. Msgr. John A. '54 (NY) New Rochelle, NY St. Joseph.
Ruwaainenyi, Deogratias M. '06 (CLV) Wickliffe, OH Our Lady of Mount Carmel.
Ruwe, Paul A. '05 (CIN)[B] Cincinnati, OH Mount St. Mary's Seminary of the West; [B] Cincinnati, OH Mount St. Mary's Seminary of the West.
Ruyechan, Matthew J. '80 (E) Oil City, PA St. Stephen; Rouseville, PA St. Venantius; Deans; College of Consultors; Presbyteral Council.
Ruygt, Hans P. '85 (PHX) Surprise, AZ St. Clare of Assisi Roman Catholic Parish; Presbyteral Council.
Ruzicka, Gary '76 (CHY) Cheyenne, WY St. Mary's Cathedral; Ex Officios, Voting; Diocese of Cheyenne, Board of Directors; Diocesan Schools Advisory Group; [G] Cheyenne, WY St. Mary's School Foundation; Building Committee; Cheyenne, WY Olivet Cemetery.
Rwegasira, Deogratias *a.j.* '96 (ALN) Elected Members; Easton, PA Our Lady of Mercy Parish; Easton – Court Easton #358.
Rweyemamu, Justinian B. '93 (NOR) Absent on Leave.
Rwezahura, Gosbertus '11 (CHI) Wilmette, IL St. Joseph.
Ryan, Adam *o.s.b.* '90 (KC) Bethany, MO Blessed Sacrament; [J] Priests Elsewhere; [A] Conception, MO Conception Seminary College.
Ryan, Alan J. *m.m.* '60 (NY)[DD] Retired.
Ryan, Albert J. '58 (FR) Retired.
Ryan, C. Duane '54 (JC) Laurie, MO Shrine of St. Patrick.
Ryan, C. Duane '54 (KC) Retired.
Ryan, Charles *f.s.s.p.* '94 (LR)[K] North Little Rock, AR Priestly Fraternity of St. Peter.
Ryan, Cornelius *c.s.c.* '66 (FTW)[H] Notre Dame Congregation of Holy Cross, United States Province of Priests & Brothers.
Ryan, Daniel J. '89 (TR) College of Consultors; Willingboro, NJ Corpus Christi; Vicars Forane (Deans).
Ryan, Daniel P. '10 (ALB) Schenectady, NY St. Paul the Apostle; Priestly Life and Ministry Council.
Ryan, David '79 (CHI) Lake Zurich, IL St. Francis de Sales.
Ryan, Denis '06 (KC)[J] Kansas City, MO Redemptorists Fathers of Kansas City, Missouri.
Ryan, Dennis K. '66 (DEN) Frisco, CO St. Mary Retired.
Ryan, Dennis M. '74 (GB) Appleton, WI St. Bernard.
Ryan, Dennis *c.ss.r.* (KC) Kansas City, MO Our Lady of Perpetual Help.
Ryan, Donald P. '63 (L)[L] Louisville, KY Bishop David Apartments Retired.
Ryan, Edmund K. *o.p.* '65 (OAK)[L] Oakland, CA Order of Preachers (Province of the Most Holy Name of Jesus – Western Dominican Province).
Ryan, Rev. Msgr. Edward A. '71 (BRK) Ridgewood, NY Our Lady of the Miraculous Medal.
Ryan, Edward J. '53 (ALB) Retired.
Ryan, Edward M. '74 (WOR) Worcester, MA Our Lady of Providence Parish.
Ryan, Eugene '69 (VEN) Retired.
Ryan, F. Lee '68 (JOL) Leave of Absence.
Ryan, Francis J. *s.j.* '56 (FgM) Watertown, MA Society of Jesus.
Ryan, Francis X. *s.j.* '84 (CLV)[B] University Heights, OH John Carroll Jesuit Community.
Ryan, Francis X. *s.j.* '84 (STL)[O] St. Louis, MO Jesuit Community Corporation at Saint Louis University – Jesuit Hall.
Ryan, G. Philip '88 (ATL) Greensboro, GA Christ Our King and Savior; Deans.
Ryan, Rev. Msgr. George J. '62 (BRK) Douglaston, NY St. Anastasia.
Ryan, Rev. Msgr. Gerald J. '45 (NY) Bronx, NY St. Luke.
Ryan, J. Patrick '76 (PAT) Totowa, NJ St. James of the Marches.
Ryan, Jack '76 (HON) Honolulu, HI Newman Center–Holy Spirit Parish; Diocesan Ecumenical Commission; Diocesan Ecumenical Interfaith Director; Presbyteral Council.
Ryan, James G. *o.s.a.* '49 (LAN) Flint, MI St. Matthew.
Ryan, James H. *s.j.* '69 (OM)[C] Omaha, NE Creighton Preparatory School.
Ryan, James M. '75 (COV) Elsmere, KY St. Henry; Judges.
Ryan, Rev. Msgr. James W. '48 (BRK)[O] Queens Village, NY Queen of Peace Residence Retired.
Ryan, John A. '70 (SFR) Burlingame, CA St. Catherine of Siena.
Ryan, John David '10 (RVC) Seaford, NY St. James.
Ryan, John J. *c.s.c.* '90 (SCR)[B] King's College; [B] Holy Cross Community; Prov. Councilors:; Provincial Councilors.
Ryan, John J. *s.j.* '67 (BUF)[N] Buffalo, NY Canisius Jesuit Community Inc.; [D] Buffalo, NY Canisius High School.
Ryan, John J. *c.s.c.* '90 (FTW)[H] Notre Dame, IN Congregation of Holy Cross, United States Province of Priests & Brothers; [H] Notre Dame Congregation of Holy Cross, United States Province of Priests & Brothers.
Ryan, John M. '64 (CHI) Waukegan, IL St. Dismas Retired.
Ryan, Rev. Msgr. John M. '55 (BUF) Buffalo, NY Assumption Retired.
Ryan, John P. '63 (NEW) Retired.
Ryan, John '74 (NO) Lafitte, LA St. Anthony.
Ryan, Rev. Msgr. John '50 (SB) Retired.
Ryan, John '54 (ALX) Retired.
Ryan, Joseph G. *o.s.a.* '87 (PH)[Y] Villanova, PA St. Thomas Monastery.
Ryan, Joseph J. '51 (STL) Retired.
Ryan, Joseph *o.s.a.* '83 (PH)[C] Villanova University.
Ryan, Rev. Msgr. Kevin E. '70 (SAT) San Antonio, TX St. Mark the Evangelist; Defenders of the Bond.
Ryan, Laurence D. *s.j.* '77 (BGP)[E] Fairfield, CT Fairfield College Preparatory School; [O] Fairfield, CT The Fairfield Jesuit Community–Fairfield University.
Ryan, Lawrence A. '42 (SAC) Retired.
Ryan, Rev. Msgr. Leo P. '54 (PAT)[Q] Chester, NJ Nazareth Village Retired.
Ryan, Michael G. '66 (SEA) Seattle, WA St. James Cathedral.
Ryan, Michael J. '72 (PH) Oreland, PA Holy Martyrs.
Ryan, Michael J. '68 (SEA) Retired.
Ryan, Milton F. *c.m.* '91 (STL) Perryville, MO St. Rose of Lima; [V] Perryville, MO St. Vincent De Paul Educational Foundation; Perryville, MO St. Vincent De Paul.
Ryan, Patrick J. *s.j.* '59 (BO)[U] Weston, MA Campion Health Center, Inc.
Ryan, Patrick J. '58 (STP) Retired.
Ryan, Patrick J. *s.j.* '68 (NY)[DD] Cardinal Spellman Hall, Jesuit Community.
Ryan, Patrick '70 (STL) St. Charles, MO St. Robert Bellarmine.
Ryan, Rev. Msgr. Paul T. '58 (BO) Senior Priests.; Norwood, MA St. Catherine of Siena Retired.
Ryan, Paul *s.m.* '45 (SAT)[K] San Antonio, TX Marianist Residence: Skilled Nursing.
Ryan, Peter F. *s.j.* '87 (BAL)[Q] Baltimore, MD Jesuit Community of Loyola University, Inc.
Ryan, Peter F. *s.j.* '87 (STL)[O] St. Louis, MO Jesuit

Community Corporation at Saint Louis University – Jesuit Hall.
Ryan, Philip V. '57 (DAV) Brooklyn, IA St. Patrick Retired.
Ryan, Philip '57 (SR) Retired.
Ryan, Raymond R. *o.s.a.* '57 (JOL)[L] New Lenox, IL Augustinian Friary; [C] New Lenox, IL Providence Catholic High School.
Ryan, Regis J. '66 (PIT) McKees Rocks, PA St. John of God Retired.
Ryan, Rev. Msgr. Richard J. '73 (STO) Stockton, CA St. Michael Church of Stockton (Pastor of); Vicar General; Vice–Officialis; Ex Officio; Diocesan Building Committee; Diocesan Finance Council; Personnel Board.
Ryan, Richard R. *c.m.* '69 (DEN)[N] Denver, CO Congregation of the Mission Western Province: De Paul House.
Ryan, Richard '77 (PHX) Retired.
Ryan, Robin *c.p.* '84 (FgM) New Rochelle, NY St. Paul of the Cross Province; New Rochelle, NY.
Ryan, Robin *c.p.* '83 (NY)[DD] Pelham Manor, NY St. Vincent's Residence.
Ryan, Stephen Desmond *o.p.* '93 (WDC)[B] Washington, DC Dominican House of Studies.
Ryan, Stephen *o.s.m.* '55 (OAK)[L] Berkeley, CA Servites Retired.
Ryan, Steve *s.d.b.* '92 (NEW)[L] South Orange, NJ Salesian Office of Youth Ministry & Vocations; [Q] Offices of Vocation and Youth Ministry; [L] South Orange, NJ Don Bosco Vocation Office.
Ryan, Rev. Msgr. T. Peter '62 (RVC) Retired.
Ryan, Terrance '77 (SFR) San Francisco, CA Old St. Mary's Cathedral.
Ryan, Thomas A. '64 (GI) Defender of the Bond; Schools; Ord, NE Our Lady of Perpetual Help.
Ryan, Thomas A. *s.j.* '71 (CIN)[Q] Milford, OH Jesuit Spiritual Center at Milford; [N] Cincinnati, OH Jesuit Community at Xavier University.
Ryan, Thomas F. '93 (MET) Sayreville, NJ Our Lady of Victories.
Ryan, Thomas J. '79 (SY) Priests' Personnel Committee; Fayetteville, NY Immaculate Conception.
Ryan, Thomas '73 (BAL) Special Assignment.
Ryan, Thomas *c.s.p.* '75 (WDC)[B] Washington, DC St. Paul's College.
Ryan, Tim '62 (ATL) Retired.
Ryan, Rev. Msgr. Timothy A. '57 (CAM) North Cape May, NJ The Parish of Saint John Neumann, North Cape May, N.J. Retired.
Ryan, Timothy K. '62 (SAV) Special Assignment.
Ryan, William A. *o.s.a.* '66 (P) Myrtle Creek, OR All Souls; [L] Myrtle Creek, OR Augustinian Community.
Ryan, William A. '59 (PEO) Retired.
Ryan, William A. '80 (WDC) On Duty Outside the Archdiocese.
Ryan, William F. '62 (CAM) Cape May Court House, NJ Retired.
Ryan, William F. *s.j.* '62 (SPK)[B] Spokane, WA Gonzaga University.
Ryan, Rev. Msgr. William H. '48 (ELP) El Paso, TX Immaculate Conception Retired.
Ryan, William P. *s.j.* '94 (BAL)[Q] Baltimore, MD Colombiere Jesuit Community.
Ryan, William '55 (JOL) Retired.
Ryan, William '68 (STO) Diamond Springs, CA Retired.
Ryba, Charles J. '69 (CLV) Columbia Station, OH St. Elizabeth Ann Seton; Grafton Correctional Institution; Lorain, OH Lorain Correctional Institution.
Rybarczyk, Melvin *c.r.* '69 (HPM) Sherman Oaks, CA St. Mary Proto–Cathedral.
Rybchuk, Bogdan (STN) Warren, MI St. Vladimir's.
Ryberg, James C. '57 (OM) Retired.
Rybicki, Daryl '79 (FTW) South Bend, IN Corpus Christi.
Rybicki, David G. '09 (LC) Wausau, WI Holy Name of Jesus.
Rybicky, Walter *o.s.b.m.* '83 (STN) Warren, MI St. Josaphat.
Rybolt, John E. *c.m.* '67 (CHI)[N] Chicago, IL DePaul Vincentian Residence.
Rydelek, Rev. Msgr. Theodore F. '89 (TYL) Buffalo, TX Blessed Kateri Tekakwitha Church.
Ryder, Joseph F. '46 (DET) Retired.
Rydzon, Walter G. '73 (PIT) Pittsburgh, PA St. Justin; Allegheny County, PA Depaul Institution; Disabilities, Dept. for Persons with.
Rye, Gary C. *o.s.a.* '65 (SD)[J] San Diego, CA Austin House.
Rykowski, Jerome A. '55 (PBL) Retired.
Rykwalder, David L. '85 (GI) Bridgeport, NE All Souls.
Ryland, Raymond '83 (STU) Retired.
Ryle, Gerald J. '68 (SAC) Sacramento, CA St. Philomene Retired.
Rymdeika, Joseph F. '82 (PH) Horsham, PA St. Catherine of Siena.
Rynes, Theodore J. *s.j.* '62 (SJ)[B] Santa Clara, CA Jesuit Community.
Rynne, Thomas J. '56 (PMB) Jensen Beach, FL St. Martin de Porres Retired.
Ryscavage, Richard J. *s.j.* '77 (BGP)[B] Fairfield, CT Fairfield University; [O] Fairfield, CT The Fairfield Jesuit Community–Fairfield University.
Ryu, Hyong–Nyol *s.j.* (ATL) Doraville, GA Korean Martyrs Catholic Church.
Rywalt, Lawrence *c.p.* '92 (FgM) New Rochelle, NY St. Paul of the Cross Province.
Rywalt, Lawrence *c.p.* '92 (BRK)[R] Jamaica, NY Immaculate Conception Monastery.
Rzadca, Janusz '95 (PAT) Whippany, NJ Our Lady of Mercy.
Rzasowski, Jerzy '85 (MO) Army Chaplains.
Rzeczkowski, Eugene M. *o.p.* '69 (WDC)[B] Washington, DC Dominican House of Studies.
Rzepiela, Thomas R. '72 (CHI) Palatine, IL St. Thomas of Villanova.
Rzeszutek, Martin *m.i.c.* '51 (SPR)[G] Stockbridge, MA Congregation of Marian Fathers of The Immaculate Conception of the Most Blessed Virgin Mary.
Rzonca, Michael W. '73 (PH) Phoenixville, PA Holy Trinity; Phoenixville, PA Sacred Heart.

S

Sa, Dominic Phan '88 (PT) Pensacola, FL St. Mary.
Saad, Hector Vazquez '08 (ORL) Oviedo, FL Most Precious Blood Catholic Church.
Saad, Chorbishop Richard D. '72 (OLL) Birmingham, AL St. Elias Maronite Catholic Church; Birmingham, AL Maronite Catholic Community of Louisiana; Saint Louis, MO St. Sharbel Maronite Catholic Mission; College of Consultors; Office of Communications; Presbyteral Council; Protopresbyters; Spiritual Director for the National Apostolate of Maronites; Personnel Board; Board of Pastors.
Saade, Bassam '92 (SAM) Orlando, FL St. Jude; Presbyteral Council.
Saade, Elie '06 (PH)[B] Springfield, PA Servants of Charity Sd.C.
Saah–Buckman, Michael *s.s.j.* '93 (NO) New Orleans, LA All Saints.
Saale, Richard T. '50 (KC) Retired.
Saato, Fred '67 (NTN) Leave of Absence.
Saavedra, Ramon '99 (NY) Manhattan, NY U.S.V.A. Medical Center.
Saavedra, Ramon '96 (MO) DEPARTMENT OF VETERANS AFFAIRS HOSPITALS AND CHAPLAINS.
Saba, Joseph J. '70 (BGP) Retired.
Saba, Joseph '74 (JUN) On Duty Outside the Diocese.
Saba, Joseph '74 (TUC) Tucson, AZ St. Mary's Hospital; [D] Tucson, AZ Carondelet St. Mary's Hospital.
Sabak, James G. *o.f.m.* '99 (WDC)[O] Silver Spring, MD Gemelli House.
Saballo, Carlito *s.o.l.t.* '96 (CHY) Saint Stephens, WY St. Stephen's; [D] Saint Stephens, WY St. Stephens Mission.
Saban, Michael J. '89 (PH) Norristown, PA Visitation B.V.M.
Sabando, Manuel '92 (DAL) Bonham, TX St. Elizabeth; Bonham, TX Sam Rayburn Memorial Veterans Center.
Sabariar, Thobias *m.c.* '92 (LEX) Middlesboro, KY St. Julian.
Sabastian, Joseph Henry (HT) Houma, LA Maria Immacolata.
Sabatini, Francis J. '63 (PH) Norristown, PA Holy Saviour Retired.
Sabatino, Rev. Msgr. Robert '56 (Y) Retired.
Sabatos, Daniel C. '62 (BRK) Retired.
Sabatté, Frank *c.s.p.* '80 (NY)[DD] New York, NY Paulist Fathers' Motherhouse.
Sabbagh, Stephen F. *o.f.m.* '59 (WDC)[O] Washington, DC Franciscan Monastery USA Inc.; Washington, DC Retired.
Sabel, David '09 (PEO) Pontiac, IL St. Mary's; Cullom, IL St. John's.
Sabella, Charles A. '94 (MET) Somerville, NJ Immaculate Conception.
Sabia, Rev. Msgr. John B. '64 (BGP) Monroe, CT St. Jude.
Sabio, Generoso T. *m.s.c.* '75 (SB) Riverside, CA St. Catherine of Alexandria; Riverside; Appointed Members; Council for Consecrated Life.
Sabio, Lennard '97 (RVC) Farmingdale, NY St. Kilian.
Sabio, Rev. Msgr. Raymundo T. *m.s.c.* (MI) Majuro, MH.
Sabio, Rev. Msgr. Raymundo T. *m.s.c.* '71 (MI) Cathedral of the Assumption; Majuro, MH Outer Island Parish; Vocations.
Sable, Rev. Msgr. Robert M. '74 (DET) On Duty Outside the Archdiocese.
Sable, Thomas F. *s.j.* '75 (SCR)[B] Scranton, PA The University of Scranton.
Sabo, Edward J. *t.o.r.* '68 (STP) Brooklyn Park, MN St. Gerard Majella; [J] Brooklyn Park, MN St. Gerard Friary.
Sabo, Gerald J. *s.j.* '80 (CLV)[B] University Heights, OH John Carroll Jesuit Community.
Sabo, Paul P. '69 (BUF) Council of Catholic Men; Holy Name Society; Adjunct Judicial Vicar; Judges; Eggertsville, NY St. Benedict.
Sabo, Steven M. '03 (RCK) Wonder Lake, IL Christ the King.
Sabog, Henry '60 (HON) Retired.
Sabol, George *o.f.m. conv.* '71 (NY)[DD] Staten Island, NY St. Francis Friary; Staten Island, NY Seaview Hospital Rehabilitation Center and Home.
Sabourin, Rev. Msgr. Gerard O. '60 (PRO) Exeter, RI Blessed Kateri Tekakwitha Catholic Community; Handicapped Persons Apostolate; Eleanor Slater Hospital.
Sabourin, Leo F. '58 (DET) Taylor, MI St. Constance.
Saburo, Rusk R. '93 (CI) Palau, PW Sacred Heart; [C] Manresa Jesuit House.
Saburo, Rusk '88 (CI) Diocesan Consultors; Palau; Defenders of the Bond.
Sacca, Raymond '79 (OAK) Deanery #1; Oakland, CA Cathedral Parish of Christ the Light; Rector of the Cathedral of Christ the Light.
Saccacio, Rev. Msgr. Robert J. '61 (RVC) Retired.
Sacco, Carmine J. *s.j.* '57 (SEA)[C] Tacoma, WA Bellarmine Preparatory School.
Sachs, John Randy *s.j.* '61 (BO)[U] Brighton, MA Noel Chabanel House.
Sack, Juan Carlos *i.v.e.* '88 (VEN) Wauchula, FL St. Michael.
Sacks, Rev. Msgr. Edward R. '64 (ALN) Bethlehem, PA Our Lady of Perpetual Help; Elected Members.
Sacks, Francis W. *c.m.* '67 (GR)[J] Spring Lake, MI St. Lazare Retreat House.
Sacks, Francis W. *c.m.* '67 (PH)[Y].
Sacksteder, Rev. Msgr. Thomas B. '73 (COV) Florence, KY St. Paul.
Sacus, Rev. Msgr. Samuel S. '66 (WH) Beckley, WV St. Francis De Sales; Diocesan Consultors; Vicars Forane.
Sadaba, Martin (ARE) Vega Baja, PR Parroquia de San Martin de Porres.
Sadek, Rev. Msgr. Ignace '57 (SAM)[A] Washington, DC Our Lady of Lebanon Maronite Seminary Retired.
Sadie, Rev. Msgr. P. Edward '57 (WH) Charleston, WV Basilica of the Co–Cathedral of the Sacred Heart; Diocesan Consultors; Vicars Forane; Catholic Conference of West Virginia; Director.
Sadlack, Robert J. '70 (BRK) East Elmhurst, NY St. Gabriel.
Sadlowski, Ronald F. '72 (SPR) Russell, MA Holy Family Parish.
Sadowski, Izydor *s.d.b.* (NOR)[H] Putnam, CT Matulaitis Nursing Home Inc.
Sadowski, Marek *c.m.* '94 (HRT) New Haven, CT St. Stanislaus.
Sadowsky, James A. *s.j.* '57 (NY)[DD] Loyola Hall, Jesuit Community.
Sadusky, Rev. Msgr. Joseph F. '70 (WDC) Washington, DC St. Peter; Pastoral Center Special Ministries; Judicial Vicars.
Saeed, Rev. Msgr. Chorbishop Saeed D. '98 (SPA) Chancellor; Director of Finance; Judicial Officer; Glendale, AZ Holy Family Mission; Scottsdale, AZ Mar Auraha Chaldean Catholic Parish.
Saelzler, Richard J. '76 (TOL)[I] Toledo, OH Ursuline Convent of the Sacred Heart.
Saengthien, Peter P. *s.j.* '06 (STL)[O] St. Louis, MO St. Matthew Jesuit Community; St. Louis, MO St. Matthew, Apostle.
Saenz, Alejandro '11 (CC) Rockport, TX Sacred Heart.
Saenz, Alonso '97 (PHX) Phoenix, AZ St. Catherine of Siena Roman Catholic Parish; Presbyteral Council.
Saenz, Christopher *s.s.c.* '00 (FgM) St Columbans, NE House of Post–Graduate Studies.
Saenz, David (CC)[D] Corpus Christi, TX.
Saenz, Fernando A. '10 (SFE) Mountainair, NM St. Alice; Rio Rancho, NM St. Thomas Aquinas.
Saenz, Francisco J. *o.p.* (TR) Freehold, NJ St. Rose of Lima.
Saenz, Jorge L. '03 (MIA) On Leave.
Saenz, José '04 (DEN) Carbondale, CO St. Vincent.
Saenz, Juan Carlos '04 (SEA) Burlington, WA St. Charles; La Conner, WA Sacred Heart; Mount Vernon, WA Immaculate Conception; Sedro Woolley, WA Immaculate Heart of Mary.
Saenz, Nestor (CHI) Chicago, IL Our Lady of Fatima.
Saenz, Roberto B. *s.j.* '57 (SPK)[J] Spokane, WA Regis Community Retired.
Saenz, Urbano *o.s.a.* '70 (BEA) Port Arthur, TX Our Lady of Guadalupe.
Saenz–Ramos, Jorge (SJN) Toa Alta, PR San Jose.
Safiejko, Edward M. '48 (MIL) Retired.
Safko, Gerard F. '90 (SCR) Montrose, PA Holy Name of Mary.
Safranek, William J. '96 (OM) Beemer, NE Holy Cross; Wisner, NE St. Joseph; [M] Ewing, NE St. Theresa Church of Clearwater Cemetery Endowment Trust Fund.
Safraniec, Joseph N. '76 (MO) Air Force Reserve Chaplains Retired.
Sagardia, Reinaldo '79 (SJN) San Juan, PR Nuestra Senora de Belen.
Saglio, Charles A. '74 (RIC) Franklin, VA St. Jude.
Sagorski, Peter A. '95 (ORL) Wildwood, FL St. Vincent de Paul.
Sagra, Rev. Msgr. Andrés '65 (DAL) Dallas, TX Mary Immaculate.
Saguto, Gerard *f.s.s.p.* '04 (SEA) Seattle, WA North

American Martyrs Personal Quasi–Parish.
Saharic, Michael C. '88 (MET) Hampton, NJ St. Ann.
Sahd, Christopher S. '01 (SCR) Archbald, PA St. Mary of Czestochowa; Archbald, PA St. Thomas Aquinas; Archbald, PA Christ the King Parish.
Saint Jean, Kidney M. '92 (MIA) Margate, FL Our Lady Queen of Heaven.
Saint Martin, Jeremy P. (BO) Newton, MA Sacred Heart.
Saint Pierre, Ronald L. '83 (BO) Tyngsborough, MA St. Mary Magdalen.
Saiz, Rafail A. '94 (ANC) Anchorage, AK Holy Cross.
Sajda, Michael *o.f.m.conv.* '79 (BUF)[N] Athol Springs, NY St. Francis of Assisi Friary; [D] Athol Springs, NY St. Francis High School; Definitors.
Sajdak, John *s.m.* '71 (DET)[K] Livonia, MI Marist Fathers & Brothers Community.
Sajdak, Ronald P. '96 (BUF) Vicars; Propagation of the Faith; Buffalo, NY St. Martin de Porres; Clergy Personnel Board.
Sajgo, Szabolcs *s.j.* '74 (ATH) Hungarian Priests' Association in Canada.
Sakano, Rev. Msgr. Donald '71 (NY) New York, NY Basilica of St. Patrick's Old Cathedral; [HH] New York, NY The Housing Fund of the Archdiocese of New York.
Sakowicz, Gregory '79 (CHI) Evanston, IL St. Mary.
Sakowski, Derek '03 (LC) Graduate Studies.
Sakowski, John J. '05 (SFR) San Francisco, CA St. Thomas the Apostle.
Sala, Manuel I. (PCE) Guayama, PR SS. Peter and Paul.
Sala, Michael J. *s.j.* '77 (NY) Metropolitan Hospital; [DD] New York, NY St. Ignatius Loyola Residence.
Salach, Conrad *o.f.m.conv.* '62 (FR) New Bedford, MA Our Lady of Perpetual Help.
Salada, Urbano '59 (SD) Retired.
Salah, Michael A. '91 (WDC) Wheaton, MD St. Catherine Laboure.
Salamone, Charles E. '75 (BO)[O] Brighton, MA Caritas St. Elizabeth's Medical Center of Boston, Inc.
Salamoni, Vincent *m.s.a.* '84 (NOR)[G] Cromwell Society of the Missionaries of the Holy Apostles.
Salanga, Victor *s.j.* '74 (NY)[DD] Loyola Hall, Jesuit Community.
Salanitro, Alfred J. '89 (OM) Bellevue, NE St. Bernadette; Deans; Deans.
Salanitro, Carl A. '70 (OM) Omaha, NE Holy Cross.
Salapata, Andrzej *s.ch.* '97 (SJ) San Jose, CA St. Brother Albert Chmielowski Polish Catholic Pastoral Mission.
Salas, Mark N.P. '11 (ELP) Presbyteral Council; El Paso, TX Most Holy Trinity.
Salas, Raul *o.m.i.* '80 (SAT)[B] San Antonio, TX George Sexton House of Studies.
Salas, Rev. Msgr. Sipio '50 (SFE) Retired.
Salatino, John C. '94 (SPR) Pittsfield, MA St. Mark's; [M] Pittsfield, MA Berkshire Community College.
Salazar, Cesar '06 (AMA) Silverton, TX Our Lady of Loretto.
Salazar, Donald *o.f.m.* '67 (FgM) New York, NY Franciscan Province of the Immaculate Conception.
Salazar, Edward '74 (ATL)[H] Atlanta, GA Ignatius House.
Salazar, Edward *s.j.* '74 (FWT)[J] Lake Dallas, TX Montserrat Jesuit Retreat House.
Salazar, Eusebio C. Fernandez '71 (SJN) San Juan, PR Santa Catalina Laboure.
Salazar, Franklin '75 (ORL) Lakeland, FL St. Joseph's.
Salazar, George '67 (SFE) LAS VEGAS: Newman Center; State Hospital; Las Vegas, NM Immaculate Conception.
Salazar, Jose A. (NY) Manhattan, NY U.S.V.A. Medical Center; New York, NY New York City Veterans Administration Hospital.
Salazar, Jose *m.s.a.* '77 (NOR)[G] Cromwell Society of the Missionaries of the Holy Apostles.
Salazar, Jose '85 (CC)[A] Houston, TX St. Mary's Seminary; On Duty Outside the Diocese.
Salazar, Jose Luis S. *s.j.* '01 (NEW)[L] Jersey City, NJ Jesuits of Saint Peter's College, Inc.; [B] Jersey City, NJ Jesuit Center.
Salazar, Mario A. '61 (YAK) Quincy, WA St. Pius X; Vicar for Priests; Clergy Personnel Board.
Salazar, Mario P. '90 (YAK) Granger, WA Our Lady of Guadalupe.
Salazar–Valero, Rogelio '08 (SJN) Rio Piedras, PR Santismo Sacramento; [B] San Juan, PR Colegio Angeles Custodios; San Juan, PR San Jose Obrero.
Salazar Castano, Jairo (SJN) Bayamon, PR Nuestra Senora de Covadonga.
Salazzo, Michael J. '76 (CHI) Chicago, IL St. Tarcissus.
Salberg, James G. '69 (PIT) Butler, PA St. Andrew.
Salca, Louis '65 (SD) Retired.
Salcedo, Luis G. '89 (WDC) Retired.
Salcedo, Reginaldo '89 (SAG) Saginaw, MI SS. Casimir & St. George; Bay City, MI Our Lady of Guadalupe.
Saldana, Jesus '82 (MIA) Miami, FL St. Kevin.
Saldana, Luis F. '99 (NY)[A] Yonkers, NY Cathedral Prep Program; [A] Yonkers, NY St. Joseph's Seminary.
Saldana, Luis *s.t.l.* '99 (BRK)[B] Douglaston, NY Cathedral Seminary Residence of the Immaculate Conception.
Saldana, Wilson '93 (PCE) Salinas, PR Our Lady of Monserrat.
Saldana–Taneco, Ermeregildo *s.t.* '94 (TUC)[I] South Tucson, AZ Blessed Kateri Tekakwitha Parish Center; Tucson, AZ Blessed Kateri Tekakwitha Roman Catholic Missions Parish – Tucson.
Saldanha, Reginald '97 (KCK) Osawatomie, KS Our Lady of Lourdes; Osawatomie, KS Sacred Heart Shrine to St. Philippine Duchesne; Osawatomie, KS St. Philip Neri.
Saldarriaga, Reinaldo A. '89 (BRK) Richmond Hill, NY Holy Child Jesus; Vice Officiale–Associate Judicial Vicar; Attorneys and Counselors at Canon Law.
Salditos, Henry '89 (LAV) Las Vegas, NV St. James the Apostle.
Salditos, Rey '83 (LAV) Las Vegas, NV Our Lady of Las Vegas; Hospital Apostolate.
Salditos, Ricardito P. '80 (MO) Air Force Chaplains.
Saldivar, Roberto *m.sp.s.* '00 (LA) Oxnard, CA Our Lady of Guadalupe Parish.
Saldua, Max E. '78 (LA) West Los Angeles, CA VA Greater Los Angeles Health System.
Saldua, Max Ernesto M. '78 (MO) DEPARTMENT OF VETERANS AFFAIRS HOSPITALS AND CHAPLAINS.
Salemi, Rev. Msgr. Cajetan P. '61 (NEW) Woodcliff Lake, NJ Our Lady Mother of the Church Retired.
Salemi, Paul S. '00 (BUF) Williamsville, NY St. Gregory the Great.
Salen, Enrique V. '90 (GAL)[S] Houston, TX The Catholic Chaplain Corps; Houston, TX St. Francis de Sales.
Salera, Alfredo J. '77 (CHI) Chicago, IL Transfiguration of Our Lord.
Salerno, Emilio J. '59 (BRK) Retired.
Salerno, Joseph A. '65 (CAM) Judges; Adjutant Judicial Vicars; Millville, NJ The Parish of All Saints, Millville, N.J.; Defenders of the Bond Retired.
Salerno, Joseph A. '80 (SY) Utica, NY Our Lady of Lourdes; Eastern Area Vicars; Presbyteral Council; Board of Diocesan Consultors.
Sales, Kenneth '04 (OAK) Priest Representatives – Alameda County; Oakley, CA St. Anthony.
Saletrik, E. George '96 (GBG) Scottdale, PA St. John the Baptist; Diocesan Catholic Scoutmaster.
Salgado, Gerardo Francisco *o.f.m.* '99 (ELP)[B] El Paso, TX St. Anthony's School of Theology.
Salgado, Manuel E. *o.ss.t.* (ARE) Isabela, PR St. Anthony.
Salgado, Raul '83 (CHK) Presbyteral Council.
Salgado, Raul '83 (CHK) Saipan, MP Santa Soledad Mission Parish; Hospital Chaplaincy (Saipan).
Salgado, Salvador *c.m.f.* '87 (SJN) Bayamon, PR San Jose.
Saliba, John A. *s.j.* '65 (DET)[K] Detroit, MI Jesuit Community at the University of Detroit Mercy.
Salibindia, Pratap Reddy '91 (WIN) Rochester, MN Pax Christi; Rochester, MN SS. Peter and Paul.
Salicone, Aniello *s.x.* '66 (MIL)[B] Franklin, WI Xaverian Missionary Fathers College Seminary.
Saliga, Christopher *o.p.* '05 (FgM) New York, NY Province of St. Joseph (Eastern).
Saligumba, Carlos *s.o.l.t.* '91 (KC) Kansas City, MO St. Louis.
Salim, Anthony J. (SAM) Olean, NY St. Joseph.
Salim, Anthony '74 (OLL) Special Assignment.
Salinas, Andres '93 (RCK) Aurora, IL St. Nicholas.
Salinas, Francisco Javier Esteban *c.o.r.c.* '97 (SB)[I] Corona, CA Confraternity of Operarios Del Reino De Cristo, C.O.R.C.
Salinas, Octavio *o.f.m.* '83 (FgM) New York, NY Franciscan Province of the Immaculate Conception.
Salinas, Rodolfo A. '11 (WDC) Silver Spring, MD St. Andrew Apostle.
Salinas, Romeo '99 (CC) Kingsville, TX St. Joseph.
Salisbury, Keith R. '06 (NU) Arlington, MN St. Mary; Gaylord, MN St. Michael; Green Isle, MN St. Brendan; Priests' Council.
Salisbury, Paschal D. *o.p.* '67 (SFR)[N] San Francisco, CA St. Dominic Priory; San Francisco, CA St. Dominic.
Saliva, Juan '90 (PCE) Police Chaplains.
Salko, John H. '60 (PBR) Scottdale, PA St. John the Baptist; Protopresbyters.
Salkovski, Varcilio Basil *o.s.b.m.* '88 (STN) Palos Park, IL Nativity of B.V.M.; Diocesan Consultors; Chicago; Presbyteral Council.
Saller, Neil *t.o.r.* '56 (PH)[Y] Fairless Hills, PA St. Anthony Friary.
Sallese, Albert J. '66 (BO) Senior Priests.; Saugus, MA Blessed Sacrament Retired.
Sallis, Steven '80 (SEA) Seattle, WA St. Benedict; Presbyteral Council; Seattle, WA St. Anne; College of Consultors.
Sallot, Steven '80 (ORG) Dana Point, CA San Felipe de Jesus; Dana Point, CA St. Edward the Confessor; Membership; Consultors; Council of Priests.
Salmani, Frank S. '82 (PRO) Warwick, RI St. William; [T] Warwick, RI.
Salmi, Richard P. *s.j.* '82 (MOB)[A] Mobile, AL Spring Hill College.
Salmon, Edward F. *s.j.* '85 (ROC)[B] Rochester, NY McQuaid Jesuit High School.
Salmon, Edward P. '59 (CHI) Oak Park, IL St. Giles Retired.
Salmon, James F. *s.j.* '64 (BAL)[B] Timonium, MD Loyola Graduate Center–Timonium Campus; [Q] Baltimore, MD Jesuit Community of Loyola University, Inc.; [B] Jesuit Community of Loyola University, Inc.
Salmon, William F. '65 (BO) Weymouth, MA Immaculate Conception.
Salmonowicz, Philip J. '03 (GR) Muskegon, MI St. Francis de Sales.
Salnicky, Michael '93 (PSC) Pocono Summit, PA St. Nicholas; [C] Cresco, PA Carpathian Village; Wyoming Valley Protopresbyterate; Saint Nicholas Shrine – Carpathian Village.
Salocks, Stephen E. '80 (BO)[A] Brighton, MA St. John Seminary.
Salois, Philip G. *m.s.* '84 (MO) DEPARTMENT OF VETERANS AFFAIRS HOSPITALS AND CHAPLAINS.
Salois, Philip *m.s.* (BO) Pastoral Care.
Salomon, Elias M. '79 (SFR) San Francisco, CA St. Elizabeth.
Salomon, Victor '98 (WDC)[B] Washington, DC Diocesan Laborer Priests, House of Studies.
Salomone, Gregory *o.p.* (NEW)[M] Summit, NJ Monastery of Our Lady of the Rosary.
Salomone, Ramon A. *s.j.* '65 (NY) New York, NY Society of Jesus; [DD] New York, NY Society of Jesus, New York Province; [DD] New York, NY St. Ignatius Loyola Residence.
Salonga, Juan S. '10 (MET) South Plainfield, NJ Sacred Heart.
Saltar, William '08 (MGZ) Mayaguez, PR Our Lady of Mt. Carmel.
Saltarin, Jose C. '67 (NEW) Retired.
Salter, Batholomew C. *c.s.c.* '71 (FTW)[H] Notre Dame Congregation of Holy Cross, United States Province of Priests & Brothers.
Salus, Jude S. *o.s.b.* '75 (PAT) Cedar Knolls, NJ Notre Dame of Mt. Carmel; [N] Morristown St. Mary's Abbey; Deans; Presbyteral Council; Clergy Personnel Office.
Salvador, Jose Maria Segura *s.j.* '11 (BO)[U] Brighton, MA Francis Xavier House.
Salvador, Stephen B. '74 (FR) Fall River, MA SS. Peter and Paul; Irving, TX National Catholic Committee on Scouting Executive Committee (1934).
Salvagna, Michael *c.p.* '69 (PIT)[O] Pittsburgh, PA St. Paul of the Cross Retreat Center.
Salvania, Leopoldo S. '11 (MET) Alpha, NJ St. Mary.
Salvas, John *o.f.m.cap.* '88 (CHL) Hendersonville, NC Immaculate Conception.
Salvatori, Chris *s.a.c.* '99 (NY) Yonkers, NY Our Lady of Mt. Carmel.
Salvi, Americo *c.r.m.* '55 (NEW) Lodi, NJ St. Joseph's.
Salvo, Enrique '10 (NY) New York, NY St. Elizabeth.
Salwowski, Andrezej '86 (BRK) Ozone Park, NY St. Stanislaus Bishop and Martyr; Ozone Park, NY Nativity of the Blessed Virgin Mary.
Saly, Rev. Msgr. Robert J. '85 (ALT) Dmitri Manor – Priests' Residence – St. Mary's Lane; [F] Hollidaysburg, PA Dmitri Manor Priests' Residence; Duncansville, PA St. Catherine of Siena.
Salz, Marvin C. '64 (DUB) St. Lucas, IA St. Luke; Waucoma, IA St. Mary; Lawler, IA Our Lady of Mt. Carmel; Deans; Protivin, IA St. John Nepomucene; Protivin, IA Assumption of the B.V.M.; Protivin, IA Holy Trinity; Vocation Awareness Advisory Committee.
Salzillo, Raphael Mary *o.p.* '09 (SEA) Seattle, WA Blessed Sacrament.
Salzmann, George S. *o.s.f.s.* '77 (BO) Cambridge, MA St. Paul; [AA] Cambridge, MA Harvard Catholic Center.
Sama, Cassian *o.p.* '11 (IND) Bloomington, IN St. Paul Catholic Center, Bloomington, Inc.
Samaha, Jeffrey F. '78 (WDC) Hospital & Nursing Home Ministries; Forestville, MD Church of the Holy Spirit.
Samaha, Rt. Rev. Victor *b.c.o.* (NTN) Retired.
Samala, Savio J. '89 (GB)[O] Green Bay, WI Society for Faith and Children's Education, Inc.
Samaniego, Eduardo *s.j.* '69 (SJ) San Jose, CA Most Holy Trinity.
Samaniego, Tarsicio *l.c.* '67 (HRT)[B] Cheshire, CT Novitiate of the Legion of Christ.
Samay, Sebastian A. *o.s.b.* '59 (GBG)[H] Latrobe, PA Saint Vincent Archabbey.
Samayoa, Emmanuel G. '89 (ROM) Detroit, MI St. John the Baptist.
Sambor, David R. '78 (SY) Special Assignment.
Sambu, Jean Olivier M. '02 (BWN) Rio Grande City Deanery; Rio Grande City, TX Immaculate Conception; Board Members.
Samela, Paul Anthony Suresh '88 (SPC) Springfield,

MO St. Elizabeth Ann Seton; Nixa, MO St. Francis of Assisi.
Samele, Christopher J. '03 (BGP)[C] Trumbull, CT St. Joseph High School; Trumbull, CT St. Catherine of Siena.
Samian, Marvin '92 (HON) Honolulu, HI Cathedral of Our Lady of Peace.
Samiano, Marvin '92 (HON) Judicial Vicar and Director of Canonical Affairs; Mission Cooperative Program.
Sammut, George '99 (PT) Chipley, FL St. Joseph the Worker; Marianna, FL St. Anne.
Sammut, Tito '52 (GB) Retired.
Samoylo, Francis J. '01 (NY) Cortlandt Manor, NY St. Columbanus.
Samperi, Charles J. '96 (GAL) Spring, TX St. James the Apostle; Priests Personnel Committee; George Bush Intercontinental Airport.
Sampson, Elric '85 (CHI)[N] Chicago, IL St. Peter's Friary.
Sampson, James *s.p.* '65 (SFE)[H] Jemez Springs, NM Our Lady of Lourdes; Albuquerque, NM Annunciation.
Sampson, Kenneth '08 (P) Astoria, OR St. Mary, Star of the Sea; Area Vicars; Finance Council.
Samra, Basil '86 (NTN) Retired.
Sams, Ronald W. *s.j.* '59 (BUF) Consultors, College of; Buffalo, NY St. Michael; Council of Priests.
Samsa, John Francis *o.f.m.cap.* '61 (GB)[J] Appleton, WI St. Fidelis Friary Retired.
Samson, Arokiaswamy '89 (HBG) Lancaster General Hospital and Lancaster Community Hospital; Lancaster, PA Sacred Heart of Jesus.
Samson, Jordan '11 (SFS) Aberdeen, SD St. Mary.
Samson, Robert J. '79 (STL) St. Louis, MO St. Gabriel the Archangel.
Samter, James W. '87 (GB) Retired.
Samuel, Francis A. *o.c.i.* '72 (RVC) Babylon, NY St. Joseph.
Samuels, Reginald Wayne '09 (GAL) Houston, TX Christ the Redeemer; Ecumenism and Interreligious Affairs Commission.
Samway, Patrick H. *s.j.* '69 (PH)[C] Jesuit Fathers; [Y] Philadelphia, PA St. Alphonsus House.
Samy, Ed '67 (SJ) Sunnyvale, CA St. Martin Retired.
Sanabria, Rafael *c.s.v.* '96 (CHI)[N] Arlington Heights Viatorian Province Center–Clerics of St. Viator.
Sanaghan, John J. '72 (CHI) Chicago, IL St. Matthias.
Sanahuja, Manuel *sch.p.* '67 (LA) Los Angeles, CA Our Lady Help of Christians (Maria Auxiliadora); Hispanic Liturgy and Ministry Coordinator; Ex Officio.
San Andres, Vito '79 (AGN) Dededo, GU Santa Barbara.
Sanchez, Adalberto '11 (RCK) Elgin, IL St. Joseph.
Sanchez, Adrian *o.praem.* '95 (ORG)[I] Silverado, CA Norbertine Fathers of Orange Inc.
Sanchez, Alejandro '93 (STV) On Duty Outside the Diocese.
Sanchez, Alejandro (SJN) Military Services.
Sanchez, Angel '90 (PCE) Villalba, PR Our Lady of Mt. Carmel.
Sanchez, Antero *m.s.c.* '65 (FRS) McFarland, CA St. Elizabeth.
Sanchez, Antonio '90 (MRY) Salinas, CA Christ the King.
Sanchez, Castor G. '61 (TR) Retired.
Sanchez, David '02 (L) Louisville, KY Holy Name; Louisville, KY St. Joseph.
Sanchez, Edgar *m.sp.s.* '97 (SEA) Mill Creek, WA St. Elizabeth Ann Seton.
Sanchez, Felix '65 (SP) Retired.
Sánchez, Rev. Msgr. Fernando Benicio Felices '82 (SJN) Trujillo Alto, PR Gruta de Lourdes.
Sanchez, Fernando *o.c.d.* (CGS) Caguas, PR San Jose.
Sanchez, German '90 (LA) Los Angeles, CA St. Sebastian.
Sanchez, Humberto '97 (GAL) Houston, TX St. Raphael the Archangel.
Sanchez, James *s.o.l.t.* '01 (SFE) Mora, NM St. Gertrude.
Sanchez, Jose M. '58 (GAL)[L] Houston, TX Pope John Paul XXIII Priests' Residence Retired.
Sanchez, Jose *c.m.f.* '95 (CHI)[N] Oak Park, IL Claretian Missionaries Community Support Trust; [N] Chicago, IL Claret House.
Sanchez, Juan Luis '84 (MIA) Miami, FL SS. Peter and Paul.
Sanchez, Luis Fernando '10 (BWN) Weslaco, TX St. Pius X.
Sanchez, Marco *s.t.* (FAJ) Loiza, PR Santiago Apostol, El Mayor.
Sanchez, Marcos '09 (B) Burley, ID St. Therese Little Flower; Catholic Liturgical Commission; Burley, ID St. Therese Little Flower.
Sanchez, Miguel Angel '98 (ELP)[A] El Paso, TX St. Charles Seminary; Vocations & Seminarians.
Sanchez, Nicolas '91 (LA) North Hollywood, CA St. Patrick.
Sanchez, Oscar '90 (FAJ) Pastoral Vicar.
Sanchez, Pablo *m.sp.s.* '05 (P) Hillsboro, OR St. Matthew; [L] Hillsboro, OR Missionaries of the Holy Spirit, M.Sp.S.
Sanchez, Rev. Msgr. Paul R. '71 (BRK) Rego Park, NY Resurrection–Ascension; Queens; Assignment Board.
Sanchez, Prudencio *c.m.* '59 (MGZ) Mayaguez, PR San Vicente.
Sanchez, Raul N. '74 (GLP) On Leave of Absence.
Sanchez, Raul '02 (OKL) Guymon, OK St. Peter's.
Sanchez, Raul '11 (FRS) Reedley, CA St. Anthony of Padua.
Sanchez, Ricardo '99 (CHL) Biscoe, NC Our Lady of the Americas.
Sanchez, Ruben D. Bedoya '91 (LAV) Las Vegas, NV Holy Family.
Sanchez, Rudolfo '01 (GAL) Houston, TX Blessed Sacrament.
Sanchez, Stephen *o.c.d.* '92 (DAL)[H] Dallas, TX Mount Carmel Center; [J] Dallas, TX Mt. Carmel Center.
Sanchez, Steve '07 (SFE) University Hospital.
Sanchez, Victor '91 (ARE) Seminario Jesus Maestro College Seminary; Retreat House, Centro Diocesano Mons. Mendez; Vocations; Diocesan Consultors; Arecibo, PR Santa Ana; Seminary Board and Vocation Program.
Sanchez, William E. '83 (SFE) Albuquerque, NM St. Edwin.
Sanchez–Espinoza, Juan '93 (CHI) Other Assignments.
Sanchez–Lopez, Oscar Alberto '90 (FAJ) Canovanas, PR San Jose.
Sanchez–Maya, Rigoberto '01 (SB) Hesperia, CA Holy Family.
Sanchez–Munoz, Alejandro '66 (MO) Army National Guard Chaplains.
Sanchez Chan, Ramiro V. *c.s.* '03 (LA)[B] Sun Valley, CA Scalabrini House of Discernment (Seminary).
Sanchez de la Torre, Flavio *o.f.m.* '90 (LAR) Hebbronville, TX Our Lady of Guadalupe.
Sanchez Muniz, Victor Rene '10 (PCE) Mercedita, PR Church of the Resurrection.
Sanchez Toledano, Nicolas '91 (LA) El Monte, CA Our Lady of Guadalupe.
Sancho, Jesus *o.c.d.* '64 (OKL) Oklahoma City, OK Our Lady of Mount Carmel and St. Therese Little Flower.
Sancho Piquer, Enrique '50 (PCE) On Duty Outside the Diocese.
Sand, John '55 (SPK) Retired.
Sandberg, Kevin J. *c.s.c.* '05 (FTW)[H] Notre Dame Congregation of Holy Cross, United States Province of Priests & Brothers.
Sandberg, Kevin J. *c.s.c.* '05 (FR)[A] North Easton, MA Holy Cross Fathers Religious.
Sandberg, Stuart '68 (NY)[HH] White Plains, NY Company of St. Paul; White Plains, NY Company of St. Paul (Lay People and Priests).
Sander, Reginald *o.s.b.* '63 (KC) Tarkio, MO St. Paul the Apostle; [J] Priests Elsewhere.
Sander, Timothy *o.s.b.* '41 (P)[L] St. Benedict, OR Mt. Angel Abbey.
Sanderfoot, Brian P. '04 (WDC) Leonardtown, MD St. Francis Xavier.
Sanders, Daniel J. '78 (MIL) Mequon, WI Lumen Christi.
Sanders, Edwin J. *s.j.* '59 (ALN)[A] Wernersville, PA Jesuit Center–Jesuit Community.
Sanders, Gary *o.s.a.* '75 (SD)[J] Office of the Provincial; [J] San Diego, CA Augustinian Provincialate; [J] San Diego, CA Monica House – Augustinian Community.
Sanders, Rev. Msgr. John C. '73 (BGP)[O] Stamford, CT The Catherine Dennis Keefe Queen of the Clergy Retired Priests' Residence Retired.
Sanders, Joseph P. '61 (ALN)[A] Wernersville, PA Jesuit Center–Jesuit Community.
Sanders, Lawrence E. '93 (TUC) Tucson, AZ Santa Catalina Roman Catholic Parish – Tucson; [G] Tucson, AZ Redemptorist Society of Arizona Redemptorist Renewal Center.
Sanders, Patrick B. '90 (NO) On Administrative Leave.
Sanders, Peter C. '84 (MRY)[F] Monterey, CA Oratorian Community–Congregation of the Oratory of Pontifical Right; Monterey, CA.
Sanders, Philip A. '05 (NEW) New Providence, NJ Our Lady of Peace.
Sanders, William F. '75 (WOR) Worcester, MA Our Lady of the Rosary; Advocates; Deans; Presbyteral Council.
Sandersfeld, Rev. Msgr. John '66 (SJ) Retired.
Sanderson, Harold (SY) Syracuse, NY Rosewood Heights Nursing Home.
Sanderson, William E. '83 (OM) Omaha, NE St. Francis Assisi; Omaha, NE St. Mary.
Sandhage, Martin J. '86 (LFT) Winamac, IN St. Peter.
Sandi, Rev. Msgr. Thomas P. '73 (NY) Shrub Oak, NY Saint Elizabeth Ann Seton.
Sandman, Gregory '80 (MRY) Administrative Committee Priests' Pension Plan; Clergy Personnel Board; Salinas, CA Madonna Del Sasso.
Sandmann, Augustus C. *o.s.a.* '47 (PH)[Y] Villanova, PA St. Thomas Monastery.
Sandor, Albert *o.f.m.cap.* '82 (DET)[K] Detroit St. Bonaventure Friary.
Sandor, George *o.f.m.conv.* '72 (SY) Binghamton, NY SS. Cyril and Method; Binghamton, NY Holy Trinity.
Sandoval, Clarence J. '87 (SLC) Layton, UT Saint Rose of Lima LLC 245.
Sandoval, Ismael '03 (CHI) Blue Island, IL St. Benedict.
Sandoval, Lazaro *o.f.m.conv.* '07 (LA) Hermosa Beach, CA Our Lady of Guadalupe.
Sandoval, Luis '74 (SAT) On Leave.
Sandoval, Norberto '05 (MIL) Fontana, WI St. Benedict.
Sandoz, Robert J. *o.f.m.* (NEW)[C] Newark, NJ Christ the King Preparatory School of Newark, N.J., Corp.; [C] Newark, NJ Christ the King Work Study Program.
Sandrick, Philip *o.s.b.m.* (STF)[E] Locust Valley, NY Provincialate of Basilian Fathers; Religious Communities, Vicar.
Sands, Joseph C. *s.j.* '92 (NY)[B] Bronx, NY Ciszek Hall.
Sands, Maurice Henry '05 (DET) Taylor, MI St. Alfred; Staff.
Sandstrom, Philip '62 (NY) On Duty Outside the Archdiocese.
Sandweg, Michael J. '79 (STL) Retired.
Sanella, Nicholas A. (BO) Presbyteral Council.
Sanfelippo, Frank J. '58 (MIL) Retired.
Sanfilippo, David '94 (PHX) Gilbert, AZ St. Anne Roman Catholic Parish; College of Consultors; Priest Personnel; Advisory Board for the Continuing Formation of Priests; Priestly Life and Ministry Board; Priests' Placement Board; Presbyteral Council; Phoenix, AZ St. Gregory Roman Catholic Parish; Priests, Vicar for.
Sanford, James R. *o.s.f.s.* '86 (TOL) Toledo, OH Sacred Heart of Jesus; Toledo, OH St. Stephen.
Sanford, L. Harold *s.j.* '75 (DET)[K] Clarkston, MI Colombiere Center.
Sanford, L. Harold *s.j.* '75 (LAN) Genesys Regional Medical Center.
Sanford, Stephen J. *s.j.* '94 (BO)[U] Boston The Society of Jesus of New England–Provincial Offices.
Sanford, Stephen J. *s.j.* '94 (RC) Pine Ridge, SD Holy Rosary/Red Cloud Indian School Inc.; [C] Pine Ridge, SD Jesuit Community of Holy Rosary Mission.
Sang, Francis D. '73 (RVC) Deer Park, NY SS. Cyril and Methodius.
Sang–Ki, Jeong '00 (BIR) Birmingham, AL Korean Catholic Community, St. Luke Hwang.
Sangermano, Rev. Msgr. Charles L. '78 (PH) Norristown, PA Holy Saviour.
Sangiovanni, William F. '77 (BGP)[C] Fairfield, CT Notre Dame Catholic High School.
San Juan, Alfonso *c.p.* '60 (SAC)[H] Citrus Heights, CA Christ the King Passionist Retreat Center.
Sankar, Paul (BGP) Norwalk, CT St. Thomas the Apostle.
Sanko, Joshua M. '06 (LFT)[B] Noblesville, IN Saint Theodore Guerin High School.
Sankoorikal, George S. '71 (BGP) Brookfield, CT St. Marguerite Bourgeoys.
Sankoorikal, Paul L. '59 (LC) Retired.
Sanks, T. Howland *s.j.* '65 (OAK)[L] Berkeley, CA Jesuit Fathers and Brothers; [A] Berkeley, CA Jesuit School of Theology of Santa Clara University (Berkeley, California Campus).
San Martin, Francisco J. *s.j.* (MOB) Sacramental Ministers.
San Martin, Javier *s.j.* '71 (MOB)[A] Mobile, AL Spring Hill College.
Sannella, Nicholas A. (BO) Lowell, MA Immaculate Conception.
Sanner, Rev. Msgr. James E. '59 (E) Retired.
San Nicasio, Julian *s.d.b.* (ARE) Orocovis, PR San Juan Bautista.
San Nicolas, Jeffrey C. '97 (AGN) Yigo, GU Our Lady of Lourdes; Formation Program for the Permanent Diaconate; Our Lady of Lourdes Parish; Archdiocesan Presbyteral Council.
Sans, Pablo '53 (BRK) Richmond Hill, NY Our Lady of the Cenacle Retired.
Sanson, Robert J. '67 (CLV) Judges in Second Instance; North Ridgeville, OH St. Peter.
Sansone, Anthony J. '80 (BRK) Brooklyn, NY Sacred Hearts of Jesus and Mary and St. Stephen.
Santa, Michael *o.s.b.* '56 (KCK)[I] Atchison, KS St. Benedict's Abbey Retired.
Santa, Thomas *c.ss.r.* '78 (CHI) Chicago, IL St. Michael in Old Town; [N] Chicago, IL The Redemptorist Fathers of Chicago.
Santa–Bibiana, Joseph *s.d.b.* '66 (PMB) Belle Glade, FL St. Philip Benizi; Religious; Episcopal Delegate.
Santaballa, Francisco Javier '02 (WDC) Bethesda, MD Our Lady of Lourdes; [A] Hyattsville, MD Redemptoris Mater Archdiocesan Missionary Seminary.
Santa Cruz, Ramon '99 (SEA) Kirkland, WA St. John Mary Vianney.
Santaella, Esteban '58 (PCE) Mercedita, PR Church of the Resurrection.
Santaliz, Edgardo Sanabria '96 (SJN) San Juan, PR Maria Madre de La Iglesia.
Santamaria, Max '56 (MRY) Retired.

Santamaria, Roberto '98 (NEW)[A] Kearny, NJ Redemptoris Mater Archdiocesan Missionary Seminary.
Santana, Edward '86 (ARE) On Duty Outside the Diocese.
Santana, Franklin *s.d.b.* '72 (MGZ) San Antonio, PR San Jose Obrero.
Santana, Sady Nelson '93 (SAT) Rocksprings, TX Sacred Heart of Mary.
Santangelo, Christopher *ss.cc.* '99 (FR) New Bedford, MA Our Lady of the Assumption.
Santangelo, Michael A. '95 (TR) Catholic Scouting.
Santarosa, Scott *s.j.* '00 (LA) Los Angeles, CA Dolores Mission.
Santeliz, William '07 (PAT) Succasunna, NJ St. Therese.
Santen, Thomas J. '70 (STL) Manchester, MO St. Joseph.
Santerre, Richard R. '82 (BO) Senior Priests. Retired.
Santhaiah, Mathew Vianney Malapati '94 (LR) Searcy, AR St. James; Searcy, AR St. Richard Church; Heber Springs, AR St. Albert Church.
Santiago, Alberto '85 (HT) Larose, LA Our Lady of the Rosary.
Santiago, Felipe *c.ss.r.* '81 (PCE) Guayama, PR St. Anthony of Padua.
Santiago, Florentino F. '78 (HT) Theriot, LA St. Eloi.
Santiago, Jose *o.p.* '93 (STL)[B] St. Louis, MO Aquinas Institute of Theology; [O] Saint Louis, MO St. Dominic Priory.
Santiago, José A. *o.ss.t.* '93 (SJN) Bayamon, PR Espiritu Santo.
Santiago, Juan José *s.j.* '64 (SJN)[D] San Juan, PR Centro Universitario Catolico; [H] San Juan, PR.
Santiago, Leoncio S. '73 (MO) DEPARTMENT OF VETERANS AFFAIRS HOSPITALS AND CHAPLAINS; Hines V.A. Hospital.
Santiago, Manuel '85 (PCE) Ponce, PR San Jose Obrero; Associate Judicial Vicars.
Santiago, Marc A. '88 (ARE) Vega–Baja, PR Holy Rosary.
Santiago, Samuel '76 (PCE) Ponce, PR Santa Maria Reina; Cursillos de Cristiandad; Police Chaplains.
Santiago, Xavier S. '94 (NY) Red Hook, NY St. Christopher.
Santiago–Mateo, Victor R. '82 (SB) Coachella, CA Our Lady of Soledad.
Santich, Jan Joseph '90 (CHY) Retired.
Santich, Jan '90 (CHY) Cheyenne, WY Holy Trinity.
Santillanes, Jose Flavio '65 (SFE) Santa Fe, NM N.S. de Guadalupe del Valle de Pojoaque.
Santilli, Francis C. '80 (PRO) Greenville, RI St. Philip; College of Consultors; Council Members.
Santin, Ricardo (CGS) Yabucoa, PR Santos Angeles Cutodios.
Santitoro, Francis E. '66 (TR) Toms River, NJ St. Maximilian Kolbe Retired.
Santo, Sergio *o.f.m.* '85 (OAK)[L] Oakland Franciscan Friars of California, (Province of St. Barbara).
Santoianni, Rolando *i.v.e.* '90 (PHX) Phoenix, AZ St. Anthony Roman Catholic Parish; Phoenix, AZ Immaculate Heart of Mary Roman Catholic Parish.
Santone, John *c.s.c.* '00 (FTW) South Bend, IN Christ the King.
Santor, John E. '65 (E) Retired.
Santora, Alexander M. '82 (NEW) Hoboken, NJ Our Lady of Grace and Saint Joseph Parish.
Santoro, David J. *o.p* '77 (DET)[L] Farmington Hills, MI Monastery of the Blessed Sacrament.
Santoro, Michael C. '80 (NEW) Jersey City, NJ St. John the Baptist; Jersey City, NJ Our Lady of Mt. Carmel.
Santorsola, Albert J. '86 (PH) Broomall, PA St. Pius X.
Santos, Angel M. '77 (ARE) Almirante Sur Station, PR The Blessed Trinity; Diocesan Consultors; Priest's Senate (Consejo Presbiteral).
Santos, Cesar E. '93 (ARE) Florida, PR Our Lady of Mercy.
Santos, Ferdinand '98 (MIA)[A] Miami, FL St. John Vianney College Seminary.
Santos, Francisco M. '97 (CHK) Presbyteral Council.
Santos, Rev. Msgr. Francisco Medina '89 (SJN) Guaynabo, PR Buen Pastor; [A] San Juan, PR ISTEPA (Instituto Superior de Teologia y Pastoral).
Santos, Gregory *o.c.s.o.* '59 (SLC)[E] Huntsville Abbey of Our Lady of the Holy Trinity of the Order of Cistercians.
Santos, J. Lawrence '91 (LA) Santa Barbara, CA St. Raphael.
Santos, John Richard F. '98 (WIL)[J] Dover, DE Oblate Apostles of the Two Hearts.
Santos, Joseph D. '89 (PRO) Providence, RI Holy Name of Jesus.
Santos, Nicky *s.j.* '00 (SJ)[B] Santa Clara, CA Jesuit Community.
Santos, Raúl '63 (CGS) Barranquitas, PR San Andres Apostol.
Santos, Tomas '95 (ARE) Morovis, PR St. Paul Apostle.
Santos, Walter Guasp '01 (CAM) Inactive.
Santos–Lecturer, Francisco Medina (PCE)[B] The Pontifical Catholic University of Puerto Rico.
Santos Rodriguez, Tomas '95 (ARE) Priest's Senate (Consejo Presbiteral).
Santre, William *t.o.r.* '61 (ALT) Altoona, PA Our Lady of Mt. Carmel Retired.
Santry, Robert '86 (HON) On Duty Outside the Diocese.
Santucci, Louis '74 (Y) Retired.
Sanvicente, Noel '85 (SJ) Gilroy, CA St. Mary.
Sanz, Florentino '65 (SJN) Retired.
Sanz, Jose A. *d.l.p.* '73 (SB)[A] Grand Terrace, CA Blessed Junipero Serra House of Formation; [I] Grand Terrace, CA Diocesan Laborer Priests, DLP; Office of Seminarians; Blessed Junipero Serra House of Formation.
Sanz, Jose *d.l.p.* '73 (WDC) On Duty Outside the Archdiocese.
Sapa, Ambrosius Sanar *ss.cc.* (HON) Kalaupapa, HI St. Francis; Kaunakakai, HI Saint Damien of Molokai Church.
Saporito, Michael A. '92 (NEW) Westfield, NJ St. Helen; Elected Members; Presbyteral Council.
Saporito, Peter M. '77 (CAM) Vineland, NJ St. Padre Pio Parish, Vineland, N.J.; Deanery Representatives.
Sappenfield, John P. '98 (NSH) Unassigned.
Sappenfield, Mark '08 (NSH) MTSU–Murfreesboro; Murfreesboro, TN St. Rose of Lima.
Saprano, Samuel '71 (STU) Shadyside, OH St. John Vianney; Shadyside, OH St. Mary's.
Sara, Solomon I. *s.j.* '63 (WDC)[O] Washington, DC The Jesuit Community at Georgetown University.
Sara, Solomon I. *s.j.* '63 (BO)[U] Boston The Society of Jesus of New England–Provincial Offices.
Sarauskas, Rev. Msgr. R. George '73 (CHI) Members; Palos Heights, IL Incarnation.
Sardina, John J. '60 (BUF)[N] Clarence, NY Regional Motherhouse of Brothers of Mercy; [M] Clarence, NY Brothers of Mercy Nursing & Rehabilitation Center; [M] Clarence, NY Brothers of Mercy Sacred Heart Home, Inc.; Cheektowaga, NY Queen of Martyrs.
Sardinas–Perez, Juan C. (TYL) Daingerfield, TX Our Lady of Fatima.
Sare, Burt '96 (RIC) Tazewell, VA Holy Family Parish.
Sarge, John S. '73 (SAG) Birch Run, MI Sacred Heart; Bridgeport, MI Assumption of the Blessed Virgin Mary.
Sargent, Anthony G. *o.s.b.* '02 (PAT)[N] Morristown, NJ St. Mary's Abbey.
Sariego, Francis *o.f.m.cap.* '69 (WIL)[J] Wilmington, DE Capuchin Franciscan Friars, St. Francis Renewal Center; [M] Wilmington, DE St. Francis Renewal Center.
Sariego, Francis *o.f.m.cap.* (PH)[T] Aston, PA Assisi House.
Sarihaddula, Silvaster '98 (BRK) Ridgewood, NY St. Matthias.
Sarkees, Reemon (SPA) Scottsdale, AZ Mar Auraha Chaldean Catholic Parish.
Sarmiento, Nicanor *o.m.i.* '99 (OAK) Oakland, CA Sacred Heart.
Sarmiento–Diaz, Carlos *o.f.m.* '99 (FgM) New York, NY Holy Name Province.
Sarnecki, Thomas G. '02 (SCR) On Duty Outside the Diocese; DEPARTMENT OF VETERANS AFFAIRS HOSPITALS AND CHAPLAINS.
Sarnicki, Piotr *o.f.m.conv.* '94 (RCK) Algonquin, IL St. Margaret Mary.
Sarno, Rev. Msgr. Robert J. '73 (BRK) Released from Diocesan Assignment.
Saroki, Anthony '05 (SD) Finance Council; San Diego, CA Ascension Catholic Parish; Priestly Vocations; [A] San Diego, CA St. Francis De Sales Center.
Sarrazin, Edward *o.f.m.* '07 (TUC) Tucson, AZ San Xavier Mission Roman Catholic Parish – Tucson.
Sarrazine, Kenneth J. '62 (FTW) Roanoke, IN St. Catharine; Roanoke, IN St. Joseph.
Sarto, Stephen Joseph *ss.cc.* '06 (FR)[F] Fairhaven National Center of the Enthronement.
Sartorelli, Otto '50 (MAR) Retired.
Sartori, Hector *c.s.* '54 (PMB) Delray Beach, FL Our Lady Queen of Peace.
Sarzynski, Rev. Msgr. Edward W. '79 (ALN)[L] Reading, PA Sacred Heart Convent; [L] Reading, PA St. Joseph Villa.
Sas, Thomas J. '76 (HRT) West Hartford, CT St. Peter Claver; Special and other Archdiocesan Assignment; Office of Ministry Enrichment for Priests; Commission for Priests' Retreats.
Sasin, Jan '77 (NEW) Newark, NJ St. Francis Xavier; North Newark Essex Deanery 19.
Sasmita, Ignatius *s.j.* '07 (OAK)[L] Berkeley, CA Jesuit Fathers and Brothers.
Saso, Michael '61 (SJ) On Duty Outside the Diocese Retired.
Sass, Pawel '09 (WDC) Gaithersburg, MD St. Martin of Tours.
Sassani, John E. '80 (BO) Newton, MA Our Lady Help of Christians; Spiritual Life; Cursillo.
Sassano, Rock '63 (P) Retired.
Sasse, John J. '02 (MAD) Cottage Grove, WI St. Patrick.
Sasso, Frank M. '73 (CHI) Chicago, IL St. Thaddeus.
Sasso, Joseph M. '58 (ROC) Retired.
Sastre, Rafael '51 (MGZ) Lajas, PR De la Merced Parish.
Sasway, Rev. Msgr. John R. '62 (ALT) Lilly, PA Our Lady of the Alleghenies.
Satoun, Arbogaste '99 (SCR) West Pittston, PA Corpus Christi Parish.
Sattler, Frederick F. '70 (ALN)[J] Bethlehem, PA Holy Family Villa Retired.
Sattler, Henry *c.ss.r.* '76 (RVC) Bethpage, NY St. Martin of Tours.
Sauber, A. Michael '69 (STP) Minneapolis, MN St. Olaf.
Saucci, Ronald R. *m.m.* '65 (FgM) Maryknoll, NY MARYKNOLL.
Sauchelli, James J. '63 (TR) Retired.
Saucier, Thomas *o.p.* '96 (JC) Columbia, MO Sacred Heart; Columbia, MO St. Thomas More Newman Center, University of Missouri; [D] Columbia, MO St. Thomas More Newman Center.
Saucier, William Patrick '01 (MOB) Chickasaw, AL St. Thomas the Apostle; Whistler, AL St. Bridget.
Saudis, Rev. Msgr. Richard T. '55 (CHI) Berwyn, IL St. Odilo; Associate Vicars.
Sauer, Anthony P. *s.j.* '71 (SFR)[E] San Francisco, CA St. Ignatius College Preparatory (Coed); [N] San Francisco, CA Jesuit Community at St. Ignatius College Preparatory.
Sauer, Bonaventure *o.c.d.* '92 (SAT) San Antonio, TX Basilica of the National Shrine of the Little Flower, Our Lady of Mt. Carmel and St. Therese Parish; [L] San Antonio, TX Discalced Carmelite Fathers of San Antonio.
Sauer, Gerard J. '01 (BRK) Pilgrimage Office; Flushing, NY St. Mel.
Sauer, James '77 (EVN) Mount Vernon, IN St. Matthew; New Harmony, IN Holy Angels.
Sauer, John M. '85 (WIN) Owatonna, MN Holy Trinity; Owatonna, MN Sacred Heart; Censors of Books and Periodicals; Divine Worship; Diocese of Winona Incardination Board; Elected Deanery Representatives.
Sauer, Simon *o.f.m.conv.* '57 (IND)[J] Mount St. Francis, IN Mount Saint Francis Friary and Retreat Center.
Sauer, Stephen J. *s.j.* '98 (NO) New Orleans, LA Immaculate Conception.
Sauer, Timothy '76 (SEA) Seattle, WA St. Bridget; Presbyteral Council; College of Consultors.
Sauerbier, Paul *c.m.* (DAL)[J] Dallas, TX Congregation of the Mission, Western Province.
Saulaitis, Antanas *s.j.* '69 (CHI) Lemont, IL Blessed Jurgis Matulaitis Mission; [N] Lemont, IL Baltic Jesuits Advancement Office.
Saumell, Amaro '92 (SB) Needles, CA St. Ann.
Saunders, Allan L. '86 (SPC) Kennett, MO St. Cecilia; Portageville, MO St. Eustachius; Region VIII; Presbyteral Council.
Saunders, Donald E. *s.j.* '84 (NO)[E] New Orleans, LA Jesuit High School.
Saunders, Rev. Msgr. Douglas William '65 (LA) Retired.
Saunders, Thomas C. *m.m.* '65 (NY)[DD] Retired.
Saunders, William P. '84 (ARL) Potomac Falls, VA Our Lady of Hope; Deans; Diocesan Consultors.
Sauppe, Timothy J. '92 (PEO) Westville, IL St. Mary's.
Sauriamakkel, Joseph '75 (SYM) Farmers Branch, TX Christ the King Syro–Malabar Knanaya Catholic Church DFW.
Sauriol, Mark A. '99 (PRO)[C] Pawtucket, RI St. Raphael Academy.
Sauser, Steve '10 (AUS) Pflugerville, TX St. Elizabeth.
Sauter, David A. *s.j.* '72 (WDC)[E] North Bethesda, MD Georgetown Preparatory School.
Sauter, John '85 (GLP) Overgaard, AZ Our Lady of Assumption; Vicars Forane; Presbyteral Council; St. Helena.
Sautner, Scott '00 (FAR) Fairmount, ND St. Anthony's Church of Fairmount; Hankinson, ND St. Philip's Church of Hankinson.
Savage, James W. '70 (BO) Cambridge, MA St. Paul.
Savage, Paul J. '57 (PIT) Retired.
Savage, Robert *s.d.b.* '46 (NY)[DD] New Rochelle, NY Salesian Provincial House.
Savage, Roger A. '77 (MIL) Bristol, WI Holy Cross.
Savage, Warren J. '79 (SPR) Agawam, MA St. John the Evangelist; Diocesan Commission for the Liturgy.
Savaia, Giuseppe '95 (PMB) North Palm Beach, FL St. Clare.
Savard, John D. *s.j.* '91 (WOR)[N] Worcester, MA Jesuits of the Holy Cross, Inc.
Savari, Thumma '93 (SCR) Mocanaqua, PA St. Mary, Our Lady of Perpetual Help.
Savariappan, M. Joseph *s.j.* '08 (SFR)[N] San Francisco, CA Loyola House Jesuit Community.
Savarimathu, Simonraj (BAL)[K] Baltimore, MD St. Agnes HealthCare, Inc.
Savarimuthu, Alphonse *m.s.f.s.* (TYL)[C] Whitehouse, TX The Missionaries of St. Francis de Sales.
Savarimuthu, Alphonse (KAL) St. Joseph, MI St. Joseph.
Savarimuthu, Amal Raj *i.m.s.* '97 (BR) Denham Springs, LA Immaculate Conception.
Savarimuthu, Arokia D. *a.l.c.p./o.s.s.* '04 (CHI) Chicago, IL St. Andrew.
Savarimuthu, Eugene K. '97 (TR) Hamilton, NJ Our

Lady of Sorrows–St. Anthony Parish.
Savarimuthu, Pancras '80 (TYL) Athens, TX St. Edward Church.
Savary, James '60 (LR) Retired.
Savastano, Rev. Msgr. Anthony J. '56 (RVC)[N] Amityville, NY St. Pius X Residence Retired.
Savchyn, Volodymyr '79 (STN) Milwaukee, WI St. Michaels.
Savela, Erwin M. *c.s.v.* '71 (CHI)[N] Arlington Heights Viatorian Province Center–Clerics of St. Viator.
Savelesky, Michael J. '73 (SPK) Spokane, WA Assumption of the Blessed Virgin Mary; Director of Deacon Formation; Censor Liborum; Members.
Savelesky, Michael '73 (SPK) Moderator of the Curia; Diocesan Business Affairs.
Savial, Joseph Clarence (LAV) Retired.
Saviano, Frederick L. '68 (BGP) Pontifical Association of the Holy Childhood; Propagation of the Faith.
Savickas, Michael G. '74 (DET) Walled Lake, MI St. William.
Savidge, Peter M. '89 (KC) Holden, MO St. Patrick's.
Savilla, Edmund '77 (SFE) Albuquerque, NM Ascension; Pilgrimage for Vocations.
Savino, Michael A. '82 (CIN) North Bend, OH St. Joseph.
Savino–Gyimah, Joseph '92 (HRT) Plainville, CT Our Lady of Mercy.
Savinski, Rev. Msgr. John M. '71 (PH) Morton, PA Our Lady of Perpetual Help.
Savio, John '67 (CHY) Douglas, WY St. James.
Savio, Michael G. '92 (MIL) Mukwonago, WI St. James.
Savitt, Alan F. '73 (PAT) On Duty Outside the Diocese.
Savoie, Johnny S. '95 (MOB) Advocate; Mobile, AL St. Pius X.
Savoree, John M. '63 (SFD) Retired.
Savundra, Edwin '72 (STP) Rush City, MN Sacred Heart.
Savyo, Dominic '99 (TOL) Toledo, OH Christ the King.
Saw, Benjamin '90 (SAL) Logan, KS St. John Parish; Phillipsburg, KS Saints Philip and James Parish; Priests' Continuing Formation Committee.
Sawicki, Grzegorz *s.d.s.* '86 (SAT) Falls City, TX Holy Trinity; Hobson, TX St. Boniface; In Rural Area; Archdiocesan Presbyteral Council; Priests Personnel Board; [L] Falls City, TX Salvatorian Fathers Community of Texas.
Sawicki, John A. *c.s.sp.* '86 (PIT)[B] Pittsburgh, PA Duquesne University of the Holy Spirit; Councilors.
Sawicki, Jonathan P. '09 (HBG) Gettysburg, PA St. Francis Xavier's.
Sawicki, Mitchell *o.f.m.conv.* '05 (BAL)[U] Ellicott City, MD AnthonyCorps, Inc.; [U] Ellicott City, MD Fr. Justin Ministry Fund, Inc.; [Q] Ellicott City Order of Friars Minor Conventual.
Sawyer, Benjamin S. '09 (WCH)[B] Wichita, KS Bishop Carroll Catholic High School; Ongoing Formation of the Clergy Committee; Wichita, KS Christ the King.
Sawyer, Rev. Msgr. Donald J. '74 (OLL) Austin, TX Our Lady's Maronite Parish; Office for Missions; Austin, TX St. Anthony of the Desert Maronite Catholic Mission/Holy Family Church.
Sawyer, Lucien A. *o.m.i.* '49 (BO)[U] Lowell, MA St. Eugene House (Residence).
Sawyer, Michael *o.s.b.* '74 (HON)[D] Waialua, HI Benedictine Monastery of Hawaii/Retreat Center; [G] Waialua, HI Benedictine Monastery of Hawaii/ Retreat Center.
Saxon, JaVan '83 (R) Laurinburg, NC St. Mary.
Say, Celestino '58 (VIC) Judges.
Say, James K. '60 (TOL) Retired.
Say, P. Celestino '58 (VIC) Victoria, TX Our Lady of Lourdes.
Sayegh, Rt. Rev. Fouad '79 (NTN) Northlake, IL St. John the Baptist; Hammond, IN St. Michael the Archangel.
Sayers, Glen W. *s.d.s.* '97 (BIR) Huntsville, AL St. Mary of the Visitation.
Sayers, James M. '58 (CHI) Homewood, IL St. Joseph Retired.
Sayers, Monty '86 (E) Clarion, PA Immaculate Conception.
Sayers, Raymond J. '64 (DET) Retired.
Sayes, Ronald E. '57 (DET) Retired.
Saylor, Brian R. '99 (ALT) Altoona, PA St. Rose of Lima.
Saylor, Rev. Msgr. Philip '55 (ALT) Retired.
Sayre, Dismas *o.p.* '08 (LA) Los Angeles, CA St. Dominic.
Sayuk, Rev. Msgr. Mitred Thomas A. '74 (SJP) On Leave; Presbyters.
Sazama, Warren J. *s.j.* '77 (MIL)[P] Milwaukee, WI Arrupe House Jesuit Community; [E] Milwaukee, WI Marquette University High School.
Sbordone, Gaetano J. '83 (BRK) Brooklyn, NY St. Frances Cabrini.
Scafidi, William A. *m.ss.a.* '83 (NY) Newburgh, NY St. Mary; Newburgh, NY Sacred Heart.
Scaglione, Paul A. '73 (L) Louisville, KY St. Barnabas.
Scagnelli, Peter J. '76 (PRO) Absent on Leave.
Scahill, James J. '74 (SPR) East Longmeadow, MA St. Michael's.
Scala, Thomas A. '73 (HBG) Milton, PA St. Joseph; Presbyteral Council.
Scalco, Joseph *c.s.j.* '79 (LA) San Pedro, CA St. Peter.
Scales, George '88 (FR) Chatham, MA Holy Redeemer.
Scalese, Mark P. *s.j.* '97 (BGP)[B] Fairfield, CT Fairfield University; [O] Fairfield, CT The Fairfield Jesuit Community–Fairfield University.
Scaletty, Thomas F. '63 (WCH) Retired.
Scalf, Kevin *c.pp.s.* '09 (LFT)[A] Rensselaer, IN Saint Joseph's College.
Scalia, Paul D. '96 (ARL) McLean, VA St. John the Beloved; Bishop's Delegate for Priests.
Scanlan, Cornelius (SAN) Retired.
Scanlan, Rev. Msgr. Edward J. '53 (BUF) Retired.
Scanlan, Francis G. '61 (CHI) Oak Forest, IL St. Damian Retired.
Scanlan, Thomas R. '57 (BAK) Retired.
Scanlan, William J. '72 (BO) Permanent Disability.
Scanlin, Joseph T. '89 (HBG) Lebanon, PA St. Cecilia; Presbyteral Council.
Scanlon, Charles *s.v.d.* '54 (CHI)[N] Techny, IL Divine Word Residence.
Scanlon, Francis P. '83 (NY) Bronx, NY St. Ann.
Scanlon, James M. *m.m.* '52 (NY)[DD] Retired.
Scanlon, Michael J. *o.s.a.* '64 (PH)[C] Villanova University; [Y] Villanova, PA St. John Stone Friary.
Scanlon, Paul *o.p.* '59 (LA) Los Angeles, CA St. Dominic.
Scanlon, Peter J. '57 (WOR)[Q] Shrewsbury, MA Campus Ministry; Campus Ministry Retired.
Scanlon, Regis *o.f.m.cap.* '72 (DEN)[N] Denver, CO St. Francis of Assisi Friary.
Scanlon, Rev. Msgr. Thomas F. '49 (NY) Mount Vernon, NY SS. Peter and Paul Retired.
Scanlon, William J. *s.j.* '70 (NY)[DD] New York, NY Murray–Weigel Hall.
Scannel, Anthony *o.f.m.cap.* '55 (LA)[F] La Canada Flintridge, CA St. Francis High School of La Canada–Flintridge.
Scannell, Timothy J. '69 (NY) Dobbs Ferry, NY Sacred Heart; Dobbs Ferry, NY Our Lady of Pompeii; [A] Yonkers, NY St. Joseph's Seminary.
Scantlebury, Neil '95 (STV) St. Thomas, VI Holy Family Parish; Chancellor; Diocesan Consultors.
Scantlin, Rev. Msgr. Joseph S. '59 (FWT) Arlington, TX Most Blessed Sacrament; Deans.
Scaramella, Renzo L. '95 (NEW) Absent on Leave.
Scaramuzzo, Peter C. '66 (NY) West Harrison, NY St. Anthony of Padua.
Scarangella, Joseph A. '92 (NEW) Montclair, NJ Immaculate Conception; Newark, NJ Cathedral Basilica of the Sacred Heart.
Scarangella, Joseph A. (NEW) Archdiocesan Liturgies for the Archdiocese of Newark.
Scarborough, Henry *o.c.s.o.* '63 (WOR)[N] Spencer, MA St. Joseph's Abbey.
Scarcella, Philip J. '77 (CHL) Charlotte, NC Our Lady of the Assumption.
Scarcella, Phillip '77 (MIA) Judges.
Scarcello, Michael S. '56 (B) Retired.
Scarcia, John J. '74 (PH) Retired.
Scardella, Joseph E. '81 (SY) Baldwinsville, NY St. Mary of the Assumption; Building Commission; Management Team.
Scarfia, Gabriel *o.f.m.* '64 (BUF)[A] East Aurora, NY Christ the King Seminary.
Scaria, Anthony *c.f.i.c.* (STP) St. Paul, MN St. Mary.
Scaria, Job Edathinatt *c.m.i.* '94 (SHP) Monroe, LA Our Lady of Fatima; [F] Monroe, LA Catholic Campus Ministry at the University of Louisiana at Monroe.
Scarlata, Ronald E. '66 (CHI) Highwood, IL St. James Retired.
Scarry, Benignus *o.f.m.cap.* (DEN)[N] Denver, CO San Antonio Friary.
Scepaniak, Russell G. '93 (WIN) Windom, MN St. Francis Xavier's; Heron Lake, MN Sacred Heart; Deans.
Scepaniak, Russell G. '93 (WIN) Brewster, MN Sacred Heart.
Scerbo, Joseph *s.a.* '70 (NY)[DD] Garrison Franciscan Friars of the Atonement, Minister General Office.
Sceski, Alfred P. '91 (HBG) Elysburg, PA Queen of the Most Holy Rosary; Deans; Presbyteral Council; [A] Coal Township, PA Our Lady of Lourdes Regional School.
Scesney, Everard *o.f.m.* '68 (GB) Birnamwood, WI St. Boniface; Birnamwood, WI St. Philomena; [J] Wausaukee, WI Villa Alverna.
Schaab, Dennis *c.pp.s.* '68 (DAV) Centerville, IA St. Mary's.
Schaab, Denny M. '76 (STL) Valley Park, MO Sacred Heart.
Schaab, R. Michael '71 (PEO) Rock Island, IL St. Pius X.
Schaab, Thomas J. '74 (STL) Clayton, MO St. Joseph.
Schabel, Joseph A. '56 (SAG) Retired.
Schabowski, Henry F. '60 (TR) Retired.
Schack, Stephen '99 (PHX) El Mirage, AZ Santa Teresita Roman Catholic Parish.
Schad, Joseph J. *s.j.* '91 (BO)[U] Boston The Society of Jesus of New England–Provincial Offices.
Schad, Joseph J. *s.j.* '91 (WDC)[O] Washington, DC The Jesuit Community at Georgetown University.
Schad, Marco Federico '08 (WDC) Bethesda, MD Our Lady of Lourdes.
Schaedel, Rev. Msgr. Joseph F. '82 (IND) Indianapolis, IN Saint Luke Catholic Church, Indianapolis, Inc.; Board of Consultors; Mission Office; [P] Indianapolis, IN Hearts and Hands Corporation of Indiana.
Schaefer, Bernard *o.s.b.* '56 (RCK)[G] Aurora, IL Marmion Abbey.
Schaefer, Rev. Msgr. Dennis R. '75 (BEL) Red Bud, IL St. John the Baptist; Red Bud, IL St. Patrick.
Schaefer, Edgar J. '54 (WIN) Retired.
Schaefer, Edward F. '75 (BEL) Carlyle, IL St. Felicitas; St. Rose, IL St. Rose.
Schaefer, James F. '61 (LC) Retired.
Schaefer, James W. '56 (STL) Saint Mary, MO Sacred Heart.
Schaefer, Rev. Msgr. Kenneth J. (BEL) Herrin, IL Our Lady of Mount Carmel; Johnston City, IL St. Paul.
Schaefer, Les F. *c.s.b.* '61 (GAL)[E] Houston, TX St. Thomas High School.
Schaefer, Martin T. '92 (WIN) Waseca, MN Sacred Heart; Deans; Appointed Members.
Schaefer, Philip *c.p.* '58 (L)[L] Louisville, KY Sacred Heart Retreat.
Schaefer, Richard L. '68 (DUB)[H] Dubuque, IA Mercy Medical Center–Dubuque.
Schaefer, Roman J. '42 (NU) Retired.
Schaefer, Thomas '82 (PBR) Pittsburgh, PA St. John the Baptist; Pittsburgh, PA St. John Chrysostom.
Schaeffer, Bradley M. *s.j.* '77 (BO)[U] Brighton, MA Alberto Hurtado House.
Schaeffer, Richard C. '83 (MAR) Leave of Absence.
Schaeffer, Richard C. '83 (GLD) Pellston, MI St. Clement; Pellston, MI Sacred Heart; Cheboygan, MI St. Mary–St. Charles.
Schaeper, Lawrence A. '09 (COV) Ludlow, KY Sts. Boniface and James; [Q] Highland Heights, KY Catholic Newman Club – Northern Kentucky University; Campus Ministry–Newman Center; Serra Club of Diocese of Covington.
Schafer, Dennis R. '89 (BIS) Williston, ND St. Joseph; Williston, ND St. John the Baptist; Presbyteral Council.
Schafer, Dennis *o.f.m.* '80 (JOL) Joliet, IL St. John the Baptist; [L] Joliet, IL St. John the Baptist Friary.
Schafer, Peter '05 (GR) Newaygo, MI St. Bartholomew's.
Schafer, Raymond E. '89 (IND) Unassigned.
Schaff, Tyrone J. '73 (SPK) Spokane, WA Our Lady of Fatima; Members.
Schaffer, Gregory J. '94 (STP) On Duty Outside the Archdiocese.
Schaffer, Rev. Msgr. Gregory T. '60 (NU) On Duty Outside the Diocese; San Lucas Mission Office.
Schaffer, J. Darrell '90 (DEN) Lakewood, CO St. Jude.
Schaffner, Mark *o.carm.* '89 (VEN) Englewood, FL St. Raphael.
Schaftlein, Steven '78 (IND) Charlestown, IN St. Michael Catholic Church, Charlestown, Inc.; Charlestown, IN St. Francis Catholic Church, Henryville, Inc.
Schaicoski, Daniel *o.s.b.m.* '95 (STN) Hamtramck, MI Immaculate Conception of B.V.M.
Schak, John R. *s.j.* '61 (MIL)[P] Milwaukee Jesuit Provincial Office, Wisconsin Province; Milwaukee, WI Society of Jesus.
Schalk, David A. '08 (COL) Columbus, OH Christ the King.
Schalk, Sebastian *o.praem.* '60 (JKS)[E] Raymond, MS Priory of St. Moses the Black.
Schall, James V. *s.j.* '63 (WDC)[O] Washington, DC The Jesuit Community at Georgetown University.
Schallberger, Meinrad *o.s.b.* '64 (B)[B] Cottonwood, ID St. Mary's Hospital; [C] Jerome, ID Monastery of the Ascension; [D] Cottonwood, ID Monastery of St. Gertrude, Motherhouse and Novitiate; Cottonwood, ID Monastery of St. Gertrude; Cottonwood, ID.
Schaller, Robert A. '87 (LC) La Crosse, WI St. James the Less; Deans.
Schamber, Richard Lee '07 (PT) Milton, FL St. Rose of Lima.
Schanberger, J. Lawrence *m.m.* '49 (FgM) Maryknoll, NY MARYKNOLL.
Schappler, Norbert *o.s.b.* '52 (KC)[J] Conception, MO Conception Abbey.
Schardt, William B. '75 (ARL) Middleburg, VA St. Stephen the Martyr.
Scharf, David E. '85 (PIT) Beaver County, PA Villa St. Joseph; [N] Baden, PA Sisters of St. Joseph; [M] Pittsburgh, PA St. John Vianney Manor.
Scharfenberger, Rev. Msgr. Edward B. '73 (BRK) Ridgewood, NY St. Matthias; Mediation and Arbitration, Board of; Lawyers.
Schariah, Abraham P. '06 (SYM) Loganville, GA St. Alphonsa Syro–Malabar Catholic Church, Atlanta.
Schartz, Kenneth E. '84 (CIN) Cincinnati, OH St. Mary.
Schatteman, Rene J. '60 (POD)[L] Pittsburgh, PA Prelature of the Holy Cross and Opus Dei; Pittsburgh.
Schatz, David A. '00 (DUB) Vocation Awareness; [A]

Dubuque, IA Seminary of St. Pius X; On Special or Other Archdiocesan Assignment.
Schatzel, John E. '61 (BO) Senior Priests. Retired.
Schatzle, Michael J. '74 (BR) Baton Rouge, LA St. George; College of Consultors; Presbyteral Council.
Schauerman, Rev. Msgr. Henry J. '51 (E) Retired.
Schaukowitch, James V. *s.j.* '79 (SFR)[E] San Francisco, CA St. Ignatius College Preparatory (Coed); [N] San Francisco, CA Jesuit Community at St. Ignatius College Preparatory.
Schaut, Gregory F. '85 (CLV) Fairview Park, OH St. Angela Merici.
Schavitz, Peter *c.ss.r.* '76 (STL)[O] Liguori, MO Liguori Mission House/Redemptorists.
Schawe, Wesley W. '04 (DOD) Presbyteral Council; Respect Life Activities; Priest Continuing Formation Commission; Office of Priestly Vocations.
Scheaffer, Rev. Msgr. Walter T. '66 (ALN) Kutztown, PA St. Mary.
Schebera, Richard *s.m.m.* '64 (BRK)[R] Ozone Park, NY Montfort Missionaries Provincialate (Missionaries of the Company of Mary).
Scheble, Carl J. '83 (STL) University City, MO Our Lady of Lourdes.
Scheckel, Roger J. '84 (LC) Richland Center, WI St. Mary (Assumption of B.V.M.); [L] La Crosse, WI Father Joseph Walijewski Orphanage Endowment Trust; Deans; Holy Childhood Association; Propagation of the Faith.
Scheckenback, Robert C. '89 (RVC) West Islip, NY Our Lady of Lourdes.
Schecker, Robert J.W. '71 (TR) College of Consultors; Fair Haven, NJ Church of the Nativity; Vicars Forane (Deans).
Scheel, Rev. Msgr. Daniel L. '69 (GAL) Houston, TX St. Jerome; Western Vicariate; Appointees; College of Consultors; Council of Catholic Women.
Scheeler, Jeffrey *o.f.m.* '80 (CIN)[N] Cincinnati, OH St. Francis Seraph Friary; Cincinnati, OH.
Scheer, Allen '95 (SAL) Salina, KS Sacred Heart Cathedral Parish; College of Consultors; Rural Life Conference; Personnel Board.
Scheer, John R. *s.a.c.* '70 (MIL)[P] Milwaukee, WI Pallotti House; Milwaukee, WI St. Vincent Pallotti; [P] Milwaukee, WI St. Vincent Community.
Scheerger, Michael Therese *c.s.j.* '07 (LAR)[D] Laredo, TX St. John Priory, F.J.; Campus Ministry.
Scheetz, Daniel L. '65 (SAL) Promoter of Justice and Guardian Retired.
Scheetz, Joseph '54 (SAL) Retired.
Schefers, Eberhard '64 (SCL) Retired.
Scheff, Philip J. '01 (VEN) Port Charlotte, FL St. Charles Borromeo.
Scheffler, Mark *c.ss.r.* (SEA) Seattle, WA Sacred Heart of Jesus; [M] Seattle, WA The Redemptionist Society of Washington.
Schehr, Timothy P. '73 (CIN)[B] Cincinnati, OH Mount St. Mary's Seminary of the West; Imprimatur Censors.
Scheib, Joseph C. '76 (PIT) Pittsburgh, PA St. Basil; Judges.
Scheible, Michael '63 (EVN)[H] Evansville, IN American–Innsbruck Alumni Association Retired.
Scheible, Ronald E. *o.s.a.* '57 (LAN) Flint, MI St. Matthew.
Scheich, Eugene '66 (L) Retired.
Scheick, James C. '63 (DET) Retired.
Scheiding, Philip '81 (MIA) Pompano Beach, FL San Isidro.
Scheidler, David *c.s.c.* '94 (FTW)[H] Notre Dame Congregation of Holy Cross, United States Province of Priests & Brothers.
Scheidt, Daniel D. '01 (FTW) Mishawaka, IN Queen of Peace; Consultors; Sacred Art and Architecture Committee.
Scheier, Steven '73 (WCH) Caldwell, KS St. Martin of Tours.
Scheierl, LeRoy '91 (SCL) Brandon, MN Church of St. Ann; Brandon, MN Seven Dolors; Parkers Prairie, MN Church of St. William; Parkers Prairie, MN Sacred Heart; Boy Scouts; Personnel Committee.
Scheiner, Richard *c.p.* '60 (BRK)[R] Jamaica, NY Immaculate Conception Monastery.
Scheinost, Douglas P. '92 (OM) Verdigre, NE St. Wenceslaus; Verdigre, NE St. William; [N] Lynch, NE Niobrara Valley House of Renewal.
Scheip, Michael A. '93 (VEN) Charismatic Renewal; Cursillo Movement; Sarasota, FL Incarnation.
Schelble, T. Michael '61 (LC) Retired.
Schelich, Theodosius A. *o.f.m.* '59 (SFD)[H] Litchfield, IL St. Francis Hospital.
Schellberg, Eugene '60 (MET) Retired.
Schellenberg, James E. '77 (SAT) San Antonio, TX Brooke Army Medical Center.
Schelling, Michael E. '74 (TOL) Retired.
Schemel, Francis *s.j.* '58 (WDC)[O] Washington, DC The Jesuit Community at Georgetown University.
Schemm, Michael '93 (WCH) Augusta, KS St. James.
Schempp, Albert *m.i.* '04 (MIL)[P] Milwaukee, WI St. Camillus Delegate House.
Schempp, Albert *m.i.* '04 (PIT) Allegheny County, PA Mercy Health System of Pittsburgh–Pittsburgh Mercy Hospital; Pittsburgh, PA St. Patrick–St. Stanislaus Kostka.
Schenck, Paul C.B. (HBG) Respect Life, Office for; Harrisburg, PA Our Lady of the Blessed Sacrament.
Schenck, Stephen *s.d.b.* '81 (NY) Port Chester, NY Our Lady of the Rosary.
Schenden, Gregory A. *s.j.* '08 (WDC) Washington, DC Holy Trinity.
Schenick, Joseph D. '51 (PRO)[O] Providence St. John Vianney Residence Retired.
Schenk, Charles (BAL) Priests Sick or Absent.
Schenk, Francis *g.h.m.* '55 (CIN)[N] Cincinnati Headquarters of Glenmary Home Missioners Retired.
Schenk, Richard *o.p.* '78 (OAK)[L] Oakland, CA Order of Preachers (Province of the Most Holy Name of Jesus – Western Dominican Province); [L] Oakland Order of Preachers (Province of the Most Holy Name of Jesus – Western Dominican Province).
Schenkel, Dennis L. '08 (MEM) Martin, TN St. Jude's Catholic Church; [H] Martin, TN Interfaith Student Center.
Schenning, Rev. Msgr. Kevin T. '81 (BAL) Baltimore, MD St. Joseph; Priest Personnel Board.
Schepers, M. B. *o.p.* '56 (FgM) New York, NY Province of St. Joseph (Eastern).
Scherba, Raymond M. '82 (BGP) Danbury, CT St. Gregory the Great.
Scherer, Gary *c.pp.s.* '67 (CIN)[N] Carthagena, OH St. Charles Retired.
Scherer, Gerald N. '54 (RC) Retired.
Scherger, Herman F. '58 (TOL) Retired.
Scherrer, Rev. Msgr. Carl E. '73 (BEL) Columbia, IL Immaculate Conception of the B.V.M.
Scherrer, Steven S. *m.m.* '72 (NY)[DD] Retired.
Scherrey, Michael *c.c.* '05 (GAL) Houston, TX Queen of Peace.
Schérschel, Michael G. '07 (CHI)[A] Chicago, IL St. Joseph College Seminary.
Schetelick, Rev. Msgr. Paul D. '76 (NEW) Bayonne Deanery 13; Bayonne, NJ St. Andrew's.
Schetter, Jerome A. '11 (TOL) Perrysburg, OH St. Rose.
Scheuerell, Charles A. '57 (MIL) Retired.
Scheuerman, Edward L. '50 (DET) Retired.
Schexnayder, Francis F. *m.m.* '64 (FgM) Maryknoll, NY MARYKNOLL.
Schexnayder, Gary '69 (LAF) Crowley, LA St. Michael Archangel; Diocesan Consultors; Council of Priests; Scouting.
Schexnayder, James '64 (OAK) Retired.
Scheyd, Rev. Msgr. William J. '65 (BGP) New Canaan, CT St. Aloysius; Vicars General; Diocesan Consultors; Presbyteral Council; Finance Council; Priest Vocation Advisory Board.
Schiavi, Giulio *pime* '63 (DET) Clinton Township, MI San Francesco Community.
Schiavo, John Lo *s.j.* '55 (SFR)[C] San Francisco, CA University of San Francisco.
Schiavo, Sylvan *c.s.j.* '63 (LA) Lancaster, CA Blessed Junipero Serra.
Schiavone, Jeldo J. '52 (LFT) Retired.
Schiavone, John '73 (LA) Long Beach, CA St. Maria Goretti.
Schiavone, Robert W. '69 (GB) On Duty Outside the Diocese.
Schiavone, Robert W. '69 (MIL)[B] Hales Corners, WI Sacred Heart School of Theology.
Schiblin, Richard *c.ss.r.* '61 (OAK)[L] Berkeley, CA Redemptorist Fathers (Denver Province).
Schichtel, Kenneth H. '62 (GR) Retired.
Schieber, Brian '99 (KCK) Topeka, KS Most Pure Heart of Mary; Vicars General; Archdiocesan Consultors; Archdiocesan Administrative Team.
Schieber, Joachim *o.s.b.* '44 (KC)[J] Conception, MO Conception Abbey.
Schiel, Nicholas E. *s.j.* '55 (MIL)[P] Milwaukee Jesuit Provincial Office, Wisconsin Province; Milwaukee, WI Society of Jesus.
Schiele, John D. '93 (PH) Hilltown, PA Our Lady of the Sacred Heart; [D] Lansdale, PA Lansdale Catholic High School.
Schierer, William '11 (ARL) Potomac Falls, VA Our Lady of Hope.
Schifalacqua, Ildebrando E. '43 (PH) Retired.
Schifano, Al '01 (TUC) Tucson, AZ Saint Thomas the Apostle Roman Catholic Parish – Tucson.
Schifano, Albert I. '01 (TUC) Special Assignment; Diocesan Consultors; Council of Priests; [I] Tucson, AZ Catholic Foundation for the Diocese of Tucson; Vicars General; Moderator of the Curia; Ex Officio; Diocesan Building Committee; Moderator of the Curia.
Schifano, James *s.c.j* '75 (MIL)[P] Franklin Sacred Heart at Monastery Lake; [P] Franklin, WI Sacred Heart at Monastery Lake.
Schiferl, David E. '01 (P) Cornelius, OR St. Alexander.
Schiffelbein, Matthew '09 (KCK) Overland Park, KS Church of the Ascension.
Schiffer, James *c.p.* '71 (ALB) Greenville, NY St. John the Baptist; Windham, NY St. Theresa of Child Jesus.
Schik, Jerome *o.s.c.* '75 (SCL) Onamia, MN St. Therese; Hillman, MN St. Rita's; Onamia, MN The Church of the Holy Cross of Onamia; Wahkon, MN Sacred Heart; [I] Onamia, MN Crosier Priory.
Schik, LeRoy '03 (SCL) Henning, MN Church of St. Edward of Henning; Battle Lake, MN Our Lady of the Lake; Underwood, MN Church of Saint James at Maine.
Schikora, Robert '11 (SAG) Lexington, MI St. Patrick; Lexington, MI St. Denis.
Schild, Eric P. '07 (TOL)[D] Oregon, OH The Kateri Catholic Academy – Kateri Catholic School System; Martin, OH Our Lady of Mt. Carmel.
Schilder, David M. '68 (COL) Retired.
Schilken, Karl '80 (FWT) Fort Worth, TX St. John the Apostle; Diocesan Pastoral Finance Committee.
Schill, Damien '87 (FAR) Veterans Administration Medical Center; On Duty Outside the Diocese.
Schill, Frederick J. '57 (TOL) Retired.
Schill, Gerald F. (Damien) '87 (MO) DEPARTMENT OF VETERANS AFFAIRS HOSPITALS AND CHAPLAINS.
Schill, Gregory *s.c.j.* '11 (JKS) Southaven, MS Christ the King; [E] Nesbit, MS St. Michael Community House; Hernando, MS Holy Spirit; Senatobia, MS St. Gregory the Great; Robinsonville, MS Good Shepherd Catholic Church.
Schill, Paul A. '63 (E) Greenville, PA St. Michael Retired.
Schiller, Francis E. '65 (NEW) Jersey City, NJ St. Patrick and Assumption/All Saints Church; [Q] Jersey City, NJ Trinity Child Care Center; [Q] Jersey City, NJ St. Patrick and Assumption All Saints Foundation.
Schiller, Thomas A. '55 (GR) Retired.
Schilli, Richard J. '77 (STL) Eureka, MO Sacred Heart.
Schillinger, James A. '84 (ATL) Atlanta, GA Immaculate Heart of Mary; Judges; College of Consultors.
Schiltz, Roger J. '68 (WIN) Retired.
Schiml, Ronald J. *c.pp.s.* '55 (LFT) Star City, IN St. Joseph.
Schimmel, Eric *c.s.c.* (FTW)[H] Notre Dame Congregation of Holy Cross, United States Province of Priests & Brothers.
Schimmel, Eric *c.s.c.* '02 (PHX)[J] Phoenix, AZ Andre House of Arizona.
Schimmelmann, Wayne *c.m.f.* '86 (CHI)[N] Oak Park, IL Claretian Missionaries USA Eastern Province.
Schimmer, Robert J. '68 (SC) Retired.
Schimscheiner, Francis M. *o.s.f.s.* '65 (BUF) Lockport, NY All Saints.
Schindler, Carl *c.ss.r.* '63 (SAT)[L] San Antonio, TX Redemptorists of Texas–San Antonio #1; Bexar County Detention Ministries.
Schindler, Paul E. '67 (CLV) Casa Parroquial Inmaculada Concepcion.
Schindler–McGraw, Kevin *o.f.m.conv.* '84 (LA) Hermosa Beach, CA Our Lady of Guadalupe.
Schineller, J. Peter *s.j.* '70 (NY)[DD] New York, NY Society of Jesus, New York Province; [DD] New York, NY "America;" Residence and publication office of the America Press.
Schineller, Peter *s.j.* (NY)[HH] New York, NY Catholic Medical Mission Board, Inc.
Schinelli, A. Giles *t.o.r.* '70 (ORL)[E] Winter Park, FL San Pedro Spiritual Development Center; Cemetery, San Pedro; San Pedro Spiritual Development Center; [F] Winter Park, FL Franciscan Friars, T.O.R., San Pedro Friary.
Schinn, Bernard *o.s.b.* '99 (PAT)[N] Clifton, NJ Holy Face of Jesus Monastery.
Schinski, Rev. Msgr. Stanley E. '51 (PAT)[Q] Chester, NJ Nazareth Village Retired.
Schipp, John H. '64 (EVN) Vincennes, IN Basilica of St. Francis Xavier; [H] Vincennes, IN Old Cathedral Library & Museum, Inc.; Advocates; Vincennes, IN St. Thomas The Apostle.
Schipp, Ralph '65 (EVN) Clergy Personnel Board Retired.
Schipper, Carl A. '68 (SFR) Retired.
Schipper, William *o.s.b.* '94 (SCL)[B] Saint John's University; [I] Collegeville, MN St. John's Abbey, of the Order of St. Benedict.
Schiro, Nicholas T. *s.j.* '57 (NO)[E] New Orleans, LA Jesuit High School.
Schiska, Paul A. '57 (MAR) Retired.
Schissel, Gregory A. *s.j.* '79 (MIL)[P] Milwaukee Jesuit Provincial Office, Wisconsin Province.
Schlachter, Eric A. '81 (JC) Absent on Leave.
Schladen, Robert '59 (PEO) Retired.
Schladheck, Regis *o.f.m.conv.* '66 (LSC) Carlsbad, NM St. Edward.
Schlaf, John E. '64 (GI) Concordia, KS Retired.
Schlafer, Joseph M. '75 (RVC) Bohemia, NY St. John Nepomucene.
Schlageter, Robert *o.f.m. conv.* '83 (HRT) Kensington, CT St. Paul.
Schlaline, Dwight D. '10 (HBG)[I] Carlisle, PA Dickinson College; Carlisle, PA Saint Patrick.
Schlangen, Louis '57 (SFD) Retired.
Schlarb, Greg '97 (PHX) Presbyteral Council.

Schlarb, Gregory J. '97 (PHX) Phoenix, AZ St. Paul Roman Catholic Parish.
Schlarb, Gregory '77 (PHX) Stewardship Office.
Schlatter, Fredric *s.j.* '56 (SPK)[B] Spokane, WA Gonzaga University.
Schlautman, Wayne W. '65 (OM) Retired.
Schlaver, David E. *c.s.c.* '71 (FTW)[H] Notre Dame Congregation of Holy Cross, United States Province of Priests & Brothers.
Schlax, Charles H. '66 (CHI) Retired.
Schlegel, Daniel F. '88 (CLV) Chagrin Falls, OH Holy Angels.
Schlegel, Rev. Msgr. George J. '66 (COL) College of Consultors Retired.
Schlegel, John P. *s.j.* '73 (OM)[J] Omaha, NE Jesuit Community at Creighton University.
Schlegel, John P. *s.j.* '73 (NY)[HH] New York, NY America Press, Inc.; [DD] New York, NY "America;" Residence and publication office of the America Press.
Schlegel, Laurence *o.s.b.* '54 (MAN)[K] Manchester, NH St. Anselm Abbey Retired.
Schleicher, Edward R. '83 (PIT)[M] Pittsburgh, PA St. John Vianney Manor Retired.
Schleisman, Jeffrey '00 (SC) Larchwood, IA St. Mary; Rock Rapids, IA Holy Name.
Schlenker, Richard J. '56 (MIL) Retired.
Schlert, Rev. Msgr. Alfred A. '87 (ALN) Hellertown, PA St. Theresa of the Child Jesus; Vicar General; Defenders of the Bond; College of Consultors; Ex Officio Members; Finance Council; Allentown Catholic Communications, Inc.
Schlesselmann, Rev. Msgr. Gregory J. '93 (FAR) Notaries; Fargo, ND St. Anthony of Padua's Church of Fargo; Permanent Diaconate.
Schleter, Edward J. '67 (TOL)[I] Fremont, OH St. Bernardine Home; Clyde, OH St. Mary.
Schleupner, Rev. Msgr. G. Michael '72 (BAL) Bel Air, MD St. Margaret.
Schlichte, Carl *o.p.* '98 (SLC)[G] Salt Lake City, UT University of Utah, Newman Center; Deans; Salt Lake City, UT Saint Catherine of Siena LLC 218.
Schlick, Regis *o.f.m.cap.* '65 (PIT)[M] Pittsburgh St. Augustine Friary.
Schliessmann, Thomas L. '89 (IND) Indianapolis, IN St. Lawrence Catholic Church, Lawrence, Inc.
Schlight, Harry J. *o.s.f.s.* '44 (FgM) Wilmington, DE OBLATES OF ST. FRANCIS DE SALES MISSIONS.
Schlim, Robert J. *s.j.* '62 (SPK)[J] Spokane, WA Regis Community.
Schlimm, Chrysostom V. *o.s.b.* '61 (GBG)[H] Latrobe, PA Saint Vincent Archabbey.
Schlitt, Dale *o.m.i.* '69 (WDC)[O] Washington, DC Provincial Offices of the United States Province of the Missionary Oblates of Mary Immaculate.
Schlitt, Rev. Msgr. Harry G. '64 (SFR)[S] San Francisco, CA Catholics for Truth & Justice Retired.
Schloeder, Paul '87 (SAC) Retired.
Schloemer, Bernard J. '60 (STL) St. Louis, MO St. Gabriel the Archangel Retired.
Schloemer, Leo *g.h.m.* '56 (CIN)[N] Cincinnati Headquarters of Glenmary Home Missioners Retired.
Schloemer, Paul *o.f.m.conv.* '04 (L)[L] Louisville, KY St. Francis of Assisi Friary.
Schloemer, Paul *o.f.m.conv.* '01 (IND)[K] Vocation Office – Our Lady of Consolation Province.
Schloemer, Thomas *s.j.* '68 (GB)[M] Oshkosh, WI Jesuit Retreat House.
Schloesser, Stephen *s.j.* '92 (CHI)[C] Chicago, IL Jesuit Community at Loyola University Chicago.
Schlosser, Richard '74 (GF) Great Falls, MT Holy Spirit; Personnel Board; Vicars Forane; Continuing Formation of Clergy.
Schloth, Brian D. *m.s.* '89 (HRT)[L] Hartford, CT Missionaries of LaSalette Province of Mary, Mother of the Americas.
Schloth, Brian *m.s.* '89 (WDC)[O] Washington, DC La Salette Formation Community.
Schludecker, Andre *o.f.m.* '64 (SFD)[L] Springfield, IL St. Francis Convent; [K] Springfield, IL Our Lady of Angels Friary.
Schluter, Rev. Msgr. O. Charles '78 (MAD) Madison, WI St. Peter; Office for the Continuing Education of Priests.
Schmalhofer, John D. '74 (HBG) New Holland, PA Our Lady of Lourdes.
Schmalzried, Bernard R. '69 (Y) Warren, OH St. Mary.
Schmeidler, John *o.f.m.cap.* '97 (KCK) Lawrence, KS St. John the Evangelist; [I] Lawrence, KS St. Conrad Friary.
Schmelz, Damian *o.s.b.* '58 (EVN) Ferdinand, IN St. Henry.
Schmelz, Damian *o.s.b.* '58 (IND)[K] Saint Meinrad St. Meinrad Archabbey.
Schmelzer, Rev. Msgr. Delbert L. '56 (MAD) Appointed; Holy Childhood, Pontifical Association; Propagation of the Faith; [F] Madison, WI Bishop O'Connor Catholic Pastoral Center Retired.
Schmelzer, Ronald '02 (SCL) Elbow Lake, MN St. Olaf; Tintah, MN St. Gall; Chokio, MN St. Charles.
Schmenk, Rev. Msgr. Cleo S. '53 (TOL) Retired.
Schmid, Wayne L. '68 (WCH) Retired.
Schmid, William '09 (PHX) Phoenix, AZ St. Theresa Roman Catholic Parish; [A] Chandler, AZ Seton Catholic Preparatory High School.
Schmidberger, Richard '57 (DET) Retired.
Schmidt, Anthony '50 (SFD) Retired.
Schmidt, Carl '50 (SFD) Retired.
Schmidt, Charles J. *m.m.* '48 (NY)[DD] Retired.
Schmidt, David R. '81 (GB) Antigo, WI SS. Mary & Hyacinth; Deerbrook, WI St. Wenceslaus; Antigo, WI St. John; Elcho, WI Holy Family; Phlox, WI St. Joseph–Holy Family Parish; Pickerel, WI St. Mary.
Schmidt, David '77 (SFD) Absent on Leave.
Schmidt, Dennis C. '80 (STL) Ste. Genevieve, MO Ste. Genevieve.
Schmidt, Donald '73 (MIL) Retired.
Schmidt, Edward P. *s.j.* '71 (FgM) Chicago, IL Society of Jesus.
Schmidt, Edward W. *s.j.* '73 (NY)[DD] New York, NY "America;" Residence and publication office of the America Press.
Schmidt, Edwin A. '63 (JC) Jefferson City, MO St. Martin; Appointed Members.
Schmidt, Florian J. '61 (DUB) Retired.
Schmidt, Francis J. '58 (MAD) Retired.
Schmidt, Rev. Msgr. Francis X. '57 (PH) Retired.
Schmidt, Rev. Msgr. George E. '70 (KNX) Chattanooga, TN Basilica of Sts. Peter and Paul; Chattanooga, TN Mount Olivet Cemetery; Deans of the Diocese; Diocesan Finance Council; Cemeteries; Ministries of the Chattanooga Deanery; Presbyteral Council.
Schmidt, Rev. Msgr. Gregory L. '61 (STL) Kirkwood, MO St. Peter Retired.
Schmidt, Henry '57 (SFD) Carrollton, IL St. John the Evangelist; Greenfield, IL St. Michael; Carrollton, IL All Saints.
Schmidt, Jan Kevin '90 (CIN) Loveland, OH St. Margaret of York.
Schmidt, Jerome J. '49 (BRK)[R] Douglaston, NY Bishop Mugavero Residence Retired.
Schmidt, John *c.ss.r.* '89 (DEN)[N] Denver, CO The Redemptorists/Denver Province.
Schmidt, Joseph F. '66 (B) College of Consultors Retired.
Schmidt, Kenneth W. '81 (KAL) Kalamazoo, MI St. Thomas More Student Parish; [H] Kalamazoo, MI Western Michigan University, Kalamazoo College, Kalamazoo Valley Community College; Priestly Life and Ministry Office; Judge.
Schmidt, Leo C. '56 (COV) Covington, KY St. Augustine.
Schmidt, Leslie *g.h.m.* '61 (RIC) Big Stone Gap, VA Sacred Heart.
Schmidt, Paul J. '64 (OAK) Pinole, CA St. Joseph; Consultors.
Schmidt, Paul Lester *s.v.d.* '81 (SB)[I] Riverside, CA Divine Word Seminary.
Schmidt, Peter *o.c.s.o.* '75 (WOR)[N] Spencer, MA St. Joseph's Abbey.
Schmidt, Raymond F. '60 (BRK) Retired.
Schmidt, Raymond F. '84 (WDC) Hollywood, MD St. John Francis Regis.
Schmidt, Richard C. *s.j.* '61 (WDC)[R] Faulkner, MD Loyola Retreat House.
Schmidt, Robert H. *s.j.* '69 (FgM) Chicago, IL Society of Jesus.
Schmidt, Rev. Msgr. Robert '57 (DAV) Retired.
Schmidt, Ronald *s.j.* '02 (LA) Tujunga, CA Our Lady of Lourdes.
Schmidt, Sebastian *o.s.b.* '60 (BIS)[A] Richardton, ND Assumption Abbey; Richardton, ND.
Schmidt, Teofilo '06 (SPP) Pago Pago, AS Sacred Heart of Jesus Parish, Vailoa; Pago Pago, AS Christ the King.
Schmidt, Thomas W. '99 (CIN) Centerville, OH St. Francis of Assisi.
Schmidt, William F. *s.a.* '59 (ARL) Sterling, VA Christ the Redeemer.
Schmidt, William T. '76 (BO) Stoneham, MA St. Patrick.
Schmied, Rev. Msgr. Michael S. '71 (RIC) Richmond, VA St. Augustine.
Schmied, Thomas *o.f.m.cap.* '69 (SAG) Saginaw, MI St. Anthony of Padua.
Schmiesing, Julian *o.s.b.* '58 (SCL)[I] Collegeville, MN St. John's Abbey, of the Order of St. Benedict.
Schmit, Arthur G. *o.s.b.* '57 (PEO)[A] Peru, IL St. Bede Abbey.
Schmit, George V. '68 (NU) Bird Island, MN St. Mary; Building Committee; Committee on Parishes; Priest Personnel Board.
Schmit, Rev. Msgr. Jerome L. '57 (LA) Altadena, CA Sacred Heart Retired.
Schmit, Kenneth A. '79 (ORG) Los Alamitos, CA St. Hedwig; Diocesan Construction Board.
Schmit, Louis *c.pp.s.* '63 (CIN)[N] Carthagena, OH St. Charles Retired.
Schmit, Roger *o.s.b.* '62 (KCK) Kansas City, KS Christ the King.
Schmit, Ronald G. '85 (OAK) Byron, CA St. Anne; Presbyteral Council.
Schmit, Ryan M. '11 (COL) Gahanna, OH St. Matthew.
Schmit, Stanley T. '94 (OM) Albion, NE St. Michael; Petersburg, NE St. John the Baptist.
Schmitmeyer, Daniel J. '06 (CIN) Sidney, OH Holy Angels.
Schmitmeyer, James M. '81 (CIN) On Duty Outside the Archdiocese.
Schmitmeyer, James '81 (AMA) Amarillo, TX St. Hyacinth's.
Schmitt, Adam '57 (FTW) Retired.
Schmitt, Bill Bernardo '68 (OM) Omaha, NE Our Lady of Guadalupe – St. Agnes Parish.
Schmitt, Bowan '97 (PEO) Pesotum, IL St. Mary; Philo, IL St. Thomas.
Schmitt, Carl E. '05 (GB) Sturgeon Bay, WI Corpus Christi; Vicariate; Maplewood, WI St. Mary; Casco, WI St. Peter–St. Hubert; College of Consultors.
Schmitt, Rev. Msgr. Carl L. '61 (DUB) Building Commission; Retired Priests' Representatives; Directors Retired.
Schmitt, Charles R. '59 (E) Retired.
Schmitt, Christopher '60 (POD) Miami.
Schmitt, Christopher '60 (MIA)[M] Miami, FL Prelature of the Holy Cross and Opus Dei.
Schmitt, Conrad *s.t.* (PAT)[N] Stirling, NJ Shrine of St. Joseph.
Schmitt, David J. '67 (WH) Point Pleasant, WV Sacred Heart Retired.
Schmitt, Eugene '00 (EVN) Celestine, IN St. Peter Celestine; Dubois, IN St. Raphael; Diocesan Council of Priests.
Schmitt, Frank J. *s.j.* '83 (FgM) St. Louis, MO Society of Jesus.
Schmitt, Gregory *c.ss.r.* '69 (CHI)[N] Chicago, IL The Redemptorist Fathers of Chicago; Chicago, IL St. Michael in Old Town.
Schmitt, Harold F. '59 (PEO)[I] Lacon, IL St. Joseph Nursing Home; Lacon, IL Immaculate Conception.
Schmitt, James C. '66 (GI) Retired.
Schmitt, James '51 (LAN) Retired.
Schmitt, Rev. Msgr. Joseph J. '55 (AUS) Retired.
Schmitt, Kent A. '73 (MAD) Madison, WI St. Dennis; Elected.
Schmitt, Michael T. '71 (ALB) Retired.
Schmitt, Phillip E. '56 (DUB) Engaged Encounter; Family Life & Marriage Advisory Committee; Mount Vernon, IA St. John the Baptist; National Marriage Encounter Retired.
Schmitt, Silverius '58 (SCL) Retired.
Schmitt, Theodore '02 (CHI) Streamwood, IL St. John the Evangelist.
Schmitt, Thomas F. '91 (BO)[A] Weston, MA Blessed John XXIII National Seminary.
Schmitt, Thomas F. '91 (SPR) On Duty Outside the Diocese.
Schmitt, William *s.s.c.* '68 (OM)[J] St. Columbans, NE Missionary Society of St. Columban.
Schmitter, Philip '71 (LAN) Flint, MI Christ the King.
Schmittgens, Kevin V. '83 (STL) Union, MO St. Joseph.
Schmitz, Aloysius F. *s.j.* '59 (MIL)[P] Wauwatosa, WI Jesuit Community at St. Camillus.
Schmitz, Bartley *s.v.d.* '44 (FgM) Techny, IL.
Schmitz, Rev. Msgr. Bernard A. '74 (DEN) Vicar for Clergy; Denver, CO Mother of God; College of Consultors; Vicar for Clergy; Pastoral Health Care.
Schmitz, Charles *s.j.* '72 (SEA)[C] Tacoma, WA Bellarmine Preparatory School.
Schmitz, Donald J. '80 (WIN) Rochester, MN Holy Spirit; Elected Deanery Representatives.
Schmitz, Rev. Msgr. Donald P. '64 (WIN) Harmony, MN The Assumption; Harmony, MN The Nativity of the Blessed Virgin; Harmony, MN St. Olaf; Diocesan Consultors; Vicar for Senior Priests.
Schmitz, George R. '69 (CIN) Cincinnati, OH St. Teresa of Avila Retired.
Schmitz, Rev. Msgr. Gerard G. '68 (HRT) Special and other Archdiocesan Assignment; [A] Bloomfield, CT St. Thomas Seminary; Office of Vicar For Priests; Ex Officio; Office of Coordinator for Retired Priests; Consultors – Canon 1742.
Schmitz, James P. '86 (CLV) West Salem, OH St. Stephen.
Schmitz, John A. '52 (MIL) Retired.
Schmitz, John J. '91 (JC) Mexico, MO St. Brendan; Priestly and Religious Vocations Committee.
Schmitz, Michael D. '96 (OM) Crofton, NE St. Andrew; Crofton, NE St. Rose of Lima.
Schmitz, Michael '03 (DUL) Campus Ministry; Department of Youth and Young Adult Ministry; [F] Duluth, MN Newman Catholic Campus Ministry.
Schmitz, Rev. Msgr. R. Michael '82 (CHI)[N] Chicago, IL Institute of Christ the King Sovereign Priest.
Schmitz, Robert A. '55 (OM) Retired.
Schmitz, Robert E. '75 (CIN) Cincinnati, OH Good Shepherd.
Schmoll, John *o.s.b. oblate* '85 (FRS) Lamont, CA St. Augustine.
Schmolt, Johnathan P. '08 (E) Erie, PA St. George; Priest Personnel Board.
Schmuhl, Lawrence R. *s.m.* '47 (ATL)[C] Atlanta, GA Marist School Retired.

Schnakenberg, Gregory *o.p.* '09 (COL) Columbus, OH St. Patrick.
Schnaubelt, Joseph C. *o.s.a.* '57 (PH)[Y] Villanova, PA St. Thomas Monastery.
Schneck, Richard J. *s.j.* '72 (FgM) Los Gatos, CA Society of Jesus.
Schneebeck, Paul O. *c.m.* '69 (STL)[O] St. Louis, MO Lazarist Residence.
Schneibel, Jeffrey A. *c.s.c.* '85 (FTW) South Bend, IN Holy Cross; South Bend, IN St. Stanislaus.
Schneible, Peter *o.f.m.* '89 (BUF)[N] St. Bonaventure, NY St. Bonaventure Friary.
Schneider, Bernard '67 (FAR) Manvel, ND St. Timothy's Church of Manvel; Altru Hospital; [I] Manvel, ND Beginning Experience Apostolate.
Schneider, Charles *s.v.d.* '46 (CHI)[N] Techny, IL Divine Word Residence.
Schneider, Daniel Mary *m. carm.* '98 (CHY)[D] Powell, WY Monks of the Most Blessed Virgin Mary of Mt. Carmel.
Schneider, Edward (ORL) Retired.
Schneider, Rev. Msgr. Ernest '77 (GR) Grand Rapids, MI St. Paul the Apostle; Deans; College of Consultors.
Schneider, Rev. Msgr. Francis J. '83 (RVC) Melville, NY St. Elizabeth; Censors of Books; Priests' Personnel Policy Board.
Schneider, Fred *o.f.m.* '49 (SFD)[K] Sherman, IL Blessed Giles Friary.
Schneider, Gilbert *o.f.m.* '64 (GLP) Navajo, NM St. Berard; Fort Defiance, AZ Our Lady of Blessed Sacrament; [E] Gallup, NM Southwest Indian Foundation; Vicars Forane; Presbyteral Council; Diocesan Consultors.
Schneider, Harold E. '62 (COL) Retired.
Schneider, Harold F. '74 (KCK) Regional Pastoral Leaders; Kansas City, KS Cathedral of St. Peter the Apostle.
Schneider, Henry W. '53 (BIS) Retired.
Schneider, Herbert *s.j.* '70 (FgM) New York, NY Society of Jesus.
Schneider, Jerzy *s.d.b.* '53 (NEW)[L] Ramsey, NJ Don Bosco Prep Salesian Residence; [C] Ramsey, NJ Don Bosco Preparatory High School Retired.
Schneider, John H. '68 (STL) Bonne Terre, MO St. Joseph's; DEPARTMENT OF VETERANS AFFAIRS HOSPITALS AND CHAPLAINS.
Schneider, John J. '11 (CLV) Parma, OH Holy Family.
Schneider, John '83 (CHL) Absent On Leave.
Schneider, Joseph M. '74 (DUB) Waukon, IA St. Patrick; Waukon, IA St. Mary; Waukon, IA St. Mary.
Schneider, Karl J. '59 (MIL) Retired.
Schneider, Kevin C. *s.j.* '94 (OM)[C] Omaha, NE Creighton Preparatory School.
Schneider, Leo J. '83 (STP) Minneapolis, MN Holy Name; Maplewood, MN St. John's Hospital.
Schneider, Michael '94 (GF) Forsyth, MT Immaculate Conception; Defender of the Bond.
Schneider, Michael '81 (SFS) Mitchell, SD Holy Spirit.
Schneider, Rev. Msgr. Nicholas A. '56 (STL) Retired.
Schneider, Nick L. '09 (BIS) Graduate Studies.
Schneider, Philip *o.f.m.conv.* '61 (FTW) Angola, IN St. Anthony; Angola, IN St. Paul Chapel.
Schneider, Ric *o.f.m.* '59 (PEO) Bloomington, IL St. Mary's.
Schneider, Rev. Msgr. Robert E. '57 (COL) Retired.
Schneider, Robert J. '81 (SP) Safety Harbor, FL Espiritu Santo; Ecumenical and Inter–Religious Affairs.
Schneider, Robert J. '78 (WIN) Madison Lake, MN All Saints; Madison Lake, MN Immaculate Conception.
Schneider, Ronald F. '67 (GR) Baldwin, MI St. Ann – St. Luther; Deans; Presbyteral Council.
Schneider, Ronald '75 (GB) Absent on Leave, Sick or Disabled.
Schneider, Terrance L. '79 (CIN) Beavercreek, OH St. Luke.
Schneider, Todd '85 (SCL) Sauk Centre, MN St. Paul's.
Schneider, Troy D. '11 (ORG) Awaiting Assignment.
Schneider, William T. '63 (TR) Retired.
Schneller, Michael J. '72 (NO) Metairie, LA St. Ann Church and Shrine; Metairie, LA St. Ann National Shrine.
Schnipke, Eugene H. *c.pp.s.* '80 (CIN) Maria Stein, OH Nativity of the Blessed Virgin Mary; Maria Stein, OH Most Precious Blood; Maria Stein, OH St. John the Baptist; Maria Stein, OH St. Rose; Maria Stein, OH St. Sebastian.
Schnipke, Ken *c.pp.s.* '90 (CIN) Celina, OH Immaculate Conception of the Blessed Virgin Mary; Rockford, OH St. Teresa; [N] Dayton Provincial Office of the Cincinnati Province of the Society of the Precious Blood.
Schnippel, Kyle E. '04 (CIN) Cincinnati, OH Our Lady of Lourdes; Vocations Office.
Schnobrich, Jon–Daniel '07 (BUR) House of Discernment; [G] Burlington, VT University of Vermont–The Catholic Center at UVM; Vocations and Seminarians.
Schnur, Edward '91 (EVN) Evansville, IN St. Wendel; Poseyville, IN St. Francis Xavier.
Schober, Robert J. '77 (BUF) North Collins, NY Epiphany of Our Lord.
Schock, Ronald A. '96 (TOL) Swanton, OH Holy Trinity; Priests' Personnel Board.
Schoeberle, Bradford C. *c.s.p.* '00 (GR) Allendale, MI St. Luke University Parish; [K] Allendale, MI St. Luke University Parish and Catholic Campus Ministry.
Schoellmann, Edward R. *m.m.* '65 (FgM) Maryknoll, NY MARYKNOLL.
Schoemann, Robert L. '66 (DM) Priests' Pension Fund Society Retired.
Schoen, Timothy *o.s.b.* '64 (KC)[A] Conception, MO Conception Seminary College; [J] Conception, MO Conception Abbey.
Schoenauer, Francis P. '73 (ALN) Nesquehoning, PA St. Francis of Assisi Parish.
Schoenbaechler, Charles *c.r.* '42 (L)[L] Louisville, KY Villa Pacis, Resurrectionist Retirement Home; Louisville, KY.
Schoenberg, Oscar *o.s.c.* '48 (SCL)[I] Onamia, MN Crosier Priory.
Schoenberger, James T. '57 (STP) Retired.
Schoenfield, Andres H. '02 (ATL) Without Archdiocesan Assignment or Faculties; On Leave of Absence.
Schoenhofen, Darr F. '82 (SY) Skaneateles, NY St. Mary of the Lake.
Schoenig, Stephen A. *s.j.* '85 (STL)[C] Saint Louis University.
Schoenig, Steven A. *s.j.* (STL)[O] St. Louis, MO Sacred Heart Jesuit Community.
Schoening, Sylvester H. '58 (PBL) Retired.
Schoenstene, Robert L. '75 (CHI)[A] Mundelein, IL University of St. Mary of the Lake/Mundelein Seminary; On Duty Outside the Diocese.
Schoepppe, F. Warren *s.j.* '58 (SJ)[M] Los Gatos, CA Sacred Heart Jesuit Center.
Scholl, Jerel A. '01 (LIN) Advocates; Diocesan Area CCD Directors.
Scholla, Robert W. *s.j.* '86 (LA)[C] Los Angeles, CA Jesuit Community; [C] Los Angeles, CA Jesuit Community.
Scholz, Mark A. '02 (KNX) Dunlap, TN Shepherd of the Valley; South Pittsburg, TN Our Lady of Lourdes.
Schomaker, Daniel Lyden '08 (COV) Diocesan Consultors.
Schommer, George P. *o.p.* '94 (WDC) Washington, DC St. Dominic Church & Priory.
Schommer, Rev. Msgr. Mark J. '63 (GB) Leo Benevolent Association Retired.
Schommer, Michael '93 (FAR) Towner, ND St. Cecilia's Church of Towner.
Schon, Randy L. '88 (SC) Boone, IA Sacred Heart; Catholic Youth Organization; Presbyteral Council.
Schonberger, Micah *o.c.s.o.* '05 (DEN)[N] Snowmass, CO St. Benedict's Monastery.
Schons, Rev. Msgr. Gerard '47 (SAC) Retired.
Schooler, Rev. Msgr. William C. '74 (FTW) Granger, IN St. Pius X; Pro–Synodal Judges; Liturgical Commission.
Schopfer, John C. '69 (SY) Syracuse, NY The Cathedral of the Immaculate Conception; Syracuse, NY Justice Center; Special Assignment; [U] Syracuse, NY Brady Faith Center, Inc.
Schopp, George L. '74 (CHI) Chicago, IL Our Lady of Grace.
Schork, John *c.p.* '76 (CHI)[N] Chicago, IL Passionist Provincial Office.
Schork, John *c.p.* '76 (L) Ex Officio; [L] Louisville, KY Sacred Heart Retreat.
Schorp, W. Franz *s.m.* '64 (SAT)[C] San Antonio, TX St. Mary's University of San Antonio, Texas; [L] San Antonio, TX Marianist Residence.
Schorr, James D. '68 (CLV) Retired.
Schorr, James '68 (SD) Scripps Mercy Hospital; [H] San Diego, CA Scripps Mercy Hospital.
Schorr, W. David '73 (PIT) Munhall, PA St. Rita; West Mifflin, PA Resurrection.
Schott, James E. '61 (NO) Retired.
Schott, Kevin J. '90 (NEW) Maywood, NJ Our Lady Queen of Peace.
Schott, Paul *s.j.* '60 (NO) New Orleans, LA Holy Name of Jesus.
Schott, Timothy R. '70 (SC) Carroll, IA St. Lawrence; Lidderdale, IA Holy Family; Deans; Presbyteral Council.
Schotzko, Philip M. '77 (NU) Saint Peter, MN Church of St. Peter; Propagation of the Faith/Holy Childhood Association; On Special or Other Diocesan Assignment; Ex Officio Members.
Schouten, Francis L. '55 (CHI) Retired.
Schrad, Merlin J. '77 (SC) Sioux City, IA Blessed Sacrament; Presbyteral Council; Diocesan Consultors; Deans.
Schrader, Dylan '10 (JC) Jefferson City, MO Immaculate Conception.
Schrader, James C. '76 (LIN) Campbell, NE St. Anne; Deaneries and Deans.
Schrader, James *c.pp.s* '56 (CIN)[N] Carthagena, OH St. Charles.
Schrader, Robert J. '78 (ROC) Rochester, NY Peace of Christ Roman Catholic Parish of Rochester, NY.
Schrader, Thomas *o.carm.* '01 (LA)[F] Encino, CA Crespi Carmelite High School; [P] Encino, CA Our Lady of Mount Carmel Priory.
Schramel, Michael J. '80 (ROC) Rochester, NY Holy Ghost; Rochester, NY St. Jude the Apostle; Rochester, NY St. Helen.
Schramm, Charles H. '71 (MIL) Hales Corners, WI St. Mary.
Schramm, Rev. Msgr. Donald C. '67 (STL) St. Charles, MO St. Charles Borromeo.
Schramm, Mark *s.v.d.* '75 (CHI)[N] Chicago, IL Edward McGuinn, S.V.D. Residence.
Schramm, Robert *o.s.f.s.* '69 (LAN) Adrian, MI St. Mary of Good Counsel.
Schratz, Martin A. *o.f.m.cap.* '83 (CHL) Charlotte, NC Our Lady of Consolation.
Schray, Karl '65 (P) North Bend, OR Holy Redeemer; Area Vicars; North Bend, OR Shutter Creek Correctional Institution.
Schreck, Rev. Msgr. Christopher J. '77 (SAV) On Duty Outside the Diocese.
Schreck, Rev. Msgr. Christopher '77 (COL)[A] Columbus, OH Pontifical College Josephinum; [A] Columbus, OH Pontifical College Josephinum.
Schreck, J. Gerard '83 (SAV) Columbus, GA St. Anne; [A] Columbus, GA St. Anne/Pacelli Catholic School; Defender of the Bond; Columbus Deanery; Presbyteral Council.
Schreck, Kim J. '07 (PIT) Beaver Falls, PA Christ the Divine Teacher; Darlington, PA St. Rose of Lima.
Schreiber, Francis '02 (GF) Poplar, MT Our Lady of Lourdes; Vicars Forane.
Schreiber, Stephen J. '99 (E) Religious Education; [A] Erie, PA St. Mark's Seminary; Vocation Office; St. Mark Seminary; Presbyteral Council.
Schreiber, William A. '79 (SC) Spencer, IA Sacred Heart.
Schreiner, Robert '89 (CR) Chancellor; Crookston, MN Cathedral of the Immaculate Conception; Finance Council; Priests' Council.
Schreiter, John P. '69 (MIL) Waukesha, WI St. John Neumann.
Schreiter, Robert *c.pp.s.* '75 (CHI)[B] Chicago, IL Catholic Theological Union.
Schreiter, Robert *c.pp.s.* '75 (CIN)[N] Dayton Provincial Office of the Cincinnati Province of the Society of the Precious Blood.
Schreitmueller, Henry '56 (NEW) Retired.
Schremmer, Robert A. '76 (DOD) Wright, KS St. Andrew Catholic Church of Wright, Kansas; Vicar General and Moderator of the Curia; Presbyteral Council; College of Consultors; Pratt, KS St. Joseph Catholic Church of Greensburg, Kansas.
Schrenger, Arthur C. '75 (MOB) Retired.
Schriber, Robert T. '96 (R) Garner, NC St. Mary, Mother of the Church.
Schriver, Ragan '95 (KNX) Seymour, TN Holy Family; Catholic Charities of East Tennessee, Inc.; Catholic Campaign for Human Development; Presbyteral Council.
Schrock, Dean (P)[J] Portland, OR Providence Health & Services–Oregon.
Schroder, John F. *s.j.* '53 (NO)[R] New Orleans, LA Ignatius Residence Retired.
Schroedel, Lawrence *c.f.r.* '07 (NY)[DD] Yonkers, NY St. Leopold's Friary.
Schroeder, Dennis A. '61 (TOL) Retired.
Schroeder, Edward H. '58 (BUF)[N] Buffalo, NY Sheehan Residence for Priests; Depew, NY Retired.
Schroeder, Eugene A. '79 (EVN) Evansville, IN St. Joseph; Cemeteries.
Schroeder, Eugene '79 (EVN) Evansville, IN Holy Trinity.
Schroeder, George J. '42 (PEO) Rock Island, IL St. Mary Retired.
Schroeder, Rev. Msgr. George '62 (DEN) Retired.
Schroeder, Rev. Msgr. George '62 (PHX) Scottsdale, AZ Blessed Sacrament Roman Catholic Parish.
Schroeder, James *s.c.j.* '70 (MIL)[P] Hales Corners Priests of the Sacred Heart.
Schroeder, Jerome *o.f.m.cap.* '70 (MIL)[S] South Milwaukee, WI The Dwelling Place; Milwaukee, WI St. Benedict the Moor; Milwaukee, WI St. Francis Institute Milwaukee.
Schroeder, Kenneth J. *c.pp.s.* '65 (CIN)[N] Carthagena, OH St. Charles.
Schroeder, Kevin M. '08 (STL) St. Charles, MO St. Joseph.
Schroeder, Matthew '02 (SJP) Miami, FL Assumption of B.V.M.; Presbyters.
Schroeder, Richard F. '45 (CHI) Retired.
Schroeder, Roger P. *s.v.d.* '79 (CHI)[B] Chicago, IL Catholic Theological Union; [N] Chicago, IL Divine Word Theologate.
Schroeder, Stephen L. '01 (TOL) Miller City, OH St. Nicholas; Miller City, OH Holy Family.
Schroeder, Tait C. '02 (MAD) Advocate/Procurator (cc.1481–1490); Graduate Studies.
Schroeder, Thomas H. '64 (MAD) Retired.
Schroeder, Timothy '88 (FAR) Grafton, ND St. John the Evangelist's Church of Grafton; Hispanic Ministry.
Schroer, Thomas A. *s.m.* '72 (CIN) Dayton, OH Queen

of Apostles; [N] Dayton, OH Mercy Siena Support Community.
Schroth, Raymond A. *s.j.* '67 (NY)[DD] New York, NY "America;" Residence and publication office of the America Press.
Schu, Walter *l.c.* '94 (HRT)[B] Cheshire, CT Novitiate of the Legion of Christ.
Schubeck, Thomas L. *s.j.* '68 (CLV)[B] University Heights, OH John Carroll Jesuit Community.
Schubert, Gerard J. *o.s.f.s.* '59 (ALN)[B] Center Valley, PA DeSales University; [K] Center Valley, PA Oblates of St. Francis de Sales.
Schubert, Gerold *o.f.m.* '54 (JOL)[L] Joliet, IL St. John the Baptist Friary Retired.
Schubert, Herbert '56 (MIL) Retired.
Schubert, Roy R. '63 (PBR) Sheffield, PA St. Michael.
Schuckenbrock, Harry *o.m.i.* '59 (BWN) Port Isabel, TX Our Lady Star of the Sea.
Schuckman, Kenneth J. '92 (WCH) Colwich, KS Sacred Heart; [K] Wichita, KS Serra Club of Wichita – Downtown.
Schudde, Derk (ORL) Winter Park, FL Saints Peter and Paul.
Schuele, Francis J. '68 (KC) Kansas City, MO St. Thomas More Retired.
Schuele, John '76 (KC) Odessa, MO St. George.
Schuelkens, Dennis R. '06 (WH) Vocations Promoters; Wheeling, WV Our Lady of Peace; Diocesan Committee on Scouting.
Schueller, Anthony *s.s.s.* '77 (NY) New York, NY St. Jean Baptiste; Cleveland, OH.
Schueller, La Verne L. '66 (DUB) Retired.
Schueller, Michael G. '97 (DUB) Manly, IA Sacred Heart; Mason City; [G] Mason City, IA Newman High School; [G] Mason City, IA Newman Elementary School; Mason City, IA Holy Family.
Schuerger, Anthony J. '77 (CLV) Cleveland, OH St. Malachi; Permanent Diaconate Formation Office.
Schuerman, James T. '86 (MIL) Delavan, WI St. Andrew; Elkhorn, WI St. Patrick; [B] Hales Corners, WI Sacred Heart School of Theology.
Schuessler, Peter *s.d.s.* '80 (MIL)[B] Hales Corners, WI Sacred Heart School of Theology; [P] Milwaukee Salvatorian Provincial Offices.
Schuessler, William R. '67 (RCK) Active Outside the Diocese.
Schuetze, John W. '97 (MO) Air Force Reserve Chaplains; Military Chaplains.
Schuetze, John W. '97 (BLX) Keesler Airforce Base.
Schuh, Rev. Msgr. John H. '65 (GB) Retired.
Schuh, Karl Christopher '09 (NOR) Absent on Leave.
Schuler, Rev. Msgr. A. John '74 (STL) Florissant, MO St. Ferdinand.
Schuler, Emeh *o.f.m.cap.* '69 (WDC)[B] Washington, DC St. Francis Friary–Capuchin College.
Schuler, Emett J. *o.f.m.cap.* '69 (MO) DEPARTMENT OF VETERANS AFFAIRS HOSPITALS AND CHAPLAINS.
Schuler, Steven *s.v.d.* '79 (TR)[N] Bordentown, NJ Society of the Divine Word.
Schulmeister, Lawrence *o.s.f.* '67 (BAL) University of Maryland– R. Adams Crowley Shock Trauma.
Schulte, Carl G. *c.m.* '48 (KC)[J] Independence, MO Vincentian Parish Mission Center.
Schulte, Francisco *o.s.b.* '79 (SCL)[I] Collegeville, MN St. John's Abbey, of the Order of St. Benedict.
Schulte, Gary W. '72 (DET) Warren, MI St. Sylvester; Absent on Leave.
Schulte, Rev. Msgr. John R. '77 (COV) Walton, KY All Saints.
Schulte, Lyle L. '60 (LC) Retired.
Schulte, Mark A. '97 (SFD) Pittsfield, IL St. Mary; Pittsfield, IL St. Mark.
Schulte, Rev. Msgr. Robert C. '75 (FTW) Fort Wayne, IN Cathedral of the Immaculate Conception; Board of Directors; Finance Council; Vicar General–Chancellor; Retired Clergy Committee; Consultors; Advisory Board; Budget Committee; Continuing Formation of Priests and Deacons; Presbyteral Council; Clergy Retirement Board; Moderator of the Curia; Permanent Diaconate.
Schulte, William P. '52 (NEW) Retired.
Schultenover, David G. *s.j.* '69 (MIL)[Y] Milwaukee, WI Theological Studies, Inc.; [P] Milwaukee, WI Jesuit Community at Marquette University.
Schultheis, Michael J. *s.j.* '65 (P)[L] Portland Jesuit Provincial Office (Society of Jesus, Oregon Prov.); Portland, OR Society of Jesus.
Schultheis, Michael *s.j.* (SPK)[B] Spokane, WA Gonzaga University.
Schultz, Blaine *o.s.b.* '60 (KCK)[A] Atchison, KS Benedictine College; [I] Atchison, KS St. Benedict's Abbey.
Schultz, Brian '82 (DUL) Retired.
Schultz, Bruce *o.p.* '88 (ATL) Atlanta, GA Our Lady of Lourdes; [F] Atlanta, GA Augustine House, Dominicans Friars of Atlanta.
Schultz, C. Raymond '91 (BEL) Caseyville, IL St. Stephen; Fairview Heights, IL Holy Trinity Catholic Church; Diocesan Consultors; Diocesan Deans.
Schultz, Charles F. '80 (SB) Retired.
Schultz, Dustin P. '08 (PEO)[B] Ottawa, IL Marquette Academy of Ottawa, Inc.; Streator, IL St. Michael the Archangel Church.
Schultz, James A. '11 (SY) Cicero, NY Sacred Heart.
Schultz, Joel P. '00 (MEM) Absent on Leave.
Schultz, John A. '65 (LC) Eau Claire, WI St. James the Greater.
Schultz, John M. '82 (E) Erie, PA St. Boniface.
Schultz, Mark A. '03 (SFE) Albuquerque, NM Holy Ghost.
Schultz, Robert '01 (CHI) Schiller Park, IL St. Beatrice.
Schultz, Stephen J. '09 (ARL) Chantilly, VA St. Timothy.
Schultz, Stephen '99 (SFE) Belen, NM Our Lady of Belen; Defenders of the Bond.
Schultz, Rev. Msgr. William F. '64 (BGP) Stratford, CT Our Lady of Grace.
Schultze, George E. *s.j.* '94 (SFR)[A] Menlo Park, CA St. Patrick Seminary and University.
Schulyer, David H. *s.m.* '60 (SLC) Judges.
Schulz, James W. *s.j.* '77 (CHI) Cicero, IL Mary, Queen of Heaven.
Schulz, Ronald '68 (PMB) Lantana, FL Holy Spirit Retired.
Schulz, Wilfred G. *o.s.b.* '53 (PAT)[N] Morristown, NJ St. Mary's Abbey.
Schumacher, Rev. Msgr. Andrew '59 (B) Defenders of the Bond; College of Consultors; Censor Librorum Retired.
Schumacher, Anthony J. '60 (MAD)[A] Madison, WI Edgewood College, Inc. Retired.
Schumacher, Jacob J. '52 (BIS)[G] Bismarck, ND Emmaus Place Retired.
Schumacher, James '95 (CHY) Laramie, WY St. Laurence O'Toole; Diocesan Schools Advisory Group; [G] Laramie, WY St. Laurence School Foundation.
Schumacher, John N. *s.j.* '57 (FgM) New York, NY Society of Jesus.
Schumacher, Rev. Msgr. Joseph A. '57 (FWT) Retired.
Schumacher, Patrick A. '93 (BIS) Dickinson, ND St. Wenceslaus; Priests' Personnel Board.
Schumacher, Paul A. '62 (NU) AIDS Ministry; Catholic Charities Advisory Committee.
Schumacher, Paul A. '62 (NU) Marshall, MN Holy Redeemer; On Special or Other Diocesan Assignment.
Schumer, Jason J. '10 (STL)[A] St. Louis, MO Cardinal Glennon College; St. Louis, MO St. Ambrose.
Schumm, Nicholas Frank '06 (PT) Quincy, FL St. Thomas the Apostle; Co Directors.
Schunk, David A. '10 (SFR) San Mateo, CA St. Gregory.
Schuster, Anthony J. '70 (GF) Retired.
Schuster, Charles G. *c.m.* '55 (FgM) Philadelphia, PA Eastern Province.
Schuster, Daniel J. '08 (GB)[N] Green Bay, WI Ecumenical Center–UWGB; Vocations; Special Assignment.
Schuster, Frank J. '00 (BIS) Underwood, ND St. Bonaventure; Underwood, ND St. Edwin's Church; Underwood, ND St. Catherine.
Schuster, Frank '99 (SEA) Woodinville, WA Blessed Teresa of Calcutta.
Schuster, Rev. Msgr. George M. '57 (BRK) Ridgewood, NY Our Lady of the Miraculous Medal; St. John's Priests Relief Society Retired.
Schuster, Paul R. '93 (FAR) Bottineau, ND St. Mark's Church of Bottineau; Bottineau, ND St. Andrew's Church of Westhope; Prison Apostolate.
Schuster, Peter L. '95 (WIN) Fairmont, MN Holy Family; Fairmont, MN St. John Vianney; Elected At–Large Representatives.
Schuster, Raymond '93 (SAT) San Antonio, TX St. John The Evangelist.
Schuster, Robert C. '95 (DET) Marine City, MI Our Lady on the River.
Schuster, Roy *o.f.m.cap* '59 (WH)[L] Charleston, WV Capuchins–St. Anthony Friary; Charleston, WV St. Anthony Retired.
Schute, Arthur B. '67 (NEW) On Duty Outside the Archdiocese Retired.
Schute, Bruce J. *s.a.c.* '60 (MIL)[P] Milwaukee, WI Pallotti House.
Schutte, James '79 (CIN) Cincinnati, OH St. Leo the Great; Cincinnati, OH St. Bernard.
Schutten, Rev. Msgr. Marion F. '45 (NO) Retired.
Schutty, John J. '83 (JC) Retired.
Schuwey, Emil *c.pp.s.* '49 (CIN)[N] Carthagena, OH St. Charles Retired.
Schuyler, David H. *s.m.* '60 (LAV) Diocesan Judges.
Schuyler, David *s.m.* '60 (SJ)[M] Cupertino, CA The Alcalde House.
Schuyler, David *s.m.* '60 (MRY) Judges.
Schuyler, David *s.m.* '60 (RNO) Advocates.
Schwab, Elwin '60 (P) Portland, OR St. Charles; Board Members.
Schwab, James '81 (JOL) Roselle, IL St. Walter.
Schwab, Joseph C. *o.m.i.* '53 (PT) Madison, FL St. Vincent de Paul.
Schwab, Joseph *o.f.m.* '08 (PHX)[G] Scottsdale, AZ Franciscan Renewal Center, Inc. (Casa de Paz Y Bien); Scottsdale, AZ Our Lady of the Angels Conventual Church.
Schwab, Joseph *o.m.i.* '53 (BO)[U] Lowell, MA Missionary Oblates of Mary Immaculate Retired.
Schwab, Steven C. '90 (IND) Indianapolis, IN Saint Thomas Aquinas Catholic Church, Indianapolis, Inc.; Indianapolis Metropolitan Police Department.
Schwaegel, Rev. Msgr. Joseph R. '65 (BEL) Retired.
Schwall, J. J. '06 (SLC) Salt Lake City, UT Our Lady of Lourdes LLC 211.
Schwalm, Donald '52 (KCK) Retired.
Schwalm, Donald (STP) Minneapolis, MN St. Hedwig Retired.
Schwan, Paul (MIL)[L] Milwaukee, WI Sacred Heart Rehabilitation Institute, Inc.; [K] Milwaukee, WI Columbia St. Mary's Hospital Ozaukee, Inc.; [K] Milwaukee, WI Columbia St. Mary's Hospital Milwaukee, Inc.
Schwanger, Rev. Msgr. Kenneth K. '90 (MIA) Miami, FL Our Lady of Lourdes; [D] Miami, FL Archbishop Coleman Carroll High School; Adjutant Judicial Vicar; Spiritual Moderators; Archdiocesan Vocations Review Board; Permanent Diaconate; Promoter of Justice.
Schwantes, John *s.j.* '69 (GB)[M] Oshkosh, WI Jesuit Retreat House.
Schwarting, J. Donald '66 (GAL) Retired.
Schwartz, Charles M. '99 (TR) Eatontown, NJ St. Dorothea.
Schwartz, Edwin V. '60 (ALN) Allentown, PA Immaculate Conception Retired.
Schwartz, Hugh F. '56 (OM) Retired.
Schwartz, James A. '68 (ROC) Penfield, NY St. Joseph; Office of Seminarians.
Schwartz, Norman R. '69 (MIL) Retired.
Schwartz, Norman (WDC)[L] Washington, DC Georgetown University Hospital.
Schwartz, Robert M. '67 (STP) Edina, MN Our Lady of Grace; Regional Vicars.
Schwartz, Rodney A. '92 (SFD) Oconee, IL Sacred Heart; Pana, IL St. Patrick.
Schwartz, Rev. Msgr. William H. *p.a.* '68 (RCK) Special Assignment; Permanent Diaconate Program Diocesan; Pro Synodal Judges.
Schwartz, William J. '68 (PIT) Beaver County, PA Heritage Valley Beaver; Beaver, PA SS. Peter and Paul; Beaver County, PA Friendship Ridge Skilled Nursing.
Schwartzlose, John A. '00 (L) Cox's Creek, KY St. Gregory; Ex Officio.
Schwarz, Elmer C. '53 (OKL) Defenders of the Bond Retired.
Schwarz, Frank L. '01 (BRK) Oakland Gardens, NY American Martyrs.
Schwarz, Joseph Patrick '08 (OKL) Anadarko, OK St. Patrick's.
Schwarz, Robert '65 (MRY) Retired.
Schwarz, Thomas J.E. *s.j.* '01 (FgM) Los Gatos, CA Society of Jesus.
Schwarzhaupt, Robert W. '86 (HON) Kamuela, HI Church of the Annunciation.
Schwebs, Daniel L. *o.s.j.* '86 (SCR)[A] Pittston, PA St. Joseph's Oblate Seminary.
Schweda, Phillip '79 (LAN) Tribunal Judges; Okemos, MI St. Martha.
Schweder, Rev. Msgr. John F. '60 (DET) Retired.
Schweers, Gregory *o.cist.* '81 (DAL)[J] Irving, TX Cistercian Abbey of Our Lady of Dallas.
Schweigardt, Erwin H. '67 (ALB) Priests Retirement Board/Priests Retirement Plan Board Retired.
Schweigardt, Erwin '67 (ALB) Priestly Life and Ministry Council Retired.
Schweiger, Troy J. '95 (LIN) Lincoln, NE St. Patrick's.
Schweikert, John *m.s.c.* '96 (RCK)[G] Aurora, IL Missionaries of the Sacred Heart Community.
Schweitzer, Rev. Msgr. Francis X. '45 (COL) Retired.
Schweitzer, Gerald H. '71 (GRY) Wanatah, IN St. Mary; Wanatah, IN Sacred Heart; Bishop's Council of Priests; Marriage Dispensations; Rural Life Conference.
Schweitzer, Joachim B. *o.s.b.* '58 (PAT)[N] Morristown, NJ St. Mary's Abbey.
Schweitzer, Paul A. *s.j.* '70 (FgM) Watertown, MA Society of Jesus.
Schweitzer, Thomas '82 (LA) Glendale, CA Church of the Incarnation; Vernon, CA Holy Angels Parish of the Deaf.
Schweizer, Paul *o.carm.* '62 (NEW) Englewood, NJ St. Cecilia's.
Schwendeman, Daniel P. '01 (LEX) Versailles, KY St. Leo.
Schwenzer, Ronald G. *c.s.b.* '68 (GAL)[E] Houston, TX St. Thomas High School.
Schwer, Albert *c.p.* '55 (L)[L] Louisville, KY Sacred Heart Retreat.
Schwermer, Paul '82 (LAN) McLaren Regional Medical Center; Hurley Regional Medical Center.
Schwertley, James F. '61 (OM) Omaha, NE St. Mary Magdalene Retired.
Schwertner, Rev. Msgr. Timothy (SAN)[C] Stanton, TX St. Vincent De Paul Society; Stanton, TX St. Joseph's.
Schwet, Edward N. '82 (CLV) Fairview General Hospital; Cleveland, OH St. Mark.

Schwinger, Rev. Msgr. William A. '58 (BUF) Retired.
Schwinghamer, David J. *m.m.* '73 (NY)[DD].
Sciacca, Guy F. '10 (BO) Needham, MA St. Joseph.
Scianna, Bernard C. *o.s.a.* (PH)[C] Villanova, PA Villanova University.
Scianna, Bernard C. *o.s.a.* '93 (FgM) Olympia Fields, IL Province of Our Mother of Good Counsel (Midwestern); Olympia Fields, IL.
Scianna, Bernard C. *o.s.a.* '93 (CHI)[N] Chicago, IL The Augustinians–Provincialate; [N] Chicago, IL St. Rita Monastery.
Sciarrotta, Paul J. '62 (CLV)[O] Chardon, OH Provincial House of the Sisters of Notre Dame, Juniorate, Novitiate Retired.
Sciberras, Ivan '99 (NEW) Belleville, NJ St. Peter's.
Sciberras, Michael J. '67 (GBG) East Vandergrift, PA Our Lady, Queen of Peace.
Sciera, Rev. Msgr. Ronald P. '61 (BUF) Retired.
Scillieri, Charles P. '73 (MET) Retired.
Scioli, Richard A. *c.s.s.* '79 (WOR) Milford, MA Sacred Heart of Jesus.
Scirghi, Thomas J. *s.j.* '86 (NY)[DD] Cardinal Spellman Hall, Jesuit Community.
Sciumbato, Michael R. '94 (SLC) Salt Lake City, UT Saint Ann LLC 215.
Sciurba, Salvatore *o.c.d.* '71 (WDC)[B] Washington, DC Discalced Carmelite Friars.
Scocco, Victor *o.ss.t.* '81 (BAL) Hanover, MD St. Lawrence Martyr; [Q] Archdiocese of Baltimore, MD – Assigned Elsewhere.
Scolamiero, Dominic A. '69 (PAT) Retired.
Scollen, Rev. Msgr. Francis J. '71 (WOR) Worcester, MA St. Peter; [Q] Worcester, MA Clark University; Diocesan College of Consultors; Black Catholics: African American.
Scordo, Joseph A. *o.p.* '69 (RIC) Charlottesville, VA St. Thomas Aquinas.
Scornaienchi, Frank *t.o.r.* '79 (ALT) Altoona, PA Our Lady of Mt. Carmel.
Scorzello, Joseph F. '69 (BO)[A] Brighton, MA St. John Seminary.
Scotchie, David '93 (ORL) Orlando, FL St. Maximilian Kolbe.
Scott, Alfonso A. '59 (LA) Retired.
Scott, Brendan T. *s.j.* '78 (NY)[DD] New York, NY Murray–Weigel Hall.
Scott, Craig *v.c.* '96 (ALX) Vicar for Clergy; Appointed Members; College of Consultors.
Scott, Delroy Thomas '86 (MGZ) Rincon, PR St. Rose of Lima; Christian Family Movement.
Scott, Derrek D. '01 (PBL) Elected.
Scott, Derrek '01 (PBL) Alamosa, CO Sacred Heart; Deans; Monte Vista, CO St. Joseph; College of Consultors; Center, CO St. Francis Jerome; Monte Vista, CO Holy Name of Mary.
Scott, Edward R. '56 (SCR)[M] Dunmore, PA Villa St. Joseph Retired.
Scott, James C. '74 (PAT) Absent on Leave.
Scott, Joe *c.s.p.* '73 (LA) Los Angeles, CA St. Paul the Apostle.
Scott, John V. '69 (GRY) Knox, IN St. Thomas Aquinas.
Scott, John *o.s.b.* '72 (SEA)[M] Lacey, WA St. Martin's Abbey.
Scott, Joseph P. *s.v.d.* '75 (SB)[I] Riverside, CA Divine Word Seminary; [I] Highland, CA.
Scott, Joseph '75 (SB)[N] San Bernardino, CA Ministerio Biblico Verbo Divino (MBVD).
Scott, Rev. Msgr. Leonard G. '64 (CAM) Mount Ephraim, NJ Emmaus Catholic Community, Mt. Ephraim, N.J.
Scott, Mark *o.c.s.o.* '87 (SAC)[A] Vina, CA Abbey of New Clairvaux, Trappist Seminary.
Scott, Mark *o.c.s.o.* (L)[L] Trappist, KY Abbey of Our Lady of Gethsemani, of the Order of Cistercians of the Strict Observance.
Scott, Michael Craig *v.c.* '96 (ALX) Alexandria, LA St. Rita; [A] Alexandria, LA Holy Savior Menard Central.
Scott, Rev. Msgr. Patrick J. '60 (PAT) Retired.
Scott, Philip P. '79 (PSC) Roswell, GA Epiphany Byzantine Church.
Scott, Philip '89 (SP) On Duty Outside the Diocese.
Scott, Raymond '48 (DAL) Retired.
Scott, Robert T. *c.s.p.* '49 (BRK)[R] Retired Retired.
Scott, Samuel V. '95 (BGP) Office for Ecumenical and Interreligious Affairs; Office for the Continuing Education of Clergy.
Scott, Timothy *o.c.s.o.* '05 (WOR)[N] Spencer, MA St. Joseph's Abbey.
Scott, Vincent J. '75 (OAK) San Leandro, CA Assumption of the Blessed Virgin Mary.
Scotti, P. Paschal *o.s.b.* '89 (PRO)[O] Portsmouth, RI Abbey of St. Gregory the Great.
Scotto, Dominic *t.o.r.* '67 (STU)[A] Steubenville, OH Franciscan University of Steubenville; [H] Steubenville, OH Holy Spirit Friary.
Scrima, Claude *o.f.m./i.c.* '61 (BO) Boston, MA St. Leonard of Port Maurice.
Scuderi, Carmen *o.f.m.* '83 (PSC) Hazleton, PA St. John the Baptist Church; [A] Sybertsville, PA Holy Dormition Friary; Presbyteral Council.
Scuderi, Michael *o.s.a.* '09 (PH) Philadelphia, PA St. Rita of Cascia.
Scull, Rev. Msgr. Edward J. '51 (BGP) Retired.
Scullin, Robert J. *s.j.* '76 (DET) Detroit, MI Gesu; Detroit, MI SS. Peter and Paul Jesuit; [K] Detroit, MI Jesuit Community at the University of Detroit Mercy; Presbyteral Council.
Scullion, James *o.f.m.* (TR) Brant Beach, NJ St. Francis of Assisi.
Scully, John J. '72 (TR) Matawan, NJ St. Clement; Tribunal Judges.
Scully, John T. *s.s.e.* '55 (BUR)[E] Colchester, VT Society of St. Edmund.
Scully, Michael G. *s.j.* '86 (HON) Laupahoehoe, HI St. Anthony; Papaikou, HI Immaculate Heart of Mary; Vicars Forane; Presbyteral Council; Clergy Personnel Board.
Scully, Michael *o.f.m.cap.* '65 (SAL) Hays, KS St. Joseph Parish.
Scully, Patrick A. '56 (SHP) Retired.
Scully, Patrick S. *s.m.* '03 (ATL) Flowery Branch, GA Prince of Peace.
Scully, Robert E. *s.j.* '96 (SY)[Q] Syracuse, NY Jesuits at LeMoyne, Inc.
Scully, Timothy R. *c.s.c.* '81 (FTW)[B] University of Notre Dame Du Lac; [H] Notre Dame, IN Holy Cross Community, Corby Hall, University of Notre Dame.
Scully, William *o.f.m.* (NY) Narrowsburg, NY St. Francis Xavier.
Scurti, Louis J. '73 (PAT) North Jersey Developmental Center; Unassigned.
Seabo, Frank J. '00 (CHL) Candler, NC St. Joan of Arc.
Seabold, John P. '88 (CLV) Grafton, OH Our Lady Queen of Peace Parish; Grafton Correctional Institution; Presbyteral Council.
Seabridge, Thomas L. '88 (SAC) Colfax, CA St. Dominic.
Seagrave, Thomas L. '68 (SFR) Retired.
Seagriff, Edward M. '81 (RVC) Massapequa Park, NY Our Lady of Lourdes.
Seaman, Cyril *o.f.m.* '56 (BO)[X] Boston, MA Saint Anthony Residence Retired.
Seaman, Cyril *o.f.m.* '56 (PAT)[N] Ringwood, NJ Holy Name Friary, Inc.
Seaman, Paul G. '85 (CHI) Chicago, IL St. Pascal; Deans.
Seamus, *o.s.a.prim.* '75 (ORL)[F] Deland, FL Augustinian Monks of the Primitive Observance.
Searby, James R. '05 (ARL) Lake Ridge, VA St. Elizabeth Ann Seton.
Searles, Lawrence P. *s.j.* '87 (SJN)[D] San Juan, PR Centro De Espiritualidad Ignaciana Pedro Arrupe (CEIPA).
Searles, Thaddeus *s.t.* '50 (MOB) Fort Mitchell, AL St. Joseph.
Searles, Rev. Msgr. Wendell H. '55 (BUR) Winooski, VT St. Stephen Retired.
Sears, Rev. Msgr. Eugene A. '58 (KAL) Presbyteral Council Members; Presbyteral Council Members Retired.
Sears, G. David '63 (SY) New Hartford, NY St. Thomas.
Sears, George A. '05 (NY) Poughkeepsie, NY St. Mary.
Sears, Gerald *o.c.s.o.* '73 (WOR)[N] Spencer, MA St. Joseph's Abbey.
Sears, Michael '94 (LA) Los Nietos, CA Our Lady of Perpetual Help.
Sears, Robert T. *s.j.* '66 (CHI)[N] Chicago, IL Woodlawn Jesuit Community.
Sears, William F. '84 (PRO) Cumberland, RI St. Aidan Retired.
Seasoltz, Kevin *o.s.b.* '56 (SCL)[I] Collegeville, MN St. John's Abbey, of the Order of St. Benedict.
Seaver, David (SY) Binghamton, NY Our Lady of Lourdes Memorial Hospital.
Seaver, Paul E. *o.p.* '59 (PRO)[O] Providence St. Thomas Aquinas Priory at Providence College.
Seavey, Michael J. '86 (PRT) Portland, ME Cathedral of the Immaculate Conception; Portland, ME St. Christopher's; Portland, ME St. Louis; Portland, ME St. Peter's; Portland, ME Sacred Heart/St. Dominic.
Seay, Robert '76 (LAF) Lafayette, LA St. Paul The Apostle.
Sebaali, Rev. Msgr. George M. '83 (SAM) Glen Allen, VA St. Anthony; Presbyteral Council; Communications; (Diocesan Newspaper) "The Maronite Voice"; College of Consultors; Board of Pastors.
Sebaali, Rev. Msgr. George (OLL) Eparchial Newsletter.
Sebahar, John '58 (JOL)[K] Naperville, IL St. John Vianney Villa Retired.
Sebastian, Angelos '01 (ORG) Huntington Beach, CA St. Bonaventure.
Sebastian, Arul '89 (NY) Rhinebeck, NY The Good Shepherd.
Sebastian, Francis *m.s.t.* '88 (CC)[D] Corpus Christi, TX CHRISTUS Spohn Hospital Corpus Christi – Shoreline.
Sebastian, Francisco J. *c.o.r.c.* '97 (SB) San Bernardino, CA Our Lady of Guadalupe.
Sebastian, George Joseph *s.j.* '01 (BAL)[Q] Baltimore, MD Jesuit Community of Loyola University, Inc.
Sebastian, Jolly *m.c.b.s.* '00 (MEM) Cordova, TN St. Francis of Assisi.
Sebastian, Joseph *s.v.d* '92 (OAK) Hayward, CA St. Joachim.
Sebastian, Pradeep Joseph *m.c.b.s.* '06 (MIL) Kenosha, WI St. Therese; [P] Kenosha, WI Missionary Congregation of the Blessed Sacrament, Inc., Zion Province.
Sebastian, Sony *s.v.d.* '92 (SB)[I] Riverside, CA Divine Word Seminary; [N] San Bernardino, CA Wordnet, Inc.; [I] Highland, CA.
Sebasty, Joseph '85 (P) Tillamook, OR Sacred Heart.
Sebaugh, Rev. Msgr. Thomas '59 (LR) Information Systems; On Special or Other Diocesan Assignment.
Sebescak, Gary '94 (BEL) Leave of Absence.
Sebesta, James A. *s.j.* '70 (STL)[C] Saint Louis University; [O] St. Louis, MO Jesuit Community Corporation at Saint Louis University – Jesuit Hall.
Sebo, Martin *s.j.* '05 (OAK)[L] Berkeley, CA Jesuit Fathers and Brothers.
Sebra, Anthony G. '72 (STA) Jacksonville Beach, FL St. Paul's.
Secor, Gary L. '77 (HON)[I] Kaneohe, HI Augustine Educational Foundation; Office of Clergy – Diocesan Screening Committee; Diocesan Board of Education; Vicar General and Moderator of the Curia; Bishops Administrative Advisory Council; College of Consultors; Diocesan Finance Council; [F] Members of the Corporation:; Members; Members; Clergy Personnel Board; Presbyteral Council; Members; Implementation Commission of Diocesan Road Map for Pastoral Program and Facility Needs; Diocesan Pastoral Council; [I] Honolulu, HI Hawaii Catholic Community Foundation.
Secora, James L. '75 (DUB) Ames, IA St. Cecilia.
Secrist, Jeremy A. '04 (JC) To The Bishop; Ministry to Priests; Secretary to the Bishop; Vice–Chancellors; Cemeteries; Historical Archives; Owensville, MO Immaculate Conception; Belle, MO St. Alexander.
Seculoff, James F. '62 (FTW) New Haven, IN St. John the Baptist; Clergy Retirement Board; Presbyteral Council; Retired Clergy Committee.
Seda, Jon M. '88 (DUB) Gilbert, IA SS. Peter and Paul; [N] Ames, IA St. Thomas Aquinas Church and Catholic Student Center (Iowa State University); Ames, IA St. Thomas Aquinas Church (and Catholic Student Center); Associate Directors.
Sedar, Adam C. '98 (ALN) Appointed Members; Minersville, PA St. Michael the Archangel Parish.
Sedita, Rev. Msgr. Vincent '72 (LKC) Judges Retired.
Sedlacek, Richard D. '79 (YAK) Benton City, WA St. Frances Xavier Cabrini; Kennewick, WA St. Joseph's; Presbyteral Council Executive Committee.
Sedlak, John A. '82 (GBG) Everson, PA St. Joseph; [K] Everson, PA Ladies of Charity; St. Vincent de Paul Society.
Sedlak, Kenneth *c.ss.r.* '72 (CHI) Chicago, IL St. Michael in Old Town; [N] Chicago, IL The Redemptorist Fathers of Chicago.
Sedley, Joseph *c.p.* '69 (PIT)[M] Pittsburgh, PA St. Paul of the Cross Monastery.
Sedlmayer, Lauro Colen '85 (MET) Port Reading, NJ St. Anthony of Padua; Woodbridge, NJ Our Lady of Mount Carmel.
Sedlock, David W. '91 (MAR) Retired.
Sedlock, Stephen J. *c.s.c.* '66 (FTW)[H] Notre Dame Congregation of Holy Cross, United States Province of Priests & Brothers.
Sedlock, Stephen J. '66 (PHX)[F] Phoenix, AZ Holy Cross Congregation/Casa Santa Cruz.
Seebauer, Joseph '11 (CLV) Westlake, OH St. Bernadette.
Seeberger, Claude *o.s.b.* '49 (BIS)[A] Richardton, ND Assumption Abbey.
Seeberger, Claude *o.s.b.* '49 (FAR)[F] Valley City, ND Sisters of Mary of the Presentation; Special Assignment.
Seed, Michael *s.a.* '86 (NY)[DD] Garrison Franciscan Friars of the Atonement, Minister General Office.
Seegar, Kenneth M. '87 (SCR) Wilkes–Barre, PA St. Andre Bessette Parish.
Seekamp, Walter J. '79 (BGP) Fairfield, CT Holy Family.
Seelman, Patrick *t.o.r.* '63 (ORL)[E] Winter Park, FL San Pedro Spiritual Development Center; [F] Winter Park, FL Franciscan Friars, T.O.R., San Pedro Friary Retired.
Seeman, Robert L. '79 (PIT) Jefferson Hills, PA St. Thomas A'Becket.
Seethaler, Scott *o.f.m.cap.* '69 (WH)[L] Wheeling, WV Capuchin Hermitage of St. Joseph.
Seeton, Philip M. '91 (OKL)[K] Lawton, OK Cameron University; Region IV.
Seeton, Philip '91 (OKL) Lawton, OK Holy Family.
Sefcik, Dennis L. '65 (SC) Retired.
Segaric, Rev. Msgr. John '48 (LA) Retired.
Segatta, Bruno '74 (B) On Duty Outside the Diocese.
Seger, Michael A. '88 (CIN)[B] Cincinnati, OH Mount St. Mary's Seminary of the West.
Seger, Oscar H. '70 (CIN) Wapakoneta, OH St. John; St. Marys, OH St. Patrick.
Segerblom, Kevin Lee '07 (RIC) Salem, VA Our Lady of Perpetual Help.

Segotta, Vincent *c.p.* '77 (PIT)[M] Pittsburgh, PA St. Paul of the Cross Monastery.
Segovia, Norman '67 (SJ) Santa Clara, CA St. Clare.
Segovia, Normandy '06 (SJ) San Jose, CA St. Francis of Assisi.
Segreve, Richard J. *c.s.c.* '61 (FR)[A] North Easton, MA Holy Cross Fathers Religious.
Segreve, Richard J. *c.s.c.* '61 (FTW)[H] Notre Dame Congregation of Holy Cross, United States Province of Priests & Brothers.
Seguin, Robert J. *c.s.b.* '69 (GAL)[O] Sugar Land Basilian Mission Center.
Segura, Anastacio '00 (ALB) Schenectady, NY Our Lady of Mt. Carmel.
Segura, Luis Alfonso *m.s.c.* '99 (FgM) Aurora, IL MISSIONARIES OF THE SACRED HEART.
Seher, Philip O. '65 (CIN) Retired.
Sehler, Michael E. *s.j.* '73 (NY)[E] New York, NY Loyola School; [DD] New York, NY "America;" Residence and publication office of the America Press.
Sehr, Bernard J. '10 (RCK) Crystal Lake, IL St. Elizabeth Ann Seton.
Seibert, Gary G. *s.j.* '73 (STL)[O] St. Louis, MO Leo Brown Jesuit Community; [C] Saint Louis University.
Seibert, James C. *c.pp.s.* '77 (CIN)[N] Carthagena, OH St. Charles; [U] Carthagena, OH The Society of the Precious Blood Senior Housing Corporation.
Seid, David K. *o.p.* '08 (NO) New Orleans, LA St. Anthony of Padua.
Seidel, George J. *o.s.b.* '58 (SEA)[M] Lacey, WA St. Martin's Abbey; [A] Lacey, WA Saint Martin's University.
Seidel, Thomas E. *c.s.c.* '57 (FTW)[H] Holy Cross House.
Seidel, Victor *s.t.* '61 (SAV) Blakely, GA Holy Family Retired.
Seidl, Larry J. '75 (GB) Neenah, WI St. Gabriel the Archangel.
Seifert, Michael D. '84 (Y) Navarre, OH Holy Family Parish.
Seifert, William N. '81 (ALN) Allentown, PA St. Stephen of Hungary; Office of Prison Ministry.
Seifert, William *s.v.d.* '67 (CHI)[N] Techny, IL Divine Word Residence; [N] Techny, IL Divine Word Novitiate.
Seifferly, Richard R. '63 (GLD) Retired.
Seifner, Thomas J. '92 (JC) Absent on Leave.
Seifried, Rev. Msgr. Kenneth A. '63 (SC) Priests' Personnel Board; Holstein, IA Our Lady of Good Counsel Retired.
Seigel, Timothy J. '91 (RCK) Genoa, IL St. Catherine of Genoa.
Seiker, Augustine *o.s.b.* '87 (SFE)[H] Abiquiu, NM Monastery of Christ in the Desert.
Seiker, Rev. Msgr. Daniel J. '87 (LIN) Priests' Continuing Education Committee.
Seiker, Leo V. '91 (LIN) Cortland, NE St. James; Building Commission; Permanent Deacon Continuing Education Committee; Pro Life.
Seiker, Mark E. '84 (LIN) North Platte, NE St. Elizabeth Ann Seton; Deaneries and Deans; Cursillo.
Seil, Paul D. '89 (BUF) Orchard Park, NY St. Bernadette.
Seiler, Andrew J. '88 (WCH) Conway Springs, KS St. Joseph.
Seiler, Gerald L. '90 (NO) Chancellor; Adjutant Judicial Vicar; Members of the Board; Censores Librorum; Canonical Permissions and Dispensations; Metairie, LA St. Edward the Confessor.
Seiler, John A. '59 (COV)[N] Fort Thomas, KY Sisters of the Good Shepherd; [I] Edgewood, KY St. Elizabeth Edgewood Retired.
Seimas, Peter '02 (SJ) Palo Alto, CA St. Thomas Aquinas.
Seipp, William J. '63 (MAD) Lancaster, WI St. Clement.
Seis, Michael '93 (GB) On Duty Outside the Diocese.
Seisser, Edward J. '98 (RCK) Rockford, IL Holy Family.
Seiter, George C. '83 (CAM) Office of Propagation of the Faith and Diocesan Missions; Cherry Hill, NJ Holy Eucharist Parish, Cherry Hill, N.J.
Seiter, Joseph A. *c.s.sp.* '62 (PIT)[O] Bethel Park, PA The Spiritan Center.
Seitz, Gilbert J. '82 (BAL) Special Assignment; Judicial Vicar.
Seitz, James J. '94 (WIN) Slayton, MN St. Ann's; Slayton, MN St. Columba's; Slayton, MN St. Mary.
Seitz, Joseph W. '58 (CHI) Evergreen Park, IL St. Bernadette Retired.
Seitz, Patrick K. '92 (BWN) Weslaco, TX San Martin de Porres; Weslaco, TX St. Pius X; Vicar for Priests; College of Consultors; Priests' Assignment Board.
Seitz, Paul F.X. '58 (CHR) Retired.
Seitz, Wolfgang *o.r.c.* '02 (DET)[K] Grosse Pointe, MI Order of Canons Regular of the Holy Cross.
Seiwert, Charles F. '99 (WCH) Defenders of the Bond; Garden City, KS St. Mary Catholic Church of Garden City, Kansas; On Duty Outside the Diocese.
Seiwert, James K. '09 (SAT) San Antonio, TX St. Francis of Assisi.
Sejba, Anthony F. '99 (CLV) Medina, OH St. Francis Xavier.
Sekellick, Rev. Msgr. John T. '69 (PSC) Jessup, PA Holy Ghost; Northern Pennsylvania/Northern New York Protopresbyterate; Judicial Vicar; Cemeteries Commission; Family Life; Presbyteral Council.
Sekere, Joseph (TOL) Lexington, OH Resurrection; Mansfield, OH St. Mary of the Snows.
Seland, John *s.v.d.* '68 (FgM) Techny, IL.
Selander, Gregg (P)[J] Newberg, OR Providence Health & Services–Oregon.
Seleccion, Romeo N. *m.s.* '82 (SB)[I] Moreno Valley, CA Missionaries of Our Lady of La Salette, MS.
Seleccion, Romeo N. *m.s.* '82 (SB) Ex Officio Member; San Bernardino Pastoral Region; San Bernardino, CA Our Lady of Hope Catholic Community, Inc.; Grand Terrace, CA Christ the Redeemer; Rancho Cucamonga, CA Our Lady of Mount Carmel; Rancho Cucamonga, CA Sacred Heart; Redlands, CA The Holy Name of Jesus Catholic Community, Inc.; Upland, CA St. Anthony; Yucaipa, CA St. Frances Xavier Cabrini; Diocesan Curia; Ex Officio; College of Consultors.
Selemobri, Efiri Matthias *m.s.p.* '91 (BWN)[I] San Juan, TX The Basilica of Our Lady of San Juan del Valle–National Shrine; San Juan, TX Basilica of Our Lady of San Juan del Valle–National Shrine.
Seli, Rev. Msgr. John J. '46 (PIT) Retired.
Seli, William F. *s.m.* '58 (WDC)[O] Washington, DC Marist Center Retired.
Selker, C. Raymond *o.f.m.* '04 (NY)[DD] New York Franciscan Friars, Holy Name Province.
Sell, Rev. Msgr. Robert L. '78 (LFT) De Motte, IN St. Cecilia; Special Assignment; [I] Board Members:; Vicar General; Chancellor and Moderator of the Curia; Diocesan Consultors; Administrative Causes; Building Commission; Corporation; Finance Council; Members; Propagation of the Faith.
Sella, Donald J. '83 (PAT) Retired.
Selladurai, Selvaraj '85 (GRY) Gary, IN St. Mary of the Lake.
Sellars, Charles *o.m.i.* '54 (NO) Medjugorje Star.
Sellars, Charles *o.m.i.* '54 (SAT)[K] San Antonio, TX Oblate Madonna Residence.
Selleck, John P. '57 (CAM) Retired.
Selleck, John '57 (PT) Panama City, FL St. Dominic; Gulf Coast Institution; Washington Correctional Institution.
Selvam, Asirvatham J. (TR) Manalapan, NJ St. Thomas More.
Selvam, Paneer (P) Roseburg, OR U.S. Veterans' Administration Hospital.
Selvam, Panneer '81 (P) Roseburg, OR St. Joseph; Roseburg, OR St. Francis Xavier.
Selvanayakam, Darnis *m.s.f.x.* '03 (BIS) Killdeer, ND St. Paul; Killdeer, ND St. Joseph.
Selvaraj, Balappa '86 (ATL) Special or Other Archdiocesan Assignment; Advocates.
Selvaraj, Bose Raja '73 (BGP) Greenwich, CT Sacred Heart.
Selvaraj, Paul Dass *o.m.i.* '04 (MIA) Miramar, FL St. Stephen.
Selvaraj, Peter '82 (NY) On Leave of Absence.
Selvaraj, Rakshaganathan '94 (AUS) Waco, TX St. Jerome.
Selvaraj Pilla, Raju B. '81 (PH) Indian Apostolate, Latin Rite.
Selvester, Guy W. '97 (MET)[I] Raritan, NJ Clairvaux House; [L] Raritan, NJ Shrine Chapel of the Blessed Sacrament; Diocesan Eucharistic League.
Selzer, Eugene P. '61 (PRM) St. Louis, MO St. Louis Mission.
Selzer, Eugene P. '61 (STL) St. Louis, MO St. Matthias Retired.
Semancik, Rev. Msgr. Joseph F. '53 (GRY) Retired.
Sember, Benjamin '07 (GB) On Duty Outside the Diocese.
Sember, Joel A. '07 (GB) Oconto Falls, WI St. Anthony; Oconto Falls, WI St. Patrick; Oconto, WI Holy Trinity.
Semeniuk, Gregory *c.m.* '89 (LA)[A] Camarillo, CA St. John's Seminary.
Semik, Leszek '94 (LA) Glendora, CA St. Dorothy.
Seminara, Ronald S. *s.j.* '74 (RC)[C] Howes, SD Kino Jesuit Community; Permanent Diaconate Program, Sioux Spiritual Center; [E] Howes, SD The Diocese of Rapid City Mahpiya na Maka Okogna.
Seminatore, Joseph '69 (CLV) Administrative Leave.
Semko, Edward '69 (PSC) Carteret, NJ St. Elias; Notaries.
Semler, Albert J. '67 (PIT) Clairton, PA St. Clare of Assisi Retired.
Semler, Andrew V. '00 (DAL) Appointed Members.
Semmer, Dean F. '79 (CHI) Antioch, IL St. Peter.
Semonin, James R. '71 (CLV) Parma Community Hospital.
Sempa, Rev. Msgr. John J. '80 (SCR) West Pittston, PA Corpus Christi Parish.
Sempko, Walter A. '50 (HBG) Retired.
Semple, James '61 (SLC) Salt Lake City, UT Retired.
Sena, Charles A. '92 (PBL) Holly, CO St. Frances of Rome; Lamar, CO St. Francis De Sales–Our Lady of Guadalupe; Springfield, CO Our Lady of the Annunciation; College of Consultors; Deans; Elected.
Sena, Sotero '81 (SFE) Clovis, NM Our Lady of Guadalupe; Defenders of the Bond.
Sendlein, Thomas *c.m.* '72 (FgM) Philadelphia, PA Eastern Province.
Senecal, Gerard *o.s.b.* '54 (KCK) Atchison, KS St. Benedict's; Atchison, KS Sacred Heart; Regional Pastoral Leaders; [I] Atchison, KS St. Benedict's Abbey.
Senetsky, Rev. Msgr. Robert '60 (PSC) Peekskill, NY SS. Peter and Paul Retired.
Senger, Rev. Msgr. Joseph '54 (FAR) Retired.
Senger, William L. *m.m.* '73 (FgM) Maryknoll, NY MARYKNOLL.
Senghas, Richard E. '98 (PRT) Ecumenical & Interreligious Services Retired.
Senior, Donald *c.p.* '67 (CHI)[B] Chicago, IL Catholic Theological Union; [B] Chicago, IL Catholic Theological Union; [N] Chicago, IL Passionist Community of St. Vincent Strambi; [W] Mundelein, IL Foundation for Adult Catechetical Teaching Aids; Consultants.
Seniw, John '82 (PHU) Berwick, PA SS. Cyril and Methodius; Protopresbyters (Deans); Board Members.
Senk, Christopher '76 (VEN) Sanibel, FL St. Isabel.
Sennik, Thomas W. '76 (NOR) Absent on Leave.
Sensat, Clinton M. '09 (LAF) Graduate Studies.
Sensat, Clinton (WDC) Hyattsville, MD St. Jerome.
Sensenig, Andrew *o.m.i.* '97 (ANC) Pastoral Team:; Pastoral Team:; Pastoral Team.
Senvello, Robert '94 (YAK) Retired.
Senz, Augustine *o.s.b.* '07 (WOR)[N] Still River, MA Benedictine Monks, St. Benedict Abbey.
Seo, Bohuo '01 (BRK) Woodside, NY Blessed Virgin Mary, Help of Christians.
Sepe, Kevin M. '86 (BO) Braintree, MA St. Francis of Assisi; Vicariate I; Elected.
Seper, John M. '83 (STL) St. Louis, MO Assumption; Archdiocesan Consultors.
Sepich, Lawrence '74 (MIL) Retired.
Sepulveda, Edgar '89 (R) Kenansville, NC Maria, Reina De Las Americas.
Sepulveda, Miguel A. '02 (MIA) Miami, FL St. Timothy.
Sepulveda, Thomas W. *c.s.b.* '74 (DET) Detroit, MI Ste. Anne de Detroit; [T] Detroit, MI Gabriel Richard Historical Society.
Sequeira, Eustace *s.j.* '75 (DEN)[N] Denver, CO Society of Jesus – St. Ignatius Loyola Jesuit Community.
Sequeira, Jose '00 (CHI) Chicago, IL St. Nicholas of Tolentine.
Sequeira, Michael '66 (NOR) Clinton, CT St. Mary of the Visitation; St. Mary of the Visitation Church – Spanish Apostolate.
Sequiera–Ruiz, Marcos '91 (NEW) Jersey City, NJ Parish of the Resurrection.
Sera, Enrique J. '78 (ORG) Costa Mesa, CA St. Joachim; Navy Reserve Chaplains; Clergy Personnel Board.
Serafin, Thomas J. '93 (MET) Three Bridges, NJ St. Elizabeth Ann Seton.
Serafini, Augustine '62 (GB)[J] Oshkosh, WI Community of Our Lady.
Seran, Augustinus *s.v.d.* '99 (LAF) St. Martinville, LA Notre Dame de Perpetuel Secours.
Serano, Joseph A. *o.praem.* '69 (PH)[B] Paoli, PA Daylesford Abbey; [Y] Paoli, PA Daylesford Abbey; Paoli, PA.
Serban, Ron '93 (SR) Lakeport, CA St. Mary Immaculate.
Serbicki, Daniel J. '11 (BUF) West Seneca, NY Queen of Heaven.
Serena, Edward T. '81 (BO) Senior Priests. Retired.
Sereno, David '86 (SD) Escondido, CA Saint Mary Catholic Parish Escondido.
Sergi, Michael '79 (ROC)[M] Canandaigua, NY Notre Dame Retreat House.
Sergoff, Joseph *o.p.* '96 (OAK)[L] Oakland, CA Order of Preachers (Province of the Most Holy Name of Jesus – Western Dominican Province).
Sergott, Joseph *o.p.* '96 (OAK)[L] Oakland, CA Order of Preachers (Province of Holy Name of Jesus – Western Dominican Province).
Sergott, Lawrence J. '01 (GLD) Mio, MI St. Mary; Cursillo; Lewiston, MI St. Francis of Assisi.
Serio, Anthony '67 (NO) Retired.
Serio, John *s.d.b.* '82 (WDC) Washington, DC Nativity; [D] Washington, DC Don Bosco Cristo Rey High School of the Archdiocese of Washington.
Sermak, Ronald *o.f.m.conv.* '60 (BUF)[N] Athol Springs, NY St. Maximilian Kolbe Friary.
Serna, Alfonso *o.ss.t.* '09 (BAL) Hanover, MD St. Lawrence Martyr; [K] Towson, MD St. Joseph Medical Center, Inc.; [Q] In Residence – Holy Trinity Monastery Baltimore.
Serna, J. Patrick '01 (CC) Banquete, TX Saint Michael the Archangel; On Duty Outside the Diocese.
Serna, Jaime Diaz *o.p.* '00 (FgM) Metairie, LA St. Martin de Porres Province (Southern Dominican Province).

Serna, Juan '00 (STO) Personnel Board; Modesto, CA Holy Family Church (Pastor of).
Sernett, Rev. Msgr. Michael D. '70 (SC) Estherville, IA St. Patrick's; Estherville, IA Immaculate Conception; Defenders of the Bond; Judges.
Serour, George J. '59 (SAG) Bay City, MI St. Maria Goretti Retired.
Serowik, James P. '87 (SY) Priests' Personnel Committee; Endicott, NY St. Anthony of Padua.
Serpa, Vincent *o.p.* '68 (OAK)[L] Oakland, CA Order of Preachers (Province of the Most Holy Name of Jesus – Western Dominican Province).
Serra, Dominic F. '72 (WDC)[C] Catholic University of America, The.
Serra, Dominic '72 (NY) On Duty Outside the Archdiocese.
Serra, Guillermo *l.c.* '04 (ATL)[F] Alpharetta, GA Legionaries of Christ, Incorporated.
Serraglio, Rev. Msgr. Mario '58 (COL) Retired.
Serraino, Fred *c.s.c.* '68 (ORL)[F] Cocoa Beach, FL Congregation of Holy Cross, United States Province Retired.
Serraino, Fred *c.s.c.* '68 (FTW)[H] Notre Dame Congregation of Holy Cross, United States Province of Priests & Brothers.
Serrano, Carlos '11 (FRS) Visalia, CA Holy Family; Visalia, CA St. Mary; Visalia, CA St. Thomas the Apostle.
Serrano, Dionisio '97 (PCE) On Duty Outside the Diocese.
Serrano, Edgar '87 (SD) San Diego, CA Metropolitan Correction Center.
Serrano, Heriberto '67 (PHX) Queen Creek, AZ Our Lady of Guadalupe Roman Catholic Parish.
Serrano, Isnardo *c.o.* '98 (SAC) Sacramento, CA St. Rose; Sacramento, CA Immaculate Conception.
Serrano, Jose A. '95 (NY) Bronx, NY St. John Vianney, Cure of Ars.
Serrano Rivera, Ivan '87 (SJN) San Juan, PR Santa Teresa de Jesus Jornet.
Serrao, Ronald *c.s.c.* '92 (SUP) Tomahawk, WI St. John the Baptist; Tomahawk, WI St. Augustine.
Serraon, Mel '82 (OAK) Union City, CA St. Anne.
Serrick, James K. *s.j.* '62 (DET)[K] Detroit, MI Jesuit Community at the University of Detroit Mercy.
Serva, Donald M. *s.j.* '78 (WH)[A] Wheeling, WV Wheeling Jesuit University.
Servatius, Rev. Msgr. Robert R. '64 (SLC) Sandy, UT Blessed Sacrament LLC 201; College of Consultors; Board of Directors; Defenders of the Bond.
Servatius, Thomas R. '03 (SY) Baldwinsville, NY St. Augustine; Vocation Formation.
Servinsky, Rev. Msgr. Michael E. '70 (ALT) Vicar General; Priests' Personnel Board; Treasurer; Altoona, PA Holy Rosary.
Serwa, Gregory P. *s.a.c.* '70 (MIL)[P] Milwaukee, WI Pallotti House.
Sescon, Albert C. '86 (KNX) Cleveland, TN St. Therese of Lisieux.
Sescon, Esteban '77 (ELP) El Paso, TX St. Francis Xavier.
Sessions, Phillip D. '80 (LAN) On Duty Outside the Diocese.
Sestito, Joseph N. '59 (OG) On Duty Outside the Diocese.
Sesto, Gennaro J. *s.d.b.* '50 (NEW) Elizabeth, NJ St. Anthony's.
Setelik, James '84 (RNO) Carson City, NV Corpus Christi.
Setonga, Mansuetus '86 (DAV)[J] Iowa City, IA O'Keefe Hall.
Setter, H. Jay '88 (WCH) Wichita, KS All Saints.
Settimo, Scott R. '06 (JUN) Ketchikan, AK Holy Name; Port Chaplains; Diocesan Consultors.
Settle, Matthew W. '04 (GB) Florence, WI Immaculate Conception; Armstrong Creek, WI St. Stanislaus Kostka; Goodman, WI St. Joan of Arc; Vicariate; Niagara, WI St. Anthony; Pembine, WI St. Margaret; Niagara, WI Sacred Heart.
Settles, Dennis F. '65 (JOL)[F] Momence, IL Good Shepherd Manor Retired.
Seubert, Xavier *o.f.m.* '71 (BUF)[A] East Aurora, NY Christ the King Seminary.
Seuferling, George '56 (KCK) Retired.
Seugwook Lim, John Chrysostom '08 (HON) Honolulu, HI Korean Catholic Community.
Seuntjens, LeRoy L. '60 (SC) Retired.
Severson, David '11 (HEL) Helena, MT Cathedral of St. Helena.
Severt, William H. '74 (CLV) University Hospitals; North Olmsted, OH St. Brendan.
Sevilla, Dennis '69 (SEA)[H] Tacoma, WA St. Joseph Medical Center.
Sevola, Frank *o.f.m.* (PAT) Pompton Lakes, NJ Our Lady of the Assumption.
Sewbert, August *o.f.m.cap.* '57 (CHI) Chicago, IL St. Simon the Apostle.
Sewell, Jack '78 (ORG) San Clemente, CA Our Lady of Fatima; Judges; Air Force Reserve Chaplains.
Sewvello, Robert '94 (GF) Glasgow, MT St. Raphael; Diocesan Consultors; Priests' Council.
Sexstone, James H. '69 (ATL) Retired.
Sexton, Rev. Msgr. Michael F. '61 (BIR) Cropwell, AL Our Lady of the Lake; Priests'/Presbyteral Council; Diocesan College of Consultors; Diocesan College of Vicars.
Seyd, Samuel '00 (HRT) West Hartford, CT St. Thomas the Apostle.
Seyer, James A. '50 (SPC) Retired.
Seyer, Lawrence '97 (LA) Los Angeles, CA Our Saviour Catholic Center; Los Angeles, CA Transfiguration; [AA] Los Angeles, CA University of Southern California.
Seymour, Rev. Msgr. Francis R. '63 (NEW) Archdiocesan/University Archives; [B] Seton Hall University; Kearny, NJ St. Cecilia's.
Seymour, James W. '87 (OG) Heuvelton, NY St. Raphael's; Committee on Assignments; Lisbon, NY SS. Philip and James; Ogdensburg, NY Riverview Correctional Facility; Ogdensburg, NY Ogdensburg Correctional Facility; Episcopal Vicar for Clergy and Director Priest Personnel and Deacons.
Seymour, John *s.t.* '70 (LA) Compton, CA Our Lady of Victory.
Seymour, Scott R. '99 (OG) Morrisonville, NY The Roman Catholic Community of St. Alexander and St. Joseph.
Sezzi, Michael J. '96 (LA) Hacienda Heights, CA St. John Vianney.
Sgarioto, Michael *o.carm.* '85 (JOL)[L] Darien Carmelite Provincial Office.
Sgarioto, Michael *o.carm.* '85 (FgM) Darien, IL Provincial Headquarters, Carmelite Provincial Office.
Shackelford, Christopher '91 (GAL) Channelview, TX St. Andrew.
Shadwell, Damian '90 (WDC) Hillcrest Heights, MD Holy Family.
Shadwell, Steven (PAT) West Milford, NJ St. Joseph.
Shaefer, Konrad *o.s.b.* '80 (FgM) Saint Benedict, OR Mount Angel Abbey.
Shafer, Rev. Msgr. Drake R. '73 (DAV) Long Grove, IA St. Ann's.
Shafer, James '75 (FTW) Fort Wayne, IN St. Elizabeth Ann Seton; Consultors; Presbyteral Council; Pro–Synodal Judges.
Shafer, Robert J. '99 (DET) Trenton, MI St. Timothy.
Shaffer, G. Scott '89 (TR) Jackson, NJ St. Aloysius; Jackson, NJ Church of St. Monica; Vicars Forane (Deans).
Shaffer, Gregory W. '06 (WDC) Washington, DC St. Stephen Martyr; Special Ministries.
Shafran, Steve *s.d.b.* '85 (WDC) Washington, DC Nativity; [D] Washington, DC Don Bosco Cristo Rey High School of the Archdiocese of Washington; [X] Washington, DC Don Bosco Cristo Rey Work–Study of the Archdiocese of Washington.
Shah, Vinod Bruno Mary *o.p.* '09 (NY) New York, NY St. Vincent Ferrer; [DD] New York, NY St. Vincent Ferrer Priory.
Shaheen, Joseph '59 (SAM) Retired.
Shaiju, Thomas *h.g.n.* '99 (OWN) Eddyville, KY St. Mark Church; Princeton, KY St. Paul; [J] Princeton, KY Heralds of Good News of St. Paul, Inc.
Shaji, Jose '92 (SFR) Menlo Park, CA St. Denis.
Shaldone, Robert *s.o.l.t.* '97 (CC)[G] Robstown, TX Society of Our Lady of the Most Holy Trinity.
Shaleta, Emanuel Hana '84 (EST) Eparchial College of Consultors.
Shaleta, Emanuel Hana '84 (EST) Shelby Twp., MI St. George Chaldean Catholic Church.
Shallbetter, Martin '69 (STP) Cologne, MN St. Bernard; Norwood, MN Ascension.
Shallow, Edmund J. '81 (MET) Carteret, NJ Divine Mercy.
Shallow, Zachary *s.o.l.t.* '04 (CC)[G] Robstown, TX Society of Our Lady of the Most Holy Trinity.
Shamleffer, Rev. Msgr. John B. '83 (STL) Judicial Vicar; Archdiocesan Consultors; Clayton, MO St. Joseph.
Shanahan, Daniel *o.p.* '62 (NO) New Orleans, LA St. Dominic.
Shanahan, John *t.o.r.* '08 (WDC)[O] Washington, DC St. Louis Friary.
Shanahan, Michael J. '92 (CHI) Chicago, IL Our Lady of Lourdes.
Shanahan, Michael *ss.cc.* '62 (FR)[E] Fairhaven, MA Our Lady's Haven of Fairhaven Inc.; [F] Fairhaven, MA Damien Residence.
Shanahan, Thomas J. *s.j.* '67 (OM)[J] Omaha, NE Jesuit Community at Creighton University.
Shananhan, Kevin *m.s.c.* '86 (SAT) San Antonio, TX St. Anthony of Padua.
Shane, Donald W. '69 (OM) Omaha, NE St. Robert Bellarmine.
Shanfelt, Thomas '78 (ALN)[J] Orwigsburg, PA St. Francis Villa for Priests.
Shangraw, Philip A. '79 (GR) Belding, MI St. Joseph's; Belding, MI St. Mary's.
Shanley, Brian J. *o.p.* '87 (PRO)[B] Providence, RI Providence College; [O] Providence St. Thomas Aquinas Priory at Providence College.
Shanley, James A. '80 (HRT) Guilford, CT St. George.
Shanley, Matthias *ss.cc.* (FR)[F] Fairhaven, MA Damien Residence.
Shanley, Owen F. '53 (ALB) Retired.
Shannon, Brendan '62 (MIA) Retired.
Shannon, Francis T. '87 (BRK) Brooklyn, NY Blessed Sacrament.
Shannon, Richard J. '59 (CHI) Lemont, IL St. Patrick Retired.
Shannon, Timothy J. '75 (STU) Vocations.
Shannon, Rev. Msgr. William H. '43 (ROC)[L] Rochester, NY Sisters St. Joseph of Rochester; Censores Librorum Retired.
Shannon, William '71 (HON) Vicars Forane; Lihue, HI Immaculate Conception; College of Consultors; Members; Presbyteral Council; Clergy Personnel Board.
Shantillo, Gerald W. '09 (SCR) Mountain Top, PA St. Jude.
Shao, Evod E. *c.s.sp.* (BAL) Baltimore, MD St. Edward.
Shapiro, Matthew *o.s.b.* '86 (TLS)[G] Hulbert, OK Our Lady of the Annunciation of Clear Creek Monastery.
Shappelle, James '48 (CIN) Cincinnati, OH St. Bernard; Cincinnati, OH Mother of Christ; Presbyteral Council; Consultors.
Sharbaugh, Jason '10 (LR) Little Rock, AR Christ the King.
Sharbel, Joseph M. '85 (KC) Kansas City, MO St. Gabriel Archangel.
Sharbel, Joseph '85 (KC) Administrative Committee.
Sharkey, Gregory C. *s.j.* '88 (BO)[U] Newton, MA The Jesuit Community at Boston College.
Sharkey, Rev. Msgr. John A. '56 (PH) Retired.
Sharkey, Peter *s.j.* '74 (CIN)[N] Cincinnati, OH Faber Jesuit Community.
Sharkey, Philip J. '98 (HRT) Hamden, CT St. Rita.
Sharkey, Rev. Msgr. Thomas F. '48 (CAM) Defenders of the Bond Retired.
Sharkey, Thomas P. *c.s.sp.* '50 (PIT)[O] Bethel Park, PA The Spiritan Center.
Sharland, David M. *y.a.* '99 (ARL)[A] Arlington, VA Marymount University; [K] Arlington, VA Marymount University; [L] McLean, VA Youth Apostles Institute, An Association of Christian Faithful.
Sharland, David '99 (FR) On Duty Outside the Diocese.
Sharman, Robert F. '84 (HBG) New Bloomfield, PA St. Bernard; Missions, Office of (Home and Foreign); Appointed; Consultors, College.
Sharon, Charles *s.a.* '72 (NY)[DD] New York, NY Atonement Friars; [DD] Garrison, NY Franciscan Friars of the Atonement, Minister General Office; General Council.
Sharp, David L. *c.s.b.* '70 (LSC)[B] Las Cruces, NM Basilian Fathers.
Sharp, Donald B. *s.j.* '71 (SFR)[E] San Francisco, CA St. Ignatius College Preparatory (Coed); [N] San Francisco, CA Jesuit Community at St. Ignatius College Preparatory Retired.
Sharp, George F. '89 (NEW) Elizabeth, NJ Elizabeth Federal Detention Center; East Orange, NJ Saint Joseph Parish; Lyndhurst, NJ St. Michael's Retired.
Sharp, James '84 (DAL) Retired.
Sharpe, Peter '09 (FAR) Fargo, ND Sts. Anne & Joachim Church of Fargo.
Sharrett, Victor F. '65 (PH) Kennett Square, PA St. Patrick.
Shatzel, Richard J. '69 (ROC) Aurora, NY Good Shepherd Catholic Community; [N] Aurora, NY Wells College, c/o Good Shepherd Catholic Community.
Shaughnessey, James *s.j.* (BO) Pastoral Care.
Shaughnessey, Rusty *o.f.m.* '73 (OAK)[N] Danville, CA San Damiano Retreat.
Shaughnessey, William G. '92 (POD) Reston.
Shaughnessy, Angelus *o.f.m.cap.* '55 (PIT)[M] Allison Park, PA St. Conrad Friary.
Shaughnessy, James M. *s.j.* '79 (BO)[U] Boston, MA Loyola House; Watertown, MA; [U] Watertown, MA The Society of Jesus of New England–Provincial Offices.
Shaughnessy, James '73 (KCK) Beattie, KS St. Malachy; Marysville, KS St. Gregory; Regional Pastoral Leaders.
Shaughnessy, Martin G. *s.j.* '63 (BO)[D] Boston, MA Boston College High School.
Shaughnessy, Paul J. *s.j.* '87 (MO) Navy Chaplains.
Shaughnessy, Paul J. *s.j.* '87 (BAL)[Q] Towson Maryland Province of the Society of Jesus.
Shaughnessy, Thomas *o.f.m.* '60 (SFD) Quincy, IL St. Francis Solanus; [K] Quincy, IL St. Francis Solanus Friary; Comite Diocesano de Ministerio Hispano – Diocesan Committee for Hispanic Ministry.
Shaughnessy, Thomas *s.s.c.* '66 (OM)[J] St. Columbans, NE Missionary Society of St. Columban.
Shaughnessy, William G. '92 (WDC)[V] Washington, DC Prelature of the Holy Cross and Opus Dei.
Shaute, Joseph '01 (ATL) Calhoun, GA St. Clement.
Shaver, James R. '89 (LAN) Jackson, MI St. John the Evangelist; Cotton Facility; Regional Vicars.
Shaw, Brian A. '66 (HRT) Milford, CT St. Ann.
Shaw, David '68 (SR) Santa Rosa, CA Resurrection; [N] Santa Rosa, CA Catholic Community Foundation; Defender of the Bond; Priests' Council; Finance

Committee; Catholic Community Foundation.
Shaw, David '06 (P) Milwaukie, OR Christ the King.
Shaw, John M. '57 (YAK) Toppenish, WA St. Aloysius; Cursillo, English; Native American; Presbyteral Council Executive Committee; Native American Ministries Retired.
Shaw, Richard D. '68 (ALB) Coxsackie Correctional Facility; Greene Correctional Facility; Special Assignment; Athens, NY St. Patrick; Catskill, NY St. Patrick.
Shaw, Thomas '01 (PEO) Walnut, IL Immaculate Conception Church; Walnut, IL St. John the Evangelist.
Shaw, William E. '57 (YAK) White Swan, WA St. Mary's.
Shayo, Barnabas *a.j.* (P)[J] Portland, OR Providence Health & Services–Oregon.
Shayo, Caroli B. *a.j.* (CLV) SouthWest General Hospital.
Shayo, Jude *a.j.* '90 (OKL) Mangum, OK Sacred Heart.
Shea, Bernard J. (BO) Melrose, MA St. Mary of the Annunciation.
Shea, Daniel B. '69 (HEL) Helena, MT Our Lady of the Valley; [B] Helena, MT Carroll College.
Shea, Daniel B. '69 (HEL) Presbyteral Council.
Shea, Rev. Msgr. Donald '62 (HEL) Bigfork, MT Pope John Paul II.
Shea, Edward *o.f.m.* '87 (CHI)[N] Chicago, IL St. Peter's Friary.
Shea, James E. *c.ss.r.* '65 (SAT) San Antonio, TX St. Gerard Majella; [L] San Antonio, TX Redemptorists of Texas–San Antonio #1.
Shea, James J. *sch.p.* '92 (PH)[F] Devon, PA Devon Preparatory School; [Y] Devon Piarist Fathers (Order of the Pious Schools).
Shea, James M. *s.j.* '75 (FgM) Towson, MD Society of Jesus; Towson, MD.
Shea, James M. *s.j.* '75 (FgM) Washington, DC National Headquarters.
Shea, James M. '65 (VEN) Venice, FL Epiphany Cathedral Retired.
Shea, James M. *s.j.* '75 (BAL)[Q] Baltimore, MD Jesuit Community of Loyola University, Inc.; [Q] Towson, MD Maryland Province of the Society of Jesus.
Shea, James P. '02 (BIS)[B] Bismarck, ND University of Mary.
Shea, John J. '61 (BO) Senior Priests. Retired.
Shea, John J. *s.j.* '75 (FgM) New York, NY Society of Jesus.
Shea, Joseph P. '78 (LA) Simi Valley, CA St. Rose of Lima; Cardinal McIntyre Fund for Charity Board of Directors.
Shea, Leo B. *m.m.* '66 (NY)[DD] Maryknoll Maryknoll Fathers and Brothers Retired.
Shea, Michael J. *c.m.* '70 (PH)[Y].
Shea, Michael J. '76 (SFE) Albuquerque, NM Prince of Peace Catholic Community.
Shea, Michael *c.ss.r.* '64 (FgM) Denver, CO Denver Province.
Shea, Peter G. *c.s.p.* '62 (SFR) San Francisco, CA Old St. Mary's Cathedral.
Shea, Rev. Msgr. Richard J. '61 (BGP) Trumbull, CT St. Catherine of Siena.
Shea, Robert F. '55 (R) Retired.
Shea, Roy *c.i.c.m.* '86 (FgM) Arlington, VA MISSIONHURST.
Shea, Thomas J. *c.s.c.* '67 (ORL)[F] Cocoa Beach, FL Congregation of Holy Cross, United States Province.
Shea, Thomas J. *c.s.c.* '67 (FTW)[H] Notre Dame Congregation of Holy Cross, United States Province of Priests & Brothers.
Shea, Thomas M. '66 (SPR) South Hadley, MA St. Patrick's; Bishop's Commission for Clergy; Presbyteral Council.
Shea, Thomas '49 (SJ) Retired.
Shea, Timothy J. '61 (BO) Woburn, MA St. Charles Borromeo.
Shea, William *s.v.d.* '64 (DUB)[B] Epworth, IA Divine Word College.
Sheaffer, John K. '93 (SPR) Lee, MA St. Mary's.
Sheahan, John A. '60 (ORG) Retired.
Sheahan, Rev. Msgr. Richard D. '69 (PRO) Cranston, RI Holy Apostles; Finance Council.
Sheahan, William T. *s.j.* '08 (KC)[D] Kansas City, MO Rockhurst High School; [J] Kansas City, MO Rockhurst Jesuit Community.
Shearer, Thomas M. '78 (CIN) Dayton, OH St. Henry.
Sheary, Pat *s.j.* '80 (LA) Long Beach, CA St. Cornelius.
Shebuski, Charles J. '65 (GB) Retired.
Shecterle, Rev. Msgr. Ross A. '86 (MIL) Consultant; Awaiting Assignment.
Shedlock, John '94 (SFE) Retired.
Sheeds, Gerald E. '68 (KCK) Retired.
Sheedy, Edward J. '72 (BUF) Olean, NY St. John.
Sheedy, Patrick J. '65 (ORL) Ocala, FL Blessed Trinity; [A] Ocala, FL Trinity Catholic High School, Inc.
Sheedy, Timothy J. '76 (DAV) Bettendorf, IA Our Lady of Lourdes.
Sheedy, Valentine '55 (ORL) Retired.
Sheehan, Augustine J. '55 (RVC) Retired.
Sheehan, Rev. Msgr. Dennis F. '63 (BO) Designated; Presbyteral Council; Newton, MA Our Lady Help of Christians.
Sheehan, Rev. Msgr. Donal C. '60 (SD) Coronado, CA Sacred Heart Catholic Parish Coronado Retired.
Sheehan, Donald P. '68 (NEW) Allendale, NJ Guardian Angel Retired.
Sheehan, Edward *s.m.* '61 (BO) Boston, MA Our Lady of Victories Retired.
Sheehan, Rev. Msgr. George F. '61 (SY)[Q] East Syracuse, NY Vianney House; Special Assignment Retired.
Sheehan, Rev. Msgr. George F. '61 (SY) Camillus, NY St. Joseph.
Sheehan, Gerard J. *s.o.l.t.* '85 (CC)[G] Robstown, TX Society of Our Lady of the Most Holy Trinity.
Sheehan, J. Peter '56 (BIR) Retired.
Sheehan, James '79 (NY)[GG] Bronx, NY Bronx Community College; [GG] Bronx, NY Hostos Community College.
Sheehan, John P. '89 (NY) Bronx, NY St. Frances of Rome.
Sheehan, John R. *s.j.* '92 (NY)[HH] New York, NY Xavier Society for the Blind; [DD] New York, NY St. Ignatius Loyola Residence.
Sheehan, Joseph A. '59 (ALN)[J] Bethlehem, PA Holy Family Villa Retired.
Sheehan, Joseph G. '48 (NEW) Holy Name Federation Retired.
Sheehan, Joseph *o.carm.* '63 (SFS)[A] Aberdeen, SD Presentation College.
Sheehan, Justin R. *o.c.s.o.* '91 (ROC)[K] Piffard, NY Abbey of the Genesee.
Sheehan, Mark S. '63 (BO) Bedford, MA St. Michael.
Sheehan, Maurice *o.f.m.cap.* '55 (PIT)[M] Pittsburgh, PA St. Augustine Friary.
Sheehan, Michael J. '78 (NEW) River Edge, NJ St. Peter the Apostle.
Sheehan, Michael J. '64 (PH) Retired.
Sheehan, Myles N. *s.j.* '94 (BO)[U] Watertown, MA The Society of Jesus of New England–Provincial Offices; [U] Newton, MA The Jesuit Community at Boston College; Watertown, MA; Watertown, MA Society of Jesus.
Sheehan, Myles *s.j.* '94 (FgM) Washington, DC National Headquarters.
Sheehan, Peter J. '04 (PRO) On Duty Outside the Diocese; Navy Chaplains.
Sheehan, Richard *o.m.i.* '61 (SAT)[K] San Antonio, TX Oblate Madonna Residence.
Sheehan, Thomas J. *s.j.* '99 (WOR) Memorial Hospital; [N] Worcester, MA Jesuits of the Holy Cross, Inc.
Sheehan, Thomas W. '70 (CLV) Retired.
Sheehan, William J. *c.s.b.* '66 (ROC)[K] Rochester Basilian Residence.
Sheehan, William *o.m.i.* '65 (BO)[U] Lowell, MA Missionary Oblates of Mary Immaculate; [U] Lowell, MA St. Eugene House (Residence).
Sheehy, Charles I. '44 (BO) Senior Priests. Retired.
Sheehy, Michael *c.m.m.* '64 (DET)[K] Vocation Office.
Sheehy, Sean O. '70 (BR) Retired.
Sheehy, Vincent J. '61 (VEN) Venice, FL Our Lady of Lourdes Retired.
Sheehy, Wilfred '60 (SR) Retired.
Sheehy, Yvon *s.c.j.* '78 (MIL)[P] Franklin, WI St. Joseph's at Monastery Lake; Franklin, WI St. Martin of Tours.
Sheekey, Philip P. '64 (WIL) Wilmington, DE St. Mary Magdalen Retired.
Sheeran, Fintan '56 (WDC) Seat Pleasant, MD St. Margaret.
Sheeran, Michael J. *s.j.* '70 (DEN)[B] Denver, CO Regis University; [N] Denver, CO Regis Jesuit Community (The Jesuits at Regis University).
Sheeran, Rev. Msgr. Robert T. '70 (SFR)[B] Seton Hall University; On Duty Outside the Archdiocese; [D] Kentfield, CA Marin Catholic College Preparatory (Coed).
Sheerin, Rev. Msgr. James O. '56 (NEW)[L] Rutherford, NJ St. John Vianney Residence for Priests Retired.
Sheerin, Philip F. *m.m.* '44 (SJ)[M] Los Altos, CA Maryknoll.
Sheets, James P. '75 (SAC) Sacramento, CA Sutter General Hospital; Sacramento, CA Sutter Memorial Hospital.
Sheets, Joseph B. '57 (IND) Retired.
Sheganoski, Fabian *t.o.r.* '65 (ALT)[G] Hollidaysburg, PA St. Bernardine Monastery Retired.
Sheil, James E. '66 (CLV) Retired.
Shelander, Donald E. '70 (CIN) Retired.
Shelby, Charles F. *c.m.* '68 (CHI)[N] Chicago DePaul Vincentian Residence.
Sheldon, Alexander J. '01 (BR) Medical Leave.
Sheldon, William W. *c.m.* '52 (PH)[Y].
Shelley, John J. '61 (PH) Willow Grove, PA St. David Retired.
Shelley, Jonathan P. '95 (STP) Hugo, MN St. John the Baptist.
Shelley, Rev. Msgr. Thomas J. '62 (NY) New York, NY St. Thomas More; On Duty Outside the Archdiocese.
Shellito, Edward D. *m.m.* '90 (FgM) Maryknoll, NY MARYKNOLL.
Shelly, Eamonn *l.c.* '02 (DAL)[D] Irving, TX The Highlands School; [J] Irving, TX Legionaries of Christ.
Shelly, Roy '78 (MRY) Spreckels, CA St. Joseph.
Shelly, Roy '78 (MRY) Vocations Director; Clergy Personnel Board; Diocesan Consultors; Diocesan Consultors; Vocations Board; Special Assignment.
Shelton, Charles M. *s.j.* '82 (DEN)[N] Denver, CO Regis Jesuit Community (The Jesuits at Regis University).
Shelton, Charles *o.f.m.conv.* '81 (MRY)[F] Arroyo Grande, CA St. Joseph Cupertino Friary.
Shelton, Henry '69 (JKS) Retired.
Shelton, James Brent '01 (KNX) Townsend, TN St. Francis of Assisi.
Shelton, Lawrence '66 (LA) Los Angeles, CA St. Anselm.
Sheltz, Rev. Msgr. George A. '71 (GAL)[S] Galveston, TX The Bishop's Palace; Chancellor and Moderator of the Curia; Vicars General; Secretariat For Administration; College of Consultors; Building and Planning Commission; Secretariat for Administration; Ex Officio Members.
Shema, George T. '67 (PAT)[Q] Chester, NJ Nazareth Village Retired.
Shemuga, Kevin C. '83 (CLV) Strongsville, OH St. Joseph.
Shen, Peter H. (BO) Boston, MA St. James the Greater.
Shen, Raphael *s.j.* '70 (DET)[K] Detroit, MI Jesuit Community at the University of Detroit Mercy.
Shenk, Rev. Msgr. Bertrand J. '37 (TOL) Retired.
Shenosky, Joseph T. '00 (PH)[A] Wynnewood, PA Theological Seminary of St. Charles Borromeo, Overbrook; Censores Librorum.
Shenoy, Leslie '76 (FRS) Retired.
Shenrock, Rev. Msgr. Joseph C. '53 (TR) Whiting, NJ St. Elizabeth Ann Seton; Tribunal Judges; [N] Trenton, NJ Villa Vianney Retired.
Shepanzyk, Thomas '09 (BRK) Brooklyn, NY Our Lady of Czestochowa–St. Casimir.
Shepard, Eugene '76 (AUS) Retired.
Shepard, Thomas B. '77 (HRT) New Haven, CT St. Brendan; New Haven, CT St. Aedan; New Haven Deanery.
Shepard, Timothy J. *s.j.* '82 (DET)[K] Clarkston, MI Colombiere Center.
Sheperd, Raymond C. '57 (TOL) Retired.
Shepley, Brian J. '92 (DAV) Brooklyn, IA St. Patrick; Victor, IA St. Bridget; DEPARTMENT OF VETERANS AFFAIRS HOSPITALS AND CHAPLAINS.
Sherba, Rev. Msgr. Girard M. '79 (R) Vicar Judicial; Ex Officio; Bishop's Delegate for Religious; Vicar Judicial & Chancellor; Diocesan Consultors; Council of Women Religious.
Sherbo, Albert '87 (DM) Retired.
Sherburne, Richard F. *s.j.* '56 (MIL)[P] Wauwatosa, WI Jesuit Community at St. Camillus.
Sherdel, Lawrence W. '81 (HBG) McSherrystown, PA Annunciation of the Blessed Virgin Mary.
Sheridan, Denis J. '81 (RVC)[N] Amityville, NY St. Pius X Residence Retired.
Sheridan, Edward J. '63 (CHL) Retired.
Sheridan, Edward M. '07 (RVC) Hampton Bays, NY St. Rosalie's.
Sheridan, Eugene F. *c.m.* '68 (PH) Philadelphia, PA St. Francis of Assisi.
Sheridan, James J. *o.s.a.* (KAL)[E] Douglas, MI Order of St. Augustine; Douglas, MI St. Peter Retired.
Sheridan, John E. '90 (BO) Salem, MA St. James.
Sheridan, John J. *o.s.a.* '85 (PH)[Y] Villanova, PA Provincial Offices of the Order of St. Augustine, Province of St. Thomas of Villanova; [Y] Villanova, PA St. Thomas Monastery; Counselors.
Sheridan, John '10 (Y) Canton, OH St. Peter.
Sheridan, Patrick L. '98 (CIN) Bellefontaine, OH St. Patrick.
Sheridan, Paul G. *s.j.* '75 (SJ)[D] San Jose, CA Bellarmine College Preparatory.
Sheridan, Rev. Msgr. Paul W. '56 (SFD) Retired.
Sheridan, Philip A. '51 (HRT) Retired.
Sheridan, Sean O. *t.o.r.* '06 (WDC)[O] Washington, DC St. Louis Friary; [C] Catholic University of America, The.
Sheridan, Thomas L. *s.j.* '57 (NEW)[B] Jersey City, NJ Jesuit Center; [L] Jersey City, NJ Jesuits of Saint Peter's College, Inc.; Elizabeth, NJ Elizabeth Federal Detention Center.
Sheridan, Thomas '64 (CHY) Green River, WY Immaculate Conception.
Sheridan, William H. '54 (CHI) Chicago, IL St. Philip Neri Retired.
Sheridan, William J. '72 (CHI) Wilmette, IL St. Francis Xavier.
Sheridan, William P. '89 (NEW) Mahwah, NJ Immaculate Conception; [O] Mahwah, NJ Ramapo College.
Sherliza, Michael S. '99 (ATL) Marietta, GA St. Joseph.
Sherlock, James C. '64 (PH) Ardmore, PA St. Colman.
Sherlock, John P. '69 (WCH) Wichita, KS Cathedral of the Immaculate Conception; Sedgwick County Adult Local Detention Facility.
Sherlock, R. Marc '79 (CIN) Tipp City, OH St. John the Baptist; Judges.

Sherman, Rev. Msgr. Anthony F. '70 (BRK) Douglaston, NY St. Anastasia.
Sherman, Daniel J. *m.m.* '47 (NY)[DD] Retired.
Sherman, Edward '56 (FAR) Native American Ministries Retired.
Sherman, Gary D. '85 (TLS)[E] Tulsa, OK St. John Medical Center, Inc.; [F] Tulsa, OK St. John Villas, Inc.; Special Assignment.
Sherman, Rt. Rev. Archimandrite Kenneth '80 (NTN) West Paterson, NJ St. Ann; Presbyteral Council.
Sherman, Richard T. '00 (SLC) Central Utah Correctional Facility; Central Valley, UT Saint Elizabeth LLC 220; [G] Ephraim, UT St. Jude Catholic Center; Correctional Institution Ministry.
Sherman, William C. '55 (FAR) Retired.
Sherrer, Charles D. *c.s.c.* '61 (P)[L] Portland, OR Holy Cross Fathers & Brothers, C.S.C. – University of Portland Retired.
Sherrer, Charles *c.s.c.* (FTW)[H] Notre Dame Congregation of Holy Cross, United States Province of Priests & Brothers.
Sherry, Robert N. '66 (RCK) McHenry, IL Church of Holy Apostles; Cursillo Movement.
Shershanovich, Rev. Msgr. Michael '74 (SPR) Pittsfield, MA St. Joseph's; Episcopal Vicars.
Sherwin, Michael S. *o.p.* '91 (OAK)[L] Oakland Order of Preachers (Province of the Most Holy Name of Jesus – Western Dominican Province).
Sherwood, Stephen K. *c.m.f.* '71 (SAT) San Antonio, TX Immaculate Heart of Mary; [C] Oblate School of Theology.
Sherwood, Timothy H. '93 (SP) St. Petersburg, FL St. Raphael.
Shetler, John '92 (PHX) Mesa, AZ Holy Cross Roman Catholic Parish.
Shetler, Joseph L. '06 (JC) Absent on Leave.
Shetter, John '57 (ORG) Retired.
Shetui, Joseph Francis (ROC) Horseheads, NY St. Mary Our Mother.
Shevlin, John *s.v.d.* '60 (LA)[D] Lakewood, CA Saint Joseph High School.
Shiahornu, David (NY) New York, NY St. Agnes.
Shidler, Anthony *o.s.b.* '64 (KC)[J] Conception, MO Conception Abbey.
Shields, David M. *s.j.* '73 (MIL)[Y] Milwaukee, WI Casa Romero Renewal Center, Inc.; [P] Milwaukee, WI Jesuit Community at Marquette University.
Shields, Rev. Msgr. Hugh Joseph '72 (PH) Philadelphia, PA St. Thomas Aquinas.
Shields, Rev. Msgr. James J. '63 (PH) North Wales, PA Mary, Mother of the Redeemer Retired.
Shields, Rev. Msgr. Maurice L. '57 (MOB) Mobile, AL St. Mary Retired.
Shields, Michael '79 (ANC) On Duty Outside Archdiocese; Magadan Mission.
Shields, Patrick J. '64 (CLV) Stow, OH Holy Family Retired.
Shields, Robert J. '64 (YAK) Retired.
Shields, Stephen L. '74 (CLV) Sheffield Lake, OH St. Thomas the Apostle.
Shields, W. Bry '84 (MOB) Mobile, AL St. Ignatius Parish, Mobile; [B] Mobile, AL McGill–Toolen Catholic High School.
Shiffer, James *s.s.c.* '65 (LA)[P] Los Angeles, CA Columban Fathers, Procure House.
Shigo, Francis L. *s.v.d.* '60 (LA)[J] San Pedro, CA Providence Little Company of Mary San Pedro Peninsula Hospital Pavilion.
Shikany, Paul M. '79 (IND) Indianapolis, IN St. Matthew Catholic Church, Indianapolis, Inc.; Adjunct Vicars Judicial; Priests' Personnel Board.
Shikaputo, Victor S. *s.s.* '94 (BAL)[Q] Baltimore Society of St. Sulpice, Province of the United States.
Shikuku, Constantine '03 (P)[J] Portland, OR Providence Health & Services–Oregon.
Shillcox, Timothy D. *o.praem.* '87 (GB) De Pere, WI Our Lady of Lourdes; [J] De Pere, WI St. Joseph Priory.
Shimek, Joseph J. '07 (MIL) Fox Point, WI St. Eugene; Whitefish Bay, WI St. Monica.
Shimkus, John Martin *o.s.b.* '03 (DET)[B] Oxford, MI St. Benedict Monastery.
Shimotsu, John M. '94 (ORG) Military Chaplains; Navy Chaplains; On Duty Outside the Diocese.
Shin, Eun Keun '79 (DEN) Aurora, CO St. Lawrence Korean Catholic Church.
Shin, Gi Hyeon (Simon) '99 (P) Portland, OR Korean Martyrs Catholic Church.
Shin, Stephen *o.f.m.cap.* '90 (WDC)[B] Washington, DC St. Francis Friary–Capuchin College.
Shine, Edward J. '57 (CIN) Harrison, OH St. John the Baptist Retired.
Shine, John V. *c.m.* '63 (LA)[P] Santa Barbara, CA St. Mary's Evangelization Center; [V] Santa Barbara, CA St. Mary's Seminary Center Retired.
Shine, Robert W. '55 (SAG) Retired.
Shinney, Robert J. *s.j.* '68 (SJ)[D] San Jose, CA Bellarmine College Preparatory.
Shinnick, Edward P. '56 (GF) Retired.
Shinnick, Lawrence E. '05 (BIR) Demopolis, AL St. Leo; Livingston, AL St. Francis of Assisi.
Shipley, Rev. Msgr. William '54 (SD) Retired.
Shipp, Edmund N. '61 (SFR) Retired.
Shipps, Bede *o.p.* '85 (WDC) Washington, DC St. Dominic Church & Priory.
Shirey, Joseph *s.j.* '56 (SPK)[J] Spokane, WA Regis Community.
Shirley, Rev. Msgr. Richard '67 (CC) Defenders of the Bond; [I] Corpus Christi, TX Journey to Damascus, Inc.
Shirley, Ronald '73 (MRY) Aptos, CA Resurrection.
Shiverski, John J. '68 (MAR) Defensore Vinculi Retired.
Shiyo, Evarist T. (B) Salmon, ID St. Charles.
Shlesinger, Bernard (Ned) '96 (R)[J] Raleigh, NC Vocations Office.
Shlesinger, Bernard E. '96 (R) Special Assignment; Office for Vocations and Seminarian Formation.
Shmaruk, Richard J. '65 (BO) Woburn, MA St. Anthony of Padua.
Shnob, Alan D. '78 (OG) Peru, NY St. Augustine; Defenders of the Bond.
Shoback, Thomas P. '77 (SCR) Unassigned or Leave of Absence.
Shober, Peter (HEL) Montana Association of Churches.
Shockey, Benjamin D. '04 (WCH) Kingman, KS St. Patrick.
Shocklee, Christopher R. '09 (LFT) Noblesville, IN Our Lady of Grace.
Shoda, D. Brian '87 (WH) Inwood, WV St. Leo.
Shoemaker, David A. '05 (BO) Absent on Leave.
Shoemaker, David M. '00 (MOB) Eufaula, AL Holy Redeemer; Ventress Correctional Institution; Bullock County Correctional Facility; Vocations.
Shoemaker, Rev. Msgr. Samuel E. '66 (PH) Yardley, PA St. Ignatius of Antioch; Archdiocesan Judges.
Shoemaker, Thomas '90 (FTW) Fort Wayne, IN St. Jude; Pro–Synodal Judges; Consultors; Presbyteral Council; Budget Committee.
Shoemaker, Victor *c.s.j.* '03 (NEW) Orange, NJ Mt. Carmel.
Shofany, Saba '95 (NTN) San Diego, CA St. Jacob Mission.
Shofner, Christopher '05 (STP) Le Center, MN St. Mary; Sharon Township, MN Church of St. Henry; Deanery 7.
Sholander, Anthony E. *s.j.* '84 (OAK)[L] Berkeley, CA Jesuit Fathers and Brothers.
Shonebarger, Thomas '69 (COL) Retired.
Shoni, Bassim '05 (OLD) Bayonne, NJ Saint Joseph Syriac Catholic Cathedral; Jamaica Plain, MA Our Lady of Mesopotamia Mission; Allentown, PA Our Lady of Mercy Parish.
Shonis, Anthony J. '71 (OWN) Deans; Henderson, KY Holy Name of Jesus; Priests' Council.
Shooner, Jeffrey P. '04 (L) Louisville, KY St. Boniface; College of Consultors; Ex Officio; Priest Personnel Office; Continuing Education for Clergy–Ministry to Priests; Vocations; Vicar for Priests; Priest Personnel Commission.
Shori, Nicholas R. '74 (Y) Office of Continuing Education and Formation of Priests; Office of Parish Planning Reconfiguration.
Short, Anthony J. *s.j.* '71 (STL)[O] St. Louis, MO Jesuit Community Corporation at Saint Louis University – Jesuit Hall.
Short, Gregory *o.m.v.* '79 (BO)[B] Boston, MA Oblate Provincialate.
Short, James M. *s.j.* '61 (STL)[O] St. Louis, MO Bellarmine House of Studies; [C] Saint Louis University.
Short, John '99 (SFS) Clark, SD St. Michael.
Shortall, Robert '74 (DAV) Retired.
Shorter, Melvin *c.p.* '86 (FgM) New Rochelle, NY St. Paul of the Cross Province.
Shortt, David J. '89 (PBR) Youngstown, OH St. Nicholas.
Shortt, Patrick J. '66 (JC) Eugene, MO Our Lady of the Snows; Senators; Iberia, MO St. Anthony; St. Elizabeth, MO St. Lawrence.
Shott, Stephen E. *o.s.f.s.* '95 (ARL) Vienna, VA Our Lady of Good Counsel.
Shoup, Steven L. '84 (CIN) Fort Loramie, OH St. Michael; Fort Loramie, OH SS. Peter and Paul; Vicarri Foranei (Deans).
Shovelton, Gerald T. '56 (FR) Retired.
Shovelton, Gerald '56 (ORL) Lady Lake, FL St. Timothy Retired.
Shovelton, William J. '46 (FR) Retired.
Showalter, Joseph L. '57 (SPK)[J] Spokane, WA Regis Community Retired.
Showalter, Rev. Msgr. Paul E. '66 (PEO) Diocesan College of Consultors; Finance Council (Canon 492); Catholic Relief Services; Clergymen's Aid, Inc.; Conciliation and Arbitration Process; Diocesan Pastoral Council; Diocesan Personnel Board; Holy Childhood Association; Priests' Eucharistic League; Propagation of the Faith; Priests' Purgatorial Society; Peoria, IL Catholic Cemetery Association of Peoria, IL; Vicars General.
Showalter, Thomas *s.o.l.t.* '97 (CC)[G] Robstown, TX Society of Our Lady of the Most Holy Trinity; Robstown, TX St. John Nepomucene.
Showers, Robert *o.f.m.conv.* '90 (STP)[M] Prior Lake, MN Franciscan Retreats.
Showfety, Rev. Msgr. Joseph '55 (CHL) Greensboro, NC Retired.
Showraiah, Marneni *o.f.m.* '90 (NSH) Franklin, TN St. Philip.
Shreenan, Timothy J. *o.f.m.* '84 (NY) New York, NY St. Francis of Assisi.
Shreve, Rev. Msgr. Thomas F. '61 (RIC) Vicar General; Building and Renovation Committee.
Shreve, Rev. Msgr. Thomas (BAL) Judicial Vicar.
Shroeder, Danielmose *o.f.m.* '91 (FgM) Washington, DC COMMISSARIAT OF THE HOLY LAND.
Shrum, Jack D. '08 (SEA) Sumner, WA St. Andrew.
Shryock, Jeremiah *c.f.r.* '11 (NY)[DD] Yonkers, NY St. Felix Friary.
Shuda, Paul R. '60 (HBG) Legion of Mary; Harrisburg, PA Retired.
Shudrak, Jaroslav '08 (SJP) On Assignment Outside the Diocese; Presbyters.
Shuey, Mark '07 (SJP) Raleigh, NC St. Basil The Great Mission; Raleigh, NC St. Nicholas Mission; Mid–Atlantic Protopresbytery; Presbyters.
Shugrue, Rev. Msgr. Michael P. '66 (R) Fayetteville, NC St. Patrick; Diocesan Consultors; Council of Priests.
Shugrue, Rev. Msgr. Timothy J. '73 (NEW) Cranford, NJ St. Michael's; Elected Members.
Shuley, Keith J. '92 (MO) Navy Chaplains.
Shuley, Keith *c.c.* '92 (CC) Military Chaplains.
Shulik, Bernard P. '74 (PIT) Absent on Sick Leave; [M] Pittsburgh, PA St. John Vianney Manor.
Shumway, Lynn M. '03 (BUF) Grand Island, NY St. Stephen.
Shuping, Kenneth J. '03 (RIC) Christiansburg, VA St. Jude.
Shuppert, William T.J. '71 (TUC) Tucson, AZ Saint Francis de Sales Roman Catholic Parish – Tucson.
Shurtleff, F. James '66 (OG) Ogdensburg, NY Notre Dame.
Shuter, Alex '91 (PSC) Williamsburg, VA Ascension of Our Lord.
Shutt, Paul–Alexander *o.s.b.* '98 (GBG)[H] Latrobe, PA Saint Vincent Archabbey.
Shutt, Paul–Alexander *o.s.b.* '98 (PBR) Latrobe, PA St. Mary.
Shuttleworth, Edward J. '90 (LC) Chippewa Falls, WI St. Charles Borromeo; Chippewa Falls, WI St. Peter; Deans.
Sia, Joseph M. '08 (DAV) Muscatine, IA SS. Mary and Mathias of Muscatine; Columbus Junction, IA St. Joseph.
Siamoo, Peter '99 (P)[J] Portland, OR Providence Health & Services–Oregon.
Sibel, John J. '72 (PH) Linwood, PA Holy Saviour.
Sibenik, Simeon B. '81 (PBR) Punxsutawney, PA SS. Peter and Paul; Consultors.
Siberski, John R. *s.j.* '07 (WDC)[O] Washington, DC The Jesuit Community at Georgetown University.
Siberski, John R. *s.j.* '07 (BO)[U] Boston The Society of Jesus of New England–Provincial Offices.
Sibilano, Joseph D. *o.s.j.* '65 (SCR)[L] Pittston, PA Our Lady of Sorrows Province of the Oblates of St. Joseph; Councilors:; [A] Pittston, PA St. Joseph's Oblate Seminary; Pittston, PA St. Joseph Marello Parish.
Sibirnij, Volodymyr '04 (STF) Troy, NY Protection of B.V.M.; Watervliet, NY St. Nicholas.
Sibley, Bryce '00 (LAF) Lafayette, LA Our Lady of Wisdom, University of Louisiana; College Ministry.
Sibley, Bryce '00 (LAF)[L] Lafayette, LA Our Lady of Wisdom Catholic Student Center.
Sica, Joseph F. '82 (SCR) Scranton, PA Immaculate Conception.
Sicard, Kenneth *o.p.* '90 (PRO)[O] Providence St. Thomas Aquinas Priory at Providence College; [B] Providence, RI Providence College.
Sicari, Rev. Msgr. Joseph J. '82 (BUF) Consultors, College of; Council of Priests; Bowmansville, NY Sacred Heart; Awaiting Assignment.
Siceloff, John C. '04 (MET) Dunellen, NJ St. John the Evangelist.
Sichko, James W. '98 (LEX) Richmond, KY St. Mark; Special Assignment; [L] Richmond, KY Catholic Campus Ministry of St. Mark; Bluegrass East.
Siciliano, Donald L. '93 (CIN) Cincinnati, OH St. Bernard.
Siciliano, Jude *o.p.* '69 (R)[F] Raleigh, NC Dominican Priory.
Sickler, Robert *m.s.a.* '87 (NOR)[G] Cromwell, CT Society of the Missionaries of the Holy Apostles.
Sickler, Thomas *m.s.* '73 (NOR) Danielson, CT St. James.
Siconolfi, Rev. Msgr. Constantine V. '59 (SCR) Retired.
Siconolfi, Michael T. *s.j.* '72 (WDC)[O] Washington, DC The Jesuit Community of St. Aloysius Gonzaga.
Siconolfi, Thomas J. *c.ss.r.* '70 (TR)[R] Long Branch, NJ San Alfonso Retreat House.
Sidera, Joseph A. *c.s.c.* '68 (FTW)[H] Notre Dame Congregation of Holy Cross, United States Province of Priests & Brothers.
Sidera, Joseph *c.s.c.* '68 (BGP) Fairfield, CT Our Lady

of the Assumption.
Sidney, Walter T. *s.j.* '78 (STL)[F] St. Louis, MO De Smet Jesuit High School; [O] St. Louis, MO De Smet Jesuit High School Community.
Sidor, Sidney '04 (PRM) Indianapolis, IN St. Athanasius Church; Priest's Pension Board Retired.
Sidoti, James *o.carm.* '92 (NY) Middletown, NY Our Lady of Mt. Carmel.
Siebenaler, John M. '61 (STP) Retired.
Siebenaler, Leonard '59 (STP) Retired.
Siebenaler, Martin '59 (STP) Retired.
Siebenand, Ambrose F. '41 (NU) Retired.
Siebenand, Paul Alcuin '60 (LA) Retired.
Sieber, Patrick *o.f.m.* '71 (PH)[Y] Philadelphia, PA Order of Friars Minor of the Province of the Most Holy Name.
Siebert, Edward J. *s.j.* '97 (LA)[BB] Culver City, CA Loyola Productions, Inc.; [P] Culver City, CA Ignatius House, The Novitiate of the California Province, Society of Jesus.
Siebert, Paul S. '86 (E) Emporium, PA St. Mark.
Siebert, Stephen A. '94 (DEN) Greeley, CO Our Lady of Peace.
Siebert, William P. '81 (DET) Retired.
Siebold, Gerald *c.ss.r.* '58 (BR)[H] Baton Rouge, LA St. Gerard Residence; [L] Baton Rouge, LA Redemptorist Fathers of Baton Rouge, Inc.
Siebor, John '58 (RVC) Hempstead, NY St. Ladislaus Retired.
Sieczynski, Jerzey '00 (SAT) On Leave.
Siedlarz, Jozef *s.ch.* '10 (DET) Sterling Heights, MI Our Lady of Czestochowa.
Siefer, Rev. Msgr. Richard R. '75 (E) Du Bois, PA St. Catherine; Clergy Continuing Education and Formation.
Siefert, John S. '89 (STL) Brentwood, MO St. Mary Magdalen.
Siefert, Ralph A. *s.m.* '73 (STL)[F] Creve Coeur, MO Chaminade College Preparatory School Inc.; [G] Creve Coeur, MO Chaminade College Preparatory; [O] Saint Louis, MO Chaminade Community.
Sieg, Leslie M. '76 (P) Tigard, OR St. Anthony; Building Commission.
Sieg, Thomas H. '71 (STP) Prior Lake, MN St. Michael; College of Consultors.
Siegel, Kenan *o.f.m.cap.* '56 (MIL)[P] Mount Calvary, WI St. Lawrence Friary Retired.
Siegert, Johannes S.A.G. '08 (BRK) Brooklyn, NY Visitation of the Blessed Virgin Mary.
Siekierski, Rev. Msgr. John J. '67 (GRY) East Chicago, IN Holy Trinity; East Chicago, IN St. Stanislaus; Defender of the Bond.
Sielski, Joseph *m.i.c.* '41 (WDC)[O] Brookeville, MD Marian Monastery–Brookeville.
Siemianowski, John S. '89 (CHI) Chicago Heights, IL St. Agnes.
Siendo, Ralph C. '97 (NEW) Jersey City, NJ St. Aloysius.
Sienkiewicz, Matthew '59 (FTW) Retired.
Siepka, Rev. Msgr. Richard W. '82 (BUF) Co–Directors; Kenmore, NY St. Andrew.
Siepker, Daniel '93 (DM) Atlantic, IA SS. Peter and Paul; Atlantic, IA St. Mary.
Sierminski, Vernon '56 (SAG) Retired.
Sierotowicz, Felicjan '90 (ROC) Auburn, NY; Moravia, NY Cayuga Correctional; Red Creek, NY Butler Correctional Facility; [I] Auburn, NY Mercy Health & Rehabilitation Center Nursing Home Co., Inc.; Auburn, NY Sacred Heart; Auburn, NY St. Hyacinth; Auburn, NY St. Francis of Assisi.
Sierra, Angel '80 (SFD) Carlinville, IL SS. Mary & Joseph.
Sierra, Luis Fermin '03 (DAL) Dallas, TX St. Augustine Catholic Church.
Sierra, Rolando A. *c.ss.r.* '99 (LA) Santa Maria, CA St. John Neumann.
Sierra–Posada, Pedro J. '76 (ALX) Lecompte, LA St. Martin.
Sievel, Thomas A. '78 (HRT) East Haven, CT St. Vincent de Paul.
Siewiera, Bogdan '98 (COS) Salida, CO St. Joseph.
Siffert, Etienne *s.m.* '58 (SFR) San Francisco, CA Notre Dame des Victoires.
Siffrin, Rev. Msgr. Robert J. '79 (Y) Finance Council; Vicar General & Moderator of the Curia; College of Consultors; Youngstown, OH St. Edward; Presbyteral Council; [P] Youngstown, OH Conference of Slovak Clergy.
Sigaran, Mamerto '60 (SFR) Retired.
Sigler, Gary L. '79 (FTW) Fort Wayne, IN Queen of Angels.
Sigler, John William '94 (LA) Hospital Chaplains.
Sigman, Anthony (PHX) Priests' Assurance Association.
Sigman, Louis Anthony '67 (PHX) Retired.
Sigmund, Andrew J. '64 (STL) Washington, MO St. Francis Borgia.
Signalness, Jason R. '11 (BIS) Bismarck, ND Saint Anne.
Signorelli, Francis *s.x.* '59 (BO)[U] Holliston, MA Xaverian Missionaries; [Z] Holliston, MA Our Lady of Fatima Shrine.
Signorelli, Jose *i.v.e.* (WDC) Chillum, MD St. John Baptist de la Salle.
Siguere, Roberto *o.f.m.* '65 (FgM) New York, NY Franciscan Province of the Immaculate Conception.
Siguere, Roberto *o.f.m.* (NY)[DD] New York Franciscan Province of the Immaculate Conception.
Sihombing, Antonius Firmansyah *s.j.* '09 (OAK)[L] Berkeley, CA Jesuit Fathers and Brothers.
Sihuay, Francis X. *o.f.m.* '51 (WDC)[O] Washington, DC Franciscan Monastery USA Inc. Retired.
Sikandar Chanan, Anthony '90 (BRK) Jackson Heights, NY St. Joan of Arc.
Siket, Bruce '07 (PRT)[M] Castine, ME Maine Maritime Academy; Ellsworth, ME St. Joseph; Ellsworth, ME Stella Maris Parish.
Siklodi, Sandor '71 (CHI) Chicago, IL St. Stephen, King of Hungary.
Sikon, Michael P. '96 (GBG) Delmont, PA St. John Baptist de La Salle; Delmont, PA St. Mary; Office for Worship.
Sikora, James R. '67 (GF)[A] Great Falls, MT University of Great Falls; [A] University of Great Falls; Special Assignment; Clerical Benefit Association.
Sikora, Stanley J. '57 (HRT)[A] In Res. at the Archbishop Daniel A. Cronin Retirement Residence at St. Thomas Seminary Retired.
Sikora, Thomas More *o.s.b.* '97 (GBG)[H] Latrobe, PA Saint Vincent Archabbey.
Sikorski, Allan '08 (RVC) Manhasset, NY St. Mary's.
Sikorski, Harold R. '56 (SAG) Retired.
Sikorski, Jeffery P. '73 (TOL) Huron, OH St. Peter.
Sikorski, Leszek '97 (MO) Navy Chaplains.
Sikorski, Leszek '97 (VEN) Military Chaplains.
Sikorski, Louis S. '64 (GAL) Retired.
Sikorsky, Charles *l.c.* '02 (WDC)[O] Potomac, MD Legionaries of Christ.
Sikorsky, Charles *l.c.* (ARL)[B] Arlington, VA The Institute for the Psychological Sciences, Inc.
Silayo, Constantine L. '82 (IND)[G] Beech Grove, IN Franciscan St. Francis Health.
Silcox, John D. '95 (PH) Drexel Hill, PA St. Dorothy.
Sileo, Joseph R. '71 (WDC) Bethesda, MD St. Bartholomew.
Sileo, Joseph (WDC) Great Mills, MD Holy Face.
Siler, Paschal *o.f.m.cap.* '60 (GF) Ashland, MT St. Labre; Lame Deer, MT Blessed Sacrament.
Siler, Rev. Msgr. Robert M. '01 (YAK) Presbyteral Council Executive Committee; Diocesan Finance Council; Moderator of the Curia; Chancellor; Campaign for Human Development; Press (Central Washington Catholic); Clergy Personnel Board; Diocesan Consultors.
Silio, Antonio R. '88 (MIA) Pembroke Pines, FL St. Boniface.
Sill, Theodore K. '89 (COL) Gahanna, OH St. Matthew.
Silloway, Michael '10 (ATL) On Duty Outside the Archdiocese; Atlanta, GA Cathedral of Christ the King.
Silos, Gerardo '07 (LAR) Zapata, TX Our Lady of Lourdes.
Silva, Alvaro '74 (POD) Chestnut Hill.
Silva, Bryan *o.m.i.* '85 (WDC)[O] Washington, DC Oblate Community; [O] Washington, DC Provincial Offices of the United States Province of the Missionary Oblates of Mary Immaculate.
Silva, Caesar '74 (MO) Air National Guard Chaplains.
Silva, Edwin Lugo '89 (MGZ) Lajas, PR Our Lady of the Purification.
Silva, Eleazar '01 (SLC) Salt Lake City, UT Cathedral of the Madeleine LLC 202; Diaconate Formation.
Silva, Ethiege *o.m.i.* (NEW) Palisades Park, NJ St. Michael's.
Silva, Francisco C. (BO) Stoughton, MA Immaculate Conception.
Silva, Frank J. '76 (BO) Appointed; Newton, MA Corpus Christi – St. Bernard.
Silva, Hilary '89 (FRS) Hilmar, CA Holy Rosary.
Silva, John '04 (EVN) On Leave.
Silva, Juan '92 (LA) Lomita, CA St. Margaret Mary Alacoque.
Silva, Langes J. '95 (SLC) Priests' Personnel Board; Salt Lake City, UT Cathedral of the Madeleine LLC 202; Vice Chancellor; Ecumenical Commission; Judicial Vicar; Judges.
Silva, Langes J. '95 (LAV) Diocesan Judges.
Silva, Luis '98 (CR) On Duty Outside the Diocese.
Silva, Miguel '84 (SAC) Yuba City, CA St. Isidore.
Silva, Raul '06 (NEW) New Milford, NJ St. Joseph's.
Silva, Raul '79 (FRS) Avenal, CA St. Joseph.
Silva, Rev. Msgr. Robert J. '65 (STO) Personnel Board; Linden, CA Holy Cross Church (Pastor of); Continuing Education of Clergy; Office for Pastoral Leadership Development; Members by Age Group.
Silva, Rolando '06 (GLD) Hillman, MI Jesus the Good Shepherd; Hillman, MI St. Augustine; Alpena, MI St. Mary.
Silva, Rosendo *l.c.* (ORG) Lake Forest, CA Santiago de Compostela.
Silva, Susith '87 (HRT) Waterbury, CT Basilica of the Immaculate Conception.
Silva, Victor T. '07 (PRO) Cranston, RI St. Matthew; Council Members.
Silva Arredondo, Raul '79 (FRS) Huron, CA St. Frances Cabrini.
Silveira, Eduino T. '87 (SAC) Vicars Forane; Sacramento, CA St. Philomene.
Silver, Bertram *o.m.i.* '54 (FgM) Washington, DC AMERICAN OBLATE MISSIONS.
Silver, Jeffrey P. '84 (CIN) Oxford, OH St. Mary Church and Catholic Campus Ministry; [R] Oxford, OH Miami University Catholic Campus Ministry.
Silver, John E. '93 (OG) Conway, SC St. James Retired.
Silveri, Donato P. '64 (PH) Spring City, PA St. Joseph; Spring City, PA Southeastern Pennsylvania Veterans Center.
Silverio, Gilbert J. *o.f.m.* '59 (FR)[F] Onset, MA St. Joseph Friary–Franciscan Friars.
Silvester, Peter *s.v.d.* '78 (CHI)[N] Techny, IL Divine Word Residence.
Silvia, Kenneth J. *c.s.c.* '64 (ORL)[F] Cocoa Beach, FL Congregation of Holy Cross, United States Province Retired.
Silvia, Kenneth J. *c.s.c.* '64 (FTW)[H] Notre Dame Congregation of Holy Cross, United States Province of Priests & Brothers.
Sim, Charles *s.j.* (STP)[J] Minneapolis, MN Markoe House Jesuit Community.
Sima, John R. *s.j.* '71 (FgM)[N] Chicago Chicago Province of the Society of Jesus–Provincial Office; Chicago, IL Society of Jesus.
Simango, Lucas K. '87 (CHY) Casper, WY St. Anthony of Padua; [C] Casper, WY St. Anthony Manor; [F] Casper, WY St. Francis Newman Center.
Simas, Rev. Msgr. Manuel C. '61 (OAK) Fremont, CA St. Joseph (Old Mission San Jose).
Simboli, Ronald L. '75 (GBG) Uniontown, PA St. Joseph.
Simburger, Joseph '79 (SFD) Altamont, IL St. Clare; Altamont, IL St. Anne; Altamont, IL St. Mary.
Simeone, Francis '61 (FRS) Retired.
Simeone, Gary F. '75 (HRT) Bristol, CT St. Gregory the Great.
Simeone, Rev. Msgr. Ronald P. '82 (PRO) Woonsocket, RI St. Anthony; Vicar for Judicial Matters; Judicial Vicar; Secretary.
Simien, Gregory M. '99 (LAF) Maurice, LA Our Lady of Perpetual Help.
Simington, Rev. Msgr. Ralph P. '62 (DUB) College of Consultors; Directors Retired.
Simko, James G. '91 (VEN) Fort Myers, FL St. Francis Xavier.
Simko, James '91 (DEN) On Duty Outside the Archdiocese.
Simlik, Frank P. '54 (PHX) Retired.
Simmons, Franklin '79 (GAL) Retired.
Simmons, Jerome S. '68 (E) Erie, PA Sacred Heart; [N] Erie, PA Sisters of Saint Joseph of Northwestern Pennsylvania; [P] Erie, PA Ecclesia Ministry.
Simmons, Joseph C. '61 (BAL) Joppa, MD Church of the Holy Spirit.
Simmons, Mark '07 (BRK) Brooklyn, NY St. Patrick.
Simmons, Matthew P. '03 (JKS) Approved Advocate and Auditors; Brookhaven, MS St. Francis; [H] Brookhaven, MS Lincoln Junior College Newman Center.
Simo, Philip *o.s.b.* '97 (WDC) Washington, DC Providence Hospital; [O] Washington, DC St. Anselm's Abbey; [L] Washington, DC Providence Hospital.
Simon, Akan S. '98 (RCK) Crystal Lake, IL St. Thomas the Apostle.
Simon, Ambrose *o.f.m.cap.* '50 (GB)[J] Appleton, WI St. Fidelis Friary Retired.
Simon, Brian '96 (SFS) Presbyteral Council.
Simon, Carl '71 (LAN) Davison, MI St. John the Evangelist.
Simon, George Howard '57 (LAF) Retired.
Simon, John L. '73 (MIL) North Fond du Lac, WI Presentation of the Blessed Virgin Mary; Eldorado, WI Our Risen Savior.
Simon, Rev. Msgr. Joseph M. '71 (STL) Oakville, MO Queen of All Saints.
Simon, Richard T. '75 (CHI) Skokie, IL St. Lambert.
Simon, Robert G. *c.s.c.* '61 (FgM)[H] Notre Dame Congregation of Holy Cross, United States Province of Priests & Brothers; New Rochelle, NY Eastern Brothers Province.
Simon, Robert J. '90 (SCR) Moscow, PA St. Catherine of Siena; Diocesan Consultors; Presbyteral Council.
Simon, Thomas *m.s.a.* '79 (NOR)[G] Cromwell, CT Society of the Missionaries of the Holy Apostles.
Simonar, Mathew J. '97 (GB) Oshkosh, WI St. Jude the Apostle; College of Consultors.
Simonds, Donald D. *m.s.* '63 (HRT)[L] Hartford, CT Missionaries of LaSalette.
Simonds, Thomas A. *s.j.* '99 (OM)[J] Omaha, NE Jesuit Community at Creighton University.
Simone, Earl Francis '77 (CIN) Dayton, OH St. Peter.
Simone, Michael A. *m.m.* '56 (NY)[DD] Maryknoll Maryknoll Fathers and Brothers Retired.
Simone, Michael M. '03 (WCH)[K] Wichita, KS Serra Club of Wichita – Metro; [K] Wichita, KS Priests'

Retirement and Education Fund of Wichita; Vocations; Wichita, KS St. Anne.
Simone, Michael *s.j.* '07 (BAL)[Q] Baltimore, MD Ferdinand Wheeler Jesuit Community.
Simoneau, Norman J. '67 (MAN) Retired.
Simoneau, Roland L. '78 (PRO) Warwick, RI St. Benedict.
Simoneaux, Jody '82 (LAF) Jeanerette, LA St. John the Evangelist.
Simonelli, Gerald '90 (JOL) Leave of Absence.
Simonetti, David J. '05 (CHI) Sauk Village, IL St. James.
Simonnet, Philippe *s.s.e.* '52 (BUR)[E] Colchester, VT Society of St. Edmund; Colchester, VT SOCIETY OF ST. EDMUND.
Simons, Derek *s.v.d.* '70 (CHI)[N] Chicago, IL Angels Studio.
Simons, James L. '00 (CIN) Bradford, OH Immaculate Conception; Covington, OH St. Teresa of the Infant Jesus.
Simons, Thomas G. '77 (GR) Alpine, MI Holy Trinity.
Simonson, Earl C. '69 (STP) Minneapolis, MN St. Clement.
Simpson, Brian L. '72 (CHI) Military Chaplains; Navy Chaplains.
Simpson, David L. *o.carm.* '70 (JOL)[L] Darien, IL St. Simon Stock Priory; [N] Darien, IL Carmelite Spiritual Center.
Simpson, Kenneth C. '78 (CHI) Chicago, IL St. Clement; Deans.
Simpson, Mauro *o.s.b.* '52 (FAJ)[B] Humacao, PR San Antonio Abad Abbey of the Order of St. Benedict.
Simpson, Robert '65 (RNO) Retired.
Simpson, Roger '52 (SFD) Retired.
Sims, John D. *o.p.* '04 (BR) Ponchatoula, LA St. Joseph.
Sims, Paul *c.r.* '86 (CHI)[N] Councilors.
Sims, Robert W. '71 (IND) Indianapolis, IN Immaculate Heart of Mary Catholic Church, Indianapolis, Inc.
Simutowe, Patrick *s.s.* '96 (BAL)[Q] Baltimore Society of St. Sulpice, Province of the United States.
Sinasac, Alvin A. *c.s.b.* '79 (GAL) Houston, TX St. Anne.
Sinatra, Leonard '67 (PHU) Retired.
Sinatra, Robert L. '04 (CAM) On Duty Outside the Diocese.
Sinatra, William D. '64 (DET) Retired.
Sinclair, Alexander B. '57 (KC) Consultors Retired.
Sindik, Rev. Msgr. George '59 (PT) Pensacola, FL Cathedral of the Sacred Heart Retired.
Sindik, Matthew A. '62 (MOB) Montgomery, AL St. Jude Parish Retired.
Singarayar, Philip *o.m.i.* '64 (OAK) Oakland, CA Sacred Heart.
Singarayer, Arulraj S. '99 (MET) Parlin, NJ St. Bernadette; Indian Apostolate.
Singareddy, Shanthi Reddy '98 (NY) Bronx, NY St. Francis Xavier.
Singelyn, Robert K. '60 (DET) Monroe, MI St. Mary Retired.
Singer, Christopher J. '03 (E) Administrative Cabinet; College of Consultors; Promoter of Justice; Pennsylvania Conference on Inter–Church Cooperation; Chancellor; Members; Directors; Erie, PA Holy Rosary; Presbyteral Council; Adjutant Judicial Vicar.
Singer, Jerome C. '63 (DET) Detroit, MI Nativity of Our Lord.
Singer, Thomas J. *o.m.i.* '57 (BEL)[F] Belleville, IL Missionary Oblates of Mary Immaculate – St. Henry's Oblate Residence.
Singler, Rev. Msgr. Charles E. '84 (TOL) Office of Vocations: Priesthood and Consecrated Life; Office of Worship and Liturgical Music; Members; Toledo, OH Queen of the Most Holy Rosary Cathedral.
Singler, James E. '82 (CLV) Cuyahoga Falls, OH Immaculate Heart of Mary.
Singler, John P. '82 (CLV) Twinsburg, OH SS. Cosmas and Damian.
Singleton, Jeremiah '65 (MIA) Fort Lauderdale, FL St. Anthony; Archdiocesan Vocations Review Board.
Singleton, Rev. Msgr. William V. '50 (RVC) East Rockaway, NY St. Raymond's Retired.
Sinibaldi, Daniel J. '96 (MAN) Farmington, NH St. Peter; Rochester, NH St. Mary.
Sinisi, Daniel *t.o.r.* '66 (ALT) Ecumenical Minister; [A] Loretto, PA St. Francis University.
Sinkler, Michael '81 (LR) Paragould, AR St. Mary; Walnut Ridge, AR Immaculate Heart of Mary.
Sinnappan, Selvaraj '97 (TYL) Canton, TX St. Therese.
Sinnema, Paul G. *o.f.m.* '63 (PAT)[N] Butler, NJ St. Anthony Friary.
Sinnerud, James A. *s.j.* '72 (OM)[C] Omaha, NE Creighton Preparatory School.
Sinnott, Andrew R. '99 (SCR) Priests' Retirement Advisory Board.
Sinnott, James P. *m.m.* '60 (FgM) Maryknoll, NY MARYKNOLL.
Sinnott, Thomas G. '00 (SCR) Unassigned or Leave of Absence.
Sinor, Michael '88 (SD) San Diego, CA Saint Didacus Catholic Parish.
Sinski, Norbert J. *c.s.c.* '77 (FTW)[H] Notre Dame Congregation of Holy Cross, United States Province of Priests & Brothers.
Sinz, Eugene R. '60 (STL) Retired.
Siok, Slawomir *s.a.c.* '90 (BUF) Niagara Falls, NY St. John de La Salle.
Sioleti, Andrew *o.f.m.* (NY) Manhattan, NY U.S.V.A. Medical Center.
Sioleti, Andrew *i.v.dei.* '84 (MO) DEPARTMENT OF VETERANS AFFAIRS HOSPITALS AND CHAPLAINS.
Sioleti, Andrew *o.f.m. conv.* '89 (BRK) Veterans Affairs Extended Care Center, St. Albans, NY.
Sioli, Joseph E. '97 (PIT) Pittsburgh, PA St. Raphael.
Siordia, Oscar O. '06 (BWN) Brownsville, TX St. Joseph.
Sipe, Robert J. '59 (STP) Retired.
Sipitkowski, James A. '74 (SPR) On Sabbatical.
Siple, Donald *o.s.m.* '92 (STL) Affton, MO Seven Holy Founders.
Siple, William P. '92 (PIT) Natrona Heights, PA St. Joseph; Natrona Heights, PA Our Lady of the Most Blessed Sacrament.
Sippel, Bernard S. '65 (MIL) Franklin, WI St. James; Judges for First Instance; Judges for Second Instance Retired.
Sippel, Edward F. '47 (MIL) Retired.
Sipperly, Edward '54 (ALB) Retired.
Sipulski, Vianney *o.f.m.* '60 (MIL)[P] Burlington, WI Queen of Peace Friary.
Siracus, Aloysius *o.f.m.* '47 (PAT)[N] Ringwood, NJ Holy Name Friary, Inc.
Siracuse, Guy F. '67 (BUF) Retired.
Sirba, Joseph A. '87 (DUL) Longville, MN St. Edward; Longville, MN St. Paul.
Sirianni, Anthony M. '89 (MET) Edison, NJ St. Helena.
Sirianni, Klaus J. '78 (WDC) Washington, DC St. Stephen Martyr.
Sirianni, Louis A. '74 (ROC) Rochester, NY St. Mark; Judicial Vicar; Judicial Vicar; Judges.
Sirianni, Richard D. '78 (P) Portland, OR St. Thomas More; Ecumenical and Interreligious Affairs; Air National Guard Chaplains; Finance Council; College of Consultors.
Sirianni, Rev. Msgr. Sam A. '89 (TR) Office of Worship.
Sirianni, Sam A. '84 (TR) Holy Trinity.
Sirico, Robert '89 (KAL) Kalamazoo, MI St. Mary.
Siriwa, Avitus Kazi *a.j.* '00 (ALN) Fountain Hill, PA St. Ursula.
Sirois, Rev. Msgr. Joseph V. '51 (WOR) Retired.
Siroki, David '93 (PSC) On Duty Outside Diocese.
Sirolli, Francis A. *o.s.a.* '65 (PH)[Y] Bryn Mawr, PA Augustinians Friars (O.S.A.); Bryn Mawr, PA Our Mother of Good Counsel.
Siroskey, Paul Larry '80 (DET) Waterford, MI St. Benedict.
Sirvent, Francisco '88 (PCE) On Duty Outside the Diocese.
Siry, Philip L. '62 (WIL) Retired.
Sis, Rev. Msgr. Michael J. '86 (AUS) Moderator of the Curia; College of Consultors; Associate Directors; Vicar General; Ex Officio; Finance Council; Clergy and Religious.
Sisk, Robert *t.o.r.* '61 (BAL) Baltimore, MD St. Elizabeth of Hungary.
Sison, Alden J. '87 (LA) Panorama City, CA St. Genevieve.
Sison, Dave Thomas N. '04 (NEW) Newark, NJ St. Anthony's.
Sison, Ronnie '03 (VEN) Naples, FL St. William.
Sistare, Juniper *c.f.r.* '03 (PRO) Greenville, RI St. Philip.
Sisul, Paul *c.m.* '72 (CHI)[N] Chicago DePaul Vincentian Residence.
Sitar, Marek '03 (CHI) Chicago, IL St. Thomas More.
Sitar, Richard T. '79 (GLD) Retired.
Sitko, Joseph S. '68 (SCR) Waymart, PA St. Mary.
Sittinger, Edward *s.t.* '77 (WDC)[O] Adelphi, MD Father Judge Missionary Cenacle.
Sitzmann, Eugene E. '62 (SC) Retired.
Sitzmann, Richard A. '62 (SC) Sioux City, IA St. Boniface; Mercy Medical Center; [C] Sioux City, IA Mercy Medical Center – Sioux City Retired.
Siu, Peter Kin Chung *s.j.* '93 (SJ) Santa Clara, CA Chinese Catholic Community; [B] Santa Clara, CA Jesuit Community.
Siu, Robert K.C. '54 (CHY) Lander, WY Holy Rosary Retired.
Siurys, Petraj *l.i.c.* '91 (LIT) Pontifical Lithuanian College of St. Casimir.
Siva, Renier C. '05 (SAC) Presbyteral Council; Portola, CA Holy Family; Vicars Forane.
Sivalon, John C. *m.m.* '65 (NY)[DD] Maryknoll Maryknoll Fathers and Brothers.
Sivillo, Rev. Msgr. Nicholas W. '64 (BRK) Middle Village, NY St. Margaret Retired.
Sivinskyi, Vasyl '92 (PHU) Baltimore, MD St. Michael's.
Siviramatu, Antony (NY) Bronx, NY St. Gabriel.
Siwek, Daniel S. '73 (CHI)[A] Mundelein, IL University of St. Mary of the Lake/Mundelein Seminary.
Sizemore, David W. '96 (COL) Sunbury, OH St. John Neumann.
Sizing, Theodore C. '55 (SY) Retired.
Skagen, Robert '70 (PHX) Priests' Assurance Association Retired.
Skaj, John P. *c.s.sp.* '63 (PIT)[O] Bethel Park, PA The Spiritan Center.
Skalsky, Ted A. '72 (DOD) Dodge City, KS Cathedral of Our Lady of Guadalupe Catholic Church of Dodge City, Kansas; College of Consultors; Deans.
Skarbek, Richard *m.s.a.* '86 (NOR)[G] Cromwell, CT Society of the Missionaries of the Holy Apostles.
Skaria, Antony *c.f.i.c.* '96 (STP)[J] St. Paul, MN Congregation of the Sons of the Immaculate Conception; Regions Medical Center.
Skarich, William '99 (DUL) Babbitt, MN St. Pius X; Ely, MN St. Anthony.
Skechus, Francis E. *s.j.* '75 (PH)[Y] Loyola Center and Manresa Hall.
Skeehan, William K. '60 (TLS) Retired.
Skehan, James W. *s.j.* '54 (BO)[U] Weston, MA Campion Health Center, Inc.
Skehan, John A. '52 (PMB) Retired.
Skehan, John R. '86 (PRT) Kittery, ME Parish of the Ascension of the Lord; Vicars Forane.
Skehan, Rev. Msgr. Martin O. '44 (YAK) Moses Lake, WA Our Lady of Fatima Retired.
Skeldon, John Robert '00 (FWT) Graduate Studies.
Skelly, Francis G. *c.ss.r.* '72 (NY) Bronx, NY Immaculate Conception.
Skelly, Rev. Msgr. John J. '53 (RVC) Manhasset, NY St. Mary's; [N] Amityville, NY St. Pius X Residence Retired.
Skelly, Rev. Msgr. Richard J. '54 (PH) Aston, PA St. Joseph Retired.
Skelskey, David A. *s.j.* '80 (FgM) Watertown, MA Society of Jesus.
Skelton, Paul H. '64 (SFD) Villa Grove, IL St. Michael; Villa Grove, IL Sacred Heart.
Skenderovic, Ivan '76 (BUF) Niagara Falls, NY St. Raphael.
Skeris, Robert A. '61 (MIL) Retired.
Skerl, Alphonse '55 (GRY) East Chicago, IN Holy Trinity.
Skertich, Mark J. '77 (PIT) Pittsburgh, PA Sacred Heart.
Skiba, Michal *s.ch.* '06 (JOL) Lombard, IL Divine Mercy Polish Mission.
Skiba, Walter F. '56 (SCR) Retired.
Skidmore, Harold G. *c.m.* '50 (PH)[Y].
Skillin, Rev. Msgr. Harmon '60 (STO) Personnel Board; Vicar for Priests; Diamond Springs, CA Retired.
Skillingstad, M. Delmar '60 (SPK)[B] Spokane, WA Gonzaga University.
Skillman, David P. '09 (STL) St. Charles, MO St. Elizabeth Ann Seton.
Skindeleski, Rev. Canon Thomas J. '71 (PMB) Delray Beach, FL St. Vincent Ferrer; Vicars Forane; Ex Officio; Knights of Columbus.
Skinner, Charles D. '53 (E) Retired.
Skirtich, John W. '90 (PIT) Pittsburgh, PA St. Maurice; College of Consultors; Clergy Personnel Board; Priest Council.
Skitzki, Francis P. '70 (SCR) Retired.
Sklar, Louis E. '01 (ALX) Elected Members; Ferriday, LA St. Patrick.
Skluzacek, Michael C. '80 (STP) New Brighton, MN St. John the Baptist; Regional Vicars.
Skok, Charles '52 (SPK) Spokane Valley, WA St. John Vianney Retired.
Skoneki, Rev. Msgr. William J. '87 (MOB) Auburn, AL St. Michael; [I] Auburn, AL Auburn University Newman Center; Archdiocesan Consultors.
Skonezny, Raymond '61 (ORG) Retired.
Skonseng, Rev. Msgr. Dennis A. '82 (FAR) Valley City, ND St. Catherine's Church of Valley City; Diocesan College of Consultors.
Skornia, Bernard L. '57 (SAG) Retired.
Skorup, Ildephonse *o.f.m.* '59 (JOL)[L] Joliet, IL St. John the Baptist Friary.
Skowron, Greg '89 (JOL) Frankfort, IL St. Anthony.
Skrobutt, Andrew '06 (RCK) Saint Charles, IL St. John Neumann.
Skrocki, Rt. Rev. Michael K. '00 (NTN) Danbury, CT St. Ann; Judges; Presbyteral Council; Sophia Press.
Skrocki, Michael K. '00 (PBR) Pro–Synodal Judges.
Skrogky, Michael '00 (BGP) Judges.
Skrypek, Gregory A. '70 (STP) Retired.
Skrzypek, Jaroslaw Z. '04 (SPC) Caruthersville, MO Sacred Heart; New Madrid, MO Immaculate Conception.
Skrzypiec, Andrzej '82 (SLC) Salt Lake City, UT Saint Ambrose LLC 214; Team; Priests' Personnel Board.
Skublics, Mate '09 (NEW) Newark, NJ St. Benedict's.
Skudlarek, William *o.s.b.* '64 (SCL)[I] Collegeville St. John's Abbey, of the Order of St. Benedict.
Skufca, Ronald J. '79 (MO) Army National Guard Chaplains.
Skupien, Rev. Msgr. Francis M. '51 (BUF)[N] Lackawanna, NY Bishop Head Residence Retired.
Skura, Mark David *o.f.m.conv.* '82 (BUF)[O] Hamburg, NY Immaculate Conception Convent; [D] Athol Springs, NY St. Francis High School; [N] Athol

Springs, NY St. Francis of Assisi Friary.
Skurla, Anthony *o.f.m.* '54 (PSC)[A] Sybertsville, PA Holy Dormition Friary.
Skurla, Robert J. '56 (PSC) Retired.
Skurla, Robert '56 (BRK)[O] Queens Village, NY Queen of Peace Residence Retired.
Slaby, Joseph A. *m.m.* '66 (FgM) Maryknoll, NY MARYKNOLL.
Slaby, Stanislaw *c.ss.r.* '99 (MET) Manville, NJ Sacred Heart of Jesus; Manville, NJ Christ the King.
Sladicka, Phillip J. '76 (SCR) Avoca, PA St. Mary's; Cursillo Movement; Avoca, PA Queen of the Apostles Parish.
Slampak, John A. '66 (RCK) North Aurora, IL Blessed Sacrament Catholic Church; Parish Services and Directors.
Slate, William '55 (SEA) Retired.
Slater, Dennis '62 (SY) Retired.
Slater, William T. '77 (RVC) New Hyde Park, NY Notre Dame.
Slatterie, Leo '51 (LAV) Retired.
Slattery, Rev. Msgr. John F. '57 (COS)[F] Colorado Springs, CO Sisters of St. Francis of Perpetual Adoration Retired.
Slattery, Kevin '86 (JKS) Gluckstadt, MS St. Joseph; Diocesan Judges; Canton, MS Sacred Heart; Diocesan Consultors; Adjutant Judicial Vicar; Continuing Formation Committee.
Slattery, Kirk '08 (COS) Cheyenne Wells, CO Sacred Heart; Presbyteral Council.
Slattery, Rev. Msgr. Michael J. '62 (LA) Santa Clarita, CA Blessed Kateri Tekakwitha.
Slattery, Michael J. *o.s.a.* '77 (CHI)[N] Chicago, IL The Augustinians–Provincialate; Chicago, IL St. Rita of Cascia; Olympia Fields, IL.
Slaughter, Martin '85 (LA) Los Angeles, CA St. Gerard Majella.
Slaven, Donald J. '67 (SC) Retired.
Sledesky, Stephen M. '93 (HRT) Manchester, CT St. Bridget; Manchester, CT St. Bartholomew.
Sledz, Stanley V. '69 (STP) Retired.
Sledziona, John S. *c.m.* '70 (MAN) Chicago, IL National Organization for Continuing Education of Roman Catholic Clergy, Inc. (NOCERCC); Office of Clergy Formation; Pelham, NH St. Patrick; Presbyteral Council.
Sleiman, Elias *m.l.m.* '98 (OLL) Los Angeles, CA Our Lady of Mt. Lebanon–St. Peter Maronite Catholic Cathedral; [A] Houston, TX The Congregation of Maronite Lebanese Missionaries; Procurator/Advocate; Office of Young Adult Ministry.
Slepicka, Rev. Msgr. Joseph J. '55 (DUB) Retired.
Slesinski, Robert F. '76 (PSC) Leave of Absence.
Slevin, Henry '62 (WDC) Washington, DC St. Francis de Sales; On Duty Outside the Archdiocese.
Slevin, Patrick C. '57 (MIA) Retired.
Sleyman, Kenneth C. *m.m.* '90 (FgM) Maryknoll, NY MARYKNOLL.
Slight, William *m.s.* (ORL) Orlando, FL Blessed Trinity.
Sliney, Michael *l.c.* '98 (WDC)[O] Potomac, MD Legionaries of Christ.
Slinger, Rev. Msgr. Joseph T. '70 (NEW) Fair Lawn, NJ St. Anne's Retired.
Slipe, Rev. Msgr. Robert H. '73 (NEW) Cedar Grove, NJ St. Catherine of Siena.
Slisz, Charles E. '71 (BUF) Tonawanda, NY St. Christopher.
Sliwinski, Philip '97 (GR) Hart, MI St. Joseph's; On Special Assignment.
Sliwinski, Richard (NOR) Middletown, CT St. Mary of Czestochowa.
Sloan, Daniel '82 (MET) Monmouth Junction, NJ St. Cecilia; College of Consultors.
Sloan, James D. *c.pp.s.* '62 (OAK)[L] Berkeley, CA Society of the Precious Blood (Kansas City Province).
Slobig, John '90 (PHX) Sun City, AZ St. Clement of Rome Roman Catholic Parish.
Sloboda, Michael J. *m.m.* '85 (FgM) Maryknoll, NY MARYKNOLL.
Slobogin, Roland D. '73 (PH) Drexel Hill, PA St. Charles Borromeo.
Slobogin, Roland D. '73 (PH) Deans; Deans.
Slodowski, Bruno '68 (MIL) Retired.
Slomba, Eugene S. '64 (BUF) Retired.
Slominski, Adam *s.ch.* '07 (JOL) Lombard, IL Divine Mercy Polish Mission.
Slominski, Fabian B. '48 (DET) Retired.
Slominski, Leon '58 (SCL) Retired.
Slomski, Joseph P. '53 (WCH) Retired.
Slon, Thomas R. *s.j.* '90 (FgM)[DD] New York, NY "America;" Residence and publication office of the America Press; [DD] New York, NY Society of Jesus, New York Province; New York, NY; New York, NY Society of Jesus.
Sloneker, Patrick L. '97 (CIN) Botkins, OH Immaculate Conception; Botkins, OH St. Lawrence; Wapakoneta, OH St. Joseph.
Slota, Frederick V. '53 (PRO) Retired.
Slovacek, Emil C. '54 (DAL) Retired.
Slovikovski, John J. '96 (ALT) On Duty Outside the Diocese.
Slovikovski, John J. '96 (BAL)[A] Baltimore, MD St. Mary's Seminary and University; [Q] Baltimore, MD St. Mary's Seminary & University.
Slovikovski, John (WDC)[A] Washington, DC Theological College of the Catholic University of America.
Slowiak, Allan L. '73 (LC) Rothschild, WI St. Mark; Deans.
Slowik, Joseph S. '72 (RIC) Retired.
Slowinski, Jerome '90 (DET) Sterling Heights, MI St. Jane Frances de Chantal; Judges.
Slowinski, Thomas F. '81 (DET) Navy Reserve Chaplains; Rochester, MI St. Andrew; Absent on Leave.
Sloyan, Gerard S. '44 (TR) Retired.
Slubecky, Rev. Msgr. David S. '73 (BUF) Finance Council; Consultors, College of; Council of Priests; Vicars General; Moderator of the Curia; The Diocese of Buffalo, N.Y.; Buffalo, NY St. Joseph Cathedral; [S] Buffalo, NY St. Joseph Investment Fund, Inc.
Slusser, Michael S. '66 (STP) Retired.
Slusz, Michael J. '03 (HRT) Naugatuck, CT St. Francis of Assisi; Cheshire–Naugatuck Deanery.
Smail, Brian E. *o.f.m.* '99 (NY)[DD] New York, NY The Franciscan Vocation Ministry of Holy Name Province; New York, NY St. Francis of Assisi.
Smaistrla, Benjamin '72 (GAL) Houston, TX St. Ambrose.
Smalarz, James A. '04 (DET) Monroe, MI St. John The Baptist.
Small, Andrew *o.m.i.* '99 (WDC)[O] Washington, DC Oblate Community.
Small, Bryan D. '02 (ATL) Decatur, GA Sts. Peter and Paul; Special or Other Archdiocesan Assignment.
Small, James *c.ss.r.* '54 (HBG)[G] Ephrata, PA St. Clement's Mission House Retired.
Small, Jeffrey '93 (PEO) On Leave of Absence.
Small, Vincent (PH)[A] Wynnewood, PA Theological Seminary of St. Charles Borromeo, Overbrook.
Small, William T. '77 (PH) Retired.
Small, William T. '77 (WIL) Lewes, DE St. Jude The Apostle Retired.
Smar, Michael J. '69 (Y) Retired.
Smarsh, Charles F. '64 (NY) On Duty Outside the Archdiocese.
Smart, Raymond W. '70 (PH) Pennsburg, PA St. Philip Neri Retired.
Smedile, Anselm *o.s.b.* '03 (MAN)[A] Manchester, NH St. Anselm Abbey Seminary; [K] Manchester, NH St. Anselm Abbey.
Smedley, Tyler '11 (SPK) Walla Walla, WA Assumption of the Blessed Virgin Mary; Walla Walla, WA St. Francis of Assisi; Walla Walla, WA St. Patrick.
Smegal, John T. '77 (SPR) Amherst, MA St. Brigid's; Continuing Education for Priests.
Smegelsky, John J. '66 (SY) Retired.
Smeltzer, Stuart M. '96 (WCH) Wichita, KS St. Joseph; Defenders of the Bond; Promoters of Justice.
Smereka, John '83 (SJP) Carnegie, PA Holy Trinity; Presbyters.
Smet, Joachim *o.carm.* '42 (WDC)[B] Washington, DC Whitefriars Hall.
Smet, Leroy R. '59 (GB) Retired.
Smetanka, Gary T. '82 (DET) Grosse Pointe, MI Our Lady Star of the Sea.
Smialek, Jeffery *o.carm.* '07 (JOL)[L] Joliet, IL St. Elias Carmelites.
Smialek, Jeffrey *o.carm.* '07 (TUC)[E] Tucson, AZ Carmelite Priory.
Smialowski, Raymond S. '82 (HRT) Bristol, CT St. Stanislaus.
Smiech, Charles *o.f.m.* '81 (CIN)[N] Cincinnati St. Francis Seraph Friary.
Smiga, George '75 (CLV) Willoughby Hills, OH St. Noel.
Smigiel, Walter J. '50 (PBL) Retired.
Smilanic, Daniel A. '73 (CHI) Park Ridge, IL St. Paul of the Cross; Canonical Services; Adjutant Judicial Vicar; Judges.
Smiley, Douglas J. '00 (R) Morehead City, NC St. Egbert.
Smit, Gerard C. '50 (LKC) Retired.
Smith, Alberic *o.f.m.* '58 (SPK) Spokane, WA St. Francis of Assisi.
Smith, Albert J. *o.s.f.s.* '65 (PH)[Y] Wyndmoor, PA Villa de Sales Oblate Residence.
Smith, Rt. Rev. Alexei R. '87 (LA) El Segundo, CA St. Andrew; Ecumenical and Interreligious Affairs; Spirituality Commission.
Smith, Rt. Rev. Alexei '87 (NTN) El Segundo, CA St. Paul; Protopresbyters; College of Eparchial Consultors; Presbyteral Council; Continuing Education of Clergy Office; Fredericksburg, VA Catholic Association of Diocesan Ecumenical and Interreligious Officers (CADEIO).
Smith, Rev. Msgr. Alfred E. '56 (BAL) Williamsport, MD St. Augustine Retired.
Smith, Andrew Charles '09 (CHI) Chicago, IL St. Ailbe.
Smith, Andrew T. *o.s.b.* '64 (PAT)[N] Morristown, NJ St. Mary's Abbey.
Smith, Anthony J. '11 (HRT) Guilford, CT St. George.
Smith, Arthur J. '71 (BUF) Buffalo Fire Department and Erie County Emergency Services; Hamburg, NY St. Mary of the Lake.
Smith, Bernard '90 (SP)[J] Tampa, FL St. Joseph's Hospital, Inc.
Smith, Brian P. '03 (BO) Foxborough, MA St. Mary.
Smith, Brian '98 (SJ) On Leave of Absence.
Smith, Charles C. '06 (ARL) Notaries; Chantilly, VA St. Veronica.
Smith, Charles D. '65 (PH) Huntingdon Valley, PA St. Albert the Great Retired.
Smith, Charles F. *s.v.d.* '88 (MO) DEPARTMENT OF VETERANS AFFAIRS HOSPITALS AND CHAPLAINS.
Smith, Christopher L. '03 (FTW) Goshen, IN St. John the Evangelist.
Smith, Christopher '78 (ORG) Vicar for Priests; Priests' Relief; Ministry to Priests; Special Assignment.
Smith, Christopher '05 (CHR) Taylors, SC Prince of Peace.
Smith, Clifford G. '96 (DAL) Plano, TX St. Mark the Evangelist.
Smith, Craig '05 (PT) Fort Walton Beach, FL St. Mary Church.
Smith, D. Stephen '73 (MAD) McFarland, WI Christ the King.
Smith, Daniel H. '10 (SFS) Yankton, SD Sacred Heart.
Smith, Daniel P. '99 (VEN) Bradenton, FL Our Lady of the Angels.
Smith, Daniel *o.carm.* '46 (JOL)[L] Darien Carmelite Provincial Office.
Smith, David A. *m.m.* '85 (NY)[HH] Maryknoll, NY Maryknoll Fathers and Brothers Apostolic Trust; [DD] Maryknoll Maryknoll Fathers and Brothers.
Smith, David L. *s.j.* '85 (DM)[J] Griswold, IA Creighton University Retreat Center.
Smith, David L. *s.j.* '85 (OM)[J] Omaha, NE Jesuit Community at Creighton University.
Smith, David W. '64 (STP)[C] St. Paul, MN University of St. Thomas; Censores Librorum Retired.
Smith, David '82 (MIA) Hialeah, FL San Lazaro.
Smith, Dean M. '99 (RCK) Stockton, IL Holy Cross.
Smith, Dennis '75 (FWT) Keller, TX St. Elizabeth Ann Seton; Presbyteral Council.
Smith, Dick (JOL)[D] Naperville, IL All Saints Catholic Academy.
Smith, Douglas *c.s.c.* '76 (FTW)[A] Notre Dame, IN Moreau Seminary.
Smith, Edmund *o.s.b.* '65 (P)[L] St. Benedict, OR Mt. Angel Abbey.
Smith, Edward J. '65 (BRK) Retired.
Smith, Edward J. '01 (CLV) Sheffield, OH St. Teresa of Avila.
Smith, Edward P. '82 (CIN) Cincinnati, OH Our Lord, Christ the King; Cincinnati, OH St. Stephen.
Smith, Elmer W. '50 (CIN) Retired.
Smith, Eugene M. *o.s.m.* '88 (STL) Affton, MO Seven Holy Founders.
Smith, Eugene P. '50 (LC) Boyd, WI Sacred Heart of Jesus–St. Joseph Retired.
Smith, F. Harold '50 (L) Retired.
Smith, Rev. Msgr. Francis J. '67 (ELP) El Paso, TX St. Raphael; Vicars General; Ex Officio Members; Advocates; Finance Council; Priests' Personnel Advisory Committee; Priests' Retirement and Disability Plan; [J] El Paso, TX Knights of Columbus; [J] El Paso, TX Knights of the Holy Sepulchre; [J] El Paso, TX Ladies of the Holy Sepulchre.
Smith, Francis J. *s.j.* '52 (DET)[K] Clarkston, MI Colombiere Center.
Smith, Francis R. *s.j.* '70 (SJ)[B] Santa Clara, CA Jesuit Community.
Smith, Gabriel J. '82 (CHR) Charleston, SC St. Joseph; Office of Tribunal.
Smith, Gary N. *s.j.* '71 (FgM)[L] Portland Jesuit Provincial Office (Society of Jesus, Oregon Prov.); Portland, OR Society of Jesus.
Smith, Gene F. '84 (CHI) Oak Lawn, IL St. Linus.
Smith, Gene F. (CHI) Retired.
Smith, Geoffrey C. '74 (HRT) Hamden, CT St. Rita; New Haven, CT Yale–New Haven Hospital; Special and other Archdiocesan Assignment.
Smith, George T. (ROC)[K] Rochester, NY Basilian Fathers.
Smith, Gerald S. '64 (PH) Retired.
Smith, Gerald '65 (AUS) Retired.
Smith, Herbert F. *s.j.* '62 (PH)[Y] Loyola Center and Manresa Hall.
Smith, Howard C. *s.m.* '72 (WDC)[O] Washington, DC Marist Center.
Smith, Ignatius E. *o.f.m.* '56 (NY) Callicoon, NY Holy Cross.
Smith, Ignatius *o.s.b.* '54 (KCK)[I] Atchison, KS St. Benedict's Abbey.
Smith, Jacob–Matthew *o.f.m.* (WDC)[O] Washington, DC Franciscan Monastery USA Inc.; Washington, DC.
Smith, James A.D. '56 (PAT)[Q] Chester, NJ Nazareth Village Retired.
Smith, James B. '85 (WIL) Hockessin, DE St. Mary of the Assumption.
Smith, James E. *c.m.* '61 (PH)[Y].
Smith, James F. *s.j.* '62 (SY)[Q] Syracuse, NY Jesuits at LeMoyne, Inc.

Smith, James G. *o.praem.* '77 (ORG)[D] Silverado, CA St. Michael's Preparatory School; [I] Silverado, CA Norbertine Fathers of Orange Inc.
Smith, James H. '63 (HRT) Retired.
Smith, James R. '67 (SC) Retired.
Smith, James T. '65 (COL) Columbus, OH St. Matthias.
Smith, Johannes Michael Mary *f.i.* '04 (SY)[Q] Maine, NY Mount St. Francis Hermitage, Inc.; [S] Maine, NY Mount St. Francis Hermitage, Inc.
Smith, Rev. Msgr. John J. '59 (FR) Retired.
Smith, John K. '04 (LUB) Olton, TX St. Peter the Apostle.
Smith, John *s.s.c.* (CHI)[N] Chicago, IL Korean Catholic Center.
Smith, John '04 (LUB) Presbyteral Council.
Smith, John *s.s.c.* '62 (OM)[J] St. Columbans Missionary Society of St. Columban.
Smith, Johnnie B. '10 (MEM) Germantown, TN Our Lady Of Perpetual Help.
Smith, Joseph A. '96 (SAV) Richmond Hill, GA St. Anne.
Smith, Joseph J. *s.j.* '57 (FgM) New York, NY Society of Jesus.
Smith, Rev. Msgr. Joseph P.T. '60 (ALN) Orefield, PA St. Joseph The Worker.
Smith, Rev. Msgr. K. Bartholomew '98 (WDC) Silver Spring, MD St. Bernadette.
Smith, Kenneth G. '84 (HBG) Abbottstown, PA Immaculate Heart of Mary.
Smith, Rev. Msgr. Kenneth J. '64 (NY) New York, NY St. Catherine of Genoa; Judges.
Smith, Kevin M. '88 (RVC) Oyster Bay, NY St. Dominic's; Nassau County, Fire Chiefs, Council of; Chaplain of the Nassau County Fire Services.
Smith, Lawrence C. *s.j.* '82 (BO)[U] Boston The Society of Jesus of New England–Provincial Offices.
Smith, Lawrence R. '76 (PIT) Pittsburgh, PA Most Holy Name of Jesus; Pittsburgh, PA St. Aloysius.
Smith, Leland J. '53 (WIN) Retired.
Smith, Leo Joseph '06 (VEN) Sarasota, FL Incarnation.
Smith, Leonard A. '91 (WH) Berkeley Springs, WV St. Vincent de Paul.
Smith, LeRoy J. '78 (BRK) Retired.
Smith, Leroy '78 (SPR) Pittsfield, MA Berkshire Medical Center.
Smith, Lester E. '75 (SY) Sherburne, NY St. Malachy; New Berlin, NY St. Theresa of the Infant Jesus.
Smith, Louis Maximilian M. *f.i.* '08 (FR)[F] New Bedford, MA Marian Friary of Our Lady, Queen of the Seraphic Order.
Smith, M. Christopher '83 (JC) On Duty Outside the Diocese.
Smith, M. Christopher '83 (KC) Lexington, MO Immaculate Conception.
Smith, Mark Leo '05 (WDC) Pomfret, MD St. Joseph.
Smith, Mark S. '96 (JC) Westphalia, MO St. Anthony of Padua; Ministry to Priests; Westphalia, MO St. Joseph; Judges; Priestly and Religious Vocations Committee; Senators.
Smith, Martin L. *o.s.a.* '77 (PH)[Y] Villanova, PA Provincial Offices of the Order of St. Augustine, Province of St. Thomas of Villanova; [Y] Villanova, PA St. Thomas Monastery.
Smith, Michael B. '74 (CLV) Akron, OH Immaculate Conception.
Smith, Michael H. '66 (SAV) Retired.
Smith, Michael M. '77 (HEL) Retired.
Smith, Michael N. *s.j.* '67 (PBL) Fruita, CO Sacred Heart.
Smith, Michael R. '00 (SP) Lecanto, FL St. Scholastica Church; Vicars Forane.
Smith, Michael S. '92 (NOR) Hebron, CT The Church of the Holy Family; Members; Continuing Education and Formation Commission for the Clergy; Advisory Board.
Smith, Nicholas P. '65 (PRO)[O] Providence St. John Vianney Residence Retired.
Smith, Nicholas W. '94 (STL) St. Louis, MO St. Joan of Arc.
Smith, Norman '50 (GLP) Retired.
Smith, Patrick A. '90 (WDC) Washington, DC St. Augustine.
Smith, Patrick '67 (PHX) Scottsdale, AZ Scottsdale Healthcare Osborn; Scottsdale, AZ Our Lady of Perpetual Help Roman Catholic Parish Retired.
Smith, Patrick '03 (JKS) Retired.
Smith, Paul F. '73 (CLV) Thompson, OH St. Patrick.
Smith, Paul O. '64 (COL) Retired.
Smith, Paul '59 (ALB) Altamont, NY St. Lucy/St. Bernadette; Albany, NY St. Francis of Assisi Parish Retired.
Smith, Paul '10 (PT) Panama City Beach, FL St. Bernadette.
Smith, Peter '01 (P) Adjutant Judicial Vicars; College of Consultors.
Smith, Peter '01 (P) Portland, OR St. Rose of Lima; [Q] Portland, OR Brotherhood of the People of Praise; Judges.
Smith, Philip A. '11 (TOL) Graduate Studies.
Smith, Philip T. *o.praem.* '84 (ORG) Costa Mesa, CA St. John the Baptist.
Smith, R. Douglas *o.s.f.s.* '62 (WIL)[J] Childs, MD Retirement and Assisted Care Facility Retired.
Smith, R. Leroy '54 (COV) Retired.
Smith, Ramon *o.f.m.* '53 (SFE)[H] Albuquerque, NM The Province of Our Lady of Guadalupe.
Smith, Richard A. '56 (MAN) Retired.
Smith, Richard L. '76 (JOL) Naperville, IL St. Elizabeth Seton; Judges.
Smith, Richard P. *m.m.* '76 (NY)[DD] Maryknoll Maryknoll Fathers and Brothers Retired.
Smith, Richard '98 (FRS) Laton, CA Shrine of Our Lady of Fatima.
Smith, Richard '84 (JKS) Booneville, MS St. Francis of Assisi; Corinth, MS St. James.
Smith, Richard '00 (WIL) Ocean City, MD St. Luke and St. Andrew.
Smith, Richard '09 (PH) Morton, PA Our Lady of Perpetual Help.
Smith, Rev. Msgr. Robert J. '70 (E)[K] Erie, PA Bishop Michael J. Murphy Residence for Retired Priests; Vicars General; Northern Vicariate; Administrative Cabinet; College of Consultors; Ex Officios; Priest Personnel Board; Members; Judicial Vicar; Matrimonial Judges; Directors; Clergy Personnel; Presbyteral Council.
Smith, Robert J. '55 (OM) Retired.
Smith, Robert J. '83 (RVC) Setauket, NY St. James; Censors of Books; Priests' Personnel Assignment Board.
Smith, Robert V. '61 (CAM) Liaison with Retired Priests Retired.
Smith, Robert '53 (ROC) Retired.
Smith, Robert '97 (FAR) Lidgerwood, ND Sts. Peter & Paul Church of Cayuga; Geneseo, ND St. Martin's Church of Geneseo; Lidgerwood, ND St. Boniface Church of Lidgerwood.
Smith, Roger J. '73 (SEA) Morton, WA Sacred Heart.
Smith, Rev. Msgr. Roger R. '76 (CC) Presbyteral Council; Judges; Corpus Christi, TX St. Patrick.
Smith, Ronald T. '73 (HRT) New Britain, CT St. Andrew; New Britain, CT St. John the Evangelist; New Britain, CT The Hospital of Central Connecticut (New Britain General Hospital); Special and other Archdiocesan Assignment.
Smith, Ronald *o.f.m.cap.* '64 (MIL)[B] Mount Calvary, WI St. Lawrence Seminary; [P] Mount Calvary, WI St. Lawrence Friary.
Smith, Russell E. '80 (RIC) Unassigned.
Smith, S. Douglas *c.s.c.* '76 (FTW)[H] Notre Dame Congregation of Holy Cross, United States Province of Priests & Brothers; [B] University of Notre Dame Du Lac; [H] Notre Dame, IN Holy Cross Community, Corby Hall, University of Notre Dame.
Smith, Rev. Msgr. Sherrill '55 (SAT)[K] San Antonio, TX Padua Place Retired.
Smith, Simon E. *s.j.* '61 (WOR)[N] Worcester, MA Jesuits of the Holy Cross, Inc.
Smith, Stephen *o.p.* '58 (R) Ex Officio; Defender of the Bond; [F] Raleigh, NC Dominican Priory; Vicar for Priests.
Smith, Terrance W. '73 (CIN) Judges; Cincinnati, OH Good Shepherd.
Smith, Terrence T. *t.o.r.* '73 (ALT) Altoona, PA Our Lady of Mt. Carmel.
Smith, Thomas A. '83 (L) Louisville, KY Holy Spirit; College of Consultors; Ex Officio.
Smith, Thomas A. *o.f.m.conv.* '79 (LSC)[D] Mesilla Park, NM Holy Cross Retreat and Friary.
Smith, Thomas E. *s.j.* '74 (NY)[DD] Loyola Hall, Jesuit Community.
Smith, Thomas E. '51 (PIT) Retired.
Smith, Thomas F. *o.c.s.o.* '58 (ATL)[F] Conyers, GA The Monastery of the Holy Spirit.
Smith, Rev. Msgr. Thomas H. '57 (HBG) Lancaster, PA St. Joseph; Cursillo Movement.
Smith, Thomas J. '60 (LC)[H] La Crosse, WI Holy Cross (Seminary) Diocesan Center Retired.
Smith, Thomas J. '82 (NOR) On Duty Outside the Diocese.
Smith, Thomas W. *c.s.c.* '72 (FTW)[H] Notre Dame Congregation of Holy Cross, United States Province of Priests & Brothers.
Smith, Thomas W. *c.s.c.* '72 (FgM) New Rochelle, NY Eastern Brothers Province.
Smith, Thomas (BAL)[B] Emmitsburg, MD Mount Saint Mary's University.
Smith, Vernon (DM) Shenandoah, IA St. Mary; Hamburg, IA St. Mary.
Smith, Vincent E. *o.s.f.s.* (CHL) High Point, NC Immaculate Heart of Mary.
Smith, Rev. Msgr. Vincent J. '55 (HBG) Mechanicsburg, PA Saint Katharine Drexel Retired.
Smith, Vincent Leo '66 (DEN) Retired.
Smith, W. Andrew '80 (LR) Jacksonville, AR St. Jude the Apostle.
Smith, Walter J. *s.j.* '72 (BO)[U] Boston The Society of Jesus of New England–Provincial Offices.
Smith, Walter J. *s.j.* '72 (NY)[DD] New York Jesuit Provincial's Office.
Smith, Wilfred T. '56 (CLV) Mentor, OH St. Mary of the Assumption Retired.
Smith, William A. '74 (BRK) South Ozone Park, NY St. Anthony of Padua.
Smith, William A. '03 (CLV) Barberton, OH St. Augustine.
Smith, William G. '79 (BRK) St. Albans, NY Our Lady of Light Roman Catholic Church.
Smith, William J. '47 (PH) Retired.
Smith, William J. '81 (MET) Port Reading, NJ St. Anthony of Padua; Woodbridge, NJ Our Lady of Mount Carmel.
Smith, William '74 (DEN) Glenwood Springs, CO St. Stephen.
Smith, Wilton S. '58 (SFR)[K] San Rafael, CA Nazareth House of San Rafael, Inc. Retired.
Smith–Soucier, Martin D. '79 (STU) On Duty Outside the Diocese; DEPARTMENT OF VETERANS AFFAIRS HOSPITALS AND CHAPLAINS.
Smith–Sourcier, Martin D. (ROC) Canandaigua, NY Veteran's Hospital.
Smithson, Thomas *s.s.s.* '02 (CHI) Chicago, IL Blessed Sacrament.
Smits, Ken *o.f.m.cap.* '64 (MIL)[P] Mount Calvary, WI St. Lawrence Friary; [P] Mount Calvary, WI St. Felix Friary.
Smits, Lee '71 (CHI)[J] Maywood, IL Loyola University Medical Center.
Smolarski, Dennis C. *s.j.* '79 (SJ)[B] Santa Clara, CA Jesuit Community.
Smolenski, Stanley '68 (HRT) On Duty Outside the Archdiocese.
Smolenski, Stanley *s.p.m.a.* '68 (CHR) Marian Programs; [J] Kingstree, SC Shrine of Our Lady of South Carolina–Our Lady of Joyful Hope.
Smoley, Rudolph F. '69 (PIT) Absent on Sick Leave; [M] Pittsburgh, PA St. John Vianney Manor.
Smolich, Thomas H. *s.j.* '86 (FgM) Washington, DC National Headquarters; Washington, DC; Washington, DC Jesuit Conference, Inc.
Smolich, Thomas H. *s.j.* '86 (WDC)[X] Washington, DC Jesuit Conference, Inc.; [O] Washington, DC Leonard Neale House.
Smolik, Peter K. '02 (BGP) Ridgefield, CT St. Mary.
Smolinski, Joseph J. '48 (NY) Retired.
Smolko, John F. '57 (BGP) On Duty Outside the Diocese Retired.
Smolley, Robert '82 (STF) Manchester, NH Protection of B.V.M.
Smuda, Alfred J. *o.s.f.s.* '66 (FgM) Wilmington, DE OBLATES OF ST. FRANCIS DE SALES MISSIONS.
Smullen, Martin J. '82 (NO) Reserve, LA St. Peter.
Smutelovic, Peter '95 (NEW) On Duty Outside the Archdiocese.
Smyka, James *o.f.m.conv.* (ALT) Johnstown, PA Memorial Medical Center; Johnstown, PA Good Samaritan Medical Center; Johnstown, PA Memorial Medical Center Lee Campus.
Smyth, James '57 (NY) Hastings–on–Hudson, NY St. Matthew Retired.
Smyth, John P. '62 (CHI)[D] Niles, IL Notre Dame College Prep.
Smyth, Joseph P. '59 (BO) Senior Priests. Retired.
Sneck, William J. *s.j.* '71 (ALN)[A] Wernersville, PA Jesuit Center–Jesuit Community; [N] Wernersville, PA Jesuit Center.
Snedeker, Arthur '74 (CLV) Absent on Sick Leave; Brooklyn, OH St. Thomas More.
Snell, Francis '91 (HRT) New Haven, CT Sacred Heart.
Snell, Roger K. '72 (FAR) Retired.
Sneyd, Derrick '70 (FTW) Auburn, IN Immaculate Conception; Consultors.
Snider, Harold *o.f.m.cap.* '89 (LA) Solvang, CA Old Mission Santa Ines.
Snider, Michael '08 (TYL) New Boston, TX St. Mary of the Cenacle; New Boston, TX Telford Unit, Texas Department of Criminal Justice.
Snieg, Peter '93 (CHI) St. Joseph College Seminary at Loyola University; The Tuite Program at St. Joseph College Seminary; [A] Chicago, IL St. Joseph College Seminary.
Sniezyk, Rev. Msgr. Richard S. '62 (SPR) Retired.
Sniosek, Jaroslaw '98 (VEN) Auditors; Bonita Springs, FL St. Leo; Judges.
Snipes, Roy Lee *o.m.i.* '80 (BWN) Mission, TX Our Lady of Guadalupe; Mission Deanery.
Sniscak, Stephen '10 (PAT)[K] Denville, NJ Saint Clare's Hospital, Inc.; Denville, NJ St. Clare Hospital; Rockaway, NJ Sacred Heart.
Snitily, Steven P. '09 (LIN) Graduate Studies.
Snock, Bernard C. '62 (GAL) Retired.
Snodgrass, Thomas A. '76 (CIN) Cincinnati, OH St. Margaret Mary; Assistant Chancellor; Judges; Cincinnati, OH Church of the Assumption.
Snoich, Stephen *o.s.b.* '72 (LFT) Lake Village, IN St. Augusta.
Snoich, Stephen *o.s.b.* '72 (IND)[K] Saint Meinrad St. Meinrad Archabbey.
Snoke, F. Richard '65 (COL) Danville, OH St. Luke.
Snopek, Charles J. '86 (CHR) Retired.
Snouffer, Philip T. '62 (BAL) Retired.
Snow, Glenn *o.carm.* '89 (TUC) Tucson, AZ Saint Cyril of Alexandria Roman Catholic Parish – Tucson.

Snow, Rev. Msgr. Harry K. '77 (OG) Norwood, NY St. Andrew; Judicial Vicar and Vicar for Canonical Affairs; Deans.
Snow, Lorn J. *s.j.* '99 (CLV) University Heights, OH Gesu; [B] University Heights, OH John Carroll Jesuit Community; Presbyteral Council; Presbyteral Conveners.
Snyder, Alexander '59 (OAK) Retired.
Snyder, Brian '79 (SEA) Renton, WA St. Stephen the Martyr.
Snyder, Chester P. '77 (HBG) Mechanicsburg, PA St. Joseph.
Snyder, Donald E. '73 (CLV) Westlake, OH St. Ladislas; Associate Judges.
Snyder, Frederick J. '52 (TOL) Swanton, OH Holy Trinity Retired.
Snyder, Frederick '52 (GI) Retired.
Snyder, Gary B. '74 (SC) Sioux City, IA St. Michael; Priests' Pension Plan – Board of Trustees.
Snyder, George T. '07 (SAC) Redding, CA St. Joseph.
Snyder, Guy Christopher *p.i.m.e.* '98 (DET)[K] Detroit, MI P.I.M.E. Missionaries; Detroit, MI All Saints.
Snyder, John F. *s.j.* '55 (STL)[O] St. Louis, MO Jesuit Community Corporation at Saint Louis University – Jesuit Hall.
Snyder, Rev. Msgr. John R. '54 (E) Retired.
Snyder, Larry J. '88 (STP) On Duty Outside the Archdiocese.
Snyder, Michael E. '97 (BLX) Picayune, MS St. Charles Borromeo.
Snyder, Michael J. *m.m.* '79 (FgM) Maryknoll, NY MARYKNOLL.
Snyders, William J. *s.j.* '66 (FgM) St. Louis, MO Society of Jesus.
Snyderwine, Rev. Msgr. L. Thomas '68 (E) Erie, PA St. Luke; Apostleship of the Sea and Chaplain to the Port of Erie; Presbyteral Council.
Snyers, Peter '53 (SCL) Retired.
So, Augustine *o.s.b.* '99 (PAT)[N] Newton, NJ St. Paul's Abbey.
Soadwah, Raphael '88 (RVC) Manhasset, NY St. Mary's.
Soares, John P. '92 (PRO) Providence, RI St. Thomas.
Soares, Rev. Msgr. Nicholas J. '64 (NY) Staten Island, NY St. Clement; Staten Island, NY St. Michael.
Soares, Stephen '87 (ALX) Pineville, LA Sacred Heart.
Sobczak, Marek W. *c.m.* '81 (BRK) Brooklyn, NY St. Stanislaus Kostka.
Soberal, Jose D. '60 (ARE) Retired.
Soberick, George J. '62 (MAN) Retired.
Sobiech, Slawomir (BRK) Springfield Gardens, NY Christ the King.
Sobiech, Stanley *o.f.m.conv.* '62 (SPR) Holyoke, MA Our Lady of the Cross.
Sobiecki, Peter S. '66 (HRT) Retired.
Sobierajski, Rev. Msgr. Edward J. '61 (BUF)[N] Tonawanda, NY O'Hara Residence Retired.
Sobierajski, Joseph A. *s.j.* '74 (WDC) Washington, DC Holy Trinity.
Sobiesiak, Rev. Msgr. Joseph R. '76 (ALN) Bethlehem, PA Holy Infancy.
Sobolewski, Edward F. '69 (CAM) Retired.
Sobolewski, Wlodzimierz *c.r.* (BO) Court Advocate/Petitioner.
Sobon, Walter A. '67 (PIT) Retired.
Sobotka, DePaul *o.f.m.* '63 (MIL)[P] Burlington, WI Queen of Peace Friary.
Sobus, James M. '86 (WH) Huntington, WV Our Lady of Fatima; Ona, WV St. Stephen.
Socha, Bogdan Mikolaj *o.s.p.p.e.* '93 (NY) New York, NY St. Stanislaus Bishop and Martyr.
Socha, Bronislaw F. *o.c.d.* '89 (GRY)[H] Munster, IN Discalced Carmelite Fathers Monastery.
Sochacki, Walter L. '68 (STP) Retired.
Sochulak, Pavol *s.v.d.* '92 (SB) Ontario, CA Our Lady of Guadalupe.
Socias, James '78 (POD) Oak Park; [V] Oak Park, IL Oak Park Study Center.
Sockol, Timothy '77 (PMB) Delray Beach, FL Emmanuel.
Socualaya, Bladi J. '01 (NY) Newburgh, NY St. Patrick.
Sodano, Thomas M. '91 (PH) Philadelphia, PA Our Lady of Ransom; [D] Philadelphia, PA St. Hubert's Catholic High School for Girls.
Sodini, Pierre G. '68 (PIT) Avella, PA St. Michael.
Sodja, Richard H. '65 (HEL) Retired.
Sodoro, Carl F. '77 (OM)[G] Omaha, NE Archbishop Bergan Mercy Medical Center; Omaha, NE St. Adalbert.
Soeherman, Miguel Marie *m.f.v.a.* '04 (BIR)[E] Birmingham, AL Franciscan Missionaries of the Eternal Word, A Public Association of the Christian Faithful.
Soehner, Mark *o.f.m.* '87 (CHI)[N] Chicago, IL St. Joseph Interprovincial Post-Novitiate Formation House.
Soerries, Denis *o.s.b.* '56 (LR) New Blaine, AR St. Scholastica; [J] New Blaine, AR Hesychia House of Prayer.
Sofie, J. Francis '94 (MOB) Mobile, AL Our Lady of Lourdes; Auditor.
Sogliuzzo, Louis P. *s.j.* '87 (SY)[T] Syracuse, NY LeMoyne College Campus Ministry; [Q] Syracuse, NY Jesuits at LeMoyne, Inc.
Soh, Christopher *s.j.* '05 (LA) Santa Barbara, CA Our Lady of Sorrows.
Soh, Mark E. '06 (BRK) Bayside, NY St. Robert Bellarmine.
Soha, Roderick N. *t.o.r.* '95 (ALT) Windber, PA St. Anthony of Padua.
Sohm, Andrew L. '05 (OM) Military Chaplains; Air Force Chaplains.
Sohm, John E. '58 (SFD) Sullivan, IL St. Columcille.
Sojka, Jeremiusz H. '95 (RIC) Blacksburg, VA St. Mary; Salem, VA Salem VA Medical Center.
Sojka, Louis L. *o.s.b.* '90 (OM)[C] Elkhorn, NE Mount Michael Benedictine School; [J] Elkhorn, NE Mount Michael Benedictine Abbey; Elkhorn, NE.
Sokalski, Marcel *o.f.m.conv.* '59 (BUF)[N] Athol Springs, NY St. Maximilian Kolbe Friary.
Sokol, Nathaniel '04 (LAN) Tribunal Judges.
Sokol, Stanislaw '85 (SPR) Springfield, MA Our Lady of the Rosary; Springfield, MA Immaculate Conception.
Sokolowski, Rev. Msgr. Robert S. '65 (WDC) On Duty Outside the Archdiocese; [C] Catholic University of America, The.
Sokolowski, Thomas J. '79 (SCR)[M] Dunmore, PA Villa St. Joseph; Unassigned or Leave of Absence Retired.
Sokolowski, William R. '65 (HRT) Wolcott, CT St. Maria Goretti.
Sokolski, John *o.m.i.* '55 (SAT)[K] San Antonio, TX Oblate Madonna Residence.
Solan, Lawrence T. '80 (COS) Colorado Springs, CO St. Patrick.
Solana, Fermin '70 (MIA) Miami, FL Our Lady of Divine Providence.
Solano, Julio R. '93 (MIA) Miami, FL Mother of Christ.
Solano-Uribe, Jose Maria '96 (SJN) Rio Piedras, PR Inmaculado Corazon de Maria.
Solari, James K. '55 (CHL) Retired.
Solarski, John E. (POD) Irving.
Solarski, John E. '76 (DAL)[I] Irving, TX Opus Dei.
Solcia, Louis M. *c.r.s.p.* '57 (SD) San Diego, CA Our Lady of the Rosary Catholic Parish; [O] San Diego, CA Magnificat (Central) San Diego Chapter.
Soler, Esteban *i.v.e.* '04 (VEN) Wauchula, FL St. Michael.
Soler, Lawrence *t.o.r.* '51 (AUS) Waco, TX Sacred Heart Catholic Church – Waco, Texas.
Soler, Manuel A. '98 (MIA) Miami, FL Our Lady of Divine Providence; Police Chaplains.
Solera, Eugenio '86 (RVC) West Babylon, NY Our Lady of Grace.
Soley, Andrew Kofi '94 (BRK) Brooklyn, NY Our Lady of Guadalupe.
Soley, Roger A. '78 (WDC) Upper Marlboro, MD Church of the Most Holy Rosary.
Solis, Francisco J. '06 (BWN) Roma, TX Sacred Heart; Roma, TX Our Lady of Refuge; Priests' Assignment Board.
Solis, Olman '97 (OAK) Oakley, CA St. Anthony; Deanery #13.
Solis, Ralph '93 (ELP) Horizon City, TX Holy Spirit.
Solis, Sergio '00 (CHI) Cicero, IL St. Anthony of Padua.
Solivan, Roberto (CGS) Caguas, PR San Pedro Apostol.
Solma, Martin A. *s.m.* '78 (STL)[O] St. Louis, MO Marianists, Province of the United States (Society of Mary); Saint Louis, MO; Saint Louis, MO Society of Mary; [O] St. Louis, MO Maryland Avenue Marianist Community.
Soloman, Louis E. *s.j.* '64 (NY)[DD] New York, NY Murray-Weigel Hall.
Solomon, Benedict M. *o.praem.* '10 (ORG)[I] Silverado, CA Norbertine Fathers of Orange Inc.
Solomon, Fernando *o.p.miss.* (SAT)[S] San Antonio, TX Deaf Ministry of San Antonio.
Solomon, John T. '11 (WIL) Elkton, MD Immaculate Conception.
Solomon, Marc J. '06 (E)[Q] Meadville, PA Allegheny College; Meadville, PA St. Mary of Grace.
Solors, Stephen '91 (DUL) Deer River, MN St. Joseph; Deer River, MN Sacred Heart.
Solorzano, Marcelo *o.p.* '95 (MIA)[H] Miami, FL Dominican Fathers of Miami, Inc.; [C] Miami, FL Barry University.
Solorzano, Mario '06 (JKS) Jackson, MS Christ the King; Jackson, MS St. Mary.
Solorzano, Miguel A. '93 (GAL) Houston, TX St. Charles Borromeo; Central Vicariate.
Soltis, John F. *m.m.* '62 (NY)[DD] Maryknoll Maryknoll Fathers and Brothers Retired.
Soltys, Daniel F. '68 (OM) Omaha, NE St. Joan of Arc.
Soltys, Raymond A. '79 (SPR) Ludlow, MA Christ the King.
Soma, Franco *f.s.c.b.* '08 (WDC) Lexington, MA; [O] Bethesda, MD Priestly Fraternity of the Missionaries of St. Charles Borromeo, Inc.
Soma, Franco *f.s.c.b.* '08 (BO)[U] Bethesda, MD House of Washington DC.
Somarriba, Marcos A. '93 (MIA) Miami, FL St. Kieran.
Sombilon, Edmundo '93 (NEW) Fort Lee, NJ Holy Trinity.
Somera, Romelo '99 (HON) Kapaa, HI St. Catherine.
Somers, Eldon K. '51 (E) Retired.
Somers, Michael '82 (GB) Absent on Leave, Sick or Disabled.
Somers, Richard '66 (JKS) Greenville, MS St. Joseph.
Somerville, Conrad *o.f.m.conv.* '54 (SY) Syracuse, NY Assumption B.V.M.
Sommer, Allan J. '66 (MIL) Retired.
Sommer, Gerald J. *m.s.c.* '47 (Y)[I] Canton, OH House of Loreto Retired.
Sommer, Harold J. *s.j.* '65 (DET)[K] Clarkston, MI Colombiere Center.
Sommer, Rev. Msgr. Jerome '40 (JC) Retired.
Sommer, Kenneth (CIN)[N] Dayton, OH Marianist Community.
Sommer, Rev. Msgr. Ralph '83 (RVC) Westbury, NY St. Brigid.
Sommermeyer, Gary H. '91 (BRK) Retired.
Son, Doan Trong *c.ss.r.* '99 (LA)[P] Baldwin Park, CA Vietnamese Redemptorist Mission.
Son, Kyungsu *m.m.* '79 (FgM) Maryknoll, NY MARYKNOLL.
Song, Jea Ho '00 (SAT) Boerne, TX Korean Martyrs Catholic Church.
Songy, David *o.f.m.cap.* '87 (DEN) Denver, CO; [N] Denver, CO Capuchin Province of Mid-America, Inc.; [N] Denver, CO St. Anthony of Padua Friary.
Songy, Rev. Msgr. James B. '54 (HT) Retired.
Sonnberger, Albert W. '56 (LC) Bloomer, WI St. John the Baptist Retired.
Sonnier, Cedric '97 (LAF) Eunice, LA St. Thomas More; Diocesan Co Chaplains.
Sonnier, Charles '64 (VIC) Sweet Home, TX St. John the Baptist; Sweet Home, TX Queen of Peace; Presbyteral Council.
Soo-Gil Chae, Cyril '04 (ATL) Norcross, GA Saint Patrick.
Soosai, Vincent *o.f.m.* '99 (NY) Staten Island, NY St. Teresa.
Soosaimanickam, Benjamin V. '90 (NOR) Colchester, CT St. Andrew; Lebanon, CT St. Francis of Assisi.
Soosairaj, Michael '88 (NY) Harrison, NY St. Gregory the Great.
Soper, Paul R. '90 (BO) Weymouth, MA St. Albert the Great.
Sopiak, Donald A. '78 (DET) Absent on Leave.
Sopoliga, Michael '79 (PSC) Fort Pierce, FL SS. Cyril and Methodius; Presbyteral Council.
Sopp, Michael '75 (SJP) On Leave; Presbyters.
Soprano, Ernest R. '79 (CAM) North Cape May, NJ The Parish of Saint John Neumann, North Cape May, N.J.
Soprych, Marion '75 (CHI) Chicago, IL St. John Fisher.
Soranno, Joseph M. '74 (SPR) Wilbraham, MA St. Cecilia's.
Sordillo, Ronald '74 (PAT)[Q] Chester, NJ Nazareth Village Retired.
Soreng, Birendra '96 (BGP) Stratford, CT St. Mark.
Sorensen, Bryan '88 (RC) Martin, SD Our Lady of the Sacred Heart; Deaneries; [E] McLaughlin, SD Priest Retirement and Aid Association/Pension Plan Board.
Sorensen, Jonathan D. '09 (GI) Grand Island, NE Cathedral of the Nativity of the Blessed Virgin Mary.
Sorenson, Kris '08 (FRS) California City, CA Our Lady of Lourdes.
Sorgie, Anthony D. '82 (NY) Carmel, NY St. James the Apostle.
Soria, Manuel B. '81 (SAC) Sacramento, CA St. Anthony.
Soriano, Arnel *m.s.* '04 (HON) Kekaha, HI St. Theresa.
Soriano, Danilo '78 (JOL) Carol Stream, IL St. Luke.
Soriano, Erasmus B. '93 (LA) Baldwin Park, CA St. John the Baptist.
Soriano, Jesus T. '70 (SAC) Vallejo, CA St. Catherine of Siena; Presbyteral Council.
Sork, Rev. Msgr. David A. '70 (LA) Rancho Palos Verdes, CA St. John Fisher.
Sormani, Daniel *c.s.sp.* '86 (FgM) Bethel Park, PA CONGREGATION OF THE HOLY SPIRIT.
Sorohan, Rev. Msgr. David V. '59 (COL) Retired.
Soroko, Kenneth *c.p.m.* '11 (L) Albany, KY Emmanuel Catholic; Glasgow, KY St. Helen.
Sorra, James L. '06 (BAL) Baltimore, MD St. Michael.
Sorrano, Rodrigo '01 (FWT) On Leave of Absence.
Sortino, Anthony *l.c.* '06 (WDC)[O] Potomac, MD Legionaries of Christ.
Sosa, Elio '03 (BRK) Brooklyn, NY Mary Mother of the Church.
Sosa, Emilio '06 (SAN) San Angelo, TX St. Joseph.
Sosa, Juan J. '72 (MIA) Miami Beach, FL St. Joseph; Committee on Popular Piety; Archdiocesan Vocations Review Board; Washington, DC Instituto Nacional Hispano de Liturgia, Inc.; Consultants.
Soseman, Rev. Msgr. Richard '92 (PEO) On Duty Outside the Diocese.
Sosing, Rev. Msgr. Romualdo '77 (RVC) Valley Stream, NY Holy Name of Mary; Oyster Bay, NY St. Dominic's.
Sosnowski, Tadevsz *c.r.* '97 (CHI)[N].
Sosnowski, Ted *c.r.* '97 (PT) Panama City Beach, FL St. Bernadette.
Sostrich, John L. '62 (SD) Retired.

Sotak, John J. *o.s.a.* '92 (TLS)[B] Tulsa, OK Cascia Hall Preparatory School.
Sotelo, A. Richard *s.j.* '87 (BAL)[Q] Towson Maryland Province of the Society of Jesus.
Sotelo, Angel '91 (FRS) Chowchilla, CA St. Columba.
Sotelo, Rev. Msgr. Antonio '58 (PHX) Phoenix, AZ Sacred Heart Roman Catholic Parish; Special Assignment; Priestly Life and Ministry Board Retired.
Sotelo, Fabio A. '99 (ATL) On Leave of Absence; Without Archdiocesan Assignment or Faculties.
Sotiroff, Stephen T. '81 (SFD) Maryville, IL Mother of Perpetual Help.
Soto, Angel Leonides (MGZ)[B] San German, PR Hospital of the Immaculate Conception.
Soto, Charles *o.f.m.* '70 (NY)[DD] New York Franciscan Province of the Immaculate Conception Retired.
Soto, Charles *o.f.m.* '70 (MO) DEPARTMENT OF VETERANS AFFAIRS HOSPITALS AND CHAPLAINS Retired.
Soto, Charles *o.f.m.* (PIT) VA Pittsburgh Health Care System.
Soto, Edward P. '58 (LA) Maywood, CA St. Rose of Lima Retired.
Soto, Jose (NY) Spring Valley, NY St. Joseph.
Soto, Randall (STL) St. Louis, MO St. Cecilia.
Soto Silvera, Calixto '85 (SJN) Toa Baja, PR San Pedro Apostol.
Soto Tanon, Carmelo '89 (SJN) Instructors.
Sottocornola, Frank *s.x.* '69 (FgM) Wayne, NJ XAVERIAN MISSIONARY FATHERS.
Sottocornula, Frank *s.x.* '59 (PAT)[N] Wayne Xaverian Missionary Fathers.
Souckar, Rev. Msgr. Michael A. '88 (MIA) Special Assignment.
Souckar, Rev. Msgr. Michael (NTN) Judges.
Soucy, A. Francis *o.f.m.* '67 (PAT)[N] Ringwood, NJ Holy Name Friary, Inc.
Soucy, Neil *s.m.* '62 (FgM) THE SOCIETY OF MARY.
Soucy, Robert P. '62 (BO) Senior Priests. Retired.
Souffrant, Claude *s.j.* '67 (CHI) Chicago, IL St. Margaret of Scotland.
Soukup, Paul A. *s.j.* '79 (SJ) Catholic Scouting; [B] Santa Clara, CA Jesuit Community.
Soule, W. Becket *o.p.* '93 (COL)[A] Columbus, OH Pontifical College Josephinum; [A] Columbus, OH Pontifical College Josephinum.
Soulliere, Richard '76 (MIA) Legion of Mary; Marian Movements & Devotions Retired.
Sousa, Edward A. '03 (PRO) Warwick, RI St. Catherine; [K] North Providence, RI St. Joseph Health Services of Rhode Island – Our Lady of Fatima Hospital.
Sousa, Manuel F. '80 (STO) Deans; Turlock, CA Our Lady of the Assumption of the Portuguese Church (Pastor of).
Sousa, Peter E. *c.ss.r.* '78 (MO) Army Reserve Chaplains.
Sousa, Peter E. *c.ss.r.* (CHR) Sumter, SC Catholic Community of Sumter.
Sousa, Peter *c.ss.r.* '78 (ORL)[F] New Smyrna Beach, FL Redemptorist Fathers of the Vice Province of Richmond.
Soutus, Anibal '06 (SJP) Presbyters; Conyers, GA Mother of God.
Soutus, Hugo '94 (STN) Phoenix, AZ Assumption of B.V.M.; Presbyteral Council.
Soutuyo, Raul S. '93 (MIA) Miami, FL St. Agatha.
Souza, Jason '98 (LA) Long Beach, CA St. Cyprian.
Sowa, Artur J. '06 (CHI) Elmwood Park, IL St. Celestine.
Sowada, Arlie '73 (SCL) Verndale, MN St. Frederick.
Sowada, Arlie '73 (SCL) Verndale, MN St. Hubert; Verndale, MN The Church of the Assumption of Our Lady of Menahga.
Soy, Esteban '52 (VEN) Retired.
Soyka, Giles *o.f.m.cap.* '50 (GB)[J] Appleton, WI St. Fidelis Friary Retired.
Spacek, Frank W. '97 (BRK) Brooklyn, NY St. Brendan; [G] Middle Village, NY Christ the King Regional High School.
Spacek, William F. '95 (BAL) Baltimore, MD St. Alphonsus, Shrine of; Special Assignment.
Spacht, Andres *c.ss.r.* '61 (CGS) San Lorenzo, PR Nuestra Senora de la Mercedes.
Spadaro, Rev. Msgr. Thomas L. '64 (RVC) Holbrook, NY Good Shepherd.
Spagnola, Michael G. '00 (CAM) On Leave of Absence.
Spagnolo, Nicholas *c.s.s.* '52 (BO)[X] Waltham, MA Stigmatine Fathers and Brothers Retired.
Spahn, James A. *o.p.* '81 (STP) Minneapolis, MN Holy Rosary/Santo Rosario; Minneapolis, MN St. Albert the Great; [J] Minneapolis, MN St. Albert the Great Priory.
Spahn, James '00 (DEN) Windsor, CO Our Lady of the Valley; Deaneries.
Spahr, Matthew D. '92 (SD)[A] San Diego, CA St. Francis De Sales Center; Priestly Formation — St. Francis Center; College of Consultors; Presbyteral Council; San Diego, CA The Immaculata Catholic Parish.
Spain, John H. *m.m.* '70 (FgM) Maryknoll, NY MARYKNOLL.
Spalatin, Christopher A. *s.j.* '71 (FgM) Milwaukee, WI Society of Jesus.
Spalding, J. Mark '91 (L) Louisville, KY Holy Trinity; Vicar General; Judicial Vicar and Director; College of Consultors; Ex Officio; L.A.M.P.; [P] Louisville, KY Catholic Bicentennial Initiative Fund, Inc.
Spalding, Leon C. '59 (L) Louisville, KY Retired.
Spanel, Hubert J. '59 (GI) Retired.
Spangenberg, George J. *c.s.sp.* '76 (PIT)[B] Pittsburgh, PA Duquesne University of the Holy Spirit.
Spangenberg, George J. *c.s.sp.* (WDC)[X] Wheaton, MD U.S. Foundation for the Congregation of the Holy Ghost and the Immaculate Heart of Mary, Inc.
Spanier, Marian '81 (NEW) Elizabeth, NJ Saint Adalbert and Saints Peter & Paul.
Spanjers, John J. '59 (SUP) Retired.
Spanley, Anthony L. '68 (GRY) Hamlet, IN Holy Cross.
Spannagel, Luke A. '03 (PEO) Rural Life Conference; Bloomington, IL St. Patrick Church of Merna; Downs, IL St. Mary's.
Spano, Philip F. '82 (BR) Baton Rouge, LA Most Blessed Sacrament.
Sparacino, Thomas A. '98 (PIT) Gibsonia, PA Saint Richard; Priest Council.
Sparklin, Paul C. '91 (BAL)[U] Baltimore, MD Johns Hopkins Hospital; Baltimore, MD Our Lady, Queen of Peace; Special Assignment.
Sparks, Kenneth A. '95 (PIT) Pittsburgh, PA St. Gabriel of the Sorrowful Virgin.
Sparks, Nathan '11 (RC) Rapid City, SD Cathedral of Our Lady of Perpetual Help.
Sparks, Richard *c.s.p.* '78 (CHI) Chicago, IL Old St. Mary.
Spatt, John *c.pp.s.* '43 (CIN)[N] Carthagena, OH St. Charles Retired.
Spaulding, Donald E. '57 (EVN) Retired.
Spaulding, Robert '09 (CHY) Cheyenne, WY St. Mary's Cathedral; Presbyteral Council.
Specht, Joseph *s.j.* '69 (SJ)[L] Los Altos, CA Jesuit Retreat Center of Los Altos.
Specht, Terry W. '96 (ARL) Diocesan Consultors; Annandale, VA Holy Spirit.
Speck, Gregory *s.c.j.* '76 (SP)[N] Pinellas Park, FL Priests of the Sacred Heart.
Speckman, Harry *o.f.m.* '61 (GLD) Indian River, MI Cross in the Woods Catholic Shrine.
Speerstra, William F. '59 (SUP) Retired.
Speicher, Charles W. '75 (PIT) Bairdford, PA St. Victor; Judges.
Speicher, David J. '86 (LAN) Howell, MI St. Joseph; College of Consultors.
Speier, Francis J. '75 (TOL) Milan, OH St. Anthony; Norwalk, OH St. Mary, Mother of the Redeemer; St. John Neumann Deanery.
Speier, Thomas *o.f.m.* '58 (CIN)[N] Cincinnati, OH St. Francis Seraph Friary.
Speiser, Thomas M. '77 (DAL) On Leave of Absence.
Speitel, Edmond J. '55 (PH) Retired.
Speitel, Mark M. '08 (HBG) Harrisburg, PA Holy Name of Jesus.
Spellerberg, Joseph R. *s.j.* '53 (NY)[DD] New York, NY Murray–Weigel Hall.
Spellman, John P. *o.s.f.s.* '66 (WIL)[B] Wilmington, DE Salesianum School.
Spellman, Paul J. '01 (LA) Los Angeles, CA Holy Name of Jesus; Deanery 15.
Spellman, Robert M. '74 (WOR) Berlin, MA St. Joseph the Good Provider.
Spenard, James *o.s.a.* '72 (ALB) Troy, NY St. Augustine.
Spencer, Gregory D. '89 (R) Havelock, NC Annunciation; Deans; Council of Priests.
Spencer, Jeremiah L. '65 (KCK) Kansas City, KS Holy Name.
Spencer, John P. *s.j.* '79 (BO)[U] Boston, MA Loyola House.
Spencer, Matthew *o.s.j.* '09 (SAC)[A] Loomis, CA Mount St. Joseph Novitiate and Seminary.
Spencer, Robert A. '98 (CHR) Military Chaplains; Navy Chaplains.
Spencer, Robert K. '85 (WCH) Bushton, KS Holy Name of Jesus; Little River, KS Holy Trinity; Lyons, KS St. Paul.
Spencer, Robert M. '82 (RIC) Richmond, VA Our Lady of Lourdes.
Spencer, William *o.f.m.* '74 (FgM) Saint Louis, MO Sacred Heart Province; Saint Louis, MO.
Spencer, William '07 (SAG) Harbor Beach, MI Our Lady of Lake Huron; Harbor Beach, MI St. Anthony.
Spencer, William *o.f.m.* '74 (STL)[O] St. Louis, MO Franciscan Friary of St. Anthony of Padua.
Spengler, Rev. Msgr. James F. '68 (BRK) Rockaway Beach, NY St. Rose of Lima.
Spenner, Jerome I. '64 (OM) Retired.
Speno, Eugene '60 (SB) Retired.
Spera, James F. '77 (NEW) Roselle Park, NJ The Assumption.
Sperger, Herbert J. '79 (PH)[AA] Malvern, PA St. Joseph's–in–the–Hills; On Special or Other Archdiocesan Assignment.
Sperl, August J. '54 (SFD) Retired.
Sperlak, Charles S. '64 (ALN) Reading, PA SS. Cyril and Methodius.
Spexarth, Aaron '08 (WCH)[B] Wichita, KS Kapaun Mt. Carmel Catholic High School; Wichita, KS Church of the Magdalen.
Spexarth, Daniel J. '84 (WCH) Presbyteral Council/College of Consultors; Wichita, KS St. Catherine of Siena.
Spexarth, James '55 (WCH) Retired.
Spexarth, Jerome J. '01 (WCH) Wichita, KS St. Patrick.
Spexarth, Joachim *o.s.b.* '65 (OKL)[I] Shawnee, OK St. Gregory's Abbey; Consultors Archdiocesan; Council of Priests Archdiocesan; Shawnee, OK.
Spezia, Leo J. '76 (STL) St. Louis, MO St. Mary Magdalen; South City Deanery PSR at St. John the Baptist Parish.
Spezia, Robert '97 (DET)[A] The College of Liberal Arts.
Speziale, Michael G. '09 (PH)[D] Philadelphia, PA Archbishop Ryan High School; Philadelphia, PA Christ the King.
Spicer, Kevin P. *c.s.c.* '92 (FR)[A] North Easton, MA Stonehill College.
Spicer, Kevin P. *c.s.c.* '92 (FTW)[H] Notre Dame Congregation of Holy Cross, United States Province of Priests & Brothers.
Spicer, Richard J. '86 (SEA) Langley, WA St. Hubert.
Spiece, Rev. Msgr. Lawrence T. '61 (E) Retired.
Spiegel, John D. '76 (DAV) Iowa City, IA St. Mary.
Spiegel, Rev. Msgr. Robert H. '66 (DAV) Military Chaplains.
Spiegel, Thomas J. '67 (DAV) Retired.
Spiekermeier, Michael J. '69 (DAV) Davenport, IA St. Paul the Apostle; [M] Davenport, IA St. Paul the Apostle Foundation.
Spieler, Joseph G. *s.j.* '75 (LA) Los Angeles, CA Blessed Sacrament; [P] Los Angeles, CA Colombiere House.
Spielman, Paul J. '61 (STL) Retired.
Spies, Dennis '02 (JOL) Steger, IL St. Liborius.
Spiess, Kevin J. '86 (JOL) Other Assignments; Joliet, IL St. Francis Xavier.
Spilka, Anthony Francis *o.f.m.conv.* '69 (ALT) Bishop's Vicar for Religious; Johnstown, PA St. Michael's; Johnstown, PA St. Francis of Assisi.
Spillane, Michael Joseph '68 (BAL) Retired.
Spillett, Thomas '64 (SP) Lecanto, FL St. Scholastica Church.
Spilly, Alphonse *c.pp.s.* '67 (CIN)[N] Dayton Provincial Office of the Cincinnati Province of the Society of the Precious Blood.
Spilly, Alphonse *c.pp.s.* (GRY)[A] Whiting, IN Calumet College of St. Joseph.
Spilly, William V. '74 (ROC) Hamlin, NY St. Elizabeth Ann Seton.
Spilman, Robert D. '96 (PEO) Spring Valley, IL Immaculate Conception; Spring Valley, IL St. Anthony; Spring Valley, IL SS. Peter and Paul's; Vicariates and Vicars; Clergymen's Aid, Inc.; Finance Council (Canon 492).
Spina, Douglas J. '76 (PRO) Warwick, RI St. Kevin.
Spinelli, Joseph A. *o.s.a.* '55 (PH)[Y] Villanova, PA St. Thomas Monastery.
Spinharney, Isaac Mary *c.f.r.* '10 (NY)[DD] New York, NY St. Joseph's Friary.
Spinler, Ruben C. '94 (WIN) Retired.
Spino, John J. '90 (NEW) Retired.
Spinosa, Rev. Msgr. Anthony '83 (OLL) Office for Missions; Office of Inter–faith/Ecumenical Affairs; [C] North Jackson, OH National Shrine of Our Lady of Lebanon; [E] North Jackson, OH Father Tobia Retirement Home.
Spiranec, Tomislav *s.j.* '09 (OAK)[L] Berkeley, CA Jesuit Fathers and Brothers.
Spirko, Nicholas A. '72 (PIT) Washington, PA Immaculate Conception.
Spisak, Stephen M. '82 (CLV) Absent on Sick Leave.
Spishak, Carl A. '59 (ALT) Altoona, PA St. Rose of Lima Retired.
Spiteri, Rev. Msgr. Laurence J. '78 (LA) On Duty Outside the Archdiocese.
Spitz, Gregory M. '67 (MIL) Milwaukee, WI Our Lady Queen of Peace.
Spitzer, Michael H. '98 (PH)[A] Wynnewood, PA Theological Seminary of St. Charles Borromeo, Overbrook.
Spitzley, Denis R. '75 (LAN) Concord, MI St. Catherine Laboure.
Splawski, Bernerd *o.f.m.* '63 (SP)[N] St. Petersburg, FL St. Anthony Friary.
Spleet, Julius A. '62 (SAG) Retired.
Spodnik, A. Leo '48 (HRT) Retired.
Spohrer, Dennis E. '03 (PEO) Alexis, IL St. Theresa's; [H] East Peoria, IL OSF Holy Family Medical Center.
Spolny, Joseph R. '78 (CLV) Fairview Park, OH St. Angela Merici.
Sponder, John '93 (JOL) Leave of Absence.
Spong, William '79 (FWT) On Duty Outside the Diocese.
Spontak, James A. '75 (PBR) Portage, PA SS. Peter and Paul; Consultors.
Sportino, Salvatore '90 (NY) Bronx, NY St. Joseph.

Spotswood, Cecil R. '97 (MOB) Special Assignment; Mobile, AL St. Ignatius Parish, Mobile.
Sprauer, Michael '72 (P) Retired.
Sprecace, Rev. Msgr. Francis A. '55 (CAM) Retired.
Sprietsma, Leo *o.f.m.* '53 (LA)[P] Santa Barbara, CA Franciscan Friary, Order of Friars Minor (Old Mission).
Spriggs, Robert '65 (SFD) Comite Diocesano de Ministerio Hispano – Diocesan Committee for Hispanic Ministry Retired.
Sprigler, William A. '75 (NU) Benson, MN St. Francis; Benson, MN St. Malachy; Benson, MN Church of the Visitation (Oratory); Murdock, MN Church of the Sacred Heart; Benson, MN St. Bridget.
Spring, Mark P. '80 (DAV) Fort Madison, IA Holy Family; Fort Madison, IA St. Joseph's.
Springer, Francis *s.m.* '55 (SFR)[N] San Francisco, CA Marist Center of the West Retired.
Springer, Lawrence F. '59 (CHI) Des Plaines, IL St. Zachary Retired.
Springer, William A. '72 (SD) San Diego, CA Mission San Diego De Alcala Catholic Parish.
Springman, Donald W. '67 (L) Retired.
Sprott, Robert *o.f.m.* '80 (CHI) Chicago, IL St. Agnes of Bohemia.
Spruill, Mark T. '07 (BIR) Fort Payne, AL Our Lady of the Valley.
Spurr, Michael R. '08 (R) Absent on Leave.
Spychala, Daniel S. '84 (ARL) Ashburn, VA St. Theresa.
Spyrka, Edward C. *o.c.d.* '62 (GRY)[H] Munster, IN Discalced Carmelite Fathers Monastery.
Squeo, Eugene P. '71 (NEW) Jersey City, NJ St. Patrick and Assumption/All Saints Church; [Q] Jersey City, NJ St. Patrick's Housing Corp.; Archdiocesan Commission for Interreligious Affairs.
Squiller, Rt. Rev. Mitred Msgr. John '56 (STF) Personnel Board Retired.
Srampical, Roy *c.p.* '96 (BRK)[R] Jamaica, NY Immaculate Conception Monastery.
Sreboth, Michael R. '86 (MOB) Montgomery, AL Our Lady Queen of Mercy; [I] Montgomery, AL Huntington College Newman Center.
Sredzinski, Joseph L. '70 (GBG) Jeannette, PA Ascension; Jeannette, PA Sacred Heart.
Srenn, Thomas E. '77 (CHI) Chicago, IL Our Lady of Mount Carmel.
Srion, Charles '78 (RVC) Franklin Square, NY St. Catherine of Sienna.
Srnec, Rev. Msgr. Stanley J. '42 (STP) Saint Paul, MN Retired.
Srode, John S. *c.pp.s.* '72 (MO) Air Force Chaplains.
Srode, John S. *c.pp.s.* '72 (CIN)[N] Dayton Provincial Office of the Cincinnati Province of the Society of the Precious Blood.
Sroka, Gerald A. '60 (GRY) Retired.
Ssebadduka, George '78 (KC) Richmond, MO Immaculate Conception.
Ssebalamu, Charles '96 (RIC) South Boston, VA St. Paschal Baylon; Clarksville, VA St. Catherine of Siena.
Ssegawa, John R. *a.j.* '94 (PHX) Glendale, AZ St. James Roman Catholic Parish.
Ssekannyo, Denis '99 (FRS) Bakersfield, CA St. Francis of Assisi.
Ssekiranda, Remigious '98 (VEN) Cape Coral, FL St. Andrew.
Ssekyole, Patrick '09 (WOR) Auburn, MA St. Joseph's.
Ssemakula, Luke '97 (OAK) Walnut Creek, CA St. John Vianney.
Ssemakula, Yozefu B. '93 (PT) On Duty Outside the Diocese.
Sseriiso, Henry M. *i.m.c.* '06 (SB) San Bernardino, CA Our Lady of the Assumption.
St–Godard, Edward G. '64 (PRO) Woonsocket, RI Holy Family.
St. Amand, Kenneth J. '69 (NEW) Retired.
St. Cyr, John *o.m.i.* '61 (FgM) Washington, DC AMERICAN OBLATE MISSIONS.
St. Fleur, Maxis '01 (ATL) On Leave of Absence; Without Archdiocesan Assignment or Faculties.
St. Forte, Elifete '08 (PMB) Elected Members; Palm Springs, FL St. Luke.
St. George, John P. *s.j.* '66 (NY)[DD] New York, NY Murray–Weigel Hall.
St. George, Peter T. '95 (CIN) Cincinnati, OH St. Ignatius of Loyola.
St. Germain, Rt. Rev. Andre '96 (NTN) Manchester, NH Our Lady of the Cedars Retired.
St. Germain, Brian '88 (PRM) Absent on Leave.
St. Hilaire, Kenneth T. '07 (SPK) Spokane, WA St. Patrick.
St. Jean, Marcel '96 (BGP) Shelton, CT St. Joseph.
St. John, George G. '52 (ALB) Albany, NY Blessed Sacrament; Ministers to Retired Priests Retired.
St. Jules, Stephen '79 (RCK) Cary, IL SS. Peter & Paul; Diocesan Consultors.
St. Laurent, Daniel A. '71 (MAN) Nashua, NH St. Aloysius of Gonzaga; Nashua Hispanic Parish Ministry Retired.
St. Louis, Richard E. '00 (MAN) Nashua, NH Immaculate Conception.
St. Marie, Denis L. '59 (CLV) Amherst, OH St. Joseph; South Amherst, OH Nativity of Blessed Virgin Mary Retired.
St. Marie, Michael '93 (B) Twin Falls, ID St. Edward The Confessor; Shoshone, ID St. Peter's; [F] Twin Falls, ID College of Southern Idaho; Gooding, ID St. Elizabeth's.
St. Martin, Jeremy P. '02 (BO) Director.
St. Martin, Robert J. '56 (HRT) Unionville, CT St. Mary Retired.
St. Martin, Robert *o.f.m.conv.* '77 (IND) Sellersburg, IN St. Joseph Hill Catholic Church, Sellersburg, Inc.; Clarksville, IN St. Anthony of Padua Catholic Church, Clarksville, Inc.
St. Paul, Michael '05 (ORG) Stanton, CA St. Polycarp; Clergy Personnel Board.
St. Peter, Dallas T. '07 (BUR) Burlington, VT St. Joseph's Co–Cathedral.
St. Romain, Irion '10 (ALX) Natchitoches, LA Immaculate Conception.
St. Vil, Romane *m.m.* '03 (NY)[DD] Maryknoll Maryknoll Fathers and Brothers.
Staab, Gregory *o.m.v.* '84 (BO)[B] Boston, MA Our Lady of Grace Seminary; [Z] Boston, MA St. Francis Chapel.
Staal, David E. '90 (OAK) Livermore, CA St. Michael; Office of the Bishop; Officers; Officers.
Staar, Robert J. '77 (NY) Port Chester, NY Our Lady of Mercy.
Stab, Herbert J. '59 (MET)[I] Somerset, NJ Maria Regina Residence; Piscataway, NJ Our Lady of Fatima Retired.
Stabeno, John M. '00 (CAM) On Sick Leave.
Stabile, Thomas *t.o.r.* '87 (FWT) Fort Worth, TX St. Andrew; Deans.
Stacer, John R. *s.j.* '63 (NO)[R] New Orleans Jesuit Provincial Office.
Stachacz, James T. '98 (RVC) Hicksville, NY St. Ignatius Loyola.
Stacherczak, Idzi '75 (CHI) Chicago, IL St. Priscilla.
Stachnik, Kenneth R. '86 (GLD) Traverse City, MI St. Francis of Assisi.
Stachowiak, Conrad P. '74 (BUF) Deaf Ministry; Cheektowaga, NY Resurrection.
Stachura, Thaddeus X. '64 (WOR) Worcester, MA Our Lady of Czestochowa; Apostleship of Prayer and Eucharistic Crusade; Diocesan Building Commission Members.
Stachurski, David *o.f.m.conv.* (TR) Delran, NJ The Church of the Resurrection, Delran Township, N.J.
Stachurski, Miroslav '03 (BGP) Shelton, CT St. Lawrence; Redding Ridge, CT St. Patrick.
Stachyra, Kenneth '01 (RCK) Rockford, IL St. Bernadette.
Stack, Daniel '82 (ATL) Cartersville, GA St. Francis of Assisi.
Stack, Gabriel D. *o.praem.* '82 (ORG)[D] Silverado, CA St. Michael's Preparatory School; [I] Silverado, CA Norbertine Fathers of Orange Inc.
Stack, James M. '86 (WDC) Hyattsville, MD St. Jerome.
Stack, Jerome P. *c.pp.s.* '72 (CIN)[N] Dayton Provincial Office of the Cincinnati Province of the Society of the Precious Blood.
Stack, John J. '88 (DAV)[G] Clinton, IA Mercy Medical Center – Clinton.
Stack, John P. *o.s.a.* '74 (PH)[C] Villanova University; [Y] Villanova, PA St. Thomas Monastery.
Stack, John P. '55 (WDC) Retired.
Stack, Rev. Msgr. Richard J. '56 (E) Erie, PA Blessed Sacrament Retired.
Stadmeyer, Raymond *o.f.m.cap.* '92 (DET) Detroit, MI St. Charles Borromeo.
Stadtmueller, Roman *s.d.s.* '54 (WDC)[B] Silver Spring, MD Salvatorian Community Retired.
Staebell, Francis J. *s.j.* '50 (NY)[DD] New York, NY Murray–Weigel Hall.
Staehler, Adrian *o.f.m.cap.* '67 (GB)[M] Appleton, WI Monte Alverno Retreat & Spirituality Center.
Staes, Robert F. *o.p.* '71 (DEN) Denver, CO St. Dominic; [N] Denver, CO Dominican Friars.
Stafford, Dennis '91 (CHI) Deerfield, IL Holy Cross; [A] Mundelein, IL Deacon Formation Program.
Stafford, Edward G. *t.o.r.* '99 (WH) Moundsville, WV St. Francis Xavier's; Glen Dale, WV St. Jude.
Stafford, James D.M. '61 (OKL) Lawton, OK Blessed Sacrament.
Stafford, Rev. Msgr. Joseph L. '57 (BRK) Flushing, NY Holy Family Retired.
Stafford, Michael *o.s.b.* '58 (PRO)[O] Portsmouth, RI Abbey of St. Gregory the Great.
Stagaman, David J. *s.j.* '66 (CHI)[C] Chicago, IL St. Joseph's Seminary; [C] Chicago, IL Jesuit Community at Loyola University Chicago.
Stagg, Robert B. '75 (NEW) Upper Saddle River, NJ Church of the Presentation; Presbyteral Council.
Stagnaro, John J. '76 (BO) Watertown, MA Sacred Heart; Laboure College.
Stahl, Allen M. '75 (ORL) On Duty Outside the Diocese Retired.
Stahl, David A. '91 (DEN) Retired.
Stahmer, Andrew J. '05 (HBG) Kulpmont, PA Holy Angels.
Stahura, Joseph L. '81 (HBG) Greencastle, PA St. Mark the Evangelist.
Staib, Donald F. '61 (R) Apex, NC St. Mary Magdalene; Council of Priests.
Staigers, P. Del '87 (CIN) Cincinnati, OH St. Veronica.
Stainwall, Bernal '80 (NY) Staten Island, NY Holy Rosary.
Stajkowski, James *m.s.* '73 (MIL)[P] Twin Lakes, WI La Salette Missionaries.
Stajkowski, Leo S. '66 (ALN) Reading, PA St. Mary.
Stake, Ronald P. '85 (CHI) Flossmoor, IL Infant Jesus of Prague; Other Assignments.
Stakem, Gary *o.f.m.cap.* '51 (PIT)[M] Butler, PA St. Mary's Friary.
Stakem, Ward G. *o.f.m.cap.* '78 (MO) Air Force Reserve Chaplains.
Stakem, Ward *o.f.m.cap.* '78 (PIT) Cabot, PA St. Joseph; Butler, PA St. Mary of the Assumption; [M] Butler, PA St. Mary's Friary.
Staley, Robert P. '95 (R) Fuquay–Varina, NC St. Bernadette.
Stalla, Michael J. '03 (CLV) Casa Parroquial San Pedro Teotepeque.
Stalter, Rev. Msgr. Cal '94 (AMA) Retired.
Stalzer, Joseph '59 (JOL) Retired.
Stammitti, Anthony O. '91 (LIN) Advocates; Apostolate to the Elderly; Health Care Facilities.
Stampiglia, Fausto *s.a.c.* '60 (VEN) Sarasota, FL St. Martha; [F] Sarasota, FL St. Martha's Housing, Inc.; [F] Sarasota, FL St. Martha's Housing II, Inc.; College of Consultors; Deans; Presbyteral Council; Theologian to the Bishop; Diaconate.
Stamschror, Robert P. '61 (WIN) Retired.
Stanbery, Stephen L. '80 (TOL) Holgate, OH St. Mary; New Bavaria, OH Sacred Heart of Jesus.
Stanchik, Dennis P. '59 (LC) Retired.
Stander, Charles *s.m.* '81 (SAT)[C] San Antonio, TX St. Mary's University of San Antonio, Texas; [L] San Antonio, TX Woodlawn Marianist Community.
Stander, Edwin L. '63 (LIN)[D] Lincoln, NE St. Elizabeth Regional Medical Center; Health Care Facilities.
Stanfield, Francis E. '80 (GLP) Retired.
Stanfield, William L. '76 (MIL)[A] St. Francis, WI Saint Francis de Sales Seminary; Special Assignment.
Stanfill, David J. '10 (RIC) Richmond, VA Holy Rosary.
Stang, Charles L. *s.j.* '67 (MIL)[P] Milwaukee, WI Pere Marquette Jesuit Community; [E] Milwaukee, WI Marquette University High School.
Stang, Mark '90 (SCL) Holdingford, MN Our Lady of Mt. Carmel; Holdingford, MN Immaculate Conception; Holdingford, MN St. Columbkille's; Diocesan Consultors; Holdingford, MN Church of All Saints.
Stang, William J. *c.pp.s.* '77 (MO) Army National Guard Chaplains.
Stang, William J. *c.pp.s.* '77 (LFT)[A] Rensselaer, IN Saint Joseph's College.
Stanganelli, Anthony M. '79 (RVC) Saint James, NY SS. Philip and James; Smithaven Deanery; Priests' Personnel Policy Board.
Stange, James R. '95 (P) Scappoose, OR St. Wenceslaus.
Stangel, Mark J. '65 (MIL) Retired.
Stanger, Edward J. '91 (STL) Ballwin, MO Holy Infant.
Stanger, Harold B. '77 (CHI) Schaumburg, IL St. Marcelline.
Stangl, Alfred '63 (SCL) Presbyteral Council Retired.
Stanibula, Christopher '95 (FR) Fall River, MA St. Anne's.
Stanichar, Rt. Rev. Joseph '68 (HPM) Seattle, WA St. John Chrysostom; Director of Evangelization.
Stanievich, J. Walter '46 (DET) Retired.
Stanis, Casimir M. '01 (SCR) Friendsville, PA St. Francis Xavier; Friendsville, PA Saint Brigid Parish.
Staniskis, Daniel '84 (PAT) Green Pond, NJ St. Simon the Apostle.
Staniszewski, Ignatius *s.s.p.* '64 (Y)[A] Canfield, OH Society of St. Paul.
Staniszewski, Stanley *c.m.* '63 (HRT)[L] Manchester, CT DePaul Provincial Residence.
Staniukiewicz, Edward *o.f.m.conv.* '87 (RCK) Rockford, IL St. Stanislaus Kostka.
Stankard, Albert H. '59 (BO) Framingham, MA St. Stephen.
Stanko, Andrew C. '71 (ALT) Allegheny Deanery; Johnstown, PA St. John Vianney's.
Stankus, Gregory A. '78 (BRK) Brooklyn, NY SS. Simon and Jude.
Stanley, Brian L. '96 (KAL) Military Chaplains; Army Chaplains.
Stanley, Charles R. '71 (BO) Peabody, MA St. Ann.
Stanley, Colm *s.s.c.* '69 (OM)[J] St. Columbans, NE Missionary Society of St. Columban.
Stanley, Cory D. '11 (OKL).
Stanley, Matthew D. '91 (SJ) Palo Alto, CA St. Thomas Aquinas; Priests' Retirement Board.
Stanley, Michael *o.s.a.* '81 (ALB) Waterford, NY St. Mary of the Assumption.
Stanley, Peter '09 (CC) Presbyteral Council; Corpus

Christi, TX SS. Cyril and Methodius.
Stanley, Richard J. *s.j.* '74 (BO)[U] Boston, MA Loyola House; [W] Gloucester, MA Eastern Point Retreat House.
Stanley, Ron '67 (NEW) Midland Park, NJ Nativity.
Stanley, Ronald *o.p.* (NY)[GG] Orangeburg, NY Dominican College; [C] Dominican College.
Stanley, Thomas *s.m.* '50 (CIN)[N] Dayton, OH Mercy Siena Woods, Nursing Care.
Stano, Luke M. *o.s.m.* '61 (CHI)[N] Chicago, IL Order of Friar Servants of Mary (Servites) United States of America Province, Inc.; [N] Chicago, IL Monastery of Our Lady of Sorrows.
Stanonik, Anthony '82 (SD) On Duty Outside the Diocese.
Stanosz, Paul A. '84 (MIL) Milwaukee, WI St. Matthias.
Stanowski, Bartlomiej *o.c.d.* '06 (GRY)[H] Munster, IN Discalced Carmelite Fathers Monastery.
Stansberry, Richard D. '92 (OKL) Oklahoma City, OK Christ the King; Judicial Vicar; Archdiocesan Finance Council.
Stansley, Rev. Msgr. Ralph W. '73 (TR) West Trenton, NJ Our Lady of Good Counsel; Tribunal Judges.
Stanton, Finbarr P. '67 (SAV) Albany, GA St. Teresa; Albany Deanery.
Stanton, Francis M. '51 (COL) Retired.
Stanton, Kyle F. '11 (MAN) Berlin, NH Good Shepherd; Gorham, NH Holy Family.
Stanton, Thomas F. (BO) Massachusetts Correctional Institution – Cedar Junction; Bay State Correctional Facility.
Stanton, Thomas J. '91 (BO) Plainville, MA St. Martha.
Stanton, Rev. Msgr. William J. '56 (SPC) St. Francis de Sales Association; Priests' Mutual Benefit Society Retired.
Stapenhorst, Verne P. '61 (SC) Retired.
Staples, Terrence R. '95 (ARL) Orange, VA St. Isidore the Farmer.
Stapleton, Gerard P. '85 (NO) Port Sulphur, LA St. Patrick.
Starasinich, James E. '99 (NEW) Lyndhurst, NJ Sacred Heart.
Starbuck, James '48 (OAK) Retired.
Starczewski, F. '04 (CHL) Mocksville, NC St. Francis of Assisi.
Stark, Paul V. *s.j.* '55 (STL)[O] St. Louis, MO Jesuit Community Corporation at Saint Louis University – Jesuit Hall; [C] Saint Louis University.
Stark, Paul *s.j.* '85 (STL)[C] Saint Louis University.
Stark, Philip M. '71 (PRO) Retired.
Stark, Robert *s.s.s.* '77 (HON) Members; Kaneohe, HI St. Ann; Resource Developer/Community Organizer; Ex Officio.
Stark, Ronald P. *o.f.m.* '66 (NY)[HH] New York, NY Franciscan Missionary Charities, Inc.
Stark, Ronald *o.f.m.* '66 (BO)[Z] Boston, MA St. Anthony Shrine.
Starkey, Brian Denis *m.afr.* '77 (FgM) Washington, DC MISSIONARIES OF AFRICA; Washington, DC; [O] Washington, DC Missionaries of Africa.
Starkey, Donald '52 (SFE) Retired.
Starkovich, Jeffery Paul '11 (LKC) Jennings, LA Our Lady Help of Christians.
Starman, Bernard '06 (OM) Omaha, NE Assumption, B.V.M.; [N] Omaha, NE Latino Catholic Scholarship Fund; [D] Omaha, NE Assumption–Guadalupe Grade School.
Starmann, Joseph W. '63 (JC) Retired.
Staron, Stanley R. '74 (HRT) Wethersfield, CT Corpus Christi; Wethersfield, CT Sacred Heart.
Starzynski, Stefan P. '96 (ARL) Fairfax, VA St. Mary of Sorrows.
Stasell, Dean '94 (LA)[P] Arcadia, CA Legionaries of Christ.
Stash, Robert '82 (PRM) Akron, OH St. Michael the Archangel.
Stashek, Brian E. '02 (LC) Leave of Absence.
Stasiak, Grzegorz '99 (BRK) Maspeth, NY Holy Cross.
Stasiak, Kurt *o.s.b.* '80 (IND)[A] Saint Meinrad, IN Saint Meinrad School of Theology; [K] Saint Meinrad, IN St. Meinrad Archabbey.
Stasik, Thaddeus '60 (NEW)[L] Rutherford, NJ St. John Vianney Residence for Priests Retired.
Stasiowski, John '65 (FWT) Lewisville, TX St. Philip the Apostle.
Stasker, Rev. Msgr. R. Louis '65 (GR) Grand Rapids, MI Basilica of St. Adalbert; Catholic Secondary Schools Pastor; On Special Assignment; Grand Rapids, MI St. James.
Staskevicius, Vytautas (LIT) Lithuanian R. Catholic Priests' League of Canada.
Staszewski, Joseph P. '64 (E) Retired.
Staszewski, Robert M. (PIT) Bulger, PA St. Ann.
Statkus, Rev. Msgr. Francis J. '46 (PH) Retired.
Statnick, Rev. Msgr. Roger A. '73 (GBG) Belle Vernon, PA St. Sebastian; Office for the Permanent Diaconate.
Statt, Thomas R. '58 (ROC) Rochester, NY St. Charles Borromeo Retired.
Stattmiller, John E. '66 (COL) College of Consultors Retired.
Statz, James '84 (SCL) Sauk Centre, MN Our Lady of the Angels; Sauk Centre, MN St. Alexius.
Statz, Jeffrey P. '05 (MAN) Woodsville, NH St. Catherine of Siena; Woodsville, NH St. Joseph; Grafton County House of Correction.
Staublin, Daniel J. '82 (IND) Deaneries and Deans.
Staublin, Daniel '82 (IND) Brownstown, IN Our Lady of Providence Catholic Church, Brownstown, Inc.; Seymour, IN St. Ambrose Catholic Church, Seymour, Inc.
Staudenmaier, John M. *s.j.* '70 (DET)[K] Detroit, MI Jesuit Community at the University of Detroit Mercy; [C] Detroit, MI Dental School.
Staudinger, Gregory '81 (GF) Columbus, MT St. Mary; [J] Great Falls, MT Big Sky Cum Christo/Cursillo; Diocesan Consultors; Priests' Council.
Staudt, Rev. Msgr. Joseph W. '78 (RVC) Cutchogue, NY Sacred Heart.
Staunton, Rev. Msgr. Patrick Joseph '60 (LA) La Puente, CA St. Joseph Retired.
Stauter, Andrew '57 (MOB)[E] Mobile, AL Little Sisters of the Poor, Home For the Aged, Inc. Retired.
Stavoy, Stephen J. '79 (MO) Navy Reserve Chaplains.
Stawarczyk, Pawel '96 (PHX) Phoenix, AZ St. Luke Roman Catholic Parish.
Stawasz, David *s.c.* '04 (LAN)[E] Chelsea, MI St. Louis Center for Exceptional Children & Adults.
Stawasz, James '53 (HON) Retired.
Stawasz, John B. '53 (HON) Kailua–Kona, HI St. Michael The Archangel Retired.
Stawiarski, Waldemar '03 (CHI) Chicago, IL St. Helen.
Staysniak, Dale W. '75 (CLV) Parma, OH St. Anthony of Padua.
Stead, Julian *o.s.b.* '52 (PRO)[O] Portsmouth, RI Abbey of St. Gregory the Great.
Stealey, Jeffrey '11 (Y) Warren, OH St. James; Warren, OH SS. Cyril and Methodius.
Stearns, Rev. Msgr. Joseph E. '72 (VEN) Sarasota, FL St. Michael the Archangel.
Steber, Rev. Msgr. Michael J. '86 (MAR) Vicar General; Consultors; Charismatic Prayer Groups; Marquette, MI St. Peter Cathedral.
Stec, John '74 (MET) Carteret, NJ Divine Mercy.
Stec, Joseph C. '57 (PH) Retired.
Stec, Mark D. '88 (BEL) Dundas, IL St. Joseph; Newton, IL Holy Cross.
Stec, Michael S. '94 (LIN) Syracuse, NE St. Paulinus; Diocesan Area CCD Directors; Deaf Ministry.
Stec, Robert G. '88 (CLV) Brunswick, OH St. Ambrose.
Stecher, John E. '72 (DAV) On Duty Outside the Diocese.
Stecher, Kenneth C. '68 (DUB)[G] Gilbertville, IA Gilbertville–Raymond Consolidation; Jesup, IA St. Athanasius; Dunkerton, IA St. Francis; Waterloo; Deanery Representatives.
Stechmann, Michael *o.a.r.* '08 (LA) Los Angeles, CA Cristo Rey.
Stechschulte, Barry J. '09 (CIN) Coldwater, OH St. Anthony; Coldwater, OH Holy Trinity; Coldwater, OH St. Mary.
Steck, Christopher W. *s.j.* '94 (WDC)[O] Washington, DC The Jesuit Community at Georgetown University.
Steckel, Gregory A. '81 (DUB) Lost Nation, IA Sacred Heart; Lost Nation, IA St. James; Oxford Junction, IA Sacred Heart.
Stecklein, Warren L. '90 (DOD) Belpre, KS St. Bernard Catholic Church of Belpre, Kansas; Larned, KS Sacred Heart of Jesus Catholic Church of Larned, Kansas; [F] Dodge City, KS The Diocese of Dodge City Priest Retirement Fund, Inc.
Steckler, Gerald G. *s.j.* '57 (SPK)[J] Spokane, WA Regis Community.
Steckler, Kenneth '96 (EVN) Absent on Medical Leave.
Stecz, Jeffrey M. '99 (PH) Philadelphia, PA St. Ignatius of Loyola; Philadelphia, PA Our Mother of Sorrows.
Steed, Mark *o.f.m.conv.* '87 (ALB) Tribes Hill, NY Sacred Heart.
Steele, John *c.s.c.* '97 (FTW) Kendallville.
Steele, Joseph S. '97 (LIN) Bellwood, NE Presentation; [C] David City, NE Aquinas/St. Mary's Schools; Presbyteral Council.
Steele, Michael L. '77 (BO) Marblehead, MA Our Lady, Star of the Sea; Presbyteral Council.
Steele, Philip G. *s.j.* '80 (DEN)[D] Aurora, CO Regis Jesuit High School Corporation; [N] Centennial, CO Regis High Jesuit Community.
Steen, Raymond *o.m.i.* '60 (BO)[X] Tewksbury, MA Immaculate Heart of Mary Residence.
Steenson, Jeffery N. '09 (SFE) On Duty Outside the Archdiocese.
Steenson, Rev. Msgr. Jeffrey N. '09 (POC).
Stefanelli, Joseph *s.m.* '51 (SJ)[M] Cupertino, CA The Marianist Center.
Stefaniak, James S. *m.m.* '50 (SJ)[M] Los Altos, CA Maryknoll.
Stefanko, Rev. Msgr. Paul F. '76 (PRT) Officialis; Office Coordinator; Diocesan Consultors; Department of Canonical Services; Cape Elizabeth, ME St. Bartholomew; Scarborough, ME St. Maximilian Kolbe; South Portland, ME Church of the Holy Cross; South Portland, ME St. John the Evangelist.
Stefanowich, Paul *i.m.c.* '72 (MET)[I] Somerset, NJ Consolata Society for Foreign Missions.
Stefanowski, Mariusz P. '04 (CHI) Chicago, IL St. Ferdinand.
Stefanski, Gery W. '79 (CHI) Other Assignments.
Steffan, Carl J. '58 (HBG) Retired.
Steffen, Arnold *s.v.d.* '57 (FgM) Techny, IL.
Steffen, Francis J. '57 (MAD) Hazel Green, WI Retired.
Steffen, Rev. Msgr. Kenneth C. '84 (SFD) Special or Other Diocesan Assignment; [H] Alton, IL Saint Anthony's Health Center; [L] Alton, IL St. Francis Convent; [N] Alton, IL Saint Anthony's Health System.
Steffen, Mark (JC)[B] Jefferson City, MO St. Mary Health Center.
Steffens, Terrence J. '82 (GRY) Dyer, IN St. Joseph.
Steffensmeier, Ralph J. '59 (OM) Cedar Rapids, NE St. Anthony; St. Edward, NE St. Edward.
Steffes, James P. '93 (WIN) Austin, MN St. Augustine's; Austin, MN St. Edward's; [A] Winona, MN Immaculate Heart of Mary Seminary.
Steffes, LuVerne W. '95 (OM) Atkinson, NE St. Joseph; Stuart, NE St. Boniface.
Steffes, Raymond *o.s.c.* '58 (SCL)[I] Onamia, MN Crosier Priory.
Steffl, Mark S. '06 (NU) Committee for Continuing Education of Clergy; Sleepy Eye, MN St. Mary; Finance Council; Morgan, MN St. Michael.
Steffy, David *l.c.* '94 (MAN)[A] Center Harbor, NH Immaculate Conception Apostolic School; Presbyteral Council.
Stefula, Salvator *t.o.r.* '74 (VEN) Bradenton, FL Sacred Heart.
Stefun, Bonaventure *o.f.m.cap.* '56 (PIT)[M] Pittsburgh St. Augustine Friary.
Steger, Francis R. *o.c.s.o.* '56 (ROC)[K] Piffard, NY Abbey of the Genesee.
Steggert, Bruce A. *s.j.* '93 (WDC)[O] Washington, DC The Jesuit Community of St. Aloysius Gonzaga; [E] Washington, DC Gonzaga College High School.
Stegman, Leonard F. '43 (ELP) Retired.
Stegman, Thomas D. *s.j.* '95 (BO)[U] Brighton, MA Walter Ciszek House.
Stegmann, Robert '95 (GB) Wautoma, WI St. Joseph; Redgranite, WI Sacred Heart of Jesus; Plainfield, WI St. Paul; Redgranite, WI St. Mark.
Stehlik, Thomas J. *c.m.* '96 (NO) New Orleans, LA St. Joseph.
Stehling, Larry '88 (AUS) Austin, TX St. Thomas More.
Stehly, Rev. Msgr. Dennis R. '77 (STL) Chesterfield, MO Ascension.
Stehly, James '83 (LA) Camarillo, CA St. Mary Magdalen.
Stehly, Mark '66 (SEA) Retired.
Stehly, Thomas J. '61 (LA) Retired.
Steier, Charles '73 (SAL) Russell, KS St. Mary Queen of Angels Parish; College of Consultors.
Steiger, Rev. Msgr. Richard A. '67 (PAT) Andover, NJ Good Shepherd Retired.
Steigmeyer, Robert C. *c.s.c.* '47 (FTW)[H] Holy Cross House Retired.
Steik, Dennis *s.m.* '69 (SFR) San Francisco, CA Notre Dame des Victoires.
Steimel, Craig E. '89 (DUB) Mason City, IA St. Joseph.
Steimel, Rev. Msgr. Paul T. '52 (DUB) Retired.
Stein, John *o.f.m.* '85 (GAL) Galveston, TX Holy Family.
Stein, Mark J. '02 (TUC) Willcox, AZ Sacred Heart of Jesus Roman Catholic Church – Willcox.
Stein, Paul '01 (CHI) Chicago, IL St. Sylvester.
Stein, Robert E. '81 (CLV) Doylestown, OH SS. Peter and Paul.
Stein, Rev. Msgr. Timothy P. '84 (ALT) "The Catholic Register"; Altoona, PA Immaculate Conception.
Steinacker, Anthony '06 (FTW) Scouting; Fort Wayne, IN St. Charles Borromeo; [C] Fort Wayne, IN Bishop Dwenger High School; Chaplains.
Steinbacher, Wil *g.h.m.* '62 (CIN)[N] Cincinnati Headquarters of Glenmary Home Missioners Retired.
Steinbauer, Joseph R. '79 (TOL) Toledo, OH Little Flower of Jesus; Members.
Steinbeisser, Joseph A. '86 (NU) Litchfield, MN St. Philip; Priests' Council.
Steinbock, Leo E. '54 (LA) Retired.
Steinbrunner, Jerome *c.pp.s.* '74 (CIN)[N] Dayton Provincial Office of the Cincinnati Province of the Society of the Precious Blood.
Steinbugler, Thomas B. *s.j.* '61 (FgM) New York, NY Society of Jesus.
Steiner, Bernard J. '61 (NU) Vicar for Retired Priests; Priests' Council Retired.
Steiner, Daniel R. '79 (CHI)[J] Chicago, IL Saints Mary and Elizabeth Medical Center.
Steiner, Edward F. '82 (NSH) Nashville, TN Cathedral of the Incarnation; Presbyteral Council; Continuing Education of Clergy.
Steiner, Rev. Msgr. John M. '69 (SPK) Defenders of the Bond.

Steiner, John W. '74 (LC) Wisconsin Rapids, WI St. Vincent de Paul; Deans.
Steiner, Rev. Msgr. John '69 (SPK) Ritzville, WA St. Ambrose; Ritzville, WA St. Agnes Retired.
Steiner, Rev. Msgr. John (GF) Billings, MT St. Pius X.
Steiner, Luke *o.s.b.* '56 (SCL)[I] Collegeville, MN St. John's Abbey, of the Order of St. Benedict.
Steiner, William H. (Carlos) *c.ss.r.* '54 (FgM) Denver, CO Denver Province.
Steingraeber, John *c.ss.r.* '74 (DEN)[N] Denver The Redemptorists/Denver Province.
Steingreaber, Paul *o.s.b.* '65 (KCK)[I] Atchison, KS St. Benedict's Abbey.
Steinhauser, Kenneth B. '70 (JC) On Duty Outside the Diocese.
Steinhauser, Michael G. '67 (BRK) On Leave/ Unassigned.
Steinhiber, Richard *s.s.c.* '51 (OM)[J] St. Columbans, NE Missionary Society of St. Columban.
Steinle, Christopher C. *o.s.a.* '98 (FgM) Olympia Fields, IL Province of Our Mother of Good Counsel (Midwestern).
Steinle, Christopher C. *o.s.a.* '98 (CHI) Chicago, IL St. Rita of Cascia.
Steinle, David G. '79 (DAV) West Burlington, IA St. Mary's; West Burlington, IA SS. Mary and Patrick; Diocesan Consultors.
Steinle, James '53 (TOL) Retired.
Steinman, Robert E. *o.s.a.* '50 (PH)[Y] Villanova, PA St. Thomas Monastery.
Steinmetz, Gerald *o.f.m.* '71 (SFE) Albuquerque, NM Holy Family; [H] Albuquerque, NM The Province of Our Lady of Guadalupe.
Steinmetz, Paul B. *s.j.* '59 (MIL)[P] Wauwatosa, WI Jesuit Community at St. Camillus.
Steinmetz, Ricardo *s.j.* '55 (FgM) St. Louis, MO Society of Jesus.
Steinmetz, Thomas P. '02 (NTN) Manchester, NH Our Lady of the Cedars; National Association of Melkite Youth; DEPARTMENT OF VETERANS AFFAIRS HOSPITALS AND CHAPLAINS.
Steinmiller, Alex *c.p.* '70 (BIR)[B] Birmingham, AL Holy Family Cristo Rey Catholic High School; Birmingham, AL Holy Family; [I] Birmingham, AL Congregation of the Passion: Holy Family Community, Inc.
Steinwachs, David *o.s.b.* '58 (SP)[N] Saint Leo, FL St. Leo Abbey.
Steller, Paul W. '65 (BUF) Lancaster, NY St. Mary of the Assumption.
Stellini, Robert J. '07 (MEM) Dyersburg, TN Holy Angels Church.
Stelmach, Jerome J. '80 (BUF) Absent on Leave.
Stelmach, Rev. Canon Michael '70 (STN) Minneapolis, MN St. Constantine; Diocesan Consultors; Minneapolis.
Stelmaszczyk, Miroslaw '77 (PIT) Creighton, PA Holy Family.
Stelten, Anthony Mary *m.f.v.a.* '00 (BIR)[E] Birmingham, AL Franciscan Missionaries of the Eternal Word, A Public Association of the Christian Faithful.
Stelten, Leo F. '50 (FAR) Retired.
Steltenkamp, Michael F. *s.j.* '76 (WH)[A] Wheeling, WV Wheeling Jesuit University.
Stelter, Richard T. '80 (RVC) Amityville, NY St. Martin of Tours.
Stelzer, Mark S. '83 (SPR) Springfield, MA Sacred Heart; Censor of Librorum.
Stembler, James '89 (CC) Kingsville, TX St. Thomas Aquinas, Catholic Center (Texas A&M University Kingsville); Kingsville, TX St. Gertrude; Diocesan Council of Catholic Women.
Stemmann, Joseph '63 (LAF)[G] New Iberia, LA Consolata Home Retired.
Stemn, Paul G. '09 (CHI) Winnetka, IL SS. Faith, Hope and Charity.
Stempora, Daniel F. '60 (JOL)[K] Naperville, IL St. John Vianney Villa Retired.
Stempsey, William E. *s.j.* '92 (WOR)[N] Worcester, MA Jesuits of the Holy Cross, Inc.
Stenberg, Jim *c.s.b.* '01 (ROC)[K] Rochester, NY Basilian Residence.
Stencil, Rallen '63 (GB) Green Bay, WI Retired.
Stengel, Rev. Msgr. Charles G. '56 (NEW)[L] Rutherford, NJ St. John Vianney Residence for Priests Retired.
Stengel, Mark *o.s.b.* '72 (LR)[A] Subiaco, AR Subiaco Abbey.
Stengel, Rev. Msgr. Paul F. '59 (BUF)[N] Lackawanna, NY Bishop Head Residence Retired.
Stengel, William J. '57 (GB) Porterfield, WI SS. Joseph & Edward Retired.
Stenger, James R. '81 (CLV) Brookpark, OH Mary Queen of the Apostles Parish; Presbyteral Council.
Stenger, Joseph *c.ss.r.* '57 (STP) Brooklyn Center, MN St. Alphonsus; [J] Brooklyn Center, MN Redemptorist Fathers of Hennepin County.
Stenson, Patrick J. *m.s.c.* '63 (CHR) Pawleys Island, SC Precious Blood of Christ.
Stenzel, Eugene F. '67 (WIN) Retired.
Stenzel, William J. '75 (CHI) Berwyn, IL St. Mary of Celle.
Stepanich, Martin *o.f.m.* '41 (CHI)[N] Lemont, IL The Slovene Franciscan Fathers, Order of Friars Minor, Commissariat of the Holy Cross.
Stepanski, Thomas K. '62 (IND) Retired.
Stephan, M. Jeffrey '01 (KC) Plattsburg, MO St. Ann's; Easton, MO St. Joseph's.
Stephan, Matthew J. '83 (CC) Falfurrias, TX Sacred Heart.
Stephen, John *c.r.* '38 (CHI)[M] Des Plaines, IL Nazarethville.
Stephens, Anthony M. *c.p.m.* '05 (OWN)[F] Auburn, KY Fathers of Mercy; Auburn, KY.
Stephens, Timothy J. *s.j.* '99 (BAL)[Q] Towson, MD Maryland Province of the Society of Jesus.
Stephenson, Alfonse J. '75 (MO) Air National Guard Chaplains.
Stephenson, Alphonse J. '75 (PAT) On Duty Outside the Diocese.
Stephenson, Alphonse J. '75 (MO) Presbyteral Council.
Stephenson, Patrick '68 (SR) Retired.
Stephenson, Robert B. '78 (SY) Tully, NY St. Leo.
Stephenson, Robert '78 (SY) Lafayette, NY St. Joseph.
Stepien, Allen F. '65 (PAT) Retired.
Stepien, Miroslaw (JOL) Frankfort, IL St. Anthony.
Steriti, Edward *o.c.s.o.* '57 (WOR)[N] Spencer, MA St. Joseph's Abbey.
Sterling, Donald A. '74 (BAL) Baltimore, MD New All Saints.
Sterling, John J. '96 (COV) Erlanger, KY St. Barbara.
Stern, Benjamin '07 (BEL) Evansville, IL St. Boniface; Ellis Grove, IL Divine Maternity of the B.V.M.
Stern, Rev. Msgr. Robert L. '58 (NY) On Duty Outside the Archdiocese.
Stern, Rev. Archimandrite Robert L. (WDC)[X] Silver Spring, MD Catholics Committed to Support the Pope.
Sternberg, Eric G. '05 (MAD) Advocate/Procurator (cc.1481–1490); Madison, WI St. Paul University Parish; Appointed; Diocesan Consultors.
Sternemann, Reinhard J. *o.s.a.* '66 (CHI)[N] Chicago, IL St. John Stone Friary.
Sterner, James M. '70 (HBG) Littlestown, PA St. Aloysius.
Sterowski, Scott P. '91 (SCR) Scranton, PA St. Francis of Assisi; Scranton, PA Saint Paul of the Cross, Scranton.
Stessman, Rev. Msgr. Gerald '59 (DM) West Des Moines, IA Retired.
Stetson, Rev. Msgr. William (POD) Los Angeles.
Stetz, Allan *o.s.b.* '66 (KC) Conception Junction, MO St. Columba; [J] Priests Elsewhere; Parnell, MO St. Joseph's.
Stetz, Mark '90 (MRY) Cambria, CA Santa Rosa.
Steuben, Rev. Msgr. Lawrence '55 (SAT)[K] San Antonio, TX Casa De Padres Retired.
Steuterman, James M. '75 (WOR) Sterling, MA St. Richard of Chichester.
Stevens, Barton K. '10 (GF)[J] Billings, MT Big Sky Marriage Encounter; Personnel Board; Billings, MT Holy Rosary; Billings, MT Little Flower; Billings, MT Our Lady of Guadalupe.
Stevens, Clifford J. '56 (OM) Boys Town, NE Immaculate Conception B.V.M. Retired.
Stevens, David E. '98 (MO) Air National Guard Chaplains.
Stevens, David '98 (SFS) Sioux Falls, SD St. Therese.
Stevens, Gladstone H. *s.s.* '00 (BAL)[Q] Baltimore, MD St. Mary's Seminary & University.
Stevens, Gladstone H. *s.s.* '00 (SFR)[A] Menlo Park, CA St. Patrick Seminary and University; [A] Menlo Park, CA St. Patrick Seminary and University.
Stevens, Gladstone H. *s.s.* '00 (L) On Duty Outside the Archdiocese.
Stevens, Shane D. '07 (SFS) Aberdeen, SD Sacred Heart.
Stevensky, Rev. Msgr. Mitred John P. '63 (SJP) St. Petersburg, FL Epiphany of Our Lord; Southern Protopresbytery; Presbyteral Council; Arbitration Board; Presbyters.
Stevenson, Dennis E. '88 (COL) Presiding Judges of First Instance; Columbus, OH St. Aloysius.
Stevenson, Francis '92 (SAC) Elk Grove, CA Good Shepherd Catholic Church.
Stevenson, Roy Anthony '81 (OWN) Hardinsburg, KY St. Mary–of–the–Woods; Hardinsburg, KY St. Anthony.
Stevenson, William J. '82 (LAN) Saline, MI St. Andrew the Apostle.
Stevenson, William '86 (SD) San Diego, CA Saint Therese Catholic Parish.
Stevko, Victor *s.v.d.* '57 (FgM) Techny, IL.
Stewart, August '94 (COS) Parker, CO Ave Maria.
Stewart, Claudio (NY) New York, NY St. Paul.
Stewart, Columba *o.s.b.* '90 (SCL)[B] Saint John's University; [I] Collegeville, MN St. John's Abbey, of the Order of St. Benedict.
Stewart, Edward R. '89 (BRK) On Leave/Unassigned.
Stewart, George R. '94 (NY) Bronx, NY St. Brendan.
Stewart, J. Patrick *s.j.* '61 (SPK)[J] Spokane, WA Regis Community.
Stewart, Keith '93 (MEM) Seminarians; Vocations; Memphis, TN St. Anne's; Formation of Permanent Deacons.
Stewart, Michael L. '75 (MEM) Judges Retired.
Stewart, Patrick F. '78 (LEX) London, KY St. William.
Stewart, Paul '73 (MO) Air Force Reserve Chaplains; On Duty Outside the Diocese.
Stewart, Robert H. '82 (KC) Lees Summit, MO St. Margaret of Scotland Catholic Church.
Stewart, Rev. Msgr. Terrence L. '70 (GR) Sparta, MI Holy Family.
Sthokal, Edward S. *s.j.* '54 (STP)[M] Lake Elmo, MN Jesuit Retreat House.
Sticco, Peter T. *s.a.c.* '69 (NEW) Fairview, NJ Our Lady of Grace; [L] South Orange, NJ Pallottine Fathers & Brothers; South Orange, NJ; [Q] South Orange, NJ Pallottine Intra–Community Operating Corporation.
Sticco, Peter T. *s.a.c.* '69 (BAL)[Q] Baltimore, MD Pallottine Center for Apostolic Causes.
Stice, Randy '07 (KNX) Worship and Liturgy; Knoxville, TN Cathedral of the Sacred Heart of Jesus.
Sticha, Cory D. '08 (GF) Worship Commission; Malta, MT St. Mary; [J] Malta, MT St. Mary's Catholic Education Trust; D.C.C.W.
Stickle, William '50 (RIC) Retired.
Stieferman, Lowell L. '63 (OKL) Retired.
Stieferman, Lowell '63 (OKL) Defenders of the Bond.
Stiefvater, Robert X. '77 (MIL) Fond du Lac, WI Holy Family.
Stiegeler, A. Francis *s.j.* '78 (SFR)[E] San Francisco, CA St. Ignatius College Preparatory (Coed); [N] San Francisco, CA Jesuit Community at St. Ignatius College Preparatory.
Stieger, Rev. Msgr. Joseph '50 (MRY) Retired.
Stiene, Paul *i.c.* '90 (PEO) Elmwood, IL St. Patrick's.
Stikel, Roman '88 (MIL) Kenosha, WI St. Elizabeth.
Stiles, J. Roy '63 (L) Vicar for Retired Clergy; Louisville, KY St. Bartholomew Retired.
Stiles, Wallis J. '61 (SAT) D'Hanis, TX Holy Cross; In Rural Area; Archdiocesan Presbyteral Council; Priests Personnel Board.
Stillmock, Martin *c.ss.r.* '58 (STP) Brooklyn Center, MN St. Alphonsus; [J] Brooklyn Center, MN Redemptorist Fathers of Hennepin County.
Stillmunks, Steven J. '77 (OM) Omaha, NE Christ the King.
Stilwell, Dennis R. '71 (GLD) Petoskey, MI St. Francis Xavier.
Stimpson, Adam '09 (PEO) La Salle, IL Resurrection; La Salle, IL St. Hyacinth's; La Salle, IL St. Patrick's; La Salle, IL Shrine of Queen of the Holy Rosary.
Stine, Robert F. '73 (BR) Baton Rouge, LA Christ the King; [K] Baton Rouge, LA Christ the King Parish and Catholic Center; Campus Ministry; Clergy Personnel; Board Members.
Stingel, Louis F. '60 (MET)[I] Somerset, NJ Maria Regina Residence Retired.
Stinson, Michael *f.s.s.p.* '09 (SAC) Sacramento, CA St. Stephen the First Martyr Parish.
Stirniman, Jeffrey D. '95 (PEO) Clergymen's Aid, Inc.; Princeton, IL St. Louis; Vicariates and Vicars.
Stirpe, Carlo C. '65 (SY) Camden, NY St. John the Evangelist; Camden, NY St. Mary.
Stiteler, Francis Michael *o.c.s.o.* '83 (ATL)[F] Conyers, GA The Monastery of the Holy Spirit; Conyers, GA.
Stites, John F. '76 (TOL) Cloverdale, OH St. Barbara; Ottoville, OH Immaculate Conception.
Stitt, Bryan D. '03 (OG) Catholic Scouting; Vocations Director; Malone, NY Notre Dame.
Stluka, Jerome D. '69 (COL) Columbus, OH Holy Cross.
Stobba, Joseph G. *o.s.a.* '59 (CHI)[N] Chicago St. Augustine Friary.
Stober, Rev. Msgr. William P. '73 (PAT) Branchville, NJ Our Lady Queen of Peace.
Stobie, Stephen A. '96 (P) Wilsonville, OR St. Cyril.
Stobie, Stephen '81 (P) Personnel Board.
Stochl, John J. *s.j.* '54 (FgM) St. Louis, MO Society of Jesus.
Stochmal, Marek '95 (DET) Absent on Leave.
Stock, Thomas E. '98 (CLV) Medina, OH St. Francis Xavier.
Stockelman, William R. '78 (CIN) Amelia, OH St. Bernadette.
Stockert, Harold R. '63 (PSC) New York, NY SS. Peter and Paul Retired.
Stockhausen, Gerard L. *s.j.* '79 (WDC)[X] Washington, DC Jesuit Conference, Inc.; [X] Washington, DC Jesuit Volunteers; [O] Washington, DC Leonard Neale House.
Stockman, Gerald W. '64 (JC) Retired.
Stockton, Marc '02 (E) Sharpsville, PA St. Bartholomew; [F] Hermitage, PA Shenango Valley Catholic School System, Inc.; [F] Hermitage, PA Blessed John Paul II Elementary School; [F] Hermitage, PA Kennedy Catholic Middle School; [F] Hermitage, PA Kennedy Catholic High School.
Stockus, Edward S. '91 (CHI) Lyons, IL St. Hugh Retired.

Stodola, Francis '80 (MO) Army National Guard Chaplains.
Stodola, Francisco '89 (LAR) Cotulla, TX Sacred Heart.
Stoeckig, Robert E. '89 (LAV) Boulder City, NV St. Andrew's.
Stoeckig, Robert '94 (LAV) Presbyteral Council for the Diocese of Las Vegas; Board of Trustees; Chancellor and Moderator of the Curia; Director of Clergy Education; Home and Foreign Missions; Information, Communications and Media; Native American and Colored People Commission; Priests' Pension Board; Vicar General.
Stoecklein, Ted D. '01 (DOD) College of Consultors; Spearville, KS St. John the Baptist Catholic Church of Spearville, Kansas; Dodge City, KS Cathedral of Our Lady of Guadalupe Catholic Church of Dodge City, Kansas; Youth/Family Ministry and Religious Formation; [F] Dodge City, KS The Diocese of Dodge City Priest Retirement Fund, Inc.
Stoegbauer, Conrad H. '82 (CAM) Retired.
Stoeger, James A. *s.j.* '74 (WDC)[X] Washington, DC Jesuit Secondary Education Association; [O] Washington, DC Leonard Neale House.
Stoeger, John D. '72 (LA) Cardinal Manning House of Prayer for Priests.
Stoeger, William R. *s.j.* '72 (TUC)[E] Tucson, AZ Jesuit Community of the Vatican Observatory.
Stoerlein, Rev. Msgr. Joseph G. '49 (CAM) Retired.
Stoetzel, Charles D. '80 (LC) La Crosse, WI St. Joseph the Workman Cathedral.
Stoffel, Richard J. '79 (MIL) Slinger, WI St. Peter; Allenton, WI Resurrection.
Stoffer, Patrick *o.f.m. conv.* (CHI)[N] Chicago, IL Sacred Heart Friary.
Stohrer, Walter J. *s.j.* '60 (MIL)[P] Milwaukee, WI Jesuit Community at Marquette University.
Stoia, Aurelius E. '09 (CHK) Saipan, MP Santa Remedios Parish; Legion of Mary; Presbyteral Council.
Stokes, David L. '02 (PRO) Censors of Books.
Stokes, Jason F. '11 (ALN) Pottsville, PA St. Patrick.
Stokes, Thomas A. *s.m.* '63 (SP) Tampa, FL Our Lady of Perpetual Help.
Stokowski, Lucjan '77 (CLV) Cleveland, OH St. John Cantius.
Stolcis, Ronald '68 (CHY) Sheridan, WY Holy Name.
Stoley, Lawrence J. '91 (LIN)[F] Waverly, NE Our Lady of Good Counsel Retreat House; Presbyteral Council; Commission for Sacred Liturgy and Sacred Music; Priests' Continuing Education Committee; Retreat Program; Schools.
Stolinski, Dennis R. '69 (OM) Retired.
Stolinski, Robert A. '70 (BUF)[N] Buffalo, NY Sheehan Residence for Priests Retired.
Stoll, Mark J. '92 (SC) Moville, IA Immaculate Conception; Vice Chancellor; Moville, IA St. Michael's.
Stollenwerk, Charles J. '73 (CLV) North Olmsted, OH St. Richard; Associate Judges.
Stoltz, John J. '90 (L) Louisville, KY St. Gabriel the Archangel; Defenders of the Bond; Ex Officio.
Stoltz, Richard L. '74 (STL) New Melle, MO Immaculate Heart of Mary.
Stolz, William K. *s.j.* '62 (SAC)[C] Sacramento, CA Jesuit High School.
Stolz, William K. *s.j.* '62 (SJ)[M] Los Gatos, CA Sacred Heart Jesuit Center.
Stolzman, William F. '71 (STP) Retired.
Stone, Bob '01 (CR) Argyle, MN St. Rose of Lima; Strandquist, MN Assumption – Church of Florian; Stephen, MN St. Stephen's.
Stone, Francis Mary *m.f.v.a.* '98 (BIR) Absent on Leave.
Stone, Harold *s.t.* (FAJ) Loiza, PR Santiago Apostol, El Mayor.
Stone, Jason '10 (JOL) Joliet, IL The Cathedral of St. Raymond.
Stone, Jeffrey E. '05 (SFD) Liberty, IL St. Brigid; Liberty, IL St. Edward; Liberty, IL St. Joseph.
Stone, Robert J. *c.m.* '77 (PH)[Y].
Stone, Robert '90 (KC) Independence, MO Nativity of Mary Parish.
Stone, Ronald G. '01 (SFE) Presbyterian Hospital; Rio Rancho, NM St. Thomas Aquinas.
Stone, Theodore '52 (CHI) Park Ridge, IL Mary, Seat of Wisdom Retired.
Stoneberg, Jeffery '90 (JOL) Channahon, IL St. Ann Parish.
Stoner, John Bosco *o.s.b.* '76 (LA)[P] Valyermo, CA St. Andrew's Abbey.
Stoner, Timothy L. '96 (GI) Chadron, NE St. Patrick's.
Stookey, Gerald L. *o.p.* '78 (DEN)[N] Denver, CO Dominican Friars; Denver, CO St. Dominic.
Stopyra, David M. *o.f.m.conv.* '60 (FR) Taunton, MA Our Lady of the Holy Rosary; [B] Taunton, MA Coyle and Cassidy High School.
Storck, Edward J. '52 (WIL) Retired.
Storey, Kevin J. *c.s.b.* '92 (GAL)[E] Houston, TX St. Thomas High School.
Storey, Richard '04 (KCK) Regional Pastoral Leaders; Overland Park, KS Holy Spirit.
Stormes, James R. *s.j.* '79 (SFR)[N] San Francisco, CA Loyola House Jesuit Community.
Stortz, Donald L. '64 (OM) Retired.
Stortz, Rev. Msgr. Mario '49 (AMA) Happy, TX Holy Name of Jesus Retired.
Stout, O. Hugh '61 (CAM) Retired.
Stout, Richard E. *c.s.c.* '71 (FgM)[H] Notre Dame Congregation of Holy Cross, United States Province of Priests & Brothers; New Rochelle, NY Eastern Brothers Province.
Stout, William *o.f.m.* '00 (JKS) Greenwood, MS St. Francis of Assisi; Greenwood, MS Immaculate Heart of Mary.
Stoviak, Leonard W. '73 (GBG) North Huntingdon, PA St. Elizabeth Ann Seton.
Stowe, Gregory P. '06 (PRO) Absent on Leave.
Stowe, John *o.f.m.conv.* '95 (ELP)[J] El Paso, TX Franciscans, Secular Order of Franciscans.
Stowe, John *o.f.m.conv.* (TOL) Carey, OH Our Lady of Consolation, Basilica–National Shrine.
Stowe, John *o.f.m.conv.* '95 (IND)[J] Mount St. Francis, IN Province of Our Lady of Consolation, Inc.
Stoyle, James '91 (FTW) Kendallville, IN Immaculate Conception.
Strabala, Matthew T.D. *o.p.* '00 (SFE) Albuquerque, NM St. Thomas Aquinas University Parish; [K] Albuquerque, NM St. Thomas Aquinas (Newman Center) University Parish.
Strachota, Michael D. '79 (MIL) Oconomowoc, WI St. Catherine; Nashotah, WI St. Joan of Arc.
Strader, Mark A. '91 (LA) Temple City, CA St. Luke the Evangelist.
Stradinger, Stephen J. '74 (MIL) Racine, WI St. Mary by the Lake.
Stradomski, Ryszard '83 (SP) Crystal River, FL St. Benedict.
Strahan, Rev. Msgr. Francis V. '59 (BO) Framingham, MA St. Bridget; Trustees.
Strain, Eugene R. '53 (DET) Retired.
Straka, Francis P. '90 (ALN) Northampton, PA Assumption of the Blessed Virgin Mary; Saint Vincent De Paul Society.
Straley, Michael '83 (PHX) Glendale, AZ Our Lady of Perpetual Help Roman Catholic Parish.
Strand, Luke N. '09 (MIL) Fond du Lac, WI Holy Family.
Strange, J. Michael *s.s.* '65 (SFR) San Francisco, CA St. Vincent de Paul.
Strange, J. Michael *s.s.* '65 (BAL)[Q] Baltimore Society of St. Sulpice, Province of the United States.
Strange, Leon Gerald '11 (NSH) Hendersonville, TN Our Lady of the Lake.
Strange, Todd O. '09 (SEA) Issaquah, WA St. Joseph.
Strano, Rev. Msgr. Edward '56 (TR) Belmar, NJ; [N] Trenton, NJ Villa Vianney Retired.
Stransky, Thomas F. *c.s.p.* '57 (WDC)[B] Washington, DC St. Paul's College Retired.
Strasser, John R. '76 (DOD) Kinsley, KS St. Nicholas Catholic Church of Kinsley, Kansas; College of Consultors; Kinsley, KS St. Joseph Catholic Church of Offerle, Kansas; Diocesan Finance Council; Diocesan Review Board; [F] Dodge City, KS The Diocese of Dodge City Priest Retirement Fund, Inc.
Strasz, James *s.m.* '80 (DET)[D] Pontiac, MI Notre Dame Preparatory School and Marist Academy.
Straten, William R. '09 (AUS) College Station, TX St. Mary.
Stratman, Joseph '77 (BEA) Retired.
Stratman, Raymond '55 (LEX) Retired.
Stratman, Thomas F. '50 (DAV)[J] Davenport, IA St. Vincent Center Retired.
Straub, David R. '94 (CHI) Lake Villa, IL Prince of Peace.
Straub, Rev. Msgr. Edward F. '65 (NY) Liberty, NY St. Peter; Sullivan.
Straughn, Daniel T. '04 (PIT) Port Vue, PA Saint Mark Parish.
Strausser, George '77 (PH) Philadelphia, PA St. Agatha–St. James.
Stravinskas, Peter M.J. '77 (B) On Duty Outside the Diocese.
Strawn, Nicholas *s.v.d.* '62 (FgM) Techny, IL.
Strazicich, Mel '07 (SEA) Kelso, WA Immaculate Heart of Mary; Castle Rock, WA St. Mary.
Strebel, Roger W. '66 (GB) White Lake, WI SS. James–Stanislaus Retired.
Strebig, John J. '52 (GRY) Retired.
Strebler, Charles F. '94 (CLV) Cleveland, OH Cathedral of St. John the Evangelist; Adjunct Judicial Vicars.
Strecok, Lubomir J. '98 (ALT) Clarence, PA Queen of Archangels.
Streichardt, Wolfgang '82 (SAG) Retired.
Streicher, Bernard J. *s.j.* '60 (CLV)[D] Cleveland, OH St. Ignatius High School.
Streifel, Keith N. '99 (BIS) Dickinson, ND St. Joseph; Associate Judges.
Streit, David *s.v.d.* '69 (FgM) Techny, IL.
Streit, Thomas G. *c.s.c.* '86 (FTW)[B] University of Notre Dame Du Lac; [H] Notre Dame, IN Holy Cross Community, Corby Hall, University of Notre Dame.
Streitenberger, Adam A. '07 (COL) Portsmouth, OH St. Mary.
Strelecki, Rev. Msgr. Richard T. '69 (NEW)[L] Rutherford, NJ St. John Vianney Residence for Priests Retired.
Strelick, Charles J. '56 (MAR) Retired.
Strelinski, Ernest '65 (PIT) Allison Park, PA St. Ursula.
Stretton, Noel '59 (DUL) Duluth, MN St. Michael; Duluth Federal Prison Retired.
Streveler, Robert A. '69 (LC) Athens, WI Holy Family; Edgar, WI St. John the Baptist; Appointed Members.
Streza, Charles V. '43 (ROM) Retired.
Strickenberger, Matthew J. '10 (E) Erie, PA St. Jude the Apostle.
Stricker, Robert A. '48 (CIN) Imprimatur Censors Retired.
Strickland, Rev. Msgr. Joseph E. '85 (TYL) Delegate of the Apostolic Administrator; College of Consultors; Judges; Priests' Pension Board; Priests' Personnel Board; Presbyteral Council; Diocesan Finance Council; Diocesan Implementation Committee On Ethics and Integrity Policy for Church Personnel; [A] Tyler, TX Bishop T. K. Gorman Regional School; Moderator of the Curia; Southern Vicariate.
Strieder, Leon '76 (AUS) On Duty Outside the Diocese.
Strieder, Leon '76 (GAL) Houston, TX St. Michael.
Striedl, Max J. '96 (RCK) Warren, IL St. Joseph; Lena, IL St. Joseph; Warren, IL St. Ann.
Striegel, Robert M. '73 (DAV) Veteran's Administration Hospital; DEPARTMENT OF VETERANS AFFAIRS HOSPITALS AND CHAPLAINS; Richland, IA Ss. Joseph and Cabrini.
Stringini, John L. '79 (RCK) Retired.
Stripe, Keith A. '96 (TOL) Maumee, OH St. Joseph; Members.
Strittmatter, Andre *t.o.r.* '61 (ALT)[G] Loretto, PA St. Francis Friary at Mount Assisi.
Strittmatter, Robert '66 (FWT) Fort Worth, TX San Mateo; Fort Worth, TX St. Mary of the Assumption.
Strmecki, Ivan M. *o.f.m.* '05 (CHI) Chicago, IL St. Jerome.
Strobl, Andrew '09 (KCK)[B] Overland Park, KS Saint Thomas Aquinas High School, Inc.; Olathe, KS Prince of Peace.
Strock, Richard M. '65 (LR)[G] Little Rock, AR St. John Manor Retired.
Strohmeyer, George E. '64 (E)[B] Erie, PA Gannon University; Priest Personnel Board; [Q] Erie, PA Gannon University.
Strollo, Charles P. *c.m.* '73 (PH) Philadelphia, PA Immaculate Conception.
Stromberg, James S. '57 (STP) Retired.
Strommer, James G. *c.p.* '70 (SAC)[H] Citrus Heights, CA Christ the King Passionist Retreat Center.
Stromski, Adam F.X. '46 (Y)[I] Canton, OH House of Loreto Retired.
Strong, Ambrose *o.cist.* '11 (DAL)[J] Irving, TX Cistercian Abbey of Our Lady of Dallas.
Strong, Barry R. *o.s.f.s.* '84 (WIL)[J] Wilmington, DE Wilmington–Philadelphia Province of the Oblates of St. Francis de Sales.
Stronkowski, John '85 (BGP) Bridgeport, CT St. Ambrose.
Stroot, Thomas J. '70 (WCH) Frontenac, KS Sacred Heart.
Strother, Michael A. '05 (BEA) Woodville, TX Our Lady of the Pines; Presbyteral Council.
Strouse, Anthony '10 (LAN) East Lansing, MI St. Thomas Aquinas.
Struginski, Rafal *s.j.* '11 (OAK)[L] Berkeley, CA Jesuit Fathers and Brothers.
Struik, Felix A.P. *o.p.* '58 (SJN)[A] Bayamon Central University.
Strumski, Matthew J. '48 (PRO) Retired.
Strupp, James A. '67 (MIL) Retired.
Strupp, Joachim *o.f.m.cap.* '63 (MIL)[P] Mount Calvary, WI St. Lawrence Friary Retired.
Strus, Walter A. '94 (CHI) Other Assignments.
Struzik, Edward J. '85 (MET)[I] Somerset, NJ Maria Regina Residence Retired.
Struzynski, Robert *o.f.m.* '63 (BUF)[P] West Clarksville, NY Mount Irenaeus, Franciscan Mountain Retreat & Holy Peace Friary; [Q] St. Bonaventure, NY St. Bonaventure University.
Struzzieri, Andrew L. '75 (BRK) Brooklyn, NY St. Matthew.
Struzzo, John A. *c.s.c.* '65 (FTW)[H] Notre Dame Congregation of Holy Cross, United States Province of Priests & Brothers.
Strycharz, Stanislaw '91 (VEN) On Administrative Leave.
Stryker, Peter *c.p.m.* (GB)[L] New Franken, WI The Shrine of Our Lady of Good Help, Inc.
Strynkowski, Rev. Msgr. John '63 (BRK) Brooklyn, NY The Cathedral–Basilica of St. James; Committee for Catholic–Protestant Relations; Vicar for Higher Education; [D] Brooklyn, NY Campus Ministers and Ministry Centers.
Strzadala, Wieslaw P. *s.d.s.* '90 (NEW) Hackensack, NJ St. Joseph's.
Strzalkowski, Dariusz '00 (DET) Taylor, MI Our Lady of the Angels.
Strzelecki, Dariusz '11 (BRK) Glendale, NY St. Pancras.

Strzok, James J. *s.j.* '70 (MIL)[P] Milwaukee Jesuit Provincial Office, Wisconsin Province.
Strzok, James J. *s.j.* '70 (FgM) Milwaukee, WI Society of Jesus.
Strzyz, Stanislaus '68 (BAK) Eastern; Health and Retirement Board; Burns, OR Holy Family; Council of Priests and Diocesan Consultors.
Stua, Ronald *c.m.f.* '81 (CHI) Oak Park, IL; [N] Chicago, IL Claret House.
Stuart, Francis *o.s.b.* '61 (JC) Retired.
Stuart, George E. '89 (WDC) Bethesda, MD Little Flower; Pastoral Center Special Ministries; Archivist; Defenders of the Bond; Vice Chancellor; Promoters of Justice.
Stubbs, Michael C. '78 (KCK) Overland Park, KS Holy Cross.
Stubeda, Anthony J. '85 (NU) Glencoe, MN St. Pius X; Silver Lake, MN Church of the Holy Family; Committee on Parishes; Winsted, MN Holy Trinity.
Stubna, Kris D. '85 (PIT) Pittsburgh, PA SS. Simon and Jude; [Q] Pittsburgh, PA Scholastic Opportunity Scholarship Program; Secretary for Catholic Education; Diocesan Development Board.
Studeny, Colman *o.f.m.cap.* '61 (FgM) Pittsburgh, PA Province of St. Augustine.
Studer, Louis *o.m.i.* '70 (STP)[M] Buffalo, MN Christ the King Retreat Center.
Studer, Louis *o.m.i.* '76 (WDC)[O] Washington, DC Oblate Community; [O] Washington, DC Provincial Offices of the United States Province of the Missionary Oblates of Mary Immaculate.
Studerus, Rev. Msgr. Gregory J. '80 (NEW) West New York, NJ St. Joseph of the Palisades.
Studniewski, Gary R. '95 (WDC) Military Chaplains; Army Chaplains.
Studzinski, Raymond *o.s.b.* '69 (IND)[K] Saint Meinrad St. Meinrad Archabbey.
Studzinski, Raymond *o.s.b.* '69 (WDC)[C] Catholic University of America, The.
Stuebben, Rev. Msgr. Lawrence J. '55 (SAT)[Q] San Antonio, TX Archdiocese of San Antonio Endowment Fund for Parishes, School and Ministries; [Q] San Antonio, TX Mary Jane Ihle Clark Endowment Fund for Ministry to Persons with Disabilities; College of Consultors Retired.
Stuempel, Robert L. '75 (L) Louisville, KY St. Bernard.
Stuglik, Robert '03 (CHI) Summit, IL St. Joseph.
Stuglik, Stanley '10 (CHI) Oak Lawn, IL St. Catherine of Alexandria.
Stuhrenberg, James A. '06 (CHL) Jefferson, NC St. Francis of Assisi.
Stump, David X. *s.j.* '71 (NEW)[B] Jersey City, NJ Jesuit Center; [L] Jersey City, NJ Jesuits of Saint Peter's College, Inc.
Stump, James M. *o.f.m.cap.* '88 (MO) DEPARTMENT OF VETERANS AFFAIRS HOSPITALS AND CHAPLAINS.
Stump, James *o.f.m.cap.* '88 (SFR)[N] Burlingame, CA Capuchin Provincial House.
Stumpf, Michael J. '01 (PIT) Pittsburgh, PA St. Mary of the Mount.
Stumpf, Walter P. '06 (GB) Crivitz, WI St. Mary; White Lake, WI SS. James–Stanislaus.
Stumpf, Rev. Msgr. William F. '85 (IND) Board of Consultors; Finance Council; Brookville, IN St. Peter Catholic Church, Franklin County, Inc.; Nashville, IN St. Agnes Catholic Church, Nashville, Inc.
Stunek, Howard *o.f.m.* '57 (MIL)[P] Burlington, WI Queen of Peace Friary.
Stunek, Leonard *o.f.m.* '60 (CLV) Cleveland, OH St. Stanislaus; [N] Cleveland, OH St. Stanislaus Friary.
Stupca, Edward L. '61 (HEL) Retired.
Sturm, Donald E. '58 (KC) Legion of Mary.
Sturm, John G. *s.j.* '50 (BUF) Buffalo, NY St. Michael.
Sturm, Jon (P)[J] Oregon City, OR Willamette Falls Hospital; [J] Portland, OR Providence Health & Services–Oregon.
Sturm, Michael O. '69 (MIL) Retired.
Sturm, Samuel L. '99 (KNX) Dayton, TN St. Bridget.
Sturn, Michael L. '77 (SB) Ontario, CA St. George.
Sturtz, Richard S. '56 (OG) Schroon Lake, NY St. Joseph; Schroon Lake, NY Our Lady of Lourdes.
Styc, Adam *s.d.s.* '96 (GRY)[H] Merrillville, IN Salvatorian Fathers (Society of the Divine Savior).
Styers, Robert (CC)[D] Beeville, TX.
Styles, Kenneth A. *s.j.* '72 (CLV)[D] Cleveland, OH St. Ignatius High School.
Suan, Charito E. '85 (SFR) San Francisco, CA St. Elizabeth; Deans.
Suarez, Carlos D. '11 (BO) Brockton, MA Our Lady of Lourdes; Brockton, MA St. Edith Stein; Brockton, MA Christ the King.
Suarez, Carlos *o.s.b.* '86 (FgM) Richardton, ND Assumption Abbey.
Suarez, Carlos *o.s.b.* '86 (BIS)[A] Richardton, ND Assumption Abbey.
Suarez, Edgar *c.s.v.* '04 (CHI)[N] Arlington Heights Viatorian Province Center–Clerics of St. Viator.
Suarez, Gildardo '92 (PRO) Providence, RI Assumption of the Blessed Virgin Mary.
Suarez, Jesus E. '86 (GAL) Houston, TX St. Philip of Jesus.
Suarez, Leo '88 (STO) Absent on Leave.
Suarez, Luke '11 (BGP) Newtown, CT St. Rose of Lima.
Suarez, Octavio '64 (TYL) Chandler, TX St. Boniface.
Suarez, Pedro A. *s.j.* '72 (MIA)[E] Miami, FL Belen Jesuit Preparatory School; [H] Miami, FL Villa Javier.
Suarez, Walter '96 (SJ) Special Assignment; Council of Priests.
Suaybaguio, Evangelio R. '75 (NY) Staten Island, NY St. Joseph, St. Thomas.
Suberlak, Donald *c.r.* '67 (KAL) Three Oaks, MI St. Mary of the Assumption.
Subiza, Innocent '01 (SAC)[K] Davis, CA Newman Catholic Student Community Davis; Davis, CA St. James.
Subler, Carl A. '04 (COL) Military Services; Army Chaplains.
Subocz, Adam C. '86 (HRT) Union City, CT St. Hedwig; [M] Hartford, CT SS. Cyril & Methodius Convent; Union City, CT St. Mary.
Subosa, Cristobal *f.i.m.* '01 (SB) San Jacinto, CA St. Anthony.
Suchan, Rev. Msgr. Aleksander '88 (DUL) Pine City, MN Immaculate Conception.
Suchan, Robert J. *s.j.* '56 (FgM) New York, NY Society of Jesus.
Sucharski, Michael M. *s.v.d.* '83 (LAF) Maurice, LA St. Joseph.
Sucher, Frederick *c.p.* '44 (L)[L] Louisville, KY Sacred Heart Retreat.
Suchnicki, Michael *o.f.m.cap.* '88 (DEN)[N] Denver, CO St. Anthony of Padua Friary.
Suchocki, James A. '62 (GLD) Retired.
Sucholet, James J. '91 (NOR) District Spiritual Advisors; Durham, CT Notre Dame; Middlefield, CT St. Colman.
Suchy, Theodore D. *o.s.b.* '67 (JOL)[A] Lisle, IL Benedictine University; [L] Lisle, IL St. Procopius Abbey; Lisle, IL.
Sudano, Glenn *c.f.r.* '84 (NEW)[L] Newark, NJ Franciscan Friars of the Renewal.
Sudario, Rev. Msgr. Antonio '69 (SB) San Bernardino, CA St. Bernardine Medical Center.
Sudarto, Gregorius Tulus '05 (LA) Monterey Park, CA St. Stephen Martyr.
Sudekum, Rev. Msgr. Edward J. '61 (STL) Retired.
Sudlik, Leonard '76 (GR) Diocesan Finance Council Membership.
Sudlik, Richard *o.m.i.* '72 (BUF) Buffalo, NY Holy Angels.
Sudol, Gerard J. '80 (NEW) Special Assignment in the Archdiocese.
Sudol, Ignatius *o.h.* (LA)[BB] Ojai, CA St. Joseph's H. & RC Foundation.
Suehr, Philip *o.s.c.* '66 (PHX)[F] Phoenix, AZ Crosier Community of Phoenix (Canons Regular of the Order of the Holy Cross) Retired.
Suellentrop, Anthony J. '73 (DOD) Retired.
Suelzer, Rev. Msgr. John N. '65 (FTW) Fort Wayne, IN St. Charles Borromeo; Budget Committee; Clergy Retirement Board.
Suelzer, Rev. Msgr. John '65 (FTW) Retired Clergy Committee.
Suenram, John Magdalene *o.c.d.* '87 (LR)[A] Little Rock, AR Marylake – Carmelite Novitiate.
Sueper, Alban *s.s.c.* '53 (OM)[J] St. Columbans Missionary Society of St. Columban Retired.
Sueper, Alban *s.s.c.* '53 (PRO)[O] Bristol, RI St. Columban's Retirement House Retired.
Suess, Milton M. '63 (GB) Luxemburg, WI Immaculate Conception; Casco, WI Holy Trinity; Censores Librorum.
Sughroue, Adam M. '11 (LIN) Lincoln, NE St. John the Apostle; Advocates.
Sughrue, Paul S. '70 (BO) Braintree, MA St. Clare.
Suglia, Dennis '11 (RVC) Deer Park, NY SS. Cyril and Methodius.
Sugrue, John F. '62 (CAM) Retired.
Sugrue, Patrick *o.c.d.* '64 (SJ)[M] San Jose, CA Carmelite Monastery, Novitiate.
Suh, Daniel '95 (BRK) Woodside, NY St. Sebastian; Graduate Studies.
Suhaka, Peter '86 (MET) Old Bridge, NJ St. Thomas the Apostle.
Suhoza, John E. '68 (PIT) Pittsburgh, PA Resurrection Retired.
Suhy, Clement *o.s.b.* '05 (DET) Lapeer, MI Immaculate Conception of the Blessed Virgin Mary.
Sui, Peter Kin Chung *s.j.* '93 (SJ) Chinese Catholic Community.
Suibielski, Kenneth J. '77 (PRO) Misquamicut, RI St. Clare; Council Members.
Suing, Benedict *o.s.b.* '54 (P)[L] St. Benedict, OR Mt. Angel Abbey.
Suire, Jared '10 (LAF) Crowley, LA St. Michael Archangel.
Suit, Robert J. '74 (STL) Valley Park, MO Sacred Heart.
Sujono, Yohanes *m.s.c.* '95 (MI) Ebeye, MH Queen of Peace; Prefecture Consultors.
Sularz, Thomas '71 (JOL) Wheaton, IL St. Daniel the Prophet Church; Deans.
Suleimanovs, Arnis G. *o.s.p.p.e.* '06 (CHI) Harwood Heights–Norridge, IL St. Rosalie.
Sulistya, Francis *o.carm* '07 (WDC)[B] Washington, DC Whitefriars Hall.
Sulkowski, Anthony P. '86 (DET) Eastpointe, MI St. Basil.
Sullins, Paul '02 (WDC) Hyattsville, MD St. Mark; [C] Catholic University of America, The.
Sullivan, Andrew A. '94 (BIR) Florence, AL St. Joseph's; [I] Florence, AL Society of St. Vincent de Paul, St. Joseph Conference; [H] Florence, AL University of North Alabama.
Sullivan, Brian '03 (PAT) Newton, NJ St. Joseph; Presbyteral Council; College of Consultors.
Sullivan, Charles D. *s.j.* '72 (NY)[E] Bronx, NY Fordham Preparatory School; [DD] Jesuit Community, Kohlmann Hall.
Sullivan, Charles J. '66 (PH) Levittown, PA St. Michael the Archangel.
Sullivan, Charles K. '64 (VEN) Retired.
Sullivan, D. Edward '42 (CHL) Retired.
Sullivan, Daniel F. '57 (CHI) Lake Villa, IL Prince of Peace Retired.
Sullivan, Daniel J. '53 (CHI) Markham, IL St. Gerard Majella Retired.
Sullivan, Daniel J. *s.j.* '61 (NY)[DD] Loyola Hall, Jesuit Community.
Sullivan, Rev. Msgr. Daniel J. '77 (PH) On Special or Other Archdiocesan Assignment; Office for Clergy; Diocesan Priests' Compensation and Benefits Committee; College of Consultors; Ex Officio.
Sullivan, Daniel J. *s.j.* '72 (PHX) Phoenix, AZ St. Francis Xavier Roman Catholic Parish; [F] Phoenix, AZ Society of Jesus.
Sullivan, Daniel James '63 (HRT) Hamden, CT Our Lady of Mt. Carmel.
Sullivan, Daniel Jeremiah '63 (HRT) South Windsor, CT St. Margaret Mary.
Sullivan, David C. '58 (STL) Retired.
Sullivan, Donal P. '90 (STA) Vicar for Priests.
Sullivan, Donal '64 (STA) Fleming Island, FL Sacred Heart.
Sullivan, E. Paul '63 (BO) Senior Priests. Retired.
Sullivan, Edward *o.f.m.* (NY)[FF] Warwick, NY Franciscan Sisters of the Poor Convent.
Sullivan, Emmanuel *s.a.* '55 (NY)[DD] Garrison, NY Franciscan Friars of the Atonement.
Sullivan, Eugene P. '68 (BO) Weymouth, MA St. Francis Xavier.
Sullivan, Rev. Msgr. Eugene '59 (CHY) St. Joseph's Society for Priests (Clergy Mutual Benefit Society) Retired.
Sullivan, Ezra *o.p.* '11 (CIN) Cincinnati, OH St. Gertrude.
Sullivan, F. Norman '62 (BUF) Retired.
Sullivan, Francis A. *s.j.* '51 (BO)[U] Newton, MA The Jesuit Community at Boston College.
Sullivan, Francis E. '88 (BO) Billerica, MA St. Mary.
Sullivan, Francis X. '48 (SPR) Retired.
Sullivan, Gael *s.d.b.* '76 (LA) Cursillo Movement.
Sullivan, Gael '76 (STO) Stockton, CA St. Luke Church of Stockton (Pastor of).
Sullivan, George *s.j.* '75 (OM)[C] Omaha, NE Creighton Preparatory School.
Sullivan, J. David *m.m.* '60 (NY)[DD] Retired.
Sullivan, J. Richard '77 (L) Louisville, KY St. Michael.
Sullivan, James B. '58 (NEW) Roseland, NJ Our Lady of the Blessed Sacrament Retired.
Sullivan, James F. '87 (PH) Drexel Hill, PA St. Andrew.
Sullivan, James M. '60 (HEL) Retired.
Sullivan, James M. '66 (STL) Chesterfield, MO Incarnate Word.
Sullivan, James M. *o.p.* '95 (CIN) Cincinnati, OH St. Gertrude; [C] Cincinnati, OH Dominican Novitiate; [N] Cincinnati, OH St. Gertrude Priory.
Sullivan, Rev. Msgr. James P. '70 (NY) Poughkeepsie, NY St. Martin de Porres.
Sullivan, James '06 (OAK) Fremont, CA Our Lady of Guadalupe.
Sullivan, Jan C. P. '91 (COL) Washington Court House, OH St. Colman.
Sullivan, Jeremiah D. *c.s.p.* '59 (NY)[DD] New York, NY Paulist Fathers' Motherhouse Retired.
Sullivan, Jeremiah '62 (HEL) Retired.
Sullivan, John D. '54 (JOL) Glen Ellyn, IL St. Petronille Retired.
Sullivan, John J. '77 (CHI) Glenwood, IL St. John.
Sullivan, John J. '67 (CLV) Wickliffe, OH Our Lady of Mount Carmel.
Sullivan, John J. '66 (DET) Retired.
Sullivan, John J. *s.m.* '65 (ATL) Atlanta, GA Our Lady of the Assumption.
Sullivan, John J. *m.m.* '60 (NY)[DD] Retired.
Sullivan, John L. '74 (BO) Canton, MA St. Gerard Majella.
Sullivan, John L. *o.p.* '49 (PRO) Providence, RI St. Pius V.
Sullivan, John L. '71 (SPR) Judges.

Sullivan, John M. '91 (BO) Melrose, MA St. Mary of the Annunciation; Courage.
Sullivan, John M. '90 (FR) Wareham, MA St. Patrick's; Tobey Hospital.
Sullivan, John P. '65 (HRT) New Haven, CT St. Joseph's.
Sullivan, John P. '72 (SAC) Presbyteral Council Retired.
Sullivan, John P. *m.s.* '70 (FR)[F] Attleboro, MA La Salette Shrine; [F] Attleboro, MA La Salette Shrine.
Sullivan, John R. '94 (LIN) Lincoln, NE Blessed Sacrament; Diocesan Finance Council; Priests' Continuing Education Committee; Presbyteral Council.
Sullivan, John *m.m.* '60 (WDC)[B] Washington, DC Maryknoll Fathers and Brothers.
Sullivan, John *o.c.d.* '68 (MIL)[P] Milwaukee, WI Provincial Offices – Discalced Carmelites.
Sullivan, Joseph D. '56 (NY) Montgomery, NY Holy Name of Mary Retired.
Sullivan, Rev. Msgr. Joseph P. '53 (SFR)[K] San Rafael, CA Nazareth House of San Rafael, Inc. Retired.
Sullivan, Joseph '03 (SPK) Colton, WA St. Gall.
Sullivan, Joseph '03 (SPK) Colton, WA St. Boniface.
Sullivan, Kenneth J. *m.m.* '57 (NY)[DD] Maryknoll Maryknoll Fathers and Brothers.
Sullivan, Kevin B. '63 (SFD) Retired.
Sullivan, Rev. Msgr. Kevin L. '76 (NY) New York, NY Corpus Christi; [H] New York, NY The Catholic Charities of the Archdiocese of New York; [H] New York, NY Roman Catholic Fund for Children and Other Purposes; [H] New York, NY Catholic Charities Alliance; [HH] New York, NY Carmel Housing Development Fund Co., Inc.; [HH] New York, NY The Housing Fund of the Archdiocese of New York; [HH] New York, NY Cor Mariae Development Fund Corporation; [HH] New York, NY Cor Mariae Housing Development Fund, Inc.; Catholic Charities; [I] New York, NY Catholic Charities Department of Housing, Housing Development Institute, Inc.
Sullivan, Lawrence F. *o.c.d.* '60 (BO)[U] Boston, MA Carmelite Monastery.
Sullivan, Lawrence F. '56 (BO) Senior Priests. Retired.
Sullivan, Lawrence J. '92 (CHI) Chicago, IL St. Christina.
Sullivan, Mervyn '69 (SJ) On Leave of Absence.
Sullivan, Michael B. *c.s.c.* '75 (FTW)[B] University of Notre Dame Du Lac; [H] Notre Dame, IN Holy Cross Community, Corby Hall, University of Notre Dame; [H] Notre Dame Congregation of Holy Cross, United States Province of Priests & Brothers.
Sullivan, Michael D. '91 (TR) Point Pleasant, NJ St. Martha.
Sullivan, Michael P. '66 (MIA) Retired.
Sullivan, Michael P. *o.s.a.* '67 (PH)[Y] Villanova, PA St. Thomas Monastery.
Sullivan, Michael *o.f.m.cap.* '84 (CHI) Chicago, IL St. Clare of Montefalco; Councilors.
Sullivan, Michael '81 (STP) Maple Grove, MN St. Joseph the Worker.
Sullivan, Michael '04 (NY) Bronx, NY St. Frances de Chantal.
Sullivan, Michael *l.c.* '09 (DAL)[J] Irving, TX Legionaries of Christ.
Sullivan, Neil S. '97 (HBG) Harrisburg, PA St. Catherine Laboure.
Sullivan, Patrick A. '82 (CR) Dilworth, MN St. Elizabeth; Hawley, MN St. Andrew.
Sullivan, Patrick J. *c.s.c.* '56 (FR)[A] North Easton, MA Holy Cross Fathers Religious.
Sullivan, Patrick J. *s.j.* '71 (NY) Staten Island, NY St. Mary of the Assumption.
Sullivan, Patrick J. *c.s.c.* '56 (FTW)[H] Notre Dame Congregation of Holy Cross, United States Province of Priests & Brothers.
Sullivan, Patrick M. *o.s.b.* '87 (MAN)[K] Manchester, NH St. Anselm Abbey.
Sullivan, Patrick T. *s.j.* '64 (NY)[DD] New York, NY Murray–Weigel Hall.
Sullivan, Patrick *o.f.m.cap.* '71 (FgM) White Plains, NY The Province of St. Mary of the Capuchin Order.
Sullivan, Patrick '09 (KCK) Frankfort, KS St. Columbkille; Frankfort, KS St. Monica – St. Elizabeth; Frankfort, KS Annunciation.
Sullivan, Patrick *c.s.c.* (BO) Labor Guild; Labor Guild.
Sullivan, Paul G. '07 (PHX) Phoenix, AZ Our Lady of Fatima Mission; Vocations Office; [H] Tempe, AZ Arizona State University; Tempe, AZ All Saints Roman Catholic Newman Center; Priests' Assurance Association.
Sullivan, Paul M. *s.j.* '83 (BO)[W] Gloucester, MA Eastern Point Retreat House.
Sullivan, Paul V. (BO) Dedham, MA St. Mary.
Sullivan, Peter J. '70 (ALB) Special Assignment; Adjutant Vicar Judicial; Judges; Bishop's Delegate for Marriage Dispensations.
Sullivan, Philip *o.c.d.* '07 (TUC)[E] Tucson, AZ Discalced Carmelite Friars of St. Margaret Mary's.
Sullivan, R. William *o.s.a.* '67 (JOL) New Lenox, IL St. Jude.
Sullivan, Randall Erza *o.p.* '11 (CIN)[N] Cincinnati, OH St. Gertrude Priory.
Sullivan, Raymond F. *m.m.* '54 (NY)[DD] Maryknoll Maryknoll Fathers and Brothers Retired.
Sullivan, Rev. Msgr. Richard J. '58 (E) Erie, PA St. Andrew.
Sullivan, Robert E. '80 (BO) On Duty Outside the Archdiocese.
Sullivan, Robert E. (FTW)[B] University of Notre Dame Du Lac.
Sullivan, Robert J. '78 (BO) Unassigned.
Sullivan, Robert J. '63 (SY) Special Assignment; Binghamton, NY Saints John & Andrew Retired.
Sullivan, Robert J. '93 (BIR) Birmingham, AL St. Francis Xavier; Navy Reserve Chaplains; Members.
Sullivan, Robert L. *s.j.* '67 (DEN)[D] Aurora, CO Regis Jesuit High School Corporation; [N] Centennial, CO Regis High Jesuit Community.
Sullivan, Sean *t.o.r.* '57 (ALT)[G] Loretto, PA St. Francis Friary at Mount Assisi.
Sullivan, Rev. Msgr. Terrence J. '64 (SJ) Retired.
Sullivan, Rev. Msgr. Thomas J. '77 (WOR) Chancery Office; Director of Catholic Relief Services; Diocesan Expansion Fund; Diocesan College of Consultors; Archivist; Diocesan Building Commission Members; Presbyteral Council; Worcester, MA Christ the King; Diocesan Expansion Fund.
Sullivan, Thomas K. '52 (STA) Retired.
Sullivan, Thomas *c.p.m.* '04 (OWN) Auburn, KY; [F] Auburn, KY Fathers of Mercy.
Sullivan, Timothy F. *c.s.p.* '85 (MEM) Memphis, TN St. Patrick's; [I] Memphis, TN St. Patrick's Center; Episcopal Vicar for Social Ministry.
Sullivan, Timothy '90 (BUR) Burlington, VT Fletcher Allen Health Care; South Burlington, VT St. John Vianney.
Sullivan, Vincent B. *s.j.* '76 (NEW)[L] Jersey City, NJ Jesuits of Saint Peter's College, Inc.; [B] Jersey City, NJ Jesuit Center; [B] Jersey City, NJ St. Aedan's: St. Peter's College Church.
Sullivan, Vincent '83 (ATL) Cleveland, GA St. Paul the Apostle.
Sullivan, Rev. Msgr. W. Jerome '61 (BUF) Promoter of Justice; Consultors, College of; Council of Priests; [N] Depew, NY Msgr. Conniff Residence; Liaison for Retired Priests Retired.
Sullivan, William F. *s.s.c.* '56 (PRO)[O] Bristol, RI St. Columban's Retirement House.
Sullivan, William J. '59 (HBG) Mechanicsburg, PA St. Joseph Retired.
Sullivan, William J. *o.s.b.* '71 (MAN)[K] Manchester, NH St. Anselm Abbey.
Sullivan, William J. *o.s.s.t.* '81 (MIA)[D] Fort Lauderdale, FL St. Thomas Aquinas High School; Fort Lauderdale, FL St. John the Baptist.
Sullivan, William J. *s.j.* '61 (MIL)[P] Wauwatosa, WI Jesuit Community at St. Camillus.
Sullivan, William M. *s.j.* '66 (NY)[DD] New York, NY Murray–Weigel Hall.
Sullivan, William M. '81 (BO) Absent on Leave.
Sullivan, William *o.ss.t.* '81 (BAL)[Q] Archdiocese of Miami, FL.
Sullivan, William '72 (FTW) Elkhart, IN St. Thomas the Apostle; Advisory Board; Presbyteral Council.
Sullivan, William *s.s.c.* '56 (OM)[J] St. Columbans Missionary Society of St. Columban.
Sumampong, Jed *c.p.* '84 (BRK)[R] Jamaica, NY Immaculate Conception Monastery; Jamaica, NY Immaculate Conception.
Sumanga, Oscar B. '95 (TR) Howell, NJ St. William the Abbot; Associate Judicial Vicars.
Sumich, Anthony *f.s.s.p.* '08 (SCR)[D] Elmhurst Twp., PA St. Gregory's Academy; [L] Elmhurst Twp., PA Priestly Fraternity of St. Peter (F.S.S.P.), North American District Headquarters.
Sumler, Kevin '82 (BEA) Retired.
Sumler, Paul '80 (BEA) Vidor, TX Our Lady of Lourdes.
Summers, Bryan F. *c.o.* '72 (GBG) Cadogan, PA St. Lawrence; Ford City, PA Christ, Prince of Peace Parish.
Summers, John '54 (Y) Retired.
Summers, Mark S. '10 (COL) Dublin, OH St. Brigid of Kildare.
Summers, Randall R. '07 (IND) Batesville, IN St. Louis Catholic Church, Batesville, Inc.; Priests' Personnel Board.
Summitt, James A. '81 (BIR) Absent on Leave.
Sumpter, Gary '79 (SR) Garberville, CA Our Lady of the Redwoods; Scotia, CA St. Patrick.
Sunberg, David A. '92 (CIN) Cincinnati, OH Our Lady of Lourdes.
Sundar, Arok *o.f.m.* (WH) Ravenswood, WV St. Matthew.
Sundaram, Manuel A. '90 (LA) Hospital Chaplains.
Sundara Raj, Irudayaraj Dominic *s.j.* '07 (OAK)[L] Berkeley, CA Jesuit Fathers and Brothers.
Sundararaj, Joseph Rajpaul '95 (STL) Florissant, MO St. Rose Philippine Duchesne.
Sundborg, Stephen V. *s.j.* '74 (SEA)[A] Seattle, WA Seattle University; [M] Seattle, WA Arrupe Jesuit Community at Seattle University.
Sunds, Rev. Msgr. Elvin '73 (JKS) Office of Vicar General; Chancellor; Propagation of the Faith; Continuing Formation Committee; Priests' Council; Diocesan Consultors; Personnel Board; Parish Pastoral Councils; Jackson, MS St. Richard of Chichester.
Sung, Hyunsang '06 (NY)[HH] Staten Island, NY Korean Catholic Apostolate of Staten Island, Inc.
Sungcad, Nemesio '76 (SD) Borrego Springs, CA Saint Richard Catholic Parish.
Sunghera, Gilbert *s.j.* '02 (DET)[K] Detroit, MI Jesuit Community at the University of Detroit Mercy.
Sunkara, Hrudayaraju '95 (NY) Pearl River, NY St. Aedan.
Sun Kim, Simon Chung '98 (ORG) Education Leave.
Sunnenberg, Scott M. '02 (SPC) Marshfield, MO Holy Trinity; [B] Springfield, MO Springfield Catholic High School; Youth Ministry; Conway, MO Sacred Heart.
Suntum, James *s.f.* '84 (SFE) Chimayo, NM Holy Family.
Sunwoo, Richard '09 (LA) Redondo Beach, CA St. Lawrence Martyr.
Su O, Chang '91 (CLV) Korean Catholic Apostolate; Cleveland, OH St. Andrew Kim Pastoral Center.
Supancheck, Norman A. '68 (LA) Sylmar, CA St. Didacus.
Suparman, Vincent *s.c.j.* '95 (RC) Lower Brule, SD St. Mary's; [C] Lower Brule, SD SCJ Community House.
Suparman, Vincent *s.c.j.* '95 (SFS) Fort Thompson, SD St. Joseph.
Suparno, Ignatius *c.m.* '99 (PH) Philadelphia, PA St. Vincent de Paul.
Super, David J. '80 (CR) Diocesan Board of Review for the Protection of Young Children; Deans; Fosston, MN St. Mary's; Bagley, MN St. Joseph.
Supnet, Romeo *o.s.a.* '84 (SD) R.J. Donovan Correctional Facility.
Suppa, F. Thomas '78 (E) Union City, PA St. Teresa of Avila.
Supple, Richard *o.carm.* '02 (NEW) Bogota, NJ St. Joseph's.
Suquilvide, Abel '55 (LA) Retired.
Surafka, Michael *o.f.m.* '91 (CLV) Cleveland, OH St. Stanislaus.
Suran, Joaquin '50 (BRK) Retired.
Surban, Denis S. '90 (NEW) Clark, NJ St. Agnes.
Suren, Richard H. '53 (STL) St. Louis, MO St. Raphael The Archangel Retired.
Surette, John E. *s.j.* '67 (BO)[U] Boston The Society of Jesus of New England–Provincial Offices.
Surette, John E. *s.j.* '67 (CHI)[C] Chicago, IL Jesuit Community at Loyola University Chicago.
Surges, Robert F. '64 (MIL) Retired.
Suriani, Raymond N. '85 (PRO) Westerly, RI St. Pius X.
Suriano, Thomas '64 (MIL) Milwaukee, WI St. Catherine Retired.
Surman, Darrell '62 (YAK) Retired.
Surman, Stanley '56 (SAG) Retired.
Surmeier, William J. '65 (SAL) Gorham, KS St. Mary Help of Christians Parish; Catholic Charities Outreach Office – Hays; Consultors.
Surowiec, Jude *o.f.m.conv.* '75 (NOR) Stafford Springs, CT St. Edward; [A] Cromwell, CT Holy Apostles College and Seminary; Ellicott City, MD.
Surprenant, Paul W. '73 (WIN) Byron, MN Christ the King; Byron, MN Holy Family; Priest Assignments Committee.
Surufka, Michael *o.f.m.* '91 (CLV)[N] Cleveland, OH St. Stanislaus Friary; [Y] Cleveland, OH Pulaski Franciscan Community Development Corp.
Survil, Bernard '67 (GBG)[F] Greensburg, PA Clelian Heights School for Exceptional Children; [I] Greensburg, PA Apostles of the Sacred Heart of Jesus.
Surwilo, Rev. Msgr. Edward R. '63 (BGP) Stamford, CT Our Lady Star of the Sea.
Susa, Robert P. '61 (E) Retired.
Susai, Barnabas Maria *i.m.s.* '90 (LR) Bella Vista, AR St. Bernard of Clairvaux.
Susaimanickam, Leon J. '79 (NOR) Dayville, CT St. Joseph.
Susann, Robert F. *m.s.* '73 (ORL) Orlando, FL Blessed Trinity; Airport Ministry, Orlando International Airport.
Suskey, Robert G. '90 (PH) Chalfont, PA St. Jude.
Susko, Rev. Msgr. Martin S. '61 (Y) Judges Retired.
Suslenko, Mark S. '86 (HRT) Prospect, CT St. Anthony's; Waterbury, CT Sacred Heart–Sagrado Corazon; [S] Waterbury, CT Spanish–Speaking Center.
Suslowski, Michael '80 (PIT) Pittsburgh, PA St. John the Baptist.
Susnik, Bernardin *o.f.m.* '59 (CHI)[N] Lemont, IL The Slovene Franciscan Fathers, Order of Friars Minor, Commissariat of the Holy Cross.
Suso, Anthony J. '09 (CLV) Akron, OH St. Francis de Sales.
Suss, Thomas J. '73 (SEA) Retired.
Sustarsic, John '52 (DUL) Retired.
Sustayta, Paul A. '91 (LA) Pasadena, CA St. Andrew.
Suszko, Robert K. '02 (NEW)[A] South Orange, NJ Immaculate Conception Seminary School of Theology; [B] Seton Hall University.
Suszynski, Michael '86 (SP) Tampa, FL Incarnation; Vicars Forane.

Sutherland, Juan Diego *c.f.r.* '07 (FWT)[H] Fort Worth, TX Community of Franciscan Friars of the Renewal Sacred Heart of Jesus Friary; [M] Fort Worth, TX Franciscan Renewal Ministries of Texas, Inc.
Sutherland, Raphael (JOL)[K] Darien, IL Carmelite Carefree Retirement Village Retired.
Sutherland, Thomas J. '60 (DET) Retired.
Sutherland, Rev. Msgr. William E. '83 (E) Co Directors.
Sutherland, William E. '83 (E)[Q] Edinboro, PA Edinboro University of PA; Edinboro, PA Our Lady of the Lake.
Sutil, Florencio '44 (SJN) On Duty Outside the Archdiocese.
Sutman, Frank I. *o.p.* '85 (PRO)[O] Providence, RI St. Pius House; Providence, RI St. Pius V.
Sutter, Conrad *o.f.m.conv.* '93 (IND)[J] Mount St. Francis, IN Mount Saint Francis Friary and Retreat Center.
Sutter, Conrad *o.f.m.conv.* '93 (L) Norton Hospitals.
Sutter, Raymond A. '73 (CLV) Parma, OH St. Matthias.
Sutter, Richard *l.c.* (ATL)[F] Atlanta, GA Legionaries of Christ.
Sutton, Brian F. '06 (WIN) Mapleton, MN St. Teresa's; Mapleton, MN St. Joseph; Mapleton, MN St. Matthew.
Sutton, Douglas B. '02 (WH) Mannington, WV St. Peter's; Mannington, WV St. Patrick's.
Sutton, ST (PAT) Wayne, NJ Our Lady of the Valley.
Sutton, Stephen '84 (BAL) Forest Hill, MD St. Ignatius.
Sutton, Thomas E. '73 (SAG) Auburn, MI St. Anthony/St. Joseph; Defenders of the Bond.
Suvakeen, John '04 (CR) Thief River Falls, MN St. Bernards.
Suvakkin, Masilamani *h.g.n.* '01 (OWN) Russellville, KY Sacred Heart.
Suwalsky, David J. *s.j.* '95 (STL)[O] St. Louis, MO Bellarmine House of Studies.
Suwalsky, David J. *s.j.* '95 (SAC)[H] Carmichael, CA Sacramento Jesuit Community.
Svarczkopf, Rev. Msgr. Mark '74 (IND) Greenwood, IN Our Lady Of The Greenwood Catholic Church, Inc.
Svida, Wayne A. '02 (CHI) Chicago Ridge, IL Our Lady of the Ridge.
Svirchuk, Taras *c.ss.r.* '06 (PHU) Newark, NJ St. John the Baptist.
Svirskas, Joseph J. '51 (BO) Senior Priests. Retired.
Svitan, Martin '79 (NY) New York, NY St. John Nepomucene.
Svobodny, Aloysius *o.m.i.* '49 (STP)[M] Buffalo, MN Christ the King Retreat Center.
Swacha, Stanley J. '79 (E) Houtzdale, PA Christ the King.
Swain, Kenneth J. '72 (ALB) Corinth, NY Holy Mother and Child Parish.
Swain, Robert *c.m.* '59 (PH)[Y].
Swalina, Rev. Msgr. Michael F. '70 (SPC) Defender of the Bond; Diocesan Consultors; Presbyteral Council; Health Leave of Absence.
Swaner, Rev. Msgr. James J. '61 (PEO) Utica, IL St. Mary.
Swanson, Charles F. '66 (OM) Retired.
Swanson, Gerald '86 (SD)[H] San Diego, CA Scripps Mercy Hospital.
Swantek, David S. '08 (TR) Censores Librorum.
Swanton, Michael J. '05 (OM) Osmond, NE St. Mary of the Seven Dolors; Randolph, NE St. Frances de Chantal.
Swarick, Joachim *o.f.m.* '52 (GB)[J] Pulaski, WI Friary Retired.
Swartvagher, Marc E. '96 (BRK)[B] Douglaston, NY Cathedral Seminary Residence of the Immaculate Conception; Graduate Studies.
Swartz, Michael R. '87 (BUF) Absent on Leave.
Sweany, Thomas M. '80 (CLV) Chesterland, OH St. Anselm.
Swearingen, Eric '87 (FRS) Fresno, CA Holy Spirit.
Sweeney, Callistus *o.f.m.* '53 (FgM) New York, NY Holy Name Province.
Sweeney, D. Gilbert *s.j.* '54 (ALN)[A] Wernersville, PA Jesuit Center–Jesuit Community.
Sweeney, Daniel *s.j.* '94 (MO) Air Force Reserve Chaplains.
Sweeney, Denis *c.ss.r* (BO) Boston, MA Our Lady of Perpetual Help.
Sweeney, E. Daniel '82 (PIT) Munhall, PA St. Therese of Lisieux; Homestead, PA St. Maximilian Kolbe.
Sweeney, Rev. Msgr. Edward A. '57 (RVC) Retired.
Sweeney, Edward '88 (AMA) Retired.
Sweeney, Eugene *s.m.* '78 (STL)[O] St. Louis, MO Marianist Community Retired.
Sweeney, Francis M. *c.s.p.* '61 (NY)[DD] New York, NY Paulist Fathers' Motherhouse Retired.
Sweeney, Frederick E. '52 (BO) Senior Priests. Retired.
Sweeney, James H. '81 (BRK) Brooklyn, NY Our Lady of the Presentation–Our Lady of Loreto; Presbyteral Council; Brooklyn, NY Holy Name.
Sweeney, John Maria *f.p.o.* '98 (BO)[U] Lawrence, MA Franciscans of Primitive Observance.
Sweeney, John P. '73 (PIT) Charismatic Prayer Groups; Glenshaw, PA St. Bonaventure.
Sweeney, John T. '70 (GBG) West Newton, PA Holy Family.
Sweeney, Kevin J. '97 (BRK) Brooklyn, NY St. Michael.
Sweeney, Kevin '94 (ORG) Military Chaplains; Navy Chaplains; On Duty Outside the Diocese.
Sweeney, Rev. Msgr. Lawrence P. '54 (SLC) Retired.
Sweeney, Luke M. '01 (NY)[A] Yonkers, NY Cathedral Prep Program; [A] Yonkers, NY St. Joseph's Seminary.
Sweeney, Michael '79 (KNX) Harriman, TN Blessed Sacrament; Lancing, TN St. Ann; Jamestown, TN St. Christopher Catholic Church.
Sweeney, Michael *o.p.* '79 (OAK)[A] Berkeley, CA Dominican School of Philosophy and Theology; Berkeley, CA St. Mary Magdalen.
Sweeney, Rev. Msgr. Patrick E. '72 (PH) Collegeville, PA St. Eleanor; [BB] Collegeville, PA Ursinus College.
Sweeney, Peter T. '61 (WDC) Damascus, MD St. Paul; Silver Spring, MD Our Lady of Grace.
Sweeney, Ricard (TR)[N] Trenton, NJ St. Lawrence Rehabilitation Center.
Sweeney, Robert J. '82 (NY) Greenwood Lake, NY Holy Rosary.
Sweeney, Rev. Msgr. Robert J. '69 (RCK) Pecatonica, IL St. Mary; Secretary for Administrative Processes; Propagation of the Faith; Special Assignment.
Sweeney, Timothy *o.s.b.* '61 (IND)[K] Saint Meinrad, IN St. Meinrad Archabbey.
Sweeney, William F. '81 (BRK)[G] Fresh Meadows, NY St. Francis Preparatory School; Oakland Gardens, NY American Martyrs.
Sweeney, William F. *s.s.c.* (BO) Readville, MA St. Anne.
Sweeney, William F. *s.s.c.* '75 (PRO)[O] Bristol, RI St. Columban's Retirement House.
Sweeney, William *s.s.c.* '75 (OM)[J] St. Columbans Missionary Society of St. Columban.
Sweeny, Daniel *s.j.* '94 (SCR)[B] Scranton, PA The University of Scranton.
Sweeny, Rev. Msgr. Edward A. '57 (RVC) Long Beach, NY St. Ignatius Martyr; Procurator & Advocates.
Sweeny, Eugene *s.m.* '78 (SAT)[K] San Antonio, TX Marianist Residence: Skilled Nursing.
Sweeny, Richard R. '86 (TR) Retired.
Sweet, Daniel J. '01 (PRO) Providence, RI St. Michael the Archangel.
Sweetser, Thomas P. *s.j.* '70 (MIL)[P] Milwaukee, WI Arrupe House Jesuit Community; Milwaukee, WI The Parish Evaluation Project.
Sweitzer, Raymond M. *s.j.* '75 (NY)[E] Bronx, NY Fordham Preparatory School; [DD] Jesuit Community, Kohlmann Hall.
Swencki, John T. '79 (BO) Middleborough, MA Sacred Heart.
Swengros, William J. '91 (SP) Valrico, FL St. Stephen; Defenders of the Bond.
Swetland, Rev. Msgr. Stuart W. '91 (PEO) On Duty Outside the Diocese.
Swetland, Rev. Msgr. Stuart W. '91 (BAL)[A] Emmitsburg, MD Mount St. Mary's Seminary; [B] Emmitsburg, MD Mount Saint Mary's University.
Swetnam, James H. *s.j.* '58 (STL)[O] St. Louis, MO Jesuit Community Corporation at Saint Louis University – Jesuit Hall Retired.
Swett, Charles J. '57 (TLS) Retired.
Swett, Rev. Msgr. Ronald '67 (FRS) Bakersfield, CA St. Philip the Apostle; Personnel Board.
Swiader, Rev. Msgr. James P. '75 (RVC) Garden City, NY St. Joseph's; Priestly Life and Ministry; Priests' Personnel Policy Board.
Swiat, James R. '67 (LAN) Retired.
Swiatek, Emil P. '65 (BUF)[N] Depew, NY Msgr. Conniff Residence Retired.
Swiatocha, Bruno '56 (RVC) Retired.
Swichtenberg, William D. '83 (GB) Algoma, WI St. Mary; Kewaunee, WI Holy Rosary.
Swickard, John L. '74 (COL) Retired.
Swiderski, Jan '94 (NOR) Higganum, CT St. Peter.
Swiderski, Stan '63 (LR) Mountain Home, AR St. Peter the Fisherman; Mountain View, AR St. Mary Church.
Swiercz, Pawel A. '94 (FR) Awaiting Assignment; [F] Fall River, MA Priests' Hostel.
Swierczynski, Joseph E. '64 (PIT) Pittsburgh, PA Immaculate Heart of Mary.
Swierz, Michael '85 (Y)[F] Youngstown, OH St. Joseph the Provider Catholic School.
Swierzbiolek, Waclaw *s.d.b.* '62 (NY)[FF] Stony Point, NY Marian Shrine; [FF] Stony Point, NY Don Bosco Retreat Center and Marian Shrine.
Swierzowski, Stanislaus J. '56 (ALB) Retired.
Swietochowski, Andrew '78 (SFS) Kimball, SD St. Margaret; Personnel Board.
Swift, Bruce *o.s.b.* '60 (KCK)[I] Atchison, KS St. Benedict's Abbey.
Swift, Daniel F. '89 (TR) Holmdel, NJ St. Benedict.
Swift, James E. *c.m.* '78 (STL)[O] St. Louis, MO Lazarist Residence.
Swift, William J. '44 (TLS) Tulsa, OK Church of St. Mary.
Swift, William V. '44 (TLS) Retired.
Swing, R. John '70 (LC) Nekoosa, WI Sacred Heart of Jesus; Port Edwards, WI St. Alexander; [L] Port Edwards, WI St. Alexander's Church, Port Edwards Endowment Trust.
Swink, Lawrence C. '06 (WDC) Huntingtown, MD Jesus the Divine Word Parish; [X] Bowie, MD Sodality Union.
Swirczynski, Gary *o.f.m.* '87 (OAK)[L] Oakland Franciscan Friars of California, (Province of St. Barbara).
Swirski, Thaddeus M. '54 (CLV) Akron, OH St. Sebastian Retired.
Swisshelm, Germain *o.s.b.* '60 (IND)[K] Saint Meinrad, IN St. Meinrad Archabbey.
Swistovich, John '98 (FWT) Bedford, TX St. Michael; Presbyteral Council; Catholic Foundation of North Texas.
Switzer, Andrew M. '11 (WH) Parkersburg, WV St. Margaret Mary.
Swoger, Rev. Msgr. John W. '63 (E) Finance Council Retired.
Swope, John W. *s.j.* '86 (BAL)[D] Baltimore, MD Cristo Rey Jesuit High School.
Swope, Mark G. '90 (PH)[Z] Huntingdon Valley, PA Sisters of the Holy Redeemer Provincialate; On Special or Other Archdiocesan Assignment.
Swope, Rev. Msgr. Timothy J. '66 (ALT) Prince Gallitzin Deanery; Ongoing Formation of the Clergy; Loretto, PA Basilica of St. Michael the Archangel; [K] Loretto, PA Office of Ongoing Formation of Clergy.
Sybertz, Donald F. *m.m.* '55 (FgM) Maryknoll, NY MARYKNOLL.
Sybirnyy, Volodymyr '04 (STF) Liturgical Commission.
Sydorovych, Roman '95 (STF) Rochester, NY Epiphany of Our Lord; Director of Religious Education for Ukrainian Heritage Schools.
Sykora, Paul M. *m.m.* '76 (FgM) Maryknoll, NY MARYKNOLL.
Sylva, Geno (PAT) Secretariat for Evangelization; Evangelization; [H] Madison, NJ St. Paul Inside The Walls: The Catholic Center for Evangelization at Bayley–Ellard.
Sylvain, Daniel *s.a.* '01 (NY)[DD] Brockton, MA Chapel of Our Savior.
Sylvain, Rubens *c.s.* (ATL) Forest Park, GA San Felipe de Jesus.
Sylvester, Emmanuel '88 (CR) Warren, MN SS. Peter and Paul; Priests' Council.
Sylvia, Albert A. '66 (BO) EnCourage.
Sylvia, Edmund J. *c.s.c.* '77 (FTW)[H] Notre Dame Congregation of Holy Cross, United States Province of Priests & Brothers.
Sylvia, William M. '08 (FR) Mansfield, MA St. Mary's.
Symolon, Lawrence S. '75 (HRT) Consultors – Canon 1742; Meriden, CT The Corporation of the Church of the Holy Angels.
Synek, Roger A. '98 (BIS) Parshall, ND St. Anthony; Parshall, ND St. Bridget; Parshall, ND St. Elizabeth; Parshall, ND Sacred Heart.
Syracuse, Ross *o.f.m.conv.* '78 (BUF) Athol Springs, NY St. Francis of Assisi; [N] Athol Springs, NY St. Maximilian Kolbe Friary.
Syrenne, Marc P. *c.c.* '97 (DET) Detroit, MI St. Scholastica.
Syring, Andrew J. '11 (OM) Schuyler, NE Divine Mercy.
Syslo, Alan M. *c.s.v.* '66 (CHI)[N] Arlington Heights Viatorian Province Center–Clerics of St. Viator.
Syverson, David '99 (FAR) Carrington, ND Sacred Heart Church of Carrington; Sykeston, ND St. Elizabeth's Church of Sykeston.
Syverstad, Daniel *o.p.* '82 (SEA) Seattle, WA Blessed Sacrament; Oakland, CA.
Szabelski, Joseph R. '70 (CHI) Retired.
Szabo, Ferenc *s.j.* '62 (ATH) "Tavlatok".
Szabo, Marcel '71 (PSC) Passaic, NJ St. Michael Cathedral; Northern New Jersey Protopresbyterate.
Szada, John A. '78 (HBG) World Apostolate of Fatima; Mount Carmel, PA Divine Redeemer.
Szakaly, Anthony V. *c.s.c.* '92 (FTW)[H] Notre Dame, IN Congregation of Holy Cross, United States Province of Priests & Brothers; South Bend, IN; Austin, TX.
Szal, George L. *s.m.* '75 (BO) Revere, MA Immaculate Conception; Trustees.
Szamocki, Piotr '91 (CAM) Bellmawr, NJ St. Joachim Parish, Bellmawr, N.J.
Szantyr, Eugene R. '78 (BGP) Bridgeport, CT St. Andrew; Bridgeport, CT Our Lady of Good Counsel.
Szanyi, Mark *o.f.m.conv.* '78 (PMB) Port St. Lucie, FL St. Lucie.
Szarek, Eugene *c.r.* '67 (CHI) Chicago, IL St. Hedwig.
Szarek, Eugene *c.r.* '67 (CHI)[N] Chicago, IL Provincial Office of the Congregation of the Resurrection; Chicago, IL.
Szarnicki, Henry A. '55 (PIT)[M] Pittsburgh, PA St. John Vianney Manor Retired.
Szaroleta, Rev. Msgr. Andrew L. '77 (MET) Edison, NJ Our Lady of Peace.
Szarwark, Stanley *c.i.c.m.* '64 (FgM) Arlington, VA MISSIONHURST.
Szatkowski, David *s.c.j.* '02 (MIL)[P] Franklin, WI Sacred Heart at Monastery Lake.

Szatkowski, John '10 (DAL) Plano, TX St. Elizabeth Ann Seton.
Szczapa, Stanley J. '71 (NOR) Vernon, CT Sacred Heart; Liturgical Commission.
Szczechowski, Glen '05 (CHY) June Priests' Retreat; Lovell, WY St. Joseph's; Powell, WY St. Barbara; [F] Powell, WY NorthWest College; College of Consultors.
Szczepanik, John '88 (MET) South River, NJ St. Stephen Protomartyr.
Szczepankiewicz, Gary J. '75 (BUF) North Tonawanda, NY Our Lady of Czestochowa.
Szczesniak, Harry F. '72 (BUF) Buffalo, NY Our Lady of Czestochowa.
Szczesnowicz, Andrzej '03 (COS) Presbyteral Council; Colorado Springs, CO Our Lady of the Pines–Black Forest.
Szczesny, John S. '75 (GBG) New Kensington, PA St. Mary of Czestochowa; New Kensington, PA St. Joseph.
Szczesny, Walter J. '90 (BUF) Vocations; [A] East Aurora, NY Christ the King Seminary.
Szczotka, Krzysztof '88 (NEW) Elizabeth, NJ Saint Adalbert and Saints Peter & Paul.
Szczur, Mark '03 (FBK)[C] Fairbanks, AK Kobuk Center.
Szczurek, Victor S. *o.praem.* '00 (ORG)[D] Silverado, CA St. Michael's Preparatory School.
Szczurek, Victor S. *o.praem.* '00 (ORG)[I] Silverado, CA Norbertine Fathers of Orange Inc.
Szczykutowicz, Rev. Msgr. Francis S. '58 (PT) Sunny Hills, FL St. Theresa; Propagation of the Faith, Office of.
Szczypula, Marcin '08 (CHI) Lemont, IL SS. Cyril and Methodius.
Szebenyi, Andrew L. *s.j.* '61 (SY)[Q] Syracuse, NY Jesuits at LeMoyne, Inc.
Szeman, Stephen J. '53 (SEA) Retired.
Szemborski, Chester *s.d.b.* '50 (NY)[FF] Stony Point, NY Don Bosco Retreat Center and Marian Shrine; [FF] Stony Point, NY Marian Shrine.
Szendrey, J. Edward *m.m.* '62 (NY)[DD] Maryknoll, NY Maryknoll Fathers and Brothers Charitable Trust; [DD] Maryknoll Maryknoll Fathers and Brothers.
Szewczyk, Grzegorz *s.d.s.* '91 (SAT) Poth, TX Blessed Sacrament; [L] Falls City, TX Salvatorian Fathers Community of Texas.
Szews, George R. '78 (LC) Eau Claire, WI Newman Community; [K] Eau Claire, WI Newman Parish.
Szippl, Richard *s.v.d.* '81 (FgM) Techny, IL.
Szivos, Charles S. '99 (NY)[A] Yonkers, NY St. Joseph's Seminary.
Szklarski, Joseph '62 (NEW) Lyndhurst, NJ St. Michael's.
Szkredka, Slawomir '02 (LA) Graduate Studies.
Szlezak, Emeric *o.f.m.* '44 (SP)[N] St. Petersburg, FL St. Anthony Friary Retired.
Szlezak, Emeric (BGP) Retired.
Szmyd, John S. '96 (CHI)[A] Mundelein, IL University of St. Mary of the Lake/Mundelein Seminary.
Szobonya, James *c.ss.r* '06 (RVC) Bethpage, NY St. Martin of Tours.
Szobonya, James *c.ss.r.* (TOL) Lima, OH St. Gerard.
Szolack, Joseph T. '88 (CAM) Deanery Representatives; Presbyteral Council; Vocation Advisory Board; Elected Members; Consultants.
Szolack, Joseph T. '88 (CAM) Woodbury Heights, NJ Infant Jesus Parish, Woodbury Heights, N.J.
Szopa, Daniel F. '76 (MAN) Retired.
Szorc, Andrzej *c.ss.r.* '86 (STV) Christiansted, VI Church of the Holy Cross.
Szparagowski, George J. '02 (PH) Blue Bell, PA St. Helena.
Szpiech, Edward P. '67 (NEW) Garfield, NJ St. Stanislaus Kostka.
Szpieg, Edmund L. '94 (PMB) Port St. Lucie, FL St. Elizabeth Ann Seton.
Szpilski, Joseph *c.m.* '56 (BRK) Brooklyn, NY St. Stanislaus Kostka.
Sztorc, Richard E. '69 (CHI) Buffalo Grove, IL St. Mary.
Sztuber, Tomasz '86 (NOR) Norwich, CT St. Joseph.
Szudarek, Ronald J. '81 (CLV) Retired.
Szudera, Ted F. '77 (GF) Stanford, MT St. Rose of Lima; Diocesan Consultors; Priests' Council.
Szufel, Adam '64 (SAV) Retired.
Szufel, Adam *o.f.m.* '64 (GB)[J] Wausaukee, WI Villa Alverna.
Szukalski, John *s.v.d.* '97 (WDC)[O] Washington, DC Society of the Divine Word/Divine Word House.
Szumilo, Julian *c.m.* '50 (HRT)[L] Manchester DePaul Provincial Residence Retired.
Szupa, Joseph '92 (PHU) Elizabeth, NJ St. Vladimir's; Procurator/Advocate; Protopresbyters (Deans); Presbyteral Council; College of Archeparchial Consultors.
Szupper, Rev. Msgr. Michael F. '57 (WIL) Retired.
Szura, John *o.s.a.* '66 (CHI)[N] Chicago, IL St. John Stone Friary.
Szura, Thomas *c.m.m.* '78 (DET)[K] Vocation Office.
Szurek, Pawel F. '05 (PAT) Priestly Life Committee.
Szuster, Jacek '01 (SAV) Augusta, GA Church of the Most Holy Trinity.
Szwach, Joseph F. '55 (WOR) Dudley, MA St. Andrew Bobola; Diocesan College of Consultors.
Szybka, Joseph P. '83 (TOL) Tiffin, OH St. Joseph; Precious Blood of Jesus Deanery.
Szybka, Stanley S. (TOL) Van Wert, OH St. Mary of the Assumption.
Szyda, Arkadiusz '99 (SAT) San Antonio, TX Holy Name.
Szydlik, Thomas R. '03 (PEO) Nauvoo, IL SS. Peter and Paul; Nauvoo, IL Immaculate Conception; Warsaw, IL Sacred Heart.
Szydlowski, Joel F. *o.f.m.* '67 (TR) St. Francis Medical Center.
Szydlowski, Joel *o.f.m.* '67 (GB)[G] Manitowoc, WI Holy Family Memorial, Inc.; [J] Green Bay, WI St. Mary of the Angels Friary.
Szydlowski, Robert L. '62 (STL) Hazelwood, MO St. Martin de Porres.
Szylar, Jan *c.m.* '94 (BRK) Brooklyn, NY St. Stanislaus Kostka.
Szymakowski, Andrew *f.s.s.p.* '04 (BAK) Nyssa, OR St. Bridget of Kildare.
Szymakowski, Andrew '04 (ARL) Alexandria, VA St. Lawrence.
Szymanski, Edward S. '99 (BAL) Special Assignment; Ellicott City, MD Resurrection.
Szymanski, Rev. Msgr. John B. '57 (MET)[I] Somerset, NJ Maria Regina Residence; Vicars General Retired.
Szymaszek, Leszek P. '97 (BGP) Stamford, CT St. Leo.
Szyszka, Michal '11 (VEN) Fort Myers, FL Church Of The Resurrection Of Our Lord.

T

Ta, Binh T. *c.ss.r.* (GAL)[R] Houston, TX Rice University/ Texas Medical Center Schools; Catholic Student Center.
Ta, Binh *c.ss.r.* (SEA) Seattle, WA Sacred Heart of Jesus; [M] Seattle, WA The Redemptionist Society of Washington.
Ta, Kiet A. '10 (ORG) Orange, CA St. Norbert.
Taabu, Simon L. '89 (PEO) Lincoln, IL Holy Family.
Tabak, Thaddeus *s.d.s.* '77 (SAT) San Antonio, TX Our Lady of Sorrows; [L] Falls City, TX Salvatorian Fathers Community of Texas.
Tabalanza, Celso *c.i.c.m.* '96 (SAT) San Antonio, TX St. Bonaventure.
Tabares, Christian '10 (SAG) Rosebush, MI St. Henry/ St. Charles; Clare, MI St. Cecilia; Coleman, MI St. Philip Neri.
Tabbert, Robert D. '79 (VEN) Fort Myers, FL Blessed Pope John XXIII.
Tabbert, Robert '79 (VEN)[F] Venice, FL Blessed Pope John XXIII Housing, Inc.
Taberski, Richard M. '64 (HRT) Goshen, CT St. Thomas of Villanova.
Tabigue, Joseph *c.r.s.p.* '05 (SD) San Diego, CA Our Lady of the Rosary Catholic Parish.
Tabios, Walter '82 (SAC) Placerville, CA St. Patrick's.
Tabo, Virgilio '05 (TUC) Coolidge, AZ Saint James Roman Catholic Parish – Coolidge.
Tabone, Marcel M. '85 (CAM) On Leave of Absence.
Tabor, Stanley '84 (JOL) Plainfield, IL St. Mary Immaculate.
Tabujara, Oscar '75 (SJ) Mountain View, CA St. Athanasius.
Tacay, Archie *c.i.c.m.* '08 (SAT) San Antonio, TX St. James the Apostle.
Tacelli, Ronald K. *s.j.* '82 (BO)[U] Newton, MA The Jesuit Community at Boston College.
Tachias, Alfred A. '59 (GLP)[D] Gallup, NM Villa Guadalupe Home for the Aged Retired.
Tack, Theodore E. *o.s.a.* '53 (TLS)[B] Tulsa, OK Cascia Hall Preparatory School.
Tackney, John P. '74 (BO) Cambridge, MA Sacred Heart.
Taddy, Jerome J. '60 (GB) Retired.
Tadena, Arnold '89 (SD) San Diego, CA Saint Charles Catholic Parish.
Tadeo, Abran R. '00 (TUC) Marana, AZ Saint Christopher Roman Catholic Parish – Marana.
Tadyszak, Leonard *s.c.j.* '51 (MIL)[P] Franklin Sacred Heart at Monastery Lake.
Tadyszak, Leonard *s.c.j.* '51 (SP)[N] Pinellas Park, FL Priests of the Sacred Heart Retired.
Tae, Jinseok '99 (COL) Columbus, OH St. Andrew Kim Taegon Korean Catholic Community.
Taft, Robert F. *s.j.* '63 (BO)[U] Boston The Society of Jesus of New England–Provincial Offices.
Taggart, Frederick H. *o.s.a.* '65 (LAN) Flint, MI St. Matthew; College of Consultors.
Taggart, James E. *o.m.i.* '85 (BO)[U] Lowell, MA Missionary Oblates of Mary Immaculate; [U] Lowell, MA St. Eugene House (Residence).
Taggart, James *o.m.i.* '85 (WDC) Washington, DC; [O] Washington, DC Provincial Offices of the United States Province of the Missionary Oblates of Mary Immaculate.
Taglianetti, Bernard J. '05 (PH) Yardley, PA St. Ignatius of Antioch.
Tah, Philip P. '96 (NY) Hartsdale, NY Sacred Heart.
Taheny, Mark V. '95 (SFR) Greenbrae, CA St. Sebastian; Deans.
Taheny, Robert R. *s.j.* '59 (SJ)[M] Los Gatos, CA Sacred Heart Jesuit Center.
Taillon, Marcel L. '94 (PRO) Narragansett, RI St. Thomas More; Ongoing Formation of Priests.
Tajak, Ralph *o.s.b.* '94 (GBG)[H] Latrobe, PA Saint Vincent Archabbey.
Tajonera, R. Joyalito F. *m.m.* '02 (FgM) Maryknoll, NY MARYKNOLL.
Takoudjou, Rodrigue *s.j.* '06 (WDC)[O] Washington, DC The Jesuit Community at Georgetown University.
Takuski, Walter J. '95 (CHI) Bartlett, IL St. Peter Damian.
Talafous, Don *o.s.b.* '52 (SCL)[I] Collegeville, MN St. John's Abbey, of the Order of St. Benedict.
Talaisis, Bernardas '52 (SP)[N] St. Pete Beach, FL Franciscan Friary; St. Pete Beach, FL St. Casimir Lithuanian Mission.
Talamo, John '98 (NO) Mandeville, LA Our Lady of the Lake Roman Catholic Church.
Talar, Charles J. '79 (GAL) Houston, TX St. John Vianney.
Talar, Charles J.T. '79 (BGP) On Duty Outside the Diocese.
Talarico, Anthony M. '70 (CHI) South Holland, IL Holy Ghost.
Talarico, Matthew L. '07 (CHI) Chicago, IL; [N] Chicago, IL Institute of Christ the King Sovereign Priest.
Talaska, Richard J. '68 (MIL) Retired.
Talavera, Carlos '96 (HT) Houma, LA St. Louis.
Talbot, Christopher '04 (DET) Ray Township, MI St. Francis of Assisi–St. Maximilian Kolbe.
Talbot, James F. *s.j.* '68 (BO)[U] Weston, MA Campion Jesuit Community.
Talbot, Ralph W. '04 (STP) Deanery 1; College of Consultors; White Bear Lake, MN St. Mary of the Lake.
Talbott, Ron *o.f.m.cap.* '81 (LA) Los Angeles, CA St. Lawrence of Brindisi.
Talcott, Peter '75 (SR) Unassigned.
Talentino, William *o.f.m. cap.* '67 (PIT)[M] Beaver, PA St. Fidelis Friary.
Talesfore, Rev. Msgr. John J. '89 (SFR) San Francisco, CA Cathedral of St. Mary (Assumption); Deans; College of Consultors.
Taliercio, Pasquale *m.s.a.* '92 (NOR)[G] Cromwell, CT Society of the Missionaries of the Holy Apostles.
Talkin, Ralph H. *s.j.* '57 (DET)[K] Clarkston, MI Colombiere Center.
Talley, Charles *o.f.m.* '99 (SD) Oceanside, CA Mission San Luis Rey Catholic Parish.
Talley, Rev. Msgr. David P. '89 (ATL) Johns Creek, GA St. Brigid.
Tallman, Gilmary *o.f.m.cap.* '60 (DEN)[N] Denver, CO St. Anthony of Padua Friary.
Tallman, John '88 (ALB) Albany, NY Parish of Mater Christi; St. Peter's Hospital; Special Assignment; [H] Albany, NY St. Peter's Hospital of the City of Albany.
Tallman, Stephen '59 (HEL) Retired.
Taluja, Stephen J. *m.m.* '09 (FgM) Maryknoll, NY MARYKNOLL.
Tam, Thomas Do Minh '50 (STP) St. Paul, MN St. Adalbert.
Tamara, Eder '90 (NY) Harriman, NY St. Anastasia.
Tamayo, Alberto W. '07 (TR) Vice Chancellors; Secretary to the Bishop.
Tamayo, Alfredo L. '77 (SAC) Vallejo, CA St. Basil.
Tamayo, Dante '93 (OAK) El Cerrito, CA St. Jerome.
Tamayo, Rev. Msgr. Elias '72 (PAT) Absent on Leave.
Tambornino, James M. *s.o.l.t.* '91 (MIL)[R] Slinger, WI Carmelite Hermit of the Trinity – CHT.
Tamburello, Dennis *o.f.m.* '80 (ALB) Mount McGregor Correctional Facility; [B] Siena College.
Tamburro, Francis J. '74 (HBG) Berwick, PA Immaculate Conception of the Blessed Virgin Mary.
Tamburro, Joseph '99 (SJP) Examiners of Clergy; Priests' Continuing Education; Presbyteral Council; Presbyters; On Leave.
Tamez, Benito '02 (DAL) Dallas, TX Baylor University Medical Center; Richardson, TX St. Paul the Apostle.
Tamiian, Calin '02 (ROM) Sherman Oaks, CA St. Mary Romanian Catholic Mission; Oxnard, CA St. John the Evangelist Romanian Catholic Mission.
Tamiian, Calin '02 (LA) Hospital Chaplains.
Tamminga, Robert G. '71 (TUC) Tucson, AZ Saint Francis de Sales Roman Catholic Parish – Tucson.
Tamoro, Briccio *s.v.d.* '72 (SB)[I] Riverside, CA Divine Word Seminary.
Tampe, Luis A. *s.j.* '02 (BO)[U] Boston The Society of Jesus of New England–Provincial Offices.
Tampe, Luis A. *s.j.* '02 (BAL)[B] Jesuit Community of Loyola University, Inc.; [Q] Baltimore, MD Jesuit Community of Loyola University, Inc.
Tanck, Norman C. *c.s.b.* '74 (ROC) Rochester, NY Kateri Tekakwitha Roman Catholic Parish.
Tancredi, Carl T. '67 (HBG) York, PA St. Rose of Lima; [I] York, PA Penn State University, York Campus; [I] York, PA York College.

Tandayu, Jonas *m.s.c.* '82 (ALN) Nazareth, PA Holy Family.
Tandoh, Francis *c.s.sp.* '93 (CIN) Dayton, OH St. Benedict the Moor; Germantown, OH St. Augustine; Dayton, OH St. Mary; Dayton, OH St. Mary.
Taneo, Teodulo G. *s.v.d.* '89 (YAK) Richland, WA Christ the King.
Tang, George Donkor '87 (CAM) Cherry Hill, NJ The Church of St. Thomas More, Cherry Hill, New Jersey.
Tang, Michael '90 (LA) Los Angeles, CA Transfiguration.
Tanghe, Warren V. '11 (BAL) Ellicott City, MD Resurrection.
Tangora, Philip–Michael (PAT) Morristown, NJ Assumption of the Blessed Virgin Mary.
Tanguay, Andre *o.m.i.* '53 (BO)[U] Lowell, MA Missionary Oblates of Mary Immaculate Retired.
Tanguay, William H. '69 (PRO) Retired.
Tank, Rev. Msgr. Thomas '67 (KCK) Overland Park, KS Church of the Ascension; Archdiocesan Consultors.
Tanon, Carmelo Soto '89 (SJN) Carolina, PR San Andres.
Tanto, Henry *s.m.m.m.* '87 (NY) Warwick, NY St. Anthony Community Hospital.
Tanto, Henry '07 (NY)[W] Warwick, NY St. Anthony Community Hospital, Inc.; [EE] Warwick, NY Mt. Alverno Center, Bon Secours Charity Health System; [Z] Warwick, NY Villa Frances at the Knolls Retired.
Tanto, Henry (PAT)[K] Denville, NJ Saint Clare's Hospital, Inc.; Dover, NJ Dover General Hospital.
Tanu, Emanuel *s.v.d.* (LKC) Bell City, LA St. John Vianney.
Tanzini, Paolo '08 (NEW) West New York, NJ Holy Redeemer.
Taormina, Rev. Msgr. Andrew C. '62 (NO) Metairie, LA St. Francis Xavier; Judges; Deans; Serra Club of Downtown New Orleans.
Taosan, John Kare *c.i.m.* (GAL) Galveston, TX Holy Family.
Tapel, Rene '84 (SP) Land O'Lakes, FL Our Lady of the Rosary.
Tapella, Joseph '78 (JOL) Joliet, IL The Cathedral of St. Raymond; Judicial Vicar; Judges; Secretary; Secretary.
Taphorn, Joseph C. '97 (OM) Moderator of the Curia and Vicar for Clergy; Judicial Vicar; Finance Council; Archbishop's Appointee; Omaha, NE St. Margaret Mary.
Tapia, Gilberto Mora '88 (SEA) Des Moines, WA St. Philomena.
Tapia, Ignacio '04 (BWN)[A] Brownsville, TX The Saint Joseph and Saint Peter Seminary; Mission, TX San Cristobal Magallanes & Companions; McAllen, TX Our Lady of Perpetual Help.
Taponi, Selwan Sulaiman '94 (OLD) Jacksonville, FL Saint Ephrem Syriac Church; Jacksonville, FL St. Ephrem Syriac Antiochian Catholic Church.
Tapp, John '84 (SP) St. Petersburg, FL Holy Family; College of Consultors; Worship, Office of; Appointed Members.
Tappe, Walter J. '85 (WDC) Greenbelt, MD Saint Hugh of Grenoble.
Tapper, John W. '61 (CHI) Hanover Park, IL St. Ansgar Retired.
Tarabay, Paul *o.m.m.* '06 (OLL) Flint, MI Our Lady of Lebanon Maronite Catholic Church; [A] Ann Arbor, MI Maronite Order of the Blessed Virgin Mary; Ann Arbor, MI.
Taran, Peter '60 (NY)[DD] Garrison, NY Franciscan Friars of the Atonement.
Tarantino, Rev. Msgr. James T. '81 (SFR) College of Consultors; Moderator of the Curia and Vicar for Administration; Archbishop's Cabinet; San Francisco, CA St. Francis of Assisi, National Shrine.
Tarantino, Rev. Msgr. James T. '81 (SFR) On Special Assignment.
Tarantino, John F. '78 (PAT) Pequannock, NJ Holy Spirit.
Taranto, James '81 (KC) Independence, MO St. Mark; Deans.
Tarasi, Carlo D. '72 (CHL) Unassigned.
Taras Miles, Michael '70 (STN) Belfield, ND St. John the Baptist; Belfield, ND St. Demetrius.
Tarazona, Ramiro '08 (AUS) Temple, TX St. Matthew; Temple, TX Our Lady of Guadalupe Catholic Church – Temple, Texas.
Targonski, George '02 (MET) Edison, NJ St. Matthew the Apostle.
Tarlton, Allen *o.s.b.* '55 (SCL)[I] Collegeville, MN St. John's Abbey, of the Order of St. Benedict.
Tarnawski, Wiktor '81 (ARE) Ciales, PR N.S. Madre del Redentor.
Tarrant, Rev. Msgr. Edward L. '50 (RVC) Hicksville, NY St. Ignatius Loyola; Mineola, NY Corpus Christi Retired.
Tarrant, Patrick J. '53 (GF) Retired.
Tarrillion, Joseph A. *s.m.* '66 (SAT)[K] San Antonio, TX Marianist Residence: Skilled Nursing.
Tarro, Michael *c.s.* '58 (PRO) Johnston, RI St. Rocco Retired.
Tartaglia, Paul '58 (ALB) Veterans' Administration Hospital Retired.
Tartaglia, Richard V. '72 (PAT) Denville, NJ St. Mary's.
Tasch, Hugh *o.s.b.* '57 (KC)[J] Conception, MO Conception Abbey; [K] Savannah, MO Sisters of St. Francis Provincial House.
Taschetta, Anthony '71 (JOL) Elmhurst, IL Mary, Queen of Heaven.
Tash, Rev. Msgr. Joseph T. '62 (AMA) Presbyteral Council; Priests' Pension Plan Retirement Committee; Amarillo, TX St. Thomas the Apostle; College of Consultors.
Tassone, Salvatore A. *s.j.* '63 (SJ)[B] Santa Clara, CA Jesuit Community.
Tassone, Thomas W. '08 (RVC) Williston Park, NY St. Aidan's Church.
Tasto, Harold J. '68 (STP) Minneapolis, MN St. Thomas the Apostle.
Tasto, John P. *o.s.a.* '67 (FgM)[N] Chicago, IL St. Rita Monastery; Olympia Fields, IL Province of Our Mother of Good Counsel (Midwestern).
Tatarczuk, Rev. Msgr. Vincent A. '49 (PRT) Retired.
Tate, Joseph H. *c.s.c.* '81 (FTW)[H] Notre Dame Congregation of Holy Cross, United States Province of Priests & Brothers.
Tatel, Orlando G. '65 (STP) Jordan, MN St. Patrick of Cedar Lake Township.
Tatman, Robert '04 (VEN) Ave Maria, FL Quasi–Parish of Ave Maria Oratory.
Taton, Thomas P. '61 (BUF) Buffalo, NY Assumption Retired.
Taton, Thomas P. '60 (BUF) Retired.
Tatro, Joseph C. '00 (WCH) On Duty Outside the Diocese.
Tatro, Joseph '00 (ARL) Alexandria, VA St. Louis.
Tatro, Kenneth J. '76 (SPR) Presbyteral Council; West Springfield, MA St. Thomas the Apostle.
Tatro, Timothy M. '99 (JC) Absent on Leave.
Tatum, Gregory T. *o.p.* '89 (OAK)[L] Oakland Order of Preachers (Province of the Most Holy Name of Jesus – Western Dominican Province).
Taube, Sylvester '64 (DET) Retired.
Tauber, Jerome A. '02 (ALN) Hellertown, PA St. Theresa of the Child Jesus; Appointed Members.
Taubitz, Leo A. '56 (KAL) Retired.
Taufen, Rev. Msgr. Daniel J. '56 (SCL) Retired.
Taugher, Timothy J. '78 (SY) Binghamton, NY St. Francis of Assisi.
Tauke, Michael L. '74 (DUB) Waverly, IA St. Mary.
Taurasi, David '88 (CC) On Duty Outside the Diocese.
Tauscher, Donald *o.s.b.* '65 (SCL)[I] Collegeville, MN St. John's Abbey, of the Order of St. Benedict.
Tavarro, Elly S. '81 (ORG)[G] Orange, CA St. Joseph Hospital of Orange.
Tavella, Thomas *c.s.p.* '81 (GR) Grand Rapids, MI Cathedral of St. Andrew; Evangelization.
Taveras, Aridio *o.s.a.* '07 (MGZ) Aguada, PR St. Francis of Assisi.
Taveras Reymoso, Julio Cesar *m.ss.cc.* (SJN) Bayamon, PR Santiago Apostol.
Tavis, Gordon *o.s.b.* '58 (SCL)[I] Collegeville, MN St. John's Abbey, of the Order of St. Benedict.
Tawiah, Rev. Msgr. Francis Yaw '81 (BRK) St. Albans, NY Our Lady of Light Roman Catholic Church.
Tawiah, Gabriel Oduro '97 (VIC) Nada, TX St. John Nepomucene.
Tawiah, Raphael Amoako '07 (NY) Hyde Park, NY Regina Coeli.
Tax, Samuel Perez '01 (NU) Benson, MN St. Francis.
Tay, Rev. Msgr. Peter P. '54 (PBR) Retired.
Tayag, Edison '08 (ROC) Rochester, NY Sacred Heart Cathedral.
Taylor, Augustus R. '66 (PIT) On Duty Outside the Diocese.
Taylor, Benedict M. *o.f.m.* '60 (NY)[DD] New York Franciscan Friars, Holy Name Province.
Taylor, Brian P. '06 (NY) Bronx, NY St. Benedict.
Taylor, Brian '06 (LAF) Basile, LA St. Augustine.
Taylor, Rev. Msgr. Charles F. '53 (CHY) Promoter of Justice Retired.
Taylor, Daniel '75 (TUC) Administrative Leave of Absence.
Taylor, David H. '74 (PIT) Pittsburgh, PA St. Charles Lwanga Parish.
Taylor, Douglas D. '97 (TOL) New London, OH Our Lady of Lourdes; Wakeman, OH St. Mary.
Taylor, Gordon A. '85 (B) Retired.
Taylor, James E. *o.m.i.* '56 (BEL)[F] Belleville, IL Missionary Oblates of Mary Immaculate – St. Henry's Oblate Residence.
Taylor, Jon '64 (GF)[A] University of Great Falls.
Taylor, Jon '64 (LAN) Retired.
Taylor, Joseph C. '53 (CHI) Chicago, IL St. Edward Retired.
Taylor, Kenneth '78 (IND) Deaneries and Deans; Commission for Multicultural Ministry; Indianapolis, IN Holy Angels Catholic Church, Indianapolis, Inc.; Board of Directors.
Taylor, Mel *o.s.b.* '67 (SCL)[I] Collegeville St. John's Abbey, of the Order of St. Benedict.
Taylor, Michael G. '93 (ARL) Chantilly, VA Corpus Christi Mission.
Taylor, Michael S. '97 (MAN) Somersworth, NH St. Mary; Somersworth, NH Saint Ignatius of Loyola; Diocesan Judges.
Taylor, Michael *o.f.m.conv.* '86 (SY) Syracuse, NY Assumption B.V.M.
Taylor, Paul R. *o.s.b.* '92 (GBG)[H] Latrobe, PA Saint Vincent Archabbey.
Taylor, Peter '74 (GB) Retired.
Taylor, Philip *s.p.* '04 (STL)[V] Dittmer, MO Servants of the Paraclete Missouri Generalate Corporation.
Taylor, Reynaldo S. '07 (CIN) Cincinnati, OH St. Joseph; On Special and Archdiocesan Assignment.
Taylor, Roger H. '64 (MAD) Retired.
Taylor, Senan *o.f.m.cap.* '70 (NY)[DD] Yonkers, NY St. Clare Friary.
Taylor, Thomas '83 (PEO) Peoria Heights, IL St. Thomas.
Taylor, William R. '67 (SAG) Saginaw, MI St. Stephen; Clergy Personnel Board Retired.
Taylor, William '64 (B) Retired.
Tcheou, Pang S. '06 (HBG)[I] Millersville, PA Millersville University.
Tchingui, Antonio Jorge '97 (HRT) Hartford, CT Our Lady of Fatima.
Te, Jesus Angelo '11 (P) Medford, OR Sacred Heart of Jesus.
Te, Jose Alvin *o.f.m.* '10 (NY)[DD] New York Franciscan Province of the Immaculate Conception.
Teague, Bruce N. '80 (BO) Pastoral Care.
Teague, Bruce '80 (SPR) Sheffield, MA Our Lady of the Valley.
Teague, James B. '87 (NY) Harrison, NY St. Gregory the Great.
Teall, Richard *c.s.c.* '50 (FTW)[H] Holy Cross House Retired.
Teater, Kristian C. '00 (STL)[A] St. Louis, MO Kenrick School of Theology.
Tebalt, Timothy D. '04 (CHR)[H] Beaufort, SC University of South Carolina, Beaufort Extension; [H] Greenwood, SC Lander University.
Tebbe, Francis S. *o.f.m.* '75 (CIN)[N] Cincinnati St. Francis Seraph Friary.
Tedesco, Joseph A. '79 (TR) On Duty Outside the Diocese.
Tedesco, Joseph P. *s.m.* '83 (CIN)[D] Dayton, OH The University of Dayton.
Tedesco, Joseph *s.m.* '83 (MIA)[E] Hollywood, FL Chaminade–Madonna College Preparatory.
Tedone, Michael G. '91 (BRK) Queens Village, NY Our Lady of Lourdes; [D] Brooklyn, NY Campus Ministers and Ministry Centers.
Tegeder, Michael '78 (STP) Office of Indian Ministry; Minneapolis, MN St. Frances Cabrini; Minneapolis, MN Church of Gichiwaa Kateri.
Tegeler, Herbert L. '53 (DUB) Retired.
Teichert, Isaiah *o.s.b.cam.* '90 (MRY)[F] Big Sur, CA New Camaldoli Hermitage.
Tejada, Franciso '95 (NY) Middletown, NY St. Joseph.
Tejada, Jose '92 (SP) Hudson, FL St. Michael the Archangel.
Teles, Dennis J. '65 (GRY) Retired.
Telesz, Rev. Msgr. Leo '39 (CLV) Retired.
Telken, Paul E. '73 (STL) Sullivan, MO St. Anthony.
Telles, John '75 (GAL)[A] Houston, TX St. Mary's Seminary.
Tellez, Eric '86 (PHX) Scottsdale, AZ St. Patrick Roman Catholic Parish.
Tellez, Jairo A. '62 (SAT) Military Chaplains.
Tellez, Jairo '62 (MIA)[G] Miami, FL Mercy Hospital.
Tellez, Tomas Vasquez '04 (YAK) Religious Education and Hispanic Catechesis.
Tellis, Cyprian *s.j.* '02 (BO)[U] Brighton, MA Noel Chabanel House.
Telnack, Methodius *o.c.s.o.* '57 (ATL)[F] Conyers, GA The Monastery of the Holy Spirit.
Telthorst, Rev. Msgr. James T. '68 (STL) St. Louis, MO Mary, Mother of the Church; Deaneries/Deans.
Temba, Camillus *a.l.c.p.* '91 (PMB) Fort Pierce, FL St. Mark the Evangelist.
Temba, Leopold *c.s.c.* '09 (FTW)[H] Notre Dame Congregation of Holy Cross, United States Province of Priests & Brothers.
Tempel, Theodore '64 (EVN)[D] Evansville, IN St. John's Home for the Aged Retired.
Templado, Josefino P. '69 (GAL) Richmond, TX Sacred Heart.
Temple, Matthew *o.carm.* '82 (ROC)[K] Rochester, NY Whitefriars Priory.
Templin, Kenneth A. *s.m.* '79 (HON)[D] Honolulu, HI Center Marianist Community Retired.
Tenbarge, Timothy '73 (EVN) St. Anthony, IN St. Anthony; Schnellville, IN Sacred Heart.
Teneza, Vicente '01 (SAC) Sacramento, CA St. Paul.
Tenhundfeld, Carl Anthony (GAL) Retired.
Tenhundfeld, Paul F. '54 (COV) Retired.
Tenorio, Michael C. *o.f.m.cap.* '99 (MO) Air Force Chaplains.
Tenorio, Michael *o.f.m.cap.* '99 (AGN)[F] Agana Heights, GU St. Fidelis Friary.
Tensi, Lawrence R. '79 (CIN) Loveland, OH St. Columban.

Tentativa, Jose '92 (NY) New York, NY St. Thomas More.
Teo, Eduardo C. '90 (LUB) O'Donnell, TX St. Pius X.
Teran, Juan Jose Sanchez '11 (ATL) Marietta, GA Church of the Transfiguration.
Terdine, Richard G. '65 (PIT)[M] Pittsburgh, PA Cardinal Dearden Center Retired.
Terembula, Tadeusz *s.v.d.* '96 (SJ) San Jose, CA Cathedral Basilica of St. Joseph.
Terga, Richard *c.i.c.m.* '73 (NY) New York, NY Our Lady of Good Counsel.
Terhes, Chris '06 (ROM) Tustin, CA St. John the Baptist Romanian Catholic Mission.
Terico, Nicholas R. *o.praem.* '89 (PH)[Y] Paoli, PA Daylesford Abbey.
Terlecky, Rt. Rev. Mitred Msgr. John '76 (STF) Ansonia, CT SS. Peter and Paul; Econome; Diocesan Consultors; Presbyteral Council; Administrative Council; Directors; Ukrainian Museum and Library of Stamford, Inc.; Diocesan Charities and Missions.
Termine, Vincent J. '44 (BRK) Retired.
Termyna, James J. '70 (PAT) Dover, NJ St. Clement, Pope and Martyr.
Ternes, Gary '79 (SFS) South Dakota State Penitentiary & Minnehaha County Correctional Centers; Tribunal Judges.
Ternullo, Joseph P. '73 (SAC) Special Assignment.
Tero, Richard D. '74 (MO) Diocesan Consultors; Air Force Reserve Chaplains.
Tero, Richard '74 (ANC) Seward, AK Sacred Heart.
Terra, J. *f.s.s.p.* '89 (PHX) Phoenix, AZ Mater Misericordiae Mission.
Terra, Rev. Msgr. Russell G. '62 (SAC) Retired.
Terranova, Robert *o.s.a.* '73 (NY) Staten Island, NY Our Lady of Good Counsel.
Terrebonne, Burnick J. '77 (NO) River Ridge, LA St. Matthew the Apostle.
Terrera, C. Bernardo '89 (SCR) On Duty Outside the Diocese.
Terrien, Douglas J. '79 (DET) Lapeer, MI Immaculate Conception of the Blessed Virgin Mary.
Terrien, Lawrence B. *s.s.* '72 (BAL)[A] Baltimore, MD St. Mary's Seminary and University; [Q] Baltimore Society of St. Sulpice, Province of the United States; [A] Baltimore, MD St. Mary's Seminary and University.
Terrien, Lawrence B. *s.s.* '72 (ARL) On Duty Outside the Diocese.
Terriquez, Enrique '63 (B) Retired.
Terry, Brian *s.a.* '97 (NY)[DD] Garrison Franciscan Friars of the Atonement, Minister General Office.
Terry, John S. '75 (SCR) Wilkes–Barre, PA Our Lady of Hope Parish; [P] Wilkes–Barre, PA Catholic Youth Center.
Terzano, John D. '74 (CLV) Peninsula, OH Mother of Sorrows.
Tesek, Albert J. '51 (CLV) Retired.
Tesfayohanneso, Musie *o.cist.* '83 (TR)[N] Mount Laurel, NJ Cistercian Monastery of Our Lady of Fatima.
Tesha, Kalist *o.f.m.cap.* '97 (CHI)[N] Chicago, IL St. Clare Friary.
Tesha, Prosper *c.s.c.* '09 (FTW)[H] Notre Dame Congregation of Holy Cross, United States Province of Priests & Brothers.
Teske, Roland J. *s.j.* '65 (MIL)[P] Milwaukee, WI Jesuit Community at Marquette University.
Teslovic, Eugene '77 (RIC) Retired.
Testa, Genaro J. '47 (HRT) Retired.
Testa, Jess '88 (JOL)[K] Naperville, IL St. John Vianney Villa Retired.
Testa, John J. '11 (TR) Monmouth Beach, NJ Church of the Precious Blood.
Testa, Richard '67 (ALB) Retired.
Testa, Rev. Msgr. Steve J. '64 (ALX) College of Consultors; Appointed Members; Deans; Holy Childhood Association; Propagation of the Faith and Foreign Mission Education; Bordelonville, LA St. Peter; Bordelonville, LA St. Michael.
Tete, James Argen *s.j.* '03 (OAK)[L] Berkeley, CA Jesuit Fathers and Brothers.
Teteh, Lawrence *c.s.sp.* '71 (FTW) Fort Wayne, IN St. Therese.
Teter, Patrick A. '92 (SPC) Mount Vernon, MO St. Susanne.
Tetherow, Gabriel Francis '02 (SCR) Unassigned or Leave of Absence.
Teti, James V. '97 (NEW) Paramus, NJ Church of the Annunciation; Office of the Permanent Diaconate; Director of Selection & Formation of Permanent Deacons.
Tetlow, John H. '84 (STA) Switzerland, FL San Juan Del Rio.
Tetlow, Joseph A. *s.j.* '60 (STL)[O] St. Louis, MO Jesuit Community Corporation at Saint Louis University – Jesuit Hall.
Tetrault, Raymond L. '60 (PRO) Retired.
Tetreault, Maynard *o.f.m.* '60 (CIN)[U] Cincinnati, OH Franciscan Central Purchasing; Councillors.
Tetreault, Maynard *o.f.m.* '60 (GAL) Galveston, TX Holy Family.
Tetreault, Raymond A. '71 (PRO) Slatersville, RI St. John the Evangelist.
Tetteh, Edward *s.v.d.* (TR) Trenton, NJ Blessed Sacrament–Our Lady of the Divine Shepherd Parish.
Tetu, Richard B. '69 (MAN) Manchester, NH St. Pius X; Manchester, NH Ste. Marie.
Teuth, Michael V. *s.j.* '71 (NY)[DD] New York, NY "America;" Residence and publication office of the America Press.
Teverzczuk, William J. '73 (PH) North Wales, PA Mary, Mother of the Redeemer.
Tewes, Edwin T. '96 (ARL) Purcellville, VA St. Francis de Sales.
Tewes, Rev. Msgr. Thomas J. '63 (BAL) Baltimore, MD St. Clare Retired.
Texada, David Ker '80 (NO) Retired.
Tezie, John M. '59 (CLV) South Amherst, OH Nativity of Blessed Virgin Mary Retired.
Thaar, Gerald *o.s.c.* '65 (PHX)[F] Phoenix, AZ Crosier Community of Phoenix (Canons Regular of the Order of the Holy Cross) Retired.
Thach, Nguyen Van *c.ss.r.* '01 (LA)[P] Baldwin Park Vietnamese Redemptorist Mission.
Thachet, Joseph '53 (KAL) Retired.
Thachil, Joy *s.a.c.* (STL) St. Louis, MO Our Lady of Sorrows.
Thadathil, Chacko *o.s.b.* '94 (LUB) Slaton, TX Our Lady of Guadalupe.
Thadathilkunnel, Benny *m.s.* '99 (GAL) Friendswood, TX Mary, Queen.
Thaden, Roy W. *s.j.* '73 (FgM) Portland, OR Society of Jesus.
Thaden, William A. '88 (CLV) Lorain, OH Sacred Heart Chapel; [V] Lorain, OH Sacred Heart Chapel.
Thagil, Matthew *m.s.f.s.* (TUC) Tucson, AZ Saints Peter and Paul Roman Catholic Parish – Tucson.
Thai, Bao Q. '03 (ORG) Orange, CA Cathedral of the Holy Family.
Thai, Joseph Nguyen '95 (ORG)[H] Santa Ana, CA Vietnamese Catholic Center.
Thai, Thomas V. '54 (LEX) Defenders of the Bond Retired.
Thai Do, (Bartholomew M.) Hoa *c.m.c.* '77 (SPC)[F] Carthage, MO Congregation of the Mother Coredemptrix, United States Assumption Province.
Thaikoottathil, James '84 (NOR) Middletown, CT St. Sebastian.
Thaiparambil, Joy Vincent (DM) Clarinda, IA Sacred Heart; Clarinda, IA St. Joseph; Clarinda, IA St. Clare.
Thai Tran, Joseph '94 (SP) Largo, FL Holy Martyrs of Vietnam.
Thakadipuram, Thomas '93 (SUP) Woodruff, WI Holy Family.
Thalakulam, Cherian *c.m.i.* '76 (CHR) North Augusta, SC St. Edward.
Thaler, Joseph L. *m.m.* '77 (FgM) Maryknoll, NY MARYKNOLL.
Thaliyan, Jesudas *c.m.i.* '70 (SFS) Platte, SD St. Peter the Apostle.
Thamert, Mark *o.s.b.* '79 (SCL)[I] Collegeville, MN St. John's Abbey, of the Order of St. Benedict.
Thames, Robert '64 (FWT) On Duty Outside the Diocese.
Than, M. Timothy Qui Van *o.cist.* '75 (SB)[I] Lucerne Valley, CA The Cistercian Congregation of the Holy Family, St. Joseph Monastery.
Thanavelil, Joseph *o.s.b.* '81 (LUB) Denver City, TX St. William.
Thang'wa, Michael *f.m.h.* '10 (SHP) Shreveport, LA St. Mary of the Pines.
Thanh, Cao Xuan *c.m.c.* (BO) Chelsea, MA St. Rose of Lima.
Thanh, Nguyen Duc *c.ss.r.* '97 (LA)[P] Baldwin Park Vietnamese Redemptorist Mission.
Thanh Vu, Joseph '85 (GAL) Ethnic Vicars.
Thanugundla, Joji '94 (CHI) Arlington Heights, IL St. James.
Than Van Liem, Joseph M. *c.m.c.* '89 (SPC) Kimberling City, MO Our Lady of the Cove.
Thapwa, Stephen M. '76 (WCH) Fredonia, KS Sacred Heart; Neodesha, KS St. Ignatius.
Tharackal, Joseph '83 (SYM) Hollis, NY Syro–Malabar Knanaya Catholic Mission of Newark New Jersey; Hollis, NY Syro–Malabar Knanaya Catholic Mission of Brooklyn, NY.
Tharackal, Joseph (BRK) Hollis, NY St. Gerard Majella.
Tharappel, Augustine *m.s.f.s.* '70 (TYL)[C] Whitehouse, TX Fransalian Center for Spirituality; [C] Whitehouse, TX The Missionaries of St. Francis de Sales.
Tharayil, Jose J. '70 (GAL) Sugar Land, TX St. Theresa.
Tharp, Larry R. '77 (CIN) Fairfield, OH Sacred Heart of Jesus; Presbyteral Council; Vicarri Foranei (Deans); Consultors; Judges.
Tharp, Shane L. '00 (OKL)[K] Chickasha, OK University of Science & Arts of Oklahoma; Chickasha, OK Holy Name.
Thayer, David D. *s.s.* '75 (HRT) On Duty Outside the Archdiocese.
Thayer, David D. *s.s.* '75 (WDC)[A] Washington, DC Theological College of the Catholic University of America; [C] Catholic University of America, The.
Thayer, David D. *s.s.* '75 (BAL)[Q] Baltimore Society of St. Sulpice, Province of the United States.
Thayil, Mathew *m.s.f.s.* '67 (TYL)[C] Whitehouse, TX The Missionaries of St. Francis de Sales.
Thayilkuzhithottu, George Kutty *m.s.f.s.* '97 (LC) Stevens Point, WI St. Stanislaus.
Thayilkuzhithottu, George *m.s.f.s.* '97 (TYL)[C] Whitehouse, TX The Missionaries of St. Francis de Sales.
Theby, James D. '08 (STL) Ellisville, MO St. Clare of Assisi.
Theempalangattu, Philip Chacko '80 (SHP)[B] Monroe, LA St. Francis Medical Center.
Thein, Edward '79 (ATL) Hapeville, GA St. John the Evangelist.
Theis, Gerald *s.v.d.* '80 (FgM) Techny, IL.
Theisen, Eugene A. *m.m.* '53 (FgM) Maryknoll, NY MARYKNOLL.
Theisen, Eugene J. '99 (MO) Air Force Chaplains.
Theisen, John J. '59 (MIL) Retired.
Theisen, Kenneth *o.s.b.* '84 (RCK) Aurora, IL; [G] Aurora, IL Marmion Abbey.
Theisen, Wilfred *o.s.b.* '56 (SCL)[I] Collegeville, MN St. John's Abbey, of the Order of St. Benedict.
Theisz, Paul '09 (HBG) Lancaster, PA St. John Neumann.
Thekkan, Pauly *c.m.i.* '89 (MET) John F. Kennedy Medical Center; Edison, NJ Our Lady of Peace.
Thekkanath, Antony *v.c.* (SYM)[B] Washington, NJ Divine Mercy Healing Center, Inc.
Thekkekara, Antony '97 (GI) Stapleton, NE St. John the Evangelist; Priests' Advisory Board (Presbyteral Council).
Thekkekara, Mathew (GI) North Platte, NE St. Patrick.
Thekkel, Hugh *o.s.b.* '76 (LUB) Post, TX Holy Cross; Seminole, TX St. James; Wilson, TX Blessed Sacrament.
Thekkemury, James Dominic '87 (SHP)[B] Monroe, LA St. Francis Medical Center.
Thekkethala, Joseph '90 (BIR) Alexander City, AL St. John the Apostle.
Thekkinen, Jolly Pappachan *o.ss.t.* '08 (BAL)[Q] Assigned in India.
Thekku, George '90 (PT) Cantonment, FL St. Jude Thaddeus.
Thekkudan, Johnson L. *c.m.i.* '02 (COV) Fort Thomas, KY St. Thomas.
Thekkumthala, Ouseph I. '75 (FWT) Hillsboro, TX Our Lady of Mercy; Abbott, TX Immaculate Heart of Mary; Penelope, TX Nativity of the Blessed Virgin Mary.
Thelakkatt, Xavier '80 (STP) Albertville, MN St. Albert; Dayton, MN St. John the Baptist.
Thelapilly, Walter *c.m.i.* (BRK) Brooklyn, NY Holy Family.
Thelappilly, Babu *s.d.v.* '08 (NEW) Newark, NJ St. Michael's.
Thelen, Albert R. *s.j.* '68 (OM)[J] Omaha, NE Jesuit Community at Creighton University.
Thelen, Frederick L. '80 (LAN) Lansing, MI Cristo Rey.
Thelen, Mathias '10 (LAN) Jackson, MI Queen of the Miraculous Medal.
Thelen, Rev. Msgr. Robert J. '70 (BRK)[B] Douglaston, NY Cathedral Seminary Residence of the Immaculate Conception; Sanitation Department; Presiding Judge of the Appellate Court; Attorneys and Counselors at Canon Law.
Thell, Richard *o.s.b.* '74 (OM)[C] Elkhorn, NE Mount Michael Benedictine School; [J] Elkhorn, NE Mount Michael Benedictine Abbey; Elkhorn, NE.
Thellikalayil, Mani George *m.c.* '94 (LEX) Cumberland, KY St. Stephen; Harlan, KY Holy Trinity; Cumberland, KY Church of the Resurrection.
Thelly, Matthew '71 (TR) Deal, NJ St. Mary of the Assumption.
Thenan, Peter (CC) Kingsville, TX Our Lady of Good Counsel.
Theneth, Thomas *c.m.i.* '84 (JOL) Winfield, IL St. John the Baptist.
Thennattil, George *t.o.r.* '76 (FWT) Fort Worth, TX St. Mary of the Assumption; Hospital Chaplaincy.
Theobald, Charles '58 (NEW) Retired.
Theophane, John '97 (FRS) Fowler, CA St. Lucy.
Theoret, Glenn J. '99 (MAR) Manistique, MI St. Francis de Sales.
Thepe, Theodore C. *s.j.* '57 (DET)[K] Clarkston, MI Colombiere Center.
The Pham, Vincent Tung '85 (PH) Philadelphia, PA Holy Innocents.
Theriault, Francis *s.v.d.* '55 (CHI)[N] Techny, IL Divine Word Residence.
Theriault, H. '60 (NY) Tivoli, NY St. Sylvia.
Theriot, Donald C. '57 (LAF) Retired.
Theroux, Bertrand L. '67 (PRO) North Kingstown, RI St. Francis De Sales.
Theroux, David *s.s.e.* '74 (BUR)[E] Colchester, VT Society of St. Edmund; Councilors.
Theroux, Denis B. '88 (DET) Northville, MI Our Lady of Victory.
Theroux, Rev. Msgr. Paul D. '77 (PRO) Wakefield, RI St.

Francis of Assisi; South County Hospital; Deans; Judges; Finance Council.
Theroux, Raymond C. '65 (PRO) Cumberland, RI St. John Baptist Mary Vianney.
Therrien, Shawn M. '87 (MAN) Claremont, NH St. Mary; Sullivan County House of Corrections.
Thesing, Gilbert J. *o.p.* '75 (CHI)[N] Chicago Dominicans (Provincial Office).
Thesing, Gilbert *o.p.* '75 (FgM) Chicago, IL Province of St. Albert the Great (Central).
Thesing, Kenneth F. *m.m.* '69 (FgM) Maryknoll, NY MARYKNOLL.
Thesing, Mark B. *c.s.c.* '86 (FTW)[B] University of Notre Dame Du Lac; [H] Notre Dame, IN Holy Cross Community, Corby Hall, University of Notre Dame.
Thesing, Robert J. *s.j.* '76 (CHI)[C] Chicago, IL Jesuit Community at Loyola University Chicago.
Thess, William C. '00 (STL) Warrenton, MO Holy Rosary.
Thessing, Charles '88 (LR) Morrilton, AR Sacred Heart; Clergy Personnel Advisory Board (Diocesan).
Thet–Kyaw, Marcian '95 (CHR) Dillon, SC St. Louis.
Theuerer, Ulrich *o.s.b.* '01 (TLS)[G] Hulbert, OK Our Lady of the Annunciation of Clear Creek Monastery.
Thevarkunnel, Anselm '57 (DUL) Retired.
Thevenin, Donelson '05 (BRK)[Q] Haitian Apostolate; Navy Chaplains; Cambria Heights, NY Sacred Heart.
Thi, Andrew '85 (NY) New York, NY Basilica of St. Patrick's Old Cathedral.
Thibault, Camillus *a.a.* '56 (BO)[U] Boston Assumptionist Center.
Thibault, Donald P. *o.p.* '68 (PRO) Providence, RI St. Pius V; [O] Providence, RI St. Pius House.
Thibault, Rodney E. '01 (FR) Judges; St. Luke's Hospital; East Freetown, MA St. John Neumann.
Thibeau, Richard *s.v.d.* '57 (FgM) Techny, IL.
Thibodeau, Andre M. '71 (MAN) Advocates Retired.
Thibodeau, Clement D. '58 (PRT) Retired.
Thibodeau, Kenneth *s.m.* '68 (BUR) White River Junction, VT St. Anthony.
Thibodeau, Raynold *o.f.m.cap.* '85 (NOR) Middletown, CT St. Pius X.
Thibodeau, Richard *c.ss.r.* '76 (NO) New Orleans, LA St. Mary's Assumption; New Orleans, LA St. Mary's Chapel; New Orleans, LA St. Alphonsus.
Thibodeau, Scott A. '98 (DET) Beverly Hills, MI Our Lady Queen of Martyrs.
Thibodeaux, Charles B. *s.j.* '59 (NO)[R] New Orleans Jesuit Provincial Office.
Thibodeaux, Mark E. *s.j.* '01 (LAF)[A] Grand Coteau, LA St. Charles College.
Thibodeaux, Paul '48 (LAF) Retired.
Thiede, John S. *s.j.* '03 (CHI)[N] Chicago Chicago Province of the Society of Jesus–Provincial Office.
Thiede, John S. *s.j.* '03 (FTW)[K] South Bend, IN Jesuit Community.
Thiel, Chris *o.f.m.cap.* '90 (LA)[F] La Canada Flintridge, CA St. Francis High School of La Canada–Flintridge.
Thiele, Richard *c.ss.r.* '54 (FgM) Denver, CO Denver Province.
Thiele, Robert A. '55 (SC) Retired.
Thielen, Jeffrey M. '74 (MIL) Retired.
Thielman, Kenneth '55 (SCL) Retired.
Thieman, Donald J. *c.pp.s.* '53 (CIN)[N] Dayton Provincial Office of the Cincinnati Province of the Society of the Precious Blood.
Thierry, Jude W. '09 (LAF) New Iberia, LA Our Lady of Perpetual Help.
Thiers, Georges G. *c.o.* '70 (PH) Philadelphia, PA St. Francis Xavier; [Y] Philadelphia, PA The Philadelphia Congregation of The Oratory of St. Philip Neri.
Thieryoung, John '96 (PEO) Aledo, IL St. Catherine's Church; Aledo, IL St. Anthony's Church.
Thiesen, Eugene '99 (STP) Military Chaplains.
Thiess, Daniel R. '90 (STL)[O] St. Louis, MO Lazarist Residence.
Thiessen, Dennis *s.d.s.* '78 (SAC)[C] Sacramento, CA Jesuit High School; Consultors:; Orangevale, CA Divine Savior.
Thimm, Donald H. '76 (MIL) New Berlin, WI Holy Apostles.
Thimmesh, Hilary *o.s.b.* '54 (SCL)[I] Collegeville, MN St. John's Abbey, of the Order of St. Benedict.
Thinh–Nguyen, Joseph *s.d.b.* '03 (LA)[F] Bellflower, CA St. John Bosco High School.
Thinnes, John M. '64 (CHI) Deerfield, IL Holy Cross Retired.
Thiruchiluvai, Roche Iruthayaraj *ss.cc.* '06 (FR)[F] Fairhaven National Center of the Enthronement.
Thirumangalam, George *c.m.i.* '76 (SAN) Menard, TX Sacred Heart; Junction, TX St. Theresa of the Child Jesus.
Thirunelliparamabil, Lukose '92 (CC) Beeville, TX Our Lady of Victory; Deans; College of Consultors; Presbyteral Council.
Thissen, Donald R. '70 (WCH) Retired.
Thoa, Ngo Dinh *c.ss.r.* '62 (LA)[P] Baldwin Park, CA Vietnamese Redemptorist Mission.
Thoennes, James '64 (SCL) Retired.
Thoennes, Roger '90 (SCL) Lowry, MN Our Lady of the Runestone; Lowry, MN St. John Nepomuk.
Thole, Simeon J. *o.s.b.* '62 (SCL)[I] Collegeville, MN St. John's Abbey, of the Order of St. Benedict.
Thole, Thomas *o.s.b.* '58 (SCL)[I] Collegeville, MN St. John's Abbey, of the Order of St. Benedict.
Tholen, John '62 (YAK) Retired.
Thoma, Steven *c.r.* '91 (LA)[A] Camarillo, CA St. John's Seminary.
Thoman, Dwayne J. '76 (DUB) Deans; Dubuque, IA Holy Spirit.
Thomas, Alan E. '92 (ALT) Johnstown, PA Resurrection Roman Catholic Church.
Thomas, Andrew R. '05 (P) Albany, OR Our Lady of Perpetual Help (St. Mary); Area Vicars.
Thomas, Anil *s.v.d.* '06 (LR) Pine Bluff, AR St. Peter.
Thomas, Antony Primal '10 (MIL) Racine, WI Cristo Rey; Racine, WI St. Patrick.
Thomas, Clyde '02 (LKC) Lake Arthur, LA Our Lady of the Lake.
Thomas, Curtis R. '87 (NO) Retired.
Thomas, David T. '52 (STL) Retired.
Thomas, Dominic *m.c.b.s.* '87 (MIL)[P] Kenosha, WI Missionary Congregation of the Blessed Sacrament, Inc., Zion Province; Kenosha, WI St. James.
Thomas, Donald K. *m.s.* '57 (HRT)[L] Hartford, CT Missionaries of LaSalette.
Thomas, Gary '83 (SJ) Saratoga, CA Sacred Heart.
Thomas, George L. '48 (SFR) Retired.
Thomas, George '97 (CC) Mathis, TX Saint Patrick Mission; Mathis, TX St. Pius X Mission – Sandia.
Thomas, Jacob '76 (ALX) Natchez, LA St. Augustine's.
Thomas, James J. '76 (ALN) On Duty Outside the Diocese.
Thomas, Jerald '56 (SR) Retired.
Thomas, Jeremy '92 (CHI) Chicago, IL St. Jerome; Presbyteral Council.
Thomas, Jesudoss *s.t.l.* '93 (TYL) Co Directors; Longview, TX St. Matthew Catholic Church.
Thomas, Joby Cheradai *m.s.* '98 (TYL) Waskom, TX St. Lawrence Brindisi.
Thomas, Joby *m.c.b.s.* '00 (ARL) Springfield, VA St. Raymond of Penafort.
Thomas, John M. '66 (SC) Armstrong, IA St. Mary's; Bancroft, IA St. John the Baptist's; Ledyard, IA Sacred Heart; Presbyteral Council; Diocesan Consultors Retired.
Thomas, John M. '93 (OWN) Madisonville, KY Christ the King; Committee for Education; Diocesan Liturgical Committee.
Thomas, John '94 (SYM) Columbus, OH St. Raphel Syro–Malabar Mission Cleveland, OH; Columbus, OH St. Mary Syro–Malabar Catholic Mission Columbus, OH.
Thomas, John '94 (COL) Columbus, OH Sacred Heart.
Thomas, Jon P. '10 (CAM) Continuing Education & Spiritual Formation of Priests (CESF).
Thomas, Jon–Peter '10 (CAM) Cherry Hill, NJ The Catholic Community of Christ Our Light, Cherry Hill, N.J.
Thomas, Jose '01 (SP) Palm Harbor, FL St. Luke the Evangelist.
Thomas, Joseph *b.s.o.* '71 (NTN) Methuen, MA Basilian Salvatorian Order.
Thomas, Joseph '11 (POD) Irving.
Thomas, Juniper J. '70 (RVC) Ronkonkoma, NY St. Joseph's.
Thomas, Kevin '88 (DET) Livonia, MI St. Aidan.
Thomas, LaVerne (Pike) '86 (SHP) Bossier City, LA St. Jude; Presbyteral Council; Diocesan Liturgy Commission; Clergy Continuing Formation Director; Master of Ceremonies, Diocese of Shreveport; College of Consultors.
Thomas, Mark A. '96 (PIT) Pittsburgh, PA St. Norbert.
Thomas, Mark L. '93 (PIT) Ellwood City, PA Holy Redeemer Parish.
Thomas, Chorbishop Michael G. '83 (SAM) Protosyncellus (Vicar General); Chancellor; Finance Council; Judges; Presbyteral Council; Fort Lauderdale, FL Heart of Jesus Catholic Church.
Thomas, Norman P. '55 (DET) Detroit, MI Sacred Heart of Jesus; Detroit, MI St. Elizabeth.
Thomas, Paschal *o.s.b.* '59 (KC)[J] Conception, MO Conception Abbey.
Thomas, Paul K. '63 (BAL) Retired.
Thomas, Paul *o.s.b.* '82 (P)[L] St. Benedict, OR Mt. Angel Abbey; President's Council.
Thomas, Phillip *o.c.d.* '79 (MIL)[P] Hubertus, WI Discalced Carmelite Monastery – Holy Hill Basilica of the National Shrine of Mary, Help of Christians, Holy Hill.
Thomas, Ralph W. '65 (CLV) Akron, OH St. Paul.
Thomas, Raymond J. '72 (Y) Ashtabula, OH Our Lady of Peace Parish.
Thomas, Richard L. '66 (GB) Green Bay, WI St. Francis Xavier Cathedral Retired.
Thomas, Robert W. '61 (BO) Senior Priests. Retired.
Thomas, Robert '61 (FgM) Boston, MA St. James the Apostle, Inc.
Thomas, Rev. Msgr. Royce R. '69 (MO) Army National Guard Chaplains.
Thomas, Scott '10 (JKS) Priests' Council; Madison, MS St. Francis of Assisi; Continuing Formation Committee.
Thomas, Sebastian Vettath '93 (CC) Skidmore, TX Immaculate Conception.
Thomas, Shaji (Jacob) *v.c.* '97 (DEN) Arvada, CO Spirit of Christ.
Thomas, Shaji R. '88 (TOL) Findlay, OH St. Michael the Archangel.
Thomas, Simon *s.m.a.* '98 (NEW)[L] Tenafly, NJ Society of African Missions, Provincialate, S.M.A. Fathers.
Thomas, Sunny *m.c.b.s.* '90 (DUL) Youth Conservation Camp; Willow River, MN St. Mary; Willow River, MN St. Isidore.
Thomas, Thomas P. '64 (MEM) Retired.
Thomas, Tom *m.s.f.s.* '98 (TYL)[C] Whitehouse, TX The Missionaries of St. Francis de Sales.
Thomas, Tom *m.s.f.s.* '98 (CHI)[J] Hoffman Estates, IL St. Alexius Medical Center.
Thomas, Wilbur N. *v.f.* '73 (CHL) Asheville, NC Basilica of St. Lawrence.
Thomas, William F. '93 (LR) Hot Springs National Park, AR St. Mary of the Springs.
Thomas, William V. '62 (CIN) Retired.
Thomasset, Alan *s.j.* '90 (BO)[U] Newton, MA The Jesuit Community at Boston College.
Thome, Edwin A. '54 (GLD) Traverse City, MI St. Joseph Retired.
Thome, Edwin J. '51 (LC) La Crosse, WI; [H] La Crosse, WI Holy Cross (Seminary) Diocesan Center Retired.
Thome, John J. '46 (SAG) Retired.
Thomlison, Steven W. '10 (LIN) Advocates; Lincoln, NE Cathedral of the Risen Christ.
Thompson, Andrew *c.ss.r.* '81 (GAL) Houston, TX Holy Ghost.
Thompson, August L. '57 (ALX) Retired.
Thompson, Augustine *o.p.* '85 (OAK)[L] Oakland, CA Order of Preachers (Province of the Most Holy Name of Jesus – Western Dominican Province); [A] Berkeley, CA Dominican School of Philosophy and Theology.
Thompson, D. Timothy '82 (FWT) Denton, TX Immaculate Conception; Consultors; Tribunal; Priests' Pension Plan Trustees.
Thompson, Dennis '89 (STP) Farmington, MN St. Michael.
Thompson, Edward C. '59 (NEW) Retired.
Thompson, Edward J. '51 (ORL) Altamonte Springs, FL St. Mary Magdalen.
Thompson, George M. '52 (PEO) Retired.
Thompson, Rev. Msgr. George P. '65 (NY) Bedford, NY St. Patrick; Northern Westchester and Putnam.
Thompson, Gregory S. '06 (ARL) Defenders of the Bond.
Thompson, J. Noel '54 (SD) Retired.
Thompson, J. Timothy *s.j.* '70 (FgM) St. Louis, MO Society of Jesus.
Thompson, James A. '44 (TR) Retired.
Thompson, James *o.s.a.* '71 (CHI)[N] Chicago, IL St. John Stone Friary; [J] Evergreen Park, IL Little Company of Mary Hospital and Health Care Centers.
Thompson, James *o.p.* '03 (SEA) Seattle, WA Blessed Sacrament.
Thompson, Jefferson M. *c.s.b.* '91 (DET)[E] Novi, MI Catholic Central High School.
Thompson, Jerald Wayne '94 (LA) Hospital Chaplains.
Thompson, Jerome H. '60 (LA) Retired.
Thompson, John *s.d.b.* '79 (FgM) New Rochelle, NY SALESIANS OF DON BOSCO.
Thompson, John *s.m.* '99 (HON)[D] Honolulu, HI Center Marianist Community.
Thompson, Kevin *o.f.m.cap.* '97 (WDC) Washington, DC Shrine of the Sacred Heart.
Thompson, Kevin '11 (RVC) Hampton Bays, NY St. Rosalie's.
Thompson, Kizito *o.c.s.o.* '70 (WOR)[N] Spencer, MA St. Joseph's Abbey.
Thompson, Matthew E. '79 (WDC) Retired.
Thompson, Melvin F. '67 (DEN) Retired.
Thompson, Michael L. *s.s.j.* '04 (BAL)[Q] Baltimore, MD St. Joseph Society of the Sacred Heart House of Central Administration.
Thompson, Michael '96 (STA) Absent or Sick Leave.
Thompson, Nicholas R. '11 (MAR) Marquette, MI St. Michael; [G] Marquette, MI Catholic Campus Ministry–Northern Michigan University.
Thompson, Rev. Msgr. Patrick G. '60 (LA) Glendale, CA Church of the Incarnation Retired.
Thompson, Philip E. '78 (DUB) Ex–Officio; [D] Cedar Rapids, IA Xavier High School Foundation; Cedar Rapids, IA St. Pius X; College of Consultors; Personnel Advisory Board; [D] Cedar Rapids, IA Xavier High School.
Thompson, Richard B. '69 (MAN) College of Consultors; Presbyteral Council; Priest Personnel Board; Institutional Ministries Office; Vicar for Clergy; Manchester, NH St. Pius X.
Thompson, Richard J. '96 (PIT) Waynesburg, PA St. Ann; [P] Waynesburg, PA Waynesburg College (Waynesburg).
Thompson, Richard R. '59 (SY) Retired.
Thompson, Richard '95 (P) Portland, OR All Saints.

Thompson, Stephen A. '10 (SFD) Springfield, IL Cathedral of the Immaculate Conception.
Thompson, Stephen '10 (SFD) Springfield, IL St. Katharine Drexel.
Thompson, Thomas A. *s.m.* '68 (CIN)[D] Dayton, OH The University of Dayton; [N] Dayton, OH Marianist Community; Dayton, OH Mariological Society of America (1949).
Thompson, Thomas E. '92 (SUP) Osceola, WI Assumption of the Blessed Virgin Mary; Osceola, WI St. Joseph; Personnel Placement Board; Vocations, Officeof; Presbyteral Council & Diocesan Consultors; Board of Directors.
Thompson, Thomas W. '64 (LAN) College of Consultors Retired.
Thompson, Thomas '82 (SD) Scripps Hospital; Thornton Hospital.
Thompson, William J. '71 (WDC) Indian Head, MD St. Mary Star of the Sea; [M] Washington, DC Cardinal O'Boyle Residence for Priests Retired.
Thompson, Rev. Msgr. William P.A. '54 (CC) Retired.
Thompson, William '08 (WIN) Dodge Center, MN St. John Baptist de La Salle; Dodge Center, MN St. Vincent de Paul; Chaplain; Dodge Center, MN St. Francis de Sales; [C] Rochester, MN Lourdes High School of Rochester, Inc.
Thoms, Jeffrey (HBG) Hanover, PA St. Vincent.
Thomsen, Steven '86 (LAN) On Leave of Absence.
Thomson, Sean P. '04 (FBK) Chaplains of Public Institutions; [C] Fairbanks, AK Peger Road House.
Thon, Andrew J. *s.j.* '74 (MIL)[P] Milwaukee, WI Jesuit Community at Marquette University.
Thoni, Rev. Msgr. Philip F. '49 (KNX) Fairfield Glade, TN St. Francis of Assisi Retired.
Thoonkuzhy, Joseph '58 (BEL) Retired.
Thoppil, Scaria T. *c.m.i.* '80 (JOL) Kankakee, IL St. Rose of Lima.
Thorburn, Rev. Msgr. Timothy J. '83 (LIN) Lincoln, NE Bishop Bonacum Chancery; [J] Lincoln, NE The Catholic Foundation of the Diocese of Lincoln; Moderator of the Curia; Vicar General; Promoters Justitiae; Defensores Vinculi; Diocesan Consultors; Presbyteral Council; Building Commission; Censores Librorum; Clergy Relief Society—The Saint John Vianney Association; Diocesan Finance Council; Diocesan Health Ministries, Inc.; Diocesan Housing Ministries, Inc.; Evangelization Committee; Insurance; Priests' Continuing Education Committee; [J] Lincoln, NE Crossing the Threshold Campaign; [J] Lincoln, NE Charity and Stewardship Appeal (DDP).
Thorn, Robert C. '99 (LC) Wausau, WI St. Matthew; Special Assignment; [C] Wausau, WI Newman Catholic Middle School at St. Matthew Parish.
Thorne, Stephen D. '98 (PH) Philadelphia, PA St. Martin De Porres; [H] Philadelphia, PA St. Martin de Porres School.
Thorne, Thomas P. '76 (BGP) Westport, CT Church of the Assumption; Diocesan Consultors; Vicariate II (Norwalk, New Canaan, Wilton, Weston, Westport); Navy Reserve Chaplains; Presbyteral Council.
Thornsberry, Michael J. '91 (BAL) Priests Sick or Absent.
Thornton, James W. *c.s.c.* '64 (PHX)[F] Phoenix, AZ Holy Cross Congregation/Casa Santa Cruz Retired.
Thornton, James *c.s.c.* (FTW)[H] Notre Dame Congregation of Holy Cross, United States Province of Priests & Brothers.
Thornton, Rev. Msgr. Michael J. '69 (BLX) Waynesboro, MS St. Bernadette; Laurel, MS Immaculate Conception; College of Consultors; Association of Priests (Diocese of Biloxi and Jackson); Promoter of Justice; South Mississippi Correctional Facility; Personnel Board; South Mississippi Correctional Institution; Defenders of the Bond.
Thornton, Rev. Msgr. Michael '69 (JKS) Association of Priests.
Thornton, William H. '09 (SFR) Novato, CA St. Anthony of Padua.
Thorsen, Henry '53 (BIR) Retired.
Thorsen, Robert J. '56 (CIN) Retired.
Thottankara, Raju '95 (MO) Gregory, TX Immaculate Conception; Navy Reserve Chaplains.
Thottapally, James J. '71 (OAK) El Sobrante, CA St. Callistus; Deanery #8.
Thottathil, Jose K. '83 (TLS) Dewey, OK Our Lady of Guadalupe; [E] Tulsa, OK Jane Phillips Health Corp.
Thottiyil, Mathew *m.s.f.s.* '78 (TYL)[C] Whitehouse, TX The Missionaries of St. Francis de Sales.
Thottiyil, Matthew *m.s.f.s.* '78 (GAL) Houston, TX St. Bernadette Soubirous.
Thottukulappananiyil, John '91 (NEW) Hackensack, NJ Holy Trinity.
Thottungal, Thomas '70 (NEW) Jersey City, NJ St. Paul's; Asian–Indian Apostolate.
Thottuvelil, Zacharias '83 (SYM) Coral Springs, FL Our Lady of Health Syro–Malabar Catholic Church (Coral Springs); Coral Springs, FL St. Joseph Syro–Malabar Catholic Mission; Coral Springs, FL St. George Syro–Malabar Catholic Mission, Miami FL.
Thottuvelil, Zacharias '83 (MIA) Indians.
Thoyalil, James *v.c.* '91 (PT) Pensacola, FL Little Flower.
Thrasher, Robert W. '62 (SPR) Vice–Chancellor; Springfield, MA Holy Cross Retired.
Thrasher, Robert W. '62 (SPR) Defenders of the Bond.
Thuerauf, Jason M. '99 (DEN) Fort Morgan, CO St. Helena; Deaneries.
Thuerauf, Jeffrey P. '89 (TUC) Leave of Absence.
Thuma, Clifton M. '96 (BO)[AA] Boston, MA The Catholic Center at Boston University; Health Leave.
Thumbi, Francis '87 (SEA) Lynnwood, WA St. Thomas More.
Thumma, Jacob '93 (NY) Staten Island, NY St. Sylvester.
Thumma, Joseph Prem (SAN) Midland, TX St. Stephen's.
Thumma, Rayappa '86 (NY) Cortlandt Manor, NY St. Columbanus.
Thundathil, Anthony '91 (SYM) Louisville, KY Syro–Malabar Catholic Mission Louisville, Kentucky.
Thundathil, Antony C. *m.s.t.* '91 (SYM) Vicar General (Protosyncellus); Eparchial Consultors.
Thundathil, Mathew '78 (MIA) Miami Beach, FL St. Patrick; Defenders of the Bond.
Thuong, Rev. Msgr. Philippe Le–Xuan '70 (GAL) Houston, TX Christ, The Incarnate Word; Archdiocesan Judges.
Thuong Tran, Joseph '05 (ORG) Garden Grove, CA St. Callistus.
Thurber, David G. '08 (PRO) Cranston, RI St. Mary.
Thurston, Anthony '82 (WH)[F] Wheeling, WV Wheeling Hospital.
Thurston, Anthony '82 (OAK) On Duty Outside the Diocese.
Thury, Gerald '67 (SFS) Retired.
Thychery, George '60 (LAF) Retired.
Thylstrup, Edward J. *s.j.* '67 (FgM) Los Gatos, CA Society of Jesus.
Tiano, Christopher M. '89 (HRT) Torrington, CT St. Francis of Assisi; Torrington, CT St. Mary; Torrington, CT St. Peter; Waterbury Vicariate; Torrington, CT Sacred Heart.
Tibakunirwa, John C. (BO) Peabody, MA St. John the Baptist.
Tibay, Ernesto C. '76 (NEW) New Milford, NJ Ascension; Filipino Apostolate.
Tibbetts, Richard K. '98 (ATL) Atlanta, GA Holy Cross.
Tibbs, Thomas T. '74 (GRY) Kouts, IN St. Mary.
Tibesar, Leo J. '68 (STP) Retired.
Tiboni, Rev. Msgr. Vito '69 (NEW) On Duty Outside the Archdiocese.
Tice, Cecil '81 (CHL) Absent On Leave.
Tichacek, Charles P. '94 (STL) Silex, MO St. Alphonsus.
Tickerhoof, Bernard *t.o.r.* '78 (ALT)[G] Loretto, PA St. Bonaventure Friary; [G] Loretto, PA St. Francis Friary at Mount Assisi.
Tickerhoof, David *t.o.r.* '67 (SFS) Marty, SD St. Paul's Church.
Ticllasuca, Rolando *m.r.s.m.* '94 (RVC) Glen Cove, NY St. Patrick's.
Ticona, Fidel Arocutipa *c.s.c.* '00 (FTW)[H] Notre Dame Congregation of Holy Cross, United States Province of Priests & Brothers.
Ticona, Fidel *c.s.c.* '00 (SCR)[B] Wilkes–Barre, PA King's College; Wilkes–Barre, PA St. Nicholas.
Tiedeman, Edmund H. '66 (SC) Retired.
Tiegs, James R. '74 (OM) Omaha, NE St. Stephen the Martyr.
Tiell, Florian *o.f.m.conv.* (TOL) Carey, OH Our Lady of Consolation, Basilica–National Shrine.
Tien, Dominic Hoang Minh '06 (PH) Philadelphia, PA Saint Cyprian.
Tiendrebeogo, Anatole A. '87 (OAK) Oakland, CA St. Leo the Great.
Tierney, Charles *o.m.i.* '73 (FgM) Washington, DC AMERICAN OBLATE MISSIONS.
Tierney, Gary M. '67 (DET) Retired.
Tierney, Rev. Msgr. James E. '50 (BO) Senior Priests. Retired.
Tierney, Joseph P. '86 (NY)[E] Bronx, NY Cardinal Hayes High School.
Tierney, Rev. Msgr. Michael J. '67 (RCK) Retired.
Tierney, Patrick J. '69 (BIR) Orland Park, IL Retired.
Tietjen, Kenneth F. *o.c.s.o.* '56 (DUB)[K] Peosta, IA New Melleray Abbey, Order of Cistercians of the Strict Observance.
Tietjen, Michael E. '06 (WDC) Avenue, MD Holy Angels.
Tiffany, Eugene W. '72 (STP) Minneapolis, MN St. Boniface; Minneapolis, MN All Saints.
Tifft, Thomas W. '69 (CLV)[A] Wickliffe, OH St. Mary Seminary and Graduate School of Theology; College of Consultors; Presbyteral Council.
Tigga, Alex (TUC) Tucson, AZ Saint Thomas the Apostle Roman Catholic Parish – Tucson.
Tigga, Jeremias *h.g.n.* '04 (FWT) Knox City, TX Santa Rosa; Munday, TX St. Joseph; Seymour, TX Sacred Heart.
Tigges, James J. '71 (SC) Humboldt, IA St. John's; Humboldt, IA St. Mary's; Humboldt, IA Sacred Heart; Council of Catholic Women.
Tighe, Dermot F. '54 (DOD)[F] Dodge City, KS The Diocese of Dodge City Priest Retirement Fund, Inc. Retired.
Tighe, James L. '70 (BRK) Flushing, NY Queen of Peace.
Tighe, Leonard J. '73 (BO) Unassigned.
Tighe, Philip M. '00 (R) Wake Forest, NC St. Catherine of Siena.
Tighe, Timothy P. *c.s.p.* '69 (BRK) Brooklyn, NY St. Saviour.
Tighe, Timothy P. *c.s.p.* '69 (NY)[DD] New York, NY Paulist Fathers' Motherhouse.
Tigreros, Ernesto *s.s.p.* '66 (NY)[B] Staten Island, NY Society of St. Paul; Staten Island, NY.
Tigyer, Jeffrey E. '00 (COL) Powell, OH St. Joan of Arc.
Tigyer, Paul '54 (PSC) Retired.
Tijerina, Richard '85 (AUS) Austin, TX St. Peter the Apostle.
Tikalsky, Russell F. '56 (MIL) Retired.
Tilford, John E. '66 (CHI) Chicago, IL St. Michael the Archangel.
Tilley, Charles J. *s.j.* '85 (SJ) Los Gatos, CA; [M] Santa Clara, CA Casa San Inigo, Jesuit Residence.
Tilley, Charles J. *s.j.* '85 (SAC)[J] Applegate, CA Jesuit Retreat Center of the Sierra.
Tillia, Marc '59 (KCK) On Duty Outside the Archdiocese.
Tillman, Rev. Msgr. Richard H. '65 (BAL) Retired.
Tillman, Richard J. '65 (STL) Special Assignment.
Tillman, Robert J. *s.j.* '77 (OM)[C] Omaha, NE Creighton Preparatory School; [J] Omaha, NE Jesuit Community at Creighton University.
Tillotson, Frederick J. *o.carm.* '69 (WDC)[X] Washington, DC Carmelite Institute; [B] Washington, DC Washington Theological Union; [B] Washington, DC Whitefriars Hall.
Tillrock, Raymond J. '69 (CHI) Chicago, IL St. Barnabas Retired.
Tilly, Charles *s.j.* '85 (SJ)[B] Santa Clara, CA Jesuit Community.
Tillyer, Rev. Msgr. Herbert K. '68 (PAT) Theological Commission; Parsippany, NJ St. Peter the Apostle; [Q] Bloomfield, NJ Riese Corporation; [Q] Paterson, NJ Martin de Porres Village Corporation; Associate Judges.
Tilp, John R. '69 (DUB) Clear Lake, IA St. Patrick.
Timar, Frank John *m.s.c.* '58 (RCK) Sycamore, IL St. Mary; [K] Sycamore, IL St. Mary's Educational Foundation, Ltd.; [G] Aurora, IL Missionaries of the Sacred Heart Community.
Timbre, Roland '61 (HT) Kenner, LA Retired.
Timby, Bryan P. '83 (MEM) Memphis, TN Our Lady of Sorrows; Memphis, TN.
Timchak, Robert M. '92 (SCR) Unassigned or Leave of Absence.
Timko, Philip S. *o.s.b.* '69 (JOL)[A] Lisle, IL Benedictine University; [L] Lisle, IL St. Procopius Abbey; Lisle, IL.
Timlin, John P. *c.m.* '79 (CHL) Greensboro, NC St. Mary.
Timm, Richard W. *c.s.c.* '49 (FgM) New Rochelle, NY Eastern Brothers Province.
Timmel, Gerald L. '56 (L)[L] Louisville, KY Bishop David Apartments Retired.
Timmerman, Bart D. '01 (MAD) Monona, WI Immaculate Heart of Mary; Appointed; Diocesan Consultors; Personnel Board.
Timmerman, Craig A. '05 (NU) Canby, MN St. Peter; St. Leo, MN St. Leo; Committee for Continuing Education of Clergy; Vocations Team; On Special or Other Diocesan Assignment.
Timmerman, David W. '87 (MAD) Cambridge, WI St. Pius X; Edgerton, WI St. Joseph; Elected.
Timmerman, Gerard *s.m.* '75 (WDC)[O] Washington, DC Marist Center.
Timmerman, Paul D. '07 (NU) Committee on Parishes; Ecumenism and Interreligious Affairs; On Special or Other Diocesan Assignment; Committee for Evangelization & Catechesis; Benson, MN St. Francis; Murdock, MN Church of the Sacred Heart.
Timmerman, Randy J. '93 (MAD) Janesville, WI St. John Vianney; Janesville; Elected.
Timmerman, Sean M. '03 (LIN) David City, NE St. Francis; [C] David City, NE Aquinas/St. Mary's Schools; [L] David City, NE Aquinas High School Endowment Fund; Advocates.
Timmermans, Rev. Msgr. John '52 (ALX) Retired.
Timmers, Jozef *o.f.m.cap.* '00 (FgM) Detroit, MI Province of St. Joseph.
Timmings, Thomas '70 (FRS) Atwater, CA St. Anthony.
Timock, Ronald K. '83 (MAR) Gladstone, MI All Saints.
Timone, Richard F. *s.j.* '64 (NY)[DD] New York, NY Murray–Weigel Hall.
Timoney, Coman (BAL)[U] Baltimore, MD Catholic War Veterans USA, Inc.
Timoney, Conan H. *c.p.* '68 (MO) DEPARTMENT OF VETERANS AFFAIRS HOSPITALS AND CHAPLAINS.
Timoney, Conan H. '68 (PSC) Baltimore, MD Patronage of the Mother of God; Syncellus; Presbyteral Council; Evangelization.
Timoney, Francis '69 (LAV) Retired.

Timony, Brian '56 (OAK) Pleasant Hill, CA Christ the King Retired.
Timp, Frederick *s.v.d.* '71 (FgM) Techny, IL.
Tinajero, Frank *s.v.d.* '88 (LA) Los Angeles, CA Metropolitan Detention Center; Los Angeles, CA St. Alphonsus.
Tindall, Harold '78 (SD) Poway, CA Saint Gabriel Catholic Parish Retired.
Tindall, William '89 (DET) Livonia, MI St. Michael; College of Consultors; Archdiocesan Pastoral Council.
Tinh, John Tran *c.m.c.* (AMA) Amarillo, TX Our Lady of Vietnam.
Tinh, Joseph Nguyen '57 (SJ) Retired.
Tinkatumire, Leo '92 (CHI) Chicago, IL St. Helena of tghe Cross.
Tinney, Richard W. '65 (BUR) Essex Junction, VT St. Pius X; Elected Members.
Tino, John '01 (BRK) Brooklyn, NY St. Dominic.
Tino, Robert F. '71 (MIL) Retired.
Tinsley, Rev. Msgr. Edmond T. '51 (WOR)[J] Leicester, MA McAuley Nazareth Home for Boys; Diocesan College of Consultors; Worcester, MA St. John's Retired.
Tintle, Raymond *o.f.m.* '69 (MRY)[F] San Miguel, CA Franciscan Friars, O.F.M.; Presbyteral Council; San Miguel, CA San Miguel.
Tiongson, Joselito S. '92 (MO) Navy Chaplains.
Tippmann, Laurence '69 (FTW) Retired.
Tipton, Prentice '08 (SAG) Munger, MI St. Norbert; Reese, MI St. Elizabeth.
Tiqual, Robert (WIL)[J] Dover, DE Oblate Apostles of the Two Hearts.
Tirabassi, Camillo '59 (FTW)[C] South Bend, IN Saint Joseph's High School; South Bend, IN Holy Family Retired.
Tirado, Orlando *c.m.* '99 (SJN) Military Services.
Tirado, Ramon Orlando '86 (SJN) San Juan, PR San Lucas; Air National Guard Chaplains.
Tirkey, Dominic '98 (GR) Edmore, MI St. Bernadette of Lourdes; Edmore, MI St. Margaret Mary.
Tirpak, Adrian *t.o.r.* '60 (ALT) Windber, PA St. Anthony of Padua.
Tiscornia, Thomas A. *m.m.* '73 (FgM) Maryknoll, NY MARYKNOLL.
Titland, Peter R. *s.j.* '70 (FgM) Portland, OR Society of Jesus.
Tito, Joseph P. '96 (CHI) Chicago, IL Our Lady of Mercy.
Tito, Joseph '88 (NOR) Baltic, CT St. Mary of the Immaculate Conception; Seminarian Advisory Board.
Tito, Rocco A. '55 (E) Retired.
Titonea, Radu N. '09 (ROM) Long Island City, NY.
Titotto, Mario *c.s.* '72 (PRO) Johnston, RI St. Rocco.
Titta, Santino '60 (ALB) Retired.
Tittler, Leo R. '63 (BAL) Retired.
Titus, Austin E. '92 (NY) Staten Island, NY Holy Family.
Titus, Fernando '05 (CI) Chuuk, FM St. Francis Assisi; [C] Tunnuk, Chuuk, FM Vicariate Residence; Chuuk, FM Assumption of the Blessed Virgin Mary.
Titus, John M. '89 (SFD) Charleston, IL St. Charles Borromeo; [M] Charleston, IL Eastern Illinois University Newman Catholic Center; Presbyteral Council.
Titus, Steven Matthew '08 (CHY) Cheyenne, WY St. Mary's Cathedral; St. Joseph's Society for Priests (Clergy Mutual Benefit Society); Presbyteral Council.
Tiu, Jim '00 (FAR)[F] Wahpeton, ND Carmel of Mary; Special Assignment.
Tivadar, Vasile '95 (STF) Brooklyn, NY St. Nicholas; Ozone Park, NY St. Mary Protectress; Brooklyn.
Tivenan, John J. '72 (BRK) Retired.
Tivy, Gerald '64 (JOL) Retired.
Tivy, Thomas A. '62 (CHI) Chicago, IL Resurrection Retired.
Tix, Michael '92 (STP) Savage, MN St. John the Baptist.
Tizio, John G. *c.ss.r.* '85 (BAL) Annapolis, MD St. Mary.
Tizio, Joseph *c.ss.r.* '75 (BRK) Brooklyn, NY Our Lady of Perpetual Help Basilica.
Tizziani, Mario J. '06 (COV) Legion of Mary; Independence, KY St. Cecilia.
Tkachuk, William '81 (CHI) Evanston, IL St. Nicholas.
Tkel, Wayne *s.j.* '02 (CI) Palau, PW St. Thomas Apostle; [C] Manresa Jesuit House.
Tkocz, Peter '01 (ALB) Cohoes, NY St. Michael.
Tlucek, Edward G. *o.f.m.* '78 (GRY) Cedar Lake, IN Holy Name; Provincial Councilors:; Bishop's Council of Priests; [H] Cedar Lake, IN Our Lady of Lourdes Friary.
Toal, Bernard E. *s.s.c.* '43 (SB) Fontana, CA St. Mary Retired.
Toal, Bernard *s.s.c.* '43 (OM)[J] St. Columbans Missionary Society of St. Columban.
Toal, Bernard *s.s.c.* '43 (PRO)[O] Bristol, RI St. Columban's Retirement House.
Toal, James F. *o.f.m.* '75 (SP)[N] St. Petersburg, FL St. Anthony Friary.
Toale, Rev. Msgr. Thomas E. '81 (DUB)[L] Dubuque, IA St. Joseph's Convent, Mount Carmel; Vicar General and Episcopal Vicar for Dubuque Region; College of Consultors; Archdiocesan Pastoral Center; The Archdiocese of Dubuque Corporate Board; Catholic Charities Board of Directors; Finance Council; Pastoral Council; Ex Officio Members; Board of Directors/Priest Pension Plan Board of Trustees; Archbishop's Cabinet; On Special or Other Archdiocesan Assignment; Archdiocese of Dubuque Deposit & Loan Fund Board; Archdiocese of Dubuque Education Fund Board; Archdiocese of Dubuque Perpetual Care Fund Board; Archdiocese of Dubuque Seminarian Education Fund Board; School Tuition Organization Board of Directors; Catholic Charities Foundation; Witness Corporate Board; Lay Formation Advisory Board.
Toan, Hoang (GAL)[L] Houston, TX Pope John Paul XXIII Priests' Residence Retired.
Toan Quang Doan, Basil M. *c.m.c.* '99 (SPC) El Dorado Springs, MO St. Elizabeth of Hungary.
Tobias, Joseph F. *m.s.c.* '66 (ALN) Nazareth, PA Holy Family; Elected Members.
Tobin, Charles P. '68 (KC) Belton, MO St. Sabina's.
Tobin, David *c.ss.r.* '63 (OAK)[L] Berkeley, CA Redemptorist Fathers (Denver Province).
Tobin, Edmund J. '72 (ORL) Melbourne, FL Ascension.
Tobin, James M. *s.m.* '69 (STL)[O] St. Louis, MO Marianist Community, Our Lady of the Pillar Parish; St. Louis, MO Our Lady of the Pillar.
Tobin, Jeremy *o.praem.* '69 (JKS) Carthage, MS St. Anne; [E] Raymond, MS Priory of St. Moses the Black; [H] Raymond, MS Hinds Community College Catholic Student Organization.
Tobin, Patrick D. *o.p.* '10 (JC)[D] Columbia, MO St. Thomas More Newman Center; Columbia, MO St. Thomas More Newman Center, University of Missouri.
Tobin, Patrick '56 (KC) Kansas City, MO St. Therese Parish Retired.
Tobin, Paul R. '64 (Y) Campbell, OH St. Joseph the Provider Retired.
Tobin, Robert V. *m.m.* '57 (FgM) Maryknoll, NY MARYKNOLL Retired.
Tobin, T. Michael '93 (L) Shelbyville, KY Annunciation of the Blessed Virgin Mary.
Tobin, Terence *o.f.m.conv.* '55 (FgM) Mount Saint Francis, IN Province of Our Lady of Consolation.
Tobin, Thomas H. *s.j.* '73 (CHI)[C] Chicago, IL Jesuit Community at Loyola University Chicago.
Tobin, Thomas '59 (GF) Finance Council; Baker, MT St. John the Evangelist.
Tobin, Tom '05 (SP) Pinellas Park, FL Sacred Heart.
Tobin, Vincent *o.s.b.* '59 (IND)[K] Saint Meinrad, IN St. Meinrad Archabbey.
Tobolski, James F. '84 (SUP) Superior, WI St. Francis Xavier; Judicial Vicar; Vicar for Canonical Affairs; Northwest Deanery; Presbyteral Council & Diocesan Consultors; Personnel Placement Board; Ecumenical Commission.
Tobolski, Robert *m.s.c.* '55 (ALN)[A] Center Valley, PA Sacred Heart Villa, Missionaries of the Sacred Heart; Reading, PA St. Mary.
Tobon, John Jaime '96 (BRK) Brooklyn, NY St. Martin of Tours–Our Lady of Lourdes.
Toborowsky, Jonathan S. '98 (MET) Laurence Harbor, NJ St. Lawrence; Deans.
Tocco, Rev. Msgr. Anthony M. '65 (DET) Bloomfield Hills, MI St. Hugo of the Hills; College of Consultors.
Tocco, Nicholas A. '11 (ORL) Orlando, FL St. James Cathedral.
Tochtrop, Randolph G. '96 (SPC) Advance, MO St. Joseph; Oran, MO Guardian Angel; Chaffee, MO St. Ambrose.
Todd, Richard *c.m.f.* '55 (MET) Perth Amboy, NJ Our Lady of Fatima.
Todd, Wilmer '63 (HT) Retired.
Toepfer, John *o.f.m.cap.* '86 (COS) Colorado Springs, CO St. Mary Cathedral; Hispanic Ministry; [E] Colorado Springs, CO Solanus Casey Friary.
Tofani, Rev. Msgr. Richard L. '79 (TR) Hainesport, NJ Our Lady Queen of Peace; Episcopal Council; New York, NY A. The Pontifical Society for the Propagation of the Faith; Burlington County.
Togni, Peter J. *s.j.* '85 (SJ)[M] Los Gatos, CA Sacred Heart Jesuit Center.
Toilolo, Damien *o.s.b.* '05 (LA) Valyermo, CA; [P] Valyermo, CA St. Andrew's Abbey.
Tokarczyk, Joseph M. '79 (NY) Florida, NY St. Joseph; Pine Island, NY St. Stanislaus.
Tokarski, Gregory '95 (DET) Farmington Hills, MI St. Clare of Assisi.
Tokarski, Stan '93 (DET) South Lyon, MI St. Joseph.
Tokarz, David J. '91 (MOB) Mobile, AL Our Savior; [J] Mobile, AL Cursillo; Ecumenical Commission.
Tokarz, Thomas M. '77 (WOR) Gardner, MA Holy Spirit; Gardner, MA St. Joseph's.
Tokaz, John *o.f.m.cap.* '78 (ROC) Trumansburg, NY St. James the Apostle; [K] Interlaken, NY St. Fidelis Friary.
Toland, Eugene W. *m.m.* '64 (FgM) Maryknoll, NY MARYKNOLL.
Toland, Terrence *s.j.* '52 (PH) Philadelphia, PA Old St. Joseph's Retired.
Tolang, Jaime '58 (SEA) Seattle, WA Immaculate Conception Retired.
Toledo, Ivan '02 (MIA) Sunrise, FL St. Bernard.
Toledo, Joseph '09 (DEN) Fort Collins, CO St. Elizabeth Ann Seton.
Tolentino, Cesar '02 (TR) Maple Shade, NJ Our Lady of Perpetual Help.
Tolentino, Rev. Msgr. Eddie E. '84 (WDC) Deans; Silver Spring, MD St. Michael; Priest Council; Archdiocesan College of Consultors.
Tolentino, Eric N. '06 (ALN) Forks of the Delaware Serra; Allentown, PA Cathedral of St. Catharine of Siena; Advocates.
Tolentino, Rommel P. '05 (LKC) Hackberry, LA St. Peter Apostle; Diocesan Consultors; Sea, Apostleship of the.
Tolentino, Virgilio T. '82 (MET) Sayreville, NJ Our Lady of Victories.
Tolentino de la Rosa, Lorenzo Maria *o.cart.* '92 (BUR)[E] Arlington, VT Carthusian Foundation in America, Inc., Charterhouse of the Transfiguration.
Tolg, Killian '04 (NO)[A] St. Benedict, LA St. Joseph Seminary College; [R] St. Benedict, LA St. Joseph Abbey.
Tollefson, Rolf R. '01 (STP) Chanhassen, MN St. Hubert; Appointees.
Tolleson, Bart (HEL) Personnel Board.
Tolleson, William Barton '07 (HEL) Frenchtown, MT St. John the Baptist.
Tollini, Frederick P. *s.j.* '65 (SJ)[B] Santa Clara, CA Jesuit Community.
Tolosa Pita, Armando '10 (MIA) Pinecrest, FL St. Louis.
Tolve, Paul *i.v.dei* '84 (NY) Valhalla, NY Westchester County Jail.
Toma, Chorbishop Sadei '95 (OLD) Phoenix, AZ Saints Behnam and Sarah Mission.
Toma, Rev. Msgr. Zouhair '68 (EST) Troy, MI St. Joseph Chaldean Parish.
Toma, Zuhair G. (ORG) Santa Ana, CA St. George (Chaldean Catholic).
Toma, Zuhair G. '00 (SPA) Campbell, CA St. Mary Assyrian–Chaldean Parish.
Tomas, Efren A. *m.s.* '81 (HON) Vicars Forane; Kahului, HI Christ the King; College of Consultors; Presbyteral Council; Clergy Personnel Board.
Tomas, Pedro Pereira *s.j.* '11 (BO)[U] Brighton, MA Isaac Jogues House.
Tomas, Peter '95 (PSC) Binghamton, NY Holy Spirit; St. Josaphat Sacerdotal Society; Presbyters.
Tomaselli, Rev. Msgr. Samuel J. '59 (ALT) Retired.
Tomasi, Lydio F. *c.s.* '63 (WDC) Washington, DC Holy Rosary.
Tomasiewicz, Edward J. *c.m.* '74 (CHI)[N] Chicago DePaul Vincentian Residence.
Tomasiewicz, Frank '65 (SCL) Retired.
Tomasiewicz, Mark A. '91 (OM) Tekamah, NE St. Patrick; Air Force Reserve Chaplains.
Tomasko, Andrew J. '91 (DET) Absent on Leave.
Tomaskovic, Emil *s.a.* '71 (NY)[DD] Garrison, NY Franciscan Friars of the Atonement.
Tomasone, Richard C. '80 (E) Falls Creek, PA St. Bernard; [C] Du Bois, PA DuBois Area Catholic School.
Tomasovich, Rev. Msgr. John A. '48 (NO) Retired.
Tomasso, Paul J. '81 (ROC) Geneva, NY Our Lady of Peace Roman Catholic Church of Geneva, NY; [N] Geneva, NY Hobart and William Smith College; [O] Rochester, NY Family Rosary For Peace, Inc.; Priests' Council; Priest Consultors.
Tomczak, Peter A. '05 (NO) Metairie, LA St. Angela Merici.
Tomei, Joseph *c.s.c.* (FTW)[H] Notre Dame Congregation of Holy Cross, United States Province of Priests & Brothers.
Tomich, Daniel W. '76 (CHI) Oak Lawn, IL St. Louis De Montfort.
Tomichek, Rev. Msgr. George *d.c.* '74 (PH) Philadelphia, PA St. Peter the Apostle.
Tomicky, Ronald '75 (CLV) Retired.
Tomiczek, Damian *s.d.s.* '82 (NEW)[L] Verona, NJ The Salvatorian Fathers.
Tomiczek, Damian *s.d.s.* (NOR) Moosup, CT All–Hallows; Wauregan, CT Sacred Heart.
Tomikeh, Tomy '88 (SPA) North Hollywood, CA St. Paul Assyrian–Chaldean Catholic Parish; North Hollywood, CA St. Paul Assyrian–Chaldean.
Tomkins, Robert J. '88 (SB) Retired.
Tomkosky, Richard B. '00 (ALT) Everett, PA St. John the Evangelist; Clearville, PA Seven Dolors B.V.M.
Tomlinson, Brian *o.f.m.cap.* '65 (NEW) Hackensack, NJ Church of St. Francis of Assisi.
Tomlinson, Richard '09 (CHR) Taylors, SC Prince of Peace.
Tompkins, John Mary *o.s.b.* '93 (GBG)[A] Latrobe, PA St. Vincent Seminary; [H] Latrobe, PA Saint Vincent Archabbey.
Tompkins, Terrence P. '82 (P)[A] St. Benedict, OR Mount Angel Seminary.
Tompkins, Terry '82 (OAK) On Duty Outside the Diocese.
Tomson, Lucas E. '07 (SPK) Okanogan, WA Our Lady of

the Valley; Members.
Tomson, Tyron J. '11 (COL) Columbus, OH St. Andrew.
Tomzik, Fred W. '84 (CHI) Chicago, IL St. Monica.
Ton, Anthony '66 (SEA) Retired.
Tonary, David *m.s.f.* '81 (SAT) Seguin, TX Our Lady of Guadalupe.
Tonelli, Robert F. '72 (CHI) Wilmette, IL St. Joseph.
Tonelotto, Walter *c.s.* '74 (NY) New York, NY St. James; New York, NY St. Joseph.
Tonelotto, Walter *c.s.* '74 (BRK)[V] Ridgewood, NY Friends of RADIO MARIA, Inc.
Toner, Oliver '71 (VEN) Fort Myers, FL Church Of The Resurrection Of Our Lord.
Toner, Patrick A. '75 (COL) Plain City, OH St. Joseph; Ohio Reformatory for Women.
Tong, Peter *o.c.s.o.* '68 (L)[L] Trappist, KY Abbey of Our Lady of Gethsemani, of the Order of Cistercians of the Strict Observance.
Tonkin, John W. '05 (CIN) Consultors; Presbyteral Council; Anna, OH Sacred Heart of Jesus.
Tonos, Joseph '94 (JKS) Approved Advocate and Auditors; Oxford, MS St. John the Evangelist; [H] Oxford, MS Ole Miss Campus Ministries.
Toof, Daniel R. '94 (ATL) Monroe, GA St. Anna.
Toohey, Richard J. '01 (E) Warren, PA St. Joseph; Deans.
Toohey, Timothy J. '65 (STL) Washington, MO Mercy Hospital Washington; [J] Washington, MO Mercy Hospital Washington Retired.
Toole, Arthur A. '58 (ALB) Troy, NY St. Michael the Archangel Retired.
Toole, Lawrence E. '67 (PRO) Cumberland, RI St. Patrick.
Toole, Patrick D. '07 (CHL) Charlotte, NC St. Matthew.
Toolis, Martin '70 (GR) Retired.
Tooman, Robert E. '77 (NEW) Jersey City, NJ Parish of the Resurrection.
Toomey, Daniel A. '03 (SCR) Dallas, PA Gate of Heaven; Harveys Lake, PA Our Lady of Victory.
Toomey, John M. '61 (BO) Senior Priests. Retired.
Toomey, Kevin G. '78 (BO) Medford, MA St. Raphael.
Topel, L. John *s.j.* '65 (SEA) Port Townsend, WA St. Mary Star of the Sea; [M] Seattle, WA Arrupe Jesuit Community at Seattle University.
Topf, Thomas J. '63 (SC) Priests' Pension Plan – Board of Trustees Retired.
Toplikar, Bostjan (BO) Brighton, MA St. Columbkille.
Topolewski, Jaroslaw P. '00 (OKL) Okeene, OK St. Anthony's.
Topper, Charles J. '68 (HBG) On Duty Outside the Diocese.
Topper, John M. *o.s.m.* '87 (CHI)[N] Chicago, IL Order of Friar Servants of Mary (Servites) United States of America Province, Inc.; Chicago, IL.
Topper, John M. *o.s.m.* '87 (P)[L] Portland, OR The Grotto, The National Sanctuary of Our Sorrowful Mother.
Topper, Rev. Msgr. Vincent J. '36 (HBG) Harrisburg, PA St. Catherine Laboure Retired.
Torak, George (NY)[EE] Sparkill, NY Dominican Convent of Our Lady of the Rosary.
Torba, Zdzislaw J. '91 (CHI) Chicago, IL St. Ferdinand.
Torborg, Elmer '55 (SCL) Retired.
Torchia, Joseph *o.p.* '01 (PRO) New York, NY; [O] Providence St. Thomas Aquinas Priory at Providence College.
Torgerson, Rev. Msgr. Lloyd A. '65 (LA) Santa Monica, CA St. Monica.
Torma, Andrew *m.s.c.* '76 (RCK)[G].
Tormey, Daniel '55 (ROC) Newly Ordained Priests Retired.
Tormey, James D. '78 (SY) Lee Center, NY St. Joseph.
Tornes, Dale F. '70 (STU) Colerain, OH St. Frances Cabrini; Deans; Members.
Torney, Rev. Msgr. John R. '39 (MET) Bernardsville, NJ Our Lady of Perpetual Help Retired.
Toro, Carlos Perez '88 (SJN) San Juan, PR Santa Rosa de Lima.
Toro–Rivas, Gabriel '02 (BRK) Brooklyn, NY St. Athanasius.
Torok, Rev. Msgr. Dezso '48 (Y) Retired.
Torok, George J. *c.o.* '58 (NY)[HH] Sparkill, NY Hallel Institute; Tappan, NY Our Lady of the Sacred Heart; [HH] Sparkill, NY New York Oratory of St. Philip Neri, Inc.
Torpey, Charles L. '69 (GI) Priests' Advisory Board (Presbyteral Council); Grand Island, NE St. Leo; Vicar General; Adjutant Vicars–Judicial; Judges; Diocesan Consultors.
Torpey, James M. '83 (ALN) Ringtown, PA St. Mary; Sheppton, PA St. Joseph.
Torpey, Matt G. *o.c.s.o.* '56 (ATL)[F] Conyers, GA The Monastery of the Holy Spirit.
Torpey, Michael J. '68 (RVC) Patchogue, NY Our Lady of Mt. Carmel.
Torquato, James R. '89 (PIT) Pittsburgh, PA St. Basil.
Torrens, Jim *s.j.* '61 (FRS) Fresno, CA St. Alphonsus.
Torrente, Lorenzo '75 (RNO) Reno, NV St. Rose of Lima; Reno, NV Renown Medical Center; Reno, NV V.A. Sierra Nevada Hospital.
Torres, A. Ernesto *c.j.m.* '08 (SD) Solana Beach, CA Saint James Catholic Parish.
Torres, Adrian '75 (PMB) Palm Springs, FL St. Luke.
Torres, Agustino Miguel *c.f.r.* (PAT)[N] Paterson, NJ Saint Michael's Friary; [Q] Clifton, NJ Casa Guadalupe.
Torres, Angel Pagan '80 (SJN) Dorado, PR Ntra. Sra. de La Salud; Del Toa y La Plata; Diocesan Consultors.
Torres, Antonio M. Soto *o.carm.* (SJN) San Juan, PR Santa Teresita Del Nino Jesus.
Torres, Rev. Msgr. Daniel A. '96 (LKC) Vicar General and Moderator of the Curia; Diocesan Consultors; Director of Seminarians; Parish Boundaries Commission; Personnel Board; Seminary Advisory Board; Vocation Director; Lake Charles, LA St. Henry; Presbyteral Council.
Torres, Ernesto '72 (DAL) Mesquite, TX Divine Mercy of Our Lord.
Torres, Fernando *sch.p.* '93 (PCE)[C] Coto Laurel, PR Colegio Ponceno.
Torres, Fernando '85 (R) Fuquay–Varina, NC St. Bernadette; Council of Priests.
Torres, Francisco Santiago '05 (PCE) Yauco, PR Santo Domingo de Guzman.
Torres, Frank D. '94 (GRY) Michigan City, IN Queen of All Saints; Valparaiso, IN St. Paul.
Torres, Fredi Gomez '02 (PEO) Mendota, IL Holy Cross; Mendota, IL SS. Peter and Paul; Diocesan Hispanic Ministry Office.
Torres, Gabriel M. (SJN)[B] San Juan, PR Nuestra Senora de la Altagracia.
Torres, Gonzalo *o.f.m.* (PAT) Pompton Lakes, NJ Our Lady of the Assumption.
Torres, Heriberto *c.r.* '04 (PBL) San Luis, CO Sangre de Cristo.
Torres, Hipólito '85 (CGS)[F] Caguas, PR Movimiento Juan XXIII; Diocesan Consultors; Caguas, PR Sagrado Corazon de Jesus.
Torres, Ivan J. '88 (MO) DEPARTMENT OF VETERANS AFFAIRS HOSPITALS AND CHAPLAINS.
Torres, Jaime Renteria *m.n.m.* '89 (SAT) San Antonio, TX St. Agnes.
Torres, Jaime V. '95 (BWN) La Joya, TX Our Lady, Queen of Angels.
Torres, Jorge '05 (ORL) Vocations.
Torres, Jose Luis *o.carm.* '04 (JOL) Joliet, IL Mount Carmel.
Torres, Jose R. *o.m.i.* '74 (BWN) Brownsville, TX Immaculate Conception Cathedral.
Torres, Juan Alberto *o.c.d.* '66 (PCE) Catholic Charismatic Renewal.
Torres, Juan M. *o.p.* '02 (GAL) Houston, TX Holy Rosary.
Torres, Juan R. '04 (MIA) Coconut Grove, FL St. Hugh.
Torres, Lonilo R. (AGN) Inarajan, GU St. Joseph.
Torres, Mario Alberto *s.j.* '01 (SJN)[B] San Juan, PR Colegio San Ignacio de Loyola; [H] San Juan, PR Comunidad Jesuita.
Torres, Mario '96 (LA) Huntington Park, CA St. Matthias.
Torres, Mark '98 (LA) Los Angeles, CA Dolores Mission.
Torres, Miguel A. *c.ss.r.* '99 (CGS)[B] Aguas Buenas, PR Casa Cristo Redentor.
Torres, Nestor '96 (CHI) Waukegan, IL Most Blessed Trinity.
Torres, Rafael *c.ss.r.* '64 (CGS) San Lorenzo, PR Nuestra Senora de la Mercedes.
Torres, Rendell '10 (ALB) Gloversville, NY Church of the Holy Spirit.
Torres, Rolando '07 (BGP) Priest Vocation Advisory Board; Stamford, CT Saint Benedict – Our Lady of Montserrat; Stamford, CT St. Mary.
Torres, Victor *o.m.i.* '95 (SJN) Toa Alta, PR San Judas Tadeo.
Torres–Pagan, William '91 (SJN) Bayamon, PR N. Sra. de la Providencia; Vicar of Ecumenism.
Torres–Rico, Rafael '07 (COS) Colorado Springs, CO St. Gabriel the Archangel.
Torres–Rivera, Gabriel Maria '95 (SJN) San Juan, PR Nuestra Senora de la Altagracia.
Torres Garzon, Jose Gabriel '00 (CHI) Waukegan, IL Most Blessed Trinity.
Torres Graciani, Ivan '88 (SJN) On Duty Outside the Archdiocese.
Torretto, Joseph '75 (RIC) Retired.
Torrez, Basil '56 (SAL) Retired.
Torrez, John '98 (KCK) Olathe, KS St. Paul.
Torsiello, Ralph C. '58 (WDC) Retired.
Torson, Daniel L. *c.pp.s.* '90 (JOL)[A] Romeoville, IL Lewis University.
Tortora, James '72 (NEW) Jersey City, NJ Our Lady of Victories.
Tortorelli, Kevin *o.f.m.* '73 (NY) New York, NY St. Francis of Assisi.
Tos, Aldo J. '53 (NY) Retired.
Toscano, Javier '07 (AUS) Cedar Park, TX St. Margaret Mary.
Toscano, Pasquale A. '44 (HRT) Retired.
Toschi, Larry *o.s.j.* '76 (FRS) Bakersfield, CA Our Lady of Guadalupe.
Tosco, Lawrence *c.s.j.* '70 (CLV)[N] Avon, OH Congregation of St. Joseph.
Tosco, Lorenzo *s.s.d.* '70 (CLV)[A] Wickliffe, OH St. Mary Seminary and Graduate School of Theology.
Tosello, Matthew '62 (PIT) Sewickley, PA St. James Retired.
Tosi, Rev. Msgr. John C. '73 (BRK) Whitestone, NY St. Luke.
Tosti, Rev. Msgr. Ronald A. '62 (FR) Retired.
Tosto, Louis F. '97 (RCK) Polo, IL St. Mary's.
Totah, Sami '71 (NY) Yonkers, NY Immaculate Conception; Good Shepherd Arabic Community of St. Mary.
Toth, Stephen J. '02 (NEW) Ridgewood, NJ Valley Hospital; Washington Township, NJ Our Lady of Good Counsel.
Tottle, Gregg '91 (SP) Clearwater, FL St. Michael The Archangel; Vicars Forane.
Totton, Joseph '04 (KC) St. Joseph, MO St. James; Deans.
Tou, Ivan *c.s.p.* (STP)[J] Minneapolis, MN Paulist Fathers; [R] Minneapolis, MN Newman Center at St. Lawrence; Minneapolis, MN St. Lawrence.
Tou, John B. '57 (NY) Retired.
Tou, Louis A. '56 (WDC)[M] Washington, DC Cardinal O'Boyle Residence for Priests Retired.
Touchette, Marc L. '57 (ALB) Retired.
Tougas, Paul J. '64 (WOR) Boylston, MA St. Mary of the Hills.
Touma, Dany N. '98 (NTN) Yonkers, NY Christ the Savior Church.
Toups, David '97 (SP) Tampa, FL Christ the King; Elected Pastors.
Toups, Mark '01 (HT) Seminarians.
Tourangeau, John M. *o.praem.* '86 (GB)[A] De Pere, WI St. Norbert Abbey; [J] De Pere, WI St. Norbert Abbey.
Tourigny, William A. '80 (SPR) Chicopee, MA St. Rose de Lima; Bishop's Commission for Clergy.
Tourville, David E. '09 (BUF) Kenmore, NY St. John the Baptist.
Tovar, Emilio *c.m.* '50 (ARE) Manati, PR La Candelaria.
Tovar, Francisco Manuel '06 (WDC) Suitland, MD St. Bernardine.
Tovar, Ireneo Lopez '50 (CAM) Retired.
Towey, Damian *c.p.* '56 (PMB)[H] North Palm Beach, FL Our Lady of Florida Spiritual Center; Promoter of Justice.
Towle, Joseph C. *s.j.* '66 (NY)[DD] New York, NY Jesuit Community of the Immaculate Conception.
Towle, Joseph W. *m.m.* '65 (NY)[DD] Maryknoll Maryknoll Fathers and Brothers Retired.
Townsend, Charles L. '91 (LIN) Wahoo, NE St. Wenceslaus; [L] Wahoo, NE Bishop Neumann High School Endowment Fund.
Townsend, Joe C. '88 (TLS) Broken Arrow, OK St. Benedict; Coweta, OK St. Vincent de Paul.
Towsley, Peter J. '91 (BGP) Bridgeport, CT St. Ann.
Toyinbo, Andrew *m.s.p.* '86 (MOB) Mount Vernon, AL St. Peter the Apostle.
Tozzi, Anthony G. '09 (CIN) Mason, OH St. Susanna.
Tozzi, Emilio C. '10 (SD) San Diego, CA Saint Brigid Catholic Parish.
Tozzi, Ross '01 (FBK) Presbyteral Council; Consultors; Vocation Director; Kotzebue, AK St. Francis Xavier Catholic Church Kotzebue; Nome, AK St. Joseph Catholic Church Nome.
Trabold, Rev. Msgr. George R. '73 (NEW) Short Hills, NJ St. Rose of Lima.
Tracey, Bernard M. *c.m.* '74 (PH)[B] Philadelphia, PA St. Vincent's Seminary; [Y] Philadelphia Congregation of the Mission.
Tracey, Michael '72 (BLX) Bay St. Louis, MS Our Lady of the Gulf; Secretaries and Ecclesiastical Notaries (Court of First Instance).
Tracey, Philip A. '88 (PRT) Diocesan Priests' Benefit Plan – Trustees.
Tracey, Thomas S. '63 (CAM) Retired.
Tracey, William *c.ss.r.* '55 (FgM) Baltimore Province.
TracPham, Michael M. *c.m.c.* (FWT) Fort Worth, TX Christ the King.
Tracy, David W. '63 (BGP) On Duty Outside the Diocese.
Tracy, Eugene '91 (SPK) Spokane, WA St. Francis Xavier.
Tracy, Rev. Msgr. James R. '60 (CAM) Members Retired.
Tracy, John P. '48 (HRT)[A] In Res. at the Archbishop Daniel A. Cronin Retirement Residence at St. Thomas Seminary Retired.
Tracy, Rev. Msgr. Joseph A. '92 (PH) Lansdale, PA St. Stanislaus.
Tracy, Laurence C. '66 (ROC) Retired.
Tracy, Philip A. '88 (PRT) Vicars Forane; Rumford, ME Parish of the Holy Savior.
Tracy, Philip Michael '60 (PRT) Retired.
Tracy, Robert D. *o.carm.* '63 (NY) FDR DVA Hospital.
Tracy, T. Shawn *o.s.a.* '66 (PH)[Y] Villanova, PA St. Augustine Friary.
Traczyk, Edward W. *s.ch.* '78 (NY) Poughkeepsie, NY St. Joseph.
Trader, William A. '74 (PH) Berwyn, PA St. Monica.
Trahan, Charles N. '81 (LAF) Retired.
Trahan, Clint James '08 (LAF) Crowley, LA St. John

the Baptist; Morse, LA Immaculate Conception.
Trahan, Harold '69 (LAF) Lafayette, LA St. Mary Mother of the Church.
Trainor, Daniel M. '61 (PRO) Providence, RI St. Joseph Retired.
Trainor, Henry J. '73 (SFR) Absent on Leave Retired.
Trainor, Michael P. *o.p.* '75 (NY)[DD] New York, NY St. Catherine of Siena Priory; Manhattan, NY Hospital for Special Surgery; Manhattan, NY Memorial Sloan Kettering Cancer Center; Manhattan, NY New York Presbyterian Hospital.
Trainor, Michael S.P. '07 (NEW) Short Hills, NJ St. Rose of Lima.
Trainor, Richard F. '75 (WOR) Fitchburg, MA St. Joseph's.
Trainor, Rev. Msgr. Robert M. '57 (NY) Bronx, NY Sacred Heart.
Tralies, Matthew J. '10 (PH) Warrington, PA St. Robert Bellarmine.
Trambley, John B. '10 (SFE) Presbyteral Council of the Archdiocese of Santa Fe; Santa Fe, NM The Cathedral Basilica of St. Francis of Assisi.
Trammell, Ian W. '05 (TR) Hamilton Square, NJ St. Gregory the Great.
Tramontin, Pedro '96 (MIL)[Y] Milwaukee, WI St. Camillus Communities, Inc. – House I.
Tran, Albert Sang V. '92 (LA) Oxnard, CA St. Anthony.
Tran, Andrew *o.praem.* '06 (ORG) Costa Mesa, CA St. John the Baptist.
Tran, Anh Q. '90 (SAT) Defenders of the Bond.
Tran, Anh '90 (FWT) Deans; Scouting; Grapevine, TX St. Francis of Assisi.
Tran, Anthony Doan '88 (BLX) Laurel, MS Immaculate Conception; Waynesboro, MS St. Bernadette.
Tran, Anthony Hung N. *o.p.* '92 (GAL)[O] Houston, TX Dominican Friars, St. Mark Priory, Inc.
Tran, Augustine '98 (ATL)[B] Roswell, GA Blessed Trinity Catholic High School.
Tran, Augustine '04 (ARL) Spotsylvania, VA St. Matthew.
Tran, Benjamin '06 (ORG) Fountain Valley, CA Holy Spirit.
Tran, Binh K. '92 (PEO) Chatsworth, IL SS. Peter and Paul.
Tran, Christopher H. '08 (OKL) Weatherford, OK St. Eugene's.
Tran, Christopher '08 (OKL)[K] Weatherford, OK Southwestern Oklahoma State University.
Tran, Cong Bang *s.v.d.* '00 (DUB)[B] Epworth, IA Divine Word College.
Tran, Dac T. *o.f.m.* '89 (NY)[DD] New York Franciscan Friars, Holy Name Province.
Tran, Dat *s.j.* (SPK)[B] Spokane, WA Gonzaga University.
Tran, Dat *c.s.p.* '11 (LA) Los Angeles, CA St. Paul the Apostle.
Tran, Dominic Dat '99 (PT) Niceville, FL Holy Name of Jesus.
Tran, Dominic Dieu *s.d.d.* '01 (PT) Panama City, FL SS. Peter & Paul Mission; Panama City, FL St. Dominic.
Tran, Dominic Hung (SAC)[H] Walnut Grove, CA Monastery of Chau Son Sacramento.
Tran, Dominic Toan '11 (PMB) West Palm Beach, FL St. Juliana.
Tran, Dominic *s.d.b.* '03 (NEW)[L] South Orange, NJ Salesian Office of Youth Ministry & Vocations; [L] South Orange, NJ Don Bosco Vocation Office.
Tran, Dominic '09 (ATL) Gainesville, GA St. Michael.
Tran, Dung Anton '02 (GR) Caledonia, MI Holy Family.
Tran, Duy John *s.v.d.* '11 (SB)[I] Riverside, CA Divine Word Seminary.
Tran, Francis Vu *s.c.j.* '05 (MIL)[P] Hales Corners Priests of the Sacred Heart.
Tran, Gregory *c.m.c.* '06 (DEN) Wheat Ridge, CO Queen of Vietnamese Martyrs.
Tran, Hieu Chi '08 (LA) Lancaster, CA Sacred Heart.
Tran, Hilary M. Nhuan *c.m.c.* '10 (STP) Minneapolis, MN Church of St. Anne – St. Joseph Hien.
Tran, Hoi '01 (SFE) Peralta, NM Our Lady of Guadalupe.
Tran, Hung Ba '98 (LA) Monrovia, CA Immaculate Conception.
Tran, Hung M. (CIN)[U] Dayton, OH Catholic Vietnamese Community of Dayton.
Tran, James Taiviet *s.j.* '04 (SEA)[M] Seattle, WA Arrupe Jesuit Community at Seattle University.
Tran, John Kha '89 (GAL) Katy, TX St. Bartholomew the Apostle.
Tran, John Lan *s.j.* '08 (STL)[F] St. Louis, MO St. Louis University High School, George H. Backer Memorial; [O] Saint Louis, MO St. Louis University High School Jesuit Community.
Tran, John Nghi '71 (LA) Avalon, CA St. Catherine of Alexandria.
Tran, John Quy V. '05 (LA) Long Beach, CA St. Lucy.
Tran, John R. '00 (L) On Duty Outside the Archdiocese.
Tran, John '95 (NY) Monticello, NY St. Peter.
Tran, John *s.v.d.* '96 (SB)[I] Riverside, CA Divine Word Seminary.
Tran, John '00 (SAV) Savannah, GA St. Peter the Apostle Church.
Tran, John–Nhan '92 (NO) La Place, LA St. Joan of Arc; Deans; Liaisons for the Vietnamese Community.
Tran, Jon Bennet '08 (STP) Brooklyn Park, MN St. Vincent de Paul.
Tran, Joseph Chuc (BAL) Baltimore, MD Our Lady of La Vang.
Tran, Joseph Chuc *m.m.* '03 (NY)[DD].
Tran, Joseph Huynh *s.v.d.* '03 (FgM) Techny, IL.
Tran, Joseph M. '95 (NO) Pointe A La Hache, LA St. Thomas.
Tran, Joseph M. Duykim N. '90 (NEW) On Duty Outside the Archdiocese.
Tran, Joseph T. Sai *s.v.d.* '03 (LAF) Eunice, LA St. Lawrence.
Tran, Joseph Thang Dinh '96 (NO) Slidell, LA St. Luke the Evangelist.
Tran, Joseph Thuong '05 (ORG) Council of Priests.
Tran, Joseph Tu '99 (HT) Terrebonne General Medical Center.
Tran, Joseph '95 (NY) Bronx, NY St. Nicholas of Tolentine; On Duty Outside the Archdiocese.
Tran, Joseph '04 (DEN) Julesburg, CO St. Anthony.
Tran, Joseph '02 (MO) Military Chaplains; Air Force Reserve Chaplains.
Tran, Joseph '05 (HRT)[J] New Britain, CT St. Lucian's Residence, Inc.; [L] New Britain Conventual Franciscans.
Tran, Joseph Thai Minh *s.s.s.* '94 (CLV)[N] Cleveland Congregation of the Blessed Sacrament Provincial House.
Tran, Kiem Van '91 (ORG) Garden Grove, CA St. Columban.
Tran, Liem Trung *o.p.* (GAL)[O] Houston, TX Vietnamese Dominican Vicariate of St. Vincent Liem.
Tran, Loc '08 (ORG) Dana Point, CA St. Edward the Confessor.
Tran, Luan Q. '94 (P) Portland, OR St. Birgitta; Vernonia, OR St. Mary of Immaculate Conception; Area Vicars; College of Consultors.
Tran, Luan Quach '94 (MO) Air Force Reserve Chaplains.
Tran, Luc Nghi '96 (SB) On Sabbatical.
Tran, Luke '01 (NEW) Linden, NJ St. John the Apostle.
Tran, Luong Quang '89 (BEA) Diocesan College of Consultors; Judicial Vicar; Diocesan Judges; China, TX Our Lady of Sorrows; Presbyteral Council.
Tran, Manh D. *s.j.* '04 (SJ)[B] Santa Clara, CA Jesuit Community.
Tran, Martin Vanban *c.m.c.* '94 (BEA) Port Arthur, TX Queen of Vietnam.
Tran, Martin '90 (ORG) Rancho Santa Margarita, CA San Francisco Solano Church.
Tran, Michael Mary Mai *c.m.c.* '93 (SB)[I] Corona, CA Congregation of the Mother Co–Redemptrix, C.M.C.
Tran, Michael X '93 (SD) Lakeside, CA Blessed Kateri Tekakwitha.
Tran, Mike '02 (HT) Raceland, LA St. Mary's Nativity; Priests Council.
Tran, Nhan *c.m.* '10 (DAL) Dallas, TX Holy Trinity; [J] Dallas, TX Congregation of the Mission, Western Province.
Tran, Nhi Dinh '71 (ARL) On Leave of Absence.
Tran, Paul M. Tai *c.m.c.* '05 (SPC)[F] Carthage, MO Congregation of the Mother Coredemptrix, United States Assumption Province.
Tran, Paul Tam X. '00 (WDC) Silver Spring, MD Our Lady of Vietnam.
Tran, Peter Duc '04 (LA) Santa Fe Springs, CA St. Pius X.
Tran, Peter Hung Viet '99 (NEW) On Duty Outside the Archdiocese.
Tran, Peter M. Khuong *c.m.c.* '10 (SPC)[F] Carthage, MO Congregation of the Mother Coredemptrix, United States Assumption Province.
Tran, Peter Tam *s.v.d.* '98 (FgM) Techny, IL.
Tran, Peter '73 (RIC) Newport News, VA Our Lady of Mount Carmel.
Tran, Peter '99 (MET) Vietnamese Apostolate; Woodbridge, NJ St. James.
Tran, Philip B. *c.m.c.* '03 (SAC) Sacramento, CA Vietnamese Martyrs Parish.
Tran, Philip '92 (NY) Absent on Sick Leave.
Tran, Phuong D. '65 (SEA) Retired.
Tran, Quan Dinh '11 (ORG) Awaiting Assignment.
Tran, Quan H. '96 (PH) Elkins Park, PA St. James; [D] Wyncote, PA Bishop McDevitt High School.
Tran, Quan M. *s.j.* '09 (P)[L] Portland Jesuit Provincial Office (Society of Jesus, Oregon Prov.).
Tran, Quang Mihn '70 (MO) DEPARTMENT OF VETERANS AFFAIRS HOSPITALS AND CHAPLAINS.
Tran, Quynh Dinh '93 (SPR) Southeast Asian Apostolate; Springfield, MA St. Paul the Apostle.
Tran, Stephen Huy *o.carm.* '07 (NY) Middletown, NY Our Lady of Mt. Carmel; [DD] Middletown, NY St. Albert's Priory.
Tran, Tam X. '00 (WDC) Forestville, MD Church of the Holy Spirit.
Tran, Thienan '05 (MO) Air Force Chaplains.
Tran, Tien '09 (NSH) Franklin, TN St. Philip.
Tran, Trong Binh '04 (DOD) Ulysses, KS St. Bernadette Catholic Church of Johnson, Kansas; On Special Diocesan Assignment; Ulysses, KS Mary, Queen of Peace Catholic Church of Ulysses, Kansas; Vietnamese Ministry.
Tran, Tuan Quoc '97 (ATL) Holy Vietnamese Martyrs.
Tran, Tung '03 (MO) Navy Chaplains.
Tran, Vang Cong *c.ss.r.* '51 (CHL) Concord, NC St. James.
Tran, Vincent '07 (GAL) Houston, TX St. Albert of Trapani.
Tran, Vu P. '04 (SEA) La Conner, WA St. Paul.
Tran, Vu Phong '04 (SEA) Anacortes, WA St. Mary.
Tran–Khac–Hy, Hilarius '57 (WDC) Retired.
Trance, F. Raymond '94 (PIT) Canonsburg, PA St. Patrick.
Tranchina, Joseph '68 (NO) Retired.
Trancone, Gerard A. '69 (WDC) Special Ministries; [U] Washington, DC Gallaudet University Catholic Community; [X] Landover Hills, MD The Center for Deaf Ministries of the Archdiocese of Washington; Chaplains.
Tranel, Daniel D. '56 (RCK) Retired.
Tranel, Don *g.h.m.* '88 (LR) Booneville, AR Church of Our Lady of the Assumption; Ratcliff, AR St. Anthony.
Tran Liem, Aloysius M. *c.m.c.* '96 (SPC)[F] Carthage, MO Congregation of the Mother Coredemptrix, United States Assumption Province.
Tran Ngoc Thoai, (Aloysius M.) *c.m.c.* '92 (SPC)[F] Carthage, MO Congregation of the Mother Coredemptrix, United States Assumption Province.
Trapani, Anthony M. '73 (RVC) Lindenhurst, NY Our Lady of Perpetual Help.
Trapasso, Rev. Msgr. Thomas J. '49 (PAT) Catholic Deaf Society; [Q] Chester, NJ Nazareth Village Retired.
Trapp, Andrew '07 (CHR) Blythewood, SC Transfiguration; Winnsboro, SC St. Theresa.
Trapp, Arthur L. *c.m.* '56 (STL)[O] Perryville, MO Congregation of the Mission.
Trapp, Daniel J. '84 (DET)[A] The School of Theology; Detroit, MI St. Augustine and St. Monica.
Trapp, Joseph J. '96 (COL) Zaleski, OH St. Sylvester; Jackson, OH Holy Trinity; Corrections Reception Center.
Trapp, Joseph L. '59 (BEL) Benton, IL St. Joseph.
Trask, David R. '86 (CLV) Solon, OH Our Lady of Guadalupe.
Traub, George W. *s.j.* '67 (CIN)[Q] Milford, OH Jesuit Spiritual Center at Milford.
Traub, Robert '39 (FTW)[F] Fort Wayne, IN Saint Anne Home & Retirement Community Retired.
Traudt, Robert *o.carm.* (NY)[DD] Middletown, NY Brandsma Priory.
Traufler, John F. '57 (WIN) Retired.
Traupman, Robert '69 (ORL) Retired.
Travaglione, Michael *o.f.m.* '66 (MO) Army Chaplains.
Travaglione, Michael *o.f.m.* '66 (NY)[DD] New York Franciscan Province of the Immaculate Conception.
Travassos, Horace J. '73 (FR) Westport, MA Our Lady of Grace.
Travers, Alan '83 (NY) Staten Island, NY Holy Child.
Travers, David O. *s.j.* '68 (BO)[U] Boston The Society of Jesus of New England–Provincial Offices.
Travers, David O. *s.j.* '68 (HON) Honolulu, HI SS Peter and Paul.
Travers, Gerard P. '65 (NY) Highland Mills, NY St. Patrick.
Travers, John J. *c.ss.r.* '59 (BRK) Brooklyn, NY Our Lady of Perpetual Help Basilica.
Travers, Luke L. *o.s.b.* '86 (PAT)[N] Morristown, NJ St. Mary's Abbey.
Travers, Luke *o.s.b.* '86 (RIC)[K] Richmond, VA Mary Mother of the Church Abbey.
Travers, Patrick J. '93 (JUN) Juneau, AK St. Paul The Apostle; Chancellor; Diocesan Consultors; Judicial Vicar; Finance Council; Air Force Reserve Chaplains.
Travers, Patrick *ss.cc.* '62 (LA)[P] La Verne, CA Congregation of the Sacred Hearts of Jesus and Mary.
Travers, Patrick '93 (FBK) Judicial Vicar.
Travers, Patrick *ss.cc* '62 (SB) Victorville, CA Holy Innocents.
Travers, Thomas J. *c.ss.r.* '62 (NY)[DD] Esopus, NY Redemptorist Priests and Brothers C.Ss.R. (Province of Baltimore); [FF] Esopus, NY Mount St. Alphonsus Redemptorist Retreat Center; Brooklyn, NY.
Traverso, Leonard '72 (SJ) Retired.
Travieso, Ernesto Fernandez *s.j.* '73 (MIA)[E] Miami, FL Belen Jesuit Preparatory School; [H] Miami, FL Villa Javier.
Travis, Adam Frederick '07 (ALX) Continuing Education of the Clergy; Alexandria, LA St. Rita; Elected Members.
Travis, Francis J. '81 (CHR) Camden, SC Our Lady of Perpetual Help; Priests' Retirement.
Travis, James M. *m.m.* '67 (NY)[DD] Maryknoll Maryknoll Fathers and Brothers Retired.
Travis, Leo *c.ss.r.* '54 (FgM) Denver, CO Denver Province.
Travis, Robert '07 (MRY) Santa Margarita, CA Santa Margarita de Cortona.

Travnikar, Rock *o.f.m.* '76 (CIN)[N] Cincinnati St. Francis Seraph Friary.
Trawick, Gregory G. '85 (OWN) Sturgis, KY St. Ambrose; Sturgis, KY St. William; Sturgis, KY St. Francis Borgia.
Traxl, William L. '60 (HRT) Retired.
Traylor, William '76 (EVN) Jasper, IN St. Joseph.
Traynor, Anthony '58 (SAC) Sacramento, CA Our Lady of Lourdes Retired.
Traynor, Scott '00 (SFS) Vermillion, SD St. Patrick; [H] Vermillion, SD University of South Dakota; Tribunal Judges; Presbyteral Council.
Treacy, Jerome F. *s.j.* '61 (DET)[K] Clarkston, MI Colombiere Center.
Treacy, John P. *s.j.* '90 (SJ)[B] Santa Clara, CA Jesuit Community.
Treacy, Paul C. '06 (STP) Minneapolis, MN Our Lady of Peace; Deanery 14.
Treacy, William '44 (SEA) Retired.
Treanor, Boniface J. *o.s.b.* '56 (NEW)[L] Newark, NJ Newark Abbey.
Trebtoske, Everett '59 (AUS) Wimberley, TX St. Mary Retired.
Treglio, Vincent (PAT) Absent on Leave.
Trejo, Alejandro E. '03 (YAK) Cashmere, WA St. Francis Xavier; Leavenworth, WA Our Lady of the Snows.
Trela, Jan '98 (BUF) Dunkirk, NY Blessed Mary Angela Parish.
Trela, Norman J. '66 (CHI) Chicago, IL St. Symphorosa and Seven Sons.
Trela, Tadeusz '82 (NEW) Irvington, NJ Sacred Heart of Jesus.
Treloar, John L. *s.j.* '70 (MIL)[Y] Milwaukee, WI Theological Studies, Inc.; Milwaukee, WI; [P] Milwaukee, WI Arrupe House Jesuit Community; [P] Milwaukee, WI Jesuit Provincial Office, Wisconsin Province.
Tremari, Albert *s.j.c.* '03 (CHI) Chicago, IL St. John Cantius; [P] Chicago, IL Canons Regular of Saint John Cantius.
Tremblay, Albert J. '97 (MAN) Priest Personnel Board; Plaistow, NH St. Luke the Evangelist Parish.
Tremblay, Eugene *o.m.i.* '74 (BO)[Z] Lowell, MA Andre Garin Residence.
Tremblay, J. Normand '53 (WOR) Charlton City, MA St. Joseph's.
Tremblay, Marc P. '80 (FR) Norton, MA St. Mary's.
Tremblay, Nellis '54 (ALB) Retired.
Tremie, Eugene R. '71 (LAF) New Iberia, LA St. Marcellus.
Treml, Richard L. '99 (DET) North Branch, MI St. Mary's Burnside; North Branch, MI SS. Peter and Paul; Presbyteral Council; Archdiocesan Vicars.
Tremmel, Benjamin *o.s.b.* '66 (KCK) Effingham, KS St. Ann; Effingham, KS St. Louis; [I] Atchison, KS St. Benedict's Abbey.
Trempe, James F. '96 (LC) Plover, WI St. Bronislava.
Trench, Rev. Msgr. Edmond J. '57 (RVC) Southampton, NY Sacred Hearts of Jesus and Mary; Procurator & Advocates Retired.
Trenchera, Manuel '80 (AGN) Mongmong, GU Nuestra Senora de las Aguas.
Trenchs, Juan *sch.p.* '40 (LA)[P] Los Angeles, CA Piarist Fathers.
Trenta, Christopher J. '09 (CLV)[V] Wooster, OH St. Mary of the Immaculate Conception; Wooster, OH St. Mary of the Immaculate Conception.
Trepanier, James R. *c.s.c.* '55 (FTW)[H] Holy Cross House Retired.
Treppa, Terence '67 (DET) Westland, MI St. Richard.
Tressic, David L. '96 (ALB) Leave of Absence.
Tressler, Rev. Msgr. David L. '85 (SCR)[C] Dunmore, PA Holy Cross High School; Carbondale, PA St. Rose of Lima; Deans; Diocesan Consultors; Presbyteral Council.
Treston, Rev. Msgr. James A. '60 (ALN) Sinking Spring, PA St. Ignatius Loyola.
Treston, Kevin *o.f.m.* '81 (WDC) Washington, DC; [O] Washington, DC Franciscan Monastery USA Inc.
Trevino, Alberto T. *m.s.f.* '84 (BWN) Donna, TX St. Joseph.
Trevino, Raciel '03 (PMB) Jupiter, FL St. Peter.
Trevizo, Raul P. '88 (TUC) Vicars General; Tucson, AZ Saint John the Evangelist Roman Catholic Parish – Tucson; Special Assignment; Diocesan Consultors; Council of Priests.
Trexler, Donald P. '98 (GBG)[G] Greensburg, PA Neumann House.
Treyes, Reynaldo B. '78 (JOL) Beaverville, IL St. Mary; Beaverville, IL St. Martin.
Tria, Maximo E. '87 (CHR) Aiken, SC St. Mary Help of Christians.
Tria, Noel '98 (CHR) Edgefield, SC St. Mary of the Immaculate Conception; Ward, SC St. William.
Tribuiani, Raymond F. '73 (PH) Oreland, PA Holy Martyrs Retired.
Trick, James F. '60 (CIN)[N] Carthagena, OH St. Charles Retired.
Triggs, Thomas J. '75 (TR) Colts Neck, NJ St. Mary's.
Trigilio, John P. '88 (HBG) Marysville, PA Our Lady of Good Counsel.
Trigueros, Raul '69 (ELP) El Paso, TX St. Mark; Catholic Communications Ministry.
Trimbur, John S. '74 (Y) Girard, OH St. Rose.
Trinchard, Paul '66 (NO) Retired.
Trindade, Leonard J. '95 (FRS) Gustine, CA Shrine of Our Lady of Miracles.
Tringhese, James D. '74 (GBG) Trafford, PA St. Regis; Bishop's Priests Council.
Trinh, Danh Ngoc '05 (ORG) Westminster, CA Blessed Sacrament.
Trinh, Hoang T. *o.f.m.* '01 (SFR) San Francisco, CA St. Boniface.
Trinh, Joseph Hoa Duc '93 (DAL) Grand Prairie, TX St. Michael the Archangel.
Trinh, Rev. Msgr. Joseph T. '91 (PH) Philadelphia, PA St. Helena; Vietnamese Apostolate.
Trinh, Joseph Truong Q. '99 (BLX) Presbyteral Council.
Trinh, Loc '92 (GR) Reed City, MI St. Philip Neri.
Trinh, Paul H. '90 (CAM) Inactive.
Trinh, Quan M. '02 (PH) Maple Glen, PA St. Alphonsus.
Trinh, Thai Paul Minh '05 (ORG) Laguna Woods, CA St. Nicholas.
Trinh, Thai Z. '90 (RIC) Unassigned.
Trinh, Truong Quang '99 (BLX) Lumberton, MS Our Lady of Perpetual Help.
Trinh, Vinh The *s.v.d.* '07 (FgM) Techny, IL.
Trinh, Vinh The *s.v.d.* '07 (CHI)[N] Techny, IL Divine Word Residence.
Trinidad, Mel *s.d.b.* '85 (LA)[V] Rosemead, CA St. Joseph's Salesian Youth Renewal Center; [F] Rosemead, CA Don Bosco Technical Institute.
Trinidad, Miguel '00 (SJN) Subcommission for Sacred Music.
Trinidad, Nelson '86 (LA) Los Angeles, CA Our Lady of Guadalupe.
Trinidad–Fonseca, Miguel Angel '00 (SJN) Toa Alta, PR San Fernando Rey.
Trinity, Rev. Msgr. Bernard J. '54 (PH) Havertown, PA St. Denis Retired.
Trinka, Joseph C. '59 (SUP) Retired.
Trinkle, Clarence M. '92 (ARL) Retired.
Tripi, Ronald *c.s.c.* '62 (FTW) South Bend, IN Christ the King; [H] Notre Dame Congregation of Holy Cross, United States Province of Priests & Brothers.
Tripole, Martin R. *s.j.* '67 (PH)[Y] Loyola Center and Manresa Hall.
Trippel, Edward G. '55 (CIN) Cincinnati, OH Retired.
Trisco, Rev. Msgr. Robert F. '54 (CHI) On Duty Outside the Archdiocese; [C] Catholic University of America, The Retired.
Triulzi, Daniel *s.m.* '81 (SJ)[M] Cupertino, CA The Marianist Center.
Trocha, Lukasz Pawel '00 (BRK) Brooklyn, NY St. Rose of Lima.
Troche, Sigfrido *m.ss.cc.* '98 (CAM) Newfield, NJ Our Lady of the Blessed Sacrament, Newfield, N.J.
Trocinski, LaVern F. '60 (WIN) Retired.
Trocio, Manuel C. '86 (AGN) Mongmong, GU Nuestra Senora de las Aguas.
Troetsch, Eliseo *c.m.* (FgM) Philadelphia, PA Eastern Province.
Troha, Michael J. '80 (CLV) Retirement Board; Translators; Willoughby, OH Immaculate Conception.
Troiano, Rev. Msgr. Leonard F. '79 (TR) College of Consultors; Lavallette, NJ The Church of St. Pio of Pietreclina, Lavallette, N.J.
Troiano, Louis *o.f.m.* '57 (NY)[DD] New York, NY Padua Friary Retired.
Trojcak, Ronald '62 (SFD) Special or Other Diocesan Assignment.
Troncale, Rev. Msgr. F. Charles '65 (MOB) Tallassee, AL St. Vincent De Paul; Group I; Vicars Forane.
Trong, John T.B. '71 (ARL) Retired.
Trosch, David '82 (MOB) Retired.
Trosley, Anthony J. '78 (PEO) Nauvoo, IL Immaculate Conception; Nauvoo, IL SS. Peter and Paul; Warsaw, IL Sacred Heart.
Trotta, Louis P. *c.m* '52 (PH)[Y].
Trouille, Alan P. '97 (LKC) Lake Charles, LA Our Lady of Good Counsel; [F] Lake Charles, LA Catholic Student Center; Presbyteral Council.
Troung, Tri Vinh '08 (CHL) Charlotte, NC St. Joseph Church.
Trout, John *s.p.s.* '89 (CHI) Libertyville, IL St. Joseph.
Trout, Richard W. '85 (ORL) Representative by Age.
Trout, Richard W. '85 (ORL) Sanford, FL All Souls; Priestly Life and Ministry.
Troutman, Richard E. '68 (TUC) Tucson, AZ Saint Odilia Roman Catholic Community – Tucson.
Trovato, Joseph A. *c.s.b.* '56 (ROC) Rochester, NY Kateri Tekakwitha Roman Catholic Parish.
Trowbridge, Jeremy '10 (RCK) Rockford, IL St. Peter Cathedral.
Troxell, Christopher '92 (LA) Claremont, CA Our Lady of the Assumption.
Troy, Gabriel (BO) Cambridge, MA St. Mary of the Annunciation.
Troyan, Rev. Archpriest Daniel '82 (PHU) Evangelization Center; Presbyteral Council; Archeparchial Museum; [F] Fox Chase Manor, PA Provincial Motherhouse of the Sisters of St. Basil the Great; Director of Evangelization; Sheptytsky Educational Center.
Trudeau, Rev. Msgr. Marc V. '81 (LA) Lomita, CA St. Margaret Mary Alacoque.
Trudel, Albert *o.p.* '94 (CIN) Cincinnati, OH St. Gertrude.
Trudell, Guy Albert *o.p.* '94 (CIN)[N] Cincinnati, OH St. Gertrude Priory.
True, Isaac *o.s.b.* '66 (KC)[J] Conception, MO Conception Abbey.
Truhan, Luke *o.c.s.o.* '82 (WOR)[N] Spencer, MA St. Joseph's Abbey.
Trujillo, Francisco '05 (PEO) Moline, IL St. Mary's.
Trujillo, Ivan R. '85 (BUF) Attica Correctional Facility; Batavia, NY Resurrection; DEPARTMENT OF VETERANS AFFAIRS HOSPITALS AND CHAPLAINS.
Trujillo, Paco (PEO) Moline, IL St. Mary's.
Trujillo, Robert '07 (STA) Presbyteral Council; Lake City, FL Epiphany.
Trujillo, Teofilo '89 (CHR) Simpsonville, SC St. Mary Magdalene; Seminary Admissions Board; Presbyteral Council; Vicar for Hispanic Ministry; Personnel Committee.
Trujillo, Vincent *o.s.b.* '82 (P)[L] St. Benedict, OR Mt. Angel Abbey; College of Consultors; Saint Benedict, OR.
Trujillo–Gonzalez, Francisco de Asis '05 (NEW) On Duty Outside the Archdiocese.
Trull, Jason '02 (STA) Jacksonville, FL Resurrection.
Trullols, Charles '06 (FTW)[G] South Bend, IN Prelature of the Holy Cross and Opus Dei.
Trullols, Charles (POD) South Bend.
Trung, Nguyen Dinh *c.ss.r.* '03 (LA)[P] Baldwin Park Vietnamese Redemptorist Mission.
Trung Dinh Hoang, Louis '95 (DOD) Fowler, KS St. Anthony Catholic Church of Fowler, Kansas; Meade, KS St. John the Baptist Catholic Church of Meade, Kansas; Plains, KS St. Patrick Catholic Church of Plains, Kansas.
Trung Thuc, John Bosco Pham (SY) Asian Apostolate.
Truong, James Thuc Van *o.s.b., c.m.c.* '62 (SPC)[F] Carthage, MO Congregation of the Mother Coredemptrix, United States Assumption Province.
Truong, Peter '99 (PMB) Boynton Beach, FL St. Thomas More.
Trupkovich, Joseph V. '97 (GBG) Leechburg, PA Christ The King.
Trupkovich, Thomas S. '97 (GBG) Priests On Leave.
Trutter, Carl B. *o.p.* '60 (NO) Retired.
Trzeciakowski, Edward J. '55 (PIT)[M] Pittsburgh, PA St. John Vianney Manor Retired.
Trzecieski, Stephen P. *c.m.* '60 (BAL) Emmitsburg, MD St. Joseph; [Q] Emmitsburg, MD Vincentian House.
Trzil, Louis J. '50 (DUB) Retired.
Tsang, Augustine H. *s.j.* '94 (FgM) Los Gatos, CA Society of Jesus.
Tsang, Peter '59 (LA) Retired.
Tsanga, Francois *s.c.* '05 (BWN) McAllen, TX McAllen Medical Hospital; Edinburg, TX Edinburg Regional Hospital; McAllen, TX McAllen Heart Hospital.
Tschakert, Gregory '82 (SFS) Dell Rapids, SD St. Mary's; Episcopal Vicar for Clergy; Judicial Vicar; Defenders of the Matrimonial Bond; Diocesan Consultors; Presbyteral Council.
Tscherne, David D. '77 (TOL) Custar, OH St. Louis; Grand Rapids, OH St. Patrick.
Tseu, Rev. Msgr. Andrew Stanislaus '56 (LA) Pomona, CA St. Madeleine Retired.
Tshibambe, Henri '81 (DEN) Denver, CO St. Mary Magdalene; Lakewood, CO Our Lady of Fatima.
Tsiquaye, Paschal B. '66 (NEW) Ho Ho Kus, NJ St. Luke's.
Tuan, Bui Quang *c.ss.r.* '97 (LA)[P] Baldwin Park Vietnamese Redemptorist Mission.
Tuan Nguyen, Camillus M. *c.m.c.* '84 (SPC)[F] Carthage, MO Congregation of the Mother Coredemptrix, United States Assumption Province.
Tubbs, Leo *o.p.* '66 (OAK)[L] Oakland, CA Order of Preachers (Province of Holy Name of Jesus – Western Dominican Province).
Tubridy, James J. '53 (NY)[DD] Bronx, NY John Cardinal O'Connor Residence Retired.
Tuchscherer, Vincent '55 (FAR) Retired.
Tucker, James A. '01 (ARL) On Leave of Absence.
Tucker, James G. '06 (NEW) Cliffside Park, NJ Epiphany.
Tucker, James S. *s.s.* '69 (SAT)[A] San Antonio, TX Assumption Seminary.
Tucker, James S. *s.s.* '69 (BAL)[Q] Baltimore Society of St. Sulpice, Province of the United States.
Tucker, James '69 (LA) On Active Leave.
Tucker, Mark E. '89 (WDC) Silver Spring, MD St. John the Evangelist; Judge.
Tucker, Patrick M. '74 (CHI) Palos Hills, IL Sacred Heart.
Tucker, Richard '58 (SY) Retired.
Tucker, Robert F. '70 (HRT) Litchfield, CT St. Anthony of Padua.
Tucker, Rev. Msgr. Robert G. '89 (LIN) Lincoln, NE Cathedral of the Risen Christ.
Tucker, Robert *s.c.j.* '82 (JKS) Southaven, MS Christ the King; Hernando, MS Holy Spirit; Senatobia, MS St. Gregory the Great; Robinsonville, MS Good

Shepherd Catholic Church; [E] Nesbit, MS St. Michael Community House.
Tucker, Thomas J. *o.s.f.s.* '66 (WIL)[J] Childs, MD Retirement and Assisted Care Facility Retired.
Tufail, Augustine '80 (ALB) Troy, NY Sacred Heart.
Tufail, Augustine '80 (MO) DEPARTMENT OF VETERANS AFFAIRS HOSPITALS AND CHAPLAINS.
Tufo, Berard *o.f.m.* '51 (BO)[U] Boston, MA St. Christopher Friary Retired.
Tufts, Donn '80 (GR) Montague, MI St. James; Twin Lake, MI St. Mary of the Woods.
Tugwell, Rev. Msgr. Michael W. '75 (PT) Tallahassee, FL Co–Cathedral of St. Thomas More; College of Consultors; Orders & Ministries, Commission for; [D] Tallahassee, FL Casa Calderon, Inc.
Tuite, Daniel '10 (NY) Yorktown Heights, NY St. Patrick.
Tuite, Howard A. '54 (CHI) Retired.
Tuite, Thomas P. '86 (RVC) Huntington, NY St. Patrick's.
Tuka, Cleophas Oseso '95 (SY)[U] Canastota, NY Catholic Diocese of Nakuru Mission Office, Inc.; Syracuse, NY St. Margaret.
Tulko, Richard *o.f.m.* '64 (GB)[A] Green Bay, WI St. Mary of the Angels Friary.
Tulko, Richard *o.f.m.* (LC) Appointed Members.
Tull, Terry *c.ss.r.* '85 (PCE) Guayama, PR St. Anthony of Padua.
Tuller, John '84 (CHL) Retired.
Tully, Eugene M. '73 (PH) Ambler, PA St. Joseph.
Tully, Gerard P. *c.s.p.* '94 (KNX) Knoxville, TN Immaculate Conception.
Tully, Henry F. '77 (IND) New Albany, IN St. Mary of the Annuciation Catholic Church, New Albany, Inc.
Tully, John P. '69 (Y) Hanoverton, OH St. John.
Tully, Rev. Msgr. Ronald J. '66 (PAT) Retired.
Tully, Thomas S. '85 (R) Hillsborough, NC Holy Family.
Tumicki, Ted F. '97 (NOR) Jewett City, CT St. Mary; Preston, CT St. Catherine of Siena; Voluntown, CT St. Thomas the Apostle; Judicial Vicar; Judges; Theological Advisor; Newspaper; Members; Diocesan Pastoral Council.
Tumino, Frank C. '98 (BRK) Woodhaven, NY St. Thomas Apostle; Diocesan Liturgy Office; Art and Architecture Commission; Liturgical Commission; Music Commission.
Tumminelli, Lawrence *b.s.o.* '96 (NTN) Methuen, MA Basilian Salvatorian Order; Methuen, MA.
Tumosa, John Joseph '69 (CAM) Retired.
Tumulty, Michael J. *c.m.* '51 (PH)[Y].
Tumusiime, Sebastian '97 (PEO) Annawan, IL Sacred Heart; Annawan, IL St. Patrick's.
Tumwesigye, Alfred '05 (CHI) Cicero, IL St. Frances of Rome.
Tunarosa, Rafael '98 (RCK) Crystal Lake, IL St. Thomas the Apostle.
Tunarosa, William (RCK) Aurora, IL Sacred Heart.
Tungol, Eugene D. '75 (SFR) San Francisco, CA Church of the Epiphany; College of Consultors; Filipino Ministry; Episcopal Vicar for Filipinos.
Tungol, Eugene '75 (SFR) On Special Assignment.
Tunink, Shawn '08 (KCK) Catholic Committee on Scouting; [B] Shawnee Mission, KS Bishop Miege High School; Leawood, KS Curé of Ars.
Tunney, Kenneth '63 (ALB) Schenectady, NY St. Gabriel the Archangel Retired.
Tunney, Michael F. *s.j.* '88 (BUF)[N] Buffalo, NY Canisius Jesuit Community Inc.; [C] Buffalo, NY Canisius College.
Tunney, Thomas P. *c.s.sp.* '60 (ARL) Arlington, VA Our Lady, Queen of Peace.
Tunnicliff, Jeffrey '07 (ROC) Penn Yan, NY Our Lady of the Lakes Catholic Community.
Tunny, Kenneth J. '63 (ALB) Retired.
Tuoc, Ignatius '71 (SP) Tampa, FL Epiphany of Our Lord.
Tuohey, John F. '81 (SPR) On Duty Outside the Diocese.
Tuong, Hoang Minh '01 (NO) Metairie, LA St. Louis King of France.
Tuozzolo, Leonard J. *c.s.sp.* '59 (PIT)[O] Bethel Park, PA The Spiritan Center.
Tupa, Allan '97 (SP) St. Pete Beach, FL St. John Vianney; Elected Parochial Vicars.
Tupa, Jerome *o.s.b.* '82 (SCL)[I] Collegeville, MN St. John's Abbey, of the Order of St. Benedict; Saint Joseph, MN St. John the Baptist.
Tupa, Michael J. '91 (SUP) Webster, WI Sacred Hearts of Jesus and Mary; Webster, WI Our Lady of Perpetual Help; Webster, WI St. John the Baptist; Presbyteral Council & Diocesan Consultors; Board of Directors; Pastoral Consultors.
Tupper, Dale E. '67 (WIN) Austin, MN Queen of Angels; Austin, MN Our Lady of Loretto.
Tuptynski, Marek S. '97 (FR) Somerset, MA St. Patrick's; Diocesan Department of Pastoral Care for the Sick.
Tupuola, Iosefo Vaitele '99 (SPP) Pago Pago, AS St. Paul.
Turalija, Dubravko '02 (WDC) Washington, DC St. Blaise.
Turano, Steven Jordan *o.p.* '04 (COL) Zanesville, OH St. Thomas Aquinas.
Turati, Fortunato *s.c.* '67 (LAN) Camp Cassidy Lake; [E] Chelsea, MI St. Louis Center for Exceptional Children & Adults; [R] Grass Lake, MI The Pious Union of St. Joseph.
Turcich, Ronald R. *o.s.a.* '58 (CHI)[N] Chicago, IL St. Rita Monastery.
Turco, Alfredo *s.x.* '88 (MIL)[B] Franklin, WI Xaverian Missionary Fathers College Seminary.
Turczany, Christopher C. '83 (BRK) Flushing, NY St. Mel; Diocesan Insurance Committee; Brooklyn, NY St. Mark.
Turek, Rev. Msgr. Michael E. '76 (STL) Deaneries/ Deans; St. Louis, MO St. Joan of Arc.
Turek, Ronald J. '74 (CLV) Orrville, OH St. Agnes; Orrville, OH Dunlap Community Hospital.
Tureman, Thomas *s.d.s.* '88 (MIL)[P] Milwaukee, WI Salvatorian Provincial Offices; Lexington, KY U.S.A. Procurator.
Turi, John J. '55 (SCR) Retired.
Turillo, B. Samuel '46 (PRO) Retired.
Turley, Sean F. '71 (WIL) Retired.
Turnbull, William '67 (ALB) Retired.
Turner, Andrew B. '06 (CLV) Strongsville, OH St. John Neumann.
Turner, Christopher M. '05 (WH) Vocations Promoters; Charleston, WV St. Agnes.
Turner, David *o.s.b.* '63 (JOL)[A] Lisle, IL Benedictine University; [L] Lisle, IL St. Procopius Abbey; Lisle, IL.
Turner, James M. *o.s.f.s.* '81 (CHL) Thomasville, NC Our Lady of the Highways.
Turner, James '84 (PHX) Glendale, AZ St. Thomas More Roman Catholic Parish.
Turner, Jerome R. '64 (MAD) Retired.
Turner, Paul '79 (KC) Cameron, MO St. Munchin.
Turner, Richard M. '80 (SPR) Chicopee, MA St. Anne's.
Turner, Richard W. '91 (R) Retired.
Turner, Robert D. '82 (SPK) Dayton, WA St. Joseph; Pomeroy, WA Holy Rosary; Dayton, WA St. Mark; Members.
Turner, Robert D. '88 (MIL) Milwaukee, WI Blessed Sacrament.
Turner, Robert G. '59 (PIT) Homestead, PA St. Maximilian Kolbe Retired.
Turner, Robert L. '11 (HRT) Madison, CT St. Margaret.
Turner, Thomas W. '82 (KC)[L] Kansas City, MO Bishop Sullivan Center.
Turner, William J. '75 (IND) Greensburg, IN Immaculate Conception Catholic Church, Millhousen, Inc.; Greensburg, IN St. Denis Catholic Church, Jennings County, Inc.; Napoleon, IN St. Maurice Catholic Church, Napoleon, Inc. Retired.
Turner, William J. '79 (LAN) Chelsea, MI St. Mary; Camp Cassidy Lake.
Turon, Louis Luke *o.p.* '55 (COL) Zanesville, OH St. Thomas Aquinas.
Turro, Rev. Msgr. James C. '48 (NEW)[B] Seton Hall University Retired.
Turro, Rev. Msgr. James '48 (NOR)[A] Cromwell, CT Holy Apostles College and Seminary.
Turyatoranwa, Julius '98 (PEO) Bloomington, IL Holy Trinity.
Turyk, Ivan '03 (PHU) Perth Amboy, NJ Assumption of B.V.M.
Tuscan, Joseph *o.f.m.cap.* '97 (WH)[L] Wheeling, WV Capuchin Hermitage of St. Joseph.
Tushar, David '76 (DUL) Carlton, MN St. Francis; Carlton, MN SS. Mary & Joseph.
Tusky, Richard J. '73 (PIT) Bellevue, PA Assumption of the Blessed Virgin Mary on the Beautiful River.
Tustin, Joseph E. *o.s.f.s.* '67 (PH) Philadelphia, PA Resurrection of Our Lord.
Tutas, Stephen *s.m.* '53 (SJ)[M] Cupertino, CA The Marianist Center.
Tutone, John J. '71 (RVC) Island Park, NY Sacred Heart; Judges for Interdiocesan Tribunal; Five Towns Deanery.
Tutor, Edwin '97 (SD) Chula Vista, CA Saint Pius X Catholic Parish Chula Vista.
Tuttle, Arthur *c.ss.r.* '65 (ALB) Saratoga Springs, NY St. Clement.
Tuttle, Charles W. '74 (BEL) Beckemeyer, IL St. Anthony; Breese, IL St. Augustine; [A] Breese, IL Mater Dei High School.
Tuttle, Patrick *o.f.m.* '94 (CHR) Greenville, SC St. Anthony of Padua; Seminary Admissions Board.
Tuttle, Richard J. '76 (STU) Retired.
Tuyn, William R. '62 (BUF) Retired.
Tuyor, Exsequel '94 (HON) Kailua, HI St. Anthony of Padua.
Tuzeneu, Rev. Msgr. Kenard J. '79 (TR) Barnegat, NJ St. Mary.
Tuzik, Robert L. '73 (CHI) Diocesan Priests' Placement Board; Chicago, IL Notre Dame de Chicago; Divine Worship, Office for.
Tvrdik, Roy *s.m.m.* '93 (RVC)[N] Eastport, NY Shrine of Our Lady of the Island; [N] Bay Shore, NY Montfort Missionaries.
Tvrdy, Julius '73 (LIN) Crete, NE Sacred Heart; Apostolate to the Spanish Speaking.
Twaddell, Gerald E. '67 (COV) Camp Springs, KY St. Joseph; Defenders of the Bond.
Twardzik, Francis M. *s.d.b.* '70 (PSC) Minersville, PA SS. Peter and Paul; Mid–Pennsylvania Protopresbyterate; Eparchial College of Consultors; Presbyteral Council.
Twardzik, Michael W.T. '70 (SPR) On Duty Outside the Diocese.
Twardzik, Michael '70 (ROC) Wayland, NY Holy Family Catholic Community.
Twarog, Jerome '82 (CHI) Chicago, IL St. Eugene.
Twele, Robert *o.f.m.conv.* '81 (BAL)[Q] Ellicott City, MD Order of Friars Minor Conventual; [U] Baltimore, MD Catholic Relief Services Foundation, Inc.
Twene, Eric (NY) Brewster, NY St. Lawrence O'Toole.
Twiggs, Matthew J. '73 (PAT) Stockholm, NJ St. John Vianney.
Twinomuhwezi, Venantius K. *a.j.* '93 (ALN) Easton, PA Our Lady of Mercy Parish.
Twinomujuni, John '01 (PIT) Pittsburgh, PA St. Bede.
Twohig, Michael J. '83 (SPR) Newman Apostolate and Campus Ministry; [M] Amherst, MA University of Massachusetts.
Twohig, Richard H. *s.j.* '65 (DET)[K] Clarkston, MI Colombiere Center.
Twohy, Patrick J. *s.j.* '70 (SEA) Seattle, WA Our Lady of Mount Virgin; [M] Seattle, WA Arrupe Jesuit Community at Seattle University; Tacoma, WA St. Leo the Great.
Twohy, Patrick J. *s.j.* '70 (P)[L] Portland, OR Jesuit Provincial Office (Society of Jesus, Oregon Prov.).
Twomey, Daniel F. '75 (BO) Unassigned.
Twomey, John E. '52 (MIL) Retired.
Ty, Jesus G. '98 (PHX) Mesa, AZ Queen of Peace Roman Catholic Parish.
Ty, Roch Keresz '60 (DAL)[B] University of Dallas.
Tybor, Karol '09 (CHI) Chicago, IL St. Christina.
Tyburski, Zbigniew '73 (PAT) Boonton, NJ SS. Cyril and Methodius.
Tyhovych, Ivan '69 (MO) Army Reserve Chaplains.
Tykhovytch, Ivan '94 (STF) Brooklyn, NY Holy Ghost.
Tylenda, Joseph N. *s.j.* '60 (SCR)[N] Scranton, PA Pascucci Family Our Lady of Peace Residence; [B] Scranton, PA The University of Scranton.
Tyler, Bernard L. '61 (GLD) Higgins Lake, MI St. Hubert; Higgins Lake, MI St. James Retired.
Tyler, Jason '05 (LR) Little Rock, AR St. Edward; Clergy Personnel Advisory Board (Diocesan).
Tyler, Thomas L. '79 (E) Force, PA St. Joseph; Deans.
Tylka, Louis '96 (CHI) North Riverside, IL Mater Christi; Presbyteral Council.
Tyma, John A. *o.s.a.* '59 (FgM) Olympia Fields, IL Province of Our Mother of Good Counsel (Midwestern).
Tyman, Gary L. '86 (ROC) Rochester, NY St. Anne; Rochester, NY Our Lady of Lourdes.
Tymko, Piotr *o.f.m.conv.* '94 (RCK) Algonquin, IL St. Margaret Mary.
Tynan, Desmond A. '67 (FgM) Society of St. James the Apostle.; Boston, MA St. James the Apostle, Inc.
Tynan, John C. *m.m.* '62 (NY)[DD] Maryknoll Maryknoll Fathers and Brothers Retired.
Tynan, Peter *o.s.b.* '11 (SEA)[M] Lacey, WA St. Martin's Abbey.
Tyrasinski, Lucius *o.s.p.p.e.* '56 (PH)[Y].
Tyrell, Wilfred *s.a.* '94 (NY)[DD] Garrison, NY Franciscan Friars of the Atonement.
Tyrrell, Bernard J. *s.j.* '65 (SPK)[B] Spokane, WA Gonzaga University.
Tyrrell, Joseph J. '89 (NY) New York, NY Cathedral of St. Patrick.
Tyrrell, Michael A. *s.j.* '76 (P)[L] Portland, OR Jesuit Provincial Office (Society of Jesus, Oregon Prov.); [L] Portland, OR Colombiere Community.
Tyrrell, Patrick *s.j.* '67 (CHI) Glenview, IL Our Lady of Perpetual Help.
Tyrrell, Wilfred *s.a.* '94 (NY)[DD] New York, NY Atonement Friars; [DD] New York, NY Atonement Friars.
Tyrrell, William *s.a.* (NY)[GG] Purchase, NY Manhattanville College.
Tyrtania, Joachim B. '83 (RCK) Rockford, IL St. James.
Tyson, David T. *c.s.c.* '75 (FTW)[H] Notre Dame, IN Congregation of Holy Cross, United States Province of Priests & Brothers; South Bend, IN; Austin, TX; [H] Notre Dame, IN Congregation of Holy Cross, United States Province, Inc.
Tyson, David T. *c.s.c.* '75 (BGP)[O] Bridgeport, CT Provincial Offices of the Priests and Brothers of Holy Cross, Eastern Province.
Tyson, Michael *o.f.m.* '67 (NY) New York, NY Holy Name of Jesus.
Tywoniak, Robert F. '83 (MIA) Oakland Park, FL Blessed Sacrament.
Tzanakas, George M. '62 (AUS) Retired.
Tzul, Max '96 (MIL) Fond du Lac, WI Holy Family.

U

Uba, Alban *s.m.m.m.* '99 (SAC) Carmichael, CA St. John the Evangelist.

Uba, Livinus '94 (WH) Huntington, WV Sacred Heart; Huntington, WV St. Peter Claver.
Ubaka, Victor O. '95 (BRK) Brooklyn, NY St. Matthew.
Ubalde, Ulysses L. '93 (MO) Navy Chaplains.
Ubalde, Ulysses '93 (NEW) Military Chaplains.
Ubanii, Angelo B. *s.m.m.m.* '97 (MO) DEPARTMENT OF VETERANS AFFAIRS HOSPITALS AND CHAPLAINS.
Ubben, Michael Luke '05 (CHI)[N] Chicago, IL St. Peter's Friary.
Ubel, John L. '89 (STP) St. Paul, MN St. Agnes; St. Paul, MN; Deanery 3; Treasurer; Archdiocesan Finance Council (AFC).
Uchendu, Clement *c.s.sp.* '94 (CHI) Chicago, IL St. Mary Magdalene.
Udahemuka, Fidelis *s.j.* '05 (SJ)[B] Santa Clara, CA Jesuit Community.
Udayar, Santiago D. '89 (SAN) Odessa, TX St. Mary's; Presbyteral Council.
Udeani, Christopher *c.m.f.* '90 (SAT)[M] San Antonio, TX Cordi–Marian Missionary Sisters.
Udegbunam, Michael '81 (SAN) Colorado City, TX St. Ann's.
Udemgia, Simon (ALB) Greenfield Center, NY St. Joseph.
Udeze, Joseph *c.m.f.* '91 (NEW) Jersey City, NJ Our Lady of Mercy.
Udeze, Kieran O. '95 (PH) African Apostolate; Philadelphia, PA Cathedral Basilica of SS. Peter and Paul.
Udick, William S. *s.j.* '55 (STL)[O] St. Louis, MO Jesuit Community Corporation at Saint Louis University – Jesuit Hall.
Udoekpo, Michael *s.t.l.* '95 (MIL)[B] Hales Corners, WI Sacred Heart School of Theology.
Udogu, Anthony '95 (NEW) Hackensack, NJ Hackensack University Medical Center.
Udoh, Emmanuel '98 (NY) Hopewell Junction, NY St. Columba.
Udoh, Michael S. '95 (BRK) South Ozone Park, NY St. Clement Pope.
Udoji, Ambrose '95 (LA) Northridge Hospital Medical Center.
Udokang, Charles (NY) Bronx, NY Our Lady of Grace.
Udomah, Justin '93 (AUS) Blanco, TX St. Ferdinand.
Udovic, Edward R. *c.m.* '84 (CHI)[C] Chicago, IL De Paul University; [N] Chicago, IL Vincentian Community, Congregation of the Mission, Western Province; [C] De Paul University.
Udulutsch, Robert *o.f.m.cap.* '56 (GB)[J] Appleton, WI St. Fidelis Friary Retired.
Udumka, Kenny '98 (PBL) Trinidad, CO Most Holy Trinity; [E] Trinidad, CO Trinidad Area Catholic Community.
Uebler, Michael G. '82 (BUF) Tonawanda, NY St. Francis of Assisi; Clergy Personnel Board.
Uehlein, Christopher *o.s.b.* '60 (SFS)[F] Marvin, SD Blue Cloud Abbey.
Uftring, Richard A. '76 (BO)[Z] Boston, MA Our Lady of the Airways Chapel; Seaport Chaplaincy; Airport Chaplaincy; Winthrop, MA St. John the Evangelist.
Ugalde, Jose *m.sp.s.* '09 (SEA) Mill Creek, WA St. Elizabeth Ann Seton.
Ugliano, Bruno A. *o.s.b.* '67 (PAT) Morristown, NJ; [N] Morristown, NJ St. Mary's Abbey.
Uglietto, Peter J. '77 (BO)[A] Weston, MA Blessed John XXIII National Seminary.
Ugo, Charles Chidindu '06 (ALT) Renovo, PA St. Joseph's.
Ugoagwu, Peter Claver '93 (NY) Cornwall, NY St. Luke's–Cornwall Hospital; Newburgh, NY St. Luke–Cornell Hospital.
Ugobueze, John '05 (MO) DEPARTMENT OF VETERANS AFFAIRS HOSPITALS AND CHAPLAINS.
Ugochukwu, Charlse '96 (BRK) Brooklyn, NY Holy Spirit.
Ugochukwu, Sebastian A. '79 (MO) DEPARTMENT OF VETERANS AFFAIRS HOSPITALS AND CHAPLAINS.
Ugochukwu, Sebastian A. (BO) Pastoral Care.
Ugwoji, Matthew '92 (NY) Bronx, NY Fulton Correctional Facility; Ossining, NY Sing Sing Correctional Facility; [E] Bronx, NY Cardinal Hayes High School.
Ugwu, Ejiofor *m.s.p.* '00 (PT) Tallahassee, FL St. Eugene, Florida A&M University; Tallahassee–Florida Agricultural & Mechanical University, St. Eugene Chapel.
Ugwu, Kenneth C. *s.s.j.* '10 (GAL) Houston, TX Our Mother of Mercy.
Ugwu, Stephen '02 (LAF) Church Point, LA Our Lady of the Sacred Heart.
Ugwuanya, Valentine C. '94 (MO) Military Chaplains; Army Chaplains.
Ugwuegbu, Ambrose '87 (SAC) Susanville, CA Sacred Heart.
Ugwuegbulem, Longinus N. '93 (NEW) Newark, NJ Blessed Sacrament–St. Charles Borromeo.
Uhde, Peter M. '81 (MO) Army Chaplains.
Uhde, Peter '81 (NEW) Military Chaplains.
Uhen, Cletus V. '42 (MIL) Retired.
Uhen, Timothy J. '96 (POD)[O] Brookfield, WI Prelature of the Holy Cross and Opus Dei Layton Study Center; Brookfield.
Uhl, Christopher W. *o.m.v.* '03 (BO)[Z] Boston, MA St. Francis Chapel.
Uhl, Christopher W. *o.m.v.* '03 (DEN) Denver, CO Holy Ghost.
Uhlenkott, Benjamin '06 (B) College of Consultors; Deans; Priest Personnel Commission; Mountain Home, ID Our Lady of Good Counsel.
Uhlenkott, Gary D. *s.j.* '80 (SPK)[B] Spokane, WA Gonzaga University.
Uhler, Carl A. '56 (CLV) West Salem, OH St. Stephen Retired.
Uhlman, Laurence *t.o.r.* '90 (STU)[H] Steubenville, OH Holy Spirit Friary; [A] Steubenville, OH Franciscan University of Steubenville.
Uhrig, A. Gregory '73 (MET)[I] Somerset, NJ Maria Regina Residence.
Uju, Ikechukwu Eliseus '03 (SB) Big Bear Lake, CA St. Joseph.
Ukaegbu, Rev. Msgr. John '72 (LA) Santa Maria, CA St. Mary of the Assumption.
Ukaegbu–Onuoha, Emmanuel '95 (SB) Norco, CA St. Mel.
Ukanide, Akama *m.s.p.* (MOB) Mobile, AL St. Francis Xavier; Prichard, AL Our Mother of Mercy.
Uko, Joseph M. '88 (BLX) Gulfport, MS St. John the Evangelist; Presbyteral Council.
Ukomadu, Linus '90 (LR) Cherokee Village, AR St. Michael; Horseshoe Bend, AR St. Mary of the Mount.
Ukwe, Stan '94 (WDC)[M] Hyattsville, MD Sacred Heart Home Inc.
Ulak, Robert T. '70 (NEW) Park Ridge, NJ Our Lady of Mercy.
Ulam, Richard *o.s.b.* '82 (GBG)[H] Latrobe, PA Saint Vincent Archabbey.
Ulam, Richard *o.s.b.* '82 (WH) Fairmont, WV Immaculate Conception.
Uline, Cyprian *o.f.m.conv.* '70 (LSC) Carlsbad, NM St. Edward; Presbyteral Council.
Ullery, Kirk J. '65 (SFR) Retired.
Ullmer, James Louis *o.s.b.* '09 (TLS)[G] Hulbert, OK Our Lady of the Annunciation of Clear Creek Monastery.
Ulloa, Daniel *o.p.* '70 (NY) Yonkers, NY St. John the Baptist.
Ulloa–Chavarry, Rodrigo *m.m.* '11 (FgM) Maryknoll, NY MARYKNOLL.
Ullrich, David *o.m.i.* '71 (FgM) Washington, DC AMERICAN OBLATE MISSIONS.
Ullrich, John R. *o.f.m.* '76 (TR) Brant Beach, NJ St. Francis of Assisi.
Ullrich, John *o.f.m.* '76 (WDC)[B] Silver Spring, MD Holy Name College.
Ullrich, Rev. Msgr. Mark C. '78 (STL) Florissant, MO Sacred Heart.
Ullrich, Peter *o.s.b.* '87 (KC) Savannah, MO St. Rose of Lima; [J] Priests Elsewhere.
Ulm, John F. '58 (GAL) Houston, TX St. Maximilian Kolbe.
Ulman, Stanley A. '73 (DET) Presbyteral Council; Rochester Hills, MI St. Mary of the Hills; Archdiocesan Vicars; College of Consultors.
Ulrich, Eugene P. '74 (BUF) Council of Priests; Elma, NY Annunciation of the Blessed Virgin Mary.
Ulrich, John *s.m* '86 (MRY) Campus Ministry Department; [F] San Luis Obispo, CA Society of Mary (Marists)–S.M.; [I] San Luis Obispo, CA California State Polytechnic Institute/Cuesta College.
Ulrich, Steve '90 (OWN) Absent on Leave.
Ulrick, Stephen D. '82 (STP) Wayzata, MN Holy Name of Jesus.
Ulshafer, Thomas R. *s.s.* '70 (BAL)[Q] Baltimore, MD Society of St. Sulpice, Province of the United States; Baltimore, MD; [U] Baltimore, MD Society of St. Sulpice Foundation US, Inc.
Ulshafer, Thomas *s.s.* '70 (WDC) On Duty Outside the Archdiocese.
Ulto, Victor A. '80 (PMB) Port St. Lucie, FL St. Bernadette.
Umana, Eduardo Pinzon *s.j.* (CHI)[N] Chicago, IL Woodlawn Jesuit Community.
Umaña, German '96 (SLC) Wendover, UT San Felipe LLC 251.
Umana, Pedro *o.f.m.* '89 (FRS) Shafter, CA St. Therese.
Umberg, Andrew J. '91 (CIN) Cincinnati, OH St. William.
Umbras, Thomas *s.v.d.* '81 (BO)[W] Duxbury, MA Miramar Retreat Center; [U] Duxbury, MA Society of the Divine Word.
Ume, Michael '93 (LA) Bellflower, CA St. Bernard.
Umekwe, Peter Obinna '01 (BAK) Condon, OR St. John.
Umeobi, Jude '97 (LA) Pastoral Team:; Montebello, CA Our Lady of the Miraculous Medal.
Umeokeke, Damian '98 (NY) Manhattan, NY Beth Israel Medical Center; New York, NY St. Stephen and Our Lady of the Scapular.
Umhoefer, Stephen J. '66 (MAD) Janesville, WI Nativity of St. Mary; Elected.
Umoenoh, Clement '96 (NY) Bronx, NY St. Joseph.
Umukoro, Fidelis *o.p.* (HBG) Lewistown, PA Sacred Heart of Jesus; Mifflintown, PA St. Jude.
Umunnakwe, Eze Venantius *c.s.sp.* '87 (CHI) Blue Island, IL St. Isidore.
Unachukwu, Arthur '11 (DAL) McKinney, TX St. Michael.
Underdahl, Mark J. '96 (STP) Lino Lakes, MN St. Joseph of the Lakes.
Underwood, Eric Christopher '06 (LFT) Lafayette, IN St. Mary Cathedral; Lafayette, IN St. Lawrence.
Underwood, Joseph '63 (BIR) Retired.
Underwood, Scott J. *o.s.b.* '76 (NO)[R] St. Benedict, LA St. Joseph Abbey; [A] St. Benedict, LA St. Joseph Seminary College.
Ungashick, Thomas '76 (Y) Newton Falls, OH St. Mary and St. Joseph Parish.
Unger, Rev. Msgr. John M. '65 (STL) Warson Woods, MO Ste. Genevieve Du Bois.
Unger, Robert P. '99 (FAR) Retired.
Unger, Steve (RVC) Stony Brook, NY Stony Brook University Hospital.
Unger, Todd '82 (BAK) Board of Education; Health and Retirement Board; [C] Bend, OR The Health and Retirement Association of the Diocese of Baker, Oregon; Redmond, OR St. Thomas.
Universal, Patrick J. '75 (BO) Boston, MA St. Stephen; [U] Boston, MA The Society of St. James the Apostle, Inc. Retired.
Universal, Patrick '75 (FgM) Boston, MA St. James the Apostle, Inc.
Unni, John J. '92 (BO) Boston, MA St. Cecilia.
Unsworth, John E. '76 (PRO) Wickford, RI St. Bernard.
Untereiner, Harry P. '72 (PSC) New Brunswick, NJ St. Joseph; Retirement Plan Board.
Unterreiner, James J. '70 (SPC) Ironton, MO Ste. Marie Du Lac; Region VI; Region VI; Diocesan Consultors; Diocesan Council of Catholic Women (DCCW).
Unverdorben, Ernest *o.c.d.* '66 (MIL)[P] Hubertus, WI Discalced Carmelite Monastery – Holy Hill Basilica of the National Shrine of Mary, Help of Christians, Holy Hill.
Unverferth, Steven R. '89 (BEL) Leave of Absence.
Unz, Thomas E. '83 (CHI) Westchester, IL Divine Providence.
Uong, Luong *c.ss.r.* '71 (DEN)[N] Denver The Redemptorists/Denver Province.
Uong, Luong *c.ss.r.* '95 (PH) Philadelphia, PA Visitation B.V.M.
Upah, William J. '98 (R) Henderson, NC St. James; Deans; Council of Priests.
Uppena, Rev. Msgr. James J. '68 (MAD) Milton, WI St. Mary.
Upson, Michael '76 (ROC) Avon, NY St. Agnes; Honeoye Falls, NY St. Paul of the Cross; Lima, NY St. Rose.
Upton, Edward F. '69 (CHI) Orland Park, IL St. Francis of Assisi; Deans.
Upton, John '83 (GAL) Spring, TX Christ the Good Shepherd.
Upton, Joseph R. '10 (PRO) Wakefield, RI St. Francis of Assisi; [C] Wakefield, RI The Prout School.
Uralikunnel, George V. '67 (MO) DEPARTMENT OF VETERANS AFFAIRS HOSPITALS AND CHAPLAINS.
Uram, Rev. Msgr. Kenneth J. '59 (STU) Retired.
Urarte, Carmelo '59 (ARE) Quebradillas, PR Sacred Heart; Diocesan Consultors.
Urassa, Rogatian '83 (BAK) Klamath Falls, OR Sacred Heart.
Urban, Anthony M. '73 (SCR) Retired.
Urban, Anthony '11 (SFS) Dell Rapids, SD St. Mary's.
Urban, Carl '66 (ALB) Retired.
Urban, Charles T. *o.praem.* '54 (PH)[Y] Paoli, PA Daylesford Abbey.
Urban, John L. '59 (MAD) Retired.
Urban, Joseph (NEW) Jersey City, NJ St. Anthony of Padua.
Urban, Rev. Msgr. Lonnie A. '67 (AUS) Taylor, TX St. Mary of the Assumption.
Urban, Peter '58 (DEN) Retired.
Urban, Reginald A. '77 (DOD) Great Bend, KS Prince of Peace Catholic Church of Great Bend, Kansas; Priest Continuing Formation Commission.
Urban, Robert M. '60 (SUP) Retired.
Urban, Thomas E. '02 (DET) Warren, MI St. Mark.
Urbanek, Raymond J. '68 (LAN) Ovid, MI Holy Family.
Urbaniak, Andrzej *o.f.m.conv.* '98 (BO) South Boston, MA Our Lady of Czestochowa; Polish; Hyde Park, MA St. Adalbert.
Urbaniak, Rev. Msgr. Bernard J. '68 (E) Erie, PA St. Stanislaus.
Urbaniak, Jan *c.m.* '71 (BRK) Brooklyn, NY St. Stanislaus Kostka.
Urbaniak, Lawrence M. '61 (RCK) Retired.
Urbaniak, Lucian '85 (SY) Cortland, NY St. Anthony of Padua; Cortland, NY St. Mary.
Urbanic, James *c.pp.s.* '71 (OAK)[L] Berkeley, CA Society of the Precious Blood (Kansas City Province).
Urbanowski, Konrad *s.ch.* '43 (DET) Sterling Heights, MI Our Lady of Czestochowa.
Urbanski, Louis '64 (P) Aloha, OR St. Elizabeth Ann Seton.

Urbina, Carlos E. *o.s.a.* (BO) Lawrence, MA St. Mary of the Assumption.
Urbonas, Rev. Msgr. Ignatius L. '35 (GRY) Lemont, IL Blessed Jurgis Matulaitis Mission Retired.
Urcia, Daniel C. '89 (SJ) Santa Clara County Jail; Detention Ministry for Juveniles; Special Assignment; Diocesan Clergy Personnel Board.
Ureel, Wayne G. '90 (DET) Dryden, MI St. Cornelius; Allenton, MI St. John the Evangelist; Capac, MI St. Nicholas.
Urell, Rev. Msgr. John '78 (ORG) Laguna Niguel, CA St. Timothy.
Urian, Thomas R. '90 (PH)[D] Drexel Hill, PA Monsignor Bonner and Archbishop Prendergast Catholic High School.
Urias, Jose Garibaldi Ballesteros '97 (PHX) Phoenix, AZ St. Augustine Roman Catholic Parish.
Uribe, Arturo *c.ss.r.* '95 (CHI) Chicago, IL St. Michael in Old Town; [N] Chicago, IL The Redemptorist Fathers of Chicago.
Uribe, Miguel Ortiz '87 (LAR) Laredo, TX San Agustin Cathedral.
Uribe, Saul de Jesus '80 (ELP) El Paso, TX Sts. Peter and Paul.
Uribe–Guzman, Francisco J. *m.n.m.* '58 (SAT) Del Rio, TX Retired.
Uribe Ramirez, Salvador E. *c.s.j.* '09 (LAR)[D] Laredo, TX St. John Priory, F.J.
Urizalqui, Rev. Msgr. Richard '77 (FRS) Tulare, CA St. Aloysius; Advocates.
Urlage, Robert J. '58 (COV) Retired.
Urmston, Benjamin J. *s.j.* '59 (CIN)[N] Cincinnati, OH Jesuit Community at Xavier University.
Urnick, Charles B. '74 (NEW) On Duty Outside the Archdiocese.
Urnick, Charles B. '74 (LAV) Laughlin, NV St. John the Baptist Catholic Church.
Uroda, Stanley *s.v.d.* '74 (CHI)[N] Chicago, IL Divine Word Theologate.
Urrabazo, Rosendo *c.m.f.* '78 (CHI)[N] Oak Park, IL Claretian Missionaries USA Eastern Province; [N] Oak Park, IL Claretian Missionaries Community Support Trust.
Urrea, Miguel A. '87 (SB) Colton, CA Arrowhead Regional Medical Center.
Urrego, Luis Ido '01 (SAC) Sacramento, CA St. Joseph's; Presbyteral Council.
Urriza, Luis *o.s.a.* '44 (BEA) Beaumont, TX Cristo Rey; Beaumont, TX.
Uschold, Raymond F. '64 (BUF)[N] Lackawanna, NY Bishop Head Residence Retired.
Useche, Teofilo '84 (VEN) Bonita Springs, FL St. Leo; Presbyteral Council.
Useda, Uriel *c.ss.r.* (BAL) Baltimore, MD Sacred Heart of Jesus.
Usenza, Robert J. '61 (BGP) Retired.
Usselmann, Gregory *l.c.* '10 (DAL)[J] Irving, TX Legionaries of Christ.
Ustaski, William B. *c.r.i.c.* '77 (LA)[P] Santa Paula, CA Canons Regular of the Immaculate Conception.
Uter, Frank M. '69 (BR) Denham Springs, LA Immaculate Conception; Judges; Cemeteries.
Uthuppu, Augustine '88 (HON) Koloa, HI St. Raphael.
Utietiang, Bekeh U. '07 (WH) Benwood, WV St. John.
Utietiang, Bekeh Ukelina '07 (WH) McMechen, WV St. James.
Utrup, Eugene E. '59 (STL) Retired.
Utser, Paul (TUC) Tucson, AZ Saints Peter and Paul Roman Catholic Parish – Tucson.
Utz, Raymond M. '63 (PIT)[M] Pittsburgh, PA Cardinal Dearden Center Retired.
Utzig, Albert R. *s.s.c.* '83 (SB) Rialto, CA St. Catherine of Siena.
Utzig, Albert *s.s.c.* '83 (OM)[J] St. Columbans Missionary Society of St. Columban.
Uvietta, Joseph *s.m.* '61 (STL)[O] St. Louis, MO Cure of Ars Marianist Community.
Uwakwe, Uzoma E. '96 (MO) Army Chaplains.
Uwamungu, Jean Bosco '06 (SHP) Bossier City, LA St. Jude.
Uwandu, Marcellinus U. '82 (MO) DEPARTMENT OF VETERANS AFFAIRS HOSPITALS AND CHAPLAINS.
Uwandu, Marcellinus '82 (ROC) Bath, NY Soldiers' Home and Veterans' Hospital.
Uwasomba, Benet '78 (RVC) Manhasset, NY North Shore Univ. Hospital.
Uzbuegbuman, Benjamin (NY) Mount Vernon, NY Sacred Heart.
Uzoh, Louis N. '73 (BRK) Rosedale, NY St. Pius X.
Uzukwu, Eugene *c.s.sp.* (PIT)[B] Pittsburgh, PA Duquesne University of the Holy Spirit.
Uzzilio, Robert A. '65 (BGP) Office for the Continuing Education of Clergy Retired.

V

V. Do, (Philip M.) Thanh *c.m.c.* '09 (SPC)[F] Carthage, MO Congregation of the Mother Coredemptrix, United States Assumption Province.
Vacca, Daniel L. '95 (WCH) Wichita, KS St. Jude; Presbyteral Council/College of Consultors.
Vaccari, Rev. Msgr. Andrew J. '86 (BRK) Brooklyn, NY St. Mary Mother of Jesus; Diocesan Judges; Attorneys and Counselors at Canon Law.
Vaccari, Rev. Msgr. Peter I. '77 (BRK) Censors of Books; Released from Diocesan Assignment.
Vaccari, Peter I. '77 (RVC) Censors of Books.
Vaccari, Rev. Msgr. Peter I. '77 (RVC)[A] Huntington, NY Diocesan Seminary of the Immaculate Conception.
Vaccaro, Christopher T. '08 (ARL) Notaries; Woodbridge, VA Our Lady of Angels.
Vaccaro, Joseph V. *o.carm.* '58 (STP)[J] Lake Elmo, MN Carmelite Hermitage of the Blessed Virgin Mary; Lake Elmo, MN.
Vacco, James *o.f.m.* '82 (BUF) Council of Priests; [N] St. Bonaventure, NY St. Bonaventure Friary; Allegany, NY St. Bonaventure.
Vacek, Carl *t.o.r.* '79 (ALT)[G] Hollidaysburg, PA St. Bernardine Monastery.
Vacek, Edward V. *s.j.* '73 (BO)[U] Brighton, MA Walter Ciszek House.
Vadakathalakal, Augustine Varghese *o.ss.t.* '08 (BAL)[Q] Assigned in India.
Vadakemuriyil, Thomas John *c.m.i.* '92 (SHP)[B] Shreveport, LA CHRISTUS Health Northern Louisiana.
Vadakkevattukula, Tomy *m.s.t.* '01 (CHI)[J] Evanston, IL Saint Francis Hospital; [J] Chicago, IL Our Lady of the Resurrection Medical Center.
Vadakin, Rev. Msgr. Royale M. '64 (LA) Moderator of the Curia and Vicar General; Cardinal McIntyre Fund for Charity Board of Directors; Members; Ex Officio Members; Ex Officio Members; Los Angeles, CA St. Anastasia.
Vadakkan, Johnny *m.s.* '00 (MAN) Enfield, NH St. Helena.
Vadakkan, Lawrence '90 (SFR) Larkspur, CA St. Patrick.
Vadakkekara, J. Philip '69 (MET) Retired.
Vadakumkara, Shijo *h.g.n.* '04 (OWN) Clinton, KY St. Jude; Fulton, KY St. Edward; Hickman, KY Sacred Heart.
Vadana, Kuriakose Chacko *m.s.t.* '81 (SYM) San Fernando, CA St. Alphonsa Syro–Malabar Catholic Church of Los Angeles; San Fernando, CA Bl. Mother Theresa Syro–Malabar Catholic Church; San Fernando, CA Bl. Chavara Syro–Malabar Catholic Mission (Bakersfield).
Vaeth, Paul *c.p.* '68 (PIT)[M] Pittsburgh, PA St. Paul of the Cross Monastery; [O] Pittsburgh, PA St. Paul of the Cross Retreat Center.
Vaghetto, Benedetto P. '78 (PIT) College of Consultors; Priest Council; [A] Pittsburgh, PA Saint Paul Seminary; Adjutant Judicial Vicar; Defenders of the Bond.
Vaghi, Rev. Msgr. Peter J. '85 (WDC)[C] Catholic University of America, The.
Vaghi, Rev. Msgr. Peter J. '85 (WDC)[X] Glen Echo, MD John Carroll Society; [X] Glen Echo, MD The John Carroll Society; Advocates; Deans; Bethesda, MD Little Flower; Archdiocesan College of Consultors; Priest Council.
Vaglienty, Felipe '00 (CHI) Chicago, IL St. Ann.
Vahi, Salvador S. '85 (BO)[T] Newton, MA Prelature of the Holy Cross and Opus Dei.
Vahi, Salvador S. (POD) Chestnut Hill.
Vail, Thomas '51 (ALB) Retired.
Vaillancourt, Joseph *o.m.i.* '46 (FgM) Washington, DC AMERICAN OBLATE MISSIONS.
Vaillancourt, Mark G. '94 (NY)[E] Somers, NY John F. Kennedy Catholic High School.
Vaillancourt, Raymond *m.s.* '89 (FR)[F] Attleboro, MA La Salette Communications Office; [F] Attleboro, MA La Salette Shrine Retired.
Vaillancourt, Raymond *m.s.* (BUR) Windsor, VT St. Francis of Assisi.
Vaillancourt, Robert C. '82 (PRT) Vocations; Special or Other Diocesan Assignment.
Vainavicz, Anthony C. '61 (GR) Diocesan Council of Catholic Women Retired.
Vakayil, Joseph Varghese '78 (CC) Pettus, TX Sacred Heart Mission.
Vakko, Justin *o.c.d.* '98 (ORL) Orlando, FL Holy Family.
Vakulskas, John A. '69 (SC) Ashton, IA St. Mary's Catholic Church; Sibley, IA St. Andrew's.
Vala, Thomas M. '09 (TR) Long Branch, NJ The Church of Christ the King, Long Branch, N.J.
Valachanath, Cyriac John '93 (SYM) Edinburg, TX Divine Mercy Syro–Malabar Catholic Church (Edinburg).
Valades, Reuben '70 (RC) Retired.
Valadez, Arturo '88 (LA) Pico Rivera, CA St. Francis Xavier.
Valainis, Vitolds '66 (DAV)[J] Iowa City, IA O'Keefe Hall; State University of Iowa Hospital.
Valan, Anthony S. *s.j.* '00 (OAK)[L] Berkeley, CA Jesuit Fathers and Brothers.
Valastro, Rev. Msgr. George J. '56 (NY) Middletown, NY St. Joseph Retired.
Valavanickal, Thomas *c.m.i.* '96 (NY) Scarsdale, NY Immaculate Heart of Mary.
Valayath, Jacob John '99 (CC) Agua Dulce, TX St. Frances of Rome.
Valayil, Bijoy Francis *o.praem.* '05 (SFE)[H] Albuquerque, NM Santa Maria de la Vid Priory; Belen, NM Our Lady of Belen.
Valcin, Fritzner '99 (COL)[K] Columbus, OH Haitian Catholic Coalition of Ohio; Haitian Catholic Coalition of Ohio; Columbus, OH St. Francis of Assisi.
Valdazo, Stephen '58 (BRK) Jackson Heights, NY St. Joan of Arc.
Valdepenas, Danilo '88 (SD) National City, CA Saint Mary Catholic Parish National City.
Valderrama, Viliulfo '96 (TUC) Tucson, AZ Our Lady of Fatima Roman Catholic Parish – Tucson; Nogales, AZ San Felipe de Jesus Roman Catholic Parish – Nogales.
Valdes, Juan Jose '91 (IND) Lanesville, IN St. Mary Catholic Church, Lanesville, Inc.
Valdez, Carlos Reynoso *o.r.c.* '96 (PCE) Adjuntas, PR St. Joachim.
Valdez, Carlos *o. carm.* '02 (JOL)[L] Darien Carmelite Provincial Office.
Valdez, John '91 (AMA) Hereford, TX St. Anthony's; Vicars Forane; Ex Officio; College of Consultors; Vocation Development Team.
Valdez, Jose Pedro '69 (LSC) Absent On Leave.
Valdez, Pat *c.r.* '75 (PBL) Cortez, CO St. Margaret Mary; Cortez, CO St. Rita; College of Consultors; Deans; Elected.
Valdez, Paul R. '82 (MRY) Marina, CA St. Jude Parish Community; Defenders of the Bond; Promoter of Justice; Administrative Committee Priests' Pension Plan; Finance Council; Insurance Committee; Vicar for Retired Priests.
Valdez, Pedro G. '98 (LA) Los Angeles, CA Our Lady of Victory.
Valdez, Rafael Padilla '03 (AUS) Bastrop, TX Ascension Catholic Church.
Valdez, Raul Adrain '04 (ORL) DeLand, FL St. Peter's Church.
Valdivia, Rev. Msgr. Adolfo '81 (SAT) San Antonio, TX Resurrection of the Lord.
Valdivia, Rev. Msgr. Antonio '63 (OAK) Pastoral Leadership Placement Board (PLPB) Retired.
Valdovinos, Francisco *s.t.* '94 (LA) Compton, CA Our Lady of Victory; Justice and Peace Commission Members 2011–2012.
Valega, John R. '98 (MIA) Key West, FL St. Mary Star of the Sea.
Valencheck, John A. '98 (CLV) Akron, OH St. Sebastian.
Valencia, Ariel A. '03 (RCK) Rockford, IL St. Rita.
Valencia, Braulio '87 (MRY) San Luis Obispo, CA San Luis Obispo.
Valencia, Carlos D. '85 (BRK) Released from Diocesan Assignment.
Valencia, Mario '10 (SR) Santa Rosa, CA St. Rose of Lima.
Valencia, Victor '93 (STP) Annandale, MN St. Ignatius.
Valenciano, Luis '77 (SD) Centinela State Prison.
Valenta, John G. '62 (STL)[O] St. Louis, MO Jesuit Community Corporation at Saint Louis University – Jesuit Hall.
Valente, Michael '58 (JOL) Joliet, IL St. Anthony Retired.
Valenti, Thomas J. '76 (ROC) On Duty Outside the Diocese.
Valenti, Thomas '76 (NY) Yonkers, NY St. John the Baptist.
Valentine, Charles R. '54 (TR) Freehold, NJ St. Robert Bellarmine Retired.
Valentine, Daniel A. '74 (PIT) Sewickley, PA St. James.
Valentine, Joseph *f.s.s.p.* '93 (JOL) Naperville, IL Sts. Peter and Paul.
Valentine, Keveny M. '73 (WDC) Hospital & Nursing Home Ministries.
Valentine, Lambert F. *o.f.m.* '43 (PAT)[N] Ringwood, NJ Holy Name Friary, Inc.
Valentine, Richard A. '74 (PRO) Georgiaville, RI St. Michael.
Valentine, Timothy S. *s.j.* '85 (MO) Army Chaplains.
Valentino, Francis P. *s.j.* '68 (NY)[DD] New York, NY Murray–Weigel Hall.
Valentino, Rev. Msgr. Frederick A. '50 (TR) Manasquan, NJ St. Denis Retired.
Valenton, Randy '06 (SJ) Palo Alto, CA St. Thomas Aquinas.
Valenzano, Rev. Msgr. Arthur F. '75 (BAL) Baltimore, MD Basilica of the National Shrine of the Assumption of the Blessed Virgin Mary.
Valenzuela, Rev. Msgr. Bayani '76 (NY) Goshen, NY St. John the Evangelist.
Valenzuela, James Paul '05 (PT) Pensacola, FL Nativity of Our Lord; Campus Ministry.
Valenzuela, Luciano '87 (SAC) Absent on Leave.
Valenzuela, Pablo '53 (SJN) San Juan, PR Corpus Christi.
Valenzuela, Ruben '06 (SD) El Centro, CA Our Lady of Guadalupe Catholic Parish El Centro.
Valera, Edmundo '02 (PBL) Grand Junction, CO St. Joseph.

Valera, Ramon G. '75 (LA) Northridge, CA Our Lady of Lourdes.
Valerio, Raymond A. '59 (MAR) Retired.
Valerio Romero, Luis '10 (CHI) Chicago, IL St. Jerome.
Valez, Victor Mauricio '08 (HON) Kihei, HI St. Theresa.
Valiquette, Hilaire *o.f.m.* '67 (SFE) Pena Blanca, NM Nuestra Senora De Guadalupe; [H] Albuquerque, NM The Province of Our Lady of Guadalupe.
Valit, Robert L. '61 (STP) Stillwater, MN St. Mary Retired.
Valiyakulathil, Jins *o.ss.t.* '10 (BAL)[Q] Assigned in India.
Valko, Rev. Msgr. George J. '77 (ALT) Retired.
Valla, Dominic J. '63 (HRT) Oxford, CT St. Thomas the Apostle.
Valladares, Alejandro E. '00 (MOB)[I] Mobile, AL Sacred Heart of Jesus Catholic Student Center at University of South Alabama; Vocations.
Vallamattam, Thomas *s.j.* '64 (BO)[U] Weston, MA Campion Jesuit Community.
Vallayil, Abraham *c.m.i.* '76 (NY) Blauvelt, NY St. Catharine.
Vallcaneras, Antonio *ss.cc.* (SJN) Bayamon, PR San Juan Bautista de la Salle.
Valle–Reyes, Tomas Del '79 (NY)[HH] New York, NY Descubriendo El Siglo XXI, Inc. (Discovering XXI Century Inc.).
Vallecorsa, Daniele '93 (PIT) Pittsburgh, PA St. Paul Cathedral; Pittsburgh, PA St. Regis; Chaplain to Latino Catholic Community.
Vallee, Robert '87 (MIA)[A] Miami, FL St. John Vianney College Seminary.
Vallejo, Amado '10 (FWT) Mansfield, TX St. Jude.
Vallejo, Rev. Msgr. Arquimedes '89 (RCK) Aurora, IL Sacred Heart; Special Assignment; Promoter of Justice; Hispanic Ministry Offices; Adjunct Judicial Vicar; Loves Park, IL St. Bridget; Defenders of the Bond.
Vallejo, Gilberto '02 (SAT) Archdiocesan Presbyteral Council; In Rural Area; Priests Personnel Board; Pleasanton, TX St. Andrew.
Vallejo, William '97 (RCK) Rochelle, IL St. Patrick.
Vallejof, Juan Diego *m.s.p.* '11 (LA) Los Angeles, CA Santa Isabel.
Vallelonga, J. Stephen '90 (WH) Weston, WV St. Patrick's.
Valleroy, Paul J. '74 (KNX) Chattanooga, TN St. Jude Retired.
Valleroy, Rickey J. '93 (STL) Farmington, MO St. Joseph.
Valley, John '60 (CLV) Retired.
Valley, Paul *s.p.* '64 (SFE)[L] Jemez Springs, NM Fitzgerald Charitable Trust; [L] Jemez Springs, NM EDSA Charitable Trust; [H] Jemez Springs, NM Our Lady of Lourdes.
Vallier, John F. '87 (GR) Grand Rapids, MI Holy Spirit.
Valliere, Timothy C. '91 (NOR) Absent on Leave.
Vallina, Rev. Msgr. Emilio '52 (MIA) Retired.
Valliparambil, Jose '83 (GF) Chinook, MT St. Gabriel.
Valliyamthadathil, Joseph *m.c.b.s.* '78 (DUL) Tower, MN St. Martin.
Vallone, Louis F. '73 (PIT) Crescent, PA St. Catherine of Siena; McKees Rocks, PA St. John of God; Clergy Personnel Board.
Valls, Richard '57 (KAL) Retired.
Valmonte, Arturo '93 (RNO) On Special Assignment; [B] Reno, NV Saint Mary's Regional Medical Center.
Valmorida, Mario '83 (SAC) Quincy, CA St. John; Westwood, CA Our Lady of the Snows.
Valomchalil, Augusty T. *m.s.s.c.c.* (HBG)[I] Gettysburg, PA Gettysburg College; Gettysburg, PA St. Joseph the Worker.
Valone, Fred W. '94 (GAL) Tomball, TX St. Anne; Northern Vicariate.
Valoret, Joseph '83 (MIA) Retired.
Vamos, Joseph E. '66 (GRY) Retired.
Vamos, Joseph L. '61 (TOL) Toledo, OH; Defenders of the Bond; Toledo, OH St. Stephen Retired.
Van Abel, John W. '72 (MIL) Retired.
Van Alstine, Mark N. '05 (SAV) Director of Vocations; Thomasville, GA St. Augustine.
Van Alstyne, Donald J. *m.i.c.* '81 (MO) Army Chaplains.
Van Alstyne, Donald *m.i.c.* '81 (SPR)[G] On Duty Outside of House.
Vanasse, Bernard '78 (FR)[E] Taunton, MA Marian Manor Inc.; [F] Fall River, MA Priests' Hostel.
Vanasse, Roman R. *o.praem.* '60 (GB)[J] De Pere, WI St. Norbert Abbey.
VanBeek, Alois '73 (MIL) Neosho, WI St. Mary; Rubicon, WI St. John.
Van Beek, Dennis E. '69 (MIL) Plymouth, WI St. John the Baptist; Elkhart Lake, WI St. Thomas Aquinas.
Van Bergen, Francis G. '56 (CLV) Retired.
Vance, Rev. Msgr. Charles P. '70 (PH) Lafayette Hill, PA St. Philip Neri.
Vance, Greg *s.j.* '98 (SPK)[D] Spokane, WA Gonzaga Preparatory School.
Vance, James L. '63 (SFE) Retired.
Vance, Rev. Msgr. Leslie A. '76 (SAT) Adjutant Judicial Vicar; [K] San Antonio, TX Casa De Padres Retired.
Van Cleve, Michael S. '01 (GAL) Houston, TX St. Jerome; [S] Houston, TX The Catholic Chaplain Corps.
Van Damme, Larry P. '93 (MAR) Marquette, MI St. Michael; [G] Marquette, MI Catholic Campus Ministry–Northern Michigan University; Consultors; St. Joseph Association; Executive Board.
Vandannoor, Joseph Augustine *m.s.t.* '81 (MAR) Rudyard, MI St. Joseph.
Vandeberg, Joseph '89 (SCL) Wheaton, MN Ave Maria; Chokio, MN St. Mary's.
van de Crommert, Paul H. '88 (NU) Olivia, MN St. Aloysius; College of Consultors; Priests' Council.
Vandegrift, J. Raymond *o.p.* '60 (WDC)[B] Washington, DC Dominican House of Studies.
Vandegrift, William S. '80 (CAM) Brigantine, NJ St. Thomas' Catholic Church, Brigantine, N.J.
Vandehey, Kelly '96 (P) Medford, OR Sacred Heart of Jesus; Adjutant Judicial Vicars; Judges; Personnel Board.
Vandehey, Scott A. '66 (P) Retired.
Van De Kreeke, William L. '63 (GB) Judges Retired.
Van Del, Curtis E. *s.j.* '65 (STL)[O] St. Louis, MO Jesuit Community Corporation at Saint Louis University – Jesuit Hall Retired.
Van De Loo, Willard J. '55 (GB) Retired.
Van De Moortell, Raymond (BO) Peabody, MA St. Adelaide; [A] Brighton, MA St. John Seminary.
Vandenakker, John A. *c.c.* '85 (GAL) Houston, TX Queen of Peace; [O] Houston, TX Companions of the Cross (Texas).
Vandenberg, Robert H. '58 (GB) Retired.
Vandenberg, Thomas L. '62 (SEA) College of Consultors; Presbyteral Council Retired.
Vanden Boogard, Steven J. *o.praem.* '88 (GB)[J] De Pere, WI St. Norbert Abbey.
VandenBossche, John V. *c.s.c.* '51 (FTW)[H] Notre Dame Congregation of Holy Cross, United States Province of Priests & Brothers.
Van Den Bussche, Hugo *o.m.i.* '53 (SAT)[L] San Antonio, TX.
Van den Eynde, Stephen *ss.cc.* '48 (HON)[D] Honolulu, HI St. Patrick's Monastery.
Vanden Hogen, Rev. Msgr. James '64 (GB) Retired.
Vanden Hogen, Paul '54 (GB) Retired.
Van De Paer, John *c.i.c.m.* '47 (PH) Parkesburg, PA Our Lady of Consolation.
Vander Heyden, William F. '70 (GB) Veterans Affairs Medical Center; On Duty Outside the Diocese; DEPARTMENT OF VETERANS AFFAIRS HOSPITALS AND CHAPLAINS.
Vanderholt, Rev. Msgr. James '57 (BEA) Silsbee, TX St. Mark the Evangelist Retired.
Vanderholt, Joseph *s.j.* '68 (SFE) Albuquerque, NM Immaculate Conception.
Vanderkolk, Peter J. '83 (LFT) Delphi, IN St. Joseph; Associate Judges; Associate Judges.
Vanderley, Louis *o.s.b.* '66 (OKL) Edmond, OK St. John the Baptist; [I] Shawnee, OK St. Gregory's Abbey.
Vanderlin, Philip *o.s.b.* '70 (BIS)[A] Richardton, ND Assumption Abbey.
Vanderlin, Philip *o.s.b.* '80 (FgM) Richardton, ND Assumption Abbey.
VanderLoop, Tony '03 (STP) Monticello, MN St. Henry.
Vander Ploeg, Jon '01 (STP) Ham Lake, MN Church of Saint Paul; [O] St. Paul, MN The Companions of Christ.
Vander Steeg, Mark P. '99 (GB) Appleton, WI St. Edward; Greenville, WI St. Mary.
Vanderweel, Richard L. *s.s.e.* '62 (BUR) Censor Librorum; [E] Colchester, VT Society of St. Edmund.
VanderWeyst, Peter '07 (SCL) Bertha, MN St. Joseph; Browerville, MN Christ the King; Clarissa, MN St. Joseph; Pastoral Council; Chokio, MN St. Mary's; Diocesan Priests Pension Plan Trustees.
Vander Woude, Thomas P. '92 (ARL) Gainesville, VA Holy Trinity.
Van Deuren, John H. '59 (GB) Luxemburg, WI St. Louis Retired.
Vandewalle, Matthew J. '00 (LIN) Colon, NE St. Joseph's; Advocates.
Van De Water, Richard '82 (LA) Pomona, CA St. Joseph.
Van Do, (Michael M.) Quang *c.m.c.* '93 (SPC)[F] Carthage, MO Congregation of the Mother Coredemptrix, United States Assumption Province.
VanDoan, Vincent '86 (MO) DEPARTMENT OF VETERANS AFFAIRS HOSPITALS AND CHAPLAINS; Milan, MI Immaculate Conception.
Van Dorn, James *o.f.m.conv.* '67 (STP)[M] Prior Lake, MN Franciscan Retreats; [J] Prior Lake, MN St. Joseph Cupertino Friary.
Van Dorpe, Raymond *c.m.* '82 (STL)[O] Earth City, MO Congregation of the Mission Western Province (Vincentians).
Van Durme, Patrick '00 (ROC) Military Chaplains; Army Chaplains.
Van Dyke, James R. *s.j.* '93 (NY)[E] New York, NY Xavier High School; [E] Bronx, NY Fordham Preparatory School.
VanDyke, James R. *s.j.* '93 (NY)[DD] Jesuit Community, Kohlmann Hall.
Van Dyke, Neil '98 (CHI) Stickney, IL St. Pius X Retired.
Vanecko, William E. '65 (CHI) Chicago, IL St. Columbanus Retired.
Vanegas, Albeyro *c.s.v.* '90 (CHI)[N] Arlington Heights Viatorian Province Center–Clerics of St. Viator.
Vanegas, Javier *sch.p.* '11 (NY) New York, NY Annunciation; [DD] New York, NY Calasanzian Fathers (Piarists).
Van Fossen, Brian F. '05 (SCR) Scranton, PA St. Paul's; Presbyteral Council.
Van Guilder, Alphonse *o.f.m.conv.* '64 (MRY) Pismo Beach, CA St. Paul the Apostle.
VanHaight, Christopher *o.f.m.* '08 (PAT) Paterson, NJ St. Bonaventure.
Van Haverbeke, Kenneth S. '91 (WCH)[G] Wichita, KS Spiritual Life Center; Ongoing Formation of the Clergy Committee; Retreats; Stewardship Office.
Van Hook, John E. *o.f.m.* '55 (ALB)[B] Siena College.
Van House, Joseph *o.cist.* '09 (DAL)[J] Irving, TX Cistercian Abbey of Our Lady of Dallas.
Vanin, Dino *p.i.m.e.* '72 (DET)[K] Detroit, MI P.I.M.E. Missionaries.
Vanissery, Matthew (SAC) Susanville, CA High Desert State Prison.
Vaniyepurackal, George (LAF) On Special Assignment.
Vankeirsbilck, Paul *e.c.* '90 (STU)[H] Bloomingdale, OH Holy Family Hermitage.
Van Kempen, Robert '93 (FTW) Bristol, IN St. Mary of the Annunciation.
Van Kuren, Corey S. '86 (SY)[T] Vestal, NY Binghamton University Newman Center; Binghamton, NY Binghamton General Hospital; Johnson City, NY Wilson Memorial Hospital.
Van Lai, Joseph Khuyen '74 (SD) Lakeside, CA Our Lady of Perpetual Help Catholic Parish Lakeside.
Van Leeuwen, Joseph *c.p.* '64 (FgM)[N] Chicago Passionist Provincial Office.
VanLente, Richard '66 (GR) Retired.
Van Liefde, Rev. Msgr. Christian M. '73 (LA) On Administrative Leave.
Van Loon, Rev. Msgr. Neil J. '79 (SCR) Laflin, PA St. Maria Goretti.
Van Massenhove, David L. '83 (SLC) Sandy, UT Saint Thomas More Catholic Church LLC 248.
Van Minh Pham, Bartholomew M. *c.m.c.* '77 (SPC)[F] Carthage, MO Congregation of the Mother Coredemptrix, United States Assumption Province.
Van Minh Pham, Bartholomew M. *c.m.c.* '77 (SPC)[I] Carthage, MO Shrine of Immaculate Heart of Mary.
Van Nguyen, James '08 (TLS) Tulsa, OK Holy Family Cathedral.
Van Nguyen, Joseph Son '82 (DAL) Carrollton, TX Sacred Heart of Jesus Christ.
Van Nguyen, Peter '60 (PMB) Boca Raton, FL Ascension; Lake Worth, FL Sacred Heart.
Van Nguyen, Thanh (HRT) Unassigned.
Van Nguyen, Tuyen '87 (ORG) Diocesan Finance Council.
Vannicola, Michael *o.s.f.s.* '06 (VEN) Naples, FL St. Ann.
Van Nquyen, Joseph Huyen '95 (SAC) Knights Landing, CA St. Paul.
Van Nuyen, Paul M. *c.m.c.* '06 (SPC)[F] Carthage, MO Congregation of the Mother Coredemptrix, United States Assumption Province.
Van Ommeren, Rev. Msgr. William '52 (SPK) Spokane, WA St. Joseph; [M] Spokane, WA Immaculate Heart Retreat Center; Defenders of the Bond Retired.
Vanoncini, Robert R. '63 (FRS) Dos Palos, CA Sacred Heart.
Vanorny, Ed '98 (RC) Rapid City, SD Cathedral of Our Lady of Perpetual Help.
Van Oss, James R. '64 (BEL) Retired.
Van Pham, Hanh '92 (CC) Corpus Christi, TX St. Philip The Apostle.
Van Pham, Phien '77 (SD) San Diego, CA Good Shepherd Catholic Parish.
Van Phuong, Rev. Msgr. Francis Pham '66 (ATL) Riverdale, GA Our Lady of Vietnam.
Vanrell, Bartolome '53 (SJN)[E] San Juan, PR Centro Medico de P.R.
vanRooyen, Pieter '10 (LAN) Lansing, MI St. Gerard.
Van Sloun, Michael '95 (STP) Anoka, MN St. Stephen; Deanery 12.
VanTassell, Malachi *t.o.r.* '04 (ALT)[A] Loretto, PA St. Francis University; [G] Loretto, PA St. Francis Friary at Mount Assisi.
Van Thanh, Louis '94 (ALB) Vietnamese Apostolate; Special Assignment.
Vanthu, Joseph N. '71 (SJ) Sunnyvale, CA Church of The Resurrection; [O] San Jose, CA Vietnamese Catholic Center; Special Assignment Retired.
Van Tran, Nhan *s.v.d.* '00 (DUB)[B] Epworth, IA Divine Word College.
Van Tran, Peter Nam '84 (NO) New Orleans, LA St. Joseph.
Van Tran, Tri '02 (JOL) Park Forest, IL St. Mary.
Van Vlaenderen, Leonard S. '88 (MIL) Retired.
Van Vliet, Charles *f.s.s.p.* (GAL) Houston, TX St. Elizabeth Ann Seton.

VanVurst, James *o.f.m.* '61 (CIN) Cincinnati, OH St. Clement.
Van Wiel, John E. *c.s.v.* '66 (CHI)[D] Arlington Heights, IL St. Viator High School; [N] Arlington Heights Viatorian Province Center–Clerics of St. Viator.
Van Winkle, Charles *c.s.c.* '78 (AUS)[G] Austin, TX Brother Andre Residence Retired.
Van Wormer, Giles *o.f.m.conv.* '57 (ALB)[L] Rensselaer, NY Provincialate, Immaculate Conception Friary – Order of Friars Minor Conventual.
Vanyo, Stephen *c.ss.r.* '62 (FgM) Baltimore Province.
Vanzillotta, Gino *o.m.* '54 (LA) Los Angeles, CA All Saints; [P] Los Angeles, CA Minim Fathers.
Vap, Rev. Msgr. Ivan F. '54 (LIN) Building Commission Retired.
Varano, Andrew R. '58 (BRK) Retired.
Varchese, Jimson *s.d.v.* (PAT) Paterson, NJ St. Michael the Archangel.
Varela, Jose *c.o.r.c.* '90 (SB) Corona, CA St. Edward; [I] Corona, CA Confraternity of Operarios Del Reino De Cristo, C.O.R.C.
Varela, Mariano O. '97 (WIN) Mankato, MN SS. Peter and Paul's; [J] Mankato, MN IVE Formation Program, Inc.
Varela–Nungaray, Enrique *o.carm.* '08 (JOL) Joliet, IL Mount Carmel.
Varettoni, Rev. Msgr. Julian B. '55 (PAT) Clifton, NJ Sacred Heart Retired.
Varga, Rev. Msgr. Andrew G. '78 (BGP) Westport, CT St. Luke; Diocesan Consultors.
Varga, Paul *o.f.m.conv.* '63 (TR) Point Pleasant Beach, NJ St. Peter's.
Varga, Wayne F. '74 (PAT) Montague, NJ St. James the Greater; Sandyston, NJ St. Thomas the Apostle.
Vargas, Alex J. '02 (PMB) Boynton Beach, FL St. Thomas More.
Vargas, Carlos '10 (ATL) Roswell, GA St. Andrew.
Vargas, Eric *s.v.d.* '75 (CHI)[N] Techny, IL Divine Word Residence.
Vargas, Gabriel '89 (SB) Chino, CA St. Margaret Mary.
Vargas, German *c.s.* (ORL) Winter Garden, FL Resurrection.
Vargas, John *c.ss.r.* '78 (DEN)[N] Denver The Redemptorists/Denver Province.
Vargas, Jose Carlos '92 (PCE) Guanica, PR St. Anthony Abbot.
Vargas, Juan Carlos '10 (NEW) Caldwell, NJ St. Aloysius; Assistant Directors.
Vargas, Lenin '06 (JKS) Pearl, MS St. Jude; Office of Vocations; Rankin County Prison; Mississippi State Hospital.
Vargas, Leonardo J. '85 (PHX) Bagdad, AZ St. Francis of Assisi Roman Catholic Parish; Yarnell, AZ St. Mary Mediatrix Mission, A Quasi Parish.
Vargas, Leonel M. '91 (ORG) Santa Ana, CA St. Joseph.
Vargas, Luis A. *t.o.r.* '98 (NEW) Newark, NJ Immaculate Heart of Mary.
Vargas, Luis A. Oyarzo *s.d.b.* '98 (MRY)[F] Watsonville, CA Saint Francis Salesian Community.
Vargas, Luis '98 (SJ) Mountain View, CA St. Joseph; College of Consultors.
Vargas, Luis '01 (WIN) Madelia, MN St. Mary; St. James, MN St. James.
Vargas–Grajales, David *o.s.a.* '02 (CHI) Chicago, IL St. Rita of Cascia.
Vargas Cruz, Gerardo A. *o.f.m.* '06 (SJN) Sabana Seca, PR San Jose Obrero.
Varghese, Abraham '03 (ALX) Marksville, LA St. Joseph's.
Varghese, Benny Mekkatt *c.f.i.c.* '04 (STP)[J] St. Paul, MN Congregation of the Sons of the Immaculate Conception; Minneapolis, MN Hennepin County Medical Center.
Varghese, Jacob *v.c.* '92 (COV) Union, KY St. Timothy.
Varghese, Josekutty '92 (HT) Priests Council; College of Consultors; Schriever, LA St. Lawrence.
Varghese, Joseph P. *v.c.* '70 (CAM) Cape May Court House, NJ The Church of Our Lady of the Angels, Cape May Court House, N.J.
Varghese, Mathew *m.s.t.* '05 (SYM) Coppell, TX St. Alphons Syro Malabar Catholic Church (Coppell).
Varghese, Peter *c.m.i.* '91 (BLX) Bassfield, MS St. Peter.
Varghese, Rejimon *s.v.d.* '02 (WDC)[O] Washington, DC Society of the Divine Word/Divine Word House.
Varghese, Shaji '94 (CC) Sinton, TX Our Lady of Guadalupe.
Varghese, Soju '03 (BRK) Ridgewood, NY Our Lady of the Miraculous Medal.
Varghese, Thunkuchan Steve *s.a.c.* (MIL)[P] Milwaukee, WI Pallotti House; South Milwaukee, WI Divine Mercy.
Varghese, TJ '95 (PRO) Chepachet, RI St. Eugene.
Varghse, Shaji (Joseph) *c.c.* '99 (SAT) Kenedy, TX Texas State Prison System–Connley Unit.
Vargo, Robert B. '89 (HRT) Poquonock, CT St. Joseph's; Special and other Archdiocesan Assignment; Judicial Vicar (Officialis).
Varickamackal, Joseph '77 (AUS) La Grange, TX Sacred Heart of Jesus.
Varkey, George *m.s.t.* '90 (SP) New Port Richey, FL St. Thomas Aquinas.
Varkey, Matthew '96 (CHI)[J] Elk Grove Village, IL Alexian Brothers Medical Center.
Varner, Rick M. '10 (SAG) Essexville, MI St. John the Evangelist; Bay City, MI St. Joseph.
Varno, John '66 (ALB) Ballston Lake, NY Our Lady of Grace Retired.
Varo, Jose Luis '56 (FRS) Visalia, CA St. Thomas the Apostle; Visalia, CA Holy Family; Visalia, CA St. Mary Retired.
Varone, Normand G. '75 (SPC) Diocesan Development Fund; Priests' Mutual Benefit Society Retired.
Varsanyi, Rev. Msgr. William I. '52 (NY)[HH] New York, NY Hungarian Catholic League of America, Inc.
Varsanyi, Rev. Msgr. William I. '46 (ATH) Providence, RI Our Lady of Charity; [L] Pawtucket, RI Jeanne Jugan Residence; Hungarian Catholic League of America, Inc.; Delegate for Canonical Affairs; Promoter of Justice; Propagation of the Faith; Catholic Relief Services; Holy Childhood Association.
Vartzelis, George D. '53 (BO) Senior Priests. Retired.
Varuvel, Paul L. '72 (BUF)[A] East Aurora, NY Christ the King Seminary.
Vas, Joseph S. '79 (OKL) Retired.
Vas, Laszlo (PAT) Passaic, NJ St. Stephen's.
Vasek, Craig J. '10 (CR) Bemidji, MN St. Philip's.
Vasek, Stephen *o.m.i.* '71 (BUF) Buffalo, NY Holy Angels.
Vashon, Rev. Msgr. Randall J. '00 (MET) Clinton, NJ Immaculate Conception; Office of Vocations; Board for Seminary Education.
Vasile, Louis A. '72 (ROC) Auburn, NY St. Alphonsus.
Vaske, Philip '06 (CHY) Kemmerer, WY St. Patrick's.
Vasko, Rev. Msgr. Christopher P. '83 (TOL) Assessors; Toledo, OH Historic Church of Saint Patrick; Toledo, OH St. Martin de Porres; Priests' Council; Judicial Vicar; Members.
Vasko, Peter *o.f.m.* '87 (FgM) Washington, DC COMMISSARIAT OF THE HOLY LAND.
Vaskov, Nicholas '09 (PIT)[P] Pittsburgh, PA Art Institute of Pittsburgh; [P] Pittsburgh, PA Point Park College.
Vasquez, Alejandro Medina *m.s.p.* (CHI) Chicago, IL Queen of the Universe.
Vasquez, James '06 (CC) On Duty Outside the Diocese.
Vasquez, James '06 (DAL)[A] Irving, TX Holy Trinity Seminary.
Vasquez, Julio '95 (NY) Yonkers, NY St. Peter.
Vasquez, Oscar *s.m.* '05 (STL)[O] Saint Louis, MO Chaminade Community.
Vasquez, Paul L. '98 (OM) Omaha, NE St. Cecilia Cathedral.
Vasquez, Pedro *o.f.m.* '71 (LA)[P] Santa Barbara, CA Franciscan Friary, Order of Friars Minor (Old Mission).
Vasquez, Pedro *o.f.m.* (OAK)[L] Oakland, CA Franciscan Friars of California, (Province of St. Barbara).
Vasquez, Perfecto L. '98 (RCK) Virgil, IL SS. Peter and Paul.
Vasquez, Rev. Msgr. Perfecto '59 (BRK) Woodside, NY St. Teresa.
Vasquez, Rodolfo D. '03 (CC) Corpus Christi, TX Saint John the Baptist.
Vasquez–Rubio, Juan *o.ss.t.* '99 (BAL)[Q] In Residence – Holy Trinity Monastery Baltimore.
Vass, Robert *s.d.v.* (PAT) Paterson, NJ St. Gerard Majella; Paterson, NJ St. Michael the Archangel.
Vassalotti, Thomas F. '07 (BRK) Assignment Board.
Vassar, Paul R. '71 (OAK) San Leandro, CA St. Leander.
Vater, Robert L. '45 (COV) Retired.
Vath, William R. '72 (LFT) Defender of the Bond; Lafayette, IN St. Boniface; Special Assignment; Defenders of the Bond.
Vathalloor, Joseph *c.m.i.* '74 (SAN) Eldorado, TX Our Lady of Guadalupe.
Vathappallil, Sojan *m.c.b.s.* '01 (SYM) West Allis, WI St. Antony Syro–Malabar Catholic Mission (Wisconsin).
Vathappallil, Thomas *m.c.b.s.* '01 (MIL)[P] Kenosha, WI Missionary Congregation of the Blessed Sacrament, Inc., Zion Province; West Allis, WI St. Aloysius Gonzaga; West Allis, WI Immaculate Heart of Mary; West Allis, WI Mary, Queen of Heaven.
Vathyiakaril–Eapen, Philip *c.m.i.* '87 (HT) Thibodaux Regional Medical Center; Thibodaux, LA St. Genevieve.
Vattakudiyil, Francis P. '63 (RVC) Kings Park, NY St. Joseph's.
Vattakunnel, James C. '88 (BGP) Wilton, CT Our Lady of Fatima.
Vattakunnel, Jose '90 (LKC) Oakdale, LA Sacred Heart; [D] Oakdale, LA Herald of Good News, Inc.
Vattapara Devasia, George *m.s.f.s.* '95 (GAL) The Woodlands, TX St. Anthony of Padua.
Vattappara, George *m.s.f.s.* '95 (TYL)[C] Whitehouse, TX The Missionaries of St. Francis de Sales.
Vatter, Joseph E. '78 (BUF) Lockport, NY All Saints.
Vaudreuil, Paul *a.a.* '64 (WOR)[N] Worcester, MA Assumptionists (Augustinians of the Assumption).
Vaughan, Rev. Msgr. Gregory D. '72 (TR)[N] Trenton, NJ Villa Vianney; Episcopal Council; Vicar General and Moderator of the Curia; Diocesan Finance Council; Ministry of Vocations.
Vaughan, James '50 (ALB) Troy, NY Sacred Heart Retired.
Vaughan, Rev. Msgr. John J. '67 (MIA) Miami Beach, FL St. Patrick.
Vaughan, John R. '74 (OWN) Owensboro, KY St. Stephen Cathedral; Judges.
Vaughan, Michael '04 (SAC) Sacramento, CA St. Joseph's.
Vaughan, Thomas *s.s.c.* '56 (OM)[J] St. Columbans Missionary Society of St. Columban Retired.
Vaughey, Rev. Msgr. James K. '65 (NY) Briarcliff Manor, NY St. Theresa; Trustees of St. Patrick's Cathedral in the City of New York, Inc.
Vaughn, John *o.f.m.* '55 (LA)[BB] Santa Barbara, CA The Cause of Blessed Junipero Serra; [P] Santa Barbara, CA Franciscan Friary, Order of Friars Minor (Old Mission).
Vaughn, Mason '50 (SAG) Retired.
Vaughn, Richard P. *s.j.* '50 (SJ)[M] Los Gatos, CA Sacred Heart Jesuit Center.
Vaughn, Robert William *o.p.* '71 (NY)[DD] New York St. Vincent Ferrer Priory.
Vaughn, Roland G. '71 (LKC) Fenton, LA St. Charles Borromeo.
Vaught, Michael '73 (OKL) Purcell, OK Our Lady of Victory.
Vavasseur, Henry C. '58 (BR) Retired.
Vaverek, Gavin N. '90 (TYL) Longview, TX St. Mary; College of Consultors; Defender of the Bond; Diocesan Building Board; Priests' Pension Board; Presbyteral Council; Diocesan Council of Catholic Women; Respect Life Program; Diocesan Implementation Committee On Ethics and Integrity Policy for Church Personnel; Diocesan Liturgical Commission; Victim Assistance Coordinator; Diocesan Christian Initiation Team.
Vaverek, Hayden J. '94 (MO) Air Force Reserve Chaplains.
Vaverek, Hayden J. '94 (NY) New York, NY St. Joseph.
Vaverek, Timothy V. '85 (AUS) Gatesville, TX Our Lady of Lourdes Catholic Church – Gatesville, Texas; Hamilton, TX St. Thomas Catholic Church – Hamilton, Texas; Gatesville, TX Texas Department of Criminal Justice; Presbyteral Council.
Vavonese, Charles S. '73 (SY) Special Assignment; Formation for Ministry and Liturgy; Public Policy; DeWitt, NY Holy Cross; Syracuse, NY St. Daniel.
Vavrak, Martin '03 (PSC) Perth Amboy, NJ St. Michael; Perth Amboy, NJ St. Nicholas.
Vavrick, Eugene B. '93 (TR) Wayside, NJ St. Anselm.
Vavrina, Kenneth P. '62 (OM) Retired.
Vayalikarottu, Antony (MCE) Elected Members; Priests – Heads of Apostolates; Malankara Catholic Children's League; Margate, FL St. Mary's Malankara Catholic Church.
Vaz, Gregorio Dafonte (CGS) Cayey, PR Nuestra Senora de la Merced.
Vaz, Richard *s.v.d.* '78 (CHI)[N] Techny, IL Divine Word Residence; [T] Techny, IL Divine Word Missionaries, Inc.
Vazhappilly, Antony *s.d.b.* '82 (OAK) Fremont, CA St. James The Apostle.
Vazhappilly, Mathew *c.m.i.* '74 (SFS) Scotland, SD St. George.
Vazneparambil, Thomas '69 (LUB) Retired.
Vazquez, Adrian '08 (B) Caldwell, ID Our Lady of the Valley.
Vazquez, Albert *c.m.f.* '55 (FRS) Fresno, CA St. Anthony Claret.
Vazquez, Antonio Jose (SJN)[E] Rio Piedras, PR Hospital del Maestro.
Vazquez, Carlos J. (CGS) Caguas, PR Nuestra Senora del Perpetuo Socorro.
Vazquez, Hector '08 (ORL)[G] Orlando, FL Catholic Campus Ministry at the University of Central Florida.
Vazquez, Jose Luis '87 (MAD) Madison, WI Cathedral Parish of St. Raphael.
Vazquez, Jose '08 (BLX) Hattiesburg, MS Sacred Heart.
Vazquez, Luis A. '91 (ARE) Vega–Baja, PR Perpetuo Socorro; Police Chaplain.
Vazquez, Manuel *m.sp.s.* '76 (LA) Huntington Park, CA St. Martha.
Vazquez, Rev. Msgr. Perfecto '56 (BRK) Retired.
Vazquez, Raymundo Chavez '00 (AUS) Bryan, TX Santa Teresa.
Vazquez, Tomas (YAK) Ellensburg, WA St. Andrew's.
Vazquez–Martinez, Jose Alberto '02 (MRY) Salinas, CA St. Mary of the Nativity.
Vazquez–Rubio, Juan *o.ss.t.* (BAL) Baltimore, MD St. Gabriel; Baltimore, MD St. Clare.
Vazquez–Vega, Edwin '95 (PCE) Juana Diaz, PR Nuestra Senora de Lourdes.
Vazquez Colon, Antonio Jose '90 (SJN)[E] San Juan, PR Centro Medico de P.R.
Vazquez Colon, Rev. Msgr. Antonio Jose '90 (SJN) Santurce, PR Ashford Presbyterian Community Hospital; Condado, San Juan, PR Stella Maris.

Vead, Victor P. '92 (ALX) On Duty Outside the Diocese.
Vebelun, Edward *o.s.b.* '04 (SCL)[I] Collegeville St. John's Abbey, of the Order of St. Benedict.
Vecchiato, Rinaldo *c.s.* '67 (BO) Framingham, MA St. Tarcisius.
Vecchio, Egidio *m.s.* '55 (LKC) Sulphur, LA Our Lady of Prompt Succor Retired.
Vecchio, Michael J. '50 (PIT) Retired.
Veda, Raphael '08 (CHI)[N] Chicago, IL Institute of Christ the King Sovereign Priest.
Veeneman, Dismas J. *o.f.m.conv.* '69 (L) Louisville, KY St. Paul.
Vega, Aglayde Rafael '06 (BWN) Board Members; Lyford, TX Prince of Peace.
Vega, Carlos '89 (MIA) Sunrise, FL St. Bernard.
Vega, Cesar '04 (YAK) Presbyteral Council Executive Committee.
Vega, Donald M. *s.j.* '65 (SJN) San Juan, PR San Ignacio de Loyola; [H] San Juan, PR Comunidad Jesuita.
Vega, Erasmo Rodriguez '72 (ELP) El Paso, TX Our Lady of Guadalupe.
Vega, Fernando *c.m.f.* '40 (LA)[V] Rancho Dominguez, CA Dominguez Seminary Inc. Retired.
Vega, Hector R. *i.sch.* '74 (CC)[I] Corpus Christi, TX Secular Institute of the Schoenstatt Fathers.
Vega, Hector R. *c.c.* '74 (MIL)[T] Waukesha, WI Secular Institute of Schoenstatt Fathers.
Vega, Hector *i.s.p.* (AUS) Austin, TX St. Paul.
Vega, Jose Antonio *s.j.* '00 (FgM) St. Louis, MO Society of Jesus.
Vega, Jose L. *o.m.* '69 (LA) Los Angeles, CA All Saints; [P] Los Angeles, CA Minim Fathers.
Vega, Jose Luis '54 (FRS) Retired.
Vega, Raymond *s.c.j.* '73 (SP)[N] Pinellas Park, FL Priests of the Sacred Heart Retired.
Vega, Richard '83 (LA) Chicago, IL The National Federation of Priests' Councils (1968); On Duty Outside the Archdiocese.
Vega, Richard (CHI) Evanston, IL St. Nicholas.
Vega, Roberto '87 (ARE) Vega-Alta, PR Immaculate Conception of Blessed Virgin Mary; Priest's Senate (Consejo Presbiteral).
Vega-Alvarenga, Salvador '01 (LR) Texarkana, AR St. Edward.
Veigas, Albert '80 (CLV) Elyria, OH St. Agnes.
Veik, Alan D. *o.f.m.cap.* '67 (MIL)[Y] Milwaukee, WI House of Peace; Sheboygan, WI St. Dominic.
Veit, David J. '98 (JC) Macon, MO Immaculate Conception; Priestly and Religious Vocations Committee.
Veith, William E. '70 (CHI)[J] Elk Grove Village, IL Alexian Brothers Medical Center.
Vela, Edison '91 (DAL) Dallas, TX St. Edward.
Vela, Fabian '56 (MRY) Retired.
Vela, Jesus *o.f.m.cap.* '98 (LA) Los Angeles, CA St. Lawrence of Brindisi; Definitors.
Vela, Rudy *s.m.* '84 (SAT)[L] San Antonio, TX Ligustrum Marianist Community; [C] San Antonio, TX St. Mary's University of San Antonio, Texas.
Velas, Vincent P. '64 (PIT) McKeesport, PA St. Patrick.
Velasco, Arturo '86 (LA) Canoga Park, CA Our Lady of the Valley.
Velasco, Fernando Rogelio '00 (SFR) Half Moon Bay, CA Our Lady of the Pillar.
Velasquez, Bernardo (PAT) Passaic, NJ Our Lady of Fatima; Passaic, NJ Holy Trinity.
Velasquez, Marcos '89 (TUC) Maricopa, AZ Our Lady of Grace Roman Catholic Parish – Maricopa.
Velasquez, Mayhel A. '11 (NEW) Belleville, NJ St. Peter's.
Velazquez, Carlos B. '90 (SAT) San Antonio, TX Holy Spirit.
Velazquez, Francisco '90 (SAC) Woodland, CA Holy Rosary.
Velazquez, Paul '06 (LA) Moorpark, CA Holy Cross.
Velazquez, Rafael '06 (NEW) Plainfield, NJ St. Mary.
Velazquez, Yamil A. '05 (CGS) Aibonito, PR Church of St. Joseph; Priests Senate.
Velez, Carlos '00 (CR) East Grand Forks, MN Sacred Heart.
Velez, Carlos (B) On Duty Outside the Diocese.
Velez, James '98 (SFR)[R] San Francisco, CA Prelature of the Holy Cross and Opus Dei.
Velez, Juan R. (POD) San Francisco.
Velez, Victor Sanchez '91 (ARE)[A] Arecibo, PR Seminario de Jesus Maestro; Priest's Senate (Consejo Presbiteral).
Velez-Cardona, Miguel '08 (KNX) Knoxville, TN All Saints Catholic Church.
Velez Lopez, Jorge Antonio '89 (ALX) Alexandria, LA St. Frances Xavier Cabrini.
Velickakathu, Varkey (LC) Fairchild, WI St. John Cantius; Fairchild, WI St. Joseph; Neillsville, WI St. Mary.
Vella, Rev. Msgr. Desmond J. '59 (NY) New York, NY Immaculate Conception; Judges.
Vella, Rev. Msgr. Desmond (NEW) Defenders of the Bond.
Vella, Joseph '68 (BRK) Brooklyn, NY St. Mark.
Vellankal, Mathew '87 (OAK) Fremont, CA Holy Spirit.
Vellaplackil, George (HRT) Windsor Locks, CT St. Robert Bellarmine; Windsor Locks, CT St. Mary.
Vellappallil, Thomas *m.s.* '94 (HRT)[L] Hartford, CT North American La Salette Mission Center; [U] Hartford, CT North American La Salette Mission Center, Inc.; Hartford, CT Missionaries of Our Lady of La Salette.
Vellappallil, Thomas *m.s.* '94 (STL)[O] Saint Louis, MO North American La Salette Mission Center.
Vellaramparampil, Aaron T. '71 (RVC) Seaford, NY St. James.
Vellardita, Guy *o.f.m.* '58 (FgM) New York, NY Franciscan Province of the Immaculate Conception.
Vellenga, R. Stephen '81 (CLV) Painesville, OH St. Mary; [V] Painesville, OH St. Mary's – Painesville; Mission Office, Society for the Propagation of the Faith; Cleveland, OH Cathedral Square Plaza.
Vellooratil, George '78 (CHI) Forest Park, IL St. Bernardine.
Velo, Rev. Msgr. Kenneth '70 (CHI) Rosemont, IL Our Lady of Hope.
Velten, Robert *o.s.b.* '54 (SP)[N] Saint Leo, FL St. Leo Abbey.
Veltri, Dennis J. '93 (E) Guys Mills, PA St. Hippolyte.
Veltrie, James V. *s.j.* '65 (STL)[C] Saint Louis University; [O] St. Louis, MO Jesuit Community Corporation at Saint Louis University – Jesuit Hall.
Veluz, Edward T. (NEW) Jersey City, NJ St. Anne's.
Vences, Marco Antonio *s.s.p.* '06 (LA) Los Angeles, CA; [P] Los Angeles, CA The Society of St. Paul.
Vendetti, Michael A. '64 (BRK) Retired.
Venditti, J. Michael '87 (MET) On Duty Outside the Diocese; Allentown, PA St. Michael.
Vendramin, Aldo *c.s.* '75 (CHI)[N] Oak Park, IL Scalabrini Development Office.
Venegas, Rafael '07 (LA) Santa Monica, CA St. Anne.
Veneklase, George L. *o.c.d.* '93 (MAR) Caspian, MI St. Cecilia; Iron River, MI St. Agnes.
Veneroso, Joseph R. *m.m.* '74 (BRK) Flushing, NY St. Paul Chong Ha-Sang Roman Catholic Chapel.
Veneroso, Joseph R. *m.m.* '78 (NY)[DD] Maryknoll Maryknoll Fathers and Brothers.
Venette, Howard *f.s.s.p.* (ATL) Mableton, GA St. Francis de Sales.
Venezia, Arthur '71 (PMB) North Palm Beach, FL St. Paul of the Cross.
Vengayil, Thomas '59 (PMB) Tequesta, FL St. Jude.
Venker, Josef V. *s.j.* '87 (SEA)[A] Seattle, WA Seattle University; [M] Seattle, WA Arrupe Jesuit Community at Seattle University.
Venne, R. Thomas '62 (MIL) Milwaukee, WI Cathedral of St. John the Evangelist Retired.
Venne, Samuel J. '78 (BUF) Awaiting Assignment.
Venner, Jonathan '11 (SFS) Sioux Falls, SD Holy Spirit.
Venneri, Michael D. '82 (SPK) Special Ministry; [F] Spokane, WA Providence Sacred Heart Medical Center & Children's Hospital (Providence Health & Services-Washington).
Vennetti, Robert C. *m.i.c.* '06 (MO) DEPARTMENT OF VETERANS AFFAIRS HOSPITALS AND CHAPLAINS.
Vennetti, Robert *m.i.c.* '06 (SPR)[G] Stockbridge, MA Congregation of Marian Fathers of The Immaculate Conception of the Most Blessed Virgin Mary.
Venni, Sebastian (LC) Ettrick, WI St. Ansgar; Ettrick, WI St. Bridget.
Vennitti, Thomas A. '73 (STU) Toronto, OH St. Francis of Assisi; Toronto, OH St. Joseph's.
Vennix, James J. '56 (GB) Retired.
Venters, Darrell '89 (OWN) Fancy Farm, KY St. Jerome; Vicar of Clergy; Vicar of Clergy; Priest Personnel Committee; Consultors; Priests' Council.
Ventiquattro, Jude '88 (ALT)[G] Loretto, PA St. Francis Friary at Mount Assisi.
Ventura, Anthony C. '78 (HRT) Retired.
Ventura, Gennaro J. '43 (ROC) Retired.
Ventura, Octavio *l.c.* '96 (SAC).
Ventura, Raul *s.t.* (PT)[E] Tallahassee, FL Missionary Servants of the Most Holy Trinity.
Ventura, William N. '06 (BO) Unassigned.
Venturini, Fabio '02 (NEW) On Duty Outside the Archdiocese.
Venvertloh, Kenneth J. '67 (SFD) Retired.
Venza, Felix F. '72 (TR) Bordentown, NJ St. Mary.
Venzor, Jesse C. '80 (FRS) Woodlake, CA St. Frances Cabrini.
Ver, Alex '67 (NEW) Jersey City, NJ St. Nicholas.
Ver'Schneider, Neil L. *s.j.* '66 (PH)[H] Philadelphia, PA The Gesu School; [Y] Philadelphia, PA Jesuit Community, Arrupe House; [Y] Philadelphia, PA Gesu School Jesuit Community and Outreach Center (S.J.).
Vera, Francisco (POD) Houston.
Vera, Francisco '07 (GAL)[N] Houston, TX Opus Dei.
Vera, Jude '89 (SP) Tampa, FL St. Mary.
Vera, Luis A. *o.s.a.* '97 (CHI)[N] Chicago, IL St. Augustine Friary.
Vera, Roberto '01 (MRY) Paso Robles, CA St. Rose; Vocations Board; Presbyteral Council; Diocesan Consultors; Diocesan Consultors.
Vera, Romulo E. *c.s.c.* '89 (FTW)[H] Notre Dame Congregation of Holy Cross, United States Province of Priests & Brothers.
Vera, Vicente Antonio '85 (TOL) Toledo, OH St. Patrick of Heatherdowns.
Vera-Perez, Jose *o.f.m.* '78 (ELP)[B] El Paso, TX Roger Bacon College.
Vera Gonzalez, P. Julio A. (PCE)[B] The Pontifical Catholic University of Puerto Rico.
Veras, Richard '96 (NY) Staten Island, NY St. Rita.
Verber, Thomas *o.s.a.* '99 (OAK) Castro Valley, CA Our Lady of Grace.
Verberg, Richard R. '71 (MIL) Retired.
Verbest, Stephen *o.c.s.o.* '98 (DUB)[K] Peosta, IA New Melleray Abbey, Order of Cistercians of the Strict Observance; Peosta, IA.
Verboomen, Willy *c.i.c.m.* '63 (SAT)[K] San Antonio, TX Padua Place Retired.
Verbryke, William *s.j.* (CIN)[N] Cincinnati, OH Jesuit Community at Xavier University.
Vercellone, Anthony '80 (RNO) Reno, NV Our Lady of the Snows; Diocesan Board of Consultors; Lists of Deans; Presbyteral Council; Priest Personnel Board.
Verdelotti, Anthony W. '86 (PRO) Cranston, RI St. Mark; Cemeteries.
Verdelotti, James J. '78 (PRO) Cranston, RI St. Mary; Deans.
Verdi, Ralph *c.pp.s.* '71 (CIN)[N] Carthagena, OH St. Charles.
Verdia Nay, Carlos '85 (SJN) San Juan, PR Ntra. Sra. de la Medalla Milagrosa.
Verdick, Jerome F. '58 (WIN) Retired.
Verdun, Gerald J. '72 (PEO) Delavan, IL St. Mary's.
Verduzco-Peregrino, Marlon M. '00 (SFR) San Mateo, CA St. Timothy.
Vereb, Jerome *c.p.* '72 (PIT)[M] Pittsburgh, PA St. Paul of the Cross Monastery.
VerEecke, Robert F. *s.j.* '78 (BO) Newton, MA St. Ignatius Loyola; [U] Newton, MA The Jesuit Community at Boston College.
Verespy, Joseph D. '79 (SCR) Dupont, PA Sacred Heart of Jesus.
Vergara, Arlon *o.s.a.* (SAC) Yuba City, CA St. Isidore.
Vergara, Armando '73 (STO) Hughson, CA St. Anthony Church of Hughson (Pastor of); Personnel Board.
Vergara, Heriberto (STA) Jacksonville, FL San Jose.
Verhagen, Norbert M. *m.m.* '39 (NY)[DD] Retired.
Verhalen, Charles J. '47 (MIL)[W] Lomira, WI Legion of Mary Retired.
Verhalen, David H. *c.s.c.* '54 (FTW)[H] Notre Dame Congregation of Holy Cross, United States Province of Priests & Brothers.
Verhalen, Peter *o.cist.* '81 (DAL)[D] Irving, TX Cistercian Preparatory School; [J] Irving, TX Cistercian Abbey of Our Lady of Dallas; Irving, TX.
Verheggen, Peter A. *o.f.m.* '49 (LSC) Tularosa, NM St. Francis de Paula.
Verhelst, Steven J. '90 (NU) Willmar, MN St. Mary; College of Consultors; Spicer, MN Our Lady of the Lakes; Kandiyohi, MN St. Patrick; Kandiyohi, MN St. Thomas More; Board of Trustees for Pension Plan for Priests; Priests' Council.
Verhoff, Melvin T. '91 (TOL) Delphos, OH St. John the Evangelist; Delphos, OH St. John the Baptist.
Verhoye, Gerard A. '49 (PEO) Retired.
Verley, Jude *o.s.c.* '79 (SCL) Hillman, MN St. Rita's; Onamia, MN The Church of the Holy Cross of Onamia; Wahkon, MN Sacred Heart; Onamia, MN St. Therese; [I] Onamia, MN Crosier Priory.
Vernon, William F. '97 (MAD) Verona, WI St. Christopher Parish.
Verona, Adam M. '11 (PIT) Graduate Studies.
Veronesi, Giulio *c.r.s.* '75 (GAL) Houston, TX Christ the King.
Verrengio, Rocco F. '70 (BRK) Retired.
Verrier, John M. '95 (PEO) Brimfield, IL St. Joseph's.
Verrill, O. Wendell '63 (BO) Senior Priests. Retired.
Verrilli, William F. '79 (BGP) Bridgeport, CT St. Andrew; Judges.
Verruni, Samuel A. '86 (PH) Norwood, PA St. Gabriel.
Verschaeve, C. Michael '77 (DET) Lake Orion, MI St. Joseph.
Verstreken, Alfred *c.j.* '73 (LA) Santa Barbara, CA Holy Cross.
Verzosa, Rev. Msgr. Antonio (STV) Charlotte Amalie, VI Cathedral of Sts. Peter and Paul.
Vesbit, Thomas '64 (GR) Retired.
Vesely, James J. '54 (CLV) Cleveland, OH St. Leo the Great; Brooklyn, OH St. Thomas More Retired.
Vesey, John E. *m.m.* '68 (FgM) Released from Diocesan Assignment; Maryknoll, NY MARYKNOLL.
Vesga, Mario '62 (SD) Chula Vista, CA Saint Rose of Lima Catholic Parish Retired.
Vessels, John L. *s.j.* '57 (ELP)[J] El Paso, TX Our Lady's Youth Center; El Paso, TX Sacred Heart.
Vetrano, Michael A. '79 (RVC) West Islip, NY Our Lady of Lourdes; Procurator & Advocates; Presbyteral Council.
Vetter, Austin '93 (BIS) Minot, ND St. Leo; Continuing Education for Clergy.
Vetter, Joseph G. '73 (R) Diocesan Consultors; Council of Priests; Wrightsville Beach, NC St. Therese.

Vetter, Rev. Msgr. Wendelyn '60 (FAR) Judges; Advocates Retired.
Vettese, Donald *s.j.* '82 (DET)[K] Detroit Detroit Province of the Society of Jesus–Provincial Office.
Vettickal, Sebastian *c.m.i.* '91 (LA) Diamond Bar, CA St. Denis.
Vettiyolil, Abraham (NY) Pelham Manor, NY Our Lady of Perpetual Help.
Vettuvelil, Stephen J. '96 (SYM) Fort Lauderdale, FL St. Jude Syro–Malabar Knanaya Catholic Mission of South Florida.
Vevik, Paul '77 (SPK) Spokane, WA Mary Queen.
Vezla, Edward *c.ss.r.* '78 (MIL)[S] Oconomowoc, WI The Redemptorist Retreat Center.
Via, Anthony P. *s.j.* '62 (SPK)[B] Spokane, WA Gonzaga University.
Viall, James A. '54 (CLV) Administrative Leave.
Viall, John L. '59 (CLV) North Royalton, OH St. Albert the Great Retired.
Vialpando, Kenneth L. '91 (SLC) Priests' Personnel Board; Ogden, UT Saint Joseph LLC 230; [C] Ogden, UT St. Joseph Catholic Elementary School; Deans; Team; Board of Directors.
Vicari, Marc A. '97 (NEW) Upper Montclair, NJ St. Cassian; Family Life Ministries; Presbyteral Council; Vicar for Family Life; Members.
Vicedo, Hermenegildo '63 (SJN) San Juan, PR Nuestra Senora de la Providencia.
Vicente, Francisco V. *o.p.* '55 (OAK) Promoter of Justice; Antioch, CA Most Holy Rosary.
Vicente, Isidore V. *o.p.* '64 (GAL) Houston, TX Holy Rosary.
Vicente, Julio '08 (B) Lewiston, ID All Saints Catholic Parish – St. James Church; College of Consultors; Lewiston, ID All Saints Catholic Parish – Our Lady of Lourdes Church; Lewiston, ID All Saints Catholic Parish – St. Stanislaus Church.
Vicentini, Joseph *c.s.* '55 (KC) Kansas City, MO Holy Rosary.
Vichich, Michael T. '74 (MAR) Spalding, MI St. John Neumann; Nadeau, MI St. Bruno.
Vicini, Andrea *s.j.* '96 (BO)[U] Newton, MA The Jesuit Community at Boston College.
Vick, James L. '99 (KNX) Chattanooga, TN Our Lady of Perpetual Help.
Vickery, Richard F. '48 (MAN) Retired.
Victor, P. R. '88 (CC) Kingsville, TX St. Martin.
Victor, Ronald J. '78 (DET) Roseville, MI St. Athanasius.
Victoria, John J. '08 (SCR) Wilkes–Barre, PA St. Nicholas.
Victoria, Jose H. (NEW) Assistant Directors.
Victoria, Robert '91 (LA) El Segundo, CA St. Anthony.
Victoria–Tovar, Jose Helber '07 (NEW) Wyckoff, NJ St. Elizabeth.
Victorino, Florentino *m.s.c.* '01 (LA) Cudahy, CA Sagrado Corazon y Santa Maria de Guadalupe.
Vida, Rev. Msgr. George N. '57 (HPM) Anaheim, CA Annunciation; Building and Sacred Arts Commission; Pension Committee.
Vidad, Gerald '97 (SB) Twentynine Palms, CA Blessed Sacrament.
Vidal, David *i.v.e.* '01 (WDC) Pastoral Center Special Ministries.
Vidal, Gregoire '92 (DEN) Denver, CO St. Catherine of Siena.
Vidal, Gustavo '97 (SLC) West Haven, UT Saint Mary LLC 237.
Vidal, Jesus Hernandez '94 (OAK) Oakland, CA St. Louis Bertrand.
Vidal, Robert S. '66 (ORG) Seal Beach, CA St. Anne's.
Vidal, Tomas '09 (YAK) Moses Lake, WA Queen of All Saints; Moses Lake, WA Our Lady of Fatima.
Vidarte, Jose Luis '08 (TYL) Center, TX St. Therese; Diocesan Liturgical Commission.
Vidmar, John C. *o.p.* '80 (PRO)[O] Providence St. Thomas Aquinas Priory at Providence College.
Vidrine, Jason '06 (LAF) Gueydan, LA St. Peter the Apostle; Diocesan Consultors.
Vidrine, Richard '95 (LAF) Washington, LA St. Peter.
Viego, Carlos M. '98 (NEW) Orange, NJ St. John's; Hispanic Curia of Essex and Union Counties.
Vieira, John S. '97 (SB) Elected At–Large Members.
Vieira, John S. '97 (SB) Ontario, CA St. Elizabeth Ann Seton; Elected Members.
Vieira, Rev. Msgr. Victor M. '67 (PRO) East Providence, RI St. Francis Xavier.
Vien, John R. (STL)[V] St. Louis, MO Archdiocesan Stewardship Education Committee.
Vien, John Rogers '93 (STL) St. Louis, MO St. Pius V.
Vientos, Luis A. Rodriguez (PCE)[B] The Pontifical Catholic University of Puerto Rico.
Viera, Manuel *o.f.m.* '82 (CIN) Judicial Vicar; [N] Cincinnati, OH St. Francis Seraph Friary.
Vierra, Theodore A. '60 (LA) Los Angeles, CA St. Paul the Apostle Retired.
Viertel, Daniel '10 (GB) Manitowoc, WI St. Francis of Assisi.
Vieson, Paul F. *s.m.* '84 (CIN)[D] Dayton, OH The University of Dayton; [N] Dayton, OH Marianist Community Retired.
Vietor, Oliver '10 (PHX) Phoenix, AZ St. Thomas the Apostle Roman Catholic Parish.
Viet Tran, Bac–Hai '84 (NO) Jefferson, LA St. Agnes.
Vieyra, Eladio '08 (B) Mountain Home, ID Our Lady of Good Counsel.
Vigil, Joe '80 (SFE) Albuquerque, NM Our Lady of Guadalupe.
Vigil, Joseph A. '06 (PBL) Pueblo, CO Our Lady of Mt. Carmel.
Vigil, Michael A. '85 (GLP) Farmington, NM St. Mary's; Presbyteral Council; Judicial Vicar; Judges.
Vigil, Paul E. '91 (LA) Los Angeles, CA St. Timothy.
Vigilanti, John A. '72 (NY)[E] Bronx, NY Academy of Mount St. Ursula; Army Reserve Chaplains; Ossining, NY St. Augustine.
Vigliotta, Thomas F. *o.f.m.* '85 (ATL)[I] Athens, GA University of Georgia – Catholic Student Center; Athens, GA Catholic Student Center at The University of Georgia; Special or Other Archdiocesan Assignment.
Vignato, Joe *s.x.* '93 (FgM)[N] Wayne Xaverian Missionary Fathers; Wayne, NJ XAVERIAN MISSIONARY FATHERS.
Vignola, Robert R. *c.m.* '50 (PH)[Y].
Vignone, John J. '75 (CAM) Egg Harbor Township, NJ The Church of Saint Katharine Drexel, McKee City, New Jersey; Appointed Members; Members.
Vigoa, Richard J. '08 (MIA) Priest Secretary to the Archbishop.
Vigues, Gabriel '93 (MIA) Miami Beach, FL St. Francis de Sales.
Vila, Carlos S. '83 (AGN) Associate Judges; Tamuning, GU St. Anthony and St. Victor.
Vila, Richard C. '02 (TR) Medford, NJ St. Mary of the Lakes; Holmdel, NJ St. Benedict.
Viladesau, Richard R. '69 (RVC) Saltaire, NY Our Lady Star of the Sea, Mission Chapel; Serving Outside the Diocese; Seaford, NY St. William the Abbot.
Vilano, Tony '96 (SAT) Archdiocesan Presbyteral Council; San Antonio, TX Cathedral of San Fernando; Vicar for Clergy; Department of Clergy and Consecrated Life.
Vilano, Tony '96 (SAT)[Q] San Antonio, TX Historical Centre Foundation.
Vilaplana, Jose *s.j.* '63 (NY)[DD] Loyola Hall, Jesuit Community.
Vilar, Juan Diaz '69 (NEW)[B] Jersey City, NJ Jesuit Center.
Vilchez, Pedro E. '11 (NEW) Lyndhurst, NJ Sacred Heart.
Vileo, Stephen L. '87 (DET) Monroe, MI St. Michael the Archangel.
Vilkauskas, Edward J. *c.s.sp.* '73 (DET) Detroit, MI St. Mary.
Villa, Eduardo '80 (BWN) Garciasville, TX St. Paul the Apostle; [A] Brownsville, TX The Saint Joseph and Saint Peter Seminary.
Villa, James *o.f.m.* '69 (NY)[DD] Mount Vernon, NY St. Bernardine of Siena Friary.
Villa, Joseph L. '97 (IND) Clinton, IN Sacred Heart Church, Clinton, Inc.; Rockville, IN St. Joseph Catholic Church, Rockville, Inc.; Universal, IN St. Joseph Catholic Church, Universal, Inc.
Villa, Leonard F. '86 (NY) Yonkers, NY St. Eugene; Westchester (Yonkers).
Villa, Richard *s.m.* '08 (FWT)[B] Fort Worth, TX Nolan Catholic High School; Presbyteral Council; [H] Fort Worth, TX Society of Mary.
Villa, Robert '02 (HRT) Waterbury, CT St. Margaret.
Villabon, German *o.s.a.* '54 (RVC) Rockville Centre, NY St. Agnes Cathedral.
Villaescusa, Gregory T. '03 (SCR) Scranton, PA St. Patrick's; Kingston, PA St. Ignatius Loyola, Kingston.
Villafan, Alberto *o.f.m.* '05 (LA) Los Angeles, CA St. Francis of Assisi.
Villafan, Alberto *o.f.m.* '05 (OAK) Oakland, CA St. Elizabeth; [L] Oakland, CA Franciscan Friars (Province of St. Barbara).
Villafan, Ignacio '99 (FRS) Tulare, CA St. Rita.
Villagomez, Jose *o.f.m.cap.* '74 (AGN)[F] Agana Heights, GU St. Fidelis Friary; Knights of Columbus; Agana Heights, GU San Francisco d'Assisi.
Villagran, Alfredo *o.f.m.* '74 (ELP)[B] El Paso, TX St. Anthony's School of Theology.
Villagran, Gonzalo *s.j.* '08 (BO)[U] Brighton, MA Miguel Pro House.
Villalobos, Alberto '85 (LA) El Monte, CA Nativity.
Villalobos, David '96 (SR) Ukiah, CA St. Mary of the Angels.
Villalobos, Jaime M. '92 (LA) South Gate, CA St. Helen.
Villalobos, Manuel *c.m.f.* '05 (CHI) Chicago, IL Our Lady of Guadalupe; [N] Oak Park Claretian Missionaries USA Eastern Province.
Villalobos–Cuellar, Efrain *m.s.p.* '08 (SB) Fontana, CA St. Joseph.
Villalon, Jose M. '89 (BWN) On Leave.
Villalta, Moises *o.f.m.cap.* '95 (WDC) Washington, DC Shrine of the Sacred Heart.
Villaluz, Anastacio *c.r.m.* '01 (NEW) Lodi, NJ St. Joseph's.
Villamide, Rev. Msgr. Aniceto '67 (BGP) Bridgeport, CT St. Peter; [W] Bridgeport, CT Hispanic Social Ministries of Fairfield County, Inc.; Diocesan Consultors; Priest Vocation Advisory Board; Cursillos of Fairfield County, Inc.
Villamor, Manuel R. '99 (FAJ) Rio Grande, PR Nuestra Senora del Carmen.
Villamor, Ronilo '83 (HT) Golden Meadow, LA Our Lady of Prompt Succor; Priests Council.
Villamthanam, George *c.s.t.* '81 (NOR) Ellington, CT St. Luke.
Villani, Rev. Msgr. Rocco D. '61 (BRK) Brooklyn, NY St. Brendan Retired.
Villano, Mark (LA)[AA] Palos Verdes Peninsula, CA Marymount College (Rancho Palos Verdes).
Villano, Richard R. '58 (STP) Minneapolis, MN St. Helena.
Villanova, Richard A. '67 (NEW) Garwood, NJ Church of St. Anne.
Villanueva, Edgar '93 (MO) Army Chaplains.
Villanueva, Edgar '08 (RNO) Lovelock, NV St. John the Baptist; Lovelock Prison.
Villanueva, Efrain '04 (AUS) Taylor, TX Our Lady of Guadalupe.
Villanueva, Felix Oliveras '82 (CGS) Naranjito, PR San Miguel Arcangel; Board of Diocesan Government; Economic Administrator.
Villanueva, Gary T. '04 (WDC) Washington, DC Holy Name; Oxon Hill, MD St. Columba.
Villanueva, Jose Antonio '63 (SAT) Dilley, TX St. Joseph's.
Villaran, P. Jose Antonio *o.f.m.cap.* '05 (PCE) Ponce, PR Santa Teresita.
Villareal, Carlos A. '01 (BWN) On Leave.
Villaroya, Ernesto '93 (DAL) Retired.
Villarreal, Louis J. *o.m.i.* '65 (BO)[U] Lowell, MA Missionary Oblates of Mary Immaculate.
Villarreal, Manuel "Meme" *o.m.i.* '78 (LA) San Fernando, CA St. Ferdinand.
Villarreal, Manuel '08 (SD) Fallbrook, CA Saint Peter the Apostle Catholic Parish.
Villarreal, Ricardo A. '98 (YAK) Chelan, WA St. Anne's; Chelan, WA St. Francis de Sales; Presbyteral Council Executive Committee.
Villarroya, Pedro *c.m.* '59 (LA)[P] Los Angeles, CA Amat Residence II.
Villarrubia, Roger '99 (HT) Vicar for Priests; Houma, LA Our Lady of the Most Holy Rosary Retired.
Villarson, Albert Gardy *o.m.i.* '86 (PH) Philadelphia, PA Incarnation of Our Lord; Haitian Apostolate.
Villaruel, Alvin M. '94 (SR) Santa Rosa, CA Cathedral of St. Eugene; [B] Santa Rosa, CA Cardinal Newman High School.
Villasenar, Francisco Leon '93 (SAC) Red Bluff, CA Sacred Heart.
Villaverde, Tirso S. '96 (CHI) Chicago, IL St. Bartholomew.
Villavicencio, Freddimir (SCL) Multicultural Ministry.
Villaviza, Catalino S. '95 (NY) Bronx, NY St. Francis Xavier.
Villegas, Diego '74 (BRK) Corona, NY St. Leo.
Villegas, Efraim *o.s.b.* '88 (FgM)[A] Richardton, ND Assumption Abbey; Richardton, ND Assumption Abbey.
Villegas, Gonzalo J. '92 (TUC) All Vicars Forane; Diocesan Consultors; Tucson, AZ Saint Augustine Cathedral Roman Catholic Parish – Tucson; Vicars Forane; Council of Priests.
Villegas, Hector '02 (STO) Newman, CA St. Joachim Church of Newman (Pastor of).
Villegas, Hernando '57 (MIA) Retired.
Villegas, Jorge *o.carm.* '97 (JOL)[L] Darien Carmelite Provincial Office.
Villegas, Juan C. *s.j.* '75 (FgM) New York, NY Society of Jesus.
Villegas, Robert *c.s.c.* '63 (LSC) Chamberino, NM San Luis Rey.
Villemaire, Arthur '51 (SP) Retired.
Villerot, Henry E. '41 (DET) Retired.
Villerot, Rev. Msgr. Thomas H. '43 (DET) Retired.
Villocillo, Carmelo '89 (MET) Basking Ridge, NJ St. James.
Villosillo, Alberto '95 (NO) Metairie, LA St. Catherine of Siena.
Villote, Augusto E. '03 (SFR) Daly City, CA Our Lady of Perpetual Help.
Vima, Benjamin A. '71 (TLS) Skiatook, OK Sacred Heart.
Vincent, David P. '64 (CIN) Versailles, OH Holy Family; Versailles, OH St. Denis.
Vincent, Jean–Marie '00 (WDC) Washington, DC Church of St. Louis.
Vincent, John *o.s.c.* '58 (SCL)[I] Onamia Crosier Priory.
Vincent, Michael A. *s.j.* '82 (CLV) University Heights, OH Gesu; Presbyteral Council.
Vincent, Rev. Msgr. Robert G. '57 (NO) Retired.
Vincenzo, Dennis J. '91 (HRT) Middlebury, CT St. John of the Cross.
Vinci, Rev. Msgr. Guy '59 (NY) Bronxville, NY St. Joseph.

Vinci, Terzo *s.a.c.* '58 (NY) Yonkers, NY Our Lady of Mt. Carmel.
Vincke, Gerald L. '99 (LAN) On Duty Outside the Diocese.
Vinh Loc Mai, Timothy M. *c.m.c.* '77 (SPC)[F] Carthage, MO Congregation of the Mother Coredemptrix, United States Assumption Province; [F] Carthage, MO Congregation of the Mother Coredemptrix, United States Assumption Province.
Vinh Ngoc Nguyen, MichaelJoseph '90 (NO) New Orleans, LA The Resurrection Of Our Lord.
Vinh Vu, Francis *c.m.c.* '00 (BEA) Port Arthur, TX Queen of Vietnam.
Vinodh–Raj, A. Pravin *sd.c.* (PH)[B] Springfield, PA Servants of Charity Sd.C.
Vinsko, John J. *m.m.* '62 (SJ)[M] Los Altos, CA Maryknoll.
Vinslauski, Robert B. '71 (SFS) Madison, SD St. Thomas Aquinas.
Vinson, Anthony *o.s.b.* '05 (IND)[K] Saint Meinrad St. Meinrad Archabbey; Saint Meinrad, IN St. Boniface Catholic Church, Fulda, Inc.; Saint Meinrad, IN St. Meinrad Catholic Church, Inc.
Viola, Jose '00 (WIL)[J] Dover, DE Oblate Apostles of the Two Hearts.
Viola, William L. '84 (BAL) Odenton, MD St. Joseph.
Viqueira, Jose Maria Valverde *s.j.* '11 (BO)[U] Brighton, MA Isaac Jogues House.
Virella, Jorge L. '97 (ARE) Arecibo, PR Church of Santa Teresita.
Virella, Miguel *s.v.d.* '96 (TR) Neptune, NJ Our Lady of Providence.
Virella Vazquez, Jorge L. '97 (ARE) Chancellor; Adjutant Judges.
Virgen, Javier G. '93 (SLC) Priests' Personnel Board; College of Consultors; Hispanic Affairs; Board For Ongoing Formation of Priests; Vocation Office.
Virginia, Stephen G. '79 (COL) Columbus, OH St. Peter; Medical Experts.
Virnig, Laurn '63 (SCL) Royalton, MN Holy Cross; Royalton, MN Holy Trinity; Directors.
Virrey, Armando '03 (ORG) Fullerton, CA St. Mary's.
Virus, Keith M. '92 (GRY) Highland, IN St. James the Less.
Visbisky, Richard W. '62 (BO)[O] Brockton, MA Caritas Good Samaritan Medical Center, Inc.; Pastoral Care.
Viscardi, Christopher J. *s.j.* '76 (MOB)[A] Mobile, AL Spring Hill College; Sacramental Ministers.
Viscaya, Natividad Acevedo '86 (SJN) Carolina, PR San Valentin.
Visich, Eduard C. '53 (BRK) Retired.
Visnovsky, Marek '04 (PRM) Brunswick, OH St. Emilian.
Visperas, Joseph '86 (LA) La Mirada, CA St. Paul of the Cross.
Vistal, Felix '87 (MO) DEPARTMENT OF VETERANS AFFAIRS HOSPITALS AND CHAPLAINS.
Visuvasam, Arul Joseph (LC) Stevens Point, WI St. Peter.
Vit, William J. '05 (MO) Sioux City, IA Cathedral of the Epiphany; Liturgy Commission; St. Joseph Education Society; Air National Guard Chaplains.
Vita, Mariano L. '42 (CHI) Retired.
Vitacolonna, Xavier *c.p.* '74 (NEW)[L] "Compassion" Magazine; [L] Union City, NJ Congregation of the Passion (Passionists)–St. Michael's Residence.
Vitaglione, Robert P. '76 (BRK) Brooklyn, NY St. Lucy–St. Patrick; Brooklyn, NY Mary of Nazareth.
Vitale, Louis *o.f.m.* '63 (OAK)[L] Oakland, CA Franciscan Friars of California, (Province of St. Barbara).
Vitali, James V. *o.s.a.* '81 (PH)[Y] Villanova, PA St. Augustine Friary.
Vitali, John *c.r.s.* '71 (MAN)[H] Allenstown, NH Pine Haven Boys Center.
Vitaliano, Dominic J. '91 (PEO) On Duty Outside the Diocese; Air Force Chaplains.
Vithanage, Denzil J. '99 (TYL) Diocesan Catholic School Advisory Council.
Vithanage, Denzil '93 (TYL) Marshall, TX St. Joseph.
Vitillo, Robert J. '72 (PAT) On Duty Outside the Diocese.
Vito, Alfred J. '84 (SCR) Gouldsboro, PA St. Rita.
Vi Tran, Gregory M. *c.m.c.* '06 (SPC)[F] Carthage, MO Congregation of the Mother Coredemptrix, United States Assumption Province.
Vitro, Thomas J. '66 (CHI) Retired.
Vitte, Jules '49 (NO) Retired.
Vittengl, Donald J. *m.m.* '56 (NY)[DD] Retired.
Vitturino, Saverio T. '67 (WDC) Retired.
Vitus, Frank '75 (JOL) Woodridge, IL Christ The Servant Parish.
Viuya, Melanio *m.j.* '95 (LA)[P] Los Angeles, CA Missionaries of Jesus, Inc.; Los Angeles, CA St. Kevin; Los Angeles, CA Precious Blood.
Viveiros, Joseph F. '74 (FR) Swansea, MA St. Dominic's.
Vivero, David P. '90 (ORL) Belleview, FL St. Theresa.
Viveros, Ricardo Henry '08 (LA) Hacienda Heights, CA St. John Vianney.
Viveros, Roberto *o.f.m.cap.* '09 (DAL)[J] Dallas, TX Capuchin Franciscan Friars, Vice Province of Texas; [M] Dallas, TX Dallas Cursillo Center; Dallas, TX Our Lady of Lourdes.
Viviano, Benedict T. *o.p.* '66 (CHI)[N] Chicago Dominicans (Provincial Office).
Viviano, Charles '89 (ORL) Winter Haven, FL St. Matthew.
Viviano, Nino '64 (ALX) Retired.
Vivona, Anthony '53 (BRK) Retired.
Vivona, Rt. Rev. Archimandrite Francis M. '69 (LAV) Diocesan Tribunal Office–Judicial Vicar; Presbyteral Council for the Diocese of Las Vegas.
Vivona, Rt. Rev. Francis M. '69 (HPM) Las Vegas, NV Our Lady of Wisdom Italo–Greek; Judicial Vicar; Censor; College of Consultors.
Vivona, Rev. Msgr. Francis M. '69 (LAV) Las Vegas, NV Shrine of the Most Holy Redeemer.
Vizcaino, Mario B. *sch.p.* '60 (MIA)[L] Miami, FL Southeast Pastoral Institute; [L] Miami, FL Southeast Regional Office for Hispanic Ministry, Inc.; [L] Miami, FL SEPI Evangelization and Education Foundation, Inc.
Vladyka, Vasyl (PHU) Carteret, NJ St. Mary's.
Vlasz, Melvyn J. '63 (RCK) Retired.
Vlaun, Rev. Msgr. James C. '88 (RVC)[Q] Uniondale, NY TELECARE of the Diocese of Rockville Centre; Television (Telecare/TV 29); Williston Park, NY St. Aidan's Church.
Vo, John K. '86 (LA) Torrance, CA St. Catherine Laboure.
Vo, Khoa '07 (ORG) Huntington Beach, CA St. Bonaventure.
Vo, Peter Son '06 (OAK) Oakland, CA St. Anthony.
Vo, Peter '88 (NEW) Rahway, NJ Divine Mercy Parish.
Vo, Quy '10 (ALB) Albany, NY Blessed Sacrament.
Vodoklys, Edward J. *s.j.* '91 (WOR)[N] Worcester, MA Jesuits of the Holy Cross, Inc.
Voelker, David A. '74 (BEL) Retired.
Voelker, Harold H. '54 (STL) Retired.
Voelker, James A. '69 (BEL) Waterloo, IL St. Michael Retired.
Voelker, Karl J. *s.j.* '72 (MIL) Milwaukee, WI Gesu Parish; [P] Milwaukee, WI Jesuit Community at Marquette University.
Voelker, Nicholas A. '02 (WCH) Hutchinson, KS St. Teresa; [K] Wichita, KS Serra Club of Reno County; Kansas State Industrial Reformatory.
Voelker, Peter H. *c.ss.r.* '61 (GAL) Houston, TX Holy Ghost.
Voellmecke, Francis W. '59 (CIN) Cincinnati, OH Our Lord, Christ the King; Judges Retired.
Vogan, Howard L. '69 (DET) Livonia, MI St. Genevieve; Livonia, MI St. Maurice.
Vogan, Robert C. '70 (PH) Aston, PA St. Joseph; Deans; Building Committee; Deans.
Vogel, Andrew P. '10 (WIN) Owatonna, MN Sacred Heart; Owatonna, MN Holy Trinity.
Vogel, Arthur '57 (SCL) Retired.
Vogel, Caleb '04 (B) Moscow, ID St. Augustine's; [F] Moscow, ID St. Augustine Catholic Center; Priest Personnel Commission; Vocations.
Vogel, David '06 (RCK) Rockford, IL Holy Family.
Vogel, Gerhard *s.v.d.* '65 (TR)[N] Bordentown, NJ Society of the Divine Word.
Vogel, John J. '86 (LA) Glendora, CA St. Dorothy.
Vogel, Joseph '87 (SFS) Sioux Falls, SD St. Katharine Drexel Catholic Church; Personnel Board.
Vogel, Kevin W. '11 (OM) Papillion, NE St. Columbkille.
Vogel, Marcel '89 (GF) Fort Shaw, MT St. Ann.
Vogel, Walter J. '58 (MIL) Retired.
Vogel, William *s.j.* '75 (YAK) Social Justice and Human Life Commission.
Vogelpohl, Daniel J. '75 (COV) Fort Mitchell, KY Blessed Sacrament.
Vogelsang, Clifford R. '63 (IND) Board of Consultors; Archdiocesan Judges; Indianapolis, IN St. Andrew the Apostle Catholic Church, Indianapolis, Inc. Retired.
Voger, William D. *s.j.* '75 (P)[L] Portland, OR Colombiere Community.
Vogl, John C. '00 (YAK) Special Assignment; Benton City, WA St. Frances Xavier Cabrini.
Vogl, Rev. Msgr. Robert R. '47 (DUB) Retired.
Vogler, J. Edward '65 (STL) St. Louis, MO Visitation–St. Ann's Shrine.
Vogler, Jean '70 (EVN) Retired.
Vogt, Emmerch *o.p.* '70 (LA)[Q] Los Angeles, CA Monastery of the Angels (Contemplative).
Vogt, Eric T. *o.s.b.* '79 (E) St. Marys, PA Sacred Heart Church.
Vogt, Eric *o.s.b.* '79 (GBG)[H] Latrobe, PA Saint Vincent Archabbey.
Vogt, Otto J. '50 (ROC) Retired.
Vogt, Richard J. *s.j.* '63 (STL)[O] St. Louis, MO Jesuit Community Corporation at Saint Louis University – Jesuit Hall.
Vogt, Robert W. '62 (BUF) Advocates Retired.
Voida, Paul '05 (ROM) McKeesport, PA St. Mary; Evangelization.
Voiss, James K. *s.j.* '88 (STL)[C] Saint Louis University; [O] St. Louis, MO Leo Brown Jesuit Community.
Voithofer, Michael B. '10 (OM) Omaha, NE St. Robert Bellarmine.
Voitus, Joshua A. '11 (CHL) Charlotte, NC St. Vincent de Paul.
Voity, Rev. Msgr. Maurice '79 (SAN) San Angelo, TX Cathedral of the Sacred Heart; Board of Directors; Judges.
Vojtek, John C. '76 (PIT) Russellton, PA Transfiguration.
Vojtik, James P. '62 (MIL) Retired.
Volavola, Simione R. '01 (PH) Ottsville, PA St. John the Baptist.
Volertas, Vytautas '93 (BRK) Maspeth, NY Transfiguration; [Q] Lithuanian.
Volk, Rev. Msgr. Marvin C. '74 (BEL) Millstadt, IL St. James; Clergymen's Aid Society.
Volk, Michael '92 (MRY) Seaside, CA St. Francis Xavier.
Volk, Norman *o.m.i.* '68 (SFS) Sisseton, SD St. Catherine; Sisseton, SD St. Peter.
Volkert, Daniel P. '01 (MIL) Greenfield, WI St. John the Evangelist.
Volkert, James T. '90 (MIL) Burlington, WI Immaculate Conception; Archdiocesan Council of Priests.
Volkmer, Michael *c.pp.s.* '68 (DAV) Albia, IA St. Mary's.
Voll, Walter Urban *o.p.* '49 (PRO)[O] Providence St. Thomas Aquinas Priory at Providence College.
Vollkommer, Andrew J. '86 (CHR) Chapin, SC Our Lady of the Lake.
Vollmer, Daniel '02 (PHX) Prescott Valley, AZ St. Germaine Roman Catholic Parish; College of Consultors; Presbyteral Council.
Vollmer, Gary L. '77 (STL) Flint Hill, MO St. Theodore.
Vollmer, William C. '58 (COS) Retired.
Vollmer, William J. '97 (CHI) Northbrook, IL St. Norbert.
Vollmer–Konig, Josef '01 (DAL) Dallas, TX St. Patrick.
Volmi, Dennis G. '75 (WIL) Retired.
Volpert, Robert C. '61 (L) Retired.
Voltaggio, Fred '71 (CAM) Retired.
Voltz, Anthony R. '85 (IND) Indianapolis, IN St. Barnabas Catholic Church, Indianapolis, Inc.
Volz, Rev. Msgr. Anthony R. '85 (IND) Archdiocesan Review Board.
Volz, Edward *o.s.p.p.e.* '88 (GBG) Freeport, PA St. Mary; [H] Kittanning, PA Pauline Fathers Monastery.
Volz, Gerald '92 (KCK) Regional Pastoral Leaders.
Volz, Jerry '92 (KCK) Topeka, KS St. Matthew.
Vomund, Jeffrey G. '97 (STL) St. Louis, MO St. Elizabeth, Mother of John the Baptist; Archdiocesan Council of Priests.
Vona, Michael S. '68 (TR) Farmingdale, NJ St. Catherine of Siena Retired.
von Arx, Jeffrey P. *s.j.* '81 (BGP)[B] Fairfield, CT Fairfield University; [O] Fairfield, CT The Fairfield Jesuit Community–Fairfield University.
von Behren, Thomas R. *c.s.v.* '83 (CHI)[N] Arlington Heights, IL Viatorian Province Center–Clerics of St. Viator.
Vonderhaar, Eugene F. '59 (CIN) Retired.
Vonderhaar, Ralph E. *s.j.* '57 (STL)[O] St. Louis, MO Jesuit Community Corporation at Saint Louis University – Jesuit Hall.
Vondras, John J. '85 (NY) Newburgh, NY St. Francis of Assisi.
von Duerbeck, Julian *o.s.b.* '76 (JOL)[A] Lisle, IL Benedictine University; [L] Lisle, IL St. Procopius Abbey; Lisle, IL.
von Emster, Ernie (SFR)[S] Tiburon, CA Catholic Charismatic Movement.
Von Essen, Pacificus *s.a.* '53 (NY)[DD] Garrison Franciscan Friars of the Atonement, Minister General Office.
Von Euw, Vincent P. '66 (BO) Senior Priests. Retired.
Von Handorf, Joseph '75 (LEX) Hispanic Ministry.
Von Kaenel, George E. *s.j.* '58 (CHY) Glenrock, WY St. Louis.
Von Kerssenbrock, Joachim *s.j.* '59 (NY)[HH] Bronx, NY American St. Boniface Society, Incorporated; [DD] New York, NY Murray–Weigel Hall.
Von Kobs, Allan G. *o.f.m.* '82 (NY) New York, NY St. Stephen of Hungary.
Von Lehmen, Jeffrey D. '85 (COV) Covington, KY St. Patrick.
von Maluski, Kris M. '01 (PRO)[B] Newport, RI Salve Regina University.
von Menshengen, Richard '00 (TUC) St. Gianna Oratory.
von Menshengen, Rev. Canon Richard '00 (TUC) Tucson, AZ Holy Family Roman Catholic Parish – Tucson.
von Nell, Boniface *o.s.b.* '91 (WDC)[O] Washington, DC St. Anselm's Abbey.
Von Tobel, James *s.j.* '67 (WIN) Jackson, MN Good Shepherd; Jackson, MN St. Luke's; Jackson, MN St. Joseph.
Voo, Won Bong '76 (SEA) Fife, WA St. Paul Chong Hasang Personal Parish.
Voor, Joseph H. '50 (L) Louisville, KY St. Brigid; Louisville, KY St. James Retired.
Voor, Rick '07 (ORL) Altamonte Springs, FL St. Mary Magdalen; [A] Orlando, FL Bishop Moore Catholic

High School Inc.
Voorhes, Rev. Msgr. Fred R. '71 (BUF) Buffalo, NY St. Thomas Aquinas; Buffalo, NY St. Martin of Tours.
Voorhies, Bennett J. '83 (SFE) Albuquerque, NM Annunciation; Vicars Forane (Deans); Presbyteral Council of the Archdiocese of Santa Fe.
Voorhies, Thomas P. '90 (LAF) Scott, LA Sts. Peter and Paul; Diocesan Consultors.
Voors, David W. '81 (FTW) Consultors; Decatur, IN St. Mary of the Assumption.
Vorderlandwehr, Adrian *o.s.b.* '67 (OKL) Konawa, OK Sacred Heart.
Voris, Francis *o.f.m.cap.* '73 (SAG) Saginaw, MI St. Joseph.
Vorwald, Aloysius J. '64 (DUB) Retired.
Vorwek, James *s.v.d.* '69 (FgM) Techny, IL.
Vorwoldt, James F. *s.j.* '71 (CHI)[D] Chicago, IL St. Ignatius Jesuit Community.
Vos, Jude '96 (FAR) Special Assignment.
Vos, Thomas *o.f.m.* '61 (GLD) Indian River, MI Cross in the Woods Catholic Shrine.
Vos, William '64 (SCL) Catholic Relief Services; Holy Childhood Association Retired.
Vosen, Gerald P. '61 (MAD) Leave of Absence.
Vosko, Richard '69 (ALB) Special Assignment.
Voss, Dennis F. '64 (BEL) Diocesan Council of Catholic Women Retired.
Voss, Donald J. '93 (PBR) McKeesport, PA St. Nicholas.
Voss, Marcus J. *o.s.b.* '71 (BIR)[E] Cullman, AL St. Bernard Abbey.
Voss, Robert D. *s.j.* '72 (FgM) St. Louis, MO Society of Jesus.
Voss, Robert J. '70 (PHX) Retired.
Voss, Steven '07 (DEN) Fort Collins, CO St. Joseph.
Vossler, Brian E. '91 (E) Ridgway, PA St. Leo the Great.
Votraw, Wilbur J. '55 (SY) Syracuse, NY St. Vincent de Paul.
Votto, Silvano P. *s.j.* '73 (SJ)[M] Los Gatos, CA Sacred Heart Jesuit Center.
Vowells, John J. *s.j.* '90 (KC) Kansas City, MO St. Francis Xavier; Presbyteral Council; Deans; Consultors; [J] Kansas City, MO Rockhurst Jesuit Community.
Vowels, G. Timothy '77 (STL) Chesterfield, MO Incarnate Word.
Voyt, Stephen A. '85 (PT) Military Chaplains; Air Force Chaplains.
Voyt, Steve '85 (HON) Military Chaplains.
Voytek, John *o.f.m.conv.* '82 (HBG) Coal Township, PA Our Lady of Hope; Trevorton, PA St. Patrick.
Voytek, Leonard E. '74 (ALT) Cambria Deanery; Windber, PA St. Elizabeth Ann Seton.
Vozzo, Gregory G. '10 (BO) Braintree, MA St. Francis of Assisi.
Vozzo, Robert A. *c.s.c.* (FTW)[H] Notre Dame Congregation of Holy Cross, United States Province of Priests & Brothers.
Vrabel, George A. '87 (CLV) Berea, OH St. Mary.
Vrana, John G. '67 (CLV) Elyria, OH St. Jude.
Vrana, John P. '56 (OKL) Retired.
Vrana, Joseph L. '65 (VIC) Nada, TX Nativity of the Blessed Virgin Mary.
Vrazel, Edward J. *o.m.i.* '58 (LAR) Laredo, TX Our Lady of Guadalupe.
Vrazel, Stephen G. '11 (MOB) Mobile, AL St. Pius X.
Vrba, James J. '77 (DAV) Solon, IA St. Mary's; Deans.
Vreteau, Robert *o.m.i.* '46 (SAT)[K] San Antonio, TX Oblate Madonna Residence.
Vu, Andy Dinh *s.v.d.* '07 (FgM) Techny, IL.
Vu, Anthony Hien T. '09 (ORG) Irvine, CA St. John Neumann.
Vu, Dat '04 (B) Meridian, ID Holy Apostles.
Vu, Diem Joseph Quang '06 (ARL) Notaries.
Vu, Duc *s.j.* '02 (SJ)[L] Los Altos, CA Jesuit Retreat Center of Los Altos.
Vu, Dustin L. '04 (DUB) Cedar Rapids, IA Blessed John XXIII; Seminary Admissions and Advisory Board; [C] Cedar Rapids, IA Mount Mercy University; Associate Directors.
Vu, Ignatius '94 (NY) Jeffersonville, NY St. George–St. Francis.
Vu, J.B Han '65 (NO) Retired.
Vu, Jack '02 (LR) Jonesboro, AR Blessed John Newman University Parish; [I] Jonesboro, AR Arkansas State University, Blessed John Newman University Parish; Jonesboro, AR Blessed Sacrament.
Vu, Joachim '63 (ORG) Retired.
Vu, John Duc (BIR) Birmingham, AL Our Lady of LaVang Parish St. John Bosco Church.
Vu, John Francis *s.j.* '97 (ORG)[H] Yorba Linda, CA Pope John Paul II Polish Center; Newman Apostolate; [M] Irvine, CA U.C.I. Interfaith Center; Council of Priests; [I] Anaheim, CA Manresa Jesuit Residence.
Vu, Joseph Dang–Hai *s.d.d.* '02 (MO) Air Force Reserve Chaplains.
Vu, Joseph Dao *s.v.d.* '88 (MEM) Memphis, TN Sacred Heart Church.
Vu, Joseph Dao *s.v.d.* (MEM)[F] Memphis, TN Society of the Divine Word (Chicago Province); Vietnamese Catholic Ministry.
Vu, Joseph Duc '70 (MO) DEPARTMENT OF VETERANS AFFAIRS HOSPITALS AND CHAPLAINS.
Vu, Joseph Phiet Trong *c.ss.r.* '95 (P) Portland, OR Our Lady of Lavang.
Vu, Joseph Q. '06 (ARL) Springfield, VA St. Bernadette.
Vu, Joseph Thanh '75 (GAL) Houston, TX Vietnamese Martyrs.
Vu, Joseph Tri Van *s.v.d.* '85 (FgM) Techny, IL.
Vu, Joseph Van '09 (LA) San Pedro, CA Holy Trinity.
Vu, Joseph '90 (BRK) College Point, NY St. Fidelis.
Vu, Lieu '91 (SJ) San Jose, CA St. Frances Cabrini.
Vu, Long '06 (ORG) Santa Ana, CA Our Lady of La Vang.
Vu, Martin *c.s.sp.* '10 (LR) Brinkley, AR St. John the Baptist; Forrest City, AR St. Francis of Assisi; Helena, AR St. Mary; Marianna, AR St. Andrew; Helena, AR St. Mary of the Lake Church.
Vu, Minh '94 (STP) St. Paul, MN St. Adalbert.
Vu, Peter Duc '96 (ATL) Riverdale, GA Our Lady of Vietnam.
Vu, Peter G. '97 (GR) Belmont, MI Assumption of the Blessed Virgin Mary.
Vu, Than N. '84 (BR) Baton Rouge, LA St. Aloysius; Vicar General/Moderator of the Curia; Defenders of the Bond; College of Consultors; Diocesan Corporation (The Roman Catholic Church of the Diocese of Baton Rouge); Presbyteral Council.
Vu, Thomas H. '01 (LAF) Franklin, LA St. Jules; Vietnamese Catholic Ministry.
Vu, Toan Quoc *s.v.d.* '06 (FgM) Techny, IL.
Vu, Tung Duc *c.ss.r.* '07 (LA)[P] Baldwin Park Vietnamese Redemptorist Mission.
Vu Dinh Hoat, Rochus '60 (BAL) Retired.
Vuelvas–Arias, David '75 (ORG) Santa Ana, CA Our Lady of Guadalupe; Cursillo Movement.
Vujs, Joseph E. '57 (HRT) Retired.
Vujs, Robert W. *m.m.* '61 (NY)[DD] Maryknoll Maryknoll Fathers and Brothers Retired.
Vujs, Robert *m.m.* (HRT) Cheshire, CT Manson Youth Institution; Cheshire, CT Cheshire Correctional Institution.
Vuky, Michael '05 (P) Banks, OR St. Francis of Assisi; Forest Grove, OR Visitation B.V.M.
Vular, Robert J. '01 (PIT) Pittsburgh, PA St. Teresa of Avila; [P] Pittsburgh, PA Community College of Allegheny County – North Hills Campus.
Vung Le, Paul *s.v.d.* '85 (LA) Metropolitan State Hospital.
Vuong, Joseph–Quoc T. '07 (STP) Wayzata, MN Holy Name of Jesus.
Vuong, Rt. Rev. M. John Lam Dinh *o.cist.* '57 (SB)[I] Lucerne Valley, CA The Cistercian Congregation of the Holy Family, St. Joseph Monastery Retired.
Vuoso, Pasquale *c.r.i.c.* '87 (LA) Santa Paula, CA St. Sebastian; [P] Santa Paula, CA Canons Regular of the Immaculate Conception.
Vurst, James Van *o.f.m.* '61 (CIN)[N] Cincinnati, OH St. Clement Friary.
Vuturo, Paul V. '73 (MIA) Sacred Art & Architecture; Members.
Vuturo, Paul '73 (MIA) Pinecrest, FL St. Louis; Consultors; Age Group II.
Vyverman, Mark J. '93 (KAL) Battle Creek, MI St. Joseph; Diocesan Consultors; Presbyteral Council Members; Presbyteral Council Members; Vicars Forane.

W

Wach, Anthony J. *s.j.* '72 (MIL)[P] Milwaukee Jesuit Provincial Office, Wisconsin Province; Milwaukee, WI Society of Jesus.
Wachala, Jon M. '79 (CHI) Chicago, IL St. Jane de Chantal; Chicago, IL St. Joseph; Chicago, IL St. Richard.
Wachdorf, Paul H. '75 (CHI) Chicago, IL St. Gregory, the Great.
Wachowiak, Duane A. '98 (GLD) Boyne City, MI St. Matthew; Boyne City, MI St. Augustine; Worship and Liturgical Formation, Secretariat for; Boyne City, MI St. John Nepomucene.
Wachter, Robert B. '76 (WCH) Iola, KS St. Joseph; Iola, KS St. John.
Wack, Neil F. *c.s.c.* '04 (FTW) South Bend, IN Christ the King; [H] Notre Dame Congregation of Holy Cross, United States Province of Priests & Brothers; Presbyteral Council; [H] Notre Dame, IN Congregation of Holy Cross, United States Province of Priests & Brothers.
Wack, William A. *c.s.c.* '94 (AUS) Austin, TX St. Ignatius Martyr; Presbyteral Council.
Wack, William *c.s.c.* (FTW)[H] Notre Dame Congregation of Holy Cross, United States Province of Priests & Brothers.
Wackerman, John F. '98 (PH) Lansdale, PA Corpus Christi.
Waclawik, Leszek J. '84 (LAR) Laredo, TX St. Joseph; Ex Officio Members.
Wadas, Rev. Msgr. Ignatius C. '53 (ALT) Retired.
Wadas, Raymond J. '72 (WDC) Takoma Park, MD Our Lady of Sorrows.
Waddell, Paul M. '84 (NY) Katonah, NY St. Mary of the Assumption.
Waddill, Dale T. '64 (P) Retired.
Wade, Ed *c.c.* '72 (GAL) Houston, TX Queen of Peace.
Wade, Edward C. '72 (CAM) Retired.
Wade, Gerald T. *s.j.* '68 (SJ)[D] San Jose, CA Bellarmine College Preparatory.
Wade, Hubert '77 (SAN) Ballinger, TX St. Mary Star of the Sea; Board of Directors; Diocesan Consultors; Presbyteral Council; Director of Seminarians.
Wade, Jarrell D. *s.j.* '65 (FgM) St. Louis, MO Society of Jesus.
Wade, John J. '56 (TLS) Retired.
Wadelton, Christopher '09 (IND) Indianapolis, IN Holy Spirit Catholic Church, Indianapolis, Inc.
Wadeson, John H. '69 (SFR) San Francisco, CA St. Charles Borromeo.
Wadowski, Stanislaw '97 (RVC) Farmingdale, NY St. Kilian.
Wafzig, James E. '55 (L) Retired.
Wagener, John M. '61 (NU) Military Chaplains Retired.
Wagenhoffer, Josef A. '65 (CAM) Cape/Atlantic Counties Retired.
Waggoner, David (P)[J] Eugene, OR Sacred Heart Medical Center.
Wagner, Alan *s.d.s.* '76 (SR)[F] Napa, CA Queen of the Valley Medical Center.
Wagner, Braden '11 (DEN) Littleton, CO St. Frances Cabrini.
Wagner, Donald '87 (SCL) Bluffton, MN St. John the Baptist; Wadena, MN St. Ann's; Personnel Committee.
Wagner, Edward *o.ss.t.* '80 (BAL)[Q] Diocese of Las Vegas, NV.
Wagner, Jay '87 (RIC) Petersburg, VA Church of the Sacred Heart.
Wagner, Rev. Msgr. John A. '49 (SAT) Retired.
Wagner, John F. '64 (SB) Temecula, CA St. Catherine of Alexandria; Elected Members.
Wagner, John J. '87 (RIC) Petersburg, VA St. John.
Wagner, John P. '62 (SY) Retired.
Wagner, Rev. Msgr. John '49 (SAT)[K] San Antonio, TX Casa De Padres; Vicar for Retired Priests; Archdiocesan Presbyteral Council; Vicar for Retired Priests Retired.
Wagner, Rev. Msgr. Joseph '65 (SFS) Retired.
Wagner, Joseph *s.j.* '98 (CIN)[N] Cincinnati, OH Jesuit Community at Xavier University.
Wagner, Joshua J. '04 (COL) Columbus, OH St. Dominic; Columbus, OH Community of Holy Rosary and St. John; Legion of Mary; Columbus, OH Christ the King.
Wagner, Leon R. '49 (CHI) Riverside, IL St. Mary Retired.
Wagner, Mark '88 (STO) Turlock, CA Sacred Heart Church of Turlock (Pastor of).
Wagner, Michael '11 (SEA) Everett, WA St. Mary Magdalen.
Wagner, Philip C. '98 (CHY) Newcastle, WY Corpus Christi; Presbyteral Council.
Wagner, Richard F. *s.s.j.* '59 (LAF) Rayne, LA Our Mother of Mercy.
Wagner, Robert J. '57 (LC)[H] La Crosse, WI Holy Cross (Seminary) Diocesan Center Retired.
Wagner, Robert J. '09 (ARL) Fairfax, VA St. Leo's; Notaries.
Wagner, Ronald F. '79 (SAG) Saginaw, MI Holy Family; Saginaw, MI St. Andrew; Vicar for Priests; Ministry to Priests; Diocesan College of Consultors.
Wagner, Ronald '79 (SAG) Saginaw, MI St. Helen.
Wagner, Thomas A. '83 (PIT) Elizabeth, PA St. Michael.
Wagner, Rev. Msgr. Van A. '61 (TUC) Tucson, AZ Saints Peter and Paul Roman Catholic Parish – Tucson; Holy Childhood Association Retired.
Wagner, Vernon *o.f.m.cap.* '53 (MIL)[P] Mount Calvary, WI St. Lawrence Friary Retired.
Wagner, Walter Cornelius *o.p.* '93 (NY) New York, NY St. Vincent Ferrer; [DD] New York, NY St. Vincent Ferrer Priory.
Wagner, William C. '73 (CIN) Cincinnati, OH St. Thomas More; Vicarri Foranei (Deans).
Wagner, William F. '63 (L) Retired.
Waguespack, Clarence J. '62 (BR) Pierre Part, LA St. Joseph the Worker.
Wah, Joseph C. '05 (LA) Pasadena, CA Assumption of the Blessed Virgin Mary.
Wahal, Stephen J. '00 (PBR) Monessen, PA Assumption of the Blessed Virgin; Donora, PA St. Michael.
Wahl, Joseph A. *c.o.* '56 (CHR) Rock Hill, SC St. Mary; [E] Rock Hill, SC Oratory of St. Philip Neri, Congregation of the Oratory of Pontifical Rite.
Wahl, Rev. Msgr. Raymond J. '52 (RCK) Pro Synodal Judges; Diocesan Consultors Retired.
Wahl, Richard A. *c.s.b.* '73 (GAL)[E] Houston, TX St. Thomas High School; Adjutant Judicial Vicar.
Wahl, Thomas *o.s.b.* '58 (SCL)[I] Collegeville St. John's Abbey, of the Order of St. Benedict; Collegeville, MN St. John's Abbey.
Wai, Thomas Than '92 (WCH) Haysville, KS St. Cecilia.
Waibel, Philip *o.s.b.* '83 (P) Mount Angel, OR St. Mary; [L] St. Benedict, OR Mt. Angel Abbey.

Wainwright, Walter L. '65 (ROC) Retired.
Waiss, John R. '87 (POD) Chicago.
Waiss, John '87 (CHI)[V] Chicago, IL Northview University Center.
Wait, Dennis '72 (KCK) Special Assignment; [M] Kansas City, KS The Cursillo Movement of the Archdiocese of Kansas City in Kansas.
Waite, James A. '04 (BUF) Lockport, NY St. John the Baptist.
Waite, Patrick J. '54 (SC) Retired.
Waitekus, Christopher J. '91 (SPR) West Stockbridge, MA St. Patrick's; Lenox, MA St. Ann; Lenox Dale, MA St. Vincent de Paul's.
Waites, Michael J. '83 (TR) Riverton, NJ Sacred Heart.
Waithaka, Paul Maina '02 (CHI) Glenview, IL St. Catherine Laboure.
Waiwood, Richard '73 (ELP) Kermit, TX St. Thomas & St. Joseph; Monahans, TX St. John the Apostle and Evangelist Retired.
Wajda, Mark R. '08 (ORL) Longwood, FL Annunciation.
Wake, John (TR)[M] Lawrenceville, NJ Morris Hall–Saint Lawrence, Inc.; [K] Lawrenceville, NJ Morris Hall/Saint Lawrence, Inc.
Wakefield, Alan '75 (LAN) Retired.
Wakefield, Michael '81 (LA) Sherman Oaks, CA St. Francis de Sales.
Wakim, Rodolph '96 (SAM) Carnegie, PA Our Lady of Victory.
Wakulich, Kerry J. '10 (TLS)[I] Tulsa, OK St. Philip Neri Newman Center at The University of Tulsa; Campus Ministry; Special Assignment.
Wal, Edward '79 (SP) St. Petersburg, FL Transfiguration.
Walck, Edward F. *m.m.* '56 (NY)[DD] Retired.
Walczak, Melvin '68 (ROC) Absent on Leave.
Walczyk, Rafal *o.s.p.p.e.* '05 (PH)[Y].
Wald, Rev. Msgr. Jeffrey '92 (FAR) Fargo, ND Holy Spirit Church of Fargo; Vice Chancellor.
Wald, Kenneth J. '57 (BIS) Retired.
Waldbilling, Brian T. '01 (LC) Leave of Absence.
Walden, Rev. Msgr. Ellsworth R. '71 (RVC) Smithtown, NY St. Patrick.
Walder, Keith A. '03 (PEO) Chillicothe, IL St. Edward.
Waldie, Paul *o.m.i.* '65 (SAT)[B] San Antonio, TX George Sexton House of Studies.
Walding, Eugene F. '66 (SC) Retired.
Waldman, Noah A. '08 (STL) St. Charles, MO Sts. Joachim and Ann.
Waldow, Rev. Msgr. Harold L. '70 (AMA) Ex Officio; Rite of Christian Initiation of Adults Commission; A.C.T.S. Movement; Continuing Education of Clergy; Moderator of the Curia; Vicar of Clergy; Ex Officio; College of Consultors; Diocesan Pastoral Council; [I] Amarillo, TX Monsignor B.A. Erpen Trust Fund; Amarillo, TX St. Mary's Cathedral.
Waldrep, Jeffrey '90 (JKS) Jackson, MS St. Peter Cathedral; [H] Jackson, MS University of Mississippi Medical Center – Newman Center; Vice Chancellor; Judicial Vicar; Engaged Encounter; Diocesan Judges; Priests' Council; [H] Jackson, MS Belhaven College Newman Center; [H] Jackson, MS Millsaps College Newman Center.
Waldrep, John W. *m.m.* '90 (FgM) Maryknoll, NY MARYKNOLL.
Waldron, Rev. Msgr. John E. '66 (BRK)[R] Douglaston, NY Bishop Mugavero Residence Retired.
Waldron, John F. '58 (ALB) Retired.
Waldron, John '66 (P) Canby, OR St. Patrick.
Waldron, Robert J. '68 (BO) Senior Priests. Retired.
Waldron, Walter J. '64 (BO) Roxbury, MA St. Patrick; Trustees.
Waldron, William '50 (PHX) Retired.
Waldrop, Gregory S. *s.j.* '99 (NY)[DD] Cardinal Spellman Hall, Jesuit Community.
Waldschmidt, Valens J. *o.f.m.* '47 (CIN)[U] Cincinnati, OH St. Dymphna Ministry; [N] Cincinnati St. Francis Seraph Friary Retired.
Walega, Stanley J. '64 (MET) Retired.
Walk, Donald J. '67 (VEN) Retired.
Walk, Edward J. '78 (E)[C] Du Bois, PA DuBois Area Catholic School.
Walka, Marcin '09 (PAT) Parsippany, NJ St. Christopher.
Walker, Anselm '56 (GAL) Retired.
Walker, Charles D. '81 (L) Elizabethtown, KY St. Ambrose; Elizabethtown, KY St. James; White Mills, KY St. Ignatius; Deans.
Walker, Rev. Msgr. David M. '64 (HRT) Branford, CT St. Therese; Special and other Archdiocesan Assignment; North Haven, CT Catholic Cemeteries Association of the Archdiocese of Hartford, Inc.; New Haven Vicariate; East Shore Deanery; Catholic Cemeteries Association.
Walker, Donald L. '58 (DET) Redford, MI St. Hilary; Dearborn Heights, MI Our Lady of Grace Retired.
Walker, Douglas '99 (FRS) Lone Pine, CA Santa Rosa.
Walker, Francisco J. '87 (BRK) Brooklyn, NY St. Agatha's.
Walker, Gerald Bernard '55 (LA) Retired.
Walker, Gerard T. '80 (BRK) Retired.
Walker, Gilbert R. *c.m.* '87 (FgM) Earth City, MO Western Province.
Walker, Henry B. *o.m.i.* '85 (GAL) Houston, TX Immaculate Conception.
Walker, J. Kenneth '81 (EVN) Special Assignment; Judicial Vicar; Diocesan Consultors; Diocesan Council of Priests; Censors of Books.
Walker, J. Patrick '88 (STO) Manteca, CA St. Anthony Church of Manteca (Pastor of); Deans.
Walker, James E. '99 (GLP) Gallup, NM St. John Vianney; Vicar General; Presbyteral Council; Diocesan Consultors.
Walker, James P. '77 (Y) Warren, OH SS. Cyril and Methodius; Warren, OH St. James.
Walker, John Paul *o.p.* '02 (WDC)[B] Washington, DC Dominican House of Studies.
Walker, Kent A. '89 (ORL) Saint Cloud, FL St. Thomas Aquinas.
Walker, Michael '62 (KC) Retired.
Walker, Mike '99 (P) Central Point, OR Shepherd of the Valley; Shady Cove, OR Our Lady of Fatima.
Walker, Paul '72 (STU) McConnelsville, OH St. James.
Walker, Robert L. *o.p.* '56 (WDC) Washington, DC St. Dominic Church & Priory.
Walker, Ronald *o.m.i.* '61 (FgM) Washington, DC AMERICAN OBLATE MISSIONS.
Walker, Thomas J. '90 (STP) Woodbury, MN Saint Ambrose of Woodbury; Deanery 5; College of Consultors.
Walker, Thomas J. '89 (MIL) Retired.
Walkowiak, David J. '79 (CLV) Chagrin Falls, OH St. Joan of Arc; Judges in Second Instance.
Wall, Antoninus *o.p.* '50 (OAK)[L] Oakland, CA Order of Preachers (Province of the Most Holy Name of Jesus – Western Dominican Province).
Wall, Augustine *s.v.d.* '91 (BLX)[D] Bay St. Louis, MS St. Augustine's Residence; [D] Bay St. Louis, MS St. Augustine's Retreat Center.
Wall, Barry W. '62 (FR) Diocesan Archives; Legion of Mary; Diocesan Consultors Retired.
Wall, Rev. Msgr. G. Warren '76 (MOB) Mobile, AL St. Mary.
Wall, Rev. Msgr. James E. '63 (BUF) Co–Directors; Priests, Vicar for; Consultors, College of; Council of Priests.
Wall, Rev. Msgr. John A. '60 (R)[I] Chapel Hill, NC Newman Catholic Student Center; Chapel Hill, NC Newman Catholic Student Center, University of North Carolina; Council of Priests Retired.
Wall, John E. '57 (CIN) Cincinnati, OH St. Ignatius of Loyola Retired.
Wall, John J. '68 (CHI) Chicago, IL Catholic Church Extension Society of the United States of America, The; [T] Chicago, IL Catholic Church Extension Society; Chicago, IL Old St. Patrick's.
Wall, Noel *o.f.m.* '61 (MIL)[P] Burlington, WI Queen of Peace Friary.
Wall, Sherman B. *o.m.i.* '57 (SPC) Willow Springs, MO Sacred Heart.
Wall, Terence Damian *c.ss.r.* '65 (SJN)[I] San Juan, PR Casa San Clemente.
Wall, Terence Damian *c.ss.r.* '65 (CGS)[B] Aguas Buenas, PR Casa Cristo Redentor.
Wallace, Basil J. *o.s.b.* '78 (PAT)[N] Morristown, NJ St. Mary's Abbey.
Wallace, Cavana '92 (SD) Oceanside, CA Saint Margaret Catholic Parish.
Wallace, Donald L. '62 (JC) Retired.
Wallace, Rev. Msgr. Francis T. '63 (LA) Burbank, CA St. Robert Bellarmine Retired.
Wallace, Francis X. '47 (FR) Retired.
Wallace, Harry C. '56 (SY) On Duty Outside the Diocese.
Wallace, James *c.ss.r.* '70 (WDC)[O] Washington, DC Holy Redeemer College.
Wallace, Jason '04 (DEN) Denver, CO Our Lady of Lourdes.
Wallace, John *f.m.s.i.* '60 (BO)[B] Framingham, MA Sylva Maria.
Wallace, Joseph D. '85 (CAM) Ecumenical and Inter–Religious Affairs; Wildwood, NJ Notre Dame de la Mer Parish, Wildwood, N.J.
Wallace, Kenneth F. '00 (CLV) Cleveland, OH Lakewood Hospital; Pastoral Care Services.
Wallace, Rev. Msgr. Murrough C. '60 (SAC) South Lake Tahoe, CA St. Theresa; Please direct all inquiries to Retired.
Wallace, Richard '86 (MO) Navy Reserve Chaplains.
Wallace, Rev. Msgr. Thomas M. '80 (SB) Palm Springs, CA St. Theresa; College of Consultors; Hemet, CA Holy Spirit; Moreno Valley, CA St. Patrick; Yucca Valley, CA St. Mary of the Valley; Ex Officio Member; Riverside Pastoral Region; Indio, CA Our Lady of Perpetual Help; Riverside, CA Our Lady of Perpetual Help; Diocesan Curia; Ex Officio.
Wallace, William J. *o.s.a.* '74 (NY) Bronx, NY St. Nicholas of Tolentine.
Wallack, Michael '04 (TR) Marlton, NJ St. Joan of Arc.
Walleman, Kenneth T. *s.j.* '59 (MIL)[P] Wauwatosa, WI Jesuit Community at St. Camillus.
Wallen, Charles L. *c.s.c.* '54 (FR)[F] North Dartmouth, MA Holy Cross Residence Retired.
Wallen, Charles L. *c.s.c.* '54 (FTW)[H] Notre Dame Congregation of Holy Cross, United States Province of Priests & Brothers.
Wallenfelsz, Scott *s.d.s.* '69 (SUP)[H] Ladysmith, WI Servants of Mary Continuing Care Trust.
Wallenfelsz, Scott *s.d.s.* '69 (MIL)[P] Milwaukee Salvatorian Provincial Offices; [Y] Milwaukee, WI Salvatorian Institute of Philosophy and Theology, Inc.; [Y] Milwaukee, WI Lay Salvatorians, Inc.; Milwaukee, WI; [Y] St. Francis, WI Canticle and Juniper Courts Foundation, Inc.
Waller, Charles J. '73 (PAT) Graduate Studies; Paterson, NJ St. Gerard Majella.
Waller, Robert C. '75 (CIN) Milford, OH St. Andrew.
Wallin, Rev. Msgr. Kevin W. '84 (BGP)[R] Bridgeport, CT Inner–City Foundation For Charity & Education.
Walling, Gerald C. *s.j.* '61 (DET)[K] Clarkston, MI Colombiere Center.
Walling, Richard W. '78 (CIN) Coldwater, OH Holy Trinity; Coldwater, OH St. Mary; Coldwater, OH St. Anthony; Imprimatur Censors.
Wallis, Jonathan '07 (FWT) Ecumenism, Office of; Graduate Studies.
Wallis, William H. '82 (SPR) Westfield, MA St. Peter and St. Casimir.
Wallisch, Scott '10 (KCK) Shawnee, KS St. Joseph; [B] Lenexa, KS Saint James Academy.
Wallner, Gerhard '89 (FBK) Leave of Absence.
Walls, John *s.m.* '72 (ATL)[C] Atlanta, GA Marist School.
Walmesley, John '74 (SEA) Seattle, WA Our Lady of Guadalupe.
Walpole, Donald *o.s.b.* '43 (IND)[K] Saint Meinrad, IN St. Meinrad Archabbey.
Walsh, Aidan J. '70 (BO) Defenders of the Bond; Milton, MA St. Elizabeth.
Walsh, Andrew J. '66 (NY) Bronx, NY St. Margaret of Cortona.
Walsh, Arthur '85 (CC) Retired.
Walsh, Brendan J. '93 (LAN) Dexter, MI St. Joseph; Regional Vicars.
Walsh, Brendan *s.c.a.* '98 (DET)[K] Wyandotte, MI Pallottine Peer Ministry; [S] Dearborn, MI Archdiocesan Catholic Campus Ministry Association, Gabriel Richard Campus Ministry Center; [S] Dearborn, MI University of Michigan–Dearborn, Henry Ford Community College Newman Center.
Walsh, Broderick M. *c.s.p.* '92 (BO)[N] Boston, MA Paulist Center; [Z] Boston, MA Chapel of the Holy Spirit.
Walsh, Rev. Msgr. Christopher J. '87 (BGP) Shelton, CT St. Joseph; Diocesan Censors.
Walsh, Christopher M. '99 (PH) Philadelphia, PA St. Raymond of Penafort.
Walsh, Clyde J. '51 (PRO)[L] Pawtucket, RI Jeanne Jugan Residence Retired.
Walsh, Daniel L. *c.ss.p.* '91 (PIT) Pittsburgh, PA St. Stephen.
Walsh, Daniel P. '68 (BUF) Gowanda, NY St. Joseph; Cattaraugus, NY St. Mary.
Walsh, Denis '66 (TYL)[C] Palestine, TX Hermitage.
Walsh, Dennis G. '92 (TOL) Toledo, OH St. Patrick of Heatherdowns; College of Consultors.
Walsh, Dennis *s.o.l.t.* '04 (DET) Detroit, MI Holy Redeemer.
Walsh, E. Corbett *s.j.* '71 (BO)[U] Weston, MA Campion Jesuit Community.
Walsh, Flannan J. '65 (STA) Retired.
Walsh, Flavian A. *o.f.m.* '56 (BO)[Z] Boston, MA St. Anthony Shrine.
Walsh, Rev. Msgr. Francis E. '66 (SPR) Retired.
Walsh, Francis M. *c.s.c.* '56 (FR)[A] North Easton, MA Holy Cross Fathers Religious.
Walsh, Francis M. '67 (WDC) On Duty Outside the Archdiocese; Washington, DC Holy Name.
Walsh, Francis M. *c.s.c.* '56 (FTW)[H] Notre Dame Congregation of Holy Cross, United States Province of Priests & Brothers.
Walsh, Francis P. '57 (CLV) Lakewood, OH St. Luke.
Walsh, Gerald G. '95 (CHI) Glenview, IL Our Lady of Perpetual Help.
Walsh, Rev. Msgr. Gerald J. '55 (BIS) Retired.
Walsh, James B. '65 (SAC) Retired.
Walsh, James F. *s.j.* '72 (BO)[U] Boston, MA Loyola House.
Walsh, James J. '93 (ALB) Formation for Priesthood/Vocation Awareness; Vocations and Vocation Awareness Program; Loudonville, NY St. Pius X.
Walsh, James J. '73 (SCR) Defenders of the Bond; Wilkes–Barre, PA St. Andrew Parish.
Walsh, James P. '73 (MAN) Retired.
Walsh, James P. *s.j.* '66 (STL)[O] St. Louis, MO Jesuit Community Corporation at Saint Louis University – Jesuit Hall.
Walsh, James P.M. *s.j.* '70 (WDC)[O] Washington, DC The Jesuit Community at Georgetown University.
Walsh, Rev. Msgr. James '69 (SJ) Retired.
Walsh, Jay Francis *c.s.b.* '65 (GAL) Houston, TX St. Anne.
Walsh, Jeffrey J. '94 (SCR) East Stroudsburg, PA St. John.

Walsh, Jerome Matthias *o.p.* (MAD) Madison, WI.
Walsh, Jerome '69 (DET) On Duty Outside the Archdiocese.
Walsh, Jim J. '68 (CIN) Cincinnati, OH St. Dominic.
Walsh, John A. '80 (E) Conneautville, PA St. Peter; Linesville, PA St. Philip.
Walsh, John A. '61 (SCR) On Duty Outside the Diocese.
Walsh, John Daly *m.m.* '56 (NY)[DD].
Walsh, John F. '76 (PIT) Allegheny County, PA Marian Manor, Inc.; [J] Pittsburgh, PA Marian Manor Corp.
Walsh, John J. *m.m.* '61 (NY)[DD] Retired.
Walsh, John J. '57 (DUB) Retired.
Walsh, John J. *s.j.* '71 (BO) Haverhill, MA St. James; Haverhill, MA St. John the Baptist.
Walsh, John P. '77 (ATL) Marietta, GA St. Joseph.
Walsh, John T. '44 (ROC) Rochester, NY Our Lady Queen of Peace Retired.
Walsh, John '77 (ATL) College of Consultors; Deans.
Walsh, John '61 (ORL) Orlando, FL Holy Cross.
Walsh, Joseph M. '86 (LIN) Hastings, NE St. Cecilia's; Presbyteral Council.
Walsh, Joseph R. '64 (SFR) South San Francisco, CA St. Veronica Retired.
Walsh, Kevin B. '92 (ARL) Falls Church, VA St. Anthony's.
Walsh, Kevin V. *o.c.s.o* '78 (CHR)[E] Moncks Corner, SC Mepkin Abbey.
Walsh, Laurence '45 (NO) Retired.
Walsh, Rev. Msgr. Lawrence '54 (SAT) San Antonio, TX Our Lady of Grace.
Walsh, Leo '94 (ANC) Anchorage, AK St. Benedict; Staff; Vocations; Anchorage, AK Holy Cross.
Walsh, Martin de Porres *o.p.* '69 (FgM) Oakland, CA Province of the Holy Name (Western Dominican Province).
Walsh, Martin *o.m.i.* '54 (BO)[Z] Lowell, MA Andre Garin Residence.
Walsh, Martin *o.p.* '69 (OAK)[L] Oakland, CA Order of Preachers (Province of the Most Holy Name of Jesus – Western Dominican Province).
Walsh, Martin *o.p.* '69 (OAK)[L] Oakland Order of Preachers (Province of the Most Holy Name of Jesus – Western Dominican Province).
Walsh, Matthew S. *s.j.* '09 (MIL)[P] Milwaukee, WI Arrupe House Jesuit Community.
Walsh, Michael F. *c.m.* '72 (LR) North Little Rock, AR St. Anne.
Walsh, Michael J. '56 (CHI) Retired.
Walsh, Rev. Msgr. Michael J. '73 (TR) Middletown, NJ St. Mary; Episcopal Council; Vicars Forane (Deans).
Walsh, Michael P. *m.m.* '88 (NY)[DD] Maryknoll Maryknoll Fathers and Brothers.
Walsh, Michael '53 (DEN) Retired.
Walsh, Michael '58 (LA)[F] La Canada Flintridge, CA St. Francis High School of La Canada–Flintridge.
Walsh, Miles D. '80 (BR) Baton Rouge, LA Our Lady of Mercy; College of Consultors; Presbyteral Council.
Walsh, Milton T. '78 (SFR) Absent on Leave.
Walsh, Patrick C. *c.s.c.* '81 (FR)[F] North Dartmouth, MA Holy Cross Residence.
Walsh, Patrick C. *c.s.c.* '81 (FTW)[H] Notre Dame Congregation of Holy Cross, United States Province of Priests & Brothers.
Walsh, Patrick E. *s.j.* '60 (MIL)[P] Wauwatosa, WI Jesuit Community at St. Camillus.
Walsh, Patrick F. '72 (P) Estacada, OR St. Aloysius; Sandy, OR St. Michael the Archangel.
Walsh, Patrick '69 (SC) Board of Education; [B] Sioux City, IA Bishop Heelan Catholic Schools.
Walsh, Peter J. *c.s.c.* '89 (ORL) Viera, FL St. John the Evangelist.
Walsh, Peter J. *c.s.c.* '89 (FTW)[H] Notre Dame Congregation of Holy Cross, United States Province of Priests & Brothers.
Walsh, Richard (Denis) L. '66 (TYL) Retired.
Walsh, Richard A. '62 (PRO)[L] Newport, RI St. Clare Home Retired.
Walsh, Richard '68 (ORL) Winter Park, FL St. Margaret Mary; Priest Personnel; Ex Officio Members.
Walsh, Robert E. '06 (WDC) Special Ministries.
Walsh, Robert T. *s.j.* '80 (SFR)[E] San Francisco, CA St. Ignatius College Preparatory (Coed); [N] San Francisco, CA Jesuit Community at St. Ignatius College Preparatory.
Walsh, Ronald J. '54 (NY) Retired.
Walsh, Seamus '66 (DUL) Grand Marais, MN St. John; Grand Marais, MN Holy Rosary.
Walsh, Sebastian *o.praem.* '05 (ORG)[D] Silverado, CA St. Michael's Preparatory School.
Walsh, Terrance G. *s.j.* '82 (BO)[U] Boston The Society of Jesus of New England–Provincial Offices.
Walsh, Terrence P. '04 (BGP) Stamford, CT The Basilica of Saint John the Evangelist.
Walsh, Theodore *c.p.* '59 (BRK)[R] Jamaica, NY Immaculate Conception Monastery.
Walsh, Thomas A. '42 (PHX) Scottsdale, AZ Blessed Sacrament Roman Catholic Parish Retired.
Walsh, Thomas E. *o.f.m.conv.* '80 (BAL) Baltimore, MD Annunciation; Baltimore, MD St. Clement Mary Hofbauer.
Walsh, Thomas F. *s.j.* '55 (PAT)[J] Morristown, NJ Loyola House of Retreats.
Walsh, Thomas F. *s.j.* '55 (NY)[DD] New York, NY Murray–Weigel Hall.
Walsh, Thomas J. '67 (BO) Marshfield, MA St. Christine.
Walsh, Thomas J. '94 (MET) East Brunswick, NJ St. Bartholomew; College of Consultors.
Walsh, Thomas J. '89 (HRT) Wallingford, CT Holy Trinity; New Britain Deanery.
Walsh, Thomas M. *s.s.c.* '57 (BUF)[M] Silver Creek, NY St. Columbans on the Lake, Home for the Aged.
Walsh, Thomas P. '86 (CHI) Chicago, IL St. Agatha.
Walsh, Thomas P. '72 (STA) Retired.
Walsh, Rev. Msgr. Thomas R. '59 (CHL) Retired.
Walsh, Thomas R. '94 (LIN) Geneva, NE St. Joseph's; Society of St. Vincent de Paul – Lincoln Council; Lincoln, NE Nebraska Penal Complex; Diocesan Area CCD Directors.
Walsh, Thomas V. '67 (WOR) Clinton, MA St. John the Guardian of Our Lady.
Walsh, Thomas *s.s.c.* '57 (OM)[J] St. Columbans Missionary Society of St. Columban Retired.
Walsh, Ulich '61 (WCH) Retired.
Walsh, Rev. Msgr. Vincent M. '62 (PH) Retired.
Walsh, William F. *o.s.f.s.* '68 (R) Kitty Hawk, NC Holy Redeemer by the Sea.
Walsh, William J. '54 (BAL)[Q] Baltimore, MD Colombiere Jesuit Community.
Walsh, William K. '49 (SAC) Rio Vista, CA St. Joseph Retired.
Walsh, William P. *s.j.* '67 (RVC)[P] Manhasset, NY St. Ignatius Jesuit Retreat House, Inisfada.
Walshe, Sebastian A. *o.praem.* '05 (ORG)[A] Silverado, CA St. Michael's Norbertine Postulancy, Novitiate and Juniorate; [I] Silverado, CA Norbertine Fathers of Orange Inc.
Walsman, Paul *o.f.m.* '58 (CIN)[N] Cincinnati St. Francis Seraph Friary.
Walter, Anthony *o.f.m.* '59 (CIN)[N] Cincinnati, OH St. John the Baptist Friary.
Walter, Chris B. '58 (BIS) Retired.
Walter, David A. '63 (STL) Retired.
Walter, Francis *o.f.m.* '77 (NY)[DD] New York Franciscan Province of the Immaculate Conception.
Walter, James A. '62 (COL) Sugar Grove, OH St. Joseph; Parochial Examiners; Deanery 11: Lancaster.
Walter, James A. '69 (BUF) Clergy Personnel Board; Springbrook, NY St. Vincent; Council of Priests.
Walter, Joseph L. *c.s.c.* '61 (FTW)[B] University of Notre Dame Du Lac; [H] Notre Dame, IN Holy Cross Community, Corby Hall, University of Notre Dame.
Walter, Marius *o.s.b.* '98 (P)[L] St. Benedict, OR Mt. Angel Abbey.
Walter, Marius *o.s.b.* '98 (BUF) Westfield, NY St. Dominic.
Walter, Mark J. '88 (CHI) Midlothian, IL St. Christopher.
Walter, Mark '10 (LFT) Carmel, IN Our Lady of Mount Carmel.
Walter, Rev. Msgr. Robert J. '45 (DAV)[J] Davenport, IA St. Vincent Center Retired.
Walter, Steven P. '77 (CIN) Cincinnati, OH St. John Fisher.
Walter, William '61 (KC) St. Joseph, MO St. Francis Xavier.
Walters, Erik T.A. '02 (MOB) On Leave from the Archdiocese.
Walters, Frederick '87 (PAT) Florham Park, NJ Holy Family.
Walters, Gary R. '79 (TOL) Sycamore, OH St. Pius X; Tiffin, OH St. Mary.
Walters, Hilarion *c.p.* '47 (FgM) New Rochelle, NY St. Paul of the Cross Province.
Walters, James *s.c.j.* '78 (MIL)[Y] Hales Corners, WI Congregation of the Priests of the Sacred Heart Support and Maintenance Trust; [B] Hales Corners, WI Sacred Heart School of Theology; [P] Hales Corners, WI Priests of the Sacred Heart.
Walters, Michael M. '81 (NEW) South Essex Deanery 18; Ministerial Development Center; Newark Ecclesial Team; South Orange, NJ Our Lady of Sorrows; Defenders of the Bond.
Walters, Michael M. '81 (PSC) Defender of the Bond.
Walters, Neil '89 (CLV) Cuyahoga County Jail; North Olmsted, OH St. Clarence.
Walters, Theodore W. *s.j.* '56 (FgM)[K] Detroit Detroit Province of the Society of Jesus–Provincial Office; Chicago, IL Society of Jesus.
Walters, Thomas *o.f.m.* (NY) New York, NY St. Francis of Assisi.
Walters, Vincent '54 (SB) Retired.
Walterscheid, Kyle '02 (FWT) Ranger, TX St. Francis Xavier; Vocations and Seminarians; Ranger, TX Holy Rosary; Ranger, TX St. Rita; Ranger, TX St. John; Fort Worth, TX St. Patrick Cathedral.
Walther, James *o.m.v.* '95 (SFD) Alton, IL St. Mary's.
Walton, James *o.f.m.* '91 (CHI)[N] Countryside, IL St. Gratian Friary, Franciscan Friars.
Walton, James *o.f.m.* '91 (JOL) Hinsdale, IL Hinsdale Hospital.
Walton, Rev. Msgr. Robert P. '74 (SAC) Sacramento, CA Sacred Heart of Jesus; Members.
Waltz, Joshua K. '07 (BIS)[C] Bismarck, ND St. Mary's Central High School; Menoken, ND St. Hildegard.
Waltz, Justin P. '08 (BIS) Minot, ND St. Leo; [I] Minot, ND Bishop Ryan High School.
Walz, Daniel '03 (SCL) Foley, MN St. John's; Sauk Rapids, MN St. Patrick.
Walz, Richard '88 (SCL) Long Prairie, MN St. Mary of Mt. Carmel; Presbyteral Council.
Walz, Richard *o.s.b.* '67 (LR)[A] Subiaco, AR Subiaco Abbey.
Walz, Rev. Msgr. W. Dean '53 (DUB) Council of Catholic Women; Judges Retired.
Wamala, Joseph '04 (RIC) Staunton, VA St. Francis of Assisi.
Wamala, Matthias M. '06 (COV) Independence, KY St. Cecilia.
Wamara, Serapio *c.s.c.* '03 (FTW)[H] Notre Dame Congregation of Holy Cross, United States Province of Priests & Brothers.
Wamayose, Bernard *a.j.* '02 (HBG) New Freedom, PA St. John the Baptist.
Wambach, John W. *s.j.* '64 (MIL)[P] Wauwatosa, WI Jesuit Community at St. Camillus.
Wambach, Joseph *s.d.s.* '67 (MIL)[P] Milwaukee Salvatorian Provincial Offices.
Wampach, Frank J. '84 (STP) Taylors Falls, MN St. Joseph's; Franconia, MN The Church of Saint Francis Xavier of Franconia.
Wanat, Mitchell *c.m.* '71 (HRT) Ansonia, CT St. Joseph.
Wanaurny, John *s.s.c.* '59 (OM)[J] St. Columbans Missionary Society of St. Columban.
Wanaurny, John *s.s.c.* '59 (FgM) St Columbans, NE House of Post–Graduate Studies.
Wanaurny, John *s.s.c.* '59 (LA)[P] Los Angeles, CA Columban Fathers, Procure House.
Wanaurny, John '59 (CHI)[N] Chicago, IL Columban Fathers Mission Center.
Wanda, Michael J. '91 (CHI) Westchester, IL Divine Infant.
Wander, Paul '90 (B) Salmon, ID St. Charles; Priest Personnel Commission.
Wandless, John H. '97 (KC) Retired.
Wang, Ignatius C. '59 (SFR) Retired.
Wang, John '54 (HEL) Retired.
Wang, John (STO) Diamond Springs, CA Retired.
Wangai, Patrick M. '07 (CHI) Forest Park, IL St. Bernardine.
Wangler, Rev. Msgr. Donald R. '57 (BUF) Retired.
Wangler, Leonard *o.s.b.* '70 (LR)[A] Subiaco, AR Subiaco Abbey; Presbyteral Council; [C] Subiaco, AR Subiaco Academy.
Wangler, Rev. Msgr. William O. '63 (BUF) Retired.
Wangwe, Fred *a.j.* '00 (HBG)[I] Lewisburg, PA Bucknell University.
Wanish, David A. '02 (MAD) Argyle, WI St. Michael; Argyle, WI St. Joseph; Argyle, WI St. Joseph; Argyle, WI St. John.
Wankar, Gabriel '04 (OAK) Oakland, CA St. Augustine.
Wankerl, Gary A. '80 (MAD) Oregon, WI Holy Mother of Consolation.
Wanser, George *s.j.* '76 (SJ) San Jose, CA Most Holy Trinity; Council of Religious.
Wantland, Thomas A. '67 (MAR) Retired.
Wapen, Francis A. '70 (SY) Taberg, NY St. Patrick.
Wapenski, Robert '05 (FAR) Anamoose, ND St. Francis Xavier Church of Anamoose; Drake, ND St. Margaret Mary.
Waraksa, Alex '90 (KNX) Morristown, TN St. Patrick.
Warburton, John *o.s.j.* '80 (MRY)[F] Shrine of St. Joseph; Santa Cruz, CA.
Warchola, Brian Lee '11 (ALT) Bellefonte, PA St. John the Evangelist's; Spring Mills, PA Blessed Kateri Tekakwitha; Bellefonte, PA State Correctional Institution – Rockview Our Lady of the Mount.
Ward, Daniel *o.s.b.* '71 (SCL)[I] Collegeville St. John's Abbey, of the Order of St. Benedict; Silver Spring, MD The Resource Center for Religious Institutes.
Ward, Daniel *o.s.b.* (WDC)[X] Silver Spring, MD National Association for Treasurers of Religious Institutes.
Ward, Donald M. *s.j.* '70 (CHL)[J] Mooresville, NC Jesuit Community; Mooresville, NC St. Therese.
Ward, Edward M. *o.m.i.* '67 (GAL) Houston, TX Immaculate Heart of Mary.
Ward, Edward *o.carm.* '73 (JOL) Darien, IL Our Lady of Mount Carmel.
Ward, Gary C. '80 (NEW) Absent on Leave.
Ward, Rev. Msgr. Gerald T. '79 (PEO) Diocesan College of Consultors; Bloomington, IL St. Patrick Church of Merna; Downs, IL St. Mary's; Vicariates and Vicars; Presbyteral Council.
Ward, Jack (BAL) Edgewood, MD Prince of Peace.
Ward, James G. *c.m.* '77 (STL)[V] Perryville, MO Association of the Miraculous Medal; [O] Perryville, MO Congregation of the Mission; [V] Perryville, MO Catholic Home Study Service.
Ward, James J. '73 (ALN) Jim Thorpe, PA Immaculate Conception; Jim Thorpe – Court Ryan #911.
Ward, Jerome A. *o.m.i.* '67 (CHR) Retired.
Ward, John B. '86 (BAL) Adjutant Judicial Vicar.

Ward, John B. '86 (MO) Judges.
Ward, John J. '55 (SFR) Retired.
Ward, John P. '65 (CAM) Retired.
Ward, Mark *c.p.* '76 (WH) Morgantown, WV St. Francis De Sales Catholic Church; Vicars Forane.
Ward, Michael G. '97 (NEW) Kearny, NJ St. Cecilia's; Kearny, NJ Our Lady of Sorrows; West Hudson Region Deanery 14; Presbyteral Council.
Ward, Paul '04 (DET) Imlay City, MI Sacred Heart.
Ward, Richard E. '68 (PIT) Bridgeville, PA St. Barbara.
Ward, Richard J. '93 (SEA) Retired.
Ward, Samuel W. '03 (LA) Secretary/Treasurer; South Gate, CA St. Helen; San Pedro Region.
Ward, Thomas I. '97 (SY) Binghamton, NY St. Mary of the Assumption; Binghamton, NY St. Paul.
Ward, Thomas '62 (KC) Retired.
Ward, Rev. Msgr. William P. '57 (SCR)[M] Dunmore, PA Villa St. Joseph Retired.
Wardanski, Rev. Msgr. Joseph V. '67 (E) Erie, PA St. Patrick; [L] Erie, PA Saint Mary's Home of Erie.
Warden, Daniel L. '66 (GAL) Houston, TX St. John Vianney; Houston, TX St. John Vianney Retired.
Warden, Joel M. *c.o.* '99 (BRK) Brooklyn, NY St. Boniface; [R] Brooklyn, NY Oratory of Saint Philip Neri, Congregation Pontifical Rite.
Warden, T. Patrick *c.s.b.* '65 (GAL)[O] Houston, TX Residence of the Basilian Fathers of the University of St. Thomas.
Wardenski, Robert W. '72 (BUF) East Aurora, NY Immaculate Conception.
Wardhana, Budi '09 (LA) Simi Valley, CA St. Rose of Lima.
Ware, Brandon M. '07 (STO) Lodi, CA St. Anne Church (Pastor of).
Ware, Donald *c.p.* '72 (PIT)[M] Pittsburgh, PA St. Paul of the Cross Monastery; [O] Pittsburgh, PA St. Paul of the Cross Retreat Center.
Wargel, William '65 (EVN) Retired.
Wargo, Rev. Msgr. Robert J. '72 (ALN) Orefield, PA St. Joseph The Worker.
Waris, Gerald R. '67 (KC) Retired.
Warkulwiz, Victor P. *m.s.s.* '91 (PH) Bensalem, PA Our Lady of Fatima; Bensalem, PA.
Warman, William C. '64 (MO) On Duty Outside the Archdiocese; U.S. Veterans Medical Center; DEPARTMENT OF VETERANS AFFAIRS HOSPITALS AND CHAPLAINS.
Warmuz, Grzegorz (CHI) Tinley Park, IL St. Stephen, Deacon and Martyr.
Warnakula, Anthony B. *c.h.s.p.* '88 (SAC) Susanville, CA California Correctional Center.
Warnakulasuriya, Edward Tissera '89 (HRT) Leave of Absence.
Warner, James P. '69 (GI) Retired.
Warner, John B. *s.j.* '74 (FgM) St. Louis, MO Society of Jesus.
Warner, Joseph A. '03 (CLV) Akron, OH Blessed Trinity.
Warnisher, Maximilian M. *f.i.* '94 (FR)[F] New Bedford, MA Marian Friary of Our Lady, Queen of the Seraphic Order.
Warnock, Damian J. *o.s.b.* '79 (GBG)[H] Latrobe, PA Saint Vincent Archabbey.
Warnstedt, Mark '96 (LA) Downey, CA Our Lady of Perpetual Help.
Warosh, James B. *s.j.* '67 (MIL)[P] Milwaukee, WI Jesuit Community at Marquette University.
Warren, Anthony *s.s.p.* '85 (Y)[A] Canfield, OH Society of St. Paul.
Warren, Arthur '63 (LAF) Retired.
Warren, Michael *o.m.v.* '08 (DEN) Denver, CO Holy Ghost.
Warren, Paul F. '78 (SFR) San Francisco, CA St. Stephen.
Warren, Robert *s.a.* '81 (NY)[DD] Garrison, NY St. Christopher's Inn; [DD] Garrison, NY St. Christopher's Friary.
Warsey, Robert J. *o.s.m.* '85 (CHI) Chicago, IL Our Lady of Sorrows, Basilica of; [N] Chicago, IL Servite Marian Center; Chicago, IL; [N] Chicago, IL National Shrine of Our Lady of Sorrows; [N] Chicago, IL Order of Friar Servants of Mary (Servites) United States of America Province, Inc.; [N] Chicago, IL Monastery of Our Lady of Sorrows.
Warsnak, Richard '07 (KCK) Emporia, KS Sacred Heart.
Wasek, Piotr '92 (RVC) Glen Head, NY St. Hyacinth; Hempstead, NY St. Ladislaus.
Waseline, Nicholas R. *o.s.f.s.* '80 (WIL)[J] Wilmington, DE Wilmington–Philadelphia Province of the Oblates of St. Francis de Sales.
Wash, Pat J. '68 (WH) Absent on Leave.
Washabaugh, Robert '78 (NOR) New London, CT St. Mary, Star of the Sea; College of Consultors; Members; St. Mary, Star of the Sea Church – Spanish Apostolate; New London.
Washburn, Thomas *o.f.m.* '00 (FR) Buzzards Bay, MA St. Margaret.
Washington, Christopher T. '06 (SCR) On Duty Outside the Diocese.
Washington, Freddy *c.s.sp.* '92 (CHI) Chicago, IL St. Ambrose; Chicago, IL St. Mary Magdalene.
Washko, Robert M. '77 (GBG) Seward, PA Holy Family.
Washko, Rt. Rev. Stephen G. '78 (HPM) Phoenix, AZ St. Stephen Cathedral; Protosyncellus (Vicar General); Ecclesiatical Notaries; Director of Ecumenical Affairs; [B] Phoenix, AZ St. Stephen Senior Citizen Apartments; College of Consultors; Finance Council; Building and Sacred Arts Commission; Pension Committee; Personnel Board.
Wasiecko, Allan *o.f.m.cap.* '68 (FgM) Pittsburgh, PA Province of St. Augustine.
Wasielewski, Henry R. '64 (PHX) Retired.
Wasikowski, Ronald S. '75 (OM) Bellevue, NE St. Matthew The Evangelist Church of Bellevue.
Wasilewski, Kenneth P. '03 (RCK) Elgin, IL St. Laurence; Ethicist for Health Care Issues, Diocesan.
Wasilewski, Thomas '10 (LAN) Adrian, MI St. Joseph; Brooklyn, MI St. Joseph Shrine.
Wasinger, Mark Shane '94 (STP) North Branch, MN St. Gregory the Great.
Waskowiak, Harlan D. P. '98 (LIN) Curtis, NE St. James; Diocesan Consultors.
Waslo, Rev. Msgr. Peter D. '86 (PHU) Protosyncellus; Chancellor; College of Archeparchial Consultors; Archeparchial Corporation; Judicial Vicar; Ecumenical Relations; The Way – Online Newspaper; Presbyteral Council; Archeparchial Council for Economic Affairs; Archdiocesan Bulletin; Director of Communication; [D] Philadelphia, PA Ascension Manor, Inc.
Wasnewski, Richard P. '53 (BO) Senior Priests. Retired.
Wasnie, Blane *o.s.b.* '66 (SCL) Avon, MN St. Benedict's; [I] Collegeville, MN St. John's Abbey, of the Order of St. Benedict.
Wasowski, Ronald *c.s.c.* '73 (P)[B] University of Portland; [L] Portland, OR Holy Cross Fathers & Brothers, C.S.C. – University of Portland.
Wasowski, Ronald *c.s.c.* (FTW)[H] Notre Dame Congregation of Holy Cross, United States Province of Priests & Brothers.
Wassef, Pafnouti '79 (MET) South River, NJ St. Mary of Ostrabrama.
Wassel, Rev. Msgr. Anthony F. '60 (ALN) Retired.
Wassell, John E. '97 (NEW) Elizabeth, NJ Our Lady of Most Holy Rosary/St. Michael; Elizabeth Deanery 25; Members; Presbyteral Council.
Wasser, James *m.s.f.* '74 (SAT)[B] San Antonio, TX MSF Formation Community.
Wassmuth, Rev. Msgr. Dennis '73 (B) Boise, ID Our Lady of the Rosary; Vicars General; Notaries; Ex Officio; Priest Personnel Commission; Finance Council; Priest Retirement Committee; McCall, ID Our Lady of the Lake; Building Commission; Catholic Liturgical Commission.
Wastag, Michael *o.carm.* '97 (NEW)[N] Mahwah, NJ Carmel Retreat.
Waszczenko, Andrew '89 (SAT) Stockdale, TX St. Ann's.
Waszczenko, Andrzej *s.d.s.* '89 (SAT) Falls City, TX Nativity of the Blessed Virgin Mary; [L] Falls City, TX Salvatorian Fathers Community of Texas.
Watanabe, Rev. Msgr. Terrence A.M. '77 (HON) Kihei, HI St. Theresa; Members.
Waterman, Gerald *o.f.m.conv.* '85 (R) Burlington, NC Blessed Sacrament; [F] Elon, NC Conventual Franciscans; [I] Elon, NC Elon University.
Waters, Bernard F. '69 (LAV) Unassigned.
Waters, Edward '77 (ORL) Lady Lake, FL St. Timothy.
Waters, J. Kevin *s.j.* '64 (SPK)[B] Spokane, WA Gonzaga University.
Waters, John J. *s.j.* '64 (DEN)[H] Denver, CO Saint Joseph Hospital; [N] Denver, CO Xavier Jesuit Center.
Waters, Joseph L. '87 (SP) Saint Petersburg, FL Cathedral of St. Jude the Apostle; Judges; Vicars Forane.
Waters, Joseph '56 (CHL) Retired.
Waters, Mark S. '90 (STA) Atlantic Beach, FL St. John the Baptist.
Waters, Philip J. *o.s.b.* '72 (NEW) Newark, NJ St. Mary's; [L] Newark, NJ Newark Abbey; Central Newark Deanery 20.
Waters, Robert E. '69 (BUF) Batavia, NY Resurrection.
Waters, Robert J. '60 (CHR) Aiken, SC St. Mary Help of Christians.
Waters, William F. *o.s.a.* '71 (BO)[AA] North Andover, MA Merrimack College Campus Ministry Center; [C] Our Mother of Good Counsel Monastery.
Wathen, Ambrose G. *o.s.b.* '65 (NO)[R] St. Benedict, LA St. Joseph Abbey.
Wathen, Daniel '06 (GF) Havre, MT St. Jude Thaddeus; [J] Havre, MT St. Jude's Education Trust; Diocesan Consultors; Clerical Benefit Association; Priests' Council.
Wathen, David *o.f.m.* '99 (FgM) Washington, DC; Washington, DC COMMISSARIAT OF THE HOLY LAND.
Wathen, David *o.f.m.* '99 (WDC)[O] Washington, DC Franciscan Monastery USA Inc.
Wathier, Douglas O. '84 (DUB)[L] Dubuque, IA Mt. Loretto Convent; [C] Loras College.
Watikha, Patrick *a.j.* '93 (LR) Charleston, AR Sacred Heart.
Watkins, Charles W. '03 (CHI) Chicago, IL St. Walter.
Watkins, Clarence N. '67 (ARL) Retired.
Watkins, Rev. Msgr. James D. '89 (WDC) Washington, DC Immaculate Conception; Deans; Priest Council.
Watkins, Mark T. '91 (CIN) Cincinnati, OH St. Lawrence.
Watkins, Paul D. *o.p.* '90 (MEM) Memphis, TN St. Peter Church.
Watson, Cletus M. *t.o.r.* '66 (SP) St. Petersburg, FL St. Mary Our Lady of Grace.
Watson, David E. *s.j.* '92 (DET)[K] Detroit, MI Jesuit Community at the University of Detroit Mercy.
Watson, Eric J. *s.j.* '09 (SEA)[A] Seattle, WA Seattle University; [M] Seattle, WA Arrupe Jesuit Community at Seattle University.
Watson, Joseph G. '92 (PH) Philadelphia, PA St. William.
Watson, Mark A. '96 (SHP) Lake Providence, LA St. Patrick; Oak Grove, LA Sacred Heart; Advocates; Presbyteral Council; Church Vocations Board & Vocations Office; College of Consultors.
Watson, Michael B. '86 (COL) Columbus, OH St. Andrew; Diocesan Finance Council.
Watson, Richard '11 (LEX) Lexington, KY Cathedral of Christ the King.
Watson, Timothy *c.ss.r.* '90 (SEA) Seattle, WA Sacred Heart of Jesus; Federal Detention Center.
Watson, Walter *s.j.* '70 (DEN)[N] Denver, CO Xavier Jesuit Center; Wheat Ridge, CO Sts. Peter and Paul.
Watson, Rev. Msgr. William A. '62 (PEO) Peoria Heights, IL St. Thomas; [B] Peoria, IL Peoria Notre Dame Scholarship Trust.
Watson, William M. *s.j.* '85 (SEA)[M] Seattle, WA Arrupe Jesuit Community at Seattle University.
Watt, Gerald *c.r.* (JOL) Westmont, IL Holy Trinity.
Watters, Timothy J. '71 (CHR) Absent On Leave.
Watters, William *s.j.* (BAL) Baltimore, MD St. Ignatius Church.
Watterson, John E. '62 (PRO) Retired.
Wattigny, Patrick B. '94 (NO) Metairie, LA St. Benilde.
Watts, Albert W. '59 (BGP) Retired.
Watts, Rev. Msgr. Roger J. '59 (BGP) Retired.
Watts, Thomas H. '57 (ROC) Owego, NY Blessed Trinity; Owego, NY St. Patrick Retired.
Watts, Trent L. '93 (R) Southport, NC Sacred Heart.
Watts, Wayne F. '90 (CHI) Chicago, IL St. John Berchmans; [G] Administration:; Associate Administrators.
Watzke, James N. *c.s.c.* '63 (FTW)[H] Notre Dame Congregation of Holy Cross, United States Province of Priests & Brothers.
Waugh, John G. '55 (PEO) Wedron, IL St. Joseph's; Illinois Industrial School for Boys.
Wawerski, Rev. Msgr. Edward '61 (RVC) Retired.
Waweru, Gabriel '07 (DUL) Hibbing, MN Blessed Sacrament; [G] Hibbing, MN Hibbing Catholic Schools Endowment Fund.
Wawryszuk, Zdzislaw F. '85 (RCK) Prophetstown, IL St. Catherine.
Wawrzycki, Andrew '70 (ORL) Retired.
Wawrzyn, Andrew '10 (CHI) Skokie, IL St. Peter.
Wawrzyniakowski, Edward J. '57 (MIL) Retired.
Waymel, Kevin G. '11 (NEW) Ridgewood, NJ Our Lady of Mount Carmel.
Wayne, Brian J. '11 (HBG) Hershey, PA St. Joan of Arc.
Wayne, David A. *s.j.* '68 (DEN)[D] Aurora, CO Regis Jesuit High School Corporation; [N] Centennial, CO Regis High Jesuit Community.
Wdowiak, Boleslaw '65 (SAC) Retired.
Wea, Raymundus *s.v.d.* '82 (SD) San Diego, CA Children's Hospital; Sharp Memorial Hospital; San Diego, CA Our Lady of the Sacred Heart Catholic Parish.
Weakley, Robert *o.f.m.* '68 (PEO) Peoria, IL Sacred Heart; Peoria, IL St. Joseph.
Weare, Kenneth M. '01 (SFR) Fairfax, CA St. Rita; Archdiocesan Board of Education; [P] San Francisco, CA Catholic Charities CYO of the Archdiocese of San Francisco.
Wearsch, Ronald '92 (CLV) Willowick, OH St. Mary Magdalene.
Weary, William M. '84 (HBG) Lewistown, PA Sacred Heart of Jesus; Mifflintown, PA St. Jude.
Weaver, Cyprian *o.s.b.* '72 (SCL) Collegeville, MN St. John's Abbey; [I] Collegeville St. John's Abbey, of the Order of St. Benedict.
Weaver, John G. '70 (HRT) Enfield, CT St. Patrick.
Weaver, Mark *o.f.m.conv.* '77 (IND) Terre Haute, IN St. Joseph University Catholic Church, Terre Haute, Inc.; [J] Mount St. Francis, IN Province of Our Lady of Consolation, Inc.
Weaver, Richard '63 (DAL) Retired.
Webb, Raymond J. '67 (CHI)[A] Mundelein, IL University of St. Mary of the Lake/Mundelein Seminary.
Webber, Rev. Msgr. Donald S. '62 (SB) Judges; Sun City, CA Retired.
Webber, Donald *c.p.* '73 (CHI)[N] Chicago, IL Passionist Provincial Office; [N] Chicago, IL Passionist Community–Immaculate Conception Community; Chicago, IL Holy Cross Province (Western).
Webber, Lawrence E. *o.f.m.cap.* '80 (DET)[K] Detroit, MI St. Mary's Friary; [T] St. Clair Shores, MI Catholic Kolping Society of America, Detroit Branch,

Inc.; [T] Detroit, MI Solanus Casey Center.
Weber, Alan '84 (SP)[S] Temple Terrace, FL Catholic Student Center, University of South Florida.
Weber, Allen *o.f.m.* '65 (BUF)[N] St. Bonaventure, NY St. Bonaventure Friary.
Weber, Arnold *o.s.b.* '52 (SCL)[I] Collegeville, MN St. John's Abbey, of the Order of St. Benedict.
Weber, Bernard *c.p.* '81 (L)[L] Louisville, KY Sacred Heart Retreat.
Weber, Christopher H. '02 (CLV) Presbyteral Convenors; Berea, OH St. Mary; Presbyteral Council.
Weber, David '77 (CLV) Administrative Leave.
Weber, Dennis M. *sd.c.* '97 (PH)[L] Springfield, PA Don Guanella School; [L] Springfield, PA Cardinal Krol Center; [Y] Springfield, PA Servants of Charity (Sd.C.); [M] Rosemont, PA St. Edmond's Home for Children; [B] Springfield, PA Servants of Charity Sd.C.
Weber, Donald E. '58 (GR) On Special Assignment; Vicar For Priests; Vicar for Clergy Retired.
Weber, Rev. Msgr. Edward J. '76 (NY) West Nyack, NY St. Francis of Assisi; Rockland; Archdiocesan Consultors.
Weber, Eric Christopher '01 (LAN) On Duty Outside the Diocese.
Weber, Fidelis F. *t.o.r.* '55 (PH)[Y] Fairless Hills, PA St. Anthony Friary.
Weber, Rev. Msgr. Francis J. '59 (LA) Mission Hills, CA San Fernando Rey Mission Retired.
Weber, Frank N. '72 (GB)[I] Kaukauna, WI St. Paul Home; Special Assignment.
Weber, Frank W. '62 (PAT) Clifton, NJ St. Brendan.
Weber, Gabriel M. *o.s.m.* '49 (DEN) Denver, CO Our Lady of Mount Carmel.
Weber, George *c.m.* '54 (NO)[R] New Orleans, LA Congregation of the Mission Western Province (Vincentians) Retired.
Weber, Gerald *o.m.i.* '62 (SAT)[K] San Antonio, TX Oblate Madonna Residence.
Weber, Herbert F. '74 (TOL) St. Katherine Drexel Deanery; Perrysburg, OH Blessed John XXIII; College of Consultors; Members.
Weber, Jamie '04 (CIN) Cincinnati, OH St. Cecilia.
Weber, Jason '10 (ARL) Arlington, VA Cathedral of St. Thomas More; Notaries.
Weber, John R. *c.s.sp.* '61 (PIT)[O] Bethel Park, PA The Spiritan Center.
Weber, John R. '09 (PH) Lansdale, PA St. Stanislaus.
Weber, John S. '73 (LSC) Finance Council; Judges; Lordsburg, NM St. Joseph.
Weber, Joseph A. '76 (PRM) St. Louis, MO St. Louis Mission.
Weber, Joseph A. '76 (STL) Sunset Hills, MO St. Justin Martyr; Air National Guard Chaplains.
Weber, Joseph O. '57 (SCR) Retired.
Weber, Keith '83 (SAL) Manhattan, KS St. Isidore Catholic Student Center Parish; [G] Manhattan, KS St. Isidore's Catholic Student Center.
Weber, Kevin '93 (SAL) Hays, KS Immaculate Heart of Mary Parish; Personnel Board; Art and Architecture Commission; Board of Trustees.
Weber, Leo F. *s.j.* '56 (DEN) Denver, CO St. Ignatius Loyola; [N] Denver, CO Society of Jesus – St. Ignatius Loyola Jesuit Community.
Weber, Mark *s.v.d.* '82 (CHI)[N] Techny, IL Divine Word Residence.
Weber, Matthew '90 (CAM) Glassboro, NJ St. Bridget's Catholic Church, Glassboro, N.J.
Weber, Michael J. *o.praem.* '77 (GB)[J] De Pere, WI St. Norbert Abbey.
Weber, Norbert B. *m.s.c.* '57 (RCK)[G] Aurora, IL Missionaries of the Sacred Heart Community.
Weber, Randall '91 (SAL) Office of Communications; Procurator and Advocate; College of Consultors; Personnel Board; Art and Architecture Commission; Ex Officio; Ex Officio; Consultors; Office of Ecumenical and Interreligious Affairs; Salina, KS Sacred Heart Cathedral Parish; Moderator of the Curia.
Weber, Robert C. '81 (SY) Holland Patent, NY St. Leo; Marcy, NY Mid–State Correctional Facility; Special Assignment.
Weber, Robert P. '65 (CAM) Delmont, NJ Southern State Correctional Facility; Bridgeton, NJ Southwoods State Prison Retired.
Weber, Robson Luis '76 (ALN) Bethlehem, PA Holy Infancy.
Weber, Samuel *o.s.b.* '96 (IND)[K] Saint Meinrad St. Meinrad Archabbey.
Weber, Terry '85 (SFS) Brandon, SD Risen Savior.
Weber, Theodore '55 (P) Retired.
Weber, Thomas L. '74 (CLV) Lyndhurst, OH St. Clare.
Weberg, Paul *o.s.b.* '03 (RCK)[G] Aurora, IL Marmion Abbey.
Weberg, Paul *o.s.b.* '03 (MO) Army National Guard Chaplains.
Webster, Robert E. '86 (ORL) Liturgy; Clermont, FL Blessed Sacrament.
Wechter, David *o.c.s.o.* '58 (WIN)[A] Winona, MN Immaculate Heart of Mary Seminary; [G] Houston, MN Hermits of St. Mary of Carmel, (H.S.M.C.); Associate Judges.
Weckerle, Leo F. '58 (BAK) Defenders of the Bond and Promoters of Justice Retired.
Weckert, Paul M. *o.s.b.* '99 (SEA) Battle Ground, WA Sacred Heart; [M] Lacey, WA St. Martin's Abbey; Presbyteral Council.
Wedeking, Patrick '88 (GLP) On Duty Outside of Diocese; Air Force Chaplains.
Wedig, James M. '93 (CIN) Wilmington, OH St. Columbkille; [R] Wilmington, OH Wilmington College Campus Ministry.
Wedig, Mark *o.p.* '86 (MIA)[C] Miami, FL Barry University; [H] Miami, FL Dominican Fathers of Miami, Inc.
Wedow, Robert L. '01 (DEN) Sterling, CO St. Anthony.
Wee, Damien (OM) Hooper, NE St. Rose of Lima.
Weeder, James M. '11 (OM) Omaha, NE St. Margaret Mary.
Weekly, Christopher S. '98 (P) Portland, OR St. Ignatius; [L] Portland, OR Colombiere Community.
Weeks, James M. *m.s.* '62 (HRT)[L] Hartford, CT Missionaries of LaSalette.
Weeks, Sean '04 (P) Ashland, OR Our Lady of the Mountain; [P] Ashland, OR Southern Oregon University (Ashland); Area Vicars; Board Members.
Weerakkody, Oliver '65 (AUS) Austin, TX St. Louis.
Weerasinghe, Felix M. '64 (RVC) Retired.
Weezorak, Dennis R. '86 (MET) South Amboy, NJ St. Mary.
Wegher, William '91 (LAN) Pinckney, MI St. Mary; Ecumenical Officer.
Weglicki, Michael '79 (LEX) Corbin, KY Sacred Heart; Williamsburg, KY St. Boniface; Defenders of the Bond; Catholic Scouting.
Wegman, Richard H. '90 (MAN) Retired.
Wegner, Gary *o.f.m.cap.* '89 (MIL)[P] Mount Calvary, WI St. Lawrence Friary; [B] Mount Calvary, WI St. Lawrence Seminary; Councilors.
Wego, Benignus Lambertus *s.v.d.* (LKC) Lake Charles Memorial Hospital; Iowa, LA St. Raphael.
Wehby, Albert *b.a.o.* '63 (NTN) North Hollywood, CA St. Anne.
Wehinger, Thomas E. '61 (TOL) Retired.
Wehman, Jack W. '80 (CIN) Wyoming, OH St. James of the Valley.
Wehmann, Mark H. '03 (STP) Lindstrom, MN St. Bridget of Sweden.
Wehmeyer, Curtis C. '01 (STP) St. Paul, MN Blessed Sacrament.
Wehn, Timothy '79 (LAV) Propagation of the Faith; Las Vegas, NV Guardian Angel Cathedral; Priests' Pension Board.
Wehner, Edwin P. '69 (BIS) Bismarck, ND Saint Anne.
Wehner, Eugene C. *o.c.d.* '75 (MIL)[P] Milwaukee Provincial Offices – Discalced Carmelites.
Wehner, James A. '95 (PIT) On Duty Outside the Diocese.
Wehner, James A. '95 (COL)[A] Columbus, OH Pontifical College Josephinum.
Wehner, James A. '95 (COL)[A] Columbus, OH Pontifical College Josephinum.
Wehnert, Donald R. *c.s.v.* '63 (JOL) Kankakee, IL St. Patrick Retired.
Wehnert, Donald R. *c.s.v.* '63 (CHI)[N] Arlington Heights Viatorian Province Center–Clerics of St. Viator.
Wehr, Arthur J. *s.j.* '90 (SAC) Sacramento, CA St. Ignatius of Loyola; [H] Carmichael, CA Sacramento Jesuit Community.
Wehri, Francis *o.s.b.* '61 (BIS)[A] Richardton, ND Assumption Abbey; Richardton, ND Assumption Abbey.
Wehrle, Jonathan '78 (LAN) Okemos, MI St. Martha; Building Commission; Priest Pension Board.
Wehrle, Peter G. '99 (NEW) North Bergen, NJ Our Lady of Fatima.
Wehrlen, Rev. Msgr. John B. '59 (PAT) Toms River, NJ Retired.
Wehrley, Charles *c.ss.r.* '01 (TUC)[G] Tucson, AZ Redemptorist Society of Arizona Redemptorist Renewal Center.
Wehrlin, Leo J. '93 (Y) Windham, OH St. Michael's; Hiram College; Garrettsville, OH St. Ambrose.
Wehrmeyer, Richard *c.m.* '91 (FgM) Earth City, MO Western Province.
Wehrs, Kenneth J. '10 (LIN) David City, NE St. Mary's; Advocates.
Wei, Luke '60 (BRK) Retired.
Weibl, Nicholas '64 (TOL) Fostoria, OH St. Wendelin.
Weible, Thomas C. '59 (LA) Retired.
Weick, Anthony *s.j.* (DAL)[D] Dallas, TX Jesuit College Preparatory School.
Weidenbenner, Joseph '07 (SPC) Diocesan Pastoral Council; West Plains, MO St. Mary; Presbyteral Council; Youth Ministry; Priests' Mutual Benefit Society.
Weider, Gregory '63 (ALB) Retired.
Weider, Henry '89 (OWN) Absent on Leave.
Weidert, Richard J. '95 (BEL) Retired.
Weidner, Halbert *c.o.* '74 (CHR)[E] Rock Hill, SC Oratory of St. Philip Neri, Congregation of the Oratory of Pontifical Rite.
Weidner, Halbert *c.o.* '74 (NOR) Middletown, CT St. Francis of Assisi; Middletown; St. Francis of Assisi Church – Spanish Apostolate; [K] Middletown, CT Wesleyan University–The University Ministry.
Weidner, Larry W. '80 (PHX) Special Assignment; Sun City, AZ Banner Boswell Medical Center.
Weidner, Mark *o.c.s.o.* '54 (P)[L] Lafayette, OR The Cistercian (Trappist) Abbey of Our Lady of Guadalupe.
Weidner, S. Anthony '05 (OM) Omaha, NE St. Peter.
Weigand, Dom Peter *o.s.b.* '70 (WDC)[E] Washington, DC St. Anselm's Abbey School, Inc.
Weigand, John J. '67 (CLV) Retired.
Weigand, Joseph C. '62 (CLV) Lagrange, OH St. Mary Retired.
Weigand, Joseph C. '62 (CLV) Cuyahoga Falls, OH Immaculate Heart of Mary Retired.
Weigand, Peter *o.s.b.* '70 (WDC)[O] Washington, DC St. Anselm's Abbey.
Weighner, James C. '07 (LC) Prairie du Chien, WI St. Gabriel; Prairie du Chien, WI St. John Nepomucene.
Weighner, Robert J. '99 (MIL) Pleasant Prairie, WI St. Anne; Archdiocesan Council of Priests.
Weigman, Joseph A. '91 (TOL)[G] Oregon, OH Sacred Heart Home Retired.
Weik, Terence P. *s.m.* '80 (BAL) Eldersburg, MD St. Joseph; [T] Sykesville, MD St. Joseph Catholic Community Endowment Trust.
Weikart, David '03 (Y) Presbyteral Council.
Weikart, G. David '03 (Y) Orwell, OH St. Mary; Rock Creek, OH Sacred Heart.
Weiksnar, William J. *o.f.m.* '94 (CAM) Camden, NJ St. Anthony of Padua Roman Catholic Church, Camden, N.J.
Weiksner, Jerome M. '55 (GBG) Retired.
Weil, Frank *o.carm.* '67 (JOL)[L] Darien Carmelite Provincial Office.
Weiler, Michael D. *s.j.* '88 (SJ)[M] Los Gatos, CA California Province of the Society of Jesus, Jesuit Provincial Office; [B] Santa Clara, CA Jesuit Community; [M] Santa Clara, CA Casa San Inigo, Jesuit Residence.
Weiler, Michael F. *s.j.* '88 (FgM) Los Gatos, CA Society of Jesus; [P] Culver City, CA Ignatius House, The Novitiate of the California Province, Society of Jesus.
Weinandy, Thomas *o.f.m.cap.* '72 (WDC)[B] Washington, DC St. Francis Friary–Capuchin College.
Weinberger, Paul L. '89 (DAL) Greenville, TX St. William; Quinlan, TX Our Lady of Fatima.
Weiner, James J. '88 (NEW) Ho Ho Kus, NJ St. Luke's.
Weiner, Rev. Mitred Archpriest Philip '91 (STF) Syracuse; Rochester, NY St. Josaphat.
Weinert, Allan *c.ss.r.* '72 (DEN)[N] Denver, CO The Redemptorists/Denver Province.
Weingartner, Derrick J. *s.j.* '10 (BR)[K] Baton Rouge, LA Martin Luther King, Jr. Catholic Student Center; Baton Rouge, LA Immaculate Conception.
Weingartz, Francis A. '54 (DET) Retired.
Weinlader, Wayne T. *m.m.* '68 (NY)[DD] Retired.
Weinzapfel, Rev. Msgr. Thomas '45 (DAL) Retired.
Weir, Bernard E. '86 (DAV) Ottumwa, IA St. Mary of the Visitation.
Weis, Anthony J. '10 (BIR) Birmingham, AL Our Lady of the Valley.
Weis, Denis P. '63 (MIL) Retired.
Weis, Eugene R. '62 (ROC) Lady Lake, FL St. Timothy Retired.
Weis, John H. '66 (PAT) On Duty Outside the Diocese.
Weis, John '66 (SAG) Pigeon, MI St. Francis Borgia; Sebewaing, MI Holy Family.
Weisbeck, Paul '70 (SJ) Santa Clara County Sheriffs Dept. Retired.
Weisbecker, Thomas W. '96 (OM) Columbus, NE St. Bonaventure; Deans; Deans; [L] Elkhorn, NE Apostolic Sodales.
Weisbrod, Daren *l.c.* (GRY)[C] Rolling Prairie, IN Sacred Heart Apostolic School, Inc.
Weiscopf, Daniel J. '90 (BRK) Retired.
Weise, Thomas D. '62 (MOB) Phenix City, AL St. Patrick; Phenix City, AL Mother Mary Parish.
Weise, Thomas L. '02 (JUN) Petersburg, AK St. Catherine of Siena; Wrangell, AK St. Rose of Lima; Diocesan Consultors.
Weisenbeck, Jude *s.d.s.* '60 (MIL)[P] Milwaukee, WI Salvatorians – Jordan Hall Retired.
Weisenberger, Gary '77 (SEA) Fife, WA St. Martin of Tours.
Weisenberger, Leon *m.s.c.* '59 (RCK)[G] Aurora, IL Missionaries of the Sacred Heart Community.
Weisenberger, Richard J. '79 (LFT) Gas City, IN Holy Family; Marion, IN St. Paul.
Weisenburger, Rev. Msgr. Edward J. '87 (OKL) Oklahoma City, OK Cathedral of Our Lady of Perpetual Help; Personnel Committee; Vicar General; Judges; Consultors Archdiocesan; Council of Priests Archdiocesan; Priests' Medical Fund; Vicar General.
Weisensel, Cyril O. '67 (MAD) Hazel Green, WI St. Francis de Sales; Hazel Green, WI St. Joseph; [F] Madison, WI Bishop O'Connor Catholic Pastoral Center Retired.
Weiser, Charles B. '66 (TR) Tribunal Judges; West End,

NJ St. Michael.
Weishaar, Leo G. '84 (MOB)[D] Mobile, AL Providence Hospital; Special Assignment.
Weishar, Paul M. '48 (MIL) Retired.
Weisman, Raymond F. '76 (WIL) Salisbury, MD St. Francis De Sales.
Weiss, Earl A. *s.j.* '54 (DET)[K] Clarkston, MI Colombiere Center.
Weiss, Erich '10 (MIL) Oconomowoc, WI St. Jerome.
Weiss, Jerome P. '77 (DUL) Grand Rapids, MN St. Joseph; Grand Rapids, MN St. John; Warba, MN St. Paul; College of Consultors.
Weiss, Joseph E. *s.j.* '85 (STP) St. Paul, MN St. Thomas More.
Weiss, Mark E. '04 (HBG) Lancaster, PA St. Philip the Apostle.
Weiss, Peter *s.s.j.* '10 (GAL) Houston, TX St. Francis Xavier.
Weiss, Richard '80 (ELP) Retired.
Weiss, Rev. Msgr. Robert E. '73 (BGP) Newtown, CT St. Rose of Lima; Diocesan Consultors.
Weiss, Robert F. *s.j.* '59 (STL)[V] St. Louis, MO The Jesuits of the Missouri Province; Saint Louis, MO; [O] St. Louis, MO The Jesuits of the Missouri Province; [O] St. Louis, MO Jesuit Community Corporation at Saint Louis University – Jesuit Hall.
Weiss, Robert *c.p.* '65 (L)[L] Louisville, KY Sacred Heart Retreat.
Weissbeck, Reinhold '72 (DEN) Longmont, CO St. John the Baptist.
Weissbeck, Reinhold '72 (DEN) Deaneries.
Weist, Edward F. '69 (CLV) Litchfield, OH Our Lady Help of Christians Parish.
Weithman, Raymond *c.ss.r.* '56 (NY)[DD] Esopus, NY Redemptorist Priests and Brothers C.Ss.R. (Province of Baltimore).
Weithman, Robert J. '55 (TOL) Retired.
Weitzel, Eugene J. *c.s.v.* '59 (CHI)[N] Arlington Heights Viatorian Province Center–Clerics of St. Viator.
Weitzel, Stephen D. '90 (HBG) Mechanicsburg, PA Saint Katharine Drexel.
Weixelman, Richard *o.m.i.* '65 (FgM) Washington, DC AMERICAN OBLATE MISSIONS.
Wekerle, Ronald '90 (B) Jerome, ID St. Jerome's.
Wekesa, Pius S. '95 (R) Roanoke Rapids, NC St. John the Baptist.
Welbers, Rev. Msgr. Thomas '68 (LA) Beverly Hills, CA Good Shepherd.
Welch, Bernard J. '81 (PRT) Retired.
Welch, Christopher J. '94 (ALB) Hancock, NY St. Paul the Apostle.
Welch, D. Michael '70 (IND) Indianapolis, IN St. Christopher Catholic Church, Indianapolis, Inc.
Welch, Gregory T. '67 (STP) Retired.
Welch, John A. *m.s.* '93 (FR)[F] Attleboro, MA La Salette Shrine.
Welch, John A. *m.s.* '93 (WDC)[O] Washington, DC La Salette Formation Community.
Welch, John E. *m.s.* '60 (NOR) Danielson, CT St. James Retired.
Welch, John *o.carm.* '65 (JOL)[L] Joliet, IL St. Elias Carmelites.
Welch, Richard L. *c.ss.r.* '80 (NY) Judges; [DD] New York, NY Redemptorist Priests and Brothers, C.Ss.R.; Associate Judicial Vicar.
Welch, Robert J. *s.j.* '60 (LA)[C] Los Angeles, CA Jesuit Community.
Welch, William J. '55 (GLP) Snowflake, AZ Our Lady of the Snows.
Weldgen, Rev. Msgr. Francis G. '59 (BUF) Council of Priests Retired.
Welding, Brian J. '91 (PIT) Judicial Vicar; Canon and Civil Law Services, Dept. for; Canonical Services, Office for; Assistant Director, Department for Canon and Civil Law Services; Vice Chancellor; Pittsburgh, PA Ascension.
Weldishofer, Bernard J. '92 (CIN) Lebanon, OH St. Francis de Sales.
Weldon, C. Michael *o.f.m.* '81 (MIL)[B] Hales Corners, WI Sacred Heart School of Theology.
Weldon, Christopher J. '05 (LFT) Muncie, IN St. Francis of Assisi; [H] Muncie, IN Newman Foundation–Ball State University; Ministry to Priests' Program; Newman Foundation, Ball State, Inc.
Weldon, Eric M. '00 (WCH) Wichita, KS St. Margaret Mary; Presbyteral Council/College of Consultors.
Weldon, James F. '98 (WCH) Wichita, KS Church of the Resurrection.
Weldon, Michael *o.f.m.* '81 (MIL)[P] Provincial Offices of the Franciscan Friars, Assumption BVM Province, Inc.
Weldu, Awte *o.cist.* '80 (TR)[N] Mount Laurel, NJ Cistercian Monastery of Our Lady of Fatima; Tribunal Judges; Mount Laurel, NJ.
Weling, John B. '81 (ORG) Newport Beach, CA Our Lady of Mount Carmel.
Welk, Thomas *c.pp.s.* '69 (WCH)[F] Wichita, KS Adorers of the Blood of Christ U.S. Region; Liberty, MO.
Welk, Thomas *c.pp.s.* '69 (KC)[A] Liberty, MO Society of the Precious Blood Provincial Offices.
Wellar, Thomas '80 (CC) Ingleside, TX Our Lady of the Assumption.
Welle, Anthony R. '07 (ORL) Indialantic, FL Holy Name of Jesus.
Wellems, Bruce L. *c.m.f.* '86 (CHI) Oak Park, IL; Chicago, IL Holy Cross/Immaculate Heart of Mary; [N] Oak Park, IL Claretian Missionaries Community Support Trust; [N] Oak Park Claretian Missionaries USA Eastern Province.
Weller, Andre *o.f.m.cap.* '63 (DET) Detroit, MI Province of St. Joseph; [K] Detroit St. Bonaventure Friary.
Weller, Joseph W. '64 (KAL) Retired.
Welles, Timothy J. '06 (LC) Rudolph, WI St. Philip; Wisconsin Rapids, WI St. Lawrence.
Wellman, Rev. Msgr. Dale L. '64 (PEO) Vicariates and Vicars; Moline, IL Sacred Heart; Diocesan College of Consultors; Catholic Women, Council of; Clergymen's Aid, Inc.
Wells, David '10 (WDC) Lexington Park, MD Immaculate Heart of Mary.
Wells, James *o.f.m.* '82 (NY)[DD] St. Peter Friary.
Wells, Rev. Msgr. Patrick R. '93 (GAL) Retired.
Wells, Peter B. '91 (TLS) On Duty Outside the Diocese.
Wells, Peter VB. '84 (PAT) Clifton, NJ St. Clare; Diocesan Cemeteries Office.
Wells, Philip J. '83 (SAC) Anderson, CA Sacred Heart.
Welsch, Gerard R. '66 (STL) Maryland Heights, MO St. John Bosco.
Welschmeyer, Joseph J. '00 (STL) Potosi, MO St. James.
Welsh, Charles A. *s.j.* '72 (FgM) Los Gatos, CA Society of Jesus.
Welsh, Christopher '82 (DET) Royal Oak, MI Beaumont Hospital.
Welsh, Garry A. '01 (OM) On Leave of Absence.
Welsh, Patrick J. '98 (CIN) Cincinnati, OH St. Bartholomew.
Welsh, Patrick J. '00 (PH)[A] Wynnewood, PA Theological Seminary of St. Charles Borromeo, Overbrook.
Welsh, Peter J. '80 (PH) Chester, PA Saint Katharine Drexel.
Welsh, Richard C. '60 (DET) Retired.
Welsh, Robert J. *s.j.* '67 (CLV)[D] Cleveland, OH St. Ignatius High School.
Welsh, Vincent F. '89 (PH) Defenders of the Bond; Norristown, PA St. Francis of Assisi.
Welsh, William P. '60 (CHI) Retired.
Welstead, Flavian *o.f.m.cap.* '67 (SFR) Burlingame, CA Our Lady of Angels.
Welter, Brian T. '05 (CHI) Archdiocesan Vocations; Chicago, IL Holy Name Cathedral.
Weltin, Richard W. '83 (SFD) Decatur, IL Our Lady of Lourdes; Decatur, IL St. Thomas the Apostle; Comite Diocesano de Ministerio Hispano – Diocesan Committee for Hispanic Ministry; Presbyteral Council.
Welzbacher, George A. '51 (STP) St. Paul, MN St. John of St. Paul; Censores Librorum.
Wempe, Richard C. '52 (KCK) Retired.
Wenani, Kizito '08 (SPC) Cape Girardeau, MO St. Vincent de Paul; Cape Girardeau Hospital Ministry.
Wendel, Alfred W. '78 (MO) Army Chaplains.
Wendel, Arthur G. *c.ss.r.* (NY) New York, NY Most Holy Redeemer.
Wendel, Fred W. '78 (ATL) Fort McPherson, GA Office of the Garrison Chaplain; Military Chaplains.
Wendel, Paul G. *c.s.c.* '55 (FTW)[H] Holy Cross House.
Wendelken, Robert M. '61 (CLV) Solon, OH St. Rita; Lyndhurst, OH St. Clare; Judges Retired.
Wendell, Richard '06 (MIL) Reeseville, WI Holy Family; Reeseville, WI St. John; Reeseville, WI St. Columbkille.
Wenderoth, Joseph R. '62 (BAL) Retired.
Wendler, Patrick J. '08 (MAD) Dodgeville, WI St. Joseph; Vicar for Permanent Deacons.
Wendling, Francis *o.f.m.* '63 (CIN)[N] Cincinnati St. Francis Seraph Friary.
Wendling, Francis *o.f.m.* '62 (SPC)[F] Ava, MO Our Lady of the Angels Friary.
Wendrychowicz, Rev. Msgr. John B. '73 (PH) Archdiocesan Boy Scouts; Sellersville, PA St. Agnes.
Wendt, Patrick '79 (MIL) Port Washington, WI St. Mary; Saukville, WI Immaculate Conception; Port Washington, WI St. Peter of Alcantara.
Wendzikowski, Rev. Msgr. Mecislaus S. '59 (BUF) Retired.
Wenger, Sean A. *c.c.* '95 (DET) Detroit, MI St. Scholastica; Adult Evangelization Coordinators.
Wenig, Laurin J. '73 (MIL) Elm Grove, WI St. Mary's Visitation.
Wenke, Leonard C. '79 (CIN) Archdiocesan Department Directors; Presbyteral Council; Vicarri Foranei (Deans); Consultors; Pontifical Mission Aid Societies; Director; Cincinnati, OH Our Lord, Christ the King.
Wenninger, Magnus *o.s.b.* '45 (SCL)[I] Collegeville, MN St. John's Abbey, of the Order of St. Benedict.
Wensing, Michael '76 (SFS) Watertown, SD Immaculate Conception; Diocesan Consultors.
Wenthe, Christopher T. '03 (STP) Special Assignment.
Wentink, William R. '70 (RCK)[D] East Peoria, IL Saint Anthony Medical Center; Special Assignment.
Wentz, Aelred W. *o.c.s.o.* '85 (ROC)[K] Piffard, NY Abbey of the Genesee.
Wenz, Robert '82 (CLV) Brunswick, OH St. Ambrose.
Wenzel, James *o.s.a.* '56 (BO)[C] North Andover, MA Merrimack College.
Wenzel, Timothy '66 (SCL) Retired.
Wenzinger, George E. '78 (TOL) Leipsic, OH St. Mary; St. George Deanery; College of Consultors.
Wenzinger, Mark Edward *o.s.b.* '95 (GBG)[H] Latrobe, PA Saint Vincent Archabbey.
Wenzinger, Rev. Msgr. Robert D. '82 (FRS) Fresno, CA St. Anthony of Padua; Advocates; Personnel Board.
Werbicki, Walter '57 (BUF) Lakeview Shock Incarceration Correctional Facility; Dunkirk, NY St. Elizabeth Ann Seton.
Weria, Theobold *a.l.c.p.* '98 (SP) Zephyrhills, FL St. Joseph Catholic Church.
Werkhoven, Michael E. '02 (MEM) Humboldt, TN St. Matthew Mission; Presbyteral Council; Search; Humboldt, TN Sacred Heart; College of Consultors.
Werling, Wolf V.K. '99 (JOL)[F] Momence, IL Good Shepherd Manor.
Werner, Benjamin '64 (LAN) Retired.
Werner, Rev. Msgr. Cyril J. '45 (OM) Retired.
Werner, George J. *s.m.m.* '57 (RVC)[N] Bay Shore, NY Montfort Missionaries; Counselors.
Werner, Gerald *o.c.d.* '74 (SR)[K] Oakville, CA Carmelite House of Prayer; [L] Oakville, CA Carmelite House of Prayer.
Werner, John J. '00 (MET) Old Bridge, NJ St. Ambrose.
Werner, Jon K. '82 (SY) Syracuse, NY St. John the Baptist.
Werner, Justin '58 (GB) Retired.
Werner, Steven '98 (SPK) Ione, WA St. Bernard; Metaline Falls, WA St. Joseph.
Werner, Steven '98 (SPK) Colville, WA Immaculate Conception; Colville, WA Sacred Heart of Jesus; Colville, WA Pure Heart of Mary; Members.
Werning, David H. '98 (WDC) Washington, DC Our Lady of Victory; Priest Council.
Wertanen, Steven A. '97 (DET) Royal Oak, MI St. Mary; Ferndale, MI St. James.
Werth, Alvin '59 (SAL) Board of Trustees Retired.
Werth, Charles M. '53 (BUF) Retired.
Werth, Frederick H. '07 (CHL) Mars Hill, NC St. Andrew the Apostle.
Werth, Joshua '09 (SAL) Hays, KS Immaculate Heart of Mary Parish.
Werth, Loren J. '56 (SAL) Retired.
Werth, Robert Thomas '79 (ROC) Monroe County Jail; Rochester, NY Roman Catholic Parish of St. Francis Xavier Cabrini.
Wertin, George P. '63 (STP) Retired.
Wertin, Matthew '06 (PBL) On Duty Outside the Diocese.
Wertman, Raymond '72 (OG) On Duty Outside the Diocese.
Wertz, Jerry *s.d.b.* '88 (SFR)[N] San Francisco, CA Salesian Provincial Residence.
Wesdock, Thomas J. '00 (PBR) Upper St. Clair, PA St. Gregory Nazianzus.
Wesely, Eugene L. '57 (CR) Detroit Lakes, MN Retired.
Wesely, Mark '93 (SAL) Herington, KS St. Columba Parish; Herington, KS St. John the Evangelist Parish; Herington, KS St. Phillip Parish.
Wesley, Andrew '80 (DET) Detroit, MI St. Ladislaus; Detroit, MI Transfiguration–Our Lady Help of Christians.
Wesley, Shaun C. '05 (LR) Berryville, AR St. Anne; Eureka Springs, AR St. Elizabeth of Hungary.
Weslin, Norman U. *o.s.* '86 (PCE) Retired.
Wesloh, Ferdinand J. '64 (STL) Hazelwood, MO St. Martin de Porres.
Wesnofske, Matthias *o.f.m.cap.* '67 (NY) New York, NY St. John the Baptist.
Wesoloski, Richard J. '72 (PIT) Pittsburgh, PA St. Bernard.
Wesolowski, Anthony P. *o.s.b.* '72 (SAV)[B] Savannah, GA Benedictine Military School; [D] Savannah, GA The Benedictine Priory.
Wesolowski, Anthony *o.s.b.* '72 (GBG)[H] Latrobe, PA Saint Vincent Archabbey.
Wesolowski, Jacek *s.ch.* '95 (PHX) Phoenix, AZ Our Lady of Czestochowa Roman Catholic Parish.
Wesolowski, Victor R. '08 (COL) Corning, OH St. Bernard; New Lexington, OH Church of the Atonement; New Lexington, OH St. Patrick; New Lexington, OH St. Rose of Lima.
Wessel, John F. '57 (CLV) Translators Retired.
Wessell, Harold (ALB) Fort Edward, NY St. Joseph.
Wesselsky, Rev. Msgr. Emil J. '56 (SAT) San Antonio, TX St. Henry.
Wessling, John E. '58 (CIN)[F] Cincinnati, OH Ursuline Academy of Cincinnati; Imprimatur Censors Retired.
West, Don J. '90 (CIN) West Chester, OH St. John.
West, H. Gregory '91 (CHR) Clemson, SC St. Andrew.
West, James P. '86 (LR) Hot Springs National Park, AR St. John the Baptist.
West, Joseph *o.f.m.conv.* '92 (IND) Clarksville, IN St. Anthony of Padua Catholic Church, Clarksville, Inc.
West, Rev. Msgr. Mauricio W. '79 (CHL) Special Assignment; [Q] Charlotte, NC Catholic Diocese of

Charlotte Housing Corp.; Vicar General, Chancellor, and Moderator of the Curia; Diocesan Consultors; Permanent Diaconate.
West, Patrick J. '81 (BRK) Brooklyn, NY Our Lady of Solace; Diocesan Insurance Committee.
West, Peter '91 (NEW) On Duty Outside the Archdiocese.
West, Samuel G. '09 (STO) Modesto, CA St. Stanislaus Church (Pastor of).
West, Stephen C. '79 (GBG) Derry, PA St. Joseph; New Derry, PA St. Martin.
West, Thomas B. *o.f.m.* '86 (SFR)[S] San Francisco, CA St. Anthony Foundation; San Francisco, CA St. Boniface.
West, Thomas *o.f.m.* '86 (OAK)[A] Berkeley, CA Franciscan School of Theology.
West, William '70 (HRT)[H] New Haven, CT Hospital of St. Raphael.
West, Rev. Msgr. Willis W. '63 (NOR) Retired.
Westbrook, J. Severyn '62 (SPK) Retired.
Westcott, Matthew J. '07 (BO) Cambridge, MA St. Paul; [AA] Cambridge, MA Harvard Catholic Center; Navy Reserve Chaplains.
Wester, Charles H. '59 (MIL) Eden, WI Shepherd of the Hills (Good Shepherd) Retired.
Wester, Donald R. '78 (STL) St. Peters, MO All Saints.
Westerhoff, Ralph A. '62 (CIN) Retired.
Westfall, Joseph B. '93 (MO) On Duty Outside the Diocese; DEPARTMENT OF VETERANS AFFAIRS HOSPITALS AND CHAPLAINS.
Westfield, Carlton J. '71 (BUF) Fredonia, NY St. Anthony.
Westhoven, Thomas *s.c.j.* '66 (MIL)[P] Franklin, WI Sacred Heart at Monastery Lake.
Weston, Michael D. '02 (WDC) On Duty Outside the Diocese; [S] Washington, DC Basilica of the National Shrine of the Immaculate Conception.
Weston, Thomas C. *s.j.* '78 (OAK)[L] Oakland, CA Jesuit Fathers and Brothers.
Westray, Kenneth M. '81 (SFR) San Francisco, CA St. Vincent de Paul; African American Ministry; Archdiocesan Board of Education.
Wetmore, John J. '73 (STL) St. Ann, MO Holy Trinity.
Wetovick, Jerry P. '10 (GI) North Platte, NE Holy Spirit.
Wetsel, Matthew '10 (ALB) Saratoga Springs, NY St. Peter.
Wetta, Augustine *o.s.b.* '03 (STL)[F] Creve Coeur, MO St. Louis Priory School; [O] St. Louis, MO The Abbey of St. Mary and St. Louis.
Wetter, Rev. Msgr. Richard L. '57 (BUF) Clergy Personnel Board; [N] Tonawanda, NY O'Hara Residence Retired.
Wetterer, Rev. Msgr. Edward V. '64 (BRK) Flushing, NY St. Michael.
Wetterholm, Lawrence E. '56 (BO) Senior Priests. Retired.
Wetzel, Steven P. *o.s.f.s.* '03 (PH) Philadelphia, PA St. Joachim.
Wetzler, Daniel '63 (SPK) Ritzville, WA St. Ambrose; Ritzville, WA St. Agnes; Charismatic Renewal Retired.
Wevita, Bede '91 (LAV) North Las Vegas, NV St. John Neumann.
Wewers, William *o.s.b.* '67 (LR) Clarksville, AR Holy Redeemer.
Wey, Richard '50 (SCL) Retired.
Weymes, Gerald '74 (ARL) Chantilly, VA St. Timothy.
Weyrens, Ronald '82 (SCL) Sauk Rapids, MN Sacred Heart; Diocesan Finance Council.
Whalen, Daniel W. '00 (PIT) Pittsburgh, PA Holy Spirit; Pittsburgh, PA St. Nicholas; Priest Council; Clergy Personnel Board.
Whalen, David M. *o.s.f.s.* '71 (TOL) Toledo, OH St. Pius X.
Whalen, Rev. Msgr. Edmund J. '84 (NY)[E] Staten Island, NY Monsignor Farrell High School; [HH] Staten Island, NY North American College of Rome, Alumni Assoc. of.
Whalen, John J. '69 (DAV) Retired.
Whalen, Joseph T. '71 (ALN) Barnesville, PA St. Richard; Elected Members.
Whalen, Joseph *m.s.* '89 (NOR) Danielson, CT St. James Retired.
Whalen, Joseph '99 (STP) Fridley, MN St. William; Fairview University Medical Center.
Whalen, Michael D. *c.m.* '83 (BRK)[R] Jamaica, NY St. Vincent's House.
Whalen, Robert B. '51 (BUR) Retired.
Whalen, Rev. Msgr. Thomas J. '67 (BGP) Shelton, CT St. Margaret Mary.
Whalen, Timothy F. '78 (PIT) On Duty Outside the Diocese.
Whalen, Timothy '78 (DET)[E] Orchard Lake, MI St. Mary's Preparatory.
Whalen, William '60 (MIL) Retired.
Wharf, Jonah *o.c.s.o.* '09 (DUB) Religious Priests Representative.
Wharff, Jonah *o.c.s.o.* '08 (DUB)[K] Peosta, IA New Melleray Abbey, Order of Cistercians of the Strict Observance; Peosta, IA.
Wharton, Paul J. '82 (WH) Bluefield, WV Sacred Heart; Princeton, WV Sacred Heart.
Whatley, Christopher '70 (BAL) Catonsville, MD St. Mark.
Whatley, Francis *o.ss.t.* '88 (LA) Hospital Chaplains.
Whatley, Frank *o.ss.t.* '88 (BAL)[Q] Archdiocese of Los Angeles, CA.
Whatley, Frank *o.ss.t.* '88 (LA) Los Angeles, CA St. Agatha.
Whealen, Martin J. *s.j.* '62 (STL)[O] St. Louis, MO Jesuit Community Corporation at Saint Louis University – Jesuit Hall Retired.
Wheatley, Carroll '75 (OWN) Absent on Leave Retired.
Wheatley, Charles '68 (MIL) Retired.
Wheatley, Dennis *o.f.m.* '84 (BO) Waltham, MA Sacred Heart; Definitors.
Wheatley, Herbert '67 (P)[J] Portland, OR Providence Health & Services–Oregon.
Wheaton, Michael F. '03 (CHI) Tinley Park, IL Saint Julie Billiart.
Wheaton, William F. '92 (SLC) Moab, UT Saint Pius X LLC 244; Monticello, UT Saint Joseph LLC 229.
Whedbee, Dominic *o.c.s.o.* '77 (WOR)[N] Spencer, MA St. Joseph's Abbey.
Whedbee, George *c.m.f.* '69 (LA)[V] Rancho Dominguez, CA Dominguez Seminary Inc. Retired.
Wheelahan, Michael '80 (OKL) Guymon, OK St. Peter's; [K] Goodwell, OK Oklahoma Panhandle State University; Region VI.
Wheelan, Mark *s.o.l.t.* '04 (FAR) Belcourt, ND St. Benedict.
Wheeland, Thomas H. '66 (ROC) Rochester, NY Holy Cross; Clergy Relief Society; Pension Committee (Lay and Priests).
Wheeler, Ambrose *c.s.c.* (FTW)[H] Notre Dame Congregation of Holy Cross, United States Province of Priests & Brothers.
Wheeler, Arthur F. *c.s.c.* '84 (P)[B] University of Portland; [L] Portland, OR Holy Cross Fathers & Brothers, C.S.C. – University of Portland.
Wheeler, Arthur *c.s.c.* (FTW)[H] Notre Dame Congregation of Holy Cross, United States Province of Priests & Brothers.
Wheeler, Charles '79 (JOL) Retired.
Wheeler, Clarence *m.s.* '54 (JC) Retired.
Wheeler, Daniel '75 (LAN) Tecumseh, MI St. Dominic Oratory; Tecumseh, MI St. Elizabeth; Regional Vicars; Finance Council.
Wheeler, James D. *s.j.* '54 (KC)[J] Kansas City, MO Rockhurst Jesuit Community.
Wheeler, James J. *s.j.* '68 (NY)[DD] New York, NY Murray–Weigel Hall.
Wheeler, James J. *s.j.* '68 (RVC)[P] Patchogue, NY St. Joseph's Prayer Center.
Wheeler, James *o.f.m.* '66 (SFD)[K] Springfield, IL Our Lady of Angels Friary.
Wheeler, Thomas F.X. *s.j.* '62 (PH)[Y] Merion Station St. Alphonsus House.
Wheeler, Wayne B. '79 (GR) Ludington, MI St. Simon's.
Wheelock, Robert *o.f.m.cap.* '64 (MIL)[P] Mount Calvary, WI St. Felix Friary.
Whelan, Rev. Msgr. Bill S. '57 (OM)[L] Omaha, NE Cor Unum Family Inc. Retired.
Whelan, Daniel '04 (L) On Duty Outside the Archdiocese.
Whelan, Dennis J. '65 (RVC) Retired.
Whelan, Edward J. *m.m.* '61 (FgM) Maryknoll, NY MARYKNOLL.
Whelan, Fintan *o.f.m.cap.* '60 (SFR)[N] Burlingame, CA Capuchin Provincial House.
Whelan, James J. '73 (PH) West Chester, PA SS. Peter and Paul.
Whelan, James P. '93 (NEW) Weehawken, NJ St. Lawrence's; Central Hudson Region Deanery 9.
Whelan, John F. '58 (RVC) Retired.
Whelan, Robert J. '83 (BRK) Bayside, NY Our Lady of the Blessed Sacrament.
Whelan, Steven *s.d.b.* '69 (OAK)[L] Berkeley Salesians of Don Bosco.
Whelton, Rev. Msgr. Daniel P. '70 (SR) Cotati, CA St. Joseph; Vicar for Priests; Judicial Vicar; Board of Consultors; Diocesan Judges; Priests' Council.
Whetstone, Richard (PHU) Adjunct Judicial Vicars.
Whetstone, Richard '83 (PBR) Retired.
Whewell, Glenn *s.o.l.t.* '01 (CC)[G] Robstown, TX Society of Our Lady of the Most Holy Trinity.
Whistle, Brad '81 (OWN) Owensboro, KY Our Lady of Lourdes; Diocesan Finance Council.
Whitaker, Cyril *s.j.* '09 (CIN)[N] Cincinnati, OH Jesuit Community at Xavier University.
White, Anthony J. '55 (NO) Retired.
White, Bernard C. '52 (CHI) Elmwood Park, IL St. Celestine; Chicago, IL St. Henry Retired.
White, Bernard L. '77 (ALT) Dudley, PA Immaculate Conception.
White, Charles H. '65 (BRK) Far Rockaway, NY St. Mary Star of the Sea and St. Gertrude Retired.
White, Charles '09 (DET) Plymouth, MI Our Lady of Good Counsel.
White, Cosmas *o.s.b.* '61 (P)[L] St. Benedict, OR Mt. Angel Abbey.
White, Daniel C. '93 (LA) Venice, CA St. Mark.
White, Daniel E. '04 (BUR) Diocesan Consultors; Vocations and Seminarians; Chancery Office; Secretary to the Most Rev. Bishop; Media Relations; Diocesan Master of Ceremonies; Members Ex Officio; Consultants; Office of Permanent Diaconate Ministry; Burlington, VT St. Joseph's Co–Cathedral; Diocesan Administrative Board.
White, Daniel P. *s.j.* '01 (STL)[O] St. Louis, MO The Jesuits of the Missouri Province.
White, Daniel *s.j.* '01 (LAF)[A] Grand Coteau, LA St. Charles College.
White, David F. *s.j.* '67 (BUF)[N] Buffalo, NY Canisius Jesuit Community Inc.
White, David P. '94 (BO) Westford, MA St. Catherine of Alexandria.
White, Denis '67 (JOL) Retired.
White, Edward Goodwin '05 (SEA) Renton, WA St. Stephen the Martyr.
White, Francis P. *c.s.v.* '44 (CHI)[N] Arlington Heights, IL Viatorian Province Center–Clerics of St. Viator.
White, Gale '56 (DAL) Retired.
White, James D. '69 (TLS) Retired.
White, Rev. Msgr. James E. '83 (NY) Mamaroneck, NY St. Vito.
White, James R. '80 (NEW) West Orange, NJ St. Joseph's; [C] West Orange, NJ Seton Hall Preparatory School.
White, James *c.ss.r.* '81 (MIL)[S] Oconomowoc, WI The Redemptorist Retreat Center.
White, John R. '81 (CIN) Greenville, OH St. Mary; Judges.
White, John V. *s.j.* '65 (CLV)[D] Cuyahoga Falls, OH Walsh Jesuit High School.
White, John '83 (RVC) Leave of Absence.
White, Joseph M. '91 (BO) South Boston, MA St. Vincent de Paul.
White, Kenneth R. '68 (PIT) Aspinwall, PA St. Scholastica.
White, Kevin R. *s.j.* '99 (FgM) Watertown, MA Society of Jesus.
White, Rev. Msgr. Lawrence E. '70 (CC) Deans; College of Consultors; Presbyteral Council; Corpus Christi, TX SS. Cyril and Methodius.
White, Rev. Msgr. Leo J. '56 (BRK) Brooklyn, NY Holy Family–Saint Thomas Aquinas Retired.
White, Mark D. '03 (WDC) On Duty Outside the Archdiocese.
White, Mark '03 (RIC) Martinsville, VA St. Joseph.
White, Michael J. '48 (BIR) Birmingham, AL Our Lady of the Valley Retired.
White, Michael '84 (BAL) Timonium, MD Church of the Nativity.
White, Michael *c.s.sp.* '83 (SD)[B] University of San Diego.
White, Morgan M. '02 (TYL) Paris, TX Our Lady of Victory; Diocesan Liturgical Commission.
White, Nathan R. '02 (STO) Diamond Springs, CA Retired.
White, Paul C. '89 (RCK) Harvard, IL St. Joseph.
White, Paul R. *c.pp.s.* '53 (LFT) Rensselaer, IN St. Francis Solano; Rensselaer, IN St. Henry; [A] Rensselaer, IN Saint Joseph's College Retired.
White, Paul T. '83 (PT) Mary Esther, FL St. Peter; Liturgy, Office of; Permanent Deacon Formation Team; Building & Renovation, Diocesan Commission for.
White, Paul *s.s.c.* '58 (LA)[P] Los Angeles, CA Columban Fathers, Procure House.
White, Paul '83 (PT) Permanent Deacon Formation Board.
White, Paul *s.s.c.* '58 (OM)[J] St. Columbans, NE Missionary Society of St. Columban Retired.
White, Peter H. '62 (WOR) Leicester, MA St. Aloysius–St. Jude.
White, Robert A. *s.j.* '62 (FgM) St. Louis, MO Society of Jesus.
White, Robert Kevin '61 (SFR) Novato, CA St. Anthony of Padua.
White, Robert L. '74 (STP) Victoria, MN St. Victoria.
White, Robert S. *c.s.s.* '73 (SPR) Springfield, MA Our Lady of Mt. Carmel; Waltham, MA.
White, Robert S. *c.s.s.* '73 (BO)[U] Waltham, MA Stigmatine Fathers & Brothers Provincial House.
White, Robert '70 (SD) On Duty Outside the Diocese.
White, Roger *o.f.m.cap.* '65 (PH) Philadelphia, PA St. John the Evangelist.
White, Seth Thomas Joseph *o.p.* '08 (WDC)[B] Washington, DC Dominican House of Studies.
White, Stephen C. '86 (PH) Retired.
White, Stephen '98 (DUL) Retired.
White, Stephen *m.s.c.* '46 (SAT)[L] San Antonio, TX Missionaries of the Sacred Heart.
White, Thomas J. '59 (JOL) Retired.
White, Thomas '64 (BLX) Ocean Springs, MS St. Alphonsus.
White, Thomas '78 (LA) Palmdale, CA St. Mary; Lancaster, CA California State Prison, L.A. County.
White, William A. '90 (NY) Pine Plains, NY St. Anthony; Bangall, NY Immaculate Conception.
Whitehead, Joseph '84 (STA) Absent or Sick Leave.

Whiteing, Richard J. '80 (OM) Fullerton, NE St. Peter; Fullerton, NE St. Peter.
Whiteside, Daniel '92 (CHI) Oak Park, IL St. Catherine of Siena–St. Lucy.
Whiteside, David '97 (PEO) Havana, IL St. Patrick's.
Whitestone, David A. '89 (ARL) Fairfax, VA St. Leo's; Diocesan Judges; Diocesan Consultors.
Whitley, John R. *c.s.b.* '54 (GAL)[O] Houston, TX Residence of the Basilian Fathers of the University of St. Thomas.
Whitley, Rufus J. *o.m.i.* '76 (CHI)[W] Chicago, IL Oblates for International Pastoral.
Whitman, Dan G. '83 (KNX) Jefferson City, TN Holy Trinity Catholic Church; [K] Knoxville, TN Diocesan Council of Catholic Women.
Whitman, David R. '05 (CHR) Columbia, SC Our Lady of the Hills.
Whitman, Glenn R. '75 (E) Sharon, PA St. Joseph; Priest Personnel Board; Presbyteral Council.
Whitman, Mark '95 (STL) Arnold, MO Immaculate Conception.
Whitman, Thomas J. '87 (E) Waterford, PA All Saints; Presbyteral Council.
Whitmore, James R. *m.m.* '59 (NY)[DD] Retired.
Whitmore, Rev. Msgr. Paul E. '54 (OG) Watertown, NY Holy Family Retired.
Whitney, John *s.j.* '94 (SEA) Seattle, WA St. Joseph; [M] Seattle, WA Jesuit House, Seattle.
Whitney, Patrick J. '68 (RVC) Port Washington, NY St. Peter of Alcantara; Priests' Personnel Assignment Board.
Whitney, Rev. Msgr. Paul J. '58 (BUF) Retired.
Whitson, Robley E. '58 (NY) Retired.
Whitt, Dwight Reginald *o.p.* '76 (STP)[C] St. Paul, MN University of St. Thomas.
Whittaker, Kenneth D. '77 (MIA) Deerfield Beach, FL Our Lady of Mercy; Defenders of the Bond.
Whittel, Joseph B. '03 (NOR) Uncasville, CT St. John the Evangelist; District Spiritual Advisors; Justice & Peace, Catholic Action for; Commission for Human Life and Justice; Advisory Ministry Evaluation Committee; Advisory Board; Oakdale, CT Our Lady of the Lakes; Quaker Hill, CT Our Lady of Perpetual Help.
Whitten, Carlton E. *s.j.* '61 (SJ)[M] Los Gatos, CA Sacred Heart Jesuit Center.
Whittier, William O. '61 (STP) Retired.
Whittingham, Jose '70 (SD) San Ysidro, CA Our Lady of Mt. Carmel Catholic Parish San Ysidro.
Whittington, Justin *s.j.* '99 (ALN)[A] Wernersville, PA Jesuit Center–Jesuit Community.
Whittington, Kenneth L. '88 (CHL) Morganton, NC St. Charles Borromeo.
Whittington, Paul De Porres *o.p.* (CHI) Chicago, IL St. Benedict the African (West).
Whittington, Shaun P. '05 (IND) Osgood, IN St. Charles Catholic Church, Milan, Inc.; Osgood, IN St. John the Baptist Catholic Church, Osgood, Inc.; Osgood, IN St. Pius V Catholic Church, Sunman, Inc.; Osgood, IN St. Mary Magdalen Catholic Church, New Marion, Inc.
Whorton, David L. '98 (LA) Santa Clarita, CA Blessed Kateri Tekakwitha.
Whorton, Jeffrey T. '08 (MO) Army National Guard Chaplains; Rio Rancho, NM St. Thomas Aquinas.
Whyte, Edmond F. '64 (MIA) Southwest Ranches, FL St. Mark.
Whyte, Michael G. '03 (HRT) West Simsbury, CT St. Catherine of Siena; Farmington Valley Deanery.
Wiant, George '61 (ROC) Penn Yan, NY Our Lady of the Lakes Catholic Community Retired.
Wiatrowski, Ralph E. '74 (CLV) Northfield, OH St. Barnabas; Vicars General; Judges in Second Instance.
Wibers, Rev. Msgr. Michael J. '72 (JC) Buildings and Properties.
Wible, Charles M. '96 (BAL) Abingdon, MD St. Francis de Sales.
Wichert, Nicholas F. '10 (SEA) Tacoma, WA Visitation.
Wichlan, David L. '57 (STL) St. Louis, MO St. Rita; Spiritual Directors.
Wichman, Edwin J. '80 (PIT) Pittsburgh, PA St. Wendelin.
Wichmanowski, Walter F. '52 (PIT) Retired.
Wicht, Robert *s.d.s.* '67 (MIL)[P] Milwaukee Salvatorian Provincial Offices.
Wickenhauser, Gerald M. *m.m.* '62 (NY)[DD] Retired.
Wicker, Paul F. '63 (COS) Colorado Springs, CO Holy Apostles; Metro–North Deanery (Colorado Springs); Calhan, CO St. Michael's; Vicars Forane.
Wickersham, Andrew '08 (OKL)[K] Alva, OK Northwestern Oklahoma State College.
Wickersham, James A. '08 (OKL) Alva, OK Sacred Heart.
Wickham, William E. *c.s.c.* '81 (P) Portland, OR Department of Veterans' Affairs Medical Center[B]; [L] Portland, OR Holy Cross Fathers & Brothers, C.S.C. – University of Portland.
Wickham, William *c.s.c.* (FTW)[H] Notre Dame Congregation of Holy Cross, United States Province of Priests & Brothers.
Wicklum, Paul R. '61 (LFT) Retired.
Wickowski, Leroy A. '66 (CHI) River Forest, IL St. Luke Retired.
Wickrematunge, Vernon P. '87 (NY) Peekskill, NY Assumption.
Wicks, W. Jared *s.j.* '62 (CLV)[B] University Heights, OH John Carroll Jesuit Community.
Widder, Matthew '10 (MIL) Hales Corners, WI St. Mary; New Berlin, WI Holy Apostles.
Widiatmoko, Tri Sunaring '03 (BRK)[R] Jamaica, NY Reverend John B. Murray, CM, House.
Widmann, Phillip A. '77 (FTW) Fort Wayne, IN St. Mary; Fort Wayne, IN St. Peter; [K] Fort Wayne, IN Cathedral Museum; Clergy Retirement Board.
Widmann, Phillip '77 (FTW) Cathedral Museum; Retired Clergy Committee.
Widner, Thomas C. *s.j.* '69 (IND)[A] Indianapolis, IN Bishop Simon Bruté College Seminary; Indianapolis, IN St. Anthony Catholic Church, Indianapolis, Inc.
Widomski, Stan *o.f.m.* '62 (SP)[N] St. Petersburg, FL St. Anthony Friary.
Wieber, Donald A. '57 (KAL) Retired.
Wieczorek, Edward R. '65 (Y) Mogadore, OH St. Joseph.
Wieczorek, Matthew S. '57 (SY) Endicott, NY St. Casimir.
Wiedel, Thomas L. '90 (LIN) Benkelman, NE St. Joseph's.
Wiederholt, Clarence E. '55 (JC) Retired.
Wiederholt, Thomas W. '63 (KC) Retired.
Wiedmann, Paul A. '63 (PH) Retired.
Wiegand, William R. '05 (DAV) Retired.
Wieging, James F. '67 (DET) River Rouge, MI Our Lady of Lourdes; Ecorse, MI St. Francis Xavier Retired.
Wieladek, Waldemar *c.ss.r.* '92 (CHI) Cicero, IL St. Mary of Czestochowa.
Wieland, Dennis J. '91 (CR) On Duty Outside the Diocese.
Wieland, Dennis J. '91 (MIL) Menomonee Falls, WI St. Anthony.
Wielgus, Rev. Msgr. Bronislaw '62 (NEW) Elizabeth, NJ Saint Adalbert and Saints Peter & Paul Retired.
Wieliczko, Andrzej '99 (MET) Somerville, NJ Somerset Medical Center; Raritan, NJ St. Joseph.
Wieling, Raymond P. '49 (SC) Retired.
Wielinski, Alan '84 (SCL) St. Cloud, MN St. Paul; St. Cloud, MN St. Peter; Presbyteral Council.
Wielunski, Rev. Msgr. Gregory C. '78 (BRK) Glendale, NY St. Pancras; Lawyers.
Wiener, Rev. Canon Michael K. '99 (STL) St. Louis, MO Oratory of St. Francis de Sales.
Wienhoff, Paul R. '78 (BEL) Dupo, IL Sacred Heart of Jesus; Promoter Justitiae; Defensores Vinculi; Cahokia, IL Holy Family; Diocesan Consultors.
Wiera, Stefan '68 (SAT) Pleasanton, TX St. Luke–Loire.
Wierichs, Paul *c.p.* '78 (PMB)[H] North Palm Beach, FL Our Lady of Florida Spiritual Center; Elected Members.
Wiering, Matthew J. '10 (NU) New Ulm, MN Cathedral of The Holy Trinity.
Wierzba, Alan P. '01 (LC) La Crosse, WI Roncalli Newman Parish; [K] La Crosse, WI Roncalli Newman Parish; Ex Officio; Consultors.
Wierzbicki, Melvin *o.f.m.* '53 (GB)[J] Pulaski, WI Friary.
Wierzchowski, Marian *s.a.c.* '87 (BRK) Brooklyn, NY St. Frances de Chantal.
Wiese, Rev. Msgr. Melvern A. '57 (OM) Retired.
Wiese, Miro *o.f.m.* '57 (GLD) Indian River, MI Cross in the Woods Catholic Shrine.
Wiese, Stephen *s.c.j.* '63 (MIL)[P] Franklin, WI Sacred Heart at Monastery Lake; [P] Franklin Sacred Heart at Monastery Lake.
Wieseler, Larry '69 (CR) Retired.
Wiesenbaugh, Robert D. *s.j.* (RIC) Richmond, VA Sacred Heart.
Wiesenbaugh, Robert D. *s.j.* '71 (ALN)[A] Wernersville, PA Jesuit Center–Jesuit Community.
Wieser, Stanley '68 (SCL) Elizabeth, MN St. Elizabeth; Pelican Rapids, MN St. Leonard's; Diocesan Priests Pension Plan Trustees; Diocesan Consultors.
Wieslaw, Strzadala *s.d.s.* '90 (NEW)[L] Verona, NJ The Salvatorian Fathers.
Wiesmann, Gary '83 (MIA)[G] Fort Lauderdale, FL Holy Cross Hospital.
Wiesner, Mark '95 (OAK) Oakland, CA St. Augustine.
Wiest, Gregory *c.ss.r.* '89 (TUC)[G] Tucson, AZ Redemptorist Society of Arizona Redemptorist Renewal Center.
Wietensteiner, Joseph M. '66 (SPK) Retired.
Wiethorn, William *o.f.m.cap.* '66 (CLV)[U] Cleveland, OH St. Paul Shrine; [N] Cleveland, OH St. Paul Friary.
Wigand, William J. '83 (STL) Ste. Genevieve, MO SS. Philip and James.
Wigand, William '83 (STL) Ste. Genevieve, MO Our Lady, Help of Christians.
Wigger, Brian K. '97 (COV) Fort Wright, KY St. Agnes; [C] Park Hills, KY Notre Dame Academy, Inc.
Wiggins, Frank '86 (RIC) Hopewell, VA St. James Church.
Wiggins, Timothy S. '02 (NY) White Plains, NY St. John the Evangelist.
Wigginton, Ellsworth T. '76 (FWT) Fort Worth, TX St. Paul the Apostle.
Wight, Jonathan C. '86 (TOL) Bellevue, OH Immaculate Conception.
Wightman, Paul *o.m.i.* '55 (SPC) Ava, MO Immaculate Heart of Mary; Mountain Grove, MO Sacred Heart.
Wigton, Matthew '01 (GLD) Charlevoix, MI St. Mary.
Wikarski, Tomasz '06 (DEN) Commerce City, CO Our Lady Mother of the Church.
Wiktorek, Wladyslaw '81 (MET) Perth Amboy, NJ Holy Trinity.
Wilber, Stewart '91 (ATL) Special or Other Archdiocesan Assignment; Marietta, GA Holy Family.
Wilbers, Rev. Msgr. Michael J. '72 (JC) Lake Ozark, MO Our Lady of the Lake; Episcopal Vicars; Diocesan Consultors; Personnel Board; Ex Officio Members; Finance Committee; Board of Trustees.
Wilborn, Jeffrey '00 (DEN) Byers, CO Our Lady of the Plains.
Wilbricht, Stephen S. *c.s.c.* '97 (FTW)[H] Notre Dame Congregation of Holy Cross, United States Province of Priests & Brothers.
Wilbricht, Stephen S. *c.s.c.* '97 (FR)[A] North Easton, MA Holy Cross Fathers Religious; [A] North Easton, MA Stonehill College.
Wilczek, Stanislaw *c.ss.r.* '98 (MET) Portuguese Apostolate; Perth Amboy, NJ Our Lady of the Rosary of Fatima.
Wild, Alexander '89 (DUB) On Special or Other Archdiocesan Assignment.
Wild, J. Jerome '81 (PH)[BB] Philadelphia, PA Temple University; On Special or Other Archdiocesan Assignment; Philadelphia, PA St. Malachy.
Wild, Jon Anthony '82 (DUL) Duluth, MN St. Elizabeth.
Wild, Jon '82 (DUL) Duluth, MN St. Margaret Mary.
Wild, Michael L. '84 (MIL) Waupun, WI St. Mary; Waupun, WI St. Joseph; Waupun, WI St. Brendan; Fox Lake, WI Annunciation.
Wild, Robert A. *s.j.* '70 (MIL)[P] Milwaukee, WI Jesuit Community at Marquette University.
Wild, Robert A. '70 (BUF) On Duty Outside the Diocese.
Wilde, Adrian *o.carm.* '72 (VEN) Englewood, FL St. Francis of Assisi.
Wilde, Denis G. *o.s.a.* '70 (PH)[Y] Philadelphia, PA Augustinian Community (O.S.A.); Philadelphia, PA St. Nicholas of Tolentine.
Wilde, Mauritius *o.s.b.* '02 (OM)[J] Schuyler, NE Benedictine Mission House.
Wilder, Daniel J. '96 (PEO) On Duty Outside the Diocese.
Wilder, Frank T. *o.a.r.* '91 (NY)[B] Suffern, NY Tagaste Monastery.
Wilder, Frank T. *o.a.r.* '91 (LA) Oxnard, CA Mary Star of the Sea; [P] Oxnard, CA Order of Augustinian Recollects (O.A.R.), St. Augustine Priory.
Wilderotter, Paul C. '74 (CHL) On Duty Outside the Diocese.
Wildes, Kevin *s.j.* '86 (NO)[C] New Orleans, LA Loyola University New Orleans.
Wiley, Leo A. '56 (OG) Watertown, NY Holy Family Retired.
Wilgenbusch, Rev. Msgr. Lyle L. '66 (DUB) On Special or Other Archdiocesan Assignment; Episcopal Vicar for Waterloo Region; College of Consultors; Continuing Formation of Priests; American Martyrs Retreat House Advisory Board; Pastoral Council; Ex Officio Members; Stewardship Committee; Archbishop's Cabinet; Archdiocesan Pastoral Center; Priestly Life and Ministry Committee.
Wilhelm, Chad F. '94 (FAR) Fargo, ND St. Mary's Cathedral of Fargo; Apostleship of Prayer.
Wilhelm, Dean E. '88 (AUS) Round Rock, TX St. William.
Wilhelm, H. Joseph *s.m.* '59 (WDC)[O] Washington, DC Marist Center Retired.
Wilhelm, Patrick R.C. '71 (NEW) Kearny, NJ Our Lady of Sorrows Retired.
Wilhelm, Paul *o.m.i.* '68 (LAR) Eagle Pass, TX Sacred Heart.
Wilhelm, Robert J. '59 (TOL) Retired.
Wilhite, Philip A. '90 (GAL) Conroe, TX Sacred Heart.
Wilimek, Louis '50 (MIL) Retired.
Wilk, Brian J. '03 (MAD) Palmyra, WI St. Mary; Advocate/Procurator (cc.1481–1490); Elected; Fort Atkinson, WI St. Joseph.
Wilk, Mitchell S. '70 (SPC) Fredericktown, MO St. Michael.
Wilk, Tomasz *o.s.p.p.e.* '05 (PH)[Y].
Wilke, David M. '95 (BEL) Fairmont City, IL Holy Rosary; Diocesan Consultors; Co Directors.
Wilke, James B. '89 (STL) Retired.
Wilkening, David F. '79 (DAV) Fort Madison, IA Holy Family; Fort Madison, IA St. Joseph's.
Wilkening, Henry '47 (JOL) Winfield, IL Central DuPage Hospital; Winfield, IL St. John the Baptist Retired.
Wilker, Ronald H. '71 (CIN) Retired.
Wilkerson, Rev. Msgr. Jerome F. '50 (STL) Retired.
Wilkerson, Wayne W. '99 (GAL) Houston, TX St.

Francis de Sales.
Wilkes, Michael '09 (DET) Bloomfield Hills, MI St. Hugo of the Hills.
Wilkie, John J. '92 (SEA) Tacoma, WA Our Lady, Queen of Heaven.
Wilkie, William E. '54 (DUB) Retired.
Wilkins, Bernard J. '61 (STL) Washington, MO St. Gertrude Retired.
Wilkinson, Bruce W. '81 (ATL) Atlanta, GA Most Blessed Sacrament.
Wilkinson, George A. '01 (WDC) College Park, MD Holy Redeemer.
Wilkinson, John H. '59 (BRK) Brooklyn, NY St. Brigid Retired.
Wilkinson, Neal *s.j.* '00 (OM) Omaha, NE Our Lady of Guadalupe – St. Agnes Parish; [J] Omaha, NE Jesuit Community at Creighton University; Omaha, NE St. Therese of the Child Jesus.
Wilkinson, Rick *c.s.c.* '79 (AUS)[A] St. Edward's University.
Wilks, Bede *o.p.* '62 (TUC) Tucson, AZ Saint Thomas More Roman Catholic Newman Parish – Tucson; [H] Tucson, AZ University of Arizona Retired.
Will, Lowell '68 (EVN) Boonville, IN St. Clement; Newburgh, IN St. Rupert.
Will, Ronald L. *c.pp.s.* '75 (KC) St. Joseph, MO St. Francis Xavier; [J] Liberty, MO Society of the Precious Blood Provincial Office; [A] Liberty, MO Society of the Precious Blood Provincial Offices.
Willard, Boniface *o.p.* '11 (SEA) Seattle, WA Blessed Sacrament.
Willard, Donald B. *c.ss.r.* '08 (LA) Whittier, CA St. Mary of the Assumption; [P] Whittier, CA Redemptorists of Whittier.
Willard, Stephen A. '93 (PEO) Champaign, IL Holy Cross.
Willcock, Christopher *s.j.* '77 (BO)[U] Newton, MA The Jesuit Community at Boston College.
Willenberg, Lukasz J. '08 (PRO) Barrington, RI St. Luke.
Willenborg, Daniel L. '05 (SFD) Nokomis, IL St. Louis; Comite Diocesano de Ministerio Hispano – Diocesan Committee for Hispanic Ministry; Presbyteral Council.
Willenbring, Mark '57 (SCL) Long Prairie, MN St. Mary of Mt. Carmel Retired.
Willenburg, Rev. Msgr. Francis J. '54 (SY) Utica, NY St. Anthony of Padua.
Willett, John *c.ss.r.* '61 (KC) Kansas City, MO Our Lady of Perpetual Help; [J] Kansas City, MO Redemptorists Fathers of Kansas City, Missouri.
Willett, William David '79 (OWN) Retired.
Willette, Donald C. '84 (MO) Air Force Reserve Chaplains.
Willette, Donald '84 (DEN) Retired.
Willey, Dennis B. '94 (CHR) Charleston, SC Church of Christ the Divine Teacher; Charleston, SC Sacred Heart; Presbyteral Council.
Willger, Gerard I. '86 (SUP) Medford, WI Our Lady of the Holy Rosary; Medford, WI Our Lady of Perpetual Help; Moderator; Presbyteral Council & Diocesan Consultors.
Willhite, Rev. Msgr. Robert J. '63 (RCK) Aurora, IL St. Joseph Retired.
William, Noel *o.f.m.* '42 (CIN)[N] Cincinnati St. Francis Seraph Friary Retired.
Williams, Anthony C. '83 (KCK) Olpe, KS St. Mary; Olpe, KS St. Joseph; Regional Pastoral Leaders.
Williams, Baykil *s.o.l.t.* '06 (PBL) Capulin, CO St. Joseph.
Williams, Benjamin '10 (PAT) Vocations Office; Dover, NJ Sacred Heart; Dover, NJ Our Lady Queen of the Most Holy Rosary.
Williams, Brady *s.o.l.t.* '04 (DET) Detroit, MI Holy Redeemer.
Williams, Brandon '10 (OWN) Owensboro, KY St. Stephen Cathedral.
Williams, Clarence E. *c.pp.s.* '78 (DET) Roseville, MI Holy Innocents–St. Barnabas; Presbyteral Council.
Williams, Clarence *c.pp.s.* '78 (CIN)[N] Dayton, OH Provincial Office of the Cincinnati Province of the Society of the Precious Blood.
Williams, Claude A. *o.praem.* '09 (ORG)[I] Silverado, CA Norbertine Fathers of Orange Inc.
Williams, Claude *o.praem.* '09 (ORG)[D] Silverado, CA St. Michael's Preparatory School.
Williams, Dennis T. '91 (NY) Mahopac, NY St. John the Evangelist.
Williams, Donald J. '83 (SCR)[B] Misericordia University; Wyoming, PA St. Frances Cabrini; Presbyteral Council.
Williams, Edward *o.m.i.* '57 (FgM) Washington, DC AMERICAN OBLATE MISSIONS.
Williams, Francis '77 (LAN) Retired.
Williams, George S. *s.j.* '72 (WDC)[E] North Bethesda, MD Georgetown Preparatory School.
Williams, George T. *s.j.* '04 (BO)[U] Boston The Society of Jesus of New England–Provincial Offices.
Williams, George T. *s.j.* '04 (SFR) California State Prison.
Williams, George *s.j.* (BO) Northeast Correctional Center; Massachusetts Correctional Institution – Concord.
Williams, Glenn *s.j.* '56 (DET)[K] Clarkston, MI Colombiere Center.
Williams, H. Brendan '65 (TR) Howell, NJ St. Veronica; Vicars Forane (Deans).
Williams, Ian J. '96 (GRY) La Porte, IN Sacred Heart.
Williams, J. Gerald *o.carm.* '80 (KCK) Garnett, KS St. Therese; Garnett, KS St. Boniface.
Williams, James J. '70 (MAR) Mackinac Island, MI Ste. Anne de Michilimackinac Retired.
Williams, James M. '97 (COS) Colorado Springs, CO Holy Trinity; Vice Chancellor; Vice Chancellor; Team.
Williams, James '65 (SEA) Retired.
Williams, Rev. Msgr. John J. '78 (R) Raleigh, NC St. Joseph.
Williams, John L. '91 (HRT) Cheshire, CT Church of the Epiphany.
Williams, Jonathan *o.f.m.cap.* '71 (FgM) Pittsburgh, PA Province of St. Augustine.
Williams, Joseph A. '02 (STP) Minneapolis, MN St. Stephen.
Williams, Kenneth '63 (SHP) Retired.
Williams, Manuel *c.r.* '87 (MOB) Montgomery, AL Resurrection Catholic Mission; Montgomery, AL Resurrection Catholic Church; [J] Montgomery, AL Resurrection Catholic Missions.
Williams, Matthew M. '03 (BO) New Evangelization of Youth and Young Adults; Holbrook, MA St. Joseph.
Williams, Matthew *o.c.d.* '90 (SB)[I] Redlands, CA Discalced Carmelites, OCD; [L] Redlands, CA El Carmelo Retreat House.
Williams, Michael A. *s.j.* '75 (MOB)[A] Mobile, AL Spring Hill College.
Williams, Michael E. '97 (OWN)[I] Bowling Green, KY Western Kentucky University Catholic Campus Center.
Williams, Michael J. '95 (LAN) Lansing, MI St. Therese.
Williams, Michael S. '64 (STA) Keystone Heights, FL St. William; Diocesan Consultors.
Williams, Michael '97 (OWN) Consultors; Priests' Council; Family Life Committee.
Williams, Michael '09 (LSC) Silver City, NM St. Francis Newman Center Parish; Presbyteral Council.
Williams, Oliver F. *c.s.c.* '70 (FTW)[B] University of Notre Dame Du Lac; [H] Notre Dame, IN Holy Cross Community, Corby Hall, University of Notre Dame.
Williams, Patrick J. '93 (NO)[A] New Orleans, LA Notre Dame Seminary Graduate School of Theology; Executive Director; Priest Personnel Office; New Orleans, LA St. Pius X; [E] New Orleans, LA Holy Cross School; Members of the Board.
Williams, Paul D. '96 (ATL) Dalton, GA St. Joseph.
Williams, Paul M. *o.f.m.* '86 (CHR) Anderson, SC St. Joseph; [H] Columbia, SC Allen University, Benedict College; Vicar for African–American Catholics; Personnel Committee.
Williams, Peter J. '04 (STP) St. Paul, MN Maternity of the Blessed Virgin; College of Consultors; Center for Ongoing Clergy Formation.
Williams, Peter Y. '87 (BUR) Springfield, VT Maternity of the Blessed Virgin Mary.
Williams, Rayner F. *o.f.m.* '56 (PAT)[N] Butler, NJ St. Anthony Friary.
Williams, Richard B. *o.p.* '71 (SAT) Defenders of the Bond.
Williams, Richard C. '65 (PH) Brookhaven, PA Our Lady of Charity Retired.
Williams, Richard *o.p.* '71 (GAL) Houston, TX Holy Rosary.
Williams, Riley J. '11 (FR) Graduate Studies.
Williams, Robert Hayes '82 (DET) Hazel Park, MI St. Justin; Adjutant Judicial Vicar.
Williams, Robert L. '68 (LFT) Anderson, IN St. Mary; Deans; Diocesan Consultors; Presbyteral Council; Anderson, IN St. Ambrose.
Williams, Robert '91 (DAL) Deans; [M] Dallas, TX Commission on Ecumenism; College of Consultors; Dallas, TX Santa Clara.
Williams, Robert *o.f.m.cap.* '09 (NY) Bronx, NY Immaculate Conception; [DD] New York, NY Immaculate Conception Friary.
Williams, Ronald '02 (CIN) Cincinnati, OH Our Lady of the Sacred Heart.
Williams, Steven T. '91 (MOB) Fairhope, AL St. Lawrence; [J] Fairhope, AL Boy Scouts; Group II.
Williams, Thomas *s.j.* '60 (SPK)[J] Spokane, WA Regis Community.
Williams, W. Ray '97 (CHL) Absent on Medical Leave.
Williams, Rev. Msgr. William E. '59 (NY) Saugerties, NY St. John the Evangelist Retired.
Williams, William G. '69 (BO) Plymouth, MA St. Peter; Presbyteral Council.
Williams, William M. '96 (ATL) Thomson, GA Queen of Angels; AACCW.
Williams, William M. '05 (IND) Beech Grove, IN Holy Name of Jesus Catholic Church, Indianapolis, Inc.
Williams, William W. *s.j.* '68 (DEN)[N] Denver, CO Xavier Jesuit Center.
Williamson, Christopher '88 (ATL) Washington, GA St. Joseph.
Williamson, G. Michael '86 (CLV) Akron, OH St. Matthew.
Williamson, John A. '00 (BAL) Baltimore, MD Ascension; Elkridge, MD St. Augustine; Priest Personnel Board.
Williamson, Rev. Msgr. Robert J. '62 (BUF) Akron, NY St. Teresa of Avila.
Williamson, Thomas '96 (CHL) Absent On Leave.
Willie, Arthur H. *m.m.* '51 (NY)[DD] Retired.
Willingham, Charles W. *o.praem.* '95 (ORG)[I] Silverado, CA Norbertine Fathers of Orange Inc.; [D] Silverado, CA St. Michael's Preparatory School.
Willis, Glen *s.d.s.* '69 (WDC)[B] Silver Spring, MD Salvatorian Community; [X] Rock Point, MD Camp St. Charles, Inc.
Willis, Kevin L. '93 (TLS) Special Assignment.
Willis, Kevin '93 (FAR) On Duty Outside the Diocese.
Willis, Kevin '93 (TLS)[F] Tulsa, OK St. John Villas, Inc.
Willis, Thomas S. '84 (STA) St. Augustine, FL Cathedral – Basilica of St. Augustine; [K] St. Augustine, FL Flagler College Newman Center; Deans; Office of Liturgy.
Willmering, John H. *s.j.* '68 (FgM) St. Louis, MO Society of Jesus.
Willoughby, Malcolm Sylvester *o.p.* '49 (WDC)[B] Washington, DC Dominican House of Studies.
Wills, Nathan D. *c.s.c.* '06 (FTW)[H] Notre Dame Congregation of Holy Cross, United States Province of Priests & Brothers.
Wilmot, John P. '77 (WIN) Mankato, MN Holy Family; Mankato, MN St. Joseph the Worker.
Wilmoth, James R. '65 (IND) Indianapolis, IN St. Roch Catholic Church, Indianapolis, Inc.; Deaneries and Deans; [C] Indianapolis, IN Roncalli High School.
Wilmsen, Gerald *s.s.c.* '59 (OM)[J] St. Columbans Missionary Society of St. Columban Retired.
Wilson, Alan *o.f.m.cap* '69 (SFR)[B] San Francisco, CA Capuchin Franciscan Order San Buenaventura Friary.
Wilson, Albert L. '51 (L)[L] Louisville, KY Bishop David Apartments Retired.
Wilson, Anthony *o.f.m.* '87 (FgM) New York, NY Holy Name Province.
Wilson, Bill '02 (SP) On Duty Outside the Diocese.
Wilson, Bill '02 (CHI) Chicago, IL St. Clement.
Wilson, C. Patrick *s.a.c.* '05 (VEN) Sarasota, FL St. Martha.
Wilson, Cedric M. *o.s.a.* '78 (ARL) Arlington, VA St. Agnes.
Wilson, Daniel *l.c.* '02 (WDC)[O] Potomac, MD Legionaries of Christ.
Wilson, David '88 (E) Johnsonburg, PA Holy Rosary; Wilcox, PA St. Anne.
Wilson, Dennis M. *o.f.m.* '92 (NY) New York, NY St. Stephen of Hungary; [DD] New York, NY Franciscan Friars, Holy Name Province.
Wilson, Edward J. '01 (PRO) Warwick, RI Sts. Rose & Clement.
Wilson, Eugene C. '00 (PH) Newtown, PA St. Andrew.
Wilson, F. Philip *o.s.b.* '53 (PRO)[O] Portsmouth, RI Abbey of St. Gregory the Great.
Wilson, Gene *c.pp.s.* (TOL)[J] Bellevue, OH Sorrowful Mother Shrine; [H] Bellevue Mary Lay Center.
Wilson, George B. *s.j.* '59 (CIN)[N] Cincinnati, OH Jesuit Community at Xavier University.
Wilson, Gregory B. '01 (CHR) Presbyteral Council.
Wilson, Gregory '01 (CHR) Aiken, SC St. Mary Help of Christians.
Wilson, Guy *s.t.* '78 (MOB) Fort Mitchell, AL St. Joseph.
Wilson, Jeffrey '11 (STO) Hughson, CA St. Anthony Church of Hughson (Pastor of).
Wilson, Joel R. '09 (TR) Belmar, NJ St. Rose; Censores Librorum.
Wilson, Jonathan F. '03 (COL) Newark, OH Church of the Blessed Sacrament.
Wilson, Joseph F. '86 (BRK) Middle Village, NY St. Margaret.
Wilson, Lawrence Clifton '09 (GAL) Houston, TX St. Thomas More.
Wilson, Method *o.f.m.* '52 (SFD)[K] Sherman, IL Blessed Giles Friary.
Wilson, Rev. Msgr. Michael '75 (WDC) Laurel, MD St. Mary; Solomons, MD Our Lady Star of the Sea; Archdiocesan College of Consultors; Priest Council.
Wilson, Richard D. '97 (FR) New Bedford Deanery; Diocesan Apostolate to Hispanics; New Bedford; New Bedford, MA Our Lady of Guadalupe.
Wilson, Robert K. '90 (NY) Amenia, NY Immaculate Conception.
Wilson, Steven *c.ss.r.* '01 (BLX) Biloxi, MS Our Mother of Sorrows; Biloxi, MS Blessed Francis Xavier Seelos; Presbyteral Council.
Wilson, Stuart T. '67 (BAL) Retired.
Wilson, Thomas R. '75 (PIT) Pittsburgh, PA St. John Vianney.
Wilson, Thomas '96 (STP) Lakeville, MN All Saints.
Wilson, William P. '69 (NEW) On Duty Outside the

Archdiocese Retired.
Wilt, George A. '59 (PIT)[M] Pittsburgh, PA St. John Vianney Manor Retired.
Wilton, David M. *c.p.m.* '93 (OWN)[F] Auburn, KY Fathers of Mercy.
Wilutis, John P. '55 (RVC)[N] Amityville, NY St. Pius X Residence Retired.
Wilwerding, Anthony P. '46 (OM) Retired.
Wilwerding, Glen '04 (DM) Osceola, IA St. Bernard; Osceola, IA St. Patrick; Osceola, IA St. Joseph.
Wilz, John C. '64 (PH) Retired.
Wimett, Leo J. '60 (SY) North Bay, NY St. John.
Wimmer, Joseph F. *o.s.a.* '64 (WDC) Beltsville, MD St. Joseph.
Wimmershoff, Simeon Frank *o.f.m.* '97 (SFE) Anton Chico, NM San Jose; Vaughn, NM St. Mary; Fort Sumner, NM St. Anthony of Padua.
Wimsatt, Michael T. '10 (L) Bardstown, KY Basilica of St. Joseph Proto–Cathedral.
Wimsett, Scott J. '88 (L) Louisville, KY Our Lady of Lourdes.
Winca, Harry S. '45 (CLV) Parkman, OH St. Lucy; Parkman, OH St. Edward Retired.
Winchel, Scott '09 (SAV) Augusta, GA St. Mary on the Hill.
Winchester, George P. *s.j.* '65 (BO)[U] Boston, MA Loyola House.
Wind, Jeremy J. '08 (SC) Schaller, IA St. Joseph's; Storm Lake, IA St. Mary's; Presbyteral Council.
Windhaus, Edward A. '72 (PH) Elkins Park, PA St. James.
Windholtz, Barry M. '88 (CIN) Cincinnati, OH St. Peter in Chains Cathedral; Cincinnati, OH St. Rose of Lima; Adjutant Judicial Vicars.
Windholtz, Barry M. '88 (COV) Judges.
Windholtz, Barry '88 (LEX) Associate Judges.
Windolph, Nestor *o.f.m.* '55 (FgM) Saint Louis, MO Sacred Heart Province.
Windsor, David E. *c.m.* '74 (MIL)[A] St. Francis, WI Saint Francis de Sales Seminary.
Windy, Jeff (PEO) On Leave of Absence.
Wingate, Arthur K. '57 (FR) Retired.
Wingert, D. William '60 (SC) Retired.
Wingert, Gerald R. '47 (SC) Retired.
Winiarski, James M. *m.s.* '66 (LKC) Sulphur, LA Our Lady of LaSalette.
Winikates, Thomas '70 (CHI) Westchester, IL Divine Infant.
Winkel, Thomas J. '71 (CLV) South Euclid, OH Sacred Heart of Jesus Parish.
Winkelbauer, Phillip J. '75 (KCK) Leavenworth, KS Sacred Heart–St. Casimir; Regional Pastoral Leaders.
Winkeljohn, James Christian '08 (PT) Tallahassee, FL Good Shepherd.
Winkelmann, Luke E. '05 (CHI) Northlake, IL St. John Vianney, Cure of Ars.
Winkels, Michael A. *o.p.* '76 (CHI)[D] Oak Park, IL Fenwick High School; [N] Oak Park, IL Dominican Community of St. Martin de Porres.
Winker, Nicklaus E. '10 (STL) Dardenne Prairie, MO Immaculate Conception.
Winkler, Chauncey '03 (PHX) Lake Havasu City, AZ Our Lady of the Lake Roman Catholic Parish; Members.
Winkler, Edward J. '86 (VIC) Schulenburg, TX St. Rose of Lima.
Winkler, Eugene '50 (MIL) Retired.
Winkler, Jude *o.f.m.conv.* '81 (BAL)[Q] Ellicott City Order of Friars Minor Conventual.
Winkowski, Michael *c.pp.s.* '70 (CIN)[N] Dayton Provincial Office of the Cincinnati Province of the Society of the Precious Blood.
Winn, Frank A. '98 (BGP) Greenwich, CT St. Paul.
Winne, George R. '83 (ALN) Reading, PA St. Joseph.
Winnicki, Tadeusz *s.ch.* '72 (JOL) Lombard, IL Divine Mercy Polish Mission.
Winshman, Alfred O. *s.j.* '65 (BO)[U] Weston, MA Campion Jesuit Community.
Winslow, Patrick J. '99 (CHL) Tryon, NC St. John the Baptist.
Winter, Donald J. *c.ss.r.* '55 (ORL)[F] New Smyrna Beach, FL St. Alphonsus Villa–Redemptorist Fathers and Brothers Retired.
Winter, Harry *o.m.i.* '64 (STP) St. Paul, MN St. Casimir.
Winterer, Rev. Msgr. Michael J. '60 (SLC) Retired.
Wintermyer, John S. '62 (WDC) Retired.
Winters, Alfred H. '62 (CLV) Lakewood, OH St. Clement Retired.
Winters, Darvin E. '99 (IND) Greencastle, IN St. Paul the Apostle Catholic Church, Putnam County, Inc.; Putnamville Correctional Facility; [O] Greencastle, IN DePauw University; Air National Guard Chaplains.
Winters, Martin N. '52 (CHI)[O] Oak Forest, IL Missionary Sisters of St. Benedict of Illinois, Inc. Retired.
Winters, Sean G. '87 (MET) Office of Hospital Chaplaincy; Perth Amboy, NJ Holy Spirit; Perth Amboy, NJ Raritan Bay Medical Center.
Winters, Vaughn P. '93 (LA) Palmdale, CA St. Mary.
Winters, William H. *o.f.m.cap.* (RVC) East Patchogue, NY St. Joseph the Worker.
Wintz, Jack R. *o.f.m.* '63 (CIN)[N] Cincinnati, OH Pleasant Street Friary.
Winzenburg, George E. *s.j.* '74 (RC) Pine Ridge, SD Holy Rosary/Red Cloud Indian School Inc.; Diocesan Consultors; [C] Pine Ridge, SD Jesuit Community of Holy Rosary Mission.
Winzerling, James L. '61 (STL) Retired.
Wiorkiewicz, Marek *s.d.s.* '89 (NEW)[L] Verona, NJ The Salvatorian Fathers.
Wippel, Rev. Msgr. John '60 (STU) On Duty Outside the Diocese; [C] Catholic University of America, The.
Wirkes, Stephen P. '80 (SY) Fulton, NY Church of the Holy Trinity.
Wirkowski, Mariusz '04 (FBK) Kotlik, AK St. Joseph Catholic Church Kotlik.
Wironen, John *c.s.c.* '79 (P)[L] Portland, OR Holy Cross Fathers & Brothers, C.S.C. – University of Portland.
Wironen, John *c.s.c.* (FTW)[H] Notre Dame Congregation of Holy Cross, United States Province of Priests & Brothers.
Wirth, Geoffrey D. '67 (RCK) Elgin, IL St. Thomas More; Diocesan Consultors.
Wirth, Jerry E. '68 (BEL) Olney, IL St. Joseph.
Wirtner, Vincent *c.pp.s.* '10 (CIN)[N] Dayton, OH Provincial Office of the Cincinnati Province of the Society of the Precious Blood; Dayton, OH Precious Blood.
Wisdom, Andrew–Carl *o.p.* '87 (CHI)[N] Chicago Dominicans (Provincial Office); [N] Chicago, IL St. Pius V Priory.
Wise, Mark *c.ss.r.* '70 (PH) Philadelphia, PA St. Peter the Apostle.
Wise, Paul C. '74 (CAM) Retired.
Wise, Richard P. '81 (ATL) Lookout Mountain, GA Our Lady of the Mount.
Wiseman, Joseph F. '52 (BRK) Flushing, NY Mary's Nativity Retired.
Wiseman, Robert A. *c.s.c.* '77 (FTW)[H] Notre Dame Congregation of Holy Cross, United States Province of Priests & Brothers.
Wiseman, Robert A. *c.s.c.* '77 (FR)[A] North Easton, MA Stonehill College; [A] North Easton, MA Holy Cross Fathers Religious.
Wiseman, Vincent *o.p.* '71 (FgM) New York, NY Province of St. Joseph (Eastern).
Wisner, John H. '72 (KCK) Roeland Park, KS St. Agnes.
Wisneski, Edward '67 (NOR) Retired.
Wisneski, John J. '64 (GR) Retired.
Wisneski, Jonathan J. '98 (GBG) Office for Clergy Vocations; North Huntingdon, PA St. Agnes.
Wisniefski, Robert W. '80 (PAT) Paterson, NJ St. Joseph's; Paterson, NJ St. George; Clifton, NJ St. Brendan.
Wisniewski, Joseph F. '07 (WIL) Wilmington, DE St. Ann.
Wisniewski, Joseph *c.m.* '65 (BRK) Brooklyn, NY SS. Cyril and Methodius.
Wisniewski, Robert W. '89 (CLV) Parma, OH St. Bridget of Kildare.
Wisniewski, Thomas S. '80 (NEW) Glen Rock, NJ St. Catharine.
Wisniewski, Thomas '76 (MIA) Parkland, FL Mary Help of Christians Church.
Wissel, Rev. Msgr. Francis C. '77 (BGP) Greenwich, CT St. Mary; [T] Bridgeport, CT St. Peter's Parish, St. Maximillian Kolbe House of Studies.
Wissler, Thomas '83 (STL) Troy, MO Sacred Heart.
Wissman, J. Patrick '64 (SPC) Bolivar, MO Sacred Heart; Region III; Region III.
Wister, Rev. Msgr. Robert J. '68 (NEW)[A] South Orange, NJ Immaculate Conception Seminary School of Theology; [B] Seton Hall University.
Wit, Mieczyslaw *o.f.m.conv.* '95 (SPR) Chicopee, MA St. Stanislaus Basilica.
Witalec, Dennis J. '82 (PH) Absent on Sick Leave; Philadelphia, PA Epiphany of Our Lord.
Witchousky, Peter *o.p.* '69 (SFD)[L] Springfield, IL Dominican Sisters of Springfield, Il.
Witcoskie, Stanley L. '93 (CAM) On Leave of Absence.
Witczak, Michael G. '77 (MIL) On Duty Outside the Archdiocese; [C] Catholic University of America, The.
With, William A. '72 (BRK) Middle Village, NY St. Margaret; Brooklyn, NY St. Ephrem.
Witherup, Ronald D. *s.s.* '76 (BAL)[Q] Baltimore, MD Society of St. Sulpice, Province of the United States.
Witherup, Ronald *s.s.* (E) On Duty Outside Diocese.
Withrow, Justin *o.s.b.* '90 (GBG) Greensburg, PA Excela Health – Westmoreland Hospital; [H] Latrobe, PA Saint Vincent Archabbey.
Witkowski, Rev. Msgr. Bernard E. '62 (PH) Philadelphia, PA Maternity B.V.M. Retired.
Witkowski, Phillip J. '75 (GR) Shelby, MI Our Lady of the Assumption; Shelby, MI Our Lady of Fatima.
Witkowski, Robert J. '61 (DET) Warren, MI St. Edmund.
Witmer, Joseph W. '67 (Y) College of Consultors; Ecumenism; Bishop's Delegate for Retired Priests Retired.
Witmer, Joseph W. '67 (Y)[I] Louisville, OH Emmaus House.
Witon, Russell F. '63 (MIL) Retired.
Witsken, Gary J. '69 (CIN) Retired.
Witt, Edward G. *s.j.* '91 (RC) White River, SD St. Ignatius; White River, SD Sacred Heart; St. Francis, SD St. Francis Mission/Rosebud Educational Society; Deaneries; [C] Howes, SD Kino Jesuit Community.
Witt, George M. *s.j.* '06 (NY)[DD] New York, NY St. Ignatius Loyola Residence; New York, NY St. Ignatius Loyola.
Witt, Michael J. '90 (STL)[A] St. Louis, MO Kenrick School of Theology.
Witt, Michael J. '75 (STL) Archdiocesan Office of the Permanent Diaconate.
Witt, Michael '90 (STL) University City, MO All Saints.
Witt, Rev. Msgr. Paul K. '71 (LIN) Valparaiso, NE Sts. Mary and Joseph's; Deaneries and Deans; Ecumenical Affairs, Commission for; Evangelization Committee.
Witte, Mark G. '95 (COV) Leave of Absence.
Witte, Steven D. '92 (BEL) Leave of Absence.
Wittenbrink, Boniface *o.m.i.* '41 (BEL)[F] Belleville, IL Shrine of Our Lady of the Snows Retired.
Witthauer, Paul G. '60 (BAL) Retired.
Wittkop, Scott '05 (SCL) Special Assignment.
Wittliff, Thomas F. '64 (MIL) Retired.
Wittman, Peter C. '75 (STP) Shakopee, MN St. Mary of the Purification; Shakopee, MN Church of St. Mary; Board of Directors; Shakopee, MN St. Mark.
Wittmann, Christopher T. *s.m.* '94 (CIN)[C] Dayton, OH Marianist Novitiate; [N] Dayton, OH Marianist Community, Novitiate.
Wittrock, Daniel L. '93 (OM) Age Groups; Winnebago, NE St. Joseph; Winnebago, NE St. Augustine's; Our Lady of Fatima; Homer, NE St. Cornelius; Consultors; Ex Officio (Consultors).
Wittstock, Joseph *o.c.s.o.* '84 (ARL)[H] Berryville, VA Cistercian Abbey of Our Lady of the Holy Cross.
Witucki, Roy R. '05 (LC) Ellsworth, WI St. Francis of Assisi.
Witz, Dennis M. '76 (MIL) West Allis, WI St. Rita.
Witzemann, B. Gerald '61 (COV) Warsaw, KY St. Joseph Retired.
Witzmann, Hugh *o.s.b.* '55 (SCL)[I] Collegeville, MN St. John's Abbey, of the Order of St. Benedict.
Wixted, Rev. Msgr. Matthew O. '62 (SLC) Apostleship of Prayer Retired.
Wleczyk, Rev. Msgr. Leo '65 (GAL) Lake Jackson, TX St. Michael; Southern Vicariate; Appointees; College of Consultors.
Wocken, Jeffrey *s.d.s.* '99 (MIL)[P] Milwaukee Salvatorian Provincial Offices; Milwaukee, WI.
Wodecki, Jeremi '07 (CHR) Charleston, SC Cathedral of St. John the Baptist.
Wodniak, John L. '43 (CHI) Chicago, IL St. James Retired.
Woempner, Michael A. '79 (MAR) Kingsford, MI St. Mary Queen of Peace; Vicars Forane; Consultors.
Woerter, Dennis C. *o.p.* '97 (CHI) River Forest, IL St. Vincent Ferrer.
Woerth, Thomas '66 (DEN) Retired.
Woerz, Chris *s.d.b.* (OAK)[E] Richmond, CA Salesian High School.
Woerz, Christian H. *s.d.b.* '76 (LA)[V] Rosemead, CA St. Joseph's Salesian Youth Renewal Center.
Woestman, William H. *o.m.i.* '56 (CHI) Associate Vicars; Promoter of Justice; Defenders of the Bond; Chicago, IL Holy Name Cathedral.
Wohinc, Karl R. '63 (WH) Shinnston, WV St. Ann's.
Wohler, Gil *o.f.m.* '62 (CIN)[N] Cincinnati St. Francis Seraph Friary.
Wohlwend, Paul W. *c.pp.s.* '54 (CIN)[N] Carthagena, OH St. Charles Retired.
Wojcicki, Miroslaus A. '62 (PIT) East Pittsburgh, PA Holy Cross.
Wojcicki, Rev. Msgr. Ted L. '75 (STL) Dardenne Prairie, MO Immaculate Conception; Deaneries/Deans.
Wojcicki, Wojciech '90 (DET) Retired.
Wojciechowski, Edward C. '81 (PRM) Retired.
Wojciechowski, Richard P. '63 (BAL) Retired.
Wojciechowski, Thomas *o.f.m.* '75 (GB)[J] Green Bay, WI St. Mary of the Angels Friary.
Wojciechowski, Thomas *o.f.m.* '75 (MIL)[P] Burlington, WI Queen of Peace Friary.
Wojciechowski, Tomasz *c.r.* '08 (CHI) Chicago, IL St. Hedwig.
Wojcik, Eugene H. '74 (BEL) Chester, IL St. Mary Help of Christians; Diaconate, Office of Permanent.
Wojcik, Grzegorz '08 (CHI) Palos Hills, IL Sacred Heart.
Wojcik, Grzegorz '11 (DEN) Fort Collins, CO St. Joseph.
Wojcik, Joseph J. '69 (CHI) La Grange Park, IL St. Louise de Marillac.
Wojcik, Przemyslaw '08 (CHI) Wilmette, IL St. Francis Xavier.
Wojcik, Richard J. '49 (CHI)[A] Mundelein, IL University of St. Mary of the Lake/Mundelein Seminary Retired.

Wojcinski, Anthony A. '85 (PBL) Pueblo, CO St. Leander.
Wojdelski, Mark *f.s.s.p.* '05 (CIN) Dayton, OH Holy Family.
Wojtan, Andrzej '83 (ORL) Mims, FL Holy Spirit.
Wojtek, Robert *c.ss.r.* (BAL) Baltimore, MD Sacred Heart of Jesus.
Wojtewicz, Eugene E. '57 (DET) Retired.
Wojtun, Daniel T. '07 (HRT) Southington, CT Immaculate Conception.
Wolak, Edmund '92 (SY) Absent on Leave.
Wolanski, Edward *c.p.* '72 (R) Greenville, NC St. Peter's.
Wolbach, Rev. Msgr. Richard A. '56 (OM) Retired.
Wolbert, Jerome *o.f.m.* '09 (PSC)[A] Sybertsville, PA Holy Dormition Friary.
Woldai, Gebriel '93 (OAK) Berkeley, CA St. Joseph The Worker; Eritrean Community.
Wolensky, Paul '94 (PHU) Scranton, PA St. Vladimir's; Scranton, PA SS. Peter and Paul.
Wolesky, John '67 (SAL) Solomon, KS St. Patrick Parish; Solomon, KS Immaculate Conception of the Blessed Virgin Mary Parish.
Wolf, Anthony J. '96 (LC) Leave of Absence.
Wolf, Dennis G. '72 (BUF) West Seneca, NY Blessed John XXIII.
Wolf, Donald J. '81 (OKL) Shawnee, OK St. Benedict; Council of Priests Archdiocesan; Region II–B.
Wolf, Eugene J. '63 (LC) Retired.
Wolf, George C. '63 (RNO) Promoter of Justice; Defenders of the Bond Retired.
Wolf, George '80 (P) Portland, OR Holy Family; College of Consultors; Board Members.
Wolf, George *o.s.b.* '44 (FgM) Collegeville, MN St. John's Abbey; [I] Collegeville, MN St. John's Abbey, of the Order of St. Benedict.
Wolf, Rev. Msgr. John V. '45 (COL) Censor of Books Retired.
Wolf, John *c.pp.s.* '69 (KC) Kearney, MO Church of the Annunciation.
Wolf, Joseph A. '68 (MIL) Retired.
Wolf, Joseph B. '54 (STL) Retired.
Wolf, Joseph D. '87 (BUF) Buffalo, NY Holy Spirit.
Wolf, Joseph M. '94 (DAV) Vice–Chancellors; Judicial Vicar; Notaries; Judges; LeClaire, IA Our Lady of the River.
Wolf, Lawrence Robert *o.s.b.m.* '75 (PSC)[A] Matawan, NJ Basilian Fathers of Mariapoch.
Wolf, Paul L. '83 (NU) Marshall, MN Holy Redeemer; Associate Judges.
Wolf, Robert '10 (P) Lake Oswego, OR Our Lady of the Lake.
Wolf, Stephen J. '97 (NSH) Nashville, TN St. Henry.
Wolfbauer, Michael '10 (SCL)[C] Saint Cloud, MN The Cathedral High School; Presbyteral Council; Sartell, MN St. Francis Xavier.
Wolfe, Allan F. '92 (HBG) Lancaster, PA Iglesia Catolica San Juan Bautista; Lancaster, PA Lancaster County Prison.
Wolfe, Joseph M. *m.f.v.a.* '93 (BIR)[E] Birmingham, AL Franciscan Missionaries of the Eternal Word, A Public Association of the Christian Faithful.
Wolfe, Michael '09 (ALT) Johnstown, PA St. Benedict's.
Wolfe, William P. '70 (LA) West Hollywood, CA St. Ambrose.
Wolfee, Robert '98 (NEW) Rochelle Park, NJ Sacred Heart; Archdiocesan Judges.
Wolfel, Daniel C. *o.s.b.* '54 (E) St. Marys, PA Queen of the World; St. Marys, PA St. Mary.
Wolfel, Daniel C. *o.s.b.* '54 (GBG)[H] Latrobe, PA Saint Vincent Archabbey.
Wolfer, Robert R. '48 (CIN) Retired.
Wolff, Alec J. '81 (CHI) Highland Park, IL Immaculate Conception; [W] Wilmette, IL Musica Pacis; Judges.
Wolff, Jim '54 (SFE) Santa Fe, NM Santa Maria de la Paz Catholic Community.
Wolff, Rev. Msgr. Robert C. '50 (CLV) Copley, OH Guardian Angels Retired.
Wolfgram, Daniel '97 (SFS) Big Stone City, SD St. Charles.
Wolford, Donald L. '79 (SFD) Moweaqua, IL St. Frances de Sales; Shelbyville, IL Immaculate Conception; Assumption, IL Assumption B.V.M.
Wolfram, Frank *s.d.b.* '62 (NY)[DD] New Rochelle, NY Salesian Provincial House.
Wolken, Louis J. *m.m.* '46 (NY)[DD] Retired.
Wolkovits, Paul Dennis '93 (LA) On Sick Leave.
Wollering, Carl J. '66 (CIN) Retired.
Wollesen, Charles A. *s.j.* '52 (SPK)[J] Spokane, WA Regis Community.
Wolnik, James G. '79 (STP) St. Paul, MN Holy Childhood.
Wolnowski, Kenneth J. '65 (CLV) Lorain, OH St. Peter Retired.
Woloszczuk, Rev. Mitred Archpriest Wolodymyr '81 (SJP) Obnova Societies; Presbyters Retired.
Wolski, Adalbert *t.o.r.* '58 (ALT)[G] Hollidaysburg, PA St. Bernardine Monastery Retired.
Wolski, Mark J. '67 (BUF) Finance Council; Hamburg, NY SS. Peter and Paul; Council of Priests.
Wolter, Richard J. '59 (STP) Retired.
Wolter, Thomas '66 (JOL)[K] Naperville, IL St. John Vianney Villa Retired.
Wolverton, R. Ambrose *o.s.b.* '65 (PRO)[O] Portsmouth, RI Abbey of St. Gregory the Great.
Won, Adrian Yu Jin (RIC) Richmond, VA St. Kim Taegon.
Won, Rev. Msgr. John P. H. '58 (LA) Retired.
Won, Raymond (STP) St. Paul, MN St. Andrew Kim.
Wonch, Charles *s.c.j.* '02 (MIL)[P] Franklin, WI Sacred Heart at Monastery Lake.
Wong, Joseph *o.s.b.cam.* '74 (MRY)[F] Big Sur New Camaldoli Hermitage.
Wong, Jules *o.f.m.* '73 (Y)[J] Youngstown, OH Mt. Alverna Friary; Youngstown, OH.
Wood, Charles A. '00 (P) Portland, OR St. Clare.
Wood, D. Mark '87 (LR) Little Rock, AR St. Theresa.
Wood, Edson J. *o.s.a.* '72 (NY) West Point, NY Catholic Chapel of the Most Holy Trinity.
Wood, Gregg D. *s.j.* '75 (FBK)[E] Bethel, AK Brother Joe Prince Jesuit Community; Superior Regular; Presbyteral Council; Consultors.
Wood, James L. '72 (RVC) Selden, NY St. Margaret of Scotland.
Wood, Kenneth E. '89 (RIC) Newport News, VA Our Lady of Mount Carmel.
Wood, Mark '87 (LR) Clergy Welfare Advisory Board; Presbyteral Council; Diocesan Consultors; Cursillo Movement.
Wood, Michael J. '11 (SPR) West Springfield, MA St. Thomas the Apostle.
Wood, Michael '84 (AMA) Retired.
Wood, Norbert J. *o.praem.* '81 (ORG) Costa Mesa, CA St. John the Baptist.
Wood, Patrick *c.ss.r.* (RVC) Bethpage, NY St. Martin of Tours.
Wood, Paul A. '80 (BRK) Maspeth, NY St. Stanislaus Kostka; Maspeth, NY Transfiguration; [D] Brooklyn, NY Campus Ministers and Ministry Centers.
Wood, Raymond B. '64 (SY) Retired.
Wood, Robert T. '87 (OKL) Guthrie, OK St. Mary's; Council of Catholic Women, Archdiocesan; Master of Ceremonies.
Wood, Robert W. '74 (BUF) Retired.
Wood, Robert *c.m.* '56 (STL)[O] Perryville, MO Congregation of the Mission.
Wood, Simon Paul *c.p.* '43 (HRT)[L] West Hartford Holy Family Monastery/Retreat.
Wood, Tyson J. '05 (MO) Military Chaplains; Army Chaplains.
Wood, William Andrew '73 (GAL) Sugar Land, TX St. Laurence.
Wood, William J. *s.j.* '65 (SJ)[M] Los Gatos, CA Sacred Heart Jesuit Center.
Woodeshick, Martin E. '69 (PH) Sharon Hill, PA Holy Spirit.
Woodhall, Jonathan A. '99 (R) Retired.
Woodland, Stephen '88 (LA) On Active Leave.
Woodland, Stephen '88 (SEA) Des Moines, WA St. Philomena.
Woodman, Gerald '78 (SEA) Woodland, WA St. Philip.
Woodruff, Mark '72 (SAN) Odessa, TX St. Elizabeth Ann Seton; Defensores Vinculi; Board of Directors.
Woodruff, William F. '82 (NY) Saugerties, NY St. John the Evangelist.
Woods, James A. *s.j.* '61 (BO)[C] Summer Session; [C] Woods College of Advancing Studies; [U] Newton, MA The Jesuit Community at Boston College.
Woods, Keith A. '95 (WDC) Morganza, MD St. Joseph; Priest Council.
Woods, Michael J. *s.j.* '04 (BAL)[Q] Towson Maryland Province of the Society of Jesus.
Woods, Michael '66 (KNX) Knoxville, TN All Saints Catholic Church; [K] Knoxville, TN Diocesan Council of Catholic Women.
Woods, Patrick F. *c.ss.r.* '75 (FgM) Brooklyn, NY AMERICAN REDEMPTORIST FATHERS.
Woods, Richard J. *o.p.* '69 (CHI)[N] River Forest, IL St. Thomas Aquinas Priory.
Woods, Samuel A. '11 (STO) Modesto, CA Holy Family Church (Pastor of).
Woods, Scott '02 (WDC) St. Inigoes, MD St. Peter Claver; St. Mary's City, MD St. Cecilia; Vocations for Men; Archdiocesan Chaplain – Catholic Committee on Boy Scouts.
Woods, Thomas F. '02 (BIR) Sylacauga, AL St. Jude; Talladega, AL St. Francis of Assisi; [H] Talladega, AL Talladega College Catholic Campus Ministry.
Woods, Thomas Matthew '05 (WDC) Absent On Leave.
Woods, Walter J. '69 (BO) Acton, MA St. Elizabeth of Hungary; Canonical Affairs Committee.
Woodward, Gregory *l.c.* '00 (SAC) Sacramento, CA Our Lady of Guadalupe Shrine.
Woodward, John *s.j.* '58 (PH)[Y] Loyola Center and Manresa Hall.
Woolever, James '74 (SY) On Duty Outside the Diocese.
Woolley, Michael J. '99 (PRO) Woonsocket, RI St. Joseph.
Woolson, Herbert '82 (LFT) Rochester, IN St. Ann; Monterey, IN St. Anne; Rochester, IN St. Joseph.
Woolway, Rev. Msgr. John S. '80 (LA) Compton, CA Sagrado Corazon, Sacred Heart.
Woost, David G. '91 (CLV) Kirtland, OH Divine Word; [Y] Kirtland, OH St. Philip Neri/Divine Word Church in the City Partnership Inc.
Woost, Michael G. '84 (CLV)[A] Wickliffe, OH St. Mary Seminary and Graduate School of Theology; [A] Wickliffe, OH Borromeo Seminary.
Woost, Thomas G. '97 (CLV) North Olmsted, OH St. Brendan.
Wooton, Jerry A. '96 (ARL) Gainesville, VA Holy Trinity.
Wopperer, Thomas J. '64 (BUF) Retired.
Woracek, Rev. Msgr. Thomas J. '46 (STL) Retired.
Worcester, Thomas W. *s.j.* '91 (WOR)[N] Worcester, MA Jesuits of the Holy Cross, Inc.
Worch, Donald P. '67 (WDC) Potomac, MD Our Lady of Mercy Retired.
Wordekemper, Thomas *o.s.b.* '94 (BIS)[A] Richardton, ND Assumption Abbey.
Workman, Jamie R. '06 (ARL) McLean, VA St. Luke; Advocates.
Workman, Joseph G. '04 (CLV) Lakewood, OH St. Clement.
Worland, Christopher J. '01 (CIN) Kettering, OH Ascension.
Worley, Jason '99 (BAL) Libertytown, MD St. Peter.
Worm, Paul F. '88 (LR) Texarkana, AR St. Edward; Ashdown, AR St. Elizabeth Ann Seton Church; Foreman, AR Sacred Heart Church; Presbyteral Council; Deans.
Worman, Jeremiah F. '67 (GB) Elcho, WI Holy Family; Pickerel, WI St. Mary Retired.
Wormek, Joseph E. '76 (STL) Crystal City, MO Sacred Heart; Herculaneum, MO Church of the Assumption of B.V.M.; Deaneries/Deans.
Woroniewicz, Michael A. '85 (DET) Dundee, MI St. Irene; Ida, MI St. Joseph.
Worry, Benedict M. *o.s.b.* '87 (PAT)[N] Morristown St. Mary's Abbey.
Worry, Benedict M. *o.s.b.* (NEW) Linden, NJ St. Elizabeth of Hungary.
Worschak, D. George '78 (PHU) Absent on Leave.
Worsley, Rev. Msgr. Stephen C. '84 (R) Sanford, NC St. Stephen The First Martyr.
Worster, John R. '87 (MO) Army National Guard Chaplains.
Worster, John '87 (B) Priest Retirement Committee; Pocatello, ID Holy Spirit Catholic Community.
Worth, James '01 (NEW) Springfield, NJ St. James the Apostle.
Worthen, Matthew Cameron '11 (PT) Pensacola, FL Cathedral of the Sacred Heart.
Worthley, Jason W. '04 (BO) Somerville, MA St. Ann; Somerville, MA St. Catherine of Genoa.
Worthy, Donald L. '62 (DET) Retired.
Wortmann, Joseph F. '58 (NEW)[B] Retired.
Worzalla, Dennis A. '50 (GB) Retired.
Woseitz, Joseph '58 (CHI) Chicago, IL Christ the King.
Wosman, Richard *s.m.* '93 (SAT)[C] San Antonio, TX St. Mary's University of San Antonio, Texas.
Woster, Rev. Msgr. Michael '82 (RC) Winner, SD St. Isidore; Winner, SD Immaculate Conception; [E] McLaughlin, SD Priest Retirement and Aid Association/Pension Plan Board; Vicar for Retired Priests.
Wotelko, Matthew S. *o.s.b.* '67 (NEW)[L] Newark, NJ Newark Abbey; Newark, NJ.
Woy, Rev. Msgr. Richard W. '79 (BAL) Vicars General; Moderator of the Curia; Special Assignment; Baltimore, MD Cathedral of Mary Our Queen; Hydes, MD St. John the Evangelist.
Woytek, Robert '91 (PSC) Leave of Absence.
Woytyna, Christopher *o.s.b.m.* '61 (STF) Long Island City, NY Holy Cross.
Wozniak, Anthony A. '59 (GBG)[G] Greensburg, PA Neumann House.
Wozniak, Casimir '68 (E)[B] Erie, PA Gannon University; The Bishop's Theological Advisory Committee.
Wozniak, James E. '97 (GRY) Crown Point, IN St. Matthias.
Wozniak, Rev. Msgr. Louis '51 (AUS) Retired.
Wozniak, Richard *c.m.f.* '52 (PHX) Prescott, AZ Sacred Heart Roman Catholic Parish.
Wozniak, Robert A. '72 (WIL) Wilmington, DE Immaculate Heart of Mary.
Wozniak, Robert A. '88 (BUF) Newfane, NY St. Brendan on the Lake; Council of Priests.
Wozniak, Ronald E. *s.j.* '77 (BO)[U] Weston, MA Campion Jesuit Community; [U] Weston, MA Campion Health Center, Inc.
Wozniak, Timothy '74 (STP) Eagan, MN St. Thomas Becket.
Woznicki, Donald C. '02 (CHI) Lake Forest, IL St. Mary; [W] Lake Forest, IL New Ethos.
Wozniczka, Stephen Z. *o.s.p.p.e.* '60 (PH)[Y].
Wozny, Jacek '88 (NY) Staten Island, NY St. Stanislaus Kostka.
Wray, Joseph M. '96 (OM) Norfolk, NE Sacred Heart.
Wrenn, Lawrence G. '53 (HRT) Hartford, CT Cathedral of St. Joseph Retired.
Wrenn, Lawrence '77 (WH) Retired.
Wright, Addison G. *s.s.* '57 (BAL)[Q] Baltimore Society of St. Sulpice, Province of the United States Retired.

Wright, Addison G. *s.s.* '60 (BGP) Retired.
Wright, Arthur J. (BO) Milton, MA St. Mary of the Hills.
Wright, Bryan B. '00 (SCR) Sayre, PA Epiphany Parish.
Wright, C. Scott '11 (CIN) Centerville, OH Incarnation.
Wright, D. Ralph *o.s.b.* '70 (STL)[F] Creve Coeur, MO St. Louis Priory School; [O] St. Louis, MO The Abbey of St. Mary and St. Louis.
Wright, David *o.p.* '68 (STL)[O] Saint Louis, MO St. Dominic Priory; [B] St. Louis, MO Aquinas Institute of Theology.
Wright, Frank *s.m.a.* '93 (WDC)[O] Takoma Park, MD Lay Missionary Program.
Wright, Frank *s.m.a.* (HEL) Butte, MT St. John the Evangelist.
Wright, Gary R. *s.j.* '80 (DET)[K] Detroit, MI Jesuit Community at the University of Detroit Mercy.
Wright, Gerald *o.m.v.* '80 (E) Erie County Prison; Veterans Administration Hospital; Erie, PA St. Joseph.
Wright, Gerald *o.m.v.* '80 (MO) DEPARTMENT OF VETERANS AFFAIRS HOSPITALS AND CHAPLAINS.
Wright, John A. '56 (CHY) Retired.
Wright, John A. '82 (MAN) Retired.
Wright, John J. '78 (CLV) University Hospitals Bedford Medical Center; Bedford, OH Our Lady of Hope.
Wright, Rev. Msgr. John M. '62 (IND) Retired.
Wright, Michael H. '95 (SEA) Seattle, WA St. Bernadette.
Wright, Michael Mary of the Trinity *m. carm.* '10 (CHY)[D] Powell, WY Monks of the Most Blessed Virgin Mary of Mt. Carmel.
Wright, Moses '06 (ROM)[A] St. Nazianz, WI Holy Resurrection Monastery.
Wright, Robert E. *o.m.i.* '74 (SAT)[C] Oblate School of Theology; [L] San Antonio, TX; [L] San Antonio, TX Joseph Gerard House; Archdiocesan Presbyteral Council.
Wright, Robert *o.m.i.* (AUS)[N] Austin, TX Texas Catholic Historical Society.
Wright, Rev. Msgr. Rupert A. '56 (BUF) Retired.
Wright, Russell *s.t.l.* '88 (VEN) Naples, FL St. Peter the Apostle.
Wright, Tennant C. *s.j.* '62 (SJ)[B] Santa Clara, CA Jesuit Community.
Wright, Warren J. *s.j.* '82 (SJ)[M] Los Gatos, CA Sacred Heart Jesuit Center.
Wright, William *c.ss.r.* '60 (FgM) Denver, CO Denver Province.
Wrightington, Charles *s.j.* '00 (NO)[C] New Orleans, LA Loyola University New Orleans; New Orleans, LA Holy Name of Jesus.
Wrightson, Mark J. *o.s.f.s.* '86 (ALN) Robesonia, PA St. Francis de Sales.
Wrigley, J. Michael '03 (BIR) Birmingham, AL St. Barnabas.
Wrobel, Charles '10 (MIL) New Berlin, WI Holy Apostles; New Berlin, WI Holy Apostles.
Wrobleski, Edward D. *c.s.p.* '62 (LA) Los Angeles, CA St. Paul the Apostle Retired.
Wroblewski, Anthony '95 (DUL) Brainerd, MN St. Andrew; Brainerd, MN St. Francis; Brainerd, MN St. Mathias; Brainerd, MN St. Thomas; Brainerd, MN All Saints; College of Consultors.
Wroblewski, Brendan *o.f.m.* '55 (GB)[J] Pulaski, WI Friary.
Wroblewski, Edward M. *m.m.* '52 (NY)[DD] Maryknoll Maryknoll Fathers and Brothers Retired.
Wroblewski, John J. '92 (NY) Staten Island, NY St. Anthony.
Wroblewski, Marion *c.r.* '65 (JOL) Westmont, IL Holy Trinity.
Wroblewski, Sergius *o.f.m.* '46 (GRY)[H] Cedar Lake, IN Our Lady of Lourdes Friary.
Wroblicky, Theodore P. '99 (STN) Sacramento, CA Holy Wisdom.
Wrona, Jacek '95 (CHI) Chicago, IL St. Ladislaus.
Wronski, John C. *s.j.* '04 (BO)[G] Jamaica Plain, MA Nativity Preparatory School; [U] Newton, MA The Jesuit Community at Boston College.
Wrozek, Timothy A. '88 (FTW) Fort Wayne, IN St. Joseph.
Wrynn, John F. *s.j.* '70 (NEW)[L] Jersey City, NJ Jesuits of Saint Peter's College, Inc.
Wrynn, John P. '70 (NEW)[B] Jersey City, NJ Jesuit Center.
Wtorek, Krzysztof '94 (CAM) Margate City, NJ Holy Trinity Parish, Margate, N.J.
Wtulich, John '72 (BRK) Belle Harbor, NY St. Francis de Sales.
Wtyklo, Jacek S. '98 (MAR) Perkins, MI St. Joseph; Rapid River, MI St. Charles Borromeo; Trenary, MI St. Rita.
Wu, Peter A. *m.m.* '61 (NY)[DD] Retired.
Wudarski, Dariusz P. '96 (SPR) Wilbraham, MA St. Cecilia's.
Wuerth, James E. *m.s.f.* '71 (STL) St. Louis, MO St. Wenceslaus.
Wuest, George *s.j.* '58 (FgM) Chicago, IL Society of Jesus.
Wulinski, Stanley F. '80 (MO) Air Force Reserve Chaplains; On Leave/Unassigned.
Wulsch, Michael A. '72 (CHI) Skokie, IL St. Peter; Deans.
Wunderlich, Dale P. '74 (STL) St. Louis, MO Shrine of St. Joseph.
Wurm, Robert L. '60 (DET) Retired.
Wurst, Wayne H. '80 (CHI) Oak Forest, IL Oak Forest Hospital.
Wurth, Elmer P. *m.m.* '56 (FgM) Maryknoll, NY MARYKNOLL.
Wurth, Richard W. '99 (COV) Leave of Absence.
Wurtz, Camillus *o.s.b.* '53 (KCK)[I] Atchison, KS St. Benedict's Abbey Retired.
Wurtz, Michael B. *c.s.c.* '04 (FTW)[H] Notre Dame Congregation of Holy Cross, United States Province of Priests & Brothers.
Wurz, George E. '60 (SY) Oswego, NY St. Peter; Oswego, NY Oswego County Jail.
Wurzel, Richard T. '59 (TOL) Retired.
Wydeven, John L. '79 (OAK) Providence, RI Veterans Administration Hospital; DEPARTMENT OF VETERANS AFFAIRS HOSPITALS AND CHAPLAINS; On Duty Outside the Diocese.
Wydeven, John '79 (PRO) Providence, RI Holy Name of Jesus.
Wyffels, Rev. Msgr. Robert J. '60 (NU) Retired.
Wymelenberg, M. John *s.j.* '60 (OM)[J] Omaha, NE Jesuit Community at Creighton University.
Wymes, John F. *m.m.* '54 (NY)[DD] Retired.
Wymes, John F. *m.m.* '54 (RVC) Malverne, NY Our Lady of Lourdes Retired.
Wynants, Paul G. *c.i.c.m.* '51 (ARL)[L] Vienna, VA Mount Tabor Society, Inc.
Wyndaele, William *c.i.c.m.* '59 (ARL)[H] Arlington, VA Missionhurst, C.I.C.M.–Central House and Provincialate.
Wyndham, Thomas F. '69 (BO) Senior Priests. Retired.
Wynne, James *o.m.i.* '55 (BEL)[F] Belleville, IL Missionary Oblates of Mary Immaculate – St. Henry's Oblate Residence.
Wynne, Robert F. *m.m.* '74 (FgM) Maryknoll, NY MARYKNOLL.
Wynnycky, John '92 (DET) Grosse Pointe Farms, MI St. Paul Catholic Church.
Wyrostek, Andrzej '00 (RC) Rapid City, SD St. Therese the Little Flower.
Wyrsch, Thomas W. '78 (STL) Florissant, MO St. Rose Philippine Duchesne.
Wyse, James B. '87 (GR) Howard City, MI Christ the King–St. Francis de Sales.
Wysochansky, Demetrius *o.s.b.m.* '59 (STN) Palos Park, IL Nativity of B.V.M.; Eparchial Censor.
Wysochansky, John '57 (PHU) Retired.
Wysochansky, Rev. Canon Walter '64 (SJP) Ambridge, PA Ss. Peter and Paul; Presbyters Retired.
Wysocki, Joseph A. '71 (SCR) Unassigned or Leave of Absence.
Wysocki, Marek B. '85 (NEW) Bloomfield, NJ Church of St. Thomas the Apostle.
Wysocki, Paul '64 (CLV) Retired.
Wysoczanski, Jaroslaw *o.f.m.conv.* (FgM) AMERICAN CONVENTUAL FRANCISCAN MISSIONS.
Wysong, William H. '72 (CIN)[J] Cincinnati, OH St. Rita School for the Deaf; Defenders of the Bond.
Wyszynski, Darius W. '58 (LAN) Retired.
Wyvill, Christopher *o.s.b.* '65 (WDC)[O] Washington, DC St. Anselm's Abbey.
Wyzykiewicz, Richard S. *sch.p.* '71 (PH)[F] Devon, PA Devon Preparatory School; [Y] Devon Piarist Fathers (Order of the Pious Schools).

X

Xavariapitchai, Udayakumar (BO) Revere, MA St. Anthony of Padua.
Xavier, Antony Pullukattu (MOB) Andalusia, AL Christ the King; Greenville, AL St. Elizabeth.
Xavier, Antony '60 (RVC) Manhasset, NY North Shore Univ. Hospital.
Xavier, Godwin '85 (SAC) Marysville, CA St. Joseph.
Xavier, Joseph *m.s.f.s.* '96 (KAL) Paw Paw, MI St. Mary; Gobles, MI St. Jude.
Xavier, Joseph *m.s.f.s.* '96 (TYL)[C] Whitehouse, TX The Missionaries of St. Francis de Sales.
Xotta, Tomas M. *o.s.m.* '64 (ELP) El Paso, TX Our Lady of Sorrows.
Xuereb, Rev. Msgr. Publius '68 (FWT) Aledo, TX Holy Redeemer Parish.

Y

Yabes, Arturo '87 (SJ) Sunnyvale, CA St. Cyprian.
Yablonsky, Gabriel '59 (Y) Retired.
Yabut, Ronald (TUC)[D] Tucson, AZ Carondelet St. Joseph's Hospital.
Yackanich, Eugene P. '65 (PBR) Munhall, PA St. Elias; Protopresbyters; Finance Advisory Council; Administrator.
Yacobi, Francis *o.f.m.cap.* '90 (PH) Philadelphia, PA St. Callistus.
Yacyshyn, Gregory '98 (RVC) Mastic Beach, NY St. Jude.
Yadron, Michael J. '83 (GRY) Munster, IN St. Thomas More; Bishop's Council of Priests; Priests' Personnel Board; Deans; Consultors.
Yadron, Raymond A. '63 (CHI) Palatine, IL St. Thomas of Villanova Retired.
Yaeger, Joseph J. '89 (R) Farmville, NC St. Elizabeth of Hungary.
Yagaza, Severine (SY) Syracuse, NY St. Joseph's Hospital Health Center; East Syracuse, NY St. Matthew.
Yagesh, Richard C. '78 (PIT) Bridgeville, PA Holy Child.
Yaghi, Milad T. *m.l.m.* '88 (OLL) Houston, TX Our Lady of the Cedars Maronite Catholic Church; [A] Houston, TX The Congregation of Maronite Lebanese Missionaries.
Yahner, Gordon A. '63 (CLV) Fairlawn, OH St. Hilary; Akron, OH St. Vincent Retired.
Yaksick, Michael L. '94 (PIT) Midland, PA St. Blaise.
Yakubu, Victor '96 (PHX) Flagstaff, AZ San Francisco de Asis Roman Catholic Parish.
Yaldo, Basel '02 (EST) Shelby Twp., MI St. George Chaldean Catholic Church.
Yali, Jacob '77 (STP) Fairview University Medical Center.
Yamauchi, James '11 (DAL) On Duty Outside the Diocese.
Yanas, John '84 (ALB) Troy, NY Sacred Heart.
Yanez, Horacio '75 (SEA) Seattle, WA Holy Family.
Yang, Benedict '07 (ORG) Placentia, CA St. Joseph; Council of Priests.
Yang, Joseph J. (HBG) Korean Ministry.
Yang, Joseph '96 (LA) Temple City, CA St. Luke the Evangelist.
Yanju, Henry M. '96 (MO) Air Force Reserve Chaplains; Military & VA Chaplains.
Yankauskas, David *o.m.v.* '88 (BO)[Z] Boston, MA St. Francis Chapel; [U] Milton, MA Oblate Residence (St. Joseph House).
Yankey, Albert '80 (VIC) El Campo, TX St. Philip the Apostle.
Yannarell, James J. *s.j.* '71 (NY)[DD] New York, NY Murray–Weigel Hall.
Yanos, Richard M. '83 (CHI) Lake Villa, IL Prince of Peace.
Yanovsky, Stepan (STF) Ansonia, CT SS. Peter and Paul.
Yanta, Timothy J. '05 (STP) Jordan, MN St. John the Baptist.
Yanus, Gary D. '81 (CLV) Cleveland, OH St. Ignatius of Antioch; Judicial Vicar.
Yanus, Gary D. (Y) Judges.
Yanus, Gary D. (TOL) Defenders of the Bond.
Yarbrough, Rev. Msgr. Michael '80 (SAT) San Antonio, TX Holy Trinity; Archdiocesan Presbyteral Council.
Yarce, Eugenio '92 (SLC) Salt Lake City, UT Sacred Heart LLC 210.
Yargeau, Rev. Msgr. Ronald G. '73 (SPR) Greenfield, MA Holy Trinity; Episcopal Vicars; Bishop's Commission for Clergy.
Yarno, Kenneth E. *c.s.v.* '59 (CHI)[N] Arlington Heights, IL Viatorian Province Center–Clerics of St. Viator Retired.
Yarno, Kenneth *c.s.v.* '59 (JOL) Retired.
Yaroch, Kenneth E. '67 (SAG) Retired.
Yaroch, Paul *o.f.m.cap.* '64 (MIL)[P] Mount Calvary, WI St. Lawrence Friary Retired.
Yarrish, Rev. Msgr. Bernard E. '76 (SCR) Retired.
Yasso, Jacob O. '60 (EST) Detroit, MI Sacred Heart Chaldean Parish; Eparchial College of Consultors.
Yastishock, Charles '77 (PSC) Toms River, NJ Our Lady of Perpetual Help; Presbyteral Council.
Yaszcz, Thomas A. '75 (SCR) On Special or Other Diocesan Assignment.
Yates, Anthony R. '10 (STL) St. Louis, MO St. Simon the Apostle.
Yates, Clark *s.m.a.* '56 (NEW)[L] Tenafly, NJ Society of African Missions, Provincialate, S.M.A. Fathers.
Yates, John L. *c.s.sp.* '54 (PIT)[O] Bethel Park, PA The Spiritan Center.
Yavarone, Mark *o.m.v.* (BO)[B] Boston, MA Oblate Provincialate.
Yavorsky, Stephen T. *s.j.* '77 (DEN) Denver, CO St. Ignatius Loyola; [N] Denver, CO Society of Jesus – St. Ignatius Loyola Jesuit Community.
Yawo Azah, Francis Perry '97 (NY) Pleasant Valley, NY St. Stanislaus Kostka.
Yaya, Louis '80 (NY) Kingston, NY Benedictine Hospital.
Ybarra, Manuel *o.f.m.* '86 (WDC) Washington, DC; [O] Washington, DC Franciscan Monastery USA Inc.
Ybarra, Paul *c.s.c.* '11 (PHX) Goodyear, AZ Saint John Vianney Roman Catholic Parish.
Ybiernas, Bernard *o.c.d.* '55 (MIL)[P] Milwaukee Provincial Offices – Discalced Carmelites.
Yeakel, James R. *o.s.f.s.* '79 (PH) Philadelphia, PA Our Mother of Consolation.
Yeazel, Rev. Msgr. J. Robert '67 (SY) DeWitt, NY Holy Cross; [F] Syracuse, NY Bishop Joseph T. O'Keefe, Inc.; [U] Syracuse, NY David W. Barry Foundation;

Vicar General; Presbyteral Council; Clerical Fund Society of the Roman Catholic Diocese of Syracuse; Finance Committee; [U] Syracuse, NY Grimes Foundation; Board of Diocesan Consultors; [U] Syracuse, NY The Robert L. McDevitt, K.S.G., K.C.H.S. and Catherine H. McDevitt, L.C.H.S. Foundation, Inc.; [U] Syracuse, NY The Syracuse Diocesan Investment Fund, Inc.; [U] Syracuse, NY The Foundation of the Roman Catholic Diocese of Syracuse.
Yeboah–Amanfo, Peter '83 (VIC) Blessing, TX St. Peter's.
Yebra, Bernardino S. '88 (MO) Army Reserve Chaplains.
Yelenc, Joseph *t.o.r.* '71 (STU)[A] Steubenville, OH Franciscan University of Steubenville; [H] Steubenville, OH Holy Spirit Friary.
Yelle, Ronald R. '79 (HRT) Appointed Retired.
Ye Myint, Sixtus '78 (WCH) Caney, KS Sacred Heart; Moline, KS St. Mary's; Moline, KS St. Robert Bellarmine.
Yender, Basil *o.s.b.* '71 (RCK)[A] Aurora, IL Marmion Abbey; [G] Aurora, IL Marmion Abbey; Aurora, IL.
Yenkevich, Daniel J. '90 (SCR) Retired.
Yennock, Rev. Msgr. Eugene M. '50 (SY) Syracuse, NY St. Daniel.
Yenushosky, Rev. Msgr. Daniel J. '77 (ALN) Whitehall, PA Holy Trinity; Vicars Forane; Serra Club of Allentown.
Yeo, Junkoo '91 (SEA) Koreans, Ministry to; Seattle, WA St. Andrew Kim Personal Parish.
Yeo, Wilfred '58 (NEW) Retired.
Yeon, Peter Yong Mo (MOB) Montgomery, AL St. Andrew Kim Taegon.
Yepes, Walter '01 (CHI) Chicago, IL St. Roman.
Yerrnini, Chinnaiah '90 (PRO) Providence, RI Rhode Island Hospital; Cranston, RI St. Matthew.
Yeruva, Lourdu Marreddy '99 (KCK) Wamego, KS Holy Family; Wamego, KS St. Joseph; Paxico, KS Sacred Heart; Wamego, KS St. Bernard.
Yesalonia, Dennis J. *s.j.* '85 (BO)[U] Watertown, MA The Society of Jesus of New England–Provincial Offices; [U] Boston, MA Loyola House.
Yesudhas, Russell Raj *o.c.d.* '96 (ARL) Clifton, VA St. Andrew the Apostle.
Yetman, Robert C. '05 (PH) Graduate Studies.
Yetsko, Robert K. *t.o.r.* '84 (PBR) Conemaugh, PA Holy Trinity.
Yetter, Robert M. '73 (BUF) Swormville, NY St. Mary.
Yi, Ju Hyung Paul '08 (BR) Donaldsonville, LA Ascension of Our Lord Jesus Christ; Donaldsonville, LA St. Francis of Assisi.
Yi, Odilo *o.s.b.* '85 (PAT)[N] Newton, NJ St. Paul's Abbey.
Yiengst, Rev. Msgr. George B. '62 (BUF) Retired.
Yiftheg, Cuthbert '89 (CI) Our Lady of Mercy.
Yim, Louis H. '57 (HON) Retired.
Yllana, Pio Antonio C. '84 (LA) Los Angeles, CA Our Lady of Guadalupe.
Ymson, Enrique *m.j.* '75 (LA)[P] Los Angeles, CA Missionaries of Jesus, Inc.; Los Angeles, CA St. Kevin; Los Angeles, CA Precious Blood.
Yncierto, Frank '75 (LAV) Las Vegas, NV Our Lady of Las Vegas.
Yoackam, Lee R. *o.s.b.* '01 (GBG)[H] Latrobe, PA Saint Vincent Archabbey.
Yoakam, Lee R. *o.s.b.* '01 (MO) Army Chaplains.
Yoakam, Lee R. *o.s.b.* '01 (GBG)[H] Latrobe Saint Vincent Archabbey.
Yoakam, Lee (KCK) Fort Leavenworth, KS St. Ignatius.
Yockey, Aelred *o.s.b.* '93 (P)[K] Mount Angel, OR Providence Health & Services–Oregon; [L] St. Benedict, OR Mt. Angel Abbey.
Yockey, John G. '70 (MIL) Oconomowoc, WI St. Jerome; Archdiocesan Consultors; Archdiocesan Council of Priests.
Yohannan, Mathai Mannoorvadakkethil '94 (WDC) Landover Hills, MD St. Mary's Catholic Church.
Yohe, Robert A. '89 (HBG) Harrisburg, PA Holy Family.
Yokum, Joseph T. '07 (COL) New Boston, OH St. Monica; Wheelersburg, OH St. Peter; Deanery 13: Scioto County; Presbyteral Council; Parochial Examiners; Presbyteral Council.
Yonas, Deebar *s.v.d.* '07 (SB) Beaumont, CA Blessed Kateri Tekakwitha Catholic Community, Inc.
Yonkovig, John R. '77 (OG) Keene, NY St. Brendan; Lake Placid, NY St. Agnes; Defenders of the Bond; Deans.
Yontz, Rev. Msgr. George W. '59 (STU) Steubenville, OH St. Peter's.
Yori, Robert O. '61 (CAM) Retired.
York, Kenneth J. '88 (BEL) East Saint Louis, IL Immaculate Conception; Fayetteville, IL St. Pancratius; Belleville, IL St. Henry; Chancellor for Canonical Affairs; Diocesan Consultors; Diocesan Finance Council.
York, Patrick G. '90 (WCH) Wichita, KS Church of the Magdalen.
York, Richard '73 (VEN) Venice, FL Epiphany Cathedral.
York, Rev. Msgr. Vincent P. '68 (ALN) Pen Argyl, PA St. Elizabeth of Hungary.
Yossa, Kenneth F. '88 (ROM) Unassigned.
Yost, Alan G. *s.j.* '06 (P)[L] Portland Jesuit Provincial Office (Society of Jesus, Oregon Prov.).
Yost, Charles *s.c.j.* '58 (SP)[N] Pinellas Park, FL Priests of the Sacred Heart Retired.
Yost, Herbert C. *c.s.c.* '75 (FTW)[H] Notre Dame Congregation of Holy Cross, United States Province of Priests & Brothers.
Yost, Richard J. *o.s.f.s.* '76 (DET)[Q] Warren, MI St. John's Deaf Center.
You, Simon (Kwanggun) '94 (ALB) Special Assignment.
Youkhanna, Sanharib (EST) Chicago, IL Mart Mariam Parish.
Younan, Andrew '04 (SPA) El Cajon, CA St. Peter Chaldean Cathedral; [A] El Cajon, CA Seminary of Mar Abba the Great.
Younes, Jean '98 (SAM) Danbury, CT St. Anthony; Presbyteral Council.
Young, Adam A. '10 (PRO) Providence, RI St. Augustine.
Young, Rev. Msgr. Bill '70 (GAL) Western Vicariate.
Young, Daniel A. '95 (BUF) North Tonawanda, NY Good Shepherd.
Young, David E. '95 (COL) West Portsmouth, OH Our Lady of Lourdes; West Portsmouth, OH Our Lady of Sorrows.
Young, David H. '02 (SEA) Black Diamond, WA St. Barbara.
Young, David J. '04 (COL) Ada, OH Our Lady of Lourdes.
Young, Dennis M. '80 (STA) Special Assignment; DEPARTMENT OF VETERANS AFFAIRS HOSPITALS AND CHAPLAINS.
Young, DeSales *o.f.m.cap.* '48 (PIT)[M] Pittsburgh, PA St. Augustine Friary.
Young, Dismas *o.f.m.cap.* '66 (WH)[D] Wheeling, WV Paul VI Pastoral Center; [L] Wheeling, WV Capuchin Hermitage of St. Joseph.
Young, Dominic G. '79 (LFT) Lafayette, IN St. Ann.
Young, Rev. Archpriest Edward Canon '83 (STF) Presbyteral Council; Censor; Diocesan Consultors.
Young, Rev. Archpriest Edward P. '83 (STF) Ludlow, MA SS. Peter and Paul; South Deerfield, MA Holy Ghost.
Young, Frank '70 (SY) Retired.
Young, Gary *c.r.* '76 (L)[M] Nazareth, KY Generalate, Motherhouse and Novitiate of the Sisters of Charity of Nazareth.
Young, Gerald A. '72 (LA) Retired.
Young, Gerard F. '63 (BR) Retired.
Young, Rev. Msgr. James E. '74 (TYL) Nacogdoches, TX Sacred Heart; College of Consultors; Deans; Diocesan Finance Council; Priests' Pension Board; Priests' Personnel Board; Presbyteral Council; Office of Clergy Development/Continuing Education.
Young, James G. '69 (PIT) Munhall, PA St. Therese of Lisieux.
Young, Jerome *o.s.b.* '86 (P)[L] St. Benedict, OR Mt. Angel Abbey.
Young, John L. *c.s.c.* '71 (HRT)[L] New Haven, CT Priests of the Congregation of Holy Cross.
Young, John L. *c.s.c.* '71 (FTW)[H] Notre Dame Congregation of Holy Cross, United States Province of Priests & Brothers.
Young, Rev. Msgr. John Melvin '47 (LA) Retired.
Young, John (KAL) Retired.
Young, Larry E. '81 (OAK) Rodeo, CA St. Patrick; Consultors; Presbyteral Council; Design Review Board.
Young, Otis W. '01 (NO) Marrero, LA St. Joseph the Worker.
Young, Park Chi (STL) University City, MO St. Andrew Kim.
Young, Peter G. '59 (ALB) Retired.
Young, Peter G. '47 (PRO) Cranston, RI St. Ann Retired.
Young, Richard A. *o.s.a.* '95 (CHI)[N] Chicago, IL St. Rita Monastery.
Young, Richard '95 (SAV) Apostleship of the Sea; Savannah, GA Sacred Heart of Jesus.
Young, Robert '94 (SP) On Duty Outside the Diocese.
Young, Robert *o.f.m.* '82 (OAK)[L] Oakland Franciscan Friars of California, (Province of St. Barbara).
Young, Ronald W. *o.m.i.* '88 (FgM) Washington, DC AMERICAN OBLATE MISSIONS.
Young, Ronald *o.m.i.* '88 (WDC)[O] Washington, DC Provincial Offices of the United States Province of the Missionary Oblates of Mary Immaculate.
Young, Samuel V. '90 (BAL) Monkton, MD Our Lady of Grace.
Young, Rev. Msgr. Terry W. '72 (ATL) McDonough, GA St. James the Apostle Retired.
Young, Valentine *o.f.m.* '50 (CIN)[N] Cincinnati, OH St. Clement Friary.
Young, Vincent J. '78 (SCR) Unassigned or Leave of Absence.
Young, William E. '90 (SFE) College of Consultors; Albuquerque, NM Queen of Heaven.
Young, Rev. Msgr. William L. '70 (GAL) Priests Personnel Committee; Houston, TX St. Vincent de Paul.
Young, William T. *s.s.s.* '64 (CLV) Cleveland Clinic Foundation; [N] Cleveland, OH Congregation of the Blessed Sacrament.
Young, William W. '76 (SFR) San Francisco, CA Most Holy Redeemer Retired.
Youngberg, Vincent *c.p.* (HRT)[L] West Hartford Holy Family Monastery/Retreat.
Youngkamp, Vincent J. *s.s.c.* '59 (FgM) St Columbans, NE House of Post–Graduate Studies.
Young Lee, Raphael Joon '08 (NEW) Part–time Staff/ Advocates/Procurators.
Youngman, Wayne M. '10 (MOB) Butler, AL St. John The Evangelist; Grove Hill, AL Sacred Heart.
Youssef, Clement *c.s.b.* '86 (MO) DEPARTMENT OF VETERANS AFFAIRS HOSPITALS AND CHAPLAINS.
Youtz, Rev. Msgr. Richard A. '66 (HBG) Lancaster, PA St. John Neumann; Deans; Diocesan Judges.
Yrlas, Raynaldo '97 (CC) Presbyteral Council.
Yrlas, Raynaldo '97 (CC) Propagation of the Faith Office; Rockport, TX Sacred Heart.
Yslas, Martin *o.s.b.* '87 (LA)[P] Valyermo, CA St. Andrew's Abbey.
Ytsen, Robert A. *s.j.* '82 (CHI)[N] Chicago Chicago Province of the Society of Jesus–Provincial Office.
Yu, Celso A. *m.f.* '92 (AUS) Bremond, TX St. Mary; [G] Bremond, TX Clerical Congregation Missionaries of Faith.
Yuantoro, Franciscus Asisi Eka *m.s.f.* '02 (BWN) Donna, TX St. Joseph.
Yudin, Raynald *o.f.m.conv.* '62 (SY) Bridgeport, NY St. Francis of Assisi; Bridgeport, NY St. Mary.
Yuenger, Paul D. '00 (WH) Oak Hill, WV SS. Peter and Paul.
Yuhaus, Cassian J. *c.p.* '51 (SCR)[L] Scranton, PA Saint Ann's Passionist Monastery; [Q] Scranton, PA Ministry for Religious Research and Consultancy.
Yulfo–Hoffman, Nestor '92 (SJN) Carolina, PR Santo Cristo de los Milagros; Carolina.
Yu Ming, Vincent Lin '01 (DAL) Plano, TX Sacred Heart of Jesus.
Yunk, Rev. Msgr. Michael J. '57 (BUF) Retired.
Yurchak, Thomas D. '76 (P) Eugene, OR St. Jude.
Yurista, Michael J. '67 (PSC) Bayonne, NJ St. John the Baptist; Retirement Plan Board; Presbyteral Council.
Yurkovic, Dale E. '91 (GF) Leave of Absence.
Yurochko, Dennis P. *s.t.l.* '02 (PIT) Graduate Studies.

Z

Zabala, Antonio *o.a.r.* '95 (NY) Bronx, NY St. John's.
Zabala, Efrain '67 (CGS) Caguas, PR Santisima Trinidad.
Zabala, Efrain (SJN) "El Visitante".
Zabala, Wilmar '03 (YAK) Vocations; [G] Ellensburg, WA Catholic Campus Ministry at Central Washington University; Youth/Young Adult Director; Presbyteral Council Executive Committee.
Zaballa, Pedro Luis '57 (SJN) San Juan, PR Nuestra Senora de la Caridad del Cobre; [E] San Juan, PR Centro Medico de P.R.
Zabarian, Georges '72 (OLN) Vicar General.
Zabelskas, John A. '56 (GAL) Friendswood, TX Mary, Queen.
Zabler, Charles G. '77 (MIL) Milwaukee, WI Our Lady of Good Hope; Archdiocesan Council of Priests.
Zaborowski, Paul *o.f.m.cap.* '97 (BAL) Baltimore, MD St. Ambrose; [Q] Baltimore, MD St. Ambrose Friary.
Zabrocki, Patrick '88 (GF) Finance Council; Plentywood, MT St. Joseph; Scobey, MT St. Philip Bonitus; Diocesan Consultors; Clerical Benefit Association; Priests' Council.
Zabrocki, Stephen J. '89 (GF) Billings, MT St. Thomas the Apostle; Vicars Forane; Worship Commission.
Zabrocki, Stephen '89 (GF) Clerical Benefit Association; Billings, MT Holy Rosary; Billings, MT Little Flower; Billings, MT Our Lady of Guadalupe.
Zaccagnigno, Raffaele '68 (BRK) Retired.
Zaccagnini, Kenneth G. '82 (GBG) Harrison City, PA St. Barbara; Deaneries; College of Consultors; Bishop's Priests Council; Yukon, PA Seven Dolors; College of Deans.
Zaccardo, Rev. Msgr. Peter J. '64 (NEW) Retired.
Zaccarelli, Herman F. *c.s.c.* (FTW)[H] Notre Dame Congregation of Holy Cross, United States Province of Priests & Brothers.
Zaccone, Paul *ss.cc.* '87 (HON)[D] Kaneohe, HI Sacred Hearts Center.
Zach, Charles E. '73 (P) Gresham, OR St. Henry; Area Vicars.
Zach, Kenneth M. '81 (RVC) Massapequa, NY St. Rose of Lima; Procurator & Advocates.
Zachariadis, Rt. Rev. Archimandrite Nicholas (ROM)[A] St. Nazianz, WI Holy Resurrection Monastery.
Zachariah, Kurian '85 (ALX) Boyce, LA St. Margaret.
Zacharias, Michael J. '02 (TOL) Fremont, OH St. Ann; Fremont, OH St. Joseph.
Zachary, John S. (ATL)[K] Covington, GA Society of Our Lady of the Most Holy Trinity.
Zacheis, Dennis B. '75 (STL) On Leave of Absence.
Zachman, Clarence *o.m.i.* '48 (BEL)[F] Belleville, IL

Missionary Oblates of Mary Immaculate – St. Henry's Oblate Residence.
Zacker, Mark '96 (COS) Colorado Springs, CO Corpus Christi; College of Consultors.
Zaczynski, Piotr F. '04 (BUF) On Duty Outside the Diocese.
Zaczynski, Piotr '04 (MAR) Sault Sainte Marie, MI St. Joseph.
Zadora, Boleslaw *s.d.s.* '74 (SAT) St. Hedwig, TX Annunciation of the Blessed Virgin Mary; [L] Falls City, TX Salvatorian Fathers Community of Texas.
Zadora, Charles J. '67 (BUF) Fredonia, NY St. Joseph.
Zadorozny, Tadeusz '99 (NOR) Oakdale, CT Our Lady of the Lakes; Quaker Hill, CT Our Lady of Perpetual Help; Uncasville, CT St. John the Evangelist.
Zadroga, Jean–Luc P. *o.s.b.* '01 (PIT) On Duty Outside the Diocese.
Zafe, Peter V. '64 (TOL) Philippine–American Catholic Council (PACC).
Zagar, Janko *o.p.* '48 (OAK)[L] Oakland, CA Order of Preachers (Province of the Most Holy Name of Jesus – Western Dominican Province).
Zagarella, John C. *o.praem.* '86 (PH) Philadelphia, PA St. Gabriel; [Y] Paoli, PA Daylesford Abbey.
Zagone, Frederick P. *s.j.* '93 (MIL)[P] Milwaukee, WI Jesuit Community at Marquette University.
Zagorc, Francis D. *c.s.c.* '58 (FTW)[H] Notre Dame Congregation of Holy Cross, United States Province of Priests & Brothers.
Zagorski, Jan '02 (MOB) Prattville, AL St. Joseph Church.
Zagst, Bernard L. '61 (ALX) Retired.
Zahler, Paul J. *o.s.b.* '62 (OKL)[I] Shawnee, OK St. Gregory's Abbey; [L] Shawnee, OK National Institute on Development Delays, Inc.
Zahn, George E. '68 (RIC) Richmond, VA St. Paul; Cemeteries.
Zahn, John '72 (IND)[D] Indianapolis, IN Cathedral High School (Cathedral Trustees, Inc.).
Zahn, Robert R. *m.m.* '55 (NY)[DD] Retired.
Zahuta, Marcin '06 (CHR)[H] Columbia, SC St. Thomas More Center.
Zahuta, Thomas '10 (ATL) Duluth, GA St. Monica.
Zaiats, Volodymyr '73 (STN) Retired.
Zaidan, Abdallah E. *m.l.m.* '86 (OLL) Los Angeles, CA Our Lady of Mt. Lebanon–St. Peter Maronite Catholic Cathedral; Thousand Oaks, CA Saints Peter and Paul Maronite Catholic Mission; [A] Houston, TX The Congregation of Maronite Lebanese Missionaries; College of Consultors; Commission for Lebanon; Procurator/Advocate; Presbyteral Council; Protopresbyters; Personnel Board; Board of Pastors; [A] Los Angeles, CA The Congregation of Maronite Lebanese Missionaries.
Zaidan, Abdallah *m.l.m.* '86 (OLL) Advisor for Priests.
Zajac, Maciej J. '07 (NEW) Bayonne, NJ St. Henry's.
Zajac, Richard E. '76 (BUF) Council of Priests; Catholic Medical Association.
Zajchowski, Zbigniew *o.f.m.conv.* '94 (RCK) Rockford, IL SS. Peter and Paul.
Zajdel, Bernard *o.f.m.conv.* '64 (FTW) Angola, IN St. Anthony.
Zajdel, Robert J. '80 (PIT) McKees Rocks, PA St. John of God; Crescent, PA St. Catherine of Siena.
Zak, Daniel '67 (TOL) Swanton, OH St. Richard.
Zak, Stanislaw '75 (OAK) Oakland, CA St. Margaret Mary.
Zak, Rev. Msgr. Steven B. '88 (LA) Glendale, CA Church of the Incarnation.
Zak, Timothy *s.d.b.* '91 (CHI) Chicago, IL St. John Bosco.
Zake, Louis J. '60 (CHI) Retired.
Zakowicz, Giles *o.f.m.conv.* (FTW)[H] Mishawaka, IN St. Francis of Assisi Novitiate.
Zakowicz, James *o.c.d.* '09 (SB)[I] Redlands, CA Discalced Carmelites, OCD; [L] Redlands, CA El Carmelo Retreat House.
Zakshesky, Francis '81 (TYL) Absent on Sick Leave Retired.
Zalacca, Joseph A. '03 (BUF) Dunkirk, NY Holy Trinity.
Zalecki, Dennis M. '76 (CHI) Mt. Prospect, IL St. Emily.
Zaleski, Daniel '80 (DET) Dearborn Heights, MI St. Albert the Great.
Zaleski, Gary A. '77 (STU) Administrative Leave.
Zalewski, Francis '78 (TR) Retired.
Zalewski, Peter Lawrence '97 (PT) Panama City, FL St. Dominic; Vicars Forane; College of Consultors; Air Force Reserve Chaplains.
Zalewski, Thomas *o.carm.* '79 (NY)[DD] Middletown, NY The National Shrine of Our Lady of Mount Carmel; [FF] Middletown, NY National Shrine of Our Lady of Mount Carmel; [DD] Middletown, NY St. Albert's Priory.
Zalewski, Tomasz '06 (VEN) Presbyteral Council; Naples, FL St. Agnes.
Zaloga, Daniel S. '67 (MAR) Iron Mountain, MI St. Mary and St. Joseph; Channing, MI St. Rose.
Zalonis, Jerome *m.i.c.* '59 (NOR)[G] Thompson, CT Marian Fathers.
Zalubski, Czeslaw *s.d.b.* '93 (MET)[K] Milford, NJ Bethany Ridge; Pittstown, NJ St. Catherine of Siena.
Zamarripa, Jesus *s.v.d.* '01 (SB) Beaumont, CA Blessed Kateri Tekakwitha Catholic Community, Inc.
Zamarripa, Jesus *s.v.d.* '01 (SD) San Diego, CA Our Lady of the Sacred Heart Catholic Parish.
Zamary, Joseph '01 (Y) Waynesburg, OH St. James.
Zamborsky, Bill '74 (ORL) Ormond Beach, FL Prince of Peace.
Zamborsky, Leonard J. '76 (CLV) Absent on Leave.
Zammit, Francis X. '66 (ORL) Retired.
Zammit, Jimmy *o.f.m.* '81 (NY)[DD] New York Franciscan Province of the Immaculate Conception.
Zammit, Rev. Msgr. Joseph J. '56 (NY) New York Police Department.
Zamora, Arnold '86 (SFR) San Francisco, CA Holy Name of Jesus.
Zamora, Clarence '05 (OAK) On Duty Outside the Diocese.
Zamora, Clarence '05 (HON) Kailua, HI St. Anthony of Padua.
Zamora, Marcos *c.s.p.* '90 (GR) Grand Rapids, MI Cathedral of St. Andrew; Evangelization.
Zamora, Noel '07 (LEX) Harrodsburg, KY St. Andrew.
Zamorano, Richard '93 (ELP) On Duty Outside of Diocese.
Zamorano, Richard '93 (TUC) Defenders of the Bond.
Zamorski, Rev. Msgr. Robert J. '72 (MET) Episcopal Vicars; College of Consultors; Metuchen, NJ Cathedral of St. Francis of Assisi.
Zampelli, Michael A. *s.j.* '93 (SJ)[B] Santa Clara, CA Jesuit Community.
Zampino, Ignatius *o.f.m.cap.* '61 (PAT) Passaic, NJ Our Lady Of Mt. Carmel.
Zanatta, Albert *c.r.s.* '74 (GAL) Central Vicariate; Houston, TX Assumption; Appointees; College of Consultors.
Zanatta, Remo *c.r.s.* (GAL) Houston, TX Christ the King.
Zancan, Robert D. '82 (BUF) Retired.
Zandri, William A. '84 (RC) Rapid City, SD St. Therese the Little Flower; Rapid City, SD St. John the Evangelist.
Zandy, Edward J. '70 (SY) Johnson City, NY Blessed Sacrament; Vestal, NY St. Vincent de Paul.
Zanetti, Gordon '06 (VEN) Marco Island, FL San Marco.
Zang, Richard P. *c.s.c.* '69 (FTW)[H] Notre Dame Congregation of Holy Cross, United States Province of Priests & Brothers.
Zang, Richard P. *c.s.c.* '69 (PHX)[F] Phoenix, AZ Holy Cross Congregation/Casa Santa Cruz.
Zaniewski, Jaroslaw '93 (NEW) Jersey City, NJ Holy Rosary.
Zaniolo, Michael G. '88 (CHI) Des Plaines, IL St. Stephen Protomartyr; Chicago, IL Chicago Airports Catholic Chaplaincy; [W] Chicago, IL Chicago Airports Catholic Chaplaincy; Chicago Airports Catholic Chaplaincy; Chicago, IL National Conference of Catholic Airport Chaplains (NCCAC).
Zanni, Frank L. '90 (Y) Vienna, OH St. Thomas the Apostle Parish, St. Vincent DePaul Church; Masury, OH St. Thomas the Apostle Parish, St. Bernadette Church.
Zanon, Romano A. '90 (BRK) Retired.
Zanon, Romano '66 (BRK) East Glendale, NY Sacred Heart.
Zanoni, Charles *c.s.* '62 (PRO) Johnston, RI St. Rocco.
Zanoni, Richard *s.j.* '75 (NY)[B] Bronx, NY Ciszek Hall.
Zanoni, Ron '05 (LAV) North Las Vegas, NV St. Christopher; Presbyteral Council for the Diocese of Las Vegas; Building Committee.
Zanotti, Rev. Msgr. Charles F. '53 (NY) Glasco, NY St. Joseph.
Zanotti, Richard *c.s.* '80 (LA) Sun Valley, CA Our Lady of the Holy Rosary.
Zanotto, Luigi *m.c.c.j.* '68 (NEW) Newark, NJ St. Lucy's; [L] Montclair, NJ Comboni Missionaries of the Heart of Jesus (Verona Fathers).
Zant, Ivan '08 (NEW) Union City, NJ St. Anthony of Padua.
Zaorski, Edward F. '90 (DET) Detroit, MI SS. Andrew and Benedict; Melvindale, MI St. Mary Magdalen.
Zapalac, David J. *c.s.b.* '93 (GAL) Manvel, TX Sacred Heart of Jesus.
Zapalac, William E. *o.m.i.* '70 (SAT)[N] San Antonio, TX Oblate Renewal Center.
Zapata, Antonio '68 (ORG) Orange, CA St. Norbert Retired.
Zapata, Carlos M. '88 (HRT) Waterbury, CT St. Margaret; Waterbury, CT Sacred Heart–Sagrado Corazon.
Zapata, Emiliano *o.p.* '95 (LUB) Lubbock, TX St. Elizabeth University Parish; Presbyteral Council.
Zapata, Juan Carlos '05 (NEW) Newark, NJ Immaculate Conception; Newark, NJ Our Lady of Good Counsel.
Zapata, Pedro '99 (ORL) Bushnell, FL St. Lawrence.
Zapata–Ramirez, Josegerman '90 (MIL) Milwaukee, WI St. Anthony of Padua.
Zapf, Albert L. '80 (PIT) Bethel Park, PA St. Valentine.
Zapfel, Rev. Msgr. Robert E. '81 (BUF) Vicars; Amherst, NY St. Leo the Great; Consultors, College of; Council of Priests; Finance Council; Bishop's Representative for Health Care; Censors—Board of Diocesan Censors of Books and Vigilance for the Faith.
Zapien, Jose B. *m.n.m.* '05 (ARE) Camuy, PR Our Lady of the Miraculous Medal.
Zapotocki, Henry E. '48 (SCR) Retired.
Zapp, John '72 (Y) Uniontown, OH Holy Spirit.
Zappa, James C. '76 (STP) Burnsville, MN Mary, Mother of the Church.
Zappitelli, Francis '62 (PHX) Retired.
Zarate, Ramon '90 (STO) Stockton, CA St. Luke Church of Stockton (Pastor of).
Zarate–Suarez, Jose Edmundo '96 (SD) National City, CA Saint Anthony of Padua Catholic Parish National City.
Zareski, Joseph S. '80 (SY) New Hartford, NY St. John the Evangelist; Priests' Personnel Committee.
Zarichny, Steven '78 (SJP) Youngstown, OH Holy Trinity; Presbyters.
Zarsky, Brion '07 (AUS) Caldwell, TX St. Mary; Caldwell, TX Holy Rosary.
Zasada, Hubert *s.ch.* '02 (DET) Hamtramck, MI St. Florian.
Zaslona, Jerzy R. '04 (NEW) Jersey City, NJ Holy Rosary.
Zastrow, John A. '56 (LIN)[E] Lincoln, NE Bonacum House Retired.
Zatalava, James D. '70 (ALT) Altoona, PA Our Lady of Fatima; DEPARTMENT OF VETERANS AFFAIRS HOSPITALS AND CHAPLAINS.
Zaucha, Finian Andrew *o.f.m.* '68 (GB) Seymour, WI St. Stanislaus; Krakow, WI St. Casimir; Pulaski, WI Assumption of the Blessed Virgin Mary.
Zavacki, Richard A. '57 (SCR) Retired.
Zavage, Michael A. '09 (PIT)[C] Pittsburgh, PA Bishop Canevin High School, Inc.; Pittsburgh, PA St. Teresa of Avila.
Zavala, Douglas A. '09 (DAL) Grand Prairie, TX Immaculate Conception.
Zavala, Genaro '97 (LA) Los Angeles, CA Santa Isabel.
Zavala, Miguel *i.v.e.* '10 (PHX) Phoenix, AZ St. Anthony Roman Catholic Parish; Phoenix, AZ Immaculate Heart of Mary Roman Catholic Parish.
Zavaski, William J. '69 (CHI) Arlington Heights, IL St. James.
Zavell, Edward '61 (PRM) Retired.
Zawacki, Robert P. *s.s.j.* '78 (NO) New Orleans, LA St. Raymond–St. Leo the Great.
Zawada, Joseph F. *o.c.d.* '64 (STA)[H] Bunnell, FL Discalced Carmelite Fathers of Florida.
Zawadzki, Ryszard *s.v.d.* '87 (LR) Little Rock, AR St. Bartholomew; Little Rock, AR Our Lady of Good Counsel.
Zawadzki, Victor C. '50 (SCR) Retired.
Zayas, Antonio '59 (PCE) On Duty Outside the Diocese.
Zborowski, Pawel '06 (DEN) Greeley, CO St. Mary.
Zborowski, Richard M. '78 (CHI) Palatine, IL St. Theresa.
Zdilla, Valentine D. '96 (HEL) Bozeman, MT Resurrection; [G] Bozeman, MT Montana State University; Personnel Board; Members.
Zebron, Samuel *o.f.m.conv.* '58 (PMB) Boynton Beach, FL St. Mark.
Zebrowski, Arnold '73 (VEN) Venice, FL Our Lady of Lourdes.
Zec, John '70 (TR)[A] Lakewood, NJ Georgian Court University.
Zeck, George '70 (DUL) Nisswa, MN St. Christopher; Pequot Lakes, MN St. Alice; Pine River, MN Our Lady of Lourdes.
Zee, Louis C. '59 (GAL) Alief, TX Ascension Chinese Mission.
Zee, Louis C. '59 (DUB) Retired.
Zegar, David E. '79 (P) Portland, OR St. Peter.
Zegeer, Eric D. '05 (MIA) Coral Gables, FL St. Augustine.
Zehler, Steven '07 (STA) Ponte Vedra Beach, FL Our Lady Star of the Sea.
Zehnle, Daren J. '05 (SFD) Springfield, IL Cathedral of the Immaculate Conception; Office for Vocations.
Zehrem, Dennis '04 (STP) Coon Rapids, MN Church of the Epiphany.
Zeid, Nadim Abou *m.l.m.* '94 (OLL) Las Vegas, NV St. Sharbel Maronite Catholic Mission; [A] Houston, TX The Congregation of Maronite Lebanese Missionaries.
Zeigler, Stephen '11 (Y) North Canton, OH St. Paul.
Zeiler, Donald '01 (DAL) Deans; McKinney, TX St. Gabriel the Archangel.
Zeimet, Richard E. *m.m.* '64 (NY)[DD] Retired.
Zeis, Gabriel *t.o.r.* '80 (ALT)[A] Loretto, PA St. Francis University.
Zeisler, Warren *o.f.m.* '50 (CIN)[N] Cincinnati, OH St. John the Baptist Friary.
Zeitler, Rev. Msgr. Edward J. '58 (E) Hermitage, PA Church of Notre Dame Retired.
Zeitler, Rev. Msgr. John W. '64 (BUF)[S] Buffalo, NY Kolping Catholic Young Men's Association of Buffalo, NY; [N] Buffalo, NY Sheehan Residence for Priests Retired.
Zelaya, Christians (TYL) Pittsburg, TX Holy Cross.

Zelik, Richard J. *o.f.m.cap.* '77 (PIT) Pittsburgh, PA St. Benedict the Moor.
Zelinski, James *o.f.m.cap.* '61 (MIL) Milwaukee, WI St. Benedict the Moor.
Zelker, Thomas '83 (ALB) Hoosick Falls, NY Immaculate Conception.
Zeller, Leonard H. '73 (BAL) Priests Sick or Absent.
Zelonis, Christopher M. '03 (ALN) Reading, PA Holy Guardian Angels.
Zemaitis, Kestutis '65 (CLV)[M] Cleveland, OH Jennings Center for Older Adults.
Zemanik, Rev. Msgr. Edward S. '81 (ALN) Easton, PA St. Anthony of Padua; Schuylkill Haven, PA St. Ambrose.
Zemczak, Pawel '05 (CHI) Chicago, IL St. Pascal.
Zemelko, John J. '87 (GRY) Valparaiso, IN Our Lady of Sorrows; Mission Office; Ministry to Deaf.
Zemlik, Edward J. *s.c.j.* '01 (JKS) Senatobia, MS St. Gregory the Great; Southaven, MS Christ the King; [E] Nesbit, MS St. Michael Community House; Hernando, MS Holy Spirit; Robinsonville, MS Good Shepherd Catholic Church.
Zemula, Antoni *s.a.c.* '78 (BRK) Brooklyn, NY St. Frances de Chantal.
Zender, Gary '86 (SEA) Renton, WA St. Anthony; Members.
Zendzian, Rev. Msgr. Peter W. '79 (BRK) Maspeth, NY Holy Cross; Presbyteral Council.
Zengierski, Patrick J. '91 (BUF) Newman Club Chaplains; [Q] Buffalo, NY Buffalo State College.
Zenk, Donald W. '54 (WIN)[F] Austin, MN Sacred Heart Care Center, Inc. Retired.
Zenk, Rev. Msgr. Richard E. '54 (SC) Promoter of Justice; Defenders of the Bond; Holy Childhood Association; Propagation of the Faith, Association of the Holy Childhood, Catholic Students' Mission Crusade Retired.
Zenkel, Edward B. '62 (ROC) Retired.
Zenorini, Henry J. *s.j.* '61 (NY)[DD] New York, NY Xavier Jesuit Community.
Zensen, Gerald F. '49 (SC) Retired.
Zenthoefer, Alex '05 (EVN)[A] Evansville, IN Reitz Memorial High School; Evansville, IN Holy Rosary; Vocation Office; Special Assignment.
Zenz, Rev. Msgr. John P. '78 (DET)[T] Detroit, MI Christ Child Society; Birmingham, MI Holy Name; College of Consultors.
Zepczyk, Gabriel C. '62 (SUP) Retired.
Zepecki, Ronald P. '95 (HRT) Wallingford, CT SS. Peter and Paul.
Zepeda, Alejandro '06 (SPK) Othello, WA Sacred Heart.
Zepeda, Jose *f.s.s.p.* '09 (SCR) Scranton, PA St. Michael's; [L] Elmhurst Twp., PA Priestly Fraternity of St. Peter (F.S.S.P.), North American District Headquarters.
Zeps, Michael J. *s.j.* '71 (MIL)[P] Milwaukee, WI Jesuit Community at Marquette University.
Zercie, David *m.s.a.* '69 (NOR)[A] Cromwell, CT Holy Apostles College and Seminary; [G] Cromwell Society of the Missionaries of the Holy Apostles.
Zeringue, Guy '75 (HT) Thibodaux, LA St. John The Evangelist.
Zerkel, Donald F. '57 (MIL) Racine, WI St. John Nepomuk Retired.
Zermeno, Joaquin '11 (BWN) San Juan, TX St. John the Baptist.
Zermeno, Joseph *o.f.m.* '68 (MRY)[F] San Miguel, CA Franciscan Friars, O.F.M.; San Miguel, CA San Miguel.
Zero, Frank '11 (RVC) Hicksville, NY Holy Family.
Zerr, Dennis P. '03 (CC) Taft, TX Holy Family.
Zerr, Gary L. '97 (P) Keizer, OR St. Edward; Area Vicars.
Zerr, Maurice J. *m.m.* '51 (NY)[DD] Maryknoll Maryknoll Fathers and Brothers Retired.
Zerucha, Christopher J. '11 (CLV) Concord Twp., OH St. Gabriel.
Zerwas, Rick '91 (SFE) Rio Rancho, NM Church of the Incarnation.
Zeth, Allen P. '86 (ALT) Vocation; [K] Loretto, PA Office of Vocations; Loretto, PA Basilica of St. Michael the Archangel.
Zettel, David H. '66 (L)[B] Louisville, KY Trinity High School Retired.
Zetzl, Ralph *o.f.m.* '65 (SFD)[H] Effingham, IL St. Anthony's Memorial Hospital; [K] Teutopolis, IL St. Francis Assisi Friary.
Zeugner, Raymond L. '67 (MAR) Retired.
Zeuner, Karl A. '71 (PH) Swarthmore, PA Notre Dame de Lourdes.
Zewe, Donald M. *s.j.* '56 (NY)[DD] New York, NY Murray–Weigel Hall.
Zeyack, John '65 (PSC) Retired.
Zglejszewski, Rev. Msgr. Andrzej '90 (RVC) Procurator & Advocates; Worship; Rockville Centre, NY St. Agnes Cathedral; Co Chancellors; Co Chancellors.
Zgunda, Ronald S. '77 (EVN) Princeton, IN St. Joseph; Oakland City, IN Blessed Sacrament; Deans; Clergy Personnel Board.
Zhai, Peter Linyong *s.v.d.* '06 (SFR) Redwood City, CA Our Lady of Mount Carmel.
Zhai, Peter *s.v.d.* '06 (LA) Rowland Heights, CA St. Elizabeth Ann Seton.
Zhang, Dehua *c.s.j.b.* '76 (BRK)[R] Elmhurst, NY Congregation of St. John the Baptist of China; [R] Elmhurst, NY Our Lady of China Chapel.
Zhang, Edward *c.s.j.b.* (BRK) Flushing, NY St. John Vianney.
Ziajka, Rafal *s.d.s.* '00 (GRY)[H] Merrillville, IN Salvatorian Fathers (Society of the Divine Savior).
Ziccardi, Rev. Msgr. C. Anthony '90 (NEW)[B] Seton Hall University; Censores Librorum.
Zidek, Vincent E. *o.s.b.* '91 (GBG)[H] Latrobe, PA Saint Vincent Archabbey.
Zidek, Vincent E. *o.s.b.* '91 (PIT) Pittsburgh, PA St. Peter.
Zidek, Vincent *o.s.b.* (PIT)[P] Pittsburgh, PA Community College of Allegheny County – Northside Campus.
Ziebacz, Wieslaw M. '92 (SCR) Unassigned or Leave of Absence.
Ziebowicz, Dariusz *s.d.s.* '88 (SAT)[L] Falls City, TX Salvatorian Fathers Community of Texas.
Ziebowicz, Dariusz *s.d.s.* '88 (AUS) Bastrop, TX Sacred Heart; Bastrop, TX St. Mary of the Assumption.
Ziegelmaier, David A. '60 (LC) Retired.
Ziegler, Ambrose M. '61 (LFT) Retired.
Ziegler, John A. '96 (ARL) Fredericksburg, VA St. Patrick.
Ziegler, Michael Tod '01 (KCK) On Sabbatical.
Ziegler, Thomas G. '69 (Y) Columbiana, OH St. Jude; East Palestine, OH Our Lady of Lourdes.
Ziegmann, Rev. Msgr. Leonard M. '59 (SC) Retired.
Zielezienski, Raymond '81 (OAK) San Ramon, CA St. Joan of Arc.
Zielinski, Brian A. *o.praem.* '71 (BAL) Baltimore, MD St. Thomas More.
Zielinski, Brian *o.praem.* '71 (WIL)[J] Middletown, DE Immaculate Conception Priory of the Canons Regular of Premontre; [J] Middletown, DE Norbertine Fathers of Delaware, Inc.
Zielinski, Chad W. '96 (GLD) Special Assignment; Air Force Chaplains.
Zielinski, Francis A. '62 (DET) Retired.
Zielinski, Martin '78 (CHI)[A] Mundelein, IL University of St. Mary of the Lake/Mundelein Seminary; [A] Mundelein, IL University of St. Mary of the Lake/ Mundelein Seminary; [A] Mundelein, IL Ongoing Formation.
Zielinski, Ryszard '83 (CC) Three Rivers, TX Sacred Heart.
Zielke, Michael *o.f.m.conv.* '89 (SPR) Chicopee, MA St. Stanislaus Basilica; Definitors.
Zielonka, Rev. Msgr. Dariusz J. '95 (BGP) Diocesan Consultors.
Ziemba, Howard '79 (Y) Maximo, OH St. Joseph; Alliance, OH Regina Coeli.
Ziemba, Rev. Msgr. Walter J. '51 (DET) Retired.
Ziemkiewicz, Frank '84 (SAV)[B] Savannah, GA Benedictine Military School; [D] Savannah, GA The Benedictine Priory.
Ziemkiewicz, Frank *o.s.b.* '84 (GBG)[H] Latrobe, PA Saint Vincent Archabbey.
Ziemniak, Jan '80 (LAR) College of Consultors; Priests Personnel Board; Laredo, TX Nuestra Senora del Rosario; Ex Officio Members.
Ziemnicki, Edward '96 (HRT) Meriden, CT St. Stanislaus.
Zientarski, Nicholas A. '03 (RVC)[A] Huntington, NY Diocesan Seminary of the Immaculate Conception; Silver Spring, MD St. Bernadette.
Zientek, Rev. Msgr. Benedict '58 (SAN) Retired.
Zientek, Rev. Msgr. Benedict '58 (AUS) Retired.
Zientek, Rev. Msgr. Boleslaus '59 (GAL) Retired.
Zientek, Theodore '00 (STN)[A] Redwood Valley, CA Holy Transfiguration Monastery.
Ziezulewicz, George F. '64 (HRT) Retired.
Zigmond, Kenneth *o.s.b.* '57 (JOL) Lisle, IL St. Joan of Arc; [L] Lisle, IL St. Procopius Abbey.
Ziliak, Jerome *s.v.d.* '47 (CHI)[N] Techny, IL Divine Word Residence.
Ziliak, Joseph '62 (EVN) Newburgh, IN St. John the Baptist; Deans; Censors of Books.
Zilimu, Johndamaseni '95 (PEO) Champaign, IL St. Matthew.
Zilliox, Robert W. '08 (BUF) On Duty Outside the Diocese; Auditor; Depew, NY St. Martha.
Zilonka, Paul *c.p.* '71 (FgM)[L] "Compassion" Magazine; New Rochelle, NY St. Paul of the Cross Province; New Rochelle, NY.
Zilonka, Paul *c.p.* '71 (BRK)[R] Jamaica, NY Immaculate Conception Monastery.
Ziminski, James C. '91 (MAR) Special Assignment; [F] Garden, MI Marygrove Retreat Center; Ongoing Formation of Priests; Cursillo; Retreats.
Zimmer, Anthony J. '86 (MIL) Pewaukee, WI St. Anthony on the Lake.
Zimmer, David L. '88 (BIS) Minot, ND St. John the Apostle; Defensor Vinculi; Priests' Personnel Board; Promoter of Justice.
Zimmer, Ellis *o.f.m.cap.* '55 (GB)[J] Appleton, WI St. Fidelis Friary Retired.
Zimmer, Eric A. *s.j.* '94 (MO) Air Force Reserve Chaplains.
Zimmer, Eric A. *s.j.* '94 (OM)[J] Omaha, NE Jesuit Community at Creighton University.
Zimmer, James '76 (SFS) Sioux Falls, SD Christ the King.
Zimmer, Matthew J. '11 (LIN) Lincoln, NE North American Martyrs; Advocates.
Zimmer, Nicholas '57 (SCL) Retired.
Zimmer, William E. '91 (CHI) Other Assignments.
Zimmerman, David M. '95 (GB) Cato, WI Immaculate Conception; Whitelaw, WI St. Michael.
Zimmerman, David '97 (SFD) Paris, IL St. Aloysius; Paris, IL St. Mary; Decatur Deanery; Presbyteral Council.
Zimmerman, Donald D. '73 (SAL) Manhattan, KS St. Thomas More Parish; Art and Architecture Commission; Personnel Board.
Zimmerman, Rev. Msgr. Donald F. '73 (DAL) At Large Members; Dallas, TX Christ the King.
Zimmerman, John M. '03 (CHR) Florence, SC St. Anne; [H] Florence, SC Francis Marion University; Priest Retirement Committee.
Zimmerman, Joseph *o.f.m.* '62 (SFD)[B] Quincy, IL Quincy University; Task Force For Racial Justice; [K] Quincy, IL Holy Cross Friary Retired.
Zimmerman, Mitchel '04 (KCK) Vocations Office; Co Directors Seminarians.
Zimmerman, Ralph '76 (SCL) Kimball, MN Holy Cross; Rockville, MN Mary of the Immaculate Conception; St. Cloud, MN St. Wendelin's.
Zimmerman, Rex A. '67 (LC) Retired.
Zimmerman, Rev. Msgr. Roland George '51 (LA) Monrovia, CA Annunciation Retired.
Zimmerschied, Daniel '97 (DEN) Denver, CO St. Vincent De Paul.
Zimodro, Slawomir '08 (RCK) Saint Charles, IL St. Patrick.
Zimpfer, Eugene A. *s.j.* '65 (BUF)[N] Buffalo, NY Canisius Jesuit Community Inc.; [D] Buffalo, NY Canisius High School.
Zina, George '86 (SAM) Springfield, MA St. Anthony.
Zingales, A. Jonathan '76 (CLV) Defenders of the Bond; Presbyteral Conveners; Promoters of Justice; Akron, OH Visitation of Mary; Presbyteral Council.
Zingaro, Joseph J. '78 (PH) Philadelphia, PA St. John Cantius.
Zink, David L. '90 (CIN) Osgood, OH St. Louis; Osgood, OH St. Nicholas; Imprimatur Censors.
Zink, William F. '68 (GR) Deans; College of Consultors; Marne, MI St. Mary's.
Zinkula, Thomas R. '90 (DUB) Episcopal Vicar for Cedar Rapids Region; Judges; Directors; Archbishop's Cabinet; Archdiocesan Pastoral Center; On Special or Other Archdiocesan Assignment.
Zinno, Henry P. '82 (PRO) Bristol, RI Our Lady of Mount Carmel; Deans.
Zins, Charles A. '77 (BIS) Mott, ND St. Vincent de Paul; Regent, ND St. Henry; Mott, ND St. John the Baptist.
Zinser, Robert E. '68 (STL) On Leave of Absence.
Zinthefer, Neil G. '69 (MIL) Campbellsport, WI St. Kilian; Campbellsport, WI St. Martin; Campbellsport, WI St. Matthew.
Zinzer, Walter W. '64 (STL) Retired.
Ziolkowski, Adam *o.f.m.conv.* '72 (HBG) Shamokin, PA Mother Cabrini.
Ziomek, Dennis A. '78 (CHI) Chicago, IL St. Barbara.
Zipay, Michael J. '68 (SCR) Luzerne, PA Holy Family.
Zirilli, David A. '08 (MIA) Vocations; Pontifical Mission Societies; Chaplain—Dade County – Serra Club; Miami, FL St. Mary's Cathedral; Society for the Propagation of the Faith; Holy Childhood Association; The Society of St. Peter Apostle; Missionary Union of Priests and Religious; Priests Purgatorial Society.
Zirimenya, Paul '07 (SFR) San Francisco, CA St. Benedict Parish at St. Francis Xavier Church[S]; San Francisco, CA St. Gabriel.
Zirnheld, Matthew J. '93 (BUF) Strykersville, NY St. John Neumann.
Zirra, Benjamin '94 (NY) Kingston, NY Benedictine Hospital; Maybrook, NY Church of the Assumption.
Zitek, Bradley '89 (LIN) Superior, NE St. Joseph's.
Ziuraitis, Gary *c.ss.r.* '78 (DEN)[N] Denver The Redemptorists/Denver Province.
Zivic, Richard A. '94 (ATL) On Leave of Absence; Without Archdiocesan Assignment or Faculties.
Zlock, Charles '94 (PH) Philadelphia, PA St. Lucy; Philadelphia, PA St. Mary of the Assumption.
Zlotkowski, Francis T. *c.s.c.* '76 (FTW)[H] Notre Dame Congregation of Holy Cross, United States Province of Priests & Brothers.
Zlotkowski, Frank *c.s.c.* '76 (AUS) Austin, TX Seton/ Brackenridge Hospital; Presbyteral Council.
Zmarlicki, Andrzej '92 (NEW) Elizabeth, NJ St. Hedwig's.
Zmozynski, Francis J. '57 (BUF) Retired.
Zmuda, Christopher J. '01 (NOR) Norwich, CT SS. Peter and Paul.
Zmudzinski, Charles *c.p.m.* '02 (L) Glasgow, KY St.

Helen; Albany, KY Emmanuel Catholic.
Zobler, Alan D. *o.s.f.s.* '07 (TOL)[H] Toledo, OH; Toledo, OH St. Clement.
Zodrow, Nathan *o.s.b.* '88 (P) Portland, OR St. Agatha.
Zoeller, Eugene '58 (L) Retired.
Zoellner, Michael *o.s.b.* '80 (KCK)[J] Leavenworth, KS Motherhouse of the Sisters of Charity of Leavenworth; [I] Atchison, KS St. Benedict's Abbey.
Zoghby, James F. '71 (MOB) Mobile, AL Corpus Christi Parish, Mobile; Vicars Forane; Archdiocesan Consultors.
Zoghby, Paul G. '93 (MOB) Foley, AL St. Margaret Queen of Scotland; Officers; Vicars Forane.
Zohlen, Ray '53 (SFR) Retired.
Zollinger, Rev. Msgr. Richard '55 (GRY) Retired.
Zoma, Rudy '09 (EST) Troy, MI St. Joseph Chaldean Parish; Eparchial College of Consultors.
Zomerfeld, Zbigniew '93 (DET) Port Huron, MI St. Mary.
Zoni, Pierino *s.x.* '61 (FgM)[N] Wayne Xaverian Missionary Fathers; Wayne, NJ XAVERIAN MISSIONARY FATHERS.
Zonneveld, Leo J. *c.i.c.m.* '58 (ARL) Culpeper, VA Precious Blood; Deans.
Zorjan, Peter '07 (PEO) Bloomington, IL St. Patrick's.
Zoromski, Herbert P. '51 (LC) Retired.
Zotter, Thomas A. '76 (SFE) Retired.
Zoubek, Ronald '89 (BAL) Retired.
Zoucha, Carl J. '98 (OM) Schuyler, NE Divine Mercy; [L] Elkhorn, NE Apostolic Sodales.
Zoufal, Michael L. '87 (CHI) Burbank, IL St. Albert the Great.
Zowada, Stanislaw *o.m.i.* '00 (LA) San Fernando, CA Santa Rosa.
Zsolczai, Raymond '83 (MIL)[P] Burlington, WI Queen of Peace Friary.
Zuber, Thaddeus F. '50 (NEW)[L] Rutherford, NJ St. John Vianney Residence for Priests Retired.
Zuberbueler, Matthew H. '96 (ARL) Dale City, VA Holy Family; Defenders of the Bond; [D] Dumfries, VA Pope John Paul the Great Catholic High School.
Zubik, Rudolf '64 (NEW)[L] Rutherford, NJ St. John Vianney Residence for Priests Retired.
Zubizarreta Mugica, Jose Ramon *c.p.* '72 (SJN) Toa Baja, PR Espiritu Santo.
Zuccaro, James E. '06 (BUR) Chester, VT St. Joseph.
Zuchowski, Robert J. '72 (GLD) Elk Rapids, MI Sacred Heart.
Zuelch, Michael Christopher '10 (DET) Novi, MI Holy Family.
Zuelke, Michael *o.f.m.cap.* '74 (MIL)[P] Mount Calvary, WI St. Felix Friary.
Zuercher, John D. *s.j.* '59 (OM)[O] Omaha, NE Christian Life Community–North Central Region (CLC).
Zuerlein, Damian J. '81 (OM) Deans; Papillion, NE St. Columbkille; Deans; Finance Council; Officers; Age Groups; [N] Papillion, NE IXIM, Spirit of Solidarity.
Zuffoletto, Michael P. '72 (BUF) Lewiston, NY St. Peter.
Zugaj, Piotr W. '04 (VEN) Venice, FL Our Lady of Lourdes.
Zugger, Christopher L. '81 (HPM) Albuquerque, NM Our Lady of Perpetual Help Retired.
Zuk, Richard P. '05 (OG) Ray Brook, NY Federal Correctional Institution; Released from Diocesan Assignment.
Zukas, Stephen P. '93 (BO) South Boston, MA St. Peter; Lithuanian.
Zukowski, Nicholas '82 (DET) New Baltimore, MI St. Mary Queen of Creation.
Zuleger, Donald M. '76 (GB) Appleton, WI St. Bernadette; Regional Vicars; Appleton, WI Sacred Heart.
Zuleta, Fernando '06 (CHI) Chicago, IL Resurrection.
Zuletta, Nondier (B) On Duty Outside the Diocese.
Zuliani, Vincent *s.d.b.* '56 (NY)[FF] Stony Point, NY Don Bosco Retreat Center and Marian Shrine; [FF] Stony Point, NY Marian Shrine.
Zuluaga, Edwin Londono '07 (SJN) Bayamon, PR Santa Teresa de Jesus.
Zulueta, Johnny *c.m.* '87 (LA)[BB] Artesia, CA Filipino Pastoral Ministry.
Zumaya, David '77 (SAT) Retired.
Zuniga, Carlos '98 (BWN) On Leave; McAllen, TX Saint Juan Diego Cuauhtlatoatzin.
Zuniga, Domingo *c.m.f.* '52 (LA) Los Angeles, CA Our Lady Queen of Angels Parish.
Zuniga, Juan M. *m.m.* '88 (FgM) Maryknoll, NY MARYKNOLL.
Zuniga, Victor *m.s.p.* (CHI) Chicago, IL Queen of the Universe.
Zunmas, Oby J. '00 (OKL) Madill, OK Holy Cross Church.
Zunno, Michael O. '53 (NY)[DD] Maryknoll Maryknoll Fathers and Brothers Retired.
Zupez, John *s.j.* '67 (OKL) Oklahoma City, OK Corpus Christi.
Zupka, Anselm *o.s.b.* '67 (CLV)[N] Cleveland Benedictine Order of Cleveland.
Zupka, Anselm *o.s.b.* '67 (Y) Walsh University; [B] North Canton, OH Walsh University.
Zurat, Hugh *o.f.m.* '62 (CHI)[N] Chicago, IL Holy Name Friary.
Zuraw, Rev. Msgr. John A. '87 (Y) Defenders of the Bond; Promoter of Justice; Office of Permanent Diaconate.
Zuraw, Rev. Msgr. John '87 (Y) Girard, OH St. Rose; Presbyteral Council.
Zurawski, Lawrence '85 (DET) Shelby Twp., MI St. Therese of Lisieux.
Zurcher, Thomas *c.s.c.* '72 (FgM) New Rochelle, NY Eastern Brothers Province.
Zurcher, Thomas *c.s.c.* (FTW)[H] Notre Dame Congregation of Holy Cross, United States Province of Priests & Brothers.
Zurek, John '04 (CHI) Orland Park, IL St. Francis of Assisi.
Zurek, Lawrence W. *o.f.m.* '85 (PEO) Peoria, IL Sacred Heart; Peoria, IL St. Joseph.
Zurovetz, Jerome G. '67 (CC) Portland, TX Our Lady of Mount Carmel.
Zuschmidt, Joseph C. *o.s.f.s.* '65 (CHL) High Point, NC Immaculate Heart of Mary.
Zuziak, Joseph R. *s.d.s.* '66 (GRY)[H] Merrillville, IN Salvatorian Fathers (Society of the Divine Savior).
Zuzik, John E. '91 (Y) Canton, OH St. Therese Little Flower.
Zvanut, Miran *s.j.* '06 (OAK)[L] Berkeley, CA Jesuit Fathers and Brothers.
Zvarych, Petro '00 (PHU) West Easton, PA Holy Ghost; West Easton, PA St. Nicholas.
Zwack, Jeffrey '84 (BIS) Dickinson, ND Queen of Peace Church.
Zwaska, Victor L. '56 (MIL) Retired.
Zwilling, Robert J. '05 (BEL) Salem, IL St. Elizabeth Ann Seton; Salem, IL St. Theresa of Avila.
Zwirn, Ralph H. '85 (CHI) Hazel Crest, IL St. Anne.
Zwolenkiewicz, Raphael *o.f.m.conv.* '79 (PAT) Clifton, NJ St. John Kanty.
Zygadlo, Mitchell '82 (ROC) Military Chaplains; Air Force Chaplains.
Zygaldo, Mitchell '82 (BLX) Keesler Airforce Base.
Zyla, Ludwik *o.cist.* '91 (CHI)[N] Willow Springs, IL Cistercian Fathers, Our Lady Mother of the Church Polish Mission; Argo, IL Our Lady, Mother of the Church Polish Mission.
Zylla, Paul '45 (SCL) Retired.
Zywan, Paul J. '86 (PIT) Wexford, PA St. Alexis.

Necrology

CARDINALS

✠ Aponte Martinez, His Eminence Luis Cardinal (SJN) Retired Archbishop of San Juan. —Died April 10, 2012

✠ Bevilacqua, His Eminence Anthony Cardinal (PH) Archbishop emeritus of Philadelphia. —Died Jan. 31, 2012

✠ Foley, His Eminence John Patrick Cardinal (PH) Grand Master emeritus of the Equestrian Order of the Holy Sepulchre of Jerusalem. —Died Dec. 11, 2011

ARCHBISHOPS

✠ Donoghue, Most Rev. John F. (ATL) Retired Archbishop of Atlanta. —Died Nov. 11, 2011

✠ Hannan, Most Rev. Philip M. (NO) Retired Archbishop of New Orleans. —Died Sept. 29, 2011

✠ Kelly, Most Rev. Thomas C., *O.P.* (L) Retired Archbishop of Louisville. —Died Dec. 14, 2011

✠ Sanchez, Most Rev. Robert F. (SFE) Retired Archbishop of Santa Fe. —Died Jan. 20, 2012

✠ Schleck, Most Rev. Charles Asa, *c.s.c.* (FgM) Official Emeritus of the Congregation for the Evangelization of Peoples. —Died July 12, 2011

BISHOPS

✠ Chedid, Most Rev. John G. (OLL) Retired Bishop of Our Lady of Lebanon of Los Angeles. —Died March 21, 2012

✠ Donovan, Most Rev. Paul V. (KAL) Retired Bishop of Kalamazoo. —Died April 28, 2011

✠ Duffy, Most Rev. Paul F., *o.m.i.* (FgM) Retired Bishop of Mongu. —Died Aug. 23, 2011

✠ Estabrook, Most Rev. Joseph W. (MO) Auxiliary Bishop for the Military Services, U.S.A. —Died Feb. 4, 2012

✠ Fernandez, Most Rev. Gilberto (MIA) Retired Auxiliary Bishop of Miami. —Died Sept. 30, 2011

✠ Mestice, Most Rev. Anthony F. (NY) Retired Auxiliary Bishop of New York. —Died April 29, 2011

✠ Negron Santana, Most Rev. Hermin (SJN) Auxiliary Bishop of San Juan, PR. —Died March 10, 2012

✠ Oliver, Most Rev. Fremiot Torres (PCE) Bishop emeritus of Ponce. —Died Jan. 26, 2012

✠ Pataki, Most Rev. Andrew (PSC) Perth Amboy, NJ St. Nicholas. —Died Dec. 8, 2011

✠ Reiss, Most Rev. John C. (TR) Retired Bishop of Trenton. —Died March 4, 2012

✠ Roman, Most Rev. Agustin A. (MIA) Retired Auxiliary Bishop of Miami. —Died April 11, 2012

✠ Schmitt, Most Rev. Bernard W. (WH) Retired Bishop of Wheeling–Charleston. —Died Aug. 16, 2011

✠ Schmitt, Most Rev. Mark F. (MAR) Retired Bishop of Marquette. —Died Dec. 14, 2011

✠ Sheridan, Most Rev. Patrick J. (NY) Retired Auxiliary Bishop of New York. —Died Dec. 2, 2011

ABBOT

✠ Rausch, Rt. Rev. Conrad R., *o.s.b.* (SEA) (Retired). —Died Aug. 9, 2011

PRIESTS

† Abell, Donald E. (BEL). —Died March 24, 2011

† Acevedo, Luis H. (ELP) (Retired). —Died July 3, 2011

† Adams, David C. (KAL) (Retired). —Died Oct. 13, 2011

† Ahler, Richard H., *s.j.* (MIL) Wauwatosa, WI Jesuit Community at St. Camillus. —Died June 8, 2011

† Aiello, John D. (MIL) (Retired). —Died July 15, 2011

† Alers, Juan (LKC) (Retired). —Died Feb. 1, 2011

† Alminde, Joseph M., *s.j.* (PH) Merion Station, PA Loyola Center & Manresa Hall. —Died March 25, 2011

† Alvares, Augustine (P) (Retired). —Died Oct. 31, 2011

† Anastasio, Thomas (BRK) (Retired). —Died Sept. 17, 2011

† Anderson, Arthur C. (RVC) (Retired). —Died Oct. 1, 2011

† Angle, Camillus, *t.o.r.* (ALT) (Retired). —Died Sept. 19, 2011

† Antus, Lawrence, *o.m.i.* (STP) (Retired). —Died May 24, 2011

† Anukam, Anselm A. (AUS) Temple, TX St. Mary. —Died May 22, 2011

† Arbanas, Harold P. (GF) (Retired). —Died Dec. 4, 2010

† Arneson, James E. (IND) (Retired). —Died Oct. 23, 2011

† Arps, Joseph W. (PRT) (Retired). —Died March 25, 2011

† Atkinson, Sean (JKS) (Retired). —Died Oct. 4, 2011

† Auen, Paul, *c.pp.s.* (CIN) (Retired). —Died Dec. 15, 2010

† Auer, Robert F. (DUB) (Retired). —Died May 23, 2011

† Augustyn, Andrew M. (GI) (Retired). —Died Nov. 22, 2010

† Avilla, William (RNO) (Retired). —Died Dec. 6, 2010

† Azevedo, Ferdinand T., *s.j.* (FgM) Society of Jesus Foreign Mission. —Died 2011

† Baeten, David (GB) (Retired). —Died Nov. 27, 2010

† Bajorek, Joseph, *s.d.b.* (NEW) (Retired). —Died Sept. 14, 2011

† Ball, Rev. Msgr. Thomas J. (BUR) Burlington, VT Cathedral of the Immaculate Conception. —Died April 19, 2011

† Banet, Paul H., *s.s.j.* (BAL) (Retired). —Died April 30, 2011

† Banfield, Lawrence, *o.p.* (P) Portland, OR Holy Rosary Priory. —Died April 11, 2011

† Barnett, Fred J. (JC) (Retired). —Died March 19, 2011

† Barragam, Feliciano Ganda (SJN). —Died Oct. 20, 2011

† Barrett, Edward F. (SCR) (Retired). —Died July 22, 2011

† Barron, Wayne, *c.m.f.* (CHI) Oak Park, IL Claretian Missionaries USA Eastern Province. —Died 2011

† Bauman, William A. (KC) (Retired). —Died April 17, 2011

† Beatty, Michael D. (CIN) Cincinnati, OH St. Simon the Apostle. —Died Dec. 14, 2011

† Beck, Erwin G., *s.j.* (NY) New York, NY Murray–Weigel Hall. —Died Dec. 15, 2010

† Beck, Richard P. (MIL) (Retired). —Died April 23, 2011

† Becka, Robert R., *s.j.* (FgM) Society of Jesus Foreign Mission. —Died 2011

† Beckman, John J., *s.j.* (CIN) Cincinnati, OH Faber Jesuit Community. —Died March 11, 2011

† Beerntsen, Harold A. (GB) (Retired). —Died Jan. 24, 2011

† Belluomini, Rev. Msgr. Ralph (FRS) Chap., Bakersfield, CA Bakersfield Memorial Hospital & San Joaquin Community Hospital. —Died June 17, 2011

† Beltrami, Robert, *o.f.m.* (OAK) Danville, CA San Damiano Retreat. —Died March 24, 2011

† Bender, Philip M. (ALT) (Retired). —Died May 23, 2011

† Benefiel, Rev. Msgr. Harry E. (LAF) (Retired). —Died March 13, 2011

† Bennett, Melvin J. (LFT) Carmel, IN St. Elizabeth Ann Seton. —Died April 19, 2011

† Bennett, Rolland, *o.m.i.* (SAT) San Antonio, TX Oblate Madonna Residence. —Died June 12, 2011

† Beshara, Rev. Msgr. Ronald (SAM) (Sabbatical). —Died Sept. 7, 2011

† Beyer, Gregory, *o.f.m.cap.* (SAL) Victoria, KS St. Fidelis Friary. —Died Dec. 9, 2010

† Bies, Michael (PEO) Odell, IL St. Paul's. —Died Dec. 16, 2010

† Bisgrove, Charles, *s.c.j.* (MIL) (Retired). —Died April 10, 2011

† Bitangjol, Albert P. (SFR) (Retired). —Died May 7, 2011

† Blinn, Richard J., *s.j.* (SJ) Los Gatos, CA Sacred Heart Jesuit Center. —Died May 11, 2011

† Bliven, Robert J., *o.s.c.* (PHX) (Retired). —Died Jan. 3, 2010

† Bochinski, Mark J. (SCR) (Retired). —Died Jan. 6, 2011

† Boeke, Anselm F. (CIN) (Retired). —Died Jan. 7, 2011

† Boileau, David A. (NO) (Retired). —Died Jan. 24, 2011

† Bolan, John, *c.pp.s.* (CIN) Cincinnati, OH Dayton Provincial Office of the Society of the Precious Blood. —Died Oct. 22, 2010

† Bollea, Richard C. (HRT) (Retired). —Died Nov. 19, 2011

† Borho, Charles D. (P) (Retired). —Died July 9, 2011

† Bouffard, Lionel A., *m.m.* (NY) (Retired). —Died July 9, 2011

† Bouska, Jerome Anthony (LA) (Retired). —Died Nov. 20, 2010

† Boyle, Rev. Msgr. Patrick J. (NY) Rye, NY Resurrection. —Died Feb. 16, 2011

† Boyle, Rev. Msgr. Raymond J. (PEO) Seneca, IL St. Patrick's. —Died Dec. 28, 2011

† Boymer, Lloyd J. (CLV) (Retired). —Died March 29, 2011

† Bozzelli, Joseph V. (WIL) (Retired). —Died June 1, 2011

† Brabandt, James Paul, *o.f.m.* (WDC) Washington, DC Franciscan Monastery. —Died 2011

† Brackley, J. Dean, *s.j.* (FgM) Jesuit Foreign Mission. —Died Oct. 16, 2011

† Bradley, Dennis J. (PIT) Pittsburgh, PA Saint John Vianney Manor. —Died Dec. 10, 2010

† Bradley, Edward C., *s.j.* (PH) Philadelphia, PA Loyola Center & Manresa Hall. —Died June 8, 2011

† Bradley, Robert (CC) (Retired). —Died March 22, 2011

† Brady, Richard J. (BO) (Retired). —Died March 30, 2011

† Brainard, Ernest B. (OAK) (Retired). —Died Dec. 14, 2010

† Brennan, George (VEN) (Retired). —Died Jan. 20, 2011

† Brennan, Joseph J., *o.s.c.* (SCL) (Retired). —Died Oct. 16, 2010

† Brentrup, Bruce, *s.d.s.* (MIL) Milwaukee, WI Milwaukee Salvatorian Provincial Offices. —Died Feb. 8, 2011

† Brenza, William J. (HRT) Plantsville, CT Mary Our Queen. —Died Dec. 22, 2010

† Brink, Joseph C. (COV) (Retired). —Died Feb. 6, 2011

† Brody, Donald, *o.f.m.cap.* (GB) (Retired). —Died Oct. 30, 2010

† Brown, Joseph E., *s.j.* (STL) St. Louis, MO Jesuit Community Corporation at Saint Louis University–Jesuit Hall. —Died Nov. 14, 2010

† Brown, Konstantin K. (ROM). —Died Dec. 30, 2010

† Bruggeman, Gerald H. (COS) (Retired). —Died April 27, 2011

† Bryl, Thaddeus J. (MIL) (Retired). —Died Dec. 2, 2010

† Bryson, John W., *s.m.* (BO) (Retired). —Died May 17, 2011

† Brzezniak, Aurelian, *o.f.m.conv.* (BUF) (Retired). —Died June 27, 2011

† Buccellato, Sebastian, *o.f.m.* (NY) New York, NY Padua Friary. —Died Nov. 4, 2010

† Buchheit, Rev. Msgr. Richard A. (STL) (Retired). —Died June 29, 2011

† Buhman, Leo T. (JC) (Retired). —Died Jan. 9, 2011

† Burke, John F. (WOR) (Retired). —Died Nov. 3, 2011

† Burke, Robert, *s.s.c.* (OM) (Retired). —Died Jan. 24, 2011

† Burns, John F. (BO) (Retired). —Died July 9, 2011

† Burton, C. Jeffries, *s.j.* (BAL) Baltimore, MD Colombiere Jesuit Community. —Died Aug. 20, 2011

† Busco, Rev. Msgr. John J. (PH) (Retired). —Died Nov. 8, 2011

† Butz, Crispin, *o.f.m.* (SFE) (Retired). —Died Nov. 7, 2011

† Byrne, James O. (CIN) (Retired). —Died July 6, 2011

† Byrne, Rev. Msgr. Laserian (FRS) (Retired). —Died May 20, 2011

† Byrne, Robert Paul (LA) (Retired). —Died July 13, 2011

† Byrnes, John P. (TR) (Retired). —Died Oct. 26, 2011

† Byron, J. Paul (R) (Retired). —Died March 15, 2011

† Caffery, James D., *m.s.* (HRT) Hartford, CT Missionaries of La Salette. —Died June 17, 2011
† Caffrey, Edward (SPK) (Retired). —Died March 20, 2011
† Cahouet, Ralph Eugene, *o.p.* (PRO) Providence, RI St. Thomas Aquinas Priory, Providence College. —Died June 21, 2011
† Caldwell, James V. (SD) (Retired). —Died Sept. 18, 2011
† Calzada, Teodoro, *c.m.* (SJN) San Juan, PR Nuestra Senora del Pilar. —Died April 27, 2011
† Campagnone, Nicholas (ALB) (Retired). —Died Jan. 14, 2011
† Cannon, Maro, *c.f.a.* (KNX) Signal Mountain, TN Alexian Village of Tennessee. —Died 2011
† Capiello, Luis Beltran Rios (SJN) Dorado, PR San Antonio de Padua. —Died June 25, 2011
† Cardoni, Albert A., *s.j.* (BO) Weston, MA Campion Center. —Died Nov. 2, 2011
† Cardoso, Luis A. (FR) (Retired). —Died June 3, 2011
† Cargill, Rev. Msgr. Eugene (GAL) (Retired). —Died Jan. 17, 2011
† Carlin, George, *s.o.l.t.* (CC) Robstown, TX Society of Our Lady of The Most Holy Trinity. —Died Oct. 17, 2011
† Carlson, Gerald J. (GI) (Retired). —Died Sept. 8, 2011
† Carolan, Thomas, *o.f.m.* (SFD) (Retired). —Died June 20, 2011
† Carpender, Thomas J. (DUB) (Retired). —Died Jan. 15, 2011
† Carroll, Gilbert A. (CHI) (Retired). —Died March 20, 2011
† Carroll, Rev. Msgr. James J. (COL) (Retired). —Died May 10, 2011
† Carroll, Michael J. (LA) (Retired). —Died May 26, 2011
† Carson, John F. (NY) Yonkers, NY St. Ann. —Died Aug. 3, 2011
† Casey, John D. (HRT) (Retired). —Died Oct. 20, 2011
† Casey, Joseph M. (PAT) (Retired). —Died July 25, 2011
† Caskey, John V., *c.ss.r.* (BAL) (Retired). —Died May 22, 2011
† Cassel, Harry A., *o.s.a.* (PH) Villanova, PA St. Thomas Monastery. —Died July 13, 2011
† Cassidy, Francis P. (CHI) (Retired). —Died Feb. 18, 2011
† Cassidy, Rev. Msgr. Thomas J. (ARL) (Retired). —Died Oct. 1, 2011
† Cavagnaro, Camillus, *o.f.m.* (TUC) Tucson, AZ Mission San Xavier del Bac. —Died March 14, 2011
† Cavanagh, Michael J. (PBL) (Retired). —Died July 13, 2011
† Cerulo, Thomas N., *o.ss.t.* (BAL) Baltimore, MD Holy Trinity Monastery. —Died Jan. 20, 2011
† Chant, William S. (BUR) (Retired). —Died Dec. 12, 2010
† Charipar, Henry W. (DUB) (Retired). —Died Oct. 14, 2011
† Chase, Charles E. (OG) (Retired). —Died Jan. 4, 2011
† Chasse, Lucien M., *s.m.* (BO) Boston, MA Marist Fathers of Our Lady of Victories. —Died July 29, 2011
† Chen, Raphael (AMA) (Retired). —Died May 4, 2011
† Chmura, Stanislaw T. (RIC). —Died Jan. 13, 2011
† Chouinard, Marcel G. (PRT) (Retired). —Died Aug. 6, 2011
† Christman, Ralph F., *m.m.* (NY) New York, NY Maryknoll. —Died March 21, 2011
† Cialone, Donald F. (NEW) Westfield, NJ Holy Trinity. —Died Feb. 9, 2011
† Cieslinski, Robert (P) (Retired). —Died Aug. 4, 2011
† Cimarrusti, Rev. Msgr. Francis A. (CHI) (Retired). —Died March 29, 2011
† Cimperman, Victor J. (CLV) (Retired). —Died Nov. 15, 2011
† Cincotta, Anthony (SY) (On Duty Outside the Diocese). —Died July 19, 2011
† Ciprian, Carl A. (CLV) (Retired). —Died Nov. 21, 2011
† Ciurej, Richard S. (OM) (Retired). —Died Jan. 2, 2011
† Clarkin, Herbert J. (HRT) (Administrative Leave). —Died Dec. 29, 2010
† Cleary, Francis X., *s.j.* (STL) St. Louis, MO Jesuit Community Corporation at Saint Louis University–Jesuit Hall. —Died Dec. 8, 2010
† Clifford, Thomas Aquinas, *o.p.* (NO) (Retired). —Died June 7, 2011
† Close, James J. (CHI) (Retired). —Died Aug. 31, 2011
† Colon Hernandez, Jose E. (PCE) (Retired). —Died June 24, 2011
† Conan, Constantine J., *c.s.sp.* (PIT) Bethel Park, PA The Spiritan Center. —Died Sept. 21, 2011
† Concha, Anthony, *s.j.* (ELP) El Paso, TX Sacred Heart. —Died Dec. 5, 2010
† Condon, Robert M. (SC) (Retired). —Died July 24, 2011
† Connell, Stephen J. (WIL) (Retired). —Died April 1, 2011
† Connolly, Rev. Msgr. Leon L. (DUB) (Retired). —Died Sept. 27, 2011
† Connolly, Thomas (SFS) (Retired). —Died Feb. 25, 2011
† Conrad, James H. (ALT) (Retired). —Died Oct. 28, 2010
† Conry, Roy, *o.carm.* (TUC) (Retired). —Died 2011
† Conti, Cornelius G., *o.f.m.* (SP) (Retired). —Died Nov. 14, 2010
† Convey, Edwin H., *s.j.* (BAL) Baltimore, MD Jesuit Community of Loyola University. —Died Oct. 18, 2010
† Conway, Laurence (MIA) (Retired). —Died May 13, 2011
† Cooper, Angus, *o.f.m.* (LA) Los Angeles, CA St. Joseph Friary. —Died Nov. 16, 2010
† Corcuera, Manuel R. (CHK) Apostolic Administrator of Chalan Kanoa. —Died Dec. 19, 2010
† Corrigan, Rev. Msgr. Bernard P. (NY) (Retired). —Died Jan. 30, 2011
† Cortney, Edward P. (GI) (Retired). —Died June 26, 2011
† Costello, Raymond, *m.s.c.* (ALN) Center Valley, PA Sacred Heart Villa. —Died July 16, 2011
† Coz, Richard T., *s.j.* (SJ) Los Gatos, CA Sacred Heart Jesuit Center. —Died Dec. 31, 2010
† Creel, Jesse (R) (Retired). —Died June 30, 2011
† Crescenzi, Rocco, *f.d.p.* (BO) East Boston, MA Don Orione Nursing Home. —Died April 9, 2011
† Croal, Thomas (ORG) (Retired). —Died May 29, 2011
† Cronin, Brian (ALB) (Retired). —Died Aug. 27, 2011
† Crossman, James (DUL) (Retired). —Died Nov. 3, 2011
† Crosthwait, Rev. Msgr. Joseph H. (GAL) (Retired). —Died Feb. 13, 2011
† Cunningham, Edward, *o.m.i.* (SAT) San Antonio, TX Oblate Madonna Residence. —Died Oct. 28, 2010
† Cunningham, Leonard, *o.c.s.o.* (CHR) Moncks Corner, SC Mepkin Abbey. —Died Dec. 5, 2010
† Cunningham, Phillip J., *c.s.p.* (SFR) (Retired). —Died March 11, 2011
† Curtin, Cornelius L., *s.j.* (DET) Clarkston, MI Colombiere Center. —Died Sept. 21, 2011
† Cusmano, John C. (DET) (Retired). —Died Oct. 29, 2011
† Daly, Rev. Msgr. Thomas J. (BO) (Retired). —Died April 4, 2011
† Daniszewski, Rev. Msgr. John D. (E) (Retired). —Died Aug. 31, 2011
† Danowski, Alexander J. (PBL) (Retired). —Died July 5, 2011
† Darby, Thomas J. (NY) (Retired). —Died Feb. 9, 2011
† Darling, Franklin (SPR) (Retired). —Died Nov. 7, 2011
† Davis, James Joseph, *o.p.* (NY) New York, NY St. Catherine of Siena. —Died Feb. 16, 2011
† Davis, Rev. Msgr. William F. (MEM) (Retired). —Died Oct. 26, 2011
† Deane, Declan (OAK) Pleasant Hill, CA Christ the King. —Died Dec. 12, 2010
† De La Garza, Jose Gerardo (SAT) (Retired). —Died July 7, 2011
† DeLellis, Francis V. (PRO) (Retired). —Died Feb. 17, 2011
† della Picca, Rev. Msgr. Paul B. (ALN) (Retired). —Died Sept. 22, 2011
† DeMarinis, Rev. Msgr. John H. (Y) Youngstown, OH St. Anthony. —Died June 12, 2011
† Dentinger, Robert (TOL). —Died Sept. 12, 2011
† DePietro, Arthur J. (BO) (Retired). —Died Oct. 31, 2011
† Desjardins, Raymond S. (MAN) (Retired). —Died Dec., 2010
† Devaney, Michael J., *o.m.i.* (BO) Tewksbury, MA Immaculate Heart of Mary Residence. —Died Aug. 7, 2011
† Dever, Rev. Msgr. Daniel J. (HON) (Retired). —Died Oct. 19, 2011
† Devore, Gerald T. (BGP) (Retired). —Died Jan. 9, 2011
† Dickman, John W. (L) (Retired). —Died May 25, 2011
† Dickrell, Cyril, *s.d.s.* (GB) (Retired). —Died Aug. 6, 2011
† Diederich, Everett A., *s.j.* (STL) St. Louis, MO Jesuit Community Corporation at Saint Louis University–Jesuit Hall. —Died April 20, 2011
† Dietzen, John J. (PEO) (Retired). —Died March 27, 2011
† DiFede, Thomas Vincent, *o.p.* (COL) Columbus, OH St. Patrick Rectory. —Died June 12, 2011
† DiFilippo, John V., *o.s.f.s.* (PH) (Retired). —Died March 28, 2011
† DiLeo, Richard, *s.c.j.* (GAL) Houston, TX Our Lady of Guadalupe. —Died July 19, 2011
† Dilgen, William, *s.m.m.* (RVC) (Retired). —Died Aug. 8, 2011
† Dillman, Alan M. (ATL) (Retired). —Died Jan. 7, 2011
† Dillon, John D. (ROC) (Retired). —Died June 2, 2011
† Dinges, Anthony (RIC) (Retired). —Died Aug. 28, 2011
† DiPietro, Rodric J. (COL) Hilliard, OH St. Brendan the Navigator. —Died Aug. 13, 2011
† Dobbin, Jay D. (GF) (Retired). —Died Nov. 8, 2011
† Dobkowski, Rev. Msgr. Paulin J. (BEL) (Retired). —Died May 12, 2011
† Dolan, Charles, *c.s.s.* (BO) Waltham, MA Stigmatine Fathers & Brothers Provincial House. —Died Jan. 18, 2011
† Doll, Rev. Msgr. William P. (PBL) (Retired). —Died May 8, 2011
† Dolski, V. Anthony (GB) (Retired). —Died Sept. 17, 2011
† Donadio, Vincent J. (TR) (Retired). —Died July 6, 2011
† Donovan, James W., *c.s.p.* (SFR) San Francisco, CA Old St. Mary's Cathedral. —Died Oct. 27, 2010
† Donovan, Patrick J., *m.m.* (NY) (Retired). —Died Jan. 22, 2011
† Donovan, Rev. Msgr. Thomas F. (BRK) (Retired). —Died March 31, 2011
† Donovan, Rev. Msgr. William L. (SCR) (Retired). —Died July 2, 2011
† Dorais, Gerald A. (WOR) Gardner, MA Our Lady of the Holy Rosary. —Died Sept. 23, 2011
† Doran, William J., *s.j.* (MIL) Wauwatosa, WI Jesuit Community at St. Camillus. —Died Jan. 31, 2011
† Dorley, Paul D. (TOL) (Retired). —Died Nov. 2, 2010
† Dougherty, Edward J. (TR) (Retired). —Died April 14, 2011
† Dougherty, William J., *o.s.f.s.* (WIL) Elsmere, DE Veteran's Hospital. —Died Feb. 27, 2011
† Douglas, Louis (ALB) (Retired). —Died May 11, 2011
† Dowd, John, *c.ss.r.* (CHI) (Retired). —Died 2011
† Doyle, John T., *o.s.f.s.* (WIL) (Retired). —Died Feb. 14, 2011
† Doyle, Thomas F. (PH) (Retired). —Died Dec. 9, 2010
† Drake, Sebastian, *o.f.m.* (OAK) Oakland, CA Franciscan Friars of California. —Died Sept. 14, 2011
† Driscoll, James E. (OAK) (Retired). —Died Oct. 29, 2011
† Driscoll, John M., *o.s.a.* (PH) Villanova, PA St. Thomas Monastery. —Died March 2, 2011
† Druding, John C. (ATL) (Retired). —Died Feb. 12, 2011
† Drupieski, Stanley R., *o.s.f.s.* (WIL) Wilmington, DE St. Anthony of Padua. —Died Sept. 25, 2011
† Duffy, George A., *s.j.* (BO) Weston, MA Campion Health Center. —Died Sept. 30, 2011
† Duffy, George Ralph (WDC) (Retired). —Died July 26, 2011
† Dumm, Wilfred M., *o.s.b.* (GBG) Latrobe, PA Saint Vincent Archabbey. —Died Sept. 23, 2011
† Dunklee, Lawrence G. (LC) (Retired). —Died Jan. 7, 2011
† Duran, Ernesto (BRK) (Retired). —Died Jan. 6, 2011
† Durkin, Patrick J., *c.s.v.* (CHI) (Retired). —Died Aug. 14, 2011
† Dusseault, Emile C., *m.s.* (HRT) Hartford, CT Missionaries of La Salette. —Died Sept. 18, 2011
† Earley, James Kiernan, *c.p.* (BRK) (Retired). —Died Nov. 11, 2011
† Eckhoff, Evan, *o.f.m.* (SFD) Springfield, IL Our Lady of Angels Friary. —Died Nov. 15, 2011
† Edelen, Richard (LEX) (Retired). —Died Feb. 28, 2011
† Egan, Rev. Msgr. Brian J. (BIR) (Retired). —Died Jan. 25, 2011
† Eikens, Leroy F. (WIN) (Retired). —Died Dec. 2, 2011
† Eisel, Howard P., *s.s.c.* (PRO) (Retired). —Died Aug. 31, 2011
† El–Hayek, Nehmatallah (SAM) (Retired). —Died May 10, 2011
† Elmer, Rev. Msgr. Charles (AUS) (Retired). —Died Sept. 4, 2011
† Endebrock, Rev. Msgr. Donald M. (MET) Carteret, NJ St. Joseph. —Died Oct. 8, 2011
† Enderlin, Joseph J. (LR) (Retired). —Died Dec. 14, 2011
† Enright, John P. (CHI) (Retired). —Died Feb. 14, 2011
† Ernest, Stephen, *s.v.d.* (OAK) Oakland, CA St. Bernard. —Died Nov. 11, 2010
† Everitt, Edward Elms, *o.p.* (BR) Hammond, LA Holy Ghost. —Died July 11, 2011
† Evers, Gerard A. (CIN) (Retired). —Died Aug. 12, 2011
† Fagan, Edward, *o.a.r.* (NY) Bronx, NY St. John. —Died Dec. 23, 2010
† Faherty, William B., *s.j.* (STL) St. Louis, MO Jesuit Community Corporation at Saint Louis University–Jesuit Hall. —Died Aug. 22, 2011
† Falvey, Edmund F. (WOR) (Retired). —Died 2011
† Famiglietti, Rocco, *o.f.m.* (FgM) Franciscan Province of the Immaculate Conception Foreign Mission. —Died Dec. 18, 2010
† Farley, Daniel H. (LC) (Retired). —Died Dec. 18, 2011
† Farrell, Thomas F. (HRT) (Retired). —Died Jan. 11, 2011

† Farrelly, John, *o.s.b.* (WDC) Washington, DC St. Anselm's Abbey. —Died June 2, 2011
† Fawcett, Brian (RC) Fort Pierce, SD St. John. —Died Oct. 9, 2011
† Fedorowich, Rev. Msgr. Michael (PHU) (Retired). —Died April 25, 2011
† Fee, George Patterson (ORG) (Retired). —Died May 30, 2011
† Felion, Jerome (CR) (Retired). —Died May 10, 2011
† Fenech, Francis X. (PMB) Lake Worth, FL Sacred Heart. —Died Jan. 27, 2011
† Fenton, Cornelius, *c.pp.s.* (CIN) (Retired). —Died May 8, 2011
† Fenton, Jerry F. (STP) (Retired). —Died Nov. 17, 2011
† Fenton, Norman Hilarion, *o.p.* (L) Louisville, KY St. Louis Bertrand Priory. —Died April 9, 2011
† Fernandez, Javier, *o.de.m.* (SJN) (Retired). —Died Aug. 26, 2011
† Fernandez, Julio, *o.de.m.* (SJN) (Retired). —Died Oct. 24, 2011
† Ferrara, Bede, *o.f.m.* (BO) Lynn, MA Franciscan Community. —Died Oct. 22, 2010
† Ferrer, Rev. Msgr. Jose Colon (PCE) (Retired). —Died Feb. 4, 2011
† Fichtner, Joseph A., *o.s.c.* (SCL) (Retired). —Died Oct. 27, 2010
† Fimbel, Duane G. (BUF) (Retired). —Died Sept. 3, 2011
† Finley, Thomas M., *c.m.* (PH) Philadelphia, PA St. Vincent's Seminary. —Died Sept. 16, 2011
† Finnane, Daniel P. (MAD) Westport, WI St. Mary of the Lake Parish. —Died June 25, 2011
† Finnerty, Peter F. (CAM) (Retired). —Died May 21, 2011
† Finnigan, Rev. Msgr. John C. (Y) Canton, OH St. Peter. —Died March 29, 2011
† Finucane, Robert (B) (Retired). —Died March 16, 2011
† Fisch, Gerald M. (SC) (Retired). —Died June 22, 2011
† Fisher, Rev. Msgr. Edward T. (BUF) (Retired). —Died June 29, 2011
† Fitzpatrick, Edmund J. (CHI) (Retired). —Died Jan. 5, 2011
† Fleming, David L., *s.j.* (STL) St. Louis, MO Ignatius House. —Died March 22, 2011
† Fleming, Thomas J. (BO) (Retired). —Died Dec. 23, 2011
† Flint, Kenneth (NOR) (Retired). —Died Sept. 10, 2011
† Flood, Rev. Msgr. James J. (PH) (Retired). —Died Jan. 17, 2011
† Flusk, Rev. Msgr. Joseph F. (NEW) (Retired). —Died July 9, 2011
† Flynn, Edward R. (SD) (Retired). —Died July 16, 2011
† Flynn, Thomas A. (SCR) (Retired). —Died Nov. 21, 2011
† Foley, Rev. Msgr. James J. (PH) (Retired). —Died June 21, 2011
† Ford, James Michael (LA) (Retired). —Died May 22, 2011
† Foster, John J. (PH) (Retired). —Died June 6, 2011
† Foster, Raymond, *o.carm.* (JOL) Joliet, IL St. Elias Carmelites. —Died 2011
† Foyo, Alexis, *o.s.b.* (SD) Oceanside, CA Prince of Peace Abbey. —Died Nov. 24, 2010
† Francis, Paul R. (BO) (Retired). —Died Oct. 16, 2011
† Franco, Robert M. (PIT) Pittsburgh, PA Saint John Vianney Manor. —Died Aug. 19, 2010
† Frank, Paul, *o.m.i.* (MIA) Fort Lauderdale, FL St. John the Baptist. —Died Oct. 5, 2011
† Freitas, Fernando P. (PRO) (Retired). —Died Feb. 19, 2011
† Frerkes, James (MRY) (Retired). —Died Sept. 8, 2011
† Friedrich, Ralph J. (Y) (Retired). —Died April 18, 2011
† Friel, James E. (PBL) (Retired). —Died Feb. 12, 2011
† Fuller, Leigh A., *s.j.* (PH) Merion Station, PA Loyola Center & Manresa Hall. —Died May 16, 2011
† Gaffney, Joseph P. (LA) (Retired). —Died April 12, 2011
† Galdon, Peter P. (NEW) (Retired). —Died Nov. 9, 2011
† Gallen, John J., *s.j.* (NY) New York, NY Murray-Weigel Hall. —Died April 17, 2011
† Galvis Rios, Hector F. (NEW) Jersey City, NJ Our Lady of Mount Carmel. —Died Jan. 31, 2011
† Gannon, Joseph (STP) (Retired). —Died July 20, 2011
† Garcia, Isidoro, *c.m.f.* (LA) (Retired). —Died Oct. 27, 2011
† Garcia, Ricardo (BWN) Brownsville, TX Mary, Mother of the Church. —Died Feb. 21, 2011
† Garlick, Thomas B. (WOR) Southborough, MA St. Anne. —Died May 22, 2011
† Garoffolo, Vincent (NEW) (Retired). —Died July 11, 2011
† Gaughan, Paul (RIC) (Retired). —Died April 5, 2011
† Gelineau, Raymond H. (WOR) (Retired). —Died Sept. 12, 2011
† Gelpi, Donald L., *s.j.* (STL) (Retired). —Died May 6, 2011
† Gentile, Emile A., *t.o.r.* (ORL) (Retired). —Died Nov. 10, 2011
† Giblin, William M. (NEW) (Retired). —Died May 13, 2011
† Gilbert, Maurice L. (WOR) Millville, MA St. Augustine. —Died July 22, 2011
† Gilgun, Bernard E. (WOR) (Retired). —Died April 25, 2011
† Gillespie, Robert B. (GR) (Retired). —Died July 30, 2011
† Gillis, Edward F. (BO) (Retired). —Died Nov. 24, 2011
† Gillis, Roger S., *s.j.* (SEA) Seattle, WA Seattle Univ. —Died Dec. 2, 2010
† Gillooly, Patrick J. (WH) (Retired). —Died June 18, 2011
† Gilmartin, Rev. Msgr. John E. (BGP) (Retired). —Died Dec. 3, 2011
† Gira, Stephen, *c.r.* (BEL) Columbia, IL Immaculate Conception of the B.V.M. —Died Dec. 6, 2010
† Girardeau, Robert A. (SAV) Americus, GA St. Mary. —Died March 20, 2011
† Gleba, Rev. Msgr. Peter W. (SY) Syracuse, NY Basilica of the Sacred Heart. —Died March 9, 2011
† Glover, George, *o.s.b.* (RCK) Aurora, IL Annunciation of the Blessed Virgin Mary. —Died Feb. 22, 2011
† Goekler, Thomas F., *m.m.* (FgM) Maryknoll Foreign Mission. —Died Nov. 24, 2010
† Goldian, Edward R., *s.j.* (STL) St. Louis MO St. Mary Magdalen. —Died March 24, 2011
† Golobich, John (DUL) (Retired). —Died June 5, 2011
† Gomez, Jorge (TLS) (Special Assignment). —Died Aug. 21, 2011
† Gondek, Joseph A. (MAR) (Retired). —Died Sept. 13, 2011
† Gonyo, Roland G. (OG) (Absent on Sick Leave). —Died Nov. 16, 2011
† Gonzalez, Rev. Msgr. Antonio (LUB) (Retired). —Died Dec. 9, 2011
† Gore, Robert D. (BEL) (Retired). —Died Jan. 20, 2011
† Gothe, Marcus (P) (Retired). —Died Dec. 20, 2010
† Graham, Joseph B. (PH) Philadelphia, PA St. Jerome. —Died Dec. 28, 2010
† Granahan, Gerry (ORL). —Died Dec. 22, 2010
† Grancini, Steven M., *c.r.s.p.* (SD) San Diego, CA Our Lady of the Rosary. —Died Jan. 2, 2011
† Grant, Frederick A. (BO) (Retired). —Died Nov. 1, 2011
† Grasso, Philip A. (MAD) (Retired). —Died July 18, 2011
† Graziano, George R., *s.j.* (FgM) Jesuit Foreign Mission. —Died March 9, 2011
† Griffin, Noel (LA) (Retired). —Died Sept. 23, 2011
† Grimes, Rev. Msgr. Kevin (COL) (Retired). —Died Oct. 15, 2011
† Guerrero, Jose (ELP) (Retired). —Died Jan. 28, 2011
† Guerrero Fernandez, Rev. Msgr. Andres (PCE) Juana Diaz, PR San Ramon Nonato. —Died March 14, 2011
† Guidry, Raymond, *s.v.d.* (CHI) (Retired). —Died June 16, 2011
† Gunn, Francis X., *o.f.m.* (ALB) Loudonville, NY Siena College. —Died Aug. 24, 2011
† Guntzelman, Louis J. (CIN) (Retired). —Died June 20, 2011
† Guth, Edward L., *s.j.* (NY) New York, NY Murray-Weigel Hall. —Died Jan. 26, 2011
† Guthrie, Paul, *o.f.m.* (PSC) Sybertsville, PA Holy Dormition Friary. —Died May 31, 2010
† Gutierrez, P. Javier, *o.de.m.* (PCE) Ponce, PR La Merced. —Died Aug. 30, 2011
† Hagenbach, George G. (PH) (Retired). —Died Aug. 1, 2011
† Haley, Joseph V., *c.m.* (STL) Perryville, MO St. Mary's of the Barrens. —Died April 28, 2011
† Haley, William J. (BO) (Retired). —Died May 14, 2011
† Halpine, Rev. Msgr. James F. (TLS) (Retired). —Died Nov. 19, 2010
† Hamernick, Joseph M., *s.j.* (BAL) Baltimore, MD Colombiere Jesuit Community. —Died Feb. 9, 2011
† Hammond, Robert (FTW) (Retired). —Died May 8, 2011
† Hanley, Francis X., *c.s.sp.* (PIT) Bethel Park, PA The Spiritan Center. —Died Dec. 23, 2010
† Hanley, Lawrence F. (CHI) (Retired). —Died June 1, 2011
† Hanlon, Rev. Msgr. Andrew J. (PH) (Retired). —Died Feb. 16, 2011
† Hansen, Howard, *o.f.m.conv.* (STP) Prior Lake, MN Franciscan Retreats. —Died April 17, 2011
† Harkins, Bernard Kenneth, *o.p.* (WDC) Washington, DC St. Dominic Priory. —Died Sept. 9, 2011
† Harnish, Lionel A. (GLD) (Retired). —Died June 10, 2011
† Harper, Henry R., *s.s.j.* (BAL) Baltimore, MD St. Peter Claver/St. Pius V. —Died March 29, 2011
† Harrigan, Philip K., *s.j.* (BO) Weston, MA Campion Health Center, Inc. —Died Dec. 30, 2011
† Hartnett, George F. (SY) (Retired). —Died Sept. 14, 2011
† Harvey, John F., *o.s.f.s.* (WIL) (Retired). —Died Dec. 27, 2010
† Haryasz, Francis S. (STA) (Retired). —Died Jan. 9, 2011
† Hasse, James W., *s.j.* (CIN) Cincinnati, OH Claver Jesuit Ministry. —Died June 19, 2011
† Hastings, William J. (CHI) Chicago, IL St. William. —Died Feb. 10, 2011
† Hawkins, Douglas W., *c.s.c.* (FR) (Retired). —Died 2011
† Hayden, Rev. Msgr. Carl T. (GI) (Retired). —Died Oct. 18, 2011
† Heaney, Joseph P. (PRO) (Retired). —Died March 17, 2011
† Heath, Thomas R., *o.p.* (FgM) Order of Preachers Foreign Mission. —Died 2011
† Hebert, Roland G. (WOR) (Retired). —Died April 3, 2011
† Hemler, Edward B. (BAL) (Retired). —Died July 27, 2011
† Hemming, Philip Michael (P) (Retired). —Died July 16, 2011
† Henry, Joseph E., *s.j.* (SCR) Scranton, PA The University of Scranton. —Died May 5, 2011
† Hertweck, Robert, *s.m.* (SJ) Cupertino, CA The Marianist Center. —Died Dec. 10, 2010
† Heuring, Rev. Msgr. Alvan P. (DUB) (Retired). —Died Dec. 8, 2010
† Heyburn, Theodore, *c.ss.r.* (BAL) (Retired). —Died Nov. 12, 2010
† Ho, Matthias (ORG) (Retired). —Died Jan. 25, 2011
† Hoctor, Thomas D. (ROC) (Retired). —Died March 22, 2011
† Hoelscher, James (SAT) (Retired). —Died May 28, 2011
† Hofto, James, *o.m.i.* (LA) (Retired). —Died Dec. 24, 2010
† Hogan, John P. (LC) (Retired). —Died July 19, 2011
† Hogan, Michael C. (ROC) (Retired). —Died Sept. 8, 2011
† Hogan, Richard (STP) (On Duty Outside Archdiocese). —Died June 14, 2011
† Hohman, Andrew, *o.f.m.cap.* (CLV) Cleveland, OH St. Paul Friary. —Died Aug. 28, 2011
† Holden, Edgar, *o.f.m.conv.* (NY) (Retired). —Died Sept. 15, 2011
† Holoman, Rev. Msgr. Thomas L. (LIN) (Retired). —Died March 19, 2011
† Homan, Daniel J., *o.s.b.* (DET) Oxford, MI St. Benedict Monastery. —Died Aug. 9, 2011
† Homann, Frederick A., *s.j.* (PH) Merion Station, PA Loyola Center & Manresa Hall. —Died Aug. 24, 2011
† Horvat, Matthew J. (KCK) (Retired). —Died Nov. 21, 2011
† Horvath, Stephen G. (TR) (Retired). —Died Nov. 2, 2011
† Houck, Peter (ANC) (Retired). —Died Jan. 19, 2011
† Hoy, Daniel J. (PH) (Retired). —Died July 25, 2011
† Hoying, Leo A. (CIN) (Retired). —Died May 22, 2011
† Hromadka, Joseph, *s.o.l.t.* (PT) (Retired). —Died June 4, 2011
† Hunkeler, Edward J. (OM) (Retired). —Died Aug. 12, 2011
† Hunt, George W., *s.j.* (NY) New York, NY Cardinal Spellman Hall. —Died Feb. 25, 2011
† Hyndman, Ernest R. (MOB) Bay Minette, AL St. Agatha Parish. —Died Aug. 2, 2011
† Hynes, Joseph P. (PRO) (Retired). —Died Oct. 7, 2011
† Idranyi, Edmund M. (HPM) (Retired). —Died Aug. 3, 2011
† Illig, A. Mark (BUF). —Died Dec. 21, 2011
† Imhof, James A., *s.m.* (SJ) Cupertino, CA Marianist Center. —Died Oct. 14, 2011
† Isacsson, Joseph Alfred, *o.carm.* (NY) Middletown, NY Our Lady of Mt. Carmel. —Died Sept. 6, 2011
† Jacobs, James T. (GB) (Retired). —Died Feb. 12, 2011
† Jakows, Ronald M. (PH) Philadelphia, PA Annunciation B.V.M. —Died Feb. 2, 2011
† Jarboe, Raymond (BAK) (Retired). —Died May 4, 2011
† Jardiniano, Rolly P. (LA) (Retired). —Died Jan. 30, 2011
† Jastrzebski, Edmund, *c.r.* (CHI) Chicago, IL St. Stanislaus Kostka. —Died May 21, 2011
† Jenkins, J. Michael (SFD). —Died Sept. 21, 2011
† John, Richard T., *o.s.c.* (SCL) Onamia, MN Crosier Priory. —Died Jan. 11, 2011
† Johnson, Rev. Msgr. Charles B. (HRT) (Retired). —Died Sept. 22, 2011
† Johnson, Stephen D. (WOR) Leicester, MA St. Pius X & St. Joseph. —Died Sept. 15, 2011
† Jones, Frank W. (GAL) (Retired). —Died July 29, 2011

† Joynes, Rev. Msgr. Joseph P. (CAM) (Retired). —Died Aug. 6, 2011
† Juras, Callistus, *o.f.m.conv.* (BAL) (Retired). —Died Feb. 15, 2011
† Juya, Filemon (CHR). —Died June 30, 2011
† Kaiser, Joseph W. (RCK) (Retired). —Died July 15, 2011
† Kaminski, Thomas J. (CHI) (Retired). —Died Feb. 12, 2011
† Kamp, Francis J., *s.v.d.* (CHI) (Retired). —Died Aug. 28, 2011
† Kanka, Robert (ROC) (Retired). —Died Oct. 19, 2011
† Kauzlarich, John J. (CHI) (Retired). —Died Sept. 20, 2011
† Kawa, Edward, *s.d.s.* (GRY) Merrillville, IN Salvatorian Fathers (Society of the Divine Savior). —Died June 3, 2011
† Keane, Edward M. (BRK) (Retired). —Died Feb. 4, 2011
† Keane, Thomas F. (BO) (Retired). —Died June 4, 2011
† Keaney, Rev. Msgr. James P. (R) (Retired). —Died Oct. 17, 2011
† Kearney, Thomas L., *o.p.* (CHI) Chicago, IL St. Pius V Priory. —Died Nov. 27, 2010
† Keefer, Hugh, *o.s.b.* (KCK) Atchison, KS St. Benedict's Abbey. —Died June 1, 2011
† Keeley, Patrick J., *c.m.* (STL) Perryville, MO St. Mary's of the Barrens. —Died Jan. 21, 2011
† Keenan, Rev. Msgr. Charles J. (LIN) (Retired). —Died July 9, 2010
† Keenan, Francis T., *s.m.* (RVC) Mineola, NY Provincial Residence and Novitiate. —Died Sept. 20, 2010
† Kegel, William M., *s.j.* (MIL) Wauwatosa, WI Jesuit Community at St. Camillus. —Died Dec. 26, 2010
† Keitz, Bernard Lawrence, *o.p.* (COL) Columbus, OH St. Patrick Rectory. —Died Oct. 16, 2010
† Kelleher, Robert N. (BO) (Retired). —Died Nov. 18, 2011
† Kelley, Edward T. (BO) (Retired). —Died Aug. 10, 2011
† Kelley, Raymond H., *m.m.* (FgM) Maryknoll Foreign Mission. —Died Dec. 22, 2010
† Kelly, Martin J. (MAN) Nashua, NH St. Patrick. —Died June 21, 2011
† Kelly, Rev. Msgr. Martin (NEW) (Retired). —Died Feb. 2, 2011
† Kelly, Maurus, *o.f.m.* (OAK) Oakland, CA Franciscan Friars of California. —Died Dec. 5, 2010
† Kelly, Thomas F. (BRK) (Retired). —Died Jan. 16, 2011
† Kelty, Matthew, *o.c.s.o.* (L) Trappist, KY Abbey of Our Lady of Gethsemani. —Died Feb. 18, 2011
† Kemme, Joseph A., *s.j.* (ALN) Wernersville, PA Jesuit Center. —Died Jan. 26, 2011
† Kemmery, Robert J. (MAN) (Retired). —Died April 21, 2011
† Kempen, Gerald Bernard, *o.praem.* (GB) (Retired). —Died Sept. 17, 2011
† Kennedy, Rev. Msgr. Edward J. (CAM) (Retired). —Died March 13, 2011
† Kennedy, Rev. Msgr. Louis J. (BRK) (Retired). —Died Aug. 13, 2011
† Kennedy, Stanley T., *m.s.* (HRT) Hartford, CT Missionaries of La Salette. —Died Oct. 20, 2011
† Kennelly, Michael F., *s.j.* (NO) (Retired). —Died Jan. 3, 2011
† Kenney, W. Henry, *s.j.* (LEX) Lexington, KY Veterans' Administration Hospital. —Died Oct. 3, 2011
† Kenny, James E. (OM) (Retired). —Died May 21, 2011
† Keppeler, Richard J. (BUF) (Retired). —Died Dec. 26, 2011
† Kern, Rev. Msgr. Joseph R. (IND) (Retired). —Died April 16, 2011
† Kidd, Wayne R. (LC) (Retired). —Died March 16, 2011
† Kiefer, R. David (GB) (Retired). —Died May 21, 2011
† Kilbridge, Robert A., *o.p.* (CHI) Chicago, IL St. Pius V Priory. —Died March 5, 2011
† Killackey, Edward R., *m.m.* (NY) (Retired). —Died April 27, 2011
† Kilmartin, John, *f.d.p.* (BO) East Boston, MA St. Joseph–St. Lazarus. —Died April 18, 2010
† Kimbrough, Conrad (CHL) (Retired). —Died July 5, 2011
† Kimecz, Aloysius J., *o.cist.* (DAL) Irving, TX Cistercian Abbey of Our Lady of Dallas. —Died Dec. 17, 2010
† King, Rev. Msgr. Charles (FWT) Denton, TX Immaculate Conception. —Died June 1, 2011
† King, Rev. Msgr. George L. (B) Orofino, ID St. Theresa's. —Died Nov. 25, 2010
† King, James E. (NTN) (Retired). —Died Nov., 2011
† Kinzer, Gary (ORG). —Died Oct. 5, 2011
† Kirsch, Gregory A. (E) Houtzdale, PA Christ the King. —Died April 28, 2011
† Kirwan, Thomas P. (DET) (Retired). —Died May 30, 2011
† Kissell, Wilbur T. (MOB) Montgomery, AL St. Andrew Kim Taegon. —Died March 14, 2011
† Klein, Bernard (STP) (Retired). —Died May 4, 2011
† Klimas, George H. (SAG) (Retired). —Died Feb. 14, 2011
† Kline, Omer U., *o.s.b.* (GBG) (Retired). —Died Jan. 17, 2011
† Kline, Robert W. (CLV) (Retired). —Died June 24, 2011
† Klink, Delbert D. (MAD) (Retired). —Died Jan. 23, 2011
† Knapp, William L. (SFR) (Retired). —Died March 20, 2011
† Kneip, Paschal N., *o.s.b.* (RIC) Chincoteague Island, VA St. Andrew the Apostle. —Died 2011
† Kobus, John J. (CHI) (On Assignment). —Died Sept. 17, 2011
† Koch, Rev. Msgr. Charles J. (EVN) (Retired). —Died Feb. 12, 2011
† Kolakowski, Marcel, *o.f.m.* (PH) (Retired). —Died April 30, 2010
† Kolinsky, Arthur J., *c.m.* (CHL) Charlotte, NC Our Lady of Guadalupe. —Died Sept. 21, 2011
† Koller, Gerold, *c.pp.s.* (CIN) (Retired). —Died Nov. 18, 2010
† Kopchik, Martin, *m.s.f.s.* (ATL) Snellville, GA St. Oliver Plunkett. —Died 2011
† Koprowski, Mitchell J. (GI) (Retired). —Died Dec. 14, 2010
† Kozminski, Rev. Msgr. Maximilian M. (BUF) (Retired). —Died Dec. 29, 2011
† Krafchak, John S. (SCR) (Retired). —Died April 20, 2011
† Krank, Michael T. (BIS) (Retired). —Died Nov. 28, 2010
† Krapfl, Daniel A. (DUB) (Retired). —Died Sept. 12, 2011
† Krejci, Rev. Msgr. Albert L. (OM) (Retired). —Died Feb. 17, 2011
† Krieg, Peter, *o.f.m.* (OAK) Oakland, CA Franciscan Friars. —Died Dec. 12, 2010
† Krische, Francis (KCK) (Retired). —Died Jan. 12, 2011
† Krudwig, William C. (SPC) (Retired). —Died Dec. 12, 2011
† Kucan, Jerome, *o.f.m.* (CHI) (Retired). —Died 2011
† Kuczynski, Edwin, *o.s.a.* (CHI) Olympia Fields, IL Tolentine Monastery at Tolentine Center. —Died 2011
† Kuenzig, Peter A. (PIT) (Retired). —Died Dec. 4, 2010
† LaCasse, John P. (DET) (Retired). —Died Sept. 29, 2011
† Lacomara, Aelred, *c.p.* (FgM) Passion Foreign Mission. —Died Sept. 14, 2011
† Lafferty, Charles L. (BAL) (Retired). —Died Aug. 17, 2011
† Lafferty, David M. (OKL) Okarche, OK Holy Trinity. —Died Feb. 2, 2011
† LaFrance, Fred P. Valerian, *o.p.* (L) Louisville, KY St. Louis Bertrand Priory. —Died March 6, 2011
† Lafrenz, James (LSC) (Retired). —Died Aug. 24, 2011
† Lakers, John J., *o.f.m.* (SFD) (Retired). —Died Nov. 4, 2011
† Lalic, Paul (BGP) (Retired). —Died July 24, 2011
† Lamitie, James F. (OG) (Retired). —Died Nov. 22, 2010
† Lanz, Mathias (FAR) (Retired). —Died April 15, 2011
† Laplante, Laurent R. (PRT) (Retired). —Died May 1, 2011
† Larkin, Donald L., *s.j.* (BO) Weston, MA Campion Health Center. —Died Jan. 20, 2011
† Larkin, Kirk S. (OKL) Lawton, OK Holy Family. —Died April 29, 2011
† Lavoy, Rev. Msgr. Elwood (LAV) (Retired). —Died April 15, 2011
† Lawlor, Joseph G. (JC) (Retired). —Died March 31, 2011
† Lechiara, Francis J. (PMB) Palm Beach, FL Saint Edward. —Died May 12, 2011
† LeClair, Lawrence J. (HRT) (Retired). —Died Feb. 21, 2011
† Lenihan, Rev. Msgr. Michael (LA) Redondo Beach, CA St. Lawrence Martyr. —Died March 23, 2011
† Lennon, Joseph Luke, *o.p.* (WDC) Washington, DC St. Dominic Priory. —Died March 13, 2011
† Leonard, Clyde A. (BO) (Retired). —Died Oct. 5, 2011
† Leonard, Patrick J. (NEW) (Retired). —Died Feb. 7, 2011
† Lesniak, Marian J. (LAN) (Retired). —Died Oct. 9, 2011
† Lester, William F., *s.j.* (SJ) Los Gatos, CA Sacred Heart Jesuit Center. —Died Oct. 17, 2010
† LeThiez, Alphonse D. (PRO) (Retired). —Died Nov. 17, 2011
† LeTure, Theodore J. (RVC) (Retired). —Died July 3, 2011
† Levesque, Rev. Msgr. Edmond R. (FR) (Retired). —Died June 5, 2011
† Lex, Henry V. (BUF) (Retired). —Died May 23, 2011
† Liebert, William, *s.v.d.* (CHI) (Retired). —Died May 5, 2011
† Lindsay, Robert E., *s.j.* (BO) Weston, MA Campion Health Center, Inc. —Died Oct. 9, 2011
† Linehan, Brian D., *o.f.m.* (PAT) Ringwood, NJ Holy Name Friary. —Died April 19, 2011
† Linehan, Cornelius (P) (Retired). —Died Feb. 26, 2011
† Linnemann, Eugene C. (BEL) (Retired). —Died March 1, 2011
† Lischaa, Rev. Msgr. Sharbel (SAM) (Retired). —Died Aug. 2, 2011
† Loftus, Joseph J. (ARL) (Retired). —Died April 2, 2011
† Lombo, German, *o.s.a.* (MGZ) Aguada, PR St. Francis of Assisi. —Died 2011
† Lopez, Rev. Msgr. Joseph A. (SAT) San Antonio, TX Assumption Seminary. —Died May 28, 2011
† Loredo, Miguel A., *o.f.m.* (SP) St. Petersburg, FL St. Anthony Friary. —Died Sept. 10, 2011
† Losito, Rev. Msgr. Felix A. (ALN) Reading, PA Holy Rosary. —Died Nov. 3, 2011
† Lott, Roger R.S., *o.s.b.* (BIR) (Retired). —Died May 22, 2011
† Luebke, Martial, *o.f.m.* (LA) (Retired). —Died May 17, 2011
† Luger, Paul P., *s.j.* (SPK) (Retired). —Died Jan. 19, 2011
† Lunnon, William (DET) (Special Assignment). —Died May 28, 2011
† Lutostanski, Anthony (BUF) (Retired). —Died March 13, 2011
† Lynam, Gerald J. (HEL) (Retired). —Died Dec. 15, 2010
† Lynch, John A. (ROC) (Retired). —Died June 4, 2011
† Lynch, John J., *s.j.* (MIL) Wauwatosa, WI Jesuit Community at St. Camillus. —Died April 14, 2011
† Lynch, Kevin A., *m.m.* (FgM) Maryknoll Foreign Mission. —Died Nov. 14, 2010
† Lynch, Patrick J. (ALB) (Retired). —Died May 25, 2011
† Lynch, Robert B. (NOR) (Retired). —Died Aug. 6, 2011
† Lynch, T. Patrick, *s.j.* (NY) New York, NY Murray–Weigel Hall. —Died Feb. 28, 2011
† Lyons, James D. (BO) (Retired). —Died May 29, 2011
† Mack, Rev. Msgr. Robert A. (BUF) (Retired). —Died Dec. 1, 2011
† MacPherson, Walter E. (BEL) (Retired). —Died July 16, 2011
† Madden, Henry L., *o.f.m.* (PAT) Ringwood, NJ Holy Name Friary. —Died May 25, 2011
† Madden, Lawrence J., *s.j.* (WDC) Washington, DC Jesuit Community at Georgetown University. —Died May 29, 2011
† Madigan, John Alphonsus, *o.p.* (PRO) Providence, RI St. Thomas Aquinas Priory, Providence College. —Died July 28, 2011
† Maher, Raymond (SJ) (Retired). —Died June 11, 2011
† Mahoney, Gordon (JOL) (Retired). —Died Feb. 3, 2011
† Mahoney, John, *o.m.i.* (SAT) San Antonio, TX Oblate Madonna Residence. —Died Aug. 7, 2011
† Mallahan, James (SEA) (Retired). —Died July 29, 2011
† Maloney, Malcolm, *o.f.m.cap.* (DET) Detroit, MI St. Bonaventure Monastery. —Died July 23, 2011
† Manning, Martin B. (DAV) (Retired). —Died May 24, 2011
† Manternach, Rev. Msgr. Albert V. (DUB) (Retired). —Died Jan. 3, 2011
† Maquire, Francis X., *c.m.* (PH) Philadelphia, PA St. Vincent's Seminary. —Died Sept. 26, 2011
† Maranto, Charles L., *c.s.v.* (CHI) (Retired). —Died March 18, 2011
† Marcotte, Wayne E. (MAR) (Retired). —Died April 30, 2011
† Mariano, John M. (BRK) (Retired). —Died Feb. 28, 2011
† Maring, William J., *s.j.* (SJ) Los Gatos, CA Sacred Heart Jesuit Center. —Died June 18, 2011
† Marino, Edward J., *c.s.* (PRO) (Retired). —Died 2011
† Marino, Vincente Fernandez (SJN). —Died Aug. 13, 2011
† Marth, Rev. Msgr. Loydell J. (FRS) (Retired). —Died April 5, 2011
† Martin, Francis T. (LAN) (Retired). —Died Sept. 23, 2011
† Martin, John F., *s.j.* (WDC) Washington, DC Jesuit Community at Georgetown University. —Died Feb. 13, 2011
† Martin, William, *o.m.i.* (BO) Tewksbury, MA Immaculate Heart of Mary Residence. —Died May 9, 2011
† Martinka, Stanley V. (NU) (Retired). —Died March 12, 2011
† Masiar, Paul E. (ALN) (Retired). —Died July 3, 2011
† Massicotte, Jean Jacques Bernard, *o.s.b.* (MRY) Big Sur, CA New Camaldoli Hermitage. —Died May 25, 2011
† Matash, Rev. Msgr. Edward M. (NEW) (Retired). —Died Feb. 15, 2011

† Maternoski, Robert (JOL) (Retired). —Died April 15, 2011
† Matteo, Rev. Msgr. James P. (PH) (Retired). —Died April 1, 2011
† McAlpin, Leonard J. (GBG) (Retired). —Died May 29, 2011
† McAskill, Kenneth F. (BO) (Retired). —Died Nov. 9, 2011
† McCaffrey, Gerald T., *o.f.m.* (PAT) Butler, NJ St. Anthony Friary. —Died Jan. 31, 2011
† McCaffrey, Patrick J. (WDC) (Retired). —Died Aug. 20, 2011
† McCasland, Howard (OG) Churubusco, NY Immaculate Heart of Mary. —Died Dec. 28, 2010
† McCauley, Daniel Thomas, *o.c.d.* (MIL) (Retired). —Died 2011
† McCauley, Walter C., *s.j.* (STL) (Retired). —Died April 28, 2011
† McCawley, William J. (SCR). —Died Aug. 3, 2011
† McCloskey, Daniel J. (WIL) (Retired). —Died Oct. 13, 2011
† McClure, John A. (TOL) (Retired). —Died June 29, 2011
† McCormley, Hugh J. (PIT) (Retired). —Died Sept. 15, 2010
† McCourt, Rev. Msgr. Robert R. (BRK) (Retired). —Died June 21, 2011
† McCune, James L. (BO) (Retired). —Died Dec. 7, 2011
† McDonald, John J., *s.j.* (NY) New York, NY Murray–Weigel Hall. —Died Sept. 16, 2011
† McDonnell, Francis P. (HRT) (Retired). —Died Nov. 30, 2011
† McFarland, Rev. Msgr. Edward J. (COL) (Retired). —Died Jan. 8, 2011
† McGarry, Thomas M. (NY) (Retired). —Died March 23, 2011
† McGee, Leo J. (PH) (Retired). —Died Oct. 15, 2111
† McGinnis, James J. (PH) (Retired). —Died Oct. 26, 2010
† McGoldrick, William J. (DET) (Retired). —Died Jan. 8, 2011
† McGovern, Donan, *o.f.m.* (BO) Boston, MA St. Anthony Shrine. —Died Oct. 12, 2010
† McGovern, John J., *m.m.* (FgM) Maryknoll Foreign Mission. —Died April 19, 2011
† McGovern, William W. (WOR) (Retired). —Died April 5, 2011
† McGuinness, Gerard J. (SB) (Retired). —Died Dec. 21, 2011
† McGuire, Anthony, *o.f.m.* (PAT) Ringwood, NJ Holy Name Friary. —Died Nov. 6, 2010
† McGuire, John C. (NY) (Retired). —Died March 23, 2011
† McHenry, John, *s.v.d.* (CHI) (Retired). —Died Nov. 11, 2011
† McHugh, Patrick Joseph (LA) (Retired). —Died July 27, 2011
† McHugh, Thomas J. (CHI) (Retired). —Died May 19, 2011
† McInnes, Val, *o.p.* (NO) (Retired). —Died Nov. 22, 2011
† McLaughlin, Anthony J. (PAT) (Unassigned). —Died Oct. 16, 2011
† McLaughlin, William J. (TR) Asbury Park, NJ Holy Spirit & St. Peter Claver. —Died Oct. 19, 2011
† McLeod, David (PAT) (Retired). —Died April 11, 2011
† McMahon, Aloysius J. (OM) (Retired). —Died May 17, 2011
† McMahon, Bernard (NY) (Retired). —Died Oct. 9, 2011
† McMahon, John Anthony, *o.p.* (WDC) Washington, DC Dominican House of Studies. —Died Jan. 27, 2011
† McNichol, Daniel (HON) (Retired). —Died July 29, 2011
† McNicholas, Stephen (ORL). —Died June 5, 2011
† McPartland, Aloysius M., *m.s.* (VEN) (Retired). —Died Jan. 1, 2011
† McShane, Patrick E. (CLV) (Retired). —Died Jan. 11, 2011
† Meehan, Rev. Msgr. Francis X. (PH) (Retired). —Died July 22, 2011
† Meik, Thomas J., *c.m.* (STL) Perryville, MO St. Mary's of the Barrens. —Died Dec. 2, 2010
† Meister, Rev. Msgr. Andrew H. (OM) (Retired). —Died April 25, 2011
† Meskill, Patrick A. (LA) (Retired). —Died Aug. 23, 2011
† Messick, Severin, *o.s.b.* (IND) Greenfield, IN St. Michael. —Died Sept. 28, 2011
† Messner, Thomas, *o.f.m.* (LA) Santa Barbara, CA Franciscan Friary. —Died Dec. 10, 2010
† Metzger, Edward C., *o.f.m.* (SP) St. Petersburg, FL St. Anthony Friary. —Died July 25, 2011
† Meyer, Rev. Msgr. Louis F. (STL) (Retired). —Died May 14, 2011
† Meznar, Robert P. (DEN) (Retired). —Died July 30, 2011
† Michalik, Bernard J., *o.f.m.conv.* (MRY) (Retired). —Died July 21, 2011
† Middendorf, Cyril, *s.m.* (CIN) Dayton, OH Mercy Siena Woods Nursing Care. —Died Feb. 19, 2011
† Middlecamp, Eric, *s.d.s.* (MIL) (Retired). —Died March 6, 2011
† Mikula, John Joseph, *o.f.m.conv.* (DET) Dearborn Heights, MI All Saints Friary. —Died March 26, 2011
† Miller, Leo, *o.m.i.* (BEL) (Retired). —Died Nov. 5, 2011
† Miller, Maurice R. (LFT) (Retired). —Died June 1, 2011
† Miller, Randall J. (LAN) Jackson, MI St. John the Evangelist. —Died March 28, 2011
† Miodowski, Leonard A. (NEW) (Retired). —Died Aug. 2, 2011
† Mitchell, William J. (PHX). —Died Dec. 23, 2010
† Mittelstadt, John, *o.f.m.* (GLP) Tohatchi, NM St. Mary. —Died March 28, 2011
† Molloy, John J., *c.p.m.* (OWN) Auburn, KY Fathers of Mercy. —Died July 15, 2011
† Molodowitz, Augustine (PHU) (Retired). —Died June 15, 2011
† Moloney, Rev. Msgr. Alphonsus (SD) (Retired). —Died June 17, 2011
† Monaghan, Joseph F., *s.j.* (PH) Merion Station, PA Loyola Center & Manresa Hall. —Died Jan. 29, 2011
† Moore, Anthony F., *o.f.m.* (NY) Yulan, NY St. Anthony of Padua. —Died Nov. 23, 2010
† Moorman, Raymond J. (STP) (Retired). —Died July 17, 2011
† Morales, Gabriel Camilo, *m.j.* (GAL) Houston, TX St. Stephen. —Died June 12, 2011
† Morales, Raul (PHX) (Retired). —Died Dec. 4, 2010
† Morales Santana, Juan Bautista (MGZ) Moca, PR Our Lady of Monserrate. —Died 2011
† Morbeck, George H. (SPK) Republic, WA Immaculate Conception; Curlew, WA St. Patrick. —Died Nov. 3, 2011
† Morgan, James F., *s.j.* (BO) Weston, MA Campion Health Center. —Died Feb. 7, 2011
† Morgan, John A. (ROC) (Retired). —Died Sept. 5, 2011
† Morgan, Thomas B. (BO) (Retired). —Died May 6, 2011
† Morris, Kenneth R., *c.s.v.* (CHI) (Retired). —Died Nov. 12, 2010
† Mounteer, Louis A., *s.j.* (NY) New York, NY Murray–Weigel Hall. —Died Nov. 25, 2010
† Moynihan, Eugene R., *s.s.j.* (BAL) (Retired). —Died Feb. 17, 2011
† Mruk, Walter, *o.f.m.conv.* (SPR) (Retired). —Died Aug. 4, 2011
† Mullally, Gerald F. (SCR) Milford, PA St. Patrick. —Died Dec. 14, 2011
† Mullen, Rev. Msgr. William J. (HRT) (Retired). —Died Feb. 2, 2011
† Mulloy, Matthew (NY) (Retired). —Died April 22, 2011
† Mulvey, John J. (NEW) (Retired). —Died Sept. 8, 2011
† Murphy, Charles J. (BO) (Retired). —Died June 11, 2011
† Murphy, Daniel G. (SY) (Retired). —Died Oct. 13, 2011
† Murphy, Harry J. (GBG) (Retired). —Died May 30, 2011
† Murphy, James E. (STL) (Retired). —Died Nov. 29, 2010
† Murphy, James J. (PH) (Retired). —Died March 7, 2011
† Murphy, Ralph, *s.d.b.* (LA) (Retired). —Died July 14, 2011
† Murphy, Thomas R. (PIT) (Retired). —Died Sept. 19, 2010
† Murphy, William T. (RVC) (Retired). —Died June 7, 2011
† Murray, Bernard, *o.c.s.o.* (FgM) Cistercian Order of the Strict Observance Foreign Mission. —Died Sept. 23, 2011
† Musonda, Francis M., *s.s.* (BAL) Baltimore, MD Society of St. Sulpice. —Died Sept., 2010
† Myers, Regis F. (ALT) (Retired). —Died Jan. 13, 2011
† Myers, Robert, *s.v.d.* (CHI) (Retired). —Died Aug. 29, 2011
† Myszel, George G. (MIL) (Retired). —Died Sept. 14, 2011
† Nardone, Richard M. (NEW) (Retired). —Died March 27, 2011
† Navin, Rev. Msgr. Cyril (LA) Encino, CA St. Cyril. —Died June 24, 2011
† Nee, Robert F., *o.f.m.* (PAT) Ringwood, NJ Holy Name Friary. —Died Jan. 19, 2011
† Nelan, Francis, *m.s.c.* (SAT) San Antonio, TX Padua Place. —Died May 2, 2011
† Neuman, Eugene C. (MIL) (Retired). —Died Aug. 19, 2011
† Nicholson, Francis J., *s.j.* (BO) Weston, MA Campion Health Center. —Died Aug. 26, 2011
† Niemier, Roch, *o.f.m.* (MIL) Franklin, WI Provincial Offices of the Franciscan Friars. —Died Dec. 31, 2010
† Noble, David H. (GAL) Houston, TX Catholic Chaplain Corps. —Died Feb. 24, 2011
† Nolan, William J. (TR) (Retired). —Died Dec. 18, 2010
† Norman, Richard W., *s.j.* (ALN) Wernersville, PA Jesuit Center. —Died Sept. 12, 2011
† Novotny, Allen P., *s.j.* (WDC) Washington, DC Jesuit Community of St. Aloysius Gonzaga. —Died Oct. 27, 2010
† Nugent, Rev. Msgr. Arthur W. (PH) (Retired). —Died Feb. 10, 2011
† O'Brien, Christian Thomas, *o.praem.* (GB) (Retired). —Died March 28, 2011
† O'Brien, Donald V., *s.j.* (NY) New York, NY Murray–Weigel Hall. —Died June 14, 2011
† O'Brien, Edward C., *s.j.* (STL) St. Louis, MO Retreat House. —Died March 1, 2011
† O'Brien, George L. (WOR) (Retired). —Died Feb. 15, 2011
† O'Brien, John E. (CHI) (Retired). —Died July 27, 2011
† O'Brien, Rev. Msgr. Martin F. (NEW) (Retired). —Died Oct. 26, 2011
† O'Brien, Richard J., *c.m.* (STL) Perryville, MO St. Mary's of the Barrens. —Died Feb. 15, 2011
† O'Connor, Donald (JOL) (Retired). —Died Nov. 15, 2011
† O'Connor, Francis J. (MAN) (Retired). —Died Dec. 1, 2010
† O'Day, Michael (SB) (Retired). —Died March 11, 2011
† O'Donnell, Rev. Msgr. Edward C. (OM) (Retired). —Died Jan. 30, 2011
† O'Donnell, Harold F.X., *s.j.* (NY) New York, NY Murray–Weigel Hall. —Died Aug. 20, 2011
† O'Halloran, Richard (MRY) (Retired). —Died Nov. 6, 2011
† O'Hara, Martin (SFD) (Retired). —Died May 8, 2011
† O'Hogan, Patrick (SEA) Forks, WA St. Anne. —Died Aug. 29, 2011
† O'Keefe, Martin D., *s.j.* (STL) St. Louis, MO Jesuit Community Corporation at Saint Louis University–Jesuit Hall. —Died Dec. 12, 2010
† O'Leary, Harold V., *c.s.b.* (GAL) Houston, TX Residence of the Basilian Fathers of the University of St. Thomas. —Died April 3, 2011
† O'Leary, Patrick D. (Y) (Retired). —Died Dec. 26, 2010
† O'Malley, John A. (BWN) (Retired). —Died Feb. 21, 2011
† O'Malley, Joseph M. (DEN) (Retired). —Died Feb. 12, 2011
† O'Neil, Patrick (SEA) (Retired). —Died Aug. 22, 2011
† O'Neill, Joseph J., *m.m.* (NY) (Retired). —Died April 22, 2011
† O'Neill, Rev. Msgr. Kevin P. (SCR) (Retired). —Died May 17, 2011
† O'Neill, Rev. Msgr. Patrick J. (SAC) (Retired). —Died Oct. 4, 2011
† O'Rourke, Edmund F., *o.s.f.s.* (WIL) (Retired). —Died April 18, 2011
† O'Shaughnessy, Richard, *s.m.* (SAT) San Antonio, TX Marianist Residence. —Died June 29, 2011
† O'Shea, Joseph (SEA) (Retired). —Died Jan. 28, 2011
† O'Sullivan, Timothy J. (SR). —Died March 5, 2011
† O'Toole, Thomas (OKL) Ardmore, OK St. Mary. —Died Jan. 12, 2011
† Obee, Gregory, *o.s.b.* (RCK) (Retired). —Died May 14, 2011
† Oehrlein, Rev. Msgr. Felix G. (MAD) Wisconsin Dells, WI St. Cecilia. —Died Nov. 25, 2011
† Okolie, Maxwell (LKC) Elton, LA St. Joseph's. —Died Oct. 3, 2011
† Okoye, Joseph (KCK). —Died April 7, 2011
† Oliver, Rev. Msgr. John A. (TUC) (Retired–Administrative Leave). —Died 2011
† Olivo, Stephen G., *s.j.* (SJ) Los Gatos, CA Sacred Heart Jesuit Center. —Died Dec. 5, 2010
† Opat, Kenneth M., *o.s.c.* (SCL) Onamia, MN Crosier Priory. —Died April 6, 2011
† Oppitz, Joseph W., *c.ss.r.* (ALB) Saratoga Springs, NY St. John Neumann Residence. —Died Oct. 6, 2011
† Orlando, Gerard A., *c.p.* (BRK) (Retired). —Died Feb. 17, 2011
† Orru, Bruno, *s.x.* (FgM) Xaverian Missionary Fathers Foreign Mission. —Died March 31, 2011
† Ortiz, Benedicto (BWN) (Retired). —Died May 14, 2011
† Ortmeier, Richard J. (SFS) (Retired). —Died June 26, 2011
† Ouellet, Maurice F., *s.s.e.* (MOB) (Retired). —Died July 25, 2011
† Paddock, Richard W. (RCK) (Retired). —Died July 20, 2011
† Parsons, Harry E. (PIT) (Retired). —Died May 9, 2011

† Parsons, Samuel, *o.p.* (OAK) Oakland, CA Siena House. —Died Oct. 4, 2011
† Partensky, Leonard J. (DET) (Retired). —Died April 14, 2011
† Pashak, Lawrence M. (SAG) Freeland, MI St. Agnes. —Died Dec. 11, 2010
† Pastore, Peter J. (CAM) (Retired). —Died April 16, 2011
† Paulits, Walter J. (BAL) (Retired). —Died June 4, 2011
† Paulshock, Emil (PSC) (Retired). —Died Feb. 15, 2011
† Payne, Arthur Joseph, *o.p.* (WDC) Washington, DC Dominican House of Studies. —Died Feb. 21, 2011
† Peacock, Francis A. (PHX). —Died July 16, 2010
† Peacock, Thomas E., *s.j.* (PH) Merion Station, PA Loyola Center & Manresa Hall. —Died Jan. 12, 2011
† Pearce, John S., *c.m.* (PH) Philadelphia, PA St. Vincent's Seminary. —Died Feb. 1, 2011
† Pekar, Athanasius B., *o.s.b.m.* (RVC) Glen Cove, NY St. Josaphat Monastery. —Died Sept. 28, 2011
† Pellegrino, Rev. Msgr. Francis B. (SLC) (Retired). —Died June 11, 2011
† Peluso, Michael J. (NY) Staten Island, NY Our Lady of Pity. —Died Sept. 27, 2011
† Pentis, William, *c.o.* (CHR) Rock Hill, SC Oratory of St. Philip Neri. —Died June 25, 2011
† Peplansky, Joseph, *c.m.f.* (CHI) Oak Park, IL Claretian Missionaries USA Eastern Province. —Died 2011
† Pesanka, Nicholas A. (PIT) (Health Leave of Absence). —Died Jan. 21, 2011
† Peterson, Francis (HON) (Retired). —Died April 14, 2011
† Petri, John C. (TR) (Retired). —Died June 10, 2011
† Pettit, Joseph (GR) (Retired). —Died July 22, 2011
† Pfaff, Joseph A. (BRK) Glendale, NY Sacred Heart. —Died May 12, 2011
† Phelan, Nicholas (SAC) (Retired). —Died Sept. 24, 2011
† Phelan, Walter M. (GI) (Retired). —Died Dec. 8, 2010
† Phillips, Rev. Msgr. George M. (OG) (Retired). —Died Oct. 28, 2011
† Pickett, Robert T. (TLS) (Retired). —Died Feb. 7, 2011
† Pied, Wilfrid L. (BO) (Retired). —Died May 29, 2011
† Pieper, Herbert, *s.m.* (SAT) San Antonio, TX Marianist Residence. —Died April 10, 2011
† Piermarini, Rev. Msgr. Louis R. (WOR) Oxford, MA St. Roch. —Died June 26, 2011
† Pierse, Rev. Msgr. James J. (ORG) Seal Beach, CA Holy Family. —Died Feb. 22, 2011
† Pilatowski, Eugene L. (NOR) (Retired). —Died June 27, 2011
† Plante, Georges J. (PRT) (Retired). —Died Aug. 9, 2011
† Plastino, James L. (MRY) (Retired). —Died July 20, 2011
† Plourde, Carroll W., *s.s.e.* (MOB) Selma, AL Our Lady Queen of Peace. —Died March 8, 2011
† Polich, James C. (DM) Des Moines, IA St. Augustin Church. —Died Nov. 20, 2011
† Pollock, Rev. Msgr. Robert C. (SLC) (Retired). —Died Dec. 2, 2010
† Ponce, Francisco (NEW) Jersey City, NJ St. Joseph. —Died June 28, 2011
† Popesh, Rev. Msgr. Bernard (DUL) (Retired). —Died Feb. 26, 2011
† Poppa, Chester, *o.f.m.cap.* (GF) Broadus, MT St. David. —Died June 14, 2011
† Powers, Isaias, *c.p.* (BRK) (Retired). —Died Oct. 26, 2011
† Prass, Charles, *o.m.i.* (BEL) (Retired). —Died July 14, 2011
† Pray, Joseph N. (BUR) (Retired). —Died June 15, 2011
† Pritzl, Kurt John, *o.p.* (COL) Columbus, OH St. Patrick Rectory. —Died July 25, 2011
† Proulx, Raymond G. (HRT). —Died May 2, 2011
† Pucci, Augusto M., *c.r.s.p.* (FgM) Clerics Regular of St. Paul Foreign Mission. —Died Dec. 11, 2010
† Puisis, John C., *c.s.v.* (CHI) (Retired). —Died Feb. 8, 2011
† Purcell, Richard, *o.f.m.* (SFR) San Francisco, CA St. Boniface. —Died Aug. 4, 2011
† Purtell, Thomas W. (DUB) (Retired). —Died Aug. 19, 2011
† Quartana, Donald F. (MIL) (Retired). —Died Sept. 25, 2011
† Quattropane, Joseph, *o.f.m.cap.* (SB) Colton, CA Immaculate Conception. —Died March 14, 2011
† Quetchenbach, Raymond, *s.v.d.* (CHI) (Retired). —Died Nov. 19, 2011
† Quevedo, Alfredo S., *s.j.* (NY) New York, NY Murray–Weigel Hall. —Died Dec. 10, 2010
† Quinlan, John J. (PAT) Swartswood, NJ Our Lady of Mt. Carmel. —Died Jan. 22, 2011
† Quinn, Donald A. (IND) Greenwood IN Our Lady Of The Greenwood Catholic Church, Inc. —Died Nov. 13, 2011
† Rager, Patrick F. (PIT) (Health Leave of Absence). —Died July 20, 2010
† Randall, John F. (PRO) (Retired). —Died June 14, 2011
† Ratermann, George H., *m.m.* (NY) (Retired). —Died Aug. 23, 2011
† Rau, Rev. Msgr. Donald E. (STL) (Retired). —Died July 14, 2011
† Reasbeck, Rev. Msgr. David E. (STU) (Retired). —Died Oct. 6, 2011
† Redden, Gerald Donald (PMB) Fort Pierce, FL San Juan Diego Pastoral Center. —Died May 20, 2011
† Regan, Francis A. (BO) (Retired). —Died Oct. 23, 2011
† Rehling, Paul L. (CIN) (Retired). —Died Feb. 7, 2011
† Reid, George B. (WDC) (Retired). —Died May 9, 2011
† Reilly, F. Joseph (STL) River aux Vases, MO Sts. Philip & James. —Died Sept. 22, 2011
† Reinhardt, Leo S. (BEL) (Retired). —Died June 3, 2011
† Reisch, Rev. Msgr. Milton L. (NO) (Retired). —Died July 18, 2011
† Reiser, Bernard A. (STP) (Retired). —Died Dec. 27, 2011
† Reisz, Leonard (OWN) (Retired). —Died Feb. 17, 2011
† Repole, Charles, *o.f.m.cap.* (BRK) Queens Village, NY Queen of Peace Residence. —Died Oct. 18, 2011
† Rezac, Robert, *i.m.c.* (BUF) Williamsville, NY Consolata Fathers. —Died Dec. 19, 2011
† Rhodes, Joseph (OWN) (Retired). —Died Dec. 6, 2010
† Riccomini, Rev. Msgr. Dino (FRS) (Retired). —Died Sept. 1, 2011
† Richardson, John M., *o.f.m.* (SP) St. Petersburg, FL St. Anthony Friary. —Died Nov. 25, 2010
† Ridella, Joseph (HPM) (Retired). —Died Feb. 26, 2011
† Riesberg, Leo L. (SC) (Retired). —Died March 18, 2011
† Riley, Patrick (SCL) (Retired). —Died Dec. 14, 2010
† Ringholz, Benedict E. (TOL) (Retired). —Died April 17, 2011
† Rischmann, Edward J. (NEW) (Retired). —Died June 7, 2011
† Ritter, Nicholas J. (LAN) (Retired). —Died April 24, 2011
† Robbins, Hugh W., *c.s.v.* (CHI) (Retired). —Died May 23, 2011
† Roetzer, Russell G. (MIL) (Retired). —Died April 28, 2011
† Rogers, Gary P. (BRK) Brooklyn, NY St. Thomas Aquinas. —Died July 19, 2011
† Rokos, Richard V. (PRT) (Retired). —Died March 22, 2011
† Ronan, Eugene T., *m.s.f.* (SAT) New Braunfels, TX Our Lady of Perpetual Help. —Died March 28, 2011
† Rooney, Rev. Msgr. Thaddeus (RVC) (Retired). —Died July 25, 2011
† Rosato, Philip J., *s.j.* (WDC) North Bethesda, MD Georgetown Preparatory School. —Died July 20, 2011
† Roth, Rev. Msgr. Joseph R. (CHR). —Died May 15, 2011
† Rothbauer, Francis (STU) (Retired). —Died Feb. 7, 2011
† Rozycki, George (SP) Zephyrhills, FL St. Joseph. —Died June 27, 2011
† Ruffolo, George, *c.m.f.* (CHI) Oak Park Claretian Missionaries USA Eastern Province. —Died 2011
† Ruggeri, Pasquale, *f.d.p.* (NY) New York, NY St. Ann. —Died Aug. 31, 2010
† Russi, Jack, *s.m.* (SJ) Cupertino, CA The Bordeaux House. —Died June 20, 2011
† Ruszel, Humphrey, *c.r.* (SB) (Retired). —Died April 9, 2011
† Ryan, Rev. Msgr. Gerald E. (DM) (Retired). —Died March 20, 2011
† Ryan, John Chrysostom, *c.p.* (BRK) (Retired). —Died 2011
† Ryan, Kenan, *s.t.* (JKS) Philadelphia, MS Holy Cross. —Died Aug. 12, 2011
† Safko, Steven (PSC) Phillipsburg, NJ SS. Peter and Paul. —Died Dec. 30, 2011
† Sahuc, Allan Fredrick, *c.m.f.* (CHI) Oak Park Claretian Missionaries USA Eastern Province. —Died 2011
† Saladna, George E. (PIT) Springdale, PA Saint Alphonsus. —Died April 17, 2011
† Sanchez, Angel Luis Figueroa (SJN). —Died Jan. 11, 2011
† Sanchez, Stephen A. (SFE) Albuquerque, NM Our Lady of Fatima. —Died April 5, 2011
† Sans, Theodore R. (L) (Retired). —Died April 21, 2011
† Santa Barbara, Robert L. (MET) New Brunswick, NJ St. Mary of Mt. Virgin. —Died Nov. 30, 2011
† Sapeta, Joseph S. (NEW) (Retired). —Died Jan. 24, 2011
† Saporito, Rev. Msgr. Cosmo G. (BRK) (Retired). —Died March 11, 2011
† Saporito, Louis R., *s.s.j.* (BAL) (Retired). —Died Dec. 21, 2010
† Sarjeant, Francis X., *s.j.* (BO) Weston, MA Campion Health Center, Inc. —Died Dec. 19, 2011
† Savage, Thomas J. (MAN) (Retired). —Died April 28, 2011
† Scheets, Francis Kelly, *o.s.c.* (PHX) Phoenix, AZ Crosier Community of Phoenix. —Died Aug. 12, 2011
† Schendt, Richard L. (CHI). —Died 2011
† Scherer, Donald R. (NEW) (Retired). —Died Dec. 3, 2010
† Schmit, Fred, *s.d.s.* (NSH) (Retired). —Died July 3, 2011
† Schmit, Rev. Msgr. Ralph R. (MIL) (Retired). —Died Nov. 10, 2011
† Schmuhl, Lawrence R., *s.m.* (ATL) (Retired). —Died Aug. 22, 2011
† Schoffelmeer, Arnold L. (SPK) (Retired). —Died March 26, 2011
† Schreck, Paul C. (BUF) (Retired). —Died Nov. 10, 2011
† Schulz, Rev. Msgr. Donald C. (COL) (Retired). —Died May 28, 2011
† Schuster, Charles G., *c.m.* (FgM) Vincentian Foreign Mission. —Died July 30, 2011
† Schuster, Rev. Msgr. Wilfred J. (MAD) (Retired). —Died March 12, 2011
† Schutter, Thomas (JOL) (Retired). —Died April 2, 2011
† Schweitzer, Robert J. (PIT) New Castle, PA Saint Joseph the Worker. —Died Aug. 25, 2010
† Scopa, Joseph, *c.s.* (PRO) (Retired). —Died May 27, 2011
† Scrincosky, Rev. Msgr. Peter (STF) (Retired). —Died Jan. 11, 2011
† Shanley, Charles M., *c.m.* (PH) Philadelphia, PA St. Vincent's Seminary. —Died Sept. 22, 2011
† Sharkey, Owen, *c.p.* (BRK) (Retired). —Died March 31, 2011
† Sharon, Norbert, *s.t.* (WDC) Adelphi, MD Father Judge Missionary Cenacle. —Died Jan. 11, 2011
† Shaum, David W. (BAL) (Retired). —Died Oct. 6, 2011
† Shaw, Charles E. (HRT) (Retired). —Died Nov. 18, 2011
† Shea, Lewis M., *o.p.* (FgM) Order of Preachers Foreign Mission. —Died 2011
† Shea, Thomas (PEO) Bloomington, IL St. Patrick Church of Merna. —Died 2011
† Sheehan, Daniel J. (BO) (Retired). —Died July 2, 2011
† Sheehan, Rev. Msgr. James M. (NEW) Newark, NJ Cathedral Basilica of the Sacred Heart. —Died Aug. 28, 2011
† Sheridan, Matthew W. (BRK) (Retired). —Died March 7, 2011
† Sheridan, Peter C., *o.f.m.* (PAT) Ringwood, NJ Holy Name Friary. —Died Nov. 3, 2010
† Sherry, Brendan (AMA) (Retired). —Died March 30, 2011
† Sherry, Bryan W. (TUC) (Retired). —Died 2011
† Shiroda, Donald L. (MAR) (Retired). —Died March 16, 2011
† Shore, Zachary J. (SFR) (Retired). —Died July 23, 2011
† Short, Redemptus, *o.c.d.* (MIL) (Retired). —Died 2011
† Siani, Angelo, *o.m.i.* (FgM) Oblates of Mary Immaculate Foreign Mission. —Died July 8, 2011
† Sierra, John, *s.f.* (WDC) (Retired). —Died April 8, 2011
† Simms, Robert A., *s.j.* (STL) St. Louis, MO Jesuit Community Corporation at Saint Louis University–Jesuit Hall. —Died June 25, 2011
† Slaven, Rev. Msgr. Frederick (Y) (Retired). —Died March 25, 2011
† Smith, Rev. Msgr. Alfred D. (TR) (Retired). —Died Sept. 12, 2011
† Smith, David L., *c.s.sp.* (PIT) Pittsburgh, PA Duquesne University of the Holy Ghost. —Died July 21, 2011
† Smith, Donald R. (SC) (Retired). —Died Feb. 22, 2011
† Smith, Francis H. (L) (Retired). —Died Jan. 27, 2012
† Smith, William P., *o.m.i.* (BO) Tewksbury, MA Immaculate Heart of Mary Residence. —Died Feb. 15, 2011
† Smochko, Rev. Msgr. Basil (PRM) (Retired). —Died May 9, 2011
† Smyth, John L., *c.ss.r* (RIC) Hampton, VA Holy Family Retreat. —Died Nov. 3, 2011
† Soileau, Charles (LKC) (Retired). —Died June 6, 2011
† Solla, P. Santiago (PCE) (Retired). —Died May 23, 2011
† Sorce, John J. (CHR) (Retired). —Died July 29, 2011
† Speice, Rev. Msgr. Lawrence T. (E) (Retired). —Died Jan. 16, 2011
† Spellerberg, Joseph R., *s.j.* (NY) New York, NY Murray–Weigel Hall. —Died Aug. 20, 2010

† Spors, Roman (DUL) (Retired). —Died March 25, 2011
† Sprute, Merlyn (B) (Retired). —Died Dec. 1, 2010
† St. Martin, Jean-Claude (PAT) Rockaway, NJ St. Cecilia's & Sacred Heart. —Died Feb. 11, 2011
† Stack, John J. (HRT) (Retired). —Died Feb. 3, 2011
† Stapleton, Edward, *s.s.s.* (SP) Holiday, FL St. Vincent de Paul. —Died Feb. 4, 2011
† Stauder, Paul W. (BEL) (Retired). —Died Nov. 16, 2011
† Steffes, Marvin J., *c.pp.s.* (CIN) (Retired). —Died Aug. 29, 2011
† Steigmeyer, Robert C., *c.s.c.* (FTW) (Retired). —Died July 16, 2011
† Stenger, William J. (WH) (Retired). —Died Feb. 8, 2011
† Stephen, John, *c.r.* (CHI) Des Plaines, IL Nazarethville. —Died July 6, 2011
† Strempeck, Rev. Msgr. Martin R. (BAL) (Retired). —Died Feb. 8, 2011
† Sullivan, Brendan V. (CAM) (Retired). —Died April 30, 2011
† Sullivan, Daniel, *c.p.* (PIT) Pittsburgh, PA St. Paul of the Cross Monastery. —Died March 3, 2011
† Sullivan, Edward Hartrick, *c.m.* (STL) Perryville, MO St. Mary's of the Barrens. —Died May 22, 2011
† Sullivan, Frederick J. (NY) (Retired). —Died Jan. 31, 2011
† Sum, Robert, *o.s.b.* (JOL) Lisle, IL St. Procopius Abbey. —Died Aug. 16, 2011
† Susi, Rev. Msgr. Joseph M. (ALX) (Retired). —Died Oct. 21, 2011
† Susin, Angelo, *c.s.* (PRO) (Retired). —Died March 2, 2011
† Sweeney, Joseph J. (PH) (Retired). —Died Oct. 16, 2011
† Sypek, Rev. Msgr. Stanislaus T. (BO) Boston, MA St. Adalbert. —Died Oct. 2, 2011
† Tagg, Joseph L. (MEM) (Retired). —Died March 19, 2011
† Taheny, Theodore T., *s.j.* (SJ) Los Gatos, CA Sacred Heart Jesuit Center. —Died Aug. 12, 2011
† Taylor, Michael J., *s.j.* (SPK) (Retired). —Died Nov. 30, 2010
† Terentieff, Robert J. (BGP) (Retired). —Died July 17, 2011
† Thomas, Charles T. (COL) Columbus, OH St. Mary Church. —Died April 24, 2011
† Thoren, S. Guy (MAR). —Died Dec. 17, 2011
† Thuer, William J. (HRT) (Retired). —Died April 21, 2011
† Tiell, Maurice J. (OWN) (Retired). —Died Oct. 11, 2011
† Tiercelin, Harry (NY) (Retired). —Died April 6, 2011
† Tlapa, Richard J. (CHI) (Retired). —Died May 28, 2011
† Toal, James Aloysius (LA). —Died June 28, 2011
† Tobin, Thomas F., *s.j.* (FgM) Jesuit Fathers and Brothers Foreign Mission. —Died July 31, 2011
† Toczek, Melchior, *o.f.m.* (SFD) (Retired). —Died March 13, 2011
† Tokarski, Stephen L. (GF) Billings, MT St. Pius X Church. —Died Oct. 4, 2011
† Tomasek, Richard A., *s.j.* (TUC) Tucson, AZ Saint Mark. —Died Aug. 6, 2011
† Toner, Edward R. (COV) (Retired). —Died July 28, 2011
† Toohy, Rev. Msgr. William J. (NY) (Retired). —Died June 12, 2011
† Toste, Frank A., *c.s.c.* (FR) (Retired). —Died 2011
† Totten, Raymond F. (COL) (Retired). —Died 2011
† Townsend, Ralph Valerian, *o.p.* (WDC) Washington, DC St. Dominic Priory. —Died July 2, 2011
† Traynor, John J. (RVC) (Retired). —Died July 11, 2011
† Tremblay, Eugene A., *o.m.i.* (BO) Lowell, MA Andre Garin Residence. —Died Feb. 20, 2011
† Trent, James F. (DET) (Retired). —Died April 28, 2011
† Trisolini, John, *s.d.b.* (FgM) Salesians of Don Bosco Foreign Mission. —Died 2011
† Tyson, Joseph V., *s.s.j.* (BAL) (Retired). —Died March 15, 2011
† Udulutsch, Irvin, *o.f.m.cap.* (GB) (Retired). —Died Dec. 11, 2010
† Valdes, Bert W. (WH) (Retired). —Died Feb. 18, 2011
† Valker, Richard J. (CHI) (Retired). —Died Oct. 27, 2011
† Vandal, Roland G., *m.s.* (HRT) Hartford, CT Missionaries of La Salette. —Died Sept. 12, 2011
† van der Beek, John, *o.s.a.* (CHI) Olympia Fields, IL Tolentine Monastery at Tolentine Center. —Died 2011
† Van der Werff, Rev. Msgr. Martin (NO) (Retired). —Died March 31, 2011
† Van Sickler, Robert (BAK) (Retired). —Died Feb. 18, 2011
† Vazquez, Carlos R. (WIL) (Retired). —Died July 16, 2011
† Verdegan, Albert L. (SUP) (Retired). —Died Feb. 22, 2011
† Vidra, Rev. Msgr. Thomas (SD) (Retired). —Died Jan. 30, 2011
† Vigeant, Wilfrid J., *s.j.* (BO) Weston, MA Campion Health Center. —Died April 28, 2011
† Vigil, Edwin (SAT) San Antonio, TX St. John the Evangelist. —Died Feb. 27, 2011
† Vogel, Philip, *s.d.s.* (BAL) (Retired). —Died Dec. 26, 2010
† Vollor, John (JKS) Clarksdale, MS St. Elizabeth. —Died Jan. 11, 2011
† Vollor, William J. (BLX) Hattiesburg, MS Holy Rosary Parish. —Died March 2, 2011
† Von Fauer, Stephen C. (BUR) (Retired). —Died Sept. 18, 2011
† Vorisek, Rudolph T., *c.s.p.* (NY) (Retired). —Died May 18, 2011
† Votruba, George L. (SUP) (Retired). —Died Jan. 22, 2011
† Vu, Joseph Duc (DET) Detroit, MI John D. Dingell Veterans Admin. Medical Center. —Died March 23, 2011
† Waickman, Thomas L. (JC) (Retired). —Died Dec. 9, 2010
† Waldron, John R. (NEW) (Retired). —Died March 27, 2011
† Walker, Earl Gordon (LA) Pastor Emeritus. —Died Oct. 26, 2010
† Wallace, Philip (SEA) (Retired). —Died Aug. 25, 2011
† Walsh, John M. (PH) (Retired). —Died March 23, 2011
† Walsh, Kenneth, *c.p.* (SCR) Scranton, PA Saint Ann's Passionist Monastery. —Died April 23, 2011
† Walsh, Rev. Msgr. Michael (LA) (Retired). —Died April 20, 2011
† Walsh, Patrick J., *s.j.* (STL) (Retired). —Died April 24, 2011
† Walsh, Peter (JC) (Retired). —Died Jan. 17, 2011
† Wang, Francis X., *s.j.* (SJ) Los Gatos, CA Sacred Heart Jesuit Center. —Died 2011
† Wannemuehler, Robert J. (EVN) (Retired). —Died Jan. 26, 2011
† Ward, Bruce, *s.t.* (FgM) Missionary Servants of the Most Holy Trinity Foreign Mission. —Died June 11, 2011
† Warren, Robert (RIC) (Retired). —Died Oct. 5, 2011
† Wasko, Anthony, *o.s.a.* (SD) (Retired). —Died Jan. 26, 2011
† Watson, James Vincent, *o.p.* (NY) New York, NY St. Vincent Ferrer. —Died Oct. 6, 2011
† Wawiorka, Raymond W. (MIL) (Retired). —Died Oct. 28, 2011
† Weaver, Patrick J. (CAM). —Died May 31, 2011
† Weber, Charles P. (BO) (Retired). —Died Nov. 2, 2011
† Werner, John P. (COV) (Retired). —Died Sept. 26, 2011
† Wesolowski, Edmund C. (PH) (Retired). —Died Jan. 7, 2011
† Wheeler, Ambrose, *c.s.c.* (FTW) Notre Dame Congregation of the Holy Cross, Indiana Province, Provincial House. —Died July 10, 2011
† Wheeler, Clarence P., *m.s.* (JC) (Retired). —Died June 9, 2011
† Whipple, Donald W., *c.s.c.* (FR) (Retired). —Died 2011
† White, Richard, *c.m.f.* (CHI) Oak Park Claretian Missionaries USA Eastern Province. —Died 2011
† Wightman, William, *s.m.* (STL) St. Louis, MO Our Lady of the Pillar. —Died April 5, 2011
† Wilger, Norbert J. (LC) (Retired). —Died March 2, 2011
† Windisch, Adolf, *s.m.* (SAT) San Antonio, TX Marianist Residence. —Died Oct. 26, 2011
† Windle, Raymond L., *s.j.* (STL) St. Louis, MO Jesuit Community Corporation at Saint Louis University–Jesuit Hall. —Died Dec. 16, 2010
† Wise, Thomas F., *c.s.v.* (CHI) (Retired). —Died Aug. 11, 2011
† Wisneski, John A. (LC) (Retired). —Died July 27, 2011
† Witt, William (Y) (Retired). —Died Feb. 22, 2011
† Wojciechowski, Robert J. (DET). —Died April 8, 2011
† Wolf, Michael H. (SAG) (Retired). —Died Jan. 5, 2011
† Wolf, Norbert G. (E) (Retired). —Died May 10, 2011
† Woodarek, Richard, *c.s.s.* (BO) Waltham, MA Stigmatine Fathers & Brothers Provincial House. —Died Aug. 5, 2011
† Wroblewski, Lawrence J., *s.j.* (ROC) Rochester, NY McQuaid Jesuit High School. —Died Jan. 1, 2011
† Wueste, Andrew, *o.m.i.* (SAT) San Antonio, TX Oblate Madonna Residence. —Died Jan. 5, 2011
† Wytrwal, Alexander J. (DET) (Retired). —Died March 11, 2011
† Xuereb, Paul D. (DET) (Retired). —Died April 27, 2011
† Yast, Robert A. (FTW) (Retired). —Died Oct. 30, 2011
† Young, Bernard L. (NO) (Retired). —Died Oct. 31, 2011
† Young, Ronald E. (DAV) (On Duty Outside Diocese). —Died Jan. 11, 2011
† Youngs, Fred A. (BR) (Retired). —Died March 7, 2011
† Zanoni, John (JOL) (Retired). —Died Feb. 14, 2011
† Zehe, Ralph, *o.f.m.cap.* (PIT) (Retired). —Died Feb. 22, 2011
† Zerfas, Rev. Msgr. Herman H. (GR) (Retired). —Died Dec. 6, 2010
† Zimmer, Ellis, *o.f.m.cap.* (GB) (Retired). —Died Jan. 3, 2011
† Zogby, Edward G., *s.j.* (NY) New York, NY Murray–Weigel Hall. —Died June 16, 2011
† Zube, Rev. Msgr. Joseph A. (PEO) (Retired). —Died April 5, 2011
† Zuercher, John D., *s.j.* (OM) Omaha, NE Jesuit Community at Creighton University. —Died May 7, 2011

2012 GENERAL SUMMARY

	*Mobile AL	Birmingham AL	ALABAMA TOTAL	*Anchorage AK	Fairbanks AK	Juneau AK	2012 U.S. GRAND TOTAL
Cardinals	–	–	–	–	–	–	**13**
Archbishops	2	–	2	2	–	–	**56**
Bishop	–	2	2	–	1	1	**394**
Abbots	–	2	2	–	–	–	**109**
Diocesan Priests	95	84	179	25	15	11	**27,125**
Religious Priests	29	28	57	11	7	2	**12,593**
Total Priests in Diocese	124	112	236	36	22	13	**39,718**
Newly Ordained Priests	2	1	3	–	1	–	**485**
Total Permanent Deacons	54	51	105	18	25	3	**17,816**
Total Brothers	10	22	32	1	2	–	**4,518**
Total Sisters	116	118	234	20	12	2	**55,045**
Number of Parishes	76	54	130	23	46	9	**18,061**
Missions	10	19	29	6	–	17	**2,627**
Pastoral Centers	3	–	3	–	2	–	**628**
New Parishes	–	–	–	–	–	–	**87**
Catholic Hospitals	1	4	5	1	–	1	**605**
Patients Assisted Annually	173,104	689,500	862,604	78,251	–	45,000	**88,519,295**
Health Care Centers	3	1	4	5	–	–	**363**
Patients Assisted Annually	5,462	39,600	45,062	10,685	–	–	**5,038,247**
Specialized Homes	5	1	6	1	–	–	**1,616**
Total Assisted Anually	1,151	20	1,171	641	–	–	**991,072**
Residential Care of Children (Orphanages)	1	–	1	2	–	–	**344**
Total Assisted Anually	65	–	65	18	–	–	**23,479**
Day Care and Extended Day Care Centers	6	–	6	–	–	1	**1,005**
Total Assisted Anually	429	–	429	–	–	100	**121,211**
Special Centers for Social Services	10	19	29	3	1	1	**3,602**
Total Assisted Anually	48,608	91,500	140,108	17,382	2,000	10,000	**32,768,652**
Diocesan Seminaries	–	–	–	–	–	–	**71**
Students	–	–	–	–	–	–	**3,346**
Religious Seminaries	–	–	–	–	–	–	**98**
Students	–	5	5	–	–	–	**1,669**
Colleges and Universities	1	–	1	–	–	–	**233**
Total Students	1,867	–	1,867	–	–	–	**812,098**
High Schools, Diocesan and Parish	3	5	8	1	1	–	**731**
Total Students	1,552	1,461	3,013	78	204	–	**327,345**
High Schools, Private	–	1	1	1	–	–	**595**
Total Students	–	153	153	42	–	–	**296,268**
Elementary Schools, Diocesan and Parish	17	18	35	3	1	1	**5,378**
Total Students	4,637	4,601	9,238	315	292	91	**1,382,539**
Elementary Schools, Private	–	1	1	1	–	–	**386**
Total Students	–	185	185	49	–	–	**106,972**
Non–residential Schools for the Disabled	–	1	1	–	–	–	**53**
Total Students	–	120	120	–	–	–	**5,729**
Religious Education High School Students	690	1,534	2,224	724	240	78	**662,914**
Religious Education Elementary Students	3,746	6,267	10,013	1,714	755	455	**2,885,785**
Priests Teaching	3	4	7	–	–	–	**1,199**
Scholastics Teaching	–	–	–	–	–	–	**422**
Brothers Teaching	2	1	3	–	–	–	**698**
Sisters Teaching	14	14	28	–	–	–	**4,026**
Lay Teachers	535	380	915	75	51	10	**162,018**
Infant Baptisms	1,182	1,821	3,003	454	323	52	**793,103**
Adult Baptisms	107	157	264	50	31	7	**43,692**
Received into Full Communion	245	414	659	54	52	6	**76,588**
First Communions	694	1,973	2,667	429	219	96	**797,582**
Confirmations	1,193	1,560	2,753	297	134	75	**618,041**
Marriages	341	338	679	88	45	20	**166,991**
Deaths	658	631	1,289	144	165	49	**419,278**
Total Catholics	68,662	90,135	158,797	37,089	13,496	10,000	**68,229,841**
Total Population	1,761,543	2,945,960	4,707,503	400,000	162,941	75,000	**307,374,682**
Catholic Population Percentage	4	3	3	9	8	13	**22**

*Indicates Archdioceses.

†Certain Diocese traverse state lines.

	ALASKA TOTAL	Samoa–Pago Pago AS	Phoenix AZ	Tucson AZ	ARIZONA TOTAL	Little Rock AR	2012 U.S. GRAND TOTAL
Cardinals	–	–	–	–	–	–	**13**
Archbishops	2	–	–	–	–	–	**56**
Bishop	2	1	3	1	4	2	**394**
Abbots	–	–	–	–	–	1	**109**
Diocesan Priests	51	16	128	90	218	73	**27,125**
Religious Priests	20	2	94	85	179	33	**12,593**
Total Priests in Diocese	71	18	222	175	397	106	**39,718**
Newly Ordained Priests	1	1	–	–	–	–	**485**
Total Permanent Deacons	46	23	231	139	370	82	**17,816**
Total Brothers	3	–	13	25	38	24	**4,518**
Total Sisters	34	9	173	170	343	171	**55,045**
Number of Parishes	78	17	92	76	168	89	**18,061**
Missions	23	–	23	46	69	38	**2,627**
Pastoral Centers	2	–	3	–	3	1	**628**
New Parishes	–	1	–	1	1	–	**87**
Catholic Hospitals	2	–	1	4	5	11	**605**
Patients Assisted Annually	123,251	–	115,355	470,000	585,355	876,711	**88,519,295**
Health Care Centers	5	–	1	1	2	5	**363**
Patients Assisted Annually	10,685	–	14,383	41,500	55,883	24,435	**5,038,247**
Specialized Homes	1	1	31	–	31	29	**1,616**
Total Assisted Anually	641	20	4,559	–	4,559	1,229	**991,072**
Residential Care of Children (Orphanages)	2	–	–	–	–	–	**344**
Total Assisted Anually	18	–	–	–	–	–	**23,479**
Day Care and Extended Day Care Centers	1	1	4	–	4	26	**1,005**
Total Assisted Anually	100	70	717	–	717	1,288	**121,211**
Special Centers for Social Services	5	1	39	2	41	5	**3,602**
Total Assisted Anually	29,382	170	1,687,416	430,000	2,117,416	44,257	**32,768,652**
Diocesan Seminaries	–	–	–	–	–	–	**71**
Students	–	4	–	–	–	–	**3,346**
Religious Seminaries	–	–	–	–	–	–	**98**
Students	–	–	–	1	1	–	**1,669**
Colleges and Universities	–	–	–	–	–	–	**233**
Total Students	–	–	–	–	–	–	**812,098**
High Schools, Diocesan and Parish	2	1	5	–	5	4	**731**
Total Students	282	273	3,516	–	3,516	1,029	**327,345**
High Schools, Private	1	–	1	6	7	2	**595**
Total Students	42	–	1,322	2,057	3,379	637	**296,268**
Elementary Schools, Diocesan and Parish	5	2	36	17	53	28	**5,378**
Total Students	698	317	9,091	4,259	13,350	5,456	**1,382,539**
Elementary Schools, Private	1	–	–	3	3	–	**386**
Total Students	49	–	–	610	610	–	**106,972**
Non–residential Schools for the Disabled	–	–	–	–	–	–	**53**
Total Students	–	–	–	–	–	–	**5,729**
Religious Education High School Students	1,042	435	4,838	2,251	7,089	1,808	**662,914**
Religious Education Elementary Students	2,924	3,085	22,066	11,278	33,344	7,225	**2,885,785**
Priests Teaching	–	4	5	–	5	1	**1,199**
Scholastics Teaching	–	–	1	–	1	–	**422**
Brothers Teaching	–	–	3	10	13	3	**698**
Sisters Teaching	–	6	40	21	61	7	**4,026**
Lay Teachers	136	61	897	436	1,333	571	**162,018**
Infant Baptisms	829	180	9,413	4,923	14,336	2,830	**793,103**
Adult Baptisms	88	90	327	243	570	220	**43,692**
Received into Full Communion	112	40	1,748	627	2,375	501	**76,588**
First Communions	744	210	8,709	4,503	13,212	3,017	**797,582**
Confirmations	506	240	9,805	2,776	12,581	1,804	**618,041**
Marriages	153	35	1,006	733	1,739	595	**166,991**
Deaths	358	40	3,050	2,014	5,064	915	**419,278**
Total Catholics	60,585	14,250	800,149	194,744	994,893	137,137	**68,229,841**
Total Population	637,941	65,000	4,369,735	1,820,667	6,190,402	2,915,918	**307,374,682**
Catholic Population Percentage	9	22	18	11	16	5	**22**

Archdioceses = 37; Dioceses = 170; Apostolates = 3

2012 GENERAL SUMMARY

	*Los Angeles CA	*San Francisco CA	Fresno CA	Monterey in California CA	Oakland CA	Orange in California CA	2012 U.S. GRAND TOTAL
Cardinals	1	–	–	–	–	–	13
Archbishops	1	3	–	–	–	–	56
Bishop	6	5	1	2	2	2	394
Abbots	2	–	–	–	–	1	109
Diocesan Priests	519	206	120	79	159	167	27,125
Religious Priests	530	168	37	32	164	87	12,593
Total Priests in Diocese	1,049	374	157	111	323	254	39,718
Newly Ordained Priests	16	4	2	–	6	9	485
Total Permanent Deacons	324	75	63	21	115	105	17,816
Total Brothers	79	38	1	–	96	8	4,518
Total Sisters	1,793	744	109	–	370	326	55,045
Number of Parishes	287	91	89	46	83	57	18,061
Missions	9	11	44	9	1	5	2,627
Pastoral Centers	14	22	–	–	8	5	628
New Parishes	–	–	–	–	–	–	87
Catholic Hospitals	14	3	3	1	–	3	605
Patients Assisted Annually	2,500,850	384,811	630,745	198,890	–	1,563,232	88,519,295
Health Care Centers	5	4	2	–	1	5	363
Patients Assisted Annually	9,804	51,224	217	–	3,381	28,376	5,038,247
Specialized Homes	10	6	–	1	8	6	1,616
Total Assisted Anually	10,849	163	–	50	18,938	623	991,072
Residential Care of Children (Orphanages)	2	1	–	–	–	–	344
Total Assisted Anually	577	80	–	–	–	–	23,479
Day Care and Extended Day Care Centers	6	3	–	–	1	2	1,005
Total Assisted Anually	490	345	–	–	514	530	121,211
Special Centers for Social Services	33	5	2	4	3	9	3,602
Total Assisted Anually	232,649	4,334	50,000	23,984	247,000	3,840,014	32,768,652
Diocesan Seminaries	1	1	–	–	–	–	71
Students	71	107	–	–	–	–	3,346
Religious Seminaries	11	1	1	–	3	–	98
Students	24	–	–	–	335	–	1,669
Colleges and Universities	4	3	–	–	2	–	233
Total Students	12,427	13,782	–	–	5,394	–	812,098
High Schools, Diocesan and Parish	26	4	–	2	3	3	731
Total Students	14,431	3,432	–	541	1,698	4,216	327,345
High Schools, Private	24	10	2	3	6	4	595
Total Students	13,000	7,848	1,178	992	4,059	2,280	296,268
Elementary Schools, Diocesan and Parish	209	51	20	11	44	32	5,378
Total Students	49,224	14,362	5,242	2,737	11,751	11,245	1,382,539
Elementary Schools, Private	9	8	–	3	2	3	386
Total Students	2,248	16,568	–	647	150	1,432	106,972
Non–residential Schools for the Disabled	–	–	–	–	–	–	53
Total Students	–	–	–	–	–	–	5,729
Religious Education High School Students	38,748	1,980	11,192	1,549	6,418	11,794	662,914
Religious Education Elementary Students	84,720	11,704	26,315	6,492	20,348	31,002	2,885,785
Priests Teaching	26	7	2	–	41	7	1,199
Scholastics Teaching	2	–	–	–	–	–	422
Brothers Teaching	13	5	–	–	33	2	698
Sisters Teaching	104	44	18	13	43	19	4,026
Lay Teachers	4,177	1,649	295	311	2,149	1,366	162,018
Infant Baptisms	76,661	6,062	19,547	6,573	8,751	13,893	793,103
Adult Baptisms	1,403	231	354	190	343	510	43,692
Received into Full Communion	6,278	350	524	1,182	475	933	76,588
First Communions	44,895	5,080	12,673	4,410	7,902	13,221	797,582
Confirmations	24,907	3,490	5,956	1,703	4,187	6,993	618,041
Marriages	7,630	1,070	1,999	858	1,009	2,121	166,991
Deaths	11,165	2,339	7,011	1,223	2,393	2,784	419,278
Total Catholics	4,233,010	432,163	1,074,901	200,469	399,546	1,291,505	68,229,841
Total Population	11,758,360	1,761,000	2,756,266	1,002,345	2,586,396	3,166,461	307,374,682
Catholic Population Percentage	36	25	39	20	15	41	22

*Indicates Archdioceses.

†Certain Diocese traverse state lines.

	Sacramento CA	San Bernardino CA	San Diego CA	San Jose in California CA	Santa Rose in California CA	Stockton CA	2012 U.S. GRAND TOTAL
Cardinals	–	–	–	–	–	–	**13**
Archbishops	–	–	–	–	–	–	**56**
Bishop	3	2	3	3	2	1	**394**
Abbots	3	1	1	–	–	–	**109**
Diocesan Priests	174	112	166	182	76	57	**27,125**
Religious Priests	70	114	85	195	10	16	**12,593**
Total Priests in Diocese	244	226	251	377	86	73	**39,718**
Newly Ordained Priests	4	6	1	3	–	2	**485**
Total Permanent Deacons	143	113	171	28	31	45	**17,816**
Total Brothers	12	19	17	52	25	3	**4,518**
Total Sisters	169	145	246	308	36	61	**55,045**
Number of Parishes	102	93	98	50	42	34	**18,061**
Missions	44	6	13	2	18	12	**2,627**
Pastoral Centers	3	5	–	4	8	–	**628**
New Parishes	–	–	–	1	–	–	**87**
Catholic Hospitals	6	2	2	2	5	1	**605**
Patients Assisted Annually	666,574	291,325	89,114	215,000	547,807	632,064	**88,519,295**
Health Care Centers	–	1	–	1	–	1	**363**
Patients Assisted Annually	–	1,200	–	100	–	9,584	**5,038,247**
Specialized Homes	2	3	6	1	1	1	**1,616**
Total Assisted Anually	344	182	3,819	140	52	1,046	**991,072**
Residential Care of Children (Orphanages)	–	–	–	–	1	–	**344**
Total Assisted Anually	–	–	–	–	119	–	**23,479**
Day Care and Extended Day Care Centers	–	–	1	1	–	–	**1,005**
Total Assisted Anually	–	–	170	101	–	–	**121,211**
Special Centers for Social Services	11	4	7	1	7	1	**3,602**
Total Assisted Anually	57,400	52,412	147,798	50,000	30,000	32,662	**32,768,652**
Diocesan Seminaries	–	1	–	–	–	–	**71**
Students	–	15	–	–	–	–	**3,346**
Religious Seminaries	2	–	–	–	–	–	**98**
Students	1	–	–	–	–	–	**1,669**
Colleges and Universities	–	–	2	1	–	–	**233**
Total Students	–	–	8,484	8,490	–	–	**812,098**
High Schools, Diocesan and Parish	3	2	3	2	2	2	**731**
Total Students	1,780	878	2,684	3,294	1,015	1,387	**327,345**
High Schools, Private	3	1	3	4	3	–	**595**
Total Students	2,333	483	1,494	3,419	928	–	**296,268**
Elementary Schools, Diocesan and Parish	40	25	44	28	10	11	**5,378**
Total Students	10,093	5,682	14,254	9,340	2,446	2,898	**1,382,539**
Elementary Schools, Private	–	1	3	2	2	–	**386**
Total Students	–	510	884	349	127	–	**106,972**
Non–residential Schools for the Disabled	–	–	1	–	–	–	**53**
Total Students	–	–	390	–	–	–	**5,729**
Religious Education High School Students	2,492	15,423	7,892	2,335	1,400	956	**662,914**
Religious Education Elementary Students	24,697	32,568	16,234	14,409	4,936	19,017	**2,885,785**
Priests Teaching	9	1	8	4	1	2	**1,199**
Scholastics Teaching	–	–	–	–	–	–	**422**
Brothers Teaching	–	–	–	3	–	1	**698**
Sisters Teaching	14	10	22	20	3	–	**4,026**
Lay Teachers	1,003	392	1,087	1,007	288	220	**162,018**
Infant Baptisms	8,987	10,479	9,447	7,255	3,017	5,901	**793,103**
Adult Baptisms	418	361	481	263	100	183	**43,692**
Received into Full Communion	1,296	507	852	282	73	687	**76,588**
First Communions	7,030	15,546	9,212	5,929	2,421	5,194	**797,582**
Confirmations	5,300	8,022	5,172	3,302	1,106	4,628	**618,041**
Marriages	1,253	1,753	1,849	947	456	772	**166,991**
Deaths	3,650	2,633	2,760	1,398	805	1,434	**419,278**
Total Catholics	979,091	929,467	982,183	585,000	174,357	227,338	**68,229,841**
Total Population	3,524,422	4,224,851	3,124,081	1,879,700	891,101	1,316,079	**307,374,682**
Catholic Population Percentage	28	22	31	31	20	17	**22**

Archdioceses = 37; Dioceses = 170; Apostolates = 3

2012 GENERAL SUMMARY

	CALIFORNIA TOTAL	The Caroline Islands CI	*Denver CO	Colorado Springs CO	Pueblo CO	COLORADO TOTAL	2012 U.S. GRAND TOTAL
Cardinals	1	–	–	–	–	–	**13**
Archbishops	4	–	–	–	–	–	**56**
Bishop	32	1	1	2	2	5	**394**
Abbots	8	–	1	–	–	1	**109**
Diocesan Priests	2,017	13	190	39	57	286	**27,125**
Religious Priests	1,508	15	103	14	17	134	**12,593**
Total Priests in Diocese	3,525	28	293	53	74	420	**39,718**
Newly Ordained Priests	53	1	10	4	1	15	**485**
Total Permanent Deacons	1,234	65	196	55	51	302	**17,816**
Total Brothers	350	2	15	1	2	18	**4,518**
Total Sisters	4,307	34	238	93	53	384	**55,045**
Number of Parishes	1,072	29	123	41	52	216	**18,061**
Missions	174	2	20	–	46	66	**2,627**
Pastoral Centers	69	–	–	2	–	2	**628**
New Parishes	1	–	4	–	–	4	**87**
Catholic Hospitals	42	–	4	2	5	11	**605**
Patients Assisted Annually	7,720,412	–	394,185	277,379	714,068	1,385,632	**88,519,295**
Health Care Centers	20	–	8	3	2	13	**363**
Patients Assisted Annually	103,886	–	27,753	147	5,000	32,900	**5,038,247**
Specialized Homes	45	–	9	3	1	13	**1,616**
Total Assisted Anually	36,206	–	2,175	147	850	3,172	**991,072**
Residential Care of Children (Orphanages)	4	–	–	–	–	–	**344**
Total Assisted Anually	776	–	–	–	–	–	**23,479**
Day Care and Extended Day Care Centers	14	–	9	–	–	9	**1,005**
Total Assisted Anually	2,150	–	704	–	–	704	**121,211**
Special Centers for Social Services	87	–	12	1	6	19	**3,602**
Total Assisted Anually	4,768,253	–	74,815	219,998	316,000	610,813	**32,768,652**
Diocesan Seminaries	3	–	2	–	–	2	**71**
Students	193	–	130	–	–	130	**3,346**
Religious Seminaries	18	–	–	1	–	1	**98**
Students	360	–	–	9	–	9	**1,669**
Colleges and Universities	12	–	2	–	–	2	**233**
Total Students	48,577	–	14,971	–	–	14,971	**812,098**
High Schools, Diocesan and Parish	52	3	2	–	–	2	**731**
Total Students	35,356	620	933	–	–	933	**327,345**
High Schools, Private	63	1	5	1	–	6	**595**
Total Students	38,014	175	2,988	333	–	3,321	**296,268**
Elementary Schools, Diocesan and Parish	525	4	36	5	3	44	**5,378**
Total Students	139,274	1,221	8,683	1,367	800	10,850	**1,382,539**
Elementary Schools, Private	33	–	2	–	1	3	**386**
Total Students	22,915	–	543	–	140	683	**106,972**
Non-residential Schools for the Disabled	1	–	1	–	–	1	**53**
Total Students	390	–	85	–	–	85	**5,729**
Religious Education High School Students	102,179	798	7,030	2,182	1,917	11,129	**662,914**
Religious Education Elementary Students	292,442	1,309	20,908	7,181	3,824	31,913	**2,885,785**
Priests Teaching	108	–	5	–	–	5	**1,199**
Scholastics Teaching	2	2	–	–	–	–	**422**
Brothers Teaching	57	2	3	–	–	3	**698**
Sisters Teaching	310	24	14	1	1	16	**4,026**
Lay Teachers	13,944	134	955	165	–	1,120	**162,018**
Infant Baptisms	176,573	1,424	9,244	1,008	1,173	11,425	**793,103**
Adult Baptisms	4,837	113	471	100	171	742	**43,692**
Received into Full Communion	13,439	–	599	158	–	757	**76,588**
First Communions	133,513	1,171	8,406	1,504	891	10,801	**797,582**
Confirmations	74,766	886	6,180	1,638	698	8,516	**618,041**
Marriages	21,717	276	1,539	203	233	1,975	**166,991**
Deaths	39,595	–	2,566	438	1,392	4,396	**419,278**
Total Catholics	11,509,030	77,733	557,049	161,770	73,264	792,083	**68,229,841**
Total Population	37,991,062	140,368	3,352,228	1,011,062	665,906	5,029,196	**307,374,682**
Catholic Population Percentage	30	55	17	16	11	22	**22**

*Indicates Archdioceses.

†Certain Diocese traverse state lines.

2012 GENERAL SUMMARY

	*Hartford CT	Bridgeport CT	† Norwich CT	CONNECTICUT TOTAL	† Wilmington DE	*† Washington DC	2012 U.S. GRAND TOTAL
Cardinals	–	–	–	–	–	3	**13**
Archbishops	2	–	–	2	–	–	**56**
Bishop	2	–	1	3	1	4	**394**
Abbots	–	–	–	–	–	2	**109**
Diocesan Priests	301	240	111	652	126	290	**27,125**
Religious Priests	85	31	59	175	70	373	**12,593**
Total Priests in Diocese	386	271	170	827	196	663	**39,718**
Newly Ordained Priests	5	1	1	7	3	5	**485**
Total Permanent Deacons	289	103	69	461	107	205	**17,816**
Total Brothers	31	–	25	56	23	107	**4,518**
Total Sisters	645	343	177	1,165	213	551	**55,045**
Number of Parishes	213	87	76	376	57	140	**18,061**
Missions	1	–	6	7	19	9	**2,627**
Pastoral Centers	–	–	8	8	–	–	**628**
New Parishes	–	–	–	–	–	–	**87**
Catholic Hospitals	3	1	–	4	1	3	**605**
Patients Assisted Annually	879,972	215,000	–	1,094,972	177,113	725,201	**88,519,295**
Health Care Centers	2	2	–	4	1	9	**363**
Patients Assisted Annually	2,772	22,405	–	25,177	175	43,707	**5,038,247**
Specialized Homes	6	16	2	24	9	50	**1,616**
Total Assisted Anually	2,974	1,206	239	4,419	585	24,779	**991,072**
Residential Care of Children (Orphanages)	2	–	1	3	–	1	**344**
Total Assisted Anually	171	–	20	191	–	260	**23,479**
Day Care and Extended Day Care Centers	9	5	–	14	3	5	**1,005**
Total Assisted Anually	456	322	–	778	151	360	**121,211**
Special Centers for Social Services	18	19	4	41	16	24	**3,602**
Total Assisted Anually	31,756	487,000	8,500	527,256	228,778	393,000	**32,768,652**
Diocesan Seminaries	1	1	–	2	–	3	**71**
Students	–	14	–	14	–	135	**3,346**
Religious Seminaries	1	–	1	2	–	10	**98**
Students	80	–	26	106	–	141	**1,669**
Colleges and Universities	2	3	1	6	–	3	**233**
Total Students	4,733	12,366	237	17,336	–	26,277	**812,098**
High Schools, Diocesan and Parish	4	5	4	13	5	2	**731**
Total Students	2,025	2,326	2,241	6,592	2,488	771	**327,345**
High Schools, Private	5	2	2	9	3	18	**595**
Total Students	2,647	1,189	424	4,260	1,654	9,438	**296,268**
Elementary Schools, Diocesan and Parish	52	32	15	99	18	65	**5,378**
Total Students	10,991	7,628	2,519	21,138	6,616	16,039	**1,382,539**
Elementary Schools, Private	2	21	–	23	4	12	**386**
Total Students	215	548	–	763	1,216	1,872	**106,972**
Non–residential Schools for the Disabled	–	2	–	2	1	1	**53**
Total Students	–	20	–	20	78	61	**5,729**
Religious Education High School Students	11,962	3,170	2,040	17,172	529	3,459	**662,914**
Religious Education Elementary Students	42,368	43,770	12,243	98,381	7,413	26,688	**2,885,785**
Priests Teaching	9	13	1	23	15	17	**1,199**
Scholastics Teaching	–	–	–	–	–	–	**422**
Brothers Teaching	4	–	4	8	6	9	**698**
Sisters Teaching	29	16	16	61	20	46	**4,026**
Lay Teachers	991	854	345	2,190	973	2,371	**162,018**
Infant Baptisms	5,710	4,212	1,587	11,509	2,367	3,871	**793,103**
Adult Baptisms	162	175	55	392	104	733	**43,692**
Received into Full Communion	291	602	262	1,155	269	548	**76,588**
First Communions	7,006	5,320	1,921	14,247	2,484	5,570	**797,582**
Confirmations	6,763	5,228	2,030	14,021	2,126	4,501	**618,041**
Marriages	1,341	1,085	463	2,889	608	1,507	**166,991**
Deaths	7,725	2,708	1,976	12,409	1,742	2,780	**419,278**
Total Catholics	600,040	410,834	238,565	1,249,439	239,017	611,019	**68,229,841**
Total Population	1,946,413	916,289	692,328	3,555,030	1,347,160	2,777,359	**307,374,682**
Catholic Population Percentage	31	45	34	35	18	22	**22**

Archdioceses = 37; Dioceses = 170; Apostolates = 3

2012 GENERAL SUMMARY

	*Miami FL	Orlando FL	Palm Beach FL	Pensacola–Tallahassee FL	St. Augustine FL	St. Petersburg FL	2012 U.S. GRAND TOTAL
Cardinals	–	–	–	–	–	–	13
Archbishops	2	–	–	–	–	–	56
Bishop	1	2	2	2	3	2	394
Abbots	–	–	–	–	–	1	109
Diocesan Priests	235	132	107	75	105	148	27,125
Religious Priests	61	71	30	14	15	116	12,593
Total Priests in Diocese	296	203	137	89	120	264	39,718
Newly Ordained Priests	2	1	2	3	–	–	485
Total Permanent Deacons	161	188	105	62	77	123	17,816
Total Brothers	48	15	1	5	2	38	4,518
Total Sisters	277	108	105	23	107	178	55,045
Number of Parishes	102	80	50	49	52	74	18,061
Missions	4	12	3	8	8	7	2,627
Pastoral Centers	1	–	1	–	–	–	628
New Parishes	2	–	–	–	–	–	87
Catholic Hospitals	4	–	–	49	2	2	605
Patients Assisted Annually	871,781	–	–	98,527	172,738	355,000	88,519,295
Health Care Centers	9	3	–	–	–	7	363
Patients Assisted Annually	19,675	1,224	–	–	–	35,000	5,038,247
Specialized Homes	10	2	5	2	2	15	1,616
Total Assisted Anually	18,238	26	436	890	42,683	969	991,072
Residential Care of Children (Orphanages)	2	–	–	–	–	–	344
Total Assisted Anually	283	–	–	–	–	–	23,479
Day Care and Extended Day Care Centers	11	5	–	–	–	16	1,005
Total Assisted Anually	3,233	146	–	–	–	1,205	121,211
Special Centers for Social Services	26	9	26	4	9	65	3,602
Total Assisted Anually	111,059	120,000	10,000	49,525	100,951	25,000	32,768,652
Diocesan Seminaries	2	–	1	–	–	–	71
Students	78	–	77	–	–	–	3,346
Religious Seminaries	–	–	–	–	–	–	98
Students	3	13	–	–	–	–	1,669
Colleges and Universities	3	–	–	–	–	1	233
Total Students	11,519	–	–	–	–	15,564	812,098
High Schools, Diocesan and Parish	9	5	3	2	4	4	731
Total Students	9,309	2,619	1,457	690	2,200	1,850	327,345
High Schools, Private	4	–	–	–	–	2	595
Total Students	3,153	–	–	–	–	1,095	296,268
Elementary Schools, Diocesan and Parish	50	30	14	7	27	26	5,378
Total Students	20,376	10,274	4,206	1,801	8,036	7,336	1,382,539
Elementary Schools, Private	2	–	2	–	–	2	386
Total Students	1,068	–	498	–	–	877	106,972
Non–residential Schools for the Disabled	1	1	–	–	1	2	53
Total Students	1,000	60	–	–	113	104	5,729
Religious Education High School Students	4,077	3,749	–	808	1,015	2,153	662,914
Religious Education Elementary Students	29,784	18,579	–	3,776	8,003	17,146	2,885,785
Priests Teaching	25	–	4	–	–	8	1,199
Scholastics Teaching	–	–	–	–	3	3	422
Brothers Teaching	19	4	–	–	–	3	698
Sisters Teaching	45	9	13	6	14	13	4,026
Lay Teachers	3,324	1,121	533	185	661	813	162,018
Infant Baptisms	12,173	5,651	3,284	994	1,890	3,676	793,103
Adult Baptisms	547	295	176	159	339	384	43,692
Received into Full Communion	880	495	335	357	430	372	76,588
First Communions	11,215	5,911	3,744	1,062	2,256	4,653	797,582
Confirmations	8,503	4,748	2,476	998	2,049	3,742	618,041
Marriages	1,899	1,143	606	323	542	922	166,991
Deaths	4,195	3,677	2,062	595	1,122	3,641	419,278
Total Catholics	733,876	393,230	243,363	63,091	175,215	432,209	68,229,841
Total Population	4,317,591	4,199,193	1,922,300	1,399,521	2,013,960	2,924,479	307,374,682
Catholic Population Percentage	17	9	13	5	9	15	22

*Indicates Archdioceses.

†Certain Diocese traverse state lines.

	Venice FL	FLORIDA TOTAL	*Atlanta GA	Savannah GA	GEORGIA TOTAL	*Agana GUAM	2012 U.S. GRAND TOTAL
Cardinals	–	–	–	–	–	–	**13**
Archbishops	–	2	1	–	1	1	**56**
Bishop	2	14	1	3	4	–	**394**
Abbots	–	1	1	–	1	–	**109**
Diocesan Priests	107	909	182	82	264	43	**27,125**
Religious Priests	65	372	69	25	94	10	**12,593**
Total Priests in Diocese	172	1,281	251	107	358	53	**39,718**
Newly Ordained Priests	2	10	7	2	9	–	**485**
Total Permanent Deacons	95	811	235	58	293	19	**17,816**
Total Brothers	14	123	33	2	35	3	**4,518**
Total Sisters	77	875	86	84	170	85	**55,045**
Number of Parishes	59	466	88	55	143	24	**18,061**
Missions	10	52	9	24	33	–	**2,627**
Pastoral Centers	1	3	–	15	15	–	**628**
New Parishes	1	3	–	–	–	–	**87**
Catholic Hospitals	–	57	5	1	6	–	**605**
Patients Assisted Annually	–	1,498,046	348,989	200,000	548,989	–	**88,519,295**
Health Care Centers	–	19	–	–	–	–	**363**
Patients Assisted Annually	–	55,899	–	–	–	–	**5,038,247**
Specialized Homes	11	47	3	–	3	1	**1,616**
Total Assisted Anually	644	63,886	95	–	95	60	**991,072**
Residential Care of Children (Orphanages)	–	2	–	–	–	–	**344**
Total Assisted Anually	–	283	–	–	–	–	**23,479**
Day Care and Extended Day Care Centers	1	33	–	–	–	4	**1,005**
Total Assisted Anually	47	4,631	–	–	–	617	**121,211**
Special Centers for Social Services	29	168	5	15	20	2	**3,602**
Total Assisted Anually	40,602	457,137	22,000	28,000	50,000	5,570	**32,768,652**
Diocesan Seminaries	–	3	–	–	–	1	**71**
Students	–	155	–	–	–	36	**3,346**
Religious Seminaries	–	–	–	–	–	–	**98**
Students	–	16	–	–	–	–	**1,669**
Colleges and Universities	1	5	–	–	–	–	**233**
Total Students	850	27,933	–	–	–	–	**812,098**
High Schools, Diocesan and Parish	3	30	3	2	5	3	**731**
Total Students	1,331	19,456	2,444	446	2,890	922	**327,345**
High Schools, Private	–	6	4	3	7	1	**595**
Total Students	–	4,248	1,363	1,016	2,379	291	**296,268**
Elementary Schools, Diocesan and Parish	10	164	15	15	30	7	**5,378**
Total Students	2,770	54,799	6,191	3,720	9,911	3,165	**1,382,539**
Elementary Schools, Private	–	6	4	–	4	–	**386**
Total Students	–	2,443	1,883	–	1,883	–	**106,972**
Non–residential Schools for the Disabled	2	7	–	–	–	–	**53**
Total Students	123	1,400	–	–	–	–	**5,729**
Religious Education High School Students	941	12,743	8,816	896	9,712	1,686	**662,914**
Religious Education Elementary Students	9,598	86,886	30,050	4,557	34,607	2,815	**2,885,785**
Priests Teaching	–	37	17	4	21	8	**1,199**
Scholastics Teaching	–	6	–	–	–	–	**422**
Brothers Teaching	–	26	3	1	4	1	**698**
Sisters Teaching	19	119	15	12	27	35	**4,026**
Lay Teachers	372	7,009	1,143	545	1,688	363	**162,018**
Infant Baptisms	3,993	31,661	7,741	1,710	9,451	1,699	**793,103**
Adult Baptisms	139	2,039	546	154	700	39	**43,692**
Received into Full Communion	264	3,133	1,166	297	1,463	248	**76,588**
First Communions	3,247	32,088	8,514	1,642	10,156	1,131	**797,582**
Confirmations	861	23,377	4,806	1,396	6,202	1,058	**618,041**
Marriages	531	5,966	1,304	414	1,718	172	**166,991**
Deaths	2,288	17,580	1,315	580	1,895	591	**419,278**
Total Catholics	226,728	2,267,712	119,235	87,718	206,953	143,650	**68,229,841**
Total Population	2,015,936	18,792,980	332,598	2,884,000	3,216,598	169,000	**307,374,682**
Catholic Population Percentage	11	12	36	3	6	85	**22**

Archdioceses = 37; Dioceses = 170; Apostolates = 3

2012 GENERAL SUMMARY

	Honolulu HI	Boise ID	*Chicago IL	Belleville IL	Joliet in Illinois IL	Peoria IL	2012 U.S. GRAND TOTAL
Cardinals	–	–	1	–	–	–	13
Archbishops	–	–	–	–	–	–	56
Bishop	1	1	10	2	4	1	394
Abbots	–	–	–	–	3	3	109
Diocesan Priests	65	83	791	107	179	189	27,125
Religious Priests	56	15	710	34	113	36	12,593
Total Priests in Diocese	121	98	1,501	141	292	225	39,718
Newly Ordained Priests	4	–	21	1	2	–	485
Total Permanent Deacons	57	70	654	27	198	120	17,816
Total Brothers	32	5	250	11	58	8	4,518
Total Sisters	169	75	1,781	309	470	202	55,045
Number of Parishes	66	52	356	117	120	157	18,061
Missions	26	28	11	–	9	25	2,627
Pastoral Centers	–	28	8	–	–	5	628
New Parishes	–	–	1	–	–	–	87
Catholic Hospitals	–	4	18	5	3	9	605
Patients Assisted Annually	–	552,297	2,811,758	524,344	864,158	2,255,991	88,519,295
Health Care Centers	3	–	2	–	–	–	363
Patients Assisted Annually	1,815	–	17,500	–	–	–	5,038,247
Specialized Homes	7	–	47	3	16	4	1,616
Total Assisted Anually	515	–	6,183	251	3,706	365	991,072
Residential Care of Children (Orphanages)	–	–	2	–	–	–	344
Total Assisted Anually	–	–	2,662	–	–	–	23,479
Day Care and Extended Day Care Centers	–	4	9	3	4	2	1,005
Total Assisted Anually	–	160	1,798	201	2,199	241	121,211
Special Centers for Social Services	1	19	100	3	5	1	3,602
Total Assisted Anually	24,939	410,000	760,236	275,000	64,524	28,305	32,768,652
Diocesan Seminaries	–	–	2	–	–	–	71
Students	2	–	196	–	–	–	3,346
Religious Seminaries	–	–	1	–	–	–	98
Students	–	–	103	–	–	–	1,669
Colleges and Universities	1	–	6	–	3	1	233
Total Students	2,850	–	50,928	–	16,429	403	812,098
High Schools, Diocesan and Parish	3	1	7	3	3	5	731
Total Students	838	680	1,082	1,129	1,886	2,640	327,345
High Schools, Private	4	–	33	–	4	–	595
Total Students	2,107	–	23,741	–	3,558	–	296,268
Elementary Schools, Diocesan and Parish	20	13	213	29	47	37	5,378
Total Students	5,447	2,286	60,707	4,971	16,231	9,452	1,382,539
Elementary Schools, Private	3	–	2	–	–	–	386
Total Students	777	–	972	–	–	–	106,972
Non–residential Schools for the Disabled	–	–	5	–	–	–	53
Total Students	–	–	450	–	–	–	5,729
Religious Education High School Students	2,117	2,313	6,925	419	4,572	1,300	662,914
Religious Education Elementary Students	5,162	5,902	83,760	4,250	38,984	10,897	2,885,785
Priests Teaching	7	–	26	6	17	13	1,199
Scholastics Teaching	–	–	–	–	–	–	422
Brothers Teaching	13	–	23	–	23	2	698
Sisters Teaching	37	1	86	8	17	10	4,026
Lay Teachers	769	209	6,757	400	466	978	162,018
Infant Baptisms	2,570	2,672	32,914	1,138	7,541	2,334	793,103
Adult Baptisms	162	216	1,585	126	205	229	43,692
Received into Full Communion	190	307	1,208	187	836	427	76,588
First Communions	1,882	2,298	26,433	1,353	9,154	2,406	797,582
Confirmations	1,307	1,219	21,745	1,475	8,177	3,170	618,041
Marriages	454	541	6,005	482	1,488	752	166,991
Deaths	1,606	808	12,920	1,194	3,529	2,066	419,278
Total Catholics	222,822	172,434	2,323,000	91,550	615,918	149,176	68,229,841
Total Population	1,360,301	1,567,582	5,956,555	860,658	1,916,361	1,492,335	307,374,682
Catholic Population Percentage	16	11	39	11	32	10	22

*Indicates Archdioceses.

†Certain Diocese traverse state lines.

	Rockford IL	Springfield in Illinois IL	ILLINOIS TOTAL	*Indianapolis IN	Evansville IN	Fort Wayne–South Bend IN	2012 U.S. GRAND TOTAL
Cardinals	–	–	1	–	–	–	**13**
Archbishops	–	–	–	1	–	–	**56**
Bishop	3	2	22	1	2	2	**394**
Abbots	2	–	8	4	–	–	**109**
Diocesan Priests	196	106	1,568	143	71	80	**27,125**
Religious Priests	42	49	984	85	5	137	**12,593**
Total Priests in Diocese	238	155	2,552	228	76	217	**39,718**
Newly Ordained Priests	7	1	32	1	–	4	**485**
Total Permanent Deacons	145	37	1,181	30	49	21	**17,816**
Total Brothers	11	27	365	30	–	113	**4,518**
Total Sisters	95	667	3,524	574	242	458	**55,045**
Number of Parishes	104	130	984	138	69	81	**18,061**
Missions	–	–	45	12	–	–	**2,627**
Pastoral Centers	–	–	13	–	8	4	**628**
New Parishes	–	1	2	–	–	1	**87**
Catholic Hospitals	3	6	44	2	2	2	**605**
Patients Assisted Annually	551,273	518,428	7,525,952	1,467,102	570,103	254,349	**88,519,295**
Health Care Centers	17	–	19	–	1	4	**363**
Patients Assisted Annually	232,132	–	249,632	–	58	57,795	**5,038,247**
Specialized Homes	7	1	78	5	3	7	**1,616**
Total Assisted Anually	3,198	90	13,793	1,281	128	2,257	**991,072**
Residential Care of Children (Orphanages)	–	1	3	–	–	–	**344**
Total Assisted Anually	–	138	2,800	–	–	–	**23,479**
Day Care and Extended Day Care Centers	1	1	20	1	1	–	**1,005**
Total Assisted Anually	36	140	4,615	72	211	–	**121,211**
Special Centers for Social Services	6	–	115	16	10	9	**3,602**
Total Assisted Anually	66,574	–	1,194,639	179,920	175,380	271,359	**32,768,652**
Diocesan Seminaries	–	–	2	1	–	–	**71**
Students	–	–	196	35	–	–	**3,346**
Religious Seminaries	–	–	1	1	–	2	**98**
Students	–	–	103	–	–	29	**1,669**
Colleges and Universities	1	2	13	2	–	5	**233**
Total Students	132	2,550	70,442	3,960	–	16,704	**812,098**
High Schools, Diocesan and Parish	6	1	25	7	4	4	**731**
Total Students	3,185	190	10,112	3,586	1,465	3,125	**327,345**
High Schools, Private	2	5	44	5	1	–	**595**
Total Students	941	1,937	30,177	2,372	16	–	**296,268**
Elementary Schools, Diocesan and Parish	40	42	408	58	24	37	**5,378**
Total Students	10,441	9,083	110,885	16,871	5,797	10,783	**1,382,539**
Elementary Schools, Private	–	1	3	1	–	–	**386**
Total Students	–	50	1,022	70	–	–	**106,972**
Non–residential Schools for the Disabled	–	–	5	–	–	–	**53**
Total Students	–	–	450	–	–	–	**5,729**
Religious Education High School Students	4,581	1,485	19,282	3,146	1,917	1,191	**662,914**
Religious Education Elementary Students	24,407	7,512	169,810	12,291	4,641	9,375	**2,885,785**
Priests Teaching	10	2	74	1	–	–	**1,199**
Scholastics Teaching	–	–	–	–	–	–	**422**
Brothers Teaching	–	3	51	2	–	–	**698**
Sisters Teaching	10	45	176	21	10	6	**4,026**
Lay Teachers	1,029	983	10,613	1,539	441	720	**162,018**
Infant Baptisms	5,748	1,742	51,417	4,131	1,153	2,680	**793,103**
Adult Baptisms	201	154	2,500	374	87	185	**43,692**
Received into Full Communion	307	319	3,284	545	162	465	**76,588**
First Communions	7,011	1,980	48,337	3,990	1,142	2,939	**797,582**
Confirmations	4,938	2,041	41,546	3,105	1,057	2,548	**618,041**
Marriages	1,020	667	10,414	1,055	396	771	**166,991**
Deaths	2,074	1,610	23,393	1,947	884	1,459	**419,278**
Total Catholics	461,297	142,847	3,783,788	227,699	83,329	159,888	**68,229,841**
Total Population	1,972,238	1,150,549	13,348,696	2,621,455	509,553	1,248,405	**307,374,682**
Catholic Population Percentage	23	12	28	9	16	13	**22**

Archdioceses = 37; Dioceses = 170; Apostolates = 3

2012 GENERAL SUMMARY

	Gary IN	Lafayette in Indiana IN	INDIANA TOTAL	*Dubuque IA	Davenport IA	De Moines IA	2012 U.S. GRAND TOTAL
Cardinals	–	–	–	–	–	–	**13**
Archbishops	–	–	1	2	–	–	**56**
Bishop	1	2	8	–	2	2	**394**
Abbots	–	–	4	2	–	–	**109**
Diocesan Priests	101	117	512	186	99	85	**27,125**
Religious Priests	37	15	279	32	2	10	**12,593**
Total Priests in Diocese	138	132	791	218	101	95	**39,718**
Newly Ordained Priests	–	4	9	2	–	1	**485**
Total Permanent Deacons	66	17	183	105	42	87	**17,816**
Total Brothers	10	3	156	23	1	–	**4,518**
Total Sisters	75	54	1,403	677	153	57	**55,045**
Number of Parishes	68	62	418	168	80	81	**18,061**
Missions	4	–	16	–	–	–	**2,627**
Pastoral Centers	6	–	18	1	–	–	**628**
New Parishes	–	–	1	1	–	1	**87**
Catholic Hospitals	6	7	19	7	3	3	**605**
Patients Assisted Annually	1,209,733	1,008,547	4,509,834	1,167,697	421,719	1,429,332	**88,519,295**
Health Care Centers	–	–	5	2	–	–	**363**
Patients Assisted Annually	–	–	57,853	256	–	–	**5,038,247**
Specialized Homes	4	1	20	4	2	2	**1,616**
Total Assisted Anually	926	590	5,182	692	397	5,527	**991,072**
Residential Care of Children (Orphanages)	2	–	2	–	–	–	**344**
Total Assisted Anually	222	–	222	–	–	–	**23,479**
Day Care and Extended Day Care Centers	2	–	4	–	–	–	**1,005**
Total Assisted Anually	500	–	783	–	–	–	**121,211**
Special Centers for Social Services	7	–	42	3	–	5	**3,602**
Total Assisted Anually	10,000	–	636,659	480	–	25,000	**32,768,652**
Diocesan Seminaries	–	–	1	1	–	–	**71**
Students	–	–	35	16	–	–	**3,346**
Religious Seminaries	–	–	3	1	–	–	**98**
Students	–	–	29	125	–	–	**1,669**
Colleges and Universities	1	3	11	3	1	1	**233**
Total Students	1,275	9,554	31,493	4,639	3,567	832	**812,098**
High Schools, Diocesan and Parish	3	2	20	7	5	2	**731**
Total Students	1,218	1,017	10,411	2,329	1,248	1,622	**327,345**
High Schools, Private	1	–	7	–	–	–	**595**
Total Students	33	–	2,421	–	–	–	**296,268**
Elementary Schools, Diocesan and Parish	20	18	157	44	13	15	**5,378**
Total Students	5,371	3,820	42,642	9,489	3,620	4,854	**1,382,539**
Elementary Schools, Private	–	–	1	–	–	–	**386**
Total Students	–	–	70	–	–	–	**106,972**
Non–residential Schools for the Disabled	–	–	–	–	–	–	**53**
Total Students	–	–	–	–	–	–	**5,729**
Religious Education High School Students	745	2,934	9,933	4,771	2,302	2,657	**662,914**
Religious Education Elementary Students	8,694	8,928	43,929	12,719	8,553	11,088	**2,885,785**
Priests Teaching	–	1	2	1	1	1	**1,199**
Scholastics Teaching	–	–	–	–	–	–	**422**
Brothers Teaching	–	3	5	–	–	–	**698**
Sisters Teaching	5	7	49	9	3	3	**4,026**
Lay Teachers	424	353	3,477	901	407	287	**162,018**
Infant Baptisms	1,573	1,791	11,328	2,456	1,297	1,667	**793,103**
Adult Baptisms	97	138	881	102	143	77	**43,692**
Received into Full Communion	173	274	1,619	291	144	210	**76,588**
First Communions	2,007	2,163	12,241	2,631	1,616	1,958	**797,582**
Confirmations	1,854	1,660	10,224	2,308	1,589	1,517	**618,041**
Marriages	483	415	3,120	868	458	462	**166,991**
Deaths	1,420	777	6,487	2,153	867	658	**419,278**
Total Catholics	185,300	95,619	751,835	202,601	97,332	94,052	**68,229,841**
Total Population	794,178	1,296,384	6,469,975	995,357	763,849	816,196	**307,374,682**
Catholic Population Percentage	23	7	12	20	13	12	**22**

*Indicates Archdioceses.

†Certain Diocese traverse state lines.

2012 GENERAL SUMMARY

	Sioux City IA	IOWA TOTAL	*Kansas City in Kansas KS	Dodge City KS	Salina KS	Wichita KS	2012 U.S. GRAND TOTAL
Cardinals	–	–	–	–	–	–	13
Archbishops	–	2	2	–	–	–	56
Bishop	2	6	–	2	2	2	394
Abbots	–	2	3	–	–	–	109
Diocesan Priests	138	508	106	32	59	121	27,125
Religious Priests	–	44	52	4	16	1	12,593
Total Priests in Diocese	138	552	158	36	75	122	39,718
Newly Ordained Priests	–	3	8	1	1	4	485
Total Permanent Deacons	41	275	22	8	7	4	17,816
Total Brothers	–	24	12	–	1	–	4,518
Total Sisters	62	949	496	72	140	258	55,045
Number of Parishes	112	441	108	48	86	90	18,061
Missions	–	–	–	1	–	–	2,627
Pastoral Centers	–	1	–	–	–	22	628
New Parishes	–	2	–	–	–	–	87
Catholic Hospitals	3	16	3	2	–	8	605
Patients Assisted Annually	262,262	3,281,010	678,671	132,135	–	510,175	88,519,295
Health Care Centers	–	2	4	1	–	2	363
Patients Assisted Annually	–	256	7,968	–	–	61,774	5,038,247
Specialized Homes	3	11	3	–	5	8	1,616
Total Assisted Anually	330	6,946	690	–	409	1,199	991,072
Residential Care of Children (Orphanages)	–	–	–	–	–	–	344
Total Assisted Anually	–	–	–	–	–	–	23,479
Day Care and Extended Day Care Centers	–	–	2	–	–	–	1,005
Total Assisted Anually	–	–	94	–	–	–	121,211
Special Centers for Social Services	5	13	6	4	–	1	3,602
Total Assisted Anually	4,321	29,801	85,000	7,656	–	24,575	32,768,652
Diocesan Seminaries	–	1	–	–	–	–	71
Students	–	16	–	–	–	–	3,346
Religious Seminaries	–	1	–	–	–	–	98
Students	1	126	1	–	–	–	1,669
Colleges and Universities	1	6	3	–	–	1	233
Total Students	1,185	10,223	4,799	–	–	3,021	812,098
High Schools, Diocesan and Parish	8	22	6	–	5	4	731
Total Students	1,685	6,884	3,362	–	656	2,565	327,345
High Schools, Private	–	–	1	–	–	–	595
Total Students	–	–	184	–	–	–	296,268
Elementary Schools, Diocesan and Parish	17	89	38	7	11	34	5,378
Total Students	4,533	22,496	11,790	989	2,142	8,106	1,382,539
Elementary Schools, Private	–	–	3	–	–	–	386
Total Students	–	–	160	–	–	–	106,972
Non–residential Schools for the Disabled	–	–	–	–	–	–	53
Total Students	–	–	–	–	–	–	5,729
Religious Education High School Students	2,653	12,383	2,686	1,421	1,667	2,058	662,914
Religious Education Elementary Students	6,697	39,057	12,514	3,645	4,011	5,981	2,885,785
Priests Teaching	5	8	–	–	4	3	1,199
Scholastics Teaching	–	–	–	–	–	–	422
Brothers Teaching	–	–	–	–	–	–	698
Sisters Teaching	8	23	14	–	1	16	4,026
Lay Teachers	566	2,161	1,124	88	229	740	162,018
Infant Baptisms	1,217	6,637	3,295	961	838	2,372	793,103
Adult Baptisms	75	397	273	40	66	208	43,692
Received into Full Communion	264	909	460	136	134	302	76,588
First Communions	1,443	7,648	3,830	1,120	914	2,576	797,582
Confirmations	1,366	6,780	3,674	845	572	2,014	618,041
Marriages	465	2,253	920	202	303	649	166,991
Deaths	1,124	4,802	1,350	369	637	1,010	419,278
Total Catholics	98,901	492,886	205,531	45,457	42,765	114,595	68,229,841
Total Population	459,279	3,034,681	1,193,425	215,895	315,983	987,240	307,374,682
Catholic Population Percentage	22	16	17	21	14	12	22

Archdioceses = 37; Dioceses = 170; Apostolates = 3

2012 GENERAL SUMMARY

	KANSAS TOTAL	*Louisville KY	Covington KY	Lexington KY	Owensboro KY	KENTUCKY TOTAL	2012 U.S. GRAND TOTAL
Cardinals	–	–	–	–	–	–	**13**
Archbishops	2	1	–	–	–	1	**56**
Bishop	6	–	2	2	2	6	**394**
Abbots	3	2	–	–	–	2	**109**
Diocesan Priests	318	137	82	52	76	347	**27,125**
Religious Priests	73	44	16	21	18	99	**12,593**
Total Priests in Diocese	391	181	98	73	94	446	**39,718**
Newly Ordained Priests	14	2	1	2	3	8	**485**
Total Permanent Deacons	41	127	35	53	5	220	**17,816**
Total Brothers	13	53	6	3	–	62	**4,518**
Total Sisters	966	602	292	74	186	1,154	**55,045**
Number of Parishes	332	102	47	49	79	277	**18,061**
Missions	1	9	6	14	–	29	**2,627**
Pastoral Centers	22	–	–	–	–	–	**628**
New Parishes	–	–	–	–	–	–	**87**
Catholic Hospitals	13	2	5	11	1	19	**605**
Patients Assisted Annually	1,320,981	263,350	849,588	1,249,529	282,290	2,644,757	**88,519,295**
Health Care Centers	7	1	–	4	–	5	**363**
Patients Assisted Annually	69,742	5,907	–	56,000	–	61,907	**5,038,247**
Specialized Homes	16	3	3	1	3	10	**1,616**
Total Assisted Anually	2,298	1,000	937	210	213	2,360	**991,072**
Residential Care of Children (Orphanages)	–	2	2	–	–	4	**344**
Total Assisted Anually	–	815	209	–	–	1,024	**23,479**
Day Care and Extended Day Care Centers	2	6	1	–	3	10	**1,005**
Total Assisted Anually	94	300	75	–	223	598	**121,211**
Special Centers for Social Services	11	7	4	1	2	14	**3,602**
Total Assisted Anually	117,231	41,000	107,344	8,000	9,030	165,374	**32,768,652**
Diocesan Seminaries	–	–	–	–	–	–	**71**
Students	–	–	–	–	–	–	**3,346**
Religious Seminaries	–	–	–	–	–	–	**98**
Students	1	–	–	–	–	–	**1,669**
Colleges and Universities	4	3	1	–	1	5	**233**
Total Students	7,820	6,242	1,886	–	681	8,809	**812,098**
High Schools, Diocesan and Parish	15	4	7	1	3	15	**731**
Total Students	6,583	2,207	2,446	807	732	6,192	**327,345**
High Schools, Private	1	5	2	1	–	8	**595**
Total Students	184	3,940	804	95	–	4,839	**296,268**
Elementary Schools, Diocesan and Parish	90	36	27	15	15	93	**5,378**
Total Students	23,027	11,440	6,333	3,045	3,016	23,834	**1,382,539**
Elementary Schools, Private	3	3	2	–	–	5	**386**
Total Students	160	514	494	–	–	1,008	**106,972**
Non–residential Schools for the Disabled	–	1	–	–	–	1	**53**
Total Students	–	65	–	–	–	65	**5,729**
Religious Education High School Students	7,832	758	276	986	846	2,866	**662,914**
Religious Education Elementary Students	26,151	5,024	3,867	2,481	3,011	14,383	**2,885,785**
Priests Teaching	7	7	1	5	4	17	**1,199**
Scholastics Teaching	–	–	–	–	–	–	**422**
Brothers Teaching	–	1	1	–	–	2	**698**
Sisters Teaching	31	23	19	7	15	64	**4,026**
Lay Teachers	2,181	1,678	720	334	317	3,049	**162,018**
Infant Baptisms	7,466	1,975	1,017	821	939	4,752	**793,103**
Adult Baptisms	587	162	135	82	122	501	**43,692**
Received into Full Communion	1,032	441	95	197	259	992	**76,588**
First Communions	8,440	2,462	1,406	994	925	5,787	**797,582**
Confirmations	7,105	2,350	1,457	759	987	5,553	**618,041**
Marriages	2,074	638	407	195	350	1,590	**166,991**
Deaths	3,366	1,565	817	285	506	3,173	**419,278**
Total Catholics	408,348	192,396	92,042	42,056	49,721	376,215	**68,229,841**
Total Population	2,712,543	1,263,368	513,971	1,578,749	879,747	4,235,835	**307,374,682**
Catholic Population Percentage	15	15	18	3	6	22	**22**

*Indicates Archdioceses.

†Certain Diocese traverse state lines.

	*New Orleans LA	Alexandria LA	Baton Rouge LA	Houma–Thibodaux LA	Lafayette LA	Lake Charles LA	2012 U.S. GRAND TOTAL
Cardinals	–	–	–	–	–	–	**13**
Archbishops	3	–	–	–	–	–	**56**
Bishop	2	1	1	1	1	2	**394**
Abbots	1	–	–	–	–	–	**109**
Diocesan Priests	202	54	73	61	158	47	**27,125**
Religious Priests	162	11	35	9	43	13	**12,593**
Total Priests in Diocese	364	65	108	70	201	60	**39,718**
Newly Ordained Priests	6	–	3	1	4	2	**485**
Total Permanent Deacons	217	6	66	40	67	26	**17,816**
Total Brothers	77	3	15	4	13	1	**4,518**
Total Sisters	429	29	95	23	136	12	**55,045**
Number of Parishes	108	44	68	39	121	38	**18,061**
Missions	10	21	–	3	29	8	**2,627**
Pastoral Centers	2	–	–	–	–	–	**628**
New Parishes	–	–	–	–	–	–	**87**
Catholic Hospitals	–	1	3	–	1	1	**605**
Patients Assisted Annually	–	205,250	625,003	–	94,065	81,969	**88,519,295**
Health Care Centers	9	1	–	–	–	–	**363**
Patients Assisted Annually	124,078	350	–	–	–	–	**5,038,247**
Specialized Homes	28	1	12	3	47	1	**1,616**
Total Assisted Anually	3,910	104	1,092	105	11,900	118	**991,072**
Residential Care of Children (Orphanages)	1	–	–	–	–	–	**344**
Total Assisted Anually	25	–	–	–	–	–	**23,479**
Day Care and Extended Day Care Centers	8	–	–	1	–	3	**1,005**
Total Assisted Anually	968	–	–	87	–	97	**121,211**
Special Centers for Social Services	264	8	8	4	6	3	**3,602**
Total Assisted Anually	353,797	925	227,093	11,474	56,798	10,021	**32,768,652**
Diocesan Seminaries	2	–	–	–	–	–	**71**
Students	173	–	–	–	–	–	**3,346**
Religious Seminaries	2	–	–	–	1	–	**98**
Students	13	–	–	–	17	2	**1,669**
Colleges and Universities	3	–	1	–	–	–	**233**
Total Students	9,781	–	1,860	–	–	–	**812,098**
High Schools, Diocesan and Parish	10	3	6	3	9	1	**731**
Total Students	4,469	691	2,197	1,873	3,496	647	**327,345**
High Schools, Private	13	–	2	–	1	–	**595**
Total Students	8,738	–	2,003	–	135	–	**296,268**
Elementary Schools, Diocesan and Parish	53	7	23	10	29	7	**5,378**
Total Students	22,298	1,771	10,927	3,846	10,492	2,019	**1,382,539**
Elementary Schools, Private	8	–	–	–	2	–	**386**
Total Students	2,173	–	–	–	744	–	**106,972**
Non–residential Schools for the Disabled	1	–	–	–	–	–	**53**
Total Students	190	–	–	–	–	–	**5,729**
Religious Education High School Students	3,691	825	3,561	2,438	13,489	1,809	**662,914**
Religious Education Elementary Students	10,424	1,836	8,338	4,997	6,352	5,040	**2,885,785**
Priests Teaching	42	–	2	–	–	–	**1,199**
Scholastics Teaching	2	–	–	–	–	–	**422**
Brothers Teaching	31	3	2	2	–	–	**698**
Sisters Teaching	46	6	10	–	1	1	**4,026**
Lay Teachers	3,544	21	945	374	977	174	**162,018**
Infant Baptisms	4,023	552	2,474	1,194	3,603	913	**793,103**
Adult Baptisms	216	41	153	33	80	69	**43,692**
Received into Full Communion	202	154	285	45	212	323	**76,588**
First Communions	4,155	593	2,487	1,174	3,630	928	**797,582**
Confirmations	3,555	423	2,040	909	2,850	758	**618,041**
Marriages	1,411	187	697	285	1,022	268	**166,991**
Deaths	3,514	599	1,702	1,225	3,259	817	**419,278**
Total Catholics	485,973	43,484	225,979	106,305	304,921	72,999	**68,229,841**
Total Population	1,214,932	383,421	969,104	202,000	568,154	292,619	**307,374,682**
Catholic Population Percentage	40	11	23	53	54	25	**22**

Archdioceses = 37; Dioceses = 170; Apostolates = 3

2012 GENERAL SUMMARY

	Shreveport LA	LOUISIANA TOTAL	Portland (in Maine) ME	Marshall Islands	*Baltimore MD	*Boston MA	2012 U.S. GRAND TOTAL
Cardinals	–	–	–	–	1	1	**13**
Archbishops	–	3	–	–	1	–	**56**
Bishop	2	10	2	–	3	8	**394**
Abbots	–	1	–	–	–	1	**109**
Diocesan Priests	33	628	143	1	249	699	**27,125**
Religious Priests	14	287	27	5	227	505	**12,593**
Total Priests in Diocese	47	915	170	6	476	1,204	**39,718**
Newly Ordained Priests	–	16	1	–	1	6	**485**
Total Permanent Deacons	20	442	43	–	168	265	**17,816**
Total Brothers	5	118	13	–	69	151	**4,518**
Total Sisters	33	757	285	10	860	1,760	**55,045**
Number of Parishes	27	445	57	5	146	289	**18,061**
Missions	13	84	18	8	7	1	**2,627**
Pastoral Centers	–	2	–	–	–	–	**628**
New Parishes	–	–	4	–	–	1	**87**
Catholic Hospitals	–	6	3	–	5	8	**605**
Patients Assisted Annually	–	1,006,287	445,575	–	1,864,800	708,219	**88,519,295**
Health Care Centers	3	13	–	–	4	3	**363**
Patients Assisted Annually	431,518	555,946	–	–	2,772	7,511	**5,038,247**
Specialized Homes	1	93	6	–	32	36	**1,616**
Total Assisted Anually	190	17,419	589	–	4,981	4,554	**991,072**
Residential Care of Children (Orphanages)	–	1	–	–	9	1	**344**
Total Assisted Anually	–	25	–	–	1,429	921	**23,479**
Day Care and Extended Day Care Centers	2	14	1	–	6	11	**1,005**
Total Assisted Anually	148	1,300	215	–	5,025	1,110	**121,211**
Special Centers for Social Services	22	315	2	1	40	43	**3,602**
Total Assisted Anually	45,132	705,240	715	270	359,747	206,000	**32,768,652**
Diocesan Seminaries	–	2	–	–	2	3	**71**
Students	–	173	–	–	247	154	**3,346**
Religious Seminaries	–	3	–	1	–	1	**98**
Students	–	32	–	2	–	33	**1,669**
Colleges and Universities	–	4	1	–	4	6	**233**
Total Students	–	11,641	3,103	–	11,315	24,900	**812,098**
High Schools, Diocesan and Parish	2	34	1	2	7	3	**731**
Total Students	683	14,056	241	180	3,384	1,150	**327,345**
High Schools, Private	–	16	2	–	13	29	**595**
Total Students	–	10,876	682	–	7,363	15,155	**296,268**
Elementary Schools, Diocesan and Parish	4	133	10	3	42	79	**5,378**
Total Students	1,245	52,598	2,088	626	16,104	24,067	**1,382,539**
Elementary Schools, Private	–	10	1	–	7	9	**386**
Total Students	–	2,917	167	–	1,111	2,264	**106,972**
Non–residential Schools for the Disabled	–	1	–	–	1	2	**53**
Total Students	–	190	–	–	116	139	**5,729**
Religious Education High School Students	445	26,258	859	82	2,430	26,624	**662,914**
Religious Education Elementary Students	1,760	38,747	5,334	382	22,589	97,419	**2,885,785**
Priests Teaching	–	44	1	–	40	7	**1,199**
Scholastics Teaching	–	2	2	–	–	–	**422**
Brothers Teaching	–	38	–	–	8	31	**698**
Sisters Teaching	1	65	4	8	64	91	**4,026**
Lay Teachers	130	6,165	246	55	2,587	3,177	**162,018**
Infant Baptisms	512	13,271	1,288	96	5,860	13,390	**793,103**
Adult Baptisms	48	640	86	–	481	250	**43,692**
Received into Full Communion	151	1,372	115	23	793	255	**76,588**
First Communions	530	13,497	1,648	81	5,828	16,786	**797,582**
Confirmations	440	10,975	1,747	26	5,299	13,305	**618,041**
Marriages	148	4,018	584	11	1,307	3,012	**166,991**
Deaths	373	11,489	2,645	22	4,167	14,426	**419,278**
Total Catholics	40,991	1,280,652	193,392	4,925	510,328	1,807,002	**68,229,841**
Total Population	812,200	4,442,430	1,274,932	52,558	3,148,690	3,764,587	**307,374,682**
Catholic Population Percentage	5	29	15	9	16	48	**22**

*Indicates Archdioceses.

†Certain Diocese traverse state lines.

	Fall River MA	Springfield in Massachusetts MA	Worcester MA	MASS. TOTAL	*Detroit MI	Gaylord MI	2012 U.S. GRAND TOTAL
Cardinals	–	–	–	1	2	–	**13**
Archbishops	–	–	–	–	1	–	**56**
Bishop	1	3	3	15	6	1	**394**
Abbots	–	–	2	3	–	–	**109**
Diocesan Priests	150	141	187	1,177	381	63	**27,125**
Religious Priests	89	43	91	728	196	6	**12,593**
Total Priests in Diocese	239	184	278	1,905	577	69	**39,718**
Newly Ordained Priests	1	3	9	19	3	1	**485**
Total Permanent Deacons	84	78	108	535	198	23	**17,816**
Total Brothers	16	20	64	251	89	–	**4,518**
Total Sisters	179	353	265	2,557	1,023	29	**55,045**
Number of Parishes	90	81	105	565	268	80	**18,061**
Missions	11	8	4	24	1	–	**2,627**
Pastoral Centers	–	1	1	2	–	–	**628**
New Parishes	–	–	1	2	–	–	**87**
Catholic Hospitals	–	1	1	10	10	3	**605**
Patients Assisted Annually	–	172,612	248,569	1,129,400	1,074,882	375,000	**88,519,295**
Health Care Centers	–	1	2	6	–	–	**363**
Patients Assisted Annually	–	7,000	226	14,737	–	–	**5,038,247**
Specialized Homes	7	9	5	57	35	–	**1,616**
Total Assisted Anually	1,196	532	215	6,497	15,438	–	**991,072**
Residential Care of Children (Orphanages)	1	–	1	3	–	–	**344**
Total Assisted Anually	200	–	12	1,133	–	–	**23,479**
Day Care and Extended Day Care Centers	1	–	21	33	–	11	**1,005**
Total Assisted Anually	45	–	1,860	3,015	–	392	**121,211**
Special Centers for Social Services	4	8	6	61	42	22	**3,602**
Total Assisted Anually	45,252	42,070	48,000	341,322	67,200	47,691	**32,768,652**
Diocesan Seminaries	–	–	–	3	2	–	**71**
Students	–	–	–	154	125	–	**3,346**
Religious Seminaries	–	–	–	1	2	–	**98**
Students	–	–	–	33	19	–	**1,669**
Colleges and Universities	1	1	3	11	3	–	**233**
Total Students	2,520	1,482	8,863	37,765	13,027	–	**812,098**
High Schools, Diocesan and Parish	5	4	4	16	10	4	**731**
Total Students	2,856	943	1,588	6,537	3,872	477	**327,345**
High Schools, Private	–	–	5	34	14	–	**595**
Total Students	–	–	1,535	16,690	6,455	–	**296,268**
Elementary Schools, Diocesan and Parish	21	15	19	134	70	16	**5,378**
Total Students	4,569	3,807	3,831	36,274	21,868	1,837	**1,382,539**
Elementary Schools, Private	–	–	3	12	1	–	**386**
Total Students	–	–	392	2,656	287	–	**106,972**
Non-residential Schools for the Disabled	–	–	1	3	–	–	**53**
Total Students	–	–	23	162	–	–	**5,729**
Religious Education High School Students	3,932	5,482	5,801	41,839	6,021	858	**662,914**
Religious Education Elementary Students	21,399	12,006	18,551	149,375	50,114	2,138	**2,885,785**
Priests Teaching	7	2	17	33	28	1	**1,199**
Scholastics Teaching	–	–	–	–	–	–	**422**
Brothers Teaching	3	–	–	34	13	–	**698**
Sisters Teaching	10	20	28	149	15	1	**4,026**
Lay Teachers	718	414	1,173	5,482	2,129	182	**162,018**
Infant Baptisms	2,883	2,267	2,333	20,873	8,784	610	**793,103**
Adult Baptisms	75	83	82	490	636	70	**43,692**
Received into Full Communion	223	173	171	822	1,040	131	**76,588**
First Communions	3,536	2,348	3,330	26,000	10,820	721	**797,582**
Confirmations	3,355	2,143	2,688	21,491	9,980	816	**618,041**
Marriages	934	665	511	5,122	2,610	242	**166,991**
Deaths	3,646	3,481	3,028	24,581	8,764	866	**419,278**
Total Catholics	313,115	226,740	301,000	2,647,857	1,378,979	58,830	**68,229,841**
Total Population	823,654	824,161	784,992	6,197,394	4,267,293	504,530	**307,374,682**
Catholic Population Percentage	38	28	38	43	32	12	**22**

Archdioceses = 37; Dioceses = 170; Apostolates = 3

2012 GENERAL SUMMARY

	Grand Rapids MI	Kalamazoo MI	Lansing MI	Marquette MI	Saginaw MI	MICHIGAN TOTAL	2012 U.S. GRAND TOTAL
Cardinals	–	–	–	–	–	2	**13**
Archbishops	–	–	–	–	–	1	**56**
Bishop	2	2	2	2	1	16	**394**
Abbots	–	–	–	–	–	–	**109**
Diocesan Priests	104	61	166	77	92	944	**27,125**
Religious Priests	16	11	45	6	6	286	**12,593**
Total Priests in Diocese	120	72	211	83	98	1,230	**39,718**
Newly Ordained Priests	1	1	3	–	4	13	**485**
Total Permanent Deacons	39	35	103	47	17	462	**17,816**
Total Brothers	1	2	3	–	–	95	**4,518**
Total Sisters	370	208	329	45	90	2,094	**55,045**
Number of Parishes	89	46	84	72	105	744	**18,061**
Missions	9	13	–	22	–	45	**2,627**
Pastoral Centers	1	1	2	1	–	5	**628**
New Parishes	–	–	–	–	–	–	**87**
Catholic Hospitals	2	3	6	1	1	26	**605**
Patients Assisted Annually	935,560	483,582	3,727,806	213,823	300,590	7,111,243	**88,519,295**
Health Care Centers	–	1	7	–	1	9	**363**
Patients Assisted Annually	–	–	104,537	–	1,406	105,943	**5,038,247**
Specialized Homes	19	27	6	1	3	91	**1,616**
Total Assisted Anually	11,762	909	503	109	376	29,097	**991,072**
Residential Care of Children (Orphanages)	–	–	–	–	3	3	**344**
Total Assisted Anually	–	–	–	–	252	252	**23,479**
Day Care and Extended Day Care Centers	–	–	1	–	–	12	**1,005**
Total Assisted Anually	–	–	100	–	–	492	**121,211**
Special Centers for Social Services	12	7	11	3	7	104	**3,602**
Total Assisted Anually	938,472	40,274	322,032	1,968	13,425	1,431,062	**32,768,652**
Diocesan Seminaries	–	–	–	–	–	2	**71**
Students	–	–	–	–	–	125	**3,346**
Religious Seminaries	–	–	–	–	–	2	**98**
Students	–	–	–	–	–	19	**1,669**
Colleges and Universities	1	–	1	–	–	5	**233**
Total Students	2,141	–	2,630	–	–	17,798	**812,098**
High Schools, Diocesan and Parish	3	3	4	–	3	27	**731**
Total Students	1,284	630	2,019	–	607	8,889	**327,345**
High Schools, Private	1	–	–	–	–	15	**595**
Total Students	181	–	–	–	–	6,636	**296,268**
Elementary Schools, Diocesan and Parish	26	19	30	9	17	187	**5,378**
Total Students	4,844	2,508	6,806	1,081	2,676	41,620	**1,382,539**
Elementary Schools, Private	1	–	2	–	–	4	**386**
Total Students	283	–	193	–	–	763	**106,972**
Non–residential Schools for the Disabled	–	–	–	–	–	–	**53**
Total Students	–	–	–	–	–	–	**5,729**
Religious Education High School Students	1,573	430	2,810	852	1,056	13,600	**662,914**
Religious Education Elementary Students	9,531	4,929	14,964	4,701	5,708	92,085	**2,885,785**
Priests Teaching	–	2	2	–	1	34	**1,199**
Scholastics Teaching	–	–	–	–	–	–	**422**
Brothers Teaching	–	1	–	–	–	14	**698**
Sisters Teaching	2	1	5	1	–	25	**4,026**
Lay Teachers	385	205	528	87	215	3,731	**162,018**
Infant Baptisms	2,334	1,291	2,307	499	805	16,630	**793,103**
Adult Baptisms	212	130	285	42	93	1,468	**43,692**
Received into Full Communion	894	142	508	123	192	3,030	**76,588**
First Communions	7,693	1,187	3,285	537	1,153	25,396	**797,582**
Confirmations	2,219	1,025	2,800	159	1,266	18,265	**618,041**
Marriages	656	304	771	232	448	5,263	**166,991**
Deaths	1,359	847	1,969	1,073	1,470	16,348	**419,278**
Total Catholics	178,000	104,386	207,023	50,410	104,726	2,082,354	**68,229,841**
Total Population	1,283,717	948,965	1,793,060	292,119	700,771	9,790,455	**307,374,682**
Catholic Population Percentage	14	11	12	17	15	22	**22**

*Indicates Archdioceses.

†Certain Diocese traverse state lines.

2012 GENERAL SUMMARY

	*St. Paul and Minneapolis MN	Crookston MN	Duluth MN	New Ulm MN	St. Cloud MN	Winona MN	2012 U.S. GRAND TOTAL
Cardinals	–	–	–	–	–	–	**13**
Archbishops	2	–	–	–	–	–	**56**
Bishop	1	2	1	1	2	2	**394**
Abbots	–	–	–	–	1	1	**109**
Diocesan Priests	337	46	72	67	110	113	**27,125**
Religious Priests	84	2	8	–	101	6	**12,593**
Total Priests in Diocese	421	48	80	67	211	119	**39,718**
Newly Ordained Priests	5	–	1	1	2	–	**485**
Total Permanent Deacons	214	18	45	4	51	30	**17,816**
Total Brothers	46	1	–	–	65	21	**4,518**
Total Sisters	643	74	97	52	463	377	**55,045**
Number of Parishes	200	66	93	76	132	114	**18,061**
Missions	2	–	–	–	–	–	**2,627**
Pastoral Centers	4	–	–	–	–	2	**628**
New Parishes	–	–	–	–	1	–	**87**
Catholic Hospitals	3	3	2	1	4	2	**605**
Patients Assisted Annually	227,315	127,751	301,963	9,701	367,136	149,850	**88,519,295**
Health Care Centers	1	–	–	1	–	1	**363**
Patients Assisted Annually	173	–	–	9,274	–	1,236	**5,038,247**
Specialized Homes	21	3	5	11	12	10	**1,616**
Total Assisted Anually	28,592	624	646	399	1,040	677	**991,072**
Residential Care of Children (Orphanages)	2	–	–	–	1	–	**344**
Total Assisted Anually	1,099	–	–	–	368	–	**23,479**
Day Care and Extended Day Care Centers	2	1	1	–	–	3	**1,005**
Total Assisted Anually	241	49	110	–	–	17,398	**121,211**
Special Centers for Social Services	2	–	–	–	67	7	**3,602**
Total Assisted Anually	37,000	–	–	–	52,625	4,392	**32,768,652**
Diocesan Seminaries	2	–	–	–	–	1	**71**
Students	100	–	–	–	–	55	**3,346**
Religious Seminaries	1	–	2	–	1	–	**98**
Students	11	–	1	1	1	–	**1,669**
Colleges and Universities	2	–	1	–	2	1	**233**
Total Students	16,178	–	4,014	–	4,096	1,372	**812,098**
High Schools, Diocesan and Parish	2	1	–	3	1	4	**731**
Total Students	853	143	–	348	650	977	**327,345**
High Schools, Private	10	–	–	–	1	–	**595**
Total Students	6,370	–	–	–	306	–	**296,268**
Elementary Schools, Diocesan and Parish	82	8	12	15	29	26	**5,378**
Total Students	21,211	1,193	1,659	1,737	4,076	4,248	**1,382,539**
Elementary Schools, Private	5	–	–	–	–	–	**386**
Total Students	811	–	–	–	–	–	**106,972**
Non–residential Schools for the Disabled	–	–	–	–	–	–	**53**
Total Students	–	–	–	–	–	–	**5,729**
Religious Education High School Students	10,285	1,747	2,734	2,536	5,263	3,385	**662,914**
Religious Education Elementary Students	29,961	2,308	3,129	5,139	10,998	6,627	**2,885,785**
Priests Teaching	5	–	1	–	24	–	**1,199**
Scholastics Teaching	–	–	–	–	–	–	**422**
Brothers Teaching	6	–	–	–	2	8	**698**
Sisters Teaching	42	–	5	3	15	4	**4,026**
Lay Teachers	2,822	104	314	189	751	334	**162,018**
Infant Baptisms	6,306	554	643	773	1,843	1,431	**793,103**
Adult Baptisms	180	20	34	15	44	35	**43,692**
Received into Full Communion	1,025	104	87	87	138	240	**76,588**
First Communions	9,126	496	644	852	2,039	1,207	**797,582**
Confirmations	7,214	399	650	841	1,819	1,327	**618,041**
Marriages	1,603	169	275	284	647	437	**166,991**
Deaths	3,338	449	903	706	1,414	776	**419,278**
Total Catholics	825,000	34,410	56,925	61,917	142,042	132,545	**68,229,841**
Total Population	2,686,763	260,616	447,042	284,768	559,865	576,284	**307,374,682**
Catholic Population Percentage	31	13	13	22	25	23	**22**

Archdioceses = 37; Dioceses = 170; Apostolates = 3

2012 GENERAL SUMMARY

	MINNESOTA TOTAL	Biloxi MS	Jackson MS	MISSISSIPPI TOTAL	*St. Louis MO	Jefferson City MO	2012 U.S. GRAND TOTAL
Cardinals	–	–	–	–	–	–	**13**
Archbishops	2	–	–	–	1	–	**56**
Bishop	9	2	2	4	2	1	**394**
Abbots	2	–	–	–	3	–	**109**
Diocesan Priests	745	51	51	102	348	87	**27,125**
Religious Priests	201	25	33	58	319	9	**12,593**
Total Priests in Diocese	946	76	84	160	667	96	**39,718**
Newly Ordained Priests	9	3	–	3	10	1	**485**
Total Permanent Deacons	362	32	7	39	265	69	**17,816**
Total Brothers	133	12	7	19	132	1	**4,518**
Total Sisters	1,706	37	156	193	1,321	44	**55,045**
Number of Parishes	681	42	75	117	188	95	**18,061**
Missions	2	9	23	32	8	15	**2,627**
Pastoral Centers	6	–	–	–	–	–	**628**
New Parishes	1	–	–	–	–	–	**87**
Catholic Hospitals	15	–	1	1	9	1	**605**
Patients Assisted Annually	1,183,716	–	134,279	134,279	2,181,270	120,756	**88,519,295**
Health Care Centers	3	–	1	1	–	14	**363**
Patients Assisted Annually	10,683	–	8,458	8,458	–	115,844	**5,038,247**
Specialized Homes	62	7	7	14	23	–	**1,616**
Total Assisted Anually	31,978	475	5,327	5,802	10,746	–	**991,072**
Residential Care of Children (Orphanages)	3	–	2	2	2	–	**344**
Total Assisted Anually	1,467	–	342	342	379	–	**23,479**
Day Care and Extended Day Care Centers	7	–	2	2	3	–	**1,005**
Total Assisted Anually	17,798	–	202	202	26,159	–	**121,211**
Special Centers for Social Services	76	7	17	24	14	2	**3,602**
Total Assisted Anually	94,017	436,810	17,897	454,707	29,172	48,073	**32,768,652**
Diocesan Seminaries	3	–	–	–	2	–	**71**
Students	155	–	–	–	107	–	**3,346**
Religious Seminaries	4	–	–	–	2	–	**98**
Students	14	–	–	–	27	–	**1,669**
Colleges and Universities	6	–	2	2	2	–	**233**
Total Students	25,660	–	20	20	16,605	–	**812,098**
High Schools, Diocesan and Parish	11	4	4	8	12	3	**731**
Total Students	2,971	1,170	1,210	2,380	4,536	937	**327,345**
High Schools, Private	11	1	–	1	16	–	**595**
Total Students	6,676	357	–	357	8,259	–	**296,268**
Elementary Schools, Diocesan and Parish	172	10	15	25	107	37	**5,378**
Total Students	34,124	2,648	3,355	6,003	27,892	6,206	**1,382,539**
Elementary Schools, Private	5	–	–	–	8	–	**386**
Total Students	811	–	–	–	2,139	–	**106,972**
Non–residential Schools for the Disabled	–	–	–	–	4	–	**53**
Total Students	–	–	–	–	179	–	**5,729**
Religious Education High School Students	25,950	908	1,310	2,218	93	1,841	**662,914**
Religious Education Elementary Students	58,162	3,638	4,097	7,735	20,380	3,634	**2,885,785**
Priests Teaching	30	–	–	–	33	9	**1,199**
Scholastics Teaching	–	–	–	–	–	–	**422**
Brothers Teaching	16	3	3	6	21	1	**698**
Sisters Teaching	69	3	10	13	79	1	**4,026**
Lay Teachers	4,514	345	437	782	3,811	545	**162,018**
Infant Baptisms	11,550	947	826	1,773	5,454	1,140	**793,103**
Adult Baptisms	328	123	76	199	272	153	**43,692**
Received into Full Communion	1,681	162	208	370	449	256	**76,588**
First Communions	14,364	967	853	1,820	6,271	1,285	**797,582**
Confirmations	12,250	673	364	1,037	6,651	1,195	**618,041**
Marriages	3,415	234	203	437	1,905	438	**166,991**
Deaths	7,586	645	437	1,082	3,995	785	**419,278**
Total Catholics	1,252,839	58,702	48,831	107,533	524,507	82,516	**68,229,841**
Total Population	4,815,338	800,165	2,111,593	2,911,758	2,211,707	910,356	**307,374,682**
Catholic Population Percentage	26	7	2	4	24	9	**22**

*Indicates Archdioceses.

†Certain Diocese traverse state lines.

	Kansas City – St. Joseph MO	Springfield – Cape Girardeau	MISSOURI TOTAL	Great Falls – Billings MT	Helena MT	MONTANA TOTAL	2012 U.S. GRAND TOTAL
Cardinals	–	–	–	–	–	–	**13**
Archbishops	–	–	1	–	1	1	**56**
Bishop	2	2	7	2	1	3	**394**
Abbots	1	2	6	–	–	–	**109**
Diocesan Priests	97	62	594	62	72	134	**27,125**
Religious Priests	82	56	466	12	6	18	**12,593**
Total Priests in Diocese	179	118	1,060	74	78	152	**39,718**
Newly Ordained Priests	2	2	15	–	1	1	**485**
Total Permanent Deacons	64	16	414	5	26	31	**17,816**
Total Brothers	33	37	203	–	2	2	**4,518**
Total Sisters	219	76	1,660	49	31	80	**55,045**
Number of Parishes	87	66	436	53	57	110	**18,061**
Missions	11	18	52	52	39	91	**2,627**
Pastoral Centers	–	4	4	–	14	14	**628**
New Parishes	–	–	–	1	–	1	**87**
Catholic Hospitals	3	8	21	2	2	4	**605**
Patients Assisted Annually	290,581	1,007,721	3,600,328	435,039	275,685	710,724	**88,519,295**
Health Care Centers	–	–	14	–	–	–	**363**
Patients Assisted Annually	–	–	115,844	–	–	–	**5,038,247**
Specialized Homes	11	1	35	2	–	2	**1,616**
Total Assisted Anually	2,335	220	13,301	80	–	80	**991,072**
Residential Care of Children (Orphanages)	–	–	2	–	–	–	**344**
Total Assisted Anually	–	–	379	–	–	–	**23,479**
Day Care and Extended Day Care Centers	8	1	12	6	3	9	**1,005**
Total Assisted Anually	1,307	29	27,495	448	97	545	**121,211**
Special Centers for Social Services	7	–	23	–	–	–	**3,602**
Total Assisted Anually	296,285	–	373,530	–	–	–	**32,768,652**
Diocesan Seminaries	1	–	3	–	1	1	**71**
Students	112	–	219	–	–	–	**3,346**
Religious Seminaries	–	–	2	–	–	–	**98**
Students	–	–	27	–	–	–	**1,669**
Colleges and Universities	2	–	4	1	1	2	**233**
Total Students	4,619	–	21,224	1,075	1,428	2,503	**812,098**
High Schools, Diocesan and Parish	4	3	22	2	2	4	**731**
Total Students	1,084	982	7,539	426	300	726	**327,345**
High Schools, Private	4	–	20	1	–	1	**595**
Total Students	2,404	–	10,663	139	–	139	**296,268**
Elementary Schools, Diocesan and Parish	26	23	193	9	4	13	**5,378**
Total Students	7,519	3,572	45,189	1,384	814	2,198	**1,382,539**
Elementary Schools, Private	1	–	9	3	–	3	**386**
Total Students	302	–	2,441	543	–	543	**106,972**
Non–residential Schools for the Disabled	–	–	4	–	–	–	**53**
Total Students	–	–	179	–	–	–	**5,729**
Religious Education High School Students	1,438	1,216	4,588	795	1,121	1,916	**662,914**
Religious Education Elementary Students	6,732	3,265	34,011	2,446	3,184	5,630	**2,885,785**
Priests Teaching	21	–	63	1	–	1	**1,199**
Scholastics Teaching	–	–	–	–	–	–	**422**
Brothers Teaching	12	1	35	3	2	5	**698**
Sisters Teaching	10	4	94	7	1	8	**4,026**
Lay Teachers	1,095	290	5,741	385	151	536	**162,018**
Infant Baptisms	2,055	882	9,531	616	457	1,073	**793,103**
Adult Baptisms	259	108	792	63	–	63	**43,692**
Received into Full Communion	461	224	1,390	160	69	229	**76,588**
First Communions	2,242	1,193	10,991	728	652	1,380	**797,582**
Confirmations	1,855	788	10,489	785	634	1,419	**618,041**
Marriages	698	299	3,340	144	133	277	**166,991**
Deaths	1,238	569	6,587	711	722	1,433	**419,278**
Total Catholics	134,173	67,950	809,146	43,731	45,278	89,009	**68,229,841**
Total Population	1,513,005	1,353,859	5,988,927	402,523	579,983	982,506	**307,374,682**
Catholic Population Percentage	9	5	14	11	8	22	**22**

Archdioceses = 37; Dioceses = 170; Apostolates = 3

2012 GENERAL SUMMARY

	Chalan Kanoa MP	*Omaha NE	Grand Island NE	Lincoln NE	NEBRASKA TOTAL	Las Vegas NV	2012 U.S. GRAND TOTAL
Cardinals	–	–	–	–	–	–	**13**
Archbishops	–	2	–	–	2	–	**56**
Bishop	1	1	1	1	3	1	**394**
Abbots	–	3	–	–	3	–	**109**
Diocesan Priests	12	185	64	150	399	37	**27,125**
Religious Priests	1	78	–	10	88	18	**12,593**
Total Priests in Diocese	13	263	64	160	487	55	**39,718**
Newly Ordained Priests	–	5	1	5	11	–	**485**
Total Permanent Deacons	–	237	6	3	246	32	**17,816**
Total Brothers	–	20	–	–	20	3	**4,518**
Total Sisters	–	266	62	148	476	–	**55,045**
Number of Parishes	12	132	36	134	302	29	**18,061**
Missions	1	15	33	1	49	6	**2,627**
Pastoral Centers	1	–	–	6	6	–	**628**
New Parishes	–	–	–	1	1	–	**87**
Catholic Hospitals	–	3	–	4	7	–	**605**
Patients Assisted Annually	–	190,489	–	170,435	360,924	–	**88,519,295**
Health Care Centers	–	–	2	–	2	–	**363**
Patients Assisted Annually	–	–	184,550	–	184,550	–	**5,038,247**
Specialized Homes	1	12	1	4	17	–	**1,616**
Total Assisted Anually	138	2,130	50	267	2,447	–	**991,072**
Residential Care of Children (Orphanages)	–	–	–	–	–	–	**344**
Total Assisted Anually	–	–	–	–	–	–	**23,479**
Day Care and Extended Day Care Centers	–	16	–	1	17	–	**1,005**
Total Assisted Anually	–	1,286	–	45	1,331	–	**121,211**
Special Centers for Social Services	2	8	–	22	30	21	**3,602**
Total Assisted Anually	3,258	83,319	–	27,439	110,758	7,500,000	**32,768,652**
Diocesan Seminaries	–	–	–	1	1	–	**71**
Students	–	–	–	34	34	–	**3,346**
Religious Seminaries	–	–	–	1	1	–	**98**
Students	–	–	–	77	77	–	**1,669**
Colleges and Universities	–	2	–	–	2	–	**233**
Total Students	–	8,793	–	–	8,793	–	**812,098**
High Schools, Diocesan and Parish	–	12	4	6	22	1	**731**
Total Students	–	2,978	505	1,704	5,187	1,268	**327,345**
High Schools, Private	1	5	–	–	5	–	**595**
Total Students	156	2,608	–	–	2,608	–	**296,268**
Elementary Schools, Diocesan and Parish	3	54	6	27	87	7	**5,378**
Total Students	169	13,899	1,071	5,257	20,227	2,704	**1,382,539**
Elementary Schools, Private	–	1	–	–	1	–	**386**
Total Students	–	62	–	–	62	–	**106,972**
Non–residential Schools for the Disabled	–	1	–	1	2	–	**53**
Total Students	–	58	–	13	71	–	**5,729**
Religious Education High School Students	697	2,448	2,046	1,722	6,216	3,274	**662,914**
Religious Education Elementary Students	663	14,786	3,662	5,312	23,760	9,775	**2,885,785**
Priests Teaching	2	28	–	24	52	1	**1,199**
Scholastics Teaching	–	3	–	–	3	–	**422**
Brothers Teaching	–	2	–	–	2	–	**698**
Sisters Teaching	2	11	2	36	49	–	**4,026**
Lay Teachers	20	1,400	117	458	1,975	229	**162,018**
Infant Baptisms	459	4,100	835	1,088	6,023	5,967	**793,103**
Adult Baptisms	20	202	71	100	373	168	**43,692**
Received into Full Communion	25	484	132	184	800	312	**76,588**
First Communions	610	4,366	851	1,535	6,752	4,177	**797,582**
Confirmations	632	3,645	665	1,515	5,825	1,664	**618,041**
Marriages	55	1,258	275	398	1,931	565	**166,991**
Deaths	127	1,844	508	693	3,045	948	**419,278**
Total Catholics	43,000	231,695	50,021	96,625	378,341	643,900	**68,229,841**
Total Population	71,850	937,293	307,587	588,641	1,833,521	1,951,000	**307,374,682**
Catholic Population Percentage	60	25	16	16	21	33	**22**

*Indicates Archdioceses.

†Certain Diocese traverse state lines.

	Reno NV	NEVADA TOTAL	Manchester NH	*Newark NJ	Camden NJ	Metuchen NJ	2012 U.S. GRAND TOTAL
Cardinals	–	–	–	–	–	–	13
Archbishops	–	–	–	2	–	–	56
Bishop	2	3	5	7	1	2	394
Abbots	–	–	1	1	–	–	109
Diocesan Priests	32	69	167	724	276	190	27,125
Religious Priests	6	24	53	167	42	36	12,593
Total Priests in Diocese	38	93	220	891	318	226	39,718
Newly Ordained Priests	–	–	1	18	3	3	485
Total Permanent Deacons	30	62	48	184	146	170	17,816
Total Brothers	3	6	20	78	12	19	4,518
Total Sisters	27	27	422	809	269	286	55,045
Number of Parishes	28	57	90	219	82	100	18,061
Missions	6	12	13	–	4	–	2,627
Pastoral Centers	–	–	–	–	–	3	628
New Parishes	–	–	1	–	22	1	87
Catholic Hospitals	1	1	2	3	1	1	605
Patients Assisted Annually	162,796	162,796	399,649	916,533	315,649	348,500	88,519,295
Health Care Centers	–	–	7	1	3	4	363
Patients Assisted Annually	–	–	1,232	11,077	18,573	27,408	5,038,247
Specialized Homes	–	–	4	9	6	9	1,616
Total Assisted Anually	–	–	124	1,571	1,613	2,133	991,072
Residential Care of Children (Orphanages)	–	–	–	–	–	–	344
Total Assisted Anually	–	–	–	–	–	–	23,479
Day Care and Extended Day Care Centers	3	3	–	4	4	2	1,005
Total Assisted Anually	263	263	–	563	474	307	121,211
Special Centers for Social Services	1	22	13	23	7	9	3,602
Total Assisted Anually	345,078	7,845,078	96,479	72,104	4,627	29,356	32,768,652
Diocesan Seminaries	–	–	–	3	–	–	71
Students	–	–	–	138	–	–	3,346
Religious Seminaries	–	–	–	–	–	–	98
Students	–	–	–	51	–	–	1,669
Colleges and Universities	–	–	4	4	–	–	233
Total Students	–	–	4,267	17,093	–	–	812,098
High Schools, Diocesan and Parish	1	2	3	10	7	3	731
Total Students	612	1,880	1,420	5,651	4,269	1,904	327,345
High Schools, Private	–	–	2	21	3	2	595
Total Students	–	–	877	7,869	1,560	1,117	296,268
Elementary Schools, Diocesan and Parish	4	11	20	76	35	28	5,378
Total Students	1,103	3,807	3,681	16,464	7,831	8,555	1,382,539
Elementary Schools, Private	–	–	4	5	–	–	386
Total Students	–	–	885	903	–	–	106,972
Non–residential Schools for the Disabled	–	–	–	–	1	1	53
Total Students	–	–	–	–	741	45	5,729
Religious Education High School Students	1,622	4,896	5,631	4,000	–	1,773	662,914
Religious Education Elementary Students	3,130	12,905	14,097	65,115	24,957	39,234	2,885,785
Priests Teaching	–	1	2	25	11	–	1,199
Scholastics Teaching	–	–	–	–	–	–	422
Brothers Teaching	–	–	1	11	6	11	698
Sisters Teaching	–	–	11	107	38	45	4,026
Lay Teachers	108	337	521	2,489	967	795	162,018
Infant Baptisms	1,615	7,582	2,260	13,362	5,018	4,430	793,103
Adult Baptisms	150	318	168	331	465	117	43,692
Received into Full Communion	501	813	121	126	245	228	76,588
First Communions	1,667	5,844	3,113	11,571	5,332	5,966	797,582
Confirmations	795	2,459	2,280	9,421	5,026	5,558	618,041
Marriages	221	786	479	2,389	1,042	992	166,991
Deaths	420	1,368	2,670	9,260	–	3,656	419,278
Total Catholics	109,579	753,479	282,745	1,318,557	511,822	631,946	68,229,841
Total Population	689,178	2,640,178	1,316,470	2,859,850	1,443,274	1,373,796	307,374,682
Catholic Population Percentage	16	29	21	46	35	46	22

Archdioceses = 37; Dioceses = 170; Apostolates = 3

2012 GENERAL SUMMARY

	Paterson NJ	Trenton NJ	NEW JERSEY TOTAL	*Santa Fe NM	† Gallup NM	Las Cruces NM	2012 U.S. GRAND TOTAL
Cardinals	–	–	–	–	–	–	13
Archbishops	–	–	2	2	–	–	56
Bishop	2	2	14	1	1	1	394
Abbots	6	–	7	1	–	–	109
Diocesan Priests	257	247	1,694	139	49	34	27,125
Religious Priests	136	66	447	77	21	40	12,593
Total Priests in Diocese	393	313	2,141	216	70	74	39,718
Newly Ordained Priests	9	6	39	1	–	–	485
Total Permanent Deacons	207	360	1,067	223	26	46	17,816
Total Brothers	46	67	222	55	8	1	4,518
Total Sisters	710	359	2,433	159	100	45	55,045
Number of Parishes	111	111	623	92	52	46	18,061
Missions	–	7	11	217	22	45	2,627
Pastoral Centers	5	–	8	4	–	1	628
New Parishes	–	–	23	–	–	–	87
Catholic Hospitals	3	2	10	1	–	–	605
Patients Assisted Annually	1,001,000	120,000	2,701,682	561,700	–	–	88,519,295
Health Care Centers	–	7	15	1	–	–	363
Patients Assisted Annually	–	4,500	61,558	2,000	–	–	5,038,247
Specialized Homes	10	8	42	3	2	–	1,616
Total Assisted Anually	1,940	680	7,937	2,025	75	–	991,072
Residential Care of Children (Orphanages)	1	2	3	–	–	–	344
Total Assisted Anually	70	25	95	–	–	–	23,479
Day Care and Extended Day Care Centers	5	5	20	1	–	1	1,005
Total Assisted Anually	1,400	490	3,234	105	–	85	121,211
Special Centers for Social Services	12	30	81	5	12	–	3,602
Total Assisted Anually	70,000	27,900	203,987	384,250	75,000	–	32,768,652
Diocesan Seminaries	1	–	4	–	–	–	71
Students	11	–	149	–	–	–	3,346
Religious Seminaries	2	–	2	–	–	–	98
Students	6	–	57	–	–	–	1,669
Colleges and Universities	2	1	7	1	–	–	233
Total Students	2,043	2,885	22,021	206	–	–	812,098
High Schools, Diocesan and Parish	3	8	31	1	1	–	731
Total Students	2,274	5,869	19,967	816	43	–	327,345
High Schools, Private	4	3	33	1	1	2	595
Total Students	1,380	1,163	13,089	709	130	357	296,268
Elementary Schools, Diocesan and Parish	36	36	211	15	11	–	5,378
Total Students	8,355	11,762	52,967	3,356	1,000	–	1,382,539
Elementary Schools, Private	3	3	11	–	1	3	386
Total Students	565	694	2,162	–	216	228	106,972
Non-residential Schools for the Disabled	–	1	3	–	–	–	53
Total Students	–	14	800	–	–	–	5,729
Religious Education High School Students	9,050	951	15,774	4,018	759	2,556	662,914
Religious Education Elementary Students	32,586	60,744	222,636	14,709	2,513	5,904	2,885,785
Priests Teaching	10	–	46	1	–	–	1,199
Scholastics Teaching	–	–	–	–	–	–	422
Brothers Teaching	6	3	37	1	–	–	698
Sisters Teaching	97	34	321	7	12	–	4,026
Lay Teachers	908	3,576	8,735	393	135	41	162,018
Infant Baptisms	6,585	7,175	36,570	4,541	639	1,828	793,103
Adult Baptisms	148	845	1,906	202	77	74	43,692
Received into Full Communion	248	282	1,129	235	80	246	76,588
First Communions	6,727	9,459	39,055	4,933	754	1,969	797,582
Confirmations	5,140	9,266	34,411	3,196	466	1,554	618,041
Marriages	1,067	1,487	6,977	931	122	309	166,991
Deaths	3,164	6,207	22,287	2,943	714	1,092	419,278
Total Catholics	425,273	856,355	3,743,953	319,467	61,990	132,646	68,229,841
Total Population	1,142,767	2,022,194	8,841,881	1,378,842	495,000	549,219	307,374,682
Catholic Population Percentage	37	42	42	23	13	24	22

*Indicates Archdioceses.

†Certain Diocese traverse state lines.

2012 GENERAL SUMMARY

	NEW MEXICO TOTAL	*New York NY	Albany NY	Brooklyn NY	Buffalo NY	Ogdensburg NY	2012 U.S. GRAND TOTAL
Cardinals	–	2	–	–	–	–	13
Archbishops	2	–	–	–	–	–	56
Bishop	3	7	1	8	3	1	394
Abbots	1	–	–	–	–	–	109
Diocesan Priests	222	630	213	507	323	121	27,125
Religious Priests	138	713	63	165	109	5	12,593
Total Priests in Diocese	360	1,343	276	672	432	126	39,718
Newly Ordained Priests	1	9	1	3	2	–	485
Total Permanent Deacons	295	379	108	216	124	70	17,816
Total Brothers	64	312	68	124	36	6	4,518
Total Sisters	304	2,666	656	872	880	104	55,045
Number of Parishes	190	369	128	188	164	99	18,061
Missions	284	–	13	–	1	7	2,627
Pastoral Centers	5	–	7	–	3	–	628
New Parishes	–	–	1	–	2	1	87
Catholic Hospitals	1	8	3	–	4	–	605
Patients Assisted Annually	561,700	450,000	1,260,500	–	1,411,218	–	88,519,295
Health Care Centers	1	2	17	–	1	–	363
Patients Assisted Annually	2,000	4,700	73,150	–	950	–	5,038,247
Specialized Homes	5	98	25	37	11	1	1,616
Total Assisted Anually	2,100	45,419	1,759	5,547	9,596	130	991,072
Residential Care of Children (Orphanages)	–	31	4	1	–	–	344
Total Assisted Anually	–	1,822	117	1,534	–	–	23,479
Day Care and Extended Day Care Centers	2	473	3	28	2	–	1,005
Total Assisted Anually	190	8,131	216	4,604	85	–	121,211
Special Centers for Social Services	17	1,238	75	92	5	4	3,602
Total Assisted Anually	459,250	284,561	90,000	110,439	610,559	20,000	32,768,652
Diocesan Seminaries	–	1	–	1	1	–	71
Students	–	43	–	20	21	–	3,346
Religious Seminaries	–	7	–	–	1	–	98
Students	–	89	–	63	–	–	1,669
Colleges and Universities	1	10	4	3	7	–	233
Total Students	206	44,412	10,000	25,587	18,071	–	812,098
High Schools, Diocesan and Parish	2	10	4	20	–	2	731
Total Students	859	4,074	1,109	14,458	–	332	327,345
High Schools, Private	4	40	3	–	15	–	595
Total Students	1,196	21,736	968	–	5,143	–	296,268
Elementary Schools, Diocesan and Parish	26	171	20	97	51	13	5,378
Total Students	4,356	47,292	4,570	30,755	10,851	1,989	1,382,539
Elementary Schools, Private	4	25	2	–	4	–	386
Total Students	444	3,822	286	–	731	–	106,972
Non–residential Schools for the Disabled	–	–	–	1	1	–	53
Total Students	–	–	–	72	325	–	5,729
Religious Education High School Students	7,333	6,973	8,267	2,742	8,457	1,121	662,914
Religious Education Elementary Students	23,126	92,074	18,662	38,446	24,072	3,939	2,885,785
Priests Teaching	1	18	–	2	36	–	1,199
Scholastics Teaching	–	–	–	–	–	–	422
Brothers Teaching	1	27	2	7	15	–	698
Sisters Teaching	19	89	12	44	70	13	4,026
Lay Teachers	569	4,035	724	3,278	1,823	181	162,018
Infant Baptisms	7,008	22,926	3,297	16,259	3,836	970	793,103
Adult Baptisms	353	1,022	74	605	143	42	43,692
Received into Full Communion	561	1,390	139	47	199	58	76,588
First Communions	7,656	21,469	3,752	11,874	4,722	918	797,582
Confirmations	5,216	18,791	3,275	10,034	4,790	875	618,041
Marriages	1,362	4,570	975	2,159	1,418	300	166,991
Deaths	4,749	12,338	4,146	8,293	6,064	1,609	419,278
Total Catholics	514,103	2,618,755	330,000	1,440,000	633,123	96,882	68,229,841
Total Population	2,423,061	5,819,455	1,392,464	4,735,422	1,544,203	497,712	307,374,682
Catholic Population Percentage	21	45	24	30	41	19	22

Archdioceses = 37; Dioceses = 170; Apostolates = 3

2012 GENERAL SUMMARY

	Rochester NY	Rockville Centre NY	Syracuse NY	NEW YORK TOTAL	Charlotte NC	Raleigh NC	2012 U.S. GRAND TOTAL
Cardinals	–	–	–	2	–	–	**13**
Archbishops	–	–	–	–	–	–	**56**
Bishop	1	5	3	29	2	2	**394**
Abbots	4	–	–	4	2	–	**109**
Diocesan Priests	171	353	220	2,538	112	90	**27,125**
Religious Priests	44	64	37	1,200	48	50	**12,593**
Total Priests in Diocese	215	417	257	3,738	160	140	**39,718**
Newly Ordained Priests	1	4	1	21	4	1	**485**
Total Permanent Deacons	134	278	85	1,394	103	57	**17,816**
Total Brothers	27	77	10	660	11	5	**4,518**
Total Sisters	443	1,112	301	7,034	123	45	**55,045**
Number of Parishes	105	133	133	1,319	73	77	**18,061**
Missions	2	1	11	35	19	18	**2,627**
Pastoral Centers	–	–	–	10	2	5	**628**
New Parishes	–	–	–	4	–	–	**87**
Catholic Hospitals	1	6	3	25	–	–	**605**
Patients Assisted Annually	99,200	648,401	675,000	4,544,319	–	–	**88,519,295**
Health Care Centers	2	3	2	27	16	–	**363**
Patients Assisted Annually	1,450	42,287	400,000	522,537	56,000	–	**5,038,247**
Specialized Homes	12	11	57	252	6	–	**1,616**
Total Assisted Anually	2,550	3,757	2,648	71,406	820	–	**991,072**
Residential Care of Children (Orphanages)	–	3	–	39	–	–	**344**
Total Assisted Anually	–	877	–	4,350	–	–	**23,479**
Day Care and Extended Day Care Centers	1	–	–	507	13	–	**1,005**
Total Assisted Anually	175	–	–	13,211	1,000	–	**121,211**
Special Centers for Social Services	74	50	2	1,540	4	10	**3,602**
Total Assisted Anually	812,108	43,167	1,750	1,972,584	29,927	56,153	**32,768,652**
Diocesan Seminaries	–	1	–	4	–	–	**71**
Students	–	46	–	130	–	–	**3,346**
Religious Seminaries	–	–	1	9	–	–	**98**
Students	–	–	14	166	–	–	**1,669**
Colleges and Universities	–	1	1	26	1	–	**233**
Total Students	–	3,037	3,502	104,609	1,734	–	**812,098**
High Schools, Diocesan and Parish	1	5	5	47	2	2	**731**
Total Students	115	4,623	1,591	26,302	1,941	1,247	**327,345**
High Schools, Private	5	5	1	69	–	1	**595**
Total Students	3,018	7,705	740	39,310	–	151	**296,268**
Elementary Schools, Diocesan and Parish	22	49	18	441	16	30	**5,378**
Total Students	4,542	17,159	3,012	120,170	5,598	7,742	**1,382,539**
Elementary Schools, Private	3	4	–	38	–	–	**386**
Total Students	334	1,337	–	6,510	–	–	**106,972**
Non–residential Schools for the Disabled	–	1	–	3	–	–	**53**
Total Students	–	98	–	495	–	–	**5,729**
Religious Education High School Students	1,502	2,503	6,315	37,880	2,841	4,362	**662,914**
Religious Education Elementary Students	11,079	94,203	20,672	303,147	24,030	16,453	**2,885,785**
Priests Teaching	2	11	1	70	–	1	**1,199**
Scholastics Teaching	–	–	–	–	–	–	**422**
Brothers Teaching	–	38	2	91	–	–	**698**
Sisters Teaching	18	46	16	308	6	5	**4,026**
Lay Teachers	647	1,794	387	12,869	627	588	**162,018**
Infant Baptisms	2,646	15,720	2,963	68,617	3,233	5,231	**793,103**
Adult Baptisms	198	598	130	2,812	293	190	**43,692**
Received into Full Communion	–	318	319	2,470	628	332	**76,588**
First Communions	3,057	17,123	3,285	66,200	5,587	5,107	**797,582**
Confirmations	2,646	16,296	3,222	59,929	3,615	2,758	**618,041**
Marriages	1,009	4,677	978	16,086	951	849	**166,991**
Deaths	3,819	10,108	4,024	50,401	1,107	1,116	**419,278**
Total Catholics	311,427	1,737,498	274,500	7,442,185	174,689	218,672	**68,229,841**
Total Population	1,510,953	3,527,942	1,170,374	20,198,525	4,801,606	4,654,373	**307,374,682**
Catholic Population Percentage	21	49	23	37	4	5	**22**

*Indicates Archdioceses.

†Certain Diocese traverse state lines.

	NORTH CAROLINA TOTAL	Bismarck ND	Fargo ND	NORTH DAKOTA TOTAL	*Cincinnati OH	Cleveland OH	2012 U.S. GRAND TOTAL
Cardinals	–	–	–	–	–	–	13
Archbishops	–	–	–	–	2	–	56
Bishop	4	2	1	3	1	5	394
Abbots	2	1	–	1	–	2	109
Diocesan Priests	202	66	132	198	275	392	27,125
Religious Priests	98	19	9	28	237	90	12,593
Total Priests in Diocese	300	85	141	226	512	482	39,718
Newly Ordained Priests	5	2	2	4	4	7	485
Total Permanent Deacons	160	77	45	122	201	220	17,816
Total Brothers	16	20	–	20	122	51	4,518
Total Sisters	168	78	114	192	878	1,025	55,045
Number of Parishes	150	98	132	230	214	174	18,061
Missions	37	–	–	–	–	1	2,627
Pastoral Centers	7	1	–	1	–	1	628
New Parishes	–	–	–	–	–	–	87
Catholic Hospitals	–	4	8	12	9	5	605
Patients Assisted Annually	–	354,819	141,077	495,896	1,564,493	650,000	88,519,295
Health Care Centers	16	–	–	–	–	1	363
Patients Assisted Annually	56,000	–	–	–	–	527	5,038,247
Specialized Homes	6	6	13	19	13	28	1,616
Total Assisted Anually	820	617	1,444	2,061	4,044	5,869	991,072
Residential Care of Children (Orphanages)	–	–	–	–	1	1	344
Total Assisted Anually	–	–	–	–	1,300	223	23,479
Day Care and Extended Day Care Centers	13	–	–	–	1	5	1,005
Total Assisted Anually	1,000	–	–	–	302	392	121,211
Special Centers for Social Services	14	4	3	7	9	17	3,602
Total Assisted Anually	86,080	500	3,197	3,697	113,186	148,956	32,768,652
Diocesan Seminaries	–	–	–	–	1	2	71
Students	–	–	–	–	39	61	3,346
Religious Seminaries	–	–	–	–	–	–	98
Students	–	–	–	–	–	6	1,669
Colleges and Universities	1	1	1	2	4	3	233
Total Students	1,734	2,971	300	3,271	20,747	7,268	812,098
High Schools, Diocesan and Parish	4	3	1	4	19	6	731
Total Students	3,188	663	325	988	9,937	3,006	327,345
High Schools, Private	1	–	–	–	4	15	595
Total Students	151	–	–	–	3,334	9,978	296,268
Elementary Schools, Diocesan and Parish	46	10	12	22	86	94	5,378
Total Students	13,340	1,620	1,598	3,218	28,003	31,400	1,382,539
Elementary Schools, Private	–	–	–	–	7	10	386
Total Students	–	–	–	–	1,989	2,398	106,972
Non–residential Schools for the Disabled	–	–	–	–	–	1	53
Total Students	–	–	–	–	–	121	5,729
Religious Education High School Students	7,203	1,529	2,128	3,657	4,797	3,662	662,914
Religious Education Elementary Students	40,483	5,127	5,234	10,361	23,662	33,070	2,885,785
Priests Teaching	1	3	1	4	12	2	1,199
Scholastics Teaching	–	–	–	–	–	–	422
Brothers Teaching	–	–	–	–	11	8	698
Sisters Teaching	11	4	3	7	41	45	4,026
Lay Teachers	1,215	206	192	398	2,655	2,856	162,018
Infant Baptisms	8,464	950	1,124	2,074	5,525	6,210	793,103
Adult Baptisms	483	36	36	72	437	416	43,692
Received into Full Communion	960	110	260	370	748	875	76,588
First Communions	10,694	870	1,049	1,919	6,899	8,461	797,582
Confirmations	6,373	980	1,142	2,122	6,839	7,661	618,041
Marriages	1,800	328	354	682	1,861	2,357	166,991
Deaths	2,223	551	920	1,471	3,928	7,672	419,278
Total Catholics	393,361	60,411	72,219	132,630	477,338	706,465	68,229,841
Total Population	9,455,979	281,619	390,972	672,591	2,994,520	2,786,680	307,374,682
Catholic Population Percentage	4	21	18	20	16	25	22

Archdioceses = 37; Dioceses = 170; Apostolates = 3

2012 GENERAL SUMMARY

	Columbus OH	Steubenville OH	Toledo OH	Youngstown OH	OHIO TOTAL	*Oklahoma City OK	2012 U.S. GRAND TOTAL
Cardinals	–	–	–	–	–	–	13
Archbishops	–	–	–	–	2	2	56
Bishop	2	2	2	1	13	–	394
Abbots	–	–	–	–	2	4	109
Diocesan Priests	153	79	179	142	1,220	78	27,125
Religious Priests	30	30	37	18	442	28	12,593
Total Priests in Diocese	183	109	216	160	1,662	106	39,718
Newly Ordained Priests	2	1	3	4	21	1	485
Total Permanent Deacons	96	6	199	77	799	95	17,816
Total Brothers	–	7	8	11	199	7	4,518
Total Sisters	233	59	500	211	2,906	90	55,045
Number of Parishes	106	58	126	94	772	66	18,061
Missions	3	3	–	1	8	45	2,627
Pastoral Centers	–	–	–	–	1	–	628
New Parishes	–	–	1	9	10	–	87
Catholic Hospitals	6	1	7	4	32	7	605
Patients Assisted Annually	809,751	231,643	1,301,302	50,461	4,607,650	331,535	88,519,295
Health Care Centers	–	–	3	32	36	2	363
Patients Assisted Annually	–	–	481	1,217,872	1,218,880	280	5,038,247
Specialized Homes	26	–	12	15	94	2	1,616
Total Assisted Anually	11,912	–	1,046	2,765	25,636	170	991,072
Residential Care of Children (Orphanages)	1	–	–	–	3	–	344
Total Assisted Anually	1,802	–	–	–	3,325	–	23,479
Day Care and Extended Day Care Centers	–	–	2	1	9	2	1,005
Total Assisted Anually	–	–	363	74	1,131	197	121,211
Special Centers for Social Services	8	1	10	16	61	–	3,602
Total Assisted Anually	520,732	28,191	150,889	45,284	1,007,238	–	32,768,652
Diocesan Seminaries	1	–	–	–	4	–	71
Students	210	–	–	–	310	–	3,346
Religious Seminaries	–	–	–	–	–	–	98
Students	–	–	–	–	6	–	1,669
Colleges and Universities	2	1	2	1	13	1	233
Total Students	4,017	2,548	3,475	2,982	41,037	734	812,098
High Schools, Diocesan and Parish	11	3	10	6	55	2	731
Total Students	4,688	466	2,881	2,163	23,141	1,099	327,345
High Schools, Private	–	–	4	–	23	–	595
Total Students	–	–	2,604	–	15,916	–	296,268
Elementary Schools, Diocesan and Parish	42	10	62	28	322	19	5,378
Total Students	11,410	1,700	12,261	5,223	89,997	3,931	1,382,539
Elementary Schools, Private	2	–	2	2	23	1	386
Total Students	232	–	326	107	5,052	239	106,972
Non-residential Schools for the Disabled	–	–	1	–	2	1	53
Total Students	–	–	49	–	170	5	5,729
Religious Education High School Students	1,241	506	4,130	3,026	17,362	3,454	662,914
Religious Education Elementary Students	13,415	1,482	21,789	10,089	103,507	9,437	2,885,785
Priests Teaching	19	1	12	4	50	4	1,199
Scholastics Teaching	–	–	7	–	7	–	422
Brothers Teaching	–	–	–	–	19	7	698
Sisters Teaching	5	5	29	5	130	18	4,026
Lay Teachers	1,146	167	1,416	489	8,729	443	162,018
Infant Baptisms	3,189	343	2,380	1,672	19,319	2,577	793,103
Adult Baptisms	358	71	357	148	1,787	198	43,692
Received into Full Communion	432	480	395	322	3,252	604	76,588
First Communions	3,681	520	3,462	2,128	25,151	2,661	797,582
Confirmations	3,666	547	3,287	2,364	24,364	1,533	618,041
Marriages	944	176	1,117	667	7,122	704	166,991
Deaths	1,426	620	2,784	2,656	19,086	800	419,278
Total Catholics	264,425	37,011	317,685	198,332	2,001,256	115,954	68,229,841
Total Population	2,580,134	514,926	1,465,561	1,195,478	11,537,299	2,069,649	307,374,682
Catholic Population Percentage	10	7	22	17	17	6	22

*Indicates Archdioceses.

†Certain Diocese traverse state lines.

	Tulsa OK	OKLAHOMA TOTAL	*Portland in Oregon OR	Baker OR	OREGON TOTAL	*Philadelphia PA	2012 U.S. GRAND TOTAL
Cardinals	–	–	–	–	–	1	**13**
Archbishops	–	2	1	–	1	1	**56**
Bishop	1	1	1	2	3	7	**394**
Abbots	–	4	5	–	5	2	**109**
Diocesan Priests	76	154	150	36	186	540	**27,125**
Religious Priests	24	52	144	9	153	356	**12,593**
Total Priests in Diocese	100	206	294	45	339	896	**39,718**
Newly Ordained Priests	2	3	7	–	7	5	**485**
Total Permanent Deacons	67	162	79	12	91	266	**17,816**
Total Brothers	28	35	78	–	78	101	**4,518**
Total Sisters	54	144	388	9	397	2,700	**55,045**
Number of Parishes	76	142	124	31	155	266	**18,061**
Missions	2	47	22	28	50	6	**2,627**
Pastoral Centers	–	–	1	–	1	17	**628**
New Parishes	–	–	–	–	–	–	**87**
Catholic Hospitals	6	13	10	4	14	6	**605**
Patients Assisted Annually	1,425,395	1,756,930	2,271,321	161,261	2,432,582	778,591	**88,519,295**
Health Care Centers	1	3	12	–	12	1	**363**
Patients Assisted Annually	5,000	5,280	22,597	–	22,597	150	**5,038,247**
Specialized Homes	6	8	15	4	19	35	**1,616**
Total Assisted Anually	594	764	3,929	189	4,118	8,001	**991,072**
Residential Care of Children (Orphanages)	–	–	–	–	–	2	**344**
Total Assisted Anually	–	–	–	–	–	419	**23,479**
Day Care and Extended Day Care Centers	–	2	4	1	5	1	**1,005**
Total Assisted Anually	–	197	2,506	20	2,526	43	**121,211**
Special Centers for Social Services	8	8	16	6	22	15	**3,602**
Total Assisted Anually	50,000	50,000	1,038,507	69,514	1,108,021	103,334	**32,768,652**
Diocesan Seminaries	–	–	1	–	1	1	**71**
Students	–	–	151	–	151	136	**3,346**
Religious Seminaries	–	–	–	–	–	11	**98**
Students	–	–	29	–	29	30	**1,669**
Colleges and Universities	–	1	2	–	2	11	**233**
Total Students	–	734	5,805	–	5,805	45,922	**812,098**
High Schools, Diocesan and Parish	1	3	3	–	3	17	**731**
Total Students	819	1,918	1,494	–	1,494	16,502	**327,345**
High Schools, Private	1	1	7	–	7	16	**595**
Total Students	568	568	4,184	–	4,184	7,537	**296,268**
Elementary Schools, Diocesan and Parish	9	28	38	5	43	163	**5,378**
Total Students	2,093	6,024	8,312	512	8,824	51,688	**1,382,539**
Elementary Schools, Private	2	3	2	–	2	18	**386**
Total Students	945	1,184	405	–	405	4,611	**106,972**
Non–residential Schools for the Disabled	–	1	–	–	–	4	**53**
Total Students	–	5	–	–	–	206	**5,729**
Religious Education High School Students	1,472	4,926	3,742	726	4,468	1,229	**662,914**
Religious Education Elementary Students	5,027	14,464	12,838	2,068	14,906	50,259	**2,885,785**
Priests Teaching	4	8	11	1	12	85	**1,199**
Scholastics Teaching	–	–	3	–	3	–	**422**
Brothers Teaching	4	11	4	–	4	31	**698**
Sisters Teaching	5	23	23	2	25	406	**4,026**
Lay Teachers	348	791	1,181	37	1,218	8,827	**162,018**
Infant Baptisms	1,345	3,922	5,794	907	6,701	12,725	**793,103**
Adult Baptisms	120	318	424	41	465	453	**43,692**
Received into Full Communion	279	883	656	122	778	378	**76,588**
First Communions	1,250	3,911	5,098	929	6,027	11,908	**797,582**
Confirmations	919	2,452	2,476	618	3,094	11,083	**618,041**
Marriages	360	1,064	964	169	1,133	4,021	**166,991**
Deaths	439	1,239	1,785	260	2,045	10,629	**419,278**
Total Catholics	62,600	178,554	415,725	34,142	449,867	1,464,263	**68,229,841**
Total Population	1,650,000	3,719,649	3,327,110	509,474	3,836,584	4,008,994	**307,374,682**
Catholic Population Percentage	4	5	12	7	12	37	**22**

Archdioceses = 37; Dioceses = 170; Apostolates = 3

2012 GENERAL SUMMARY

	Allentown PA	Altoona–Johnstown PA	Erie PA	Greensburg PA	Harrisburg PA	Pittsburgh PA	2012 U.S. GRAND TOTAL
Cardinals	–	–	–	–	–	–	**13**
Archbishops	–	–	–	–	–	–	**56**
Bishop	2	2	1	2	1	3	**394**
Abbots	–	–	–	1	–	–	**109**
Diocesan Priests	204	120	187	107	137	376	**27,125**
Religious Priests	67	56	7	65	35	97	**12,593**
Total Priests in Diocese	271	176	194	172	172	473	**39,718**
Newly Ordained Priests	1	3	1	–	1	4	**485**
Total Permanent Deacons	107	36	62	2	69	84	**17,816**
Total Brothers	11	8	–	32	1	34	**4,518**
Total Sisters	320	70	321	196	335	1,072	**55,045**
Number of Parishes	104	88	117	85	89	208	**18,061**
Missions	2	5	21	–	8	–	**2,627**
Pastoral Centers	26	–	–	–	–	–	**628**
New Parishes	–	–	–	–	–	–	**87**
Catholic Hospitals	2	–	1	–	1	1	**605**
Patients Assisted Annually	510,945	–	440,600	–	248,646	221,990	**88,519,295**
Health Care Centers	2	1	–	–	–	1	**363**
Patients Assisted Annually	4,760	253	–	–	–	–	**5,038,247**
Specialized Homes	13	3	7	2	7	13	**1,616**
Total Assisted Anually	1,039	288	1,816	194	536	32,740	**991,072**
Residential Care of Children (Orphanages)	–	–	–	–	1	–	**344**
Total Assisted Anually	–	–	–	–	611	–	**23,479**
Day Care and Extended Day Care Centers	1	–	1	–	–	–	**1,005**
Total Assisted Anually	152	–	216	–	–	–	**121,211**
Special Centers for Social Services	6	2	24	6	14	7	**3,602**
Total Assisted Anually	30,537	26,678	56,046	16,398	2,872	115,178	**32,768,652**
Diocesan Seminaries	–	–	1	–	–	1	**71**
Students	–	–	22	–	–	21	**3,346**
Religious Seminaries	–	–	–	1	–	–	**98**
Students	–	–	–	24	–	–	**1,669**
Colleges and Universities	2	2	2	2	–	3	**233**
Total Students	5,809	4,379	8,741	4,166	–	13,630	**812,098**
High Schools, Diocesan and Parish	7	–	6	2	7	8	**731**
Total Students	3,513	–	1,646	679	3,391	3,281	**327,345**
High Schools, Private	–	4	1	–	–	4	**595**
Total Students	–	1,005	630	–	–	694	**296,268**
Elementary Schools, Diocesan and Parish	38	20	32	14	39	85	**5,378**
Total Students	8,926	4,482	4,852	2,421	8,133	16,539	**1,382,539**
Elementary Schools, Private	–	–	1	3	2	3	**386**
Total Students	–	–	221	258	82	723	**106,972**
Non–residential Schools for the Disabled	3	–	–	–	–	2	**53**
Total Students	186	–	–	–	–	163	**5,729**
Religious Education High School Students	229	2,589	4,768	1,876	1,445	3,803	**662,914**
Religious Education Elementary Students	16,226	6,080	7,148	7,153	15,188	38,533	**2,885,785**
Priests Teaching	2	5	7	31	1	2	**1,199**
Scholastics Teaching	–	331	–	–	–	–	**422**
Brothers Teaching	–	1	–	4	–	11	**698**
Sisters Teaching	28	7	10	7	29	55	**4,026**
Lay Teachers	807	327	568	440	750	1,635	**162,018**
Infant Baptisms	2,780	925	1,530	1,235	2,024	5,043	**793,103**
Adult Baptisms	135	75	130	53	326	260	**43,692**
Received into Full Communion	2,915	134	65	321	418	478	**76,588**
First Communions	3,513	1,154	1,800	1,502	2,738	6,438	**797,582**
Confirmations	3,694	1,427	1,700	675	2,817	6,635	**618,041**
Marriages	807	452	610	556	718	2,017	**166,991**
Deaths	2,854	1,538	2,400	2,213	2,255	7,795	**419,278**
Total Catholics	271,482	90,507	221,550	152,689	249,238	634,736	**68,229,841**
Total Population	1,272,222	652,258	855,252	659,596	2,224,542	1,915,363	**307,374,682**
Catholic Population Percentage	21	14	26	23	11	33	**22**

*Indicates Archdioceses.

†Certain Diocese traverse state lines.

2012 GENERAL SUMMARY

	Scranton PA	PENN. TOTAL	*San Juan, Puerto Rico	Arecibo, Puerto Rico	Caguas, Puerto Rico	Fajardo–Humacao Puerto Rico	2012 U.S. GRAND TOTAL
Cardinals	–	1	–	–	–	–	13
Archbishops	–	1	1	–	–	–	56
Bishop	4	22	1	2	2	1	394
Abbots	–	3	–	–	–	–	109
Diocesan Priests	280	1,951	121	72	48	19	27,125
Religious Priests	60	743	106	49	34	11	12,593
Total Priests in Diocese	340	2,694	227	121	82	30	39,718
Newly Ordained Priests	1	16	4	1	–	–	485
Total Permanent Deacons	71	697	161	1	102	26	17,816
Total Brothers	7	194	18	7	–	6	4,518
Total Sisters	488	5,502	331	139	95	27	55,045
Number of Parishes	108	1,065	143	59	34	21	18,061
Missions	18	60	143	241	–	–	2,627
Pastoral Centers	–	43	–	–	–	–	628
New Parishes	10	10	–	–	–	–	87
Catholic Hospitals	4	15	5	–	–	–	605
Patients Assisted Annually	639,244	2,840,016	17,699	–	–	–	88,519,295
Health Care Centers	2	7	3	–	–	–	363
Patients Assisted Annually	297,982	303,145	76,944	–	–	–	5,038,247
Specialized Homes	13	93	24	5	2	–	1,616
Total Assisted Anually	2,130	46,744	82,056	269	362	–	991,072
Residential Care of Children (Orphanages)	5	8	8	3	–	–	344
Total Assisted Anually	698	1,728	936	57	–	–	23,479
Day Care and Extended Day Care Centers	9	12	1	–	–	1	1,005
Total Assisted Anually	419	830	85	–	–	26	121,211
Special Centers for Social Services	13	87	8	2	–	1	3,602
Total Assisted Anually	209,834	560,877	46,467	1,952	–	27	32,768,652
Diocesan Seminaries	–	3	1	1	2	–	71
Students	–	179	19	–	–	–	3,346
Religious Seminaries	–	12	6	–	–	–	98
Students	–	54	11	–	–	–	1,669
Colleges and Universities	4	26	2	1	–	–	233
Total Students	14,503	97,150	8,995	690	–	–	812,098
High Schools, Diocesan and Parish	4	51	15	7	2	6	731
Total Students	1,460	30,472	3,234	1,306	–	1,676	327,345
High Schools, Private	1	26	28	6	7	–	595
Total Students	838	10,704	6,323	1,809	–	–	296,268
Elementary Schools, Diocesan and Parish	16	407	21	7	2	5	5,378
Total Students	4,725	101,766	6,391	1,583	–	1,243	1,382,539
Elementary Schools, Private	–	27	37	5	7	–	386
Total Students	–	5,895	13,247	5,388	–	–	106,972
Non–residential Schools for the Disabled	1	10	1	–	–	–	53
Total Students	27	582	120	–	–	–	5,729
Religious Education High School Students	4,790	20,729	9,557	3,454	–	–	662,914
Religious Education Elementary Students	23,100	163,687	19,638	12,089	–	215	2,885,785
Priests Teaching	3	136	12	9	–	–	1,199
Scholastics Teaching	–	331	52	–	–	–	422
Brothers Teaching	–	47	23	4	–	–	698
Sisters Teaching	21	563	331	23	–	–	4,026
Lay Teachers	312	13,666	1,961	390	–	–	162,018
Infant Baptisms	2,827	29,089	3,161	3,860	3,326	588	793,103
Adult Baptisms	87	1,519	766	305	359	85	43,692
Received into Full Communion	122	4,826	12	4,515	–	–	76,588
First Communions	3,422	32,475	4,609	4,481	3,398	529	797,582
Confirmations	3,776	31,807	3,520	3,903	4,215	392	618,041
Marriages	923	10,104	953	323	438	97	166,991
Deaths	5,428	35,112	–	3,045	2,219	381	419,278
Total Catholics	293,061	3,377,526	897,325	370,000	350,000	97,869	68,229,841
Total Population	1,120,162	12,708,389	1,281,893	603,469	503,000	293,000	307,374,682
Catholic Population Percentage	26	27	70	61	70	33	22

Archdioceses = 37; Dioceses = 170; Apostolates = 3

2012 GENERAL SUMMARY

	Mayaguez, Puerto Rico	Ponce, Puerto Rico	PUERTO RICO TOTAL	Providence RI	Charleston SC	Rapid City SD	2012 U.S. GRAND TOTAL
Cardinals	–	–	–	–	–	–	13
Archbishops	–	–	1	1	–	–	56
Bishop	2	1	9	6	2	1	394
Abbots	–	–	–	3	–	–	109
Diocesan Priests	47	81	388	271	86	37	27,125
Religious Priests	26	36	262	108	43	17	12,593
Total Priests in Diocese	73	117	650	379	129	54	39,718
Newly Ordained Priests	–	–	5	2	4	1	485
Total Permanent Deacons	24	106	420	90	124	27	17,816
Total Brothers	2	3	36	71	20	4	4,518
Total Sisters	112	185	889	458	119	39	55,045
Number of Parishes	30	43	330	142	92	88	18,061
Missions	–	–	384	6	23	29	2,627
Pastoral Centers	–	248	248	1	1	4	628
New Parishes	1	–	1	1	–	–	87
Catholic Hospitals	1	–	6	1	3	1	605
Patients Assisted Annually	38,911	–	56,610	200,000	313,244	15,918	88,519,295
Health Care Centers	–	7	10	–	–	–	363
Patients Assisted Annually	–	336,690	413,634	–	–	–	5,038,247
Specialized Homes	4	12	47	9	1	1	1,616
Total Assisted Anually	397	325,342	408,426	44,654	26	5,820	991,072
Residential Care of Children (Orphanages)	–	1	12	–	–	1	344
Total Assisted Anually	–	26	1,019	–	–	6	23,479
Day Care and Extended Day Care Centers	5	2	9	2	–	1	1,005
Total Assisted Anually	267	10,052	10,430	115	–	40	121,211
Special Centers for Social Services	1	4	16	6	9	6	3,602
Total Assisted Anually	14,938	52,823	116,207	62,300	20,561	21,297	32,768,652
Diocesan Seminaries	–	1	5	1	–	–	71
Students	–	24	43	27	–	–	3,346
Religious Seminaries	–	2	8	–	–	–	98
Students	–	9	20	–	–	–	1,669
Colleges and Universities	1	1	5	3	–	–	233
Total Students	1,810	9,908	21,403	7,841	–	–	812,098
High Schools, Diocesan and Parish	4	11	45	4	2	1	731
Total Students	408	1,683	8,307	2,003	1,103	235	327,345
High Schools, Private	6	4	51	8	2	1	595
Total Students	900	680	9,712	3,535	646	200	296,268
Elementary Schools, Diocesan and Parish	5	17	57	31	28	1	5,378
Total Students	1,035	5,028	15,280	7,570	5,368	466	1,382,539
Elementary Schools, Private	6	4	59	4	–	1	386
Total Students	1,685	1,183	21,503	1,418	–	333	106,972
Non–residential Schools for the Disabled	–	–	1	–	–	–	53
Total Students	–	–	120	–	–	–	5,729
Religious Education High School Students	310	2,469	15,790	7,456	1,697	894	662,914
Religious Education Elementary Students	2,989	7,606	42,537	21,590	12,180	2,944	2,885,785
Priests Teaching	–	12	33	28	4	1	1,199
Scholastics Teaching	–	–	52	–	–	2	422
Brothers Teaching	1	–	28	13	3	–	698
Sisters Teaching	5	6	365	38	25	3	4,026
Lay Teachers	287	227	2,865	1,160	599	114	162,018
Infant Baptisms	3,674	2,980	17,589	3,508	2,882	436	793,103
Adult Baptisms	129	414	2,058	158	137	26	43,692
Received into Full Communion	81	–	4,608	327	412	65	76,588
First Communions	3,253	3,511	19,781	4,479	3,348	425	797,582
Confirmations	3,729	3,423	19,182	4,667	2,372	306	618,041
Marriages	307	549	2,667	1,138	644	160	166,991
Deaths	708	–	6,353	4,761	1,253	493	419,278
Total Catholics	342,899	424,263	2,482,356	621,015	196,658	24,075	68,229,841
Total Population	489,857	565,683	3,736,902	1,052,567	4,625,364	227,211	307,374,682
Catholic Population Percentage	70	75	66	59	4	11	22

*Indicates Archdioceses.

†Certain Diocese traverse state lines.

2012 GENERAL SUMMARY

	Sioux Falls SD	SOUTH DAKOTA TOTAL	Knoxville TN	Memphis TN	Nashville TN	TENNESSEE TOTAL	2012 U.S. GRAND TOTAL
Cardinals	–	–	–	–	–	–	13
Archbishops	–	–	–	–	–	–	56
Bishop	1	2	1	1	1	3	394
Abbots	3	3	–	–	–	–	109
Diocesan Priests	122	159	62	66	43	171	27,125
Religious Priests	28	45	13	13	24	50	12,593
Total Priests in Diocese	150	204	75	79	67	221	39,718
Newly Ordained Priests	5	6	1	3	1	5	485
Total Permanent Deacons	35	62	59	61	69	189	17,816
Total Brothers	9	13	11	27	1	39	4,518
Total Sisters	247	286	37	52	2	91	55,045
Number of Parishes	146	234	47	42	53	142	18,061
Missions	–	29	2	5	3	10	2,627
Pastoral Centers	3	7	2	–	2	4	628
New Parishes	–	–	–	–	–	–	87
Catholic Hospitals	11	12	1	–	3	4	605
Patients Assisted Annually	750,000	765,918	99,681	–	614,000	713,681	88,519,295
Health Care Centers	–	–	1	–	–	1	363
Patients Assisted Annually	–	–	278	–	–	278	5,038,247
Specialized Homes	9	10	3	3	2	8	1,616
Total Assisted Anually	–	5,820	733	100	320	1,153	991,072
Residential Care of Children (Orphanages)	–	1	–	–	–	–	344
Total Assisted Anually	–	6	–	–	–	–	23,479
Day Care and Extended Day Care Centers	–	1	–	2	3	5	1,005
Total Assisted Anually	–	40	–	430	580	1,010	121,211
Special Centers for Social Services	10	16	7	1	8	16	3,602
Total Assisted Anually	52,000	73,297	62,776	1,200	55,800	119,776	32,768,652
Diocesan Seminaries	–	–	–	–	–	–	71
Students	–	–	–	–	–	–	3,346
Religious Seminaries	–	–	–	–	–	–	98
Students	–	–	–	–	–	–	1,669
Colleges and Universities	2	2	–	1	1	2	233
Total Students	1,937	1,937	–	1,641	1,080	2,721	812,098
High Schools, Diocesan and Parish	3	4	2	4	2	8	731
Total Students	988	1,223	1,101	1,741	1,536	4,378	327,345
High Schools, Private	–	1	–	3	1	4	595
Total Students	–	200	–	1,210	256	1,466	296,268
Elementary Schools, Diocesan and Parish	21	22	8	21	16	45	5,378
Total Students	4,056	4,522	2,192	4,768	3,774	10,734	1,382,539
Elementary Schools, Private	1	2	–	1	2	3	386
Total Students	228	561	–	562	628	1,190	106,972
Non–residential Schools for the Disabled	–	–	–	–	–	–	53
Total Students	–	–	–	–	–	–	5,729
Religious Education High School Students	4,291	5,185	1,005	551	988	2,544	662,914
Religious Education Elementary Students	7,353	10,297	3,408	4,648	6,763	14,819	2,885,785
Priests Teaching	–	1	2	–	–	2	1,199
Scholastics Teaching	1	3	–	–	–	–	422
Brothers Teaching	–	–	–	20	1	21	698
Sisters Teaching	3	6	13	8	9	30	4,026
Lay Teachers	339	453	200	857	293	1,350	162,018
Infant Baptisms	1,430	1,866	1,094	1,260	1,849	4,203	793,103
Adult Baptisms	–	26	82	79	195	356	43,692
Received into Full Communion	278	343	243	206	303	752	76,588
First Communions	1,539	1,964	1,116	1,470	1,802	4,388	797,582
Confirmations	1,655	1,961	655	1,213	1,597	3,465	618,041
Marriages	510	670	278	305	399	982	166,991
Deaths	1,017	1,510	415	470	473	1,358	419,278
Total Catholics	120,204	144,279	61,827	59,041	77,736	198,604	68,229,841
Total Population	569,926	797,137	2,364,692	1,562,650	2,418,763	6,346,105	307,374,682
Catholic Population Percentage	21	18	3	4	3	22	22

Archdioceses = 37; Dioceses = 170; Apostolates = 3

2012 GENERAL SUMMARY

	*Galveston - Houston TX	*San Antonio TX	Amarillo TX	Austin TX	Beaumont TX	Brownsville TX	2012 U.S. GRAND TOTAL
Cardinals	1	–	–	–	–	–	13
Archbishops	1	2	–	–	–	–	56
Bishop	2	3	2	2	1	2	394
Abbots	–	–	–	–	–	–	109
Diocesan Priests	198	152	40	142	46	81	27,125
Religious Priests	224	179	4	54	23	29	12,593
Total Priests in Diocese	422	331	44	196	69	110	39,718
Newly Ordained Priests	4	1	1	2	–	3	485
Total Permanent Deacons	402	359	60	168	32	91	17,816
Total Brothers	12	85	–	43	3	16	4,518
Total Sisters	449	702	87	96	22	103	55,045
Number of Parishes	146	139	38	101	44	69	18,061
Missions	7	34	11	22	4	45	2,627
Pastoral Centers	18	–	–	4	–	2	628
New Parishes	–	–	–	–	–	–	87
Catholic Hospitals	4	5	–	5	3	–	605
Patients Assisted Annually	234,274	400,000	–	1,836,646	406,107	–	88,519,295
Health Care Centers	8	5	–	–	–	1	363
Patients Assisted Annually	102,000	37,800	–	–	–	137	5,038,247
Specialized Homes	9	11	6	4	–	2	1,616
Total Assisted Anually	10,716	981	731	344	–	256	991,072
Residential Care of Children (Orphanages)	4	3	–	–	–	–	344
Total Assisted Anually	958	469	–	–	–	–	23,479
Day Care and Extended Day Care Centers	36	10	1	2	–	1	1,005
Total Assisted Anually	3,498	977	89	300	–	17	121,211
Special Centers for Social Services	10	8	1	4	7	6	3,602
Total Assisted Anually	770,911	12,828	300	27,000	4,723	139,944	32,768,652
Diocesan Seminaries	1	2	–	–	–	1	71
Students	81	91	–	–	–	8	3,346
Religious Seminaries	–	6	–	–	1	–	98
Students	10	28	–	–	7	–	1,669
Colleges and Universities	1	5	–	1	–	–	233
Total Students	3,754	15,498	–	5,285	–	–	812,098
High Schools, Diocesan and Parish	–	5	1	4	1	–	731
Total Students	–	1,283	136	1,054	431	–	327,345
High Schools, Private	9	6	–	2	–	3	595
Total Students	4,419	2,402	–	475	–	968	296,268
Elementary Schools, Diocesan and Parish	44	30	4	16	5	8	5,378
Total Students	11,584	8,101	568	3,348	1,167	2,292	1,382,539
Elementary Schools, Private	6	7	–	1	–	3	386
Total Students	2,107	1,561	–	863	–	912	106,972
Non-residential Schools for the Disabled	–	–	–	–	–	–	53
Total Students	–	–	–	–	–	–	5,729
Religious Education High School Students	17,801	10,511	2,149	9,149	1,622	8,497	662,914
Religious Education Elementary Students	68,029	29,769	3,532	27,621	6,221	28,374	2,885,785
Priests Teaching	7	34	2	3	–	4	1,199
Scholastics Teaching	4	–	–	–	–	–	422
Brothers Teaching	–	20	–	–	–	6	698
Sisters Teaching	27	51	6	4	1	12	4,026
Lay Teachers	1,377	1,595	62	507	135	297	162,018
Infant Baptisms	10,071	8,772	1,052	7,984	1,381	8,846	793,103
Adult Baptisms	1,894	392	59	394	178	290	43,692
Received into Full Communion	854	1,337	116	722	249	901	76,588
First Communions	20,719	9,206	1,086	7,707	1,289	8,238	797,582
Confirmations	11,093	6,457	686	4,291	1,004	3,924	618,041
Marriages	3,260	1,917	206	1,421	244	1,445	166,991
Deaths	3,843	4,540	307	1,600	710	2,695	419,278
Total Catholics	1,170,403	716,269	50,237	518,940	72,117	1,074,477	68,229,841
Total Population	6,099,524	2,363,714	427,927	2,809,636	616,838	1,264,091	307,374,682
Catholic Population Percentage	19	30	12	18	12	85	22

*Indicates Archdioceses.

†Certain Diocese traverse state lines.

	Corpus Christi TX	Dallas TX	El Paso TX	Fort Worth TX	Laredo TX	Lubbock TX	2012 U.S. GRAND TOTAL
Cardinals	–	–	–	–	–	–	13
Archbishops	–	–	–	–	–	–	56
Bishop	3	5	–	–	1	1	394
Abbots	–	1	–	–	–	–	109
Diocesan Priests	132	100	79	74	30	49	27,125
Religious Priests	26	75	40	53	21	9	12,593
Total Priests in Diocese	158	175	119	127	51	58	39,718
Newly Ordained Priests	3	6	2	3	–	1	485
Total Permanent Deacons	79	152	25	109	31	52	17,816
Total Brothers	3	8	13	11	7	–	4,518
Total Sisters	142	118	121	81	74	24	55,045
Number of Parishes	69	69	57	89	32	62	18,061
Missions	32	5	19	2	17	–	2,627
Pastoral Centers	–	3	–	–	–	–	628
New Parishes	–	–	–	–	–	–	87
Catholic Hospitals	6	–	–	–	–	2	605
Patients Assisted Annually	486,633	–	–	–	–	297,315	88,519,295
Health Care Centers	8	–	2	–	1	20	363
Patients Assisted Annually	77,751	–	56,919	–	25,000	58,324	5,038,247
Specialized Homes	2	2	1	4	1	–	1,616
Total Assisted Anually	285	252	230	348	855	–	991,072
Residential Care of Children (Orphanages)	–	–	–	–	1	–	344
Total Assisted Anually	–	–	–	–	49	–	23,479
Day Care and Extended Day Care Centers	1	1	–	–	–	–	1,005
Total Assisted Anually	56	163	–	–	–	–	121,211
Special Centers for Social Services	1	4	3	19	3	1	3,602
Total Assisted Anually	195,090	59,579	34,065	110,199	314,159	30,000	32,768,652
Diocesan Seminaries	–	2	1	–	–	–	71
Students	–	87	2	–	–	–	3,346
Religious Seminaries	–	1	1	–	–	–	98
Students	–	13	13	–	–	–	1,669
Colleges and Universities	–	1	–	1	–	–	233
Total Students	–	2,861	–	8	–	–	812,098
High Schools, Diocesan and Parish	1	3	–	4	1	1	731
Total Students	424	2,850	–	1,319	390	53	327,345
High Schools, Private	1	4	3	–	–	–	595
Total Students	318	2,391	1,145	–	–	–	296,268
Elementary Schools, Diocesan and Parish	14	28	8	16	5	2	5,378
Total Students	2,384	9,737	2,487	4,502	1,223	377	1,382,539
Elementary Schools, Private	2	2	2	1	1	–	386
Total Students	489	487	446	140	500	–	106,972
Non–residential Schools for the Disabled	–	1	–	–	–	–	53
Total Students	–	150	–	–	–	–	5,729
Religious Education High School Students	3,719	6,700	7,407	8,028	4,208	1,516	662,914
Religious Education Elementary Students	9,329	40,919	11,657	35,402	8,829	4,935	2,885,785
Priests Teaching	3	15	–	–	2	–	1,199
Scholastics Teaching	–	3	–	–	–	–	422
Brothers Teaching	–	4	7	1	2	–	698
Sisters Teaching	23	13	9	18	11	1	4,026
Lay Teachers	291	1,238	268	486	145	53	162,018
Infant Baptisms	2,050	15,390	4,908	5,982	2,672	1,276	793,103
Adult Baptisms	172	986	112	342	63	84	43,692
Received into Full Communion	317	529	218	–	94	142	76,588
First Communions	2,723	11,620	5,218	6,360	3,073	1,356	797,582
Confirmations	1,604	8,151	4,282	3,403	1,715	946	618,041
Marriages	624	1,907	779	1,053	452	291	166,991
Deaths	1,832	1,328	2,166	1,208	1,051	639	419,278
Total Catholics	397,449	1,165,415	686,037	710,000	299,573	80,742	68,229,841
Total Population	571,987	3,770,433	858,546	3,260,246	352,439	494,458	307,374,682
Catholic Population Percentage	69	31	80	22	85	16	22

Archdioceses = 37; Dioceses = 170; Apostolates = 3

2012 GENERAL SUMMARY

	San Angelo TX	Tyler TX	Victoria in Texas TX	TEXAS TOTAL	Salt Lake City UT	Burlington VT	2012 U.S. GRAND TOTAL
Cardinals	–	–	–	1	–	–	13
Archbishops	1	–	–	4	–	–	56
Bishop	–	–	1	23	1	2	394
Abbots	–	–	–	1	4	–	109
Diocesan Priests	51	83	54	1,311	56	91	27,125
Religious Priests	11	8	5	761	12	36	12,593
Total Priests in Diocese	62	91	59	2,072	68	127	39,718
Newly Ordained Priests	2	6	–	34	–	1	485
Total Permanent Deacons	87	94	35	1,776	76	49	17,816
Total Brothers	–	1	1	203	9	23	4,518
Total Sisters	22	50	79	2,170	35	95	55,045
Number of Parishes	47	45	50	1,057	48	76	18,061
Missions	22	27	17	264	19	35	2,627
Pastoral Centers	–	1	–	28	–	1	628
New Parishes	–	2	–	2	–	1	87
Catholic Hospitals	–	3	–	28	–	–	605
Patients Assisted Annually	–	1,165,343	–	4,826,318	–	–	88,519,295
Health Care Centers	–	–	–	45	–	–	363
Patients Assisted Annually	–	–	–	357,931	–	–	5,038,247
Specialized Homes	–	–	1	43	–	4	1,616
Total Assisted Anually	–	–	59	15,057	–	290	991,072
Residential Care of Children (Orphanages)	–	–	–	8	–	–	344
Total Assisted Anually	–	–	–	1,476	–	–	23,479
Day Care and Extended Day Care Centers	–	–	–	52	16	–	1,005
Total Assisted Anually	–	–	–	5,100	564	–	121,211
Special Centers for Social Services	–	9	–	76	3	1	3,602
Total Assisted Anually	–	25,000	–	1,723,798	542,500	3,493	32,768,652
Diocesan Seminaries	–	–	–	7	–	–	71
Students	–	–	–	269	–	–	3,346
Religious Seminaries	–	–	–	9	3	–	98
Students	–	–	–	71	–	2	1,669
Colleges and Universities	–	–	–	9	–	2	233
Total Students	–	–	–	27,406	–	2,879	812,098
High Schools, Diocesan and Parish	–	1	2	24	3	2	731
Total Students	–	256	178	8,374	1,728	465	327,345
High Schools, Private	–	–	1	29	–	–	595
Total Students	–	–	316	12,434	–	–	296,268
Elementary Schools, Diocesan and Parish	3	5	12	200	13	9	5,378
Total Students	705	810	2,353	51,638	3,693	1,329	1,382,539
Elementary Schools, Private	–	–	1	26	–	2	386
Total Students	–	–	302	7,807	–	353	106,972
Non–residential Schools for the Disabled	–	–	–	1	–	–	53
Total Students	–	–	–	150	–	–	5,729
Religious Education High School Students	4,203	796	2,059	88,365	2,033	1,412	662,914
Religious Education Elementary Students	7,013	8,097	6,091	295,818	8,170	4,319	2,885,785
Priests Teaching	–	–	–	70	–	4	1,199
Scholastics Teaching	–	–	–	7	1	–	422
Brothers Teaching	–	–	–	40	–	–	698
Sisters Teaching	–	–	10	186	1	–	4,026
Lay Teachers	54	29	198	6,735	526	251	162,018
Infant Baptisms	1,810	2,383	1,109	75,686	3,278	764	793,103
Adult Baptisms	224	75	70	5,335	284	74	43,692
Received into Full Communion	157	265	89	5,990	506	105	76,588
First Communions	1,751	1,664	1,126	83,136	3,404	911	797,582
Confirmations	1,288	2,035	882	51,761	2,228	905	618,041
Marriages	349	290	346	14,584	529	332	166,991
Deaths	854	288	835	23,896	576	1,384	419,278
Total Catholics	84,555	54,746	102,860	7,183,820	270,000	118,000	68,229,841
Total Population	831,998	1,396,736	277,995	25,396,568	2,763,885	625,000	307,374,682
Catholic Population Percentage	10	4	37	28	10	19	22

*Indicates Archdioceses.

†Certain Diocese traverse state lines.

	St. Thomas Virgin Islands	Arlington VA	Richmond VA	VIRGINIA TOTAL	*Seattle WA	Spokane WA	2012 U.S. GRAND TOTAL
Cardinals	–	–	–	–	–	–	13
Archbishops	–	–	–	–	3	–	56
Bishop	2	1	2	3	1	2	394
Abbots	–	1	–	1	2	1	109
Diocesan Priests	14	160	144	304	199	81	27,125
Religious Priests	4	61	25	86	87	72	12,593
Total Priests in Diocese	18	221	169	390	286	153	39,718
Newly Ordained Priests	1	3	2	5	6	4	485
Total Permanent Deacons	27	61	86	147	110	48	17,816
Total Brothers	1	11	7	18	19	7	4,518
Total Sisters	16	132	160	292	369	156	55,045
Number of Parishes	8	68	146	214	147	58	18,061
Missions	1	6	4	10	27	21	2,627
Pastoral Centers	–	1	–	1	6	–	628
New Parishes	–	–	–	–	–	–	87
Catholic Hospitals	–	–	10	10	11	6	605
Patients Assisted Annually	–	–	700,000	700,000	2,273,059	373,143	88,519,295
Health Care Centers	–	1	–	1	2	–	363
Patients Assisted Annually	–	239	–	239	12,800	–	5,038,247
Specialized Homes	–	2	20	22	25	5	1,616
Total Assisted Anually	–	600	2,000	2,600	8,568	1,730	991,072
Residential Care of Children (Orphanages)	–	–	–	–	221	1	344
Total Assisted Anually	–	–	–	–	505	31	23,479
Day Care and Extended Day Care Centers	–	31	2	33	3	1	1,005
Total Assisted Anually	–	2,253	200	2,453	443	182	121,211
Special Centers for Social Services	4	11	2	13	126	17	3,602
Total Assisted Anually	787	43,998	–	43,998	52,146	222,244	32,768,652
Diocesan Seminaries	–	–	–	–	–	1	71
Students	–	–	–	–	–	13	3,346
Religious Seminaries	–	–	–	–	–	–	98
Students	–	–	–	–	–	–	1,669
Colleges and Universities	–	3	–	3	2	1	233
Total Students	–	4,961	–	4,961	9,566	7,701	812,098
High Schools, Diocesan and Parish	2	4	5	9	5	1	731
Total Students	136	3,775	1,747	5,522	2,429	114	327,345
High Schools, Private	–	2	3	5	6	2	595
Total Students	–	539	880	1,419	3,659	1,070	296,268
Elementary Schools, Diocesan and Parish	3	38	22	60	57	14	5,378
Total Students	453	11,904	5,958	17,862	15,654	3,343	1,382,539
Elementary Schools, Private	–	1	3	4	5	–	386
Total Students	–	214	1,000	1,214	1,102	–	106,972
Non–residential Schools for the Disabled	–	–	–	–	–	–	53
Total Students	–	–	–	–	–	–	5,729
Religious Education High School Students	103	2,885	5,653	8,538	5,800	763	662,914
Religious Education Elementary Students	438	31,572	15,259	46,831	26,500	2,846	2,885,785
Priests Teaching	–	6	1	7	11	–	1,199
Scholastics Teaching	–	–	–	–	–	–	422
Brothers Teaching	1	–	4	4	8	–	698
Sisters Teaching	2	34	18	52	25	–	4,026
Lay Teachers	68	1,275	912	2,187	1,646	225	162,018
Infant Baptisms	196	5,035	3,088	8,123	6,633	1,391	793,103
Adult Baptisms	11	1,274	47	1,321	449	94	43,692
Received into Full Communion	12	695	–	695	522	147	76,588
First Communions	144	8,161	3,323	11,484	6,488	1,783	797,582
Confirmations	108	6,852	3,688	10,540	3,869	1,850	618,041
Marriages	52	1,551	708	2,259	1,311	311	166,991
Deaths	192	1,569	1,664	3,233	2,662	577	419,278
Total Catholics	30,000	453,916	231,859	685,775	580,000	106,003	68,229,841
Total Population	120,917	2,968,486	4,982,668	7,951,154	5,262,350	815,409	307,374,682
Catholic Population Percentage	25	15	5	9	11	13	22

Archdioceses = 37; Dioceses = 170; Apostolates = 3

2012 GENERAL SUMMARY

	Yakima WA	WASHINGTON TOTAL	Wheeling–Charleston WV	*Milwaukee WI	Green Bay WI	La Crosse WI	2012 U.S. GRAND TOTAL
Cardinals	–	–	–	–	–	–	**13**
Archbishops	–	3	–	2	–	–	**56**
Bishop	2	5	1	2	3	1	**394**
Abbots	–	3	–	4	2	–	**109**
Diocesan Priests	75	355	106	339	180	155	**27,125**
Religious Priests	2	161	51	345	99	12	**12,593**
Total Priests in Diocese	77	516	157	684	279	167	**39,718**
Newly Ordained Priests	–	10	2	6	2	–	**485**
Total Permanent Deacons	44	202	45	177	133	51	**17,816**
Total Brothers	2	28	11	71	34	3	**4,518**
Total Sisters	30	555	137	1,252	457	393	**55,045**
Number of Parishes	41	246	110	205	157	165	**18,061**
Missions	3	51	18	–	2	–	**2,627**
Pastoral Centers	1	7	4	–	18	–	**628**
New Parishes	–	–	–	–	–	–	**87**
Catholic Hospitals	–	17	3	10	8	9	**605**
Patients Assisted Annually	–	2,646,202	633,117	1,891,652	943,303	603,842	**88,519,295**
Health Care Centers	1	3	–	1	–	–	**363**
Patients Assisted Annually	65,925	78,725	–	11,071	–	–	**5,038,247**
Specialized Homes	–	30	6	22	17	15	**1,616**
Total Assisted Anually	–	10,298	16	35,390	10,584	8,546	**991,072**
Residential Care of Children (Orphanages)	–	222	1	–	–	–	**344**
Total Assisted Anually	–	536	16	–	–	–	**23,479**
Day Care and Extended Day Care Centers	1	5	2	4	2	2	**1,005**
Total Assisted Anually	174	799	200	601	98	143	**121,211**
Special Centers for Social Services	5	148	11	11	8	2	**3,602**
Total Assisted Anually	49,389	323,779	41,723	169,789	217,325	5,678	**32,768,652**
Diocesan Seminaries	–	1	–	1	–	1	**71**
Students	–	13	–	32	–	–	**3,346**
Religious Seminaries	–	–	–	3	1	–	**98**
Students	–	–	–	149	8	–	**1,669**
Colleges and Universities	–	3	1	5	2	1	**233**
Total Students	–	17,267	1,372	24,906	3,532	3,000	**812,098**
High Schools, Diocesan and Parish	–	6	7	6	5	7	**731**
Total Students	–	2,543	1,430	2,939	1,470	1,565	**327,345**
High Schools, Private	1	9	–	7	1	–	**595**
Total Students	176	4,905	–	3,646	736	–	**296,268**
Elementary Schools, Diocesan and Parish	6	77	22	93	54	63	**5,378**
Total Students	1,644	20,641	4,505	23,883	8,458	7,138	**1,382,539**
Elementary Schools, Private	–	5	–	4	–	–	**386**
Total Students	–	1,102	–	1,118	–	–	**106,972**
Non–residential Schools for the Disabled	–	–	–	1	–	–	**53**
Total Students	–	–	–	20	–	–	**5,729**
Religious Education High School Students	2,135	8,698	766	12,958	6,364	3,798	**662,914**
Religious Education Elementary Students	5,852	35,198	4,142	27,390	14,120	12,471	**2,885,785**
Priests Teaching	–	11	2	26	–	10	**1,199**
Scholastics Teaching	–	–	–	–	–	–	**422**
Brothers Teaching	2	10	2	–	–	–	**698**
Sisters Teaching	3	28	1	99	16	17	**4,026**
Lay Teachers	171	2,042	567	4,037	940	832	**162,018**
Infant Baptisms	3,412	11,436	836	6,726	3,408	1,991	**793,103**
Adult Baptisms	96	639	190	223	135	142	**43,692**
Received into Full Communion	147	816	164	404	209	219	**76,588**
First Communions	2,683	10,954	955	7,374	3,555	2,329	**797,582**
Confirmations	1,027	6,746	897	5,377	3,007	2,323	**618,041**
Marriages	468	2,090	211	1,762	1,080	655	**166,991**
Deaths	514	3,753	1,006	4,913	2,989	1,992	**419,278**
Total Catholics	72,980	758,983	83,129	625,765	332,200	180,305	**68,229,841**
Total Population	681,556	6,759,315	1,819,777	2,327,812	1,006,668	901,157	**307,374,682**
Catholic Population Percentage	11	11	5	27	33	20	**22**

*Indicates Archdioceses.

†Certain Diocese traverse state lines.

	Madison WI	Superior WI	WISCONSIN TOTAL	† Cheyenne WY	EASTERN RITE *Philadelphia	EASTERN RITE *Pittsburgh	2012 U.S. GRAND TOTAL
Cardinals	–	–	–	–	–	–	13
Archbishops	–	–	2	–	2	–	56
Bishop	1	2	9	2	–	–	394
Abbots	1	–	7	–	–	1	109
Diocesan Priests	133	70	877	55	48	55	27,125
Religious Priests	21	6	483	5	5	9	12,593
Total Priests in Diocese	154	76	1,360	60	53	64	39,718
Newly Ordained Priests	2	7	17	–	–	–	485
Total Permanent Deacons	20	71	452	22	7	21	17,816
Total Brothers	8	–	116	1	–	2	4,518
Total Sisters	399	73	2,574	19	49	69	55,045
Number of Parishes	120	104	751	32	66	76	18,061
Missions	–	–	2	39	–	2	2,627
Pastoral Centers	1	–	19	–	–	2	628
New Parishes	4	–	4	–	–	–	87
Catholic Hospitals	3	6	36	–	–	–	605
Patients Assisted Annually	488,203	253,592	4,180,592	–	–	–	88,519,295
Health Care Centers	2	1	4	–	–	–	363
Patients Assisted Annually	145,038	155	156,264	–	–	–	5,038,247
Specialized Homes	6	12	72	2	2	2	1,616
Total Assisted Anually	773	377	55,670	102	279	548	991,072
Residential Care of Children (Orphanages)	–	–	–	1	–	–	344
Total Assisted Anually	–	–	–	242	–	–	23,479
Day Care and Extended Day Care Centers	22	2	32	–	–	–	1,005
Total Assisted Anually	1,104	233	2,179	–	–	–	121,211
Special Centers for Social Services	25	4	50	4	–	–	3,602
Total Assisted Anually	53,051	381	446,224	14,859	–	–	32,768,652
Diocesan Seminaries	–	–	2	–	1	1	71
Students	–	–	32	–	3	10	3,346
Religious Seminaries	–	–	4	–	–	–	98
Students	–	–	157	–	–	–	1,669
Colleges and Universities	1	–	9	–	1	–	233
Total Students	2,650	–	34,088	–	969	–	812,098
High Schools, Diocesan and Parish	–	–	18	–	–	–	731
Total Students	–	–	5,974	–	–	–	327,345
High Schools, Private	3	–	11	–	1	–	595
Total Students	685	–	5,067	–	324	–	296,268
Elementary Schools, Diocesan and Parish	42	15	267	7	4	–	5,378
Total Students	6,766	2,508	48,753	961	567	–	1,382,539
Elementary Schools, Private	3	–	7	–	–	–	386
Total Students	461	–	1,579	–	–	–	106,972
Non–residential Schools for the Disabled	–	–	1	–	–	–	53
Total Students	–	–	20	–	–	–	5,729
Religious Education High School Students	6,168	1,948	31,236	907	96	271	662,914
Religious Education Elementary Students	12,352	4,455	70,788	3,015	409	652	2,885,785
Priests Teaching	–	–	36	–	2	–	1,199
Scholastics Teaching	–	–	–	–	–	–	422
Brothers Teaching	1	–	1	–	–	–	698
Sisters Teaching	29	5	166	2	12	–	4,026
Lay Teachers	699	222	6,730	91	78	–	162,018
Infant Baptisms	2,600	726	15,451	942	232	133	793,103
Adult Baptisms	112	37	649	117	3	6	43,692
Received into Full Communion	200	134	1,166	122	9	33	76,588
First Communions	2,598	921	16,777	862	191	157	797,582
Confirmations	2,081	881	13,669	846	233	143	618,041
Marriages	706	255	4,458	231	72	60	166,991
Deaths	1,723	1,085	12,702	563	519	–	419,278
Total Catholics	281,438	74,697	1,494,405	54,129	15,779	58,200	68,229,841
Total Population	1,015,451	439,182	5,690,270	563,626	–	–	307,374,682
Catholic Population Percentage	28	17	26	10	–	–	22

Archdioceses = 37; Dioceses = 170; Apostolates = 3

2012 GENERAL SUMMARY

	Holy Protection of Mary	Lady of Deliverance	Lady of Lebanon	Lady of Nareg	Newton	Parma	2012 U.S. GRAND TOTAL
	EASTERN RITE (cont)						
Cardinals	–	–	–	–	–	–	13
Archbishops	–	–	–	–	–	–	56
Bishop	1	1	1	2	2	1	394
Abbots	–	–	1	–	–	–	109
Diocesan Priests	22	13	35	4	47	40	27,125
Religious Priests	1	–	15	10	14	1	12,593
Total Priests in Diocese	23	13	50	14	61	41	39,718
Newly Ordained Priests	1	–	–	–	–	–	485
Total Permanent Deacons	12	4	19	1	58	16	17,816
Total Brothers	2	–	–	–	–	–	4,518
Total Sisters	3	–	6	10	5	8	55,045
Number of Parishes	19	9	30	9	36	29	18,061
Missions	1	7	9	–	7	5	2,627
Pastoral Centers	–	–	–	–	–	1	628
New Parishes	–	–	–	–	–	–	87
Catholic Hospitals	–	–	–	–	–	–	605
Patients Assisted Annually	–	–	–	–	–	–	88,519,295
Health Care Centers	–	–	–	–	–	–	363
Patients Assisted Annually	–	–	–	–	–	–	5,038,247
Specialized Homes	–	–	–	–	–	–	1,616
Total Assisted Anually	–	–	–	–	–	–	991,072
Residential Care of Children (Orphanages)	–	–	1	–	–	–	344
Total Assisted Anually	–	–	20	–	–	–	23,479
Day Care and Extended Day Care Centers	–	–	–	–	–	1	1,005
Total Assisted Anually	–	–	–	–	–	28	121,211
Special Centers for Social Services	–	–	–	–	–	5	3,602
Total Assisted Anually	–	–	–	–	–	16,500	32,768,652
Diocesan Seminaries	–	–	–	–	–	–	71
Students	–	–	–	–	–	–	3,346
Religious Seminaries	–	–	–	–	1	–	98
Students	–	–	–	–	2	–	1,669
Colleges and Universities	–	–	–	–	–	–	233
Total Students	–	–	–	–	–	–	812,098
High Schools, Diocesan and Parish	–	–	–	1	–	–	731
Total Students	–	–	–	389	–	–	327,345
High Schools, Private	–	–	–	–	–	–	595
Total Students	–	–	–	–	–	–	296,268
Elementary Schools, Diocesan and Parish	–	–	–	–	–	1	5,378
Total Students	–	–	–	–	–	161	1,382,539
Elementary Schools, Private	–	–	1	4	–	–	386
Total Students	–	–	39	542	–	–	106,972
Non–residential Schools for the Disabled	–	–	–	–	–	–	53
Total Students	–	–	–	–	–	–	5,729
Religious Education High School Students	77	94	349	35	122	107	662,914
Religious Education Elementary Students	325	400	1,509	85	636	339	2,885,785
Priests Teaching	–	–	–	1	–	–	1,199
Scholastics Teaching	–	–	–	–	–	–	422
Brothers Teaching	–	–	–	–	–	–	698
Sisters Teaching	–	–	–	1	–	–	4,026
Lay Teachers	–	–	1	146	–	–	162,018
Infant Baptisms	72	76	381	161	317	55	793,103
Adult Baptisms	6	4	28	–	12	8	43,692
Received into Full Communion	15	40	12	–	2	21	76,588
First Communions	91	80	288	132	180	48	797,582
Confirmations	99	15	394	–	203	60	618,041
Marriages	19	26	106	69	182	25	166,991
Deaths	38	18	171	–	128	143	419,278
Total Catholics	2,402	22,500	46,000	37,500	21,000	8,659	68,229,841
Total Population	–	–	–			–	307,374,682
Catholic Population Percentage							22

*Indicates Archdioceses.

†Certain Diocese traverse state lines.

2012 GENERAL SUMMARY

	EASTERN RITE (cont)						
	Passaic	Romanian	St. Josaphat	St. Maron	St. Nicholas	St. Peter the Apostle	2012 U.S. GRAND TOTAL
Cardinals	–	–	–	–	–	–	13
Archbishops	–	–	–	–	–	–	56
Bishop	–	1	2	2	2	1	394
Abbots	–	1	–	1	3	–	109
Diocesan Priests	67	19	48	48	43	15	27,125
Religious Priests	10	2	1	13	12	5	12,593
Total Priests in Diocese	77	21	49	61	55	20	39,718
Newly Ordained Priests	–	1	1	–	3	–	485
Total Permanent Deacons	26	7	8	16	11	10	17,816
Total Brothers	1	5	3	7	–	–	4,518
Total Sisters	16	4	2	2	–	10	55,045
Number of Parishes	84	15	38	34	38	9	18,061
Missions	4	4	4	8	4	–	2,627
Pastoral Centers	–	–	–	–	–	–	628
New Parishes	–	–	–	–	–	–	87
Catholic Hospitals	–	–	–	–	–	–	605
Patients Assisted Annually	–	–	–	–	–	–	88,519,295
Health Care Centers	–	–	–	–	–	–	363
Patients Assisted Annually	–	–	–	–	–	–	5,038,247
Specialized Homes	–	–	–	–	–	2	1,616
Total Assisted Anually	–	–	–	–	–	92	991,072
Residential Care of Children (Orphanages)	–	–	–	–	–	–	344
Total Assisted Anually	–	–	–	–	–	–	23,479
Day Care and Extended Day Care Centers	–	–	–	–	–	–	1,005
Total Assisted Anually	–	–	–	–	–	–	121,211
Special Centers for Social Services	–	–	–	–	–	–	3,602
Total Assisted Anually	–	–	–	–	–	–	32,768,652
Diocesan Seminaries	–	–	–	1	–	–	71
Students	–	–	–	5	–	–	3,346
Religious Seminaries	–	–	–	–	–	–	98
Students	–	–	–	–	–	–	1,669
Colleges and Universities	–	–	–	–	–	–	233
Total Students	–	–	–	–	–	–	812,098
High Schools, Diocesan and Parish	–	–	–	–	–	–	731
Total Students	–	–	–	–	–	–	327,345
High Schools, Private	–	–	–	–	–	–	595
Total Students	–	–	–	–	–	–	296,268
Elementary Schools, Diocesan and Parish	–	–	–	–	2	–	5,378
Total Students	–	–	–	–	245	–	1,382,539
Elementary Schools, Private	–	–	–	–	–	–	386
Total Students	–	–	–	–	–	–	106,972
Non–residential Schools for the Disabled	–	–	–	–	–	–	53
Total Students	–	–	–	–	–	–	5,729
Religious Education High School Students	164	45	32	329	40	–	662,914
Religious Education Elementary Students	509	78	101	1,441	105	–	2,885,785
Priests Teaching	–	–	–	–	1	–	1,199
Scholastics Teaching	–	–	–	–	–	–	422
Brothers Teaching	–	–	–	–	–	–	698
Sisters Teaching	–	–	–	–	2	–	4,026
Lay Teachers	–	–	–	–	20	–	162,018
Infant Baptisms	144	37	48	350	250	447	793,103
Adult Baptisms	3	1	1	8	5	9	43,692
Received into Full Communion	16	7	110	14	5	–	76,588
First Communions	149	37	50	330	120	437	797,582
Confirmations	133	38	54	404	256	447	618,041
Marriages	52	22	7	94	85	154	166,991
Deaths	457	15	109	240	200	109	419,278
Total Catholics	14,729	5,675	8,500	31,800	10,500	60,000	68,229,841
Total Population	–	–	–	–	–	–	307,374,682
Catholic Population Percentage							22

Archdioceses = 37; Dioceses = 170; Apostolates = 3

2012 GENERAL SUMMARY

	EASTERN RITE (cont) St. Thomas the Apostle	St. Thomas Syro-Malabar	Stamford	Syro-Malankara	EASTERN RITE TOTAL	*Military Archdiocese	2012 U.S. GRAND TOTAL
Cardinals	–	–	–	–	–	–	13
Archbishops	–	–	–	–	2	2	56
Bishop	1	1	2	1	21	5	394
Abbots	–	–	–	–	7	–	109
Diocesan Priests	21	38	39	12	614	–	27,125
Religious Priests	–	15	10	1	124	–	12,593
Total Priests in Diocese	21	53	49	13	738	–	39,718
Newly Ordained Priests	1	–	1	–	8	–	485
Total Permanent Deacons	120	–	10	–	346	–	17,816
Total Brothers	–	–	1	–	21	–	4,518
Total Sisters	10	18	42	33	287	–	55,045
Number of Parishes	9	27	51	12	591	–	18,061
Missions	1	37	3	4	100	–	2,627
Pastoral Centers	–	–	–	–	3	–	628
New Parishes	1	5	–	–	6	–	87
Catholic Hospitals	–	–	–	–	–	–	605
Patients Assisted Annually	–	–	–	–	–	–	88,519,295
Health Care Centers	–	–	–	–	–	–	363
Patients Assisted Annually	–	–	–	–	–	–	5,038,247
Specialized Homes	1	–	1	–	8	–	1,616
Total Assisted Anually	60	–	26	–	1,005	–	991,072
Residential Care of Children (Orphanages)	–	–	–	–	1	–	344
Total Assisted Anually	–	–	–	–	20	–	23,479
Day Care and Extended Day Care Centers	–	–	1	–	2	–	1,005
Total Assisted Anually	–	–	48	–	76	–	121,211
Special Centers for Social Services	1	–	–	–	6	–	3,602
Total Assisted Anually	150	–	–	–	16,650	–	32,768,652
Diocesan Seminaries	–	–	1	–	4	–	71
Students	–	–	2	–	20	–	3,346
Religious Seminaries	–	–	–	–	1	–	98
Students	–	–	–	4	6	–	1,669
Colleges and Universities	–	–	–	–	1	–	233
Total Students	–	–	–	–	969	–	812,098
High Schools, Diocesan and Parish	–	–	1	–	2	–	731
Total Students	–	–	210	–	599	–	327,345
High Schools, Private	–	–	–	–	1	–	595
Total Students	–	–	–	–	324	–	296,268
Elementary Schools, Diocesan and Parish	–	–	2	–	9	–	5,378
Total Students	–	–	198	–	1,171	–	1,382,539
Elementary Schools, Private	–	–	–	–	5	–	386
Total Students	–	–	–	–	581	–	106,972
Non-residential Schools for the Disabled	–	–	–	–	–	–	53
Total Students	–	–	–	–	–	–	5,729
Religious Education High School Students	–	962	218	–	2,941	–	662,914
Religious Education Elementary Students	–	3,181	642	–	10,412	–	2,885,785
Priests Teaching	–	–	–	–	4	–	1,199
Scholastics Teaching	–	–	–	–	–	–	422
Brothers Teaching	–	–	–	–	–	–	698
Sisters Teaching	–	–	–	–	15	–	4,026
Lay Teachers	–	–	–	–	245	–	162,018
Infant Baptisms	978	303	171	–	4,155	4,155	793,103
Adult Baptisms	7	69	7	–	177	844	43,692
Received into Full Communion	–	97	9	–	390	335	76,588
First Communions	680	669	151	–	3,790	3,149	797,582
Confirmations	985	766	178	–	4,408	3,253	618,041
Marriages	328	86	44	–	1,431	883	166,991
Deaths	269	57	213	–	2,686	–	419,278
Total Catholics	125,000	87,000	13,783	–	569,027	–	68,229,841
Total Population	–	–	–	–	–	–	307,374,682
Catholic Population Percentage	–	–	–	–	–	–	22

*Indicates Archdioceses.

†Certain Diocese traverse state lines.

2012 GENERAL SUMMARY

					2002 GRAND TOTAL	2011 GRAND TOTAL	2012 U.S. GRAND TOTAL
Cardinals	–	–	–	–	11	14	**13**
Archbishops	–	–	–	–	49	60	**56**
Bishop	–	–	–	–	377	396	**394**
Abbots	–	–	–	–	113	109	**109**
Diocesan Priests	–	–	–	–	29,715	27,284	**27,125**
Religious Priests	–	–	–	–	14,772	12,978	**12,593**
Total Priests in Diocese	–	–	–	–	44,487	40,271	**39,718**
Newly Ordained Priests	–	–	–	–	449	480	**485**
Total Permanent Deacons	–	–	–	–	14,106	17,433	**17,816**
Total Brothers	–	–	–	–	5,568	4,650	**4,518**
Total Sisters	–	–	–	–	74,698	57,113	**55,045**
Number of Parishes	–	–	–	–	19,484	18,201	**18,061**
Missions	–	–	–	–	2,988	2,604	**2,627**
Pastoral Centers	–	–	–	–	1,069	577	**628**
New Parishes	–	–	–	–	44	70	**87**
Catholic Hospitals	–	–	–	–	585	554	**605**
Patients Assisted Annually	–	–	–	–	83,921,898	89,501,723	**88,519,295**
Health Care Centers	–	–	–	–	477	357	**363**
Patients Assisted Annually	–	–	–	–	5,249,083	5,535,260	**5,038,247**
Specialized Homes	–	–	–	–	1,534	1,541	**1,616**
Total Assisted Anually	–	–	–	–	778,623	1,031,215	**991,072**
Residential Care of Children (Orphanages)	–	–	–	–	226	418	**344**
Total Assisted Anually	–	–	–	–	714,253	28,941	**23,479**
Day Care and Extended Day Care Centers	–	–	–	–	1,117	963	**1,005**
Total Assisted Anually	–	–	–	–	136,000	91,009	**121,211**
Special Centers for Social Services	–	–	–	–	3,044	3,671	**3,602**
Total Assisted Anually	–	–	–	–	20,032,104	30,172,406	**32,768,652**
Diocesan Seminaries	–	–	–	–	70	73	**71**
Students	–	–	–	–	3,251	3,394	**3,346**
Religious Seminaries	–	–	–	–	143	117	**98**
Students	–	–	–	–	1,271	1,853	**1,669**
Colleges and Universities	–	–	–	–	237	235	**233**
Total Students	–	–	–	–	749,512	804,826	**812,098**
High Schools, Diocesan and Parish	–	–	–	–	824	732	**731**
Total Students	–	–	–	–	386,764	324,384	**327,345**
High Schools, Private	–	–	–	–	552	608	**595**
Total Students	–	–	–	–	299,887	306,203	**296,268**
Elementary Schools, Diocesan and Parish	–	–	–	–	6,773	5,497	**5,378**
Total Students	–	–	–	–	1,872,848	1,413,481	**1,382,539**
Elementary Schools, Private	–	–	–	–	369	361	**386**
Total Students	–	–	–	–	98,546	104,227	**106,972**
Non–residential Schools for the Disabled	–	–	–	–	85	61	**53**
Total Students	–	–	–	–	18,535	59,160	**5,729**
Religious Education High School Students	–	–	–	–	767,739	678,273	**662,914**
Religious Education Elementary Students	–	–	–	–	3,582,943	3,012,244	**2,885,785**
Priests Teaching	–	–	–	–	1,596	1,383	**1,199**
Scholastics Teaching	–	–	–	–	33	102	**422**
Brothers Teaching	–	–	–	–	1,021	821	**698**
Sisters Teaching	–	–	–	–	7,389	4,977	**4,026**
Lay Teachers	–	–	–	–	161,775	155,665	**162,018**
Infant Baptisms	–	–	–	–	1,005,490	830,937	**793,103**
Adult Baptisms	–	–	–	–	81,013	42,338	**43,692**
Received into Full Communion	–	–	–	–	82,292	73,395	**76,588**
First Communions	–	–	–	–	897,635	825,917	**797,582**
Confirmations	–	–	–	–	637,705	619,697	**618,041**
Marriages	–	–	–	–	241,727	170,165	**166,991**
Deaths	–	–	–	–	477,702	423,275	**419,278**
Total Catholics	–	–	–	–	66,407,105	68,301,775	**68,229,841**
Total Population	–	–	–	–	290,446,533	313,369,375	**307,374,682**
Catholic Population Percentage	–	–	–	–	22	22	**22**

Archdioceses = 37; Dioceses = 170; Apostolates = 3

U.S. Census Bureau estimate of Total Population as of Jan. 1, 2012: 313,391,478
U.S. Census Bureau estimate of Total Population as of Jan. 1, 2011: 311,276,073
U.S. Census Bureau estimate of Total Population as of Jan. 1, 2002: 285,828,934

Catholic Dioceses

2300 Wisconsin Ave NW Suite 400
Washington, DC 20007
cara.georgetown.edu

in the United States

This map shows boundaries of the Latin Rite dioceses whose bishops belong to the United States Conference of Catholic Bishops (USCCB). Archdioceses are indicated by capital letters and Ecclesiastical Provinces are grouped by color. USCCB regions are shown within maroon lines and indicated by Roman numerals. Dashed lines show where dioceses cross state lines. This map does not show the Diocese of St. Thomas in the U.S. Virgin Islands, which is part of the Ecclesiastical Province of Washington, or the Archdiocese for the Military Services.

The Official Catholic Directory®

Products and Services Guide

Index to Advertisers

AUDIO & VIDEO—General

Lighthouse Catholic Media, NFP
303 E. State St.
Sycamore, IL 60178
Tel: 866-767-3155 (Toll Free)
Fax: 815-895-0333 Fax
E-mail: Tim@LighthouseCatholicMedia.org
Website: www.LigthouseCatholicMedia.org

Type of Business

Lighthouse Catholic Media, NFP is a not-for-profit organization dedicated to providing high quality Catholic audio CDs, mp3 downloads as an affordable and convenient way for parishioners to hear faith-filled presentations from the best Catholic speakers of our day.

These recordings provide an easy and effective way to foster catechesis, and provide parishioners with a powerful way to reach out to their family members, friends, etc.

"These CDs helped make the Mass come alive and left me with a hunger to learn more. What a blessing!"

Our **FAITHRAISER Kiosk Program** is proven effective, with approximately 5,000 parish customers, and the program is primarily self-funding.

We have over 150 CD titles available in English and Spanish, and our Starter Kit comes complete with a beautiful display stand, CDs, pamphlets, and now great books too! We also provide a proven success plan, support, and assistance to make your program a success.

For more information, please call 866-767-3155.

Personnel:

Mark Middendorf (President, Board of Directors)
Terry Barber (Chairman of the Board)
Dave Durand (VP of Sales)
Tim Truckenbrod (VP of Marketing and Operations)

Cassettes, Audio & Video

Holy Cross Family Ministries
Family Rosary
Family Theater Productions
Father Peyton Family Institute
Family Rosary International
518 Washington Street
North Easton, MA 02356
Tel: 508-238-4095
Fax: 508-238-3953
Website: www.hcfm.org

Type of Business:

Continuing the mission of our founder, Servant of God Father Patrick Peyton, C.S.C., Holy Cross Family Ministries serves Jesus Christ and His Church throughout the world by promoting and supporting the spiritual well-being of the family through products and programs.

Personnel:

Fr. John Phalen, C.S.C. (President)
Susan Wallace (Director of External Relations)
Beth Mahoney (Mission Director)

BUSINESS & FINANCE—General

United States Conference of Catholic Bishops
Office of National Collections
3211 Fourth Street, N.E.
Washington, DC 20017
Tel: 202-541-3400
Website: www.usccb.org/nationalcollections

Type of Business:

The national collections administered by the United States Conference of Catholic Bishops (USCCB) have been established by either the Holy Father or the bishops of the United States. The national collections support the Church's works of social justice, evangelization, and education, both domestically and around the globe.

Every Catholic participates in a global community of faith by contributing and acting as faithful stewards of the gifts God has given them. The national collections of the USCCB are a powerful way to express your solidarity with this community.

Capital Campaigns

Guidance in Giving, Inc.
Full Service Stewardship, Development and Campaign Consultants
225 Snedecor Avenue
Bayport, NY 11705
Tel: 888-757-5444; Cell: 631-553-9064
E-mail: mcusack@guidanceingiving.com
Website: www.guidanceingiving.com

Type of Business:

Guidance In Giving, Inc. is a Catholic organization that truly understands the mission of the Catholic Church. Serving as stewardship, development and campaign counsel to dioceses, parishes and schools, our firm has extensive experience in conducting capital campaigns and implementing stewardship throughout the United States. In all of our development efforts, we utilize techniques that are continuously tested and refined. Services include: diocesan capital campaigns; diocesan annual appeals; diocesan development audits and feasibility studies; parish capital campaigns; offertory enhancement, implementing stewardship; parish feasibility studies, school development audits, school feasibility studies, major gifts solicitations and school capital campaigns. Additionally, the firm has an Hispanic and Multicultural Division and offers bilingual services. To discuss your individual situation or to get a cost free analysis of your potential, please contact Michael R. Cusack, Chairman and CEO at 888-757-5444.

Personnel:

Michael R. Cusack (Chairman and CEO)
Michael V. Goodwin (President, Diocesan Division)
Joseph W. Zamorano (President, Parish Division)
Stephen A. Babcock (Executive Vice President, Parish Division)
Joseph E. Neville (Senior Vice President)
Carlos H. Proaño (Executive Vice President, Hispanic and Multicultural Division)

Computers & Software

parishSupport Growth Software
271 South Ellsworth Avenue
Salem, OH 44460
Tel: 877.393.3330
Fax: 330.337.5990
E-mail: info@parishsupport.com
Website: www.parishsupport.com

Type of Business:

Parish management software designed by Catholics for Catholics to effortlessly engage, enlighten and ultimately empower parishioners to grow Catholic. parishSupport utilizes everyday parish staff functions like contribution recording, calendar developing and census data and effortlessly releases valuable information to leadership and parishioners. parishSupport has effectively designed an online census program that helps save a great deal of office personnelís time and efforts. Built in electronic giving capabilities allow parish staff to have electronic giving records be illustrated, charted and displayed with all other giving methods for accurate information.

PowerChurch Software
601 Alliance Court
Asheville, NC 28806
Tel: 800-486-1800
Fax: 828-665-1999
E-mail: info@powerchurch.com
Website: www.powerchurch.com

Type of Business:

PowerChurch Software provides church management software to help centralize the administrative duties of managing your Membership, Contributions, Accounting, and Event scheduling. You can record comprehensive membership information, keep track of activity participation, and attendance of church services or events. Track contributions, pledges, and prepare statements for mailing or e-mailing. Manage your financial records with a complete fund accounting system specially designed for churches. Plan upcoming events by reserving rooms and equipment, avoiding any scheduling conflicts. Visit www.powerchurch.com to download a free, full-working demo or request one on CD. There you can also learn about other products offered such as PowerChurch Online and Check In system.

Consultants

Arthur J. Gallagher & Co.
Religious Practice Group
Two Pierce Place, The Gallagher Center
Itasca, IL 60143
Tel: 888-285-5106, ext. 3898; Fax: 630-345-9623
E-mail: Peter_Persuitti@ajg.com; Website: www.ajg.com/religious

Type of Business:

Our Commitment to Religious Organizations

Since 1927, Gallagher has been serving the needs of churches as consultant, insurance broker, agent, loss control specialist and claims advocate. For more than fifty years we have worked closely with the Roman Catholic faith traditions (dioceses, religious orders).

We help dioceses and archdioceses with risk management challenges, gaps in coverage, consultative benefit plan analysis and 403(b) audits by forging innovative and collaborative programs. Our consultative approach is our hallmark and a valued resource for church finance councils and boards. We encourage you to log-in to the premiere resource for the Church www.gallagherpost.com

We are a leader in helping the Church reclaim dollars for ministry through innovative self-insurance, unbundling of claims, data and exposure management, proactive risk control training, specialized allocation and billing services and investments in appraisals.

We also are a premiere advisor for international and domestic mission services through Gallagher Charitable International Insurance Services (GCIIS). We encourage a diocese to set up its own World Youth Day 2011 Madrid insurance program by engaging our GCIIS team.

Of the more than 11,500 employees we have globally, more than 20 percent of our work force touch the serving of our religious and nonprofit clients, many living in your community or region.

Personnel:

Peter A. Persuitti Managing Director, Gallagher Religious Practice

Guidance in Giving, Inc.
Full Service Stewardship, Development and Campaign Consultants
225 Snedecor Avenue, Bayport, NY 11705
Tel: 888-757-5444; Cell: 631-553-9064
E-mail: mcusack@guidanceingiving.com
Website: www.guidanceingiving.com

Type of Business:

Guidance In Giving, Inc. is a Catholic organization that truly understands the mission of the Catholic Church. Serving as stewardship, development and campaign counsel to dioceses, parishes and schools, our firm has extensive experience in conducting capital campaigns and implementing stewardship throughout the United States. In all of our development efforts we utilize techniques that are continuously tested and refined. Services include: diocesan capital campaigns; diocesan annual appeals; diocesan development audits and feasibility studies; parish capital campaigns; offertory enhancement, implementing stewardship; parish feasibility studies, school development audits, school feasibility studies, major gifts solicitations and school capital campaigns. Additionally, the firm has an Hispanic and Multicultural Division and offers bilingual services. To discuss your individual situation or to get a cost free analysis of your potential, please contact Michael R. Cusack, Chairman and CEO at 888-757-5444.

Personnel:

Michael R. Cusack (Chairman and CEO)
Michael V. Goodwin (President, Diocesan Division)
Joseph W. Zamorano (President, Parish Division)
Stephen A. Babcock (Executive Vice President, Parish Division)
Joseph E. Neville (Senior Vice President)
Carlos H. Proaño (Executive Vice President, Hispanic and Multicultural Division)

Rohn & Associates Design, Inc.
1113 Creedmoor Avenue
Pittsburgh, PA 15226
Tel: 412-561-1228; 800-245-1288; Fax: 412-561-1201
E-mail: rolfrohn@rohndesign.com; Website: www.rohndesign.com
Blog: http://catholicliturgicalarts.blogspot.com/
Facebook: Catholic Liturgical Arts Journal

Type of Business:

Liturgical Designers, Artists & Artisans
TRADITION. Over the past 58 years, we have assisted the Catholic Church by designing, budgeting and implementing liturgical spaces.
COLLABORATION. We work side-by-side with our clients and collaborators to design and create appropriate and quality sacred art, interior finishes, lighting systems, acoustical systems, liturgical furnishings and appointments to create a rich devotional experience for your parishioners.
EXPERIENCE. We draw upon decades of experience and from a rich treasury of designers, architectural staff and contributing artists.
SCOPE OF SERVICES: Liturgical Design; Interior Design & Decorating; Sacred Artwork; Mosaics; Art Glass; Statuary; Liturgical Appointments; Liturgical Furniture; Metalwork.
ADDITIONAL LOCATIONS: 719 S. Flores St., Suite 200, San Antonio, TX 78204. Tel.: 210-231-0377; Fax: 210-231-0366
Contact us to arrange a complimentary project review.

Personnel:

Rolf R. Rohn (President - Liturgical Designer-Consultant)
Kathleen L. Maglicco (Vice President, Design)
Francesca Lofaro (Director, Sales)

Conventions & Trade Fairs

KOINÈ

Koinè World Fair of Church Supplies, Liturgical and Ecclesiastical Art
Vicenza Fair, Italy 13-16 April 2013 Organized by Conference Service Srl
Via de' Buttieri 5/a
40125 Bologna - Italy
Tel: +39.0514298311; Fax: +39.051.4298312
E-mail: info@koinexpo.com; Website: www.koinexpo.com

THE WORLDWIDE FAIR FOR THE RELIGIOUS INDUSTRY

Type of Business:

Koinè keeps focused on market trends and new industry developments: Buyers and traders from all over the world are coming to Vicenza to meet with church manufacturers showcasing new, contemporary and classic products and services and to learn and get inspired about the latest liturgical trends and designs in sacred art and furniture, technical apparels and ecclesiastical supplies.
Serving the ecclesiastical market worldwide.
In the jewel of renaissance Vicenza, north east of Italy, since 1989, Koinè gathers together the worldwide industry: distribution channel and Church players, craftsmen, artists, designers, church architects, combined with THE highest quality manufacture labeled made in Italy and the leading international suppliers.
Koinè Research 2013: celebrating 50 years of Vatican II Sacrosanctum Concilium with research on sacred art, liturgical trends, renovation and construction of spaces of worship
Koinè is the landmark for the religious industry, convincing in all aspects: more exhibitors, more visitors and higher degree of internationalism and professionalism.
Over 320 exhibitors giving the chance to 12.000 visitors attending coming from the 5 continents to discover and compare the full spectrum of new products you could not see anywhere else.

National Catholic Development Conference
86 Front Street
Hempstead, NY 11550
Tel: 1-888-TRY-NCDC (879.6232)
Fax: 516.489.9287
Website: www.ncdc.org

Our Mission:

NCDC leads the Catholic development community toward excellence in the ministry of ethical fundraising through education, resources, networking, and advocacy.
The National Catholic Development Conference is the United States' largest membership association of charitable religious fundraisers. Our nonprofit membership consists of religious communities of men and women, shrines, social service agencies, schools, parishes, dioceses, seminaries and international relief agencies. Corporate partnership is available to businesses wishing to promote the interests and purposes of the Conference. NCDC affirms the mission of each of its member organizations by working for and with them in the context of fundraising as a ministry.
Membership in NCDC (subject to approval by the Board of Directors) is open to Catholic and non-Catholic nonprofit organizations as well as businesses that service nonprofit organizations. NCDC membership is organizationally-based, meaning all members of the fundraising staff of a member organization are entitled to member benefits. The same applies for members of a Corporate Partner's staff.
Special Membership rates are available for qualifying organizations.

Personnel:

Sr. Georgette Lehmuth, OSF (President/CEO glehmuth@ncdc.org)

Donor Walls & Trees of Life

W & E Baum
89 Bannard Street
Freehold, NJ 07728
Tel: 800-922-7377; 732-866-1881
Fax: 732-866-8978
E-mail: info@webaum.com
Website: www.webaum.com/Church-Products.html

Type of Business:

W&E BAUM, celebrating 92 years and three generations, specializes in the design and fabrication of symbols of recognition and generosity. Additional income for churches can be generated by using many of our innovative products. Our Donor Walls, Bronze Memorials, Giving Trees, Plaques, Awards, Sculptures and more, promote fund-raising efforts and acknowledge gifts of all kinds. Quality, creativity and personal attention to detail are the elements that capture the attention of potential contributors in today's sophisticated world.
To thank, to honor, to reward, to commemorate, to memorialize, W & E Baum stands ready to help you translate your vision into reality.
Our Bronze Memorial Designs are a new and innovative way for your parishioners to permanently memorialize their loved ones. These memorials provide a steady stream of income for many years.
Contact us for more details.

Personnel:

Richard Baum (President)
Maurice Zagha (CEO)
Heshy Spira (Vice President)

Financial Services/Insurance

Arthur J. Gallagher & Co.
Religious Practice Group
Two Pierce Place, The Gallagher Center, Itasca, IL 60143
Tel: 888-285-5106, ext. 3898; Fax: 630-345-9623
E-mail: Peter_Persuitti@ajg.com; Website: www.ajg.com/religious

Type of Business:

Our Commitment to Religious Organizations
Since 1927, Gallagher has been serving the needs of churches as consultant, insurance broker, agent, loss control specialist and claims advocate. For more than fifty years we have worked closely with the Roman Catholic faith traditions (dioceses, religious orders).
We help dioceses and archdioceses with risk management challenges, gaps in coverage, consultative benefit plan analysis and 403(b) audits by forging innovative and collaborative programs. Our consultative approach is our hallmark and a valued resource for church finance councils and boards. We encourage you to log-in to the premiere resource for the Church www.gallagherpost.com
We are a leader in helping the Church reclaim dollars for ministry through innovative self-insurance, unbundling of claims, data and exposure management, proactive risk control training, specialized allocation and billing services and investments in appraisals.
We also are a premiere advisor for international and domestic mission services through Gallagher Charitable International Insurance Services (GCIIS). We encourage a diocese to set up its own World Youth Day 2011 Madrid insurance program by engaging our GCIIS team.
Of the more than 11,500 employees we have globally, more than 20 percent of our work force touch the serving of our religious and nonprofit clients, many living in your community or region.

Personnel:

Peter A. Persuitti Managing Director, Gallagher Religious Practice

Investment Advisors

Christian Brothers Investment Services, Inc.
777 Third Avenue, 29th Floor
New York, NY 10017
Tel: 800-592-8890 or 212-490-0800
Fax: 212-490-6092
Website: www.cbisonline.com

Type of Business:

Christian Brothers Investment Services, Inc. (CBIS) manages approximately $4.0 billion for Catholic organizations seeks to combine faith and finance through the responsible stewardship of Catholic assets. CBIS' combination of premier institutional asset managers, diversified product offerings, and careful risk-control strategies constitutes a unique investment approach for Catholic institutions and their fiduciaries. CBIS strives to integrate faith-based values into the investment process through a disciplined approach to socially responsible investing that includes principled purchasing (stock screens), active ownership strategies (proxy voting, dialogues, and shareholder resolutions), and community investing. The firm contributes a portion of all profits to support the Church's educational and social ministry.
For Catholic organizations seeking to unify faith and finance, CBIS welcomes the opportunity to serve you.
Please contact Fred Devlin at 877-550-2247 ext. 4721 or e-mail: fdevlin@cbisonline.com.

Personnel:

Michael W. O'Hern, FSC (President & CEO)
Fred Devlin (Vice President)

Planned Giving

Delivering Food, Shelter and Hope to the Poorest of the Poor

Formerly known as Cross International Catholic Outreach

2700 N. Military Trail, Suite 240, PO Box 273908
Boca Raton, FL 33427-3908 • **www.CrossCatholic.org**

Cross Catholic Outreach
2700 North Military Trail, Suite 240 ; P.O. Box 273908
Boca Raton, FL 33427-3908
Tel: 800-914-2420 x 141 or x121; Fax: 561-288-4397
E-mail: ejurczak@crosscatholic.org
Website: www.crosscatholic.org

Type of Business:

Cross Catholic Outreach (CCO) is a relief and development ministry founded to support Catholic programs for the poor in nearly 30 locations, including Haiti, the Philippines, and more than 20 countries in Africa, Latin America and Asia. Cardinal Edwin F. O'Brien is the organization's patron, and several prominent U.S. Bishops serve on its board of directors, providing leadership and strong financial accountability. Cross Catholic Outreach's primary goals are to serve the poorest of the poor and to educate American parishes about the international efforts of the Church. The ministry's Catholic outreach is extensive, including feeding programs, water projects, clinic and school construction, housing initiatives, educational and job training projects, programs benefitting orphans and more. It also has an official relationship with the Pontifical Council ***Cor Unum***, allowing it to collaborate on special projects directed by the Holy Father.

Personnel:

Most Rev. Sam Jacobs (Chairman, Board of Directors)
James Cavnar (President)
Msgr. Ted Bertagni (Director of Clergy and Diocese Relations)
Evelyn Jurczak (Manager of Parish Services)
Cecile Erlsten (Director of Outreach Priests)

CHURCH ART—General

Botti Studio of Architectural Arts, Inc.
919 Grove Street
Evanston, IL 60201
Tel: 800-524-7211; 847-869-5933 ; Fax: 847-869-5996
E-mail: botti@bottistudio.com; Website: www.bottistudio.com

Type of Business:

Since 1864, Botti Studio has specialized in serving the ecclesiastic environment through design, fabrication, delivery, and installation. Experts on staff in new design commissions, repair, restoration, conservation, and repair provide a source for experienced project management – from conception through completion. Services include: stained, faceted, sandblasted, carved and painted glass, wood / metal / stone frames / protective glazing, murals, marble, mosaics, bronze, statuary, gilding, painting and decorating, complete interiors, new and restorations, historic discovery, documentation and consultation to owner / architect.

Our staff of 45 includes internationally recognized ecclesiastic artists / designers working in conjunction with highly skilled craftspeople / artisans / conservators.

Locations: New York, NY / (212) 362-6085, LaPorte, IN / (219) 362-5934, Chicago, IL / (847) 869-5933, San Diego, CA / (760) 753-0705, Sarasota, FL / (941) 951-0978, Nassau, Bahamas / (242) 327-2992, Agropoli, Italy / (800) 524-7211.

Personnel:

Ettore Christopher Botti (Principal)
Ethlyn Panzironi Botti (Principal)

Conrad Schmitt Studios Inc.

Excellence in Artistry Since 1889

Conrad Schmitt Studios, Inc.
2405 S. 162nd Street
New Berlin, WI 53151
Tel: 800-969-3033; 262-786-3030
Fax: 262-786-9036
E-mail: studio@conradschmitt.com
Website: www.conradschmitt.com

Type of Business:

Since 1889, our Studio has been privileged to have decorated and restored churches of all sizes and styles throughout the country. Due to our extensive scope of work, we have the ability to be a single source to provide a variety of services. Our experienced, full-time staff of artists and craftsmen is skilled in various decorative painting, restoration and conservation techniques, including the investigation and documentation of original decorative schemes, plaster and scagliola conservation, gilding, glazing, marbleizing, stenciling and trompe l'oeil. Our Studio has been designing and executing new stained glass and conserving historic stained glass for over a century. We also design and conserve murals, statuary, sculpture and fitments. The Studio can help generate enthusiasm and financial support by assisting projects in the early stages with renderings, decorative samples and fundraising materials. We enjoy working as part of a team, to create the best projects in terms of function, longevity and aesthetics.

Gaspard, Inc.
(formerly The Robert Gaspard Company, Inc.)
200 N. Janacek Road
Brookfield, WI 53045
Tel: 800-784-6868 (toll free)
Fax: 800-784-7567
E-mail: info@gaspardinc.com
Website: www.gaspardinc.com

Type of Business:

For more than five decades customers have looked to Gaspard for fine quality, handcrafted vestments and paraments made in the USA. Offerings include the exquisite Castle Craft® collection; wardrobe essentials such as albs, surplices, cassocks, robes, and clergy shirts; extensive metalware offerings, fair linens, altar accessories, and communion ware.

Because your vestment and parament selections are made to order in our one and only location in Brookfield, Wisconsin, special sizes and custom designs are not a problem. One of our friendly Customer Service Representatives will be happy to help you find just the right size and style to enhance your spiritual expression. Please visit us online or call for a free catalog.

Personnel:

Jason R. Gaspard (President)
Joann Gaspard (Vice President)

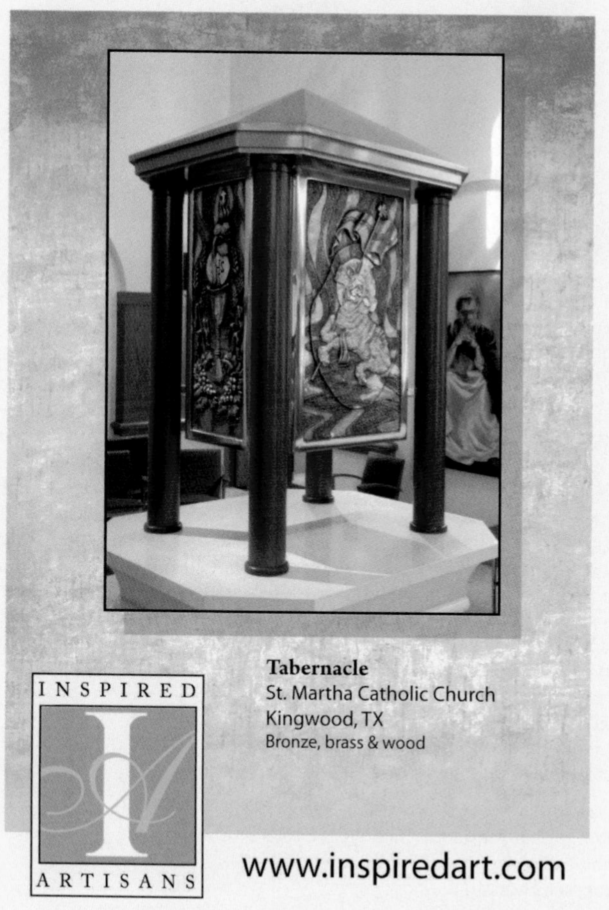

Tabernacle
St. Martha Catholic Church
Kingwood, TX
Bronze, brass & wood
INSPIRED
ARTISANS
www.inspiredart.com

67 Mountain Spring Drive
Sparta, NJ 07871
Tel: 973-726-0835
E-mail: yuri@uasrestoration.com
Website: uasrestoration.com

Type of Business:

HISTORICAL RESTORATION — CONSERVATION OF ART

With very few exceptions we shall repair any object of aesthetic, ecclesiastical, spiritual, historical, sentimental or simply monetary value. We offer following services: Complete restoration projects, including: architectural planning, management and execution. Design and fabrication of church furnishings and fixtures. Restoration of paintings, including: murals, frescoes, Greek or Russian icons. Canvas repairs, relining, cleaning, stretching. Custom framing. Goldleafing. Repairs of statuary made of gypsum, marble, wood, composit materials. Repairs of mosaics, tile, ceramics, plaster, terrazzo. Restoration of antique furniture and woodcarvings.

Our Art Gallery creates a range of fine art from ecclesiastical to contemporary, to church interiors, to decoration of living space.

Honestly, Yuri Mironoff

RAMBUSCH
SINCE 1898

Rambusch
160 Cornelison Avenue
Jersey City, NJ 07304
Tel: 201-333-2525
Fax: 201-433-3355
Website: www.rambusch.com

Type of Business:

Creativity and Quality are Rambusch Hallmarks. A small, highly personal business, where everything is custom. Each inquiry is handled by a principal, who guides the client through a myriad of possibilities. The chosen solution is then made tangible by our supremely skilled craftspeople.

Rambusch creates complete interiors, shrines, individual art works, stained glass and mosaics. New work, renovations, and restorations all receive the same attention, resulting in beautiful, fitting solutions for your unique commission. Our design rooms, art metal workshops and stained glass studios are in-house, ensuring seamless crafting of all designs. Rambusch-patented lighting fixtures, the recognized industry standard for church lighting, are individually built on our own worktables. Rambusch custom engineered lighting systems make everything look its best!

Call/or come visit our intriguing design rooms and workshops for an initial courtesy consultation. We look forward to hearing from you. Remember Rambusch – on time, within budget, designed just for you.

Personnel:

Edwin P. Rambusch
Martin V. Rambusch
Viggo B.A. Rambusch, Senior Advisor

Art, Statuary & Decorations

Conrad Schmitt Studios Inc.
Excellence in Artistry Since 1889

Conrad Schmitt Studios, Inc.
2405 S. 162nd Street
New Berlin, WI 53151
Tel: 800-969-3033; 262-786-3030
Fax: 262-786-9036
E-mail: studio@conradschmitt.com
Website: www.conradschmitt.com

Type of Business:

Since 1889, our Studio has been privileged to have decorated and restored churches of all sizes and styles throughout the country. Due to our extensive scope of work, we have the ability to be a single source to provide a variety of services. Our experienced, full-time staff of artists and craftsmen is skilled in various decorative painting, restoration and conservation techniques, including the investigation and documentation of original decorative schemes, plaster and scagliola conservation, gilding, glazing, marbleizing, stenciling and trompe l'oeil. Our Studio has been designing and executing new stained glass and conserving historic stained glass for over a century. We also design and conserve murals, statuary, sculpture and fitments. The Studio can help generate enthusiasm and financial support by assisting projects in the early stages with renderings, decorative samples and fundraising materials. We enjoy working as part of a team, to create the best projects in terms of function, longevity and aesthetics.

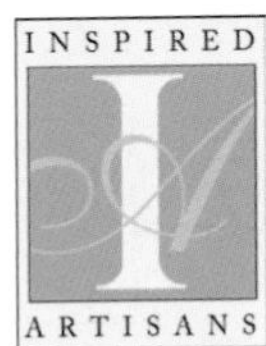

Inspired Artisans, Ltd.
816 W. National Avenue
Milwaukee, WI 53204
Tel: 888-442-9141
Fax: 414-672-9479
E-mail: gianfranco@inspiredart.com
Website: www.inspiredart.com

Type of Business:

Inspired Artisans, Ltd. has been serving the Catholic Church in the design and creation of sacred art since 1997. Our mission is to create beautiful works of art that meet the needs and visions of our clients. We take great satisfaction in our commitment to maintain a close relationship with each client.
Recent commissions in Art and Statuary:
Georgetown University, Washington DC; OFM General Curia, Rome, Italy; College of the Holy Cross, Worchester SC; St. Augustine of Canterbury, Toronto, Canada; St. Raphael Cathedral, Madison WI; St. Mary's Cathedral, Cheyenne WY; St. Martha Catholic Church, Kingwood TX; St. Mary Mother of God Catholic Church, Yatesboro PA; Immaculata Monastery, Norfolk NE; St. Justin Martyr Catholic Church, Seminole FL; Immaculate Conception/St. Joseph Catholic Church, Leavenworth KS; see our ad under Church Art.
We invite you to visit our website for a full introduction to our studio, a complete list of commissions or to request a portfolio.

Personnel:

Gianfranco Tassara
Irene Perez
Gino Tassara

LP Bronze International, Inc.
100 Sunrise Avenue, Unit 101/152
Toronto, ON M4A 1B3
Canada
Tel: 1-888-572-2645
Fax: 1-877-572-2645
E-mail: info@lpbronze.com
Website: www.lpbronze.com

Type of Business:

LP Bronze International has been serving the Catholic Cemeteries community in North America for over 25 years. LP Bronze International is renowned for designing, creating and delivering many of the finest Italian and Spanish style statuary to North America.
With a highly skilled team of artists, it offers a wide array of religious statuary and a large selection of various size saints. Statuary can be created in a variety of materials bronze, marble, Fiber-Marble™, and FiberBronze™ to suit any budget.
LP Bronze offers standard and customized features. Its custom statuary are "Unique Works of Art". Each piece is renowned for its attention to detail and authenticity. Religious and historical accuracy is researched and incorporated into all LP's artistic commissions.
The statue of Pope John Paul II created by LP Bronze International is an authentic replica of the bronze statue approved by His Holiness John Paul II on June 19th, 2002. A replica of this feature now resides in the "Sala Clementina" in the Vatican.

Personnel:

Andrew Krawczyk, President
Laura Peraboni-Krawczyk, President

Rohn & Associates Design, Inc.
1113 Creedmoor Avenue
Pittsburgh, PA 15226
Tel: 412-561-1228; 800-245-1288
Fax: 412-561-1201
E-mail: rolfrohn@rohndesign.com; Website: www.rohndesign.com
Blog: http://catholicliturgicalarts.blogspot.com/
Facebook: Catholic Liturgical Arts Journal

Type of Business:

Liturgical Designers, Artists & Artisans
TRADITION. Over the past 58 years, we have assisted the Catholic Church by designing, budgeting and implementing liturgical spaces.
COLLABORATION. We work side-by-side with our clients and collaborators to design and create appropriate and quality sacred art, interior finishes, lighting systems, acoustical systems, liturgical furnishings and appointments to create a rich devotional experience for your parishioners.
EXPERIENCE. We draw upon decades of experience and from a rich treasury of designers, architectural staff and contributing artists.
SCOPE OF SERVICES: Liturgical Design; Interior Design & Decorating; Sacred Artwork; Mosaics; Art Glass; Statuary; Liturgical Appointments; Liturgical Furniture; Metalwork.
ADDITIONAL LOCATIONS: 719 S. Flores St., Suite 200, San Antonio, TX 78204. Tel.: 210-231-0377; Fax: 210-231-0366
Contact us to arrange a complimentary project review.

Personnel:

Rolf R. Rohn (President - Liturgical Designer-Consultant)
Kathleen L. Maglicco (Vice President, Design)
Francesca Lofaro (Director, Sales)

Sacred Spaces Liturgical Design Studios, Inc.
312 Montgomery Street, Suite 100
Alexandria, VA 22314
Tel: 703-519-9800; 1-888-519-4599 (toll free)
Fax: 703-519-4599
E-mail: info@sacredspacesinc.com
Website: www.SacredSpacesInc.com

Type of Business:

Sacred Spaces is a liturgical design studio with a team of international artists and master craftsmen with experience spanning four decades in the design of worship environments: new construction, renovation and restoration. Our Services include Liturgical Design Consulting, Custom Design, Appointments, Removals, Consignments and Facsimiles. Specializing in marble, bronze and stone, we custom design altars, ambos, tabernacle thrones and baptismal fonts. We also offer Master Planning Services and Educational Programs for pastoral teams and parish-wide Town Hall meetings. Sacred Spaces - Excellence in Liturgical Design, Artistry and Craftsmanship.

Personnel:

J. Michael Carrigan (President/CEO)
John Grosvenor (Project Director)

Gold Leafing & Painted Murals

Conrad Schmitt Studios Inc.

Excellence in Artistry Since 1889

Conrad Schmitt Studios, Inc.
2405 S. 162nd Street
New Berlin, WI 53151
Tel: 800-969-3033; 262-786-3030
Fax: 262-786-9036
E-mail: studio@conradschmitt.com
Website: www.conradschmitt.com

Type of Business:

Since 1889, our Studio has been privileged to have decorated and restored churches of all sizes and styles throughout the country. Due to our extensive scope of work, we have the ability to be a single source to provide a variety of services. Our experienced, full-time staff of artists and craftsmen is skilled in various decorative painting, restoration and conservation techniques, including the investigation and documentation of original decorative schemes, plaster and scagliola conservation, gilding, glazing, marbleizing, stenciling and trompe l'oeil. Our Studio has been designing and executing new stained glass and conserving historic stained glass for over a century. We also design and conserve murals, statuary, sculpture and fitments. The Studio can help generate enthusiasm and financial support by assisting projects in the early stages with renderings, decorative samples and fundraising materials. We enjoy working as part of a team, to create the best projects in terms of function, longevity and aesthetics.

67 Mountain Spring Drive
Sparta, NJ 07871
Tel: 973-726-0835
E-mail: yuri@uasrestoration.com
Website: uasrestoration.com

Type of Business:

HISTORICAL RESTORATION — CONSERVATION OF ART

With very few exceptions we shall repair any object of aesthetic, ecclesiastical, spiritual, historical, sentimental or simply monetary value. We offer following services: Complete restoration projects, including: architectural planning, management and execution. Design and fabrication of church furnishings and fixtures. Restoration of paintings, including: murals, frescoes, Greek or Russian icons. Canvas repairs, relining, cleaning, stretching. Custom framing. Goldleafing. Repairs of statuary made of gypsum, marble, wood, composit materials. Repairs of mosaics, tile, ceramics, plaster, terrazzo. Restoration of antique furniture and woodcarvings.

Our Art Gallery creates a range of fine art from ecclesiastical to contemporary, to church interiors, to decoration of living space.

Honestly, Yuri Mironoff

Mosaics

Baker Liturgical Art, LLC

Church Restoration / Church Renovation

Baker Liturgical Art, LLC
1210 Meriden Waterbury Road
Plantsville, CT 06479
Tel: 860-621-7471
Fax: 860-621-7607
E-mail: bakerart@sbcglobal.net
Website: www.bakerliturgicalart.com

Type of Business:

Baker Liturgical Art, LLC offers a full range of construction and renovation services. These services encompass architectural specifications and liturgical design as well as sound system and lighting design.

Our liturgical design talents result in beautiful altar furnishings of hand-carved wood or of fine imported Italian marble. Stained glass and sacred artwork (painted, wood-carved or chiseled from marble) are the final accents to complete prayerful settings in every worship space from the smallest Chapel to the grandest Cathedral! Baker Liturgical Art, LLC prides itself in offering uncompromising quality in its products and services.

Our Services Include: Liturgical Design, Architectural Services, Liturgical Furnishings, Sculpture & Artwork, Flooring, Millwork, Multi-Media Systems, Stained Glass Fabrication & Restoration.

Additional location: 9427 S. Ocean Drive, Jensen Beach, FL 34957. Tel: 860-919-2119.

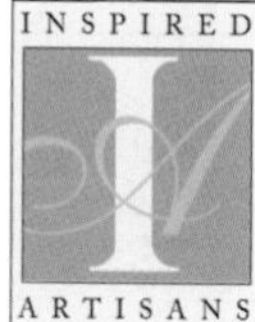

Inspired Artisans, Ltd.
816 W. National Avenue
Milwaukee, WI 53204
Tel: 888-442-9141
Fax: 414-672-9479
E-mail: gianfranco@inspiredart.com
Website: www.inspiredart.com

Type of Business:

Inspired Artisans, Ltd. has been serving the Catholic Church in the design and creation of sacred art since 1997. Our mission is to create beautiful works of art that meet the needs and visions of our clients. We take great satisfaction in our commitment to maintain a close relationship with each client.

Recent commissions in mosaics:

St. Joseph Catholic Church, South Bend IN; Santa Maria Mediatrice, Rome, Italy; OFM Curia, Rome, Italy; Holy Cross Greek Orthodox, Middletown NY; Annunciation Greek Orthodox, Milwaukee WI; Marquette University, Milwaukee WI; Holy Sepulchre Cemetery, Coram NY; St. Martha Catholic Church, Kingwood TX; Kimisis Tis Theotokou Greek Church, Racine, WI; Maryrest Catholic Cemetery, Mahwah, NJ; see our ad under Church Art.

We invite you to visit our web site for a full introduction to our studio, a complete list of commissions, or to request a portfolio.

Personnel:

Gianfranco Tassara
Irene Perez
Gino Tassara

RAMBUSCH

SINCE 1898

Rambusch
160 Cornelison Avenue
Jersey City, NJ 07304
Tel: 201-333-2525
Fax: 201-433-3355
Website: www.rambusch.com

Type of Business:

Creativity and Quality are Rambusch Hallmarks. A small, highly personal business, where everything is custom. Each inquiry is handled by a principal, who guides the client through a myriad of possibilities. The chosen solution is then made tangible by our supremely skilled craftspeople.

Rambusch creates complete interiors, shrines, individual art works, stained glass and mosaics. New work, renovations, and restorations all receive the same attention, resulting in beautiful, fitting solutions for your unique commission. Our design rooms, art metal workshops and stained glass studios are in-house, ensuring seamless crafting of all designs. Rambusch-patented lighting fixtures, the recognized industry standard for church lighting, are individually built on our own worktables. Rambusch custom engineered lighting systems make everything look its best!

Call/or come visit our intriguing design rooms and workshops for an initial courtesy consultation. We look forward to hearing from you. Remember Rambusch – on time, within budget, designed just for you.

Personnel:

Edwin P. Rambusch
Martin V. Rambusch
Viggo B.A. Rambusch, Senior Advisor

Sculpture

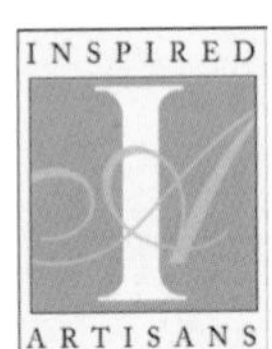

Inspired Artisans, Ltd.
816 W. National Avenue
Milwaukee, WI 53204
Tel: 888-442-9141
Fax: 414-672-9479
E-mail: gianfranco@inspiredart.com
Website: www.inspiredart.com

Type of Business:

Inspired Artisans, Ltd. has been serving the Catholic Church in the design and creation of sacred art since 1997. Our mission is to create beautiful works of art that meet the needs and visions of our clients. We take great satisfaction in our commitment to maintain a close relationship with each client.

Recent commissions in sculpture:
St. Anthony Shrine, Ellicott City MO; Poor Clares Monastery, Roswell NM; St. Gertrude Mausoleum, Newark NJ; Brescia University, Owensboro KY; Cuore Immacolato di Maria, San Marino; Catholic Cemeteries, Denver CO; Catholic Cemeteries, Syracuse NY; Catholic Cemeteries, Newark, NJ; St. Francis of Assisi Catholic Church, Orland Park, IL; Holy Family Catholic Church, St. Petersburg, FL; St. Louis University High School, St. Louis, MO; St. Vincent de Paul Catholic Church, Austin, TX; St. Henry Catholic Church, Owasso, OK; Trustees of St. Patrick Cathedral, New York, NY; see our ad under Church Art.

We invite you to visit our web site for a full introduction to our studio, a complete list of commissions, or to request a portfolio.

Personnel:

Gianfranco Tassara
Irene Perez
Gino Tassara

Stations
Crucifixes
Saints
Angels
Fine bronzes...

Kircher & Associates, Inc.
Sculpture Studio
P.O. Box 53
Jaroso, CO 81138
Tel: 719-672-3063
Website: www.kirchersculpture.com

Type of Business:

Since 1992 we have installed over 200 sculptures in 15 states, 2 foreign countries and the Vatican Collection. Drawing upon classical themes, careful research and the contemporary aspirations of parish leaders, Lynn Kircher crafts his sculptures first in clay and then in bronze using the lost wax process in US foundries and local craftsmen. Professionally trained, gifted and dedicated to his art, Lynn brings powerful expression to each piece. This work is designed to inspire, uplift and create wonder. Your new facilities or the renovation of your existing ones benefit from the freshness of superior custom bronzes. Lynn's existing portfolio of crucifixes, angels and saints contains a selection of sculptures suitable for indoor and outdoor spaces. Commissions for new works are available. The Kircher studio is located at the Colorado – New Mexico border. We welcome clients and visitors by appointment.

Personnel:

Lynn Kircher (Sculptor)
Jane Kircher (Patination & Business)
Jennifer Hunt (Studio Assistant)

Imagine Create Deliver

LP Bronze International, Inc.
100 Sunrise Avenue, Unit 101/152
Toronto, ON M4A 1B3
Canada
Tel: 1-888-572-2645
Fax: 1-877-572-2645
E-mail: info@lpbronze.com
Website: www.lpbronze.com

Type of Business:

LP Bronze International has been serving the Catholic Cemeteries community in North America for over 25 years. LP Bronze International is renowned for designing, creating and delivering many of the finest Italian and Spanish style statuary to North America.

With a highly skilled team of artists, it offers a wide array of religious statuary and a large selection of various size saints. Statuary can be created in a variety of materials bronze, marble, Fiber-Marble™, and FiberBronze™ to suit any budget.

LP Bronze offers standard and customized features. Its custom statuary are "Unique Works of Art". Each piece is renowned for its attention to detail and authenticity. Religious and historical accuracy is researched and incorporated into all LP's artistic commissions.

The statue of Pope John Paul II created by LP Bronze International is an authentic replica of the bronze statue approved by His Holiness John Paul II on June 19th, 2002. A replica of this feature now resides in the "Sala Clementina" in the Vatican.

Personnel:

Andrew Krawczyk, President
Laura Peraboni-Krawczyk, President

RAMBUSCH
SINCE 1898

Rambusch
160 Cornelison Avenue
Jersey City, NJ 07304
Tel: 201-333-2525
Fax: 201-433-3355
Website: www.rambusch.com

Type of Business:

Creativity and Quality are Rambusch Hallmarks. A small, highly personal business, where everything is custom. Each inquiry is handled by a principal, who guides the client through a myriad of possibilities. The chosen solution is then made tangible by our supremely skilled craftspeople.

Rambusch creates complete interiors, shrines, individual art works, stained glass and mosaics. New work, renovations, and restorations all receive the same attention, resulting in beautiful, fitting solutions for your unique commission. Our design rooms, art metal workshops and stained glass studios are in-house, ensuring seamless crafting of all designs. Rambusch-patented lighting fixtures, the recognized industry standard for church lighting, are individually built on our own worktables. Rambusch custom engineered lighting systems make everything look its best!

Call/or come visit our intriguing design rooms and workshops for an initial courtesy consultation. We look forward to hearing from you. Remember Rambusch – on time, within budget, designed just for you.

Personnel:

Edwin P. Rambusch
Martin V. Rambusch
Viggo B.A. Rambusch, Senior Advisor

Rohn & Associates Design, Inc.
1113 Creedmoor Avenue
Pittsburgh, PA 15226
Tel: 412-561-1228; 800-245-1288
Fax: 412-561-1201
E-mail: rolfrohn@rohndesign.com
Website: www.rohndesign.com
Blog: http://catholicliturgicalarts.blogspot.com/
Facebook: Catholic Liturgical Arts Journal

Type of Business:

Liturgical Designers, Artists & Artisans

TRADITION. Over the past 58 years, we have assisted the Catholic Church by designing, budgeting and implementing liturgical spaces.

COLLABORATION. We work side-by-side with our clients and collaborators to design and create appropriate and quality sacred art, interior finishes, lighting systems, acoustical systems, liturgical furnishings and appointments to create a rich devotional experience for your parishioners.

EXPERIENCE. We draw upon decades of experience and from a rich treasury of designers, architectural staff and contributing artists.

SCOPE OF SERVICES: Liturgical Design; Interior Design & Decorating; Sacred Artwork; Mosaics; Art Glass; Statuary; Liturgical Appointments; Liturgical Furniture; Metalwork.

ADDITIONAL LOCATIONS: 719 S. Flores St., Suite 200, San Antonio, TX 78204. Tel.: 210-231-0377; Fax: 210-231-0366

Contact us to arrange a complimentary project review.

Personnel:

Rolf R. Rohn (President - Liturgical Designer-Consultant)
Kathleen L. Maglicco (Vice President, Design)
Francesca Lofaro (Director, Sales)

Baker Liturgical Art, LLC
Church Restoration / Church Renovation

Baker Liturgical Art, LLC
1210 Meriden Waterbury Road
Plantsville, CT 06479
Tel: 860-621-7471
Fax: 860-621-7607
E-mail: bakerart@sbcglobal.net
Website: www.bakerliturgicalart.com

Type of Business:

Baker Liturgical Art, LLC offers a full range of construction and renovation services. These services encompass architectural specifications and liturgical design as well as sound system and lighting design.

Our liturgical design talents result in beautiful altar furnishings of hand-carved wood or of fine imported Italian marble. Stained glass and sacred artwork (painted, wood-carved or chiseled from marble) are the final accents to complete prayerful settings in every worship space from the smallest Chapel to the grandest Cathedral! Baker Liturgical Art, LLC prides itself in offering uncompromising quality in its products and services.

Our Services Include: Liturgical Design, Architectural Services, Liturgical Furnishings, Sculpture & Artwork, Flooring, Millwork, Multi-Media Systems, Stained Glass Fabrication & Restoration.

Additional location: 9427 S. Ocean Drive, Jensen Beach, FL 34957. Tel: 860-919-2119.

RAMBUSCH
SINCE 1898

Rambusch
160 Cornelison Avenue
Jersey City, NJ 07304
Tel: 201-333-2525
Fax: 201-433-3355
Website: www.rambusch.com

Type of Business:

Creativity and Quality are Rambusch Hallmarks. A small, highly personal business, where everything is custom. Each inquiry is handled by a principal, who guides the client through a myriad of possibilities. The chosen solution is then made tangible by our supremely skilled craftspeople.

Rambusch creates complete interiors, shrines, individual art works, stained glass and mosaics. New work, renovations, and restorations all receive the same attention, resulting in beautiful, fitting solutions for your unique commission. Our design rooms, art metal workshops and stained glass studios are in-house, ensuring seamless crafting of all designs. Rambusch-patented lighting fixtures, the recognized industry standard for church lighting, are individually built on our own worktables. Rambusch custom engineered lighting systems make everything look its best!

Call/or come visit our intriguing design rooms and workshops for an initial courtesy consultation. We look forward to hearing from you. Remember Rambusch – on time, within budget, designed just for you.

Personnel:

Edwin P. Rambusch
Martin V. Rambusch
Viggo B.A. Rambusch, Senior Advisor

Rohn & Associates Design, Inc.
1113 Creedmoor Avenue
Pittsburgh, PA 15226
Tel: 412-561-1228; 800-245-1288
Fax: 412-561-1201
E-mail: rolfrohn@rohndesign.com
Website: www.rohndesign.com
Blog: http://catholicliturgicalarts.blogspot.com/
Facebook: Catholic Liturgical Arts Journal

Type of Business:

Liturgical Designers, Artists & Artisans
TRADITION. Over the past 58 years, we have assisted the Catholic Church by designing, budgeting and implementing liturgical spaces.
COLLABORATION. We work side-by-side with our clients and collaborators to design and create appropriate and quality sacred art, interior finishes, lighting systems, acoustical systems, liturgical furnishings and appointments to create a rich devotional experience for your parishioners.
EXPERIENCE. We draw upon decades of experience and from a rich treasury of designers, architectural staff and contributing artists.
SCOPE OF SERVICES: Liturgical Design; Interior Design & Decorating; Sacred Artwork; Mosaics; Art Glass; Statuary; Liturgical Appointments; Liturgical Furniture; Metalwork.
ADDITIONAL LOCATIONS: 719 S. Flores St., Suite 200, San Antonio, TX 78204. Tel.: 210-231-0377; Fax: 210-231-0366
Contact us to arrange a complimentary project review.

Personnel:

Rolf R. Rohn (President - Liturgical Designer-Consultant)
Kathleen L. Maglicco (Vice President, Design)
Francesca Lofaro (Director, Sales)

Altars, Tabernacles, etc.

RAMBUSCH
SINCE 1898

Rambusch
160 Cornelison Avenue
Jersey City, NJ 07304
Tel: 201-333-2525
Fax: 201-433-3355
Website: www.rambusch.com

Type of Business:

Creativity and Quality are Rambusch Hallmarks. A small, highly personal business, where everything is custom. Each inquiry is handled by a principal, who guides the client through a myriad of possibilities. The chosen solution is then made tangible by our supremely skilled craftspeople.
Rambusch creates complete interiors, shrines, individual art works, stained glass and mosaics. New work, renovations, and restorations all receive the same attention, resulting in beautiful, fitting solutions for your unique commission. Our design rooms, art metal workshops and stained glass studios are in-house, ensuring seamless crafting of all designs. Rambusch-patented lighting fixtures, the recognized industry standard for church lighting, are individually built on our own worktables. Rambusch custom engineered lighting systems make everything look its best!
Call/or come visit our intriguing design rooms and workshops for an initial courtesy consultation. We look forward to hearing from you. Remember Rambusch – on time, within budget, designed just for you.

Personnel:

Edwin P. Rambusch
Martin V. Rambusch
Viggo B.A. Rambusch, Senior Advisor

Sacred Spaces Liturgical Design Studios, Inc.
312 Montgomery Street, Suite 100
Alexandria, VA 22314
Tel: 703-519-9800; 1-888-519-4599 (toll free)
Fax: 703-519-4599
E-mail: info@sacredspacesinc.com
Website: www.SacredSpacesInc.com

Type of Business:

Sacred Spaces is a liturgical design studio with a team of international artists and master craftsmen with experience spanning four decades in the design of worship environments: new construction, renovation and restoration. Our Services include Liturgical Design Consulting, Custom Design, Appointments, Removals, Consignments and Facsimiles. Specializing in marble, bronze and stone, we custom design altars, ambos, tabernacle thrones and baptismal fonts. We also offer Master Planning Services and Educational Programs for pastoral teams and parish-wide Town Hall meetings. Sacred Spaces - Excellence in Liturgical Design, Artistry and Craftsmanship.

Personnel:

J. Michael Carrigan (President/CEO)
John Grosvenor (Project Director)

Baptismal Fonts

RAMBUSCH
SINCE 1898

Rambusch
160 Cornelison Avenue
Jersey City, NJ 07304
Tel: 201-333-2525
Fax: 201-433-3355
Website: www.rambusch.com

Type of Business:

Creativity and Quality are Rambusch Hallmarks. A small, highly personal business, where everything is custom. Each inquiry is handled by a principal, who guides the client through a myriad of possibilities. The chosen solution is then made tangible by our supremely skilled craftspeople.
Rambusch creates complete interiors, shrines, individual art works, stained glass and mosaics. New work, renovations, and restorations all receive the same attention, resulting in beautiful, fitting solutions for your unique commission. Our design rooms, art metal workshops and stained glass studios are in-house, ensuring seamless crafting of all designs. Rambusch-patented lighting fixtures, the recognized industry standard for church lighting, are individually built on our own worktables. Rambusch custom engineered lighting systems make everything look its best!
Call/or come visit our intriguing design rooms and workshops for an initial courtesy consultation. We look forward to hearing from you. Remember Rambusch – on time, within budget, designed just for you.

Personnel:

Edwin P. Rambusch
Martin V. Rambusch
Viggo B.A. Rambusch, Senior Advisor

Bells, Carillons, Etc.

he Verdin Co.
44 Reading Road
Cincinnati, OH 45202
00-543-0488 (toll free)
el: 513-241-4010; Fax: 513-241-1855
-mail: info@verdin.com
Vebsite: www.verdin.com

ype of Business:

America's Bell Ringer
For 170 years The Verdin Company has been the world's premier manufacturer and restorer of bells, carillons and clocks. We distinguish ourselves by blending innovative technology with superior customer service. Today, we feature the same high quality bells and clocks as our fathers and grandfathers before us. Our Verdin legacy is the sound of bells ringing from more than 50,000 installations all over the world.
Family owned for six generations, The Verdin Company emphasizes honesty, integrity and trust while bringing the sound of bells to parishioners everywhere.

ersonnel:

Robert J. Verdin (CEO)
James R. Verdin (President)
David E. Verdin (Vice President)
Suzanne Sizer (Marketing Manager)

Bishop's Regalia

C.M. Almy
Three American Lane, P.O. Box 2644
Greenwich, CT 06836-2644
Tel: 800-225-2569
Fax: 800-426-2569
E-mail: almyaccess@almy.com
Website: www.almy.com
Showroom in Old Greenwich, CT

Type of Business:

Almy was founded in 1892. We design and make virtually all of our products in our Maine shop. It is our mission to design furnishings that will grace your worship and to ensure their value by making them with the highest quality materials and craftsmanship. We make a complete line of liturgical vestments, clergy apparel, choir robes, candles, communion bread, linens, processional and altar appointments, and eucharistic vessels. We also offer custom design and fabrication of all Almy products, and repair and refurbishing of old metal appointments. Quik Ship© delivery of many popular items. All orders backed by The Almy Guarantee. Call, write, or e-mail for a free catalog.

Interior Design/Restoration

Baker Liturgical Art, LLC
1210 Meriden Waterbury Road
Plantsville, CT 06479
Tel: 860-621-7471
Fax: 860-621-7607
E-mail: bakerart@sbcglobal.net
Website: www.bakerliturgicalart.com

Type of Business:

Baker Liturgical Art, LLC offers a full range of construction and renovation services. These services encompass architectural specifications and liturgical design as well as sound system and lighting design.
Our liturgical design talents result in beautiful altar furnishings of hand-carved wood or of fine imported Italian marble. Stained glass and sacred artwork (painted, wood-carved or chiseled from marble) are the final accents to complete prayerful settings in every worship space from the smallest Chapel to the grandest Cathedral! Baker Liturgical Art, LLC prides itself in offering uncompromising quality in its products and services.
Our Services Include: Liturgical Design, Architectural Services, Liturgical Furnishings, Sculpture & Artwork, Flooring, Millwork, Multi-Media Systems, Stained Glass Fabrication & Restoration.
Additional location: 9427 S. Ocean Drive, Jensen Beach, FL 34957. Tel: 860-919-2119.

Conrad Schmitt Studios Inc.
Excellence in Artistry Since 1889

Conrad Schmitt Studios, Inc.
2405 S. 162nd Street
New Berlin, WI 53151
Tel: 800-969-3033; 262-786-3030
Fax: 262-786-9036
E-mail: studio@conradschmitt.com
Website: www.conradschmitt.com

Type of Business:

Since 1889, CSS has been privileged to decorate and restore churches of all sizes and styles throughout the country. Our experienced staff assists projects in the early stages to help assemble the master plan, communicate the vision and generate the enthusiasm and funding needed to make the plan a reality. Some of the tools used to accomplish these goals include renderings, on-site samples, budgetary estimates and fundraising materials.
Our comprehensive scope of services allows us to be a single source for a variety of needs, creating the best projects in terms of function, longevity and aesthetics. Our services include the investigation and documentation of original decorative schemes, gilding, glazing, marbleizing, stenciling, trompe l'oeil and faux finishing.
Recent decorating commissions include the Cathedral of the Immaculate Conception, Springfield, IL; St. Mary Magdalen Catholic Church, Abbeville, LA; St. Joseph Cathedral, Sioux Falls, SD; and St. John Neumann Catholic Church, Knoxville, TN.

RAMBUSCH

SINCE 1898

Rambusch
160 Cornelison Avenue
Jersey City, NJ 07304
Tel: 201-333-2525
Fax: 201-433-3355
Website: www.rambusch.com

Type of Business:

Creativity and Quality are Rambusch Hallmarks. A small, highly personal business, where everything is custom. Each inquiry is handled by a principal, who guides the client through a myriad of possibilities. The chosen solution is then made tangible by our supremely skilled craftspeople.

Rambusch creates complete interiors, shrines, individual art works, stained glass and mosaics. New work, renovations, and restorations all receive the same attention, resulting in beautiful, fitting solutions for your unique commission. Our design rooms, art metal workshops and stained glass studios are in-house, ensuring seamless crafting of all designs. Rambusch-patented lighting fixtures, the recognized industry standard for church lighting, are individually built on our own worktables. Rambusch custom engineered lighting systems make everything look its best!

Call/or come visit our intriguing design rooms and workshops for an initial courtesy consultation. We look forward to hearing from you. Remember Rambusch – on time, within budget, designed just for you.

Personnel:

Edwin P. Rambusch
Martin V. Rambusch
Viggo B.A. Rambusch, Senior Advisor

Lighting of Liturgical Space

RAMBUSCH

SINCE 1898

Rambusch
160 Cornelison Avenue
Jersey City, NJ 07304
Tel: 201-333-2525
Fax: 201-433-3355
Website: www.rambusch.com

Type of Business:

Creativity and Quality are Rambusch Hallmarks. A small, highly personal business, where everything is custom. Each inquiry is handled by a principal, who guides the client through a myriad of possibilities. The chosen solution is then made tangible by our supremely skilled craftspeople.

Rambusch creates complete interiors, shrines, individual art works, stained glass and mosaics. New work, renovations, and restorations all receive the same attention, resulting in beautiful, fitting solutions for your unique commission. Our design rooms, art metal workshops and stained glass studios are in-house, ensuring seamless crafting of all designs. Rambusch-patented lighting fixtures, the recognized industry standard for church lighting, are individually built on our own worktables. Rambusch custom engineered lighting systems make everything look its best!

Call/or come visit our intriguing design rooms and workshops for an initial courtesy consultation. We look forward to hearing from you. Remember Rambusch – on time, within budget, designed just for you.

Personnel:

Edwin P. Rambusch
Martin V. Rambusch
Viggo B.A. Rambusch, Senior Advisor

Liturgical Design

Baker Liturgical Art, LLC
1210 Meriden Waterbury Road
Plantsville, CT 06479
Tel: 860-621-7471
Fax: 860-621-7607
E-mail: bakerart@sbcglobal.net
Website: www.bakerliturgicalart.com

Type of Business:

Baker Liturgical Art, LLC offers a full range of construction and renovatio services. These services encompass architectural specifications an liturgical design as well as sound system and lighting design.

Our liturgical design talents result in beautiful altar furnishings of hand carved wood or of fine imported Italian marble. Stained glass and sacre artwork (painted, wood-carved or chiseled from marble) are the fina accents to complete prayerful settings in every worship space from th smallest Chapel to the grandest Cathedral! Baker Liturgical Art, LLC pride itself in offering uncompromising quality in its products and services.

Our Services Include: Liturgical Design, Architectural Services, Liturgica Furnishings, Sculpture & Artwork, Flooring, Millwork, Multi-Medi Systems, Stained Glass Fabrication & Restoration.

Additional location: 9427 S. Ocean Drive, Jensen Beach, FL 34957. Tel 860-919-2119.

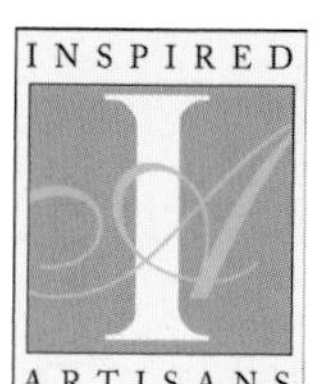

Inspired Artisans, Ltd.
816 W. National Avenue
Milwaukee, WI 53204
Tel: 888-442-9141
Fax: 414-672-9479
E-mail: gianfranco@inspiredart.com
Website: www.inspiredart.com

Type of Business:

Inspired Artisans, Ltd. has been serving the Catholic Church in the design and creation of sacred art since 1997. Our mission is to create beautiful works of art that meet the needs and visions of our clients. We take great satisfaction in our commitment to maintain a close relationship with each client.

Recent commissions in liturgical design:

Marquette University High School, Milwaukee WI; St. Anne Catholic Church, Barrington IL; St. Mary Cathedral, Cheyenne WY; Bellarmine Jesuit Retreat Center, Barrington IL; Poor Clares Monastery, Palos Park IL; Santa Marianita, Galapagos, Ecuador; St. Joseph Catholic Church, Vancouver WA; All Saints Cemetery, Des Plaines IL; St. Catherine Catholic Church, Portage MI; Basilica of St. Josaphat, Milwaukee WI; Church of the Holy Child, Wilmington DE; St. Katherine Drexel Catholic Church, Sugar Grove, IL; Old St. Mary Catholic Church, Milwaukee, WI; see our ad under Church Art.

We invite you to visit our web site for a full introduction to our studio, a complete list of commissions, or to request a portfolio.

Personnel:

Gianfranco Tassara
Irene Perez
Gino Tassara

RAMBUSCH

SINCE 1898

Rambusch
160 Cornelison Avenue
Jersey City, NJ 07304
Tel: 201-333-2525
Fax: 201-433-3355
Website: www.rambusch.com

Type of Business:

Creativity and Quality are Rambusch Hallmarks. A small, highly personal business, where everything is custom. Each inquiry is handled by a principal, who guides the client through a myriad of possibilities. The chosen solution is then made tangible by our supremely skilled craftspeople.

Rambusch creates complete interiors, shrines, individual art works, stained glass and mosaics. New work, renovations, and restorations all receive the same attention, resulting in beautiful, fitting solutions for your unique commission. Our design rooms, art metal workshops and stained glass studios are in-house, ensuring seamless crafting of all designs. Rambusch-patented lighting fixtures, the recognized industry standard for church lighting, are individually built on our own worktables. Rambusch custom engineered lighting systems make everything look its best!

Call/or come visit our intriguing design rooms and workshops for an initial courtesy consultation. We look forward to hearing from you. Remember Rambusch – on time, within budget, designed just for you.

Personnel:

Edwin P. Rambusch
Martin V. Rambusch
Viggo B.A. Rambusch, Senior Advisor

Rohn & Associates Design, Inc.
1113 Creedmoor Avenue
Pittsburgh, PA 15226
Tel: 412-561-1228; 800-245-1288; Fax: 412-561-1201
E-mail: rolfrohn@rohndesign.com; Website: www.rohndesign.com
Blog: http://catholicliturgicalarts.blogspot.com/
Facebook: Catholic Liturgical Arts Journal

Type of Business:

Liturgical Designers, Artists & Artisans

TRADITION. Over the past 58 years, we have assisted the Catholic Church by designing, budgeting and implementing liturgical spaces.

COLLABORATION. We work side-by-side with our clients and collaborators to design and create appropriate and quality sacred art, interior finishes, lighting systems, acoustical systems, liturgical furnishings and appointments to create a rich devotional experience for your parishioners.

EXPERIENCE. We draw upon decades of experience and from a rich treasury of designers, architectural staff and contributing artists.

SCOPE OF SERVICES: Liturgical Design; Interior Design & Decorating; Sacred Artwork; Mosaics; Art Glass; Statuary; Liturgical Appointments; Liturgical Furniture; Metalwork.

ADDITIONAL LOCATIONS: 719 S. Flores St., Suite 200, San Antonio, TX 78204. Tel.: 210-231-0377; Fax: 210-231-0366

Contact us to arrange a complimentary project review.

Personnel:

Rolf R. Rohn (President - Liturgical Designer-Consultant)
Kathleen L. Maglicco (Vice President, Design)
Francesca Lofaro (Director, Sales)

SACRED SPACES INC
LITURGICAL DESIGN STUDIOS

Sacred Spaces Liturgical Design Studios, Inc.
312 Montgomery Street, Suite 100
Alexandria, VA 22314
Tel: 703-519-9800; 1-888-519-4599 (toll free)
Fax: 703-519-4599
E-mail: info@sacredspacesinc.com
Website: www.SacredSpacesInc.com

Type of Business:

Sacred Spaces is a liturgical design studio with a team of international artists and master craftsmen with experience spanning four decades in the design of worship environments: new construction, renovation and restoration. Our Services include Liturgical Design Consulting, Custom Design, Appointments, Removals, Consignments and Facsimiles. Specializing in marble, bronze and stone, we custom design altars, ambos, tabernacle thrones and baptismal fonts. We also offer Master Planning Services and Educational Programs for pastoral teams and parish-wide Town Hall meetings. Sacred Spaces - Excellence in Liturgical Design, Artistry and Craftsmanship.

Personnel:

J. Michael Carrigan (President/CEO)
John Grosvenor (Project Director)

Plaques & Memorials

W&E
BAUM
Designers and Manufacturers
Donor Walls • Plaques • Awards • Memorials

W & E Baum
89 Bannard Street
Freehold, NJ 07728
Tel: 800-922-7377; 732-866-1881
Fax: 732-866-8978
E-mail: info@webaum.com
Website: www.webaum.com/Church-Products.html

Type of Business:

W&E BAUM, celebrating 92 years and three generations, specializes in the design and fabrication of symbols of recognition and generosity. Additional income for churches can be generated by using many of our innovative products. Our Donor Walls, Bronze Memorials, Giving Trees, Plaques, Awards, Sculptures and more, promote fund-raising efforts and acknowledge gifts of all kinds. Quality, creativity and personal attention to detail are the elements that capture the attention of potential contributors in today's sophisticated world.

To thank, to honor, to reward, to commemorate, to memorialize, W & E Baum stands ready to help you translate your vision into reality.

Our Bronze Memorial Designs are a new and innovative way for your parishioners to permanently memorialize their loved ones. These memorials provide a steady stream of income for many years.

Contact us for more details.

Personnel:

Richard Baum (President)
Maurice Zagha (CEO)
Heshy Spira (Vice President)

CHURCH GLASS—General

Conrad Schmitt Studios Inc.

Excellence in Artistry Since 1889

Conrad Schmitt Studios, Inc.
2405 S. 162nd Street
New Berlin, WI 53151
Tel: 800-969-3033; 262-786-3030
Fax: 262-786-9036
E-mail: studio@conradschmitt.com
Website: www.conradschmitt.com

Type of Business:

CSS, in its 121 years of existence, has contributed to the art glass heritage of America through both creation and conservation. The Studio continually works to preserve and advance the techniques that facilitate work in the industry. Clients have commissioned work in a variety of styles. Many recent requests have been for new, traditional-style windows to complement more classically inspired architecture. Contemporary designs are also created in figural, geometric and abstract compositions. Full-time artisans conserve and restore stained glass, including priceless windows by John La Farge, Louis Comfort Tiffany, Mayer of Munich, Thomas O'Shaughnessy, and McCully and Miles.

Recent new stained glass commissions include St. John the Baptist Catholic Church, Costa Mesa, CA; the University of Notre Dame, Notre Dame, IN; and St. Anne Catholic Church, Sherman, TX.

Recent stained glass conservation projects include St. Vincent de Paul Catholic Church, Petaluma, CA and St. Mary Magdalen Catholic Church, Abbeville, LA.

Glass Heritage, llc
3113 Hickory Grove Road
Davenport, IA 52806
Tel: 877-324-4300
Fax: 563-324-4321
E-mail: info@glassheritage.com
Website: www.glassheritage.com

Type of Business:

Specializing in restoration, design and fabrication of custom stained glass windows for ecclesiastical environments, the team at Glass Heritage, llc is dedicated to the standard of excellence in glass. Our goal is to create a finished work of art that enhances the spiritual mission of your church and creates a space of meditative enrichment. While we specialize in historic restorations and maintenance of leaded glass, Glass Heritage also supplies custom design and fabrication services for stained and leaded glass, faceted glass, etched glass and custom blown glass.

When you choose Glass Heritage, llc, you choose a team of creative, dedicated craftsmen who will meet the needs of your sacred space. All our glasswork is handcrafted, never manufactured. Our reputation for personalized and affordable service is unsurpassed.

Glass Heritage, llc is a Fully Accredited studio member of The Stained Glass Association of America.

RAMBUSCH

SINCE 1898

Rambusch
160 Cornelison Avenue
Jersey City, NJ 07304
Tel: 201-333-2525
Fax: 201-433-3355
Website: www.rambusch.com

Type of Business:

Creativity and Quality are Rambusch Hallmarks. A small, highly personal business, where everything is custom. Each inquiry is handled by a principal, who guides the client through a myriad of possibilities. The chosen solution is then made tangible by our supremely skilled craftspeople.

Rambusch creates complete interiors, shrines, individual art works, stained glass and mosaics. New work, renovations, and restorations all receive the same attention, resulting in beautiful, fitting solutions for your unique commission. Our design rooms, art metal workshops and stained glass studios are in-house, ensuring seamless crafting of all designs. Rambusch-patented lighting fixtures, the recognized industry standard for church lighting, are individually built on our own worktables. Rambusch custom engineered lighting systems make everything look its best!

Call/or come visit our intriguing design rooms and workshops for an initial courtesy consultation. We look forward to hearing from you. Remember Rambusch – on time, within budget, designed just for you.

Personnel:

Edwin P. Rambusch
Martin V. Rambusch
Viggo B.A. Rambusch, Senior Advisor

Rohn & Associates Design, Inc.
1113 Creedmoor Avenue
Pittsburgh, PA 15226
Tel: 412-561-1228; 800-245-1288
Fax: 412-561-1201
E-mail: rolfrohn@rohndesign.com
Website: www.rohndesign.com
Blog: http://catholicliturgicalarts.blogspot.com/
Facebook: Catholic Liturgical Arts Journal

Type of Business:

Liturgical Designers, Artists & Artisans

TRADITION. Over the past 58 years, we have assisted the Catholic Church by designing, budgeting and implementing liturgical spaces.

COLLABORATION. We work side-by-side with our clients and collaborators to design and create appropriate and quality sacred art, interior finishes, lighting systems, acoustical systems, liturgical furnishings and appointments to create a rich devotional experience for your parishioners.

EXPERIENCE. We draw upon decades of experience and from a rich treasury of designers, architectural staff and contributing artists.

SCOPE OF SERVICES: Liturgical Design; Interior Design & Decorating; Sacred Artwork; Mosaics; Art Glass; Statuary; Liturgical Appointments; Liturgical Furniture; Metalwork.

ADDITIONAL LOCATIONS: 719 S. Flores St., Suite 200, San Antonio, TX 78204. Tel.: 210-231-0377; Fax: 210-231-0366

Contact us to arrange a complimentary project review.

Personnel:

Rolf R. Rohn (President - Liturgical Designer-Consultant)
Kathleen L. Maglicco (Vice President, Design)
Francesca Lofaro (Director, Sales)

WILLET HAUSER
Architectural Glass, Inc.

Willet Hauser Architectural Glass, Inc.
811 East Cayuga Street
Philadelphia, PA 19124
Tel: 800-533-3960; Fax: 877-495-9486
Website: www.willethauser.com

Type of Business:

Since 1896 Willet Hauser Architectural Glass has a century-old legacy of stained glass design and over six decades of renowned restoration. Willet Hauser is the preeminent stained glass studio in the country and operates facilities in Winona, Minnesota, and Philadelphia, Pennsylvania. Willet Hauser has created or restored over 15,000 projects, including some of the most magnificent stained glass windows for religious buildings within the United States and in 14 countries around the world.

The proof of our artistry is in the projects that we have designed and restored. Here are just a few prominent examples of the thousands of churches and institutions that have been our clients during the last century:

The National Cathedral, Washington, DC; The Church Center, United Nations, NY; The Cathedral of St. Mary of the Assumption, San Francisco, CA; Cathedral of Mary Our Queen, Baltimore, MD; Princeton University Chapel; The Cadet Chapel, United States Military Academy, West Point; Arlington National Cemetery Chapel; The Cathedral of Christ the King, Atlanta, GA.

When you choose Willet Hauser to create or preserve your legacy in stained glass, you are placing it in the experienced hands of artists, designers and craftspeople whose sole purpose is to ensure that every detail reflects your unique vision in a tribute of glass, color, and light.

...You can trust your legacy to our legacy.

Antiqued Stained Glass

WILLET HAUSER
Architectural Glass, Inc.

Willet Hauser Architectural Glass, Inc.
811 East Cayuga Street
Philadelphia, PA 19124
Tel: 800-533-3960; Fax: 877-495-9486
Website: www.willethauser.com

Type of Business:

Since 1896 Willet Hauser Architectural Glass has a century-old legacy of stained glass design and over six decades of renowned restoration. Willet Hauser is the preeminent stained glass studio in the country and operates facilities in Winona, Minnesota, and Philadelphia, Pennsylvania. Willet Hauser has created or restored over 15,000 projects, including some of the most magnificent stained glass windows for religious buildings within the United States and in 14 countries around the world.

The proof of our artistry is in the projects that we have designed and restored. Here are just a few prominent examples of the thousands of churches and institutions that have been our clients during the last century:

The National Cathedral, Washington, DC; The Church Center, United Nations, NY; The Cathedral of St. Mary of the Assumption, San Francisco, CA; Cathedral of Mary Our Queen, Baltimore, MD; Princeton University Chapel; The Cadet Chapel, United States Military Academy, West Point; Arlington National Cemetery Chapel; The Cathedral of Christ the King, Atlanta, GA.

When you choose Willet Hauser to create or preserve your legacy in stained glass, you are placing it in the experienced hands of artists, designers and craftspeople whose sole purpose is to ensure that every detail reflects your unique vision in a tribute of glass, color, and light.

...You can trust your legacy to our legacy.

Etched Glass

WILLET HAUSER
Architectural Glass, Inc.

Willet Hauser Architectural Glass, Inc.
811 East Cayuga Street
Philadelphia, PA 19124
Tel: 800-533-3960; Fax: 877-495-9486
Website: www.willethauser.com

Type of Business:

Since 1896 Willet Hauser Architectural Glass has a century-old legacy of stained glass design and over six decades of renowned restoration. Willet Hauser is the preeminent stained glass studio in the country and operates facilities in Winona, Minnesota, and Philadelphia, Pennsylvania. Willet Hauser has created or restored over 15,000 projects, including some of the most magnificent stained glass windows for religious buildings within the United States and in 14 countries around the world.

The proof of our artistry is in the projects that we have designed and restored. Here are just a few prominent examples of the thousands of churches and institutions that have been our clients during the last century:

The National Cathedral, Washington, DC; The Church Center, United Nations, NY; The Cathedral of St. Mary of the Assumption, San Francisco, CA; Cathedral of Mary Our Queen, Baltimore, MD; Princeton University Chapel; The Cadet Chapel, United States Military Academy, West Point; Arlington National Cemetery Chapel; The Cathedral of Christ the King, Atlanta, GA.

When you choose Willet Hauser to create or preserve your legacy in stained glass, you are placing it in the experienced hands of artists, designers and craftspeople whose sole purpose is to ensure that every detail reflects your unique vision in a tribute of glass, color, and light.

...You can trust your legacy to our legacy.

Faceted Glass

WILLET HAUSER
Architectural Glass, Inc.

Willet Hauser Architectural Glass, Inc.
811 East Cayuga Street
Philadelphia, PA 19124
Tel: 800-533-3960; Fax: 877-495-9486
Website: www.willethauser.com

Type of Business:

Since 1896 Willet Hauser Architectural Glass has a century-old legacy of stained glass design and over six decades of renowned restoration. Willet Hauser is the preeminent stained glass studio in the country and operates facilities in Winona, Minnesota, and Philadelphia, Pennsylvania. Willet Hauser has created or restored over 15,000 projects, including some of the most magnificent stained glass windows for religious buildings within the United States and in 14 countries around the world.

The proof of our artistry is in the projects that we have designed and restored. Here are just a few prominent examples of the thousands of churches and institutions that have been our clients during the last century:

The National Cathedral, Washington, DC; The Church Center, United Nations, NY; The Cathedral of St. Mary of the Assumption, San Francisco, CA; Cathedral of Mary Our Queen, Baltimore, MD; Princeton University Chapel; The Cadet Chapel, United States Military Academy, West Point; Arlington National Cemetery Chapel; The Cathedral of Christ the King, Atlanta, GA.

When you choose Willet Hauser to create or preserve your legacy in stained glass, you are placing it in the experienced hands of artists, designers and craftspeople whose sole purpose is to ensure that every detail reflects your unique vision in a tribute of glass, color, and light.

...You can trust your legacy to our legacy.

Stained Glass

Baker Liturgical Art, LLC
1210 Meriden Waterbury Road
Plantsville, CT 06479
Tel: 860-621-7471
Fax: 860-621-7607
E-mail: bakerart@sbcglobal.net
Website: www.bakerliturgicalart.com

Type of Business:

Baker Liturgical Art, LLC offers a full range of construction and renovation services. These services encompass architectural specifications and liturgical design as well as sound system and lighting design.

Our liturgical design talents result in beautiful altar furnishings of hand-carved wood or of fine imported Italian marble. Stained glass and sacred artwork (painted, wood-carved or chiseled from marble) are the final accents to complete prayerful settings in every worship space from the smallest Chapel to the grandest Cathedral! Baker Liturgical Art, LLC prides itself in offering uncompromising quality in its products and services.

Our Services Include: Liturgical Design, Architectural Services, Liturgical Furnishings, Sculpture & Artwork, Flooring, Millwork, Multi-Media Systems, Stained Glass Fabrication & Restoration.

Additional location: 9427 S. Ocean Drive, Jensen Beach, FL 34957. Tel: 860-919-2119.

Botti Studio of Architectural Arts, Inc.
919 Grove Street
Evanston, IL 60201
Tel: 800-524-7211; 847-869-5933
Fax: 847-869-5996
E-mail: botti@bottistudio.com
Website: www.bottistudio.com

Type of Business:

Since 1864, Botti Studio has specialized in serving the ecclesiastic environment through design, fabrication, delivery, and installation. Experts on staff in new design commissions, repair, restoration, conservation, and repair provide a source for experienced project management – from conception through completion. Services include: stained, faceted, sandblasted, carved and painted glass, wood / metal / stone frames / protective glazing, murals, marble, mosaics, bronze, statuary, gilding, painting and decorating, complete interiors, new and restorations, historic discovery, documentation and consultation to owner / architect.

Our staff of 45 includes internationally recognized ecclesiastic artists / designers working in conjunction with highly skilled craftspeople / artisans / conservators.

Locations: New York, NY / (212) 362-6085, LaPorte, IN / (219) 362-5934, Chicago, IL / (847) 869-5933, San Diego, CA / (760) 753-0705, Sarasota, FL / (941) 951-0978, Nassau, Bahamas / (242) 327-2992, Agropoli, Italy / (800) 524-7211.

Personnel:

Ettore Christopher Botti (Principal)
Ethlyn Panzironi Botti (Principal)

Conrad Schmitt Studios Inc.
Excellence in Artistry Since 1889

Conrad Schmitt Studios, Inc.
2405 S. 162nd Street
New Berlin, WI 53151
Tel: 800-969-3033; 262-786-3030
Fax: 262-786-9036
E-mail: studio@conradschmitt.com
Website: www.conradschmitt.com

Type of Business:

CSS, in its 121 years of existence, has contributed to the art glass heritage of America through both creation and conservation. The Studio continually works to preserve and advance the techniques that facilitate work in the industry. Clients have commissioned work in a variety of styles. Many recent requests have been for new, traditional-style windows to complement more classically inspired architecture. Contemporary designs are also created in figural, geometric and abstract compositions. Full-time artisans conserve and restore stained glass, including priceless windows by John La Farge, Louis Comfort Tiffany, Mayer of Munich, Thomas O'Shaughnessy, and McCully and Miles.

Recent new stained glass commissions include St. John the Baptist Catholic Church, Costa Mesa, CA; the University of Notre Dame, Notre Dame, IN; and St. Anne Catholic Church, Sherman, TX.

Recent stained glass conservation projects include St. Vincent de Paul Catholic Church, Petaluma, CA and St. Mary Magdalen Catholic Church, Abbeville, LA.

Glass Heritage, llc
3113 Hickory Grove Road
Davenport, IA 52806
Tel: 877-324-4300
Fax: 563-324-4321
E-mail: info@glassheritage.com
Website: www.glassheritage.com

Type of Business:

Specializing in restoration, design and fabrication of custom stained glass windows for ecclesiastical environments, the team at Glass Heritage, llc is dedicated to the standard of excellence in glass. Our goal is to create a finished work of art that enhances the spiritual mission of your church and creates a space of meditative enrichment. While we specialize in historic restorations and maintenance of leaded glass, Glass Heritage also supplies custom design and fabrication services for stained and leaded glass, faceted glass, etched glass and custom blown glass.

When you choose Glass Heritage, llc, you choose a team of creative, dedicated craftsmen who will meet the needs of your sacred space. All our glasswork is handcrafted, never manufactured. Our reputation for personalized and affordable service is unsurpassed.

Glass Heritage, llc is a Fully Accredited studio member of The Stained Glass Association of America.

HIEMER & COMPANY
Stained Glass Studio

Hiemer & Company Stained Glass Studio
141 Wabash Avenue
Clifton, NJ 07011
Tel: 973-772-5081
Fax: 973-772-0325
E-mail: jevanwie@hiemco.com
Website: www.hiemco.com

Type of Business:

Bold Liturgical statements and traditional Biblical portrayals are executed in magnificent color schemes by the artists and craftsmen at Hiemer & Company. Four generations of the Hiemer family have dedicated their careers to excellence in stained glass and promotion of faith through art. The studio members are highly skilled and experienced with large scale restorations, artistic replications and window renovations. The permanent staff works from concept to installation to the client's complete satisfaction. Over 1,100 Churches served in North America. Fabricators of stained, faceted, and etched glass. Exceptional figure portrayals are a specialty. Information and quotations submitted without obligation.

Personnel:

Gerhard E. Hiemer (C.E.O.)
Judith Hiemer Van Wie (President)
James E. Van Wie (Vice President)

ROHLF'S STAINED & LEADED GLASS STUDIO, INC.

DEDICATED TO STAINED GLASS EXCELLENCE

WOOD REPLICATION,
NEW MAHOGANY FRAMES

DIVERSITY IN STAINED GLASS ART

ESTABLISHED 1920

ROHLF'S

STAINED AND LEADED GLASS, INC.
783 SOUTH THIRD AVE.
MOUNT VERNON, NY 10550
(800) 969-4106 FAX: (914) 699-7091
E-MAIL: ROHLF 1@AOL.COM WEB SITE: WWW.ROHLFSTUDIO.COM

EST. 1920 ROHLF STUDIO

PAYNE STUDIOS OF NEW JERSEY
An Affiliate of Rohlf's Studio, Inc

TRADITIONAL • CONTEMPORARY • RESTORATION

RAMBUSCH
SINCE 1898

Rambusch
160 Cornelison Avenue
Jersey City, NJ 07304
Tel: 201-333-2525
Fax: 201-433-3355
Website: www.rambusch.com

Type of Business:

Creativity and Quality are Rambusch Hallmarks. A small, highly personal business, where everything is custom. Each inquiry is handled by a principal, who guides the client through a myriad of possibilities. The chosen solution is then made tangible by our supremely skilled craftspeople.

Rambusch creates complete interiors, shrines, individual art works, stained glass and mosaics. New work, renovations, and restorations all receive the same attention, resulting in beautiful, fitting solutions for your unique commission. Our design rooms, art metal workshops and stained glass studios are in-house, ensuring seamless crafting of all designs. Rambusch-patented lighting fixtures, the recognized industry standard for church lighting, are individually built on our own worktables. Rambusch custom engineered lighting systems make everything look its best!

Call/or come visit our intriguing design rooms and workshops for an initial courtesy consultation. We look forward to hearing from you. Remember Rambusch – on time, within budget, designed just for you.

Personnel:

Edwin P. Rambusch
Martin V. Rambusch
Viggo B.A. Rambusch, Senior Advisor

Rohlf's Stained & Leaded Glass Studio, Inc.
783 South Third Avenue
Mt. Vernon, NY 10550
Toll Free: 800-969-4106
Tel: 914-699-4848
Fax: 914- 699- 7091
E-mail: rohlf1@aol.com
Website: www.rohlfstudio.com

Type of Business:

For Three Generations our family owned and operated Studio together with our affiliate, George L. Payne Studio have been dedicated to excellence in Stained Glass Art. Our team of International designers and Master Craftspersons have created stained glass windows for over a thousand Churches and Institutions Worldwide. Our reputation and experience in the field of Restoration, Replication and Preservation is well known. We would be pleased to assist you in the early stages of planning and design, working with your Architect and/or committee to achieve your desired goals. From concept to completion, we are dedicated to serve you.

Personnel:

Peter A. Rohlf (Chairman & CEO)
Peter Hans Rohlf (President)
Gregory Rohlf (Vice President)

WILLET HAUSER
Architectural Glass, Inc.

Willet Hauser Architectural Glass, Inc.
811 East Cayuga Street
Philadelphia, PA 19124
Tel: 800-533-3960
Fax: 877-495-9486
Website: www.willethauser.com

Type of Business:

Since 1896 Willet Hauser Architectural Glass has a century-old legacy of stained glass design and over six decades of renowned restoration. Willet Hauser is the preeminent stained glass studio in the country and operates facilities in Winona, Minnesota, and Philadelphia, Pennsylvania. Willet Hauser has created or restored over 15,000 projects, including some of the most magnificent stained glass windows for religious buildings within the United States and in 14 countries around the world.

The proof of our artistry is in the projects that we have designed and restored. Here are just a few prominent examples of the thousands of churches and institutions that have been our clients during the last century:

The National Cathedral, Washington, DC; The Church Center, United Nations, NY; The Cathedral of St. Mary of the Assumption, San Francisco, CA; Cathedral of Mary Our Queen, Baltimore, MD; Princeton University Chapel; The Cadet Chapel, United States Military Academy, West Point; Arlington National Cemetery Chapel; The Cathedral of Christ the King, Atlanta, GA.

When you choose Willet Hauser to create or preserve your legacy in stained glass, you are placing it in the experienced hands of artists, designers and craftspeople whose sole purpose is to ensure that every detail reflects your unique vision in a tribute of glass, color, and light.

...You can trust your legacy to our legacy.

CLERICAL APPAREL—General

C.M. Almy
Three American Lane, P.O. Box 2644
Greenwich, CT 06836-2644
Tel: 800-225-2569
Fax: 800-426-2569
E-mail: almyaccess@almy.com
Website: www.almy.com
Showroom in Old Greenwich, CT

Type of Business:

Almy was founded in 1892. We design and make virtually all of our products in our Maine shop. It is our mission to design furnishings that will grace your worship and to ensure their value by making them with the highest quality materials and craftsmanship. We make a complete line of liturgical vestments, clergy apparel, choir robes, candles, communion bread, linens, processional and altar appointments, and eucharistic vessels. We also offer custom design and fabrication of all Almy products, and repair and refurbishing of old metal appointments. Quik Ship© delivery of many popular items. All orders backed by The Almy Guarantee. Call, write, or e-mail for a free catalog.

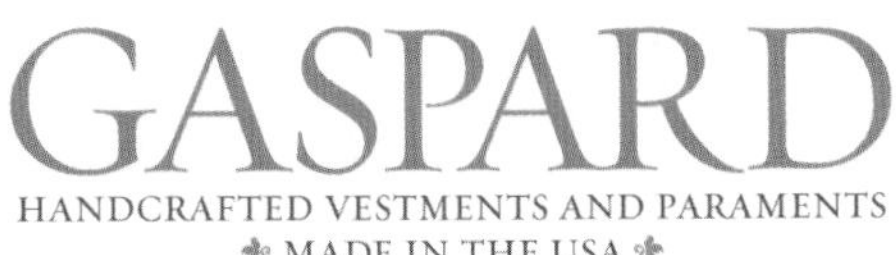

aspard, Inc.
ormerly The Robert Gaspard Company, Inc.)
)0 N. Janacek Road
ookfield, WI 53045
l: 800-784-6868 (toll free)
x: 800-784-7567
mail: info@gaspardinc.com
ebsite: www.gaspardinc.com

pe of Business:

or more than five decades customers have looked to Gaspard for fine quality, handcrafted vestments and paraments made in the USA. Offerings nclude the exquisite Castle Craft® collection; wardrobe essentials such s albs, surplices, cassocks, robes, and clergy shirts; extensive metalware fferings, fair linens, altar accessories, and communion ware.

ecause your vestment and parament selections are made to order in ur one and only location in Brookfield, Wisconsin, special sizes and ustom designs are not a problem. One of our friendly Customer Service epresentatives will be happy to help you find just the right size and style o enhance your spiritual expression. Please visit us online or call for a ree catalog.

rsonnel:

ason R. Gaspard (President)
oann Gaspard (Vice President)

Renzetti - Magnarelli Clergy Apparel, Inc.

enzetti – Magnarelli Clergy Apparel, Inc
216 S. Broad Street
hiladelphia, PA 19145
el: 1-888-439-0164 (toll free); 215-339-0558
ax: 215-463-0161
Vebsite: www.clergyapparel.com

ype of Business:

Renzetti – Magnarelli Clergy Apparel has been serving the vesturing needs of various religious orders and church organizations since 1945. Renzetti – Magnarelli is known for its high quality garments at extremely reasonable prices. We custom manufacture a complete line of cassocks, clerical vests, rabots and vestments. Our garments are made with Old World craftsmanship passed down from generation to generation and are made according to your individual measurements and specifications at a cost that is less than ready made garments, a value we feel cannot be matched.

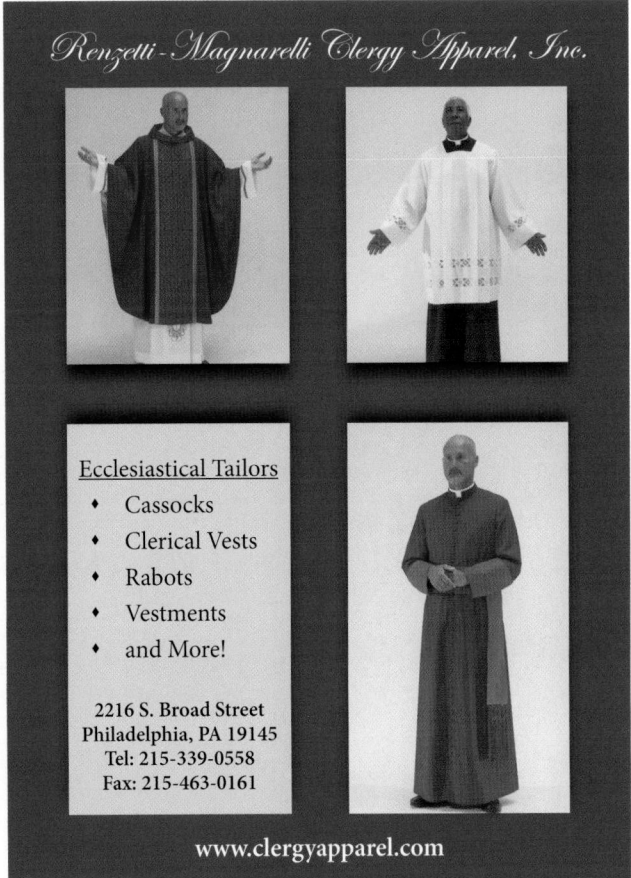

Robes, Vestments, etc.

Art Studio Slabbinck
Headquarters:
L. Bauwensstraat 18
8200 Brugge, Belgium
Tel: +32-50-312557
Fax: +32-50-318358
Website: www.slabbinck.com

Type of Business:

Since 1903, Slabbinck is a family owned business that made church vestments in Bruges, Belgium. We make chasubles, stoles, albs, copes, deaconstoles, dalmatics, altar and lectern covers, altar linens and cloths, tapestries and banners. Chalices, ciboria, patens and pyxes are also available. "Slabbinck Speed Service", which allows delivery within 48 hrs, is offered for many items in our catalog. For more information, a free catalog, or a dealer nearest you, visit www.slabbinck.be, e-mail us at info@ slabbinck.be , call us at 1-800-423-3224 or fax us at 1-800-284-9000.

C.M. Almy
Three American Lane, P.O. Box 2644
Greenwich, CT 06836-2644
Tel: 800-225-2569
Fax: 800-426-2569
E-mail: almyaccess@almy.com
Website: www.almy.com
Showroom in Old Greenwich, CT

Type of Business:

Almy was founded in 1892. We design and make virtually all of our products in our Maine shop. It is our mission to design furnishings that will grace your worship and to ensure their value by making them with the highest quality materials and craftsmanship. We make a complete line of liturgical vestments, clergy apparel, choir robes, candles, communion bread, linens, processional and altar appointments, and eucharistic vessels. We also offer custom design and fabrication of all Almy products, and repair and refurbishing of old metal appointments. Quik Ship© delivery of many popular items. All orders backed by The Almy Guarantee. Call, write, or e-mail for a free catalog.

Renzetti - Magnarelli Clergy Apparel, Inc.

Renzetti – Magnarelli Clergy Apparel, Inc
2216 S. Broad Street
Philadelphia, PA 19145
Tel: 1-888-439-0164 (toll free); 215-339-0558
Fax: 215-463-0161
Website: www.clergyapparel.com

Type of Business:

Renzetti – Magnarelli Clergy Apparel has been serving the vesturing needs of various religious orders and church organizations since 1945. Renzetti – Magnarelli is known for its high quality garments at extremely reasonable prices. We custom manufacture a complete line of cassocks, clerical vests, rabots and vestments. Our garments are made with Old World craftsmanship passed down from generation to generation and are made according to your individual measurements and specifications at a cost that is less than ready made garments, a value we feel cannot be matched.

Suits, Coats & Cassocks

Renzetti - Magnarelli Clergy Apparel, Inc

Renzetti – Magnarelli Clergy Apparel, Inc
2216 S. Broad Street
Philadelphia, PA 19145
Tel: 1-888-439-0164 (toll free); 215-339-0558
Fax: 215-463-0161
Website: www.clergyapparel.com

Type of Business:

Renzetti – Magnarelli Clergy Apparel has been serving the vesturin needs of various religious orders and church organizations since 194 Renzetti – Magnarelli is known for its high quality garments at extreme reasonable prices. We custom manufacture a complete line of cassock clerical vests, rabots and vestments. Our garments are made with Ol World craftsmanship passed down from generation to generation and ar made according to your individual measurements and specifications a cost that is less than ready made garments, a value we feel cannot b matched.

CONSTRUCTION, MAINTENANCE & RENOVATION—General

Baker Liturgical Art, LLC
Church Restoration/Church Renovation

Baker Liturgical Art, LLC
1210 Meriden Waterbury Road
Plantsville, CT 06479
Tel: 860-621-7471
Fax: 860-621-7607
E-mail: bakerart@sbcglobal.net
Website: www.bakerliturgicalart.com

Type of Business:

Baker Liturgical Art, LLC offers a full range of construction and renovatio services. These services encompass architectural specifications an liturgical design as well as sound system and lighting design.

Our liturgical design talents result in beautiful altar furnishings of hand carved wood or of fine imported Italian marble. Stained glass and sacre artwork (painted, wood-carved or chiseled from marble) are the fina accents to complete prayerful settings in every worship space from th smallest Chapel to the grandest Cathedral! Baker Liturgical Art, LLC pride itself in offering uncompromising quality in its products and services.

Our Services Include: Liturgical Design, Architectural Services, Liturgica Furnishings, Sculpture & Artwork, Flooring, Millwork, Multi-Medi Systems, Stained Glass Fabrication & Restoration.

Additional location: 9427 S. Ocean Drive, Jensen Beach, FL 34957. Tel 860-919-2119.

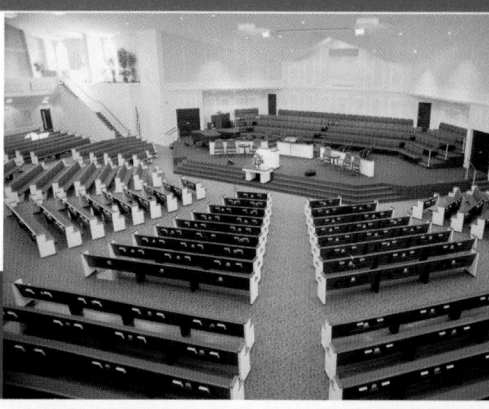

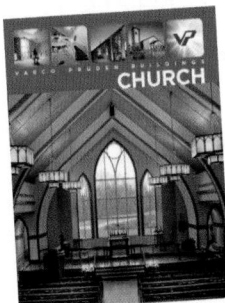

Guidance in Giving, Inc.
Full Service Stewardship, Development and Campaign Consultants
225 Snedecor Avenue
Bayport, NY 11705
Tel: 888-757-5444; Cell: 631-553-9064
E-mail: mcusack@guidanceingiving.com
Website: www.guidanceingiving.com

Type of Business:

Guidance In Giving, Inc. is a Catholic organization that truly understands the mission of the Catholic Church. Serving as stewardship, development and campaign counsel to dioceses, parishes and schools, our firm has extensive experience in conducting capital campaigns and implementing stewardship throughout the United States. In all of our development efforts we utilize techniques that are continuously tested and refined. Services include: diocesan capital campaigns; diocesan annual appeals; diocesan development audits and feasibility studies; parish capital campaigns; offertory enhancement, implementing stewardship; parish feasibility studies, school development audits, school feasibility studies, major gifts solicitations and school capital campaigns. Additionally, the firm has an Hispanic and Multicultural Division and offers bilingual services. To discuss your individual situation or to get a cost free analysis of your potential, please contact Michael R. Cusack, Chairman and CEO at 888-757-5444.

Personnel:

Michael R. Cusack (Chairman and CEO)
Michael V. Goodwin (President, Diocesan Division)
Joseph W. Zamorano (President, Parish Division)
Stephen A. Babcock (Executive Vice President, Parish Division)
Joseph E. Neville (Senior Vice President)
Carlos H. Proaño (Executive Vice President, Hispanic and Multicultural Division)

Rohn & Associates Design, Inc.
1113 Creedmoor Avenue
Pittsburgh, PA 15226
Tel: 412-561-1228; 800-245-1288
Fax: 412-561-1201
E-mail: rolfrohn@rohndesign.com
Website: www.rohndesign.com
Blog: http://catholicliturgicalarts.blogspot.com/
Facebook: Catholic Liturgical Arts Journal

Type of Business:

Liturgical Designers, Artists & Artisans
TRADITION. Over the past 58 years, we have assisted the Catholic Church by designing, budgeting and implementing liturgical spaces.
COLLABORATION. We work side-by-side with our clients and collaborators to design and create appropriate and quality sacred art, interior finishes, lighting systems, acoustical systems, liturgical furnishings and appointments to create a rich devotional experience for your parishioners.
EXPERIENCE. We draw upon decades of experience and from a rich treasury of designers, architectural staff and contributing artists.
SCOPE OF SERVICES: Liturgical Design; Interior Design & Decorating; Sacred Artwork; Mosaics; Art Glass; Statuary; Liturgical Appointments; Liturgical Furniture; Metalwork.
ADDITIONAL LOCATIONS: 719 S. Flores St., Suite 200, San Antonio, TX 78204. Tel.: 210-231-0377; Fax: 210-231-0366
Contact us to arrange a complimentary project review.

Personnel:

Rolf R. Rohn (President - Liturgical Designer-Consultant)
Kathleen L. Maglicco (Vice President, Design)
Francesca Lofaro (Director, Sales)

Varco Pruden Buildings — A BlueScope Steel Company
3200 Players Club Circle
Memphis, TN 19085-1603
Tel: 901-748-8000; 800-238-3246 (toll free)
E-mail: vpsales@vp.com; sales@vp.com
Website: www.vp.com

Type of Business:

VP Buildings is a world leader in pre-engineered steel systems construction. Working closely with architects, engineers, and contractors, we offer buildings that combine extraordinary aesthetic appeal with optimum functionality. Steel systems construction is ideal for churches, retreat houses, sanctuaries, schools, office complexes and more. We can incorporate glass, brick, stone, or pre-cast concrete for special purposes and to add distinctive, artistic appeal. Our network of more than 1,000 independent Authorized VP Builders offers state-of-the-art design/build services in local communities across the United States and Canada, as well as throughout Central and South America, Europe, and Asia.

WILLET HAUSER
Architectural Glass, Inc.

Willet Hauser Architectural Glass, Inc.
811 East Cayuga Street
Philadelphia, PA 19124
Tel: 800-533-3960
Fax: 877-495-9486
Website: www.willethauser.com

Type of Business:

Since 1896 Willet Hauser Architectural Glass has a century-old legacy of stained glass design and over six decades of renowned restoration. Willet Hauser is the preeminent stained glass studio in the country and operates facilities in Winona, Minnesota, and Philadelphia, Pennsylvania. Willet Hauser has created or restored over 15,000 projects, including some of the most magnificent stained glass windows for religious buildings within the United States and in 14 countries around the world.

The proof of our artistry is in the projects that we have designed and restored. Here are just a few prominent examples of the thousands of churches and institutions that have been our clients during the last century:
The National Cathedral, Washington, DC; The Church Center, United Nations, NY; The Cathedral of St. Mary of the Assumption, San Francisco, CA; Cathedral of Mary Our Queen, Baltimore, MD; Princeton University Chapel; The Cadet Chapel, United States Military Academy, West Point; Arlington National Cemetery Chapel; The Cathedral of Christ the King, Atlanta, GA.
When you choose Willet Hauser to create or preserve your legacy in stained glass, you are placing it in the experienced hands of artists, designers and craftspeople whose sole purpose is to ensure that every detail reflects your unique vision in a tribute of glass, color, and light.
...You can trust your legacy to our legacy.

Architects & Builders

DUNCAN G. STROIK ARCHITECT LLC

Duncan G. Stroik Architect
218 West Washington Street, Suite 1200
South Bend, IN 46601
Tel: 574-232-1783
Fax: 574-232-1792
E-mail: stroik@stroik.com
Website: www.stroik.com

Type of Business:

Duncan G. Stroik Architect LLC is nationally known for its classical churches in the Roman Catholic tradition. Stroik is considered a leader in the renaissance of sacred architecture through his design work, publications, teaching, lectures, and editorship of the journal Sacred Architecture. During the past twenty years the firm has designed and completed a large number of ecclesiastical projects including parish churches, schools, college chapels, monasteries, a national shrine, and cathedrals. Projects range from Connecticut to California, Texas to Minnesota and all states in between. Budgets for renovations from $400 thousand to $10 million and new buildings from $5 million to $35 million. The firm has also produced masterplans for religious communities, seminaries, and colleges.

FRANCK & LOHSEN
ARCHITECTS
FRANCKLOHSEN.COM ~ (202) 223-9449

Franck & Lohsen Architects Inc
1715 N Street, N.W.
Washington, DC 20036-2801
Tel: 202-223-9449
Fax: 202-223-9484
E-mail: art@francklohsen.com
Website: www.francklohsen.com

Type of Business:

Architectural design, Master Planning, new construction, historic renovations and additions of Churches and Religious facilities. Design of liturgical elements and furnishings including mosaics, altars, lighting fixtures, statuary, custom vestments, interiors, etc. Our firm provides services nationally from our offices in Washington, DC as well as in Italy. We are dedicated to producing the highest quality work through a thoughtful and sophisticated combination of classical approaches and modern sensibilities in keeping with the established traditions and norms of the Church. Please feel free to inquire with any questions.

Personnel:

Arthur Lohsen, AIA, LEED, NCARB, RIBA (President)
Michael Franck, AIA, NCARB, RIBA (Vice President)

Varco Pruden Buildings — A BlueScope Steel Company
3200 Players Club Circle
Memphis, TN 19085-1603
Tel: 901-748-8000; 800-238-3246 (toll free)
E-mail: vpsales@vp.com; sales@vp.com
Website: www.vp.com

Type of Business:

VP Buildings is a world leader in pre-engineered steel systems construction. Working closely with architects, engineers, and contractors, we offer buildings that combine extraordinary aesthetic appeal with optimum functionality. Steel systems construction is ideal for churches, retreat houses, sanctuaries, schools, office complexes and more. We can incorporate glass, brick, stone, or pre-cast concrete for special purposes and to add distinctive, artistic appeal. Our network of more than 1,000 independent Authorized VP Builders offers state-of-the-art design/build services in local communities across the United States and Canada, as well as throughout Central and South America, Europe, and Asia.

Artists & Decorators

Botti Studio of Architectural Arts, Inc.
919 Grove Street
Evanston, IL 60201
Tel: 800-524-7211; 847-869-5933
Fax: 847-869-5996
E-mail: botti@bottistudio.com
Website: www.bottistudio.com

Type of Business:

Since 1864, Botti Studio has specialized in serving the ecclesiastic environment through design, fabrication, delivery, and installation. Experts on staff in new design commissions, repair, restoration, conservation, and repair provide a source for experienced project management – from conception through completion. Services include: stained, faceted, sandblasted, carved and painted glass, wood / metal / stone frames / protective glazing, murals, marble, mosaics, bronze, statuary, gilding, painting and decorating, complete interiors, new and restorations, historic discovery, documentation and consultation to owner / architect.

Our staff of 45 includes internationally recognized ecclesiastic artists / designers working in conjunction with highly skilled craftspeople / artisans / conservators.

Locations: New York, NY / (212) 362-6085, LaPorte, IN / (219) 362-5934, Chicago, IL / (847) 869-5933, San Diego, CA / (760) 753-0705, Sarasota, FL / (941) 951-0978, Nassau, Bahamas / (242) 327-2992, Agropoli, Italy / (800) 524-7211.

Personnel:

Ettore Christopher Botti (Principal)
Ethlyn Panzironi Botti (Principal)

Conrad Schmitt Studios Inc.

Excellence in Artistry Since 1889

Conrad Schmitt Studios, Inc.
2405 S. 162nd Street
New Berlin, WI 53151
Tel: 800-969-3033; 262-786-3030
Fax: 262-786-9036
E-mail: studio@conradschmitt.com
Website: www.conradschmitt.com

Type of Business:

Since 1889, CSS has been privileged to decorate and restore churches of all sizes and styles throughout the country. Our experienced staff assists projects in the early stages to help assemble the master plan, communicate the vision and generate the enthusiasm and funding needed to make the plan a reality. Some of the tools used to accomplish these goals include renderings, on-site samples, budgetary estimates and fundraising materials.

Our comprehensive scope of services allows us to be a single source for a variety of needs, creating the best projects in terms of function, longevity and aesthetics. Our services include the investigation and documentation of original decorative schemes, gilding, glazing, marbleizing, stenciling, trompe l'oeil and faux finishing.

Recent decorating commissions include the Cathedral of the Immaculate Conception, Springfield, IL; St. Mary Magdalen Catholic Church, Abbeville, LA; St. Joseph Cathedral, Sioux Falls, SD; and St. John Neumann Catholic Church, Knoxville, TN.

Bronze Memorials

Designers and Manufacturers

Donor Walls • Plaques • Awards • Memorials

W & E Baum
89 Bannard Street
Freehold, NJ 07728
Tel: 800-922-7377; 732-866-1881
Fax: 732-866-8978
E-mail: info@webaum.com
Website: www.webaum.com/Church-Products.html

Type of Business:

W&E BAUM, celebrating 92 years and three generations, specializes in the design and fabrication of symbols of recognition and generosity. Additional income for churches can be generated by using many of our innovative products. Our Donor Walls, Bronze Memorials, Giving Trees, Plaques, Awards, Sculptures and more, promote fund-raising efforts and acknowledge gifts of all kinds. Quality, creativity and personal attention to detail are the elements that capture the attention of potential contributors in today's sophisticated world.

To thank, to honor, to reward, to commemorate, to memorialize, W & E Baum stands ready to help you translate your vision into reality.

Our Bronze Memorial Designs are a new and innovative way for your parishioners to permanently memorialize their loved ones. These memorials provide a steady stream of income for many years.

Contact us for more details.

Personnel:

Richard Baum (President)
Maurice Zagha (CEO)
Heshy Spira (Vice President)

Restoration/Refinishing

Botti Studio of Architectural Arts, Inc.
919 Grove Street
Evanston, IL 60201
Tel: 800-524-7211; 847-869-5933
Fax: 847-869-5996
E-mail: botti@bottistudio.com; Website: www.bottistudio.com

Type of Business:

Since 1864, Botti Studio has specialized in serving the ecclesiastic environment through design, fabrication, delivery, and installation. Experts on staff in new design commissions, repair, restoration, conservation, and repair provide a source for experienced project management – from conception through completion. Services include: stained, faceted, sandblasted, carved and painted glass, wood / metal / stone frames / protective glazing, murals, marble, mosaics, bronze, statuary, gilding, painting and decorating, complete interiors, new and restorations, historic discovery, documentation and consultation to owner / architect.

Our staff of 45 includes internationally recognized ecclesiastic artists / designers working in conjunction with highly skilled craftspeople / artisans / conservators.

Locations: New York, NY / (212) 362-6085, LaPorte, IN / (219) 362-5934, Chicago, IL / (847) 869-5933, San Diego, CA / (760) 753-0705, Sarasota, FL / (941) 951-0978, Nassau, Bahamas / (242) 327-2992, Agropoli, Italy / (800) 524-7211.

Personnel:

Ettore Christopher Botti (Principal)
Ethlyn Panzironi Botti (Principal)

Conrad Schmitt Studios Inc.

Excellence in Artistry Since 1889

Conrad Schmitt Studios, Inc.
2405 S. 162nd Street
New Berlin, WI 53151
Tel: 800-969-3033; 262-786-3030
Fax: 262-786-9036
E-mail: studio@conradschmitt.com
Website: www.conradschmitt.com

Type of Business:

Since 1889, CSS has been privileged to decorate and restore churches of all sizes and styles throughout the country. Our experienced staff assists projects in the early stages to help assemble the master plan, communicate the vision and generate the enthusiasm and funding needed to make the plan a reality. Some of the tools used to accomplish these goals include renderings, on-site samples, budgetary estimates and fundraising materials.

Our comprehensive scope of services allows us to be a single source for a variety of needs, creating the best projects in terms of function, longevity and aesthetics. Our services include the investigation and documentation of original decorative schemes, gilding, glazing, marbleizing, stenciling, trompe l'oeil and faux finishing.

Recent decorating commissions include the Cathedral of the Immaculate Conception, Springfield, IL; St. Mary Magdalen Catholic Church, Abbeville, LA; St. Joseph Cathedral, Sioux Falls, SD; and St. John Neumann Catholic Church, Knoxville, TN.

RAMBUSCH

SINCE 1898

Rambusch
160 Cornelison Avenue
Jersey City, NJ 07304
Tel: 201-333-2525
Fax: 201-433-3355
Website: www.rambusch.com

Type of Business:

Creativity and Quality are Rambusch Hallmarks. A small, highly personal business, where everything is custom. Each inquiry is handled by a principal, who guides the client through a myriad of possibilities. The chosen solution is then made tangible by our supremely skilled craftspeople.
Rambusch creates complete interiors, shrines, individual art works, stained glass and mosaics. New work, renovations, and restorations all receive the same attention, resulting in beautiful, fitting solutions for your unique commission. Our design rooms, art metal workshops and stained glass studios are in-house, ensuring seamless crafting of all designs. Rambusch-patented lighting fixtures, the recognized industry standard for church lighting, are individually built on our own worktables. Rambusch custom engineered lighting systems make everything look its best!
Call/or come visit our intriguing design rooms and workshops for an initial courtesy consultation. We look forward to hearing from you. Remember Rambusch – on time, within budget, designed just for you.

Personnel:

Edwin P. Rambusch
Martin V. Rambusch
Viggo B.A. Rambusch, Senior Advisor

Rohlf's Stained & Leaded Glass Studio, Inc.
783 South Third Avenue
Mt. Vernon, NY 10550
Toll Free: 800-969-4106
Tel: 914-699-4848
Fax: 914- 699- 7091
E-mail: rohlf1@aol.com
Website: www.rohlfstudio.com

Type of Business:

For Three Generations our family owned and operated Studio together with our affiliate, George L. Payne Studio have been dedicated to excellence in Stained Glass Art. Our team of International designers and Master Craftspersons have created stained glass windows for over a thousand Churches and Institutions Worldwide. Our reputation and experience in the field of Restoration, Replication and Preservation is well known. We would be pleased to assist you in the early stages of planning and design, working with your Architect and/or committee to achieve your desired goals. From concept to completion, we are dedicated to serve you.

Personnel:

Peter A. Rohlf (Chairman & CEO)
Peter Hans Rohlf (President)
Gregory Rohlf (Vice President)

67 Mountain Spring Drive
Sparta, NJ 07871
Tel: 973-726-0835
E-mail: yuri@uasrestoration.com
Website: uasrestoration.com

Type of Business:

HISTORICAL RESTORATION — CONSERVATION OF ART
With very few exceptions we shall repair any object of aesthetic, ecclesiastical, spiritual, historical, sentimental or simply monetary value. We offer following services: Complete restoration projects, including: architectural planning, management and execution. Design and fabrication of church furnishings and fixtures. Restoration of paintings, including: murals, frescoes, Greek or Russian icons. Canvas repairs, relining, cleaning, stretching. Custom framing. Goldleafing. Repairs of statuary made of gypsum, marble, wood, composit materials. Repairs of mosaics, tile, ceramics, plaster, terrazzo. Restoration of antique furniture and woodcarvings.
Our Art Gallery creates a range of fine art from ecclesiastical to contemporary, to church interiors, to decoration of living space.
Honestly, Yuri Mironoff

WILLET HAUSER

Architectural Glass, Inc.

Willet Hauser Architectural Glass, Inc.
811 East Cayuga Street
Philadelphia, PA 19124
Tel: 800-533-3960
Fax: 877-495-9486
Website: www.willethauser.com

Type of Business:

Since 1896 Willet Hauser Architectural Glass has a century-old legacy of stained glass design and over six decades of renowned restoration. Willet Hauser is the preeminent stained glass studio in the country and operates facilities in Winona, Minnesota, and Philadelphia, Pennsylvania. Willet Hauser has created or restored over 15,000 projects, including some of the most magnificent stained glass windows for religious buildings within the United States and in 14 countries around the world.

The proof of our artistry is in the projects that we have designed and restored. Here are just a few prominent examples of the thousands of churches and institutions that have been our clients during the last century:
The National Cathedral, Washington, DC; The Church Center, United Nations, NY; The Cathedral of St. Mary of the Assumption, San Francisco, CA; Cathedral of Mary Our Queen, Baltimore, MD; Princeton University Chapel; The Cadet Chapel, United States Military Academy, West Point; Arlington National Cemetery Chapel; The Cathedral of Christ the King, Atlanta, GA.
When you choose Willet Hauser to create or preserve your legacy in stained glass, you are placing it in the experienced hands of artists, designers and craftspeople whose sole purpose is to ensure that every detail reflects your unique vision in a tribute of glass, color, and light.
...You can trust your legacy to our legacy.

EDUCATION—GENERAL

National Catholic Development Conference
86 Front Street
Hempstead, NY 11550
Tel: 1-888-TRY-NCDC (879.6232)
Fax: 516.489.9287
Website: www.ncdc.org

Our Mission:

NCDC leads the Catholic development community toward excellence in the ministry of ethical fundraising through education, resources, networking, and advocacy.

The National Catholic Development Conference is the United States' largest membership association of charitable religious fundraisers. Our nonprofit membership consists of religious communities of men and women, shrines, social service agencies, schools, parishes, dioceses, seminaries and international relief agencies. Corporate partnership is available to businesses wishing to promote the interests and purposes of the Conference. NCDC affirms the mission of each of its member organizations by working for and with them in the context of fundraising as a ministry.

Membership in NCDC (subject to approval by the Board of Directors) is open to Catholic and non-Catholic nonprofit organizations as well as businesses that service nonprofit organizations. NCDC membership is organizationally-based, meaning all members of the fundraising staff of a member organization are entitled to member benefits. The same applies for members of a Corporate Partner's staff.

Special Membership rates are available for qualifying organizations.

Personnel:

Sr. Georgette Lehmuth, OSF (President/CEO glehmuth@ncdc.org)

Educational Opportunities

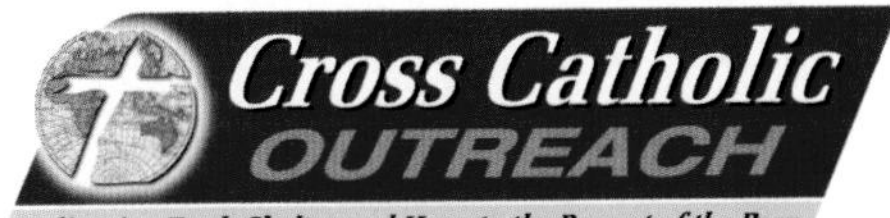

Formerly known as Cross International Catholic Outreach

2700 N. Military Trail, Suite 240, PO Box 273908
Boca Raton, FL 33427-3908 • **www.CrossCatholic.org**

Cross Catholic Outreach
2700 North Military Trail, Suite 240; P.O. Box 273908
Boca Raton, FL 33427-3908
Tel: 800-914-2420 x 141 or x121; Fax: 561-288-4397
E-mail: ejurczak@crosscatholic.org
Website: www.crosscatholic.org

Type of Business:

Cross Catholic Outreach (CCO) is a relief and development ministry founded to support Catholic programs for the poor in nearly 30 locations, including Haiti, the Philippines, and more than 20 countries in Africa, Latin America and Asia. Cardinal Edwin F. O'Brien is the organization's patron, and several prominent U.S. Bishops serve on its board of directors, providing leadership and strong financial accountability. Cross Catholic Outreach's primary goals are to serve the poorest of the poor and to educate American parishes about the international efforts of the Church. The ministry's Catholic outreach is extensive, including feeding programs, water projects, clinic and school construction, housing initiatives, educational and job training projects, programs benefitting orphans and more. It also has an official relationship with the Pontifical Council ***Cor Unum***, allowing it to collaborate on special projects directed by the Holy Father.

Personnel:

Most Rev. Sam Jacobs (Chairman, Board of Directors)
James Cavnar (President)
Msgr. Ted Bertagni (Director of Clergy and Diocese Relations)
Evelyn Jurczak (Manager of Parish Services)
Cecile Erlsten (Director of Outreach Priests)

GUEST HOUSE INSTITUTE

Guest House Institute
1601 Joslyn Road
Lake Orion, MI 48360
Tel: 800-626-6910; 248-391-4445
Fax: 248-391-0210
E-mail: crichards@guesthouse.org
Website: www.guesthouseinstitute.org

Type of Business:

We offer FREE workshops for Catholic Clergy and Religious. Highly qualified professionals are available as part of our Guest House Institute Speakers Bureau. These services are offered in the spirit of healing, through education and understanding. They are designed to lessen the damages of addictive disorders and emotional problems experienced by those in ministry and those served.

The mission of Guest House Institute is to promote health and spiritual wellness of Catholics by providing educational services regarding alcoholism and other addictions, and by promoting and providing research in alcoholism and other addictions affecting the Catholic Church.

Personnel:

Denise Bertin-Epp (President & Chief Operating Officer)
Colleen Richards (Project Coordinator)

National Catholic Council on Addictions
1601 Joslyn Road
Lake Orion, MI 48360
Tel: 248-391-4445, ext. 1200
Fax: 248-391-0210
E-mail: ncca@guesthouse.org
Website: www.nccatoday.org

Type of Business:

The NCCA, affiliated with the U.S. Conference of Catholic Bishops, and under the auspices of Guest House, Inc., is dedicated to the promotion of adequate treatment for all clergy, men and women religious, and laity who are suffering from alcoholism and other drug dependencies. NCCA also provides educational programs including workshops for dioceses, an annual Conference, also educational and "Spirituality Support" resources, including a free booklet: "Prayers for Addicted Persons and Their Loved Ones"; also a publication: "When They Won't (or Can't) Quit Alcohol or Drugs". The NCCA seeks to help those struggling to overcome an addiction and those engaged in pastoral ministry, including outreach to the nation's jail and prison ministries.

Seton Hall University
Immaculate Conception Seminary School of Theology
400 South Orange Avenue
South Orange, NJ 07079
Tel: 973-761-7491; Fax: 973-761-9577
E-mail: theology@shu.edu; Website: theology.shu.edu

Type of Business:

Immaculate Conception Seminary School of Theology (ICSST) is the school of theology of Seton Hall University and the major seminary of the Catholic Archdiocese of Newark. With a 152-year tradition of preparing committed Catholics for service to the Church, ICSST admits both seminarians studying for the Catholic priesthood and lay students. ICSST offers three graduate degree programs—the Master of Arts in Theology, the Master of Arts in Pastoral Ministry and the Master of Arts in Divinity—in addition to a Bachelor of Arts in Catholic Theology. The School also offers a number of certificate programs, including Christian Spirituality, Great Spiritual Books, Scripture Studies and Seminary's Theological Education for Parish Service (STEPS). Since Fall 2011, the School's Center for Diaconal Formation has provided graduate-level intellectual formation for permanent diaconate candidates.

Personnel:

Rev. Monsignor Robert F. Coleman, J.C.D. (Rector and Dean)
Rev. Robert K. Suszko, M.B.A., M.Div. (Vice Rector, Director of Formation and Business Manager)
Rev. Christopher M. Ciccarino, S.S.L., S.T.D. (Associate Dean)
Dianne M. Traflet, J.D., S.T.D. (Associate Dean)
Rev. Douglas J. Milewski, S.T.D. (Associate Dean for Undergraduate Programs)
Rev. Monsignor Joseph R Chapel, S.T.D. (Director of the Center for Diaconal Formation)

Spiritual Enrichment

Formerly known as Cross International Catholic Outreach
2700 N. Military Trail, Suite 240, PO Box 273908
Boca Raton, FL 33427-3908 • www.CrossCatholic.org

Cross Catholic Outreach
2700 North Military Trail, Suite 240; P.O. Box 273908
Boca Raton, FL 33427-3908
Tel: 800-914-2420 x 141 or x121; Fax: 561-288-4397
E-mail: ejurczak@crosscatholic.org; Website: www.crosscatholic.org

Type of Business:

Cross Catholic Outreach (CCO) is a relief and development ministry founded to support Catholic programs for the poor in nearly 30 locations, including Haiti, the Philippines, and more than 20 countries in Africa, Latin America and Asia. Cardinal Edwin F. O'Brien is the organization's patron, and several prominent U.S. Bishops serve on its board of directors, providing leadership and strong financial accountability. Cross Catholic Outreach's primary goals are to serve the poorest of the poor and to educate American parishes about the international efforts of the Church. The ministry's Catholic outreach is extensive, including feeding programs, water projects, clinic and school construction, housing initiatives, educational and job training projects, programs benefitting orphans and more. It also has an official relationship with the Pontifical Council ***Cor Unum***, allowing it to collaborate on special projects directed by the Holy Father.

Personnel:

Most Rev. Sam Jacobs (Chairman, Board of Directors)
James Cavnar (President)
Msgr. Ted Bertagni (Director of Clergy and Diocese Relations)
Evelyn Jurczak (Manager of Parish Services)
Cecile Erlsten (Director of Outreach Priests)

Holy Cross Family Ministries
Family Rosary
Family Theater Productions
Father Peyton Family Institute
Family Rosary International
518 Washington Street
North Easton, MA 02356
Tel: 508-238-4095
Fax: 508-238-3953
Website: www.hcfm.org

Type of Business:

Continuing the mission of our founder, Servant of God Father Patrick Peyton, C.S.C., Holy Cross Family Ministries serves Jesus Christ and His Church throughout the world by promoting and supporting the spiritual well-being of the family through products and programs.

Personnel:

Fr. John Phalen, C.S.C. (President)
Susan Wallace (Director of External Relations)
Beth Mahoney (Mission Director)

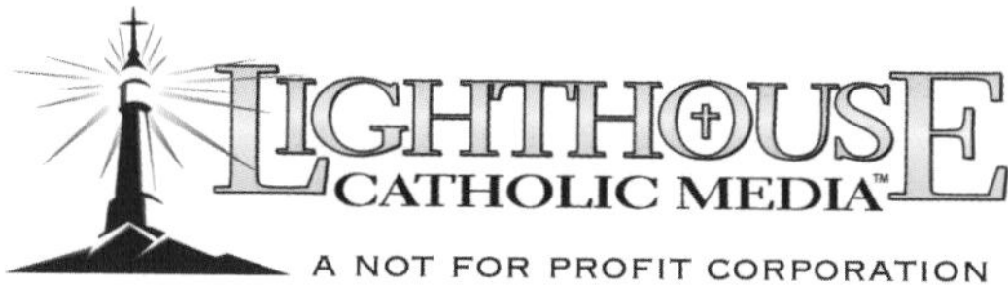

Lighthouse Catholic Media, NFP
303 E. State St.
Sycamore, IL 60178
Tel: 866-767-3155 (Toll Free)
Fax: 815-895-0333 Fax
E-mail: Tim@LighthouseCatholicMedia.org
Website: www.LigthouseCatholicMedia.org

Type of Business

Lighthouse Catholic Media, NFP is a not-for-profit organization dedicated to providing high quality Catholic audio CDs, mp3 downloads as an affordable and convenient way for parishioners to hear faith-filled presentations from the best Catholic speakers of our day.
These recordings provide an easy and effective way to foster catechesis, and provide parishioners with a powerful way to reach out to their family members, friends, etc.

"These CDs helped make the Mass come alive and left me with a hunger to learn more. What a blessing!"

Our **FAITHRAISER Kiosk Program** is proven effective, with approximately 5,000 parish customers, and the program is primarily self-funding.
We have over 150 CD titles available in English and Spanish, and our Starter Kit comes complete with a beautiful display stand, CDs, pamphlets, and now great books too! We also provide a proven success plan, support, and assistance to make your program a success.
For more information, please call 866-767-3155.

Personnel:

Mark Middendorf (President, Board of Directors)
Terry Barber (Chairman of the Board)
Dave Durand (VP of Sales)
Tim Truckenbrod (VP of Marketing and Operations)

ercy Center
pirituality & Conference Center
300 Adeline Drive
urlingame, CA 94010-5540
el: 650-340-7474
ax: 650-340-1299
mail: mc@mercyburl.org
ebsite: www.mercy-center.org and on Facebook

ype of Business:

Mercy Center Burlingame Conference and Retreat Center
We are known worldwide for pioneering work in spiritual direction, Taizé prayer and East-West meditation. Educational and spiritual conferences, retreats and training programs are offered year round on our beautiful, wooded campus. We offer summer internships in spiritual direction, on-going training in Centering Prayer, directed retreats and a personal sabbatical program. We will be glad to spend time with you finding the right program or retreat that fits your need. Limited scholarships available. Check out the videos on our website www.mercy-center.org to find out what our past program participants say about our transformational contemplative programs. Contact Colleen Shannon Soracco 650-340-7495 in our Program office for assistance.

ersonnel:

Suzanne Buckley (Director)
Colleen Shannon Soracco (Program Office)

National Catholic Development Conference
86 Front Street
Hempstead, NY 11550
Tel: 1-888-TRY-NCDC (879.6232)
Fax: 516.489.9287
Website: www.ncdc.org

Our Mission:

NCDC leads the Catholic development community toward excellence in the ministry of ethical fundraising through education, resources, networking, and advocacy.
The National Catholic Development Conference is the United States' largest membership association of charitable religious fundraisers. Our nonprofit membership consists of religious communities of men and women, shrines, social service agencies, schools, parishes, dioceses, seminaries and international relief agencies. Corporate partnership is available to businesses wishing to promote the interests and purposes of the Conference. NCDC affirms the mission of each of its member organizations by working for and with them in the context of fundraising as a ministry.
Membership in NCDC (subject to approval by the Board of Directors) is open to Catholic and non-Catholic nonprofit organizations as well as businesses that service nonprofit organizations. NCDC membership is organizationally-based, meaning all members of the fundraising staff of a member organization are entitled to member benefits. The same applies for members of a Corporate Partner's staff.
Special Membership rates are available for qualifying organizations.

Personnel:

Sr. Georgette Lehmuth, OSF (President/CEO glehmuth@ncdc.org)

FUNDRAISING—General

Lifetouch®
Connecting You through Family Photography

ifetouch Church Directories and Portraits
1000 Viking Drive, Suite 200
den Prairie, MN 55344
el: 800.303.0054
Website: www.lifetouch.com

ype of business

Connect your community! A customized pictorial family album program makes it easy for your parish to connect your members and reach out to the community. Lifetouch delivers the highest quality portraits and directories quickly and at NO COST to your parish. Every family photographed receives a FREE pictorial directory PLUS a free 8x10 portrait. Also, Lifetouch can share exclusive, proven techniques for reactivation. Partner with us on our community give-back programs such as Feed the Need where Lifetouch has provided funds for over 1.7 million meals donated back to local communities. Our standard program also includes our Online Community, outreach and fundraising support, directory design software, digital images of your members on CD, online scheduling for your members, and our Connections Calling Service – ALL FREE. Contact Lifetouch today for our special offers and fundraising opportunities.

Fundraising Counseling

CCS
461 Fifth Avenue
New York, NY 10017
Tel: 800-223-6733
Fax: 212-967-6451
E-mail: catholic@ccsfundraising.com
Website: www.fundingcatholiccauses.com

Type of Business:

Since 1947, CCS has played a vital role in assisting Catholic institutions address critical pastoral, educational, and charitable priorities. One of the largest, most widely recommended firms, CCS provides fundraising counsel and management services to Catholic institutions worldwide. Our methodology, combined with an emphasis on the precepts and principles of stewardship, has helped to shape some of the most successful and complex fundraising campaigns in the Catholic world, including the Archdioceses of Baltimore, Hartford, Philadelphia, St. Louis, and Washington D.C., and the Dioceses of Arlington, Austin, Biloxi, Brooklyn, Cleveland, Honolulu, Springfield, Stockton, and Tucson, among many others. CCS successfully plans and manages campaigns and stewardship initiatives for dioceses, parishes, universities, colleges, high schools, hospitals, homes for the aged, social service agencies, seminaries, and religious communities. CCS offices are located in New York, Boston, Baltimore, Washington D.C., Chicago, St. Louis, Seattle, San Francisco, Los Angeles, Toronto, London, and Dublin. To learn more visit www.fundingcatholiccauses.com or contact us at catholic@ccsfundraising.com or (800) 223-6733.

National Catholic Development Conference
86 Front Street
Hempstead, NY 11550
Tel: 1-888-TRY-NCDC (879.6232)
Fax: 516.489.9287
Website: www.ncdc.org

Our Mission:

NCDC leads the Catholic development community toward excellence in the ministry of ethical fundraising through education, resources, networking, and advocacy.

The National Catholic Development Conference is the United States' largest membership association of charitable religious fundraisers. Our nonprofit membership consists of religious communities of men and women, shrines, social service agencies, schools, parishes, dioceses, seminaries and international relief agencies. Corporate partnership is available to businesses wishing to promote the interests and purposes of the Conference. NCDC affirms the mission of each of its member organizations by working for and with them in the context of fundraising as a ministry.

Membership in NCDC (subject to approval by the Board of Directors) is open to Catholic and non-Catholic nonprofit organizations as well as businesses that service nonprofit organizations. NCDC membership is organizationally-based, meaning all members of the fundraising staff of a member organization are entitled to member benefits. The same applies for members of a Corporate Partner's staff.

Special Membership rates are available for qualifying organizations.

Personnel:

Sr. Georgette Lehmuth, OSF (President/CEO glehmuth@ncdc.org)

Fundraising Services

CCS
461 Fifth Avenue
New York, NY 10017
Tel: 800-223-6733
Fax: 212-967-6451
E-mail: catholic@ccsfundraising.com
Website: www.fundingcatholiccauses.com

Type of Business:

Since 1947, CCS has played a vital role in assisting Catholic institutions address critical pastoral, educational, and charitable priorities. One of the largest, most widely recommended firms, CCS provides fundraising counsel and management services to Catholic institutions worldwide. Our methodology, combined with an emphasis on the precepts and principles of stewardship, has helped to shape some of the most successful and complex fundraising campaigns in the Catholic world, including the Archdioceses of Baltimore, Hartford, Philadelphia, St. Louis, and Washington D.C., and the Dioceses of Arlington, Austin, Biloxi, Brooklyn, Cleveland, Honolulu, Springfield, Stockton, and Tucson, among many others. CCS successfully plans and manages campaigns and stewardship initiatives for dioceses, parishes, universities, colleges, high schools, hospitals, homes for the aged, social service agencies, seminaries, and religious communities. CCS offices are located in New York, Boston, Baltimore, Washington D.C., Chicago, St. Louis, Seattle, San Francisco, Los Angeles, Toronto, London, and Dublin. To learn more visit www.fundingcatholiccauses.com or contact us at catholic@ccsfundraising.com or (800) 223-6733.

Guidance in Giving, Inc.
Full Service Stewardship, Development and Campaign Consultants
225 Snedecor Avenue
Bayport, NY 11705
Tel: 888-757-5444; Cell: 631-553-9064
E-mail: mcusack@guidanceingiving.com
Website: www.guidanceingiving.com

Type of Business:

Guidance In Giving, Inc. is a Catholic organization that truly understanc the mission of the Catholic Church. Serving as stewardship, developme and campaign counsel to dioceses, parishes and schools, our firm ha extensive experience in conducting capital campaigns and implementir stewardship throughout the United States. In all of our development effor we utilize techniques that are continuously tested and refined. Service include: diocesan capital campaigns; diocesan annual appeals; diocesa development audits and feasibility studies; parish capital campaign offertory enhancement, implementing stewardship; parish feasibilit studies, school development audits, school feasibility studies, majc gifts solicitations and school capital campaigns. Additionally, the fir has an Hispanic and Multicultural Division and offers bilingual service To discuss your individual situation or to get a cost free analysis of you potential, please contact Michael R. Cusack, Chairman and CEO at 888 757-5444.

Personnel:

Michael R. Cusack (Chairman and CEO)
Michael V. Goodwin (President, Diocesan Division)
Joseph W. Zamorano (President, Parish Division)
Stephen A. Babcock (Executive Vice President, Parish Division)
Joseph E. Neville (Senior Vice President)
Carlos H. Proaño (Executive Vice President, Hispanic and Multicultural Division)

National Catholic Development Conference
86 Front Street
Hempstead, NY 11550
Tel: 1-888-TRY-NCDC (879.6232)
Fax: 516.489.9287
Website: www.ncdc.org

Our Mission:

NCDC leads the Catholic development community toward excellence in the ministry of ethical fundraising through education, resources, networking, and advocacy.

The National Catholic Development Conference is the United States largest membership association of charitable religious fundraisers. Our nonprofit membership consists of religious communities of men and women, shrines, social service agencies, schools, parishes, dioceses, seminaries and international relief agencies. Corporate partnership is available to businesses wishing to promote the interests and purposes of the Conference. NCDC affirms the mission of each of its member organizations by working for and with them in the context of fundraising as a ministry.

Membership in NCDC (subject to approval by the Board of Directors) is open to Catholic and non-Catholic nonprofit organizations as well as businesses that service nonprofit organizations. NCDC membership is organizationally-based, meaning all members of the fundraising staff of a member organization are entitled to member benefits. The same applies for members of a Corporate Partner's staff.

Special Membership rates are available for qualifying organizations.

Personnel:

Sr. Georgette Lehmuth, OSF (President/CEO glehmuth@ncdc.org)

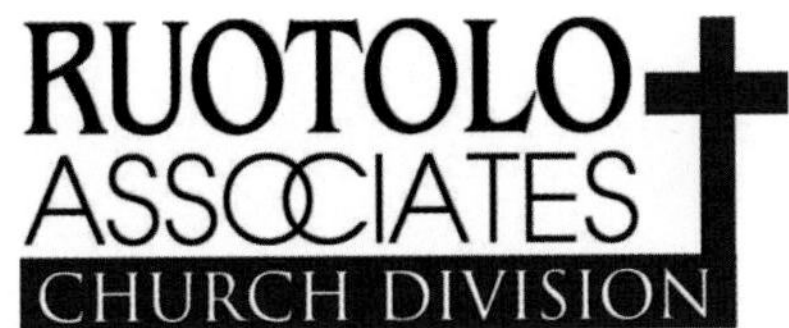

uotolo Associates Inc.
orizon Square
9 Broadway, Suite 210
resskill, NJ 07626
el: 800-786-8656
ax: 201-568-8783
-mail: info@ruotoloassoc.com
Vebsite: www.ruotoloassociates.com

ype of Business:

Since 1979, Ruotolo Associates has provided fundraising and public relations counsel to Catholic dioceses, parishes, schools, religious orders and social service agencies nationwide. Our services include: Stewardship efforts, feasibility/planning studies, comprehensive development programs, capital campaigns, annual funds, planned giving, strategic planning, marketing, public relations, executive search, student/membership recruitment, staff/volunteer training, seminars/workshops, TESS (Temporary Executive Staffing Services). Please call us to discuss an individualized creative strategy and solution for your advancement requirements.

ersonnel:

George C. Ruotolo, Jr., CFRE (Chairman and CEO)
Theresa A. Shubeck (Executive Vice President)
Douglas R. Held (Vice President)
Milissa S. Else, (Vice President and Director, Church Division)

LITURGICAL & CHURCH GOODS—General

Church Budget Envelope & Mailing Company
71 South Ellsworth Avenue
Salem, OH 44460
Tel: 800-446-9780
Fax: 330-337-5990
E-mail: info@churchbudget.com
Website: www.churchbudget.com

Type of Business:

An offering envelope company in Touch with the needs of todayís Catholic Parish! Since 1917, we have provided appealing offering envelope products that effectively translate the images and readings of the Catholic traditions. CBE has recently released a full line of 52 full color changing lectionary verses that can be printed on any of the product lines. This leading technology has witnessed a 35% savings in cost to each parish over traditional black ink.

Offertory Products include:

Annual Boxed Sets, Periodic Mail Services, Mailback Return Booklets, Prestige Series Holy Day Envelopes, Children Collection Envelopes, Diocesan Mailing Services, Full Color Print Capability, Electronic Giving Services, Parish Growth Software, NCOA Services, 24/7 Emergency Customer Service

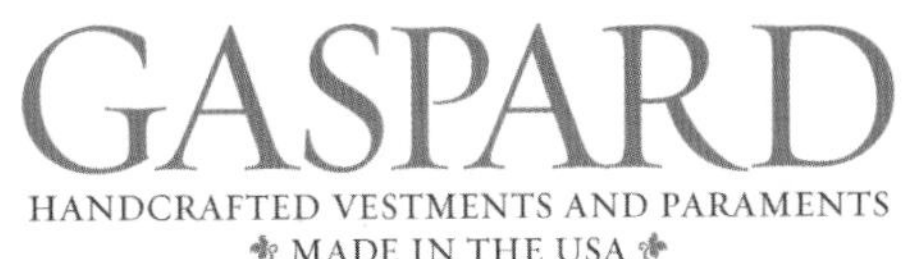

Gaspard, Inc.
(formerly The Robert Gaspard Company, Inc.)
200 N. Janacek Road
Brookfield, WI 53045
Tel: 800-784-6868 (toll free)
Fax: 800-784-7567
E-mail: info@gaspardinc.com
Website: www.gaspardinc.com

Type of Business:

For more than five decades customers have looked to Gaspard for fine quality, handcrafted vestments and paraments made in the USA. Offerings include the exquisite Castle Craft® collection; wardrobe essentials such as albs, surplices, cassocks, robes, and clergy shirts; extensive metalware offerings, fair linens, altar accessories, and communion ware.

Because your vestment and parament selections are made to order in our one and only location in Brookfield, Wisconsin, special sizes and custom designs are not a problem. One of our friendly Customer Service Representatives will be happy to help you find just the right size and style to enhance your spiritual expression. Please visit us online or call for a free catalog.

Personnel:

Jason R. Gaspard (President)
Joann Gaspard (Vice President)

Bibles, Hymnals, Missalettes

American Bible Society
Scripture Provision Program
1865 Broadway
New York, NY 10023
Tel.: 1-888-239-3976
Fax: 1-866-570-2077
E-mail: abscast@americanbible.org
Website: www.bibles.com

Type of Business:

American Bible Society offers an affordable variety of English, Spanish and international language Bibles for Catholic readers, including the New American Bible Revised Edition (NABRE), the Good News Translation, the New Revised Standard Version, the New Jerusalem Bible, Dios Habla Hoy and more. There are outstanding resources for children, youth and adults, as well as multimedia and academic resources. Call for a free Scripture Resource catalog.

Personnel:

Brian Sherry (Executive Director)

Candles, Incense

The A.I. Root Company d/b/a Root Candles
623 W Liberty Street
Medina, OH 44256
Tel: 800-289-7668
Fax: 330-725-5624
E-mail: church@rootcandles.com
Website: www.rootcandles.com

Type of Business:

Since 1869, every Root candle has been made using premium waxes featuring the finest beeswax and natural woven wicks for pure, clean flames that burn nearly one-third longer than ordinary liturgical altar candles. Root's devotion to purity, honesty and uncompromising quality has created "The Best Liturgical Candle in America."

Root's Full Line of Liturgical Candles, Church Goods & Services:

- **Altar, Sacramental, Hand-Decorated Paschals, Advent, Special Occasions, Votives, Devotional, Sanctuary Lights.**
- **Altar Bread & Wine, Palms & Ashes, Inspirational Gifts. Replating & Refinishing Services.**
- **Patron Saint & Custom Decal Candles for Grottos, Shrines or Chapels.**

Two factory locations: Medina, OH & San Antonio, TX.
Free 200+ page color catalog. 800-BUY-ROOT

Personnel:

Brad Root (President)

Cathedral Candle Corp/eximious ®
Website: www.cathedralcandles.com

Type of Business:

Classical symbolism and expressive liturgical design in the luxurious hand decorated artistry of SCULPTWAX, created and mastercrafted here in the United States... exclusively at Cathedral Candle Co.
Now in stock at your nearest church goods dealer.

C.M. Almy
Three American Lane, P.O. Box 2644
Greenwich, CT 06836-2644
Tel: 800-225-2569
Fax: 800-426-2569
E-mail: almyaccess@almy.com
Website: www.almy.com
Showroom in Old Greenwich, CT

Type of Business:

Almy was founded in 1892. We design and make virtually all of our products in our Maine shop. It is our mission to design furnishings that will grace your worship and to ensure their value by making them with the highest quality materials and craftsmanship. We make a complete line of liturgical vestments, clergy apparel, choir robes, candles, communion bread, linens, processional and altar appointments, and eucharistic vessels. We also offer custom design and fabrication of all Almy products, and repair and refurbishing of old metal appointments. Quik Ship© delivery of many popular items. All orders backed by The Almy Guarantee. Call, write, or e-mail for a free catalog.

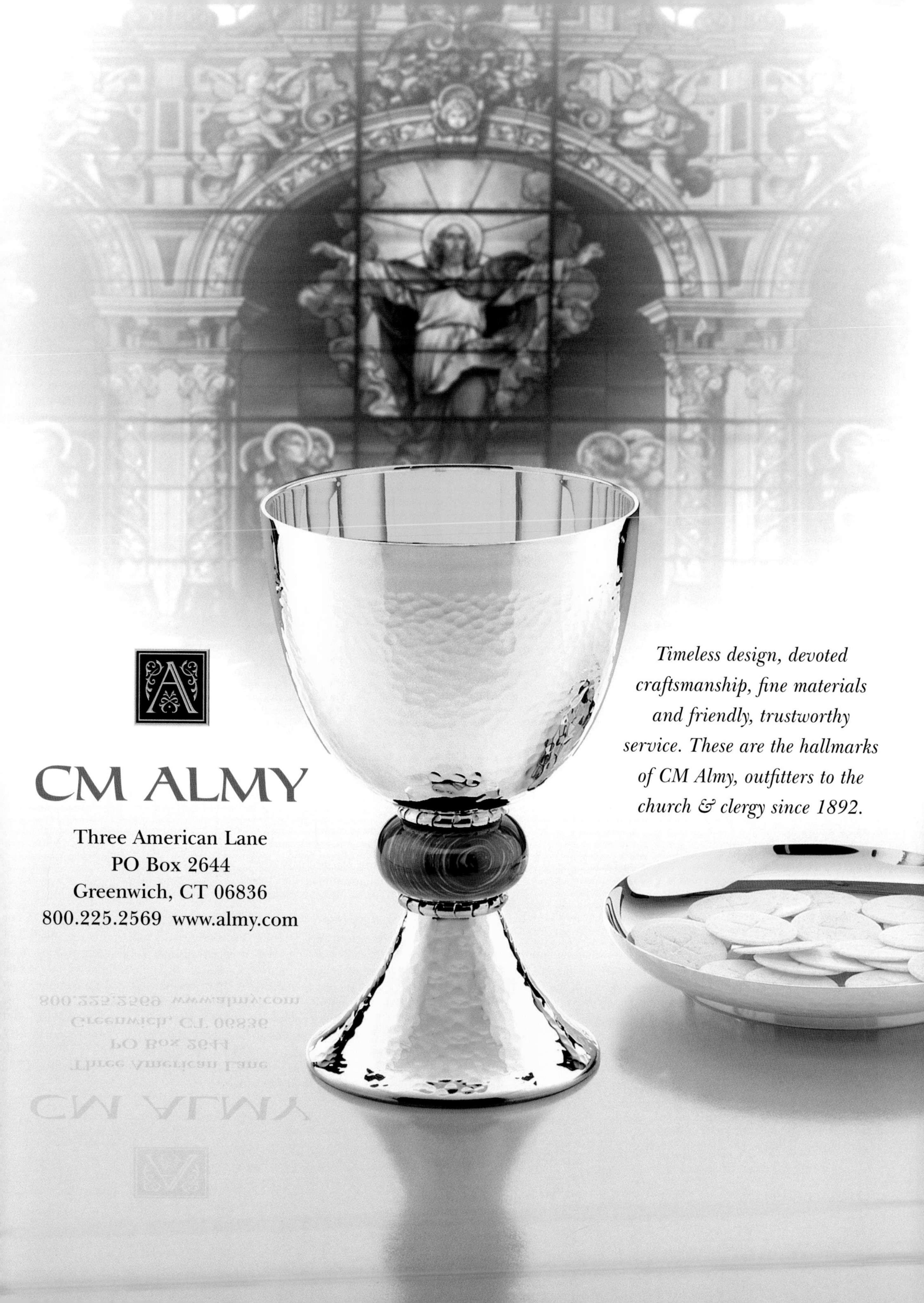
CM ALMY
Three American Lane
PO Box 2644
Greenwich, CT 06836
800.225.2569 www.almy.com
Timeless design, devoted craftsmanship, fine materials and friendly, trustworthy service. These are the hallmarks of CM Almy, outfitters to the church & clergy since 1892.

Chalices, Crosses & Metalware

C.M. Almy
Three American Lane, P.O. Box 2644
Greenwich, CT 06836-2644
Tel: 800-225-2569
Fax: 800-426-2569
E-mail: almyaccess@almy.com
Website: www.almy.com
Showroom in Old Greenwich, CT

Type of Business:

Almy was founded in 1892. We design and make virtually all of our products in our Maine shop. It is our mission to design furnishings that will grace your worship and to ensure their value by making them with the highest quality materials and craftsmanship. We make a complete line of liturgical vestments, clergy apparel, choir robes, candles, communion bread, linens, processional and altar appointments, and eucharistic vessels. We also offer custom design and fabrication of all Almy products, and repair and refurbishing of old metal appointments. Quik Ship© delivery of many popular items. All orders backed by The Almy Guarantee. Call, write, or e-mail for a free catalog.

Liturgical Certificates

Wolfson Creative
12872 E. Mexico Avenue
Aurora, CO 80012
Tel: 303-525-4991
E-mail: orders@wolfsoncreative.com
Website: www.wolfsoncreative.com

Type of Business:

Wolfson Creative offers electronic certificates (baptism and confirmation) for congregational use. The Wolfson Certificates are designed to teach (with Scripture and artwork) the marvelous treasure of the Gospel. They are designed to be keepsakes, framed and hung on the wall in the nursery, dining room or the office, as a constant reminder that we are baptized and confirmed, the heirs of the Lord's promises. It is our hope that these certificates help the Lord's children rejoice in the gifts of life, salvation and the forgiveness of sins. The unlimited prints makes offering these beautiful certificates very practical for every congregation.

Personnel:

Rev. Bryan Wolfmueller (bryan@wolfsoncreative.com)
Jason Hanson (jason@wolfsoncreative.com)

Offering Envelopes

Church Budget Envelope & Mailing Company
271 South Ellsworth Avenue
Salem, OH 44460
Tel: 800-446-9780
Fax: 330-337-5990
E-mail: info@churchbudget.com
Website: www.churchbudget.com

Type of Business:

An offering envelope company in Touch with the needs of todayís Catholic Parish! Since 1917, we have provided appealing offering envelope products that effectively translate the images and readings of the Catholic traditions. CBE has recently released a full line of 52 full color changing lectionary verses that can be printed on any of the product lines. This leading technology has witnessed a 35% savings in cost to each parish over traditional black ink.

Offertory Products include:

Annual Boxed Sets, Periodic Mail Services, Mailback Return Booklets, Prestige Series Holy Day Envelopes, Children Collection Envelopes, Diocesan Mailing Services, Full Color Print Capability, Electronic Giving Services, Parish Growth Software, NCOA Services, 24/7 Emergency Customer Service

Sacred Vessels

C.M. Almy
Three American Lane, P.O. Box 2644
Greenwich, CT 06836-2644
Tel: 800-225-2569
Fax: 800-426-2569
E-mail: almyaccess@almy.com
Website: www.almy.com
Showroom in Old Greenwich, CT

Type of Business:

Almy was founded in 1892. We design and make virtually all of our products in our Maine shop. It is our mission to design furnishings that will grace your worship and to ensure their value by making them with the highest quality materials and craftsmanship. We make a complete line of liturgical vestments, clergy apparel, choir robes, candles, communion bread, linens, processional and altar appointments, and eucharistic vessels. We also offer custom design and fabrication of all Almy products, and repair and refurbishing of old metal appointments. Quik Ship© delivery of many popular items. All orders backed by The Almy Guarantee. Call, write, or e-mail for a free catalog.

PROFESSIONAL ASSOCIATIONS & ORGANIZATIONS —General

Catholic Relief Services
228 W. Lexington Street
Baltimore, MD 21201-3443
Donations address:
P.O. Box 17090
Baltimore, MD 21203-7090
Tel: 877-435-7277; E-mail: webinfo@crs.org
Website: www.crs.org
Type of Business:

Catholic Relief Services is the official international humanitarian agency of the Catholic community in the United States. CRS alleviates suffering and provides assistance to people in need in nearly 100 countries, without regard to race, religion or nationality. The agency is called to save lives, address the root causes and effects of poverty, promote the sacredness and dignity of human life, and help build more just and peaceful societies outside the United States. CRS' relief and development work is accomplished through programs of emergency response, HIV, health, agriculture, education, microfinance and peacebuilding. CRS is efficient and effective. Ninety-five percent of the agency's expenditures go directly to programs that benefit the poor overseas. CRS programs touch more than 100 million lives.

Personnel:

Dr. Carolyn Y. Woo (President & CEO)
Mr. Sean Callahan (Executive Vice President, Overseas Operations)
Mr. Mark Palmer (Executive Vice President, Chief Financial Officer)
Ms. Joan Rosenhauer (Executive Vice President, U.S. Operations)

CFCA®

Christian Foundation for Children and Aging (CFCA)
1 Elmwood Avenue
Kansas City, KS 66103
Tel: 913-384-6500 or 800-875-6564
Fax: 913-384-2211
E-mail: mail@cfcausa.org
Website: www.hopeforafamily.org
Type of Business:

Christian Foundation for Children and Aging is an international nonprofit working in 22 developing countries to help families break the cycle of poverty. CFCA's Hope for a Family sponsorship program helps provide basic resources, opportunities and encouragement to children, youth, the elderly and their families through the generous support of individual sponsors. CFCA sponsorship helps provide food, education, health care and livelihood programs. Moreover, it gives families hope that they can create a path out of poverty for their children. CFCA seeks to provide a viable and trustworthy way for the Catholic faithful to participate in the Church's preferential option for the poor and vulnerable. Founded by lay Catholics acting on the Gospel call to serve those living in poverty, CFCA works with and serves persons of all faith traditions.

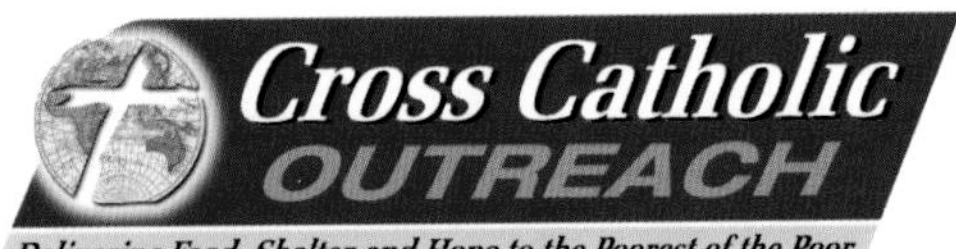

Delivering Food, Shelter and Hope to the Poorest of the Poor

Formerly known as Cross International Catholic Outreach

2700 N. Military Trail, Suite 240, PO Box 273908
Boca Raton, FL 33427-3908 • **www.CrossCatholic.org**

Cross Catholic Outreach
2700 North Military Trail, Suite 240
P.O. Box 273908
Boca Raton, FL 33427-3908
Tel: 800-914-2420 x 141 or x121; Fax: 561-288-4397
E-mail: ejurczak@crosscatholic.org
Website: www.crosscatholic.org

Type of Business:

Cross Catholic Outreach (CCO) is a relief and development ministry founded to support Catholic programs for the poor in nearly 30 locations, including Haiti, the Philippines, and more than 20 countries in Africa, Latin America and Asia. Cardinal Edwin F. O'Brien is the organization's patron, and several prominent U.S. Bishops serve on its board of directors, providing leadership and strong financial accountability. Cross Catholic Outreach's primary goals are to serve the poorest of the poor and to educate American parishes about the international efforts of the Church. The ministry's Catholic outreach is extensive, including feeding programs, water projects, clinic and school construction, housing initiatives, educational and job training projects, programs benefitting orphans and more. It also has an official relationship with the Pontifical Council ***Cor Unum***, allowing it to collaborate on special projects directed by the Holy Father.

Personnel:

Most Rev. Sam Jacobs (Chairman, Board of Directors)
James Cavnar (President)
Msgr. Ted Bertagni (Director of Clergy and Diocese Relations)
Evelyn Jurczak (Manager of Parish Services)
Cecile Erlsten (Director of Outreach Priests)

FOOD FOR THE POOR, INC.
Saving Lives... Transforming Communities... Renewing Hope

Food for the Poor Inc.
6401 Lyons Road
Coconut Creek, FL 33073
Tel: 954-427-2222; Fax: 954-570-7654
Website: www.FoodForThePoor.org

Type of Business:

Food For The Poor, named by The Chronicle of Philanthropy as the largest international relief and development organization in the United States, serves the destitute in 17 countries of the Caribbean and Latin America through churches and missionaries. Since its founding in 1982, Food For The Poor has distributed more than 59,610 containers of lifesaving aid to the region and maintains an operating expense ratio under 4%. Food For The Poor provides food, housing, health care, water projects, education, emergency relief and micro-enterprise assistance to millions of the poor in the region.

Personnel:

Robin G. Mahfood (President/CEO)
Angel A. Aloma (Executive Director)
Vicki Kaufmann (Director, Speakers Bureau)
Joan C. Vidal (Manager, Church Relations)

National Catholic Development Conference
86 Front Street
Hempstead, NY 11550
Tel: 1-888-TRY-NCDC (879.6232)
Fax: 516.489.9287
Website: www.ncdc.org

Our Mission:

NCDC leads the Catholic development community toward excellence in the ministry of ethical fundraising through education, resources, networking, and advocacy.

The National Catholic Development Conference is the United States' largest membership association of charitable religious fundraisers. Our nonprofit membership consists of religious communities of men and women, shrines, social service agencies, schools, parishes, dioceses, seminaries and international relief agencies. Corporate partnership is available to businesses wishing to promote the interests and purposes of the Conference. NCDC affirms the mission of each of its member organizations by working for and with them in the context of fundraising as a ministry.

Membership in NCDC (subject to approval by the Board of Directors) is open to Catholic and non-Catholic nonprofit organizations as well as businesses that service nonprofit organizations. NCDC membership is organizationally-based, meaning all members of the fundraising staff of a member organization are entitled to member benefits. The same applies for members of a Corporate Partner's staff.

Special Membership rates are available for qualifying organizations.

Personnel:

Sr. Georgette Lehmuth, OSF (President/CEO glehmuth@ncdc.org)

National Federation of Priest' Councils
333 N. Michigan, Suite 1205
Chicago, IL 60601
Tel: 312-442-9700
Fax: 312-442-9709
E-mail: nfpc@nfpc.org
Website: www.nfpc.org

Type of Business:

Since 1968, the NFPC has been the only organization of its kind to support member Presbyteral Councils, Associations and Affiliates through collaboration, communication, continuing formation, research and the voicing of priestly concerns. The organization collaborates with bishops, deacons, religious, laity and national church organizations to further the spiritual renewal of priestly life. Programs, publications, annual conferences and research help promote fraternity among United States priests.

Priests for Life
P.O. Box 141172
Staten Island, NY 10314
Tel: 888-735-3448; 718-980-4400; Fax: 718-980-6515
E-mail: mail@priestsforlife.org
Website: www.priestsforlife.org

Type of Business:

Priests for Life is the largest ministry in the Catholic Church working exclusively to end abortion and euthanasia. Priests for Life helps both clergy and laity to present the pro-life message effectively, and to work strategically to advance the protection of life. We provide Resources, Networking with Priests Worldwide, Seminars on Abortion, Regular Newsletter, Pro-Life Strategies, Consultation and assist with Organizing Activities. Subscribe to our biweekly column (free) at: subscribe@priestsforlife.org.

Fraternal Organizations

Knights of Columbus
1 Columbus Plaza
New Haven, CT 06510
Tel: 203-752-4000; Customer service (insurance): 800-380-9995
Website: kofc.org

Type of Business:

The Knights of Columbus is the world's largest Catholic fraternal organization. Founded by Father Michael J. McGivney in 1882 as a fraternal benefit society, the K of C has maintained its original mission to render financial assistance to members and their families. In addition, social and supportive fellowship is promoted among members through a variety of educational, charitable, religious, community and other service programs and initiatives. The K of C has more than 1.8 million members throughout North and Central America, the Philippines, the Caribbean, Poland, Guam and Saipan.

The organization's history shows the foresight of Father McGivney, whose cause for sainthood is under consideration by the Holy See. Father McGivney's ideals have helped families obtain financial security through fraternal programs for 130 years. Beyond this, the Knights of Columbus contributes time and money worldwide to service to the Church and charitable initiatives. Last year, Knights contributed more than $154 million and over 70 million volunteer service hours to worthy causes across the globe.

Prayer & Devotional Groups

Circle of Prayers
P.O. Box 373
Depew, NY 14043
Tel: 716 352-7971
E-mail: comments@circleofprayers.com
Website: www.circleofprayers.com

Type of Business:

Come pray with us. Establish your own Parish Online Prayer Community at CircleofPrayers.com.

Membership is FREE.

Form an online prayer group and bolster your connection with your parishioners, expand the power of their prayers and help strengthen their faith. Join with your parishioners, and others around the world, in prayers selected by you and your group members. Post prayer requests for your parishioners, for the sick and the needy, friends and family.

At CircleofPrayers.com, you can also post prayer memorials, and utilize our email prayer reminder service to keep in touch with members. And, it is easy to use. Also explore our prayer activities for youth, videos and audios, and our prayer blog and forum. CircleofPrayers.com is available in 5 languages.

Private Associations of Lay Faithful

The Coming Home Network International
P.O. Box 8290
Zanesville, OH 43701
Tel: 740-450-1175
E-mail: info@chnetwork.org
Website: www.chnetwork.org

Type of Business:

The Coming Home Network International (CHNI) exists to help inquiring clergy as well as laity of other traditions to return home and then be at home in the Catholic Church.

Our goal is to assist the Church in fulfilling its mission of evangelization and its call for Christian unity, as proclaimed by Pope John Paul II in his encyclical, "That They May Be One" (Ut Unum Sint).

We offer contacts, assistance and fellowship, along with resources such as books, audio/video presentations, a monthly newsletter, and online discussion groups. In addition, we produce "The Journey Home" television show and "Deep in Scripture" radio show weekly in partnership with the Eternal Word Television Network (EWTN) for broadcast worldwide.

Personnel:

Marcus Grodi (President and Founder)
Kevin Lowry (Executive Vice President/COO)
Jim Anderson (Senior Adviser, History and Theology)
Ann Moore (Financial Coordinator)

Pioneer Total Abstinence Association of the Sacred Heart
International Headquarters:
Pioneer Total Abstinence Association
27 Upper Sherrard Street
Dublin 1
IRELAND
Tel: 00 353 1 874 94 64
E-mail: pioneer@jesuit.ie
Website: www.pioneerassociation.ie
Founded December 28th 1898, St Francis Xavier Church, Dublin, Ireland

Type of Business:
The chief end of the Association is the promotion of sobriety. Members consecrate their total abstinence from alcohol combined with daily intercessory prayer in honour of the Sacred Heart for the benefit of relatives and friends suffering from the effects of addiction. Among the glories of the Association is Venerable Matt Talbot, the reformed alcoholic and candidate for canonisation.

Personnel:
Father Bernard J McGuckian, SJ (Central Spiritual Director)

PUBLISHERS—General

Convivium Press, Inc.
7661 N.W., 68th Street, Suite 108
Miami, FL 33166
Tel: 305-889-0489, 786-866-9718; Fax: 305-887-5463
E-mail: convivium@conviviumpress.com, sales@conviviumpress.com, ventas@conviviumpress.com
Website: www.conviviumpress.com

Type of Business:
Convivium Press provides a significant contribution to religious studies through English and Spanish translations of classic authors and contemporary voices for academic and non-academic readers.
In the spirit of its name, Convivium Press books enrich conversation, understanding, and appreciation among religions and cultures. They inspire a dialogue at the interface of ethics and social problems, with a solid theological perspective. And they encourage reconciliation and cooperative endeavors through printed and online publications and social networking.We publish new works and superlative and accessible translations of recognized international authors, including N. T. Wright, Albert Vanhoye, Luis F. Ladaria, José Antonio Pagola, Bernard Sesboüé, Tormas Spidlik, John Main, Antoine Vergote, Sergio Bastianel, Hosffman Ospino, Roberto Goizueta, and José Ignacio González Faus.
Our books are the result of key collaborations with the International Society for the Studies of Biblical and Semitic Rhetoric, the Pontifical Gregorian University, the Institute for Hispanic/Latino Theology and Ministry at Barry University, and the World Community for Christian Meditation. Convivium Press books support the religious formation of Hispanic/Latino communities in the U.S. through the establishment of joint editorial projects.

Personnel:
Dr. Rafael Luciani (Editor in Chief, rluciani@conviviumpress.com)
Dr. Felix Palazzi (Spanish Market Director, fpalazzi@conviviumpress.com)
Alan Fisboin (Sales Executive, English, afisboin@conviviumpress.com)
Beatriz Méndez L., (Sales Manager, Spanish, bmendez@conviviumpress.com)

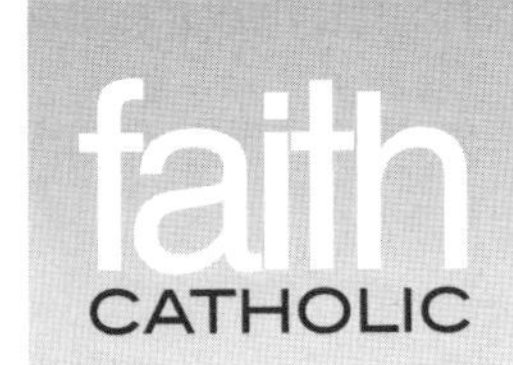

FAITH Catholic
1500 East Saginaw Street
Lansing, MI 48906
E-mail: pobrien@faithcatholic.com
Website: www.faithcatholic.com

Type of Business:
FAITH Catholic specializes in partnering with dioceses and Catholic entities to create effective custom magazines. We make it easy. With FAITH Catholic, it's your magazine. You have 100% control. Our proven magazine format is unique in that it reaches adults of all ages. Our purchasing power makes publishing a magazine affordable. Contact FAITH Catholic for turn-key marketing solutions in any combination of the following areas: editorial, graphic design, printing, mailing, online and data services.

Personnel:
Patrick O'Brien (President and CEO)
Elizabeth Martin Solsburg (Editorial Director)
Cynthia Vandecar (Marketing Manager)

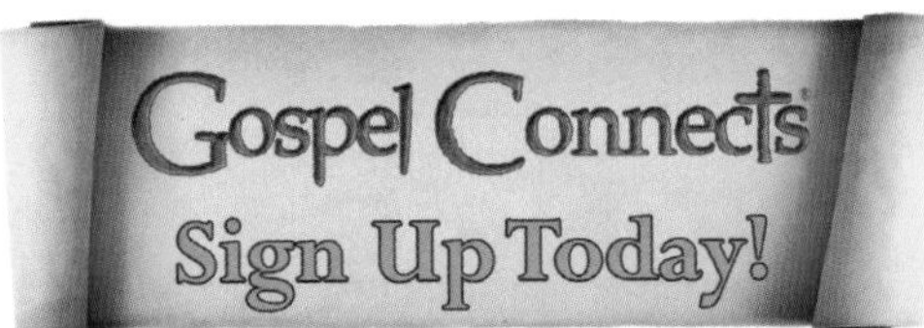

Gospel Connects®
Tel: 770-335-1822
E-mail: Richard@gospelconnects.com
Free Preview sign up go to www.previewgc.com
For more information go to www.gospelconnects.com

Type of Business:
◈ Gospel Connects, is an easy, inexpensive and efficient tool for Pastors to use as they guide their parishioners to become well-formed Catholic men and women who are prepared to confront the challenges posed by our growing secular culture.

◈ Helps Pastors develop a more personal relationship with their parishioners and shepherd them closer to our Lord.

◈ Diocese and Parish specific with each Pastor and individual in the parish having their own secure personal account that can be reached at anytime, anywhere, on any Internet device.

◈ The weekly Communiqué consists of the "Sunday Gospel", a "Conversation with the Pastor," taken in part from the previous Sunday's Homily, a "Resolution" for the week, special parish "News" section and "Going Deeper" section for more in-depth reading on that week's Gospel.

OCP
(Oregon Catholic Press)
5536 NE Hassalo
Portland, OR 97213
Tel: 1-800-LITURGY (548-8749)
Fax: 1-800-462-7329
E-mail: liturgy@ocp.org
Website: ocp.org

Type of Business:

Do you want to **engage, unite** and **inspire** your assembly in worship? Join over two-thirds of the U.S. Catholic churches who turn to OCP for resources to serve the needs of their community. These include: seasonal and annual missals (*Today's Missal, Breaking Bread w/Readings, Misal del Día, Unidos en Cristo/United in Christ*); hymnals with intergenerational and multicultural music for liturgy and prayer (*Journeysongs; Spirit & Song; Flor y Canto; One Faith, Una Voz; Thán Ca Dân Chúa*); contemporary music for Catholic worship (spiritandsong.com); choral music; liturgy planning tools (Today's Liturgy, Liturgia y Canción); online resources (Liturgy.com, LicenSingOnline.org) and Pastoral Press books. OCP, a not-for-profit organization based in Portland, Oregon, has been in operation for over 80 years, is distributed worldwide and known for excellent customer service. Call us today to find out why! Custom workshops, conferences and events are also available (English, Spanish and bilingual).

Personnel:

John J. Limb (Publisher)
Tim Dooley (Customer Service Manager)
Mónica Rada (Marketing Manager)

St Pauls/Alba House Publishing
2187 Victory Boulevard
Staten Island, NY 10314
Tel: 800-343-ALBA (2522)
Fax: 718-698-8390
E-mail: orders@stpauls.us or sales@stpauls.us
Website: www.stpauls.us

Type of Business

ST PAULS/Alba House Publishing is a ministry of the Society of St. Paul. The specific mission of the Pauline Family (6 religious congregations and 4 secular institutes worldwide) is evangelization through the media of social communications. ST PAULS/Alba House is one of the instruments used for propagation of the faith. We are ministers who are responsible for accompanying the people of God towards His Kingdom, following the teaching of the universal and local Church.

Personnel:

Rev. Edmund C. Lane, SSP (Editor)
Rev. Matthew Roehrig. SSP (Marketing Director)
Rev. Arcangel Cardenas, SSP (Spanish Editor/Distribution)
Bro. Peter Lyne, SSP (Promotion)

spiritandsong.com
5536 NE Hassalo
Portland, OR 97213
Tel: 1-800-LITURGY (548-8749)
Fax: 1-800-462-7329
E-mail: support@spiritandsong.com
Website: spiritandsong.com

Type of Business:

If you are looking to reach youth and young adults with the best contemporary songs for Catholic worship, look no further. A division of OCP, spiritandsong.com is the place for the latest releases from both big name composers (including Steve Angrisano, Josh Blakesley, Tom Booth, Sarah Hart, Matt Maher, Jesse Manibusan) and emerging talents (including Jackie François and Ike Ndolo). It is also home to the popular streaming video program The Commons, giving visitors live, in-studio performances, artist interviews and a behind-the-scenes look at their favorite songs. OCP, a not-for-profit organization based in Portland, Oregon, has been in operation for over 80 years and is distributed worldwide. Nearly all Catholic churches in the United States turn to OCP for innovative solutions to engage, unite and inspire their multicultural and intergenerational congregation in worship.
More information is available at ocp.org and 1-800-548-8749.

Personnel:

Robert Feduccia (General Manager)
Tom Booth (Associate Director, Artists and Repertoire)
Mónica Rada (Marketing Director)

Magazines & Journals

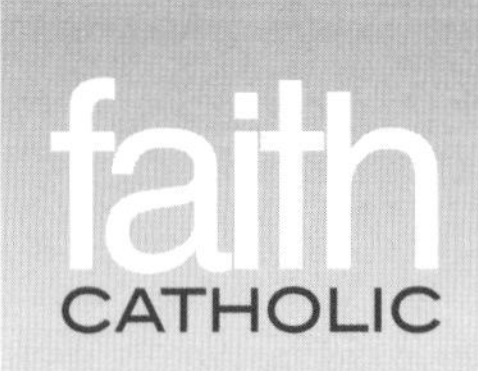

FAITH Catholic
1500 East Saginaw Street
Lansing, MI 48906
E-mail: pobrien@faithcatholic.com
Website: www.faithcatholic.com

Type of Business:

FAITH Catholic specializes in partnering with dioceses and Catholic entities to create effective custom magazines. We make it easy. With FAITH Catholic, it's your magazine. You have 100% control. Our proven magazine format is unique in that it reaches adults of all ages. Our purchasing power makes publishing a magazine affordable. Contact FAITH Catholic for turn-key marketing solutions in any combination of the following areas: editorial, graphic design, printing, mailing, online and data services.

Personnel:

Patrick O'Brien (President and CEO)
Elizabeth Martin Solsburg (Editorial Director)
Cynthia Vandecar (Marketing Manager)

National Catholic Reporter
115 E. Armour Blvd.
Kansas City, MO 64111
Tel: 800-333-7373
Website: NCRonline.org

Type of Business:

Established in 1964, *National Catholic Reporter (NCR)* began as a newspaper and is now a print and web news source that stands as one of the few truly independent journalistic outlets for Catholics and others who struggle with the complex moral and societal issues of the day. *NCR* is a religious news source with worldly interests; we report and comment on the church in the modern world and also cover the religious, political and social forces shaping public policies and institutions. *NCR* is committed to providing a forum for open and informed discussion on Church issues by concerned people of faith.

Twelve-time winner of the general excellence award from the Catholic Press Association, *NCR* is an essential tool for American Catholics who care about the church and want to further its mission in the world.

Parish Directories

Lifetouch®
Connecting You through Family Photography

Lifetouch Church Directories and Portraits
11000 Viking Drive, Suite 200
Eden Prairie, MN 55344
Tel: 800.303.0054
Website: www.lifetouch.com

Type of business

Connect your community! A customized pictorial family album program makes it easy for your parish to connect your members and reach out to the community. Lifetouch delivers the highest quality portraits and directories quickly and at NO COST to your parish. Every family photographed receives a FREE pictorial directory PLUS a free 8x10 portrait. Also, Lifetouch can share exclusive, proven techniques for reactivation. Partner with us on our community give-back programs such as Feed the Need where Lifetouch has provided funds for over 1.7 million meals donated back to local communities. Our standard program also includes our Online Community, outreach and fundraising support, directory design software, digital images of your members on CD, online scheduling for your members, and our Connections Calling Service – ALL FREE. Contact Lifetouch today for our special offers and fundraising opportunities.

SPECIAL CARE FACILITIES—General

Guest House, Inc.
1601 Joslyn Road
Lake Orion, MI 48360
Tel: 800-626-6910; 248-391-4445; Fax: 248-391-0210
E-mail: info@guesthouse.org
Website: www.guesthouse.org

Type of Business:

Guest House, Inc. is a lay-owned, lay-operated nonprofit corporation established in 1956. With the approbation of the Catholic hierarchy, it operates special residential treatment centers for Catholic priests, deacons, brothers, sisters and seminarians with addictions from all over the world. The facilities are licensed and accredited.

GUEST HOUSE FOR WOMEN RELIGIOUS Tel.: 800-626-6910; 248-391-3100; Fax: 248-393-0186; E-mail: ghousemi@guesthouse.org

GUEST HOUSE FOR CLERGY AND MEN RELIGIOUS Tel.: 800-634-4155; 507-288-4693; Fax: 507-288-1240; E-mail: ghousemn@tds.net

Personnel:

Denise Bertin-Epp (President and Chief Operating Officer)

The St. Louis Consultation Center
2039 N. Geyer Road
St. Louis, MO 63131
Tel: 314-909-4620
E-mail: information@stlconsult.org
Website: www.stlconsult.org

Type of Business:

The Saint Louis Consultation Center is an internationally recognized treatment center founded in 1992 for clergy and vowed men and religious women. The Consultation Center provides (a) a comprehensive assessment process for behavioral and/or psychological issues; (b) a six-month intensive behavioral treatment program; and (c) a two year Aftercare program to monitor progress over the long-term. All of our services are conducted in collaboration with religious leadership. Our experienced staff of lay and religious professionals provides results-oriented services to priests and vowed religious men and women in a respectful, practical, and cost-effective manner which recognizes the central role spirituality plays in the treatment process. We specialize in the out-patient treatment of alcoholism, behavioral problems, anger management, sexual misconduct, compulsive behavior, vocational discernment, and acculturation. We are also available for candidate assessments for those considering religious life or priesthood. Please visit our website for detailed information about our programs and services: www.stlconsult.org.

Personnel:

Dr. Paul M. Midden (Clinical Director)

Best Catholic Pilgrimages™

"The Most Trusted & Respected Name in Catholic Group Travel"

Best Catholic Pilgrimages™
500 N. Michigan Avenue
Chicago, IL 60611
Tel: 800-908-2378; Fax: 888-647-2378
E-mail: info@religious-travel.com
Website: www.gobestcatholic.com

Type of Business:

Best Catholic Pilgrimages™ "Serving Generations of Catholics" is not a retail travel agency. We are a tour operator and Wholesale Land Destination Management Company that specializes in Catholic Tours to Shrines and Holy Sites Worldwide. Whether a small group of 15 people, a large group of 500+, a Consistory, Pallium, Ad Limina, Conference, Special Event, Youth Group, or a Choir Group, we have a proven satisfaction record! There are no third parties commissions to increase the cost to your group. Our professional staff will handle all the administrative details. Best Catholic Pilgrimages is accustomed to serving the needs requirements and demands of clientele with high expectations.

Round trip air from major Airports, Hotels from Religious to 5 Star Deluxe Hotels, Breakfast Daily, Lunch and Dinners per itinerary, Private Deluxe Motor Coaches, Professional Tour Manager, Hospitality Desk in Hotel Lobby, Licensed Local Guides, All entrance fees on sightseeing, All transfers per Itinerary, Luggage Porterage, Land and Road Taxes, Hotel taxes and service charges, Mass Daily

"Travel with Peace of Mind"

Personnel:

Susan Mary Ives (President)
Fred Davidson (Vice President)

"The Most Trusted Name in Religious Group Travel"

Catholic Travel Centre
4444 Riverside Drive, Ste. 301
Burbank, CA 91505
Tel: 800-553-5233; 818-848-9449
Fax: 818-848-0712
E-mail: Groups@GoCatholicTravel.com
Website: www.GoCatholicTravel.com

Type of Business:

A reputation for extraordinary quality has made Catholic Travel Centre the choice of groups that demand exacting service and exceptional attention to detail. With meticulous detail, we will plan a one-of-a-kind pilgrimage tour catering to your group's specific interests. We can work within the constraints of any budget.

Our client list includes prestigious Catholic institutions nationwide, returning year-after-year to Catholic Travel Centre. To start planning your tour please call 800-553-5233 or visit our web site at GoCatholicTravel.com.

Go with Catholic Travel Centre, "The most trusted name in customized religious group travel."

Personnel:

J. Scott Scherer (President)
Inga Duranovic (Director of Operations)

The Leo House
332 West 23rd Street
New York, NY 10011
Tel: 212-929-1010; Fax: 212-366-6801

For reservations requests you can:

- Call 212-929-1010, ext. 219
- E-mail: lhreservations@332west23nyc.org
- Go to our new secure website: leohousenyc.org

Type of Business:

Centrally located in Manhattan, The Leo House is a quiet, not-for-profit, Catholic Christian Guesthouse with an old world charm. We provide Christian hospitality to travelers of all races and religions, both foreign and domestic. The dedicated staff includes the Sisters of St. Agnes and lay personnel. We offer single and double rooms with private or shared baths (all rooms have a sink and toilet). Rooms are equipped with color cable TV and we have a new telephone system. A wonderful buffet-style breakfast is served every day except Sunday (7:30 to 10:30 am) at a cost of $9 per person. We also have an a la carte breakfast menu. Baking is performed on premises. Relax in our peaceful garden, meditate or pray in our chapel; we also have Wi-Fi in several locations in the guesthouse.

The Chelsea neighborhood offers a wide variety of entertainment, reasonably priced restaurants, and is in walking distance to Broadway's theater district, Madison Square Garden and the Fashion District. Transportation to many other tourist attractions such as, Greenwich Village, Little Italy and Chinatown, is within half a block walking distance. Single and double rooms are $105 to $140 per night. **WE RECOMMEND RESERVATIONS TWO and 1/2 MONTHS IN ADVANCE.** We only accept Visa and Mastercard. **Cash, Travelers Checks, Personal Checks or Money Orders will be not accepted.**

Personnel:

Frank J. Castro (Executive Director)
Lucy Morales (Front Desk Manager)

Nawas International Travel
The Leader in Catholic Pilgrimages for 63 years

Nawas International Travel
777 Post Road, Suite 305
Darien, CT 06820-4721
Tel: 800-221-4984
E-mail: George@Nawas.com; Website: www.NAWAS.com

On the West Coast:

1100 Alma Street, Suite 100
Menlo Park, CA 94025-3344
Tel: 800-288-2688; E-mail: Sami@Nawas.com

Type of Business:

NAWAS INTERNATIONAL proudly celebrates 63 years of operating inspiring and affordable pilgrimages to the Holy Land, Rome and Italy, and other important Catholic Shrines.

Since 1949 Nawas has also been designing and operating pilgrimages to the Holy Land, Italy, Lourdes, Fatima, Santiago de Compostela, the Shrines of Europe, Ireland, Poland, Greece, Turkey with the Steps of St. Paul, and more. We are dedicated to delivering high quality programs and the finest pilgrimages available at the most competitive prices. Plus, we offer excellent tour host benefits—you can travel FREE with as few as 6 or 8 paying passengers! Thousands of Catholic leaders have organized their travel plans through Nawas. Call us toll free and we'll show you how to promote your pilgrimage and travel FREE!

Personnel:

Soli Nawas (President)
George Khoury (Executive Vice President (Darien, CT))
Sami Nawas (Vice President)
Neil Dellis (Vice President)

John XXIII Retreat Center
407 W. McDonald Street
Hartford City, IN 47348
Tel: 765-348-4008; 888-882-1391
E-mail: john23rd@sbcglobal.net
Website: www.john23rdretreatcenter.com

Type of Business:

John XXIII Retreat Center provides a safe, nurturing, hospitable and homelike environment open to all people of all faiths. Founded under the inspiration of the Blessed Pope John XXIII, and sponsored by the Diocese of Lafayette-in-Indiana. The Center is a place of learning, renewal and spiritual growth. The ministry of the Center is rooted in scripture, prayer and community building which results in healing and forgiveness.

Located within the city limits of rural farming community the Center offers the opportunity to "Be Still and Know that I Am".

Mercy Center
Spirituality & Conference Center
2300 Adeline Drive
Burlingame, CA 94010-5540
Tel: 650-340-7474
Fax: 650-340-1299
E-mail: mc@mercyburl.org
Website: www.mercy-center.org and on Facebook

Type of Business:

Mercy Center Burlingame Conference and Retreat Center
Experience peace, tranquility and gracious hospitality for all of your meeting and conference needs.
Close to SF airport and downtown, transportation. We accommodate groups from 4-200. 85 guest rooms; 2 dining rooms, chapel, Labyrinth garden, internet, A/V and more.
Discounts for first time groups and weekday events. www.mercy-center.org

Personnel:

Suzanne Buckley (Director)
Constance Quirk (Conference Services/Reservations)

Pilgrimages

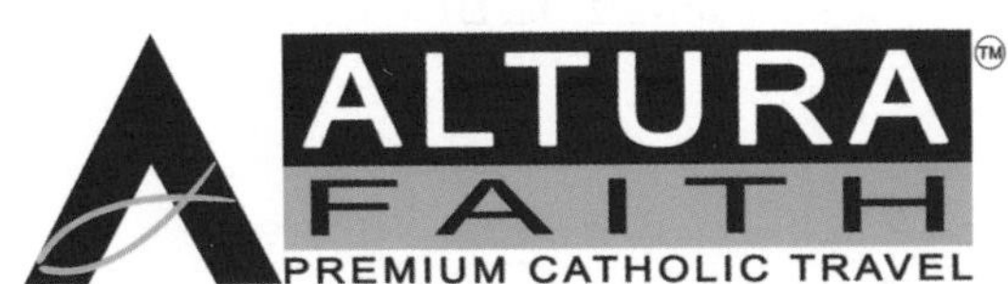

tura Faith (Part of Altura Tours Inc.)
60 Brickell Avenue, Suite 1801
iami, FL 33131
l: 800-242-4122; 305-374-7007 (local)
x: 305-374-7024
mail: info@alturafaith.com
ebsite: www.alturafaith.com

pe of Business:

ltura Tours Religious Department has been providing meaningful spiritual xperiences to Catholic Pilgrims around the World for over 20 years. ebranded as Altura Faith, an enhanced and dedicated team of travel rofessionals is ready to assist you in planning all aspects of your trip. Ve carefully design our itineraries with special consideration to devotion, rayer and reflection, including reliable schedule flights, comfortable, ccommodations, experienced tour directors, comprehensive sightseeing, leluxe land transportation and exceptional meals.

roup travel is an excellent way to raise funds, and a Pilgrimage Tour an serve this purpose. The group organizer can travel free of cost and he participants are rewarded with a memorable spiritual experience and group benefits not possible with independent travel.

et us take you and your group on your next Pilgrimage of joy and peace o experience a journey of a lifetime!

rsonnel:

Diego Linares Dimperio (President)
vonne Gero (Vice President Operations – Groups)

"THE MOST TRUSTED NAME IN RELIGIOUS GROUP TRAVEL"

Worldwide Tours & Pilgrimages

atholic Travel Centre
444 Riverside Drive, Ste. 301
urbank, CA 91505
el: 800-553-5233; 818-848-9449
ax: 818-848-0712
-mail: Groups@GoCatholicTravel.com
Vebsite: www.GoCatholicTravel.com

ype of Business:

A reputation for extraordinary quality has made Catholic Travel Centre the choice of groups that demand exacting service and exceptional attention to detail. With meticulous detail, we will plan a one-of-a-kind pilgrimage tour catering to your group's specific interests. We can work within the constraints of any budget.

Our client list includes prestigious Catholic institutions nationwide, returning year-after-year to Catholic Travel Centre. To start planning your tour please call 800-553-5233 or visit our web site at GoCatholicTravel.com.

Go with Catholic Travel Centre, "The most trusted name in customized religious group travel."

ersonnel:

J. Scott Scherer (President)
Inga Duranovic (Director of Operations)

Friendly Planet Travel Pilgrimages
500 Old York Road, Suite 200
Jenkintown, PA 19046
Tel: 888-795-8003
E-mail: fppilgrimages@friendlyplanet.com
Website: www.friendlyplanet.com/pilgrimages

Type of Business:

We are wholesale tour operators with more than 30 years of experience operating pilgrimage programs throughout the world. Over the years, we have learned to be excellent stewards of our passengers' budgets while delivering a fine, upscale travel program to every destination we serve. We are members of ASTA (the American Society of Travel Agents), IATAN (the International Airlines Travel Agent Network), and CLIA (Cruise Line International Association). We are bonded, licensed, and we carry all the appropriate insurance necessary to protect both our clients and ourselves, and we are proud of our excellent BBB and Dunn & Bradstreet ratings.

It is our experience in arranging pilgrimage travel, our excellent pricing for all aspects of your trip, and personal commitment to making your tour the experience of a lifetime, that is your assurance of the very best pilgrimage experience available anywhere. We offer shared departures that individuals are invited to join that are accompanied by a priest as spiritual leader, and we offer a full array of private group services at excellent prices.

Personnel:

Peggy M. Goldman (President)

Nawas International Travel
The Leader in Catholic Pilgrimages for 63 years

NAWAS INTERNATIONAL TRAVEL
777 Post Road, Suite 305
Darien, CT 06820-4721
Tel: 800-221-4984
E-mail: George@Nawas.com
Website: www.NAWAS.com

On the West Coast:

1100 Alma Street, Suite 100
Menlo Park, CA 94025-3344
Tel: 800-288-2688
E-mail: Sami@Nawas.com

Type of Business:

NAWAS INTERNATIONAL proudly celebrates 63 years of operating inspiring and affordable pilgrimages to the Holy Land, Rome and Italy, and other important Catholic Shrines.

Since 1949 Nawas has also been designing and operating pilgrimages to the Holy Land, Italy, Lourdes, Fatima, Santiago de Compostela, the Shrines of Europe, Ireland, Poland, Greece, Turkey with the Steps of St. Paul, and more. We are dedicated to delivering high quality programs and the finest pilgrimages available at the most competitive prices. Plus, we offer excellent tour host benefits—you can travel FREE with as few as 6 or 8 paying passengers! Thousands of Catholic leaders have organized their travel plans through Nawas. Call us toll free and we'll show you how to promote your pilgrimage and travel FREE!

Personnel:

Soli Nawas (President)
George Khoury (Executive Vice President (Darien, CT))
Sami Nawas (Vice President)
Neil Dellis (Vice President)

REGINA TOURS

Regina Tours
494 Eighth Avenue, 22nd Floor
New York, NY 10001
Tel: 800-CATHOLIC (800-228-4654)
Fax: 212-594-7073
E-mail: regina@groupist.com
Website: www.1800CATHOLIC.com

Type of Business:

Regina Tours has been the leader in Catholic Pilgrimages since 1984. Our Pilgrimages start at $1,498 and include Fatima, Lourdes, the shrines of Italy (Assisi, Florence, Rome, San Giovanni Rotondo - Padre Pio - Pompeii, & Sicily), Greece (following St. Paul), Mexico (Our Lady of Guadalupe), Poland, Ireland, Israel, the Holy Land, with Jordan extension, Canonizations, World Youth Day, Year of Faith and any Church celebrations.

We understand the true meaning of a Pilgrimage and will provide our expertise for you and your Pilgrims. Contact us for our free color brochure. Learn how you can travel for free and/or use travel as a fundraiser. For more information, visit our website or contact us today.

Personnel:

Nicholas Mancino (President)
Angela Scharf (Custom Groups)
Sharon, Benni, Bill, Maria, Loretta, Lucille, & Zelda (Travel Experts)

206 Tours
333 Marcus Blvd.
Hauppauge, NY 11788
Tel: 631-361-4644; Toll Free: 800-206-TOUR (8687)
E-mail: sales@206tours.com; Website: www.206tours.com

Type of business:

206 Tours is a highly respected Catholic pilgrimage operator. We have been in business for over 25 years. Our offers include; regularly scheduled all-inclusive pilgrimages to unforgettable sacred sites and Marian shrines. 206 Tours also offers personalized services for individuals, private groups and conferences.

Each one of our clients is handled with care, attention and respect.

For all of our tours, you will be provided with; Mass daily, a personal spiritual director (Catholic priest), superior accommodations, meals, air and ground arrangements and much more. We offer an incomparable sightseeing schedule and knowledgeable tour guides throughout your journey.

Upon request, we can provide you with a free, color brochure, which covers every detail of what we do and explains our policies. For a complete list of our pilgrimages, please visit our website- www.206tours.com.

Interested in being a group leader or spiritual director? Learn how you can travel for FREE! www.206tours.com/groups

Why travel with 206 Tours?

When you choose 206 Tours, you can rest assured that we will emphasize the highest quality and care for every traveler.

We are proud to share letters from our past clients– www.206tours.com/letters.

Mention this listing and receive a $100 discount on your next Pilgrimage!

Personnel:

Milanka M. Lachman (President)
Eva Manise-Relyea (Vice President)
Sandra Lippold (Director of Operations)
Linda Antonelle (Group Development)

"THE MOST TRUSTED NAME IN RELIGIOUS GROUP TRAVEL"

Worldwide Tours & Pilgrimages

Catholic Travel Centre
4444 Riverside Drive, Ste. 301
Burbank, CA 91505
Tel: 800-553-5233; 818-848-9449
Fax: 818-848-0712
E-mail: Groups@GoCatholicTravel.com
Website: www.GoCatholicTravel.com

Type of Business:

A reputation for extraordinary quality has made Catholic Travel Centre the choice of groups that demand exacting service and exceptional attention to detail. With meticulous detail, we will plan a one-of-a-kind pilgrimage tour catering to your group's specific interests. We can work within the constraints of any budget.

Our client list includes prestigious Catholic institutions nationwide returning year-after-year to Catholic Travel Centre. To start planning your tour please call 800-553-5233 or visit our web site at GoCatholicTravel.com.

Go with Catholic Travel Centre, "The most trusted name in customized religious group travel."

Personnel:

J. Scott Scherer (President)
Inga Duranovic (Director of Operations)

Nawas International Travel
The Leader in Catholic Pilgrimages for 63 years

Nawas International Travel
777 Post Road, Suite 305
Darien, CT 06820-4721
Tel: 800-221-4984
E-mail: George@Nawas.com; Website: www.NAWAS.com

On the West Coast:
1100 Alma Street, Suite 100
Menlo Park, CA 94025-3344
Tel: 800-288-2688; E-mail: Sami@Nawas.com

Type of Business:

NAWAS INTERNATIONAL proudly celebrates 63 years of operating inspiring and affordable pilgrimages to the Holy Land, Rome and Italy, and other important Catholic Shrines.

Since 1949 Nawas has also been designing and operating pilgrimages to the Holy Land, Italy, Lourdes, Fatima, Santiago de Compostela, the Shrines of Europe, Ireland, Poland, Greece, Turkey with the Steps of St. Paul, and more. We are dedicated to delivering high quality programs and the finest pilgrimages available at the most competitive prices. Plus, we offer excellent tour host benefits—you can travel FREE with as few as 6 or 8 paying passengers! Thousands of Catholic leaders have organized their travel plans through Nawas. Call us toll free and we'll show you how to promote your pilgrimage and travel FREE!

Personnel:

Soli Nawas (President)
George Khoury (Executive Vice President (Darien, CT))
Sami Nawas (Vice President)
Neil Dellis (Vice President)

Tours

206 Tours
333 Marcus Blvd.
Hauppauge, NY 11788
Tel: 631-361-4644; Toll Free: 800-206-TOUR (8687)
E-mail: sales@206tours.com; Website: www.206tours.com

Type of business:

206 Tours is a highly respected Catholic pilgrimage operator. We have been in business for over 25 years. Our offers include; regularly scheduled all-inclusive pilgrimages to unforgettable sacred sites and Marian shrines. 206 Tours also offers personalized services for individuals, private groups and conferences.

Each one of our clients is handled with care, attention and respect.

For all of our tours, you will be provided with; Mass daily, a personal spiritual director (Catholic priest), superior accommodations, meals, air and ground arrangements and much more. We offer an incomparable sightseeing schedule and knowledgeable tour guides throughout your journey.

Upon request, we can provide you with a free, color brochure, which covers every detail of what we do and explains our policies. For a complete list of our pilgrimages, please visit our website- www.206tours.com.

Interested in being a group leader or spiritual director? Learn how you can travel for FREE! www.206tours.com/groups

Why travel with 206 Tours?

When you choose 206 Tours, you can rest assured that we will emphasize the highest quality and care for every traveler.

We are proud to share letters from our past clients– www.206tours.com/letters.

Mention this listing and receive a $100 discount on your next Pilgrimage!

Personnel:

Milanka M. Lachman (President)
Eva Manise-Relyea (Vice President)
Sandra Lippold (Director of Operations)
Linda Antonelle (Group Development)

"The Most Trusted Name in Religious Group Travel"

Catholic Travel Centre
4444 Riverside Drive, Ste. 301
Burbank, CA 91505
Tel: 800-553-5233; 818-848-9449
Fax: 818-848-0712
E-mail: Groups@GoCatholicTravel.com
Website: www.GoCatholicTravel.com

Type of Business:

A reputation for extraordinary quality has made Catholic Travel Centre the choice of groups that demand exacting service and exceptional attention to detail. With meticulous detail, we will plan a one-of-a-kind pilgrimage tour catering to your group's specific interests. We can work within the constraints of any budget.

Our client list includes prestigious Catholic institutions nationwide, returning year-after-year to Catholic Travel Centre. To start planning your tour please call 800-553-5233 or visit our web site at GoCatholicTravel.com.

Go with Catholic Travel Centre, "The most trusted name in customized religious group travel."

Personnel:

J. Scott Scherer (President)
Inga Duranovic (Director of Operations)

Nawas International Travel
The Leader in Catholic Pilgrimages for 63 years

Nawas International Travel
777 Post Road, Suite 305
Darien, CT 06820-4721
Tel: 800-221-4984
E-mail: George@Nawas.com
Website: www.NAWAS.com

On the West Coast:
1100 Alma Street, Suite 100
Menlo Park, CA 94025-3344
Tel: 800-288-2688
E-mail: Sami@Nawas.com

Type of Business:

NAWAS INTERNATIONAL proudly celebrates 63 years of operating inspiring and affordable pilgrimages to the Holy Land, Rome and Italy, and other important Catholic Shrines.

Since 1949 Nawas has also been designing and operating pilgrimages to the Holy Land, Italy, Lourdes, Fatima, Santiago de Compostela, the Shrines of Europe, Ireland, Poland, Greece, Turkey with the Steps of St. Paul, and more. We are dedicated to delivering high quality programs and the finest pilgrimages available at the most competitive prices. Plus, we offer excellent tour host benefits—you can travel FREE with as few as 6 or 8 paying passengers! Thousands of Catholic leaders have organized their travel plans through Nawas. Call us toll free and we'll show you how to promote your pilgrimage and travel FREE!

Personnel:

Soli Nawas (President)
George Khoury (Executive Vice President (Darien, CT))
Sami Nawas (Vice President)
Neil Dellis (Vice President)

Circle of Prayers
P.O. Box 373
Depew, NY 14043
Tel: 716 352-7971
E-mail: comments@circleofprayers.com
Website: www.circleofprayers.com

Type of Business:

Come pray with us. Establish your own Parish Online Prayer Community at CircleofPrayers.com.

Membership is FREE.

Form an online prayer group and bolster your connection with your parishioners, expand the power of their prayers and help strengthen their faith. Join with your parishioners, and others around the world, in prayers selected by you and your group members. Post prayer requests for your parishioners, for the sick and the needy, friends and family.

At CircleofPrayers.com, you can also post prayer memorials, and utilize our email prayer reminder service to keep in touch with members. And, it is easy to use. Also explore our prayer activities for youth, videos and audios, and our prayer blog and forum. CircleofPrayers.com is available in 5 languages.

Convivium Press, Inc.
7661 N.W., 68th Street, Suite 108
Miami, FL 33166
Tel: 305-889-0489, 786-866-9718; Fax: 305-887-5463
E-mail: convivium@conviviumpress.com, sales@conviviumpress.com, ventas@conviviumpress.com
Website: www.conviviumpress.com

Type of Business:

Convivium Press provides a significant contribution to religious studies through English and Spanish translations of classic authors and contemporary voices for academic and non-academic readers.

In the spirit of its name, Convivium Press books enrich conversation, understanding, and appreciation among religions and cultures. They inspire a dialogue at the interface of ethics and social problems, with a solid theological perspective. And they encourage reconciliation and cooperative endeavors through printed and online publications and social networking.We publish new works and superlative and accessible translations of recognized international authors, including N. T. Wright, Albert Vanhoye, Luis F. Ladaria, José Antonio Pagola, Bernard Sesboüé, Tormas Spidlik, John Main, Antoine Vergote, Sergio Bastianel, Hosffman Ospino, Roberto Goizueta, and José Ignacio González Faus.

Our books are the result of key collaborations with the International Society for the Studies of Biblical and Semitic Rhetoric, the Pontifical Gregorian University, the Institute for Hispanic/Latino Theology and Ministry at Barry University, and the World Community for Christian Meditation. Convivium Press books support the religious formation of Hispanic/Latino communities in the U.S. through the establishment of joint editorial projects.

Personnel:

Dr. Rafael Luciani (Editor in Chief, rluciani@conviviumpress.com)
Dr. Felix Palazzi (Spanish Market Director, fpalazzi@conviviumpress.com)
Alan Fisboin (Sales Executive, English, afisboin@conviviumpress.com)
Beatriz Méndez L., (Sales Manager, Spanish, bmendez@conviviumpress.com)

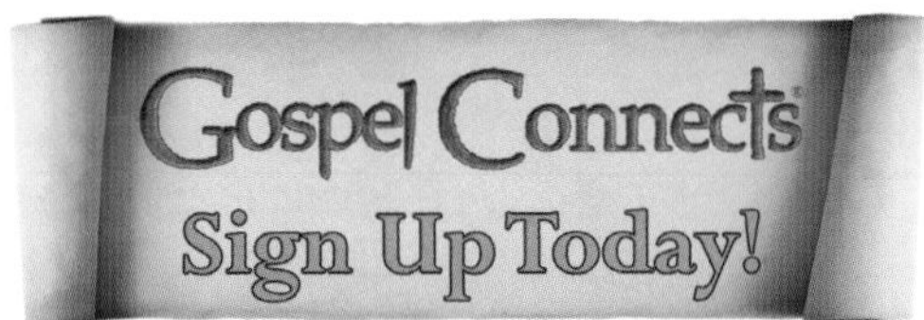

Gospel Connects®
Tel: 770-335-1822
E-mail: Richard@gospelconnects.com
Free Preview sign up go to www.previewgc.com
For more information go to www.gospelconnects.com

Type of Business:

◈ Gospel Connects, is an easy, inexpensive and efficient tool for Pastors to use as they guide their parishioners to become well-formed Catholic men and women who are prepared to confront the challenges posed by our growing secular culture.

◈ Helps Pastors develop a more personal relationship with their parishioners and shepherd them closer to our Lord.

◈ Diocese and Parish specific with each Pastor and individual in the parish having their own secure personal account that can be reached at anytime, anywhere, on any Internet device.

◈ The weekly Communiqué consists of the "Sunday Gospel", a "Conversation with the Pastor," taken in part from the previous Sunday's Homily, a "Resolution" for the week, special parish "News" section and "Going Deeper" section for more in-depth reading on that week's Gospel.

Wolfson Creative
12872 E. Mexico Avenue
Aurora, CO 80012
Tel: 303-525-4991
E-mail: orders@wolfsoncreative.com
Website: www.wolfsoncreative.com

Type of Business:

Wolfson Creative offers electronic certificates (baptism and confirmation) for congregational use. The Wolfson Certificates are designed to teach (with Scripture and artwork) the marvelous treasure of the Gospel. They are designed to be keepsakes, framed and hung on the wall in the nursery, dining room or the office, as a constant reminder that we are baptized and confirmed, the heirs of the Lord's promises. It is our hope that these certificates help the Lord's children rejoice in the gifts of life, salvation and the forgiveness of sins. The unlimited prints makes offering these beautiful certificates very practical for every congregation.

Personnel:

Rev. Bryan Wolfmueller (bryan@wolfsoncreative.com)
Jason Hanson (jason@wolfsoncreative.com)